Complete Baronetage

KU-314-186

Complete Baronetage

Edited by G.E.C.

With a new introduction by
HUGH MONTGOMERY-MASSINGBERD

BERKSHIRE COUNTY LIBRARY
C

ALAN SUTTON
1983

Alan Sutton Publishing Limited
17a Brunswick Road
Gloucester GL1 1HG

This Microprint® edition first published 1983

© Copyright in Reprint Alan Sutton Publishing Limited
© Copyright in Introduction Hugh Montgomery-Massingberd

British Library Cataloguing in Publication Data

Cokayne, G.E.
The complete baronetage.
1. Great Britain—Peerage
I. Title
929.7'2 CS424

ISBN 0 86299 004 1

READING CENTRAL LIBRARY
REFERENCE DEPARTMENT
CLASS 929.72 COK
ADDED 9/85 PRICE £75.00
DISPOSED OF/FILED

Printed in Great Britain
by Redwood Burn Limited,
Trowbridge

PUBLISHERS' NOTE

George Edward Cokayne's *Complete Baronetage* was published in six volumes (the last comprising an *Index*) between 1900 and 1909. All six volumes are here reprinted photographically in reduced format enabling the complete work to be published as one, conveniently-sized volume.

Inevitably, errors, omissions and inconsistencies have been retained. The effects of original variations in inking and out of true page make-up have been minimized wherever possible. Some damaged characters have had to be allowed to stand.

In general the pages are reduced to approximately eighty percent of their original size and arranged in fours, even numbered pages on the left and odd numbered pages on the right. The omission of some blank pages accounts for any apparent breaks in numerical sequence and the occasional departure from this policy.

INTRODUCTION

Sir Walter Elliot, of Kellynch-hall, in Somersetshire, was a man who, for his own amusement, never took up any book but the Baronetage; there he found occupation for an idle hour, and consolation in a distressed one; there his faculties were roused into admiration and respect, by contemplating the limited remnant of the earliest patents; there any unwelcome sensations, arising from domestic affairs, changed naturally into pity and contempt, as he turned over the almost endless creations of the last century — and there, if every other leaf were powerless, he could read his own history with an interest which never failed — this was the page at which the favourite volume always opened:

'ELLIOT OF KELLYNCH-HALL . . .'

Thus Jane Austen introduces us to that vain snob Sir Walter Elliot, Bt, in *Persuasion* (first published 1817). She goes on to summarize 'the history and rise of the ancient and respectable family':

> how it had first been settled in Cheshire; how mentioned in Dugdale — serving the office of High Sheriff, representing a borough in three successive parliaments, exertions of loyalty, and dignity of baronet in the first year of Charles II, with all the Marys and Elizabeths they had married; forming altogether two handsome duodecimo pages, and concluded with the arms and motto . . .

It is not clear to which particular version of the *Baronetage* Sir Walter was so attached; Debrett's have impudently claimed that honour but the notes on other *Baronetages* in the first volume of *The Complete Baronetage* show that there was more than one in the field.

It seems unlikely that Sir Walter would have found quite the same comfort in *The Complete Baronetage* (published in five volumes, plus an index volume, 1900–09) had it been available a century or so earlier. The two great works of George Edward Cokayne ('G.E.C.'), *The Complete Peerage* and *The Complete Baronetage*, applied more rigorous standards of scholarship to subjects where human vanity had hitherto been allowed a ludicrously liberal vein.

The eighteenth century had seen the appearance of works on the peerage and baronetage by Collins which were full of fairy-tales. Most of the pride of popular *Peerages* in the nineteenth century were to copy these legends. It was the golden age of bad genealogy: a whole shoddy industry propped up the pretensions of the parvenus to social status by supplying bogus evidence of gentility. There was also the craving for medieval romanticism and to satisfy the families (or, let us face it, the customers) some lamentable exercises in 'Gothick phantasie' were perpetrated. Mythological twaddle was put into the pedigrees, which would often begin with the dread phrase 'The origins of this ancient family are lost in the mists of antiquity . . .' whereas it was often more likely — social mobility being one of the key factors in tracing a genealogy — that the origins were lost in the dust thrown up by their carriage wheels. The sorry effect of all this was that genealogy became almost irredeemably tainted with the stigma of snobbery.

Happily the late nineteenth to early twentieth centuries were marked by a veritable renaissance in genealogy. Cokayne (born 1825) was of an older generation than the ruthlessly reforming school of genealogists led by the brilliant medievalist J. H. Round (born 1854) who turned the subject on its head, but G.E.C. can be affectionately regarded as the elder statesman in this revolutionary pantheon. *The Complete Peerage* (first published in eight volumes, 1887–98, and later replaced in the light of further scholarship by a new edition over thirteen volumes, from 1910 to 1959*) and *The Complete Baronetage* certainly belong to this new objective tradition of recording genealogy.

The Cokaynes, Viscounts Cullen and later Lords Cullen of Ashbourne, established themselves in Derbyshire in medieval times. G.E.C. himself was only a Cokayne in the female line; his mother, Mrs Adams, being one of ten daughters of William Cokayne, brother of the 6th (and last) Viscount Cullen (see pp 561–65 of Volume III of *The Complete Peerage*). Another of the ten daughters, incidentally, married the Reverend Robert Austen — presumably a kinsman of the author of *Persuasion*. G.E.C.'s father, William Adams, was one of the counsel for the Crown in the trial of Queen Caroline in 1820. After graduating from Exeter College, Oxford, young George Edward followed his father into the legal profession, becoming a Barrister-at-law of Lincoln's Inn in 1853. He then went to the College of Arms, being appointed Rouge Dragon Pursuivant in 1859, Lancaster Herald 1870, Norroy King of Arms 1882 and Clarenceux King of Arms 1894. He became a Fellow of the Society of Antiquaries in 1866 and published several other genealogical works apart from *The Complete Peerage* and *The Complete Baronetage*. Upon his mother's death in 1873, he assumed by Royal Licence, in compliance with his mother's will, the surname and arms of Cokayne in lieu of those of Adams.

G.E.C.'s sister Louisa married the banker Henry Gibbs (later 1st Lord Aldenham) and their son Vicary was later to revise his uncle's work on *The Complete Peerage*. G.E.C. then married the 1st Lord Aldenham's sister, Mary, to whose memory he dedicated the final (index) volume of *The Complete Baronetage* ('My much loved and loving wife', who 'though eight years my junior was taken from me . . . on 11 March 1906'). In a note to the index volume Cokayne refers to his health and advancing years — 'if the health of the Editor [now, 1909] in his 85th year should permit . . .' — and he was to die on 6 August 1911. G.E.C. had had a good innings of eighty-six years.

The Cokaynes lived at Exeter House (presumably named after his old college), Roehampton, then, and doubtless now, a fashionable suburb of London. Their eldest surviving son, Brien, did well in the maternal family bank and ended up as Governor of the Bank of England and a Lieutenant of the City of London. He was created Lord Cullen of Ashbourne in 1920 and this peerage is now held by his son, sometime amateur champion of the arcane game of 'real' tennis.

'G.E.C.', as he modestly styled himself on the title pages of his monumental tomes, was in the best traditions of the dedicated editor. Like the lexicographer Eric Partridge he worked alone, preferring to make his own mistakes. He originated and compiled single-handed the first editions of the two most authoritative books of reference on their subjects. *The Complete Peerage* was subsequently revised, but *The Complete Baronetage* remains, as reprinted here, all his own work. In five volumes and an index, it covers the baronetcies created from 1611 to 1800.

The word 'baronet' suggests a 'mini-baron' and it has been claimed that it was first used in Britain to denote a baron who had lost the right to be summoned to Parliament — in effect, a second-class baron. In his admirable little general history of *The Baronetage* (second edition, 1979), the late Sir Martin Lindsay of Dowhill, Bt, gives various examples of baronets being created in the fourteenth, fifteenth and sixteenth centuries. But G.E.C. is not having any of this, going along with the view expressed by Fuller (famous for his *Worthies*):

---

* Reprinted in a Microprint edition, Alan Sutton Publishing, 1982.

> We meddle not with ancient Baronets, finding that word promiscuously blended with Bannerets . . .

The Complete Baronetage sticks soundly to the titles created after the Order of the Baronetage was instituted by James I in 1611.

In fact, the baronets are definitely not peers, rather the holders of an hereditary order of knighthood. They have never had any legislative powers and they are styled the same as any knight, with the prefix 'Sir' before their Christian name. On the outside of envelopes, and in formal contexts, the word baronet is written after the surname, nowadays usually abbreviated to 'Bt' ('Bart' has sadly rather gone out of fashion). The suffix 'Bt,' or 'Bart', is as unobtrusive as the prefix 'Honourable' (borne, for instance by G.E.C.'s grandfather); one would be most unlikely to find a real life baronet being called 'Bart' by members of his family in the way that Galsworthy's Sir Lawrence Mont is in *The Forsyte Saga*. The wife of a baronet, like the wife of a knight, bears the title of 'Lady' before her surname, with no intervening Christian name — unless, of course, she happens to be the daughter of an earl, marquess or duke; though present-day journalists often seem as persistent in referring to baronets' and knights' wives who are not dukes', marquesses' or earls' daughters as 'Lady Jane Smith' as they are in referring to people like Lady Charlotte Curzon as 'Lady Curzon'. The children of baronets have no courtesy title or prefix at all; but the eldest son succeeds to the baronetcy when his father dies.

The vast majority of the existing baronetcies can pass only to direct male heirs, despite the recent efforts of Miss Eleanor Dixie, elder daughter of the late Sir Wolstan Dixie, 13th (and last) Bt of Market Bosworth, to apply the modern sex equality legislation retroactively. However, the seventeenth and early eighteenth-century Scottish creations do include a few with unusual remainders, such as descent through the female line. There is, for instance, one Scottish baronetess at the present time, Lady Dunbar of Hempriggs. And, on one occasion, a woman actually received the dignity herself. In 1635 Dame Mary Bolles was created a baronet; her grandson succeeded to the title, after which it died out.

The original purpose of the Order of the Baronetage was to help in the colonization of Ireland. The baronets were made to pay the equivalent of thirty soldiers' wages for three years in return for the new dignity. This connexion between the baronetage and colonization was extended by Charles I to the New World when he instituted the Baronetage of Nova Scotia in 1625 — charging those who joined this Scottish Order (Nova Scotia had been annexed to Scotland in 1621) £3,000. In return, they were to receive not just a baronetcy, but also a grant of land in Sir William Alexander's North American colony. These grants of land soon ceased; and the idea that a new recruit to the baronetage should pay a substantial sum of money towards colonization in Ireland, Nova Scotia or anywhere else was likewise dropped.

Since the baronetage was instituted as a means of raising money, it was originally limited to substantial county landowners with estates that brought in at least £1,000 a year. Sir Walter Elliot doubtless approved of such a qualification: 'You mislead me by the term *gentleman*', he once said, 'I thought you were speaking of some man of property'. Landowners of such standing had, in the past, almost invariably been knighted — so that their elevation to the baronetage simply meant that the knighthood which had formerly been given to successive heads of their family as a matter of course would in future come to them by hereditary right.

The territorial qualification for becoming a baronet was afterwards abandoned. Baronetcies, unlike peerages, were frequently given to gentlemen possessing neither a landed estate nor any other form of endowment. And so the baronetage increased through the centuries, becoming much more broadly based than the peerage. Not only were baronets of later creation on the whole people of more modest means than the original ones — as Sir Walter noted with 'pity and contempt' — but the preponderance of great county magnates in the baronetage grew still less as the descendants of many of the early seventeenth-century baronets were themselves made peers.

In his invaluable *Index of Baronetage Creations* (Institute of Heraldic and Genealogical Studies, Canterbury, 1967), C. J. Parry lists 3,482 baronetcies created between 1611 and 1964. The ranks of the baronetage were swollen by the creation of 740 baronetcies at a fairly even rate after 1911. There are today over 1,350 baronets — one cannot be exact — and by no means all of these appear on the Official Roll of Baronets maintained by the Home Office to which proofs of succession should be submitted. Over 200 baronetcies are now held by peers. This has usually come about by a baronet being advanced to the peerage, though there have also been instances of a baronet inheriting the peerage of an ancestor.

There are five classes of creation in the Baronetage: of England; of Ireland; of Scotland (and Nova Scotia); of Great Britain; and of the United Kingdom. G.E.C. covers the first four in order of creation. The Baronets of England were created between 1611 and 1707; the present premier baronet, Sir Nicholas Bacon, descends from the first baronet created on 22 May 1611, Sir Nicholas Bacon (half-brother of the great Francis). The Baronets of Ireland were created between 1619 and 1801; the premier Irish baronet is now the Viscount Valentia (holder of the Annesley baronetcy created in 1620). The Baronets of Scotland and Nova Scotia were created between 1625 and 1707; the Duke of Roxburghe holds the senior baronetcy, created for Sir Robert Innes of New Innes. Following the Act of Union in 1707, no futher baronets of England or Scotland were made and the style was changed to 'Baronets of Great Britain'. The first so created was Sir Francis Dashwood of West Wycombe, whose descendant and namesake is the premier.

After G.E.C.'s closing date of 1800 came the Act of Union with Ireland in 1801 which brought the creation of Baronets of Ireland to an end. Creations of baronetcies from that date onwards were styled 'Baronets of the United Kingdom'. Lord De Saumarez holds the senior baronetcy of this class of creation.

Although G.E.C. did not manage to cover any Baronets of the United Kingdom, he gave due notice to the baronetcies created by Oliver Cromwell and, in an appendix, the Jacobites. In his *Index of Baronetage Creations*, Parry lists five creations by the Protector of the Commonwealth and twenty-five created between 1688 and 1784 by James II in exile, the titular James III and the titular Charles III.

Surprisingly enough, some of Oliver's baronets were re-created by Charles II after his Restoration. Among them, I am happy to say, was my own ancestor Sir Henry Massingberd. The family has always been rather keen to cover up this little detail; faithful historians have studiously omitted to notice the existence of the patent of 1658. One herald obligingly asserted that Sir Henry (indicted for high treason in 1643) had maintained 'an inviolable allegiance to his lawfull Sovereign' and even G.E.C. missed the Massingberd Cromwellian creation from the main body of the text of Volume III of *The Complete Baronetage* — though it is mentioned in the Corrigenda to that volume. The patent is still preserved, bearing the initial of Oliver's Christian name, encircling a good likeness of him (warts and all), on a robe of ermine. The preamble states that the honour is conferred

> as well for his faithfulness and good affection to us and his country, as for his descent, patrimony, ample estate and ingenious education, every way answerable, who out of a liberal mind hath undertaken to maintain thirty foot soldiers in Ireland for three whole years . . .

This baronetcy was duly forfeited in May 1660, but Sir Henry Massingberd was then re-created a baronet by Charles II in August (at about the same time as Sir Walter Elliot's ancestor received the honour).

Sir Walter's vanity must be infectious as it saddens me to record not only that the Massingberd baronetcy died out in 1723, but that my great-grandfather turned down the offer of a baronetcy two centuries later. Such idle boasts are, of course, the stock in trade of arch-bores; though there is documentary evidence to support this one. My great-grandfather, a

Northern Ireland Privy Councillor, was noted as an advocate of religious toleration in public life but refused the hereditary honour after his grandson and eventual heir had become a Catholic. By so doing, the old boy inadvertently deprived his Protestant descendants (not to put too fine a point on it, *me*) of a title, for the Catholic grandson never married and in later life became a priest. A baronetcy is such a modest dynastic ambition, after all!

Certainly from the second half of the nineteenth century onwards, a baronetcy did not seem to be beyond the reach of professional 'achievers'. As landless baronets became more numerous, it was natural that there should have been some of them living by their wits. This is what probably gave rise to the tradition of the 'Bad Bold Bart' in Victorian melodramas — a character not wholly to be trusted on the Turf or where a lady's virtue is concerned. No doubt because it is such a uniquely British institution, the baronetage occupies a special place in the national folklore. As well as the Villainous Baronet, with his twirling moustaches and a wicked glint in his eye, there is also a Heroic Baronet, a fine, upstanding, soldierly figure more romantic than any Lord. The latter is likely to have had his origin in the large number of landless baronets who followed a military career.

'Baronets are so boring', one 1950s debutante was heard to observe. 'They are all descended from Lord Mayors'. The reason why so many baronets of nineteenth and twentieth-century creation are indeed descended from Lord Mayors is that, until the end of 1964, when baronetcies ceased to be created, it was customary for a baronetcy to be given to every Lord Mayor of London towards the end of his year of office. Since that year in the Mansion House usually represents several decades of service to the City and its charities and also entails large-scale entertaining towards the cost of which each Lord Mayor is expected to contribute something between £20,000 and £100,000 out of his own pocket, the Lord Mayor's baronetcy was in the great majority of cases very well earned.

The conferring of baronetcies on Lord Mayors was also a way of honouring the leading City families. In the same way, the giving of baronetcies to eminent members of the legal, medical and other professions, which was customary in the nineteenth and early-twentieth centuries, conferred an hereditary distinction on leading professional families. This emphasized the fact that such families, though they may be landless, are just as much part of the hereditary aristocracy as the owners of ancestral acres. And what was most useful, the granting of baronetcies enabled successful men in all walks of life to be rewarded with a title which they could hand on to their sons without swelling the ranks of the hereditary peerage.

G.E.C. discusses some of the rights and privileges of the baronetage in his preface that follows. It is worth noting some of the progress made in this direction since the beginning of this century. The campaign to be allowed 'supporters' to their coats of arms, for which the baronets have petitioned the College of Arms on many occasions, has not been successful — in spite of the anomaly whereby the Lord Lyon King of Arms has granted supporters to most of the Scottish baronets. The Scots have also long enjoyed the use of a neck badge; this was finally granted to the other four classes of creation in 1928 after the then Home Secretary (Sir William Joynson-Hicks) had intervened on behalf of his fellow baronets. The major achievement since G.E.C.'s remarks were written was, of course, the institution of the official Baronets' Roll which the Home Office inaugurated in the year of G.E.C.'s death, 1911.

The setting-up of this authoritative process was due to the efforts of the Standing Council of the Baronetage. The story is nicely told in that definitive work *The Baronetage* by Sir Martin Lindsay, who has some well-reasoned criticisms to make over the trouble caused by claims to titles having to go through the College of Arms. The Standing Council (of which Sir Martin was Vice-Chairman) is very much active in safeguarding the interests of the Order; it helps those who are having difficulty in establishing their claim to a baronetcy and reprints the official Roll of Baronets.

One unhappy episode concerning which G.E.C. would certainly have had something to say was the notorious honours broking at the beginning of the 1920s. It could be argued that there was nothing new about the 'sale' of honours as such, but Sir Martin Lindsay does not mince words; no excuse, he says, can be made for the man

> who brought the system into total disrepute by the wholesale manner in which he sold honours for funds of which he was the sole beneficiary, the usual price being £100,000 for a peerage, £40,000 for a baronetcy and £10,000 for a knighthood. In eighteen months, from January, 1921, to June, 1922, he was responsible for seventy-four baronetcies, many of which must be considered tainted.

Lloyd George, though, had an answer. 'You and I know', he told J. C. C. Davidson (later 1st Viscount Davidson)

> that the sale of honours is the cleanest way of raising money for a political party. The worst of it is you cannot defend it in public. In America the steel trusts support one political party, and the cotton people support another. This places political parties under the domination of great financial interests and trusts. Here a man gives £40,000 to the party and gets a baronetcy. If he comes to the leader of the party and says, I subscribe largely to the party funds, you must do this or that, we can tell him to go to the devil.

Note the example L.G. chose was a baronetcy; with one or two exceptions the sale of honours was limited to baronetcies and knighthoods.

This sorry state of affairs led to the appointment after Lloyd George's downfall, of an Honours Scrutiny Committee in 1923 and the Honours (Prevention of Abuses) Act of 1925 to prevent the sale of honours. Ironically, the man who paid £30,000 to shut the mouth of Lloyd George's honours broker Maundy Gregory when he came out of prison was himself duly given a baronetcy in 1934 — Sir Julien Cahn, the millionaire furnishing tycoon and fanatical sportsman. Controversial awards of honours have continued to be made, such as Sir Harold Wilson's Resignation List of 1976.

However, since 31 December 1964 no baronetcies have been created — nor, of course, have any hereditary peerages since the following day, 1 January 1965 — and it seems that Sir Graeme Finlay, Bt, is to have the melancholy distinction of being the holder of the last baronetcy. In *The Baronetage* Sir Martin Lindsay notes that 'since about eight baronetcies become extinct each year, actuaries could tell us that within less than two hundred years the Order may well have disappeared'. It is a mystery why such a harmless honour as the baronetcy has fallen out of official favour as it does not — unlike a peerage — confer any legislative power. Is it simply a question of the 'hereditary principle' now being regarded as unacceptable to the prim nostrils of our modern masters? In which case, one might ask: what about the Monarchy?

HUGH MONTGOMERY-MASSINGBERD

Complete Baronetage

VOLUME ONE
1611–1625

Complete Baronetage.

EDITED BY

G. E. C.

VOLUME I.

1611—1625.

EXETER :
WILLIAM POLLARD & Co. LTD., 39 & 40, NORTH STREET.
1900.

CONTENTS.

I

PREFACE.

This work is intended to set forth the entire Baronetage, giving a short account of all holders of the dignity, as also of their wives, with (as far as can be ascertained) the name and description of the parents of both parties. It is arranged on the same principle as *The Complete Peerage* (eight vols., 8vo., 1884-98), by the same Editor, save that the more convenient form of an alphabetical arrangement has, in this case, had to be abandoned for a chronological one; the former being practically impossible in treating of a dignity in which every holder may (and very many actually do) bear a different name from the grantee.([a])

Baronetcies, will, accordingly, be here treated of according to the date of their creation; thus, the reign of James I will be first dealt with and will comprise the *English* Baronetcies (1611-1625) and the *Irish* Baronetcies (1619-1625) conferred by that King; then will follow the reign of Charles I, which will comprise the *English, Irish* and *Scotch* (or Nova Scotia) Baronetcies (these last having been first instituted in this reign in 1625) conferred (1625-1649) by that King. See fuller prospectus on p. 272.

The date of creation is put within square brackets after each Baronet, inasmuch as the territorial description of a grantee (a description which, in many cases,([b]) does not exist) is not, by

([a]) Besides the cases (more numerous than would be imagined) where the heir, by royal licence, or otherwise, has changed his name, there are many Baronetcies granted with special remainder to families of a different name to that of the grantee, *e.g.*, FOOTE, *cr.* 1660, with rem. to ONSLOW; BOWYER, *cr.* 1678, with rem. to GORING; BARROW, *cr.* 1784, with rem. to CRAWLEY-BOEVEY, etc.

([b]) Thus for instance, the description of Francis Cottington, *cr.* a Bart. by James I, 15 Feb. 1622/3, is simply "Secretary to Charles, Prince of Wales"; that of Thomas Aylesbury, *cr.* a Bart. by Charles I, 29 April 1627, is "one of the Masters of Requests," while, later on, in 1746, William Gooch was *cr.* a Bart. as "Lieut. Governor of Virginia"; in 1755, Horatio Mann as "Envoy at

the grant of a Baronetcy, made hereditary. In a few cases where two Baronetcies of the *same* name have been created in the *same* year, the numerals "1" and "2" are added after such date, thus, in the case of the two Baronetcies of Molyneux, "[1611(1)]" signifies that it was the *first* of that name created in that year, and "[1611(2)] that it was the *second* so created.

The letters "[S.]" *and* "[I.]" put before the date of creation, denote severally that the Baronetcy is one of "Scotland" (or Nova Scotia) or of Ireland. The letters "[E.]" for England,

the Court of Florence"; in 1764, George Brydges Rodney as "Vice Admiral"; in 1765, Charles Knowles as "Admiral of the Blue"; in 1766, John Moore as "Admiral of the Red." Thus in a single year, 1813, we have the Baronetcies of Sheaffe, "Major General"; of Duckworth, "Admiral of the Blue"; of Oakes, "Lieut. General"; of Rowley, "Capt, R.N."; of Broke, "Capt. R.N."; and of Hewett, "General in the Army." In the next year, 1814, we have the Baronetcies of Beresford, "Capt. R.N."; of Grey, "Capt. R.N."; of Wylie, "Physician to the Emperor of Russia"; of Blackwood, "Rear Admiral"; of Collier, "Capt. R.N."; of Hoste, "Capt. R.N." In the next year, 1815, we have those of Hamilton, "Lieut. Gen."; of Campbell, "Lieut. Gen."; of McMahon, "Master of the Rolls in Ireland"; of Campbell, "Lieut. Colonel." In the next year, 1816, those of Ochterlony "Major General"; of Brownrigg, "Lieut. General"; of Ogle, "Admiral of the Red"; of Floyd, "General in the Army," and of Elphinstone, "Lieut. Colonel." In 1660, the territorial description "of London" was given to Gould, Adams, Allen, Humble, Robinson, Brown, Backhouse, Cutler, Foote, and Gardiner, grantees of Baronetcies; in like manner, that "of Westminster," in 1662, to Long; in 1698, to Germaine; in 1723, to Frederick; etc. In many cases (probably most) the estate by which the grantee is described, has been alienated by one of his successors in the dignity, as, for instance (to go no further than the first Baronetcy), was that "of Redgrave, co. Suffolk," about 1690, by Sir Robert Bacon, the 5th Baronet [1611]. In that family the following curious incident occurred as to the territorial designation "of Gillingham, co. Norfolk," being that of Nicholas Bacon, the grantee of a Baronetcy in 1662. That Baronetcy became extinct in 1685, when the *estate* of Gillingham devolved on the last holder's cousin, Sir Henry Bacon, 3d Bart. [1627], whose ancestor had been *cr. a Bart.* in 1627, as "of Mildenhall, co. Suffolk." The estate of Mildenhall, however, had been alienated before 1685, at which date the holder of the Baronetcy of Bacon, which, in 1627, was "of Mildenhall" became (by possession of the estate) "*of Gillingham,*" though the Baronetcy of Bacon, which, in 1662, was "of Gillingham," was extinct. In 1755, the Baronetcy of Bacon, which, in 1611, was "of Redgrave" (an estate which had long since been alienated) devolved on the 8th Baronet of the creation of 1627, and the two Baronetcies (1611 and 1627) became united and continue to be so held by his posterity.

"[G.B.]" for Great Britain, and "[U.K.]" for the United Kingdom, are sometimes used (when required for the sake of clearness), but must be understood when absent.

The index at the end of each volume will shew the surname of every holder (being a Commoner) of any Baronetcy created during the period treated of therein, while a general index at the end of the work (the incorporation of all these several indexes) will shew the same during the entire period.

As to the term "BARONET," it is here used in the same sense as it was by Thomas Fuller in his *Worthies*, who (under Sir John Darell, Bart., of Berkshire) writes, "We meddle not with ancient BARONETS, finding that word promiscuously blended with BANNERETS (Sir Ralph Fane in a patent([a]) passed unto him [by Edward VI in 1550] is expressly termed a Baronet) but insist on their new erection in [1611] the ninth of King James."([b])

Baronetcies of England were instituted (as above stated) by James I, on 22 May 1611, who also, on 30 Sep. 1619, instituted *Baronetcies of Ireland*, while *Baronetcies of Scotland*, or *of Nova Scotia*, were instituted by Charles I on 26 May 1625. The creation of the last two classes ceased respectively at the date of the Union with Scotland, 1 May 1707, and with Ireland, 1 Jan. 1801. After the first date, *Baronetcies of Great Britain* took the place of English and Scotch Baronetcies till the last date, since which, *all* creations are styled *Baronetcies of the United Kingdom.*

Much interesting and original information respecting "the institution and early history of the dignity of Baronet" is given in *The Herald and Genealogist* (vol. iii, pp. 193-212, 341-352, 449-458) in an article, so headed, contributed by its learned and

([a]) In the *Genealogical Magazine* (vol. iii, p. 55) this grant (Pat. Roll, 4 Ed. VI) of the "order, state, rank, honour and dignity of a Baronet," is set out in full.

([b]) Besides Sir Ralph Fane, or Vane, above mentioned, whose dignity seems to have been but *personal*, William de la Pole *and his heirs* had (according to Sir Robert Cotton, the Antiquary) letters patent of 13 Ed. III [1339], conferring on them the dignity of a Baronet *in return for a sum of money;* a precedent more in accordance with the Baronetcies conferred by James I. "By the statutes of Richard II, every Archbishop, Bishop, Abbot, Prior, Duke, Earl, Baron, *Baronet* and Knight of the Shire, was commanded to appear in Parliament, according to ancient usage, and in an attaint, under Henry VI, one of the jury challenged himself because his ancestors had been *Baronets and Seigneurs des Parlements.*" [Debrett's *Baronetage*, etc., p. xxxiii, edit. 1900].

accomplished editor, John Gough Nichols. In this it is stated (p. 346) that though James I engaged "for himself, his heirs and successors," that the number of Baronets in the Kingdom of England should never exceed 200, and that, though he eventually created 204 (or 205, if Vavasour, a creation of 22 June 1631, with the *precedency* of 29 June 1611, be reckoned) yet "he did not depart from his bargain, inasmuch as five vacancies had arisen, not by extinction, but by promotion to the peerage, *viz.*, Sir Robert Dormer to an English Barony in 1615; Sir Thomas Ridgeway, Sir William Maynard and Sir William Hervey to Irish Baronies in 1616 and 1620, and Sir Thomas Beaumont to an Irish Viscountcy in 1622." This mode, however, of reckoning mergers as *equivalent* to extinctions is not necessary, for six *actual* extinctions occurred in the lifetime of James I, four of them being before 1623, in which year the last English Baronetcies created by him were conferred. These extinctions were (1) St. Paul, 28 Oct. 1613; (2) Bigg, 11 June 1621; (3) Clere, 21 Aug. 1622; (4) Forster, in or about 1623; (5) Ashby, 23 Dec. 1623, and (6) Courteen, in or about 1624. Whether, however, the King was aware of these extinctions, or of these mergers in the peerage, before he proceeded to create English Baronetcies above the number of 200, is very questionable. It is more probable that, like his son and his other successors, he would, had he lived longer, have disregarded the stipulated limitation altogether, as he certainly did one clause thereof which stipulated that, failing the heir male of the body of the grantee, "the first number of 200 should thereby be allowed to *decrease* and be reduced to a lesser number."

The precedency of the Scotch and Irish Baronetcies in relation to those of England and Great Britain is left undetermined by the respective acts of Union with Scotland and Ireland. The general opinion, held for more than half a century after the Irish Union, was that, by analogy, they followed the precedency assigned under those acts to other hereditary dignities, *i.e.*, Peerages. One thing, however, is certain, *viz.*, that either they *were*, or they *were not*, affected by these acts. If the former, the precedency *in England, Scotland and Ireland* of the Scotch Baronets is next after those of England and before those of Great Britain, while the precedency, as above, of the Irish Baronets is next after those of Great Britain, and before those of the United Kingdom. If, however, Scottish and Irish

Baronetcies were not (analogously) so affected, their precedency *in England* would (still) be in the case of Scotch Baronetcies below those of England, and in the case of Irish Baronetcies below those of Great Britain (such having been their precedence *in England* at the time of the respective Unions), but there would be this difference, that *in Scotland* (and in Scotland alone) the Scotch Baronets would precede all others, and *in Ireland* (and in Ireland alone) the Irish Baronets would, also, precede all others, such having been the precedency that existed in each of those Kingdoms before the respective acts of Union. Sir Charles George Young, Garter (1842-69), probably the best authority in all matters of "*precedence*," writes (9 June 1863) as under, "By the act of Union in 1801, no direct provision is made for the precedence of Baronets of Ireland any more than in the prior case for those of Scotland, which, though hereditary dignities, were overlooked in these acts. By analogy (and no other reason can be applied) their rank must be determined by those rules which govern superior hereditary dignities . . . so that, regard being had to the ranking of the Baronets of Scotland and Ireland after those of England, Sir James [should be 'Charles'] Coote, although he may retain his precedence of 1620 among Baronets of Ireland as a class, would, nevertheless, give place to Sir James Fergusson [whose ancestor was], created a Baronet of England [*sic*, but doubtless a misprint for 'of Scotland'] in 1703,(a) upon occasions where the respective orders are ranked in public proceedings, and this analogy is recognised and admitted in the *Roll of Precedence in Ireland*, issued by 'Ulster' [Sir John Bernard Burke] himself from Dublin Castle in 1854." It appears, however, that "Ulster" changed his views some nine years later, for he writes, on 9 June 1863, in answer to "Garter," as under, "To the doctrine insisted on by Sir Charles Young, that an act of Parl. which alters the precedence of one body of men [*i.e.*, Peers] can, by analogy, be made to take

(a) This *Scotch* Baronetcy is, apparently, quoted, as the letter has reference to the relative precedence of Scotland and Ireland only. The relative precedency of the Baronets of the *three* Kingdoms would have been better illustrated, by the substitution of "Stirling" (in lieu of "Fergusson"), that dignity *cr.* 15 Dec. 1800, being the last creation of a Baronetcy *of Great Britain* and, accordingly, one which, at the date of the Irish Union (1 Jan. 1801), ranked unquestionably *in England* next immediately above all *Irish* Baronetcie

away the precedence of others not named in it, I demur *in toto* . . . Baronets of England, Ireland and Scotland, hold at this moment the exact precedence granted to them by their respective patents, according to the priority and seniority of their creations unaffected by the acts of Union, which acts do not name Baronets at all. Consequently, Sir Charles Coote, Baronet of Ireland, does retain his precedence of 1620, and should not give place to Sir James Ferguson [whose ancestor was], created a Baronet of Scotland in 1703" [See *Herald and Genealogist*, vol. i, pp. 555-558, in an article on the relative precedence of the cities of Dublin and Edinburgh]. It is difficult to follow the late(a) "Ulster's" argument. No doubt the Baronetcy of Coote retains "the exact precedence" granted to it by its patent, one which places it (with the exception of Annesley) probably above all other existing *Irish* Baronetcies. Irish Baronetcies may possibly (perhaps probably) rank *in Ireland* (as they did previous to the Irish Union) before all other Baronetcies whatsoever, but *neither* by express words, *nor* by analogy, does the act of Union give them a precedency in England or Scotland over the Baronetcies of England, Scotland, or Great Britain, which they previously had never enjoyed.(b)

The great difficulty which presents itself in a work treating of Baronetcies is to ascertain the persons who, *by succession*, are entitled to that dignity. There is, however, in many cases, no little difficulty in determining as to whether, or no, the fact of the *creation* itself may fairly be assumed. The enrollment of the patent on the patent rolls is, of course, the best evidence (next to the actual production of the original) of the creation of the dignity, but its non-enrolment by no means *disproves* its existence. Passing over the later years of the reign of Charles I (when, owing to the Civil War, such enrolments were the exception rather than the rule) it is astonishing to find that no less than twenty English Baronetcies (of whose existence there has never been any doubt) are

(a) Sir John Bernard Burke, C.B., the well known editor of Burke's *Peerage and Baronetage*, Burke's *Extinct Peerage*, Burke's *Extinct Baronetage*, and numerous other genealogical works, was Ulster King of Arms, from 1853 to 1892, and died 12 Dec. 1892, aged 80.

(b) "Until the Union of 1801 all Baronets of Ireland ranked in England after English Baronets of whatever creation." [J. G. Nichols on the "Dignity of Baronet" in the *Herald and Genealogist*, vol. iii, p. 347.]

in that plight out of the 204 that were created by James I. These are (1) Napier; (2) Bayning; (3) Temple; (4) Penyston, all four created 24 Sep. 1611; (5) Blakiston, created 27 May 1615; (6) Grey; (7) Salisbury; (8) Mill; (9) Phelipps; (10) Foulis; (11) Hervey; (12) Mackworth; (13) Ley; (14) Villiers; (15) Hicks; (16) Beaumont; (17) Dryden; (18) Airmyn; (19) Forster; and (20) Chester, of which the last named fifteen were created in 1619 or 1619/20. With respect to the first nine of these, there being no signet bill or other document respecting their creation, their names do not appear in the valuable list of the *Creation of Baronets*, 1611-1646, in the appendix to the 47th Report of the Deputy Keeper of the Public Records. The names, however, of the other eleven *do* so appear, as the signet bills for their creations (in one case, Beaumont, being only a fragment) exist, besides, also, that in one case, Foulis, there is the "warrant for granting receipt of £1,100 on his creation as Baronet."

The compiler, has, however, endeavoured to include *all*, who, rightly, or wrongly, have assumed the title of Baronet, though when he himself is not satisfied with their right thereto he has ventured to call attention to the want (or possible want) of proper evidence. No check, however, exists to anyone assuming a Baronetcy and such assumptions unfortunately, in rapidly increasing number, pass muster but too frequently in Society, and even (it is believed) at Court, while Official gazetting of naval, military, and other appointments given to "*soi-disant Baronets*," are (it is feared) not uncommon. The withholding of Royal and Official recognition until proper proof is given of the succession to a Baronetcy seems the only practical method of restraining these ever increasing and, in many cases, preposterous assumptions.(a) It may, of course, be a question as to the desirability of withholding recognition from the *existing* holders of (doubtful or fictitious) Baronetcies, but, at all events, no hardship would be caused by a notice that no person, who *succeeded* to the dignity of a Baronet on or after a certain date next ensuing, would be recognised as such, until proper

(a) In Foster's *Baronetage* for 1883, no less than sixty-five Baronets (then living) are relegated to the part of that work called "Chaos," as being among "the more questionable assumptions," to which statement is added the remark that "it is, however, more than probable that there are weak points in some of the other titles which I have not discovered."

proof of his right to such succession had been given. This would gradually and effectively (without any violent measures having to be adopted) effect the purpose, though it would not interfere with the *existing* style of any person, save of those who, after due warning and *in defiance of such notice*, had assumed the dignity, without having proved their right thereto. The heir apparent of a Baronetcy (unlike the heir apparent to a peerage) has no distinctive title (such as "Honble.," or "Lord"), so that he would, by this measure, be only *detained in the position he had always occupied*, instead of being recognised at once in a new one to which he had not *proved* himself to be entitled.(a) The Baronets themselves have recently become alive to the want of a proper court to determine the claim of succession to that dignity, and are endeavouring to obtain one. It is to be hoped that whatever may be the measures that they are able to *enforce against* the *existing* pretenders they will not fail to obtain the power by some such method as this to bar any *future* assumptions of the title.

(a) See *Herald and Genealogist*, vol. iv, p. 285, for an almost similar suggestion made in Jan. 1867, by "a non-practising Barrister," accompanied with some remarks thereon by (J. G. Nichols) the well known editor of that work.

LIST OF PRINTED BARONETAGES,(a)

PREVIOUS TO 1900.

[*Note.*—Those works which contain merely the existing holder of the dignity, with no account of his predecessors therein, are excluded. Such are the second (1819) and all later editions of Stockdale's *Present Baronetage*; such also Dod's (most useful) *Peerage, Baronetage and Knightage*, first issued in 1841, and, with three exceptions (1843, 1845 and 1847), continued annually to the present date, the vol. for 1900 being the fifty-seventh issue; and such also, since 1840, Debrett's *Baronetage*, etc., of which the edition for this year (1900) is stated to be the "ninety-second year."]

A.D. 1720.—"*The Baronettage of England*, etc., by Arthur Collins" [the well known editor of Collins' *Peerage*]. 2 vols., 8vo. This work is incomplete, dealing only with the creations of James I, and containing but three-quarters or so of them, as it ends with Palmer, a creation of 29 June 1621. It, however, unlike any of its successors, comprises *all* the creations (whether existing or extinct) within the period of which it treats, save only those which were then (1720) merged in an English peerage, and of which its editor had accordingly treated in his *Peerage*. This work was re-issued in 1742, with (merely) a new title page.

1727. "*The English Baronets*," etc. [edited by and] printed for Thomas Wotton.(b) 3 vols., 12mo.; comprising the then existing Baronetcies.

1741.—"*The English Baronetage*, containing a genealogical and historical account of all the English Baronets now existing . . . [with] an account of *such Nova Scotia Baronets* as are of English families now resident in England" [edited by and] printed for Thomas Wotton.(b) 4 vols. (the third vol. being in two parts and usually bound in two vols.), 8vo. This is the same work, but greatly enlarged, as the one next above. Its editor, in the preface, acknowledges his obligations to "Arthur Collins, Esq., the author of

(a) See *Herald and Genealogist*, vol. ii, p. 358; also "*Catalogue of Works on the Peerage and Baronetage*, etc., in the library of Chas. Geo. Young, York Herald [afterwards, 1820-42, Garter], MDCCCXVII."

(b) Wotton "possessed the best materials which then existed, and even now exist for such a purpose—the collections made by Peter le Neve, Esq., Norroy" [1704-27]. These, as far as they relate to the *Baronetage*, are now in the library of the College of Arms, and W. Courthope [Somerset Herald, 1854-66] had "free access to them" when compiling his *Extinct Baronetage* [1839], so that such Baronetcies as are not noticed by Wotton, from having been extinct before his period, are dealt with, by Courthope, in this work. See preface to Courthope's work.

the *Peerage of England*."(a) [see above, under A.D. 1720.] This work, which contains numerous monumental inscriptions, etc., is still "the fullest source of information upon many of the families which it commemorates."

1769.—"*A New Baronetage of England*, or a genealogical and historical account of the present English Baronets," printed for J. Almon.(b) 3 vols., 12mo.

1771.—"*The Baronetage of England* containing a genealogical and historical account of all the English Baronets now existing," etc., with "an account of *such Nova Scotia Baronets*, as are of English families," by E. Kimber and R. Johnson. 3 vols., 8vo. This is an abridgement of Wotton's valuable work (1741) which (in a meagre form) is here continued up to date.

1801-05.—"*The Baronetage of England* or the history of English Baronets [*i.e.*, of those then existing] and such Baronets of Scotland as are of English families, by the Rev. William Betham.(c) 5 vols., 4to.

1804 to 1840.—In 1804 the work, well known afterwards as *Debrett's Baronetage* was first issued under the name of *A New Baronetage of England*, etc., "printed for William Miller. 1 vol., 12mo. The second edition in 1808, and all subsequent ones were "edited by John Debrett," the third edition was in 1815, the fourth in 1819, the fifth (after Debrett's death) in 1824, and the sixth in 1828; all these being in 2 vols. 12mo. The seventh edition, greatly augmented, was edited by W. Courthope [afterwards, 1839-66, Rouge Croix Pursuivant and Somerset Herald] and published in 1835, in 1 vol., 8vo.; the eighth edition, ed. by G. W. Collen [afterwards, 1841-78, Portcullis Pursuivant], was published in 1840, in the same form. After that date this work ceased to contain more than the notice of such members of the Baronetage and their collaterals as were then living.

1809-12.—*British Family Antiquity*, by William Playfair, of which (the first five vols. relating solely to the Peerage) vols. vi and vii contain the *English Baronetage* then existing; vol. viii, *The Baronetage of Scotland*, and vol. ix, *The Baronetage of Ireland*.(d) These all relate only to such dignities as were existing at that date.

(a) Collins is often credited with being the actual author of this work, an error which obtained great circulation from the well known Sir Egerton Brydges having stated in the preface to his valuable edition (1812) of Collins' *Peerage*, that Arthur Collins "reprinted and completed, in 1741 in 5 vols., 8vo., his incomplete Baronetage of 1720," to which [erroneous] statement Brydges adds (most justly) that this Baronetage of 1741 is "an admirable work."

(b) John Almon, celebrated as a publisher of political pamphlets, printed the *Peerage of Scotland*, 1767; the *Peerage of Ireland*, 1768, and that of England, Scotland and Ireland, 1769. John Debrett, was, in or before 1802, his successor.

(c) For a full account of these 5 vols., see Moule's *Bibliotheca Heraldica*, p. 498. Betham contributed also to a smaller Baronetage published by W. Miller in 1804, being the first edition of Debrett's *Baronetage*.

(d) This bulky (though uncritical) work is especially valuable for the Irish Baronetage, which had never before been dealt with, as also was the case in regard to that of Scotland, other then as to certain families *settled in England*, who had obtained Scotch Baronetcies.

1827-1900.—In 1827 the work so well known as *Burke's Peerage and Baronetage* first appeared under the name of *A Genealogical and Heraldic Dictionary of the Peerage and Baronetage of the United Kingdom for MDCCCXXVI*, by "John Burke, Esq.," 8vo. It was claimed for this work, which "inaugurated the encylopedic form in treating of our aristocratic genealogy," that in it "all the [existing] British hereditary dignities were then, for the first time, brought together and combined in one alphabetical arrangement" [*i.e.*, Baronetcies were for the first time intermingled alphabetically with peerages]. In the second edition (1828) "the [existing] Baronets of Ireland and Nova Scotia, which [said the editor] are not to be found in any other book of reference(a), are inserted. The fourth edition (1832) was (alone of all the series) in 2 vols., all subsequent editions being in one large vol. of increasing bulk, till in the sixty-first edition (1899) the number of pages amounted to (cxxxvi + 1848) 1984, and in the sixty-second edition (1900) to (clxvi + 1916), 2082. After the death of the first editor, John Burke (27 March 1848, aged 61) his son, the well known Sir John Bernard Burke, C.B., Ulster King of Arms (1853-92), who had been for some years joint editor with his father, continued the work with great success till his death (12 Dec. 1892, aged 80), when his sons succeeded him therein, the last (1900) edition, however, being edited by "Ashworth P. Burke" [alone]. This was of a yet larger size than the previous ones.

1880 to 1883.—"*The Baronetage and Knightage of the British Empire*" (as then existing), by Joseph Foster. 1 vol., 8vo. The first edition appeared (together with the Peerage) in 1880, and the last (pp. 786) in 1883. This work is chiefly remarkable for the "Chaos" [pp. 693-708], in which persons are placed "claiming the dignity of Baronet, but regarding whose claims there does not appear to be accessible the *primâ facie* evidence, which would justify their inclusion among those whose titles are unquestioned."

The above works, excepting the fragmentary one of 1720 (dealing only with creations during the first ten years of the existence of the dignity of a Baronet), deal only with Baronetcies *then existing*, but the two following, excluding the *existing* Baronetcies, deal with Baronetcies *then extinct*, viz.—

1835.—"*Synopsis of the Extinct Baronetage of England*, containing the date of the creation with succession of Baronets and their respective marriages and time of death, by William Courthope, Esq., editor of the improved editions of Debrett's *Peerage and Baronetage*" [and, afterwards, 1839-54, Rouge Croix Pursuivant, and, 1854-66, Somerset Herald]. Small 8vo., pp. (xii + 256) 358.

1838 is the date on the illuminated title page of *The Extinct and Dormant Baronetcies of England*, by John Burke and John Bernard Burke."(b) 1 vol., 8vo. A second edition (none has since been issued) of this most valuable work has on the title page the date of 1844, though the preface is dated "July 1841." At the end of it are added *The Extinct and Dormant Baronetcies of Ireland and Scotland*, as also some "addenda" (pp. 509-604) and an unpaged "supplement" of four pages, of which last but twenty-five copies were printed.

(a) This, however, was not the case. See the Baronetage of these two Kingdoms in Playfair's *British Family Antiquity*, 1809-12.

(b) See as to these writers under the dates 1827-1900, above.

ABBREVIATIONS

USED IN THIS WORK.

Besides those in ordinary use the following may require explanation.

admon., administration of the goods of an intestate
ap., apparent.
b., born.
bap., baptised.
bur., buried.
cr., created.
d., died.
da., daughter.
h., heir.
m., married.
M.I., Monumental Inscription.
pr., proved.
s., son.
s.p., sine prole.
s.p.m., sine prole masculo.
s.p.m.s., sine prole masculo superstite
s.p.s., sine prole superstite.
suc., succeeded.

Baronetcies of England.

1611—1707.

CREATIONS BY JAMES I.

22 May 1611 to 27 March 1625.

BACON

(Premier Baronetcy):

cr. 22 May 1611.

[*Note.*—With this Baronetcy the Baronetcy of Bacon, *cr.* 29 July 1627, has been united since 30 April 1755.]

I. 1611. "NICHOLAS BACON, of Redgrave, co. Suffolk, Knt.,"(a) s. and h. of Sir Nicholas Bacon, Lord Keeper of the Great Seal (1559-79), by his 1st wife, Jane, da. of William FERNLEY, of West Creting, Suffolk, and of London (being elder br., of the half blood, to the still more celebrated Lord Chancellor, Francis Bacon,(b) afterwards Baron Verulam and Viscount St. Albans), was *b.* about 1540; Pensioner of Gonville and Caius Coll., Cambridge, Nov. 1554; student of Gray's Inn, 1562; Sheriff of Suffolk, 1581-82, and of Norfolk, 1597-98; M.P. for Beverley, 1563-67; and for Suffolk, 1572-83; *Knighted* by Queen Elizabeth, at Norwich, 22 May 1578; suc. his father, 20 Feb. 1578/9; Sheriff of Suffolk (again) 1581, and was *cr. a Bart.*, as above, at the institution of that Order, 22 May 1611, being the 1st person(b) ever advanced to that dignity.(c) He *m.* 1564, Anne, da. and

(a) The style of each grantee (here given in inverted commas), and the date of creation, during the reigns of James I and Charles I, are taken from the *Creations of Peers and Baronets*, 1483 to 1646, in the 47th Rep. of the D.K. of the Public Records.

(b) It appears to have been by Francis Bacon's advice, given in 1606 (some five or six years before it was carried into effect) that the order of Baronets was instituted; so that "it is not surprising to find that the first of the new dignity was Sir Nicholas Bacon," his eldest brother, and the head of the family. *See Notes and Queries*, 3d S., xii, 168.

(c) He was the first of a batch of eighteen persons with whom the order originated. This was followed, about five weeks later (29 June 1611), by a larger batch of fifty-two (53 according to Dugdale and others, who, erroneously, include "DALLISON" therein), and, subsequently, on 24 Sep. by one of four, and on 25 Nov. following by one of seventeen, after which creations (91 in all, ending with that of Holte, all being in 1611), each creation in this reign, and for the most part in those following, is dated on a separate day. There were "twenty-two patents originally intended for the first seal (22 May 1611), of which four "were stayed" viz., those for (1) SIR GEORGE TRENCHARD, of Wolverton, Dorset; (2) his son in law, SIR JOHN STRANGWAYS, of Melbury in that county, "subsequently conspicuous for his opposition to the measures of the Court;" (3) SIR THOMAS WALSINGHAM, of Scadbury, Kent, who *d.* 1639, aged 69; (4) Sir Thomas' cousin german (by the mother), SIR THOMAS BARNARDISTON, of Ketton, Suffolk, who *d.* 23 Dec., 1619, two of whose great grandsons were, in 1663, created Baronets. See a fuller account in *Her. et Gen.*, iii, 208—212.

h. of Edmund BUTTS, of Thornage, Norfolk, by Anne, da. and coheir of Henry BURES or BUERS, of Barrow, co. Suffolk. She *d.* 19 Sep. 1616, aged 68. He *d.* 12 or 22 Nov. 1624, at Cutford, Suffolk. Both *bur.* at Redgrave. M.I. His will pr. 1624.

II. 1624. SIR EDMUND BACON, Bart. [1611], of Redgrave aforesaid, s. and h., *b.* about 1570; M.P. for Eye, 1588-89; and for Norfolk, 1593 and 1625; *suc. to the Baronetcy.* He *m.* Philippa, da. of Edward (WOTTON), 1st BARON WOTTON OF MARLEY, by his 1st wife, Hester, da. and coheir of Sir William PUCKERING. She, who was *bap.* 7 June 1576, at Boughton Malherbe, Kent, *d.* 1 and was *bur.* 6 Oct. 1626, at Redgrave. He *d.* s.p. 10 April 1649 and was also *bur.* there. M.I. Will pr. 1649.

III. 1649. SIR ROBERT BACON, Bart. [1611], of Redgrave aforesaid, and of Ryburgh, Norfolk, br. and h.; M.P. for St. Ives, 1621-22; *suc. to the Baronetcy*, 10 April 1649. He *m.* firstly, Ann, da. of Sir John PEYTON, 1st Bart. [1611], of Iselham, by Alice, da. of Sir Edward OSBORNE, sometime Lord Mayor of London. She was *bur.* 27 Sep. 1640, at Ryburgh. M.I. He *m.* secondly Katherine. She is mentioned in a deed of settlement 20 May 1650. He was *bur.* 16 Dec. 1655, at Ryburgh. M.I. Will pr. 1656.

IV. 1655. SIR EDMUND BACON, Bart. [1611], of Redgrave aforesaid, grandson and h., being s. and h. of Robert BACON, by Catharine, da. of Grave VIOLET, of Pynkney House, Taterford, Norfolk, which Robert was s. and h. ap. of the last Bart., by his 1st wife, but *d.* v.p. 25 Aug. 1652. He was admitted, 1616, to Gray's Inn; was B.A., Oxford, from Clare Hall, Cambridge, and incorp. 10 July 1627, as M.A.; *suc. to the Baronetcy*, Dec. 1655; Sheriff of Suffolk, 1665-66. He *m.*, before May 1650, Elizabeth, 4th da. and coheir of Sir Robert CRANE, Bart. [1626], of Chilton by Susan, 3d da. of Sir Giles ALINGTON. He *d.* s.p.m. (though he had had five sons and ten daughters) 12 and was *bur.* 14 Sep. 1685, at Redgrave, aged 52. M.I. Will pr. Feb. 1686. His widow, who was *b.* 18 Aug. and *bap.* 2 Sep. 1634, at Chilton, Suffolk, *m.* (Lic. Fac. 10 Jan. 1686/7), John TATE, Serjeant at Law. She *d.* 6 and was *bur.* 10 Dec. 1690, at Redgrave, aged 57. M.I. Will dat. 25 Dec. 1689, pr. 21 Jan. 1702/3.

V. 1685. SIR ROBERT BACON, Bart. [1611], of Egmore, co. Norfolk, and of Redgrave aforesaid, and, subsequently, of Garboldisham, in the said county, cousin and h. male, being s. and h. of Butts BACON, by Catharine, da. and coheir of Sir John TRACY, of Stanhow, Norfolk, which Butts, who *d.* Jan. 1662, was 2d s. of the 3d Bart., by his 1st wife. He *suc. to the Baronetcy*, 12 Sep. 1685, but sold the family estate of Redgrave to Chief Justice Holt, and removed to Garboldisham, in Norfolk. He *m.* Elizabeth, da. of Daniel CHANDLER, of London. She *d.* 21 Dec. 1686, and was *bur.* at Wyghton, Norfolk. M.I. He *d.* 31 Jan. and was *bur.* 3 Feb. 1704, aged 52, at All Saints', Garboldisham. M.I. Admon. 16 April 1705.

VI. 1704. SIR EDMUND BACON, Bart. [1611], of Garboldisham aforesaid, s. and h.; *suc. to the Baronetcy*, 31 Jan. 1704; M.P. for Thetford, 1710-13; for Norfolk, 1728-41. He *m.* 27 Nov. 1712, at Ubbeston, Suffolk, Mary, da. of Sir Robert KEMP, 3d Bart. [1642], of Gissing, and sole heir of her mother (his first wife), Lætitia, da. of Robert KING, of Great Thurlow, Suffolk. She *d.* 14 and was *bur.* 17 Sep. 1727, at Garboldisham. He *d.* s.p.m. 30 April 1755. Will pr. 1755.

VII *and* VIII. 1755. SIR RICHARD BACON, Bart. [1611 and 1627], of Colchester, cousin and h. male, being 8th Bart. of the creation of 29 July 1627. He was br. of the 5th and 7th Bart. of that creation (which see) all three being sons of Sir Edmund BACON, 4th Bart. [1627], s. and h. of Sir Henry BACON, 3d Bart. [1627], s. and h. of Sir Henry BACON, 2d Bart. [1627], s. and h. of Sir Butts BACON, 1st Bart., so *cr.* 29 July 1627, who was yr. s. of Sir Nicholas BACON, of Redgrave, *cr.* a Bart. 11 May 1611 as aforesaid. He was *b.* 22 Feb. and *bap.* 5 March 1695, at Gillingham, Norfolk. He *suc.*, on the death of his brother, 10 April 1753, *to the Baronetcy, cr.* in 1627, and on the death of his cousin (as aforesaid), 30 April 1755, *to the Baronetcy, cr.* in 1611. He *m.* firstly, 29 Dec. 1720, at St. Mary's, Colchester, Bridget, da. of (—) MAYHEW, of

Colchester. She *d.* 6 Jan. 1725/6, and was *bur.* in Trinity church, Colchester. He *m.* secondly, 18 July 1729, at St. Paul's, Covent Garden, Lucy,(a) 1st da. of Thomas GARDINER, of Tollesbury, Essex, by Lucy, 2d da. and coheir of Henry MILDMAY, of Graces in that co. She, who was *b.* 30 Jan. and *bap.* 12 Feb. 1691, at Little Baddow, Essex, *d.* s.p. 17 and was *bur.* 22 Aug. 1765, at Trinity church aforesaid. He *d.* s.p.s. 26 March, and was also *bur.* there 11 April 1773. Will dat. 21 Jan. 1773, pr. 14 April 1773.

VIII *and* IX. 1773. SIR EDMUND BACON, Bart. [1611 and 1627], of Raveningham Hall, Norfolk, nephew and h., being s. and h. of Castell BACON, of the same, by Elizabeth, da. of Richard DASHWOOD, of Cley, Norfolk, which Castell was a yr. s. (1st s. *by the 2d wife*, Mary, da. of John CASTELL, of Raveningham aforesaid) of Sir Edmund BACON, 4th Bart. of the creation of 29 July 1627, he being a yr. br. of Sir Richard BACON, 8th Bart. of *that* creation, and 7th Bart. of the creation of 11 May 1611, abovenamed. This Edmund was *b.* 14 Oct. 1749, at Raveningham, in which estate he suc. his father, 13 April 1770, three years before the death, 26 March 1773, of his uncle (of the half blood), whereby he *suc. to the Baronetcies.* He *m.* 29 Jan. 1778, at St. Marylebone, Anne, 1st da. of Sir William BEAUCHAMP-PROCTOR, 1st Bart. [1745], and K.B., by his 1st wife, Jane, da. of Christopher TOWER, of Iver, Bucks. She, who was *b.* 8 Aug. 1749, *d.* 26 Aug. 1813, and was *bur.* at Raveningham. He *d.* 5 Sep. 1820, and was *bur.* there. Will pr. Oct. 1820.

IX *and* X. 1820. SIR EDMUND BACON, Bart. [1611 and 1627], of Raveningham Hall aforesaid, s. and h.; *b.* 6 July 1779, at Raveningham, and *bap.* there; *suc. to the Baronetcies*, 5 Sep. 1820. He *m.* 27 Aug. 1801, at Ottery St. Mary, Devon, Mary Anne Elizabeth, da. of his paternal uncle, Dashwood BACON, of Ottery St. Mary, by Anne Barbara, da. of (—) OGILVIE, of the island of St. Christopher, planter. She *d.* 24 Oct. 1820, and was *bur.* at Raveningham. He *d.* s.p.m.s. 30 May 1864, at Raveningham Hall, aged 84.

X *and* XI. 1864. SIR HENRY HICKMAN BACON, Bart. [1611 and 1627], of Thonock Hall, near Gainsborough, co. Lincoln, nephew and h. male, being s. and h. of Nicholas Bacon, of Blundeston, Suffolk, by Jane, 2d da. of Alexander BOWKER, of Lynn, which Nicholas (who *d.* 1863, aged 77), was yr. br. of the last Bart. He was *b.* 5 April 1820, at Blundeston and *bap.* there; ed. at Sandhurst, was sometime Capt. in the 3d Dragoon Guards; *suc. to the Baronetcies*, 30 May 1864; Sheriff of Lincolnshire, 1867. He *m.* 17 March 1853, at Corringham, Elizabeth, yst. da. and coheir of Sir Thomas BECKETT, 3d Bart. [1813], of Somerby Park, by Caroline, da. of Joseph BECKETT, of Barnsley, co. York. He *d.* 14 Nov. 1872, at Thonock Hall, aged 52. His widow *d.* there, 29 Nov. 1885, aged 59. Both *bur.* at Raveningham.

XI *and* XII. 1872. SIR HICKMAN BECKETT BACON, Bart. [1611 and 1627], of Thonock Hall aforesaid, s. and h. He was *b.* 14 April 1855, at Thonock, and *bap.* at Gainsborough. He *suc. to the Baronetcies*, 14 Nov. 1872; Lieut. Gren. Guards, 1877-78; Sheriff for Lincolnshire, 1887. F.S.A.

Family Estates.—These, in 1883, were 3,377 acres in Lincolnshire, worth £5,358 a year. *Seat.*—Thonock Hall, near Gainsborough, co. Lincoln.

MOLYNEUX:

cr. 22 May 1611,

afterwards, 1628-1771, VISCOUNTS MOLYNEUX OF MARYBOROUGH [I.],

and subsequently, since 1771, EARLS OF SEFTON [I.].

I. 1611. "RICHARD MOLYNEUX, of Sefton, co. Lancaster, Knt.," s. and h. of William MOLYNEUX, by Bridget, da. of John CARYLL of Warnham, co. Sussex, which William (who *d.* v.p. 1567), was 1st s. and h. ap. of

(a) This Lucy, in 1756, on the death of Benjamin (Mildmay) Earl FitzWalter, became one of the three coheirs of the Barony of FitzWalter, and was so declared by the House of Lords, 18 July 1844.

Sir Richard MOLYNEUX, of Sefton aforesaid; suc. his grandfather in 1568, being then but 8 years old; was *Knighted*, 24 June 1586 by Queen Elizabeth; M.P. for Lancashire, 1584-85, 1593 and 1604-11; Sheriff thereof, 1588-89 and 1596-97, and was *cr. a Bart.*, as above, at the institution of that Order, 22 May 1611. He *m.*, about 1590, Frances, sister of Thomas, 1st BARON GERARD OF GERARD'S BROMLEY, 1st da. of Sir Gilbert GERARD, of Sudbury, co. Suffolk, Master of the Rolls (1581-92), by Anne, da. of Thomas RATCLIFFE. She was *bur.*, 19 Feb. 1620, at Sefton. He was *bur.* there, 8 Feb. 1622. Will pr. 1623.

II. 1622. SIR RICHARD MOLYNEUX, Bart. [1611(1)](a), s. and h., of Sefton aforesaid; born about 1594; mat. at Oxford (Brasenose Coll.), 24 Nov. 1609, at the age of 15; *Knighted*, 27 March 1613; M.P. for Wigan, 1614; for Lancashire, 1625 and 1628-29; *suc. to the Baronetcy*, 8 Feb. 1622. He *m.* about 1618, Mary, 1st da. and coheir of Sir Thomas CARYLL. She was living when he was *cr.*, 22 Dec. 1628, VISCOUNT MOLYNEUX OF MARYBOROUGH, in the Queens County [I.], in which peerage this *Baronetcy* then *merged*, and so continues. The 9th Viscount was *cr.*, 30 Nov. 1771, EARL OF SEFTON [I.]. See *Peerage*.

MANSELL, *or* MAUNSELL:

cr. 22 May 1611,

afterwards, 1712-50, BARONS MANSELL OF MARGAM;

ex. 29 Nov. 1750.

I. 1611. "THOMAS MAUNSELL [*i.e.* MANSELL] of Morgan [*i.e.* Margam], co. Glamorgan, Knt.," s. and h. of Sir Edward MANSEL, of the same, by Jane, yst. da. of Henry (SOMERSET), 2d EARL OF WORCESTER; was Sheriff of Glamorganshire, 1593-94, 1603-04, and 1622-23; suc. his father, 5 Aug. 1595, and, having been *Knighted* before 1593, was *cr. a Bart.*, as above, at the institution of that Order, 22 May 1611. He *m.* firstly, 30 May 1582, at Chelsea, Mary, da. of Lewis MORDAUNT, 3d LORD MORDAUNT, by Elizabeth, da. of Sir Arthur DARCY, Knt. He *m.* secondly, Jane, widow of John BUSSEY, and formerly of John FULLER, da. of Thomas POLE, or POWELL, of Bishop Hall, Midx. He *d.* 20 Dec. 1631, and was *bur.* 1 March 1631/2, at Margam. Funeral cert. at Coll. of Arms. Will pr. 10 March 1631/2.

II. 1631. SIR LEWIS MANSEL, Bart. [1611], of Margam aforesaid, s. and h., by 1st wife; *b.* about 1594; mat. at Oxford (Bras. Coll.), 30 Jan. 1600/1, aged 16; adm. to Linc. Inn, 5 Feb. 1602/3; *Knighted*, 23 July 1603, at Whitehall, and *suc. to the Baronetcy*, 20 Dec. 1631: Sheriff of Glamorganshire, 1636-37. He *m.* firstly, after 1603, Katharine, da. of Robert (SYDNEY), 1st EARL OF LEICESTER, by his 1st wife, Barbara, da. and h. of John GAMAGE. She *d.* s.p. He *m.* secondly, Katharine, da. of Sir Edward LEWIS, of Vann, co. Glamorgan. She *d.* s.p.m. He *m.* thirdly, 25 Aug. 1627, at Totteridge, Herts, Elizabeth, 1st da. of Henry (MONTAGU), 1st EARL OF MANCHESTER, by his 1st wife, Catharine, da. of Sir William SPENCER, of Yarnton, Oxon. He *d.* 4 April 1638, at Margam, and was *bur.* there. Funeral cert. at Coll. of Arms. Will pr. 1638. His widow *m.* secondly, Sir Edward SEBRIGHT, 1st Bart. [1626], but *d.* in his lifetime before Feb. 1657/8.

III. 1638. SIR HENRY MANSEL, Bart. [1611], of Margam aforesaid, 1st s. and h.; *suc. to the Baronetcy*, 4 April 1638, being then aged 8 years. He *d.* in infancy soon afterwards.

IV. 1640? SIR EDWARD MANSEL, Bart. [1611], of Margam aforesaid, only br. and h., aged 1 year in 1638; *suc. to the Baronetcy*, about

(a) In the rare event (which, however, among the numerous creations of this year, 1611, occurs two or three times) of there having been *two* Creations of the same name in the same year, they are distinguished by the numerals "(1)" and "(2)," put immediately after the date, thus the Baronetcy of Molyneux of Sefton, *cr.* in *May* 1611, is denoted by "[1611 (1)]," and that of Molyneux of Teversall, *cr.* in *June* 1611, by "[1611 (2)]."

1640; M.P. for Glamorgan, 1660, 1670-79, 1681 and 1685-87; Sheriff, Jan. 1688, but, apparently, declined to act. He *m.*, about 1665, Martha, da. and coheir of Edward CARNE, of Ewenny, co. Glamorgan, by Martha, da. and coheir of Sir Hugh WYNDHAM, Bart. [1641], of Pilsden, Dorset. He *d.* 17 Nov. 1706, aged 70.

V. 1706. SIR THOMAS MANSEL, Bart. [1611], of Penrice and Margam aforesaid, 2d but 1st surviving s. and h.(a); *b.* about 1668; matric. at Oxford (Jesus Coll.), 7 March 1684/5, and then aged 17; Sheriff of Glamorgan, 1700-01; M.P. for Cardiff, 1689-98, and for Glamorgan, 1699-1712; Comptroller of the Household to Queen Anne, 1704-08 and 1711-12; one of the Commissioners of the Treasury, 1710-11; one of the Tellers of the Exchequer, 1712-14; Vice Admiral of South Wales, and a Privy Councillor, 1704. He *suc. to the Baronetcy*, 17 Nov. 1706. He *m.* (while under age), 18 May 1686, at Westm. Abbey (Lic. Vic. Gen.), Martha, only da. and h. of Francis MILLINGTON, of London, Merchant, one of the Commissioners of Customs to Charles II, by Martha, da. of Samuel VYNER, also of London. She was living when he was *cr.* 1 Jan. 1711/2, BARON MANSELL OF MARGAM, in which peerage this *Baronetcy* then *merged* and so continued till the death, 29 Nov. 1750, of the 4th Baron and 7th Baronet, when it, as well as the peerage, became *extinct*. See *Peerage*.

SHIRLEY:

cr. 22 May 1611,

sometime, 1677—1711, LORD FERRERS [OF CHARTLEY],

and subsequently, since 1711, EARLS FERRERS.

I. 1611. "GEORGE SHIRLEY, of Stanton, co. Leicester, Esq.," s. and h. of John SHIRLEY, by Jane, da. and sole h. of Thomas LOVETT, of Astwell, co. Northampton, which John (who *d.* v.p. 12 Sep. 1570) was s. and h. ap. of Francis SHIRLEY, of Staunton Harold aforesaid; was *b.* 23 April 1559, at Staunton; suc. his said grandfather, 27 July 1571; matric. at Oxford (Hart Hall), 1573, aged 15; served in Holland, under the Earl of Leicester, in 1585; was Sheriff of Northamptonshire, 1603, and was *cr. a Bart.*, as above, at the institution of that Order, 22 May 1611. He *m.* firstly (settlm. 21 Feb. 1586/7, her portion being £2,500), Frances, 2d da. of Henry (BERKELEY), LORD BERKELEY, by Katharine, da. of (the celebrated) Henry HOWARD, *styled* EARL OF SURREY. She *d.* 29 Dec. 1595, aged 31, and was *bur.* at Bredon on the Hill, co. Leicester. M.I. He *m.* secondly, Dorothy, widow of Sir Henry UNTON, of Farringdon, Berks (who *d.* 23 March 1596), da. of Sir Thomas WROUGHTON, of Wilcot, Wilts. He *d.* at Astwell aforesaid, 27 April 1622, aged 63, *bur.* 28 at Bredon. M.I. Orig. will (never proved) dat. 20 Jan. (1599/600), 42 Eliz. His widow, by whom he had no issue. was living at Astwell, 1633. Her will pr. 1635.

II. 1622. SIR HENRY SHIRLEY, Bart. [1611], of Staunton Harold aforesaid, 1st surviving s. and h.(b), by 1st wife; *b.* about 1588, being 34 years old at his father's death, when he *suc. to the Baronetcy*, 27 April 1622; Sheriff of Leicestershire, 1624-25, when he proclaimed Charles I as King. He *m.* 1 Aug. 1616, at Staunton Harold, Dorothy, youngest sister (whose issue became coheir) of Robert (DEVEREUX), 3d EARL OF ESSEX, 4th VISCOUNT HEREFORD, and 12th LORD FERRERS OF CHARTLEY (who *d.* s.p. 14 Sep. 1646), da. of Robert, 2d EARL OF ESSEX, by Frances, da. and h. of Sir Francis WALSINGHAM. Her jointure was £3,000. He *d.* 8 Feb. 1632/3, and was *bur.* at Bredon. Inq. p.m., at Leicester, 18 April 1633. Will dat. 5 Sep. 1629, to 9 Aug. 1632, proved 2 April 1633. His widow *m.* 1634, William STAFFORD, of Blatherwick, co. Northampton (who *d.* 6 July 1637), by whom she had no issue. She *d.* 30 March and was *bur.* 5 April 1636, at Blatherwick.

(a) Edward Mansel, the eldest son, *d.* v.p. 20 and was *buried* 22 June 1681, in Westm. Abbey, aged 15.

(b) His youngest br. was Sir Thomas SHIRLEY, the celebrated antiquary.

III. 1633. SIR CHARLES SHIRLEY, Bart. [1611], of Staunton Harold, and of Astwell aforesaid, s. and h., *b.* 9 Sep. 1623; *suc. to the Baronetcy*, 8 Feb. 1632/3; matric. at Oxford (Merton Coll.), 2 March 1639/40. By an ordnance of Parl., 12 Aug. 1645, he had to pay a fine of £600 for his estate. He *d.*, unm., aged 23, at Essex House, Strand, Middlesex, 7 June and was *bur.* 3 July 1646, at Bredon. Admon. 14 Aug. and 26 Nov. 1646, and again 1 June 1650.

IV. 1646. SIR ROBERT SHIRLEY, Bart. [1611], of Staunton Harold, and of Astwell aforesaid, and of Chartley Castle, co. Stafford, br. and h.; matric. at Oxford (Corpus Christi), 12 Aug. 1645, as a Gentleman Commoner; *suc. to the Baronetcy*, 7 June 1646. On the death (14 Sep. 1646) of his uncle, the 3d EARL OF ESSEX (above mentioned), he suc. to a moiety of the estates of the DEVEREUX family, including Chartley Castle. He was the first Protestant of his race, and rebuilt the church at Staunton Harold. He was a zealous Royalist, and was imprisoned no less than seven times, dying a prisoner, "not without suspicion of poison," in the Tower of London. He *m.* 1647, Catharine, da. of Humphrey OKEOVER, of Okeover, co. Stafford, by Martha, da. of Sir Oliver CHENEY. He *d.*, as aforesaid, 6 Nov. 1656, and was *bur.* 22 Dec. at Bredon, but, in 1661, his remains were removed to Staunton Harold. Will dat. 29 Nov. 1654, pr. 1657. His widow *d.* 18 Oct. 1672, at Astwell, and was *bur.* 20 at Staunton. Her will proved 1673.

V. 1656. SIR SEYMOUR SHIRLEY, Bart. [1611], of Staunton Harold and of Chartley Castle aforesaid, s. and h.; *b.* 23 Jan. 1646/7; *suc. to the Baronetcy*, 6 Nov. 1656; matric. at Oxford (Ch. Ch.), 20 March 1660; M.A., 12 Sep. 1661. He *m.*, 29 Jan. 1666, Diana, da. of Robert (BRUCE), 1st EARL OF AILESBURY, by Diana, da. of Henry (GREY), 1st EARL OF STAMFORD. He *d.* 16 July 1667 in his 20th year, and was *bur.* at Staunton. Admon. 13 March 1666/7. His widow *m.* 10 Nov. 1671, at the chapel at Ampthill, Beds. (as the 2d of his 3 wives) John MANNERS, styled LORD DE ROS, then s. and h. ap. of John, 8th EARL OF RUTLAND. She *d.* s.p.s. 15 July 1672 at Belvoir Castle, and was *bur.* at Bottesford, co. Leicester. Her husband, who in 1679, after her death, *suc.* as 9th EARL OF RUTLAND, and was *cr.*, 29 March 1703, DUKE OF RUTLAND, *d.* 10 Jan. 1710/1, aged 72.

* * * * * * * *

VI. 1668. SIR ROBERT SHIRLEY, Bart. [1611], posthumous and only child, s. and h.; *b.* Jan. 1667/8, and *suc. to the Baronetcy* on his birth; *d.* an infant, aged 14 months, and was *bur.* 11 March 1668/9 at Staunton Harold. Admon. 8 April 1669.

VII. 1669. SIR ROBERT SHIRLEY, Bart. [1611], of Staunton Harold and of Chartley Castle aforesaid, uncle and h.; *b.* at East Sheen, Surrey, during his father's imprisonment, and *bap.* 20 Oct. 1650 at Mortlake; matric. at Oxford (Ch.Ch.) 3 May 1667, and was M.A. 15 July 1669, having meanwhile *suc. to the Baronetcy* in March 1668/9. He *m.* firstly, 28 Dec. 1671, at her age of 15, Elizabeth, da. and h. of Laurence WASHINGTON, of Garesden, Wilts, by Eleanor, da. of William GUISE, of Elmore, co. Gloucester. She was living when, on 14 Dec. 1677, the abeyance of the BARONY OF FERRERS [OF CHARTLEY] (of which, in right of his grandmother abovenamed, he represented a moiety) was terminated in his favour. He, accordingly, on 28 Jan. 1677/8, took his place in the House of Lords as LORD FERRERS in the precedency of the writ of summons issued to the first Lord, 6 Feb. (27 Ed. I) 1298/9. On 3 Sep. 1711 he was *cr.* EARL FERRERS. In that Barony and, subsequently, in that Earldom this *Baronetcy* then *merged*, and in the latter still so continues. See *Peerage*.

STRADLING:

cr. 22 May 1611;

ex. 27 Sep. 1738.

I. 1611. "JOHN STRADLING, of St. Donates, co. Glamorgan, Knt.," s. and h. of Francis STRADLING, of St. George's, near Bristol (*d.* 1589), by Mary, da. of Bartholomew MITCHELL, was *b.* 1563; matric. at Oxford (Brasenose)

18 July 1580; B.A. (Mag. Hall) 7 Feb. 1583/4; Sheriff of Glamorgan, 1607-08, and 1607 and 1620; *Knighted*, 15 May 1608 (as "of Salop") at Whitehall; suc. to the castle and estate of St. Donats aforesaid, on the death, s.p., 15 May 1609, of his second cousin, Sir Edmund Stradling,(a) shortly after which he was *cr. a Bart.*, as above, at the institution of that Order, 22 May 1611; was M.P. for St. Germans, 1624/5; for Old Sarum, 1625, and for Glamorgan, 1625/6. He was also an author of some note as a Historian and a Poet. He *m.*, in or before 1600, Elizabeth, da. and h. of Edward GAGE (5th son of Sir Edward GAGE, of Firle, Sussex), by Margaret, da. of John SHELLEY, of Mitchelgrove, co. Sussex. He *d.* 9 and was *bur.* 11 Sep. 1637, at St. Donats, aged about 73. Funeral certif. in Coll. of Arms. Will pr. 1637.

II. 1637. SIR EDWARD STRADLING, Bart. [1611], of St. Donats aforesaid, s. and h.,(b) *b.* 1601; matric. at Oxford (Bras. Coll.) 16 June 1615; *suc. to the Baronetcy*, 9 Sep. 1637; M.P. for Glamorgan, April to May 1640; was concerned in several business undertakings; was Col. of a Reg. of foot, on behalf of the King, at Edgehill, in Oct. 1642, where he was taken prisoner, but was soon released. He *m.*, about 1620, Mary, da. of Sir Thomas MANSEL, 1st Bart. [1611] of Margam, by his second wife Jane, da. of Thomas POLE. He *d.* while attending the King at Oxford, and was *bur.* 21 June 1644, in the chapel of Jesus College in the parish of St. Michael's there. His widow gave protection to Bishop Ussher, at St. Donats, in July 1645.

III. 1644. SIR EDWALD STRADLING, Bart. [1611], of St. Donats aforesaid, s. and h., *b.* about 1624; *Knighted*, at Oxford, 13 June 1643; *suc. to the Baronetcy* in June 1644; fought for the Royal cause(c) at the battle of Newbury, Oct. 1644. He *m.* about 1642 Catherine, da. of Hugh PERRY, Alderman and Sheriff (1632-33) of London. He *d.* (it is said "of consumption") before 1661. His widow *m.* Bussey MANSEL, of Briton Ferry, co. Glamorgan.

IV. 1660? SIR EDWARD STRADLING, Bart. [1611], of St. Donats aforesaid, s. and h., *b.* about 1643; *suc. to the Baronetcy* before 1661; matric. at Oxford (Jesus Coll.) 26 Oct. 1660, and *cr.* M.A. 12 Sep. 1661, being then a Baronet. He *m.* 20 Nov. 1667, at St. Giles' in the Fields (Lic. Vic. Gen., he about 24, she about 18, with consent of her mother) Elizabeth, da. of Anthony HUNGERFORD, of Farley Castle, co. Somerset. He *d.* 5 Sep. 1685.

V. 1685. SIR EDWARD STRADLING, Bart. [1611], of St. Donats aforesaid, s. and h., *b.* about 1672; matric. at Oxford (Ch. Ch.), 18 July 1684, aged 12; *suc. to the Baronetcy*, 5 Sep. 1685; M.P. for Cardiff in five Parls., 1698—1701 and 1710-22; Sheriff of Glamorgan, 1709-10. He *m.* Elizabeth, sister of Thomas, 1st BARON MANSEL OF MARGAM, da. of Sir Edward MANSEL, 3d Bart. [1611], by Martha, da. of Edward CARNE. He *d.* 8 April 1735. Will pr. 1735.

(a) This Edward Stradling, who died at the age of about 80, was s. and h. of Sir Thomas S. (*d.* 1571, aged about 73), s. and h. of Sir Edward S. (*d.* 8 May 1535), s. and h. of Thomas S. (*d.* 1480, aged 24), which Thomas was father of Henry S.; father of Francis and grandfather of the legatee. He was an author, antiquary, and a great genealogist.

(b) He was one of six brothers, all of whom were distinguished Loyalists, viz.:—(1) He himself; (2) Thomas, who was Lieut.-Col. under him; (3) John, Capt. in the Expedition to Rhee; (4) Sir Henry, Capt. of a Man of War, and one of the two naval officers, whom the Parl. could not bring over; (5) Francis, a Capt. in Ireland, who, however, *d.* before the rebellion; (6) George, who, as a Fellow of All Souls' Coll., Oxford, served in the army during the Civil War, and who afterwards (1672-88) was Dean of Chichester.

(c) His brothers John and Thomas were on the same side, and were implicated in the Glamorganshire risings, 1647-48. John died a prisoner in 1648.

VI. 1735, to 1738. SIR THOMAS STRADLING, Bart. [1611], of St. Donats aforesaid, 2d but only surv. s. and h.; *b.* 24 July 1710; *suc. to the Baronetcy*, 5 April 1735. He *d.* unm., at Montpelier, in the south of France, 27 Sep. 1738, aged 37,(a) when *the Baronetcy became extinct.*(b) Will dat. 4 March 1735; pr. 15 Dec. 1738.

LEKE, *or* LEAKE:

cr. 22 May 1611,

sometime, 1625-45, BARON DEINCOURT,

and subsequently, 1645—1736, EARLS OF SCARSDALE;

ex. 17 July 1736.

I. 1611. "FRANCIS LEAKE [or LEKE] of Sutton, co. Derby, Knt.," s. and h. of Sir Francis LEKE, of Sutton in Scarsdale aforesaid, by his first wife, Frances, da. and coheir of Robert SWIFT, of Bayton, co. York, was *b.* before 1581; M.P. for Derbyshire, 1601; Sheriff thereof, 1604-05; *Knighted* 14 March 1603/4, and was *cr. a Bart.*, as above, at the institution of that Order, 22 May 1611. He *m.* 16 Sep. 1607, at Great Berkhampstead, Herts, Anne, sister of Henry, 1st VISCOUNT FALKLAND [S.], 6th da. of Sir Edward CAREY, of Aldenham, Herts. She was living when he was *cr.* 26 Oct. 1624, BARON DEINCOURT OF SUTTON, co. Derby, and subsequently, 11 Nov. 1645, EARL OF SCARSDALE. In that peerage this *Baronetcy* then *merged*, and so continued till on the death, 17 July 1736, of the 4th Earl, Baron, and Baronet, *it* and all other his honours became *extinct*. See *Peerage.*

PELHAM:

cr. 22 May 1611,

sometime, 1706-14, BARONS PELHAM OF LAUGHTON,

afterwards, 1714-15, EARL OF CLARE,

and, 1715-68, DUKE OF NEWCASTLE,

subsequently, 1768—1801, BARON PELHAM OF STANMER,

and finally, since 1801, EARLS OF CHICHESTER.

I. 1611. "THOMAS PELHAM, of Lawghton, co. Sussex, Esq.," 2d s. of Sir Nicholas PELHAM, of Halland in Laughton aforesaid (whose will, dat. 6 Feb. 1559/60, was pr. 31 March 1561), by Anne, da. of John SACKVILLE, of Chiddingleigh, in that county, was *b.* about 1540; suc. his nephew, Oliver Pelham, 19 Jan. 1584, in the family estates; was M.P. for Lewes, 1584-85, and for Sussex, 1586-90; Sheriff of that county 1589, and was *cr. a Bart.*, as above, at the institution

(a) "The estate of St. Donats Castle was bequeathed to the Drakes of Shardeloes, and is now [1838] possessed by Thomas Tyrwhitt Drake, Esq.; Merthymawr and Monknash passed to Hugh Bowen, Esq., and Penlline Lampey and Cwm Hawey to Bussey Mansel, Esq." [Burke's *Extinct Baronetcies.*] Jane, the great aunt of the last Baronet (da. of the 3d Bart.), had *m.* George Bowen, of Kettlehill, co. Glamorgan, and Dame Catharine Mansel, widow of the 3d Bart., had *m.* Bussey Mansel. The disposition of the property in the will gave rise to a Chancery suit, which lasted sixty years from 1738, at the close of which, the valuable library, furniture, etc., of St. Donats Castle were sold. [*N. & Q.*, 3d S., xi, 153.]

(b) In Walford's *County Families* (2d edit. 1864), under "Nicholl-Carne, of Nash Manor, co. Glamorgan," the following very extraordinary statement appears. *The dormant Baronetage of Stradling of St. Donats is centred in and claimed by this family.* The writer of an article, signed "N.O." [*Herald and Genealogist*, vol. iv, p. 234], justly ridicules "the notion of claiming a Baronetcy by virtue of female descent in the case of a dignity in which "all the male heirs of the grantee included in the remainder are well known to be exhausted."

of that Order, 22 May 1611.(a) He *m.* in or before 1590 Mary, da. of Sir Thomas WALSINGHAM, of Scadbury in Chislehurst, Kent, by Dorothy, da. of Sir John GULDEFORD. He *d.* 2 Dec. 1624, and was *bur.* (in state) at Laughton. Inq. p.m. at Lewes 5 Sep. 1625. Will (directing his burial to be at St. Michael's, Lewes), dat. 14 April 1620, pr. 5 Feb. 1624/5. His widow was *bur.* 7 March 1634, at Laughton.

II. 1624. SIR THOMAS PELHAM, Bart. [1611], of Halland in Laughton aforesaid, only s. and h., *bap.* 22 Sep. 1597, at East Hoathley, Sussex; being 27 at his father's death, when he *suc. to the Baronetcy*, 2 Dec. 1624, He had previously been M.P. for East Grinstead, 1621-22; for Sussex, 1624-25, 1625, April to May 1640, again 1640 till secluded in 1648, and 1654 till his death. He *m.* firstly, in or before 1623, Mary, da. and coheir of Sir Roger WILBRAHAM, Master of Requests, by Mary, da. of Edward BARBER, of Tew, co. Somerset, Serjeant at Law. She was *bur.* 7 March 1634, at Laughton. He *m.* secondly, in 1637, Judith, widow of John SHURLEY, of Lewes, 1st da. of Sir Robert HONYWOOD, of Pett in Charing, co. Kent, by Alice, da. of Sir Robert BARNHAM. She, who was *b.* 5 July 1602, at Hollingbourne, co. Kent, was *bur.* 21 Nov. 1638, at Laughton. He *m.* thirdly, Margaret, da. of Sir Henry VANE, Treasurer of the Household, by Frances, da. of Thomas DARCY, of co. Essex. He, who lived a retired life, during the Usurpation, was *bur.* 28 Aug. 1654, at Laughton, aged 57. Will dat. 13 Jan. 1652/3, pr. 13 Nov. 1654. His wife, who probably survived him, was living Jan. 1652/3.

III. 1654. SIR JOHN PELHAM, Bart. [1611], of Halland in Laughton aforesaid, s. and h. by first wife, *b.* about 1623, being aged 9 and upwards in 1633; *suc. to the Baronetcy* in Aug. 1654; was M.P. for Hastings, Oct. 1645 till secluded in 1646; for Sussex, 1654-55, 1656-58, 1660, as also in six succeeding Parls. till 1698. He *m.* 20 Jan. 1647, at Penshurst, Kent, Lucy, 2d da. of Robert (SYDNEY), 2d EARL OF LEICESTER, by Dorothy, da. of Henry (PERCY), EARL OF NORTHUMBERLAND. She was *bur.* 19 Oct. 1685 at Laughton. He *d.* at his residence at Halland, and was *bur.* 20 Jan. 1702/3 at Laughton aforesaid, aged about 80. Will dat. 16 Nov. 1702, pr. 3 March 1702/3.

IV. 1703. SIR THOMAS PELHAM, Bart. [1611], of Halland in Laughton aforesaid, s. and h., *b.* about 1650; M.P. for East Grinstead, 1678 and 1678/9; for Lewes, 1679—1702; and for Sussex, 1702-05; a promoter of the Revolution; a Commissioner of the Customs, 1689; a Lord of the Treasury, 1689-94, and, again, 1701-02; *suc. to the Baronetcy*, Jan. 1702/3, and was *cr.*, 16 Dec. 1706, BARON PELHAM OF LAUGHTON, co. Sussex. He *m.* firstly, at St. Giles' in the Fields, 18 March 1679/80 (Lic. Vic. Gen., he about 26, and she about 15), Elizabeth, da. and h. of Sir William JONES, of Ramsbury, Wilts, Attorney General, by Elizabeth, da. of Edmund ALLEYNE, of Hatfield Peverell, co. Essex. She *d.* s.p.m. in childbed in London, and was *bur.* 13 Oct. 1681 at Laughton. He *m.* secondly (Lic. Vic. Gen. 21 May 1686, he about 33 and she about 18), Grace, sister of John, DUKE OF NEWCASTLE, 4th and yst. da. of Gilbert (HOLLES), 3d EARL OF CLARE, by Grace, da. of the Hon. William PIERREPONT. She *d.* 13 Sep. 1700 and was *bur.* at Laughton. He *d.* of apoplexy, at Halland aforesaid, 23 Feb. and was *bur.* 8 March 1711/2 at Laughton. Will pr. March 1712.

V. 1712. THOMAS (PELHAM-HOLLES, *formerly* PELHAM), 2d BARON PELHAM OF LAUGHTON [1706] and 5th Baronet [1611], s. and h., *b.* 1 July 1693; took the additional name of *Holles* on succeeding to the estates of that family, by the death of his maternal uncle John, Duke of Newcastle, 15 July 1711, and *suc. to the titles*, as above, 8 March 1711/2. He was *cr.*, 19 Oct. 1714, EARL OF CLARE, co. Suffolk, etc., and 11 Aug. 1715, DUKE OF NEWCASTLE-UPON-TYNE, etc. There being, however, after the death, 6 March 1754, of his br., the Rt. Hon. Henry Pelham, no heir to succeed to his peerage dignities he was *cr.*, 17 Nov. 1756, DUKE OF NEWCASTLE-UNDER-LYNE, with a spec. rem. in favour of the family of Clinton, and was also *cr.*, 4 May 1762, BARON PELHAM OF STANMER, co. Sussex, with a spec. rem. in favour of his heir male Thomas Pelham, of Stanmer aforesaid. He d. s.p. 17 Nov. 1768 aged 75, when the Barony

(a) The good actions of his family are recited in the patent. See *Collins' Peerage* (Edit. 1812), vol. v, p. 513.

of 1706, the Earldom of 1714, and the Dukedom of 1715 became extinct, while the Dukedom of 1756 devolved (under the spec. rem.) on the Clinton family, and the Barony of 1762 devolved in like manner on his cousin and heir male as under. See fuller particulars in *Peerage*, under "Newcastle."

VI. 1768. THOMAS (PELHAM), BARON PELHAM OF STANMER [1762], and 6th Baronet [1611], cousin and h. male, being s. and h. of Thomas PELHAM, of Stanmer aforesaid (d. 1737), 3d s. (but the only one that had issue) of Henry PELHAM, Clerk of the Pells (*d.* 1 April 1721), who was yr. br. of Thomas, 1st BARON PELHAM OF LAUGHTON, both being sons of Sir John PELHAM, 3d Bart. [1611]. He was *b.* 28 Feb. 1727/8, and *suc. to the titles*, as above (to the *Baronetcy* as heir male of the body of the grantee, and to the *peerage* under the spec. rem. of that dignity), 17 Nov. 1768. He was *cr.* 22 June 1801, EARL OF CHICHESTER. In those peerages this *Baronetcy* then *merged*, and still so continues. See *Peerage*, under "Chichester."

HOGHTON, *or* HOUGHTON:

cr. 22 May 1611,

sometime, 1835-62, BOLD-HOGHTON,

afterwards, since 1862, DE HOGHTON.

I. 1611. "RICHARD HOUGHTON [*or* HOGHTON], of Houghton Tower, co. Lancaster, Knt.," s. and h. of Thomas HOGHTON, of the same, by Ann, da. of Henry KIGHLEY, of Kighley, co. York, *b.* Sep. 1570; suc. his father, 21 Nov. 1589, being then under age; was *Knighted* in Jan. 1600, by Queen Elizabeth; was Sheriff of Lancashire, 1598-99, and M.P. for that county in 1601 and 1604-05; and was *cr. a Bart.*, as above, at the institution of that order, 22 May 1611. In 1617, he entertained James I at Hoghton Tower, on his progress to Scotland. He *m.*, in or before 1590, Catharine, da. of Sir Gilbert GERARD, of Gerards Bromley, co. Stafford, Knt., Master of the Rolls (1581-92), by Anne, da. of William RATCLIFFE, of Wimersley, co. Lancaster. She *d.* 17 Nov. 1617, aged 48 years and 6 months. He *d.* 12 Nov. 1630, aged 60 years, 6 weeks, and 2 days.

II. 1630. SIR GILBERT HOGHTON, *or* HOUGHTON, Bart. [1611], of Hoghton, or Houghton, Tower aforesaid, s. and h., *b.* 1591; *Knighted*, 21 July 1604, at Whitehall; *suc. to the Baronetcy*, 12 Nov. 1630; was M.P. for Clitheroe, 1614, for Lancashire, 1621-22, 1626, and April to May 1640; and was greatly distinguished for his loyalty during the Civil Wars, in which his castle of Hoghton was partially destroyed. He *m.* Margaret, 1st da. and coheir of Sir Roger ASTON, of Cranford, Middlesex, Master of the Wardrobe to James I, by Mary, da. of Andrew (STEWART), LORD OCHILTREE [S.]. He *d.* April 1647. His widow *d.* 23 Dec. 1657.

III. 1647. SIR RICHARD HOGHTON, Bart. [1611], of Hoghton Tower aforesaid, 2d but 1st surv. s. and h., aged 48 in 1664 (*Visit. of Lanc.*); *suc. to the Baronetcy*, April 1647; M.P. for Lancashire, 1646 till secluded in 1648, and 1656-58; Sheriff, 1658-59. He *m.* Sarah, da. of Philip (STANHOPE), 1st EARL OF CHESTERFIELD, by his first wife Catherine, sister of Henry (HASTINGS), 5th EARL OF HUNTINGDON. He *d.* 3 Feb. 1677/8. His widow was *bur.* at Walton, 21 May 1698.

IV. 1678. SIR CHARLES HOGHTON, Bart. [1611], of Hoghton Tower aforesaid, 5th but 1st surv. s. and h., aged 13 in 1664; *suc. to the Baronetcy*, Feb. 1677/8; was three times M.P. for Lancashire, 1679-81, 1681, and 1689-90. He *m.* (articles dat. 8 March 1676, fortune £5,000) Mary, 1st da. of John (SKEFFINGTON) 2d VISCOUNT MASSEREENE [I], by Mary, da. and h. of John (CLOTWORTHY), 1st VISCOUNT MASSEREENE [I.]. He *d.* at Hoghton Tower 10 June 1710, in his 67th year. His widow *d.* 30 April 1732, aged 76. Both *bur.* at Walton on the Hill, co. Lancaster. M.I.

V. 1710. SIR HENRY HOGHTON, Bart. [1611], of Walton Hall, co. Lancaster, and Hoghton Tower aforesaid, 2d but 1st surv. s. and h.,(a) *b.* 1679; *suc. to the Baronetcy*, 10 June 1710; was M.P. for Preston, 1710-13 and 1715-22; for East Looe, 1724-27, and for Preston (again), 1727-41. For his services in opposing at Preston the Jacobite rising of 1715, he was made one of the Commissioners for the Forfeited Estates, and, subsequently, Advocate General or Judge Martial of the Land Forces. He *m.* firstly, Oct. 1710, Mary, 1st da. of Sir William BOUGHTON, 4th Bart. [1641] of Lawford, by his 1st wife, Mary, da. of John RAMSEY, Alderman of London. She *d.* at Dover, 23 Feb. 1719/20, in her 33d year. He *m.* secondly, 14 April 1721, Elizabeth, widow of Lord James RUSSELL (*d.* 22 June 1712), da. of (—) LLOYD, and Tryphena, his wife, afterwards widow of Robert GROVE. She *d.* at Reading, on her journey from Bath, 1 Dec. 1736. Will dat. 14 Nov. 1735, pr. 29 March 1737. He *m.* thirdly, Susanna, 1st da. of Thomas BUTTERWORTH, of Manchester. He *d.* s.p. at Walton Hall, 23 Feb. 1768, aged 89. Will pr. May 1771. His widow *d.* 16 Oct. 1772, aged 63. All three were *bur.* at Preston.

VI. 1768. SIR HENRY HOGHTON, Bart. [1611], of Walton Hall, etc., aforesaid, nephew and h., being s. and h. of Philip HOGHTON, by his 1st wife, Elizabeth, da. of Thomas SLATER, of Denham, co. Lancaster, which Philip was 3d but 2d surv. s of the 4th Bart. He was *b.* 22 Oct. 1728, at Lancaster; was a Dissenter from the Church of England; was, for thirty years, M.P. for Preston in five Parls., 1768-95, and *suc. to the Baronetcy*, 23 Feb. 1768. He *m.* firstly, 1761, Elizabeth, only da. and h. of William ASHURST, of Hedingham Castle, Essex. She *d.* s.p.m., in childbed, 1762,(b) and was *bur.* at Castle Hedingham. He *m.* secondly, 8 July 1766, at Shenfield, Essex, Fanny, 1st da. and coheir of Daniel BOOTH, of Hutton Hall, Essex, a Director of the Bank of England. He *d.* 9 March 1795, aged 67, and was *bur.* at Walton. M.I. at Walton. Will pr. May 1795. His widow *d.* April 1803, and was *bur.* in Bunhill fields, Midx.

VII. 1795. SIR HENRY PHILIP HOGHTON, Bart. [1611], of Walton Hall, etc., aforesaid, s. and h., by 2d wife, *b.* 12 June 1768; M.P. for Preston, 1795-1802; *suc. to the Baronetcy*, 9 March 1795. He was a Dissenter; Colonel of the 3d Royal Lancashire Militia. He *m.*, 13 Nov. 1797, Susanna, widow of Thomas Townley PARKER, only da. and h. (1787) of Peter BROOKE, of Astley Hall, co. Lancaster, by Susanna, da. of James CROOKALL, of Clifton, in that county. He *d.* 27 Nov. 1835, at Walton Hall, aged 67; *bur.* at Walton. M.I. His widow *d.* 8 Dec. 1852, at Astley Hall aforesaid, and was *bur.* at Chorley, aged 90, having survived her first husband more than 59 years.

VIII. 1835. SIR HENRY BOLD-HOGHTON, Bart. [1611], of Walton Hall, etc., aforesaid, only s. and h., *b.* 3 Jan. 1799, at Walton, and *bap.* there; took by royal licence, 15 Feb. 1835, the surname of *Bold* before that of *Hoghton*; Sheriff of Lancashire, 1829, and sometime Colonel of the 3d Royal Lancashire Militia; *suc. to the Baronetcy*, 27 Nov. 1835. He *m.* firstly, 23 May 1820, at St. Geo. Han. sq., Dorothea, 2d but eventually eldest surv. da. and coheir of Peter Patten BOLD, of Bold, co. Lancaster. She *d.* 7 Dec. 1840, at Bold Hall, and was *bur.* at Tarnworth. He *m.* secondly, 13 Nov. 1847, Harriet Sarah, 1st da. of John SMITH, of Norwich. He *d.* 19 July 1862, at Anglesea, near Gosport, Hants, and was *bur.* there. M.I. at Walton. His widow *d.* 25 Oct. 1866.

IX. 1862. SIR HENRY BOLD-HOGHTON, *afterwards* DE HOGHTON, Bart. [1611], of Walton Hall, etc., aforesaid, s. and h. by 1st wife, *b.* 2 Aug. 1821, at Walton Hall; Sheriff for Cardiganshire 1849; *suc. to the Baronetcy*, 19 July 1862; took, by royal licence, 6 Aug. 1862, as did the other issue of his father, the name of "*De Hoghton*" in lieu of that of "*Bold-Hoghton.*" He *m.* firstly, 14 Aug. 1845, Louisa Josephine, 4th da. and coheir of Joseph SANDERS. This marriage was

(a) His elder br., John, was of the Middle Temple, but *d.* unm. and v.p., being *bur.* 23 Feb 1698/9 in the Temple Church, London, aged 21.

(b) Elizabeth, her only da. and h., *m.* 15 July 1783, Lewis MAJENDIE, who became, in her right, possessed of Hedingham Castle, and *d.* 13 Aug. 1833, leaving issue.

dissolved by Act of Parl. 1849. He *m.* secondly, 1 July 1851, at Watford, co. Northampton, Aline, 3d da. of Sir Henry Meredyth Jervis WHITE-JERVIS 2nd Bart. [I., 1797], by Marian, da. of William CAMPBELL. She *d.* 29 Dec. 1852, at Leamington, aged 22. He *m.* thirdly, 6 Sep. 1854, at Hafod, co. Cardigan, Ellen Anne, only child of Ralph HARVEY, of Lincoln's Inn. He *d.* s.p.m.(a), 2 Dec. 1876, at 13 Cockspur street, Westminster, aged 55. His widow living 1899.

X. 1876. SIR CHARLES DE HOGHTON, Bart. [1611], of Walton Hall, etc., aforesaid, br. (of the whole blood) and h. male, *b.* 20 Nov. 1823; sometime Captain in the 73d Foot; *suc. to the Baronetcy*, 2 Dec. 1876. He *m.*, in 1863, Florence, da. of Louis MOYARD, of Morges, Canton de Vaud, Switzerland. She *d.* 1872. He *d.* s.p. of pneumonia, 12 April 1893, at Hoghton Tower aforesaid, aged 69.

XI. 1893. SIR JAMES DE HOGHTON, Bart. [1611], br. (of the half blood) and h. male, being 5th son of the 8th Bart., 3d son by his 2d wife. He was *b.* 2 Feb. 1851; served in the Ashantee war, 1873-74 (medal with clasp); sometime Major Lincolnshire Reg.; Instructor of Musketry; Hon. Lieut. Col. 4th Battalion Linc. Reg. of Militia; *suc. to the Baronetcy*, 12 April 1893. He *m.*, 27 June 1878, Aimée, Jane, da. of John GROVE, of Mudeford, Hants (br. of Sir Thomas Fraser GROVE, 1st Bart. [1874]), by Clara Cicely Sarah, da. of Joseph Ashton BURROW, of Carleton Hall, Cumberland.

Family Estates.—These, in 1883, consisted of 4,700 acres in Lancashire, valued at £13,397 a year (ground rents not included), and were, at that date, vested in the trustees of Sir Henry de Hoghton, decd.; the then Baronet, Sir Charles, being "only part owner."

HOBART:

cr. 11 May 1611,

subsequently, 1728-46, BARON HOBART OF BLICKLING,

and, since 1746, EARLS OF BUCKINGHAMSHIRE.

I. 1611. "HENRY HOBART, of Intwood, co. Norfolk, Knt.," 2d s. of Thomas HOBART(b), of Plumstead (*d.* 28 March 1560), by Audrey, da. of William HARE, of Beeston, both in that county; was admitted to Lincoln's Inn, 10 Aug. 1575; Barrister, 24 June 1584; Lent Reader, 1601 and 1603; was M.P. for St. Ives in Cornwall, 1588-89; for Yarmouth, 1597 and 1601; and for Norwich, 1604 to 1611; Steward of Norwich, 1595; was, on the accession of James I, *Knighted* (with his cousin, John Hobart), 23 July 1603; Serjeant at Law, 1603, till exonerated in 1606; Attorney of the Court of Wards (for life), 1605; Attorney Gen., 1606-13, being, when such, *cr. a Bart.*, as above, at the institution of that order, 11 May 1611. He was Chancellor to Henry, Prince of Wales, and, subsequently (1617), to Charles, Prince of Wales; was Chief Justice of the Court of Common Pleas, 1613 till his death in 1625. He purchased the estate of Intwood in 1596 and that of Blickling, co. Norfolk, in 1616, where he built a stately mansion. He *m.*, 21 April 1590, at Blickling, Dorothy, da. of Sir Robert BELL, of Beaupre Hall, in Outwell, Norfolk, Chief Baron of the Exchequer (1577), by Dorothy, da. of Edmund Beaupre, of Beaupre Hall aforesaid. They had no less than twelve sons and four daughters. He *d.* 29 Dec. 1625, and was *bur.* 4 Jan. 1625/6 at Blickling. Will dat. 26 July 1625, pr. 7 March 1625/6. His widow, who was *bap.* at Outwell, 19 Oct. 1572, *d.* in Covent Garden, Midx., and was *bur.* 30 April 1641 at Blickling. Will pr. April 1643.

II. 1625. SIR JOHN HOBART, Bart. [1611], of Blickling, co. Norfolk, 2d but 1st surv. s. and h., *b.* 19 April 1593, at Norwich; was *Knighted*, 1 Nov. 1611, at Whitehall; M.P. for Cambridge, 1621-22; for Lostwithiel,

(a) Cecil, his only son (by his 1st wife), *d.* unm. and v.p., 24 July 1874, at Brussels, aged 25.

(b) See a good pedigree in the *Norfolk Visitation* of 1563 (vol. ii.) pub. by the Norf. Arch. Soc.

1624-25; for Brackley, 1626; and for Norfolk, Dec. 1645 to 1647, having *suc. to the Baronetcy*, 26 Dec. 1625. He *m.* firstly, Philippa, da. of Robert (SYDNEY), 1st EARL OF LEICESTER, by Barbara, da. of John GAMAGE. She *d.* in London 24 Sep. and was *bur.* 5 Oct. 1620, at Blickling. He *m.* secondly, Feb. 1621, Frances, 1st da. of John (EGERTON), 1st EARL OF BRIDGWATER, by Frances, da. of Ferdinando (STANLEY), EARL OF DERBY. He *d.* s.p.m.s., after a long illness, at Norwich 20 and was *bur.* 29 April 1647, at Blickling. Will dat. 17 Jan. 1645; pr. 14 Oct. 1647. His widow *d.* at Chapplefield, in Norwich, 27 Nov. 1664, and was *bur.* at Blickling. Will dat. 26 Oct. 1664, pr. at Norwich.

III. 1647. SIR JOHN HOBART, Bart. [1611], of Blickling aforesaid, nephew and h. male, being only s. and h. of Miles HOBART, of Intwood aforesaid, by his 1st wife, Frances, 6th da. of Sir John PEYTON, 1st Bart. [1611], which Miles (who was *bur.* 6 Dec. 1639, at St. Paul's, Covent Garden,(a) aged 44) was 2d surv. son of the 1st Baronet. He was *bap.* 20 March 1627/8, at Ditchingham, and *suc. to the Baronetcy*, 20 April 1647; was M.P. for Norfolk, 1654-55 and 1656-58, being called by writ, 11 Dec. 1657, to Cromwell's "House of Lords," 1657-58; Sheriff of Norfolk, 1665-66, and was again M.P. for Norfolk, Feb. 1673, 1678-79, and 1681. He entertained Charles II at his house at Blickling in Sep. 1671. He *m.* firstly, Philippa, da. and h. of his uncle, Sir John HOBART, 2d Bart., by his 2d wife, Frances, da. of John (EGERTON), EARL OF BRIDGWATER. She was *bap.* 12 Oct. 1635, at Blickling, and was *bur.* there, 19 Jan. 1654/5. Her admon., as of St. Paul's, Covent Garden, Midx., dat. 25 Jan. 1654/5. He *m.* secondly, at St. Giles' in the Fields, June 1656, Mary, widow of Col. Robert Hammond (*d.* Oct. 1654), 6th da. of John HAMPDEN,(b) of Great Hampden, Bucks (called "the Patriot"), by his 1st wife, Elizabeth, da. and h. of Edward SIMEON, of Pirton, Oxon. He *d.* 22 and was *bur.* 30 Aug. 1683 at Blickling. Will dat. 18 Feb. 1662, pr. 20 Sep. 1683; the will of his widow, who was *bap.* 1 May 1630, at Great Hampden, dat. 7 Jan. 1686, pr. 2 May 1689.

IV. 1683. SIR HENRY HOBART, Bart. [1611], of Blickling aforesaid, s. and h., by 2d wife, *b.* about 1658, being *Knighted*, when about 13, by Charles II, at Blickling, 29 Sep. 1671. He, who *suc. to the Baronetcy*, 22 Aug. 1683, had been (with his father) M.P. for Lynn, 1681; for Norfolk, 1689-90; for Beeralston, 1694-95, and for Norfolk (again), 1695-98; being a strenuous supporter of the Revolution; was Gen. of the Horse to Will. III, whom he attended at the battle of Boyne, 1 July 1690. He *m.* 9 July 1684, at St. Giles' in the Fields (Lic. Fac., he about 25, and she about 17), Elizabeth, 1st da. and coheir of Joseph MAYNARD (s. and h. ap. of the well known Sir John MAYNARD, Serjeant at Law), by Mary, da. of Sir Edward Mosley, 1st Bart. [1640], of Hough. He was killed in a duel at Cawston heath,(c) 21 Aug. 1698, and *bur.* 26 at Blickling. Will dat. 21 Aug. 1698, pr. 11 Aug. 1699. His widow *d.* of consumption, 22 Aug. 1701, at Gunnesbury, in Ealing, Midx., and was *bur.* at Blickling. Admon. 13 Oct. 1701, to a creditor.

V. 1698. SIR JOHN HOBART, Bart. [1611], of Blickling aforesaid, only s. and h.; *b.* 11 Oct. 1693; *suc. to the Baronetcy*, 21 Aug. 1698; ed. at Clare Hall, Cambridge; M.P. for St. Ives, 1715-27, and for Norfolk, 1727-28; Vice Admiral of Norfolk, 1719; one of the Lords of Trade, 1721; K.B., 27 May 1725; Treasurer of the Chamber, 1727-44. He *m.* firstly, 8 Nov. 1717, at Thorpe Market, Norfolk, Judith, da. and coheir of Robert BRITTIFFE, of Baconsthorpe, Recorder of Norwich. She *d.* 7 Feb. 1727, and was *bur.* at Blickling. He *m.*

(a) He is generally confused with the well known *Sir* Miles Hobart (the opponent of Charles I), who *m.* 17 Aug. 1627, at St. Ann's, Blackfriars, "Margaret Dudley," but *d.* at Marlow, Bucks, without issue, 29 June 1632. See *Gent. Mag.*, April 1849, Sep. and Oct. 1851, where their separate identity is proved. See also p. 12, note "b."

(b) It was in consequence of this match that the estates of the Hampden family were inherited, 5 Oct. 1824, by their descendant, in the fifth generation, George Robert, 5th Earl of Buckinghamshire, who consequently took the name of Hampden.

(c) Oliver Le Neve, his antagonist was found guilty of manslaughter.

secondly, 10 Feb. 1728, Elizabeth, da. of Robert BRISTOW, M.P., by Catharine, da. of Robert Woolley, of London. She was living when he was *cr.*, 28 May 1728, BARON HOBART OF BLICKLING, co. Norfolk, being subsequently *cr.*, 5 Sep. 1746, EARL OF BUCKINGHAMSHIRE. In these peerages this *Baronetcy* then *merged*, and still so continues. See *Peerage*.

BOOTH:

cr. 22 May 1611,

sometime, 1661-90 and 1758-70, BARONS DELAMER OF DUNHAM MASSEY,

and, from 1690 to 1758, EARLS OF WARRINGTON;

ex. 7 Nov. 1797.

I. 1611. "GEORGE BOUTHE [*i.e.* BOOTH], of Dunham Massey, co. Chester, Knt.," s. and h. of Sir William BOOTH, of the same, by Elizabeth, da. of Sir John WARBURTON, of Arley, Cheshire; *b.* 20 Oct. 1566; suc. his father (when under age), 28 Nov. 1579; was *Knighted*, 1599; was Sheriff of Cheshire, 1621-22; Sheriff of Lancashire, 1622-23, and was *cr. a Bart.*, as above, at institution of that order, 22 May 1611. He *m.* firstly, 18 Feb. 1577/8, Jane, da. and h. of John CARINGTON, of Carington, Cheshire, by Ellen, da. of Thomas HOLFORD, of Holford. She, who was *bap.* 10 Dec. 1562, at Bowdon, co. Chester, *d.* s.p., but her lands were inherited by her husband and his descendants. He *m.* secondly, about 1590, Katharine, da. of Sir Edmund ANDERSON, L. Ch. Justice of the Common Pleas [1582—1605], by Magdalen, da. of Christopher SMITH, of Annables, Herts. She was *bur.* 26 Feb. 1638/9, at Bowdon. He *d.* 24 Oct. and was *bur.* there, 18 Nov. 1652, aged 86. Admon. 28 Feb. 1655/6.

II. 1652. SIR GEORGE BOOTH, Bart. [1611], of Dunham Massey aforesaid, grandson and h., being s. and h. of William BOOTH, by Vere, 2d da. and coheir of Sir Thomas EGERTON (the 1st s. and h. ap. of the celebrated Lord Chancellor), which William was 1st s. and h. ap. of the 1st Bart. (by his 2d wife), but *d.* v.p. 26 April 1636. He was *b.* 18 Dec. 1622; was M.P. for Cheshire, March 1646, till secluded in 1648; 1654-56, and 1656-58; for Lancashire 1659, and for Cheshire (again), 1660; was Com. in Chief, for the King, of all the forces in Cheshire, Lancashire, and North Wales; was imprisoned by the Parliamentarians in the Tower of London; and *suc. to the Baronetcy*, 24 Oct. 1652. He *m.* firstly, 30 Nov. 1639, at St. Mary's, Colechurch, London (Lic. London), Catharine, 1st da. of Theophilus (CLINTON), 4th EARL OF LINCOLN, by his 1st wife, Bridget, da. of William (FIENNES), VISCOUNT SAY AND SELE. She *d.* in childbed s.p.m., and was *bur.* 5 Aug. 1643, at Bowdon. He *m.* secondly (Lic. London, 14 Dec. 1644, he 26 [*sic*] and she 22), Elizabeth, 1st da. of Henry (GREY), 1st EARL OF STAMFORD, by Anne, da. and coheir of William (CECIL), 2d EARL OF EXETER. She was living when he (who was one of the twelve members, chosen in 1660 to recall the King) was *cr.*, 20 April 1661, BARON DELAMER OF DUNHAM MASSEY, co. Chester. He *d.* 8 Aug. 1684, aged 61. For fuller particulars of him, after his accession to the Peerage, as also of his widow, see *Peerage*.

III. 1684. HENRY (BOOTH), 2d BARON DELAMER OF DUNHAM MASSEY [1661], and 3d Baronet [1611], s. and h.; *b.* 13 Jan. 1652; *suc. to the titles*, as above, 8 Aug. 1684, and was *cr.*, 19 April 1690, EARL OF WARRINGTON, co. Lancaster. He *d.* 2 Jan. 1693/4.

IV. 1694. GEORGE (BOOTH), 2d EARL OF WARRINGTON [1690], 3d BARON DELAMER OF DUNHAM MASSEY [1661], and 4th Baronet [1611], s. and h., *b.* 2 May 1675; *styled* LORD DELAMER, 1690-94; *suc. to the titles*, as above, 2 Jan. 1693/4. He *d.* s.p.m., 2 Aug. 1758, when the *Earldom of Warrington* became *extinct*.

[III and IV:] See fuller particulars in *The Peerage*, under "WARRINGTON."

V. 1758. NATHANIEL (BOOTH), 4th BARON DELAMER OF DUNHAM MASSEY [1661], and 5th Baronet [1611], cousin and h., being 4th but only surv. s. and h. of the Hon. Robert BOOTH, D.D., Dean of Bristol, who was s. of the 1st Lord and 2d Baronet, by his 2d wife. He was *b.* 1709, and *suc. to the dignities*, as above, 2 Aug. 1758. He *d.* s.p.s. 9 Jan. 1770, aged 60, when the *Barony of Delamer of Dunham Massey* became *extinct*. For fuller particulars of him and his widow, see *Peerage*.

VI. 1770, to 1797. SIR GEORGE BOOTH, Bart. [1611], of Ashton-under-Line, co. Lancaster, cousin and h. male, being only s. and h. of John BOOTH, of Clerkenwell, Midx. (*d.* 1725, aged 58), by Mary, da. of Gilbert PICKERING, of London, Merchant, which John was 4th s. of Nathaniel BOOTH, of Mottram Andrew, co. Chester (*d.* 1692, aged 65), who was 4th s. of William Booth abovenamed, the s. and h. ap. of the 1st Bart. He was *b.* 20 March 1724; was in Holy Orders, being Chaplain to his cousin, Nathaniel, 4th Lord Delamer; was Rector of Ashton-under-Line, co. Lancaster, 1758; and *suc. to the Baronetcy*, 9 Jan. 1770. He *m.*, about 1745, Hannah, da. of Henry TURNER, of Botwell in Hayes, Midx. She *d.* before him. Admon. July 1789. He *d.* s.p.s. 7 Nov. 1797, aged 73, when the *Baronetcy* became *extinct*. Will pr. Jan. 1798.

PEYTON:

cr. 22 May 1611,

doubtful after 1720;

probably *extinct* before 1840.

I. 1611. "JOHN PEYTON,(a) of Iselham, co. Cambridge, Knt.," 2d surv s. and h. of Robert PEYTON of the same (*d.* 19 Oct. 1590), by Elizabeth da. of Thomas (RICH), 1st BARON RICH, LORD CHANCELLOR (1547-51); was *b.* about 1560; Sheriff for Cambridgeshire, 1593-94; being M.P. for that shire, 1593 and 1604-11; was *Knighted*, 1 Nov. 1596, and was *cr. a Bart.*, as above, at the institution of that order, 22 May 1611. He *m.*, 9 June 1580, at St. Dionis Backchurch, London, Alice, 1st da. of Sir Edward OSBORNE, Lord Mayor of London (1583), by Anne, da. and h. of Sir William HEWETT, also (1559) Lord Mayor of that city. He was *bur.* 19 Dec. 1616, at Iselham. Will dat. 21 Nov. 1615, pr. 14 May 1617, by his widow. She, who was *bap.* 4 March 1562/3, at St. Dionis aforesaid, directs in her will, dat. 29 Jan. 1625/6, pr. 6 Dec. 1626, to be *bur.* at Iselham.

II. 1616. SIR EDWARD PEYTON, Bart. [1611(a)], of Iselham aforesaid, and of Great Bradley, Suffolk, 1st s. (of seven) and h.; ed. at Bury School and at Cambridge; was *Knighted*, 18 March 1611,(b) at Whitehall; admitted to Gray's Inn, 16 Aug. 1611; *suc. to the Baronetcy*, Dec. 1616; was M.P. for Cambridgeshire, 1621-22; 1624-25; 1625 and 1626; Sheriff of Camb. and Hunts., 1622-23. Taking an active part with the Presbyterians in the Civil Wars, he so impoverished

(a) See R. E. Chester Waters's *Family of Chester, of Chicheley*, for an account of this family, correcting many previous inaccuracies. See also *Herald and Genealogist*, vol. vi, pp. 53—74 and 344—345, as also J. J. Howard's *Visitation of Suffolk, 1561*, pp. 109—131.

(b) There appear to have been two Knights dubbed within a few weeks of each other, each being called "Edward Peyto," *viz.*, (1) one, in Feb. 1610/1, who (see Philipot's *List of Knights*) is described of "co. Warwick," and who doubtless, therefore, was the Sir Edward Peyto, who was of Chesterton, co. Warwick, and (2) the other, 28 March 1611, to whom there is *no* designation of County, and who, presumably, is the Edward Peyton, of the text. It is certain that this Edward Peyton was Knighted between Nov. 1607 (when he is called "Esq." in the baptismal register of his son, at Iselham), and before Aug. 1611, when he is admitted, as a "Knight" to Gray's Inn.

himself that he ruined his whole estate and (probably) had to sell Iselham. He *m.* firstly, 24 April 1604, at Streatham, Surrey, Martha, da. of Robert LIVESEY, of Tooting, Surrey. She, who was *bap.* 25 Oct. 1584, was *bur.* 30 Oct. 1613, at Iselham. He *m.* secondly, 6 June 1614, at St. Barth. the Less, London, Jane, widow of Sir Henry THIMBLETHORPE, da. of Sir James CALTHORPE, of Cockthorpe, Norfolk. He *m.* thirdly, 13 Dec. 1638 (being then about 50), at St. James', Clerkenwell, Dorothy MINSHAW, of that parish, aged 21, Spinster (Lic. London). She is, however, called (in the *Visit. Camb.* of 1688) da. [possibly meaning *step* da.] of Edward BALL, of Stockwell, Surrey. He *d.* at Wicken, co. Cambridge, April 1657, and was *bur.* at St. Clement's Danes. Admon. 1 July 1657. His widow *m.* Rev. Edward LOWE, Vicar of Brighthelmstead, Sussex, who long survived her. She was *bur.* there 10 April 1681. Admon. 14 Oct. 1681.

III. 1657. SIR JOHN PEYTON, Bart. [1611(1)], possibly sometime of Iselham aforesaid(a); s. and h., by 1st wife, *bap.* 2 Nov. 1607, at Iselham; admitted, 6 Nov. 1627, to Gray's Inn; *suc. to the Baronetcy*, April 1657. He *m.* firstly, 31 Jan. 1630/1, Mary, da. of Sir Edward BELLINGHAM. She *d.* s.p., was *bur.* 29 Jan. 1633, at Iselham. He *m.* secondly Dorothy, da. and coheir of Robert HOBART, of Clifford's Inn, London, by Elizabeth, da. of Alan HORD of Ewell, Surrey. She, who was *b.* about 1617, was *bur.* 8 Feb. 1640/1, at Iselham.(b) He *m.* thirdly, Anne, who survived him, but who was dead before 5 July 1693. He *d.* "about 1665" (*Visit. Camb.* 1688) at St. Giles' in the Fields, Midx., and is said(c) to be *bur.* there. Admon. 5 July 1693.

IV. 1666 to 1720. SIR JOHN PEYTON, Bart. [1611(1)], 2d but 1st surv. s. and h., by 2d wife; *suc. to the Baronetcy* (apparently) in 1666; an officer in the Army; served at Tangier; was Lieut. in Buckingham's Foot in 1672; Quartermaster, 1673; went into Ireland in 1674; and was living at St. Stephen's Green, Dublin, in 1688 (*Visit. Camb.*); was attainted by James II, but restored by William III; Governor of Ross Castle, co. Kerry, *temp.* Anne. He *m.* firstly, (—), widow of Kana O'HARA, da. of (—) NEWMAN. He *m.* secondly, (—), widow of Richard BARRY, da. of (—) LLOYD, of Morton Hall, in Wales. He *m.* thirdly, Rebecca, widow of Rev. Daniel TOMLINSON, da. of (—) WILLIAMS of Liverpool. He *d.* s.p. 23 March 1719/20, in Great Britain street, Dublin, and was *bur.* 3 May 1720, at St. Audoen's in that city. Will pr. 1720 at Dublin. His widow was *bur.*, at St. Audoen's aforesaid 19 Sep. 1730. Her will pr. 1730 at Dublin.

[After his death the succession seems very doubtful(d), but the title was assumed and is recognised in Wotton's (1741) *Baronetage*, as below.]

(a) In the admon. of 1693, he is described "of Iselham," though as having died at St. Giles in the Fields, but the sale of Iselham was probably before 1657. See *Her. and Gen.*, vol. vi, p. 97, note 2.

(b) This, apparently, is the last entry in the Iselham register of the name of Peyton.

(c) Wotton's [1741] *Baronetage*, as also the earlier one (1720) of Arthur Collins, where the date of death is given as 1666. There seems no reason to question this date, as letters of admon. are frequently granted many years after the death. It is certain that he was dead before 1673, and probably before 1672, as his son was appointed a Lieut., as "*Sir* John" in June 1672, and a Quartermaster, as "*Bart.*" in 1673. His burial at St. Giles, however, is not in the extracts from those registers in Col. Chester's collection. See note "a."

(d) The male issue of his father (the 3d Bart.) was probably extinct, his only surv. brother, presumably, the "Lieut. Thomas Peyton," who was *bur.* 3 March 1674/5 at St. Martin's in the Fields, being said to have *d.* s.p.—but, of his uncles, (1) Edward the 2d son of the 2d Bart., was living in 1632, was in Holy Orders, and left three sons (Edward, Robert, and Henry), of whom no more is known. (2) Robert, the 3d son of the said 2d Bart., bap. at Bromley, Kent, 23 July 1611, was living 1632; (3) Thomas the 4th son (the only son of the second wife), is the ancestor (through his *third* son, Charles), of Yelverton Peyton, who, in 1720, assumed the title, and through his *second* son Robert, of the family of Peyton, settled in Virginia, who, presumably, were the rightful heirs of the Baronetcy in and after 1720.

V. 1720. SIR YELVERTON PEYTON, Bart. [1611(1)], *assumed the Baronetcy* as cousin and h. male in March 1719/20, being s. and h. of Charles PEYTON, of Grimston and Swannington, Norfolk, by Elizabeth, da. of William BLADWELL of Swannington, in that co., which Charles (living 1688 with issue) was *third*(a) surv. s. of Thomas PEYTON, of Rougham, Norfolk(b), (*d.* 1683, aged 67), who was 3d s. (eldest s., by his 2d wife) of the 2d Bart. He was Capt. of the "Hector" Man of War. He *m.* Flower, da. of Philip FACY, of Plymouth. He *d.* s.p.s. 10 Oct. 1748, at North Runcton, Norfolk. Will pr. 1748. The admon. of his widow, as of North Runcton, 29 Oct. 1748, granted to her br. John Facey, the only next of kin.

VI. 1748. SIR CHARLES PEYTON, Bart. [1611(1)], nephew and h., being only s. and h. of Bladwell PEYTON, by Mary, da. of William PROBART, of Court Evangewenge, co. Radnor, which Bladwell was next br. of the late user of the title, on whose death, 10 Oct. 1748, he *assumed the Baronetcy.* He *m.* 14 March 1747, Ruth, da. of Henry Box (*d.* April 1718) of Hammersmith, Middlesex, and of the Inner Temple, s. of Alderman Sir Ralph Box. She was *bap.* 5 Feb. 1709/10, at Hammersmith, and *bur.* there 4 March 1748/9. Admon. 28 Sept. 1751, as of St. Clement Danes, Midx. He *d.* s.p. 6 Nov. 1760 at Hammersmith. Will pr. 1765.

VII. 1760. SIR JOHN PEYTON, Bart. [1611(1)], cousin and h., being s. and h. of John PEYTON, of Fleet street, London, distiller, by his 1st wife Dorothy, da. of James ALTHAM, of Markshall, in Latton, Essex, which John last named (who *d.* 22 Oct. 1741) was youngest br. of Yelverton Peyton who *assumed the Baronetcy* in 1720. He *assumed the Baronetcy* 6 Nov. 1760. He *d.* unm. 6 July 1772 in Villiers street, Strand.

VIII. 1773, to 1815. SIR YELVERTON PEYTON, Bart. [1611(1)], of Lynn, co. Norfolk, br. of the half blood, and h., being son of John PEYTON, Citizen of London abovenamed, by his 2d wife, Susan, da. of Peter CALVERT, of Hunsdon, Herts; *b.* about 1739; *assumed the Baronetcy* 6 July 1772. He *m.* 19 March 1773, at St. George the Martyr, Queen square, Midx., Rebecca, widow of Felix CALVERT, da. of Thomas BAYLY, of Arley, co. Warwick. She *d.* 20 Sep. 1812, aged 87. He *d.* s.p. 18 Oct. 1815, aged 76, when the issue male of Charles Peyton, of Grimston, Norfolk, ancestor of the holders of this Baronetcy after 1720, became *extinct.* Will pr. Nov. 1815.

(a) Of three elder sons (1) Thomas *d.* in 1637, aged but 6 weeks; (2) William Peyton, of Dublin, *m.* in 1686 Frances Lunsford, and *d.* s.p.s. about 1656; but (3) Robert Peyton, called "Major Robert Peyton," who settled in Virginia (about 1665, and was there living with issue 1688), is said to have had no less than five sons, Benjamin, Thomas, Robert, William and Ambrose, of whom the 2d son Thomas Peyton *m.* Frances Tabb, and had issue, "SIR JOHN PEYTON, of Isleham in Gloucester, county Virginia, who had issue JOHN PEYTON, only surv. s., *m.* Anne, da. of Henry Washington, and *d.* s.p.m." See *Her. and Gen.*, vol. vi, pp. 344—345, correcting (in many respects) the account therein, pp. 66—74, and stating positively that the male descendants, in Virginia, of the Peyton Baronets are *extinct*, and that Col. John Lewis Peyton (said to claim that title) is only collaterally related to the 1st Bart., he being 9th in descent (as there shewn) from Thomas Peyton, from whom the said 1st Bart. was 5th. It is not, however, very clear whether the successor in Virginia to Robert, the first settler (*d.* 1685) was not (as in page 68 of that work) "his eldest son SIR JOHN PEYTON, of Isleham" [Virginia], who *d.* s.p.m. legit., and was suc. by his nephew (son of his br. Robert) "SIR JOHN PEYTON, Bart., of Isleham. In this line the title and estate remained till 1776," when, "after the declaration of American independence the title was dropped. The estate of Isleham, however, remained in this line till about 1830, when, the male line failing, it was sold for distribution among the female descendants of the late Baronet (by hereditary right) who died in that year."

(b) By Elizabeth, da. of Sir William YELVERTON, 2d Bart. [1620], of Rougham aforesaid, which match introduced the christian name of 'Yelverton" to this family.

TOLLEMACHE, *or* TALLEMACH, *or* TALMACHE:
cr. 22 May 1611,
subsequently, 1696—1821, EARLS OF DYSART [S.];
ex. 9 March 1821.

I. 1611. "LIONEL TALLEMACH, of Hellingham [*i.e.* Helmingham], co. Suffolk, Esq.," s. and h. of Lionel TOLLEMACHE, of Helmingham aforesaid (*d.* 11 Dec. 1575, aged 30), by Susanna, da. of Sir Ambrose JERMYN, of Rushbrooke, Suffolk, was *bap.* 14 Dec. 1562(a), at Helmingham; Sheriff of Suffolk 1592-93, 1608-09, and again 1616-17, and was *cr. a Bart.*, as above, at the institution of that order, 22 May 1611(b), being subsequently *Knighted* at Whitehall, 24 May 1612(c). He *m.* 10 Feb. 1580-1, at North Elmham, Katharine, da. of Henry (CROMWELL) BARON CROMWELL, by Mary, da. of John (PAULETT), 2d MARQUESS of WINCHESTER. She *d.* 24 March 1620(d). He was living 1617, but *d.* before 1621.

II. 1620? SIR LIONEL TOLLEMACHE, Bart. [1611], of Helmingham, aforesaid, s. and h., *b.* 1 and *bap.* 15 Aug. 1591, at Helmingham, was *Knighted* v.p. 15 Nov. 1612, at Whitehall; *suc. to the Baronetcy* before 1621, being "as a Bart.," M.P. for Orford, 1621-22 and 1628-29; Privy Councillor to James I. and Charles I. He *m.* about 1620, Elizabeth, da. (whose issue in 1675 became coheir) of John (STANHOPE), 1st BARON STANHOPE OF HARRINGTON, by his 2d wife, Margaret, da. of Henry MACWILLIAMS. He *d.* 6 Sep. 1640, in his 49th year, and was *bur.* at Helmingham. M.I. Admon, 2 Nov. 1640. His widow (by whom he had thirteen children) *d.* about 1661. Will pr. 1661.

III. 1640. SIR LIONEL TOLLEMACHE, Bart. [1611], of Helmingham aforesaid, s. and h., *suc. to the Baronetcy*, 6 Sep. 1640. He *m.* before 22 May 1651, Elizabeth, *suo jure* COUNTESS OF DYSART, &c. [S.], by whom he had eleven children. He was *bur.* 25 March 1669, at Helmingham. Will pr. 1669. His widow, who was da. and h. of William (MURRAY), 1st EARL OF DYSART and LORD HUNTINGTOWER [S.], by Catharine, da. of (—) BRUCE, *m.* (as his second wife) 17 March 1671/2, being then "about 44," at Petersham, Surrey, John (MAITLAND), 1st DUKE OF LAUDERDALE [S.], who *d.* 24 Aug. 1682, aged 66. Her Grace *d.* 5 and was *bur.* 16 June 1698, at Petersham. Will pr. 1698.

IV. 1669. SIR LIONEL TOLLEMACHE, Bart. [1611], of Helmingham aforesaid; 1st surv. s. and h.; *b.* 30 Jan. 1648/9, at Helmingham; aged 15 in 1664 (*Visit. Suffolk*); *suc. to the Baronetcy* in March 1669; was M.P. for Suffolk, 1673-74; for Orford, 1678-79 and 1685-87; and for Suffolk (again) 1698 till 1707, when, as a Scotch Peer, he was by the Act of Union [S.], no longer eligible. He *m.* in 1680, shortly before 1 Nov., Grace, da. and coheir of Sir Thomas WILBRAHAM, 3d Bart. [1621], by Elizabeth, da. and h. of Edward MITTON. She survived him. On the death, 5 June 1698, of his mother, the Dow. DUCHESS OF LAUDERDALE [S.], he succeeded as EARL OF DYSART, &c. [S.] With this title the Baronetcy remained united till the death, s.p., of his great great grandson Wilbraham (TOLLEMACHE), EARL OF DYSART, &c. [S.], and 7th Bart. [1611], when it became *extinct*, though the Peerage [S.], devolved on his sister and heir of line.

(a) This is the child to whom at his baptism, "Aug. 1561" [*sic*], Queen Elizabeth is said (see Strickland's *Queens*) to have been godmother, presenting the mother with a lute, which is still at Helmingham. It has, however, been clearly shewn by "John A. C. Vincent," that the visit of Aug. 1561 was to Castle *Hedingham* (the Earl of Oxford's) and not to Helmingham, and that no Tollemache was bap. there in 1561. [*Genealogist*, N.S., vol. 1, pp. 82, 90, and p. 183; vol. ii, p. 192.]

(b) See an interesting account of the creation of this "favoured client of the Lord Privy Seal" in the *Her. and Gen.*, vol. iii, pp. 206-207.

(c) In 1612, no less than ten of the Baronets, who in the previous year had been as "Esquires" raised to that dignity, were Knighted. These were, on 9 April 1612, Sir Thomas Brudenell, Sir Lewis Tresham, and Sir John Shelley; on 24 May 1612, Sir Lionel Tollemache and Sir Thomas Spencer; on 8 June 1612, Sir John Molyneux, Sir George Gresley, and Sir Thomas Puckering; on 21 July 1612, Sir Robert Napier; and, on 19 Aug. 1612, Sir Edward Devereux.

CLIFTON
cr. 22 May 1611,
afterwards, 1837-69, JUCKES-CLIFTON;
ex., presumably, 30 May 1869,
assumed since 1880.

I. 1611. "JERVASE CLIFTON, of Clifton, co. Nottingham, Knight," posthumous s. and h. of George Clifton (who *d.* v.p. 1 Aug. 1587, in his 21st year), by Winifred, da. of Sir Anthony THOROLD, of Marston, co. Lincoln, and grandson and h. of Sir Gervase Clifton, of Clifton Hall in Clifton aforesaid (who was popularly known as "Gervase the Gentle"), suc. his said grandfather 20 Jan. 1587/8, being then aged 4 months and 11 days; was made K.B. at the coronation, 25 July 1603, (being then aged 16) and was *cr. a Bart.*, as above, at the institution of that order, 22 May 1611. He was Sheriff of Notts, 1610-11; served in nine Parliaments, being M.P. for Notts, 1614-25; for Nottingham, 1626; for Notts (again), 1628-29; for Retford, 1640, till disabled in 1644; and for Notts (again) 1661-66. He was distinguished for his loyalty, having to pay as much as £7,625 to the sequestrators of estates of delinquents, as a composition. He *m.* no less than seven times,(a) viz.:—firstly, in or shortly before 1613, Penelope, 2d da. of Robert (RICH), 1st EARL OF WARWICK, by his first wife Penelope, da. of Walter (DEVEREUX), EARL OF ESSEX. She *d.* 26 Oct. 1613, aged 23, and was buried in Clifton church. M.I. He *m.* secondly, about 1614, Frances, 2d da. of Francis (CLIFFORD) 4th EARL OF CUMBERLAND, by Grissel, da. of Thomas HUGHES. She *d.* 22 Oct. 1627, aged 33, and was *bur.* 23d at Clifton church aforesaid. M.I. He *m.* thirdly, 5 May 1629, at St. Giles', Cripplegate, Mary, widow of Sir Frances LEKE, da. of John EGIOKE, of Egioke, co. Worcester, and Anne his wife. By her, however, he had no issue. She *d.* 19 and was *bur.* 22 Jan. 1630/1, at St. Giles, Cripplegate, London. M.I. in Clifton church. Admon. 28 Jan. 1630/1. He *m.* fourthly, 17 May 1632, at St. Gregory's by St. Paul's, London, Isabel, widow of John HODGES, Alderman and sometime (1622-23) Sheriff of London, da. of Thomas MEEKE, of Wolverhampton. She *d.* s.p., and was *bur.* 10 July 1637, at Clifton aforesaid. Admon. 17 Aug. 1637, to her husband. He *m.* fifthly Anne, da. of Sir Francis SOUTH, of Kelsterne, co. Lincoln. She *d.* s.p. and was *bur.* 1 June 1639, at Clifton aforesaid. He *m.* sixthly, 17 Feb. 1639, at Rampton, Notts, Jane, da. of Anthony EYRE, of Rampton. She, who was *bap.* at Rampton 23 Nov. 1618, *d.* in London, and was *bur.* 17 March 1655, at Clifton aforesaid. He *m.* seventhly, 17 Dec. 1656, at St. Andrew's Undershaft, London (reg. at St. Giles' in the Fields), Alice, da. of Henry (HASTINGS), 5th EARL OF HUNTINGDON, by Elizabeth, da. and coheir of Ferdinando (STANLEY) 5th EARL OF DERBY. He *d.* 28 June 1666, aged 80, and was *bur.* 2 Aug., with great solemnity, attended by the Heralds, at Clifton aforesaid(b). His widow *d.* s.p. a few months after him, and was *bur.* 29 March 1667, at St. Giles' in the Fields, Midx. Will pr. 1667.

II. 1666. SIR GERVASE CLIFTON, Bart. [1611], of Clifton Hall in Clifton aforesaid, s. and h. by first wife, *b.* about 1612; *suc. to the Baronetcy*, 28 June 1666. He *m.* Sarah, da. of Timothy PUSEY, of Selston, Notts. She *d.* at Norton, Cheshire, 22 Jan. 1652. He *d.* s.p. 14 Jan. 1675. Both *bur.* at Clifton aforesaid. M.I.

III. 1675. SIR WILLIAM CLIFTON, Bart. [1611], of Clifton Hall aforesaid, nephew and h., being s. and h. of Sir Clifford Clifton, by Frances, da. of Sir Heneage FINCH, Recorder of London, which Clifford (who *d.* 22 June 1670), was s. of the 1st Bart. by his 2d wife. He was *bap.* 7 April 1663, at Kensington; *suc. to the Baronetcy* in Jan. 1675. He *d.* unm. in France, and was *bur.* 8 June 1686, at Clifton. Will pr. June 1686.

(a) See *Herald and Genealogist*, vol. vii, p. 568, for an account of another husband of *seven* wives. King Henry VIII had but six.

(b) An interesting account of his death is given in Thoroton's *Notts*, and copied thence in the Baronetages of *Wotton*, *Betham*, etc.

IV. 1686. Sir Gervase Clifton, Bart. [1611], of Clifton Hall aforesaid, cousin and h., being s. and h. of Robert Clifton, by Sarah, da. of Nathaniel Parkhurst, of Woodford, Essex, which Robert was third s. (the only s. by his 6th wife) of the 1st Bart. He *suc. to the Baronetcy* in 1686, was aged 27 in 1693, and was a Roman Catholic. He *m.* Anne, da. of Dudley Bagnall, of Newry, in Ireland. He *d.* 27 Feb. or 6 March 1730/1, and was *bur.* at Clifton, having had no less than fifteen sons, of whom, however, ten *d.* unm. Will pr. April 1731. His widow *m.* Sep. 1734, William Blackburne, of Ongar, Essex, and *d.* at Boulogne.

V. 1731. Sir Robert Clifton, Bart. [1611], of Clifton Hall aforesaid, s. and h., who v.p. had been made K.B. on the revival of that Order, 27 May 1725. He was *b.* and *bap.* 1690, at Clifton; *suc. to the Baronetcy*, 27 Feb. 1730/1; was M.P. for East Retford, 1727-34 and 1734-41. He *m.* firstly, 28 Aug. 1723, Frances, da. and h. of Nanfan (Coote), Earl of Bellomont [I.], by Lucia Anna, da. of Henry, Count of Nassau. She *d.* s.p.m. 14 and was *bur.* 17 April 1733 at Clifton(a). He *m.* secondly, 2 June 1740, Hannah, 1st da. and coheir of Sir Thomas Lombe, Alderman and sometime [1727-28] Sheriff of London, by Elizabeth, da. of John Turner, of Heden, co. Kent. She *d.* 16 and was *bur.* 27 May 1748, at Clifton. He *m.* thirdly, 11 Feb. 1756, at St. John's the Evangelist, Westminster, Judith, da. of Capt. Thwaites, of the East India Company, by Judith (afterwards Dame Judith Leighton), da. of John Elwick, a director of the East India Company. He *d.* 7 and was *bur.* 12 Dec. 1762, at Clifton. His widow *d.* 13 May 1765, and was *bur.* there. Her will pr. 1766.

VI. 1762. Sir Gervase Clifton, Bart. [1611], of Clifton Hall aforesaid, s. and h. by 2d wife, *b.* 31 May 1744; *suc. to the Baronetcy* before April 1766; Sheriff of Notts, 1767-68. He *m.*, 14 April 1766, at St. Marylebone, Frances Egerton, da. and h. of Richard Lloyd, of Aberbrachar, co. Denbigh, and Trelydon, co. Montgomery, by Dorothy, sister of the Rev. Juckes Egerton, of Trelydon aforesaid. She, who was *bap.* 18 Sep. 1746 at Guilsfield, co. Montgomery, *d.* (of putrid fever caught by attending on her sons) 11 and was *bur.* 17 Sep. 1779, at Clifton. He *d.* 26 Sep. 1815, aged 71. Will pr. 1815.

VII. 1815. Sir Robert Clifton, Bart. [1611], of Clifton Hall aforesaid, s. and h., *b.* June 1767; ed. at Rugby School, 1782; *suc. to the Baronetcy*, 26 Sep. 1815; Sheriff of Notts, 1820. He *d.* unm., 29 April 1837, at Clifton aforesaid, aged 70. Will pr. May 1837.

VIII. 1837. Sir Juckes-Granville Juckes-Clifton, Bart. [1611], of Clifton Hall and Trelydon aforesaid, br. and h., *b.* 1769; ed. at Rugby School, 1782; took the name of *Juckes* only, by Royal lic., 2 Sep. 1790, under the will (dat. and pr. Feb. 1772) of his great uncle, the Rev. Jukes Egerton aforesaid, on suc. to the estate of that family; *suc. to the Baronetcy*, 29 April 1837, and thereon assumed the addit. name of *Clifton*, which was confirmed by Royal lic. 6 Dec. 1837. He *m.*, firstly, 1794, Margaret, da. of James de Lancy, of Bath, co. Somerset. He *m.*, secondly, 21 Aug. 1821, Marianne Margarita, da. of John Swinfen, of Swinfen, co. Stafford, by his second wife Anne, sister of Sir Francis Ford, 1st Bart. [1798]. He *d.* 1 Oct. 1852, at Clifton Hall, aged 83. Will pr. April 1853. His widow *d.* 20 Dec. 1860, at 20, Bruton street, St. Geo., Han. sq., aged 69. Both *bur.* at Clifton.

IX. 1852, to 1869. Sir Robert Juckes-Clifton, Bart. [1611], of Clifton Hall aforesaid, s. and h. by 2d wife, *b.* 24 Dec. 1826, and *bap.* 20 Jan. 1827, at Guilsfield, co. Montgomery; educated at Eton and at Christ Church, Oxford; matric. 14 Nov. 1844; *suc. to the Baronetcy*, 1 Oct. 1852; M.P. for Nottingham, 1861-66, and again 1868-69; author of a pamphlet called *Turkey in 1860*, for which he obtained the Order of the Medjidie from the

(a) Frances, her only da. and h., *m.*, March 1747 George, (Carpenter) 1st Earl of Tyrconnel [I.], which family inherited the Coote and Nanfan estates in Worcestershire.

Sultan. He *m.*, 4 March 1863, at St. James', Westm., Geraldine Isabella, da. of Colonel John O'Meara. He *d.* s.p. of typhoid fever, at Clifton Hall, 30 March and was *bur.* 7 April 1869, aged 42, at Clifton, when *the Baronetcy* became, apparently, *extinct.*(a) His widow living in 1899, at Dawlish, Devon.

In the annual issue of Dod's *Peerage and Baronetage*, 1870 to 1884, *no* mention is made of this title, but in that from 1885 to 1887 it is stated that "*this title*, which is presumed to have become *extinct* in 1869, has been *assumed* by Mr. Francis Clifton, of The Hollies, Fulham, S.W." From the issue in 1888 of that work, and the subsequent ones, the following information is obtained.

XI.(b) *1880* "Sir Francis Clifton," 11th [*sic*] Bart.(b) [1611], 1st s. of Marshall Waller Clifton(c), F.R.S. [M.L.C. and J.P. of the Colony of Australia], by Elinor, da. of Daniel Bell, of Wandle House, Surrey; *b.* 1812; *suc. his cousin* in this Baronetcy, 1880. He *m.* firstly, 1840, Eleanor Louisa, da. of Major John Martin. He *m.* secondly, 1861, Marion Fergus, da. of Alexander Manson, of Paisley. She *d.* 1882. [He *d.* s.p.m. 13 Jan. 1892, aged 79, at Silverdale, Putney, the residence of his br., George.]

XII. 1892. "Sir Waller Clifton, 12th Bart." [(1611) br. and heir male to the late holder of the Baronetcy, being a yr.], s. of Marshall Waller Clifton, Chief Commissioner of Australia; *b.* 1813; was for many years in the Admiralty; J.P. of Westminster. He, who resided at "The Hollies, Fulham, S.W.," *d.* s.p.m. [unm. ?] 3 Jan. 1894, aged 80.

XIII. 1894. "Sir Robert Symmons Clifton, 13th Bart." (1611) nephew and h. male to the late holder of the Baronetcy, being s. of William Pearce Clifton, Resident Magistrate of Bunbury, West Australia, by Amy, da. of Charles Symmons, Police Magistrate, of Fremantle, West Australia; *b.* 1879; "*suc. his uncle*, 1893" [*sic*, but should be 1894].

GERARD, *or* GERRARD:
cr. 22 May 1611;
afterwards, since 1876, Barons Gerard of Bryn.

I. 1611. "Thomas Gerrard, of Brynne,(d) co. Lancaster, Knt.," s. and h. of Sir Thomas Gerard, of Bryn aforesaid, by Elizabeth, 1st da. and coheir of Sir John Port, of Etwall, co. Derby, *b.* 1560; matric. at Oxford

(a) His uncle, Gen. Sir Arthur Benjamin Clifton, G.C.B., the heir presumptive to the Baronetcy, died unm. but a few days before him, 7 March 1869, at 52 Old Steyne, Brighton, in his 99th year. The representation of the family devolved on the late Baronet's only sister and h., Marianne-Margaret, who *m.*, 12 June 1842, Sir Henry Hervey Bruce, 4th Bart. [1804], and had issue. The estates, however, passed to Henry Robert Markham (grandson and h. of the Ven. Robert Markham, Archdeacon of York, by Frances, the only sister of the 7th and 8th Barts.), who, by royal lic. dat. 6 Aug. 1869, took the name of Clifton.

(b) It is to be observed that the existence of a 10th Bart., who enjoyed the title from 1869 to 1880, is, here presumed, who (in the edit. of Dod's *Peerage*, etc., of 1893) is said to have been "the heir male of the 4th Bart.," and that on his death, and the consequent failure of issue male from the 4th Bart., it was "claimed by the present holder and his predecessors [*sic*] as descendants of the 1st Baronet.'

(c) No indication is given as to the descent of this gentleman from any of the Clifton Baronets (or even as to his parentage), but as the issue male of the 4th Bart. is said to have failed (see note next above), and as the 3d and 2d Barts. *d.* s.p., it must have been through the 1st Bart. only.

(d) "Le Bryn" is in the parish of Winwick, in the hundred of West Derby, co. Lancaster.

(Bras. Coll.), 20 July 1578, aged 18; Student of the Inner Temple, 1579; suc. his father in the family estates, Sep. 1601; *Knighted*, 18 April 1603, and was *cr. a Bart.* as above, at the institution of that order, 22 May 1611, the £1,000, that was due to the Crown for such creation, being returned in consideration of his Father's sufferings in the cause of Mary, Queen of Scotland, the King's mother; M.P. for Liverpool, 1597-98; for Lancashire 1614, and for Wigan 1621. He *m.*, firstly, about 1580, Cecily, da. of Sir Walter Manney, of Staplehurst.(a) He *m.*, secondly, after 1606, Mary, widow of Sir Robert Lee (sometime, 1602, 03, L. Mayor of London), and formerly of William Smith, of that city, da. of Sir James Hawes, sometime (1574-75) L. Mayor thereof, by Audrey, da. of John Copwood. By her he had no issue.(a) He *m.*, thirdly, Mary, widow of Sir Edward Uvedale (*d.* 1606), and formerly of the Hon. Anthony Browne (*d.* v.p. 29 June 1592), da. of Sir William Dormer, of Wing, Bucks, by Dorothy, da. of Anthony Catesby. By her, also, he had no issue. He *d.* and was *bur.* 16 Feb. 1620/4, at St. Margaret's, Westm. Inq. p.m. 1621. Will dat. 13 Feb. 1620/1, pr. 5 May 1621. The will of his widow, as "of Riverpark, in the parish of Tilleton, co. Sussex, in which she directs to be bur. at Midhurst in that county, dat. 20 July, and pr. 23 Nov. 1637.

II. 1621. Sir Thomas Gerard, Bart. [1611], of Bryn and of Etwall aforesaid, s. and h., by 1st wife; *b.* about 1584, being 36 when he *suc. to the Baronetcy* in Feb. 1620/1; M.P. for Liverpool, 1624-25. He *m.*, about 1610, Frances, sister of Richard, 1st Viscount Molyneux of Maryborough [I.], da. of Sir Richard Molyneux, 1st Bart. [1611(1)], of Sefton, co. Lanc., by Frances, da. of Sir Gilbert Gerard, Master of the Rolls. She is, presumably, "the wife of Mr. Thomas Gered," stated to have been *bur.* 28 Feb. 1613/4, at Winwick, co. Lancaster. He *d.* 15 May 1630 (*Visit. Lanc.*, 1665).

III. 1630? Sir William Gerard, Bart. [1611] of Bryn and Etwall aforesaid, s. and h., *b.* in 1612; *suc. to the Baronetcy* on his father's death; Gov. of Denbigh Castle. He expended considerable sums (said to amount to £100,000) in the cause of Charles I, and sold the estate of Etwall in Derbyshire. His lands were sequestrated. Entered his ped. in 1665 (*Visit. Lanc.*), being then aged 53. On 37 Feb. 1671/2 was admitted to Lincoln's Inn. He *m.*, in or before 1638, Elizabeth, 1st da. of Sir Cuthbert Clifton, of Lytham, co. Lancaster, by his 1st wife Ann, da. of Thomas Tildersley, of Morley, in that county. He was *bur.* 7 April 1681, at Winwick.

IV. 1681. Sir William Gerard, Bart. [1611], of Bryn, aforesaid, and of Garswood, co. Lancaster, s. and h.; *b.* 1638; aged 27 in April 1665; *suc. to the Baronetcy*, April 1681. He. *m.*, firstly, in or shortly before 1662, Anne, da. of Sir John Preston, 1st Bart. [1644] of Furness, by Jane, da. and coheir of Thomas Morgan, of Weston, co. Warwick. He *m.*, secondly, Mary, widow of James Poole, of Poole, co. Chester, sister of Sir Edward Mostyn, 1st Bart. [1670], and da. of John Mostyn, of Talacre, co. Flint, by Anne, da. of Henry Fox, of Lehurst, Salop. By her he had no issue. He was *bur.* 16 April, 1702, at Winwick. She (as "Lady Mary Gerard, widow, of Birchley") was *bur.* there 30 Jan. 1717/8.

V. 1702. Sir William Gerard, Bart. [1611], of Bryn and Garswood aforesaid) s. and h. by 1st wife, *bap.* 22 June 1662 at Winwick; aged 3 in 1665; *suc. to the Baronetcy* in April 1702; was one of the English Catholic nonjurors in 1715. He *m.*, in or before 1697, Mary, 2d da., but eventually sole h. of John Causfield, of Causfield, by Elizabeth, da. of James Anderton, of Birchley. She was *b.* 22 June (her husband's birthday), 1671. He was *bur.* 29 May 1721, at Winwick. His widow was *bur.* there 18 July 1726.

VI. 1721. Sir William Gerard, Bart. [1611], of Bryn and Garswood aforesaid, and sometime of Richmond, co. Surrey, s. and h., *b.* 27 Dec. 1697; *suc. to the Baronetcy* in 1721. He *m.*, about 1720, Elizabeth, 4th da.

(a) The burial of "My Ladie Gerrard," 1 Oct. 1612, at Winwick, may apply to her.

of Thomas Clifton, of Lytham, co. Lancaster, by Eleanora Alathea, da. of Richard Walmesley. He *d.* 9 Dec. 1732 at Ghent, in Flanders. Admon. 17 May 1733, his widow being then living.(a)

VII. 1732. Sir William Gerard, Bart. [1611], of Bryn and Garswood aforesaid, s. and h., *b.* 4 Sep. 1721; *suc. to the Baronetcy*, 9 Dec. 1732. He *d.* a minor and unm., 22 March 1740.

VIII. 1740. Sir Thomas Gerard, Bart. [1611], of Bryn and Garswood aforesaid, br. and h., *b.* about 1723; *suc. to the Baronetcy* 22 March 1740. He *m.* Elizabeth, da. of (—) Tasburgh. "Lady Gerard, wife of Sir Thomas, Bart.," *d.* 1768 (*Gent. Mag.*). He *d.* s p.m.(b) in Upper Seymour street, Marylebone, and was *bur.* 7 July 1780, at Winwick, aged 57. Will pr. July 1783.

IX. 1780. Sir Robert-Cansfield Gerard of Bryn and Garswood aforesaid, br. and h. male, *b.* about 1725; *suc. to the Baronetcy* 1780. He *m.*, about 1770, Catherine, da. of William Anderton, of Euxton Hall, co. Lancaster, by Mary, relict of Thomas Clifton of Lytham, and da. of Richard (Molyneux), 5th Viscount Molyneux of Maryborough [I.], by Mary, da. of Francis Brudenell, *styled* Lord Brudenell. He *d.* 6 and was *bur.* 11 March 1784, at Winwick, aged 59. Will pr. May, 1784. His widow *d.* at Richmond. co. York, 13 and was *bur.* 22 Jan. 1821, at Winwick, aged 79. Will pr. 1821.

X. 1784. Sir Robert-Clifton Gerard, Bart. [1611], of Bryn and Garswood aforesaid, s. and h.; *suc. to the Baronetcy* 6 March 1784. He *d.* a minor and unm., 26 Aug. 1791, at Liege.

XI. 1791. Sir William Gerard, Bart. [1611], of Bryn and Garswood aforesaid, br. and h., *b.* 12 July 1773; *suc. to the Baronetcy* 25 Aug. 1791. He *m.*, 21 Dec. 1795, Anna-Maria, da. of William Stapylton, of Richmond, co. York. She *d.* 13 and was *bur.* 20 Sep. 1808 at Winwick, aged 31. He *d.* s.p. 2 and was *bur.* 9 Aug. 1826, at Winwick, aged 73.

XII. 1826. Sir John Gerard, Bart. [1611], of Bryn and Garswood aforesaid, nephew and h., being s. and h. of John Gerard, of Windle Hall, co. Lancaster, by Elizabeth, da. of Edward Ferrers, of Baddesley Clinton, co. Warwick, which John was 3d s. of the 9th Bart., and *d.* 22 May 1882. He was *b.* 8 Dec. 1804; *suc. to the Baronetcy*, 2 Aug. 1826; was Col. of the 3d Regt. of Royal Lancashire Militia. He *m.*, 3 Dec. 1827, Monica, da. of Thomas Strickland-Standish, of Standish, co. Lancaster, by his 1st wife, Anastacia, da. and coheir of Sir John Lawson, Bart. He *d.* s.p. 21 Feb. 1854, at Lower Grove House, Roehampton, aged 50. His widow *d.* 4 May 1865, at Brighton, aged 60, and was *bur.* in the Rom. Cath. cemetery at East Sheen, Surrey.

XIII. 1854. Sir Robert-Tolver Gerard Bart. [1611], of Bryn and Garwood aforesaid, br. and h.; *b.* 12 May 1808, at Sutton, co. Lancaster; sometime (1828-37) an officer in the Army; *suc. to the Baronetcy*, 21 Feb. 1854; Sheriff of Lancashire, 1859. He *m.*, 14 Feb. 1849, at the Rom. Cath. church, St. John's Wood, Midx., Harriet, da. of Edward Clifton, of Clifton and Lytham, co. Lancaster, by Elizabeth, da. of Thomas Scarisbrick-Eccleston. She was living when he was *cr.*, 18 Jan. 1876, BARON GERARD OF BRYN, co. Lancaster, in which peerage this *Baronetcy* then *merged*, and still so continues. See *Peerage*.

(a) "Lady Elizabeth Gerard, of London," *bur.* 1 Sep. 1783, at Winwick; will pr. Sep. 1783.

(b) Of his two daughters and coheirs, Clare, the youngest, *d.* 1798, bequeathing a large portion of her fortune to the poor.

ASTON:

cr. 22 May 1611,

afterwards, 1627-1751, LORDS ASTON OF FORFAR [S.];

ex. 24 Aug. 1751.

I. 1611. "WALTER ASTON, of Tixall, co. Stafford, Knt.," 1st surv. s. and h. of Sir Edward ASTON,(a) of the same, by his 2d wife, Anne, da. of Sir Thomas LUCY, of Charlecote, co. Warwick; was *bap.* at Charlecote, 9 July 1584; suc. his father, 1598; was made K.B. at the coronation, 25 July 1603, and was *cr. a Bart.*, as above, at the institution of that order, 22 May 1611. Gent. of the Privy Chamber to Charles I. He *m.*, about 1607, Gertrude, only da. of Sir Thomas SADLEIR, Knt., of Standon, Herts, by his 2d wife, Gertrude, da. of Robert MARKHAM, of Cotham, Notts. She was living 1616. He was *cr.*, 28 Nov. 1627, LORD ASTON OF FORFAR [S.], with rem. to his heirs male for ever, bearing the name of Aston. In that peerage this *Baronetcy* then *merged*, and so continued till the death of the 5th Lord and 5th Baronet, 24 Aug. 1751, when *the Baronetcy became extinct*, though the peerage [S.] was assumed, possibly lawfully, by the collateral heir male till 21 Jan. 1845, since which date it has been dormant. See *Peerage*.

KNYVETT:

cr. 22 May 1611;

ex. 9 Oct. 1699.

I. 1611. "PHILIP KNYVETT, of Bucknam, co. Norfolk, Esq.," s. and h. of Sir Thomas KNYVETT, of Buckenham Castle, co. Norfolk, by Katharine, da. of Sir Thomas LOVELL, of East Harling in that county; was *cr. a Bart.*, as above, at the institution of that order, 22 May 1611. He alienated the castle and estate of Buckenham. He *m.* Katharine, da. and h. of Charles FORD, of Butley Abbey, Suffolk (disinherited by his father, 1600), by Elizabeth, da. and h. of John JERNEGAN, of Somerleyton. She was *bur.* 25 Sep. 1647, at St. Martin's in the Fields. Admon. 1647 and 27 March 1650. He, who sold his estate of Buckenham before 1650, *d.* in Baldwin's Gardens, and was *bur.* 28 Feb. 1654/5, at St. Andrew's, Holborn. Admon. 13 March 1654/5.

II. 1655, to 1699. SIR ROBERT KNYVETT, Bart. [1611], s. and h.; *suc. to the Baronetcy* in Feb. 1654/5. He *m.* firstly, Elizabeth, da. of William LUDLEY, of Middleham, co. York. He *m.* secondly, Dorothy, da. of William THORNBOROUGH, of Salstead, Westmorland. He *m.* thirdly, Philippa, da. of Thomas RUSSELL, of Barsham, Norfolk. He *d.* s.p. and was *bur.* 9 Oct. 1699, at St. Giles' in the Fields, Midx., when the *Baronetcy* became *extinct*. Will, as of St. Clement Danes, Midx., dat. 14 July 1696, and pr. 19 Oct. 1699, by Philippa, the relict.

SAINT JOHN:

cr. 22 May, 1611,

afterwards, 1716-51, VISCOUNTS ST. JOHN,

and subsequently, since 1751, VISCOUNTS BOLINGBROKE AND ST. JOHN.

I. 1611. "JOHN ST. JOHN, of Lideard Tregos, co. Wilts, Knt.," s. and h. of Sir John ST. JOHN, of the same, by Lucy, da. and h. of Sir Walter HUNGERFORD, of Farley, in that county; matric. at Oxford (Trin. Coll.) 3 April 1601; was admitted to Lincoln's Inn, 1604; *Knighted* at Whitehall, 2 Feb. 1608/9, and was *cr. a Bart.*, as above, at the institution of that order, 22 May 1611. He was M.P. for Wilts, 1624-25. By the death of his uncle Oliver (ST. JOHN), 1st VISCOUNT GRANDISON [I.], he *suc.* 30 Dec. 1630, to the manors of Battersea and Wandsworth, Surrey. Sheriff of Wilts, 1632-33. He was zealously attached to the Royal cause, in which three of his sons were slain during the Civil

Wars. He *m.* firstly, Anne, da. of Sir Thomas LEIGHTON, of Feckenham, co. Worcester. He *m.* secondly, Margaret, widow of Sir Richard GRUBHAM. She *d.* before 24 Nov. 1637, when admon. of her goods was granted. He was *bur.* 1648, at Battersea (though there is no entry thereof in the register) with such unusual pomp that his executor was prosecuted by the College of Arms. Will pr. 1648.

II. 1648. SIR JOHN ST. JOHN, Bart. [1611], of Lydiard Tregoze aforesaid, grandson and h., being s. and h. of Oliver ST. JOHN, by Catharine, da. and coheir of Horatio (VERE), BARON VERE of Tilbury which Oliver, who was s. and h. ap. of the 1st Bart., *d.* v.p. Nov. 1641, aged about 28. He was *b.* about 1637, and *suc. to the Baronetcy* in 1648. He *d.* unm., 1657, aged 20 years and 9 months. Will pr. 1657.

III. 1657. SIR WALTER ST. JOHN, Bart. [1611], of Lydiard Tregoze and Battersea aforesaid, uncle and h., *b.* about 1622; *suc. to the Baronetcy* in 1657; M.P. for Wilts, 1656-58 and 1659; for Wotton Bassett, 1660-79; for Wilts (again), 1679-81 and 1690-95. He was famed for "piety and moral virtues." He *m.*, in or before 1651, Johanna, da. of Oliver ST. JOHN, of Longthorpe, co. Northampton, Lord Chief Justice of the Common Pleas (1648-60) by his 1st wife Johanna, da. and h. of Sir James ALTHAM. Her will pr. Feb. 1705. He *d.* 3 and was *bur.* 9 July 1708, at Battersea, in his 87th year. Will pr. July 1708.

IV. 1708. SIR HENRY ST. JOHN, Bart. [1611], of Battersea aforesaid, only s. and h.; *b.* about 1652, at Battersea; Fellow Comm. of Caius Coll., Cambridge, 29 May 1668, aged 16; M.A. (St. John's Coll.) per lit. regias 1669; incorporated at Oxford, 13 July 1669, where he was *cr.* D.C.L. 27 Aug. 1702; was M.P. during 21 years, for Wootton Basset, 1679-95; for Wilts, 1695-98; and for Wootton Basset (again) 1698-1700. He *suc. to the Baronetcy*, 3 July 1708. He *m.* firstly, 11 Dec. 1673, at Lees, co. Essex, Mary, 2d da. and coheir of Robert (RICH), 2d EARL OF WARWICK, by his second wife, Anne, da. of Sir Thomas CHEEKE. He *m.* secondly, 1 Jan. 1686/7, at St. Anne's, Soho (Lic. Vic. Gen., she aged 20) Angelica Magdelina Wharton, widow, da. of George PELISSARY, Treasurer of the Navy to Louis XIV of France. She was living when, on 2 July 1716, he was *cr.* VISCOUNT AND BARON ST. JOHN OF BATTERSEA, co. Surrey, with *spec. rem.* to his 2d and 3d sons respectively, and finally to the heirs male of his own body. In that peerage this *Baronetcy* then *merged* and so continues, the 3d Viscount and 6th Baronet becoming, by inheritance, 15 Dec. 1751, VISCOUNT BOLINGBROKE (*cr.* 1712), a peerage of some 4 years greater antiquity. See *Peerage*.

SHELLEY:

cr. 22 May 1611.

I. 1611. "JOHN SHELLEY, of Michelgrove, co. Sussex, Esq.," s. and h. of John SHELLEY, of the same, by Eleanor, da. of Sir Thomas LOVELL, of East Harling, Norfolk, was *cr. a Bart.* 22 May 1611, as above, being the 18th and last of the eighteen Baronets with whom that order was instituted. He was subsequently, 9 April 1612, *Knighted* at Whitehall.(a) He *m.* Jane, da. of Sir Thomas RERESBY, of Thribergh, co. York, by Mary, da. of Sir John MONSON, of South Carlton, co. Lincoln. Both *d.* in or before 1644. His admon., 14 Nov. 1644, and hers, as a widow, 15 Nov. 1644.

II. 1644? SIR CHARLES SHELLEY, Bart. [1611], of Michelgrove aforesaid, grandson and h., being s. and h. of Sir William Shelley (Knt.), by Christiana Maria, da. of Sir James VANTELET, which William, who was s. and h. ap. of the 1st Bart., *d.* v.p. 1635, his admon. being dated 22 Nov. 1639. He *suc. to the Baronetcy* in or about 1644. He *m.* firstly, 2 March 1651/2, at St. Dionis Backchurch, London, Elizabeth, da. of Hon. Benjamin WESTON (4th s. of

(a) See p. 18, note "c," *sub* "Tollemache," as to several Baronets so Knighted.

Richard, EARL OF PORTLAND), by Elizabeth, Dow. COUNTESS OF ANGLESEY, da. of William SHELDON, of Hornby, co. Leicester. He *m.* secondly, after 1666, Mary, Dow. BARONESS ABERGAVENNY, da. of Thomas GIFFORD, M.D., of Dunton Waylett, Essex, by Anne, da. and h. of Gregory BROOKSBY, of Burstall, co. Leicester. He *d.* 1681, and was *bur.* at Rouen in France. His widow, by whom he had no issue, *d.* and was *bur.* from St. Giles' in the Fields 14 Nov. 1699 at St. Pancras, Midx.

III. 1681. SIR JOHN SHELLEY, Bart., [1611], of Michelgrove aforesaid, 1st surv. s. and h. by first wife; *b.* after 1662(a); *suc. to the Baronetcy* about 1681. He *m.* firstly, Winifred, only da. of George (NEVILLE), LORD ABERGAVENNY, by Mary, da. of Thomas GIFFORD, both abovementioned. She, whose issue became heir (in 1695) to her brother George, LORD ABERGAVENNY, *d.* s.p.m. and was *bur.* 24 May 1687 at Clapham, Sussex. He *m.* secondly, about 1690, Mary, da. and eventually coheir of Sir John GAGE, 4th Bart. [1622], of Firle, co. Sussex, by his 1st wife, Mary, da. of Robert MIDDLEMORE, of Edgbaston, co. Warwick. He *d.* 25 and was *bur.* 28 April 1703 at Clapham, Sussex. Will dat. 2 June 1702, pr. 1703. His widow *m.* George MATHEW, of Thurles, co. Tipperary, and was living April 1717. Her will pr. 1722.

IV. 1703. SIR JOHN SHELLEY, Bart. [1611], of Michelgrove aforesaid, s. and h. by second wife, *b.* 5 and *bap.* 6 March 1691/2, at Clapham aforesaid; *suc. to the Baronetcy*, 25 April 1703. He conformed to the established religion, 26 Feb. 1716. Was M.P. for Arundel, 1727-41, and for Lewes, Dec. 1743 to 1747. He *m.* firstly, 21 May 1717, Catharine, da. of Sir Thomas SCAWEN, Alderman of London, by Martha, his wife. She *d.* s.p.m. through a fall from her horse, and was *bur.* 3 Oct. 1726, at Clapham aforesaid, aged 32. He *m.* secondly, 16 March 1726/7, at St. Giles' in the Fields, Margaret, sister of Thomas, 1st DUKE OF NEWCASTLE, 5th da. of Thomas (PELHAM), 1st BARON PELHAM OF LAUGHTON, by Grace, da. of Gilbert (HOLLES,) EARL OF CLARE. She *d.* 24 Nov. 1758, aged 58. Admon. 3 Feb. 1759. He *d.* 6 Sep. 1771, aged 81. Both *bur.* at Clapham aforesaid. Will pr. Feb. 1771.

V. 1771. SIR JOHN SHELLEY, Bart. [1611], of Michelgrove aforesaid, only s. and h. by 2d wife; *b.* about 1730; *suc. to the Baronetcy*, 6 Sep. 1771; was M.P. for East Retford, Dec. 1751 to 1758, and for Newark, 1768-74. Keeper of the Records in the Tower of London, Clerk of the Pipe in the Exchequer, Treasurer of the Household, 1766-77, and P.C., 1766. He *m.* 27 Aug. 1769, Wilhelmina, da. of John NEWNHAM, of Maresfield Park, Sussex. She *d.* 21 March 1772, aged 23, and was *bur.* at Clapham. He *m.* secondly, 14 Feb. 1775, at Stoke Newington, Middlesex, Elizabeth, da. of Edward WOODCOCK, of Lincoln's Inn. He *d.* 11 Sep. 1783. Will pr. Oct. 1783. His widow *m.* 18 Sep. 1790, at Castle Malwood in Binstead, Hants, John STEWART, M.D., of Southampton. She *d.* 22 Dec. 1808, and was *bur.* at Southampton.

VI. 1783. SIR JOHN SHELLEY, Bart. [1611], of Michelgrove, and subsequently (1814) of Maresfield Park aforesaid, s. and h., by 1st wife; *b.* 3 March 1772, at Michelgrove; *suc. to the Baronetcy*, 11 Sep. 1783; ed. at Winchester and at Eton; Ensign, Coldstream Guards, 1790; Lieut., 1793-94, having served at Famars and (1793) at Valenciennes. M.P. for Helston, April to Oct. 1806, and for Lewes, 1816-31. He *m.*, 4 June 1807, at St. Geo. Han. sq., Frances, da. and h. of Thomas WINCKLEY, of Brockholes, co. Lancaster, by Jacintha, da. of Hew DALRYMPLE. He *d.* 28 March 1852, at Lonsdale House, Fulham, Midx., and was *bur.* at Clapham aforesaid, in his 81st year.(b) Will pr. June 1852.(c) His widow *d.* 24 Feb. 1873, in her 86th year, at Maresfield Lodge, East Cowes, Isle of Wight.

(a) His elder brothers, but not he himself, are in the Visit. of Sussex for 1662.

(b) Was well known on the turf, and was twice (with "Phantom" in 1811 and with "Cedric" in 1824) winner of the Derby.

(c) He was claimant as a coheir (one out of a vast number) of the Barony of Sudeley, which had been in abeyance nearly 500 years. The claim was one of those in the early years of Queen Victoria's reign, 1838 to 1841, a period distinguished for the rapid termination of many ancient abeyances. [See *Complete Peerage*, by G.E.C., vol. i, p. 288, note "b," *sub* "Beaumont."]

VII. 1852. SIR JOHN VILLIERS SHELLEY, Bart. [1611], of Maresfield Park aforesaid, s. and h., *b.* 18 March 1808, in Charles Street, Berkeley Square, and *bap.* at St. Geo. Han. sq.; ed. at Charterhouse; *suc. to the Baronetcy*, 28 March, 1852; M.P. for Gatton, 1830-31; for Grimsby, 1831-32; and for Westminster, 1852—1865. Lieut.-Col. 46th Middlesex Rifle Volunteers, 1864-67. Chairman of the Bank of London. He *m.* 13 Aug. 1832, at Welwyn, Herts, Louisa Elizabeth Anne, only child of Rev. Samuel Johnes KNIGHT, of Henley Hall, Salop, Rector of Welwyn aforesaid, and Vicar of Allhallows, Barking, London. He *d.* s.p.m.(a) 28 Jan. 1867, at Maresfield Park aforesaid, aged 58. His widow *d.* there 15 March 1895.

VIII. 1867. SIR FREDERIC SHELLEY, Bart. [1611], of Shobrooke Park, Devon, br. and h. male; *b.* 1809; in Holy Orders; Rector of Beerferris, Devon, 1844; *suc. to the Baronetcy*, 28 Jan. 1867. He *m.*, 4 Feb. 1845, at Bath, Charlotte Martha, da. of the Rev. Henry HIPPESLEY, of Lambourne place, Berks, by Anne, da. and coheir of Lock ROLLINSON, of Chadlington, Oxon. He *d.* 19 March 1869, at Shobrooke Park aforesaid, aged 58. His widow *d.* 20 May 1893, at Posbury House, Crediton, Devon, aged 82.

IX. 1869. SIR JOHN SHELLEY, Bart. [1611], of Shobrooke Park, s. and h., *b.* 31 Aug. 1848; ed. at Marlborough School; matric. at Oxford (Univ. Coll.) 19 Oct. 1867; B.A. 1872; student of the Inner Temple, 1871; *suc. to the Baronetcy*, 19 March 1869; Sheriff of Devon, 1895. He *m.*, 29 June 1892, at St. Mark's, North Audley street, Marion Emma, 1st da. of Richard BENYON (formerly FELLOWES), of Englefield House, Berks, by Elizabeth Mary, da. of Robert CLUTTERBUCK, of Watford, Herts.

Family Estates.—These, in 1883, were 6,500 acres in Devon, worth £7,300 a year, belonging to Sir John Shelley, Bart., besides 3,865 acres (worth £3,685 a year) in Sussex, and 1,187 acres (worth £2,338 a year) in Lancashire, belonging to "Lady Shelley, of Maresfield Park, Uckfield."

SAVAGE:

cr. 29 June 1611,(b)

afterwards, 1626-40, VISCOUNTS SAVAGE,

and subsequently, 1640 to about 1735, EARLS RIVERS;

ex. about 1735.

I. 1611. "JOHN SAVAGE, of Rock Savage, co. Chester, Knt.," 1st surv. s. and h. of Sir John SAVAGE, of Clifton, otherwise Rock Savage aforesaid, by his 1st wife, Elizabeth, da. of Thomas (MANNERS), 1st EARL OF RUTLAND; suc. his father, 5 Dec. 1597; *Knighted* in Ireland 1599; Mayor of Chester, 1607; Sheriff of Cheshire, 1606-07; was *cr. a Bart.*, as above, 29 June 1611. He *m.*, before 1582, Mary, da. and coheir of Richard ALLINGTON, by Jane, sister and h. of Sir William CORDELL, of Long Melford, Suffolk, sometime Master of the Rolls. He was *bur.* 14 July 1615, at Macclesfield. The admon. of his widow as "of Bostock, Cheshire," dat. 16 May 1636.

II. 1615. SIR THOMAS SAVAGE, Bart. [1611], of Rock Savage aforesaid, 2d but 1st surv. s. and h.,(c) *b.* about 1586; *Knighted*, at Edinburgh, 2 July 1617; *suc. to the Baronetcy* in July 1615. He *m.* 14 May 1602, Elizabeth, da. of Thomas (DARCY), EARL RIVERS. She was living when he was *cr.*,

(a) His only da. and h., who *m.* 13 Nov. 1874, Hervey Charles Pechell, inherited the estate of Maresfield; as also such right as her grandfather possessed to a coheirship of the Barony of Sudeley.

(b) He was first of the 56 Baronets created at that date, that being the second batch of such creations, one more than three times the number of the inaugural batch (18) of the 22 May preceding. See p. 1, note "c," under Bacon.

(c) John, the eldest son of the 1st Bart. (who *d.* v.p.), is, presumably, the "John Savage, of Cheshire, Gent.," who matric. at Oxford (Brasenose Coll.) 13 Oct. 1598, aged 13.

4 Nov. 1626, VISCOUNT SAVAGE. In this peerage *the Baronetcy* then *merged*, the 2d Viscount becoming, 21 Feb. 1639/40, by inheritance, EARL RIVERS [1626]. On the death, however, of the 5th Earl, 5th Viscount, and 6th Baronet, about 1735, it and all his other honours became *extinct*. See *Peerage*.

BARRINGTON:
cr. 29 June 1611;
ex. 26 Sep. 1833.

I. 1611. "FRANCIS BARRINGTON, of Barrington Hall [in Hatfield Broadoak], co. Essex, Knt.," s. and h. of Sir Thomas BARRINGTON, of the same, by Winifred, relict of Sir Thomas HASTINGS, yst. da. and coheir of Henry (POLE), LORD MONTAGU(a); *b.* about 1570; suc. his father in 1586; was 30 years old, 1598-99; M.P. (in seven Parls.) for Essex, 1601-28; was *Knighted* at Theobalds, 7 May 1603; admitted to Gray's Inn, 19 March 1605/6, and was *cr.* a Bart., as above, 29 June 1611. He opposed the Court measures and in 1627 refused to contribute to the loan. He *m.* Joan (aunt to Oliver Cromwell, the Protector), da. of Sir Henry CROMWELL, *otherwise* WILLIAMS, of Hinchinbrook, co. Huntingdon, by Joan, da. of Sir Ralph WARREN, sometime Lord Mayor of London. He *d.* 3 July 1628. Will pr. 12 July 1628; that of his relict as "of Hatfield, Essex, widow," pr. 14 Dec. 1641.

II. 1628. SIR THOMAS BARRINGTON, Bart. [1611], of Barrington Hall aforesaid, s. and h.; *Knighted*(b) in his father's lifetime, before 1621; *suc. to the Baronetcy*, 3 July 1628; was M.P. for Newtown, 1621-29; for Essex, April to May 1640; and for Colchester, 1640 to death, opposing the Court measures. He took the Protestation in 1641 and the Covenant in 1643, and was a Lay Assessor in the Assembly of Divines,(b) 12 June 1643. He *m.* firstly, in or before 1605, Frances, da. and coheir of John GOBERT, of Coventry. He *m.* secondly, Judith, widow of Sir George SMITH, da. of Sir Rowland LYTTON, of Knebworth, Herts (*d.* June 1616), by Anne, da. of Oliver (ST. JOHN), 1st BARON ST. JOHN OF BLETSHO. He *d.* about Sep. 1644. His widow *d.* in or before 1657, aged 65. Will as "of Barrington Hall, Essex," pr. 22 Sep. 1657.

III. 1644. SIR JOHN BARRINGTON, Bart. [1611], of Barrington Hall aforesaid, s. and h. by first wife, *b.* 1605; aged 19 years in 1634; admitted, to Gray's Inn, 6 Nov. 1635; *Knighted* at Whitehall, 8 May 1638; *suc. to the Baronetcy* in 1644. M.P. for Newport, Isle of Wight, Nov. 1645, till secluded Dec. 1648; being re-elected 1660 and 1661-79; was one of the Parliamentary Committee for that Island and for Essex; nominated one of the members of the "High Court of Justice" to try King Charles, but refused to attend its meetings or to sign the warrant for the King's execution; Sheriff of Essex and Herts, 1654-55. He *m.*, in or before 1643, Dorothy, da. of Sir William LYTTON of Knebworth, Herts. (*d.* Aug. 1660, aged 70), by his 1st wife, Anne, da. and h. of Stephen SLANEY of Norton, Salop. He *d.* 24 March 1682/3, and was *bur.* 3 April 1683, at Hatfield aforesaid. Admon. 11 April 1683. His widow *d.* 27 Oct. 1703, at St. Mary's, Woolnoth, London, and was *bur.* at Hatfield aforesaid. Will pr. Nov. 1703.

IV. 1683. SIR JOHN BARRINGTON, Bart. [1611], of Barrington Hall aforesaid, grandson and h., being s. and h. of Thomas Barrington, by Anne,(c) da. and coheir of Robert (RICH), EARL OF WARWICK, which Thomas was s. and h. of the last Bart., and *d.* v.p. 31 Jan. 1681/2, aged 38. He was *b.* 16 Oct. 1670; ed. at Trin. Coll., Cambridge; *suc. to the Baronetcy*, 24 March 1682/3. He *d.* unm. at St. Clement, Danes, Midx., of the small pox, 26 Nov. 1691, and was *bur.* at Hatfield aforesaid. M.I. Admon. 18 Dec. 1691, and, again, 16 Nov. 1693.

(a) He was s. and h. of Sir Richard Pole, K.G., by Margaret, *suo jure* Countess of Salisbury, da. of George (Plantagenet), Duke of Clarence, br. to Edward IV.
(b) Noble's *Cromwell*.
(c) They were married in Lees chapel, 8 Nov. 1664.

V. 1691. SIR CHARLES BARRINGTON, Bart. [1611], of Barrington Hall aforesaid, br. and h., was a minor when he *suc. to the Baronetcy*, 26 Nov. 1691; M.P. for Essex in seven Parls., Feb. 1694 to 1715; Vice-Admiral of that county. He *m.* firstly, 20 April 1693, at St. Bride's London (Lic. Vic.-Gen., he 21, she 19, with consent of their respective mothers), Bridget, da. and h. of Sir John MONSON, K.B., by Judith, da. of Sir Thomas PELHAM, 2d Bart. [1611]. She *d.* Dec. 1699. He *m.* secondly (Lic. Fac. 23 May 1700, she 23), Anna Marie, da. of William (FITZWILLIAM), 1st EARL FITZWILLIAM [I.], by Anne, da. of Edmund CREMOR, of West Winch, Norfolk. He *d.* s.p. 29 Jan. 1714/5, and was *bur.* at Hatfield aforesaid.(a) Will dat. 2 July 1714, pr. Dec. 1715. His widow *d.* at Bath, July 1717, aged 41, and was *bur.* at Marham, co. Northampton. Admon. 7 Aug. 1717.

VI. 1715. SIR JOHN BARRINGTON, Bart. [1611], of Hitchin, Herts, of Swainston in the Isle of Wight, and of Dunmow Park, Essex, cousin and h., being only s. and h. of John BARRINGTON, of Dunmow Park aforesaid, by Elizabeth, da. of Edward HAWKINS, of Bishop's Stortford, Essex, which John was 3d s. of the 3d Bart. He *suc. to the Baronetcy*, 29 Jan. 1714/5. He *m.* Susan, sister of George Draper of Lilly, Herts, da. of George DRAPER, of Hitchin, Herts. He *d.* Aug. 1717, aged about 44, and was *bur.* at Hitchin. Will dat. 26 March 1716/7, pr. 7 Nov. 1717. His widow *d.* about 1750, and was *bur.* at Hitchin. Will pr. Oct. 1750.

VII. 1717. SIR JOHN BARRINGTON, Bart. [1611], of Swainston and Hitchin aforesaid, s. and h., *suc. to the Baronetcy*, Aug. 1717. M.P. for Newtown, Isle of Wight, in seven Parls., 1727-75. He *m.* Mary, da. of Patricius ROBERTS, by Elizabeth, da. of John WESTON, of Ockham, Surrey. She *d.* 17 June 1752. He *d.* s.p. 4 May 1776, and was *bur.* at Lilly, Herts. Will dat. 3 April 1770 pr. May 1776.

VIII. 1776. SIR FITZWILLIAM BARRINGTON, Bart. [1611], of Swainston, and Hitchin aforesaid, br. and h., *b.* 9 May 1708, at Hitchin, and *bap.* there. By the death of his uncle, George Draper, of Lilly, abovenamed, he, in 1745, inherited that estate; Sheriff of Herts, 1754-55; *suc. to the Baronetcy*, 9 May 1776. He *m.* firstly, 18 June 1741, in Ely chapel, St. Andrew's, Holborn (being then of St. Michael's, Bassishaw, London), Sarah, da. and h. of Thomas MEADE, R.N. She *d.* 1 Aug. 1746, and was *bur.* at Hitchin. He *m.* secondly, 24 Feb. 1749/50, at Westm. Abbey (Lic. Vic. Gen., she of St. Clement, Danes, about 25, spinster), Jane, da. of Matthew HALL, of Horsham, Surrey. He *d.* in Great James street, London, after ten years of palsy, 24 Sep. 1792, in his 85th year. Will, directing his burial to be at Hatfield Broadoak, dat. 25 Aug. and pr. 2 Oct. 1792. His widow *d.* in Great James street, 13 April 1797, aged 75. Her will pr. April 1797.

IX. 1792. SIR JOHN BARRINGTON, Bart. [1611], of Swainston aforesaid, 1st surv. s. and h., by 2d wife, *b.* 8 Dec. 1752, in Red Lion street, and *bap.* 3 Jan. 1753, at St. Andrew's, Holborn; M.P. for Newtown, Isle of Wight, 1780-96; *suc. to the Baronetcy*, 24 Sep. 1792. He *d.* unm. 5 Aug. 1818, in his 66th year. Will pr. 1819.

X. 1818, to 1832. SIR FITZWILLIAM BARRINGTON, Bart. [1611], of Swainston aforesaid, and of Calbourne, also in the Isle of Wight, br. and h., *b.* in Red Lion street, 2 and *bap.* 22 March 1755, at St. Andrew's, Holborn; *suc. to the Baronetcy*, 5 Aug. 1818. He *m.*, 8 July 1789, at St. Geo., Han. sq. (mar. lic. at Winchester, 9 Oct. 1764), Edith Mary, da. of Sir

(a) "A fast friend to the Church and Monarchy, and a courteous affable gentleman, as much esteemed as any in the county he lived in, and died generally lamented by all his friends." [Wotton's *Baronetage*]. He resided at "The Priory," a house attached to the east end of the parish church at Hatfield, the original residence of the family, "Barrington Hall" [now a farm] being 1½ mile therefrom. He devised the greater part of the Essex estates to his sister, Anne, wife of Charles Shales (Goldsmith to Queen Anne), whose sons, after her death, 17 Nov. 1729, took the name of Barrington.

Samuel MARSHALL, R.N., by Elizabeth, da. of Sir Edward WORSLEY, of Gatcombe, in the Isle of Wight. He *d.* s.p.m. 26 Sep. 1832,(a) at Swainston, aged 77, when the *Baronetcy* became *extinct*. Will pr. Oct. 1832. His widow *d.* at Exeter, and was *bur.* in the cathedral there. Admon. March 1845.

BERKELEY, *or* BERKLEY:
cr. 29 June 1611;
ex. about 1630.

I. 1611, to 1630? "HENRY BERKLEY, of Wymondam, co. Leicester, Esq.," only s. and h. of Maurice BERKELEY, of Wymondham aforesaid, by Mary, da. of John HALL, of Grantham, co. Lincoln, was *b.* about 1566; suc. his father in 1600, and was *cr. a Bart.*, as above, 29 June 1611. He *m.* firstly (—), da. of (—) MYNNE. He *m.* secondly, Katharine, widow of Anthony BYRON, da. of Nicholas BEAUMONT, of Cole Orton, co. Leicester, by Anne, da. of William SAUNDERS, of Welford. He sold the estate of Wymondham to Sir William Sedley, Bart., and *d.* s.p. about 1630, when the *Baronetcy* became *extinct*.

WENTWORTH:
cr. 29 June 1611,
sometime, 1628-39, BARONS AND VISCOUNTS WENTWORTH,
afterwards, 1639-41 and 1662-95, EARLS OF STRAFFORD,
subsequently, 1695-1711, BARON RABY,
and finally, 1711-99 (again), EARLS OF STRAFFORD;
ex. 7 Aug. 1799.

I. 1611. "WILLIAM WENTWORTH, of Wentworth Woodhouse, co. York, Esq.," only s. and h. of Thomas WENTWORTH, of the same, sometime (1583) Sheriff of Yorkshire, by Margaret, da. and h. of William GASCOIGNE, of Gawthorpe in that county, was *bap.* 3 July 1562, at Wentworth; suc. his father, 14 Feb. 1587; Sheriff of Yorkshire, 1601-02, and was *cr. a Bart.*, as above, 29 June 1611. He *m.*, in or before 1591, Anne, da. of Robert ATKINSON, of Stowell, co. Gloucester, Barrister of the Inner Temple, by Joyce, da. of Humphrey ASHFIELD, of Heythrop, Oxon. She was *bur.* at Wentworth, 23 July 1611. He was *bur.* there 10 Sep. 1614.

II. 1614, to 1641. SIR THOMAS WENTWORTH, Bart. [1611 (1)], 1st surv. s. and h., *b.* in Chancery lane, 13 and *bap.* 22 May 1593, at St. Dunstan's in the West; ed. at St. John's Coll., Cambridge; admitted to the Inner Temple, Nov. 1607; *Knighted*, 6 Dec. 1611; *suc. to the Baronetcy* in Sep. 1614; Custos Rot. for West Riding of Yorkshire, 1615-26; M.P. for York, 1614; for Yorkshire, 1621-22; for Pontefract, 1624, and for Yorkshire, again, 1625 and 1628; Councillor of the North, 1623 and 1625; Sheriff of Yorkshire, 1625-26. He was *cr.*, 22 July 1628, BARON WENTWORTH OF WENTWORTH WOODHOUSE, being (five months later) *cr.*, 13 Dec. 1628, VISCOUNT WENTWORTH, and (subsequently) *cr.*, 12 Jan. 1639/40, BARON RABY with a spec. rem., and EARL OF STRAFFORD with the usual remainder. He *m.* firstly, 22 Oct. 1611, at Londesborough, Margaret, 1st da. of Francis (CLIFFORD), 4th EARL OF CUMBERLAND, by Grisel, da. of Thomas HUGHES. Her burial, 21 Sep. 1622, is reg. at St. Olave's, York, and at Wentworth. He *m.* secondly, 24 Feb. 1625, Arabella, 2d da. of John (HOLLES), 1st EARL OF CLARE, by Anne, da. of Sir Thomas STANHOPE. She was living when he was raised to the Peerage. By his execution, 12 May 1641, in his 49th year, this *Baronetcy* and *all other his honours* became *forfeited*. For his well known career, as LORD WENTWORTH and as EARL OF STRAFFORD, see *Peerage*.

* * * * * *

(a) Of his five daughters and coheirs, the eldest *m.* Sir Richard Godin Simeon, 2d Bart. [1815], and inherited the estate of Swainston.

III. 1662. WILLIAM (WENTWORTH), EARL OF STRAFFORD, etc., only s. and h., by 2d wife; *b.* 8 June 1626; was, in the same year of his father's execution, *cr.* 1 Dec. 1641, EARL OF STRAFFORD, etc. By Act of Parl., 19 May 1662, the attainder of his father was reversed, and he, accordingly, *inherited the Peerage dignities and the Baronetcy* [1611 (1)] which had been thereby *forfeited*. He *d.* s.p. 16 Oct. 1695, aged 70, when all the Peerage honours conferred on himself, as also on his father, became *extinct*, excepting the Barony of Raby, which devolved, with the Baronetcy, as below.

IV. 1695. THOMAS (WENTWORTH), BARON RABY, and *4th Baronet*, cousin and h. male; being 2d but 1st surv. s. and h. of Sir William WENTWORTH (*d.* July 1693), s. and h. of another Sir William WENTWORTH (slain at Marston Moor, 3 July 1644), who was next br. to Thomas, EARL OF STRAFFORD (so *cr.* 1640), both being sons of Sir William WENTWORTH, the 1st Bart. He was *bap.* 17 Sep. 1672, and *suc.*, 16 Sep. 1695, *to the Peerage*, as BARON RABY, under the spec. rem. in the creation [1640] of that dignity, and to *the Baronetcy* [1611 (1)], as heir male of the body of the 1st Bart. He was *cr.*, 29 June 1711, EARL OF STRAFFORD, etc., with a spec. rem. He *d.* 15 Nov. 1739, aged 67.

V. 1739. WILLIAM (WENTWORTH), EARL OF STRAFFORD, etc., and *5th Baronet*, only s. and h.; *b.* 1722; *suc. to the above dignities*, 15 Nov. 1739. He *d.* s.p. 10 March 1791, aged 70.

VI. 1791, to 1799. FREDERICK THOMAS (WENTWORTH), EARL OF STRAFFORD, etc. [1711], BARONY RABY [1640] and *6th Baronet*, cousin and h. male, being only surv. s. and h. of William WENTWORTH (*d.* June 1776, aged 76), only surv. s. and h. of Peter WENTWORTH (*d.* Feb. 1738/9), next br. to Thomas, EARL OF STRAFFORD last named, who had been so *cr.* in 1711. On 10 March, 1791, he *inherited the Peerage* (under the spec. rem. in the creation of the Earldom, etc., in 1711, and of the Barony in 1640), and *the Baronetcy* [1611(1)] as heir male of the body of the 1st Bart. He *d.* s.p. 6 Aug. 1799, aged 67, when this *Baronetcy and all other his honours* became *extinct*.

(See fuller particulars in the *Peerage*, under "STRAFFORD.")

MUSGRAVE:
cr. 29 June 1611.

I. 1611. "RICHARD MUSGRAVE of Hartley, co. Westmoreland, Knt.," s. and h. of Christopher MUSGRAVE, by Joan, da. of Sir Henry CURWEN, of Workington, co. Cumberland, suc. his grandfather, Sir Simon MUSGRAVE, of Hartley and of Edenhall, co. Cumberland; was made K.B., 25 July 1603, at the coronation of James I; was M.P. for Westmorland, 1604-11, and was *cr. a Bart.*, 29 June 1611, as above. He *m.* (at the age of 14) Frances, 3d da. of Philip (WHARTON), 3d BARON WHARTON, by Frances, da. of Henry (CLIFFORD), EARL OF CUMBERLAND. He *d.* at Naples 6 Nov. 1615, aged 30, and is *bur.* in the Cathedral there.

II. 1615. SIR PHILIP MUSGRAVE, Bart. [1611], of Hartley and of Edenhall aforesaid, 2d but 1st surv. s. and h, aged 7 years at his father's death in 1615, when he *suc. to the Baronetcy*; admitted to Gray's Inn, 1627. He was M.P. for Westmorland, April to May 1640, and Nov. 1640, till disabled in Feb. 1643; was a distinguished Royalist, fought at Marston Moor, etc.; was Commander in Chief of the counties of Westmorland and Cumberland; Governor of Carlisle, 1648, and again, 1660; Governor of the Isle of Man, 1651, and is said to have had a warrant creating him BARON MUSGRAVE OF HARTLEY CASTLE, but never to have taken out the patent. He *m.* Julian, youngest da. of Sir Richard HUTTON, of Goldsborough, co. York, one of the Justices of the Common Pleas (1617-39), by Agnes, da. and h. of Thomas BRIGGS, of Cawmire, co. Westmorland. She *d.* 5 March 1659, in her 53d year. He *d.* at Edenhall, 7 Feb. 1677/8, aged 70. Both *bur.* at St. Cuthbert's Edenhall. M.I.

III. 1678. SIR RICHARD MUSGRAVE, Bart. [1611], of Edenhall, etc., aforesaid, s. and h., was of an infirm constitution; *suc. to the Baronetcy*, 7 Feb. 1677/8. He *m.* Margaret, da. of Sir Thomas HARRISON, of Allerthorpe, co. York, Knt., by Margaret, da. of Conyers (DARCY), LORD DARCY AND CONYERS. He *d.* s.p.m. about 1687, but certainly before 1689.

IV. 1687? SIR CHRISTOPHER MUSGRAVE, Bart. [1611], of Edenhall, aforesaid, br. and h. male; matric. at Oxford (Queen's Coll.), 10 July 1651; B.A., same date; Student of Gray's Inn, 1654. He, as a young man, was active in the Royal cause; Captain of the Guards before 1661; M.P. for Carlisle in six Parls., 1661-90; for Westmorland, 1690-95; for Appleby, 1695-98; for Oxford Univ., 1698—1700; for Westmorland (second time), 1700-01; for Totnes, 1701-02, and for Westmorland (the third time), 1702-04; *Knighted* in 1671; Mayor of Carlisle, 1672; Gov. of Carlisle, 1677; *suc. to the Baronetcy* about 1687; was made, by Queen Anne, one of the four tellers of the Exchequer. He *m.* firstly, 31 May 1660, Mary, eldest da. and coheir of Sir Andrew COGAN, of East Greenwich, co. Kent. She *d.* in childbed at Carlisle Castle, 8 July 1664, in her 28th year. *Bur.* at St. Cuthbert's, Edenhall. M.I. He *m.* secondly (Lic. Fac. 16 April 1671), Elizabeth (then aged 23), sister of Sir Richard FRANCKLYN, 1st Bart. [1660], da. of Sir John FRANCKLYN, of Willesden, co. Midx., by Elizabeth, da. of George PUREFOY, of Wadley, Berks. She *d.* 11 April 1701, and was *bur.* at Edenhall aforesaid. M.I. He *d.* of apoplexy, at St. James', Westm., 29 July 1704, in his 73d year, and was *bur.* at Trinity Minories, London. M.I. at Edenhall. Will pr. Aug. 1704.

V. 1704. SIR CHRISTOPHER MUSGRAVE, Bart. [1611], of Edenhall aforesaid, grandson and h., being only s. and h. of Philip MUSGRAVE, by Mary, 1st da. of George (LEGGE), 1st LORD DARTMOUTH, which Philip was 1st s. of the 4th Bart., by his 1st wife, but *d.* v.p. 2 July 1689; *b.* 25 Dec. 1688, in London; *suc. to the Baronetcy*, 29 July 1704; ed. at Eton and at Ch. Ch., Oxford, where he matric. 4 March 1705/6, aged 17. Clerk of the Privy Council 1710, in succession to his uncle, Christopher Musgrave; M.P. for Carlisle, 1713-15; and for Cumberland, 1722-27. He *m.* 21 June 1711, Julia, sister of Sir John CHARDIN, Bart. [1720], and da. of Sir John CHARDIN, of Kempton Park, Middlesex, by Esther, da. of (—) DE LARDINIERE PEIGNE, of Rouen, in France. He *d.* 3 Jan. 1735/6, at the house of his friend, Henry Fleetwood, at Penwortham, co. Lancaster; *bur.* in the church there. M.I. The will of his widow pr. 1763.

VI. 1736. SIR PHILIP MUSGRAVE, Bart. [1611], of Edenhall aforesaid, s. and h. He was also of Kempton Park, in Sunbury, co. Middlesex, with which estate he was presented, in 1746, by his uncle, Sir John Chardin, Bart. abovenamed; ed. at Eton and at Oriel College, Oxford; matric. 8 Jan. 1732/3, aged 20; *suc. to the Baronetcy*, 3 Jan. 1735/6; M.P. for Westmorland, 1741-47. He *m.* 1742, Jane, da. of John TURTON, of Orgreave, co. Stafford. He *d.* 5 July 1795, at Kempton Park, aged 84, and was *bur.* in Sunbury Church. M.I. at Edenhall. Will dat. 5 April 1779, pr. with six codicils, 27 July 1795. The will of his widow pr. 1802.

VII. 1795. SIR JOHN CHARDIN MUSGRAVE, Bart. [1611], of Edenhall aforesaid, *b.* 15 Jan. 1757; matric. at Oxford (Oriel Coll.) 27 Jan. 1775, aged 18; *cr.* M.A. 14 Nov. 1777; *suc. to the Baronetcy*, 5 July 1795. He *m.*, 13 July 1791, Mary, 1st da. of Rev. Sir Edmund FILMER, 6th Baronet [1674], by Annabella Christiana, da. of Sir John HONYWOOD, Bart. He *d.* 24 July 1806, at Tunbridge Wells, and was *bur.* at Sudbury aforesaid. M.I. at Edenhall. Will pr. 1806. His widow, who was *bap.* 8 March 1761, at Crundale, co. Kent, *d.* 9 Jan. 1838, at Brighton. M.I. at Edenhall. Will pr. May 1838.

VIII. 1806. SIR PHILIP MUSGRAVE, Bart. [1611], of Edenhall aforesaid, s. and h., *b.* 12 July 1794, at Marylebone; matric. at Oxford (Ch. Ch.), 17 March 1813, aged 18; M.P. for Petersfield, 1820-25; for Carlisle, 1825-27; *suc. to the Baronetcy*, 24 July 1806. He *m.* 21 Oct. 1824, at Ayston, co. Rutland, Elizabeth, 3d da. of George FLUDYER, of Ayston, by Mary, da. of John, 9th EARL OF WESTMORLAND. He *d.* s.p.m. 16 July 1827. M.I. at Edenhall. His widow *d.* 21 Aug. 1861, in Albemarle street, Midx., aged 66.

IX. 1827. SIR CHRISTOPHER JOHN MUSGRAVE, Bart. [1611], of Edenhall aforesaid, br. and h. male; matric at Oxford (Ch. Ch.), 24 May 1816, aged 18; B.A. (from St. Alban's Hall), 1821; M.A., 1823. In Holy Orders; Rector of Crundale, co. Kent, 1826-34; *suc. to the Baronetcy*, 16 July 1827. He *m.* Sep. 1825, Mary Anne, d. of Edward HASELL, of Dalemain, co. Cumberland. He *d.* s.p.m. 11 May 1834. M.I. at Edenhall. Will pr. Dec. 1834 and Sep. 1838. Admon. of his widow dat. Oct. 1835 and Jan. 1853.

X. 1834. SIR GEORGE MUSGRAVE, Bart. [1611], of Edenhall aforesaid, br. and h. male, *b.* 14 June 1799, at Kempton Park aforesaid; sometime an officer in the 5th Hussars; *suc. to the Baronetcy*, 11 May 1834; Sheriff of Cumberland, 1840. He *m.* 26 June 1828, at Christ Church, Marylebone, Charlotte, 7th da. of Sir James GRAHAM, 1st Bart. [1783], of Netherby, by Catherine, da. of John (STEWART), 7th EARL OF GALLOWAY [S.] He *d.* 29 Dec. 1872, in Albemarle street, aged 73. His widow *d.* 26 June 1873, at 27 Eaton place.

XI. 1872. SIR RICHARD COURTENAY MUSGRAVE, Bart. [1611], of Edenhall aforesaid, 2d. but only surviving s. and h., *b.* 21 Aug. 1838; sometime an officer in the 71st Highland Light Infantry; *suc. to the Baronetcy*, 29 Dec. 1892; M.P. for East Cumberland, 1880-81; L. Lieut. of Westmorland, 1876-81. He *m.* 17 Jan. 1867, Adora Frances Olga, only da. of Peter WELLS, of Forest farm, Windsor, by his 2d wife, Adora Julia, da. of Sir John Hesketh LETHBRIDGE, 3d Bart. [1804]. He *d.* 13 Feb. 1881, of pleurisy, at 17 Cavendish square. His widow *m.* 18 April 1882, at St. Paul's, Knightbridge, Henry Charles (BROUGHAM), 3d BARON BROUGHAM AND VAUX OF BROUGHAM, and was living 1899.

XII. 1881. SIR RICHARD GEORGE MUSGRAVE, Bart. [1611], s. and h., *b.* 11 Oct. 1872; sometime Lieut. in the Argyll and Sutherland Highlanders; *suc. to the Baronetcy*, 13 Feb. 1881. He *m.*, 9 Feb. 1895, Eleanor, 7th da. of Charles (HARBORD), 5th BARON SUFFIELD, by Cecilia Annetta, da. of Henry BARING. She was *b.* 7 Jan. 1868.

Family Estates.—These, in 1883, consisted of 10,543 acres in Cumberland, 3,121 in Westmorland, and 1,785 in Durham. *Total*, 15,449 acres, worth £15,016 a year, exclusive of mine rents.

SEYMOUR:

cr. 29 June 1611,

afterwards, since 1750, DUKES OF SOMERSET.

I. 1611. "EDWARD SEYMOUR, of Bury Castle, co. Devon, Esq.," s. and h. of Sir Edward SEYMOUR, generally styled LORD SEYMOUR(a), by Jane, da. of Jonn WALSH, of Cathanger, co. Somerset, one of the Justices of the Common Pleas (1563-72), *b.* about 1563; suc. his father, 6 May 1593, being then aged 30 and upwards; was M.P. for Devon, 1590, 1601 and 1604-11; Sheriff, 1595-96 and 1605-06, and was *cr. a Bart.*, 29 June 1611,(b) as above. He *m.*, 19 or 30 Sep. 1576,

(a) He was the 1st s. (by his 1st wife) of the famous DUKE OF SOMERSET (LORD PROTECTOR, *temp.* Edw. VI), but was *not* the h. ap. to his Peerage, which was conferred with a *spec. rem.* to the heirs male of the body of the grantee, by his *second* wife, failing which, to his like heirs by his *first* or any other wife. In the "*Inq. post mortem*," taken at Totnes, 20 Sep. 1593, he is called "Edward Seymour, Knt., Lord Seymour."

(b) "Two letters, which, at this period, Mr. Seymour [grandson of the Duke of Somerset, the Protector, and by seniority of birth actually his male heir] addressed to the Lord Treasurer, are preserved in the State Papers' office, and the terms in which he expresses his appreciation of the honour [of a Baronetcy] conferred upon him by his admission into 'the new order' are very remarkable as coming from a person of his birth.

In the earlier letter, dated 'Lupton, 12th June 1611,' he desires to 'intymate how much I standye further charged to your Lordship for your honbly conceaved good

F

at Dartington, Devon, Elizabeth, da. of Sir Arthur CHAMPERNOWNE, of Dartington, by Mary, da. of Sir Henry NORRIS, of Rycote, Oxon. He *d.* 11 April and was *bur.* in great state, 27 May 1613, from the Castle, at Bury Pomeroy. Admon. 6 Sep. 1613. His widow was then living. She was *bur.* at Bury Pomeroy. M.I.

II. 1613. SIR EDWARD SEYMOUR, Bart. [1611], of Bury Castle aforesaid in Bury Pomeroy, co. Devon, s. and h., *b.* about 1580. He was *Knighted* at Greenwich, 22 May 1603, and was sent by James I on an embassy to Denmark; was M.P. for Penrhyn, 1601; for Newport, 1604-11; for Lyme Regis, 1614; for Devon, 1621-22; for Callington, 1624-25, and for Totnes, 1625; *suc. to the Baronetcy*, 11 April 1613. Joining the Royal cause, his castle at Bury Pomeroy was reduced to ruins in the civil wars. He and his son were captured at Plymouth, and had to pay £1,200 to the sequestrators of estates. He *m.* 15 Dec. 1600, at St. Margaret's, Lothbury, London, Dorothy, da. of Sir Henry KILLEGREW, of Laroch, Cornwall, by his first wife, Katharine, da. of Sir Anthony COOKE, of Gidea Hall, Essex. She was *bur.* 30 June 1643 at Bury Pomeroy. He *d.* there 5 Oct. 1659.

III. 1659. SIR EDWARD SEYMOUR, Bart. [1611], of Bury Pomeroy aforesaid, s. and h., *bap.* 10 Sep. 1610 at Bury Pomeroy. Like his father he was a sufferer for the Royal cause. M.P. for Devon, April to May 1640, and 1640 till disabled in 1644; re-elected July to Dec. 1660; for Totnes (in four Parls.) 1661-87; *suc. to the Baronetcy*, 5 Oct. 1659. Sheriff of Devon, 1679-80; Vice-Admiral of Devon. He *m.* about 1630, Anne, da. of Sir John PORTMAN, Bart., 1st Bart. [1611], by Anne, da. of Sir Henry GIFFORD. He *d.* 7 Dec. 1688. His widow *d.* 1695. Both *bur.* at Bury Pomeroy.

IV. 1688. SIR EDWARD SEYMOUR, Bart. [1611], of Maiden Bradley, Wilts, and of Bury Pomeroy aforesaid, *b.* 1633. He was an active politician during four several reigns. M.P. for Hindon, 1661-78; for Devon, 1678-79; for Totnes, 1679-81; for Exeter (in three Parls.), 1685-95; for Totnes, again, 1695-98; and for Exeter, again (in five Parls.), 1698 to death. Clerk of the Hanaper, 1667-1708. Speaker of the House of Commons, 15 Feb. 1672/3 till 1679; P.C. 1673; and is said to have refused a Peerage for himself, though he obtained one for his younger son. Treasurer of the Navy, 1673-81. He was mainly instrumental in passing the "Habeas Corpus" act. He *suc. to the Baronetcy*, 7 Dec. 1688; was Commissioner of the Treasury, 1691-94, and Comptroller of the Household, 1702-04. He *m.* firstly (Lic. Fac. 7 Sep. 1661), Margaret, da. and coheir of Sir William WALE, of North Luffenham, co. Rutland, Alderman of London. He *m.* secondly, in 1674, Lætitia, sister of Sir Francis POPHAM, K.B., da. of Alexander POPHAM of Littlecot, Wilts, by his 1st wife, Lætitia, da. of William CARRE, Groom of the Bedchamber. He *d.* 17 Feb. 1707/8, in his 76th year, at Maiden Bradley, and was *bur.* there. M.I. Admon. 2 Dec. 1708, 13 May 1710, and 10 Nov. 1714. His widow(a) *d.* 16 March 1714. Her admon. as "of Woodlands, Dorset, widow," dat. 5 April 1715.

---

opinion of me and my house as to deeme me worthie to be ranckt amongst that newe intended order of Baronettes, which (as it should seeme) is ment to none but such as are well deservinge.'

Again, writing from Exeter, on the 21st of July [1611], a similar letter of thanks, Sir Edward Seymour a second time expresses his gratitude 'in that yt pleased yor LoP to holde me worthy to be ranckt in the number of Baronettes, and in that havinge precedencye of many worthie gentlemen of the same creation, wch I cannot but be sensible to be by yor hoble meanes.'

When it is remembered that the writer was grandson to a Duke; in remainder to the (then dormant) Dukedom, and to the existing Earldom of Hertford, and that his descendant (the 6th Bart.) actually succeeded to both those dignities in 1750, these passages are certainly worthy of notice in proof of the estimation in which the dignity of Baronet was held in some quarters at its first institution." [*Herald and Genealogist*, vol. iii, p. 351, being part of an article "on the dignity of Baronet," by its accomplished editor, John Gough Nichols.]

(a) Francis SEYMOUR, 2d but 1st surv. s. of this Lady, took the additional name of CONWAY, and was ancestor of the MARQUESSES OF HERTFORD.

V. 1708. SIR EDWARD SEYMOUR, Bart. [1611], of Maiden Bradley and of Bury Pomeroy aforesaid, s. and h., by 1st wife; *b.* about 1663 at Maiden Bradley; matric. at Oxford (Ch. Ch.), 8 Sep. 1679, aged 16; *suc. to the Baronetcy*, 17 Feb. 1707/8. M.P. for West Looe, 1690-95; for Totnes, 1708-10, and for Great Bedwyn, 1711-15. He *m.* Lætitia, only da. of his maternal uncle, Sir Francis POPHAM, K.B., of Littlecot, Wilts, by Helena, da. and h. of Hugh ROGERS, of Cunnington, Somerset. She *d.* 1738. He *d.* 29 Dec. 1740, aged 80. Will pr. 1741.

VI. 1740. SIR EDWARD SEYMOUR, Bart. [1611], of Maiden Bradley and of Bury Pomeroy aforesaid, s. and h.; *bap.* 17 Jan. 1694/5, at Easton, Wilts; matric. at Oxford (Mag. Coll.), 15 March, 1711/2; *suc. to the Baronetcy*, 29 Dec. 1740. M.P. for Sarum, 1741-47. He *m.* 8 March 1716, Mary, da. and h. of Daniel WEBB, of Monckton Farley and Melksham, Wilts, by Elizabeth, da. of John, sister and heir of Edward Somner, of Seend, in that county. She was living when, on 7 Feb. 1749/50, he *suc. to the Peerage* as DUKE OF SOMERSET, etc., by the death of his father's fifth cousin, Algernon, the 7th Duke, and the consequent failure of issue male, by the *second* wife of the 1st Duke.(a) He was, consequently, on 23 Nov. 1750, summoned to Parl. in that dignity. In that Dukedom this *Baronetcy* then *merged*, and has ever since so continued. See *Peerage.*

FINCH:

cr. 29 June 1611,

afterwards, since 1634, EARLS OF WINCHILSEA.

I. 1611. "MOYLE FINCH, of Eastwell, co. Kent, Knt.," s. and h. of Sir Thomas FINCH,(b) of the same, and of the Moat, near Canterbury, by Catherine, da. and coheir of Sir Thomas MOYLE, of Eastwell aforesaid; *b.* about 1550; suc. his father in or before Feb. 1563; admitted to Gray's Inn, 1568, being, presumably, afterwards called to the Bar thereof; M.P. for Weymouth 1575-83; for Kent, 1593; and for Winchelsea 1601; *Knighted* at Greenwich, 7 May 1584; suc. his mother in the Eastwell estate, 9 Feb. 1586/7, being then aged 35; Sheriff of Kent, 1596-97, and 1606-07; and was *cr. a Bart.*, as above, 29 June 1611.(c) He *m.* in or before 1573, Elizabeth, da. and h. of Sir Thomas HENEAGE, of Copt Hall, co. Essex, Chancellor of the Duchy of Lancaster, by his 1st wife, Anne, da. of Sir Nicholas POYNTZ, of Acton, co. Gloucester. He *d.* 18 Dec. 1614, aged about 64, and was *bur.* at Eastwell. M.I. Funeral certificate in Coll. of Arms. Will pr. 1615. His widow, who was *b.* about 1557, was *cr.*, 8 July 1623, VISCOUNTESS MAIDSTONE, and on 11 July 1628, COUNTESS OF WINCHILSEA, with, in each case, a rem. of the dignity to the heir male of her body. She *d.* at Eastwell, 23 March 1633/4, aged about 76, and was *bur.* there, 5 April 1634. M.I. Funeral certificate in Coll. of Arms. Will pr. 1634.

II. 1614. SIR THEOPHILUS FINCH, Bart. [1611], of Eastwell aforesaid, 1st s. and h., *b.* about 1573; matric. at Oxford (Mag. Coll.), 25 Oct. 1588, aged 15; B.A., 1 Feb. 1591/2; *Knighted*, 30 July 1599; *suc. to the Baronetcy*, 18 Dec. 1614; M.P. for Great Yarmouth, Norfolk, 1614; admitted to Gray's Inn, 2 Aug. 1618. He *m.*, 16 July 1596, at Blickling, Agnes, da. of Sir Christopher HEYDON, of Baconsthorpe, co. Norfolk, by Agnes, da. of Robert CRANE, of Chilton, co. Suffolk. He *d.* s.p. between Aug. 1618 and 1620,(d) and was *bur.* in St. Paul's Cathedral, London, near his maternal grandfather. His widow was *bur.* 16 Feb. 1620/1, at St. Anne's, Blackfriars, London. Burial entry at Blickling.

(a) See p. 33, note "a."

(b) An interesting account of the Finch family, in 1620, drawn up by "Jo. Philipott, Rouge Dragon," is in the *Mis. Gen. et Her.*, 1st series, vol. ii, pp. 325—337.

(c) It is said that he "by reason of his great prudence in the management of public affairs would have been more highly dignified in case his death had not prevented it." [Collins' *Peerage*, edit. 1812, vol. iii, p. 382, quoting "Lord Bacon in the *Cabala*."]

(d) His death is mentioned by Philipott [1620]; see note "b," above.

I

III. 1619? SIR THOMAS FINCH, Bart. [1611], of Eastwell aforesaid, br. and h.; b. about 1575; *Knighted*, 8 Jan. 1608/9, at Whitehall; *suc. to the Baronetcy*, between 1618 and 1620(a); M.P. for Winchilsea, 1621-22, and for Kent, 1628-29; was *styled* VISCOUNT MAIDSTONE, after 11 July 1628. He *m.*, in 1609, Cicely, sister of Sir John WENTWORTH, Bart., da. of John WENTWORTH, of Gosfield, co. Essex, by Cicely, da. and coheir of Sir Edward UNTON. She was living, when, by the death of his mother, 23 March 1633/4, he *suc. to the Peerage*, as EARL OF WINCHILSEA, etc., in which title this *Baronetcy* then *merged*, and has ever since so continued. See *Peerage*.

COPE:

cr. 29 June 1611.

I. 1611. "ANTHONY COPE, of Hanwell, co. Oxford, Knt.," s. and h. of Edward Cope, of the same, by Elizabeth, da. and h. of Walter MOHUN, of Wollaston, co. Northampton, which Edward was s. and h. of Sir Anthony Cope, of Hanwell aforesaid, and of Banbury, Oxon; Vice-Chamberlain to Katharine Parr, the Queen Consort; Sheriff of Oxon, 1582-83, 1591-92, and 1603-04; M.P. for Banbury, in seven Parls., 1571—1601; and for Oxon, 1606-11 and 1614; was committed to the Tower, 27 Feb. to 23 March 1586/7, for presenting to the Speaker a Puritan version of the Prayer-book and a bill to abrogate ecclesiastical law; was *Knighted* by Queen Elizabeth, 1590; admitted to Gray's Inn, 19 March 1605/6; was *cr. a Bart.*, as above, 29 June 1611. He twice (1606 and 1612) entertained the King at his house at Hanwell, and was noted for his hospitality. He *m.* firstly, Frances, da. of Sir Rowland LYTTON, of Knebworth, Herts., by his 2d wife, Anne, da. of George CARLETON, of Brightwell, Oxon. She was *bur.* 13 Jan. 1600/1, at Hanwell. He *m.* secondly, Ann, widow of Sir Nicholas L'ESTRANGE, and formerly of Sir George CHAWORTH, da. of Sir William PASTON, of Paston, Norfolk, by Frances, da. of Sir Francis CLERE, of Stokesby. He *d.* and was *bur.* 23 July 1615, at Hanwell, aged 66. M.I. Will dat. 9 June 1613, pr. 14 Feb. 1615/6. His widow was *bur.* there 2 Aug. 1637.

II. 1615. SIR WILLIAM COPE, Bart. [1611], of Hanwell aforesaid, s. and h. by 1st wife; *Knighted* by James I, 11 May 1603, at the Charterhouse; *suc. to the Baronetcy*, 23 July 1615; admitted to Lincoln's Inn 8 Aug. following. M.P. for Banbury, 1604-11, 1614, and 1621-22; for Oxon, 1624-25; and again for Banbury, 1625; Sheriff of Oxon, 1619-20. He *m.* 8 April 1602, at Hanwell, Elizabeth, da. and h. of Sir George CHAWORTH, of Wiverton, Notts, by the abovenamed Anne, da. of Sir William PASTON, which Anne *m.* thirdly, Sir Anthony COPE, 1st Bart., abovenamed. With her he acquired the estate of Marneham, Notts. She was *bur.* 24 Aug. 1635, at Hanwell. He *d.* 2 and was *bur.* 22 Aug. 1637, at Hanwell aforesaid. Will pr. 1637.

III. 1637. SIR JOHN COPE, Bart. [1611], of Hanwell aforesaid, s. and h., *bap.* 28 Aug. 1608, at Hanwell; was B.A. of Oxford (Queen's Coll.) 22 June 1625; *suc. to the Baronetcy* in Aug. 1637. He *m.* firstly (Lic. Lond. 11 Nov. 1626) Mary (then aged 17), da. of Sir John WALTER, Lord Chief Baron of the Exchequer, by his first wife Margaret, da. of William OFFLEY, of London. She *d.* s.p.m. He *m.* secondly, Elizabeth, da. of Francis (FANE), 1st EARL OF WESTMORLAND, by Mary, da. and h. of Sir Anthony MILDMAY, of Apethorpe, co. Northampton. He was *bur.* 25 Oct. 1638, at Hanwell. Will pr. 1638. His widow *m.* William COPE, of Icombe, co. Gloucester, 4th s. of Richard COPE, a younger s. of the 1st Bart.

IV. 1638. SIR ANTHONY COPE, Bart [1611], of Hanwell aforesaid, s. and h., by 2d wife; said to have been ed. at Oriel Coll., Oxford; M.P. for Banbury 1660, and for Oxon, 1661-75; *suc. to the Baronetcy* in Oct. 1638. He *m.* his cousin, Mary, da. of Dutton (GERARD), 3d BARON GERARD OF BROMLEY, by

(a) See p. 35, note "d."

his 1st wife, Mary, da. of Francis (FANE), 1st EARL OF WESTMORLAND aforesaid. He *d.* s.p.m., and was *bur.* 12 June 1675, at Hanwell. Funeral certificate at Coll. of Arms. Will dat. 10 May and pr. 26 Oct. 1676.

V. 1675. SIR JOHN COPE, Bart. [1611], of Hanwell aforesaid, br. and h.; matric. at Oxford (Queen's Coll.), 10 Nov. 1651; had a command at Dunkirk, when that fortress was delivered up to the French in 1662; *suc. to the Baronetcy* in June 1675; M.P. for Oxon (in three Parls.), 1679-90, and for Banbury, 1699—1700. He *m.* Anne, da. of Philip BOOTH. He *d.* 11 Jan. 1721, and was *bur.* at Eversley, Hants. Will, directing his burial to be there, dat. 12 Nov. 1712; pr. May 1726.

VI. 1721. SIR JOHN COPE, Bart. [1611], of Hanwell aforesaid, s. and h., *bap.* 1 Dec. 1634, at Hanwell; matric. at Oxford (Oriel Coll.) 22 Oct. 1689; was *Knighted* by William III, on 28 Nov. 1695; M.P. for Plympton, 1705-08; for Tavistock (in three Parls.), 1708-27; for Hants, 1727-34; and for Lymington, 1734-41. He purchased the manor and estate of Bramshill,(a) in Eversley, Hants, between 1695 and 1713. He *suc. to the Baronetcy*, 11 Jan. 1721. He *m.* 1696, Alice, da. of Sir Humphrey MONNOUX, 2d Bart. [1660], by Alice, da. of Sir Thomas COTTON, 3d Bart. [1611], of Connington. She *d.* Feb. 1728. He *d.* 8 Dec. 1749. Will pr. 1749.

VII. 1749. SIR MONNOUX COPE, Bart. [1611], of Bramshill and Hanwell aforesaid, s. and h.; *suc. to the Baronetcy* 8 Dec. 1749. M.P. for Banbury, 1722-27, and for Newport, 1741-47. He *m.* Penelope, da. of Lieut. Gen. the Hon. Henry MORDAUNT by his 2d wife, Penelope, da. and h. of William TIPPING, of Ewelme, Oxon, which Henry was br. to Charles, 2d EARL OF PETERBOROUGH. She *d.* Dec. 1737; admon. 29 Oct. 1760. He *d.* 24 June, 1763, aged 67. Will pr. 1763.

VIII. 1763. SIR JOHN MORDAUNT COPE, Bart. [1611], of Bramshill aforesaid, s. and h.; *b.* at Ewelme, Oxon; matric. at Oxford (Trin. Coll.). 18 March 1748/9, aged 17; *cr.* M.A., 15 June 1752, and D.C.L., 2 July 1772; *suc. to the Baronetcy*, 24 June 1763. He *d.* unm. 7 March 1779. Will pr. March 1779.

IX. 1779. SIR RICHARD COPE, Bart. [1611], of Bramshill aforesaid, cousin and h., being s. and h. of the Rev. Galen Cope, Rector of Eversley, Hants, by Anne, da. of Richard ONSLOW, of Drungwick, Sussex, which Galen was 4th s. of the 5th Bart. He was ed. at Clare Hall, Cambridge; B.A., 1743; M.A., 1747; D.D., 1763; was in Holy Orders; Preb. of Westminster, 1754—1806. He *suc. to the Baronetcy*, 7 March 1779. He *m.* firstly, Anne, da. of Thomas WYNDHAM, of Yateley, Hants, by Elizabeth, da. and h. of John HELYAR, of Yateley aforesaid. He *m.* secondly, Catherine, widow of John BURTON, of Owlerton, Notts, da. and h. of John LAW, of Northeram, co. York. Her will pr. 1807. He *d.* s.p. 6 Nov. 1806.

X. 1806. SIR DENZIL COPE, Bart. [1611], of Bramshill aforesaid, nephew and h., being s. and h. of William Cope, Solicitor, of Bridgen place, in Bexley, co. Kent, Chapter Clerk and Registrar to Westm. Abbey (1763—1803), by Anne, da. and h. of Benjamin GREENWOOD, of St. Mary's Cray, Kent, which William (who *d.* Sep. 1803) was yr. br. of the late Baronet. He was *b.* 18 June and *bap.* 14 July 1766, at Westm. Abbey; admitted to Lincoln's Inn, 15 Jan. 1784; *suc. to the Baronetcy*, 6 Nov. 1806. He *m.*, 13 Sep. 1810, at St. Geo. Han. sq. (spec. lic.), Elizabeth Dorothea, da. of (—) FRANCIS, she being then of Park place, St. James', Westm. He *d.* s.p. 30 Dec. 1812, aged 46, and was *bur.* at Eversley. M.I. Will dat. 16 Oct. 1810, pr. 12 Jan. 1813. His widow *m.*, 30 Aug. 1820, Henry RUSH, of Heckfield, Hants, and *d.* 16 Sep. 1840, being *bur.* at Eversley. Will pr. 1840.

(a) The magnificent mansion of Bramshill Park was probably the work of Thorpe, who built Holland House, in 1607, for Sir Walter Cope, br. of the 1st Bart. It was erected between 1600 and 1625, for Lord Zouche, who died there.

XI. 1812. SIR JOHN COPE, Bart. [1611], of Bramshill aforesaid, br. and h.; *b.* 22 July and *bap.* 17 Aug. 1768, at Westm. Abbey; was sometime, till 1806, a Solicitor. He *suc. to the Baronetcy*, 30 Dec. 1812; and was well known as a Master of Foxhounds and owner of several celebrated horses on the turf. He is said to have *m.* a lady, who *d.* before him, but *d.* s.p.s. 18 Nov. 1851, at Bramshill Park, aged 83, and was *bur.* at Eversley. Will pr. Feb. 1852.

XII. 1851. SIR WILLIAM HENRY COPE, Bart. [1611], of Bramshill aforesaid, 5th cousin and h., being s. and h. of Lieut. Gen. Edmund Reily COPE, of Valenciennes, in France, by Maria, da. of James FURBER, of Woolcombe, Dorset, which Edmund (who *d.* 18 Aug. 1835) was s. and h. of William COPE, of Dublin, s. and h. of Joseph COPE, also of Dublin (*d.* 1754), yr. s., whose issue became h. male of William COPE, of Dublin (*d.* 1715), s. and h. of Anthony COPE, who was yr. s. of Anthony COPE, who first settled in Ireland, the 2d s. of the 1st Bart. He was *b.* 27 Feb. 1811; ed. at Trinity Coll., Dublin; B.A., 1831; incorporated, 24 Oct. 1839, at Oxford (Mag. Coll.); M.A., 1840; was sometime an officer in the Rifle Brigade; took Holy Orders; Minor Canon and Librarian of Westm. Abbey, 1842 to 1853; Chaplain of Westm. Hospital, 1843-51; author of several works; *suc. to the Baronetcy* (and, by devise, to the estate), 18 Nov. 1851. He *m.* firstly, 12 Aug. 1834, Marianne, 5th da. of Henry GARNETT, of Green Park, co. Meath, by Alice, da. of the abovenamed William COPE, of Dublin. She *d.* 20 Dec. 1862, at Monckstown, co. Dublin. He *m.* secondly, 30 Aug. 1865, at St. George's, Dublin, Henriette Margaret, 2d da. of Robert Jaffray HAUTENVILLE, of Vesey place, Monkstown aforesaid. He *d.* 7 Jan. 1892, at Lennox tower, Southsea, in his 81st year, and was *bur.* at Eversley. His widow living 1899.

XIII. 1892. SIR ANTHONY COPE, Bart. [1611], of Bramshill aforesaid, 3d but 1st surv. s., by 1st wife; *b.* 9 March 1842; served in the Ashantee war (medal and clasp), 1873-74; sometime Col. of the Rifle Brigade; *suc. to the Baronetcy*, 7 Jan. 1892. He *m.*, Oct. 1870, Mary Leckonby, widow of Rev. Henry TUDWAY, da. of John Lewis PHIPPS, of Leighton, Wilts.

Family Estates.—These, in 1883, consisted of 3,833 acres in Hants; 1,120 in Oxon; 231 in Northamptonshire; 154 in Warwickshire, and 74 in Berks. *Total*, 5,442 acres, worth £6,797 a year. *Principal Seat.*—Bramshill Park, near Winchfield, Hants.

MONSON, *or* MOUNSON:

cr. 29 June 1611,

afterwards, since 1728, BARONS MONSON OF BURTON,

being sometime, 1886-98, VISCOUNT OXENBRIDGE OF BURTON.

I. 1611. "THOMAS MOUNSON, of Carlton, co. Lincoln, Knt.," 1st surv. s. and h. of Sir John MONSON, of South Carlton aforesaid, by Jane, da. of Robert DIGHTON, of Little Sturton, in that county; was *b.* about 1565; matric. at Oxford (Mag. Coll.), 9 Dec. 1579, aged 15; *cr.* M.A., 30 Aug. 1605, having been *Knighted* between 1598 and 1604; admitted to Gray's Inn, 1583; suc. his father, 20 Dec. 1593; M.P. for Lincolnshire, 1597-98; for Castle Rising, 1604-11; and for Cricklade, 1614; Master of the Armoury and Master Falconer, 1605; was *cr. a Bart.*, as above, 29 June 1611. He was twice tried on suspicion of being concerned in the poisoning of Sir Thomas Overbury, but was acquitted. He was an author of some religious works. He *m.*, in July 1590,(a) Margaret, da. of Sir Edmund Anderson, of Eyworth, Beds.; L. Ch. Justice of the Common Pleas (1582—1605), by Magdalen, da. of Christopher SMYTH, of Annables, Herts. She was *bur.* 3 Aug. 1630, at South Carlton. He was *bur.* there, 29 May 1641. Admon.(b) 10 Feb. 1642/3, as late of St. Martin's in the Fields, Midx., to his son, William, Viscount Castlemaine.

(a) *Ex. inform.* A. S. Larken (Richmond Herald, 1882-89), who took it from a deed in the family custody.
(b) He is erroneously styled therein, "Sir *William*," instead of "Sir *Thomas*."

II. 1641. SIR JOHN MONSON, Bart. [1611], of South Carlton aforesaid, and of Broxbourne, Herts, s. and h.,(a) was *b.* 1599, in the parish of St. Sepulchre's, London; studied the Law; M.P. for Lincoln, 1625, and for Lincolnshire, 1626; K.B. at the coronation of Charles I, 2 Feb. 1626/7; *suc. to the Baronetcy* in May 1641; retired to Oxford on the breaking out of the Civil War, and was concerned in the surrender of the garrison there to the Parl. in 1646; was *cr.* D.C.L., 1 Nov. 1642. He *m.*, about 1625, Ursula, da. and h. of Sir Robert OXENBRIDGE, of Hurstbourne, Hants, by Elizabeth, da. and coheir of Sir Henry COCK, of Broxbourne aforesaid. By her, he, in 1645, acquired the estate of Broxbourne, where he afterwards resided. He was *bur.* 29 Dec. 1683, at South Carlton, aged 84.(b) His widow was *bur.* there, 10 Dec. 1692. His will pr. 19 Jan. 1683/4, and that of his widow, 3 Jan. 1692/3.

III. 1683. SIR HENRY MONSON, Bart. [1611], of Burton, co. Lincoln, grandson and h., being 1st surv. s. and h. of Sir John MONSON, K.B., by Judith, da. of Sir Thomas PELHAM, 2d Bart. [1611], which John was only s. and h. ap. of the late Baronet, but *d.* v.p. 14 Oct. 1674, aged 46. He was *bap.* 17 Sep. 1653, at Burton, co. Lincoln; was M.P. for Lincoln (in five Parls.), 1675-89, but vacated on refusal to take the oaths to Will. and Mary. He *suc. to the Baronetcy*, 29 Dec. 1683. He *m.*, 4 March 1674/5, at Westm. Abbey (Lic. Fac.), Elizabeth, da. of Charles (CHEYNE), 1st VISCOUNT NEWHAVEN [S.], by his 1st wife, Jane, da. of William (CAVENDISH), DUKE OF NEWCASTLE. He *d.* s.p. 6 and was *bur.* 18 April 1718, at South Carlton. Will dat. 22 May 1706/7 to 9 Aug. 1710, pr. 26 April 1718. His widow, who was *bap.* 18 May 1656, at Chelsea, *d.* 20 and was *bur.* 29 May 1725, at South Carlton. Will pr. May 1725.

IV. 1718. SIR WILLIAM MONSON, Bart. [1611], of Burton aforesaid, and of Broxbourne, Herts, br. and h., *b.* about 1655; M.P. for Lincoln, 1695-98; for Heytesbury, 1703-08; for Hertford, 1708-10; and for Aldborough, 1715-22; *suc. to the Baronetcy*, 6 April 1718. He *m.* (Lic. Fac. 2 April 1688) Lætitia (then aged 22), da. of John (POULETT), 3d BARON POULETT OF HINTON ST. GEORGE, by his 1st wife, Essex, da. of Alexander POPHAM. He *d.* s.p. 7 March 1726/7. Will dat. 15 Dec. 1726, pr. 20 March 1726/7. His widow *d.* 25 April 1734.

V. 1726. SIR JOHN MONSON, Bart. [1611], of Burton and Broxbourne aforesaid, nephew and h., being s. and h. of George MONSON, by Anne, da. and h. of Charles WREN, of the Isle of Ely, which George (who was *b.* 27 Feb. and *bap.* 5 March 1657/8, at Burton, and who *d.* 16 Oct. 1726) was yr. br. of the late Baronet. He was *b.* about 1693; matric. at Oxford (Ch. Ch.), 26 Jan. 1707/8, aged 15; was M.P. for Lincoln, 1722-28; inv. K.B., 27 May and inst. 17 June 1725, being one of the original Knights at the restoration of that order; *suc. to the Baronetcy*, 7 March 1726/7. He *m.*, 8 April 1725, at St. Geo. the Martyr, Queen sq., Midx., Margaret, 4th and yst. da. of Lewis (WATSON), 1st EARL OF ROCKINGHAM, by Catharine, da. and coheir of George (SONDES), EARL OF FEVERSHAM. She was living when he (two months after his succession to the Baronetcy) was *cr.*, 28 May 1728, BARON MONSON OF BURTON, co. Lincoln. In that Barony this *Baronetcy* then *merged*, and still so continues, the 7th Baron being *cr.*, in 1886, VISCOUNT OXENBRIDGE OF BURTON, which title became *extinct* on his death in 1898. See *Peerage*, under "MONSON."

(a) His yr. br., William Monson, was cr. in 1628 Viscount Monson of Castlemaine [I.], being, as a Regicide, degraded for high treason in 1661.
(b) In Sir Joseph Williamson's *Lincolnshire Families, temp. Charles II* [*Herald and Genealogist*, ii, 116—126], the estate of this family "at Burton, neare Lincoln," is put at £4,000 a year.

GRESLEY:

cr. 29 June 1611.[a]

I. 1611. "George Gresley, of Drakelow,[b] co. Derby, Esq.," s. and h. of Sir Thomas Gresley, of the same, by his 1st wife, Dorothy, da. of Sir Thomas Walsingham, of Scadbury, co. Kent, *b.* about 1580; matric. at Oxford (Ball. Coll.), Nov. 1594, aged 14; suc. his father, Sep. 1610, and was *cr. a Bart.*, 29 June 1611, as above; being, subsequently,[c] 3 June 1612, *Knighted*. He was M.P. for Newcastle-under-Lyne, 1628-29; Sheriff of Derbyshire (appointed by Parl.), 1644-45; and was a great patron of learning.[d] He *m.*, 17 Dec. 1600, at Walton on Trent, Susan, da. of Sir Humphrey Ferrers, of Tamworth, co. Warwick, by Anne, da. of Sir Humphrey Bradborne. Her admon. 23 Nov. 1626. He was *bur.* in the Temple church, London, 5 Feb. 1650/1.

II. 1651. Sir Thomas Gresley, Bart. [1611], of Drakelow aforesaid, grandson and h., being s. and h. of Thomas Gresley, by Bridgett, da. of Sir Thomas Burdett, 1st Bart. [1619], of Foremark, which Thomas Gresley was s. and h. ap. of the 1st Bart. He *suc. to the Baronetcy* in Feb. 1650/1; was Sheriff of Derbyshire 1662-63. He *m.*, about 1648, Frances, da. and coheir of Gilbert Morewood, of London, and of Netherseale, co. Leicester, by Frances, da. of (—) Salmon. He *d.* 5 June 1699, aged 70, and was *bur.* at Gresley, co. Derby. M.I. Will pr. 11 May 1700. The will of his widow, who was *bap.* 16 March 1630, at Seale, pr. Oct. 1711.

III. 1699. Sir William Gresley, Bart. [1611], of Drakelow aforesaid, s. and h., *b.* 8 Nov. 1661[e]; matric. at Oxford (Trin. Coll.), 10 June 1681, aged 17 [*Qy.* 19]; *suc. to the Baronetcy*, 5 June 1699; Sheriff of Derbyshire, 1703-04. He *m.*, 2 Sep. 1696, at Bishop's Castle, Barbara, widow of Richard Oakeley, of Oakeley, Salop, and da. of John Walcot, of Walcot, in that county, by Elizabeth, da. of (—) Clarke. He *d.* 17 Oct. 1710, in his 48th year. Admon. (as of Oakeley, co. Salop), 7 Nov. 1710. That of his widow (as of Ludlow, co. Salop), 28 April 1724.

IV. 1710. Sir Thomas Gresley, Bart. [1611], of Drakelow aforesaid, only s. and h., *b.* about 1699; matric. at Oxford (Ball. Coll.), 7 May 1716, aged 17; *suc. to the Baronetcy*, 17 Oct. 1710; Sheriff of Derbyshire, 1723-24. He *m.* firstly, 5 April 1719, at Biddulph, Dorothy, da. and coheir of Sir William Bowyer, 4th Bart. [1660], of Knipersley, co. Stafford (which estate she brought into this family), by Anne, da. of George Dale. She *d.* 31 July 1736, and was *bur.* at Gresley. M.I. He *m.* secondly, 11 June 1739, at Haddon Chapel, Gertrude, da. and coheir of John Grammer, of Pledwick, co. York, by Mary, da. of George Beaumont. He *d.* 1746. Admon. 18 Feb. 1746/7. The will of his widow pr. Dec. 1790.

V. 1746. Sir Thomas Gresley, Bart. [1611], of Drakelow aforesaid, s. and h., by 1st wife; *b.* about 1723; matric. at Oxford (Ball. Coll.), 24 May 1739, aged 16; Sheriff of Derbyshire, 1751-52; M.P. for Lichfield, Nov. to Dec. 1753; *suc. to the Baronetcy* in 1746. He *m.*, in 1749, Wilmot, da.

(a) Before this creation, and next after that of Monson, is the precedency of the Baronetcy conferred (in the following reign), 23 June 1631, on Charles Vavasour, of Killingthorpe, co. Lincoln, according to the words contained in the creation of that dignity. In like manner, the precedency of 29 June 1611 had been previously granted by James I to the Baronetcy of Dallison, *cr.* 27 Oct. 1624. See that dignity.

(b) A valuable account of *The Gresleys of Drakelowe*, by Falconer Madan, M.A. (Oxford), was issued to subscribers in 1899, from which many of the dates, etc., in this article are kindly furnished by its editor.

(c) See p. 18, note "c," *sub* "Tollemache," as to several recently created Baronets, who were subsequently knighted.

(d) By him Sir William Dugdale was introduced to Thomas, the well known Earl of Arundel, Earl Marshal of England, from whom he obtained his subsequent appointment in the College of Arms.

(e) Mr. Madan (see note "b" above) states that "this date is undoubtedly right," though "it is odd that the Oxford Register should be at fault about his age."

and h. of (—) Hood, an Alderman of Leicester. He *d.* of small pox, s.p.m., 23 Dec. 1753.[a] Admon. 4 Jan. 1754, to his widow. Her will pr. Dec. 1797, and again, Sep. 1838.

VI. 1753. Sir Nigel Gresley, Bart. [1611], of Knipersley aforesaid, br. and h. male; sometime an officer, R.N.; *suc. to the Baronetcy*, 23 Dec. 1753; Sheriff of Staffordshire, 1759-60. He *m.*, 18 May 1752, at Astbury, Cheshire, Elizabeth, da. of Rev. Ellis Wynn, of Cheshire, by Elizabeth, da. of Leftwich Oldfield. He *d.* at Bath, 17 and was *bur.* 21 April 1787, in Bath Abbey, aged 60.[b] His widow was *bur.* there, 22 May 1793.

VII. 1787. Sir Nigel-Bowyer Gresley, Bart. [1611], of Knipersley, and, afterwards, of Drakelow aforesaid, s. and h.; *suc. to the Baronetcy*, 17 April 1787. He *m.* firstly, 26 Jan. 1776, at Croxall, co. Derby, his cousin, Wilmot, da. and h. of Sir Thomas Gresley, 5th Bart., by Wilmot, da. and h. of (—) Hood aforesaid. By her he acquired the estate of Drakelow. She *d.* s.p.m. 4 Dec. 1790. He *m.* secondly, 26 June 1796, at St. James', Westm., Maria Elizabeth, da. and h. of Caleb Garway, of Worcester. He *d.* 26 March 1808. Will pr. 1808. The admon. of his widow dat. Dec. 1840.

VIII. 1808. Sir Roger Gresley, Bart. [1611], of Drakelow aforesaid, and of Netherseale, co. Leicester, only surv. s. and h., by 2d wife, *b.* 27 Dec. 1799; matric. at Oxford (Ch. Ch.), 17 Oct. 1817, aged 17; *suc. to the Baronetcy*, 26 March 1808; M.P. for City of Durham, 1830-31; for Romney Marsh, 1831-32, and for South Derbyshire, 1835-37. He *m.*, 2 June 1821, at St. Geo. Han. sq., Sophia-Catherine, yst. da. of George William (Coventry), 7th Earl of Coventry, by his 2d wife, Peggy, da. and coheir of Sir Abraham Pitches, Knt. He *d.* s.p. 12 Oct. 1837, aged 37. Will pr. 1838. His widow *m.*, 16 July 1839, Sir Henry-William Des Voeux, 3d Bart. [I. 1787], who *d.* 4 Jan. 1868. She *d.* s.p. 29 March 1875.

IX. 1837. Sir William-Nigel Gresley, Bart. [1611], of Drakelow, and Netherseale aforesaid, cousin and h. male, being s. and h. of Rev. William Gresley, B.A., Rector of Seale, co. Leicester [1798—1829], by his 1st wife, Louisa-Jane, da. of Sir Nigel Gresley, 6th Bart., which William (who *d.* 3 Oct. 1829, aged 69) was s. and h. of Rev. Thomas Gresley, D.D., also Rector of Seale aforesaid (*d.* 18 April 1785), the s. and h. of John Gresley, of Netherseale, who was s. and h. of Thomas Gresley, of the same, yr. br. of the 3d Bart., both being sons of the 2d Bart. He was *b.* 25 March 1806; matric. at Oxford (Ch. Ch.), 4 May 1824, aged 18; B.A. (St. Mary Hall), 1829; Rector of Seale, 1830-47; *suc. to the Baronetcy*, 12 Oct. 1837. He *m.*, 25 March 1831, in Lichfield Cathedral, Georgina-Anne, 2d da. of George Reid, of Watlington Hall, Norfolk, and of Bunker's Hill, and Friendship in Jamaica, by Louisa, da. of Sir Charles Oakeley, 1st Bart. [1790]. He *d.* 3 Sep. 1847, at Netherseale Hall, in his 42d year. Will pr. Jan. 1848. His widow living 1899.

X. 1847. Sir Thomas Gresley, Bart. [1611], of Drakelow aforesaid, s. and h., *b.* at Netherseale Hall, 17 June 1832; ed. at Rugby; *suc. to the Baronetcy*, 3 Sep. 1847; Capt. 1st Dragoon Guards, 1853—1858; sometime Aide-de-Camp to the Viceroy of Ireland; M.P. for South Derbyshire, 1868 till death; Lieut. Col. of Derbyshire Rifle Volunteers, 1860. He *m.*, 28 Feb. 1854, at the Chapel Royal, Dublin, Laura-Anne, 1st da. of Robert Griffiths Williams, Capt. in the Army (2d s. of Sir Robert Williams, 9th Bart. [1661]), of Penryn, by Mary-Anne, da. of Piers Geale, of Dublin. He *d.* 18 Dec. 1868, at Shipley Hall, co. Derby, after a short illness, aged 36. His widow living 1899.

XI. 1868. Sir Robert Gresley, Bart. [1611], of Drakelow aforesaid, only s. and h., *b.* 1 Feb. 1866, in Upper Grosvenor street, Midx., and *suc. to the Baronetcy*, 18 Dec. 1868; ed. at Eton. He *m.*, 6 June 1893, at St. Margaret's, Westm., Frances Louisa, 1st da. of George Charles (Spencer-Churchill), Duke of Marlborough, by his 1st wife, Frances Albertha Anne, da. of James (Hamilton), 1st Duke of Abercorn [I.]. She was *b.* 15 Sep. 1870.

(a) Wilmot, his only da. and h., inherited the estate of Drakelow. See 7th Bart.

(b) See *Gent. Mag.*, 1787, for his character, reprinted, with some verses to his memory, in Betham's *Baronetage*, 1801.

Family Estates.—These, in 1883, consisted of 3,241 acres in Derbyshire, and 506 in Leicestershire. *Total*, 3,747 acres, worth £8,511 a year. *Principal Residence.*—Drakelowe Hall, near Burton-on-Trent, co. Derby.

TRACY:

cr. 29 June 1611;

ex. 28 Feb. 1677.

I. 1611. "Paul Tracye, of Stanwaye, co. Gloucester, Esq.," s. and h. of Richard Tracy,[a] of Stanway aforesaid, by Barbara, da. of Thomas Lucy, of Charlecote, co. Warwick; was *b.* about 1550; suc. his father, 1569; was, possibly, "(—) Tracie, of co. Gloucester, Esq.," who was M.A., Oxford (from Univ. Coll.), in or before 1572, and then aged 24; was Sheriff of co. Gloucester, 1586-87 and 1610-11, and was *cr. a Bart.*, as above, 29 June 1611. He *m.* firstly, in or before 1580, Anne, da. and h. of Ralph Shakerley, of Aynho on the hill, co. Northampton, by Alice, da. and h. of Hugh Radcliffe.[b] She, by whom he had ten sons and ten daughters, *d.* 1615. He *m.* secondly, 19 Aug. 1619, at St. James', Clerkenwell, Anne, widow of William Dutton, da. of Sir Ambrose Nicholas, sometime (1575) L. Mayor of London. She, by whom he had no issue, was *bur.* 10 Aug. 1625 (with her first husband), at Sherborne, Dorset. He *d.* 4 March 1625/6. Will pr. 1626.

II. 1626. Sir Richard Tracy, Bart. [1611], of Stanway aforesaid, 1st surv. s. and h., *b.* about 1581; matric. at Oxford (Queen's Coll.), 14 Oct. 1597, aged 16; Student of the Middle Temple, 1600; *Knighted*, 23 July 1603; *suc. to the Baronetcy*, 4 March 1625/6; Sheriff of Gloucestershire, 1628-29. He *m.* (settl. 20 July 1608) Anne, 3d da. of Sir Thomas Coningsby, of Hampton Court, co. Hereford, by Philippa, da of Sir William Fitzwilliam, L. Deputy of Ireland. He was *bur.* at Stanway, 25 Aug. 1637. Inq. p.m. Will pr. 1637. Will dat. 17 July and pr. 6 Dec. 1637. His wife survived him.

III. 1637. Sir Humphrey Tracy, Bart. [1611], of Stanway aforesaid, s. and h., *b.* about 1611; matric. at Oxford (Queen's Coll.), 21 Nov. 1628, aged 17; Student of the Middle Temple, 1629; *suc. to the Baronetcy* in Aug. 1637; Sheriff of Gloucestershire, 1639-40; a great sufferer in the Royal cause, his estate being sequestrated and he being fined £1,560 as composition money.[c]. He *m.* Elizabeth, da. of (—). He was *bur.* 15 Jan. 1657/8, at Stanway. Will dat. 15 Jan. 1657, and pr. 27 Feb. 1657/8.

IV. 1658. Sir Richard Tracy, Bart. [1611], of Stanway aforesaid, and of Hadley, co. Midx., s. and h.; *suc. to the Baronetcy* in Jan. 1657/8. He *d.* s.p. unm. and was *bur.* 6 July 1666, at Monken Hadley aforesaid. Admon. 11 Aug. 1666, to Sir John Tracy, Bart., uncle and next of kin.[d]

(a) This Richard was yr. br. of William Tracy, of Todington, co. Gloucester, ancestor of the Viscounts Tracy of Rathcoole [I.], both being sons of Sir William Tracy, of Todington aforesaid, a grantee of several ecclesiastical estates at the Reformation.

(b) Margaret, da. of Philip Moss [or Moyse], of Cannon [in Banstead], co. Surrey, who would appear to have been his wife, from a (grammatical) reading of the M.I. to Paul Tracy, his *grandson* (who *d.* 1 June 1618), was the wife of his *son*, Paul Tracy, the father of the child commemorated. [See Lodge's *Irish Peerage*, edit. 1789, vol. v, p. 7, compared with the Visit. of co. Gloucester, 1623.]

(c) By him the monument in St. Peter's, Gloucester, of Robert of Normandy (1st son of William I.), which had been broken up by the Parl. soldiers was preserved. After the Restoration it was consequently able to be re-erected.

(d) In all the printed accounts this Richard is made brother of the 2d and 4th Baronets. There was, indeed, a brother named Richard, who is mentioned in the Glouc. Visit. of 1623, as being between them, but not only does the admon. of the 4th Bart. shew that John, the 5th Bart., was his uncle, but the said Sir John in his will mentions lands "late the property of my brother, Sir Humphrey Tracy, Bart., which, *by the death of his son*, Sir Richard Tracy, Bart., descended to me."

V. 1666, to 1678. Sir John Tracy, Bart. [1611], of Stanway aforesaid, uncle and h.; *bap.*, 3 Aug. 1862, at Hasfield; *suc. to the Baronetcy* in July 1666. He *m.* before 10 Sep. 1663, Juliana, da. of Sir Erasmus de la Fontaine, of Kirby Bellers, co. Leicester, by Mary, da. of Edward (Noel), 2d Viscount Campden. He *d.* s.p., 28 Feb. and was *bur.* 17 March 1677/8, at Stanway, when the *Baronetcy* became *extinct*. Will dat. 13 June 1673, pr. by his widow, 10 May 1678.[a].

WENTWORTH:

cr. 29 June 1611;

ex. Oct. 1631.

I. 1611, to 1631. "John Wentworth, of Gosfield, co. Essex, Knt.," s. and h. ap. of John Wentworth, of the same, by Cicely, da. of Sir Edward Unton, of Wadley, was *b.* about 1583; *Knighted* at Belvoir Castle, 22 April 1603; was Gent. of the Bedchamber in 1610 to Henry, Prince of Wales, whose funeral he, in 1613, attended; having been previously *cr. a Bart.*, as above, 29 June 1611. He suc. his father, 10 Feb. 1613/4. In June 1620 he joined the expedition in support of the Elector Palatine. In 1622 he alienated the family estate at Gosfield. He *m.* Catharine, da. of Sir Moyle Finch, 1st Bart. [1611], by Elizabeth, *suo jure* Countess of Winchilsea. He *d.* s.p.m.s.[b], Oct. 1631, when the *Baronetcy* became *extinct*. His admon., as "of St. Clement Danes, Midx., Knt." 26 Jan. 1632/3, to a creditor. His widow was *bur.* 26 Sep. 1639, at Epping. Her will pr. 29 Sep. 1639.

BELLASIS, *or* BELASYSE:

cr. 29 June 1611,

afterwards, 1627-43. Barons Fauconberg of Yarm,

and, 1643-89, 1700-56 and 1802-15,

Viscounts Fauconberg of Henknoll,

being sometime, 1689-1700, and 1756-1802, Earls Fauconberg;

ex. 24 June 1815.

I. 1611. "Henry Bellasis, of Newborough, co. York, Knt." 2d but 1st surv. s. and h. of Sir William Bellasis, or Belasyse, of the same, by Margaret, da. of Sir Nicholas Fairfax, of Gilling, in Walton, co. York; was *bap.* 14 June 1555, at Coxwold; signed the pedigree (as "Henry Belassis") in the Heralds' Visit. of Yorkshire, 1584; was *Knighted* at York, 17 April 1603; Sheriff of Yorkshire, 1603-04; suc. his father (who died aged 81), 13 April 1604, and was *cr. a Bart.* as above, 29 June 1611. He was renowned for great hospitality. He *m.* Ursula, 1st da. of Sir Thomas Fairfax of Denton, co. York, by Dorothy, da. of George Gale, sometime L. Mayor of York. He was *bur.* 19 August 1624, at St. Saviour's, York. M.I. in York Minster. Will dat. 25 Feb. 1622 to 16 Aug. 1624, pr. at York. His widow *m.* William Mallory, and *d.* 25 Aug. 1633. Her will dat. 7 Dec. 1631, pr. 6 June 1633, at York.

II. 1624. Sir Thomas Belasyse, Bart. [1611], of Newborough aforesaid, only s. and h.; *b.* 1577; M.P. for Thirsk, 1597-98, 1614, 1621-22, and 1624-25; *Knighted*, 9 July 1603; *suc. to the Baronetcy* in Aug. 1624. He

(a) In it he leaves the Stanway estate to his distant cousin, the Hon. Ferdinando Tracy (2d son of John, 3d Viscount Tracy of Rathcoole [I.], whose descendants in the male line possessed it for two generations.

(b) Of the two survivors of his four daughters and coheirs (1) Cicely, *m.*, in or before 1627, William (Grey) 2d Baron Grey of Werke; (2) Lucy, *m.* in 1638, as his second wife, her kinsman Thomas (Wentworth), Earl of Cleveland, by whom she had a da., her only child.

m. about 1600, Barbara, 1st da. of Sir Henry CHOLMLEY, of Whitby, co. York, by Margaret, da. of Sir William BABTHORPE. She was living, when he was *cr.*, 25 May 1627, BARON FAUCONBERG OF YARM, co. York, and subsequently, 31 Jan. 1642/3, VISCOUNT FAUCONBERG OF HENKNOWLE, in the Bishopric of Durham. The 2d Viscount and 3d Bart. was *cr.*, 2 April 1689, EARL FAUCONBERG, which dignity became *extinct* at his death, 31 Dec. 1700. The 4th Viscount and 5th Bart. was *cr.*, 16 June 1756, EARL FAUCONBERG OF NEWBOROUGH, co. York, which dignity became *extinct* on the death of his son, 23 March 1802. The Viscountcy and Barony of Fauconberg [1643 and 1627], together with this *Baronetcy* became *extinct*, 24 June 1815. See *Peerage.*

CONSTABLE:

cr. 29 June 1611;

ex. 15 June 1655.

I. 1611, to 1655. "WILLIAM CONSTABLE, of Flambrough, co. York, Esq.,"(a) s. and h. of Sir Robert CONSTABLE,(b) of the same and of Holme in that county, by Anne, da. and h. of John HUSSEY, of Duffield, was *b.* about 1580; served under the Earl of Essex in Ireland, by whom, probably,(a) he was *Knighted*, at Dublin, 12 July 1599; was involved in the treasonable plot of that Earl, but admitted to bail, in 1601; suc. his father, 1601, in the family estates, and was *cr. a Bart.*, as above, 29 June 1611. He was M.P. for Yorkshire, 1626; for Scarborough, 1628-29; and for Knaresborough (by an unjust return), Nov. 1641 to 1653. He took an active part against the Court measures, raised a reg. of foot, of which he was colonel, and fought against the King at Edgehill, Burlington, Whitby, Malton, etc., was Joint Guardian over the King 1648, and subsequently, one of the Regicide Judges, being one who signed the death warrant. He was Governor of Gloucester, 1648-51. His debts had, however, constrained him to sell his estate of Holme in 1633 and that of Flamborough in 1636. He was member of the 1st, 2nd, and 4th Councils of State under the Commonwealth, being twice President of the 4th Council. He *m.* 15 Feb. 1608, at Newton Kyme, co. York, Dorothy, da. of Thomas (FAIRFAX), 1st LORD FAIRFAX OF CAMERON [S.], by Ellen, da. of Robert ASKE. He *d.* s.p.s., 15, and was *bur.* 21 June 1655 in Westm. Abbey, *when the Baronetcy* became *extinct.* Will dat. 13 Dec. 1654, pr. 18 July 1655. His widow, who was *b.* 13 July 1590, at Denton, co. York, *d.* (a few months after his death), 9, and was *bur.* 11 March 1655/6, at St. Mary's, Bishophill, York. By his death before the Restoration he escaped attainder for high treason, but his body was one of the 21 that were, by warrant, 9 Sep. 1661, exhumed (as the bodies of traitors) from Westm. Abbey,(c) and his estates (which had been excepted from the act of grace) confiscated.

LEIGH, *or* LEGH:

cr. 29 June 1611,

afterwards, 1643—1786, BARONS LEIGH OF STONELEIGH;

ex., 4 June 1786.

I. 1611. "THOMAS LEGH, of Stonelly [*i.e.* Stoneleigh], co. Warwick, Knt.," 3d s. of Sir Thomas LEIGH, Lord Mayor of London (1558), by Alice, da. of John BARKER, *alias* COVERALL, of Hagmond in Wolverton, Salop; was Sheriff of Warwickshire, 1581-82 and 1595-96; *Knighted* by Queen Elizabeth before 1595, and was *cr. a Bart.*, 29 June 1611, as above. He was Custos

(a) Though called "Esq." when *cr. a Bart.*, he is said in almost all accounts of him to have been *Knighted*, 12 July 1599, at Dublin, by the Earl of Essex.

(b) This Robert, who was son of Sir Robert Constable, of Flamborough, by Dorothy, Widdrington (afterwards), his 2d wife, was born in the lifetime of his father's *first* wife. He, however, succeeded to the family estates.

(c) See a list of these in Col. Chester's *Registers of Westminster Abbey*, p. 521.

Rotulorum for co. Warwick. He *m.*, about 1570, Katharine, 4th da. of Sir John SPENCER, of Wormleighton, co. Warwick, by Katharine, da. of Sir Thomas KITSON, of Hengrave, co. Suffolk. He *d.* 1 Feb. 1625/6, and was *bur.* at Stoneleigh. Will pr. 1626. His widow *d.* Jan. 1639, and was also *bur.* there.(a) Will pr. 1639.

II. 1626. SIR THOMAS LEIGH, Bart. [1611], of Stoneleigh aforesaid, grandson and h., being only s. and h. of Sir John LEIGH, by his 1st wife, Ursula, da. and h. of Sir Christopher HODDESDON, of Leighton Buzzard, Beds., which John, who was only s. and h. ap. of the 1st Bart., *d.* v.p. He was *b.* about 1595; matric. at Oxford (Mag. Coll.), 4 Nov. 1608, aged 13; was possibly (unless it was his uncle) *Knighted*, at Theobalds, 21 Dec. 1616, and *suc. to the Baronetcy*, 1 Feb. 1625/6; was M.P. for Warwickshire, 1628-29; Sheriff of Warwickshire, 1636-37. He distinguished himself for his intrepid loyalty,(a) and entertained the King (when the gates of Coventry were shut against him) at Stoneleigh. He *m.*, about 1615, Mary da. and coheir of Sir Thomas EGERTON (s. and h. ap. of Thomas, 1st VISCOUNT BRACKLEY and BARON ELLESMERE), by Elizabeth, da. of Thomas VENABLES, of Kinderton.(b) She was living, when he was *cr.*, 1 July 1643, BARON LEIGH OF STONELEIGH, co. Warwick, in which Peerage this *Baronetcy* became *merged*, and so continued till both became *extinct*, 4 June 1786, by the death of the 5th Baron and 6th Baronet. See *Peerage.*

NOEL, *or* NOELL:

cr. 29 June, 1611,

afterwards, 1617-29, BARON NOEL OF RIDLINGTON,

subsequently, 1629-82, VISCOUNTS CAMPDEN,

and finally, 1682-1798, EARLS OF GAINSBOROUGH;

ex. 8 April 1798.

I. 1611. "EDWARD NOELL, of Brooke, co. Rutland, Knt.," s. and h. of Sir Andrew NOEL, of Dalby, co. Leicester, and of Brooke aforesaid, by Mabel, da. of Sir James HARINGTON, of Exton, co. Rutland, was M.P. for Rutland, 1601, *Knighted* at Dublin Castle, 13 May 1602; suc. his father, 9 Oct. 1607; was Sheriff of Rutland, 1608-09 and 1615-16, and was *cr. a Bart.*, as above, 29 June 1611. He *m.* 20 Dec. 1605, at Leyton, co. Essex, Juliana, 1st da. and coheir of Baptist (HICKS), 1st VISCOUNT CAMPDEN (so *cr.* 5 May 1628), by Elizabeth, da. of Richard MAY, of London. She was living when he was *cr.* 23 March 1616/7, BARON NOEL OF RIDLINGTON, co. Rutland. In Oct. 1629, he suc. (on the death of his wife's father) as 2d VISCOUNT CAMPDEN, his grandson, the 4th Viscount, being *cr.* 1 Dec. 1682, EARL OF GAINSBOROUGH. In these titles, respectively, *this Baronetcy merged*, till they and it became *extinct*, 8 April 1798, by the death of the 6th Earl, 9th Viscount, and 8th Baronet. See *Peerage.*

COTTON:

cr. 29 June, 1611;

ex. 27 March 1752.

I. 1611. "ROBERT COTTON, of Cunington [*i.e.* Conington]. co. Huntingdon, Knt.," s. and h. of Thomas COTTON, of the same, by his 1st wife, Elizabeth, da. of Francis SHIRLEY, of Staunton Harold, co. Leicester, was *b.* 22, and *bap.* 27 Jan. 1570/1, at Denton, near Conington aforesaid; ed. at Westm. School, and at Jesus Coll., Cambridge; B.A. 1585; devoted himself to literature, and began in 1588 to collect (chiefly from the monastic libraries recently dispersed) the

(a) On 14 Dec. 1647, he was fined £5,642.

(b) Their da., Alice, wife of Sir Robert DUDLEY, a Duke of the Empire, was *cr.* DUCHESS DUDLEY, 1644, and *d.* 13 Jan. 1668/9, aged 90.

manuscripts afterwards so well known as "the Cottonian MSS."(a) He was *Knighted* 11 May 1603(b) at the Charterhouse; was M.P. for Newtown (I.W.), 1601; for Huntingdon, 1604-11. Being presumably the most profound antiquary of his period, he was consulted by the Crown as to the prerogative of raising money by royal authority alone. The creation of Baronets, and the taking a fine for each creation appears to have had its origin from his suggestion.(c) He was accordingly himself *cr. a Bart.*, as above, 29 June 1611, being one of the second set of persons so advanced. He again (after eleven years' absence) entered Parl. as M.P. for Old Sarum, 1624-25; for Thetford, 1625, and for Castle Rising, 1628-29, but advocating the King's duty to consult Parl., he became obnoxious to the Court, was accused before the Star Chamber of being the author of a seditious pamphlet, and was refused access to his valuable library. He *m.*, about 1592, Elizabeth, da. and coh. of William BROCAS, of Theddingworth, co. Leicester. He *d.*, after two days' illness, 6 May 1631, in his 61st year, at his house at Westminster, and was *bur.* with great pomp, at Connington. M.I. Will pr. 1631. Admon. of his widow, 18 May 1658.

II. 1631. SIR THOMAS COTTON, Bart. [1611], of Conington aforesaid, only s. and h., *b.* 1594; matric. at Oxford, 16 April 1613; B.A. (Broadgates Hall), 24 Oct. 1616; M.P. for Great Marlow, 1624-5 and 1625; for St. German's, 1628-29, and for Huntingdonshire, April to May 1640; Sheriff of Hunts, 1636-37; *suc. to the Baronetcy*, 6 May 1631. He took no active part during the Civil War, but, in 1650, removed for safety his father's books and manuscripts from Westminster to Stratton, Beds. He *m.* firstly, in or before 1620, Margaret, da. of Lord William HOWARD, of Naworth Castle, Cumberland, by Elizabeth, sister and coheir of George (DACRE), LORD DACRE OF GILLESLAND. He *m.* secondly (Lic. Lond. 17 April 1640), Alice, widow of Edmund ANDERSON, of Eyworth, Beds., da. and h. of Sir John CONSTABLE, of Dormanby, co. York, by Dorothy, da. and coheir of Benedict BARNHAM, Alderman of London. He *d.* 13 May 1662, aged 68, and was *bur.* at Conington. M.I. Admon. 25 Jan. 1674/5, probate of will having been renounced.

III. 1662. SIR JOHN COTTON, Bart. [1611], of Conington aforesaid, s. and h., by 1st wife; *b.* 1621; being aged 63 at the Heralds' Visit. of Cambridgeshire in 1683; Gent. of the Privy Chamber, 1661; M.P. for Huntingdon, 1661-79, and for Hunts, 1685-87; *suc. to the Baronetcy*, 13 May 1662. He *m.* firstly, Dorothy, da. and sole h. of Edmund ANDERSON, of Stratton and Eyworth, both co. Beds., by Alice, da. of Sir John CONSTABLE, which Alice was afterwards wife of Sir Thomas COTTON, 2d Bart., as abovestated. He *m.* secondly, 20 Oct. 1658, at Mark's Hall, Essex, Elizabeth, sister and h. of John Lamotte Honywood (who *d.* s.p. 1693), da. of Sir Thomas HONYWOOD, of Mark's Hall, Essex, by Hester, da. and coheir of John LAMOTTE, of London. She was *bap.* 20 Aug. 1637, at Mark's Hall, and *d.* 3 April 1702, in her 55th year, at Cotton House, Westminster. He *d.* 12 Sep. 1702, in his 81st year, at Stratton, Beds. Will dat. 11 April 1701 to 8 April 1702, pr. 15 Sep. 1702. Both *bur.* at Conington. M.I.

IV. 1702. SIR JOHN COTTON, Bart. [1611], of Conington aforesaid, grandson and h., being s. and h. of John COTTON, by Frances, da. of Sir George DOWNING, 1st Bart. [1663], which last named John was s. and h. ap. of the last Bart. by his 1st wife, but *d.* v.p. 1681, aged 31. He *suc. to the Baronetcy*, 12 Sep. 1702; was M.P. for Huntingdon, 1705 till unseated, 22 Jan. 1705/6, and for Huntingdonshire, 1710-13. He *m.*, in 1708, Elizabeth, da. of James HERBERT, of Kinsey, Oxon, by Catherine, da. of Thomas (OSBORNE), 1st DUKE OF LEEDS. She *d.* 11 Feb. 1721/2, aged 42, and was *bur.* at Conington. M.I. He *d.* s.p., 5 Feb. 1730/1, in North street,

(a) These, by the direction (1700) of his grandson, the 3d Bart., were transferred to the nation, together with Cotton House, Westminster, for £4,500, paid in 1707 to the then (4th) Baronet, 1731; nearly a fifth part of them were destroyed or injured by a fire on 23 Oct. 1731, and in 1754 they were removed to the library of the British Museum.

(b) Henceforward, having been called "cousin" by the King, owing to his descent from the Bruce family "he signed himself 'Robert Cotton Bruceus,' and designated himself Robert Bruce Cotton" [*Nat. Biogr.*]. See pedigree in Camden's *Visitation of Huntingdonshire*, 1613.

(c) See the interesting account of the Institution of that dignity in the *Herald and Genealogist* (vol. iii), written by its learned editor, John Gough Nichols.

Red Lion square, Midx., and was *bur.* in the burial ground of St. George the Martyr near Lamb's Conduit Midx. M.I. there. Will pr. 1731.(a).

V. 1731. SIR ROBERT COTTON, Bart. [1611], of Gidding, co. Huntingdon, uncle and h. male, being only surviving s. of the 3d Bart. by his second wife; ed. at Trin. Coll., Cambridge. He *suc. to the Baronetcy*, 5 Feb. 1730/1. He *m.* firstly, Elizabeth, da. of (—) WIGSTON. She *d.* 1745, aged 63. He *m.* secondly, Sarah, widow of (—) MORTON. He *d.* 12 July 1749, aged 80. Will pr. 1748. His widow *d.* 1753. Will pr. 1753.

VI. 1749, to 1752. SIR JOHN COTTON, Bart. [1611], of Gidding aforesaid, s. and h. by 1st wife. He *suc. to the Baronetcy*, 12 July 1749. He *m.* Jane, da. of Sir Robert BURDETT, 3rd Bart. [1619], of Bramcote, by his 2d wife, Magdalene, da. of Sir Thomas ASTON, 1st Bart. [1628], of Aston. He *d.* s.p.m.s. 27 March 1752, when the *Baronetcy* became *extinct.* Will pr. 1752. The will of his widow pr. 1769.

CHOLMONDELEY:

cr. 29 June 1611,

afterwards, 1628-46, VISCOUNT CHOLMONDELEY OF KELLS [I.],

and *subsequently*, 1646-59, EARL OF LEINSTER [I.];

ex. 2 Oct. 1659.

I. 1611, to 1659. "ROBERT CHOLMONDELEY, of Cholmondeley, co. Chester, Esq.," s. and h. of Sir Hugh CHOLMONDELEY, of the same, by Mary, da. and h. of Christopher HOLFORD, of Holford, in that county; *b.* 26 June 1584, at Cronchend, Highgate, Midx.; matric. at Oxford (Queen's Coll.), 24 Oct. 1600; suc. his father, in the family estates, 23 July 1601, and was *cr. a Bart.*, as above, 29 June 1611; Sheriff of Cheshire, 1619-20; M.P. for Cheshire, 1625. He *m.* Catharine, da. of John (STANHOPE), 1st BARON STANHOPE OF HARRINGTON, by Margaret, da. and coheir of Henry MAC-WILLIAMS. She was living when he was *cr.*, 2 July 1628, VISCOUNT CHOLMONDELEY OF KELLS, co. Meath [I.], being subsequently *cr.*, 1 Sep. 1645, BARON CHOLMONDELEY OF WICHE MALBANK, co. Chester [E.], and finally, 3 March 1645/6, EARL OF LEINSTER. In these titles, respectively, this *Baronetcy* then *merged* till they and it became *extinct* on his death, s.p. legit., 2 Oct. 1659. For further particulars see *Peerage.*

MOLYNEUX:

cr. 29 June 1611;

ex. 9 June 1812.

I. 1611. "JOHN MOLYNEUX, of Tevershalt [*i.e.*, Teversall], co. Nottingham, Esq.,"(b) s. and h. of Thomas MOLYNEUX, of Teversall, Hawton, and Aslacton in that county, by Alice, da. and coheir of Thomas CRANMER, of Aslacton aforesaid, suc. his father in 1597; was Sheriff of Notts, 1609-10 and 1611-12, and was *cr. a Bart.*, as above, 29 June 1611, being subsequently,(a) 3 June 1612, *Knighted.* He lived in so great style that he was forced to alienate much of his estate in Yorkshire and Notts. He *m.*, firstly, in or before 1602, Isabel, da. of John MARKHAM of Sedgebrooke, by his 1st wife, Mary, da. of Sir Anthony THOROLD. He *m.* secondly, Anne, widow of Thomas FOLJAMBE, da. of Sir James HARINGTON, of Ridlington, co. Rutland, by Lucy, da. of Sir William SIDNEY. He *d.* before 1618. The will of his widow pr. Dec. 1644.

(a) Conington House was pulled down in 1753.

(b) See p. 18, note "c," *sub* "Tollemache," as to many Baronets so *Knighted.* There was a "John Molineux, Notts," *Knighted* in Nov. 1608, who was doubtless the "Sir John Mullynoxe, Prisoner in the Fleet," who was buried at St. Bride's, London, 1 Sep. 1625, whose admon., dat. 23 Aug. 1633, was granted to Dame Lucy, his widow.

II. 1614? SIR FRANCIS MOLYNEUX, Bart. [1611(²)],(a) of Teversall and Hawton aforesaid, s. and h. by 1st wife, *b.* 1602; *suc. to the Baronetcy* before 1618; Sheriff of Notts. 1648-49. He *m.* (Lic. Lincoln, 4 Jan. 1619/20, he aged 18 and a Baronet, and she 17), Theodosia, da. of Sir Edward HERON, K.B., of Cressy Hall, co. Lincoln, by Ann, da. of Sir Henry BROOKE. He *d.* 12 Oct. 1674, aged 72, at Kneveton manor, and was *bur.* at Teversall. M.I. His wife survived him.

III. 1674. SIR JOHN MOLYNEUX, Bart. [1611(²)], of Teversall and Hawton aforesaid, s. and h., *b.* 1625, *suc. to the Baronetcy*, 12 Oct. 1674, aged 62 in 1687.(b) He *m.* Lucy, widow of Robert HESKETH, of Rufford, co. Lancaster, da. of Alexander RIGBY, of Middleton, in the said county, one of the Barons of the Exchequer. She *d.* Aug. 1688. He *d.* Oct. 1691, aged 66, both being *bur.* at Teversall. M.I.

IV. 1691. SIR FRANCIS MOLYNEUX, Bart. [1611(²)], of Teversall and Hawton aforesaid, s. and h., *b.* 1656; aged 31 in 1687(b); *suc. to the Baronetcy* in Oct. 1691; was M.P. for Newark, 1693—1700; for Notts, 1701-02 and 1702-06. He *m.*, before 1687, Diana, sister of Scrope, 1st VISCOUNT HOWE [I.], da. of John Grubham HOWE, of Langar, Notts, by Annabella, illegit. da. of Emanuel (SCROPE), EARL OF SUNDERLAND. She *d.* 8 Jan. 1718, in her 60th year. He *d.* 12 March 1741/2, aged 86. M.I. to both at Teversall.

V. 1742. SIR CHARLES MOLYNEUX, Bart. [1611(²)], of Teversall aforesaid, *suc. to the Baronetcy*, 12 March 1741/2, 5th but 1st surv. s. and h. male. Sheriff of Notts. He *d.* unm., 28 July 1764, at Teversall. Will pr. 1764.

VI. 1764. SIR WILLIAM MOLYNEUX, Bart. [1611(²)], of Teversall aforesaid; br. and h., *suc. to the Baronetcy*, 28 July 1764; sometime one of the Verdurers of Sherwood Forest. He *m.*, in or before 1737, Anne, da. and h. of William CHALLAND, of Wellow, Notts. He *d.* May 1781.

VII. 1781, to 1812. SIR FRANCIS MOLYNEUX, Bart. [1611(²)], of Wellow, Notts, s. and h.; *b.* before 1737. He was made Gentleman Usher of the Black Rod in 1765, and was *Knighted* 18 Sep. 1765; *suc. to the Baronetcy*, May 1781; *cr.* D.C.L. of Oxford, 4 July 1793. He *d.* unm. 9 June 1812, aged 75, when the title became *extinct*.(c) Will pr. 1812.

WORTLEY:

cr. 29 June 1611;

ex. 14 March 1665.

I. 1611. "FRANCIS WORTLEY of Wortley, co. York, Knt.," s. and h. of Sir Richard WORTLEY, of the same, by Elizabeth (*afterwards* COUNTESS OF DEVONSHIRE), da. of Edward BOUGHTON, of Cawston, co. Warwick, *b.* about 1592; suc. his father in the family estates, 25 July 1603; matric. at Oxford (Mag. Coll.), 17 Feb. 1608/9, aged 17; *Knighted*, 15 Jan. 1610/1, at Theobald's, being *cr. a Bart.*, as above, 29 June 1611. He was admitted to Gray's Inn, 1 Aug. 1624; was M.P. for East Retford (in three Parls.), 1624-26; was a devoted adherent of the Royal cause during the Civil Wars; raised a troop of horse, fortified his house at Wortley, and was taken prisoner in 1644 at Wotton House, near Wakefield. His estates were

(a) The figure "(2)" is put after the date of creation [1611], inasmuch as this is the second of two Baronetcies of the same name which were created in the same year. See p. 4, note "a."

(b) Visit. of London, 1687.

(c) The estates passed to his nephew, Henry Thomas Howard (afterwards Lord Henry Thomas Molyneux-Howard), br. of the Duke of Norfolk, both being children of his sister, Juliana (Molyneux), by Henry Howard, of Glossop, co. Derby.

sequestrated,(a) being fined £500 on 24 April 1647. He *m.* firstly, Grace, da. of Sir William BROUNCKER, of Melksham, Wilts. He *m.* secondly, after 1615, Hester, widow of Christopher EYRE, Alderman of London, da. of George SMITHES, Alderman and sometime (1611-12), Sheriff of London, by Sarah, da. of Anthony WOOLHOUSE, of Chapwell, co. Derby. She probably (not being mentioned in his will), died before him. He *d.* Sep. 1652. Nunc. will as "of Carleton, co. York," directing his burial to be, by his father, at Windsor, dat. 9, and pr. 18 Sep. 1652.

II. 1652, to 1665. SIR FRANCIS WORTLEY, Bart. [1611], of Wortley aforesaid, only s. and h. by first wife; admitted to Gray's Inn, 16 March 1640/1, and again 22 April 1657; *suc. to the Baronetcy* in Sep. 1652; "served Deputy Lieut., Justice of the Peace and all other offices suiting his condition, in the West Riding of Yorkshire, *temp.* Car. II."(b) He *m.* Frances, da. and coheir of Sir William FAUNTE, of Foston, co. Leicester, by Lucy, da. of Sir James HARINGTON, of Ridlington. He *d.* s.p. legit.(c) 14 March 1665, when *the Baronetcy* became *extinct*. Will pr. 1668. His widow was *bur.* from Holborn, 22 Jan. 1683/4, at St. Giles' in the Fields. Will dat. 2 Oct. 1683, pr. 3 Jan. 1683/4.

SAVILE:

cr. 29 June 1611,(d)

sometime, 1668-79, VISCOUNT HALIFAX,

subsequently, 1679-82, EARL OF HALIFAX,

and afterwards, 1682—1700, MARQUESSES OF HALIFAX;

ex. 10 Jan. 1784.

I. 1611. "GEORGE SAVILE,(e) of Thornehill, co. York, Sen. Knt.," s. and h. of Henry SAVILE, of Lupset in the said county, by his 2d wife, Joan, relict of Sir Richard BOZOM, da. and h. of William VERNON, of Barrowby, co. Lincoln, was *b.* about 1550; ed. at St. John's Coll., Oxford, in or before 1566; Student of Linc. Inn, 1568; M.P. for Boroughbridge, 1586-87, and for Yorkshire, 1592; *Knighted* in Holland, 1587; was of Barrowby, co. Lincoln aforesaid, till he suc. to the estate of Thornhill, on the death of his cousin, Edward SAVILE, in Feb. 1602/3, and was *cr. a Bart.*, as above, 29 June 1611.(d) He was Sheriff of Yorkshire, 1613-14. He *m.* firstly, in or before 1600, Mary,(f) da. of George (TALBOT), 6th Earl of SHREWSBURY, by his 1st wife, Gertrude, da. of Thomas (MANNERS), EARL OF RUTLAND. He *m.*, secondly, Elizabeth, widow of George SAVILE, of Wakefield, da. of Sir Edward AYSCOUGH, of South Kelsey, co. Lincoln, Knt., by Hester, da. of Thomas GRANTHAM, of Goltho', in that county. He *d.* 12 Nov. 1622, in his 72d year, and was *bur.* 19 Nov. in Thornhill Church. M.I. Admon. 20 Dec. 1622. His widow was *bur.* 25 Jan. 1625/6, at Horbury.

(a) He was an author of poems and of various essays, his most known work being his *Characters and Elegies*.

(b) Collins' *Baronetage*, 1720.

(c) He devised his vast estates to the Hon. Sidney Montague (2d son of Edward, 1st Earl of Sandwich), who had married his illegit. da. Anne Newcomen, otherwise Wortley, on condition of his taking the name of Wortley, which he accordingly did. These afterwards passed to their son and then to their grandaughter Mary, Countess of Bute, [S.], *cr.*, in 1761, Baroness Mount Stuart of Wortley, whose second son inherited them and took the name of Wortley, being ancestor of the Barons and Earls of Wharncliffe, the present [1899] owners thereof.

(d) "The warrant for Sir George Savile, of Thornhill, did not pass until 2 July 1611, and that for Sir George St. Paul not until the 5th of that month, but warrants were issued to date their patents of creation on the 29th of June last past, notwithstanding the statute 18 Hen. VI, and they were ranked respectively as the 39th and 48th in order of creation." [*Her. and Gen.*, vol. iii, p. 352.]

(e) See J. W. Clay's *Dugdale's Visit. of Yorkshire*, with additions.

(f) By her the estate of Rufford, Notts., came into the Savile family.

H

II. 1622. SIR GEORGE SAVILE, Bart. [1611], of Thornhill aforesaid, grandson and h., being s. and h. of Sir George SAVILE, by his 2d wife, Ann, da. of Sir William WENTWORTH, 1st Bart. [1611], which last named George (*Knighted* 11 May 1603), was s. and h. ap. of the late Bart. (by his 1st wife), and *d.* v.p., being *bur.* at Thornhill, 24 Aug. 1614, aged 31. He was *b.* about 1611; *suc. to the Baronetcy*, 12 Nov. 1622. He matric. at Oxford (Univ. Coll.), 5 May 1626, aged 15, and *d.* there unm., 19 Dec. following, being *bur.* 20 Jan. 1626/7 at Thornhill.

III. 1626. SIR WILLIAM SAVILE, Bart. [1611], of Thornhill aforesaid, brother and h., *b.* about 1612; matric. at Oxford (Univ. Coll.), 8 Dec. 1626, aged 14; *suc. to the Baronetcy* (a few days later), 19 Dec. 1626; Student of Gray's Inn, 1628; M.P. for Yorkshire, April to May, 1640, and for Old Sarum, about Feb. 1641, till disabled in Sep. 1642; Governor of York. He was a great sufferer for the Royal cause, and was in command of a Reg. of Foot. He *m.* Anne, da. of Thomas (COVENTRY), 1st BARON COVENTRY OF AYLESBOROUGH, Lord Keeper of the Great Seal, by his 2d wife, Elizabeth, da. of John ALDERNEY. He *d.* at York, 24 Jan. and was *bur.* 15 Feb, 1643/4, at Thornhill. Will dat. 18 July 1642, pr. 31 Jan. 1643/4. His widow,(a) (who was even more zealous than her husband for the King's cause in the Civil Wars), *m.* Thomas CHICHELEY of Whimple, co. Cambridge, afterwards (7 June 1670), *Knighted*. She *d.* at Whimple about 1661, and was *bur.* there.

IV. 1644. SIR GEORGE SAVILE, Bart. [1611], of Thornhill aforesaid, s. and h., *b.* 11, and *bap.*, 28 Nov. 1633, at Thornhill, *suc. to the Baronetcy*, 24 Jan. 1643/4; M.P. for Pontefract, 1660; Capt. of a troop of Horse, etc. He *m.*, firstly, 1 Dec. 1656, at St. Giles' in the Fields, Dorothy, da. of Henry (SPENCER), 1st EARL OF SUNDERLAND, by Dorothy, da. of Robert (SIDNEY), EARL OF LEICESTER. She was living, when he (presumably on account of the zeal of his parents in the Royal cause) was raised to the peerage, being *cr.*, 13 Jan. 1668, VISCOUNT HALIFAX, co. York, etc.; on 16 July 1679, EARL OF HALIFAX, and on 17 Aug. 1682, MARQUESS OF HALIFAX. He *d.* 5 April 1695, aged 61. For a fuller account of him, who afterwards was one of the greatest statesmen of his time, see *Peerage*.

V. 1695. WILLIAM (SAVILE), 2d MARQUESS OF HALIFAX, etc., and 5th Bart. [1611], only surv. s. and h., by 1st wife; *b.* 1665; *suc. to the Peerage and Baronetcy*, 5 April 1695. He *d.* s.p.m., 31 Aug. 1700, when the *Peerage* became *extinct*, but the Baronetcy devolved as under. For fuller account of him, see *Peerage*.

VI. 1700. SIR JOHN SAVILE, Bart. [1611], of Lupset, co. York, cousin and h. male, being s. and h. of Sir John SAVILE, of Lupset aforesaid, by his 2d wife, Anne, da. of Sir John SOAME, which John Savile last named, (who was *bur.*, 8 May 1660, at Horbury), was s., by his 2d wife, of the 1st Bart. He was *bap.* 15 Feb. 1650/1, at Horbury; *suc. to the Baronetcy*, 31 Aug. 1700, on the death of his cousin, the 2d Marquess of HALIFAX. He *d.* unm. about 1704.

VII. 1704? SIR GEORGE SAVILE, Bart. [1611], of Thornhill aforesaid, and of Rufford, Notts., cousin and h. male, being s. and h. of Rev. John SAVILE, Rector of Thornhill aforesaid (1670-1700), by his 2d wife, Barbara, da. of Thomas JENNISON of Newcastle upon Tyne, which John was the only s. that left issue of Henry SAVILE, of Bowling, co. York (aged 67 in 1666), the 3d. s. (by his 1st wife), of the 1st Bart. He was *bap.* 18 Feb. 1678, at Thornhill; matric. at Oxford (Ch. Ch.), 4 July 1696; Student of the Middle Temple, 1691; *suc. to the Baronetcy* about 1704, having previously inherited (1700), the family estates; was Sheriff of Notts, 1706-07; M.P. for Yorkshire, 1728-34; F.R.S., etc. He *m.*, 19 Dec. 1722, at St. James', Westminster, Mary, da. of John PRATT, of Dublin, by Honoretta, da. of Sir John BROOKES, 1st Bart. [1676], of York. He *d.* 16, and was *bur.* 25 Sep. 1743, at Thornhill. M.I. Will pr. (in London) 1743, and in Dublin, 1744.

(a) See her life by Dr. Barwick. She effected the escape of the loyal Sir Marmaduke Langdale, and was herself besieged by the insurgents in Sheffield Castle. Kimber's *Baronetage*, 1771, vol. iii, p. 420.]

VIII. 1743, to 1784. SIR GEORGE SAVILE, Bart. [1611], of Thornhill and of Rufford aforesaid, only s. and h., *b.* about 1727; *suc. to the Baronetcy*, 16 Sep. 1743. He was M.P. for Yorkshire, 1758-83, and Col. of the 1st Battalion of the West Riding Militia. F.R.S., and Vice President of the Society of Arts and Sciences. He *d.* unm., 10 Jan. 1784, in his 58th year, when the *Baronetcy* became *extinct*.(a) Will pr. 3 Feb. 1784.

KNIVETON *or* KNYVETON:

cr. 29 June 1611;

ex. about 1706.

I. 1611. "WILLIAM KNYVETON, of Myrcaston, co. Derby, Esq.," s. and h. of Thomas KNIVETON, of Mircaston aforesaid, by Joan, 1st da. and coheir of Ralph LEECH, of Chatsworth, co. Derby; was Sheriff of Derbyshire, 1587-88, and again, 1614-15; M.P. for that county, 1604-11, and was *cr. a Bart.*, as above, 29 June 1611. He *m.*, about 1580, Matilda, da. and h. of John ROLLESLEY, of Rollesley. He *d.* about 1632. Admon., 14 July 1632.

II. 1632? SIR GILBERT KNIVETON, Bart. [1611], of Mircaston aforesaid, and of Bradley, co. Derby, s. and h.; entered at Gray's Inn, 22 Nov. 1602; *Knighted*, 29 May 1605, at Greenwich; *cr.* M.A. of Oxford, 30 Aug. 1605; M.P. for Derby, 1614; Sheriff of Derbyshire, 1623-24; *suc. to the Baronetcy*, in or shortly before 1632. He *m.* firstly, Mary, da. and coheir of Andrew GREY, of co. Hertford, and Essex. He *m.* secondly, 30 May 1634, at St. Swithin's, London, Frances, da. of the well known Sir Robert DUDLEY, by Alice, *suo jure* DUCHESS DUDLEY, da. of Sir Thomas LEIGH. Her will pr. April 1641. He *d.* about 1641, certainly before Nov. 1646.(b)

III. 1641? SIR ANDREW KNIVETON, Bart. [1611], of Mercaston aforesaid, s. and h., admitted to Gray's Inn, 10 Oct. 1634; *suc. to the Baronetcy* before Nov, 1646, when he petitions for discharge of his sequestration. He *m.* Alice. He *d.* s.p., and was *bur.* 24 Dec. 1669, at St. Giles' in the Fields, Middlesex. Admon., 5 Jan. 1669/70, to Alice, the relict.

IV. 1669, to 1706? SIR THOMAS KNIVETON, Bart. [1611], of Mercaston aforesaid, br. and h., *suc. to the Baronetcy*, and appears to have disposed of the estates. He was one of the Gentlemen Pensioners to Charles II, James II, William III, and Anne. He *m.*, before 1658, Elizabeth, 1st da. and coheir of Carew STURY, of Rossall, Salop, by Mary, da. of Thomas BROWNE of Shredicot, Salop. He *d.* s.p.s., about 1706, when *the Baronetcy* became *extinct*.(c) His will pr. March 1706.

WODEHOUSE, *or* WOODHOUSE:

cr. 29 June 1611,

afterwards, 1797—1866, BARONS WODEHOUSE OF KIMBERLEY,

and subsequently, since 1866, EARLS OF KIMBERLEY.

I. 1611. "PHILIP WOODHOUSE, of Kymberley Hall, Norfolk, Knt.," s. and h. of Sir Roger WODEHOUSE, of the same, by Mary, da. of John CORBET, of Sprowston, Norfolk; was M.P. for Castle Rising, 1586-87; suc. his

(a) The estates devolved on his sisters or their representatives, that of Rufford passing to his sister Barbara, Countess of Scarbrough, whose 4th son, John, afterwards (1832-35), 7th Earl, inherited them and took the name of Savile.

(b) There is, at St. Giles' in the Fields, a burial, 9 Feb. 1656/7, of "Mr. Gilbert Knifton."

(c) His son, Stury Knyveton, also a Gentleman Pensioner (1694), *d.* v.p., and was *bur.* 17 Sep. 1709, at St. Marylebone. His three sisters, or their issue, were the coheirs of the family, viz., (1) Mary, *m.* Sir Aston Cokayne, Bart.; (2) Katharine, *m.* Thomas Pegg, of Yeldersley, co. Derby, being mother of Katharine Pegg, mistress to Charles II; (3) Elizabeth, *m.* William NEVILL, of Holt, co. Leicester.

father, 4 April 1588 : Sheriff of Norfolk, 1594-95; served both in Spain and Portugal; was *Knighted* by the Earl of Essex, at Cadiz, in 1596, and was *cr. a Bart.*, as above, 29 June 1611. He *m.*, 22 Dec. 1582, at Kimberley, Grisell, widow of Hamon L'Estrange, of Hunstanton, Norfolk, da. of William Yelverton, of Rougham, in that county, by Jane, da. of Edward Cocket, of Ampton, Suffolk. He *d.* 30 Oct. 1623. Admon. 2 Oct. 1624. His widow *d.* 4 Aug. 1635. Both *bur.* at Kimberley.

II. 1623. Sir Thomas Wodehouse, Bart, [1611], of Kimberley aforesaid, s. and h., *b.* about 1585 ; was *Knighted*, when only 18, in July 1603; Gentleman of the Chamber to Henry, Prince of Wales ; *suc. to the Baronetcy*, 30 Oct 1623 ; Sheriff of Norfolk, 1624-25 ; was twice M.P. for Thetford, *viz.*, April to May 1640, and 1640-53. He *m.*, 16 June 1605, at Hunsdon, Herts, Blanche, widow of Christopher Peyton, 2d da. of John (Carey), 3d Baron Hunsdon, by Mary, da. of Leonard Hyde. She *d.* 6 Nov. 1651. He *d.* 18 March 1658, and was *bur.* at Kimberley. M.I. Will pr. 1658.

III. 1658. Sir Philip Wodehouse, Bart. [1611], of Kimberley aforesaid s. and h.; *bap.* there, 24 July 1608; *suc. to the Baronetcy*, 18 March 1658. He was a man of great learning and a skilled musician ; M.P. for Norfolk, 1654-55 and 1656-58; and for Thetford, 1660. He *m.* Lucy, da. of Sir Thomas Cotton, 2d Bart. [1611], of Conington, by his 1st wife, Margaret, da. of Lord William Howard. He *d.* 6 May 1681. His widow *d.* 26 June 1684. Both *bur.* at Kimberley. M.I.

IV. 1681. Sir John Wodehouse, Bart. [1611], of Kimberley aforesaid, grandson and h., being only s. and h. of Sir Thomas Wodehouse, by Anne, da. and h. of Sir William Airmine, 2d Bart. [1619], which Thomas, who was *Knighted*, 2 Nov. 1666, was s. and h. ap. of the 3d Bart., but *d.* v.p. 29 April 1671 (of the small pox), aged about 35. He was *b.* at Kimberley. 23 March 1669 ; *suc. to the Baronetcy*, 6 May 1681 ; was M.P. for Thetford, 1695-98, 1701-02, and 1705-08 ; for Norfolk, 1710-13; Recorder of Thetford. He *m.* firstly (Lic. Fac. 17 June 1700, he 25 [*sic*] and she above 21, parents deceased), Elizabeth, sister of Robert, Baron Bingley (so *cr.* 1713), da. of Robert Benson, of Wrenthorpe, co. York, by Dorothy, da. of Tobias Jenkins. She *d.* s.p. 5 Jan. 1700/1, and was *bur.* at Kimberley. M.I. He *m.* secondly, Mary, da. of William (Fermor), 1st Baron Lempster, by his 2d wife, Catharine, da. of John (Poulett), 3d Baron Poulett of Hinton St. George. She *d* 24 Oct. 1729. He *d.* 9 Aug. 1754. Will pr. 1754. Both *bur.* at Kimberley.

V. 1754. Sir Airmine Wodehouse, Bart. [1611], of Kimberley aforesaid, 2d but 1st surv. s. and h., by 2d wife, *b.* 1714 ; M.P. for Norfolk in five Parliaments from 1737 to 1768. Col. of the East Norfolk Militia ; *suc. to the Baronetcy*, 9 Aug. 1754. He *m.* Lætitia, da. and h. of Sir Edmund Bacon, 6th Bart. [1611], of Garboldisham, co. Norfolk, by Mary, da. of Sir Robert Kemp, Bart. [1642]. She *d.* March 1759. He *d.* 21 May 1777. Will pr. 1777.

VI. 1777. Sir John Wodehouse, Bart. [1611], of Kimberley aforesaid, 2d but 1st surv. s. and h., *b.* 4, and *bap.*, 25 April 1741, at St. James', Westm.; matric. at Oxford (Ch. Ch.), 6 Feb. 1758; *suc. to the Baronetcy*, 21 May 1777 ; Recorder of Falmouth ; M.P. for Norfolk, 1784-97. He *m.*, 30 March 1769, at South Audley chapel, St. Geo., Han. sq., Sophia, only da. and h. of Hon. Charles Berkeley, of Bruton Abbey, Somerset, by Frances, da. of Col. John West. She, who was *b.* 6 Aug. 1747, and who, in 1773, became heir to her uncle John, 5th and last Baron Berkeley of Stratton, was living, when on 26 Oct. 1797 he was *cr.* a Peer, as BARON WODEHOUSE OF KIMBERLEY, co. Norfolk. In that Barony this *Baronetcy* then *merged* and still so continues, the 3d Baron and 8th Baronet being, on 1 June 1866, *cr.* EARL OF KIMBERLEY, co. Norfolk. See *Peerage*.

POPE :

cr. 29 June 1611,

subsequently, 1628-68, Earls of Downe [I.] ;

ex. 18 May 1668.

I. 1611. "William Pope, of Willcott, co. Oxford, Knt.," only surv. s. and h. of John Pope, of the same (who was yr. br. of Sir Thomas Pope, the Founder, 1555, of Trinity College, Oxford), by his 2d wife,

Elizabeth, da. of Sir John Brocket, of Brocket, Herts., was *bap.* 15 Oct. 1573, at Wroxton, co. Oxford ; suc. his father 24 June 1583 ; was made K.B. 25 July 1603, at the Coronation of James I, and was *cr. a Bart.*, as above, 29 June 1611. He *m.*, in 1595, Anne, widow of Henry (Wentworth), 3d Lord Wentworth (who *d.* 1593), da. of Sir Owen Hopton, Lieut. of the Tower of London, by Anne, da. and h. of Sir Edward Itchingham. She was *bur.* 10 May 1625, at Wroxton. He was *cr.*, 16 Oct. 1628, EARL OF DOWNE, etc. [I.], in which peerage this *Baronetcy* became *merged* till by the death of the 4th Earl and 4th Baronet, 18 May 1668, they both became *extinct*. See *Peerage*.

HARINGTON, *or* HARRINGTON :

cr. 29 June 1611,

sometime, 1661-80, *under forfeiture*.

I. 1611. "James Harrington, of Ridlington, co. Rutland, Knt.," br. of John, 1st Baron Harington of Exton, co. Rutland, being the 3d s. of Sir James Harington, of Exton (*d.* 1592), by Lucy, da. of Sir William Sidney, of Penshurst, Kent ; was Sheriff of Rutland, 1593-94, and 1601-02, and of Oxon, 1605-06 ; *Knighted* at Grimston, 18 April 1603, and was *cr. a Bart.*, as above, 29 June 1611. He *m.* firstly, Frances, da. and coheir of John Sapcote, of Elton, co. Huntingdon, by (—), his 2d wife. She *d.* Sep. 1599, and was *bur.* at Ridlington. He *m.* secondly, Anne, widow of John D'Oyley, of Merton, Oxon, da. of Frances Bernard, of Abington, co. Northampton. He *d.* 2 Feb. and was *bur.* 10 March 1613/4, at Ridlington (Reg. at Merton aforesaid). Will dat. 21 July 1613, pr. 14 Feb. 1613/4.

II. 1614. Sir Edward Harington, Bart. [1611], of Ridlington aforesaid, s. and h., by 1st wife ; *Knighted* 11 May 1603, at the Charter House ; *suc. to the Baronetcy*, 2 Feb. 1613/4 ; Sheriff of Rutland, 1621-22 and 1636-37. He *m.*, 24 Sep. 1601, at Merton, Oxon, Margery, 1st da. and coheir of the said John D'Oyley, of Merton, by Ann (second wife of his father), da. of Francis Bernard, abovenamed. He *d.* 1653. Will, without date, pr. 15 May 1653. His widow *d.* in London, 12 and was *bur.* 23 Dec. 1658, aged about 80, at Merton. M.I. Admon. as of St. Bride's, London, 27 Feb. 1660/1.

III. 1653, to 1661. Sir James Harington, Bart. [1611], of Ridlington, and Merton aforesaid, and sometime of Swakeleys, co. Midx., s. and h. ; *bap.* 30 Dec. 1607, at Merton ; *Knighted* at Oxford, 23 Dec. 1628. M.P. for Rutland, July 1646 to 1653 ; and for Midx., 1654-55. Taking part against Charles I in the Civil Wars, he was named one of the Commissioners for trying the King, but only attended one day (23 Jan.) and did not sign the death warrant. He was in the Council of State 1649 to 1653, and in 1660, being, in 1653, Joint Master of the Mint. He *suc. to the Baronetcy* in 1653. After the Restoration he, by Act of Parl., 13 Car. II (1661), was excepted out of the general pardon, his real and personal estate forfeited to the Crown, and he, himself, *degraded* from all honour, dignity, and pre-eminence, and *from the title of Baronet, Knight, Esquire*, or *Gentleman*, and from any coat of arms, being also sentenced to be drawn with a rope round his neck through the streets of London, and to be imprisoned in the Tower of London [a] The *Baronetcy* was consequently *forfeited* at that date (1661) during his life. He *m.*, 2 Aug. 1632, at St. Peter's, St. Alban's, Herts, Catharine, da. and coheir of Sir Edmund Wright, of Swakeleys[b] in Ickenham, Midx., sometime (1640) L. Mayor of London, by his 1st wife, Martha, da. of (—) Barnes. She *d.* 15 and was *bur.* 20 June 1675, at Merton, æt. 58. He *d.* April 1680, and was *bur.* there. M.I.

* * * * *

[a] No mention is made of *his issue* in this Act, and a mere forfeiture for felony is not sufficient of itself to bar the Baronetcy, being an estate tail. An act was passed in 1660 for the *attainder* of several persons guilty of high treason for the murder of Charles I, in which, however, Sir James' name does not occur.

[b] He built the house there, which, with the manor, was sold by this Sir James Harington and his wife to Sir Robert Vyner, Bart.

IV. 1680. Sir Edmund Harington, Bart. [1611], of Merton aforesaid, s. and h., *b.* about 1635 ; admitted to the Inner Temple, 7 June 1654 He *suc. to the Baronetcy* (notwithstanding the forfeiture of his father) on his father's death in April 1680.[a] He *m.* firstly (settl., 20 Aug. 1679), Sarah, da. and h. of Penning Alston, Citizen and Grocer of London. She *d.* s.p. He *m.* secondly, 6 April 1697, at St. Antholin's, London, Abigail, da. of Joseph Vennour, of St. Benet's, Gracechurch. Settlement after marriage dat. 12 April 1697. He *d.* s.p.m.s. 1708, and was *bur.* at Reigate. Will dat. 21 Feb. 1704/5, pr. 3 Sep. 1708. His widow was *bur.* 31 Aug. 1709, at Stoke Newington, Midx. Will dat. 25 June and 19 Aug. 1709, pr. 5 Sep. following.

V. 1708. Sir Edward Harington, Bart. [1611], of Merton aforesaid, br. and h., *bap.* 10 Oct, 1639, at St. Peter le Poor, London ; *suc. to the Baronetcy* in 1708, and is described as a Baronet in Nov. 1709. He *d.* s.p. 27 March and was *bur.* 10 April 1716, aged 76, at Merton. M.I.[b]

VI. 1716. Sir James Harington, Bart. [1611], of Merton, aforesaid, and of Bourton on the Water, Oxon, great nephew and h. being s. and h. of Richard Harrington, of Iver, Bucks, by Margaret,[c] da. of William Lane, of Cowley, Midx., which Richard (who *d.* 13 June 1717, aged 33), was s. and h. of Henry Harrington, of St. Michael's, Cornhill, London, merchant (living Feb. 1704/5), who was br. to the 5th and 4th and son of the 3d Bart., and who *d.* Oct. 1705. He was *b.* about 1706, and *suc. to the Baronetcy*, 27 March 1716. He matric. at Oxford (Ball. Coll.), 15 June 1724. He *m.* firstly, Catharine, da. of William Boucher, Barrister of the Middle Temple, London. She was *bur.* 19 April 1732, at Merton. He *m.* secondly, (—), widow of (—) Moore. She *d.* s.p. He *m.* thirdly, Elizabeth, da. of William Wright, of Little Ilford, Essex, and of Blakesley Hall, co. Northampton. He *d.* 24 Jan., was *bur.* at Merton, 6 Feb. 1782, aged 77. His widow *m.* Rev. John Chaunter. She *d.* s.p. at Bourton on the Water, 16, and was *bur.* 28 Oct. 1794, at Merton. Will dat. 8 Oct. 1794, proved 3 Nov. following by her said husband.

VII. 1782. Sir James Harington, Bart. [1611], of Penpound, co. Monmouth, s. and h. by 1st wife, *b.* 6 Aug. and *bap.* 4 Sep. 1726, at Merton aforesaid ; *suc. to the Baronetcy*, 24 Jan. 1782. He *m.* Anna, only da. of James Ashenhurst of Park Hall, co. Stafford. He *d.* 17 Jan. 1793. His widow *d.* 26 June 1812, aged 82. Both *bur.* at Abergavenny. His will dat. 31 March 1786, proved 10 April 1793. Her will dat. 1 Nov. 1806, proved 6 Aug. 1812.

VIII. 1793. Sir John Edward Harington, Bart. [1611], 1st surv. s. and h., *b.* 1760. Was in the Civil Service of the E.I.C. at Fort William in Bengal ; *suc. to the Baronetcy*, 17 Jan. 1793. He *m.* 10 April 1787 at Fort William aforesaid, Marianne, da. of Thomas Philpot. She *d.* 20 Dec. 1824. He *d.* 9 June 1831, in 72d year, in Berkeley square, Midx. Will pr. June 1831. Both *bur.* at Richmond, Surrey.

IX. 1831. Sir James Harington, Bart. [1611], s. and h., *b*, 30 Sep. and *bap.* 13 Nov. 1788 at Fort William aforesaid ; matric. at Oxford 24 Oct. 1806, aged 18. Senior Magistrate and sometime a Judge at Patna in

[a] The general impression, doubtless, was that the title had been altogether forfeited. Collins (*Baronetage*, 1720) says that "by reason of the aforesaid degradation the title expired, though his descendants are yet possessed of Merton in com. Oxon." Wotton, who only deals with the [then] existing Baronetage, omits "Harington" altogether in his valuable work of 1741 ; Kimber, however, includes it in his work of 1771, but makes the then Bart., Sir James's father, Richard (whom, however, he does not style a Baronet), to be eldest son and successor [in 1680] of the degraded Baronet.

[b] There is an entry among the burials at Bath Abbey, 11 Aug. 1709, of "Sir Richard Harrington, Bart., died suddenly ; carrd away."

[c] She was *m.* 2 March 1705/6 at St. Peter le Poor, London.

the East Indies ; *suc. to the Baronetcy*, 9 June 1831. He *m.*, 2 April 1817, at Bhangulpore in Bahar, Bengal, Sophia, da. of Charles Steer, of Chichester and of London. He *d.* at Patna aforesaid, and was *bur.* there 5 Jan. 1835 aged 46. Will pr. Oct. 1839. His widow *d.* 21 Oct. 1859, in Halkin street west, Midx. Will pr. Nov. 1850.

X. 1835. Sir John Edward Harington, Bart. [1611], of Eaton Place, Midx., only s. and h., *b.* 22 May 1821, and *bap.* 3 Jan. 1822, at Jessore, in Bengal ; *suc. to the Baronetcy*, 5 Jan. 1835 ; ed. at Christ Church, Oxford ; B.A., 1842 ; Lieut. Coldstream Guards, 1841 ; Capt. 48th Foot, 1848. He *m.* 26 Oct. 1846, at St. Paul's, Knightsbridge, Jane Agnes, youngest da. of John Studholme Brownrigg, M.P. for Boston, by Elizabeth Rebecca, da. of James Henry Casamajor. He *d.* s.p., 9 Feb. 1877, at Paris, aged 54. His widow *d.* 17 April 1891, at 40 Wilton Place, Midx., aged 72, and was *bur.* at Ashford.

XI. 1877. Sir Richard Harington, Bart. [1611], of Whitbourne Court, co. Worcester, cousin and h., being s. and h. of the Rev. Richard Harington, D.D., Principal of Brasenose College, Oxford [1842-53], by his 1st wife, Cecilia, 4th da. of the Rev. Samuel Smith, D.D., Dean of Christ Church, Oxford, [1824-31], which Richard last named (who *d.* 13 Dec. 1853, aged 53), was 3d son of the 8th Bart. He was *b.* 20 May 1835, at Old, co. Northampton ; ed. at Eton, and at Christ Church, Oxford ; Student, 1853-60 ; Slade Exhibitioner, 1853 ; 2d class Classics in Mods. 1853 ; B.A., 2d class Classics and 1st class Law and Modern History, 1857 ; Vinerian Law Scholar, 1858 ; M.A., 1860 ; B.C.L., 1863 ; Barrister (Linc. Inn), 1858, with a first class certificate of honour ; *suc. to the Baronetcy*, 9 Feb. 1877 ; one of the Metrop. Police Magistrates Nov. 1871 to Jan. 1872 ; a Judge of the County Courts since 1872 ; Chairman of Quarter Sessions in Herefordshire, 1880. He *m.*, 5 June 1860, Frances Agnata, 2d da. of Rev. Robert Biscoe, Rector of Whitbourne, Herefordshire and Prebendary of Hereford.

Family Estates.—These have long since been alienated. *Residence.*—Whitbourne Court, co. Worcester.

SAVILE :

cr. 29 June 1611 ;

ex. 23 June 1632.

I. 1611, to 1632. "Henry Savile, of Metheley, co. York, Knt.," s. and h. of Sir John Savile, of Bradley Hall, near Halifax, in that county, one of the Barons of the Exchequer (1598—1606), by his 1st wife, Jane, da. of Richard Garth, of Morden, Surrey ; was *b.* in London, 1579 ; matric. at Oxford (Merton Coll.), 4 Feb. 1593/4, aged 14 ; admitted to the Middle Temple, 1593 ; *Knighted*, 23 July 1603, at the coronation of James I ; suc. his father, 2 Feb. 1606/7, and was *cr. a Bart.*, as above, 29 June 1611. He was M.P. for Aldborough (Yorkshire), 1604-11 and 1611 ; and for Yorkshire, 1629 ; was several times Vice President of the Council of the North, and was Col. of the York Militia. He *m.* Mary, da. and coheir of John Dent, Citizen of London. He *d.* s.p.s.[a] at Methley, 23 June 1632, in his 53d year, and was *bur.* there, when the *Baronetcy* became *extinct*.[b] M.I. Will dat. 13 June and pr. 29 July 1632. His widow *m.* (Lic. Lond. 23 Sep. 1634, he 45, widower, she 46, widow) Sir William Sheffield, whose will was pr. 1646.

[a] Of his many children, all of whom *d.* before him, John Savile, a young man of great promise, *d.* in France in 1631, in his 21st year.

[b] The estate of Methley devolved on his brother of the half blood, John Savile, who *d.* 1651, whose great grandson, Sir John Savile, K.B., was *cr.*, in 1753, Baron Pollington [I.], and, in 1766, Earl of Mexborough [I.], with whose descendants (the present Earls) it still remains.

WILLOUGHBY, *or* WILLUGHBY:
cr. 29 June 1611;
ex. 20 Nov. 1649.

I. 1611, to 1649. "HENRY WILLUGHBY, of Risley, co. Derby, Esq.," s. and h. of Sir John WILLOUGHBY, of the same, by Frances, da. and h. of Henry HUN, of Helgay, co. Norfolk; was *b.* 14 Sep. 1579, and was *cr. a Bart.*, as above, 29 June 1611. He *m.* firstly, Elizabeth (25 years old in 1604), da. and coheir of Sir Henry KNOLLYS, of Rotherfield Grays, Oxon, by Margaret, da. and h. of Sir Ambrose CAVE. He *m.* secondly, in 1621, Lettice, 2d da. and coheir of Sir Francis DARCY, of Bramford, Midx. He *d.* s.p.m.(a) 20 Nov. 1649, aged 70, and was *bur.* at Wilne, co. Derby, when the *Baronetcy* became *extinct*. Will pr. 1654.

TRESHAM:
cr. 29 June 1611;
ex. (—) 1642?

I. 1611. "LEWIS TRESHAM, of Rushton, co. Northampton, Esq.," yr. br. of Francis TRESHAM, of the same (well known as a conspirator in and betrayer of the gunpowder plot, who *d.* in the Tower, 30 Nov. 1605), both being sons of Sir Thomas TRESHAM (who *d.* two months previously, 11 Sep. 1605), by Muriel. da. of Sir Thomas THROCKMORTON, of Coughton, co. Warwick, was *b.* about 1575, and (probably owing to an entail) suc. to Rushton(b) and other estates, notwithstanding the attainder of his brother, and was *cr. a Bart.*, as above, 29 June 1611, being subsequently,(c) 9 April 1612, *Knighted* at Whitehall. He *m.* 4 March 1602/3, at St. Barth. by the Exchange, London (Lic. Lond. 3 March), "Mrs. Marie PEREZ," aged 23, spinster, da. of Mrs. MOORE, wife of John MOORE, Alderman of London. She, who was a native of Bilboa, and a natural born Spaniard both by father and mother, was apparently the da. of Don Ricardo PEREZ. He *d.* 1639. Admon. as "of Liveden, co. Northampton," granted 13 Sep. 1639 to Mary, his widow. The will of his widow, who directs her burial to be at St. Pancras, Midx., was pr. 1643/4 in the Commissary Court of London by "Sir don Alonzo de Cardenas, Knt," the executor.

II. 1639, to 1642? SIR WILLIAM TRESHAM, Bart. [1611], of Liveden, co. Northampton, only s. and h., *suc. to the Baronetcy* in 1639. He *m.* Frances, 1st da. of Sir John GAGE, 1st Bart. [1622] of Firle, co. Sussex, by Penelope, da. of Thomas (DARCY), Earl RIVERS. He *d.* s.p., it is said, in 1642, when *the Baronetcy* became *extinct.*(d) Admon. 22 Feb. 1650/1 to his kinsman and principal creditor. His widow *m.* George GAGE, who, presumably, was buried 14 Jan. 1688/9, from St. Giles' in the Fields. Her burial from St. Giles' in the Fields was recorded 1 Jan. 1696. Admon. 20 May 1696.

(a) He had five daughters and coheirs, *viz.* (by 1st wife) (1), Mary, *b.* 24 May 1605, *m.* Sir Henry Griffith, 1st Bart., and *d.* s.p.; (2) Frances, *b.* 14 Oct. 1607, *d.* unm.; (3) Anne, *m.* firstly, Hon. Anchitel Grey, of Risley, who *d.* there, 9 July 1602, and secondly, Sir Thomas Aston, 1st Bart., of Aston. By his 2d wife he had (4) Catherine, *m.* firstly, Sir James Bellingham, 2d Bart., and secondly, George Purefoy; (5) Elizabeth, *m.* firstly, Sir Simon Dewes, 1st Bart., and, secondly, Sir John Wray, 3d Bart.

(b) The estate of Rushton was sold not long afterwards to Sir William Cokayne, who greatly added to the grand old Elizabethan mansion (commenced in 1570 under the auspices of John Thorpe), and who died possessed thereof in 1626. It remained with his descendants, the Viscounts Cullen, for more than 200 years later.

(c) See p. 18, note "c," *sub* "Tollemache" as to the knighting of recently created Baronets.

(d) It has been conjectured (*Northants, N. and Q.*, vol. vii, pp. 41, et seq.) that he was succeeded by his brother, "Sir Maurice Tresham, Bart." There is, however, apparently no proof of such statement beyond the fact that Betham in his *Baronetage* (vol. i, p. 474), *sub* "Williamson," states that "Elizabeth, da. of Sir Maurice Tresham, *Bart.*" married Lyon Falconer, whose da. Elizabeth, married Ferdinand Hudleston, whose granddaughter married [in 1748] Sir Hedworth Williamson, 5th Bart. Muriel, sister of Sir Lewis Tresham, 1st Bart. da. of Sir Thomas Tresham of Rushton and Muriel, his wife, married Maurice Tresham, of Geddington, co. Northampton, and had a son, Maurice, born in 1618. Probably this accounts for the confusion. There are several other persons named Maurice Tresham, among the family settled at Newton and Pilton, co. Northampton.

BRUDENELL:
cr. 29 June 1611,
afterwards, 1628-61, BARON BRUDENELL OF STONTON,
subsequently, 1661—1868, EARLS OF CARDIGAN,
and finally, since 1868, MARQUESSES OF AILESBURY.

I. 1611. "THOMAS BRUDENELL, of Deene, co. Northampton, Esq.," s. and h. of Robert BRUDENELL, of Doddington, co. Huntingdon, (*d.* 4 July 1599), by Catharine, da. and h. of Geoffrey TAYLARDE, s. and h. ap. of Sir Laurence TAYLARDE, of Doddington aforesaid, *b.* about 1583; suc. to the estate of Deane, 16 Oct. 1606, on the death of his paternal uncle, and was *cr. a Bart.*, as above, 29 June 1611, being, subsequently,(a) 9 April 1612, *Knighted* at Whitehall. He *m.*, in or before 1607, Mary, da. of Sir Thomas TRESHAM, of Rushton, co. Northampton, by Muriel, da. of Sir Robert THROCKMORTON, of Coughton, co. Warwick. She was living when he was *cr.*, 26 Feb. 1627/8, BARON BRUDENELL OF STONTON, co. Leicester, being, subsequently, *cr.*, 20 April 1661, EARL OF CARDIGAN. All these dignities devolved, 27 March 1868, on the MARQUESS OF AILESBURY. See *Peerage*, under these titles, in which, since 1628, this *Baronetcy* has been *merged*.

SAINT PAUL:
cr. 29 June 1611(b);
ex. 28 Oct. 1613.

I. 1611, to 1613. "GEORGE ST. PAUL, of Snarford, co. Lincoln, Knt.," only s. and h. of Thomas ST. PAUL, of the same, by Faith, da. of Vincent GRANTHAM, of Lincoln; suc. his father, 29 Aug. 1582, was Sheriff of Lincolnshire, 1588-89; M.P. for that county, 1588-89 and 1593; and for Grimsby, 1604-11; and, having been *Knighted* before 1593, was *cr. a Bart.*, as above, 29 June 1611.(b) He *m.* Frances, da. of Sir Christopher WRAY, of Glentworth, co. Lincoln, Lord Chief Justice of the Queen's Bench, by Anne, da. of Nicholas GIRLINGTON, of Normanby, co. York. He *d.* s.p.s. 28 Oct. 1613, aged 51 years, and was *bur.* at Snarford, when the *Baronetcy* became *extinct*. M.I.(c) Will, as "of Mellwood, co. Lincoln," dat. 1612, pr. 2 June 1614, and confirmed 10 June 1615. His widow *m.*, 14 Dec. 1616, at St. Barth. the Great, London, Robert (RICH), 1st EARL OF WARWICK, who *d.* 24 March 1618/9. She *d.* at Hackney, and was carried thence, 15 Aug. 1634, to be *bur.* at Felstead, Essex, with her late husband. Will pr. 1634.

TYRWHITT, *or* TIRWHITT:
cr. 29 June 1611;
ex. 22 Aug. 1760.

I. 1611. "PHILIP TIRWHITT, of Stainfeild, co. Lincoln, Knt.," s. and h. of Edward TIRWHITT, of the same, by Anne, da. of William DALLYSON, of Laughton, co. Lincoln, was admitted t Lincoln's Inn, 23 April 1572; Sheriff of Lincolnshire, 1595-96; *Knighted*, 23 April 1603, at Belvoir Castle, and was *cr. a Bart.*, as above, 29 June 1611. He *m.*, in or before 1576, Martha, da. of Sir Anthony THOROLD, of Marston, co. Lincoln, by Margaret, da. of Henry SUTTON, of Wellingore, in that county. He *d.* 5 Feb. 1624. Will pr. 1628.

(a) See p. 18, note "c," *sub* "Tollemache," as to several Baronets being subsequently knighted.

(b) The warrant, however, did not pass till 5 July 1611. See p. 49, note "d," *sub* "Savile, of Thornhill."

(c) His heir at law was his sister's son, Philip Tirwhitt, whose father, Sir Edward (afterwards the 2d Bart.), opposed (on his behalf) the said will, by which, most of the estates were devised in the male line to the family of St. Paul.

I

II. 1624. SIR EDWARD TYRWHITT, Bart. [1611], of Stainfield, aforesaid, s. and h., *bap.* 23 March 1576/7, at St. Margaret's, Lincoln; was *Knighted*, 23 April 1603, the same day and place as his father, and *suc. to the Baronetcy*, 5 Feb. 1624. He *m.* firstly, in or before 1598, Faith, sister and coheir of Sir George ST. PAUL, Bart. (so *cr.* 1611), da. of Sir Thomas ST. PAUL, of Snarford, co. Lincoln, by Faith, da. of Vincent GRANTHAM. He *m.* secondly (settlmt. 25 March 1602), Elizabeth, widow of Robert FITZWILLIAMS, of Mabethorpe, da. of George CHUTE, of Bethersden, Kent, by Elizabeth, da. of James GAGE, of Bentley, Sussex. He *d.* 4 March 1628. Inq. p.m. at Lincoln, 8 Sep. 1628. The will of Dame Elizabeth Tyrwhitt was pr. 1649.

III. 1628. SIR PHILIP TYRWHITT, Bart. [1611], of Stainfield aforesaid, s. and h., by 1st wife, *bap.* 23 Sep. 1598, at St. Mark's, Lincoln; *suc. to the Baronetcy* about 1628. He was a great sufferer in the Royal cause during the Civil Wars, paying as much as £3,488 15s. 0d. composition to the sequestrators. He *m.* (Lic. Lond. 2 Aug. 1627, he 27, and she 28), Anne, 2d da. of Nicholas (SAUNDERSON), 1st VISCOUNT CASTLETON [I.], by Mildred, da. and h. of John ELLTOFT, of Boston. He *d.* about 1667. Admon. 2 May 1667.

IV. 1667? SIR PHILIP TYRWHITT, Bart. [1611], of Stainfield aforesaid, s. and h., *bap.* 3 Dec. 1633, at Aylesby, co. Lincoln; aged 1 year at the Visit. of Lincolnshire, 1634; Sheriff of Lincolnshire, 1660-61; M.P. for Grimsby, Oct. till unseated in Nov. 1667; *suc. to the Baronetcy* about 1667; was a Roman Catholic.(a) He *m.*, in or before 1663, Penelope, da. of Sir Erasmus DE-LA-FOUNTAIN, of Kirkby Bellers, co. Leicester. He was *bur.* 15 July 1688, at Stainfeild. Will dat. 10 March 1687/8, pr. 31 July 1688. The will of his widow pr. March 1709.

V. 1688. SIR JOHN TYRWHITT, Bart. [1611], of Stainfield aforesaid, only surv. s. and h., *suc. to the Baronetcy*, 15 July 1688; M.P. for Lincoln, 1715-22 and 1722-27. He *m.* firstly, 24 Feb. 1690/1, at St. Michael's, Bassishaw, London (Lic. Fac., he 27, and she 21), Elizabeth, da. and coheir of Francis PHILIPS, of Kempton Park, in Sunbury, Midx., by Anne, his wife. She *d.* s.p.m. He *m.* secondly (Lic. Fac. 5 Aug. 1704, she aged 24), Mary, da. of Sir William DRAKE, of Shardloes, Bucks, by Elizabeth, da. and coheir of William MONTAGUE, L. Ch. Baron of the Exhequer. She *d.* Nov. 1738. He *d.* Nov. 1741. Will pr. March 1742.

VI. 1741, to 1760. SIR JOHN-DE-LA-FOUNTAIN TYRWHITT, Bart. [1611], of Stainfield, only surv. s. and h. by 2d wife, *suc. to the Baronetcy*, Nov. 1738. M.P. for Lincoln, 1741-47. He *d.* unm. 22 Aug. 1760, when the *Baronetcy* became *extinct*.(b) Will pr. 1761.

(a) In Sir Joseph Williamson's *Lincolnshire Families, temp. Car. II*, it is said of him, "Sir Philipp hath £2,500 per ann. Sold much. . . . hathe a young sone. A retired man; a good fellow;—yᵉ son, good naturall parts but desbauched." [*Her. and Gen.*, vol. ii, p. 126].

(b) Under his will his maternal kinsman, Thomas DRAKE of Shardloes, inherited the estates to the exclusion of the issue of his sister and half sisters. This Thomas assumed, in 1776, the name of TYRWHITT before that of DRAKE. He was, however, not descended from the Tyrwhitt family.

CARR, *or* CARRE:(a)
cr. 29 June 1611;(b)
ex. in 1695.

I. 1611. "EDWARD CARRE, of Sleford, co. Lincoln, Knt.," 4th and yst. s. of Robert Carre of the same (one of the largest landed owners in that county), by his first wife, Elizabeth, da. of (—) CAWDRON, the King's Bailiff at Heckington, co. Lincoln, was *Knighted* at Belvoir Castle, 23 April 1603; suc. his only surv. brother, Sir William Carre, of Aswerbie, co. Lincoln, in or before April 1608 in the family estates, and was *cr. a Bart.*, as above, 20 June 1611; Sheriff of Lincolnshire, 1614-15. He *m.* firstly, Katharine, da. of Charles BOLLE, of Hough, co. Lincoln, by his 2d wife, Bridget, da. of George FANE. She *d.* s.p. He *m.* secondly, before 1613, Anne, da. of Sir Richard DYER, of Stoughton, co. Huntingdon, by Mary, da. of Sir William FITZWILLIAM. He *d.* 1 Oct. 1618, and was *bur.* at Sleford. M.I. Will, pr. 1618. His widow *m.* Col. Henry CROMWELL, of Hinchinbrooke, co. Huntingdon. She *d.* 1639 [Qy. if her will pr. in 1657?].

II. 1618. SIR ROBERT CARR, Bart. [1611], of Aswarby aforesaid, 1st s. and h., by 2d wife; *suc. to the Baronetcy*, 1 Oct. 1618. On coming of age in 1636 he founded the Sleaford Hospital, but was "of very weak understanding." He *m.* 30 April 1629 at St. James', Clerkenwell, Mary, da. and coh. of Sir Richard GARGRAVE(c) of Kingsley Park and Nostell, co. York, by Catharine, sister of Henry, EARL OF DANBY, da. of Sir John DANVERS. He *d.* 14 and was *bur.* 29 Aug. 1667 at New Sleaford. Admon. 6 Nov. 1667, 15 Nov. 1675 and 18 July 1685. His widow, who became involved in a series of law suits occasioned by several forged documents, *d.* 1675. Will pr. 1675.

III. 1667. SIR ROBERT CARR, Bart. [1611], of Aswarby aforesaid, only s. and h., *suc. to the Baronetcy*, 14 Aug. 1667. M.P. for Lincolnshire in several Parls., 1664/5—1681, having been *Knighted* before Jan. 1664/5; adm. to Gray's Inn, 1671/2; Chancellor of the Duchy of Lancaster, 1672-82, and P.C. 1672. He was designated as a Knight of the (intended) order of the Royal Oak.(d) He *m.*(e) Elizabeth, sister of Henry, 1st EARL OF ARLINGTON, da. of Sir John BENNET, of Dawley, by Dorothy, da. of Sir John CROFTS of Saxham. He was *bur.* 17 Nov. 1682, æt. 45, at New Sleaford.(f). Will pr. 1682 by his widow. She *d.* 1696. Will pr. 1696.

(a) See an interesting account of this family by Mr. P. Moore, read 1863, at Sleaford, printed in the *Transactions of the Lincoln Architectural Society*.

(b) Among the 52 Baronets created 29 June 1611, "SIR ROGER DALLISON, of Laughton, Lincolnshire, Knt." (making the number 53), is erroneously placed in Dugdale's *List* between those of Tyrwhitt and Carr, all three being of the same county, *i.e.* Lincolnshire [List in *Her. and Gen.*, vol. iii, p. 350]. As undoubtedly the precedency of 29 June 1611 was granted (though the grant was *after* the said Sir Roger's decease) to his son, on the creation of the Baronetcy, 27 Oct. 1624, this precise place among the numerous creations of 29 June 1611 would probably have been that of the dignity *if* the patent to the father had been sealed at that date. See under "Dallison," *cr.* 27 Oct. 1624.

(c) This Richard wasted the whole of his immense estates by gambling, and was found dead in the stable of a small inn, resting his head on the saddle of his pack horse.

(d) The list of these is given in Dugdale's *Ancient Usage of Arms* (ed. by T. C. Banks, 1812), as also in Burke's *Commoners* (edit. 1837, vol. i, pp. 688-697). The annual value of £4,000 (a sum that, in that list, is in very few instances exceeded) is ascribed to the estate of Sir Robert Carr.

(e) "Robert Carr and Isabel Falkingham" were married 13 July 1662 at New Sleaford.

(f) Sir Joseph Williamson in his *Lincolnshire Families, temp. Car. II*, writes "Carre of Sleford originally, and at Aswerby; about £5,000 or £6,000 per an.; raised from a kind of an Auditor at the dissolution of the monasteries, and, on that fall, made advantage and by consequence most of their estates in church land save some part which he gott of yᵉ Lord Hussey's estate, to whom he was a kind of servant; Sir Edward; Sir Robert; Sir Robert, Knt.; Mr. Rochester Carre, madd and without

IV. 1682. Sir Edward Carr, Bart. [1611], of Aswarby aforesaid, only s. and h.; *suc. to the Baronetcy* in Nov. 1682. He *d.* unm. 28 Dec. 1683, æt. 18, and was *bur.* 6 Jan. at New Sleaford.(a)

V. 1683, to 1695. Sir Rochester Carr, Bart. [1611], great uncle and h., being 2d and yst. s. of the 1st Bart, by his 2d wife. In 1637 he was found a lunatic, and so continued till his death. He *suc. to the Baronetcy*, 28 Dec. 1683, but *d.* unm. in or shortly before 1695, in Chancery lane, London, when the *Baronetcy* became *extinct.* Admon. 7 May 1695, to Elizabeth Carr Fox (wife of Charles Fox, Esq.), great niece, by the sister and next of kin.

HUSSEY:

cr. 29 June 1611;

ex. 14 Feb. 1729/30, *or* (possibly) 1 April 1734.

I. 1611. "Edward Hussey,(b) of Honington, co. Huntingdon [*sic*, but should be co. Lincoln], Knt.," s. and h. of Sir Charles Hussey, of the same, by Ellen (*m.* 6 July 1582), da. of John Birch, Lord Chief Baron of the Exchequer, was *bap.* 10 Oct. 1585, at Blankney; admitted to Gray's Inn, 6 Nov. 1607; *Knighted*, 29 March 1608, at Whitehall; suc. his father, 30 Jan. 1609, and was *cr. a Bart.*, as above, 29 June 1611. He was Sheriff of Lincolnshire, 1618-19 and 1636-37; M.P. for that county, 1640; was a great sufferer in the Royal cause during the Civil Wars, and was one of those named, in 1644, to be removed from the King's councils. In Dec. 1647, he paid £4,500, part of £9,000 imposed on him as a "delinquent." He *m.*, in or before 1610, Elizabeth, da. of George Anton, Recorder of Lincoln and M.P. for that city, by Jane, da. of Thomas Taylor, of Doddington Pigot, co. Lincoln. He *d.* 22 March 1648, and was *bur.* at Honington. Admon. 12 May 1648. His widow, who was *bap.* 15 Jan. 1591, at St. Martin's, Lincoln, suc. to the estate of Doddington in 1653, on the death of her maternal uncle, Thomas Taylor, and *d.* between Jan. and May 1658, being *bur.* at Honington. Will dat. 25 Jan. 1657/8, pr. 22 May 1658.

II. 1648. Sir Thomas Hussey, Bart. [1611], of Honington, and afterwards of Doddington aforesaid, grandson and h., being s. and h. of Thomas Hussey, by Rhoda(c), da. and coheir of Thomas Chapman, of London, which last named Thomas Hussey, sometime (1637) M.P. for Grantham, was 1st s. and h. ap. of the 1st Bart., but *d.* v.p. shortly before 25 March 1641. He was *bap.* 14 Jan. 1638/9, at Doddington; *suc. to the Baronetcy*, 22 March 1648.(d) He resided at the grand old mansion of Doddington(e); was Sheriff of Lincolnshire, 1668-69; M.P. for Lincoln, 1681, and for Lincolnshire (in four Parls.), 1685-95.(f) He *m.*, 21 Feb. 1660/1 (Bishop Saunderson of Lincoln officiating), at Great St. Helen's, London (Lic. Fac.), Sarah, da. of Sir John Langham, 1st Bart. [1660], by Mary, da. of

child, placed at Aswerby. To him Sir Robert, Knt., will inherit £800 per ann." [*Her. and Gen.*, vol. ii, p. 120, the editor (John Gough Nichols) adding in a note that the story about the Hussey estates "was probably scandal. The estates of the attainted Lord were granted by Hen. VIII to Lord Clinton, of whom the same were purchased by Carr."]

(a) Isabella, his only sister and h., *m.*, 1 Nov. 1688, John (Hervey), 1st Earl of Bristol, to whose descendants the family estates passed.

(b) See a good account of this family in Cole's *History of Doddington, co. Lincoln*, of which copious use has here been made.

(c) They were *m.*, 11 Dec. 1633, at St. Mary's, Woolnoth, London.

(d) As he was a Baronet in 1648, he presumably was not the "Thomas Hussey, Esq.," who matric. at Oxford (Trin. Coll.), 10 March 1656/7.

(e) An engraving thereof, between 1686 and 1706, is in Kip's *Brittania Illustrata.*

(f) Sir Joseph Williamson, in his *Lincolnshire Families, temp. Car. II*, "Hussey, originally of the county . . . at Honington anciently—Sir Edward, Caythorpe, Donington, Honington; each branch hath about £2,500 per an." [*Her. and Gen.*, vol. ii, p. 122].

James Bunce. She *d.* 19 July 1697, aged 62. He *d.* s.p.m.s.(a) 19 Dec. 1706. Both were *bur.* at Honington. M.I. His admon., 8 Feb. 1706/7, to his daughters, Sarah and Elizabeth.

III. 1706. Sir Edward Hussey, Bart. [1611 and 1661], of Caythorpe and Welbourne, co. Lincoln, cousin and h. male, being s. and h. of Sir Charles Hussey, Bart. [so *cr.* 21 July 1611], of Caythorpe aforesaid, by Elizabeth, da. of Sir William Brownlow, 1st Bart. [1641], of Humby in that county, which Charles was yr. son of the 1st Baronet of the creation of 29 June 1611. He, in or shortly before 1680, *suc.*, on the death of his br., Sir Charles Hussey, 2d Bart. [1661], *to the Baronetcy* conferred on his father, *21 July 1661*, and, about twenty-six years later, *suc. to the Baronetcy* conferred on his grandfather, 29 June 1611. He was M.P. for co. Lincoln (in five Parls.), 1689—1705. He *m.* firstly, in or before 1684, Charlotte, only child of (—) Brevint, D.D., Dean of Lincoln. She *d.* s.p m. 30 Aug. 1695, in her 31st year. He *m.* secondly, 31 May 1698, at St. Sepulchre's, London, Elizabeth,(b) da. and h. of Sir Charles De Vic, 2d Bart. [1649]; Mar. Lic., Vic. Gen., she of St. James', Westm., about 22, spinster. He *d.* 19 Feb. 1724/5, aged 65. His widow *d.* 21 Jan. 1750, aged 78. M.I. at Caythorpe. Will pr. 1750.

IV. 1725, to 1730. Sir Henry Hussey, Bart. [1611 and 1661] of Caythorpe aforesaid, s. and h., by 2d wife. He *suc. to the Baronetcies*, 19 Feb. 1724/5. He *d.* s.p. 14 Feb. 1729/30, aged 27.(c) M.I. at Caythorpe. At his death *both these Baronetcies*, in all probability, became *extinct*. He is, however, generally said to have been succeeded as below.

V. 1730, to 1734. Sir Edward Hussey, Bart. [1611 and 1661], of Caythorpe aforesaid, br. and h.,(d) is said to have *suc. to the Baronetcies*, 19 Feb. 1724/5, and to have *d.* s.p. 1 April 1734, when (if not before) *both these Baronetcies* became *extinct.*

MORDAUNT, *or* MORDANT:

cr. 29 June 1611.

I. 1611. "Le Straunge Mordant, of Massingham Parva, co. Norfolk, Esq.," s. and h. of Henry Mordaunt,(e) of King's Lynn in that county, by Ann, da. of (—) Poley, of Beds, was *b.* at Lynn, 1572; distinguished

(a) Sarah, da. and eventually sole heir, *bap.* 7 June 1672, at Doddington, *m.*, in 1700, Robert Apreece, of Washingley, co. Huntingdon, and had issue, who inherited the Lincolnshire estates of Doddington and Honington.

(b) Called "Anne" (by mistake) in mar. reg. at St. Sepulchre's.

(c) Charlotte, sister of the half blood to the last Bart., da. of the 3d Bart., by his *first* wife, *m.* Thomas Pochin, of Barkby, co. Leicester. Their da., Charlotte, *m.* Charles James Packe, of Prestwold Hall, and eventually inherited the Caythorpe estates.

(d) On the M.I. at Caythorpe, to the 3d Bart, it is stated that he had eleven children by his 1st wife, all of whom, save Charlotte and Sarah, died unm., and that he had three sons and one daughter by his 2d wife, viz., "Anne-Charlotte, Henry, Robert and Edward"; that "Sir Edward died Feb. 19, 1724/5, æt. 65; Henry succeeded him, and died unmarried, Feb. 14, 1729, æt. 27; Anne-Charlotte, Robert *and Edward* died young. This monument erected by the widow, Elizabeth."

It would therefore seem that Edward died before his brother, Henry. In Collins' *Baronetage* (1720) it is stated that of the three sons by the 2d wife "only Henry and Edward are living."

(e) This Henry was son of Robert Mordaunt, of Hempsted, co. Essex, by Barbara, da. and h. of John L'Estrange, of Massingham, co. Norfolk, and Anne, da. and coheir of Thomas L'Estrange, of Walton, co. Warwick, whereby both those estates came into the Mordaunt family. The said Robert was s. and h. of William Mordaunt, Prothonotary of the Common Pleas, 1495. a younger brother of Sir John Mordaunt, of Turvey, Beds, the ancestor of the Lords Mordaunt, Earls of Peterborough, and Earls of Monmouth.

himself as a soldier in the Low Countries and, subsequently, in Ireland, was Sheriff of Norfolk, 1606-07 and 1623-24, and was *cr. a Bart.*, as above, 29 June 1611. He *m.* firstly, Margaret, da. of Peter de Charles, of Antwerp. He *m.* secondly, Frances, widow of Thomas Sotherton, of Norwich, da. of Robert Cheeke, of Debenham, Suffolk. He *d.* 1627, and was *bur.* at Massingham, aged 55. Admon., as "of Congham, Norfolk," 10 Oct. 1627.

II. 1627. Sir Robert Mordaunt, Bart. [1611], of Massingham aforesaid, of Walton, co. Warwick, and of Hempsted, Essex, s. and h., by 1st wife; *Knighted*, v.p., 2 Jan. 1618/9, at Whitehall; *suc. to the Baronetcy* in 1627. He *m.*, in or before 1615, Amy, da. of Sir Austin Southerton, of Norfolk. He *d.* 23 Aug. 1638, and was *bur.* at Hempsted aforesaid. Admon., as "of Ipswich, Suffolk, Knt.," 7 Feb. 1638/9, to a creditor. His widow *m.*, 18 June 1639, at Croydon, Surrey, Basset Cole. She was *bur.* 26 March 1668, at St. Paul's, Covent Garden.

III. 1638. Sir Charles Mordaunt, Bart. [1611], of Massingham aforesaid, s. and h., *b.* about 1615; *suc. to the Baronetcy*, 23 July 1638. He was a great sufferer in the Royal cause; was shut up at Lynn during the siege. His estates were sequestrated. He *m.*, in or before 1638, Catharine, da. of Sir Lionel Tollemache, 2d Bart., by Elizabeth, da. of John (Stanhope), Baron Stanhope of Harrington. He *d.* in London, 10 July 1648, aged 33, and was *bur.* at Massingham. M.I. Admon. 8 Aug. 1648, and 24 July 1663. His widow *m.* (as the 2d of his four wives) Sir Charles Lee, of Billesley, co. Warwick, who *d.* 18 Oct. 1700, aged 80. She *d.* about 1653, before July 1663.

IV. 1648. Sir Charles Mordaunt, Bart. [1611], of Massingham aforesaid, s. and h., *b.* about 1638; *suc. to the Baronetcy*, 10 July 1648. He *m.* (Lic. Vic. Gen., 18 Dec. 1663, he 25 and she 18) Elizabeth, da. and coheir of Nicholas Johnson, of St. Gregory's, London, by (—), sister of Sir William Turner, sometime (1668-69) Lord Mayor of London. He *d.* s.p. 24 April 1665, aged 25, and was *bur.* at Massingham. M.I. His widow *m.* Francis Godolphin, of Colston, Wilts. Her admon., as of St. Clement Danes, Midx., widow, 10 Nov. 1687, to Sir William Turner, Knt., uncle and next of kin.

V. 1664. Sir John Mordaunt, Bart. [1611], of Walton D'Evile, co. Warwick, and of Massingham aforesaid, br. and h., *b.* about 1650; *suc. to the Baronetcy*, 24 April 1665; M.P. for Warwickshire (in eight Parls.), 1698—1715. He *m.* firstly, 13 June 1678 (Lic. Vic. Gen., he 21 and she 17), at Blunham, Beds, Anne, da. and h. of William Risley, of the Friary, Bedford, by Mary, his wife. She *d.* s.p.m. June 1692, aged 30, and was *bur.* at Wellesbourne Hastang, co. Warwick. M.I. He *m.* secondly (Lic. Fac. 8 June 1695), Penelope (then aged 22), da. of Sir George Warburton, 1st Bart. [1660], of Arley, by his 2d wife, Diana, da. of Sir Edward Bishopp, 2d Bart. [1620], of Parham, Bart. He *m.* thirdly, 1 July 1715, at St. James', Clerkenwell, Elizabeth Floyd, widow. He *d.* 6 Sep. 1721. Will pr. 1722. The will of his widow pr. 1734.

VI. 1721. Sir Charles Mordaunt, Bart. [1611], of Walton and of Massingham aforesaid, s. and h. by 2d wife, *b.* about 1698; matric. at Oxford, 8 June 1714, aged 16; admitted to Lincoln's Inn, 21 May 1718; *suc. to the Baronetcy*, 6 Sep. 1721; M.P. for Warwickshire, 1734-74; *cr.* D.C.L. (Oxford), 3 July 1759. He *m.* firstly, 1 Dec. 1720 (—), da. of John Conyers, of Walthamstow, Essex. She *d.* s.p.m. March 1725/6. He *m.* secondly, 7 July 1730, at St. Marylebone, Sophia, da. of Sir John Wodehouse, 4th Bart. [1611], by Mary, da. of William (Fermor), 1st Baron Lempster. She *d.* April 1738. He *d.* 11 March 1778. Will pr. 1778.

VII. 1778. Sir John Mordaunt, Bart. [1611], of Walton D'Evile and of Massingham aforesaid, s. and h., by 2d wife, *b.* about 1735; matric. at Oxford (New Coll.), 26 Feb. 1752, aged 17; *cr.* M.A., 8 July 1756, and D.C.L., 8 July 1763; *suc. to the Baronetcy*, 11 March 1778; M.P. for Warwickshire (in three Parls.), 1793—1802. One of the Grooms of the Royal Bedchamber. He *m.*,

8 Jan. 1769, Elizabeth, da. and eventually coheir of Thomas Prowse(a), of Compton Bishop and Axbridge, co. Somerset, by Elizabeth, da. of John Sharpe, of Grafton park, co. Northampton. He *d.* 18 Nov. 1806, at Walton, aged 73. Will pr. 1807. His widow, who was *b.* 25 Sep. 1749, *d.* at Hampstead 5 Oct. 1826, aged 77. Will pr. Feb. 1827.

VIII. 1806. Sir Charles Mordaunt, Bart. [1611], of Walton D'Evile and of Massingham aforesaid, only surv. s. and h., *b.* about 1771; ed. at Eton; matric. at Oxford (Ch. Ch.), 1 Dec. 1788, aged 17; B.A., 1791; M.P. for Warwickshire (in six Parls.), 1804-20; *suc. to the Baronetcy*, 18 Nov. 1806. He *m.*, 1807, Marianne, 1st da. of William Holbech, of Farnborough, co. Warwick, by Anne, da. of William Woodhouse, M.D., of Lichfield. He *d.* 30 May 1823. Will pr. 1823. His widow *d.* 1842. Will pr. July 1842.

IX. 1823. Sir John Mordaunt, Bart. [1611], of Walton and of Massingham aforesaid, only s. and h., *b.* 24 Aug. 1808, at Farnborough; ed. at Eton; *suc. to the Baronetcy*, 30 May 1823; matric. at Oxford, 23 May 1826, age 17; B.A., 1829; M.A., 1832; M.P. for South Warwickshire, 1835-45. He *m.*, 7 Aug. 1834, at Bromley Palace, Kent, Caroline Sophia, 2d da. of George Murray, Bishop of Rochester (grandson of John, 3d Duke of Atholl [S.]), by Sarah Maria, 2d da. of Robert-Auriol (Drummond-Hay), 9th Earl of Kinnoull [S.]. He *d.* 27 Sep. 1845, at Walton aforesaid, aged 37. Will pr. 1846. His widow, who was *b.* 10 July 1814, at Castle Mona, Isle of Man, *m.*, 25 April 1853, at St. Michael's, Chester square, Midx., Gustavus Thomas Smith, of Goldicote, co. Worcester, who *d.* 8 Jan. 1875. She was living 1899.

X. 1845. Sir Charles Mordaunt, Bart. [1611], of Walton aforesaid, 1st s. and h., *b.* 28 April 1836, in Grosvenor Place; ed. at Eton; matric. at Oxford (Ch. Ch.), 8 June, 1854; *suc. to the Baronetcy*, 27 Sep. 1845; M.P. for South Warwickshire, 1859—1868; Sheriff of that co., 1879; Hon. Lieut.-Col. Warwickshire Yeomanry. He *m.*, firstly, 7 Dec. 1866, at St. John's Episc. Church, Perth, his cousin, Harriet Sarah, 4th da. of Sir Thomas Moncreiffe, 7th Bart. [S.], by Louisa Drummond-Hay, 1st da. of Thomas Robert, 10th Earl of Kinnoull [S.]. From her, by whom he had no male issue, he obtained a divorce. 11 March 1875. He *m.*, secondly, 24 April, 1878, at Adlestrop, co. Gloucester, Mary Louisa, 2d da. of Rev. the Hon. Henry Pitt Cholmondeley, Rector of Adlestrop (3d s. of Thomas, 1st Baron Delamere of Vale Royal), by Mary, da. of Chandos (Leigh), 1st Baron Leigh of Stoneleigh. He *d.* 15 Oct. 1897, aged 61, in London. Will pr. at £370,490. His widow living 1899.

XI. 1897. Sir Osbert L'Estrange Mordaunt, Bart. [1611], of Walton aforesaid, only s. and h., by 2d wife; *b.* 27 Jan. 1884; *suc. to the Baronetcy*, 15 Oct. 1897.

Family Estates.—These, in 1883, consisted of 4,123 acres in Somerset (worth £8,057 a year) and 3,325 in Warwickshire. *Total*, 7,448 acres, worth £12,792 a year. *Principal Residence.*—Walton Hall, near Wellesbourne, Warwickshire.

BENDISH, *or* BENDISHE:

cr. 29 June 1611;

ex. 4 Sep. 1717.

I. 1611. "Thomas Bendishe, of Steple Bumpsted, co. Essex, Esq.," s. and h. of Thomas Bendish, of Steeple Bumstead aforesaid, by his 1st wife, Eleanor, da. and h. of John Foord, of Frating and Great Horkesley, in that county, *b.* about 1568; suc. his father, 23 Feb. 1603, being then 35 years old, and was *cr. a Bart.*, as above, 29 June 1611. Sheriff of Essex, 1618-19, and 1630-31.

(a) See pedigree of Prowse in *Mis. Gen. et Her.*, N. S., vol. iii, pp. 165—169. The mother of this Thomas Prowse was a da. of the well known George Hooper, Bishop of Bath and Wells.

He *m.* Dorothy, yst. da. of Richard CUTTS, of Arkesden and Debden, co. Essex, and of the Inner Temple, London. He *d.* 26 March 1635, at Bower Hall, in Steeple Bumstead, where he was *bur.*, aged 71. Will dat. 15 June 1635, pr. 26 May 1636. His wife, who probably survived him, living June 1635.

II. 1636. SIR THOMAS BENDISH, Bart. [1611], of Bower Hall, aforesaid, s. and h., *b.* about 1607; being 7 years old in 1614, and 29 years when he *suc. to the Baronetcy*, 26 March 1636; was a zealous Royalist in the Civil Wars, sending £3,000 to the King at Newcastle. His estates were accordingly sequestrated, he being fined £1,500 in Aug. 1644. In 1647 he was sent as Ambassador to Constantinople, continuing there for about fourteen years.[a] He *m.*, about 1627, Anne, da. and coheir of Henry BAKER, of Shoeberry, co. Essex. She *d.* before him at Constantinople, but was *bur.* at Steeple Bumstead. He *d.* at Bower Hall aforesaid, about 1674.

III. 1674? SIR JOHN BENDISH, Bart. [1611], of Bower Hall aforesaid, 2d but 1st surv. s. and h., *b.* about 1630; *suc. to the Baronetcy* about 1674. He *m.*, about 1664, Martha, da. of Robert BETTESON, or BATSON, of London, Merchant, by Sarah, da. of Richard FORD. She *d.* 5 and was *bur.* 20 Dec. 1705, at Steeple Bumstead. M.I. Her will pr. Jan. 1706. He *d.*, a prisoner for debt in the Fleet prison, London, 22 April and was *bur.* 3 May 1707, at Steeple Bumstead, aged 78.

IV. 1707, to 1717. SIR HENRY BENDISH, Bart [1611], of Bower Hall aforesaid, 6th and yst. but only surv. s. and h., *b.* about 1674; *suc. to the Baronetcy*, 22 April 1707; el. Sheriff of Essex, Nov. 1610, but did not act. He *m.*, Feb. 1706/7, at St. Paul's Cathedral, London, Catharine, da. of Sir William GOSTLIN, of Ealing, Midx., sometime (1684-85) Sheriff of London. He *d.* s.p.s. 4 and was *bur.* 11 Sep. 1717, at Steeple Bumstead, aged 43, when the *Baronetcy* became *extinct*. Will dat. 13 Feb. 1713, to 6 July 1717, pr. 1 Oct. 1717. His widow *d.* about 1738. Her admon., as "of Steeple Bumstead," granted 20 March 1738/9, to "Charles Gostlin, Esq.," br. and next of kin.

WYNN:

cr. 29 June 1611;

ex. 7 Jan. 1719.

I. 1611. "JOHN WYNN, of Gwydder, co. Carnarvon, Knt.," s. and h. of Maurice WYNN, of Gwydir aforesaid, by Jane, da. of Sir Richard BULKELEY, of Beaumorris, co. Anglesey; was *Knighted* at Whitehall, 14 May 1606, and was *cr. a Bart.*, as above, 29 June 1611. He, who was a great collector of Welsh antiquities, was author of a history of the "Gwedir family." He *m.*, about 1575, Sidney, da. of Sir William GERRARD, L Chancellor of Ireland (1576), by whom he had 11 sons and 2 daughters. He *d.* 1 March 1626, and was *bur.* at Llanwryst. M.I. Will pr. 1627. The Admon. of his widow, dat. 2 July 1632, to her son Sir Richard Wynn, Bart.

II. 1626. SIR RICHARD WYNN, Bart., [1611], of Gwydir aforesaid, 1st surv. s. and h.,[b] *b.* about 1588. He was one of the Gentlemen of the Privy Chamber to Charles, Prince of Wales, whom he accompanied in his journey to Spain,[c] being, after that prince's accession to the throne, Treasurer to the Queen Consort Henrietta. He was M.P. for Carnarvonshire, 1619; for Ilchester, 1621-22, 1624-25 and 1625; for Andover, April to May 1640, and for Liverpool, Nov. 1640, till his death. He *suc. to the Baronetcy* (presumably)[b] 1 March 1626. He *m.* 16 June 1616, at Greenwich, Anne, da. and coheir of Sir Francis DARCY, of Isleworth, co. Midx. He *d.* s.p. 19 July 1649. Will pr. 1649.

(a) There is an elaborate account of his career in that post in Collins' *Baronetage* (1720), reproduced in Burke's *Extinct Baronetage* and elsewhere.

(b) John Wynn (who probably was the "Sir John Wynn, of Carnarvon," who was *Knighted* at Whitehall, 19 May 1613) is mentioned in Collins' *Baronetage* (1720) as the eldest son of the 1st Bart., it being there stated that "he succeeded to the title and estate, but dying unmarried, was succeeded by Richard, his brother."

(c) Of this journey he wrote an account, which is printed in Hearne's *Tracts*.

III. 1649. SIR OWEN WYNN, Bart. [1611], of Gwydir aforesaid, br. and h.; *suc. to the Baronetcy* in 1649. He *m.* Grace, da. of Hugh WILLIAMS, of Werg. co. Carnarvon. He *d.* about 1660. Admon. 28 Nov. 1660, to his widow. Her will pr. 1680.

IV. 1660? SIR RICHARD WYNN, Bart. [1611], of Gwydir aforesaid, s. and h.; M.P. for Carnarvonshire, Jan. 1647, till secluded in Dec. 1648; also, in 1661, till death; Sheriff of the same, 1657-58; *suc. to the Baronetcy* about 1660. He *m.* Sarah, sister of Thomas MIDDLETON, 1st Bart. [1660], 5th da. of Sir Thomas MIDDLETON, of Chirk, co. Denbigh, by his 2d wife, Mary da. of Sir Robert NAPIER, 1st Bart. [1611]. He *d.* s.p.m.s.[a] in 1674, before 18 Nov.

V. 1674, to 1719. SIR JOHN WYNN, Bart. [1611], of Watstay (afterwards Wynnstay), co. Denbigh, cousin and h. male, being only s. of Henry WYNNE, who was 10th son of the 1st Bart. He was *b.* about 1628, and *suc. to the Baronetcy* about 1674; was Sheriff of Carnarvonshire, 1674-75; M.P. for Merioneth, 1678-79, 1679-81, 1685-87, 1689-90, and 1690-95. He *m.* Jane, da. and h. of Eyton EVANS, of Watstay aforesaid, by whom he acquired that estate.[b] She *d.* before him. He *d.* s.p. 7 Jan. 1718/9, aged 91, when the *Baronetcy* became *extinct*. Will pr. May 1719.

THROCKMORTON:

cr. 29 June 1611;

ex. June 1682.

I. 1611. "WILLIAM THROCKMORTON,[c] of Tortworth, co. Gloucester, Knt.," s. and h. of Sir Thomas THROCKMORTON[d], of the same, sometime (1588 and 1601) Sheriff of Gloucestershire, by Elizabeth, his 1st wife, da. of Sir Richard BERKELEY, of Stoke, was *b.* about 1579; matric. at Oxford (New Coll.), 10 Oct. 1594, aged 15; suc. his father in 1607; was *Knighted*, and was afterwards *cr. a Bart.*, as above, 29 June 1611. He *m.* firstly, Cicely (aged 25 in 1611), 1st. da. and coheir of Thomas BAYNHAM, of Clowerwall in Newland, co. Gloucester, by Mary, da. of Sir William WINTER, of Lydney, in that county. He *m.*, secondly, Alice, da. of (—) MORGAN. He *m.* thirdly, Sarah, da. of (—) HALL. He *d.* in his 50th year, 18 and was *bur.* 20 July 1628, at Newland. M.I. Inq. p.m. 8 Car.

II. 1628. SIR BAYNHAM THROCKMORTON, Bart. [1611], of Clowerwall aforesaid, s. and h. by 1st wife; *b.* about 1606; *suc. to the Baronetcy* 18 July 1628, being then aged 22 and more. He *m.*, about 1626, Margaret, sister and coheir of Ralph, BARON HOPTON OF STRATTON, da. of Robert HOPTON, of Witham, co. Somerset, by Jane, da. of Rowland KEMEYS. He *d.* 28, and was *bur.* 29 May 1664, at St. Margaret's, Westm. Funeral certificate at Coll. of Arms.

(a) Mary his only da. and h., whose estates at Gwydir and elsewhere were computed at £6,000 or £7,000 a year, *m.*, 30 July 1678, Robert (Bertie), 1st Duke of Ancaster and Kesteven, and in their descendants they continue, being now (1899) held by Earl Carrington.

(b) By his will he devised the Wynnstay estate to his first cousin twice removed, viz., Watkin Williams, s. of Sir William Williams, 2d Bart. [1688], by Jane, da. and coheir of Edward Thelwall and Sidney his wife, who was the only child that had issue of William Wynn, Prothonotary of Wales, the 6th son of Sir John Wynn, 1st Bart. The said Watkin Williams thereupon assumed the additional name of Wynn, and succeeded to the Baronetcy [1688] on the death of his father in 1740, being ancestor of the present family of Williams-Wynn, Baronets.

(c) See *Bristol and Gloucester Arch. Soc. Publications*, vol. vii, p. 293.

(d) He was s. and h. of Sir Thomas Throckmorton (*d.* 1586), who was s. and h. of William Throckmorton, s. and h. of Christopher Throckmorton, s. and h. of John Throckmorton, s. and h. of another John Throckmorton, who was younger br. of Thomas Throckmorton, of Coughton, co. Warwick, ancestor of the Throckmortons, Barts. (1642), of Coughton, aforesaid.

III. 1664. SIR BAYNHAM THROCKMORTON, Bart. [1611], of Clowerwall aforesaid, s. and h., *b.* about 1628; M.P. for Gloucestershire, 1656-58; for Wotton Bassett, 1660, and for Gloucestershire (second time), Dec. 1664 to 1669; *Knighted* at Rochester, 28 May 1660; *suc. to the Baronetcy*, 28 May 1664. He *m.* firstly, in or before 1661, Mary, da. and h. of Giles GARTON, of Billinghurst, Sussex. She *d.* s.p.m. 2 and was *bur.* 4 April 1666, in her 29th year, at Newland, M.I. He *m.* secondly, 11 Dec. 1669, at St. Dunstan's in the West, London (reg. at Newland; Lic. Vic. Gen., she aged 19), Katharine, da. of Piers EDGCUMBE, of Mount Edgcumbe, Devon, by Mary, da. of Sir John GLANVILE, of Broadclyst, co. Devon. He *d.* s.p.m. Will dat. 16 July 1680, pr. 3 Feb. 1681/2. The will of his widow pr. 1685.

IV. 1681? to 1682. SIR WILLIAM THROCKMORTON, Bart. [1611], of Hewelsfield, co. Gloucester, cousin and h. male, being s. and h. of Sir Nicholas THROCKMORTON, of Hewelsfield aforesaid (*d.* June 1664), who was younger s. by his 1st wife of the 1st Bart.; *b.* 1658; ed. at Westm., School; matric. at Oxford (Ch. Ch.) 4 Dec. 1677, aged 19; admitted to the Inner Temple, 1681, *suc. to the Baronetcy*, about 1681. He *d.* unm. June, and was *bur.* 1 July 1682, at St. Margaret's Westm., being killed in a duel, when the *Baronetcy* became *extinct*. Admon. 7 June 1686, to his three sisters.

WORSLEY, *or* WORSELEY:

cr. 29 June 1611,

afterwards, 1805—1825, WORSLEY-HOLMES;

ex. 10 Jan. 1825.

I. 1611. "RICHARD WORSELEY, of Appledorecombe, co. Southampton, Knt.," s. and h. of Thomas WORSLEY, of Apuldercombe in the Isle of Wight, by Barbara da. of William ST. JOHN, of Farley, Hants. *b.* about 1589; suc. his father. 1604; matric. at Oxford (Mag. Coll.), 10 May 1605, aged 16; *Knighted*, 8 Feb. 1610/1, at Whitehall, and was *cr. a Bart.*, as above, 29 June 1611. M.P. for Newport (Isle of Wight), 1614, and Jan. 1620/1, to his death June 1621. Sheriff of Hants, 1616-17. He *m.* about 1610, Frances, 2d da. of Sir Henry NEVILLE, of Billingbeare, Berks, by Anne, da. of Sir Henry KILLIGREW. He *d.* 27 June 1621, and was *bur.* at Godshill, Isle of Wight. Admon. 17 Oct. 1621. The will of his widow, dat. 18 Oct. 1659, pr. 27 May 1661.

II. 1621. SIR HENRY WORSLEY, Bart. [1611], of Apuldercombe aforesaid, s. and h., *b.* 1612; *suc. to the Baronetcy*, 27 June 1621; M.P. for Newport (Isle of Wight), April to May 1640, and 1640, till secluded in Dec. 1648; for Newton (Isle of Wight), 1660, and 1661 till death; Sheriff of Hants, 1658. He *m.*, 1634, Bridget, 4th da. of Sir Henry WALLOP, of Farley Wallop, Hants, by Elizabeth, da. and h. of Robert CORBET, of Moreton Corbet. He *d.* 11 Sep. 1666, at Compton, Hants. Admon. 31 Jan. 1666/7 and 18 July 1677. The will of his widow pr. 1676.

III. 1666. SIR ROBERT WORSLEY, Bart. [1611], of Apuldercombe aforesaid, s. and h., *b.* 1643; was *Knighted* at Whitehall, 29 Dec. 1664, and *suc. to the Baronetcy*, 11 Sep. 1666. M.P. for Newton (Isle of Wight), Nov. 1666 till death. He *m.*, 1667, Mary, da. of Hon. James HERBERT, of Kingsey, Bucks (2d s. of Philip, 4th EARL OF PEMBROKE), by Jane, da. of Sir Robert SPILLER, of Laleham, co. Midx. He *d.* 1676. Will pr. 22 Feb. 1676/7. His widow *m.* (as his 2d wife) Edward (NOEL), 1st EARL OF GAINSBOROUGH, who *d.* Jan. 1688/9. She *d.* 6 April 1693, aged 44, and was *bur.* at Great Mintern, Dorset. M.I.

IV. 1676. SIR ROBERT WORSLEY, Bart. [1611], of Apuldercombe aforesaid, and of Chilton Candover, Hants, s. and h., *b.* 1669; *suc. to the Baronetcy* in 1676; matric. at Oxford (Ch. Ch.), 17 Dec. 1684, aged 15; M.P. for Newton (Isle of Wight), 1715-22. He *m.* (Lic. Fac., 13 Aug. 1690, he about 21, she about 17), Frances, da. of Thomas (THYNNE), 1st VISCOUNT WEYMOUTH, by

Frances, da. of Heneage (FINCH), EARL OF WINCHILSEA. He *d.* s.p.m.s. in New Burlington street, Midx., 29 July 1747, aged 80.[a] Will pr. 1747 His widow *d.* April 1750.[b] Will pr. 1750.

V. 1747. SIR JAMES WORSLEY, Bart. [1611], of Pilewell, Hants, cousin and h. male, being s. and h. of Sir James WORSLEY, of Pilewell aforesaid, by Mary, da. of Sir Nicholas STUART, 1st Bart. [1660], of Hartley Mauduit, which James, last named (who *d.* 17 March 1695), was 2d surv. s. of the 2d Bart. He was *b.* 1672; matric. at Oxford (New Coll.) 15 June 1688, aged 16; admitted to the Inner Temple, 1691; was M.P. for Newton, Isle of Wight, in nine Parls., 1695-1701, 1705-22, and 1727-41, and *suc. to the Baronetcy*, 29 July 1747. He *m.*, 25 Feb. 1713/4, at St. Paul's cathedral, London, Rachael, da. of Thomas MERRICK. He *d.* 12 June 1756, aged 86. Will pr. 1756.

VI. 1756. SIR THOMAS WORSLEY, Bart. [1611], of Apuldercombe, aforesaid, s. and h., *b.* 22 April 1728, matric. at Oxford (Corpus Col.), 14 March 1744/5, aged 16; *cr.* D.C.L. 2 July 1754; *suc. to the Baronetcy* 12 June 1756. He *m.*, 4 March 1749, Elizabeth, 1st da. of John (BOYLE), 5th EARL OF CORK [I.], by his 1st wife, Henrietta, da. of George (HAMILTON), EARL OF ORKNEY [S.]. He *d.* 23 Sep. 1768. Will pr. Oct. 1768. His widow, who was *b.* 7 May 1731, *d.* 16 Jan. 1800.

VII. 1768. SIR RICHARD WORSLEY, Bart. [1611], of Apuldercombe, aforesaid, only s. and h., *b.* 13 Feb., and *bap.* 17 March 1751; matric. at Oxford (Corpus Coll.) 9 April 1768, aged 17; *suc. to the Baronetcy*, 23 Sep. 1768; M.P. for Newport, Isle of Wight, 1774-84; for Newton, 1790-93 and 1796-1802; Clerk of the Privy Council, Comptroller of the Board of Green Cloth, 1777, and sometime Comptroller of the Household. P.C. 1779; Capt.-Gen. and Vice-Admiral of the Isle of Wight; F.R.S.; F.S.A., etc., being well known as an antiquary. In 1793, he was Minister to the Republic of Venice till its reduction by the French in 1797. He *m.*, 20 Sept. 1775, Seymour, da. and coheir of Sir John FLEMING, Bart. [1763], of Brompton Park, Midx., by Jane, da. of William COLEMAN. He *d.* s.p.m., 5 Aug. 1805.[c] Will pr. 1807.

VIII. 1805. SIR HENRY WORSLEY-HOLMES, Bart. [1611], Clerk in Holy Orders, 4th cousin and h. male, being s. and h. of Thomas (sometimes called Robert) WORSLEY, of Pidford, in the Isle of Wight, by Jane, sister of Thomas, BARON HOLMES OF KILMALLOCK [I. 1760], da. of Henry HOLMES, of Newport, Isle of Wight, which Thomas was s. and h. of Rev. John WORSLEY, Vicar of Gatcombe, the s. and h. of George WORSLEY, who was s. and h. of Thomas WORSLEY, of Bembridge, 3d s. of the 1st Bart. He was *b.* 1756; matric. at Oxford (St. Mary Hall), 24 Nov. 1771, aged 21; B.C.L. and D.C.L., 1791. In 1804, he assumed the name of HOLMES, after that of WORSLEY, pursuant to the will of his maternal uncle, the said Thomas, LORD HOLMES. He *suc. to the Baronetcy* (but not to the paternal estates), 5 April 1805. He *m.* Elizabeth Troughear, widow of Edward Meux WORSLEY, of Gatcombe, Isle of Wight, and 1st da. of Leonard (HOLMES), LORD HOLMES, *formerly* TROUGHEAR, BARON HOLMES [I. 1797], by Elizabeth, da. of the Rev. (—) TERRELL. He *d.* 7 April 1811. Will pr. 1811. His widow *d.* 20 Jan. 1832, at Newport aforesaid, aged 73. Will pr. Aug. 1832.

(a) Frances, his only surv. da. and h., *m.* John (THYNNE), LORD CARTERET, who, after her death, was *cr.* EARL GRANVILLE, and had issue.

(b) It is said (Collins's *Peerage*, edit. 1812, *sub* "Bath") of this lady that to her "illustrious descent were added a fine person and delicate understanding."

(c) The estate of Apuldercombe was inherited by his niece, Henrietta-Anna-Maria-Charlotte (da. and h. of his sister, Henrietta-Frances, by the Hon. John Bridgeman-Simpson), wife of Charles (Anderson Pelham), 2d Baron Yarborough, who, in 1837, was *cr.* BARON WORSLEY OF APULDERCOMBE in the Isle of Wight, and EARL OF YARBOROUGH.

IX. 1811. to 1825. SIR LEONARD-THOMAS WORSLEY-HOLMES, Bart. [1611], of Westover, Isle of Wight, s. and h., *b.* 16 July 1787; matric. at Oxford (Ch. Ch.), 24 Oct. 1805, aged 18; M.P. for Newport (Isle of Wight), 1809-25; *suc. to the Baronetcy*, 7 April 1811; Recorder of Newport. He *m.*, 5 June 1813, Anne-Redstone, da. of John DELGARNO, of Newport aforesaid, by (—), sister of Leonard (HOLMES formerly TROUGHEAR), BARON HOLMES [I. 1797] aforesaid. He *d.*, s.p.m., 10 Jan. 1825, at his mother's house at Newport aforesaid, aged 38, when the *Baronetcy* became *extinct*([a]). Will pr. Aug. 1825. His widow *d.* at Newport aforesaid, 1 April 1857, aged 64. Admon., June 1857.

FLEETWOOD:
cr. 29 June 1611;
ex. 10 Dec. 1802.

I. 1611. "RICHARD FLEETWOOD, of Calwish, co. Stafford, Esq.," s. and h. of Thomas Fleetwood, of Calwiche, in the parish of Ellaston, co. Stafford, and of Penwortham, near Preston, co. Lancaster, by Mary, da. of Sir Richard SHIRBURNE, of Stonyhurst, in that county, was *cr. a Bart.*, as above, 29 June 1611; Sheriff of Staffordshire, 1614-15. He *m.*, in or before 1609, Anne, 1st da. of Sir John PESHALL, 1st Bart. [1611], of Horsley, by Anne, da. of Ralph SHELDON, of Beoley, co. Worcester. He *d.* 1649. Will pr. 1654. His widow *d.* 1650. Her admon., as "of Wotton, co. Stafford," 27 Feb. 1650/1, to a creditor.

II. 1649. SIR THOMAS FLEETWOOD, Bart. [1611], of Calwiche aforesaid, s. and h., *b.* 1609, being aged 54 at the Visit of Staffordshire, 2 April 1663; *suc. to the Baronetcy* in 1649. He *m.*, in or before 1628, Gertrude, da. of Thomas EYRE, of Ash,([b]) co. Derby. He was living 2 April 1663. [*Visit. of Staffordshire.*]

III. 1670? SIR RICHARD FLEETWOOD, Bart. [1611], of Calwiche aforesaid, s. and h., *b.* 1628, being aged 38 in the Visit. of Staffordshire, 2 April 1663. He *m.* firstly, in or before 1660, Anne, da. of Sir Edward GOLDING, 1st Bart., of Colston Bassett, Notts, by Eleanor, da. of John THROCKMORTON. She was *bur.* 10 Sep. 1700, at Colston Bassett, aged 56. He *m.* secondly, (—), da. and h. of Christopher BANISTER. He *d.*, s.p.m.s.([c]).

IV. 1700? SIR THOMAS FLEETWOOD, Bart. [1611], of Martin Sands, co. Chester, nephew and h., being s. and h. of Thomas FLEETWOOD (by his 1st wife, Elizabeth, da. of (—) COYNEY, Esq.), which last named Thomas, was 2d s. of the 2d Bart. He *m.* Magdalen, da. of Thomas BERINGTON, of Moat Hall, Salop. He *d.* s.p. Dec. 1739, and was *bur.* at Newchurch, Cheshire. Will dat. 14 Jan. 1735, enrolled (Exch.) 13 and 14 Geo. II. The will of his widow pr. 1741.

V. 1739. SIR JOHN FLEETWOOD, Bart. [1611], of Prestwood,([d]) in Ellaston, co. Stafford, br. of the half blood and h., being s. of Thomas FLEETWOOD, last abovenamed by (—), his 2d wife. He *m.* Philippa, da. of William BERINGTON, of Shrewsbury, niece of Magdalen Berington abovenamed, the wife of his brother. He *d.* 1741. Will dat. 17 March 1740/1, enrolled (1745-46) 19 Geo. II.

([a]) Elizabeth, his only surv. da. and h., *m.*, 3 Oct. 1833, the Hon. William Henry Ashe A'Court, who, by royal lic., on the 14th of the same month, took the name of HOLMES after that of A'COURT, and who, in 1860, *suc.* his father as (2d) BARON HEYTESBURY.

([b]) In *Barrett's MSS.* (fol. 129) she is said to be da. of Rowland Eyre, of Hassop. [*Ex. inform.* W. Farrer.]

([c]) His granddaughter and h., Elizabeth, da. and h. of Thomas Fleetwood (aged 3 in 1663, who *d.* v.p.), *m.* Thomas LEGH, younger br. of Peter Legh, of Lyme, Cheshire. The estate of Calwiche passed to the family of Granville.

([d]) This estate he inherited from his uncle, Rowland Fleetwood (3d son of the 1st Bart.) who *d.* s.p.

VI. 1741, to 1802. SIR THOMAS FLEETWOOD, Bart. [1611], s. and h.; *b.* 1741, and *suc. to the Baronetcy* in that year. He *m.* 4 Nov. 1771, at St. George the Martyr, Queen square, Midx., Mary Winifred, 1st da. of Richard BOSTOCK, of Queen square aforesaid. He *d.* s.p.([a]) and was *bur.* 10 Dec. 1802, in Bath Abbey, aged 61, when the *Baronetcy*, presumably, became *extinct*. Will dat. 12 May 1798, pr. 24 March 1803, by his widow, to whom he left all his land in Cheshire, Staffordshire, Essex, and elsewhere. She *m.*, Nov. 1804, COUNT ST. MARTIN DE FRONT, Envoy from the King of Sardinia. She *m.* thirdly, Thomas WRIGHT, and was living 8 Feb. 1812.

SPENCER:
cr. 29 June 1611;
ex. before 1711.

I. 1611. "THOMAS SPENCER,([b]) of Yardington, co. Oxford, Esq.," s. and h. of Sir William SPENCER, of Yarnton aforesaid, by Margaret, da. of Francis BOWYER, Alderman of London (which William was the 3d s. of Sir John SPENCER, of Althorpe, co. Northampton, ancestor of the Earls of Sunderland, Dukes of Marlborough, Earls Spencer, etc.), matric. at Oxford (Bras. Coll.), 8 June 1599, aged 13; B.A., 18 June 1602; Student of Lincoln's Inn, 1604; M.P. for Woodstock, 1604-11; Sheriff of Oxon, 1616-17; suc. his father, 19 June 1608; and was *cr. a Bart.*, as above, 29 June 1611, being subsequently *Knighted*([c]), 4 May 1612, at Whitehall. He *m.*, about 1605, Margaret, da. of Richard BRAINTHWAIT, Sergt. at Law. He *d.* 7 and was *bur.* 18 Aug. 1622, at Yarnton. Will pr. 1622. His widow *m.* after 1625, as his 3d wife, Richard (BUTLER), 3d VISCOUNT MOUNTGARRET [I.], who *d.* 1651. She *d.* at St. Giles' in the Fields, 16, and was *bur.* 21 Dec. 1655, at Yarnton. Will pr. 1657.

II. 1622. SIR WILLIAM SPENCER, Bart. [1611], of Yarnton aforesaid, s. and h., aged 14 when he *suc. to the Baronetcy*, 17 Aug. 1622; *Knighted* (as his father had been), after he had become a Bart., by Charles I., at Oxford, 27 Aug. 1629. On the death s.p.m. of his great uncle Thomas SPENCER, of Claverdon, co. Warwick, he *suc.* to that estate. He *m.* about 1635, Constance, 1st da. of Sir Thomas LUCY, of Charlecote, co. Warwick, by Alice, only da. and h. of the said Thomas SPENCER, of Claverdon aforesaid. She was aged 5 in 1619. He *d.* May 1647. Will dat. 13 and pr. 26 May 1647 and 1651. His widow *m.* Sir Edward SMITH, of Whitchurch, Bucks, Chief Justice of the Common Pleas in Ireland, 1665-69.

III. 1647. SIR THOMAS SPENCER, Bart. [1611], of Yarnton and Claverdon aforesaid, s. and h., *b.* 1 Jan. 1638/9; *suc. to the Baronetcy*, May 1647. M.P. for Woodstock, 1660 and 1661-79. He *m.* 24 Jan. 1654/5, at St. Paul's, Covent Garden, Jane, da. of Sir John GARRARD, 2d Bart. [1622], of Lamer, by Jane, da. of Sir Moulton LAMBARD. He *d.*, s.p.m.s.,([d]) 6 March 1684/5, aged 46. *Bur.* at Yarnton. M.I. Will pr. June 1687. His widow *d.* 30 March 1712, aged 74, and was *bur.* at Yarnton. Will pr. July 1712.

IV. 1685. SIR THOMAS SPENCER, Bart. [1611], of Erdington, co. Salop, cousin and h. male, being s. and h. of Richard SPENCER, by Anne, da. of (—) WAGSTAFFE, which Richard (*bap.* 2 Feb. 1616/7, at Yarnton) was 4th s. of the 1st Bart. He *suc. to the Baronetcy* (but not to the estates), 6 March 1684/5. He *m.* Elizabeth, da. of Ancor PALMER, of Bricklehampton, co. Worcester. He *d.* about 1722.

([a]) It is stated both in Courthope's and in Burke's *Extinct Barts.*, that he *d.* unm. in Jan. 1780, when the title is supposed to have been extinct, but was assumed by a Thomas Fleetwood, who died in 1802. These *two* Thomas Fleetwoods, however, appear to be *one and the same person*, for the marriage, in 1771, is that of "*Sir Thomas Fleetwood, Bart.*," to Mary Bostock, and the will of the Baronet, who died in 1802, mentions his cousins, Rev. Charles Berington and Rev. Thomas Berington, doubtless relatives of his mother, the wife of the 5th Bart. No Baronet of the name of Thomas Fleetwood appears to have died in Jan. 1780.

([b]) See Baker's *Northamptonshire*, vol. i., p. 752.

([c]) See p. 18, note "c," *sub* "Tollemache."

([d]) See Baker's *Northamptonshire*, as in note "b" above for names and descriptions of his daughters and coheirs.

V. 1722? SIR HENRY SPENCER, Bart. [1611], of Erdington aforesaid, s. and h. He *d.* s.p., at Stratford-upon-Avon, Warwick, 1726.

VI. 1726. SIR WILLIAM SPENCER, Bart. [1611], br. and h. He *m.* Elizabeth, da. of Thomas DEE, of Bridgnorth, Salop. He *d.* s.p.m.

VII. 1735? to 1775? SIR CHARLES SPENCER, Bart. [1611], cousin and h. male, being s. and h. of Charles SPENCER, of Lyons Hall, co. Hereford, by Anne, da. of Francis PEMBER, of Elston, Wilts, which Charles last named, was next br. to the 4th Bart. He was living as a Baronet and a minor 1741, but *d.* s.p., before 1771, when the *Baronetcy* became *extinct*.

TUFTON:
cr. 29 June 1611,
afterwards, 1626—1628, BARON TUFTON OF TUFTON, co. Sussex,
and *subsequently*, 1628—1849, EARLS OF THANET;
ex. 12 June 1849.

I. 1611. "JOHN TUFTON, of Hothfeild, co. Kent. Knt.," s. and h. of John TUFTON, of Hothfield aforesaid, and of Northiam, co. Sussex, (Sheriff of Kent, 1562), by Mary, 1st da. of Sir John BAKER, of Sisinghurst, in that county (sometime Recorder of London), suc. his father, 10 Oct. 1567; was Sheriff of Kent, 1575-76; was *Knighted*, 11 May 1603, and, being a person of great abilities, was *cr. a Bart.* as above, 29 June 1611. He *m.* firstly, Olympia, da. and sole h. of Christopher BLORE, of Blores place and Sileham, in Rainham and of Pope's in Hartlip, co. Kent. She *d.* s.p.m. He *m.* secondly, 10 Dec. 1575, at Terling, co. Essex, Christian, da. and coheir of Sir Humphrey BROWNE, of Ridley Hall, in Terling, sometime (1542-62) one of the Justices of the Common Pleas, by Ann, da. of John (HUSSEY), LORD HUSSEY DE SLEFORD. He *d.* 2 and was *bur.* 5 April 1624, at Hothfield, but was removed to Rainham aforesaid. M.I. Will pr. 1624.

II. 1624. SIR NICHOLAS TUFTON, Bart. [1611], of Hothfield aforesaid, s. and h., by 2d wife; *bap.* 19 Jan. 1577/8, at Terling aforesaid; matric. at Oxford (Hart Hall), 15 Oct. 1591, aged 14; student of Lincoln's Inn, 1596. He was *Knighted* (shortly before his father) 13 April 1603, at Newcastle upon Tyne, upon the first arrival of James I, in England. M.P. for Peterborough 1601, and for Kent 1624-25; *suc. to the Baronetcy*, 2 April 1624. He *m.* about 1605, Frances, 7th da. of Thomas (CECIL) 1st EARL OF EXETER, by his 1st wife Dorothy, da. of John (NEVILLE) LORD LATIMER. She was living when, on 1 Nov. 1626, he was *cr.* BARON TUFTON OF TUFTON, co. Sussex, being two years later *cr.*, 5 Aug. 1628, EARL OF THANET, in which titles this *Baronetcy* then *merged*, and so continued till the death, 12 June 1849, of the 11th Earl and 12th Baronet, when *all* his dignities became *extinct*. See *Peerage*, under "Thanet."

PEYTON:
cr. 29 June 1611,
ex. 11 Feb. 1683/4.

I. 1611. "SAMUEL PEYTON, of Knowlton, co. Kent, Knt.," s. and h. of Sir Thomas PEYTON, of the same, by Ann, da. of Sir Martin CALTHORPE, twice (1579 and 1589) Lord Mayor of London, was *b.* about 1590; matric. at Oxford (Ex. Coll.), 23 Jan. 1606/7, aged 16; was *Knighted*, 15 May 1608, at Whitehall; adm. to Gray's Inn, 1609; suc. his father in April 1611, and was *cr. a Bart.*, as above, 29 June 1611. He was M.P. for Sandwich, 1614. He *m.* about 1610, Mary, 2d da. and coheir of Sir Roger ASTON, of Cranford, co. Midx., Master of the Wardrobe to James I, by Mary, da. of Andrew (STEWART) LORD OCHILTREE [S.] He *d.* 1623. His widow *m.*, 1626, Edward CHOLMELEY.

II. 1623. to 1684. SIR THOMAS PEYTON, Bart. [1611(2)]([a]), of Knowlton aforesaid, 1st s. and h., *b.* about 1613; *suc. to the Baronetcy* in 1623, was an active Royalist during the Civil Wars, being eight years in prison for that cause, and having to compound for his estate for £1,000, on 6 March 1645; M.P. for Sandwich, 1640, till disabled, 5 Feb. 1643/4; for Kent, 1661-79. He joined the Royalist rising in 1659, and after the Restoration was M.P. and a Commissioner of prizes, receiving a grant of a third part of the revenue of the duty on coals. He *m.* firstly, 21 May 1636, at St. Bride's, London, Elizabeth, da. of Sir Peter OSBORNE, of Chicksand, Beds, by Dorothy, da. of Sir John DANVERS, of Dauntsey, Wilts. She *d.* 10 Sep. 1642.([b]) He *m.* secondly (Lic. Lond., 18 Jan. 1647/8, she aged 33), Cecilia, widow of Sir William SWAN. She *d.* 26([b]) and was *bur.* 30 Oct. 1661, at Southfleet, co. Kent. He *m.* thirdly (Lic. Fac., 28 Feb. 1666/7), "Dame Jane THORNHILL," widow of (—) SWIFT, and formerly of (—) MATTHEWS, and, before that, of Sir Timothy THORNHILL, da. of Sir William MONINS, 1st Bart. [1611], by Jane, da. of Roger TWISDEN. She was *bur.* 8 Feb. 1671/2, at St. Bride's, London. He *d.* s.p.m.s.([c]) 11 and was *bur.* 15 Feb. 1683/4, in Westm. Abbey, aged about 70, when *the Baronetcy* became *extinct*. Admon., as "late of Barham, co. Kent," 14 May 1684.

MORRISON:
cr. 29 June 1611;
ex. 20 Aug. 1628.

I. 1611, to 1628. "CHARLES MORRISON, of Caishobury [Cashiobury], co. Hertford, Knt.," only s. and h. of Sir Charles MORRISON, of Cashiobury, in Watford, Herts, aforesaid, sometime [1579-80] Sheriff of that county, by Dorothea, da. of Nicholas CLARK, was *b.* 18 April 1587; suc. his father, 31 March 1599; and was *cr. a Bart.*, as above, 29 June 1611. He was made K.B. at the coronation of James I in 1603; M.P. for Herts, 1621-22; for St. Albans, 1625-26; and for Hertford, 1628-29. He *m.*, 4 Dec. 1606, at Low Leyton, co. Essex, Mary, yst. da. and coheir of Baptist (HICKS), 1st VISCOUNT CAMPDEN, by Elizabeth, da. of Richard MAY, of London. He *d.* s.p.m.s.([d]) 20 Aug. 1628, and was *bur.* at Watford, when the *Baronetcy* became *extinct*. Will pr. 1628. His widow *m.*, as his 2d wife, Sir John COOPER, 1st Bart. [1622], of Rockbourne, Hants, who *d.* 23 March 1631. She *m.* thirdly Sir Richard ALFORD.

BAKER:
cr. 29 June 1611;
ex. 28 March 1661.

I. 1611. "HENRY BAKER, of Sissinghurst, co. Kent, Knt.," s. and h. of John BAKER, of the same, by Mary, da. of Sir Thomas GULDEFORD, of Hempstead, in that county (which John was s. and h. of Sir Richard BAKER, who, in July 1573, entertained Queen Elizabeth at Sissinghurst aforesaid), was *b.* at Cranbrook, co. Kent, about 1587; matric. at Oxford (Mag. Coll.), 6 June 1600, aged 13; B.A., 31 May 1603; Student of the Middle Temple, 1604; *Knighted*, 15 July 1606, at Oatlands, and was *cr. a Bart.*, as above, 29 June 1611. He *m.*, in

([a]) The number "(2)" after the date "1611" denotes that this was the second Baronetcy of this surname created in this year.

([b]) See "a 17th century note book" [*Genealogist*, N.S., vol. viii, pp. 101-104.] The date of 1661 (as in the text) is there given as 1660, but see Chester's "Westm. Abbey Registers," p. 209, note 1.

([c]) His four daughters and coheirs (three by his first and one by his second wife) are set forth in Collins' *Baronetage* [1720]. By his second wife he had a son Thomas who *d.* of the small pox when young.

([d]) Elizabeth, his only surv. da. and h., *m.* Arthur (Capell), 1st Baron Capell of Hadham, and *d.* 26 Jan. 1660/1, being mother of Arthur, 1st Earl of Essex, in whose descendants the estate of Cashiobury still continues.

or before 1608, Catharine, sister of Thomas, 1st VISCOUNT STRANGFORD [I.], 1st da. of Sir John SMYTHE, of Ostenhanger, co. Kent, by Elizabeth, da. and h. of John FINEAUX. He *d.* and was *bur.* 4 Dec. 1623, at Cranbrook. Will pr. 1624.

II. 1623. SIR JOHN BAKER, Bart. [1611], of Sissinghurst aforesaid, s. and h., aged 11, at the Heralds' Visitation of Kent 1619, *suc. to the Baronetcy*, 4 Dec. 1623; M.P. for Hastings, April to May, 1640; Sheriff of Kent, 1633-34; a zealous Royalist, being fined £3,000, as such, 22 April 1644. He *m.* Eleanor, d. of Sir Robert PARKHURST, sometime (1634-35) Lord Mayor of London, by Eleanor, da. of William BABINGTON, of Chorley, Surrey. She *d.* 1639. He *d.* 15 Jan. 1653.(a)

III. 1653, to 1661. SIR JOHN BAKER, Bart. [1611], of Sissinghurst, aforesaid, only s. and h.; *suc. to the Baronetcy*, 15 Jan. 1653. He *m.* Elizabeth, only da. and h. of Sir Robert NEWTON, Bart [so *cr.* 15 Jan. 1660/1], of London, by Elizabeth, da. and coheir of Francis LONGSTON, of the same. He *d.* s.p.m. (b), 28 March 1661, when the *Baronetcy* became *extinct*. His widow *m.* 23 April 1668, at St. Martin's in the Fields (Lic. Lon.), Sir Philip HOWARD.

APPLETON :
cr. 29 June 1611 ;
ex. 7 Nov. 1708.

I. 1611. "ROGER APPLETON, of Southbernfleet [*i.e.* South Benfleet], co. Essex, Esq.," s. and h. of Henry APPLETON, of Jarvis Hall, in South Benfleet aforesaid, by Faith, da. of William CARDINALL, of Great Bromley, Essex (which Henry was s. and h. of Sir Roger APPLETON, also of Jarvis Hall aforesaid), suc. his father, 2 Nov. 1606, was Sheriff of Essex, 1608-09, and was *cr. a Bart.*, as above, 29 June 1611. He *m.* Anne, da. of Sir Thomas MILDMAY, of Moulsham, Essex, by Frances, da. of Henry (RATCLIFFE), EARL OF SUSSEX. He was *bur.* 16 Jan. 1612/3 at South Benfleet. Will dat. 17 July 1607, pr. 17 June 1613. His widow *m.* John PASCHALL, of Great Badow, Essex, and was (apparently) *bur.* 6 Aug. 1628 at South Benfleet.

II. 1613. SIR HENRY APPLETON, Bart. [1611], of Jarvis Hall aforesaid, s. and h.; *suc. to the Baronetcy* in Jan. 1612/3, being subsequently(c) *Knighted* at Greenwich, 27 June 1613. He was a distinguished Royalist, and, as such, was present at the defence of Colchester, in 1648. He *m.* firstly, Joan, da. of Edward SHELDON, of Beoley, co. Worcester, by Elizabeth, da. of Thomas MARKHAM, of Ollerton, Notts. She was *bur.* 22 Feb. 1624/5, at South Benfleet. He *m.* secondly, 11 Aug. 1628, at St. Catharine's Coleman, London (Lic. Lond., he about 30, widower, and she about 22, spinster), Alice, da. of William RIPPINGHAM, or RIPLINGHAM, of St. James', Clerkenwell. She *d.* s.p., and was *bur.* 8 Nov. 1631, at South Benfleet. He *m.*, thirdly, Magdalen, widow of William BRYAN, of Wrotham, co. Kent, da. of Sir John WATTS, sometime (1606-07) Lord-Mayor of London, by Magdalen, da. of Sir James HAWES. She was *bur.* 1638, at South Benfleet. He *d.* in reduced circumstances. Admon. 16 Nov. 1649, granted to "Sir Henry Mildmay, Knt., Lord Fitzwalter," the principal creditor.

III. 1649. SIR HENRY APPLETON, Bart. [1611], of Jarvis Hall, and Great Badow aforesaid, s. and h. by 1st wife; *suc. to the Baronetcy* in 1649. He *m.* firstly, Sarah, da. of Sir Thomas OLDFIELD, of Spalding, co. Lincoln. He *m.* secondly, Mary, widow of Sir Thomas WISEMAN. He *d.* Jan. 1669/70, and was *bur.* at Great Badow. Will dat. 15 Nov. 1669, pr. 4 March 1669/70. His wife survived him.

(a) Admon. 4 Jan. 1631/2, of goods of Lady Mary Gray, of St. Giles' in the Fields, Midx., was granted to "Sir John Baker, Bart., grandson, by the son of deceased" [nepoti ex filio], but was renounced and fresh admon. granted on the 16th inst. to Andrew, Lord Gray, the husband. There seems some mistake in the above.

(b) The estate passed to his four daughters and coheirs, from whose heirs they were purchased by the family of Mann.

(c) See p. 18, note "c" as to such subsequent Knighthoods.

IV. 1670. SIR HENRY APPLETON, Bart. [1611], of Jarvis Hall aforesaid, only s. and h. by 1st wife, *suc. to the Baronetcy* in Jan. 1669/70. He *m.* (Lic. Vic. Gen. 17 May 1675, he about 28 and she about 19), Mary, da. of John RIVET, of Beeston, Suffolk, and of London, merchant. He *d.* s.p.m., Feb. 1678/9. His widow living 1695.(a)

V. 1679. SIR WILLIAM APPLETON, Bart. [1611], of Jarvis Hall aforesaid, and of Shenfield, near Brentwood, Essex, uncle and h., being s. of the 2d Bart., by his 1st wife; *b.* about 1630, being 12 years old in 1642; *suc. to the Baronetcy* in Feb. 1678/9. He *m.* Dorothy, da. of John HATT, of Orsett, Essex, and of London, Attorney at Law. He *d.* 15 and was *bur.* 21 Nov. 1705, aged 77, at South Benfleet. His widow *d.* 16 and was *bur.* 21 Dec. 1719, aged 84, at the same place. M.I.

VI. 1705, to 1708. SIR HENRY APPLETON, Bart. [1611], of Jarvis Hall, and of Shenfield aforesaid, 2d but only surviving s. and h., *suc. to the Baronetcy*, 15 Nov. 1705. He *m.* Elizabeth.(b) He *d.* s.p., and was *bur.* 7 Nov. 1708, at South Benfleet, when the *Baronetcy* became *extinct*.(c) Will dat. 30 Oct. 1708, pr. 3 Feb. 1709/10, by the relict and universal legatee.

SEDLEY, *or* SIDLEY :
cr. 29 June 1611;
ex. 20 Aug. 1701.

I. 1611. "WILLIAM SEDLEY, of Alisford [*i.e.* Aylesford], co. Kent, Knt.," s. and h. of John SEDLEY, or SIDLEY, of Southfleet in that county, by Ann, da. of John COLEPEPER, of Aylesford aforesaid, was *b.* about 1558; matric. at Oxford (Hart. Hall.), 1574, aged 16; was of Ball. Coll., 1575; B.A., 11 Feb. 1574/5; M.A., 1 July 1577. Barrister (Lincoln's Inn), 1584; Treasurer of Lincoln's Inn, 1608; *Knighted*, 30 July 1605, at Oxford, and was *cr. a Bart.*, as above, 29 June 1611. He was Founder of the Sidleian Lecture of Natural Philosophy at Oxford, 1621. He *m.*, in or after 1587, Elizabeth, Dowager BARONESS ABERGAVENNY, da. and coheir of Stephen DARRELL, of Spelmonder, Kent, by Philippa, da. of Edward WELDON. She was living Feb. 1601/2. He *d.* 27 Feb. 1618, and was *bur.* at Southfleet. Funeral certificate. Will pr. 1619.

II. 1618. SIR JOHN SEDLEY, Bart. [1611], of Aylesford and Southfleet aforesaid, s. and h., *b.* about 1597; matric. at Oxford (Mag. Coll.), 3 April 1609, aged 13; B.A., 19 March 1611/2; M.A., 8 July 1613; *Knighted*, 3 July 1616, at Oatlands; *suc. to the Baronetcy*, 27 Feb. 1618; High Sheriff of Kent, 1620-21. He *m.* in 1613, Elizabeth,(d) da. and h. of the celebrated Sir Henry SAVILE, Provost of Eton, etc., by Margaret, da. of George DACRES, of Cheshunt, Herts. He *d.* 13 Aug. 1638, at his residence, Mount Mascall, in North Cray, and was *bur.* at Southfleet, Kent. Funeral certificate in Public Record Office. Will pr. 1638.

III. 1638. SIR HENRY SEDLEY, Bart. [1611], of Southfleet aforesaid, s. and h., *b.* about 1623; matric. at Oxford (St. John's Coll.), 14 June 1630, aged 16. He *d.* unm. 1641. Will pr. Nov. 1641.

(a) Possibly the "Dame Mary Ash, *alias* Appleton, of St. James', Westm., widow," whose admon., 29 March 1721, was granted to her brother Charles Bateman.

(b) "He *m.* a mean woman, and, as I am informed, run out the whole estate, and departing this life about 1709, left a son, an infant, whose name I cannot learn." [Collins' *Baronetages*, 1720.] This son presumably died *before* his father.

(c) The estates of the family passed to his only sister Elizabeth, who *m.* Richard VAUGHAN (in her right), of Shenfield place, Essex.

(d) Waller wrote on her death :—

"Here lies the learned Savile's heir—
So early wise and lasting fair,
That none, except her years they told,
Thought her a child, or thought her old."

IV. 1641. SIR WILLIAM SEDLEY, Bart. [1611], of Southfleet, aforesaid, br. and h., of whom Anthony A. Wood says "that when he was a young man he lived very high in London." He *suc. to the Baronetcy* in 1641. He *m.*, 9 Oct. 1655, at St. Mildred's, Poultry (Banns pub. at St. Bride's, London), Jane, Dowager BARONESS CHANDOS, 2d da. of John (SAVAGE), EARL RIVERS, by his first wife, Catharine, da. of William (PARKER), LORD MORLEY. He *d.* s.p. 1656. Will pr. 1656. His widow *m.* (for her 3d husband) George PITT, of Strathfield Saye, Hants, who *d.* 27 July 1694. She herself *d.* 6 June 1676.

V. 1656, to 1701. SIR CHARLES SEDLEY, Bart. [1611], of Southfleet, aforesaid, br. and h.; *b.* (posthumous) in Shoe Lane, and *bap.* 30 March 1639 at St. Clement Danes; matric. at Oxford (Wad. Coll.) 22 March 1655/6, aged 17; *suc. to the Baronetcy* in 1656; was distinguished as a wit, a writer(a) and a gallant. M.P. for New Romney in eight Parls., 1668-81, 1690-95, 1696-1701. Though he had received many favours from James II(b) he took an active part against him. He *m.* 23 Feb. 1657, at St. Giles' in the Fields, Catharine, 3d da. of the said John (SAVAGE), EARL RIVERS, and Catherine, his first wife. He *d.* s.p.m., legit.,(c) 20 Aug. 1701, at Haverstock Hall, Hampstead, when the *Baronetcy* became *extinct*. Will pr. Aug. 1701.

TWISDEN, *or* TWYSDEN :
cr. 29 June 1611.

I. 1611. "WILLIAM TWISDEN, of East Peckham, co. Kent, Knt.," s. and h. of Roger TWISDEN, of Roydon Hall, in East Peckham aforesaid, by Anne, 1st da. of Sir Thomas WYATT, of Allington Castle in that county, admitted to Gray's Inn, 28 Oct. 1584; M.P. for Clitheroe, 1593; for Helston, 1601; for Thetford, 1606-11 and 1614, and for Winchelsea, 1628 till death; was *Knighted* at the Charter House, 11 May 1603; suc. his father, Nov. 1603, and was *cr. a Bart.*, as above, 29 June 1611. He was a great collector of MS., being learned in Hebrew, Greek, and other languages. He *m.* Anne, da. of Sir Moyle FINCH, 1st Bart., by Elizabeth *suo jure* COUNTESS OF WINCHILSEA. He *d.* 8 Jan. 1627/8, in his 63d year. Will pr. 1629. His widow *d.* 14 Nov. 1638, aged 64. Both *bur.* at East Peckham. M.I.

II. 1628. SIR ROGER TWISDEN, Bart. [1611], of Roydon Hall aforesaid, s. and h.(d) *b.* 21 Aug. 1597; admitted to Gray's Inn, 2 Feb. 1602/3; was M.P. for Winchelsea, 1625 and 1626, and for Kent, April to May 1640; *suc. to the Baronetcy*, 8 Jan. 1627/8. He, also, was much distinguished for his learning, and assisted John Philipot in his *Survey of Kent*, besides being himself the author of some ecclesiastical works. He was a zealous Royalist (as was his wife), and suffered

(a) His plays and poems are now almost forgotton, save the charming madrigal commencing "Phillis is my only joy."

(b) It is said that he disapproved of his only da. and h., Catharine (*b.* 21 Dec. 1657), being the mistress of that king, by whom she was *cr.* COUNTESS OF DORCHESTER. This incident is alluded to by Dr. Johnson (when speaking of the wish for beauty) he writes in his *Vanity of Human Wishes* "And Sedley cursed the form that pleased a King." Her *lack* of beauty was, however (as a matter of fact), notorious, and it is doubtful whether her father (one of the most licentious men of his age) would feel any real resentment at the Royal honours (though of a somewhat questionable kind) thus conferred on his daughter.

(c) By Catharine Ayscough, of Yorkshire (with whom he is said to have celebrated a marriage during his wife's lifetime) he had a natural son, Sir Charles Sedley, who was knighted (when under age) at Whitehall, 12 March 1688, to whom his father left all his estates, making no mention of the Countess of Dorchester, his legitimate da. and heiress. That son *m.* Frances, da. of Sir Richard Newdigate, Bart., but *d.* before 30 June 1701 (Admon. of that date), shortly before his father, leaving issue, of whom Charles Sedley inherited the estate of Southfleet, and was *cr. a Bart.* 10 July 1702.

(d) His yr. br., Sir Thomas Twysden, of Bradbourne, Kent, a Justice of the King's Bench, was *cr. a Bart.*, 13 June 1666, but this dignity became *extinct* 1 Jan. 1841.

imprisonment no less than seven years for that cause, besides a fine, in 1644, of £3,000 reduced, in Jan. 1650, to £1,300 to the sequestrators. He *m.*, 1 June 1620, at Greenwich, Isabella, yst. da. and coheir of Sir Nicholas SAUNDERS, of Ewell, Surrey. She *d.* 11 March 1656/7, aged 52.(a) He *d.* 27 June 1672, in his 75th year. Both *bur.* at East Peckham. M.I. His will pr. 1673.

III. 1672. SIR WILLIAM TWISDEN, Bart. [1611], of Roydon Hall aforesaid, s. and h., *b.* 1635; *suc. to the Baronetcy*, 27 June 1672; was M.P. for Kent, 1685-87, and for Appleby, 1695 till his death. He *m.* (Lic. Fac. 8 June 1665, he 27 and she 16), Frances, da. and h. of Josiah CROSS, of St. Swithin's, London, by Frances, his wife. He *d.* in London, 27 Nov. 1697, and was *bur.* at East Peckham. Will pr. 1697. His widow's will was pr. Aug. 1731.

IV. 1697. SIR THOMAS TWISDEN, Bart. [1611], of Roydon Hall aforesaid, 1st surviving s. and h., aged 21; when he *suc. to the Baronetcy*, 27 Nov. 1697. He *m.* 1710, Catharine, da. and sole h. of Sir Francis WYTHENS, of Southend in Eltham, co. Kent, one of the Judges of the Court of King's Bench, (1683-87), by Elizabeth, sister of Sir Thomas TAYLOR, 1st Bart. [1665], of Park House, in Maidstone. He *d.* s.p.m., 10 Oct. 1712. Will pr. Jan. 1713. His widow *m.*, 14 Nov. 1713, at Maidstone, Brig. Gen. George JOCELYN (who *d.* Nov. 1727), and *d.* April 1730.

V. 1712. SIR WILLIAM TWISDEN, *otherwise* TWYSDEN, Bart. [1611], of Roydon Hall aforesaid, br. and h.; *suc. to the Baronetcy*, 10 Oct. 1712. He *m.* Jane, da. of Francis TWISDEN [5th s. of Sir Thomas TWISDEN, 1st Bart. (1666), of Bradbourne], by Rebecca sometime widow of (—) HALE. He *d.* 20 Aug. 1751. Will pr. 1751.

VI. 1751. SIR WILLIAM TWYSDEN, Bart. [1611], of Roydon Hall aforesaid, s. and h..(b) *suc. to the Baronetcy*, 20 Aug. 1751. He *m.* in or before 1760, Mary, da. of George JERVIS. He *d.* 8 and was *bur.* 14 July 1767, aged 60, at East Peckham. M.I. Will pr. Jan. 1768. His widow *d.* 4 June 1818, aged 87. Will pr. 1818.

VII. 1767. SIR WILLIAM-JERVIS TWYSDEN, Bart. [1611], of Roydon Hall aforesaid, s. and h., *b.* 13 May 1760; *suc. to the Baronetcy*, 8 July 1767. Educated at Westm. School. He *m.* 7 May 1786, Frances, da. of Alexander WYNCH, Governor of Madras. He *d.* 3 Feb. 1834. Will pr. May 1834. His widow *d.* abroad. Her admon. March 1849.

VIII. 1834. SIR WILLIAM TWYSDEN, Bart. [1611], of Roydon Hall aforesaid, s. and h., *b.* 1 Dec. 1788, at Marylebone, Middlesex; *suc. to the Baronetcy* 3 Feb. 1834. He *m.* firstly 24 March 1831, Eliza, widow of Rev. John Bosanquet POLHILL, M.A., sister of Walter-Barton MAY, of Hadlow Castle, Kent, only da. of Walter-Barton MAY. She *d.* s.p. 12 July 1863, at 6 Sussex square, Brighton. He *m.* secondly, 18 Feb. 1869, Annie Browne, widow of Aaron HERDE. He *d.* s.p. 22 June 1879, in his 91st year, at 2 Aberdeen place, Maida Hill, Midx.

IX. 1879. SIR LOUIS-JOHN-FRANCIS TWYSDEN, Bart. [1611], of Crowborough, co. Sussex, nephew and h. male, being only s. and h. of John TWYSDEN, by his 1st wife, Cecilia, da. of Louis BAZALGETTE, of Eastwick Park, Surrey, which John (who *d.* 1863, aged 55) was 3d and yst. s. of the 7th Bart. He was *b.* 1830, at Roydon Hall aforesaid, sometime Lieut. 2d Dragoons; *suc. to the Baronetcy*, 22 June 1879. He *m.*, 1856, his maternal cousin, Helen, sister of Sir Joseph William BAZALGETTE, C.B., da. of Joseph William BAZALGETTE, Capt. R.N.

Family Estates.—These were, in 1876, under 3,000 acres.

(a) "A lady of rare patience and prudence in struggling through many troubles and hardships, in assisting her husband in his long imprisonment." (Collins' *Baronetage*, 1720).

(b) His yr. br. Philip Twysden, D.C.L., was Bishop of Raphoe, 1746-52. He *d.* 2 Nov. 1752, aged 38, being more famous as a sportsman and bold rider than for his clerical learning.

HALES:

cr. 29 June 1611;

ex. 15 March 1829.

I. 1611. "EDWARD HALES, of Woodchurch, co. Kent, Knt.," s. and h. of William HALES,(a) of Tenterden, by Elizabeth, da. of Paul JOHNSON, of Fordwich, co. Kent, was *b.* 1576; *Knighted*, 12 July 1603, at Sir W. Fleetwood's; Sheriff of Kent, 1608-09; M.P. for Hastings, 1605-11 and 1614; for Queenborough, 1625; for Kent, 1626; for Queenborough (again), April to May 1640, and 1640 till disabled, 18 April 1648, having been *cr. a Bart.*, as above 29 June 1611. Being zealous for the liberty of the subject, he took part in the Civil Wars against his King, being five years imprisoned in the Tower of London, and (30 Oct. 1643) fined £6,000 He *m.* firstly, Debora, da. and h. of Martin HARLACKENDEN, of Woodchurch aforesaid, by whom he acquired that estate. He *m.* secondly, Martha, widow of Sir James CROMER, of Tunstall, Kent, da. of Sir Matthew CAREW. He *d.* Sep. 1654, aged 78, *bur.* at Tunstall. M.I. Will dat. 15 Oct. 1651, pr. 1 Nov. 1659 (*Arch. Cant*, xiv).

II. 1654. SIR EDWARD HALES, Bart. [1611], of Tunstall, Kent, grandson and h., being only s. and h. of Sir John HALES (Knt.), by Christian, da. and coheir of the said Sir James CROMER, of Tunstall, which John was s. and h. ap. of the 1st Bart., but *d.* v.p. in or before 1652. He was *b.* about 1626; matric. at Oxford (Mag. Coll.) 20 May 1642, aged 16; *suc. to the Baronetcy* in Sep. 1654. He was a devoted Royalist, and risked his life in endeavouring to rescue Charles I from his imprisonment at Carisbrooke; was M.P. for Maidstone, Aug. to Dec. 1660. He *m.* Anne, 4th da. and coheir of Thomas (WOTTON), 2d BARON WOTTON OF MARLEY, by Mary, da. and coheir of Sir Arthur THROCKMORTON. She was as zealous for the King as her husband. He *d.* in France, about 1660, before 1661.

III. 1660? SIR EDWARD HALES, Bart. [1611], of Hackington, *otherwise* St. Stephen's, Kent, s. and h., *suc. to the Baronetcy* before 1661; M.P. for Queenborough in three Parls., 1661-81. He was Col. of a Reg. of Foot, being one of the Roman Catholic officers, who, by the King's dispensary power (confirmed, in this case, by the Court of King's Bench), was enabled to refuse taking the oath of supremacy. His fidelity to James II was unshaken, and he was one of the last who remained in attendance on that King, and was his sole companion on his memorable flight, 12 Dec. 1688, when he threw the Great Seal into the Thames. He was one of the Lords of the Admiralty, 1679-85, Deputy Governor of the Cinque Ports, and Lieutenant Governor of the Tower of London, 1685-86. By James II, when in exile, he was *cr.*, 3 May 1692, BARON HALES OF EMLEY, co. Kent, VISCOUNT TUNSTALL and EARL OF TENTERDEN, but these dignities, having been conferred after the King had been deposed, were, of course, not allowed. He *m.* (Lic. Vic. Gen., 12 July 1669, he about 24, and she about 23), Frances,(c) da. of Sir Francis WINDEBANK, of Oxford, Sec. of State to Charles I. She *d.* 1693. He *d.* in France, 1695, and was *bur.* at St. Sulpice, in Paris. Will pr. April 1708.

IV. 1695. SIR JOHN HALES, Bart. [1611], of Hackington aforesaid, 1st surv. s. and h.,(d) *suc. to the Baronetcy* in 1695. He *m.* firstly

(a) This William was grandson to John HALES, a Baron of the Exchequer, *temp.* Hen. VIII.

(b) The curious preamble to this patent is given in Betham's *Baronetage* (vol. i, p. 135, edit. 1801.) He was to have a "cap of honour," "a golden coronet," "a golden rod," etc. The rem. of the dignity, failing his issue male, was to his brothers, John and Charles.

(c) She apparently was the "Mrs. Frances Wyndebanke, of Oxford, about 17," who, with consent of her parents, had lic. (Vic. Gen.), 24 May 1666, to marry "Matthew Loveday of Oxford, Gent., about 21, Bachelor"—a marriage which, presumably, never took place.

(d) Edward Hales, his eldest br. was killed at the battle of the Boyne, fighting for James II.

Helen, da. of Sir Richard BEALING, of Ireland, Secretary to Katharine, Queen dowager of Charles II. He *m.* secondly, Helen, da. of Dudley BAGNAL, of Newry in Ireland. She *d.* at Luckly, near Wokingham, Berks, Nov. 1737. He *d.* 1744.

V. 1744. SIR EDWARD HALES, Bart. [1611], of Hale's Place, in Hackington aforesaid, grandson and h., being s. and h. of Edward HALES, by (—) relict of (—) PARKER, granddaughter of Sir Richard BULSTODE, which Edward was s. and h. ap. of the 4th Bart., by his 1st wife, and *d.* v.p. He was aged about 14, when he *suc. to the Baronetcy* in 1744. He *m.* firstly, in or before 1758, Barbara Mabella, da. and h. of John WEBB (s. and h. ap. of Sir John WEBB, 3d Bart. [1644]), by Mabella, da. and coheir of Sir Henry Joseph TICHBORNE, 4th Bart. [1621]. She *d.* 1770. He *m.* secondly (—) widow of (—) PALMER, of Ireland. She *d.* s.p. He *d.* Aug. 1802. Will pr. 1803.

VI. 1802, to 1829. SIR EDWARD HALES, Bart. [1611], of Hale's Place aforesaid, s. and h., *b.* 1758; *suc. to the Baronetcy* in Aug. 1802. He *m.* 1789, Lucy, 2d da. of Henry DARELL, of Calehill, Kent, by Elizabeth, da. of Sir Thomas GAGE, Bart. He *d.* s.p., at Hales Place, 15 March 1829, in 72d year, when the *Baronetcy* became *extinct*. Will pr. June and Aug. 1829. His wife survived him.

Family Estates.—Hales Place, near Canterbury (and 57 acres), many years the residence of Miss Mary Barbara Felicite Hales, heiress of the estates of that family (whose grandmother was da. of the 5th Bart. [see *Arch. Cant.*, vol. xiv], and who *d.* 18 April 1865, in her 50th year, at Sarre court, near Ramsgate), was sold in Aug. 1880, for £24,000, for a Jesuit College. The famous collection of china, pictures, plate and furniture had been sold a few months before.

MONYNS, *or* MONINS:

cr. 29 June 1611;

ex. 1678.

I. 1611. "WILLIAM MONINS, of Walwarshar, co. Kent, Esq.," only s. and h. of Sir Edward MONYNS, of Waldershare aforesaid, by Elizabeth, da. of Thomas LOVELACE, suc. his father in 1602, and was *cr. a Baronet*, as above, 29 June 1611. He *m.* firstly, (—), who *d.* s.p. He *m.* secondly, in or before 1600, Jane, sister of Sir William TWISDEN, 1st Bart. [1611], 1st da. of Roger TWISDEN, of East Peckham, co. Kent, by Anne, da. of Sir Thomas WYAT. He *d.* 24 Feb. 1642/3.

II. 1643. SIR EDWARD MONYNS, Bart. [1611], of Waldershare aforesaid, 1st s. and h. by 2d wife, *b.* about 1600; matric. at Oxford (Univ. Coll.), 8 Nov. 1616, aged 16; *suc. to the Baronetcy*, 24 Feb. 1642/3; was Sheriff of Kent, 1645-46. He *m.* Elizabeth, 1st da. of Sir Thomas STYLE, 1st Bart. [1627], of Wateringbury, by Elizabeth, da. of Robert FOULKES. He *d.* s.p.m.,(a) in 1663. Will pr. in 1666. His widow *d.* 1703. Will pr. 1703 and 1706.

III. 1663, to 1678. SIR THOMAS MONYNS, Bart. [1611], br. and h. male, *b.* about 1604; matric. at Oxford (Wadham Coll.), 17 June 1621, aged 17; Student of Lincoln's Inn, 1623; was probably the "Capt. Thomas Munnings, of Dover," who, though Treasurer to the Parl. sequestrators of Canterbury Cathedral, was a "Royalist at heart." He *m.* Elizabeth, widow of Robert BROMFIELD, of Tilmanstone, da. of James DARELL, of Calehill, co. Kent, by Catharine, da. of (—) Wade, of Colchester. He *d.* s.p., 1678, when the *Baronetcy* became *extinct*. Will pr. 1678.

(a) Susan, his 1st da. and coheir *m.* the Hon. Peregrine Bertie, by whom she had two daughters and coheirs, who inherited the estate of Waldershare, which they sold to Sir Henry Furnese, Bart.

MILDMAY:

cr. 29 June 1611;

ex. 13 Feb. 1625/6.

I. 1611, to 1626. "THOMAS MILDMAY, of Mulsham, co. Essex, Esq.," 1st s. and h. of Sir Thomas MILDMAY, of the same, by Frances, da. of Henry (RATCLIFFE), EARL OF SUSSEX, was M.P. for Malden, 1593; suc. his father, 20 July 1608, and was *cr. a Baronet*, as above, 29 June 1611. He *m.* firstly, Elizabeth, sister of Sir Thomas PUCKERING, 1st Bart. [1611], da. of Sir John PUCKERING, sometime Keeper of the Great Seal, by Anne, da. of George CHOWNE, of co. Kent. He *m.* secondly (Lic. Lond., 18 March 1616/7, he 44, she 36, and a spinster), Anne, da. of Thomas SAVILE, of Wrenthorpe in Wakefield, co. York. He *d.* s.p., 13 Feb. 1625/6, when the *Baronetcy* became *extinct*. Admon. 31 March 1626.

MAYNARD:

cr. 29 June 1611,

subsequently, 1620-1766, BARONS MAYNARD OF WICKLOW [I.],

and 1628-1766, BARONS MAYNARD OF ESTAINES [E.],

afterwards, 1766-1775, VISCOUNT MAYNARD [G.B.];

ex. 30 June 1775.

I. 1611. "WILLIAM MAYNARD, of Eston Parva, co. Essex, Knt.," s. and h. of Henry MAYNARD, of Little Easton aforesaid (Sec. to the L.-Treasurer Burleigh), by Susan, da. and coheir of Thomas PIERSON (Usher of the Star Chamber), was *b.* before 1589; ed. at St. John's Coll., Cambridge; was Gent. of the Privy Chamber about 1608; *Knighted*, 7 March 1608/9; M.P. for Penrhyn, 1609-11, and for Chippenham, 1614; suc. his father, 11 May 1610, and was *cr. a Baronet*, as above, 29 June 1611. He *m.* firstly, Frances, da. of William (CAVENDISH), 1st BARON CAVENDISH OF HARDWICK (subsequently, 1618, EARL OF DEVONSHIRE), by his 1st wife Anne, da. and coheir of Henry KEIGHLEY. She *d.* v.p. and s.p.m., 1 Sep. 1613, aged 20, and was *bur.* at Little Easton. He *m.* secondly, Anne, da. and heir of Sir Anthony EVERARD, of Great Waltham, Essex, by his 1st wife Anne, da. of Sir Thomas BARNARDISTON, of Kedington, Suffolk. She was living when he was *cr.*, 30 May 1620, BARON MAYNARD OF WICKLOW [I.], and, a few years later, 14 March 1627/8, BARON MAYNARD OF ESTAINES [E.]. In this peerage the *Baronetcy* then *merged*, the 6th and last Baron and Baronet being *cr.*, 28 Oct. 1766, VISCOUNT MAYNARD OF EASTON LODGE, co. Essex, with a spec. rem. On the death, however, of the said Viscount, unm., 30 June 1775, the *Baronetcy* and the Baronies [I. and E.] of 1620 and 1628 became *extinct*, though the Viscountcy remained.

LEE:

cr. 29 June 1611,

afterwards, 1674-1776, EARLS OF LICHFIELD;

ex. 4 Nov. 1776.

I. 1611. "HENRY LEE, of Quarrendon, co. Bucks, Esq., s. and h. ap. of Sir Robert LEE, of Hulcott, in that county (who *d.* 20 Aug. 1616, aged 71), by Lucy, da. of Thomas PIGOTT, of Beachampton, Bucks; *suc.* to the estate of Quarrendon, on the death, s.p.s., in 1610, of his cousin, Sir Henry Lee, K.G.,

(a) His brother, Sir Henry Mildmay, was his heir, whose grandson Benjamin Mildmay was in 1669, sum. to Parl. in the Barony of Fitzwalter by right of descent from the family of Ratcliffe, Earls of Sussex and Lords Fitzwalter.

and was *cr. a Bart.* as above, 29 June 1611, being subsequently *Knighted*(a) 18 Aug. 1614, at Woodstock. Sheriff of Oxon, 1613-14, and Sheriff of Bucks, 1620-21, having suc. his father, 20 Aug. 1616. He *m.* Eleanor, da. of Sir Richard WORTLEY, of Wortley, co. York, by Elizabeth, da. of Edward BOUGHTON. He was *bur.* 8 April 1631, at Spelsbury, Oxon. M.I. Will pr. 5 May 1631. His widow *m.* (as his 3d wife) 22 May 1634, at St. Andrew's, Holborn (Lic. Fac.), Edward (RATCLIFFE), 5th EARL OF SUSSEX, who *d.* s.p. Aug. 1643. She *m.* (for the third time) as his 3d wife, Robert (RICH), 3d EARL OF WARWICK, who *d.* 18 April 1658. Finally (for the fourth time), she *m.* in July 1649, as the 4th of his five wives, Edward (MONTAGU), 2d EARL OF MANCHESTER, who *d.* 5 May 1671, aged 68. She was *bur.* 31 Jan. 1666, at Kimbolton, co. Huntingdon. Will dat. 5 June 1665, pr. 2 Feb. 1666/7.

II. 1631. SIR FRANCIS HENRY LEE, Bart. [1611], of Quarrendon aforesaid, and of Ditchley, co. Oxford, 2d but only surv. s. and h.(b); *bap.* 3 March 1615/6, at Spelsbury; *suc. to the Baronetcy* in April 1631. He *m.*, 2 Oct. 1632, at Battersea, co. Surrey, Ann, da. of Sir John ST. JOHN, 1st Bart. [1611], of Lydiard Tregoz, Wilts, by his 1st wife Ann, da. of Sir Thomas Leighton. He *d.* 23 July 1639. Will pr. 10 Aug. 1639. His widow *m.*, before 7 Jan. 1644/5, as his 2d wife, Henry (WILMOT), 1st EARL OF ROCHESTER, who *d.* 19 Feb. 1657, aged 45, and was *bur.* at Spelsbury, Oxon. She, who was *b.* 6 Nov. 1614, was *bur.* (with both her husbands), 18 March 1695/6 at Spelsbury. Will dat. 1 June 1683 to 23 March 1692, pr. 1 April 1696.

III. 1639. SIR HENRY LEE, Bart. [1611] of Quarrendon and Ditchley aforesaid, s. and h., *bap.* 18 Dec. 1637, at Spelsbury; *suc. to the Baronetcy*, 13 July 1639. He *m.* (reg. 30 May 1655 at Spelsbury and 1 June 1655 at West Lavington, Wilts) Ann, 2d da. and coheir of Sir John DANVERS, of Chelsea, one of the Regicide Judges, by his 2d wife, Elizabeth, da. of Ambrose DAUNTSEY, and grandchild and heir of Sir John DAUNTSEY, of Lavington, Wilts. He *d.* s.p.m.(c) and was *bur.* 31 March 1658, at Spelsbury. Will dat. 18 May 1658, pr. 16 Feb. 1659. The will of his widow, dat. 15 June to 31 July 1659, pr. 22 Dec. following.

IV. 1658. SIR FRANCIS HENRY LEE, Bart. [1611], of Quarrendon and Ditchley aforesaid, br. and h. male, *bap.* 17 Jan. 1638/9, at Spelsbury; *suc. to the Baronetcy* in March 1658; *cr.* M.A. at Oxford, 28 Sep. 1663; M.P. for Malmesbury, 1660, and 1661-67. He *m.*, in or before 1663, Elizabeth, da. and coheir of Thomas (POPE), 2d EARL OF DOWNE [I.], by Lucy, da. and coheir of John DUTTON, of Sherborne, Dorset. He *d.* 4 Dec. 1667. His widow *m.*, as his 3d wife, Robert (BERTIE), 3d EARL OF LINDSEY, who *d.* 8 May 1701. She *d.* 1 July 1719. Will dat. 20 June, and pr. 26 Sep. 1719.

V. 1667. SIR EDWARD HENRY LEE, Bart. [1611], of Quarrendon and Ditchley aforesaid, s. and h., *b.* 4 Feb. 1662/3, *suc. to the Baronetcy*, 4 Dec. 1667, and, having *m.* 6 Feb. 1666/7 (when both were very young), the "LADY CHARLOTTE FITZROY," illegit. da. of Charles II, by Barbara, *suo jure* DUCHESS OF CLEVELAND, was *cr.* by the King, his father in law, 5 June 1674 (when under 12 years of age), EARL OF LICHFIELD, co. Stafford, etc. In that peerage, this *Baronetcy* continued *merged* till, on the death of the 4th Earl and 8th Baronet, it and all other his dignities became *extinct*.

(a) See p. 18, note "c," *sub* "Tollemache."

(b) Sir Henry Lee, *Knighted* at Theobalds, 20 Dec. 1611, the eldest son and h. ap., *d.* v.p. and unm.

(c) Eleanor, his 1st da. and coheir, *bap.* 3 June 1658, at Spelsbury, *m.* James (Bertie), 1st Earl of Abingdon, and had issue.

NAPIER:

cr. 24 Sep. 1611(a);

ex. 2 Jan. 1747/8.

I. 1611. "ROBERT NAPIER, of Luton Hoo, co. Bedford, Knt.," 2d s. of Alexander NAPIER, *otherwise* SANDY,(b) of Exeter, by his 3d wife, Ann, da. of Edward BIRCHLEY, of Herts; was admitted to Gray's Inn, 10 Aug. 1600; and was *cr. a Bart.*, as above, 24 Sep. 1611,(a) being subsequently,(c) *Knighted*, 21 July 1612. He was M.P. for Beds, 1611-12, and for Corfe Castle, 1626-28. He purchased the estate of Luton Hoo, a fine mansion with a park in the parish of Luton, co. Bedford. He *m.* firstly, Mary, da. of Richard BARNES, citizen and mercer of London. She *d.* s.p. He *m.* secondly, Ann, da. of Richard STAPLES, of London. She also d. s.p. He *m.* thirdly, in or before 1603, Margaret, da. of John ROBINSON, of London, merchant of the Staple. He was *bur.* 22 April 1637, at Luton. Will pr. 1637. His widow was *bur.* 12 Feb. 1637/8, at Luton aforesaid.

II. 1637. SIR ROBERT NAPIER, Bart. [1611], of Luton Hoo aforesaid, s. and h. by 3d wife; *b.* about 1603; matric. at Oxford (Ex. Coll.), 17 Dec. 1619, aged 16; admitted to Gray's Inn, 1620; *Knighted* at Whitehall, 30 April 1623; M.P. for Weymouth, 1628-9; for Peterboro', 1640, till secluded in 1648; *suc. to the Baronetcy* in April 1637. He *m.* firstly, in or before 1623, Frances, da. of Sir William THORNHURST, of Agincourt, Kent, by Anne, da. and coheir of Hon. Charles LYTE-HOWARD, s. of Thomas, VISCOUNT BINDON. She was *bur.* 29 April 1626, at Luton aforesaid. He *m.* secondly, in or before 1633, Penelope, da. of John (EGERTON), 1st EARL OF BRIDGWATER, by Frances, da. and coheir of Ferdinando (STANLEY), EARL OF DERBY. She was *bur.* 16 July 1658, at Luton. He surrendered the patent of his Baronetcy, with the intent that it should be regranted with the date of the old precedency (24 Sep. 1611), to himself and his issue male by his *second* marriage.(d) A patent to that effect was accordingly granted, dated 4 March 1660/1, the date, however, being but three days before his burial. He was *bur.* 7 March 1660/1, at Luton. Will pr. 26 April 1661.

III. 1661. SIR ROBERT NAPIER, Bart. [1611], grandson and h., being s. and h. of Robert NAPIER,(e) by Margaret, da. of Sir Edward LITTLETON, 1st Bart. [1627], which Robert last named, who was s. and h. ap. (by his 1st wife), of the 1st Bart. *d.* v.p., and was *bur.* 2 Oct. 1656, at Luton. He of right would have *suc. to the Baronetcy*(d) in March 1660/1, but, as he appears to have been disinherited by his grandfather, as to the estates, probably never assumed the title. He *d.* unm. and under age, and was *bur.* as "Mr. Robert Napire," 5 April 1675, at Luton.

IV. 1675. SIR JOHN NAPIER, Bart. [1611 and 1661], of Luton Hoo aforesaid, uncle and h. male of the half blood, being 2d s. (but 1st

(a) None of the four Baronetcies (Napier, Bayning, Temple, and Penyston), which were *cr.* on 24 Sep. 1611, are enrolled on the Patent Rolls, and, consequently, do not appear among the *Creations, 1483—1646*, in the Appendix of the 47th Report of the Deputy Keeper of the Public Records. The compiler thereof (R. Douglas Trimmer) states (27 May 1899) that they are not either in the indexes "of the Privy Seals and Signed bills (Chancery) or of the Signet bills (Chapter House) under date, September 1611." The description of the four grantees of these Baronetcies is therefore taken from Collins' *Baronetage* of 1720. These four Baronetcies (as well as the next batch of seventeen created on 25 Nov. following) are frequently misattributed to 1612 instead of to 1611.

(b) This Alexander, who was second of the two sons (each named Alexander) of Sir Alexander Napier, of Merchistoun, in Scotland, was the first of his race, who settled in England, where he was popularly known as Sandy."

(c) See p. 18, note, "c," *sub* "Tollemache."

(d) This surrender by the holder (the 2d Bart.) of an English hereditary dignity, defeating the vested rights of posterity, is here treated as inoperative, it being doubtless illegal.

(e) This Robert Napier, matric. at Oxford (Oriel Coll.), 24 July 1652, as "equitis fil. nat. max."; B.A., 17 Feb 1656 [*i.e.*, 1655/6].

I

surv. s. by the 2d wife), of the 2d Bart., was *bap.* 5 July 1636, at Luton aforesaid. He *suc.* his father 4 March 1660/1, in the family estates, and in *the Baronetcy*, *cr.* 4 March 1660/1, with the *precedency* of 24 Sep. 1611, as above stated.(a) By the death of his nephew in April 1675, he *suc. to the Baronetcy* of the actual creation of 24 Sep. 1611, as heir male to his father. He entered his pedigree in the Visit. of Beds, 1669, being then aged 30, and a Baronet; was M.P. for Bedfordshire, May 1664 to 1679, but afterwards became a lunatic, and had a commission awarded against him in Hilary term, 1710. He *m.* (Lic. Fac. 25 Aug. 1666), Elizabeth, da. of Sir Theophilus BIDDULPH, 1st Bart. [1664], by Susanna, da. of Zachary HIGHLAND, of London. He *d.* Aug. 1711. Admon. 3 April 1714, to Elizabeth his relict, and again, 9 Dec. 1721. The will of his widow pr. 1721.

V. 1711. SIR THEOPHILUS NAPIER, Bart. [1611 and 1661], of Luton Hoo, aforesaid, 1st surv. s. and h., *b.* 25 Oct. 1672, and *bap.* at Luton, aforesaid; *suc. to the two Baronetcies* in Aug. 1711; Sheriff of Beds, 1716-17. He *m.* Elizabeth, da. of John ROTHERAM, of Much Waltham, Essex. He *d.* s.p. 1719. Will pr. May 1719. His widow *m.* 25 Jan. 1721/2, as his 2d wife, Thomas (HOWARD), 6th BARON HOWARD OF EFFINGHAM, who *d.* 13 July 1725. She *m.* as her 3d husband (settl. dat. 11 Sep. 1728), as his 2d wife, Sir Conyers DARCY, K.B., who *d.* 1 Dec. 1758. She *d.* 30 Nov. 1741, aged 51, and was *bur.* at Lingfield. Will pr. 2 Jan. 1741/2.

VI. 1719 to 1748. SIR JOHN NAPIER, Bart. [1611 and 1661], of Luton Hoo, aforesaid, nephew and h., being s. and h. of Archibald NAPIER, by Sarah, relict of (—) ANGIER, which Archibald (who was *bap.* 6 Oct. 1678, at Luton, aforesaid), was 2d son of the 4th Bart. He *suc. to the two Baronetcies* in 1719; was Sheriff of Beds, 1729-30. He *d.* unm., at Luton Hoo, 2 Jan. 1747/8, when both *this Baronetcy* [1611] and the *Baronetcy* [1661] became *extinct.*(b) Will pr. 1748.

BAYNING:

cr. 24 Sep. 1611,(c)

afterwards, 1628-38, BARONS AND VISCOUNTS BAYNING;

ex. 11 June 1638.

I. 1611. "PAUL BAYNING, of Bentley parva, co. Essex, Esq.,(c) s. and h. ap. of Paul BAYNING, Alderman and sometime (1592), Sheriff of London, by his 2d wife, Susanna, da. and coheir of Edward NORDEN, of Mistley, co. Essex, was *bap.* 28 April 1588, at St. Olave's, Hart street, London, and was, v.p., *cr. a Bart.*, as above, 24 Sep. 1611,(c) being subsequently, 19 July 1614, *Knighted*(d) at Audley End. He suc. his father in the family estates, 1 Oct. 1616, and was Sheriff of Essex, 1617-18. He *m.*, in or before 1613, Anne, da. of Sir Henry GLEMHAM, of Glemham, co. Suffolk, by Anne, da. of Thomas (SACKVILLE), 1st EARL OF DORSET. She was living when he was *cr.* 27 Feb. 1657/8, BARON BAYNING OF HORKESLEY, co. Essex, and a few days later, 8 March 1627/8, VISCOUNT BAYNING OF SUDBURY, co. Suffolk. In this peerage, this *Baronetcy* then *merged* till on the death of the 2d Viscount and 2d Baronet, 11 June 1638 *it*, as well as the peerage dignities, became *extinct*. See *Peerage*.

(a) See p. 80, note "d."

(b) He devised Luton Hoo to his aunt, Frances NAPIER, who devised it to Francis HERNE, of Harrow, Middlesex, by whom it was sold to John (STUART), 3d EARL OF BUTE [S.], the well known statesman.

(c) See p. 80, note "a," *sub* "Napier."

(d) See p. 18, note "c," *sub* "Tollemache."

M

TEMPLE:

cr. 24 Sep. 1611(a);

sometime, 1714-18, BARON COBHAM,

and afterwards, 1718-49, VISCOUNT COBHAM;

dormant, 15 Nov. 1786;

though assumed ever since that date.

I. 1611. "SIR THOMAS TEMPLE,(b) of Stowe, co Buckingham, Knt."(a) 1st s. and h. of John TEMPLE,(c) of Stowe aforesaid (who purchased that manor in 1590, and *d.* 9 May 1603, aged 61), and of Burton Dassett, co. Warwick, by Susan, da. and h. of Thomas SPENCER, of Everdon, co. Northampton, was *bap.* 9 Jan. 1566/7; matric. at Oxford (Univ. Coll.), 22 June 1582, aged 16; admitted to Lincoln's Inn, 1583; M.P. for Andover, 1588-89; suc. his father 9 May 1603; was *Knighted*, shortly afterwards, July 1603, at Salden, Bucks, and was *cr. a Bart.*, as above, 24 Sep. 1611(a); Sheriff of Oxon, 1606-07; of Bucks, 1616-17; and of Warwickshire, 1620-21. He *m.*, about 1595, Hester, da. of Miles SANDYS, of Latimers, and of Eton, Bucks, Master of the King's Bench office, by Hester, da. of William CLIFTON, of Brimpton, co. Somerset. He was living Feb. 1632, but *d.* before March 1636/7, at Burton Dasset, and was *bur.* there. Will dat. 4 Feb. 1632, pr. 13 March 1636/7. His widow *d.* 1656.(d)

II. 1636? SIR PETER TEMPLE, Bart. [1611], of Stowe aforesaid, 1st s. and h., *bap.* 10 Oct. 1592, at Stowe; *suc. to the Baronetcy* about 1636; Sheriff of Bucks, 1634-5; M.P. for Buckingham, April to May 1640, and 1640-53(e) He *m.* firstly, 5 July 1614, at Paulerspury, co. Northampton, Ann, 2d da. and h. of Sir Arthur THROCKMORTON, of Paulerspury, by Ann, da. of Thomas LUCAS, of Colchester. She *d.* s.p.m.,(f) and was *bur.* 23 Jan. 1619/20, at Stowe. He *m.* secondly, 20 May 1630, at Kensington, Christian, da. and coheir of Sir John LEVESON, of Haling, co. Kent, and Lilleshall, co. Stafford, by Frances, da. and h. of Sir Thomas SONDES, of Throwley, co. Kent. He was *bur.* 12 Sep. 1653, at Stowe. Admon. 6 Jan. 1653/4, to a creditor. His widow was *bur.* at Stowe, 3 April 1655.

(a) See p. 80, note "a," *sub* "Napier."

(b) The family of Temple is ably dealt with in the *Her. and Gen.* (vol. iii, pp. 305-410, pp. 530-544, vol. iv, pp. 8-13, and vol. viii, pp. 510-514), where it is shewn that, notwithstanding their alleged descent in the male line from the Saxon Earls of Mercia (see Edmondson's *Baronagium* [vol. iii, p. 278], etc.), they "did not rise above the rank of small gentry until the latter part of the fifteenth century," and it was not till the seventeenth century that any member obtained the rank of knighthood.

(c) His yr. br., Anthony Temple, of Coughton, co. Warwick, is said, but whether truly or not is very doubtful (see *Nat. Biogr.* under "Temple, Sir William"), to have been father of Sir William Temple, Provost of Trinity College, Dublin, (1609-1627), who undoubtedly, by his son Sir John Temple, Master of the Rolls in Ireland, (1640-1677), was grandfather of Sir William Temple, Bart. (so *cr.* 31 Jan. 1665), the celebrated Statesman, and of Sir John Temple, the father of Henry, 1st Viscount Palmerston [I.]

(d) "She had four sons and nine daughters, which lived to be married, and so exceedingly multiplied, that this lady saw 700 extracted from her body" [Fuller's *Worthies*]. If this is true, she far exceeds Mrs. Honywood (*d.* 11 May 1620, aged 93), who had but 376 descendants at her death (see *Top. and Gen.*, vol. i, pp. 397-411, and 568-576), but it should be noted that the Honywood case is well authenticated, whereas that of Temple rests merely on Dr. Fuller's statement.

(e) He was, at first, a zealous partisan of the Parl., and was actually nominated one of the Judges for the King's trial, but he abstained from attendance thereat, and, after the King's executien, threw up his commission in the Army. He is often confused both (1) with his cousin, Peter Temple, one of the Regicide Judges (who, having signed the death warrant, was condemned to be hanged, 16 Oct. 1660, and died a prisoner, 20 Dec. 1663, aged 63), as also (2) with his nephew, Sir Peter Temple (Knt.), of Stanton Bury, Bucks, ancestor of the 5th, 6th, and 7th Baronets.

(f) Ann, her only surv. child, *bap.* 26 Jan. 1619/20, *m.* Thomas (Roper), Viscount Baltinglass [I.], and *d.* in the Fleet prison, London, 1696.

III. 1653. SIR RICHARD TEMPLE, Bart. [1611], of Stowe aforesaid, only s. and h., by 2d wife, *b.* 1634; admitted to Gray's Inn, 6 Nov. 1648; *suc. to the Baronetcy* in Sep. 1653; M.P. for Warwickshire, 1654-55; for Buckingham, 1659; and for Bucks, 1660 till his death, having been made K.B. at the coronation of Charles II in 1661, and taking a leading part against the Popish plot, and for the exclusion of James, Duke of York, from the Crown; one of the Council for foreign plantations, 1671, and a Commissioner of Customs, 1672-94.(a) He *m.*, in or before 1675, Mary, da. and coheir of Henry KNAPP, of Weston, co. Oxford. He was *bur.* at Stowe, 12 May 1697. Will pr. 1697. His widow was *bur.* there, 15 May 1726. Will pr. 1727.

IV. 1697. SIR RICHARD TEMPLE, Bart. [1611], of Stowe aforesaid, s. and h., *b.* 24 Oct. and *bap.* 1 Nov. 1675, at St. Paul's, Covent Garden; entered the Army in 1685, and distinguished himself at the siege of Lille in 1708, becoming, subsequently (1742), Field Marshal; *suc. to the Baronetcy* in May 1697; was M.P. for Buckingham (five Parls.), 1697-1704; for Bucks, 1704-08, and for Buckingham (again), 1708-13; Envoy to Vienna, 1714-15. He was *cr.*, 19 Oct. 1714, BARON COBHAM(b) of Cobham, co. Kent, being subsequently, 23 May 1718, *cr.*, BARON AND VISCOUNT COBHAM(c) of Cobham, co. Kent, with (in this case), a spec. rem. failing his issue male, in favour of two of his sisters; P.C., 1716; Gov. of Jersey, 1723-49. He *m.* Anne, da. of Edmund HALSEY, of Stoke Pogis, Bucks, and of Southwark, Surrey, Brewer. He *d.* s.p. 13 and was *bur.* 18 Sep. 1749, at Stowe, when the *Barony of Cobham*, created 1714, became *extinct*, but the *Barony and Viscountcy of Cobham*, created 1718, devolved on his sister(c) (according to the spec. rem. in its creation), as did also the estate of Stowe and the other estates of the Temple family, while the Baronetcy devolved on his cousin and heir male, as below. His widow *d.* 20 March 1760. For fuller particulars of him and his wife, see "Peerage."

V. 1749. SIR WILLIAM TEMPLE, Bart. [1611], of Nash House in Kempsey, co. Worcester, cousin and h. male, being 1st s. and h. of William TEMPLE, of Lillingston Dayrell, Bucks, by Mary, da. of (—) Green, of co. Kent, which William last named (who was *bur.* at Buckingham, 27 Aug. 1706), was 5th and yst. s. of Sir Peter TEMPLE, of Stanton Bury, Bucks, which Peter (who was *b.* 1613; *Knighted* 6 June 1641, and *bur.* at St. Peter's, Mancroft, Norwich, 14 Jan. 1659/60), was 1st s. and h.(d) of Sir John TEMPLE, of

(a) This Sir Richard Temple rebuilt the house at Stowe, originally built by Peter Temple, *temp.* Eliz. Lord Cobham, son of Sir Richard, built a new front and added the wings, which front was again rebuilt in a more stately form by his nephew and successor, Earl Temple.

(b) His connection with the family of Cobham was somewhat remote. His paternal grandmother, Christian, being 2d da. and coheir of Sir John Leveson, by Frances, da. of Sir Thomas Sondes, and Margaret, his wife, sister, but not heir or coheir, of Henry (Brooke), Lord Cobham, attainted in 1603, whose nephew and representative, Sir William Brooke, K.B. (died in 1643), left issue.

(c) Hester Grenville, widow of Richard Grenville, of Wootton, Bucks. She was *cr.* (a few days later), 14 Oct. 1749, Countess Temple, with rem. of that dignity to her issue male. This and her other peerage dignities continued in such issue, till, by the death s.p.m., 28 March 1889, of the Duke of Buckingham and Chandos, 5th in descent from her, and the last of her issue male, the Earldom of Temple (1749) became extinct, but the Barony and Viscountcy of Cobham (1718) passed (under the spec. rem. in its creation) to Baron Lyttelton of Frankley, heir male of the body of Dame Christian Lyttelton, the other sister of Richard (Temple), 1st Viscount Cobham, who was in remainder to that title. The 2d Duke of Buckingham and Chandos had, however, obtained an *Earldom of Temple of Stowe*, co. Buckingham, *cr.* 4 Feb. 1822, with a spec. rem., in fault of his issue male, to his daughter and her issue male. This rem. took effect on the death, abovementioned, of the 3d Duke in 1889, when William Stephen Gore-Langton, the son and heir of such daughter, became Earl Temple of Stowe (1822), though he neither inherited the estate of Stowe, nor in any way represented the family of Temple, of which (though a descendant), he was not even a junior coheir.

(d) This Sir Peter Temple had three younger brothers, THOMAS, EDMUND and PURBECK, all under age and unm. at their father's death in 1632. (See his funeral certificate). Of these three (i) SIR THOMAS TEMPLE, *bap.* 10 Jan. 1614, was Gov. of

Stanton Bury aforesaid (by his 1st wife, Dorothy, da. and coheir of Edmund LEE, of Stanton aforesaid), which John (who was *Knighted* 21 March 1612/3, in his 20th year, and *d.* 23 Sep. 1632), was 2d s. of the 1st Baronet. He was *b.* April 1694; *suc.* his father in Aug. 1706; was sometime of Buckingham and of North Crawley; purchased, about 1738, the estate of Nash House abovenamed, and *suc. to the Baronetcy* 15 Sep. 1749, on the death of his cousin, Viscount Cobham. He *m.* firstly, May 1718, Elizabeth, da. and h. of Peter PAXTON, M.D., of Buckingham, by Elizabeth, his wife. She *d.* 1729, and was *bur.* at Martin Hussentree, co. Warwick. He *m.* secondly, Nov. 1731, Elizabeth, da. of Hugh ETHERSEY, of Leckhampstead, Bucks. He *d.* s.p.m.s.(a) 1760, aged 66, and was *bur.* at Kempsey. M.I. His widow *d.* 2 Dec. 1762, aged 67, and was *bur.* there.

VI. 1760. SIR PETER TEMPLE, Bart. [1611], br. and h. male, sometime of Buckingham, but afterwards of Draycot, co. Oxford, *suc. to the Baronetcy*, 7 April 1760. He *m.* firstly, 1719, Elizabeth BROUGHTON, of Longdon, co. Stafford. She *d.* 1726. He *m.* secondly, 1729, Elizabeth, da. of John MOLD, of Charlton, Oxon. She *d.* June 1759, and was *bur.* at Draycot. He *d.* (within a year of his succession to the title), 15 Nov. 1761, and was *bur.* at Draycot. Will pr. 1761.

VII. 1761, to 1786. SIR RICHARD TEMPLE, Bart. [1611], of Nash House, in Kempsey aforesaid, only surv. s. and h., by 2d wife,(b) *b.* 1 June 1731; *suc. to the Baronetcy*, 15 Nov. 1761; a Commissioner of the Navy, 1761; Comptroller of Excise, 1763-86. He *m.*, 24 June 1758,

Acadia, or Nova Scotia, 1656-70, and was *cr. a Bart.* [S.], 7 July 1662. He *d.* unm. 27 March 1674, and was *bur.* at Ealing, Midx. The children of his br. Edmund are wrongly attributed to him in Le Neve's MS., *Baronets*, and in Nichols' *Leicestershire.* (ii) SIR PURBECK TEMPLE, 4th and yst. br., was of Addiscombe, co. Surrey, Knighted 3 Sep. 1660, *m.*, but *d.* s.p. Aug. 1695, and was *bur.* at Islington. He and his brother Edmund are mentioned as living in the will of their stepmother, Dame Frances Temple, dat. 3 Aug. 1642, and pr. 9 Aug. 1647. (iii) EDMUND TEMPLE, the 3d brother, *bap.* 6 June 1622, at Stowe; was a Col. in the Parl. service, and was of Sulby Priory, in the parish of Welford, co. Northampton, where he was *bur.* 9 March 1667/8, naming in his will three sons, STEPHEN, JOHN and EDMUND. Of these three (1) STEPHEN TEMPLE, of Sulby, *d.* s.p., and was *bur.* 26 Oct. 1672, naming in his will his brother John (as his heir at law), and his brother Edmund. (2) JOHN TEMPLE, of Sibbertoft, co. Northampton, was *bur.* at Welford, 22 Feb. 1701/2, aged 52, having had by Martha his wife (who *d.* 1723), two sons, viz. RICHARD, *b.* in 1683, of whom nothing more is known, and PURBECK. This PURBECK TEMPLE, *b.* 1689, was of Sibbertoft aforesaid, and *d.* 16 May 1763, aged 74, leaving, by Mary his wife (who *d.* 1771), one son, EDWARD.

"*There appears every probability that* the last named EDWARD [TEMPLE] *was the Baronet for the last ten years of his life* [1786-96], unless there was any issue in the male line existing, from his uncle Richard. At any event, *it is clear that till his decease* [15 Sep. 1796], *the dignity could not have devolved on any younger branch of the family.*" [*Her. and Gen.* iii, 542.] This Edward Temple, presumably the *de jure* Baronet, *d.* unm., 15 Sep. 1796.

(3) EDMUND TEMPLE, 3d and yst. s. of Col. Edmund Temple, of Sulby Abbey aforesaid (who was yr. br. of Sir Peter Temple, "Knt." grandfather of the 5th and 6th Baronet), was living 22 Aug. 1683, being then father of a son named Purbeck; was of Leicester in 1690, soon after which date he appears to have died, leaving Ellen, his widow. His son, PURBECK TEMPLE, was living 14 July 1693, being mentioned in the will of that date of his great uncle and godfather, Sir Purbeck Temple. The male issue of this Edmund Temple, of Leicester, is not, improbably, still in existence.

(a) By his 2d wife, he had an only child, who *m.* her cousin, the 7th Baronet. By his 1st wife he had a son, Paxton Temple, *b.* April 1720, who *d.* in London unm. and v.p. 1743; and a da., Henrietta, *b.* Dec. 1723, who *m.* William Dicken, of Shenton, co. Salop. John Dicken, their s. and h., who subsequently inherited the Nash estate, took the name and arms of "Temple" by royal lic., 23 Sep. 1796. Their grandson and heir, Richard Temple, of Nash aforesaid, was *cr. a Bart.*, 16 Aug. 1876.

(b) His elder br. of the half blood, Peter Temple, was in the Royal Navy, but *d.* unm., v.p., of the small pox, 1748, at Portsmouth.

at Kempsey aforesaid, Anna Sophia, yst. da. and coheir of his uncle, Sir William TEMPLE, 5th Bart. [1611], by his 2d wife, Elizabeth, da. of Hugh ETHERSEY. He *d.* s.p.s. at Bath, 15 and was *bur.* 20 Nov. 1786, at Bath Abbey, aged 55. Will pr. Nov. 1786. His widow *d.* 4 Oct. 1805, and was *bur.* at Kensington. Will pr. 1805. At his death the *Baronetcy* became *dormant*; the heir male of the body of the grantee (for such heir undoubtedly existed), not assuming it.(a) It was, however, assumed as under.

VIII. 1786. "SIR JOHN TEMPLE, Bart.," assumed the dignity of a Baronet [1611] in Nov. 1786 (being at that date Consul Gen. of New York), as heir male of the body of the grantee.

Various descents are assigned to him [I]. A memorandum in his own handwriting gives his descent from Sir Peter Temple, the 2d Bart., as being "the son of Robert, eldest son of Thomas, the son of Purbeck, who was 2d son of the aforementioned Sir Peter Temple, Bart.,(b) of Stowe." He is accordingly "stated in editions of the *Baronetage*, published before 1828, to have descended from the *second* Baronet. This [however] could not have been the fact, or his branch would have inherited the dignity [in 1749] before those of Stanton Bury [whose descent was from *a younger brother* of the said 2d Bart.] Other lines of descent have, subsequently, been suggested for him, but none has been actually ascertained" [*Her. and Gen.*, iii, 396]. [II] A conjecture in Debrett's *Baronetage*, of 1835 (edited by W. Courthope), that the descent might be from Col. Edmund Temple (one of the sons of Sir John Temple, 2d son of the 1st Bart.), is, in Burke's *Baronetage* (1841), adopted as a certainty, though the precise descent is not given.(c) [III] An American genealogist makes the said John to be son of Robert, son of Thomas, son of Sir Purbeck Temple, a younger son of Sir John Temple, of Stanton Bury, the 2d son of the 1st Bart. [*New England Hist. and Gen. Reg.*, vol. x]. It is, however, quite certain that the said Sir Purbeck died without issue. [IV] The descent (as in Burke's *Peerage*, 1899) is from the Rev. Thomas Temple, D.C.L. [1633], said (therein) to be Rector of Bourton on the Water, co. Gloucester,(d) which Thomas, who was *bap.* 8 April 1604, at Stowe, was 3d son of the 1st Bart. This Thomas is stated to have had "a grandson" [the child's *parentage*, a most important part in the pedigree, is apparently unknown], named Thomas

(a) Failing any nearer heir male (and none such, apparently, existed), Edward Temple was entitled to the Baronetcy, from 1786 to 1796. He was son of Purbeck Temple (*d.* 1763, aged 71), son of John Temple (*d.* 1702, aged 52), son of Col. Edmund Temple (*d.* 1668, aged 46), son of Sir John Temple (Knt.), of Stantonbury (*d.* 1632), who was 2d son of the 1st Baronet. See p. 83, note "d."

(b) The remarkable letter to "Sir John Temple, Bart., Consul Gen., New York," from the Marquess of Buckingham, dated "Stowe, 3 Dec. 1786" [printed in the *Her. and Gen.*, vol. iv, p. 8], states that on the recent death of Sir Richard Temple, Bart., "the title devolves upon you as heir male to Sir Peter Temple, my great great grandfather and your great grandfather." His Lordship does not say that this Sir Peter was a *Baronet*, and possibly does not mean Sir Peter Temple, *Bart.* (*i.e.*, the 2d Bart.), the person claimed by the said John for a *great* great (not great) grandfather. This Peter, the 2d Bart., was great grandfather (not, as stated, to the *writer* himself, but) to the *writer's father*, through that father's mother, Hester, Countess Temple, wife of Richard Grenville. Another Sir Peter Temple [Knt., not Bart.] may possibly be meant, who was the lineal ancestor of the lately deceased Bart., and who was great grandfather (not, as stated, to the writer himself but) to the writer's father, the Rt. Hon. George Grenville, son of Richard Grenville (by Hester, Countess Temple above named) and grandson of another Richard Grenville, by Elinor, da. of the last named Sir Peter Temple.

(c) The male issue of this Edmund is dealt with on p. 83, note "d," among which was Edward Temple, who was not improbably the rightful Baronet in 1786.

(d) In the Visit. of Surrey for 1662, "Sir Ralph Freeman, of Lee, co. Surrey, Knt., 1662," is said to have *m.* "Margaret, da. of Collonell Tho. Temple, of Stow in co. Bucks, Dr. of the Civil Law." This is, unquestionably, the 3d son of the 1st Bart., called in the Visit. of 1634, "Thomas Temple, Dr. of the Civil Law," and is important as shewing that the said Thomas married and had issue.

Temple, who resided in Ireland, and who, by the sister of Nathaniel White, was father of Robert Temple, of Boston in America (*b.* 1694), who was father of John, who, in 1786, assumed the [1611] Baronetcy. As to these last two named descents, neither of them would, even if genuine, justify John Temple in assuming the Baronetcy while issue male remained, which it undoubtedly did till 1796, of Col. Edmund Temple, *elder* brother of Sir Purbeck Temple, and a descendant of the *second* son of the 1st Baronet.

JOHN TEMPLE, who (as abovestated) assumed the Baronetcy in 1786 was, undoubtedly, 3d son, and (after 1781), heir male of Robert TEMPLE, of Boston, in New England, "descended from Ireland,"(a) by Mehitabel (*m.* 11 Aug. 1721), da. of John NELSON, of Boston aforesaid, which John Nelson was "executor of the will of his uncle, Sir Thomas(b) Temple,"(a) being s. of Robert NELSON, of Gray's Inn, Midx., by Mary, 3d da. of Sir John TEMPLE (ancestor of the 5th, 6th and 7th Barts.), 2d s. of Sir Thomas Temple the 1st Bart. His *maternal* descent from that Baronet is, therefore, undoubted, and the cousinship thus existing with the *Temple* Baronets may have given rise to the idea that it was one. in the male line, *through Temple*, instead of one in the female line, *through Nelson*. His *paternal* lineage, however, is, even if allowed as far as his grandfather, altogether conjectural beyond that period. His father, "Capt. Robert Temple," *b.* 1694, emigrated from the north of Ireland to Boston, in New England, in Sep. 1717, and *d.* 14 April 1754, at Charlestown, aged 60, being, probably, son of a Thomas TEMPLE, who *d.* in Ireland, by [—], da. of [—] WHITE,(c) in Ireland, the parentage of the said Thomas Temple (said to have been a ship's carpenter), being unproved.(d) He himself, the second s.(e) of his parents, was *b.* at Noddle's island (afterwards East Boston), and *bap.* 16 April 1732, at Boston aforesaid; was Surveyor Gen. of the Customs in the Northern District of America, 1761-67; a Commissr. of Revenue, 1767-74; Lieut. Gov. of New Hampshire, 1768-74, and Consul General for Great Britain in America, 1786-98, being the first so appointed after the declaration of the independence. He *m.* 20 Jan. 1767, Elizabeth, da. of James BOWDOIN, Gov. of the State of Massachusetts. He *d.* in the city of New York, 17 Nov. 1798, aged 67, and was *bur.* in St. Paul's church there. M.I. Will pr. Feb. 1799.

IX. 1798. SIR GRENVILLE TEMPLE, Bart.(f) [1611], s. and h. *b.* 16 Oct. 1768; suc. his father, and *assumed the Baronetcy*, 17 Nov. 1798. He *m.* firstly, 20 March 1797, Elizabeth, da. of Col. George WATSON, of Boston aforesaid. She *d.* 4 Nov. 1809. He *m.* secondly, 9 June 1812, Maria Augusta Dorothea, widow of Col. Frederick MANNERS, da. of Sir

(a) See pedigree of Nelson recorded in the College of Arms in 1769.

(b) *i.e.*, Sir Thomas Temple, Bart. [S.], who *d.* unm. 27 March 1674. See page 83, note "d."

(c) She was sister of Nathaniel White, of Plymouth, merchant, living there, Sep. 1717.

(d) A conjectural father for this Thomas is given in a draft pedigree among the private MSS. of Sir Isaac Heard, Garter ["J.P., 89," in the Coll. of Arms], as "Edmund Temple, Col. of a Regt.," which Edmund, by subsequent additions, is suggested to have been a "younger son of Peter, son of Sir Thomas, the 1st Bart." These suggestions are, however, very unhappy. If Edmund Temple, of Sulby, co. Northampton, who was, undoubtedly, a Colonel, is meant, he had no son named Thomas (see p. 83, note "d") neither was his father named Peter. The 1st Bart. had, indeed, a son Peter, viz., his son and heir, the 2d Bart., which Sir Peter Temple, Bart., left but one son, Sir Richard, the 3d Bart., whose male issue failed in 1749.

(e) Robert Temple, of Ten Hills, near Boston, the elder br., *d.* s.p.m., 1781, aged 53, leaving three daughters and coheirs, of whom the second *m.* Hans Blackwood, afterwards 2d Baron Dufferin and Clandboye [I.]

(f) On the supposition that the assumption of the Baronetcy [1611], by John Temple, in 1786, was a legal one. For some period it was generally considered as not existing, *e.g.*, "it is not to be found in Debrett's *Baronetage* of 1840, but gradually it has reappeared and made its way into Debrett, Burke, Dod and the Court Kalendar." [*Her. and Gen.*, iv, 284].

Thomas RUMBOLD, 1st Bart. [1779], by his 2d wife, Joanna, da. of Edmund LAW, BISHOP OF CARLISLE. He *d.* 18 Feb. 1829, at Florence, aged 60. Will pr. Feb. 1830. His widow, by whom he had no issue, *d.* 14 Feb. 1852, at Tours, in France. Admon. June 1582.

X. 1829. SIR GRENVILLE TEMPLE, Bart.(a) [1611], s. and h. by 1st wife, *b.* 20 July 1799; an officer in the army, 15th Hussars, becoming Lieut. Col. in Nov. 1841; suc. his father, and *assumed the Baronetcy*, 18 Feb. 1829. He *m.* 5 May 1829, at Florence, Mary, da. of George BARING, by Harriet Rochfort, da. of Sir John Hadley D'OYLY, 6th Bart. [1663]. He *d.* very suddenly, 7 June 1847, aged 48, at Constance, in Switzerland. His widow *d.* there, 10 May 1863.

XI. 1847. SIR GRENVILLE LEOFRIC TEMPLE, Bart.(a) [1611], s. and h., *b.* at Florence, 3 Feb. 1830; was sometime an officer in the Royal Navy; suc. his father, and *assumed the Baronetcy*, 7 June 1847. He *m.* 22 July 1856, at Hermandstadt, Transylvania, Marie, 2d da. of (—) ARON VAN BISTREN, or DE BISTROY, Minister of Finance for Transylvania. He *d.* 3 March 1860, at Thulgarten, near Constance aforesaid. His widow *d.* at Constance, 12 June 1865.

XII. 1860. SIR GRENVILLE LOUIS JOHN TEMPLE, Bart.(a) [1611], only s. and h., *b.* 5 Jan. 1858, at Chateau de Salenstein, Switzerland; suc. his father, and *assumed the Baronetcy*, 3 March 1860; sometime Lieut. 20th Foot.

Family Estates.—Those of the first Baronets, including the princely seat at Stowe, in Bucks, passed, in 1749, on the death of Viscount Cobham, the 4th Bart., to the Grenville family. That of Kempsey, co. Worcester, purchased by the 5th Baronet, passed, in 1786 or 1805, to the family of Dicken (descendants and representatives in the female line of the said Baronet), who took the name of Temple, and acquired a Baronetcy in 1876.

PENYSTON:

cr. 24 Sep. 1611;(b)

ex. 24 Dec. 1705.

I. 1611. "THOMAS PENYSTON, of Leigh, co. Essex, Esq.,"(c) only s. and h. of Thomas PENYSTON, of Deane, co. Oxford, by Mary, da. and coheir of John SOMER, of Newland, co. Kent, was *b.* about 1592; matric. at Oxford (Queen's Coll.), 13 March 1606/7, aged 15; B.A. (from St. Edm. Hall), 15 June 1599; Student of the Inner Temple, 1609, being then of Rochester; was *cr. a Baronet*, as above,(b) 24 Sep. 1611. He was Sheriff of Oxon, 1637-38; was M.P. for Westbury, April to May, 1640. He *m.* firstly, Ann, 4th da. of Sir William STONEHOUSE. He *m.* secondly, in or before 1612, Martha, 4th da. of Sir Thomas TEMPLE, 1st Bart. [1611], of Stowe, Bucks, by Hester, da. of Miles SANDYS. She was *bur.* at Stowe, 24 Jan. 1619. He *m.* thirdly, Elizabeth, widow of Sir William POPE (who *d.* v.p. 1624), da. and h. of Sir Thomas WATSON, of Halstead, co. Kent. He *d.* probably shortly after 17 Sep. 1642, the date of his will,(d) which was proved, 7 July 1647, a prior admon. being dated 18 March 1645/6. In both of these he is described as of Cornwell, co. Oxford.

(a) See p. 86, note "f."

(b) See p. 80, note "a," *sub* "Napier."

(c) This Thomas, who *d.* v.p., was s. and h. ap. of Thomas Penyston, of Hawridge, Bucks, which estate he sold in 1572, though it had been for many generations in the family.

(d) He devises his "lands in Wales, Suffolk and Lincolnshire," to his son Thomas, but makes no mention of any lands in Oxon or Bucks.

II. 1642? SIR THOMAS PENYSTON, Bart. [1611], of Cornwell aforesaid, only surv. s. and h. by 3d wife; *suc. to the Baronetcy* about 1642, being a minor as late as July 1647. He *m.* 31 Aug. 1647, Elizabeth, da. and h. of Sir Cornelius FAIRMEDOW, of St. Martin's in the Fields (who *d.* in or before April 1638), by Dyonisia his wife. He was *bur.* 29 May 1674 at Cornwell aforesaid. Will dat. 15 Oct. 1672, pr. 3 July 1674. His widow was *bur.* there 31 May 1705. Will as "of Adlestrop, co. Glouc.," dat. 21 Jan. 1704, pr. July 1705.

III. 1674. SIR THOMAS PENYSTON, Bart. [1611], of Cornwell aforesaid, 1st s. and h., *b.* about 1648; matric. at Oxford (Oriel Coll.) 3 March 1664/5, aged 16; Student of Gray's Inn 1666; aged 20 (Visit. of Oxon) 1668; *suc. to the Baronetcy* in May 1674. He *d.* unm. in or before 1679, and was *bur.* at St. Dunstan's in the West. Admon. 11 July, 1679.

IV. 1679? to 1705. SIR FAIRMEDOW PENYSTON, Bart. [1611], of Cornwell aforesaid, br. and h., *b.* 1656; *suc. to the Baronetcy* in or before 1679; was Sheriff of Oxon, April to Nov. 1689. He *m.* firstly, Elizabeth, da. of Sir Compton READE, 1st Bart. [1660], of Shipton, Oxon, by Mary, da. of Sir Gilbert CORNWALL, of Burford. She was *bur.* 2 March 1685, at Cornwell. Admon. 25 May 1688. He *m.* secondly (Lic. Vic. Gen. 17 Dec. 1687, each being then aged 32), Mary, widow of Sir William PAUL, of Bray, co. Berks, 1st da. of John POWNEY, of Old Windsor in that county. He *d.* s.p. 24 and was *bur.* 27 Dec. 1705, at Cornwell aforesaid, in his 50th year, when the *Baronetcy* became *extinct*. His widow *d.* and was *bur.* 13 Jan. 1714, at Cornwell, in her 66th year. Will dat. 30 July 1714, pr. 12 Feb. 1714/5.

DEVEREUX, *or* DEVOREUX:(a)

cr. 25 Nov. 1611,(b)

afterwards, since 1646, VISCOUNTS HEREFORD.

I. 1611. "EDWARD DEVOREUX, of Castle Bramwitch [*i.e.* Bromwich], co. Warwick, Esq.," 4th s. of Walter (DEVEREUX), 1st VISCOUNT HEREFORD, LORD FERRERS OF CHARTLEY, etc., being his only s., by his 2d wife, Margaret, da. of Robert GARNISH, of Kenton, Suffolk, was M.P. for Tamworth, 1588-89; Sheriff of Warwickshire, 1593-94, and was *cr. a Bart.,* as above, 25 Nov. 1611,(b) and, subsequently,(c) *Knighted,* 19 Aug. 1612. He *m.* Katharine, 1st da. of Edward ARDEN, of Park Hall, co. Warwick, by Mary, da. of Sir Robert THROGMORTON. He *d.* 22 Sep. 1622. Will pr. 1622. His widow *d.* 20 Nov. 1627. Will pr. 1628. Both are *bur.* at Aston, co. Warwick.

(a) This is the first in order of the seventeen creations of this date, which are here dealt with, as placed in the *Creations, 1483—1646,* in app. 47th rep. of the D.K. Pub. Records. The order in Collins' *Baronetage* of 1720, and in most other printed lists, is as under (1) Portman, (2) Saunderson, (3) Sandys, (4) Gostwick, (5) Puckering, (6) Wray, (7) Ayloffe, (8) Wyvill, (9) Pershall, (10) Englefield, (11) Ridgway, (12) Essex, (13) Gorges, (14) Devereux, (15) Mohun, (16) Grimston, and (17) Holte.

(b) The error of attributing the last seventeen creations in 1611 to the year 1612 is thus dealt with by J. Gough Nichols. "In all lists of the Baronets these creations will be found placed under the date, 25 Nov. 1612, instead of 1611. This error crept into the lists on some very early occasion, and has never hitherto been duly corrected. As regards Sir Marmaduke Wyvill it was detected 'from examination of the original patent the date whereof has hitherto been erroneously printed (by Dugdale, and in other catalogues of Baronets) Nov. 25, 1612. Ex. inf. Dom. Mar. Wyvill, Bar.' [*The English Baronetage,* 1741, vol. i, p. 232]. But this discovery, being confined to the Wyvill patent, the only result was an undue removal [in the Baronetage of 1741] of the article of Wyvill from its proper precedence to a place before that of Gostwick, and in the Baronetage [by Kimber] of 1771, Wyvill is further advanced before Temple, *cr.* Sep. 12, 1611; the latter being misassigned to 1612." [*Her. and Gen.,* vol. iii, p. 449].

(c) See p. 18, note "c," *sub* "Tollemache."

II. 1622. SIR WALTER DEVEREUX, Bart. [1611], of Castle Bromwich aforesaid, 2d but 1st surv. s. and h., *Knighted,* v.p., apparently, 23 July 1603. M.P. for Stafford, 1614; for Marlboro', 1621-22; for Worcestershire, 1624-26; for Worcester, 1625, and for Lichfield, 1640. Sheriff of Warwickshire, 1616-17; of Worcestershire, 1625-26; *suc. to the Baronetcy,* 22 Sep. 1622.(a) He *m.* firstly, Elizabeth, da. and h. of Robert BASPOLE, of Aldeby, Norfolk. She *d.* s.p. He *m.* secondly, before 1615, Elizabeth, widow of Thomas MARTIN, 2d da. of Thomas KNIGHTLEY, of Burgh Hall, co. Stafford, by Elizabeth, da. of John SHUCKBURGH, of Naseby, co. Northampton. She *d.* before him. On the death s.p., 14 Sep. 1646, of his cousin, Robert (Devereux), 4th Viscount Hereford and 2d Earl of Essex (the Parliamentary General), to whom he was heir male, he *suc.* him as 5th VISCOUNT HEREFORD, in which Viscountcy this *Baronetcy* has ever since continued to be *merged.* See *Peerage.*

RIDGEWAY, *or* RIDGWAY:

cr. 25 Nov. 1611,(b)

subsequently 1616-22, BARON GALLEN RIDGEWAY [I.],

and afterwards 1622-1714, EARLS OF LONDONDERRY [I.];

ex. 7 March 1713/4.

I. 1611. "THOMAS RIDGWAY, of Torr, co. Devon, Knt.," s. and h. of Thomas RIDGEWAY, of Tor Mohun aforesaid, by Mary, da. of Thomas SOUTHCOTE, of Bovey Tracey in the said county, was *b.* about 1565, suc. his father, 27 June 1597, and, having served in Ireland, was *Knighted* in 1600, being Sheriff of Devon, 1599—1600; was M.P. for Devon, 1604-06, and employed in the Colonization of Ulster; Vice Treasurer of War [I.], 1603-06; Treasurer [I.], 1606-16; P.C. [I.], and was *cr. a Bart.,* as above, 25 Nov. 1611.(b) M.P. [I.] for Ballynakill, 1613, and for Tyrone, 1613. He *m.* Cicely (sometime maid of honour to Queen Elizabeth), sister and coheir of Henry MACWILLIAM. He was *cr.* 25 May 1616, LORD RIDGEWAY, BARON OF GALLEN RIDGEWAY [I.], and subsequently, 23 Aug. 1623, EARL OF LONDON DERRY [I.] In these peerages this *Baronetcy* then *merged,* and so continued till on the death of the 4th Earl and 4th Baronet, 7 March 1713/4, it and all other his honours became *extinct.* See *Peerage.*

SANDYS:

cr. 25 Nov. 1611;(b)

ex. 23 Feb. 1653/4.

I. 1611. "MILES SANDYS, of Wilberton, in the Isle of Ely, co. Cambridge, Knt.," 3d s. of Edwin SANDYS, Archbishop of York [1578-88], by his 2d wife, Cecilia, da. of Sir Thomas WILFORD, of Cranbrook, co. Kent, was *b.* 29 March 1563; ed. at Merchant Taylors' school (with his brothers, Edwin and Samuel), 1571; *Knighted,* 11 May 1603, at the Charterhouse, and was *cr. a Bart.,* as above, 25 Nov. 1611.(b) He was M.P. for the Univ. of Cambridge, 1614; for Huntingdon, 1621-22, and for Cambridgeshire, 1628-29; Sheriff of Camb. and Hunts, 1615-16.(c) He *m.* firstly, Elizabeth, da. of Edward COOKE, of North Cray, co. Kent, by whom he had seven sons, all of whom *d.* s.p. He *m.* secondly, 28 Nov. 1626, at St. Mary, Aldermanbury, London (Lic. Lond., he 64, and she 40), Mary WEST, widow. He *d.* 1645. Will pr. April 1645.

(a) He must not be confounded with Sir Walter Devereux (base son of the 2d Earl of Essex) who was *Knighted* at Ashby de la Zouch, 2 Sep. 1617, being (as "Esq.") M.P. for Pembroke, 1614, and (as "Knt.") 1624-25; for Tamworth, 1626, and 1628-29; for Lichfield, April to May 1640, and 1640 till his death, about Aug. 1641. [*Ex. inform.* W. D. Pink].

(b) See p. 88, notes "a" and "b," *sub* "Devereux."

(c) "A gentleman of polite parts and learning." Collins' *Baronetage,* 1720.

N

II. 1645, to 1654. SIR MILES SANDYS, Bart. [1611], of Wilberton aforesaid, s and h.; was *Knighted* v.p., at Whitehall, 9 Dec. 1626, and *suc. to the Baronetcy* in 1645. He *m.* Elizabeth, da. and coheir of Thomas PARK, of Wisbeach, in the Isle of Ely, by Audrie, da. of John CROSSE. He *d.* s.p., and was *bur.* 23 Feb. 1653/4, in the Temple church, London, when the *Baronetcy* became *extinct.* Admon. 24 March 1653/4, to Samuel Sandys, the next of kin.

PORTMAN:

cr. 25 Nov. 1611;(a)

ex. April 1690.

I. 1611. "JOHN PORTMAN, of Orchard, co. Somerset, Knt," s. and h. of Sir Henry PORTMAN, of Orchard Portman aforesaid, by Jane, da. of Thomas MICHELL; suc. his father in 1590; was *Knighted,* 3 Feb. 1604/5, at Whitehall; was Sheriff of Somerset, 1606-07, and was *cr. a Bart.,* as above, 25 Nov. 1611.(a) He *m.,* about 1600, Anne, da. of Sir Henry GIFFORD, of Hants. He *d.* 4 Dec. 1612. Will pr. 1613. His widow *m.* Thomas NEVILL, who was living Jan. 1651/2. Her admon. as "of Orchard, co. Somerset," 15 Jan. 1651/2.

II. 1612. SIR HENRY PORTMAN, Bart. [1611], of Orchard Portman aforesaid, s. and h., was *b.* about 1595; *suc. to the Baronetcy,* 4 Dec. 1612. M.P. for Somerset, 1621-22. He *m.,* 20 July 1615, at St. Margaret's, Westm., Anne, da. of William (STANLEY), 6th EARL OF DERBY, by Elizabeth, da. of Edward (VERE), EARL OF OXFORD. He *d.* s.p. Feb. 1623/4. Will pr. 1624. His widow, who was *b.* at Hackney, Midx., about 1600, *m.* Robert (KERR), 1st EARL OF ANCRAM [S.], who *d.* at Amsterdam in Dec. 1654. She *d.* at St. Paul's, Covent Garden, and was *bur.* 15 Feb. 1656/7, in Westm. abbey. Admon. 9 June 1657.

III. 1624, Feb. SIR JOHN PORTMAN, Bart. [1611], of Orchard Portman aforesaid; br. and h., *b.* about 1605; matric. at Oxford (Wadham Coll.), 27 June 1623, aged 18; *suc. to the Baronetcy,* Feb. 1623/4; *d.* unm. at Wadham Coll., 12 and was *bur.* 23 Dec. 1624, in the chapel there. M.I. Will pr. 1625.

IV. 1624, Dec. SIR HUGH PORTMAN, Bart. [1611], of Orchard Portman aforesaid, br. and h., *b.* about 1608; matric. at Oxford (Exeter Coll.), 25 June, 1624, aged 16; *suc. to the Baronetcy,* 12 Dec. 1624; M.P. for Taunton, 1625 and 1628-29. He *d.* unm. 1632. Will pr. 14 May 1632.

V. 1632. SIR WILLIAM PORTMAN, Bart. [1611], of Orchard Portman aforesaid, br. and h.; *b.* about 1610; matric. at Oxford (Wadham Coll.), 30 June 1626, aged 16; admitted to the Middle Temple, 1627; *suc. to the Baronetcy* in 1632; Sheriff of Somerset, 1637-38; M.P. for Taunton, April to May 1640, and again, 1640, till disabled in Feb. 1643/4. He was a Royalist and was taken prisoner at Naseby. His estate was sequestrated for £20,000. He *m.,* in or before 1644, Elizabeth, da. and h. of John COLLES, of Barton, co. Somerset, by Elizabeth, da. of Humphrey WYNDHAM, of Wiveliscombe. He *d.,* a prisoner in the Tower, in Sep. 1645, and was *bur.,* by order of the House (16 Sep.), at Orchard Portman. Will pr. 17 Oct. 1648.

VI. 1645, to 1690. SIR WILLIAM PORTMAN, Bart. [1611], of Orchard Portman aforesaid, only s. and h., *b.* 1644; *suc. to the Baronetcy* in Sep. 1645; matric. at Oxford (All Souls), 26 April 1659; K.B. at the coronation of Charles II in April 1661; M.P. for Taunton, 1661-79 and 1678-79; for Somerset, 1679-81; for Taunton (again), 1685-87, 1689-90, and 1690 till his death. He was also F.S.A. He *m.* firstly, (—), 2d da. and coheir of Sir John CUTLER, 1st Bart. [1660], of London, yst. and only child, by his 2d wife, Elizabeth

(a) See p. 88, notes "a" and "b," *sub* "Devereux."

da. and coheir of Sir Thomas FOOTE, 1st Bart. He *m.* secondly, Elizabeth, da. of Sir Thomas SOUTHCOLE, of Buckland All Saints', Devon. He *m.* thirdly, Mary, da. and h. of Sir John HOLMAN. He *d.* s.p. 1690, when *the Baronetcy* became *extinct.*(a) Will pr. 8 April 1690.

ENGLEFIELD, *or* ENGLEFEILD:

cr. 25 Nov. 1611;(b)

ex. 21 March 1822.

I. 1611. "FRANCIS ENGLEFEILD, of Wootton Basset, co. Wilts, Esq.," only s. and h. of John ENGLEFIELD, of the same, by Margaret, da. of Sir Edward FITTON, of Gawsworth, Cheshire, sometime Lord President of Connaught, was *b.* about 1561; suc. his father, 1 April 1567; becoming the head of his family on the death of his uncle, Sir Francis ENGLEFIELD,(c) about 1596, and was *cr. a Bart.,* as above, 25 Nov. 1611.(b) He *m.* Jane, sister of Anthony Mary, 2d VISCOUNT MONTAGUE, da. of the Hon. Anthony BROWNE, by Mary, da. of Sir William DORMER. He *d.* 26 Oct. 1631, aged 69 years, 3 months and 27 days, and was *bur.* at Englefield, Berks. M.I. Will pr. 3 Nov. 1631. His widow *d.* about 1650. Admon. 16 Jan. 1650/1, which was revoked, and will pr. Jan. 1651/2.

II. 1631. SIR FRANCIS ENGLEFIELD, Bart. [1611], of Wotton Basset aforesaid, 1st surv. s. and h., *Knighted,* v.p., 10 Aug. 1622, at Easthampstead, and *suc. to the Baronetcy,* 26 Oct. 1631. He had a dispensation from the penalties of a "Popish Recusant," on 6 Dec. 1634. He *m.* Winifred, da. and coheir of William BROOKSBY, of Sholeby, co. Leicester. He *d.* 1 May 1656. The will of his widow pr. 1672.

III. 1656. SIR FRANCIS ENGLEFIELD, Bart. [1611], of Wotton Basset aforesaid, only s. and h., *suc. to the Baronetcy,* 1 May 1656. He *m.* 2 March 1656/7 (reg. at St. Giles' in the Fields, Midx., as also at Henley on Thames, Oxon.), Honora, yst. da. and coh. of Henry (O'BRIEN), 5th EARL OF THOMOND [I.], by Mary, da. of William (BRERETON), 1st BARON BRERETON, OF LEIGHLIN [I.] He *d.* s.p., May 1665, and was *bur.* at Englefield. M.I. His will dat. 27 Sep. 1660, pr. 30 May 1665 by his widow. She *m.* (as the 2d or 3d of his four wives), the Hon. Sir Robert HOWARD, Auditor of the Exchequer (6th s. of Thomas, 1st EARL OF BERKSHIRE), who *d.* 3 Sep. 1698, aged 73.

IV. 1665. SIR THOMAS ENGLEFIELD, Bart. [1611], of Wotton Basset aforesaid, uncle and h., *suc. to the Baronetcy* in May 1665. He *m.* firstly, Mary, da. and coheir of Sir Henry WINCHCOMBE, 1st Bart. [1661]. She *d.* s.p. He *m.* secondly, in or before 1670, Mary, da. of George HUNTLY, of co. Gloucester. His admon. as "of St. Giles' in the Fields, Midx.," 21 Feb. 1677/8, granted to Mary, the relict. Her admon. 11 July 1728.

(a) He devised his vast estates to his first cousin. Henry Seymour, 5th son of Sir Edward Seymour, 4th Bart. [1611], by Anne, da. of Sir John Portman, 1st Bart., which Henry, took the name of Portman, but *d.* s.p. in Feb. 1727/8, being suc. therein by William Berkeley, another cousin of the testator, being grandson of William Berk ley, of Pylle, by Philippa, only da. of George Speke and Joan, his wife, another da. of the said Sir John Portman, 1st Bart. This William Berkeley (the grandson) also took the name of Portman, and is ancestor of the Viscounts Portman, who still possess the estate of Orchard Portman.

(b) See p. 88, notes "a" and "b," *sub* "Devereux."

(c) This Sir Francis Englefield, Master of the Wards and P.C. to Queen Mary, was of Englefield, Berks, which estate, said to have been in the family since A.D. 803, was, owing to his having been attainted, in 1586, for high treason, forfeited to and retained by Queen Elizabeth. He *d.* s.p. in banishment, at Valladolid in Spain, about 1596. His father, Sir Thomas Englefield, was (1527-37) one of the Justices of the Court of Common Pleas.

V. 1678. SIR CHARLES ENGLEFIELD, Bart. [1611], of Wotton Basset aforesaid, only s. and h. by 2d wife, *b.* about 1670; *suc. to the Baronetcy* about Feb. 1677/8. He *m.* 23 Feb. 1685/6, at St. James', Westm., (Lic. Fac., he being about 16, bachelor, she about 14, spinster), Susan COLEPEPER, illegit. da. of Thomas (COLEPEPER), 2d BARON COLEPEPER OF THORESWAY, by Mrs. Susan Willis. Her will pr. 6 Dec. 1720. He *d.* s.p.s., 21 April 1728, and was *bur.* at Englefield. Will dat. 25 Jan. 1727/8, pr. 1728

VI. 1728. SIR HENRY ENGLEFIELD, Bart. [1611], of White Knights, in the parish of Sonning, Berks, cousin and h. male, being s. and h. of Henry ENGLEFIELD, of White Knights aforesaid, by Catharine Day, da. of Benjamin POOLE, of London, which Henry, last named, was 4th s. (but the only one out of ten who had issue), of Anthony ENGLEFIELD, of the same, who was s. and h. of another Anthony ENGLEFIELD, also of White Knights aforesaid (*d.* about 1665), who was 5th s. of the 1st Bart. He *suc. to the Baronetcy*, 21 April 1728. He *m.* firstly, 1742, Mary, da. of Thomas BERKELEY, of Spetchley, co. Worcester, by Mary, da. and h. of (—) DAVIS, of Clytha, co. Monmouth. She *d.* s.p.m., at Clytha aforesaid. Admon. 14 April 1744. He *m.* secondly, in 1751, Catharine, sister and coheir of Sir Charles BUCK, 4th Bart., da. of Sir Charles BUCK, 3d Bart. [1660], by Anne, da. of Sir Edward SEBRIGHT, 3d Bart. [1626]. He *d.* 25 May 1780. Will pr. June 1780. His widow *d.* 31 May 1805, in her 80th year, in Tylney street, Mayfair. Will pr. 1805.

VII. 1780, to 1822. SIR HENRY CHARLES ENGLEFIELD, Bart. [1611], of White Knights aforesaid, s. and h. by 2d wife; *b.* 1752; ed. at one of the English colleges abroad; F.R.S., 1778; F.S.A., 1779, of which Society he was, subsequently, Vice-President for many years, and was elected President, but not so confirmed, owing to his being a Roman Catholic. He *suc. to the Baronetcy*, 25 May 1780, and was well known as an Antiquary and Astronomer. He *d.* unm. (having been blind for many years), 21 March 1822, in his 70th year, in Tylney street aforesaid, and was *bur.* at Englefield, when the *Baronetcy* became *extinct*. Will pr. June 1822.

MOHUN:

cr. 25 Nov. 1611,(a)

afterwards, 1628—1712, BARONS MOHUN OF OKEHAMPTON;

ex. 15 Nov. 1712.

I. 1611. "REGINALD MOHUN of Buckonnock [*i.e.*, Boconnoc], co. Cornwall, Knt.," s. and h. of Sir William MOHUN, of the same, by his 1st wife Elizabeth, da. and h. of John HORSEY, was *b.* about 1564; suc. his father 6 April 1587, being then aged 23 years and more; was *Knighted* 25 March 1599, and was *cr. a Bart.*, as above, 26 Nov. 1611.(a) M.P. for East Looe, 1614, and for Lostwithiel, 1625. He was Recorder of East Looe, 1620. He *m.* firstly (Lic. Lond. 7 Sep. 1589), Mary, da. of Sir Henry KILLEGREW, by his 1st wife, Katharine, da. of Sir Anthony COOKE, of Giddy Hall, co. Essex. He *m.* secondly, before 1593, Philippa, da. of John HELE, of Wembury, Devon, by Margaret, da. and coheir, of Ellis WARWICK, of Batsborow. He *m.* thirdly, before 1604, Dorothy, sister of Sir George Chudleigh, 1st Bart. [1622], da. of John CHUDLEIGH, of Ashton, Devon, by Elizabeth, da. of Sir George SPEKE. He entered and signed his pedigree in the Visitation of Cornwall in 1620. He *d.* 26 Dec. 1639. Inq. p.m., 16 Charles I. Will dat. 30 Jan. 1638/9; pr. 30 April 1640 by Dorothy the widow.

II. 1639. SIR JOHN MOHUN, Bart. [1611], of Boconnoc aforesaid, 2d but eldest surv. s. and h., being 1st s. by 2d wife, *b.* 1595, being aged 25 in 1620; M.P. for Grampound, 1624-25 and 1625. He *m.*, about 1614, Cordelia,(b) widow of Sir Roger ASTON, da. of Sir John STANHOPE, of Shelford, Notts, by his 2d wife, Catherine, da. of Thomas TRENTHAM, of Rocester Priory, co. Stafford. She was living when he was *cr.* 15 April 1628 (in his father's lifetime), BARON MOHUN OF OKEHAMPTON, co. Devon. He subsequently *suc. to the Baronetcy*, 26 Dec. 1639, which then became *merged* in the peerage, and so continued till both became *extinct*, 15 Nov. 1712, on the death of the 4th Baron and 5th Baronet. See *Peerage*.

(a) See p. 88, notes "a" and "b," *sub* "Devereux."

(b) She was aunt to Sir Aston Cokayne, Bart., who received the name of "Aston" (at his baptism 20 Dec. 1608) from her first husband, his godfather.

GORGES:

cr. 25 Nov. 1611,(a)

afterwards, 1620-1712, BARONS GORGES OF DUNDALK [I.];

ex. Sep. 1712.

I. 1611. "EDWARD GORGES, of Langford, co. Wilts, Knt.," 1st surv. s. and h. of Sir Thomas GORGES, of the same, by Helena, DOWAGER MARCHIONESS OF NORTHAMPTON, da. of Wolfgang von SUAVENBERG, of Sweden, was *b.* about 1582, in co. Kent; matric. at Oxford (Mag. Coll.), 23 March 1598/9, aged 16; was *Knighted*, 9 April 1603, at Widdrington; suc. his father, 30 March 1610, and was *cr. a Bart.*, as above, 25 Nov. 1611.(a) He *m.* firstly (Lic. Lond. 3 July 1605, he of Malden, co. Essex, aged 22), Katharine, widow of Edward HASELWOOD, of Woodham Wallers, in that county, da. and h. of Sir Robert OSBORNE, of Kelmarsh, co. Northampton, by Margaret, da. and h. of John FREEMAN, of Great Billing, in that county. She, who was *bap.* at Moulton, 14 Oct. 1582, was living when he was *cr.*, 13 July 1620, BARON GORGES OF DUNDALK, co. Louth [I.], in which peerage this *Baronetcy* continued *merged*, until they both became *extinct* on the death of the 2d Baron and Baronet in Sep. 1712.

PUCKERING:

cr. 25 Nov. 1611;(a)

ex. 20 March 1636.

I. 1611, to 1636. "THOMAS PUCKERING, of Weston, co. Herts, Esq.," only s. and h. of Sir John PUCKERING, of the same, Serjeant at Law, sometime (1586), Speaker of the House of Commons, and (1592-96), Lord Keeper of the Great Seal, by Anne, da. of George, or Nicholas, CHOWNE, of co. Kent, suc. his father, 30 April 1596, and was *cr. a Bart.*, as above, 25 Nov. 1611,(a) being *Knighted* subsequently,(b) 3 June 1612. M.P. for Tamworth, 1621-22, 1625, 1626, and 1628-29; Sheriff of Warwickshire, 1625. He resided latterly at his estate of the Priory, near Warwick. He *m.* 2 July 1616, at St. Barth. the Less, London, Elizabeth, da. of Sir John MORLEY, of Halnaker, co. Sussex, by Cicely, da. of Sir Edward CARRILL, of Harting, in that county. He *d.* s.p.m.(c) 20 March 1636, and was *bur.* at St. Mary's, Warwick. M.I. At his death the *Baronetcy* became *extinct*. Will pr. 1637. His widow *d.* 1652.

AYLOFFE:

cr. 25 Nov. 1611;(a)

ex. 19 April 1781.

I. 1611. "WILLIAM AYLOFFE, of Braxted Magna, co. Essex, Knt.," s. and h. of William AYLOFFE, of Brittains in Hornchurch, in that county, one of the Justices of the Court of Queen's Bench [1577-85], by Jane, da. of Eustace SULYARD, of Flemings, also in co. Essex, was *b.* 1563; suc. his father, 8 Nov. 1585; Sheriff of Essex, 1594-95; *Knighted* at the Charter House, 5 May 1603, and was *cr. a Bart.*, as above, 25 Nov. 1611.(a) M.P. for Stockbridge, 1621-22. He *m.* firstly, Catherine, da. and coheir of John STERNE, of Melbourne, co. Cambridge. He *m.* secondly, Barbara, da. and h. of Thomas SEXTON. She was *bur.* 16 Dec. 1617, at Hornchurch. He *m.* thirdly (Lic., 4 Dec. 1621, Dean and Chapter of Westminster), Alice, da. of James STOKES, of Stoke, near Coventry. He *d.* 5 Aug. 1627, (leaving issue by all three wives), and was *bur.* at Great Braxted. His widow was *bur.* 17 April 1652, at Hornchurch.

(a) See p. 88, notes "a" and "b," *sub* "Devereux."

(b) See p. 18, note "c," *sub* "Tollemache."

(c) Jane, his only surv. da. and h., *m.* Sir John Bale, Bart. (so. *cr.* 1643), and *d.* s.p. 1651, when the Puckering estates were inherited by her cousin, Sir Henry Newton, 3d Bart. [1620], who consequently assumed the name of Puckering.

II. 1627. SIR BENJAMIN AYLOFFE, Bart. [1611], of Great Braxted aforesaid, s. and h. by 1st wife; *bap.* 29 Aug. 1592, at Hornchurch; *suc. to the Baronetcy*, 5 Aug. 1627; was Sheriff of Essex, *temp.* Car. I, to whose cause he adhered, and was consequently imprisoned, his estates being sequestrated and himself obliged to sell that of Brittains. He was fined, 29 May 1649, £2,000, increased to £3,000; was M.P. for Essex, 1661 till his death. He (like his father) *m.* three times, viz., firstly, about 1611, Alice, da. of Martin AVONDALE. She *d.* s.p.m. and was *bur.* 28 Nov. 1612, at Hornchurch. He *m.* secondly, 9 May 1616, at Barking, Essex, Margaret, 5th da. of Thomas Fanshawe, of Jenkins in Barking, Remembrancer of the Exchequer, by his 2d wife, Joan, da. of Thomas SMITH, of Ostenhanger, co. Kent. He *m.* thirdly, Margaret, sister of George PORTER. He *d.* 1662, and was *bur.* at Braxted. Will dat. 19 Feb. 1658, proved Nov. 1662. His widow *m.* (Lic. Fac., 3 Dec. 1666), John WALL, of St. Clement Danes, Midx. Her will, as "of Bow, near London, widow," dat. 15 Sep. 1681 to 20 Jan. 1681/2, pr. 13 March 1681/2.

III. 1662. SIR WILLIAM AYLOFFE, Bart. [1611], of Great Braxted, aforesaid, s. and h. by 2d wife, *bap.* 3 Dec. 1618, at Hornchurch. Was, with his father, in the service of Charles I, and was Colonel of a Regiment at the siege of Colchester; *suc. to the Baronetcy* in 1662. He *m.* Anne, widow of Frederick DE LA TREMOUILLE, COUNT DE LAVAL AND BENON, sister of Sir Thomas ORBY, 1st Bart. [1658], 1st da. of Peter ORBY, of Burton Penwardine, co. Lincoln, and of Chertsey, Surrey, by Elizabeth, da. of Robert HORSEMAN, of Burton Penwardine aforesaid. He *d.* s.p.s. 1675, and was *bur.* at Braxted. M.I. Will pr. 1676. His widow, who was *b.* before 16 Oct. 1609, and unm. 18 Oct. 1633, *d.* 8 Nov. 1683, and was *bur.* there. Her will dat. 12 March 1679, pr. 7 Feb. 1683/4.

IV. 1675. SIR BENJAMIN AYLOFFE, Bart. [1611], of Great Braxted aforesaid, br. and h. of the whole blood. He, who was a merchant in London, *suc. to the Baronetcy* in 1675. He *m.*, 21 Sep. 1669, at North Ockendon, Essex, Martha, da. of Sir John TYRRELL, of Heron, Essex, by his 2d wife, Margaret, da. of Sir Laurence WASHINGTON. He *d.* s.p.m. 5 March 1722, aged 91. Will pr. 1722.

V. 1722. SIR JOHN AYLOFFE, Bart. [1611], of Stanford Rivers, co. Essex, nephew and h., being s. and h. of Henry AYLOFFE, of Pandets, Captain of a troop of Horse, by Dorothy, da. and h. of Richard BULKELEY, of Cheadle, Cheshire, which Henry (who *d.* 1708), was yst s. of the 2d Bart., by his 2d wife. He was ed. at Peterhouse, Cambridge; B.A., 1691; M.A., 1695, and, taking Holy Orders, was Rector of Stanford Rivers, 1707-30. He *suc. to the Baronetcy*, 5 March 1722. He *d.* unm. 10 Dec. 1730, and was *bur.* at Braxted. His will dat. 13 Sep. 1728, pr. in the Consistory Court of the Bishop of London, 26 Jan. 1730/1, by Anne Ayloffe, sister, extrix. and residuary legatee.

VI. 1730, to 1781. SIR JOSEPH AYLOFFE, Bart. [1611], of Framfield, co. Sussex, and of Acton, co. Midx., cousin and h. male, being s. and h. of Joseph AYLOFFE, of Gray's Inn, Barrister at Law (1689), by Mary, da. of Bryan AYLIFFE, Citizen and Merchant of London, which Joseph last named, who *d.* 1726, was s. and h. of another Joseph AYLOFFE, also of Gray's Inn (admitted Oct. 1646), who was yst. s. of the 1st Bart., by his 3d wife. He was *b.* 1709; ed. at Westm. school; Student of Lincoln's Inn, 1724; and *suc. to the Baronetcy*, 10 Dec. 1730. F.S.A., 1732, of which Society he was many years Vice President; F.R.S. (also), 1732; and a prominent member of the literary club, called "the Gentlemen's Society at Spalding"; one of three Keepers of the State Paper Office, 1763; and a well known writer.(a) He *m.*, about 1734, Margaret, da. and h. of Thomas RAILTON, of Carlisle, co. Cumberland. He *d.* s.p.s.(b) at his house at Kensington, 19 April 1781, aged 72, when the *Baronetcy* became *extinct*. His will, as "of Wharton in the parish of Framfield, Sussex," dat. 30 April 1772, leaving all to his wife, who pr. the same, 18 May 1781. She *d.* 8 March 1797, aged 92. Her will pr. March 1797. Both are *bur.* at Hendon, co. Midx. M.I.

(a) See p. 88, notes "a" and "b," *sub* "Devereux."

WRAY:

cr. 25 Nov. 1611;(c)

ex. 27 Aug. 1809.

I. 1611. WILLIAM WRAY,(d) of Glentworth, co. Lincoln, Knt." only s. and h. of Sir Christopher WRAY, of the same, Lord Chief Justice of the Queen's Bench [1575-92], by Anne, da. of Nicholas GIRLINGTON, of Normanby, co. York, was *b.* about 1555; suc. his father, 8 May 1592, in which year he was Sheriff of Lincolnshire; was M.P. for Grimsby, 1584-85 and 1604-11, and for Lincolnshire, 1601; Sheriff of that county, 1594-95; was *Knighted* in 1596, and was *cr. a Bart.*, as above, 25 Nov. 1611.(c) He *m.* firstly, 6 April 1580, at St. Benet's Fink, London, Lucy, 1st da. of Sir Edward MONTAGU, of Boughton, co. Northampton, by Elizabeth, da. of Sir John HARRINGTON, of Exton, Rutland. She (by whom he had fifteen children), *d.* at Lincoln, 1 March 1599, and was *bur.* in the Cathedral there. M.I. He *m.* secondly, Frances, widow of Sir Nicholas CLIFFORD, sister and coheir of Sir Robert DRURY, of Hawsted, Suffolk [*d.* 1615], being 1st da. of Sir William DRURY, Lord Deputy of Ireland, by Elizabeth, da. of Sir William STAFFORD, of Blatherwick, co. Northampton. He *d.* 13 Aug. 1617, at Ashby, co. Lincoln, and was *bur.* there. M.I. Admon. 2 Jan. 1617/8. His widow, who was *b.* 8 and *bap.* 13 June 1576, at Hawsted, was also *bur.* there. Her will dat. 27 May 1637, pr. 15 Jan. 1641/2.

II. 1617. SIR JOHN WRAY, Bart. [1611], of Glentworth aforesaid, s. and h. by 1st wife; *bap.* at Louth, 27 Nov. 1586; was M.P. for Grimsby, 1614, and for Lincolnshire, 1625, 1628-29, April to May 1640, and 1640 till secluded in Dec. 1648; *Knighted* at Whitehall, 7 June 1612; *suc. to the Baronetcy*, 13 Aug. 1617; Sheriff of Lincolnshire, 1625-26, and M.P. for that county in three Parliaments. During the Civil War he took the side of the Parliament. He *m.*, Sep. 1607, Grisel, d. and h. of Sir Hugh BETHELL, of Ellerton, co. York, by Anne, da. of Sir William MALLORY, of Studley in that county. She was *bur.* 26 Jan. 1653/4, at Glentworth. He was *bur.* there, 31 Dec. 1655.

(a) He was editor (in 1772) of *Calendars of the Ancient Charters, etc., and of the Welsh and Scottish Rolls in the Tower of London*, and of many other antiquarian publications; among others of the magnificent work called *Edmondson's Baronagium*, six vols., folio, 1764 to 1784, which contains the pedigree of the Peers of England existing at that date. These were, in a great measure, abridged from Segar's valuable MSS. *Baronagium* in the College of Arms, London, which, however, comprises the *extinct* as well as the *extant* peerage down to the date of its compilation.

(b) Joseph, his only child, *d.* of the small pox, at Trin. Hall, Cambridge, 19 Dec. 1756, unm., aged 21. M.I. at Hendon, Midx.

(c) See p. 88, notes "a" and "b," *sub* "Devereux."

(d) In vol. i of the *History of the Wrays, of Glentworth*, by Charles Dalton (1880), some account is given of the 1st and 2d Barts. See also an article by the Rev. Geo. Wray, LL.D. in the *Genealogist* (1880), vol. iv, p. 278.

III. 1655. SIR JOHN WRAY, Bart. [1611], of Glentworth aforesaid, s. and h., *bap.* there 21 Sep. 1619. He was Capt. of horse in the Parl. forces, and taken prisoner at Newark in 1645. He *suc. to the Baronetcy* in Dec. 1655. M.P. for Lincolnshire, 1654-55. He *m.* firstly, about 1654, Elizabeth, widow of Sir Symonds D'EWES, 1st Bart [1641], 5th and yst. da. and coheir of Sir Henry WILLOUGHBY, Bart. [1611], of Risley, co. Derby, by his 2d wife, Lettice, da. and coheir of Sir Francis DARCY. She was *bur.* at Glentworth, 3 Nov. 1655,(a) her only child dying a few months later. Admon. 7 Feb. 1655/6. He *m.* secondly, Sarah, da. of Sir John EVELYN, of West Dean, Wilts, by Elizabeth, da. and coheir of Robert COCKES, of London. He *d.* s.p.m.,(b) and was *bur.* 29 Oct. 1664, at Glentworth. Admon. 15 Oct. 1664, to his widow. She *m.* before 1666/7, Thomas (FANSHAWE), 2d VISCOUNT FANSHAWE OF DROMORE [I.], who *d.* May 1674, aged 42. She *m.*, 14 Feb. 1674/5, at the Temple Church, London (for her 3d husband), George (SAUNDERSON), 5th VISCOUNT CASTLETON [I.], who *d.* 27 May 1714. Her will dat. 29 May 1714, proved 12 Nov. 1717.

IV. 1664, Oct. SIR CHRISTOPHER WRAY, Bart. [1611], br. and h. male, *bap.* 29 March 1621, at Glentworth; matric. at Oxford (Mag. Hall), 14 July 1637, aged 16; admitted to Lincoln's Inn, 1638; *suc. to the Baronetcy* in Oct. 1664. He *m.*, 24 Dec. 1646, at Glentworth, his cousin Frances, da. and h. of Sir Francis FOLJAMBE, Bart. (so *cr.* 1622), by his 1st wife, Elizabeth, da. of Sir William WRAY, 1st Bart., of Glentworth. He *d.* s.p., within a month of succeeding to the Baronetcy, and was *bur.* 25 Nov. 1664, at Glentworth. Admon. 14 Feb. 1664/5. His widow *m.* John TROUTBECK, M.D., of Lincoln (whom she predeceased), and was *bur.* 2 Nov. 1667, at Glentworth.

V. 1664, Nov. SIR BETHELL WRAY, Bart. [1611], br. and h. male,(c) *bap.* 30 Jan. 1632/3, at Blyton, co. Lincoln. He *suc. to the Baronetcy* in Nov. 1664, but was found a lunatic, 23 May 1666. He *d.* unm., at St. Giles', Cripplegate, London (*Qy.* at Bedlam) and was *bur.* thence, 19 Feb. 1671/2, at St. Giles' in the Fields, Midx. Admon. 4 March 1671/2, to his sisters, Dame Theodosia BARKER and Grisel THOROLD.

VI. 1672. SIR CHRISTOPHER WRAY, Bart. [1611 and 1660], of Ashby, co. Lincoln, cousin and h. male, being s. and h. of Sir William WRAY, 1st Bart., of Ashby, co. Lincoln [so *cr.* 27 June 1660], by Olympia, da. of Sir Humphrey TUFTON, 1st Bart. [1641], which Sir William (who *d.* 17 Oct. 1669), was s. and h. of Sir Christopher WRAY, of Ashby aforesaid (*d.* Feb. 1645/6), yr. s. (being 1st s. by 2d wife) of Sir William WRAY, 1st Bart. [1611], abovementioned. He was *b.* about 1652; matric. at Oxford (Univ. Coll.), 19 Dec. 1668, aged 16. He *suc.*, on the death of his father, 17 Oct. 1669, *to the Baronetcy* of 1660, and on the death of his cousin, in Feb. 1671/2, *to the Baronetcy* of 1611. M.P. for Grimsby, 1675-79.

(a) "Lady D'Ewes, ux. John Wray, Arm."

(b) Elizabeth, his only da. and h., by 2d wife, *bap.* at Glentworth, 27 Feb. 1663, *m.* Hon. Nicholas SAUNDERSON, s. and h. ap. of George, 5th VISCOUNT CASTLETON [I.] She inherited Glentworth and the whole of the Wray estates, worth £3,500 a year. See "Williamson's Notes" in *the Herald and Genealogist*, vol. ii, p. 126. She *d.* at York, s.p.s., 7 April 1714, having, however, entailed some part of the estates on the Wray family, whereby the 10th Bart. *suc.* to Branston, etc., co. Lincoln.

(c) In Sir Joseph Williamson's notes (see note "b" above), it is stated under Wray of Glentworth that "Ye 3 last brothers, Sir Jo., Sir Chr. and Sir Theoph. succeeded in ye Bartcy one to another and dyed almost all mad in ye compasse of few months." The following entry of burial from Winteringham, co. Lincoln, contradicts the supposition that Theophilus (who was indeed the next br. to Christopher, having been *bap.* at Glentworth, 8 July 1624), did so succeed, although it is *just* possible he may have done so (for a day or so) unknown to the person who entered his burial. "Theophilus Wray, *Generosus*, filius dom. Johis W., Mil. and Bar., phreneticus, qui se submersit, Novembris 21, 1664," *i.e.*, three days BEFORE the burial of his elder br., at Glentworth. It is, however, more probable that Theophilus is confused with Bethell Wray, who, also, was dead long before the notes were written, and who is not mentioned, though (if it were true of the three others), he would make a fourth brother who was insane, and who suc. to the title?

He *d.* unm. and was *bur.* 31 Aug. 1679 (with his brother and their grandparents),(a) at St. Giles' in the Fields, Midx. Admon. 14 Dec. 1682 (in the Court of Delegates, and again, 28 March 1695.

VII. 1679. SIR WILLIAM WRAY, Bart. [1611 and 1660], of Ashby aforesaid, and of Louth, co. Lincoln, br. and h.; *suc. to the two Baronetcies* in Aug. 1679. He *d.* unm. 1686-87, when the *Baronetcy, conferred* on his father *in 1660*, became *extinct*, though the one *cr.* in 1611 devolved as below. Will, as "of Louth," dat. 9 March 1685/6, pr. 8 Nov. 1687, 9 Feb. 1694/5, and 30 June 1711.

VIII. 1687? SIR BAPTIST EDWARD WRAY, Bart. [1611], of Barlings, co. Lincoln, cousin and h. male, being only s. and h. of Edward WRAY, of Barlings aforesaid, by Dorothy, relict of the Hon. George FANE, da. and h. of James HORSEY, of Honingham, co. Warwick, which Edward, who *d.* 23 Jan. 1684/5, was next br. to Sir William WRAY, 1st Bart. [1660], of Ashby, both being sons of Sir Christopher WRAY, of Ashby, yr. s. of the 1st Bart. [1611], of Glentworth. He *suc. to the Baronetcy*(b) about Oct. 1687, and *d.* unm. before 18 Nov. 1689.

IX. 1689? SIR DRURY WRAY, Bart. [1611], of Rathcannon Castle and Ballygaedy Casey, both in co. Limerick, uncle and h. male, being 3d s. of Sir Christopher WRAY (abovementioned) of Ashby, co. Lincoln, by Albinia, 2d da. and coheir of Edward (CECIL), 1st VISCOUNT WIMBLEDON, which Christopher (who *d.* Feb. 1645/6) was yr. s., being 1st s. by the 2d wife, of Sir William Wray, 1st Bart. [1611], of Glentworth. He was *b.* 29 July 1633, in Lincolnshire; was Sheriff of Limerick, 1685; Capt. in a Jacobite regiment, 1690; was attainted in 1691, lived sometime abroad, returning to Ireland about 1702, having *suc. to the Baronetcy*, apparently, about 1689. He *m.* Anne, da. and h. of Thomas CASEY, of Rathcannon Castle and Ballygaedy Casey aforesaid, by Bridget, da. and coheir of Sir John DOWDALL, of Kilfinny, co. Limerick. She, who brought him a large estate in Ireland, *d.* 22 April 1697. He *d.* 30 Oct. 1710, and was *bur.* in the church of Clonara, Limerick.(c).

X. 1710, Oct. SIR CHRISTOPHER WRAY, Bart. [1611], of Rathcannon Castle aforesaid, s. and h., *b.* before 1672; Lieut. Col. in the Army. He fought at the battle of the Boyne for William III, and served in Flanders, Spain, Portugal, and at the siege of Ostend. He *suc. to the Baronetcy*, 30 Oct. 1687, but *d.* unm., a few days after his father, at Portsmouth, while preparing to embark with the fleet for Spain, 21 Nov. 1710, and was *bur.* in the church there. Will dat. 8 July 1710, pr. 7 Dec. following.

(a) Burials at St. Giles' aforesaid—
1645/6. Feby 13. Sir Christopher Wray.
1659/60. Jany 30. The Lady Albinia Wray.

(b) This Edward is said, in Dalton's ***Wray Family***, in *Wotton's Baronetage*, and elsewhere, to have suc. to the Baronetcy [1611] on the death of Sir William. The abstract of the title deeds of Barlings (in a vol. in Mr. Ross's collections) do not, however, speak of him as a Baronet, but merely as "Edward Wray," both when (as son and heir of Edward Wray, Esq., and Dorothy) he, on 5 and 6 March 1683/4, mortgages that estate, and also when, on 18 Nov. 1689, Dorothy Wray is mentioned as his sister and heir. This Dorothy, by will, 27 Nov. 1694, left that estate to her brother of the half blood, Sir Henry Fane, K.B.

(c) He had several daughters, whose issue became his coheirs. Of these, Jane *m.* William Twigge, Archdeacon of Limerick, and had two daughters and coheirs, viz.: (I) Jane, *m.* Rev. Stackpole Pery, by whom she was mother of (1) Edmund Sexten Pery, *cr.*, in 1785, VISCOUNT PERY [I.], and (2) of William Cecil Pery, Bishop of Limerick, *cr.*, in 1796, BARON GLENTWORTH [I.] (although that estate had ceased to belong to the Wray family since 1664), whose son, the 2d Lord, was *cr.* EARL OF LIMERICK [I.]; and (II) Anne, *m.* Thomas Maunsell, of Thorpe Malsor, co. Northampton, being grandmother of Thomas Philip MAUNSELL, of the same, many years (1835-57), M.P. for North Northamptonshire.

XI. 1710, Nov. SIR CECIL WRAY, Bart. [1611], of Rathcannon Castle aforesaid, br. and h.; was sometime Capt. in his eldest brother's Regiment; *suc. to the Baronetcy*, 21 Nov. 1710. By the death of his cousin,(a) the Hon. Elizabeth Saunderson (*née* Wray), 7 April 1714, he inherited the estate of Branston, co. Lincoln, and other estates [not however including that of Glentworth(b)] which had belonged to the Wray family. He was Sheriff of Lincolnshire, 1715-16. He *m.*, 30 Nov. 1721, at St. Martin's in the Fields, Mary, widow of Benjamin COLUMBINE, da. of Edward HARRISON, of Morely, co. Antrim, by Joanna, da. of Jeremy TAYLOR, Bishop of Dromore. He *d.* s.p., 9 and was *bur.* 13 May 1736, at Branston, aged 57. Will dat. 21 Jan. 1735/6, pr. 21 May 1736, at Lincoln.(c) His widow *d.* 18 Dec. 1745.

XII. 1736. SIR JOHN WRAY, Bart. [1611], of Sleningford, in the West Riding of co. York, and of Helgay Woodhall, Norfolk, cousin and h. male, being s. and h. of William WRAY, by Isabella, da. and coheir of John ULLITHORNE, of Sleningford aforesaid, which William was only s. and h. of Cecil WRAY, the 4th son of Sir Christopher WRAY (abovenamed), of Ashby, co. Lincoln, Knt. (*d.* Feb. 1645/6), who was yr. s. (by his 2d wife), of the 1st Bart. He was *b.* 24 Oct. 1689, and *suc. to the Baronetcy*, 9 May 1736, as also (as heir male to the Wray family) to the estates of Fillingham, co. Lincoln, and other family estates under the will of Elizabeth Saunderson (*née* Wray) abovementioned. He *m.*, 4 March 1727/8, at Ripon, co. York, Frances, sister and h. of Thomas NORCLIFFE, of Langton, in the East Riding, and of Heslington, co. York, da. of Fairfax NORCLIFFE, of Langton aforesaid, by Mary, yst. da. and coheir of Thomas HESKETH, of Heslington aforesaid. He *d.* 26 Jan. 1752, and was *bur.* at Ripon minster. Will pr. 1752. His widow, who was *b.* 16 Sep. 1700, at Heslington, *d.* 4 July 1770, at Sleningford, and was *bur.* at Ripon minster. M.I. Will pr. Jan. 1771.

XIII. 1752. SIR CECIL WRAY, Bart. [1611], of Fillingham aforesaid, only surv. s. and h., *b.* 3 Sep. 1734; *suc. to the Baronetcy*, 26 Jan. 1752. In Michaelmas, 1755, he barred the entail as settled by Hon. Mrs. SAUNDERSON,(d) of Fillingham, and the other family estates. He was M.P. for East Retford, 1768-74, and 1774-80, and for Westminster, June 1782 to 1784, being a zealous opponent of Fox's ministry. Capt. of the Lincolnshire militia, 1778. He *m.* Esther, da. of James (?) SUMMERS, of Fillingham aforesaid. He *d.* s.p. 10 Jan. 1805, and was *bur.* at Fillingham. Will pr. 1805. His widow *d.* 1 Feb. 1825, at "Summers Castle," in Fillingham (a place built by her husband in her honour), aged 88. Will pr. March 1825.

XIV. 1805. SIR WILLIAM ULLITHORNE WRAY, Bart. [1611], Rector of Darley, co. Derby (1761), 1st cousin and h. male, being only s. and h. of Cecil WRAY, of Enfield, Midx., by Frances, da. of John HOLMES, which Cecil was br. to the 12th Bart.; was *b.* Aug. 1721; matric. at Oxford (Hart Hall), 6 April 1739, aged 17; B.A. (Hert. Coll.), 1742; M.A., 1760; Rector [and Patron] of Darley aforesaid, 1764—1808; *suc. to the Baronetcy*, 10 Jan. 1805. He *m.*, 2 Feb. 1765, Frances, da. of the Rev. Francis BROMLEY, D.D., Rector of Wickham, Hants, and Rebecca, his wife. He *d.* 9 Aug. 1808, in his 87th year. His widow, who was *bap.* 7 Dec. 1740, at Wickham aforesaid, *d.* 22 June 1816, at Kenwick, near Worcester. Will pr. 1816.

(a) See p. 95, note "d."

(b) The estate of Glentworth passed on her death, to her husband's family, that of Saunderson, and from them to the family of Lumley.

(c) In this he leaves £14,000 and all his estates to his illegitimate da., Ann CASEY, spinster, who *m.*, soon afterwards, Lord Vere BERTIE, and had issue.

(d) See p. 95, note "d." He entailed the estate of Sleningford on John DALTON, 2d son of his sister, Isabella, who had *d.* 29 May 1780. The eldest s., Thomas DALTON, who, in 1807, took the name of NORCLIFFE, inherited the estate of the Norcliffe family at Langton, co. York.

XV. 1808, to 1809. SIR WILLIAM JAMES WRAY, Bart. [1611], only surv. s. and h.,(a) *b.* about 1771; matric. at Oxford (Ball. Coll.), 28 June 1788, aged 17; B.A., 1792; sometime Major in the North Lincolnshire Militia; *suc. to the Baronetcy*, 9 Aug. 1808. He *m.*(b) but *d.* s.p., after a short illness, at the King's Head Inn, Coventry, 27 Aug. 1809, in his 40th year, when the *Baronetcy* became *extinct*. Will pr. 1812. His wife survived him.(b)

ESSEX:

cr. 25 Nov. 1611;(c)

ex. about 1645.

I. 1611, to 1645? "WILLIAM ESSEX, of Bewcott co. Berks, Esq.," only s. and h. of Thomas ESSEX, of Bewcott, or Becket, in Shrivenham, by Joan (*m.* Nov. 1573), da. of Thomas HARRISON, being grandson of Sir Thomas ESSEX, of Bewcot aforesaid, (who *d.* 1558, and was *bur.* at Lambourn, Berks), was *b.* about 1575; matric. at Oxford (Ch. Cb.), 13 July 1587, aged 12; was possibly M.P. for Arundel, 1597-98; and for Stafford, 1601; and was *cr. a Bart.*,(d) as above, 25 Nov. 1611.(c) He *m.* Jane, da. of Sir Walter HARCOURT, of Stanton Harcourt, Oxon, by Dorothy, da. of William ROBINSON, of Drayton Bassett. Having wasted his vast inheritance(e) he became Captain of a company of Foot in one of the regiments organised by the Parl. against the King, of which regiment his only son, Charles Essex, was the Colonel. The said son was slain and the father was taken prisoner at the battle of Edgehill, 23 Oct. 1642. He *d.*, soon afterwards, s.p.m.s. (1645 ?), when the *Baronetcy* became *extinct*.

SAUNDERSON:

cr. 25 Nov. 1611(c),

afterwards, 1627—1720, VISCOUNTS CASTLETON [I.],

being subsequently, 1716-20, VISCOUNT CASTLETON OF SANDBECK [G.B.],

and *finally*, 1720-23, EARL CASTLETON OF SANDBECK [G.B.];

ex. 23 May 1723.

I. 1611. "NICHOLAS SAUNDERSON, of Saxbie, co. Lincoln, Knt.," s. and h. of Robert SAUNDERSON, of the same, and of Fillingham, in that county, by Catherine, yst. da. of Vincent GRANTHAM, of St. Katharine's, Lincoln, was *b.* about 1560; suc. his father, 2 Nov. 1583, being then aged 21; was Sheriff of Lincolnshire, 1592-93 and 1613-14; M.P. for Grimsby, 1593, and for Lincolnshire, 1626; ***Knighted*** at Belvoir Castle, 23 April 1603, and was *cr. a Bart.*, as above, 25 Nov. 1611.(c) He *m.*, before 1599, Mildred, da. and h. of John ELLTOFT, or HILTOFT, of Boston, co. Lincoln. He was *cr.*, 11 July 1627, VISCOUNT CASTLETON,

(a) His elder br., Cecil Bromley Wray, *b.* 1768; admitted to Lincoln's Inn, 1787; matric. at Oxford (Ball. Coll.), 28 Oct. 1788, aged 20; *d.* v.p. and s.p. 1794.

(b) Dalton's *Wray Family*, see p. 95, note "b."

(c) See p. 88, notes "a" and "b," *sub* "Devereux."

(d) In the *Her. and Gen.*, vol. iii, p. 450, is a letter, dated 14 Aug. 1611, from Robert Bowyer, Clerk of the Parliament, to Sir Robert Cotton, "to entreate you to have commended my cosen Essex his name to be in the list of the next Baronetts and one chiefe point of ours is that he mai be ranked as high as by your good meanes mai be, which we hope maie be foremost of anie of his counterie because as yet none of that shire, *viz.* Barkeshire, is come in."

(e) In Fuller's *Worthies* he is spoken of (*sub* "Berks) as "a Baronet with the revenues of a Baron, but" [adds the writer] "riches endure not for ever if providence be not as well used in preserving as attaining them." This alludes doubtless to his having, as early as 1621, alienated the estate of Becket with the manor of Shrivenham.

co. Limerick, etc. [I.], in which peerage this *Baronetcy* continued *merged* till the death, 23 May 1723, of the 6th Viscount [I.] and 6th Baronet (who had previously been made in 1714 a Viscount [G.B.], and afterwards in 1720, EARL CASTLETON, OF SANDBECK, co. Lincoln [G.B.]), when it and all the said peerage honours became *extinct*.

GOSTWICK:

cr. 25 Nov. 1611;(a)

ex. or *dormant*, May 1766.

I. 1611. "WILLIAM GOSTWICK,(b) of Willington, co. Bedford, Esq.," s. and h. of John GOSTWICK, of the same, by Elizabeth, da. of Sir William PETRE, of Ingatestone, Essex, was *bap.* 2 Dec. 1565, at St. Mary's, Bedford; Sheriff of Beds, 1595-96, and was *cr. a Bart.*, as above, 25 Nov. 1611.(a) He *m.* in or before 1588, Jane, da. and h. of Henry OWEN, of Wotton, Beds, who survived him. He *d.* 19 and was *bur.* 20 Sep. 1615, at Willington, in his 50th year. M.I. Admon. 16 April 1638.

II. 1615. SIR EDWARD GOSTWICK, Bart. [1611], of Willington aforesaid, s. and h., *b.* 1588; *Knighted*, v.p., 3 May 1607, at Whitehall; *suc. to the Baronetcy*, 19 Sep. 1615. Sheriff of Beds, 1626-27. He *m.* clandestinely, at her father's house in Gosfield, 2 April 1608, Anne, sister of Sir John WENTWORTH, Bart. (so *cr.* 1611), da. of John WENTWORTH, of Gosfield, Essex, by Cicely, da. of Edward UNTON. He *d.* 20 Sep. 1630, æt. 42. His widow *d.* 6 July 1633, æt. 42. Will dat. 15 May, pr. 8 July 1633. Both *bur.* at Willington. M.I.

III. 1630. SIR EDWARD GOSTWICK, Bart. [1611], of Willington aforesaid, s. and h., was deaf and dumb at his birth, 1619, and was 11 years old at his father's death in 1630,(c) when he *suc. to the Baronetcy*. He *m.*, 8 Sep. 1646, at Knebworth, Herts, Mary, da. of Sir William LYTTON, of Knebworth aforesaid, by his 1st wife, Anne, da. of Stephen SLANEY. She was *bap.* there, 7 Feb. 1622. He was living Aug. 1659.

IV. 1665? SIR WILLIAM GOSTWICK, Bart. [1611], of Willington aforesaid, 2d but 1st surv. s. and h., *bap.* 21 Aug. 1650, at Willington; *suc. to the Baronetcy*, on his father's death;(d) Sheriff of Beds, 1679-80. M.P. for Beds (in seven Parls.), 1698 to 1713. He *m.*, 17 Sep. 1668, at Walton Woodhall, Herts, Mary, da. of Sir Philip BOTELER, K.B., of Walton Woodhall aforesaid, by Elizabeth, da. and coheir of Sir John LANGHAM, 1st Bart. [1660]. She *d.* 1691. He wasted all his estate, and *d.* at St. Martin's in the Fields, Midx., being *bur.* 24 Jan. 1719/20, at Willington, in his 70th year. Will pr. 1723.

V. 1720, to 1766. SIR WILLIAM GOSTWICK, Bart. [1611], of Willington(e) aforesaid, and afterwards of North Tawton, Devon, grandson and h., being s. and h. of John GOSTWICK, by Martha, da. of Anthony HAMMOND, of Cambridge, which John, who was s. and h. ap. of the 4th Bart., *d.* v.p., and was *bur.* 8 March 1715, at Willington. He *suc. to the*

(a) See p. 88, notes "a," and "b," *sub* "Devereux."

(b) See *Bedfordshire Notes and Queries*, vol. ii, pp. 178-191, and vol. iii, pp. 44-47, for a good account of this family, as also of the family of Gostwick, of North Tawton, Devon, being that of the wife of the 5th and last Baronet.

(c) Visit. of Beds, 1634. The baptism, 5 Feb. 1625, at Colmworth, Beds, of "Edward Gostwick, son of Edward and Ann," presumably applies (not to him, but) to some child of his paternal aunt Ann, by (her cousin), Capt. Edward Gostwick.

(d) His elder br., "Edward Gostwick, Esq., s. and h. to Sir Edwd., Bart.," was *bur.* 13 Aug. 1659, at Willington.

(e) The estate of Willington, which had been 400 years in the family, was sold in 1731 to the old Duchess of Marlborough, in consequence of the debts of the 4th Bart. The 5th Bart. in his will (dat. 1760), states that "I have, thro' the improvidence of grandfather, succeeded to no part of a very large family estate."

Baronetcy, 24 Jan. 1719/20; was an officer in the Irish service. He *m.*, after 16 Sep. 1760, Loveday, da. of Edward GOSTWICKE, formerly of Northampton, but afterwards of North Tawton aforesaid, "mercer and shopkeeper," by Margery his wife. He *d.* s.p., and was *bur.* 6 May 1766, at North Tawton, since which time the *Baronetcy* has not been claimed, and is presumably *extinct*. Will, before marriage, dat. 16 Sep. 1760, pr. 9 June and 4 July 1766, by the widow, and (save as to £30), universal legatee. She, who was *bap.* 18 Feb. 1727, at North Tawton, *d.* 1786. Will dat. 1786, pr. June 1786.(a)

PESHALL:

cr. 25 Nov. 1611;(b)

probably *ex.* 29 Feb. 1712;

but *assumed* about 1770 to 1838.

I 1611. "JOHN PESHALL, of Horseley, co. Stafford, Esq." s. and h. of Thomas PESHALL, of Horsley aforesaid, by Joanna, relict of Anthony Windsor, da. and coheir of Sir Edmund FETTIPLACE, of Berks, was *b.* 22 Feb. 1562; suc. his father, 28 Nov. 1608, and was *cr. a Bart.*, as above, 25 Nov. 1611.(b) He was Sheriff of Staffordshire, 1615-16. He *m.* Anne, da. of Ralph SHELDON, of Beoley, co. Worcester, by Ann, da. of Sir Robert THROCKMORTON. She *d.* 30 March 1613, and was *bur.* at Eccleshall. He *d.* 13 Jan. 1646, aged 84, at Sugnal,(c) and was *bur.* at Eccleshall. Will pr. 1647.

II. 1646. SIR JOHN PESHALL, Bart. [1611], of Sugnal aforesaid, grandson and h., being s. and h of Thomas PESHALL, by Bridget, da. of Sir William STAFFORD, of Blatherwick, co. Northampton, which Thomas (*b.* 3 April 1596 at Horsley Hall), was s. and h. ap. of the 1st Bart., but *d.* v.p. He was *b.* 30 Sep. 1628, and *suc. to the Baronetcy*, 13 Jan. 1646. He *m.*, 1660, Frances, da. of Col. Thomas LEIGH, of Adlington, co. Chester. He *d.*, 1701.

III. 1701, to 1712. SIR THOMAS PESHALL, Bart. [1611], of Sugnal aforesaid, only s. and h., *suc. to the Baronetcy* in 1701. He *m.* (—), da. of (—) MEDCALF. She *d.* at Great Sugnal, and was *bur.* 29 Nov. 1705. He *d.* s.p.m.s.,(d) and was *bur.* there 29 Feb. 1712, when the *Baronetcy*, presumably, became *extinct*.(e) Will pr. Feb. 1713.

The title was assumed about 1770 by the Rev. John Pearsall, descended from a yeoman family of that name, seated at Hawn, in Halesowen, co. Worcester, who asserted that his father and grandfather were entitled thereto, the latter being grandson (as alleged) of Humphrey Pershall,(f) who (according to an inscription to him placed by his said great great grandson in Halesowen church) was "fil. dni Johis de Horsley Hall in agro' Staff. B'ti," and died 1650, æt. 51, an age which agrees (possibly being for that very purpose adopted) with the birth (1 Nov. 1599), of Humphrey(f) a son of the 1st Bart. See *Her. and Gen.*, vol. vii, pp. 270-272.

(a) In it she makes her nephew, Edward GOSTWICKE (only s. of her br. Edward), her residuary legatee. He *d.* s.p., 18 Oct. 1797, having had five married sisters, of whom four left issue.

(b) See p. 88, notes "a" and "b," *sub* "Devereux."

(c) The hall at Horsley had been burnt down some time before.

(d) John Peshall, his s. and h. ap., *m.* 15 May 1690, at St. Edmund the King, London (Lic. Lond., he 21), was M.P. for Newcastle-under-Lyne, 1701-02, and *d.* v.p. and s.p.m. in 1706.

(e) It is stated in Collins' *Baronetage* [1720], that on the death [1712] of Sir Thomas, the 3d Bart., "the title of Baronet ceased in this family," and the dignity is omitted accordingly in Wotton's (existing) *Baronetage* of 1741. In Kimber's *Baronetage*, however, dated 1771, the succession after 1712 is given as in the text.

(f) No such Humphrey appears among the children existing in 1614 of the 1st Baronet, which were eight daughters (three of them married) and four sons, viz.,

IV. 1712. THOMAS PEARSALL, of Halne, in Halesowen, co. Stafford, *should* (according to his grandson's statement) *have suc. to the Baronetcy* in Feb. 1712. He was s. and h. of John PEARSALL, of Halesowen aforesaid, by his 2d wife, Mary, da. and h. of Richard DOLMAN, of Clent, co. Stafford, which John (*b.* 7 Jan. 1620) is stated to have been s. and h. of Humphrey PESHALL, the 2d s. of the 1st Bart. He was *b.* 15 June 1652, matric. at Oxford (Pemb. Coll.), 26 March 1670, aged 17. He *m.* Elizabeth, da. and h. of John GROVE, of Hasberry, in Halesowen, by Mary, da. of R. PRINCE, of Clungerford, Salop. He *d.* at Halne 20 and was *bur.* 22 March 1714, at Halesowen, in his 63d year. M.I., as "Thomas Peshall, Gent.," the word "Peshall" having, it appears, been "originally engraved Pearsall." His widow *m.* Edward CARTWRIGHT, of Womburne, co. Stafford, and was *bur.* there.

V. *1714.* THOMAS PEARSALL, of Halne or Hawn aforesaid, only surv. s. and h., *b.* 9 June 1694; matric. at Oxford (Trin. Coll.), 20 Oct. 1711, aged 17. He, according to his son's statement, *should have suc. to the Baronetcy*, 20 March 1714. He *m.*, 15 April 1714, Anne, da. and coheir of Samuel SANDERS, by Elizabeth, da. and h. of J. Higgens, of Hasbery aforesaid. He *d.* 14 Sep. 1759, aged 65, and was *bur.* at Halesowen. His widow *d.* at Halne aforesaid, 6 July 1770, under the designation of "Lady Peshall."

VI. *1759,* and 1770. JOHN PEARSALL, of Guildford, co. Surrey, 2d but 1st surv. s. and h.;(a) *b.* at Halne, 27 Jan. 1718; matric. at Oxford (Pemb. Coll.), 15 April 1736, aged 18; B.A., 1739; M.A., 1745; in holy orders; sometime a schoolmaster at Highgate. In or shortly before 1770, he *assumed the Baronetcy* (on the ground of the descent abovementioned), and, changing his name to *Peshall*, styled himself "SIR JOHN PESHALL, Bart." [1611]. He *m.*, 12 July 1753, Mary, da. and coheir of the Rev. James ALLEN, Vicar of Thaxted, Essex, by Anne, da. of Peter PEERS, merchant. He *d.* Nov. 1778. Will pr. 1778. The will of his widow, pr. 1801.

VII. 1778. SIR JOHN PESHALL, Bart.(b) [1611], 2d but 1st surv. s. and h., *b.* 27 Dec. 1759, and *bap.* at Trinity, Guildford; *suc. to the Baronetcy*,(b) in Nov. 1778. He *m.* (—). He *d.* at his apartments, in Chelsea Hospital, 21 Nov. 1820, in his 61st year. Admon. Jan. 1838. His widow *d.* at an advanced age, 25 May 1842.

VIII. 1820, to 1838? SIR CHARLES JOHN PESHALL, Bart.(b) [1611], presumably s. and h.(c) Of him no more is known, but that he *d.* abroad, and that his will was pr. Jan. 1838. Since his death there has not, apparently, been any assumption of this Baronetcy.

Thomas, then aged 18, William, John, and Robert. Of these four, Thomas was *b.* 1596, William in 1601, John in 1606, and Robert in 1608. There are said to have been (Kimber's *Baronetage*, vol. i, p. 119) two others, viz., Humphrey, *b.* 1 Nov. 1599, and Ralph, *b.* 3 June 1600, but as neither of them is mentioned by their father in the pedigree entered by him in the pedigree entered by him in the Visit. of Staffordshire in 1614, the presumption is that they died young and before that date.

(a) Thomas, his elder br., *b.* 5 July 1716, *d.* s.p., a few months before his father, 6 Jan. 1759, and was *bur.* at Halesowen.

(b) According to the assumption of that dignity in 1770.

(c) The deceased had apparently no *brother* named "Charles." His elder br., Thomas, *b.* 31 Aug. 1758, *d.* v.p., 25 Jan. 1764, and was *bur.* in Trinity church, Guildford; Sparry, a yr. br., *b.* 10 Jan. 1760, *m.*, *d.* s.p., 24 Dec. 1803; Samuel 4th and yst. s. of his parents, was *b.* 28 Dec. 1761, but of him no more is known.

WYVILL, *or* WYVELL:

cr. 25 Nov. 1611;(a)

dormant since 23 Feb. 1774.

I. 1611. "MARMADUKE WYVELL, of Constable Burton, co. York, Knt.," s. and h. of Christopher WYVILL, of the same (will dat. 26 March 1577), by Margaret, da. of Hon. John SCROPE, of Hameldon, Bucks., yr. s. of Henry, LORD SCROPE DE BOLTON, was *b.* 1540; entertained Queen Elizabeth at Constable Burton; was Vice Chamberlain of the Queen's household; M.P. for Richmond, co. York, 1584-85, and 1597-98; was *Knighted*, June 1608, at Sion House, Midx., and was *cr. a Bart.*, as above, 25 Nov. 1611.(c) He *m.* Magdalen, da. of Sir Christopher DANBY, of Thorpe Place and Farnley, co. York, by Elizabeth, da. of Richard (NEVILLE), LORD LATIMER. He *d.* 9 Jan. 1617/8, aged 76, and was *bur.* at Masham, co. York. M.I.

II. 1618. SIR MARMADUKE WYVILL, Bart. [1611], of Constable Burton aforesaid; grandson and h., being s. and h. of Christopher WYVELL, by Jane, da. of Sir Robert STAPLETON, of Wighill, co. York, which Christopher was s. and h. ap. of the 1st Bart., but *d.* v.p., and was *bur.* at Masham, 22 July 1694, aged 52. He was *Knighted*, at Auckland, 19 April 1617, and *suc. to the Baronetcy*, 1 Jan. 1617/18; was Sheriff of Yorkshire, 1634, and was a distinguished Royalist and a great sufferer in the Royal cause, having to pay £1,343 composition to the sequestrators of estates. He *m.*, 23 Dec. 1611, at Richmond, co. York, Isabel, da. and sole heir of Sir William GASCOIGNE, of Sedbury, co. York, by Barbara, da. and coheir of Henry ANDERSON, of Haswell Grange. He *d.* about 1648.

III. 1648? SIR CHRISTOPHER WYVILL, Bart. [1611], of Constable Burton aforesaid, son and h., *bap.* at Wycliffe, 6 Dec. 1614; *suc. to the Baronetcy* about 1648; was M.P. for Richmond, co. York, 1659 and 1660. He *m.* Ursula, da. of Conyers (DARCY), 1st EARL OF HOLDERNESSE, by Grace, da. and h. of Thomas ROKEBY, of Skyers, co. York. He was *bur.* 8 Feb. 1680/1, at Masham.

IV. 1681. SIR WILLIAM WYVILL, Bart. [1611], of Constable Burton aforesaid, 4th but 1st surv. s. and h., *b.*, 1645, being aged 20 in 1665; *suc. to the Baronetcy*, 8 Feb. 1680/1. He *m.* Anne, sister of Sir John BROOKES, Bart. (so *cr.* 1676), da. of James BROOKES, of Ellingthorpe, co. York, sometime L. Mayor of York. He *d.* about 1684.

V. 1684? SIR MARMADUKE WYVILL, Bart. [1611], of Constable Burton aforesaid, s. and h.; *suc. to the Baronetcy* about 1684; was M.P. for Richmond, co. York, 1695-98. One of the Commissioners of the Salt Duties and a Commissioner of the Excise, 1702-10. He *m.*, 29 March 1688, at Snaith, co. York, Henrietta-Maria (maid of honour to the Queen Consorts of Charles II and James II), da. of Sir Thomas YARBURGH, of Balne Hall and Snaith aforesaid, by Henrietta-Maria, da. of Col. Thomas BLAGUE, of Hollinger, Suffolk. He *d.* in Great Ormond street, 2 and was *bur.* thence 7 Nov. 1722, at St. Andrew's, Holborn. Admon. 23 Nov. 1722. His widow, who was *bap.* 8 Oct. 1667, at Snaith, *d.* 15 and was *bur.* 17 Aug. 1738, at St. Lawrence's Church, York, aged 71.

VI. 1722. SIR MARMADUKE WYVILL, Bart. [1611], of Constable Burton aforesaid, s. and h.; *b.* 1692; *suc. to the Baronetcy* in Nov. 1722. M.P. for Richmond aforesaid, 1727 till unseated in April 1736; Postmaster Gen. of Ireland, 1736-54. He *m.* in 1716, Carey, sister of Thomas COKE, 1st EARL OF LEICESTER, (1744), da. of Edward COKE, of Holkham, co. Norfolk, by Carey, da. of Sir John NEWTON, 3d Bart. [1660]. She *d.* 11 June 1734. He *d.* s.p. 27 Dec. 1754. Will pr. 1754.

(a) See p. 88, notes "a" and "b," *sub* "Devereux," in which last note especial mention is made of this Baronetcy.

VII. 1754, to 1774. **Sir Marmaduke-Asty Wyvill**, Bart. [1611], of Constable Burton aforesaid, nephew and h., being only surv. s. and h. of Christopher Wyvill, by his 2d wife, Henrietta, 2d da. and coheir of Francis Asty, of Black Notley, Essex, Hamburgh Merchant, which Christopher, was 3d s. of the 5th Bart., and *d.* 26 April 1752. He was *b.* 10 Sep. 1740; *suc. to the Baronetcy*, 27 Dec. 1754; was Sheriff of Yorkshire, 1773-74. He *d.* unm., at Bath, 23 Feb. and was *bur.* 2 March 1774, in the Abbey there, since which time the *Baronetcy* has remained *dormant*.(a) Will pr. 9 March 1774.

The right to the Baronetcy(b) after 1774 appears to have been as below.

VIII. 1774. **Marmaduke Wyvill**, of Anne Arundel county in Maryland, United States of America, cousin and h. male, being s. and h. of William Wyvill, of the same (aged 13 on 14 June 1719, emigrated from England, and was lost at sea on a return voyage in 1750), who was 1st s. and h. of Darcy Wyvill, Collector of Excise at Derby (*d.* there 4 Jan. 1735), who was 2d s. of the 4th Bart. He appears to have been on 23 Feb. 1773, *entitled to the Baronetcy* [1611]. He *m.* firstly, 15 March 1764, at St. James' church in Anne Arundel county aforesaid, Harriet Rateby, by whom he had two sons and three daughters. He *m.* secondly there, 15 Oct. 1775, Susanna Burgers, by whom he had two other sons and six daughters. He *d.* 7 Sep. 1784, and was *bur.* at St. James' aforesaid.

IX. 1784. **Darcy Wyvill**, of Anne Arundel county aforesaid, 1st s. and h., by 1st wife, *b.* April 1766, is presumed to have survived his father, and accordingly to have become, on 7 Sep. 1784, *entitled to the Baronetcy* [1611]. He *m.* (—).

X. 1790? **Robert Wyvill**, of Anne Arundel county aforesaid, only s. and h., is presumed to have survived his father, and consequently to have become, on his death, *entitled to the Baronetcy* [1611]. He *d.* s.p.

XI. 1800? **Marmaduke Wyvill**, of Anne Arundel county aforesaid, uncle and h., being 2d s. of the 8th (*de jure?*) Bart., by his 1st wife, *b.* 5 Feb. 1771; became (presumably on his nephew's death) *entitled to the Baronetcy* [1611]. He *m.*, in or before 1807, (—). He *d.* s.p.m.(c) in 1808, and was *bur.* at St. James' church aforesaid.

(a) The estates on his death passed to his only surv. sister (of the half blood), Elizabeth, the 1st wife of the Rev. Christopher Wyvill, Rector of Black Notley, Essex. She *d.* s.p.s. 23 July 1783, and her husband appears to have suc. to them. He by a second wife, is ancestor of the present (1899) family of Wyvill, of Constable Burton. He *d.* 8 March 1822 aged 82, being, probably, the "Christopher Wyvill" who was LL.B., Cambridge (Queen's Coll.), 1764. He is said to have been only son of Edward Wyvill, Supervisor of Excise at Edinburgh (*d.* at York, 12 March 1791), *second* son of Darcy Wyvill, Collector of Excise at Derby (*d.* there 4 Jan. 1735), who was 2d son of the 4th Baronet. If so, it is of course obvious, that he would have been, in 1774, entitled to the Baronetcy, failing any nearer heirs male. Such, however, appear to have existed among the descendants of William Wyvill, *eldest* son of Darcy Wyvill abovenamed, as set forth in the text.

(b) The editor is indebted to W. Duncombe Pink for the information as to the American branch of the family.

(c) Hannah-Rateby, his only da., *b.* 7 March 1807, *m.*, in or before 1827, Robert Garraway Pindell, and *d.* 1 Dec. 1886, leaving issue.

XII. 1808. **Walter Wyvill**, of Calvert county, in Maryland aforesaid, br. and h. male, being 3d s. (1st s. by 2d wife) of the 8th (*de jure*) Bart., *b.* 4 Feb. 1780; became, in 1808, *entitled to the Baronetcy* [1611]. He *m.*, 3 June 1811, at St. James' aforesaid, Anne Wood.

XIII. 1840? **Edward Hale Wyvill**, of Calvert county aforesaid, only s. and h., *b.* 14 Sep. 1812; became, on his father's death, *entitled to the Baronetcy* [1611]. He *m.*, 29 Nov. 1832, Mary Davis. He was living 1890, his heir ap. being his 1st son, Walter Davis Wyvill, *b.* 8 May 1834, then a merchant at Washington, in the United States of America.

HOLTE, *or* HOLT:
cr. 25 Nov. 1611;(a)
ex. 13 March 1782.

I. 1611. "**Thomas Holt**, of Aston, *juxta* Birmingham, co. Warwick, Knt.," s. and h. of Edmund Holte, of Aston aforesaid (who *d.* Jan. 1592/3), by Dorothy, da. of John Ferrers, of Tamworth Castle, was *b.* about 1571; matric. at Oxford (Mag. Coll.), 9 Feb. 1587/8, aged 17; admitted to the Inner Temple, 1590; Sheriff of Warwickshire, 1599—1600; *Knighted* at Grimston, 18 April 1603, and was *cr. a Bart.*, as above, 25 Nov. 1611.(a) Being a person of great learning and influence, he was named by Charles I as Ambassador to Spain, but was excused owing to his great age. In the Civil War he assisted the King by raising supplies, entertained him at Aston for two nights before the battle of Edgehill (23 Oct. 1642), and sent his son to fight in his cause. He was imprisoned, his house plundered, and his estates mulcted, the loss sustained being computed at £20,000. He *m.* firstly, Grace, da. of William Bradbourne, of Hough, co. Derby, by (presumably) Frances, da. of John Preist. He *m.* secondly, Ann, sister of Sir Edward Littleton, 1st Bart. [1627], da. of Sir Edward Littleton, of Pillaton, co. Stafford, by Mary, da. of Sir Clement Fisher. By her he had no issue. He *d.* 14 Dec. 1654, aged 83, and was *bur.* at Aston. M.I.

II. 1654. **Sir Robert Holte**, Bart. [1611], of Aston aforesaid, grandson and h., being s. and h. of Edward Holte, Groom of the Bedchamber to Charles I, by Elizabeth, da. of John King, Bishop of London, which Edward, who was s. and h. ap. of the 1st Bart., by his 1st wife, *d.* during the siege of Oxford, and was *bur.* 30 Aug. 1643, at Christchurch, there. He *suc. to the Baronetcy*, 14 Dec. 1654; was active in promoting the Restoration; was Sheriff of Warwickshire, 1658 to 1660, and M.P. for that county in 1661-79. He *m.* firstly, 23 May 1648, at St. Barth. the Less, London, Jane, sister (whose issue, became in 1722, coheir), of William, 2d Baron Brereton of Leighlin [I.], da. of the Hon. Sir John Brereton (who *d.* v.p., 1629), by Ann, da. of Sir Edward Fitton, Bart. [1617]. She *d.* in childbed, about 1649, and was *bur.* at St. Clement Danes, Midx. He *m.* secondly, Mary, da. of Sir Thomas Smith, of Hough, Cheshire. She was *bur.* at St. Clement Danes aforesaid, 18 June 1679. Her admon. 1 Aug. 1691. He *d.* 3 Oct. 1679, and was *bur.* at St. Clement's aforesaid. Admon. 12 April 1695.

III. 1679. **Sir Charles Holte**, Bart. [1611], of Aston aforesaid, s. and h., being the only child by first marriage; *b.* about 1649; matric. at Oxford (Mag. Coll.), 29 Oct. 1666, aged 17; B.A., 11 Feb. 1668/9; M.A., 1 July 1671; *cr.* Doctor of Med. 9 Nov. 1695; *suc. to the Baronetcy*, 3 Oct. 1679; M.P. for Warwickshire, 1685-87; a man of great learning and consideration. He *m.* (Lic. Vic. Gen., 3 Aug. 1680, he aged 30, and she 18), Anne, da. and coheir of Sir John Clobery, of Winchester, and of Bradstone, co. Devon, by Anne, da. of William Cranmer, of London. He *d.* 20 June 1722, and was *bur.* at Aston. Will pr. 1723. His widow *d.* March 1737/9, at Aston Hall, aged nearly 90. Will pr. March 1738.

(a) See p. 88, notes "a" and "b," *sub* "Devereux."

IV. 1722. **Sir Clobery Holte**, Bart. [1611], of Aston aforesaid, s. and h., *b.* about 1682; matric. at Oxford (Mag. Coll.), 6 June 1694, aged 12; B.A., 3 March 1696/7; M.A., 16 June 1699; Proctor, 1716; *cr.* D.C.L., 18 June 1721; *suc. to the Baronetcy*, 20 June 1722. He *m.* Barbara, da. and h. of Thomas Lister, of Whitfield, co. Northampton. He *d.* at Aston Hall, 25 July 1729, and was *bur.* at Aston. Will pr. 1729.

V. 1729. **Sir Lister Holte**, Bart. [1611], of Aston Hall, s. and h., *b.* about 1721; *suc. to the Baronetcy*, 25 July 1729; matric. at Oxford (Mag. Coll.), 4 Feb. 1736/7, aged 15; *cr.* D.C.L., 13 April 1749; M.P. for Lichfield, 1741-47. He *m.* firstly, Oct. 1739, Anne, yst. da. of William (Legge), 1st Earl of Dartmouth, by Anne, da. of Heneage (Finch), Earl of Aylesford. She *d.* s.p., July 1740, and was *bur.* at Aston. He *m.* secondly, 18 July 1742, Mary, yst. da. of Sir John Harpur, 4th Bart. [1626], of Calke, co. Derby, by Catharine, da. and coheir of Thomas (Crew), 2d Baron Crew of Stene. She *d.* 1752, and was *bur.* at Aston. He *m.* thirdly, 1754, Sarah, da. of Samuel Newton, of Kings Bromley, co. Stafford. He *d.* s.p., at Aston Hall, 21 April 1770. Will pr. May 1770. That of his widow, pr. April 1794.

VI. 1770, to 1782. **Sir Charles Holte**, Bart. [1611], of Aston Hall(a) aforesaid, br. and h., *b.* about 1722; matric. at Oxford (Mag. Coll.), 13 Feb. 1738/9, aged 17; *suc. to the Baronetcy*, 21 April 1770; M.P. for Warwickshire, 1774-80. He *m.*, in 1754, Anne, da. of Pudsey Jesson, of Langley, co. Warwick. He *d.* s.p.m.,(b) 13 March 1782, when the *Baronetcy* became *extinct*. Will pr. March 1782. That of his widow pr. July 1799.

GRIMSTON:
cr. 25 Nov. 1611(b);
ex. Oct. 1700.

I. 1611. **Harbottle Grimston**, of Bradfield, co. Essex, Knt." s. and h. of Edward Grimston, of the same, by Joan, da. and coheir of Thomas Risby, of Lavenham, Suffolk (which Edward was s. and h. of Sir Edward Grimston, Comptroller of Calais), was *Knighted* at the Tower, 14 March 1603/4; suc. his father, 15 Aug. 1610, and was *cr. a Bart.*, as above, 25 Nov. 1611.(c) He was Sheriff of Essex, 1614-15; M.P. for Harwich, 1614; for Essex, 1626 and 1628-29; for Harwich (again), April to May, 1640, and Nov. 1640 till his death. He was of Puritanical sentiments, and was imprisoned, 1627, for refusing to contribute to the (forced) loan of that year. He *m.* Elizabeth, da. of Ralph Coppinger, of Stoke, co. Kent. He *d.* 19 Feb. 1647/8, aged 78. Will pr. 1648.

II. 1648. **Sir Harbottle Grimston**, Bart. [1611], of Bradfield aforesaid, and, afterwards, of Gorhambury, Herts, s. and h., *b.* 27 Jan. 1602/3, at Bradfield Hall; was a "Pensioner" at Emman. Coll., Cambridge, in 1619, and subsequently a Barrister of Lincoln's Inn; M.P. for Harwich, 1628; for Colchester, April to May, 1640, and 1640 till secluded in 1648; for Essex, 1656-58, and for Colchester (again) in five Parls., 1660-81. Recorder of Harwich, 1634; of Colchester, 1638-53, and of Harwich (again), 1660. He, at first, took part against the King, but, afterwards, espoused his side. He *suc. to the Baronetcy*, 19 Feb. 1647/8, and retired to the continent, 1653-56. At the Restoration he was made Speaker of the House of Commons (25 April 1660) in the Convention Parl.; P.C. Master of

(a) Aston Hall was built by the 1st Bart., being commenced about 1618 According to Dugdale (*Warwickshire*), it "much exceeds for beauty and state any in those parts." By Act of Parl., 1817, it was sold to satisfy the claims of the reversioners under the will of the 5th Bart.

(b) He left an only da. and h., Mary, who *m.*, in 1775, Abraham Bracebridge, of Atherstone Hall, co. Warwick, but her issue became extinct with her grandson.

(c) See p. 88, notes "a" and "b," *sub* "Devereux."

the Rolls, 1660 to 1685; High Steward of St. Albans, 1664. He purchased, in 1652, from Henry Meautys (cousin of his second wife, who had a life interest therein), the reversion of the estate of Gorhambury, Herts, which he thenceforth made his principal residence. He *m.* firstly, 16 April 1629, at St. Dunstan's in the West, London, Mary, da. of Sir George Croke, of Waterstoke, Oxon, Justice of the Common Pleas (1625-28), and of the King's Bench (1628-40), by Mary, da. of Sir Thomas Bennet, sometime (1603-04) Lord Mayor of London. He *m.* secondly, before 1652, Anne, widow of Sir Thomas Meautys, of Gorhambury, Herts, da. and at length h. of Sir Nathaniel Bacon, K.B., of Culford, Suffolk, by Jane, da. of Hercules Meautys, she being niece of the celebrated Francis Bacon, of Gorhambury aforesaid, Baron Verulam and Viscount St. Albans. By her, who was *bur.* 20 Sep. 1680, at St. Michael's, in St. Albans, he had no surviving issue. He *d.* 2 Jan. 1684/5, aged 82, and was *bur.* at St. Michael's aforesaid. Will pr. Jan. 1685.

III. 1685, to 1700. **Sir Samuel Grimston**, Bart. [1611], of Gorhambury, Herts, only surv. s. and h.,(a) by 1st wife, *b.* 7 Jan. 1643; *suc. to the Baronetcy*, 2 Jan. 1684/5; M.P. for St. Albans, in seven Parls., 1668-81, and 1689—1700. He *m.* firstly, Elizabeth, da. of Heneage (Finch), 1st Earl of Nottingham, Lord High Chancellor, by Elizabeth, da. of William Harvey. She *d.* s.p.m.(b) He *m.* secondly, in or before 1674, Anne, da. of John (Tufton), 2d Earl of Tufton, by Margaret, da. and coheir of Richard (Sackville), Earl of Dorset. By her he had no issue. He *d.* s.p.m. Oct. 1700, æt. 52, when the title became *extinct*.(b) Will pr. March 1701. His widow *d.* 22 Nov. 1713, in her 60th year, and was *bur.* at Tewin, Herts. M.I. Will pr. Dec. 1713.

["After these creations (25 Nov. 1611) there were no more for three years and a half. During that interval considerable difficulties arose from two causes. The first was a warmly disputed question of precedence; the other an effort made in the Parl. of 1614 to overthrow and unmake the new Order altogether." *Her. and Gen.*, iii, 451.]

BLAKISTON, *or* BLACKSTONE:(c)
cr. 27 May 1615;(d)
ex. 1630.

I. 1615, to 1630. **Thomas Blakiston**, of the manor of Blakiston, in the parish of Norton, in the Bishopric of Durham, Esq.,(d) s. and h. ap. of Sir William Blakiston, of the same (who was *b.* 1553, and living 1618), by Alice, 2d da. and coheir of William Claxton, of Winyard, was *bap.* at Norton, 8 July 1582, and was *cr.* a Bart., as above, 27 May 1615. He probably was, subsequently,(e) *Knighted* at Greenwich 10 June following. He *m.* about 1610, Mary, sister of Henry, 1st Viscount Dunbar [S.], da. of Henry

(a) George Grimston, his elder br., matric. at Oxford (Bras. Coll.) 6 Nov. 1650, and was a student of Lincoln's Inn, 1652. He *d.* v.p. and was *bur.* 5 June 1655, at S. Michael's aforesaid, aged 23.

(b) Elizabeth, his only da. and h. (by 1st wife), *m.* William (Savile), 2d Marquess of Halifax, and had issue; but (to the exclusion of his own descendants) he left his estates to his great nephew, William Luckyn, afterwards 5th Bart., who, in 1719, was *cr.* Viscount Grimston [I.], and is ancestor of the present Earls of Verulam.

(c) As was the case with the four Baronetcies *cr.* 24 Sep. 1611 (see p. 80, note "a") no patent is enrolled, and no signet bill exists of the creation of Blakiston, 27 May 1615; of Grey, 15 June 1619; of Salisbury, 10 Nov. 1619; of Mill, 31 Dec. 1619, and of Phelips, 16 Feb. 1619/20. They are, consequently, omitted in the list of "*Creations, 1483—1646*, in Ap. 47th Rep. D.K. Pub. Records."

(d) This date is given in Dugdale's list, etc., as also in Collins' *Baronetage* of 1722, where the grantee is called "No. 94. Sir [*sic*] Thomas Blackston, of Blackston, Esq. [*sic*], Durh." The designation of the grantee, as in the text, is, consequently, only conjectural.

(e) See p. 18, note "c," *sub* "Tollemache."

CONSTABLE, of Burton Constable, co. York, by Margaret, da. of Sir William DORMER, of Ethorp, Bucks. He, having sold his estate of Blakiston as long ago as 1615, *d.* s.p.m. in 1630, aged 48, when *the Baronetcy* became *extinct*. The will of his widow, dat. 17 April 1669, was pr. at York.

DORMER:

cr. 10 June 1615,

afterwards, since 20 June 1615, Barons Dormer of Wyng.

I. 1615. "ROBERT DORMER, of Whynge, co. Bucks, Knt., Keeper of the Royal Hawks, Falcons, etc.," s. and h. of Sir William DORMER, K.B., of Wyng aforesaid, by his 2d wife, Dorothy, daughter of Anthony CATESBY, of Whiston, co. Northampton; was M.P. for Tregony, 1571, and for Bucks, 1593; suc. his father, 17 May 1575; was *Knighted*, 1591, and was *cr. a Bart.* as aforesaid, 10 June 1615. He *m.* Elizabeth, da. of Anthony (BROWNE), 1st VISCOUNT MONTAGU, by his 2d wife, Magdalen, da. of William (DACRE)) LORD DACRE DE GILLESLAND. She was living when (ten days after he had received his Baronetcy), he was *cr.*, 20 June 1615, BARON DORMER OF WYNG. co. Buckingham. In this dignity this *Baronetcy* then *merged*, and so continues. See *Peerage*.

EGERTON:

cr. 5 April 1617,

sometime, 1784-1801, BARON GREY DE WILTON,

and *subsequently*, 1801-1814, EARL OF WILTON;

afterwards, since 1815, GREY-EGERTON.

I. 1617. "ROLAND EGERTON, of Egerton, co. Chester, Knt.," s. and h. of Sir John EGERTON ("black Sir John"), of Egerton and Oulton, co. Chester, of Wrinehill, co. Stafford, and of Farthingho, co. Northampton, by his 1st wife, Margaret, da. of Sir Rowland STANLEY, of Hooton, co. Chester, suc. his father, 27 April 1614; was *Knighted*, 14 March 1616/7, at Whitehall, and was *cr. a Bart.*, as above, 5 April 1617. M.P. for Wotton Basset, 1624-25. Though too aged to join the camp, he was a great promoter of the Royal cause during the Civil Wars. He *m.* Bridget, sister and coheir of Thomas (GREY), LORD GREY DE WILTON (attainted 1603 and *d.* 1614), da. of Arthur, LORD GREY DE WILTON, sometime Chief Gov. of Ireland, by his 2d wife, Jane Sibella, da. of Sir Richard MORRISON. He *d.* suddenly, and was *bur.* 3 Oct. 1646, at Farthingho. Will pr. Oct. 1646. His widow *d.* 28 July 1648, and was *bur.* at Farthingho. Will pr. 1648.

II. 1646. SIR JOHN EGERTON, Bart. [1617], of Wrinehill and Farthingho aforesaid 1st surv. s. and h.(a); *suc. to the Baronetcy*, 4 Oct. 1646. He *m.* Anne, da. of George WINTOUR, of Dyrham, co. Gloucester. He *d.* at Wrinehill, and was *bur.* 1674, at Madeley, Salop. Will pr. 1674. His widow's will dat. 21 Nov. 1680, pr. 2 Nov. 1681.

III. 1674. SIR JOHN EGERTON, Bart. [1617], of Wrinehill and Farthingho aforesaid, *b.* about 1658; matric. at Oxford (Bras. Coll.) 5 May 1673, aged 15; *suc. to the Baronetcy*, in 1674. He *m.* firstly, Elizabeth, sister and heir of Edward HOLLAND, of Heaton and Denton, co. Lancaster, da. of William

(a) His elder br., Thomas Egerton, who was *b.* in Bucks, matric. at Oxford (Mag. Coll.), 28 Jan. 1632/3, aged 18; B.A. 29 Jan. 1632/3, and *d.* v.p. and s.p.

HOLLAND, of the same. She *d.* 31 May 1701, and was *bur.* at Madeley. He *m.* secondly, Anne, da. and sole heir of Francis WOLFERSTAN (or WOLFERSTON), of Statfold, co. Stafford, by his 1st wife, Hester, da. of John BOWYER, of Biddulph. She *d.* s.p.s., 12 April 1726. He *d.* at Wrinehill aforesaid, 4 Nov. 1729, aged 73. Will pr. 1730.

IV. 1729. SIR HOLLAND EGERTON, Bart. [1617], of Heaton and Farthingho aforesaid, s. and h., by 1st wife; *b.* about 1689: matric. at Oxford (Bras. Coll.), 10 Oct. 1704, aged 15; *suc. to the Baronetcy*, 4 Nov. 1629. He was a distinguished antiquary. He *m.*, 27 March 1712, at Thorpe Mandeville, Northants, Eleanor, yst. da. of Sir Roger CAVE, 2d Bart. [1641], by his 2d wife, Mary, da. of Sir William BROMLEY, K.B. He *d.* at Heaton, 25 April 1730, and was *bur.* at Madeley, aged 44. Will dat. 12 to 21 April 1730, pr. 9 Dec. following. His widow *m.*, 1732, John BROOKE, s. of Sir Thomas BROOKE, of Norton, 3d Bart. [1662]. She *d.* at Heaton, 26 Sep. 1734.

V. 1730. SIR EDWARD EGERTON, Bart. [1617], of Heaton and Farthingho aforesaid, 4th but 1st surv. s. and h., *b.* about 1719; *suc. to the Baronetcy*, 25 April 1730; matric. at Oxford (Bras. Coll.), 30 Nov. 1736, aged 17. He *d.* unm. 16 Feb. 1743/4. Admon. 26 May 1744.

VI. 1744. SIR THOMAS GREY EGERTON, Bart. [1617], of Heaton and Farthingho aforesaid, br. and h., *b.* about 1721; a minor in 1741; *suc. to the Baronetcy*, 16 Feb. 1743/4. M.P. for Newton, 1747-54. He *m.*, 14 June 1748, Catharine, da. of Rev. John COPLEY, of Batley, co. York, Rector of Thornhill and Wakefield, in that county. He *d.* 7 Aug. 1756, aged 35, and was *bur.* at Prestwich, co. Lancashire. His widow *d.* 30 May 1791.

VII. 1756. SIR THOMAS EGERTON, Bart. [1617], of Heaton and Farthingho,(a) aforesaid, only surv. s. and h., *b.* 14 Aug. 1749, at Heaton; *suc. to the Baronetcy*, 7 Aug. 1756; ed. at Westm. and at Ch. Ch., Oxford; matric. 1 Feb. 1767; *cr.* M.A., 14 Feb. 1769; was M.P. for Lancashire, in three Parls., 1772-84; being, on 15 May 1784, *cr.* a Peer, as BARON GREY DE WILTON, co. Hereford; and being, subsequently, 26 June 1801, *cr.* (with a *spec. rem.*, failing his issue male, to the 2d and yr. sons of his da. in tail male respectively) VISCOUNT GREY DE WILTON and EARL OF WILTON of Wilton Castle, co. Hereford. He *m.*, 12 Sep. 1769, at Middleton, co. Lancaster, his cousin, Eleanor, yst. da. and coheir of Sir Ralph ASSHETON, 3d Bart. [1660], of Middleton, by his 2d wife, Eleanor, da. and coheir of the Rev. John COPLEY, abovenamed. He *d.* s.p.m.s., 23 Sep. 1814, aged 65, at Heaton House, and was *bur.* at Prestwich, when the *Barony* became *extinct*, but the *Earldom*, etc., descended to the issue of his daughter,(b) while the Baronetcy devolved on the heir male of the body of the grantee, as below. Will pr. 1815. His widow *d.* there, 3 Feb. 1816, aged 66. Admon. April 1816.

VIII. 1814. SIR JOHN EGERTON, afterwards, 1815, GREY-EGERTON, Bart. [1617], of Oulton Park, co. Chester, cousin and h. male, being s. and h. of Philip EGERTON, of Oulton aforesaid, by Mary, sister and heir of Sir John Haskyn EYLES-STYLES, 4th Bart, da. of Sir Francis Haskyn EYLES-STYLES, 3d Bart. [1714], which Philip (*bur.* 15 May 1786, aged 54) was s. and h. of John EGERTON, of Broxton, co. Chester, the 2d s. of Rev. Philip EGERTON, D.D., Rector of Astbury, Cheshire (*d.* 6 March 1726), who was 3d s. of Sir Philip EGERTON, of Egerton and Oulton aforesaid (*bur.* 15 Aug. 1698, at Little Budworth), the 3d s. of the 1st Bart. He was *b.* 11 July 1776; suc. his father, 15 May 1786; was Sheriff of Cheshire, 1793-94; M.P. for Chester, 1807-12, and 1812-16; *suc. to the Baronetcy* 23 Sep. 1814; and by royal lic., 17 Oct. 1815, took the name of *Grey* before that of

(a) In 1789, he sold the manorial estate and advowson of Farthingho to George Rush.

(b) Eleanor, Marchioness of Westminster, whose 2d son thus became the 2d Earl of Wilton, and in 1821, took the name of Egerton in lieu of that of Grosvenor.

Egerton. He *m.*, 9 April 1795, Maria, da. and sole heir of Thomas-Scott JACKSON, one of the Directors of the Bank of England. He *d.* s.p. 24 May 1825. Will pr. Nov. 1825. His widow was *bur.* 23 Aug. 1830. Will pr. Sep. 1830.

IX. 1825. SIR PHILIP EGERTON, *afterwards* GREY-EGERTON, Bart. [1617], of Oulton Park aforesaid, br. and h., *b.* 6 Jan. 1767; Rector of Tarporley, and of the higher mediety of Malpas. He *suc. to the Baronetcy*, 24 May 1825, and, by Royal lic., 21 July following, took the name of *Grey* before that of *Egerton*. He *m.*, 14 Sep. 1804, Rebecca, yst. da. of Josias DU PRE, of Wilton Park, Bucks, by Rebecca, sister of James, 1st EARL OF CALEDON [I.], da. of Nathaniel ALEXANDER. He *d.*, after three days' illness, 13 Dec. 1829, at Oulton Park, aged 63. Will pr. March 1830. His widow *d.* 11 June 1870, aged 90, at Knolton Hall, co. Flint.

X. 1829. SIR PHILIP-DE-MALPAS GREY-EGERTON, Bart. [1617], of Oulton Park aforesaid, s. and h., *b.* 13 Nov. 1806, at Malpas; ed. at Eton and at Ch. Ch., Oxford; B.A., 1828; *suc. to the Baronetcy*, 13 Dec. 1839. Lieut. Col. of Cheshire Yeomanry Cavalry, 1847; M.P. for Chester, 1830-31; for South Cheshire, 1835-68; and for West Cheshire, 1868-81; a Trustee of the British Museum. He *m.*, 8 March 1832, Anna-Elizabeth, 2d da. of George John LEGH, of High Legh, Cheshire. He *d.*, 5 April 1881, at 28 Albemarle street. His widow *d.* there, 26 Nov. 1882.

XI. 1881. SIR PHILIP LE BELWARD GREY-EGERTON, Bart. [1617], of Oulton Park aforesaid, s. and h., *b.* 28 March 1833, in Chester street, Pimlico; ed. at Eton; entered Rifle brigade, 1852; sometime, 1857-61, Capt. Coldstream Guards; *suc. to the Baronetcy*, 5 April 1881. He *m.*, 18 July 1861, at St. Martin's in the Fields, Henrietta Elizabeth Sophia, da. of Albert (DENISON, *formerly* CONYNGHAM), 1st BARON LONDESBOROUGH, by his 1st wife, Henrietta Maria, da. of Cecil Weld (FORESTER), 1st BARON FORESTER. He *d.* 2 and was *bur.* 5 Sep. 1891, at Little Budworth. Will pr. at £26,730 gross. His widow, who was *b.* 25 Dec. 1836, living 1899.

XII. 1891. SIR PHILIP HENRY BRIAN GREY-EGERTON, Bart. [1617], 1st and only surv. s. and h., *b.* 29 April 1864, sometime Capt. 4th batt. Cheshire regiment; *suc. to the Baronetcy*, 2 Sep. 1891. He *m.*, 4 Jan. 1893, at St. Peter's, Eaton square, May Carolyn Campbell, da. of Major J. Wayne CUYLER, of Baltimore, in the United States, America.

Family Estates.—These, in 1883, consisted of 8,840 acres in Cheshire, worth £14,676 a year. *Residences.*—Oulton Park, near Tarporley, and Broxton Old Hall, near Chester, Cheshire.

TOWNSHEND:

cr. 16 April 1617,

afterwards, 1661-82, BARON TOWNSHEND OF LYNN REGIS,

subsequently, 1682—1787, VISCOUNTS TOWNSHEND OF RAYNHAM,

and finally, since 1787, MARQUESSES TOWNSHEND OF RAYNHAM.

I. 1617. "ROGER TOWNSHEND, of Raynham, co. Norfolk, Esq.," s. and h. of Sir John TOWNSHEND,(a) of the same, sometime M.P. for Norfolk, by Anne, 1st da. and coheir of Sir Nathaniel BACON, of Stiffkey, in that county, was *b.* about 1596; suc. his father, 2 Aug. 1603, and was *cr. a Bart.*, as above, 16 April 1617. He was M.P. for Orford, 1621-22, and for Norfolk, 1628-29;

(a) See ped. in Norfolk Visit., 1563, enlarged and pub. by the Norfolk Arch. Soc., vol. i.

Sheriff, 1629-30, and was much esteemed for his charity and munificence. He erected (the architect being the celebrated Inigo Jones) the stately mansion called Raynham Hall. He *m.*, in or before 1628, Mary, 2d da. and coheir of the well-known Horatio (DE VERE), BARON VERE OF TILBURY, by Mary, da. of Sir John TRACY. He *d.* 1 Jan. 1636/7, aged 41, and was *bur.* in the church of East Raynham. Will dat. 31 Dec. 1636, pr. 10 June 1637. His widow *m.*, 21 June 1638, at Hackney, Midx. (Lic. Lond., he 33, and she 30), Mildmay (FANE), 2d EARL OF WESTMORLAND, who *d.* 12 Feb. 1665/6, aged about 63. She who was *b.* in the Netherlands, but naturalised by Act of Parl., 21 Jac. I, *d.* at Mereworth, co. Kent, Nov. 1669. Admon. 2 Dec. 1669.

II. 1636. SIR ROGER TOWNSHEND, Bart. [1617], of Raynham Hall, aforesaid, s. and h., *b.* 21 Dec. 1628; *suc. to the Baronetcy*, 1 Jan. 1636/7; was a Ward of the Crown. He *d.* abroad, a minor and unm., about 1648. Admon. 13 July and 11 Oct. 1648, to his grandmother, Mary, Lady Vere, during the minority of his brother.

III. 1648. SIR HORATIO TOWNSHEND, Bart. [1617], of Raynham Hall aforesaid, br. and h., *b.* about 1630; ed. at Cambridge, being *cr.* M.A. 27 Nov. 1645; *suc. to the Baronetcy* in 1648. Though under age when the Civil War began, he engaged subsequently in many measures to promote the Restoration, such as the design for surprising Lynn, in 1659, the address from Norfolk to demand a free Parl., etc. M.P. for Norfolk, 1656-58, 1659 and 1660; one of the Council of State, May to Dec. 1659, and was nominated by the House to invite the return of the King from the Hague. He *m.* firstly, probably before 1658, Mary, da. and h. of Edward LEWKNOR, of Denham, co. Suffolk, by Elizabeth, da. of Sir William RUSSELL, of Chippenham, co. Cambridge. She was living when, on 20 April 1661, he was *cr.* a Peer, as BARON TOWNSHEND OF LYNN REGIS, co. Norfolk, and, subsequently, 2 Dec. 1682, was *cr.* VISCOUNT TOWNSHEND OF RAYNHAM, co. Norfolk. In this peerage this *Baronetcy* continues *merged*, the 6th Viscount and 8th Baronet being *cr.* in 1787, MARQUESS TOWNSHEND OF RAYNHAM. See *Peerage*.

CLARKE:

cr. 1 May 1617;

dorm. or *ex.* 9 Feb. 1898.

I. 1617. "SIMON CLARKE, of Salford, co. Warwick, Esq.," s. and h. of Walter CLARKE,(a) of Ratcliffe, Bucks, and of Buxford in Great Chart, Kent, by Elizabeth, da. of Simon EDOLPH, of St. Radigan's, in the same county, was *cr. a Bart.*, as above, 1 May 1617. In the Civil Wars he adhered to the King, and was fined £800 by the sequestrators of the estates of the loyalists. He was also "a great encourager" of Sir William Dugdale in writing his history of Warwickshire. He *m.* firstly, Margaret, da. and coheir of John ALDERFORD, of Abbots Salford, co. Warwick, by Elizabeth, da. of Peter DORMER, of Newbottle, co. Northampton. She *d.* 2 May 1617, and was *bur.* at Salford. M.I. He *m.* secondly, Dorothy, widow of Thomas HAY, da. of Thomas HOBSON, of Cambridgeshire, but by her he had no issue. He was living 1631, but *d.* about 1642, and was *bur.* at Salford aforesaid. M.I. His widow *d.* 8 Nov. 1699, aged 84, and was also *bur.* at Salford. M.I.

II. 1642? SIR JOHN CLARKE, Bart. [1617], of Salford aforesaid, s. and h., by 1st wife, *suc. to the Baronetcy* about 1642. He *m.* Ann, sister of Sir Edmund WILLIAMS, Bart. [1642], da. of John WILLIAMS, of Marnehull, Dorset. She *d.* 1 Sep. 1653, and was *bur.* at Sunning, Berks. He survived her, but *d.* s.p. in or before 1679. Will pr. 1679.

(a) The family claim a male descent from Sir Simon Woodchurch, who, in the wars with Scotland, *temp.* Ed. I, was called "Malleus Scotorum," and who bore the arms (Gu., three swords erect in pale, arg.) used by his descendants. His wife, Susan, da. and h. of Henry Clarke, of Munsidde, brought so large an inheritance to the family, that her descendants adopted her name. The descent is set forth in a series of tablets erected by the 1st Baronet to his ancestors at Salford Priors church.

III. 1679. Sir Simon Clarke, Bart. [1617], nephew and h., being s. and h. of Peter Clarke, a Captain in the Low Countries, by Elizabeth, da. of (—) Corbyson, of co. Warwick, which Peter was 2d s. of the 1st Bart., by his 1st wife, and was killed, in 1639, by Lord Morley. He was *b.* 1635, at Dunkirk in Flanders, and was an officer in the Army. He *suc. to the Baronetcy* about 1679. He *m.* Mercy, da. of Philip Brace, of Doverdale, co. Worcester. He *d.* 10 Nov. 1687, aged 52. His widow *d.* 22 Dec. 1698, aged 56. Both *bur.* at Salford Priors. M.I.

IV. 1687. Sir Simon Clarke, Bart. [1617], s. and h., *b.* about 1662; matric. at Oxford (Mag. Coll.), 25 May 1683. He *m.* (Lic. Lond. 19 Jan. 1702/3, he being then "of Clarke Hall, co. Warwick," aged 40, bachelor, and she 27, spinster) Elizabeth, sister of Henry Castell, of Greenford, Midx., da. of the Rev. (—) Castell. He *d.* 1718.(a)

V. 1718. Sir Simon Peter Clarke, Bart. [1617], only s. and h., *suc. to the Baronetcy* in 1718. He was an officer of the Royal Navy, but was transported to Jamaica(b) for highway robbery, having been convicted at the Lent assizes of 1730, held at Winchester. He *d.* s.p.m. 1736. Will pr. 1737.

VI. 1736. Sir Simon Clarke, Bart. [1617], of St. Catherine's, Kingston, in Jamaica, cousin and h., being s. and h. of Philip Clarke, by Arabella Lucy, his wife, which Philip was 2d s. of the 3d Bart. He settled in Jamaica, and, in 1722, was Clerk of the Crown, being M.P. in several Parls., and in 1730, a Member of the Council there; *suc. to the Baronetcy* in 1736. He *m.* Mary, da. of Philip Bonny, of Jamaica. She *d.* 1762. He *d.* 7 Feb. 1770, at Kingston, and was *bur.* the next day at St. Catherine's in that island.

VII. 1770. Sir Simon Clarke, Bart. [1617], of Hanover, in Jamaica aforesaid, s. and h., *b.* 2 Nov. 1727, in Jamaica; *suc. to the Baronetcy*, 7 Feb. 1770. He *m.*, 21 July 1760, Anne, 2d and yst. da. and coh. of Philip Haughton, a wealthy Jamaica planter, by Catherine, da. of Joseph Tharpe, of Bachelor's Hall, in that island. With her he obtained £100,000, an estate called "Retirement," in St. James', and other lands in Hanover, Jamaica. He *d.* 2 Nov. 1777, on his 50th birthday, and was *bur.* at St. Lucia. M.I. Monument by Flaxman. Will pr. May 1783. His widow *d.* 1800. Will pr. 1800.

VIII. 1777. Sir Philip Haughton Clarke, Bart. [1617], of Kingston, in Jamaica aforesaid, s. and h., *b.* 1761; *suc. to the Baronetcy*, 2 Nov. 1777; matric. at Oxford (Queen's Coll.), 16 May 1778, aged 16. He *d.* unm., 12 May 1798. Will pr. June 1798.

IX. 1798. Sir Simon Haughton Clarke, Bart. [1617], of Kingston, in Jamaica aforesaid, and of Oak Hill, in East Barnet, Herts., br. and h., *b.* 7 Nov. 1764; *suc. to the Baronetcy*, 12 May 1798; M.P. for St. James', Jamaica, 1807. He *m.*, 9 April, 1814, Catherine Haughton, 2d da. of his uncle, John Haughton James, of Burnt Ground, in Hanover aforesaid. He *d.* 28 Aug. 1832, at Oak Hill aforesaid. Will pr. Oct. 1832. His widow *d.* 13 Aug. 1837. Will pr. Jan. 1839.

(a) He (though his death was as early as 1718) is apparently the person mentioned in Collins' *Baronetage* (1722) as "Sir Simon Clarke, the present Baronet [is] as I am informed, very poor, the estate in Warwickshire being out of the family."

(b) It is probable that interest was made that he should be sent to Jamaica, where his cousin, afterwards the 6th Bart., was established and in some authority. See *History of St. James' Parish in Jamaica*, by John Roby, Kingston, 1844, of which (apparently) only three parts (66 pages) were published. The notes are full of genealogical history of various Jamaica families.

X. 1832. Sir Simon Haughton Clarke, Bart. [1617], of Oak Hill, aforesaid, s. and h., *b.* 7 April 1818; matric. at Oxford (Ball. Coll.), 16 Dec. 1837, aged 19; *suc. to the Baronetcy*, 28 Aug. 1832. He *d.* unm. 28 April 1849, at Guernsey, aged 31.

XI. 1849, to 1898. Sir Philip Haughton Clarke, Bart. [1617], of Oak Hill, aforesaid, and sometime of Aldwick Place in Bognor, co. Sussex, br. and h.; *b.* 11 April 1819; was sometime Capt. 9th Lancers; *suc. to the Baronetcy*, 28 April 1849. He *m.* 24 July 1895, at St. Geo., Han. sq., Rose, da. of Charles Drummond Bailey, of Charlton Musgrave, co. Somerset. He *d.* s.p. 9 Feb. 1898, at Paultons, Southampton, when the *Baronetcy* became *dormant* or *extinct*. His widow living 1899.

FITTON, *or* PHYTTON:

cr. 2 Oct. 1617;

ex. Aug. 1643.

I. 1617. "Edward Phytton [*i.e.* Fitton], of Gowseworth [*i.e.* Gawsworth], co. Chester, Esq.," s. and h. of Sir Edward Fitton, of Gawsworth, sometime President of Munster, by Alice, da. and sole heir of John Holcroft, of Holcroft, co. Lancaster, was *b.* 3 Dec. 1572; suc. his father, 4 March 1605/6, and was *cr. a Bart.*, as above, 2 Oct. 1617. He *m.* Anne, da. and coheir of James Barret, of South Wales. He *d.* 10 May 1619, aged 46, and was *bur.* at Gawsworth. M.I. His widow *d.* 1644.

II. 1619, to 1643? Sir Edward Fitton, Bart. [1617], of Gawsworth aforesaid, 1st surv. s. and h., *bap.* at Gawsworth, Aug. 1603; *suc. to the Baronetcy*, 10 May 1619; matric. at Oxford (Trin. Hall), 15 Oct. 1619, aged 16; Student of Gray's Inn, 1622; Sheriff of Cheshire, 1632-33. He was an officer (of some distinction) in the King's service. He *m.* firstly, 13 Oct. 1622, Jane, da. of Sir John Trevor, of Plas Teg, co. Denbigh. She was *bur.* 9 June 1638, at Gawsworth. He *m.* secondly, Felicia, 6th da. of Ralph Sneyd, of Keel, co. Stafford, by Felicia, da. of Nicholas Archbold. He *d.* s.p., shortly after the taking of Bristol, Aug. 1643, when the *Baronetcy* became *extinct*. Admon. 13 Nov. 1651. Will pr. May 1661. His widow *m.* Sir Charles Adderley, of Lea Marston, co. Warwick.

LUCY:

cr. 11 March 1617/8;

ex. 19 Nov. 1759.

I. 1618. "Richard Lucy, of Broxborne, co. Herts, Knt.," 2d s. of Sir Thomas Lucy, of Charlecote, co. Warwick, by his 2d wife, Constance, da. and h. of Richard Kingsmill, of High Clere, Hants, was *b.* about 1592; matric. at Oxford (Mag. Coll.), 19 June 1607, aged 15; B.A. (Ex. Coll.), 4 July 1611; admitted to Lincoln's Inn, 1608; *Knighted* at Whitehall, 8 Jan. 1617/8, and was, shortly afterwards, *cr. a Bart.*, as above, 11 March 1617/8. He was M.P. for Old Sarum, 1647-53; and for Herts, 1654-55, and 1656-58. He *m.* firstly, Dame Elizabeth Oxenbridge, widow of the Hon. Robert West, and formerly of Sir Robert Oxenbridge, da. and coheir of Sir Henry Cock, of Broxbourne aforesaid, Cofferer of the Royal Household, by Ursula, da. of Jacob Bury, of Hampton Poyle, Oxon. By her, who *d.* 1645, he had a *life* interest in the estate of Broxbourne. He *m.* secondly, Rebecca, widow of Sir Thomas Playters, 3d Bart. [1623] (who *d.* 1651, aged 35), da. and coheir of Thomas Chapman, of Wormley, Herts. He *d.* 6 and was *bur.* 12 April

Q

1667, at Broxbourne. Will dat. 4 and pr. 22 April 1667. His widow *m.* (as his 2d wife), in or before 1662, Sir Rowland Lytton, of Knebworth, Herts (who *d.* 1 Nov. 1674, aged 59), and *d.* 23 May 1685, being *bur.* at Aynho, co. Northampton.(a)

II. 1667. Sir Kingsmill Lucy, Bart. [1618], of Facombe and Netley, co. Hants, s. and h., by 1st wife, *b.* about 1649; *suc. to the Baronetcy*, 6 April 1667; *cr.* D.C.L. of Oxford, 6 Aug. 1667; admitted to Lincoln's Inn, 1667; was M.P. for Brecknock, 1661 till void 17 May, and for Andover, 1673-78; was F.R.S. He *m.*, 14 May 1668, at St. James', Clerkenwell (Lic. Fac., he 19, and she 18), Theophila, 2d da. of George (Berkeley), 1st Earl of Berkeley, by Elizabeth, da. and coheir of John Massingberd. He was *bur.* 20 Sep. 1678, aged 29, at Facombe aforesaid. Will dat. 19 Sep., pr. 5 Oct. 1678. His widow, who was *b.* 1650, *m.*, 23 Nov. 1682, Robert Nelson (*b.* 22 June 1656), the well known author of the *Festivals and Fasts of the Church*, who *d.* 16 Jan. 1714/5. She *d.* 26 and was *bur.* 21 Jan. 1706/7, at Cranford, Midx.

III. 1678, to 1759. Sir Berkeley Lucy, Bart. [1618], of Facombe and Netley aforesaid, only surv. s. and h., *b.* about 1672; *suc. to the Baronetcy*, 20 Sep. 1678. He was F.R.S. He *m.* Catharine, 2d da. of Charles Cotton, of Beresford, co. Stafford, by Isabella, da. of Sir Thomas Hutchinson, of Owthorpe in that county. She was *bur.* 22 June 1740, at Facombe. He *d.* s.p.m.,(b) 19 and was *bur.* 26 Nov. 1759, at Facombe, aged 87, when the *Baronetcy* became *extinct*. Will dat. 18 June 1759, pr. 21 Nov. following.

BOYNTON:

cr. 15 May 1618.

I. 1618. "Matthew Boynton, of Barmston, co. York, Knt." s. and h. of Sir Francis Boynton, of the same, by Dorothy, da. and coheir of Sir Christopher Place, of Halnaby, co. York was *bap.* 26 Jan. 1591, at Barmston; suc. his father, 9 April 1617; was *Knighted*, at Whitehall, 9 May 1618, being, six days afterwards, *cr. a Bart.*, as above, 15 May 1618; M.P. for Heydon, co. York, 1620, and for Scarborough, 1645-47; Sheriff of Yorkshire, 1628-29, and again, 1643 to 1645. He sided with the Parl. in the Civil War and aided in the capture of Sir John Hotham, who was planning to surrender Hull to the King. He was Gov. of Scarborough Castle and Col. of a troop of horse. He *m.* firstly (Lic. at York, 1613, the settl. dat. 27 Sep. 1614) Frances, da. of Sir Henry Griffith, 1st Bart. [1627], of Burton Agnes, co. York, by Elizabeth, da. of Thomas Throckmorton, of Coughton, co. Warwick. She *d.* July 1634, in her 30th year and was *bur.* at Rousby. M.I. He *m.* secondly, Katharine, widow of Robert Stapleton, of Wighill, co. York, 3d da. of Thomas (Fairfax), 1st Viscount Fairfax of Emley [I.], by his 2d wife, Catharine, da. of Sir Henry Constable. He *d.* at Highgate, Midx., and was *bur.* 12 March 1646/7, in the chancel of St. Andrew's, Holborn. Will pr. 1647. His widow, by whom he had no issue, *m.* Sir Arthur Ingram, who *d.* 4 July 1655. She *m.*, for her 4th husband, William Wickham and *d.* 23 Feb. 1666, being *bur.* at Rousby. M.I.

II. 1647. Sir Francis Boynton, Bart. [1618], of Barmston and afterwards [1654] of Burton Agnes aforesaid, s. and h. by 1st wife, *b.* about 1618, *suc. to the Baronetcy* in March 1646/7, and suc. to the estate of Burton Agnes, 20 Feb. 1654, on the death s.p. of his maternal uncle, Sir Henry Griffith, 2d Bart. [1627]. He was aged 47 in the Her. Visit. of Yorkshire, 1665; was Col. of a Reg. of Militia, etc. He *m.* (Sunday) 7 March 1637, Constance, da. of William (Fiennes),

(a) So says Clutterbuck in his *Herts*, vol. ii, p. 377, but elsewhere her burial is given as having been with her last husband, at Knebworth, where probably she died.

(b) Of his daughters and coheirs (1) Mary, *bap.* 9 Nov. 1709, at St. Andrew's, Holborn, *m.*, 14 Aug. 1727, Hon. Charles Compton, s. of George, 4th Earl of Northampton, and was mother of the 7th and 8th Earls. (2) Elizabeth, *m.* 20 July 1765, Edward Plowden, of Plowden, co. Stafford, and had issue.

1st Viscount Say and Sele, by Elizabeth, da. of Thomas Temple, of Stowe, Bucks. She was *bur.* 2 Sep. 1692 at Barmston. He *d.* 9 and was *bur.* 16 Sep. 1695 at Barmston aforesaid, aged 76.

III. 1695. Sir Griffith Boynton, Bart. [1618], of Burton Agnes and Barmston aforesaid, grandson and h., being s. and h. of Lieut. Col. William Boynton (who was M.P. for Hedon, 1680-81), by Elizabeth, da. and coheir of John Bernard, Alderman of Kingston-upon-Hull, which William was s. and h. ap. of the last Bart., by his 1st wife, but *d.* v.p. Aug. 1689. He was *b.* 8 Dec. 1664, at Burton Agnes, and *suc. to the Baronetcy*, 9 Sep. 1695. He was founder of an almshouse at Barmston and improved the mansion at Burton Agnes. He *m.* firstly, in 1712, at Chamlesford, co. York, Adriana, da. and coheir of John Sykes, of Dort, merchant. She *d.* 19 Nov. 1724, aged 69, in Pall Mall, Midx., and was *bur.* at Burton Agnes. He *m.* secondly, Nov. 1728, in London, Rebecca, da. of John White, of Tuxford, Notts, sometime M.P. for that county. He *d.* s.p. 22 Dec. 1731, in Ormond street, Midx., and was *bur.* at Burton Agnes. Will pr. April 1732. His widow *d.* at Wallingwells, Notts, 8 and was *bur.* 27 Oct. 1732, at Burton aforesaid, aged 35. M.I. Her will pr. May 1733.

IV. 1731. Sir Francis Boynton, Bart. [1618], of Burton Agnes aforesaid, cousin and h. being s. and h. of the Rev. Henry Boynton, M.A., Rector of Barmston aforesaid, by his 1st wife, Dorothy, da. of Alexander Amcotts, of Pensbire in Houghton le Spring, co. Durham, which Henry was 3d s. of the 2d Bart. by his 1st wife, and *d.* 29 May 1719, aged 73. He was *bap.* at Barmston, 17 Nov. 1677, ed. at St. John's Coll., Cambridge; *suc. to the Baronetcy*, 22 Dec. 1731, Barrister at Law; Recorder of Beverley, 1733; M.P. for Heydon aforesaid, 1734 till his death. He *m.* 8 April 1703, at Beverley, Frances, da. of James Heblethwayte, of Norton, in the East Riding, co. York, by Bridget, da. and h. of Sir William Cobb, of Otteringham and Beverley aforesaid, whose heir Lady Boynton became. She was *bap.* 19 May 1677 and *d.* 1 April 1720, aged 43, at Beverley, being *bur.* at St. Mary's, Beverley. M.I. He *d.* 16 Sep. 1739, in his 62d year and was *bur.* at Burton Agnes. Will pr. 1744 in the Prerog. Court [I.].

V. 1739. Sir Griffith Boynton, Bart. [1618], of Burton Agnes aforesaid, 1st surv. s. and h., *b.* 24 May and *bap.* 5 June 1712 at Beverley; admitted to Gray's Inn, 1730; *suc. to the Baronetcy*, 16 Sep. 1739; Sheriff for Yorkshire, 1750-51. He *m.* 5 April 1742, in Audley Street Chapel, St. Geo. Han. sq., Anne, 2d da. of Thomas White, of Wallingwells and Tuxford, Notts, Clerk of the Ordnance, by Bridget, da. and coheir of Richard Taylor, of Wallingwells, in that county. She *d.* in childbed 27 Feb. 1744/5, aged 34, at Wallingwells and was *bur.* at Burton Agnes. He *d.* 18 Oct. 1761, at Burton Agnes, and was *bur.* there. M.I.

VI. 1761. Sir Griffith Boynton, Bart. [1618], of Burton Agnes aforesaid, only s. and h., *b.* 22 and *bap.* 29 Feb. 1744/5, at Walling Wells aforesaid, ed. at Corpus Christi Coll., Cambridge; *suc. to the Baronetcy*, 18 Oct. 1761; F.S.A., 1771; Sheriff of Yorkshire, 1771-72; M.P. for Beverley, May 1772 to 1774. He *m.* firstly, 9 May 1762, at York Minster, Charlotte, 1st da. of Francis Topham, D.C.L., Judge of the Prerog. Court of York, by Charlotte Oswald his wife. She *d.* in childbed, s.p.s., 9 and was *bur.* 15 Sep. 1767, at Burton Agnes, in her 26th year. He *m.* secondly, 1 Aug. 1768, at Burton Agnes aforesaid, Mary, 1st da. of James Heblethwayte, of Norton and Bridlington, in the East Riding, co. York. He *d.* of fever in St. James' street, Midx., 6 and was *bur.* 20 Jan. 1778, at Burton Agnes. M.I.(a) Will pr. Jan. 1778. His widow, who was *b.* 5 Jan. 1749, at Bridlington, co. York, *m.* at Burton Agnes, about 1784, John George Parkhurst, of Catesby Abbey, co. Northampton (who *d.* June 1823) and *d.* 13 May 1815.

VII. 1778. Sir Griffith Boynton, Bart. [1618], of Burton Agnes aforesaid, s. and h., by 2d wife, *b.* 17 July 1769, at Burton Agnes, *suc. to the Baronetcy*, 6 Jan. 1778; ed. at Cheam School, Surrey, at Eton, and at

(a) This was composed by (the poet) Rev. W. Mason.

Trin. Coll., Cambridge; M.A., 1789. Though eminently accomplished and learned, he totally excluded himself from society for many years before his death. He *m.* 30 July 1790 (as soon as he came of age), at Winchester, Anna Maria, sister of his step father above named, da. of Capt. Robert (or Richard) Parkhurst. He *d.* s.p., 10 July 1801, at Epsom, Surrey, and was *bur.* at Burton Agnes. His widow, who was *b.* 12 Aug. and *bap.* 25 Sep. 1763, at Shenstone, co. Stafford, *m.* Rev. Charles Drake Barnard, Rector of Bigby, co. Lincoln. She *d.* 17 March 1853, in Connaught square, Paddington, aged 89, and was *bur.* at Bigby. Will pr. April 1853.

VIII. 1801. Sir Francis Boynton, Bart. [1618], of Burton Agnes aforesaid, br. and h., *b.* 28 March 1777, in Berners street, and *bap.* at St. Marylebone; ed. at Eton; Capt. in the North York Reg. of Militia; *suc. to the Baronetcy*, 10 July 1801. He *m.* 10 June 1815, at St. Paul's, Covent Garden, Sally Bucktrout, of that parish, spinster. He *d.* s.p. at Burton Agnes, 19 Nov. 1832, aged 55. His widow *m.* (as his second wife) 1837, Walter Strickland, of Cokethorpe Park, Oxon, and *d.* 11 Oct. 1877, at Brighton, in her 87th year.

IX. 1832. Sir Henry Boynton, Bart. [1618], of Burton Agnes aforesaid, br. and h., being posthumous s. of the 6th Bart., *b.* 22 March 1778, in St. James street, Midx.; ed. at Eton and at Trin. Coll., Cambridge; B.A., 6 July 1799; M.A., 1803; *suc. to the Baronetcy*, 14 Nov. 1832. He *m.* 1 Jan. 1810, Mary, da. of Capt. (—) Gray, by (—), sister of William Watson, of Dover, Capt. R.N. He *d.* 28 Aug. 1854, at Burton Agnes, aged 76. His widow *d.* 26 June 1877, aged 90, in Manor street, Bridlington Quay.

X. 1854. Sir Henry Boynton, Bart. [1618], of Burton Agnes aforesaid, s. and h. *b.* 2 March 1811, at Nafferton Hall, East Riding, co. York; *suc. to the Baronetcy*, 28 Aug. 1854. He *m.* firstly, 2 Nov. 1833, Louisa, 2d da. of the abovenamed Walter Strickland, of Cokethorpe Park, Oxon., by his 1st wife. She *d.* s.p. He *m.* secondly, 7 Feb. 1843, Harriet, 2d da. of Thomas Lightfoot, of Sevenoaks, Kent and Old Burlington street, Midx. He *d.* 25 June 1869, at Burton Agnes aforesaid, aged 58. His widow *d.* 13 Sep. 1889, at the Mount, York.

XI. 1869. Sir Henry Somerville Boynton, Bart. [1618], of Burton Agnes aforesaid, only s. and h., by 2d wife, *b.* 23 June 1844, at Burton Agnes, ed. at Mag. Coll., Cambridge; *suc. to the Baronetcy*, 25 June 1869. He *m.* 27 July 1876, at St. James,' Westm., Mildred Augusta, da. of the Rev. Thomas Bradley Paget, Vicar of Welton, co. York, and Canon of York, by Sophia, da. of Sir Edmund Beckett, 4th Bart. He *d.* s.p.m.,(a) at Burton Agnes aforesaid, 11 and was *bur.* there 14 April 1899, in his 55th year. Will pr. at £76,698 gross and £65,620 personalty net. His widow living 1899.

XII. 1899. Sir Griffith Henry Boynton, Bart. [1618], of Burton Agnes aforesaid, cousin and h. male, being s. and h. of the Rev. Griffith Boynton, Rector of Barmston aforesaid (1860-98), by Selina, 3d da. of William Watkins, of Badby House, co. Northampton, which Griffith, last named (who *d.* 19 May 1898, aged 82), was 2d s. of the 9th Bart. He was *b.* 31 May 1849, and *suc. to the Baronetcy*, 11 April 1899.

Family Estates.—These, in 1883, consisted of 9,300 acres in the East Riding of Yorkshire, valued at £10,000 a year. *Residence.*—Burton Agnes Hall, near Hull.

(a) To his only da. and h., Cicel Mabel, b. 1 May 1877, he left considerable property, and directed that her future husband should, if a commoner, take the name of Boynton.

LYTTELTON, *or* LITTLETON:

cr. 25 June 1618,

sometime, 1757—1779, Barons Lyttelton of Franckley,

afterwards, since 1779, Barons Westcote of Ballymore [I.],

and, since 1794 (again), Barons Lyttelton of Franckley,

being finally, since 1889, Viscounts Cobham.

I. 1618. "Thomas Littleton, of Franckley, co. Worcester, Esq.," s. and h. of John Littleton, of the same, by Muriel (mar. lic. 12 Dec. 1590), da. of Sir Thomas Bromley, Lord Chancellor (1579-87), was *b.* about 1593; suc. his father (who was convicted of high treason, 20 Feb. 1600/1, and whose attainder was not reversed till 1 Jac. I) on 25 July 1601; matric. at Oxford (Ball. Coll.), 22 June 1610, aged 14; B.A. (Broadgates Hall), 2 July 1614; admitted to the Inner Temple, 1613; was *cr. a Bart.*, as above, 25 June 1618, being, shortly afterwards, *Knighted* at Whitehall, 3 Nov. 1618.(b) He was M.P. for Worcestershire, 1621-22, 1624-25, 1625, 1626, and April to May 1640. Compounded 23 Oct. 1644; fined £4,000, 6 May 1645; was an active Royalist and Colonel of all the troops raised in Worcestershire, but was taken prisoner in 1645, at Bewdley, and sent to the Tower, his estate being sequestrated and his seat at Frankley (garrisoned by Prince Rupert), being burnt. He *m.* Catharine, da. and h. of Sir Thomas Crompton, of Driffield, co. York, and of Hounslow, Midx., by Muriel, sister of Henry, 1st Viscount Falkland, [S.], da. of Sir Edward Carey, of Aldenham, Herts. He *d.* 22 Feb. 1649/50, aged 57, at Newcastle House, Clerkenwell, Midx. His widow *d.*, "full of yeares and good workes," 24 June 1666. Both *bur.* in Worcester Cathedral. M.I.

II. 1650. Sir Henry Lyttelton, Bart. [1618], of Hagley Park, co. Worcester, s. and h.; *b.* about 1624; matric. at Oxford (Ball. Coll.), 12 Sep. 1640, aged 16; *suc. to the Baronetcy*, 22 Feb. 1649/50. He fought on the King's side in the battle of Worcester, 3 Sep. 1651, and was taken prisoner. Was Sheriff of Worcestershire, 1654-55, and was, after the Restoration, M.P. for Lichfield, Feb. 1678 to Jan. 1679, and March to July 1679. He *m.* firstly, Philadelphia, da. and coheir of Robert (Carey), 2d Earl of Monmouth, by Martha, da. of Lionel (Cranfield), Earl of Middlesex. She, who had been Maid of Honour to Katharine, the Queen Consort, *d.* s.p., of a fever, 2 Aug. 1663, æt. 32, at Tunbridge, Kent, and was *bur.* in the church there. M.I. He *m.* secondly, Elizabeth, 1st da. of Francis (Newport), 1st Earl of Bradford, by Diana, da. of Francis (Russell), Earl of Bedford. He *d.* s.p. 24 June 1693, aged 69, at Over Arley, co. Stafford, and was *bur.* there. M.I. Will pr. 1693. His widow *m.* Edward Harvey, of Combe, co. Surrey.

III. 1693. Sir Charles Lyttelton, Bart. [1618], of Hagley Park aforesaid, br. and h., *b.* 1629. He was likewise an active Royalist, and was at the siege of Colchester; imprisoned in the Tower, but escaped to France, where, in 1650, he was Cupbearer to Charles II; was *Knighted* about 1662; was a Major in the Army, 5 Nov. 1664; Lieut. Col., 15 July 1665; Colonel, 15 Feb. 1668; distinguished himself at Solebay (1672) and at Maestricht (1676), being then a Brigadier General; was Lieut. Gov. of Jamaica, 1662; Gov., 1663-64; Gov. of Harwich and Languard Fort, 1667-52; Gov. of Sheerness, 1680; M.P. for Bewdley, 1685-87, but resigned all his places at the Revolution, retiring to Sheen, in Surrey, till he *suc. to the Baronetcy*, and the family estates, 24 June 1693. He *m.* firstly, Catharine, widow of (—) Lister, da. of Sir William Fairfax, of Steeton, co. York. She *d.* s.p.s. 26 Jan. 1662, and was *bur.* in the Rod Church, Jamaica. M.I. He *m.* secondly (Lic. Vic. Gen., 23 May 1666, he 36 and she 17), Anne, sister and coheir of Richard Temple, of Frankton, co. Warwick, da. of Thomas Temple, of the same, by Rebecca, da. of

(a) Lineal descendant and heir male of the celebrated Sir Thomas Lyttelton, K.B., one of the Judges of the Court of Common Pleas, author of the "*treatise on tenures*," who *d.* at Frankley, Aug. 1481, at a great age. The Judge was a *maternal* descendant of that family, being s. of Thomas Westcote, Eschaetor of Worcestershire, 29 Hen. VI, who, having *m.* Elizabeth, da. and h. of Thomas Lyttelton, of Frankley, took the name of Lyttelton.

(b) See p. 18, note "c," *sub* "Tollemache."

Sir Nicholas Carew, of Beddington, Surrey. He *d.* at Hagley, 2 May 1716, in his 87th year, and was *bur.* at Over Arley. M.I. Will pr. Feb. 1717. His widow *d.* 22 Aug. 1718.

IV. 1716. Sir Thomas Lyttelton, Bart. [1618], of Hagley Park, aforesaid, only surv. s. and h., by 2d wife; *suc. to the Baronetcy*, 2 May 1716; M.P. for Worcester in three Parls., March 1721 to 1734, and for Camelford, 1734-41; one of the Lords of the Admiralty, 1727-1741. He *m.* 8 May 1708, Christian, sister to Richard, 1st Viscount Cobham, so *cr.* 23 May 1718 (with a spec. rem. of that dignity in favour, ultimately, of the heirs male of his said sister's body), da. of Sir Richard Temple, 3d Bart. [1611], of Stowe, by Mary, da. and coheir of Henry Knapp. She was Maid of Honour to Queen Anne. He *d.* 14 Sep. 1751, and was *bur.* at Hagley. Will dat. 4 March 1750, pr. 20 Nov. 1751.

V. 1751. Sir George Lyttelton, Bart. [1618], of Hagley Park, aforesaid, *bap.* 17 Jan. 1708/9, at St. James', Westm.; matric. at Oxford (Ch. Ch.), 11 Feb. 1725/6; M.P. for Okehampton in four Parls., March 1735 to 1756; Prin. Sec. to the Prince of Wales, 1737; a Lord of the Treasury, 1744-54; *suc. to the Baronetcy*, 14 Sep. 1751; P.C. 1754; Cofferer of the Household, 1754-55; Chancellor of the Exchequer and one of the Commissioners of the Treasury, Nov. 1755 to Nov. 1756, being *cr.* 18 Nov. 1756, BARON LYTTELTON OF FRANCKLEY, co. Worcester. F.S.A. He *m.* firstly, June 1742, Lucy, sister of Matthew, 2d Baron Fortescue of Castle Hill, da. of Hugh Fortescue, of Filleigh, co. Devon, by his 2d wife, Lucy, da. of Matthew (Aylmer), 1st Baron Aylmer of Balrath [I.]. She *d.* 19 Jan. 1746/7, aged 29, and was *bur.* at Over Arley, co. Stafford. M.I. at Hagley. He *m.* secondly, 10 Aug. 1749, Elizabeth (then aged 33, with a fortune of £20,000), da. of Field Marshal Sir Robert Rich, 4th Bart. [1676], by (—), da. and coheir of Col. (—) Griffin, Clerk to the Board of Green Cloth. He *d.* of inflammation of the bowels, 22 Aug. 1773, aged 64, at Hagley, and was *bur.* there. M.I. Will pr. 1772. His widow *d.* s.p. in Portugal street, 17 Sep. 1795. Will pr. Sep. 1795.

VI. 1773. Thomas (Lyttelton, 2d Baron Lyttelton of Franckley [1756], and 6th Baronet [1618], s. and h., by 1st wife; *b.* 30 Jan. 1744; *suc. to the Peerage and Baronetcy*, 22 Aug. 1773 and *d.* s.p. 27 Nov. 1779, when the *Peerage* became *extinct*, but the Baronetcy devolved as below.

VII. 1779. William Henry (Lyttelton), Baron Westcote of Ballymore [I.], uncle and h. male, being 4th s. of the 4th Bart., *b.* 24 Jan. 1724/5, and was *cr.* 29 April 1776, BARON WESTCOTE(a) OF BALLYMORE, co. Longford [I.] He *suc. to the Baronetcy*, 27 Nov. 1779. He was *cr.* 13 Aug. 1794, LORD LYTTELTON, BARON OF FRANCKLEY, co. Worcester. In these Peerages, this *Baronetcy* became *merged* and so continued till the 5th Baron succeeded, 26 March 1889, as VISCOUNT COBHAM. See *Peerage*, under the Barony of Lyttelton, and, after 1889, under the Viscountcy of Cobham.

[VI.–VII.:] See fuller particulars in *Peerage*.

LEIGH:

cr. 24 Dec. 1618,

afterwards, 1628-44, Baron Dunsmore,

and subsequently, 1644-53, Earl of Chichester;

ex. 21 Dec. 1653.

I. 1618, to 1653. "Francis Leigh, of Newneham Regis, co. Warwick, Knt.," s. and h. of Sir Francis Leigh, K.B., of the same, by Mary, da. of Thomas (Egerton), Viscount Brackley (better known as Lord Chancellor Ellesmere); was *Knighted* at Newmarket, Jan. 1612/3, and *cr. a Bart.*, as above, 24 Dec. 1618. M.P. for Warwick, 1625 and 1626.

(a) See p. 117, note "a," as to the paternal descent of the family from Westcote.

He *m.* firstly, 31 July 1617, at St. Dunstan's, Stepney, Susan Banning, widow, of St. Gabriel's, Fenchurch, da. and h. of Richard Northam. She *d.* s.p. shortly afterwards. He *m.* secondly, in 1618, Audrey, widow of Sir Francis Anderson (who *d.* 22 Dec. 1616), sister and coheir of William (Boteler), Lord Boteler of Brantfield, being 1st da. of John, 1st Lord Boteler, by Elizabeth, sister of the celebrated favourite George, Duke of Buckingham, da. of Sir George Villiers. After this alliance his advance was rapid. She was living when he was *cr.*, 31 July 1628, BARON DUNSMORE, co. Warwick, and when, subsequently, he was *cr.*, 3 June 1644, EARL OF CHICHESTER, both with a spec. rem. In these peerages this *Baronetcy merged* in 1628, till on his death s.p.m. 21 Dec. 1653, *it* (together with the Barony of Dunsmore) became *extinct*. See *Peerage*, *sub* "Chichester."

BURDETT:

cr. 25 Feb. 1618/9.

I. 1619. "Thomas Burdett, of Bramcott, co. Warwick, Esq.," s. and h. of Robert Burdett, of the same, by Mary, da. of Thomas Wilson, D.D., Dean of Durham and Sec. of State, was *b.* 3 Aug. 1585; suc. his father, 27 March 1603; matric. at Oxford (Ball. Coll.), 6 May 1603, aged 18; was Sheriff of Derbyshire, 1610-11, and was *cr. a Bart.*, as above, 25 Feb. 1618/9. He *m.*, in 1602, Jane, da. and h. of William Francis, of Foremark (near Repton), co. Derby, by Elizabeth, da. of William Francis, of Ticknall. He *d.* about 1647, and was *bur.* at Repton. Will pr. 22 May 1647. His widow afforded an asylum at Bramcote to Archbishop Sheldon during the exile of Charles II. She was *bur.* at Repton.

II. 1647? Sir Francis Burdett, Bart [1619], of Foremark aforesaid, s. and h.; *b.* 10 Sep. 1608; matric. at Oxford (Linc. Coll.), 31 Oct. 1628, aged 20; Barrister (Inner Temple) 1637; *suc. to the Baronetcy* about 1647; was Sheriff of Derbyshire, 1649-50. He *m.*, 1635, Elizabeth, da. of Sir John Walter, Lord Chief Baron of the Exchequer, by Margaret, da. of William Offley. They, who were renowned for their hospitality and charity, rebuilt and re-endowed the church at Foremark. He *d.* 30 Dec. 1696, in his 89th year, and was *bur.* at Repton. M.I. Will pr. 8 Feb. 1697. His widow, who was *b.* Sep. 1613, *d.* 17 April 1701, in her 88th year. Her will pr. 14 May 1701. Both were *bur.* at Foremark. M.I.

III. 1696. Sir Robert Burdett, Bart. [1619], of Foremark aforesaid, s. and h., *b.* 11 Jan. 1640; matric. at Oxford (Queen's Coll.) 21 March 1658/9; admitted to Gray's Inn, 1662; M.P. for Warwickshire, 1679 and 1679-81, and for Lichfield, in three Parls., 1689-98; *suc. to the Baronetcy*, 30 Dec. 1696. He *m.* firstly, Mary, da. of Gervase Pigot, of Thrumpton, Notts, by (—), da. and coheir of John St. Andrew, of Gotham, in that county. She *d.* s.p.m. 31 Aug. 1668, in her 27th year. He *m.* secondly, Magdalen, da. of Sir Thomas Aston, 1st Bart. [1628], of Aston, by his 2d wife, Anne, da. and h. of Sir Henry Willoughby, Bart. [1611], of Risley. He *m.* thirdly, Mary, da. of Thomas Brome, of Croxhall, co. Derby. He *d.* 18 Jan. 1715/6, in his 76th year. His last wife, by whom he had no surviving issue, survived him.

III.(*bis*) 1716. Walter Burdett, of the Inner Temple, London, Barrister, and afterwards of Knoyle Hill, co. Derby, is said to have *assumed the Baronetcy* during the pregnancy of the mother of the 4th Bart. He *d.* 1732.

IV. 1716. Sir Robert Burdett, Bart. [1619], of Foremark aforesaid, grandson and h., being posthumous s. and h. of Robert Burdett, by Elizabeth, da. of William (Tracy), 4th Viscount Tracy of Rathcoole [I.], which

Robert last named was s. and h. ap. of the 3d Bart., but *d.* v.p. 2 Jan. 1715/6, a few days before him. He was *b.* 28 May 1716, and *suc. to the Baronetcy* at his birth; matric. at Oxford (New Coll.) 13 April 1733, aged 16; was *cr.* D.C.L., 14 April 1749; M.P. for Tamworth, in three Parls. 1748-68. He *m* firstly, 6 Nov. 1739, Elizabeth, da. of Sir Charles SEDLEY, of Southfleet, by (—), da. and h. of (—) COLLINGE, of Nutball, Notts. She *d.* 24 Aug. 1747. Admon Jan. 1812. He *m.* secondly, 17 July 1753, Caroline, widow of Sir Henry HARPUR, 5th Bart., da. of John (MANNERS), 2d DUKE OF RUTLAND, by his 2d wife, Lucy, da. of Bennet (SHERARD), 2d BARON SHERARD OF LEITRIM [I.]. She, by whom he had no issue, *d.* 10 Nov. 1769, at Foremark Will pr. Jan. 1770. He *d.* 13 Feb. 1797. Will pr. May 1797.

V. 1797. SIR FRANCIS BURDETT, Bart. [1619], of Foremark aforesaid, and of Ramsbury Manor, Wilts, grandson and h., being s. and h. of Francis BURDETT, by Eleanor, da. and coheir of William JONES, of Ramsbury Manor aforesaid, which Francis last named was s. and h. ap. of the 4th Bart., but *d.* v.p. 3 Feb. 1794, aged 50. He was *b.* 25 Jan. 1770; ed. at Westm. School and at Ch. Ch. Oxford; matric. 13 Dec. 1785, aged 15; *suc. to the Baronetcy,* 13 Feb. 1797; was M.P. for Boroughbridge, 1796-1802; for Midx., 1802 till void July 1804, and again, March 1805 till void Feb. 1806; for Westminster, in nine Parls., 1807-37, and (in the Conservative interest) for North Wilts in two Parls., 1837 till his death in 1844; well known in his early career as a leading politician and advocate for reform, he was imprisoned in the Tower, 1810, for a breach of parliamentary privilege, and, in 1819, was fined £1,000 for a libel on the Government and imprisoned for three months. He *m.*, 5 Aug. 1793, Sophia, yst. da. of Thomas COUTTS, of the Strand, Midx., the well known banker, by his 1st wife, Susan, da. of (—) STARKIE. She, who had long been an invalid, *d.* 12 Jan. 1844, at 25 St. James' Place, where (nine days afterwards) he *d.* 23 Jan. 1844 (within two days of his birthday of 74), both being bur. on the same day at Ramsbury.(a) His will pr. March, and hers April 1844.

VI. 1844. SIR ROBERT BURDETT, BART. [1619], of Foremark and Ramsbury aforesaid, s. and h., *b.* 26 April 1796, in Piccadilly, St. Geo. Han. sq.; matric. at Oxford (Bras. Coll.), 23 June 1813, aged 17; Col. in the Army; *suc. to the Baronetcy,* 23 Jan. 1844; Sheriff of Derbyshire, 1848. He *d.* unm. 7 June 1880,(b) at his chambers in the Albany, Piccadilly, aged 84. Admon. 14 Aug. 1880.

VII. 1880. SIR FRANCIS BURDETT, Bart. [1619], of Foremark and Ramsbury aforesaid, and of Ancaster House, in Richmond, co. Surrey, cousin and h. male, being s. and h. of William Jones BURDETT, of Copt Hall in Twickenham, Midx., by Sarah Holmes (who, in 1807, when unm., took the name of BRENT), da. of Capt. HODGKINSON, R.N., which William (who *d.* 2 Oct. 1840, aged 68) was yr. br. of the 5th Bart. He was *b.* 23 March 1813; ed. at Charterhouse School and at Trin. Coll., Cambridge; entered the Army, 1834, being sometime Lieut. Col. 17th Lancers; *suc. to the Baronetcy,* 7 June 1880; Sheriff of Surrey, 1880. He *m.* firstly, 22 Oct. 1842, Amelia Eliza, da. of Major James SHARP, of Kincarrathie, co. Perth. She *d.* s.p.m. 14 April 1866. He *m.* secondly, 22 Aug. 1867, Mary Dorothy, da. of John SMYTH, of Cleatlam, co. Durham. He *d.* 31 May 1892, at his daughter's house, 6 Chesham Place, and was *bur.* at Foremark, aged 79. Will pr. at £80,613 gross, and £69,304 net. His widow living 1899.

(a) Their 5th and yst. da., Angela Georgina, *b.* 25 April 1814, inherited the greater part of the large fortune of her maternal grandfather (Thomas Coutts) under the will of his 2d wife and widow, Harriet, da. of Matthew Mellon, once a celebrated actress, who had remarried, 16 June 1827 (as his second wife) the Duke of St. Albans, and who *d.* s.p. 6 Aug. 1837. She accordingly took the additional name of Coutts, and was *cr.*, 9 June 1871, Baroness Burdett-Coutts.

(b) He was a petitioner for the termination, in his favour, of the abeyance of the Barony of Scales, of which he was a coheir (representing, however, but a small fraction), through the families of Tracy, Devereux, Withipool, Cornwallis, Nevill Lord Latimer), Vere, Howard, and Scales.

VIII. 1892. SIR FRANCIS BURDETT, Bart. [1619], only s. and h., by 2d wife, *b.* 1869; ed. at Eton and Trin. Coll., Cambridge; Lieut. 4th Dragoon Guards, 17th Lancers; *suc. to the Baronetcy,* 8 May 1892.

Family Estates.—These, in 1883, consisted of 5,923 acres in Derbyshire (worth £12,065 a year), 6,541 in Berkshire, 3,958 in Wilts, 2,258 in Leicestershire, 1,885 in Warwickshire, and 419 in Staffordshire. *Total,* 20,984 acres, worth £29,385 a year. *Principal Residence.*—Foremark Hall, near Repton, Derbyshire, and Ramsbury Manor, Wilts.

MORTON:
cr. 1 March 1618/9;
ex. 8 Jan. 1698/9.

I. 1619. "GEORGE MORTON, of St. Andrewes, Milborne, co. Dorset, Esq.," s. and h. of Sir George MORTON, of Milborne, St. Andrew's aforesaid, by Joan, da. of (—) HOLLOWAY, of Walton, suc. his father in 1611, and was *cr. a Bart.,* as above, 1 Mar. 1618/9. He was M.P. for Dorset, 1626, and was a faithful Royalist. He *m.* firstly Catharine, da. of Sir Arthur HOPTON, of Witham, co. Somerset. He *m.* secondly Anne, widow of Sir Rotherham WILLOUGHBY (who *d.* in or before July 1634), da. of Sir Richard WORTLEY, of Wortley, co. York, by Elizabeth, da of Edward BOUGHTON. He *d.* 1661. Will pr. 1671.

II. 1611, to 1699. SIR JOHN MORTON, Bart. [1619], of Milborne St. Andrew's aforesaid, s. and h., by 2d wife, was *b.* about 1627; Gent. of the Privy Chamber, 1660; *suc. to the Baronetcy* in 1661; was M.P. for Poole, 1661-79; for Weymouth and Melcomb Regis (in four Parls.), 1679-90. He *m.* firstly, before 1664, Eleanor, da. of John FOUNTAIN, Serjeant at Law (1658). She *d.* 1671, s.p.m., and was *bur.* at Milborne. He *m.* secondly (Lic. Vic. Gen., 24 Feb. 1675/6, he above 40, widower, and she of Mudge Hall, Wilts, about 25, spinster) Elizabeth da. of the Rev. Benjamin CULME, D.D., Dean of St. Patrick's, Ireland, by Deborah, da. of Sir Charles PLEYDELL, of Mudge Hall aforesaid. He *d.* s.p.m. 8 Jan. 1698/9, aged 71, and was *bur.* at Milborne when the *Baronetcy* became *extinct.* M.I. Will dat. 22 Oct. 1697, pr. 20 May 1699. His widow *d.* 15 Sep. 1715 in her 70th year, and was *bur.* at Milborne aforesaid. M.I. Will pr. Nov. 1715.

HERVEY, *or* HERVY:
cr. 31 May 1619,(a)
afterwards, 1620-42, BARON HERVEY OF ROSSE [I.],
being subsequently, 1628-42, BARON HERVEY OF KIDBROOKE [E.];
ex. July 1642.

I. 1619, to 1642. WILLIAM HERVEY, of St. Martin's in the Fields, co. Middlesex, Knt.," s. and h. of Henry HERVEY (a yr. s. of Sir Nicholas HERVEY, of Ickworth, co. Suffolk), by Jane, da. of John THOMAS, of Llanvihangell, signalized himself in the action against the Armada,

(a) This is the date of the patent as in Dugdale's *List,* and elsewhere, but it is not enrolled; the date of the signet bill for the creation (one, of course, a few days in advance thereof) is the one given in the list of *Creations, 1483—1646,* in ap. 47th Rep. D.K. Pub. Records. This Baronetcy is one of no less than ten of this period not so enrolled, which are similarly dealt with in that work, the dates given therein (as below) being that of the signet bills, viz., (1) Hervey, 29 May 1619; (2) Mackworth, 29 May 1619; (3) Villiers, 15 July 1619; (4) Ley, 15 July 1619; (6) Hickes, 18 July 1619; (7) Beaumont [fragment, no date]; (8) Dryden, 11 Nov. 1619; (9) Forster, 4 March 1619/20; and (10) Chester, 12 March 1619/20. Another contemporary Baronetcy, which also was not so enrolled, *viz.,* that of Foulis, in Feb. 1619/20, is given in that work on the authority of the receipt of the creation money.

was *Knighted* at Cadiz (by the Earl of Essex), 27 June 1596; served afterwards in Ireland; was M.P. for Horsham, 1601, and for Petersfield, 1604-11, and was *cr. a Bart.,* as above, 31 May 1619,(a) "for life, with reversion to his son, WILLIAM HERVY, Esq., and the heirs male of his body; rem. to any other heirs male of the body of the said William, the father and the heirs male of their bodies."(b) He *m.* firstly, May 1597, Mary, Dow. COUNTESS OF SOUTHAMPTON, widow of Sir Thomas HENEAGE, and formerly of Henry (WRIOTHESLEY), 2d EARL OF SOUTHAMPTON, da. of Anthony (BROWNE), 1st VISCOUNT MONTAGU, by his 1st wife, Jane, da. of Robert (RATCLIFFE), EARL OF SUSSEX. She, by whom he had no issue, *d.* 1607. Will dat. 22 April, pr. 14 Nov. 1607. He *m.* secondly, 5 Feb. 1607, Cordell, da. of Brian ANNESLEY, of Lee and Kidbrooke, co. Kent, gentleman-pensioner, by Audrey, da of (—) TIRRELL, of co. Essex, Warden of the Fleet Prison. She was living when he was *cr.,* 5 Aug. 1620, BARON HERVEY OF ROSSE, co. Wexford [I.], and subsequently, 27 Feb. 1627/8, BARON HERVEY OF KIDBROOKE, co. Kent [E.] In these peerages this *Baronetcy* then *merged* and so continued till, on his death s.p.m.s., in July 1642, it and all his other honours became *extinct.*

MACKWORTH:
cr. 4 June 1619(a);
ex. 1 Aug. 1803.

I. 1619. "THOMAS MACKWORTH, of Normanton, co. Rutland, Esq.," s. and h. of George MACKWORTH, of the same, by his 1st wife, Grace, da. of Ralph ROKEBY. Serjeant at Law; was Sheriff of Rutland, 1599—1600, 1598/9 and 1609-10, and was *cr. a Bart.,* as above, 4 June 1619.(a) He *m.* Margaret, da. of Henry HALL, of Gretford, co. Lincoln, and sole h. to her mother (—), da. and coheir of Francis NEALE, of Tugby, in the said county. He *d.* March 1625/6. Admon. 10 May 1626.

II. 1626. SIR HENRY MACKWORTH, Bart. [1619], of Normanton aforesaid, s. and h., *suc. to the Baronetcy* in March 1625/6. Sheriff of Rutland, 1627-28. He re-built the manor house at Normanton. He *m.* Mary, widow of Sir Thomas HARTOPP, sister and coheir of Ralph, BARON HOPTON OF STRATTON, da. of Robert HOPTON, of Witham, Somerset, by Jane, da. and h. of Rowland KEMEYS, of Vaudry, co. Monmouth. He *d.* Aug. 1640. Will pr. 1640.

III. 1640. SIR THOMAS MACKWORTH, Bart. [1619], of Normanton and Empingham aforesaid, s. and h.; *suc. to the Baronetcy* in Aug. 1640; was fined as a delinquent, 9 March 1647/8; Sheriff of Rutland, 1666-67, and M.P. thereof (in five Parls.), 1679 to 1694. He *m.* firstly, Dorothy, da. of Capt. George DARELL, of Calehill, Kent. She *d.* s.p.m. He *m.* secondly Anne, da. of Humphrey MACKWORTH, of Betton, Salop, by his 1st wife, Anne, da. of Thomas WALLER, of Beaconsfield, Bucks. He *d.* Nov. 1694. Will pr. 1695.

IV. 1694. SIR THOMAS MACKWORTH, Bart. [1619], of Normanton and Empingham aforesaid, only surv. s. and h. by second marriage; *suc. to the Baronetcy,* Nov. 1694; M.P. for Rutland, 1694-95, and, in four Parls., 1701-08; for Portsmouth, 1713-15, and for Rutland, again, 1721-27. Sheriff of that county, 1696-7. He *d.* unm. Feb. 1744/5.(c) Will pr. 1745.

V. 1745. SIR THOMAS MACKWORTH, Bart. [1619], of Huntingdon, cousin and h. male, being only s. and h. of Robert Mackworth, of Huntingdon, by Mary, da. of William DOWSE of Huntingdon aforesaid merchant, which Robert was 2d s. of Robert Mackworth, of Empingham aforesaid (*d.* 1 Feb.

(a) No patent is enrolled, but the signet bill exists. See p. 121, note "a," *sub* "Hervey."

(b) *Creations,* 1483—1646, in ap. 47th Rep. D.K. Pub. Records.

(c) John WINGFIELD, of Tickencote, co. Rutland, grandson of his half sister, Dorothy, became eventually his sole representative.

1717/8, aged 95), 2d s. of the 2d Bart. He was an apothecary at Huntingdon, and Alderman of that borough. He *suc. to the Baronetcy,* but to none of the estates in Feb. 1744/5. He *m.* firstly, about 1737, Elizabeth, da. of John MAULE, of Ecton, co. Northampton. She *d.* s.p.m. He *m.* secondly Mary, widow of Rev. (—) WALLER, of Great Stoughton, co. Huntingdon, da. of Rev. Leonard RERESBY, of Thribergh, co. York, but had no issue by her. He *d.* 17 Oct. 1769.

VI. 1769. SIR HENRY MACKWORTH, Bart. [1619], cousin and h. male, being s. and h. of Henry Mackworth, by Katharine, da. of (—) ROBERTS, of Empingham aforesaid, which Henry was s. and h. of another Henry Mackworth, the 3d s. of the 2d Bart. He *suc. to the Baronetcy,* 17 Oct. 1769. He *m.* Elizabeth, da. of Rev. Edward LAMB, Rector of Acle, co. Norfolk. He *d.* 14 Jan. 1774. Will pr. July 1774.

VII. 1774, to 1803. SIR HENRY MACKWORTH, Bart. [1619], s. and h., *b.* about 1728; *suc. to the Baronetcy,* 14 Jan. 1774. He was admitted, 7 Nov. 1786, as one of the Almsmen in the Charter House, London, where he *d.* s.p. 1 being *bur.* there 5 Aug. 1803, aged 75, when the *Baronetcy* became *extinct.*

GREY:
cr. 15 June, 1619,(a)
afterwards, 1624-1706, BARONS GREY OF WERKE,
and *sometime,* 1695-1701, EARL OF TANKERVILLE;
ex. 20 June 1706.

I. 1619. "WILLIAM GREY, Esq., s. and h. of Sir Ralph GREY, of Chillingham, co. Northumberland, Knt.,"(b) by Isabel, da. and h. of Sir Thomas GREY, of Horton, co. Northumberland, was *cr. a Bart.,* 15 June 1619.(a) Having suc. to the estates of Chillingham and Werke, he was *cr.,* 11 Feb. 1623/4 BARON GREY OF WERKE, co. Northumberland, in which peerage this *Baronetcy merged* (the 3d Baron being *cr.,* 11 June 1695, EARL OF TANKERVILLE, a dignity which became *extinct* at his death, 24 June 1701), till the death unm. of the 4th Baron and Baronet, 20 June 1706, when *all his dignities* became *extinct.* See *Peerage.*

VILLIERS:
cr. 19 July 1619(c);
ex. 27 Feb. 1711/2.

I. 1619. "WILLIAM VILLIERS, of Broukesby [*i.e.,* Brokesby], co. Leicester, Esq.," brother, of the half blood, of George, DUKE OF BUCKINGHAM, (the celebrated favourite of James I), being s. and b.(d) of Sir George

(a) This is the date of the patent as in Dugdale's *List* and elsewhere, but it is not enrolled. Neither is there any signet bill, so that it is not given in the list of *Creations 1483—1646* in ap. 47 Rep. D.K. Pub. Records. It is one of four creations of that period similarly omitted, viz. (1), Grey, 15 June 1619; (2) Salisbury, 10 Nov. 1619; (3) Mill, 31 Dec. 1619; and (4) Phelipps, 16 Feb. 1619/20. See p. 107, note "c," as to "Blakiston," *cr.* 27 May 1615, and p. 80, note "a," as to four Baronetcies *cr.* 24 Sep. 1611, all five of which (like these four) are similarly omitted.

(b) So described in Collins' *Baronetage.*

(c) No patent is enrolled, but the signet bill exists. See p. 121, note "a," *sub* "Hervey."

(d) He was the eldest of five brothers, of whom the 2d, Sir Edward Villiers, was ancestor of the Earls of Jersey; the 3d (eldest of the half blood), John, was *cr.* Viscount Purbeck; the 4th, George, was *cr.* Duke of Buckingham; and the 5th, Christopher, was *cr.* Earl of Anglesey.

VILLIERS, of Brokesby aforesaid, by his *first* wife Audrey, da. and h. of William SAUNDERS, of Harrington, co. Northampton, was *b.* about 1575; suc. his father, 4 Jan. 1605; was Sheriff of Leicestershire, 1608-09; and was *cr. a Bart.*, as above, 19 July 1619.(a) He in 1628 acquired the estate (11,614 acres) of Dromahaire in the English plantation of Leitrim,(b) and is said to have refused a peerage. He *m.* firstly, Anne, da. of Sir Edward GRIFFIN, **K.B.**, of Dingley and Braybrooke, co. Northampton, by Lucy, da. of Reginald CONYERS. She *d.* s.p.m. He *m.* secondly, about 1614, Elizabeth (not Anne), da. of Richard (Fiennes), LORD SAY AND SELE, by his 1st wife, Constance, da. of Sir Richard KINGSMILL. She *d.* s.p.m. He *m.* thirdly, before 1618, Rebecca, 2d da. of Robert ROPER, of Heanor, co. Derby, by Elizabeth, da. of William NOTT, of Imber court in Thames Ditton, Surrey. He *d.* 12 June 1629, aged 54. Will of that date, pr. 27 Aug. 1629. His widow, who was *bap.* at St. Peter's, Derby, 17 Jan. 1590/1, *m.* Francis CAVE, of Ingarsby, co. Leic., Capt. of Horse in the army of Charles I, who *d.* at Brokesby, 1646. She, who retained Brokesby Hall for her life, *d.* a widow 1661.

II. 1629. SIR GEORGE VILLIERS, Bart. [1619], of Goadby Marwood, co. Leicester, and afterwards [1661], of Brokesby aforesaid, only s. and h. by 3d wife, *b.* Feb. 1619/20; *suc. to the Baronetcy*, 12 June 1629. He was a staunch Royalist, and suffered much in that cause. He *m.* 17 June 1641, at Boarstall, Bucks, Margaret, 3d da. of Sir George DYNHAM of Boarstall, by Penelope, da. of Richard (WENMAN), 1st VISCOUNT WENMAN OF TUAM [I.]. She was *bur.* at Goadby, 24 July 1668. He *m.* secondly, Mary, da. of Thomas GOLDING, of Newhouse in Poslingford, Suffolk, by Frances, da. of Thomas BEDINGFIELD, of Darsham. He was living 11 Oct. 1681, but *d.* the next year. His widow *d.* s.p. suddenly in London 14 and was *bur.* 25 Nov. 1699 at Poslingford. Will dat. 4 Oct. and pr. 1 Dec. 1699.

III. 1682, to 1712. SIR WILLIAM VILLIERS, Bart. [1619], of Brokesby aforesaid, only s. and h. by 1st wife, *b.* 1645; *suc. to the Baronetcy* in 1682; was M.P. for Leicester, in two Parls., 1698-1701. He sold the estate of Brokesby to his wife's cousin, Sir Nathan Wright, retaining the manor and lands of Hoby in the same county of Leicester. He *m.*, 16 April 1668, at Chelsea (Lic. Fac., he 22 and she 20), Ann, da. and h. of Charles POTTS, of Mannington, co. Norfolk, by Susanna, sister of Sir Benjamin WRIGHT, 1st Bart. [1661], of Cranham, Essex. She *d.* 31 July 1711. He *d.* s.p. seven months later, 27 Feb. 1711/2, aged 66, when the *Baronetcy* became *extinct*. Both were *bur.* at Brokesby. M.I. His will, as of St. Andrew's, Holborn, dat. 26 Feb. pr. 6 March 1711/2.

LEY:
cr. 20 July 1619(a);
afterwards, 1623-26, BARON LEY of Ley, co. Devon,
and subsequently, 1626-79, EARLS OF MARLBOROUGH;
ex. 1679.

I. 1619. "JAMES LEY, of Westbury, co. Wilts, Knt.," 6th and yst. s. of Henry LEY, of Teffont Ewyas, Wilts (*d.* 7 June 1574), by Dyonisia DE ST. MAYNE, was *b.* there 1552; ed. at Brasenose Coll., Oxford; B.A., 3 Feb. 1573/3; Barrister (Lincoln's Inn), 11 Oct. 1584; Bencher, 1600; was M.P. for Westbury, 1597-98, 1604-05, and 1609-10; for Bath, 1614; for Westbury (again), 1621; was Justice of Carmarthen, Pembroke, and Cardigan, June 1603; *Knighted*, 8 Oct, 1603, at Wilton, Wilts; Serjeant at Law, Nov. 1603; Ch. Justice of the King's Bench in Ireland, 1603-08, being, from April to Nov. 1605, a Commissioner of the Great Seal in Ireland. Returning to England he was made Attorney of the Court of Wards, Nov. 1608,

(a) No patent is enrolled, but the signet bill exists. See p. 121, note "a," *sub* "Hervey."

(b) This was sold, 3 March 1664/5, for a trifling sum by his son to Sir George Lane, afterwards Viscount Lanesborough [I.].

and was *cr. a Bart.*, as above, 20 July 1619(a). He was Ch. Justice of the King's Bench, 1621-24; Speaker of the House of Lords and Joint Commissioner of the Great Seal, May to July 1621; P.C., 1624; LORD HIGH TREASURER, 1624-28, during which period he was raised to the peerage as below. He *m.* firstly, before 1593, Mary, 1st da. of John PETTIE, of Stoke Talmage, Oxon, by Elizabeth, da. and h. of Thomas (or Edward) SNAPE, of Fawler, near Witney. By her he had eleven children. He *m.* secondly (Lic. Lond. 13 Feb. 1617/8, he 60 and she 40) Mary, widow of Sir William BOWYER, of Denham, Bucks, da. and coheir of Thomas PIERSON, Usher of the Court of Star Chamber. By her, who was *bur.* at Westbury aforesaid, 5 Oct. 1618, aged about 40, he had no issue. He *m.* thirdly, 4 July 1621, Jane (then aged 17), 3d da. of John (BOTELER), 1st BARON BOTELER OF BRANTFIELD by Elizabeth, sister (of the half blood) to George, DUKE OF BUCKINGHAM (the well known Court favourite), da. of Sir George VILLIERS. She was living when he was *cr.*, 31 Dec. 1625, BARON LEY of Ley, co. Devon, and when, a few weeks later, he was *cr.*, 5 Feb. 1625/6, EARL OF MARLBOROUGH. In these peerages the *Baronetcy merged* till on the death, 1679, of the 4th Earl and 4th Baronet, it and all his other honours, became *extinct*. See *Peerage*.

HICKS, *or* HICKES:
cr. 21 July 1619(a);
afterwards, since 1834, HICKS-BEACH.

I. 1619. "WILLIAM HICKS, of Beverston Castle, co. Gloucester," and also of Ruckholts, in the parish of Low Layton, Essex, only s. and h. of Sir Michael HICKES, of Beverstone aforesaid and of Witcombe, co. Glouc.; Secretary to the Lord Treasurer Burghley, by Elizabeth, relict of Henry PARVIS, of Buckholts aforesaid, da. of Gabriel COULSON, of London, and Low Layton aforesaid, merchants, was *b.* at his father's house on St. Peter's Hill, London, 1596, being named "William" after his godfather, the said LORD BURGHLEY; was ed. at Trin. Coll. Cambridge; suc. his father (who *d.* aged 65) 15 Aug. 1612, and was *cr. a Bart.*, as above, 21 July 1619(a). He was M.P. for Marlow, 1626; for Tewkesbury, 1628-29, and for Marlow, again, April to May 1640. He distinguished himself in the Royal cause, was imprisoned for six weeks by Parliament, and fined £1,000 in 1649. He *m.*, 8 Sep. 1620, at Drayton, Midx., Margaret, 1st da. of William (PAGET) 4th LORD PAGET OF BEAUDESERT, by Lettice, da. and coheir of Henry KNOLLYS. She *d.* at Westminster, and was *bur.* 10 Sep. 1652, in the Abbey there. He *d.* at Ruckholts aforesaid, 9 Oct. 1680, aged 84, and was *bur.* at Low Layton. M.I. Will dat. 9 Feb. 1677, pr. 15 Feb. 1680/1.

II. 1680. SIR WILLIAM HICKES, Bart. [1619], of Beverstone and Ruckholts aforesaid, s. and h., *b.* Dec. 1629; ed. at Trin. Coll., Cambridge; is said to have been *Knighted* at Ruckholts by Charles II; *suc. to the Baronetcy*, 9 Oct. 1680; Sheriff of Essex, 1684-85. He *m.* (Lic. Vic. Gen., 7 Feb. 1661/2, he 22 and she 21), Marthagnes, 1st da. and coheir of Sir Harry CONINGSBY, of the Wild in Shenley, Herts, by Hester, da. of Robert CAMBELL, Alderman and sometime [1630-31] Sheriff of London. He *d.* 22 April 1703, aged 73; *bur.* at Low Layton. M.I. Will pr 1702. His widow *d.* 1723, aged 80. Will pr. 1724.

III. 1703. SIR HENRY, *or* HARRY HICKES, Bart. [1619], of Ruckholts(b) aforesaid, s. and h., *b.* about 1666, being aged 21 in 1687; *suc. to the Baronetcy*, 22 April 1703. He *m.* firstly, Elizabeth, da. of Sir John HOLMES, Admiral R.N. She *d.* 14 Jan. 1705, aged 29; *bur.* at Low Layton. M.I. He *m.* secondly, before 1721, Barbara, da. of Joseph JOHNSON, of Walthamstow, Essex. She was *bur.* 8 Aug. 1746, at Low Layton. He *d.* 28 Oct. 1755, at his house called the Bowling Green, in Chigwell. Will dat. 25 Nov. 1754, pr. 11 Nov. 1755.

(a) No patent is enrolled, but the signet bill exists. See p. 121, note "a," *sub* "Hervey."

(b) He sold this estate, *circa* 1720, to Benjamin COLLIER, who resold it to EARL TYLNEY.

IV. 1755. SIR ROBERT HICKES, Bart. [1619], only s. and h. by second wife; *suc. to the Baronetcy*, 28 Oct. 1755. He was blind, and consequently disinherited by his father in favour of his younger br. Michael, whom however, he survived, when he inherited (March 1764) the estates. He *d.* unm. 1768.

V. 1768. SIR JOHN BAPTIST HICKES, Bart. [1619], cousin and h., being s. and h. of Charles Hickes of Kensington, by (—), da. of (—) CONINGSBY, which Charles was 2d s. of the 2d Bart., and *d.* 1760. He *suc. to the Baronetcy*, 1768. He *d.* s.p. 23 Nov. 1792.

VI. 1792. SIR HOWE HICKS, Bart. [1611], of Witcombe, co. Gloucester, cousin and h., being s. and h. of Howe HICKS, of the same (*d.* 1723), by Mary, da. of Jeffrey WATTS, of Essex, which Howe last named was s. and h. of Sir Michael Hicks, of Witcombe aforesaid (*m.* Aug. 1679 and *d.* 4 May 1710, aged 65), who was 2d s. of the 1st Bart. He was *b.* 8 Aug. 1722; *suc. to the Baronetcy*, 23 Nov. 1792. He *m.* 28 July 1739, at Bustleton, Martha, da. of Rev. John BROWNE, Rector of Coberley, co. Gloucester. He *d.* Aug. 1801, aged 79. Will pr. 1802.

VII. 1801. SIR WILLIAM HICKS, Bart. [1619], of Williamstrip Park, co. Gloucester, s. and h., *b.* 29 Oct. 1754; *suc. to the Baronetcy*, Aug. 1801. Sheriff of co. Gloucester, 1812-13. He *m.* firstly, 12 May 1785, Judith, 3d da. and coheir of Edward WHITCOMBE, of Orleton. She *d.* s.p.s. 5 March 1787. He *m.* secondly, 7 Oct. 1793, Anne Rachel, 1st da. of Thomas Lobb CHUTE, of the Vine, Hants. He *d.* s.p.m.(a) 23 Oct. 1834. Will pr. Nov. 1834. His widow(a) *d.* 13 April 1839, at Witcombe Park, aged 83.

VIII. 1834. SIR MICHAEL HICKS HICKS-BEACH, Bart. [1619], of Williamstrip Park and Netheravon aforesaid, great nephew and h. male, being s. and h. of Michael Beach HICKS-BEACH, of Netheravon, Wilts, by Caroline Jane, 1st da. of William MOUNT, of Wasing place, Berks, which Michael (who *d.* v.p. 27 Sep. 1817, aged 37) was s. and h. ap. of Michael HICKS-BEACH,(b) of Beverstone Castle aforesaid (*d.* 5 Jan. 1830), the 2d s. of the 6th Bart., aged 70. He was *b.* 25 Oct. 1809, at Netheravon House aforesaid; matric. at Oxford (Ch. Ch.), 8 Dec. 1827, aged 18; *suc. to the Baronetcy*, 23 Oct. 1834; M.P. for East Gloucestershire, Jan. 1854 till his death; Lieut. Col. of the North Gloucester Militia, 1844. He *m.*, 14 Aug. 1832, at Farthinghoe, co. Northampton, Harriett Victoria, 2d da. of John STRATTON, of Farthinghoe Lodge. He *d.* of gastric fever, 22 Nov. 1854, at Williamstrip Park aforesaid, aged 45. His widow living 1899.

IX. 1854. SIR MICHAEL EDWARD HICKS-BEACH, Bart. [1619], of Williamstrip Park and Netheravon aforesaid, s. and h., *b.* 23 Oct. 1837, in Portugal street, Midx.; ed. at Eton and at Christ Church, Oxford; B.A. and 1st class Law and Modern History, 1858; M.A., 1861; *cr.* D.C.L., 1878; *suc. to the Baronetcy*, 22 Nov. 1854; M.P. for East Gloucestershire, in five Parls., 1864-85, and for West Bristol since 1885; Sec. to Poor Law Board, 1868; Under Sec. Home Dept., 1868; Chief Sec. for Ireland, 1874-78; P.C. [G.B. and I.], 1874; Sec. for the Colonies, 1878-80; Chancellor of the Exchequer, 1885-86; Chief Sec. for Ireland (second time) 1886-87; President of the Board of Trade, 1888-92; Church Estates Commissioner, 1892-95; Chancellor of the Exchequer (second time) since 1895. He *m.* firstly, 6 Jan. 1864, at Colesbourne, co. Gloucester, Caroline Susan, 1st da. of John Henry ELWES, of Colesbourne Park. She *d.* s.p. 14 Aug. 1865, in childbirth, at 41 Portman square, aged 21. He *m.* secondly, 3 Sep. 1874, Lucy Catherine, 3d da. of Hugh (FORTESCUE), 3d EARL FORTESCUE, by Georgiana Augusta Charlotte Caroline, da. of the Rt. Hon. George Lionel DAWSON-DAMER. She was *b.* 27 March 1851.

(a) Anne Rachel, their only da. and h., *b.* 11 Sep. 1794, *m.*, 16 March 1816, Sir Lambert CROMIE, Bart. [S.], against the wish of both her parents, so that she inherited the property of neither.

(b) He had taken the name of BEACH, after that of HICKS, by royal lic. dat. 23 June 1790, on inheriting the estates of that family through his mother, Henrietta Maria, da. and h. of William BEACH, of Netheravon, Wilts.

Family Estates.—These, in 1883, consisted of 7,199 acres in Wiltshire (worth £4,982 a year) and 4,135 in Gloucestershire (worth £5,485 a year). *Total*, 11,334 acres, worth £10,467 a year. *Principal Residences.*—Williamstrip Park, near Fairford, co. Gloucester, and Netheravon House, near Amesbury, co. Wilts.

BEAUMONT:
cr. 17 Sep. 1619(a),
afterwards, 1622—1702, VISCOUNTS BEAUMONT OF SWORDS [I.];
ex. 11 June 1702.

I. 1619. "SIR THOMAS BEAUMONT, of Cole Orton, co. Leicester, Knt.,"(b) s. and h. of Sir Henry BEAUMONT, of the same, by Elizabeth, sister and heir of Humphrey LEWIS, da. of John LEWIS, citizen of London; was *Knighted*, 23 April 1603, at Belvoir Castle; was M.P. for Leicestershire, 1604-11 and 1621 till void 7 Feb. 1621/2; Sheriff of that county, 1610-11, and was *cr. a Bart.*, as above, 17 Sep. 1619.(a) He *m.*, in or before 1614, Elizabeth, da. and h. of Henry SAPCOTE, of Bracebridge, co. Lincoln, by Eleanor, da. and coheir of Henry SAPCOTE, of Elton, co. Huntingdon. She was living when he was *cr.*, 20 May 1622, VISCOUNT BEAUMONT OF SWORDS, co. Dublin [I.]. In this peerage the *Baronetcy* continued to be *merged*, till on the death of the 3d Viscount and Baronet,(c) 11 June 1702, both became *extinct*. See *Peerage*.

SALUSBURY, *or* SALISBURY:
cr. 10 Nov. 1619(d);
ex. 23 May 1684.

I. 1619. "HENRY SALISBURY, of Lleweny, co. Denbigh, Esq.,"(e) s. and h. of Sir John SALUSBURY, or SALISBURY, of the same (called "the Strong," many years M.P. for Denbigh), by Ursula, said to be da. of Henry (STANLEY), EARL OF DERBY; suc. his father in 1613, and was *cr. a Bart.*, as above, 10 Nov. 1619(d). Sheriff of Denbighshire, 1627-28. He *m.* firstly Hester, 1st da. of Sir Thomas MIDDLETON, of Chirk Castle, co. Denbigh, sometime (1613) Lord Mayor of London, by his 2d wife, Elizabeth, da. of James DANVERS, of London. She (by whom he had seven children) *d.* 26 Jan. 1614, and was *bur.* at Stansted Montfichet, co. Essex. He *m.* secondly, in or before 1617, Elizabeth, widow of Sir Edward MOORE, da. of John (VAUGHAN), EARL OF CARBERY [I.]. He *d.* 2 Aug. 1632, at his Hall at Lleweny, and was *bur.* at Whitechurch, co. Denbigh. Funeral certificate at the Coll. of Arms. Admon. 14 Oct. 1632. His widow *d.* at St. Martin's in the Fields. Her will (directing her burial to be with her first husband "in the church in Aldermanbury") dat. 13 Aug. 1640, pr. 21 May 1642.

II. 1632. SIR THOMAS SALUSBURY, Bart. [1619], of Llewenny aforesaid, s. and h. by 1st wife; ed. at Jesus Coll., Oxford; admitted to Inner Temple, Nov. 1631; *suc. to the Baronetcy*, 2 Aug. 1632; Alderman of Denbigh, 1634-39; M.P. for Denbighshire, April to May 1640; was acting in the King's cause,

(a) No patent is enrolled, but a fragment of the signet bill is given in the *Creations, 1483—1646*, in ap. 47th Rep. D.K. Pub. Records. See p. 121, note "a," *sub* "Hervey."

(b) So described in Collins' *Baronetage*, 1720.

(c) He devised the estate of Cole Orton to his cousin and heir male, Sir George Beaumont, 4th Bart. [1661] of Stoughton, co. Leicester.

(d) No patent is enrolled, neither is there any signet bill. See p. 123, note "a," *sub* "Grey."

(e) So described in the (useful) lists of creations of Baronets [1611—1769] in Kimber's *Baronetage* (vol. iii, pp. 287—343) of 1771, as also, though *without* the word "Esq.," in Collins' *Baronetage*.

and was impeached by the Parl., 22 Sep. 1642; *cr.* D.C.L. of Oxford, 1 Nov. 1642.(a) He *m.*, before Aug. 1632, Hester, widow of Sir Peter LEMAIRE, da. of Sir Edward TYRRELL, 1st Bart. [1627] of Thornton, Bucks, by his 1st wife, Elizabeth, da. of Sir William KINGSMILL. He *d.* Aug. 1643, and was *bur.* at Whitchurch, co. Denbigh. Admon. 21 Oct. 1646 to his widow. She *m.* (for her 3d husband) her cousin, Thomas TYRRELL, of Hanslope, Bucks.

III. 1643. SIR THOMAS SALISBURY, Bart. [1619], of Llewenny aforesaid, s. and h., *b.* 8 June 1634; *suc. to the Baronetcy* in Aug. 1643; matric. at Oxford (Queen's Coll.), 4 Nov. 1651. He *d.* unm. 1658. Admon. 18 Nov. 1658.

IV. 1658, to 1684. SIR JOHN SALUSBURY, Bart. [1619], of Llewenny aforesaid, only br. and h., a minor when he *suc. to the Baronetcy* in 1658; was M.P. for Denbighshire, in four Parls., 1661-81. He *m.* Jane, da. of Edward WILLIAMS, of Weige, co. Carnarvon. He *d.* s.p. 23 May 1684, when *the Baronetcy* became *extinct.* Will dat. 14 March 1683/4, pr. 14 April 1685, by his widow.(b)

DRYDEN, *or* DRIDEN:

cr. 16 Nov. 1619(c);

ex. 21 March 1770.

I. 1619. "ERASMUS(d) DRIDEN, of Canons Ashbie, co. Northampton, Esq.," s. and h. of John DRYDEN, of the same, by Elizabeth, da. of Sir John COPE, also of Canons Ashby aforesaid,(e) was *b.* 20 Dec. 1553; matric. at Oxford (Mag. Coll.), 1571, aged 18; Demy. of Mag. Coll., 1571-75; Fellow, 1575-80; B.A., 11 June 1577; admitted to Inner Temple, 1577; suc. his father, 13 Sep. 1584, and was *cr. a Bart.*, as above, 16 Nov. 1619.(c) Sheriff of Northamptonshire, 1598-99 and 1619-20; M.P. for Banbury, 1624-25. He *m.* in or before 1580, Frances, 2d sister and coheir of Robert WILKES, da. of William WILKES, of Hodnell, co. Warwick. She *d.* 16 Feb. 1630/1. He *d.* 22 May 1632. Both *bur.* at Canons Ashby. M.I. His admon. 6 June 1632.

II. 1632. SIR JOHN DRYDEN, Bart. [1619], of Canons Ashby aforesaid, s. and h.; *b.* about 1580; matric. at Oxford (Broadgates Hall), 29 Oct. 1596, aged 16; admitted to Inner Temple, 1602; *suc. to the Baronetcy*, 22 May 1632; Sheriff of Northamptonshire, 1634-35; M.P. for that county, 1640-53 and 1654-55. He *m.* three times, viz., firstly Priscilla, sister of Sir Robert QUARLES, da. of James QUARLES, of Romford, Essex. She *d.* s.p.s. He *m.* secondly, Anna, da. of Henry PARVIS, of Ruckholts in Low Layton, Essex, by Elizabeth, da. of Gabriel COLSON, of London. She *d.* s.p. 20 Feb. 1630/1. He *m.* thirdly, 3 July 1632, at St. Mary Wolnoth, London (Lic. London, he 52, widower, and she 22, spinster), Honor, da.

(a) He was author of a poem called "*the History of Joseph.*"

(b) He devised his estates, after the death of his wife, to his only sister, Dame Hester Cotton and her issue, and they accordingly passed to the family of Cotton, of Combermere in Cheshire, now Viscounts Combermere.

(c) No patent is enrolled but the signet bill exists. See p. 121, note "a," *sub* "Hervey."

(d) He was so named after his maternal uncle, Erasmus Cope, who *d.* (v.p.) before 1558, and who is said to have been godson of the famous Erasmus, who *d.* 1536. The story of Erasmus Dryden's father having been a schoolmaster is highly improbable. [See Wotton's *Baronetage* (1741), vol. i, p. 350].

(e) It is shewn in Baker's *Northamptonshire* (vol. ii, p. 5) that the notion that the Dryden property in Ashby was a portion of the Cope estate is wrong. The bulk of Sir John Cope's estate, including the site of the monastery at Ashby, descended to Edward Cope, his grandson, but it was purchased by Sir Robert Dryden, in 1665.

and coheir of Sir Robert BEVILL, K.B., of Chesterton, co. Huntingdon, by Mary, da. and coheir of (—) COLES, of Preston, co. Northampton. She, who was *bap.* 3 Oct. 1609, at Chesterton, *d.* before him. He *d.* about 1658. Will dat. 20 Jan. 1656/7, pr. 11 Nov. 1658.

III. 1658? SIR ROBERT DRYDEN, Bart. [1619], of Canons Ashby aforesaid, s. and h. by 3d wife, *b.* about 1638; matric. at Oxford (Wad. Coll.), 14 Nov. 1650; admitted to Middle Temple, 1654; *suc. to the Baronetcy* in 1658; purchased the site of the Priory at Canons Ashby in 1655. Sheriff of Northamptonshire, 1666-67, and of Warwickshire, 1669-70; was aged 42 in 1681. He *d.* unm. 19 and was *bur.* 30 Aug. 1708, in his 76th year, at Canons Ashby.(a) M.I. Will dat. 5 July, pr. Dec. 1708.

IV. 1708. SIR JOHN DRYDEN, Bart. [1619], of West Farndon in Woodford, co. Northampton, cousin and h., being s. and h. of William DRYDEN, of the same, by his 1st wife, (—), da. of (—) CAVE, of co. Leicester, which William (sometime a woollen draper in St. Paul's Churchyard, but *bur.* at Woodford, 24 Dec. 1660, aged 68) was 2d s. of the 1st Bart. He was *b.* about 1635; *suc. to the Baronetcy*, but not to the estate, 19 Aug 1708. He *m.* (Lic. Vic. Gen., 15 June 1663, he of St. Bride's, London, about 27, bachelor, she of St. Dunstan's in the West, about 22, spinster, Elizabeth, da. of (—) LUCK, of co. Northampton. He *d.* s.p.m.s.(b) and was *bur.* at Woodford, 23 May 1710.

V. 1710, May. SIR ERASMUS HENRY DRYDEN, Bart. [1619], of Tichmarsh, co. Northampton, cousin and h., being 3d but only surv. child and h. of John DRYDEN, the celebrated POET LAUREATE, by Elizabeth, da. of Thomas (HOWARD), 1st EARL OF BERKSHIRE, which John, who *d.* 1 May 1700, aged 68, was s. and h. of Erasmus DRYDEN, of Tichmarsh aforesaid (*bur.* there 18 June 1654, aged 66), the 3d s. of the 1st Bart. He was *b.* 2 May 1669; was a scholar at Charterhouse, being "elected to the University" 1685; studied at Douay; entered the Noviciate of the Dominicans, 1692; was ordained Priest, 1694; Sub-Prior of the Convent of Holy Cross, Bornheim, 1697—1700. He, who in his last years appears to have been imbecile, *suc. to the Baronetcy* in May 1710; *d.* unm. six months later, and was *bur.* 4 Dec. 1710, at Canons Ashby.

VI. 1710, Dec. SIR ERASMUS DRYDEN, Bart. [1619],(c) uncle and h., being next br. to the Poet, both being sons of Erasmus DRYDEN abovenamed, 3d s. of the 1st Bart. He was *b.* 1636; was sometime a Grocer in King street, Westm.; *suc. to the Baronetcy* in Dec. 1710. He *m.*, 27 Aug. 1667, at Highgate, Midx. (Lic. Vic. Gen., he of St. Marg., Westm., "Grocer," aged 28, bachelor, she about 23), Elizabeth, da. of Edward MARTYN, of King street aforesaid, citizen and Grocer. She *d.* before him. He *d.* 3 and was *bur.* 16 Nov. 1718, at Canons Ashby, aged 82. Will, dat. 28 Oct. 1718, pr. 17 Feb. 1718/9.

VII. 1718, to 1770. SIR JOHN DRYDEN, Bart. [1619], of Canons Ashby aforesaid grandson and h., being s. and h. of Edward Dryden, of the same, by Elizabeth, sister of Sir Thomas ALLEN, da. of Edward ALLEN, of Finchley, which Edward Dryden, who in 1708 had inherited the estate of Canons and who *d.* v.p. Nov. 1717, aged 49, was s. and h. ap. of the 6th Bart. He was *b.* about 1704; *suc. to the Baronetcy*, 3 Nov. 1718; matric. at Oxford (Ch. Ch.), 16 Jan. 1719/20; and was *cr.* D.C.L., 11 July 1733; Sheriff of Northamptonshire, 1727-28. He *m.* firstly, June 1724, Frances, da. and h. of Thomas INGRAM, of Barraby, co. York, and Freeston, co. Lincoln. She *d.* s.p. and was *bur.* 30 Jan. 1724/5, at Canons Ashby. He *m.* secondly, 22 Sep. 1726, at St. Marg.,

(a) He devised that estate to his cousin, Edward Dryden, son of the 6th and father of the 7th Baronet.

(b) John Dryden, his only son, an attorney, *d.* v.p. and s.p. by a fall from his horse.

(c) He resided at Canons Ashby after 1708, in which year it had devolved (under the will of the 3d Bart.) on his son, Edward Dryden, father of the 7th Bart.

Westm. (Lic. Vic. Gen., she of St. Giles' in the Fields about 19, spinster), Elizabeth, da. of John ROPER, of Berkhampstead, Berks. He *d.* s.p. 21 March, at Canons Ashby, and was *bur.* there 2 April 1770, when the *Baronetcy* became *extinct.*(a) Will pr. 11 May 1797. His widow *d.* 7 May 1791, aged 85. Will pr. May 1791.

ARMYNE, AIRMYN, *or* AYRMINE:

cr. 28 Nov. 1619(b);

ex. 1668.

I. 1619. "WILLIAM ARMYNE, Esq., son of William ARMYNE, of Osgodby, co. Lincoln, Knt.," by Martha, da. of William (EURE), LORD EURE, was *b.* 11 Dec. 1593, at Osgodby, and was v.p. *cr. a Bart.*, as above, 28 Nov. 1619.(b) He suc. his father (who *d.* in his 60th year) 22 Jan. 1621/2. M.P. for Boston, 1621-22 and 1624-25; for Grantham, 1625; for Lincolnshire, 1626 and 1628-29, and for Grantham (again), April to Dec. 1641. Sheriff of Lincolnshire, 1629-30, and of Hunts, 1639-40. Took a most active part in the Civil War against the King, one of whose judges he was elected, though he refused to sit; was one of the Council of State, 1649-51. He *m.* firstly, 14 Dec. 1619, Elizabeth, da. of Sir Michael HICKS, of Beverstone Castle, co. Gloucester, and of Ruckholts, in Low Leyton, Essex, by Elizabeth, relict of Henry PURVIS, of Ruckholt aforesaid, and da. of Gabriel COULSON, of London. He *m.* secondly, 28 Aug. 1628, Mary, widow of Thomas HOLCROFT, of Vale Royal, da. and coheir of the Hon. Henry TALBOT (4th s. of George, 6th EARL OF SHREWSBURY), by Elizabeth, da. of Sir William REYNER, of co. Huntingdon. He *d.* 10 April 1651, and was *bur.* at Lavington, otherwise Lenton, co. Lincoln. Admon., 10 Dec. 1651, to his widow. She *d.* s.p.s. in St. Martin's lane, Middlesex, 6 March 1674/5, aged above 80, and was *bur.* at Orton Longueville, co. Huntingdon. Funeral certificate. Will dat. 31 Aug. 1654 and 26 June 1674, pr. 26 March 1675.

II. 1651. SIR WILLIAM ARMYNE, Bart. [1619], of Osgodby aforesaid, s. and h., by 1st wife, *b.* 14 July 1622, at Ruckholt aforesaid; admitted to Gray's Inn, 18 Nov. 1639; M.P. for Cumberland, March 1646 to 1653; *suc. to the Baronetcy*, 10 April 1651. He *m.*, 26 Aug. 1649, at Chilton, co. Suffolk, Anne, da. and coh. of Sir Robert CRANE, Bart. [so cr. 1626] of Chilton, by his 2d wife, Susan, da. of Sir Giles ALINGTON. He *d.* s.p.m.,(c) in London, 2 and was *bur.* 17 Jan. 1657/8, at Lenton aforesaid. Will dat. 19 Dec. 1657, pr. 16 Feb. 1657/8. His widow *m.* (as the second of his three wives) 11 July 1659, at St. Vedast's, London, John (BELASYSE), 1st BARON BELASYSE OF WORLABY, who *d.* 10 Dec. 1689. She *d.* 11 and was *bur.* 20 Aug. 1662 at St. Giles' in the Fields.

III. 1658, to 1668. SIR MICHAEL ARMYNE, Bart. [1619], of Osgodby aforesaid,(d) br. and h. male, *b.* 21 Sep. 1625, at Osgodby; *suc. to the Baronetcy*, 2 Jan. 1657/8. He was executor to his brother's will; was Sheriff of Lincolnshire, 1666-67. He *m.* Mary, 2d da. of John (CHAWORTH), 2d VISCOUNT CHAWORTH OF ARMAGH [I.], by his 1st wife, Penelope, da.

(a) The estates devolved, after the death of his widow, in 1791, on his niece, Elizabeth, da. of Bevill Dryden. She *m.*, in 1781, John TURNER, who, in 1791, took the name of *Dryden* only, and was *cr. a Bart.* in 1795.

(b) No patent is enrolled, but the signet bill exists. See p. 121, note "a," *sub* "Hervey."

(c) Of his two daughters and coheirs, (1) Susan, who apparently inherited the estate of Osgodby, *m.*, 29 Oct. 1662, Sir Henry Belasyse, and was *cr.* BARONESS BELASYSE OF OSGODBY in 1674, but *d.* s.p. 6 March 1712/3; (2) Anne, *m.* firstly Sir Thomas Wodehouse, secondly Thomas (Crewe) 2d Baron Crewe of Steyne, and thirdly Arthur (Herbert) Earl of Torrington. She had issue by her first two husbands.

(d) "Armyn, at Osgodby, an ancient family £4,000 per annum" is included in Sir Joseph Williamson's *Lincolnshire Families, temp. Car. II.* [*Her. and Gen.*, vol. ii, 120].

of Edward (NOEL), VISCOUNT CAMPDEN. She *d.* 1667, and was *bur.* at Lenton aforesaid. He *d.* a widower and s.p. in 1668, when the *Baronetcy* became *extinct.*(a) Will dat. 30 March to 12 April, and pr. 4 Dec. 1668.

BAMBURGH:

cr. 1 Dec. 1619;

ex. 12 Dec. 1631.

I. 1619. "WILLIAM BAMBURGH, of Howson [*i.e.*, Howsham], co. York, Knt.," s. and h. of Thomas BAMBURGH, of Howsham aforesaid, by Catharine, da. of Matthew THIMELBY, of Poleham, co. Lincoln, was *Knighted* 18 April 1603, at Grimston; Sheriff of Yorkshire, 1607-08, and was *cr. a Bart.*, as above, 1 Dec. 1619. He *m.* in or before 1606, Mary, da. of Robert FORD, of Butley, co. Suffolk (Sheriff, 1569), by Frances, da. of Edward GLEMHAM, of Glemham. He *d.* 18 July 1623. Will dat. 25 Jan. 1622 3, pr. 19 Jan. 1623/4, at York. His widow *m.* (articles 1 Jan. 1626/7), as his 2d wife, Thomas (FAIRFAX), 1st VISCOUNT FAIRFAX OF EMLEY [I.], who *d.* at Howsham, 23 Dec. 1636, aged 62. She *d.* March 1638/9. Will pr. at York, 22 of that month.

II. 1623. SIR THOMAS BAMBURGH, Bart. [1619], of Howsham aforesaid, 1st s. and h., *suc. to the Baronetcy* 28 July 1623, being then aged 16 years 5 months and 16 days. He *d.* s.p. 3 June 1624. Will dat. 13 May and pr. 4 Oct. 1624, at York.

III. 1624, to 1631. SIR JOHN BAMBURGH, Bart. [1619], of Howsham aforesaid, only br. and h., *suc. to the Baronetcy*, 3 June 1624, being then aged 11 years 5 months and 5 days. He *d.* unm. and a minor, 12 Dec. 1631, when the *Baronetcy* became *extinct.*(b)

HARTOPP:

cr. 3 Dec. 1619;

ex. 13 Jan. 1762.

I. 1619. "EDWARD HARTOPP, of Freathbie, co. Leicester, Esq.," s. and h. of William HARTOPP, of Burton Lazers, in that county, by Eleanor, da. and h. of (—) ADCOCK, suc. his father, 2 Sep. 1586; served in the Low Countries under the Earl of Leicester; was Sheriff of Leicestershire, 1617-18; and was *cr. a Bart.*, as above, 3 Dec. 1619. He was M.P. for Leicester, 1628-29. He *m.* Mary, 2d da. of Sir Erasmus DRYDEN, 1st Bart. [1619], by Frances, da. and coheir of William WILKES. He *d.* 1652.

II. 1652. SIR EDWARD HARTOPP, Bart. [1619], of Freathby aforesaid, and of Buckminster, co. Leicester, s. and h., *b.* 1608; was *Knighted* at Belvoir, 26 July 1634. He raised a regiment for the service of the Parliament against the King. He *suc. to the Baronetcy* in 1652. He *m.* Mary, da. of Sir John COKE, of Melbourne, co. Derby, Sec. of State to Charles I, by Mary, da. of (—) POWELL, of Presteign, co. Radnor. He *d.* 1657. His widow *m.* 14 Jan. 1663/4, at St. Anne's, Blackfriars (for his third wife), Charles FLEETWOOD, of Feltwell, Norfolk, the Parliamentary General (Lic. Fac., he about 50, widower, she, of Stoke Newington, Midx., about 40, widow). Her will pr. 1693.

(a) He mentions his uncle "Evers Armyne, Esq.," as living, to whom and to whose issue male he leaves his manors of Peekworth and Willoughby, co. Lincoln.

(b) His coheirs were (1) his sister Katherine (*d.* 22 Aug. 1634, aged 31), relict of Sir Thomas Norcliffe, and then wife of Sir John Hotham, Bart.; (2) Thomas Wentworth, of North Elmsall, son of his deceased sister, Mary; (3) William Robinson, of Newby, son of his decd. sister, Anne or Amy ["Fairfaxiana," by "C.B.N.," in *Her. and Gen.*, vol. viii, p. 225].

III. 1657. Sir John Hartopp, Bart. [1619], of Freathby aforesaid, s. and h., *bap.* 21 Oct. 1637, at Buckminster; matric. at Oxford (St. John's Coll.) 25 July 1655; admitted to Lincoln's Inn, 1656; *suc. to the Baronetcy* in 1657; was a zealous Nonconformist; M.P. for Leicestershire in three Parls., 1679-81.(a) He *m.*, 8 Nov. 1666, at Feltwell, Norfolk, Elizabeth, da. of the abovenamed Charles Fleetwood (son in law of the Protector Cromwell), by his 1st wife, Frances, da. and h. of Thomas Smith, of Winston, Norfolk. She was *bur.* 26 Nov. 1711 ("in woollen") at Stoke Newington, Middlesex. He *d.* 1 and was *bur.* there 11 April 1722 ("in linen"), æt. 85.

IV. 1722, to 1762. Sir John Hartopp, Bart. [1619], of Freathby aforesaid, s. and h., *b.* 1680; *suc. to the Baronetcy* 1 April 1722. He *m.* firstly, 1716, Sarah, da. of Sir Joseph Wolfe, of Hackney, Middlesex, Alderman of London. She was *bur.* ("in a velvet coffin") at Stoke Newington, 22 Sep. 1730. He *m.* secondly, Sarah, da. of (—), Marsh. He *d.* s.p. at Bath, 13, and was *bur.* 28 Jan. 1762, at Stoke Newington, aged 82, when the *Baronetcy* became *extinct.*(b) Will pr. 1762. The will of his widow pr. 1763.

MILL:

cr. 31 Dec. 1619,(c)

sometime, 1766-80, Mill-Hoby;

ex., presumably, 6 Feb. 1835;

assumed in 1844.

I. 1619. "John Mill, of Camois Court, co. Sussex, Esq.,"(d) and of Newton Berry in Eling, Hants, 2d but 1st surv. s. and h. of Lewknor Mill, of the same, by Cecily, da. of John Crook of Southampton, suc. his father in 1587, and was *cr. a Bart.* as above, 31 Dec. 1619(c); was M.P. for Southampton, 1624-25, 1625, 1626, and April to May 1640; Sheriff of Hants, 1627-28; was a Royalist; petitioned to compound in 1648, which was effected in Nov. 1650 (after his death), for £1,350. He, on the death, in 1623, of Dame Mary Mill, widow of his cousin Sir Richard Mill, of Nursling, inherited that estate. He *m.* firstly, 24 Feb. 1604/5, Elizabeth, da. of Sir George More, of Loseley, co. Surrey, by Ann, da. and h. of Sir Adrian Poynings. She *d.* s.p. and was *bur.* 10 March 1605/6, at Loseley. He *m.* secondly, Ann, da. of Sir Thomas Fleming, Lord Chief Justice of the King's Bench (1607-13), by Dorothy (or Mary), da. of Sir Henry Cromwell, of Hinchingbroke. He *d.* at Oxford, July 1648. Will pr. 1648.

II. 1648? Sir John Mill, Bart. [1619], of Newton Berry aforesaid, grandson and h., being only s. and h. of Sir John Mill, by Philadelphia, da. of Sir Henry Knollys, of Grove Place, Hants, which Sir John was s. and h. ap. of the 1st Bart. (by his 2d wife), but was slain v.p. "by one Slatford," near Oxford, 1642. He *suc. to the Baronetcy* about 1648. He *m.*, in or before 1660, Margaret, sister of Edwin, Lord Sandys of the Vine, who *d.* s.p. in 1700, 4th da. of Col. Henry Sandys, by Jane, da. of Sir William Sandys, of Missenden, co. Gloucester. He *d.* 1670, in his 28th year. Will pr. July 1671. His widow *d.* 1707. Will pr. Sep. 1707.

(a) He is often (erroneously) stated to have been an Alderman of London, being, possibly, confused with *Thomas* Hartopp, Alderman of Coleman, 1686 to 1687. [*Ex. inform.* W. D. Pink]

(b) The estates eventually centered in his granddaughter, Anne, only child of Sarah (*bur.* at Stoke Newington, 4 April 1766), his eldest da. (by his 1st wife) by Joseph Hurlock, Governor of Bencoolen, who was *bur.* at Stoke Newington, 15 Aug. 1793, aged 78. This Anne also suc. to the Fleetwood property in Norfolk, under the will of her cousin, Jane Fleetwood. She *m.* Edmund Bunny, who took the name of Cradock-Hartopp, and was *cr.* a Bart. in 1796.

(c) No patent is enrolled, neither is there any signet bill. See p. 123, note "a," *sub* "Grey."

(d) So described in Collins' *Baronetage* (1720).

III. 1670. Sir John Mill, Bart. [1619], of Newton Berry aforesaid and afterwards [1700], of Mottisfont, co. Southampton (which last estate he inherited from his uncle, Lord Sandys aforesaid) only, s. and h.; *b.* 1 June 1661. He was living June 1692, but *d.* about 1697; matric. at Oxford (St. John's Coll.), 2 Aug. 1677, aged 16; *suc. to the Baronetcy* in 1670; Sheriff of Hants, 1684-85. He *m.* 17 June 1679, at Woolbeding, Sussex (Lic. Fac., he about 21 and she about 18) Margaret, da. and h. of Thomas Grey, of Woolbeding aforesaid, by Mary, da. of Humphrey Steward, of Milland in Trotton, Sussex. She was dead before Oct. 1692.(a)

IV. 1697? Sir John Mill, Bart. [1619], of Mottisfont, Newton Berry and Woolbeding aforesaid, 1st s. and h.; *bap.* 9 July 1681 at Woolbeding; *suc. to the Baronetcy* about 1697. He *d.* unm. Admon. 2 Feb. 1705/6, and again 24 July 1722.

V. 1706? Sir Richard Mill, Bart. [1619], of Mottisfont, etc., aforesaid, br. and h., *b.* 1690; *suc. to the Baronetcy* in 1706; matric. at Oxford (St. John's Coll.), 12 March 1707/8, aged 18; M.P. for Midhurst, Nov. 1721 to 1722, and Feb. 1729 to 1734; for Penrhyn, 1734-41; and for Horsham, 1741-47. Sheriff of Hants, 1723-24. He *m.*, 12 March 1712, Margaret, 1st da. of Robert Knollys, of Grove Place, in Nutshelling, Hants. She *d.* 11 Oct. 1744, aged 56, *bur.* at Woolbeding. M.I. He *d.* 16 and was *bur.* there 23 May 1760, aged 70. Will pr. 14 June 1760.

VI. 1760. Sir Richard Mill, Bart. [1619], of Mottisfont, etc., aforesaid, s. and h., *b.* 1717; matric. at Oxford (New Coll.), 17 Feb. 1734/5, aged 18; *cr.* M.A., 12 July 1738; *suc. to the Baronetcy*, 16 May 1760; M.P. for Hants, 1765-68. He *m.*, Aug. 1760, Dorothy, da. and h. of Richard Warren, of Redcliff, co. Somerset, by Henrietta, da. of Charles Yate, of Arlingham Court, co. Gloucester. He *d.* s.p.m. 17 March 1770, and was *bur.* at Mottisfont. Will pr. March 1770. His widow *d.* June 1811. Admon. Nov. 1811, and again Aug. 1852.

VII. 1770. Sir John Hoby Mill-Hoby, Bart. [1619], of Mottisfont, etc., br. and h. male, *bap.* 20 May 1719, at Woolbeding; matric. at Oxford (Ch. Ch.), 16 June 1738, aged 19; was subsequently of Clare Hall, Cambridge; B.A., 1743; *suc. to the Baronetcy*, 17 March 1770. In 1766 he assumed the additional surname of Hoby, under the will of his 1st cousin, the Rev. Sir Philip Hoby, 5th Bart. [1666], whose estate, at Bisham, Berks, he inherited. He *m.* Elizabeth, da. of (—) Comyn. He *d.* s.p. July 1780. Will pr. July 1780. His widow sold the Bisham estate, and *m.* (—) Oxlade. Her will pr. May 1792.

VIII. 1780. Sir Henry Mill, Bart. [1619], of Mottisfont, etc., aforesaid, br. and h., *bap.* 5 Jan. 1729; ed. at Clare Hall, Cambridge, LL.B., 1748; in Holy Orders; Rector of Woolbeding, and of Kingston Bowsey by Sea, both in co. Sussex; *suc. to the Baronetcy*, July 1780. He *d.* unm., Nov. 1781. Will pr. Feb. 1782.

IX. 1781. Sir Charles Mill, Bart. [1619], of Mottisfont, etc., aforesaid, br. and h., *bap.* 8 July 1722; ed. at Clare Hall, Cambridge; LL.B., 1748; in Holy Orders; *suc. to the Baronetcy*, Nov. 1781. He *m.* 17 Nov. 1763, Mary, da. of (—) Windover. He *d.* 19 July 1792. Will pr. Aug. 1792. His widow *d.* 1800. Will pr. July 1800.

X. 1792, to 1835. Sir Charles Mill, Bart. [1619], of Mottisfont, etc., aforesaid, only s. and h., *b.* 1765; *suc. to the Baronetcy* 19 July 1792. Sheriff of Hants, 1804-05. He *m.*, Jan. 1800, Selina, 1st da. of Sir John Morshead, 1st Bart. [1784], by Elizabeth, da. and coheir of Sir Thomas Frederick, 3d Bart. [1723]. He *d.* s.p. in Dover street, Piccadilly,

(a) See will of Humphrey Steward, pr. at Chichester, Oct. 1692.

25 Feb. 1835, aged 70, when the *Baronetcy* is presumed to have become *extinct.* Will pr. April 1835. His widow *m.*, 15 Aug. 1839, at St. Geo. Han. sq., William Henry Ashurst, of Waterstock, Oxon, and was apparently living 1862.(a)

> The title was, however, assumed, in or soon after 1844, as below.
>
> *XI. 1835.* John Frederick Mill, who *never assumed the Baronetcy*, though, according to his brother's statement, he was, in 1839, heir male of the body of the grantee, as being s. and h. of the Rev. John Mill, by Sarah, da. of John Guiver, which John Mill (who *d.* 1828, aged 72) was only s. and h. of another John Mill (*d.* 1776), only s. and h. of another John Mill (*d.* 1738, aged 72), s. and h. of Thomas Mill (*d.* 1706), s. and h. of Thomas Mill, of Nutshelling, Hants (*m.* 1628, and *d.* 1664), who was 2d s. of the 1st Bart. He was *b.* 29 March 1810, and *d.* unm. 1844.
>
> XII. 1844. "Sir George Mill, Bart." [1619], who *assumed this Baronetcy* in, or soon after, 1844, br. and h., *b.* 17 May 1812, and was living 1860.

RADCLYFFE, RADCLIFF, *or* RATCLIFFE:

cr. 31 Jan. 1619/20,

afterwards, 1688-1716, Earls of Derwentwater;

forfeited 24 Feb. 1715/6.

I. 1620. "Francis Radcliff, of Darentwater (*i.e.*, Derwentwater), co. Cumberland, Esq.," being also of Dilston, co. Northumberland, s. and h. of Sir George Radclyffe, of the same, by Catharine, da. of Sir John Mallory, *b.* 1569; matric. at Oxford (Queen's Coll.), 22 Nov. 1588, aged 19; was *cr. a Bart.*, as above, 31 Jan. 1619/20. He *m.* Isabel, da. of Sir Ralph Grey, of Chillingham, co. Northumberland, by Isabel, da. and coheir of Sir Thomas Grey, of Horton, in that county.

II. 1640? Sir Edward Radclyffe, Bart. [1620], of Derwentwater and Dilston aforesaid, 1st surv. s. and h.; *suc. to the Baronetcy* on his father's death. He *m.* in or before 1615, Elizabeth (living unm. 1612), da. and h. of Thomas Barton, of Wenby, co. York, by Alice, da. of Thomas Braithwaite, of Burneside. He *d.* at Dilston 13 and was *bur.* there 18 Dec. 1663. Will dat. 29 June 1657, pr. at Durham. His widow *d.* at Dilston and was *bur.* there 19 Dec. 1668. Will dat. 18 Dec. 1668, pr. at Durham.

III. 1663. Sir Francis Radclyffe, Bart. [1620], of Derwentwater and Dilston aforesaid, only surv. s. and h., *b.* 1625; Capt. in Vane's Reg. of Foot, 1667; *suc. to the Baronetcy*, 13 Dec. 1663. He *m.*, in or before 1665, Catherine, widow of Henry Lawson, of Brough, co. York (slain 1644), da. and coheir of Sir William Fenwick, of Meldon, co. Northumberland, by Isabel, da. and coheir of Sir Arthur Grey, of Shindlestone in that county. She was living when he was *cr.*, 7 March 1687/8, EARL OF DERWENTWATER. In that peerage this *Baronetcy* then *merged* and so remained till, by the attainder and execution, 24 Feb. 1715/6, of the 3d Earl and 5th Baronet, *it* and all other his dignities were *forfeited*. See "Peerage."

(a) Dod's *Peerage*, etc., of 1862, her name not appearing in the edition for 1863.

FOULIS:

cr. 6 Feb. 1619/20(a);

ex. 7 Oct. 1875.

I. 1620. "Sir David Foulis, of Ingleby, co. York, Knt.,"(b) 3d s. of James Foulis, of Colinton, co. Edinburgh, was in the service of James I. (before his accession); was *Knighted* at the Tower of London, 13 May 1603; admitted to Gray's Inn, 1603; was a Gent. of the King's privy chamber, being then of the Inner Temple, 28 Feb. 1604/5; M.A. of the Univ. of Oxford, 30 Aug. 1605, being incorp. at Cambridge, 1608; purchased in 1609, from Lord Eure, the estate of Ingleby manor in Cleveland, co. York; was one of the King's Council in the North, Cofferer to Prince Henry and subsequently to Prince Charles, and was *cr. a Bart.*, as above, 6 Feb. 1619/20(a). In 1632, having resisted the Commission for compulsory Knighthood, he was fined £800, deprived of all official employment, and committed to the Fleet prison. He *m.* in 1604, at Great Missenden, Bucks, Cordelia, da. of Sir William Fleetwood, Sergeant at Law and Recorder of London, by Anne, da. of Ralph Barton, of Smithells, co. Lanc. He was *bur.* 24 Aug. 1642 at Ingleby.

II. 1642. Sir Henry Foulis, Bart. [1620], of Ingleby Manor aforesaid, s. and h., *b.* in London about 1607; matric. at Oxford (Mag. Coll.), 28 Jan. 1624/5, aged 17: admitted to the Inner Temple, 1626; Lieut. Gen. of Horse, being in command (on the King's side) at the taking of Leeds. He was fined (£500) and imprisoned with his father; *suc. to the Baronetcy*, Aug. 1642. He *m.*, in or before 1633, Mary, 1st da. of Sir Thomas Layton, of Sexhowe, co. York, by Mary, da. of Thomas (Fairfax), 1st Viscount Fairfax of Emley [I]. He *d.* 13 Sep., and was *bur.*, 11 Oct. 1643, at Boston, co. Lincoln.(c) Admon. 13 Aug. 1646 to a creditor. His widow was *bur.* 21 Nov. 1657, at Ingleby. Will pr. 1658.

III. 1643. Sir David Foulis, Bart. [1620], of Ingleby Manor aforesaid, s. and h., *bap.* 14 March 1632/3, at Ingleby; *suc. to the Baronetcy*, 13 Sep. 1643; was aged 32 at the Her. Visit of York, 13 Sep. 1665; M.P. for North Allerton, 1685-88. He *m.*, in or before 1658, Catharine, 1st da. of Sir David Watkins, of Midx. He *d.* 13 and was *bur.* 20 March 1694/5, at Ingleby, in his 62d year. Will pr. 1 June 1695, at York. His widow *d.* 1717. Her will dat. 18 Aug. 1716, pr. at York.

IV. 1694. Sir William Foulis, Bart. [1620], of Ingleby Manor aforesaid, 1st surv. s. and h., *bap.* 9 March 1658/9, at Ingleby; matric. at Oxford (Mag. Coll.), 2 July 1675, aged 16; admitted to Middle Temple, 1678; *suc. to the Baronetcy*, 13 March 1694/5. He *m.*, 2 Aug. 1688, at St. Mary Aldermary, London, Anne, widow of Sir Lumley Robinson, 2d Bart. [1682], of Kentwell Hall, and da. and h. of John Lawrence, of St. Ives, co. Huntingdon, by Amy, da. of Richard Williams, of Chichester. She, who was *b.* about 1658, was *bur.*, as "the Lady Anne Robinson," 13 Dec. 1690, at Westm. Abbey, with her parents and her 1st husband. He was *bur.* 7 Oct. 1741, at Ingleby, aged 83.

V. 1741. Sir William Foulis, Bart. [1620], of Ingleby Manor aforesaid, only s. and h., *b.* probably about 1680; *suc. to the Baronetcy*, in Oct. 1741. He *m.*, 1721, Mildred, 1st da. of Henry (Dawnay), 2d Viscount Downe [I.], by Mildred, da. of William Godfrey. He was *bur.* 11 Dec. 1756, at Ingleby.

(a) No patent is enrolled, and no signet bill exists, but in the list of *Creations* 1483—1646 (ap. 47th Rep. D.K. Pub. Records,) is the "Warrant, 14 Feb. 1619/20, for granting receipt for £1,000 to David Foulis, of Ingleby, co. York, Knt., on his creation as Baronet," in the "Signet bills, Chapter House, 17 Jas. I." See p. 121, note "a," *sub* "Hervey."

(b) Such is his description in Collins' *Baronetage* (1720).

(c) His 2d son, Henry Foulis, Fellow of Lincoln College, Oxford, was author of several works on divinity. He *d.* 24 Dec. 1669, aged 33, and was *bur.* at St. Michael's, Oxford.

Will dat. 2 July 1745, pr. 10 Jan. 1757, at York. His widow was *bur.* 6 Feb. 1780, at Ingleby. Will pr. May 1781.

VI. 1756. SIR WILLIAM FOULIS, Bart. [1620], of Ingleby Manor aforesaid, only s. and h., *b.* 1729; matric. at Oxford (Hert. Coll.), 4 Nov. 1741, aged 17; *suc. to the Baronetcy*, in Dec. 1756; Sheriff of Yorkshire, 1764-65. He *m.*, 1758, Hannah, only da. of John ROBINSON, of Buckton, in the East Riding, co. York. He was *bur.*, 17 June 1780, at Ingleby. Will pr. 18 Nov. 1780, at York. The will of his widow pr. June 1812.

VII. 1780. SIR WILLIAM FOULIS Bart. [1620], of Ingleby Manor aforesaid, s. and h.; *bap.* 30 April 1759 at Ingleby; matric. at Oxford (Univ. Coll.), 17 March 1777, aged 17; *suc. to the Baronetcy* in June 1780; Sheriff of Yorkshire, 1802, but died during his tenure of office. He *m.*, 1789, Mary-Anne, 2d da. of Edmund TURNOR, of Panton House, co. Lincoln. He *d.* 5 Sep. 1802, at Ingleby Manor. Admon. 23 Oct. 1802. His widow *d.* 18 Oct. 1831. Will pr. Nov. 1831.

VIII. 1802. SIR WILLIAM FOULIS, Bart. [1620], of Ingleby Manor aforesaid, s. and h., *bap.* 29 May 1790, at Ingleby; *suc. to the Baronetcy*, 5 Sep. 1802; matric. at Oxford (Ch. Ch.), 21 Oct. 1808, aged 18. He *m.*, 11 May 1825, Mary Jane, da. of Gen. Sir Charles ROSS, of Balnagowan, 6th Bart. [S. 1672], by his 2d wife, Mary, da. of William-Robert (FITZGERALD), 2d DUKE OF LEINSTER [I.]. He *d.* s.p.m.(a) 7 Nov. 1845, in Grosvenor place, aged 65. Will pr. Aug. 1846. His widow *d.* 11 June 1852, in Grosvenor place. Admon. July 1852.

IX. 1845, to 1876. SIR HENRY FOULIS, Bart. [1620], br. and h. male, *b.* at Ingleby Manor, and *bap.* 15 Sep. 1800, at Ingleby; ed. at St. John's Coll., Cambridge; B.A., 1823; took Holy Orders; Rector of Great Brickhill, Bucks, 1834-76; Preb. of Lincoln, 1844-76; *suc. to the Baronetcy*, 7 Nov. 1845. He *d.* unm., 7 Oct. 1876, at Ampthill, aged 76, when the *Baronetcy* became *extinct*.

[In Burke's *Baronetage* of 1877 and elsewhere, the 9th Baronet is stated to have been succeeded in the Baronetcy by his cousin, John Robinson FOULIS, an officer, R.N., grandson of the 6th Bart. This cousin, however, *d.* unm. as long ago as 1815, aged 18, in the lifetime of his father (another) John Robinson Foulis, of Buckton, co. York, who *d.* s.p.m.s. 29 April 1826, aged 64.]

PHELIPPS, *or* PHILLIPS:

cr. 16 Feb. 1619/20;(b)

ex. 1 March 1689/90.

I. 1620. "SIR THOMAS PHILLIPS [*or* PHELIPPS], of Barrington, co. Somerset, Knt.,"(c) s. and h. of Sir Thomas PHELIPPS of Barrington(d) aforesaid (who purchased that estate in 1605 and *d.* 28 June 1618) by Jane, da. of Sir John CLIFTON (which Thomas last named, was 2d s. of Thomas PHELIPPS, of Montacute, in that county, who *d.* Nov. 1588), was *bap.* 15 June 1590, at Montacute; *Knighted* in Ireland, 24 March 1606/7, by the L. Deputy, and was *cr. a Bart.*, as above, 16 Feb. 1619/20; was M.P. for Winchester, 1625. He *m.* Charity (aged 23 in 1618-19), 1st da. and coheir of William WALLER,

(a) Mary, his da. and h., *b.* 19 May 1826, *m.*, 23 April 1850, Philip (Sidney) 2d Baron de L'Isle and Dudley, and *d.* 14 June 1891, leaving issue, who inherit the Ingleby estate.

(b) No patent is enrolled, neither is there any signet bill. See p. 123, note "a," *sub* "Grey."

(c) So described in Collins' *Baronetage* (1720).

(d) See an admirable account of this family in J. J. Howard's *Catholic Families*

of Oldstoke, Hants, and Stoke Charity, co. Somerset, by his 1st wife, Anne, relict of (—) TREGONELL, da. of (—) SOMESTER, of co. Devon. He, who latterly resided at Winchester, *d.* 29 April 1627. Will (without date) pr. 26 May 1627, by his relict, who had already *m.* (a few weeks after his death) Sir William OGLE, *cr.* 23 Dec. 1645, VISCOUNT OGLE OF CATHERLOUGH [I.], who *d.* s.p.m. 14 July 1682, and was *bur.* at Michelmarsh. She, however, *d.* 5 Oct. 1645, shortly before such creation, and was *bur.* at Stoke Charity.

II. 1627. SIR THOMAS PHELIPPS, Bart. [1620], of Barrington and Stoke Charity aforesaid, 1st s. and h.; *b.* March 1620/1. He *m.* before 12 Jan. 1639/40, Grace, widow of Arthur PYNE, of Cathanger, Somerset, da. of Thomas BARLEY, of Elsingham, Essex. He *d.* s.p. and was *bur.* 5 March 1644, at Stoke aforesaid. His widow *m.* (as her 3d husband), before 19 May 1652, Cressy TASBURY, of Bodney, co. Norfolk. Both were living 3 Nov. 1653.

III. 1644. SIR JAMES PHELIPPS, Bart. [1620], of Barrington and Stoke Charity aforesaid, br. and h., *b.* about 1625; *suc. to the Baronetcy* in March 1644, and, being a Royalist, was fined £700. He *m.* (settlement after marriage 6 May 1651) Elizabeth, da. of Sir Richard TICHBORNE, 2d Bart. [1620], of Tichborne, Hants, by his 2d wife, Susan, 2d da. and coheir of William WALLER, of Oldstoke and Stoke Charity aforesaid. He *d.* 28 and was *bur.* 29 Oct. 1652, at Stoke Charity. M.I. Will dat. 20 July 1652, pr. 22 June 1653. His widow, living at Winchester 1690, *d.* 25 and was *bur.* 30 March 1693, at Stoke Charity. Will dat. 13 Sep. 1690, pr. 7 June 1693.

IV. 1652, to 1690. SIR JAMES PHELIPPS, Bart. [1620], of Stoke Charity aforesaid, s. and h.; *bap.* 16 July 1650, at Stoke Charity; *suc. to the Baronetcy*, 28 Oct. 1652; settled in Ireland, Jan. 1688/9. He *m.* 1 May 1671, at Stoke Charity, Marina, da. of Col. William MITCHELL, by Marina, relict of Sir Henry HUNLOKE, 1st Bart. [1693], da. of Dixie HICKMAN. Her birth, 12 March 1635, is reg. at St. Clement Danes. He *d.* s.p.s. at Cork, 1 March 1689/90, when the *Baronetcy* became *extinct*. Will dat. 4 Oct. 1689, pr. 18 July 1690. His widow *d.* at Bath, 19 Sep. 1700. Will dat. 20 May 1698, pr. 6 May 1701.

FORSTER:

cr. 7 March 1619/20;(a)

ex. about 1623.

I. 1620, to 1623? "CLAUDE FORSTER, of Bambrough Castle, co. Northumberland, Knt.," and of Blanchland in the said county, s. and h. of Nicholas FORSTER,(b) of the same, by Jane, da. and h. of Cuthbert RATCLIFFE, of Blanchland aforesaid; suc. his father in 1613; was Sheriff of Northumberland, 1612-13, and having, subsequently to that date, been *Knighted*, was *cr. a Bart.*, as above, 7 March 1619/20.(a) He *m.* Elizabeth, 1st da. of Sir William FENWICK, of Wallington, co. Northumberland, by his 2d wife, Margaret, da. of William SELBY, of Newcastle upon Tyne. He *d.* s.p. about 1623,(c) when the *Baronetcy* became *extinct*. The admon., 10 Jan. 1672/3, of "Dame Elizabeth Forster, of Blenchland, co. Northumberland, widow, granted to her nephew (by the sister), Sir William Foster, Knt. and Bart.," apparently refers to his said wife.

(a) No patent is enrolled, but the signet bill exists. See p. 121, note "a," *sub* "Hervey."

(b) This Nicholas is said to have been a natural son of Sir John Forster, of Bamborough Castle, L. Warden of the Middle Marches, who died 1602.

(c) Visit. of Northumberland, 1666.

T

CHESTER:

cr. 23 March 1619/20;(a)

ex. 17 May 1769.

I. 1620. "ANTHONY CHESTER,(b) of Chitchley [*i.e.*, Chicheley], co. Bucks, Esq.," s. and h. of William CHESTER, citizen and Draper of London, being only child of his father's 1st wife, Judith, da. and coheir of Anthony CAVE, of Chicheley aforesaid (*d.* 9 Sep. 1558), which William (who *d.* 14 April 1608) was s. and h. of Sir William CHESTER, sometime (1560) Lord Mayor of London, was *b.* in Lime street, and *bap.* at St. Dionis, London, 10 April 1566; suc. (his mother having died in July 1570) to the whole of the Chicheley estates on the death of his maternal grandmother in Aug. 1577; raised a troop of horse in 1588; was Sheriff of Bucks, 1602-03,(c) and was *cr. a Bart.*, as above, 23 May 1619/20.(a) He made extensive purchases in Northamptonshire and Beds., and was Sheriff of Beds, 1628-29, obtaining a licence to reside out of that county. He *m.* firstly, 24 Oct. 1589, at St. Giles', Cripplegate, Elizabeth, sister of John, 1st BARON BOTELER OF BRANTFIELD, da. of Sir Henry BOTELER, of Hatfield Woodhall, Herts, by his 1st wife, Catharine, da. of Robert WALLER, of Beaconsfield. She *d.* 5 April 1629, aged 63, and was *bur.* at Chicheley. M.I. He *m.* secondly, 5 Sep. 1631 (settl. 31 Aug. 1631), Mary (some forty years his junior), only da. of John ELLIS, of Kidall and Rothwell, co. York, by Elizabeth, da. of William PLOMPTON, of Plompton. He *d.* at Chicheley 1 and was *bur.* 3 Dec. 1635 there, in his 70th year. Will dat. 25 Nov., pr. 9 Dec. 1635. Inq. p.m. at Olney, 7 Oct. 1636. His widow *m.*, 8 June 1658, at St. Peter's, Paul's Wharf, London, Samuel LODINGTON, Barrister of the Inner Temple and Clerk of the Midland Circuit, who was *bur.* in the Temple Church, 29 Jan. 1662/3. She, herself, was *bur.* 24 Sep. 1692, at St. Martins' in the Fields. Will dat. 19 July 1677 to 10 Sep. 1692, pr. 26 Sep. 1692.

II. 1635. SIR ANTHONY CHESTER, Bart. [1620], of Chicheley aforesaid, s. and h. by 1st wife; *bap.* there 25 March 1593; admitted to Gray's Inn, 25 Oct. 1615; *suc. to the Baronetcy* in Dec. 1635, but only to a small part of the estate. Sheriff of Bucks, 1636-37. He joined the Royal army in the Civil War, and commanded a troop of horse at Naseby, his house at Chicheley being consequently sacked and his rents sequestrated, so that in 1646 he fled to Holland to escape arrest. He *m.*, in 1623 (without his father's consent), Elizabeth, da. of Sir John PEYTON, of Doddington, co. Cambridge, by Alice, da. of Sir John PEYTON, 1st Bart. [1611], of Iselham. He returned home in 1650, and was *bur.* 15 Feb. 1651/2, at Chicheley. His widow, by whom he had thirteen children, *d.* (40 years later) 3 and was *bur.* 4 July 1692, at Chicheley, in her 89th year. M.I.

III. 1652. SIR ANTHONY CHESTER, Bart. [1620], of Chicheley aforesaid, 2d but 1st surv. s. and h., *b.* about 1632, being 19 years old when he *suc. to the Baronetcy*, in Feb. 1651/2, and to a much encumbered estate. By his marriage, in 1657, and by the death s.p.s. of his uncle, Sir Henry Chester, **K.B.**, 18 Aug. 1669 (aged 72), he inherited the estates of Liddington Park and Tilsworth Manor, in Beds and elsewhere.(d) He was Sheriff of Bucks, 1668-69; M.P. for Bedford,

(a) No patent is enrolled, but the signet bill exists. See p. 121, note "a," *sub* "Hervey."

(b) See pedigree and account of this family in R. E. Chester Waters' masterly work entitled *The Family of Chester of Chicheley*, 2 vols., 4to, 1878. Its author (who was 5th in descent from the 4th Baronet, through the families of Toller and Methold) died, after many years illness, 25 Nov. 1898, aged 68, at 11 Clarendon road, Notting Hill, and was buried at Kensal Green.

(c) As he is called "Esquire" both in 1615 (when his son was admitted to Gray's Inn) and in 1620 (when *cr.* a Bart.), he cannot be the "Anthony Chester, *Heref.* [*Qy.* Herts], who was *Knighted*, 27 June 1603, at Easton Neston. This, possibly, may be the "Anthony Chester" admitted in 1582/3, to Gray's Inn, who is not mentioned in Chester Waters' work.

(d) He had, however, during a long period, to provide for the jointures of three Dowager Ladies Chester, who were all living at the same time, their united ages amounting to 256 years. The first to die was his uncle's widow, who *d.* April. 1684, aged 80; the next was his mother, who *d.* June 1692, aged 90; and the last his step-grandmother, in Sep. 1692, aged 88.

1685-87. He *m*, 21 May 1657, at Chicheley, Mary, only da. (whose issue became sole heir) of Samuel CRANMER, of Astwoodbury, Bucks, Alderman and sometime (1631) Sheriff of London, by his 2d wife, Mary (who *m.* secondly, Sir Henry Chester, **K.B.**, abovementioned), sister of Sir Henry WOOD, Bart. [1642 ?], of Loudham, co. Suffolk. He *d.* at Chicheley, 15 and was *bur.* there 19 Feb. 1697/8, aged 65. M.I. His widow, by whom he had sixteen children, *d.* 21 and was *bur.* 26 May 1710, at Chicheley, aged 75. Will dat. 3 Feb. 1709-10, pr. at Oxford, 18 Aug. 1710.

IV. 1698. SIR JOHN CHESTER, Bart. [1620], of Chicheley aforesaid, 2d but 1st surv. s. and h.(a); *b.* 24 June and *bap.* 6 July 1666, at Chicheley; *suc. to the Baronetcy*, 15 Feb. 1697/8, shortly after which he rebuilt (1699—1704) Chicheley Hall at a great cost, and restored the parish church. He was a well known sportsman, and was one of the Gentlemen of Queen Anne's Privy Chamber. He *m.* firstly, 2 Nov. 1686, at Shenton, co. Leicester (when under age), Anne (£10,000 portion), 1st da. and coheir of William WOLLASTON, of Shenton Hall, by Elizabeth, only child of Capt. Francis CAVE, of Ingarsby. She, who was five years his senior, and by whom he had eleven children, was *bap.* 13 May 1668, at Shenton, where she *d.* in childbed, 3 and was *bur.* 11 Oct. 1704, at Chicheley. M.I. He *m.* secondly, April 1714, Frances, widow of Sir Charles SKRIMSHIRE, and formerly of Ralph SNEYD, of Keele, co. Stafford, da. of Sir William NOEL, 2d Bart. [1660], of Kirkby Mallory, and only child of his 2d wife, Frances, da. of Humble (WARD), 1st BARON WARD OF HIMLEY. He *d.* 6 and was *bur.* 16 Feb. 1725/6, at Chicheley, in his 60th year. His will (not proved in C.P.C.) was disputed in Chancery. His widow, who was *b.* at Himley Hall and *bap.* 14 April 1673, at Himley, co. Stafford, *m.*, for her 4th husband (as his 2d wife), Charles ADDERLEY, of Hams Hall, co. Warwick, who *d.* 2 Feb. 1746, aged 82. She *d.* Feb. 1751, in her 78th year. Will dat. 24 Oct. 1747, pr. 21 Jan. 1752.

V. 1726, Feb. SIR WILLIAM CHESTER, Bart. [1620], of Chicheley aforesaid (where, however, he never resided), 1st s. and h., *b.* at Shenton Hall aforesaid, 5 and *bap.* 8 Sep. 1687, at Shenton; matric. (with his br. Thomas) at Oxford (Ch. Ch.) 18 May 1705, as a Gent. Commoner; *suc. to the Baronetcy*, 6 Feb. 1725/6, but not to the greater part of the estates.(b) He *m.*, 6 March 1716/7, at Shenton, co. Leicester, Penelope, only da. of George HEWETT, of Stretton and Great Glen, co. Leicester, by Penelope, da. of Sir William JESSON, and Penelope, da. of Sir George VILLIERS, 2d Bart. [1619]. He *d.* s.p.m.(c) at Great Glen aforesaid (only thirty-two days after his father) 10 and was *bur.* 19 March 1725/6, at Chicheley, aged 38. His widow *m.*, 5 April 1736, at the Mercer's Chapel, London (Lic. Fac.), James MONTAGUE, of Newbold, co. Leicester, widower (grandson of the 1st EARL OF SANDWICH), who *d.* s.p. 8 Nov. 1748. She *d.* before him, between May 1739 and Dec. 1744.

VI. 1726, March. SIR JOHN CHESTER, Bart. [1620], of Chicheley aforesaid, br. and h. male, *b.* at Shenton Hall, 23 April and *bap.* 16 May 1693, at Shenton aforesaid; ed. at Christ's Coll., Cambridge, as a Fellow Commoner, 1709; B.A., 1712; M.A., 1716; admitted to the Inner Temple, 6 June 1713; *suc. to the Baronetcy*, and to the Chicheley estate, 10 March 1725/6, having, in the preceding month, on his father's death, suc. to the Bedfordshire estates; was M.P. for Beds, 1741-47. He *m.*, 15 Feb. 1718/9, at Blithfield, co. Stafford, Frances, da. of Sir Edward BAGOT, 4th Bart. [1627], by Frances, da. and h. of Sir Thomas WAGSTAFFE. He *d.* 8 and was *bur.* 13 Feb. 1747/8, at Chicheley, aged 54. Admon. 27 May 1748. His widow *d.* at St. Margaret's, Westm., 17 and was *bur.* 21 Feb. 1748/9, at Chicheley. Will dat. 5 Feb. 1748/9, pr. 19 July 1749.

(a) His elder br., Anthony Chester, *b.* 6 and *bap.* 20 Oct. 1663, at Chicheley; matric. at Oxford (Ch. Ch.), 17 Dec. 1679; B.A., 7 July 1682; *d.* unm. v.p., and was *bur.* 10 July 1685, at Chicheley, in his 22d year.

(b) His father devised (just as the 1st Baronet had done) the estates in Bedfordshire to a yr. son, viz., John, afterwards the 6th Baronet.

(c) He left, including a posthumous child, six daughters and coheirs, who were most inadequately provided for; the Chicheley estate having been settled in tail male on their father's marriage.

VII. 1748. SIR CHARLES BAGOT CHESTER, Bart. [1620], of Chicheley aforesaid, 1st s. and h., *b.* 1724; ed. at Westm. School and at St. John's Coll., Oxford; matric. 4 Nov. 1741, and was *cr.* D.C.L., 14 April 1749; *suc. to the Baronetcy*, 8 Feb. 1747/8, as also to the whole of the family estates, the entail of which he cut off, leaving them, as well as the residue of his personalty (excluding both his sister as also his heir male) to his maternal cousin, Charles Bagot.(a) He *d.* unm. and s.p. legit.(b) 25 and was *bur.* 29 May 1755, at Chicheley, in his 31st year. Will dat. 21 and pr. 27 May 1755.

VIII. 1755. SIR FRANCIS CHESTER, Bart. [1620], uncle and h. male, *b.* 3 and *bap.* 9 May 1694, at Shenton aforesaid; was sometime a Merchant in London. He *m.*, 4 March 1717/8, Bertha (ten years his senior), da. and coheir of Thomas WEBB, otherwise WOOD (nephew and coheir of Sir Henry WOOD, Bart., abovenamed), by Susanne, his wife. She, who was *bap.* 29 Jan. 1683/4, at Chelsea, and who inherited, a few days before her death, a considerable property (on the death of her cousin, Charles CRANMER, otherwise WOOD), *d.* 29 Sep., and was *bur.* 5 Oct. 1743, at St. Augustine's, Hackney, in her 60th year. M.I. He, on his wife's death, became deranged, and *d.* s.p.m.s.,(c) in a lunatic asylum, at Chelsea, 18 and was *bur.* 30 Oct. 1766, at Hackney aforesaid, in his 74th year. M.I.

IX. 1766, to 1769. SIR ANTHONY CHESTER, Bart. [1620], of East Haddon, co. Northampton, cousin and h. male, being only s. and h. of Henry CHESTER, of East Haddon aforesaid, by Theodocia, da. of Thomas TOWER, of Haddenham, in the Isle of Ely, which Henry (who was *b.* 14 and *bap.* 29 Sep. 1668, at Chicheley, and *d.* 6 May 1726) was 3d s. and 10th child of the 3d Bart. He was *b.* at Astwoodbury, and *bap.* 26 June 1706, at Astwood, Bucks; matric. at Cambridge (Em. Coll.) as a Pensioner, 10 July 1724; B.A., 1727; M.A., 1731, in which year he took Holy Orders; Chaplain of the Mercers' Company in 1734. He *m.* (Lic. Fac. 18 Jan. 1750/1) Elizabeth BURT, of St. Mary Arden, co. Leicester, then above 25, spinster. He *d.* s.p.m. of paralysis, 17 and was *bur.* 23 May 1769, at East Haddon, aged 62, when the *Baronetcy* became *extinct*. His widow *d.* at Northampton, 13 and was *bur.* 20 June 1808, at East Haddon aforesaid, aged 88. M.I. Will pr. 1808.

TRYON:

cr. 29 March 1620;

ex. 24 April 1724.

I. 1620. "SAMUEL TRYON, of Laire Marney, co. Essex, Knt.," 2d s. of Peter TRYON, of St. Christopher's by the Exchange, London, Merchant (a refugee, who brought with him above £6,000, from the Low Countries, and who *d.* April 1611), by Mary, his wife; was *Knighted*, 25 April 1615, at Newmarket; purchased the manor of Layer Marney aforesaid, and afterwards that of Halstead, Essex, where he erected a mansion called Boys' Hall. He is said to have *m.* firstly, Mary, da. of Edward GULDEFORD, of Hemsted, co. Kent. He *m.* Elizabeth, da. of John ELDRED, Citizen of London. He *d.* at Boys' Hall, 8 March 1626/7, aged 46, and was *bur.* at Halsted, Essex. M.I. Will pr. 26 April 1627. His widow (Elizabeth) *m.* Edward WORTLEY, yr. br. of Sir Francis WORTLEY, 1st Bart. [1611].

(a) He, who was *b.* 1 Sep. 1730, and who was the devisee's school fellow at Westm., suc. to them accordingly in 1755 (being then a Wine Merchant in Oporto). He took the name of Chester. He *d.* 2 April 1793, leaving issue, who still possess the greater part of them.

(b) He had children by two mistresses "whom he kept to the day of his death" and appears to have been a drunken spendthrift, thus called by Cole (the Antiquary) "a thorough accomplished gentleman, universally esteemed by his acquaintance."

(c) Francis Chester, only surv. son, *b.* 17 and *bap.* 25 July 1724, at Hackney; *d.* unm. and v.p. 18 and was *bur.* 24 Dec. 1757 there.

II. 1627. SIR SAMUEL TRYON, Bart. [1620], of Boys' Hall aforesaid, s. and h., *b.* in London, 1615; *suc. to the Baronetcy*, 8 March, 1626/7, and was in ward to his stepfather, Sir Edward Wortley; was admitted to St. John's Coll., Cambridge, as a Fellow Commoner, 26 April 1634, and then called 17. Sheriff of Essex, 1649-50. He *m.* firstly, Eleanor,(a) da. of Sir Henry LEE, 1st Bart. [1611], of Quarendon, by Eleanor, sister of his said stepfather, da. of Sir Richard WORTLEY. He *m.* secondly, Susan, da. of John HARVEY, of Newton, co. Suffolk. He *d.* 1665. Will pr. 1665. His widow (who was a celebrated beauty) *m.* Timothy THORNBURY, of London, Gent., and *d.* Michaelmas, 1684, being *bur.* in Crutched Friars.

III. 1665. SIR SAMUEL TRYON, Bart. [1620], of Boys Hall aforesaid, s. and h. by 1st wife; *suc. to the Baronetcy* about 1665. He *d.* unm., about 1672. Admon. 2 Oct. 1672, to his sister, Dame Eleanor Frankelyn.

IV. 1672, to 1724. SIR SAMUEL JOHN TRYON, Bart. [1620], br., of the half blood and h. male, being s. of the 2d Bart. by his 2d wife; *suc to the Baronetcy* about 1671. He *m.* Mary, da. of Robert BOWNDS, of Chelmsford, Draper. He *d.* s.p.m., 24 April 1724, when the *Baronetcy* became *extinct*.

NEWTON:

cr. 2 April 1620,

afterwards, 1652-1700, PUCKERING;

ex. 22 Jan. 1700.

I. 1620. "ADAM NEWTON, of Charlton, co. Kent., Esq.," Tutor, (1599), and Treasurer to Henry, afterwards Prince of Wales, and, subsequently, to his br., Prince Charles; was, though a layman, Dean of Durham, 1606-20; purchased, in May 1607, for £4,500, the manor of Charlton, co. Kent; and was *cr. a Bart.*, as above, 2 April 1620. He *m.* Katharine, da. of Sir John PUCKERING, L.-Keeper of the Seal, 1592-96, by Anne, da. of George CHOWNE, of Kent. She was living May 1606, but *d.* before him. He *d.* 13 Jan. 1629/30, and was *bur.* at Charlton. M.I. Will dat. 9 Jan. 1629, pr. 3 Dec. 1630.

II. 1630. SIR WILLIAM NEWTON, Bart. [1620], of Charlton aforesaid, s. and h.; *suc. to the Baronetcy* in 1629. He *d.* unm., before March 1635/6.(b)

III. 1635? to 1700. SIR HENRY NEWTON, *afterwards* (1652) PUCKERING, Bart. [1620], of Charlton aforesaid, br. and h., *bap.* 13 April 1618, at St. Dunstan's in the West, London; *suc. to the Baronetcy* before March 1635/6.(b) He suc. to the Priory in Warwick and the other estates of his maternal uncle, Sir Henry PUCKERING, Bart. [so *cr.* 25 Nov. 1611, who *d.* 20 March 1636], after the death s.p.s., 27 Jan. 1652, of Dame Jane Bale, only surv. child of the said Henry, and *assumed* in consequence, the name of *Puckering*. He fought for the royal cause at Edgehill, and was, 20 July 1646, fined £1,910, reduced to £1,273 on 3 Dec. following. He was M.P. for Warwickshire, 1661-79, and for Warwick, 1679; was Paymaster Gen. of the forces to Charles II. In 1658 he sold the manor of Charlton for £8,500. He *m.*, in or before 1645, Elizabeth, da. of Thomas MURRAY. He *d.* s.p.s., 22 Jan. 1700, aged 83, and was *bur.* at St. Mary's, Warwick, M.I., when the *Baronetcy* became *extinct*.(c) Admon., 19 May 1701, to Dame Jane Bowyer, widow, principal creditor.

(a) Whom, however, "he affected not, which was the unfortunate occasion of ruining a fine estate." [Collins' *Baronetage*.]

(b) "Sir *Henry* Newton, Bart.," presented to the Rectory of Charlton in March 1635/6.

(c) He left his estates for life to his wife's niece, Jane, widow of Sir John Bowyer, Bart., of Knipersley, da. and coheir of Henry Murray, Groom of the Bedchamber, with rem. to Vincent Grantham, of Goltho', co. Lincoln.

BOTELER:

cr. 12 April 1620,

afterwards, 1628-47, BARONS BOTELER OF BRANTFIELD;

ex. 1647.

I. 1620. "JOHN BOTELER, of Hatfield Woodhall, co. Herts, Knt.," s. and h. of Sir Henry BOTELER, of the same, and of Brantfield in the said county, by his 1st wife, Catharine, da. of Robert WALLER, of Hadley, Midx., *b.* about 1565; was *Knighted* at Greenwich, July 1607; suc. his father, 20 Jan. 1608/9, being then aged 43, and having *m.*, before 1609, Elizabeth, sister of the half blood to George, DUKE OF BUCKINGHAM (the all powerful favourite of the King), da. of Sir George VILLIERS, of Brokesby, co. Leicester, by his 1st wife, Audrey, da. and h. of William SAUNDERS, of Harrington, co. Northampton, was *cr. a Bart.*, as above, 12 April 1620; was M.P. for Herts, 1625, and was *cr.*, 30 July 1628, BARON BOTELER OF BRANTFIELD, co. Hertford. In that Barony this *Baronetage* then *merged* till both became *extinct* on the death of the 2d holder in 1647. See "Peerage."

GERARD, *or* GERRARD:

cr. 13 April 1620;

ex. Feb. 1715/6.

I. 1620. "GILBERT GERRARD,(a) of Harrow-on-the-hill, co. Middlesex, Esq.," s. and h. of William GERRARD, *or* GERARD, of Flamberds in that parish, by Dorothy, da. of John RATCLIFFE, of Langley, suc. his father in that estate, 15 April 1583; admitted to Gray's Inn, 3 Aug. 1592; and was *cr. a Bart.*, as above, 13 April 1630. He was M.P. for Middlesex (in five Parls.), 1621-48, and for Lancaster in the conv. Parl. of 1660; Sheriff of Berks, 1626-27; Treasurer of War, 1642, and one of the Council of War to Parl. in 1643; Chancellor of the Duchy of Lancaster, 1649 and 1659. He *m.*, in or before 1620, Mary, da. of Sir Francis BARRINGTON, 1st Bart. [1611], by Joan, da. of Sir Henry CROMWELL. She inherited the Manor of Aston Clinton, Bucks, and was *bur.*, 4 May 1666, at Harrow. He *d.* 6 and was *bur.* there 20 Jan. 1669/70. Will dat. 11 June 1668, pr. 2 March 1669/70.

II. 1670. SIR FRANCIS GERARD, Bart. [1620], of Flamberds aforesaid, s. and h., *b.* about 1620; M.P. for Seaford, 1641-48; for Midx., 1659, and for Bossiney in the conv. Parl. of 1660; was *Knighted* v.p., 8 June 1660, at Whitehall; *suc. to the Baronetcy* in Jan. 1669/70. He *m.*, in or before 1650, Isabel, da. of Sir Thomas CHEEKE, of Pirgo, Essex, by his 2d wife, Essex, da. of Robert (RICH), EARL OF WARWICK. He was living 1681, but was dead in 1685.

III. 1684? SIR CHARLES GERARD, BART. [1620], of Flamberds aforesaid, s. and h., *b.* about 1654; Sheriff of Berks, 1681-82; *suc. to the Baronetcy* on the death of his father. He was M.P. for Midx., 1685-95, and for Cockermouth, 1695-98. He *m.*, 10 Feb. 1675/6, at St. Michael's, Cornwall (Lic. Vic. Gen., he about 22, and she about 17), Honora, sister of Charles, 6th DUKE OF SOMERSET, da. of Charles (SEYMOUR), 2d BARON SEYMOUR OF TROWBRIDGE, by his 2d wife, Elizabeth, da. of William (ALINGTON), 1st BARON ALINGTON OF KILLARD [I]. He *d.* s.p.m.s.(b) at Harrow in 1701. Admon., 26 July 1701 and again 7 Feb. 1735, to Elizabeth Stapleton, only child of deceased. His widow *d.* at Hampstead, and was *bur.* 10 May 1731, at Harrow. Will pr. May 1732.

(a) See in "N. and Q.," 8th S., p. 243, a good account of this branch of the family, by W. Duncombe Pink.

(b) His son, Francis, died v.p. and s.p. Admon., 7 Feb. 1735. Elizabeth, his da. and h., *m.* firstly, Warwick Lake (by whom she was ancestress of the Viscounts Lake), and secondly, Miles Stapleton. She, on the death of her uncle, the 4th and last Bart., inherited in Feb. 1715/6, the estate of Flamberds.

IV. 1701. SIR FRANCIS GERARD, Bart. [1620], of Flamberds aforesaid, br. and h. male; *suc. to the Baronetcy*, 1701. He *m.* (—). He *d.* s.p.m.,(a) and was *bur.* 1 Sep. 1704, at Harrow.

V. 1704, to 1716. SIR CHEEKE GERARD, Bart. [1620], of Flamberds aforesaid, br. and h. male, *b.* 2 July 1662, at Harrow; *suc. to the Baronetcy*, Aug. 1704. He *d.* unm. and was *bur.* 9 March 1715/6, at Harrow, when the *Baronetcy* became *extinct*. Admon., 20 March 1715/6, to Elizabeth Lake, widow, great aunt and next of kin.

LEE, *or* LEA:

cr. 3 May 1620;

ex. April 1660.

I. 1620. "HUMFREY LEE, of Langley, co. Salop, Esq.," and of Acton Burnell in that county, s. of Richard LEE, of Langley, by Eleanor, da. of Walter WROTTESLEY, of Wrottesley, co. Stafford, was *b.* about 1569; matric. at Oxford (Hart Hall), 17 Dec. 1576, aged 17; admitted to Inner Temple (as H. Lea), 1578; was Sheriff of Shropshire, 1599—1600; and was *cr. a Bart.*, as above, 3 May 1620, being the first Shropshire gentleman so advanced. He *m.*, in or before 1600, Margaret,(b) da. of Reginald CORBETT, of Stoke, co. Salop, one of the Justices of the Court of King's Bench (1559-66), by Alice, da. of John GRATTWOOD. He was *bur.* 4 Oct. 1631, at Acton Burnell.

II. 1631, to 1660. SIR RICHARD LEE, Bart. [1620], of Langley and Acton Burnell aforesaid, s. and h., *b.* about 1600; matric. at Oxford (Queen's Coll.), 10 May 1616, aged 16; *suc. to the Baronetcy*, probably about 1630; Sheriff of Salop, 1638-39; was M.P. for Salop, 1640, till disabled in 1642. He suffered much in the royal cause, and attended the King at Oxford, 1643, and was a compounder, 11 Feb. 1651 (on final review) for £2,966. He *m.*, 17 June 1626, at St. Helen's, Bishopsgate, Elizabeth,(c) da. of Edward ALLEN, Alderman, and sometime (1620-21) Sheriff of London, by his 1st wife, Judith, da. of William BENNETT, of London. He *d.* s.p.m.s. April 1660, when the *Baronetcy* became *extinct*.(d)

BERNEY:

cr. 5 May 1620.

I. 1620. "RICHARD BERNEY, of Parkehall in Redham, co. Norfolk, Esq.," 3d s., but eventually h. of Sir Thomas BERNEY, of the same, by Juliana, da. of Sir Thomas GAWDY, of Redenhall, co. Norfolk, one of the Justices of the Common Pleas, suc. his father in 1616, and was *cr. a Bart.*, as above, 5 May 1620. Sheriff for Norfolk, 1622-23. He *m.* Anne, da. of Michael SMALPAGE, of Chichester, Sussex. He *d.* 1668. Will pr. 21 Jan. 1669 and 25 June 1701.

(a) Of his two daughters and coheirs (1) [—], *m.* [—] Lethieullier, (2) Isabella, *m.* firstly, Sir John Fryer, Bart., who *d.* Sep. 1726, and secondly, Henry (Temple), 1st Viscount Palmerston [I.], who *d.* 1757. She, however, *d.* s.p.

(b) The admon., 25 May 1648, of Dame Margaret Leigh, *alias* Devett, *alias* Dale, of Tixover co. Rutland, to her husband, "Thomas Levett, Esq.," may possibly relate to this Margaret.

(c) The will of "Dame Elizabeth Leigh" is pr. 1665, and may possibly be that of this Elizabeth.

(d) See account of his two surv. daughters and their descendants in Burke's *Extinct Baronetage*. He had three sons, of whom, Humphrey, the eldest, is said (presumably in error), in Collins' *Baronetage* (1720), to have suc. to the title.

II. 1668. Sir Thomas Berney, Bart. [1620], of Norwich, s. and h.; *suc. to the Baronetcy*, but not to the estate(a), in 1668. He *m.* [secondly ?] Sarah, daughter of Thomas Tyrrel, Governor of Landguard Fort. He *d.* 1693. Will dat. 6 Nov. 1693, pr. 5 Feb. 1713/4.

III. 1693. Sir Richard Berney, Bart. [1620], of Kirby Bedon,(b) co. Norfolk, s. and h.; *suc. to the Baronetcy* in 1693. He *m.* Dorothy, da. of William Branthwayte, of Hethel, co. Norfolk. He *d.* May 1706. His will dat. 10 Sep. 1705 to 29 April 1706, pr. in the consistory court of Norwich, 1706, and again, in London, 5 Feb. 1713/14, His wife survived him.

IV. 1706. Sir Richard Berney, Bart. [1620], of Kirby Bedon aforesaid, s. and h.; *suc. to the Baronetcy* in May 1706. He *d.* unm. in 1710, aged 22.

V. 1710. Sir Thomas Berney, Bart. [1620], of Kirby Bedon aforesaid, br. and h.; *suc. to the Baronctcy* in 1710. He *m.* Elizabeth, da. and h. of Simon Folkes of (—), co. Suffolk, by Elizabeth, da. and coheir of Samuel Hanson, of Barbadoes. By her he acquired a good estate, viz., a plantation in that island called "Hansons." He *d.* 1742.

VI. 1742. Sir Hanson Berney, Bart. [1620], of Kirby Bedon aforesaid, s. and h.; Sheriff of Norfolk, 1762-63. He *m.*, 8 April 1756, at Somerset House chapel, Midx., Catharine, da. and h. of William Woodball, of Walthamstow, Essex. He *d.* at Kensington, Midx., 1778. Admon. 16 April 1778. His wife survived him.

VII. 1778. Sir John Berney, Bart. [1620], of Kirby Bedon aforesaid, s. and h.; *suc. to the Baronetcy* in 1778. He *m.*, 9 Sep. 1779, Henrietta, da. of George (Nevill), 1st Earl of Abergavenny, by Henrietta, da. of Thomas Pelham. He *d.* 4 Sep. or Oct. 1825, at Bruges, aged 68. His widow, who was *b.* 24 May 1756, *d.* 2 April 1833, at Auderlecht, near Brussels, aged 77. Both were *bur.* in the English cemetery, at Bruges. M.I.

VIII. 1825. Sir Hanson Berney, Bart. [1620], of Kirby Bedon aforesaid, and of Twycross, co. Leicester, s. and h., *b.* 3 Dec. 1780, at Kirby Bedon aforesaid; *suc. to the Baronetcy* in 1825. He *m.* firstly, April 1811, Anne, 1st. da. of Henry Tahourdin, of Sydenham, Kent. She *d.* s.p. 14 Jan. 1838. He *m.* secondly, 10 Oct. 1843, Agnes, da. of Thomas Peek. He *d.* Sep. 1870, at 2 Castle street, Beaumaris. His widow *d.* 6 Oct. 1870.

IX. 1870. Sir Henry Hanson Berney, Bart. [1620], of Barton Bendish, co. Norfolk, s. and h., by 2d wife, *b.* 30 Nov. 1843, at Twycross aforesaid; ed. at Trin. Hall, Cambridge; LL.B., 1865; *suc. to the Baronetcy*, Sep. 1870. He *m.*, 31 Jan. 1866, Jane Dorothea, da. of the Rev. Andrew Bloxam, then Vicar of Twycross, but afterwards Rector of Harborough Magna, co. Warwick.

Family Estates.—These, in 1883, consisted of 3,148 acres in Norfolk, worth £4,181. *Seat.*—Barton Bendish. *Residence.*—Woodlands, in Windermere, co. Westmorland.

(a) He was disinherited by his father, who left Park Hall and all his estates (about £7,000 a year), to the second son, Richard, whose s. and h. Richard Berney, Sheriff of Norfolk, 1692, alienated them, and *d.* s.p., having squandered nearly all his fortune.

(b) "A very handsome seat," which he purchased with money left him by his uncle Richard. [Collins' *Baronetage*, 1770].

FORSTER, *or* FORESTER:
cr. 20 May 1620;
ex. Dec. 1711.

I. 1620. "Humfrey Forster, of Aldermaston, co. Berks, Esq.," only s. and h. of Sir William Forster, K.B., of the same, by Mary, da. of Sir Mark Stewart, of Ely; suc. his father, 1618; was Sheriff of Berks, 1619-20, and was *cr. a Bart.*, as above, 20 May 1620; was a Royalist and a compounder for £1,000. He *m.*, about 1616, Anne, da. of Sir William Kingsmill, of Sidmanton, Hants. He *d.* 1663, æt. 68, and was *bur.* at Aldermaston. Will pr. 1663. His widow, by whom he had sixteen children, *d.* 12 Oct. 1673, and was *bur.* at Aldermaston. M.I.

II. 1663, to 1711. Sir Humphrey Forster, *or* Forester,(a) Bart. [1620], of Aldermaston aforesaid, grandson and h., being s. and h. of William Forster, by Elizabeth, da. of Sir John Tyrell, of Heron, Essex, which William was s. and h. ap. of the 1st Bart., but *d.* v.p. 1661. He *suc. to the Baronetcy* in 1663; was M.P. for Berks, in seven Parls., 1677—1701; Sheriff of Berks, 1704. He *m.*, 26 Nov. 1672, at St. Margaret's, Westm. (Lic. Vic. Gen., he 23 and she 18), Judith, da. and coheir of Sir Humphrey Winch, Bart. (so *cr.* 1660), by Rebecca, da. of Martin Browne, Alderman of London. He *d.* s.p.s. Dec. 1711, when the *Baronetcy* became *extinct*.(b) Will pr. 1712. His widow *d.* 1720.

BIGGS, *or* BIGG, *or* BYGGS:
cr. 26 May 1620;
ex. 11 June 1621.

I. 1620, to 1621. "Thomas Byggs, of Lenchwicke, co. Worcester, Esq.," s. and h. of Sir Thomas Bigg, or Biggs, of the same, by Ursula, da. of Clement Throckmorton, of Haseley, co. Warwick, *b.* about 1577; matric. at Oxford (Queen's Coll.), 8 Nov. 1594, aged 17; admitted to Middle Temple, 1597; suc. his father, 4 May 1613; was M.P. for Evesham, 1614 and 1621; and was *cr. a Bart.*, as above, 26 May 1620. He *m.* Anne, da. of William Witham, of Leadstone, co. York. He *d.* s.p. 11 June 1621, in his 45th year, and was *bur.* at Norton, co. Worcester, when the *Baronetcy* became *extinct*. M.I. Admon. 26 June 1621, to a creditor, and again, 25 Feb. 1655/6, to his sister's children and next of kin.(c) His widow *m.* (as his 2d wife), 18 July 1622, at Isleworth, Midx., Sir John Walter, Ch. Baron of the Exchequer, who *d.* 17 Nov. 1630, and was *bur.* at Woolvercott, Oxon, leaving her surviving.

BELLINGHAM:
cr. 30 May 1620;
ex. Oct. 1650.

I. 1620. "Henry Bellingham, of Helsington, co. Westmorland, Esq.," s. and h. of Sir James Bellingham, of the same, by Agnes, da. of Sir Henry Curwen, was *cr. a Bart.*, as above, 30 May 1620, being *Knighted*, the next day,(d) at Theobalds; was M.P. for Westmorland, 1625-26, April to May 1640, and Nov. 1640 till disabled in Oct. 1645; was a Royalist; a compounder in July 1646; and was fined £3,228 in Feb. 1647, and £1,971 more in May 1649. He *m.* Dorothy, da. of Sir Francis Boynton, of Barington, co. York. He *d.* early in Oct. 1650.

(a) He subscribes himself as "Forester" to his marr. lic. in 1672.

(b) The estate of Aldermaston devolved on Elizabeth, Baroness Stawell, da. of his sister Elizabeth, by her first husband, William Pert. She *d.* in 1721. To its subsequent devolution, as given in Burke's *Extinct Baronetage*, may be added its purchase, in 1899, by Charles Keyser.

(c) Cecilia, his da. and h., *m.*, before 1644, William Standish, of Standish, co. Lancaster, and *d.* 19 Jan. 1719/20, leaving issue.

(d) See p. 18, note "c," *sub* "Tollemache."

II. 1650, 10 ? to 26 Oct. Sir James Bellingham, Bart. [1620], of Helsington aforesaid, s. and h.; *bap.* 8 Sep. 1623; admitted to Gray's Inn, 7 May 1640; M.P. for Westmorland, Jan. 1646 till secluded in Dec. 1648; was a compounder, and was, 19 May 1649, fined £200; *suc. to the Baronetcy* in Oct. 1650. He *m.* Catharine, 4th da. and coheir of Sir Henry Willoughby, Bart. (so *cr.* 1611), of Risley, co. Derby, by his 2nd wife, Lettice, da. and coheir of Sir Francis Darcy. He *d.* s.p. a few days after his father, and was *bur.* 26 Oct. 1650, at Heversham, when the *Baronetcy* became *extinct*. Will pr. 1651. His widow *m.* in or before 1656, George Purefoy, of Whalley, Berks, who *d.* in or before Jan. 1671, being, by her, father of Sir Henry Purefoy, Bart., so *cr.* 1686. She survived her 2d husband, and *d.* at Oxford. Admon. 30 June 1673, and again, 2 May 1676.

YELVERTON:
cr. 31 May 1620;
ex. 15 Nov. 1649.

I. 1620. "William Yelverton,(a) of Rougham, co. Norfolk, Esq.," s. and h. of Henry Yelverton,(b) of the same (*d.* 26 April 1601), by Bridget, da. of Sir William Drury, of Hawsted, Suffolk; was *b.* about 1558, being aged 43, on 12 Aug. 1601, and was *cr. a Bart.*, as above, 31 May 1620. Sheriff of Norfolk, 1621-22. He *m.* (settl. 12 March 1586/7), Dionysia, 1st da. and coheir of Richard Stubbes, of Sedgeford, co. Norfolk. He *d.* 30 Oct. 1631. Inq. p.m., 1 April 1636. Admon. 10 July 1635.

II. 1631. Sir William Yelverton, Bart. [1620], of Rougham aforesaid, s. and h., *b.* probably about 1590, though said to be aged about 30 (12 Car. I) 1636. He *m.* (settlement 12 June 1614) Ursula, 1st da. of Sir Thomas Richardson, Lord Chief Justice of the King's Bench, 1631-34, by his 1st wife, Ursula, da. of John Southwell, of Barham, co. Suffolk. He *d.* 19 July 1648. His widow *d.* 20 March 1657.

III. 1648, to 1649. Sir William Yelverton, Bart. [1620], of Rougham aforesaid, s. and h.; *suc. to the Baronetcy*, 19 July 1648; was a Royalist, and was, 27 Sep. 1649, fined £1,545. He *d.* unm. 15 Nov. 1649, when the *Baronetcy* became *extinct*.(c) Will pr. 1650.

SCUDAMORE:
cr. 1 June 1620,
afterwards, 1628—1716, Viscounts Scudamore of Sligo [I.];
ex. 2 Dec. 1716.

I. 1620. "John Scudamore, of Honelacy [*i.e.*, Holme Lacy], co. Hereford, Esq., son and heir, of James Scudamore, Knt. decd.," being his s. by Anne, da. of Sir Thomas Throckmorton (which James, who *d.* v.p. 14 April 1619, was s. and h. ap. of Sir John Scudamore, of Holme Lacy aforesaid), was *bap.* there 22 March 1600/1; matric. at Oxford (Mag. Coll.), 8 Nov. 1616; admitted to Middle Temple 1617, and was *cr. a Bart.*, as above, 1 June 1620. M.P. for Herefordshire, 1621-22 and 1624-25; for Hereford, 1625 and 1628-29. He

---

(a) See pedigree in *Visit. of Norfolk*, 1563, as published by the Norfolk Arch. Soc. (vol. i, p. 265).

(b) This Henry was 4th in descent from Sir William Yelverton, K.B., of Rougham and of Rackheath in the same county, one of the Judges both in the court of King's Bench and Common Pleas, *temp.* Hen. VI and Ed. IV. See note "a" above.

(c) Of his two sisters and coheirs (1) Elizabeth, *m.* Thomas Peyton (4th s. of Sir Edward Peyton, 2d Bart. [1611] of Iselham), and was ancestor of the Peytons of Virginia, as also of Yelverton Peyton who assumed that Baronetcy in 1721. She *d.* 15 June 1668. (2) Ursula, *m.* (—) Shipdam, clerk in holy orders.

suc. his said grandfather in the family estate, 1623; was one of the Council of the Marches, 25 Aug. 1623; Ambassador to Paris, 1634-39; was a Royalist compounder, being, 19 Sep. 1648, fined £2,690. He *m.* 12 March 1614/5 (Reg. at Holme Lacy), Elizabeth da. and h. of Sir Anthony Porter, of Lanthony, co. Gloucester, by Ann, da. of John Danvers, of Dauntsey, Wilts. She was living when he was *cr.*, 1 July 1628, VISCOUNT SCUDAMORE OF SLIGO [I.] In this peerage this *Baronetcy* then *merged*, till, by the death s.p.m., 2 Dec. 1716, of the 3d Viscount and Baronet, it and all other his honours became *extinct*. See *Peerage*.

GOWER *or* GORE:
cr. 2 June 1620,
afterwards, since 1689, Leveson-Gower,
being, since 1703, Barons Gower of Stittenham,
afterwards, since 1746, Earls Gower,
subsequently, since 1786, Marquesses of Stafford,
and *finally*, since 1833, Dukes of Sutherland.

I. 1620. "Thomas Gore [*i.e.*, Gower], of Stittnam, co. York, Knt.," s. and h. of Thomas Gower, of Stittenham aforesaid, by Mary, da. of Gabriel Fairfax, of Steeton, was 8 weeks old in Sep. 1584, and was, after having been previously *Knighted*, *cr. a Bart.*, as above, 2 June 1620. Sheriff of Yorkshire, 1620-21; was a Royalist, and was, 3 Dec. 1646, fined £730. He *m.* 28 May 1604, Anne, da. and coheir of John D'Oyley, of Merton, co. Oxford, by Anne, da. of Frances Bernard, of Abington. She *d.* 28 Oct. 1633, and was *bur.* at St. Clement's Danes, Midx. He was living 12 Nov. 1652, and probably 20 April 1655, but was certainly dead before 12 June 1655.

II. 1655 ? Sir Thomas Gower, Bart. [1620], of Stittenham aforesaid, s. and h., *b.* about 1605; matric. at Oxford (Wad. Coll.), 7 Nov. 1617, aged 12; admitted to Gray's Inn, 1621; was *Knighted*, 24 June 1630, at Whitehall; *suc. to the Baronetcy* probably in 1655; was a considerable sufferer for his fidelity to the Royal cause, for which he raised a regiment of Dragoons. Twice Sheriff of co. York. M.P. for Malton, 1661-72. He *m.* firstly, Elizabeth, sister of Charles, 1st Earl of Carlisle, da. of Sir William Howard, of Naworth Castle, by Mary, da. of William (Eure), Lord Eure. She *d.* s.p. He *m.* secondly, Frances, da. and coheir of Sir John Leveson, of Haling, co. Kent and Lilleshall, co. Stafford, by Frances, da. and h. of Sir Thomas Sondes, of Throwley, co. Kent. He *d.* 1672. Admon. 31 March 1683.

III. 1672. Sir Thomas Gower, Bart. [1620], of Stittenham aforesaid, grandson and h., being only s. and h. of Edward Gower, by Dorothy, da. of Thomas Wentworth, of Elmshall, co. York; which Edward was s. and h. ap. of the late Baronet by his 2d wife, but *d.* v.p. He was *b.* about 1666; *suc. to the Baronetcy* in 1672; matric. at Oxford (Univ. Coll.), 15 July 1681, aged 15; was a Col. of Foot. He *d.* unm. at the Camp at Dundalk, 28 Oct. 1689. Will dat. there same day, pr. 3 Nov. 1692, devising his estate to his cousin "Lt.-Col. James Gower," etc.

IV. 1689. Sir William Leveson-Gower, Bart. [1620], of Lilleshall and Stittenham aforesaid, uncle and h. male, being 3d and yst. s. of the 2d Bart., by his 2d wife. He inherited from his great uncle, Sir Richard Leveson, K.B. (who *d.* about 1668, his widow dying in 1691), the vast estate of Trentham, co. Stafford, and thereupon assumed the additional name of *Leveson*; was M.P. for Merton, Feb. to March 1673; for Newcastle-under-Lyne, in three Parls., April 1675 to 1681; for Shropshire, 1681, and for Newcastle (again) 1689-91; was one of the Duke of Monmouth's bail in 1683; *suc. to the Baronetcy*, 28 Oct. 1689. He *m.* Jane (whose issue in 1711 became coheir to her family), 1st da. of John (Granville), 1st Earl of Bath, by Jane, da. of Sir Peter Wyche. He *d.* Dec. 1691. Will pr. Dec. 1691. His widow *d.* 27 Feb. 1696. Admon. 24 March 1696/7, 26 Jan. 1705/6 and 11 July 1712.

V. 1691. Sir John Leveson-Gower, Bart. [1620], of Lilleshall and Stittenham aforesaid, 1st s. and h., *b.* 7 Jan. 1674/5; *suc. to the Baronetcy,* Dec. 1691. M.P. for Newcastle-under-Lyne, 1692—1702; P.C. 1702; Chancellor of the Duchy of Lancaster, 1702-6. He *m.* in Sep. 1692, Catherine, da. of John (Manners), 1st Duke of Rutland, by his 3d wife, Catherine, da. of Baptist (Noel), Viscount Camden. She, who was *b.* 19 May 1675, was living when, on 15 March 1702/3, he was *cr.* BARON GOWER OF STITTENHAM, co. York. In that peerage this *Baronetcy* then *merged,* and so continues, the 2d Baron and 6th Baronet being *cr.*, 8 July 1746, EARL GOWER; the 2d Earl, 3d Baron and 7th Baronet, being *cr.*, 1 March 1786, MARQUESS OF STAFFORD, and the 2d Marquess, 3d Earl, 4th Baron and 8th Baronet, being *cr.*, 28 Jan. 1833, DUKE OF SUTHERLAND. See *Peerage.*

PAKINGTON:
cr. 22 June 1620;
ex. 6 Jan. 1830.

I. 1620. "John Pakington, of Alisbury [*i.e.*, Aylesbury], co. Bucks, Esq.," s. and h. ap. of Sir John Pakington, K.B., of Westwood Park, co. Worcester (sometime L. Lieut. of that county, who *d.* 18 Jan. 1625), by Dorothea, relict of Benedict Barnham, Alderman of London, da. of Ambrose Smith, of London, Mercer, was *b.* about 1600; admitted to Gray's Inn, 2 Feb. 1618/9, and was, when but 20 years of age, and in the lifetime of his father, *cr. a Bart.*, as above, 22 June 1620. He was M.P. for Aylesbury, 1624 till death. He *m.* Frances, da. of Sir John Ferrers, of Tamworth, by Dorothy, da. of Sir John Puckering, sometime Lord Keeper of the Great Seal. He *d.* v.p., and was *bur.* 29 Oct. 1624, aged 24, at Aylesbury. Admon. 25 May 1625. His widow *m.*, 29 Dec. 1626, at St. Antholins, London, "Robert Leasly [Leslie?], gent."(a)

II. 1624. Sir John Pakington, Bart. [1620], only s. and h., *suc. to the Baronetcy* in Oct. 1624, and, on the death of his grandfather, 18 Jan. 1625, to Westwood Park aforesaid, being then aged 4 years. He was M.P. for Worcestershire, April to May 1640; for Aylesbury, 1640 till disabled Aug. 1642, and for Worcestershire (again), 1661-79. In 1642, he raised troops for the Royal cause in Worcestershire, but was taken prisoner and fined £5,000, his estates sequestrated, and his house in Bucks destroyed. His total losses were estimated as above £20,000. At the battle of Worcester he again joined the Royal cause with a troop of horse, was again taken prisoner and fined £7,670, being thereby forced to alienate some of his estates. He *m.* about 1648, Dorothy, da. of Thomas (Coventry), 1st Baron Coventry of Aylesborough, Lord Keeper of the Great Seal (in whose guardianship he had been during his minority), by his 2d wife, Elizabeth, da. of John Aldersey. She(b) was *bur.* 13 May 1679, at Hampton Lovett, co. Worcester. He was *bur.* there 3 Jan. 1679/80. Admon. 5 March 1679/80.

III. 1680. Sir John Pakington, Bart. [1620], of Westwood Park aforesaid, s. and h., *b.* about 1649; matric. at Oxford (Ch. Ch.), 3 May 1662, aged 13; *suc. to the Baronetcy* in Jan. 1679/80; M.P. for Worcestershire, 1685-87; being a steady supporter of Church and State. He *m.*, 17 Dec. 1668 (Lic. Vic. Gen., she aged 21), Margaret, da. of Sir John Keyt, 1st Bart. [1660], of Iberton [Ebrington], co. Gloucester, by Margaret, da. and h. of William Taylor, of Bricksworth, co. Northampton. He was *bur.* 28 March 1688, at Hampton Lovett. Will pr. April 1689. The Admon. of his widow dat. 19 Nov. 1690.

IV. 1688. Sir John Pakington, Bart. [1620], of Westwood Park aforesaid, only s. and h., *b.* 16 March 1671; *suc. to the Baronetcy,* 28 March 1688; matric. at Oxford (St. John's Coll.), 11 Oct. 1688, aged 17; M.P.

(a) In Douglas' *Peerage of Scotland* [1816], her second husband is [erroneously] given as Alexander (Leslie), the 1st Earl of Leven [S.], whose only wife, Agnes, did not die till June 1651.

(b) She was much esteemed for her learning and piety, and was said to have been the Authoress of the well-known treatise called *The Whole Duty of Man.*

for Worcestershire when only 19 years old, and so continued during eleven Parls., 1690-95 and 1698—1727, being thus in every Parliament, but one which he declined, until his death. Recorder of Worcester, 1721-27. He was a strenuous asserter of the rights of the subject.(a) He *m.* firstly (Lic. Vic. Gen., 28 Aug. 1691, he 21 and she 18), Frances, da. of Sir Henry Parker, 2d Bart. [1681], of Honington, co. Warwick, by Margaret, da. of Alexander Hyde, Bishop of Salisbury. She, who was aged 11 in 1682, *d.* s.p.m.v. He *m.* secondly (Lic. Fac., 26 Aug. 1700, he and she both 28, Hester, da. and sole h. of Sir Herbert Perrot, of Haroldstone, co. Pembroke, by his 2d wife, Hester, da. of William Barlow, of Slebitch, co. Pembroke. She *d.* 1715. He *d.*, 13 Aug. 1727, aged 65, *bur.* at Hampton Lovett. M.I. Will dat. 10 Aug., and pr. 27 Oct. 1727.

V. 1727. Sir Herbert Perrot Pakington, Bart. [1620], of Westwood Park aforesaid, only surv. s. and h. by 2d wife; *b.* about 1701; *suc. to the Baronetcy,* 13 Aug. 1727. M.P. for Worcestershire, 1727-34 and 1734-41. He *m.* June 1721, at Somerset House Chapel, Elizabeth, da. of John Conyers, of Walthamstow, Essex, King's Counsel, by Mary, da. and h. of George Lee, of Stoke, co. Salop. He *d.* 24, and was *bur.* 30 Sep. 1748, in the College Church at Leyden, in Holland, aged 47. His widow was *bur.*, 14 July 1758, at Hampton Lovett.

VI. 1748. Sir John Pakington, Bart. [1620], of Westwood Park aforesaid, s. and h., *b.* about 1722; *suc to the Baronetcy,* 24 Sep 1748. He *m.* 1761, Mary, da. of Henry Bray, of Bromyard, co. Hereford. He *d.* s.p., 30 Nov. 1762, aged 40, and was *bur.* at Hampton Lovett. Will pr. 1763. His widow *d.*, 23 Feb. 1812, and was *bur.* there. Will dat. 17 Sep. 1810, pr. 25 March 1812.

VII. 1762. Sir Herbert Perrot Pakington, Bart. [1620], of Westwood Park aforesaid, br. and h.; *suc. to the Baronetcy,* 30 Nov. 1762. He *m.*, 1759, Elizabeth, widow of Herbert Wylde, of Ludlow, Salop, sister of Sir Cæsar Hawkins, 1st Bart. [1778], da. of Cæsar Hawkins, by (—) da. of (—) Bright. She *d.* June 1783. He *d.* at Bath, 2 May 1795. Will dat. 26 May 1791, pr. 3 June 1795. Both *bur.* at Hampton Lovett.

VIII 1795, to 1830. Sir John Pakington, Bart. [1620], of Westwood Park aforesaid, Knt., s. and h., *b.* 1760; matric. at Oxford (Worc. Coll.), 8 July 1778, aged 18; B.C.L. (from All Souls' Coll.), 1786; *suc. to the Baronetcy,* 2 May 1795. In 1802 he sold the manor of Aylesbury and the estate there.(b) He *d.* s.p. 6 Jan. 1830, in his 70th year, at Hampton Lovett, when the *Baronetcy* became *extinct.*(c) Will pr. July 1830.

ASSHETON, *or* ASHTON:
cr. 28 June 1620;
ex. 9 June 1696.

I. 1620. "Ralph Ashton, of Leverr [*i.e.*, Great Lever], co. Lancaster, Esq.," being also of Whalley Abbey and of Downham, all in that county, s. and h. of Ralph Assheton, of the same (Sheriff for Lancashire, 1594), by his 1st wife, Johanna,(d) da. of Edward Radclyffe, of Todmorden, in the said county,

(a) He is said to have been the original of Addison's "Sir Roger de Coverley" in *The Spectator,* which also has been attributed to Sir Roger Burgoyne, 2d Bart. (1641), who *d.* 1716. The matter is discussed in A. W. Crawley-Boevey's *Perverse Widow.*

(b) This had been inherited by the Pakington family in 1545, on the death of Sir John Baldwin, whose da. and coheir had *m.* Robert Pakington.

(c) The estates devolved on his nephew, John Somerset Russell, who thereupon took the name of Pakington, and was *cr. a Bart.*, 13 July 1846, being, subsequently, 6 March 1874, raised to the peerage as Baron Hampton of Hampton Lovett and Westwood, co. Worcester.

(d) She, in right of her mother, became a coheir of the well known family of Radclyffe, of Wimmerley

was *b.* about 1581; matric. at Oxford (Bras. Coll.), 16 Feb. 1598/9, being then aged 17; admitted to Gray's Inn, 1601; suc. his father, 8 May 1616, and was *cr. a Bart.*, as above, 28 June 1620. In 1629, he sold his paternal estate of Great Lever to John Bridgeman, Bishop of Chester. He *m.* firstly (sett. dat. 19 Aug. 1604), Dorothy, sister of Sir Henry Bellingham, 1st Bart. [1620], da. of Sir James Bellingham, of Levens, Westmorland, by Agnes, da. of Sir Henry Curwen. He *m.* secondly, April 1610, Eleanor, 2d da. of Thomas Shuttleworth, of Smethells, co. Lancaster, by Anne, da. of Richard Lever. He *d.*, 18 Oct. 1644, and was *bur.* at Whalley. His widow, who inherited, for life, the manor of Downham, *d.* s.p.-1658.

II. 1644. Sir Ralph Assheton, Bart. [1620], of Whalley Abbey and of Downham, aforesaid, s. and h. by 1st wife, was aged 10 at the Heralds' Visitation of Lancashire in 1613; matric. at Oxford (Univ. Coll.) 21 Feb. 1622/3, aged 17; admitted to Gray's Inn, 7 May 1624. Sheriff of Lancashire, 1632-33; M.P. for Lancashire, 1640 till secluded in 1648; for Clitheroe, 1660, and 1661 till void Feb. 1662; 1678-99, and 1679 till decease; *suc. to the Baronetcy,* 18 Oct. 1644. He pulled down the old Abbey Church and tower at Whalley; was a Receiver of the revenue of the Duchy of Lancaster, 1642-44. He *m.* firstly (Lic. at Canterbury, 17 April 1630), Dorothy, 3d da. of Nicholas (Tufton), 1st Earl of Thanet, by Frances, da. of Thomas (Cecil), 1st Earl of Exeter. She *d.* 28 Jan. 1635, aged 29, and was *bur.* at Downham. M.I. He *m.* secondly, 3 Feb. 1643/4, at St. Martin's in the Fields, Elizabeth, da. of Sir Sapcote Harington, of Royde, co. Lincoln. He *d.* s.p.s. in London, 30 Jan. and was *bur.* 3 March 1679/80 at Downham. M.I. Will dat. Aug. 1679, pr. 4 May 1680. His widow, who inherited for life the manor of Downham, *d.* 8 June 1686, and was *bur.* in the New Chapel at Westminster. M.I. at Downham. Will dat. 7 Aug. 1684, pr. 25 June 1686.

III. 1680. Sir Edmund Assheton, Bart. [1620], of Whalley Abbey, etc., aforesaid, next br. and h., *b.* 1620; admitted to Gray's Inn, 3 Nov. 1648, *suc. to the Baronetcy* in Jan. 1679/80. He *d.* unm. and intestate, 31 Oct. 1695, at Whalley aforesaid, aged 75.

IV. 1695, to 1696. Sir John Assheton, Bart. [1620], of Whalley Abbey, etc., aforesaid, only surv. br. and h., being 10th and yst. s. of the 1st Bart., by his 1st wife, *b.* 1624; *suc. to the Baronetcy,* 31 Oct. 1695. He *m.* Catharine, widow of Thomas Lister, of Arnoldsbiggin, co. York, da. of Sir Henry Fletcher, of Hutton. She was *bur.* 20 May 1676, at Gisburne, aged 64. M.I. He *d.* s.p. 9 and was *bur.* 18 June 1696, at Gisburne, aged 76, when the *Baronetcy* became *extinct.*(a). M.I.

HICKS *or* HICKES:
cr. 1 July 1620,
afterwards, 1628-29, Viscount Campden;
ex. Oct. 1629.

I. 1620, to 1629. "Baptist Hickes, of Campden, co. Gloucester, Knt.," 3d and yst. s. (b) of Robert Hicks, of St. Pancras Lane, Cheapside, London, Mercer, by Julia, da. of William Arthur, of Clapton-in-Gordano, Somerset, was *b.* about 1560; amassed a large fortune in trade; was *Knighted* 22 July 1603, and in 1607 maintained his right to keep a shop

(a) The estate of Whalley devolved on his nephew, Sir Ralph Assheton, 2d Bart. [1660], of Middleton, he being s. and h. of his eldest sister, Anne; that of Downham went (as directed by his eldest br., Sir Ralph Assheton, the 2d Bart.) to Richard Assheton, of Cuerdale in Walton, co. Lancaster, the heir male of this family, he being grandson and h. of Radclyffe Assheton, of Cuerdale aforesaid, next br. of the 1st Bart. His descendant in the male line, Ralph Assheton, of Downham Hall and of Cuerdale aforesaid, sometime M.P. for Clitheroe, is the present (1899) possessor.

(b) The eldest son, Sir Michael Hicks, was the father of William Hicks, *cr. a Bart.* 21 July 1619, a dignity still (1899) existing.

in London after such Knighthood; was financial agent to the king; elected Alderman of London (Bread street), 12 Nov. 1611, but was fined and discharged the same month; built "Hicks Hall" in Clerkenwell, founded a market house and hospital at Campden, co. Glouc., and was *cr. a Bart.* as above, 1 July 1620; was M.P. for Tavistock, 1621-22, and for Tewkesbury, in four Parls., 1624-28. He was *cr.* 5 May 1628, BARON HICKS OF ILMINGTON, co. Warwick, and VISCOUNT CAMPDEN of Campden, co. Gloucester, with a spec. rem., failing his issue male, to his daughter's husband. He *m.*, 6 Sep. 1584, at Allhallows, Bread street, London, Elizabeth, sister of Sir Humphrey May, Master of the Rolls (1629), da. of Richard May, of London, Merchant Taylor, by Mary, da. of (—) Hillersdon, of Devon. He *d.* s.p.m., at his house in St. Laurence, Jewry, 18, 20 or 28 Oct. 1629, and was *bur.* at Campden, when the Peerage devolved on his son in law, Baron Noel of Ridlington, according to the spec. rem. in the patent, but the *Baronetcy* became *extinct.*(a) Will pr. 1629. His widow *d.* between 25 April and 26 June 1643. Will dat. 14 Feb. 1642/3, pr. 11 Aug. 1643.

ROBERTS, *or* ROBERTES:
cr. 3 July 1620;
ex. 7 July 1745.

I. 1620. "Thomas Robertes, of Glassenbury, co. Kent, Knt.," s. and h. of Walter Roberts, of Glassenbury in Cranbrook, by Frances,(b) da. and h. of John Maynard, Alderman of London, was *b.* about 1561, suc. his father in 1579, being then 18; was *Knighted* at Whitehall, 23 July 1603, and was *cr. a Bart.*, as above, 3 July 1620. He was Sheriff of Kent, 1621-22. He is described as "hospitable without excess, and charitable without ostentation." He *m.* Frances, da. of Martyn James, of Smarden, Kent. He *d.* 21 and was *bur.* 23 Feb. 1627/8, at Cranbrook, aged 67. His widow *d.* Feb. 1648.

II. 1628. Sir Walter Roberts, Bart. [1620], of Glassenbury aforesaid, s. and h., *Knighted* at Greenwich, 7 May 1624; *suc. to the Baronetcy,* Feb. 1627/8. He *m.* Margaret, da. and h. of George Roberts, of Brenchley, Kent, by (—) da. of (—) Sheaf. She brought her husband a great accession of property. She *d.* April 1644. He was living July 1652, but *d.* before 1660, and was *bur.* in London.

III. 1655? Sir Howland Roberts, Bart. [1620], of Glassenbury aforesaid, grandson and h., being s. and h. of Thomas Roberts, of Warbleton, Sussex, by Elizabeth, da. of Sir Matthew Howland, and sister and h. of Sir John Howland, of Streatham, Surrey, which Thomas was s. and h. ap. of the 2d Bart., and *d.* v.p. 23 Jan. 1638. He was *b.* about 1634; matric. at Oxford (Ex. Coll.), 27 July 1652; entered Gray's Inn, 1654; *suc. to the Baronetcy* about 1655. He *m.*, 16 Dec. 1656, in London, Bridget, da. of Sir Robert Jocelyn, of Hyde Hall, Herts, by Bridget, da. of Sir William Smith, of Hill Hall, Essex. He *d.* Nov. 1661, aged 27, and was *bur.* at Cranbrook. Will pr. 1662. His widow, who was *b.* and *bap.* at Sawbridgeworth, 23 Aug. 1626, *d.* April 1706, aged 79. Will dat. 2 Dec. 1706, pr. 4 May 1711.

IV. 1661. Sir Thomas Roberts, Bart. [1620], of Glassenbury aforesaid, s. and h., *b.* 2 and *bap.* 7 Dec. 1658 in the private chapel there; *suc. to the Baronetcy* in Nov. 1661. He opposed the measures of James II; was M.P.

(a) His two coheirs are said (by Stowe) to have had £100,000 each. Of these (1) Juliana *m.* Edward (Noel) 1st Baron Noel of Ridlington, and 2d Viscount Campden, as abovenamed (honours which became *extinct* on the death of Henry Noel, 6th Earl of Gainsborough and 9th Viscount Campden, 1798), and (2) Mary, *m.*, firstly, Sir Charles Morrison, of Cashiobury, Herts, Knt. (ancestor of the family of Capell, Earls of Essex), secondly, Sir John Cooper, Bart., and thirdly, Sir Edward Alford, Knt.

(b) She was *b.* when the Emperor Charles V was in England, who honoured her by being her godfather.

for Kent, Nov. 1691 to 1695, and 1695-98; for Maidstone, 1702 till void soon afterwards. He *m.*, 31 May 1683, at St. Dionis Backchurch, London, Jane, 1st da. and coheir of Sir John BEALE, Bart. (so *cr.* 1660), by his 2d wife, Jane, da. of Richard DUKE, of Maidstone. She *d.* 25 July 1692, aged 28. He *d.* 20 Nov. 1706, in his 48th year. Will pr. Feb. 1707.

V. 1706. SIR THOMAS ROBERTS, Bart. [1620], of Glassenbury aforesaid, 2d but 1st surv. s. and h., *b.* 27 June 1689; *suc. to the Baronetcy*, 20 Nov. 1706. He *m.*, 1714, Elizabeth, da. and sole h. of Samuel NEWBERY, Citizen of London. She *d.* 30 July 1727, aged 35. Will pr. Nov. 1727. He *d.* s.p. 5 Jan. 1729/30, aged 40. Will pr. 1730. Both *bur.* at Cranbrook.

VI. 1730, to 1745. SIR WALTER ROBERTS, Bart. [1620], of Glassenbury aforesaid, br. and h., *b.* March 1690/1; *suc. to the Baronetcy*, 5 Jan. 1729/30. He *m.* 1726, Elizabeth, only da. and h. of William SLAUGHTER, of Rochester, Kent. She *d.* 15 and was *bur.* 25 July 1744, at Cranbrook, aged 42. Admon. 24 Oct. 1745. He *d.* s.p.m. 7 and was *bur.* 15 July 1745, at Cranbrook, aged 54, when the *Baronetcy* became *extinct.*(a). Will pr. 1745.

HANMER:
cr. 8 July 1620;
ex. 5 May 1746.

I. 1620. "JOHN HANMER, of Hanmer, co. Flint, Esq.," s. and h. of Sir Thomas HANMER, of the same, by his 2d wife, Catherine, da. of Sir Thomas MOSTYN, was *b.* about 1591; matric. at Oxford (Oriel Coll.), 13 March 1606/7, aged 15; B.A., 2 July 1608; admitted to Lincoln's Inn, 1610; suc. his father, 18 April 1619, and was *cr. a Bart.*, as above, 8 July 1620. He was M.P. for Flintshire, 1624 till his death. He *m.* Dorothy, da. and coheir of Sir Richard TREVOR, of Trewallyn, co. Denbigh. He *d.*, in the flower of his age, 1624. Will pr. 1625.

II. 1624. SIR THOMAS HAMNER, Bart. [1620], of Hanmer aforesaid, s. and h., *suc. to the Baronetcy* in 1624; M.P. for Flint, April to May 1640, and for Flintshire, Nov. 1669 till decease; was probably the "Thomas Hanmore" *cr.* D.C.L. at Oxford, 1 Nov. 1642, and was a Royalist compounder, being, 18 Nov. 1645, fined £984. He *m.* firstly, Elizabeth, da. of Sir Thomas BAKER, sister and h. of Thomas BAKER, of Whittingham Hall, Suffolk. She, who had been Maid of Honour to Anne, Queen of James I, *d.* in France. Admon. 9 Nov. 1650. He *m.* secondly, Susan, da. of Sir William HERVEY, of Ickworth, Suffolk, by his 1st wife, Susan, da. of Sir Robert JERMYN, of Rushbrooke, Suffolk. He *d.* 1678. Will pr. 1688.

III. 1678. SIR JOHN HANMER, Bart. [1620], of Hanmer and of Whittingham Hall aforesaid, s. and h. by 1st wife; was *Knighted*, v.p. 9 Aug. 1660; was M.P. for Flint, 1659; for Evesham, Oct. 1669 to 1679; for Flintshire, 1681, and for Flint (again), 1685-87 and 1689-90; Sheriff of Gloucestershire, 1664-65; *suc. to the Baronetcy* in 1678; Col. of the 11th Foot, 1688—1701;

(a) Jane, his da. and eventually his sole h., *m.*, 23 Oct. 1752, George (BEAUCLERK) 3d DUKE OF ST. ALBANS, but *d.* s.p. Dec. 1788, and was *bur.* at Cranbrook. The manor of Glassenbury passed, under her will, to Thomas ROBERTS of the co. of Cork, her Grace being apparently under the impression that he was of her family, inasmuch as his great great grandfather, the Rev. Thomas Roberts, Chancellor of the diocese of Cork (*d.* 1664, aged about 74), was, in a pedigree (by Hawkins, Ulster, 22 June 1775), made identical with Thomas, 2d s. of the 1st Bart. The last mentioned Thomas, however, *d.* s.p. in 1644. Had such descent been proved, it would have carried with it the Baronetcy of 1611 and the right to the Coat of Arms borne by those Baronets. That pedigree, however, was rejected by the Heralds' College, a new Coat of Arms was granted to him, and the Grantee was *cr. a Bart.* 20 Sep. 1809, he being described as "of Glassenbury, co. Kent and Brightfieldston, co. Cork."

Major-General in the Army and Col. of the 11th Foot, serving at the battle of the Boyne on the side of William III. He *m.* Mary, da. and h. of Joseph ALSTON, of Netherhall, Suffolk. He *d.* s.p. 1701. The admon. of his widow, as "of Kensington," granted 26 Dec. 1709 to her cousin and next of kin, Samuel Alston.

IV. 1701, to 1746. SIR THOMAS HANMER, Bart. [1620], of Hanmer aforesaid, and of Mildenhall, Suffolk, nephew and h., being only s. and h. of William Hanmer, by Peregrina, da. of Sir Henry NORTH, 1st Bart. [1660], of Mildenhall aforesaid, sister and coheir of the 2d Bart., which William Hanmer was s. of the 2d Bart. by his 2d wife. He was *b.* at Bettisfield, 24 Sep. 1677; matric. at Oxford (Ch. Ch.), 17 Oct. 1693, aged 17; LL.D. Cambridge (comitiis regiis), 16 April 1705; *suc. to the Baronetcy* in 1701; was M.P. for Thetford, 1701-02; for Flintshire, 1702-05; for Thetford (again), 1705-08; and finally, 1708-27, for Suffolk. He was, in 1713, unanimously chosen SPEAKER OF THE HOUSE OF COMMONS. He was, also, distinguished in the literary world. He *m.* firstly (Lic. Lond. 14 Oct. 1698, he 24, she 25) Isabella, widow of Henry (FITZROY) 1st DUKE OF GRAFTON, da. and h. of Henry (BENNET) 1st EARL OF ARLINGTON, by Isabella, da. of Louis DE NASSAU, COUNT OF BEVERWART AND AUVERQUERQUE in Holland. She, who by her father's death, 28 July 1685, had become *suo jure*, COUNTESS OF ARLINGTON, *d.* 9 Feb. 1722/3 in her 56th year. He *m.* secondly, Elizabeth, only da. and h. of Thomas FOLKES, of Barton and of Bury St. Edmunds, Suffolk. The will of "Dame Eliz. Hanmer" was pr. 1741. He *d.* s.p. 7 May 1746, aged 68, and was *bur.* in Hanmer church, when the *Baronetcy* became *extinct.*(a) Will pr. 1746.

OSBORNE:
cr. 13 July 1620,
afterwards, since Feb. 1672/3, VISCOUNTS OSBORNE OF DUNBLANE [S.],
being, shortly afterwards, since Aug. 1673, VISCOUNTS LATIMER OF DANBY,
and, since 1674, EARLS OF DANBY,
subsequently, since 1689, MARQUESSES OF CARMARTHEN,
and, since 1694, DUKES OF LEEDS.

I. 1620. "EDWARD OSBORNE, of Keeton, co. York,"(b) 1st s. and h. of Sir Hewett(c) OSBORNE, of Kiveton, *otherwise* Keeton aforesaid (in the parish of Harthill), and of Parsloes, in Dagenham, co. Essex, by Joyce, da. of Thomas FLEETWOOD, of the Vache, co. Bucks, was *bap.* 12 Dec. 1596, at St. Benet's, Gracechurch, London; suc. his father (when an infant) in Sep. 1599; sold the estate of Parsloes, to the Fanshawe family, in Feb. 1618/9, for £1,150, and was *cr. a Bart.*, as above, 13 July 1620. He was M.P. for East Retford, 1628-29; for York, April to May 1640, and for Berwick, 1640 till void 7 Dec. 1640; was Vice-President of the Council of the North, 1629, and, in 1641, was Lieut.-Gen. of the Yorkshire Forces raised for the King; was a Compounder, 29 Nov. 1645, and was fined £1,649 in April 1647. He *m.* firstly, 13 Oct. 1618, at Coxwold, Margaret, 1st da. of Thomas (BELASYSE), 1st VISCOUNT

(a) He was "a high church Hanover-Tory statesman." The estate of Hanmer devolved, by settlement, on the (very remote) heir male of the family, whose descendant, Walden Hanmer was *cr. a Bart.* 21 May 1774, as of Hanmer, co. Flint. The Mildenhall property in Suffolk, which came to the 4th Bart. through his mother, went to his nephew, William BUNBURY, afterward Sir William Bunbury, 5th Bart. [1681].

(b) No designation whatever, such as "Knt." or "Esquire" is given him.

(c) This Hewett Osborne, who was *bap.* 13 March 1566/7, affords one of the earliest instances of a surname given as a Christian name, which, in pre-Reformation times, was invariably either a Scripture name or the name of a Saint. He was s. and h. of the well known Sir Edward Osborne, Lord Mayor of London, 1583, by Anne, da. and h. of Sir William Hewett, Lord Mayor 1559, who had purchased the estates in Yorkshire, Notts, Derbyshire, and Essex, which were inherited by his descendants.

FAUCONBERG OF HENKNOWLE, by Barbara, da. of Sir Henry CHOLMLEY, of Roxby, co. York. She *d.* 7 Nov. 1624, and was *bur.* at Harthill. He *m.* secondly, in or before 1630, Anne, widow of William MIDELTON, of Stockeld, co. York, 2d da. (but not heir or coheir) of Thomas WALMESLEY, of Dunkenhalgh, co. Lancaster, by his 1st wife Eleanor, sister of Henry, EARL OF DANBY, da. of Sir John DANVERS, and Elizabeth, his wife, sister and coheir of John (NEVILL), LORD LATIMER.(a) He *d.* 9 Sep. 1647, and was *bur.* at Harthill, aged 50. Admon. 16 Nov. 1657. His widow was *bur.* 20 Aug. 1666, at Harthill aforesaid. Will dat. 16 Aug. 1666, pr. at York, 4 May 1667.

II. 1647. SIR THOMAS OSBORNE, Bart. [1620], of Kiveton, aforesaid, 2d and 1st surv. s. and h.,(b) being 1st s. by the 2d wife; *b* 1631; *suc. to the Baronetcy*, 2 Sep. 1647; Sheriff of Yorkshire, 1661; M.P. for York, Jan. 1665 till 1673; Joint Com. of Pub. Account, 1667; Joint Treasurer of the Navy, 1668; Treasurer of the Navy, 1671. He *m.*, in 1651, Bridget, 2d da. of Montagu (BERTIE), 2d EARL OF LINDSEY, by his 1st wife, Martha, sister of Charles, 1st VISCOUNT CULLEN [I,], da. of Sir William COKAYNE. She, who was *bap.* 2 June 1629, at St. Peter-le-Poor, London, was living when he was *cr.*, 2 Feb. 1672/3, VISCOUNT OSBORNE OF DUNBLANE [S.], obtaining, a few months later, an English peerage, when he was *cr.*, 15 Aug. 1673, VISCOUNT LATIMER OF DANBY, co. York. He was subsequently *cr.*, on 27 June 1674, EARL OF DANBY, co. York; on 9 April 1689, MARQUESS OF CARMARTHEN, and finally, on 4 May 1694, DUKE OF LEEDS. In these titles this *Baronetcy* became consequently *merged*, and still so continues. See *Peerage*.

CHALONER:
cr. 20 July 1620;
ex. about 1641.

I. 1620. to 1641? "WILLIAM CHALONER, of Guisborough, co. York, Esq.," s. of Sir Thomas CHALONER, of Steeple Clayton, Bucks, and of Guisborough aforesaid, by his 1st wife, Elizabeth, da. of William FLEETWOOD, Sergeant at Law and Recorder of London, was *bap.* 24 March 1587/8, at St. Olave's, Silver street, London; suc. his father, 17 Nov. 1615; matric. at Oxford (Mag. Coll.), 22 Feb. 1604/5, aged 17; B.A. 8 July 1607; incorp. at Cambridge, 1608, and was *cr. a Bart.* as above, 20 July 1620. He *d.* s.p. at Scanderoon, in Turkey, about 1641, when the *Baronetcy* became *extinct*. Will pr. Aug. 1642.

FELTON:
cr. 20 July 1620;
ex. 18 Nov. 1719.

I. 1620. "HENRY FELTON, of Playford, co. Suffolk, Esq.," s. and h. of Sir Anthony FELTON, K.B., of Playford aforesaid, by Elizabeth, da. of Henry (GREY), 1st BARON GREY OF GROBY; suc. his father in or shortly before 1614, and was *cr. a Bart.*, as above, 20 July 1620. He *m.* Dorothy, widow of Sir Bassingborne GAWDY (who *d.* 1606), da. of Sir Nicholas BACON, of Redgrave, by Anne, da. and h. of Edmund BUTTS, of Thornage, Norfolk. He *d.* 18 Sep. 1624. His admon. 21 Oct. 1624. His widow *d.* 1653.

(a) This descent (though it was one without any representation) gave rise to the titles of Latimer and Danby, two out of the many selected by the 2d Baronet on five creations of peerage which culminated in that of the Dukedom of Leeds.

(b) Edward Osborne, only s. by the first wife, *d.* a minor, unm. and v.p., being killed by a fall of some chimneys at York Manor house, 31 Oct. 1638. He was *bur.* in York Minster.

II. 1624. SIR HENRY FELTON, Bart. [1620], of Playford aforesaid, s. and h., *suc. to the Baronetcy* about 1624. M.P. for Suffolk, 1656-58, 1659, 1660, and 1661-79. He *m.* Susanna, 3d da. of Sir Lionel TOLLEMACHE, 2d Bart. [1611], by Elizabeth, da. of John (STANHOPE), BARON STANHOPE OF HARRINGTON. He *d.* 1690. Will pr. Nov. 1690.

III. 1690. SIR ADAM FELTON, Bart. [1620], of Playford aforesaid, s. and h.; M.P. for Thetford, 1689, and 1690 till void, and for Orford, 1695, till decease; *suc. to the Baronetcy* in 1690. He *m.*, 1673-76, Elizabeth, relict [1] of Sir Francis FOLJAMBE, Bart.; [2] of Edward HORNER; and [3] of William (MONSON) VISCOUNT MONSON OF CASTLEMAINE [I.] (who *d.* 1673), da. of Sir George RERESBY, of Thribergh, co. York, by Elizabeth, da. and coheir of John TAMWORTH, of Shervile Court, Hants. She, who was *bap.* 24 Feb. 1613, at Thribergh, *d.* at Bury St. Edmunds 26 Feb. 1695. Admon. 24 July 1696. He *d.* s.p. Feb. 1696/7. Will dat. 25 Jan., pr. 19 Feb. 1696/7.

IV. 1697. SIR THOMAS FELTON, Bart. [1620], of Playford aforesaid, br. and h., one of the Grooms of the Bedchamber to Charles II. and Comptroller of the household to the Queen Consort; M.P. for Orford (two Parls.), 1690-98, and 1690 till void Feb. 1700; for Bury (four Parls.), 1701-09; *suc. to the Baronetcy* in Feb. 1696/7. He *m.* Elizabeth, 2d da. and coheir of James (HOWARD), 3d EARL OF SUFFOLK, LORD HOWARD DE WALDEN, she being his only da. by his 2d wife, Barbara, da. of Sir Edward VILLIERS. She *d.* Dec. 1681, aged 25, and was *bur.* at Walden. Her admon. 30 May 1682. He *d.* s.p.m. 2 March 1708/9.(a) Will pr. March 1709.

V. 1708, to 1719. SIR COMPTON FELTON, Bart. [1620], of Ipswich, br. and h. He *m.* Frances FINCH, of Playford aforesaid, spinster. He d. s.p.(b) 18 Nov. 1719, at his house in Ipswich, aged 69, when the *Baronetcy* became *extinct*.

FRERE, *or* FRYER:(c)
cr. 22 July 1620;(d)
ex. 2 Nov. 1629.

I. 1620, to 1629. "EDWARD FRYER [*or* FRERE], of Water Eaton, co. Oxford, Esq.," s. and h. of Walter FRERE, of the same, Justice of the Peace (1574), by Mary (*m.* 12 Nov. 1560), da. and coheir of William BAMFIELD, of Turnworth, co. Dorset, was *b.* about 1564; matric. at Oxford (Trin. Coll.), 20 Sep. 1574, aged 10, and was *cr. a Bart.*, as above, 22 July 1620.(d) He *m.* Mary, da. of John STAFFORD, of Blatherwicke, co. Northampton. She was *bur.* 23 Nov. 1623, at St. Andrew's, Holborn. He *d.* s.p.m.s.,(e) at Erith, co. Kent, and was *bur.*, 29 Sep. 1629, at St. Andrew's aforesaid, when the *Baronetcy* became *extinct*. Admon. 2 Nov. 1629. Will pr. 1630.

(a) Elizabeth, his only da. and h., *m.* John HERVEY, 1st EARL OF BRISTOL, and is ancestress of the MARQUESSES OF BRISTOL (her heirs male), and of the LORDS HOWARD DE WALDEN (her heirs general), who, through her, inherit that Barony.

(b) Elizabeth, his niece, only da. and h. of John Felton, of Worlingham, *m.* John PLAYTERS, of Worlingham aforesaid [Collins' *Baronetage*, 1720].

(c) In the Visit. of Oxon it is spelt "FRERE," but in the M.I's. at All Saints', Oxford, "Freurs."

(d) 22 July is the date in the *Creations*, 1483—1646 as in the 47th Rep. D.K. Pub. Records, though 11 July is the generally given date.

(e) William Frere, his only son, *d.* unm. v.p., in his 24th year.

BISHOPP :

cr. 24 July 1620,
afterwards, 1780? to 1870, BISSHOPP,
sometime, 1815-1828, LORD ZOUCHE ;
ex. 27 Jan. 1870.

I. 1620. "THOMAS BISHOPP,(a) of Parham, co. Sussex, Knt," s. and h. of Thomas BISHOPP, of Henfield in that county, by Elizabeth, relict of William SCOTT, illegit. da. of Sir Edward BELKNAP, was *b.* about 1550 ; admitted to the Inner Temple as "of Henfield, Sussex," 1573 ; was aged 30 in 1579 ; Sheriff of Surrey and Sussex, 1584-85 and 1601-02; M.P. for Gatton, 1584-85; for Steyning, 1586-87 and 1604-11 ; purchased, in 1597, the estate of Parham aforesaid ; was *Knighted* at Theobalds, 7 May 1603, and was *cr. a Bart.* as above, 24 July 1620. He *m.* firstly, 19 Sep. 1577, Anne, da. of William CROMER, of Tunstall, Kent. She *d.* s.p. He *m.* secondly Jane, da. of Sir Richard WESTON, of Sutton, co. Surrey, by Jane, da. and h. of John DISTER, of Bergholt, Essex. He *d.* 1626, aged 77. Will pr. 1627.

II. 1626. SIR EDWARD BISHOPP, Bart. [1620], of Parham aforesaid, s. and h. by 2d wife, b. about 1601 ; matric. at Oxford (Trin. Coll.) 22 Oct. 1619, aged 18; admitted to the Inner Temple, 1620 ; *Knighted*, 18 Dec. 1625, at Hampton Court, and *suc. to the Baronetcy* in 1626 ; M.P. for Steyning, 1626, and for Bramber, 1640 till void 16 Dec. 1640 ; Sheriff of Sussex, 1636-37 ; Governor of Arundel Castle for the King, 1643, on whose side he fought, his estates being consequently sequestrated ; was a Compounder, Oct. 1644 ; fined £7,500 in Oct. 1645, which subsequently was reduced to £4,790. He *m.*, about 1626, Mary, 4th da. of Nicholas (TUFTON), 1st EARL OF THANET, by Frances, da. of Thomas (CECIL), 1st EARL OF EXETER. He *d.* in April 1649. His widow *d.* 1663.

III. 1649. SIR THOMAS BISHOPP, Bart. [1620], of Parham aforesaid, s. and h., bap. there 3 Dec. 1627 ; aged 7 in 1634 ; *suc. to the Baronetcy* in 1649, but *d.* unm. in 1652.

IV. 1652. SIR CECIL BISHOPP, Bart. [1620], of Parham aforesaid, br. and h. ; *b.* about 1635 ; *suc. to the Baronetcy* in 1652 ; M.P. for Bramber, Jan. 1662 to 1679. He *m.*, 17 June 1666, at Culham, Oxon, Sarah, da. and h. of George BURY, of Culham aforesaid. She was *b.* 11 and *bap.* 12 Sep. 1650, at Culham, and was *bur.* there 12 March 1679. He *d.* 3 and was *bur.* 6 June 1705, at Parham. Will dat. 31 July 1699, pr. at Chichester, 11 June 1711.

V. 1705. SIR CECIL BISHOPP, Bart. [1620], of Parham aforesaid, s. and h., *suc. to the Baronetcy*, 3 June 1705. He *m.* Elizabeth, da. and h. of Henry DUNCH, of Newington, Oxon. He *d.* 25 Oct. 1725, at Parham. Will dat. 19 Oct. 1724, pr. 10 Nov. 1725. The will of his widow pr. 1751.

VI. 1725. SIR CECIL BISHOPP, Bart. [1620], of Parham aforesaid, s. and h., *suc. to the Baronetcy*, 25 Oct. 1725 ; M.P. for Penryn, 1727-34 ; for Boroughbridge, March 1755 to 1761, and 1761-68 ; Superintendent of H.M.'s Founderies, Aug. 1755. He *m.*, in 1726, Anne, 2d da. of Hugh (BOSCAWEN), 1st VISCOUNT FALMOUTH, by Charlotte, da. and coheir of Charles GODFREY. She, who was *b.* 17 Feb. 1703/4, was *bur.* 11 May 1749, at Parham. He *d.* 15 June 1778. Will pr. June 1778.

(a) See *Top. and Gen.*, iii., 365-370, for some remarks on the *Sussex* families of Bishop. In Playfair's *Brit. Fam. Antiq.* is a pedigree of this family, deducing it from Pockington, co. York, which is ably confuted in the *Her. and Gen.*, viii., pp. 11-12.

VII. 1778. SIR CECIL BISHOPP, Bart. [1620], of Parham aforesaid and of Fridley manor, co. Surrey (which last he had purchased in 1762), s. and h., *suc. to the Baronetcy*, 15 June 1778. He *m.*, 8 Jan. 1750, Susan, 1st da. and only child that had issue of Charles HEDGES, of Finchley, co. Midx., by Catherine, 1st da. of Bartholomew TATE, of Delapre, co. Northampton. He was *bur.* 10 Sep. 1779, at Bath Abbey. Will dat. 31 Aug. and pr. 3 Nov. 1779. His widow *d.* 1 Dec. 1791.

VIII. 1779. SIR CECIL BISHOPP, *or* BISSHOPP,(a) Bart. [1620], of Parham aforesaid, s. and h., *b.* 29 Dec. 1753 ; *suc. to the Baronetcy* in Sep. 1779 ; M.P. for New Shoreham, 1780-90 and 1796—1806 ; F.R.S. ; D.C.L., Oxford, 5 July 1810. He established his claim, made 7 Feb. 1804 (in right of his mother, through the families of Hedges, Tate and Zouche) as a coheir of the Barony of Zouche (*cr.* 1308, but *in abeyance* since 1625), and (the abeyance of that ancient title having been determined in his favour) was, accordingly, sum. to the House of Lords, by writ, 27 Aug. 1815, as LORD ZOUCHE DE HARYNGWORTH. He *m.*, 27 June 1782, at St. Martin's in the Fields, Harriet Anne, only da. and h. of William SOUTHWELL, of Frampton, co. Gloucester, by his 2d wife, Arabella, da. of Henry PYE, of Faringdon Berks. He *d.* s.p.m.s. 11 Nov. 1828, at Parham, aforesaid, when the *Barony of Zouche* fell again into *abeyance*(b) between his two daughters and coheirs, while the Baronetcy (but not, however, the family estate) devolved on the heir male. His will pr. 1828. His widow *d.* 10 Dec. 1839, at Hyde Park place west, aged 79, and was *bur.* at Parham. Will pr. Jan. 1840.

IX. 1828. SIR GEORGE WILLIAM BISSHOPP, Bart. [1620], Dean of Lismore in Ireland, cousin and h. male, being only s. and h. of Edward BISHOPP,(c) of Chiswick, Midx., by Jane, da. of William ATKINSON, of Pall Mall, Midx., which Edward was 3d s. of the 6th Bart. He was *b.* 5 July 1791 ; matric. at Oxford (Pemb. Coll.), 9 May 1809 ; B.A. (Queen's Coll.), 1813 ; M.A. 1817. In holy orders ; Archdeacon of Aghadoe, 1816-34 ; Dean of Lismore, 1831-34 ; was also Sub-Dean of Dublin Castle Chapel, having *suc. to the Baronetcy*, 11 Nov. 1828. He *m.*, 17 May 1820, Catherine Elizabeth, 3d da. of Andrew SPROULE, Capt. R.N. She *d.* 1832. He *d.* at Cheltenham, co. Glouc., 22 March 1834, aged 42. Will pr. April 1734.

X. 1834. SIR CECIL AUGUSTUS BISSHOPP, Bart. [1620], s. and h., *b.* 6 July 1821, at St. Peter's, Dublin; *suc. to the Baronetcy*, 22 March 1834 ; ed. at Merton Coll., Oxford ; B.A , 1843 ; M.A., 1845. In holy orders ; Archdeacon of Malta and Chaplain to the Bishop of Gibraltar. He *m.*, Jan. 1843, Mary Bickerton, 1st da. of Rear Admiral Sir James HILLYAR, K.C.B. and K.C.H., of Tor House, Devon, by Mary, 2d da. of Nathaniel TAYLOR, Naval Storekeeper at Malta. He *d.* s.p.m.s. 22 Jan. 1849, at Malta, aged 28. Will pr. June 1849. His widow *m.*, 15 April 1857, Walter LONG, of Rood Ashton, Wilts, who *d.* 1867. She *d.* 1 March 1891.

XI. 1849. SIR GEORGE CURZON BISSHOPP, Bart. [1620], br. and h., *b.* 10 April 1823 ; *suc. to the Baronetcy* 22 Jan. 1849 ; sometime Capt. in the 12th Foot, but retired in 1853. He *d.* unm. at St. Michael's, Hastings, Sussex, 15 Dec. 1865.

(a) This eccentric method of spelling was not adopted in 1771 (when Kimber's *Baronetage* was published), but crops up soon afterwards.

(b) It was, however, soon again terminated. in Jan. 1829, in favour of his eldest da., Harriet Anne, wife of the Hon. Robert Curzon, who thus became Baroness Zouche, and *d.* 15 May 1870, aged 82, leaving issue. She inherited the estate of Parham, co. Sussex, being that of the former Baronets.

(c) In Betham's *Baronetage*, vol. i, p. 195, it is stated that this Edward Bisshopp *d.* 1792, "leaving one legitimate son, *Henry*, now [1801] at Storington, Sussex, a Col. in the Cheshire fencibles."

XII. 1865, to 1870. SIR EDWARD CECIL BISSHOPP, Bart. [1620], br. and h., *b.* 23 Feb. 1826 ; was an officer R.N. ; served through the Syrian war, and was, in 1840, at the bombardment of St. Jean d'Acre ; *suc. to the Baronetcy*, 15 Dec. 1865. He *m.*, 13 April 1847, Mary, only da. of (—) TAYLOR, Rear-Admiral in the Brazilian Navy. He *d.* s.p. 27 Jan. 1870, in his 44th year, when the *Baronetcy* became *extinct*. His widow *m.*, in 1880, COUNT QUARTO, of Italy. She was living, 1899, at Colle Felice, Maddaloni, near Naples.

VINCENT :

cr. 26 July 1620.

I. 1620. "SIR FRANCIS VINCENT, of Stoke, Dawbernon [*i.e.*, D'Abernon], co. Surrey, Knt.," s. and h. of Sir Thomas VINCENT, of the same and of Barnack, co. Northampton, by Jane, only da. and h. of Thomas LYFIELD,(a) of Stoke D'Abernon aforesaid, was *b.* about 1568 ; matric. at Oxford (Ch. Ch.), 12 Oct. 1582, aged 14 ; was *Knighted* 23 July 1603 ; suc. his father, 14 Dec. 1613, and was *cr. a Bart.*, as above, 26 July 1620. He was M.P. for Surrey, 1626 ; was elected Sheriff of Surrey, 1636, but did not act. He *m.* firstly, Sarah, da. of Sir Amyas POULETT, Governor of Guernsey and Jersey (*d.* 1588), by Catharine, da. and h. of Anthony HARVEY. She *d.* 13 June 1608, aged 37, and was *bur.* at Stoke. M.I. He *m.* secondly, Mary, da. of Sir Henry ARCHER, of Essex. By her he had no issue. He *m.* thirdly, Eleanor, widow of Sir Arthur ACLAND, of Killerton, Devon (who *d.* 1614), da. and sole h. of Robert MALET, of Woolleigh in that county. He *d.* 1640. Will dat. 2 April 1639, pr. 15 May 1640. The will of his widow pr. Oct. 1645.

II. 1640. SIR ANTHONY VINCENT, Bart. [1620], of Stoke D'Abernon aforesaid, only surv. s. and h. by 1st wife, *b.* 1594 ; was *Knighted* at Rycott, 11 Sep. 1617 [as "*Arthur* Vincent"] ; was [as a Knight] Sheriff of Surrey and Sussex, 1636-37 ; *suc. to the Baronetcy* in 1640 ; was a great sufferer, during the civil war, for the Royal cause. He *m.* Elizabeth, da. of the said Sir Arthur ACLAND, by (his step-mother) the said Eleanor, da. of Robert MALET. He *d.* 1642. Will pr. 1656.

III. 1642. SIR FRANCIS VINCENT, Bart. [1620], of Stoke D'Abernon, aforesaid, only s. and h., *b.* in co. Devon about 1621 ; matric. at Oxford (Ex. Coll.) 12 May 1637, aged 16 ; *suc. to the Baronetcy* in 1642 ; M.P. for Dover, 1661 till his death. He *m.* firstly, in or before 1645, Catharine, da. of George PITT, of Harrow-on-the-hill, Midx., Serjeant at Law. She *d.* 16 Feb. 1653/4, and was *bur.* at Stoke. M.I. He *m.* secondly, Elizabeth, da. of Sir Henry VANE, of Hadlow, Kent, by Frances, da. of Thomas DARCY, of co. Essex. He *d.* about 1670. Will pr. June 1670. The will of his widow pr. 1680.

IV. 1670? SIR ANTHONY VINCENT, Bart. [1620], of Stoke D'Abernon aforesaid, s. and h. by 1st wife, *b.* about 1645 ; matric. at Oxford (Mag. Coll.), 16 July 1661, aged 16 ; *suc. to the Baronetcy* about 1670. He *m.* Anne, da. of Sir James AUSTEN, of Southwark, by Margaret, da. and h. of Anthony CARLETON, of Sevenoaks, Kent. He *d.* s.p.m. 1674. By will dat. 10 Aug. and pr. Sep. 1674, he devised his real estate (subject to £5,000 for his da. and an annuity to his widow) to his successor in the title. His widow *m.* Thomas FOWKES, who survived her. Her will pr. July 1682.

V. 1674. SIR FRANCIS VINCENT, Bart. [1620], of Stoke D'Abernon aforesaid, br. of the whole blood and h. male, *b.* about 1646; admitted to Lincoln's Inn, 1661 ; matric. at Oxford (St. Mary Hall), 21 June 1662, aged 16 ; *suc. to the Baronetcy* in Sep. 1674 ; M.P. for Surrey, 1690-95 and 1710-13. He *m.* Rebecca, da. of Jonathan ASHE, of London, merchant. She *d.* 19 Aug. 1725, aged 80. He *d.* 10 Feb. 1735/6, aged 90. Will pr. 25 Feb. 1736. Both were *bur.* at Stoke. M.I.

(a) He inherited this estate in right of his wife, Frances, da. of Edmund (BRAYE), 1st LORD BRAYE, and sister and coheir of the 2d Lord.

VI. 1736. SIR HENRY VINCENT, Bart. [1620], of Stoke D'Abernon aforesaid, s. and h., *b.* about 1685 ; matric. at Oxford (Corpus Coll.), 11 Oct. 1703, aged 18 ; B.A. 1707 ; M.P. for Guildford, Feb. 1728 to 1734 ; *suc. to the Baronetcy*, 10 Feb. 1735/6. He *m.* Elizabeth, da. of Bezaleel SHERMAN, of London, Turkey merchant. She *d.* 1751, aged 66. He *d.* 10 Jan. 1757, aged 72. Admon. 11 Dec. 1767. Both were *bur.* at Stoke. M.I.

VII. 1757. SIR FRANCIS VINCENT, Bart. [1620], of Stoke D'Abernon aforesaid, s. and h. ; M.P. for Surrey (1761-75) ; *suc. to the Baronetcy*, 10 Jan. 1757. He *m.* firstly, 25 Aug. 1741, Elizabeth, da. and sole h. of David KILMAINE, of the Strand, Middlesex, banker. She, who brought him a great fortune, *d.* s.p. 22 Nov. 1744 in her 26th year, and was *bur.* at Stoke. M.I. He *m.* secondly, 13 March 1745/6, Mary, da. of Lieut. Gen. the Hon. Thomas HOWARD, of Great Bookham, co. Surrey (yr. s. of Francis, BARON HOWARD OF EFFINGHAM), by Mary, da. of William MORTON, BISHOP OF MEATH in Ireland. She *d.* 16 Aug. 1757, and was *bur.* at Stoke. M.I. He *m.* thirdly, Arabella, widow of Anthony-Langley SWIMMER, da. and coheir of Sir John ASTLEY, 2d Bart. [1662], of Patshull, by Mary, da. and h. of Francis PRYNCE. By her he had no issue. He was *bur.* at Stoke, 28 May 1775. Admon. 22 Dec. 1775. His widow *d.* 20 June 1785. Will pr. June 1785.

VIII. 1775. SIR FRANCIS VINCENT, Bart. [1620], of Stoke D'Abernon aforesaid, s. and h., by 2d wife, *bap.* 11 Oct. 1747 ; *suc. to the Baronetcy* in May 1775 ; was Resident Consul at Venice. He *m.*, 12 July 1779, at St. Geo. Han. sq., Mary, da. of Richard MUILMAN-TRENCH CHISWELL, of Debden, co. Essex (who, being a lunatic, shot himself there, 3 Feb. 1797), by (—), da. of James JURIN, M.D. He *d.* 17 Aug. 1791, at Vicenza, near Venice. Admon. March 1796. His widow *d.* 8 Jan. 1826. Will pr. Feb. 1826.

IX. 1791. SIR FRANCIS VINCENT, Bart. [1620], of Stoke D'Abernon and Debden Hall aforesaid, s. and h., b. 24 July 1780; ed. at Pembr. Coll., Cambridge ; M.A., 1799 ; *suc. to the Baronetcy*, 17 Aug. 1791 ; was Under Foreign Secretary, 1806-07. He *m.*, 16 Jan. 1802, Jane, da. of Hon. Edward BOUVERIE (2d s. of Jacob, 1st VISCOUNT FOLKESTONE), by Harriot, only da. of Everard FAWKENOR. She, who was *b.* 15 Jan. 1781, *d.* 15 April 1805. He *d.* 17 Jan. 1809.(a) Admon. March 1809.

X. 1809. SIR FRANCIS VINCENT, Bart. [1620], of Debden Hall aforesaid, s. and h., *b.* 3 March 1803, in Charlotte street, Bloomsbury, Middlesex ; *suc. to the Baronetcy*, 17 Jan. 1809 ; M.P. for St. Albans, 1832-35. He *m.* 10 May 1824, at St. Geo. Han. sq , Augusta-Elizabeth, only child of Hon. Charles HERBERT (2d s. of Henry, 1st EARL OF CARNARVON), by Bridget-Augusta, da. of John (BYNG), 5th VISCOUNT TORRINGTON. She *d.* 3 April 1876, at Morpeth terrace. He *d.* s.p.m., 6 July 1880, in his 78th year.(b)

XI. 1880. SIR FREDERICK VINCENT, Bart. [1620], cousin and h. male, being 2d and yst. s. of Henry Dormer VINCENT, of Lily Hill, in Bracknell, Berks, by Isabella, da. of the Hon. Felton HERVEY (10th s. of John, 1st EARL OF BRISTOL), which Henry (who *d.* 22 May 1833, aged 82) was 2d s. of the 7th Bart. He was *b.* 8 Jan. 1798, in London ; matric. at Oxford (Bras. Coll.) 1 Nov. 1815; B.A. 1819; M.A. 1823; took holy orders; was Vicar of Hughenden, Bucks, 1826; Rector of Slinfold, Sussex, 1844-69 ; Preb. of Chichester, 1860 ; *suc. to the Baronetcy*, but not to the family estates, 6 July 1880, being then in his 83d year. He *m.* firstly, 26 Oct. 1826, Louisa, da. and coheir of John NORRIS, of Hughenden manor, Bucks. She *d.* 23 May 1841. He *m.* secondly, 4 Sep. 1844, Maria Copley, da. of Robert Herries YOUNG, of Auchenskeugh, Dumfries. He *d.* 9 Jan. 1883, at Villa Flora, Cannes, in France, aged 85, and was *bur.* in the cemetery of Route de Grasse there. Will pr. 15 Feb. 1883, under £230,000. His widow *d.* 29 Nov. 1899, at 8 Ebury street, Pimlico, in her 80th year, and was *bur.* at Esher, co. Surrey.

(a) It is said by Capt. Gronow that he was a victim to high play at the Salon des Etrangers.

(b) The estate of Debden Hall passed to his da. Blanche, who *m.*, 10 Jan. 1871, John Raymond Cely TREVILIAN, sometime an officer in the 3d Buffs, who *d.* in 1884.

XII. 1883. SIR WILLIAM VINCENT, Bart. [1620], s. and h. by 1st wife, b. 20 Sep. 1834, at Hughenden aforesaid; ed. at Marlborough and at Ch. Ch. Oxford; matric. 19 Oct. 1853, aged 19; B.A. 1857; M.A., 1860; in holy orders; Rector of Postwick, Norfolk, 1864-87; *suc. to the Baronetcy*, 9 Jan. 1883. He *m.* firstly, 24 May 1860, Margaret, yst. da. of Henry David (ERSKINE), EARL OF BUCHAN [S.], by his 2d wife, Elizabeth Rae, da. of John HERVEY. She, who was *b.* 15 Nov. 1834, *d.* 22 Nov. 1872, in Lowndes square. He *m.* secondly, 10 May 1882, at Harlwood, co. Hereford, Hester Clara, widow of Major Gen. STUBBS, yst. da. of the Rev. Edward Burdett HAWKSHAW, Rector of Weston-under-Penyard, by Catherine Mary Jane, da. of Sir Hungerford HOSKYNS, 7th Bart. [1676].

Family Estates.—Those of the 10th Bart., in 1878, consisted of 3,259 acres in Essex, worth £3,433 a year.(a) *Residence.*—Debden Hall, near Saffron Walden, Essex.

CLERE:

cr. 26 Feb. 1620/1;

ex. 22 Aug. 1622.

I. 1621, to 1622. "HENRY CLERE, of Ormesbye, co. Norfolk, Esq., s. and h. ap. of Edward CLERE,(b) of Thetford in the same county, Knt.," being 1st s. by his 1st wife, Margaret, da. of William YAXLEY, of Yaxley, co. Suffolk, was *b.* about 1599, being aged 12 years and 5 months, on 21 March 1611; and, having been *Knighted*, 11 May 1603; was v.p. *cr. a Bart.*, as above, 26 Feb. 1620/1. He *m.*, Sep. 1619, Muriel, 1st da. of Sir Edmund MUNDEFORD, of Feltwell, Norfolk, by Abigail, da. of Sir Thomas KNEVITT, of Ashwellthorpe. He *d.* s.p.m.(c) and probably v.p. 22 Aug. 1622, and was *bur.* at Ormsby, when the *Baronetcy* became *extinct*. Inq. p. mort. 16 Jan. 1638. His widow is said to have *m.* Sir (—) MANWOOD.

TICHBORNE, *or* TITCHBURNE:

cr. 8 March 1620/1,

sometime, 1845-53, DOUGHTY,

afterwards, since 1853, DOUGHTY-TICHBORNE.

I. 1621. "BENJAMIN TITCHBURNE [*or* TICHBORNE] of Titchburne, [near Alresford], co. Southampton, Knt.," s. and h. of Nicholas TICHBORNE, of Tichborne Park, by Elizabeth, his 2d wife, sister and coheir of James RYTHE, of Rythe, was *b.* about 1540; Sheriff of Hants, 1579-80 and 1602-03. M.P. for Petersfield, 1588-89, and for Hants, 1593; *Knighted* by Queen Eliz. at Tichborne on her way to Basing in 1601(a); was again Sheriff of Hants, 1602, in which capacity he proclaimed at Winchester the accession of James I in March 1602/3; was Gentleman of the Privy Chamber to that King, who honoured him with several visits at Tichborne, and gave him the Castle of Winchester in fee farm, and by whom, having been long before *Knighted*,(a) he was *cr. a Bart.*, as above, 8 March 1620/1. He *m.* firstly, (—), da. of (—) SHELLEY, of Maple Durham, Oxon She *d.* s.p. He *m.* secondly (Lic. Lond. 17 May 1571), Amphillis, da. of Richard WESTON, of Skreens in Roxwell, Essex, Justice of the Common Pleas (1559-72), by his 1st wife, Wiburga, da. of Michael CATESBY, of Seaton, co. Rutland. He *d.* 6 Sep. 1629, and was *bur.* at Tichborne, aged 89. M.I. Will dat. 23 Feb. 1628, pr. 14 Nov. 1629. His wife survived him.

(a) The property at Stoke D'Abernon, which was in possession of the 9th Bart. in 1800, had apparently been alienated by him.

(b) See a well worked up pedigree, by Aug. Jessopp, D.D., in the *Genealogist*, vol. iii, p. 292, reproduced, with additions, in vol. ii. of the *Norfolk Visitations* of 1563, pub. by the Norf. Arch. Soc. This Edward, whose father, Sir Edward Clere, was *bur.* at Blickling, 14 Aug. 1606, was *bap.* there 1 Jan. 1563/4; was "in such esteem at the French Court that he was elected one of the Knights of the Gallick Order of St. Michael. Affecting much grandeur, he contracted a debt on his estate, and was obliged to sell Blickling to Sir John Hobart" [Collins' *Baronetage*, 1720]. He was, and had been, in 1620, for some time a prisoner in the Fleet prison for debt, and was living 1626. The pedigree in Blomefield's *Norfolk* is "a mass of confusion," and the earlier generations are disproved by Walter Rye in the *Genealogist*, vol. iv, p. 97.

(c) Henry, his only son, *d.* v.p. and was *bur.* 29 June 1621, at Feltwell; Abigail, his only da. and h,, *m.* John Cromwell, 2d s. of Sir Oliver Cromwell, of Hinchenbrooke, co. Huntingdon.

I

II. 1629. SIR RICHARD TICHBORNE, Bart. [1621], of Tichborne aforesaid, 1st s. and h.,(b) *b.* about 1578. He was M.P. for Lyme Regis, 1597-98; for Hants, 1614; and for Winchester (five Parls.), 1621-29; was *Knighted*, 11 May 1603, at the Charter House; *suc. to the Baronetcy*, 11 Sep. 1629; was Gent. of the Bedchamber to Charles I, by whom he was sent as Ambassador to the Queen of Bohemia, and for whom he held Winchester Castle during the civil wars, his estates being accordingly sequestrated, 30 Sep. 1650. He *m.* firstly, Ellen, da. and coheir of Robert WHITE, of Aldershot, Hants (s. of Sir John WHITE, Lord Mayor of London, 1563), by Mary, da. and h. of William FORSTER, of London, and of Bradley, co. Derby. She *d.* s.p.m. 18 May 1606, aged 27. He *m.* secondly, in or before 1616, Susan, 2d da. and coheir of William WALLER, of Oldstoke and Stoke Charity, Hants, by his 1st wife, (—), da. of (—) SOMESTER. He *d.* April 1652, aged 74. His widow, who was *b.* 1597, was living 1657.

III. 1652. SIR HENRY TICHBORNE, Bart. [1621], of Tichborne aforesaid, 3d and yst. but only surv. s. and h.; fought at Cheriton and elsewhere for the cause of the King; *suc. to the Baronetcy* in April 1652. From Nov. to Dec. 1678, he was imprisoned for supposed complicity in the plot denounced by Titus Oates, but was, in 1685, made Lieut. of the New Forest by Charles II, and subsequently, 1687-88, Lieut. of the Ordnance by James II. He *m.* Mary, only da. of Hon. William ARUNDELL, of Horningsham, Wilts (2d s. of Thomas, 1st BARON ARUNDELL OF WARDOUR), by Mary, da. of Anthony Maria (BROWNE), 2d VISCOUNT MONTAGU. He *d.* April 1689, aged 65 (c) His widow *d.* 24 Dec. 1698.

IV. 1689. SIR HENRY JOSEPH TICHBORNE, Bart. [1621] of Tichborne aforesaid, s. and h.; *suc. to the Baronetcy* in April 1689. He *m.* (settl. 29 July 1689) Mary, da. of Anthony KEMP, of Slindon, Sussex, by Mary, da. of Sir Thomas GAGE, 2d Bart. [1622], of Firle. He *d.* s.p.m.s. 15 July 1743.(d) Will dat. 11 May 1742, pr. 14 Jan. 1744. The will of his widow pr. 20 Jan. 1755.

V. 1743. SIR JOHN HERMENGILD TICHBORNE, Bart. [1621], br. and h. male, a Priest of the Society of Jesus; *suc. to the Baronetcy*, 15 July 1743, and *d.* unm. at Ghent, 5 May 1748.

(a) See *Her. and Gen.*," vol. iv., pp. 64-71. All his four sons were Knighted by James I, viz., Richard and Walter, both on 11 May 1603, at the Charterhouse; Benjamin, 2 Sep. 1618, at Aldershot (*d.* s.p. 21 Aug. 1665); and Henry, 29 Aug. 1623, also at Tichborne. Another "Walter Tichborne, of Hants" is said to have been Knighted, 16 Nov. 1604, at Whitehall.

(b) His yr. br., Sir Henry, was grandfather of Henry Tichborne, *cr. a Bart.* 12 July 1697, being subsequently *cr.*, 26 Sep. 1715, Baron Ferrard of Beaulieu [I.].

(c) In 1670 Giles Tilbury, an eminent Flemish painter, painted him (then aged 45), his wife, three children, and several other persons, standing in front of the old manor house and distributing the well known "Tichborne dole." [See *Her. and Gen*, vol. iv, p. 65].

(d) He left three daughters and coheirs, of whom, Frances Cecily *m.* George Brownlow Doughty, of Snarford Hall, co. Lincoln, and died, as his widow, 20 Aug. 1765, aged 72, leaving a da., who inherited that estate, which she left to her cousin, Edward Tichborne, afterwards (1826) Doughty, who in 1845 inherited the Tichborne Baronetcy.

X

VI. 1748. SIR HENRY TICHBORNE, Bart. [1621], of Tichborne aforesaid, cousin and h. male, being s. and h. of James TICHBORNE, of Aldershot, Hants, by Mary, da. of (—) RUDYARD, which James was s. and h. of White TICHBORNE (*d.* 30 Aug. 1700) the s. and h. of Francis TICHBORNE (*d.* July 1671, aged 68), the s. and h. of Sir Walter TICHBORNE,(a) all of Aldershot aforesaid, which Walter (who *d.* 1640) was 2d s. of the 1st Bart. He was *bap.* at Fumley, co. Surrey, 14 Oct. 1710; matric. at Oxford (Queen's Coll.), 3 June 1728, aged 17, and *suc. to the Baronetcy*, 5 May 1748. He *m.*, 1742-43, his cousin, Mary, da. of Michael BLOUNT, of Mapledurham, Oxon, by Mary-Agnes, da. and coheir of Sir Henry-Joseph TICHBORNE, 4th Bart. He *d.* 16 July 1785. Will pr. Aug. 1785. His widow *d.* 10 Feb. 1799. Will pr. May 1799.

VII. 1785. SIR HENRY TICHBORNE, Bart. [1621], of Tichborne aforesaid, s. and h., *b.* 6 Sep. 1756; *suc. to the Baronetcy*, 16 July 1785. He *m.*, 1778, Elizabeth-Lucy, 1st da. of Edmund PLOWDEN, of Plowden, Salop, by Lucy, da. and coheir of William THOMPSON. He *d.* 14 June 1821. Will pr. 1821. His widow *d.* 24 Jan. 1829, at Southampton, aged 71.

VIII. 1821. SIR HENRY TICHBORNE, Bart. [1621], of Tichborne aforesaid, s. and h., *b.* 8 Jan. 1779; *suc. to the Baronetcy*, 14 June 1821. Sheriff of Hants, 1831-32. He *m.*, 23 April 1806, Anne, 4th da. of Sir Thomas BURKE, 1st Bart. [I. 1797], of Marble Hill, by Christian, da. of James BROWNE, of Limerick. He *d.* s.p.m. 3 June 1845, at Tichborne Park, aged 66. Will pr. Jan. 1846 and Aug. 1856. His widow *d.* 12 Aug. 1853, at Woodstock. Admon. Nov. 1853.

IX. 1845. SIR EDWARD DOUGHTY, Bart. [1621], of Tichborne aforesaid, and of Snarford Hall and West Barkworth, co. Lincoln, br. and h. male, *b.* 27 March 1782, at Tichborne Park. By royal lic., 29 May 1826, he took the name of *Doughty* in lieu of that of *Tichborne*, having suc. to the estates of that family under the will of his cousin, Miss Doughty, of Snarford Hall aforesaid.(b) Sheriff of Dorset, 1834; *suc. to the Baronetcy*, 3 June 1845. He *m.*, 26 June 1827, at Wardour Castle, Katharine, da. of James-Everard (ARUNDELL), 9th BARON ARUNDELL OF WARDOUR, by his 1st wife, Mary-Christiana, da. and coheir of Henry (ARUNDELL), 8th BARON ARUNDELL OF WARDOUR. He *d.* s.p.m.s. 5 March 1853, at Tichborne Park, in his 71st year. Will pr. June 1853. His widow *d.* there 12 Dec. 1872.

X. 1853. SIR JAMES-FRANCIS TICHBORNE, *afterwards* DOUGHTY-TICHBORNE, Bart. [1621], of Tichborne aforesaid, br. and h. male, *b.* 3 Oct. 1784, at Tichborne Park. He *suc. to the Baronetcy* (and estates), 5 March 1853, and by royal lic., 6 May 1853, took the name of *Doughty* before that of *Tichborne*. He *m.*, 1 Aug. 1827, Henriette Felicité, da. of Henry SEYMOUR, of Knoyle, Wilts, by his 2d wife, Louise, CONTESSE DE PANTHOU, in France. He *d.* 11 June 1862. His widow *d.* suddenly 12 March 1868, at Howlett's Hotel, Manchester street, Marylebone, and was *bur.* at Tichborne.

The Baronetcy was assumed, about 1866, by ARTHUR ORTON (s. of George ORTON, of 69 High street, Wapping, Shipping-butcher), who pretended to be "Roger Charles," 1st s. and h. ap. of the late Bart., which Roger (*b.* 5 Jan. 1829) had *d.* unm. v.p. in the spring of 1854, being lost in the ship "Bella," at sea, off South America, though his mother remained incredulous as to his death. "The Claimant" (as he was generally called)

(a) This Walter *m.*, 7 May 1597, Mary, da. and coheir of Robert WHITE abovenamed (s. of Sir John White, Lord Mayor of London, 1563), with whom he acquired the estate of Aldershot. See as to her sister, Ellen, *sub* 2d Bart.

(b) See p. 161, note "d."

was *b.* (five years later) 20 March 1834; deserted from his ship, 1849; resided in Australia (as a Butcher, at Wagga-Wagga), 1853-66, when, having read the Dow. Lady Tichborne's advertisements for her missing son, he met her, at Paris in Jan. 1867, and was acknowledged by her as such son; came to London, styled himself "SIR ROGER CHARLES DOUGHTY-TICHBORNE, BART.," and laid claim to the Tichborne estates, valued at £24,000 a year. The trial for this purpose, 11 May 1871 to 6 March 1872, went against him, as also did one for perjury, 23 April 1872 to 28 Feb. 1874 [the Queen *v.* Thomas Castro, *alias* Arthur Orton, *alias* Sir Roger Tichborne], and he was sentenced to fourteen years hard labour. He was released 20 Oct. 1884 (weighing then ten and a half stone instead of twenty-five stone as in 1874); kept a tobacconist's shop at Islington; published a confession of his imposture in 1895, in *The People* (a London weekly paper) and *d.* 1 April 1898, at 21 Shouldham street, being *bur.* in Paddington cemetery, aged 64. The cost of these trials, about £90,000 was, by Act of Parl., paid out of the estates.

XI. 1862. SIR ALFRED-JOSEPH DOUGHTY-TICHBORNE, Bart. [1621], of Tichborne aforesaid, 1st surv. s. and h., *b.* 4 Sep. 1839, in Paris; *suc. to the Baronetcy*, 11 June 1862. He became a bankrupt. He *m.*, 17 June 1861, Theresa-Mary, 1st da. of Henry-Benedict (ARUNDELL), 11th BARON ARUNDELL OF WARDOUR, by his 3d wife, Theresa, da. of William (STOURTON), BARON STOURTON. He *d.* at Fencote Hall, near Bedale, co. York, 22 Feb, and was *bur.* 2 March 1866, at Tichborne. His widow, who was *b.* 5 Oct. 1840, *m.*, 24 Feb. 1873, at the Roman Catholic chapel, Warwick street, Henry Lampleigh WICKHAM, sometime Capt. Rifle Brigade.

* * * * * * *

XII. 1866. SIR HENRY-ALFRED-JOSEPH DOUGHTY-TICHBORNE, Bart. [1621], of Tichborne aforesaid, posthumous s. and h., *b.* 28 May 1866, at Fencote Hall aforesaid, and *suc. to the Baronetcy* at his birth; Sheriff of Hants, 1892. He *m.*, 8 Sep. 1887, at the Roman Catholic church of St. Osburg, Coventry, Mary Gwendoline, da. of Edward Henry PETRE, of Whitley Abbey, co. Warwick, by Gwendoline, sister of Bertram Arthur (TALBOT), 17th EARL OF SHREWSBURY.

Family Estates.—These, in 1883, consisted of 7,270 acres in Hants; 1,984 in Lincolnshire; 1,092 in Dorset, and 661 in Bucks. *Total*, 11,007 acres, worth £8,716 a year. *Principal Residences.*—Tichborne Park, near Alresford, Hants, and Upton House, Dorset.

WILBRAHAM:

cr. 5 May 1621;

ex. Aug. 1692.

I. 1621. "RICHARD WILBRAHAM, of Woodhey, co. Chester, Knt., only s. and h. of Thomas WILBRAHAM, of the same, by Frances, da. of Sir Hugh CHOLMONDELEY, of Cholmondeley, was *b.* 1579; suc. his father, 12 July 1610; was *Knighted* at Christ Church, Dublin, 4 Sep. 1603, by Sir George Carey, L. Deputy [I.]; was Sheriff of Cheshire, 1615-16, and was *cr. a Bart.*, as above, 5 May 1621. He *m.*, in or before 1601, Grace, sister of Thomas, 1st VISCOUNT SAVAGE, da. of Sir Thomas SAVAGE, 1st Bart. [1611], of Rock Savage, by Mary, da. and coheir of Richard ALLINGTON. He *d.* April 1643.

II. 1643. SIR THOMAS WILBRAHAM, Bart. [1611], of Woodhey aforesaid, s. and h.; *b.* about 1601, being aged 13 in 1614; *suc. to the Baronetcy* about 1642; distinguished himself in the Royal cause during the civil war; was fined £2,500, his estate being sequestrated. He *m.* (Lic. London 2 Feb. 1612/3, he about 11 and she about 10), Elizabeth, da. and coheir of Sir Roger WILBRAHAM, one of the Masters of the Court of Requests (*d.* 1616). He *d.* 31 Oct. 1660. The will of his widow pr. 1680.

III. 1660, to 1691. SIR THOMAS WILBRAHAM, Bart. [1621], s. and h.; *b.* about 1630, being 38 in 1668; *suc. to the Baronetcy*, 31 Oct. 1660; Sheriff of Staffordshire, 1654-55; of Cheshire, 1663-64; was nom. a Knight of the (intended) order of the Royal Oak(a); was M.P. for Stafford, 1679-81. He *m.* Elizabeth, da. and h. of Edward MITTON, of Weston under Lyzcard, co. Stafford. He *d.* s.p.m.(b), and was *bur.* at Woodhey, 19 Aug. 1692, when the *Baronetcy* became *extinct*. Will pr. 1692.

DELVES:
cr. 8 May 1621; *ex.* 12 Sep. 1727.

I. 1621. "THOMAS DELVES, of Dudington [*i.e.*, Dodington], co. Chester, Knt.," s. and h. of Henry DELVES, of the same, by Frances, da. of Thomas STANLEY, of Alderley in that county, was *bap.* at Alderley 30 Nov. 1571; was ed. at Bras. Coll., Oxford,(c) to which he was a benefactor; *Knighted* 10 July 1609 at Whitehall; suc. his father 8 Oct. 1606, and was *cr. a Bart.*, as above, 8 May 1621; Sheriff of Cheshire, 1636-37; was a Royalist, being, 27 June 1646, fined £1,878 (afterwards reduced to £1,300), and his estate sequestrated. He *m.* firstly, in or before 1598, Mary, sister of Sir Richard WILBRAHAM, 1st Bart. [1621], da. of Thomas WILBRAHAM, of Woodhey, co. Chester, by Frances, da. of Sir Hugh CHOLMONDELEY. She was *bur.* 22 June 1603, at Wybunbury. He *m.* secondly, Mary, widow of Sir Roger WILBRAHAM, da. of Edward BABER, of Chew, co. Somerset, Serjeant at Law. She was *bur.* 6 Jan. 1644, at Wybunbury. He *d.* 23 and was *bur.* there 24 April 1658.

II. 1658. SIR HENRY DELVES, Bart. [1621], of Dodington aforesaid, s. and h., by 1st wife; *bap.* 24 May 1579, at Wybunbury; matric. at Oxford, 1 July 1613; B.A. (Bras. Coll.), 29 Jan. 1615/6; Sheriff of Cheshire, 1649-50(d); *suc. to the Baronetcy*, 23 April 1658. He *m.* firstly, in or before 1630, Catherine, da. and coheir of Sir Roger WILBRAHAM abovenamed. She was *bur.* 28 Aug. 1630, at Wybunbury. He *m.* secondly, Mary, da. of Randal LEICESTER, of Chester, Citizen of London. He *d.* 23 May 1663, aged 64, and was *bur.* at Wybunbury. M.I. His widow, by whom he had no issue, *d.* 1 Feb. 1690, aged 68, and was *bur.* at St. Michael's, Chester. M.I.

III. 1663. SIR THOMAS DELVES, Bart. [1621], of Dodington aforesaid, 3d and yst. but only surv. s. and h., by 1st wife; *bap.* 28 Aug. 1630, at Dodington; matric. at Oxford (Mag. Coll.), 3 Feb. 1650/1, being B.A. the next day and M.A. 21 June 1653; *suc. to the Baronetcy*, 23 May 1663; Sheriff of Cheshire, 1664-65. He *m.*, in or before 1652, Elizabeth, only child of Hall RAVENSCROFT, of Horsham, co. Sussex, by Elizabeth, da. of John STAPLEY, of Twineham in that county. She *d.* in childbirth, 2 Dec. 1654, in her 26th year, and was *bur.* at Horsham. M.I. He *m.* secondly (Lic. Vic. Gen., 20 Dec. 1683, she about 23, spinster), Rachel, da. of Francis FORRESTER, of Watling street, in Wellington, co. Salop. He *d.* 15 May 1713.

IV. 1713, to 1727. SIR THOMAS DELVES, Bart. [1621], s. and h., by 1st wife; *b.* 4 Oct. 1652; matric. at Oxford (Bras. Coll.), 21 Oct. 1670, aged 19; nom. Sheriff of Cheshire, 1685 and 1697, but did not act; was Sheriff, 1698-99; *suc. to the Baronetcy*, 15 May 1713. He *m.* firstly, 13 Aug. 1674, at Fawsley, co. Northampton (Lic. Vic. Gen., she about 21), Jane, da. of Sir Richard KNIGHTLEY, K.B., of Fawsley, co. Northampton, by his 2d wife, Anne,

---

(a) See a list of these in Dugdale,s *Antient Usage of Arms*, edit. 1812.

(b) The estates devolved on his three daughters and coheirs, of whom (1) Elizabeth *m.* Sir Thomas Myddelton, 2d Bart. [1660] of Chirk Castle; (2) Grace, *m.* Lionel (Tollemache), Earl of Dysart [S.]; (3) Mary, *m.* Richard (Newport), 2d Earl of Bradford.

(c) Collins' *Baronetage*, 1720.

(d) "Unless the son were of different politics from the father it is difficult to understand his nomination. In the list of Sheriffs he is styled *Knight*, but I find no record of his Knighthood." [W. D. Pink].

da. of Sir William COURTEEN, of London. She *d.* s.p.m.,(a) and was *bur.* 24 Dec. 1692, at Wybunbury. He *m.* secondly, 16 Feb. 1696, Elizabeth, da. of Henry (BOOTH), 1st EARL OF WARRINGTON, by Mary, da. and h. of Sir James LANGHAM, 2d Bart. [1660]. She *d.* s.p. and was *bur.* 13 Oct. 1697, at Wybunbury. He *m.* thirdly, 1 May 1699, Elizabeth, da. of Andrew BARKER, of Fairford, co. Gloucester, by Elizabeth, da. of William ROBINSON, of Cheshunt, Herts. He *m.* fourthly (Lic. Worcester, 25 Oct. 1725), Rhoda, da. of Sir John HUBAND, 2d Bart. [1661], by Rhoda, da. of Sir Thomas BROUGHTON, 2d Bart. [1660]. He *d.* s.p.m.s.(b) 12 Sep. 1727, aged 75, when the *Baronetcy* became *extinct*. His will pr. 17 Nov. 1730. The will of his widow pr. 11 Feb. 1772.

WATSON:
cr. 23 June 1621, *afterwards*, 1644—1782, BARONS ROCKINGHAM, *and*, sometime, 1714-46, EARLS OF ROCKINGHAM, *subsequently*, Feb. 1746 to 1782, EARLS OF MALTON, *and finally*, April 1746 to 1782, MARQUESSES OF ROCKINGHAM; *ex.* 1 July 1782.

I. 1621. "LEWIS WATSON, of Rockingham Castle, co. Northampton, Knt.," 1st s. and h. of Sir Edward WATSON, of the same, by Anne, da. of Kenelm DIGBY, of Stoke Dry, co. Rutland, was *bap.* 14 July 1584, at Rockingham; matric. at Oxford (Mag. Coll.), 24 May 1590; *Knighted*, 19 Aug. 1608, at Grafton; M.P. for Lincoln, 1621-22, and 1624-25; suc. his father, 4 March 1616; acquired from the Crown the fee of Rockingham Castle and the lands thereof, formerly held on lease, and was *cr. a Bart.*, as above, 23 June 1621; Sheriff of Northants, 1632-33; Verderer of Rockingham and Brigstock, 1638. He *m.* firstly, in 1609, Catherine, da of Robert (BERTIE), LORD WILLOUGHBY DE ERESBY, by Mary, da. of John (VERE), EARL OF OXFORD. She *d.* s.p.m. in childbirth, 15 Feb. 1610, and was *bur.* at Spilsby, co. Lincoln. M.I. He *m.* secondly, 3 Oct. 1620, Eleanor, sister of John, 8th EARL OF RUTLAND, da. of Sir George MANNERS, of Haddon Hall, co. Derby, by Grace, da. of Sir Henry PIERREPONT. She was living, when he, for his services to the Royal cause, was *cr.*, 29 Jan. 1644/5, BARON ROCKINGHAM, co. Northampton. See fuller particulars in *Peerage*. In that Barony this *Baronetcy* then *merged*, the 3d Baron and Baronet being *cr.*, 19 Oct. 1714, EARL OF ROCKINGHAM (a dignity which became extinct by the death, 26 Feb. 1745/6, of the 3d Earl, 5th Baron and Baronet), his successor to the said Barony and Baronetcy, being, at that date, 26 Feb. 1745/6, EARL OF MALTON, and being *cr.*, 19 April 1746, MARQUESS OF ROCKINGHAM. On the death of his son, the 2d Marquess, 7th Baron and Baronet, this *Baronetcy*, as well as all the peerage dignities, became *extinct*.

PALMER:
cr. 29 June 1621; *ex.* 19 Feb. 1838; *assumed* (by two parties) after 1838.

I. 1621. "THOMAS PALMER,(c) of Wingham, co. Kent, Knt.," s. and h. of Sir Henry PALMER, of the same, by Jane, da. of Sir Richard

---

(a) Elizabeth, her only child, *b.* 4 Dec. 1670, *m.*, 16 Feb. 1696, her cousin, Sir Bryan Broughton, 3d Bart. [1660], and was ancestress of the family of Delves-Broughton, Barts., of Dodington.

(b) Henry, his only s. and h. ap. (by his 3d wife), *b.* 18 July 1700 (whom Collins, in his *Baronetage* [1720], calls "the 15th in a genealogical series from John de Delves, of Delves Hall, co. Stafford"), *d.* unm. and v.p. at Warwick, on his return from France, in April 1725.

(c) Pedigree (made in 1672, but continued in some places to 1750) in *Mis. Gen. et Her.*, vol. i, pp. 105—122. This is reviewed in the *Her. and Gen.*, vol. v, pp. 377-79.

WINDEBANK, of Guisnes, was *b.* 1540; suc. his father (who was slain in his 70th year, at the siege of Guisnes) in 1558; was Sheriff of Kent, 1595-96; *Knighted* by the Earl of Essex, 1596, at the taking of Cadiz; was Gent. of the Privy Chamber to James I, and was *cr. a Bart.*, as above, 29 June 1621. He was famed for his hospitality, keeping no less than sixty "open Christmasses." He *m.*, about 1562, Margaret, da. of John POLEY, of Badley, Suffolk, by Anne, da. of Thomas (WENTWORTH), LORD WENTWORTH. He *d.* 7 Jan. 1624/5, aged 85. His widow *d.* Aug. 1625, aged 83. Both were *bur.* at Wingham. M.I.(a)

II. 1625. SIR THOMAS PALMER, Bart. [1621], of Wingham aforesaid, grandson and h., being s. and h. of Sir Thomas PALMER, by Margaret, da. of Herbert PELHAM, of Buxsteep, Sussex, which Thomas last named, who was s. and h. ap. of the 1st Bart., *d.* v.p. and was *bur.* 10 Sep. 1608, at Wingham. He *suc. to the Baronetcy*, 7 Jan. 1624/5. He suffered much for his loyalty to the Royal cause, being imprisoned, his estates sequestrated, and himself fined £1,000 in July 1651. He *m.*, before 1627, Elizabeth (*b.* 1599), da. and coheir of Sir John SHURLEY, or SHIRLEY, of Isfield, Sussex, by his 1st wife, Anne, da. of Sir Thomas SHIRLEY, of Wiston. He was *bur.* 20 April 1656, at Wingham.

III. 1656. SIR HENRY PALMER, Bart. [1621], of Wingham aforesaid, s. and h., who, like his father, was a zealous Royalist; *suc. to the Baronetcy* in April 1656; Sheriff of Kent, 1690-91. He *m.* Ann, da. of Sir William LUCKYN, 1st Bart. [1661], of Waltham, Essex, by Winifred, da. of Sir Richard EVERARD, 1st Bart. [1629]. He *d.* s.p. 19 and was *bur.* 24 Sep. 1706, at Wingham. Will dat. 5 March 1701/2, pr. 13 Nov. 1706.

IV. 1706. SIR THOMAS PALMER, Bart. [1621], of Wingham aforesaid, nephew and h., being s. and h. of Herbert PALMER, by Dorothy, da. and h. of John PINCHEON, of Writtle, Essex, which Herbert was 3d s. of the 2d Bart., and *d.* 1699-1700, aged 70. He was *bap.* 5 July 1682, at St. Paul's, Covent Garden, and *suc. to the Baronetcy*, 19 Sep. 1706; M.P. for Kent, 1708-10, and for Rochester, 1715-22, and 1722 till death, being also a Commissioner for stating the debts of the Army. He *m.* firstly, in or before 1707, Elizabeth, sister of Robert, 1st BARON ROMNEY, da. of Sir Robert MARSHAM, 4th Bart. [1663], by Margaretta, da. of Thomas BOSVILE. She was *bur.* 29 July 1714, at Wingham. He *m.* secondly, Susanna "*Mrs. Cox*." She was *bur.* 15 Jan. 1721, at Wingham. He *m.* thirdly, Elizabeth, widow of (—) MARKHAM. He *d.* s.p.m. legit.(b) 8 and was *bur.* 16 Nov. 1723, at Wingham, aged 42. Will dat. 6 Aug. 1723, pr. 11 Feb. 1724 and 21 May 1725, mentioning his wife, Elizabeth; his son [*i.e.*, illegit. son], Herbert Palmer, by late wife, and his four daughters, Elizabeth, Mary, Anne and Frances.(c) His widow *m.*, in or before 1732, Thomas HAY, and *d.* before May 1765.

V. 1723. SIR CHARLES PALMER, Bart. [1621], of Dorney Court, Bucks, cousin and h. male, being s. and h. of Charles PALMER, of the same, by Jane, da. of John JENYNS, of Hayes, co. Midx., which Charles, last

---

(a) By his third son, Sir James Palmer, of Dorney Court, Bucks, Chancellor of the Order of the Garter (*d.* 15 March 1657, in his 73d year), he was grandfather of Roger, Earl of Castlemaine [I.] (husband of Barbara, Duchess of Cleveland), as also of Sir Philip Palmer, of Dorney Court aforesaid, ancestor of the 5th Bart., which Philip is (erroneously) said to have been *cr. a Bart.* between 1657 and 1669.

(b) "A man of pleasure and very extravagant in all things. He left his estate (which was not settled on his daughters) to Herbert Palmer, his son, by Mrs. Cox, before he married her." [See p. 165, note "b."]

(c) Three of these daughters were by the first wife, *viz.* (1), Elizabeth, *bap.* 21 Aug. 1709, at Wingham, *m.* the Hon. Charles Finch, and was grandmother to George William, Earl of Winchilsea; (2) Mary, *bap.* 23 Aug. 1712, at Wingham, *m.* Daniel (Finch), Earl of Winchilsea; (3) Ann, *bap.* 26 July 1714, at Wingham, *m.*, firstly, Sir Brook Bridges, Bart., and, secondly, the Hon. Charles Feilding. The other da., Frances, was apparently, by the third wife. She *d.* unm. and was *bur.* "from Wickham" 13 Aug. 1770 at Wingham.

named (*b.* 1651; *d.* 1712) was 4th and yst. but only s. that left surv. issue of Sir Philip PALMER, of Dorney aforesaid, Cupbearer to Charles II (sometimes, but apparently erroneously, called a Baronet),(a) which Philip (*b.* 1615, *d.* 1683) was s. and h. of Sir James PALMER, Chancellor of the Order of the Garter, of Dorney Court (who acquired that estate with his 1st wife, Martha, da. of Sir William GARRARD), which James (*d.* 15 March 1657, aged 73) was 3d s. of the 1st Bart. He *suc. to the Baronetcy* in Nov. 1723. He *m.*, June 1729, Anne, da. of Richard HARCOURT, of Wigsel, Sussex, and of the Inner Temple, London, by Elizabeth, sister of Simon, 1st VISCOUNT HARCOURT, da. of Sir Philip HARCOURT. He *d.* 8 and was *bur.* 13 Nov. 1773, at Dorney. Will pr. Nov. 1773. His widow *d.* 20 and was *bur.* there 27 May 1774, aged 63. Will, as "of Somerset street, Marylebone, widow," dat. 4 Jan. to 11 April 1774, pr. 26 May 1774, by "Richard Harcourt, Esq.," her brother.

VI. 1773, to 1838. SIR CHARLES HARCOURT PALMER, Bart. [1621], of Dorney Court aforesaid, grandson and h., being s. and h. of Charles Palmer, an officer in the East India Company's military service, by Sarah, da. of Thomas CLACK, of Wallingford, which Charles was s. and h. ap. of the 6th Bart., and *d.* v.p. in Sumatra, 1764, aged 33. He was *b.* 1760; *suc. to the Baronetcy*, 8 Nov. 1773; matric. at Oxford (Mag. Coll.), 14 Nov. 1777, aged 17. He *d.* unm. at Dorney Court, 19 and was *bur.* 27 Feb. 1838, at Dorney, aged 77, when the *Baronetcy* became apparently *extinct*.(b) Will, dat. 24 Sep. 1835 to 13 Feb. 1838, proved 10 March 1838, by John Palmer, *Esquire* [*sic*], Rev. Henry Palmer, Clerk in Orders, and Philip Palmer, Esq., sons and executors.(c)

[This Baronetcy has, however, been assumed by two several parties, viz. (1) by the son of one of the illegitimate sons of the 6th Bart. and (2) by some members of an Irish family purporting to descend in the male line from the grantee.]

VII. 1838. JOHN PALMER, of Dorney Court aforesaid, 1st of the three illegit. sons of the 6th Bart., by Caroline BONIN, spinster, *b.* 1795; matric. at Oxford (Bras. Coll.), 6 Nov. 1812, aged 17. He, according to the assumption of the title by his nephew, (in or soon after 1865,) would have been the 7th Bart. [1621] in Feb. 1838, at which date he suc. to the family estates by the will of the late Bart. He *d.* s.p. and was *bur.* at Dorney 1 Sep. 1852, as "John Palmer, Esq."(d)

(a) It is quite evident that his father, Charles, had not been so created, so that the dignity could not have been one, granted (as were several) during the rebellion by Charles I, of which grants no record exists. There is no evidence that he ever styled himself a Baronet, but he is so styled in his mar. lic. (Vic. Gen.) 15 Nov. 1669, as also in his admon., 28 Nov. 1681, though apparently erroneously. His son and successor does not appear to have assumed it.

(b) Kimber, in his *Baronetage* (A.D. 1771), vol. i, p. 210, says that Philip PALMER, of Richmond, Surrey [a younger br. of Sir Charles Palmer, Bart., of Dorney Court], by his wife Jane, da. and h. of John THOMPSON, of Nettleden, Bucks, and of Ludgate Hill, London, mercer (*m.* before 1741), "has had three sons and two daughters, viz., Philip, John, Charles, Jane, and Anna, all now (A.D. 1771) living. This is the *only remaining branch of the male line*." In the "Addenda" to Burke's *Extinct Baronets* (edit. 1844), it is stated that all these sons and one of their sisters Jane, *d.* unm., while Anna *m.* James LANDON, of Cheshunt, Herts, and had issue.

(c) They were (together with a da. named Angelica, who *m.*, before 1835, William Watts WILSON, R.N.) his illegit. children, by his cousin, Caroline BONIN, spinster, da. of Goussé Bonin, of Antigua, by Dorothy, da. of Sir Charles PALMER, the 5th Bart. He left his estates to his three illegit. sons successively in tail male, with remainders over. He had also left in his will of 1835 (though he revoked it in the codicil of 1888) £4,000 to his "*cousin*, Caroline BONIN." The will of the said "CAROLINE BONIN, of Dorney Court, Bucks, gentlewoman, dat. 10 May 1849, was proved 17 Feb. 1852, by Angelica FINCH, wife of William FINCH, Esq., heretofore Angelica WILSON (relict of William Watts WILSON), executrix and residuary legatee.

(d) See p. 165, note "b."

VIII. 1852. REV. HENRY PALMER, of Dorney Court aforesaid, 2d of the three illegit. sons abovenamed, *b.* 1798 ; matric. at Oxford (Ch. Ch.), 27 Jan. 1814, aged 16 ; B.A., 1817 ; M.A., 1820 ; in Holy Orders ; Vicar of Dorney, Bucks, 1832-56 ; suc. to the family estates, 1 Sep. 1852, when, according to the assumption of the title by his son, he would have been the 8th Bart. [1621]. He *d.* 20 and was *bur.* 27 Nov. 1865, at Dorney, as "the Rev. Henry Palmer."(a)

IX. 1865, to 1895. "SIR CHARLES JAMES PALMER, Bart." [1621] (according to his own designation), of Dorney Court aforesaid, only surv. s. and h. of the above ; *b.* 1829 ; ed. at the Coll. Bourbon, Paris ; admitted to Inner Temple, 1 May 1860 ; Barrister, 17 Nov. 1863 ; suc. to the family estates, 20 Nov. 1865, when, or shortly after which, he *assumed this Baronetcy.* F.S.A. He *m.*, in 1862, Katherine Millicent, da. of Peter HOOD, M.D., sometime of Windmill Hills, Durham, and of Watford, Herts. From him she obtained a judicial separation, 23 Jan. 1874. He *d.* 11 July 1895, at 2 Sinclair road, Kensington, and was *bur.* at Dorney, aged 66. Will pr. at £35,064. His widow was living 29 July 1896, when, by Royal licence, she and her children by the said Charles James Palmer (therein described as "Esquire") were authorised to bear the surname of Palmer and to have arms established thereto. The eldest s. and h., Charles Dayrell Palmer, *discontinues the assumption of this Baronetcy.*

Another assumption of this Baronetcy took place (on the ground of a male descent from a younger son of the grantee), as under :—

VII. 1838. THOMAS PALMER stated(b) to have *assumed* the *Baronetcy of Palmer* [1621], on the ground of a descent from Henry Palmer,(c) the yst s. of the 1st Bart., was s. and h. of Patrick PALMER, LL.D., of Glanmore, co. Longford, by Catharine, 1st da. and coheir of Edward SMYTH, of Callow hill, co. Fermanagh, the parentage or remoter ancestry of the said Patrick, not being set forth. He *d.* s.p.m., 1847.

VIII. 1847. "SIR WILLIAM PALMER, Bart." [1621] (according to his own designation), of Streamstown, near Mullingar, co. Westmeath, and of Invermore, co. Mayo, br. and h., *b.* 1776 ; was an officer of the 53d Foot. In 1862, if not before (*Qy.* 1847), he *assumed this Baronetcy.* He *m.* firstly, 1802, Helen, da. of J. Gratrix HILL, of Fieldtown, co. Westmeath. He *m.* secondly, 1844, Charlotte, da. of Colonel PATTON. He *d.* 30 Dec. 1865, aged 89. His widow (called "Lady Palmer") *d.* 27 Feb. 1885, at Hastings, in her 85th year.

IX. 1865, to 1885. "SIR WILLIAM PALMER, Bart." [1621] (according to his own designation), Vicar of Whitchurch Canonicorum, Dorset, s. and h. by 1st wife. He was *b.* 14 Feb. 1803 ; ed. at Trin. Coll., Dublin ; B.A., 1824, and, having taken Holy Orders, was incorp. at Oxford (Mag. Hall.), 1828 ; M.A., 1829 ; Fellow of Worc. Coll., Oxford; author, in 1832, of the well-known *Origines Liturgicæ* and other works; Vicar of Whitchurch, 1846-65; Vicar of Monckton Wyld, 1864-69; Prebendary of

(a) See p. 165, note "b."

(b) *N. and Q.*, 4th S., ii, 47, but such assumption seems doubtful, and is attributed to his brother in 1862 in Walford's *County Families* (1864), the Editor thereof adding that the title "was not assumed between 1838 and 1862." [*Her. and Gen.*, vol. iv, pp. 283-284, where is a note by the Editor thereof that, "In the 3d edit. [1865] of Walford's *County Families*, Mr. Palmer of Streamstown is reduced to the rank of Esquire ; but we find that there are other Irish cousins claiming descent from the Palmers of Wingham, whose claim is not challenged," etc.]

(c) This Henry PALMER, however, is stated to have "died young." See M.I. at Wingham, Kent, to the 1st Bart. [*Mis. Gen. et Her.*, vol. i, p. 179.]

Sarum, 1849-58 ; *assumed the Baronetcy* in 1865. He *m.* in Oct. 1839, Sophia Mary Bonne, 1st da. of Admiral Sir Francis BEAUFORT, K.C.B. She *d.* 11 June 1872, at 62 Montagu square, Marylebone. He *d.* in London, Oct. 1885, aged 83, leaving one son, who, it is believed, *discontinued the assumption of this dignity.*(a)

ROBARTES, *or* ROBERTS :

cr. 3 July 1621,

afterwards, 1625—1757, BARONS ROBARTES OF TRURO,

and *finally*, 1679—1757, EARLS OF RADNOR ;

ex. 15 July 1757.

I. 1621. "RICHARD ROBERTS [or ROBARTES], of Trewro [*i.e.*, Truro], co. Cornwall, Knt.," only s. and h. of John ROBARTES, of Truro aforesaid, by Philip, 2d da. of John GAVERIGAN, of Gaverigan, co. Cornwall, was *b.* in or before 1585; was, v.p., Sheriff of Cornwall, 1614-15; suc. his father, 21 March 1615, being then aged 30 and upwards ; *Knighted* at Whitehall, 11 Nov. 1616, and was *cr. a Bart.*, as above, 3 July 1621. He *m.* (settlm. 5 Jan. 1598) Frances, da. and coheir of John HENDER, of Botreux Castle, Cornwall, by Jane, da. of (—) THORNE, of co. Northampton. She was living when he was *cr.*, 26 Jan. 1624/5, BARON ROBARTES OF TRURO, co. Cornwall, in which peerage this *Baronetcy* then *merged*, the 2d Baron and Baronet being *cr.*, 23 July 1679, EARL OF RADNOR, till by the death of the 4th Earl, 5th Baron and Baronet, 15 July 1757, it, and all his peerage dignities, became *extinct.*

RIVERS :

cr. 19 July 1621,

sometime, 1760—1805, RIVERS-GAY ;

ex. 31 Oct. 1870.

I. 1621. "JOHN RIVERS, of Chafford, co. Kent, Esq.," s. and h. ap. of Sir George RIVERS, of the same, by Frances, da. and coheir of William BOWYER, of co. Sussex, which George (whose will dat. 3 Dec. 1627(b) was pr. 5 June 1630) was s. and h. of Sir John RIVERS, of Chafford, sometime (1573-74) L. Mayor of London, was *b.* about 1579 ; matric. at Oxford (St. Mary Hall), 14 Oct. 1596, aged 17 ; admitted to Inner Temple, 1600, and was v.p. *cr. a Bart.*, as above, 19 July 1621. He *m.* firstly, in or before 1602,(c) Dorothy, da. and coheir of Thomas, POTTER,(d) of Well street in Westerham, co. Kent. She was *bur.* there 13 Jan. 1627. He *m.* secondly, Dulcibella, widow of Nicholas LOVE, D.D., Warden of Winchester, da. of Barnabas COLNETT, of Combley, in the Isle of Wight, by Elizabeth, sister of Sir Richard MILLS. He *d.* about 1651. Admon. 2 Oct. 1651. His widow *d.* 22 May 1657, aged 68, and was *bur.* at Crondall, Hants. M.I.(e)

(a) See a letter of "Ed. Marshall," and various references in *N. and Q.*, 7th S., vol. vii, as to this assumption.

(b) In it he twice mentions "my unkind son, Sir John Rivers, Bart." [*Her. and Gen.*, iv, 133].

(c) His son, Potter, was *bap.* 11 Aug. 1602, and *bur.* 12 Aug. 1621, at Westerham.

(d) The marriage of "Thomas Potter Esq. and my Lady Rivers," 23 Nov. 1591, at Westerham, is presumably that of her widowed father with the widowed grandmother of her husband.

(e) *Coll. Top. et Gen.*, vii, 220.

II. 1651. SIR THOMAS RIVERS, Bart. [1621], of Chafford aforesaid, grandson and h., being s. and h. of James RIVERS, by Charity, da. and coheir of Sir John SHURLEY, of Isfield, co. Sussex (by his 1st wife, Anne, da. of Sir Thomas SHIRLEY, of Wiston), which James (*bap.* 15 Dec. 1603, at Westerham) was M.P. for Lewes, 1640-41, but *d.* v.p. 8 June 1641, and was *bur.* at St. Barth. the Great, London. He *suc. to the Baronetcy* about 1651 ; was M.P. for Sussex, 1654-55, and 1656 till death. He *d.* unm. 1657. Will pr. 1658.

III. 1657. SIR JOHN RIVERS, Bart. [1621], of Chafford aforesaid, br. and h., *suc. to the Baronetcy* in 1657. He *m.*, 26 Feb. 1662/3, at St. Barth. the Great, London (Lic. Vic. Gen.), Anne, sister and coheir of George, VISCOUNT HEWETT OF GOWRAN [I.], da. of Sir Thomas HEWETT, 1st Bart. [1660], of Pishobury, Herts, by his 2d wife, Margaret, da. of Sir William LYTTON. He *d.* about 1679. Admon. 28 March 1678/9, and 10 Feb. 1689/90. The will of his widow pr. April 1689.

IV. 1679 ? SIR GEORGE RIVERS, Bart. [1621], of Chafford aforesaid, 1st s. and h., *b.* 1 and *bap.* 2 April 1665, at St. Martin's in the Fields(a) ; *suc. to the Baronetcy* about 1679. He *m.* (Lic. Fac. 29 Jan. 1688/9) Dorothea (she aged 18 and he 24), da. of Sir William BEVERSHAM, of Holbrooke Hall, Suffolk, one of the Masters in Chancery, by Dorothy, his wife. He *d.* s.p.m.s.,(b) and was *bur.* 9 Aug. 1734, at Falkenham, Suffolk. Will pr. 1734.

V. 1734. SIR JOHN RIVERS, Bart. [1621], nephew and h. male, being s. and h. of Rev. Thomas RIVERS, D.C.L., Prebendary of Winchester (1702) and Rector of Easton, Hants (1723-31), by Mary, da. of Richard HOLBROOKE, of the Isle of Wight, which Thomas was 3d s. of the 3d Bart., and *d.* 8 Sep. 1731, aged 63. He was *b.* about 1718 ; *suc. to the Baronetcy* in Aug. 1734 ; matric. at Oxford (Ch. Ch.), 4 Feb. 1736/7, aged 18 ; B.A., 1741. He *d.* unm. 24 March 1742/3.

VI. 1743. SIR PETER RIVERS, *afterwards* (about 1760) RIVERS-GAY, Bart. [1621], br. and h., *b.* about 1721 ; matric. at Oxford (Ch. Ch.), 15 Oct. 1737, aged 18 ; B.A. (Mag. Coll.), 1741 ; M.A., 1744, having *suc. to the Baronetcy*, 24 March 1742/3 ; was in Holy Orders ; Rector of Buttermere, Wilts, 1745-52; Rector of Woolwich, 1752 ; *assumed* the *additional name of Gay* about 1760; Prebendary of Hereford, 1760 ; Prebendary of Winchester, 1766 ; Rector of Chelmsford, 1774-90. He *m.*, 1768, Martha, sister of the Rev. William COXE, the historian, da. of William COXE, M.D., Physician to the Household, by Martha his wife. He *d.* 20 July 1790, aged about 69. Will pr. Dec. 1790. His widow, who was *b.* in Dover street, 9 Sep., and *bap.* 2 Oct. 1749, at St. James' Westm., *d.* about 1835. Will pr. March, 1835.

VII. 1790. SIR THOMAS RIVERS-GAY, Bart., [1621], s. and h., *b.* about 1770 ; *suc. to the Baronetcy*, 20 July 1790. He *d.* unm. 3 Feb. 1805, in the Close, Winchester. Will pr. 1805.

VIII. 1805. SIR James RIVERS, Bart. [1621], br. and h., *b.* at Winchester, and *bap.* there 11 June, 1772 ; scholar of Winchester College, 1783 ; matric. at Oxford (St. Mary Hall), 16 Nov. 1790, aged 18 ; B.A., 1794; Captain 3d Dragoon Guards ; *suc. to the Baronetcy*, 3 Feb. 1805, and, *d.* unm., seven months later, 27 Sep. 1805, being accidentally shot.

IX. 1805. SIR HENRY RIVERS, Bart. [1621], br. and h., *b.* about 1779 ; ed. at St. John's Coll., Camb. ; B.A., 1801; M.A., 1805 ; *suc. to the Baronetcy*, 27 Sep. 1805 ; was in Holy Orders; Rector of Martyr Worthy,

(a) The name of his father is wrongly given therein as "George."

(b) The estates passed to his numerous daughters and coheirs.

Hants, 1817. He *m.*, 2 May 1812, at St. Geo. Han. sq., Charlotte, da. of Samuel EALES, of Cranbury Hants. He *d.* 7 July 1851, aged 72. Will pr. July 1851. His widow *m.* Henry William COBB, of Salisbury, where she *d.* 28 March 1870.

X. 1851. SIR JAMES FRANCIS RIVERS, Bart. [1621], 2d but 1st surv. s. and h., *b.* 30 Dec. 1822, at Winchester ; ed. at Winchester School, 1834-36 ; sometime an officer in the army ; *suc. to the Baronetcy*, 7 July 1851. He *m.*, 12 Jan. 1859, Sarah Elizabeth, 1st da. of George GAMBIER, of Orange street, Canterbury. She *d.* 1865. He *m.* secondly, 1 Oct. 1867, at Exeter Cathedral, Catherine, widow of R. D. EASTCOTT, of Camden square, Midx. He *d.* s.p., 5 Nov. 1869, at Salisbury, aged 47. His widow *d.* apparently in 1871.(a)

XI. 1869, to 1870. SIR HENRY CHANDOS RIVERS, Bart. [1621], of Beaconhill, Bath, br. and h., being 5th of the six sons of the 9th Bart. ; *b.* 1834, at Winchester ; *suc. to the Baronetcy*, 5 Nov. 1869, and *d.* unm., 31 Oct. 1870, aged 36, when the *Baronetcy* became *extinct.*

JERNINGHAM, *or* JERNEGAN :

cr. 16 Aug. 1621 ;

afterwards, since 1825, BARONS STAFFORD.

I. 1621. "HENRY JERNEGAN, of Cossey, *alias* Cossese, co. Norfolk, Esq.," s. and h. of Henry JERNEGAN, *or* JERNINGHAM, of the same, by his 1st wife Eleanor, da. of William (DACRE), LORD DACRE OF GILLESLAND, and grandson of Sir Henry JERNEGAN, *or* JERNINGHAM,(b) of Cossey aforesaid, and Huntingfield, co. Norfolk, Vice-Chamberlain to Queen Mary ; suc. his father, 15 June 1619, and was *cr. a Bart.*, as above, 16 Aug. 1621. He suffered severely during the Civil Wars, his park and mansion being let to farm and suffered to fall to decay. He *m.* (settlement 31 Jan. 1591/2) Eleanor, da. of Thomas THROCKMORTON, of Coughton, co. Warwick, by Margaret, da. and coheir of William Whorwood, Attorney-General to Henry VIII. He *d.* 1 Sep. 1646, and was *bur.* at Cossey. His admon. 9 Feb. 1647/8 to a creditor. The admon. of his widow dat. 2 Dec. 1648.

II. 1646. SIR HENRY JERNEGAN, *or* JERNINGHAM, Bart. [1621], of Cossey aforesaid, grandson and h., being s. and h. of John JERNEGAN, *or* JERNINGHAM, by Anne, da. of Sir Francis MOORE, of Fawley, Berks, which John was s. and h. ap. of the 1st Bart., but *d.* v.p. 1636, aged 38. He was *b.* in or soon after, 1620, and *suc. to the Baronetcy*, 1 Sep. 1646. He *m.* Mary, da. of Benedict HALL, of High Meadow, co. Gloucester. She *d.* 30 April 1653, and was *bur.* at Bookham, Surrey. M.I. He *d.* 6 Oct. 1680.

III. 1680. SIR FRANCIS JERNEGAN, *or* JERNINGHAM, Bart. [1621], of Cossey aforesaid, 2d but 1st surv. s. and h., *b.* about 1650 ; *suc. to the Baronetcy*, 6 Oct. 1680. He *m.* (Lic. Vic. Gen., 29 June 1675, he 25 and she 20) Anne, da. of Sir George BLOUNT, 2d Bart. [1642], of Sodington, by Mary, da. of Richard KIRKHAM. He *d.* 26 Aug. 1730, aged 80; and was *bur.* at Cossey. Will pr. 1730. His widow *d.* 13 and was *bur.* there 17 Feb. 1735.

(a) She is included in Dod's *Baronetage* of that year, but is omitted in the next.

(b) "It seems as if Sir Henry varied the spelling of the name that his family might be distinguished from the Somerly Jernegans" [Blomefield's *Norfolk*]. The matter of this change is treated of by "A. Jessop, D.D.," and as also by "Hermentrude," in *N. and Q.* (7th S., vii, 89), who considers that "Jerningham was always the correct spelling, and Jernegan a colloquialism."

IV. 1730. SIR JOHN JERNEGAN, *or* JERNINGHAM, Bart. [1621], of Cossey aforesaid, s. and h., *bap.* 6 Sep. 1678, at Cossey ; *suc. to the Baronetcy,* 26 Aug. 1730. He *m.* 1704, Margaret, da. of Sir Henry BEDINGFELD, 2d Bart. [1661], by his 2d wife, Elizabeth, da. of Sir John ARUNDELL. He *d.* s.p., 14 and was *bur.* 17 June 1737, at Bath Abbey, in his 55th year. M.I. Will dat. 12 Sep. 1732, pr. 1737. His widow *d.* at Winchester, and was *bur.* with her husband, 23 Dec. 1756. Will dat. 22 Nov. 1756, pr. 22 Jan. 1757.

V. 1737. SIR GEORGE JERNEGAN, *or* JERNINGHAM, Bart. [1621], of Cossey aforesaid, br. and h., *bap.* 2 June 1680, at Cossey ; *suc. to the Baronetcy,* 14 June 1737. He *m.*, in 1733 (being then aged 53), Mary, da., and eventually sole h., of Francis PLOWDEN, of Plowden, co. Worcester, by Mary, sister of John Paul, 4th and last EARL OF STAFFORD, da. of the Hon. John STAFFORD-HOWARD.(a) He *d.* 21 Jan. 1774, at Cossey Hall, in his 94th year, and was *bur.* at Cossey. His widow *d.* in London, 1785. Will pr. Oct. 1785.

VI. 1774. SIR WILLIAM JERNINGHAM, Bart. [1621], of Cossey aforesaid, s. and h., was *b.* 7 March 1736 ; *suc. to the Baronetcy,* 21 Jan. 1774. He *m.*, 16 June 1767, Frances, 1st da. of Henry (DILLON), 11th VISCOUNT DILLON OF COSTELLO GALLEN [I.], by Charlotte, da. of George Henry (LEE), 2d EARL OF LICHFIELD. He *d.* 14 Aug. 1809, aged 73. Admon. March 1813. His widow, who was *b.* 17 Oct. 1747, *d.* 2 March 1825.

VII. 1809. SIR GEORGE WILLIAM JERNINGHAM, Bart. [1621], of Cossey aforesaid, s. and h. He was *b.* 27 April 1771 ; *suc. to the Baronetcy,* 14 Aug. 1809. In right of his grandmother, the said Mary PLOWDEN, he claimed the BARONY OF STAFFORD (*cr.* 1640(b)), which claim (after the reversal, 17 June 1824, of the attainder of his ancestor, William, VISCOUNT AND BARON STAFFORD) was allowed by the House of Lords, 6 July 1825, and he consequently became BARON STAFFORD. By royal lic., 5 Oct. 1826, he took the name of *Stafford* before that of *Jerningham.* He *m.* firstly, 24 Dec. 1799, Frances Henrietta, yst. da. and coheir of Edward SULYARDE, of Haughley Park, Suffolk, by Susanna, 1st da. and coheir of George RAVENSCROFT, of Wickham, co. Lincoln. She was living when he inherited the peerage as above, 6 July 1825.(c) He *d.* 4 Oct. 1851, aged 80. For fuller particulars see *Peerage.*

VIII. 1851. HENRY VALENTINE (STAFFORD-JERNINGHAM), 3d BARON STAFFORD [1640] and 8th Bart. [1621], s. and h., by 1st wife, was *b.* 3 Jan. 1802; *suc. to the titles,* 4 Oct. 1851; *d.* s.p. 30 Nov. 1884.

IX. 1884. AUGUSTUS FREDERICK FITZHERBERT (STAFFORD-JERNINGHAM), 4th BARON STAFFORD [1640] and 9th Bart. [1621], nephew and h., was *b.* 28 June 1830 ; *suc. to the titles,* 30 Nov. 1884 ; *d.* unm. 16 April 1892.

X. 1892. FITZHERBERT (STAFFORD-JERNINGHAM), 5th BARON STAFFORD [1640] and 10th Bart. [1621], only br. and h., was *b.* 17 July 1833 ; *suc. to the titles,* 15 April 1892.

[For fuller particulars see *Peerage.*]

(a) He was yr. s. (his issue becoming sole heir) of the unfortunate William (HOWARD), VISCOUNT STAFFORD, who, together with his wife, Mary, sister and h. of Henry (STAFFORD), LORD STAFFORD, was raised to the peerage, he being *cr.*, 12 Sep. 1640, BARON, and she BARONESS, STAFFORD, with rem. of the Barony (failing the heirs male) to the heirs *general* of their bodies. He, who was subsequently *cr.* VISCOUNT STAFFORD, was *attainted* 3 June 1678, and beheaded 29 Dec. 1680.

(b) See note "a" above.

(c) It is singular that this family held no public office between 1658 and 1830, when the s. and h. ap. of the 7th Bart. (then Lord Stafford) became M.P. for Pontefract.

DARNELL :

cr. 6 Sep. 1621 ;

ex. in or before 1639.

I. 1621, to 1638? "THOMAS DARNELL, of Healing, co. Lincoln, Esq.," s. and h. of Sir Thomas DARNELL, of the same, by Helen, da. of (—) ; suc. his father in or before Feb. 1608/9, and was *cr. a Bart.*, as above, 6 Sep. 1621. He *m.* Sarah, sister of Sir Thomas FISHER, Bart. (so *cr.* 1627), da. of Thomas FISHER. He *d.* s.p.m.,(a) about 1638, when the *Baronetcy* became *extinct.* Admon. (as of St. Mary's Savoy, Midx.) granted 1 Feb. 1638/9, to a creditor. The will of his widow, living Oct. 1638, pr. 1639.

SEDLEY, *or* SIDLEY :

cr. 24 Sep. 1621 ;

ex. between 1741 and 1771.

I. 1621. "ISAACK SIDLEY, of Great Charte, co. Kent, Knt.," s. and h. of Nicholas SIDLEY, by Jane, da. and h. of Edward IZAACKE (which Nicholas was 3d s. of William SIDLEY, of Scadbury in Southfleet, in that county, the grandfather of Sir William SIDLEY, 1st Bart. [1611], of Aylesford), was *Knighted,* at Enfield, 6 Dec. 1606, and was *cr. a Bart.*, as above, 24 Sep. 1621. Sheriff of Kent, 1625-26. He *m.*, about 1600, (—), da. and h. of (—) HOLDITCH, of Ranworth and Foulden, Norfolk. He *d.* 1627. Will pr. 1627.

II. 1627. SIR JOHN SIDLEY, *or* SEDLEY, Bart. [1621], of St. Cleres in Ightham, co. Kent, s. and h., *b.* about 1600 ; B.A. (Corpus Coll.) Oxford, 17 May 1613 ; *suc. to the Baronetcy,* 1627 ; was (at one time) Col. in the Parl. army, but is said to have been a Compounder in 1651. He sold certain estates in Norfolk and purchased that of Ightham, co. Kent, where he erected "the magnificent pile" called St. Cleres. He *m.* firstly (—). He *m.* secondly (Lic. Vic. Gen., 28 Dec. 1663, he 60, widower, she 22, parents dead), Mary, da. of (—) BRADSHAW, of Exeter. He was *bur.* at Ightham, 21 Nov. 1673. Admon. 2 Dec. 1673, in the Court of Arches, London, to Mary, the relict.

III. 1673. SIR ISAAC SEDLEY, *or* SIDLEY, Bart. [1621], of St. Clere's aforesaid, s. and h., by 1st wife ; was *Knighted* v.p., 9 Aug. 1641, at Whitehall, and was a Royalist ; *suc. to the Baronetcy* in Nov. 1673. He *m.* firstly, (—). She *d.* s.p.m. He *m.* secondly (Lic. Fac., 3 June 1663, he 40, widower, she 18, spinster) Cecily, da. of John MARSH, of Lincoln's Inn. He *d.* before 1695. His widow *m.* Reginald PECK, of Yalding, Kent.

IV. 1690? SIR CHARLES SEDLEY, *or* SIDLEY, Bart. [1621], of St. Clere's aforesaid, only s. and h. by 2d wife ; *suc. to the Baronetcy* before 1695. He *d.* unm. and was *bur.* Oct. 1702, at Ightham.

V. 1702. SIR JOHN SEDLEY, *or* SIDLEY, Bart. [1621], uncle and h. male ; *suc. to the Baronetcy,* Oct. 1702. He *m.*, in or before 1664, Mary, da. of (—) NICHOLS, of Kemsing, Kent. She *d.* 1701.

VI. 1710? SIR GEORGE SEDLEY, *or* SIDLEY, Bart. [1621], of (—), near Lewes, Sussex, s. and h. ; *bap.* 27 Feb. 1665, at Kemsing ; *suc. to the Baronetcy* on the death of his father. He *d.* before 12 Oct. 1722.(b)

(a) A da. named Susan was living 1638. See will of her grandmother, Dame Helen Darnell, of Stickford, co. Lincoln, widow, dat. 8 Oct. and pr. 6 Dec. 1638.

(b) At that date a M.I. in Kemsing church records the death of Mary Hopkins, aged 29, *sister* to Sir George Sedley, Bart.

VII. 1720? SIR GEORGE SEDLEY, *or* SIDLEY, Bart. [1621], s. and h., *suc. to the Baronetcy* before 12 Oct. 1722.(a) He *d.* unm., and was *bur.* 5 Aug. 1737, at Kemsing, Kent.

VIII. 1737, to 1760? SIR CHARLES SEDLEY, *or* SIDLEY, Bart. [1621], br. and h., *suc. to the Baronetcy,* 5 Aug. 1737 ; was living 1741 [Wotton's *Baronetage* of that date], but *d.* s.p. *ante* 1771 [Kimber's *Baronetage* of that date], when the *Baronetcy* became *extinct.*(b)

BROWNE :

cr. 21 Sep. 1621 ;

ex. about 1662.

I. 1621. "ROBERT BROWNE, of Walcott, co. Northampton, Esq.," 2d s. of Robert BROWNE,(c) of the same, by Margaret, relict of Sir Bernard WHETSTONE, da. of Philip BARNARD, of Akenham, suc. to the family estate in 1603, on the death of his elder br., Sir William BROWNE, **K.B.**, and was *cr. a Bart.*, as above, 21 Sep. 1621. He *m.* firstly, Anne, da. of Roger CAPSTOCK. She *d.* s.p. He *m.* secondly, Elizabeth, widow of Francis HARBY (who *d.* 1607), sister of Sir Anthony COPE, 1st Bart. [1611], da. of Edward COPE, of Hanwell, Oxon, by Elizabeth, da. of Walter MOHUN. He *d.* about 1624. Will pr. 1624. His widow *m.* (as his 2d wife) Sir Guy PALMES, of Ashwell, co. Rutland, and was living 1633 (as was her husband) but dead before 14 June 1658.

II. 1624. SIR THOMAS BROWNE, Bart. [1621], of Walcot aforesaid, s. and h., by 2d wife ; *suc. to the Baronetcy* in 1624. He *m.* Annie, da. of Sir Guy PALMES above mentioned, by his 1st wife, Anne, da. of Sir Edward STAFFORD. He *d.* s.p.m.(d) 16 April 1635. Admon. 11 May 1635. Inq. p.m., 6 June 1635. His widow *m.* (as the second of his three wives) Robert (SUTTON), 1st BARON LEXINGTON OF ARAM, who *d.* 13 Oct. 1668. She *d.* before 1661, and was *bur.* at Aram, Notts.

III. 1635, to 1662? SIR ROBERT BROWNE, Bart. [1621], br. and h. male ; *suc. to the Baronetcy,* 16 April 1635. He was living 1647, but *d.* unm. about 1662, when the *Baronetcy* became *extinct.*

(a) See p. 173, note "b." "Robert, son of Susan Muckwine and Sir George Sidley, Bart.," was *bap.* 2 Dec. 1723, at Kemsing.

(b) In the *Gent. Mag.* is this notice ; 1737 April 24, "died at his lodgings in Tottenham Court Road, Sir John Sidley, Bart., Major of the Red Regiment of the city trained bands. At his death the Baronetcy became extinct, and the estate fell to a niece." This John was, presumably, next brother to (being a year younger than) the 6th Bart., whose issue, probably, he (rightly or wrongly) considered illegitimate, and consequently himself assumed the Baronetcy.

(c) This Robert was great grandson of Robert Browne, who *d.* 1506-07, possessed of the manor of Walcot in the parish of Barnack, co. Northampton. That Robert was s. of Sir John Browne, Lord Mayor of London, 1480, and br. of Sir William Browne, Lord Mayor, 1507.

(d) Anne, his 2d da. and coheir, *b.* posthumously 10 July 1635, *m.* about 1660 (as his 2d wife), John (Poulett), 2d Baron Poulett of Hinton, who *d.* 15 Sep. 1665, aged 49. See Bridges' *Northamptonshire,* vol. ii, p. 498. The estate of Walcot Hall, over 1,200 acres has recently (Feb. 1891) been sold for £45,000.

HEWET, *or* HEWETT :

cr. 11 Oct. 1621 ;

ex. 7 June 1822.

I. 1621. "JOHN HEWETT, of Headly Hall, co. York, Esq." and, afterwards, of Waresley, co. Huntingdon, s. and h. of John HEWITT, of Headly aforesaid, by Elizabeth, da. of Sir Robert HAMPSON, Alderman of London ; was *b.* about 1598 ; suc. his father in 1602, and was *cr. a Bart.*, as above, 11 Oct. 1621 ; Sheriff of Northants, 1631-32 ; of Hunts, 1637-38. He was a great sufferer for his loyalty to his King during the Civil Wars, being fined £2,158. He *m.* Katharine, sister and heir of Sir Robert BEVILE, **K.B.**, da. of another Sir Robert BEVILE, also **K.B.**, of Chesterton, co. Huntingdon, by Mary, da. of (—) COLES, of Preston, co. Northampton. She *d.* 12 Feb. 1638. He *d.* 14 Nov. 1657, aged 59. Both *bur.* at Waresley. M.I. His will pr. 1658.

II. 1657. SIR JOHN HEWET, Bart. [1621], of Waresley aforesaid, s. and h., *suc. to the Baronetcy,* 14 Oct. 1657 ; Sheriff of Cambs and Hunts, 1661-62. He *m.* Frances, da. of Sir Toby TYRELL, 3d Bart. [1627], of Thornton, by his 1st wife, Edith, da. of Sir Francis WINDEBANK. He *d.* 30 Sep. 1684. Will pr. 1684. His widow *m.* Philip COTTON, of Connington, co. Cambridge.

III. 1684. SIR JOHN HEWET, Bart. [1621], of Waresley aforesaid, s. and h. ; *suc. to the Baronetcy,* 30 Sep. 1684 ; Sheriff of Cambridgeshire and Huntingdonshire, 1684-85. He *m.* firstly, Anne, da. of Francis STOKES, of Tiderton, Wilts. He *m.* secondly, Eleanor, 1st da. of Sir John OSBORN, 2d Bart. [1662], of Chicksands, by his 2d wife, Martha, da. of Sir John KELYNGE. She *d.* s.p. 1728. Will pr. 1728. He *d.* s.p.m.s. 3 Feb. 1737. Will pr. 1740.

IV. 1737. SIR WILLIAM HEWET, Bart. [1621], of Potton, Beds, nephew and h., being s. and h. of William HEWET, of St. Neots, who was 7th s. of the 2d Bart. He was Captain of the "Colchester," man of war. He *suc. to the Baronetcy,* but not to the family estates, 3 Feb. 1737. He *m.* Elizabeth, da. of (—) LEVEMORE, of Gosport, Hants. He *d.* 1749. Will pr. 1749. The admon. of his widow, as "of Potton, Beds," 10 April 1778.

V. 1749. SIR WILLIAM HEWET, Bart. [1621], of Potton aforesaid, s. and h. ; *suc. to the Baronetcy* in 1749, and was (like his father) a Captain, R.N. He *d.* unm., being lost (together with his br., Levemore HEWET, Lieut. R.N.) before Pondicherry, 1 Jan. 1761, in the "Duc d' Aquitaine," of which ship he was in command. Will pr. 1762.

VI. 1761. SIR TYRRELL HEWET, Bart. [1621], of Potton, aforesaid, uncle and h. male ; *suc. to the Baronetcy,* 1 Jan. 1761. He *m.* (—), da. of Roberts GEDDING, of the Post Office. He *d.* 17 Feb. 1770.

VII. 1770. SIR BYNG HEWET, Bart. [1621], s. and h., *b.* about 1752 ; *suc. to the Baronetcy,* 17 Feb. 1770, having previously gone to India in the East India Company's Service, 1768, where he *d.* unm., being killed about 1770.

VIII. 1770? to 1822. SIR THOMAS HEWET, Bart. [1621], br. and h., *b.* about 1756, at Potton, ; matric. at Oxford (Merton Coll.), 30 March 1773, aged 18 ; B.A., 1778 ; took Holy Orders ; was Rector of Sudborough, Northamptonshire ; *suc. to the Baronetcy* about 1770. He *m.* Mary, da. of (—) TEBBUTT, of Sudborough aforesaid. He *d.* s.p., at Sudborough, 7 June 1822, in his 66th year, when the *Baronetcy* became *extinct.* The will of his widow pr. Dec. 1826.

HYDE:

cr. 8 Nov. 1621;

ex. 18 May 1665.

I. 1621. "NICHOLAS HYDE, of Albury, co. Herts, Knt.," s. and h. of Robert HYDE, of the same, was probably the "Nicholas Hyde, fil. Gen., London," who matric. at Oxford (Queen's Coll.), 3 Aug. 1578, aged 17; was Sheriff of Herts, 1619-20, and, having been *Knighted* before 1619, was *cr. a Bart.*, as above, 8 Nov. 1621. He *m.* Bridget, da. of Miles SANDYS, of Latimers, Bucks. He *d.* about 1625. Admon. 4 April 1625. The admon. of his widow 29 March 1654.

I. 1625? to 1665. SIR THOMAS HYDE, Bart. [1621], of Albury aforesaid, s. and h.; *suc. to the Baronetcy* about 1625; Sheriff of Herts, 1627-28. He *m.*, 11 June 1660, at North Mimms, Mary, da. of John WHITCHURCH, of Walton, near Aylesbury, Bucks. He *d.* s.p.m.(a) 18 May 1665, aged 71, when the *Baronetcy* became *extinct*. Will pr. 1665. His widow *m.*, as his 2d wife, Sir Robert VYNER, Bart. [so *cr.* 1666], who survived her. Her admon. 12 Jan. 1674/5, and 31 July 1689.

PHILIPPS, *or* PHILLIPPS:

cr. 9 Nov. 1621,

sometime, 1776-83, BARON MILFORD [I.],

and *subsequently*, from 1823 to 1857, PHILIPPS-LAUGHARNE-PHILIPPS.

I. 1621. "JOHN PHILLIPPS, of Pickton [*i.e.*, Picton], co. Pembroke, Esq.," s. and h. of Morgan PHILIPPS, of Picton aforesaid, by Elizabeth, da. of Richard FLETCHER, of Bangor, was Sheriff of co. Pembroke, 1594-95 and 1610-11; of co. Cardigan, 1622-23; was M.P. for co. Pembroke, 1597-98 and 1601, and was *cr. a Bart.*, as above, 9 Nov. 1621. He *m.* firstly, Anne, da. of Sir John PERROT, of Haroldstone, co. Pembroke, Lord-Deputy of Ireland, by his 2d wife, Jane, da. of Sir Lewis POLLARD. He *m.* secondly, Margaret, da. of Sir Thomas DENNIS, of Bicton, Devon. He *d.* 27 March 1629. Will pr. 1629.

II. 1639. SIR RICHARD PHILIPPS, Bart. [1621], of Picton, aforesaid, s. and h., by 1st wife; was Sheriff of co. Pembroke, 1632-33, and of co. Carmarthen, 1640-41; *suc. to the Baronetcy*, 27 March 1629; garrisoned Picton Castle, on behalf of Charles I. He *m.* Elizabeth, da. of Sir Erasmus DRYDEN, 1st Bart. [1619], by Frances, da. and coheir of William WILKES, of Hodnell, co. Warwick. He *d.* about 1648. Admon. 7 Aug. 1648. Will pr. 1649.

III. 1648. SIR ERASMUS PHILLIPS, Bart. [1621], of Picton aforesaid, s. and h., *b.* about 1623; *suc. to the Baronetcy* about 1648; Sheriff of co. Carmarthen, 1649-50; of co. Pembroke, 1655-56; M.P. thereof, 1654-55 and 1659; Custos Rotulorum for co. Pembroke. He *m.* firstly, Cecily, da. of Thomas (FINCH), EARL OF WINCHILSEA, by Cicely, da. of John WENTWORTH. She *d.* s.p.m.s. He *m.* secondly (Lic. Fac., 1 Sep. 1660, he 37, she 19), Catharine, da. and coheir of the Hon. Edward DARCY, by Elizabeth, da. of Philip (STANHOPE), 1st EARL OF CHESTERFIELD. He *d.* 18 Jan. 1696/7. Will pr. 1697. The will of his widow pr. 1713.

IV. 1697. SIR JOHN PHILIPPS, Bart. [1621], of Picton aforesaid, s. and h. by 2d wife; *suc. to the Baronetcy*, 18 Jan. 1696/7; M.P. in four Parls. for Pembroke, 1695-1702, and for Haverfordwest, 1718-22; Custos

(a) Bridget, his only da. and h., *m.* 25 April 1682, Peregrine (OSBORNE), 2d DUKE OF LEEDS, and is ancestress of the succeeding Dukes.

Rotulorum for Pembrokeshire; one of the Commissioners for building fifty new churches near London. He *m.*, 12 Dec. 1697, Mary, da. and h. of Anthony SMITH, East India merchant. She, who was *b.* at Surat, in India, *d.* 18 Nov. 1722, at Bath, in her 47th year. M.I. at Prendergast. He *d.* in London, 5 and was *bur.* 28 Jan. 1736/7, at St. Mary's, Haverfordwest, in his 77th year. M.I. Will pr. 7 Feb. 1736/7.

V. 1737. SIR ERASMUS PHILIPPS, Bart. [1621], of Picton aforesaid, s. and h., *b.* about 1700; matric. at Oxford (Pemb. Coll.), 4 Aug. 1720, aged 20; M.P. for Haverfordwest in four Parls., 1726-43; *suc. to the Baronetcy*, 5 Jan. 1736/7. Sheriff of Carmarthen town, 1726-27. He *d.* unm., 15 Oct. 1743, being drowned in the Avon, near Bath, and *bur.* in Bath Abbey. Admon. 29 Feb. 1743/4.

VI. 1743. SIR JOHN PHILIPPS, Bart. [1621], of Picton aforesaid, formerly of Kilgetty, in the parish of St. Issells, co. Pembroke, br. and h., *b.* about 1701; matric. at Oxford (Pemb. Coll.), 4 Aug. 1720, aged 19; *cr.* D.C.L., 12 April 1749; Barrister at law; *suc. to the Baronetcy*, 15 Oct. 1743; M.P. for Carmarthen, 1741-47; for Petersfield, 1754-61; and for Pembrokeshire, 1761-64; Commissioner of Board of Trade, 1744-46; Privy Councillor, 1763. He *m.*, at Whitehall chapel, 22 Sep. 1725, Elizabeth, da. of Henry SHEPHERD, of London, by Mary, da. of Thomas ALLESTRE, of Alvaston, co. Derby. He *d.* 23 June 1764, aged 63, and was *bur.* at Haverfordwest. Will pr. 1764. His widow *d.* 28 Sep. and was *bur.* 4 Oct. 1788, at Kingston on Thames, aged 88. Will pr. 1789.

VII. 1764. SIR RICHARD PHILIPPS, Bart. [1621], of Picton aforesaid, only s. and h., *b.* at Kilgetty aforesaid; matric. at Oxford (Pemb. Coll.), 3 Feb. 1761, aged 18; *suc. to the Baronetcy*, 23 June 1764; was M.P. for Pembrokeshire, 1765-70; for Haverfordwest, 1784-86, and for Pembrokeshire (again), 1786-1812; Custos Rotulorum of Haverfordwest, 1764-70; L. Lieut. thereof 1770-1823; was *cr.*, 29 June 1776, BARON MILFORD in Ireland [I.]; L. Lieut. of Pembrokeshire, 1780-1824. He *m.* 2 June 1764, Mary, da. of James PHILIPPS, of Pontypark, co. Pembroke. She *d.* at Picton Castle, 26 Aug. 1815. Admon. April 1817. He *d.* s.p., at Picton Castle, 28 Nov. and was *bur.* 8 Dec. 1823, at St. Mary's, Haverfordwest, when his *Peerage* became *extinct*, but the *Baronetcy* (though not the Picton estates)(a) devolved on his distant cousin and h. male, as under. Will dat. 21 Jan. 1820, pr. 3 Feb. 1824.

VIII. 1823. SIR ROWLAND HENRY PHILIPPS-LAUGHARNE-PHILIPPS, Bart. [1621], *formerly* Rowland Henry PHILIPPS-LAUGHARNE, of Orlandon, co. Pembroke, cousin and h. male, being s. and h. of John PHILIPPS-LAUGHARNE, of St. Brides, Pembroke, by Elizabeth, da. of Joseph ALLEN, which John was s. and h. of Rowland PHILIPPS-LAUGHARNE (who assumed the additional name of *Laugharne* on his marriage, in 1750, with Annie, da. of Rev. James LAUGHARNE), the said Rowland being s. and h. of Rowland PHILIPPS (*d.* 1768), s. of Charles PHILIPPS, s. and h. of Richard PHILIPPS, s. and h. of Hugh PHILIPPS, of Martletwyo and Sandyhaven, co. Pembroke (*d.* 1651/2), who was 2d s. of the 1st Bart. He was *b.* Jan. 1788, at Neeslin, in the parish of Harbrandston, co. Pembroke; *suc. to the Baronetcy*, 28 Nov. 1823, when he appears to have re-assumed his patronymic of *Philipps* as the final surname. He *m.*, 21 Jan. 1812, at Marston Bigott, co. Somerset, Elizabeth, da. of James FRAMPTON, of Frome, Somerset. He *d.* s.p. 23 April and was *bur.* 1 May 1832, at St. John's, Horsley Down, co. Surrey. His widow *d.* 26 Aug. and was *bur.* 3 Sep. 1834, at Frome aforesaid.

IX. 1832. SIR WILLIAM PHILIPPS-LAUGHARNE-PHILIPPS, Bart. [1621], of Orlandon aforesaid, *formerly* William PHILIPPS-LAUGHARNE, br. and h., was *b.* 2 Oct. 1794, at Orlandon aforesaid; matric. at Oxford (Jesus Coll.), 14 Dec. 1813, aged 19; *suc. to the Baronetcy*, 23 April 1832, when he assumed the final name of *Philipps*. He *m.*, at Usk, co. Monmouth, 13 Oct. 1829, Elizabeth, da. of George WHITE. He *d.* 17 Feb. 1850, at Haverfordwest. Will pr. Sep. 1857. His widow, who was *b.* 1 Nov. 1808, *d.* 1865.

(a) See notice of "*Family Estates*" on p. 178, at the end of this article.

Z

X. 1850. SIR GODWIN PHILIPPS-LAUGHARNE-PHILIPPS, of Orlandon aforesaid, only s. and h., was *b.* 10 Jan. 1840; *suc. to the Baronetcy*, 17 Feb. 1850. He *d.* unm. 12 Feb. 1857, at Valley St. David's, aged 17.

XI. 1857. SIR JAMES EVANS PHILIPPS, Bart. [1621], cousin and h. male, being s. of William Hollingworth PHILIPPS, Captain in the Notts Militia, by Harriett, 1st da. of Anthony FONBLANQUE, of London, merchant, which William (*d.* 9 May 1839, aged 81) was s. and h. of William PHILIPPS, Captain, R.N., s. and h. of Cosby PHILIPPS, Captain in the Army, s. and h. of Lieut. Gen. Richard PHILIPPS, Governor of Nova Scotia (*d.* 14 Oct. 1750, aged 90), 2d s. of Richard PHILIPPS abovenamed, who was s. and h. of Hugh PHILIPPS, also abovenamed, the 2d s. of the 1st Bart. He was *bap.* 16 Nov. 1793, at Lynn, Norfolk; matric. at Oxford (Queen's Coll.), 8 July 1813, aged 19; B.A., 1817; M.A., 1820; in Holy Orders; Vicar of Osmington, Dorset, 1832-73; *suc. to the Baronetcy*, 17 Feb. 1850. He *m.*, 4 July 1822, Mary Anne, da. of Benjamin BICKLEY, of Bristol, merchant. She *d.* 20 March 1833. He *d.* 14 Feb. 1873, at Osmington Vicarage, in his 80th year.

XII. 1873. SIR JAMES ERASMUS PHILIPPS, Bart. [1621], only s. and h., *b.* 23 Oct. 1824, at Boyton, Wilts; matric. at Oxford (Ch. Ch.), 19 Oct. 1842; B.A., 1847; M.A., 1853; in Holy Orders; Vicar of Warminster, Wilts, and Warden of St. Boniface's Missionary College there, 1859-97; Prebendary of Salisbury, 1870; *suc. to the Baronetcy*, 14 Feb. 1873. He *m.* 5 May 1859, at Abbot's Anne, Hants, Mary Margaret, 1st da. of Rev. the Hon. Samuel BEST, Rector of Abbot's Anne (yr. sister of the 1st BARON WYNFORD), by his 2d wife Emma, da. of Lieut. Col. Charles DUKE. She was *b.* 10 May 1836.

Family Estates.—The Picton estate (consisting, in 1883, of 23,084 acres in the counties of Pembroke and Carmarthen, worth £23,815 a year), which belonged to the earlier Baronets, passed, on the death of Lord Milford [I.], the 7th Bart., to R. B. P. Grant, whose mother was da. of James Child by the da. and heir of Bulkeley Philipps, s. of the 4th Bart. He took the name of Philipps, was *cr. a Bart.* in 1828, and was subsequently *cr.* in 1847, Baron Milford of Picton Castle [U.K.]. He, however, *d.* s.p., 3 Jan. 1857, when all his honours became *extinct*, and the estates devolved on his half brother (the son of his mother by a second marriage), the Rev. J. H. A. Gwyther, who also took the name of Philipps. He *d.* s.p.m., 3 Dec. 1875, when they devolved on his eldest da., wife of C. E. G. Fisher, who, having taken the name of Philipps, and, being in possession of the Picton estates, was *cr. a Bart.*, 23 July 1887, as "of Picton Castle, co. Pembroke."

STEPNEY:

cr. 24 Nov. 1621;

ex. 12 Sep. 1825.

I. 1621. "JOHN STEPNEY, of Prendergast, co. Pembroke, Knt.," s. and h. of Alban STEPNEY,(a) of the same, Registrar of the diocese of St. Davids, by his 2d wife, Mary, da. and coheir of William PHILIPPS, of Picton Castle, co. Pembroke, was *b.* about 1581; matric. at Oxford (St. John's Coll.), 24 Nov. 1598, aged 17; admitted to Lincoln's Inn, 1599; Sheriff of Pembrokeshire, 1613-14; *Knighted*, 30 June 1618, and was *cr. a Bart.*, as above, 24 Nov. 1621. He *m.* Jane, da. of Sir Francis MANSEL, 1st Bart. [1622] of Muddlescombe, by his 2d wife, Dorothy, da. of Alban STEPNEY, abovenamed. He *d.* Aug. 1624.(b) Will pr. 1626. His widow living Jan. 1628/9.

(a) He had acquired the estate of Prendergast with his *first* wife, Margaret, da. and coheir of Thomas CATHARN. She, however, *d.* s.p., and it was inherited by her husband and subsequently by his children.

(b) In Betham's *Baronetage* the date is given as "Aug. 1634," reference being made to "*Goff's Notes*, 146." His will and the admon. of his son shew this date to be an error.

II. 1624. SIR ALBAN STEPNEY, Bart. [1621], of Prendergast aforesaid, s. and h.; *suc. to the Baronetcy* in 1624. He *d.* unm. Admon. 5 Jan 1628/9, to his mother.

III. 1628? SIR JOHN STEPNEY, Bart. [1621], of Prendergast aforesaid, br. and h.; *suc. to the Baronetcy* in or before Jan. 1628/9; was Sheriff of Pembrokeshire, 1636-37; M.P. for Pembroke, April to May 1640; and for Haverfordwest, Nov. 1640, till disabled in April 1643; was Governor thereof for the King when taken prisoner at Hereford, Dec. 1648; was a compounder and fined in Dec. 1646 £1,250, which was reduced in 1649, he being discharged 3 May 1650. He *m.* Magdalen, da. and coheir of Sir Henry JONES, Bart. (so *cr.* 1643), of Albemarlis, co. Carmarthen, by Elizabeth, da. of Sir John SALUSBURY. He was living May 1650, but *d.* s.p.m.(a) The will of his widow pr. Aug. 1689.

IV. 1650? SIR JOHN STEPNEY, Bart. [1621], of Prendergast aforesaid, nephew and h. male, being s. and h. of Thomas STEPNEY, by Price, the other da. and coheir of Sir Henry JONES, Bart, and Elizabeth his wife, abovenamed, which Thomas (*b.* about 1610), was 3d s. of the 1st Bart., but *d.* v.p. before 1634. He was *b.* about 1632; *suc. to the Baronetcy* in or soon after 1650. He *m.* in 1653 (at her age of 12), Justina Maria Anna, da. and h. of Sir Anthony VANDYKE (the celebrated painter), by Mary Catharine, da. of the Hon. Patrick RUTHVEN, yr. s. of William, 1st EARL OF GOWRIE [S.]. He *d.* at St. Martin's in the Fields, in or before 1681. Admon. 12 Sep. 1681. His widow, who was *b.* 4 and *bap.* 9 Dec. 1641 (the day of her father's death), at St. Anne's, Blackfriars, *m.* Martin DE CARBONEL, who survived her. Her admon. 26 Nov. 1688 and 1 Oct. 1703.

V. 1681? SIR THOMAS STEPNEY, Bart. [1621], of Prendergast aforesaid, only s. and h. *b.* about 1668; *suc. to the Baronetcy* about 1681; Sheriff of Pembrokeshire, 1696-97; M.P. for Carmarthenshire, 1717-22. He *m.* (settlement 1691) Margaret, sister and coheir of Walter VAUGHAN, of Llanelly, co. Carmarthen. She *d.* 1 Nov. 1733, aged 73. M.I. He was *bur.* at Llanelly 19 Jan. 1744/5, aged 76. M.I.

VI. 1745. SIR JOHN STEPNEY, Bart. [1621], of Prendergast and Llanelly aforesaid, s. and h., *bap.* 1692/3 at Llanelly; matric. at Oxford (Jesus Coll.), 27 June 1711, aged 17; *suc. to the Baronetcy* 24 Feb. 1744/5. He *m.* Eleanor, da. and h. of John LLOYD, of Buckleithwen, co. Carmarthen. She *d.* 3 Jan. 1733, aged 32. M.I. He was *bur.* 14 March 1747/8, at Llanelly, aged 56. M.I.

VII. 1748. SIR THOMAS STEPNEY, Bart. [1621], of Prendergast and Llanelly aforesaid, s. and h., *b.* 12 and *bap.* 24 Oct. 1729, at Llanelly; *suc. to the Baronetcy* in 1748. He *m.* Elizabeth, da. and h. of Thomas LLOYD, of Dan-yr-alt, in Llangadock, by Elizabeth, da. of John VAUGHAN, of Court Derlyss, both in co. Carmarthen. He *d.* 7 Oct. 1772. Admon. Aug. 1801. His widow *d.* June 1795, and was *bur.* at Bath. Will pr. July 1795.

VIII. 1772. SIR JOHN STEPNEY, Bart. [1621], of Prendergast and Llanelly aforesaid, only s. and h., *b.* 19 Sep. and *bap.* 6 Oct. 1743, at Llanelly; *suc. to the Baronetcy*, 7 Oct. 1772; M.P. for Monmouth, 1767-88; Envoy Extraordinary to Dresden, 1775, and to Berlin, 1782. He *d.* unm., at Temeswar, in Hungary, 3 Oct. 1811. Will dat. 9 Aug. 1802 to 7 Dec. 1810, pr. 28 Jan. 1812.

IX. 1811. to 1825. SIR THOMAS STEPNEY, Bart. [1621], of Prendergast and Llanelly aforesaid, br. and h.; Groom to the Bedchamber to H.R.H., the Duke of York; *suc. to the Baronetcy* in Oct. 1811. He was *b.* 11 Feb. and *bap.* 8 March 1760, at Llanelly. He *m.* 8 June 1813, at Edinburgh, Catharine, widow of Russell MANNERS, and da. of Rev. Thomas POLLOK, D.D., Rector of Grittleton, Wilts, by Susanna, da. of Charlton PALMER, of London. He *d.* s.p.m. 12 Sep. 1825, aged 65, when the *Baronetcy* became *extinct*. Will pr. Oct. 1825, and June 1835. His widow, who was the authoress of several works of fiction, *d.* 14 April, 1845, in Henrietta street, Cavendish square.

(a) Frances, his only da. and h., *m.* Henry MANSEL, and was mother of Sir Edward Mansel, 1st Bart. [1697], of Trimsaran.

WAKE:
cr. 5 Dec. 1621,
sometime, 1748-55, WAKE-JONES.

I. 1621. "BALDWIN WAKE, of Clevedon, co. Somerset, Esq.," s. and h. of John WAKE, by Margaret, da. and h. of Robert GOODWIN, of Portbury, Somerset, was *cr. a Bart.*, as above, 5 Dec. 1621. He *m.* firstly, 11 Nov. 1600, at St. Margaret's, Westm., Abigail, da. of Sir George DIGBY, of Coleshill, co. Warwick, by Abigail, da. of Sir Arthur HEVENINGHAM, Knight Banneret. He *m.* secondly, Elizabeth. He *d.* about 1627. Admon. 11 Jan. 1627/8, as "of Piddington, co. Northampton," Elizabeth, the relict, being then living.

II. 1627 ? SIR JOHN WAKE, Bart. [1621], of Piddington aforesaid, s. and h., *suc. to the Baronetcy* about 1627. He raised a troop of horse of which he was Colonel, for the service of Charles I, and mortgaged his estates to serve the Royal cause. He *m.* firstly, Bridget, da. and coheir of Henry SANDYS, of Plumpton, co. Northampton. He *m.* secondly, Anne, da. and coheir of Gregory BROKESBY, of Fritbley, co. Leicester. She was *bur.* 17 Jan. 1641/2, at St. Mary's, Aldermanbury, London. Will pr. Jan. 1642. He *d.* about 1663. Will pr. 1663.

III. 1663 ? SIR WILLIAM WAKE, Bart. [1621], of Piddington aforesaid, s. and h, by 1st wife; *suc. to the Baronetcy* about 1663. He *m.* Diana, only da. of Sir Drue DRURY, 2d Bart. [1627], of Riddlesworth Hall, Norfolk, by Susan, da. of Isaac JONES, of London, which Susan was sister and heir of Sir Samuel JONES, of Waltham Holy Cross and Nazing, Essex, and of Courteenhall, co. Northampton. Her issue became heir, 27 April 1712, to her brother, Sir Robert DRURY, 3d Bart. [1627]. She *d.* 25 Jan. 1674, and was *bur.* at Piddington aforesaid. He *d.* Jan. 1697/8. Will pr. 1698.

IV. 1698. SIR JOHN WAKE Bart. [1621], s. and h., was *b.* 1660; matric. at Oxford (Merton Coll.), 19 July 1679, aged 17; admitted to Gray's Inn, 1679; *suc. to the Baronetcy*, Jan. 1697/8. He *d.* s.p. 1714.

V. 1714. SIR BALDWIN WAKE, Bart. [1621], br. and h.; *suc. to the Baronetcy* in 1714. He *m.* firstly (Lic. Fac. 10 July 1686, he of Furnival's Inn, aged 22, bachelor, and she 21), Anne DERHAM, spinster, da. of Elizabeth READ, *alias* DERHAM, widow. He *m.* secondly (Lic. Lond. 24 June 1697, he of Whitechapel, aged 30, widower, and she 30, spinster), Mary, da. of (—) HART, of Burford, Oxon. Will of Dame Mary Wake pr. June 1717. His will pr. 1748.

VI. 1748. SIR CHARLES WAKE-JONES, Bart. [1621], of Courteenhall and of Waltham and Nazing aforesaid, *formerly* Charles WAKE, grandson and h., being s. and h. of Baldwin WAKE, by Mary, da. and coheir of Edward LANE, of Hanslope, Bucks, which Baldwin was s. and h. ap. of the late Bart., but *d.* v.p. 14 March 1734/5. On the death of his paternal uncle, Charles WAKE-JONES, 22 March 1739/40, he became entitled to the estates of Waltham and Nazing and of Courteenhall abovenamed, and assumed the additional surname of *Jones*. He, subsequently, *suc. to the Baronetcy* in 1748; was Sheriff of Northamptonshire, 1752-53. He *m.* Mary, sister of Samuel JACKSON. He *d.* s.p. Jan. 1755. Will pr. 1755. The admon. of his widow dat. 30 March 1758.

VII. 1755. SIR WILLIAM WAKE, Bart. [1621], of Riddlesworth Hall, Norfolk, cousin and h. male, being only surv. s. and h. of Rev. Robert WAKE, Dean of Bocking, in Essex, and Rector of Buxtead with Cuckfield, Sussex, by Elizabeth, da. of William GREENFIELD, of Marlborough, which Robert

(living 1725) was 4th s. of the 3d Bart. He *suc. to the Baronetcy* and the greater part of the family estates in Jan. 1755. He *m.*, 19 April 1738, at St. Giles' in the Fields, Sarah WALKER, of Weston, co. York, spinster. He *d.* Sep. 1765. Will pr. Oct. 1765. That of his widow pr. Feb. 1794.

VIII. 1765. SIR WILLIAM WAKE, Bart. [1621], of Courteenhall, and of Waltham and Nazing aforesaid, s. and h., was *b.* 1742; ed. at Trin. Coll., Cambridge; M.A., 1767, having *suc. to the Baronetcy* in Jan. 1755; Sheriff of Northamptonshire, 1771-72; M.P. for Bedford, 1774-84. He *m.*, June 1765, Mary, da. and sole h. of Richard FENTON, of Bank Top, co. York. He *d.* 29 Oct. and was *bur.* 6 Nov. 1785, from Courteenhall, aged 43. Will pr. Oct. 1786. His widow *d.* 10 Dec. 1823. Will pr. 1824.

IX. 1785. SIR WILLIAM WAKE, Bart. [1621], of Courteenhall aforesaid, s. and h., was *b.* 5 April 1768; ed. at Trin. Coll., Cambridge; M.A., 1789; *suc. to the Baronetcy*, 29 Oct. 1785; Sheriff of Northamptonshire, 1791-92. He *m.* firstly, 1 July 1790, at St. Geo. Han. sq., Mary, only da. of Francis SITWELL, *formerly* HURT, of Renishaw, co. Derby, by Mary, da. of the Rev. (—) WARNEFORD. She *d.* 22 Nov. 1791. He *m.* secondly, 22 April 1793, at St. James', Westm., Jenny, da. of Vice Admiral James GAMBIER, by his 2d wife, Jane, da. of Col. MOMPESSON. She *d.* 7 May 1837. He *d.* 28 Jan. 1846. Will pr. March 1846.

X. 1846. SIR CHARLES WAKE, Bart. [1621], of Courteenhall aforesaid, s. and h., by 1st wife, was *b.* 21 Nov. 1791, in Clarges street, Middlesex; sometime Captain in North Hants militia; *suc. to the Baronetcy*, 18 Jan. 1846. He *m.* firstly, 21 Aug. 1815, Mary Alice, 1st da. of his maternal uncle, Sir Sitwell SITWELL, 1st Bart. [1808], by his 1st wife, Alice, da. of Thomas PARKES. She *d.* s.p. 3 Feb. 1816. He *m.* secondly, 1 June 1822, Charlotte, sister of Archibald Campbell TAIT, ARCHBISHOP OF CANTERBURY (1868-82), 2d da. of Craufurd TAIT, of Harriestoun, co. Clackmannan, by Susan, 4th da. of Sir Islay CAMPBELL, 1st Bart. [1808]. He *d.* 23 Sep. 1864, at Brighton, aged 73. His widow *d.* 31 March 1888, at Pitsford House, Northampton, in her 88th year, and was *bur.* from Courteenhall.

XI. 1864. SIR WILLIAM WAKE, Bart. [1621], of Courteenhall aforesaid, s. and h., by 2d wife, was *b.* 1823, at Renishaw Hall, co. Derby; ed. at Rugby School; sometime an officer in the Army and Captain in the West Essex Yeomanry Cavalry; *suc. to the Baronetcy*, 23 Sep. 1864. He *m.*, 21 Sep. 1844, Margaret-Anne, 1st da. of Henry FRICKER, of Southampton. He *d.* 13 April 1865, of bronchitis, on board his yacht, off Southampton, aged 42.(a) His widow *d.* 12 Dec 1866, at Kensington.

XII. 1865. SIR HEREWARD WAKE, Bart. [1621], of Courteenhall aforesaid, s. and h., was *b.* 6 July 1852, at Southampton; ed. at Eton; *suc. to the Baronetcy*, 13 April 1865; Sheriff of Northamptonshire, 1869. He *m.*, 14 April 1874, at St. Geo. Han. sq., Catharine, sister of John, 1st BARON ST. LEVAN OF ST. MICHAEL'S MOUNT, yst. da. of Sir Edward ST. AUBYN, 1st Bart. [1866], by Emma, da. of Gen. William KNOLLYS.

Family Estates.—These, in 1883, consisted of 1,629 acres in Northamptonshire, and 1,512 in Essex. *Total*, 3,141 acres, valued at £5,810 a year. *Principal Residence.*—Courteenhall, co. Northampton.

(a) Author of *My Escape and Imprisonment*, and other works.

MASHAM:
cr. 20 Dec. 1621,
afterwards, 1711-76, BARONS MASHAM OF OTES;
ex. 14 June, 1776.

I. 1621. "WILLIAM MASHAM, of High Laver, co. Essex, Esq.," s. and h. of William MASHAM, of Otes, in High Laver aforesaid, by Alice(a), da. of (—) CALTON, was *b.* about 1592; matric. at Oxford (Mag. Coll.), 13 Feb. 1606/7, aged 15; admitted to Inner Temple (as "of Creetingham, co. Suffolk") 1610; *cr. a Bart.*, as above; 20 Dec. 1621; was M.P. for Maldon, 1624-26; for Colchester, 1628-29, April to May 1640, and for Essex, 1640-53 and 1654-55; took a leading part against the King, for whose trial he was a commissioner, but did not act; was in the Council of State, 1649-52. He *m.* Elizabeth, widow of Sir James ALTHAM, da. of Sir Francis BARRINGTON, 1st Bart. [1611], by Joan, da. of Sir Henry CROMWELL. He *d.* about 1656. Will pr. 1656. His widow living Feb. 1662/3.

II. 1656 ? SIR WILLIAM MASHAM Bart. [1621], of Otes aforesaid, grandson and h., being s. and h. of William MASHAM, by Elizabeth, da. of Sir John TREVOR, which William, last named (who was M.P. for Shrewsbury, 1645-53), was s. and h. ap. of the late Bart., by his 1st wife, but *d.* v.p. He *suc. to the Baronetcy*, about 1656. He *d.* unm., in France, about 1662. Admon., 20 Feb. 1662/3.

III. 1662 ? SIR FRANCIS MASHAM, Bart. [1621], of Otes aforesaid, br. and h.; *b.* about 1646; *suc. to the Baronetcy* about 1663; M.P. for Essex (eight Parls.), 1690-1710. He *m.* firstly, 1 Nov. 1666, at Richmond, Surrey (Lic. Fac., he about 20, she of Kew, Surrey, about 17), Mary, da. of Sir William SCOTT, 1st Bart. [1653], of Rouen in Normandy, Marquis de la Mezansene in France, by Elizabeth or Catherine, da. of Samuel FORTREY, of Kew. He *m.*, secondly, 25 June 1685, at St. Andrew's, Holborn (Lic. Vic. Gen., he 36 and she 21), Damaris, da. of the Rev. Ralph CUDWORTH, D.D., of Cambridge. She, who was *b.* 18 Jan. 1658/9, *d.* 20 April 1708, and was *bur.* in Bath Abbey. He *d.* 7 Feb. 1722/3,(b) and was *bur.* at High Laver, aged 77. Will dat. 1 Jan. 1718/9, pr. 21 March 1722/3.

IV. 1724. SAMUEL (MASHAM), BARON MASHAM OF OTES, and 4th Bart. [1621], 8th but 1st surv. s. and h. male by 1st wife. He, who had v.p. been *cr.*, 31 Dec. 1711, BARON MASHAM OF OTES, co. Essex, *suc. to the Baronetcy*, 7 Feb. 1723/4, which thus became *merged* in the peerage title, till by the death s.p. 14 June 1776, of the 2d Baron and 5th Baronet, *both dignities* became *extinct*. See *Peerage*.

COLBRAND, *or* COLBROND:
cr. 21 Dec. 1621;
ex. 2 June 1709.

I. 1621. "JOHN COLBROND, of Borham, co. Sussex, Esq," s. and h. of John COLBROND, *or* COLBRAND, of Chichester, by Martha, da. of Oliver (ST. JOHN), 1st BARON ST. JOHN OF BLETSO; suc. his father, 21 Oct. 1600, and was *cr. a Bart.*, as above, 21 Dec. 1621. He *m.* firstly, Ann, da. of (—) WILSON.

(a) This Alice *m.* secondly, 17 Dec. 1606, Sir Francis Castillion.

(b) His death is frequently, but erroneously, given as in March 1703, and that of *his successor* in the Baronetcy as Feb. 1723, that successor being called Francis Masham, his grandson, s. and h. of his 4th son (another Francis), who *d.* v.p. The 3d Bart., however, in his will, dated 1719, makes no mention of any such Francis, though he therein entails his estates somewhat strictly.

He *m.* secondly, Sarah, da. of (—) NEEDHAM, of Derbyshire. He *d.* 1627. Will dat. 20 Dec. 1627 (as "of Southover, Sussex"), pr. 20 March 1627/8. His widow *m.* Humphrey NEWTON, of Axmouth, Devon.

II. 1627. SIR JAMES COLBRAND, Bart. [1621], of Boreham aforesaid, s. and h.. by the 2d wife, *suc. to the Baronetcy* in 1627, living 1634, at Lewes. He *m.*, in or before 1631, Margaret, da. of Richard AMHERST, Serjeant at Law, by Margaret, da. of Sir Thomas PALMER, 1st Bart. [1611], of Wingham. She was *bur.* at Tonbridge 26 July 1666 as "the Lady Margt. Colbrand."

III. 1640 ? SIR RICHARD COLBRAND, Bart. [1621], of Boreham aforesaid, 1st surv. s. and h.; said to have been a Colonel in the King's Army; was admitted to Gray's Inn, 24 Nov. 1660, being then a Baronet. He *d.* unm., and was *bur.* at Tonbridge, 14 March 1664.

IV. 1664. SIR CHARLES COLBRAND, Bart. [1621], of Boreham aforesaid, br. and h., *suc. to the Baronetcy* March 1664. He *d.* unm. of the small pox, and was *bur.* at Tonbridge 19 March 1667. Will pr. 1668.

V. 1667, to 1709. SIR ROBERT COLBRAND, Bart. [1621], of Boreham aforesaid, uncle and h. male, being 5th and yst. s. of the 1st Bart., by his 2d wife; *suc. to the Baronetcy* in March 1667. He *m.* Mary, da. of Thomas SOUTHLAND, of Lee, co. Kent. He *d.* s.p. 2 June 1709, in London, when the *Baronetcy* became *extinct*. Will pr. June 1709.

HOTHAM:
cr. 4 Jan. 1621/2,
sometime, 1771-94, HOTHAM-THOMPSON,
afterwards, since 1811, BARONS HOTHAM OF SOUTH DALTON [I.]

I. 1622. "JOHN HOTHAM, of Scarborough, co. York, Knt.," s. and h. of John HOTHAM, of the same, by his 3d wife, Jane, da. and coheir of Richard LEGARD, of Riseholme in Holderness: suc. his father about 1605, was *Knighted* at York, 11 April 1617, and was *cr. a Bart.*, as above, 4 Jan. 1621/2. He was M.P. for Beverley, 1625, 1626, 1628-29, April to May 1640, and 1640 till disabled 7 April 1643; was Sheriff of Yorkshire, 1634-35; was Governor of Hull, during the Civil Wars, on behalf of the Parliament, and actually shut the gates of that town against the King, but being suspected, subsequently, of intriguing with the Royalist party, was taken prisoner, found guilty at a court martial at Guildhall, 30 Nov. 1644, and, as was also his eldest son, Col. John Hotham, beheaded. He *m.* no less than five times, and had issue by all his wives *viz.*, firstly, he *m.*, 16 Feb. 1606/7, at the Belfry Church, York, Catharine, da. of Sir John RODES, of Barlborough, co. Derby, by his 2d wife, Frances, da. of Marmaduke CONSTABLE, of Holderness. He *m.* secondly, 16 July 1614, at St. John's Beverley, Anne, only child of Ralph ROKEBY, of York, Secretary for the North, by his 2d wife, Joan, da. of John PORTINGTON, of Portington. She, who was *bap.* 15 July 1593, at the Belfry Church, York, *d.* about 1624. He *m.* thirdly, Frances, da. of John LEGARD, of Ganton, co. York, by Elizabeth, da. of Sir William MALLORY. He *m.* fourthly, Catharine, widow of Sir Thomas NORCLIFFE, da. of Sir William BAMBURGH, Bart. [1619], of Howsham, co. York, by Mary, da. of Robert FORDE. She *d.* 22 Aug. 1634. He *m.* fifthly, 7 May 1635, at Etton, co. York, Sarah, da. of Thomas ANLABY, of Etton, by his 2d wife, Sarah, da. of Gervase CRESSY, of Birkin. He *d.* 2 Jan. 1644/5, being beheaded (as aforesaid) the day after his son. Both *bur.* at Allhallows Barking, London.(a)

(a) Extracts from the Burial Register at Allhallows Barking—
1644 Jany 1. "John HOTHAM, Esquire beheaded for betraying his trust to ye state."
1644 Jany 2. "Sir John HOTHAM, Knight beheaded for betraying his trust to the Parliament."
1645 June 17. "Dorathie HOTHAM, daur of Sir John Hotham, Knight, and the Ladie Eliza. [*sic.*, but should be 'Sarah'] his wife."

II. 1645. Sir John Hotham, Bart. [1622], of Scarborough aforesaid, and afterwards of South Dalton, co. York, grandson and h., being s. and h. of Col. John Hotham above named, by his 1st wife, Frances, da. of Sir John Wray, 2d Bart. [1611], of Glentworth, which John Hotham, last named, was s. and h. ap. of the 1st Bart., by his 1st wife, but was beheaded v.p., 1 Jan. 1644/5 as aforesaid, aged 34. He was *bap.*, 21 March 1631/2, at Glentworth; and *suc. to the Baronetcy*, 2 Jan. 1644/5. He was M.P. for Beverley (in six Parls.), 1660-81, and 1689 till his death. He *m.*, 8 Aug. 1650, at Burton, co. Lincoln, Elizabeth, da. of Sapcote (Beaumont), 2d Viscount Beaumont of Swords [I.], by his 1st wife, Bridget, da. of Sir Thomas Monson, 1st Bart. [1611]. He was *bur.* 29 Dec. 1689, at South Dalton. His widow, who was *bap.* at Burton, co. Lincoln, 20 March 1632/3, and who was sister and h. (11 June 1702) of Thomas, 3d and last Viscount Beaumont of Swords [I.], was *bur.* at South Dalton, 10 Dec. 1697.

III. 1689. Sir John Hotham, Bart. [1622], of South Dalton aforesaid, s. and h. *b.* 2, and *bap.* 10 Aug. 1655, being aged 10 at the Visit. of York, 1665. He was M.P. for Beverley, May 1689 to Feb. 1690, and *suc. to the Baronetcy* in Dec. 1689. He *m.* at St. John's, Beverley, 5 Feb. 1678/9, Catherine, da. of John Heron of Beverley aforesaid. He *d.* s.p. 1691. His widow *m.* at Kilnwick, 26 Aug. 1692, John Moyser, and was *bur.* at St. Mary's, Beverley, 5 Jan. 1727/8.

IV. 1691. Sir Charles Hotham, Bart. [1622], of South Dalton aforesaid, cousin and h. male, being s. and h. of Charles Hotham, Rector of Wigan, Lancashire (ejected in 1662), by Elizabeth, da. of Stephen Thompson, of Humbleton, co. York, which Charles (who *d.* in the West Indies), was 3d s. of the 1st Bart., being 1st son by his 2d wife. He *suc. to the Baronetcy* in 1691; was Colonel of the King's own Regiment of Dragoons; was M.P. for Scarborough (five Parls.), April 1695 to 1702, and for Beverley (seven Parls.). 1702 till his death. He *m.*, firstly, 9 Sep. 1690 at Bishop's Burton, co. York, his first cousin, Bridget, da. of William Gee, of Bishop's Burton, by Frances, da. (by his 1st wife) of Sir John Hotham, 1st Bart. She was *bur.* at Scarborough, 14 Aug. 1707. He *m.* secondly, Mildred, widow of Sir Uvedale Corbet, 3d Bart. [1642], yst. da. of James (Cecil), 3d Earl of Salisbury, by Margaret, da. of John (Manners), Earl of Rutland. He *d.* 8 Jan. 1722/3. Will pr. 1723. His widow *d.* 18 Jan. 1726/7 and was *bur.* at St. Margaret's, Westminster. M.I.

V. 1723. Sir Charles Hotham, Bart. [1622], of South Dalton aforesaid, s. and h. by 1st wife, *bap.* 27 April 1693, at Scarborough; *suc. to the Baronetcy*, 8 Jan. 1722/3; Colonel of the 1st troop of Horse Grenadier Guards and Groom of the Bedchamber to George II; M.P. for Beverley (three Parls.), 1723 till his death. He *m.* 1724, Gertrude, 1st da. of Philip (Stanhope), 3d Earl of Chesterfield, by Elizabeth, da. of George (Savile), Marquess of Halifax. He was *bur.* 25 Jan. 1737/8 at South Dalton. Will pr. 1738. His widow *d.* 12, and was *bur.* there 24 April 1775, aged 29. Her will pr. April 1775.

VI. 1738. Sir Charles Hotham, Bart. [1622], of South Dalton aforesaid, only s. and h.; *suc. to the Baronetcy*, Jan. 1737/8. Groom of the Bedchamber to George III. He *m.* Clara Anne, only surv. da. and h. of Thomas Clutterbuck, of Mill Green, Essex. She was *bur.* 13 July 1759, at South Dalton. He *d.* s.p. at Stavelo, near Spa, Germany, in Oct., and was *bur.* 6 Dec. 1767 at South Dalton. Will pr. Oct. 1767.

VII. 1767. Sir Beaumont Hotham, Bart. [1622], of South Dalton aforesaid, uncle and h., being 2d s. of the 4th Bart. by his 1st wife. Was a Commissioner in H.M.'s Customs, 1737-63; *suc. to the Baronetcy*, Oct. 1767. He *m.* Frances, aunt and h. (Aug. 1771) of Lillingston Thompson, of Humbleton, co. York, da. of the Rev. Stephen Thompson, of Thornthorpe in that county, by Hannah, da. of the Rev. Stephen Clarke. He was *bur.* 9 Sep. 1771 at South Dalton. Will pr. Sep. 1771. His widow was *bur.* there 29 Nov. following.

VIII. 1771. Sir Charles Hotham-Thompson, Bart. [1622], of South Dalton and of Humbleton aforesaid, s. and h. *b.* May 1729; assumed the addit. surname of *Thompson* on succeeding to the estate of that family; *suc. to the Baronetcy* in Sep. 1771; K.B. 15 Jan. 1772. General in the Army, and Colonel of the 15th Reg. of Foot; Groom of the Bedchamber to George III, 1761; M.P. for St. Ives, 1761-68. He *m.* 21 Oct. 1752, at Duke Street Chapel, Westm., Dorothy, da. of John (Hobart), 1st Earl of Buckinghamshire, by his 1st wife, Judith, da. of Robert Britiffe. He *d.* s.p.m. 25 Jan. 1794. Will pr. Feb. 1794. His widow *d.* in London, 1 June 1798. Will pr. June 1798. Both were *bur.* at South Dalton.

IX. 1794. Sir John Hotham, Bart. [1622], Lord Bishop of Clogher [I.], br. and h. male, *b.* 16 March 1734; ed. at Trin. Coll., Cambridge; B.A., 1756; M.A., 1760; in Holy Orders; Vicar of Northall, Midx., 1763-79; Vicar of Shoreditch, 1767-80; Prebendary of St. Paul's, London, 1763-80; Archdeacon of Midx., 1764-80; Chaplain in ordinary to the King; Bishop of Ossory [I.], 1779; Bishop of Clogher [I.], 1782; *suc. to the Baronetcy*, 25 Jan. 1794. He *m.*, 11 April 1765, Susanna, sister of Sir Herbert Mackworth, 1st Bart. [1619], da. of Herbert Mackworth, of Gnoll, co. Glamorgan, by Juliana, da. of William (Digby), 5th Baron Digby of Geashill [I.] She was *b.* 25 July 1738. He *d.* 3 Nov. 1795. Will pr. Dec. 1795.

X. 1795. Sir Charles Hotham, Bart. [1622], of South Dalton aforesaid, and of Ebberston Lodge, co. York, only s. and h., *b.* 25 May 1766. He *m.*, 16 Nov. 1804, Elizabeth, 4th da. of Owen Meyrick. He *d.* s.p. 18 July 1811. Will pr. 1811. His widow *m.*, 20 Oct. 1812, George Morgan, and *d.* Aug. 1834.

XI. 1811. William (Hotham) Baron Hotham of South Dalton [I. 1797], and 11th Bart. [1622], uncle and h. male, being 3d s. of the 7th Bart., *b.* 8 April 1736; was Admiral R.N., and was, for his victory over the French squadron (14 March 1795), *cr.* 17 March 1797, BARON HOTHAM OF SOUTH DALTON [I.], with a spec. rem., failing the issue male of his body, to that of his father. He *suc. to the Baronetcy*, 18 July 1811, which accordingly then *merged* in this peerage, and still so continues. See *Peerage*.

MANSEL, *or* MANSELL:

cr. 14 Jan. 1621/2.

I. 1622. "Francis Mansell, of Mudlescombe [in Kidwelly], co. Carmarthen, Esqre.," yr. br. of Sir Thomas Mansell, Bart. (so *cr.* 1611), both being sons of Sir Edward Mansell, of Margam, co. Glamorgan [*d.* 5 Aug. 1595], by Jane, yst. da. of Henry Somerset, 2d Earl of Worcester. Was Sheriff of co. Carmarthen 1594-95 and 1610-11, and was *cr. a Bart.*, as above, 14 Jan. 1621/2. He *m.* firstly, Catharine, da. and coheir of Henry Morgan, of Muddlescombe aforesaid. He *m.* secondly, Dorothy, sister of Sir John Stepney, 1st Bart. [1621], da. of Alban Stepney, of Prendergast, co. Pembroke, by his 2d wife, Mary, da. of William Philipps, of Picton in that county. He *d.* about 1628. Admon. 2 Dec. 1628, 27 June 1631, and 3 April 1641.(a) His widow (Dorothy) was living Dec. 1628. In the calendar of the (now missing) admons. for 1662 are two of "Dame Dorothy Mansell," one in April as of "co. Carmarthen," and the other in July as of "co. Pembroke," both being, presumably, those of this lady.

II. 1628? Sir Walter Mansel, Bart. [1622], of Muddlescombe aforesaid, s. and h. by 1st wife; *b.* about 1588; matric. at Oxford (Oriel Coll.), 22 May 1601, aged 13; B.A., 15 July 1603; adm. to Linc. Inn, 1605; *suc. to the Baronetcy* about 1628. He *m.* (settlmt. 2 Aug. 1623) Elizabeth [often, erroneously, called Mary], sister of Sir John Fotherby, da. of Charles Fotherby,

(a) The first and second are to the son, "Sir Walter Mansell, *Bart.*," and the last is to "Sir Anthony Mansell, *Knt.*, Britton Ferry, co. Glamorgan, son of decd., the said Sir Walter being now deod."

Dean of Canterbury, by Cecilia, da. and h. of Ralph Waller. He *d.* s.p. and was *bur.* at Kidwelly, 12 April 1640. Admon. 10 Feb. 1640/1, to Elizabeth, his widow. She, who, presumably, was *bap.* at Canterbury Cathedral, 24 April 1614 (though, in that case, she would be somewhat under 10 years at her marriage), *d.* at the house of Mr. George Norbury, at Great St. Bartholomew's, London, 11, was carried thence 18 and *bur.* 20 Sep. 1643, in the cathedral aforesaid. Will dat. 10 Sep. and pr. 29 Nov. 1643, at the Prerog. Court, then at Oxford.

III. 1640. Sir Francis Mansel, Bart. [1622], of Muddlescombe aforesaid, only s. and h.; *suc. to the Baronetcy* in April 1640. He was living 10 Sep. 1643, being then a minor, and under the age at which he could make choice of his guardian. He *d.* s.p.m., most probably unm. and under age.

[The succession to this Baronetcy is obscure during the period of nearly fifty years, *viz.*, between 1643 and the death of Sir Richard Mansel, Bart. in 1691. There is a pedigree entered at the College of Arms, shewing (in full) the first four sons of the 1st Bart. and the issue of the 4th son, Richard Mansel, of Ischoed (*d.* before 1636), whose grandson, Sir Richard Mansel abovenamed was the first of that issue who inherited the Baronetcy, and was progenitor of all the succeeding Baronets. The third of those sons, Francis Mansell, D.D., Principal of Jesus College, Oxford, *d.* unm. 1 May 1665, not having inherited the title, which must, therefore, have vested between 1643 and 1665, and probably later, in Francis, the 3d Bart., or his issue (he being the *only* son of Walter, the 2d Bart., the eldest son), or in Anthony, the second son, therein stated to have been slain (*ex. parte Regis*) at Newbury, 27 Oct. 1644,(a) or his issue. In this pedigree no issue, or mark of issue, is given either to the said Walter or Anthony, though there is no express statement that they *d.* without issue. Anthony is described as a "Knight" (only), not as a "Baronet." Le Neve, however, in his (MS.) *Baronetage*, makes (correctly) Walter, the 2d Bart., to be father (of a da., Elizabeth,(b) and) of "Sir Francis Mansell, Bart., ob. s.p." He also makes the said Anthony to have issue, "Sir Edward Mansell, Francis, and Arthur, a Barrister," of whom, he states, Sir Edward was father of "Sir Edward Mansell, 1694."(c) Sir Edward Mansel, *Bart.*, is, however (with more probability), made the *son* (not grandson) of this Anthony in Prothero's *Welsh Pedigrees*. The account in Wotton's *Baronetage* is strangely inaccurate, the 2d and 3d Barts. being totally ignored. The suggested succession as to the next holder is as under].

IV? 1650? Sir Edward Mansel, Bart. [1622], of Muddlescombe aforesaid, cousin and h. male, being (presumably) s. and h. (possibly, however, grandson and h., as being s. and h. of *another* Sir Edward Mansel, said to have been s. and h.) of Sir Anthony Mansel (by Jane, da. of William Price, of Britton Ferry, co. Glamorgan), which Anthony (who was *Knighted*, 19 July 1629, and was Sheriff of Glamorgan 1630-31), was 2d s. of the 1st Bart. (by his 1st wife), and was living 3 April 1641, but is said to have been slain in the Royal cause at Newbury, 27 Oct. 1644.(a) He *suc. to the Baronetcy* about 1650, and was Sheriff of co. Carmarthen, 1661. He *m.* Jane, widow of Sir Roger Lort, 1st Bart. [1662], da. of Humphrey Windham, of Dunraven, co. Glamorgan. He *d.* s.p.m.

V? 1680? Sir Richard Mansel, Bart. [1622], of Ischoed, in St. Ishmaell's, co. Carmarthen, cousin and h. male, being next br. and h. of Anthony Mansel, of Ischoed (*d.* s.p. and was *bur.* 4 April 1679, at Margam), both being sons of Anthony Mansel, of Ischoed, by Mary, da. of Edward Carne, of Cowbridge, which last named Anthony (*b.* 1613, and living May 1666) was eldest s. and h. of Richard Mansel, also of Ischoed, by Catherine, da. and h. of Rees Morgan, of Ischoed aforesaid, the said Richard (whose will, dat. 1634 was pr. 17 March 1635/6) being 4th s. (by his 1st wife) of the 1st Bart. He was *bap.* 6 Jan. 1641, at St. Ishmaell's; *suc. to the Baronetcy*, on his cousin's death, at some date after 4 April

(a) It should be mentioned that Le Neve, in his *Barts.*, says "slain at Newby, co. York," which statement Wotton (in his *Baronetage*) follows, adding, however, "temp. Car. I," but neither of them say that it was in a battle.

(b) She, who became heir to her br., *m.* (—) Brome, Serjeant-at-Law.

(c) *Sic*, but the date of 1694 is apparently a few years too late, as Sir *Richard* Mansell, Bart., who *d.* Aug. 1691, must have inherited the title before that date.

1679, being that of the death of his own *elder* brother, abovenamed. He *m.* Alice, da. and h. of Rees Davies, of Pentre-yr-istill, in Swansea, co. Glamorgan. She was *bur.* 11 Dec. 1689, at St. Ishmaell's. He was *bur.* 28 Aug. 1691, at Kidwelly.

VI? 1691. Sir Richard Mansel, Bart. [1622], of Ischoed aforesaid, s. and h., is said(a) to have *suc. to the Baronetcy* on the death of his father, and to have *d.* in London unm.

VII? 1700? Sir William Mansel, Bart. [1622], of Ischoed aforesaid, and of Clognakilly in Ireland, br. and h.; *bap.* 15 March 1670, at Kidwelly; *suc. to the Baronetcy* on the death of his brother. He *m.* 18 Oct. 1700, Amy, 4th da. of Sir Richard Cox, 1st Bart. [I. 1706], Lord Chancellor of Ireland, 1703-07, by Mary, da. of (—) Bourne. She, who was *b.* 29 June 1684, *d.* before him. He *d.* about 1732. His admon. 5 May 1733, was revoked and regranted 9 Aug. 1733, to "Sir William [*sic*, but apparently should be "Richard"] Mansell, Bart., his son."

VIII? 1732? Sir Richard Mansel, Bart. [1622], of Pembrey, co. Carmarthen, of Ischoed aforesaid, and of Woodstone, co. Cork, s. and h., *suc. to the Baronetcy* about 1732. He *m.* firstly (Lic. at Cork, 1732) Susanna Warner. He *m.* secondly (Lic. at Cork, 1737) Rebecca, 1st da. of William Ware, of Farranalough, co. Cork. He was *bur.* at Kidwelly, 20 Feb. 1749. Admon. 5 Jan. 1752, at Carmarthen. His widow was *bur.* there 8 Dec. 1791.

IX? 1749. Sir William Mansel, Bart. [1622], of Ischoed and Woodstone aforesaid, only s. and h. by second wife, *b.* 1 March 1738/9; *suc. to the Baronetcy* in Feb. 1749; was presumably (though described as "of Ischoed, Esq."), Sheriff for co. Carmarthen 1781-82; M.P. for that county, 1784. He *m.* 26 Aug. 1765, at St. Ishmaell's, Mary, only sister and coheir of George Philipps, of Coedgaing, co. Carmarthen, da. of John Philipps, of the same. He was *bur.* at St. Ishmaell's, 14 Jan. 1804, aged 66. Admon. 3 Feb. 1804. His widow *d.* 27 Dec. 1811, and was *bur.* at St. Peter's, Carmarthen. Will dat. 14 May 1811, pr. 5 Dec. 1812.

X? 1804. Sir William Mansel, Bart. [1622], of Ischcoed aforesaid, s. and h., *b.* 29 April 1766; *suc. to the Baronetcy*, 14 Jan. 1804. He *m.* Dec. 1790, Elizabeth, da. and h. of John Bell, of Harefield, Midx. He *d.* 20 May 1829, aged 63. His widow *d.* 12 Aug. 1843, at Wrotham Heath, Kent, in her 73d year. Will pr. Nov. 1843.

XI? 1829. Sir John Bell William Mansel, Bart. [1622], of Ischoed aforesaid, 2d but 1st surv. s. and h. male; *b.* 5 Oct. 1806; *suc. to the Baronetcy*, 1829. Barrister at Law (Lincoln's Inn), 1831; Sheriff for co. Carmarthen, 1846. He *m.* 31 July 1832, at St. Mary le bone, Mary Georgiana, sister of Sir Henry Dymoke, Bart. (so *cr.* 1841), da. of Rev. John Dymoke, Rector of Scrivelsby, co. Lincoln, by Amelia Jane Alice, da. of John Elphinstone, Capt. R.N., Admiral in the Russian Navy. He *d.* s.p.m., 14 April 1883, at Wrotham Heath House, co. Kent., aged 76. Will, wherein he devised his real estate to his daughters,(b) pr. 17 Aug. 1883, above £9,000. His widow, who was *b.* 7 Feb. 1801 and *bap.* at Scrivelsby, *d.* at Wrotham Heath aforesaid, 18 Oct. 1888, aged 81.

XII? 1883. Sir Richard Mansel, Bart. [1622], of Coedgaing, co. Carmarthen, cousin and h. male, being only s. and h. of Courtenay Mansell, formerly Philipps, of Coedgaing, sometime Major 15th Hussars, by Eliza, da. of the Rev. John Sidney, which Courtenay (who resumed the name of Mansel only by Royal lic. 12 May 1866, and *d.* 9 Sep. 1875, aged 74) was 1st s. of Richard Philipps, formerly Mansel, of Coedgaing, Commander R.N. (who, by Royal lic. 24 Jan. 1793,

(a) The absence of any date in any part of his career renders it somewhat problematical. His death is stated in Wotton's *Baronetage* to have been "in London."

(b) Maria, the only daughter who married, was wife of Sir Edward Bradford Medlycott, 4th Bart. [1808].

took the name of PHILIPPS in lieu of that of MANSEL, and who *d.* 20 Aug. 1844, aged 67), the 2d s. of Sir William MANSEL [9th ?], Bart., by Mary, only da. of John PHILIPPS, of Coedgaing aforesaid. He was *b.* 2 Dec. 1850 in Sussex square, Paddington; ed. at Eton; *suc. to the Baronetcy*, but not to the family estates, 4 April 1883, and was a bankrupt(a) in Aug. following, being then "of the Grange, Wimbledon, Surrey." He *m.* firstly, 4 Sep. 1878, Maud Margaretta Bowen, da. of John JONES, of Maes-y-Crugian, co. Carmarthen. She *d.* 12 Sep. 1885. He *m.* secondly, Ada Alice LEA, spinster, late of the music-hall stage. He *d.* July 1892. His widow living 1899.

XIII? 1892. SIR COURTENEY CECIL MANSELL, Bart. [1622], only s. and h., by 1st wife, *b.* 25 Feb. 1880; *suc. to the Baronetcy* in July 1892.

POWELL:
cr. 18 Jan. 1621/2;
ex. 1653.

I. 1622, to 1654. "EDWARD POWELL, of Penkelley [*i.e.*, Pengethly], co. Hereford, Esq.," s. and h. of Edmund POWELL, of Mustow in Fulham, co. Midx., and of Pengethly aforesaid, by Katharine, da. of (—) YOUNG (mar. lic. 26 Jan. 1577/8), was *b.* about 1580; matric. at Oxford (Merton Coll.), 23 July 1596, aged 16; B.A., 8 May 1599; M.A., 7 July 1602; admitted to Middle Temple, 1601; was one of the Masters of the Requests, and was *cr. a Bart.*, as above, 18 Jan. 1621/2. He *m.* Mary, said to have been a da. of Sir Peter VANLORE. Her admon. 15 Jan. 1651/2 and 17 Oct. 1674. He *d.* s.p. in Chelsea, 1653, when the *Baronetcy* became *extinct*.(b) Will, as "of Chelsea," dat. 6 Feb. 1651/2, pr. 22 May 1653.

GARRARD:
cr. 16 Feb. 1621/2;
ex. 1 July 1767.

I. 1622. "JOHN GARRARD, of Lamer [in Wheathampstead], co. Herts., Knt.," s. and h. ap. of Sir John GARRARD, of Lamer aforesaid, sometime (1601-02) Lord Mayor of London, by Jane, da. of Richard PARTRIDGE, of London, Citizen and Haberdasher, which John (who *d.* 7 May 1625, aged 79) was 3d s., but eventually h. male of Sir William GARRARD, of Dorney, Bucks, and of Lamer aforesaid, also sometime (1555-56), Lord Mayor of London; was *b.* about 1590; matric. at Oxford (Ch. Ch.), 31 Oct. 1605, aged 15; B.A., 13 April 1608; admitted to Middle Temple, 2 Feb. 1608/9; *Knighted* at Whitehall, 26 Feb. 1614/5, and was *cr. a Bart.*, as above, 26 Feb. 1621/2. He suc. his father, 7 May 1625. He *m.* firstly, 6 May 1611, at St. Mary Aldermary, Elizabeth, 1st da. of Sir Edward BARKHAM, of Southacre, Norfolk, sometime (1621-22) Lord Mayor of London, by Jane, da. of John CROUCH, of Cornbury, Herts. She (who was mother of fourteen children) *d.* 17 April 1632, in her 39th year, and was *bur.* at Wheathampstead, Herts. M.I. He *m.* secondly, 3 June 1636,(c) at Westcombe, co. Kent (reg. also at St. Mary's Wolnoth), Jane, widow of Sir Moulton LAMBARDE, of Sevenoaks, Kent, 4th da. of Sir Thomas LOWE, sometime (1604-05), Lord Mayor of London, by Anne, da. of Gabriel COULSTON, of that city. He *d.* (less than a year afterwards) 1637. Will dat. 8 April to 20 May, and pr. 21 June 1637. His widow, who was *bap.* 16 March 1592/3, at St. Peter le Poor, London, was *bur.* there 22 Feb. 1672/3. Will pr. 1673.

(a) Debts secured, £37,000; unsecured, £3,645; the assets being £9,800.
(b) He devised his estates to his nephew, "William Powell, *alias* Hinson, of the Middle Temple, Esq.," who was *cr. a Bart.*, 23 Jan. 1660/1, as of Pengethly, co. Hereford, but who *d.* s.p.m. 1680-81.
(c) See "The Lambarde Diary" in *Mis. Gen. et Her.*, 1st S., vol. ii, pp. 99—114.

II. 1637. SIR JOHN GARRARD, Bart. [1622], of Lamer aforesaid, s. and h., by 1st wife; *suc. to the Baronetcy* in 1637; Sheriff of Herts, 1643-45. He *m.* in or before 1638, Jane, da. of Sir Moulton LAMBARDE, and Jane, his wife (his own stepmother), both above named. He *d.* 11 March 1685/6, and was *bur.* at Wheathampstead. His widow, who was *b.* at Putney, Surrey, 12 June 1617, *d.* 5 and was *bur.* 9 April 1692, at Wheathampstead, in her 75th year. Will pr. 17 June 1692.

III. 1685. SIR JOHN GARRARD, Bart. [1622], of Lamer aforesaid, s. and h., *b.* 1638; matric. at Oxford (Ch. Ch.), 13 March 1656/7; Sheriff of Herts, 1670-71; M.P. for Ludgershall, 1679-81 and 1681; and for Amersham, 1698—1700, and 1700 till death; *suc. to the Baronetcy*, 11 March 1685/6. He *m.* (Lic. Vic. Gen., 6 May 1669, he 25 and she 23), Katharine, widow of Sir George BUSWELL, Bart. [1660], da. and coheir of Sir James ENYON, Bart. [1642] of Flore, by Jane, da. of Sir Adam NEWTON, 1st Bart. [1620] of Charlton. He *d.* s.p.m.,(a) 13 Jan. 1700/1, aged 62, and was *bur.* at Wheathampstead. M.I. Will dat. 17 June 1700, pr. 20 Jan. 1700/1. His widow *d.* 16 April 1702, aged 60, and was *bur.* (with her first husband) at Clipston, co. Northampton. M.I. Will pr. June 1702.

IV. 1701. SIR SAMUEL GARRARD, Bart. [1622], of Lamer aforesaid, br. and h. male, *suc. to the Baronetcy*, 13 Jan. 1700/1; Sheriff of London, 1702-3; Alderman of Aldersgate, 1702-22, and of Bridge Without, 1722 till death; Lord Mayor, 1709-10, becoming, finally, the senior Alderman of that city. President of Bethlehem and Bridewell Hospitals. M.P. for Amersham, 1701 and 1702-10; *cr.* D.C.L. of Oxford, 12 June 1707. He *m.* firstly (Lic. Fac., 16 Oct. 1675, he 24 and she 19), Elizabeth, da. of George POYNER, of Coddicotebury, Herts, by Cecilia, his wife. She *d.* s.p. He *m.* secondly (Lic. Fac., 22 Jan. 1688/9, she 20), Jane, da. of Thomas BENET of Salthrop, Wilts. He *d.* 10, and was *bur.* 17 March 1724/5, at Wheathampstead, in his 74th year. M.I. Will pr. 1725. That of his widow pr. 1746.

V. 1725. SIR SAMUEL GARRARD, Bart. [1622], of Lamer aforesaid, s. and h. by 2d wife, *b.* 31 July 1692; *suc. to the Baronetcy*, 10 March 1724/5. He *d.* unm., 1 Dec. 1761, and was *bur.* at Wheathampstead. Will pr. 1761.

VI. 1761, to 1767. SIR BENET GARRARD, Bart. [1622], of Lamer aforesaid, yst. br.(b) and h.; *suc. to the Baronetcy*, 1 Dec. 1761. M.P. for Amersham, 1762 till death. He *d.* unm. 1 July 1767, aged 63, and was *bur.* at Wheathampstead, when the *Baronetcy* became *extinct*. Will pr. July 1767.

GROSVENOR:
cr. 23 Feb. 1621/2,
afterwards, since 1761, BARONS GROSVENOR OF EATON,
and, since 1784, EARLS GROSVENOR,
subsequently, since 1831, MARQUESSES OF WESTMINSTER,
and *finally*, since 1874, DUKES OF WESTMINSTER.

I. 1622. "RICHARD GROSVENOR, of Eaton, co. Chester, Knt.," s. and h. of Richard GROSVENOR, of the same, by his 1st wife, Christian, da. of Richard BROOKE, of Norton in the said county; was *b.* 9 Jan. 1584/5; matric. at

(a) Jane his da. and sole h. (*b.* 1675, *d.* 1 April 1724), *m.* Montagu DRAKE, of Shardeloes, Bucks, and was great grandmother of Charles DRAKE-GARRARD, who inherited Lamer in 1767 under the will of the 6th and last Bart.
(b) Thomas Garrard, another br. was made Common Sergeant of London in 1729. He *d.* s.p. 10 Feb. 1758, in his 60th year, and was *bur.* at Wheathampstead.

Oxford (Queen's Coll.), 26 Nov. 1599, aged 14; B.A., 30 June 1602; *Knighted*, 24 Aug. 1617; suc. his father, 18 Sep. 1619, and was *cr. a Bart.*, as above, 23 Feb. 1621/2. M.P. for Cheshire, 1621-22, 1626, and 1628-29; Sheriff of Cheshire, 1623-24; Sheriff of Denbighshire, 1624-25; sometime Mayor of Chester. He *m.* firstly, Lettice, sister of Robert, EARL OF LEINSTER [I.], 2d da. of Sir Hugh CHOLMONDELEY, of Cholmondeley, Cheshire, by Mary, da. and h. of Christopher HOLFORD, of Holford. She was *bur.* at Eccleston, 20 Jan. 1611. He *m.* secondly, 1614, Elizabeth, da. of Sir Thomas WILBRAHAM, of Woodhey, Cheshire, by his 1st wife, Frances, da. of Sir Hugh CHOLMONDELEY. She was *bur.* at Eccleston, 26 June 1621. He *m.* thirdly, Elizabeth, widow of Sir Thomas STANLEY, of Alderley, da. and h. of Sir Peter WARBURTON, of Grafton, Justice of the Common Pleas, by his 1st wife, Margaret, da. and h. of George BARLOW. She *d.* 12 March 1627/8. Inq. p.m. 5 Car. I. He *d.* 14 Sep. 1645, aged 61, and was *bur.* at Eccleston.

II. 1645. SIR RICHARD GROSVENOR, Bart. [1622], of Eaton aforesaid, s. and h. by 1st wife; Sheriff of Cheshire (for the King), 1643-44, when he raised the "Posse Comitatus" to oppose the Parliamentary army under Fairfax; *suc. to the Baronetcy*, 14 Sep. 1645; was a Compounder, and was fined £2,590 on 18 Sep. 1646. Continuing faithful to the royal cause, he was expelled from his house at Eaton, and his estates sequestrated. He *m.* 1628, Sidney, da. of Sir Roger MOSTYN, of Mostyn, co. Flint, by Mary, da. of Sir John WYNNE, 1st Bart. [1611], of Gwydyr. He *d.* 31 Jan. 1664, aged 60, and was *bur.* at Eccleston. Will pr. 1665.

III. 1664. SIR THOMAS GROSVENOR, Bart. [1622], of Eaton aforesaid, grandson and h., being s. and h. of Roger GROSVENOR, by Christian, da. of Sir Thomas MYDDLETON, which Roger was s. and h. ap. of the 2d Bart., but *d.* v.p. 22 Aug. 1661, aged 33, being killed in a duel.(a) He was *b.* about 1656; *suc. to the Baronetcy*, 31 Jan. 1664. He was M.P. for the city of Chester (in six Parls.), 1679—1700; Mayor of Chester, 1685; and Sheriff of the county, 1688-89. He was in command at the camp at Hounslow in 1688, and is said to have refused a peerage sooner than assent to the repeal of the penal laws and the test act. He *m.* (Lic. London 8 Oct. 1677, he 21 and she 13) Mary,(b) da. and h. of Alexander DAVIS, *or* DAVIES,(c) of Ebury, Middlesex, and of London, Scrivener, by Mary, da. of Richard DUKESON, D.D., Rector of St. Clement Danes. He *d.* June and was *bur.* 2 July 1700, at Eccleston, aged 44. Will pr. Sep. 1700. His widow *d.* 12 and was *bur.* there 15 Jan. 1729/30, aged 65. Admon. 6 Feb. 1729/30.

IV. 1700. SIR RICHARD GROSVENOR, Bart. [1622], of Eaton, aforesaid, 2d but 1st surv. s. and h.; *b.* 26 June 1689; *suc. to the Baronetcy* in June 1700. Mayor of Chester, 1715, and M.P. for that city (in three Parls.), 1715 till his death. He was Grand Cupbearer at the coronation of George II, as being Lord of the Manor of Wymondeley, Herts. He *m.* firstly, 1708, Jane, da. of Sir Edward WYNDHAM, 2d Bart. [1611], of Orchard Wyndham, by Catharine, sister of John, 1st BARON GOWER OF STITTENHAM, da. of Sir William LEVESON-GOWER, 4th Bart. [1620]. She was *bur.* 6 Feb. 1719, at Eccleston. He *m.* secondly, 1724, Diana, da. and h. of Sir George WARBURTON, 3d Bart. [1660], of Arley, by Diana, da. of William (ALINGTON), 2d and 1st BARON ALINGTON [I. and E.]. She *d.* s.p. 18 and was *bur.* 28 Feb. 1729/30, at Eccleston, aged 27. He *d.* s.p.s. 12 and was *bur.* 18 July 1732, at Eccleston, aged 44. Will pr. 1732.

(a) This Roger was one of thirteen gentlemen of Cheshire nominated, in 1660, to be Knights of the Royal Oak.
(b) She was heiress of the enormous estate in Westminster and St. George's Hanover square, still possessed by her descendants.
(c) This Alexander Davis *d.* of the plague 3 July 1665. He was a br. of Sir Thomas Davis, Lord Mayor in 1677, both being sons of John Davis, of London, Draper, by Eliz., da. and h. of Stephen Peacock and coheir of her mother, Elizabeth, sister and coheir of the celebrated Hugh Audley, the usurer. See pedigree (by E. Green, Rouge Dragon) in *Middx. and Herts N. and Q.*, vol. ii, p. 189.

V. 1732. SIR THOMAS GROSVENOR, Bart. [1622], of Eaton aforesaid, br. and h., *b.* 7 Dec. 1693, and *bap.* at Eccleston; matric. at Oxford (Bras. Coll.), 21 Oct. 1712. Alderman of Chester and M.P. for that city, 1727, till his death; *suc. to the Baronetcy*, 12 July 1732. He *d.* unm. of consumption, at Naples, 31 Jan. 1732/3, and was *bur.* 28 May 1733, at Eccleston. Will pr. June 1733.

VI. 1733. SIR ROBERT GROSVENOR, Bart. [1622], of Eaton aforesaid, br. and h., *b.* 7 and *bap.* 16 May 1695, at Eccleston; matric. at Oxford (Bras. Coll.), 21 Oct. 1712, aged 16; *suc. to the Baronetcy*, 31 Jan. 1732/3; admitted to Inner Temple, 1716; M.P. for Chester (in six Parls.), 1733 till his death; Mayor of that city, 1737. He *m.*, 21 May 1730, Jane, only surv. child of Thomas WARRE, of Swell Court and Shipton Beauchamp, Somerset, and of Sandhall, Hants. He *d.* 1 and was *bur.* 12 Aug. 1755, at Eccleston. Will pr. 1755. His widow was *bur.* 25 May 1791, at Eccleston, aged 86. Will pr. June 1791.

VII. 1755. SIR RICHARD GROSVENOR, Bart. [1622], of Eaton, aforesaid, s. and h., *b.* 18 June 1731; ed. at Oriel Coll., Oxford; *cr.* M.A., 2 July 1751 and D.C.L., 2 July 1754; M.P. for Chester, 1754-61; *suc. to the Baronetcy*, 1 Aug. 1755; Mayor of Chester, 1759. He was unmarried when, on 8 April 1761, he was *cr.* a Peer as BARON GROSVENOR OF EATON, co. Chester, being subsequently *cr.*, 5 July 1784, EARL GROSVENOR. In these peerages this *Baronetcy* then *merged* and still so continues, the 2d Earl and Baron and 8th Bart. being *cr.*, 13 Sep. 1831, MARQUESS OF WESTMINSTER, and the 3d Marquess, 4th Earl and Baron, and 10th Baronet, being *cr.*, 27 Feb. 1874, DUKE OF WESTMINSTER. See *Peerage*.

MOODY *or* MODY:
cr. 11 March 1621/2;
ex., presumably, 1661.

I. 1622. "HENRY MODY, of Garesdon, co. Wilts, Knt.," s. of Richard MOODY, of Lee and Whitchurch-cum-Milborne, Wilts, and of Garesdon aforesaid (*d.* 30 Nov. 1612, aged 70), by Christiana, da. and coheir of John BARWICK, of Wilcot, Wilts, was *b.* about 1582, being aged 30 and more in 1612; *Knighted* at Whitehall 18 March 1605/6; was Sheriff of Wilts, 1618-19; M.P. for Malmesbury, 1625, 1626, and 1628-29, and was *cr. a Bart.*, as above, 11 March 1621/2. He *m.*, 20 Jan. 1605/6, Deborah, da. of Walter DUNCH, of Avebury, Wilts, by Deborah, da. of James PILKINGTON, BISHOP OF DURHAM. He *d.* 23 April 1629, at Garesdon. Inq. p.m. 8 Car. I. Admon. 1 Feb. 1630/1. His widow, being a Nonconformist, emigrated in 1636, with her son, to Massachusetts, but in 1643 removed to the Dutch settlement in Long Island, where, at Gravensonde, she *d.* between Dec. 1654 and May 1659.(a)

II. 1629, to 1661. SIR HENRY MOODY, Bart. [1622], of Garesdon aforesaid, s. and h., *b.* about 1607; matric. at Oxford (Mag. Coll.), 2 Nov. 1621, aged 14; B.A., 7 Feb. 1623/4; *cr.* D.C.L.; *suc. to the Baronetcy*, 23 April 1629, and was aged 23 in 1632. His estate was sequestrated but discharged 28 Nov. 1646, he not being worth £200. He sold the estate of Garesdon, and emigrated to Massachusetts; was, in 1660, on an embassy to Virginia. He *d.* in debt, at the house of Col. Morrittson in Virginia, soon after 20 Sep. 1661, presumably unm., when the *Baronetcy*, in all probability, became *extinct*.(a) Admon. (now lost) Dec. 1662.

(a) See *N. and Q.*, 7th S., vol. v, p. 415. A discourse on "Lady Deborah Moody," by James W. Gerard, is printed by the New York Hist. Soc.

BARKER:
cr. 17 March 1621/2;
ex. 3 Jan. 1766.

I. 1622. "JOHN BARKER, of Grimston Hall, in Trimley [St. Martin's], co. Suffolk, Esq.," s. and h. of Sir Robert BARKER, K.B., of the same, by his 1st wife, Judith, da. of George STODDART, of Mottingham, co. Kent; suc. his father 8 Oct. 1618, and was *cr. a Bart.*, as above, 17 March 1621/2. He was Sheriff of Suffolk, 1634-35. He *m.* Frances, da. of Sir John JERMY, K.B., of Brightwell. co. Suffolk, by Margaret, da. and h. of Sir Thomas SAYE. She apparently *d.* before him. He *d.* 1652. His will dat. 11 May, pr. 17 June 1652.

II. 1652. SIR JOHN BARKER, Bart. [1622], of Grimston Hall aforesaid, s. and h., *suc. to the Baronetcy*, in 1652; was Sheriff of Suffolk, 1654-55. He *m.*, about 1654, Winifred, da. of Sir Philip PARKER, of Arwalton, co. Suffolk, by Dorothy, da. and h. of Sir Robert GAWDY. He *d.* 1664. Will pr. 1664. His widow *m.* (Lic. Vic. Gen., 15 Dec. 1665, he 32, bachelor, and she 30, widow), Anthony GAWDY, of St. Margaret's, Westm.

III. 1664. SIR JERMY BARKER, Bart. [1622], of Grimston Hall aforesaid, s. and h.; *suc. to the Baronetcy*, in 1664. He *m.* Winifred, but *d.* s.p. in 1665, and was *bur.* at Trimley. Admon. 5 May 1665 to his widow.

IV. 1665. SIR JOHN BARKER, Bart. [1622], of Grimston Hall aforesaid, br. and h.; *b.* about 1656; matric. at Oxford (Merton Coll.), 10 Feb. 1672/3, aged 18; *suc. to the Baronetcy* in 1665; was M.P. for Ipswich (six Parls.), 1680-81, 1685-87, and 1689-96. He *m.* (Lic. at Ipswich) Bridget, da. of Sir Nicholas BACON, K.B., of Shrubland, co. Suffolk. He *d.* July 1696, at Ipswich. Will pr. 1697. His widow *m.* (Lic. Fac. 4 Oct. 1698, he 30, bachelor) John ELLIS, of Gray's Inn, Barrister at Law.

V. 1696. SIR WILLIAM BARKER, Bart. [1622], of Ipswich and of Sproughton, co. Suffolk, only s. and h., *b.* about 1680; *suc. to the Baronetcy* in July 1696; was M.P. for Ipswich, 1708-10 and 1710-13; for Thetford, 1713-15; for Suffolk, 1722-27, and 1727 till death. He *m.* firstly, Mary, da. and h. of John BENCE, of Heveningham, co. Suffolk, by Catherine, da. and h. of Sir Thomas GLEMHAM, of Glemham. She *d.* 1 Jan. 1715/6. He *m.* secondly, 9 Feb. 1731, at St. Marylebone, Anne, widow of Edward SPENCER, of Rendlesham. He *d.* 23 July 1731. Will pr. Aug. 1731. His widow, by whom he had no issue, *d.* about 1760. Admon. as "of Sproughton, co. Suffolk, widow," 21 April 1760.

VI. 1731. SIR JOHN BARKER, Bart. [1622], of Sproughton aforesaid, s. and h., by 1st wife; *suc. to the Baronetcy*, 23 July 1731; Sheriff of Suffolk, 1742-43. He *m.*, 28 Oct. 1740, at Morden College (reg. at Charlton, co. Kent), Alice, sister and h. (1736) of Sir William FYTCHE, 3d Bart. [1688], of Eltham, co. Kent, da. of Sir Comport FYTCHE, 2d Bart., by Anne, da. of Sir Lumley ROBINSON, 2d Bart. [1682], of Kentwell, co. Suffolk. He *d.* 7 June 1757, and was *bur.* at Trimley. Will pr. 14 June 1757. The will of his widow pr. Nov. 1771.

VII. 1757, to 1766. SIR JOHN FYTCHE BARKER, Bart. [1622], of Sproughton aforesaid, only s. and h.; *b.* 25 July 1741; *suc. to the Baronetcy*, 7 June 1757. He *m.* Lucy, da. of Sir Richard LLOYD, of Hintlesham, co. Suffolk. He *d.* s.p. at Sproughton, 3 Jan. 1766, when the *Baronetcy* became *extinct*. Will dat. 10 Dec. 1762, pr. 26 Feb. 1766.(a) The admon. of his widow dat. Feb. 1785.

(a) In it he devises his lands, failing his issue, to his wife for life, with rem. to George Nassau (yst. son of Richard Savage Nassau, of Euston, co. Suffolk) in fee.

BUTTON:
cr. 18 March 1621/2;
ex. 29 Nov. 1712.

I. 1622. "WILLIAM BUTTON, of Alton, co. Wilts, Knt." s. and h. of William Button, of Alton aforesaid, and of Tockenham Court in Lyneham, Wilts, by Jane, da. of John LAMB, of that county, which William last named was br. and h. male of Sir Ambrose BUTTON, of Alton aforesaid (*d.* 1613), was *b.* about 1584; matric. at Oxford (Queen's Coll.), 13 Feb. 1600/1, aged 16; *Knighted* at Whitehall, 15 July 1605; was Sheriff of Wilts, 1611-12; M.P. for Morpeth, 1614, and for Wilts, 1628-29; was, possibly,(a) admitted to Gray's Inn, 2 Feb. 1617/18, and was *cr. a Bart.*, as above, 18 March 1621/2. Was a Royalist, and was fined £2,380 on 2 Jan. 1647. He *m.* Ruth, da. of Walter DUNCH, of Avebury, Wilts, by Deborah, da. of James PILKINGTON, BISHOP OF DURHAM. He *d.* 16 Jan. 1654/5, and was *bur.* at Wraxall, Wilts. M.I. Will dat. 29 Dec. 1654, pr. 10 March 1654/5.

II. 1655. SIR WILLIAM BUTTON, Bart. [1622], of Tockenham Court aforesaid, s. and h., aged 9 in 1623; *suc. to the Baronetcy*, 16 Jan. 1654/5. He *m.*, 6 April 1640, at Petrockstowe (Lic. 17 Aug. 1639), Anne (aged 4 in 1620), da. of Sir Henry ROLLE, of Stevenstone, Devon, by Anne, da. and coheir of Thomas DENNIS, of Holcombe. He *d.* s.p. 8 March 1659/60, and was *bur.* at Wraxall. M.I. Will dat. 6 March 1659/60, pr. Feb. 1661. His widow *d.* 4 Feb. 1665, and was *bur.* at Wraxall.

III. 1659. SIR ROBERT BUTTON, Bart. [1622], of Tockenham Court aforesaid, br. and h., *b.* 1622; matric. at Oxford (Exeter Coll.), 24 May 1639, aged 16; *suc. to the Baronetcy*, 8 March 1659; Sheriff of Wilts, 1670-71. He *m.* Eleanor, da. of William COMPTON, of Hartbury, co. Gloucester, by Eleanor, da. of Sir John MEUX. He *d.* s.p. about 1679. Will dat. 20 July 1677, pr. 1679. That of his widow pr. 1707.

IV. 1679? to 1712. SIR JOHN BUTTON, Bart. [1622], of Ogbourne St. George, Wilts, br. and h., *suc. to the Baronetcy* before 5 May 1679. He *m.* firstly, (—), da. of (—) NORTON, of co. Huntingdon. He *m.* secondly, Mary, da. of Thomas BENNET, of Salthorp, Wilts. She *d.* before him. He *d.* s.p., 29 Nov. 1712, and was *bur.* at Wroughton, Wilts, when the *Baronetcy* became *extinct*. Will dat. 30 Sep. 1707 to 5 April 1711, pr. 16 Dec. 1713.

GAGE:
cr. 26 March 1622,
afterwards, since 1744, VISCOUNTS GAGE OF CASTLE ISLAND [I].

I. 1622. "JOHN GAGE, of Firley (*i.e.*, Firle), co. Sussex, Esq.," s. and h. of Thomas GAGE,(b) by Elizabeth, da. of Sir Thomas GULDEFORD, of Hemstead, Kent, suc. his uncle, John GAGE, of Firle aforesaid, 1595, and was *cr. a Bart.*, as above, 26 March 1622. He *m.* (settl. 28 June 1611), Penelope,(c) widow of Sir George TRENCHARD, 3d da. and coheir of Thomas (D'ARCY), EARL RIVERS, by Mary, da. and coheir of Sir Thomas KITSON, of Hengrave, co. Suffolk. He *d.* 3 and was *bur.* 8 Oct. 1633, at West Firle. Will dat. 3 June, and pr. 5 Oct. 1633. His widow *m.* (for her 3d husband), 1642, Sir William HERVEY, of Ickworth, Suffolk, who *d.* 30 Sep. 1660, and was *bur.* there. She was *bur.* at Hengrave aforesaid. Will dat. 30 June 1656, pr. 2 July 1661.

(a) Probably, however, this was William Button, *Knighted* 15 Dec. 1606, the description being "London" in that Knighthood, as it is in this admission. He was brother to Thomas, the Arctic navigator, *Knighted* in 1616, being 2d s. of Miles Button, of Glamorgan. [*Ex inform.* W. D. Pink].

(b) He was s. of Sir Edward Gage, K.B., the s. and h. of the celebrated Sir John Gage, K.G., both of Firle aforesaid.

(c) She was aged only 17 at the time of her second marriage. She is said to have promised her three husbands to marry them all in their turn.

II. 1633. SIR THOMAS GAGE, Bart. [1622], of Firle aforesaid, s. and h.; *suc. to the Baronetcy*, 3 Oct. 1633. He *m.* about 1635, Mary, 1st da. and coheir of John CHAMBERLAIN, of Sherborne Castle, Oxon, by Katherine, da. of Francis PLOWDEN. He *d.* 2 July 1654, and was *bur.* at Firle. Will pr. 1654. His widow *m.*, before May 1661, Sir Henry GORING, 2d Bart. [1622], of Burton, co. Sussex (who *d.* May 1683), and *d.* 1694, being *bur.* at Burton aforesaid.

III. 1654. SIR THOMAS GAGE, Bart. [1622], of Firle aforesaid, s. and h.; *suc. to the Baronetcy*, 2 July 1654. He *d.* unm. 22 Nov. 1660, "in the flower of his age," at Rome, and was *bur.* in the chapel of the English College there. M.I. Admon. 11 May 1661 to his mother, Dame Mary Goring.

IV. 1660. SIR JOHN GAGE, Bart. [1622], of Firle aforesaid, br. and h., *b.* about 1642; *suc. to the Baronetcy*, 22 Nov. 1660; Sheriff of Sussex, 1687-88. He *m.* firstly, Mary, da. and sole h. of Robert MIDDLEMORE, of Edgbaston, co. Warwick, by Henrietta-Maria, da. of Sir Maurice DRUMMOND. She *d.* s.p.m., 28 July 1686. He *m.* secondly, Mary, da. of Sir William STANLEY, 1st Bart. [1661], of Hooton, Cheshire, by Charlotte, da. of Richard (MOLYNEUX), 1st VISCOUNT MOLYNEUX OF MARYBOROUGH [I.]. He *d.* 27 May 1699, in his 58th year.

V. 1699. SIR JOHN GAGE, Bart. [1622], of Firle aforesaid, s. and h. by 2d wife. He *d.* Jan. 1699/700, aged about 8 years.

VI. 1700. SIR THOMAS GAGE, Bart. [1622], of Firle aforesaid, br. and h. He *d.* unm., in France, Oct. 1713, in his 20th year, and was *bur.* at Blaye, in Guienne.

VII. 1713. SIR WILLIAM GAGE, Bart. [1622], of Firle aforesaid, br., and h., *b.* 1695. He conformed to the Church of England, and was M.P. for Seaford (four Parls.), 1727 till his death; was *cr.* K.B. at the re-institution of that order, being installed 11 July 1725. He *d.* unm., 23 April 1744.(a) Will pr. 1744.

VIII. 1744. THOMAS (GAGE), 1st VISCOUNT GAGE OF CASTLE ISLAND [I.], and 8th Bart. [1622], cousin and h. male, being s. and h. of Joseph GAGE, of Sherborne Castle, co. Oxford, by Elizabeth, da. of Sir George PENRUDDOCK, which Joseph was 4th s. of the 2d Bart. He was *cr.* VISCOUNT GAGE OF CASTLE ISLAND, co. Kerry [I.], 14 Sep. 1720, and *suc. to the Baronetcy*, 28 April 1744, which accordingly then *merged* in this peerage, and still so continues. See *Peerage*.

GORING, *or* GORINGE:
cr. 14 May 1622;
ex. 29 Feb. 1723/4.

I. 1622. "WILLIAM GORINGE, Esq., s. and h. ap. of Henry GORINGE,(b) of Burton, co. Sussex, Knt.," being such son by Elenor, da. of Sir William KINGSMILL, of Hants, was v.p., *cr. a Bart.*, as above, 14 May 1622. He suc. his father, 16 July 1626. M.P. for Sussex, 1628-29. He *m.* Eleanor or Bridget, da. and h. of Sir Edward FRANCIS. He was *bur.* 25 Feb. 1657/8, at Burton. Admon. 20 June 1658.

(a) His two sisters, of the half blood (daughters of the 4th Bart., by his 1st wife), became his coheirs; (1) Mary, *m.* Sir John SHELLEY, 3d Bart.; (2) Bridget, *m.* Thomas (BELASYSE), 3d VISCOUNT FAUCONBERG.

(b) This Henry was grandson of another Sir Henry Goring, of Burton (*d.* 1594), who was uncle of George, Baron Goring and Earl of Norwich, and who (by his second son, Edward), was great grandfather of Henry Goring, of Highden, in Washington, co. Sussex, the 2d Bart. in succession to a Baronetcy, conferred in 1678, on Sir James Bowyer.

II. 1658. SIR HENRY GORING, Bart. [1622], of Burton aforesaid, s. and h.; was fined, as a Royalist, £500, on 24 Oct. 1645; *suc. to the Baronetcy* in Feb. 1657/8. He *m.* Mary, widow of Sir Thomas GAGE, 2d Bart. [1622], of Firle, da. and coheir of John CHAMBERLAINE, of Sherborne Castle, Oxon, by Katherine, da. of Francis PLOWDEN. He *d.* 8 June 1671, aged 52. Admon. 8 Sep. 1671. His widow *d.* 1694, and was *bur.* at Burton. Her admon., 23 May 1715.

III. 1671, to 1724. SIR WILLIAM GORING, Bart. [1622], of Burton aforesaid, s. and h., *b.* about 1659; *suc. to the Baronetcy*, 8 June 1671. He *m.* Dorothy, widow of Philip DRAYCOT, da. of Edmund PLOWDEN, of Plowden, co. Salop, by Penelope, da. and coheir of Sir Maurice DRUMMOND. He, who was a Roman Catholic, *d.* s.p. 29 Feb. 1723/4, aged 65, when the *Baronetcy* became *extinct*.(a). Will dat. 22 Jan. 1721, pr. 17 March 1723/4.

NORTON:
cr. 18 May 1622.
ex. 9 Jan. 1686/7.

I. 1622. "RICHARD NORTON, of Rootherfeild [*i.e.*, Rotherfield in East Tisted], co. Southampton, Knt.," s. and h. of Sir Richard NORTON, of the same (will dat. 31 Aug. 1610, pr. 12 Nov. 1611), by Mabell, da. of Henry BECHER, Alderman of London, was *b.* 1582; matric. at Oxford (Queen's Coll.), 14 Oct. 1597, aged 15; entered Middle Temple, 1602; *Knighted* at Hampton Court, 10 Jan. 1610/1; M.P. for Petersfield, 1621-22; and was *cr. a Bart.* as above, 18 May 1622; Sheriff of Hants, 1596-97 and 1613-14. He was a sufferer in the royal cause, and was imprisoned in July 1644, and fined £1,000, reduced to £500. He *m.* Amy, da. of Thomas BILSON, BISHOP OF WINCHESTER (1597-1616). He *d.* before 27 Aug. 1645. Admon. 30 May, 1661. His widow *d.* before 1655. Her admon. 19 Nov. 1655, to her son, Sir John Norton.

II. 1645? SIR RICHARD NORTON, Bart. [1622], of Rotherfield, 1st s. and h.,(b) *b.* 1619; matric. at Oxford (Mag. Coll.), 1 March 1635/6, aged 17; *suc. to the Baronetcy* in 1645, and compounded for his delinquency, 28 Aug. 1645, by a fine of £100. He *m.* Elizabeth. He *d.* s.p.m.(c) Will dat. 26 July and pr. 5 Oct. 1652. His widow *m.* as his 3d wife (Lic. Vic. Gen., 11 Feb. 1660/1, he 50, widower, and she 30, widow), Sir Humphrey BENNET, of Petersfield, Hants, who *d.* Dec. 1667.

III. 1652, to 1687. SIR JOHN NORTON, Bart. [1622], of Rotherfield aforesaid, br. and h. male, *b.* 1620; matric. at Oxford (Corp. Coll.), 23 June 1637, aged 17; adm. to Middle Temple, 1641; *suc. to the Baronetcy* in 1652; M.P. for Hants, 1661-68, and for Petersfield, 1678-87. He, with his father, was a sufferer in the Royal cause. He *m.* before Sep. 1670, Dorothy, da. and h. of Thomas MARCH, of Ely, co. Camb., who *d.* 1670. He *d.* s.p. 9 Jan. 1686/7, aged 67, and was *bur.* at East Tisted, when the *Baronetcy* became *extinct*. M.I. Will dat. 30 Dec. 1686, pr. 14 Feb. 1686/7. The will of his widow (who directs her burial to be at East Tisted, Hants) dat. 22 Dec. 1701, pr. 25 Nov. 1703.

(a) The Burton estate (which had been in the family of Goring for eight generations) passed to the Biddulph family, descendants of his sister Anne, by Richard Biddulph, of Biddulph, co. Stafford.

(b) His sister, Mabella, *m.*, 14 Oct. 1656, at St. Margaret's, Westm. (a match which has given rise to great confusion in the Norton pedigree), Sir Henry NORTON, 2d Bart. [I. 1624], who, apparently, was no blood relation. Both were living 1661.

(c) Elizabeth, his posthumous da. and h., *m.* (Lic. Vic. Gen. 20 May 1674) Francis Paulet, of Awport (aged 40 in 1686, when he recorded his pedigree), and had issue. He was grandson of the 4th and grandfather of the 12th Marquess of Winchester.

COURTEN, *or* COURTENE:
cr. 18 May 1622;
ex. (—) 1624.

I. 1622 to 1624. "PETER COURTEN, of Addington, *alias* Aunton, co. Worcester, Esqr.," s. and h. ap. of Sir William COURTEN,(a) of St. Andrew's Hubbard, London (who *d.* May 1636), by his 1st wife Margaret, da. of Peter CROMLYN, of Flanders, was aged 22 in 1620, and was, v.p., *cr. a Bart.*, as above, 18 May 1622. He was, subsequently,(b) 22 Feb. 1623/4, *Knighted* at Whitehall. He *m.* Jane, da. of Sir John STANHOPE, of Elvaston, co. Derby, by his 2d wife, Catherine, da. of Thomas TRENTHAM, of Rocester, co. Stafford. He *d.* s.p.m. and v.p. 1624, when the *Baronetcy* became *extinct.* Will pr. 1624. His widow *m.* as his second wife, Francis (ANNESLEY), 1st VISCOUNT VALENTIA [I.], who *d.* Nov. 1660. She *d.* 12 and was *bur.* 15 March 1683, at St. Mary's, Nottingham.

LEVENTHORPE:
cr. 30 May 1622;
ex. 30 Aug. 1680.

I. 1622. "JOHN LEVENTHORPE, of Shingle [*i.e.*, Shingey] Hall, co. Herts, Knt.," s. and h. of Edward LEVENTHORPE, of Shingey Hall, in Sawbridgeworth aforesaid, by Mary, da. of Sir Henry PARKER (s. and h. ap. of Henry, LORD MORLEY), suc. his father 8 Oct. 1566, being then aged six years; was *Knighted* at Theobalds, 7 May 1603; Sheriff of Herts, 1593-94 and 1607-08; and was *cr. a Bart.*, as above, 30 May 1622. He *m.* Joan, 1st da. of Sir John BROGRAVE, of Hamells, in Braughing, Herts, Attorney Gen. of the Duchy of Lancaster, by Margaret, da. of Simeon STEWARD, of Lackenheath, Suffolk. He *d.* 23, and was *bur.* 25 Sep. 1625, at Sawbridgeworth. Will pr. 1626. His widow was *bur.* there 1 March 1627/8. Her admon. 24 June 1650.

II. 1625. SIR THOMAS LEVENTHORPE, Bart. [1622], of Shingey Hall aforesaid, 2d but 1st surv. s. and h., *bap.* 18 May 1592 at Sawbridgeworth; *suc. to the Baronetcy*, 25 Sep. 1625. He *m.* Dorothy, da. of Sir Giles ALINGTON, of Horseheath, co. Cambridge, by Dorothy, da. of Thomas (CECIL), EARL OF EXETER. He *d.* 30 April, and was *bur.* 2 May 1636 at Sawbridgeworth. Admon. 20 Nov. 1636 and 19 June 1650. His widow, who was *bap.* 9 Jan. 1603 at Horseheath, *m.* (—) HOLFORD, of Cheshire. She was *bur.* 26 Sep. 1643 at Sawbridgeworth. Admon. 29 Sep. 1654.

III. 1636. SIR JOHN LEVENTHORPE, Bart. [1622], of Shingey Hall aforesaid, 1st s. and h., *bap.* 30 July 1629, at Sawbridgeworth; *suc. to the Baronetcy*, 30 April 1636. He *d.* unm. of the small pox, in Chancery lane, London, 29 Nov. and was *bur.* 2 Dec. 1649, at Sawbridgeworth.

IV. 1649. SIR THOMAS LEVENTHORPE, Bart. [1622], of Shingey Hall aforesaid, br. and h.; *b.* 30 Nov. and *bap.* 7 Dec. 1635, at Sawbridgeworth; *suc. to the Baronetcy*, 29 Nov. 1649. He *m.*, 2 Jan. 1654/5, Mary, da. and coheir of Sir Capell BEDELL, Bart. [so *cr.* 1622], of Hamerton, co. Huntingdon, by Alice, da. of Sir Henry FANSHAWE, of Ware, Herts. He *d.* s.p.m.,(a) being killed by a kick from a horse, at Elvaston, co. Derby, 27 July and was *bur.* 2 Aug. 1679, at Sawbridgeworth. His widow *d.* in London, 30 April and was *bur.* 2 May 1683, at Sawbridgeworth.

(a) This William was s. of William Courten of Leye, in Flanders, who emigrated thence owing to the Duke of Alva's persecution. He entered his ped. in the Visit. of London 1634.

(b) See p. 18, note "e," *sub* "Tollemache," for several such Knighthoods.

V. 1679, to 1680. SIR CHARLES LEVENTHORPE, Bart. [1622], uncle and h. male; *bap.* 15 Sep. 1594, at Sawbridgeworth; was in Holy Orders; Rector of White Roding, co. Essex, 1617. He *d.* unm. 30 Aug. 1680, when the *Baronetcy* became *extinct.*

BEDELL:
cr. 3 June 1622;
ex. Dec. 1643.

I. 1622, to 1643. "CAPELL BEDELL, of Hamerton, co. Huntingdon, Esq.," only s. and h. of Sir Thomas BEDELL, of the same (*bur.* there 11 July 1613), by Winifred, da. of Sir Arthur CAPELL, of Hadham, Herts, was aged 11 years in 1613 (*Visit. Hunts*), and was *cr. a Bart.*, as above, 3 June 1622. M.P. for Hertford, 1626, and for co. Huntingdon, 1628-29, and April to May 1640; Sheriff of co. Cambridge and co. Huntingdon, 1632-33. He *m.*, in or before 1623, Alice, sister of Thomas, 1st VISCOUNT FANSHAWE OF DROMORE [I.], da. of Sir Henry FANSHAWE, of Ware Park, Herts. by Elizabeth, da. of Thomas SMYTHE, of Ostenhanger, co. Kent. He *d.* s.p.m., and was *bur.* 14 Dec. 1643, at Hamerton, when the *Baronetcy* became *extinct.* Admon. 28 May 1646, and 23 Dec. 1663. His widow, who was *bap.* 3 June 1602, at Dronfield, co. Derby, was *bur.* 12 Jan. 1666, at Hamerton. Admon. 6 April 1667.

DARELL:
cr. 13 June 1622;
ex. in or before 1657.

I. 1622, to 1657? "JOHN DARELL, of West Woodhey, co. Berks, Esq.," s. of Thomas Darell, of Hungerford in that County (which Thomas was 2d s. of Sir Edward Darell, of Littlecote, Wilts), was *cr. a Bart.*, as above, 13 June 1622. He was Sheriff of Berks, 1625-26. He *m.* firstly, Anne, da. of Sir Thomas CHAMBERLAIN, Justice of the Court of King's Bench, by Elizabeth, da. of Sir George FERMOR. He *m.* secondly, Anne, da. of William YOUNG, of East Woodhey, Hants, "Ignobilis." He, who was living 1643, at Barton Court, Berks, *d.* s.p.m. in or before 1657, and was *bur.* at Kentbury, Berks, when the *Baronetcy* became extinct.(b) Admon. 17 June 1657. His widow *m.* William SANDYS, who survived her. Her admon., as "of Edmonton, Midx.," 6 Sep. 1660.

WILLIAMS:
cr. 15 June 1622;
ex. 1695-97.

I. 1622. "WILLIAM WILLIAMS, of Vaynoll, co. Carnarvon, Esq.," s. and h. of Thomas WILLIAMS(c) of the same, by Jane, da. of William STANLEY, of Hooton, co. Chester; was *cr. a Bart.*, as above, 15 June 1622.

(a) Mary, his da. and h., *m.*, 15 June 1672, John Coke, of Melbourne, co. Derby, whose son sold Shingey Hall (which had been for ten generations in the family of Leventhorpe) to Ralph Freeman.

(b) West Woodhey passed into the family of RUDYERD, and thence into that of SLOPER.

(c) He was 2d br. of William Williams, of Cochwillan, whose s. Edmund Williams, of Conway, was father of John Williams, Archbishop of York, Lord Keeper of the Great Seal, and of Robert Williams, the father of Griffith Williams, of Penrhyn, *cr. a Bart.* 1661.

He *m.* firstly, his cousin, Ellen, da. of William WILLIAMS, of Cochwillan (s. and h. of his uncle, William WILLIAMS, of the same), by his 1st wife, Agnes, da. of John WYNN ap Meredith, of Gwydyr. He *m.* secondly, Dorothy, da. of Edward DYMOCK, of Willington, co. Flint. She, apparently, *d.* before 24 May 1625. He *d.* about 1630, and was *bur.* at Bangor. Will dat. 24 May 1625, pr. 20 May 1630.

II. 1630? SIR THOMAS WILLIAMS, Bart. [1622], of Vaynol aforesaid, s. and h., *suc. to the Baronetcy* about 1630. He *m.* Katharine, da. of Robert WYNNE.

III. 1650? SIR WILLIAM WILLIAMS, Bart., [1622], of Vaynol aforesaid, s. and h., *suc. to the Baronetcy* on his father's death. He *m.* firstly, Margaret, da. of John WYNNE, of Mell. He *m.* secondly, Margaret, da. and h. of Richard JONES, of Castle March. He *d.* about 1659. Will pr. 1659.

IV. 1659? SIR GRIFFITH WILLIAMS, Bart. [1622], of Vaynol aforesaid, s. and h., *suc. to the Baronetcy* on his father's death. He *m.*(a) Penelope, da. of Thomas (BULKELEY), 1st VISCOUNT BULKELEY OF BEAUMARIS [I.] He *d.* about 1663. Will pr. 1663.

V. 1663? SIR THOMAS WILLIAMS, Bart. [1622], of Vaynol aforesaid, s. and h., *suc. to the Baronetcy* about 1663. He *d.* a minor and unm.

VI 1670? to 1696. SIR WILLIAM WILLIAMS, Bart., of Vaynol aforesaid, br. and h., *suc. to the Baronetcy* on the death of his brother. He was M.P. for co. Carnarvon (in three Parls.), 1689 till his death. He *m.* Ellen, da. of Robert (BULKELEY), 2d VISCOUNT BULKELEY OF BEAUMARIS [I.]. He *d.* s.p. about 1696, when the *Baronetcy* became *extinct.* Will dat. 25 June 1695, pr. 2 Feb. 1696/7.

ASHBY:
cr. 18 June 1622;
ex. 23 Dec. 1623.

I. 1622, to 1623. "FRANCIS ASHBY, of Harfield [*i.e.*, Harefield], co. Midx., Knt.," s. and h. of Sir Robert ASHBY,(b) of Breakspears, in Harefield aforesaid, by Dorothy, da. of Francis HAYDON, of the Grove, in Watford, Herts, was *bap.* 10 Oct. 1595, at Harefield; matric. at Oxford (Corpus Coll.), 9 Feb. 1609/10, aged 16; B.A. (Trin. Coll.), 2 July 1612; was of Gray's Inn, 1607; *Knighted*, 2 Sep. 1617, at Ashby de la Zouch; suc. his father, 20 March 1617/18; and was *cr. a Bart.*, as above, 18 June 1622. He *m.* Joane. He *d.* s.p.m. 23 Dec. 1623, aged 31, and was *bur.* 23 Feb. 1622/4, at Harefield, when the *Baronetcy* became *extinct.* M.I. Will dat. 23 Feb. and pr. 7 March 1623/4. His widow was *bur.* 17 March 1634/5, at Harefield aforesaid.

ASHLEY:
cr. 3 July 1622;
ex. 13 Jan. 1627/8.

I. 1622, to 1628. "ANTHONY ASHLEY, of St. Giles', Wimborn, co. Dorset, Knt.," s. and h. of Anthony Ashley, of Damerham, by Dorothy, da of John LYTE, of Lyte's Carey, Somerset, inherited eventually the family estates; was M.P. for Tavistock, 1588-89, and for Old Sarum,

(a) No such match appears in the Bulkeley pedigree as given in Lodge's *Irish Peerage* (1789), vol. v, pp. 26-27.

(b) See pedigree in *Coll. Top. et Gen.*, vol. v, pp. 128-141.

1593-94; Secretary to the Council of War; Clerk of the Privy Council, *temp.* Eliz.; *Knighted*, at Cadiz, June 1596; Sheriff of Dorset, 1619-20, and was *cr. a Bart.*, as above, 3 July 1622. He *m.* firstly, Jane, widow of Thomas COKAYNE, of Ravenston Grange in Bradburne, co. Derby (*d.* s.p. 15 Jan. 1587), da. and h. of Philip OKEOVER, of Okeover, co. Stafford, by Margaret, da. of William DETHICK, of Newhall, co. Derby. He *m.* secondly, Philippa, da. of (—) WESTON, but by her had no issue. He *d.* s.p.m. 13 Jan. 1627/8, aged 86, when the *Baronetcy* became *extinct.*(a) Will dat. 22 Aug. 1625, pr. 1 Feb. 1627/8 and 27 Nov. 1635. The will of his widow (who directs her burial to be at West Horsley) dat. 23 April, pr. 20 June 1674.

COOPER, *or* COUPER:
cr. 4 July 1622,
afterwards, since 1661, BARONS ASHLEY OF WIMBORNE ST. GILES,
and, since 1672, EARLS OF SHAFTESBURY.

I. 1622. "JOHN COUPER, of Rockbourne, co. Southampton, Esq.," s. and h. of Sir John COOPER, of the same, by Margaret, da. of Anthony SKUTT, of Stanton Drew, co. Somerset, suc. his father, 24 Nov. 1610, and was *cr. a Bart.*, as above, 4 July 1622. He was M.P. for Poole, 1625 and 1628-29. He *m.* firstly, Anne, da. and h. of Sir Anthony ASHLEY, Bart. [so *cr.* 1622], of Wimborne St. Giles, Dorset, by his 1st wife, Jane, da. and h. of Philip OKEOVER, of Okeover, co. Stafford. She *d.* 20 July 1628, a few months after her father. He *m.* secondly, Mary, widow of Sir Charles MORRISON, of Cashiobury, Herts, 2d da. and coheir of Baptiat (HICKS), 1st VISCOUNT CAMPDEN, by Elizabeth, da. of Richard MAY, of London. He *d.* 23 March 1630/1, and was *bur.* at Rockbourne. Inq. p.m. at Basingstoke, 11 May 1631. His widow *m.* (for her 3d husband) Sir Richard ALFORD.

II. 1631. SIR ANTHONY ASHLEY COOPER, Bart. [1622], of Wimborne St. Giles, etc., aforesaid, s. and h., *b.* 22 July 1621, at Wimborne; *suc. to the Baronetcy* and to estates, valued at £7,000 a year, 23 March 1630/1; matric. at Oxford (Exeter Coll.) 24 March 1636/7; admitted to Lincoln's Inn, 18 Feb. 1638; M.P. for Tewkesbury, April to May 1640; for Downton, Dec. 1640; for Wilts (in five Parls.), 1653-60; Sheriff of Dorset, 1643-44; Sheriff of Wilts (nom. by Parl.), 1646-48, having declared for the Royal Cause, 1643, but for that of Parl. 1644; was at the taking of Wareham 20 Aug. 1644, being made Field Marshal and Com. in Chief of the Parl. forces in Dorset, when he effected the capture of Sturminster and Shaftesbury; Councillor of State, 1653-60, to the Protector, whose measures, however, he, in 1656, opposed, assuming then the lead of the Presbyterians and Republicans; was first Commissioner of the Tower of London, 1659-60, which he held against Gen. Lambert, and was one of the twelve deputed, 7 May 1660, to invite the return of the King, by whom he was made P.C., Col. of Reg. of Horse, and, in 1661, a Peer. He *m.* firstly, 25 Feb. 1639, Margaret, da. of Thomas (Coventry), 1st BARON COVENTRY OF AYLESBOROUGH, sometime Lord Keeper of the Great Seal, by his 2d wife Elizabeth, da. of John ALDERSEY, of Spurston, Cheshire. She *d.* s.p. 11 Sep. 1646. He *m.* secondly, 25 April 1650, at St. Anne's, Blackfriars, London, Frances, da. of David (Cecil) 3d EARL OF EXETER, by Elizabeth, da. of John (EGERTON), 1st EARL OF BRIDGWATER. She *d.* 1654. He *m.* thirdly, 30 Aug. 1655, at St. Paul's, Covent Garden, Margaret, da. of William (SPENCER), 2d BARON SPENCER OF WORMLEIGHTON, by Penelope, 1st da. of Henry (WRIOTHESLEY), 3d EARL OF SOUTHAMPTON. She (who was *bap.* 19 July 1627, at Brington, co. Northampton) was living when he was *cr.*, 20 April 1661, BARON ASHLEY OF WIMBORNE ST. GILES', co. Dorset, being, subsequently, *cr.* 23 April 1672, EARL OF SHAFTESBURY. In these peerages *this Baronetcy* then *merged* and still so continues. See *Peerage*, under "Shaftesbury."

(a) Anne, his only da. and h. by his first wife, *m.* Sir John COOPER, 1st Bart. [1622], and was mother of Anthony Ashley (COOPER), EARL OF SHAFTESBURY, who inherited the estates of the Ashley family.

PRIDEAUX:
cr. 17 July 1622;
ex. 11 Feb. 1875.

I. 1622. "EDMUND PRIDEAUX, of Netherton [in the parish of Farway], co. Devon, Esq.," 2d s. of Roger PRIDEAUX, of Soldon, in that county, by Philippa, da. of Roger YORKE, Serjeant at Law (being yr. br. of Sir Nicholas PRIDEAUX, of Soldon aforesaid), was *b.* about 1555; was a barrister of some repute; Autumn Reader of the Inner Temple, 1598; Treasurer, 1609; Double Reader, 1616; and, having acquired considerable estates in Devon and Cornwall, was *cr. a Bart.*, as above, 17 July 1622. He *m.* firstly, in or before 1590, Bridget, 7th da. of Sir John CHICHESTER, of Raleigh, Devon, by Gertrude, da. of Sir William COURTENAY, of Powderham. She *d.* s.p.m. He *m.* secondly, in or before 1596, Catharine, da. of Piers EDGCUMBE, of Mount Edgcumbe, by Margaret, da. of Sir Andrew LUTTRELL, of Dunster, co. Somerset. He *m.* thirdly, 22 July 1606, at Ugborough, Devon, Mary, widow of Arthur FOWELL, of Fowelscombe, Devon, da. of Richard REYNELL, of East Ogwell, by Agnes, da. of John SOUTHCOTT, of Bovey Tracey, both in that county. He *d.* at Netherton, 28 Feb., and was *bur.* 12 March 1628/9, at Farway, Devon, aged 74. M.I. Inq. p.m., 5 Charles I. The will of his widow, dat. 30 July 1630, was pr. 15 Jan. 1630/1, in the Probate Registry at Exeter.

II. 1629. SIR PETER PRIDEAUX, Bart. [1622], of Netherton aforesaid, 1st surv. s. and h.(a), by 2d wife, *b.* 1596; aged 24 in 1620; *suc. to the Baronetcy*, 28 Feb. 1628/9; M.P. for Honiton, 1661; Sheriff of Devon, 1662. He *m.* Susanna, sister of John, 1st BARON POULETT OF HINTON, da. of Sir Anthony POULETT, of Hinton, co. Somerset, by Catharine, da. of Henry (NORRIS), LORD NORRIS. She was *bur.* 10 Oct. 1673, at Farway. He was *bur.* there 3 Feb. 1681/2. Will dat. 21 Jan., pr. 15 Feb. 1681/2, at Exeter.

III. 1682. SIR PETER PRIDEAUX, Bart. [1622], of Netherton aforesaid, 4th but 1st surv. s. and h., *bap.* 13 July 1626, at Farway; M.P. for Liskeard, 1661-79, and for St. Mawes, 1685-87; *suc. to the Baronetcy* in Feb. 1681/2. He *m.*, 17 Nov. 1645, at Kilkhampton, co. Cornwall, Elizabeth, sister of John, 1st EARL OF BATH, da. of the famous Sir Bevill GRANVILLE, or GRENVILLE, of Stow, co. Cornwall, by Grace, da. of Sir George SMITH, of Exeter. She (to whom by Royal lic., 27 Aug. 1675, the precedency of the da. of an Earl was granted) was *bur.* 28 May 1692, at Farway. He *d.* 22 and was *bur.* 24 Nov. 1705, at Farway, aged 79. M.I. Will dat. 11 Sep. and pr. 29 Dec. 1705.

IV. 1705. SIR EDMUND PRIDEAUX, Bart. [1622], of Netherton aforesaid, 1st s. and h.; *b.* 1647; matric. at Oxford (Oriel Coll.), 18 April 1663, aged 16; M.P. for Tregony, 1713-20; Barrister (Inner Temple), 1680; *suc. to the Baronetcy*, 22 Nov. 1705. He *m.* firstly (Lic. Fac. 23 Nov. 1672), Susanna, widow of John AUSTIN, of Derhams, near Barnet, Midx., 1st da. of James WINSTANLEY, of Braunston, co. Leicester. She was *bur.* 29 Nov. 1687, at Great Stanmore, Midx. Admon. 8 Nov. 1687. He *m.* secondly, in or before 1695, Elizabeth, da. and coheir of the Hon. George SAUNDERSON, of Thoresby, co. Lincoln (3d s. of Nicholas, 1st VISCOUNT CASTLETON, [I.]), by his (—) wife. She was *bur.* 14 May 1702, at Great Stanmore. Admon. 22 May 1702. He *m.* thirdly, 5 Sep. 1710, at St. Andrew's Plymouth, Mary, widow of Sir John ROGERS, 1st Bart. [1699], of Wisdom, da. of Spencer VINCENT, Alderman of London. By her he had no issue. He *d.* 6 Feb. and was *bur.* 1 March 1719/20, at Great Stanmore. Will dat. 24 Jan. 1716/7, pr. 4 Jan. 1720/1. His widow *m.*, 31 Jan. 1722/3, at St. Martin's in the Fields, for her third husband, John ARUNDELL, Col. in the army. She *d.* 12 March following, aged about 80. Will dat. 10 and pr. 21 March 1723/4, by her husband and universal legatee.

(a) His next br., Edmund Prideaux (*b.* Sept. 1601), Attorney Gen., 1649-59, was *cr. a Baronet* by Cromwell, 31 May 1658, but *d.* next year, 19 Aug. 1659. He left male issue, who, however, never assumed the title.

V. 1720. SIR EDMUND PRIDEAUX, Bart. [1622], of Netherton aforesaid, 1st s. and h., by 1st wife; *b.* 13 and *bap.* 21 Nov. 1675, at St. Giles' in the Fields; matric. at Oxford (Exeter Coll.), 19 May 1694; *suc. to the Baronetcy*, 6 Feb. 1619/20. He *m.* firstly (settlm. 20 and 21 Feb. 1709/10), Mary, da. of Samuel REYNARDSON, of Hillingdon, Middlesex. She *d.* 12 and was *bur.* 22 Aug. 1712, at St. Giles' in the Fields. He *m.* secondly (Lic. 6 May 1714), Anne, da. of Philip HAWKINS, of Pennans, co. Cornwall. He *d.* s.p.m.s. 26 Feb. and was *bur.* 22 March 1728/9, in Westm. Abbey, aged 53. Will dat. 3 April 1722, pr. 3 May 1729 and 10 Oct. 1743. His widow *d.* 10 May 1741. Will dat. 20 Feb. 1738/9, pr. 14 Jan. 1741/2.

VI. 1729. SIR JOHN PRIDEAUX, of Netherton aforesaid, br. of the half blood and h. male, being s. (only s. by the 2d wife) of the 4th Bart.; *b.* 17 and *bap.* 24 June 1695, at St. James', Westm.; *suc. to the Baronetcy*, 26 Feb. 1728/9. He *m.*, 4 Feb. 1718/9, at St. Anne's, Blackfriars, London, Anne, 1st da. of John (VAUGHAN), 1st VISCOUNT LISBURNE [I.], by Mallet, 3d da. of John (WILMOT), 2d EARL OF ROCHESTER. He was *bur.* 29 Aug. 1766, at Farway. Will dat. 13 March 1763, pr. 24 Dec. 1766. His widow *d.* 5 Dec. 1767. Will dat. 11 Feb. 1767. pr. 4 Nov. 1770.

VII. 1766. SIR JOHN WILMOT PRIDEAUX, Bart. [1622], of Netherton aforesaid, grandson and h., being s. and h. of General John PRIDEAUX, by Elizabeth, da. of Edward Rolt, and sister of Sir Edward BAYNTUM-ROLT, 1st Bart. [1762], which John last named, was s. and h. ap. of the late Bart., and *d.* v.p., being slain at the siege of Niagara, 19 July 1759, aged 38. He was *b.* 13 Feb. and *bap.* 6 March 1747/8, at St. Geo. Han. sq., and *suc. to the Baronetcy*, 29 Aug. 1766; was an officer in the Army, 1771. He *m.* firstly, 4 June 1778 (Lic. Lond.), at St. James' Westm., Harriet Webb, of that parish. She *d.* s.p. He *m.* secondly, 28 Jan. 1791, at Farway aforesaid, Anne Phœbe, da. of William PRIDDLE, of that place. She *d.* 2 Sep. 1793, aged 28. M.I. at Farway. He *m.* thirdly, 19 May 1804, at Farway, Sarah, widow of (—) ELLIS, da. of (—) SMITH, of that place. He *d.* 4 and was *bur.* 10 March 1826 at Farway, aged 72. M.I. His widow *d.* 22 and was *bur.* 27 Sep. 1851, at Sidbury, Devon, aged 79.

VIII. 1826. SIR JOHN WILMOT PRIDEAUX, Bart. [1622], of Netherton aforesaid, s. and h. by 2d wife; *b.* 29 Sep. 1791. Captain in the East India Company's service, and served with distinction; *suc. to the Baronetcy*, 4 March 1826. He *d.* unm. at Calcutta, 13 May 1833. M.I. at Farway.

IX. 1833, to 1875. SIR EDMUND SAUNDERSON PRIDEAUX, Bart. [1622], of Netherton aforesaid, br. of the whole blood and h. He was *b.* 17 Jan. and *bap.* 8 April 1793 at Farway aforesaid; was sometime an officer in the Army, retiring as Major; *suc. to the Baronetcy*, 13 May 1833; Hon. Col. of the Exeter and South Devon Volunteer Rifles, 1862. He *m.* firstly, 19 Jan. 1832, at Awliscombe, Devon, Frances Mary Anne, 3d da. of Rev. William Edward FITZ THOMAS, of Awliscombe, by Anna Maria, da. of William HOLLAND, M.D., of Retford, Notts, and of Hinckley, co. Leicester. She, who was *b.* 15 Jan. 1814, and *bap.* at Kelvedon, Essex, *d.* 1 and was *bur.* 9 June 1836, at Farway. M.I. He *m.* secondly, 29 April 1841, at Sidmouth, Caroline, da. of Rev. James BERNARD, or BARNARD, Rector of Comb Flory. She *d.* 3 and was *bur.* 10 Aug. following, at Farway, aged 45. M.I. Will pr. Nov. 1841 in C.P.C. He *m.* thirdly, 6 Oct. 1842, at Walcot, near Bath, Frances, da. of Edmund Lamplugh IRTON, of Irton Castle, co. Cumberland. She *d.* 17 Nov. 1852. M.I. at Farway. He *m.* fourthly, 7 Aug. 1855, at St. James' Westm., Louisa, widow of George WATLINGTON, of Caldecote House, in Aldenham, Herts, yst. da. and coheir of Robert BODLE, of Woolston Hall, Essex. He *d.* s.p.s.(a) 11 Feb. 1875, in his 82d year, at 3 Hesketh Crescent, Torquay, and was *bur.* at Farway, when the *Baronetcy* became *extinct*. His widow (on whose death Netherton place passed under her husband's will to the collateral heir male of the first Baronet) *d.* at the same place, 19 Dec. 1878, aged 78, and was *bur.* at Farway.

(a) John Rolle PRIDEAUX, his last surviving son, *b.* 13 June 1835, Lieut. 23d Foot, *d.* v.p., unm., 14 May 1855, on his passage from India to the Crimea.

HASILRIGG, *or* HESILRIGE:
cr. 21 July 1622,
afterwards, since 1818, HAZLERIGG.

I. 1622. "THOMAS HASILRIGG, of Nosely, co. Leicester, Knt.," s. and h. of Thomas HESILRIGE, *or* HASILRIGG, of Noseley Hall, in Noseley aforesaid, by Ursula, da. of Sir Thomas ANDREWES, of Charwelton, co. Northampton, was *b.* 1564; matric. at Oxford (Univ. Coll.), 17 March 1581/2, aged 17; *Knighted*, 19 June 1608; was Sheriff of Leicestershire, 1612-13; M.P. thereof, 1614 and 1624-25, and was *cr. a Bart.*, as above, 21 July 1622. He *m.* Frances, da. and h. of William GORGES, of Alderton, co. Northampton (*d.* 2 June 1589), and Cecilia, his wife. He *d.* 11 Jan. 1629, aged 66. Admon. 25 Nov. 1630, and 20 Nov. 1649. His widow *d.* 1638.

II. 1629. SIR ARTHUR HESILRIGE, Bart. [1622], of Noseley Hall aforesaid, s. and h., *suc. to the Baronetcy*, 11 Jan. 1629; was M.P. for Leicestershire, April to May 1640, and 1640-45; for Leicester (in three Parls.), 1654-59, and, being a staunch Puritan, served in almost every important office on the ante-Royalist side from 1642 to 1660. He was named as one of the Regicide Judges, but declined to act; was a member of the Council of State, 1649-53, being President thereof, Jan. to Feb. 1651/2, and again a member, 1659-60. He was Colonel of a reg. of Cuirassiers, called "The Lobsters," which was very efficient against the King's party. He was Governor of Newark, 1647, and (with his son) obtained many additions to his estate during the Commonwealth.(a) He *m.* firstly, in or before 1625, Frances, da. of Thomas ELMES, of Lilford, co. Northampton, by Christian, da. and h. of William HICKLING, of Greens Norton. She *d.* 1632. He *m.* secondly, Dorothy, sister of Robert, 2d BARON BROOKE OF BEAUCHAMPS COURT, da. of Fulke GREVILLE, of Burton Latimer, by Mary, da. of Christopher COPLEY. She *d.* 28 Jan. 1650. He, who was excepted from the Act of Pardon, 1660, *d.*, a prisoner in the Tower of London, 7 and was carried thence 12 Jan. 1660/1.

III. 1661. SIR THOMAS HESILRIGE, Bart. [1622], of Noseley Hall aforesaid, s. and h., by 1st wife; *b.* about 1625; *suc. to the Baronetcy* 7 Jan. 1660/1. He *m.*, in or before 1664, Elizabeth, da. and coheir of George FENWICK, of Brunton Hall, Northumberland. She *d.* 30 May 1673. He *d.* 24 Feb. 1680, aged 55.

IV. 1680. SIR THOMAS HESILRIGE, Bart. [1622], of Noseley Hall aforesaid, s. and h.; *suc. to the Baronetcy* in 1680; Sheriff of Leicestershire, 1686-87; M.P. thereof, 1690-95. He *d.* unm. 11 July 1700, aged 36.

V. 1700. SIR ROBERT HESILRIGE, Bart. [1622], of Noseley Hall aforesaid, uncle and h., being only surv. s. (by his 2d wife) of the 2d Bart.; *b.* about 1640; *suc. to the Baronetcy*, 11 July 1700. He *m.* (Lic. Fac. 3 May 1664, he 24 and she 21) Bridget, da. of Sir Samuel ROLLE, of Heanton, Devon, by his 2d wife, Margaret, da. of Sir Thomas WISE, of Sydenham, Devon. She *d.* 26 July 1697. He *d.* 22 May 1713.

VI. 1713. SIR ROBERT HESILRIGE, Bart. [1622], of Noseley Hall aforesaid, s. and h.; *suc. to the Baronetcy*, 22 May 1713; Sheriff of Leicestershire, 1715-16. He *m.* (Lic. Fac. 29 July 1696, he 28 and she 22) Dorothy, 2d da. of Banaster (MAYNARD), 3d BARON MAYNARD OF ESTAINES, by Elizabeth, da. of Henry (GREY), 10th EARL OF KENT. He *d.* 19 May 1721. Will pr. 1721. His widow *d.* 11 Sep. 1748, and was *bur.* at Noseley.

(a) He purchased the estate of Bishops Auckland for £6,103; that of Easingwood for £5,833, and that of Wolsingham for £6,704, all being part of the lands of the Bishopric of Durham.

VII. 1721. SIR ARTHUR HESILRIGE, Bart. [1622], of Noseley Hal aforesaid, only s. and h.; *suc to the Baronetcy*, 19 May 1721. He *m.*, June 1725, Hannah(a), da. of (—) STURGES. He *d.* 23 April 1763. Will pr. 1763. His widow *d.* 27 Feb. 1765.

VIII. 1763. SIR ROBERT HESILRIGE, Bart. [1622], s. and h., who was dis inherited by his father in favour of a yr. br., Charles(b) Hesilrige; admitted to Middle Temple, 9 Feb. 1738; *suc. to the Baronetcy* (but not to the estates) in 1763. He *m.* Sarah, da. of Nathaniel WALLER, of Roxburgh in New England, in which country he was residing in 1776, being living in 1787.(c)

IX. 1790? SIR ARTHUR HESILRIGE, Bart. [1622], s. and h., was in the East India Company's service, being collector of customs at Jessore; *suc. to the Baronetcy*, on his father's death. He *m.* firstly, Elizabeth CHARNAND, of Smyrna. She *d.* 1797, at Calcutta. He *m.* secondly, Charlotte Elizabeth, da. of Capt. F. E. S. GRAY. He *d.* s.p., 1805, in Bengal. His widow *m.* Capt. Henry William WILKINSON, B.N.I., and *d.* at sea 8 Jan. 1817, in her 35th year. M.I. at South Park street Burial ground, Calcutta.

X. 1805. SIR THOMAS MAYNARD HESILRIGE, Bart. [1622], of Hoxne Hall, co. Suffolk, uncle and h., *suc to the Baronetcy* in 1805. He *m.* firstly, 1805, Mary, da. of Edmund TYRELL, of Gipping Hall, co. Suffolk. She *d.* very suddenly, 13 Feb. 1809. He *m.* secondly, 30 Nov. 1811, Letitia, 2d da. of John (WODEHOUSE), 1st BARON WODEHOUSE OF KIMBERLEY, by Sophia, da. and h. of Charles BERKELEY, of Bruton. He *d.* s.p. 24 April 1817. Will pr. 7 June 1817. His widow *m.*, 15 Aug. 1842, Frederick FIELDING, Barrister, and *d.* 3 March 1864.

XI. 1817. SIR ARTHUR GREY HESILRIGE, *afterwards* HAZLERIGG, Bart. [1622], of Noseley Hall aforesaid, nephew and h., being s. and h. of Col. Grey HESILRIGE, by Bridget,(d) da. of Rev. Richard BUCKLEY, Rector of Seagoe, co. Armagh, which Grey (*d.* Oct. 1810, aged 61) was 5th and yst. s. of the 7th Bart. He *suc. to the Baronetcy*, 24 April 1817. He inherited Noseley Hall and the other family estates from his uncle, Charles HESILRIGE, who *d.* s.p. By royal lic., 8 July 1818, he took the name of *Hazlerigg* in lieu of that of *Hesilrige*.(e) He *m.*, 26 July 1811, Henrietta Anne, da. of John BOURNE, of Stanch Hall, Hants. He *d.* 24 Oct. 1819. Will pr. 1820. His widow *d.* 25 Oct. 1868, at Southfields, Leicester, in her 85th year.

XII. 1819. SIR ARTHUR GREY HAZLERIGG, Bart. [1622], of Noseley Hall aforesaid, s. and h.; *b.* 20 Oct. 1812, at Whitchurch, co. Hereford; *suc. to the Baronetcy*, 24 Oct. 1819; ed. at Eton; matric. at Oxford (Ch. Ch.), 1 Nov. 1830, aged 18; Sheriff of Leicestershire, 1837. He *m.*, 14 July 1835, Henrietta, 5th da. of Charles Allen PHILLIPPS, of St. Bride's Hill, co. Pembroke. She *d.* 13 Dec. 1883, at Noseley Hall. He *d.* there 11 May 1890, aged 77.

(a) She is said to have been the person from whom Richardson drew the character of "Pamela."

(b) This Charles Hesilrige was Sheriff of Leicestershire in 1770, which office he served with unusual state, "the six fine blood chesnut horses" which drew his carriage, costing, it was said, £500. He *m.* but *d.* s.p., leaving the estates back to the then Baronet.

(c) Royal Kalendar for 1776 and 1787. The date of his death and that of his wife was enquired for in *N. and Q.* (8th S.I. 495) with no result. It is there stated that "the early registers and papers at Noseley Hall were all dispersed or destroyed in the last century by some careless owner of the estate."

(d) It is stated (*N. and Q.*, 8th S., i, 495) that she was his niece, being the da. of his sister, Elizabeth, and that it was thought that an Act of Parl. was passed to legitimate their nine children. None such, however, would be needed, for the marriage, though *voidable* in the lifetime of both of the parties, was not of itself *void*, and would, *unless* so set aside, be *valid* after the death of either of them.

(e) "Having," he states, "reason to consider that the original orthography of the name of the antient family from which he derives his descent was *Hazlerigg*."

XIII. 1890. Sir Arthur Grey Hazlerigg, Bart. [1622], of Noseley Hall aforesaid, grandson and h., being only s. and h. of Arthur Grey Skipwith, Major Royal Scots Fusileers, by Janet Edith, da. of Sir Archibald Orr-Ewing, 1st Bart. [1886], which Arthur last named (who had served in the Crimean and Zulu campaigns) *d. v.p.* 16 July 1880, aged 43. He was *b.* 18 Nov. 1878, and *suc. to the Baronetcy*, 11 May 1890.

Family Estates.—These, in 1883, consisted of 2,162 acres,(a) worth £3,837 a year. *Seat.*—Noseley Hall, near Tugby, co. Leicester.

BURTON:

cr. 22 July 1622;

ex. 1720-50?

I. 1622. "Thomas Burton, of Stockerston, co. Leicester, Knt.," s. and h. of John Burton, of the same, by Anne, da. and h. of John Digby, of Coats and Luffenham in the same county, was, presumably, the "Thomas Burton, of co. Leicester, Gent.," who matric. at Oxford (Linc. Coll.), 10 Oct. 1597, aged 17. He was *Knighted*, 5 Oct. 1605, by the Lord Deputy [I.], at Dublin, and was *cr. a Bart.*, as above, 22 July 1622. Sheriff of Leicestershire, 1633-34. He *m.* firstly, Philippa, widow of Walter Calverley, da. of Sir Henry Brooke, *otherwise* Cobham (yst. s. of George, 4th Lord Cobham), by Anne, da. of Sir Henry Sutton. She *d.* s.p., and was *bur.* 28 Sep. 1613, at Stokeston. He *m.* secondly, before 1618, Anne, widow of Thomas Havers, of the Custom House, London, da. of Robert Reynolds, of London, and of Stockerston aforesaid. She was *bur.* at Stockerston, 9 July 1634. He *m.* thirdly (Lic. Lond. 13 Jan. 1644/5, he about 60, widower), Frances Turville, of St. Andrew's, Holborn, about 50, widow. He was *bur.* at Stockerston, 4 Sep. 1655. Will pr. 1656; that of Dame Frances Burton pr. the same year.

II. 1655. Sir Thomas Burton, Bart. [1622], of Stockerston aforesaid, 2d but 1st surv. s. and h., by 2d wife, *b.* before 1618. He distinguished himself in the Civil Wars on the part of the King, and was, v.p., in the first Commission of Array for co. Leicester, in 1641, suffering sequestration and imprisonment; *suc. to the Baronetcy* in 1655. He *m.* in or before 1657, Elizabeth, da. of Sir John Pretyman, 1st Bart. [S. 1641], of Loddington, co. Leicester, by Elizabeth, da. and h. of George Turpin, of Knapstoft. He *d.* 3 April 1659. Will pr. 1659. His widow *m.*, before 1663, Sir William Halford, of Welham, co. Leicester. Her will pr. 27 July 1698.

III. 1659. Sir Thomas Burton, Bart. [1622], of Stockerston aforesaid, s. and h., *bap.* there 4 July 1657, and *suc. to the Baronetcy*, 3 April 1659; Sheriff of co. Leicester, 1682-83. He sold, about 1690, the estate of Stockerston to Sir Charles Duncombe. He *m.* (Lic. Fac., 26 June 1680, he about 23 and she about 21) Anne, 1st da. of Sir Thomas Clutterbuck, of Blakesware, Herts, Alderman of London, and sometime Consul at Leghorn, by Martha, da. of George Swanley, of Hackney, Midx. He *d.* at Newark, Notts, and was *bur.* there 14 Nov. 1705. Will pr. Dec. 1705. His widow was *bur.* at Newark, 7 April 1720.

(a) The property must have been greatly diminished since 1741, when Wotton, in his *Baronetage* [1741], gave the following note to Robert, the 5th Bart.—"In Sir Robert's time [1700-13] (—) Hesilrige, of Swarland in Northumberland, Esq., a younger branch of the family, died, and left the manor of Swarland to Sir Robert, which is also enjoyed by the present [1721-63] Sir Arthur, his grandson, with all the old estates of the family, *viz.*, Wettislade, East-Brunton, West-Brunton, Fawdon, Dinington, Widcopen and Witchet in Northumberland, Nosely and Ilston in com. Leicester."

IV. 1705, to 1750? Sir Charles Burton, Bart. [1622], 1st . and h.; *b.* before 1688(a); *suc. to the Baronetcy* in Nov. 1705. He *m.*, 4 Aug. 1720, at St. Andrew's, Holborn, Mary Reynolds, of St. Giles' in the Fields. In 1710, he was a prisoner for debt, and (twelve years later), 12 Sep. 1722, was convicted for stealing and sentenced to transportation [*Hist. Reg.* for 1722].(b) He *d.* s.p.(c) and the *Baronetcy* is presumed to have become *extinct* at his death.

FOLJAMBE:

cr. 24 July 1622;

ex. 17 Dec. 1640.

I. 1622, to 1640. "Francis Foljambe, of Walton, co. Derby, Esq.," s. and h. of Francis Foljambe, of Aldwark, in the West Riding of Yorkshire, by Frances, da. of Thomas Burdett, of Birthwaite, and grandson of Sir James Foljambe, of Walton and Aldwark aforesaid; suc. his father, 1600, and was *cr. a Burt.*, as above, 24 July 1622. He was M.P. for Pontefract, 1626, and Sheriff of Derbyshire, 1633-34; was "a man of a profuse temper and excessive hospitality," and was forced to part with Walton and other family estates. He *m.* firstly, 21 Oct. 1614, Elizabeth, da. of Sir William Wray, 1st Bart. [1611], by his 1st wife, Lucy, da. of Sir Edward Montagu. She *d.* s.p.m., and was *bur.* 19 April 1638, at Glentworth, co. Lincoln. He *m.* secondly, 22 May 1638, at Rotherham, Elizabeth, da. of Sir George Reresby, of Thribergh, co. York, by Elizabeth, da. and coheir of John Tamworth, of Shervile Court, Hants. By her he had no issue. He *d.* s.p.m. at Bath, co. Somerset, 17 Dec. 1640, when the *Baronetcy* became *extinct*.(d) His widow, who was *bap.* 24 Feb. 1613, at Thribergh, *m.* Edward Horner, of Mells, co. Somerset, who *d.* before 1660. She *m.* thirdly, before Sep. 1665 (as his 3d wife), William (Monson), Viscount Monson of Castlemaine [I.], who was degraded of his honours, 12 July 1661, and *d.* s.p.m.s. in 1673. She *m.*, before 1676, as her 4th husband, Sir Adam Felton, 3d Bart. [1620], who *d.* Feb. 1696/7. She *d.* 26 Dec. 1695, at Bury St. Edmunds. Admon. 24 July 1696.

YATE:

cr. 30 July 1622;

ex. 1690.

I. 1622. "Edward Yate, of Buckland, co. Berks, Esq.," s. and h. of Edward Yate, of the same, being possibly the "Edward Yate" who was B.A., Oxford (Corpus Coll.), 26 March 1602, and M.A., 2 May 1606, was *cr. a Bart.*, as above, 30 July 1622. Sheriff of Berks, 1628-29; was a recusant in

(a) In that year his *younger* br., John (an Ensign in the Army, 1711), was *bap.* at Stockerston.

(b) He is mentioned in Kimber's *Baronetage*, 1771, as "the present Baronet," but, if then living, must have been of great age. His brother, Thomas, was living in 1741 [Wotton's *Baronetage*]. If these two *d.* s.p.m. the title would probably have become extinct. In a pedigree (of no authority) in which many dates, from 1730 to 1738, occur, mention is made of a s. and h. of Sir Charles, *viz.*, Sir William Burton, the present [1738?] Baronet." See *N. and Q.*, 5th S., iv, 200, 213 and 279, as to the claim of Admiral Ryder Burton, to this Baronetcy, and see also several letters, *circa* 1875, of the wife of the celebrated African traveller, afterwards Sir Richard Francis Burton, K.C.M.G. (*d.* 1890), as to that Richard being ("if we can only prove it") entitled thereto. Sir Richard's grandfather was the Rev. Edward Burton, Rector of Tuam, co. Galway.

(c) Blore's *Rutland*.

(d) Frances, his only da. and h., by his 1st wife, *m.* firstly, 24 Dec. 1646, at Glentworth, co. Lincoln, Sir Christopher Wray, 4th Bart., who *d.* s.p. Nov. 1664. She *m.* secondly, John Troutbeck, M.D., and *d.* s.p., and was *bur.* 2 Nov. 1667, at Glentworth aforesaid.

1644. He *m.* Catharine, sister of Sir Henry Baker, 1st Bart. [1611], da. of John Baker, of Sisinghurst, co. Kent, by Mary, da. of Sir Thomas Guldeford. He *d.* Feb. 1645. Will pr. March 1645.

II. 1645. Sir John Yate, Bart. [1622], of Buckland aforesaid, s. and h.; *suc. to the Baronetcy* in 1645. He *m.* Mary, da. and coheir of Humphrey Packington, of Chaddesley Corbet, co. Worcester. He *d.* about 1658. Admon. 28 Feb. 1658/9, to Mary, the relict.

III. 1658? Sir Charles Yate, Bart. [1622], of Buckland aforesaid, s. and h.; *suc. to the Baronetcy* about 1658. He *m.* Frances, da. of Sir Thomas Gage, 2d Bart. [1622], of Firle, by Mary, da. and coheir of John Chamberlain. He *d.* about 1680. Will pr. 1680.

IV. 1680? to 1690. Sir John Yate, Bart. [1622], of Buckland aforesaid, only s. and h.; *suc. to the Baronetcy* about 1680. He *d.* unm. at Paris, 1690, when the *Baronetcy* became *extinct*.(a) Will pr. March 1691.

CHUDLEIGH, *or* CHUDLEIGHE:

cr. 1 Aug. 1622;

ex. 1 Aug. 1745.

I. 1622. "George Chudleighe, of Ashton, co. Devon, Esq.," s. and h. of John Chudleigh, of the same, by Elizabeth, da. of George Speke, of West Lackington, co. Somerset, which John (*d.* 6 Oct. 1589) was s. and h. of Christopher (*d.* 1 Oct. 1570), s. and h. of Sir Richard Chudleigh (*d.* 26 Aug. 1558), all of Ashton aforesaid; was *b.* about 1578; suc. his father when eleven years old; matric. at Oxford (New Coll.), 26 Nov. 1596, aged 18; was M.P. for St. Michael's, 1601; for East Looe, 1614; for Lostwithiel, 1621-22; for Tiverton, 1624-25, and for Lostwithiel (again), 1625, being *cr. a Bart.*, as above, 1 Aug. 1622. He, at first, opposed the King, but afterwards (with his son) took up arms on his behalf, and published, in 1643, a declaration of his reasons for so doing. He is said (Prince's *Worthies of Devon*) "to have paid dear" for his loyalty. He *m.*, in or before 1606, Mary, da. of Sir William Strode, of Newnham, Devon, by his 1st wife, Mary, da. of Thomas Southcott, of Bovey Tracey. She, who was *bap.* at Bovey Tracey, 30 July 1586, was living 1644, but *d.* before her husband, and was *bur.* at Ashton. He *d.* about 1657. Will dat. 20 Sep. 1655, pr. 1 July 1658.

II. 1657? Sir George Chudleigh, Bart. [1622], of Ashton aforesaid, 2d but 1st surv. s. and h.(b), *b.* 1612, being aged 8 in 1620; *suc. to the Baronetcy* about 1657. He *m.*, 16 Aug. 1637, at Wear Gifford, Elizabeth, da. of Hugh Fortescue, of Filleigh, Devon, by Mary, da. of Robert Rolle, of Heanton. She was *bap.* 8 Sep. 1616, at Petrockstowe. He *d.* 1691.

III. 1691. Sir George Chudleigh, Bart. [1622], of Ashton aforesaid, 2d but 1st surv. s. and h.; matric. at Oxford (Exeter Coll.), 17 March 1653/4; admitted to Inner Temple, 1656; *suc. to the Baronetcy* in 1691. He *m.* (Lic. Vic. Gen. 21 Feb. 1673/4, he 30 and she 17) Mary,(c) da. of Richard Lee, of Winslade, Devon, and of Westminster. She, who was an authoress and poet, *d.* 1710, at Ashton, and was *bur.* there. He *d.* in 1718. Will dat. 13 Aug. 1715, pr. 9 Feb. 1718/9.

(a) His only sister and heir, Mary, *m.* Sir Robert Throckmorton, 3d Bart. [1642], of Coughton, co. Warwick, and brought the estate of Buckland into that family.

(b) John, the eldest br., was *bap.* 20 July 1606, at Plympton St. Mary; was M.P. for East Looe, 1626, but *d.* unm. v.p. Admon. 10 May 1634.

(c) The marriage is said to have been an unhappy one.

IV. 1718. Sir George Chudleigh, Bart. [1622], of Ashton aforesaid, s. and h.; *suc. to the Baronetcy* about 1719. He *m.* Frances, da. and coheir of Sir William Davie, 4th Bart. [1641], of Creedy, by his 2d wife, Abigail, da. of John Pollexfen. He *d.* s.p.m. at Ashton, 10 Oct. 1738. Will dat. 19 Aug. 1734, pr. 21 July 1739, 27 Jan. 1747, and 30 March 1749. His widow, who was *bap.* 12 June 1697, at Sandford, *d.* about 1748. Admon., as of "Hall Down, Devon," 11 Jan. 1748/9 20 April 1751, and 17 March 1752.

V. 1738. Sir Thomas Chudleigh, Bart. [1622], of Ashton aforesaid, nephew and h. male, being s. and h. of Col. Thomas Chudleigh, by Harriet, his wife, which Thomas last named (*d.* 1719-34), was 2d s. of the 3d Bart. He *suc. to the Baronetcy*, 10 Oct. 1738; was a Lieutenant in Lord James Cavendish's Regiment of Foot. He *d.* unm. at Aix la Chapelle, 23 June and was *bur.* 12 July 1741, at Chelsea, Midx.(a) Will pr. Feb. 1742.

VI. 1741, to 1745. Sir John Chudleigh, Bart. [1622], of Chalmington, Dorset, cousin and h. male, being s. and h. of George Chudleigh, by Isabella, da. of (—) Garnier, of Pall Mall, Westm., which George (who *d.* 1739) was 2d s. but eventually h. of Hugh Chudleigh, of Westm. (*d.* 1707), 2d surv. s. of the 2d Bart. He *suc. to the Baronetcy*, June 1741. He *d.* unm., being killed at Ostend, 1 Aug. 1745, when the *Baronetcy* became *extinct*. Admon., as "late of St. George's Hanover square," 4 Dec. 1745, to his mother, "Dame Isabella Chudleigh, widow."(b)

DRAKE:

cr. 2 Aug. 1622;

ex. 22 Feb. 1794.

I. 1622. "Francis Drake, of Buckland, co. Devon, Esq.," s. and h. of Thomas Drake, of Buckland Monachorum aforesaid, by Elizabeth, da. of (—) Gregory, of Plympton St. Mary (which Thomas was br. and h. of the celebrated navigator, Admiral Sir Francis Drake(c)), was *bap.* 16 Sep. 1588, at Buckland; matric. at Oxford (Exeter Coll.), 23 Nov. 1604, aged 15; admitted to Lincoln's Inn, 1606; suc. his father, 4 April 1606, and was *cr. a Bart.*, as above, 2 Aug. 1622. He was M.P. for Plympton, 1624-25, and for Devon, 1628-29; Sheriff of Devon, 1662-33. He *m.* firstly, 22 Sep. 1602, at Buckland aforesaid, Jane, da. of Sir Amyas Bamfylde, of Poltimore, Devon, by Elizabeth, da. of Sir John Clifton, of Barrington, Somerset. She *d.* s.p.m. and was *bur.* 26 Feb. 1612/3, at Buckland. He *m.* secondly (Lic. Exeter, 5 Oct. 1615, and settlm. after marriage, dat. 17 Jan. 1627), Joan, da. of Sir William Strode, of Newnham, Devon, by his 1st wife, Mary, da. of Thomas Southcott, of Bovey Tracey. He *d.* 11 March 1637. Admon. 14 April 1637, to relict. His widow *m.*, 21 Aug. 1639, at Buckland, as his 2d wife, John Trefusis, of Trefusis.

II. 1637. Sir Francis Drake, Bart. [1622], of Buckland aforesaid, s. and h., by 2d wife; *bap.* 25 Sep. 1617, at Buckland; *suc. to the Baronetcy*, 11 March 1637; was Col. of the Plymouth Reg. of Horse for the Parl.; Sheriff of Devon, 1645-46; M.P. for Beeralston, Jan. 1646 till secluded, Dec. 1648, and for Newport, 1660, and 1661 till his death. He *m.*, 18 Jan. 1640, at S.

(a) Elizabeth, his only sister and h., *b.* 1720; *m.* firstly, 4 Aug. 1744, Augustus John (Hervey), 3d Earl of Bristol, and secondly, in the Earl's lifetime, 8 March 1769, Evelyn (Pierrepont), Duke of Kingston, for which she was found guilty of bigamy.

(b) The will of "Sir John Chudleigh, Bart., Dorset," is pr. May 1783, in the C.P.C.

(c) He *d.* s.p. 28 Jan. 1595/6. His widow *m.* William Courtenay, of Powderham, Devon.

Margaret's, Westm., Dorothy, da. of John PYM, of Brymore, Somerset, a noted Parliamentarian. She was *bur.* 16 May 1661, at Dunster, in that county. Admon. May 1662. He *d.* s.p. 6 and was *bur.* 10 June 1661, at Buckland. Will pr. 9 April 1662.

III. 1661. SIR FRANCIS DRAKE, Bart. [1622], of Buckland aforesaid, nephew and h., being s and h. of Thomas DRAKE, Major of Horse for the Parliament, by Susan, da. of William CRIMES, of Buckland Crimes, which Thomas (*bap.* 18 July 1620, and *d.* before 1661) was 2d s. of the 1st Bart., by his 2d wife. He is said(a) to have been *bap.* 1 May 1642, at Buckland; *suc. to the Baronetcy*, 6 June 1661; matric. at Oxford (Exeter Coll.), 3 June 1663, aged 16 [*sic*]; *cr.* M.A., 28 Sep. 1663; Sheriff of Devon, 1662-63; M.P. for Tavistock (four Parls.), 1673-81 and (four Parls.) 1689-1700. He *m.*. 6 Feb. 1664/5, at Beere Ferrers (settlm. after marriage dat. 30 Aug. 1673), Dorothy, da. of Sir John BAMFYLDE, 1st Bart. [1641], by Gertrude, da. of Amyas COPLESTONE, of Warleigh. She *d.* s.p.m., and was *bur.* 30 Jan. 1679, at Buckland. He *m.* secondly (Lic. Exeter, 21, and settlm. dat. 25 Oct. 1680), Anne, da. and coheir of John BOONE, of Mount Boone, Devon. She *d.* s.p., and was *bur.* 22 Dec. 1685, at Buckland. He *m.* thirdly (Lic. Vic. Gen. 17 Feb. 1689/90), Elizabeth, 1st da. of Sir Henry POLLEXFEN, of Nutwell Court, Devon, Lord Chief Justice of the Common Pleas, by Mary, da. of George DUNCOMBE, of Shalford, Surrey. She was *bur.* 25 March 1717, at Meavy. He was *bur.* there 15 Jan. 1718. Will dat. 26 Aug. and 26 Oct. 1717, pr. 1 March 1718, and again, 1731.

IV. 1718. SIR FRANCIS HENRY DRAKE, Bart. [1622], of Buckland and of Nutwell Court aforesaid, s. and h., by 3d wife; *bap.* 2 March 1693/4, at Buckland; *suc. to the Baronetcy*, Jan. 1718; M.P. for Tavistock, (three Parls.), 1716-34, and for Beeralston (six Parls.), 1734-41, 1747-71 and 1774-80; Master of the Household, 1771. He *m.*, 27 March 1720, Anne, sister of Sir William HEATHCOTE, 1st Bart. [1733], da. of Samuel HEATHCOTE, of Hursley, Hants, by Mary, da. of William DAWSON, of Hackney, Midx. He *d.* 26 Jan. and was *bur.* 15 Feb. 1739/40, at Buckland, aged 46. Will dat. 11 April 1721, pr. 11 March 1739/40. His widow was *bur.* 5 Nov. 1768, at Hackney. Will dat. 20 July 1751, pr. 17 Nov. 1768.

V. 1740, to 1794. SIR FRANCIS HENRY DRAKE, Bart. [1622], of Buckland and of Nutwell Court aforesaid, s. and h.; *bap.* 3 Sep. 1723, at Meavy; *suc. to the Baronetcy*, 26 Jan. 1639/40; M.P. for Beeralston, Jan. 1771 to 1774; Ranger of Dartmoor; Comptroller of the Court of Green Cloth. He *d.* unm. 22 Feb. 1794, at his house in St. James' place, Westm., aged 70, when the *Baronetcy* appears to have become *extinct*. Will dat. 1 Dec. 1792, pr. 22 March 1794.(b)

VI. 1794, to 1839. "SIR FRANCIS HENRY DRAKE, Bart. [1622], of Cheltenham, co. Gloucester, *assumed the Baronetcy*, 22 Feb. 1794, as nephew and h. male, he being s. (tho' apparently illegit.) of Vice Admiral Francis William DRAKE, Governor of Newfoundland, by Grace America, da. of Col. Samuel GREDHILL, Governor of Placentia, Newfoundland, which Francis William (who *d.* 1787, aged 63) was yst. br. of the late Bart. He was *b.* 1756, but the marriage of his parents is doubtful. He *m.* Anne Frances, da. of Thomas MALTBY. He *d.* 4 July 1839, at Cheltenham, aged 83, apparently s.p.m., as the *Baronetcy* has *not been assumed* since his death. Will dat. 25 Jan. 1836, pr. Sep. 1839. His widow *d.* 1840. Will pr. 1840.

(a) Col. Vivian's *Visitations of co. Devon.*

(b) He left his estates to his nephew, Francis Augustus (ELIOTT), 2d BARON HEATHFIELD OF GIBRALTAR, s. and h. of his sister, Anne Pollexfen, by the celebrated Lord Heathfield. His Lordship *d.* unm. 26 Jan. 1813, when they passed to his nephew, Thomas Trayton FULLER, who took the name of FULLER-ELIOTT-DRAKE, and was *cr. a Bart.*, 1821. See that creation.

MEREDITH:

cr. 13 Aug. 1622;

ex. Jan. 1738/9.

I. 1622. "WILLIAM MEREDITH, of Stanstye [*i.e.*, Stansley], co. Denbigh, Esq.," s. and h. of Sir William MEREDITH, of the same, and of Leeds Abbey, co. Kent, by Jane, da. of Sir Thomas PALMER, 1st Bart. [1611], of Wingham; was *cr. a Bart.*, as above, 13 Aug. 1622. He *m.* firstly, Susan, da. and h. of Francis BARKER, of London, by whom he had twelve children. He *m.* secondly, Mary, widow of Thomas AYNSCOMBE, sister of Sir Henry GORING, 1st Bart. [1622], da. of Sir Henry GORING, of Burton, Sussex, by Elinor, da. of Sir William KINGSMILL, but by her had no issue. He *d.* 10 and was *bur.* 13 April 1675, aged 72, at Leeds. M.I. Will pr. May 1675. His widow *d.* about 1688. Will dat. 19 March 1684, pr. 7 March 1688/9.

II. 1675. SIR RICHARD MEREDITH, Bart. [1622], of Leeds Abbey aforesaid, s. and h.; M.P. for Kent, 1656-58, and for Sandwich, 1659; *suc. to the Baronetcy*, 10 April 1675. He *m.*, 8 April 1655, at Acton, Midx., Susanna, sister of Sir Philip SKIPPON, of Stratford, co. Suffolk, yst. da. of the well known Parliamentary General, Philip SKIPPON, of Tobsham, Norfolk. He was *bur.* 5 Sep. 1679, at Leeds. His widow living 19 March 1684.

III. 1679. SIR WILLIAM MEREDITH, Bart. [1622], of Leeds Abbey aforesaid, s. and h., *b.* about 1666; *suc. to the Baronetcy*, Sep. 1679; *d.* unm., and was *bur.* at Leeds, 28 May 1681. Will dat. 25 May 1681, pr. 28 Aug. 1682.

IV. 1681. SIR RICHARD MEREDITH, Bart. [1622], of Leeds Abbey aforesaid, next surv. br. and h. male; *suc. to the Baronetcy* in May 1681. He *d.* unm. and was *bur.* 29 Aug. 1723, at Leeds.

V. 1723, to 1739. SIR ROGER MEREDITH, Bart. [1622], of Leeds Abbey aforesaid, next surv. br. and h. male, being 6th and yst. s. of the 2d Bart.; *b.* about 1673; matric. at Oxford (Linc. Coll.), 19 Oct. 1693, aged 16; B.A., 1697; Fellow of All Souls' Coll., and M.A., 1701; Barrister (Middle Temple), 1703; *suc. to the Baronetcy*, Aug. 1723; was M.P. for Kent, 1727-34. He *m.*, 22 Sep. 1728, Mary, widow of Samuel GOTT, da. of Francis TYSSEN, of Shacklewell, in Hackney, by his 2d wife, Mary, da. of Thomas WESTERN, of Rivenhall, Essex. He *d.* s.p. and was *bur.* 28 Jan. 1738/9, at Leeds, when the *Baronetcy* became *extinct*. Will pr. 1739. His widow, who was *bap.* 15 Dec. 1699, at the Dutch church, London, was *bur.* 26 April 1742, at Leeds. Will pr. May 1742.

MIDDLETON, MIDLETON, *or* MYDDELTON:

cr. 22 Oct. 1622;

dormant, or *ex.*, about 1757.

I. 1622. "HUGH MIDLETON,(b) of Ruthin, co. Denbigh, Esq., Citizen and Goldsmith of the city of London," yr. br. of Sir Thomas MIDDLETON, Lord Mayor of London, (1613-14), being 6th s. of Richard MIDDLETON, Governor of Denbigh Castle (*d.* 8 Feb. 1575/6, aged 67), by Jane, da. of Hugh DRYHURST, of Denbigh, was *b.* about 1555, at Galch Hill, in Henllan, near Denbigh; became free of the Goldsmith's Company, London, and traded as a Goldsmith, a Cloth Manufacturer, and an Engineer; was M.P. for Denbigh, 1604-11, 1614,

(a) He left Leeds Abbey to his niece and heir at law, Susan, da. of his 2d br., Col. Henry Meredith. She *d.* unm. 3 Feb. 1758, and it was sold, in 1765, to John Calcraft.

(b) See *Cheshire Courant*, July to Nov. 1891, for an able and exhaustive account of this family (of which this branch is especially obscure) by W. Duncombe Pink.

1621-22, 1624-25, 1625, 1626, and 1628-29; was one of the Royal Jewellers in 1605, and, having acquired considerable wealth from mining transactions in Cardiganshire, commenced, in 1609, the well known "NEW RIVER," to bring water to London from Amwell, Herts (twenty-two miles), which achievement was effected on Michaelmas Day, 1613. The cost, however, was ruinous,(a) and he was not even *Knighted* as a reward, though, some nine years later, he was *cr. a Bart.*, as above, 22 Oct. 1622. He was, of course, the first Governor of the New River Company. He *m.* firstly, Anne, widow of Richard EDWARDS, of London, da. of Richard COLLINS, of Lichfield. She *d.* s.p. 11 Jan. 1596/7, and was *bur.* at St. Matthew's, Friday street, London He *m.* secondly, in or before 1598, Elizabeth, da. and coheir of John OLMSTEAD, of Ingatestone, co. Essex, by Elizabeth, da. and coheir of James DANVERS, of London, she being stepda. of his br., Sir Thomas Middleton above mentioned. He *d.* at Basinghall street, 7 and was *bur.* 10 Dec. 1631, at St. Matthew's aforesaid, aged 71. Will dat. 21 Nov. and pr. 21 Dec. 1631. His widow *d.* 19 Dec. 1643, aged 63, and was *bur.* from Bush Hill, Edmonton. M.I. Will dat. 8 Jan. 1639 to 19 June 1643, pr. 15 Sep. 1643.

II. 1631. SIR WILLIAM MIDDLETON, *or* MYDDELTON, Bart. [1622], of Hoddesdon, Herts, 3d but 1st surv. s. and h.(b); *bap.* 10 April 1603, at St. Matthew's, Friday street, London; M.P. for Denbigh, 1630 and 1647; *suc. to the Baronetcy*, 7 Dec. 1631, and was, like his father, Governor of Denbigh Castle and of the New River Company; entered his pedigree in the Visit. of London, 1633, signing it as "Wm. Myddelton." He *m.*, in or before 1632, Eleanor, da. of Sir Thomas HARRIS, 1st Bart. [1622], of Boreatton. She, apparently, *d.* before May 1651. His will, as "of Hodsdon, Herts," dat. 12 May 1651, pr. 26 March 1652.

III. 1652? SIR HUGH MIDDLETON, Bart. [1622], of Gloucester, s. and h., *b.* in or before 1633; *suc. to the Baronetcy*, 1651-52; was Gent. Usher to the Duke of York in 1665. He *m.* firstly, 10 Nov. 1650, at Croydon, Frances, da. of Thomas MORTON, of Whitehorse, in Croydon, by his 1st wife, Frances, da. of Francis POULTON, of Twickenham. She was *bur.* at Croydon, 3 July 1655 He *m.* secondly (pub. May 1657, at St. Paul's, Covent Garden), Jane, widow of Charles GORGES, of St. Clement's Dane. He *m.* thirdly, Elizabeth, who survived him. He was *bur.* 11 Dec. 1675, at St. Martin's in the Fields. Will dat. 13 Nov. 1675, pr. 8 Jan. 1675/6, by Elizabeth, the widow.

IV. 1675. SIR HUGH MIDDLETON, Bart. [1622], s. and h.; *b.* and *bap.* 6 April 1653, at Croydon.(c) He, who is not mentioned in his father's will, *suc. to the Baronetcy* in Dec. 1675, and was sworn a Burgess of Denbigh, 31 Aug. 1681; M.P. for Denbigh, 1681 and 1692; Gent. of the Privy Chamber, 1685. He *m.*, 6 March 1682/3, in Westm. Abbey, Elizabeth, da. and coheir of Henry HALL, of Gretford and Burton Coggles, co. Leicester, by Elizabeth, da. of Sir Edward HARTOPP, 1st Bart. [1619]. He was *bur.* 2 Feb. 1700/1, at St. Peter's, Nottingham. His widow was *bur.* there 7 March 1732/3. Will dat. 30 April 1731, pr. 8 Jan. 1735/6.

V. 1701. SIR HUGH MIDDLETON, Bart. [1622], s. and h.; *suc. to the Baronetcy* in Feb. 1700/1; was Capt., R.N., 1 Jan. 1712/3, being dismissed by Court Martial, 1727, but restored. He *m.*, 8 May 1716, at St. Bennet's

(a) The total cost was £500,000; of this, Sir Hugh had spent £160,000 before parting with half to the King, who thereupon contributed half the remaining expenses. He, subsequently, sold half of his remaining half, reserving but a quarter for himself and his heirs.

(b) Hugh, an elder br., *bap.* 20 Sep. 1601, at St. Matthew's, was, about 1620, described as "of London, son and heir," *i.e.* heir apparent.

(c) It should be mentioned that Le Neve (in his MS. "Baronets") states this Hugh to be a son of the *third* wife, Elizabeth, and that also, about two years later there occurs among the burials at Croydon on 22 June 1655, "Sir Hugh Midlton's sonne." This may refer to the Hugh, *bap.* 6 April 1653, but may equally well refer to some yr. child (possibly unbaptized) born shortly before such burial. See Col. Chester's *Westm. Abbey Reg.* (p. 21), as to a mention in 1694 of Sir Hugh Middleton, Bart., as son of Sir Hugh Middleton, of Ruthyn.

Paul's wharf, London (being then of St. Margaret's, Westm.), Anne COMYNS, of Chigwell, Essex, spinster. He was *bur.* 16 Nov. 1756, at Chigwell. His widow (who lived in the Rookery there on £100 a year) was *bur.* there 31 Dec. 1764.

VI. 1756, to 1757? SIR HUGH MIDDLETON, Bart. [1622], only s. and h.; *bap.* at Chigwell, 1 Dec. 1723; *suc. to the Baronetcy* in Nov. 1756. He *d.* unm. in extreme poverty(a) in a barn belonging to the White Hart Inn, at Chigwell about 1757,(b) when the *Baronetcy*, which has never since been assumed, became *dormant*.

The right to the Baronetcy appears(c) to have devolved as under.

VII. 1757? HENRY MIDDLETON, of London, Doctor of Physic, cousin and presumably h. male, being s. and h. of Starkey MIDDLETON, Citizen and Surgeon of London, by his 2d wife, Dinah, which Starkey (*bap.* 3 April 1688, at St. Olave's, Hart street, London, and *bur.* at Bath Abbey, 24 June, 1755), was s. and h. of Henry MIDDLETON, of St. Olave's aforesaid, Surgeon, by his 1st wife, Anne, da. of Philip STARKEY, Citizen and Cook of London, the said Henry last named (*b.* 1662, and *d.* 14 May 1745, aged 83), being 2d but 1st surv. s. of Henry MIDDLETON, Sergeant of Mace, 1647 (*bap.* 14 June 1607, at St. Matthew's, Friday street; *d.* about 1675, certainly before 1678), who was 6th but 2d surv. s. of the 1st Bart. He was *b.* about 1720; was M.D. of St. Andrew's, Scotland, and Licentiate of the College of Physicians, London, both in April 1755. He *d.* unm., 4 Sep. 1759, in Cateaton street, London.

VIII. 1759. STARKEY MIDDLETON, br. and h.; *bap.* at Abingdon, Berks, 16 Sep. 1724. He *d.* unm. in the West Indies in 1768.

IX. 1768. STARKEY MIDDLETON, of Hoxton, Midx., cousin and h. male, being s. and h. of Henry MIDDLETON, of West Ham, co. Essex, which Henry (*bap.* 20 July 1691, *d.* 30 Nov. 1726), was 2d s. of Henry MIDDLETON and Ann, da. of Philip STARKEY, all three abovenamed. He was *b.* 7 June 1719, at West Ham. He *m.*, 2 March 1741, at St. Luke's, Old street, Midx., Sarah ROBERTS. He *d.* a few months after his cousin abovenamed. Will dat. 23 Aug., pr. 22 Oct. 1768.

X. 1768. JOSEPH MIDDLETON, of West Ham aforesaid, s. and h.; *b.* 16 Jan. 1742; *m.* firstly, 9 May 1774, at West Ham, Mary BARD, who was *bur.* there 1 April 1778. He *m.* secondly, 22 Sep. 1778, also at West Ham, Mary SHEPHERD. He was *bur.* there 24 May 1787.

XI. 1787. JOSEPH RICHARD MIDDLETON, only surv. s. and h. by 2d wife; *bap.* 22 June 1786, at Barking; *d.* young, and was *bur.* 24 May 1797, at West Ham.

XII. 1797, to 1828. JABEZ MIDDLETON, of High street, Hoxton aforesaid, uncle and h. male; was 17 years old on 29 May 1774, having previously *m.* Christian SHORT. He had a pension of £52 a year from the Corporation of London, in consideration of his descent from the founder of the New River Company. He *d.* s.p.m., 27 May 1828, when *the male descendants of the 1st Bart.* appear to have become *extinct*.(d)

(a) An annual allowance from the New River Company was his whole support. [*Gent. Mag.*, 52, p. 74].

(b) See *Gent. Mag.* for 1792 (p. 720) as to this date. He is there called "a tall, thin man, very profligate, and addicted to all manner of low vice."

(c) *Ex. inform*, W. D. Pink. See p. 209, note "b."

(d) Jane Boyer or Bowyer, one of his daughters, who, in 1828, petitioned for the continuation to her of her father's pension, states him to have been "the last male representative of Sir Hugh Middleton."

THORNHURST:
cr. 12 Nov. 1622;
ex. 16 Dec. 1627.

I. 1622, to 1627. "GIFFORD THORNHURST, of Agnes Court, co. Kent., Esq.," s. and h. of Sir William [*Qy.* Stephen] THORNHURST, of Agnes, or Aghne Court, in Romney Marsh, by Anne, da. of Charles LYTE, *otherwise* HOWARD, yr. son of Thomas (HOWARD), 1st VISCOUNT HOWARD OF BINDON, was *cr. a Bart.*, as above, 12 Nov. 1622. He *m.*, 16 Sep. 1627, at Allington, co. Kent, Susan, da. of Sir Alexander TEMPLE. He *d.* s.p.m.(a) 16 Dec. 1627, and was *bur.* at Allington aforesaid, when the *Baronetcy* became *extinct.* M.I. His admon. 28 Feb. 1627/8 (he being, erroneously, therein called "Geoffrey") as "of Allington Castle, co. Kent," granted to Susan, the widow. His widow *m.*, about 1636, Sir Martin LISTER, of Thorpe Arnold, co. Leicester, who *d.* 1670, aged about 67. She was living 1651, having a large family by that husband.

HERBERT:
cr. 16 Nov. 1622,
afterwards, 1656—1748, BARONS POWIS,
subsequently, 1674-1748, EARL OF POWIS,
and finally, 1687—1748, MARQUESSES OF POWIS.

I. 1622. "PERCY HERBERT, Esq., s. and h. ap. of William HERBERT, of Redcastle, co. Montgomery, **K.B.**," afterwards (2 April 1629) *cr.* BARON POWIS of Powis, co. Montgomery, by Eleanor, da. of Henry (PERCY), EARL OF NORTHUMBERLAND, was *b.* shortly before 1600; M.P. for Shaftesbury, 1621-22, and for Wilton, 1624-25; was, apparently, *Knighted*, 7 Nov. 1622,(b) at Theobalds, and was, v.p., *cr. a Bart.*, as above, 16 Nov. 1622, three days before his marriage. He was Councillor of Wales, 1633. Being a Royalist his estate was sequestrated, and, in 1650, was ordered to be sold. He *m.*, 19 Nov. 1622, at St. Andrew's Undershaft, London, Elizabeth, sister (whose issue became coheir) of William, 1st EARL OF CRAVEN, 1st surv. da. of Sir William CRAVEN, sometime Lord Mayor of London, by Elizabeth, sister of Sir George WHITMORE, also Lord Mayor of London. She, who was *bap.* 7 Jan. 1599/1600, at St. Antholin's, London, was living when, by the death of his father, 7 March 1655/6, he became BARON POWIS. In that peerage this *Baronetcy* then *merged*, the 2d Baron and Baronet being *cr.*, 4 April 1674, EARL OF POWIS, and subsequently *cr.*, 24 March 1687, MARQUESS OF POWIS. By the death, 8 March 1747/8, of the 3d Marquess (3d Earl, 4th Baron and Baronet), this *Baronetcy* and all other his honours became *extinct.*

FISHER:
cr. 7 Dec. 1622;
ex. 1739.

I. 1622. "ROBERT FISHER, of Packington, co. Warwick, Knt.," s. and h. of Sir Clement FISHER, of the same, by Mary, da. of Francis REPINGTON, of Amington, in that county, was *b.* 29 Nov. and *bap.* 2 Dec. 1579(c);

(a) Of his two daughters and coheirs, Frances and Barbara, the former *m.* Richard Jenyns, and was mother of "La belle Jenyns," Duchess of Tyrconnel [I.], and of Sarah, the famous Duchess of Marlborough.

(b) It is possible that the date should be "17" or "27" Nov. 1622, *i.e.*, a date subsequent to the Baronetcy, he being styled "Esq.," when so created. See p. 18, note "c," under "Tollemache."

(c) See various entries as to the family of Fisher in *Mis. Gen. et Her.*, 2d S., vol. iii, p. 108.

matric. at Oxford (Ball. Coll.), 14 Jan. 1596/7, aged 18; was *Knighted* at Whitehall, 26 June 1609; suc. his father, 1619, and was *cr. a Bart.*, as above, 7 Dec. 1622; Sheriff of Warwickshire, 1627-28; was fined, as a Royalist, £3,006, afterwards reduced to £2,006. He *m.* Elizabeth, da. of Sir Anthony TYRINGHAM, of Tyringham, Bucks, by Eleanor, da. of Sir Robert THROCKMORTON. He *d.* 29 March 1647, and was *bur.* at Packington. Admon. 12 April 1647, to Elizabeth, the relict.

II. 1647. SIR CLEMENT FISHER, Bart. [1622], of Great Packington aforesaid, s. and h., who, with his father, had suffered much from the rebels during the usurpation; *suc. to the Baronetcy*, 29 March 1647; was fined £1,711, 24 Jan. 1648, reduced to £1,140; M.P. for Coventry, 1661-79. He *m.*, 8 Dec. 1662 (the Archbishop of Canterbury officiating)(a), the celebrated "*Jane Lane*," who assisted so materially in the escape of Charles II, after the battle of Worcester, Sep. 1651, for which she received (after the Restoration) £1,000 a year for life. This Jane was da. of Thomas LANE, of Bentley, co. Stafford, by Anne, sister of Sir Harvey BAGOT, 1st Bart. [1627], da. of Walter BAGOT, of Blithfield, in that county. He *d.* s.p. 15 April 1683. Will pr. July 1683. His widow *d.* 9 Sep. 1689, both *bur.* at Packington.

III. 1683. SIR CLEMENT FISHER, Bart. [1622], of Packington aforesaid, nephew and h., being s. and h. of Thomas FISHER, of Walsh Hall in Meriden, co. Warwick, by Dorothy, da. of James LACON, of West Copies, Salop, which Thomas was 2d s. of the 1st Bart., and *d.* 1681. He was *b.* about 1657; matric. at Oxford (Mag. Coll.), 14 May 1675, aged 18; admitted to Inner Temple, 1677; *suc. to the Baronetcy*, 15 April 1683; chosen Sheriff of Warwickshire, 1703, but did not act. He *m.*, 16 Feb. 1685, at Sheldon,(a) Anne, da. of Anthony JENNENS, of Erdington, co. Warwick. She *d.* 17 Jan. 1707. He *d.* s.p.m. 9 April 1729.(b) Will pr. 1729.

IV. 1729, to 1739. SIR ROBERT FISHER, Bart. [1622], br. and h.; *suc. to the Baronetcy*, 9 April 1729. He *m.* Anne, da. of Jacques WISEMAN, of London. He *d.* s.p. 1739, when the *Baronetcy* became *extinct.* Will pr. 1739.

WASTENEYS, *or* WASTNEYS:
cr. 18 Dec. 1622;
ex. 17 Dec. 1742.

I. 1622. "HARDOLPH WASTENEYS, of Headon, co. Notts, Esq.," s. and h. of Gervase WASTNEYS, of the same, by Jane, da. of Lionel RERESBY, of Thribergh, co. York, was *cr. a Bart.*, as above, 18 Dec. 1622. He was Sheriff of Notts, 1635-36. He *m.* Jane, da. of Gervase EYRE, of Kiveton, co. York. He *d.* May 1649.

II. 1649. SIR HARDOLPH WASTNEYS, *or* WASTENEYS, Bart. [1622], of Headon aforesaid, s. and h., aged 2 years in 1614. Being well versed in the law, he was made Steward of East Retford, Notts; *suc. to the Baronetcy* in May 1649; Sheriff of Notts, 21 to 25 Nov. 1653. He *m.* Anne, da. of Sir Thomas CHICHELEY, of Whimple, co. Cambridge. He *d.* s.p. 1673.

III. 1673. SIR EDMUND WASTNEYS, Bart. [1622], of Headon aforesaid, nephew and h., being the only s. that left issue of John WASTNEYS, of Tolwick, co. York, by (—), da. of (—) IRELAND, of Lancashire, which John was 2d s. of the 1st Bart. He *m.* Catharine, da. of Col. William SANDYS, of Askham, co. York. He *d.* 12 March 1678.

(a) See p. 212, note "c."

(b) He re-erected the mansion of Packington, which passed to his only da. and h., Mary, who *m.*, 9 Dec. 1712, Heneage (FINCH), 2d EARL OF AYLESFORD.

IV. 1678, to 1742. SIR HARDOLPH WASTNEYS, Bart. [1622], of Headon aforesaid, s. and h. He *m.* Judith, da. and h. of Col. Richard JOHNSON, of Bilsby, co. Lincoln. She *d.* at Newark, Notts, and was *bur.* 22 Sep. 1727, at Headon. Burial registered at Newark. He *d.* s.p. 17 Dec. 1742, when the *Baronetcy* became *extinct.*(a)

The Baronetcy was assumed, in Jan. 1887, by WILLIAM WASTENEYS, who [in Debrett's *Baronetage* for 1893] is styled "the 5th Bart.," and said to have been *b.* 6 Feb. 1851; ed. at Trin. Coll., Cambridge; B.A., 1874; M.A. and LL.B., 1877; Barrister (Middle Temple), 1873. He *m.*, in 1878, Julia Marianne, da. of Charles FARDELL, of Holbech lodge, co. Lincoln. In an advertisement in the *Morning Post*, for 3 Aug. 1887, he sets forth the grounds of his claim, by stating that he is fifth in lineal male descent from Simon WASTENEYS, which Simon, he states, was (though he omits to tell us how) "the direct male issue of the grantee." His advertisement is as follows:—"ASSUMPTION of TITLE.—Whereas King James the First, by his Patent, dated the 18th day of December 1622, granted the dignity and title of a Baronet of England unto Hardolph Wasteneys, of Headon, in the county of Notts, esquire, and the heirs male of his body lawfully begotten; and Whereas Sir Hardolph Wasteneys, fourth baronet, great grandson of the first mentioned Baronet, died without male issue, and all other collateral male issue being extinct, the title vested in the cousin and heir-at-law of the said fourth baronet, that is to say, in Simon Wasteneys, of Edlington, in the county of York, who was also the direct male issue of the grantee of the title. And Whereas the said Simon left one son only, William, who left one son only, William (deceased), who had two sons and no more, William Parslove and Hardolph, whereof the elder, William Parslove is dead, leaving me, William Wasteneys, his only son and heir-at-law surviving; and Whereas I am advised and believe that it is expedient that I should reassume the title and dignity of baronet to which I am entitled as aforesaid. NOW I HEREBY DECLARE THAT IT IS MY INTENTION HENCEFORTH TO ASSUME AND BEAR SUCH DIGNITY AND TITLE, AND TO BE DESIGNATED in all Legal Documents and Otherwise as SIR WILLIAM WASTENEYS, BARONET; and I hereby request all persons whom it may concern so to call and designate me. As witness my hand this 28th day of January, 1887. W. WASTENEYS. Witness to the signature of the said Sir William Wasteneys, Baronet, ARTHUR D. BENNETT, Notary Public, Auckland, New Zealand."

SKIPWITH:
cr. 20 Dec. 1622.

I. 1622. "HENRY SKIPWITH, of Prestwould, co. Leicester, Knt.," s. and h. of Sir William SKIPWITH, of Cotes, in the said county, by Margaret,(b) da. of Roger CAVE, of Stanford, co. Northampton, was *Knighted* at Whitehall, 19 July 1609; suc. his father, 3 May 1610, and was *cr. a Bart.*, as above, 20 Dec. 1622. He was one of the Commissioners of Array for Leicestershire; Sheriff of that county, 1636-37; Gent. of the Privy Chamber, 1641; was a zealous Royalist; entertained Charles I, 28 May 1645, at his house, at Cotes; was fined £1,114 by Parl., and was so much impoverished by his expenditure

(a) The estates passed to his great niece, Judith-Lætitia, da. and h. of John BURY, of Nottingham, by Catharine, da. and h. of Edward HUTCHINSON, who was 2d s. of Samuel HUTCHINSON, of Boston, co. Lincoln, by Catharine, only da. of the 3rd Bart. She *m.*, at Headon, 1755, Anthony EYRE, of Grove, Notts, and was living 1786.

(b) Her mother, Margaret, da. of Richard CECIL, was sister of the famous LORD BURLEIGH.

in the Royal cause, that, before 1653, he was forced to sell his estate of Prestwould and others. He *m.*, in or before 1616, Tresham, 3d da. and coheir of Sir Thomas KEMP, of Kent. He *m.* secondly, 2 May 1639, at St. Mary's, Woolnoth, London, Blandina ACTON, widow.(a) He *d.* about 1658. Her admon as "of Greenwich, widow," 3 Dec. 1660, to her son, Edward Acton.

II. 1658? SIR HENRY SKIPWITH, Bart. [1622], of Cotes aforesaid, s. and h., by 1st wife, *b.* about 1616; matric. at Oxford (Univ. Coll.), 27 May 1632, aged 16; entered the Inner Temple, 1633; *suc. to the Baronetcy* about 1658. He *d.* unm. soon after his father. Admon. 9 Nov. 1663, to a creditor.

III. 1663? SIR GREY SKIPWITH, Bart. [1622], br. and h. During the Civil Wars he had emigrated to Virginia, in America, where he *m.* and *d.*,(b) having *suc. to the Baronetcy* in or shortly before 1663.

IV. 1680? SIR WILLIAM SKIPWITH, Bart. [1622], of Virginia, only s. and h., *b.* about 1670; *suc. to the Baronetcy* about 1680. He *m.* (—), da. of J. PEYTON, and was living in Virginia, 1730, aged about 60.(b).

V. 1730? SIR GREY SKIPWITH, Bart. [1622], of Virginia, s. and h., *b.* about 1700. He *suc. to the Baronetcy* about 1730 [?] and is said to have *d.* s.p.m. in Virginia, where he was living 1730, aged about 30.(b)

VI. 1750? SIR WILLIAM SKIPWITH, Bart. [1622], of Prestwould, in Virginia,(c) br. and h., *b.* 1708; *suc. to the Baronetcy* about 1750 [?]. He *d.* 26 Feb. 1764, at Prestwould aforesaid.(c)

VII. 1764. SIR PEYTON SKIPWITH, Bart. [1622], of Prestwould in Virginia aforesaid,(c) s. and h.; *suc. to the Baronetcy*, 26 Feb. 1764. He *m.* firstly, Anne, da. of Hugh MILLER, of Green Crofts in Virginia. He *m.* secondly Jane, sister of his 1st wife. He *d.* 9 Oct. 1805, in Virginia.

VIII. 1805. SIR GREY SKIPWITH, Bart. [1622], of Hampton Lucy, co. Warwick, and afterwards, of Newbold Hall, in that county,(d) s. and h., by 1st wife, *b.* 17 Sep. 1771, at Prestwould, in Virginia aforesaid; *suc. to the Baronetcy*, 9 Oct. 1805; was M.P. for Warwickshire, 1831-32, and for South Warwickshire, 1832-35. He *m.*, 22 April 1801, Harriet, 3d da. of Gore TOWNSEND, of Honington Hall, co. Warwick, by whom he had twenty children, of whom eighteen attained full age. She *d.* 7 July 1830. Will pr. Sep. 1830. He *d.* 13 May 1852, at Hampton Lucy aforesaid, aged 81. Will pr. Sep. 1852.

IX. 1852. SIR THOMAS GEORGE SKIPWITH, Bart. [1622], of Newbold Hall, and of Hampton Lucy aforesaid, s. and h., *b.* 9 Feb. 1803, at Barford, co. Warwick; ed. at Rugby, 1813; sometime Capt. in the Army; *suc. to the Baronetcy*, 13 May 1852; Lieut. Col., 2d Warwickshire Militia, 1853-58. He *m.* firstly, 15 July 1840, Emma, da. of Thomas HATTON, of Liverpool. She *d.* s.p. 14 June 1842. He *m.* secondly, 21 May 1853, Jane, 2d da. of Hubert Butler MOORE, of Shannon View and Anaghbeg, co. Galway. She *d.* 3 May 1862, at Coton House, co. Warwick, aged 34. He *d.* 30 Nov. 1863, at Leamington Spa, co. Warwick, aged 60.

(a) "Sir Henry Skipwith, of Coats, co Leicester, Bart., and Blandina Acton, widow."

(b) Wotton' (*Baronetage*, 1740) states the information to be "by a letter from Virginia." It is evident that to establish (in the absence of any authentic dates) the correct succession to this dignity (though there is no reason to doubt its existence) further evidence is required.

(c) Kimber's *Baronetage*, 1771. See note "b," next above.

(d) He apparently succeeded to the estates of Newbold on the death, 28 March 1832, at Newbold Hall (in her 80th year), of Selina, widow of Sir Francis George Skipwith, 4th and last Bart. [1670], of Newbold aforesaid, who *d.* s.p. 1790, and who was a very remote cousin.

X. 1863. SIR PEYTON ESTOTEVILLE[a] SKIPWITH, Bart. [1622], s. and h., *b.* 12 Feb. 1857 ; *suc. to the Baronetcy*, 30 Nov. 1863 ; Hon. Major, 2d Warwick Militia, 1879. He *m.*, 6 Feb. 1879, at St. James', Paddington, Alice Mary, only da. of Col. Benjamin Bousfield HERRICK, Royal Marines Light Infantry. He *d.* 12 May 1891, at Leamington Hastings, co. Warwick, aged 34. His widow *m.*, 1 June 1892, John Broughton LEIGH.

XI. 1891. SIR GRAY HUMBERSTON ESTOTEVILLE[a] SKIPWITH, Bart. [1622], 1st s. and h., *b.* 1 Dec. 1884 ; *suc. to the Baronetcy*, 12 May 1891.

Family Estates.—These, which were in Leicestershire, were alienated by the 1st Baronet as early as 1653, the family emigrating to Virginia, and there remaining for several generations. The estate of Newbold, co. Warwick,[b] which, in 1832, devolved on the 8th Bart., was apparently sold by his son or grandson.

HARRIS :
cr. 22 Dec. 1622 ;
ex. 26 May 1693.

I. 1622. "THOMAS HARRIS, of Boreaton, co. Salop, Esq.,"[c] 2d s. of Roger HARRIS, of Shrewsbury, Draper, and grandson of William HARRIS, of Wheathill, in Condover, Yeoman; was admitted to Shrewsbury School in Jan. 1571/2 ; lived in Shrewsbury ; purchased, 20 Nov. 1617, the Boreatton and Onslow estates, Salop ; was Sheriff of that County, 1618-19, and was *cr. a Bart.*, as above,[d] 22 Dec. 1622. He *m.* firstly, Sara KYFFIN. He *m.* secondly, Sara, da. of William JONES, Alderman of Shrewsbury. He was *bur.* 27 Jan. 1627/8, at Baschurch, Salop. Will pr. 1630.

II. 1629. SIR PAUL HARRIS, Bart. [1622], of Boreatton aforesaid, 2d but 1st surv. s. and h., *bap.* 30 Dec. 1595, at St. Julian's, Shrewsbury, admitted to Lincoln's Inn, 24 Nov. 1613 ; *Knighted* at Whitehall, 30 April 1625 ; Surveyor of Ordnance, 1627 ; *suc. to the Baronetcy* in Jan. 1628/9 ; Sheriff of Shropshire, 1636-37 ; was, during the Civil Wars, an active Commissioner of Array on the side of the King, but was "not well beloved by the ancient gentry of the county, neither by the common people."[e] He *m.*, in or before 1634/5, Ann, widow of Richard PAUL, sister of Sir Alexander BRETT, a Col. in the Royal Army, da. of William BRETT, of Rotherby, co. Leicester. He *d.* July 1644, and was *bur.* at Baschurch. Will pr. May 1645. The will of his widow pr. 1676.

III. 1644. SIR THOMAS HARRIS, Bart. [1622], of Boreatton aforesaid, s. and h., *b.* about 1629 ; admitted to Shrewsbury School in Oct. 1643 ; *suc. to the Baronetcy* in July 1644 ; was taken prisoner at the capture of Shrewsbury in Feb. 1644/5, and was, for his father's delinquency, fined £1,572. In 1655, he was concerned in a general rising against Cromwell's government, and undertook to seize Shrewsbury, but the attempt was frustrated. He *m.* Mary, da. of Thomas MYTTON, of Halston, Salop. He was living in 1660, but *d.* s.p. soon afterwards.

(a) The family claim a male descent from Robert de Estoteville, feudal Lord of Cottingham, *temp.* Will. I.

(b) See p. 214, note "e"

(c) See an article in the *Shropshire Arch. Transactions*, 2d Series, vol. xi, as to this family.

(d) He was impleaded in the Court of Chivalry by Capt. Simon LEEKE as being, by descent, unworthy of the distinction of the Baronetcy. He is sometimes (probably erroneously), said to have been a Master in Chancery, which office, presumably, was held by Thomas Harris, Sergeant at Law, 1589, possibly, the "(—) Harris, LL.D.," Master in Chancery (1582-83), 25 Eliz.

(e) See "Gough," as quoted in Burke's *Extinct Baronets.*

IV. 1661 ? SIR GEORGE HARRIS, Bart. [1622],[a] br. and h. ; *bap.* 31 Oct. 1631, at Baschurch ; *suc. to the Baronetcy* about 1661. He *d.* s.p. between 1660 and 1666.

V. 1664 ? SIR PAUL HARRIS, Bart. [1622],[a] br. and h. ; *bap.* 8 April 1634, at Baschurch ; admitted to Gray's Inn, 1650, and matric. at Oxford (Queen's Coll.), 2 April 1652 ; *suc. to the Baronetcy* about 1664. He *d.* s.p., and was *bur.* at St. Chad's, Shrewsbury, 19 July 1666.

VI. 1666. SIR ROGER HARRIS, Bart. [1622],[a] uncle and h., being 4th s. of the 1st Bart. ; *bap.* 7 Oct. 1601, at St. Julian's, Shrewsbury ; *suc. to the Baronetcy* in July 1666. He *d.* s.p. 1685.

VII. 1685, to 1693. SIR ROBERT HARRIS, Bart. [1622], br. and h., being 7th s. of the 1st Bart. ; *bap.* 24 May 1612, at St. Julian's, Shrewsbury, in which town he appears to have been a draper ; *suc. to the Baronetcy* in 1685. He *d.*, apparently, s.p. and was *bur.* 26 May 1693, in Shrewsbury Abbey, when, presumably, the *Baronetcy* became *extinct.*

TEMPEST :
cr. 23 Dec. 1622 ;
ex. 31 May 1742.

I. 1622. "NICHOLAS TEMPEST, of Stella, in the Bishopric of Durham, Knt.," s. and h. of Thomas TEMPEST, by Elizabeth, da. of Rowland PLACE, of Halnaby, co. York ; was *Knighted*, 14 March 1603/4, at the Tower of London, and was *cr. a Bart.*, as above, 23 Dec. 1622. He *m.* Isabel, da. of Robert LAMBTON, of Lambton, co. Durham. He *d.* 26 March 1626, aged 73.

II. 1626. SIR THOMAS TEMPEST, Bart. [1622], of Stella aforesaid, s. and h. ; *suc. to the Baronetcy*, 26 March 1626. He *m.* Troth, da. of Sir Richard TEMPEST, of Bracewell and Bolling, by Elizabeth, da. of Sir Francis RODES, one of the Judges of the Common Pleas. He *d.* Aug. 1641.

III. 1641. SIR RICHARD TEMPEST, Bart. [1622], of Stella aforesaid, s. and h., *b.* about 1620 ; matric. at Oxford (Queen's Coll.), 2 Dec. 1636 aged 16 ; admitted to Lincoln's Inn, 1626 ; *suc. to the Baronetcy*, Aug. 1641 ; was fined £134, as a Royalist, in May 1649 ; was Col. of a Reg. of Horse in the service of Charles I. He *m.*, 9 Oct. 1641, at Sevenoaks, Kent, Sarah, da. of Thomas CAMBELL (3d s. of Sir Thomas CAMBELL, Lord Mayor of London, 1609-10), by his 1st wife, Sarah, sister of Obediah SPARKES. He *d.* Jan. and was *bur.* 5 Feb. 1662, at St. Giles', co. Durham.

IV. 1662. SIR THOMAS TEMPEST, Bart. [1622], of Stella aforesaid, s. and h. ; *suc to the Baronetcy*, Jan. 1662. He *m.* Alice, 2d da. and coheir of William HODGSON, of Hepburn, co. Durham, by Margaret, da. of Sir Thomas HAGGERSTON, 1st Bart. [1643]. He *d.* Aug. 1692, aged 50.

V. 1692. SIR FRANCIS TEMPEST, Bart. [1622], of Stella aforesaid, s. and h. ; *suc. to the Baronetcy*, Aug. 1692. He *d.* unm., at Montpelier, in France, 1698.[b]

(a) The estate of Boreatton had been sold about 1661, to Thomas HUNT, of Shrewsbury.

(b) Jane, his sister and sole heir, inherited the family estates. She *m.* William (WIDDRINGTON), 4th and last BARON WIDDRINGTON, and *d.* 9 Sep. 1714. Her husband (after having been convicted of high treason, but, subsequently, pardoned) *d.* 1743.

VI. 1698, to 1742. SIR NICHOLAS TEMPEST, Bart. [1622], cousin and h. male, being 3d s. of Thomas TEMPEST, by Jane, da. of Sir Jordan METHAM, of Metham, co. York, which Thomas was 3d s. of the 2d Bart. He was *b.* about 1664) and *suc. to the Baronetcy* (though not to the estates) in 1698. He was in an impoverished condition, but was allowed £240 a year from his cousin's husband,[a] the LORD WIDDRINGTON. He *m.* Ann, da. of (—) PRICE. He *d.* s.p. 31 May, and was *bur.* 4 June 1742, at Tanfield, Durham, aged 78, when the *Baronetcy* became *extinct.*

COTTINGTON, *or* COTTINGTAM :
cr. 16 Feb. 1622/3 ;
afterwards, 1631-53, BARON COTTINGTON ;
ex. 19 June 1652.

I. 1623, to 1652. "FRANCIS COTTINGTAM [*i.e.*, COTTINGTON], Esq., Secretary to Charles, Prince of Wales," 4th s. of Philip COTTINGTON, of Godmanston, Somerset, by Jane, da. of Thomas BIFLETE, of that county, was *b.* about 1579 ; Clerk of the Council to James I ; Secretary to Charles, Prince of Wales, and was *cr. a Bart.*, as above, 16 Feb. 1622/3 ; was M.P. for Camelford, 1624-25 ; for Bossiney, 1625, and for Saltash, 1628-29 ; Chancellor and Under Treasurer of the Exchequer, 1628-35. He *m.*, in 1622, Anne, widow of Sir Robert BRETT, da. of Sir William MEREDITH, of London, Treasurer of Flushing, by Jane, da. of Sir Thomas PALMER, 1st Bart. [1611], of Wingham. She was living when he, having been made Ambassador to the Court of Madrid, 1630, for negotiating a peace, was *cr.*, 10 July 1631, BARON COTTINGTON OF HAMWORTH [*i.e.*, HANWORTH], co. Midx., in which peerage *this Baronetcy* then *merged*, and so continued till by his death, s.p.s., 19 June 1652, in his 74th year, it, together with the peerage, became *extinct.* For further particulars of him and his wife after July 1631 see *Peerage.*

HARRIES :
cr. 12 April 1623 ;
ex. about 1649.

I. 1623, to 1649 ? "THOMAS HARRIES, of Tong Castle, co. Salop, Serjeant at Law," s. and h. of John HARRIES, of Cruckton, in that county, by Eleanor, da. of Thomas PROWDE, of Sutton, co. Salop, was M.P. for Shrewsbury, 1586-87 and 1604 till void, 26 Nov. 1604 ; and, being an eminent lawyer, was made Serjeant at Law, Feb. 1603/4. He, having purchased Tong Castle (from Sir Edward Stanley), was *cr. a Bart.*, as above, 12 April 1623. He *m.* Eleanor, da. of Roger GIFFORD, M.D., of London, Physician to Queen Elizabeth. He *d.* s.p.m.s.[b] about 1649, when the *Baronetcy* became *extinct.* Will pr. 1649.

(a) See p. 217, note "b."

(b) Francis, his s. and h. ap. (who *d.* v.p. and s.p.), was living 1623, and then aged 24. Elizabeth, da. and eventually sole h., *m.* Hon. William PIERREPONT, and was grandmother of Evelyn (PIERREPONT), 1st DUKE OF KINGSTON, whose son, the last Duke, sold the castle and estate of Tong to George DURANT.

BARKHAM :
cr. 26 June 1623 ;
ex. 28 Dec. 1695.

I. 1623. "EDWARD BARKHAM, of Southacre, co. Norfolk, Esq., son and heir apparent of Edward BARKHAM, of London, Knt.," sometime [1621-22] Lord Mayor of London, by Jane, da. of John CROUCH, of Cornbury, Herts, was *b.* about 1595, and was v.p. *cr. a Bart.*, as above, 26 June 1623, being, two days afterwards, *Knighted*[a], 30 June 1623 at Greenwich. He was M.P. for Boston, 1625-26 ; and suc. his father 15 Jan. 1633/4. He entered and signed his pedigree at the Visit. of London 1634 ; was Sheriff of Norfolk, 1635-36. He *m.*, 31 July 1622, at Tottenham, Midx., Frances, sister of Sir Richard BERNEY, 1st Bart. [1620], da. of Sir Thomas BERNEY, of Reedham, Norfolk, by Juliana, da. of Sir Thomas GAWDY, one of the Judges of the Court of Common Pleas. She *d.* 1 July and he (four weeks later) 2 Aug. 1667 at his house at Tottenham, both being *bur.* at Southacre. His will pr. 1667.

II. 1667. SIR EDWARD BARKHAM, Bart. [1623], of Southacre aforesaid ; *b.* 1628, being aged 6 in 1634 ; *suc. to the Baronetcy*, 1 Aug. 1667 ; Sheriff of Norfolk, 1667-68. He *m.* firstly, Grace, da. of Lewis (WATSON), 1st BARON ROCKINGHAM, by his 2d wife, Eleanor, da. of Sir George MANNERS. She was *bur.* at Southacre 30 March 1658. He *m.* secondly, Frances, da. of Sir Robert NAPIER, 2d Bart. [1611], of Luton, by his 2d wife, Penelope, da. of John (EGERTON), 1st EARL OF BRIDGWATER. He *d.* s.p. 1688. Will pr. Aug. 1688. His widow *m.* Henry (RICHARDSON), 3d BARON CRAMOND [S.], who *d.* s.p. 5 Jan. 1701 in his 51st year. She *d.* at Norwich, and was *bur.* 10 Nov. 1706, at Didlington, Norfolk.

III. 1688, to 1695. SIR WILLIAM BARKHAM, Bart. [1623], of East Walton, co. Norfolk, and of Hatton Garden, London, br. and h. ; *bap.* 28 Feb. 1638/9, at Tottenham aforesaid ; *suc. to the Baronetcy* in 1688. He *m.* Judith, da. of Sir John HALSEY, of Gaddesden, Herts, one of the Masters of the Court of Chancery, by Judith, da. of James NECTON. He *d.* s.p.m.[b] and was *bur.* at Southacre 28 Dec. 1695, aged 56, when the *Baronetcy* became *extinct.* Will pr. Jan. 1696. His widow *m.* 19 June 1697, at Westm. Abbey, John HOLSWORTHY, who survived her, but *d.* before Dec. 1735. She was *bur.* 19 March 1723/4 at Woolwich. Admon. 15 Dec. 1735.

CORBET, *or* CORBETT :
cr. 4 July 1623 ;
ex. 1661.

I. 1623. "JOHN CORBETT, of Sprowston, co. Norfolk, Esq.," s. and h.[c] of Sir Thomas CORBET of the same, sometime (1611) Sheriff of Norfolk, by Anne, da. of Edward BARRET, of Belhouse, Essex, was *b.* about 1591 ; suc. his father (who *d.* aged 54) in 1617, and was *cr. a Bart.* as above, 4 July 1623 ; M.P. for Norfolk, 1624-25 ; for Great Yarmouth, 1625 and 1626. He *m.* Anne, da. of Sir Arthur CAPELL, of Hadham, Herts, by Margaret, da. of the Lord John GREY OF PIRGO, Essex. She *d.* between Sep. 1624 and Feb. 1624/5. He *d.* 19 Jan. 1627/8, aged 37. His will, dat. 1 Sep. 1624 to 5 Feb. 1624/5, proved 12 Nov. 1628.

(a) See p. 18, note "c," *sub* "Tollemache."

(b) Edward Barkham, s. of the 3d Bart., was *bur.* at Southacre the same day as his father.

(c) His yr. br., Miles Corbet, of Lincoln's Inn, one of the Registrars in Chancery, was one of the Regicide Judges, and was executed accordingly, 19 April 1662.

II. 1628. SIR JOHN CORBET, Bart. [1623], of Sprowston aforesaid, s. and h., *suc. to the Baronetcy*, 19 Jan. 1627/8. He *d.* unm. before 1649.

III. 1640? to 1661. SIR THOMAS CORBET, Bart. [1623], br. and h., *suc. to the Baronetcy* on his brother's death; was a zealous Royalist, and suffered much in consequence, being fined £1,247. He sold the estate of Sprowston.(a) He *d.* unm. 1661, when *the Baronetcy* became *extinct*. Will pr. 1661.

PLAYTERS:
cr. 13 Aug. 1623;
ex. 23 Sep. 1832.

I. 1623. "THOMAS PLAYTERS,(b) of Sotterlye, co. Suffolk, Knt.," s. and h. of William PLAYTERS, of the same, by his 2d wife, Elizabeth, da. of Thomas TIMPERLEY, of Hintlesham, Suffolk, suc. his father, June 1584; was Sheriff of Suffolk, 1605-06; *Knighted*, 19 Oct. 1606, at Newmarket, and was *cr. a Bart.*, as above, 13 Aug. 1623. He *m.* firstly, Ann, da. of Sir William SWAN, of Southfleet, Kent. She was *bur.* 14 Oct. 1594, at Sotterley. He *m.* secondly, in or before 1596, Anne, da. of Sir Anthony BROWNE, of Elsing, Norfolk. He *d.* 18 and was *bur.* 20 May 1638, at Sotterley. Will dat. 2 Jan. 1637, pr. 1 June 1638. His 2d wife survived him. Her will pr. Oct. 1642.

II. 1638. SIR WILLIAM PLAYTERS, Bart. [1623], of Sotterley aforesaid, s. and h., by 1st wife; *bap.* 17 Jan. 1590, at Sotterley; *Knighted*, 12 Sep. 1623, at Wanstead, and *suc. to the Baronetcy*, 18 May 1638. He was Col. of a Reg. of Foot; D.L. and Vice-Admiral of Suffolk, but was turned out of all his employments by "the Rebellious Parliament." He *m.*, 16 July 1615, at Sotterley, Frances, da. and h. of Christopher LE GRYS, of Billingford, Norfolk. She *d.* s.p.m.s.(c) 9 Sep. 1659, at Billingford, and was *bur.* in Dickleburgh Church, Norfolk. M.I. He *d.* at Westminster, and was *bur.* 24 April 1668, at Sotterley. Will dat. 6 April and pr. 28 May 1668.

III. 1668. SIR LYONEL PLAYTERS, Bart. [1623], of Sotterley aforesaid, br. of the half blood, and h. male, being s. of the 1st Bart., by his *second* wife; *bap.* 4 March 1605, at Sotterley; was in Holy Orders, and was sometime Rector of Sotterley, and of Uggeshall, co. Norfolk; *suc. to the Baronetcy*, in 1651. The persecution he underwent during the Rebellion is described in Walker's *Sufferings of the Clergy* (p. 334), etc. He *m.* Elizabeth, da. of John WARNER, of Brandon, Norfolk. He *d.* 5 and was *bur.* 6 Oct. 1679, at Sotterley, aged 74. M.I. His widow *d.* 1699. Will dat. 20 Dec. 1694, as "of North Glemham, Suffolk," pr. at Saxmundham, 28 July 1699.

(a) The purchaser was Sir Thomas Adams, 1st Bart. [1660].
(b) See "Notes on the family of Playter or Playters, of Suffolk," in the *Genealogist* N.S., vol. i, by the Rev. T. P. Wadley.
(c) Thomas Playters, his only s. and h. ap. (often, erroneously, said to have been the 3d Bart.), was *bap.* 11 Sep. 1617, at Sotterley; was Col. of a Reg. of five hundred Cuirassiers in behalf of Charles I, in 1643, and was Admiral of six ships commissioned by Don Juan, of Austria, 1650. He *m.*, but *d.* s.p. and v.p. at Messina, in Sicily, 1651. Will dat. 1 Aug. 1649, pr. 24 Sep. 1651.

IV. 1679. SIR JOHN PLAYTERS, Bart. [1623], of Sotterley aforesaid, s. and h., *bap.* 21 April 1636, at Uggeshall; *suc. to the Baronetcy*, 5 Oct. 1679. He *m.* firstly, 31 Jan. 1662/3, at Bardwell, co. Suffolk, Jane, da. of Thomas READ, of Bardwell, by Bridget, da. of Sir Charles CROFTS, also of Bardwell. She was *bap.* there 4 April 1645. He *m.* secondly, Isabel, da. and h. of Thomas HALL, of London, merchant. She was *bur.* 31 Dec. 1720 at Sotterley. He *d.* s.p.s. and was *bur.* there 25 Aug. 1721.

V. 1721. SIR JOHN PLAYTERS, Bart. [1623], of Sotterley aforesaid, and afterwards of Ellough and Worlingham, co. Suffolk, nephew and h., being s. and h. of Lyonel PLAYTERS,(a) of Ellough aforesaid, by Martha, da. of Talmash CASTEL, of Raveningham, co. Norfolk, which Lyonel (*bap.* at Uggeshall, 22 June 1643, and *bur.* 16 Sep. 1699, at Sotterley) was next br. of the late Bart. He was *bap.* 18 May 1680, at Ellough; *suc. to the Baronetcy* in Aug. 1721; was Sheriff of Suffolk, 1727-28, and sold the estate of Sotterley in 1744.(b) He *m.*, 2 Aug. 1710, at Playford, Elizabeth, da. and h. of John FELTON, of Worlingham, co. Suffolk, s. of Sir Henry FELTON, of Playford in that county. By her he obtained the estate of Worlingham. She *d.* 14 and was *bur.* 16 Nov. 1748, at Worlingham, aged 58. M.I. He *d.* at Ellough Hall, 11 and was *bur.* 16 Dec. 1768, at Ellough, aged 88. Will dat. 8 June 1762, pr. 26 Dec. 1768.

VI. 1768. SIR JOHN PLAYTERS, Bart. [1623], of Worlingham aforesaid, grandson and h., being s. and h. of John PLAYTERS, by his 1st wife, Anne Caroline, da. and coheir of John TURNER (s. and h. ap. of Sir Charles TURNER, 1st Bart. [1727], of Warham), which lastnamed John Playters was s. and h. ap. of the 6th Bart., but *d.* v.p. He was *bap.* 26 Sep. 1742, at Weston near Beccles; was an officer in the 24th foot, and *suc. to the Baronetcy*, 11 Dec. 1768. He *d.* unm. 26 May 1791, at Ingatestone, Essex. Admon. 10 June 1791.

VII. 1791. SIR CHARLES PLAYTERS, Bart. [1623], of East Bergholt, Norfolk, br., of the whole blood, and h.; *suc. to the Baronetcy*, 26 May 1791. He *d.* unm., at Haynford, co. Norfolk, 1806. Admon. May 1834.

VIII. 1806, to 1832. SIR WILLIAM JOHN PLAYTERS, Bart [1623], of Yelverton, Norfolk, br., of the half blood, and h. male, being s. of the abovenamed John PLAYTERS (s. and h. ap. of the 6th Bart.), by his 2d wife, Elizabeth, da. of Joshua LEWIS, of Great Faringdon, Berks. He *suc. to the Baronetcy* in 1806. He *m.* firstly, 1782, Patena CLARKE, spinster. She *d.* s.p. 14 Aug. 1825. He *m.* secondly, Anne WRIGHT, spinster. He *d.*, at Norwich, s.p. legit.,(c) 23 Sep. 1832, when the *Baronetcy* became *extinct*. Will dat. 20 Nov. 1826, pr. 27 Feb. 1833. His wife survived him. Her will pr. June 1845.

DALYSON:
cr. 27 Oct. 1624;
ex. 14 June 1645.

I. 1624, to 1645. "THOMAS DALYSON.—A special warrant, granted on petition of THOMAS, son and heir male of the body of SIR ROGER DALLISON, of Laughton, co. Lincoln, Knt., deceased, to John, Bishop of London, Lord Keeper of the Great Seal of England for making, passing and sealing letters patent to bear date 29 June [1611], 9 Jac. I, in

(a) This Lionel is generally made to have suc. his brother John in the Baronetcy. His burial as an "Esq.," and his will as such (dat. 25 April and pr. 8 Dec. 1699, at Norwich), in which he mentions his brother "Sir John," shew this not to be the case. See Wadley's *Notes* as in note "a."
(b) The purchaser was "Miles Barne, Esq."
(c) See an account in Burke's *Extinct Baronets*, 1844 (referring to one in the *Gent. Mag.*), of his illegitimate da., Elizabeth WRIGHT, to whom he devised his estate in Norfolk. She *m.*, before Nov. 1826, Robert Moore, an Officer in the Army.

consequence of the omission to seal the original letters patent of that date, creating the said Sir Roger, a Baronet."(a) The abovenamed THOMAS DALLISON, of Laughton, co. Lincoln, s. and h. of the abovenamed Sir Roger DALLISON, of the same, Lieut. Gen. of the Ordnance, by his 2d wife, Elizabeth, da. of (—) TIRWHITT, was *bap.* 4 June 1591, at Laughton aforesaid; suc. his father in or before Jan. 1622/3,(b) and was *cr. a Bart.*, 27 Oct. 1624, as above, with a direction that the said patent should be pre-dated 29 June 1611, being the date of the dignity intended for his said father, but of which the patent was never sealed. He *d.* s.p., presumably unm.,(c) being slain at Naseby, fighting on the King's side, 14 June 1645, when the *Baronetcy* became *extinct*.

A Baronetcy of Dallison, presumably one purporting to be of this creation (27 Oct. 1624) was assumed as under.

1677. "SIR ROBERT DALLYSON, Bart., of Greetwell, co. Lincoln," had lic. (Vic. Gen.), 17 April 1677, to marry at Swinderly, co. Lincoln, Mrs. Alice ANDREWES, of the city of Lincoln, widow.

1713. "SIR THOMAS DALLISON, Bart., of St. Paul's, Covent Garden, Midx., Bachr.," admon., 25 June 1713, of his goods to the principal creditor, "DAME ALICE DALLISON, mother of decd., having renounced."

1714. "SIR JAMES DALYSON, Bart., of Chelsea, Midx., above 25, Bachr.," had lic. (Vic. Gen.), 13 April 1714, to marry at St. Bride's or St. Mary le Bow, London, Anne SYMONDS, of Chelsea, aged 18, spinster, with consent of her mother, Anne Symonds, of the same, wife of John Symonds, now at Barbadoes.

(a) The exact position attributed by Dugdale, and followed in all succeeding lists, to this Baronetcy, among the 53 creations of the date of 29 June 1611, is between Tirwhitt and Carre, numbers 31 and 32 of that batch of creations. Probably the warrant or sign manual, which directed the said dignity to be conferred on Sir Roger, allots it such a place. "Sir *Roger* Dallison" figures in these lists as a Baronet, but inasmuch as he was dead before Jan. 1622/3, nearly two years before the patent was granted to his son, Thomas, the pre-dating of that patent (though possibly granting the *precedence* of such pre-date) cannot be construed as raising a dead man to a Baronetcy. A clause (equally unjust to the previous patentees) in the patent, 22 June 1631, of the Vavasor Baronetcy, grants it the precedency of this same date of 29 June 1611, between numbers 9 and 10 of that batch of creations. See p. 40, note "a," *sub* "Gresley." The *practical* effect of each patent seems the same.
(b) The Baronet's father (who was Sheriff of Lincolnshire, 1601-02) was dead before 21 Jan. 1622/3, when his admon. as that of "Sir Roger Dallison, *Knight*, of St. Bride's, Fleet street, London" [be being possibly a debtor in the Fleet prison] was granted to a creditor.
(c) Ann, his sister and h., *m.* Sir Thomas Wolstenholme, 1st Bart. [1665], and *d.* 21 Nov. 1661. Her husband *d.* 4 July 1670, aged 74, both being *bur.* at Stanmore.

Baronetcies of Ireland,(a)
1619—1800.

CREATIONS BY JAMES I,
30 July 1619 to 27 March 1625.(b)

[Instituted by letters under the Privy Signet, dat. at Apthorpe, 30 July [1619] 17 Jac. I, and by letters patent at Dublin, 30 Sep. following. In the warrant, 24 Jan. 1620/1, for the creation of the Baronetcy of Coote, the King thus refers to his reasons for extending that dignity to Ireland:—"Having cast our eyes upon that kingdom, we find, to our comfort and the glory of that age, that Ireland, which was heretofore a place of rebellions and troubles, is now by the happy peace which it hath enjoyed under our government, become as our other kingdoms replenished with many worthy and well deserving men; and to the end that they may not want encouragement from us, we did purposely institute *the dignity of Baronets in that realm* to be conferred upon them, that their virtues and our grace might be made known both to the present, and succeeding times."]

SARSFIELD:
cr. 30 Sep. 1619,
afterwards, 1625-27, VISCOUNT KINGSALE [I.],
and subsequently, 1627-91, VISCOUNTS SARSFIELD OF KILMALLOCK [I.];
forfeited July 1691.

I. 1619. "SIR DOMINICK SARSFIELD, Knt., Chief Justice of the Common Pleas [I.], of Carrickleamlery, co. Cork,"(b) 3d and yst. s. of Edmund SARSFIELD, of Cork, Alderman; was *Knighted*, at Dublin Castle, 10 Feb. 1604/5; Justice of the King's Bench [I.], 1609; Chief Justice of the Common Pleas [I.], 1616, till deprived by the Star Chamber, 1634, and was, by patent dat. at Dublin, 30 Sep. 1619 (Privy Seal dat. at Apthorpe, 30 July previous), *cr. a Bart.* [I.],

(a) For a vast quantity of original and valuable information (mostly obtained from hitherto unexplored sources) respecting these Baronetcies, the editor is indebted to George Dames Burtchaell, M.A., LL.B., Barrister at Law, now (1900) of the Office of Arms, Dublin, author of a very valuable and critical work, entitled *The Genealogical Memoirs of the M.P.'s for Kilkenny* (1888). Sir Arthur Vicars, Ulster, has kindly and very fully replied to several queries concerning them, while C. M. Tenison (of Hobart, Tasmania) has contributed a considerable amount of facts from his copious genealogical collection.
(b) The description of each grantee and (down to 1772) the date of each creation is taken from the list in a bulky work (two huge vols., folio) entitled *Liber Munerum Publicorum Hiberniæ, 1152—1827*, published by the Irish Record Commissioners (1832). As far as 27 July 1772, that date being (as stated) the end of Lodge's *Baronetage*, this list seems to furnish full particulars, but not so between that date and 1800, during which period the date of the year only is given. *After* the Union, however, the exact date and description is given of some forty-five Baronetcies, from that of "Crofton," 9 July 1801, to that of "James," 11 Jan. 1822, conferred on natives of Ireland, all of which, of course, were Baronetcies (not of Ireland, but) of the *United Kingdom*. This circumstance throws some doubt on to the acumen of the editor, or editors, of these vols., in dealing with other Irish matters. It appears to have been (erroneously) assumed that because by a *special* clause in the Irish Union Act the Crown was enabled to continue the creations of Peers of a non-existing kingdom, the same anomalous power was therein granted to it (and actually excercised) as to Baronetcies.

as above, this being the first Irish Baronetcy that was conferred. He *m.*, probably, before 1600, and his wife was living when he was *cr.*, 2 April 1625, VISCOUNT KINGSALE, co. Cork [I.], etc., being subsequently *cr.*, 17 Sep. 1627 (in substitution), VISCOUNT SARSFIELD OF KILMALLOCK, co. Limerick [I.] In these peerages this *Baronetcy* then *merged*, and so continued, till by the death, 12 July 1691, and attainder of the 3d Viscount and Baronet, it and all other his honours became *forfeited*. See *Peerage*.(a)

ANNESLEY:

cr. 7 Aug. 1620;

afterwards, since 1629, Barons Mountnorris [I.],

and *subsequently*, since 1642, Viscounts Valentia [I.];

being *sometime*, 1661-1761, Earls of Anglesey [E.],

and, 1793-1844, Earls of Mountnorris [I.].

I. 1620. "Sir Francis Annesley, Knt., of Mountnorris, co. Armagh," said(b) to be s. of Robert Annesley, one of the Undertakers of the plantation of Munster, by Beatrix, da. of John Cornwall, of Moore park, Herts, was, possibly, s. of Thomas Annesley, High Constable of Newport hundred, Bucks, and (as such) *bap.* at Newport Pagnell, 2 Jan. 1585/6; was in Ireland as early as 1606, taking an active part in the colonization of Ulster, and receiving a grant of the fort of Mountnorris, etc.; was M.P. [I.] for co. Armagh, 1613; *Knighted* at Theobald's, 16 June 1616; was Prime Sec. of State [I.], 1616-34, and was, by patent dat. at Dublin 7 Aug. 1620 (privy seal dat., at Greenwich, 26 June previous) *cr. a Bart.* [I.], as above. He obtained, 11 March 1621/2, the reversionary grant of the VISCOUNTCY OF VALENTIA [I.] on the death of the then Viscount; was Vice Treasurer and Receiver General of the Revenue [I.] in 1625; M.P. for Carmarthen, 1625, and for Newton (co. Lancashire), 1628-29. He *m.* firstly, about 1608, Dorothea, da. of Sir John Philipps, 1st Bart. [1611], of Picton, by his 1st wife Anne, da. and coheir of Sir John Perrot, sometime Viceroy of Ireland. She *d.* 3 and was *bur.* 4 May 1624 at St. John's, Dublin. Funeral cert. in Ulster's office. He *m.* secondly, after 1624, Jane, widow of Sir Peter Courtene, Bart. (so *cr.* 1622), da. of Sir John Stanhope, of Elvaston, co. Derby, by his 2d wife, Catharine, da. of Thomas Trentham. She was living (probably being already married) when he was *cr.*, 8 Feb. 1628/9, BARON MOUNTNORRIS of Mountnorris, co. Armagh [I.], and when, on 25 May 1642, he became (by the death of the former holder of the dignity) VISCOUNT VALENTIA [I.]. In these peerages this Baronetcy then *merged*, and still so continues, the 2d Viscount being *cr.*, 20 April 1661, EARL OF ANGLESEY [E.], a dignity which became, extinct 14 Feb. 1761, and the 8th Viscount being *cr.*, 3 Dec. 1793, EARL OF MOUNTNORRIS [I.], a dignity which became extinct, 23 July 1844. See *Peerage*, under "Valentia."

BLUNDELL *or* BLUNDEL:

cr. 13 Oct. 1620;

afterwards, 1620—1756, Viscounts Blundell of Edenderry [I.];

ex. 19 Aug. 1756.

I. 1620. "Sir Francis Blundel, Knt., Secretary for the affairs of Ireland," being according to some accounts(c) son of William Blundell, but generally said to be a yr. br. of Sir George Blundell, of Cardington, Beds, both of them sons of John Blundell, by Catharine, da. and coheir of Roger Budoxshyde,

(a) The grantee (afterwards the 1st Viscount) died Dec. 1636, and was buried at Christ Church, Cork, 17 Jan. 1636/7. [*Ex. inform.* G. D. Burtchaell; see p. 223, note "a."]

(b) Lodge's *Peerage* [I.] and elsewhere.

(c) *Ex. inform.* C. M. Tenison. See p. 223, note "a."

was probably the "Francis Blundell, of Bucks, pleb.," who matric. at Oxford (Broadgates Hall), 14 Oct. 1596, aged 17; being B.A. (Ch. Ch.), 7 July 1600; M.A., 28 June 1603, and incorp. at Cambridge, 1604; was Clerk to the Commission for remedy of defective titles [I.], 1612; Constable of Limerick Castle; obtained grants of land in King's County, which he erected into the Manor of Blundell; was M.P. [I.] for Lifford, 1613-15; M.P. for Oxford, 1621 till void, 9 Feb. 1621; was *Knighted* at Newmarket, 30 Jan. 1617/18; admitted to Gray's Inn, 1 March 1617/8; made Secretary for Ireland, P.C., Vice-Treasurer and Receiver General, 1619, and was by patent dat. at Dublin, 13 Oct. 1620 (Privy Seal dat. at Broadlands, Hants, 27 Aug. previous), *cr. a Bart.* [I.], as above, and had letters patent in 1622, to nominate two Baronets [I.] He *m.* Joyce, da. of William Sergeant, of Waldridge in Dinton, Bucks. He *d.* 26 April and was *bur.* 5 May 1625, at Christ Church, Dublin. Funeral certificate in Ulster's office. His will, as "of Waldridge, Bucks," dat. 17 May 1622, pr. 9 Dec. 1625. His widow *m.* Nicholas White.

II. 1625. Sir George Blundell, Bart. [I. 1620], of Blundell Manor, King's County, 1st surv. s. and h.(a); *suc. to the Baronetcy*, 26 April 1625; was a Commissioner of Customs and Excise [I.], and was M.P. [I.] for Dingle, 1639-48, and for Philipstown, 1661-66. He *m.*, in or before 1642, Sarah, da. (whose issue became heir) of Sir William Colley, of Edenderry, by Elizabeth, sister of Sir John Giffard, of Castle Jordan. He was Sheriff of King's County, 1657, and was living, probably, long afterwards.(b) His widow *d.* 25 Feb. 1701, and was *bur.* at Monasteroris. M.I.

III. 1665? Sir Francis Blundell, Bart. [I. 1620], of Blundell manor and Edenderry aforesaid, s. and h., *b.* 30 Jan. 1643; *suc. to the Baronetcy* about 1665; was attainted, 1689, by the Parl. of James II, but was afterwards M.P. [I.] for the King's County from 1692, till his death. He *m.* firstly, 1 Dec. 1670 or 1671, Ursula, da. of Sir Paul Davys, Sec. of State [I.], by his 3d wife, Mary, da. of Sir William Crofton. She *d.* s.p., and was *bur.* 23 May 1673 at St. Audoen's, Dublin, leaving 884 acres to charitable uses. He *m.* secondly, in 1675, Anne, only da. of Sir Henry Ingoldsby, 1st Bart. [1661], of Beggstown, co. Meath, by Anne, da. of Sir Hardress Waller. She *d.* 14 and was *bur.* 16 July 1705 at St. Bride's, Dublin. Funeral certificate in Ulster's office [I.]. He *d.* about 1707. His will pr. 1707 in the Prerog. Court [I.](c).

IV. 1707? to 1756. Sir Montague Blundell, Bart. [I. 1620], of Blundell manor and Edenderry aforesaid, s. and h. by second wife; *b.*, 1689; *suc. to the Baronetcy* about 1707; was M.P. for Haslemere, 1714. He was *cr.* 22 Nov. 1720 (the Privy Seal being dated 27 June previous, at Herrenhausen, in Hanover), BARON AND VISCOUNT BLUNDELL OF EDENDERRY, in King's County [I.]. He *m.*, Sep. 1707, Mary, da. of John Chetwynd, of Grendon, co. Warwick. He *d.* s.p.m.s.(d) 19 Aug. 1756, when *all his honours*, apparently, became *extinct*.(e) Will pr. Sep. 1756. His widow *d.* 9 Dec. following. Her admon. as "of St. Geo. Han. sq." 31 Dec. 1756.

(a) Thomas, the 1st son, *d.* young, 15 June 1623, as did Francis, the 2d son, 29 July 1624. Funeral certificates in Ulster's Office. Another son, Arthur, was *bap.* at St. Werburgh's, Dublin, 28 Oct. 1622. He also *d.* young and v.p., and, consequently, was not the Sir Arthur Blundell, a Capt. in Ormonde's Reg. in Ireland, who *d.* 1650, and was *bur.* at St. Werburgh's aforesaid.

(b) He must not be confounded with his distant cousin, Sir George Blundell, of Cardington, Beds, Knighted 17 April 1661, and named as one of the Knights of the proposed order of the Royal Oak. As to the latter, who was *bur.* 14 Nov. 1688, at Cardington, see the Visit. of Beds, 1669, and Blaydes' *Genealogia Bedfordiensis.*

(c) He was acquitted in 1674 of the murder of the 3d and last Viscount Tara [I.].

(d) Montague Blundell, his only son, *d.* s.p. and v.p. 21 Jan. 1732/3. Mary, his only da. that had issue, *m.*, 4 June 1733, William Trumbull. Their only child, Mary, *m.* Col. the Hon. Martin Sandys, and had an only child, Mary, *cr.*, in 1802, Baroness Sandys, being ancestress of the present Barons Sandys and of the Marquesses of Downshire [I.].

(e) It is to be observed, however, that William Blundell, who *d.* 1732, being 2d son of the 2d Bart., had two sons, of whom nothing seems to be known.

PARSONS:

cr. 10 Nov. 1620;

afterwards, 1681—1764, Viscounts Rosse [I.];

and finally, 1718-64, Earls of Rosse [I.];

ex. 27 Aug. 1764.

I. 1620. "Sir William Parsons, Knt.,(a) Surveyor General," emigrated to Ireland, about 1590, from Norfolk, being, apparently, s. of William Parsons, of that county; was a Commissioner of Plantation, obtaining considerable grants from the Crown; was Surveyor Gen. [I.] in 1602, and was, in 1611, joint Supervisor of the Crown lands with his br., Laurence Parsons, ancestor of the Baronets [I.], so *cr.* 1677, subsequently (since 1807), Earls of Rosse [I.]. He was *Knighted* in Ireland, 7 June 1620, by the Lord Deputy [I.], and was by patent dat. at Dublin, 10 Nov. 1620 (Privy Seal dat. at Westm., 10 Oct. previous) *cr. a Bart.* [I.], as above. He was M.P. [I.] for Newcastle (co. Dublin), 1613-15, and for co. Wicklow, 1639-48, and was, in 1640, Joint Lord Justice of Ireland, being, however, removed in 1643, charged with treason and imprisoned. He *m.* Elizabeth, said(b) to be niece of Sir Geoffrey Fenton, 1st da. of John Lany, Alderman of Dublin (*d.* 22 Sep. 1624), by Katharine Bostocke. She *d.* on Easter Sunday, 5 and was *bur.* 10 April 1640, at St. Patrick's, Dublin. He *d.* at Westm., and was *bur.* at St. Margaret's there 2 March 1649/50. Will, without date, pr. 18 Feb. 1650/1. The will of Dame Eliz. Parsons pr. 1663.

II. 1650. Sir William Parsons, Bart. [I. 1620], of Bellamont, co. Dublin, grandson and h., being s. and h. of Richard Parsons, sometime M.P. [I.] for Fethard, 1634-39, and for the town of Wicklow, 1639-42, by his 1st wife, Lettice, da. of Sir Adam Loftus, of Rathfarnham, which Richard was living 1639 as s. and h. ap. of the 1st Bart., but *d.* v.p. He *suc. to the Baronetcy*, 2 March 1649/50. He *m.* Catherine, 1st da. of Arthur (Jones), 2d Viscount Ranelagh [I.], by Catherine, da. of Richard (Boyle), 1st Earl of Cork [I.]. He *d.* 31 Dec. 1658. Will pr. 1658, in Prerog. Court [I.] His widow *m.*, as his 2d wife, Hugh (Montgomery), 1st Earl of Mount Alexander [I.]. Her will pr. 1675 in the Prerog. Court [I.].

III. 1658. Sir Richard Parsons, Bart. [I. 1620], of Bellamont, aforesaid, only surv. s. and h., *b.* about 1656; *suc. to the Baronetcy*, 31 Dec. 1658. He *m.* firstly (Lic. Fac., 27 Feb. 1676/7, he aged 19 and she 17), Anne, da. of Thomas Walsingham, of Chesterford, co. Essex, by Anne, da. of Theophilus (Howard), Earl of Suffolk. She *d.* s.p. He *m.* twice afterwards, but each time subsequently to 2 July 1681, when he was *cr.* VISCOUNT ROSSE, co. Wexford [I.], etc. In that peerage this *Baronetcy* then *merged*, the 2d Viscount being *cr.* 16 June 1718, EARL OF ROSSE [I.], but, on the death s.p., 27 Aug. 1764, of the 2d Earl, 3d Viscount and 5th Baronet, it and all other his honours became *extinct*. See *Peerage*.

COOTE:

cr. 2 April 1621,

sometime, 1660—1802, Earls of Mountrath [I.].

I. 1621. "Sir Charles Coote, Knt.," of Castle Cuffe, in Queen's county, 1st s. of Sir Nicholas Coote, of Blownorton, co. Norfolk, by his 1st wife, Anne, da. of Thomas Cooper, of Thurgarton, in that

(a) See O'Donovan's *Annals of Four Masters*, p. 2021, note.

(b) *Lodge.*

county,(a) landed in Ireland in 1600, joining the war against O'Neil; was, in 1602, at the siege of Kingsale; was made Provost Marshal of Connaught for life in 1605; Sheriff for co. Cork, 1606; was *Knighted* by the Lord Deputy [I.], 5 Nov. 1616; made Vice President of Connaught, 1620, and was, by patent dat. at Dublin, 2 April 1621 (Privy Seal(b) dat. at Westm., 24 Jan. 1620/1), *cr. a Bart.* [I.], as above,(c) and also a P.C. [I.]. He was M.P. [I.] for Queen's County, 1639 till his death in 1642. In 1641 he greatly distinguished himself against the Irish rebels, being, at one time, forty-eight hours on horseback, when, in April 1642, effecting the famous passage through Mountrath woods for the relief of Birr. He *m.*, before 1617, Dorothea, yr. da. and coheir of Hugh Cuffe, of Cuffe's Wood, co. Cork. He *d.* 7 May 1642, being slain in a sally to protect the town of Trim.

[For fuller particulars, see *Peerage*, under "Mountrath," Earldom [I.], *cr.* 1660; *ex.* 1802.]

II. 1642. Sir Charles Coote, Bart. [I. 1621], of Castle Cuffe aforesaid, 1st s. and h.,(d) was *b.* about 1610; was *Knighted* in Ireland, 4 June 1626; was v.p. M.P. [I.] for co. Leitrim, 1634-35 and 1639-48, as also for Galway and Mayo, 1654-55, 1656-58, and 1659; *suc. to the Baronetcy*, 7 May 1642, in which year he was made Provost Marshal of Connaught, being, on 16 Oct. 1644, made President of that province; P.C. [I.] 4 Jan. 1647. He was confirmed in the post of President by Parl., which he accordingly assisted in reducing Ireland to subjection, being in 1652 First Commissioner for Connaught, and in Jan. 1659(e) one of the Commissioners of Government. Shortly afterwards he, with Lord Broghill, entered into measures for the restoration of the King, by whom he was, 30 July 1660, confirmed in the post of Lord President of Connaught, etc. He *m.* firstly, Mary, 2d da. and eventually coheir of Sir Francis Ruish, of Castle Jordan and of Ruish Hall in Queen's County. He *m.* secondly, before May 1645, Jane, da. of Sir Robert Hannay, Bart. [S.], which lady was living when he was *cr.*, 6 Sep. 1660, EARL OF MOUNTRATH(f) in Queen's County, etc. [I.]. He *d.* 18 Dec. 1661.

III. 1661. Charles (Coote), 2d Earl of Mountrath, etc., and 3d Bart. [I.], s. and h. by 1st wife, *b.* about 1630; *suc. to the titles*, 19 Dec. 1661; *d.* 30 Aug. 1672.

IV. 1661. Charles (Coote), 3d Earl of Mountrath, etc., and 4th Bart. [I.], s. and h., *b.* about 1635; *suc. to the titles*, 30 Aug. 1672; *d.* 29 May 1709.

V. 1709. Charles (Coote), 3d Earl of Mountrath, etc., and 5th Bart. [I.], s. and h., *b.* about 1680; *suc. to the titles*, 29 May 1709; *d.* unm., 14 Sep. 1715.

(a) *Ex. inform.* G. D. Burtchaell. See p. 223, note "a." With respect to the Coote Baronetcy he remarks that there is a "full pedigree in Ulster Office. *Lodge*, in the earlier portion, is all wrong."

(b) This is given in full in Playfair's *Baronetage*, and is somewhat curious as setting forth the reason the King gives for these Irish creations. See p. 223.

(c) Most of the existing Baronetages state that Coote is the *premier* Baronetcy of Ireland. This honour, even if one grants that the premier *creation*, viz., Sarsfield (which undoubtedly is under forfeiture), is *extinct*, would appear to belong (not to the *fifth*, but) to the second creation, viz., Annesley, and to be now vested in Viscount Valentia [I.].

(d) The 2d son, Chidley Coote, was ancestor of the 9th and all the succeeding Baronets, as also of the Barons Castle-Coote [I.], a Barony which became extinct in 1827. The third son, Richard Coote, was *cr.* in 1660 Baron Coote of Coloony [I.], a dignity which became extinct, together with the Earldom of Bellamont [I.], in 1800.

(e) "Coote was the ablest friend of the Commonwealth in Ireland, and enjoyed the implicit trust of the Parliamentary party, even after the death of Cromwell" [*Nat. Biogr.*].

(f) In recognition of his father's famous passage through Mountrath woods.

VI. 1715. HENRY (COOTE), 4th EARL OF MOUNTRATH, etc., and 6th Bart. [I.], br. and h., *b.* 4 Jan. 1683/4; *suc. to the titles*, 14 Sep. 1715; *d.* 27 March 1720.

VII. 1720. ALGERNON (COOTE), 5th EARL OF MOUNTRATH, etc., and 7th Bart. [I.], br. and h., *bap.* 6 June 1689; *suc. to the titles*, 27 March 1720. He *d.* 27 Aug. 1744.

VIII. 1744. CHARLES HENRY (COOTE), 6th EARL OF MOUNTRATH, etc., and 8th Bart. [I.], only s. and h., *b.* about 1725; *suc. to the titles*, 27 Aug. 1744. He having no legit. issue was *cr.*, 31 July 1800, BARON CASTLE COOTE [I.], with a spec. rem., failing his issue male to a distant cousin. He *d.* unm., 1 March 1802, when the EARLDOM OF MOUNTRATH, etc. [I.], became *extinct*, and the BARONY OF CASTLE COOTE devolved according to the spec. rem.(a), but the *Baronetcy* devolved on the h. male of the body of the grantee, as below.

For fuller particulars, see *Peerage*, under "MOUNTRATH," Earldom [I.], *cr.* 1660; *ex.* 1802.

IX. 1802. SIR CHARLES HENRY COOTE, Bart. [I. 1621], of Ballyfin, Queen's County, and formerly of Ash Hill, co. Limerick, cousin and h. male, being s. and h. of Chidley COOTE, of Ash Hill aforesaid, by his 2d wife, Elizabeth Anne, da. of the Rev. Ralph Carr, of Alderly, co. Chester, which Chidley (who *d.* 6 June 1799) was s. and h. of Robert COOTE, of Ash Hill aforesaid and Ballyclough (*d.* Dec. 1745), who was s. and h. of the Rev. Chidley COOTE, D.D., also of Ash Hill aforesaid (*m.* 31 Jan. 1702 and *d.* 2 Aug. 1720), s. and h. of Lieut.-Col. Chidley COOTE, of Kilmallock, co. Limerick (attainted in 1689 and living 1702), who was s. and h. of Col. Chidley COOTE(b), of Killester, co. Dublin (by Anne, da. and coheir of Sir Thomas PHILIPS, of Newtown Limavady, co. Derry, which Chidley, who *d.* 19 Nov. 1668, was 2d s. of the 1st Bart. He was *b.* 2 Jan. 1792; suc. his father, 6 Aug. 1799, and *suc. to the Baronetcy*, 1 March 1802, on the death of his cousin, the EARL OF MOUNTRATH [I.]; was M.P. for Queen's County in ten parls., 1821-47 and 1852-59; Col. of the Queen's County Militia. He *m.*, 1814, Caroline, da. of John WHALEY, of Whaley Abbey, co. Wicklow, by Anne, da. of John (MEADE), 1st EARL OF CLANWILLIAM [I.]. She *d.* 1837. He *d.* 8 Oct. 1864, at 5 Connaught place, Paddington.

X. 1864. SIR CHARLES HENRY COOTE, Bart. [I. 1621], of Ballyfin aforesaid, s. and h., *b.* Sep. 1815 at Ballyfin; ed. at Eton and at Trin. Coll., Cambridge; Sheriff of Queen's County, 1838; *suc. to the Baronetcy*, 8 Oct. 1864. He *d.* unm. at 5 Connaught place aforesaid, 15 Nov. 1895, aged 80.

XI. 1895. SIR ALGERNON COOTE, Bart. [I. 1621], of Ballyfin aforesaid, next surv. br. and h., being 3d s. of the 9th Bart.; *b.* 29 Sep. 1817; ed. at Eton and Bras. Coll., Oxford; matric., 25 May 1836; B.A., 1840; M.A., 1844; in holy orders; Rector of Marsh Gibbon, Bucks, 1844-56; Vicar of Nonington, Kent, 1856-71; *suc. to the Baronetcy*, 15 Nov. 1895; Sheriff of Queen's County, 1897. He *m.* firstly, 12 Feb. 1847, Cecilia Matilda, da. of John Pemberton PLUMPTRE, of Tredville, Notts. She *d.* 24 May 1878. He *m.* secondly, 25 Sep. 1879, Constance, only surv. da. of T. H. HEADLAM, of Wavertree, Tunbridge Wells. He *d.* 21 Nov. 1899 at Ballyfin aforesaid, aged 82. His widow living 1900.

XII. 1899. SIR ALGERNON CHARLES PLUMPTRE COOTE, Bart. [I. 1621], of Ballyfin aforesaid, 1st s. and h., *b.* 14 Dec. 1847; ed. at Eton and at St. John's College, Cambridge; B.A., 1872; M.A., 1875; sometime

(a) The Barony also became extinct in 1827.
(b) Sir Philips Coote, of Mount Coote, co. Limerick, 2d s. of this Chidley Coote and Anne Philips, his wife, was *bap.* 10 March 1658 and fought for William III, at the battle of the Boyne. By his 2d wife, Elizabeth BRABAZON, 1st da. and coh. of William (Brabazon), 3d EARL OF MEATH [I.], he was ancestor of the family of Coote, now (1900) of Mount Coote aforesaid.

Secretary to the British and Foreign Bible Society, and to the Orphan Working School; *suc. to the Baronetcy*, 21 Nov. 1809. He *m.* firstly, 28 Aug. 1873, Jean, 3d da. of John TROTTER, of Dyrham Park, Herts, by Charlotte Amelia, da. of Thomas Henry (LIDDELL), 1st BARON RAVENSWORTH. She *d.* 15 April 1880. He *m.* secondly, 21 April 1882, Ellen Melesina, 2d da. of Philip Charles Chenevix TRENCH, of Botley Hill, Hants, by Ellen Maria, da. of Thomas TURNER, of the East India Company's Service.

Family Estates.—These, in 1883, consisted of 47,571 acres in Queen's County, 1,017 in co. Roscommon, 878 in co. Kildare, and 340 in co. Limerick. *Total.*—49,686 acres, worth £19,255 a year. *Principal Residence.*—Ballyfin, near Mountrath, Queen's County.

WILMOT, *or* WILLMOTT:
cr. 1 Oct. 1621;
ex. 13 March 1628/9.

I. 1621, to 1629. "ARTHUR WILLMOTT, Esqr.," yr. br. of Edward Wilmot, (the father of Charles, 1st VISCOUNT WILMOT OF ATHLONE [I.], President of the Province of Connaught), both being sons of Edward WILMOT, of Witney, Oxon, formerly of Derwent, co. Gloucester, was, for his services in Ireland, *cr. a Bart.* [I.], as above, by patent, dat. 1 Oct. 1621, at Dublin, the Privy Seal being dat. at West, 5 Sep. previous. He was Sheriff of Hants, 1624-25. He *d.* s.p. legit.,(a) presumably unm., 13 and was *bur.* 20 March 1628/9, at St. James', Clerkenwell, Midx., when the *Baronetcy* became *extinct*. Will, as "of Weld, co. Southampton," dat. 23 Feb. and pr. 16 March 1628/9, by Charles, Viscount Wilmot abovenamed, the nephew. Funeral certificate at the College of Arms.

COURTENAY, *or* COURTNEY:
cr. Jan. 1621/2?;
ex. about 1651?

I. 1622? "GEORGE COURTNEY, Esq., of Newcastle, co. Limerick," was *cr. a Bart.* [I.], as above, presumably(b) in Jan. 1621/2, the Privy Seal being dat. at Westm., 10 Dec. 1621. He, apparently, was the George COURTENAY who was 4th of the seven sons of Sir William COURTENAY, of Powderham, co. Devon (one of the undertakers, in 1585, for the plantation of Ireland), by his 1st wife, Elizabeth, da. of Henry (MANNERS), EARL OF RUTLAND, which George was *b.* about 1580-85, and *m.*, in or before 1616, Catharine, da. of Francis BERKELEY, of Askeaton, co. Limerick, by whom he had three sons, William, Francis and Morris, aged 4, 3 and 2 respectively in 1620 [*Visit. of Devon*]. Of these sons, William and Morris are said(c) to have died s.p.

(a) His illegit. da., Dorothy Wilmot, *m.* firstly, 1 Jan. 1613/4, at St. James' Clerkenwell, Arnold Warren, formerly Waring, of Thorpe Arnold, co. Leicester, and secondly, 27 April 1647, at St. Barth.-the-less, London, Nicholas Lanyon, of Cornwall. By her first husband she was ancestress of the family of Warren, of Stapleford Hall, Notts, which became extinct, 27 Feb. 1822, by the death of Admiral Sir John Borlase Warren, Bart., G.C.B.
(b) No patent is enrolled, but the date of Privy Seal is the same as that of the two succeeding Baronetcies, the patents of which are dated, 14 and 25 Jan. 1621/2 respectively.
(c) Additions "by Parker," as in the copy of the *Visit. of Devon*, 1620, printed by the Harleian Soc., vol. vi, p. 76.

II. 1640? to 1651? SIR WILLIAM COURTENAY, Bart. [I. 1622], 1st s. and h., *b.* 1616; is presumed to have *suc. to the Baronetcy* on his father's death,(a) and to have *d.* s.p.m. about 1651, when the *Baronetcy* became *dormant* or *extinct*.

NUGENT:
cr. 14 Jan. 1621/2;
forfeited 1700?
but assumed till 1775 or later.

I. 1622. "THOMAS NUGENT, Esq., son and heir to Sir Christopher NUGENT, of Moyrath, co. Westmeath," by Elizabeth, da. of Richard LUTTRELL, of Luttrellstown, suc. his father, 19 Dec. 1620, being then above 21, and was *cr. a Bart.* [I.], as above, by patent dat. at Dublin, 14 Jan. 1621/2, the Privy Seal being dat. at Westm., 10 Dec. 1621, having been *Knighted* in Ireland (between these dates, *viz.* on) 11 Jan. 1621/2. He had, in Nov. 1641, a commission for the government of co. Wicklow and was comprehended in the articles made at Kilkenny, 12 May 1652. He *m.* Alison, da. and h. of Robert BARNEWALL, of Robertstown, co. Meath, and was living 1662.

II. 1665? SIR ROBERT NUGENT, Bart. [I. 1622], of Moyrath, aforesaid, and of Taghmon. 2d but 1st surv. s. and h.; *suc. to the Baronetcy* on the death of his father, having been declared innocent of the Rebellion, and, in 1662, restored to the estate when his father should die; had a grant of lands in 1666. He *m.* Thomazine, da. of Patrick EVERS, of Ballygardon, co. Meath, by Elizabeth, da. of Edward NANGLE, of Kildalkey, both in co. Meath.(b) He *d.* 1675.

III. 1675, to 1710. SIR THOMAS NUGENT, Bart., [I. 1622], s. and h.; *suc. to the Baronetcy* in 1675. He was in command of a regiment for James II, whom he followed into France, where he was made Col. of a regiment. He *m.*, 25 March 1675, Anne, yr. da. of Carey (DILLON), 5th EARL OF ROSCOMMON [I.], by Catharine, da. of JOHN WERDEN. At his death, his two sons, John (called "SIR JOHN NUGENT, of Farragh") and Richard having been attainted for treason, the *Baronetcy* became *forfeited*. His widow was *bur.* 18 Nov. 1726, at St. Bride's, Dublin. Will pr. 1726, in Prerog. Court [I.].

The right to this dignity, save for the attainder, was apparently as below.(b)

IV. 1710? "SIR JOHN NUGENT, of Farragh," who, but for the attainder, would have been a Baronet [I. 1622], s. and h. He and his br., Richard, seem to have *d.* s.p., when the title was assumed by

V. 1730? "SIR JAMES NUGENT, of Taghmon," who, but for the attainder, would have been a Baronet [I. 1622], cousin and h. male, being 1st s. and h. of Christopher NUGENT, of Dardistown, M.P. [I.] for Fore in the non-recognised Parl. of 1689, and again, 1692-95, a Col. of Cavalry,

(a) In a letter in the Maryland archives respecting an entry, 25 Nov. 1655, of a power of Attorney from Sir William Courtenay, of Newhouse, co. Wilts, Bart.," to sell lands at Maryland, the writer [as to whom see fuller particulars later on in this work among the "*Creations, 1641-48?* the date of whose patent is unknown," *sub* "Courtenay"], states (to distinguish between three contemporary Baronets all of the name of William Courtenay), that "Sir William Courtenay, of Newcastle, born in 1616, died about four years [*i.e.*, about 1651] before the date [25 Nov. 1655] of the power of Attorney."
(b) *Ex. inform.* G. D. Burtchaell. See p. 223, note "a."

under James II, and a Gen. in France, by Bridget, da. of Robert (BARNEWALL), BARON TRIMLESTOWN [I.], which Christopher was s. and h. of Francis NUGENT, of Dardistown aforesaid, 2d s. of the 1st Bart. He was Col. of a Cavalry Reg. in France, and was Knight of the Military Order of St. Louis, in that kingdom. He *m.* Elizabeth Bridget, da. of Peter REDMOND, of the Hall, co. Wexford, Knight of the Order of Christ in Portugal. He *d.* s.p.m.(a)

VI. 1750? to 1780? "SIR PETER NUGENT," calling himself Baronet [I. 1622], br. and h. male; was "General of the Imperial Cavalry(b)," and apparently unm. in 1764.(c) See pedigree in Ulster's Office; living 1775.

AYLMER:
cr. 25 Jan. 1621/2.

I. 1622. "SIR GERALD AYLMER, Knt., of Donedea [*i.e.*, Donadea], co. Kildare," appears to have been the Gerald Aylmer who was 3d s. of Richard AYLMER, of Lyons, co. Kildare, by Elinor, da. of George FLEMING. He was possibly, however, the Gerald Aylmer "of Castletown," 1st s. and h. of George AYLMER, of Cloncurries, by Mary, da. of Patrick HUSSEY, of Galtrim, which Gerald was 9 years old and no more at his father's death, 26 Dec. 1582, the said George being the 2d son of Richard Aylmer abovenamed. He was *Knighted*, 17 [not 8] June 1598, at Christ Church, Dublin, by the Lord Justices [I.], and was *cr. a Bart.* by patent at Dublin, 25 Jan. 1621/2(d), the Privy Seal being dat. at Westm. 10 Dec. 1621. He *m.* firstly, Mary, widow of James (EUSTACE), 3d VISCOUNT BALTINGLASS [I.] (who *d.* 1583), da. and coheir of Henry TRAVERS (s. and h. of Sir John TRAVERS, Master of the Ordnance), by Janet, da. of Jenico (PRESTON), VISCOUNT GORMANSTON [I.]. She *d.* s.p. 28 Nov. 1610, and was *bur.* (with her father) at Monkstown. He *m.* secondly, Julia, da. of Christopher (NUGENT), LORD DELVIN [I.], by Mary, da. of Gerald (FITZGERALD), EARL OF KILDARE [I.]. She *d.* 12 Nov. 1617. He *d.* 19 Aug. 1634. Both are *bur.* at Donadea. M.I. Funeral certificates [I.].

II. 1634. SIR ANDREW AYLMER, Bart. [I. 1622], of Donadea aforesaid, only s. and h. by 2d wife, *b.* between 1610 and 1617; said to have been *Knighted* v.p.; *suc. to the Baronetcy* 19 Aug. 1634. He *m.*, in 1634, Ellen, sister of James, 1st DUKE OF ORMONDE, da. of Thomas BUTLER, *styled* VISCOUNT THURLES, by Elizabeth, da. of Sir John POYNTZ. He was living April 1670 and 24 May 1671, but *d.* before 1681.

III. 1681? SIR FITZGERALD AYLMER, Bart. [I. 1622], of Donadea aforesaid, grandson and h., being only s. and h. of Capt. Garret AYLMER, by Jane, da. and h. of Philip FITZGERALD, of Alloone, co. Kildare, which Garret was s. and h. ap. of the late Bart., but *d.* v.p. 20 and was *bur.* 23 Dec. 1663, at Christ Church, Dublin. Funeral certificate [I.].(e) He was *b.* 1663; *suc. to the Baronetcy* in or before 1681. He spent great part of the family estate. He *m.* June 1681, Helen, 2d da. of Luke (PLUNKETT), 3d EARL OF FINGALL [I.], by

(a) Anna Joanna, his only da., *m.*, July 1761, Edmund Rothe.
(b) His services, entirely in the French army, are set forth in O'Callaghan's *Irish Brigades*, p. 613.
(c) At that date his yr. br., Patrick Nugent, Capt. of Foot, was dead s.p.
(d) In Playfair's *Baronetage* this creation is spoken of as "Premier Baronet of Ireland," and is placed before that of Coote, its creation being given as "25 Jan. 1621," while that of the latter is given as "2 April 1621." This last date was probably (from ignorance of the old style) thought to be later than the former.
(e) *Ex. inform.* G. D. Burtchaell. See p. 223, note "a."

Margaret, da. of Donough (MACCARTHY), 1st EARL OF CLANCARTY [I.]. He *d.* of the small pox, 9 and was *bur.* 11 June 1685, at Donadea, being not quite 22. Funeral certificate [I.]. His widow *m.* 1694, Michael FLEMING, of Staholmock, co. Meath, having £500 a year jointure.

IV. 1685. SIR JUSTIN AYLMER, Bart. [I. 1622], of Donadea aforesaid, s. and h., *b.* 24 Feb. 1681; *suc. to the Baronetcy*, 11 June 1685; educated in France; outlawed (with his mother) by James II, which outlawry was, however, reversed 9 Aug. 1692. In 1706 he was worth £500 a year. He *m.*, in 1702, Ellice, 1st da. of Sir Gerald AYLMER, 2d Bart. [I. 1662], of Balrath, by Mary, da. of Sir John BELLEW, of Willystown, co. Louth. He *d.* 1711. His widow *m.* firstly, Philip ROCHE; secondly, in March 1714, Luke DILLON, of Clonbrock; and thirdly (for her 4th and last husband) in May 1718, John DILLON, of Mile Abbey, co. Kildare. She *d.* 27 Aug. 1741.

V. 1711. SIR GERALD AYLMER, Bart. [I. 1622], of Donadea aforesaid, s. and h. He *suc. to the Baronetcy* at an early age, in 1711, and to estates worth about £1,750 a year. He *m.*, Oct. 1726, Lucy, da. of Sir John NORRIS, of Hempstead, Kent, Admiral of the Fleet, with whom he had £3,000 portion and £600 a year jointure. He *d.* in Dublin, 6 Jan. 1736/7. Will dat. 25 April 1735, proved in Prerog. Court [I.] 1736. His widow *m.*, Nov. 1737, Robert FISHER.

VI. 1737. SIR FITZGERALD AYLMER, Bart. [I. 1622], of Donadea aforesaid, s. and h., *b.* 14 Sep. 1736; *suc. to the Baronetcy*, in his infancy, 6 Jan. 1736/7; was Sheriff of co. Kildare, 1761; M.P. [I.] for Roscommon, 1761-68; for Old Leighlin, 1769-76; for Kildare, 1776-83, and for Harristown (in two parls.), 1783-94. He *m.*, 15 Sep. 1764, Elizabeth, da. and h. of Fenton COLE, of Silver Hill, co. Fermanagh, by Dorothy, da. of Alexander SANDERSON, of Drumkeevil, co. Cavan. He *d.* Feb. 1794. His will pr. 1794, and that of his widow, 1797, in the Prerog. Court [I.].

VII. 1794. SIR FENTON AYLMER, Bart. [I. 1622], of Donadea, aforesaid, s. and h., *b.* at Donadea, Nov. 1770; ed. at Trin. coll., Dublin; B.A., 1788; *suc. to the Baronetcy*, Feb. 1794; Sheriff of co. Kildare, 1795. He *m.*, 4 June 1795, Jane-Grace, sister of John, 6th BARON CARBERY [I.], da. of Sir John EVANS-FREKE, 1st Bart. [I. 1768], by Elizabeth, da. of Arthur (GORE), 1st EARL OF ARRAN [I.]. He *d.* 23 May 1816. His widow *d.* 31 Dec. 1827.

VIII. 1816. SIR GERALD-GEORGE AYLMER, Bart. [I. 1622], of Donadea aforesaid, s. and h., *b.* 15 Sep. 1798, at Carnarvon; sometime Lieut. in the 1st Dragoon Guards; *suc. to the Baronetcy*, 23 May 1816; Sheriff of co. Kildare, 1827. He *m.*, 24 April 1826, Maria, 1st da. and coh. of James HODGSON, of Carlisle, Col. in the East India Company's Service. He *d.* 8 Feb. 1878, at Donadea Castle, aged 79. His widow *d.* 9 May 1879.

IX. 1878. SIR GERALD GEORGE AYLMER, Bart. [I. 1622], of Donadea aforesaid, only s. and h., *b.* 26 May 1830, in Dublin; ed. at Sandhurst Coll.; Sheriff of co. Kildare, 1854; *suc. to the Baronetcy*, 8 Feb. 1878. He *m.*, 6 April 1853, Alice Hester Caroline, 4th da. of Conway Richard DOBBS, of Castle Dobbs, co. Antrim, by Charlotte Maria, da. and coheir of William SINCLAIR, of Fortwilliam, in that county. He *d.* 25 June 1883, aged 53. His widow living 1900.

X. 1883. SIR JUSTIN GERALD AYLMER, Bart. [I. 1622], of Donadea aforesaid, only s. and h., *b.* 17 Nov. 1863; *suc. to the Baronetcy*, 25 June 1883; having entered Trin. Coll., Cambridge in Oct. 1882, where he *d.* unm. 15 March 1885 (from the effects of a fall from his bicycle), aged 21.(a)

(a) The estate of Donadea Castle devolved on his only sister and heir, Caroline Maria. This, in 1883, consisted of 15,396 acres in co. Kildare, worth £6,890 a year. The 9th Bart. had, also, lands in Cumberland (acreage not stated) worth £500 a year.

I

XI. 1885, March. SIR ARTHUR PERCY AYLMER, Bart. [I. 1622], great uncle and h. male, being 2d s. of the 7th Bart., *b.* 31 Aug. 1801; ed. at Trin. Coll., Dublin; B.A., 1823; M.A., 1826. He *m.*, 12 Dec. 1833, Martha, da. of Richard REYNELL, of Killynon, co. Westmeath. He *suc. to the Baronetcy*, 15 March 1885, and *d.* at Cork, a few weeks later, 7 May 1885, aged 83. His widow *d.* 3 Feb. 1887, at Park View, Cork, in her 78th year.

XII. 1885, May. SIR ARTHUR PERCY FITZ-GERALD AYLMER, Bart. [I. 1622], grandson and h., being s. and h. of Fenton John AYLMER, Capt. 97th Foot, by Isabella Eleanor, da. of George DARLING, of Fowberry tower, Northumberland, which Fenton, who *d.* v.p. (of illness contracted in the Crimean war) 9 April 1862, aged 26, was s. and h. ap. of late Bart. He was *b.* 2 March 1858, and *suc. to the Baronetcy*, 7 May 1885. He *m.* firstly, 27 Nov. 1878, Annie, yst. da. of John SANGER of London. She *d.* 1884. He *m.* secondly, in 1885, Anne, divorced wife of George STELLE, of Chicago, da. of J. Douglas REID, of New York, which marriage was dissolved in 1886.

GORE:

cr. 2 Feb. 1621/2;

sometime, 1741-46, GORE-ST. GEORGE;

also sometime, 1764—1802, BARON GORE OF MANOR GORE [I.],

and, 1768—1802, VISCOUNT BELLISLE [I.];

being subsequently, 1772—1802, EARL OF ROSS [I.].

I. 1622. "CAPTAIN PAUL(a) GORE, of Magharabeg [*i.e.*, Magherabegg], co. Donegal," stated to be a yr. br. of Sir John GORE, Lord Mayor of London (1624-25), being 8th and yst. s. of Gerard GORE, Alderman of London (*d.* 18 Dec. 1607, aged 91, by Helen, da. of Ralph DAVENANT, of Essex, was Commander of a troop of horse in Ireland, being entrusted in Nov. 1602 with Queen Elizabeth's protection to Rory O'Donnell, whom he accordingly brought to Athlone for his submission to the Lord Deputy [I.], and received in recompense the Barony of Boylagh and Bannagh, co. Donegal, which was exchanged, 3 Jan. 1610, for the estate (1348 acres) of Magherabegg in the same county; was M.P. [I.] for Ballyshannon, 1613-15, and was *cr. a Bart.* [I.] as above by patent dat. at Dublin 2 Feb. 1621/2, the Privy Seal being dat. 8 Sep. 1621 at Windsor. He *m.*, after 1607, Isabella, da. of Francis WYCLIFFE, said(b) to be "niece to Sir Thomas WENTWORTH, after EARL OF STRAFFORD." He *d.* Sep. 1629, and was *bur.* in the Abbey church at Donegal. Will dat. 19 Sep., pr. Nov. 1629, in Prerog. Court [I.]. Funeral certificate [I.].

II. 1629. SIR RALPH GORE, Bart. [I. 1622], of Magherabegg, otherwise Manor-Gore, aforesaid, 1st s. and h.(c); *suc. to the Baronetcy* in Sep. 1629; was M.P. [I.] for co. Donegal, 1639-48. His house was captured by the Irish rebels, for whose suppression he was, 10 Nov. 1641, made Col. of a Reg. of

(a) The name is "Poule," both in his will and funeral certificate, and in various contemporary documents he is so described; sometimes, indeed, as "Powel," or "Powle." [*Ex. inform.* G. D. Burtchaell. See p. 223, note "a".]

(b) Lodge's *Peerage of Ireland*, 1789, vol. iii, p. 278. The statement, however, appears to be untrustworthy.

(c) Of his younger brothers, Arthur Gore, of Newton Gore, co. Mayo, the 2d son, was *cr. a Bart.* [I.], 10 April 1662, his grandson and heir, being *cr.* 12 April 1762, Earl of Arran [I.], ancestor of the present Earl; Sir Francis Gore, of Artaman, co. Sligo, the 4th son, was great grandfather of Booth Gore, of Lissadell in that county, who was *cr. a Bart.* [I.] 30 Aug. 1760, and is ancestor of the present Baronet.

five hundred men. He *m.* (Lic. 1640) Anne, 2d da. of William (CAULFEILD), 2d BARON CAULFEILD OF CHARLEMONT [I.], by Mary, da. of Sir John KING. He *d.* about 1661. Inq. p.m. at Enniskillen, 1 Feb. (1661/2), 12 Car. II. His widow *m.* Sir Paul HARRIS, and subsequently (as her 3d husband) Sir John WROTH.

III. 1661? SIR WILLIAM GORE, Bart. [I. 1622], of Manor Gore aforesaid, only s. and h.; ed. at Trin. Coll., Dublin, 1657; *suc. to the Baronetcy* about 1661; M.P. [I.] for Banagher, 1661-66; Sheriff of co. Fermanagh, 1668; of co. Donegal, 1673; LL.D., Dublin, 1676; P.C. [I.] to Charles II; Custos Rotulorum of co. Leitrim, 1684. He *m.* Hannah, niece to Gustavus, 1st VISCOUNT BOYNE [I.], elder da. and coheir of James HAMILTON, of Manor Hamilton, co. Leitrim, by Catherine, da. of Claud (HAMILTON), 1st BARON STRABANE [I.]. He *d.* about 1703. Will dat. 1 March 1703, pr. 12 May 1705, in Prerog. Court [I.] His widow *d.* 16 May 1733, and was *bur.* at St. Mary's, Dublin.

IV. 1703? SIR RALPH GORE, Bart. [I. 1622], of Manor Gore and Manor Hamilton aforesaid, s. and h.; ed. at Trin. Coll. Dublin, 1693; *suc. to the Baronetcy* about 1703; M.P. [I.] for Donegal, 1703-13; for co. Donegal, in two parls., 1713-27, and for Clogher, 1727-33; Sheriff of co. Leitrim, 1710; P.C. [I.], 1714 and 1728; Chancellor of the Exchequer [I.], 1717; LL.D., Dublin, 1718; SPEAKER OF HOUSE OF COMMONS [I], 1729, and one of the LORDS JUSTICES [I.], 1730 and 1732 till his death. He *m.* firstly (Lic. 1705), Elizabeth, da. of Sir Robert COLVILLE, of Newtown, co. Leitrim. She *d.* s.p.m. He *m.* secondly, Elizabeth, sister and h. (Jan. 1721) of St. George ASHE, only da. of St. George ASHE, Bishop of Clogher, by Jane, sister and coh. (1726) of Richard ST. GEORGE, of Dunmore, co. Galway, da. of George ST. GEORGE, of Dunmore aforesaid. He *d.* 23 Feb. 1732-3, and was *bur.* in Christ Church, Dublin. Will dat. 5 Feb. 1726, pr. 29 March 1733, in Prerog. Court [I.]. His widow *d.* 7 Dec. 1741, and was *bur.* with him.

V. 1733. SIR ST. GEORGE GORE, *afterwards* (1741) GORE-ST. GEORGE, Bart. [I. 1622], of Manor Gore and Dunmore aforesaid, 1st s. and h., *b.* 25 June 1722; *suc. to the Baronetcy*, 23 Feb. 1732/3, and to the estate of Dunmore on the death, 7 Dec. 1741, of his mother. In 1726, when he assumed the name of *St. George* after that of *Gore*, was M.P. [I.] for co. Donegal, 1741-46; Sheriff of co. Fermanagh, 1746; Gov. of co. Donegal, 1748. He *m.* 22 Sep. 1743, Anne, only sister of Francis Pierpoint (CONYNGHAM, *formerly* BURTON), 2d BARON CONYNGHAM OF MOUNT CHARLES [I.], da. of the Rt. Hon. Francis BURTON, of Buncraggy, co. Clare, by Mary, sister of Henry, EARL CONYNGHAM OF MOUNT CHARLES [I.], da. of Major-Gen. Henry CONYNGHAM. She *d.* at Bath, 23 April 1745. He *d.* s.p. 25 Sep. 1746, and was *bur.* at Castletown, co. Kildare.

VI. 1746. SIR RALPH GORE, Bart. [I. 1622], of Manor Gore and Dunmore aforesaid, next br. and h., *b.* 23 Nov. 1725 at Bellisle,(a) co. Fermanagh; ed. at Trin. Coll., Dublin; *suc. to the Baronetcy*, 25 Sep. 1746; was M.P. [I.] for co. Donegal, in two parls., 1747-64; Joint Gov. of that county. He had (previously) joined the Army, as Lieut. 33d Foot, Nov. 1744; was severely wounded at the battle of Fontenoy, 30 April 1745, and distinguished himself, as Captain, at the battle of Laffeldt, 2 July 1747, being thanked next day at the head of his regiment; was Lieut.-Col. com. of the 92d Reg. (Donegal Light Infantry); Sheriff of co. Donegal, 1755; of co. Fermanagh, 1760. He *m.* firstly, 23 Feb. 1754, Catharine, sister of the Rt. Hon. Thomas CONOLLY, 1st da. of William CONOLLY, by Anne, da. of Thomas (WENTWORTH), EARL OF STRAFFORD. She was living when he was *cr.*, 30 June 1764, BARON GORE OF MANOR GORE, co. Donegal [I.], being subsequently *cr.*, 25 Aug. 1768, VISCOUNT BELLISLE of Bellisle, co. Fermanagh [I.], and, on 4 Jan. 1772, EARL OF ROSS, co. Fermanagh [I.]. He *d.* s.p.s.(b) in 1802 (before 16 Sep.), when the *peerage* titles became *extinct*. See fuller particulars in *Peerage*.

(a) It appears (Lodge's *Peerage of Ireland*, 1789, vol. iii, p. 283) that the 4th Bart., who in right of his mother possessed the estates of Manor Hamilton, co. Leitrim, "adorning the island of Ballymacmanus, in Lough Earne, co. Fermanagh, with many elegant improvements, gave it the name of *Belle Isle*."

(b) His only child, Ralph Gore, *styled* Viscount Bellisle, *b.* 3 Oct. 1774, *d.* unm. 1789.

VII. 1802. SIR RALPH GORE, Bart. [I. 1622], of Manor Gore aforesaid, nephew and h., being s. and h. of Richard GORE, of Sandymount, co. Wicklow, by Martha, da. of the Rev. Thomas FIOTT, of Guernsey, which Richard (*b.* 16 Oct. 1728, *d.* 1785-92) was 3d s. of the 4th Bart. He was *b.* 3 Dec. 1758, and *suc. to the Baronetcy* in 1802. He *m.*, 22 May 1802, Grace, da. of Barry (MAXWELL), 1st EARL OF FARNHAM [I.], by his 2d wife, Grace, da. of Arthur BURDETT, of Ballymaney. He *d.* 25 March 1842, at Brunswick square, Brighton, in his 83d year. His widow *d.* 19 June 1866, at Horsham park, aged 94.

VIII. 1842. SIR ST. GEORGE GORE, Bart. [I. 1622], of Manor Gore aforesaid, only s. and h.; *b.* 28 April 1811, at Dublin; matric. at Oxford (Oriel Coll.), 17 June 1830. He *d.* unm. 31 Dec. 1878, at Inverness, aged 67.

IX. 1878. SIR ST. GEORGE RALPH GORE, Bart. [I. 1622], of Kingsholm House, Brisbane, in Queensland, cousin and h. male, being s. and h. of St. George Richard GORE, of Lyndhurst, in Queensland aforesaid, by Frances, da. of Edward CALDWELL, of Lyndhurst, Hants, which St. George Richard (who *d.* 16 Aug. 1871, aged 59) was s. and h. of the Rev. Thomas GORE, Rector of Mulrancan, in the diocese of Ferns (*d.* 4 June 1834, aged 66), who was yr. br. of the 7th Bart. He was *b.* 21 Sep. 1841; was an emigration agent in Queensland, and *suc. to the Baronetcy*, 31 Dec. 1878. He *m.*, 6 April 1876, Eugenia Marion, da. of the Hon. Eyles Irwin Caulfeild BROWNE, Solicitor, Member of the Legislative Council of Queensland. He *d.* 17 Oct. 1887, at Dunrobin, Brisbane, aged 46.

X. 1887. SIR RALPH ST. GEORGE CLAUDE GORE, Bart. [I. 1622], of Kingsholm house aforesaid, 1st s. and h., *b.* 12 May 1877; *suc. to the Baronetcy*, 17 Oct. 1887; entered the Army 1898.

Family Estates.—These, in 1878 (see De Burgh's *Landowners of Ireland*, of that date), consisted of 2,592 acres, co. Galway; 488, co. Limerick, and 96, co. Dublin. *Total*, 3,176 acres, valued at £1,384 a year.

LEIGH:

cr. Feb. 1621/2?(a);

ex. 30 July 1638.

I. 1622? "DANIEL(b) LEIGH, Esq.," was, by Privy Seal, dat. at Westm. 10 Dec. 1621, *cr. a Bart.* [I.], as above, presumably by patent dat. Feb. 1621/2(a), the Privy Seal being dat. at Westm. 10 Dec. 1621. He was *Knighted* in Ireland (about the same date), 2 Feb. 1621/2, by the Lord Deputy [I.]; was Sheriff of co. Tyrone, 1624. He *m.* Mary, da. of John STANTON, of (—), in England. His admon. (as "Daniel Leigh, *Knt.*"), 1 Feb. 1633, at Prerog. Court [I.], granted to "Arthur Leigh, Bart.," his son. The will of "Mary CHESWICK, *alias* Dame Mary LEIGH, of Omagh, co. Tyrone, widow," is pr. 1659, in the Prerog. Court [I.].

(a) The Privy Seals for the Baronetcies [I.] of Gore, Leigh and Fish, bear date, respectively, 8 Sep. 1621, 10 Dec. 1621, and 21 Dec. 1621, the patent for Gore dates 2 Feb. 1621/2, and that for Fish 12 Feb. 1621/2. It may, therefore, be presumed that the patent for Leigh is also in Feb. 1621/2.

(b) "John, Edmund and Daniel Leigh, three brothers, came to Ulster under the auspices of Sir Henry Bagenall." [Hill's *Plantation in Ulster*, p. 543].

II. 1633, to 1638. SIR ARTHUR LEIGH, Bart. [I. 1622], of Omagh and Fentenagh, co. Tyrone, only s. and h., *suc. to the Baronetcy* in 1633. He *m.* Elizabeth, 1st da. of Sir William RYVES, one of the Justices of the King's Bench [I.]. He *d.* s.p. 30 July 1638,(a) at (—), co. Londonderry, when the *Baronetcy* became *extinct.* Funeral certificate at Ulster's office. Will dat. 27 Feb. 1635, pr. at Prerog. Court [I.], 1638.

FISH(b):
cr. 12 Feb. 1621/2;
ex. about 1670.

I. 1622. "JOHN FISH, Esq.,(c) of Lissameon, co. Cavan," as also of Southill, Beds, only s. and h. of George FISH, of Southill aforesaid, by his 2d wife, Judith, da. of John HAMBY, Auditor of the Prest; was M.P. [I.] for co. Cavan, 1613-15; Sheriff of co. Cavan, 1616, and was *cr. a Bart.* [I.], as above, by patent dat. 12 Feb. 1621/2, at Dublin, the Privy Seal being dat. 21 Dec. 1621, at Westm. He *m.* Mary, da. of Edward PULTER, of Great Wymondley and Bradfield, Herts, by Mary, relict of Thomas HARLESTONE, da. of Sir Rowland LYTTON. He *d.* (Tuesday) 9 March 1623. Funeral certificate [I.]. His widow *m.* (as his second wife) Sir John PHILPOTT, 3d Justice of the Common Pleas [I.], 1621-37.

II. 1623. SIR EDWARD FISH, Bart. [I. 1622], of Southill aforesaid, only s. and h.; admitted to Lincoln's Inn, 18 May 1620; *suc. to the Baronetcy*, Feb. 1623, being then aged 24. He *m.*, before 1623, Elizabeth, da. and coheir of Martin HETON, Bishop of Ely, 1599-1609. She was *bur.* 23 Nov. 1657, at St. James', Clerkenwell. He was *bur.* there 28 July 1658. Admon., as "of Chertsey, Surrey," 10 Nov. 1658.

III. 1658, to 1670? SIR EDWARD FISH, Bart. [I. 1622], only s. and h., was 6 years old in May 1635; *suc. to the Baronetcy* in July 1658, when he was administrator to his father. He *d.* s.p., probably, about 1670, when the *Baronetcy* became *extinct.*(d)

BROWNE:
cr. 16 Feb. 1621/2,
afterwards, 1689—1798, *titular* VISCOUNTS KENMARE [I.],
being, since 1798, *actual* VISCOUNTS KENMARE [I.],
and, since 1801, EARLS OF KENMARE [I.].

I. 1622. "VALENTINE BROWNE, Esq., of Mohaliffe [Molahiffe], co. Kerry," s. and h. of Sir Nicholas BROWNE, of Rosse Castle, in that county, by Sheela, or Julia, da. of O'Sullivan BEAR, of co. Cork; was admitted to

(a) Mary, his only sister and heir, *m.* "George Arundell, Esq.," who testified the truth of the funeral certificate.
(b) *Ex. inform.* G. D. Burtchaell. See p. 223, note "a."
(c) "This undertaker came from Bedford, as one of Sir Francis Anderson's company, and represented himself as worth £300 per annum." [Hill's *Plantation in Ulster* (p. 281), where it is said that his Baronetcy cost him more than £1,000. The statement therein that he had been previously Knighted is erroneous]. His sister, Dorothy, was wife of Michael Boyle, Bishop of Waterford, 1619-35, which may account for his connection with Ireland.
(d) His sisters became his coheirs, of whom (1) Alice, *m.* (—) Harington, of co. Lincoln, and (2) Anne, *b.* 16 Feb. 1623, *m.* Sir Thomas Raymond, one of the Justices of the King's Bench, and was mother of Robert, 1st Baron Raymond of Abbots Langley, Chief Justice of the King's Bench, 1725-32.

Gray's Inn, 12 March 1611/2, having previously suc. his father, 12 Dec. 1606, in the vast family estates (including the celebrated lakes of Killarney) in both those counties(a) (which were confirmed to him, 28 May 1618), and was *cr. a Bart.* [I.], as above, by patent dat. 16 Feb. 1621/2, at Dublin; the Privy Seal being dat. 21 Dec. 1621, at Westm.; was Sheriff of co. Kerry, 1623. He *m.* firstly, Ellice, da. of Gerald (FITZGERALD), EARL OF DESMOND [I.], the "rebel Earl," by his 2d wife, Eleanor, da. of Edmund (BUTLER), BARON DUNBOYNE [I.]. He *m.* secondly, Sheela, da. of Charles (MACCARTY), 1st VISCOUNT MUSKERRY [I.], by Margaret, da. of Donough (O'BRIEN), 4th EARL OF THOMOND [I.]. She *d.* 21 Jan. 1633. He *d.* 7 Sep. 1633, and was *bur.* in the church of Killarney. Funeral certificate [I.].

II. 1633. SIR VALENTINE BROWNE, Bart. [I. 1622], of Molahiffe aforesaid, 1st s. and h., by 1st wife; *suc. to the Baronetcy* in Sep. 1633; was M.P. [I.] for co. Kerry, 1634-35 and 1639 till December. He *m.* Mary (sister of his stepmother), da. of Charles (MACCARTY), 1st VISCOUNT MUSKERRY [I.], by Margaret, da. of Donough (O'BRIEN), 4th EARL OF THOMOND [I.]. He *d.* 25 April and was *bur.* 6 July 1640, in the church of Killarney. Funeral certificate [I.]. His widow *m.* Edward FITZGERALD, of Ballymallon.

III. 1640. SIR VALENTINE BROWNE, Bart. [I. 1622], of Molahiffe aforesaid, 1st s. and h., *b.* 1638, being but 2 years old at his father's death,(b) when he *suc. to the Baronetcy*, 25 April 1640; was, in Feb. 1687, a Commissioner of Oyer and Terminer, co. Kerry; P.C. [I.] to James II, to whom, he was Col. of a Reg. of Foot, and a staunch adherent, and by whom, after his deposition, 11 Dec. 1688, by the *English* Parl. (but when he was in full possession of all his rights as King of Ireland), he was *cr.*,(c) 20 May 1689,(d) BARON CASTLEROSSE and VISCOUNT KENMARE [I.]. He was taken prisoner, 12 July 1691, at the battle of Aughrim, by the English and Dutch forces, and was (together with his eldest son) apparently, attainted in consequence. He *m.* Jane, da. and h. of the Hon. Sir Nicholas PLUNKETT, of Balrath, co. Meath (3d s. of Christopher, BARON KILLEEN [I.]), by (—), his 1st wife, da. and coheir of William TURNER, Alderman of Dublin. He *d.* 1694. Will dat. 7 June 1690, pr. 23 June 1691, in Prerog. Court [I.].

IV. 1694. SIR NICHOLAS BROWNE, Bart. [I. 1622], *titular* VISCOUNT KENMARE, etc. [I.], s. and h.; was Sheriff for co. Cork, 1687; M.P. [I.] for co. Kerry, 1689, in the Parl. of James II, and was Col. of a Reg. of Foot in the army of that King, being, together with his father, apparently, attainted, whereby, during their lives, the estates were forfeited. He *suc. to his father's designation* in 1604. He accompanied James II to St. Germain. He *m.*, in 1684, his cousin, Helen, 1st da. and coheir of Thomas BROWNE, of Hospital, co. Limerick (a yr. s. of the 1st Bart. by his 2d wife), by his cousin, Elizabeth, da. and h. of Sir John BROWNE, of Hospital aforesaid. She was *bur.* (as "Mrs. Ellen Browne, w.") 16 July 1700, at St. James', Westm. Admon. (as "Dame Helen Browne, *alias* Viscountess Kenmare") 22 July 1700. He *d.* at Brussels, April 1720.

(a) The reversion to these estates, formerly those of the family of McCarthy More, had been purchased, 28 June 1588, by his grandfather, Sir Valentine Browne, on the death s.p.m. of Donald, Earl of Clancare [I.], which happened in or shortly before 1601.
(b) See *McGillycuddy Papers*, by M. Brady, D.D., 1867, p. 181, in the petition of Sir V. Browne, to the Duke of Ormonde, to whom his wardship had been granted.
(c) This was one of seven Irish Peerages so created, viz. (1), the Dukedom of Tyrconnell, etc., 30 March 1689; (2) the Barony of Fitton of Gosworth, 1 April 1689; (3) the Barony of Bourke of Bophin, 2 April 1689; (4) the Barony of Nugent of Riverston, 3 April 1689; (5) the Viscountcy of Kenmare, etc., 20 May 1689; (6) the Viscountcy of Mountcashell, etc., 23 May 1689, and (7) the Viscountcy of Mount Leinster, 23 Aug. 1689. All these creations were duly inscribed on the patent rolls of Ireland, from which they have never been erased.
(d) See the preamble to this creation in Lodge's *Peerage of Ireland*, edit. 1789, vol. vii, p. 55, *sub* "Aylmer," where there is a full account of this family.

V. 1720. SIR VALENTINE BROWNE, Bart. [I. 1622], *titular* VISCOUNT KENMARE, etc. [I.], s. and h., *b.* 1695; *suc. to his father's designation* in April 1720, and appears to have recovered the family estates. He *m.* firstly, Nov. 1720, Honora, 2d da. of Col. Thomas BUTLER, of Kilcash, by Margaret, DOWAGER VISCOUNTESS MAGENNIS [I.], da. of William (BOURKE), 7th EARL OF CLANRICARDE [I.]. She *d.* of small pox, 1730. He *m.* secondly, Oct. 1735, Mary, DOWAGER COUNTESS OF FINGALL [I.], da. of Maurice FITZGERALD, of Castle Ishen, co. Cork. He *d.* 30 June 1736. His widow *m.* (for her 3d husband and as the second of his three wives), John (BELLEW), 4th BARON BELLEW OF DULEEK [I.], who *d.* s.p.m. in 1770. She *d.* in London, 1792.

VI. 1736. SIR THOMAS BROWNE, Bart. [I. 1622], *titular* VISCOUNT KENMARE, etc. [I.], 2d but only surv. s. and h. by 1st wife, *b.* 1726; *suc. to his father's designation*, 30 June 1736. He *m.*, Dec. 1750, Anne, da. of Thomas COOKE, of Painstown, co. Carlow, by Helen, da. of Nicholas PURCELL. She *d.* before him. He *d.* at Killarney, 9 Sep. 1795. Will pr. 1795 at Prerog. Court [I.].

VII. 1795. SIR VALENTINE BROWNE, Bart. [I. 1622], *titular* VISCOUNT KENMARE, etc. [I.], only s. and h.; *b.* Jan. 1754; *suc. to his father's designation*, 9 Sep. 1795. He *m.* firstly, 7 July 1777, Charlotte, da. of Henry (DILLON), 11th VISCOUNT DILLON OF COSTELLO-GALLEN [I.], by Charlotte, da. of George Henry (LEE), 3d EARL OF LICHFIELD. She, who was *b.* 11 Sep. 1755, *d.*, s.p.m., 15 Aug. 1782, at Cambray. He *m.* secondly, 24 Aug. 1785, at Lyons, co. Kildare, Mary, 1st da. of Matthew AYLMER, of Lyons aforesaid, by Margaret, da. of George MATHEW, of Bowastown, co. Tipperary. She was living when he (as "*Sir Valentine Browne, Bart.*," the peerage conferred, in 1689, by James II, not being recognised) was *cr.*, 12 Feb. 1798, BARON CASTLEROSSE and VISCOUNT KENMARE [I.], that being the same title as the one conferred on his ancestor by James II, as abovementioned. He was subsequently *cr.*, 3 Jan. 1801, EARL OF KENMARE, etc. [I.]. In these peerage titles this *Baronetcy* then *merged*, and still so continues. See *Peerage.*

BROWNE(a):
cr. 30 March 1622;
ex. probably soon after 1682.

I. 1622. "RICHARD BROWNE, Esq., of Kishack [now Kishoge], co. Dublin," and afterwards of Bellanemore [now Ballynamore], co. Longford, s. and h. of Patrick BROWNE(b), of Kishoge, Alderman of Dublin (*d.* 1613), by Margaret, sister of Thomas GERROTT, also Alderman of that city, was himself Sheriff of Dublin, 1605, being Mayor thereof, 1614, 1615, and 1620, and was *cr. a Bart.* [I.], as above, by patent, 30 March 1622, at Dublin, the Privy Seal being dat. at Westm., 17 Jan. 1621/2; was Sheriff of co. Longford, 1623. He *m.* firstly, before 1607, Margaret, da. of John MALONE, Alderman of Dublin. She *d.* 9 Jan. 1612, and was *bur.* at St. Audoen's, Dublin. He *m.* secondly, Mary, widow of James O'FERRALL BOY, sister of Lucas, 1st EARL OF FINGALL [I.], 3d da. of Christopher (PLUNKETT), LORD KILLEEN [I.], by Janet, da. of Sir Lucas DILLON, Chief Baron of the Exchequer [I.]. He *d.* in 1642, and was *bur.* at Christ Church, Ballynamore. Will dat. 14 Sep. 1642, pr. 1642, in Prerog. Court [I.]. The will of his widow (as "Dame Mary Browne, *alias* Plunkett"), dat. 1 March 1645, pr. there 1645.

(a) *Ex. inform.* G. D. Burtchaell (see p. 223, note "a"), some of the particulars herein being supplemental to an article on this family contributed by him to the Journal of the Royal Soc. of Antiquaries [I.].
(b) The pedigree, going back for several generations, is in the *Visit. of Dublin*, 1607.

II. 1642. SIR SILVESTER BROWNE, Bart. [I. 1622], of the city of Dublin, 2d but 1st surv. s. and h.(a) by 1st wife; *suc. to the Baronetcy* in 1642. He *m.* Mary, da. of (—) ROCHE. He *d.* s.p.m.(b) 8 and was *bur.* 10 May 1657. Funeral entry. Will dat. 23 Feb. 1643, pr. 3 Nov. 1663 in the Prerog. Court [I.] by the widow, who was living 1666.

III. 1657, to 1690? SIR RICHARD BROWNE, Bart. [I. 1622], of Ballynamore aforesaid, br. (of the half blood) and h. male, being only 3d and yst. s. of the 1st Bart. and only son by 2d wife; *suc. to the Baronetcy*, 8 May 1657. He was living 3 Nov. 1682(c) as "an insolvent and fugitive person," in consequence of judgment against him for £23 8s. 3d. at suit of William Jans, of Dublin, gent. It is presumed that he *d.* s.p.m., and that, consequently, the *Baronetcy* became *extinct.*

EVERARD(d):
cr. 30 April 1622;
ex. 1740-46.

I. 1622. "RICHARD EVERARD, Esq., of Balliboye,(e) co. Tipperary," 2d s. of Sir John EVERARD, of Fethard, in that county, second Justice of the King's Bench [I.], 1602-06 (*Knighted*, in Ireland, 10 or 20 Feb. 1604/5; M.P. [I.] for co. Tipperary, 1613-15, and *d.* 14 Sep. 1624), by Catharine, da. of (—) PLUNKETT, was *cr. a Bart.* [I.], as above, by patent dat. at Dublin, 30 April 1622, the Privy Seal being dat. at Westm., 15 March 1620/1. He was one of the confederate Catholics, 1646; his estates were forfeited, and he was condemned, though not put to death, by Ireton, when, in 1650, the latter took Limerick. He *m.*, about 1627, Catherine, da. of John TOBIN, of Killaghy and Compshinagh, co. Tipperary. He, his wife, Catherine, and his son, Redmond, were all living, 10 June 1657, when they were "transplanted" into Connaught.

II. 1660? SIR REDMOND EVERARD, Bart. [I. 1622], of Fethard aforesaid, s. and h., *suc. to the Baronetcy* on his father's death, to whose forfeited lands, in recognition of his own services beyond the sea, he was restored by Act of Parl. He *m.* Elizabeth, da. of Richard BUTLER, of Kilcash (br. to the 1st DUKE OF ORMONDE), by Frances, da. of Mervyn (TOUCHET), 2d EARL OF CASTLEHAVEN [I.]. He *d.* in Dublin, 20 Feb. 1686, and was *bur.* in Trinity Church, Fethard. Funeral certificate [I.]. Will dat. 19 Feb. 1686/7, pr. 12 July 1687, in Prerog. Court [I.]. His widow living 1687.

III. 1687. SIR JOHN EVERARD, Bart. [I. 1622], of Fethard aforesaid, s. and h.; *suc. to the Baronetcy* in Feb. 1686/7, was M.P. [I.] for Fethard, 1689, in the Parl. of James II. He *m.*, after Feb. 1686/7, Eleanor, da. of Pierce (BUTLER), 4th BARON CAHER [I.], by Elizabeth da. of Toby MATHEW. He was killed 12 July 1690, at the battle of Aughrim, on the side of James II. Admon. of his widow, 1 July 1707, in Prerog. Court [I.]

(a) Patrick Browne, his elder br., *d.* v.p. and s.p.
(b) Margaret his da. and h., *m.*, 1659 (as 1st wife), Thomas Newcomen, afterwards (1669) 5th Bart. [I.]
(c) Exchequer bill of that date, Jans *v.* Browne.
(d) Almost all the information in this article is supplied by G. D. Burtchaell, though some particulars are from C. M. Tenison. See p. 223, note "a."
(e) *Qy.* if not the same as "Everard's Castle, co. Tipperary."

IV. 1690, to 1740? SIR REDMOND EVERARD, Bart. [I. 1622], of Fethard aforesaid, 1st surv. s. and h. male; *suc. to the Baronetcy*, 12 July 1690; was M.P. [I.] for co. Tipperary, 1703; for Kilkenny city, 1709-13, and for Fethard, 1713-14; D.C.L. (Oxford), 22 Sep. 1715. He was a Jacobite, residing principally abroad, and was a witness to the will, 31 Dec. 1725, of Bishop Atterbury, who speaks of him as "the Knight of Chaton." He was *cr. a Viscount* (VISCOUNT EVERARD?) in or about 1722, *by the titular King, James III*. He *m.*, 15 June 1721, at Westm. Abbey, Mary, only da. of Montagu DRAKE, of Shardeloes, Bucks, by Jane, da. and h. of Sir John GARRARD, 3d Bart. [1622], of Lamer. He *d.* s.p. in France, about 1740, when the *Baronetcy* became *extinct*. Will[a] dat. 10 March 1739/40, pr. in the Prerog. Court [I.] 15 April 1746, after the death of his widow. She, who was *b.* 15 and *bap.* 25 June 1694, at Amersham, Bucks, *d.* intestate before April 1746.

CONNOR, *or* O'CONNOR[b]:

Privy Seal dat. 11 May 1622;

ex. 21 July 1625.

I. 1622 to 1625. "CHARLES [*otherwise* "Callough"] CONNOR, Esq., of Sligo, co. Sligo," s. and h. of Donal, *otherwise* Daniel O'CONNOR (*d.* between 1609 and 1611), the br. and h. of Sir Donogh O'CONNOR-SLIGO (*d.* 1609), both being sons of Sir Donal, *otherwise* Daniel, O'CONNOR-SLIGO (*d.* 1 Jan. 1587), was in ward to Faithful Fortescue, 27 Jan. 1611/2, and was, by Privy Seal dated at Westm. 11 May 1622, *nominated a Bart.* [I.], as above, and was subsequently, 8 June 1622, *Knighted* as "Sir Charles O'Connor, Bart.," by the Lords Justices of Ireland. A match was intended, 4 Jan. 1624/5,[c] between him and a da. of the Earl of Antrim [I.], but it never took place, and, some six months later, he *d.* unm. at Sligo, 21 July 1625, when the *Baronetcy* became *extinct*. Inq. p.m. 23 Sep. 1625.[d]

ALEN, *or* ALLEN[b]:

cr. 7 June 1622;

ex. 8 March 1627.

I. 1622, to 1627. "THOMAS ALEN (great nephew to John ALEN, L.C.) of St. Wolstons, co. Kildare," was s. and h. of John ALLEN, *or* ALEN, of St. Wolstons, *otherwise* Allen's *or* Alen's Court aforesaid, by Anne, da. of Thomas DILLON, of Riverstown[e]; was *b.* about 1566, being aged 50 and unm. at his father's death, 29 Sep. 1616, and was, "in consideration of the great services rendered to the State by (his great-uncle) Archbishop Alen," *cr. a Bart.* [I.] as above, the patent being dat. at Dublin, 7 June 1622, and the Privy Seal at Westm., 12 May 1622, and was subsequently, 8 June 1622, *Knighted*, as "Sir Thomas Allen, Bart.," by the Lord Justices of Ireland. He *m.* firstly, after 1616, Mary, sister of Christopher (FLEMING), LORD SLANE [I.]. She *d.* s.p., 18 Nov., and was *bur.*, 3 Dec. 1623, at Donacomper, co. Kildare. He *m.* secondly, Mary, da. of Jenico (PRESTON), 5th VISCOUNT GORMANSTON [I.], by Margaret, da. of Nicholas (ST. LAWRENCE), LORD HOWTH [I.]. He *d.* s.p. 7 March 1626/7, and was *bur.* at Donacomper, when the *Baronetcy* became *extinct*. Funeral certificate [I.]. Will dat. 1 March 1626, pr. 18 April 1627, in the Prerog. Court [I.]. His widow *m.*, before Nov. 1634, Simon LUTTRELL, of Luttrellstown. Her will, dat. 9 March 1665, pr. 18 June 1666.

(a) He leaves his estate (failing his issue), after his wife's death, to James Long, second son of his second cousin, John Long, of Killoran, with a direction to take the name of Everard; a direction which, apparently, indicates that the *male* descendants of the 1st Bart. were extinct.

(b) The whole of the information in this article is given by G. D. Burtchaell (see p. 223, note "a")

(c) Letter of that date among the State Papers [I.].

(d) The lady destined for him, viz., Sarah, da. of Randal (Macdonell), 1st Earl of Antrim [I.], *m.* his brother and heir, Donogh O'Connor, of Sligo. This Donogh *d.* s.p. 14 May 1634, and was suc. by his uncle, Teige O'Connor-Sligo.

(e) His parentage is thus given by G. D. Burtchaell (see p. 223, note "a"), but in Burke's *Landed Gentry* (vol. ii, p. 363, edit. 1837, where an elaborate pedigree of the family is given) he is made to be son of "John Alen, Esq., of St. Wolstans," by "a da. of the Lord Slane," the said John being son of another John, son of Francis, elder br. of John, Archbishop of Dublin, murdered 28 July 1534.

LYNCH:

cr. 8 June 1622;

afterwards, since 1762, LYNCH-BLOSSE.

I. 1622. "HENRY LYNCH, Esq., of Galway," eldest of the twelve sons of Nicholas LYNCH, Mayor of Galway, was himself sometime Mayor thereof, and was *cr. a Bart.* [I.], as above, by patent dat. 8 June 1622, at Dublin, the Privy Seal being dat. 12 May 1622, at Westm. He was M.P. [I.] for Galway, June to Dec. 1634. He *m.*, in or after 1603, Elizabeth, widow of James DARCY, Vice President of Connaught, da. of Richard MARTIN, of Galway. He *d.* 21 Feb. and was *bur.* 6 March 1634/5, in the church of St. Nicholas, Galway. Will pr. 1635, in the Prerog. Court [I.].

II. 1635. SIR ROBERT LYNCH, Bart. [I. 1622], of Galway, s. and h., *suc. to the Baronetcy* in Feb. 1634/5; was M.P. [I.] for Galway, 1639 till expelled, June 1642. He was resident Counsel of Connaught during the Rebellion. He *m.* Ellice, da. of Sir Peter FRENCH, of Galway (*d.* 27 Feb. 1631), by Mary, da. of Geffrey BROWNE, of the same. He *d.* 1667.

III. 1667. SIR HENRY LYNCH, Bart. [I. 1622], of Galway, s. and h., *suc. to the Baronetcy* in 1667; admitted to King's Inn, Dublin, 8 July 1674; one of the Barons of the Exchequer [I.], 1687-90; accompanied James II in his exile. He *m.* firstly, Margaret, da. of Theobald (BOURKE), 3d VISCOUNT MAYO [I.], by his 1st wife, Elinor, da. of Thomas TALBOT. She *d.* s.p. He *m.* secondly, Mary, da. of Nicholas BLAKE, of Cromlee. He *d.* at Brest, 1691. His widow *d.* 1712. Will pr. at Prerog. Court [I.], 1712.

IV. 1691. SIR ROBERT LYNCH, Bart. [I. 1622], of Corandalen, co. Galway, s. and h., by 2d wife, *suc. to the Baronetcy* in 1691. He *m.* Catharine, da. of Henry BLAKE, of Lehynch, co. Mayo.

V. 1720? SIR HENRY LYNCH, Bart. [I. 1622], of Castle Carra, co. Mayo, s. and h., *suc. to the Baronetcy* on the death of his father. He *m.* Mary, da. and coheir of John MOORE, of Brees, co. Galway. He *d.* 1762.

VI. 1762. SIR ROBERT LYNCH-BLOSSE, Bart. [I. 1622], of Castle Carra aforesaid, s. and h.; Sheriff of co. Mayo, 1760; *suc. to the Baronetcy* in 1762. He *m.*, 14 July 1749, Jane, da. and h. of Francis BARKER, of Sibton, Suffolk, which lady was heiress of Tobias BLOSSE, of Little Belstead, in that county. He accordingly *assumed the name of Blosse* after his patronymic. She *d.* 1756. He *d.* 1775. Will dat. 17 June 1771, pr. May 1776.

VII. 1775. SIR HENRY LYNCH-BLOSSE, Bart. [I. 1622], of Castle Carra aforesaid, s. and h., *b.* 14 Oct. 1749; matric. at Oxford (Ch. Ch.), 27 April 1768, aged 18; *suc. to the Baronetcy* in 1775; was M.P. [I.] for Tuam, 1776-83. He *d.* s.p. legit. in 1788. Will pr. 1788, in Prerog. Court [I.].

VIII. 1788. SIR ROBERT LYNCH-BLOSSE, Bart. [I. 1622], of Athaville, co. Mayo, nephew and h., being s. and h. of Francis LYNCH-BLOSSE, 14th Light Dragoons, by Hatton, da. of John Smith, of Rathcorney, co. Cork, which Francis, who was 2d s. of the 6th Bart., *d.* before 1788. He was *b.* 23 Feb. 1774; *suc. to the Baronetcy*, in 1788. He *m.* firstly, Elizabeth, da. of John GORMAN, of Carlow. He *m.* secondly, 13 March 1807, Charlotte, da. of John RICHARDS, of Cardiff. He d. Jan. 1818. Will pr. March 1818 and June 1837. His widow *d.* 3 Oct. 1834. Admon. Nov. 1834.

IX. 1818. SIR FRANCIS LYNCH-BLOSSE, Bart. [I. 1622], of Athaville aforesaid, s. and h. by first wife; *b.* Aug. 1801; *suc. to the Baronetcy* in Jan. 1818; ed. at Trin. Coll., Dublin; M.A. 1823; was in Holy Orders. He *m.*, 5 April 1824 Elizabeth, da. of William Conyngham (PLUNKET), 1st BARON PLUNKET OF NEWTOWN, by Catherine, da. of John MACCAUSLAND. He *d.* 5 July 1840, at Perrin Castle, in his 39th year. His widow *d.* 3 April 1885, at 22 Clyde Road, Dublin, in her 86th year.

X. 1840. SIR ROBERT LYNCH-BLOSSE, Bart. [I. 1622], of Athaville aforesaid, s. and h., *b.* 15 Feb. 1825, at St. Stephen's Green, Dublin; ed. at Rugby School and at Trin. Coll., Cambridge; *suc. to the Baronetcy*, 5 July 1840; Sheriff for co. Mayo, 1847. He *m.*, 31 March 1853, Harriet, 4th da. of Howe Peter (BROWNE), 2d MARQUESS OF SLIGO [I.], by Louisa Catherine, da. of Richard (HOWE), EARL HOWE. He *d.* 3 Dec. 1893, at Athaville aforesaid. His widow, who was *b.* 16 Feb. 1827, living 1900.

XI. 1893. SIR HENRY LYNCH-BLOSSE, Bart. [I. 1622], s. and h.; *b.* 21 April 1857; ed. at Eton; *suc. to the Baronetcy*, 3 Dec. 1893.

Family Estates.—These, in 1883, consisted of 22,658 acres in co. Mayo, worth £9,274 a year. *Principal Seat*—Athaville, near Castlebar, co. Mayo.

TUITE[a]:

cr. 16 June 1622.

I. 1622. "OLIVER TUITE, Esq., of the Sonnagh, co. Westmeath," s. and h. of John TUITE, of the same (who *d.* 1597, aged 30), by Margaret, da. of Edward NUGENT, of Dysert, was *b.* about 1588; suc. his father, 1597, and was *cr. a Bart.* [I.], as above, by patent, dat. at Dublin, 16 June 1622, the Privy Seal being dat. at Westm., 12 May 1622. Sheriff of co. Westmeath, 1634. He *m.* Mabel, da. of Sir Gerald AYLMER, 1st Bart. [I. 1622], by his 2d wife, Julia, da. of Christopher (NUGENT), BARON DELVIN [I.]. He *d.* 1642. Inq. p.m.

II. 1642. SIR OLIVER TUITE, Bart. [I. 1622], of Sonnagh aforesaid, grandson and h., being s. and h. of Thomas TUITE, by Martha, da. of Thomas LUTTRELL, of Luttrellstown, which Thomas TUITE was s. and h. ap. of the late Bart., but *d.* v.p. Oct. 1634, and was *bur.* in the Abbey of Multifornham. He was 8 years old in 1641, and *suc. to the Baronetcy* in 1642. He *m.* Elinor, da. of Roger O'FERRALL, of Mornine, co. Longford, by Alice, da. of James (DILLON), 1st EARL OF ROSCOMMON [I.]. He *d.* Aug. 1661. Inq. p.m. Admon. 2 Sep. 1665. His widow *m.* Major Owen O'CONNOR, of Belanagar, co. Roscommon.

III. 1661. SIR JAMES TUITE, Bart. [I. 1622], of Sonnagh aforesaid, only s. and h.; *suc. to the Baronetcy* in Aug. 1661. He *d.* s.p. and under age, Feb. 1664. Inq. p.m.

(a) See p. 240, note "b."

IV. 1664. SIR HENRY TUITE, Bart. [I. 1622], of Sonnagh aforesaid, uncle and h. male, being 3d and only surv. s. of the 1st Bart.; *suc. to the Baronetcy*, Feb. 1664. He served in the wars in Flanders, *temp.* Car. II. He *m.* Diana, da. of Kympton MABBOTT, by Susan, sister of Edward (HYDE), 1st EARL OF CLARENDON, da. of Henry HYDE, by Mary, da. of Edward LANGFORD. He *d.* May 1679. Inq. p.m. His widow *m.* Rev. John TWELLS.

V. 1679 SIR JOSEPH TUITE, Bart. [I. 1622], of Sonnagh aforesaid only s. and h.; *b.* 1677; *suc. to the Baronetcy* in May 1679. He *m.* in May 1706, Mary, da. of John PERCEVAL, of Knightsbrook, by Martha, da. of Edward KNIGHT, of Culvin, co. Westmeath. He *d.* 1727, and was *bur.* at Churchtown, in that county. His will dat. 4 April 1727, pr. 28 Oct. 1728, in Prerog. Court [I.]. His widow *d.* May 1749. Her will dat. 18 May, pr. (as above) 20 Nov. 1749.

VI. 1727. SIR HENRY TUITE, Bart. [I. 1622], of Sonnagh aforesaid, only s. and h., *b.* about 1708; matric. at Oxford (Bras. Coll.), 2 Oct. 1724, aged 16; *suc. to the Baronetcy* in 1727; Sheriff of co. Westmeath, 1733. He *m.* firstly, in 1728, Mary, sister of Robert, 1st EARL OF BELVIDERE [I.], da. of the Rt. Hon. George ROCHFORT, of Gaulstown, co. Westmeath, by Elizabeth, da. of Henry (MOORE), 3d EARL OF DROGHEDA [I.]. She *d.* 25 Feb. 1729, and was *bur.* at Gaulstown. He *m.* secondly, 6 July 1741, Mary da. of Marcus Anthony MORGAN, of Cotlestown, co. Sligo. He *d.* at Bath, and was *bur.* in the Abbey there, 9 April 1765. Will dat. 18 March 1758, pr. 24 May 1765, at Prerog. Court [I.].

VII. 1765. SIR GEORGE TUITE, Bart. [I. 1622], of Sonnagh aforesaid, s. and h., being only child by 1st wife; *b.* 20 Feb. 1729; *suc. to the Baronetcy* in April 1765. He *d.* unm., being murdered 12 Feb. 1782, in his house at Sonnagh. Admon. 10 March 1782, to his br., Mark Anthony Tuite.

VIII. 1782 SIR HENRY TUITE, Bart. [I. 1622], of Sonnagh aforesaid, br. (of the half blood) and h., being s. of the 6th Bart., by his 2d wife; *b.* 1743; was sometime a Lieut. in the Royal Navy; *suc. to the Baronetcy*, 17 Feb. 1782. He *m.*, Nov. 1784, Elizabeth, 2d da. of Thomas COBBE, of Newbridge, co. Dublin, by Elizabeth Dorothea, da. of Marcus (BERESFORD), 1st EARL OF TYRONE [I.]. He *d.* s.p. Aug. 1805. Will pr. at Prerog. Court [I.], 1805. His widow *d.* at Bath in May 1850, aged 85. Will pr. July 1850.

IX. 1805. SIR GEORGE TUITE, Bart. [I. 1622], of Lissievoolin, co. Westmeath, nephew and h., being only s. and h. of Mark Anthony TUITE, Capt., 9th Dragoons, by Patience, da. of Marlborough STIRLING, Prothonotary of the Court of Common Pleas [I.], which Mark Anthony, who was *b.* Dec. 1745, was next br. to the late Bart. He was *d.* 8 June 1778, and *suc. to the Baronetcy* in Aug. 1805. He *m.*, 8 June 1807, at St. Geo. Han. sq., Janet, widow of Thomas WOODHALL, Major, 12th Reg. He *d.* 15 June 1841, aged 63, in Wyndham place, St. Marylebone. Will pr. Oct. 1841. His widow *d.* 21 Feb. 1845. Admon. June 1845.

X. 1841. SIR MARK ANTHONY HENRY TUITE, Bart. [I. 1622], of Kilruane, co. Tipperary, s. and h., *b.* 24 March 1808; *suc. to the Baronetcy*, 15 June 1841; sometime Capt., 19th Reg., 1842-48. He *m.*, 18 Nov. 1854. Charlotte, da. of Richard Hugh LEVINGE, of Levington park, co. Westmeath, by Jane, da. of Thomas CHILD, of Brookfield, co. Cork. She *d.* 9 April 1878, at Kilruane house. He *d.* there s.p. March 1898, in his 80th year.

XI. 1898. SIR MORGAN HARRY PAULET TUITE, Bart. [I. 1622], of Kilruane aforesaid, nephew and h., being s. and h. of Major Gen. Hugh Manley TUITE, Royal Artillery, by Frances Maria, da. of Lieut. Col. Richard WILLIAMS, which Hugh, who *d.* 4 Jan. 1889, was br. to the late Bart. He was *b.* 27 Oct. 1861; was sometime Lieut., 9th Batt. Rifle Brigade, and *suc. to the Baronetcy* in March 1898.

Family Estates.—These, in 1883, were under 2,000 acres.

PIERCE,(a) *or* PEIRSE:

cr. 21 June 1622;

ex. about Aug. 1649.

I. 1622. "HENRY PIERCE, Esq. (Principal Secretary to the Lord Deputy Chichester for eleven years), of Pierce Court, co. Cavan," whose parentage has not been ascertained, was M.P. [I.] for Baltimore, 1613-15, and was *cr. a Bart.* [I.] as above, by patent dat. 21 June 1622, at Dublin, the Privy Seal being dat. 6 June 1622, at Westm. He was, shortly afterwards, *Knighted*, in Ireland, 24 Dec. 1622. He *m.* Eleanor, 1st da. of Sir Francis STAFFORD, Privy Councillor [I.]. He *d.* 6 Nov. and was *bur.* 13 Dec. 1638, in the church of Knockbride, co. Cavan. Funeral certificate [I.]. His widow *m.* (Lic. 14 Aug. 1639) Richard FITZWILLIAM, of Merrion, co. Dublin, and was living in July 1662.

II. 1638, to 1649? SIR GEORGE PIERCE, *or* PEIRSE, Bart. [I. 1622], only s. and h., *suc. to the Baronetcy*, 6 Nov. 1638, being then aged 14 years, 6 months and 12 days. He had previously *m.* (at the age of 10 years,(b) 7 months, and 6 weeks), Thomazine, da. of Henry (BLAYNEY), 2d BARON BLAYNEY OF MONAGHAN [I.], but this marriage was (in the presence of the Archbishop of Armagh, etc.) absolutely repudiated by that lady, 7 March 1639, when she became of the age of 12, the valid age for a contract.(c) He *d.* s.p. about 16 Aug. 1649, when the *Baronetcy* became *extinct.*(d) Inq. p.m. 20 July 1662.

BLAKE:

cr. 10 July 1622.

I. 1622. "VALENTINE BLAKE,(e) Esq., of Galway," s. and h. of Walter BLAKE, Mayor of Galway (1547 and 1562), by Juliana, da. of Thomas BROWNE, was Mayor of Galway, 1611, and again, 1630, was M.P. [I.] for Galway, 1613-15, and was *cr. a Bart.* [I.], as above,(f) by patent dat. 10 July 1622, at Dublin, the Privy Seal being dat. 11 May 1622, at Westm. He was, shortly afterwards, *Knighted*, in Ireland, 29 Nov. 1622. He *m.* firstly, Margaret, da. of Robuck (or Robert) FRENCH, of Galway. He *m.* secondly, Annabel, da. of James LYNCH, by whom he had no issue. He *d.* 2 and was *bur.* 6 Jan. 1634, in St. Francis' Abbey, Galway. Funeral certificate [I.]. Will pr. 1634, in Prerog. Court [I.].

II. 1634. SIR THOMAS BLAKE, Bart. [I. 1622], of Galway aforesaid, s. and h., by 1st wife; *suc. to the Baronetcy*, 2 Jan. 1634; M.P. [I.] for Galway borough, 1634-35; Mayor of Galway, 1637. He *m.* Julian, da. of Geoffrey BROWNE, of Carro-Browne, and of Castle-ma-Garret.

III. 1640? SIR VALENTINE BLAKE, Bart. [I. 1622], of Galway aforesaid, s. and h.; admitted to Middle Temple, London, 19 July 1628; M.P. for co. Galway, 1634-35; for Galway borough, 1639, till expelled in 1642; was *Knighted*, 3 Oct. 1629; *suc. to the Baronetcy* on the death of his father. He *m.*, before 1634, Eleanor, 3d da. of Sir Henry LYNCH, 1st Bart. [I. 1622], by Elizabeth, da. of Richard MARTIN, of Galway. His will dat. 1 June 1651, was pr. 1654, in Dublin.

(a) See p. 240, note "b."

(b) As to this early age, see F. J. Furnivall's "Child-Marriages," etc., in the *Early English Text Society* (1897), p. 108.

(c) She, subsequently, *m.* Joseph Fox, of Graige, co. Tipperary.

(d) His next heir was Henry Peirse, son of Thomas, a yr. br. of the 1st Bart.

(e) He is called in the corporation books of Galway "Valentine Blake Fitzwalter Fitzthomas."

(f) On the nomination of Sir Francis Blundell, Bart. [I.], by deed poll, 6 July 1622, he having, by Privy Seal dat. 11 May 1622, the power to nominate two persons of quality to the Baronetage.

IV. 1651? SIR THOMAS BLAKE, Bart. [I. 1622], of Galway aforesaid, and of Menlough, co. Galway, s. and h.; *suc. to the Baronetcy* on the death of his father. He *m.* firstly, in 1649, Mary, da. of Richard MARTIN. She *d.* s.p. He *m.* secondly, Maria, da. of Marcus FRENCH, of Abbert. He was living 1668 (20 Car. II), when he made a settlement of his estate of Menlough.

V. 1670? SIR VALENTINE BLAKE, Bart. [I. 1622], of Menlough aforesaid, s. and h., by 2d wife; *suc. to the Baronetcy* on the death of his father. He *d.* unm., soon after his father, being treacherously killed in a duel at Galway.

VI. 1672? SIR WALTER BLAKE, Bart. [I. 1622], of Menlough aforesaid, br. and h., *suc. to the Baronetcy* on the death of his brother. He was M.P. [I.] for co. Galway, 1689, in the Parl. of James II, but was the first Roman Catholic of any distinction that joined William III in his invasion of Ireland, where he raised and maintained a regiment at his own expense. He *m.* firstly, 10 Aug. 1687, Anne, da. of Sir John KIRWAN, of Castle Hacket, co. Galway. He *m.* secondly, his cousin, Agnes, da. of John BLAKE. He *d.* May 1748, in Marlborough street, Dublin. His will pr. 14 May 1748, in Prerog. Court [I.], that of his widow being pr. there in the same year.

VII. 1748. SIR THOMAS BLAKE, Bart. [I. 1622], of Somerville, co. Galway, and of Menlough aforesaid, s. and h., by 1st wife; *suc. to the Baronetcy* in May 1748. He *m.*, 1716, Elizabeth, da. of Ulick BURKE, of Tyaquin, a lady of some little note as a poetess. By his will, dat. 1748, pr. 1749, in Prerog. Court [I.], he devised his estates in tail male to his son, rem. to Maurice Blake and John Blake, both of Galway, rem. to Thomas Blake, of Brendrum, which last rem. took effect in 1766.

VIII. 1749? SIR ULICK BLAKE, Bart. [I. 1622], of Somerville, and of Menlough aforesaid, only s. and h.; admitted to the Middle Temple, London, 15 July 1738; *suc. to the Baronetcy* about 1749. He *m.* Mary, da. and sole h. of Richard BLAKE, of Newgrove, and of Ardfry, co. Galway, by Anastatia, da. of Denis DALY, Justice of the Common Pleas [I.] He *d.* s.p.m. in June 1766.(a) Will pr. at Prerog. Court [I.] 1766. His widow, living 1769, sold the estate of Ardfry to her cousin, Joseph Blake (ancestor of the Barons Wallscourt [I.]), and *d.* at her estate of Trainbane, co. Galway.

IX. 1766. SIR THOMAS BLAKE, Bart. [I. 1622], of Menlough aforesaid, cousin and h. male, being s. and h. of Thomas BLAKE, of Brendrum abovenamed, by Mary, da. of Peter LYNCH, which Thomas lastnamed, was only s. and h. of Henry BLAKE, the 2d s. of the 3d Bart. He *suc. to the Baronetcy* in 1766, when he returned to Ireland from Bordeaux, and, by payment of £8,000 to Mrs. Foster, the da. and h. of the last Bart., obtained peaceful possession of the Menlough estate. He *m.*, 1730, Eleanor, da. of (—) LYNCH. He *d.* s.p.m. 3 March 1787. His widow *d.* 3 March 1791.

X. 1787. SIR WALTER BLAKE, Bart. [I. 1622], of Menlough aforesaid, br. and h.; *suc. to the Baronetcy*, 3 March 1787. He *m.*, 10 April 1751, Barbara, da. of Myles BURKE, of Ower, co. Galway, by Mary, da. of (—) LYNCH. He and his wife (both of whom were *b.* and *m.* in the month of *April*) *d.* on the same day in *April* 1802.

(a) Anastatia, his only da. and h., *m.* Francis Foster, of Ashfield, co. Galway, and was ancestress of the family of Blake-Foster.

XI. 1802. SIR JOHN BLAKE, Bart. [I. 1622], of Menlough aforesaid, s. and h., *b.* 15 July 1753; *suc. to the Baronetcy* in April 1802. He *m.* firstly, 12 May 1779, his cousin, Eleanor, da. of Edward LYNCH, by Mary, only da. and h. of Sir Thomas BLAKE, 9th Bart. [I.] abovenamed. He *m.* secondly, 20 Oct. 1800, Rose, da. of Edward BRICE, of Kilroot, co. Antrim, by Theodora, 1st da. of Thomas (MULLINS), 1st BARON VENTRY [I.]. He *d.* 1834.

XII. 1834. SIR VALENTINE JOHN BLAKE, Bart. [I. 1622], of Menlough aforesaid, s. and h., by 1st wife, *b.* 23 June 1780; *suc. to the Baronetcy* in 1834; M.P. for Galway borough, 1812-20 and 1841 till his death in 1847. He *m.* firstly, 8 Aug. 1803, Eliza, 1st da. of Joseph DONELLAN, of Killagh, co. Galway, by Ellis, da. of Charles LAMBERT, of Cregclare. She *d.* 8 May 1836. He *m.* secondly, 8 April 1843, Julia Sophia, da. of Robert MACDONNELL, M.D. He *d.* Jan. 1847, in Paris. His widow *m.*, 10 Oct. 1850, John CUXSON, of Shifnal, Salop, and *d.* 11 March 1883.

XIII. 1847. SIR THOMAS EDWARD BLAKE, Bart. [I. 1622], of Menlough aforesaid, s. and h., by 1st wife, *b.* 25 May 1805, at Killagh aforesaid; *suc. to the Baronetcy*, Jan. 1847. He *m.*, 29 May 1830, Lætitia Maria, only da. and h. of Ulick O'BRIEN, of Waterview, co. Galway. He *d.* 3 Jan. 1875, at Menlough Castle, and was *bur.* at Menlough. His widow *d.* 18 Jan. 1879.

XIV. 1875. SIR VALENTINE BLAKE, Bart. [I. 1622], of Menlough aforesaid, only s. and h., *b.* 2 Dec. 1836, at Menlough Castle; Sheriff of the county of the town of Galway, 1872; *suc. to the Baronetcy*, 3 Jan. 1875; Hon. Major of the Galway Militia. He *m.*, 25 June 1864, Camilla Eugenia, yst. da. of Harvey COMBE, of the Madras Civil Service.

Family Estates.—These, consisting of 3,403 acres, are estimated as worth but £763 a year. *Principal Seat.*—Menlough Castle, co. Galway.

FITZHARRIS(a):

cr. 4 Nov. 1622;

ex., presumably, in 1704.

I. 1622. "EDWARD FITZHARRIS, Esq., of Killinan [*i.e.*, Kilfinane], co. Limerick," 2d s. of Matthew FITZHARRIS, *or* FITZHENRY, of Moghmayne, co. Wexford, sometime (1584) M.P. [I.] for co. Wexford by Margaret, da. of Sir Walter BROWNE, of Mulrankin, was admitted to the King's Inns, Dublin, 24 June 1607, and, having obtained a grant of the castle and estate of Kilfinane, was *cr. a Bart.* [I.], as above, by patent dat. 4 Nov. 1622, at Dublin, the Privy Seal being dat. 11 Sep. previous at Westm. He was M.P. [I.] for co. Limerick, 1634-35 and 1639 till his death. He *m.* Gyles [*i.e.*, Julia], da. and h. of John ROCHE, of Kilfinane aforesaid, by whom he had seven sons. He *d.* 3 March 1640, at Clonodfoy, co. Limerick, and was *bur.* at Kilfinane. Funeral certificate [I.].

II. 1640. SIR EDWARD FITZHARRIS, Bart. [I. 1622], grandson and h., being 1st s. and h. of George FITZHARRIS, by Joan, da. of Thomas (FITZMAURICE), 18th BARON KERRY [I.], which George was elder s. and h. ap. of the late Bart., but *d.* v.p. 17 March 1626, and was *bur.* at Kilfinane. He *suc. to the Baronetcy*, 3 March 1640. He signed, in 1661, the remonstrance of the Catholic nobility and gentry [I.] to Charles II. He *m.*, before March 1640, Ellen, da. of Thomas FITZGERALD, of co. Limerick, called "the Knight of the Valley." He *d.* before Oct. 1700.

(a) See p. 240, note "b."

III. 1690? to 1704? SIR WILLIAM FITZHARRIS, Bart. [I. 1622], presumably s. and h.,(a) and *b.* between March 1640 and 1648; *suc. to the Baronetcy* probably about 1690, but certainly before 12 Oct. 1700, when he *m.*, at St. George's, Canterbury, Mary WILLS, of Deal, widow. He appears to have *d.* abroad, s.p.m. in or before Oct. 1704, when the *Baronetcy* became *dormant*, or *extinct.* Will pr. Oct. 1704.

TUFTON:

cr. 18 Jan. 1622/3;

ex. March 1663/4.

I. 1622 "WILLIAM TUFTON, Esq., of Vintners [in the parish of Boxley], co. Kent," yr. br. of Sir Humphrey TUFTON, 1st Bart. [1644], of the Mote, co. Kent, being 5th s. of Sir John TUFTON, 1st Bart. [1611], of Hothfield, by his 2d wife, Christian, da. and coheir of Sir Humphrey BROWN, was *cr. a Bart.* [I.], as above, by patent dat. 18 Jan. 1622/3, at Dublin, the Privy Seal being dat. 30 Dec. 1622. He was Governor of Barbadoes. He *m.*, 30 Jan. 1620/1, at Greenwich, Ann, da. of Cecil CAVE, of co. Leicester. She *d.* 1649, and was *bur.* at Foot's Cray, Kent. M.I. Her burial registered 2 April 1649, at Greenwich. He *d.* at Barbadoes, 1650.(b)

II. 1650. SIR BENEDICT TUFTON, Bart. [I. 1623], of Sittingbourne, co. Kent, s. and h.; *suc. to the Baronetcy* in 1650. He *d.* s.p. about 1655. His admon., 21 May 1655, to his "only br., Sir Charles Tufton, Knt."

III. 1655? to 1664. SIR CHARLES TUFTON, Bart. [I. 1623], of Vintners aforesaid, only br. and h. He *d.* unm. and was *bur.* 12 March 1663/4, at Greenwich, when the *Baronetcy* became *extinct.*(c) Admon. 14 May 1664, to his sister, Dame Vere Beaumont.

TALBOT, *or* TALBOTT:

cr. 4 Feb. 1622/3;

ex., presumably, 24 Dec. 1724.

I. 1623. "WILLIAM TALBOTT, Esq., of Carton, co. Kildare," s. and h. of Robert TALBOT, of the same, who was 3d s. of Sir Thomas TALBOT, of Malahide, co. Dublin (aged 28 in 1529), was M.P. [I.] for co. Kildare, 1613-15, and was *cr. a Bart.* [I.], as above, by patent dat. 4 Feb. 1622/3, at Dublin, the Privy Seal being dat. 16 Dec. 1622, at Westm. He *m.* Alison, da. of John NETTERVILLE, of Castleton, co. Meath. He *d.* 16 March 1633/4, and was *bur.* 1 April 1634, in the church of Maynooth, having had eight sons(d) and eight daughters. Funeral certificate [I.]. Will pr. at Dublin, 1636.

(a) The notorious Edward Fitzharris, *b.* about 1648, who was executed for high treason, 1 July 1681, was a younger son of the 2d Bart. His widow (a da. of William Finch, Commander in the Royal Navy) and two children were living 1689.

(b) The admon., 16 Oct. 1631, of the goods of Sir William Tufton, Knt. (granted to a creditor), who died beyond the seas, a bachelor, cannot, presumably, apply to him.

(c) Vere, his only sister and h., *m.* firstly, Sir Thomas BEAUMONT, 3d Bart. [1627], of Gracedieu, who *d.* 7 July 1686, and secondly, George LANE.

(d) Of these, the youngest, Richard (the well known "lying Dick Talbot"), was *cr.*, 20 June 1685, Earl of Tyrconnell [I.], being, subsequently, after the expulsion of James II, *cr.* by that King, 30 March 1689, Duke of Tyrconnell.

II. 1633. SIR ROBERT TALBOT, Bart. [I. 1623], of Carton aforesaid, 1st s. and h., b. about 1610(a); *suc. to the Baronetcy* in March 1633. M.P. [I.] for co. Wicklow, June to Oct. 1634(b). He *m.* Grace, da. of George (CALVERT), 1st BARON BALTIMORE [I.], by Anne, da. of George MYNNE. He *d.* s.p.m.(c) probably about 1670. Admon. [I.] 13 May 1671.

III. 1670? to 1724. SIR WILLIAM TALBOT, Bart. [I. 1623], nephew and h. male, being s. and h. of Garrett TALBOT, by Margaret, da. of Henry GAYDON, of Dublin, which Garrett (who *d.* before May 1671) was yr. br. of the late Baronet. He *suc. to the Baronetcy* at some date previous to May 1671. He was M.P. [I.] for co. Meath, 1689, in the Parl. of James II, and P.C. [I.]. On the death s.p.m., 14 Aug. 1691, of his yst. uncle, Richard, EARL OF TYRCONNEL [I.], he would have been, but for the attainder of the grantee, entitled to that Earldom, under the spec. rem. in its creation, 20 June 1685,(d) and, accordingly, styled himself COMTE (*or* CONDÉ) DE TYRCONNEL. He appears to have resided in France, or Spain. He *d.* 26 Dec. 1724, in his 82d year, when the *Baronetcy* is presumed to have become *extinct.*

BOULEN:
cr. 14 Feb. 1622/3;
ex., presumably, about 1660.

I. 1623, to 1660? "PETER BOULEN, Esq., a Dutch gentleman," was *cr. a Bart.* [I.], as above, by patent dat. 14 Feb. 1622/3, at Dublin, the Privy Seal being dat. 24 Dec. 1622, at Westm. Nothing more has been ascertained respecting him, and on his death, probably about 1660, the *Baronetcy* is presumed to have become *extinct.*

BARNEWALL:
cr. 21 Feb. 1622/3;
sometime, 1790—1821, *dormant.*

I. 1623. "PATRICK BARNEWALL, Esq., of Crickstown, co. Meath." s. and h. of Sir Richard BARNEWALL, of the same, by Elizabeth, da. of Sir Oliver PLUNKETT, of Rathmore, co. Meath, was *cr. a Bart.* [I.], as above, 21 Feb. 1622/3, the Privy Seal being dat. at Westm., 11 May 1622. He *m.* firstly, in or before 1602, Cecilia, da. of William (FLEMING), 5th LORD SLANE [I.], by Elinor, da. and coheir of Thomas (FLEMING), 4th LORD SLANE [I.]. He *m.* secondly, Elizabeth, whom, in June 1624, he made his executrix. He *d.* 21 June 1624. Inq. p.m. 18 Oct. 1624.(a) Will dat. 24 March 1615, 26 March 1616, and June 1624.(b) His widow is said to have *m.* Patrick BARNEWALL, of Kilbrew.

(a) Peter Talbot, Archbishop of Dublin, 1669-80, one of the yr. brothers, was *b.* in 1620; the ages of the eight daughters are unknown.

(b) On 30 Oct. 1634, Bryan Byrne was elected Member for co. Wicklow, "vice Talbot deceased." This, however, is presumably an error. [*Ex. inform.* W. D. Pink].

(c) Frances, his da. and h., *m.* her cousin, Richard Talbot, of Malahide (who *d.* 1703), by whom she was grandmother of Richard Talbot, whose wife was *cr.*, in 1831 Baroness Talbot de Malahide [I.].

(d) The limitation of this Earldom was, failing heirs male of the body of the grantee, to his nephews, "Sir William Talbot, of Carton, Bart., and William Talbot, of Haggardstone, Esq."

II. 1624. SIR RICHARD BARNEWALL, Bart. [I. 1623], of Crickstown aforesaid, s. and h., b. 21 Dec. 1602; *suc. to the Baronetcy,* 21 June 1624, and had, 15 July 1629, special livery of his estate; M.P. [I.] for co. Meath, 1639-48; was a zealous Royalist, being in command of hundred horse; was one of the Council of Kilkenny; was excepted from Cromwell's act of grace, 12 Aug. 1652; was attainted, but restored after the Restoration, though despoiled of all but two thousand acres. He *m.* firstly, 1621, Thomazina, da. of Edward DOWDALL, of Athlumney, co. Meath. She *d.* s.p.m. 1628. He *m.* secondly, Julia, da. of Sir Gerald AYLMER, 1st Bart. [I. 1622]. He *d.* 6 July 1679. Admon. [I.] 12 July 1679.

III. 1679. SIR PATRICK BARNEWALL, Bart. [I. 1623], of Crickstown aforesaid, and of Newcastle, co. Meath, s. and h., by 2d wife; *b.* about 1630; *suc. to the Baronetcy* in July 1679. He was confirmed in the estate of Crickstown; had a grant of 1,261 acres in co. Galway; was granted a pension of £150 a year, by Charles II, which, in 1687, was charged on the establishment, and was M.P. [I.] for co. Meath, 1689, in the Parl. of James II. He *m.* Frances, da. of Richard BUTLER, of Kilcash, by Frances, da. of Mervyn (TOUCHET), 2d EARL OF CASTLEHAVEN [I.]. His will dat. 26 March 1695, pr. 1702, in Prerog. Court [I.]. His widow was *bur.* 1 Feb. 1709, at St. James', Dublin.

IV. 1702? SIR GEORGE BARNEWALL, Bart. [I. 1623], of Crickstown Castle aforesaid, only s. and h. He *d.* s.p. 22 Oct. 1735.(c) Will dat. 18 Aug. 1735, pr. 29 Jan. 1735/6, in Prerog. Court [I.].

V. 1735. SIR GEORGE BARNEWALL, Bart. [I. 1623], cousin and h. male, being 2d but 1st surv. s. of Barnaby BARNEWALL, of Ballyard, by Jane, da. of Kedagh GEOGHEGAN, of Carne and Jamestown, which Barnaby was s. of James BARNEWALL, of Roskeen, Queen's County (*d.* 1692), who was s. of John BARNEWALL, of Athronan, the 2d s. of the 2d Bart. Having established in the College of Arms, Dublin, 28 Aug. 1744, his pedigree and (consequently) his right to the *Baronetcy to which he had suc.*, 22 Oct. 1735, he returned to Germany, where he had previously resided. He *d.* s.p. after June 1770.(d)

(a) The names of his sons, as given in Lodge's *Irish Peerage,* 1789 (*sub* "Kingsland"), are Richard, John, George and Michael. These four and no others, in his will, dat. 24 March 1615, are the devisees of his land in tail male, with rem. to his two brothers, to his uncle, and to a variety of cousins. This devise is *unaltered* by the subsequent codicils, and seems to preclude the birth of a younger son, James, "born subsequent to March 1615" [Burke's *Peerage* etc., 1899], who would thus be disinherited. There is, however, an entry in Ulster's Office (being, apparently, the draft of a proposed funeral certificate), wherein the fourth and last named son of the said Sir Patrick is called "James" instead of "Michael." This entry, however, is both undated and uncertified. It is printed (with notes thereon) in Foster's *Collect. Gen.*

(b) "It is to be observed that the original will does not exist. In the copy inserted in the *inq. p.m.* engrossed on a separate skin, in a different handwriting, and sewn in, the engrosser writes the date of the last codicil xxxth June, while the jurors found the testator died on the 21st. This last codicil is nuncupative, and certainly mentions the wife, *Elizabeth.* Could this be a mistake? but, on the other hand, why this codicil, if not to make provision for another wife? The second wife is admitted in the pedigrees in Ulster's office." [G. D. Burtchaell, see p. 223, note "a."]

(c) His sisters inherited the lands at Crickstown, said to have been for twelve generations in the Barnewall family. Of these, Ellinor, Countess of Mount Alexander [I.], *d.* s.p., and the three others *d.* unm. before 1758.

(d) "Sir George, the 5th Bart., is supposed to have died after June 1770, as the will of John Barnewall, only child of George Barnewall, the eldest br. of Sir Thomas, the 6th Bart., is dated 15 Feb. and pr. 22 June 1770, as appears in the pedigree registered [I.] in 1884 of the then Baronet.' [G. D. Burtchaell, see p. 223, note "a."]

VI. 1771? SIR THOMAS BARNEWALL, Bart. [I. 1623], cousin and h. male, being only surv. s. of James BARNEWALL (*d.* 20 Nov. 1709), by Margaret, da. of Kedagh GEOGHEGAN abovenamed, which James was br. to Barnaby BARNEWALL abovenamed, the father of the 5th Bart. He *m.* (—), da. of (—) MULHALL, of Kilcauligar Castle, Queen's County. He *suc. to the Baronetcy* after June 1770, but not to any of the family estates. He *d.* s.p.m. 1790.

* * * * * *

After 1790 this *Baronetcy* was, for more than thirty years, generally considered *extinct*, and, as such, is consequently omitted in Playfair's (extensive) *Baronetage of Ireland* (1809-12). Its devolution, however, as below, is in Burke's *Peerage and Baronetage* of 1871 (possibly in those for 1868-70), though, in that work, from 1828 to 1867, a different pedigree had been given, *viz.*, one deducing the then Baronet from *Michael* Barnewall, 4th s. of the 1st Bart., which Michael (*not* James) is therein made the father of Bartholomew Barnewall, of Ballyhost, hereafter named. According to that work (1841 and 1871) *each* of these two contradictory descents had "full recognition by the College of Arms in Ireland."(a) It appears, however, "that this is not so," and that "*the descent* from Michael is *not* registered in any of the pedigrees registered in Ulster's Office. His name only occurs in one of them, but nothing further," and "that pedigree only comes down to Sir George, the 5th Bart" [G. D. Burtchaell, see p. 223, note "a"]. In Burke's edition of 1871, the account runs thus:—

"From the period of the decease of Sir George [the 5th Bart.], the Baronetcy remained *dormant* until revived in Nov. 1821, in favour of the late SIR ROBERT BARNEWALL, by a full recognition of his right by the College of Arms in Ireland. The immediate line of this gentleman we shall now trace. (1) James Barnewall, Esq.,(b) 4th s. of the 1st Bart., left an only s. and h. (2) Bartholomew Barnewall, Esq.,(c) of Ballyhost, co. Westmeath, who *m.* Jane, da. of Kidagh GEOGHEGAN, Esq., of Castletown Geoghegan, and, dying in 1732, was *suc.* by (3) his eldest son, Robert Barnewall, Esq., of Mograth, co. Meath, *m.* Bridget, widow of Richard BARNEWALL, Esq., of Mograth, da. of Henry PIERS, Esq., of Lisloughan, and had (4) Bartholomew, his successor." This Bartholomew Barnewall is the *de jure* Baronet of 1790, as set forth in the succession given below.

VII. 1790. BARTHOLOMEW BARNEWALL, of Greenanstown, co. Westmeath, who, according to the above pedigree, was cousin and h. male, and, as h. male of the body of the grantee, the *de jure* 7th Bart. [I.], being s. and h. of Robert BARNEWALL, of Moyrath, co. Meath, by Bridget, da. of Henry PIERS, of Lisloughan, which Robert (*b.* 1702; *m.* 1723) was s. and h. of Bartholomew BARNEWALL,(c) of Ballyhost, co. Westmeath (*d.* 1736), said to be s. of James BARNEWALL, Lieut.-Col. of Horse, said to be the 4th s. of the 1st Bart. He, who was *b.* about 1724, *never assumed the Baronetcy,* to which his right, as above, would have accrued in 1790.(d) He *m.* (settlm. 16 April 1748), Mary, sister and h. of Isaac Brand COLT, of Brightlingsey Hall, Essex, 2d da. of John Colt. She *d.* 24 March 1802. He *d.* also in 1802.

(a) These words occur in the edition of Burke's work in 1841, where the descent of the then Baronet is deduced from *Michael* Barnewall, as well as in that of 1871, where the deduction is from *James* Barnewall.

(b) As to this James being such 4th son, see p. 249, note "a," but G. D. Burtchaell (see p. 223, note "a") states that "there are numerous proofs given for the descent of the present Bart. from *James* in the pedigree registered [I.] in 1884."

(c) "Bartholomew Barnewall, who married Mrs. of Castletown's daughter, who lives, or did live, in co. Westmeath," is mentioned in the will of Sir George, the 4th Bart., dat. 18 April 1735, as having lent testator £10. No relationship to the testator is, however, mentioned, and certainly the affiliation of the said Bartholomew (as son of James and grandson of the 1st Bart.) cannot be conjectured therefrom.

(d) Assuming the male descent from the grantee to be sufficiently proved. See note "b," next above.

VIII. 1802. SIR ROBERT BARNEWALL, Bart. [I. 1623],(a) of Greenanstown, co. Meath, s. and h., *b.* 6 Oct. 1757; *suc. to the Baronetcy* in 1802,(a) to which, in Nov. 1821, his right was recognised by, and registered in, the College of Arms, Dublin. He *m.* firstly (settlm. 2 Nov. 1786), Catharine Rose, 1st da. and eventually coheir of Charles AYLMER, of Painstown, co. Kildare. She *d.* 10 Feb. 1790. He *m.* secondly (Lic. 3 Oct. 1795), Margaret Jane, 1st da. of George PALMER, of Dublin, Governor of the Bank of Ireland. He *d.* 27 Aug. 1836. His widow *d.* 1844.

IX. 1836. SIR AYLMER JOHN BARNEWALL, Bart. [I. 1623],(a) of Greenanstown aforesaid, only s. and h., by 1st wife, *b.* 30 Dec. 1789; was Lieut. in the 35th Foot, serving, in 1815, at the battle of Waterloo. He *suc. to the Baronetcy,*(a) 27 Aug. 1836. He *m.*, 29 Sep. 1836, Esmay Mary Catherine, 1st da. of Christopher BARNEWALL, of Meadstown, co. Meath, by Anne, da. of Charles AYLMER, of Painstown, co. Kildare. He *d.* 22 Jan. 1838. His widow *d.* 5 March 1879, at 4 Green street, Grosvenor square, in her 85th year.

X. 1838. SIR REGINALD AYLMER JOHN DE BARNEVAL BARNEWALL, Bart. [I. 1623],(a) of Greenanstown aforesaid, posthumous s. and h., *b.* 16 Feb. 1838; *suc. to the Baronetcy*(a at his birth; ed. at the Catholic University of Dublin.

Family Estates.—These, in 1883, were under 3,000 acres.

STEWART(b):
cr. 2 May 1623,
sometime, 1683—1769, VISCOUNTS MOUNTJOY [I.],
and, 1745—1769, EARL OF BLESINGTON [I.].

I. 1623. "SIR WILLIAM STEWART, Knt., of Ramalton, co. Donegal," elder brother of Sir Robert STEWART, of Culmore, Governor of Derry (1643), their parentage being, apparently, unknown(c); being undertaker of escheated lands in Wexford, 1612, was made a free denizen of Ireland, 7 July 1613; had considerable grants of land in co. Donegal and co. Tyrone; was M.P. [I.] for co. Donegal, 1613-15 and 1634-35; Capt. of fifty foot soldiers in Ireland, 1616; *Knighted,* at Royston, Oct. 1619, and was *cr. a Bart.* [I.], as above, by patent dat. at Dublin, 2 May 1623, the Privy Seal being dat. 10 April 1623; was P.C. [I.] to James I and Charles I; distinguished himself during the rebellion of 1641, in the defeat of O'Neill, at Strabane. He *m.* Frances, 2d da. of Sir Robert NEWCOMEN, 1st Bart. [I. 1623], by his 1st wife, Catherine, da. of Thomas MOLYNEUX. His will dat. 8 Oct. 1646, pr. 28 July 1647, in Prerog. Court [I.].

II. 1647? SIR ALEXANDER STEWART [I. 1623], of Ramalton aforesaid, 1st s. and h.; *suc. to the Baronetcy* about 1647; was a Covenanter, and was head of the Lagan forces. He *m.*, about 1648, his cousin, Catherine, da. of

(a) See p. 250, note "d."

(b) Chiefly *ex inform.* G. D. Burtchaell. See p. 223, note "a."

(c) They are said to be descended from Archibald Stewart, of Fintallach, son of another Archibald Stewart, Parson of Kirkmahoe, 1507-21, who was 2d s. of Sir Alexander Stewart, of Garlies, ancestor of the Earls of Galloway [S.], according to Wood's *Douglas's Peerage of Scotland,* but, according to Burke's *Peerage,* etc. (edit. 1899), from "Walter, the 3d surv. son of Sir William Stewart, of Dalswinton and Garlies," living 1479, whose 1st son, Alexander, was ancestor of the Earls of Galloway [S.], and whose 2d son, Thomas, was ancestor of the Lords Blantyre [S.]. The first Baronet is there called "of Castlewigg and Tonderghie, Wigtownshire," being called in Playfair's *Baronetage* "of Aughentean and of Newtown Stewart, co. Tyrone."

Sir Robert NEWCOMEN, 2d Bart. [I. 1623], by his 1st wife, Anne, da. of (—) BOLEYN. He was slain at the battle of Dunbar, 3 Sep. 1653. His widow *m.* Arthur (FORBES), 1st EARL OF GRANARD [I.], who *d.* 1695. She *d.* in Dublin, 8 Dec. 1714, both being *bur.* at Newtown Forbes.

III. 1653. SIR WILLIAM STEWART, Bart. [I. 1623], of Ramalton aforesaid, posthumous s. and h., was *b.* in Oct. 1653 (six weeks after his father's death), and *suc. to the Baronetcy* on his birth; was in ward, in 1660, to his stepfather, then Sir Arthur Forbes, afterwards 1st EARL OF GRANARD [I.] Custos Rotulorum of co. Donegal, 1678. He *m.*, probably before 1680, Mary, 1st da. of Richard (COOTE), 1st BARON COOTE OF COLOONY [I.], by Mary, da. of Sir George ST. GEORGE. She was living when he was *cr.*, 19 March 1682/3, BARON STEWART OF RAMALTON, co. Donegal, and VISCOUNT MOUNTJOY, of co. Tyrone [I.]. He was slain at the battle of Steinkirk, 24 Aug. 1692, aged 38.

IV. 1692. WILLIAM (STEWART), 2d VISCOUNT MOUNTJOY, etc. [I.], and 3d Bart. [I. 1623], 1st s. and h.; *suc. to his father's dignities*, 24 Aug. 1692, in his minority. He *d.* 10 Jan. 1727/8.

V. 1728. WILLIAM (STEWART), 3d VISCOUNT MOUNTJOY, etc. [I.], and 4th Bart. [I. 1623], only surv. s. and h., *b.* 7 April 1709; *suc. to his father's dignities*, 10 Jan. 1727/8. He was *cr.*, 7 Dec. 1745, EARL OF BLESINGTON, co. Wicklow [I.]. He *d.* s.p.s. 14 Aug. 1769, when *all his peerage dignities* became *extinct*, but the Baronetcy devolved on the heir male of the body of the grantee, as under.

For fuller particulars, after 1688, see Peerage.

VI. 1769. SIR ANNESLEY STEWART, Bart. [I. 1623], of Fort Stewart near Ramalton (or Rathmelton), co. Donegal, cousin and h. male, being only surv. s. and h. of Ezekiel STEWART, of the same, by Anne,(a) da. of Charles WARD, which Ezekiel (who *d.* Oct. 1734) was s. and h. of William STEWART, of Fort Stewart, Col., 9th Reg., Sheriff (1697) of co. Donegal (*d.* July 1713), only s. of Thomas STEWART, of the same, who was 2d surv. s. of the 1st Bart. He was *b.* 1725; was M.P. [I.] for Charlemont (in five Parls.), 1763-97; *suc. to the Baronetcy* on the death of his cousin, the EARL OF BLESINGTON, [I.], 14 Aug. 1769; was, in 1776, a Banker at 19 Mary's Abbey, Dublin, probably in partnership with W. Gleadowe. He *m.*, in Sep. 1755, Mary, da. of John MOORE, of Drumbanagher. He *d.* March 1801. Will dat. 1792, pr. 21 Jan. 1802, in Prerog. Court [I.].

VII. 1801. SIR JAMES STEWART, Bart. [I. 1623], of Fort Stewart aforesaid, s. and h.; *b.* about 1760; was M.P. [I.] for Enniskillen, 1783-90, and [U.K.] for co. Donegal, 1802-18; Sheriff of co. Donegal, 1799; *suc. to the Baronetcy* in March 1801. He *m.* 19 Dec. 1778, Mary Susanna, da. of Richard Chapell WHALEY, of Whaley Abbey, co. Wicklow, by his 2d wife Anne, da. of the Rev. Bernard WARD. He *d.* 20 May 1827.

VIII. 1827. SIR JAMES ANNESLEY STEWART, Bart. [I. 1623], of Fort Stewart aforesaid, only s. and h.; *b.* 1798; sometime an officer in the Inniskilling Dragoons; *suc. to the Baronetcy*, 20 May 1827; Sheriff of co. Donegal, 1830; Hon. Col. Donegal Artillery Militia, 1855; Vice-Lieut. of that county, 1866. He *m.*, in Oct. 1830, Jane, da. of FRANCIS MANSFIELD, of Castle Wray, co. Donegal. He *d.* s.p. 13 April 1879. His widow *d.* 15 Jan. 1886, at Fort Stewart.

(a) The mother of this Anne, was Deborah, da. of James Annesley, whence the name of Annesley was introduced into the family.

IX. 1879. SIR AUGUSTUS ABRAHAM JAMES STEWART, Bart. [I. 1623], of Fort Stewart aforesaid, cousin and heir male, being s. and h. of William Augustus STEWART, Capt. 58th Foot, by Anna, da. of William MOLLOY, of Blackford, co. Tipperary, which William Augustus (who *d.* 23 Aug. 1867, aged 70), was s. of Rev. Abraham Augustus STEWART, D.D., Rector of Donabate, co. Dublin (*d.* Jan. 1812, aged 50), s. of Abraham STEWART, Capt. in the Army (*m.* 4 May 1761), only surv. s. of Rev. Robert STEWART, D.D., Prebendary of Kilkenny (*d.* 1772, aged 72), which Robert was next br. to Ezekiel STEWART abovementioned, father of the 6th Bart. He was *b.* 29 April 1832; was a Barrister (Inner Temple), 1874, being some time in practice at Calcutta; *suc. to the Baronetcy*, 13 Sep. 1879; Sheriff of co. Donegal, 1883. He *d.* unm. 26 Aug. 1889, aged 57.

X. 1889. SIR WILLIAM AUGUSTUS ANNESLEY STEWART, Bart. [I. 1623], of Fort Stewart aforesaid, nephew and h., being s. and h. of William Molloy STEWART, by Ellen, relict of Francis Berkeley DRUMMOND, da. of W. H. URQUHART, which William Molloy, who *d.* 1889, aged 56, was next br. to the late Bart. He was *b.* 1865; *suc. to the Baronetcy*, 26 Aug. 1889. He *d.* unm. 4 Jan. 1894, at Calcutta, aged 28.

XI. 1894. SIR HARRY JOCELYN URQUHART STEWART, Bart. [I. 1623], of Fort Stewart aforesaid, br. and h.; *b.* 1872; *suc. to the Baronetcy*, 4 Jan. 1894; Capt. in the Donegal Artillery Militia. He *m.*, 12 Aug. 1896, Isabel Mary, da. of Col. F. S. MANSFIELD, of Castle Wray, co. Donegal.

Family Estates.—These, in 1883, consisted of 7,547 acres in co. Donegal, then worth £4,486 a year. *Principal Seat.*—Fort Stewart, near Rathmelton, co. Donegal.

DUNGAN, or DONGAN(a):

cr. 23 Oct. 1623,

sometime, 1662-91, VISCOUNT DUNGAN OF CLANE [I.],

afterwards, 1686-91, EARL OF LIMERICK [I.];

presumably forfeited, 1691.

I. 1623. "WALTER DUNGAN, Esq., of Castletowne, co. Kildare," 1st s. and h. of John DUNGAN, or DONGAN, of Dublin, Alderman (who *d.* 8 Aug. 1582, and was *bur.* in St. John's church, Dublin), by Margaret, da. of Walter FOSTER, Merchant and Alderman of Dublin; suc. his father, 8 Aug. 1592; was under age in 1597; passed patent for the manor of Kildrought (*i.e.*, Castletown), in 1616, and was *cr. a Bart.* [I.], as above, by patent dat. at Dublin, 23 Oct. 1623, the Privy Seal being dat. at Westm., 8 July previous. He was Sheriff of Dublin City, 1624. He *m.* Jane, da. of Robert ROCHFORT, of Kilbride. He *d.* 21 Dec. 1626. Will pr. 11 Feb, 1627, in Prerog. Court [I.].

II. 1626. SIR JOHN DUNGAN, Bart. [I. 1623], of Castletown aforesaid, s. and h.; *suc. to the Baronetcy* in 1626, being then aged 23; was M.P. [I.] for Newcastle, co. Dublin, 1634-35, and 1639 till expelled, 9 Aug. 1642, "for non-attendance," *i.e.*, for being in rebellion. He *m.*, before 1626, Mary, 1st da. of Sir William TALBOT, 1st Bart. [I. 1623], of Carton, by Alison, da. of John NETTERVILLE, of Castleton, co. Meath. His will dat. 26 July 1642, pr. 27 Jan. 1663, in the Prerog. Court [I.]. He *d.* before 21 May 1656, when his widow had 1,500 acres in Connaught allotted to her.

(a) Chiefly *ex inform.* G. D. Burtchaell. See p. 223, note "a."

III. 1650? SIR WALTER DUNGAN, Bart. [I. 1623], of Castletown aforesaid, 1st s. and h.; *b.* about 1625; was Capt. of a Reg. in 1641, and was, in 1646, one of the confederate Catholics assembled in Kilkenny. He *suc. to the Baronetcy* in or before 1656, in which year (19 July) he was "transplanted" to Connaught, having 1500 acres allotted to him there in full satisfaction. He *d.* s.p.

IV. 1686? to 1691. WILLIAM (DUNGAN), EARL OF LIMERICK [I.], etc., br. and h; *b.* about 1630; was *cr.* 14 Feb. 1661/2, VISCOUNT DUNGAN OF CLANE, co. Kildare [I.], and, subsequently, 2 Jan. 1685/6, EARL OF LIMERICK [I.], with rem. (failing male issue) to his br. Thomas. He *suc. to the Baronetcy* on the death of his brother, which, accordingly, became thenceforth *merged* in the peerage. He *d.* s.p.m.s. in France, Dec. 1698, having been attainted in 1691, when, presumably, *all his honours* were *forfeited*.(a)

See Peerage, under Limerick Earldom cr. 1686; attainted 1691.

NEWCOMEN(b):

cr. 30 Dec. 1623;

ex. 27 April 1780.

I. 1623. "SIR ROBERT NEWCOMEN, Knt., of Kenagh, co. Longford," 3d s. of Charles NEWCOMEN,(c) of London, an Officer in the Exchequer, by Jane, da. and coheir of Richard NIGHTINGALE, of Brentwood, co. Essex; settled in Ireland, where, at Dublin Castle, he was *Knighted*, 9 June 1605, by the L. Deputy [I.], and was *cr. a Bart.* [I.], as above, by patent dat. 30 Dec. 1623, at Dublin, the Privy Seal being dat. 10 April previous at Westm.; was Sheriff of co. Dublin, 1612; M.P. [I.] for Kilbeggan, 1613-15. He *m.* firstly, in or before 1600, Catherine, 2d da. of Thomas MOLYNEUX, Chancellor of the Exchequer [I.], by Catherine, da. of Lodowick SALABOERTE, Governor of Bruges. He *m.* secondly, Elizabeth, widow of Christopher (ST. LAWRENCE), LORD HOWTH [I.] (*d.* in Oct. 1619), da. of (—) WENTWORTH, "of the house of Pockring." She *d.* 1627. He *m.* thirdly, Alice, widow of Christopher PEYTON, Auditor at Wars and of the Revenue [I.], formerly (1593) widow of Nathaniel DILLON, of Dublin, da. of William NEWMAN, Alderman of that city. Will dat. 29 April 1627, in the Prerog. Court [I.]. He *d.* 28 Sep. 1629. Funeral certificate [I.]. Admon. 26 April 1632. His widow *d.* 1632. Funeral certificate [I.].

II. 1629. SIR BEVERLEY NEWCOMEN, Bart. [I. 1623], of Kenagh aforesaid, 1st s. and h., by 1st wife. He was M.P. [I.] for Kilbeggan 1613-15; *Knighted*, v.p., 24 March 1616/7, by the L.-Deputy [I.]; was Commander of *The Swallow* man-of-war, and Admiral of the Irish Seas (Patent 18 Feb. 1618); *suc. to the Baronetcy*, 28 Sep. 1629. He *m.* Margaret, 3d da. of Sir William USSHER,

(a) Thomas, his next surv. br. and heir male, assumed the Earldom on his death in Dec. 1698, to which (under the spec. rem.) he would have been entitled, as also would he have been to the Baronetcy, save for the attainder. He appears to have been generally recognised as an Earl, but *d.* s.p. 14 Dec. 1715, aged 81, when *all his honours* became, presumably, *extinct*. The first Bart. had, besides his successor, six younger sons, one of whom was, apparently, the father of the John Dongan hereafter named. The second Bart. had, besides his two successors (Walter and William), six younger sons, Edward, Robert, Michael, Jerome, Thomas, and James, of whom all, presumably but Thomas, were dead s.p. before the creation, 2 Jan. 1685/6, of the Earldom of Limerick [I.], which was granted with a spec. rem. firstly in favour of the said Thomas, with, secondly, a further spec. rem. in favour of the Earl's cousin, John Dongan.

(b) Chiefly *ex inform.* G. D. Burtchaell. See p. 223, note "a."

(c) This Charles was son of Brian Newcomen, of Saltfletby, co. Lincoln. There is a full pedigree of Newcomen registered in Ulster's office.

Clerk of the Council [I.], by Isabella, da. of Adam LOFTUS, Archbishop of Dublin and L. Chancellor [I.]. He *d.* s.p.m.s.,(a) being drowned (with Arthur, his only son), 28 April 1637, at Passage, near Waterford. His widow *d.* 18 and was *bur.* 27 Aug. 1645, at St. Audoen's, Dublin. Funeral certificate.

III. 1637. SIR THOMAS NEWCOMEN, Bart. [I. 1623], of Kenagh aforesaid, br. of the whole blood and h.; M.P. [I.] for Enniscorthy, 1634-35; *suc. to the Baronetcy*, 28 April 1637. He *m.* Elizabeth, da. of Sir Charles PLEYDELL, of Midge hill, Wilts, by his 1st wife, Catherine, da. and coheir of Thomas BOURCHIER, of Barnesley, co. Gloucester. He *d.* s.p., and was *bur.* at St. Catherine's, Dublin, 29 April 1642. His widow *d.* 1669, and was *bur.* at Lydiard, Wilts. Will pr. 1669.

IV. 1642. SIR ROBERT NEWCOMEN, Bart. [I. 1623], of Kenagh aforesaid, br. of the whole blood and h.; *suc. to the Baronetcy* in 1642; Provost Marshal of Connaught, 11 July 1645; M.P. [I.] for co. Longford, 1646-49, and for Mullingar, 1661-66. He *m.* firstly, Anne, da. of (—) BOLEYN, or BULLEIN, called "Consanguinea Elizabethæ, Reginæ Angliæ." He *m.* secondly, 31 March 1650, Katharine, da. of (—) VERSCHOYLE, but by her (of whom no notice is taken in his funeral certificate) had no issue. He *d.* 12 and was *bur.* 13 Aug. 1677, at St. Catherine's aforesaid. Funeral certificate. Will (nuncupative) dat. 5 Aug. 1667, pr. 28 May 1668, in Prerog. Court [I.].

V. 1667. SIR THOMAS NEWCOMEN, Bart. [I. 1623], of Kenagh aforesaid, only s. and h. by 1st wife; was *Knighted*, v.p., in 1664, by the L. Deputy [I.]; *suc. to the Baronetcy*, 12 Aug. 1667. He *m.* firstly (banns pub. 31 Aug. 1659 in Newgate Market, Dublin), Margaret, da. and h. of Sir Silvester BROWNE, 2d Bart. [I. 1622], of Ballynamore, co. Longford, by Mary, da. of (—) ROCHE. She *d.* s.p.m. He *m.* secondly, in or before 1664, Sarah, 6th and yst. da. of Sir George ST. GEORGE, of Carrickdrumrusk, co. Leitrim (*d.* 5 Aug. 1660), by Catherine, da. of Capt. Richard GIFFORD, of Ballymagarett, co. Roscommon. He was killed at the siege of Enniskillen in 1689.

VI. 1689. SIR ROBERT NEWCOMEN, Bart. [I. 1623], of Mosstown, co. Longford, 1st s. and h. by 2d wife; *b.* 1664; entered Trin. Coll., Dublin, as a Fellow Comm., 9 Nov. 1679, aged 15; B.A., 1683; *suc. to the Baronetcy* in 1689; was LL.D. of the Univ. of Dublin (spec. gra.) 10 March 1718; was Sheriff for co. Longford, 1699; M.P. [I.] for that county (in six Parls.), 1692 till his death in 1734. He *m.* Mary, da. of Arthur (CHICHESTER), 2d EARL OF DONEGALL [I.], by Jane, da. of John ITCHINGHAM. He *d.* 6 March 1734. Will dat. 17 Jan. 1734, pr. 5 June 1736, in Prerog. Court. [I.].

VII. 1734. SIR ARTHUR NEWCOMEN, Bart. [I. 1623], of Mosstown aforesaid, only s. and h.; Sheriff of co. Longford, 1732; *suc. to the Baronetcy*, 6 March 1734; was M.P. [I.] for co. Longford, 1734 till his death. He *m.*, firstly (articles 4 July 1724), Sarah, only da. of William GORE, by Katharine, only da. of Sir Thomas NEWCOMEN, 5th Bart. [I. 1623], which William was 3d s. of Sir Arthur GORE, 1st Bart. [I. 1662], of Newtown Gore. He *m.* secondly (Lic. 29 Nov. 1736), Elizabeth, 3d da. of Sir Thomas MOORE, of Marlfield, co. Tipperary. She *d.* 6 and was *bur.* 9 April 1744, at Mosstown. He *d.* 25 Nov. 1759. Will dat. 16 Oct. 1758, pr. 25 March 1761, in Prerog. Court [I.].

(a) Katherine Newcomen, his da. and h. was his administatrix in 1637. Sir Beverley had an illegit. son (by — Niell), Sir Thomas Newcomen, of Sutton, co. Dublin, *Knighted* about 1680, who was P.C. [I.]. He *m.* twice, and had issue by both wives. His will dat. 16 Feb. 1694. That of his widow, Jane, was pr. 1740, in the Prerog. Court [I.].

VIII. 1759, to 1789. SIR THOMAS NEWCOMEN Bart. [I. 1623], of Mosstown aforesaid, s. and h. by 2d wife; *b.* 1740; *suc. to the Baronetcy,* 26 Nov. 1759; was sometime Sheriff of co. Longford; M.P. [I.] thereof, 1759-60, and for Longford borough, 1761-68. He *m.* (Lic. 26 Sep. 1760) Margaret, da. of John (BOURKE), 1st EARL OF MAYO [I.], by Margaret, da. and coheir of Joseph DEANE, L.-Ch. Baron of the Exchequer [I.]. She *d.* before him. He *d.*, s.p., 27 April 1789, when *the Baronetcy* became *extinct.* Will pr. 1789, in Prerog. Court [I.].

ARRAGH, *or* MAC-BRIAN-ARRAGH, *or* O'BRIEN ARRAGH.(a):
cr. 28 Feb. 1623/4;
ex. 28 March 1626.

I. 1624, to 1626. "TERENCE, *alias* TIRLAGH, MAC-BRIAN-ARRAGH, Esq., of Dough-Arragh, co. Tipperary," s. and h. of Mortogh or Morietagh MAC-BRIAN-ARRAGH, *or* MAC-I-BRIEN ARRAGH, *or* O'BRIEN ARRAGH(b) of the same (a Chieftain of such power that Queen Elizabeth, in 1570, made him Bishop of Killaloe, which office he held till a year before his death, 30 April 1613), by Slaney, da. of (—) BUTLER; was *cr. a Bart.* [I.], as above, by patent dat. at Dublin, 28 Feb. 1623/4, the Privy Seal being dat. at Westm., 13 April 1623. He *m.* Ellis, 9th and yst. da. of Walter (BUTLER), EARL OF ORMOND [I.], by Helen, da. of Edmund (BUTLER), 2d VISCOUNT MOUNTGARRET [I.]. She *d.* 10 Feb. 1625. He *d.* s.p. 28 March 1626, when *the Baronetcy* became *extinct.* Both are *bur.* in St. Mary's church, on the island of Iniscaltra, in the river Shannon, under a monument erected by his mother, "the Ladye Slany Ry Brien." Will, in which he is styled "*Sir Terlogh O'Brien*, Knt. and Bart., of Castle Arra, co. Tipperary," dat. 19 March 1625 [*Qy.* 1625/6], pr. 1626, in the Prerog. Court [I.].

CHEVERS(a):
Warrant dat. 25 June 1623.

CHRISTOPHER CHEVERS, of Macetown, co. Meath, 1st s. and h. of John CHEVERS, of the same (who *d.* 30 April 1599), by his 1st wife, Catherine, da. and h. of Henry TRAVERS, of Monkstown, co. Dublin, had a *warrant for a Baronetcy* [I.], by letters, 25 June 1623, addressed to Viscount Falkland [S.], the Lord Deputy [I.],(c) but not only does no patent for the creation now exist, but it may reasonably be supposed *never* to have existed, from the fact of the dignity having never been assumed. He *m.* firstly, Eleanor, sister of Richard (NUGENT), 1st EARL OF WESTMEATH [I.], 4th da. of Christopher, BARON DELVIN [I.]. She (by whom he had six sons and three daughters) *d.* 31 Aug. and was *bur.* 19 Oct. 1636, at St. Nicholas, Macetown. Funeral certificate [I.], He *m.* secondly, Jane, da. of Jerome BATH, of Edickstown, co. Meath, by whom he had three sons. He *d.* 7 and was *bur.* 9 Nov. 1640, in the chapel at Macetown.(d) Funeral certificate [I.].

(a) Chiefly *ex inform.* G. D. Burtchaell, etc. See p. 223, note "a."
(b) A descendant in the male line from the family of O'Brien, Princes of Thomond.
(c) Cal. State Papers [I.].
(d) "The heir male of his body is John Joseph Chevers, of Killyan, co. Galway, J.P., D.L., living 1900. Pedigree registered in Ulster's office." [G. D. Burtchaell, see p. 223, note "a."

CROOKE.(a)
cr. 19 April 1624.
ex., presumably, March 1665/6.

I. 1624. "THOMAS CROOKE, late Esq., now Knight, of Baltimore, co. Cork," son of Thomas CROOKE, S.T.D., "Minister of the Word of God" in the Society of Gray's Inn, was *b.* about 1584(b); was admitted to Gray's Inn, 1 March 1596/7(c); established a Protestant colony at Baltimore, co. Cork, and procured a charter of incorporation for that town, being its first "Sovereign"; was M.P. [I.] thereof, 1613-15; had large grants in co. Cork(d); was *Knighted* at Theobalds, 4 March 1623/4, and was *cr. a Bart.* [I.], as above, by patent 19 April 1624, at Dublin, the Privy Seal being, 5 March 1623/4, at Westm. He *m.*, before 1615, Mary, da. of (—). He *d.* 1630. Will, dat. 27 Feb. 1629/30, pr. by his widow on 7 May 1630, in the Commissary Court of London, and on 6 May 1631, in the Prerog. Court [I.].

II. 1630, to 1666? SIR SAMUEL CROOKE, Bart. [I. 1624], of Baltimore aforesaid, 1st surv. s. and h.(e); adm. to Gray's Inn, 6 March 1624/5; *suc. to the Baronetcy* in 1630. He *m.* Judith, both being living s.p. in 1635, when he made a will. He *d.* s.p. and intestate about March 1665/6, when the *Baronetcy* is presumed to have become *extinct.*(f) Admon. 11 March 1665/6 in Prerog. Court [I.], to his relict Dame Judith, then dwelling in England.

NORTON.(g)
cr. 27 April 1624;
ex., presumably, about 1690.

I. 1624. "GREGORY NORTON, Esq., of Charlton, co. Berks," possibly a son of Gregory NORTON, a Capt in Queen Elizabeth's army in Ireland (who was s. of Sir Dudley NORTON); was *cr. a Bart.* [I.], as above, by patent 27 April 1624, at Dublin, the Privy Seal being 20 Feb. 1623/4, at Westm.; was admitted to Gray's Inn, 3 Aug. 1649, being then "of Hampden's, Bucks, Knt."; was M.P. for Midhurst, 1645 till his death; was one of the most extreme of the ante-Royalist party; served on every principal Committee of Parl., 1648-49; sat (Jan. 1648/9) every day but two, as one of the King's judges, and signed the death warrant. He was rewarded in 1649 with a grant (at a nominal sum) of Sheen palace, in

---

(a) Chiefly *ex inform.* G. D. Burtchaell, C. M. Tenison, etc. See p. 223, note "a."
(b) In his will, dat. 17 Feb. 1629/30, he calls himself aged 56 "or thereabouts," mentions his brothers, "Dr. Helkiah Crooke," Richard Crooke and Samuel Crooke, Rector of Wrington, co. Somerset, and various other relatives. The arms on the seal, are a fess engrailed between three eagles displayed, and testator is called late of St. Stephen's Coleman street, London.
(c) The identity of the Thomas so admitted with the future Baronet is shewn by the admissions of two of his sons at Gray's Inn, *viz.*, 5 Aug. 1620, "Thomas Crooke, s. and h. of Thomas Crooke, late of Gray's Inn, now of Ireland, Esq.," and, 6 March 1624/5, "Samuel Crooke, son of Thomas Crooke, of Baltimore, co. Cork, Knt. and Bart. (extra hosp. Oct. 13, 1626; *Stet*; for this gent. was mistaken for his brother Thomas erased)."
(d) The statement that "Crookhaven" in that district was called after him is supported by its having been so styled as early as 1577 (Elizabethan fiats).
(e) See note "c," next above, as to an elder br., Thomas, being alive in Aug. 1620.
(f) He had a yr. br. James, whom he mentions in his will of 1665, who, or whose issue male, if living after his death, would have been entitled to the Baronetcy.
(g) Chiefly *ex inform.* C. M. Tenison, etc. See p. 223, note "a."

Richmond, Surrey. He *m.* Martha, da. of (—). He was *bur.* 26 March, 1652, at Richmond aforesaid. Will dat. 12 March 1651/2, pr. 24 Sep. 1652, by his widow. She *m.*, 20 Oct. 1655, at St. Paul's, Covent Garden, Robert (GORDON), 4th VISCOUNT KENMURE [S.], who *d.* s.p. 1663. Her will pr. Nov. 1671.

II. 1652, to 1690? SIR HENRY NORTON, Bart. [I. 1624], only s. and h.; *suc. to the Baronetcy*, 26 March 1652, but was disinherited by his father as to the estates. He was admitted to Gray's Inn, 10 March 1657/8, being then of Richmond aforesaid; was M.P. for Petersfield, 1659, but had been "unduly elected." He *m.*, 14 Oct. 1656, at St. Margaret's, Westm., Mabella, da. of Sir Richard NORTON, 1st Bart. [1622], of Rotherfield, Hants, by Amy, da. of Thomas BILSON, Bishop of Winchester. She petitions, as his wife, in Sep. 1660, for £300 a year, setting forth that he had been disinherited for his loyalty by his father, and mentioning the services of her own father and brother in the Royal cause. He was living 31 Dec. 1661, but nothing further is known of him; but at his death, say about 1690, the *Baronetcy* is presumed to have become *extinct.*

GALWEY, *or* GALWAY(a):
cr. probably in April 1624(b);
ex. probably about 1700.

I. 1624. "GEFFREY GALWAY, Esq., of Kallwollin, co. Limerick," 1st s. of James GALWEY, of Kingsale and of Limerick, Alderman; was admitted to Gray's Inn (as "of Limerick, gent.") 13 Aug. 1590;(c) was Mayor of Limerick, 1600; M.P. [I.] thereof, 1613, and Governor of Limerick, and was *cr. a Bart.* [I.], as above, the patent, however, not being enrolled but the Privy Seal bearing date 6 March 1623/4(b) at Westm. He was M.P. [I.] for Limerick city, 1634-35. He *m.* firstly, Anne, da. of Nicholas COMYN, Alderman and (1583) Mayor of Limerick. He *m.* secondly, Mary, da. of Morogh MCSHEEHY, of Ballyallevan, co. Limerick. He *m.* thirdly, Moare, da. of Morogh O'BRIEN, of Tuagh, co. Limerick. He *d.* 28 March 1636, at Kingsale, and was *bur.* there. Funeral certificate [I.]. Will dat. that day, and pr. 12 May 1636, in the Prerog. Court [I.]. His widow *m.* John BROWNE, of Kilcomen, co. Kerry, who *d.* s.p. 20 June 1689. Funeral certificate [I.].

II. 1636. SIR GEOFFREY GALWEY *or* GALWAY, Bart. [I., 1624], grandson and h., being s. and h. of John GALLWEY, by Elizabeth, da. of (—) BETTS, of co. Norfolk, which John was 1st s. and h. ap. of the late Bart, by his 1st wife, but *d.* v.p.; *suc. to the Baronetcy*, 28 March 1636, being then aged 19. He *m.* Eleanor. He was outlawed 1641; attainted 1642 as "of Tyssaxenbeg," at the reduction of Limerick, and was, with nineteen others, excepted as to life and property in the articles, 27 Oct. 1651. He succeeded in making his escape,(d) but *d.* before 1653, when his widow, then aged 26, was "transplanted" to co. Clare. She, by the description of "Dame Eleanor Galway, relict of Sir Geoffrey, the younger," was confirmed in the lands in that county, 4 Nov. 1676, by the Commissioners of Claims.

(a) G. D. Burtchaell and C. M. Tenison (see p. 223, note "a") have kindly supplied nearly all the information in this article.
(b) The date of the Privy Seal for this creation (6 March 1623/4) is the same as that for Crooke, of which the patent was dated 19 April 1624.
(c) "Spent many years in England studying the common law, and returning to Ireland about 1597 did so pervert the city of Limerick that by his malicious council and perjurious example he withdrew the Mayor, Aldermen, and generally the whole city from coming to church."
(d) Thomas Dineley's *Limerick*, 1681.

III. 1652? to 1700? SIR JAMES GALWEY, Bart. [I., 1624], only s. and h., *suc. to the Baronetcy* in 1650; was "transplanted" to Connaught 26 Aug. 1656 (being then of co. Clare), and had 366 acres allotted to him; was appointed a Justice of the Peace of co. Limerick in 1688. He *m.* Jan. 1684, Margaret, da. of John BLUNT, of Ballycullane, co. Limerick. He was living 1690, but *d.* s.p.m.s.(a) probably about 1700, when *the Baronetcy* became *extinct.*

STYLE, *or* STYLES:
cr. 13 Sep. 1624,
afterwards, 20 May 1627, *cr.* a BARONET OF ENGLAND;
ex. 10 Nov. 1659.

I. 1624, to 1659. "SIR HUMPHRY STYLE, *alias* STYLES, Knt., one of the Gentlemen of the Privy Chamber in ordinary," was *cr. a Bart.* [I.] as above by patent, 13 Sep. 1624, at Dublin, the Privy Seal being 20 July 1624, at Westm. He was subsequently cupbearer to Charles I, by whom, 20 May 1627, he was *cr. a Bart. of England.* He *d.* s.p. 10 Nov. 1659, in his 64th year, when *both the Baronetcies* [I. and E.] *became extinct.* See fuller particulars under "CREATIONS [E.] by CHARLES I."

(a) He had a son Patrick, living 1663, who, apparently, *d.* young. Catherine, his da. and eventually sole heir, born 5 Jan. 1690, *m.*, 4 Feb. 1705, Simon Ronan, and *d.* at Ballingoran, co. Waterford, 7 April 1767, leaving issue.

I

CORRIGENDA ET ADDENDA.

p. 12; lines 26 and 38, *for* "11 May," *read* "22 May."

p 14; line 1, *for* "1728," *read* "1727/8, at St. Paul's, London."

p. 40; line 4, *for* "1st," *read* "2d"; line 25, *after* "Barbara," *add* "(*b.* 31 Jan. 1661/2)"; line 38, *for* "*d.*," *read* "was *bur.* at Gresley, 11 Oct."; line 41, *for* "about 1723," *read* "12 July 1722, at Drakelow."

p. 41; line 2, *after* "widow," *add* "She *d.* in Hertford street, Mayfair, 12 and was *bur.* 26 June 1797, at Gresley"; line 5, *after* "male," *add* "*b.* 11 Jan. 1725/6, and *bap.* 27 at Walton"; line 11, *after* "s. and h.," *add* "*b.* 18 March 1753; ed. at Manchester Grammar School; Sheriff of Derbyshire, 1780"; line 14, *after* "She," *add* "(who was *b.* at Drakelow, 17 Aug. and *bap.* 5 Oct. 1750, at Walton)"; line 16, *after* "1808," *add* "of dropsy, at Bath, and was *bur.* in the Abbey there. M.I."; line 17, *for* "The admon. of his widow," *read* "His widow *d.* at Cheltenham, 9 Nov. 1840, in her 70th year. Admon."

p. 49; line 26, *dele* "relict of Sir Richard Bozom"; line 32, *for* "1600," *read* "1583"; line 34, *after* "secondly," *add* "in or before 1599"; line 36, *for* "Goltho'," *read* "Goltho." Note (f), *after* "came," *add* "on the death of the 8th Earl in 1617."

p. 50; line 15, *for* "Alderney," *read* "Aldersey, of Spurstow"; line 36, *dele* "of Lupset, co. York"; line 37, *for* "s. and h.," *read* "2d s."; line 38, *for* "aforesaid," *read* "co. York"; line 40, *after* "Horbury," *add* "He did not succeed to the estate of Lupset on the death s.p., about 1670, of his elder br., Thomas, but"; line 45, *for* "of Thomas Jennison," *read* "and coheir of Thomas Jenison"; line 46, *for* "by his 1st," *read* "2d s. by his 2d"; last line, *conclude* "His widow, from whom he had been separated in Oct. 1735,(b) *m.*, May 1744, Capt. Wallis, and subsequently (as her 3d husband) Charles Morton, M.D., F.R.S., Librarian of the British Museum, who outlived her, and *d.* 10 Feb. 1799." *Add as a note* "(b) She appears to have intrigued with the Duke of Kingston."

p. 101; line 12, *for* "1838," *read* "1834."

p. 102; in margin, *for* "1838?" *read* "1834"; in text, line 3 from bottom, *for* "*d.* abroad," *read* "who was sometime British Consul for North Carolina, *d.* abroad early in Aug. 1834."

p. 104; line 6, *after* "1740," *add* "and *bap.* 1 Feb. 1741, at St. Geo., Queen sq., Midx."

p. 109; line 3, from bottom, *for* "1776," *read* "1766."

p. 126; line 35, *for* "living 1899," *read* "*d.* Jan. 1900, at Penlergare, near Swansea, aged 87."

p. 132; in margin, *for* "1648?" *read* "1648"; in text, line 34, *for* "July," *read* "16 May"; line 39, *for* "about 1648," *read* "16 May 1648."

p. 133; line 17, *for* "1712," *read* "1712/3, at Nursling, Hants"; line 18, *for* "Nutshelling, Hants," *read* "Nursling aforesaid, by Margaret, da. of Edward Fleming, of Stoneham. She, who was *bap.* at Nursling, 28 June 1688, and

whose issue (in Dec. 1752) became heir to her father"; line 21, *for* "etc.," *read* "and Grove place aforesaid"; line 37, *for* "1729," *read* "1720"; line 44, *for* "da. of (—) Windover," *read* "Windover, of Stockbridge"; *after* "1792," *add* "and was *bur.* at Kingsomborne"; line 45, *for* "1800," *read* "3 July 1800, and was *bur.* there."

p. 134; line 3, *for* "and was apparently living 1862(a)," *read* "who *d.* June 1846, aged 67. She *d.* s.p. March 1862, aged 83." *Dele* note "(a)."

p. 142; line 21, *after* "Dorothy," *add* "(*m.* 26 Sep. 1581, at Harrow)"; line 22, *dele* "15 April 1583"; line 26, *for* "1620," *read* "1617"; line 32, *for* "*b.* about 1620," *read* "*bap.* 12 Oct. 1617, at Harrow"; line 34, *for* "1650," *read* "1648"; line 38, *for* "about 1654," *read* "16 Aug. 1653, and *bap.* at Harrow." Note (a), line 1, *after* "8th S.," *add* "vol. ii."

p. 159; line 8, *for* "(1761-75)," *read* ", 1761-75."

p. 160; note (b), lines 8 and 9, *for* "and was living 1626," *read* "was living in 1626, and was *bur.* 10 May 1633, in Bath Abbey."

p. 170; line 37, *for* "about 1835," *read* "Feb. 1835, aged 80."

p. 185; line 24, *for* "Aug.," *read* "at the Vicarage Stoke Milburg, Salop, May."

p. 212; between lines 19 and 20, *insert* "*ex.* 8 March 1747/8."

p. 216; note (b), *for* "214," note 'a,'" *read* "215, note 'd.'"

p. 218; line 11, *for* "1631-53, Baron Cottingham," *read* "1631-52, Baron Cottington of Hamworth."

p. 224; line 2, *for* "and his," *read* "Joan. da. of Edmund Tirry, Alderman of Cork. He *m.* secondly, Anne, widow of Sir Dudley Loftus, da. of Sir Nicholas Bagenall. His."

p. 225; in margin, *for* "1665?" *read* "1675?"; in text, line 25, *for* "was living probably long afterwards," *read* "*d.* between 8 Nov. 1673 and 2 Nov. 1678"; line 29, *for* "1665," *read* "1675." Note (b), *commence* "At the former date he himself, and at the latter, his successor (as Sir F. B., *Bart.*) was a Commissioner in King's County for disarming Roman Catholics ['Ormond Papers,' *Hist. MSS. Com.*, vol. ii, pp. 338 and 353]."

p. 239; note (d), *conclude* "The pedigree of Everard was recorded, in 1716, in Ulster's office."

p. 240; line 2, *dele* "surv."

p. 246; note (a), *conclude* "In April 1690 (shortly after this article was in type) there appeared in the *Genealogical Magazine* (vol. iii), 'Notes on Extinct Irish Baronetcies, by T.' These (which are to be continued) contain Fitzharris, *cr.* 1622; MacMahon, *cr.* 1628, and Magrath, *cr.* 1629, or 1630. They, however, contain no additional information as to Fitzharris, save as to the collateral branches."

INDEX

TO THE SURNAMES OF THE SEVERAL HOLDERS OF THE BARONETCIES CREATED BY JAMES I,

including not only those of the grantees themselves but of their successors; to which is added the local or, failing that, personal description of each grantee. The name of any Peerage dignity held with such Baronetcy is not included in the alphabetical arrangement, neither is the surname of the holder of any such peerage, when different(a) from that of any Baronet who was a Commoner.

(a) Thus the surname of the Earl of Winchilsea, who, 2 Aug. 1826, succeeded his kinsman in that peerage and in the Baronetcy of Finch (*cr.* 29 June 1611) was Finch-Hatton, but the name of "Hatton" is not given in this index in connection with this Baronetcy. So also as to the names of "Hampden" and "Bruce" in connection with the Baronetcies of Hobart (*cr.* 22 May 1611) and of Brudenell (*cr.* 29 June 1611), though the surname of the Earls of Buckinghamshire, who enjoy the former, has been, since 1878, "Hobart-Hampden," while that of the Marquesses of Ailesbury, who, in 1868, inherited the latter, is "Brudenell-Bruce."

PROSPECTUS

OF THE

Complete Baronetage,

Extant, Extinct, or Dormant,

EDITED BY

G. E. C.

EDITOR OF THE

"Complete Peerage."

Vol. i., BARONETCIES (English and Irish), created by JAMES I., 1611 to 1625; issued (April 1900), **at 14s. to** Subscribers; price, after publication, £1 1s. net.

To be followed in the course of 1901, by

Vol. ii., BARONETCIES (English, Irish and Scotch) created by CHARLES I., 1625 to 1649. This Vol. to be issued at £1 1s to Subscribers; price, after publication, £1 11s. 6d. net.

Vols. iii. and iv., will contain BARONETCIES (as next above) created 1649 to 1707 (the date of the Union with Scotland), each Vol. to be issued on the same terms as Vol. ii.

Vols. v. and vi. will contain the BARONETCIES of Great Britain and those of Ireland, 1707 to 1800 (the date of the Union with Ireland), while the remaining Vols. will deal with those of the United Kingdom, viz., 1801 to the date of publication.

[APRIL, 1900].

LIST OF SUBSCRIBERS.

Aldenham, Lord, St. Dunstan's, Regent's Park, N.W.
Amherst of Hackney, Lord, per Sotheran & Co., 140, Strand, W.C.
Annesley, Lieut. Gen. A. Lyttelton, Templemere, Weybridge, Surrey.
Antrobus, Rev. Frederick, The Oratory, South Kensington, S.W.
Armytage, Sir George, Bart., F.S.A., Kirklees Park, Brighouse.
Arnold, Charles T., Stamford House, West Side, Wimbledon.
Assheton, Ralph, Downham Hall, Clitheroe.
Astley, John, Moseley Terrace, Coundon Road, Coventry.
Athill, Charles H., F.S.A., Richmond Herald, College of Arms, E.C.

Batten, John, Aldon, Yeovil.
Bedford, Duke of, per Sotheran & Co., 140, Strand, W.C.
Bools, W. E., Enderby, 13, Vernon Road, Clapham, S.W.
Boyle, Colonel the Hon. R. E., 6, Summer Terrace, London, S.W.
British Museum, Department of MSS., per Sotheran & Co., 140, Strand, W.C.
Brooking-Rowe, J., Castle Barbican, Plympton.
Burke, Ashworth P., per Harrison & Sons, 59, Pall Mall, S.W.
Burke, Henry Farnham, Somerset Herald, College of Arms, E.C.
Burnard, Robert, 3, Hillsborough, Plymouth.

Carington, R. Smith, Ashby Folville Manor, Melton Mowbray.
Carlton Club, Pall Mall, per Harrison & Sons, 59, Pall Mall, S.W.
Carmichael, Sir Thomas D. Gibson, Bart., M.P., Castlecraig, Dolphinton, N.B.
Chadwyck-Healey, C. E. H., per Sotheran & Co., 140, Strand, W.C.
Clements, H. J. B., Killadoon, Cellridge, co. Kildare, Ireland.
Codrington Library, All Souls' College, Oxford.
Conder, Edward, F.S.A., The Conigree, Newent, Gloucester.
Cooper, Samuel J., Mount Vernon, near Barnsley.
Crawford and Balcarres, Earl of, per Sotheran & Co. 140, Strand, W.C.
Crisp, F. A., Grove Park, Denmark Hill, London, S.E.
Cust, Lady Elizabeth, 13, Eccleston Square, London, S.W.

Dalrymple, Hon. Hew., Oxenfoord Castle, Dalkeith.
Davies, Seymour G. P., English, Scottish, and Australian Bank Ltd., Melbourne, Australia.
Davison, R. M., Grammar School, Ilminster.
Douglas, David, 10, Castle Street, Edinburgh.
Duckett, Sir George, Bart., Oxford and Cambridge Club, Pall Mall, S.W.
Duleep Singh, His Highness Prince, per Sotheran & Co., 140, Strand, W.C.
Dunkin, E. H. W., Rosewyn, 70, Herne Hill, London, S.E.

Edwardes, Sir Henry H., Bart., per Harrison & Sons, 59, Pall Mall, S.W.
Exeter Royal Albert Memorial Museum (J. Dallas, Librarian), Exeter.

Foley, P., Prestwood, Stourbridge, per A. & F. Denny, 304, Strand, W.C.
Foster, Joseph, 21, Boundary Road, London, N.W.
Fox, Charles Henry, M.D., 35, Heriot Row, Edinburgh.
Fox, Francis F., Yate House, Chipping Sodbury, Gloucester, per W. George's Sons, Top Corner, Park Street, Bristol.
Fry, E. A., 172, Edmund Street, Birmingham.

Gatty, *see* Scott-Gatty.
George's Sons, William, Top Corner, Park Street, Bristol.
Gibbs, Antony, Tyntesfield, near Bristol.
Gibbs, H. Martin, Barrow Court, Flax Bourton, Somerset, per W. George's Sons, Top Corner, Park Street, Bristol.
Gibbs, Rev. John Lomax, Speen House, near Newbury, Berks.
Gibbs, Hon. Vicary, M.P., St. Dunstan's, Regent's Park, London, N.W.
Gough, Henry, Sandcroft, Redhill, Surrey.
Graves, Robert Edmund, B.A., British Museum, W.C. (2).

Hanson, Sir Reginald, Bart., M.P., 4, Bryanston Square.
Hardy & Page, 21, Old Buildings, Lincoln's Inn, London, W.C.
Harrison & Sons, 59, Pall Mall, London, S.W.
Haslewood, Rev. F. G., Chislet Vicarage, Canterbury.
Hatchards, 187, Piccadilly, London, W. (6)
Hawkesbury, Lord, per Sotheran & Co., 140, Strand, W.C. (2)
Healey, *see* Chadwyck-Healey.
Hesilrige, Arthur G. M., 160A, Fleet Street, London, E.C.
Hofman, Charles, 16, Grosvenor Street, London, W.
Hovenden, R., Heathcote, Park Hill Road, Croydon.
Hughes of Kinmel, H. R., Kinmel Park, Abergele, North Wales, per Sotheran & Co., 140, Strand, London, W.C.
Hull Subscription Library (A. Milner, Librarian), Royal Institution, Hull.

Incorporated Law Society (F. Boase, Librarian), 103, Chancery Lane, W.C.
Inner Temple Library, per Sotheran & Co., 140, Strand, London, W.C.
Iveagh, Lord, per Sotheran & Co., 140, Strand, London, W.C.

Johnston, G. Harvey, 22, Garscube Terrace, Murrayfield, Edinburgh, per W. & A. K. Johnston, 5, White Hart Street, Warwick Lane, London, E.C.

Kildare Street Club, Dublin.
King's Inns Library, Dublin, per Hodges, Figgis & Co., Dublin.

Larpent, Frederic de H., 16, St. Helen's Place, London, E.C.
Lea, J. Henry, 18, Somerset Street, Boston, Mass., U.S.A.
Leeds Library (Charles W. Thonger, Librarian), Commercial Street, Leeds.
Lincoln's Inn Library (A. F. Etheridge, Librarian), London, W.C.
Lindsay, Leonard C. C., 87, Cadogan Gardens, London, S.W.
Lindsay, W. A., Q.C., Windsor Herald, College of Arms, London, E.C.
Littledale, Willoughby A., F.S.A., 26, Cranley Gardens, S.W.

Macdonald, W. R., Carrick Pursuivant, Midpath, Weston Coates Avenue, Edinburgh.
Maddison, Rev. Canon, Vicars' Court, Lincoln.
Magrath, Rev. John Richard, D.D., Queen's College, Oxford.
Manchester Free Library, per J. E. Cornish, 16, St. Ann's Square, Manchester.
Marshall, George W., LL.D., Sarnesfield Court, Weobley, R.S.O.
Marshall, Julian, London, N.W., per T. Carver, 8, High Town, Hereford.
Marsham-Townshend, Hon. Robert, Frognal, Foots Cray, Kent.
Maskelyne, Anthony Story., Public Record Office, Chancery Lane, W.C.
Mitchell Library (F. T. Barrett, Librarian), 21, Miller Street, Glasgow.
Murray, Keith W., F.S.A., 37, Cheniston Gardens, Kensington, London, W.

National Library of Ireland, Dublin, per Hodges, Figgis & Co., Dublin.
Newberry Library, Chicago, per H. Grevel & Co., 33, King Street, Covent Garden, London, W.C.

O'Connell, Sir Ross., Killarney, per Bickers & Son, 1, Leicester Square, London, W.C.
Oxford & Cambridge Club, Pall Mall, per Harrison & Sons, 59, Pall Mall, S.W.

Paul, Sir James Balfour, Lyon King of Arms, 30, Heriot Row, Edinburgh.
Penfold, Hugh, Rustington, Worthing.
Phillimore, W. P. W., 124, Chancery Lane, London.

Ramsay, Sir James H., Bart., Banff, Alyth, N. B.
Reform Club, Pall Mall, per Jones, Yarrell & Co., 8, Bury Street, S.W.

Richardson, W. H., 2, Lansdown Place, Russell Square, W.C.
Royce, Rev. David, Nether Swell Vicarage, Stow on Wold, Gloucestershire.
Rye, Walter, St. Leonard's Priory, Norwich.

Schomberg, Arthur, Seend, Melksham.
Scott-Gatty, A. S., York Herald and Acting Registrar, College of Arms, London, E.C.
Seton, Bruce Maxwell, Bart., Durham House, Chelsea, London, S.W.
Shadwell, Walter, H. L., F.S.A., Trewollack, Bodmin.
Shelley, Spencer, 37, Bathwick Hill, Bath.
Sherborne, Lord, 9, St. James's Square, London, S.W.
Smith, J. Challenor, F.S.A., Whitchurch, Oxon. (2)
Sotheran & Co., 140, Strand, London, W.C. (9)
Strange, Hamon le, Hunstanton Hall, Norfolk.
Stoddart, A. R., Fishergate Villa, York.

Tempest, Sir Robert T., Bart., Tong Hall, Drighlington, Bradford, Yorks.
Tenison, C. M., Hobart, Tasmania.
Thompson, W. N., St. Bees, Cumberland.
Townshend, *see* Marsham-Townshend.
Toynbee, Paget, Dorney Wood, Burnham, Bucks.

Wedderburn, Alexander, 47, Cadogan Place, London, S.W.
Weldon, William H., Norroy, College of Arms, London, E.C.
Were, Francis, Gratwicke Hall, Flax Bourton, Somerset.
Wood, F. A., Highfields, Chew Magna, Somerset.
Woods, Sir Albert W., K.C.B., Garter, 69, St. George's Road, S.W.

Yarborough, Countess of, 17, Arlington Street, Piccadilly, W., per H. Sotheran & Co., 140, Strand, W.C.

Complete Baronetage

VOLUME TWO
1625–1649

Complete Baronetage.

EDITED BY

G. E. C.

EDITOR OF THE

"Complete Peerage."

VOLUME II.

1625—1649.

EXETER:
WILLIAM POLLARD & Co. Ltd., 39 & 40, NORTH STREET.
1902.

CONTENTS.

LIST OF SUBSCRIBERS.

Adams, Rev. H. W., Normanhurst, Eton Avenue, Hampstead, N.W.
Aldenham, Lord, St. Dunstan's, Regent's Park, N.W.
Amherst of Hackney, Lord, F.S.A., per Sotheran & Co., 140, Strand, W.C.
Anderson, J. R., 84, Albert Drive, Crosshill, Glasgow.
Annesley, Lieut.-Gen. A. Lyttelton, Templemere, Weybridge, Surrey.
Anstruther, Sir R., Bt., Balcaskie, Pillenweena, Scotland.
Antrobus, Rev. Frederick, The Oratory, South Kensington, S.W.
Armytage, Sir George, Bt., F.S.A., Kirklees Park, Brighouse.
Arnold, Charles T., Stamford House, West Side, Wimbledon.
Assheton, Ralph, Downham Hall, Clitheroe.
Astley, John, Moseley Terrace, Coundon Road, Coventry.
Athenæum Club, per Jones, Yarrell, & Poulter, Booksellers, 8, Bury Street, S.W.
Athill, Charles H., F.S.A., Richmond Herald, College of Arms, E.C.

Bain, J., Bookseller, 1, Haymarket, S.W. (4).
Baronetage, The Hon. Society of the, per Sotheran & Co., 140, Strand, W.C.
Batten, H. B., Aldon, Yeovil.
Beaven, Rev. A. B., Greyfriars, Leamington.
Bedford, Duke of, per Sotheran & Co., 140, Strand, W.C.
Bell & Sons, York Street, Covent Garden, W.C.
Boase, F., 28, Buckingham Gate, S.W.
Bools, W. E., Enderby, 13, Vernon Road, Clapham, S.W.
Boyle, Colonel the Hon. R. E., 6, Summer Terrace, S.W.
British Museum, Department of MSS., per Sotheran & Co., 140, Strand, W.C.
Brooking-Rowe, J., Castle Barbican, Plympton.
Bruce Bannerman, W., F.S.A., The Lindens, Sydenham Road, Croydon, Surrey.
Burke, Ashworth P., per Harrison & Sons, 59, Pall Mall, S.W.
Burke, Henry Farnham, F.S.A., Somerset Herald, College of Arms, E.C.
Burnard, Robert, 3, Hillsborough, Plymouth.

Carington, R. Smith, F.S.A., Ashby Folville Manor, Melton Mowbray.
Carlton Club, Pall Mall, per Harrison & Sons, 59, Pall Mall, S.W.
Carmichael, Sir Thomas D. Gibson, Bt., Castlecraig, Dolphinton, N.B.
Cazenove & Son, C. D., Booksellers, 26, Henrietta Street, Covent Garden, W.C.
Chadwyck-Healey, C. E. H., F.S.A., per Sotheran & Co., 140, Strand, W.C.
Clarke, C. L., Homewood, Stevenage, Herts.
Clements, H. J. B., Killadoon, Cellridge, co. Kildare, Ireland.
Codrington Library, All Souls College, Oxford.
Colyer-Fergusson, T. C., Ightham Mote, Ivy Hatch, near Sevenoaks.
Conder, Edward, F.S.A., The Conigree, Newent, Gloucester.
Cooper, Samuel J., Mount Vernon, near Barnsley.
Craigie, Edmund, The Grange, Lytton Grove, Putney Hill, S.W.
Crawford and Balcarres, Earl of per Sotheran & Co., 140, Strand, W.C.
Crawley-Boevey, A. W., 24, Sloane Court, S.W.
Cresswell, L., Wood Hall, Calverley, Leeds.
Crisp, F. A., F.S.A., Grove Park, Denmark Hill, S.E.
Crompton, S. Douglas, per Sotheran & Co., 140, Strand, W.C.
Culleton, Leo., 92, Piccadilly, W.
Cullum, G. M. G., 4, Sterling Street, Montpelier Square, S.W.
Cust, Lady Elizabeth, 13, Eccleston Square, S.W.

Dalrymple, Hon. Hew., Oxenfoord Castle, Dalkeith.
Davies, Seymour G. P., English, Scottish, and Australian Bank Ltd., Melbourne, Australia.
Davison, R. M., Grammar School, Ilminster.
Douglas, David, 10, Castle Street, Edinburgh.
Douglas & Foulis, 9, Castle Street, Edinburgh (6).
Duckett, Sir George, Bt., Oxford and Cambridge Club, Pall Mall, S.W.
Duleep Singh, His Highness Prince, per Sotheran & Co., 140, Strand, W.C.
Dunkin, E. H. W., Rosewyn, 70, Herne Hill, S.E.

Edwardes, Sir Henry H., Bt., per Harrison & Sons, 59, Pall Mall, S.W.
Eland, H. S., Bookseller, High Street, Exeter.
Exeter Royal Albert Memorial Museum, Exeter.

Foley, P., F.S.A., Prestwood, Stourbridge, per A. & F. Denny, 304, Strand, W.C.
Foster, Joseph, 21, Boundary Road, N.W.
Fox, Charles Henry, M.D., 35, Heriot Row, Edinburgh.
Fox, Francis F., Yate House, Chipping Sodbury, Gloucester, per W. George's Sons, Top Corner, Park Street, Bristol.
Fry, E. A., 172, Edmond Street, Birmingham.

George, William Edwards, Downside, Stoke Bishop, near Bristol, per George's Sons, Bristol.
George's Sons, William, Top Corner, Park, Street, Bristol.
Gibbs, Antony, Tyntesfield, near Bristol.
Gibbs, H. Martin, Barrow Court, Flax Bourton, Somerset, per W. George's Sons, Top Corner, Park Street, Bristol.
Gibbs, Rev. John Lomax, Speen House, near Newbury, Berks.
Gibbs, Hon. Vicary, M.P., St. Dunstan's, Regent's Park, N.W.
Glencross, R. M., The Office of Arms, Dublin Castle, Ireland.
Gough, Henry, Sandcroft, Redhill, Surrey.
Graves, Robert Edmund, Lyndhurst, Grange Park, Ealing, W. (2).
Green & Sons, W., Law Booksellers, Edinburgh.
Guildhall Library (per C. Welch), E.C.

Hanson, Sir Reginald, Bt., 4, Bryanston Square, W.
Hardy & Page, 21, Old Buildings, Lincoln's Inn, W.C.
Harrison & Sons, 59, Pall Mall, S.W. (3).
Haslewood, Rev. F. G., Chislet Vicarage, Canterbury.
Hatchards, 187, Piccadilly, W. (6).
Hawkesbury, Lord, per Sotheran & Co., 140, Strand, W.C. (2).
Head, Christopher, 6, Clarence Terrace, Regent's Park, N.W.
Hesilrige, Arthur G. M., 160A, Fleet Street, E.C.
Hodge, Figgis & Co., Booksellers, 104, Grafton Street, Dublin.
Hofman, Charles, 16, Grovenor Street, W.
Hovenden, R., F.S.A., Heathcote, Park Hill Road, Croydon.
Hughes of Kimmel, H. R., Kimmel Park, Abergele, North Wales, per Sotheran & Co., 140, Strand, W.C.
Hull Subscription Library (William Andrews, Librarian), Royal Institution, Hull.

Incorporated Law Society (F. Boase, Librarian), 103, Chancery Lane, W.C.
Inner Temple Library, per Sotheran & Co., 140, Strand, W.C.
Iveagh, Lord, F.S.A., per Sotheran & Co., 140, Strand, W.C.

Johnston, G. Harvey, 22, Garscube Terrace, Murrayfield, Edinburgh, per W. & A. K. Johnston, 5, White Hart Street, Warwick Lane, E.C.

Kildare Street, Club, Dublin.
King's Inns Library, Dublin, per Hodges, Figgis & Co., Dublin.

Larpent, Frederic de H., 11, Queen Victoria Street, E.C.
Lawton, William F., Librarian, Public Libraries, Hull.
Lea, J. Henry, 18, Somerset Street, Boston, Mass., U.S.A.
Lee, W. D., Seend, Melksham.
Leeds Library (Charles W. Thonger, Librarian), Commercial Street, Leeds.
Lincoln's Inn Library (A. F. Etheridge, Librarian), W.C.
Lindsay, Leonard C. C., 87, Cadogan Gardens, S.W.
Lindsay, W. A., K.C., F.S.A., Windsor Herald, College of Arms, E.C.
Littledale, Willoughby A., F.S.A., 26, Cranley Gardens, S.W.
Loraine, Sir Lambton, Bt., 7, Montagu Square, W.

Macdonald, W. R., Carrick Pursuivant, Midpath, Weston Coates Avenue, Edinburgh.
Mackenzie, Sir E. M., Bt., Naval & Military Club, Melbourne, Australia.
MacLehose & Sons, J., 61, St. Vincent Street, Glasgow.
Macmillan & Bowes, Cambridge.
Maddison, Rev. Canon, F.S.A., Vicars' Court, Lincoln.
Magrath, Rev. John Richard, D.D., Queen's College, Oxford.
Malcolm, J. W. Hoveton Hall, Norwich.
Manchester Free Library, per J. E. Cornish, 16, St. Ann's Square, Manchester.
Marshall, George W., L.L.D., F.S.A., Sarnesfield Court, Weobley, R.S.O.
Marshall, Julian, 13, Belsize Avenue, N.W.
Marsham-Townshend, Hon. Robert, F.S.A., Frognal, Foots Cray, Kent.
Maskelyne, Anthony Story, Public Record Office, Chancery Lane, W.C.
Mitchell Library (F. T. Barrett, Librarian), 21, Miller Street, Glasgow.
Montagu, Col. H., 123, Pall Mall, S.W.
Moseley, Sir O., Rolleston Hall, Burton-on-Trent.
Murray, Keith W., F.S.A., 37, Cheniston Gardens, Kensington, W.
Myddelton, W. M., Spencer House, St. Albans.

National Library of Ireland, Dublin, per Hodges, Figgis & Co., Dublin.
National Portrait Gallery, per Eyre & Spottiswoode, 5, Middle New Street, E.C.
Newberry Library, Chicago, per H. Grevel & Co., 33, King Street, Covent Garden, W.C.
Nudd, W. A., Bookseller, 2, The Haymarket, Norwich.

O'Connell, Sir Ross., Killarney, per Bickers & Son, 1, Leicester Square, W.C.
Office of Arms, Dublin Castle, Ireland.
Oxford & Cambridge Club, Pall Mall, per Harrison & Sons, 59, Pall Mall, S.W.

Parker & Co., J., Booksellers, 27, Broad Street, Oxford.
Paul, Sir James Balfour, Lyon King of Arms, 30, Heriot Row, Edinburgh.
Penfold, Hugh, Rustington, Worthing.
Phillimore, W. P. W., 124, Chancery Lane, W.C.
Pixley, F. W., per Sotheran & Co., 140, Strand, W.C.
Public Record Office, per Eyre and Spottiswoode, 5, Middle New Street, E.C.

Ramden, J. C., Willinghurst, Guildford, Surrey.
Ramsay, Sir James H., Bt., Banff, Alyth, N.B.
Reform Club, Pall Mall, per Jones, Yarrell & Poulter, 8, Bury Street, S.W.
Rich, Sir Charles H. Stuart, Bt., F.S.A., Devizes Castle.
Richardson, W. H., F.S.A., 2, Lansdown Place, Russell Square, W.C.
Rimell & Son., J., Booksellers, 91 Oxford Street, W. (2).
Royce, Rev. David, Nether Swell Vicarage, Stow on Wold, Gloucestershire (2).
Rye, Walter, St. Leonard's Priory, Norwich.
Rylands, J. Paul. F.S.A., 2, Charlesville, Birkenhead.
Rylands Library, The John, Manchester, per Sotheran & Co., 140, Strand, W.C.
Rylands, W. H., F.S.A., 37, Great Russell Street, Bloomsbury, W.C.

Schomberg, Arthur, Seend, Melksham.
Scott-Gatty, A. S., F.S.A., York Herald and Acting Registrar, College of Arms, E.C.
Seton, Bruce Maxwell, Bt., Durham House, Chelsea, S.W.
Shadwell, Walter H. L., F.S.A., Trewollack, Bodmin.
Shaw, W. A., 3, Rusthall Park, Tunbridge Wells.
Shelley, Spencer, 37, Bathwick Hill, Bath.
Sherborne, Lord, 9, St. James's Square, S.W.
Simpkin, Marshall, Hamilton, Kent, & Co., Ltd., 4, Stationers' Hall Court, E.C.
Smith, J. Challenor, F.S.A., Whitchurch, Oxon. (2).
Sotheran & Co., 140, Strand, W.C. (9).
Stevens, Son, & Stiles, Booksellers, 39, Great Russell Street, W.C.
Stewart, C. P., Chesfield Park, Stevenage.
Strange, Hamon le, Hunstanton Hall, Norfolk.
Stoddart, A. R., Fishergate Villa, York.
St. Leger, James, White's Club, St. James's Street, S.W.

Tempest, Sir Robert T., Bt., Tong Hall, Drighlington, Bradford, Yorks.
Tenison, C. M., Hobart, Tasmania.
Thompson, W. N., St. Bees, Cumberland.

Tooke Hales, J. B., Copdock, Ipswich.
Toynbee, Paget, Dorney Wood, Burnham, Bucks.
Turnbull, Alex H., per Sotheran & Co., 140, Strand, W.C.

United University Club, 1, Suffolk Street, Pall Mall East, London.

Wedderburn, Alexander, K.C., 47, Cadogan Place, S.W.
Weldon, William H., F.S.A., Norroy, College of Arms, London, E.C.
Were, Francis, Gratwicke Hall, Flax Bourton, Somerset, per George's Sons, Bristol.
Wilson, Sir S. M., Fitzjohn, near Rugby.
Wood, F. A., Highfields, Chew Magna, Somerset, per George's Sons, Bristol.
Wood, H. J. T., Fingest Cottage, near High Wycombe, Bucks.
Woods, Sir Albert W., K.C.B., F.S.A., Garter, 69, St. George's Road, S.W.

Yarborough, Countess of, 17, Arlington Street, Piccadilly, W., per H. Sotheran & Co., 140, Strand, W.C.

ABBREVIATIONS

USED IN THIS WORK.

Besides those in ordinary use the following may require explanation.

admon., administration of the goods of an intestate.
ap., apparent.
b., born.
bap., baptised.
bur., buried.
cr., created.
d., died.
da., daughter.
h., heir
m., married.
M.I., Monumental Inscription.
pr., proved.
s., son.
s.p., sine prole.
s.p.m., sine prole masculo.
s.p.m.s., sine prole masculo superstite.
s.p.s., sine prole superstite.
suc., succeeded.

Baronetcies of England.

1611—1706.

SECOND PART,

VIZ.,

CREATIONS BY CHARLES I.

27 March 1625 to 30 Jan. 1648/9.

The number of Baronetcies of England that had been created by James I was 204, not reckoning therein the Baronetcy of Vavasour, which was in fact created by his successor, 22 June 1631, tho' with *the precedency* of 29 June 1611. James had undertaken that the number should not exceed 200, and, allowing for six which had become extinct, they did not exceed 198 at his death. "Charles I, however, had not been long on the throne, when, relying on his royal prerogative as the Fountain of Honour, he disregarded the stipulated limitation of the number of Baronets." [*Her. and Gen.*, vol. iii, p. 346.]

ASHFIELD, *or* ASHFEILD:

cr. 20 June 1626;

ex., apparently, March 1713/4.

I. 1626. "JOHN ASHFEILD, of Harkestead Netherhall, co. Suffolk, Knt., one of the Gentlemen of the Privy Chamber," s. of Sir Robert Ashfield, of the same and of Stow Langtoft,(a) in the said county, by Anne, da. of Sir John TASBURGH, of Flixton, Suffolk, was *b.* about 1597; ***Knighted***, at Theobalds, 3 June 1615; suc. his father, Oct. 1624; entered his pedigree at the Her. Visit. of London, 1624; was one of the Gentlemen of the Privy Chamber to Charles I, 1637, and was *cr. a Bart.* as aforesaid 20 June 1626, being the first person on whom Charles I conferred that dignity. He *m.* (Lic. Lond. 30 April 1627, he 30 and she 27) Elizabeth, widow of Sir James ALTHAM, of Oxey, Herts, da. and h. of Sir Richard SUTTON, one of the Auditors of the Imprest. He *d.* 1635. Admon. as of St. Botolph, Aldersgate, London, 30 Nov. 1638. His widow *m.* 12 Nov. 1655, at St. Giles' in the Fields, Sir Richard MINSHALL, widower.

II. 1635. SIR RICHARD ASHFIELD, Bart. [1626], of Harkestead Netherhall aforesaid, s. and h.; *b.* about 1630; *suc. to the Baronetcy* in 1635. He was Sheriff of Gloucestershire, 1668-69. He *m.* firstly, in or before 1654, (—), da. and coh. of Sir Richard ROGERS, of Eastwood, co. Gloucester. He *m.* secondly, 20 Feb. 1673/4, at St. Mary Mag., Old Fish street, London (Lic. Lond. 30 Dec. 1673, he 44) Dorcas BURCHETT, widow, da. of James HORE, of the Mint, in the Tower of London. He *d.* about 1684. Will pr. 1684.

(a) This Sir Robert sold in 1614 the estate of Stow Langtoft (which had belonged to the Ashfield family from the time of Edward III) to Paul D'EWES, ancestor of the D'Ewes, Barts., of that place.

III. 1684? to 1714. SIR JOHN ASHFIELD, Bart. [1626], of Harkestead Netherhall, and of Eastwood, both aforesaid, s. and h. by 1st wife; *bap.* 8 Dec. 1654, at Hillesden, Bucks; *suc. to the Baronetcy* about 1684. He *m.* Anne, da. of James HORE abovenamed, being sister to his stepmother. She was *bur.* 13 Dec. 1702, at St. Giles' in the Fields. He was living 1692, as was also his son Charles (a minor of the age of 14), but the estates had been alienated. He was *bur.* 9 March 1713/4, at St. Giles' aforesaid, when apparently the *Baronetcy* became extinct,(a) which, it is stated,(b) to have been before 1727.

HARPUR, *or* HARPER:

cr. 8 Dec. 1626;

afterwards, since 1808, HARPUR-CREWE.

I. 1626. "HENRY HARPER, of Calke, co. Derby, Esq.," 3d s. of Sir John HARPUR, of Swarkeston, in that co., by Isabel, da. of Sir George PIERREPONT, of Holme, Notts, which John (who *d.* 7 Oct. 1622), was s. and h. of Richard HARPUR, one of the Justices of the Court of Common Pleas (*d.* 29 Jan. 1573), was *b.* about 1585; matric. at Oxford (Bras. Coll.) 20 Feb. 1595/6, aged 17; admitted to the Inner Temple, 1598, and was *cr. a Bart.*, as above, 8 Dec. 1626. He *m.* Barbara, widow of Sir Henry BEAUMONT, of Grace Dieu, co. Leicester, da. of Anthony FAUNT, of Foston, by Elizabeth, da. of Andrew NOELL, of Dalby, both in co. Leicester. He *d.* 1638. Will pr. 1639. His widow *d.* 2 July 1649, aged 69, and was *bur.* at All Saints', Derby. M.I.

II. 1638. SIR JOHN HARPUR, Bart. [1626], of Calke Abbey, in Calke aforesaid, s. and h.; *b.* about 1616; *suc. to the Baronetcy* in 1638; Sheriff of Derbyshire, 1641-42; was sequestrated and fined £110, from May 1646. He *m.*, probably about 1640, Susan, da. of (—) WEST, Citizen of London. He *d.* 1669, aged 53. Will pr. Feb. 1670.

III. 1669. SIR JOHN HARPUR, Bart. [1626], of Calke Abbey aforesaid, s. and h.; *b.* probably about 1645; matric. at Oxford (Queen's Coll.), 26 Oct 1660; *suc. to the Baronetcy* in 1669 and to the estate of Swarkeston, co. Derby, under the will of his cousin, Sir John HARPUR,(c) of Swarkeston, who *d.* s.p. in 1677. He *m.* 17 Sep. 1674, at Swarkeston, Anne, 3d da. of William (WILLOUGHBY), 6th BARON WILLOUGHBY OF PARHAM, by Anne, da. of Sir Philip CAREY, of Aldenham, Herts. She was *b.* at Stansteadbury, Herts, 15 Dec. 1652, her birth being regd. at Hunsdon. He *d.* 1681. Will pr. 1681.

IV. 1681. SIR JOHN HARPUR, Bart. [1626], of Calke Abbey aforesaid, s. and h., *b.* 23 March 1679; *suc. to the Baronetcy* in 1681; mat. at Oxford (Mag. Coll.) 6. July 1697. Sheriff of Derbyshire, 1702. He *m.*, in or before 1709, Catherine, yst. da. and coheir of Thomas (CREWE), 2nd BARON CREWE OF STENE, by his 2d wife, Anne, da. and coheir of Sir William AIRMYN,

(a) "Richard Ashfeild, of St. Giles' in the Fields, Esq., Bachr., about 22" (evidently a yr. s. of the 2d Bart.), had lic. (Vic. Gen.) 26 Dec. 1677, to marry "Mrs. Mary Gunning, of St. Dunstan's in the West, about 22, spinster." This Richard mat. at Oxford (Mag. Coll.), 27 Feb. 1673/4, aged 17, as "son of Richard, of Eastwood, co. Glouc., Bart.," and became a Barrister of the Middle Temple, 1682. Among the baptisms at St. Giles' are some of the children of Sir Richard Ashfield and Dame Dorcas, viz., Thomas, 22 Feb. 1674/5; Charles, 9 Sep. 1676; and James, 27 Dec. 1677. Among the burials is that of "Charles Ashfield, Esq.," 14 Sep. 1694.

(b) In Courthope's as well as in Burke's *Extinct Baronetcies*.

(c) This Sir John had *m.* (Lic. Fac. 3 June 1661) Frances Willoughby, elder sister to Anne, the wife of his cousin and devisee, the 3d Bart. This lady, afterwards Countess of Bellomont [I.], who probably held the principal part of the Swarkeston estates for life, *d.* s.p. 25 May 1714, in her 72d year, and was *bur.* at Swarkeston.

2nd Bart. [1619]. He *d.* suddenly at Calke Abbey, 24 and was *bur.* 30 June 1741, at Calke. Will pr. 1741. His widow, who was *bap.* 28 Oct. 1682 at St. Martin's in the Fields, was *bur.* at Calke, 24 Jan. 1744/5. Will pr. 1745.

V. 1741. SIR HENRY HARPUR, Bart. [1626], of Calke Abbey, aforesaid, s. and h., *b.* about 1709; matric. at Oxford (Bras. Coll.), 10 May 1725, aged 16; *suc. to the Baronetcy*, 24 June 1741; M.P. for Worcester, 1744-47, and for Tamworth, 1747 till his death. He *m.* (Spec. Lic. Fac. 2 Oct. 1734) Caroline, da. of John (MANNERS), 2nd DUKE OF RUTLAND, by his 2d wife, Lucy, da. of Bennet, (SHERARD), 2nd BARON SHERARD OF LEITRIM [I.]. He *d.* 7 June 1748. Admon. July 1748. His widow *m.*, 18 July 1753, Sir Robert BURDETT, 4th Bart. [1619], who *d.* 13 Feb. 1797. She *d.* 10 Nov. 1769, at Foremark, co. Derby. Will pr. Jan. 1770.

VI. 1748. SIR HENRY HARPUR, Bart. [1626], of Calke Abbey aforesaid; s. and h., *suc. to the Baronetcy*, 7 June 1748; M.P. for Derbyshire, 1761-68, and Sheriff, 1774-75. He *m.* 17 July 1762, Frances Elizabeth, 2nd da. of Francis (GREVILLE), 1st EARL BROOKE and EARL OF WARWICK, by Elizabeth, da. of Lord Archibald HAMILTON. He *d.* 10 Feb. 1789. Will pr. 1789. His widow, who was *b.* 11 May 1744, *d.* 6 April 1825. Will pr. May 1825.

VII. 1789. SIR HENRY HARPUR, *afterwards*, since 1808, HARPUR-CREWE, Bart. [1626], of Calke Abbey aforesaid, s. and h.; *b.* 13 May 1763; matric. at Oxford (Ch. Ch.) 23 June 1781, aged 17; *suc. to the Baronetcy*, 10 Feb. 1789. Sheriff of Derbyshire, 1794-95. By royal lic., 11 April 1808, he took the name of CREWE,(a) being that of his great grandmother, the wife of the 4th Bart. He *m.*, 4 Feb. 1792, at Calke (spec. lic.), Anne or Nanny HAWKINS, of Calke aforesaid, spinster. He *d.* 7 Feb. 1819, at his residence, Boreham Wood, Elstree, Herts, owing to an accidental fall from his coach box. Admon. April 1819. His widow *d.* 20 March 1827, at East Moulsey Park, Surrey, aged 61. Will pr. April 1827.

VIII. 1829. SIR GEORGE HARPUR-CREWE, Bart. [1626], of Calke Abbey aforesaid, s. and h.; *b.* 1 Feb. 1795; entered Rugby School, 30 May 1806; *suc. to the Baronetcy*, 7 Feb. 1819; Sheriff of Derbyshire, 1820-21; M.P. for South Derbyshire, 1835-43. He *m.*, 9 Sep. 1819, Jane, 1st da. of Rev. Thomas WHITAKER, M.A., Vicar of Mendham, Norfolk. He *d.* at Calke Abbey, 1 and was *bur.* 9 Jan. 1844, at Calke. Will pr. July 1844. His widow *d.* 10 Feb. 1880, aged 81, at 13 Queen's Gate Gardens, Kensington, and was *bur.* at Calke.

IX. 1844. SIR JOHN HARPUR-CREWE, Bart. [1626], of Calke Abbey aforesaid, s. and h.; *b.* there 18 Nov. 1824; ed. at Rugby and at Ex. Coll. Oxford; matric. 16 Nov. 1843, aged 18; *suc. to the Baronetcy*, 1 Jan. 1844. Sheriff of Derbyshire, 1853. He *m.*, 20 Nov. 1845, at St. Geo. Han. sq., his cousin, Georgiana Jane Henrietta Eliza, 2d da. of Vice Admiral William Stanhope LOVELL, K.H., by Selina, da. of Sir Henry HARPUR, *afterwards* HARPUR-CREWE, 7th Bart. abovenamed. He *d.* 1 March 1886, after a lingering illness, at Calke Abbey, in his 62d year. His widow living 1900.

X. 1886. SIR VAUNCEY HARPUR-CREWE, Bart. [1626], of Calke Abbey aforesaid, 1st s. and h.; *b.* 14 Oct. 1846; *suc. to the Baronetcy*, 1 March 1886. He *m.*, 20 April 1876, at Lea Marston, co. Warwick, Isabel, 6th and yst. da. of Charles Bowyer (ADDERLEY), 1st BARON NORTON, by Julia Anna Eliza, da. of Chandos (LEIGH), 1st BARON LEIGH OF STONELEIGH. She was *b.* 28 Oct. 1852.

Family Estates.—These, in 1883, consisted of 14,256 acres in Staffordshire, 12,923 in Derbyshire, and 877 in Leicestershire. *Total*, 28,050 acres, worth £36,366 a year. *Principal Residences.*—Calke Abbey, Repton Park, and Warslow Hall (near Ashbourne), all in co. Derby.

(a) The lic. is to take the name of Crewe *only* and to bear the arms of Crewe quarterly with those of Harpur.

SEBRIGHT, *or* SEABRIGHT:

cr. 20 Dec. 1626.

I. 1626. "EDWARD SEABRIGHT, of Besford, co. Worcester, Esq.," s. and h. of John SEBRIGHT,[a] of Blackshall in Wolverley, in that county, by Anne, da. of Richard BULLINGHAM; was *b.* about 1585; matric. at Oxford (Bras. Coll.), 11 Dec. 1601, aged 16; suc. his uncle, William SEBRIGHT (Town Clerk of London, 1573-1612, M.P. for Droitwich, 1572-83), in the estate of Besford, 27 Oct. 1620; was Sheriff of Worcestershire, 1621, and was *cr. a Bart.*, as above, 20 Dec. 1626, being subsequently,[b] 10 April 1627, *Knighted* at Whitehall. He was a faithful Royalist, and was fined £1,809 by the sequestrators accordingly. He *m.* firstly, in or before 1611, Theodocia, da. of Gerard WHORWOOD, of Compton, co. Stafford, by Dorothy, da. and h. of Edward BARBOUR, of Flashbrook. He *m.* secondly, in or after 1638, Elizabeth, widow of Sir Lewis MANSEL, 2nd Bart. [1611], of Margam, da. of Henry (MONTAGU), 1st EARL OF MANCHESTER, by his first wife Catharine, da. of Sir William SPENCER, of Yarnton, Oxon. She *d.* before him. His admon. 11 Feb. 1657/8 and 20 Feb. 1669.

II. 1658? SIR EDWARD SEBRIGHT, Bart. [1626], of Besford Court, in Besford aforesaid, 1st surv. s. and h.[c] by second wife; *b.* about 1645[d]; *suc. to the Baronetcy* about 1658; matric. at Oxford (St. John's Coll.), 13 Sep. 1661, aged 16; *cr.* M.A. 9 Sep. 1661. He *m.* (Lic. Lond. 15 Feb. 1664/5, he 20 and she 15) Elizabeth, da. of Sir Richard KNIGHTLEY, K.B., of Fawsley, co. Northampton, by 2d wife, Ann, da. of Sir William COURTEEN. He *d.* 11 Sep. 1679, aged 34, and was *bur.* at Besford. His will pr. 1679. His widow *d.* 30 Sep. 1685, aged 34. Her will pr. 1685.

III. 1679. SIR EDWARD SEBRIGHT, Bart. [1626], of Besford Court aforesaid, s. and h., *b.* 1668; matric. at Oxford (Jesus Coll.), 7 March 1684/5, aged 17; *suc. to the Baronetcy*, 11 Sep. 1679; el. Sheriff of Worcestershire, 1685. He *m.* (Lic. Lond. 24 March 1687/8, he 21 and she 24) Anne, da. and h. of Thomas SAUNDERS,[e] of Beechwood, in Flamsted, Herts, by Ellen, da. and h. of Robert SADLEIR, of Sopwell in that county. He *d.* 15 Dec. 1702, in his 36th year and was *bur.* at Besford. M.I. Will pr. March 1703. His widow, who was *b.* and *bap.* 27 April 1670, at Flamsted, *m.* Charles LYTTELTON (s. and h. ap. of Sir Charles Lyttelton, 3d Bart. [1618], of Franckley), who *d.* v.p., 16 Aug. 1712. She *d.* 25 Dec. 1718. Will pr. May 1719.

IV. 1702. SIR THOMAS SAUNDERS SEBRIGHT, Bart. [1626], of Beechwood and of Besford Court aforesaid, s. and h., *b.* 11 May and *bap.* 8 June 1692, at Flamsted; matric. at Oxford (Jesus Coll.), 3 June 1705, aged 13; *cr.* M.A., 28 April 1708; D.C.L., 19 Aug. 1732, having *suc. to the Baronetcy*, 15 Dec. 1702. M.P. for Herts in four Parls., 1715 till decease. He *m.* Henrietta, da. of Sir Samuel DASHWOOD, sometime Lord Mayor of London, by Anne, da. of John SMITH, of Tedworth, Hants. He *d.* 12 and was *bur.* 20 April 1736, at Flamsted. Will pr. 1736. His widow *d.* 21 and was *bur.* 28 March 1772, at Flamsted. Will pr. March 1772.

V. 1736. SIR THOMAS SAUNDERS SEBRIGHT, Bart. [1626], of Beechwood and of Besford Court aforesaid, s. and h., *bap.* 21 Dec. 1723 in London, ed. at Westminster School, matric. at Oxford (Ch. Ch.), 10 Feb. 1741/2, aged 18; *suc. to the Baronetcy*, 12 April 1736. He *d.* unm. 30 Oct., and was *bur.* 4 Nov. 1761 at Flamsted. Admon. 12 Dec. 1761.

---

[a] See Clutterbuck's *Herts*, vol. i, p. 362.

[b] See vol. i, p. 18, note "c," *sub* "Tollemache."

[c] Of his two elder brothers of the half blood (William and John), John was aged 16 in 1627.

[d] He was under age, (his uncle, the Earl of Manchester, being his "curator,") 11 Feb. 1657/8, but had attained full age 20 April 1669.

[e] See pedigree in Clutterbuck's *Herts*, vol. i, p. 362, and see also notes in Playfair's *Baronetage*, under Sebright, as to the families of Saunders and Sadleir.

VI. 1761. SIR JOHN SEBRIGHT, Bart. [1626], of Beechwood and of Besford Court aforesaid, br. and h., *bap.* 19 Oct. 1725 at Flamsted, ed. at Westminster School; *suc. to the Baronetcy*, 30 Oct. 1761; Colonel of the 18th Regt. of Foot; Lieut. Gen. in the army; M.P. for Bath in three Parls. 1763-68. He *m.*, 15 May 1766, at St. Geo. Han. sq., Sarah, 3d da. of Edward KNIGHT, of Wolverley, co. Worcester, by Elizabeth, da. of (—) JAMES, of Olton End, co. Warwick. He *d.* 23 Feb., and was *bur.* 4 March 1794, at Flamsted. Will pr. March 1794. His widow was *bur.* there 4 Jan. 1813. Will pr. 1813.

VII. 1794. SIR JOHN SAUNDERS SEBRIGHT, Bart. [1626], of Beechwood and of Besford Court aforesaid, s. and h., *b.* 23 May 1767 in Sackville street, St. James' Westm.; *suc. to the Baronetcy*, 23 Feb. 1794; M.P. for Herts in eight Parls. 1807-35; Sheriff of Herts, 1797-98. He *m.*, 6 Aug. 1793, Harriet, only da. and h. of Richard CROFTS, of West Harling, Norfolk, by Harriet, da. and coh. of John DARELL, of York street, St. James' Westm. She *d.* Aug. 1826. Will pr. March 1827. He *d.* 15 April 1846. Will pr. July 1846.

VIII. 1846. SIR THOMAS GAGE SAUNDERS SEBRIGHT, Bart. [1626], of Beechwood and of Besford Court aforesaid, only s. and h., *b.* 1802, *suc. to the Baronetcy*, 15 April 1846. He *m.* firstly, 17 Nov. 1842, Sarah Anne, 2d da. of (—) HOFFMAN, Capt., R.N. She *d.* 14 Feb. 1846. He *m.* secondly, in 1850, Olivia, yst. da. of John Joseph HENRY, of Straffan, co. Kildare, by Emily Elizabeth, da. of William Robert (FITZGERALD), 2d DUKE OF LEINSTER [I.]. She *d.* 27 June 1859, in Wilton crescent, aged 44. He *d.* 29 Aug. 1864, at Beechwood, aged 62.

IX. 1864. SIR JOHN GAGE SAUNDERS SEBRIGHT, Bart. [1626], of Beechwood and of Besford Court aforesaid, s. and h. by 1st wife; *b.* 20 Aug. 1843, in Paris; Ensign 4th Herts Rifle Volunteers, 1860; matric. at Oxford (Ch. Ch.), 23 May 1861, aged 17; *suc. to the Baronetcy*, 29 Aug. 1864; Sheriff of Herts, 1874; Hon. Major in the Beds Militia, 1881. He *m.*, 27 Aug. 1865, Olivia Amy Douglas, yst. da. of John Wilson (FITZPATRICK), 1st BARON CASTLETOWN, by Augusta, only da. of Rev. Archibald Edward DOUGLAS, Rector of Cootehill, Ireland. He *d.* 15 Nov. 1890, at Caddington Hall, Beds, aged 47. His widow *d.* 22 May 1895, at 101 Eaton Place, Midx.

X. 1890. SIR EGBERT CECIL SAUNDERS SEBRIGHT, Bart. [1626], of Beechwood aforesaid, only s. and h.; *b.* 12 June 1871, in Chesham place, Midx.; *suc. to the Baronetcy*, 15 Nov. 1890. He d., unm., off Batavia, Java, 1 April and was *bur.* 5 June 1897, at Flamsted, aged 25.

XI. 1897. SIR EDGAR REGINALD SAUNDERS SEBRIGHT, Bart. [1626], of Beechwood aforesaid, uncle and h., being 2d s. (1st s. by the 2d wife) of the 8th Bart.; *b.* 27 May 1854; ed. at Eton and at Mag. Coll., Oxford; matric. 24 Jan. 1874, aged 19; sometime Col. 4th Batt. Beds. Militia; Equerry to H.R.H. the Duchess of Teck; *suc. to the Baronetcy*, 1 April 1897.

Family Estates.—These, in 1883, consisted of 3,886 acres in Herts; 2,929 in Worcestershire; 394 in Beds, and 1 (worth £736 a year) in Surrey. *Total*, 7,210 acres, worth £13,567 a year. *Residences.*—Beechwood, near Dunstable, Herts, and Besford Court, near Pershore, co. Worcester.

BEAUMONT:

cr. 31 Jan. 1626/7;

ex. 7 July 1686.

I. 1627. "JOHN BEAUMONT, of Gracedieu [in Belton], co. Leicester, Esq.," 2d s., but eventually h. male of Francis BEAUMONT, of Gracedieu Priory, sometime (1592-98) one of the Justices of the Court of Common Pleas, by Anne, relict of Thomas THOROLD, da. of Sir George PIERREPONT, of Holme Pierrepont, Notts, was *b.* about 1582; matric. at Oxford (Broadgates Hall), 4 Feb. 1596/7, aged 14; admitted to Inner Temple, 1598, and suc.

to the family estates on the death of his elder br., Sir Henry BEAUMONT, s.p.m., 13 July 1605, and was *cr. a Bart.*, as above, 31 Jan. 1627/8. He was a poet of some merit.[a] He *m.* Elizabeth, da. of John FORTESCUE. He was *bur.* 19 April 1627[b], in Westm. Abbey. Admon. 3 Jan. 1628/9. His widow was living 16 April 1652.

II. 1627. SIR JOHN BEAUMONT, Bart. [1627], of Gracedieu Priory aforesaid, s. and h.; *b.* 24 June 1607; *suc. to the Baronetcy* in April 1627. He, who was a man of extraordinary strength, was a Col. in the Army, distinguishing himself in the royal cause. He *d.* unm., being slain at the siege of Gloucester, in Sep. 1643. Limited Admon. 27 April 1652.

III. 1643, to 1686. SIR THOMAS BEAUMONT, Bart. [1627], of Gracedieu Priory aforesaid, br. and h., *b.* 29 April 1620; *suc. to the Baronetcy* in Sep. 1643; was fined £1,190 on 25 Dec. 1649. He *m.* Vere, only da. of Sir William TUFTON, 1st Bart. [I. 1622], of Vintners, co. Kent, by Anne, da. of Cecil CAVE, of Leicestershire. He *d.* s.p.m.[c], 7 July 1686, aged 66, when the *Baronetcy* became *extinct*. His widow *m.* George LANE.

DERING:

cr. 1 Feb. 1626/7.

I. 1627. "EDWARD DERING, of Surrenden, co. Kent, Knt.," s. and h. ap. of Sir Anthony DERING, of Surrenden Dering, in Pluckley, co. Kent, Deputy Lieut. of the Tower of London, by his 2d wife, Frances, da. of Sir Robert BELL, Lord Chief Baron of the Exchequer, was *b.* 28 Jan. 1598, in the Tower of London; ed. at Mag. Coll., Cambridge; was *Knighted*, 22 Jan. 1618/9, at Newmarket, and was *cr. a Bart.*, as above, 1 Feb. 1626/7. He suc. his father in 1636; was Lieut. of Dover Castle; M.P. for Hythe, 1629, and for Kent, 1640, till disabled, 2 Feb. 1642. He, tho' he had presented a bill for extirpating Bishops, Deans and Chapters, joined the King at Oxford, was sent prisoner to the Tower of London, suffered sequestration,[d] and was fined. He was well known for antiquarian research and his collection of valuable MS. He *m.* firstly, 29 Nov. 1619, at St. Dionis Backchurch, London, Elizabeth, da. of Sir Nicholas TUFTON, 2d Bart. [1611], who, in 1628 (six years after her death) was *cr.* EARL OF THANET, by Frances, da. of Thomas (CECIL), 1st EARL OF EXETER. She *d.* s.p.s., 24 Jan. 1622. He *m.* secondly, Anne, 3d da. of Sir John ASHBURNHAM, of Ashburnham, Sussex, by Elizabeth,[e] da. of Sir Thomas BEAUMONT, of Staughton, co. Leicester. She *d.* 1628. He *m.* thirdly, 16 July 1629, also at St. Dionis Backchurch, Unton, da. of Sir Ralph GIBBES, of Honington, co. Warwick, by Gertrude, da. of Sir Thomas WROUGHTON. He *d.* 22 June 1644, in his 46th year. Inq. p.m. at Maidstone 8 Aug. 1645. Admon. 19 Oct. 1648, to his son, Sir Edward Dering, Bart. His widow was *bur.* 10 Nov. 1676.

II. 1644. SIR EDWARD DERING, Bart. [1627], of Surrenden Dering aforesaid, only s. and h., by 2d wife; *b.* 8 Nov. 1625, at Pluckley; *suc. to the Baronetcy*, 22 June 1644. M.P. for Kent, 1660; for East Retford, Nov. 1670; for Hythe, 1678-79, 1679-81, and 1681; was one of the Lords Commissioners of the Navy. He *m.*, 5 April 1648, at St. Bartholomew's the Less, London,

---

[a] Of his poems "for the first time collected and edited" by the Rev. A. B. Grosart, 156 copies were printed for private circulation in 1869 in the "Fuller Worthies Library." His younger brother Francis Beaumont is well known as a dramatist.

[b] It has been suggested that this date may be erroneous. Anthony A'Wood and others state his death to have been "in the winter time of 1628."

[c] See as to his five married daughters and coheirs in Nichols' *Leicestershire*, vol. iii, p. 640, where also is a good account of Gracedieu Priory.

[d] In Wotton's *Baronetage*, vol. ii, p. 17, etc., is an interesting account of his tergiversations, and a spirited letter in defence of his conduct.

[e] This Elizabeth, afterwards wife of L. Ch. Justice Sir Thomas Richardson, was (in his lifetime) in 1628 *cr.* Baroness Cramond [S.].

Mary, da. of Daniel HARVEY,[a] of Coombe in Croydon, Surrey, and of Folkestone, by Elizabeth, da. of Henry KYNNERSLEY, of London, merchant. He *d.* 24 and was *bur.* 28 June 1684 at Pluckley. Will dat. 24 Feb. 1682/3, pr. 4 July 1684. His widow, who was *bap.* 3 Sep. 1629 at St. Lawrence, Pountney, London, *d.* 7 and was *bur.* 12 Feb. 1703/4 at Pluckley, M.I.

III. 1684. SIR EDWARD DERING, Bart. [1627], of Surrenden Dering aforesaid, s. and h., *b.* 1650; *suc. to the Baronetcy*, 24 June 1684; M.P. for Kent, 1678-79, 1679-81, and 1681. He *m.* Elizabeth, sister and coh. of Sir Hugh CHOLMELEY, 3d Bart. [1641], 1st da. of Sir William CHOLMELEY, 2d Bart., of Whitby, by his 2d wife, Catharine, da. of John SAVILE, of Methley, co. York. He *d.* 1689, aged 39, and was *bur.* at Pluckley. His widow *d.* 1704, aged 47, and was *bur.* there. Will pr. Dec. 1704.

IV. 1689. SIR CHOLMELEY DERING, Bart. [1627], of Surrenden Dering aforesaid, s. and h., *b.* 23 June; and *bap.* 16 July, 1697, at Pluckley; *suc. to the Baronetcy*, 24 June 1684; matric. at Oxford (New Coll.), 4 Feb. 1696/7, aged 17; admitted to Middle Temple 1696. M.P. for Kent, 1705-08; for Saltash, 1708-10, and for Kent again, 1710-11. He *m.*, 17 July 1704, at St. Andrew's, Holborn, Mary, only da. and h. of Edward FISHER, of Fulham, co. Midx. He *d.* 9 May 1711, being killed by Richard Thornhill in a duel[b] at Tothill Fields, Westminster. Will dat. 11 Nov. 1707, pr. 1 July 1711.

V. 1711. SIR EDWARD DERING, Bart. [1627], of Surrenden Dering aforesaid, s. and h., *b.* about 1706; *suc. to the Baronetcy*, 9 May 1711; matric. at Oxford (Oriel Coll.), 31 Jan. 1721/2, aged 15; *cr.* M.A. 17 Dec. 1725; D.C.L. 3 July 1759; M.P. for Kent in three parls, 1733-54. He *m.* firstly, 24 Feb. 1727/8, at St. Geo. the Martyr, Queen sq., Midx., Mary, da. and coh. of Edward HENSHAW, of Well Hall in Eltham, Kent, by Elizabeth, da. and h. of Edward ROPER[c], of Well Hall aforesaid and of St. Dunstan's, Canterbury. She *d.* March 1734/5, and was *bur.* at Pluckley. He *m.* secondly, 11 Sep. 1735, at St. Anne's, Soho, Mary ("£30,000") widow of Henry MOMPESSON, 1st da and coh. of Charles FOTHERBY, Capt. R.N., of Barham Court, Kent, by Mary, da. of George ELCOCKE.[d] He *d.* 15 April 1762. Will pr. April 1762, June 1821, May 1835, and Oct. 1843.

VI. 1762. SIR EDWARD DERING, Bart. [1627], of Surrenden Dering aforesaid, s. and h. by 1st wife; *b.* 28 Sep. 1732; *suc. to the Baronetcy*, 15 April 1762; M.P. for New Romney (in five parls.). He *m.* firstly, 8 April 1755, Selina, sister of the half blood and coheir of Sir Henry FURNESE, 3rd Bart. [1707], 2d da. and coh. of Sir Robert FURNESE, 2d Bart., of Waldeshere, Kent, by his 3d wife, Selina, da. of Robert (SHIRLEY), 1st EARL FERRERS. She *d.* 29 March 1757. He *m.* secondly, 1 Jan. 1765, Deborah, only da. of John WINCHESTER, of Nethersole, Kent, formerly a Surgeon in London. He *d.* 8 Dec. 1798. Will pr. Dec. 1798. His widow *d.* 20 March 1818. Will pr. 1818.

VII. 1798. SIR EDWARD DERING, Bart. [1627], of Surrenden Dering aforesaid, s. and h. by 1st wife, *b.* 16 Feb. 1757; *suc. to the Baronetcy* 8 Dec. 1798. He *m.*, 16 April 1782, Anne, da. of William HALE, of King's Walden, Herts, by Elizabeth, da. of Sir Charles FARNABY, 1st Bart. [1726]. He *d.* 30 June 1811. Will pr. 1811. His widow *d.* 17 July 1830. Will pr. Aug. 1830.

---

[a] See Harvey pedigree in *Mis. Gen. et Her.*, 2d s., vol. iii, pp. 329-336, where it is added that this Mary is "said to have clandestinely married (*c.* 1646) her father's apprentice, her second cousin William, son of John Halke, but which marriage was (*c.* 1647) declared null and void."

[b] This was fought with pistols that were discharged within sword's length. Thornhill was found guilty of manslaughter.

[c] He, who was well-known as a sportsman, was the last male of the senior line of the Roper family, of which, on his death (by a fall from his horse when hunting), 24 March 1723/4, aged 84, the Lords Teynham then became the representatives. An interesting account, among the Dering MSS. in 1719, of the births, deaths, etc., of the Roper family of Eltham, is printed in Sprots' *Chronica* and reproduced (with notes) in *The Genealogist*, N.S., vol. xiii, pp. 140-144.

[d] See an account of the Fotherby family in Playfair's *Baronetage*, under "Dering."

II

VIII. 1811 SIR EDWARD CHOLMELEY DERING, Bart. [1627], of Surrenden Dering aforesaid, grandson and h., being s. and h. of Edward Dering, by Henrietta, 1st da. and coh. of Richard NEVILLE, *formerly* JONES, of Furnace, co. Kildare, which Edward last named was 1st s. and h. ap. of the 7th Bart., but *d.* v.p. 19 Sep. 1808, aged 25. He was *b.* 19 Nov. 1807 at Barham, co. Kent; *suc. to the Baronetcy*, 30 June 1811; matric. at Oxford (Ch. Ch.), 17 Oct. 1827, aged 19; was M.P. for Wexford, 1829-30 and 1830-31; for Romney, 1831, and for East Kent, 1852-57 and 1863-68. Lieut. Col. in the East Kent Yeomanry Cavalry, 1861. He *m.*, 10 April 1832, at Haydor, co. Lincoln, Jane, 3d da. of William (EDWARDES), 2d BARON KENSINGTON [I.], by Dorothy, da. of Richard THOMAS. He *d.* 1 April 1896, at Surrenden Dering, aged 89. His widow *d.* 1 Sep. 1897, at "The Ashes," Hothfield, Kent, aged 85.

IX. 1896. SIR HENRY NEVILL DERING, Bart. [1627], of Surrenden Dering aforesaid, 4th but 1st surv. s. and h.,(a), *b.* 21 Sep. 1839; ed. at Harrow; entered the Diplomatic Service 1859; Chargé d'Affairs, at Coburg; Sec. of Legation at Buenos Ayres, 1882; Sec. of Embassy at St. Petersburg and at Rome; Consul Gen. in Bulgaria, 1892-94; Minister in Mexico since 1894; C.B., 1896; *suc. to the Baronetcy* 1 April 1896; was sometime Major East Kent Yeomanry Cavalry. He *m.* 20 Oct. 1862, Rosa Anne, da. of Joseph UNDERWOOD, of London and of co. Kent.

Family Estates. These, in 1883, consisted of 7,280 acres in Kent, worth £12,000 a year. *Residence*, Surrenden Dering,(b) in Pluckley, near Ashford, co. Kent.

KEMP, *or* KEMPE:
cr. 5 Feb 1626/7;
ex. 1667.

I. 1627, to 1667. "GEORGE KEMPE, of Pentlowe, co. Essex, Esq.," s. and h. of John KEMP,(c) of the same, and of Colts Hall, in Cavendish, Suffolk, by Eleanor, da. of John DREWE, of Devon, one of the Exigenters of the Court of Common Pleas, was *bap.* 12 Nov. 1602, at Finchingfield, Essex; *suc.* his father (who *d.*, aged 48), 7 Jan. 1609, and was *cr. a Bart.*, as above, 5 Feb. 1626/7. He *m.* Thomazine, da. of (—) BROOKE. He *d.* s.p.m.,(d) 1667, when the *Baronetcy* became *extinct*. Will dat. 30 March 1663, pr. 22 Jan. 1666/7. His wife was living March 1663.

BRERETON:
cr. 10 March, 1626/7;
ex. 7 Jan. 1673/4.

I. 1627. "WILLIAM BRERETON, of Hanforde, co Chester, Esq.," s. and h. of William BRERETON,(e) of Hanforde, Handforth or Honford aforesaid, by Margaret, da. and coh. of Richard HOLLAND, of Denton, co. Lancaster; was *bap.* 1604 at Manchester; suc. his father 18 Feb. 1610, was adm. to Gray's Inn, 29 Jan. 1622/3, and was *cr. a Bart.*, as above, 10 March 1626/7; M.P. for Cheshire, 1628-29, Apr. to May 1640, and 1640-53; a zealous Puritan and an active supporter of the Parl., on whose side he was, in 1642, Com.-in-Chief of the Cheshire Forces against the King, to whose overthrow in those parts he

(a) His eldest br., Edward Cholmeley Dering, sometime an officer in the 88th and 44th foot, *m.* twice, but *d.* s.p. and v.p., 17 Nov. 1874, aged 41.

(b) John Dering, of Westbrooke, Kent., who *d.* 1425, lineal ancestor of the 1st Baronet, acquired the estate of Surrenden, by his marriage with Christian, da. and coheir of James Hant, of Pluckley, by Joan, da. and h. of John Surrenden [Philpot's *Kent*], and this has been inherited by their posterity ever since The 5th Baronet enclosed the park with a brick wall about 1750.

(c) See J. J. Howard's *Suffolk Visitation*, 156, vol. ii, p. 1-8.

(d) Of his two daughters and coheirs, the younger *m.* Sir John WINTER. The estate of Pentlowe, however, went to his nephew and h. male John KEMPE, who also *d.* s.p.m.

(e) Pedigree in Ormerod's *Cheshire*, vol. iii, p. 644.

greatly contributed. He was appointed one of the King's Judges, but did not act; was on the Council of State, Feb. to Dec. 1651, and Dec. 1652 to April 1653, and was liberally rewarded by various grants, that of Croydon palace (taken from the Archbishopric of Canterbury) being among them.(a) He *m.* firstly, in or before 1627, Susan, da. of Sir George BOOTH, 1st Bart. [1611] of Dunham, by his 2d wife, Catharine, da. of L. Ch. Justice Sir Edmund ANDERSON. She *d.* May 1637, and was *bur.* at Bowdon, Cheshire. He *m.* secondly, Cicely, widow of Edward MYTTON, da. of Sir William SKEFFINGTON, 1st Bart. [1627], by Elizabeth, da. of Richard DERING. Her admon., dat. 11 Dec. 1649. He *d.* at Croydon palace, 7 and was removed thence 9 April 1661, for burial at Cheadle.(b) Admon. 27 July 1661. Will dat. 6 April and pr. 27 July 1661, 12 Oct. 1677, and 1 May 1678.

II. 1661, to 1674. SIR THOMAS BRERETON, Bart. [1627], of Honford aforesaid, only s. and h., by 1st wife; *b.* 1632, being aged 32, in the Her. Visit. of Cheshire, 1664; *suc. to the Baronetcy*, 7 April 1661. He *m.* before 1664, Theodosia, 2d da. of Humble (WARD), 1st BARON WARD OF BIRMINGHAM, by Frances, *suo jure*, BARONESS DUDLEY. He *d.* s.p., 7 Jan. 1673/4, and was *bur.* at Cheadle, when the *Baronetcy* became *extinct*. Admon. 23 March 1677/8. His widow, who was *b.* at the Wren's nest house, Dudley, and *bap.* 15 May 1642, at St. Edmunds, Dudley, *m.*, before Feb. 1677, Charles BRERETON; was living March 1677/8, and *d.* at Brereton after childbirth, probably not long afterwards, being *bur.* at Cheadle 18 Jan. 1678 [1678/9 ?]

RUSSELL:
cr. 12 March 1626/7;
ex. 23 Jan. 1705.

I. 1627. "WILLIAM RUSSELL, of Wytley, co. Worcester, Esq.," s. and h. [*i.e.*, h. ap.] of Thomas RUSSELL, Knt.," of Strensham in the same county, by Elizabeth, da. of Sir William SPENCER, of Yarnton, Oxon; was *b.* about 1602; matric at Oxford (Wad. Coll.) 12 May 1620, aged 18; admitted to Middle Temple, 1621; to Gray's Inn, 1631; M.P. for Worcestershire, 1625, and was *cr. a Bart.*, as above, 12 March 1626/7. He was Treasurer of the Navy, 1631; *suc.* his father, 29 Dec. 1632; Sheriff of Worcestershire, 1635-36 and 1642-43, and was a zealous supporter of the Royal Cause in the Civil Wars, having to compound with the Sequestrators for £1,800 besides £50 a year. At the Restoration, however, his estate was valued at £3,000 a year, and he was one of the Knights nominated for the projected order of "*the Royal Oak*."(c) He *m.* in or before 1639, Frances, sister of Sir John READE, 1st Bart., [1642], da. of Sir Thomas READE, of Barton, Berks, by Mary, da. and coh. of Sir John BROCKETT, of Brockett Hall, Herts. He *d.* 30 Nov. 1669, and was *bur.* at Strensham. M.I. Admon. 28 Dec. 1669.

II. 1669 to 1705. SIR FRANCIS RUSSELL, Bart. [1627], of Strensham aforesaid, 1st surv. s. and h.;(d) *suc. to the Baronetcy*, 30 Nov. 1669; was M.P. for Tewkesbury (six Parls.), 1673-90. He entered his pedigree in the Visit. of Worcestershire, 1683, being then 45. He *m.* (Lic.

(a) The diary of his travels, 1634-35, in England, Ireland, Holland, and the United Provinces, has been published by the Chetham Society.

(b) There is no entry in the Cheadle registers of such burial, and the tradition is that in crossing a river the coffin was swept away.

(c) A list of these proposed knights (687 in number) arranged in counties, is given in Dugdale's *Ancient usage of Arms* [edit. 1812, pp. 160-172], as also in Burke's *Commoners* [edit. 1837, vol. i, pp. 688-694]. The annual value of Russell's estate, £3,000, is much above the average and, though equalled by one person in his own county (Lyttelton, of Franckley, co. Worcester), is exceeded by but eleven out of the 687 persons, *viz.*, Cornwall, of Herefordshire, £6,000; Knightley, of London, and Stawell, of Somerset, each of which three were £5,000; Boscawen, of Cornwall; Legh, of Lyme, co. Chester; Freke, of Dorset; Mostyn, of Flintshire; Hall, of Gloucestershire; Carr, of Lincolnshire; Morgan, of Monmouthshire; and Lowther, of Westmoreland, all eight of which were £4,000.

(d) His eldest br., Thomas Russell, *d.* v.p. and s.p., and was *bur.* 1 March 1657/8, at St. Peter's, Paul's Wharf, London.

C

Fac. 8 July 1662, he 23 and she 20), Anne, da. of Sir Rowland LYTTON, of Knebworth, Herts, by his 1st wife, Judith, da. of Sir Humphrey EDWARDS, of London. He *d.* s.p.m., 24 Jan., and was *bur.* 2 Feb. 1705/6, at Strensham, aged 68, when the *Baronetcy* became *extinct*. Will pr. March 1706. The will of his widow pr. June 1710.

CURWEN, *or* CURWENN:
cr. 12 March 1626/7;
ex. 1664.

I. 1627, to 1664. "PATRICK CURWENN, of Workington, co. Cumberland, Esq.," s. and h. of Sir Henry CURWEN, of the same, sometime (1621-22) M.P. for Cumberland, by his 1st wife, Catherine, da. and coh. of Sir John DALSTON; suc. his father in 1623; was M.P. for Cumberland, 1625-26, 1628-29, Apr. to May 1640; Nov. 1640 till disabled in March 1644; and 1661 till death, having been *cr. a Bart.* as above, 12 March 1626/7; Sheriff of Cumberland, 1636-37. He *m.* Isabel, da. and coh. of George SELBY, of Whitehouse, co. Durham. He *d.* s.p. 1664, when the *Baronetcy* became *extinct*.(a)

SPENCER:
cr. 14 March 1626/7;
ex. Sep. 1633.

I. 1627, to 1633. "JOHN SPENCER, of Offley, co. Herts, Esq.," s. and h. of Sir Richard SPENCER, of the same, by Helen, 4th da. and coh. of Sir John BROCKET, of Brocket Hall in that county (which Richard was 4th s. of Sir John SPENCER, of Althorpe, co. Northampton); suc. his father in Nov. 1624, and was *cr. a Bart.* as above, 14 March 1626/7. He *m.*, in or before 1618, Mary, da. of Sir Henry ANDERSON, Alderman, and sometime [1601-02] Sheriff of London, by Elizabeth, sister of Sir William BOWYER, of Denham, Bucks, da. of Francis BOWYER, Alderman, and sometime [1577-78] Sheriff of London. She was *bap.* 29 Feb. 1595/6, at St. Olave's, Jewry, London. He *d.* s.p.m. Aug. 1633 and was *bur.* at Offley, when the *Baronetcy* became *extinct*.(b) Funeral certificate at Coll. of Arms.

ESTCOURTE:
cr. 17 March 1626/7;
ex. about 1684.

I. 1627. "GILES ESTCOURTE, of Newton, co. Wilts, Knt.," s. and h. of Sir Edward ESTCOURT, of Salisbury, by Mary, da. of John GLANVILE, of Tavistock, Devon; was *b.* about 1601, matric. at Oxford (Wad. Coll.), 8 May 1618, aged 17; admitted to Lincoln's Inn, 1618; *Knighted* 3 Dec. 1622, at Newmarket, Sheriff of Wilts, 1626-27, and was *cr. a Bart.*, as above, 17 March 1626/7. He was M.P. for Cirencester, 1628-29. He *m.* Anne, or Amy, da. of Sir Robert MORDAUNT, 2d Bart. [1611], by Amy, da. of Sir Augustine SOUTHERTON.

II. 1650 ? SIR GILES ESTCOURT, Bart. [1627], of Newton aforesaid, s. and h.; *suc. to the Baronetcy* on the death of his father. He *d.* unm., about 1676, being slain in Italy. Admon. 2 May 1676.

(a) The estates passed to his two brothers in succession, and are still (1900) in possession of the heirs male of the body of the younger one.

(b) A fresh Baronetcy was, however, granted, 26 Sep. 1642, to his only br. and h. male, Brocket Spencer, who succeeded to the Offley estate.

III. 1676 ? to 1684 ? SIR WILLIAM ESTCOURT, Bart. [1627], of Newton aforesaid, br. and h., *suc. to the Baronetcy* about 1676. He *d.* unm., being slain in a duel by Henry St. John, at the Globe Tavern, St. Bride's parish, London, about 1684, when the *Baronetcy* became *extinct*. Admon. 23 May 1684.(a)

AYLESBURY:
cr. 19 April 1627;
ex. in 1657.

I. 1627, to 1657. "THOMAS AYLESBURY, Esq., one of the Masters of Requests,"(b) s. of William AYLESBURY, of St. Andrew's, Holborn, London (*d.* Dec. 1620), by his 1st wife, Anne, da. of John POOLE, and niece to Sir Henry POOLE, of Saperton; was *b.* in London 1576; sometime Master of the Requests and of the Mint; and was *cr. a Bart.*, as above, 19 April 1627. He fled to Antwerp after the execution of Charles I, and resided there some years. He *m.* (Lic. Lond. 3 Oct. 1611) Anne, widow of William DARELL (*d.* 1610), da. and coh. of the Rev. Francis DENMAN, Rector of West Retford, Notts (1578-95), by Anne, relict of Nicholas TOWERS and da. of Robert BLOUNT, of Eckington, co. Derby. He *d.* at Breda, 1657, aged 81.(c) in which year the *Baronetcy* become *extinct*. His widow was *bur.* 13 Nov. 1661 (in the Hyde vault) in Westm. Abbey.

II. 1657. WILLIAM AYLESBURY, only surv. son, *bap.* 13 July 1612, at St. Margaret's Lothbury, London. He went out to Jamaica, as Secretary to the Governor there, in Cromwell's second expedition, and *d.* there s.p. in 1657, but whether shortly before or shortly after his father is not certain. In the latter case he would, of course, have *suc. to the Baronetcy* for a short time. In 1657, however, the *Baronetcy* was *extinct*.

STYLE:
cr. 21 April 1627.

I. 1627. "THOMAS STYLE, of Watringbury [*i.e.*, Wateringbury], co. Kent, Esq.," s. and h. of Oliver STYLE,(d) of the same, Alderman and sometime (July to Nov. 1605) Sheriff of London, by Susanna, da. of John BULL, of London, was *b.* 1587; matric. at Oxford (St. Alban Hall), 18 May 1604, aged 17; admitted to Middle Temple, 1606; suc. his father, 4 March 1621/2, and was *cr. a Bart.*, as above, 21 April 1627. Sheriff of Kent, 1632-33. He *m.*, in or before 1615, Elizabeth, da. and sole. h. of Robert FOLKES, of Mountnessing, co. Essex. He *d.* 18 Oct. 1637, in St. John's lane, Smithfield. Will pr. 1637. Funeral certificate at Coll. of Arms. His widow *d.* 20 May 1660. Both *bur.* at Wateringbury.

(a) Granted to Sir John Mordaunt, Bart., a creditor; the sisters of the decd. Amy, wife of Alexander Haddon, and Anne Estcourt renouncing.

(b) Like the previous creation, of Cottington, 16 Feb. 1622/3, no territorial description is given to the grantee.

(c) Out of his five children, Frances, *bap.* 25 Aug. 1617, at St. Margaret's, Westminster, *m.* Edward (HYDE), 1st EARL OF CLARENDON, by whom she was grandmother of Mary and Anne, Queens of England.

(d) This Oliver was younger br. of Edmund Style, of Langley in Beckenham, Kent, grandfather of Sir Humphrey STYLE, of Langley, Bart. (so *cr.* 20 May 1627), both being sons of Sir Humphrey STYLE, of Langley aforesaid, one of the Esquires of the body to Henry VIII.

II. 1637. SIR THOMAS STYLE, Bart. [1627], of Wateringbury aforesaid, only s. and h. ; b. in St. John's lane, Smithfield, Christmas 1624 ; *suc. to the Baronetcy*, 18 Oct. 1637 ; matric. at Oxford (Merton Coll.), 15 April 1641, aged 15 ; M.P. for Kent, 1656-58 and 1659. He *m.* firstly, Elizabeth, da. of Sir William AIRMYNE, 1st Bart. [1619], of Osgodby, co. Lincoln, by his 1st wife, Elizabeth, da. of Sir Michael HICKS. She *d.* 10 Dec. 1679, and was *bur.* at Wateringbury. M.I. He *m.* secondly, Margaret, da. of Sir Thomas TWISDEN, 1st Bart. [1666], of Bradbourne, by Jane, da. of John TOMLINSON. He *d.* 19 Nov. 1702, in his 78th year. Will pr. 1703. His widow *d.* 5 Dec. 1718, aged 71. Both *bur.* at Wateringbury. M.I.

III. 1702. SIR OLIVER STYLE, Bart. [1627], of Wateringbury aforesaid, 4th but 1st surv.(a) s. and h., by 1st wife ; *suc. to the Baronetcy*, 19 Nov. 1702 ; sometime President in Smyrna. He *d.* s.p., 12 Feb. 1702/3, aged 42, and was *bur.* at Wateringbury. M.I. Admon. 15 April 1703.

IV. 1703. SIR THOMAS STYLE, Bart. [1627], of Wateringbury aforesaid, br. of the half blood, and h., being s. of the 2d Bart., by his 2d wife ; *suc. to the Baronetcy*, 12 Feb. 1702/3 ; rebuilt the mansion of Wateringbury ; was Sheriff of Kent, 1709-10 ; M.P. for Bramber, 1715, till void, 1 June. He *m.* Elizabeth, 1st da. of Sir Charles HOTHAM, 4th Bart. [1622], by his 1st wife, Bridget, da. of William GEE. She *d.*, 25 Oct. 1737, in Hanover street, Midx., aged 43 He *d.* 11 Jan. 1769. Will pr. 1769.

V. 1769. SIR CHARLES STYLE, Bart. [1627], of Wateringbury aforesaid, s. and h. ; an officer in the 5th Regt. of Dragoons ; *suc. to the Baronetcy* 11 Jan. 1769. He *m.* 7 March 1770, Isabella, da. of Richard (WINGFIELD), 1st VISCOUNT POWERSCOURT [I.], by his 2d wife Dorothy, da. of Hercules ROWLEY. He *d.* 18 April 1774. Will pr. April 1774. His widow *d.* 24 Sep. 1808.

VI. 1774. SIR CHARLES STYLE, Bart. [1627], of Wateringbury aforesaid, s. and h. ; *suc. to the Baronetcy*, 18 April, 1774. He *m.*, 29 March, 1794, Camilla, 1st da. of James WHATMAN, of Vintners, in Boxley, Kent, by his 1st wife, Sarah, da. of Edward STANLEY, Sec. to H.M.'s Customs. He *d.* 5 Sep. 1804. Will pr. 1805, in Prerog. Court, Dublin. His widow *d.* 17 Sep. 1829. Admon. Oct. 1829.

VII. 1804. SIR THOMAS STYLE, Bart. [1627], of Wateringbury aforesaid, s. and h. ; ed. at the Royal Military College, Marlow ; was sometime Ensign in 1st Foot Guards ; *suc. to the Baronetcy*, 5 Sep. 1804. He *d.* unm. in Spain, 5 Nov. 1813. Admon. April 1814.

VIII. 1813. SIR THOMAS CHARLES STYLE, Bart. [1627], of Wateringbury aforesaid, br. and h., *b.* 21 Aug. 1797 ; *suc. to the Baronetcy*, 5 Nov. 1813 ; Sheriff of co. Donegal, 1824 ; M.P. for Scarborough, 1837-41. He sold the estate of Wateringbury. He *m.*, 28 Oct. 1822, Isabella, da. of Sir George CAYLEY, 6th Bart. [1661], of Brompton, by Sarah, da. of the Rev. George WALKER, of Nottingham. He *d.* s.p.s. 23 July 1879, at 102 Sydney place, Bath, in his 82d year. His widow *d.* 27 Dec. 1882, aged 84.

IX. 1879. SIR WILLIAM-HENRY-MARSHAM STYLE, Bart. [1627], of Glenmore, co. Donegal, cousin and h. male, being s. and h. of William STYLE, of Bicester, Oxon, Capt. R.N., by Charlotte, da. of the Rev. the Hon. Jacob MARSHAM, D.D. (yr. s. of Robert, 2d BARON ROMNEY), which William (who *d.* 24 Feb. 1868, aged 82) was 2d s. of the Rev. Robert STYLE, Vicar of Wateringbury and Rector of Mereworth, co. Kent (*d.* 5 June 1800), who was yr. br. of the 5th and son of the 4th Bart. He was *b.* 3 Sep. 1826, at Kirkby Overblow, co. York ; ed. at Eton and Merton Coll., Oxford ; matric. 26 June 1844, aged 17 ; B.A., 1848 ; M.A. 1852 ; Sheriff for co. Donegal, 1856 ; *suc. to the Baronetcy*, 23 July 1879. He *m.* firstly, 18 Dec. 1848, at Bassaly church, Rosamond Marion, da. of Charles Morgan Robinson

(a) His elder br., Thomas Style, *m.* (Lic. Vic. Gen. 11 Dec. 1671, he 22 and she 16) Mary, da. of Sir Stephen Langham, but *d.* s.p.s. and v.p., 30 Aug. 1672.

(MORGAN), 1st BARON TREDEGAR, by Rosamond, da. of Gen. Godfrey Basil MUNDY. She *d.* 15 Jan. 1883, at the Mansion house, Brecon, aged 53. He *m.* 2dly, 2 June 1885, at St. Saviour's, Chelsea, Ellen Catherine, widow of Henry Hyde Nugent BANKES and formerly widow of the Rev. Charles Henry BARHAM, da. of Edward Taylor MASSY, of Cottesmore, co. Pembroke, by Helen, da. of Jonathan PEEL, of Cottesmore aforesaid.

Family Estates.—These, in 1883, consisted of 39,564 acres in co. Donegal, worth £4,000 a year. *Residence.*—Glenmore, co. Donegal.

CORNWALLIS, *or* CORNEWALLIS :

cr. 4 May 1627,

afterwards, 1661—1852, BARONS CORNWALLIS OF EYE,

subsequently, 1753-1852, EARLS CORNWALLIS,

being sometime, 1792—1823, MARQUESSES CORNWALLIS ;

ex. 21 May 1852.

I. 1627. "FREDERICK CORNEWALLIS, of Broomehall, co. Suffolk, Esq.," 3d s. of Sir William CORNWALLIS, of the same, by his 2d wife, Jane, da. of Hercules MEWTAS, was *b.* 14 March 1610 ; was, when young, in the household of Henry, and afterwards of Charles, Princes of Wales ; suc. to the family estates on the death of his elder br. (of the half blood), Thomas CORNWALLIS, in 1626, and was, in his 17th year, *cr. a Bart.* as above, 4 May 1627, being subsequently (a) *knighted* 30 Dec. 1630 ; M.P. for Eye, April to May 1640, and Nov. 1640 till disabled 23 Sep. 1642, and subsequently, M.P. for Ipswich, Oct. to Dec. 1660. Opposing the violent measures of the predominant party, he accompanied the King to Oxford and sat among the members assembled there in Jan. 1643/4. He distinguished himself in many of the battles against the rebels, particularly in that of Cropredy bridge, Oxon (30 June 1644), where he rescued Lord Wilmot from being made prisoner. His estates were consequently sequestrated, he was fined £800 on 21 Feb. 1648, and followed Charles II into exile. He *m.* firstly, about 1630, Elizabeth, da. of Sir John ASHBURNHAM, of Ashburnham, Sussex, by Elizabeth, *suo jure* BARONESS CRAMOND [S.], da. of Sir Thomas BEAUMONT. She *d.* at Oxford and is said to have been *bur.* in Christ Church Cathedral there. He *m.* secondly, before 1641, Elizabeth, sister (of the half blood) to William, BARON CROFTS OF SAXHAM, da. of Sir Henry CROFTS, of Saxham, co. Suffolk, by his 2d wife, Elizabeth, da. of Sir Richard WORTLEY, of Wortley, co. York. She (who *d.* s.p.m.) was living when he, having accompanied the King in his triumphant entry through London 29 May 1660, was *cr.* 20 April 1661 (3 days before the coronation) BARON CORNWALLIS OF EYE, co. Suffolk. In that peerage this *Baronetcy* then *merged*, the 5th Baron being *cr.* 30 June 1753, EARL CORNWALLIS, and the 2d Earl (6th Baron and Baronet) being *cr.* 8 Oct. 1792 MARQUESS CORNWALLIS. This Marquessate became *extinct* 9 Aug. 1823, on the death of the 2d Marquess, but the Baronetcy, together with the Earldom and Barony, continued till 21 May 1852, when on the death of the 5th Earl, 9th Baron and Baronet, it, and the other honours became *extinct*. See *Peerage*.

DRURY, *or* DRURIE :

cr. 7 May 1627 ;

ex. 27 April 1712.

I. 1627. "DRUE DRURIE, of Riddlesworth, co. Norfolk, Esq.," s. and h. of Sir Drue DRURY,(b) of Hedgerley, Bucks, and of Linstead, co. Kent, Gentlemen Usher to Queen Elizabeth, by his 2d wife, Catharine, only da. and h. of William FINCH, of Linstead aforesaid, was *b.* 1588 ; suc. his father (who *d.*

(a) See vol. i, p. 18, note "c," as to these subsequent Knighthoods.

(b) See pedigree of Drury in J. J. Muskett's *Suffolk Manorial Families*.

aged 99) in 1617 ; was M.P. for Norfolk, 1621-22, and for Thetford, 1624-25, and was *cr. a Bart.*, as above, 7 May 1627. He *m.*, 28 June 1608, Anne, 1st da. and coh. of Edward WALDEGRAVE, of Lawford, co. Essex, by his 1st wife, (—), da. and h. of Bartholomew AVERELL, of Essex. He *d.* 23 April 1632, and was *bur.* at Riddlesworth. M.I. Will dat. 23 Jan. 1630, pr. 31 Oct. 1632. Inq. p.m. 23 May 1632, at Bury St. Edmunds. His widow *m.* (—) GLEANE, of Hardwick, co. Norfolk. Her will pr. May 1642.

II. 1632. SIR DRUE DRURY, Bart. [1627], of Riddlesworth aforesaid, 1st s. and h., by 1st wife ; *b.* 17 Jan. 1611 ; *suc. to the Baronetcy*, 23 April 1632. He was fined £957, reduced to £629. He *m.* firstly, Susan, da. of Isaac JONES, of London, and sister and coh. of Sir Samuel JONES, of Courteen Hall, co. Northampton. He *m.* secondly, 7 Aug. 1641, at Maidstone, Mary, widow of John REYNOLDS, da. of John BOYS. He *d.* 13 July 1647. Admon. 29 July 1647, and 1 Jan. 1650/1. His widow *d.* 1649. Will dat. 10 Nov. 1647, pr. 11 Feb. 1650/1.

III. 1647 to 1712. SIR ROBERT DRURY, Bart. [1627], of Riddlesworth aforesaid, s. and h., by 1st wife ; *suc. to the Baronetcy*, 13 July 1647. He *m.* firstly, Elizabeth, da. and h. of Edward DUNSTON, of Worlingworth and Waldingfield, co. Suffolk, by Elizabeth, da. and eventually heir of John MAYHEW. He *m.* secondly, Eleanor, widow of William MARSHAM, of Stratton, co. Norfolk, da. of Samuel HARSNET, of Great Fransham in that county. She was killed in the hurricane of 1703. He *m.* thirdly, Diana, da. of George VILET, of Pinkney Hall, Norfolk. He *d.* s.p. 27 April 1712, aged 78, when the *Baronetcy* became *extinct*.(a) M.I. at Riddlesworth. His widow living 1736.

SKEFFINGTON :

cr. 8 May 1627,

afterwards, 1665-1816, VISCOUNTS MASSEREENE [I.],

and subsequently, 1756-1816, EARLS OF MASSEREENE [I.] ;

ex. 25 Feb. 1816.

I. 1627. "WILLIAM SKEFFINGTON, of Fisherwicke, co. Stafford, Esq.," s. and h. of John SKEFFINGTON,(b) of the same, by Alice, da. of Sir Thomas CAVE, of Stanford, co. Northampton, was *cr. a Bart.* as above, 8 May 1627. He *m.*, in or before 1590, Elizabeth, sister of Sir Anthony DERING, of Surrenden Dering, co. Kent, by Margaret, da. of William TWYSDEN, of East Peckham in that county. He was *bur.* 16 Sep. 1635 at St. Michael's, Lichfield.

II. 1635. SIR JOHN SKEFFINGTON, Bart. [1627], of Fisherwick aforesaid, s. and h., *b.* about 1590, being aged 30 in 1619 ; was M.P. for Newcastle under Lyne, 1626 ; *suc. to the Baronetcy* in Sep. 1635. Sheriff of Staffordshire, 1637-38 ; was, in Nov. 1650, fined £1,152, reduced to £961. He *m.* Cicely, sister and coh. of Sir John SKEFFINGTON, of Skeffington, co. Leicester. He *d.* 19 and was *bur.* 20 Nov. 1651, at Skeffington.

III. 1651. SIR WILLIAM SKEFFINGTON, Bart. [1627], of Fisherwick and Skeffington aforesaid, only s. and h. ; *suc. to the Baronetcy*, 19 Nov. 1651. He *m.* Ursula. He *d.* s.p., and was *bur.* 7 April 1652, at Skeffington. Admon. 23 June 1652, to Ursula the relict.

IV. 1652. SIR JOHN SKEFFINGTON, Bart. [1627], of Fisherwick aforesaid, cousin and h., being s. and h. of Sir Richard SKEFFINGTON, sometime (1646-47) M.P. for Staffordshire, by Anne, da. of Sir John NEWDIGATE, of

(a) Diana, his only sister and h., *m.* Sir William WAKE, 3d Bart. [1621], whose descendants inherited, accordingly, Riddlesworth Hall, co. Norfolk, and Courteen Hall, co. Northampton.

(b) This John was great grandson of Sir William Skeffington, the well known Lord Deputy of Ireland, *temp.* Hen. VIII.

Arbury, co. Warwick, which Richard, who had been *Knighted* 24 Aug. 1624, and who *d.* 2 June 1647, was yst. s. of the 1st Bart. He *suc. to the Baronetcy* in April 1652 ; was M.P. [I.], for the town of Antrim, 1659, and for co. Antrim, 1661-65. He *m.*, 20 July 1654, at St. Paul's, Covent Garden, Mary, only child of John (CLOTWORTHY), VISCOUNT MASSEREENE [I.], by Margaret, da. of Roger (JONES), 1st VISCOUNT RANELAGH [I.], which John had been *cr.* Viscount Massereene, 21 Nov. 1660, with a spec. rem. (failing heirs male of his body), to his son-in-law, the said Sir John SKEFFINGTON, who, accordingly, on the Viscount's death, s.p.m., 23 Sep. 1665, became VISCOUNT MASSEREENE [I.] In that peerage, consequently, this *Baronetcy* became *merged*, the 5th Viscount being *cr.* EARL OF MASSEREENE [I.], which Earldom, together with this *Baronetcy* became *extinct* on the death of the 4th Earl, 8th Viscount and 11th Baronet, 25 Feb. 1816, though the Viscountcy (according to the spec. rem. in its creation) devolved on his da. and heir as heir general.

CRANE :

cr. 11 May 1627 ;

ex. Feb. 1642/3.

I. 1627, to 1643. "ROBERT CRANE, of Chilton, co. Suffolk, Knt.," s. of Robert Crane, of the same (*d.* 12 Sep. 1591), by Bridget, da. of Sir Thomas JERMYN, of Rushbrooke in that county ; was *Knighted* at Newmarket, 27 Feb. 1604/5 ; was M.P. for Sudbury, 1614 ; for Suffolk, 1621-22 ; for Sudbury (again) 1624-25 and 1625 ; for Suffolk (again) 1626 and for Sudbury (again) 1628-29 ; April to May 1640, and Nov. 1640 till decease, having been *cr. a Bart.*, as above, 11 May 1627 ; Sheriff of Suffolk, 1631-32. He *m.* firstly, 19 Jan. 1606/7, at St. Anne's, Blackfriars, London, Dorothy, 1st da. of Sir Henry HOBART, 1st Bart. [1611], Lord Chief Justice of the Common Pleas, by Dorothy, da. of Sir Robert BELL. She, who was *b.* 14 March 1591/2, d. 11 and was *bur.* 13 April 1624, at Chilton. He *m.* secondly, 21 Sep. 1624, at Chilton, Susan, da. of Sir Giles ALINGTON, of Horseheath, co. Cambridge, by Dorothy, da. of Thomas (CECIL), 1st EARL OF EXETER. He *d.* s.p.m.,(a) in London, 17 Feb. 1642/3, and was *bur.* at Chilton, aged 58, when the *Baronetcy* became *extinct*. Will dat. 13 and pr. 23 Feb. 1642/3. His widow *m.* Isaac APPLETON, of Waldingfield Parva, co. Suffolk. She was *bur.* 14 Sep. 1681, at Chilton. Her will, dat. 18 Aug. 1676, pr. in Arch. Court of Sudbury.

BRYDGES, *or* BRIDGES :

cr. 17 May 1627,

afterwards, 1676-1789, BARONS CHANDOS OF SUDELEY,

subsequently, 1714-89, EARLS OF CARNARVON,

and finally, 1719-89, DUKES OF CHANDOS ;

ex. 29 Sep. 1789.

I. 1627. "GILES BRIDGES, of Wilton, co. Hereford, Esq.," s. and h. of the Hon. Charles BRYDGES, of Wilton Castle in Bridstow in the said county, by Jane, da. of Sir Edward CARNE, of Ewenny, co. Glamorgan, which Charles (who *d.* at a great age, 9 April 1619, being 3d but 2d surv. s. of John, 1st BARON CHANDOS OF SUDELEY) was, presumably, the "Giles Brugges, of co. Gloucester, Arm. fil.," who matric. at Oxford (St. Alban Hall), 27 Nov. 1590, being then aged 17 ; was M.P. for Tewkesbury, 1621-22 ; for Herefordshire, 1625-29 ; Sheriff of Herefordshire, 1625-26 ; and was *cr. a Bart.*, as above, 17 May 1627. He *m.* Mary, da. of Sir James SCUDAMORE, of Holme Lacy, co. Hereford, by Anne da. of Sir Thomas THROCKMORTON. She *d.* before Sep. 1634 and was *bur.* at Peterstowe, co. Hereford. He *d.* 12 Sep. 1637 and was *bur.* there. Will dat. 4 Sep. 1634, pr. 22 Nov. 1637, Inq. p.m. 31 Oct. 1637.

(a) Of his four daughters and coheirs (1) Mary *m.* Sir Ralph HARE, 1st Bart. [1641] ; (2) Jane *m.* firstly, 28 Aug. 1649, at Chilton, Sir William AIRMYNE, 2d Bart. [1619], and secondly, John (BELASYSE), 1st Baron Belasyse of Worlaby ; (3) Susan *m.* Sir Edward WALPOLE, K.B. ; and (4) Katherine *m.* Sir Edmund BACON, 4th Bart. [1611].

II

II. 1637. SIR JOHN BRYDGES, Bart. [1627], of Wilton Castle aforesaid s. and h., *b.* 1623; matric. at Oxford (Bras. Coll.), 4 May 1638, aged 14; *suc. to the Baronetcy*, 12 Sep. 1637. His castle at Wilton having been burnt by the Royalists he took part with their opponents and was instrumental in the surprise of Hereford by the Parl. army. He *m.* Mary, only da. and h. of James PEARLE, of Dewsal and Aconbury, co. Hereford. He *d.* of the small pox, in Bridges street, Covent Garden, Midx., 21 Feb. 1651/2, and was *bur.* at Peterstowe aforesaid, aged 29. Admon. 10 March 1651/2. His widow *m.*, as his 1st wife, Sir William POWELL, *otherwise* HINSON, Bart. (so *cr.* 23 Jan. 1660/61), of Pengethly, co. Hereford, who *d.* 1681. She was *bur.* at Aconbury aforesaid.

III. 1652. SIR JAMES BRYDGES, Bart. [1627], of Aconbury aforesaid, only s. and h., *b.* Sep. 1642; *suc. to the Baronetcy*, 21 Feb. 1651/2; matric. at Oxford (St. John's Coll.), 15 June 1657; Sheriff of Herefordshire, 1667-68. He *m.* before 1673, Elizabeth, 1st da. and coh. of Sir Henry BARNARD, of London, by Emma, da. of Robert CHARLTON, of Whitton Court, Salop. She was living, when, on 22 Aug. 1676, he suc. on the death of his cousin to the peerage as 8th BARON CHANDOS OF SUDELEY (a Barony *cr.* 8 April 1554), taking his seat as such, 15 Feb. 1676/7. In that peerage this *Baronetcy* continued *merged*; the 9th Baron being *cr.*, 19 Oct. 1714, EARL OF CARNARVON, etc., and, subsequently, 29 April 1719, DUKE OF CHANDOS, etc. By the death, 29 Sep. 1789, of James, 3d Duke of Chandos, 11th Baron Chandos of Sudeley, and 6th Baronet, this *Baronetcy* and all other the said peerage honours became *extinct*.

COLEPEPER, *or* COLEPEPYR:

cr. 17 May 1627;

ex. 18 May 1723.

I. 1627. "WILLIAM COLEPEPYR, of Prestonhall [in Aylesford], co. Kent, Esq.," s. and h. of Sir Thomas COLEPEPER, of the same, by Mary, da. of Thomas PYNNER, of Mitcham, Surrey, Chief Clerk comptroller to Queen Elizabeth; was *b.* about 1588; suc. his father, 12 Oct. 1604; matric. at Oxford (St. Alban Hall) 31 Oct. 1606, aged 18; B.A., 11 May 1609; admitted to Gray's Inn, 1611, and was *cr. a Bart.*, as above, 17 May 1627; Sheriff of Kent, 1635-36. He *m.* Helen, 1st da. of Sir Richard SPENCER, of Offley, Herts, by Helen, da. of Sir John BROCKET, of Brocket Hall in that county. He *d.* 1651. Will dat. 23 Dec. 1648, pr. 5 Nov. 1651. The will of his widow, dat. 10 Oct. 1663, pr. 19 Feb. 1678.

II. 1651. Sir RICHARD COLEPEPER, Bart. [1627], of Prestonhall aforesaid, s. and h.; *suc. to the Baronetcy* in 1651. He *m.*, in or before 1653, Margaret REYNOLDS. He was *bur.* 10 Jan. 1659/60, at Aylesford. Will pr. Sep. 1660. His widow was *bur.* there 26 Sep. 1691.

III. 1660, to 1723. SIR THOMAS COLEPEPER, Bart. [1627], of Prestonhall aforesaid, only surv. s. and h.; *b.* about 1657; *suc. to the Baronetcy*, in Jan. 1659/60; matric. at Oxford (Mag. Hall), 15 June 1672, aged 15; Sheriff of Kent, 1703-04; M.P. for Maidstone, in five Parls., 1705-13, and 1715, till his death. He *m.* Elizabeth (—), of (—). She was *bur.* 5 Feb. 1708, at Aylesford. He *d.* s.p.(a) at Prestonhall, 18 and was *bur.* 24 May 1723, at Aylesford, when the *Baronetcy* became *extinct*.(b) Will dat. 16 Feb. 1710/1, pr. 27 May 1723.

(a) Alice, his sister and sole h., *m.*, for her 4th husband, John MILNER, M.D., on whom she settled Preston Hall. She *d.* s.p. 1734, and her said husband devised the estate to the Milner family.

(b) The burial, in the Temple church, London, 2 April 1663, of "Sir Cheney Culpeper, Bart. [*sic*], of the Middle Temple," refers, apparently, to Sir Cheney Colepeper, of Hollingbourne, co. Kent, *Knt.*, whose admon. (to a creditor) is dat. 19 Dec. 1666 and 10 March 1690/1.

WINGFIELD, *or* WINGFEILD:

cr. 17 May, 1627;

ex. soon after 1727.

I. 1627. "ANTHONY WINGFEILD, of Godwyns, co. Suffolk, Esq.," only s. and h. of Sir Thomas WINGFIELD, of Letheringham, in that county, by his 2d wife, Elizabeth, da. of Sir Drue DRURY, of Riddlesworth, was *b.* about 1585; suc. his father 22 Jan. 1609, and was *cr. a Bart.*, as above, 17 May 1627. He was Sheriff of Suffolk, 1637-38. He *m.* Anne, da. of Sir John DEANE, of Deane's Hall, in Great Maplestead, co. Essex, by Anne, da. of Sir Drue DRURY, abovenamed. He *d.* 30 July 1638, aged 53. Fun. certif. in Coll. of Arms. The will of his widow pr. May 1642.

II. 1638. SIR RICHARD WINGFIELD, Bart. [1627], of Letheringham aforesaid, and of Easton, s. and h.; *suc. to the Baronetcy*, 30 July 1638. He *m.* firstly, 11 June 1649, at St. Dionis, Backchurch, London, Susanna, da. of Sir John JACOB, 1st Bart. [1665], by his 1st wife, Elizabeth, da. of John HALLIDAY. He *m.* secondly, Mary, da. of Sir John WINTOUR, of Lidney, co. Gloucester, by Mary, da. of Lord William HOWARD, s. of Thomas, DUKE OF NORFOLK. He *d.* about 1656. Admon. 28 Dec. 1656. The will of his widow pr. 1657.

III. 1656? SIR ROBERT WINGFIELD, Bart. [1627], of Letheringham aforesaid, 1st s. and h., by 1st wife; *b.* about 1652; *suc. to the Baronetcy* about 1656. He *d.* abroad at Strasbourg a minor and unm. about 1671. Admon. 17 July 1671, 14 Feb. 1671/2, and 18 May 1678.

IV. 1671? SIR HENRY WINGFIELD, Bart. [1627], of Easton, co. Suffolk and Letheringham aforesaid, br. (of the half blood) and h., being s. of the 2d Bart. by his 2d wife, was *b.* about 1655; *suc. to the Baronetcy* about 1671. He *m.* Mary, da. of Mervyn (TOUCHET) 4th EARL OF CASTLEHAVEN [I.], by Mary, da. of John (TALBOT), EARL OF SHREWSBURY. She *d.* 15 Oct. 1675, and was *bur.* at East Soham, Suffolk. M.I. He *d.* abroad in Lorraine, 1677. Admon. 23 June 1677.

V. 1677. SIR HENRY WINGFIELD, Bart. [1627], of Letheringham aforesaid, s. and h.; *b.* about 1673; *suc. to the Baronetcy* in 1677. He sold the estate of Letheringham,(a) and followed James II to France after his expatriation. He *m.* (—) GUARIGUES, of Toulouse. He *d.* abroad, s.p., 1712.

VI. 1712, to 1730? SIR MERVYN WINGFIELD, Bart. [1627], br. and h.; *b.* about 1675; *suc. to the Baronetcy* in 1712. He *m.* Mary, da. of Theobald DALTON, of Greenan, co. Westmeath. He *d.* s.p.m.(b) after (probably not long after) 1727, when the *Baronetcy* became *extinct*.

KYRLE, *or* KIRLE:

cr. 17 May 1627;

ex. 4 Jan. 1679/80.

I. 1627. "JOHN KYRLE, of Much Marcle, co. Hereford, Esq.," s. and h. of Thomas KYRLE, of the same, by Frances, da. and h. of John KNOTSFORD, of Malvern, was *cr. a Bart.*, as above, 17 May 1627. He was twice Sheriff of Herefordshire, 1608-09 and 1628-29. He *m.* Sybill, da. and h. of Philip SCUDAMORE. He *d.* 1650.

(a) The estate of Letheringham had been the chief seat of the head of this most ancient family for very many centuries.

(b) Mary, his da. and h., *m.* Francis Dillon, of Proudstown, co. Meath, who was *cr.* a Baron of the Holy Roman Empire in 1767.

D

II. 1650, to 1680. SIR JOHN KYRLE, Bart. [1627], of Much Marcle aforesaid, grandson and h. being s. and h. of Francis KYRLE (Sheriff of Herefordshire, 1647-48), by Hester, da. of Sir Paul TRACY, 1st Bart. [1611], which Francis, who was s. and h. ap. of the late Bart., *d.* v.p., 1649; *b.* about 1617; matric. at Oxford, 25 Nov. 1636, aged 19; adm. to Inner Temple, 1638; *suc. to the Baronetcy* in 1650, and was M.P. for Herefordshire, Sep. 1668 to 1678. He *m.* 16 Dec. 1647, Rebecca, da. of (—) VINCENT. He *d.* s.p.m., 4 Jan. 1679/80, when the *Baronetcy* became *extinct*.(a) His widow *m.* John BOOTH, of Letton, co. Hereford, who was living 1 July 1693. Her admon. 1 July 1693.

STYLE, *or* STYLES:

cr. 20 May 1627;

ex. 20 Nov. 1659.

I. 1627, to 1659. "HUMFREY STYLES [more correctly STYLE], of Becknam, co. Kent, Knt.," Cupbearer to the King, s. and h. of William STYLE,(b) of Langley in Beckenham, aforesaid, by his 1st wife, Anne, da. of John EVERSFIELD, of Denn, Sussex, was one of the Gentlemen of the Privy Chamber to James I, and was (after having been *Knighted*, 11 Aug. 1622, at Farnham), under that designation, *cr. a Bart. of Ireland*,(c) 13 Sep. 1624, by that King. He was made Cup bearer to Charles I, by whom he was *cr. a Bart. of England*, as above, 20 May 1627.(d) He was Colonel of the trained bands of Horse in Kent. He *m.* Elizabeth, widow of Sir Robert BOSVILE, of Eynesford, da. and h. of Robert PESHALL, *or* PERSHALL, of Eccleshall, co. Stafford, and of Lincoln's Inn, London. He *d.* s.p. 10 Nov. 1659, in his 64th year and was *bur.* at Beckenham, when *both the Baronetcies* [E. and I.] became *extinct*.(e) Will pr. April 1660. His widow *m.* John SCOTT, Gentleman of the Privy Chamber, who *d.* 8 April 1670, in his 45th year, and was *bur.* at Hayes, Kent. M.I.

MOORE:

cr. 21 May 1627;

ex. 10 April 1807.

I. 1627. "HENRY MOORE, of Falley [*i.e.*, Fawley], co. Berks, Esq.," s. and h. of (the learned) Sir Francis MOORE, of the same, Serjeant at Law, by Ann, da. of William TWITTY, of Boreham, Essex, suc. his father, 20 Nov. 1621, and was *cr. a Bart.*, as above, 21 May 1627. He *m.* Elizabeth, da. of William BEVERLEY, of Kenoe, Beds. He *d.* about 1633. Admon. 19 March 1633/4, and again 4 May 1635. His widow living May 1635.

(a) Vincentia, his da. and h., *b.* 2 Oct. 1651; *m.*, 6 Dec. 1674, Sir John ERNLE, of Buryton, Wilts. In her descendants (the family of KYRLE-MONEY), the estate of Much Marcle became vested. See "KYRLE-MONEY," Bart., *cr.* 1838. John KYRLE, the celebrated "Man of Ross," *b.* May 1637, *d.* unm. 7 Nov. 1724, was of this family.

(b) This William was s. and h. of Edmund Style, of Langley, who was elder br. of Oliver, the father of Sir Thomas STYLE, 1st Bart., of Wateringbury, so *cr.* 21 April 1627.

(c) It will be observed, however, that no notice is made of his Irish creation when he was *cr. a Bart.* [E.], 20 May 1627.

(d) A curious document relating to his various services is in Wotton's *Baronetage*, vol. ii, p. 22, edit. 1741.

(e) The estate of Langley went to his br. (of the half blood) William STYLE, Barrister at Law. This William *d.* Dec. 1699, aged 80, and was *suc.* by his s. Humphrey Style, whose only da. and h., Elizabeth, *m.* firstly, Sir John Elwill, 2d Bart. [1709], and secondly, Henry BARTELOTT, of West Wickham, Kent, who sold the estate, May 1732 (a few months before his death) for £6,500 to Hugh RAYMOND.

II. 1633. SIR HENRY MOORE, Bart. [1627], of Fawley aforesaid, s. and h; was a minor when he *suc. to the Baronetcy* in 1633. He *m.* firstly, Judith, da. of (—) CAMBELL,(a) Alderman of London. He *m.* secondly, Mary, da. of William HITCHCOCK, of Kinteley, Bucks. He *d.* about 1685. Will pr. Nov. 1690.

III. 1685? SIR RICHARD MOORE, Bart. [1627], of Fawley aforesaid, grandson and h., being s. and h. of Francis MOORE, by Frances,(b) da. and h. of Alexander JERMIN, of Lordington, Sussex, which Francis was s. and h. ap. of the 2d Bart., but *d.* v.p. He *suc. to the Baronetcy* about 1685. He *m.* Anastacia Jane, da. and coheir(c) of John AYLWARD, of London. He *d.* 10 Dec. 1737. Will pr. 1738. That of his widow, who *d.* abroad, pr. Aug. 1742.

IV. 1737. SIR RICHARD MOORE, Bart. [1627], of Fawley aforesaid, s. and h., *suc. to the Baronetcy*, 10 June 1737. He *d.* unm. 15 June 1738. Will pr. 1738.

V. 1738. SIR JOHN MOORE,(d) Bart. [1627], of Fawley aforesaid, br. and h., *suc. to the Baronetcy*, 15 June 1738. He *d.* s.p. 25 Aug. 1790. Will pr. Sep. 1790.

VI. 1790, to 1807. SIR THOMAS MOORE, Bart. [1627], br. and h., *suc. to the Baronetcy* (but not to the estate), 25 Aug. 1790. He *d.* s.p. 10 April 1807, when the *Baronetcy* became *extinct*. Will pr. 1807.

HELE, *or* HEALE:

cr. 28 May, 1627;

ex. 1677;

assumed 1677-83.

I. 1627. "THOMAS HEALE,(e) of Fleet [near Modbury], co. Devon, Esq.," eldest surv. s. and h. of Thomas HELE, of the same, sometime Sheriff of Devon, by Bridget, da. of Sir Henry CHAMPERNOWNE, of Modbury aforesaid, suc. his father, 7 Nov. 1624, and was *cr. a Bart.*, as above, 28 May 1627. He was Sheriff of Devon, 1635-36; was M.P. for Plympton, 1626, 1628-29, April to May 1640 and Nov. 1640 till disabled Jan. 1644; for Okehampton, 1661 till his death; attended the king at Oxford, Jan. 1643; was one of the chief commanders of the Royal forces at the siege of Plymouth, Sep. to Dec. 1648; compounded for his estate at £2 834, and a yearly sum of £80. He *m.* firstly, in or before 1629, Penelope, da. and coheir of Emorbe JOHNSON, of Wigborow, Somerset, by whom he had Thomas, who inherited that estate, but *d.* v.p. and s.p. 13 Nov. 1665, aged 36. He *m.* secondly, 16 July 1632, at Kensington, Elizabeth, da. of Edward ELWAYES. He is also said to have *m.* Elizabeth, da. of (—) CURSON, of Oxon. His 2d or 3d wife was *bur.* 14 March 1646, at Holberton church, Devon. He *d.* intestate 7 and was *bur.* 16 Nov. 1670, at Holberton. Admon. 8 June 1683 to his da., Dame Honora Bonython, *otherwise* Hockmore.

(a) Probably Judith, unm. in 1638, da. of Robert Cambell, sometime (1631) Master of the Ironmongers' Company, who was 2d s. of Sir Thomas Cambell, sometime (1609-10) Lord Mayor of London.

(b) This Lady was by royal warrant, 1686, raised to the same rank as if her husband had *suc.* to the Baronetcy. The only other instance, apparently, of such a warrant, in the case of a Baronetcy, is that of KEYT, in or soon after 1702.

(c) Mary, the other coheir, *m.* Charles HOWARD and was mother of Charles, 10th DUKE OF NORFOLK, who *d.* s.p. 16 Dec. 1815.

(d) In 1765 he sold the estate of Fawley to the family of VANSITTART, who in 1778 resold it to Bartholomew TIPPING, whose niece and h., Mary Anne, *m.* Rev. Philip WROUGHTON.

(e) An elaborate account of the Hele family and their descendants is given in Burke's *Extinct Baronetcies*, 1844. See also Vivian's *Visitations of Devon*.

II. 1670. SIR SAMUEL HELE, Bart. [1627], of Flete aforesaid, 6th s. (by 2d wife) and h.; *suc. to the Baronetcy*, 16 Nov. 1670. He *m.* 28 April 1668, at St. Martin's in the Fields, Midx., Mary, sister of Sir Edward HUNGERFORD, K.B., da. of Anthony HUNGERFORD, of Farley Castle, Somerset, by Rachel, da. of (—) JONES. She *d.* in his lifetime. He *d.* s.p.m., and was *bur.* 18 Jan. 1672 at Holberton. Will dat. 4 March 1671, pr. 4 Jan. 1675/6, entailing the Flete estates on the heirs male of his family.

III. 1672. to 1677. SIR HENRY HELE, Bart. [1627], of Flete aforesaid, br. and h. male; *suc. to the Baronetcy* in Jan. 1672. He *m.*, 13 July 1676 at St. German's, Cornwall, Susan, da. of John ELIOT, of Port Eliot, by Honora, da. of Sir Daniel NORTON, of Southwick, Hants. She was *bap.* 27 April 1648. He *d.* s.p., April 1677, when the *Baronetage* became *extinct*.

On the death of the 3rd Baronet in April 1677 the estate of Fleet passed under the will of the 2d Baronet to the heir male. This was RICHARD HELE, only s. and h. of Richard HELE, by Mary (*m.* 16 July 1645 at Holberton) da. of Richard HILLERSDON, which Richard Hele last named, who *d.* 1679 was a yr. br. of the 1st Bart. He *m.* (Lic. Exeter 24 May 1678) Judith, da. of George CARY, D.D., Dean of Exeter. He is *said to have assumed the style of Baronet* on succeeding to the estates. He *d.* 29 July 1682 at Fleet.(a) His widow *d.* May 1784.

CARLETON:
cr. 28 May 1627;
ex. 1650.

I. 1627. "JOHN CARLETON, of Holcum [*i.e.*, Holcombe], co. Oxford, Esq.," s. and h. ap. of George CARLETON, of Holcombe aforesaid, by Elizabeth, da. and coheir of Sir John BROCKETT, of Brockett Hall, Herts, was B.A. Oxford (Ch. Ch.), 10 Feb. 1609/10, and was *cr. a Bart.*, as above, 28 May 1627. He suc. his father, 8 March 1627/8; was M.P. for Cambridgeshire, 1628-29. On the death, 15 Feb. 1631/2, of his uncle Dudley (CARLETON), VISCOUNT DORCHESTER, he inherited the estate of Brightwell, co. Oxford; Gent. of the Privy Chamber, 1633; Sheriff of Cambridgeshire, 1636-37. He *m.*, 1625, Anne, widow of Sir John COTTON, of Lanwade, co. Cambridge, da. of Sir Richard Hoghton, 1st Bart [1611], by Catharine, da. of Sir Gilbert GERARD, Master of the Rolls. He *d.* in London, 7 Nov. 1637, and was *bur.* at Brightwell. Will as of "Cheavley, co. Cambridge," dat. 21 Sep. 1635 to 1 Nov. 1637, pr. 24 Nov. 1637. Inq. p.m. at Oxford, 5 April 1638. His widow *d.* 17 May 1671, and was *bur.* with her first husband at Lanwade. Admon., as "of Cheaveley, co. Cambridge," 5 June 1671, to her son, Sir John Cotton, Bart.

II. 1637, to 1650. SIR GEORGE CARLETON, Bart. [1627], of Brightwell and Holcombe aforesaid, only s. and h., aged 12 on 5 April 1638, having *suc. to the Baronetcy*, 7 Nov. 1637. He *d.* unm., 1650, at Cheveley, co. Cambridge, and was *bur.* at Brightwell, when the *Baronetcy* became *extinct*.(b) Admon. 27 Feb. 1650/1, to his sisters Anne, wife of George Garth, "Esq.," and Catherine Carlton.

(a) He was succeeded in the estates, but not in the assumption of the Baronetcy, by his only s. and h., Richard Hele, sometime M.P. for Plympton and for West Looe, who *d.* Dec. 1709 at Fleet, and was suc. by his only s. and h., James Modyford Hele, the last in the male line of the family of Hele of Fleet. He *d.* a minor in London Aug. 1716, when, under the will of his father, the estate passed to James Bulteel, of Tavistock, an entire stranger in blood to the family.

(b) The estates passed to his two sisters and coheirs, of whom (1) Anne *m.* George Garth, of Morden, co. Surrey, and *d.* 1655, leaving issue; (2) Catharine, *m.* John Stone, whose son, John Stone, inherited Brightwell, and *d.* 1722 s.p., leaving it to his cousin Francis Lowe, ancestor of the family of Lowndes-Stone, of that place.

ISHAM:
cr. 30 May 1627.

I. 1627. "JOHN ISHAM, of Lamport, co. Northampton, Knt.," s. and h. of Thomas ISHAM, of the same, by Elizabeth, da. of Christopher NICHOLSON, of Cambridge, was *b.* 27 July 1582; *suc.* his father 3 Dec. 1605, was *Knighted*, 29 March 1608; was Sheriff of Northamptonshire, 1611-12, and was *cr. a Bart.*, as above, 30 May 1627. He *m.*, 19 Oct. 1607, Judith, sister to Sir Justinian LEWIN, da. of William LEWIN, D.C.L., Judge of the Prerogative Court of Canterbury, of Ottringden, Kent, by Anne, da. of Francis GOULDSMITH, of Crayford, co. Kent. She *d.* 25 June 1625, aged 34. He *d.* 8 July 1651, in his 69th year. Both *bur.* at Lamport. M.I.

II. 1651. SIR JUSTINIAN ISHAM, Bart., [1627], of Lamport aforesaid, only s. and h., *b.* 20 Jan. 1610. Fellow Commoner of Christ's College, Cambridge, 18 April 1627. Adm. to Middle Temple, 11 Oct. 1628. For his zeal in the Royal Cause he suffered imprisonment and had to compound for his estate at Shangton, co. Leicester (which he possessed, v.p.) for £1,106; *suc. to the Baronetcy*, 8 July 1651; was M.P. for Northampton, 1661 till his death. He *m.* firstly, 10 Nov. 1634, Jane, da. of Sir John GARRARD, 1st Bart. [1622], of Lamer, Herts, by his 1st wife, Elizabeth, da. of Sir Edward BARKHAM. She *d.* s.p.m., 3 March 1638, aged 25 years and 10 months, and was *bur.* at Lamport. M.I. He *m.* secondly, 1653, Vere, da. of Thomas (LEIGH), 1st BARON LEIGH OF STONELEIGH, by Mary, da. and coheir of Sir Thomas EGERTON, s. and h. ap. of Thomas, 1st BARON ELLESMERE and VISCOUNT BRACKLEY. He *d.* at Oxford 2 March 1674/5, in his 65th year, *bur.* at Lamport. M.I. His widow *d.* 29 Oct. 1704.

III. 1675. SIR THOMAS ISHAM, Bart. [1627], of Lamport aforesaid, s. and h., by 2d wife, *b.* 15 March 1656; matric. at Oxford (Ch. Ch.), 4 June 1675, aged 18; *suc. to the Baronetcy*, 2 March 1674/5. He *d.* (while on the point of marriage) in London, 26 July 1681, in his 24th year. Admon. 31 Oct. and 30 Nov. 1681.

IV. 1681. SIR JUSTINIAN ISHAM, Bart. [1627], of Lamport aforesaid, br. and h.; *b.* 11 Aug. 1658; matric. at Oxford (Ch. Ch.), 4 Dec. 1674, aged 18; adm. to Linc. Inn, 1677; *suc. to the Baronetcy*, 26 July 1681. M.P. for Northampton, 1685-87; 1689-90; March to Oct. 1695 and 1695-98; for Northants (in eleven Parls.), 1698 till his death. He was one of the troop formed at Nottingham as a guard for the Princess Anne of Denmark to enable her to desert her father, James II. He *m.* 16 July 1683, at St. Giles' in the Fields (Lic. Fac., he 24 and she 18), Elizabeth, only da. of Sir Edmund TURNER, of Stoke Rochfort, co. Lincoln, by Margaret, da. of Sir John HARRISON, of Balls, Herts. She *d.* 22 Aug. 1713, in her 47th year. He *d.* 13 May 1730, aged 72. Both *bur.* at Lamport. M.I. Will pr. 1731.

V. 1730. SIR JUSTINIAN ISHAM, Bart. [1627], of Lamport aforesaid, s. and h., *b.* 20 July 1687; *suc. to the Baronetcy*, 13 May 1730; M.P. for Northamptonshire. 1730-37; Commissioner of land and window tax and for the duty on hides. He was a good antiquary and a great lover of literature. He *m.* Mary, only surv. child of Lisle HACKET, of Moxhill, co. Warwick, by Dorothy, da. of Sir John BRIDGEMAN, 2d Bart. [1660]. He *d.* s.p. suddenly, 5 March 1736/7, in his 50th year, in London. Will pr. 1737. That of his widow pr. 1744.

VI. 1737. SIR EDMUND ISHAM, Bart. [1627], of Lamport aforesaid, br. and h., *b.* 18 Dec. 1690; ed. at Rugby School and at Wadham Coll., Oxford; matric. 10 Oct. 1707; demy of Magdalen Coll., 1710-20; B.A., 1711; M.A., 1714; fellow, 1720-36; D.C.L., 1723; member of the Coll. of Advocates (Doctors Commons), London, 1 Dec. 1724; Judge Advocate for the Court of Admiralty, 1731-41; assessor to the Dep. Earl Marshal; *suc. to the Baronetcy*, 5 March 1736/7; M.P. for Northamptonshire (six Parls.), 1737 till his death. He *m.* firstly, in 1734, Elizabeth, 1st da. of Edward WOOD, of Littleton, Middlesex, by Elizabeth, da. and h. of Henry BRIDGER, of Guildford. She, who was

b. 18 Aug. 1699, *d.* 19 July 1748, aged nearly 49. Admon. May 1750. He *m.* secondly, 4 May 1751, at St. Geo. the Martyr, Queen's sq., Midx., Philippa, only da. of Richard GEE, of Orpington, Kent. He *d.* s.p. 16 Sep. 1772. Will pr. Feb. 1773. His widow *d.* 11 Dec. 1786. Will pr. Dec. 1786.

VII. 1772. SIR JUSTINIAN ISHAM, Bart. [1627], of Lamport aforesaid, nephew and h., being s. and h. of the Rev. Euseby ISHAM, D.D., Head of Lincoln Coll., Oxford, and Rector of Lamport and Haselbeech, co Northampton, by Elizabeth, da. of the Rev. Matthew PANTING, D.D., Head of Pembroke College, Oxford, which Euseby (who *d.* 17 June 1755) was 3d s. of the 4th Bart. He was *b.* 8 July 1740, and *bap.* 1 Aug. at All Saints', Oxford; matric. at Oxford (Linc. Coll.), 11 May 1758; *cr.* M.A., 8 July 1763, D.C.L., 4 July 1793; *suc. to the Baronetcy*, 11 Dec 1772; was Sheriff of Northants, 1776-77. He *m.* 9 Sep. 1766, Susanna, da. of Henry BARRET, of London, merchant. He *d.* 1 April 1818. Will pr. May 1818 and Feb. 1847. His widow *d.* 31 Jan. 1823.

VIII. 1818. SIR JUSTINIAN ISHAM, Bart. [1627], of Lamport aforesaid, and of Elm park, Ireland, s. and h., *b.* 24 April 1773; *suc. to the Baronetcy*, 1 April 1818. He *m.* May 1812, Mary, 1st da. of Rev. Samuel CLOSE, of Drumbanagher and Elm park, co. Armagh, by (—), da. of Rev. Arthur CHAMPAGNÉ, Dean of Clonmacnoise [I.] He *d.* at Lamport Hall, 26 March 1845, in his 72d year. Will pr. April 1845 and Jan. 1847. His widow *d.* 26 Jan. 1878, in her 90th year, at Lamport Hall.

IX. 1845. SIR JUSTINIAN VERE ISHAM, Bart. [1627], of Lamport Hall aforesaid, s. and h., *b.* 7 Nov. 1816; ed at Eton and at Ch.Ch., Oxford; matric. 22 Oct. 1835; *suc. to the Baronetcy*, 26 March 1845. He *d.* unm., suddenly, 25 Aug. 1846, at Cheltenham, in his 30th year. Will pr. Dec. 1846.

X. 1846. SIR CHARLES EDMUND ISHAM, Bart. [1627], of Lamport Hall aforesaid, br. and h., *b.* 16 Dec. 1819, at Lamport; ed. at Rugby and at Brasenose Coll., Oxford; matric. 25 Jan. 1840; *suc. to the Baronetcy*, 25 Aug. 1846. Sheriff of Northamptonshire, 1851. He *m.* 26 Oct. 1847, at St. Geo. Han. sq., Emily, youngest da. of the Right Hon. Sir John VAUGHAN, one of the Justices of the Common Pleas, by Louisa, Dowager BARONESS ST. JOHN, 1st da. of Sir Charles William ROUSE-BOUGHTON, 9th Bart. [1641]. She *d.* 6 Sep. 1898, at Lamport Hall, after a long illness, aged 74.

Family Estates.—These, in 1883, consisted of 3,112 acres in Northamptonshire and 1,118 in Leicestershire. *Total*—4,230 acres, worth £7,373 a year. *Principal Seat*—Lamport Hall, co. Northampton.

MAPLES,
cr. 30 May 1627;
ex. 1634/5.

I. 1627, to 1635. "THOMAS MAPLES, of Stowe, co. Huntingdon, Esq.," of whom very little seems to be known, was *cr. a Bart.* as above, 30 May 1627. He *d.* s.p.m.s.,(a) 1634/5, when the *Baronetcy* became *extinct*. Will pr. 1635.

(a) His da. and h. (or coheir) *m.* Edward Hinde, of Madingley, co. Cambridge, and was mother of Jane, who *m.* Sir John Cotton, 1st Bart. [1641], of Lanwade.

POLLARD, *or* POLLARDE:
cr. 31 May 1627;
ex. June 1701.

I. 1627. "LODOVICK (LEWIS) POLLARDE, of Kings Nimpton, co. Devon, Esq." s. and h. of Sir Hugh POLLARD,(a) of the same, by his first wife, Dorothy, da. of Sir John CHICHESTER, of Yolston, in that county, was presumably the "Lewis Pollarde, of Devon, Gent.," who matric. at Oxford (Broadgates Hall), 12 Dec. 1595, aged 17, and was *cr. a Bart.*, as above, 31 May 1627. He *m.* Margaret, da. of Sir Henry BERKELEY, of Bruton, co. Somerset, by Margaret, da. of William LYGON. He *d.* after 1641, but before 20 Nov. 1657, at which date the admon. of his widow was granted to her son, George Pollard.

II. 1645? SIR HUGH POLLARD, Bart. [1627], of Kings Nympton aforesaid, s. and h., *b.* about 1610; *suc. to the Baronetcy*, on the death of his father. He was M.P. for Berealstone, 19 Nov. 1640. till expelled 9 Dec. 1641, as privy to the Army plot, being imprisoned till 1646; M.P. for Callington, 1660, and for Devon, 1661, till his death; was a staunch royalist, and held for some time Dartmouth, of which he was Governor, against the Parliament, and surrendered it on good terms. He was fined £518, by the sequestrators; was P.C., 1660; Gov. of Guernsey; Comptroller of the household to Charles II, 1663 till his death, and was known for his magnificent hospitality, which was the cause of his selling the estate of Kings Nympton. He *m.* firstly, Bridget, widow of Francis (NORRIS) EARL OF BERKSHIRE, da. of Edward (DE VERE), EARL OF OXFORD, by his first wife, Anne, da. of William (CECIL), 1st BARON BURGHLEY. He *m.* secondly, probably about 1650, Mary, widow of Henry ROLLE, of Stevenstone, co. Devon, da. of William STEVENS, of Great Torrington, by Grace, da. and h. of John HUDDLE, of the same, Vintner. She, who was *bap.* 30 Oct. 1619 at Great Torrington, *d.* before him. Admon. 8 Dec. 1657. He *d.* s.p.m., 27 Nov. and was *bur.* Dec. 1666 in Westm. Abbey. Admon. 18 Dec. 1666 to a creditor.

III. 1666, to 1701. SIR AMYAS POLLARD, Bart. [1627], br. and h. male, *b.* about 1617; *suc. to the Baronetcy* in Dec. 1666, but to little, if any, of the estate. He *d.* unm. and s.p. legit.,(b) in his 85th year, being *bur.* 7 June 1701, at Abbots Bickington, when the *Baronetcy* became *extinct*. M.I.

BAGOT:
cr. 31 May 1627;
afterwards, since 1780, BARONS BAGOT OF BAGOTS BROMLEY.

I. 1627. "HERVEY BAGOTT, of Blithfield, co. Stafford, Esq.," s. and h. of Walter BAGOT, of the same, by Elizabeth, da. of Roger CAVE, of Stanford, co. Northampton, and Margaret, sister of the well-known William (CECIL), BARON BURGHLEY, was *b.* 8 Feb. 1590/1; matric. at Oxford (Trin. Coll.), 18 Nov. 1608; suc. his father 16 March 1622; was Sheriff of Staffordshire, 1626-27; and was *cr. a Bart.*, as above, 31 May 1627. He was M.P. for that county 1628-29 and April 1641, till disabled in Nov. 1642; was a great sufferer in the Royal cause, being fined £1,340, by the sequestrators reduced to £1,004. He *m.* firstly in or before 1616, Katharine, da. of Humphrey ADDERLEY, of Weddington, co. Warwick. She *d.* 16 Feb. 1622 and was *bur.* at Blithfield. He *m.* secondly, Anne, widow of Sir Thomas DILKE, of Maxtock, co. Warwick, da. of Sir Clement FISHER, of Packington, by Mary, da. of Francis REPINGTON, of Arnington, both in that county. He *d.* 27 Dec. 1660, aged 69, and was *bur.* at Blithfield. M.I.

II. 1660. SIR EDWARD BAGOT, Bart. [1627], of Blithfield, aforesaid, s. and h. by 1st wife; *b.* 23 May 1616; matric. at Oxford

(a) This Hugh was great grandson to Sir Lewis Pollard, of Kings Nympton, one of the Judges of the Court of Common Pleas, 1515.

(b) Thomas Pollard, his illegit. son, *d.* s.p. 9 Dec. 1710, aged 29, having *m.* 25 June 1702, at Encombe, Sarah, da. of Jonathan Prideaux.

(Trin. Coll.), 20 Feb. 1634/5; adm. to the Middle Temple, 1635; M.P. for co. Stafford, in the Convention Parl. of 1660; "a true assertor of Episcopacy in the church and hereditary monarchy in the state"(a); *suc. to the Baronetcy*, 27 Dec. 1660. He *m.* 9 May 1641, at Buckingham, Mary, widow of John CRAWLEY, of Someries, Beds., da. and h. of William LAMBARD, Bailiff of Buckingham. He *d.* 30 March 1673, in his 57th year. His widow (by whom he had 17 children) *d.* 22 Oct. 1686, aged 67. Both *bur.* at Blithfield. M.I. Her will pr. July 1687.

III. 1673. SIR WALTER BAGOT, Bart. [1627], of Blithfield aforesaid, s. and h.; *b.* 21 March 1644; matric. at Oxford (Ch. Ch.), 26 Nov. 1662; adm. to the Middle Temple, 1666; *suc. to the Baronetcy*, 30 March 1673; M.P. for co. Stafford in six Parls., 1678-81, 1685-90, and 1693-95; was a "Noble Promoter" of Plot's *History of Staffordshire*. He *m.* (Lic. Vic. Gen., 25 June 1670, he about 22 and she about 20, with the consent of her mother), Jane, da. and h. of Charles SALUSBURY, of Bachymbydd, co. Denbigh, and Iland Lloyd, co. Flint. She *d.* 20 July 1695 in her 45th year. He *d.* 15 Feb. 1704 in his 60th year. Both *bur.* at Blithfield. M.I. His will pr. Oct. 1705.

IV. 1704. SIR EDWARD BAGOT, Bart. [1627], of Blithfield aforesaid, s. and h.; *b.* 21 Jan. 1673/4; matric. at Oxford (Ch. Ch.), 15 Dec. 1691; adm. to the Middle Temple, 1692. He was M.P. for co. Stafford, in five Parls., 1698—1708, having *suc. to the Baronetcy*, 15 Feb. 1704. He *m.* 15 April 1697, Frances, d. and h. of Sir Thomas WAGSTAFFE, of Tachbrooke, co. Warwick. He *d.* May 1712, and was *bur.* at Blithfield. Will pr. June 1712. His widow *m.* her cousin, Adolphus OUGHTON (who, after her death, was, in 1718, *cr. a Bart.*), and *d.* about 1714. Admon., as of Tachbrooke, 24 July 1714.

V. 1712. SIR WALTER WAGSTAFFE BAGOT, Bart. [1627], of Blithfield aforesaid, only surv. s. and h., *b.* 23 Aug. 1702; *suc. to the Baronetcy*, May 1712; matric. at Oxford (Mag. Coll.), 27 April 1720; D.C.L. thereof by diploma, 17 May 1737; M.P. for Newcastle-under-Lyne, 1724-27; for co. Stafford, in four Parls., 1727-61, and for the Univ. of Oxford, 1762-68. He *m.* 27 July 1724, Barbara, 1st da. of William (LEGGE), 1st EARL OF DARTMOUTH, by Anne, da. of Heneage (FINCH), EARL OF AYLESFORD. She *d.* 29 Oct. 1765. He *d.* 20 Jan. 1768. Both *bur.* at Blithfield. His will pr. 1768.

VI. 1768. SIR WILLIAM BAGOT, Bart. [1627], of Blithfield, aforesaid, s. and h., *b.* 28 Feb. 1728; matric. at Oxford (Mag. Coll.), 28 Feb. 1746/7, aged 17; *cr.* M.A., 12 April 1749, and D.C.L., 2 July 1754; was M.P. for Staffordshire, in four Parls., 1754-80, having *suc. to the Baronetcy*, 20 Jan. 1768. He *m.* 20 Aug. 1760, Elizabeth Louisa, 1st da. of John (St. John), 2d VISCOUNT ST. JOHN, by his 1st wife, Anne, da. and eventually coheir of Sir Robert FURNESE, 2d Bart. [1707]. She was living when, on 17 Oct. 1780, he was *cr.* BARON BAGOT OF BAGOTS BROMLEY, co. Stafford, in which dignity this *Baronetcy* became henceforth *merged*. See *Peerage*.

MANNOCK, *or* MANNOCKE:
cr. 1 June 1627;
ex. 3 June 1787.

I. 1627. "FRANCIS MANNOCKE, of Gifford Hall, in Stoke juxta Neilond [*i.e.*, Neyland], co. Suffolk, Esq.," s. and h. of William MANNOCK, of the same, by Etheldred, da. of Ferdinando PARYS, of Linton, co. Cambridge, suc. his father, 15 March 1616/7, being then aged above 30, and was *cr. a Bart.*, as above, 1 June 1627. He *m.* Dorothy, da. of William SAUNDERS, of Welford, co. Northampton, and of Blofield, Norfolk, by Anne, da. of Rees MORGAN, of Michelchurch. He *d.* 20 Nov. 1634 and was *bur.* in the Mannock Chapel, at Stoke by Neyland. Will pr. 1634.

(a) See his M.I. at Blithfield.

II. 1634. SIR FRANCIS MANNOCK, Bart. [1627], of Gifford Hall aforesaid, s. and h., *suc. to the Baronetcy* in Nov. 1634. He *m.* 1636, Mary, 1st da. of Sir George HENEAGE, of Hainton, co. Lincoln, by Elizabeth, da. of Francis TRESHAM, of Rushton, co. Northampton. By her he had 22 children. He *d.* 26, and was *bur.*, 30 April 1687, in the Mannock Chapel aforesaid. Will dat. 22 April 1687, pr. 25 May following, and 24 Jan. 1690/1.

III. 1687. SIR WILLIAM MANNOCK, Bart. [1627], of Gifford Hall aforesaid, s. and h., *suc. to the Baronetcy*, 26 April 1687. He *m.* (Lic. Lond., 2 Feb. 1672 3, she of Claxby, co. Lincoln, aged 21), Ursula, da. of Henry NEVILL, *otherwise* SMITH, of Holt, co. Leicester. He *d.* 26 Jan., and was *bur.* 1 Feb. 1713/4, in the Mannock chapel aforesaid. His widow *bur.* there 30 Dec. 1727.

IV. 1714. SIR FRANCIS MANNOCK, Bart. [1627], of Gifford Hall aforesaid, s. and h., *bap.* 20 Jan. 1675, at Stoke by Neyland; *suc. to the Baronetcy* 26 Jan. 1713/4. He *m.* Frances, da. and h., of George YEATES, of North Waltham, Hants. He *d.* 27 Aug., and was *bur.* 4 Sep. 1758 in the Mannock chapel aforesaid. Will pr. 1758. His widow *d.* 18 and was *bur.* there 21 May 1761. Her will dat. 13 Nov. 1758, pr. 30 May 1761.

V. 1758. SIR WILLIAM MANNOCK, Bart. [1627], of Great Bromley Hall, Essex, and of Gifford Hall aforesaid, s. and h.; *suc. to the Baronetcy*, 27 Aug. 1758. He *m.* firstly, Teresa, da. of Anthony WRIGHT, of Wealdside, Essex, and of Covent Garden, Midx, Banker. She *d.* s.p.s., and was *bur.*, 13 July 1750, in the Mannock chapel aforesaid. He *m.* secondly, Elizabeth, da. and coheir of Robert ALLWYN, of Treford, Sussex. He *d.* 16 March 1764 and was *bur.* in the Mannock chapel aforesaid. Will dat. 1 Jan. 1762, pr. 18 May 1764. His widow *d.* 1774. Her will dat. 10 Dec. 1773, pr. 19 Jan. 1775.

VI. 1764. SIR WILLIAM ANTHONY MANNOCK, Bart. [1627], of Gifford Hall aforesaid, only surv. child and h., by 2d wife, *b.* 28 May 1759; *suc. to the Baronetcy*, 16 March 1764; was residing at Liége, in Belgium, in 1775, being then aged 16. He *d.* unm., 24 March 1776. Will pr. March 1776.

VII. 1776. SIR FRANCIS MANNOCK, Bart. [1627], of Gifford Hall aforesaid and of Sevington, Hants, uncle and h., *b.* 17 Sep., 1710; *suc. to the Baronetcy*, 24 March 1776. He *m.* Elizabeth Mary, 4th da. of Thomas STONOR, of Watlington Park, and of Stonor, Oxon. He *d.* s.p., 17 Sep. 1778. Will dat. 3 June 1777, and pr. 2 Oct. 1778. His widow (who was *b.* 10 June 1714 at Watlington park aforesaid) *d.* 1789. Her will dat. 26 May and 6 Sep. 1789, pr. 31 Dec. following.

VIII. 1778. SIR THOMAS MANNOCK, Bart. [1627], of Gifford Hall aforesaid, br. and h., *suc. to the Baronetcy*, 12 Sep. 1778. He *m.* firstly, 1 March 1756, at St. Geo., Queen's sq., Midx., Mary, da. of George Brownlow DOUGHTY, of Snarford Hall, co. Lincoln. She *d.* s.p, and was bur. in the Mannock chapel. Admon. 12 Feb. 1781, granted to her husband. He *m.* secondly, 17 April 1780, Anastacia, da. of Mark BROWNE, of Eastbourne, Sussex, by his second wife, Anastacia, da. of Sir Richard MOORE, 3d Bart. [1627], of Fawley, Berks. He *d.* s.p., 2 Sep. 1781. Will dat. 20 Jan. 1781, pr. 19 Sep. following. His widow, who was *b.* 10 May 1749, *d.* at Windsor, Berks, 8 April 1814. Will pr. 1814.

IX. 1781, to 1787. SIR GEORGE MANNOCK, Bart. [1627], of Great Bromley Hall aforesaid, br. and h., *suc. to the Baronetcy*, 2 Sep. 1781. He *d.* s.p., being killed by the overturning of the Dover mail coach, 3 June 1787, when the *Baronetcy* became *extinct*.(a) Will pr. June 1787.

(a) Of his four sisters, three, *viz.*, Etheldred, Mary, and Anne were unm. in 1761, while the eldest, Ursula, *m.*, before 1749, James NIHILL, M.D., of Limerick, to whom she took out admon. in 1753.

GRIFFITH:
cr. 7 June 1627;
ex. 1656.

I. 1627. "HENRY GRIFFITH, of Agnes Burton, co. York, Esq." s. and h. of Sir Henry GRIFFITH, of the same (admon. 2 Oct. 1621), by Elizabeth, da. of Thomas THROCKMORTON, of Coughton, co. Warwick, was aged 9 at the Visit. of Yorkshire in 1612, and was *cr. a Bart.*, as above, 7 June 1627; Sheriff of Staffordshire, 1633-34. He *m.* Mary, 1st da. and coheir of Sir Henry WILLOUGHBY, Bart. [so *cr.* 1611], of Risley, co. Derby, by his 1st wife, Elizabeth, da. and coheir of Sir Henry KNOLLYS. She was *b.* 24 May 1603.(a) He *d.* before Oct. 1644.

II. 1640? to 1656. SIR HENRY GRIFFITH, Bart. [1627], of Burton Agnes aforesaid, s. and h., *suc. to the Baronetcy*,(a) on the death of his father; was fined £7,457, in Oct. 1647. He *m.* Margaret, da of Sir Francis WORTLEY, 1st Bart. [1611], by his 1st wife, Grace, da. of Sir William BROUNCKER. He *d.* s.p.s., 1656, when *the Baronetcy* became *extinct*. Admon. 25 June 1656, to "Gustavus Boynton, Esq.," nephew and next of kin.

DYER, *or* DEYER:
cr. 8 June 1627;
ex. Nov. 1669.

I. 1627, to 1669. LODOWICK DEYER [*i.e.*, DYER], of Staughton, co. Huntingdon, Esq.," s. and h. of Sir William Dyer, of the same, by Catharine, da. and coheir of John DOYLEY, of Merton, Oxon, was aged 8 at the Visit. of co. Huntingdon, in 1613, suc. his father (who *d.* aged 39), 29 April 1621, and was *cr. a Bart.*, as above, 8 June 1627; was fined £1,500. He *m.*, in or before 1637, Elizabeth, da. of Sir Henry YELVERTON. He *d.* s.p.s.(b) and was *bur.* 15 Nov. 1669, at Colmworth, Beds., when the *Baronetcy* became *extinct*. Nunc. will, as "of Colmworth," dat. 26 Oct. 1669, pr. 4 Feb. 1669/70.

STEWKLEY, STEWKELEY, *or* STUKELEY:
cr. 9 June 1627;
ex. in 1719.

I. 1627. "HUGH STEWKLEY, of Hinton, co. Southampton, Knt.," s. and h. of Sir Thomas STEWKLEY, of Marsh, co. Somerset, and of Hinton aforesaid (living 1623), by Elizabeth, da. and coh. of John GOODWIN, of Over Wichingdon, Bucks., matric. at Oxford (Wadh. Coll.), 3 July 1618, aged 14; adm. to Middle Temple, 1621; was *Knighted*, at Whitehall 20 June 1626, and was *cr. a Bart.*, as above, 9 June 1627; Sheriff of Hants, 1640-41. He *m.* Sarah, da. and coheir of Ambrose DAUNTSEY, of Lavington, Wilts. He *d.* 1642. Will pr. Oct. 1642.

II. 1642, to 1719. SIR HUGH STEWKELEY, Bart. [1627], of Hinton, *otherwise* Hinton Ampner aforesaid, s. and h., *suc. to the Baronetcy* in 1642; Sheriff of Hants, 1661-62. He *m.* firstly, Catherine, da. and h. of Sir John TROTT, Bart. [so *cr.* 1660] of Leverstoke, Hants, by Elizabeth, da. and coheir of Sir Edmund WRIGHT, sometime (1640) Lord Mayor of London. Her admon. 14 May 1679 to her husband. He *m.* secondly Mary, da. of John YOUNG, of Exton. He *d.* s.p.m.(c) in 1719, when the *Baronetcy* became *extinct*. Will dat. 17 March 1718/9, pr. July 1719 by dame Mary, the relict.

(a) "Henry Griffith, of Agnes Burton, co. York, Bart.," was adm. to Gray's Inn, 16 March 1640/1, being probably, but not certainly, the 2d Bart.
(b) His only son, Henry, *d.* an infant, 22 Sep. 1637.
(c) Charles, s. and h. ap., living 1686, *d.* s.p. and v.p. Catherine, da. by his first wife, *m.* before 1686, Sir Charles Shuckburgh, 2d Bart. [1660].

STANLEY:
cr. 26 June 1627,
afterwards, since 1 Feb. 1735/6, EARLS OF DERBY.

I. 1627. "EDWARD STANLEY, of Biggarstaffe, co. Lancaster, Esq.," s. and h. of Henry STANLEY, by Margaret (*m.* 26 Sep. 1563), da. and h. of Peter STANLEY,(a) of Bickerstaff, otherwise Biggarstaffe, aforesaid, in the parish of Ormskirk, suc. his father, 23 July 1598; was Sheriff of Lancashire, 1614-15 and 1626-27; of Cheshire, 1627-28, and of Lancashire (again), 1638-39, having been *cr. a Bart.*, as above, 26 June 1627. He *m.* firstly, Katherine, da. of Sir Randal MAINWARING, of Over Peover, co. Chester, by his first wife Margaret, da. of Sir Edward FITTON, of Gawsworth. She *d.* s.p.m. He *m.* secondly, in or before 1616, Isabel, da. and coheir of Peter WARBURTON, of Warburton and Arley, co. Chester, by Mary, da. of Sir John HOLCROFT, of Holcroft. She was aged 36 at her father's death in 1628. He *d.* May 1640.

II. 1640. SIR THOMAS STANLEY, Bart. [1627], of Bickerstaffe aforesaid, s. and h., by second wife, *bap.* 22 Oct. 1616, at Ormskirk; *suc. to the Baronetcy*, May 1640. He *m.*, in or before 1643, Mary, da. of Peter EGERTON, of Shaw, co. Lancaster, by Elizabeth, da. and coheir of Leonard ASHAWE. He *d.* May 1653. Will pr. 1654. His widow *m.* Capt. Henry HOGHTON.

III. 1653. SIR EDWARD STANLEY, Bart. [1627], of Bickerstaffe aforesaid, *b.* 1643; *suc. to the Baronetcy* in May 1653; matric. at Oxford (Brasenose Coll., 4 Dec. 1661, aged 18; M.A., 12 Sep. 1661. He *m.* 25 Dec. 1663, Elizabeth, da. and coheir of Thomas BOSVILE, of Warmsworth, co. York, by his first wife, Barbara, da. of John BABINGTON. He *d.* 16 Oct. 1671.

IV. 1671. SIR THOMAS STANLEY, Bart. [1627], of Bickerstaffe aforesaid, only s. and h.; *b.* 27 Sep. 1670; *suc. to the Baronetcy*, in his infancy, 16 Oct. 1671; was M.P. for Preston 1695. He *m.* firstly, 16 Aug. 1688, Elizabeth, da. and h. of Thomas PATTEN, of Preston aforesaid (who *d.* 1697, aged 61), by (—) da. and coheir of (—) DOUGHTY, of Coln Hall, co. Lancaster. She *d.* 1694. He *m.* secondly, Margaret, widow of Sir Richard STANDISH, 1st Bart. [1677], da. of Thomas HOLCROFT, of Holcroft, co. Lanc. He *d.* 7 May 1714. His widow, by whom he had no issue, *d.* 14 Oct. 1735, at a great age.

V. 1714. SIR EDWARD STANLEY, Bart. [1627], of Bickerstaffe aforesaid, 1st s. and h., by 1st wife, *b.* 17 Sep. 1689, at Knowsley in Hayton, co. Lancaster; *suc. to the Baronetcy*, on the death or his father, 7 May 1714; Sheriff of Lancashire, 1722-23; M.P. thereof, 1727-36. He *m.* 14 Sep. 1714, Elizabeth, da. and h. of Robert HESKETH, of Rufford, co. Lancaster, by Elizabeth, da. of the Hon. William SPENCER, of Ashton Hall, in that county, 3d s. of William, 2d BARON SPENCER OF WORMLEIGHTON. She was living when, on the death, 1 Feb. 1735/6, of his 6th cousin, James STANLEY, 10TH EARL OF DERBY, he became EARL OF DERBY. In that peerage (*cr.* 27 Oct. 1485) this *Baronetcy* then *merged*, and so continues. See *Peerage*.

LITTLETON, *or* LITLETON:
cr. 28 June 1627,
ex. 18 May 1812.

I. 1627. "EDWARD LITTLETON, of Pileton [Pillaton] Hall, co. Stafford, Esq.," s. and h. ap. of Sir Edward LITTLETON,(b) of the same, by Mary, da. of Sir Clement FISHER, of Packington, co. Warwick, was *b.* about 1599; mat. at Oxford, 28 March 1617, aged 18; adm. to Inner Temple, 1618, and was *cr. a Bart.*, as above, 28 June 1627. He *suc.* his father, 25 Aug. 1630; was Sheriff of Stafford-

(a) This Peter was 3d s. of Sir William Stanley, of Hooton, co. Chester, the elder line of the family of Stanley.
(b) This Sir Edward was fourth in descent from Richard LITTLETON, who *m.* Alice, da. and h. of William WINESBURY, of Pillaton aforesaid, which Richard, was 2d s. of Sir Thomas Littleton, K.B., of Frankley, co. Worcester, the celebrated Judge.

shire, 1636-37; M.P. thereof, April to May 1640 and Nov. 1640, till disabled, 4 March 1643/4. He was an ardent Royalist, and had to pay £1.347 6s. 8d. to the sequestrators of estates. He *m.* Hester, da. of Sir William COURTEEN, of London, by his second wife, Hester, sister of Sir Samuel TRYON. He was living 11 June 1649,(a) when he petitions to compound, owning to having "deserted the Parl." and gone to Oxford, which fact precludes the petition from being that of his son. He possibly may be the "Sir Edward Littleton, Knt.," who was *bur.* 3 Aug. 1657 at St. Edward's, Romford, and, again, the admon., 5 Feb. 1657/8, of "Sir Edward Littleton, of Ferant, co. Montgomery, Bart.," granted, however, to the widow, "*Catherine*" [*sic*], may refer to him. His widow is said to have *m.* Thomas THORNE, of Shelrock, Salop, and to have been *bur.* at Ryton church, Salop, 12 Dec. 1674.

II. 1657? SIR EDWARD LITTLETON, Bart. [1627], of Pillaton Hall aforesaid, s. and h.; *suc. to the Baronetcy* on the death of his father; M.P. for Staffordshire, 1663-78. He *m.* firstly, about 1650, Mary, da. of Sir Walter WROTTESLEY, 1st Bart. [1642], by Mary, da. of John GREY of Enville, co. Stafford. By her he had five children. He *m.* secondly, before 1674, his cousin, Joyce, da. of (—) LITTLETON, of Teddesley Hay. By her he had eight children. He *d.* in 1709.

III. 1709. SIR EDWARD LITTLETON, Bart. [1627], of Pillaton Hall aforesaid, grandson and h., being s. and h. of Edward LITTLETON (Sheriff of Staffordshire, 1680-81, and M.P. thereof, 1685-87), by Susannah (*m.* Jan. 1670/1), da. of Sir Theophilus BIDDULPH, 1st Bart. [1664], which Edward last-named was s. and h. ap. of the 2d Bart. by his 1st wife, and *d.* v.p. 24 Jan. 1704, aged about 55. He *suc. to the Baronetcy* in 1709. He was Sheriff of Staffordshire, 1712-13. He *m.* Mary, only da. of Sir Richard HOARE, Lord Mayor of London (1712-13), by Susanna, da. of John AUSTIN, of Brittons, Essex. He *d.*, s.p., 2 Jan. 1741/2. His widow *d.* 18 April 1761. Will pr. 1761.

IV. 1742, to 1812. SIR EDWARD LITTLETON, Bart. [1627], of Pillaton Hall aforesaid, and afterwards of Teddesley Park, near Penkridge, co. Stafford, nephew and h., being s. and h. of Fisher LITTLETON, by Frances, 1st da. and coheir of James WHITEHALL, of Pipe Ridware, co. Stafford, which Fisher was br. of the 3d Bart., and *d.* May 1740. He was *b.* about 1725, and *suc. to the Baronetcy* 2 Jan. 1741/2; was Sheriff of Staffordshire, 1762-63, and M.P. thereof in six Parliaments, 1784-1807. He raised a Company during the rebellion of 1745, being Captain thereof. He *m.* Frances, 1st da. of Christopher HORTON, of Catton, co. Derby, by Frances, only da. and h. of Sir Eusebius BUSWELL, Bart., so *cr.* 1713/4. He *d.* s.p. 18 May 1812, aged 86, when the *Baronetcy* became *extinct*.(b)

BROWNE:
cr. 7 July 1627;
ex. 3 Nov. 1690.

I. 1697. "AMBROSE BROWNE, of Bettsworth Castle, co. Surrey, Esq.," s. and h. of Sir Matthew BROWNE, of the same,(c) by Jane, da. of Sir Thomas VINCENT, of Stoke D'Abernon, co. Surrey, suc. his father, 4 Aug. 1603;

(a) He cannot, therefore, be the Sir Edward Littleton who was slain at Naseby fight (four years before) and *bur.* 19 June 1645, at St. Sepulchre's, Northampton.

(b) His estates develved on his great nephew Edward John WALHOUSE, only s. and h. of Moreton WALHOUSE, of Hatherton, co. Stafford, who was only s. and h. of another Moreton WALHOUSE, by Frances, only sister of the said Sir Edward Littleton. He took the name of LITTLETON, and was *cr.* a Peer, 11 May 1835, as BARON HATHERTON.

(c) This Matthew was s. and h. of Sir Thomas Browne, the grandson and h. of Sir Matthew Browne, s. and h. of Sir George Browne, all of Bettsworth, or Bechworth, Castle aforesaid, the said George being s. and h. of Sir Thomas Browne, Treasurer of the Household of Henry VI, by Eleanor, da. and h. of Sir Thomas Fitzalan, *alias* Arundel, of Bechworth Castle aforesaid, br. of John, Earl of Arundel. The 4th s. of the said Sir Thomas Browne and Eleanor his wife, was Sir Anthony Browne, Standard Bearer of England, the ancestor of the Viscounts Montagu.

was ed. at Jesus College, Cambridge; admitted to Gray's Inn, 12 March 1624/5; Sheriff of Surrey and Sussex, 1628-29, and was *cr. a Baronet*, as above, 7 July 1627. He was M.P. for Surrey, 1628-29, April to May 1640, and Nov. 1640, till secluded in Dec. 1648; was one of "the members of the House of Commons that advanced horse, etc., for defence of the Parl.," June 1642 (*N. and Q.*, 1st S., xii., p. 358), undertaking to "finde 2 horses well furnisht"; was one of the Surrey Sequestrators Committee, 1643. He *m.*, 1 Oct., 1607, at Fulmere, co. Cambridge, Elizabeth, da. of William ADAM, of Saffron Walden, Essex. She was *bur.* at Dorking, 19 Oct. 1657. Admon. 19 Dec. 1661, to her son, Sir Adam Browne, Bart. He *d.* 16 Aug. 1661, and was *bur.* 23d at Dorking.

II. 1661, to 1690. SIR ADAM BROWNE, Bart. [1627], of Bettsworth Castle aforesaid, s. and h.; was fined, 30 June 1648, as a delinquent £60, increased to £240; *suc. to the Baronetcy*, 16 Aug. 1661. M.P. for Surrey, 1661-79 and 1685-87. He *m.*, before 1658, Philippa, da. of Sir John COOPER, 1st Bart. [1622], of Wimborne, by Anne, da. of Sir Anthony ASHLEY, Bart. [1622]. He *d.* s.p.m.s., and was *bur.*, 3 Nov. 1690,(a) at Dorking, when the *Baronetcy* became *extinct*. Will pr. Dec. 1690. His widow *d.* 20 May 1701, aged 77. Will pr. May 1701.

CROWE:
cr. 8 July 1627;
ex. 21 June 1706.

I. 1627. "SACKVILLE CROWE, of Lanherne [*i.e.*, Laugharne], co. Carmarthen, Esq., Treasurer of the Fleet," s. of William Crowe, of Sacketts, co. Kent, by Anne, da. and coh. of John SACKVILLE, of Chiddingstone, co. Sussex; was M.P. for Hastings, 1625, and for Bramber, 1628-29, and was *cr. a Bart.* as above, 8 July 1627. In April 1648 he was sent as prisoner to the Tower. He *m.*, in or before 1674, Mary, sister of John, 8th EARL OF RUTLAND, da. of Sir George MANNERS, of Haddon, co. Derby, by Grace, da. of Sir Henry PIERREPONT. She was *b.* 1 Jan. 1612. He *d.* in the Fleet prison, London, 1683. Admon. 28 May 1683, to his son John.

II. 1683, to 1706. SIR SACKVILLE CROWE, Bart. [1627], of Laugharne afsd., s. and h., *b.* about 1674; *suc. to the Baronetcy* in 1683, matric. at Oxford (Jesus Coll.), 6 June 1689, aged 15; adm. to Lincoln's Inn, 1692. He *m.* firstly (Lic. Worcester, 23 Feb. 1670), Ann, da. of Sir [Thomas?] ROUSE, Bart. She *d.* 13 Dec. 1679, æt 38, and was bur. at Laugharne.(b) He *m.* secondly, Elizabeth, widow of Sir Henry Vaughan, of Derwitt, co. Carmarthen, da. of William HERBERT, of Llangattock, co. Monmouth. She, by whom he had no issue, *d.* 6 Aug. 1694, æt 56. Admon. 13 June 1695, granted to her husband. He *d.* s.p.m.s. 21 June 1706, æt 69, when *the Baronetcy* became *extinct*. Both were *bur.* at Laugharne.

LIVESEY, *or* LYVESEY:
cr. 11 July 1627,
attainted 1660.

I. 1627, to 1660. "MICHAEL LYVESEY, of Eastchurch, within the Isle of Sheppy, co. Kent, Esq.," only s. and h. of Gabriel LIVESEY, of Hollingbourne and Minster, in that county, by his second wife Anne, da. of Sir Michael SONDES, of Throwley, co. Kent, was *b.* 1611; suc. his father 18 March 1622, and was, when a minor, *cr. a Bart.*, as above, 11 July

(a) His son, Ambrose Browne, matric. at Oxford (Trin. Coll.), 4 Nov. 1673, aged 14; was M.P. for Bletchingley 1685-87, but *d.* unm. and v.p., and was *bur.* 24 July 1688, at Dorking. Margaret, the only da. and h., *m.* in 1691, William Fenwick, but *d.* s.p., and was *bur.* 6 May 1726, at Dorking, when the estates of Bechworth passed by sale, to the families of Tucker, Mildmay, and (in 1798) Peters.

(b) Sackville Crowe, their only son, *d.* unm. and v.p., 15 Feb. 1700, aged 28. Their only da. and h., Jane, *m.* Francis Cornwallis.

1627; was Sheriff of Kent, 1643-44, 1655-56, and 1656-57. At the outbreak of the Civil War he took an active part against the King, was Col. of Horse in the Parl. army, and was at the battle of Cheriton Down, 29 March 1644, where, however, "he deliberately ran away";(a) was M.P. for Queenborough in the long Parl. 1645 till its dissolution; was one of the Regicide Judges, attending every day of the trial and signing the death warrant. He escaped into the Low Countries at the Restoration, was one of the thirty living Regicides excluded from the act of oblivion, was attainted for high treason in 1660, whereby the *Baronetcy* was *forfeited*. He *m.* Elizabeth. He was living in Oct. 1663, but *d.* probably soon afterwards, presumably s.p.m.(b) The admon. of his widow as "Dame Elizabeth Livesey, of Maidstone, Kent, widow," was granted 27 Feb. 1665/6, to her da., Deborah Livesey.(c)

BENNETT:
cr. 17 July 1627,
ex. 21 Aug. 1631.

I. 1627, to 1631. "SIMON BENNETT, of Benchampton [*i.e.*, Beachampton], co. Bucks, Esq.," 2d s. and h. of Sir Thomas BENNET *or* BENNETT, of the same, sometime (1603-04) Lord Mayor of London, by Mary, da. of Robert TAYLOR, of London, mercer, was *b.* about 1584; matric. at Oxford (Univ. Coll.) 15 Oct. 1602, aged 18; adm. to Inner Temple, 1605, and was (soon after his father's death, 16 Feb. 1626/7), *cr. a Bart.*, as above, 17 July 1627. He suc. his elder br., Ambrose Bennett (who apparently was excluded from the family estates), 22 March 1630/1. He *m.*, before Dec. 1624, Elizabeth, da. of Sir Arthur INGRAM, of London, by his 1st wife Susan, da. of Richard BROWN, of London. He *d.* s.p. 21 and was *bur.* 22 Aug. 1631, at Beachampton, when the *Baronetcy* became *extinct*. M.I.(d) Funeral certificate at the Coll. of Arms. Will dat. 15 Aug., pr. 3 Sep. 1631. His widow *d.* 13 and was *bur.* 30 June 1636, at St. Barth. the Great, London. Funeral certificate as above.

FISHER:
cr. 19 July 1627;
ex. 7 Oct. 1707.

I. 1627. "THOMAS FISHER, of the parish of St. Giles, co. Midx., Knt.," only s. of Thomas FISHER,(e) of London, citizen and skinner, by Susan, da. of Sir Thomas TYNDALL, of Hockwold, co. Norfolk, suc. his father early in 1613; was *Knighted* at Whitehall, 12 March 1616/7, and was *cr. a Bart.* as above, 19 July 1627. He *m.*, 2 March 1619/20, at Islington, Sarah, 1st da. and coh. of Sir Thomas FOWLER, Bart. [1628], of Barnsbury, in Islington, by Elizabeth, da. and h. of William PIERSON. He *d.* 22, and was *bur.*, 25 May 1636, at Islington. Will pr. 1636. That of his widow, who was living 1649, pr. 1666.

II. 1636. SIR THOMAS FISHER, Bart. [1627], of Barnsbury aforesaid, s. and h.; *b.* about 1623; *suc. to the Baronetcy*, 22 May 1636. He *m.*, before 1643, Jane, da. of Sir John PRESCOT, of Hoxne, Suffolk. He was *bur.* 9 Sep. 1670, at Islington. Admon. 21 Oct. 1670. His widow *m.*, after Nov. 1671, (as his 1st wife), the Hon. William MAYNARD, 2d s. of William, 2d BARON MAYNARD, and *d.* 1 March 1675.

(a) *Nat. Biogr.*, it being there added that "his cowardice and incapacity made him generally disliked."

(b) Said to have been cut to pieces by the Dutch boors on being denounced as one of the King's murderers [*Hist. MSS. Com.*, 5th Rep., p. 174]. Gabriel Livesey, M.P. for Queenborough, 1657-58, was probably his brother.

(c) Anne, another da., *m.* Sir Robert Sprignell, 2d Bart. [1641], who *d.* s.p. 1690.

(d) Erected at Beachampton 128 years after his death by Univ. Coll., Oxford, to which he had been a liberal benefactor.

(e) See ped. of Fisher in Chester Waters's *Family of Chester of Chisheley*, p. 278.

III. 1670. SIR THOMAS FISHER, Bart. [1627], of Barnsbury afsd., s. and h., *b.* about 1643; *suc. to the Baronetcy* in Sep. 1670. He had lic. (Faculty office) dat. 16 Nov. 1666(a) (he about 23, bachelor, she about 17, spinster), to marry his cousin Elizabeth, da. of Sir Henry DUCIE, K.B., by Sarah, da. of Sir Thomas FISHER, 1st Bart., but *d.* unm. He was *bur.* 14 April 1671, at Islington. Admon. 8 Nov. 1671 (as a bachelor) to his uncle Sir Richard Fisher, Bart.

IV. 1671, to 1707. SIR RICHARD FISHER, Bart. [1627], of Barnsbury afsd., uncle and h., *bap.* 22 Jan. 1629, at Islington, admitted to Middle Temple, 1647, *suc. to the Baronetcy* in April 1671. He *m.* firstly, Anne LEIGH, of St. John's Close, Clerkenwell, spinster. She was *bur.* 29 April 1693 at Islington. He *m.* secondly (Lic. Fac., 31 July 1704), Browne, widow of Sir George DALSTON, da. of Sir William RAMSDEN, of Longley, co. York. He *d.* s.p. 7, and was *bur.* 14 Oct. 1707 at Islington, when the Baronetcy became *extinct*.(b) Will pr. Oct. 1707. His widow was *bur.* 24 March 1740 at Islington. Will pr. 1740.

BOWYER:
cr. 23 July 1627;
ex. Feb. 1679/80.

I. 1627. "THOMAS BOWYER,(c) of Leyghthorne [in North Mundham], co. Sussex, Esq.," s. and h. of Thomas BOWYER, of the same, and of the Middle Temple, London, by his second wife, Jane, da. of John BIRCH, one of the Barons of the Court of Exchequer, was *b.* 28 Nov., and *bap.* 4 Dec. 1586, at Mundham; suc. his father 7 March 1594/5; was M.P. for Midhurst, 1614, and for Bramber (7 successive Parls.), 1621 to 1642, when he was disabled; was Sheriff of Surrey and Sussex, 1626-27, and was *cr. a Bart.*, as above, 23 July 1627; was fined £2,033 as a delinquent, 18 May 1650. He *m.* firstly, in or before 1610, Anne, da. and coheir of Adrian STOUGHTON, of West Stoke, co. Surrey, Recorder of Chichester. He *m.* secondly, before 1634, Jane, widow of Sir George STOUGHTON, and formerly of Samuel AUSTEN, of Stratford, da. and h. of Emery CRANLEY, of co. Surrey. She was *bur.* 10 April 1640 at North Mundham. He *m.* thirdly, in or before 1642, Anne. He was *bur.* 28 Feb. 1650 at Mundham, leaving a widow and thirteen children.(d) Will dat. 20 Jan. 1648/9, pr. 9 April 1652. His widow was *bur.* 11 May 1683 at St. Margaret's, Westm. Will dat. 21 March 1682, pr. 5 Dec. 1683.

II. 1650. SIR THOMAS BOWYER, Bart. [1627], of Leythorne aforesaid, 1st s. and h. by 1st wife; matric. at Oxford (Trin. Coll.), 9 June 1626, aged 16; was aged 24 and upwards in 1634 and unm.; *suc. to the Baronetcy* in Feb. 1650. He *m.* firstly, Katherine, da. and coheir of Richard STANY, of Elston, Sussex, by Bridget, da. and h. of Richard ERNLY, of Rackham. She was living 1648. He *m.* secondly, Margaret. He *d.* s.p.m.(a) Will dat. 13 June 1659, pr. 21 Dec. 1659 by his widow. Her will as "of Chichester," dat. 26 July 1687, pr. 22 Nov. 1693.

III. 1659, to 1680. SIR JAMES BOWYER, Bart. [1627], of Leythorne aforesaid, brother of the half-blood and h. male, being s. of the 1st Bart. by his 3rd wife; *bap.* at North Mundham; elected a scholar at Winchester in 1656, and then aged 11(e); *suc. to the Baronetcy* in 1659; matric. at Oxford (New Coll.), 14 Feb. 1661/2, and then aged 17; Fellow, 1663-65;

(a) In this he is called "Bart.," and "of Islington," yet "Sir Thomas Fisher, the elder Knt. and Bart. of Islington" afsd. is therein spoken of as alive. There is, however, another lic. (Vic. Gen. office), 31 Oct. 1670, of a "Sir Thomas Fisher" (not however called "Bart."), of St. Giles in the Fields, bachelor, about 23 [Qy., if the same man?] to marry "Mrs. Anne Askew, spinster, about 24."

(b) Ursula his sister *m.* as second wife, Sir William HALTON, 1st Bart. [1642], and her son, the 3d Bart., inherited the manor of Barnsbury, which was devised by his son, the 4th Bart. (*d.* s.p., 12 Feb. 1754), to the family of TUFNELL.

(c) *N. and Q.* 7th S., xii, 285 and 422. See also an article by the Rev. J. H. Cooper, in vol. xlii of the pubs. of the Sussex Arch. Soc.

(d) Cat. of Compounders, vol. ii, p. 833.

(e) *N. and Q.*, 8th S., i, 136.

adm. to the Middle Temple, London, 1665. Having wasted all his estate, and having no issue, he obtained a new patent of Baronetcy, dated 18 May 1678 (said to have been granted with the precedency of the former creation, on a surrender(a) of the patent of 1627), with rem., failing heirs male of his body, to Henry Goring, of Highden, Sussex.(b) He *d.* s.p. in London, and was *bur.* 28 Feb. 1679/80. Admon. 27 April 1682 to Henry Bellingham, cousin and next of kin. At his death *the Baronetcy*, of 23 July 1627, became *extinct*, but that of the recent creation (18 May 1678) devolved according to the spec. rem. in the patent thereof. See "BOWYER" Baronetcy, *cr.* 18 May 1678.

BACON:

cr. 29 July 1627;
merged 30 April 1758
into the Baronetcy of Bacon, *cr.* 22 May 1611.

I. 1627. "BUTTS BACON, of Mildenhall, co. Suffolk, Esq.," yr. s. of Sir Nicholas BACON, 1st Bart. [1611] of Redgrave, by Anne, da. and h. of Edmund BUTTS, of Thornage, Norfolk, was *cr. a Baronet*, 29 July 1627. He *m.* Dorothy, widow of William JERMYN, da. of Sir Henry WARNER, of Parham and Mildenhall, Suffolk. She *d.* 4 Sep. 1655, and was *bur.* at Blundeston, Norfolk. He *d.* 29 May 1661, and was *bur.* there. M.I. Will, as of Heringfleet, dat. 18 March 1660, pr. at Norwich, 30 Jan. 1661/2.

II. 1661. SIR HENRY BACON, Bart. [1627], of Heringfleet aforesaid, s. and h.; *suc. to the Baronetcy*, 29 May 1661. He *m.* Barbara, da. of William GOOCH, of Mettringham, Suffolk. He *d.* before 1671.

III. 1670? SIR HENRY BACON, Bart. [1627], of Heringfleet aforesaid and of Gillingham, Norfolk, s. and h., which last estate he inherited from his sister's husband, Sir Richard Bacon, 3rd Bart. [1662] of Gillingham aforesaid; *suc. to the Baronetcy* (on the death of his father), about 1670. He *m.*, 29 June 1671, at Sturston, Suffolk, Sarah, da. of Sir John CASTLETON, 2d Bart. [1641], by Margaret, da. and h. of Robert MORSE, of Sturston aforesaid. He was *bur.*, 13 Jan. 1685/6, at Gillingham. His widow *d.* 3 and was *bur.* 7 Feb. 1727, at Gillingham.

IV. 1686. SIR EDMUND BACON, Bart. [1627], of Gillingham aforesaid, s. and h. He was *bap.* 6 April 1672, at Sturston aforesaid; *suc. to the Baronetcy* in Jan. 1685/6; M.P. for Orford (four Parls.), 1700-08. He *m.* firstly, at Redgrave, about Christmas 1688, Philippa, 4th da. and coheir of Sir Edmund BACON, 4th Bart. [1611] of Redgrave, by Elizabeth, da. and coheir of Sir Robert CRANE, Bart. [1643]. She, who was *bap.* 29 July 1672, was *bur.*, 12 July 1710, at Gillingham. He *m.* secondly, 16 April 1713, at Raveningham, Norfolk, Mary, da. of John CASTELL, of Raveningham aforesaid. He *d.* 10 and was *bur.* 17 July 1721, at Gillingham.

(a) Such surrender, however would have been invalid, according to the decision, 1678, in the case of the Viscountcy of Purbeck. See note sub "STONEHOUSE" Baronetcy, *cr.* 7 May 1628.

(b) This transaction is supposed to have been effected in consequence of a bribe from Goring to the needy baronet, who (save for such bribe), gained nothing whatever by it. There appears to have been no relationship between the parties, and the connection between them is so ludicrously remote as hardly to be worth any consideration. A certain Sir Henry Bowyer married (as her first husband) Dorothy, da. of George Goring, of Danny, co. Sussex, and died childless in 1606, his widow promptly remarrying. That Henry was great grandson of William Bowyer, from whom, by another of his sons, the grantee of 1678 was a great great great grandson. The said Dorothy was granddaughter of Sir William Goring, of Burton (*d.* 1553), from whom Henry Goring, the successor to the Baronetcy created in 1678, was (by another son), 4th in descent. Thus James Bowyer, the grantee of 1678 was 2d cousin twice removed to a man who died above seventy years ago, without issue, leaving a *widow*, who was first cousin (also) twice removed to Henry Goring, the remainder man and subsequent inheritor of the Baronetcy thus created.

V. 1721. SIR EDMUND BACON, Bart. [1627], of Gillingham aforesaid, s. and h. by 1st wife. He was *b.* 7 and *bap.* 14 Aug. 1693 at Gillingham; *suc. to the Baronetcy*, 10 July 1721; M.P. for Thetford, in 3 parliaments, 1727 to 1738. He *m.* 7 Nov. 1724, at the Chapel Royal, Whitehall, Susan, da. of Sir Isaac REBOW, of Colchester. He *d.* at Bath 4 and was *bur.* 16 Oct. 1738 at Gillingham. Will pr. 1739. His widow, who was *b.* Sep. 1687, was living 1771.

VI. 1738. SIR EDMUND BACON, Bart. [1627], of Gillingham aforesaid, s. and h.; *b.* 7 and *bap.* 17 Aug. 1725 at Gillingham; *suc. to the Baronetcy*, 5 Oct. 1738; ed. at Westm. School, 1741. He *d.* unm 6, and was *bur.* 12 April 1750 at Gillingham. Admon. 7 June 1750.

VII. 1750. SIR HENRY BACON, Bart. [1627], of Gillingham aforesaid, uncle and h., being 2d s. of the 4th Bart. by his 1st wife. He was *b.* 5 and *bap.* 8 Oct. 1693 at Gillingham; *suc. to the Baronetcy*, 6 April 1750. He *d.* unm., and was *bur.* 10 April 1753 at Gillingham.

VIII. 1753. SIR RICHARD BACON, Bart. [1627], of Colchester, Essex, br. and h., being 3d s. of the 4th Bart., by his 1st wife. He was *b.* 22 Feb., and *bap.* 5 March 1695, at Gillingham; *suc. to the Baronetcy*, 10 April 1753. By the death of his cousin, Sir Edmund BACON, 6th Bart. [1611] of Garboldisham, co. Norfolk, he *suc. to the Baronetcy*, conferred, 22 May 1611, on his ancestor (Sir Nicholas BACON, of Redgrave, co. Suffolk), becoming thus the *premier Baronet*. See "BACON," *cr.* 22 May 1611, under the 7th Baronet.

CORBET, *or* CORBETT:

cr. 19 Sep. 1627;
ex. 7 May 1750.

I. 1627. "JOHN CORBETT, of Stoke, co. Salop, Esq.," s. and h. of Richard CORBET,(a) of the same and of Adderley in that county, by Anne, da. of Sir Thomas BROMLEY, Lord Chancellor of England, was *bap.* 20 May 1594, at Ferne, co. Salop, and was *cr. a Bart.*, as above, 19 Sep. 1627. In that same year, however, he was conspicuous in his opposition to the loan required by the King, being, it is said,(b) "one of those five illustrious patriots worthy of the eternal gratitude of their country" who did so. He was Sheriff of Shropshire, 1628-29; M.P. for that county 1640 till secluded in 1648, and was one of the Salop Com. of Sequestrators, April 1643. He *m.*, in or before 1620, Anne, da. of Sir George MAINWARING, of Ightfield, Salop. He *d.* July 1662, aged 68, having had ten sons and ten daughters, and was *bur.* at Market Drayton, Salop. M.I. Admon. 1662. His widow, who was known as "the good Lady Corbet," *d.* 29 Oct. 1682, aged nearly 80, and was *bur.* with him. M.I. Her will, dat. 23 Oct. 1682, proved 31 Jan. 1682/3.

II. 1662. SIR JOHN CORBET, Bart. [1627], of Stoke and Adderley aforesaid, and h.; *b.* about 1620; matric. at Oxford (St. Alban's Hall), 25 Nov. 1636, aged 16; *suc. to the Baronetcy* in July 1662.(c) He *m.*, in or before 1645, Lætitia, da. of Sir Robert KNOLLYS, of Gray's Court, Oxon, by Joanna, da. of Sir John WOLSTENHOLME. He was *bur.* 24 Feb. 1664/5 at Westminster Abbey. The will of his widow, dat. 5 Oct. 1669, was pr. 20 July 1670.

III. 1665. SIR JOHN CORBET, Bart. [1627], of Stoke and Adderley aforesaid; s. and h., *b.* about 1645; *suc. to the Baronetcy* in Feb. 1664/5; was Sheriff of Shropshire, 1675-76. He *m.* firstly, 28 Nov. 1658, at Woodford, co.

(a) This Richard was s. and h. of Reynold Corbet, of Stoke, one of the Justices of the Court of Common Pleas, *temp* Eliz. who was 2d s. of Sir Robert Corbet, of Moreton Corbet, Salop, ancestor of the Corbets of that place, *cr. Barts.* in 1642 and 1808 respectively.

(b) Blakeway.

(c) He was not the M.P. for Bishop's Castle, 1645-53, named as one of the King's Judges. [*Ex inform.*, W. D. Pink].

F

Essex, Theophila, da. and h. of John CAMPBELL, of Woodford, by Theophila, da. of John (MOHUN), 1st BARON MOHUN OF OKEHAMPTON. She *d.* at Woodford. Admon. 12 June 1672. He *m.* secondly (Lic. London, 29 July 1672, he 27 and she about 17), Frances, da. and coheir of Major-General Randolph EGERTON, of Betley, co. Stafford. He *d.* in 1695. His widow *m.* Sir James POOLE, 1st Bart. [1677], of Poole, co. Chester.

IV. 1695. SIR ROBERT CORBET, Bart. [1627], of Stoke and Adderley aforesaid, only surviving s. and h. by first wife, *b.* about 1670; matric. at Oxford (Ch. Ch.) 6 July 1687, aged 17; admitted to Inner Temple, 1688; *suc. to the Baronetcy* in 1695; was Sheriff of Shropshire, 1700-01; M.P. for Salop, 1705-10 and 1715-22; Clerk of the Board of Green Cloth and Commissioner of Customs to George I, 1720. He *m.* (Lic. Fac. 21 June 1693, he 23 [?], she 16) Jane, da. of William HOOKER, s. and h. of Sir William HOOKER, sometime (1673-74), Lord Mayor of London. He *d.* 3 Oct. 1740, aged 80 [70?]. Will pr. 1740. Admon. to his widow, as of St. James', Westminster, 7 April 1748, and again Sep. 1811.

V. 1740. SIR WILLIAM CORBET, Bart. [1627], of Stoke and Adderley aforesaid, s. and h.; *suc. to the Baronetcy*, 3 Oct. 1740; M.P. for Montgomery, 1727-41, and for Ludlow, 1741 till death. Clerk of the Pipe, May 1748 till death. He *m.* Harriot, sister of William, 1st EARL OF CHATHAM, da. of Robert PITT, of Boconnock, Cornwall, by Harriet, sister of John (VILLIERS) EARL OF GRANDISON [I.] He *d.*, s.p., 15 Sep. 1748. Will pr. Oct. 1748, May 1750, June 1784, and Nov. 1847.

VI. 1748, to 1750. SIR HENRY CORBET, Bart. [1627], br. and h.; probably the Henry Corbet, of Queen's Coll., Cambridge, who was B.A. 1730 and M.A. 1734; was in holy orders; sometime Rector of Adderley aforesaid; *suc. to the Baronetcy*, 15 Sep. 1748. He *d.* unm. 7 May 1750, when the *Baronetcy* became *extinct*.(a) Will pr. 1750.

TYRRELL, *or* TIRRELL:

cr. 31 Oct. 1627;
second patent, 19 Feb. 1638/9;
ex. 20 Jan. 1749.

I. 1627, and 1639. "EDWARD TYRRELL, of Thorneton, co. Bucks, Knt.," s. and h. of Sir Edward TYRRELL,(b) of the same, by his 1st wife, Mary, da. of Benedict LEE, of Hulcote, Bucks, suc. his father 29 Jan. 1605/6; was *Knighted* at Windsor, 8 Sep. 1607, was Sheriff of Bucks, 1612-13, and was *cr. a Bart.*, as above, 31 Oct. 1627. Wishing, however, to debar his eldest son, Robert, (possibly a lunatic) from succeeding to that dignity, he obtained, under the same description as above,(c) a new Baronetcy, 19 Feb. 1638/9, containing a clause granting the precedency of the former (*i.e.*, precedence of all creations since 31 Oct. 1627), and with a spec. rem. in the first instance to his two younger sons (Toby and Francis) in tail male respectively. For this purpose he surrendered, though such surrender must be considered as invalid,(d) the former patent. He *m.* firstly, in or before 1608, Elizabeth, da. of Sir William KINGSMILL, of Sidmanton, Hants. She *d.* 1 Sep. 1621, and was *bur.* at Thornton. He *m.* secondly, Elizabeth, widow of Sir John NEEDHAM, of Lichborough, co. Northampton, da. of Sir Edward WATSON, of Rockingham Castle in that county, by Anne, da. of Kenelm DIGBY. She was *bur.* 26 June 1637, at Thornton. He *d.* 2 July 1656, and was *bur.* there. Will dat. 29 April and pr. 22 Sep. 1656.

(a) The estate passed to his nephew, Corbet D'Avenant, who took the name of Corbet, and was *cr. a Bart.* 1786.

(b) Humphrey Tyrrell, the grandfather of this Edward, married Jane, da. and heir of Robert Ingleton, of Thornton, and by her acquired this and thirty other manors.

(c) *i.e.*, not being described as a *Baronet*, but simply as a *Knight*.

(d) Decision, 1678, in the case of the Viscountcy of Purbeck. See note, *sub* "STONHOUSE," Baronetcy, *cr.* 7 May 1628.

II. 1656. SIR TOBY TYRELL, Bart. [1627 and 1639], of Thornton aforesaid, 1st surv. s. and h., *suc. to both Baronetcies*, 2 July 1656, his elder br. Robert Tyrrell(a) having died unm. in his father's lifetime. He *m.* firstly, 1 Dec. 1638, at St. Giles' in the Fields, Edith, da. of Sir Francis WINDEBANK, Sec. of State to Charles I. She *d.* s.p.m. He *m.* secondly, about 1645, Lucy, widow of William CHENEY, of Chesham, Bucks, and da. of Sir Thomas BARRINGTON, 2d Bart. [1611], by his 1st wife, Frances, da. of John GOBERT. He *d.* at Waresley, co. Huntingdon, 1 and was *bur.* 7 Oct. 1671, at Thornton. Will dat. 8 Oct. 1670, pr. 7 Nov. 1671. His widow *d.* 1691, aged 70, and was *bur.* at Chesham Boys. Admon. 10 June 1691.

III. 1671. SIR THOMAS TYRRELL, Bart. [1627 and 1639], of Thornton aforesaid, 1st surv. s. and h. by 2d wife; matric. at Oxford (St. Edm. Hall), 6 June 1660; *suc. to the Baronetcies*, 1 Oct. 1671. He *m.* in 1666, Frances, da. of Sir Henry BLOUNT, of Tittenhanger, Herts, by Hester, da. and coheir of Christopher WASE, of Upper Holloway, Middlesex. She was *b.* 25 Oct. 1648, *d.* 7 and was *bur.* 11 June 1699, at Thornton. He *d.* 10, and was *bur.* 14 Oct. 1705, at Thornton.

IV. 1705. SIR HARRY TYRRELL, Bart. [1627 and 1639], of Thornton aforesaid, s. and h.; *b.* about 1670; *suc. to the Baronetcies*, 10 Oct. 1705. He *m.*, 21 Oct. 1692, at Banbury, Oxon, Hester, 1st da. and h. of Charles BLOUNT, of Blounts Hall, co. Stafford, by Eleanora, 4th da. of Sir Timothy TYRRELL, of Oakley, Bucks, and of Shotover, Oxon. He *d.* 6 Nov. 1708, and was *bur.* at Thornton. Will pr. 1712. His widow, who was *b.* 27 Dec. 1673, inherited Blounts Hall aforesaid, in April 1729, as h. to her br. Charles Blount. She *d.* 3 May 1752. Will pr. 1752.

V. 1708. SIR THOMAS TYRRELL, Bart. [1627 and 1639], of Thornton aforesaid, s. and h., *b.* about 1693; *suc. to the Baronetcies*, 6 Nov. 1708; matric. at Oxford (New Coll.), 7 Feb. 1710/1. He *d.*, unm., 25 Dec. 1718, aged 25, and was *bur.* at Thornton. Admon. 1 Dec. 1719 and 4 July 1722.

VI. 1718. SIR HARRY TYRRELL, Bart. [1627 and 1639], of Thornton aforesaid, br. and h.; *b.* about 1695; matric. at Oxford (New Coll.), 25 Sep. 1711; admitted to Inner Temple, 1711; *suc. to the Baronetcies*, 25 Dec. 1718. He *d.*, unm., 7 or 9 Nov. 1720, aged 25, and was *bur.* at Thornton. Will pr. 1722.

VII. 1720, to 1749. SIR CHARLES TYRRELL, Bart. [1627 and 1639], of Thornton aforesaid, only surv. br. and h., *b.* shortly after his father's death in Nov. 1708; *suc. to the Baronetcies* in Nov. 1720. He *m.*, in 1726, at Geneva, Jane-Elizabeth, only da. of John SELLON, of that city, merchant. He *d.* s.p.m. 20 Jan. 1749, when *both the Baronetcies became extinct*.(b) Will pr. 1749.

DIXWELL:

cr. 18 Feb. 1627/8;
ex. 28 Dec. 1642.

I. 1628, to 1642. "BASIL DIXWELL, of Terlingham, *alias* Gerelingham, co. Kent, Esq.," 4th s. of Charles DIXWELL, of Coton Hall, co. Warwick (*d.* 1591), by Abigail, da. of Henry HERDSON, of Stourton, co. Lincoln, was *b.* 27 Dec. 1585; inherited considerable estates near Folkestone and elsewhere in Kent from his maternal uncle, John Herdson; was

(a) This Robert was *bap.* 4 May 1609, at Thornton, and *d.* v.p. 20 May 1644.

(b) His only da. and h., Hester-Maria, *m.* 16 Oct. 1755, Rev. William COTTON, of Crakemarsh Hall, co. Stafford, and *d.* 1778, leaving an only da. and h., Elizabeth, who *m.* Thomas SHEPPARD, who was *cr. a Bart.* 29 Sep. 1809, as "COTTON-SHEPPARD, of Thornton Hall, Bucks."

M.P. for Hythe, 1626; Sheriff of Kent, 1626-27, and was *cr. a Bart.*, as above, 18 Feb. 1627/8, being *Knighted*, at Whitehall, the same day. He subsequently built a stately house at Broome in that county. He *d.* unm. 28 Dec. 1642 at Folkestone, aged 57 years and a day, and was *bur.* 12 Jan. 1642/3, at Barham, co. Kent, when *the Baronetcy* became *extinct.*(a)

YOUNG, *or* YOUNGE:

cr. 10 March 1627/8;

ex. March 1650/1?

I. 1628, to 1651? "RICHARD YOUNGE, Knt., one of the Gentlemen of the Privy Chamber," being, perhaps, the "Richard YONGE, of London, Esq.," who was admitted to Gray's Inn, 9 Aug. 1591; was *Knighted*, 9 Jan. 1617/8; was M.P. for Worcester, 1621-22 and 1624-25, and was *cr. a Bart.*, as above, 10 March 1627/8. On 29 April 1647, being then of Aldermanbury, London, he was fined £73. He *m.* Martha, sister of Sir William FORTH. He *d.* s.p., when *the Baronetcy* became *extinct*. It is presumed that the burial of "Sir Richard Young, out of the Fleet" [prison] at St. Bride's 19 March 1650/1, and the admon. of "Sir Richard Younge, Knt., of St. Bride's, London," granted 24 Oct. 1652, to John Felton, the principal creditor, relate to him.

PENNYMAN:

cr. 6 May 1628;

ex. 22 Aug 1643.

I. 1628, to 1643. "WILLIAM PENNYMAN, junior, of Maske, *alias* Marske, co. York, Esq.," s. and h. of William PENNYMAN, of St. Albans, Herts, one of the Six Clerks in Chancery(b), by Anne, da. of Richard TOTTLE, was *b.* about 1607; matric. at Oxford (Ch. Ch.), 31 Oct. 1623, aged 16; admitted to Inner Temple, 1623, and was *cr. a Bart.*, as above, 6 May 1623. He was Sheriff of Yorkshire, 1635-36; a Bencher of Gray's Inn, 1639; was M.P. for Richmond, co. York, April to May 1640 and Nov. 1640, till disabled in Aug. 1642. He was a zealous royalist, maintaining two troops of horse and one company of foot at his own expense during the Civil Wars, and was, in April 1643, made Governor of Oxford by Charles I. He *m.* Anne, d. and h. of William ATHERTON, of Skelton, co. York. He *d.*, s.p., 22 Aug. 1643, at Oxford, when the *Baronetcy* became *extinct*. His widow *d.* 13 July 1644. Both were *bur.* in Christ Church Cathedral, Oxford. M.I. His admon. in Commissary Court of London "as of St. Giles' in the Field, co. Midx., Bart.," 20 July 1644, to William Nelson, cousin and creditor, and (apparently) again 8 Sep. 1649 (in C.P.C.) as "of Marke, co. York, Kt." His widow's will pr. Feb. 1645.

STONHOUSE, *or* STONEHOUSE:

cr. 7 May 1628,

sometime [*Qy.* 1866-76], VANSITTART.

I. 1628. "WILLIAM STONEHOUSE, of Radly, co. Berks, Esq.," s. and h. of George STONEHOUSE of the same, and of Little Peckham, Kent, one of the clerks of the Green Cloth to Queen Elizabeth (*d.* 1573) by his 2d wife, Elizabeth, da. of David WOODROFFE, Alderman and sometime [1554-55] Sheriff of London, was *b.* about 1556; ed. at Merchant Taylors' School, London, 1572;

(a) He left his estates to his nephew, Mark Dixwell (younger s. of William Dixwell, of Coton Hall, co. Warwick), whose son, Basil Dixwell, was *cr. a Bart.* 18 June 1660, as "of Broom house, co. Kent."

(b) Stated to have been a natural son of James Pennyman, of Ormsby, the grandfather of James Pennyman, cr. a Bart., 22 Feb. 1663/4.

admitted to Inner Temple, 1574; matric. at Oxford (Univ. Coll.) 10 Jan. 1574/5, aged 18; M.A. 1583, and was *cr. a Bart.*, as above, 7 May 1628. He *m.* (Lic. Lond., 7 June 1592), Elizabeth, da. and h. of John POWELL, of Pengethley, co. Hereford, and Fulham, co. Midx., by Ann, da. of Richard DOD, of Salop. He *d.* 5 Feb. 1631/2, aged 76, and was *bur.* at Radley. M.I. His will pr. March 1632. That of his widow pr. 1655.

II. 1632. SIR JOHN STONHOUSE, Bart. [1628], of Radley aforesaid, s. and h., *b.* about 1602; matric. at Oxford (Trin. Coll.), 21 March 1616/7, aged 15; was a Demy of Mag. Coll., Oxford, 1618-22; admitted to Gray's Inn, London, 1619, was aged 21, at the Visit. of Berks, 1623; M.P. for Abingdon, 1628-29; Gentleman of the Bedchamber to Charles I, by whom he was *Knighted* at Abingdon, 28 Aug. 1629; *suc. to the Baronetcy*, 5 Feb. 1621/2. He *d.* unm. (a few months after his father) 14 June 1632, aged 31, and was *bur.* at Radley. M.I. Funeral certif. in Coll. of Arms.

III. 1622. SIR GEORGE STONHOUSE, Bart. [1628], of Radley aforesaid, br. and h., *suc. to the Baronetcy*, 14 June 1632; aged about 25 in 1633; Sheriff of Berks, 1637-38; M.P. for Abingdon, April to May 1640 and Nov. 1640, till disabled in Jan. 1643/4; re-elected 1660, and 1661 till death. He was a zealous Royalist and was, 31 Dec. 1646, fined £2,705, reduced in Aug. 1649 to £1,460. Wishing to debar his eldest son from the succession to his estate and title, he obtained a new patent of Baronetcy, 5 May 1670, with a clause granting the precedency of 7 May 1628 to himself for life, but with a *spec. rem.* to his 2d and younger sons and the heirs male of their bodies respectively, having, for that purpose, surrendered (or rather endeavoured to surrender) the Baronetcy of the last named date.(a) He *m.* (lic., Archdeaconry of Berks, 22 April 1633, she about 18, to marry at Hurley) Margaret, da. of Richard (LOVELACE), 1st BARON LOVELACE OF HURLEY, by his 2d wife Margaret, da. and h. of William DODSWORTH. He *d.* about 1675. Will pr. 1675. That of his widow pr. 1693.

IV. 1675? SIR GEORGE STONHOUSE, Bart. [1628], 1st s. and h., *b.* about 1638. He was disinherited "for marrying without his father's consent" [Le Neve's *Baronetage*], as above stated, but claimed and enjoyed the title of Baronet under the patent of 7 May 1628 (notwithstanding the purported surrender thereof), *succeeding to the Baronetcy* on his father's death about 1675. He *m.* "Mrs. Anne SCARLETT, of an ancient family, but no fortune."

V. 1700? SIR GEORGE STONHOUSE, Bart. [1628], s. and h., *suc. to the Baronetcy* on the death of his father. He *m.* Anne. da. of James ASHTON, "of an ancient family in Lancashire." He *d.* in Fetter lane, London, 24 Feb. 1736/7. Will dat. 18 Aug. 1729, pr. 7 March 1736/7, by Ann, the relict.(b)

VI. 1737. SIR JOHN STONHOUSE, Bart. [1628], only surv. s. and h., *suc. to the Baronetcy*, 24 Feb. 1736/7. He *d.* unm. July 1740, when the issue male of his grandfather, the 4th Bart. [1628], the first and disinherited son of the 3d Bart. became extinct.

VII and IV. 1740. SIR JOHN STONHOUSE, Bart. [1628 and 1670], of Radley aforesaid, cousin and h. male, being s. and h. of Sir John STONHOUSE, 3d Bart. [1670] of Radley aforesaid, by his second wife, Penelope, da. of Sir Robert DASHWOOD, 1st Bart. [1684], of Northbrooke, Oxon, which Sir John last named (who *d.* 10 Aug. 1733) was s. and h. of Sir John STONHOUSE, 2d Bart.

(a) It being, however, contrary to *English* law (as adjudged by the House of Lords in the case of the Viscountcy of Purbeck) to bar any title of honour, this surrender was invalid. A similar attempt to debar the eldest son was made Feb. 1638/9, in the case of the Tyrell Baronetcy, *cr.* 31 Oct. 1627. See also the purported surrender in 1678 of the Baronetcy of Bowyer, *cr.* 23 July 1627.

(b) In this will he mentions "that wicked family the Stonhouses of Radley," as also how that his father was by his parents disinherited, "though he never gave them any provocation, and it was for no other reason but by their having taken an antipathy against him."

[1670], the said Sir John last named [who *d.* 1700] being 2d son of Sir George STONHOUSE, 3d Bart. [1628] and 1st Bart. [1670] abovenamed, but heir (according to the spec. rem.) to the Baronetcy conferred on his said father 5 May 1670. He was *b.* about 1710; matric. at Oxford (St. John's Coll.) 9 May 1729, aged 18; *suc. to the Baronetcy* [1670] on the death of his said father, 10 Aug. 1733, and *suc. to the older Baronetcy* [1628] on the death of his cousin, the 6th Bart., in July 1740. He *d.* unm. Will dat. 23 Aug. 1736 [*sic*], proved 13 Oct. 1767 in the Archdeaconry Court of Berks, by his brother, Sir William Stonhouse, Bart.

VIII. and V. 1767? SIR WILLIAM STONHOUSE, Bart. [1628 and 1670], of Radley aforesaid, br. and h.; *b.* about 1714; matric. at Oxford (St. John's Coll.), 22 May 1732, aged 18; admitted to the Middle Temple, London, 6 May 1732; was Sheriff of Berks, 1771-72. He *suc. to the Baronetcies* on the death of his brother. He *d.* unm. before 1777. Will pr. May 1780.

IX. and VI. 1776? SIR JAMES STONHOUSE, Bart. [1628 and 1670], of Radley aforesaid, br. and h.; *b.* about 1719; matric. at Oxford (St. John's Coll.), 7 June 1736, aged 17; B.C.L. 26 Jan. 1742/3, D.C.L. 1747; in Holy Orders; Rector of Clapham, Surrey, 1753-92; *suc. to the Baronetcies* about 1776. He *d.*, unm., at Radley, 13 April 1792, aged 74.(a) Will pr. May 1792.

X and VII. 1792. SIR JAMES STONHOUSE [1628 and 1670], cousin and h. male, being s. of Richard STONHOUSE, of Tubney, Berks (*d.* 1776), who was s. of James STONHOUSE (*d.* aged 88), 3d s. of the 3d Bart. [1628], the grantee of the Baronetcy of 5 May 1670. He was *b.* 9 July 1716; matric. at Oxford (St. John's Coll.) 15 Jan. 1732/3, aged 16; B.A., 1736; M.A., 1739; B. Med., 1743; D. Med. 14 Jan. 1745/6; was more than 20 years Physician to the Infirmary at Northampton, but afterwards took Holy Orders, and was (1763-95) Rector of Great and Little Cheverel, Wilts. He, who was an eminent preacher, *suc. to the Baronetcies*, 3 April 1792. He *m.* firstly, in or before 1744, Anne (maid of honour to the Queen Consort), da. of John NEALE, of Allesley, co. Warwick. She *d.* 1 Dec. 1747. He *m.* secondly, in or before 1758, Sarah, only da. and h. of Thomas EKINS, of Chester on the Water, Northants. She *d.* 10 Dec. 1788. He *d.* 8 Dec. 1795, aged 79, and was *bur.* in the Chapel at the Hot Wells, Bristol. M.I. Will pr. Dec. 1795.

XI and VIII. 1795. SIR THOMAS STONHOUSE, Bart. [1628 and 1670], s. and h. by 1st wife, *b.* about 1744; *suc. to the Baronetcies*, 8 Dec. 1795. He *d.* unm. 1810, aged 66. Admon. March 1811.

XII and IX. 1810. SIR JOHN BROOKE STONHOUSE, Bart. [1628 and 1670], nephew, of the half blood, and h., being s. and h. of John STONHOUSE, of the East India Service at Bengal, by Sarah, da. of Richard STEPHENS, Capt. in the Army, which John lastnamed (who *d.* 1803, aged 44), was s., by the 2d wife, of the 10th Bart. He was *b.* between 1796 and 1798, and was sometime Registrar of the Zilla Court of Ghazepoore in the Bengal Civil Service. He *suc. to the Baronetcies* in 1810. He *d.* unm. 2 Dec. 1848, in York Crescent.

XIII and X. 1848. SIR TIMOTHY VANSITTART STONHOUSE, Bart. [1628 and 1670], br. and h., *b.* 26 Jan. 1799; entered the Madras Civil Service, 1815, became Accountant General, and (June 1850) a Provisional Member of the Council, retiring in 1858. He *suc. to the Baronetcies*, 9 Dec. 1848. He *m.* 1825, Mary Diana, 1st da. of Rev. George William Milner Mordaunt STURT, Rector of More Crichell, Dorset, by Mary Louisa, da. of (—) EARLE. He *d.* 30 Jan. 1866, aged 67, at Somerset House, Ryde, Isle of Wight. His widow *d.* 31 Dec. 1878, at Arundel House, Southsea.

(a) At his death the estate of Radley devolved on his niece Penelope, BARONESS RIVERS, for her life, with *spec. rem.* to his nephew, George BOWYER, in fee, who was *cr. a Bart.* 8 Sep. 1794, as "of Radley," and who, in April 1799, suc. to the older Baronetcy of Bowyer, which (as "Bowyer, of Denham Court, Bucks,") had been *cr.* 25 June 1660.

XIV and XI. 1866. SIR HENRY VANSITTART STONHOUSE, Bart. [1628 and 1670], sometime [*Qy.* from 1866 to 1876] VANSITTART (only), only s. and h., *b.* 6 May 1827; an officer, 1848-54, in 94th and 74th Reg.; *Aide-de-Camp* to the Gov. of Madras, 1850-55; *suc. to the Baronetcies*, 30 Jan. 1866, and appears for some time to have dropped the surname of *Stonhouse* for that of *Vansittart*. He *m.* 18 June 1851, Charlotte, 4th da. of John Beattie WEST, M.P. for Dublin, by (—), da. of Hon. Mr. Justice BURTON [I.] She *d.* 21 Aug. 1857. He *d.* 13 Nov. 1884, at Trial, Berkley county, in the United States of America, of malarial fever, and was *bur.* there.(a)

XV. and XII. 1884. SIR ERNEST HAY STONHOUSE, Bart. [1628 and 1670], 3d and yst. but only surv. s. and h., *b.* 27 June 1855; ed. at Cheltenham Coll.; *suc. to the Baronetcies*, 13 Nov. 1884. He *m.* 4 Nov. 1897, Louisa Catherina, da. of Lodowick William REES, of Cheltenham.

FOWLER:

cr. 21 May 1628;

ex. 1656.

I. 1628, to 1656. "THOMAS FOWLER, of Islington, co. Midx., Knt.," s. and h. of Sir Thomas FOWLER, of Barnsbury manor in Islington aforesaid,(b) one of the Governors of Highgate School, by his second wife, Jane, only da. of Gregory CHARLET, Citizen and Tallowchandler, of London, was *b.* after [probably soon after] 1586; was *knighted*. at Whitehall, 23 July 1603; suc. his father 14 Jan. 1624/5, and was *cr. a Bart.*, as above, 21 May 1628. He *m.* in or before 1602, Elizabeth. da. and h. of William PIERSON, of the Inner Temple. She, by whom he had twelve children, *d.* 19 Sep. 1618. He *d.* s.p.m.s.(c) 1656, when *the Baronetcy* became *extinct*. Will pr. 1656.

FENWICK:

cr. 9 June 1628;

extinct 27 Jan. 1696/7.

I. 1628. "JOHN FENWICK, of Fenwick, co. Northumberland, Knt.," s. and h. of Sir William FENWICK, of Fenwick and Wallington in that county, by his first wife Grace, da. and coheir of Sir John FORSTER, of Edderstone and Hexham, co. Northumberland, Warden of the Middle Marches, was *b.* about 1578; was *Knighted* at Royston, 18 Jan. 1604/5; suc. his father in 1613, being then 35 years old; was M.P. for Northumberland, 1624-25, 1625, 1626, 1628-29, and April to May 1640; for Cockermouth, 1640-42, and for Northumberland, again, Jan. 1642 till disabled as a Royalist, Jan. 1643/4, being, however, restored June 1646 till again secluded, Dec. 1648, having been (20 years before the last date); *cr. a Bart.*,

(a) His later career is thus described in F. Boase's *Modern English Biography*, 1850—1900. "Officer of a negro regiment in Charlestown, U.S.A., during the war; tried, convicted, and sent to gaol for defrauding a negro of his pension, 1866; dropped name of *Stonhouse* and called himself *Vansittart* for some time; Magistrate and teacher of a coloured school at St. Stephen's, Berkley county; lived in great poverty at Pineville; clerk, then book-keeper and postmaster, with P. F. Murphy, at Trial in Berkley county; discharged for carelessness."

(b) See an account of this family, by E. Chester Waters, in *The Herald and Genealogist*, vol. ii, p. 559.

(c) Besides four sons who *d.* in infancy, he had a son John, *bap.* 2 Sep. 1605 at Islington, who *m.* Elizabeth, da. and h. of Aunselyn Fowler, of Gloucestershire, and *d.* v.p. and s.p. 1 Sep. 1638. Of his seven daughters, the eldest, Sarah, *m.* 2 March 1619/20, at Islington, Sir Thomas Fisher, 1st Bart. [1627], and inherited the manor of Barnsbury.

as above, 9 June 1628. He *m.* firstly (Lic. 1603) Katharine,(a) 4th da. of Sir Henry SLINGSBY, of Scriven, co. York, by Frances, da. of William VAVASOUR, of Weston. She was *bap.* 31 July 1584 at Knaresborough. He *m.* secondly, in or before 1621, Grace, da. of Thomas LORAINE, of Kirkharle, Northumberland. He *m.* thirdly (—), da. of (—) BOND. He *d.* 1658, aged 79.

II. 1658. SIR WILLIAM FENWICK, Bart. [1628], of Fenwick, Wallington and Hexham aforesaid, 1st surviving s. and h., by 2d wife; *b.* about 1621, being aged 45 in 1666. He was admitted to Gray's Inn, 10 Feb. 1635/6; was M.P. for Northumberland, Nov. 1645 till, apparently (tho' a decided Parliamentarian), secluded in Dec. 1648. He *suc. to the Baronetcy* in 1658. He *m.*, in or before 1644, Jane, da. of Henry STAPLETON, of Wighill, co. York, by Mary, illegit. da. of Sir John FORSTER, of Alnwick.(b) She was executrix to her father's will in March 1657. He *d.*, about 1682, aged about 61. Admon. 6 Feb. 1681/2.

III. 1682? to 1697. SIR JOHN FENWICK, Bart. [1628], of Fenwick, Wallington and Hexham aforesaid, s. and h., aged 10 in 1654. He was M.P. for Northumberland (in five Parls.) 1677-87, having *suc. to the Baronetcy* about 1682. He, in 1685, brought up the bill of attainder against the Duke of Monmouth. He was so prodigal of his wealth that he was forced to alienate nearly all his estates. His fidelity to the hereditary royal race of Stuart was unbounded. He was concerned in a scheme for the restoration of James II, in which it is said that Lord Marlborough, the Duke of Shrewsbury, Admiral Russell and many others who held posts under the established government were implicated. He was apprehended at New Romney, committed to the Tower, and indicted for high treason 28 May 1696. The great national influence of the other conspirators made it good policy to ignore their backslidings, and, though narrowly watched, they were continued in the Government employment, but Sir John Fenwick, being a ruined man and desperate Jacobite, it was thought fit to make an example of him. It was, however, against the law of the land to convict a person of high treason on the oath of only one witness,(c) but an *ex post facto* law was made to apply to this case (the majority in the Commons being 33, out of 345, and that in the Lords only 7, besides that 40 Peers protested against it), which act promptly, and even it is said gladly(d) received the Royal assent. He was thus legally murdered by an act "which cannot be too much condemned as a breach of the most sacred and unalterable rules of justice." He *d.* s.p.s., being beheaded on Tower Hill 27 Jan. 1696/7, aged 52. He was *bur.* the day following in the church of St. Martin's in the fields. *The Baronetcy* at his death became *extinct*, but it was not forfeited, as all execution of the act of attainder (excepting only that of the beheading) had been remitted by writ of the 18th inst. He *m.* 14 July 1663, at St. James', Clerkenwell (Lic. London, he about 19, she about 16), Mary, 1st da. of Charles (HOWARD), 1st EARL OF CARLISLE, by Anne, da. of Edward (HOWARD), 1st BARON HOWARD OF ESCRICK. She, who had been unremitting in her exertions to save her husband's life, *d.* 27 Oct. 1708, aged 60, and was *bur.* at York Minster. M.I.

(a) Her only s. John Fenwick, aged 3 years in 1615, was M.P. for Morpeth, 1640 till disabled in Jan. 1643/4, was a Colonel of Dragoons, and *d.* s.p., v.p., being slain at the battle of Marston Moor, 2 July 1644.

(b) Elizabeth Radcliffe, aged above 5 years in 1626, sister of Francis (Radcliffe), 1st Earl of Derwentwater, is said to have *m.* "Sir William Fenwick, Baronet" [*Mis. Gen. et Her.*, N.S., vol. ii, p. 297]. That William was, however, only a *knight*, being of Meldon, co. Northd., and a younger br. of Sir John, the 1st Bart [*Genealogist*, O.S., pt, ii, p. 17]. His admon 2 May 1653 was granted to Elizabeth, the widow.

(c) This witness was a certain Capt. George Porter, who, it is said, had taken a bribe of £300.

(d) It appears he was personally obnoxious to *both* their Majesties—(1) to William, for some remarks made on his conduct while serving in the army in Holland; and (2) to Mary (whom, doubtless, he considered a modern "Tullia") for ostentatiously refusing to take off his hat to her when he met her as Queen in the park.

WREY, *or* WRAY:

cr. 30 June 1628.

I. 1628. "WILLIAM WRAY, of Trebich [in St. Ives], co. Cornwall, Knt.," 2d s. of John WRAY *or* WREY, of Northrussell, co. Devon (*d.* April 1577), by Blanche, da. and h. of Henry KILLIGREW, of Trebeigh *or* Trebich aforesaid, and of Wolston, Cornwall, was *Knighted* 27 July 1603, suc. his elder br. John Wrey (aged 40 in 1596) before 1620, probably before 1612; was Sheriff of Cornwall, 1612-13, and was *cr. a Bart.*, as above, 30 June 1628.(a) He is described in Carew's "Survey of Cornwall," as "a man of hospitality and a general welcomer of his friends and neighbours." He *m.*, in or before 1600, Elizabeth, 3d da. of Sir William COURTENAY, of Powderham, Devon, by his 1st wife, Elizabeth, da. of Henry (MANNERS), EARL OF RUTLAND. She was living in Dec. 1634. He *d.* June 1636. Will dat. 24 Dec. 1634, pr. 11 Dec. 1636. The admon. presumably of his widow,(b) is dated 30 June 1670.

II. 1636. SIR WILLIAM WREY, *or* WRAY, Bart. [1628], of Trebich aforesaid, s. and h., *b.* about 1600; was aged 20 in 1620 [*Visit. of Devon*]; was *Knighted*(c) v.p. before 24 Dec. 1634, and *suc. to the Baronetcy*, June 1636. He *m.* (Lic. Exeter, 6 Oct. 1624), Elizabeth, da. of Edward (CHICHESTER), 1st VISCOUNT CHICHESTER OF DONEGAL [I.], by his 1st wife Ann, da. and h. of John COPLESTONE, of Eggesford, Devon. She was *b.* 29 June 1607. He *d.* Aug. 1645.

III. 1645. SIR CHICHESTER WREY, Bart. [1628], of Trebich aforesaid, 1st and only surv. s. and h., *b.* 1628. He was a faithful follower of Charles I during the Civil War; was *Knighted* at Bristol 3 Aug. 1643; *suc. to the Baronetcy* in Aug. 1645; was a Gent. of the Privy Chamber; was fined £552 (when a minor), 4 March 1649; was, after the Restoration, made Col. of the Duke of York's Regiment and Governor of Sheerness; was M.P. for Lostwithiel, 1661 till death. He *m.*, in or before 1653, Anne,(d) widow of James (CRANFIELD), 2d EARL OF MIDDLESEX (who *d.* s.p.m. in Sep. 1651), 3d da. and coheir of Edward (BOURCHIER), 4th EARL OF BATH, by his 1st wife, Dorothy, da. of Oliver (ST. JOHN), 3rd BARON ST. JOHN OF BLETSHO. She, who was *b.* 1628, was *bur.* 9 Sep. 1662 at St. Giles' in the Fields, Middlesex. He was *bur.* there 17 May 1668. Will dat. 4 and 8, pr. 16 May 1668, and again 8 Aug. 1670.

IV. 1668. SIR BOURCHIER WREY, Bart. [1628], of Tawstock Court, North Devon, s. and h. He was (v.p.) made **K.B.** 23 April 1661, at the Coronation of Charles II, and *suc. to the Baronetcy* in May 1668, being then aged 15 years. He served under the Duke of Monmouth at the siege of Maestricht (1676), and commanded a Regiment of Horse at Torbay in 1690; was M.P. for Liskeard, Feb. 1677/8 to Jan. 1678/9; for Devon, 1685-87; and for Liskeard, again (three Parls.),

---

(a) In many accounts, this Baronetcy is stated to have been given to Sir William, the *son* and successor of this Sir William. Such, however, was not the case, as this last named William, in his will, dated 1634, calls himself "*Knt. and Bart.*," and describes his son William [*not* as "Bart.," but] as "Knt."

(b) Admon. 30 June 1670, "Dame Elizabeth Wrey, late of St. Martin's in the Fields, Midx., but formerly of Treleigh, in St. Ives, co. Cornwall," granted to Mary Courtney, niece or grandchild ["nepti"] and next of kin. This admon. probably refers to Elizabeth, da. of Sir William Courtenay, wife of the 1st Bart. She, however, was a mother as early as, or earlier than 1600, and certainly left issue. It is possible (considering the date), that the admon. may refer to Elizabeth (Chichester), born 1607, wife of the 2d Bart.

(c) He is not the "Sir William Wray," who was one of seven persons, all of the Bishopric of Durham, who were Knighted there, 24 April 1617. That William was "of Beamish," and was *bur.* 1 Jan. 1628, at Tanfield, Durham.

(d) This lady brought the estate of Tawstock, near Barnstaple, in North Devon, to the Wrey family, which henceforth became their chief seat. She and her two sisters, on the death of their father, the Earl of Bath, 2 March 1636/7, became coheirs to the ancient Barony of Fitzwarine, *cr.* by writ, 1295. Of these two sisters, Elizabeth, COUNTESS OF DENBIGH, *d.* s.p. 22 Sep. 1670, while Dorothy *m.* (1) Thomas GREY *styled* LORD GREY OF GROBY, and (2) Gustavus Mackworth, and left issue.

1689 till death. He *m.*, 3 May 1681, at St. Giles' in the Wood, Florence, da. of Sir John ROLLE, K.B., of Marrais, and afterwards of Stevenstone, Devon, by Florence, 1st da. of Dennis ROLLE, of Stevenstone aforesaid. He was wounded in a duel with James Pound, in May, from the effects of which he *d.* 28 July, and was *bur.* 13 Aug. 1696, at Tawstock. Will, dat. 16 and 18 Aug. 1694, pr. 7 June 1697. His wife, living Aug. 1694, probably survived him.

V. 1696. SIR BOURCHIER WREY, Bart. [1628], of Tawstock Court aforesaid, s. and h.; *b.* about 1683; *suc. to the Baronetcy*, 28 July 1696; matric. at Oxford (Ch. Ch.), 12 July 1700, aged 17; M.P. for Camelford, 1712-13. He *m.*, 28 Feb. 1707/8, at St. Peter's, Cornhill, London (Lic. Fac.), his first cousin, Diana, widow of John SPARKE, of Plymouth, da. of John ROLLE, of Stevenstone aforesaid, by Christian, da. of Robert (BRUCE), 1st EARL OF AILESBURY. She was *bap.* 12 July 1683. He was *bur.* 12 Nov. 1726 at Tawstock.

VI. 1726. SIR BOURCHIER WREY, Bart. [1628], of Tawstock Court aforesaid, s. and h., *b.* about 1715; matric. at Oxford (New Coll.), 21 Oct. 1732, aged 17; *suc. to the Baronetcy* in Nov. 1726; M.P. for Barnstaple, 1749-54; Col. of the Devon Militia, 1759. He *m.* firstly, 1749, Mary, da. of John EDWARDS, of Highgate, Midx. She *d.* s.p., and was *bur.* 3 Sep. 1751 at Tawstock, aged 27. He *m.* secondly, 1 May 1755, at Chippenham, Ellen, da. of John THRESHER, of Bradford, Wilts (who *d.* 1741, aged 52), by Ellen, da. of Henry LONG, of Melksham, in that county. He *d.* 13, and was *bur.* 22 April 1784 at Tawstock, aged 69. Will pr. May 1784, and in Ireland 1787. His widow *d.* Nov. 1813. Will pr. 1814.

VII. 1784. SIR BOURCHIER WILLIAM WREY, Bart. [1628], of Tawstock Court aforesaid, s. and h. by 2d wife; *b.* 22 and *bap.* 23 Feb. 1757 at Tawstock; matric. at Oxford (New Coll.), 5 Nov. 1774, aged 17; Fellow of All Souls' College and, when such, B.A., 30 May 1782; M.A., 31 Oct. 1786; having *suc. to the Baronetcy* 13 April 1784. He *m.* firstly, 14 May 1786, at Shottesbrooke, Berks, Ann, da. of Sir Robert PALK, 1st Bart. [1782], by Anne, da. of Arthur VANSITTART. She *d.* Sep. 1791. He *m.* secondly, 1793, Anne, da. of John OSBORNE, of Alderley, co. Gloucester. He *d.* 20 Nov. 1826. Will pr. March 1827. His widow *d.* 26 Jan. 1816.

VIII. 1826. SIR BOURCHIER PALK WREY, Bart. [1628], of Tawstock Court aforesaid, s. and h. by 1st wife, *b.* 10 Dec. 1788, at Haldon House, near Exeter; matric. at Oxford (Oriel Coll.), 10 June 1807, aged 18; Barrister (Linc. Inn), 1815; *suc. to the Baronetcy*, 20 Nov. 1826. He *m.* firstly, 14 March 1818, at Christ Church, London, and again 10 July 1832, at St. Geo., Han. sq., Ellen Caroline RIDDLE, widow.(a) She *d.* s.p.m., 23 July 1842, aged 50, and was *bur.* at Tawstock. He *m.* secondly, 11 Sep. 1843, Eliza COLES, spinster. She *d.* s.p., 11 May 1875. He *d.* s.p.m.,(b) 11 Sep. 1879, at Quayfield House, Ilfracombe (of which place he was Lord of the Manor), and was *bur.* 18 at Tawstock, in his 91st year.

(a) In this last entry she is called "Ellen Caroline Wrey, formerly Riddle," the place and date of the previous marriage being recited, and it being added "doubts having arisen as to the validity of such marriage." In the *North Devon Journal*, 25 Sep. 1879 (quoting the *Western Times* for the 22 and 23 inst.), is a long account of the marriages of this Baronet. His first wife is stated to have been an Irish woman "of rare beauty, who bore the name of the widow Johnson, *née* Ellen O'Brien," and who was nurse to the eldest child of Mrs. Hartopp, his sister. The marriage of 1818 is said to have been in the belief of the death of the said Ellen's first husband, who had not been heard of for seven years. His existence, however, is said to have been afterwards discovered, as also that his name was not Johnson but Riddle: that he had "been a groom to Lord Adare," and that his death took place in 1826. The second wife is said to have been daughter of the lodge keeper at Tawstock and lady's maid to the first. There are, apparently, some inaccuracies in this newspaper account, as *e.g.*, that the first marriage in 1818 was "at St. Anne's, Holborn," the second one "at Brighton," etc.

(b) Ellen Caroline, his 1st daughter, and, eventually, sole heir, *b.* 1819, *m.* 9 Aug. 1838, Edward Joseph Weld, of Lulworth Castle, co. Dorset, and *d.* 13 Oct. 1866, leaving issue, among whom (if the said Ellen can be proved to have been legitimate) the coheirship of the Barony of Fitzwarine is vested.

IX. 1879. SIR HENRY BOURCHIER WREY, Bart. [1628], of Tawstock Court aforesaid, br. of the half blood, and h. male, being s. of the 7th Bart. by his 2d wife, *b.* at Tawstock Court, 5 June 1797. Ed. at Eton and at Ball. Coll., Oxford; matric. 11 May 1815; B.A., 28 Jan. 1819; M.A., 27 June 1821; in Holy Orders; Vicar of Okehampton, 1822; Rector of Tawstock, 1840-82; *suc. to the Baronetcy*, 11 Sep. 1879. He *m.* firstly, 27 Sep. 1827, Ellen Maria, only da. of Nicholas Roundell TOKE, of Godington, Kent. She *d.* 1 March 1864. He *m.* secondly, 5 Jan. 1865, Jane, widow of John STEAVENSON, of Newcastle-on-Tyne, da. of H. LAMB, of Ryton House, co. Durham. He *d.* 23 Dec. 1882, aged 85, at Corffe, near Barnstaple. His widow *d.* 26 July, 1889, aged 76.

X. 1882. SIR HENRY BOURCHIER TOKE WREY, Bart. [1628], of Tawstock Court aforesaid, 1st s. and h., *b.* 27 June 1829, at Sandgate, co. Kent; matric. at Oxford (Trinity Coll.), 3 Nov. 1847, aged 18; B.A. 1851; sometime Capt. and Hon. Major 4th Batt. of the Devonshire Regiment of Militia; *suc. to the Baronetcy*, 23 Dec. 1882; Sheriff of Devon, 1891. He *m.*, 6 July 1854, Marianna Sarah, da. and h. of Philip Castell (SHERARD), 9th BARON SHERARD OF LEITRIM [I.], by Anne, da. of Nathaniel WEEKES, of Barbadoes. She *d.*, 16 Feb. 1896, at Tawstock Court, aged 68. He *d.* 10 March 1900 at Ventnor, Isle of Wight, aged 70. Will pr. at £155,838, the net personalty being £54,253.

XI. 1900. SIR ROBERT BOURCHIER SHERARD WREY, Bart. [1628], of Tawstock Court aforesaid, 1st s. and h., *b.* 23 May 1855; served in the Royal Navy; Lieut., 1879; Com., 1894; served with distinction in the Zulu war, 1879; in the Egyptian campaign, 1882, and in Burmah, 1885-86; *suc. to the Baronetcy*, 10 March 1900.

Family Estates. These, in 1883, consisted of 7,393 acres in Devon, 373 in Cornwall and 220 in Dorset. *Total*, 7,985 acres, worth £9,269 a year. "By the late Baronet's will the Ilfracombe estate is gone to Mr. Weld of Lulworth" [note in Bateman's "Great Landowners," edit. 1883.] *Principal seat.*—Tawstock Court, near Barnstaple, North Devon.

TRELAWNY:

cr. 1 July 1628;

afterwards, since 1802, SALUSBURY-TRELAWNY.

I. 1628. "JOHN TRELAWNY, of Trelawny, co. Cornwall, Esq.," s. and h. of Sir Jonathan TRELAWNY, of the same, sometime Sheriff and M.P. for that county, by Elizabeth, 2d da. of Sir Henry KILLIGREW, was *b.* at Hall 24 April, and *bap.* 7 May 1592, at Fowey, Cornwall; suc. his father 21 June 1604; matric. at Oxford (Merton Coll.), 23 Oct. 1607, aged 15; opposed the validity of the election of Sir John Eliot as M.P. for Cornwall, and was accordingly committed to the Tower by the House of Commons, 13 May 1628; was released by the King, 26 and *Knighted*(a) 29 June 1628, at Whitehall, being, three days afterwards, *cr. a Bart.*, as above, 1 July 1627; Sheriff of Cornwall, 1630-31; was (with his son) a Compounder, May 1649. He *m.* firstly, in or before 1617, Elizabeth, da. of Sir Reginald Mohun, 1st Bart. [1611], of Boconnoc, by Philippa, da. of Sir John HELE. She, who was *bap.* 10 Feb. 1593, at St. Pinnock, was living Jan. 1639. He *m.* secondly, Douglas, widow of Sir William COURTENAY, of Saltash, da. and coheir of Tristram GORGES, of Budockshead. She, who was *bap.* 13 Sep. 1586 at Budeaux, *d.* in or before 1660. Admon. 1 Oct. 1660. He was *bur.* 16 Feb. 1664, at Pelynt.

II. 1664. SIR JONATHAN TRELAWNY, Bart. 1628, of Trelawny aforesaid, s. and h. by 1st wife; *b.* about 1623; matric. at Oxford (Ex. Coll.), 14 Dec. 1640, aged 17; was fined (with his father) £629, in May 1649; Gent. of the Privy Chamber, 1660; *suc. to the Baronetcy*, 26 Feb. 1664; M.P. for East Looe, 1660; for Cornwall, 1661-78; for East Looe, again, 1678-79 and for Liskeard, 1679-81. He is said(b) to have been "sequestered, imprisoned, and ruined for loyalty during the Civil War." He *m.* Mary, 6th da. of Sir Edward SEYMOUR, 2d

---

(a) It will be observed, however, that he was not described as a Knight in the patent of Baronetcy.

(b) *Dict. Nat. Biogr.*

Bart. [1611], by Dorothy, da. of Sir Henry KILLIGREW abovenamed. She was *bap.* 19 Dec. 1619, at Berry Pomeroy. He was *bur.* 5 March 1680/1, at Pelynt. Will dat. 30 Dec. 1680, pr. 9 April 1681, in Archd. Court of Cornwall.

III. 1681. SIR JONATHAN TRELAWNY, Bart. [1628], of Trelawny aforesaid, 3d but eldest surv. s. and h.;(a) ; *b.* at Pelynt [*Qy.* if not at Coldrinick], 24 March 1650 ; ed. at Westm. School ; matric. at Oxford (Ex. Coll.), 5 Aug. 1668, aged 18 ; Student of Ch. Ch., 1669 ; B.A., 22 June 1672 ; M.A., 29 April 1665 ; took Holy Orders, 4 Sep. 1673 ; Rector of St. Ives and Vicar of Southill, co. Cornwall, 1677-89. He *suc. to the Baronetcy* in March 1680/1 ; distinguished himself in his opposition to Monmouth's rebellion in 1685, and was, in that year, made BISHOP OF BRISTOL, being, as such, one of the seven Bishops committed to the Tower, 8 June 1688, by James II,(b) and one of the two out of those seven who took the oaths to William and Mary. He accordingly was made BISHOP OF EXETER in 1689 (the Archdeaconry of Totnes, 1693—1694, and that of Exeter, 1704-1707, being added "*in commendam*") and finally, 1707-1721, BISHOP OF WINCHESTER. He *m.* in 1684, Rebecca, da. and coheir of Thomas HELE, of Bascombe, by Elizabeth, da. and coheir of Matthew HALS, of Efford, both in co. Devon. She, by whom he had 12 children, *d.* 11 Feb. 1710. He *d.* at Chelsea 19 July and was *bur.* 10 Aug. 1721, with his ancestors, at Pelynt, aged 71. Admon. 6 Dec. 1721.

IV. 1721. SIR JOHN TRELAWNY, Bart. [1628], of Trelawny aforesaid, s. and h., *b.* about 1691, at Trelawny ; matric. at Oxford (Ch. Ch.), 26 Jan. 1707/8, aged 16 ; M.P. for West Looe, April to Aug. 1713 and 1713-15 ; for Liskeard, 1715-22, for West Looe, again, 1722-27, and for East Looe, 1727-34 ; *suc. to the Baronetcy*, 19 July, 1721. He *m.* Agnes, da. of (—) BLACKWOOD, of (—), in Scotland. He *d.* s.p., 1756. Will dat. 23 Feb. to 26 Nov. 1754, pr. 9 March 1756. His widow *d.* in Edinburgh, 8 April 1777.

V. 1756. SIR HARRY TRELAWNY, Bart. [1628], of Trelawny aforesaid, cousin and h. male, being s. and h. of Henry TRELAWNY, of Whitleigh, co. Devon, by his 1st wife, Rebecca, da. and coheir of the abovenamed Matthew HALS, of Efford aforesaid, which Henry, who was Brig. General in the Army, and Governor of Plymouth, and who *d.* 1702, was 7th s. of the 2d Bart. He was *bap.* 15 Feb. 1687, at Egg Buckland ; matric. at Oxford 19 Jan. 1702/3, aged 15 ; was sometime *Aide-de-Camp* to the Duke of Marlborough ; M.P. for East Looe, 1708-10 ; *suc. to the Baronetcy*, 1756. He *m.* in or before 1720, his cousin(c) Lætitia, da. (whose

(a) John Trelawny, the eldest son, *d.* s.p. and v.p. in 1680.

(b) The feeling roused by this arbitrary act is well set forth in a spirited poem by the Rev. Robert Stephen Hawker (41 years Vicar of Morwenstow, Cornwall, *d.* 15 Aug. 1875, aged 70), entitled "*The Song of the Western Men*," who (the head of one of their leading families, being a prisoner) may naturally be supposed to have been especially affected. It commences as below—

"A good sword and a trusty hand,
A merry heart and true,
King James's men shall understand
What CORNISH LADS can do.
And have they fixed the Where and When,
And shall TRELAWNY die?
Then twenty thousand Cornish men
Will know the reason why!
What! will they scorn TRE, POL and PEN?
And shall TRELAWNY die?
Then twenty thousand underground
Will know the reason why!"

The whole of this long passed for an original song dating from 1688, and its author (when he declared himself) states from local tradition that the *refrain* ["And shall Trelawny die," etc.] was so, but "Hawker's testimony is not quite conclusive. There is some ground for believing that the cry was first raised in 1628, owing to the fears of Cornishmen for the life of Sir John Trelawny, 1st Bart., *at the hands of the House of Commons*" [*Dict. Nat. Biogr.*].

(c) Their ten years' courtship is recounted in the "Love Letters of Myrtilla and Philander, 1706-36." The match was opposed by the bride's father.

issue became coheir) of Sir Jonathan TRELAWNY, 3d Bart., by Rebecca, da. and coheir of Thomas HELE. He d. s.p.m.s., 7 April 1762, aged about 75. His widow was *bur.* 6 June 1775, at Egg Buckland. Will pr. June 1775.

VI. 1762. SIR WILLIAM TRELAWNY, Bart. [1628], of Trelawny aforesaid, nephew and h. male, being s. and h. of William TRELAWNY, Capt. in the Army (*bap.* 13 Nov. 1696, at St. Margaret's, Westm.), who was br. to the last Bart. He, who was sometime of Budshed, in St. Budeaux, co. Devon, was a Capt. R.N. ; was M.P. for West Looe, May 1757-61 and 1761-67 ; *suc. to the Baronetcy*, 7 April 1762, and was appointed Governor of Jamaica, 1767. He *m.*, in or before 1756, his cousin Lætitia, da. and sole h. of Sir Harry TRELAWNY, 5th Bart., by Lætitia, da. of Sir Jonathan TRELAWNY, 3d Bart., BISHOP OF WINCHESTER. She, who was *bap.* 16 June 1728, at St. Budeaux, *d.* 24 Aug. 1772. He *d.* in Spanish town, Jamaica, 11 and was honoured with a public funeral there (costing 1,000 guineas) 13 Dec. 1772. Will pr. May 1773.

VII. 1772. SIR HARRY TRELAWNY, Bart. [1628], of Trelawny aforesaid, only s. and heir ; *b.* at Budshed and *bap.* 26 June 1756, at St. Budeaux ; ed. at Westminster ; *suc. to the Baronetcy*, 11 Dec. 1772 ; matric. at Oxford (Ch. Ch.), 2 July 1773, aged 17 ; B.A., 1776 ; M.A., 1781 ; joined the Methodists soon after 1776, and subsequently the Calvinists. He, however, subsequently took Holy Orders in the Church of England ; was Preb. of Exeter, 1789, Vicar of St. Austell, 1791, and of Egloshayle, Cornwall, 1793. He *m.*, 28 Feb. 1778, Anne, da. of Rev. James BROWN, Rector of Portishead and Vicar of Kingston, Somerset. She *d.* 18 Nov. 1822. He *d.* 24 Feb. 1834, at Laveno in Italy (having, apparently, become a Roman Catholic), aged 77. Will pr. June 1834.

VIII. 1834. SIR WILLIAM LEWIS SALUSBURY-TRELAWNY, Bart. [1628], of Trelawny aforesaid, s. and h. ; *b.* at Runcorn, Cheshire, 4 July 1781 ; ed. at Westm. ; matric. at Oxford (Oriel Coll.) 18 Feb. 1799, aged 17. By royal lic., 11 Dec. 1802, he took the name of *Salusbury* before that of *Trelawny*, under the will of his cousin Owen SALUSBURY-BRERETON ; was Sheriff of Cornwall, 1811-12 ; M.P. for East Cornwall, 1832-1837 ; *suc. to the Baronetcy*, 24 Feb. 1834 ; L. Lieut. of Cornwall, 1840, and subsequently Custos Rotulorum. He *m.*, 24 Aug. 1807, Patience Christian, da. of John Phillips CARPENTER, of Mount Tavy, Devon. He *d.* 15 Nov. 1856 at Harewood, near Tavistock, Devon. Will pr. Jan. 1857. His widow *d.* 20 June 1857. Will pr. July, 1857.

IX. 1856. SIR JOHN-SALUSBURY SALUSBURY-TRELAWNY, Bart. [1628], of Trelawny aforesaid, s. and h. ; *b.* 2 June 1816, at Harewood aforesaid ; ed. at Westm. and at Trin. Coll., Cambridge : B.A. 1839 ; Barrister (Mid. Temple), 1841 ; M.P. for Tavistock, 1843—1852, and 1857—1865 ; for East Cornwall, 1868—1874 ; sometime (1840) Capt. Royal Rangers and Dep. Warden of the Stannaries. He *m.* firstly, 25 Jan. 1842, at St. Ewe, Cornwall, Harriet Jane, 1st da. of John Hearle TREMAYNE, of Heligan, in that county. She *d.* 5 Nov. 1879. He *m.* secondly, 19 May 1881, "in London," Harriet Jacqueline, widow of Col. E. G. W. KEPPEL, 5th and yst. da. of Sir Anthony BULLER, of Pound, co. Devon, Judge of the Supreme Court of Bengal, by Isabella Jane, da. of Sir William LEMON, 1st Bart. [1774]. He *d.* 4 Aug. 1885, in his 70th year. Will pr. 5 Feb. 1886, over £7,000. His widow living 1900.

X. 1885. SIR WILLIAM LEWIS SALUSBURY-TRELAWNY, Bart. [1628], of Trelawny aforesaid, only s. and h., by 1st wife ; *b.* 26 Aug. 1844, at the Royal Clarence Baths, Devonport ; ed. at Eton and at Trin. Coll., Cambridge ; sometime Capt. Royal Cornwall Rangers Militia ; *suc. to the Baronetcy*, 4 Aug. 1885 ; Sheriff of Cornwall, 1895. He *m.* firstly, 14 July 1868, Jessy Rose Mary, only da. of John MURRAY, of Philipshaugh. She *d.* 23 Nov. 1871. He *m.* secondly, 17 Dec. 1872, at Morval, co. Cornwall, Harriet Buller, 1st da. of the Rev. James Buller KITSON, Vicar of Morval.

Family Estates.—These, in 1883, consisted of 8,000 acres in Cornwall, valued at £6,000 a year. *Principal seat.*—Trelawne [or Trelawny], near Liskeard, co. Cornwall.

CONYERS, *or* CONNIERS:

cr. 14 July 1628 ;

ex. 15 April 1810.

I. 1628. "JOHN CONNIERS, of Norden [*i.e.*, Horden], in the Bishopric of Durham, gent.," s. and h. of Christopher CONYERS, of the same, by his 2d wife Anne (*m.* 4 Nov. 1586), da. of Sir Ralph HEDWORTH, of Harraton, co. Durham, was *cr. a Bart.*, as above, 14 July 1628. In Aug. 1648, he was fined £651. He *m.*, about 1606, Frances, da. of Thomas GROVES, citizen of York. He was *bur.* 6 Dec. 1664, at Easington, co. Durham.

II. 1664. SIR CHRISTOPHER CONYERS, Bart. [1628], of Horden aforesaid, 2d but 1st surv. s. and h., *bap.* 28 March 1621, at Easington ; admitted to Gray's Inn (with his elder br. Richard Conyers), 12 Feb. 1637/8 ; *suc. to the Baronetcy*, in Dec. 1664. He *m.* firstly, 28 Sep. 1648 at Long Ditton, Surrey, (Lic. Fac.), Elizabeth (then of Putney, Surrey, aged 19), da. of William LANGHORNE, of London, merchant, and sister (whose issue became heir) of Sir William LANGHORNE, Bart. [1668]. She *d.* in childbed, 27 April, and was *bur.* 1 May 1654, at St. Giles' in the Fields, Midx. M.I. He *m.* secondly (Lic. Fac. 3 Nov. 1666), Julia, widow of Alexander JERMYN, of Lordington, Sussex, da. of Richard (LUMLEY), 1st VISCOUNT LUMLEY OF WATERFORD [I.], by Frances, da. of Henry SHELLEY. He *d.* Oct. 1693. Will pr. March 1706.

III. 1693. SIR JOHN CONYERS, Bart. [1628], of Horden aforesaid, only s. and h., by 1st wife ; *b.* about 1649 ; matric. at Oxford (New Inn Hall), 14 Dec. 1666, aged 17 ; *suc. to the Baronetcy* in Oct. 1693. He, in Feb. 1714, inherited the estate of Charlton, Kent, and other estates from his uncle, the said Sir William Langhorne, Bart. He *m.* (Lic. Vic. Gen. 9 Nov. 1675, he about 26, she about 22), Mary, 1st da. and coheir of Edward NEWMAN, of Folkesworth, Norman Cross, near Peterborough, by Christian, da. of (—) MATTHEWS. By her he acquired the estate of Baldwins in Great Stoughton, co. Huntingdon. She was *bap.* 1 Sep. 1647, at Folkesworth, and *d.* 24 Oct. 1714, aged 67. He *d.* 14 Sep. 1719, aged 75. Both *bur.* at Great Stoughton. M.I. His will pr. 1720.

IV. 1719. SIR BALDWIN CONYERS, Bart. [1628], of Horden and Great Stoughton aforesaid, only surv. s. and h. ; *b.* about 1681 ; *suc. to the Baronetcy*, 14 Sep. 1719. He *m.* firstly, in or before 1710, Sarah, only da. and h. of Edward CONYERS, of Blaston, co. Leicester, by whom he acquired the manor of Bradley in that county. He *m.* secondly, Margaret, 1st da. and coh. of Henry NEVILL, *otherwise* SMITH, of Holt, co. Leicester, by Margaret, da. of George NAPIER, of Holywell, Oxon. He *d.* s.p.m.s.,(a) 17 April 1731, in 51st year, and was *bur.* at Great Stoughton. M.I. Will pr. 1731.(b) His widow living 1741. Her will pr. Jan. 1758.

V. 1731. SIR RALPH CONYERS, Bart. [1628], of Chester le street, co. Durham, cousin and h. male, being s. and h. of John Conyers, of Chester le street aforesaid, who is stated to have been s. of John Conyers [*bap.* at Easington 20 Sep. 1622, and *d.* 1687], who was 2d s. of the 1st Bart. He was *bap.* 20 June 1697 at Chester le street, in which town he was afterwards a glazier, and *suc. to the Baronetcy*, 17 April 1731, but to none of the family estates. He *m.*, about 1726, Jane, da. of Nicholas Blakiston, of Shieldsrow, co. Durham, by Jane, da. of (—) PORTER, which Nicholas was br. to Sir Ralph Blakiston, *cr. a Bart.* 1642. He *d.* 22 Nov. 1767.(c) His widow living 1771.

(a) His only son, John, *d.* 4 Sep. 1729 in his 19th year.

(b) The estate of Horden was sold by his daughters and coheirs to Rowland BURDON, while that of Charlton in Kent, went (according to an entail) to the family of GAMES, and afterwards to that of MARYON, whence it descended to that of Wilson, afterwards Maryon-Wilson.

(c) In the *Chronicon Mirabile* there is an entry of the burial of "Sir Ralph Conyers, Bart.," 19 Aug. 1751, at Chester le Street. *Query*, if this is correct, and if the date of 22 Nov. 1767 (as given in the text) is an error.

VI. 1767. SIR BLAKISTON CONYERS, Bart. [1628], s. and h., Captain of the Marines, 1757, and Collector of the Customs at Newcastle ; *suc. to the Baronetcy*, 22 Nov. 1767. He *d.* unm. Oct. 1791.

VII. 1791. SIR NICHOLAS CONYERS, Bart. [1628], br. and h., *bap.* 27 July 1729, at Chester le Street; sometime Comptroller of the Customs at Glasgow ; *suc. to the Baronetcy*, in Oct. 1791. He *m.* (—). He *d.* s.p. 1796. His widow *m.* (—) CAMPBELL.

VIII. 1796. SIR GEORGE CONYERS, Bart. [1628], s. and h., *suc. to the Baronetcy* in 1796. He, who is said to have "squandered" his fortune "in scenes of the lowest dissipation,"(a) *d.* s.p.

IX. 1800? to 1810. SIR THOMAS CONYERS, Bart. [1628], uncle and h., *bap.* 12 Sep. 1731, at Chester le Street, *suc. to the Baronetcy* on the death of his nephew. He *m.* Isabel, da. of James LAMBTON, of Whitehall, co. Durham. He *d.* s.p.m., in great indigence, at Chester le Street, where for many years he had been in the workhouse,(a) 15 April 1810, aged 79, when the *Baronetcy* became *extinct.*

BOLLES, *or* BOLLE:

cr. 24 July 1628 ;

ex. 23 Dec. 1714.

I. 1628. "JOHN BOLLES, of Scumpton [*i.e.*, Scampton], co. Lincoln, Esq.," s. and h. of Sir George BOLLES, *or* BOLLE,(b) sometime [1617-18], L. Mayor of London, by Joan, da. and coheir of Sir John HART, of Scampton aforesaid, sometime [1588-89], L. Mayor of London ; was *b.* about 1680, and *bap.* at St. Swithin's, London ; suc. his father 1 Sep. 1621 ; was Sheriff of Lincolnshire, 1626-27, and was *cr. a Bart.*, as above, 24 July 1628. He *m.*, in or before 1612, Katharine, 1st da. and eventually coheir of Thomas CONYERS, of Brodham, co. Lincoln, and of East Barnet, Herts. She *d.* 20 and was *bur.* 21 Sep. 1644, at Scampton, aged 55. He *d.* 8 and was *bur.* there 9 March 1647/8, aged 67. M.I. Will. pr. 1651.

II. 1648. SIR ROBERT BOLLES, Bart. [1628], of Scampton aforesaid, 3d but 1st surv. s. and h. ; *bap.* there 11 April 1619 ; was fined £1,500 in Jan. 1646 ; *suc. to the Baronetcy*, 9 March 1647/8 ; was, in 1661, one of the Grand Jury for trying the Regicides ; M.P. for Lincoln, 1661 till death ; a munificent patron of the fine arts and literature. He *m.* 14 Oct. 1637, at Honington, co. Lincoln, Mary, da. of Sir Edward HUSSEY, 1st Bart. [1611], by Elizabeth, da. of George ANTON. He *d.* 3 Aug. 1663, aged 44, and was *bur.* (by torch light) at St. Swithin's, London. Will dat. 8 to 14 July 1663, pr. 22 March 1663/4, at Lincoln. His widow, who was *bap.* 16 July 1617, at Honington, was *bur.* 30 Nov. 1672, at St. Swithin's aforesaid. Will pr. 1672.

III. 1663. SIR JOHN BOLLES, Bart. [1628], of Scampton aforesaid, s. and h., *bap.* there 21 June 1641 ; *suc. to the Baronetcy*, 3 Aug. 1663.(c) He *m.* firstly, 3 Dec. 1663, at St. Andrew's, Holborn (Lic. Vic.-Gen., he 23 and she 20), Elizabeth, da. and coheir of John PYNSENT, of that parish, Prothonotary of the Common Pleas. She *d.*, s.p.m., and was *bur.* 9 Sep. 1664, at St. Swithin's. He *m.* secondly, May 1667, Elizabeth, 1st da. of Sir Vincent CORBET, 1st Bart. [1642], by Sarah, *suo jure* VISCOUNTESS CORBET, da. of Sir Robert MONSON. She *d.*

(a) See Burke's *Vicissitudes of Families*, 2nd Series, pp. 1-29, for an account of these Baronets. The names of the husbands ("all working men in the little town of Chester le Street") of the three daughters of the last Bart. are there given.

(b) See "anecdotes of the family of Bolles," in Illingworth's *Scampton, co. Lincoln* [4to, 1808], where in some few copies is a folding tabular pedigree.

(c) In Sir Joseph Williamson's account of "*Lincolnshire Families, temp. Car. II,*" his estates there and in Yorkshire are estimated at £3,000 a year. [*Her. and Gen.*, vol. ii, p. 120.]

at St. Andrew's, Holborn, and was *bur.* 8 Aug. 1676, at St. Swithin's aforesaid. Admon. 18 Aug. 1676. He *d.* 3 and was *bur.* there 8 March 1685/6. Will dat. 23 Feb. 1680, pr. March 1687.

IV. 1686, to 1714. SIR JOHN BOLLES, Bart. [1628], of Scampton aforesaid, only surv. s. and h., by 2d wife; *b.* July 1669; matric. at Oxford (Ch. Ch.), 23 Jan. 1682/3, aged 13; admitted to Gray's Inn, 1680; *suc. to the Baronetcy*, 3 March 1685/6; M.P. for Lincoln (in five Parls.) 1690—1702. He is said to have lived in great state. He *d.* unm. 23 Dec. 1714, aged 44, and was *bur.* at St. Swithin's aforesaid, when the *Baronetcy* became *extinct*. Admon. 29 Jan. 1714/5, to his [only] sister Sarah Bolle.(a)

ASTON:

cr. 25 July, 1628;

ex. 22 March 1815.

I. 1628. "THOMAS ASTON, of Aston [in the parish of Runcorn], co. Chester, Esq.," s. and h. of John Aston, of the same (Server to Anne, Queen of James I), by Maud, da. of Robert NEEDHAM, of Shavington, Salop (which John was s. and h. of Sir Thomas Aston, of Aston aforesaid), was *b.* 29 Sep. 1600 in Shropshire; suc. his father 13 May 1615; matric. at Oxford (Bras. Coll.), 28 March 1617, aged 16; B.A. 8 July 1619; admitted to Lincoln's Inn, 1620; and was *cr. a Bart.*, as above, 25 July 1628. He was Sheriff of Cheshire, 1635-36; M.P. thereof, April to May 1640; Captain of a troop of Horse, which he raised for the service of Charles I, being a zealous supporter of the Crown. He was defeated by Sir William Brereton, the Parliamentary General, near Nantwich, 28 Jan. 1642; made a prisoner soon afterwards and brought to Stafford, where he died, in consequence of a blow received when attempting to escape from prison. He *m.* firstly, in 1627, Magdalen, sister and coheir of John POULTENEY, of Misterton, co. Leicester, da. of Sir John POULTENEY, of the same. She *d.*, s.p.s., 2 June 1635, and was *bur.* at Aston. M.I. Admon. 30 June 1636, to her husband. He *m.* secondly, in 1639, Anne, widow of the Hon. Anchitel GREY, da. and coheir of Sir Henry WILLOUGHBY, Bart. [so *cr.* 1611], of Risley, co. Derby, being sole heir of his first wife Elizabeth, da. and coheir of Henry KNOLLYS. He *d.* at Stafford (as abovesaid), 24 March 1645/6, and was *bur.* at Aston. Will pr. 1668. His widow *d.* 2 June 1688, aged 74, and was *bur.* (with her father) at Wilne, co. Derby.

II. 1646. SIR WILLOUGHBY ASTON, Bart. [1628], of Aston aforesaid, s. and h., by 2d wife; *b.* 5 July 1640; *suc. to the Baronetcy*, 24 March 1645/6; aged 22 in 1662; Sheriff of Cheshire, 1680-81 and 1690-91. He built a magnificent mansion at Aston, a short distance from the old residence. He *m.*, in or before 1665, Mary, da. of John OFFLEY, of Madeley, co. Stafford, by Mary, da. of Thomas BROUGHTON, of Broughton, in that county. He *d.* 14 Dec. 1702, and was *bur.* at Aston. M.I. His widow, who was *b.* 3 Feb. 1649/50, and by whom he had eight sons and thirteen daughters, *d.* 22 Jan. 1711/2, and was *bur.* at Aston. M.I.

III. 1702. SIR THOMAS ASTON, Bart. [1628], of Aston aforesaid, s. and h.; *b.* 17 Jan. 1665/6; *suc. to the Baronetcy*, 14 Dec. 1702; Sheriff of Cheshire, 1723. He *m.* (Lic. Lond. 22 Oct. 1703, he 30 and she 25), Catharine, yst. da. and coheir of William WIDDRINGTON. He *d.* 16 Jan. 1724/5, and was *bur.* at Aston. M.I. Will, dat. 6 Feb. 1723/4, proved 8 Dec. 1725. His widow, who was *b.* Nov. 1676, *d.* 10 April 1752, and was *bur.* at Aston. M.I. Will pr. May 1752.

IV. 1725. SIR THOMAS ASTON, Bart. [1628], of Aston aforesaid, only s. and h.; *b.* about 1705; matric. at Oxford (Corp. Christi Coll.), 1 March 1721/2, aged 17; *suc. to the Baronetcy*, 16 Jan. 1724/5; was M.P. for Liverpool, May 1729 to 1734, and for St. Albans, 1734-41. He *m.*, March

(a) She *d.* unm. 7 Nov. 1746, when the Scampton estate devolved on his coheirs (descendants of the 2d Bart.), who in 1749 sold it to William Cayley.

1735/6, Rebecca, da. of John SHISHE, of Greenwich, Kent. She, who was *b.* 25 Nov. 1717, *d.* 16 May 1737, and was *bur.* at Aston. M.I. He *d.* s.p., in France, and was *bur.* at Aston, 17 Feb. 1743/4.(a) Admon. 11 May 1744, to mother, Dame Catharine Aston, widow.

V. 1744. SIR WILLOUGHBY ASTON, Bart. [1628], of Risley, co. Derby aforesaid, cousin and h., being s. and h. of Richard ASTON, of Wadley, Berks, by Elizabeth, da. of John WARREN, of Wantage, in that county, and of Priory Court, Oxon, which Richard (who *d.* 24 Nov. 1741), was 6th s. of the 2d Bart. He was *b.* about 1715; matric. at Oxford 7 Jan. 1729/30 (Oriel Coll.); B.A. (All Souls' Coll.), 14 Jan. 1735; M.A., 20 Oct. 1739; admitted to Linc. Inn, 19 Nov. 1731; *suc. to the Baronetcy*, 17 Feb. 1743/4. He was M.P. for Nottingham 1754-61; Col. of the Berkshire Militia 1759. He *m.* 14 May 1744, at St. Geo. the Martyr, Midx., Elizabeth, 4th da. of Henry PYE, of Farringdon, Berks, by Anne, sister of Allen, 1st EARL BATHURST, da. of Sir Benjamin BATHURST. He *d.* 24 and was *bur.* 27 Aug. 1772, at Bath Abbey.

VI. 1772, to 1815. SIR WILLOUGHBY ASTON, Bart. [1628], of Risley aforesaid, only s. and h., *b.* about 1748, *suc. to the Baronetcy*, 24 Aug. 1772. He *m.* Jane, 3d da. of Robert (HENLEY), 1st EARL OF NORTHINGTON (Lord Chancellor, 1761-66), by Jane, da. of Sir John HUBAND. He *d.* s.p., 22 March 1815, aged 67, when the *Baronetcy* became *extinct*. Admon. April 1815. The will of his widow pr. Feb. 1823.

JENOURE:

cr. 30 July 1628;

ex. 15 Aug. 1755.

I. 1628. "KENELM JENOURE of [Bygotts in] Much Dunmowe, co. Essex, Esq.," s. and h. of Andrew JENOURE, of the same, by Crysogona, da. and h. of Thomas SMITH, of Campden, co. Gloucester, suc. his father in Dec. 1622; was *cr. a Bart*, as above, 30 July 1628. He *m.* Jane, da. of Sir Robert CLARKE, Baron of the Exchequer [1587-1607], by Margaret (relict of Sir Edward OSBORNE), daughter of John MAYNARD. He *d.* in 1629. Will dat. 25 Aug. and pr. 30 Oct. 1629. His widow living 1640.

II. 1629. SIR ANDREW JENOURE, Bart, [1628], of Great Dunmow aforesaid, s. and h., *suc. to the Baronetcy* in 1629. He *m.* firstly, in or before 1632, Margaret, da. of Richard SMITH, of Strixton, co. Northampton, Citizen of London. She d. s.p. He *m.* secondly, 4 March 1678/9, at Roxwell, Essex, Mary, da of Sir John BRAMSTON, K.B., of Skreens in that parish, by Alice, da. of Anthony ABDY, Alderman of London. His will dat. 26 Feb. 1690, pr. 9 April 1692 in the Archdeaconry of Middlesex. His widow, who was *b.* 15 Aug. 1638, *d.* s.p. 17 and was *bur.* 22 Aug. 1692 at Roxwell. Her will, as of St. Ann's, Westm., dat. 12 Aug. and pr. 3 Sep. 1692 by her father abovenamed.

III. 1692? SIR MAYNARD JENOURE, Bart. [1628], of Great Dunmow aforesaid, grandson and h., being s. and h. of Andrew JENOURE, by Sarah, da. of Robert MILBORN of Markshall, in Dunmow aforesaid, which Andrew was s. and h. ap. of the 1st Bart by his first wife. He was *b.* about 1667, and *suc. to the Baronetcy* about 1692. He *m.* (Lic. Vic.-Gen., 19 June 1693, he above 21, she about 17) Elizabeth, only da. of Sir John MARSHALL, of Sculpons in Finchingfield, Essex, by Dorothy, da. and coheir of John MEAD of the same.

(a) He devised Aston Hall and other estates to his eldest sister Catherine, wife of Rev. the Hon. Henry Hervey, D.D., who took the name of *Aston*, after that of *Hervey*, by Act. of Parl., and in whose descendants they still continue.

IV. 1710? SIR JOHN JENOURE, Bart. [1628], s. and h., *suc. to the Baronetcy*, on the death of his father. He *m.* Joan, da. and sole h. of Richard DAY, of Northweald, Essex. He *d.* 28 April 1739. Will pr. 1743. Admon. of his widow, as of Great Easton, co. Essex, granted 1 Dec. 1764 to John Reeve, cousin and next of kin.

V. 1739. SIR RICHARD DAY JENOURE, Bart. [1628], s. and h., *b.* about 1718; *suc. to the Baronetcy*, 17 April 1739; admitted to Linc. Inn 19 Jan. 1740/1. He *d.* s.p. 23 March 1743/4, aged 26. Will pr. 1744.

VI. 1744, to 1755. SIR JOHN JENOURE, Bart, 1628], cousin and h. male,(a) being s. and h. of Joseph JENOURE, Surveyor Gen. of South Carolina (1731) by Anne, da. of John SANDFORD, of Bishops Stortford, which Joseph was 3d s. of the 3d Bart. He, who was sometime a Capt. in the Guards, *suc. to the Baronetcy* 23 March 1743/4. He *d.* s.p. (probably unm.) 15 Aug. 1755, when the *Baronetcy* became *extinct*. Will pr. 1755.

PRYCE, *or* PRICE:

cr. 15 Aug. 1628;

ex. 28 June 1791.

I. 1628. "JOHN PRYCE of Newtowne, co. Montgomery, Esq.," s. and h. of Edward PRYCE, of the same, by Julian, da. of John VAUGHAN, of Llwydyarth in the same county, was *cr. a Bart* as above, 15 Aug. 1628. He was M.P. for Montgomeryshire, Nov. 1640, till disabled in Oct. 1645; re-elected 1654-55; was Gov. of Montgomery Castle, 1643-45 for the Parl., but was accused of intending to betray his trust, his estate being accordingly sequestrated, though freed therefrom 31 March 1652. He *m.* Catharine, da. of Sir Richard PRYSE, of Gogerddan, co. Cardigan, by Gwenllian, da. and h. of Thomas PRYSE, of Aberbychan, co. Montgomery. He *d.* in or before 1657. Admon. 16 Nov. 1657.

II. 1657? SIR MATTHEW PRYCE, Bart. [1628], of Newtown aforesaid, only surv. s. and h.(b), *suc. to the Baronetcy*, in or before 1657. He *m.* in or before 1661, Jane, da. of Henry Vaughan, of Kilkenain, co. Cardigan. Will pr. 1674.

III. 1674? SIR JOHN PRYCE, Bart. [1628], of Newtown aforesaid, s. and h., *b.* about 1662; *suc. to the Baronetcy* on his father's death; matric. at Oxford (Ch. Ch.), 3 May 1679, aged 17; Sheriff of Montgomeryshire, March to April 1689. He *m.* (Lic. Fac. 30 June 1680, he about 20), Anna Maria, da. of Sir Edmund Warcup, of Northmore, Oxon. He *d.* s.p.m.s. in 1699. Will dat. 19 June and pr. 17 Nov. 1699. That of his widow pr. 1732.

IV. 1699. SIR VAUGHAN PRYCE, Bart. [1628], of Newtown aforesaid, br. and h. male, admitted to Gray's Inn 14 Jan. 1680/1; *suc. to the Baronetcy* in 1699; Sheriff of Montgomeryshire 1708-09. He *m.* Ann, sister to Sir Thomas POWELL, Bart. [so *cr.* 1698] da. of Sir John POWELL, of Broadway, near Laugharne, co. Carmarthen, one of the Justices of the Court of King's Bench. He *d.* about 1720. Will pr. Nov. 1720. That of his widow pr. Oct. 1723.

V. 1720? SIR JOHN PRYCE, Bart. [1628], of Newtown aforesaid, s. and h., *suc. to the Baronetcy* about 1720; Sheriff of Montgomeryshire, 1748-49. He *m.* firstly Elizabeth, da. and eventually sole h. of the said Sir Thomas POWELL, Bart. [so *cr.* 1698], by Judith, da. and h. of Sir James HERBERT, of Colebrook, co. Monmouth. She *d.* 22 April 1731 in her 33d year and was *bur.* at Newtown. M.I. He *m.* secondly, Mary, 1st da. of John MORRIS, of Wern Goch in Beriew, co. Mont-

(a) See Morant's "*Essex*" vol. ii, 426. The late Baronet had a yr. br., John, who, in some accounts, is made to be the "John" who succeeded him in 1744.

(b) Edward Pryce, his elder br. served with distinction in the Royal army during the Civil War, but *d.* unm. and v.p. being slain in a tumult.

gomery, by Mary, da. of Oliver JONES, of Gwern-yr-Ychen, in Llandyssil, in that county. She *d.* s.p.m. 3 Aug. 1739, aged 24 years, 1 month and 2 days, and was *bur.* at Newtown. M.I. He *m.* thirdly, Eleanor, widow of Roger JONES, of Buckland, Brecon, but by her had no issue. He *d.* 1761.(a)

VI. 1761. SIR JOHN POWELL PRYCE, Bart. [1628], of Newtown aforesaid, only s. and h. by 1st wife, *suc. to the Baronetcy* in 1761. He *m.* Elizabeth, da. and h. of Richard MANLEY, of Earleigh Court in Sunning, Berks. He *d.* 4 July 1776, in the King's Bench prison. Will pr. 1789. The will of "Dame Elizabeth Price" was pr. 1805.

VII. 1776, to 1791. SIR EDWARD MAMLEY PRYCE, Bart. [1628], of Newtown aforesaid s. and h.; *suc.* to the *Baronetcy* 4 July 1776. He *m.* (—), da. of (—) FLINN, of Norfolk street, Strand, Middlesex. He *d.* s.p. legit.(b) 28 June 1791, at Pangbourne, Berks, when the *Baronetcy* is presumed to have become *extinct*.

BEAUMONT:

cr. 15 Aug. 1628;

ex. 28 Oct. 1631.

I. 1628, to 1631. "RICHARD BEAUMONT, of Whitley, co. York, Knt.," s. and h. of Edward BEAUMONT, of Whitley Beaumont aforesaid, by Elizabeth, da. of John RAMSDEN, *suc.* his father 3 Jan 1574/5; was *Knighted* 23 July 1603, at Whitehall; was in command of 200 train-band soldiers in 1613; was M.P. for Pontefract 1625 till void 28 May, and was *cr. a Bart.*, as above, 15 Aug. 1628. He *d.* unm. 28 Oct. 1631, when the *Baronetcy* became *extinct*. By his will, dat. 22 Aug. 1631, he devised his estates to his cousin Sir Thomas Beaumont, maternal grandson of his maternal aunt, Rosamond, by (her husband and distant relative) William Beaumont, of Lassells Hall, co York.(c)

WISEMAN:

cr. 29 Aug. 1628.

I. 1628. "WILLIAM WISEMAN of Canfeilde Hall, co. Essex, Esq.," 2d s. of Thomas Wiseman(d) of the same, by Alice, da. and h. of Robert MYLES, of Sutton, Suffolk, *suc.* his elder br. Robert Wiseman in the estate of Great Canfield, 1628, and was *cr. a Bart.* as above 29 Aug. 1628. He was Sheriff of Essex, 1638-39. He *m.* 6 Nov. 1628, at Hadham Parva, Herts, Elizabeth, sister of Arthur, 1st BARON CAPELL OF HADHAM, da. of Sir Henry CAPELL, of Hadham, Herts, by his first wife Theodosia, da. of Sir Edward MONTAGU. He *d.* at Oxford, and was *bur.* 1 July 1643 at St. Peter's in the East, in that city. Will pr. July 1643 and Nov. 1644. His widow, who was *b.* 26 Jan. 1612, *d.* 6 April 1660 and was *bur.* at Great Canfield. M.I. Will pr. Nov. 1660.

II. 1643. SIR WILLIAM WISEMAN, Bart. [1628(1)],(e) of Canfield Hall aforesaid, s. and h., aged 4 years in 1634 (Visit. of Essex); *suc. to the Baronetcy* in 1643; Sheriff of Essex, 1659-60. He *m.* firstly, 26 Oct. 1659 at St. Mary Magdalen's, Milk street, London, Anne, da. and coheir of Sir John PRESCOT, of

(a) *Gent. Mag.*, but Kimber's *Baronetage* says "Oct. 1748."

(b) According to Courthope's "*Extinct Baronetage*" [1835], "Sir Edward left an illegitimate son, who assumed the title."

(c) See Burke's "*Commoners*" (edit. 1837), vol. ii, p. 321.

(d) He was grandson of Sir John Wiseman, one of the Auditors of the Exchequer temp. Hen. VIII, who was *Knighted* at the battle of the Spurs.

(e) See vol. i, p. 4, note "a."

Hoxton, and of Bromley, Kent. She *d.* s.p., 11 May 1662, aged 24, and was *bur.* at Great Canfield. M.I. Admon. Nov. 1662. He *m.* secondly, 18 May 1664, at St. Martin's in the Fields (Lic. Fac., he about 33, she about 17), Arabella, sister, of the whole blood, and coheir of George, VISCOUNT HEWETT OF GOWRAN [I.], 5th da. of Sir Thomas HEWETT 1st Bart. [1660], by his 2d wife, Margaret, da. of Sir William LYTTON. He *d.* 14 and was *bur.* 23 Jan. 1684/5, at Great Canfield, aged 55. M.I. Will pr. Feb. 1685. That of his widow pr. Aug. 1705.

III. 1685. SIR THOMAS WISEMAN, Bart. [1628(1)], of Canfield Hall aforesaid, s. and h. by 2d wife; *suc to the Baronetcy*, 14 Jan. 1684/5. He sold the estate of Great Canfield. He *d.* unm. 1 May 1731. Will pr. May 1733.

IV. 1731. SIR CHARLES WISEMAN, Bart. [1628(1)], br. of the whole blood and h., *bap.* 27 Aug. 1676 at St. Andrew's, Holborn, *suc. to the Baronetcy*, 1 May 1731. He *d.* unm. 3 June 1751. Will pr. 1751.

V. 1751. SIR WILLIAM WISEMAN, Bart. 1628(1)], nephew and h., being s. and h. of John Wiseman, of the Temple, London, Barrister, by Penelope, his wife, which John (who was *bap.* 14 Dec. 1679, at St. Andrew's, Holborn), was younger br. of the 3d and 4th Barts. He *suc to the Baronetcy* 3 June 1751. He was Lieut. Col. of a Company of the Coldstream Guards, 1759. He *d.* s.p. 25 May 1774. Will pr. June 1774.

VI. 1774. SIR THOMAS WISEMAN, Bart. [1628(1)], cousin and h., being only surv. s. and h. of Edward WISEMAN, of Tewkesbury, by his 1st wife, Mary, da. of (—) Jones, of Worles, which Edward (who was *b.* 21 Dec. 1700 and *d.* at Jersey about 1767) was s. and h. of Edmund W., of Tewkesbury (*d.* 1741), the only s. of Sir Edmund WISEMAN, of London (*d.* 8 May 1704, aged 74), who was 2d s. of the 1st Bart. He was *b.* 30 Jan. 1731 and *suc. to the Baronetcy* 25 May 1774. He *m.* firstly, 1 Dec. 1757, Mary, da. of Michael GODDEN, Master Attendant of the Dock Yard at Chatham. She *d.* 11 June 1766. He *m.* secondly, 2 Dec. 1769, Sarah, da. of Thomas KING, of Gravesend, Kent, but by her had no male issue. She *d.* 4 Dec. 1777. He *d.* 27 Jan. 1810.

VII. 1810. SIR WILLIAM SALTONSTALL WISEMAN, Bart. [1628(1)], grandson and h., being s. and h. of Edmund WISEMAN, by Jemima, da. of Michael ARNE, of London, which Edmund was s. and h. ap. of the 6th Bart. by his first wife, and *d.* v.p. 7 May 1787, aged 28. He was *b.* 5 March 1784 and was sometime a Captain R.N. He *suc. to the Baronetcy* 27 Jan. 1810. He *m.* firstly, 8 Jan. 1812, at Bagdad in Persia, Catharine, 2d da. of Right Hon. Sir James MACKINTOSH, Recorder of Bombay. She was divorced by Act of Parl. 22 June 1825. He *m.* secondly, 5 April 1827, Eliza, 1st da. of Rev. George DAVIES, B.D., Rector of Cranfield, Beds. He *d.* 1 July 1845. Will pr. July 1845. His widow *d.* s.p. 27 Oct. 1862, at Hillingdon End, Uxbridge, aged 74.

VIII. 1845. SIR WILLIAM SALTONSTALL WISEMAN, Bart. [1628(1)], s. and h. by 1st wife, *b.* 4 Aug. 1814 at Bombay; entered Royal Navy; *suc. to the Baronetcy* 1 July 1845; Capt. R.N. 1854. Commodore on the Australian station; Vice President Ordnance Select Committee, 1863; granted a "good service" pension, 1866, becoming finally (1869) Rear Admiral, and retiring in 1870. C.B. 1864; K.C.B. 1867. He *m.* 25 Oct. 1838, at Widley, Hants, Charlotte Jane, only da. of Charles William PATERSON, of East Cosham House, Hants., Admiral R.N. He *d.* suddenly 14 July 1874, in his 60th year, at the Saunders House, St. Joseph Missouri, in the United States of America, and was *bur.* in Mount Mora cemetery.(a) His widow *d.* 23 May 1891, at 70, Eaton terrace, and was *bur.* in the cemetery at Bedford.

IX. 1874. SIR WILLIAM WISEMAN, Bart. [1628(1)], only s. and h., *b.* 23 Aug. 1845 at Cosham House aforesaid; entered the Royal Navy, 1859, serving in the New Zealand war, 1864-65; Lieut. 1867; served in the Niger Expedition, 1869; Commander, 1871; Capt. 1882, having *suc. to the Baronetcy,*

(a) See *The Times*, 19 Aug 1874 as to his having registered his name as "William Chambers, Lincoln, Neb."

14 July 1874. He *m.* 20 Sept. 1878, at Putney, co. Surrey, Sarah Elizabeth, 3d da. of Lewis LANGWORTHY, of "Ellesmere," Putney Hill. He *d.* 11 Jan. 1893, at 4, Elliot Terrace, Plymouth and was *bur.* in the cemetery at Bedford. Admon. £1,367 gross. His widow living 1900.

X. 1893. SIR WILLIAM GEORGE EDEN WISEMAN, Bart. [1628(1)], only s. and h., *b.* 1 Feb. 1885; *suc. to the Baronetcy* 11 Jan. 1893.

Family Estates.—These appear to have been long since alienated; that of Great Canfield was sold about 1710 by the 3d Bart.

NIGHTINGALE:

cr. 1 Sep. 1628;

dormant (for 70 years), 1722 to 1791.

I. 1628. "THOMAS NIGHTINGALE, of Newport Pond, co. Essex, Esq.," as also of Langley in that county, and of Kneesworth in Bassingbourn, co. Cambridge, s. and h. of Geoffrey NIGHTINGALE, of Newport Pond aforesaid, Double Reader of Gray's Inn, London, by Katharine, da. and h. of John CLAMPS, of Huntingdon, was admitted to Gray's Inn, 1 March 1591/2; suc. his father, 23 Feb. 1619; was Sheriff of Essex, 1627-28, and was *cr. a Bart.*, as above, 1 Sept. 1628. He *m.* firstly, in or before 1606, Millicent, da. of Sir Robert CLERK, of Pleshy and of Newarks in Good Easter, Essex, one of the Barons of the Exchequer, by Dorothy, da. of John MAYNARD. He *m.* secondly, in or before 1617, Catharine, 1st da. of Sir Robert CHESTER, of Cockenhatch, Herts, by Anne, da. of Sir Henry Capell, of Hadham. She was *bur.* 3 March 1635/6, at Newport. He *m.* thirdly, Elizabeth, da. of (—). He *d.* Jan. 1644/5. His will, dat. 4 and proved 24 Jan. 1644/5. His widow *d.* s.p.m., 23 and was *bur.* 25 Aug. 1686, at Newport, Essex, aged 74. M.I.

II. 1645. SIR THOMAS NIGHTINGALE, Bart. [1628], of Langley, Essex, and of Stevenage, Herts, grandson and h., being s. and h. of Robert Nightingale, by Theodosia, 3d da. of Sir Robert CHESTER, abovenamed, which Robert Nightingale was s. and h. ap. (by his 1st wife) of the 1st Bart., and *d.* v.p. 30 April 1636, aged 29. He was *b.* 15 Oct. 1629, and *suc. to the Baronetcy* in Jan. 1644/5. He *m.* 30 May 1655, at St. Olave's, Southwark, Jane, da. of George SHIERS, of London and of Slyfield House in Great Bookham, Surrey, aunt and eventually heir of Sir George SHIERS, Bart. so *cr.* 1684. He *d.* s.p.m.s.(a) and was *bur.* at Newport, Essex, 19 Oct. 1702. Admon. 13 Dec. 1703, *pendente lite* between Sir Bridges Nightingale, Bart. and others. His widow *d.* 1705. Her will dat. 19 July 1704, proved 22 May 1705.

III. 1702. SIR BRIDGES NIGHTINGALE, Bart. [1628], of Enfield, Middlesex, nephew and h., being s. and h. of Geoffrey NIGHTINGALE, of Enfield aforesaid and of Hamburgh, Merchant, by Anne da. of John BRIDGES, of St. Gile's Cripplegate, London, Citizen, and Pinmaker, which Geoffrey (who was *bur.* at Enfield 23 July 1690), was yr. br. of the 2d Bart. He *suc. to the Baronetcy*, in Oct. 1702. He *d.* unm. and was *bur.* at Enfield.

IV. 1715? SIR ROBERT NIGHTINGALE, Bart. [1628], of Enfield, aforesaid br. and h.; *suc. to the Baronetcy* on the death of his brother. He was one of the Directors of the East India Company. He *d.* unm. and was *bur.* 24 July 1722, at Enfield. Will dat. 23 May, and proved 16 July 1722.(b)

[After his death the *Baronetcy*, remained *dormant* for about 70 years, the right thereto being as below.]

(a) His only s. and h. ap. Sir Robert Nightingale [often, erroneously said to have suc. him in the Baronetcy], was *Knighted* at Whitehall, 12 Dec. 1685; Sheriff of Norfolk, 1685-86; *d.* s.p., and v.p., 3 and was *bur.* 11 July 1697, at Newport aforesaid.

(b) He left his estates to his cousin Robert GASCOYNE, younger s. of the Rev. Joseph GASCOYNE, Vicar of Enfield, by Anne, da. of Francis THEOBALD, of Barking, Suffolk, and Anne, his wife, sister of Sir Thomas NIGHTINGALE, the 2d Bart. This Robert GASCOYNE *d.* unm. (of the small pox), 2 Nov. 1722 and was *bur.* at Enfield.

V. 1722. EDWARD NIGHTINGALE, of Kneesworth aforesaid, cousin and h. male, being s. and h. of Geoffrey Nightingale, of the same, by his 1st wife, Elizabeth, da. of Sir William LUCKYN, of Essex, which Geoffrey (who *d.* 9 May 1681, aged 64), was s. of the 1st Bart. by his 2nd wife. He was *bap.* 27 Aug. 1658. He *suc. to the Baronetcy* on the death of his cousin, in July 1722, but *never assumed the title.* He *m.* Anne Charlotte, da. of Sir Arthur SHINGSBY, of Bifrons, 1st Bart. [1657], by his wife, a native of Flanders. She was *bap.* 4 Jan. 1664, at Patrixbourne, in Kent. He *d.* 2 July 1723. Will dat. 20 April 1722, pr. 1723.

VI. 1723? GAMALIEL NIGHTINGALE, s. and h., admitted to Gray's Inn, 4 May 1710; mentioned in his father's will April 1722, whom he probably survived,(a) thereby *succeeding to the Baronetcy*, though *not assuming the title.* He *d.* a lunatic, and unm.

VII. 1730? EDWARD NIGHTINGALE, of Kneesworth aforesaid, br. and h.,(a) *b.* 1696; admitted to Gray's Inn, 5 April 1720. His elder br. having died s.p., he *suc. to the Baronetcy* on his (or, possibly, on their father's) death, but *never assumed the title.* He *m.* Eleanora, da. of Charles ETHELSTON of London. He *d.* at Bath 20 Oct. 1750. Will dat. 26 Sep. and proved 31 Oct. 1750. His widow *d.* 14 Sep. 1771, aged 71, and was *bur.* at Bassingbourne. Her will dat. 22 Sep. 1765, pr. 24 Sep. 1771.

VIII. 1750? EDWARD NIGHTINGALE, of Kneesworth aforesaid, s. and h., *b.* 4 Sept 1726, *suc. to the Baronetcy*, presumably on 20 Oct. 1750, but *never assumed the title.* He *d.* unm. at Town Malling, Kent, July 1782. Admon. 1 Aug. 1782.

IX. 1782. GAMALIEL NIGHTINGALE, of Kneesworth aforesaid, br. and h., *b.* 15 Feb. 1731. Captain R.N., was in command of a frigate in 1761, when he captured a French ship of superior force off the Land's End; *suc. to the Baronetcy* in July 1782, but *never assumed the title.* He *m.* Maria, da. of Peter CLOSSEN, of Hamburgh, Merchant, a native of Mecklenburg Schwerin. She *d.* 20 Feb. 1789, aged 50, and was *bur.* at Bassingbourne. He *d.* Jan. 1791. Will dat. 20 Aug. 1789, proved 27 Jan. 1791.

X. 1791. SIR EDWARD NIGHTINGALE, Bart. [1628], of Kneesworth aforesaid, only s. and h., *b.* 14 Oct. 1760, at Gosport, Hants; *suc. to the Baronetcy* in Jan. 1791, and consequently *assumed the title of Baronet* as heir male of the body of the 1st Bart., having recorded a pedigree, proving that fact, in the College of Arms. London, which he signed, 12 Aug. 1797. He *m.* once at Gretna Green, Scotland, and again at Bassingbourne, Eleanor, da. and sole h. of his uncle Robert NIGHTINGALE, of Kneesworth aforesaid, by (his cousin), Mary, da. of Charles ETHELSTON, of London. He *d.* 4 Dec. 1804. Will pr. 1805. His widow *d.* 20 Jan. 1825. Will pr. Feb. 1825.

XI. 1804. SIR CHARLES ETHELSTON NIGHTINGALE, Bart. [1628], of Kneesworth aforesaid, 1st surviving s. and h., *b.* 1 Nov. 1784. Lieut. 3d Foot Guards; *suc. to the Baronetcy* 4 Dec. 1804. He *m.* Dec. 1805, his cousin, Maria, only da. of Thomas Lacy DICKONSON, of West Retford, Notts, by Maria Eleanor, sister of Sir Edward NIGHTINGALE, 10th Bart. abovenamed. He *d.* 5 July 1843, aged 59, at Bath, leaving it was said, all his property to Dr. Greville, his physician.(b) His widow *d.* 8 Dec. 1846, at Boulogne-sur-mer. Admon. May 1847.

XII. 1843. SIR CHARLES NIGHTINGALE, Bart. [1628], s. and h., *b.* at West Retford, 30 April 1809; sometime a Midshipman in the Royal navy; served also in Sir de Lacy Evans' brigade in Spain; *suc. to the Baronetcy*, 5 July 1843. He *m.* 2 Feb. 1829, Harriet Maria, da. of Edward Broughton FOSTER, of Ayleston co.

(a) Whether Gamaliel survived his father, or was himself survived by his brother Edward, must remain uncertain, till the date of death of Gamaliel is ascertained.

(b) See obituary in *Ann. Reg.* as to the suspicion by his son, of his having been poisoned. The verdict however, after the *post mortem* was "hæmatemis, by the Visitation of God."

Leicester, and of Kingston-on-Thames, Capt. in the army, niece of Lieut. Gen. TRAPAUD. He *d.* 17 Sep. 1876, aged 67, at Ludham. His widow *d.* 22 Dec. 1881, aged 81, at Hounslow.

XIII. 1876. SIR HENRY DICKONSON NIGHTINGALE, Bart. [1628], only s. and h., *b.* 15 Nov. 1830, at Bruges, in Belgium; entered the Royal Marines, 1849; served throughout the Burmese war of 1852 in H.M.S. "Fox"; First Lieut. 1853; Captain, 1861. Capt. and Paymaster, 45th Foot, 1864-82, retiring as Hon. Lieut. Col.; *suc. to the Baronetcy*, 17 Sep. 1876. He *m.* 14 Aug. 1855, Mary, da. of Thomas Spark, Capt. R.N.

Family Estates.—These appear to have totally alienated, after the death, in July 1843 of the 11th Bart., who for some time resided at Kneesworth Hall. He possibly may have disposed of them even in his lifetime.

JAQUES, *or* JACQUES:

cr. 2 Sep. 1628;

ex. Jan. 1660/1.

I. 1628. to 1661. "JOHN JAQUES, of (—), co. Middlesex, Esq., one of H.M.'s Gentlemen Pensioners," was *b.* about 1599, (being, presumably the "John Jaques, s. and h. of John JAQUES, of Highgate, co. Midx., Esq.," who, 20 Oct. 1623, was admitted to Gray's Inn), was *cr. a Bart.*, as above, 2 Sep. 1628. He was sometime student at Sion College; was M.P. for Haslemere, April to May 1640, and Nov. 1640, till void shortly afterwards. On 14 Sep. 1642 he had lic. from the Bishop of London's office (being then of St. Helen's, London, about 43, bachelor) to marry Jane DIXON, of Great St. Bartholomew, about 50, widow. He apparently *m.* (secondly?) Mary.(a) The will of "Dame Mary Jaques" is pr. 1657. He *d.* s.p. and was *bur.* 15 Jan. 1660/1, at St. Christopher le Stocks, London, when the *Baronetcy* became *extinct.*

VAN LORE, *or* VAULOOR:

cr. 3 Sep. 1628;

ex. 1644/5.

I. 1628, to 1645. "PETER VAULOOR [*i.e.*, VAN LORE], of Tylehurst,(b) co. Berks, Esq.," s. of Sir Peter VAN LORE, of Fenchurch Street, London, Merchant,(c) a Protestant refugee from Utrecht (who with "Jacoba(d) Van Lore, of Ixea [*Qy.* Ixem] in Flanders," presumably his wife, had settled in London; being *Knighted*, 5 Nov. 1621, at Whitehall, and who *d.* 6 Sep. 1627, aged 80), was probably *b.* about 1580, and was *cr. a Bart.*, as above, 3 Sep. 1628. He *m.* firstly, Susan, da. of Laurence BECKE, of Antwerp. He *m.* secondly, Katharine, who survived him. He *d.* s.p.m.(e) about 1644/5, when the *Baronetcy* became *extinct.* Will dat. 18 Aug. 1644, pr. 6 March 1644/5, and 1663. His second wife survived him. Her will pr. 1663.

(a) In Courthope's *Extinct Baronetage*, "Mary" is the *only* wife attributed to him.

(b) It is stated in Burke's *Extinct Baronetcies* that he "is supposed to have had a temporary interest in the manor of Tylehurst by some alliance with the Kendrick family."

(c) In 1618-19 he was among the wealthy Dutch merchants sued in the Star chamber by James I. for exporting the large sums made in business from the realm. He was fined no less than £7,000. See Moens' introduction to the *Austen Friars Registers.*

(d) She, apparently, is the "Jacomynken" wife of "Pieter Van Loore," living 11 Dec. 1608 [Crawley-Boevey's *Boevey Family*, p. 14].

(e) Of his three daughters and coheirs—(1) Jacoba, *m.* Henry Alexander, *otherwise* Zinzan, of Tilehurst, and *d.* 22 June 1677; (2) Susanna, *m.* 29 July 1634, at St. Andrew's, Holborn, Sir Robert Crooke; and (3) Mary, *m.* Henry (Alexander), Earl of Stirling [S.].

DILLINGTON:
cr. 6 Sep. 1628;
ex. 4 July 1721.

I. 1628. "ROBERT DILLINGTON, of [Knighton in the parish of Newchurch, in] the Isle of Wight, co. Southampton, Esq.," only s. and h. of Tristram DILLINGTON, of Newchurch aforesaid, by Jane, da. of Nicholas MARTIN, of Achilhampton, co. Dorset, suc. his father in Feb. 1593/4, and his uncle, Sir Robert Dillington, in Dec. 1604, and was *cr. a Bart.*, as above, 6 Sep. 1628; M.P. for Isle of Wight, Nov. 1654 to 1655. He *m.* firstly, Mabell, da. of Sir Humphrey FORSTER, of Berks. He *m.* secondly, Catharine [Frances?] sister of Richard (GORGES), BARON GORGES OF DUNDALK [I.], da. of Sir Thomas GORGES, of Langford, Wilts, by Helena, Dow. Marchioness of Northampton, da. of Wolfgang VON SUAVENBURG, of Sweden. He *d.* 1664. Admon. 31 Oct. 1665 to Sir Robert Dillington, Bart., *pendente lite.* His relict, "Dame Frances Dillington," was living 7 June, 1688.

II. 1664. SIR ROBERT DILLINGTON, Bart. [1628], of Knighton aforesaid, grandson and h., being s. and h. of Robert Dillington, of Mottistone, in the Isle of Wight (admitted to Gray's Inn, 18 May 1631; M.P. for Newport, 1659 and 1660), who was 2d but 1st surv. s. and h. ap. of 1st Bart. by his 1st wife, and *d.* v.p. He matric. at Oxford (Queen's Coll.), 9 Dec. 1653; was admitted to Gray's Inn, 1 Nov. 1654, and *suc to the Baronetcy* in 1664; was M.P. for Newport (Isle of Wight), in four Parls., 1670-81. He *m.* firstly, Jane, da. of John FREKE, of Shrowton. She was *bur.* at Newchurch. He *m.* secondly (Lic. Vic. Gen., 28 May 1678, he about 30, widower, she about 18, spinster), Hannah, da. of William WEBB, of Throgmorton street, St. Bartholomew, near the Exchange, London, citizen. He *d.* 25 April 1687, aged 53, and was *bur.* at Newchurch. Will dat. 2 Feb. 1682/3, pr. 10 June 1687.

III. 1687? SIR ROBERT DILLINGTON, Bart. [1628], of Knighton aforesaid, s. and h. by 1st wife; was *b.* about 1665; matric. at Oxford (Queen's Coll.) 1 June 1682, aged 17; *suc. to the Baronetcy* about 1687; was M.P. for Newport (Isle of Wight) for some months in 1689, till his death. He *d.* unm. 1689, and was *bur.* at Newchurch. Will dat. 7 June 1688, pr. 17 Dec. 1689.

IV. 1689. SIR JOHN DILLINGTON, Bart. [1628], of Knighton aforesaid, br. and h.; under 21 in Feb. 1682/3; *suc. to the Baronetcy* about 1689. He *d.* s.p. 5 March 1705/6, and was *bur.* at Newchurch. Will dat. 9 Nov. 1705, pr. 24 July 1712.

V. 1706 to 1721. SIR TRISTRAM DILLINGTON, Bart. [1628], of Knighton aforesaid, half br. and h., being s. of the 2d Bart. by his 2d wife; *suc. to the Baronetcy* about 1706. He was sometime a Major in the Guards. He *d.* s.p., 7 July 1721, aged 43, and was *bur.* at Newchurch, when the *Baronetcy* became *extinct.* Will dat. 11 June 1706, pr. 5 Sep. 1721.

PILE:
cr. 12 Sep. 1628;
ex. about 1780.

I. 1628. "FRANCIS PILE, of Compton [*i.e.*, Compton-Beauchamp], co. Berks, Esq.," s. and h. of Sir Gabriel PILE, of Bubton, Wilts, by Anne, da. of Sir Thomas PORTER, of Newark, co. Gloucester, was *b.* 15 June 1589; aged 34 in 1623; suc. his father 7 Nov. 1626 and, for his service to the Crown, was *cr. a Bart.* as above, 12 Sep. 1628. He *m.*, in or before 1617, Elizabeth, 2d da. of Sir Francis POPHAM, of Littlecott, Wilts, by Amy, da. of John DUDLEY, of Stoke Newington. He *d.* 1 and was *bur.* 8 Dec. 1635, at Collingbourne Kingston, Wilts. Will pr. 1636. His widow *d.* 7 Oct., and was *bur.* 5 Nov., 1658, at Collingbourne. Will pr. 1658.

II. 1635. SIR FRANCIS PILE, Bart. [1628], of Compton Beauchamp aforesaid, s. and h., was *b.* about 1617; aged 6 in 1623; matric. at Oxford (Univ. Coll.), 22 Nov. 1633, aged 16; admitted to Middle Temple, 1637; *suc. to the Baronetcy*, 1 Dec. 1635. Sheriff of Berks, 1643-45; M.P. thereof, July 1646 till death. He *m.* firstly, 9 June 1634, Mary, only da. of Samuel DUNCH, of Pusey, Berks, by Dulcibella, his wife. She, who was *b.* 25 June 1596, *d.* s.p.s., Sep. 1655, and was *bur.* at Pusey. M.I. He *m.* secondly, Jane, said(a) to be da. of John STILL, Bishop of Bath and Wells (1593-1608), by his second wife, Jane, da. of Sir John HORNER. He *d.* s.p.m.,(b) 12 Feb. 1648/9. Will pr. April 1649. His widow *d.* 25 July and was *bur.* 4 Aug. 1692, at Collingbourne, aged 80. Will pr. 1692.

III. 1649. SIR SEYMOUR PILE, Bart. [1628], of Axford in Ramsbury Wilts, br. and h. male; matric. (with his brother) at Oxford (Univ. Coll.), 22 Nov. 1633, aged 15; admitted to Middle Temple, 1635; *suc. to the Baronetcy*, 12 Feb. 1648/9. He *m.* in or before 1661, Elizabeth, 2d da. of Sir Henry MOORE, 1st Bart. [1627], of Fawley, by Elizabeth, da. of William BEVERLEY, of Kenoe, Beds. His widow was living 25 Nov. 1689.

IV. 1670? SIR FRANCIS PILE, Bart. [1628], of Axford aforesaid, s. and h., *suc. to the Baronetcy* on the death of his father. He *m.* Frances, da. of Sir Bulstrode WHITELOCK, of Chilton, Berks, sometime Lord Keeper of the Great Seal, by his 2d wife Frances, da. of William (WILLOUGHBY), 3d BARON WILLOUGHBY OF PARHAM. She *d.* before him. He *d.* about 1689. Admon. 25 Nov. 1689.

V. 1689? SIR SEYMOUR PILE, Bart. [1628], of Axford aforesaid s. and h., *suc. to the Baronetcy* about 1689, being then a minor. He *m.* Jane, only da. of John LAWFORD, of Stapleton, co. Gloucester. She *d.* July 1726.

VI. 1730? to 1761. SIR FRANCIS SEYMOUR PILE, Bart. [1628], of North Stoneham, and of Somerley, Hants, s. and h., unm. in 1741;(c) *suc. to the Baronetcy*, on his father's death. He *m.* Anne, widow of Richard FLEMING, da. of Sir Ambrose CROWLEY, of GREENWICH, Alderman, and sometime, 1706-07, Sheriff of London, by Mary, da. of Charles OWEN. The will of "Dame Ann Pill" [*sic*] is pr. 1761. He *d.* apparently s.p.m.s., 4 May 1761, when the *Baronetcy*, presumably,(d) became *extinct.*

POLE:
cr. 12 Sep. 1628;
subsequently, 1790-99, *and since* 1874, DE-LA-POLE;
being, *sometime*, 1847-1874, REEVE-DE-LA-POLE.

I. 1628. "JOHN POLE, of Shutt [*i.e.*, Shute], co. Devon, Esq.," s. and h. ap. of Sir William POLE, of Colcomb in that county, the celebrated Antiquary, by his 1st wife Mary, 1st da. and coheir of Sir William PERIAM, Lord Chief Baron of the Exchequer, was M.P. for Devon, 1626; Sheriff thereof, 1638-39, and was v.p. *cr. a Bart.*, as above, 12 Sep. 1628. He *suc.* his father (who *d.* aged 74) 9 Feb. 1635; took arms for the Parl. and was one of the sequestrators for

(a) In the Bishop's funeral certificate, 4 April 1607, no such da. is mentioned. It is there stated that by Jane his 2d wife he had one son Thomas Still, then 12 years old. The two sons and four daughters (Sarah, Anne, Elizabeth, and Mary) by the 1st wife and their husbands are fully set out. The age of Dame Jane Pile at death is inconsistent with such parentage, as the Bishop died 26 Feb. 1607/8; possibly it should be 84 or 85, and possibly she was a posthumous child.

(b) Of his three daughters and coheirs by his 2d wife, (1) Ann *m.* Francis (HOLLES), 2d BARON HOLLES OF IFIELD; (2) Elizabeth *m.* Sir Thomas STRICKLAND, Bart., of Boynton; (3) Jane *m.*, 13 Nov. 1672, at Collingbourne, Edward RICHARDS, of Yaverland, Isle of Wight, and their issue inherited Compton Beauchamp.

(c) Wotton's *Baronetage*, 1741.

(d) According, however, to Kimber's *Baronetage*, 1771, he left a son and successor, Sir Seymour Pile, the present Baronet, who is a minor."

I

Devon, 1643. He *m.* firstly, 5 Jan. 1613/4, at Shute, Elizabeth, da. and h. of Roger How, of London, Merchant, by Jane, da. of William SYMES, of Chard, which Jane *m.*, for her 2d husband (as his 2d wife), Sir William POLE abovenamed. He *m.* secondly, Mary, widow of William LOCKLAND, of Bromley St. Leonard's, Midx. He *d.* at Bromley aforesaid, 16 April, and was *bur.* 13 July 1658, at Colyton. Admon. 24 June 1658, his widow, Mary, being then living.

II. 1658. SIR COURTENAY POLE, Bart. [1628], of Shute aforesaid, 2d but 1st surv. s. and h. male(a); *bap.* 17 Feb. 1618/9, at Colyton; adm. to Lincoln's Inn, 16 June 1635; took arms for the King; *suc. to the Baronetcy* in April 1658; M.P. for Honiton, 1661-79. Sheriff of Devon, 1681-82. He *m.*, in or before 1649, Urith, da. of Thomas SHAPCOTE, of Shapcote. He was *bur.* 13 April 1695, at Shute.

III. 1695. SIR JOHN POLE, Bart. [1628], of Shute aforesaid, only surviving s. and h.; *b.* and *bap.* 17 June 1649, at Allhallows, Goldsmith street, Exeter; registered at Colyton; M.P. for Lyme Regis, 1685-87, and 1689-90; for Bossiney, 1698-1700; for Devon, 1701-02; for East Looe, 1702-05, and for Newport, co. Cornwall, 1705-08; having *suc. to the Baronetcy* in April 1695. He *m.* Anne, sister of Sir William MORICE, 1st Bart. [1661], da. of Sir William MORICE, of Werrington, Devon, Secretary of State to Charles II, by Elizabeth, da. of Humphrey PRIDEAUX, of Soulden in that county. He *d.* 13 and was *bur.* 20 March 1707/8, at Colyton. Will pr. May 1708. His widow was *bur.* there 1 March 1713/4. Will pr. March 1714.

IV. 1708. SIR WILLIAM POLE, Bart. [1628], of Shute aforesaid, s. and h. *bap.* 17 Aug. 1678; matric. at Oxford (New Coll.) 7 July 1696, aged 18; M.P. for Newport, 1701-02; for Camelford, 1704-08; for Newport (again), 1708-10; for Devon, 1710-12; for Bossiney, 1713-15; for Honiton, 1716-27 and 1731-34; having *suc. to the Baronetcy*, 13 March 1707/8. Master of the Royal Household, 1713. He is said to have married(b) Elizabeth WARRY or WARREN, of Colyton, spinster, sometimes called da. of Robert WARRY. He *d.*, of the gout, 31 Dec. 1741. Will pr. May 1742. His widow was *bur.* 12 April 1758.

V. 1741. SIR JOHN POLE, Bart. [1628], of Shute aforesaid, only s. and h., *b.* about 1733; *suc. to the Baronetcy*, 31 Dec. 1741; matric. at Oxford (New Coll.) 19 April 1750, aged 17. He *m.* firstly, Elizabeth, da. and coheir of John Mill, of Woodford, Essex. She *d.* 10 Aug. 1758, aged 21. He *m.* secondly, Maria, da. of Rev. (—) PALMER, of Combe Raleigh, Devon. He *d.* 19 Feb. 1760, aged 27. Will pr. 1760. His widow *m.* George CLAVERING (by whom she was mother of Sir Thomas John Clavering, 8th Bart.), and *d.* in or before 1777; admon. 2 Aug. 1777, as "of St. Marylebone, Midx." granted to her said husband.

VI. 1760. SIR JOHN WILLIAM POLE, *afterwards* (1790-99), DE-LA-POLE, Bart. [1628], of Shute aforesaid, only s. and h. by first marriage, *b.* at Salisbury and *bap.* 27 June 1757, at Shute; matric. at Oxford (Corpus Christi Coll.), 8 June 1776, aged 18; *suc. to the Baronetcy*, 19 Feb. 1760. Sheriff of Devon, 1782-83. By Royal Lic. 1790, he took the name of DE-LA-POLE in lieu of POLE. M.P. for West Looe, 1790-96. He *m.*, 9 Jan. 1781, Anne, only da. of James TEMPLER, of Stover House, Devon. He *d.* 30 Nov. 1799. Will pr. Aug. 1800. His widow *d.* 12 Feb. 1832.

VII. 1799. SIR WILLIAM TEMPLER POLE, Bart. [1628], of Shute aforesaid, s. and h. *b.* 2 Aug. and *bap.* 20 Sep. 1782 at Shute; ed. at Eton; *suc. to the Baronetcy* 30 Nov. 1799; matric. at Oxford (Ch. Ch.), 24 April 1801, aged 18; *cr.* M.A., 13 June 1804, and D.C.L., 5 July 1810; admitted to Lincoln's Inn,

(a) Sir William Pole, the eldest s. and h. ap., was *bap.* 6 Dec. 1614, at Colyton; was M.P. for Honiton, 1640-42; *Knighted* 19 April 1641; married two wives and had seven children, of whom the three sons died unm. before their grandfather. He, himself, *d.* v.p. and was *bur.* 30 Jan. 1648/9 at Colyton. Admon., as "of Shute, co. Devon," 2 Nov. 1656, to his principal creditor. That of his widow Katherine "as of Burford, Wilts," 18 Feb. 1657/8.

(b) The date [presumably in or before 1733] and place of this marriage are unknown, as also are any proofs afforded by settlements or otherwise.

21 Feb. 1803 as "POLE," not having availed himself of the licence (to his father) to bear the name of DE-LA-POLE. Sheriff of Devon, 1818-19. He *m.* firstly, 24 Aug. 1804, Sophia Anne, only da. of his maternal uncle, George TEMPLER, of Shapwick House, Somerset, by Jane, da. of Henry PAUL, of West Monckton. She *d.* 17 March 1808. He *m.* secondly, 31 July 1810, Charlotte Frances, only da. of John FRASER, by (—), sister of John FARQUHAR, of Fonthill Abbey, Wilts. He *d.* 1 April 1847, at Shute House, aged 65. Will, as "Pole *alias* De-la-Pole," pr. July 1847. His widow *d.* 2 Oct. 1877, at Bayford Grange, Herts, in her 91st year.

VIII. 1847. SIR JOHN GEORGE REEVE-DE-LA-POLE, Bart. [1628], of Shute aforesaid, s. and h. by 1st wife; *b.* 21 Jan. 1808 at Shute House; educated at Winchester and at Sandhurst. By Royal Lic., 5 Oct. 1838, he took the name of REEVE before that of DE LA POLE in compliance with the will of Anna Maria, widow of Sir George Trenchard, da. and coheir of Sir Thomas Reeve. He *suc. to the Baronetcy*, 1 April 1847. He *m.* firstly, 26 March 1829, Margaretta, 2d da. of Henry BARTON, of Saucethorpe Hall, co. Lincoln. She *d.* June 1842. He *m.* secondly, 2 Feb. 1843, Mlle. Josephine Catherine Denise CARRÉ, of Anse, Rhone, in France. He *d.* s.p.m., 19 May 1874, in Jermyn street, Midx. His widow *m.*, 1881, Mons. Antoine Pierre ROUPE and was living at Paris, 1900.

IX. 1874. SIR WILLIAM EDMUND DE-LA-POLE, Bart. [1628], of Shute House aforesaid, br., of the half blood, and h., being s. by his 2d wife, of the 7th Bart. He was *b.* 3 July 1816 in Weymouth street, Marylebone; ed. at Winchester; matric. at Oxford (Ch. Ch.), 17 Oct. 1833, aged 17; Student, 1834-41; B.A., 1837; M.A., 1840; admitted to Lincoln's Inn, 18 Nov. 1837; Barrister, 1841; *suc. to the Baronetcy*, 19 May 1874. He *m.*, 26 April 1841, Margaret Victoriosa, 2d da. of Admiral the Hon. Sir John TALBOT, G.C.B. (son of Margaret, *suo jure* BARONESS TALBOT OF MALAHIDE [I.]), by Juliana, da. of James Everard (ARUNDELL), 9th BARON ARUNDELL OF WARDOUR. She *d.* 23 Nov. 1886, at Colcombe, Mount Ephraim road, Streatham, aged 69. He *d.* 21 March 1895, at Shute House, after a long illness. Will pr. at £8,604 gross.

X. 1895. SIR EDMUND REGINALD TALBOT DE-LA-POLE, *formerly* POLE, Bart. [1628], of Shute aforesaid, 1st s. and h.; *b.* 22 Feb. 1844; ed. at Winchester; *suc. to the Baronetcy*, 21 March 1895, on which occasion he assumed the name of *De La Pole.* He *m.* firstly, 25 Sep. 1877, at South Benfleet, Essex, Mary Ann Margaret, widow of John Ormsby PHIBBS, 3d Hussars, only child of Capt. Hastings SANDS, King's Dragoon Guards. She *d.* 10 May 1878. He *m.* secondly, 18 Dec. 1884, Elizabeth Maria, da. of Charles RHODES, of "Lyndhurst," in Sidcup, co. Kent.

Family Estates.—These, in 1883, consisted of 5,846 acres in Devon, valued at £7,416 a year, and of (—) acres in Berks, of the annual value of £370. *Principal Seat.*—Shute House, near Axminster, Devon.

LEWIS:
cr. 14 Sep. 1628;
ex. 1677.

I. 1628, to 1677. "WILLIAM LEWIS, of Langors [*i.e.*, Llangorse], co. Brecon, Esq.," s. and h. of Lodowick LEWIS, of Trewalter in that county, by (—), da. and coheir of William WATKINS, of Llangorse aforesaid, was Sheriff of Brecon, 1619-20, and again 1636-37; was M.P. for Petersfield, April to May 1640, and Nov. 1640 till (being one of the eleven Presbyterian members impeached in 1647) he was secluded Dec. 1648; M.P. for Breconshire, 1660, and for Lymington, 1661 till death, having been *cr. a Bart.*, as above, 14 Sep. 1628. He, who resided principally at Borden, Hants, was Gov. of Portsmouth, for the Parl., 1642; served in most of the Parl. Committees, and was Commissioner of the

Admiralty in Oct. 1645. He *m.*, in or after Feb. 1621/2, Mary, widow of Sir Thomas NEALE, of Warneford, Hants, da. of Robert CALTON, of Goring, Oxon. She was *bur.* 22 Feb. 1635/6, at Warneford aforesaid with her first husband. He *d.* s.p.m.s.,(a) 1677, when the *Baronetcy* became *extinct*. Will dat. 4 March 1674/5, pr. 28 Nov. 1677.

COLEPEPER, *or* CULPEPER:

cr. 20 Sep. 1628;

ex. 28 March 1740.

I. 1628. "WILLIAM CULPEPER, of Wakehurst, co. Sussex, Esq.," 2d but 1st surv. s. and h. of Sir Edward CULPEPER, *or* COLEPEPER, of the same, by Elizabeth, da. of William FERNFOLD, of Nashin, Sussex, was admitted to Lincoln's Inn 1623, and was *cr. a Bart.*, as above, 20 Sep. 1628; Sheriff of Surrey and Sussex, 1634-35; M.P. for East Grinstead 1640, till void 24 Dec. He *m.*, in or before 1629, Jane, da. and eventually h. of Sir Benjamin PELLETT, of Bolney, Sussex. He *d.* about 1651. Will pr. 1651.

II. 1651? SIR BENJAMIN COLEPEPER, Bart. [1628], of Wakehurst aforesaid, s. and h., aged 5 at the visitation of Sussex in 1634; *suc. to the Baronetcy* about 1651. He *m.* Catherine, da. and coheir of Goldsmith HUDSON. He *d.* s.p.m.

III. 1670? SIR EDWARD COLEPEPER, Bart. [1628], of Wakehurst aforesaid, br. and h., *b.* about 1632. He *suc. to the Baronetcy* on the death of his brother. He *m.* (—).

IV. 1700? to 1740. SIR WILLIAM COLEPEPER, Bart. [1628], of Wakehurst aforesaid, grandson and h., being s. and h. of Benjamin COLEPEPER by Judith, da. of Sir William WILSON, 1st Bart. [1660], of Eastbourne, which Benjamin was s. and h. ap. of the late Bart., but *d.* v.p. He was *b.* 23 Nov. 1668, at Wakehurst; *suc. to the Baronetcy* on the death of his grandfather. He *d.*, unm. 28 March, and was *bur.* 6 April 1740, at St. James', Westm., when the *Baronetcy* became *extinct*.(b)

LAWRENCE, *or* LAURENCE:

cr. 9 Oct. 1628;

ex. April 1714.

I. 1628. "JOHN LAURENCE, of [Delaford in] Iver, co. Bucks, Knt.," s. and h. of Thomas LAWRENCE,(c) of Chelsea, citizen and goldsmith of London (*d.* 28 Oct. 1593, aged 54), by Martha, da. of Sir Anthony CAGE, of London, was *b.* about 1589; matric. at Oxford (St. John's Coll.), 27 May 1603, aged 14; B.A. (from Oriel Coll.), 29 Oct. 1604; M.A. (from St. Edm. Hall), 7 July 1615; was *Knighted* at Royston, 26 Jan. 1609/10, and was *cr. a Bart.*, as above, 9 Oct. 1628. He *m.*, in or before 1610, Grisel, da. and coheir of Jarvis GIBBON, of Benenden, co. Kent. He *d.* 13 and was *bur.* 14 Nov. 1638, at Chelsea, aged 50. Funeral certificate in Public Record office. Will pr. 1639. His widow was *bur.* 22 March 1675, at Chelsea. Will pr. 1679.

(a) His only son, Lodowick Lewis, *d.* v.p., leaving three daughters and coheirs, one of whom was ancestress of the families of Pryse and Loveden, afterwards Pryse, by whom, in 1806, the greater part of the Llangorse estate was sold.

(b) In the Temple Church, London, occurs the burial, 2 April 1663, of "Sir Cheney Culpeper, Bart." The word "Bart.," however, is clearly a mistake for "Knt." He was of Hollingbourne, co. Kent; matric. at Oxford (Hart. Hall), 6 Nov. 1618, aged 17; admitted to Middle Temple, 1621. Mar. lic. (London) 24 Oct. 1632, aged 28, and a bachelor. Admon. 19 Dec. 1666 and 10 March 1690/1.

(c) See *Coll. Top. et Gen.*, vol. iii, p. 281.

II. 1638. SIR JOHN LAWRENCE, Bart. [1628], of Chelsea aforesaid, s. and h.; *b.* about 1610; matric. at Oxford (St. Edm. Hall), aged 17; admitted to Inner Temple, 1631; *suc. to the Baronetcy*, 13 Nov. 1638.(a) He *m.*, in or before 1646, Mary, da. of Sir Thomas HAMPSON, 1st Bart. [1642], of Taplow, Bucks, by Anne, da. and coheir of William DUNCOMBE. She was *bur.*, 11 Oct. 1664, at Chelsea. He was living 28 Dec. 1680, but *d.* before 19 Feb. 1710/1.(b)

III. 1690? to 1714. SIR THOMAS LAWRENCE, Bart. [1628], of Chelsea aforesaid, s. and h.; *b.* about 1645; matric. at Oxford (St. John's Coll.), 20 Nov. 1661, aged 16; B.A. 23 Feb. 1664/5; M.A. (Univ. Coll.), 1668; admitted to Middle Temple, 1664; *suc. to the Baronetcy* on his father's death. He, having spent all his estate, emigrated to Maryland, where he was Secretary to Gov. Seymour in 1696. He *m.* (Lic. Vic. Gen. 18 May 1674, he about 28 and she about 20) Anne ENGLISH, of St. Clement Danes, spinster. He *d.* s.p.m.s.(c) and was *bur.* at Chelsea, 25 April 1714,(d) when the *Baronetcy* became *extinct*. His widow was *bur.* 2 Nov. 1723 at Chelsea.

SLINGSBY:

cr. 22 Oct. 1628;

ex. 1630.

I. 1628, to 1630. ANTHONY SLINGSBY, of Screvin [*i.e.*, Scriven], co York, Esq.," s. of Peter SLINGSBY,(e) of the same, being Gov. of Zutphen, in the Low Countries, was *cr. a Bart.*, as above, 22 Oct. 1628. He *d.* s.p. 1630, when the *Baronetcy* became *extinct*.

VAVASOUR:

cr. 24 Oct. 1628;

ex. 27 Jan. 1826.

I. 1628. "THOMAS VAVASOUR, of Hesselwood [*i.e.*, Haslewood], co. York, Esq.," s. and h. of William Vavasour, of the same, by Anne, da. of the Hon. Sir Thomas MANNERS, younger s. of Thomas, 1st EARL OF RUTLAND, was *cr. a Bart.*, as above, 24 Oct. 1628. He was Knight Marshal of the King's Household. He *m.* Ursula, da. of Walter GIFFARD, of Chillington, co. Stafford, by Philippa, da. of Richard WHITE, of South Warnborough, Hants. He *d.* before March 1635/6.

II. 1630? SIR WALTER VAVASOUR, Bart. [1628], of Haslewood aforesaid, s. and h.; *suc. to the Baronetcy* before March 1635/6. He raised a regiment in the Civil Wars for the service of his King, serving as Colonel under the Marquess of Newcastle. He was, accordingly, nominated in 1660 one of the Knights

(a) In Faulkner's *Chelsea* he is incorrectly identified with Sir John Laurence, of St. Helen's, Bishopsgate, L. Mayor of London, 1664-65, who *d.* 26 Jan. 1691/2.

(b) His son (in the burial of a child named "Giles") is spoken of as "Mr. Thomas Laurence, Esq.," 28 Dec. 1680, and his son's wife (in the burial of her mother, "Mrs. Elizabeth English"), as "Lady Laurence," 19 Feb. 1710/1. See burials of those dates at Chelsea.

(c) John Laurence, his s. and h. ap., was *bap.* at Chelsea, 5 Nov. 1676; matric. at Oxford (Univ. Coll.), 24 May 1694; B.A. 26 Feb. 1697/8; *m.* Elizabeth, who was *bur.* at Chelsea 7 Aug. 1701; sold an estate at Chelsea, 26 March 1706, to William, Lord Cheyne, and *d.* s.p.m. and v.p.

(d) It is, however, stated in *N. and Q.* (4th S., xii, 512) that "there is positive proof that he died in Maryland in 1712," but query if this does not relate to John Laurence, his son and heir apparent.

(e) This Peter was s. of Simon Slingsby, a yr. br. of Thomas Slingsby (ancestor of the family seated at Scriven, who were Baronets [S.] 1635 to 1869), both being sons of John Slingsby, of Scriven, who *d.* 1513.

of the intended order of the Royal Oak. He *m.* (Lic. Lon., 8 March 1635/6, he 23 and she 18), Ursula, da. of Thomas (BELASYSE), 1st VISCOUNT FAUCONBERG OF HENKNOWLE, by Barbara, da. of Sir Henry CHOLMLEY, of Whitby. He was living 13 Aug. 1666, being then aged 53.

III. 1670? SIR WALTER VAVASOUR, Bart. [1628], of Haslewood aforesaid, only surv. s. and h., aged 22 on 13 Aug. 1666; *suc. to the Baronetcy* on the death of his father. He *m.* Jane, 2d da. of Sir Jordan CROSSLAND, of Newby, co. York, by Bridget, da. of John FLEMING. She, who was *bap.* at Helmsley, 26 Dec. 1649, was living 1696. He *d.* s.p. 16 Feb. 1712/3.

IV. 1713. SIR WALTER VAVASOUR, Bart. [1628], of Haslewood aforesaid, cousin and h. male, being s. and h., of Peter VAVASOUR, M.D., by Elizabeth, da. of Philip LANGDALE, of Lanthorpe, co. York, which Peter, who was *bur.* at York 26 Nov. 1659, was youngest s. of the 1st Bart. He was *b.* about 1659, and *suc. to the Baronetcy*, 16 Feb. 1712/3. He *d.* unm., May 1740, aged about 80, in Lancashire.

V. 1740. SIR WALTER VAVASOUR, Bart. [1628], of Haslewood aforesaid, nephew and h., being s. and h. of Peter VAVASOUR, of York, which Peter, who *d.* 6 June 1735, aged 68, was next br. of the late Bart. He *suc. to the Baronetcy* in May 1745. He *m.* firstly, Elizabeth, da. of Peter VAVASOUR, of Willitoft, in the East Riding, co. York. She *d.* s.p.s. He *m.* secondly, April 1741, Dorothy, da. of Marmaduke (LANGDALE), 4th BARON LANGDALE OF HOLME, by Elizabeth, da. of William (WIDDRINGTON), BARON WIDDRINGTON OF BLANCKNEY. She *d.* 25 April 1751, at Haslewood. He *d.* 13 April 1766.

VI. 1766. SIR WALTER VAVASOUR, Bart. [1628], of Haslewood aforesaid, s. and h. by 2d wife; *b.* 16 Jan. 1744; *suc. to the Baronetcy*, 13 April 1766. He *m.*, Sep. 1797, Jane, only da. and h. of William LANGDALE, of Langthorpe, co. York. He *d.* s.p. 3 Nov. 1802, and was *bur.* at Haslewood.

VII. 1802, to 1826. SIR THOMAS VAVASOUR, Bart. [1628], of Haslewood aforesaid, br. and h. He *d.* unm., at Haslewood Hall, 20 Jan. 1826, aged about 80, when the *Baronetcy* became *extinct*.(a)

WOLSELEY:

cr. 24 Nov. 1628.

I. 1628. ROBERT WOLSELEY, of Morton, co. Stafford, Esq.," Clerk of the King's Letters Patent, 2d s.(b) of John Wolseley, of Stafford, by Isabella, da. of John PORTER, of Chillington in that county, was *b.* about 1587, and was *cr. a Bart.*, as above, 24 Nov. 1628. He was a Col. in the King's Army and suffered sequestration accordingly. He *m.*, in or before 1630, Mary, 2d da. of Sir George WROUGHTON, of Wilcot, Wilts. He *d.* in London, 21 Sep. 1646, aged 59, and was *bur.* in Colwich church, co. Stafford. M.I.

II. 1646. SIR CHARLES WOLSELEY, Bart. [1628], of Wolseley, co. Stafford, s. and h., *b.* about 1630, being aged 33 at the *Visit. of Staffordshire* on 4 April 1663; *suc. to the Baronetcy*, 21 Sep. 1646, his (late) father's estate being fined £2,500 in Oct. 1647; was M.P. for Oxon, 1653; for Staffordshire, 1654-55 and 1655-58, and for Stafford, 1660. He enjoyed favour with the Commonwealth authorities, and was one of Cromwell's "House of Lords." He *m.*, in or before 1649, Anne, youngest da. of William (FIENNES), 1st VISCOUNT SAY AND SELE, by Elizabeth, da. of John TEMPLE, of Stow. He d. 9 Oct. 1714, aged 85, and was *bur.* at Colwich aforesaid. M.I.

(a) The Vavasour estates passed, under his will, to his maternal relative, Edward Marmaduke STOURTON, 2d s. of Charles-Philip, BARON STOURTON, by Mary, da. and coheir of his maternal uncle, Marmaduke (LANGDALE), BARON LANGDALE. This Edward took the name of Vavasour in 1826, and was *cr. a Bart.* 14 Feb. 1828. He, however, has not any descent from the family of Vavasour.

(b) The elder br., William Wolseley, a Capt. in Ireland, was living 1614 (*Visit. of Stafford*) with a son and h. ap. named Charles, then five years old.

III. 1714. SIR WILLIAM WOLSELEY, Bart. [1628], of Wolseley aforesaid, 4th but 1st surv. s. and h.(a); *b.* about 1660; *suc. to the Baronetcy*, 9 Oct. 1714. He *d.* unm., 8 July 1728, in his 69th year (being drowned in his chariot, while crossing a brook at Long, near Lichfield), and was *bur.* at Colwich aforesaid. M.I.

IV. 1728. SIR HENRY WOLSELEY, Bart. [1628], of Wolseley aforesaid, br. and h.; *suc. to the Baronetcy*, 8 July 1728. He *d.* unm. 1730. Admon. 14 Jan. 1730/1.

V. 1730. SIR WILLIAM WOLSELEY, Bart. [1628], of Wolseley aforesaid, nephew and h., being s. and h.(b) of Capt. Richard WOLSELEY, of Mount Arran, afterwards Mount Wolseley, co. Carlow, by Frances, da. and h. of John BURNESTON of Ireland, which Richard was 6th s. of the 1st Bart. He *suc. to the Baronetcy* in 1730. He *m.*, in or before 1740, (—), da. of (—). He *d.* 12 May 1779. Will pr. July 1779.

VI. 1779. SIR WILLIAM WOLSELEY, Bart. [1628], of Wolseley aforesaid, s. and h.; *b.* 24 Aug. 1740; *suc. to the Baronetcy*, 12 May 1779. He *m.* firstly, 2 July 1765, (—), da. of (—) CHAMBERS, of Wimbledon, Surrey. He *m.* secondly, Anna, widow of John WHITLEY, only da. of William NORTHEY, of Compton Bassett, Wilts. He *d.* 5 Aug. 1817. His widow *m.* John ROBINS, and subsequently (for her 4th husband) (—) HARGRAVE.

VII. 1817. SIR CHARLES WOLSELEY, Bart. [1628], of Wolseley aforesaid, s. and h. by first wife; *b.* 20 July 1769; *suc. to the Baronetcy*, 5 Aug. 1817. He *m.* firstly, 13 Dec. 1792, Mary, da. of Hon. Thomas CLIFFORD, of Tixall, Salop, by Barbara, da. and coheir of James (ASTON), 5th LORD ASTON [S.]. She *d.* 16 July 1811. He *m.* secondly, 2 July 1812, Anne, youngest da. of Anthony WRIGHT, of Wealdside, Essex, by Anne, da. (whose issue become coheir) of John BIDDULPH, of Biddulph, co. Stafford. She *d.* 24 Oct. 1838. He *d.* 3 Oct. 1846, at Wolseley Hall, in his 78th year.(c) Will pr. Oct. 1846.

VIII. 1846. SIR CHARLES WOLSELEY, Bart. [1628], of Wolseley aforesaid, s. and h. by 2d wife; *b.* 6 May 1813, at Wolseley Hall; *suc. to the Baronetcy*, 3 Oct. 1846. He *m.*, 23 Sep. 1839, Mary Anne, 1st da. of Nicholas SELBY, of Acton House, Middlesex. He *d.* 15 May 1854. Will pr. June 1854. His widow *d.* 18 Jan. 1873, at the Convent, Kensington square, aged 56.

IX. 1854. SIR CHARLES-MICHAEL WOLSELEY, Bart. [1628], of Wolseley aforesaid, 2d but 1st surv. s. and h.; *b.* 4 July 1846 in Paris; *suc. to the Baronetcy*, 15 May 1854; matric. at Oxford (Ch. Ch.), 20 Jan. 1866, aged 19; sometime Lieut. in the Staffordshire Yeomanry Cavalry; served with the 9th Lancers in the Afghan Campaign, 1879. He *m.*, 17 July 1883, at the pro-cathedral, Kensington, Anita Theresa, da. of Daniel T. MURPHY, of San Francisco, in California.

Family Estates.—These, in 1883, consisted of 2,111 acres in Staffordshire, worth £2,789 a year. *Principal Seat.*—Wolseley Hall, near Rugeley, co. Stafford.

(a) His eldest br., Robert Wolseley, aged 14 in 1663; admitted to Lincoln's Inn, 14 May, 1667; was by William III sent as envoy at Brussels, and *d.* unm. v.p. 1697.

(b) His yst. br., Richard Wolseley, who inherited the Irish estates of their father, was *cr. a Bart.* [I.], 19 Jan. 1744, as of Mount Wolseley, co. Carlow.

(c) His extraordinary career as a demagogue, his imprisonment for a year, and subsequently (March 1820) for 18 months, etc., are set forth in the Annual Register for 1846.

RUDD:

cr. 8 Dec. 1628;

ex. 15 July 1739.

I. 1628. "RICHARD RUDD, of Aberglasine [*i.e.*, Aberglassney], co. Carmarthen, Esq.," 2d but only son that had issue of Anthony RUDD, BISHOP OF ST. DAVID'S, 1593-1614 (who purchased a good estate in the parish of Llangathen, co. Carmarthen, erected a mansion thereon called Aberglassney, and *d.* 7 March 1614), by Alice, formerly Alice DALTON his wife, was *cr. a Bart.*, as above, 8 Dec. 1628. Sheriff of co. Carnarvon, 1636-37; was a Royalist and was fined £581 in Oct. 1648. He *m.* firstly, Jane, da. of Thomas AP RICE, of Richeston, co. Pembroke. He *m.* secondly, Elizabeth, sister of Sir John AUBREY, 1st Bart. [1660], da. of Sir Thomas AUBREY, of Llantrithed, co. Glamorgan, by Mary, da. and h. of Anthony MANSELL. She *d.* s.p. He *d.* May 1664.

II. 1664. SIR RICE RUDD, Bart. [1628], of Aberglassney aforesaid, grandson and h., being only s. and h. of Anthony RUDD, by Judith, da. and h. of Thomas RUDD, of Higham Ferrers, co. Northampton, which Anthony (who matric. at Oxford 4 Dec. 1635, aged 16) was s. and h. ap. of the 1st Bart., by his first wife, but *d.* v.p. He was *b.* about 1643; *suc. to the Baronetcy* in May 1664; was M.P. for Higham Ferrers, 1678-79, 1679-81, and 1681; and for co. Carmarthen (5 Parls.), 1689, till death. He *m.* 7 Dec. 1661, at St. Bartholomew the Less, London (Lic. Fac., each being about 18), Dorothy, da. of Charles CORNWALLIS, of High Holborn. He *d.* s.p. and a widower, July 1701, at St. Anne's, Soho. Admon. 1 Sep. 1701, 9 Feb. 1701/2, 26 Feb. 1704/5, and 14 March 1718/9.

III. 1701. SIR ANTHONY RUDD, Bart. [1628], of Aberglassney aforesaid, cousin and h. male, being s. and h. of Thomas RUDD, who was yst. s. of the 1st Bart. by his first wife. He *m.* firstly Magdalen, da. of Sir Henry JONES, Bart. [so *cr.* 1643], of Abermarles, co. Carmarthen, by Elizabeth, da. of Sir John SALISBURY. She *d.* s.p. He *m.* secondly, Beatrice, da. of Sir John BARLOW, 1st Bart. [1677], of Slebech, co. Pembroke, sole heir of her mother, his first wife, Beatrice, da. and eventually (1674) heir of Sir John LLOYD, 1st Bart. [1662], of Woking. He *d.* 25 Dec. 1725. His widow *m.* Griffith LLOYD, and *d.* Feb. 1735/6. Her will pr. 1737.

IV. 1725, to 1739. SIR JOHN RUDD, Bart. [1628], of Aberglassney aforesaid, s. and h. by 2d wife; *suc. to the Baronetcy* on the death of his father, 25 Dec. 1725. He *m.* Mary, da. of (—). He *d.* s.p. 15 July 1739, when the *Baronetcy* became *extinct.* Admon. 9 Aug. 1739 to the widow. Her will pr. 1802.

WISEMAN:

cr. 18 Dec. 1628;

ex. 1654.

I. 1628, to 1654? "RICHARD WISEMAN, of Thundersley, co. Essex, Esq.," s. and h. of Robert Wiseman,[a] of Stondon in that county, by Barbara, da. of William BETHELL, was aged 7 in 1608, matric. at Oxford (Wadham Coll.), 17 June 1621, aged 20; admitted to Lincoln's Inn, 1622, and was *cr. a Bart.*, as above, 18 Dec. 1628. He was living at Stondon aforesaid, 1634. He *d.* s.p. about 1654, when the *Baronetcy* became *extinct.* Will pr. 1654.

[a] This Robert was 2d s. of Sir Ralph Wiseman, of Rivenhall, Essex, and br. of Sir Thomas Wiseman of the same, whose grandson, William Wiseman, was *cr. a Bart.* 15 June 1660.

FERRERS:

cr. 19 Dec. 1628;

ex. 1675.

I. 1628. "HENRY FERRERS, of Skellingthorpe,[a] co. Lincoln, Esq."; was *cr. a Bart.*, as above, 19 Dec. 1628. He resided at St. Leonard's, Bromley, Midx. He *m.* Anne, da. of James SCUDAMORE. He *d.* 1663.[b]

II. 1663, to 1675. SIR HENRY FERRERS, Bart. [1628], of Skellingthorpe aforesaid, s. and h.; *b.* about 1630; *suc. to the Baronetcy*, in 1663 He *d.* s.p., 1675, aged 45, when the *Baronetcy* became *extinct.*

ANDERSON:

cr. 3 Jan. 1628/9;

ex. 1630.

I. 1629, to 1630. "JOHN ANDERSON, of St. Ives, co. Huntingdon, Esq.," yst. s. of Sir Francis Anderson,[c] of Eyworth, Beds (*d.* 22 Dec. 1615), being only s. by his 2d wife, Audrey, 1st da. and coheir of John (BOTELER), 1st BARON BOTELER OF BRANTFIELD (by Elizabeth, da. of George VILLIERS, and sister to George, the celebrated DUKE OF BUCKINGHAM), was *cr. a Bart.*, as above, 3 Jan. 1628/9. He *d.* unm. at Apscourt,[d] in the parish of Walton upon Thames, Surrey, 1630, when the *Baronetcy* became *extinct.* Admon. 2 Aug. 1630 to his mother, Audrey, Lady Baroness Dunsmore.

RUSSELL:

cr. 9 or 19 Jan. 1628/9[e];

ex., presumably, 25 April 1804.

I. 1629. "WILLIAM RUSSELL, of Chippenham, co. Cambridge, Knt.," s. and h. of William RUSSELL, of Yaverland in the Isle of Wight, was *Knighted* at Theobalds, 29 April 1618; M.P. for Windsor, 1626; and was *cr. a Bart.*, as above, 9 or 19 Jan. 1628/9.[e] He was Treasurer of the Royal Navy, 1618-27 and 1630-39; was (as such) admitted to Gray's Inn, 1 March 1630/1, and was a great benefactor to the church of Deptford, Kent. He *m.* firstly, Elizabeth, da. of Sir Francis CHERRY, of Camberwell, Surrey, by his 1st wife, Margaret, da. of Harry HAYWARD. She was *bap.* 28 July 1588, and *d.* s.p. He *m.* secondly, in or before 1616, Elizabeth, da. of Thomas GERARD, of Burwell, co. Cambridge. She was *bur.* 14 Oct. 1626 at Chippenham. He *m.* thirdly, 12 April 1628, Elizabeth, widow of John WHEATLEY, of Catsfield, Sussex, Barrister, da. and coheir of Michael SMALLPAGE, of Chichester, by Catharine, da. and coheir of William DEVENISH, of Hellingleigh, Sussex. She probably *d.* before him. He was *bur.* 3 Feb. 1653/4 at Chippenham. Admon. (to his son) 16 Feb. 1654/5, and, again, 5 May 1663.

[a] "Mrs. Ellinor Ferrers" was buried at Skellingthope, 25 Feb. 1640/1, and "William Ferrers, Esq.," 4 Oct. 1646.

[b] Under the name of "Sir Henry Ferrers, *Knt.*," he (or possibly his son) was indicted for abetting in the murder of "one Stone" by one "Nightingale." He pleaded that he was never *Knighted*, and the indictment was made out *de novo* to "Sir Henry Ferrers, *Baronet.*"

[c] This Francis was s. and h. of Sir Edmund Anderson, Lord Chief Justice of the Common Pleas, 1582 to 1605, ancestor of the Andersons, of Broughton *cr.* Barts. 1660, and of the Andersons, of Eyworth *cr.* Barts. 1664.

[d] This was the seat of his mother's 2d husband, Sir Francis LEIGH, Bart. (*cr.* 1618), who was *cr.* BARON DUNSMORE, 1628, and EARL OF CHICHESTER, 1644.

[e] The usual date is "19 Jan.," but "9 Jan." is that given in the "*Creations, 1485-1646*" in ap. 47th Report, D.K. Pub. Records.

II. 1654. SIR FRANCIS RUSSELL, Bart. [1629], of Chippenham aforesaid, s. and h. by 2d wife; *b.* about 1616; matric. at Oxford (Wadham Coll.), 28 Jan. 1630/1, aged 14; admitted to Gray's Inn, 15 Aug. 1633, and to the Inner Temple, 1635; was M.P. for Cambridgeshire, 1645-53, 1654-55, and 1656-58; was a Col. in the Parl. army; Gov. of Ely, 1645, and of Lichfield, and afterwards, 1648, of the Channel Islands; *suc. to the Baronetcy* in Feb. 1653/4; was one of Cromwell's "Upper House." He *m.* 19 Sep. or Dec. 1631, at Chippenham, Catharine, da. and h. of John WHEATLEY, by Elizabeth, da. and coheir of Michael SMALLPAGE, all abovenamed, the said Elizabeth being the 3d wife of the 1st Bart. abovenamed. He was *bur.* 30 April 1664 at Chippenham.[a]

III. 1664. SIR JOHN RUSSELL, Bart. [1629], of Chippenham aforesaid, s. and h.; *bap.* there 6 Oct. 1640; *suc. to the Baronetcy* in April 1664. He *m.* (Lic. Fac., 22 April 1663, he about 21, bachelor, she of Holy Trinity. London, about 22, widow) Frances, widow of the Hon. Robert RICH (who *d.* s p, 16 Feb. 1657/8, aged 23), yst. da. of OLIVER CROMWELL, the "LORD PROTECTOR," by Elizabeth, da. of Sir James BOURCHIER, of Felstead, co. Essex. He was *bur.* 24 March 1669, at Chippenham. Will pr. June 1670. His widow, who was *bap.* 6 Dec. 1638 at St. Mary's, Ely, *d.* 27 Jan. 1720, aged above 80. Will pr. 1720.

IV. 1669. SIR WILLIAM RUSSELL, Bart. [1629], of Chippenham aforesaid, s. and h.; *suc. to the Baronetage* in March 1669. He spent the remainder of what once was a considerable fortune in raising troops at the time of the Revolution, and sold the estate of Chippenham. He *m.* Catharine, da. of (—) GORE, of Ireland. He, who was latterly of Hampton, co. Midx., was *bur.* 16 Sep. 1707 at Kingston-on-Thames, Surrey. Admon. 12 Nov. 1707. The admon. of his widow, as of St. Anne's, Westm., 18 July 1713, was granted to Dame Frances Russell, grandmother of her children, then minors.

V. 1707. SIR WILLIAM RUSSELL, Bart. [1629], s. and h.; *suc. to the Baronetcy* in Sep. 1707; was a minor in July 1713. He *d.* unm. May 1738, at Passage, near Waterford, Ireland.

VI. 1738. SIR FRANCIS RUSSELL, Bart. [1629], br. and h.; *suc. to the Baronetcy* in May 1738; was one of the Council at Fort William, in Bengal. He *m.* in 1725 Anne, da. of (—) GEE, merchant.

VII. 1750? SIR WILLIAM RUSSELL, Bart. [1629], only s. and h.; *suc. to the Baronetcy* on his father's death; Lieut. in the 1st Regt. of Foot Guards. He *d.* unm. 1757. Admon., as of "St. Geo. Han. sq.," 16 Jan. 1758.

VIII. 1757. SIR JOHN RUSSELL, Bart. [1629], of Checquers Court, in Ellesborough, Bucks, cousin and h. male, being s. and h. of Col. Charles RUSSELL, 34th Foot, by Mary Johanna Cutts,[b] da. of Col. RIVETT, which Charles (who *d.* 20 Nov. 1754, aged 53) was s. and h. of John RUSSELL, Governor of Fort William, Bengal (*b.*, posthumously, 14 Oct. 1670, and *d.* 5 Dec. 1735), who was 3d s. of the 3d Bart. He was *b.* 31 Oct. 1741; *suc. to the Baronetcy* in 1757; matric. at Oxford (Ch. Ch.) 24 May 1758, aged 17; B.A. 1762; M.A. 1765; Barrister (Lincoln's Inn), 1766. He *m.* 25 Oct. 1775 Catharine, da. of Gen. the Hon. George CARY, of Skutterskelfe, co. York (2d s. of Lucius Henry, 6th VISCOUNT FALKLAND [S.]), by Isabella, da. and h. of Arthur INGRAM. She *d.* 26 Dec. 1782, in her 34th year, and was *bur.* at Ellesborough. M.I. He *d.* 7 Aug. 1783 at Sir Henry Oxenden's house, in Kent, and was *bur.* at Ellesborough in his 42d year. M.I. Will pr. Aug. 1783.

[a] Elizabeth, their 1st da., *m.* Henry CROMWELL, Lord Deputy of Ireland, yst. s. of the "LORD PROTECTOR."

[b] By her the estate of Checquers came to the Russell family; her mother, Johanna, being da. and h. of John Thurbane, Serjeant at Law (1689), who had acquired it by marriage.

IX. 1783. SIR JOHN RUSSELL, Bart. [1629], of Checquers Court aforesaid, s. and h.; *b.* 6 May 1777 at Knightsbridge, Midx.; *suc. to the Baronetcy*, 7 Aug. 1738: matric. at Oxford (Ch. Ch.), 29 Oct. 1795, aged 18. He *d.* unm. 11 June 1802, and was *bur.* at Ellesborough. M.I. Will pr. 1802.

X. 1802, to 1804. SIR GEORGE RUSSELL, Bart. [1629], of Checquers Court aforesaid, br. and h.; *b.* 15 April 1780 at Knightsbridge, Midx.; matric. at Oxford (Ch. Ch.), 24 Oct. 1798, aged 17; admitted to Lincoln's Inn, 5 May 1802; *suc. to the Baronetcy*, 11 June 1802. He *d.* s.p. 25 April 1804, in London, and was *bur.* at Ellesborough. M.I. At his death the *Baronetcy* is presumed to have become *extinct.*[a] Will pr. 1804.

POWELL:

cr. 21 Jan. 1629/30;

ex., presumably, about 1700.

I. 1630. "THOMAS POWELL, of Berkenhead, co. Chester, Esq.," s. and h. of Thomas POWELL, of Horsley, co. Denbigh, and of the Priory of Birkenhead, co. Chester, by Dorothy, da. of Morris WYNNE, of Gwydir, was, presumably, as "Thomas Powell, of co. Denbigh, gent.," admitted to Lincoln's Inn, 23 Oct. 1602, was Sheriff of Denbighshire, 1615-16 and 1638-39; of Cheshire, 1639-40, having been *cr. a Bart.*, as above, 21 Jan. 1629/30. He *m.* Margaret (*b.* 2 and *bap.* 6 Sep. 1584), da. of Sir John EGERTON, of Egerton and Oulton, by Margaret, da. of Sir Rowland STANLEY, of Hooton. His burial as "Sir Thomas Powell, Knt.," is registered 25 Sep. 1647, both at Long Ditton and at Barnes, co. Surrey.

II. 1647? to 1700? SIR THOMAS POWELL, Bart. [1630], of Horsley and Birkenhead aforesaid, grandson and h. being s. and h. of John POWELL, by Margaret, da. of Edward PULESTON, of Allington, which John was s. and h. ap. of the 1st Bart., but *d.*, v.p., Dec. 1642. He was *b.* 1631, being aged 18 in 1649; he *suc. to the Baronetcy* on the death of his father. He was Sheriff of Denbighshire, 1656-57. He *m.* firstly, in or before 1650,[b] Mary, da. of William CONWAY, of Bodryddan, co. Carnarvon. He *m.* secondly, Jane, da. of Robert RAVENSCROFT, of Bretton, co. Flint. He was living 1694, aged 63, but *d.* s.p.m.s.[c] it is presumed shortly afterwards (1700?) certainly before 1710,[d] when the *Baronetcy* appears to have become *extinct.*

EVERARD:

cr. 29 Jan. 1628/9;

ex. 1745.

I. 1629. "RICHARD EVERARD, of [Langleys in] Much Waltham, co. Essex, Esq.," s. and h. ap. of Hugh EVERARD, of the same, by Mary, da. of Thomas BRAND, *otherwise* BOND, of Great Hormead, Herts (which Hugh

[a] In the event of William Russell (who *d.* s.p. abroad about the same date) having survived him, he would have been entitled to the dignity, as being s. of Thomas Russell (*b.* 27 Feb. 1724, sometime an officer in the army), s. of Francis Russell (*bap.* 19 Jan. 1691 at Fordham, co. Suffolk), s. of William Russell, of Fordham (*bur.* 26 June 1701), s. of Gerald Russell of the same (*d.* 7 Dec. 1682, aged 63), who was a yr. s. of the 1st Bart, by his 2d wife.

[b] The date of "28 May 1629" [*Qy.* 1649], is given for this marriage in the ped. in Ormerod's *Cheshire*, but it is manifestly erroneous. See note "b" below.

[c] His only son, Thomas Powell, of Horsley aforesaid, who matric. at Oxford (Jesus Coll.), 5 July 1667, aged 17; was Sheriff of Denbighshire, 1683-84, and of Cheshire, April 1689; *m.* twice, but *d.* v.p. before 1694, having had by his 2d wife three daughters, but by his 1st wife "male issue" [see ped. in Ormerod's *Cheshire*, taken from Le Neve's MS. peds. of Baronets], which, presumably, was extinct before the death of his father, the 2d Bart.

[d] In 1710 the estate of Birkenhead Priory was sold to John Cleiveland, presumably after the extinction in the male line of the Powell family.

was next br. and h. male (1614) to Sir Anthony Everard, of Langleys aforesaid), was, v.p., *cr. a Bart.*, as above, 29 Jan. 1628/9. He suc. his father, 24 Aug. 1637; was a committee-man on the side of the Parl., 1643-45, and for raising and maintaining the new model, Feb. 1645; was Sheriff of Essex, 1644-45. He *m.* firstly, 1 Nov. 1621, at St. Barth. the Less, London, Joan, da. of Sir Francis BARRINGTON, 1st Bart. [1611], by Joan, da. of Sir Henry CROMWELL. He *m.* secondly, 11 Sep. 1653, at St. Anne's, Blackfriars, London, Frances, widow of Sir Gervas ELWES, of Woodford, Essex, da. of Sir Robert LEE, of Billesley, co. Warwick, by Anne, da. of Sir Thomas LOWE, sometime (1604-05), Lord Mayor of London. By her, who *d.* in St. Martin's in the Fields and was *bur.* 2 Dec. 1676 at St. Andrew's, Undershaft, he had no issue. He *d.* about 1680. His will pr. 1680 at the Archdeaconry Court of Essex.

II. 1680? SIR RICHARD EVERARD, Bart. [1629], of Langleys aforesaid, s. and h. by 1st wife; *b.* about 1625; was possibly the "Sir Richard Everard, Knt." (who, apparently, was of Boreham, Essex), who was M.P. for Westm., 1661-78; *suc. to the Baronetcy* about 1680. He *m.* firstly, in or before 1654, Elizabeth, 1st da. and coheir of Sir Henry GIBB, Bart. [S. 1634], by Anne, da. of Sir Ralph GIBBS, of Honiton, co. Warwick. He *m.* secondly, Jane, da. of Sir John FINET, Master of the Ceremonies. By her he had no issue. He *d.* 29 Aug. 1694, aged 69, and was *bur.* at Waltham.

III. 1694. SIR HUGH EVERARD, Bart. [1629], of Langleys aforesaid, only surv. s and h. by 1st wife; *b.* about 1654. In early life he distinguished himself in the army in Flanders; was Receiver General of the Land tax for Essex; *suc. to the Baronetcy* in Aug. 1694, but much encumbered his estate. He *m.*, in or before 1683, Mary, da. of John BROWNE, M.D., of Salisbury. He *d.* 2 Jan. 1705/6, aged 51, and was *bur.* at Waltham. Will pr. May 1707. His widow was living 1707.

IV. 1706. SIR RICHARD EVERARD, Bart. [1629], of Bromfield Green, co. Essex, s. and h.; *b.* about 1683; *suc. to the Baronetcy* in Jan. 1705/6, and sold the estate of Langleys; was Governor of North Carolina, 1724, under the Lords Proprietor. He *m.* (Lic. Lond. 21 Dec. 1705, he aged 22) Susanna, only child that had issue of Richard KIDDER, D.D., Bishop of Bath and Wells [1691-1703]. He *d.* 17 Feb. 1732/3, in Red Lion street, Holborn. Will pr. 1733. His widow *d.* 12 Sep. 1739. Will pr. 1739.

V. 1733. SIR RICHARD EVERARD, Bart. [1629], of Bromfield Green aforesaid, s. and h.; admitted to Gray's Inn, 14 Aug. 1731; *suc. to the Baronetcy*, 17 Feb. 1732/3. He *d.* a widower and s.p. 7 March 1741/2. Admon., as of St. Martin's in the Fields, Midx., 11 May 1743, to his br. and next of kin as below.

VI. 1742, to 1745. SIR HUGH EVERARD, Bart. [1629], only br. and h.; *suc. to the Baronetcy*, 7 March 1741/2. He emigrated to Georgia, where he *m.* Mary, da. of (—). He *d.* s.p. 1745,(a) when the *Baronetcy* became *extinct*. Will dat. 2 March 1744/5, and pr. 31 Aug. 1745, by his relict and universal legatee.

LUCKYN:

cr. 2 March 1628/9;

afterwards, since 1737, VISCOUNTS GRIMSTON [I.];

and subsequently, since 1815, EARLS OF VERULAM [U.K.]

I. 1629. "WILLIAM LUCKYN, of Little Waltham, co. Essex, Esq.," s. and h. of William LUCKYN, of Shinges, *otherwise* Mascalls, in Great Baddow in that county, by Margaret, da. of Thomas JENNY, of Bury St. Edmunds, was *b.* 1594; *suc.* his father, 13 Dec. 1610; was admitted to Lincoln's Inn, 6 Feb.

(a) His sister, Susanna, had *m.* in Virginia before 1741, (—) WHITE, a considerable merchant and planter there.

1613/4, and was *cr. a Bart.*, as above, 2 March 1628/9; was Sheriff for Essex, 1637-38. He *m.* firstly, in or before 1620, Mildred, 3d da. of Sir Gamaliel CAPELL, of Raynes, co. Essex, by Jane, da. and coheir of Weston BROWNE, of Rookwoods in that county. He *m.* secondly, 1 Dec. 1634, at St. Bride's, London (Lic. Lond., he 30 and she 20), Elizabeth, da. of Sir Edward PYNCHON, of Writtle, by Dorothy, da. of Sir Jerome WESTON, of Roxwell, both in co. Essex. His will, dat. 2 July 1658, pr. 28 Feb. 1660/1. His widow *d.* 7 July 1667.

II. 1660? SIR CAPELL LUCKYN, Bart. [1629], of Messing Hall, Essex, s and h. by 1st wife; aged 13 in 1634; admitted to Lincoln's Inn, 17 June 1640; *Knighted*, 2 June 1660; *suc. to the Baronetcy* about 1660; M.P. for Harwich, April 1648 till secluded in Dec.; re-elected 1680 and April 1664-79. He *m.* 20 Jan. 1647/8, at Hackney, Midx., Mary, 1st da. of Sir Harbottle GRIMSTON, 2d Bart. [1611], of Bradfield Hall, Essex, and afterwards of Gorhambury, Herts, by Mary, da. of Sir George CROKE, Justice of the Common Pleas. He *d.* about 1680. Will pr. 1680. His widow *d.* 18 and was *bur.* 24 March 1719, at Messing, aged 86.

III. 1680? SIR WILLIAM LUCKYN, Bart. [1629], of Messing Hall aforesaid, surv. s. and h.; *suc. to the Baronetcy* about 1680. He *m.* 1 Dec. 1681, at St. Peter's, Cornhill, Mary, da. of William SHERRINGTON, Fishmonger and Alderman of London (*bur.* 15 Nov. 1706, at St. Peter's aforesaid), by Elizabeth his wife. He *d.* about 1708. Admon. 11 Feb. 1708/9 and 11 Feb. 1735/6. His widow, who was *bap.* 4 June 1663, at St. Peter's aforesaid, was *bur.* 24 Nov. 1749, at Messing. Will pr. 1750.

IV. 1708? SIR HARBOTTLE LUCKYN, Bart. [1629], of Messing Hall aforesaid, s. and h.; *bap.* 16 Jan. 1683/4 at St. Peter's, Cornhill, London; *suc. to the Baronetcy* about 1708; was Cupbearer to Queen Anne and to George I and II. He *d.*, unm., 4 and was *bur.* 15 Feb. 1736/7, at Messing. M.I. Will pr. 1737.

V. 1737. WILLIAM (GRIMSTON), VISCOUNT GRIMSTON [I.] and Bart. [1629], br. and h.; *b.* about 1664; suc., in Oct. 1700, on the death of his great uncle, Sir Samuel Grimston, 3d Bart. [1611], to the estate of Gorhambury, Herts, when he took the name of *Grimston* in lieu of that of his patronymic of *Luckyn*; was M.P. for St. Albans, 1710-22 and 1729-34, and was *cr.*, 29 Nov. 1719, BARON DUNBOYNE, of co. Meath, and VISCOUNT GRIMSTON [I.] By the death of his elder br., 4 Feb. 1736/7, he *suc. to the Baronetcy*, which has since continued to be united with the Viscountcy of Grimston [I.], as also, since 1815, with the Earldom of Verulam, the 4th Viscount having been *cr.*, 24 Nov. 1815, EARL OF VERULAM [U.K.]. See *Peerage* under "GRIMSTON" and "VERULAM."

GRAHAM, *or* GRAHME,(a) of Eske, co. Cumberland [E.],

cr. 29 March 1629;

sometime, 1681-90 *and* 1690-1739, VISCOUNTS PRESTON [S.];

forfeited 1690;

but, possibly, *restored* in 1691.

I. 1629. "RICHARD GRAHAM, of Eske, co. Cumberland, Esq.," and also of Netherby in that county, 2d s. and h. male of Fergus GRAHAM, or GRAHME, of Plomp, in that county, by Sibill, da. of William BELL, of Godsbrigg, in Scotland, was Gentleman of the Horse to James I, was M.P. for Carlisle 1626 and 1628-29, and was *cr. a Bart.*, as above, 29 March 1629. He adhered to the Royal cause with great fidelity and was severely wounded at the Battle of Marston Moor, 2 July 1644. He purchased the estate of Netherby and the Barony of Liddell, co. Cumberland. He

(a) The name is frequently spelt "Grahme," and appears to have been so used by the earlier Baronets.

m., in or before 1624, Catharine, da. of Thomas MUSGRAVE, of Cumcatch, co. Cumberland, by Susanna, his wife. She *d.* 23 and was *bur.* 27 March 1649, at Wath, co. York, in her 48th year. M.I. He *d.* 28 Jan. and was *bur.* 11 Feb. 1653/4, at Wath.(a) Will dat. 26 March 1653, and pr. 30 Jan. 1653/4.

II. 1654. SIR GEORGE GRAHAM, *or* GRAHME, Bart. [1629], of Netherby aforesaid., s. and h.,(b) *b.* about 1624; *suc. to the Baronetcy* 28 Jan. 1653/4. He *m.* Mary, da. of James (JOHNSTONE), 1st EARL OF HARTFELL [S.], by his 1st wife, Margaret, 1st da. of William (DOUGLAS), 1st EARL OF QUEENSBERRY [S.]. He *d.* 19 March 1657/8, aged 33, and was *bur.* at Arthuret, co. Cumberland, M.I. Will dat. 19 March 1657/8, pr. 3 March 1658/9. His widow *m.* Sir George FLETCHER, 2d Bart. [1641], of Hutton, who *d.* 23 July 1700, aged 67.

III. 1658, to 1690. SIR RICHARD GRAHAM, Bart. [1629], of Netherby aforesaid, s. and h.; *b.* 24 Sep. 1648, at Netherby; *suc. to the Baronetcy*, 19 March 1657/8; ed. at Westm. and at Ch. Ch., Oxford; matric. 20 June 1664, aged 15; M.A. 4 Feb. 1666/7; admitted to the Inner Temple, 1664; was 16 years old at the Heralds' Visitation, 29 March 1665; M.P. for Cockermouth (4 Parls.), 1675-81, and for co. Cumberland, 1685-87, having meanwhile been *cr.* a Scotch peer, 12 May 1681, as VISCOUNT PRESTON and LORD GRAHAM OF ESK [S]. He *m.*, 2 Aug. 1670, Anne, 2d da. of Charles (HOWARD), 1st EARL OF CARLISLE, by Anne, da. of Edward (HOWARD), BARON HOWARD OF ESCRICK. As an adherent of James II, he was found guilty of high treason and condemned to death by the English Parl., 17 Jan. 1689/90, under the designation of a Baronet, whereby the *Baronetcy* [E.], and his English estates were *forfeited*, though "the attainder could not affect his Scottish peerage, as no act of forfeiture passed against him in Scotland."(c) He was, however, subsequently pardoned by Royal Sign Manual.(d) dated June 1691. He *d.* 22 Nov. 1695, and was *bur.* at Nunnington, co. York, aged 47. His widow living 5 Feb. 1706. See fuller particulars of him in *Peerage*.

* * * * * *

[If the pardon granted to the 1st Viscount Preston had the effect of reversing the attainder of 1690, the Baronetcy would on his death, 22 Nov. 1695, descend as below.]

IV. 1695. EDWARD (GRAHAM), 2d VISCOUNT PRESTON, [S.], and a Bart.(e) [1629], 3d but 1st surv. s. and h., *b.* 1679; *suc. to the peerage*, 22 Nov. 1695; *d.* 1710.

V. 1710. CHARLES (GRAHAM), 3d VISCOUNT PRESTON, [S.], and a Bart.(e) [1629], s. and h.; *b.* 25 March 1706; *suc. to the peerage* in 1710; *d.* s.p. 23 Feb. 1738/9, when the *peerage* [S.] became *extinct*, but the right to the Baronetcy, so far as it was not affected by the attainder of 1690, devolved as below.(f)

[See fuller particulars in *Peerage*.]

(a) See copious extracts from these registers, with notes by the Rev. John Ward, illustrating this family, in the *Top. and Gen.*, vol. iii, pp. 414-436.

(b) Richard Graham, the 2d s., *bap.* 11 March 1635/6, at Wath, was *cr. a Bart.* 17 Nov. 1662, as of Norton Conyers, co. York, a dignity which still (1900) exists.

(c) Wood's *Douglas's Peerage of Scotland.*

(d) In an article by Peter Burke, Serjeant at Law [*Her. and Gen.*, vol. iv, p. 369], it is stated that, before pronouncing positively as to whether this Baronetcy is affected or not by the attainder of 1690, "it will be necessary to find out whether the attainting judgment was of record and what was the exact nature of the pardon granted to Viscount Preston."

(e) On the assumption that the forfeiture of 1690 was invalid or had been reversed. See note "d" above.

(f) The estate of Netherby and the other large estates of the family devolved on his lordship's aunts, the two daughters of the 1st Viscount. Of these, Mary *d.* unm., 18 Oct. 1753, and her surv. sister, Catharine, Dowager Baroness Widdrington (who *d.* s.p. 1757) devised them to her cousin, Robert Graham, D.D., 2d s. of William Graham, Dean of Wells, who was 4th s. of the 2d Bart., and consequently br. of the 1st Viscount. His s. and h., James Graham, was *cr. a Bart.* in 1782 as "of Netherby."

VI. 1739. SIR WILLIAM GRAHAM, Bart.(a) [1629], cousin and h. male, being s. and h. of the Rev. Charles GRAHAM, Rector of Southchurch, Essex, by Priscilla, da. of Case BILLINGSLEY, of Tottenham, Midx., merchant, which Charles (*d.* April 1734) was s. and h. of William Graham, D.D., Dean of Wells (*d.* Feb. 1711/2), yr. br. of Richard, 1st VISCOUNT PRESTON [S.], both being sons of the 2d Bart. He was *b.* 1730, at Tottenham aforesaid., and appears to have *assumed*, 23 Feb. 1738/9, not *only the Baronetcy* [E.] but also the *Viscountcy of Preston* [S.].(b) He is said to have been ed. at St. John's Coll., Cambridge, and was in Holy Orders. He *m.* 7 Nov. 1761 at St. Botolph's, Aldgate, London, Susanna, widow of Richard FRENCH, of Battle, Sussex, da. of (—) REEVE, of Ashburnham, in that county. He *d.* 21 Sep. 1774, aged 44, and was *bur.* at Carmarthen.(c) Admon. (*query* at Carmarthen). Feb. 1775. His widow *d.* at Edinburgh, 1788, and was *bur.* there.

VII. 1774. SIR CHARLES GRAHAM, Bart.(a) [1629], s. and h.; *bap.* at Battle aforesaid, 11 Nov. 1764, as "the Hon. Charles Grayham, s. of the Rev. William G., Lord Viscount Preston." He *suc. to the Baronetcy*,(a) 21 Sep. 1774. He *d.* unm. 26 Nov. 1795, and was *bur.* at St. Martin's in the Fields.

VIII. 1795. SIR ROBERT GRAHAM, Bart.(a) [1629], of Dulwich and Putney, Surrey, and afterwards of Dursley, co. Gloucester, br. and h.; *bap.* 1 Nov. 1769, at Battle aforesaid. He *suc. to the Baronetcy*,(a) 26 Nov. 1795. He was one of the claimants of the EARLDOM OF ANNANDALE [S.] as heir gen. of Lady Mary JOHNSTONE, eldest sister of James, 1st Earl, and wife of the 2d Bart. He *m.*, 25 April 1810, in Bloomsbury square, St. Geo., Bloomsbury, Middlesex (by spec. lic.), Elizabeth, only da. of John YOUNG, of Battle aforesaid, surgeon. He *d.* 27 Jan. 1852, at Dursley aforesaid, aged 82. Will pr. Nov. 1852. His widow *d.*, 16 Dec. 1859, at Bayswater, aged 70.

IX. 1852. SIR EDWARD GRAHAM, Bart.(a) [1629], 4th but 1st surv. s. and h., *b.* 1 and *bap.* 20 Jan. 1820, at Dulwich aforesaid, regd. at St. Giles', Camberwell, *suc. to the Baronetcy*,(a) 27 Jan. 1852; appointed in 1855 to the Turkish Contingent with local rank as Assistant Commissary of the 1st Class. He *m.* firstly, 5 June 1841, (—) widow of Charles HENDERSON, of St. John's terrace, Oxford, but by her had no issue. He *m.* secondly, 3 Aug. 1844, Adelaide Elizabeth, yst. da. of James Dillon TULLY, M.D., Deputy Inspector-Gen. of Army Hospitals in Jamaica. She *d.* 12 March 1852, from a fall downstairs, aged 30. He *m.* thirdly, 20 Jan. 1855, Amelia Ellen, da. of William John AKERS. He *d.* 27 May 1864, at Montreal, in Canada, aged 44. His widow *m.*, 1870, James R. JOHNSTON, and *d.* April 1877.

X. 1864. SIR ROBERT JAMES STUART GRAHAM, Bart.(a) [1629], s. and h. by 2d wife, *b.* 2 Dec. 1845, in London, *suc. to the Baronetcy*(a) 27 May 1864. He *m.* 1 Aug. 1874, at New York, U.S.A., Eliza Jane, da. of Charles BURNS, of Brooklyn.

Family Estates.—These were, in 1757, devised to the cadet line of the family of Graham, afterwards, since 1783, Baronets, of Netherby. *Residence.*—Brooklyn, New York, U.S.A.

(a) See p. 70, note "e."

(b) "Neither as a Peer or a Baronet is the existence of this person or his posterity admitted in Wood's edit. (1813) of Douglas's *Peerage of Scotland*, nor is he inserted [in Wotton's *Baronetage*, 1741] in Kimber and Johnson's *Baronetage*, 1771, either in a distinct article or in the account of this family given in relation to the Norton Conyers branch, which is also descended from the first Baronet of Esk. In the *Baronetage* of 1819 an article for "Graham of Esk" is inserted, and thenceforward the title [*i e.*, that Baronetcy] is recognised by all subsequent works of that class, but we have failed to discover anywhere that the attainder of 1690 has actually been reversed." [*Her. and Gen.*, vol. iv., p. 278.]

(c) In the *Gent. Mag.* for 1777 his death is thus recorded: "Sep. 21, at Mr. Lewis', in Carmarthen, the Rt. Hon. and Rev. William Graham, Lord Viscount Preston," which notice is followed by an erroneous statement that he was son and successor of the Viscount who died in 1739. That [erroneous] affiliation is, however, ascribed to him in the old (1764) edit. of *Douglas's Peerage of Scotland*, though not in the subsequent one of 1816.

TWISLETON:

cr. 2 April 1629;

ex. Oct. 1635.

I. 1629, to 1635. "GEORGE TWISLETON, of Barly, co. York, Esq.," s. and h. of Christopher TWISLETON, of the same, by Alice, da. of (—) HASELWOOD, of Maidwell, co. Northampton; was aged 7 at the Visit. of Yorkshire in 1612, and was *cr. a Bart.*, as above, 2 April 1629. He *m.* Catharine, da. of Henry STAPYLTON, of Wighill, co. York, by Mary, illegit. da. of Sir John FORSTER, of Alnwick. He *d.* s.p. Oct. 1635. Will pr. 1635, when the *Baronetcy* became *extinct.*(a) His widow *m.* Sir Henry CHOLMELEY, of West Newton. She was *bur.*, 14 June 1672, at Oswaldkirk.

ACTON:

cr. 30 May 1629;

ex. 1651.

I. 1629, to 1651. "WILLIAM ACTON, of the city of London, Esq.," s. and h. of Richard ACTON(b) of the same, citizen and mercer, by Margaret, da. of (—) DANIEL, also of London, was apprenticed, 7 Sep. 1593, in the Merchant Tailors Company; made free, 18 Jan. 1601; was on the livery, 5 July 1616; Alderman of Aldersgate, 12 Feb. 1627/8; Sheriff of London, 1628-29, and was, during office, *cr. a Bart.*(c) as above, 30 May 1629, being *knighted* the subsequent day. He was, subsequently, 1640, Lord Mayor of London, but was discharged from his office, 6 Oct. 1640, (shortly after his election), as also from being Alderman, by the House of Commons on account of his favouring the party of the King. He *m.* firstly, Anne, da. and h. of James BILL, of Astwell, Herts. He *m.* secondly, Jane, widow of Sir William BIRD, D.C.L., Judge of the Admiralty Court (who *d.* Aug. 1624), da. of (—) JOHNSON. She was *bur.*, 1 March 1644/5, at St. Peter's Cheap, London. Her will dat. 3 Dec. 1640, pr. 28 Feb. 1644/5. He *d.* s.p.m.(d) 22 Jan. 1650/1, when the *Baronetcy* became *extinct.* Will, in which he directs his burial to be at Edmonton, dat. 30 May 1650, pr. 26 March 1651 and 5 Feb. 1672/3.

LE STRANGE, L'ESTRANGE, *or* STRANGE:

cr. 1 June 1629;

ex. 21 April 1762.

I. 1629. "NICHOLAS LE STRANGE, of Hunstanton, co. Norfolk, Esq.," s. and h. ap.(e) of Sir Hamon LE STRANGE, of Hunstanton aforesaid, by Alice, da. and coheir of Richard STUBBE, of Sedgeford, in that county,

(a) The estates passed to his uncle, John Twisleton, of Drax, co. York, ancestor, in the male line, of the Lords Saye and Sele.

(b) This Richard was 2d s. of William Acton, of Aldenham, Salop, ancestor of the ACTONS, Barts., so *cr.* 17 Jan. 1643/4.

(c) This is the first Baronetcy conferred on a City dignitary, and it is to be noted that the recipient, in this case, had not, as yet, attained the Mayoralty.

(d) Elizabeth, his only da. and h. (by his 1st wife), *m.* 16 April 1635, at Leyton, co. Essex, Sir Thomas WHITMORE, Bart. (so *cr.* 1641), to whom she brought her mother's estate of Astwell aforesaid.

(e) His younger br., Sir Roger Le Strange, *otherwise* LESTRANGE, attempted to reduce Lynn for Charles I, but was taken prisoner and condemned to death. He became, subsequently, well known as a voluminous writer, and was "Licenser of the press." He *d.* 11 Dec. 1704, aged 87, and was *bur.* at St. Giles' in the Fields. M.I.

was *bap.* 27 March 1604, at Hunstanton, and was v.p., *cr. a Baronet*,(a) as above, 1 June 1629;(a) suc. his father, 1654. He *m.*, 26 Aug. 1630, at St. Stephen's Norwich, Ann, da. of Sir Edward LEWKENOR, of Denham, Suffolk, by Mary, da. of Sir Henry NEVILL, of Billingbere, Berks. He *d.* 24 July 1655 and was *bur.* at Hunstanton, aged 52. M.I. Admon. 15 May 1656. His widow *d.* 15 July 1663, aged 51, and was *bur.* at Hunstanton.

II. 1655. SIR HAMON LE STRANGE, Bart. [1629], of Hunstanton aforesaid, s. and h., *bap.* there 8 Dec. 1631; *suc. to the Baronetcy*, 24 July 1655, but *d.* s.p., seven months afterwards, 15 Feb. 1655/6 and was *bur.* at Hunstanton.

III. 1656. SIR NICHOLAS LE STRANGE, *otherwise* L'ESTRANGE, Bart. [1629], of Hunstanton aforesaid, br. and h.; *bap.* there 17 Oct. 1632; *suc. to the Baronetcy*, 15 Feb. 1655/6. He *m.* firstly, Mary, da. of John COKE, of Holkham, Norfolk, by Muriel, da. and h. of Anthony WHEATLEY, Prothonotary of the Court of Common Pleas. Her admon. June 1662. He *m.* secondly, 16 Oct. 1662, at Stowlangtoft, Elizabeth, da. of Sir Justinian ISHAM, 2d Bart. [1627] by his 1st wife, Jane, da. of Sir John GARRARD, 1st Bart. [1622]. He *d.* 13 and was *bur.* 15 Dec. 1669, at Hunstanton. Admon. 17 June 1670. His widow, who was *b.* 22 Aug. and *bap.* 7 Sep. 1636, at Lamport, co. Northampton, was *bur.*, 6 Aug. 1689, in Westm. Abbey. Will dat. 13 May and pr. 6 Aug. 1689.

IV. 1669. SIR NICHOLAS L'ESTRANGE, Bart. [1629], of Hunstanton aforesaid, s. and h., by 1st wife, *b.* 2 Dec. 1661, *suc. to the Baronetcy*, 13 Dec. 1669; matric. at Oxford (Ch. Ch.), 23 May 1677, aged 15. Col. of the Yellow Regiment of Trained Bands, 1683; M.P. for Castle Rising, 1685-87. He *m.*, 2 Dec 1686, at St. Giles' in the Fields (Lic. Fac., he 25 and she 18), Anne, da. of Sir Thomas WODEHOUSE, of Kimberley, Norfolk (s. and h. ap. of the 3d Bart.), by Ann, da. and coheir of Sir William ARMYNE, 2d Bart. [1619]. He *d.*, 18 Dec. 1724, at Gressenhall, co. Norfolk. Will dat. 8 March 1722, pr. 14 May 1725. His widow *d.* 1727. Will pr. 12 June 1727.

V. 1724. SIR THOMAS L'ESTRANGE, Bart. [1629], of Hunstanton aforesaid, eldest surv. s. and h.,(b) *b.* 1689; *suc. to the Baronetcy*, 18 Dec. 1724. He *m.*, 27 July 1721, Anne, da. and, at length, sole h. of Sir Christopher CALTHORPE, K.B., of East Barsham, Norfolk, by Dorothy, da. of Sir William SPRING, 1st Bart. [1641]. She *d.* 1743. He *d.* s.p. 8 and was *bur.* 10 Nov. 1751, at Hunstanton.

VI. 1751. SIR HENRY L'ESTRANGE, Bart. [1629], of Hunstanton aforesaid, and of Gressenhall, co. Norfolk, br. and h., *suc. to the Baronetcy* in 1751. He *m.* Mary, 3d da. of the Rt. Hon. Roger NORTH, of Rougham, Norfolk (s. of Dudley, Lord North), by Mary, da. of Sir Robert GAYER, of Stoke Pogis. He *d.* s.p. 2 Sep. 1760,(c) and was *bur.* at Hunstanton. Admon. 2 Oct. 1760, and, again, May 1826. The will of his widow was pr. at Norwich, 19 Nov. 1781.

(a) The patent was, in 1900, in the muniment room at Hunstanton. It has, at the foot, a quaint inscription in the handwriting of Sir Hamon le Strange, the father of the 1st Baronet, as follows:—"Md that I, Hamon le Strange, Knt, father of the within-named Sr Nichs, was Knighted at the coronācon of King James, ão 1604, and, because the dignitie of Baronet would give mee small exceedence, therefore I purchased the same for my sonn Nichs and bestowed the same upon him ão 5o Caroli, wch. cost in money 300 li., and in charges 100 li; all witnessed by this subscription of my name, under myne hande, Hamon le Strange." [*Ex inform.* Hamon le Strange, Hunstanton Hall, Norfolk.]

(b) Hamon, his elder br., *b.* 1687; *d.* unm. and v.p. in 1715, on his travels.

(c) Of his sisters and coheirs (1), Armyne, the eldest, *m.* Nicholas STYLEMAN, of Snettisham, Norfolk, and their descendants (STYLEMAN-LE STRANGE) inherit the estate of Hunstanton; (2), Lucy, the youngest, *m.* Sir Jacob ASTLEY, 3d Bart. [1660], and their great grandson was, in 1841, as her representative, summoned to the House of Peers, in the BARONY OF HASTINGS, of which she and her elder sister abovenamed represented the junior coheir.

VII. 1760, to 1762. SIR ROGER L'ESTRANGE, Bart. [1629], cousin and h. male,(a) being only surv. s. of Roger L'ESTRANGE, of Hoe, near East Dereham, co. Norfolk, by his 2d wife, Susan, da. and coheir of Francis LANE, of Thuxton, which Roger last named (who *d.* 29 Oct. 1706, aged 63) was a yr. s. of the 1st Bart. He was *b.* 1682, and was living at Harleston in 1703. He *suc. to the Baronetcy*, but not to the family estate, 2 Sep. 1760, when nearly 80. He *m.* firstly, Lettice, da. of Richard COGSDELL, of Harleston. He *m.* secondly, in 1713, Sarah NIXON, of Wymondham, co. Norfolk, spinster. He *m.* thirdly, in or before 1717, Elizabeth, da. of Thomas REDE, of Weston, co. Suffolk. He *d.*, s.p.m.s., at Beccles, 21 and was *bur.* 25 April 1762, at Weston, when the *Baronetcy* became *extinct.* Will dat. 26 Oct. 1761, pr. 1 June 1762, in Archdeaconry of Suffolk. His widow was *bur.* 17 Nov. 1779, at Weston.

HOLLAND:

cr. 15 June 1629;

ex. 17 Feb. 1728/9.

I. 1629. "JOHN HOLLAND, of Quidenham, co. Norfolk, Esq.," s. and h. of Sir Thomas HOLLAND of the same (living 1625), by Mary, da. of Sir Thomas KNYVET, was *b.* Oct. and *bap.* Nov. 1603, and was *cr. a Baronet*, as above, 15 June 1629; was M.P. for Norfolk, April to May 1640, for Castle Rising, Nov. 1640 till secluded in Dec. 1648, and for Aldborough, 1661-79; was a Presbyterian and an energetic supporter of the Parl. measures, serving on many important Committees, 1642-47, and being a Col. in the Parl. army; was one of the New Council of State, Feb. to May 1660. He *m.*, between Nov. 1629 and Dec. 1632, Alathea, widow of William (SANDYS), LORD SANDYS OF THE VINE, 1st da. and testamentary coheir of John PANTON, of Brynnelkib, in Henthlan, co. Denbigh, by Helenor, da. of Sir William BOOTH, of Dunham Massey, co. Chester. She *d.* 22 May 1679. He *d.* 19 Jan. 1701, aged 98, and was *bur.* at Langley. Will pr. March 1705.

II. 1701. SIR JOHN HOLLAND, Bart. [1629], of Quidenham aforesaid, grandson and h., being son and h. of Col. Thomas HOLLAND, who *d.* v.p. 28 Dec. 1698, by Elizabeth, da. of Thomas MEADE, of Loftus, Essex. He *suc. to the Baronetcy*, 19 Jan. 1701; was M.P. for Norfolk (four Parls.), 1701-10; P.C., 2 June 1709, and Comptroller of the Household to Queen Anne, 1709-11. He *m.*, May 1699, Rebecca, 2d and ygst. da. and coheir of William (PASTON), 2d and last EARL OF YARMOUTH, by his 1st wife, Charlotte Jemima Henrietta Maria BOYLE, *or* FITZROY, illegit. da. of King CHARLES II. She was *b.* 14 Jan. 1681. He *d.* about 1724. Admon., as of Bury St. Edmunds, 22 July 1724, his widow being then alive.

III. 1724? to 1729. SIR WILLIAM HOLLAND, Bart. [1629], of Quidenham aforesaid, s. and h., was *b.* 17 April 1700; *suc. to the Baronetcy* about 1724. He *m.* Mary, da. of Arthur UPTON, merchant. He *d.* s.p. 17 Feb. 1728/9, when the *Baronetcy* became *extinct.* Admon., 1 April 1729, to his widow, and, again, Feb. 1815. Her will pr. May 1771.

ALEYN, *or* ALLEN:

cr. 24 June 1629;

ex. 15 Sep. 1759.

I. 1629. "EDWARD ALEYN, of Hatfield, co. Essex, Esq.," s. and h. of Edmund ALEYN, of the same, by Martha, da. and coheir of John GLASCOCK, of Pewters Hall, in Witham, Essex, was *b.* about 1586; suc. his father,

(a) See ped. by G. A. Carthew in the *Visitation of Norfolk*, 1563, vol. i, pp. 444-445, as published by the Norfolk Arch. Soc. See also Carthew's *History of Laundith*, part ii, pp. 444-447.

12 Sep. 1616, being then aged 30; and was *cr. a Baronet*, as above, 24 June 1629. He was Sheriff for Essex, 1629-30. He *m.* Elizabeth, da. and coheir of George SCOTT, of Little Leighs, Essex. He *d.* Nov. 1638. Will pr. 1638.

II. 1638. SIR EDMUND ALEYN, Bart. [1629], of Hatfield aforesaid, grandson and h., being s. and h. of Edmund ALEYN, by Mary, da. of Nicholas MILLER, of Wrotham, Kent, which Edmund last-named, who *d.* v.p. 1633, was 1st s. of the late Bart. He was aged about 2 years in 1634, and *suc. to the Baronetcy* in Nov. 1638. He *m.*, 1 May 1651, at St. Giles' in the Fields, Midx. (marriage also reg. at Birdbrook, Essex), Frances, only da. and h. of Thomas GENT, of Moynes in Steeple Bumpsted, Essex, and of Lincoln's Inn, Barrister at Law. He *d.* s.p.m. 2 Nov. 1656. His widow, who was *b.* 1636 and who brought her husband an estate of about £600 a year, *d.* 16 Jan. 1657. Both *bur.* at Hatfield Church.(a) Her will dat. 15 Jan. 1657, pr. 1 Feb. 1657/8.

III. 1656. SIR EDMUND ALEYN, Bart. [1629], of Hatfield aforesaid, s. and h., *suc. to the Baronetcy*, 2 Nov. 1656 and *d.* soon afterwards, young and unm.

IV. 1658? SIR GEORGE ALEYN, Bart. [1629], of Little Leighs aforesaid, great-uncle and h. male, being br. of the 2d and grandson of the 1st Bart.; *suc. to the Baronetcy* on the death of his nephew. He *m.* firstly, Elizabeth, da. of (—) HALL, of co. Lincoln. She *d.* s.p.m. He *m.* secondly, Martha, da. of Roger JONES, of co. Monmouth. He *m.* thirdly, (—). He *d.* 1664, and was *bur.* at Little Leighs.

V. 1664. SIR GEORGE ALEYN, Bart. [1629], of Little Leighs aforesaid, s. and h. by 2d wife, *suc. to the Baronetcy* in 1664. He *m.* Mercy, yst. da. of John CLOPTON, of Little Waltham, Essex. He *d.* 1702 and was *bur.* at Little Leighs.

VI. 1702. SIR CLOPTON ALEYN, Bart. [1629], of Little Leighs afore said, s. and h., *suc. to the Baronetcy* in 1702. He *d.* unm. 8 Sep. 1726 and was *bur.* at Little Leighs.(b)

VII. 1726. SIR GEORGE ALEYN, Bart. [1629], of Little Leighs aforesaid, br. and h., *suc. to the Baronetcy* on the death of his brother. He *d.* unm. about 1746. Will pr. 1746.

VIII. 1746? to 1759. SIR EDMUND ALEYN, Bart. [1629], of Little Leighs aforesaid, nephew and h., being s. and h. of Edward ALEYN, by Mary, da. of the Rev. (—) TROTT, Vicar of Great Saling, Essex, which Edward was 3d s. of the 5th Bart. He *suc. to the Baronetcy* about 1746 and *suc.* to the family estates in 1751 under the will of his cousin, the Hon. Mrs. Howard(c); was Sheriff of Essex, 1752-53. He *d.* unm. 15 Sep. 1759, at Bath, co. Somerset, when the *Baronetcy* became *extinct.* Will pr. 1759.

(a) Arabella, their only da., who was h. to her br., the 3d Bart., eventually inherited their large estates. She *m.* firstly, Francis THOMPSON; secondly, the Hon. George HOWARD. Under her will, dat. 20 June 1746, these estates passed in 1751 (after the death of Arthur Dobbs to whom she had conveyed them for life) to her cousin, Sir Edmund Aleyn, the 8th Bart.

(b) Query if "*Sir Edmund Alen, Bart.*," who was *bur.* "from Barnards Inn" 27 Dec. 1726, at St. Andrew's, Holborn, may not have been next br. and successor to the 6th Bart.

(c) See note "a" above. These estates passed on his death to his sister Arabella, wife of the Rev. James CHALMERS, M.A., Vicar of Earls Colne and Rector of Little Waltham, Essex.

EARLE, *or* ERLE:

cr. 2 July 1629;

ex. 13 Aug. 1697.

I. 1629. "RICHARD ERLE, of Straglethorpe co. Lincoln, Esq.," s. and h. ap. of Augustine ERLE, *or* EARLE, of the same, by Frances (*m.* 22 Jan. 1599), sister of Sir Thomas CONY, of Bassingthorpe in that county, was admitted to Gray's Inn 27 Jan. 1626/7, and was, v.p., *cr. a Baronet*, as above, 2 July 1629. He suc. his father in Nov. 1637(a); was a prisoner of war to the King in 1645; one of the English hostages for the treaty with Scotland, 17 Dec. 1646; Sheriff of Lincolnshire, 1647-48. He *m.*, in or before 1629, Frances, da. of Sir Edward HARTOPP, 1st Bart. [1619], by Mary, da. of Sir Erasmus DRYDEN, 1st Bart. [1619]. He *d.* 25 March 1667, aged 60, and was *bur.* at Straglethorpe. M.I. Will dat. 3 Oct. 1665, pr. 14 May 1667. His widow, by whom he had 12 children, *d.*(b) aged 80, and was *bur.* at Sturton, Notts. M.I. erected by her da. Elizabeth, wife of John Thornhagh.

II. 1667. SIR RICHARD EARLE, *or* ERLE, Bart. [1629], of Straglethorpe aforesaid, grandson and h., being s. and h. of Augustine EARLE, by (—), da. of (—) NODES, which Augustine (aged 5 years in 1634) was elder s. of the late Bart., but *d.* v.p. He *suc. to the Baronetcy*, 25 March 1667, but *d.* unm., of the small-pox, probably soon afterwards.

III. 1670? SIR RICHARD EARLE, *or* ERLE, Bart. [1629], of Straglethorpe aforesaid, uncle and h., *suc. to the Baronetcy* on his nephew's death. He *m.*, in or before 1673, Ellena, da. of William WELBY, of Denton, co. Lincoln; was Sheriff of Lincolnshire, 1675-76. He *d.* about 1680. Will pr. 1680. His widow *m.* Edward PAYNE, of Hough on the Hill, co. Lincoln, who survived her and was *bur.* there 30 Dec. 1728. She *d.* 2 and was *bur.* there, 10 March 1726/7.

IV. 1680? to 1697. SIR RICHARD EARLE, *or* ERLE, Bart. [1629], of Straglethorpe aforesaid, s. and h., *b.* about 1673; *suc. to the Baronetcy* about 1680. He *d.* unm. at Kensington 13 Aug. 1697, aged 24, and was *bur.* at Straglethorpe, when the *Baronetcy* became *extinct.*(c) M.I. there. Will dat. 9 Aug. 1697, pr. 3 June 1699.(d)

(a) Among Sir Joseph Williamson's "*Lincolnshire Families, temp. Car. II,*" he is noticed as "son of Anthony [should be "Augustine"] an Atturney, from an Atturney at Stragglethorpe, near Newark; £1,500; a retired man." [*Her. and Gen.*, vol. ii, p. 121.]

(b) The date of her death, which had been inscribed on the monument, was illegible when a copy, about 1870, of the inscription was made by Lord Hawkesbury. The parish register is, unfortunately, defective about that period.

(c) The Rev. W. Earle, Curate of St. Clement Danes, Westm., was, in 1900, a claimant of this Baronetcy.

(d) He "gave his estate to [his maternal cousin] William Welby, the younger, of Denton, and in case of no issue to Thomas, yst. s. of Edward Payne, on condition to change the name to Earle." [Le Neve's *Baronets.*] The will was contested by Elizabeth, wife of John Thornhagh, of Fenton in Sturton, and of Osberton, Notts she being heir at law, as only da. of the 1st Bart. but a compromise was effected, [*Ex inform.* Lord Hawkesbury.]

DUCIE:

cr. 28 Nov. 1629;

sometime, 1661? to 1679, VISCOUNT DOWNE [I.];

ex. May 1703.

I. 1629. "ROBERT DUCIE, Esq., Alderman of the city of London," 1st surv. s. of Henry DUCIE, of London, and of Little Aston, co. Stafford, merchant (*d.* Nov, 1587), by Mary (*m.* 2 July 1571, at St. Lawrence Jewry), da. and eventually h. of Robert HARDY, of London, was *bap.* 29 May 1575 at St. Lawrence Jewry, London; admitted Free of the Merchant Taylors' Company; Sheriff of London, 1620-21; Alderman of Farringdon Without, 1620-25; of Billingsgate, 1625-27, and of Bassishaw, 1627 till death, being *cr. a Baronet*, as above, 28 May 1629. He was subsequently, 1630-31, Lord Mayor of London, and was *Knighted*, during office, at Greenwich 5 June 1631. He is said to have been banker to Charles I, and to have advanced to him £80,000, but to have been worth some £400,000 notwithstanding. He *m.*, before 1609, Elizabeth, da. of Richard PYOTT, citizen and grocer of London, sometime, 1610-11, Sheriff of that city, by Margaret, da. of Richard FLOYER, of Uttoxeter. He *d.* 12 and was *bur.* 22 July 1634, at St. Lawrence Jewry. Inq. p.m. 12 Aug. 1634, at Tedbury. Will pr. 1634. His widow was *bur.* 9 Feb. 1635/6 at St. Lawrence aforesaid.

II. 1634. SIR RICHARD DUCIE, Bart. [1629], of Tortworth, co. Gloucester, 1st s. and h., *b.* about 1609; matric. at Oxford (Hart Hall) 27 Jan. 1625/6, aged 16; admitted to Middle Temple, 1627; aged 23 years and more when he *suc. to the Baronetcy*, 12 July 1634; Sheriff of Gloucestershire, 1636-37. In 1638 he was an inhabitant of St. Michael's Bassishaw, London. He was a sufferer in the cause of Charles I, and was taken prisoner by Gen. Waller; sequestrated, Oct. 1643, and fined £3,346. He *d.* unm. at his manor house at Tortworth 7 March 1656/7, and was *bur.* 10 April 1657 at Tortworth. Admon. 19 June 1657.

III. 1657. SIR WILLIAM DUCIE, Bart. [1629], of Tortworth aforesaid, br. and h.; *b.* about 1612; *suc. to the Baronetcy*, 7 March 1656/7; was Sheriff of Gloucestershire, 1660-61; made K.B., at the coronation of Charles II, 23 April 1661, and was, probably not long afterwards, *cr.*(a) BARON CLONEY and VISCOUNT DOWNE [I.]. He *m.* (Lic. Fac. 23 June 1662, he 40 and she 27), Frances, da. and coheir of Francis (SEYMOUR), 1st BARON SEYMOUR OF TROWBRIDGE, by his 1st wife, Frances, da. and coheir of Sir Gilbert PRYNNE. He *d.* s.p. 9 Sep. 1679, at Charlton, co. Kent, and was *bur.* at Tortworth, when the *peerage* became *extinct.*(b) Admon. 26 Sep. 1679. His widow, who was *bap.* (at the Lodge in the Great Park) at Great Bedwyn, Wilts, 27 April 1673, was *bur.* there 20 Sep. 1699.

IV. 1679. SIR WILLIAM DUCIE, Bart. [1629], of Islington, co. Midx., nephew and h. male, being s. and h. of Sir Hugh DUCIE, K.B., of Islington aforesaid, which Hugh, who *d.* in or before March 1661/2, was yr. s. of the 1st Bart. He was a minor at his father's death, but was of full age on 1 June 1680, having *suc. to the Baronetcy*, 9 Sep. 1679. He *m.* Judith, da. of (—), of co. Hertford. He *d.* s.p. in the Fleet prison, about 1691.

(a) Sir John Reresby, in his "*Memoirs*," states this creation to have been made at the instance of Lord Halifax, who received on that account £25,000 from the grantee.

(b) His estates devolved on his niece, Elizabeth, only da. and h. of his br., Robert Ducie. She *m.* Edward MORETON, of Moreton, co. Stafford, and was mother of Matthew Ducie Moreton, *cr.* 9 June 1720, LORD DUCIE, BARON OF MORETON, co. Stafford.

V. 1691? to 1703. SIR ROBERT DUCIE, Bart. [1629], of Islington aforesaid, br. and h.; *suc. to the Baronetcy* about 1691. He *d.* unm. May 1703, when the *Baronetcy* became *extinct.* Admon. 15 April 1704.

[After the date of the above creation, 28 Nov. 1629, a very remarkable cessation takes place in the creation of Baronetcies. In the space of somewhat more than *eleven years*, that ensued therefrom, down to 1 Jan. 1640/1, there are but *four creations*, while during *seven years* of that period, 1632 to 1638 inclusive, there are *none*.]

GRENVILE, *or* GRANVILLE:

cr. 9 April 1630;(a)

ex. 1658.

I. 1630, to 1658. "RICHARD GRENVILE, of Killegarth, co. Cornwall, Knt. and Colonel," 2d s. of Sir Barnard GRENVILE *or* GRANVILLE, of Stow, in Kilkhampton, co. Cornwall, by Elizabeth, da. and h. of Philip BEVILE, of Killegarth or Kellygarth aforesaid, was *bap.* 26 June 1600, at Kilkhampton, being aged 20 at the Visit. of Devon in 1620; was one of the Captains in the expedition of the Duke of Buckingham; *Knighted*, 20 June 1627, at Portsmouth; was M.P. for Fowey, 1628-29, and was *cr. a Baronet*, as above, 9 April 1630. He was thanked by the House of Commons, 30 Sep. 1643, for his services "against the Papist rebels in Ireland," but, soon afterwards, distinguished himself as "the King's General in the West"(a) on the Royalist side, being "excepted as to life and estate" in the propositions to the King, Sep. 1644, Nov. 1645, and Nov. 1648; was banished, and his estate confiscated, 16 March 1648/9. He *m.*, in Oct. 1629, "a rich widow," *viz.*, Mary, widow of Sir Charles Howard (4th s. of the 1st EARL OF SUFFOLK), formerly widow of the Hon. Thomas DARCY, and, before that, of Sir Allen PERCY, K.B., da. of Sir John FITZ, of Fitzford, Devon, by Bridget, da. of Sir William COURTENAY. She, who was *bap.* 1 Aug. 1596, at Whitchurch, obtained a separation from him in Feb. 1631. He *d.* s.p.m.(b) 1658, at Ghent, when the *Baronetcy* became *extinct.* His admon. as "late of Tavistock, Devon, but died beyond the seas," 17 Aug. 1661. The admon. of his widow, 20 Oct. 1671, her will being subsequently pr. May 1672.

VAVASOUR, *or* VAVASOR:

cr. 22 June 1631,

with a spec. clause as to precedency;(c)

ex. Feb. 1643/4.

I. 1631, to 1644. "CHARLES VAVASOR, of Killingthorpe, co. Lincoln, Esq.," 3d but 1st surv. s. and h. of Sir Thomas VAVASOUR, of Copmanthorpe, co. York, by Mary, da. and h. of John DODGES, of Cope, co. Suffolk, suc. his father in Nov. 1620; and was *cr. a Baronet*, as above, 22 June 1631, "to take precedence(c) next after Thomas Mounson and next before George Greisley, who were created Baronets in the year 1611," *i.e.*, 29 June 1611. He attended the King at Oxford, where he *d.* unm. Feb. and was *bur.* 1 March 1643/4, at St. Mary's, Oxford, when the *Baronetcy* became *extinct.* Admon. April 1662 and 11 March 1664/5.

(a) These words are on his monument in Ghent. See *Nat. Biogr.*, and see also a letter of "W. D. Pink" in *N. and Q.*, 7th S., xi, 276.

(b) Elizabeth, his da. and h., *m.* Col. William Lennard, and was administratrix to her father, 17 Aug. 1661.

(c) This clause was presumably invalid. It is certainly contrary to the Act of Parl. 31 Hen. VIII for settling the precedency *of Peers* "according to their ancienty and times of creation." See also vol. i, p. 40, note "a."

TYRRELL, *or* TIRRELL:

cr. 9 Feb. 1638/9;

ex. 20 Jan. 1749.

I. 1639. "EDWARD TYRRELL, of Thorneton, co. Bucks, Knt.," who had, however, been *cr. a Baronet* previously, *viz.*, on 31 Oct. 1627, wishing to disinherit his eldest son, was, after, it is said, a resignation(a) of the Baronetcy of 31 Oct. 1627, *cr. a Baronet*, as above, 9 Feb. 1638/9, with, however, a spec. rem., *viz.*, "to hold the dignity for life, with rem. to his son, Tobias Tyrell, Esq., in tail male; rem. to Francis Tyrell, another son in tail male; rem. to the heirs male of the body of the said Edward in tail male. To take precedence of Baronets created since 31 Oct. [1627] 3 Chas. I."(b) He *d.* 2 July 1656.

II. 1656. SIR TOBY TYRRELL, Bart. [1627 and 1639], of Thornton aforesaid, 2d but 1st surv. s. and h.; *suc. to both Baronetcies*, 3 July 1656, his eldest br., Robert Tyrrell (who was the h. ap. to the Baronetcy of 1627), having *d.* v.p. unm. 20 May 1644. Both Baronetcies, however, became *extinct*, 20 Jan. 1749.

[See fuller particulars under "Tyrrell," Baronetcy *cr.* 31 Oct. 1627.]

MOSLEY, *or* MOSELEY:

cr. 10 July 1640;

ex. 14 Oct. 1665.

I. 1640. "EDWARD MOSELEY, of Rowleston [*i.e.*, Rolleston], co. Stafford, Esq.," s. and h. of Rowland MOSELEY, *or* MOSLEY,(a) of the Hough in that county (Sheriff thereof, 1615-16), by his 2d wife, Anne, sister and coheir of Richard SUTTON, da. of Francis SUTTON, both of Sutton, co. Chester (which Rowland was s. and h. of Sir Nicholas MOSLEY, sometime, 1599—1600, Lord Mayor of London), was *bap.* at Didsbury, Sep. 1616, inherited the manor of Manchester, on the death, 23 Feb. 1616/7, of his father, and that of Rolleston on the death, 1638, of his uncle (Sir Edward Mosley, Attorney Gen. of the Duchy of Lancaster), and was *cr. a Baronet*, as above, 10 July 1640; was Sheriff of Staffordshire, 1641-43; was a zealous Royalist and was taken prisoner at Middlewich, 13 March 1642/3. He was fined £4,200, as also £64 a year; his estates were confiscated, but restored on payment of £4,874, on 21 Sep. 1647. He was, subsequently, charged with rape, but acquitted 28 Jan. 1647/8; lived many years in embarrassed circumstances. He *m.*, 15 Nov. 1636, at Chorlton chapel, Mary, da. of Sir Gervase CUTLER, of Steinborough Hall, co. York, and h. of her mother, Elizabeth, da. and h. of Sir John BENTLEY, of Bradsal Park, co. Derby. He was *bur.* at Didsbury 4 Dec. 1657. Admon. 5 Nov. 1658 to principal creditor. The admon. of his widow as "of St. Martin's in the Fields, Midx.," 15 Nov. 1658.

II. 1657, to 1665. SIR EDWARD MOSLEY, Bart. [1640], of Rolleston aforesaid, s. and h., matric. at Oxford (Bras. Coll.), 28 March 1655, and *suc. to the Baronetcy* in Dec. 1657. He was aged 25 at the Visit. of Lancashire in 1664; was Sheriff of Lancashire, Nov. to Dec. 1660; M.P. for St. Michael's, 1661 till death; purchased the estate of Hulme in 1661. He *m.*

(a) The resignation of this *Dignity* was, apparently, invalid. In the case of the Viscountcy of Purbeck, 1678, it was laid down that "a dignity cannot be surrendered to the Crown to the prejudice of the next heir, for it is annexed to the blood, and nothing but a deficiency or corruption of the blood can hinder the descent." See also p. 37, note "a," *sub* "Stonhouse."

(b) See p. 78, note "c."

(c) In Booker's "*Didsbury*" [Chetham Society, vol. xlii] is a pedigree of the Mosley family, copies of several of their wills, etc.

April 1665, Katharine, yr. da. of William (GREY), 1st BARON GREY OF WERKE, by Priscilla, or Cecilia, da. of Sir John WENTWORTH. He *d.* s.p. at Hough 14, and was *bur.* 21 Oct. 1665 at Didsbury, when the *Baronetcy* became *extinct.*(a) His wills dat. respectively 18 Dec. 1660, and 13 Oct. 1665, were disputed. His widow, who enjoyed the estate of Rolleston in dower, *m.* (Lic. Vic. Gen., 6 April 1667, he about 25 and she about 23) Charles NORTH, who, presumably, in consequence of that alliance (though his wife was not heir or coheir to her father) was sum. to Parl., 24 Oct. 1673, as LORD GREY DE ROLLESTON, and who suc. his father as LORD NORTH DE KIRTLING. He *d.* Jan. 1690 in his 56th year, and was *bur.* at Kirtling. She *m.* thirdly (Lic. Vic. Gen., 30 April 1691, he above 30, she about 40), Col. Francis RUSSELL, who *d.* in Barbadoes about 1 Oct. 1696. She *d.* there before him in or before Jan. 1694/5. Admon. 18 June 1695.

LUMLEY, *or* LOMLEY:

cr. 8 Jan. 1640/1;

ex. 11 Dec. 1771.

I. 1641. "MARTIN LUMLEY,(b) of Bardfield Magna, co. Essex, Esq.," s. and h. of Sir Martin LUMLEY, *or* LOMLEY, sometime, 1623-24, Lord Mayor of London, by his 1st wife, Mary, da. and h. of Robert WITHORNE *or* WITHAM, of Yorkshire, Citizen and Upholsterer of London, was *b.* about 1596, being aged 23 at the death of his mother in 1619; was Sheriff of Essex, 1639-40; suc. his father, 3 July 1634: was M.P. for Essex in the Long Parliament,(c) Feb. 1641, till secluded in Dec. 1648, and was *cr. a Baronet*, as above, 8 Jan. 1640/1, being *Knighted* at Whitehall on the day following. He was a Presbyterian and a supporter of the Parl. measures, serving on several important committees, 1643-46. He *m.* firstly, 15 Jan. 1620/1, at St. Andrew's Undershaft, London, Jane, da. and h. of John MEREDITH, of co. Denbigh. She was living 15 Oct. 1624,(d) but *d.* s.p.m. within three years of that date. He *m* secondly, 29 May 1627, at St. Andrew's aforesaid, Mary, da. of Edward ALLEN, of Finchley, Midx., Alderman and sometime, 1620-21, Sheriff of London, by his 1st wife, Judith, da. of William BENNETT, of London. He *d.* about 1651. Will pr. 1651. His widow was *bur.* 2 Oct. 1678, at Great Bardfield. Will pr. 1678.

II. 1651? SIR MARTIN LUMLEY, Bart. [1641], of Great Bardfield aforesaid, s. and h. by 2d wife, aged 6 in 1634; *suc. to the Baronetcy* about 1651; Sheriff of Essex, 1662-63. He *m.*, 16 July 1650, at St. Helen's, Bishopsgate (Lic. Fac. she aged 18), Anne, da. of Sir John LANGHAM, 1st Bart. [1660], by Mary, da. of James BUNCE, of London. She was *bur.* 20 Sep. 1692 at Great Bardfield. He was *bur.* there 11 Sep. 1702, aged 74.

III. 1702. SIR MARTIN LUMLEY, Bart. [1641], of Great Bardfield aforesaid, s. and h.; *bap.* there 27 March 1662; *suc. to the Baronetcy* in Sep. 1702; Sheriff of Essex, Jan. to Nov. 1710. He *m.* firstly, 3 June 1683, at St. Dionis Backchurch (Lic. Fac., he 21 and she 15), Elizabeth, da. of Sir Jonathan

(a) The Lancashire estates devolved on his uncle, Sir Edward Mosley, of Hulme, co. Lancaster, who *d.* s.p.m. 1695. The estate of Rolleston devolved, after his widow's death, on his 1st cousin, Oswald Mosley (son of his uncle, Nicholas Mosley), who eventually inherited the manor of Manchester, and who *d.* 1726, being father of Oswald Mosley, *cr. a Bart.* 18 June 1720. The nieces and heirs at law of the 2d Bart. appear to have been passed over. These were the two daughters and coheirs of his sister, Mary, wife of Joseph Maynard, of whom (1) Elizabeth *m.* Sir Henry Hobart, Bart. [1611], and (2) Mary *m.* Henry (GREY), Earl of Stamford.

(b) See pedigree in *Mis. Gen. et Her.*, N.S., vol. i, p. 474.

(c) His name appears among "the members of the House of Commons that advanced horse, money, and plate for the defence of the Parl." June 1642 [*N. and Q.* 1st S., xii, 358], to which object, also, he contributed four horses.

(d) See funeral cert. of her sister Prudence, whose heir she was.

DAWES, of Allhallows, Staining, Alderman and sometime, 1671-72, Sheriff of London, by Anne, da. of Sir Thomas BENDISHE, 2d Bart. [1611]. She *d.* s.p.m.s., and was *bur.* 21 Aug. 1691, at Great Bardfield. He *m.* secondly, 17 Jan. 1695, at Great Bardfield, Elizabeth, da. of Richard CHAMBERLAYNE, of Gray's Inn, Midx. She was *bur.* 20 April 1704, at Great Bardfield. He *m.* thirdly, Elizabeth, da. of Clement RAWLINSON, of Sanscute, co. Lancaster, but by her had no issue. He *d.* 12 and was *bur.* 19 Jan. 1710/1, at Great Bardfield.

IV. 1711, to 1771. SIR JAMES LUMLEY, Bart. [1641], of Great Bardfield aforesaid, only surv. s. and h. by 2d wife; *b.* about 1697; *suc. to the Baronetcy*, 12 Jan. 1710/1; matric. at Oxford (Ch. Ch.), 15 March 1713/4, aged 17; was declared a lunatic, 29 June 1725, and that he had been one for four years; commission under the Great Seal granted, 17 July 1725, to Elizabeth NEVILLE, widow.(a) He *d.* unm. 11 Dec. 1771, when the *Baronetage* became *extinct.*

DALSTON:

cr. 15 Feb. 1640/1;

ex. 7 March 1765.

I. 1641. "WILLIAM DALSTON, of Dalston, co. Cumberland, Esq.," s. and h. ap. of Sir George Dalston, of the same and of Heath Hall, near Wakefield, co. York, (sometime M.P. and Sheriff for Cumberland), by Catharine, da. and coheir of John THORNWORTH, of Halsted, co. Leicester, was admitted to Gray's Inn, 7 Dec. 1631, and was *cr. a Baronet*, as above, 15 Feb. 1640/1, being *Knighted* at Whitehall, 31 July 1641; was M.P. for Carlisle, April to May 1640; and Nov. 1640 till disabled in Jan. 1644; was Col. of Horse in the King's service. During the rebellion both he and his father were great sufferers, paying as much as £3,700 to the sequestrators. He suc. his father in Sep. 1657. He *m.* Anne, da. of Thomas BOLLES, of Osberton, Notts, by Mary, da. of William WYTHAM, of Ledstone, co. York, which Mary (after her husband's death) was *cr.* a Baronetess [S.] in 1635, as "Dame Mary Bolles, widow." He *d.* 13 Jan. 1683.

II. 1683. SIR JOHN DALSTON, Bart. [1641], of Dalston and Heath Hall aforesaid, 1st surv. s. and h. male; *Knighted* (with his 1st br., George Dalston) at Whitehall 16 Feb. 1663/4, *suc. to the Baronetcy*, 13 Jan. 1683; Sheriff of Cumberland, 1686-87. He *m.* Margaret, 2d da. of Sir William RAMSDEN, of Byrom and Longley, co. York, by Elizabeth, da. and h. of George PALMES, of Naburn. She was *bap.* at Almondbury 9 Jan. 1656. He *d.* at Heath Hall, 1711.

III. 1711. SIR CHARLES DALSTON, Bart. [1641], of Dalston and Heath Hall aforesaid, s. and h., *suc. to the Baronetcy* in 1711; was Sheriff of Cumberland, 1712-13. He *m.* firstly (—), da. and coheir of Sir Francis BLAKE, of Whitney, Oxon. He *m.* secondly, in or after 1716, Anne, widow of Sir Lyon PILKINGTON, 4th Bart. [S. 1635], da. of Sir Michael WENTWORTH, of Woolley, co. York, by Dorothy, da. of Sir Godfrey Copley, 1st Bart. [1661]. He *d.* 5 March 1723. His widow, who was *b.* 16 and *bap.* 18 March 1663, at Woolley (by whom he had no surv. issue), *m.* for her 3d husband, 1 Dec. 1730, at Horbury, John MAUDE, of Alverthorpe Hall, and of Wakefield, co. York. She *d.* at Chevet 15 Aug. 1764, and was *bur.* at Wakefield.

IV. 1723, to 1765. SIR GEORGE DALSTON, Bart. [1641], of Dalston and Heath Hall aforesaid, only s. and h., by 1st wife, *suc. to the Baronetcy* 5 March 1723. In 1740, being then unm., he was a volunteer on board Admiral Haddock's squadron; Sheriff of Cumberland, 1752-53; Lieut.-Col. of the Yorkshire Militia, 1759; sold the estate of Dalston in 1761. He *m.* 28 Oct. 1742, Anne, da. of George HUXLEY. He *d.* s.p.m.(b) 7 March 1765, when the *Baronetcy* became *extinct.* His widow *d.* 2 Nov. 1776, at St. Omer's.

(a) *Qy.* if she was not his stepmother.

(b) His only da. *m.* a French gentleman of the name of Dillon.

M

According however to Kimber's *Baronetage* [1771], the 4th Bart. left a son

V. 1765. SIR WILLIAM DALSTON, "the present [1771] Bart." Of him, however, nothing is known, and it is conjectured that, if he ever existed, he probably was illegitimate.(a)

COLE:

cr. 15 Feb. 1640/1;

ex. 25 March 1720.

I. 1641. "NICHOLAS COLE, of Branspeth Castle, co. pal. of Durham, Knt.," s. and h. ap. of Ralph COLE, of Newcastle on Tyne, merchant (Mayor, 1633, and the purchaser, in 1636, of Brancepeth Castle, who *d.* Nov. 1655), was thrice, 1640-42 and 1643-44, Mayor of Newcastle, and was, while such, *Knighted* at Whitehall 11 Feb. 1640/1, and four days afterwards, *cr. a Baronet*, as above, 15 Feb. 1640/1. Being a zealous Royalist, he was excepted from pardon in 1644 and 1645 and was fined £312 in June 1649. He *m.*, in or before 1641, Mary, da. of Sir Thomas LIDDELL, 1st Bart. [1642], by Isabel, da. of Henry ANDERSON. He apparently was *bur.* 12 Aug. 1660 [1669?], at Brancepeth.

II. 1660? SIR RALPH COLE, Bart. [1641], of Brancepeth Castle aforesaid, s. and h.; *suc. to the Baronetcy* on the death of his father; was M.P. for Durham, March 1678 to Jan. 1679, and March to July 1679. He *m.* firstly, (—), da. of (—) WINDHAM. He *m.* secondly, Katharine, da. of Sir Henry FOULIS, 2d Bart. [1620], of Ingleby, co. York, by Mary, da. of Sir Thomas LAYTON. She was *bap.* at Ingleby, 23 Sep. 1637. He sold the Brancepeth estates on 19 April 1701,(b) for £16,800, with a life annuity of £500 and one for £200 for his wife if she survived him. He *d.* 9 Aug. 1704. His widow *d.* in Durham 29 Sep. and was *bur.* 2 Oct. 1704, at Brancepeth.

III. 1704. SIR NICHOLAS COLE, Bart. [1641], grandson and h., being s. and h. of Nicholas COLE, by Elizabeth, da. of Sir Mark MILBANKE, 1st Bart. [1661], which Nicholas last named was s. and h. ap. of the late Bart.,(c) but *d.* v.p. He was *bap.* 9 June 1685, at St. Nicholas', Newcastle, and *suc. to the Baronetcy*, on the death of his grandfather, 9 Aug. 1704. He *m.* firstly, Anne, da. of Collier CAMPBELL. He *m.* secondly (Lic. Fac. 16 July 1705) Anne, sister of Sir George SAVILE, 7th Bart. [1611], da. of Rev. John SAVILE, by his second wife, Barbara, da. and h. of Thomas JENISON. He *d.* s.p. 1710/1. His widow *m.* a Belgian adventurer called "BARON DOGNYES."(d)

(a) In the obituary of the *Annual Register* for 1771 there occurs the death, 1 Oct. 1771, "at his seat at Acorn Bank in Westmoreland [*sic*] SIR WILLIAM DALTON [*sic*] Bart." [*sic*]. The family of *Dalston* of Acornbank, co. *Cumberland*, recorded their pedigree in the Visitation of that County in 1664, being 6th in descent from Thomas Dalston, of Dalston, the lineal ancestor of the Baronets. No member of the Acornbank branch of the family of Dalston and no one of the name of *Dalton* was apparently ever created a Baronet.

(b) Hutchinson's *Durham.*

(c) Another son of the 2d Bart., viz., "Ralph Cole, s. of Ralph, of Kepier, co. Durham, Bart.," matric. at Oxford (Linc. Coll.) 2 March 1679/80, aged 17, and became B.A. 1683; M.A. 1686.

(d) MS. diary of Miss Gertrude Savile [*ex inform.* Lord Hawkesbury].

IV. 1711, to 1720. SIR MARK COLE, Bart. [1641], br. and h. He was *bap.* 8 Nov. 1687, at St. Nicholas', Newcastle; *suc. to the Baronetcy* in 1711, but *d.* s.p. and was *bur.* 25 March 1720, at St. Margaret's, Durham, when the *Baronetcy* became *extinct.*

FLETCHER:

cr. 19 Feb. 1640/1;

ex. 19 May 1712.

I. 1641. "HENRY FLETCHER, of Hutton in le Forest, co. Cumberland, Esq.," only s. and h. of Sir Richard Fletcher, of the same, formerly of Cockermouth in that county, merchant, by his 2d wife, Barbara, da. of Henry CRACKENTHORPE, of Newbiggen, suc. his father between 1630 and 1637, and was *cr. a Baronet*, as above, 19 Feb. 1640/1. He was twice Sheriff for Cumberland, 1641-43. He raised a regiment for the Royal service, at the head of which he fell at the skirmish at Rowton Heath, near Chester, 24 Sep. 1645. He *m.*, about 1638, Catharine, sister of Sir William DALSTON, 1st Bart. [1641], da. of Sir George DALSTON, of Dalston, Cumberland, by Catharine, da. and coheir of John THORNWORTH. He was slain as above-mentioned in 1645. Admon. 27 May 1650 to his widow. She, who endured, with great spirit, sequestration, incarceration, etc., from the Parl., *m.* Thomas SMITH, D.D., BISHOP OF CARLISLE, 1684—1702, who *d.* 12 April 1702, aged 88.

II. 1645. SIR GEORGE FLETCHER, Bart. [1641], of Hutton aforesaid, only surv. s. and h., *b.* about 1633, *suc. to the Baronetcy* 1645; was fined in May 1647, for his father's delinquency, £2,200, afterwards reduced to £714; was Sheriff of Cumberland 1657-58 and 1679-80; M.P. thereof, 1661-79, 1681, 1689-90, 1690-95, 1695-98, and 1698-1700. He *m.* firstly, 27 Feb. 1654/5, at Totteridge, Herts, Alice, da. of Hugh (HARE), 1st BARON COLERAINE [I.], by Lucy, da. of Henry (MONTAGU), 1st EARL OF MANCHESTER. She, who was *bap.* 20 Oct. 1633, at Totteridge, was *bur.* at Hutton. He *m.* secondly, before 1665, Mary, widow of Sir George GRAHAM, 2d Bart. [1629], da. of James (JOHNSTONE, 1st EARL OF HARTFELL [S.], by his 1st wife, Margaret, da. of William (DOUGLAS), 1st EARL OF QUEENSBERRY [S.]. He *d.* 23 July 1700, and was *bur.* at Hutton, aged 67.

III. 1700, to 1712. SIR HENRY FLETCHER, Bart. [1641], of Hutton aforesaid, s. and h. by 1st wife, *b.* about 1661, being 3 years and 11 months old at the Visit. of Cumberland, 27 March 1665; matric. at Oxford (Queen's Coll.), 10 June 1678, aged 16; M.P. for Cockermouth, 1689-90; *suc. to the Baronetcy*, 23 July 1700. He settled his estate on his distant cousin, Thomas Fletcher, of Moresby,(a) and retired into a monastery of English monks at Douay, in France, where he *d.* unm. 19 May 1712, when the *Baronetcy* became *extinct.* He was *bur.* in a magnificent chapel at Douay, built at his own expense. Will pr. May 1712.

PYE:

cr. 23 April 1641;

ex. 28 April 1673.

I. 1641, to 1673? "EDMUND PYE, of Leckamsteed, co. Bucks, Esq.," s. and h. of Edmund PYE, of the same and of St. Martin's, Ludgate, London, scrivener, by Martha, "sister of Alderman ALLEN of London,"(b) (both living May 1635); was *b.* about 1607, and was *cr. a Baronet*,

(a) After much litigation it was arranged that, if this Thomas Fletcher *d.* s.p. (which event took place), the estates should go to Henry VANE, 2d s. of Lionel Vane, by Catharine, one of the sisters (of the whole blood) and coheirs of the 3d Bart. This Henry VANE, *suc.* to the Hutton estate, took the additional name of Fletcher, and *d.* unm. 1761. His br., Walter Vane, afterwards Walter Fletcher-Vane, then *suc.* thereto, and was father of Lionel Wright FLETCHER-VANE, *cr. a Bart.* 1786.

(b) See pedigree of Pye in *Visit. of London, 1634.*

as above, 23 April 1641, being *Knighted* at Whitehall four days later. He was voted a delinquent by Parl. and fined £3,065. He acquired the manor and estate of Bradenham, Bucks, where he chiefly resided; was M.P. for High Wycombe, 1661. He *m.* (Lic. Lond., 7 May 1635, he 28 and she 18), Catherine, sister of John, 1st BARON LUCAS OF SHERFIELD, da. of Thomas LUCAS, of Colchester, by Elizabeth, da. and h. of John LEIGHTON. He *d.* s.p.m.(a) and was *bur.* 28 April 1673, at Bradenham, about 1673, when the *Baronetcy* became *extinct.* Will pr. 1673. His widow *d.* 1701, aged 89. Will pr. 1702.

Memorandum.—In an dafter May 1641 down to the end of the reign of Charles I the enrolment of any patent was the exception. Among the 116 Baronetcies that are given in the *Creations, 1483—1646* (ap. 47th Rep. D.K. Pub. Records) as having been created during that period, no patents, in as many as 85 cases, are enrolled, though, as to 67, the date of the signet bill, warrant, or privy seal is therein given as under, *viz.*, Every, 21 May 1641; Napier, 23 June 1641; Yelverton, 27 June 1641; Cave, 28 June 1641; Hatton, 2 July 1641; Boteler, 3 July 1641; Abdy, 5 July (Qy. June) 1641; Cotton, 10 July 1641; Bamfeild, 12 July 1641; Thynne, Dewes, and Burgoyne, 13 July 1641; Drake, 14 July 1641; Rous, 16 July 1641; Pratt, and Sydenham, 19 July 1641; Norwich, and Nichols, 22 July 1641; Brownlow, 23 July 1641; Hare, Northcote, and [another] Brownlow, 24 July 1641; Strickland, 29 July 1641; Windham, Maleverer, Knatchbull, Chichester, and Boughton, 31 July 1641; Wolryche, 2 Aug. 1641; Pryse, and Carew, 5 Aug. 1641; Cholmeley, Spring, and Castleton, 7 Aug. 1641; Trevor, 11 Aug. 1641; Davie, 11 Aug. 1641; Bindlosse, 13 Aug. 1611; Meux, 8 Dec. 1641; Willys, 13 Dec. 1641; Halford, 16 Dec 1641; Cowper, and Thomas, 28 Feb. 1641/2; Dawney and Hamilton, 3 May 1642; Morgan, Kemeys, and Williams, 11 May 1642; Reresby, 14 May 1642; Moore, 16 May 1642; Hampson, 20 May 1642; Hardres and Williamson, 22 May 1642; Denny, 26 May 1642; Alston, 28 (?) May 1642; Lowther, 31 May 1642; Middleton, 10 June 1642; Payler, 15 June 1642; Corbett, [—] June 1642; Rudston, 6 Aug. 1642; Hungate, and Thorold, 10 Aug. 1642; Anderson, 30 June 1643; Jones, 24 July 1643; Bate, 2 Nov. 1643; O'Neale, 9 Nov. 1643; Hickman, 11 Nov. 1643, and Boteler, 30 Nov. 1643. To the above 67 Baronetcies must be added the 18 (with which the abovenamed list of *Creations, 1483—1646* concludes), of which neither patent, signet bill, warrant nor privy seal are enrolled, though the *docquet* of the creation is noticed in a publication generally known as *Black's Docquets.*(b) These are as under, *viz*:—Vavasour, 17 July 1643; Waldegrave, 1 Aug. 1643; Pate, 28 Oct. 1643; Acton, 17 Jan. 1643/4; Hawley, 14 March 1643/4; Preston, 1 April 1644; Prestwich, 25 April 1644; Williams, 4 May 1644; Thorold and Lucas, 14 June 1644; Bard, 8 Oct. 1644; Van Colster, 28 Feb. 1644/5; De Boreel, 21 March 1644/5; Carteret, 9 May 1645; Windebanke, 25 Nov. 1645; Wright, 7 Feb. 1645/6; Charlton, 6 March 1645/6; and Willis, 11 June 1646.

"A CATALOGUE OF THE BARONETS OF ENGLAND" was (according to a statement made in Dugdale's *Ancient Usage of Arms*), "*published by authority* in 1667," being revised some "12 years and more" later [1681 ?]. This purports to be a "*catalogue* of such, touching whom the docquet books remaining with the Clerk of the Crown in Chancery do take notice."(c) In this *catalogue* there are

---

(a) Of his two daughters and coheirs, (1) Margaret *m.* John (Lovelace), 3d Baron Lovelace of Hurley, and had issue, who inherited the Bradenham estate; (2) Elizabeth, *m.* the Hon. Charles West, but *d.* s.p.

(b) "Docquets of letters patent and other instruments passed under the Great Seal of King Charles I, at Oxford in the years 1642, 1643, 1644, 1645 and 1646," edited by Mr. Black, an assistant keeper of the Public Records, from the original Crown office docquet book at that time preserved in the Ashmolean Museum, at Oxford.

(c) It is as well, perhaps, to quote Dugdale's own words from his "Preface" to the said *catalogue*, as given in the edition [p. 67] of his *Ancient Usage of Arms*, edited by "T. C. Banks, Esq." (folio 1812):—"Whereas in the year 1667, a catalogue of the Baronets of England was by authority published, to the end that such as had

as many as nineteen Baronetcies (whose existence for the most part has never been questioned) which are not named in the abovementioned list of the *Creations, 1483—1646.* These are:—Strutt, 5 March 1641/2; St. Quintin, 8 March 1641/2; Kempe, 14 March 1641/2; Reade, 16 March 1641/2; Enyon, 9 April 1642; Williams, 19 April 1642; Wintour, 29 April 1642; Borlase, 4 May 1642; Knollys, 6 May 1642; Ingelby, 17 May 1642; Widdrington [of Widdrington], 9 July 1642; Valckenburg and Constable, 20 July 1642; Blakiston, *or* Blackstone, 30 July 1642; Widdrington [of Cartington], 8 Aug. 1642; Markham and Lennard, 15 Aug. 1642; Bland, 30 Aug. 1642, and Throckmorton, 1 Sep. 1642. It is accordingly thought better, on and after the date of May 1641 when the enrolments are so very irregular, to follow this official (or semi-official) *Catalogue* as given by Dugdale (referring to it as "*Dugdale's Catalogue*"), which includes the above-named nineteen Baronetcies, indispersed among those mentioned in the list of *Creations*, 1483—1646. There are, however, many other Baronetcies conferred during the Civil Wars which are *not* comprehended in this *Catalogue* (*e.g.*, Bathurst, Cokayne, Courtenay, Haggerston, Lloyd, etc.) which will be here dealt with at the end of those given by Dugdale.

EVERY:

cr. 26 May 1641.(a)

I. 1641. "SIMON EVERY, of Eggington, co. Derby, Esq.," only s. and h. of John EVERY, of Chardstock, co. Somerset, and of Oxford, by Elizabeth, sister of William LAMBERT, of Oxford, was *b.*, about 1603, in Northamptonshire; matric. at Oxford (Wadham Coll.), 27 Nov. 1618, aged 15; admitted to Middle Temple, 1620; pr. his father's will 29 Oct. 1623; was M.P. for Leicester, April to May 1640, and, having been a great sufferer in the Royal cause and a steady adherent of Charles I, was *cr. a Baronet*, as above, 26 May 1641,(a) being *Knighted* at Whitehall 4 June following. He was a Compounder. He *m.* in or before 1629, Anne, 1st da. and coheir, and eventually sole heir of Sir Henry LEIGH, of Eggington or Egginton aforesaid, by Catherine, da. of (—) HORTON, of Catton in that county. He *d.* about 1647. Will pr. 1649.

II. 1647? SIR HENRY EVERY, Bart. [1641], of Egginton aforesaid, s. and h., *bap.* there 15 Nov. 1629, *suc. to the Baronetcy* about 1647. He, like his father, was a great sufferer for his loyalty to his King. He *m.* in or before 1653, Vere, 1st da. of Sir Henry HERBERT, Master of the Revels to Charles I

---

obtained patents for that honour, which were not enrolled, should, by descerning an omission of their names therein, take care to supply that defect, so that upon a second impression thereof they might be inserted. Now, whereas, after 12 years and more, no enrollments are yet to be found for sundry persons which have assumed this title, which causeth some to doubt whether they can make any justifiable claims thereto. Whereas, therefore, no person [*sic*] whatsoever ought to take upon them [*sic*] this title of dignity, but such as have been really advanced thereto by letters patent under the Great Seal of England, it is thought fit by the Rt. Hon. Robert, Earl of Aylesbury, who, now excerciseth [*i.e.* as a Joint Commissioner, 30 June 1673] the office of Earl Marshall of England, that this present catalogue of such touching whom the Docquet books remaining with the Clerk of the Crown in Chancery do take notice, shall be published, to the end that those, of whom no memorial upon record is to be found to justifie their right to the title, may be known; and care henceforth taken in commissions of the peace and otherwise that it be not given unto them until they shall manifest the same unto the Lord Chancellor of England and have speciall order from his Lordship to enroll such patents where they pretend title to that dignity. As also that regard be had of giving credit to any other catalogues of the Baronets which are already publisht, or that shall be publisht, than what is taken from the authority of those Docquet books above mentioned or the enrollment of their patents."

(a) The patent is not enrolled. The date here given is that in Dugdale's *Catalogue*, See *Memorandum* on p. 84. The date of the signet bill is 21 May 1641.

and Charles II, by his 1st wife (—), da. of (—). He *d.* 29 Sep. and was *bur.* 3 Oct. 1700, at Egginton. His widow, who was *b.* 29 Aug. 1627, was *bur.* there 26 Feb. 1706/7.

III. 1700. SIR HENRY EVERY, Bart. [1641], of Egginton aforesaid, s. and h., *b.* about 1653, *suc. to the Baronetcy*, 29 Sep. 1700. He *m.* firstly, (Lic. Vic. Gen., 30 April 1685, he about 30, she about 20), Mary, da. of John (TRACY), 3d VISCOUNT TRACY OF RATHCOOLE [I.], by Elizabeth, da. of Thomas (LEIGH), 1st BARON LEIGH OF STONELEIGH. She was *bur.* at Egginton, 16 March 1692. He *m.* secondly, Anne, widow of Richard LYGON, of Madresfield Court, co. Worcester (*d.* s.p. 15 April 1687, aged 49), 1st da. and coheir of Sir Francis RUSSELL, 2d Bart. [1627] of Whitley and Strensham, by Anne, da. of Sir Rowland LYTTON. He *d.* s.p. Sep. 1709, and was *bur.* at Newton Solney, co. Derby. Will dat. 14 May 1709, pr. 10 March 1710. His widow *m.* (as her 3d husband) Sir John GUISE, 3d Bart. [1661], who *d.* 16 Nov. 1732. She *d.* 22 Feb. 1734/5.

IV. 1709. SIR JOHN EVERY, Bart. [1641], of Egginton aforesaid, br. and h., *b.* about 1654. He was sometime Captain of the "Queen," man-of-war, and served in the cause of William III, with some distinction; *suc. to the Baronetcy* in Sep. 1709; was Sheriff of Derbyshire, 1717-18. He *m.* firstly, 28 April 1704, at Knightsbridge Chapel, Midx., Martha, da. of John (THOMPSON), 1st BARON HAVERSHAM, by Frances, da. of Arthur (ANNESLEY), 1st EARL OF ANGLESEY. She *d.* 9 and was *bur.* 14 Feb. 1715, at Egginton. Her admon. 10 July 1717. He *m.* secondly, Dorothy, da. of Godfrey MEYNELL, of Bradley, co. Derby. He *d.* s.p.s. 1 and was *bur.* 4 July 1729, at Egginton, aged 75. Will pr. 1730. His widow *d.* 1749. Will pr. 1749.

V. 1729. SIR SIMON EVERY, Bart. [1641], of Egginton aforesaid, br. and h., *b.* about 1658; ed. at Christ's Coll., Cambridge, of which he was sometime Fellow; B.A., 1683; M.A., 1687; in Holy Orders; Rector of Navenby, co. Lincoln; *suc. to the Baronetcy* 1 July 1729. He *m.* in or before 1708, Mary, da. of Rev. Joshua CLARKE, Rector of Somerby, co. Lincoln, and Prebendary of Lincoln. She *d.* 10 Aug. 1723, aged 34. He *d.* 12 and was *bur.* 17 Jan. 1753, at Egginton, aged 95.

VI. 1753. SIR HENRY EVERY, Bart. [1641], of Egginton aforesaid, 1st s. and h., *b.* 25 Oct. 1708; Sheriff of Derbyshire, 1749-50; *suc. to the Baronetcy* 12 Jan. 1753. He *m.* 1 July 1741, Frances, sister of Sir Henry IBBETSON, Bart. [1740], da. of James IBBETSON, of Leeds, co. York, by Elizabeth, da. of John NICHOLSON, M.D. She *d.* 21 Sep. 1754 and was *bur.* at Egginton, aged 52. He *d.* s.p. 31 May and was *bur.* 12 June 1755 at Egginton. Admon. 20 Aug. 1755.

VII. 1755. SIR JOHN EVERY, Bart. [1641], of Egginton aforesaid, br. and h.; *b.* 17 Oct. 1709; ed. at Christ's Coll., Cambridge; B.A., 1729; M.A., 1733; in Holy Orders; Rector of Waddington and Vicar of Bracebridge, both co. Lincoln; *suc. to the Baronetcy*, 31 May 1755. He *m.*, 1 Dec. 1767, at Egginton, Dorothy PAKEMAN. She was *bur.* there 29 Aug. 1769. He *d.* s.p. 29 June and was *bur.* 5 July 1779, at Egginton. Admon. 24 July 1779 to his cousin german and next of kin, Edward Every; further admon. Feb. 1787.

VIII. 1779. SIR EDWARD EVERY, Bart [1641], of Egginton aforesaid, cousin and h. male, being only s. and h. of John EVERY, of Derby, by Mary LUNN, his wife, which John (*bap.* at All Saints', Derby, 20 Jan. 1724/5, and *bur.* 1 April 1767 at Egginton) was 1st s. of Henry EVERY, of St. Peter's, Derby (*bap.* 3 April 1701 and *bur.* 15 March 1775 at All Saints' aforesaid), only s. of John EVERY, of Castle Donington, co. Leicester and All Saints', Derby (*d.* 4 April 1746, aged 74), only s. of Francis EVERY, of Castle Donington aforesaid (*d.* Sep. 1708), 3d s. of the 1st Bart. He was *bap.* 15 Aug. 1754, at All Saints', Derby; *suc. to the Baronetcy*, as also to the family estate, 29 June 1779; Sheriff of Derbyshire, 1783, and rebuilt

the mansion at Egginton. He *m.* 4 Sep. 1776, at St. Alkmund's, Derby, Mary, widow of Joseph BIRD, of Loughborough, and formerly of William ELLIOT, of Derby, da. of Edward MORLEY, of Horsley, co. Derby. He was *bur.* 4 Jan. 1786, at Egginton. Will pr. 1786. His widow *m.* (for her 4th husband) 10 March 1790, at Egginton, Ashton-Nicholas MOSLEY, of Park Hill, co. Derby (who *d.* 2 April 1830, aged 62), and *d.* 9 March 1826.

IX. 1786. SIR HENRY EVERY, Bart. [1641], of Egginton aforesaid, s. and h.; *b.* 4 June and *bap.* 7 July 1777, at St. Alkmund's, Derby; *suc. to the Baronetcy* in Jan. 1786; was Sheriff of Derbyshire, 1804-05. He *m.* firstly, 22 Dec. 1726, at Egginton, Penelope, 4th da. of Sir John-Parker MOSLEY, 1st Bart. [1781], by Elizabeth, da. of James BAYLEY. She (who was sister to her husband's step-father abovenamed) *d.* 30 Aug. 1812. He *m.* secondly, Elizabeth, da. of William SOAR, of Little Chester, near Derby, yeoman. She *d.* s.p.s. a few months before him, and was *bur.* at Barrow upon Trent. He *d.* 28 Dec. 1855, at Egginton Hall, in his 79th year. Will pr. Feb. 1856.

X. 1855. SIR HENRY FLOWER EVERY, Bart. [1641], of Egginton Hall aforesaid, grandson and h., being s. and h. of Henry EVERY, of Beaumont Lodge, near Windsor, Berks, sometime an officer in the Life Guards, by his 2d wife, Caroline, da. of Henry (FLOWER), 4th VISCOUNT ASHBROOK [I.], which Henry Every was s. and h. ap. of the 9th Bart., but *d.* v.p., 27 Feb. 1853, aged 53. He was *b.* 25 Dec. 1830, in London; ed. at Cheltenham; was sometime an officer in the 90th foot; *suc. to the baronetcy*, 28 Dec. 1855; Sheriff of Derbyshire, 1863. He *m.* firstly, 8 Feb. 1855, Gertrude, 5th da. of Hon. and Rev. Baptist-Wriothesley NOEL (yr. br. of Charles, 1st EARL OF GAINSBOROUGH), by Jane, da. of Peter BAILLIE, of Dochfour. She *d.* 26 Feb. 1858. He *m.* secondly, 12 Oct. 1859, Mary-Isabella, 1st da. of Rev. Edmund HOLLAND, of Benhall Lodge, near Saxmundham, Suffolk, by Isabella, 12th da. of Sir John ROBINSON, 1st Bart. [1819], of Rokeby Hall, co. Louth. He *d.* 26 Feb. 1893, at Egginton Hall, aged 62. Will pr. at £14,678. His widow living 1900.

XI. 1893. SIR EDWARD OSWALD EVERY, Bart. [1641], of Egginton Hall aforesaid, grandson and h., being 1st but only surv. s. and h. of Henry Edmund EVERY, Captain South Wales Borderers, by Leila Frances Harford, da. of the Rev. Henry Adderley BOX, which Henry was 1st s. and h. ap. of the late Bart. by his 2d wife, but *d.* v.p. 1 Dec. 1892, aged 32. He was *b.* 14 Jan. 1886 and *suc. to the Baronetcy*, 26 Feb. 1893.

Family Estates.—These, in 1883, consisted of 2,231 acres in Derbyshire, worth £4,930 a year. *Principal seat.*—Egginton Hall, near Burton on Trent, co. Derby.

LANGLEY:

cr. 29 May 1641.

I. 1641. "WILLIAM LANGLEY, of Hygham Gobion, co. Bedford, Esq.," as also of Stainton, co. York, s. and h. of George LANGLEY, of Stainton aforesaid, by Jane, da. of John HALL, of Sherbourn, co. York, became possessed of the manor of Higham Gobion in 1639, and was *cr. a Baronet*, as above, 29 May 1641. He *m.* Elizabeth, sister of Richard, 1st VISCOUNT LUMLEY OF WATERFORD [I.], da. of Roger LUMLEY, by Anne, da. of (—) KURTWICH. He *d.*, at Mrs. Eliz. Threkill's house in High Holborn, 21 and was *bur.* 23 Aug. 1653, at St. Andrew's, Holborn. Will p. 1654. His widow *m.* before 24 March 1659, Roger GUNTER, of Isleworth, co. Midx. Her will, dat. 24 March 1659, pr. 7 Dec. 1681, by her said husband.

II. 1653. SIR ROGER LANGLEY, Bart. [1641], of Sheriff Hutton Park, co. York, s. and h., *b.* about 1627 ; *suc. to the Baronetcy*, 21 Aug. 1653 ; was Sheriff of Yorkshire, 1663-64, and was aged 38 at the Visit. of Yorkshire in 1665. He sold the manor of Higham Gobion to Arabella, Countess of Kent. He was Foreman of the Jury at the trial of the seven Bishops in 1688, and was a Commissioner of the Prize Office, *temp.* William III. He *m.* firstly (Lic. Fac., 26 April 1647, he being then of Enfield, Midx., about 20 and she about 17), Mary, da. of Thomas KEIGHLEY, of Hertingfordbury, Herts. He *m.* secondly (Lic. Fac., 10 April 1672), Barbara, widow of (—) HOBSON, da. and coheir of (—) CHAPMAN, of Foxton, co. Leicester, Serjeant at Law. By her he had no issue. He had lic. to marry (Lic. London, 1 April 1684, being then aged 58 and a widower) Mary REND, of St. John's, Walbrook, widow, aged 34. He *m.* shortly after that date (a da. being *bap.* Feb. 1684/5, at St. Andrew's, Holborn) Sarah, da. of John NEALE, of Malden Ash, Essex. He was *bur.* 4 Jan. 1698/9, at St. Margaret's, Westminster. His will, dat. 27 April 1697 and 17 Oct. 1698, pr. 10 Jan. 1698/9 and again 4 Sep. 1716. His widow was *bur.* 4 Nov. 1701, at St. Margaret's aforesaid. Will pr. June 1702.

III. 1699. SIR ROGER LANGLEY, Bart. [1641], grandson and h., being s. and h. of William LANGLEY, by Isabella, da. of Sir John Griffith, of Erith, Kent, which William (aged 18 in 1665) was s. and h. ap. of the 2d Bart., by his 1st wife, and *d.* v.p. 1689. He *suc. to the Baronetcy* in Jan. 1698/9. He *m.* Mary, da. of Stanislaus BROWNE, of Eastbourne, Sussex. He *d.* s.p.s. 19 Sep. 1721. The will of his widow pr. 1758.

IV. 1721. SIR THOMAS LANGLEY, Bart. [1641], br. and h., *suc. to the Baronetcy*, 19 Sep. 1721. He *m.* (—), 2d da. of Capt. Robert EDGWORTH, of Longwood, co. Meath. He *d.* s.p.m.s., 1 and was *bur.* 6 Dec. 1762, with his parents at St. Margaret's, Westm., aged, it is said, 98.(a)

V. 1762. SIR HALDANBY LANGLEY, Bart. [1641], nephew and h. male, being 1st surv. s. of Haldanby LANGLEY, by Mary, da. of Charles PECK, of Gildersley, co. Derby, which Haldanby lastnamed was yst br. of the 3d and 4th Barts., and *d.* 30 May 1728. He *suc. to the Baronetcy*, 1 Dec. 1762. The time of his death has not been ascertained, but he is stated to have left a son and h., "but whether such were really the case has not been ascertained."(b)

VI? 1770? to 1820? "SIR HENRY LANGLEY, Bart. [1641], called s. and h.,"(b) who, if so, would have *suc. to the Baronetcy* on his father's death. He, who was living 1818, "is presumed to have *d.* s.p., *when the title became extinct*."(b)

PASTON :

cr. 7 June 1641(c) ;

sometime, 1673-1732, VISCOUNTS YARMOUTH ;

and subsequently, 1679-1732, EARLS OF YARMOUTH ;

ex. 25 Dec. 1732.

I. 1641. "WILLIAM PASTON, of Oxnead, co. Norfolk, Esq.," s. and h. of Sir Edmund PASTON, of Paston and Oxnead, by Catharine, da. of Sir Thomas KNEVITT, of Ashwelthorpe, all in co. Norfolk, was *b.* about 1610 ; suc. his father (who *d.* aged 48) in 1632 ; was Sheriff of Norfolk, 1636-37, and was *cr. a*

(a) According, however, to the *Gent. Mag.*, "Sir Thomas Langley, Bart., Uxbridge," died 1740, and another Sir Thomas Langley, Bart., aged 98, grandson of Sir Robert [*sic*] of 1688 [*sic*], "died in Westminster 1762."

(b) Courthope's *Extinct Baronetage* [1835].

(c) But, according to Dugdale's *Catalogue* (see *memorandum* on p. 84) the patent was dated *8* June 1641.

Baronet, as above, 7 June 1641. He *m.* firstly, in or before 1631, Catharine, 1st da. of Robert (BERTIE), 1st EARL OF LINDSEY, by Elizabeth, da. of Edward (MONTAGU), 1st BARON MONTAGU OF BOUGHTON. She *d.* 3 Jan. 1636, and was *bur.* at Oxnead. He *m.* secondly, Margaret, sister of Sir George HEWITT. He *d.* 22 Feb. 1662/3. Will pr. 1663. His widow *m.* George STRODE. Her admon., as of St. Giles' in the Fields, Midx., 23 Dec. 1669, granted to her said husband.

II. 1663. SIR ROBERT PASTON, Bart. [1641], of Paston and Oxnead aforesaid, 1st s. and h. by 1st wife, *b.* 29 May 1631 ; ed. at Westm. School and at Trin. Coll. Cambridge ; *Knighted*, 26 May 1660 ; was M.P. for Thetford, 1660, and for Castle Rising, 1661-78 ; *suc. to the Baronetcy*, 22 Feb. 1662/3 ; F.R.S., 20 May 1663 ; a Gent. of the Privy Chamber, 1666/7. He *m.*, about 1650, Rebecca, 2d da. of Sir Jasper CLAYTON, of St. Edmund the King, by Mary, da. of William TOMSON, of Tinmouth Castle, Cumberland. She was living when he was *cr.*, 19 Aug. 1673, VISCOUNT YARMOUTH, co. Norfolk, etc., and subsequently, 30 July, 1679, EARL OF YARMOUTH. In these peerages this Baronetcy thenceforth merged, till it and the other honours became *extinct*, 25 Dec. 1732, on the death of the 2d Earl and 3d Baronet.

STONHOUSE, *or* STONEHOUSE :

cr. 10 June 1641(a) ;

ex. 13 April 1695.

I. 1641. "JAMES STONEHOUSE of Amerden Hall [in Debden] co. Essex, Esq.," s. and h. of Sir James STONHOUSE, of the same (who was the yst. br. of Sir William STONHOUSE, of Radley, 1st Bart. [1628]), by his 2d wife, Anne, da. of Sir Humphrey WELD, suc. his father (who *d.* aged 73) 1 Dec. 1638, and was *cr. a Baronet*, as above, 10 June 1641.(a) His estate was sequestrated in 1651 and he was fined £3,000 on 16 Sep. 1652. He *m.* (—).(b)

II. 1652? SIR JAMES STONHOUSE, Bart. [1641], of Amerden Hall aforesaid, s. and h.,(c) *suc. to the Baronetcy* on the death of his father. He *m.* Mary, d. of (—) BLEWITT, of Holcombe, Devon. His admon. as "late of Amerden Hall, but decd. at St. Gregory's, London," granted 2 May 1654, to his widow. She (who was living June 1669) *m.* Sir John LENTHAL, of Besilden Lee, Berks, and was *bur.* there.

III. 1654? SIR BLEWET STONHOUSE, Bart. [1641], of Amerden Hall aforesaid, s. and h., *suc. to the Baronetcy* in his infancy about 1654 ; matric. at Oxford (Ch. Ch.) 29 June 1669, aged 15 ; *cr.* M.A. 9 July following ; admitted to Lincoln's Inn, 1669. He *d.* unm. probably about 1670.(d)

IV. 1670? SIR GEORGE STONHOUSE, Bart. [1641], of Amerden Hall aforesaid, br. and h., *suc. to the Baronetcy* on his brother's death. He *m.* (—), da. of (—) HAMILTON.(e)

(a) But, according to Dugdale's *Catalogue* (see *Memorandum on* p. 84), it was 8 June 1641.

(b) Neither his own burial nor that of any of his descendants took place apparently at Debden.—"Lady Stonehouse" [*Qy.* his wife or widow] is there buried 20 March 1651/2, and his father, Sir James, 3 Dec. 1638. The will of "Dame Elizabeth Stonehouse" is pr. 1655.

(c) The statement of his succession is from Morant's *Essex*. It is, however, possible that the 1st and 2d Baronets are in reality but one person. The pedigree is very obscure and confused.

(d) In Morant's *Essex* the date of his death is given as 1693, but the date seems much too late.

(e) The will of "Dame Margaret Stonehouse," possibly being that of this lady, is pr. 1692.

N

V. 1675? SIR JOHN STONHOUSE, Bart. [1641], of Amerden Hall aforesaid, and of Bishops Itchington, co. Warwick, s. and h., *suc. to the Baronetcy* on the death of his father. He *m.* Elizabeth, da. of George COLE, of Buckish, Devon, and of Enstone, Oxon. Will as "of the city of York, Bart.," dat. 31 July 1681, pr. 12 Jan. 1681/2, by Elizabeth, the widow.

VI. 1681, to 1695. SIR GEORGE STONHOUSE, Bart. [1641], of Amerden Hall aforesaid, s. and h., *bap.* 14 Jan. 1678/9, at Debden, *suc. to the Baronetcy* in 1681 ; matric. at Oxford (Glouc. Hall) 14 Feb. 1693/4, aged 15. He *d.* a minor and unm. 13 April 1695, when the *Baronetcy* became *extinct*.(a)

PALGRAVE :

cr. 24 June 1641 ;

ex. 3 Nov. 1732.

I. 1641. "JOHN PALGRAVE, of Norwood Barningham, co. Norfolk, Esq.," s. and h. of Sir Augustine PALGRAVE,(b) of the same (*d.* Nov. 1639, aged 72), by Elizabeth, sister of Sir Henry WILLOUGHBY, Bart. [1611], 1st da. of Sir John Willoughby, of Risley, co. Derby, was *bap.* 26 June 1605, at Norwood Barningham, and was *cr. a Baronet*, as above, 24 June 1641, being *Knighted* at Whitehall four days later. He was M.P. for Norfolk, Nov. 1647, till secluded in Dec. 1648, and for Great Yarmouth, 1660, till void on 18 May ; was a Colonel in the Parliamentary army ; served on the Committee of Sequestrators for Norfolk, 1643, and of the "New Model," 1645. He *m.* firstly, in or before 1629, Elizabeth, da. of John JERMY, of Gunton, co. Norfolk, Chancellor of Norwich, by his 1st wife, Mary, da. of Thomas MOULETON. She was *bur.* 19 Dec. 1634, at Norwood Barningham. He *m.* secondly, at Merton, co. Norfolk, Anne, widow of Cotton GASCOIGNE, of Illington, co. Norfolk, da. of Sir William DE GREY, of Merton, co. Norfolk, by Anne, da. of Sir James CALTHORPE. He was *bur.* 26 April 1672, at Norwood Barningham. His widow *d.* 25 Nov. 1676, and was *bur.* at St. Peter's, Hungate, Norwich. Will dat. 15 Sep. 1673, pr. 2 Sep. 1678, in Arch. Court, Norwich.

II. 1672. SIR AUGUSTINE PALGRAVE, Bart. [1641], of Norwood Barningham aforesaid, s. and h. by 1st wife ; *bap.* 1 Dec. 1629 ; Gent. of the Privy Chamber ; *suc. to the Baronetcy* in April 1672 ; was Sheriff of Norfolk, 1690-91. He *m.* firstly, Barbara, da. and h. of the said Cotton GASCOIGNE and Anne, da. of Sir William DE GREY abovenamed. He *m.* secondly (Lic. Vic. Gen. 13 Aug. 1685, he about 47 and she, therein called "Katharine LEMQUEL," about 37), Katharine, widow, of Capt. (—) LAWRENCE, of Brockdish, Herts, da. of Sir William SPRING, 1st Bart. [1641], by Elizabeth, da. of Sir Hamon LE STRANGE. She *d.* 1 and was *bur.* 6 Sep. 1682, at Norwood Barningham. He *m.* thirdly, 21 May 1686, at St. Martin's in the Fields (Lic. Fac. she about 30, spinster), Anne, da. of Sir Richard Grubham HOWE, 2d Bart. [1660], by Anne, da. of John KING, BISHOP OF LONDON. He *d.* 13 March 1710/1, and was *bur.* at Norwood Barningham, aged 83. His widow *d.* 8 Aug. 1714, and was *bur.* there, aged 69.

III. 1711, to 1732. SIR RICHARD PALGRAVE, Bart. [1641], of Norwood Barningham aforesaid, only surv. s. and h. by 3d wife ; *bap.* there 6 Oct. 1688 ; *suc. to the Baronetcy*, 13 March 1710/1. He *d.* unm. in Norwich gaol 3 and was bur. 6 Nov. 1732, at Norwood Barningham, aged 44, when the *Baronetcy* became *extinct*. Admon. 21 June 1735(c) to a creditor.

(a) Elizabeth, his only sister, *m.* Thomas JERVOISE, of Herriard, Hants, who sold the estate of Amerden Hall to Thomas Sclater BACON.

(b) See a good pedigree in the *Visit. of Norfolk, 1563*, with copious additions, pub. by the Norfolk Arch. Soc., vol. ii, pp. 23-34.

(c) The estate was sold under a decree in Chancery (by his heirs (of the whole blood), who were the four daughters of Samuel Smith of Colkirk, Norfolk, whose mother Ursula, was da. of the 1st Bart. [*N. and Q.*, 7th S., xii, 326].

NAPIER, *or* NAPER :

cr. 25 June 1641(a) ;

ex. 25 Jan. 1765.

I. 1641. "GERRARD NAPER [*i.e.*, NAPIER], of Middlemerth [*i.e.*, Middlemarsh] Hall [near Sherbourne], co. Dorset, Esq.," s. and h. of Sir Nathaniel NAPIER,(b) of the same, and of More Critchell in that county, sometime Sheriff and M.P. for Dorset, by Elizabeth, da. and h. of John GERARD, of Hyde, in the Isle of Purbeck, was *bap.* 19 Oct. 1606 at Steeple ; was M.P. for Wareham, 1628-29 ; suc. his father in 1635, and was *cr. a Baronet*, as above, 25 June 1641,(a) being *Knighted* at Whitehall four days later. He was afterwards, 1640, M.P. for Melcomb Regis, till disabled in Jan. 1644/5, having sat in the King's Parl. at Oxford, though, on 20 Sep. 1644, he took the National Covenant. He was fined £3,514 on 19 Dec. 1645, which was reduced, 21 June 1649, to £988, but his estates in Dorset and Kent being sequestrated, his losses during the Civil Wars were estimated at more than £10,000. He was Sheriff of Dorset, 1650-51. In 1665 he entertained the King and Queen at More Critchell. He *m.* Margaret, da. and coh. of John COLLES, of Barton, Somerset. She *d.* in 1660. Admon. 19 June 1665. He *d.* 14 May 1673. Both *bur.* at Mintern Magna. M.I. His will dat. 12 Nov. 1667 to 9 May 1673, pr. 21 Oct. 1673.

II. 1673. SIR NATHANIEL NAPIER, Bart. [1641], of Middlemarsh Hall and of More Critchell aforesaid, only surv. s. and h., *b.* about 1638 ; matric. at Oxford (Oriel Coll.), 16 March 1653/4 ; *Knighted* 16 Jan. 1661 ; *suc. to the Baronetcy*, 14 May 1673 ; was M.P. for Dorset, April 1677, till void 21 May ; for Corfe Castle (four Parls.), 1679-81 and 1685-87 ; for Poole (three Parls.) 1689-98, and for Dorchester, Feb. to July 1702, and 1702-05 ; elected Sheriff of Dorset (but did not act), Nov. 1688. He was a good linguist and well versed in architecture and painting, and wrote a journal of his travels. He *m.* firstly, 20 Dec. 1657, at St. Bride's, Fleet Street, London, Blanche, da. and coh. of Sir Hugh WYNDHAM, of Sylton, co. Dorset, Justice of the Court of Common Pleas, by his 1st wife, Jane, da. of Sir Thomas WODEHOUSE, 2d Bart. [1611]. She *d.* in 1695 and was *bur.* at Mintern aforesaid. He *m.* secondly, 9 March 1696/7, at St. Dionis Backchurch, London (Lic. Fac., he about 45, she about 21, with consent of her mother, Mrs. Ann ARNOLD, widow), Susanna, da. of the Rev. (—) GUISE, of co. Gloucester. He *d.* at Critchell Jan. 1708/9, aged 72, and was *bur.* at Mintern aforesaid. Will pr. June 1709. The will of his widow, by whom he had no issue, pr. Feb. 1711.

III. 1709. SIR NATHANIEL NAPIER, Bart. [1641], of Middlemarsh Hall and of More Critchell aforesaid, only surv. s. and h., by 1st wife, *b.* about 1669 ; admitted to Lincoln's Inn, 1683 ; matric. at Oxford (Trin. Coll.) 10 April 1685, aged 16 ; M.P. for Dorchester (9 Parls.), 1695—1708 and 1710-22 ; *suc. to the Baronetcy* in Jan. 1708/9. He *m.* firstly, Jane, da. of Sir Robert WORSLEY, 3d Bart. [1611], by Mary, da. of Hon. James HERBERT, s. of Philip, EARL OF PEMBROKE. She *d.* s.p., soon afterwards. He *m.* secondly, 28 Aug. 1694, at Isleworth, Midx. (Lic. Fac., he about 25, bachelor [*sic*], she of Hammersmith, spinster), Catharine, da. of William ALINGTON, 1st BARON ALINGTON OF WYMONDLEY, by his 3d wife Diana, da. of William (RUSSELL), 1st DUKE OF BEDFORD. She, who was *b.* 27 Sep. 1677, and who was in Sep. 1691, coheir of her brother, the 2d Baron, *d.* 13 April 1724, and was *bur.* at Mintern. He *d.* 24 Feb. 1727/8. Will pr. 1728.

IV. 1728. SIR WILLIAM NAPIER, Bart. [1641], of Middlemarsh Hall and of More Crichell aforesaid, s. and h., by 2d wife, *b.* about 1696 ; *suc. to the Baronetcy*, 24 Feb. 1727/8 ; Sheriff of Dorset, 1732-33. He *d.* unm. 27 Jan. 1753. Will pr. 1753.

(a) The patent is not enrolled. The date here given is that in Dugdale's *Catalogue*. See *Memorandum* on p. 84. The date of the signet bill is 23 June 1641.

(b) This Nathaniel was s. and h. of Sir Robert Napier, who purchased Middlemarsh in 1592, was Lord Chief Baron of the Exchequer of Ireland, 1593, and Sheriff of Dorset, 1606. The said Robert was 3d s. of James Napier, of Puncknoll, Dorset, 3d s. of John Napier, of Swyre, in that county, who was a yr. s. of Sir Alexander NAPIER, of Merchistoun, in Scotland.

f

V. 1753. SIR GERARD NAPIER, Bart. [1641], of Middlemarsh Hall and of More Critchell aforesaid, br. and h., *b.* about 1701; matric. at Oxford (Ball. Coll.), 11 May 1719, aged 18; *suc. to the Baronetcy*, 27 Jan. 1753. He *m.*, in or before 1740, Bridget, da. of Edward PHELIPS, of Montacute, Somerset. She *d.* in 1758, aged 51. He *d.* 23 Oct. 1759, aged 59. Will pr. 1761.

VI. 1759, to 1765. SIR GERARD NAPIER, Bart. [1641], of Middlemarsh Hall and of More Critchell aforesaid, only s. and h., *b.* about 1740; matric. at Oxford (Trin. Coll.), 13 April 1758, aged 18; *suc. to the Baronetcy*, 23 Oct. 1759; was M.P. for Bridport, 1761-65. He *m.* Elizabeth, da. of Sir John OGLANDER, 4th Bart. [1665], by Margaret, da. of John COXE. He *d.* s.p., 25 Jan. 1765, aged 26, when the *Baronetcy* became *extinct.*(a) Will pr. Feb. 1765. His widow *m.* in 1779, James WEBB, and *d.* 16 Oct. 1814 at Bath.

WHITMORE:

cr. 28 June 1641;

ex. March 1699.

I. 1641. "THOMAS WHITMORE, of Apley, co. Salop, Esq.," 2d but 1st surv. s. and h. ap. of Sir William WHITMORE, of the same (who had purchased that estate and was Sheriff of Salop in 1620), by his second wife, Dorothy, da. of William WELD, of London, was *b.* 28 Nov. 1612, in London; matric. at Oxford (Trin. Coll.), 29 Jan. 1629/30, aged 17; B.A., 10 May 1631; Barrister (Mid. Temple), 1639; M.P. for Bridgnorth, April to May 1640, and 1640 till disabled in Feb. 1644, and was *cr. a Baronet*, as above, 28 June 1641, and *Knighted* the same day at Whitehall. He suc. his father Dec. 1648;(b) was a Compounder in Jan. 1648/9; fined £5,315 on 3 April 1649, reduced in May 1650 to £5,000. He *m.*, 16 April 1635, at Leyton, co. Essex, Elizabeth, da. and h. of Sir William ACTON, Bart. (so *cr.* 30 May 1629), Alderman and sometime [1640] Lord Mayor of London, by his first wife Anne, da. and h. of James BILL, of Astwell, Herts. He *d.* 1653. Will pr. 1664. His widow, who inherited her mother's estate of Astwell, d. 1666. Will pr. 1667.

II. 1653, to 1699. SIR WILLIAM WHITMORE, Bart. [1641], of Apley aforesaid, s. and h.; *b.* 8 April 1637; *suc. to the Baronetcy* in 1653; was M.P. for Shropshire, 1660; for Bridgnorth (nine Parls.), 1661, till decease. He m., about Aug. 1658, Mary, da. of Eliab HARVEY, of St. Lawrence Pountney, London, Turkey Merchant, by Mary, da. of Francis WEST, of London.(c) He *d.* s.p. March 1699, and was *bur.* at Stockton, Salop, when the *Baronetcy* became *extinct.*(d) Will dat. 12 Nov. 1695, pr. 11 Nov. 1700. His widow, who was *bap.* 15 Nov. 1637, at St. Lawrence's aforesaid, *d.* 30 Jan. and was *bur.* 15 Feb. 1710/1 (with her parents), at Hempstead, co. Essex. Will dat. 1 May 1710, pr. 21 Feb. 1710/1.

(a) The estates devolved on his cousin and h., Humphrey STURT, of Horton, Dorset, only s. and h. of Humphrey Sturt, of the same (who *d.* at Bath, 1 Feb. 1739/40), by Diana, only da. of the 3d Bart.

(b) The admon. of this William was granted 11 Feb. 1658/9 to his grandson, "Sir [—] Whitmore, Bart.," the sons of the deceased, Richard Whitmore and George Whitmore having renounced.

(c) See an elaborate ped. of Harvey in *Mis. Gen. et Her.*, 2d S., vol. iii, pp. 329, 362, and 381.

(d) The estate of Apley passed to his first cousin (once removed) and heir male, William Whitmore, of Lower Slaughter, co. Glouc., whose descendants still hold it.

MAYNEY, *or* MAYNE:

cr. 29 June 1641;

ex. 1706.

I. 1641. "JOHN MAYNE [or MAYNEY], of Lynton, co. Kent, Esq.," s. and h. of Walter MAYNEY, of Linton aforesaid, was *b.* about 1608 and was *cr. a Baronet*, as above, 29 June 1641, being *Knighted* at Whitehall the same day. He was a zealous Royalist, was fined £1,600 on 22 March 1648 and £1,970 on 1 Aug. 1649; and, being eventually ruined in that cause, sold his estate of Linton to Sir Francis Withens. He *m.*, before 1634, Mary, da. of Sir Peter RICAUT, of AYLESFORD, co. Kent and of London, merchant, by Mary, da. of Roger VERCOLCIA. He d. about 1676, aged 68.

II. 1676? to 1706. SIR ANTHONY MAYNEY, Bart [1641], s. and h.; *suc. to the Baronetcy* about 1676. He *d.* unm. (his death said to have been caused by actual want(a)) in 1706, when the *Baronetcy* became *extinct.*

CAVE:

cr. 30 June 1641(b);

sometime, in 1810, CAVE-BROWNE,

and afterwards, since 1810, CAVE-BROWNE-CAVE.

I. 1641. "THOMAS CAVE, Junior, of Stanford, co. Northampton, Knt.," s. and h. ap. of Sir Thomas CAVE, of Stanford on Avon aforesaid, by Elizabeth, da. of Sir Herbert CROFT, of Croft Castle, co. Hereford, was *b.* about 1622; matric. at Oxford (St. John's Coll.), 28 April 1637, aged 15; *Knighted* at Whitehall, 24 June 1641, and, a few days later, was *cr. a Baronet*, as above, 30 June 1641.(b) He, as well as his father, was a strenuous supporter of the cause of his King. He suc. his father between June 1663 and Feb. 1666/7. He *m.* firstly, Katharine, da. of Sir Anthony HASLEWOOD, of Maidwell, co. Northampton, by Elizabeth, da. of Sir William WILLMER, of Sywell, in that county. She *d.* s.p. He *m.* secondly, in or before 1651, Penelope, 2d da. and coheir of Thomas (WENMAN), 2d VISCOUNT WENMAN OF TUAM [I.], by Margaret, da. and h. of Edmund HAMPDEN. Her will dat. 2 Feb. 1665, pr. 27 March 1666. His will pr. Feb. 1671.

II. 1671? SIR ROGER CAVE, Bart. [1641], of Stanford aforesaid, s. and h., by 2d wife, *b.* about 1651, *suc. to the Baronetcy* about 1671; was Sheriff of Northants., 1679-80; M.P. for Coventry, 1685-87 and 1689-90. He *m.* firstly (Lic. Vic. Gen., 24 Feb. 1675/6, each aged about 21), Martha, da. and h. of John BROWNE, of Eydon, co. Northampton, Clerk of the Parliament, by Elizabeth, 1st da. of John PACKER, of Shillingford, Berks, one of the Clerks of the Privy Seal. She *d.* before 1691. He *m.* secondly, Mary, sister of William BROMLEY, Speaker of the House of Commons, da. of Sir William BROMLEY, K.B., of Bagington, co. Warwick. He *d.* 11 Oct. 1703, aged 49. His widow *d.* 22 Nov. 1721.

III. 1703. SIR THOMAS CAVE, Bart. [1641], of Stanford aforesaid, s. and h., by 1st wife, *b.* about 1682, matric. at Oxford (Ch. Ch.), 27 Jan. 1698/9, aged 16; *suc. to the Baronetcy* 11 Oct. 1703; M.P. for Leicestershire (three Parls.), 1711 till his death in 1719. He *m.* 20 Feb. 1703, at St. Giles' in the Fields, Margaret, sister of Ralph, 1st EARL VERNEY [I.], da. of John (VERNEY), 1st VISCOUNT

(a) His brother, from a like cause, had previously, in 1694, committed suicide.

(b) The patent is not enrolled. The date here given is that in Dugdale's *Catalogue*. See *Memorandum* on p. 84. The date of the signet bill is 28 June 1641.

FERMANAGH [I.], by his 1st wife, Elizabeth, da. of Ralph PALMER. He *d.* 21 April 1719, in his 39th year, and was *bur.* at Stanford. M.I. Will dat. 20 Jan. 1718-19, pr. 23 July 1719. His widow (whose issue, in 1810, became heir to the family of Verney) *d.* 17 May 1774. Her will pr. May 1774.

IV. 1719. SIR VERNEY CAVE, Bart. [1641], of Stanford aforesaid, s. and h., *b.* 4 and *bap.* 18 Jan. 1704/5, at St. Martin's in the Fields; *suc. to the Baronetcy*, 21 April 1719; matric. at Oxford (Balliol Coll.), 29 March 1722, aged 15. He *d.* unm., 13 Sep. 1734, aged 29, and was *bur.* at Stanford. M.I. Admon., 24 Oct. 1734, to br., Sir Thomas Cave, Bart.

V. 1734. SIR THOMAS CAVE, Bart. [1641], of Stanford aforesaid, br. and h., *b.* 27 May and *bap.* 4 June 1712, at St. Martin's in the Fields; matric. at Oxford (Ball. Coll.), 3 Nov. 1729, aged 17; *suc. to the Baronetcy*, 13 Sep. 1734; Barrister (Inner Temple), 1735; M.P. for Leicestershire, 1741-47, 1762-68 and 1768-74; *cr.* D.C.L. of Oxford, 7 April 1756. He *m.*, 1736, Elizabeth, da. and sole surv. issue of Griffith DAVIES, M.D., of Theddingworth, co. Leicester, and of Birmingham, co. Warwick, by Elizabeth, da. of Sir John BURGOYNE, 3d Bart. [1641], of Sutton. She *d.* 15 May 1760. He *d.* 7 Aug. 1778, aged 67. Both *bur.* at Stanford.

VI. 1778. SIR THOMAS CAVE, Bart. [1641], of Stanford aforesaid, s. and h., *b.* 22 Aug. 1737; matric. at Oxford (Balliol Coll.), 1 April 1756, aged 18; *cr.* D.C.L., 8 July 1773; F.R.S., F.S.A., 1799; *suc. to the Baronetcy*, 7 Aug. 1778; Sheriff for Leicestershire, Feb. to June 1780. He *m.* in 1765 (it is said, at St. Lawrence Jewry, London), Sarah, da. and coh. of John EDWARDS, merchant, of London and Bristol, by his wife, Sarah HOLFORD. He *d.* 31 May 1780, and was *bur.* at Stanford. Will pr. July 1780. His widow d. July 1819. Will pr. 1819.

VII. 1780. SIR THOMAS CAVE, Bart. [1641], of Stanford aforesaid, only s. and h., *b.* 6 Oct. 1766; matric. at Oxford, 28 Oct. 1785, aged 19; *suc. to the Baronetcy*, 31 May 1780; M.P. for Leicestershire, 1790, till his death in 1792. He *m.*, 3 June 1791, Lucy, da. of Robert (SHERARD), 4th EARL OF HARBOROUGH, by his 2d wife, Jane, da. of William REEVE. He *d.* s.p. 16 Jan. 1792, and was *bur.* the 27th at Stanford.(a) Will pr. Feb. 1792. His widow, who was *b.* 13 Oct. 1769, at Southwell, Notts, *m.* 20 Aug. 1798, at St. Geo. Han. sq., Hon. Philip BOUVERIE, afterwards PUSEY, who *d.* 14 April 1828, aged 81. She *d.* 27 March 1858, aged 89.(b)

VIII. 1792. THE REV. SIR CHARLES CAVE, Bart. [1641], uncle and h., being 2d and yst, s. of the 6th Bart., was *b.* about 1747; matric. at Oxford (Balliol Coll.] 7 March 1766, aged 19; B.A., 1769; M.A. (St. Mary Hall), 1772; in Holy Orders; Rector of Finedon, co. Northampton, and Vicar of Theddingworth, co. Leicester; F.S.A., 1781; *suc. to the Baronetcy*, 16 Jan. 1792. He *d.* unm., 21 March 1810, and was *bur.* at Stanford. Will pr. May 1810.

(a) The estate of Stanford, the paternal inheritance of the Cave family, devolved on his sister and heir, Sarah, *b.* 2 July 1768. She *m.*, 25 Feb. 1790, Henry Otway, of Castle Otway, co. Tipperary, who *d.* 13 Sep. 1815, and, a quarter of a century after his death, obtained a peerage (not apparently for any services rendered by him, herself, or any of her family, but) as being the representative of one of six coheirs of a Barony (that of Braye) which had been in abeyance for about 300 years, and of which she did not inherit a single manor. See as to this pernicious practice (which prevailed during the earlier years of Queen Victoria's reign) the "*Complete Peerage*," by G.E.C., vol. i, p. 288, note "b," and p. 289, note "c," and, as to "BRAYE," vol. ii, pp. 11-13.

(b) By her second husband she had nine children, of whom the second son was the well-known "Dr. Pusey" [Edward Bouverie Pusey, D.D., Regius Professor of Hebrew and Canon of Christ Church, Oxford], who *d.* 16 Sep. 1882, aged 82.

IX. 1810. SIR WILLIAM CAVE-BROWNE, afterwards CAVE-BROWNE-CAVE, Bart. [1641], of Stretton Hall, in Stretton en-le-field, co. Derby, cousin and h., being s. and h. of John CAVE-BROWNE, of Stretton Hall aforesaid, by his second wife, Catherine, da. and h. of Thomas ASTELEY, of Wood Eaton, co. Stafford, and Asteley, co. Salop, which John (who by Act of Parl., 1752, took the name of *Browne*, as a final surname, on inheriting the Stretton estates from his maternal grandfather, and who *d.* 2 Oct. 1798), was 2d s., but the only son that had issue, of Roger CAVE, of Eydon, co. Northampton, and Raunston, co. Leicester (by Catherine, da. and coheir of William BROWNE, of Stretton Hall aforesaid), which Roger (who *d.* March 1741) was s. of Sir Roger CAVE, 2d Bart. by his 2d wife. He was *b.* 19 Feb. 1765 and *bap.* 25 March, at Stretton aforesaid. He *suc. to the Baronetcy*, 21 March 1810, and soon afterwards assumed the name of CAVE after that of CAVE-BROWNE, which surnames were confirmed to his issue male by Royal Lic. dat. 18 Jan. 1839. He *m.* firstly, 13 Oct. 1788, at Croxall, co. Derby, Sarah, da. of Thomas PRINSEP, of Croxall. She *d.* s.p. and was *bur.* 21 June 1790, at Stretton aforesaid. He *m.* secondly, 4 Jan. 1793, at Stretton, Louisa, 4th da. of Sir Robert Meade WILMOT, 2d Bart. [1759], of Chaddesden, by Mary, da. and h. of William WOOLLETT. She, who was *b.* 8 Feb. 1771 and *bap.* at Chaddesden, *d.* 23 and was *bur.* 30 April 1824, at Stretton. He *d.* 24 and was *bur.* 29 Aug. 1838, at Stretton, aged 73. Will pr. Nov. 1838.

X. 1838. SIR JOHN ROBERT CAVE-BROWNE-CAVE, Bart. [1641], of Stretton Hall aforesaid, s. and h., *b.* 4 March and *bap.* 10 May 1798, at Stretton; *suc. to the Baronetcy*, 24 Aug. 1838; was confirmed in the surname of *Cave-Browne-Cave*. by Royal Lic. 18 Jan. 1839; Sheriff of Derbyshire, 1844. He *m.* 22 Nov. 1821, at Kenilworth, co. Warwick, Catharine Penelope, yst. da. and coheir of William MILLS, of Barlaston Hall, co. Stafford. He *d.* 11 Nov. 1855. Will pr. Jan. 1856. His widow, who was *b.* 25 June and *bap.* 10 Oct. 1799, at Basford, co. Stafford, *d.* 13 March 1871, at Kenilworth, aged 71.

XI. 1855. SIR MYLLES CAVE-BROWNE-CAVE, Bart. [1641], of Stretton Hall aforesaid, s. and h., *b.* 1 Aug. and *bap.* 31 Nov. 1822 at Kenilworth, sometime an officer in the 11th Hussars; *suc. to the Baronetcy* 11 Nov. 1855. He *m.* 15 May 1855, at Stretton en le field, Isabelle, yst. da. of John TAYLOR, of "The Newarke," Leicester.

Family Estates.—The estate of Stanford, co. Northampton, passed away from the family in 1792; see p. 94, note "a." That now held by the Baronet, being at Stretton en le field, co. Derby, came into the family by the marriage, in 1721, of Roger Cave (s. of the 2d and grandfather of the 9th Bart.) with Catharine, da. and coheir of William Browne, of Stretton. This estate appears to have been in 1878 under 8,000 acres. *Seat.*—Stretton Hall, near Ashby de la Zouche, co. Derby.

YELVERTON:

cr. 30 June 1641(a);

afterwards, 1676-1799, LORDS GREY DE RUTHIN;

subsequently, 1690-1799, VISCOUNTS LONGUEVILLE,

and *finally*, 1717-99, EARLS OF SUSSEX;

ex. 22 APRIL 1799.

I. 1641. "CHRISTOPHER YELVERTON, of Easton Manduyt [*i.e.*, Mauduit], co. Northampton, Knt.," s. and h. of Sir Henry YELVERTON,(b) of the same, one of the Judges of the Common Pleas (1625-30), by Margaret, da. of Robert BEALE, Clerk of the Council to Queen Elizabeth, was admitted to Gray's Inn, 28 Feb. 1606/7; was M.P. for Newport, 1626 and 1528-29; for Bossiney, 1640 till secluded Dec. 1648; *Knighted*, 29 Jan. 1629/30; suc. his father,

(a) The patent is not enrolled. The date here given is that in Dugdale's *Catalogue*. See *Memorandum* on p. 84. The date of the signet bill is 27 June 1641.

(b) This Henry was s. and h. of Sir Christopher Yelverton, a Judge of the King's Bench, who purchased the estate of Easton Mauduit, and who *d.* there, 1607.

in 1630; was Sheriff of Northants, 1639-40; and was *cr. a Baronet*, as above, 30 June 1641.(a) He *m.* 20 April 1630, at St. Giles', Cripplegate, Anne, yst. da. of Sir William TWISDEN, 1st Bart. [1611], by Anne, da. of Sir Moyle FINCH, 1st Bart. [1611]. He *d.* 4 Dec. 1654, and was *bur.* at Easton Mauduit. M.I. Will pr. 1655. His widow *d.* 3 Dec. 1670, aged 67, and was *bur.* at Easton Mauduit. M.I. there and at East Peckham, co. Kent. Will pr. Nov. 1671.

II. 1654. SIR HENRY YELVERTON, Bart. [1641], of Easton Mauduit aforesaid, only s. and h., *bap.* there 6 July 1633, matric. at Oxford (Wad. Coll.), 12 Nov. 1651; *suc. to the Baronetcy* 4 Dec. 1654; was M.P. for Northamptonshire, 1660, and March 1664, till his death. He *m.* in or before 1657, Susan, *suo jure* BARONESS GREY DE RUTHIN, da. and h. of Charles (LONGUEVILLE), LORD GREY DE RUTHIN, by Frances, da. and coheir of Edward NEVILL, of Keymer, co. Sussex. He *d.* 3 Oct. 1670. Will pr. 1671. His widow *d.* 28 Jan. 1676. Both *bur.* at Easton Mauduit.

III. 1670. SIR CHARLES YELVERTON, Bart. [1641], of Easton Mauduit aforesaid, 1st s. and h., *b.* there 21 Aug. 1657, *suc. to the Baronetcy* in Oct. 1670; matric. at Oxford (Ch. Ch.), 1 July 1673, aged 16. By the death of his mother, 28 Jan. 1676, he became LORD GREY DE RUTHIN, in which peerage this *Baronetcy* then *merged*. His br. and h. (the 4th Bart.) was *cr.* 21 April 1690, VISCOUNT LONGUEVILLE, whose s. and h. (the 2d Viscount and 5th Bart.) was *cr.* 26 Sep. 1717, EARL OF SUSSEX. On the death s.p.m., 22 April 1799, of the 3d Earl, 4th Viscount, and 7th Baronet, *this Baronetcy*, as also the said Earldom and Viscountcy, became *extinct*, though the Barony devolved on the Earl's da. and h. general. See *Peerage*, under "Grey de Ruthin."

BOTELER:

cr. 3 July 1641;(b)

ex. 22 Jan. 1772.

I. 1641. "WILLIAM BOTELER, of Telton [*i.e.*, of Barham Court, in Teston], co. Kent, Esq.," 3d but only surv. s. and h. of Sir Oliver BOTELER, of the same and of Shernbrooke, Beds, by Anne, da. and h. of Thomas BARHAM, of Barham Court aforesaid, was admitted to Gray's Inn, 22 May 1622; suc. his father, 1632, and was *cr. a Baronet*, as above, 3 July 1641.(b) He raised a regiment for the King, and was slain, at the head of it, at the battle of Cropredy bridge, 29 June 1644. He *m.*, 1 May 1631, Joan, sister of Thomas, 1st VISCOUNT FANSHAWE OF DROMORE [I.], da. of Sir HENRY FANSHAWE, of Ware Park, Herts, by Elizabeth, da. of Thomas SMYTHE, of Ostenhanger, co. Kent. He *d.*, as aforesaid, 29 June and was *bur.* 4 July 1644, at Oxford. Will pr. March 1645. His widow, who, in Dec. 1647, was fined £2,782 for her late husband's delinquency, *m.*, in 1646, Sir Philip WARWICK (who *d.* 15 Jan. 1682, in his 74th year), and *d.* before 5 June 1672, being *bur.* at Chislehurst, Kent. M.I. Her admon. 5 June 1672.

II. 1644. SIR OLIVER BOTELER, Bart. [1641], of Barham Court aforesaid, s. and h., aged 10 in 1647; *suc. to the Baronetcy*, 29 June 1644. He *m.* firstly, 1665,(c) Anne, da. of Sir Robert AUSTEN, 1st Bart. [1660], of Bexley, by his 2d wife, Anne, da. of Thomas MUNS. He *m.* secondly, Anne, da. of Jacob UPHILL, of Dagenham, Essex, and Anne his wife. He *d.* about 1689. Admon. 21 Jan. 1689/90. His widow was *bur.* 26 Jan. 1712/3, at Dagenham. M.I. Will dat. 22 Dec. 1712, pr. 1 Feb. 1713/4.

(a) *Vide* p. 95, note "a."

(b) The patent is not enrolled. The date here given is that in Dugdale's *Catalogue*. See *Memorandum* on p. 84. The date of the signet bill is [the same date, *viz.*] 3 July 1641.

(c) There is a licence at the Fac. office, 12 March 1660/1, for Sir Edward Boteler, Knt. and *Bart.*, of St. Paul's, Covent Garden, about 20, bachelor, son of Sir Allen Boteler, deceased, and Dame Katharine Boteler, to marry Jane Russell, about 21, a spinster. It is, however, difficult to identify the abovenamed Baronet. His father was *Knighted* 16 Feb. 1645/6, at Oxford, as "of Bucks."

III. 1689? SIR PHILIP BOTELER, Bart. [1641], of Barham Court aforesaid, s. and h., *b.* about 1674; *suc. to the Baronetcy* about 1689; M.P. for Hythe (seven Parls.), 1690—1708. He *m.* (Lic. Vic. Gen. 17 Dec. 1690, he about 26, she about 22) Anne, sister of Sir William DES BOUVERIE, 1st Bart. [1714], da. of Sir Edward DES BOUVERIE, of Cheshunt, Herts, by Anne, da. and coheir of Jacob DE LA FORTERIE, of London, merchant. She *d.* 1717, and was *bur.* at Teston, Admon. 9 Oct. 1717. He *d.* April 1719, and was *bur.* at Teston aforesaid. Will dat. 29 March 1708 [*sic*], pr. 10 June 1719.

IV. 1719, to 1772. SIR PHILIP BOTELER, Bart. [1641], of Barham Court aforesaid, only s. and h., *b.* about 1695; matric. at Oxford (Ch. Ch.), 10 Oct. 1712, aged 17; *suc. to the Baronetcy* in April 1719. He *m.* May 1720, at St. Anne's, Blackfriars, Elizabeth, da. and h. of Thomas WILLIAMS, of Cabalva, co. Radnor. She *d.* 8 Oct. 1752, and was *bur.* at Teston. He *d.* s.p.s. 22 Jan. 1772, aged about 77, and was *bur.* at Teston aforesaid, when the *Baronetcy* became *extinct*. Will pr. Feb. 1772.(a)

HATTON:

cr. 5 July 1641(b);

ex. 19 Sep. 1812.

I. 1641. "THOMAS HATTON,(c) of Long Stanton, co. Cambridge, Knt." 3d s. of John HATTON, of the same, by Jane, da. of Robert SHUTE, one of the Barons of the Exchequer, was *b.* about 1583; admitted to Gray's Inn, 2 Feb. 1606/7; *Knighted*, at Bletsho, 26 July 1616; M.P. for Corfe Castle, 1621-22; for Malmesbury, 1624-25 and 1625; for Stamford, 1628-29, and April to May 1640, and was *cr. a Baronet*, as above, 5 July 1641.(b) He *m.* Mary, 6th da. of Sir Giles ALINGTON, of Horseheath, co. Cambridge, by Dorothy, da. of Thomas (CECIL), EARL OF EXETER. He *d.* 23 Sep. 1658, aged about 75. Will pr. 1659. His widow, who was *bap.* 19 Oct. 1612, at Horseheath, was *bur.* 27 Aug. 1674 at Long Stanton. Will dat. 3 Oct. 1670, pr. 2 Sep. 1674.

II. 1658. SIR THOMAS HATTON, Bart. [1641], of Long Stanton aforesaid, s. and h.; *suc. to the Baronetcy*, 23 Sep. 1658; was Sheriff of Cambridgeshire and Hunts, 1662-63. He *m.* before 1660, Bridget, da. of Sir William GORING, 1st Bart. [1621], of Burton, by Eleanor, da. and h. of Sir Edward FRANCIS. He was *bur.* 19 April 1682, at Long Stanton. Admon. 24 April 1682 to his widow.

III. 1682. SIR CHRISTOPHER HATTON, Bart. [1641], of Long Stanton aforesaid, s. and h., *suc. to the Baronetcy* 19 April 1682.(d) He *d.* young and was *bur.* 26 Sep. 1683, at Long Stanton.

(a) He devised one moiety of his real and personal estate to the Dow. Viscountess Folkestone for her life, with rem. to her stepson, William, 1st Earl of Radnor, grandson and h. of his uncle, Sir William Des BOUVERIE, Bart., abovenamed; the other moiety (in which was the manor of Teston) he devised to Elizabeth Des Bouverie, of Chart Sutton, Kent, Spinster, da. of another uncle, Sir Christopher des Bouverie.

(b) The patent is not enrolled. The date here given is that in Dugdale's *Catalogue*. See *Memorandum* on p. 84. The date of the signet bill is 2 July 1641.

(c) His eldest br., Sir Christopher HATTON, of Kirby, co. Northampton (*bur.* 11 Sep. 1619 at Westm. Abbey), inherited the great estates of the LORD CHANCELLOR HATTON, whose h. male he was. His son was *cr.* BARON HATTON, 1643, and his grandson, VISCOUNT HATTON, 1706, titles which became *extinct* in 1762, the estates passing to the family of FINCH, afterwards FINCH-HATTON, EARLS OF WINCHELSEA, the 6th Earl of Winchilsea having *m.* the Hon. Anne HATTON, sister and coheir of William, 2d and last VISCOUNT HATTON. These estates, including the magnificent but dilapidated Hall at Kirby, were for sale in 1880.

(d) The marriage, 24 Dec. 1682, of "Sir John Hatton and Mary Hinton," at Knightsbridge Chapel, does not, apparently, relate to any of these Baronets.

IV. 1683. SIR THOMAS HATTON, Bart. [1641], of Long Stanton aforesaid, br. and h., *suc. to the Baronetcy* in Sep. 1683. He *d.* young and was *bur.* 15 March 1684/5 at Long Stanton.

V. 1685. SIR CHRISTOPHER HATTON, Bart. [1641], of Long Stanton aforesaid, uncle and h. male, *suc. to the Baronetcy*, 15 March 1684/5. He *m.* 14 July 1674, at Westm. Abbey (Lic. Vic. Gen., he about 23 and of the Middle Temple, and she about 20), Elizabeth, da. of Thomas BUCK, of Westwick, co. Cambridge, by his 1st wife Rebecca, da. of Thomas LOVERING, of Norwich. She *d.* July 1710. He *d.* Oct. 1720.

VI. 1720. SIR THOMAS HATTON, Bart. [1641], of Long Stanton aforesaid, s. and h.; *suc. to the Baronetcy* in Oct. 1720; was Sheriff of Cambridgeshire and Hunts, 1725-26. He *m.* firstly, Elizabeth, da. and h. of Cooper ORLEBAR, of Henwick, Beds. She *d.* 5 May 1732, aged 44. He *m.* secondly, Henrietta, da. of Sir James ASTRY, of Woodend in Harlington, Beds, by Anne, 2d da. of Sir Thomas PENYSTONE, 1st Bart. [1611]. He *d.* s.p. at Woodend aforesaid, 23 June 1733, and was *bur.* at Long Stanton. M.I. Will pr. 1733.

VII. 1733. SIR JOHN HATTON, Bart. [1641], of Melbourne, co. Cambridge, br. and h., *suc. to the Baronetcy*, 23 June 1733. He *m.* Mary, widow of William HITCH, da. of Thomas HAWKES. He *d.* 1 July 1740. Will pr. 1740. The will of Dame Mary Hatton pr. 1760.

VIII. 1740. SIR THOMAS HATTON, Bart. [1641], of Long Stanton aforesaid, s. and h., *b.* 14 Sep. 1728, *suc. to the Baronetcy* 1 July 1740. He *m.* 26 April 1752, at Ely Chapel, Holborn (Lic. Lond., he above 21 and she above 17), Harriet, da. of Dingley ASKHAM, of Connington, co. Cambridge. He *d.* 7 and was *bur.* 14 Nov. 1787, at Long Stanton, aged 59. Will pr. 1788. His widow *d.* 20 and was *bur.* 28 March 1795, aged 60, at Long Stanton. Will pr. April 1795.

IX. 1787. SIR JOHN HATTON, Bart. [1641], of Long Stanton aforesaid, s. and h., *suc. to the Baronetcy* 7 Nov. 1787. He *m.* in 1798 (—), da. of (—) BRIDGEMAN, an American refugee. He *d.* s.p. 29 July 1811.

X. 1811, to 1812. SIR THOMAS DINGLEY HATTON, Bart. [1641], of Long Stanton aforesaid, br. and h., *b.* about 1771, *suc. to the Baronetcy* 29 July 1811. He *d.* unm. (in consequence of a fall from his curricle) 19 and was *bur.* 29 Sep. 1812, at Long Stanton, aged 41, when the *Baronetcy* became *extinct*. Admon. May 1813.

ABDY:

cr. 14 July 1641;(a)

ex. 16 April 1868.

I. 1641. "THOMAS ABDY, of Felix Hall [in Kelvedon], co. Essex, Esq.," s. and h. of Anthony ABDY, of St. Andrew Undershaft, Alderman and sometime, 1630-31, Sheriff of London, by Abigail, da. of Sir Thomas CAMBELL, sometime, 1609-10, Lord Mayor of London, was *b.* about 1612; admitted to Lincoln's Inn, 29 Jan. 1631/2; suc. his father, 10 Sep. 1640, and was *cr. a Baronet*,(b) as above, 14 July 1641,(a) having, apparently, been previously, 8 July 1641, *Knighted*.(c) He *m.* firstly, 1 Feb. 1637/8, at St. Peter le Poor, London (Lic. London, he 25, she

(a) The patent is not enrolled. The date here given is that in Dugdale's *Catalogue*. See *Memorandum* on p. 84. The date of the signet bill is 5 July 1641; the date of the Warrant [June ?] 1641.

(b) He was one of three brothers, all of whom obtained Baronetcies, *viz.*, (1) Thomas, 14 July 1641, *extinct* 16 April 1868; (2) Robert, 9 June 1660, *extinct* 2 April 1759; and (3) John, 22 June 1660, *extinct* about 1662.

(c) He is, however, not designated a Knight in the patent of 14 July 1641.

21), Mary, 9th da. and coheir of Lucas CORSELLIS, of London, merchant. She *d.* s.p.m. 6 April 1645, aged 27, and was *bur.* at Kelvedon. M.I. He *m.* secondly, 16 Jan. 1646/7, at St. Barth. the Less, Anne, 1st da. and coheir of Sir Thomas SOAME, of Throcking, Herts, Alderman and sometime, 1635-36, Sheriff of London, by Joane, da. of William FREEMAN, of Aspeden, Herts. She *d.* 19 June 1679, aged 56. He *d.* 14 Jan. 1685/6, aged about 74. Both *bur.* at Kelvedon. M.I. His will dat. 15 Oct. 1682, pr., with a codicil, 11 Feb. 1685/6.

II. 1686. SIR ANTHONY ABDY, Bart. [1641], of Felix Hall aforesaid, s. and h. by 2d wife, *b.* about 1655; *suc. to the Baronetcy*, 14 Jan. 1685/6. He *m.*, in or before 1690, Mary, only da. and h. of Richard MILWARD, D.D., Rector of Great Braxted, Essex, and Canon of Windsor, by Mary, da. of Sir Anthony THOMAS, of Chobham, Surrey, aunt and h. of Gainsford THOMAS, of Chobham aforesaid. He *d.* 2 April 1704, aged about 49, and was *bur.* at Kelvedon. M.I. Will pr. 1704. His widow *d.* 18 Aug. 1744, aged 86, and was *bur.* at Chobham. M.I. Will dat. 2 April 1743 to 16 July 1744, pr. 12 Oct. 1744.

III. 1704. SIR ANTHONY-THOMAS ABDY, Bart. [1641], of Felix Hall aforesaid, s. and h., *b.* about 1690; *suc. to the Baronetcy*, 2 April 1704; matric. at Oxford (Trin. Coll.), 19 April 1707, aged 17; admitted to Lincoln's Inn, 1708. He *m.* firstly, Mary, da. and sole h. of Hope GIFFORD, of Colchester, Essex. She *d.* s.p. 1718. He *m.* secondly, in 1720, Charlotte, 3d da. and coheir of Sir Thomas BARNADISTON, 3d Bart. [1663], of Ketton, by Anne, da. and coheir of Sir Richard ROTHWELL, Bart., so *cr.* in 1661. She *d.* s.p.m. 19 Feb. 1731. He *m.* thirdly, Anne, da. and h. of Thomas WILLIAMS, of Tendring Hall, Suffolk, by Elizabeth, da. of Sir Thomas BARNADISTON, 1st Bart. [1663], of Ketton. He *d.* s.p.m.(a) 11 June 1733, aged about 43. Will pr. June 1733. His widow *d.* s.p. 21 Sep. 1745, and was *bur.* at Kelvedon. Will dat. 26 Dec. 1744, pr. 7 Nov. 1745.

IV. 1733. SIR WILLIAM ABDY, Bart. [1641], of Chobham Place, Surrey, and of Golden sq., St. James' Westm., br. and h. male, *suc. to the Baronetcy* (but not to the Essex estates), 11 June 1733. He *m.* about 1720, Mary, only da. and h. of Philip STOTHERD, of Terling, Essex. She *d.* 6 April 1743. He *d.* 18 Jan. 1749/50. Admon. 5 Feb. 1749/50, and again 25 Feb. 1777.

V. 1750. SIR ANTHONY-THOMAS ABDY, Bart. [1641], of Chobham Place aforesaid, 1st s. and h., *b.* about 1720; admitted to Lincoln's Inn, 1738; Barrister at Law (Lincoln's Inn), and finally King's Counsel; *suc. to the Baronetcy*, 18 Jan. 1749/50; suc., in 1759, to the estate of Albyns, in Stapleford Abbots, Essex, under the will of Sir John Abdy, 4th and last Bart. [1660], of Albyns aforesaid; M.P. for Knaresborough, 1763 till decease. He *m.* 13 Aug. 1747, at St. Paul's Cathedral, London, Catharine, da. and coheir of William HAMILTON, of Chancery Lane, London. He *d.* s.p. 7 April 1775, aged about 55. Will pr. April 1775. His widow *d.* 1792. Will pr. Oct. 1792.

VI. 1775. SIR WILLIAM ABDY, Bart. [1641], of Chobham Place aforesaid, br. and h., *b.* about 1732; Captain, R.N.; *suc. to the Baronetcy*, 7 April 1775. He *m.* 1771, Mary, only da. of James BREBNER-GORDON (formerly James BREBNER), of More Place, Herts, by Ann LAVINGTON, his wife. He *d.* 21 July 1803, aged 71, and was *bur.* at Chobham. M.I. Will pr. 1803 and again Dec. 1835. His widow, who was *b.* in Antigua, was aunt (her issue, in 1854, becoming heir) to James-Adam GORDON, of Knockespock, co. Aberdeen, Naish House in Wraxall, co. Somerset, and Stocks in Aldbury, Herts, who *d.* s.p. March 1854, aged 63. She *d.* 4 March 1829. Will pr. June 1829.

VII. 1803, to 1868. SIR WILLIAM ABDY, Bart. [1641], of Chobham Place aforesaid (which he sold in 1809), s. and h., *b.* at Marylebone, 1779; ed. at Eton; matric. at Oxford (Ch. Ch.), 22 Jan. 1796, aged 17; *suc. to the Baronetcy*, 21 July 1803. He *m.* 3 July 1806, by spec. lic.,

(a) Felix Hall went to his 1st da., who *m.* in 1744 John Williams, by whom it was rebuilt, but afterwards, in 1761, sold.

at Hyde Park Corner, Anne WELLESLEY, natural da. of Richard (WELLESLEY), MARQUESS WELLESLEY [I.], by Hyacinthe-Gabrielle ROLAND, spinster, da. of Monsieur Pierre ROLAND. She was divorced by Act of Parliament, 25 June 1816.[a] He *d.* s.p. 16 April 1868, at 20 Hill street, Berkeley square, when the *Baronetcy* became *extinct.*

COTTON:
cr. 14 July 1641;[b].
ex. 25 Jan. 1863.

I. 1641. "JOHN COTTON, of Landwade, co. Cambridge, Knt.," s. and h. of Sir John COTTON, of the same, by his 3d wife, Anne, da. of Sir Richard HOGHTON, 1st Bart. [1611], was *b.* Sep. 1615; suc. his father (when only five years old), 5 March 1620; was *Knighted* at Whitehall, 26 June and was *cr. a Baronet,* as above, 14 July 1641.[b] He was Sheriff of Cambridgeshire when the rebellion broke out, and proclaimed the Earl of Essex as a traitor in every market town in that county. He took up arms for the King, to whom, when at Oxford, he conveyed the plate sent by the University of Cambridge. During the Usurpation he was forced to reside abroad. He *m.* Jane, da. and sole h. of Edward HINDE, of Madingley Hall, co. Cambridge, by (—), da. and h. of Sir Thomas MAPLES, Bart. [so *cr.* 1627], of Stow, co. Huntingdon. She brought the Madingley estate to the Cotton family. He *d.* in 1689,[c] aged about 74. Will pr. June 1689.

II. 1689. SIR JOHN COTTON, Bart. [1641], of Madingley Hall aforesaid, s. and h.; *suc. to the Baronetcy* in 1689; Recorder of Cambridge and M.P. for that town (seven Parls.), 1689-90, 1690-95, and Nov. 1696 to 1708. He *m.* 14 Jan. 1678/9, at Westm. Abbey, Elizabeth, da. and coheir of Sir Joseph SHELDON, sometime, 1675-76, Lord Mayor of London, by his 1st wife, Elizabeth, daughter of William CLIFTON, of St. Paul's, Covent Garden. He *d.* 20 and was *bur.* 23 Jan. 1712/3, at Landwade. Admon. 24 April 1716. His widow surv. him, but *d.* before 1716.

III. 1713. SIR JOHN HINDE COTTON, Bart. [1641], of Madingley Hall aforesaid, s. and h.; was *cr.* M.A. of Cambridge Univ. [*comitiis regiis*], 1705; *suc. to the Baronetcy,* 20 Jan. 1712/3; was M.P. for the town of Cambridge (four Parls.), 1708-22; for Cambridgeshire, 1722-27; for Cambridge, again (two Parls.), 1727-41, and for Marlborough (two Parls.), 1741 till decease. One of the Lords Commissioners of trade and plantations, 1712; Treasurer of the Chamber, 1744. He *m.* firstly, Lettice (portion £10,000), 2d da. of Sir Ambrose CROWLEY, of Greenwich, Kent, sometime, 1706-07, Sheriff of London, by Mary, da. of Charles OWEN, of Condover, Salop. She *d.* Aug. 1718. He *m.* secondly, Margaret, widow of Samuel TREFUSIS, 3d da. of James CRAGGS, Joint Postmaster General, by (—), da. of "Brigadier" RICHARDS, of Westminster. She *d.* s.p. 23 Aug. 1734. Will pr. 1737. He *d.* 4 Feb. 1752, in his 64th year, and was *bur.* at Landwade, with his two wives. Will pr. 1752.

IV. 1752. SIR JOHN HINDE COTTON, Bart. [1641], of Madingley Hall aforesaid, only surv. s. and h. by 1st wife; M.P. for St. Germains, 1741-47; for Marlborough (two Parls.), 1752-61; and for Cambridgeshire (three Parls.), 1764-80; *suc. to the Baronetcy,* 4 Feb. 1752; *cr.* D.C.L. of Oxford, 7 July 1763. He *m.* Aug. 1754, his cousin Anne, 2d da. of Humphrey PARSONS, of Reigate, Surrey, twice (1730-31 and 1740-41), Lord Mayor of London, by Sarah, 3d da. of Sir Ambrose CROWLEY, abovenamed. She *d.* in or before 1769. Admon. 26 June 1769, under £1,000. He *d.* 23 Jan. 1795.

[a] She *m.* 16 July following, Lieut. Col. Lord William-Charles-Augustus CAVENDISH-BENTINCK, being his 2d wife. He *d.* 28 April 1826, aged 46, and she *d.* 19 March 1875.

[b] The patent is not enrolled. The date here given is that in Dugdale's *Catalogue.* See *Memorandum* on p. 84. The date of the signet bill is 10 July 1641.

[c] His son John, was returned as "Esq." to the Convention of 1689, but as "Baronet" to the Parl. of 1690.

V. 1795. SIR CHARLES COTTON, Bart. [1641], of Madingley Hall aforesaid, s. and h., *b.* about 1758; was Post Capt. in the Royal Navy, 1779; was in command of the "Majestic" in the battle of 1 June 1794; *suc. to the Baronetcy,* 23 Jan. 1795; obtained a flag in 1797, serving in the Channel Fleet under Lord St. Vincent, and, in 1807, in the expedition against Portugal; became Admiral in 1808 and Commander in Chief of the Channel Fleet. He *m.* 27 Feb. 1798, Philadelphia, 1st da. of Admiral Sir Joshua ROWLEY, 1st Bart. [1786], by Sarah, da. and h. of Bartholomew BURTON. He *d.* 24 Feb. 1812, at Stoke, near Plymouth. Will pr. 1812. His widow *d.* 5 April 1855, aged 92, at Madingley Hall aforesaid. Will pr. July 1855.

VI. 1812, to 1863. SIR ST. VINCENT COTTON, Bart. [1641], of Madingley Hall aforesaid, s. and h., born there 6 Oct. 1801; *suc. to the Baronetcy,* 24 Feb. 1812; ed. at Westm. and at Ch. Ch., Oxford; sometime an officer in the 10th Hussars, 1827 to 1830, when he retired on half pay; well-known in the hunting, racing, shooting, cricket and pugilistic world, and also as a celebrated "whip," driving, in 1836 and many years subsequently, the "Age" coach from Brighton to London; was also a great gambler and dissipated all his property. He *m.* (by spec. lic.) in his own dwelling house, a few days before his death, Hephzibah, da. of (—) DIMMICK. He *d.* s.p. 25 Jan. 1863, at 5, Hyde Park terrace, Kensington Road, aged 61, when the *Baronetcy* became *extinct.* His widow *d.* 12 May 1873, at Finborough Road, West Brompton.

BAMFYLDE, BAMFEILD, *or* BAMPFIELD:
cr. 14 July 1641;[a]
afterwards, since 1831, BARONS POLTIMORE.

I. 1641. "JOHN BAMFEILD, Junior, of Poltimore, co. Devon, Esq.," s. and h. ap. of John BAMPFIELD of the same (s. and h. of Sir Amyas Bamfield, who *d.* 9 Feb. 1625/6, aged 67), by Elizabeth, da. of Thomas DRAKE, of Buckland, Devon, was *b.* about 1610; matric. at Oxford (Wadham Coll.), 30 Oct. 1629, aged 19; admitted to Middle Temple, 1630; was M.P. for Penrhyn, 1640 till decease, and was *cr. a Baronet,* as above, 14 July 1641.[a] He, who was one of the "Extremists" or "Independents," suc. his father after Aug. 1644. He *m.* 3 May 1637, Gertrude, sister and coheir of John COPLESTONE, of Coplestone and Warleigh in Tamerton Foliot, Devon, 4th da. of Amyas COPLESTONE, of the same, by Gertrude, da. of Sir John CHICHESTER. He *d.* April 1650, and was *bur.* at Poltimore. M.I. His widow *d.* 1658. Her will dat. 8 Nov. 1657, pr. 29 Nov. 1658.

II. 1650. SIR COPLESTONE BAMFYLDE, Bart. [1641], of Poltimore aforesaid, s. and h., was *b.* 1638; *suc. to the Baronetcy* in April 1650, in his minority; matric. at Oxford (Corpus Coll.), 20 March 1650/1, as a Gent. Commoner; was an active Royalist, joining in a remonstrance to the "Rump" Parl.; presented to Gen. Monk a "petition of right" from the co. of Devon, for which he was imprisoned; was M.P. for Tiverton, 1659; Sheriff of Devon, 1660-61, and subsequently M.P., 1671-79 and 1685-87, for that county; Col. of the Devon Militia. He *m.* firstly, Margaret, da. of Francis BULKELEY, of Burgate, in Fordingbridge, Hants. She was living Nov. 1657. He *m.* secondly (Lic. Vic. Gen. 21 Oct. 1674, he about 30 and she about 20), Jane, da. of Sir Courtenay POLE, 2d Bart. [1628], of Shute, by Urith, da. of Thomas SHAPCOTE. He *d.* at Warleigh aforesaid, 9 Feb. 1691/2, aged 54, and was *bur.* at Poltimore. Will, dat. 24 Aug. 1691, pr. 2 May 1692. His widow, by whom he had no issue, *m.* Edward GIBBONS, of Whitechapel, Devon. Her will, dat. 2 Sep., pr. 5 Oct. 1710 in the Cons. Court of Exeter.

[a] The patent is not enrolled. The date here given is that in Dugdale's *Catalogue.* See *Memorandum,* on p. 84. The date of the signet bill is 12 July 1641.

III. 1692. SIR COPLESTONE WARWICK BAMFYLDE, Bart. [1641], of Poltimore aforesaid, grandson and h., being s. and h. of Col. Hugh Bamfylde, of Wareley, Devon, by Mary, da. of James CLIFFORD, of Kingsteignton in that county, which Hugh, who was s. and h. ap. of the last Bart. by his 1st wife, *d.* v.p. 16 June 1691, aged 28. He was *b.* about 1690; *suc. to the Baronetcy,* 9 Feb. 1691/2, in his infancy; matric. at Oxford (Ch. Ch.), 26 Jan. 1707/8, aged 18; was M.P. for Exeter, 1710-13, and subsequently, 1713 till his death, for Devon. He *m.*, in or before 1718, Gertrude, widow of Godfrey COPLEY, 2d Bart. [1661], da. of Sir John CAREW, 2d Bart. [1641], of Antony, by his 3d wife Mary, da. of Sir William MORICE, 1st Bart. [1661]. He *d.* 7 and was *bur.* 14 Oct. 1727, at Poltimore. His widow *d.* 14 and was *bur.* 23 April 1736 with him. Will pr. 1736.

IV. 1727. SIR RICHARD WARWICK BAMFYLDE, Bart. [1641], of Poltimore aforesaid, only s. and h.; *bap.* 21 Nov. 1722, at Poltimore; *suc. to the Baronetcy,* 7 Oct. 1727, in his infancy; matric. at Oxford (New Coll.), 16 May 1739, aged 17; *cr.* M.A., 4 July 1741; M.P. for Exeter, 1743-47, and for Devon (six Parls.), 1747 till his death. He *m.* 8 Aug. 1742, at Somerset House chapel, Midx., Jane, da. and h. of Col. John CODRINGTON, of Charlton House in Wraxall, Somerset, by Elizabeth, only da. and h. of Samuel GORGES, of Wraxall aforesaid. He *d.* 15 and was *bur.* 25 July 1776, at Poltimore. Will pr. Aug. 1776, and at Dublin in 1807. His widow, who was *b.* 14 Oct. and *bap.* 15 Nov. 1720, at Wraxall, *d.* 15 and was *bur.* there 24 Feb. 1789. Admon. March 1789.

V. 1776. SIR CHARLES WARWICK BAMFYLDE, Bart. [1641], of Poltimore aforesaid and of Hardington Park, Somerset, s. and h., *b.* and *bap.* 23 Jan. 1753, at St. Augustine's, Bristol; matric. at Oxford (New Coll.), 6 Jan. 1770, aged 16; M.P. for Exeter in seven Parls., 1774-90 and 1796-1807; *suc. to the Baronetcy,* 15 Aug. 1776. He *m.* 9 Feb. 1776, at St. James', Westm., Catharine, 1st da. and coheir of Admiral Sir John MOORE, Bart. [*cr.* 1766] and K.B., by Penelope, da. of Gen. William MATHEW. He *d.* in Montagu square, Midx., 19 April 1823, from a pistol shot received from one Morland (formerly his servant), on the 7th and was *bur.* the 25th, at Hardington. Will pr. 1823. His widow (from whom he had been separated for many years) *d.* 20 March 1832, aged 78, at Egham, Surrey. Will pr. April 1832.

VI. 1823. SIR GEORGE WARWICK BAMFYLDE, Bart. [1641], of Poltimore, etc., aforesaid, only s. and h., *b.* 23 March and *bap.* 20 April 1786, at St. James', Westm.; matric. at Oxford (Bras. Coll.), 10 Oct. 1804, aged 18; *suc. to the Baronetcy,* 19 April 1823. He *m.* firstly, 2 May 1809, at St. Geo., Han. sq., his cousin, Penelope, 3d da. of the Rev. Ralph SNEYD, Chaplain to Geo. IV, by Penelope, 2d da. and coheir of Admiral Sir John Moore, Bart., and K.B. abovenamed. She, who *d.* s.p.m., was living when he was *cr.*, 10 Sep. 1831,[a] BARON POLTIMORE of Poltimore, co. Devon. In that peerage this *Baronetcy* then became *merged,* and still so continues. See *Peerage.*

THYNNE:
cr. 15 July 1641[b];
afterwards, since 1682, VISCOUNTS WEYMOUTH;
and *subsequently,* since 1789, MARQUESSES OF BATH.

I. 1641. "HENRY-FREDERICK THYNNE, of Course [*i.e.*, Caus] Castle, co. Salop, Esq.," being also of Kempsford, co. Gloucester, 4th s. of Sir Thomas THYNNE, of Longleate, Wilts, being his 1st s., by Catharine his 2d

[a] This was a coronation peerage. The Annual Register of 1858 (in his obituary) speaks of it as given "for zealous services rendered in the cause of Reform"—but though the zeal might have been great, the actual service of a man who was never in Parliament and never held any public office must have been somewhat small.

[b] The patent is not enrolled. The date here given is that in Dugdale's *Catalogue.* See *Memorandum* on p. 84. The date of "warrant for granting receipt for £1,095 to Henry Frederick Thynne of Course Castle, co. Salop, Esq., on his creation as Baronet" is 13 July 1641.

wife, da. and coheir of Hon. Charles LYTE-HOWARD, (yr. s. of Thomas, 1st VISCOUNT HOWARD OF BINDON,) was *b.* 1 March 1615 (the Queen-Consort being his godmother, who gave him the additional name of "Frederick," being that of her father, the King of Denmark); matric. at Oxford (Ex. Coll.), 13 Nov. 1632, aged 17; admitted to Lincoln's Inn, 1634, and was *cr. a Baronet,* as above, 15 July 1641.[a] He *m.* Mary, da. of Thomas (COVENTRY), 1st BARON COVENTRY OF AYLESBOROUGH, sometime Lord Keeper of the Great Seal, by Elizabeth, his 2d wife, da. of John ALDERSEY. He *d.* at Oxford 6 March 1680, aged 66 years and 5 days, and was *bur.* at Kemsford. M.I. Will pr. 1680.

II. 1680. SIR THOMAS THYNNE, Bart. [1641], of Drayton, Salop, and afterwards, 1682, of Longleate, Wilts, s. and h., *b.* about 1640; matric. at Oxford (Ch. Ch.), 21 April 1657, having the famous Dr. John Fell for his tutor; F.R.S. 23 Nov. 1664; M.P. for Oxford University, 1674-79, and for Tamworth (three Parls.), 1679-81; *suc. to the Baronetcy,* 6 March 1680; was High Steward of Tamworth, 1681. By the death of his 1st cousin, Thomas THYNNE, of Longleate, who was murdered in his coach in Pall Mall, 12 Feb. 1681/2, and the consequent extinction of all elder issue male of his grandfather, he *suc.* to that estate and became the representative of his family. He *m.* in or before 1675, Frances, 1st da. of Heneage (FINCH), 2d EARL OF WINCHILSEA, by his 2d wife, Mary, da. of William (SEYMOUR), 2d DUKE OF SOMERSET. She was living when he was *cr.* 11 Dec. 1682, VISCOUNT WEYMOUTH, co. Dorset, etc., with a *spec. rem.*, failing his issue male, to his two yr. brothers and the heirs male of their bodies respectively. In that peerage this Baronetcy then merged and so continues, the 3d Viscount Weymouth being *cr.* 18 Aug. 1789, MARQUESS OF BATH. See *Peerage* under those titles.

D'EWES:
cr. 15 July 1641;[b]
ex. 21 April 1731.

I. 1641. "SIMON [*i.e.*, SIMONDS] D'EWES, of Stow Hall [in Stowlangtoft], co. Suffolk, Knt.," s. & h. of Paul D'Ewes, of the same, by Cecilia, only da. and h. of Richard SIMONDS, or SYMONDS, of Coxden, co. Dorset; was *b.* 18 Dec. 1602, at Coxden; was a student of St. John's Coll., Cambridge; Barrister (Middle Temple), 27 June 1623; was *Knighted* at Whitehall, 6 Dec. 1626, suc. his father, 14 March 1630/31; was Sheriff of Suffolk, 1639-40; M.P. for Sudbury, 1640, till secluded Dec. 1648; and was *cr. a Baronet,* as above, 15 July 1641.[b] He gave £100 to aid the Earl of Essex, 11 Oct. 1642, and served in the "New Model" Feb. 1645. His knowledge of history and antiquity was very great. He was the author of "*The Journals of all the Parliaments, temp. Eliz.,*" and other valuable works.[c] He *m.* firstly, 24 Oct. 1626, at St. Anne's, Blackfriars, London, Anne, da. and eventually h. of Sir William CLOPTON, of Kentwell, Suffolk, by his 1st wife, Anne, da. of Sir Thomas BARNADISTON, of Clare, Suffolk. She, who was *bap.* at Clare, 2 March 1612, *d.* s.p.m. in 1641. He *m.* secondly, Elizabeth, 5th and yst. da. and coh. of Sir Henry WILLOUGHBY, Bart. (so *cr.* 1611), of Risley, by his 2d wife, Lettice, da. and coheir of Sir Francis DARCY. He *d.* 18 April and was *bur.* 7 June 1650, at Stowlangtoft, aged 48. Will pr. 1650 and 1652. His widow *m.* about 1654, as his 1st wife, John WRAY, of Glentworth, co. Lincoln (who shortly after her death became 3d Bart. [1611]), and was *bur.* 3 Nov. 1655, at Glentworth aforesaid. Her admon. 7 Feb. 1655/6 to her said husband.

[a] *Vide* note "b," p. 102.

[b] The patent is not enrolled. The date here given is that in Dugdale's *Catalogue.* See *Memorandum,* on p. 84. The date of the signet bill is 13 July 1641.

[c] The "*Autobiography of Sir Simonds D'Ewes*" was edited by J. O. Halliwell, 2 vols., 1845. Extracts from the registers of Stowlangtoft, relating to the family of D'Ewes, are in *N. and Q.*, 3d series. ix, 294 and x, 33.

II. 1650. SIR WILLOUGHBY D'EWES, Bart. [1641], of Stowlangtoft Hall aforesaid, only s. and h., by 2d wife; *b.* about 1650; *suc. to the Baronetcy*, 18 April 1650, when an infant; matric. at Oxford (Ch. Ch.), 23 April 1664, aged 14; Sheriff of Suffolk, 1677-78. He *m.* Priscilla, da. of Francis CLINTON, *otherwise* FIENNES, of Stourton Parva, co. Lincoln, by Priscilla, da. of John HILL. He *d.* at Stow Hall, 13 and was *bur.* 16 June 1685, at Stowlangtoft. Admon. 14 July 1685, to the widow. She *d.* 1719. Her will, dat. 6 Feb. 1718/9, pr. 31 Aug. 1719.

III. 1685. SIR SIMONDS D'EWES, Bart. [1641], of Stowlangtoft Hall aforesaid, s. and h., *b.* about 1670; *suc. to the Baronetcy*, 13 June 1685. He *m.* firstly, in or before 1687, Delariviere, 5th da. and coheir of Thomas (JERMYN), 2d BARON JERMYN OF ST. EDMUNDSBURY, by Mary, da. of Henry MERRY. She *d.* at St. Anne's, Westm., and was *bur.* 12 Feb. 1708/9, at Stowlangtoft. Admon. 19 Dec. 1709 to her husband. He *m.* secondly, 21 March 1709/10, at St. Bride's, London (Lic. Vic. Gen., he about 41 and she about 24), Elizabeth KIEFE, of St. Margaret's, Westm., spinster. He *d.* in May 1722. Will pr. 1722.

IV. 1722, to 1731. SIR JERMYN D'EWES, Bart. [1641], of Stowlangtoft Hall aforesaid, 1st s. and h., by 1st wife; *bap.* 2 April 1688, at Stowlangtoft; *suc. to the Baronetcy* in May 1722. He *d.* unm. 21 April 1731, when the *Baronetcy* became *extinct*.(a) Will pr. 1732.

BURGOYNE:

cr. 15 July 1641.(b)

I. 1641. "JOHN BURGOYNE, of Sutton, co. Bedford, Esq.," as also of Wroxhall and Honiley, co. Warwick, s. and h. of Roger BURGOYNE, of the same, by his 1st wife, Margaret, da. of Thomas WENDY, of Haslingfield, co. Cambridge, was *bap.* at Haslingfield, 29 Jan. 1591; *suc.* his father, 28 June 1636; was Sheriff of Beds, 1640-41; M.P. for Warwickshire, Oct. 1645, till secluded Dec. 1648, and was *cr. a Baronet*, as above, 15 July 1641.(b) He served on several important Committees, on the side of the Parl., 1643-47. He *m.* about 1617, Jane, da. and h. of William KEMPE, of Spain's Hall in Finchinfield, co. Essex, by Philippa, da. and coheir of Francis GUNTER, of Aldbury, Herts. He was *bur.* at Sutton 9 Oct. 1657. Admon. 25 May 1663 to his son.

II. 1657. SIR ROGER BURGOYNE, Bart. [1641], of Sutton and Wroxhall aforesaid, s. and h., *bap.* 10 March 1618 at Wroxall; admitted to Lincoln's Inn, 11 Nov. 1637; *Knighted*, v.p. 14 July 1641, at Whitehall; M.P. for Bedfordshire, April to May 1640, and Jan. 1641, till secluded in Dec. 1648; for Warwickshire, 1656-58. He (like his father) served on several important Committees on the side of the Parl., 1643-45; *suc. to the Baronetcy* in Oct. 1657; was Sheriff of Beds, 1661-62. He *m.* firstly, about 1650, Anne, da. and h. of Charles SNELLING, of London. She was *bur.* at Sutton 1658. He *m.* secondly, Anne, da. of John ROBINSON, of Dighton, co. York, by Elizabeth, da. of Sir Thomas HUTTON, of Poppleton. He *d.* 16 and was *bur.* 21 Sep. 1677 at Sutton aforesaid, aged 59. M.I. Will dat. 13 Sep. and pr. 26 Nov. 1677. His widow *d.* s.p.m.s., 5 Feb. 1693/4, aged 51, and was *bur.* at Wroxall. M.I. Will pr. 1694.

III. 1677. SIR JOHN BURGOYNE, Bart. [1641], of Sutton Park and Wroxhall aforesaid, only s. and h., by 1st wife, *suc. to the Baronetcy*, 16 Sep. 1677. He *m.* (Lic. Fac., 18 July, and Lic. Vic. Gen., 4 Nov. 1677, he about 25 and she about 19) Constance, da. of Richard LUCY, of Charlecote, co. Warwick, by Elizabeth, da. and h. of John URRY, of Thorley, in the Isle of Wight. He *d.* 9 and was *bur.* 16 April 1709 in his 58th year at Sutton. Will dat. 29 Jan. 1705, pr. 4 July 1709. His widow *d.* 22 and was *bur.* 30 April 1711, aged 52, also at Sutton. M.I.

(a) See the names and alliances of his four sisters and coheirs in Burke's "*Extinct Baronetage*."

(b) The patent is not enrolled. The date here given is that in Dugdale's *Catalogue*. See *Memorandum* on p. 84. The date of the signet bill is 13 July 1641.

IV. 1709. SIR ROGER BURGOYNE, Bart. [1641], of Sutton Park and Wroxhall aforesaid, s. and h., ed. at Rugby 1695, *suc. to the Baronetcy*, 9 April 1709. He *m.* 22 June 1703, at St Andrew's, Holborn (Lic. Lon., 21 and settl. 10 June 1703) Constance, da. of Sir Thomas MIDDLETON, of Stansted Mountfichet, co. Essex, by Mary, da. and h. of Sir Stephen LANGHAM, of Quentin, co. Northampton. He *d.* 1716. His will dat. 2 Nov. 1710, pr. 29 March 1716. His widow *m.* 8 March 1715, at Cople, Beds, Christopher WREN, afterwards of Wroxhall aforesaid (s. of the celebrated Sir Christopher Wren), and *d.* 23 May 1734.

V. 1716. SIR JOHN BURGOYNE, Bart. [1641], of Sutton Park aforesaid, 1st s. and h., *b.* about 1705; *suc. to the Baronetcy* in 1716. He *d.* young and unm. only six months after his father.

VI. 1716. SIR ROGER BURGOYNE, Bart. [1641], of Sutton Park aforesaid br. and h., *b.* about 1710, *suc. to the Baronetcy* in 1716; M.P. for Beds, 1734-41 and 1741-47. He *m.* Jan. 1738/9, Frances, 1st da. of George (MONTAGU), 1st EARL OF HALIFAX, by his 2d wife, Mary, da. of Richard (LUMLEY), EARL OF SCARBROUGH. He *d.* 31 Dec. 1780 aged 70. Will dat. 19 Feb. 1755, pr. (with five codicils) 22 Jan. 1781. His widow *d.* in Harley street, Marylebone, 24 July 1788. Will dat. 31 Jan. 1784, pr. 5 Aug. 1788.

VII. 1780. SIR JOHN BURGOYNE, Bart. [1641], of Sutton Park aforesaid, s. and h., *b.* 21 Sep. 1739; entered the army, becoming finally Lieut.-Gen.; was Col. of the 58th Foot and of the 19th Light Dragoons, having *suc. to the Baronetcy*, 31 Dec. 1780. He *m.* 13 July 1772, Charlotte Frances, 1st da. of (—) JOHNSTONE, of Overstone, co. Northampton, General in the Army. He *d.* 23 Sep. 1785, in the East Indies. Will pr. 1787. His widow *m.* Lieut.-Gen. Eyre Power FRENCH, and *d.* 14 April 1820. Her admon. dat. 26 May 1820.

VIII. 1785. SIR MONTAGU ROGER BURGOYNE, Bart. [1641], of Sutton Park aforesaid, s. and h., *b.* 2 May 1773; *suc. to the Baronetcy*, 23 Sep. 1785. He entered the army, becoming finally Major-Gen. He *m.* 1 Nov. 1794 (by spec. lic.), at Bramshill, Catherine, da. of John BURTON, of High House in Sheffield, and of Bramley Hall, in Harasworth, co. York. He *d.* 11 Nov. 1817, at his mother's residence in Oxford. Will, dat. 13 Oct. 1810, pr. 6 Nov. 1817. His widow, who was *b.* 25 Feb. 1773, at Bramley Hall aforesaid, *d.* in Eaton square 1 May 1855, aged 82. Will pr. June 1855.

IX. 1817. SIR JOHN MONTAGU BURGOYNE, Bart. [1641], of Sutton Park aforesaid, s. and h., *b.* there 17 Oct. 1796; *suc. to the Baronetcy*, 11 Nov. 1817; entered the army, becoming, finally, Col. in the Grenadier Guards, 1846, but retired 1848; Sheriff of Bedfordshire, 1820, but did not act, and again 1852. He *m.*, 20 Dec. 1831, Mary Harriet, 1st da. of William GORE-LANGTON, *formerly* GORE, of Newton Park, co. Somerset, by Bridget, da. and h. of Joseph LANGTON, of Newton Park aforesaid. He *d.* 17 March 1858, aged 61. His widow *d.* 1 April 180, aged 84, at 9 Eaton place.

X. 1858. SIR JOHN MONTAGU BURGOYNE, Bart. [1641], of Sutton Park aforesaid, only s. and h., *b.* 23 Oct. 1832, in London; ed. at Eton; entered the army 1850, being severely wounded at the Alma in the Crimean War; Lieut.-Col. Grenadier Guards, 1860, but retired in 1861, having *suc. to the Baronetcy*, 17 March 1858; Sheriff of Beds, 1868. He *m.* 10 Nov. 1858, Amy, only da. of Henry Nealson SMITH, Capt. Royal Engineers. She *d.* 12 Oct. 1895, at Cowes, Isle of Wight.

Family Estates.—These, in 1883, consisted of 2,375 acres in Bedfordshire, worth £3,547 a year. *Residence*—Sutton Park, near Biggleswade, Beds.

NORTHCOTE:

cr. 16 July 1641;(a)

afterwards, since 1885, EARLS OF IDDESLEIGH.

I. 1641. "JOHN NORTHCOTE, of Haine [*i.e.*, Hayne, in Newton St. Cyres], co. Devon, Esq.," 1st surv. s. and h. of John Northcote, of Upton, in that county, by his 2d wife, Susanna, da. of Sir Hugh POLLARD, of Kingsnympton, Devon, was *b.* about 1600; matric. at Oxford (Exeter Coll.), 9 May 1617, aged 16; admitted to Middle Temple 1618; is stated to have been 21 in 1620 (Visit. of Devon); was Sheriff of Devon, 1626-27; suc. his father in Dec. 1632; was M.P. for Ashburton, 1640, till secluded in Dec. 1648; for Devon, 1654-55, 1656-58, 1659 and 1660; and for Barnstaple, 1667 till his death, having been *cr. a Baronet*, as above, 16 July 1641.(a) He was an active Parliamentarian, was Col. of a Reg. of 1,200 men in Sep. 1643, was excepted from pardon by the King but joined in the Restoration(b). He *m.*, in or before 1627, Grace,(c) da. and coheir of Hugh HALSEWELL, of Halsewell, co. Somerset, by Elizabeth, da. of Sir William BROUNKARD. She, who was aged 14 in 1623 (Visit. of Somerset), was *bur.* 19 July 1675, at Newton St. Cyres. He was *bur.* there 24 June 1676, aged 77. Will pr. 2 Dec. 1676.

II. 1676. SIR ARTHUR NORTHCOTE, Bart. [1641], of Kingsnympton aforesaid, s. and h., *bap.* 25 March 1628, at Newton St. Cyres; *suc. to the Baronetcy* in June 1676. He *m.* firstly, Elizabeth, da. and h. of James WELSH, of Alverdiscott. She *d.* s.p. He *m.* secondly, probably in or before 1650, Elizabeth, 1st da. of Sir Francis GODOLPHIN, K.B., of Godolphin, co. Cornwall, by Dorothy, da. of Sir Henry BERKELEY, of Yarlington, co. Somerset. He *d.* in or before July 1688. Will pr. July 1689. His widow, who was *bap.* 8 Feb. 1635 at Breage, *d.* in or before 1707. Admon. 30 Oct. 1707.

III. 1688. SIR FRANCIS NORTHCOTE, Bart. [1641], of Kingsnympton aforesaid, 1st surv. s. and h., by 2d wife, *b.* about 1659, *suc. to the Baronetcy* in or before July 1688. He *m.* 26 July 1688, at St. Bennet Fink, London (Lic. Vic. Gen., he about 29, and she 22), Anne, da. of Sir Christopher WREY, 3d Bart. [1628], of Trebitch, by Anne, COUNTESS DOWAGER OF MIDDLESEX, 3d da. and coheir of Edward (BOURCHIER), EARL OF BATH. He *d.* s.p. 1709. Admon. 25 May 1711 to a creditor, his widow, Anne, renouncing. Her will pr. 1730.

IV. 1709. SIR HENRY NORTHCOTE, Bart. [1641], of Corfe, near Barnstaple, Devon, br. and h., *b.* about 1667; matric. at Oxford (Exeter Coll.), 7 March 1686/7, aged 19; Fellow, 1689-1704; B.A. 1693; M.A. 1695; B. Med. 1697; D. Med. 1701; *suc. to the Baronetcy* in 1709. He *m.* in or before 1711, Penelope, da. and coheir of Robert LOVETT, of Liscombe, Bucks, and of Corfe aforesaid, by his 2d wife, Joan, da. and h. of James HEARLE, of Tawstock, Devon. He *d.* at Corfe aforesaid, Feb. 1729-30. Will pr. 1730. That of his widow pr. 1732.

V. 1730. SIR HENRY NORTHCOTE, Bart. [1641], of Pynes, in Upton Pyne, near Exeter, Devon, only s. and h., *bap.* at Tawstock, 1710; matric. at Oxford 23 April 1729, aged 18; *suc. to the Baronetcy*, Feb. 1729/30; M.P. for Exeter, 1735, till his death. He *m.* 16 Aug. 1732 at Uffculme, Bridget Maria, only surv. da. and h. of Hugh STAFFORD, of Pynes aforesaid, by Bridget, da. of John KELLAND, of Painsford. He was *bur.* 28 May 1743 at Newton St. Cyres. His widow, who was *b.* 21 Jan. and *bap.* 5 Feb. 1711/12 at Upton Pyne, *m.* there 11 Sep. 1754, Richard MADDON, of Exeter, and *d.* 15 being *bur.* 19 Aug. 1773, at Newton St. Cyres. Her will pr. Aug. 1773.

(a) The patent is not enrolled. The date here given is that in Dugdale's *Catalogue*. See *Memorandum* on p. 84. The date of the signet bill is 24 [*sic*] July 1641, which possibly is a mistake, but more probably the error is in the date of the patent. That date, however, is also assigned to it in Wotton's *Baronetage*, where it is placed between Burgoyne, 15 July, and Hare, 23 July 1641.

(b) The proof of his authorship of the well known "Note Book," attributed to him is doubtful. See a note of W. D. Pink, in *N. and Q.*

(c) Her sister Jane *m.* John TYNTE, of Chelvey, Somerset, and had a son and h., Halsewell TYNTE, who suc. to the estate of Halsewell and was *cr. a Bart.* 1674.

VI. 1743. SIR STAFFORD NORTHCOTE, Bart. [1641], of Pynes aforesaid, s. and h., *bap.* 6 May 1736, at Upton Pyne, *suc. to the Baronetcy* in May 1743. He *m.* 17 Oct. 1761, Catharine, da. of Rev. George BRADFORD, M.A., Rector of Talaton, Devon. He *d.* 11 and was *bur.* 12 March 1770, at Newton St. Cyres. His widow *d.* Jan. 1802. Will pr. 1802.

VII. 1770. SIR STAFFORD HENRY NORTHCOTE, Bart. [1641], of Pynes aforesaid, s. and h., *b.* 6 Oct. 1762, *suc. to the Baronetcy*, 11 March 1770; Sheriff of Devon, 1803-04. He *m.* 6 May 1791, Jacquetta, da. of Charles BARING, of Larkbeer, Devon, by Margaret, da. and h. of William Drake GOULD, of Lew Trenchard in that county, which Charles was br. to Francis BARING, *cr. a Bart.* in 1793. She, who was *b.* 3 June 1768, *d.* 22 Jan. 1841 at Newton St. Cyres. He *d.* 17 March 1851, aged 89. Will pr. May 1851.

VIII. 1851. SIR STAFFORD HENRY NORTHCOTE, Bart. [1641], of Pynes aforesaid, grandson and h., being s. and h. of Henry Stafford NORTHCOTE, by his 1st wife, Agnes Mary, only da. of Thomas COCKBURN (East India Company's service), of Portland place, Marylebone, which Henry was s. and h. ap. of the 7th Bart, but *d.* v.p., 22 Feb. 1850, aged 57. He was *b.* in Portland place aforesaid, 27 Oct. 1818, and *bap.* at Upton Pyne the year following; ed. at Eton and at Balliol Coll. Oxford; matric. 3 March 1836, aged 17; Scholar, 1836-42; B.A. (1st Class classics and 3d mathematics), 1839; M.A. 1842; Private Sec. to Pres. of the Board of Trade (W. E. Gladstone), 1843-45; Barrister (Inner Temple), 1847; *suc. to the Baronetcy*, 17 March 1851; C.B., 1851. M.P. for Dudley, 1855-1857; for Stamford, 1858-1866; and for North Devon, 1866, till created a Peer. He was Financial Sec. to the Treasury, Jan. to June 1859; *cr.* D.C.L. of Oxford, 27 June 1863; P.C. 1866; President of the Board of Trade, 1866-67; Sec. of State for India and President of the Council for India, 1867-68; a member of the High Joint Commission at Washington, Feb. 1871; Chancellor of the Exchequer and *Leader of the House of Commons*, 1874-1880; G.C.B., 20 April 1880; FIRST LORD OF THE TREASURY, June 1885 to Feb. 1886, during which period he was created a Peer, as stated below. He *m.* 5 Aug. 1853, at Trinity Church, Marylebone, Cecilia Frances, sister of Thomas, 1st BARON FARRER OF ABINGER, da. of Thomas FARRER, of Lincoln's Inn Fields, solicitor, by Cecilia, da. of Richard WILLIS, of Halsnead, co. Lancaster. She was living when he was raised to the peerage, being *cr.*, 3 July 1885, EARL OF IDDESLEIGH, etc. In that peerage this *Baronetcy* then *merged*, and so continues. See "*Peerage*."

DRAKE:

cr. 17 July 1641;(a)

ex. 28 Aug. 1669.

I. 1641, to 1669. "WILLIAM DRAKE, of Sherdelowes, co. Bucks, Knt.," s. and h. of Francis Drake, of Esher, co. Surrey, one of the Gentlemen of the Privy Chamber, by Joan, 1st da. and coheir of William TOTHILL, of Shardeloes aforesaid, was *bap.* 28 Sep. 1606; suc. his father, 17 March 1633; was Chirograbper to the Court of Common Pleas; was *Knighted* at Whitehall, 14 and was *cr. a Baronet*, as above, 17 July 1641.(a) He was M.P. for

(a) The patent is not enrolled. The date here given is that in Dugdale's *Chronicle*. See *Memorandum* on p. 84. The date of the signet bill is 14 July 1641.

Amersham, April to May 1640, 1640 till secluded Dec. 1648, and 1661 till his death; was *cr.* M.A. of Oxford, 15 July 1669. He *d.* unm. 28 Aug. and was *bur.* 29 Sep. 1669, at Amersham, aged 63, when the *Baronetcy* became *extinct.*(a) Will pr. 8 Sep. 1669.

ROUS, *or* ROUSE:
cr. 23 July 1641;(b)
ex. 29 Dec. 1721.

I. 1641. "THOMAS ROUS, of Rouslench, co. Worcester, Esq.," s. and h. ap. of Sir John ROUS, of the same, by Esther, da. of Sir Thomas TEMPLE, of co. Warwick, was *b.* 1608; matric. at Oxford (Bras. Coll.), 20 Oct. 1626, aged 18; B.A. (Corpus Coll.), 31 Jan. 1627/8; admitted to Middle Temple, 1628; was *cr. a Baronet*, as above, 23 July 1641,(b) but was, notwithstanding, a great opponent of the Royal cause. He suc. his father, 1645; was Sheriff of Worcestershire, 1647-48; M.P. thereof 1654-55, 1656-58; and for Evesham, 1660; Sheriff of Warwickshire, 1667-68. He *m.* firstly, Jane, da. of Sir John FERRERS, of Tamworth Castle, by Dorothy, da. of Sir John PUCKERING, L. Keeper of the Great Seal. He *m.* secondly, Frances, da. of David MURRAY. He *m.* thirdly, Anne, da. of (—). He *d.* 27 May 1676, aged 68. Will pr. 1679.

II. 1676. SIR EDWARD ROUSE, Bart. [1641], of Rouselench aforesaid, s. and h., by 1st wife; matric. at Oxford (Trin. Coll.), 12 Dec. 1654; admitted to Inner Temple, 1656; *suc. to the Baronetcy*, 27 May 1676. He *m.* Elizabeth, da. of John LISLEY, of Moxhall, co. Warwick. He *d.* s.p. 5 Nov. 1677. Will pr. 1678. That of his widow pr. 1692.

III. 1677. SIR FRANCIS ROUSE, Bart. [1641], of Rouselench aforesaid, br. of the half-blood and h., being s. of the 1st Bart by his 2d wife, *suc. to the Baronetcy*, 5 Nov. 1677. He *m.* (Lic. Worc., 7 Aug. 1682) Frances, da. of Thomas ARCHER, of Umberslade, co. Warwick, by Anne, his wife. He *d.* s.p., 31 July 1687. His widow *m.* John CHAPLIN, of Taishwell, co. Lincoln, who *d.* before June 1715. Her will dat. 25 June 1715, pr. 2 June 1719.

IV. 1687, to 1721. SIR THOMAS ROUSE, Bart. [1641], of Rouselench aforesaid, br. of the full blood and h.; *b.* 1664; *suc. to the Baronetcy*, 31 July 1687. He *m.* Anne, da. of Charles HOOKER. He *d.* s.p.s., 29 Dec. 1721, aged 57, when the *Baronetcy* became *extinct.*(c) Will pr. 1722.

(a) The estates devolved on his nephew and h., Sir William Drake (s. and h. of Francis Drake, of Walton upon Thames, Surrey), ancestor of the family of TYRWHITT-DRAKE, of Shardeloes aforesaid.

(b) The patent is not enrolled. The date here given is that in Dugdale's *Chronicle.* See *Memorandum* on p. 84. The date of the signet bill is 16 July 1641.

(c) The estate passed to his sister Elizabeth, who *d.* unm. 1729, when Thomas Philipps succeeded to them and took the name of Rouse only, being Sheriff of Worcestershire, 1733. He was grandson of Elizabeth Phillips, by Mary, da. of Sir Thomas Rouse, 1st Bart., by his 1st wife. He *d.* unm. 30 Dec. 1768, leaving the estate to Charles William Boughton, who also took the name of Rouse, and was *cr.* a Baronet in 1791, succeeding, however, in 1794 (as 9th Baronet) to the Baronetcy *cr.* in 1641. This Charles was 2d son of Shuckburgh Boughton, by Mary (*d.* 1786, aged 72), da. of the Hon. Algernon Greville and Catharine, da. of Lord Arthur Somerset, by Mary, da. of Sir William Russell, Bart. [*cr.* 1660], and Hester, his wife, da. of Sir Thomas Rouse, 1st Bart., by his 1st wife. See "Boughton," Baronetcy, *cr.* 4 Aug. 1641.

HARE:
cr. 23 July 1641;(a)
ex. 18 March 1764.

I. 1641. "RALPH HARE, of Stow Bardolf, co. Norfolk, Esq.," s. and h. of Sir John HARE, of the same, by Margaret, da. of Thomas (COVENTRY), 1st BARON COVENTRY OF AYLESBOROUGH, sometime L. Keeper of the Great Seal, was *b.* about 1614; matric. at Oxford (Mag. Coll.), 14 Sep. 1638, aged 14; suc. his father, in or shortly before 1638, and was *cr. a Baronet*, as above, 23 July 1641.(a) He was Sheriff of Norfolk, 1650-51; M.P. thereof 1654-55, 1656-58; for King's Lynn, 1660, and for Norfolk, again, 1661 till his death. He *m.* firstly (Lic Fac, 26 Oct. 1647, he about 23 and she about 18), Mary, 1st da. and coheir of Sir Robert CRANE, Bart. [so *cr.* 1626], of Chilton, co. Suffolk, by his 2d wife, Susan, da. of Sir GILES ALINGTON. She was *b.* and *bap.* 19 March 1628, at Chilton. He *m.* secondly, 30 Aug. 1660, at St. Christ. le Stocks, London (Lic. Vic. Gen., he about 34, she about 19), Vere, sister of Horatio, 1st VISCOUNT TOWNSHEND OF RAYNHAM, da. of Sir Roger TOWNSHEND, 1st Bart. [1617], by Mary, 2d da. and coheir of Horatio (DE VERE), BARON VERE OF TILBURY. She *d.* s.p. He *m.* thirdly (Lic. Vic. Gen., 12 July 1671, he about 47, widower, she of Westm., about 31, spinster), Elizabeth, da. of (—) CHAPMAN, of Suffolk, by Mary, his wife. He *d.* Feb. 1671/2. Will pr. 1674. The will of his widow, dat. 19 Feb. 1680, was pr. 11 April 1684 by Mary Chapman, her mother.

II. 1672. SIR THOMAS HARE, Bart. [1641], of Stow Bardolph aforesaid, s. and h., by 1st wife, *b.* about 1658, *suc. to the Baronetcy* in Feb. 1671/2; was M.P. for Norfolk (soon after he came of age), 1685-87. He *m.* Elizabeth, sister of Sir Robert DASHWOOD, 1st Bart. [1684], da. of George DASHWOOD, Alderman of London, by Margaret, da. of William PERRY, of Thorpe, co. Surrey. He *d.* 1 Jan. 1693, aged 35, and was *bur.* at Stow Bardolph. M.I. His widow *d.* at Bush Common, Essex, 1750, aged 90. Will pr. 1750.

III. 1693. SIR RALPH HARE, Bart. [1641], of Stow Bardolph aforesaid, s. and h., *suc. to the Baronetcy*, 1 Jan. 1693. He *m.* Susan, da. and coheir of Walter NORBONNE, of Calne, Wilts. She was *bur.* 15 July 1730, at St. James' Westm. Admon. 21 Nov. 1730 to her husband. He *d.* s.p. 22 Sep. 1732, aged 51. Will pr. 1734.

IV. 1732. SIR THOMAS HARE, Bart. [1641], of Stow Bardolph aforesaid, br. and h., *b.* about 1688; matric. at Oxford (Oriel Coll.), 18 March 1702/3, aged 15; *suc. to the Baronetcy*, 22 Sep. 1732. He *m.* Rosamond, da. of Charles NEWBY, of Hooton, co. York. He *d.* s.p.m. 21 Feb. 1760, aged about 72.(b) Will pr. 1760. His widow *d.* 1773. Will pr. 1773.

V. 1760, to 1764. SIR GEORGE HARE, Bart. [1641], of Stow Bardolph aforesaid, br. and h., b. about 1701; a Major of Dragoons; *suc. to the Baronetcy*, 21 Feb. 1760. He *d.* unm. 18 March 1764, aged 63, when the *Baronetcy* became *extinct.* Will pr. 1764.

(a) The patent is not enrolled. The date here given is that in Dugdale's *Chronicle.* See *Memorandum*, on p. 84. The date of the signet bill is 24 [*sic*] July (*i.e.*, the day *after* the patent), so that there is, apparently, an error in the date of one of them.

(b) Of his children, two daughters were living 1741, *viz.*, Elizabeth, who is supposed to have *d.* unm., and Mary, who *m.* Sir Thomas HARRIS, sometime [1764-65], Sheriff of London, who *d.* 15 June, 1782. She, apparently, inherited Stow Bardolph in 1760, on the death of her uncle, the 5th and last Bart. She *d.* a widow at Finchley, Midx., at a great age, on 24 March 1791. On her death the estates went to Thomas LEIGH, grandson and h. of Thomas LEIGH, of London, Turkey merchant, by Mary, the only da. that left issue, of Sir Thomas HARE, 2d Bart. This Thomas Leigh took the name of *Hare* and was *cr. a Baronet*, in 1818.

NORWICH
cr. 24 July 1641(a);
ex., presumably, Jan. 1741/2.

I. 1641. "JOHN NORWICH, of Brampton, co. Northampton, Knt.," s. and h. of Sir Simon NORWICH, of the same, by his 1st wife, Ann, da. of Sir William WILLOUGHBY, of Marlow, Bucks, was *bap.* 19 Sep. 1613 at Great Marlow; ed. at Oundle School; *suc.* his father, 10 Feb. 1624; was *Knighted* 19 July 1641, at Whitehall, and was *cr. a Baronet*, as above, 24 July 1641.(a) He was a Parliamentarian and served on several Committees, 1643-45; was Sheriff of Northants, 1645-46; M.P. thereof 1654-55, and for Northampton 1660 and 1661, till void 22 May 1661. He *m.* firstly, in or before 1636, Anne, da. of Sir Roger SMITH, of Edmundthorpe, co. Leicester, by his 2d wife, Anna, da. of Thomas GOODMAN, of London. She was *bur.* 23 July 1650 at Brampton. He *m.* secondly, Mary, sister of Sir Richard ATKINS, 1st [Bart. 1660], da of Sir Henry ATKINS, of Cheshunt, Herts, by Annabella, da. of John HAWKINS, of Chiddingstone, Kent. He was *bur.* 19 Oct. 1661, at Brampton. Will pr. 1661. That of his widow pr. 1693.

II. 1661. SIR ROGER NORWICH, Bart. [1641], of Brampton aforesaid, s. and h., by 1st wife, *bap.* 29 Sep. 1636 at Brampton, *suc. to the Baronetcy* in Oct. 1661; M.P. for Northamptonshire, 1679 and 1685-87. Verdurer of the Forest of Rockingham, but resigned that post, *temp.* James II, with whose measures he disagreed. In July 1666 he obtained the royal pardon for having slain one Roger Halford. He *m.* 12 May 1663, at Brampton, Catharine, widow of Sir John SHUCKBURGH, Bart. [1660], da. of Sir Hatton FERMOR, of Easton Neston, co. Northampton, by Anne, da. of Sir William COKAYNE, of Rushton in that county, sometime, 1619-20, Lord Mayor of London. She *d.* in St. Paul's, Covent Garden, and was *bur.* 28 May 1681 at Brampton. Admon. 16 March 1681/2. He was *bur.* at Brampton 24 Sep. 1691. Admon. 14 Aug. 1693 and 31 Jan. 1693/4.

III. 1691. SIR ERASMUS NORWICH, Bart. [1641], of Brampton aforesaid, s. and h. He was *b.* and *bap.* 24 July 1668, at Brampton; *suc. to the Baronetcy* in Sep. 1691; Sheriff of Northants, 1704-05. He *m.* firstly, Annabella, yst. da. of Thomas (SAVAGE), EARL RIVERS, by Elizabeth, da. and coheir of Thomas (DARCY), 3d BARON DARCY OF CHICHE. She *d.* s.p. and was *bur.* 3 Feb. 1702/3, at Brampton. Admon. 1 June 1703. He *m.* secondly (Lic. Fac., 6 April 1704), Jane,(b) da. and h. of William ADAMS, of Sprowston Hall, Norfolk (s. and h. ap. of Sir William ADAMS, 2d Bart. [1660]), by Mary, relict of Francis BULLER, da. and sole heir of Sir John MAYNARD, of Isleham, co. Cambridge. He *d.* Aug. 1720, and was *bur.* at Brampton. Will pr. Sep. 1720.

IV. 1720, to 1742. SIR WILLIAM NORWICH, Bart. [1641], of Brampton aforesaid, only surv. s. and h., by 2d wife. He was *b.* and *bap.* 11 Nov. 1711 at St. Anne's, Westm., though registered at Brampton. He *suc. to the Baronetcy*, Aug. 1720, but is said to have ruined the family by gambling, and to have sold the family estates. He *d.* unm. Jan. 1741/2, at Market Harboro', when the *Baronetcy* is presumed to have become *extinct*,(c) unless any issue male of the younger sons of the 1st Bart. was still in existence.(d) Admon. April 1742 to his sister and next of kin, Arabella Catharine, wife of "Henry Barwell, Esq."

(a) The patent is not enrolled. The date here given is that in Dugdale's *Catalogue.* See *Memorandum* on p. 84. The date of "warrant for granting receipt for £1,095 to John Norwich, of Brampton, co. Northampton, Knt, on his creation as Baronet" is 22 July 1641.

(b) On the death of her uncle, Sir Charles ADAMS, 3d Bart. [1660], who *d.* s.p. 12 Aug. 1716, she inherited Sprowston Hall and other estates in Norfolk.

(c) He had three sisters, (1) Arabella Catharine, *m.* in 1738, Henry BARWELL, of Marston, Trussell, co. Northampton. (2) Annabella, unm. in 1741. (3) Jane, *m.* (—) NICHOLS, of Hiltoft, near Edgworth, Midx.

(d) The will of "Sir Erasmus Norwich," proved 1750, seems to indicate a successor of that name to the Baronetcy.

The title seems to have been assumed as under:—

V. 1742. "SIR JOHN NORWICH, Bart.," said to have been br. and h. of the late Bart. He was a pensioner of the Dukes of Montagu.(a)

VI. 1780? "SIR JOHN NORWICH, Bart.," s. and h. He *d.* in the Workhouse at Kettering, co. Northampton.

VII. 1820? "SIR SAMUEL NORWICH, Bart." s. and h. He was a sawyer, at Kettering aforesaid. His widow "very poor and very ignorant"(b) *d.* there 21 June 1860.(a)

VIII. 1850? "SIR WILLIAM NORWICH, Bart." [*Qy.* s. and h. of above], "the present [1863] heir of the family now in America.(b)

BROWNLOW, *or* BROWNLOWE:
cr. 26 July 1641(c);
ex. 23 Nov. 1679.

I. 1641, to 1679. "JOHN BROWNLOWE of Belton, near Grantham, co. Lincoln, Esq.," s. and h. of Richard BROWNLOW, of Kirby Underwood in that county, chief Prothonotary of the Court of Common Pleas, by Katharine, da. of John PAGE, of Wembly, co. Midx., a Master in Chancery, was *b.* about 1594; matric. at Oxford (St. Mary Hall), 26 June 1607, aged 13; B.A. (Univ. Coll.), 28 April 1610; admitted to Inner Temple, 1608; suc. his father in 1638; was Sheriff of Lincolnshire, 1639-40, and again (but did not act) 1665, and was *cr. a Baronet*, as above, 26 July 1641.(c) He was indicted at Grantham for high treason April 1643. He *m.* Alice, 2d da. but eventually h. of Sir John PULTENEY, of Misterton, co. Leic. He *d.* s.p. 23 Nov. 1679,(d) when the *Baronetcy* became *extinct.* Will pr. 1680.

BROWNLOW, *or* BROWNLOWE:
cr. 27 July 1641(e);
sometime, 1718-54, VISCOUNT TYRCONNEL [I.];
ex. 27 Feb. 1754.

I. 1641. "WILLIAM BROWNLOWE, of Humby, co. Lincoln, Esq.," yr. br. of Sir John Brownlow, Bart. [1641], next abovenamed, was *b.* about 1595; matric. at Oxford (St. Mary Hall), 26 June 1607 (the same day as

---

(a) Sir Bernard Burke's *Vicissitudes of Families*," 3d series [1863], pp. 13-16.

(b) *Northampton Herald*, (—) Nov. 1862.

(c) The patent is not enrolled. The date here given, as also the description of the grantee, is that in Dugdale's *Catalogue.* See *Memorandum* on p. 84. The date of the "warrant for granting receipt for money paid on creation, filed on the same bundle of signet bills," is 23 July 1641, but the christian name of "William" is erroneously given for that of "John."

(d) In Sir J. Williamson's "Notes on Lincolnshire Families," *temp.* Car. II [*Her. and Gen.*, vol. ii, p. 120] he and his estates are thus mentioned, "At Belton, near Grantham; at Rinxton, near Bourne; Snarford, near Lincoln; £8,000 per annum; rich, about £20,000 in purse; beares 10 horses in ye militia."

(e) The patent is not enrolled. The date here given is that in Dugdale's *Catalogue.* See *Memorandum* on p. 84. The date of the signet bill is 24 July 1641.

his elder brother), aged 12; B.A. (Univ. Coll.), 28 Jan. 1610/1; Barrister (Inner Temple), 1617; and was *cr. a Baronet*, as above, 27 July 1641(a), on the day following the creation of his brother, as a Baronet. He was a Parliamentarian, serving on several committees, 1643-45; was M.P. for Lincolnshire, 1653.(b) He *m.*, in or before 1624, Elizabeth, da. and coheir of William DUNCOMBE, of London, Haberdasher, by Agnes, da. of Sir Thomas BENNET, sometime, 1603-04, L. Mayor of London. He *d.* 1666. Will pr. 1668.

II. 1666. SIR RICHARD BROWNLOW, Bart. [1641], of Humby aforesaid and of Rippingale, co. Lincoln, s. and h.; admitted to Gray's Inn, 21 Jan. 1645/6; *suc. to the Baronetcy* in 1666. He *m.* Elizabeth, da. of John FREKE, of Ewern Courtney, Dorset, by his 2d wife, Jane, da. and coheir of Sir John SHIRLEY, of Ifield, co. Sussex. He *d.* 30 Aug. and was *bur.* 5 Sep. 1668 at Rippingale, co. Lincoln, in his 40th year. Admon. 24 Oct. 1668. His widow *d.* 2 Feb. 1683/4 and was *bur.* at Somerby, co. Lincoln, in her 51st year. M.I.

III. 1668. SIR JOHN BROWNLOW, Bart. [1641], of Humby aforesaid, s. and h., *b.* 26 June and *bap.* 6 July 1659 at Rippingale aforesaid; *suc. to the Baronetcy*, 30 Aug. 1668. On 23 Nov. 1679, by the death of his great uncle, Sir John Brownlow, Bart. [*cr.* 25 July 1641], of Belton, he *suc.* to Belton and the other family estates in co. Lincoln; was Sheriff of Lincolnshire, 1688-89; M.P. for Grantham, 1689-90, 1690-95, and 1695 till death. He *m.* (at the age of 16) 27 March 1676, at Westm. Abbey (Lic. Dean of Westm.), Alice, sister to Sir John Sherard, 1st Bart. [1674], 1st da. of Richard SHERARD, of Lobthorpe, co. Lincoln, by Margaret, da. of Lumley DEWE, of Upton Bishop, co. Hereford. He *d.* s.p.m. 16 July 1697, and was *bur.* at Belton. Will, as "of Belton," dat. 29 July 1689, pr. 2 Sep. 1697.(c) His widow *d.* 27 June 1721. Will pr. 1721.

IV. 1697. SIR WILLIAM BROWNLOW, Bart. [1641], of Belton and Humby aforesaid, br. and h. male, *b.* 5 and *bap.* 10 Nov. 1665 at Rippingale aforesaid; *suc. to the Baronetcy*, 16 July 1697; was M.P. for Peterborough, 1689-90, 1690-95, and 1695-98; for Bishops Castle 1698 till unseated 4 Feb. 1700. He *m.* firstly, Dorothy (aged 3 in 1668), 1st da. and coheir of Sir Richard MASON, of Sutton, Surrey, Clerk of the Green Cloth, by Anne Margaret, da. of Sir James LONG, of Draycott, Wilts. Her will pr. May 1700. He *m.* secondly, Henrietta. He *d.* at St. Martin's in the Fields, 6 March 1700/1. Admon. 20 March 1700/1, and again 16 Sep. 1714. His widow living March 1700/1.

V. 1701, to 1754. SIR JOHN BROWNLOW, Bart. [1641], of Belton and Humby aforesaid, s. and h. by 1st wife; *suc. to the Baronetcy*, 6 March 1700/1; was of full age in Sep. 1714; M.P. for Grantham 1713-15; for Lincolnshire, 1715-22, and for Grantham again (3 parls.) 1722-41; was *cr.* 23 June 1718, BARON CHARLEVILLE, co. Cork, and VISCOUNT TRYCONNEL [I.]; was made K.B. on the revival of that order, 27 May 1725. He *m.* firstly, Eleanor, 4th da. and coheir of his uncle Sir John BROWNLOW, 3d Bart. [1641] by Alice, da. of Richard SHERARD, all abovenamed. She *d.* s.p. 11 Sep. 1730. He *m.* secondly, 24 Jan. 1731/2, at Marnham, Notts, Elizabeth, da. of William Cartwright, of Marnham aforesaid. He *d.* s.p. 27 Feb. 1754, at Belton aforesaid, when *all his honours* became *extinct.*(d) Admon 1 Feb. 1755. His widow *d.* at Buxton, 17 July 1780.

(a) *See* p. 111, note "e."

(b) His estate was "At Humby, near Grantham; £1,600" [*i.e.*, a year]. See Williamson's notes, as on p. 111, note "b."

(c) All of his four daughters and coheirs *m.* noblemen, *viz.*, (1) Jane, *m.* Peregrine (Bertie), 2d Duke of Ancaster; (2) Elizabeth, *m.* John (Cecil), 6th Earl of Exeter; (3) Alicia, *m.* Francis (North), 2d Baron Guilford; and (4) Elizabeth, *m.* her cousin, John (Brownlow), Viscount Tyrconnel [I.], and 5th Bart. [1641], as mentioned in the text.

(d) His sister, Ann, *m.* Sir Richard Cust, 2d Bart. [1677], and their son, Sir John Cust, 3d Bart. Speaker of the House of Commons, inherited the estate of Belton. Sir John's s. and h. was (for his father's services) in commemoration of his descent from the Brownlow family, *cr.* BARON BROWNLOW OF BELTON in 1776, and left a son who, in 1815, was *cr.* EARL BROWNLOW.

SYDENHAM:
cr. 28 July 1641(a);
ex. 10 Oct. 1739.

I. 1641. "JOHN SYDENHAM, of Brimpton, co. Somerset, Esq.," s. and h. of John SYDENHAM, of the same, by Alice, sister and heir of Sir William HOBY, da. of William HOBY, of Hales, co. Glouc., was *b.* about 1620; suc. his father, 10 March 1626; and was *cr. a Baronet*, as above, 28 July 1641.(a) He *m.* in 1638, Anne, sister of Sir Ralph HARE, 1st Bart. [1641], 2d da. of Sir John HARE, of Stow Bardolph, co. Norfolk, by Elizabeth, da. of Thomas (COVENTRY), 1st BARON COVENTRY OF AYLESBOROUGH. He *d.* 1643, and was *bur.* at Stow Bardolph. Will pr. 1643.

II. 1643. SIR JOHN SYDENHAM, Bart. [1641], of Brimpton aforesaid, posthumous s. and h., *b.* 1643, and *suc. to the Baronetcy* on his birth; was M.P. for Somerset, Nov. 1665, till void 9 Nov. 1666; again, Nov. 1669 to 1679, and 1679. He *m.* firstly, Elizabeth, da. of John (POULETT), 2d BARON POULETT OF HINTON ST. GEORGE, by his 1st wife, Catherine, da. of Horatio (DE VERE), BARON VERE OF TILBURY. She *d.* s.p.s. and was *bur.* at Brimpton in 1669. M.I. He *m.* secondly, Mary, 2d da. of Philip (HERBERT), 5th EARL OF PEMBROKE, by Penelope, da. and h. of Sir Robert NAUNTON. She, who was *bap.* 7 May 1650, *d.* 1686, and was *bur.* at Brimpton. M.I. He *d.* 1696 in his 54th year. Admon. 18 Jan. 1696/7 and 4 March 1697/8.

III. 1696, to 1739. SIR PHILIP SYDENHAM, Bart. [1641], of Brimpton aforesaid, 2d but 1st surv. s. and h., was *b.* about 1676; *suc. to the Baronetcy* in 1696; was of full age in March 1697/8. He, who was sometime M.P. for Helston, 1700-01; for Somerset, 1701-02 and 1702-05; wasted an estate of £4,000 a year, and sold Brimpton to his cousin, Humphrey Sydenham. He *d.* unm. 10 and was *bur.* 25 Oct. 1739, at Barnes, co. Surrey, aged about 63, when the *Baronetcy* became *extinct.*

PRATT:
cr. 28 July 1641(b);
ex. 17 Jan. 1673/4.

I. 1641. "HENRY PRATT, of Coleshull, co. Berks, Esq.," s. of Henry PRATT, of Cirencester, Clothier, was *b.* about 1573; apprenticed, 8 Dec. 1587, in the Company of Merchant Taylors; was on the Livery, 16 July 1610; 3d Warden, 17 July 1627; 2d Warden, 13 July 1630; Master, 4 Aug. 1630; Alderman of Bridge Ward, 4 July 1633 to March 1641(c); Sheriff of London, 1631-32; purchased, in 1626, the estate of Coleshill, Berks, and was *cr. a Baronet*, as above, 28 July 1641, being *Knighted* subsequently at Whitehall, 26 [*sic*, but query] July 1641.(b) He *m.*, in or before 1605, Mary, da. of Thomas ADAMS, of Wisbeach, co. Cambridge. He *d.* 6 April, and was *bur.* 9 May 1647 at Coleshill, aged 75. M.I. Will, dat. 2 July 1645, pr. 16 April 1649. His widow *d.* before 6 April 1672.

(a) The patent is not enrolled. The date here given is that in Dugdale's *Catalogue.* See *Memorandum* on p. 84. The date of the signet bill is 19 July 1641.

(b) The patent is not enrolled. The date of Baronetcy here given is that in Dugdale's *Catalogue* (see *Memorandum* on p. 84), and also in the Visit. of Berks, 1664, but as the Grantee was Knighted, *as* a Baronet, two days previously, there is, apparently, some mistake. The date of the signet bill is 19 July 1641.

(c) Clode's *London during the Great Rebellion*, p. 28.

II. 1647. SIR GEORGE PRATT, Bart. [1641], of Coleshill aforesaid,(a) s. and h.; *b.* about 1605; matric. at Oxford (Mag. Hall), 27 June 1623, aged 18; admitted to Gray's Inn, 1626; *suc. to the Baronetcy*, 6 April 1647; was Sheriff of Berks, 1654-55. He entered his pedigree in the Visit. of Berks., 1665, being then aged 58. He *m.*, in or before 1650, Margaret, da. of Sir Humphrey FORSTER, 1st Bart. [1620], of Aldermaston, Berks, by Anne, da. of Sir William KINGSMILL. He was *bur.* 11 May 1673 at Coleshill. Will dat. 6 April 1672, pr. 21 June 1673. His widow was *bur.* there 24 March 1698/9.

III. 1673, to 1674. SIR HENRY PRATT, Bart. [1641], of Coleshill aforesaid, only s. and h.; *b.* about 1650; matric. at Oxford (Trin. Coll.), 15 July 1665, aged 15; admitted to Inner Temple, 1667; *suc. to the Baronetcy* in May 1673. He *d.* s.p., probably unm., and was *bur.* 17 Jan. 1673/4, at Coleshill, when *the Baronetcy* became *extinct.*(b) Will pr. 1674.

NICHOLS, *or* NICOLLS:
cr. 28 July 1641;(c)
ex. 1717.

I. 1641. "FRANCIS NICHOLS, of Hardwick, co. Northampton, Esq.," s. and h. of Francis NICHOLS, of the same, Gov. of Tilbury Fort, 1588, by Anne, da. of David SEYMOUR, being nephew and h. of Sir Augustine NICOLLS, *or* NICHOLS, of Faxton, co. Northampton, one of the Judges of the Court of Common Pleas, was *b.* about 1587; matric. at Oxford (Bras. Coll.), 15 Oct. 1602, aged 15; admitted to Middle Temple, 1602; suc. his father, 1 April 1604, and suc. his said uncle (in the estate of Faxton), 3 Aug. 1616; was M.P. for Bishop's Castle, 1621-22, and for Northamptonshire, 1628-29; Sheriff thereof, 1630-31; Sec. to the Elector Palatine in 1640; and was *cr. a Baronet*, as above, 28 July 1641.(c) He *m.* in or before 1618, Mary, da. of Edward BAGSHAW, of London. She *d.* 10 July 1634, in her 47th year, and was *bur.* at Faxton. M.I. He *d.* 4 March 1641/2, and was *bur.* at Hardwick. M.I.

II. 1642. SIR EDWARD NICHOLS, *or* NICOLLS, Bart. [1641], of Faxton aforesaid, only s. and h.; *b.* about 1619; matric. at Oxford (Linc. Coll.), 8 May 1635, aged 15; admitted to Middle Temple, 1637; *suc. to the Baronetcy*, 4 March 1641/2; was on the Northants. Committee, Aug. 1644; Sheriff of that county, 1657-58. He *m.* firstly, Judith, da. of the Hon. Sir Rowland ST. JOHN, K.B., by Sibylla, da. of John VAUGHAN. She, by whom he had seven daughters, was *bur.* 15 June 1663, at St. Leonard's Shoreditch. He *m.* secondly, 20 Feb. 1664/5, at St. Margaret's, Westm. (Lic. Dean and Chapter of Westm.). Jane, sister of Sir Peter SOAME, 2d Bart. [1685], 8th da. of Sir Stephen SOAME, of Heydon, Essex, by Elizabeth, da. of Sir Thomas PLAYTERS, 1st Bart. [1623]. He *d.* 28 Feb. 1682/3, aged 63 years and 4 months, and was *bur.* at Faxton. M.I. His widow resided at Old, co. Northampton. Her admon. 19 June 1707, 4 May 1719, and 10 Dec. 1720.

III. 1683, to 1717. SIR EDWARD NICHOLS *or* NICOLLS, Bart. [1641], of Faxton aforesaid, only s. and h., by 2d wife, *suc. to the Baronetcy*, 20 Feb. 1682/3. He *d.* s.p. 1717, when the *Baronetcy* became *extinct.* Will pr. 1717.

(a) The house at Coleshill was rebuilt in 1650, the well known Inigo Jones being the architect.

(b) His only sister, Mary, *m.* 16 Feb. 1666/7, at Coleshill, Thomas Pleydell, of Shrivenham, and their great grandson, Mark Stuart Pleydell, of Coleshill, was *cr. a Baronet* in 1732.

(c) The patent is not enrolled. The date here given is that in Dugdale's *Catalogue.* See *Memorandum* on p. 84. The date of the signet bill is 22 July 1641.

STRICKLAND:
cr. 30 July 1641(a);
sometime, 1865-74, CHOLMLEY.

I. 1641. "WILLIAM STRICKLAND, of Boynton, co. York, Knt.," s. and h. of Walter STRICKLAND, of the same, by Frances, da. of Peter WENTWORTH, of Lillingston Dayrell, Bucks, was *b.* about 1596, being aged 16 in 1612 (Visit. of Yorkshire); admitted to Gray's Inn, 21 May 1617; *Knighted*, 24 June 1630; suc. his father in 1635, and was *cr. a Baronet*, as above, 30 July 1641.(a) He was a vehement Parliamentarian, serving on nearly every important Committee, 1641-59, save that of the king's trial, and being in command at Hull in July 1643. He was M.P. for Hedon 1640-53, and for the East Riding of Yorkshire, 1654-55 and 1656, and was summoned by Cromwell to "*the other house*" (as it was then called) under the designation of LORD STRICKLAND (b); was P.C. (to Richard Cromwell) 1659. He was, however, unmolested at and after the Restoration. He *m.* firstly, 18 June 1622, at St. Leonard's, Shoreditch (Lic. London, he 23 and she 18), Margaret, da. of Sir Richard CHOLMLEY, of Whitby, co. York, by his 1st wife, Susanna, da. of John LEGARD. She *d.* s.p.m. 1629, and was *bur.* at Whitby. He *m.* secondly, 3 May 1631, at St. George's, Canterbury, Frances, 1st da. of Thomas (FINCH), 1st EARL OF WINCHELSEA, by Cicely, da. of John WENTWORTH. He *d.* 1673.

II. 1673. SIR THOMAS STRICKLAND, Bart. [1641], of Boynton aforesaid, only s. and h., by 2d wife, *b.* about 1639; was M.P. for Beverley, 1659; aged 26 in 1665 (Visit. of Yorkshire); *suc. to the Baronetcy* in 1673. He *m.* 19 Nov. 1659 at Kensington, Elizabeth, 2d da. and coheir of Sir Francis PILE, 2d Bart. [1620], by his 2d wife, Jane,(c) said to be yst. da. of John STILL, Bishop of Bath and Wells. He *d.* 20 Nov. 1684.

III. 1684. SIR WILLIAM STRICKLAND, Bart. [1641], of Boynton aforesaid, s. and h., *b.* March 1665; matric. at Oxford (Ex. Coll.), 12 Nov. 1680, aged 15; *suc. to the Baronetcy* in 1684; was M.P. for Malton (in seven Parls., 1689-98, 1700-08, and 1722-24; for Yorkshire, 1708-10, and for Old Sarum, 1716-22. Commissary General of the Musters to George I. He *m.* 28 Aug. 1684, at St. Michael's, Malton, Elizabeth, da. and eventually sole h. of William PALMES, of Malton aforesaid, and of Lindley, co. York, by Mary, da. and coheir of Col. the Hon. Sir William EURE, yr. s. of William, 4th BARON EURE. He *d.* 12 May 1724, aged 59. The will of his widow was pr. 1740.

IV. 1724. SIR WILLIAM STRICKLAND, Bart. [1641], of Boynton aforesaid, s. and h., was a Commissioner of the Revenue [I.], 1709; M.P. for Malton (three Parls.), 1708-15; for Carlisle, 1715-22, and for Scarborough (three Parls.), 1722 till death; *suc. to the Baronetcy*, 12 May 1724; was one of the Lords of the Treasury, 1725-27; Treasurer to the Queen's household; Secretary at War, 1730-35; P.C., 11 June 1730. He *m.* Catharine, da. of Sir Jeremy SAMBROOKE, of Gobions, Herts, by Judith, da. of Nicholas VANACKER, of London, Merchant. He *d.*, at Boynton, 1 Sep. 1735. Will pr. 1736. The will of his widow pr. Feb. 1767.

V. 1735. SIR GEORGE STRICKLAND, Bart. [1641], of Boynton aforesaid, s. and h., *b.* March 1729; *suc. to the Baronetcy*, 1 Sep. 1735; Sheriff of Yorkshire, 1768-69. He *m.* 25 Nov. 1751, at Wragby, Elizabeth Lætitia, 5th da. of Sir Rowland WINN, 4th Bart. [1660], of Nostell, co. York, by Susanna, da. of Edward HENSHAW, of Eltham, co. Kent. He *d.* 13 Jan. 1808. Will pr. 1809. His widow *d.* at Hildenley Hall, co. York, 1813, aged 79. Will pr. 1813.

(a) The patent is not enrolled. The date here given is that in Dugdale's *Catalogue.* See *Memorandum* on p. 84. The date of the signet bill is 29 July 1641.

(b) His 2d br., Walter, was, also, one of Cromwell's Lords, under the designation of "LORD WALTER STRICKLAND." He, like his brother, was unmolested at and after the Restoration.

(c) See p. 57, notes "a" and "b," *sub* "PILE."

VI. 1808. SIR WILLIAM STRICKLAND, Bart. [1641], of Boynton aforesaid, s. and h., *b.* 12 March 1753; *suc. to the Baronetcy*, 13 Jan. 1808. He *m.* 15 April 1778, Henrietta, 3d da. and coheir of Nathaniel CHOLMLEY, of Whitby Abbey and of Howsham, co. York, by his 2d wife, Henrietta-Catharine, da. of Stephen CROFT, of Stillington. She, who was *b.* 28 Aug. 1760 at Howsham, *d.* 26 March 1827. He *d.* 8 Jan. 1834 at Boynton, in his 81st year. Will pr. 1834.

VII. 1834. SIR GEORGE STRICKLAND, *afterwards* (1865-74), CHOLMLEY, Bart. [1641], of Boynton and Hildenley Hall aforesaid, and of Hildenby Hall, co. York, s. and h.; *b.* 26 Nov. 1782, at Welburn, Kirby Moorside, co. York; Barrister (Lincoln's Inn), 1810; M.P. for Yorkshire, 1831; for West Division of Yorkshire, 1832-41; and for Preston, 1841-57; *suc. to the Baronetcy*, 8 Jan. 1834. By royal lic., 17 March 1865, he took the name of CHOLMLEY, in lieu of that of STRICKLAND. He *m.* firstly, 30 March 1818, at Sigglesthorne, Mary, only child of Rev. Charles CONSTABLE, of Wassand, co. York. She *d.* 10 Jan. 1865, at Walcot, co. Lincoln, aged 67. He *m.* secondly, 25 May 1867 (being then aged 85), at St. Martin's in the Fields, Jane, 1st da. of Thomas LEAVENS, of Norton's Villas, Yorkshire. He *d.* 23 Dec. 1874, in his 92d year, at Newton Hall, Boynton. His widow *d.* 19 Oct. 1898, in her 89th year, at 139 North Marine Road, Scarborough. Will pr. at £95,811, the net personalty being £52,364.

VIII. 1874. SIR CHARLES WILLIAM STRICKLAND, Bart. [1641], of Boynton and of Hildenley Hall aforesaid, s. and h., by 1st wife; *b.* at Hildenley Hall, 6 Feb. 1819; ed. at Rugby: B.A., Cambridge (Trin. Coll.), 1842; M.A., 1847; Barrister (Lincoln's Inn and Middle Temple), 1847; *suc. to the Baronetcy*, 23 Dec. 1874; Sheriff of the North Riding of Yorkshire, 1880. He *m.* firstly, 19 Feb. 1850, Georgina Selina Septima, da. of Sir William Mordaunt Stuart MILNER, 4th Bart. [1717], by his 2d wife, Harriet Elizabeth, da. of Lord Edward Charles CAVENDISH-BENTINCK. She *d.* 13 June 1864,. He *m.* secondly, 22 May 1866, at Thorney, Notts, Anne Elizabeth, yst. da. of Rev. Christopher NEVILE, of Thorney aforesaid. She *d.* 7 April 1886, aged 42, at Hildenley.

Family Estates.—These, in 1883, consisted of 16,000 acres in the North, East, and West Ridings of Yorkshire, worth 17,000 a year. *Principal Seats.*—Hildenley Hall, near Malton; Boynton, near Bridlington; Whitby Abbey and Howsham, all in co. York.

WINDHAM, *or* WYNDHAM:

cr. 4 *Aug.* 1641.(a)

ex. 1663.

I. 1641, to 1663. "HUGH WINDHAM, of Pilsden Court, co. Dorset, Esq.," 4th surv. s. of Edmond WINDHAM, of Kentsford, in St. Decumans, Somerset (2d s. of Sir John WYNDHAM, of Orchard Wyndham), by Margaret, da. and eventually coheir of Richard CHAMBERLAIN, Alderman of London, was living at Aldermanbury, London, as a merchant in 1626; entered and signed his pedigree in the Visit. of London, 1634, and was *cr. a Baronet*, as above, 4 Aug 1641,(a) being *Knighted* the 10th following; was a Compounder (with his father) in 1645, being, in Nov. 1651, fined £692; was Sheriff of Dorset, 1651-52; He *m.*, in or before 1625, Mary, da. of Christopher ALANSON, of London. She *d.* before Sep. 1661. He *d.* s.p.m.s., in 1663,(b) when the *Baronetcy* became *extinct.* Will dat. 17 Sep. 1661, pr. 18 July 1663, directing his burial to be at Pilsden.

(a) The patent is not enrolled. The date here given is that in Dugdale's *Catalogue.* See *Memorandum* on p. 84. The date of the signet bill is 31 July 1641.

(b) The Sir Hugh Windham, who was M.P. for Minehead, 1661, till his death in 1671, was his great nephew, being s. and h. ap. of Sir Edmund Windham (who survived his said son), s. and h. of Sir Thomas Windham, all of Kentsford aforesaid.

MAULEVERER:

cr. 4 Aug. 1641(a);

ex. 27 March 1713.

I. 1641. "THOMAS MAULEVERER, of Allerton Maulever [*sic*] co. York, Esq.," s. and h. of Sir Richard MAULEVERER, of the same, by his 2d wife, Katherine, da. of Sir Ralph BOURCHIER, was *bap.* 9 April 1599; admitted to Gray's Inn, 22 Oct. 1617; was M.P. for Boroughbridge, 1640-53, and, though he had opposed the King's party, was *cr. a Baronet*, as above, 4 Aug. 1641.(a) He shortly afterwards raised two regiments of foot and a troop of horse for the Parl.; fought at the battle of Atherton in 1643; served on several important Committees, 1643-46; was one of the Regicide Judges, attending every day and signing the death warrant. He *m.* firstly, Mary, da. of Sir Richard HUTTON, Chief Justice of the Common Pleas, but by her had no issue. He *m.* secondly, about 1622, Elizabeth, da. of Thomas WILBRAHAM, of Woodhey, Cheshire, by his 2d wife, Mary, da. of Peter WARBURTON, of Arley, in that county. She was *bur.* 10 March 1652/3 in Westm. Abbey.(b) He *d.* about June 1655. Admon. 9 June 1655 and 13 Feb. 1656/7. He, though dead, was, after the Restoration, excepted out of the bill of pardon.

II. 1655. SIR RICHARD MAULEVERER, Bart. [1641], of Allerton Mauleverer aforesaid, s. and h., by 2d wife, *b.* about 1623, was, in opposition to his father, a zealous loyalist; was admitted to Gray's Inn, 12 July 1641, and was *Knighted* v.p. at Christ Church, Oxford, 27 March 1645; was fined £3,287 by Parl. in 1649, his estate sequestered, 1650, and declared an outlaw in 1654. He *suc. to the Baronetcy* about June 1655; was in Lord Wilmot's rising, 1655, and was taken prisoner to Chester, 1655, but escaped thence to the Hague; returned to London, 1659, and was again imprisoned for some months; was confirmed in title and estate by Charles II, and made Gent. of the Privy Chamber and Captain of Horse in 1660; M.P. for Boroughbridge, 1661, till death; was a Commissioner for licensing hackney coaches, 1665; Sheriff of Yorkshire, 1667-68. He *m.* 10 Aug. 1642, at St. Giles' in the Fields (Lic. Lond., he about 19, and she about 20). Anne, da. of Sir Robert CLERKE,(c) of Pleshey, Essex, by Judith, da. of Sir William DANIEL, of London. He was *bur.* 25 July 1675 in Westm. Abbey.

III. 1675. SIR THOMAS MAULEVERER, Bart. [1641], of Allerton Mauleverer aforesaid, 1st s. and h., *b.* about 1643; *suc. to the Baronetcy* in July, 1675; was M.P. (four Parls.) for Boroughbridge, 1679, till death; held a command, 1685, against the rebels under the Duke of Monmouth; sold "Armley Hall" and other Yorkshire estates. He *m.* Katherine, da. and h. of Sir Miles STAPLETON, of Wighill, co. York, by Mary, da. of Sir Ingram HOPTON. He *d.* s.p. legit.(d) and was *bur.* 13 Aug. 1687, in Westm. Abbey. Will dat. 10 June, pr. 16 Aug. 1687, by Richard, his br. and universal legatee. His widow, with whom he had lived unhappily, *m.* her cousin, John HOPTON, of Ingersgill, and *d.* s.p. and intestate, 31 Jan. 1703/4, being *bur.* at Nether Poppleton.

IV. 1687. SIR RICHARD MAULEVERER, Bart. [1641], of Allerton Mauleverer aforesaid, br. and h., *suc. to the Baronetcy* in Aug. 1687. He *m.* (Lic. Vic. Gen., 10 April 1688, he 22 [*sic*, but query if not 42] and she 19) Barbara, da. of Sir Thomas SLINGSBY, 2d Bart. [S. 1635], of Scriven, co. York, by Dorothy, da. and coheir of George CRADOCK. He was *bur.* 11 May 1689 in Westm. Abbey. Will dat. 15 Oct. 1688, pr. 13 June 1689. His widow *m.* (as 2d wife) 14 Feb. 1692/3, at Allhallows', Staining, London (Lic. Vic. Gen., she about 25), John (ARUNDELL), 2d BARON ARUNDELL OF TRERICE, who was *bur.* 23 June 1698 at St. James', Westm., aged 49. She *m.* (for her 3d husband and his 2d wife) 21 Sep. 1708, at St. James'

(a) *Vide* p. 116, note "a."

(b) See note in Col. Chester's *Registers of Westm. Abbey*, as to her being generally called "Mary"—also as to her husband's intended marriage, July 1659, with Susanna Raylton, of Fulham, widow.

(c) See Col. Chester's *Westm. Abbey Registers*, p. 186, note 11, as to the error in calling her da. of "Sir *Henry* Clerke, *Bart.*"

(d) His illegit. son, Thomas Newsham, *otherwise* Mauleverer, was well provided for under the will of the 4th Bart.

aforesaid, Thomas (HERBERT), 3d EARL OF PEMBROKE, who *d.* 22 Jan. 1732/3. She *d.*, and was *bur.* 9 Aug. 1721, in Salisbury Cathedral. Admon. 8 May 1733 and 30 April 1759.

V. 1689, to 1713. SIR RICHARD MAULEVERER, Bart. [1641], of Allerton Mauleverer aforesaid, only s. and h., *b.* 18 and *bap.* 25 March 1689 at St. Martin's in the Fields; *suc. to the Baronetcy* a few months later, in May 1689. He *d.* unm. of the small pox, at the Earl of Pembroke's house, and was *bur.* 27 March 1713, in Westm. Abbey, aged 24, when the *Baronetcy* became *extinct.*

KNATCHBULL:

cr. 4 Aug. 1641.(a);

sometime, 1746-63, KNATCHBULL-WYNDHAM.

I. 1641. "NORTON KNATCHBULL, of Mersham Hatch,(b) co. Kent, Esq.," s. and h. of Thomas Knatchbull, of the same, by Eleanor, da. and eventually coheir of John ASTLEY, of Maidstone (by Margaret, da. and h. of Lord Thomas GREY, br. of Henry, DUKE OF SUFFOLK), which Thomas was br. and h. to Sir Norton KNATCHBULL, of Mersham Hatch, was *b.* about 1602, at Mersham; suc. his father, 1623, and was *cr. a Baronet*, as above, 4 Aug. 1641.(a) He was M.P. for Kent, April to May 1640; for New Romney, 1640 till secluded in Dec. 1648, and again 1660 and 1661-77; was somewhat inclined to the Parl. side, though sequestrated in 1643, and fined 1,000 marks; was esteemed a person of great learning. He *m.* firstly (Lic. at Canterbury, 22 Oct. 1630, he aged 23), Dorothy, da. of Thomas WESTROW, Alderman and sometime (1625) Sheriff of London by Mary (who subsequently *m.* the abovementioned Sir Norton KNATCHBULL), da. of, John ALDERSEA, of Spurgrove, co. Chester. By her he had thirteen children. He *m.* secondly, 27 Nov. 1662, at St. Martin's in the Fields (Lic. Vic. Gen., he about 50 and she about 40), Dorothy, widow of Sir Edward STEWARD, da. of Sir Robert HONYWOOD, of Pett, in Charing, Kent, by Alice, da. of Sir Martin BARNHAM, of Hollingbourne. He *d.* 5 Feb. 1684/5, aged about 83, and was *bur.* at Mersham. M.I. Will dat. 30 June 1682, pr. 7 Aug. 1685. His widow, who was *b.* 30 Aug. and *bap.* 8 Sep. 1611, at Charing, and by whom he had no issue, was *bur.* 2 May 1694, at Mersham.

II. 1685. SIR JOHN KNATCHBULL, Bart. [1641], of Mersham Hatch aforesaid, s. and h., by 1st wife, was a Commissioner for the office of Lord Privy Seal, 1650-51; M.P. for New Romney, 1660; for Kent (three Parls.), 1685-95; *suc. to the Baronetcy*, 5 Feb. 1684/5. He *m.* 17 Jan. 1659, Jane, da. of Sir Edward MONINS, 2d Bart. [1611], by Elizabeth, da. of Sir Thomas STYLE, 1st Bart. [1627], of Wateringbury. He *d.* s.p.m.s., 15 Dec. 1696, aged 60. His widow *d.* 7 June 1699, aged 59. Both *bur.* at Mersham. M.I.

III. 1696. SIR THOMAS KNATCHBULL, Bart. [1641], of Mersham aforesaid, br. and h.; *suc. to the Baronetcy*, 15 Dec. 1696. He *m.* Mary, da. of Sir Edward DERING, 2d Bart. [1627], by Mary, da. of Daniel HARVEY, of Coombe, co. Surrey. He *d.* about 1712. Will dat. 12 Dec. 1711. His widow was living 1724.

IV. 1712? SIR EDWARD KNATCHBULL, Bart. [1641], of Mersham Hatch aforesaid, s. and h., *suc. to the Baronetcy*, on the death of his father; was M.P. for Rochester, 1702-05; for Kent, 1713-15 and 1722-27, and for Lostwithiel, 1728 till death. He *m.* about 1698, Alice, sister of Thomas, BARON WYNDHAM OF FINGLASS [I.], sometime [1726-39] Lord Chancellor of Ireland, 1st da. of Col. John WYNDHAM,(c) of Norrington, Wilts, by Alice, da. of Thomas FOWNES. She, who was *b.* 11 April 1676, *d.* 15 and was *bur.* 16 April 1723, at Mersham. He *d.* in Golden square, Midx. 3 April 1730. Will pr. 1730.

(a) *Vide* p. 116, note "a."

(b) Mersham Hatch was purchased by Richard Knatchbull in 1485, and has ever since remained with his descendants.

(c) See *Mis. Gen. et Her.*, 2d series, vol. iv, for many interesting particulars of the Wyndham family, together with some of that of Knatchbull as connected therewith.

V. 1730. SIR WYNDHAM KNATCHBULL, *afterwards* (1746-49), KNATCHBULL-WYNDHAM, Bart. [1641], of Mersham Hatch aforesaid, s. and h., *suc. to the Baronetcy*, 3 April 1730; was Sheriff of Kent, June to Dec. 1733; took the addit. name of *Wyndham*, by act of Parl. 1746. He *m.*, 23 June 1730, Catharine, da. of James HARRIS, of Salisbury, only child of his 1st wife, Catherine, da. of Charles COCKS, of Worcester. She *d.* 6 Jan. 1740/1, at St. James', Westm. Admon. 27 June 1751. He *d.* 3 July 1749. Will pr. 1749.

VI. 1749. SIR WYNDHAM KNATCHBULL-WYNDHAM, Bart. [1641], formerly (1737-46), KNATCHBULL, of Mersham Hatch aforesaid, s. and h., *b.* in Golden square, 16 Feb. 1737; *suc. to the Baronetcy*, 3 July 1749; was M.P. for Kent, 1760-61, and 1761 till death. He *d.* unm., 26 Sep. 1763. Will pr. 1763.

VII. 1763. SIR EDWARD KNATCHBULL, Bart. [1641], of Mersham Hatch aforesaid, uncle and h., *b.* 12 Dec. 1704, or 17 Dec. 1705; was M.P. [I.] for Armagh, 1727-60) *suc. to the Baronetcy*, 26 Sep. 1763. He *m.* Grace, 2d da. of William LEGGE, of Salisbury. Her admon. April 1788. He *d.* 21 Nov. 1789, aged 85. Will pr. 1789.

VIII. 1789. SIR EDWARD KNATCHBULL, Bart. [1641], of Mersham Hatch aforesaid, only surv. s. and h., *b.* about 1760; matric. at Oxford (Ch. Ch.), 25 Jan. 1777, aged 17; Sheriff of Kent, 1785; *suc. to the Baronetcy*, 21 Nov. 1789; M.P. for Kent in six Parls., 1785-86, 1790-1802, and 1806 till his death; was a zealous supporter of Pitt's administration; *cr.* D.C.L. of Oxford, 6 July 1810. He *m.* firstly, July 1780, Mary, da. and one of the two coheirs of William Western HUGESSEN, of Provenders, near Faversham, co. Kent, by Thomazine, da. of Sir John HONYWOOD, 3d Bart. [1660]. She *d.* 24 May 1784. He *m.* secondly, 4 June 1785, Frances, da. of John GRAHAM, Lieut. Governor of Georgia. She *d.* 23 Nov. 1799. He *m.* thirdly, 13 April 1801, at St. Geo. Han. sq., Mary, da. and coheir of Thomas HAWKINS, of Nash Court, in Boughton under Blean, Kent, by Mary Theresa only da. of John BRADSHAW, of Stretton, Cheshire. He *d.* 21 Sep. 1819, in his 61st year. Will pr. 1819. His widow *d.* 19 Dec. 1850, at Dover. Will pr. Jan. 1851.

IX. 1819. SIR EDWARD KNATCHBULL, Bart. [1641], of Mersham Hatch aforesaid, s. and h. by 1st wife, *b.* 20 Dec. 1781; matric. at Oxford (Ch. Ch.) 5 Feb. 1800, aged 18; admitted to Lincoln's Inn, 1803; *suc. to the Baronetcy*, 21 Sep. 1819; M.P. for Kent, 1819-31; for East Kent, 1833-45; P.C. 16 Dec. 1834; Paymaster General of the Forces, 1834-35 and 1841-45. He *m.* firstly, 25 Aug. 1806, Annabella Christiana, 2d da. of Sir John HONYWOOD, 4th Bart. [1660], by Frances, da. of William (COURTENAY), 2d VISCOUNT COURTENAY. She *d.* 4 April 1814. He *m.* secondly, 24 Oct. 1820, Fanny Catherine, 1st da. of Edward KNIGHT, *formerly* AUSTEN, of Godmersham Park, Kent, by Elizabeth, da. of Sir Brook BRIDGES, 3d Bart. [1718]. He *d.* 24 May 1849,(a) at Mersham Hatch, aged 67. Will pr. July 1849. His widow *d.* 24 Dec. 1882, at Provenders, in her 90th year.

X. 1849. SIR NORTON JOSEPH KNATCHBULL, Bart. [1641], of Mersham Hatch aforesaid, s. and h. by 1st marriage, *b.* 10 July 1808, at Provenders aforesaid; ed. at Winchester and at Christ Church, Oxford; matric. 20 Nov. 1826, aged 18; *suc. to the Baronetcy*, 24 May 1849. He *m.* 31 May 1831, Mary, 1st da. of Jesse WATTS-RUSSELL, *formerly* RUSSELL, of Ilam Hall, co. Stafford, and of Biggin, co. Northampton, by Mary, da. and h. of David Pike WATTS, of Portland Place, Marylebone. He *d.* 2 Feb. 1868, at 3 Chesham place. His widow *d.* 3 Sep. 1874, at Maidstone.

(a) His sixth son (the 1st son by his 2d wife), Edward Hugessen Knatchbull, *afterwards* (1849), Knatchbull-Hugessen, who inherited the Hugessen estates belonging to his grandmother's family, was *cr.* 26 May 1880, BARON BRABOURNE of Brabourne, co. Kent.

II

XI. 1868. SIR EDWARD KNATCHBULL, Bart. [1641], of Mersham Hatch aforesaid, 1st s. and h., *b.* 26 April 1838; Barrister at Law; *suc. to the Baronetcy* 2 Feb. 1868. He *d.* unm. 30 May 1871, at Mersham Hatch, aged 33.

XII. 1871. SIR WYNDHAM KNATCHBULL, Bart. [1641], of Mersham Hatch aforesaid, only br. and h., *b.* 9 Aug. 1844; ed. at Eton; Barrister at Law; sometime a Civil servant in the Gen. Post Office; *suc. to the Baronetcy*, 30 May 1871; M.P. for East Kent, 1875-76.

Family Estates.—These, in 1883, consisted of 4,638 acres in Kent, valued at £7,224 a year, besides 483 acres (let at £930), belonging to the Dowager Lady Knatchbull. *Seat.*—Mersham Hatch, near Ashford, Kent.

CHICHESTER:

cr. 4 Aug. 1641.(a)

I. 1641. "JOHN CHICHESTER, of Raleigh [in Pilton] co. Devon, Esq.," s. and h. of Sir Robert Chichester,(b) K.B., of Raleigh aforesaid, by his 2d wife, Mary, da. of Robert HILL, of Shilston, in that county, was *b.* 23 April 1623, suc. his father, 24 April 1624, and was *cr. a Baronet*, as above, 4 Aug. 1641;(a) was M.P. *for* Barnstaple 1661 till death. He *m.* firstly, Elizabeth, da. of Sir John RAYNEY, 1st Bart. [1642], by his 1st wife, Catharine, da. of Thomas STYLE. She *d.* 1654. He *m.* secondly, 18 July 1655, at St. Anne's, Blackfriars, Mary WARCUP, widow, of that parish. He *d.* 1667.

II. 1667. SIR JOHN CHICHESTER, Bart. [1641], of Raleigh aforesaid, and of Youlston, near Barnstaple, co. Devon, 2d but 1st surv. s. and h., *b.* about 1658, matric. at Oxford (Ex. Coll.), 8 May 1675, aged 17; *suc. to the Baronetcy* in 1677; admitted to Inner Temple, 1679. He *m.* (Lic. Vic. Gen., 4 Nov. 1679) Elizabeth, 1st da. of Sir Charles BICKERSTAFFE, of the Wilderness, in the parish of Sele, co. Kent, by Elizabeth, his wife. They *d.* s.p., both being taken ill the same day, and *bur.* 16 Sep. 1680, at Sele aforesaid, he aged 22 years and 3 months and she aged 21 years and 3 months. M.I. His will dat. 6 and pr. 11 Sep. 1680.

III. 1680. SIR ARTHUR CHICHESTER, Bart. [1641], of Youlston aforesaid, br. and h., *suc. to the Baronetcy* in Sep. 1680; M.P. for Barnstaple, 1685-87, 1689-90, 1713-15, and 1715 till death. He *m.* Elizabeth, da. of Thomas DREWE, of the Grange, Devon. He *d.* 3 Feb. 1717/8.

IV. 1718. SIR JOHN CHICHESTER, Bart. [1641], of Youlston aforesaid, s. and h., *bap.* 2 Jan. 1688/9; *suc. to the Baronetcy*, 3 Feb. 1717/8; M.P. for Barnstaple, 1734 till death. He *m.* firstly, in or before 1718, Anne, da. of John LEIGH, of Newport, in the Isle of Wight. She was *bur.* 16 July 1623, at Sherwell, co. Devon, aged 28. M.I. He *m.* secondly, Frances, who survived him. He *d.* 2 and was *bur.* 10 Sept. 1740, at Sherwell. Will dat. 4 Feb. 1736, pr. 22 Nov. 1740.

V. 1740. SIR JOHN CHICHESTER, Bart. [1641], of Youlston aforesaid, s. and h. by 1st wife, *bap.* 26 March 1721 at Sherwell; matric. at Oxford (Balliol Coll.) 13 April 1739, aged 18; *suc. to the Baronetcy*, 2 Aug. 1740; Sheriff of Devon, 1753-54. He *m.*, in or before 1752, Frances, 2d da. and coh. of Sir George CHUDLEIGH, 4th Bart. [1622], by Frances, da. and coh. of Sir William DAVIE, 4th Bart. [1641]. Her admon., 14 March 1752, to her said husband. He *d.* in London 18 and was *bur.* 30 Dec. 1784, at Ashton, near Exeter. Admon. Feb. 1785.

(a) *Vide* p. 116, note "a."

(b) This Robert was s. and h. of Sir John Chichester, yr. br. of (1) Arthur Chichester, Lord Deputy of Ireland, 1603, who was *cr.* BARON BELFAST [I.], 1612 (which Barony became *ex.* in 1624], and (2) of Edward Chichester, *cr.* VISCOUNT CHICHESTER [I.], who was ancestor of the EARLS AND MARQUESSES OF DONEGALL [I.]

VI. 1784. SIR JOHN CHICHESTER, Bart. [1641], of Youlston aforesaid, only s. and h., *b.* about 1752; matric. at Oxford (Mag. Coll.), 29 March 1771, aged 19; *suc. to the Baronetcy*, 18 Dec. 1784; Sheriff of Devon, 1788-89. He *d.* unm., at Wickham, co. Kent, 30 Sep. and was *bur.* 16 Oct. 1808, at Ashton aforesaid. Will pr. 1809.

VII. 1808. SIR ARTHUR CHICHESTER, Bart. [1641], of Youlston aforesaid, cousin and h. male, being s. and h. of John CHICHESTER, of Hart. (*d.* 1 Aug. 1800, aged 48), by Elizabeth, da. of (—) CORY, of Newton, which John was only s. of the Rev. William CHICHESTER, Rector of Georgeham and Sherwell, both co. Devon (*d.* Sep. 1770, aged 48), who was 2d and yst. s. of the 4th Bart., was *b.* 25 April 1790; *suc. to the Baronetcy*, 30 Sep. 1808; Sheriff of Devon, 1816-17. He *m.* 8 Sep. 1819, at Clovelly, Charlotte, youngest da. of Sir James HAMLYN-WILLIAMS, 2d Bart. [1795], by Diana Anne, da. of Abraham WHITAKER. She *d.* 18 and was *bur.* 25 Aug. 1834, at Sherwell, aged 36. M.I. He *d.* at Youlston 30 May, and was *bur.* 6 June 1842 at Sherwell, aged 52. Will pr. Aug. 1842 and Oct. 1843.

VIII. 1842. SIR ARTHUR CHICHESTER, Bart. [1641], of Youlston aforesaid, s. and h., *b.* there 4 Oct. 1822; ed. at Eton, *suc. to the Baronetcy*, 30 May 1842; Capt., 7th Dragoons, 1847; Lieut. Col. of North Devon Yeomanry Cavalry, 1862. He *m.* firstly, 20 Nov. 1847, Mary, 1st da. of John NICHOLETTS, of South Petherton, Somerset. She *d.* 28 June 1879 at Youlston. He *m.* secondly, 23 Jan. 1883, Rosalie, widow of Sir Alexander Palmer Bruce CHICHESTER, 2d Bart. [1840], of Arlington, Devon, da. of Thomas CHAMBERLAYNE, of Cranbury Park, Hants. He *d.* 13 July 1898 at Youlston, aged 75. Will pr. at £106,673 gross, and £4,831 net personalty. His widow living 1900.

IX. 1898. SIR EDWARD CHICHESTER, Bart. [1641], of Youlston aforesaid, 2d but 1st surv. s. and h., *b.* 20 Nov. 1849 and *bap.* 24 Jan. 1850 at Sherwell; entered the royal navy, served in the Egyptian campaign in 1882 (medal and bronze star); Capt., R.N., being transport officer in Natal, 1899; *suc. to the Baronetcy*, 13 July 1898; C.M.G., 1899; aide-de-camp to Queen Victoria, 1899. He *m.* 12 Oct. 1880, Catharine Emma, 1st da. of Robert Charles WHYTE, of Instow, Devon, Commander, R.N.

Family Estates.—These, in 1883, consisted of 7,022 acres in Devon, worth £6,051 a year. *Residence.*—Youlston, near Barnstaple, Devon.

BOUGHTON:

cr. 4 Aug. 1641;(a)

afterwards, since 1794, ROUSE-BOUGHTON.

I. 1641. "WILLIAM BOUGHTON of Lawford Parva, co. Warwick, Esq.," s. and h. of Edward Boughton, of the same, and of Hillmorton and Bilton in the same county, by Elizabeth, da. and h. of Edward CATESBY, of Lapworth Hall, co. Warwick, was *b.* about 1600; matric. at Oxford (Queen's Coll.), 28 April 1615, aged 15; admitted to Mid. Temple, 1617; suc. his father 9 Aug. 1625; was Sheriff of Warwickshire, 1633, and was *cr. a Baronet*, as above, 4 Aug. 1641.(a) He *m.* Abigail, 1st da. and coheir of Henry BAKER, of South Shoebury, Essex. She *d.* 21 Feb. 1634/5 and was *bur.* at Newbold upon Avon. M.I. He *d.* in 1656, and was *bur.* there, aged about 56. Will dat. 30 Aug. 1655, pr. 4 Dec. 1656.

II. 1656. SIR EDWARD BOUGHTON, Bart. [1641], of Lawford Hall in Lawford Parva aforesaid, s. and h., *b.* about 1628, *suc. to the Baronetcy* in 1656; was Sheriff of Warwickshire, 1660-61; M.P. thereof, 1678/9 and 1679 till death. He *m.* firstly, Mary, da. of Thomas (POPE), 3d EARL OF DOWNE [I.], by Beata, da. of Sir Henry Poole. She *d.* s.p. He *m.* secondly, Anne, da. of Sir John HEYDON, Governor of the Bermudas. He *d.* s.p. 1680, aged about 52. Will pr. Feb. 1681.

(a) *Vide* p. 116, note "a."

R

III. 1680. SIR WILLIAM BOUGHTON, Bart. [1641], of Lawford Hall aforesaid, br. and h., *b.* about 1632, *suc. to the Baronetcy* in 1680; was aged about 50 at the Visit. of Warwickshire in 1682. He *m.* Mary, da. of Hastings INGRAM, of Little Woolford, co. Warwick. He *d.* 12 Aug. 1683, aged 53, and was *bur.* at Newbold. Will pr. Aug. 1683. His widow *d.* 24 Feb. 1693 and was *bur.* there. M.I. Will pr. 1693.

IV. 1683. SIR WILLIAM BOUGHTON, Bart. [1641], of Lawford Hall aforesaid, s. and h., *b.* about 1663; matric. at Oxford (Mag. Coll.), 1 Dec. 1681, aged 17; *suc. to the Baronetcy*, 12 Aug. 1683; nom. Sheriff of Warwickshire, Nov. 1688, but did not act till April (to Nov.) 1689; M.P., for that county, 1712-13; is said to have declined being raised to the Peerage. He *m.* firstly (Lic. Vic. Gen., 28 Feb. 1684/5, he about 22, she about 16 and an orphan), Mary, da. of John RAMSEY, Alderman of London. She *d.* in or before July 1694; admon. 7 July 1694. He *m.* secondly, Catharine, da. of Sir Charles SHUCKBURGH, 2d Bart. [1660], by his 1st wife, Catharine, da. of Sir Hugh STEWKLEY, or STUKELEY, 2d Bart. [1627]. He *d.* 22 July 1716, aged 53, and was *bur.* at Newbold aforesaid. M.I. Will pr. Aug. 1716. His widow *d.* about 1725. Will pr. 1725.

V. 1716. SIR EDWARD BOUGHTON, Bart. [1641], of Lawford Hall aforesaid, s. and h., by 1st wife, *b.* about 1689, *suc. to the Baronetcy* 22 July 1716; Sheriff of Warwickshire, 1720-21. He *m.* about 1718, Grace, 1st da. of Sir John SHUCKBURGH, 3d Bart. [1660] (br. of the whole blood to his step-mother), by Abigail, da. of George GOODWIN. He *d.* 12 Feb. 1721/2, aged 33. Will pr. 1722. His widow *m.*, in or before 1723, Matthew LISTER, of Burwell, co. Lincoln. She *d.* before him, Feb. and was *bur.* 4 March 1779, at Burwell, aged 77.

VI. 1722. SIR EDWARD BOUGHTON, Bart. [1641], of Lawford Hall aforesaid, s. and h., *b.* about 1719, *suc. to the Baronetcy*, 12 Feb. 1721/2; matric. at Oxford (Mag. Coll.), 22 July 1736, aged 17; Sheriff for Warwickshire, 1748-49. He *m.* firstly, after 1741, (—), da. of (—) BRIDGES, of co. Somerset. She *d.* s.p. He *m.* secondly, in or before 1760, Anna Maria, da. and coheir of John BEAUCHAMP, of co. Warwick. He *d.* suddenly 3 March 1772 and was *bur.* at Newbold. Will dat. 3 May 1759, pr. 22 May 1772. His widow, who was living 1781, *d.* at Bath in or before 1787. Admon. Sep. 1787.

VII. 1772. SIR THEODOSIUS EDWARD ALLESLEY BOUGHTON, Bart. [1641], of Lawford Hall aforesaid, s. and h., by 2d wife, *b.* Aug. 1760, *suc. to the Baronetcy*, 3 March 1772. He *d.* a minor and unm., 29 Aug. 1780, aged 20, at Lawford Hall, having been poisoned by "laurel water," administered to him by his sister's husband, Capt. John Donellan.(a) He was *bur.* in the family vault at Newbold. Will pr. 1780.

VIII. 1780. SIR EDWARD BOUGHTON, Bart. [1641], of Lawford Hall aforesaid, and of Poston Court, co. Hereford cousin and h. male, being s. and h. of Shuckburgh BOUGHTON, of Poston Court aforesaid, by Mary, da. of the Hon. Algernon GREVILLE, 2d s. of Fulke, 5th BARON BROOKE OF BEAUCHAMP'S COURT, which Shuckburgh Boughton (who *d.* 1763, aged 60) was s. of the 4th Bart., by his 2d wife, Catherine, da. of Sir Charles SHUCKBURGH, 2d Bart. [1660]. He was *b.* about 1742; *suc. to the Baronetcy*, 29 Aug. 1780; pulled down Lawford Hall and sold most of the estates in Warwickshire and Leicestershire to enlarge those at Poston Court,

(a) Donellan was executed for murder, at Warwick, 2 April 1781, the trial having caused the greatest sensation. He had *m.*, in June 1777, Theodosia Beauchamp, only sister and (by this murder) sole heir of the unfortunate Baronet, by whom he had a son and a daughter, both of whom took the name of Beauchamp (being that of their maternal grandmother, Lady Boughton) in lieu of Donellan, and died unm. (See order of the Lord Chancellor, 21 Nov. 1816, in "Hume *v.* King *et al.*") The widow *m.* secondly, Sir Egerton Leigh, 2d Bart. [1772]. She *m.* thirdly, 10 Feb. 1823, Barry E. O'Meara, surgeon R.N. (the attendant of Napoleon at St. Helena), who survived her. She *d.* 14 Jan. 1830.

etc., in Herefordshire, which had been purchased by his father. He was Sheriff for Herefordshire, 1786-87. He *d.* unm. s.p. legit.(a) 26 Feb. 1794, in his 53d year, and was *bur.* in Vow church, co. Hereford. Will pr. April 1794.

IX. 1794. / I. 1791. SIR CHARLES WILLIAM ROUSE-BOUGHTON, Bart. [1641] *formerly* BOUGHTON-ROUSE, Bart. [1791], of Rouse Lench, near Evesham, co. Worcester, and of Downton Hall, near Ludlow, Salop, br. and h., was *b.* in the parish of St. Nicholas, Worcester. In 1765 he went to India in the Bengal Civil Service, and was a Judge in several Courts there. In 1769 he took the name of ROUSE after that of BOUGHTON on succeeding to the estates of the Rouse family at Rouse Lench abovenamed.(b) M.P. for Evesham, 1780-84, and 1784-90, and for Bramber, 1796-99. Secretary to the Board of Control for Indian Affairs, 1784 to 1791. On 13 May 1791 he obtained a Royal lic. to use the name of Rouse either *before* or *after* that of Boughton, and a few days afterwards, 28 July 1791, was *cr. a Baronet* under the surname of BOUGHTON-ROUSE (the mode in which, since 1769, the names had been used), and the description "of Rouse Lench, co. Worcester, and Downton Hall, co. Salop." When, however, on 26 Feb. 1794, he *suc. to the* more ancient (1641) *Baronetcy* of Boughton (though to none of the family estates), he transposed the order of these names to ROUSE-BOUGHTON. In 1799 he was one of the Commissioners for auditing public accounts. He was also Commander of the Chiswick Volunteers. He *m.* 3 June 1782, at St. James', Westm., Catharine, da. and h. of William PEARCE, *otherwise* HALL, of Downton Hall aforesaid, which estate she inherited. She *d.* 14 Aug. 1808. He *d.* 26 Feb. 1821, in Devonshire place, Marylebone. Will pr. March 1821. Both were *bur.* at Rouse Lench.

X. and II. 1821. SIR WILLIAM EDWARD ROUSE-BOUGHTON, Bart. [1641 and 1791], of Rouse Lench and of Downton Hall aforesaid, only s. and h., *b.* 14 Sep. 1788, in Lower Grosvenor street; matric. at Oxford (Ch. Ch.), 21 Jan. 1806, aged 17; B.A., 1808; M.P. for Evesham, 1818-19 and 1820-26; *suc. to the Baronetcies*, 26 Feb. 1821; F.R.S. He *m.* 24 March 1824, at St. Marylebone, Charlotte, yst. of the three daughters and coheirs of Thomas Andrew KNIGHT, of Downton Castle, co. Hereford (*d.* 11 May 1838, in his 80th year), by Frances, da. of H. FELTON. She *d.* 14 May 1842, aged 41, at Downton Hall. He *d.* 22 May 1856, aged 67. Will pr. Aug. 1856. Both were *bur.* at Rouse Lench.

XI. and III. 1856. SIR CHARLES HENRY ROUSE-BOUGHTON, Bart. [1641 and 1791], of Downton Hall aforesaid, s. and h., *b.* 16 Jan. 1825, at Henley Hall, near Ludlow, and *bap.* at Bitterley, Salop; ed. at Harrow; an officer in the 52d foot, 1843-50; *suc. to the Baronetcies*, 22 May 1856; Capt. 10th Shropshire Rifle Volunteers, 1860; Sheriff for Salop, 1860. He *m.* 23 Aug. 1852, at Thenford, co. Northampton, Mary Caroline, 2d da. of John Michael SEVERNE, of Thenford aforesaid and of Wallop Hall, Salop, by Anna Maria, da. of Edmund Meysey WIGLEY, of Shakenhurst, co. Worcester. She was *b.* 12 Dec. 1832.

Family Estates.—These, in 1883, consisted of 5,456 acres in Shropshire, valued at £7,645 a year; in 1878 the amount was 4,891 acres in Shropshire, and 14 (valued at £58 a year) in Herefordshire; it being added that "the return mentions some property in Worcestershire, since sold," the total, at that date, being 4,905 acres, valued at £6,000 a year; in 1876 the amount stands as 4,891 acres in Shropshire, 2,325 (valued at £3,170) in Worcestershire, and 14 in Herefordshire, the total (at that date) being 7,230 acres, valued at £9,170 a year. *Residence.*—Downton Hall, near Ludlow, Salop.

(a) His illegit. da., Eliza, *m.* Sir George Charles Braithwaite, 2d Bart. [1802], who took the name of Boughton.

(b) These estates came to him, 30 Dec. 1768, under the will of his cousin, Thomas Phillips-Rouse (formerly Thomas Phillips) of Rouse Lench aforesaid; see p. 108, note "c."

WOLRYCHE :

cr. 4 Aug. 1641(a) ;

ex. 25 June 1723.

I. 1641. "THOMAS WOLRYCHE, of Dudmaston, co. Salop, Knt.," s. and h. of Francis WOLRYCHE, of the same, by Margaret, da. of George BROMLEY, of Hatton, in the said county, was *b.* at Worfield in 1598 ; suc. his father in 1614 ; ed. at Cambridge Univ. ; admitted to Inner Temple, 11 Oct. 1615 ; M.P. for Wenlock, 1621-22, 1624-25 and 1625 ; was Col. in the Royal Army, during the Civil Wars ; a zealous supporter of the King by whom he was made Governor of Bridgnorth ; was *Knighted* at Whitehall, 22 July 1641, and *cr. a Baronet*, as above, 4 Aug. 1641. He was twice sequestered, once imprisoned and was, 11 March 1647, fined £730. He *m.*, in or before 1628, Ursula, da. of Thomas OTLEY, of Pichford, Salop, by Mary, da. of Roger GIFFORD, M.D., Physician to Queen Elizabeth. He *d.* 4 and was *bur.* 9 July 1668 at St. Chad's, Shrewsbury, in his 71st year. M.I. at Quatt, co. Salop. Will dat. 21 Dec. 1662 to 2 Feb. 1662/3, pr. 7 Nov. 1668, by Ursula, his widow.

II. 1668. SIR FRANCIS WOLRYCHE, Bart. [1641], of Dudmaston aforesaid, s. and h., *b.* about 1627, was aged 35 in 1663 [*Visit. of Salop*]; *suc. to the Baronetcy*, 4 July 1668. He *m.* Elizabeth, 1st da. of Sir Walter WROTTESLEY, 1st Bart. [1642], by Mary, da. of Ambrose GREY, of Enville, co. Stafford. He *d.* s.p.m. 12 and was *bur.* 15 June 1688 at Quatt, in his 62d year. M.I. Admon. 3 Sep. 1689. The will of his widow dat. 7 April 1711, pr. 2 May 1713.

III. 1688. SIR THOMAS WOLRYCHE, Bart. [1642], of Dudmaston aforesaid nephew and h. male, being 1st s. and h. of John WOLRYCHE, of Dudmaston, by Mary, da. of the Rev. Matthew GRIFFITH, D.D., Chaplain to Charles I, which John (who was *cr.* D.C.L. of Oxford 1670, and who *d.* before June 1688, his admon. being dat. 8 April 1690) was yr. s. of the 1st Bart. He was *bap.* 14 April 1672, at Quatt and *suc. to the Baronetcy*, 12 June 1688. He *m.* 26 Nov. 1689, Elizabeth, 1st da. of George WELD, of Willey, Salop, Lieut. of the Tower, by Mary, da. of Sir Peter PINDAR, 1st Bart. [1662]. He *d.* 3 and was *bur.* 6 May 1701, at Quatt, aged 29. M.I. His widow (who survived him 64 years) *d.* 1 and was *bur.* 5 April 1765, at Quatt, aged 93. M.I. Will dat. 12 June 1753, pr. 26 April 1765.

IV. 1701, to 1723. SIR JOHN WOLRYCHE, Bart. [1641], of Dudmaston aforesaid, only s. and h., *b.* about 1691, *suc. to the Baronetcy*, 3 May 1701 Sheriff of Salop, 1715-16. He *d.* unm., being drowned in the Severn while endeavouring to cross it on horseback, 25 and was *bur.* 26 June 1723, at Quatt, aged 32, when the *Baronetcy* became *extinct*. M.I. Will dat. 15 Aug. 1722, pr. 26 July 1723.(b)

PRYSE, *or* PRICE :

cr. 9 Aug. 1641 ;(c)

ex. 1694.

I. 1641. "RICHARD PRYSE, of Gogarthan [*i.e.*, Gogerddan], co. Cardigan, Knt.," s. and h. of Sir John PRYSE, of the same, by Mary, da. of Sir Henry BROMLEY, of Shawardine Castle, co. Salop, was, having previously (after 1639) been *Knighted*, *cr. a Baronet*, as above, 9 Aug. 1641.(c) He was

(a) The patent is not enrolled. The date here given is that in Dugdale's *Catalogue*. See *Memorandum* on p. 84. The date of the signet bill is 2 August 1641.

(b) The Dudmaston estates were held by his mother and sisters till the death of the survivor of the latter, Mary Wolryche, spinster, 21 June 1771, in her 78th year, under whose will they devolved for 4 years on Lieut. Col. Thomas Weld, and, at his death in 1774, on William Whitmore, great grandson of Richard Whitmore, of Slaughter, co. Gloucester, by Anne, sister of George Weld, her maternal grandfather. In that family (which has no descent from that of Wolryche) they still remain.

(c) The patent is not enrolled. The date here given is that in Dugdale's *Catalogue* See *Memorandum* on p. 84. The date of the signet bill is 5 August 1641.

Sheriff of Cardiganshire, 1639-40 ; was M.P. thereof, Aug. 1646, till secluded in Dec. 1648. He *m.* firstly, Hester, 5th da. of the well known Sir Hugh MIDDLETON, 1st Bart. [1622], by his 2d wife, Elizabeth, da. and coheir of John OLMSTEAD. She was *bap.* 10 Jan. 1612/3, at St. Matthew's, Friday street, London. He *m.* secondly, Mary, widow of Sir Anthony VANDYKE (the famous painter, who *d.* Dec. 1641), da. of the Hon. Patrick RUTHVEN, yr. s. of William, 1st EARL OF GOWRIE [S.]. She *d.* before him. Her admon. 8 May 1651 and 12 Jan. 1651/2. He was *bur.* 21 Oct. 1651 in Westm. Abbey. Admon. 27 Nov. 1651.

II. 1651. SIR RICHARD PRYSE, Bart. [1641], of Gogerddan aforesaid, 1st s. and h. by 1st wife ; *suc. to the Baronetcy* in Oct. 1651; was Sheriff of Cardiganshire, 1656-57. He *d.* s.p. and probably unm.

III. 1680? SIR THOMAS PRYSE, Bart. [1641], of Gogerddan aforesaid, br. of the whole blood and h. ; was Sheriff of Cardiganshire (as "Esq.") 1675-76 ; *suc. to the Baronetcy* on the death of his brother. He *d.* s.p., probably unm., in May 1682. Will pr. 1682.

IV. 1682, to 1694. SIR CARBERY PRYSE, Bart. [1641], of Gogerddan aforesaid, nephew and h., being only s. and h. of Carbery PRYSE, by Hester, da. of Sir Bulstrode WHITLOCK, which Carbery last named was yr. br., of the whole blood, to the 3d and 2d Barts., *suc. to the Baronetcy* in May 1682. In 1690, mines of immense value were discovered on his estate, as to the working of which he obtained two acts of Parl. He *d.* s.p., probably unm., in 1694, when the *Baronetcy* became *extinct*.(a). Will pr. Jan. 1694 [1694/5 ?], revoked and admon. granted, 8 Aug. 1696, to his mother, Hester SCAWEN, *alias* PRYSE.

CAREW :

cr. 9 Aug. 1641(b) ;

ex., presumably, 24 March 1748 ;

but *assumed* after that date.

I. 1641. "RICHARD CAREW, of Antony, co. Cornwall, Esq.," s. and h. of Richard CAREW, of the same (the celebrated antiquary and the author of the "Survey of Cornwall"), by Julian, da. of John ARUNDELL, of Trerice, co. Cornwall, was *b.* about 1580; matric. at Oxford (Merton Coll.), 20 Oct. 1594, aged 14 ; admitted to Middle Temple, 1597 ; suc. his father, 6 Nov. 1620 ; was M.P. for Cornwall, 1614, and for St. Michael's, 1621-22, and was *cr. a Baronet*, as above, 9 Aug. 1641.(b) He *m.* firstly, in or before 1609, Bridget, da. of John CHUDLEIGH, of Ashton, Devon, by Elizabeth, da. of Sir George SPEKE. He *m.* secondly, 18 Aug. 1621, at Petrockstowe, Grace, da. of Robert ROLLE, of Heanton, Devon, by Joane, da. of Thomas HELE, of Fleet, in that county. He was *bur.* 14 March 1642/3 [presumably] at Antony aforesaid.

II. 1643. SIR ALEXANDER CAREW, Bart. [1641], of Antony aforesaid, s. and h. by 1st wife, *b.* 30 Aug. and *bap.* 1 Sep. 1609 at Antony, being aged 10 at the Visit. of Devon, 1620 ; M.P. for Cornwall, 1640, till disabled 4 Sep. 1643, and, at that time, a great supporter of the Parl. measures ; *suc. to the Baronetcy*, 14 March 1642/3. He agreed to surrender the isle of St. Nicholas, near Plymouth, to the royal forces, but was discovered, committed to the Tower of London, 5 Dec. 1643, and condemned "for adhering to the King and betraying his trust" and was executed on Tower Hill, 23 Dec. 1644, being *bur.* the same day at Hackney, aged 35. His estate was freed from sequestration, 27 Nov. 1645. Will dat.

(a) The estates passed eventually to his kinsmen of the name of Pryse, of whom Lewis Pryse *d.* s.p.m.s. 12 March 1798, leaving Pryse Loveden (son of his da. Margaret) as his grandson and heir, who assumed the surname of Pryse, and whose grandson was *cr. a Baronet* in 1866.

(b) See p. 124, note "c," *sub* "Pryse."

20 to 22 and pr. 28 Dec. 1644. He had *m.*, 17 Dec. 1631 at Petrockstowe (Lic. Exeter), Jane, sister of Grace Rolle abovenamed, being da. of Robert ROLLE, by Joan, da. of Thomas HELE, all abovenamed. His widow, who was *bap.* 25 Jan. 1605/6, at Petrockstowe, was *bur.* 28 April 1679 at Antony. Will dat. 18 Nov. 1678, pr. 3 Nov. 1679.

III. 1644. SIR JOHN CAREW, Bart. [1641], of Antony aforesaid, s. and h., *b.* about 1633, *suc. to the Baronetcy*, 23 Dec. 1644 ; M.P. for Cornwall, 1660, for Bodmin, 1661-79, for Lostwithiel, 1679, 1679-81 and 1681 ; for Cornwall, again, 1689-90, and for Saltash, 1690 till death ; el. Sheriff of Cornwall, Nov. 1688, but did not act. He *m.* firstly, before 8 Aug. 1664, Sarah, da. of Anthony HUNGERFORD, of Farley Castle, Wilts. She, who was living at that date, *d.* s.p.m.(a) He *m.* secondly, Elizabeth, 1st da. of Richard NORTON, of Southwick, Hants. She, who *d.* s.p., was *bur.* 14 Aug. 1679 at Antony. He *m.* thirdly, in or before 1682, Mary, da. of Sir William MORICE, 1st Bart. [1661], of Werrington, by Gertrude, da. of Sir John BAMFYLDE, 1st Bart. [1641]. He was *bur.* 6 Aug. 1692, at Antony. Will dat. 29 Oct. 1691, pr. 7 Dec. 1692. His widow was *bur.* there, 8 June 1698.

IV. 1692. SIR RICHARD CAREW, Bart. [1641], of Antony aforesaid, s. and h., by 3d wife, *bap.* 2 March 1683, at Antony, *suc. to the Baronetcy* in Aug. 1692. He *d.* unm. in 1703 or 1704. Will dat. 24 June, 1703, pr. 9 May 1704.

V. 1704? SIR WILLIAM CAREW, Bart. [1641], of Antony aforesaid, br. of the whole blood and h., *b.* about 1689; matric. at Oxford (Ex. Coll.) 4 Sep. 1707, aged 18, having previously *suc. to the Baronetcy* ; was M.P. for Saltash 1711-13, and for Cornwall (six Parls.) 1713 till death ; was *cr.* D.C.L. of Oxford, 22 May 1736. He *m.* (Lic. Worc., 31 Dec. 1713, he 24 and she 18) Anne only da. and h. of Gilbert (COVENTRY), 4th EARL OF COVENTRY, by his 1st wife, Dorothy, da. of Sir William KEYT, 2d Bart. [1660]. She *d.* before him. He *d.* 8 March 1743/4. Admon. 27 April 1744, 11 Aug. 1750, and 22 Dec. 1762.

VI. 1744, to 1748. SIR COVENTRY CAREW, Bart. [1641], of Antony aforesaid, only s. and h., *b.* about 1717; matric. at Oxford (Balliol Coll.) 21 Feb. 1734/5, aged 18 ; *suc. to the Baronetcy*, 8 March 1743/4 ; was M.P. for Cornwall 1744 till death. He *m.* 1 July 1738 at St. George the Martyr, Queen Square, Midx., his cousin, Mary, only da. of Sir Coplestone Warwick BAMFYLDE, 2d Bart., [1641] by Gertrude, sister of the whole blood of Sir William CAREW, 5th Bart., abovenamed. He *d.* s.p. 24 March 1748, when the *Baronetcy* probably became *extinct*. Will pr. 1748. His widow *m.* before 1750 Francis BULLER, of Morval, Cornwall (who *d.* s.p. 1766) and *d.* before Dec. 1762. Will pr. 1763.

According to Burke's *Extinct Baronetage*, on the death, in 1748, of the 6th Bart. the Baronetcy reverted to his kinsman.

SIR ALEXANDER CAREW, (who was "in Holy Orders") in right of his descent from "Thomas CAREW, of Harrowbear, 2d s. of Sir Alexander, the 2d Bart.," and that at his death without issue it became extinct.

This, apparently, is a mistake. Thomas Carew, abovenamed, had, by Wilmot his wife, two sons, of whom the yr. son, John Carew, living 1691, *d.* s.p., while the elder son, Alexander, living 1678 and 1691, who was in Holy Orders and Vicar of St. Wenn, *d.* (also) s.p. in 1709.(b) This Alexander appears to be the person presumed (erroneously) to be living in 1748, and consequently then entitled to the Baronetcy. Sir Thomas Carew, of Barley, co. Devon (a yr. s. of the 1st Bart. by his 2d wife), had by Elizabeth, da. of John Cooper, several children, on some of whose descendants, if such there were, the Baronetcy is more likely to have devolved.

(a) Jane, her eldest da., *m.* Jonathan Rashleigh, whose da. and h., Sarah, *m.* the Rev Carolus Pole and was grandmother of Reginald Pole who, after the death, s.p.m., of John Carew, of Camerton, inherited the estate of Antony and took the name of Carew (under the will of the 6th Bart.), being ancestor of the family of Pole-Carew.

(b) Vivian's *Visitations of Cornwall*.

CASTLETON :

cr. 9 Aug. 1641 ; (a)

ex. 17 Nov. 1810.

I. 1641. "WILLIAM CASTLETON, of St. Edmondsbury, co. Suffolk, Esq.," s. and h. of William CASTLETON, of the same and of Clopton Hall in Woolpit and Rattlesden in that co., by Anne, da. of William HILL, of St. Edmundsbury aforesaid, was *b.* about 1590 ; *suc.* his father 24 May 1616, being then aged 26, and was *cr. a Baronet*, as above, 9 Aug. 1641 ;(a) Sheriff of Suffolk, 1641-42. He *m.* (—), widow of (—) BACON, of Hesset, co. Suffolk, da. of (—) MASSAM, of the said county. He *d.* about 1643.

II. 1643? SIR JOHN CASTLETON, Bart. [1641], of Shipdam, co. Norfolk, and of Sturston, co. Suffolk, s. and h., *suc. to the Baronetcy* about 1643 ; Sheriff of Suffolk, 1660-61. He *m.* 26 April 1642, at Sturston,(b) Margaret, da. and h. of Robert MORSE, of Hoo Margarets in Sturston aforesaid, by Margaret, da. of Henry BEDINGFIELD. He was *bur.* 20 Nov. 1677 at Sturston. His widow was *bur.* there 12 Aug. 1702.

III. 1677. SIR JOHN CASTLETON, Bart. [1641], of Sturston Hall, in Sturston aforesaid, s. and h. ; *bap.* 4 Aug. 1644, at Sturston ; ed. at Botesdale and Eye schools; admitted to Caius Coll., Cambridge, as Fellow Commoner, 29 June 1661, aged 16 ; admitted to Gray's Inn, 2 May 1662 ; *suc. to the Baronetcy* in Nov. 1677 ; el. Sheriff of Suffolk, in Nov. 1686, but did not act. He *m.* 8 Nov. 1677, at Bardwell, Suffolk, Bridget, sister of Sir Charles CROFTS READ, of Bardwell, da. of Thomas READ, of Wrangle, co. Lincoln, by Bridget, da. of Sir Charles CROFTS, of Bardwell aforesaid. He *d.* s.p. and was *bur.* 14 June 1705, at Sturston. Will pr. March 1706. His widow, who was *bap.* at Bardwell, 3 Jan. 1649/50, was *bur.* 24 March 1726, at Sturston aforesaid.

IV. 1705. SIR ROBERT CASTLETON, Bart. [1641], of Sturston Hall aforesaid, br. and h. ; *bap.* 6 Nov. 1659, at Sturston ; *suc. to the Baronetcy* in June 1705. He *d.* unm.

V. 1710? SIR PHILIP CASTLETON, Bart. [1641], of Sturston Hall aforesaid, br. and h. ; *bap.* 26 July 1663, at Sturston ; *suc. to the Baronetcy* on the death of his brother. He *m.* 6 May 1708, at Sturston, Elizabeth, da. of Osborn CLARKE, of that place. He *d.* s.p.s. and was *bur.* 1 Aug. 1724, at Sturston, aged 61. His widow was *bur.* there 13 Nov. 1748.

VI. 1724. SIR CHARLES CASTLETON, Bart. [1641], Rector of Gillingham, Norfolk, cousin and h., being surv. s. and h. of William CASTLETON, of Oakley, co. Suffolk, by Sarah, da. of (—) SIDNEY, *or* SYDNOR,(c) which William was 2d s. of the 1st Bart. He was *bap.* at Sturston, 4 Sep. 1659 ; ed. at Thetford and Bury schools ; admitted to Caius Coll., Cambridge, as sizar, 16 April 1678, aged 18 ; scholar, 1678-83 ; B.A., 1682 ; M.A., 1685 ; took Holy Orders ; Rector of Gillingham aforesaid, 1692-1745 ; *suc. to the Baronetcy*, 1 Aug. 1724. He *m.* in 1693, Elizabeth, 2d da. of Edward TAVERNER, of St. Olave's Abbey, in Heringfleet, Suffolk. He *d.* Sep. 1745, aged 86.

VII. 1745. SIR CHARLES CASTLETON, Bart. [1641], s. and h. ; *suc. to the Baronetcy* in Sep. 1745 and *d.* unm. 22 Oct. 1749.

(a) The patent is not enrolled. The date here given is that in Dugdale's *Catalogue*. See *Memorandum* on p. 84. The date of the signet bill is 7 August 1641.

(b) There are copious extracts from the Parish Register of Sturston in the *East Anglian*, vol. iii, which illustrate this pedigree.

(c) They were *m.* 7 Aug. 1655, at Sturston.

VIII. 1749. SIR JOHN CASTLETON, Bart. [1641], Vicar of Gorleston and Hopton, Suffolk, br. and h.; *b.* about 1698, at Gillingham; ed. at Woodbridge school; admitted, as sizar, to Caius Coll., Cambridge, Oct. 1715, aged 18; scholar, 1715-20; B.A. 1720. In Holy Orders; Vicar of Gorleston, Suffolk, 1722-77; Vicar of Hopton in said county, 1725-77; *suc. to the Baronetcy,* 22 Oct. 1749. He *m.* but *d.* s.p., 7 Nov. 1777. M.I. at Gorleston to him and his wife.

IX. 1777, SIR WILLIAM CASTLETON, Bart. [1641], br. and h., *b.* about 1701, *suc. to the Baronetcy,* 7 Nov. 1777. He *m.* (—) He *d.* at Hingham, Norfolk, 16 Jan. 1788, aged 87.

X. 1788, Jan. SIR JOHN CASTLETON, Bart. [1641], only s. and h., *suc. to the Baronetcy,* 16 Jan. 1788, and *d.* s.p. a few months later, 11 June 1788.

XI. 1788. June. SIR EDWARD CASTLETON, Bart. [1641], Rector of Thornham cum Holme, Norfolk, uncle and h., *b.* about 1706 at Gillingham, ed. at Beccles and Woodbridge schools, admitted as Sizar to Caius Coll., Cambridge 1725, aged 18; B.A., 1729; in Holy Orders; Rector of Thornham aforesaid, 1761-94; *suc. to the Baronetcy,* 11 June 1788. He *m.* (—). He *d.* 15 Oct. 1794 in his 89th year. M.I. at Ringstead.

XII. 1794, to 1810. SIR EDWARD CASTLETON, Bart. [1641], of Lynn, Norfolk, s. and h., *suc. to the Baronetcy,* 15 Oct. 1794, but being in reduced circumstances, did not for some time assume the title. He *d.* s.p. 17 Nov. 1810, aged 58, when the *Baronetcy* became *extinct.* Will pr. 1810.

CHOLMLEY, *or* CHOLMELEY:

cr. 10 Aug. 1641(a);

ex. 9 Jan. 1688/9.

I. 1641 "HUGH CHOLMELEY, of Whitby, co. York, Knt.," s. and h. of Sir Richard CHOLMELEY, *or* CHOLMLEY, of the same,(b) by his 1st wife Susanna, da. of John LEGARD, of Ganton, co. York, was *b.* 22 July 1600, at Roxby, near Thornton; *Knighted* at Whitehall, 29 May 1626; suc. his father (who *d.* aged 51), 3 Sept. 1631; was M.P. for Scarborough, 1624-25, 1625, 1626, April to May 1640, and 1640 till disabled in April 1643, and was *cr. a Baronet,* as above, 10 Aug. 1641.(a) He was, in 1643, "for the public liberties," and fought against the Royalists at Malton and Gainsborough, but in that year declared for the King, by whom he was made General of the Northern parts of England and Governor of Scarborough Castle, which he held for more than a year and only surrendered on highly honourable terms in 1645. His estate was sequestrated and he went into exile until he compounded for £850 on 27 June 1649.(c) He *m.* 10 Dec. 1622, at St. Mary Magdalen, Milk Street, London, Elizabeth, 1st da. of Sir William TWYSDEN, 1st Bart. [1611], of Peckham, by Anne, da. of Sir Moyle FINCH, 1st Bart. [1611]. She, with whom he had £3,000 portion, was *b.* 18 Aug. 1600, *d.* 17 April 1655, in Bedford Street, Covent Garden in her 55th year. He d. 20 Nov. 1657 in his 58th year. Both were *bur.* at East Peckham, co. Kent. M.I. His will pr. Nov. 1660.

II. 1657. SIR WILLIAM CHOLMLEY, *or* CHOLMELEY, Bart. [1641], of Whitby Abbey in Whitby aforesaid, s. and h., *b.* Dec. 1625 and *bap.* at East Peckham, Kent, *suc. to the Baronetcy,* 20 Nov. 1657. He *m.* firstly, 17 Aug. 1654, Katharine, yst. da. of Sir John HOTHAM, 1st Bart. [1622], by his 5th wife, Sarah, da. of Thomas ANLABY, of Etton, co. York. She *d.* s.p.s. in childbed, 15 June

(a) The patent is not enrolled. The date here given is that in Dugdale's *Catalogue.* See *Memorandum* on p. 84. The date of the signet bill is 7 Aug. 1641.

(b) In *Mis. Gen. et Her.,* Orig. Series, vol. ii, p. 218, is a good account of this family.

(c) One hundred copies of his life and adventures, with particulars of his family (from a MS. in his handwriting, in possession of Nathaniel Cholmley, of Whitby and Howsham, in 1787) were printed in 1870.

1655 and was *bur.* at Whitby. He *m.* secondly, April 1657, Katharine, da. of John SAVILE, of Methley, co. York, by his 2d wife, Margaret, da. of Sir Henry GARRAWAY, Alderman, and sometime, 1639-40, Lord Mayor of London. He *d.* at Mitcham, co. Surrey, 11 Oct. 1663, and was *bur.* at East Peckham aforesaid. M.I. Nunc. will dat. 11 Oct., pr. 13 Nov. 1663. His widow *m.* after July 1665, Sir Nicholas STRODE, of Chipsted House, Kent, and *d.* in 1710.

III. 1663. SIR HUGH CHOLMLEY, Bart. [1641], of Whitby Abbey aforesaid, only s. and h., *suc. to the Baronetcy,* 11 Oct. 1663. He *d.* in infancy at Mitcham, Surrey, 2 July 1665, aged 3 years, and was *bur.* at East Peckham aforesaid. M.I. Admon. 28 July 1665.

IV. 1665, to 1689. SIR HUGH CHOLMLEY, Bart. [1641], of Whitby Abbey aforesaid, uncle and h., *b.* 21 July 1632 at Fyling Hall, co. York, *suc. to the Baronetcy,* 2 July 1665. In 1665 he was Governor of Tangier, in Morocco, where he resided many years and directed the building of the mole there; was M.P. for Northampton, 1679; for Thirsk, 1685-87. He *m.* 19 Feb. 1665/6, at Hamerton, co. Hunt., Anne, 1st da. of Spencer (COMPTON), 2d EARL OF NORTHAMPTON, by Mary, da. of Sir Francis BEAUMONT. He *d.* s.p.m.(a) at Whitby 9 Jan. 1688/9, aged 56, when the *Baronetcy* became *extinct.* His widow *d.* there 26 May 1705, aged 68. Both were *bur.* in Whitby Church.

SPRING:

cr. 11 August 1641(b);

ex. 17 August 1769.

I. 1641. "WILLIAM SPRING, of Pakenham, co. Suffolk, Esq.," 2d but only surv. s. and h. of Sir William SPRING,(c) of the same, by Elizabeth, sister of Sir Thomas SMITH, 1st Bart. [1661] of Hill Hall, da. of Sir William SMITH, of Theydon, co. Essex, was *bap.* 13 March 1613, at Stanton All Saints; suc. his father, 1638; was Sheriff of Suffolk, 1640-41, and was *cr. a Baronet,* as above, 11 Aug. 1641.(b) He was a Parliamentarian, serving on several important committees, 1643-46; was M.P. for Bury St. Edmunds, 1646 till secluded, Dec. 1648; for Suffolk, 1654 till death in that year. He *m.,* in or before 1642, Elizabeth, sister of Sir Nicholas L'ESTRANGE, 1st Bart. [1629], da. of Sir Hamon L'ESTRANGE, of Hunstanton, co. Norfolk, by Alice, da. and coheir of Richard STUBBS. He *d.* 17 Dec. 1654, and was *bur.* at Pakenham. Will dat. 18 Oct. 1653, pr. 1655. His widow, who was *b.* 10 March 1613, *d.* 21 March 1678, and was *bur.* there.

II. 1654. SIR WILLIAM SPRING, Bart. [1641], of Pakenham aforesaid, 1st and only surv. s. and h., *b.* May 1642; *suc. to the Baronetcy,* 17 Dec. 1654. Sheriff of Suffolk, 1674-75; M.P. thereof, 1679-81 and 1681. He *m.* firstly (Lic. Fac., 11 Oct. 1661, both aged 21), Mary, da. of Dudley (NORTH), 4th LORD NORTH DE KIRTLING, by Anne, da. of Sir Charles MONTAGU. She *d.,* in childbirth, 23 Oct. 1662 and was *bur.* at Pakenham. He *m.* secondly, in or before 1670, Sarah, da. of Sir Robert CORDELL, 1st Bart. [1660], by Margaret, da. and coheir of Sir Edmund WRIGHT. He *d.* 30 April and was *bur.* 3 May 1684, at Pakenham. Will pr. 1684. His widow *d.* 2 Aug. 1689 and was *bur.* there.

(a) Mary, the only child that survived infancy, *b.* 21 Sep. 1667, *m.,* for her first husband, 16 Oct. 1683, at Whitby, her cousin, Nathaniel Cholmley, of London, merchant, who *d.* 20 April 1687 (in her father's lifetime), by whom she was ancestress of the family of Cholmley, of Whitby and Howsham, co. York, extinct in the male line, March 1791.

(b) The patent is not enrolled. The date here given is that in Dugdale's *Catalogue.* See *Memorandum* on p. 84. The date of the signet bill is 7 Aug. 1641.

(c) In J. J. Howard's *Visitations of the County of Suffolk* (vol. i, pp. 166-206) is a good account of this family.

III. 1684. SIR THOMAS SPRING, Bart. [1641], of Pakenham aforesaid, 1st surv. s. and h., by 2d wife, *b.* 1 and *bap.* 12 Dec. 1672, at Pakenham, *suc. to the Baronetcy,* 30 April 1684. He *m.* 28 May 1691, at Rushbrooke, co. Suffolk, Merolina, 5th da. and coheir of Thomas (JERMYN), 2d BARON JERMYN OF ST. EDMUNDSBURY, by Mary, da. of Henry MERRY. He *d.* 5 and was *bur.* 6 April 1704, at Pakenham, aged 31. Admon. 20 Sep. 1710 and 28 Nov. 1727. His widow *m.* as his 2d wife, Sir William GAGE, 2d Bart. [1662] of Hengrave, co. Suffolk, who *d.* 8 Feb. 1726/7. She *d.* at Hengrave and was *bur.* 5 Sep. 1727, at Pakenham. Admon. 28 Nov. 1727.

IV. 1704. SIR WILLIAM SPRING, Bart. [1641], of Pakenham aforesaid, only surv. s. and h., *bap.* Jan. 1696/7, at Pakenham, *suc. to the Baronetcy,* 5 April 1704. He *d.* unm. and was *bur.* 22 March 1735/6, at Pakenham. Admon. 9 April 1737 and Oct. 1811.(a)

V. 1736. SIR JOHN SPRING, Bart. [1641], of Coney Weston, co. Suffolk, uncle and h. male, *b.* 14 and *bap.* 15 Jan. 1673/4, at Pakenham, *suc. to the Baronetcy* in March 1736. He *m.* 24 June 1704, at Gazeley, co. Suffolk, Mary [*or* Elizabeth], da. of Joseph NIGHTINGALE, of Cambridge. He was *bur.* 30 May 1740 at Pakenham, aged 66.

VI. 1740, to 1769. SIR JOHN SPRING, Bart. [1641], s. and h., *suc. to the Baronetcy* in May 1740, resided in Bolton street, Piccadilly. He *m.* Anne, da. of Charles Barlow, of Worksop, Notts. He *d.* s.p. in Vere street, 17 and was *bur.* 25 Aug. 1769, at St. Marylebone, when the *Baronetcy* became *extinct.* Will pr. 1769. His widow was *bur.* there 5 Jan. 1776. Will pr. Jan. 1776.

TREVOR:

cr. 11 Aug. 1641(b);

ex. 5 Feb. 1676.

I. 1641, to 1676. "THOMAS TREVOR, of Enfield, co. Middlesex, Esq.," only s. and h. ap. of Sir Thomas TREVOR, one of the Barons of the Court of Exchequer (1625-49), by his 1st wife, Prudence (*d.* 1614), da. of Henry BUTLER, was *b.* about 1612; was M.P. for Monmouth, 1640 till void, 29 Nov. 1644; for Tregony, Feb. 1647 till excluded, Dec. 1648, and was *cr. a Baronet,* as above, 11 Aug. 1641(b); was *Knighted* at Whitehall 12 Dec. following; was Auditor of the Duchy of Lancaster, and suc. his father, 21 Dec. 1656. At the coronation of Charles II, 23 April 1661, he was made K.B. He *m.* firstly (Lic. Lond., 15 May 1632, he 20 and she 15), Anne, da. of Robert JENNER, of St. Leonard's, Foster Lane, London. He *m.* secondly (Lic. Fac., 16 July 1647, he 35 and she 24), Mary, da. of Samuel FORTREY of Kew, co. Surrey, by Catherine, da. of John DE LATFEUR, of Heynalt. He *d.* s.p. 5 Feb. 1676, when the *Baronetcy* became *extinct.*(c) Will pr. 1677. His widow *m.* (as the 2d of his three wives) Lieut.-Gen. the Hon. Sir Francis COMPTON, of Hamerton, co. Huntingdon, who *d.* 20 Dec. 1716, aged 87, and was *bur.* at Fulham. She *d.* between June 1694 and April 1696. Her will, in which she directs to be *bur.* at Leamington-Hastings, co. Warwick, dat. 1 June 1694, pr. 20 Jan. 1698/9.

(a) The estates devolved on his sisters and coheirs, of whom (1) Merolina, *m.* Thomas Discipline and had issue, and (2) Mary *m.* Rev. John Symonds, D.D., and had issue.

(b) The patent is not enrolled. The date here given is that in Dugdale's *Catalogue.* See *Memorandum* on p. 84. The date of the signet bill is *also* 11 Aug. 1641.

(c) He settled the inheritance of the estate of Leamington-Hastings, co. Warwick (which had been purchased by his father) on his cousin, Sir Charles Wheler, 2d Bart. [1660], who was s. and h. of William Wheler, by Eleanor, da. and h. of Edward Puleston and Winifred his wife, only sister of Sir Thomas Trevor, his father, which Eleanor (who *d.* 1 June 1678, aged 85) survived the testator by a few years.

OWEN:

cr. 11 Aug 1641(a);

afterwards, 1844-51, OWEN-BARLOW;

ex. 25 Feb. 1851.

I. 1641. "HUGH OWEN, of Orielton, co. Pembroke, Esq.," s. and h. of John OWEN, of the same, who was yr. s. of Sir Hugh OWEN, of Bodowen, co. Anglesey and of Orielton aforesaid, by Elizabeth, da. and h. of George WYRRIOT, of Orielton, was M.P. for Pembroke, 1626 and 1628-29; for Haverfordwest, April to May 1640; for Pembroke (again), Nov. 1640 till secluded in Dec. 1648, and for Pembrokeshire, 1660. He was Sheriff of Pembrokeshire, 1633-34, 1653-54, and 1663-64, and was *cr. a Baronet,* as above, 11 Aug. 1641,(a) having apparently being *Knighted* (as a Baronet) the day before. His estate was sequestrated 6 May 1651. He *m.* firstly, Frances, da. of Sir John PHILIPPS, 1st Bart. [1621], of Picton, by Anne, da. and coheir of Sir John PERROT, Lord Deputy of Ireland. He *m.* secondly, Catharine, widow of John LEWIS, of Prescoed, da. of Evan LLOYD, of Yale, co. Denbigh. He *d.* 1670. Will pr. June 1671.

II. 1670. SIR HUGH OWEN, Bart. [1641], of Orielton aforesaid, 1st surv. s. and h., by 2d wife, was *b.* about 1645; matric. at Oxford (Ch. Ch.), 7 Dec. 1660, aged 15; admitted to Inner Temple 1672; *suc. to the Baronetcy* in 1670. M.P. for Pembroke, 1676-79; for Pembrokeshire (four Parls.), 1679-81 and 1689-95: Sheriff of Anglesey, 1688, but did not act. He *m.* firstly, Anne, da. and sole h. of his paternal uncle, Henry OWEN, of Bodowen aforesaid. He *m.* secondly, Catharine, widow of Lewis AMWELL, of Park, da. of William GRIFFITH, of Len, but by her he had no issue. He *d.* 1698/9. Will pr. 1699. The admon. of his widow, as of "Long Shipping, co. Pembroke," 9 June 1699, was granted to her son "William Lewis Amwell, Esq."

III. 1699. SIR ARTHUR OWEN, Bart. [1641], of Orielton and Bodowen aforesaid, and of Llansillin, co. Denbigh, s. and h. by 1st wife, *suc. to the Baronetcy* in 1699; was M.P. for Pembrokeshire (five Parls.), 1695—1705; for Pembroke, 1708-10 and 1710 till unseated in 1712; for Pembrokeshire, again, 1715-22 and 1722-27. Lord Lieutenant of Pembrokeshire. He voted for the Hanoverian succession, thereby making the number equal, which, by the vote of Mr. Rice (M.P. for Carmarthenshire), was turned into a majority. He is said to have been offered a Peerage by George I. He *m.* Emma, only da. of Sir William WILLIAMS, 1st Bart. [1688], of Anglesey, sometime Speaker of the House of Commons, by Margaret, da. and coheir of Watkin KYFFIN, of Glascoed, co. Denbigh. He *d.* 6 June 1753. Will pr. 1754.

IV. 1753. SIR WILLIAM OWEN, Bart. [1641], of Orielton and Bodowen aforesaid. s. and h., *b.* about 1697; matric. at Oxford (New Coll.) 16 June 1713, aged 15. M.P. for Pembroke, 1722-47; for Pembrokeshire, 1747-61, and for Pembroke again 1761-74; *suc. to the Baronetcy,* 6 June 1753; Lord Lieutenant of Pembrokeshire. He *m.* firstly, Elizabeth, da. and sole h. of Thomas LLOYD, of Grove, co. Pembroke. She *d.* s.p.m. He *m.* secondly, Elizabeth, da. of John WILLIAMS, of Chester. He *d.* 7 May 1781. Will pr. June 1781.

V. 1781. SIR HUGH OWEN, Bart. [1641], of Orielton and Bodowen aforesaid, s. and h., by 2d wife, *suc. to the Baronetcy,* 7 May 1781; was M.P. for Pembrokeshire (four Parls.), 1770 till death, being sometime Lord Lieutenant of that county. He *m.* 1775, Anne, da. of John COLBY. He *d.* 16 Jan. 1786. Will pr. Jan. 1786. Will of Dame Anne Owen pr. 1823.

VI. 1786. SIR HUGH OWEN, Bart. [1641], of Orielton and Bodowen aforesaid, only child and h., *b.* 12 Sep. 1782, ed. at Eton, *suc. to the Baronetcy,* 16 Jan. 1786; matric. at Oxford (Ch. Ch.) 28 Jan. 1801, aged 18; Sheriff of Pembrokeshire, 1804-05; M.P. for Pembroke, 1809, till his death in that year. He *d.* unm. 8 Aug. 1809. Will pr. 1809.(b)

(a) This patent, unlike many of the preceding ones (including all those in the month of July) is enrolled, as are also many more in and after the month of Aug. 1641.

(b) He devised Orielton and other family estates to his second cousin, John LORD, who took the name of OWEN, and was *cr. a Baronet,* 1813. This John was s. and h. of Joseph Lord, by Corbetta, sister of Sir Arthur Owen, 7th Bart., da. of Lieut

VII. 1809. SIR ARTHUR OWEN, Bart. [1641], cousin and h. male, being s. and h. of Lieut. General John OWEN, by Anne, his cousin, da. of Charles OWEN, of Nash, which John, who *d.* Jan. 1776, was 2d s. of the 3d Bart. He, who was a Colonel in the army and sometime Adjutant General in the East Indies, *suc. to the Baronetcy*, 8 Aug. 1809. He *d.* unm. 4 Jan. 1817, in his 77th year.

VIII. 1817, to 1851. SIR WILLIAM OWEN, *afterwards* (1844-51) OWEN-BARLOW, Bart. [1641], of Lawrenny, co. Pembroke, nephew and h., being s. and h. of Brig.-Gen. William OWEN, by Ann, da. of John TRIPP, Barrister, which William (who *d.* 1795) was next br. to the late Bart. He was *b.* 11 April 1775; was Barrister (1799) and subsequently Bencher of the Middle Temple, Attorney-General of the Carmarthen circuit, and "Postman" of the Court of Exchequer. He *suc. to the Baronetcy* (but to none of the Owen estates) 4 Jan. 1817. By royal lic., Aug. 1844, he took the name of BARLOW after that of OWEN on succeeding, for life, to the estate of Lawrenny, on the death of his aunt, Emma Anne, widow of Hugh Barlow, of Lawrenny aforesaid. He *d.* unm. 25 Feb. 1851, at his chambers in Fig Tree Court, Temple (where he lived more than half-a-century), and was *bur.* 1 March, in the Middle Temple vault, Temple church, London, aged 76, when the *Baronetcy*, presumably, became *extinct.*(a) Will pr. March 1851.

CURZON:

cr. 11 Aug. 1641(b);

having been previously, 18 June 1636, *cr.* a Baronet [S.];

afterwards, since 1761, BARONS SCARSDALE.

I. 1641. "JOHN CURZON, of Kedleston, co. Derby, Baronet of Scotland," 1st s. and h. of John Curzon, of Kedleston aforesaid, by Millicent, da. of Sir Ralph SACHEVERELL, of Stanton, co. Derby, was *b.* about 1599; matric. at Oxford (Mag. Coll), 12 June 1618, aged 18; admitted to Middle Temple, 1620; M.P. for Brackley, 1628-29; for Derbyshire, April to May 1640, and 1640 till secluded in 1648; Sheriff of Derbyshire, 1637-38, having been *cr. a Baronet of Nova Scotia*, 18 June 1636, and subsequently, 11 Aug. 1641,(a) *a Baronet of England* as aforesaid, after having been *Knighted* at Whitehall three days previously. He was a Parliamentarian, and served on several important committees, 1643-46. He *m.* Patience, sister of John, 1st BARON CREWE OF STENE, da. of Sir Thomas CREWE, of Stene, co. Northampton, by Temperance, da. and coh. of Reginald BRAY, of Stene aforesaid. She *d.* 30 March 1642. He *d.* 13 Dec. 1686 in his 89th year. Will pr. Feb. 1687, Both were *bur.* at Kedleston. M.I.

General John Owen (*d.* Jan. 1776), a yr. s. of the 3d Bart. Inasmuch, however, as the said Corbetta had a brother, Brigadier General William Owen (*d.* 1795), who was father not only of the 8th Bart. (who *d.* unm.), but of Frances, who *m.* Rev. Charles Tripp and had issue, the family of Tripp (and not that of Lord) represented these Baronets.

(a) A petition was presented, soon after 1851, to the Crown, by the Rev. Henry Tripp, M.A., Fellow of Worcester College, Oxford, eldest s. of Charles Tripp, D.D., Rector of Silverton, Devon, by Frances, sister and coheir (being the only sister who left issue) of Sir William Owen-Barlow, 8th and last Bart. [1641], praying that the dignity of a Baronet should be conferred on him "in consideration of his being the heir-in-blood of the ancient Baronets [of Owen] of Orielton," adding that this had been recently done in the cases of Pakington [*cr.* 1846], Barker-Mill [*cr.* 1836], and Mackenzie, afterwards Douglas of Glenbervie [*cr.* 1831]. To this the petitioner thought fit to add several very irrelevant statements, *e.g.*, that his grandfather, the Rev. John Tripp, Rector of Spofforth, Yorkshire, was a friend of George (O'Brien), Earl of Egremont, and was the son of Dr. Tripp, Barrister at Law, Deputy Recorder of Taunton, the family being traditionally descended "from a scion of the illustrious house of Norfolk, whose arms they bear in addition to the scaling ladder which was substituted for their bend by Henry V, when their name was changed from Howard to Tripp." The ridiculous statements thus set forth by the petitioner failed, naturally enough, to gain him his object. His eldest son, however, Owen Howard Tripp, took by royal licence in 1898 the name of Owen, though he inherited none of the estates of that family, which had been devised to the family of Lord. In the *Times* of (22 or 23 ?) August 1900 he advertised his *intention to assume this Baronetcy* of 1641 [one, it is to be observed, limited to heirs *male* of the body of the grantee] as being grandson of Frances, *sister* of the late Baronet, and consequently his heir, not however stating that, though (through this *female* descent) he was heir *general*, he was *not* the *heir male*, to whom only the succession was limited.

(b) See p. 131, note "a," under "Owen."

II. 1686. SIR NATHANIEL CURZON, Bart. [E. 1641 and S. 1636], of Kedleston aforesaid, only surviving s. and h., *b.* about 1640; was a merchant of London in 1671; *suc. to the Baronetcies*, 13 Dec. 1686. Sheriff of Derbyshire, 1691-92. He *m.* (Lic. Vic. Gen., 5 July 1671, he about 30 and she about 16) Sarah, da. of William PENN, of Penn, Bucks. He *d.* 4 March 1718/9. Will pr. March 1719. His widow *d.* 4 June 1727/8. Will pr. 1728. Both were *bur.* at Kedleston. M.I.

III. 1719. SIR JOHN CURZON, Bart. [E. 1641 and S. 1636], of Kedleston aforesaid, s. and h., *b.* about 1674; matric. at Oxford (Trin. Coll.), 18 July 1690, aged 16; B.A. 1693; admitted to Inner Temple, 1692; M.P. for Derbyshire (eight Parls.), 1701-27; *suc. to the Baronetcies*, 4 March 1718/9. He *d.* unm. 6 Aug. 1727 and was *bur.* at Kedleston. Will dat. 10 May 1725, pr. 13 Sep. 1727.

IV. 1727. SIR NATHANIEL CURZON, Bart. [E. 1641 and S. 1636], of Kedleston aforesaid, br. and h., *b.* about 1676; matric. at Oxford (Trin. Coll.), 2 July 1692, aged 16; Barrister (Inner Temple), 1700; M.P. for Derby, 1713-15; for Clitheroe, 1722-27, and for Derbyshire (four Parls.), 1721-54; *suc. to the Baronetcies*, 6 Aug. 1727. He *m.* Mary, da. and coh. of Sir Ralph ASSHETON, 2d Bart. [1660], of Middleton, co. Lancaster, by his 1st wife, Mary, da. and h. of Thomas VAVASOUR. With her he acquired the estate of Whalley Abbey, co. Lanc.(b) He *d.* 18 Nov. 1758. Admon. 5 Dec. 1758 and Jan. 1789. His widow *d.* 18 March 1776, aged 81, and was *bur.* at Kedleston. Her will pr. May 1776.

V. 1758. SIR NATHANIEL CURZON, Bart. [E. 1641 and S. 1636], of Kedleston aforesaid, surviving s. and h., *b.* in Queen Square, and *bap.* 19 Jan. 1726/7, at St. Geo. the Martyr, Midx.; matric. at Oxford (Ch. Ch.), 14 Feb. 1744/5, and was *cr.* D.C.L. 14 April 1749; was M.P. for Clitheroe 1748-54, and for Derbyshire 1754-61; *suc. to the Baronetcies*, 18 Nov. 1758. He *m.* 27 Oct. 1750 at St. Geo. Han. sq., Caroline, 1st da. of Charles (COLYEAR), 2d EARL OF PORTMORE [S.], by Juliana, Dow. DUCHESS OF LEEDS, da. and coheir of Roger HALE. She was living when he was *cr.* 9 April 1761 BARON SCARSDALE, co. Derby, in which peerage these *Baronetcies* then *merged* and still so continue. See *Peerage*.

SANDFORD:

cr. 11 Aug 1641(c);

ex. 2 April 1723.

I. 1641. "THOMAS SANDFORD, of Howgill Castle, co. Westmorland, Esq.," s. and h. ap. of Sir Richard SANDFORD, of the same (whose will, dat. 2 Oct. 1660, was pr. 25 Aug. 1663), by Anne, da. of Henry CRACKENTHORPE, of Newbiggin, was v.p. *cr. a Baronet*, as above, 11 Aug. 1641.(c)

(a) See p. 131, note "a," under "Owen."

(b) This estate passed to their 3d and youngest s. Assheton Curzon, *b.* 2 Feb. 1733, *cr.* BARON CURZON OF PENN, in 1794 and VISCOUNT CURZON OF PENN, in 1802. He *d.* 1820 and was *suc.* by his grandson, Richard William Penn CURZON HOWE, *b.* 11 Dec. 1796, *cr.* EARL HOWE, in 1821, who sold the property.

(c) See p. 131, note "a" under "Owen." The date of the patent in this instance is given as 12 Aug. but in the *Creations, 1483-1646* [ap. 47th Rep. D.K. Pub. Records] it is given as 11 Aug. 1641.

He was M.P. for Cockermouth, April 1642 till disabled in 1644; was a Col. in the Royalist Army; was sequestrated and fined £600, on 18 Jan. 1649. He *m.* Bridget, da. of Sir George DALSTON, of Dalston, co. Cumberland, by Catherine, da. and coheir of John THORNWORTH, of Halsted, co. Leicester. He *d.* v.p. before 2 Oct. 1660. His widow living 25 Aug. 1663.

II. 1655? SIR RICHARD SANDFORD, Bart. [1641], of Howgill Castle aforesaid, s. and h.; *suc. to the Baronetcy* on the death of his father. He *m.* Mary (aged 15 in 1666), da. of Sir Francis BOWES, of Thornton, co. Durham, by his third wife, Margaret, da. and coheir of Robert DELAVAL. He was murdered(a) in Whitefriars 8 and was *bur.* 11 Sep. 1675 in the Temple church, London. The admon. of his widow, as "of St. George the Martyr, Midx.," is dated 22 June 1734.

III. 1675, to 1724. SIR RICHARD SANDFORD, Bart. [1641], of Howgill Castle aforesaid, only s. and h., *b.* 8 Sep. 1675, said to have been at the hour of his father's death; *suc. to the Baronetcy* at his birth; ed. at Christ's College, Cambridge; was M.P. for Westmorland (three Parls.), 1695-1700; for Morpeth, 1701; for Westmorland, again, 1701-02; for Morpeth, again (three Parls.), 1705-13, and for Appleby (three Parls.), 1713 till death. He *d.* unm. 2 April 1723, when the *Baronetcy* became *extinct.*(b) Admon. 19 May 1724.

BRIGGES:

cr. 12 Aug. 1641;(c)

ex., presumably, 27 Oct. 1767;

but *assumed* till 1816 or later.

I. 1641. "MORTON BRIGGES, of Haughton [in Shiffnal], co. Salop, Esq.," s. and h. of Humphrey BRIGGES, of Ernestry Park, near Ludlow, in that co. (Sheriff, 1605), by Anne, 1st da. and coheir of Robert MORETON, of Haughton aforesaid, was *b.* about 1587; matric. at Oxford (Exeter Coll.), 18 March 1602/3, aged 16; B.A., 23 Oct. 1605; admitted to Lincoln's Inn, 1606; and was *cr. a Baronet*, as above, 12 Aug. 1641.(c) He *m.*, about 1610, Chrisogena, da. of Edward GREY (living 1601), of Buildwas, Salop. She *d.* aged 97.(d)

II. 1650? SIR HUMPHREY BRIGGES, Bart. [1641], of Haughton aforesaid, s. and h., *b.* about 1615; admitted to Lincoln's Inn, 1 Nov. 1631; said to have been *Knighted*, v.p.; *suc. to the Baronetcy* on his father's death between 1641 and 1665; M.P. for Wenlock, July 1646 till secluded in Dec. 1648. Sheriff of Salop, 1665-66. He *m.* four times, *viz.*, firstly, about 1630, Elizabeth, da. of Sir Philip Carey, of Aldenham, Herts (br. to Henry, 1st VISCOUNT FALKLAND [S.]), by Elizabeth, da. of Richard BLAND, of Carlton, co. York. She was *bap.* 1 Sep. 1611, at Great Berkhampstead, Herts. He *m.* secondly, about 1648, Elizabeth, yst. da. of Sir Richard WILBRAHAM, 1st Bart. [1621], by Grace, da. of Thomas (SAVAGE), 1st VISCOUNT SAVAGE OF ROCKSAVAGE. He *m.* thirdly (Lic. Fac., 30 June 1665, he 50 and she 47), Anne, widow of Richard MORETON, of co. Montgomery, but by her had no issue. He *m.* fourthly, Magdalen, da. of Sir John CORBET, 1st Bart. [1627], of Stoke, by Ann, da. of Sir George MAINWARING, but by her, also, he had no issue. He was *bur.* at Shrewsbury, 21 May 1691. Admon. 16 June 1691, and 13 Jan. 1709/10. His widow living June 1691, but dead before 1693. Will pr. 10 Nov. 1693.

(a) The assassins, Henry Symbal and William Jones, suffered death soon afterwards.

(b) The estates devolved on his only sister, Mary, who had *m.*, between 1694 and 1696, Robert Honywood, of Markshall, Essex, Col. of a Reg. of Foot, who was *bur.* there 26 Jan. 1734/5. She, also, was *bur.* there 11 Aug. 1745, leaving issue, which became extinct on the death of her 5th and yst. son, Philip Honywood, 20 Feb. 1785, aged 73.

(c) See p. 131, note "a," under "Owen."

(d) Note to *Visit. of Salop 1623*, pub. by the Harleian Society.

III. 1691. SIR HUMPHREY BRIGGES, Bart. [1641], of Haughton aforesaid, only surv. s. and h. by 2d wife, *b.* about 1650; admitted to Lincoln's Inn, 25 Nov. 1687; *suc. to the Baronetcy*, 21 May 1691. He *m.* Barbara, da. of Sir Wadham WYNDHAM, of Norrington, Wilts, one of the Justices of the Court of King's Bench, by Barbara, da. of Sir George CLARKE, of Watford, co. Northampton. She, who was *b.* 7 Nov. 1649,(a) *d.* before him. He *d.* 1699, aged 49. Admon. 6 May 1700.

IV. 1699. SIR HUMPHREY BRIGGES, Bart. [1641], of Haughton aforesaid, s. and h., *b.* about 1670; matric. at Oxford (Wadham Coll.), 3 July 1687, aged 17; admitted to Lincoln's Inn, 1687; *suc. to the Baronetcy* in 1699; M.P. for Salop, 1700-01; for Bridgnorth, 1702-10, and for Wenlock, 1716-27. He *d.* unm. 8 Dec. 1734, at Haughton. Will pr. Feb. 1735.

V. 1734, to 1767. SIR HUGH BRIGGES, Bart. [1641], of Haughton aforesaid, br. and h., *b.* about 1684; matric. at Oxford (Wadham Coll.), 17 Dec. 1708, aged 16; *suc. to the Baronetcy*, 8 Dec. 1734; Sheriff for Salop, 1747-48. He *d.* unm. 27 Oct. 1767, when the *Baronetcy* became *extinct.*(b) Will pr. Nov. 1767.

The title, however, was assumed as under.

VI. 1767. SIR JONATHAN BRIGGS, styling himself "Baronet," as being descended from a younger branch of the family. He was Surveyor of Excise at Milford Haven. He *d.* 3 Dec. 1774.

VII. 1774, to 1816. SIR JOHN BRIGGS, styling himself "Baronet," s. and h. of above. He was of Blackbrook, co. Monmouth; was plaintiff in a cause tried at Hereford in 1795. He *d.* in Dublin, 3 Oct. 1816. Doubtless the will of "Sir John Briggs, Bart.," pr. 1819, refers to him.(c)

HEYMAN:

cr. 12 Aug. 1641(d);

ex. 20 Nov. 1808.

I. 1641. "HENRY HEYMAN, of Somerfeilde [in Sellinge], co. Kent., Knt.," s. and h. of Sir Peter HEYMAN, of the same (sometime M.P. for Hythe), being only s. by his 1st wife, Sarah, da. and coheir of Peter COLLET, of London, merchant, was *b.* 20 Nov. 1610, at Selling; suc. his father in or before March 1640/1; M.P. for Hythe, April to May 1640, and 1640-53; was a pronounced Parliamentarian, serving on several important committees, 1642-49; was *Knighted*, 7 July 1641, at Whitehall, and, a few weeks later, was *cr. a Baronet*, as above, 12 Aug. 1641.(d) He *m.* Mary, da. and h. of Daniel HOLFORD, of West Thurrock, co. Essex. She *d.* before him. He *d.* at Grays, co. Essex, 1658, and was *bur.* at Sellinge.(e) Admon. 7 Dec. 1658.

(a) *Mis. Gen. et Her.*, 2d S., vol. iv, p. 55, where an interesting account of this branch of the Wyndham family is given.

(b) The estates passed to the descendants of his three sisters; that of Houghton devolving on those of Elizabeth, who *m.* Leigh Brooke, of Blacklands, co. Stafford. By act of Parl., 1800, a more regular partition of these estates was made.

(c) The will of "Sir John Briggs, Bart., Guernsey," proved April 1842, and the admon. of "Dame Tamar Priscilla Briggs, Guernsey," May 1827, doubtless refer to other persons who assumed this Baronetcy.

(d) See p. 131, note "a," under "Owen."

(e) Philipot, in his *History of Kent*, speaks of his great obligations to him.

II. 1658. SIR PETER HEYMAN, Bart. [1641], of Somerfield aforesaid, s. and h., *b.* 10 and *bap.* 21 July 1642, at St. Anne's, Blackfriars, London; *suc. to the Baronetcy* in 1658. He dissipated all the family inheritance. He *m.* Mary, da. of (—) RICH, of Clapham, Surrey. The will of "Dame Mary Hayman, Surrey," was pr. June 1711. He *d.* at Canterbury, 5 Oct. 1723, and was *bur.* (as was his wife) at St. Alphage's, in that city.

III. 1723. SIR BARTHOLOMEW HEYMAN, Bart. [1641], s. and h., *b.* about 1690; *suc. to the Baronetcy*, 5 Oct. 1723. His eyesight, having been impaired in his youth by gunpowder, rendered him unfit for military service. He was one of the Poor Knights at Windsor, Berks. He *m.*, about 1720, Elizabeth, da. of Thomas NELSON, of Sandwich, Kent, merchant. He *d.* 9 June 1742, and was *bur.* in St. George's chapel, Windsor, aged 52. M.I.

IV. 1742. SIR PETER HEYMAN, Bart. [1641], of Windsor aforesaid, only s. and h., *b.* about 1720, and *suc. to the Baronetcy*, 9 June 1742. He was an officer in the army. He *m.*, when aged only 17, in 1737, (—), only child of (—) KEMPE, of Plymouth. He *d.*, a widower, s.p.s., July 1790, aged 70.(a)

V. 1790, to 1808. SIR HENRY PIX HEYMAN, Bart. [1641], cousin and h. male, being s. and h. of Henry HEYMAN, of Stroud, by Elizabeth, da. of Hatch UNDERWOOD, which Henry last named was s. and h. of the Rev. Peter HEYMAN, Rector of Headcorn, Kent, 2d s. of the 2d Bart.; was ed. at Emmanuel Coll. Cambridge, of which he was sometime Fellow; B.A., 1784; M.A., 1787; B.D., 1794; *suc. to the Baronetcy*, in July 1790; was Rector of Fressingfield, Suffolk, 1797. He *d.* s.p. 20 Nov. 1808, when the *Baronetcy* became *extinct.*

GOODRICK, *or* GOODRICKE:
cr. 14 Aug. 1641(b);
ex. 9 March 1839.

I. 1641. "JOHN GOODRICK, of Ribston, co. York, Esq.," s. and h. of Sir Henry GOODRICK, of the same,(c) by Jane, da. of Sir John SAVILE, of Methley, one of the Barons of the Exchequer, is said to have been *b.* 20 April 1617 and *bap.* 31 Aug. 1620, at St. Mary's, York; suc. his father, 22 July 1641, and was, the next month, *cr. a Baronet*, as above, 14 Aug. 1641.(b) During the Civil Wars he was a great sufferer in the Royal cause, and was imprisoned at Manchester and afterwards in the Tower of London, being fined £1,508, (or £1,200, with £40 a year,) on 23 Nov. 1646. He was aged 48 at the Visit. of Yorkshire in 1665, and was M.P. for Yorkshire, 1661 till death. He *m.* firstly, 7 Oct. 1641, at Trinity, Micklegate, York, Katharine, da. and coheir of Stephen NORCLIFFE, of York, by (—), da. of (—) UDALL. She was *bap.* 31 Aug. 1620, at St. Mary's Castlegate, York. He *m.* secondly, before 1665, Elizabeth, Dow. VISCOUNTESS FAIRFAX OF ELMLEY [I.], da. of Alexander SMITH, of Stutton, co. Suffolk. He *d.* Nov. 1670. Will dat. 19 Sep. 1669, pr. at York 25 Nov. 1670. The will of his widow dat. 4, pr. 15 June 1692, in London and 13 Sep. following at York.

II. 1670. SIR HENRY GOODRICK, *or* GOODRICKE, Bart. [1641], of Ribston aforesaid, s. and h. by 1st wife, *b.* 24 Oct. 1642; aged 22 at the Visit of Yorkshire in 1665; *suc. to the Baronetcy*, Nov. 1670; was M.P. for Boroughbridge (ten Parls.), Nov. 1673 to 1705; was Envoy Extraordinary, from Charles I, to Charles II, King of Spain; Lieut. Gen. of the Ordnance, 1668-1702, and

(a) He was in such reduced circumstances that, in 1783, a concert was got up for his benefit. See an interesting account of this in Burke's *Extinct Baronets*, edit. 1841.

(b) See p. 131, note "a," under "Owen."

(c) See an account of this family in Dugdale's *Visitation of Yorkshire, 1665*, as edited by J. W. Clay, F.S.A., with copious additions.

P.C. 13 Feb. 1689/90, to William III. He *m.* Mary, sister of George, 1st BARON DARTMOUTH, da. of Col. William LEGGE, by Elizabeth, da. of Sir William WASHINGTON. He *d.* s.p., at Brentford, Midx., 5 March 1704/5, and was *bur.* at Ribston. Will dat. 2, pr. 24 March 1704/5. His widow *d.* aged 70, and was *bur.* (with her father) at Trinity Minories, London. Her will dat. 13 Feb. 1714/5, was pr. 9 April 1715, at the Archdeaconry of Midx.

III. 1705. SIR JOHN GOODRICKE, Bart. [1641], of Ribston aforesaid, br. of the half blood and h., being s. of the 1st Bart. by his 2d wife, *b.* 16 Oct. 1654; aged 10 at the Visit. of Yorkshire, 1665; *suc. to the Baronetcy*, 5 March 1704/5. He *m.* Sarah, da. of Sir Richard HOPKINS, of Coventry, Serjeant at Law. He *d.* 10 Dec. 1705. Will dat. 21 Nov. 1705, pr. at York 22 Sep. 1706. The will of his widow dat. 24 Feb. 1731, pr. at York 5 March 1732.

IV. 1705. SIR HENRY GOODRICKE, Bart. [1641], of Ribston aforesaid, s. and h., *b.* 8 Sep. 1677; *suc. to the Baronetcy*, 10 Dec. 1705. He *m.* 26 April 1707, at York Minster, Mary, only da. and h. of Tobias JENKINS, of Grimston, co. York, by his 1st wife, Mary, da. of Charles (PAULET *or* POWLETT) 1st DUKE OF BOLTON. He *d.* 21 July 1738, and was *bur.* at Ribston. Will dat. 11 Feb. 1737/8, pr. at York 31 July 1738.

V. 1738. SIR JOHN GOODRICKE, Bart. [1641], of Ribston aforesaid, s. and h., *b.* 20 May 1708 at Ribston; *suc. to the Baronetcy*, 21 July 1738. P.C. 1 Sep. 1773; M.P. for Pontefract, 1774-80 and for Ripon, Dec. 1787 till death; Comiss. Board of Trade, Aug. 1788; Envoy Extraordinary to Stockholm, where he chiefly resided. He *m.* 28 Sep. 1731, at Hendon, Mary JOHNSON, *afterwards* BENSON, spinster, illegitimate da. of Robert (BENSON), BARON BINGLEY, by (—), da. of James SILL, of Wakefield, mercer. He *d.* 3 Aug. 1789, and was *bur.* at Hunsingore. Will dat. 20 May 1788, pr. at York 29 Aug. 1789.

VI. 1789. SIR HENRY GOODRICKE, Bart. [1641], of Ribston aforesaid, grandson and h., being 2d but only surv. s. and h. of Henry GOODRICKE, of Groningen, in Holland, by Levina Benjamina, da. of Peter SESSTER, of Namur,(a) which Henry was only s. and h. ap. of the late Baronet, but *d.* v.p. 9 July 1784. He was *b.* 12 Oct. 1765, at Groningen; was M.P. for Lymington, Dec. 1778 to 1780; *suc. to the Baronetcy*, 3 Aug. 1789. He *m.*, 30 Nov. 1796, at Mold, Charlotte, sister to William Charles, 2d VISCOUNT CLERMONT [I.], 2d da. of Rt. Hon. James FORTESCUE, of Ravensdale park, co. Louth, by Henrietta, da. of Thomas Orby HUNTER, of Croyland, co. Lincoln. He *d.* 23 March 1802, and was *bur.* at Hunsingore. Will dat. 9 Dec. 1801, pr. at York 31 July 1802. His widow *d.* 10 Aug. 1842. Will pr. Oct. 1842.

VII. 1802. SIR HENRY-JAMES GOODRICKE, Bart. [1641], of Ribston aforesaid, only s. and h., *b.* 26 Sep. at Dublin and *bap.* 23 Oct. 1797 at St. Thomas', in that city; *suc. to the Baronetcy*, 23 March 1802, at the age of 4 years; ed. at Rugby; matric. at Oxford (Ch. Ch.), 19 Oct. 1816, aged 19. In March 1829 he suc. to the vast estates in Ireland of his maternal uncle, abovenamed, the 2d and last VISCOUNT CLERMONT [I.]. His income is said to have been £40,000 a year; was Sheriff of Yorkshire, 1831-32. "Sir Harry" was well known in the sporting world, and was, from 1831 till his death in 1833, Master of the Quorn Hunt, the whole expenses of which he defrayed. He *d.* unm., after an illness of forty-eight hours, at Ravensdale park, co. Louth, in his 36th year, 22 Aug. 1833, and was *bur.* at Hunsingore. Will dat. 25 July, and pr. 27 Oct. 1833, devising Ribston Hall and his other English estates to Francis Lyttleton HOLYOAKE,(b) one of his sporting friends, who was, however, in no way connected with the family, thereby excluding his three aunts, who were his coheirs, as well as his heir male.

(a) They were married in, or shortly before, 1764, at Woldhuysen, in East Friesland.

(b) He took the additional name of GOODRICKE, after that of HOLYOAKE, and was *cr. a Baronet*, 31 March 1835 (some few years before the extinction of the old Baronetcy of that name) as "of Ribston, co. York," etc., a title which became extinct on the death of his son, the 3d Bart., 11 Aug. 1888.

VIII. 1833, to 1839. SIR THOMAS FRANCIS HENRY GOODRICKE, Bart. [1641], cousin and h. male, being 2d but last surv. s. of Lieut. Col. Thomas GOODRICKE, 25th Regt., by Elizabeth, da. of James BUTTON, of Rochester, which Thomas last named (who was *b.* 12 March 1711/2) was 2d surv. s. of the 4th Bart. He was *b.* 24 Sep. 1762, at Rochester; *suc. to the Baronetcy* (but to none of the estates), 22 Aug. 1833. He *m.* April 1794, at Hunsingore, his cousin Harriet, sister of the 6th Bart., 1st da. of Henry GOODRICKE, of Groningen, by Levina Benjamina, da. of Peter SESSTER, all abovenamed. She was *b.* 20 Oct. 1767, at Hunsingore. He *d.* s.p. in London, 9 March 1839, and was *bur.* at Kensal Green, aged 76, when the *Baronetcy* became *extinct.* Will dat. 8, and pr. 23 March 1839.

POTTS:
cr. 14 Aug. 1641;
ex. 14 Jan. 1731/2.

I. 1641. "JOHN POTTS, of Mannington, co. Norfolk, Knt.," s. and h. of John POTTS, of Lincoln's Inn, London, by Anne, da. and coheir of John DODGE, of Mannington aforesaid; was admitted to Gray's Inn, 10 Oct. 1634; was M.P. for Norfolk, 1640, till secluded in Dec. 1648, and for Great Yarmouth 1660; was *Knighted*, 9 Aug. 1641, at Whitehall, being, a few days later *cr. a Baronet*, as above, 14 Aug. 1641; was a Parliamentarian, serving on several important Committees, 1643-48, and was on the Council of State, Feb. to April 1660. He *m.* firstly, apparently when a minor,(a) (—), da. of (—) GOODSILL. She *d.* s.p.m. He *m.* secondly, Ursula, widow of (—) SPELMAN, da. of Sir Henry WILLOUGHBY, of Risley, co. Derby. Banns of marriage were pub. May 1654, between him (then a widower) and "Mrs. Mary HANGER, of Enfield, Midx., widow." He *d.* 1673. Admon. 19 Nov. 1673 to a creditor.

II. 1673. SIR JOHN POTTS, Bart. [1641], of Mannington aforesaid, s. and h. by 2d wife, was admitted to Gray's Inn, 10 Oct. 1624; *suc. to the Baronetcy* in 1673. He *m.* firstly, in or before 1640, Susan, da. of Sir John HEVENINGHAM, of Heveningham, Norfolk. He *m.* secondly, Elizabeth, da. of Sir Samuel BROWNE, of Arlesley, Beds., one of the Justices of the Common Pleas, (1660-68), by Elizabeth, da. of John MEADE, of Finchingfield, Essex. She survived him many years.

III. 1690? SIR ROGER POTTS, Bart. [1641], of Mannington aforesaid, only s. and h., *b.* about 1641, aged 23 in 1664; *suc. to the Baronetcy* on the death of his father. He *m.*, in or before 1675, Mary, da. and h. of William DAVY, of Great Ellingham, Norfolk, by Margaret, da. of Thomas GOURNAY, of West Barsham. She *d.* 8 March 1701/2 (the same day and hour as King William III), and was *bur.* at Ellingham. He *d.* 14 Oct. 1711, aged 70.

IV. 1711. SIR ALGERNON POTTS, Bart. [1641], of Mannington aforesaid, 1st s. and h., *b.* in or before 1675; *suc. to the Baronetcy*, 14 Oct. 1711. He *m.* Frances, widow of Thomas CRANE, of Norwich, merchant, da. and coheir of (—) CALIBUT, of Saham Toney. He *d.* s.p., 17 Sep. 1716. His widow *d.* Nov. 1717.

V. 1716, to 1732. SIR CHARLES POTTS, Bart. [1641], of Mannington aforesaid, br. and h., *b.* 1676; was a Citizen and Merchant Taylor, and sometime a merchant in London; *suc. to the Baronetcy*, 17 Sep. 1716. He *m.* firstly, Elizabeth, only sister of William *or* Thomas NEWMAN, of Baconsthorpe, Norfolk. She *d.* at Kensington, 21 Sep. 1706, and was *bur.* at Great Ellingham. He *m.* secondly Mary, da. of Thomas SMITH, of London, merchant. He *d.* s.p. 14 Jan. 1731/2, aged 56, and was *bur.* at Mannington, when the *Baronetcy* became *extinct.*(b) Will pr. 1732. His widow, who had the estate of Mannington for her life, *d.* 7 Feb. 1735/6 and was *bur.* at Mannington. Admon. 21 Feb. 1735/6.

(a) An old writer in the time of the Court of Wards says that "He was obliged to marry a da. of (—) Goodsill, Esq., a favourite at Court, with a small fortune." [Burke's *Extinct Baronetcies.*]

(b) There is, however, the will of a "Sir Roger Potts," proved in 1751, which possibly may be that of some one who (rightly or wrongly) assumed this Baronetcy.

RODES:
cr. 14 Aug. 1641;
ex. presumably, Oct. 1743.

I. 1641. "FRANCIS RODES,(a) of Balbrough [Barlborough], co. Derby, Knt.," 2d s. but h. (by entail) of Sir John RODES,(b) of the same, being his 1st s. by his 3d wife Frances, da. of Marmaduke CONSTABLE, of Holderness, was *b.* about 1595; admitted to Gray's Inn, 21 May 1617; suc. his father in his estates, Sep. 1639; was *Knighted* at Whitehall, 9 Aug. 1641, and a few days afterwards was *cr. a Baronet*, as above, 14 Aug. 1641. He *m.* Elizabeth, da. and h. of Sir George LASCELLES, of Sturton and Gateford, Notts. He *d.* 8 Feb. 1645/6. Admon. 27 May 1646. His widow, who was aged 19 in 1614, *m.* Allan LOCKHART. She *d.* 5 and was *bur.* 6 Dec. 1666 at Barlborough.

II. 1646. SIR FRANCIS RODES, Bart. [1641], of Barlborough aforesaid, 2d but 1st surv. s. and h.; *suc. to the Baronetcy*, 8 Feb. 1645/6. Was fined, as a Royalist, £500 on 25 March 1650. He *m.* Ann, da. of Sir Gervase CLIFTON, 1st Bart. [1611], by his 2d wife, Frances, da. of Francis (CLIFFORD), EARL OF CUMBERLAND. He *d.* 3 May 1651. Admon. 10 June 1651.

III. 1651. SIR FRANCIS RODES, Bart. [1641], of Barlborough Hall aforesaid, only s. and h.; *suc. to the Baronetcy*, 3 May 1651; aged 14 at the Visit. of Derby, 1662; Sheriff of Notts, 1670-71. He *m.* (Lic. Fac. 1 May 1665, each being about 20), Martha, da. of (his guardian), William THORNTON, of Grantham, co. Lincoln. He *d.* 14 March 1675, in his 28th year. His widow *d.* 25 Oct. 1719, in her 77th year. Both *bur.* at Barlborough. M.I.

IV. 1675, to 1743. SIR JOHN RODES, Bart. [1641], of Barlborough Hall aforesaid, only s. and h., *b.* about 1670, being aged 25 on 28 July 1695, having *suc. to the Baronetcy*, 14 March 1675. He *d.* unm. Oct. 1743, when, presumably, the *Baronetcy* became *extinct.* Will dat. 12 March 1731,(c) pr. 1744.

SPRIGNELL:
cr. 14 Aug. 1641;
ex. Aug. 1691.

I. 1641. "RICHARD SPRIGNELL, of Coppenthorp, in the county of the city of York, Esq.," only s. and h. of Robert SPRIGNELL,(d) of Hornsey, co. Midx. (lessee of the Rectory of Copmanthorpe aforesaid), by Susan his

(a) Pedigree in Glover's *Derbyshire*, vol. ii, p. 83.

(b) This John was s. and h. of the learned Francis RODES, one of the Justices of the Common Pleas, *temp.* Eliz., by whom the stately Elizabethan mansion of Barlborough Hall was erected in 1583.

(c) In this he entails the estates, on failure of issue male of his sister, Frances HEATHCOTE (which issue, however, inherited the estates and took the name of RODES), to his cousin, John RODES, of Northgate in Horbury. This John RODES (if no nearer heir existed) would have been, if alive in 1743, entitled to the Baronetcy. He was s. of William RODES (aged 6 in Feb. 1694/5), who was the only s. (that survived infancy) of John RODES, of Cornhill, London, linen draper (living 1695), the s. and h. of John RODES, of Sturton, Notts, 4th s. of the 1st Bart. Of the two other (younger) sons of the said John RODES, of Sturton, Francis RODES emigrated to Maryland, *m.* twice, and had issue living 1695; and Charles RODES also *m.*, having emigrated to Virginia. See MS. notes by Brooke (*Somerset Herald*) in his own copy of Wotton's *Baronetage.*

(d) This Robert was only s. of Richard Sprignell, Citizen and Barber Surgeon of London, whose curious will (apologising for his last marriage) is dat. 12 and pr. 27 Feb. 1602/3.

wife, suc. his father between 1618 and 1624; matric. at Oxford (Bras. Coll.), 28 Jan 1619/20, aged 20; B.A. 28 Feb. 1621/2, and was *cr. a Baronet*, as above, 14 Aug 1641. He *m.* Anne, only da. of Gideon DE LAUNE, of Sharsted, co. Kent, and of London, apothecary, by Judith, da. of Henry CHAMBERLAINE, of London. He resided at Highgate, co. Midx., and was *bur.* there, 19 Jan. 1658/9. Will dat. 13 Aug. 1656, pr. 12 Feb. 1658/9. His widow was *bur.* at Highgate, 9 May 1661.

II. 1659. SIR ROBERT SPRIGNELL, Bart. [1641], of Coppenthorp aforesaid, 1st s. and h.; *suc. to the Baronetcy* in Jan. 1658/9. He *m.* Anne, da. of Sir Michael LIVESEY, Bart. [1627], the regicide. He *d.* s.p. before Nov. 1688.

III. 1680? to 1691. SIR WILLIAM SPRIGNELL, Bart. [1641], of London, br. and h.; *suc. to the Baronetcy* on the death of his brother. He *d.* unm. and was *bur.* 6 Sep. 1691, at Highgate, when the *Baronetcy* became *extinct.* Will dat. 12 Nov. 1688, pr. 3 Sep. 1691 in the Commissary Court of London.

BINDLOSSE:

cr. 16 Aug. 1641;(a)

ex. Nov. 1688.

I. 1641, to 1688. "ROBERT BINDLOSSE, of Borwick, co. Lancaster, Esq.," s. and h. of Sir Francis BINDLOSSE (only s. and h. ap. of Sir Robert BINDLOSSE, of the same,) by his 2d wife, Cecilia, da. of Thomas (WEST), LORD DELAWARR, was *bap.* 8 May 1624; suc. his father (who *d.* v.p. aged 26) 25 July 1629, and was *cr. a Baronet*, as above, 16 Aug. 1641.(a) He was M.P. for Lancaster, 1646, till secluded in Dec. 1648 and for Lancashire, 1660; Sheriff of that county, 1657-58, 1671-72, and 1672-73. He *m.* Rebecca, 3d and yst. da. and coheir of Hugh PERRY, Alderman and sometime [1632-33] Sheriff of London, by Catharine, da. of Richard FENNE, of London, merchant. He *d.* s.p.m.(b) and was *bur.* 15 Nov. 1688, at Wharton, co. Lancaster, when the *Baronetcy* became *extinct.*(c) His widow was *bur.* 17 June 1708, at Wharton aforesaid.

The dignity was, however, assumed many years afterwards (on what grounds is unknown) by EDWARD BINDLOSSE, who was a J.P. for Westminster. He *d.* s.p. in or before 1789. The will of "Sir Edward Bindlosse, Bart., Midx.," is proved May 1789.

LAWLEY:

cr. 16 Aug. 1641;

sometime, 1831-32, BARON WENLOCK;

afterwards, since 1851, BARONS WENLOCK.

I. 1641. "THOMAS LAWLEY, of St. Poonell [*i.e.*, Spoonhill], co. Salop, Esq.," 2d s. of Francis LAWLEY, of the same, by Elizabeth, da. and h. of Sir Richard NEWPORT, of High Ercall, Salop, suc. his eldest br., Richard LAWLEY, of Spoonhill aforesaid, in 1623, and was *cr. a Baronet*, as above,

(a) The patent is not enrolled. The date here given is that in Dugdale's *Catalogue*. See *Memorandum* on p. 84. The date of the "privy seals and signed bills, Chancery," is 13 Aug. 1641.

(b) Cecilia, his da. and h., *m.* William Standish, of Standish, co. Lancaster (who *d.* 8 June 1705), and *d.* 19 Jan. 1729/30, leaving issue.

(c) The will of a "Sir Robert Bindlosse" is proved 1655.

16 Aug. 1641. He was M.P. for Wenlock, 1625, 1626 and 1628-29. He *m.* Anne, da. and coheir of John MANNING, of Hackney, Midx., and of Cralle, Sussex. He *d.* 19 Oct. 1646. Will, without date, pr. 16 Dec. 1646. His widow *m.* (for his 2d wife) Sir John GLYNNE, Lord Chief Justice of the Upper Bench, 1655, who *d.* 15 Nov. 1666. Her will, directing her burial to be with her parents at St. Andrew's, Undershaft, London, dat. 23 Jan. 1666, pr. 19 Dec. 1668.

II. 1646. SIR FRANCIS LAWLEY, Bart. [1641], of Spoonhill aforesaid, s. and h., *suc. to the Baronetcy*, 19 Oct. 1646; was M.P. for Wenlock, 1659 and 1660 and for Salop 1661-79; Gent. of the Privy Chamber, 1660; a Comis. of Customs, 1675-79; el. Sheriff of Staffordshire, 1688, but did not serve. He purchased Canwell Priory, co. Stafford. He *m.*, about 1650, Anne, 1st da. of Sir Thomas WHITMORE, 1st Bart. [1641], by Elizabeth, da. and h. of Sir William ACTON, Bart. [1629]. He *d.* Oct. 1696. Will dat. 15 May 1693 to 31 July 1696, pr. 28 Oct. 1696. The will of his widow dat. 29 June 1713 to 25 Oct. 1715, pr. 18 Dec. 1718.

III. 1696. SIR THOMAS LAWLEY, Bart. [1641], of Canwell Priory and Spoonhill aforesaid, s. and h., *b.* about 1650; was M.P. for Wenlock, 1685-87; *suc. to the Baronetcy* in Oct. 1696. He *m.* firstly, Rebecca, 2d da. and coheir of Sir Humphrey WINCH, Bart. [1660], by Rebecca, da. of Martin BROWNE, Alderman of London. By her he had fourteen children. He *m.* secondly, 3 March 1711/2, at St. Paul's Cathedral, London, Elizabeth, widow of (—) PERKINS. He *d.* 30 Sep. 1729, aged about 80. Will dat. 6 Dec. 1727/8 to 22 Oct. 1729, pr. 31 Dec. 1729. His widow *m.* 22 Feb. 1730, in Somerset House Chapel, Mark HALFPENN, and *d.* 28 Jan. 1739/40. Will dat. 27 May 1739, pr. 17 May 1740.

IV. 1729 SIR ROBERT LAWLEY, Bart. [1641], of Canwell Priory aforesaid, s. and h. by 1st wife; *suc. to the Baronetcy*, 30 Sep. 1729. Sheriff of Staffordshire, 1743-44. He *m.* in 1726, Elizabeth, 1st da. of Sir Lambert BLACKWELL, 1st Bart. [1718], by Elizabeth, da. of Sir Joseph HERNE. She *d.* 21 March 1774. Her will dat. 17 Nov. 1770, pr. 6 April 1774. He *d.* 28 Nov. 1779. Will dat. 15 March 1776, pr. 19 Jan. 1780.

V. 1779. SIR ROBERT LAWLEY, Bart. [1641], of Canwell Priory, etc., aforesaid, only surv. s. and h., *bap.* 22 March 1735/6; *suc. to the Baronetcy*, 28 Nov. 1779; M.P. for Warwickshire, 1780-93. He *m.* 11 Aug. 1764, Jane, only da. (whose issue became sole heir) of Beilby THOMPSON, of Esrick, co. York, by Janet, relict of Sir Darcy DAWES, 5th Bart. [1663], da. and coheir of Richard ROUNDELL, of Hutton Wansley, co. York. He *d.* 11 March 1793. Will dat. 10 Feb. 1792, pr. 28 March 1793. His widow *d.* Nov. 1816. Will pr. 1816.

VI. 1793. SIR ROBERT LAWLEY, Bart. [1641], of Canwell Priory, etc., aforesaid, *b.* 1768; *suc. to the Baronetcy*, 11 March 1793; was an officer in the Guards; Equerry to H.R.H. the Duke of Cumberland; Sheriff of Staffordshire, 1797-98; was M.P. for Newcastle under Lyne, 1802-06; and was, 10 Sep. 1831, *cr.* a Peer as BARON WENLOCK of Wenlock, co. Salop, it being one of the "Coronation" Peerages of William IV. He *m.* 16 Sep. 1793, at Seamer, co. York, Anna Maria, da. of Joseph DENISON, of Denbies, co. Surrey, and of St. Mary's Axe, London, Banker, by his 2d wife, Elizabeth, da. of William BUTLER, of Lisbon, merchant. He *d.* s.p., at his villa near Florence, 10 April, and was *bur.* 19 Aug. 1834, at Hints, co. Stafford, aged 66, when the *Peerage* became *extinct.* Will pr. June 1834. His widow *d.* 20 Aug. 1850, in Carlton house terrace. Will pr. Oct. 1850.

VII. 1834. SIR FRANCIS LAWLEY, Bart. [1641], of Middleton Hall, co. Warwick, br. and h., *b.* about 1782; matric. at Oxford (Ch. Ch.), 20 Oct. 1800, aged 18; Fellow of All Souls' College, Oxford, till 1815; B.C.L., 1808; D.C.L. 1813; M.P. for Warwickshire, 1820-32; *suc. to the Baronetcy*, 10 April 1834; sometime Lieut. Col. of the Warwickshire Yeomanry Cavalry, resigning in 1848. He *m.* 18 May 1815, Mary Anne, 1st da. and coheir of George TALBOT, of Temple Guiting, co. Gloucester, by Charlotte Elizabeth, da. and coheir of Rev. Thomas DRAKE, D.D., of Amersham, Bucks. He *d.* s.p., 30 Jan. 1851, at Middleton Hall aforesaid, aged 68. Will pr. June 1851. His widow *d.* 21 Dec. 1878, at 10 Chichester terrace, Kemp town, Brighton.

VIII. 1851. PAUL BEILBY (LAWLEY-THOMPSON), 1st BARON WENLOCK [1839] and 8th Bart. [1641], br. and h., was, in his elder brother's lifetime, *cr.*, 13 May 1839, BARON WENLOCK of Wenlock. co. Surrey, and, afterwards, *suc. to the Baronetcy*, 30 Jan. 1851, which thenceforth became *merged* in that peerage. See *Peerage.*

WALTER:

cr. 16 Aug. 1641;

ex. 20 Nov. 1781.

I. 1641. "WILLIAM WALTER, of Larsdenn [*i.e.*, Sarsden], co. Oxford, Esq.," s. and h. of Sir John WALTER, of Wolvercot, Oxon, Lord Chief Baron of the Exchequer (1625-30), by his 1st wife, Margaret, da. of William OFFLEY, of London, was *b.* about 1604; matric. at Oxford (Ch. Ch.), 16 March 1620/1, aged 17; Barrister (Inner Temple), 1630; suc. his father, 18 Nov. 1630, and was *cr. a Baronet*, as above, 20 Nov. 1641. He was *cr.* D.C.L. of Oxford, 2 Nov. 1642; was M.P. for Weobley, 1628-29 and for Oxfordshire, April 1663 till declared void; was a Compounder and was fined £1,430 in Aug. 1646; Sheriff of Oxon, 1656-57. He *m.* (Lic. Lond. 20 Dec. 1632, he said to be 23 and she 20), Elizabeth, sister of John, 1st BARON LUCAS OF SHENFIELD, da. of Thomas LUCAS, of St. John's, near Colchester, by Elizabeth, da. and h. of John LEIGHTON. He *d.* 23 and was *bur.* 27 March 1675, at Sarsden. Admon. 24 Nov. 1675 to his widow. She was *bur.* 12 May 1691, at Sarsden. Her admon. 6 July 1691, registered in Oxford Act book.

II. 1675. SIR WILLIAM WALTER, Bart. [1641], of Sarsden aforesaid, s. and h., *b.* probably about 1635; matric. at Oxford (Queen's Coll.), 2 Oct. 1652, being, presumably, *cr.* M.A., 28 Sep. 1663; admitted to Inner Temple, 1649; *suc. to the Baronetcy*, 23 March 1674-5. Sheriff of Oxon, 1688-89. He *m.* firstly, in or before 1671, Mary, da. of John (TUFTON), 2d EARL OF THANET, by Margaret, da. and coheir of Richard (SACKVILLE), EARL OF DORSET. She was *bur.* 7 Feb. 1673/4, at Sarsden. He *m.* secondly (settlement 22 March 1677/8), Mary, 4th da. of Robert (BRUCE), 2d EARL OF ELGIN [S.] and 1st EARL OF AILESBURY, by Diana, da. of Henry (GREY), 1st EARL OF STAMFORD. He *d.* 5 and was *bur.* 8 March 1693/4, at Sarsden. Will dat. 5 May 1692, pr. 14 Feb. 1697/8. His widow, who was *b.* 31 Dec. 1657, was *bur.* 15 May 1711, at Sarsden.

III. 1694. SIR JOHN WALTER, Bart. [1641], of Sarsden aforesaid, 2d but 1st surv. s. and h. by 1st wife, *b.* about 1673;(a) matric. at Oxford (Queen's Coll.), 21 Aug. 1691, and was *cr.* D.C.L., 27 Aug. 1702, having *suc. to the Baronetcy*, 5 March 1693/4. He was M.P. for Appleby, 1694-95 and 1697-1700; for Oxford (six Parls.), 1706 till death. Clerk of the Green Cloth. He *m.* Elizabeth, da. of Sir Thomas VERNON, of Twickenham park, Midx. He *d.* s.p. 11 and was *bur.* 16 June 1722, at Sarsden. His widow *m.* 30 Sep. 1724, in Oxfordshire (as his 3d wife), Simon (HARCOURT), 1st VISCOUNT HARCOURT OF STANTON HARCOURT, who *d.* 28 July 1727, aged 66. She *d.* 12 July 1748 and was *bur.* at Sarsden. Will dat. 13 Feb. 1747, pr. 22 July 1748.

IV. 1722, to 1731. SIR ROBERT WALTER, Bart. [1641], of Sarsden aforesaid, br. of the half blood and h. male, being s. of the 2d Bart. by his 2d wife; was *b.* 29 Aug. and *bap.* 3 Sep. 1680, at Ampthill, Beds; matric. at Oxford (New Coll.), 15 Sep. 1693, aged 13; admitted to the Inner Temple, 1695; *suc. to the Baronetcy*, 11 June 1722. He *m.* Elizabeth Louisa, 1st da. of the Hon. Henry BRYDGES, D.D., Archdeacon of Rochester (br. of James, 1st DUKE OF CHANDOS), by Annabella, da. of Henry ATKINS. He *d.* s.p. 20 Nov. 1731, and was *bur.* at Churchill, Oxon, when the *Baronetcy* became *extinct.* Will dat. 7 Oct. and pr. 6 Dec. 1731 and 22 June 1748. His widow *m.* John BARNEVAL, "Esq.," and *d.* in or near Paris, 1740. Admon. 21 May 1746, her said husband being then alive.

(a) His elder br., William, who *d.* v.p. and unm., was *b.* 1671.

FERMOR, FARMOR, *or* FARMER:

cr. 6 Sep. 1641;

subsequently, 1692-1867, BARONS LEOMINSTER, *or* LEMPSTER;

afterwards, 1721-1867, EARLS OF POMFRET, *or* PONTEFRACT;

ex. 8 June 1867.

I. 1641. "WILLIAM FARMER, of Easton Neston, co. Northampton, Esq.," 1st s. and h. of Sir Hatton FARMER, *or* FERMOR, of the same, by Anne, sister of Charles, 1st VISCOUNT CULLEN [I.], da. of Sir William COKAYNE, of Rushton, co. Northampton, sometime (1618-19) Lord Mayor of London, was *b.* at Cokayne House, Broad street, and *bap.* 7 Nov. 1621, at St. Peter le Poor, London; matric. at Oxford (Ex. Coll.), 1 June 1636, aged 14; suc. his father (who had distinguished himself in the royal cause) 28 Oct. 1640; and was, a few months later, *cr. a Baronet*, as above, 6 Sep. 1641. Col. of Horse for the King; a Compounder and was fined £1,400 in Aprill 1645. He was made K.B. at the Coronation of Charles II, in 1661; was M.P. for Brackley, 1661, till void 18 July; P.C. 1660. He *m.* 8 Sep. 1646, at North Luffenham, Rutland, Mary, widow of the Hon. Henry NOEL (who *d.* s.p.), da. and coheir of Hugh PERRY, Alderman and sometime (1632-33) Sheriff of London, by Catharine, da. of Richard FENNE, of London, merchant. He *d.* of the small pox, "at the house of Mr. Hill, a tailor, at the 'Sign of the Lyon's Head,' in Covent Garden," 14 and was *bur.* 22 May 1661, at Easton Neston. Nunc. will, dat. 14, pr. 21 May 1661 and 3 June 1673. His widow *d.* in London 18 July, and was *bur.* 5 Aug. 1670, at Easton aforesaid. Will dat. 9 July 1670, pr. 1 Aug. 1671.

II. 1661. SIR WILLIAM FERMOR, *or* FARMOR, Bart. [1641], 2d but 1st surv. s. and h.; *b.* 3 and *bap.* 18 Aug. 1648, at Easton Neston; *suc. to the Baronetcy*, 14 May 1661; matric. at Oxford (Mag. Coll.), 20 June 1664, aged 15, and was *cr.* M.A., 17 April 1667; was M.P. for Northampton, 1670-79 and 1678-79. He *m.* firstly, in London (Lic. Vic. Gen., 21 Dec. 1671), Jane, da. of Andrew BARKER, of Fairford, co. Glouc., by Elizabeth, da. of William ROBINSON, of Cheshunt, Herts. She *d.* s.p.m. 10 and was *bur.* 12 Aug. 1673, at Easton Neston. He *m.*, secondly, June 1682, Catherine, 1st da. of John (POULETT), 3d BARON POULETT OF HINTON ST. GEORGE, by his 1st wife, Essex, da. of Alexander POPHAM. She, who was *b.* 9 and *bap.* 15 March 1664, at Hinton St. George, co. Somerset, *d.* also s.p.m. He *m.* thirdly, 5 March 1691/2 (Lic. Vic. Gen., 8 Feb.), his 2d cousin, Sophia, widow of Donough O'BRIEN, *styled* LORD O'BRIEN, 6th da. of Thomas (OSBORNE), 1st DUKE OF LEEDS, by Bridget, da. of Montagu (BERTIE), 2d EARL OF LINDSEY. She was living when he was *cr.*, 12 April 1692, BARON LEOMINSTER, co. Hereford. In that peerage this *Baronetcy* then *merged*, the second Baron being *cr.*, 27 Dec. 1721, EARL OF POMFRET, *or* PONTEFRACT, but *all these honours* became *extinct*, 8 June 1867, on the death of the 5th Earl, 6th Baron, and 7th Baronet.

DAVIE:

cr. 9 Sept. 1641;(a)

ex. 12 Jan. 1846.

I. 1641. "JOHN DAVIE, of Creedie [in Sampford and of Crediton], co. Devon, Esq.," s. and h. of John DAVIE, of the same, by Margaret, da. of George SOUTHCOTE, of Calverley, Devon, was *b.* about 1589; matric. at Oxford (Ex. Coll.), 22 Feb. 1604/5, aged 16, as an "Esq."; was living with four children, 1620 (Visit. of Devon, 1620); was M.P. for Tiverton 1621-22; Sheriff of Devon, 1629-30; and was *cr. a Baronet*, as above, 2 Sep. 1641.(a) He *m.* firstly, Juliana, 5th da. of Sir William STRODE, of Newnham, co. Devon, by his 1st wife, Mary, da. of Thomas SOUTHCOTE, of Bovey Tracey. She *d.* 14 and was *bur.* 25 May, 1627, at Sandford. He *m.* secondly, Isabel, da. of (—) HELE, of Gnaton, Devon. He was *bur.* 13 Oct. 1654, at Sandford. His widow, who *d.* s.p.m. was *bur.* there 28 Oct. 1656.

(a) The patent is not enrolled. The date here given is that in Dugdale's *Catalogue*. See *Memorandum* on p. 84. The date of the "privy seals and signed bills chancery" is 11 Aug. 1641.

II

II. 1654. SIR JOHN DAVIE, Bart. [1641], of Creedie aforesaid, s. and h. by 1st wife; *bap.* 6 Dec. 1612, at Sandford; aged 8 at the Visit. of Devon, 1620; matric. at Oxford (Ex. Coll.), 2 Dec. 1631, aged 19; *suc. to the Baronetcy* in Oct. 1654; was M.P. for Tavistock, May to Dec. 1661; Sheriff of Devon, 1670-71.(a) He *m.* firstly, Eleanor, da. of Sir John ACLAND, 1st Bart. [1644], by Elizabeth, da. of Sir Francis VINCENT, 1st Bart. [1620]. She *d.* s.p. He *m.* secondly, in or before 1645, Triphena, da. and coheir of Richard REYNELL, of Lower Creedy, Devon, by Margaret, da. and coheir of John PERYAM. She was *bur.* 1 Feb. 1658/9, at Sandford. He *m.* thirdly, Amy, da. of Edmund PARKER, of Burrington, Devon. She, by whom he had no issue, was *bur.* 25 April 1670, at Sandford. He *d.* s.p.s.(b) and was *bur.* there 31 July 1678. Will pr. 1678.

III. 1678. SIR JOHN DAVIE, Bart. [1641], of Creedie aforesaid, nephew and h. male, being s. and h. of William DAVIE, of Dura, co. Devon, Barrister at Law, by Margaret, da. of Sir Francis CLARKE, of Putney, Surrey, which William, (who was *bur.* 28 Nov. 1663, at Sandford, aged 49), was 2nd s. of the 1st Bart. He was *b.* 1660; matric. at Oxford (Ex. Coll.), 21 March 1677/8, aged 17; *suc. to the Baronetcy* in July 1678; was M.P. for Saltash 1679-81 and 1681; el. Sheriff of Devon 1689, but did not serve. He *d.* unm. 30 Sep., and was *bur.* 1 Oct. 1692, at Sandford, aged 32. M.I. Will pr. 1693.

IV. 1692. SIR WILLIAM DAVIE, Bart. [1641], of Creedie aforesaid, br. and h.; *bap.* 1 July 1662, at Sandford; matric at Oxford (Ex. Coll.), 30 March 1680, aged 17; *suc. to the Baronetcy*, 30 Sep. 1692.' Sheriff of Devon, 1697-98. He *m.* firstly, in or before 1688, Mary, da. and h. of (—) STEDMAN, of Downside, Somerset. She was *bur.* 4 March 1690/1, at Sandford. He *m.* secondly, in or before 1694, Abigail, da. of John POLLEXFEN, of Wembury, Devon. He *d.* s.p.m. and was *bur.* 24 March 1706/7, at Sandford, aged 44. M.I. Will pr. May 1707. The will of his widow pr. April 1725.

V. 1707. SIR JOHN DAVIE, Bart. [1641], of Creedie aforesaid, cousin and h. male, being s. and h. of Humphrey DAVIE, formerly of London, but afterwards (about 1662) of New England, merchant, by Mary, sister of Edmund WHITE, of Clapham, Surrey, merchant, which Humphrey (who was *bap.* 24 Aug. 1625, at Sandford) was yst. s. of the 1st Bart. He was B.A. of the University of Cambridge in New England, and was a merchant there till he *suc. to the Baronetcy* in March 1706/7, as well as to the family estates. He is said to have been much respected for his piety and generosity. He *m.* in or before 1700, "Mrs. Elizabeth RICHARDS," of New England. She was *bur.* 3 Dec. 1713, at Sandford. He was *bur.* there 29 Dec. 1727. Will dat. 25 April 1727, pr. 13 July 1728.

VI. 1727. SIR JOHN DAVIE, Bart. [1641], of Creedie aforesaid, s. and h., *b.* 1700; *suc. to the Baronetcy* in Dec. 1727. He *m.* 3 May 1726, at Broad Clyst, Devon, Elizabeth, da. of John ACLAND, of Kelleton, by Elizabeth, da. of Richard ACLAND, of Barnstaple. He was *bur.* 3 Sep. 1737, at Sandford. Admon. 8 May 1738 and 7 April 1744 to the curators of his four minor children. His widow was *bur.* 25 March 1738, at Sandford. Will pr. 1738.

VII. 1737. SIR JOHN DAVIE, Bart. [1641], of Creedie aforesaid, s. and h.; *bap.* 4 Aug. 1734, at Sandford; *suc. to the Baronetcy*, in his infancy, in Sep. 1737; matric. at Oxford (Mag. Coll.), 9 April 1750, aged 16; *cr.* M.A., 21 Nov. 1754; Sheriff of Devon, 1761-62. He *m.*, in or before 1764, Catherine, da. of John STOKES, of Rill, co. Devon. She was *bur.* 24 Dec. 1776, at Sandford. Will pr. 1790. He was *bur.* 26 Sep. 1792, at Sandford, aged 58. Admon. July 1797, March 1815, and March 1840.

VIII. 1792. SIR JOHN DAVIE, Bart. [1641], of Creedie aforesaid, 2d but 1st surv. s. and h., *bap.* 9 April 1772, at Sandford; matric. at Oxford (Mag. Coll.), 20 Feb. 1790, aged 18; *suc. to the Baronetcy* in Sep. 1792. Sheriff of Devon, 1802-03. He *m.* 6 Sep. 1796, Anne, 1st da. of Sir William LEMON, 1st Bart. [1774], by Jane, da. of James BULLER, of Morval, co. Cornwall. He was *bur.* 16 May 1803, at Sandford, aged 31. Will pr. 1803. His widow was *bur.* there 12 Dec. 1812, aged 46.

(a) He is, however, described only as an "Esq." on the list.

(b) John Davie. his only son (by 2d wife), matric. at Oxford (Ex. Coll.), 3 June 1663, aged 18, *d.* v.p. and unm. and was *bur.* 11 Jan. 1667/8, at Sandford.

IX. 1803. SIR JOHN DAVIE, Bart. [1641], of Creedie aforesaid, s. and h., *bap.* (with his twin brother) 28 March 1798, at Sandford; *suc. to the Baronetcy*, 16 May 1803; matric. at Oxford (Ex. Coll.), 26 Jan. 1818, aged 19. He *d.* unm. 18 Sep. 1824.(a) Will pr. 1824.

X 1824, to 1846. SIR HUMPHREY PHINEAS DAVIE, Bart. [1641], of Creedie aforesaid, uncle and h. male, *b.* 12 Jan. and *bap.* 5 April 1775, at Sandford; matric. at Oxford (Ch. Ch.), 1 Feb. 1793, aged 18; Colonel in the army; *suc. to the Baronetcy*, 18 Sep. 1824. He *d.* unm. 12 Jan. 1846, at Sandford, aged exactly 71, when the *Baronetcy* became *extinct*. M.I. Will pr. Feb. 1846.

PETTUS:

cr. 23 Sep. 1641;

ex. 31 July 1772.

I. 1641. "THOMAS PETTUS, of Rackheath, co. Norfolk, Esq.," s. and h. of Sir Augustine PETTUS,(b) of the same, by his 1st wife, Mary, da. of Henry VYLETT. of Lynn; was *cr. a Baronet*, as above, 23 Sep. 1641. He was a zealous Loyalist. He *m.* firstly, Elizabeth, da. of Sir Thomas KNYVETT, of Ashwelthorpe, Norfolk. She *d.* 1653. He *m.* secondly, Anne, da. of Arthur EVERARD, of Stow Park, Suffolk. He *d.* 21 Nov 1654 His widow *m.* 18 Feb. 1657/8, at St. Dionis Backchurch, London (Banns pub. at St. Paul's, Covent Garden), Francis WARNER, of Parham, Suffolk. She *d.* 1662.

II. 1654. SIR THOMAS PETTUS, Bart. [1641], of Rackheath aforesaid, s. and h., by 1st wife; *suc. to the Baronetcy*, 21 Nov. 1654; Sheriff of Norfolk, 1664-65. He *m.*, in or before 1640, Elizabeth, da. of William OVERBURY, of Barton, co. Warwick. He *d.* s.p.m.s., 1671. Admon. 9 May 1672, to Elizabeth, the relict. Will pr. Nov. 1673, but subsequently revoked and admon. granted 7 March 1676/7, and 6 Nov. 1684. His widow *m.* (—) PODE. Her admon. as of St. Mary's Savoy, widow, 25 June 1687.

III. 1671. SIR JOHN PETTUS, Bart. [1641], of Rackheath aforesaid, br. of the whole blood, and h. male, *b.* about 1640; *suc. to the Baronetcy* in 1671. He was Cup bearer to Charles II, James II, and William III; and one of the Commissioners of Appeal. F.R.S.(c) He *m.* (Lic. Vic. Gen., 27 May 1670, he about 30 and she about 20), Mary, da. and coheir of Nicholas BURWELL, of Gray's Inn, Midx., brother of Sir Geoffrey BURWELL, of Rougham, Suffolk. He *d.* 29 Oct. 1698, aged 58.

IV. 1698. SIR HORATIO PETTUS, Bart. [1641], of Rackheath aforesaid, s. and h.; *b.* about 1672; *suc. to the Baronetcy*, 29 Oct. 1698. He *m.* (Lic. Fac., 1 May 1701, he about 29 and she about 21), Elizabeth, yst. da. of Sir Thomas MEERS, of Kirton, co. Lincoln. He *d.* 9 March 1730/1, aged 63. The will of his widow dat. 22 Sep. 1744, pr. 17 Aug. 1746, and 4 Jan. 1768.

V. 1731. SIR JOHN PETTUS, Bart. [1641], of Rackheath aforesaid, 1st surv. s. and h., *suc. to the Baronetcy*, 9 March 1730/1. His mother, in her will, mentions having paid £5,500 for his debts and those of his father. He *m.* 4 Dec. 1744, Rebecca, da. of Edmund PRIDEAUX, of Padstow, Cornwall, by Hannah, da. of Sir Benjamin WRENCH, of Norwich. He *d.* s.p.m. May 1743. His widow *d.* 17 Nov. 1780, aged 50, and was *bur.* at Rackheath.

(a) Frances Juliana, his only surv. sister and h., *m.* 20 March 1823, Henry Robert FERGUSON, and suc. to the family estates, on her uncle's death, in Jan. 1846. Her husband took the name of DAVIE after that of FERGUSON, and was *cr. a Baronet*, 9 Jan. 1847.

(b) There was a "Thomas Pettus, s. of Sir John, Knt. of Norwich," admitted, 29 May 1609, to Lincoln's Inn; also a "John Pettus, 2d s. of Sir Augustine, Knt. of Rackheath, co. Norfolk, Knt., deceased," who was so admitted 13 May 1635. This John, who was Knighted, 21 Nov. 1641, was M.P. for Droitwich, 1670; was of Chesterton Hall, Suffolk, and *d.* s.p.m. about 1690. He is often confused with the 3d Baronet, and *he* possibly (and not that Baronet, as stated in the text) was "F.R.S."

(c) See note "b" above, *ad finem.*

U

VI. 1743, to 1772. SIR HORATIO PETTUS, Bart. [1741], br. and h. male; *suc. to the Baronetcy* in May 1743; was Sheriff of Norfolk, 1746-47. He *d.* s.p. 31 July 1772, when the *Baronetcy* became *extinct*. Admon. Dec. 1808.

MEUX:

cr. 11 Dec. 1641;(a)

ex. 6 March 1705/6.

I. 1641. "JOHN MEUX, of the Isle of Wight, co. Southampton, Esq.," only s. and h. of Sir William MEUX, of Kingston, in that island, by his 1st wife, Winifred, da. of Sir Francis BARRINGTON, 1st Bart. [1611], was admitted to Gray's Inn, 11 Feb. 1629/30, and was *cr. a Baronet*, as above, 11 Dec. 1641.(a) M.P. for Newtown (Isle of Wight) April to May 1640 and Nov. 1640 till disabled. 5 Feb. 1643/4; was a Compounder, April 1646, and fined £375 in Oct. 1646. He *m.* Elizabeth, da. of Sir Richard WORSLEY, 1st Bart. [1611], by Frances, da. of Sir Henry NEVILLE. She was *bur.* 28 Dec. 1652, at Kingston aforesaid. He was *bur.* there 12 Feb. 1657.

II. 1657. SIR WILLIAM MEUX, Bart. [1641], of Kingston aforesaid, 1st s. and h., *suc. to the Baronetcy* in Feb. 1657. He *m.* firstly (Banns pub. 1657, at Kingston), Mabel, sister of Sir Robert DILLINGTON, 2d Bart. [1628], da. of Robert DILLINGTON, of Knighton, in the Isle of Wight. She *d.* s.p.m.s. and was *bur.* 19 Sep. 1670, at Kingston. He *m.* secondly, in or before 1681, Elizabeth, da. of George BROWNE, of Buckland, co. Surrey. He *d.* about 1697. Will dat. 24 June 1693, pr. 11 May 1697. His widow was *bur.* 29 Jan. 1731/2, at St. Margaret's, Westm. Will dat. 31 Aug. 1730, pr. 9 June 1732.

III. 1697? to 1706. SIR WILLIAM MEUX, Bart. [1641], of Kingston aforesaid, 1st surv. s. and h., by 2d wife, *bap.* 25 June 1683, at St. Paul's, Covent Garden; *suc. to the Baronetcy* about 1697. He *d.* unm. 6 and was *bur.* 13 March 1705/6, at Kingston, aged 22, when the *Baronetcy* became *extinct*.(b)

ANDREWE, *or* ANDREWS:

cr. 11 Dec. 1641.

ex. 1804.

I. 1641. "WILLIAM ANDREWE, of Deinton, *alias* Little Doddington, co. Northampton, Esq.," was *cr. a Baronet*, as above, 11 Dec. 1641; was a Royalist, and a Compounder, Feb. 1648. He *m.* (—) da. of (—) PARIS, of Linton, co. Cambridge. By her he had five sons, of whom three fell at the battle of Worcester, fighting for their King. He *d.* of the gout, in or before Jan. 1649, and was *bur.* at Bury St. Edmunds, Suffolk. Will pr. 1649.

II. 1649? SIR JOHN ANDREWE, Bart. [1641], of Deinton *otherwise* Denton aforesaid, s. and h.; *suc. to the Baronetcy* in or before 1649. He *d.* s.p.m.(c)

(a) The patent is not enrolled. The date here given is that in Dugdale's *Catalogue*. See *Memorandum* on p. 84. The date of the signet bill is 8 Dec. 1641.

(b) His sister Elizabeth, the only one that was married, was *bap.* 19 July 1677, at Kingston; *m.* 2 May 1710, at St. Dunstan's in the West, London, Sir John Miller, 2d Bart. [1705], and had issue. Another Baronetcy was conferred, 30 Sep. 1831, on Henry Meux, of Theobald's Park, Herts (a descendant of Bartholomew Meux, br. of the 1st Bart.), but this, in Jan. 1900, became, also, extinct.

(c) His only da. died unm.

III. 1665? SIR WILLIAM ANDREWE, *or* ANDREWS, Bart. [1641], of Denton aforesaid, br. and h., *suc. to the Baronetcy* on his brother's death. He *m.* Eleanor, da. and h. of Edward ATSLOW, of Downham Hall, Essex (aged 30 in the Visit. of Essex of 1634, and unm.), by (—), da. of (—) PARIS. He *d.* 15 Aug. 1684, and was *bur.* at Downham aforesaid. Will pr. 1684.

IV. 1684. SIR FRANCIS ANDREWS, Bart. [1641], of Denton and Downham aforesaid, s. and h.; *suc. to the Baronetcy*, 15 Aug. 1684. He sold the estate of Downham under an Act of Parl. dat. 1698. He *m.* Bridget, da. and coheir of Sir Thomas CLIFTON, Bart. [1660], of Clifton, co. Lancaster, by his 2d wife, Bridget, da. of Sir Edward HUSSEY. He *d.* at Chelsea, Middlesex, 3 April 1759.

V. 1759, to 1804. SIR WILLIAMS ANDREWS, Bart. [1641], only s. and h.; *suc. to the Baronetcy*, 3 April 1759. He *d.* s.p. in 1804, when the *Baronetcy* became *extinct*.

GURNEY, *or* GOURNEY:

cr. 14 Dec. 1641;

ex. 6 Oct. 1647.

I. 1641, to 1647. "RICHARD GOURNEY, Knt., now Mayor of the City of London," 2d s. of Bryan GOURNARDE,(a) GOURNEY, *or* GURNEY, of Croydon, Surrey (*bur.* there 24 Aug. 1602), by Magdalen (*m.* 27 April 1567, at Croydon), da. of (—) HEWET, was *bap.* 8 March 1577/8, at Croydon;(b) was apprenticed to R. Coleby, a silk mercer in Cheapside, who left him his shop and £6,000; became Free of the Clothworkers' Company; was Sheriff of London, 1633-34, in which year he entered and signed (as "Richard Gurney") his pedigree in the *Heralds' Visit.* of that city; was Alderman of Bishopsgate, 1634-37, and of Dowgate, 1637 till ejected, 11 Aug. 1642; was (after a severe contest, he being a sturdy Loyalist) Lord Mayor, 1641-42 (though ejected by Parl., 11 Aug. 1642), being, during office, *Knighted*, 25 Nov. 1641, at Kingsland, near Shoreditch, on the King's return from Scotland, whom, next day, he entertained at Guildhall, and was *cr. a Baronet*, as above, a few weeks later, 14 Dec. 1641. He was, by the Commons, committed to the Tower (where he remained upwards of five years), 11 July 1642, and ejected from office 11 Aug. following. On 6 March 1644/5 he was fined £5,000. He *m.* firstly, probably before 1620, Elizabeth, da. of Henry SANDFORD, of Birchington, in the Isle of Thanet, co. Kent. He *m.* secondly, in Oct. 1632, Elizabeth, widow of Robert SOUTH, da. of Richard GOSSON, of Odiham, Hants, and of London, goldsmith. He *d.* s.p.m.s.,(c) 6 and was *bur.* 8 Oct. 1647, at St. Olave's, Jewry, aged about 70, when the *Baronetcy* became *extinct*. Will pr. 1647. His widow, by whom he had no issue, was *b.* at Odiham aforesaid, and living 1652, at Pointer's Grove, in Totteridge, Herts.

(a) See pedigree in *Visit. of London, 1634*, amplified by G. S. Steinman, in *Coll. Top. et Gen.*, vol. iv, p. 91, and see copy of the donation of land at Fulham, Midx., 18 Feb. 1633, by Elizabeth, his wife, to the poor of Odiham, Hants, in vol. viii, p. 233.

(b) In Steinman's pedigree (see note "a" above) he is said to have been "born at Croydon, 17 April 1577; *bap.* there 8 March 1578," but query the authority for his birth nearly a year before his own baptism, and but four months after the baptism of his brother John.

(c) Richard Gurney, only s. and h. ap. by 1st wife, was living 1633, but *d.* v.p. and s.p.

WILLIS, *or* WILLYS:

cr. 15 Dec. 1641;(a)

ex. 14 April 1732.

I. 1641. "THOMAS WILLYS, of Fenn Ditton, co. Cambridge, Esq.," s. and h. of Richard WILLYS, of the same, and of Exhall and Horningsey, in the same county, by Jane, da. and h. of William HENMARSH, of Balls, in Ware, co. Herts, was *b.* about 1614, (being aged about 72 at the *Her. Visit. of Cambridgeshire, 1684*); suc. his father, 16 Oct. 1628; and was *cr. a Baronet*, as above, 15 Dec. 1641.(a); M.P. for Cambridgeshire, 1659; for Cambridge, 1660; Sheriff of Cambridgeshire and Hunts., 1665-66. He *m.*, about 1633, Anne, 1st da. and coheir of Sir John WYLD, of Mystole and of St. Martin's, Canterbury, Kent, by Anne, da. of Robert HONYWOOD, of Charing, in that county. She, who was *b.* at her maternal grandfather's house, at Markshall, co. Essex, *d.* 20 Oct. 1685, aged 75. He *d.* 17 Nov. 1701, aged 87. Will dat. 13 and pr. 25 Nov. 1701.

II. 1701. SIR JOHN WILLYS, Bart. [1641], of Fen Ditton aforesaid, 2d but 1st surv. s. and h. *b.* about 1635 (aged 49 in 1684); *suc. to the Baronetcy*, 17 Nov. 1701. He *m.* Mary, da. of Thomas SAVAGE, of Elmley Court, co. Worcester, by Mary, da. of Sir John HARE, of Norfolk. He was *bur.* 9 Aug. 1704, aged 68, at Fen Ditton. Will dat. 28 Oct. 1701 to 14 Oct. 1703, pr. 4 Oct. 1704. His widow *d.* 1709. Her will dat. 26 Oct. 1708, pr. 5 April 1709.

III. 1704. SIR THOMAS WILLYS, Bart. [1641], of Fen Ditton aforesaid, s. and h., *b.* there about 1674 (aged 9 years in 1684); *suc. to the Baronetcy* in Aug. 1704. He *m.*, in or before 1704, Frances, da. of (—) RIX. He *d.*, of the small pox, 17 June 1705. Admon. 25 July 1705. His widow *m.* the Rev. Matthew BAINES, and was living, as his wife, in 1724.

IV. 1705. SIR THOMAS WILLYS, Bart. [1641], of Fen Ditton aforesaid and of St. Mary's, Islington, Midx., only surv. s. and h., *b.* about 1704, and *suc. to the Baronetcy* in his infancy, 17 June 1705. He *d.* unm. about 1724, aged 20. Admon. 14 April 1724, granted to his mother.

V. 1724? SIR THOMAS WILLYS, Bart. [1641], of Fen Ditton aforesaid and of Hackney, Midx., cousin and h. male, being s. and h. of William WILLYS, of Austin Friars, London, Hamburg merchant, by his 2d wife, Catharine, da. of Robert GORE, of London, merchant, which Thomas (who was *bur.* at Fen Ditton 9 Aug. 1606, aged about 66) was 3d s. of the 1st Bart. He was *b.* about 1680, and *suc. to the Baronetcy* about 1724. He *d.* unm. 17 July 1726, aged 46, and was *bur.* at Nackington, Kent. Will dat. 13 April 1713, pr. 5 Aug. 1726 and 9 Feb. 1732.

VI. 1726, to 1732. SIR WILLIAM WILLYS, Bart. [1641], of Fen Ditton aforesaid, only br and h.; *b.* about 1685; *suc. to the Baronetcy*, 17 July 1726. M.P. for Newport (Isle of Wight) Jan. to July 1727, and for Great Bedwyn, 1727 till death. He *d.* unm. 14 April 1732, when the *Baronetcy* became *extinct*.(b) Will pr. 1732.

(a) The patent is not enrolled. The date here given is that in Dugdale's *Catalogue*. See *Memorandum* on p. 84. The date of the signet bill is 13 Dec. 1641.

(b) The estate of Fen Ditton was purchased in 1733 from his six sisters and coheirs by Sarah, the famous DUCHESS OF MARLBOROUGH, for her grand-daughter, Lady Mary GODOLPHIN, whose husband, the DUKE OF LEEDS, sold it, in 1749, to Thomas PANTON, of Newmarket.

ARMYTAGE:

cr. 15 Dec. 1641;

ex. 12 Oct. 1737.

I. 1641. "FRANCIS ARMYTAGE,(a) of Kirklees [in the parish of Hartshead], co. York, Esq.," 2d but 1st surv. s. and h. ap. of John ARMYTAGE,(b) of the same (Sheriff of Yorkshire, 1615), by Winifred, da. and h. of Henry KNIGHT, of Knighthill and Brockholes, in Lambeth, co. Surrey, was *b.* about 1600; was Bow Bearer of the Free Chase of Mashamshire, 1632; and was v.p., *cr. a Baronet*, as above, 15 Dec. 1641. He suc. his father, in July 1650. He *m.*, in 1629, Catherine, da. of Christopher DANBY, of Farnley, near Leeds, and of Thorpe Perrow, co. York, by Frances, da. of Edward (PARKER), LORD MORLEY. He *d.* v.p., and was *bur.* 12 June 1644, in York Minster. His widow, who was *bap.* at Leeds, 29 Feb. 1611/2, was *bur.* 13 Jan. 1666, at Wakefield.

II. 1644. SIR JOHN ARMYTAGE Bart [1641], of Kirklees aforesaid, s. and h., *bap.* 15 Dec. 1629, at Hartshead; *suc. to the Baronetcy* in June 1644, and to the estates (on the death of his grandfather), in July 1650; aged 38 at the *Heralds' Visitation of Yorkshire, 1666*; Sheriff of Yorkshire, 1668-69; Capt. of a Troop of Volunteer Horse. He *m.* in or before 1651, Margaret, 2d da. of Thomas THORNHILL, of Fixby, co. York, by Ann, da. and coheir of Thomas TRIGOT. By her he had eight sons and five daughters. He was *bur.* 9 March 1676/7, at Hartshead. His widow, who was *bap.* 1 Feb. 1633/4, at Elland, was *bur.* 10 Feb. 1695, at Hartshead.

III. 1677. SIR THOMAS ARMYTAGE, Bart. [1641], of Kirklees aforesaid, s. and h., *bap.* 10 May 1652, at Hartshead: *suc. to the Baronetcy* in March 1676/7; matric. at Oxford (Univ. Coll.), 19 Dec. 1668, aged 16. He *d.* unm. between Feb. and May 1694. Will dat. 23 Feb. 1693/4, pr. at York, 26 May 1694.

IV. 1694. SIR JOHN ARMYTAGE, Bart. [1641], of Kirklees aforesaid, br. and h., *bap.* 14 April 1653, at Hartshead; *suc. to the Baronetcy* in 1694. He *d.* unm. 2, and was *bur.* 7 Dec. 1732, at Hartshead, aged about 80. Will dat. 17 April 1732, pr. at York, 22 March 1732/3.(c)

V. 1732. SIR GEORGE ARMYTAGE, Bart. [1641], of Kirklees aforesaid, and of Mirfield, br. and h., being 7th and only surv. s. of the 2d Bart., *bap.* 23 Aug. 1660, at Hartshead; *suc. to the Baronetcy*, 2 Dec. 1732. He *d.* unm. and was *bur.* 24 April 1736, at Hartshead,(b) aged 75.

VI. 1736, to 1737. SIR THOMAS ARMYTAGE, Bart. [1641], of South Kirkby, co. York, cousin and h. male, being only surv. s. and h. of Francis ARMYTAGE, of South Kirkby aforesaid, by Mary, da. of Robert TRAPPES, of Nidd, in that county, which Francis (who was *bap.* 3 Jan. 1631/2, at Hartshead, and who *d.* between Nov. 1695 and Oct. 1728) was 2d s. of the 1st Bart. He, who was *bap.* 31 July 1673, at South Kirkby, *suc. to the Baronetcy*, 24 April 1736. He *d.* unm. 12 Oct. 1737, aged 64; and was *bur.* at South Kirkby, when the *Baronetcy* became *extinct*. M.I. at South Kirkby.

(a) Though the name is apparently enrolled as "Armitage" it is spelt "Armytage" in the patent (which is now in possession of Sir G. J. Armytage, 6th Bart. [1738]), and is so signed by the grantee and all his successors.

(b) See *Mis. Gen. et Her.*, orig. series, vol. ii, pp. 87-94, as to this family.

(c) He left Kirklees and other estates. after the death of his br., George, to his cousin Samuel Armytage, who was *cr. a Baronet*, 4 July 1738, and whose descendants still enjoy that estate and title.

HALFORD:

cr. 18 Dec. 1641;(a)

ex. 21 July 1780.

I. 1641. "RICHARD HALFORD, of Wistowe, co. Leicester, Esq.," s. and h. of Edward HALFORD, of Langham, co. Rutland, by Dionysia, da. of (—) BURY, of co. Rutland, was *b.* about 1580; was Sheriff of Rutland, 1619-20; of Leicestershire, 1621-22, and of Rutland (again), 1631-32; greatly distinguished, in the time of the Civil Wars, for his loyalty to the King, whom he entertained at his house of Wistow, and by whom he was *cr. a Baronet*, as above, 18 Dec. 1641,(a) being subsequently *Knighted*, 8 Jan. 1641/2, at Whitehall. He was very heavily fined, viz., £5,000 on 27 July 1644, and £2,000 on 16 Aug. 1645. He *m.* firstly, *circa* 1602, Isabel, da. of George BOWMAN, of Medbourne, co. Leicester. He *m.* secondly, Joan, widow of Thomas ADAMS and formerly of (—) LEAVER, da. of (—) ARCHER. He *d.* 1658, aged 78, *bur.* at Wistow. Will dat. 4 June 1657, pr. 17 Nov. 1658, and again 1698. His widow, by whom he had no issue, *d.* 1665. Will, as "of Sheavesby, co. Leicester, widow," dat. 2 Oct. 1664, pr. 16 Jan. 1665.

II. 1658. SIR THOMAS HALFORD, Bart. [1641], of Wistow aforesaid, grandson and h., being s. and h. of Andrew HALFORD, by his 1st wife Elizabeth, da. of Sir George TURPIN, of Knaptoft, co. Leicester, which Andrew was s. and h. ap. of the 1st Bart. (by his 1st wife) but *d.* v.p. 1657, aged 54(b). He *suc. to the Baronetcy* in 1658. He *m.* Selina, 1st da. of William WELBY, of Denton, co. Lincoln, by whom he had 22 children. He *d.* 1679, and was *bur.* at Wistow. Admon. 4 July 1679. That of his widow 1st April 1698.

III. 1679. SIR THOMAS HALFORD, Bart. [1641], of Wistow aforesaid, s. and h.; *suc. to the Baronetcy* in 1679; M.P. for Leicestershire, 1689-90. He *d.* unm. 1690, and was *bur.* at Wistow. Will dat. 5 Feb. 1689, pr. 30 May 1690.

IV. 1690. SIR WILLIAM HALFORD, Bart. [1641], of Wistow aforesaid, br. and h., *suc. to the Baronetcy* in 1690, being then under 21. He *m.* Judith, da. of Thomas BOOTHBY, of Tooley Park, co. Leicester. He *d.* s.p. 1695, and was *bur.* at Wistow. Will dat. 18 May 1695, proved by his br. Richard the same year.

V. 1695. SIR RICHARD HALFORD, Bart. [1641], of Wistow aforesaid, br. and h.; was probably B.A. of Cambridge (Queen's Coll.), 1700, and M.A., 1704; was in Holy Orders. He *suc. to the Baronetcy* in 1695, and purchased the Manor of Kibworth Harcourt in Leicestershire. He *m.* Mary, da. of Rev. William COTTON, Rector of Broughton Astley, Leicestershire. He *d.* 5 Sep. 1727, and was *bur.* at Wistow.

VI. 1727. SIR WILLIAM HALFORD, Bart. [1641], of Wistow aforesaid, s. and h., *b.* 1709; matric. at Oxford (Lincoln Coll.), 10 May 1723, aged 14; B.A. 26 Jan. 1726/7; M.A. 1730, having *suc. to the Baronetcy*, 5 Sep. 1727. At the coronation of George II he claimed the office of "Great Pannater." Sheriff of Leicestershire, 1760-61. He *d.* unm. 1768. Will pr. May 1768.

VII. 1768, to 1780. SIR CHARLES HALFORD, BART. [1641], of Wistow aforesaid, nephew and h., being 4th but 1st surv. s. and h. of Thomas HALFORD, by Elizabeth, da. of Thomas PALMER, of Leicester, which Thomas was 2d s. of the 5th Bart. He *suc. to the Baronetcy* in 1768; was Sheriff of Leicestershire, 1769-70. He *m.* Sarah, yst. da. of Edward FARNHAM, of Quorndon House, co. Leicester. He *d.* s.p. 21 July 1780, when

---

(a) The patent is not enrolled. The date here given is that in Dugdale's *Catalogue*. See *Memorandum* on p. 84. The date of the signet bill is 16 Dec. 1641.

(b) It is said that this Andrew was condemned to death by Cromwell, for having hanged a party of rebels against the King, but that his life was spared for a bribe of £30,000.

the *Baronetcy* is presumed to have become *extinct*(a). He was *bur.* at Wistow. Will dat. 13 Sep. 1777; pr. 13 Dec. 1780. His widow *m.* 21 July 1783, at Wistow (as his 2d wife), Basil (FEILDING), 6th EARL OF DENBIGH, who *d.* 14 July 1800. She, who was *b.* 25 Oct. 1741, *d.* s.p. 2 Oct. 1814, at Brighton, and was *bur.* at Wistow(b). Will pr. 1815.

TUFTON:

cr. 24 Dec. 1641;

ex. 14 Oct. 1685.

I. 1641. "HUMFREY TUFTON, of Le Mote, in the parish of Maidstone, co. Kent, Knt.," being also of Bobbing Court in that county, yr. br. to Nicholas, 1st EARL OF THANET, and to Sir William TUFTON, 1st Bart. [I. 1622], being 3d s. of Sir John TUFTON, 1st Bart. [1611], of Hothfield, in that county, by his 2d wife Christian, da. and coheir of Sir Humphrey BROWN, was *b.* 1584; matric. at Oxford (Univ. Coll.), 30 June 1598, aged 14; admitted to the Inner Temple, 1601; *Knighted*, 18 Jan. 1613/4; was M.P. for Maidstone in the long Parl. 1640, till secluded Dec. 1648; and was *cr. a Baronet*, as above, 24 Dec. 1641. He was a Parliamentarian, serving on several important Committees, 1642-45; was Sheriff of Kent, 1654-55. He *m.* Margaret,(c) 1st da. and coheir of Herbert MORLEY, of Glynd, co. Sussex, a Colonel in the Parliament Service, by Anne, da. of Sampson LENNARD, and Margaret, (*suo jure*) BARONESS DACRE. He *d.* at Bobbing Court, Oct. 1659, aged 76, and was *bur.* at Bobbing. Admon. 8 Oct. 1659. The will of his widow pr. 1667.

II. 1659, to 1685. SIR JOHN TUFTON, Bart. [1641], of the Mote and of Bobbing Court aforesaid, 2d but eldest surv. s. and h., *b.* 1623; matric. at Oxford (Univ. Coll.), 29 April 1636, aged 13; *Knighted*, 21 Dec. 1641, at Whitehall; *suc. to the Baronetcy*, Oct. 1659. He *m.* firstly, Margaret, 3d da. and coheir of Thomas (WOTTON), 2d BARON WOTTON OF MARLEY, by Mary, da. and coheir of Sir Arthur THROCKMORTON. He *m.* secondly, Mary, da. and coheir of Sir James ALTHAM, of Marks Hall, in Latton, co. Essex, by Alice, da. and h. of Sir John SPENCER, Bart. [1626], of Offley, Herts. He *d.* s.p. 11 Oct. 1685, aged 62, and was *bur.* in Maidstone Church, when the *Baronetcy* became *extinct*(d). Will pr. June 1686.

COKE:

cr 30 Dec. 1641;

ex. 26 Aug. 1727.

I. 1641. "EDWARD COKE, of Langford, co. Derby, Esq." s. and h. of Clement COKE, by Sarah, da. and h. of Alexander REDDISH, of Reddish, co. Lancaster, and of Langford aforesaid (which Clement was 7th and

---

(a) See *N. and Q.*, 6th S. vii., 387, for some conjectures as to this not being the case.

(b) On her death, the Halford estates passed under the will of her late husband, the last Baronet, to his great nephew Sir Henry HALFORD, Bart., formerly Henry VAUGHAN, M.D. See the Baronetcy of Halford, *cr.* 27 Sep. 1809.

(c) See a curious account of her intimacy (Platonic, or otherwise) with the Hon. Sir Christopher NEVILL (s. of LORD ABERGAVENNY) in Pocock's Memorials of the family of Tufton—small 8vo., Greenwich, 1800; p. 34, etc.

(d) He directed Bobbing Court to be sold for payment of his debts, but left "The Mote" (which had been purchased by his father of Thomas CÆSAR) to his niece Tufton, da. of Sir William Wray, 1st Bart [1660], of Ashby, by his sister Olympia, whose issue became sole heir of her family. She *m.* Sir James MONTAGU, Lord Chief Baron of the Exchequer, and sold that estate to Sir John MARSHAM Bart., ancestor of the EARLS OF ROMNEY, who resided there till the 4th Earl sold it, May 1897, to Alderman Samuel.

yst. s. of the celebrated Lord Chief Justice Sir Edward Coke), suc. his father, 23 May 1629, and was *cr. a Baronet*, as above, 30 Dec. 1641. He was Sheriff of Derbyshire, Jan. to Dec. 1646. He *m.* in or before 1645, Catherine, da. and coheir of Sir William DYER, of Great Stoughton, co. Huntingdon. His will pr. 1669.

II. 1669? SIR ROBERT COKE, Bart. [1641], of Langford aforesaid, s. and h., *bap.* 29 April 1645, at Langford. Sheriff of Derbyshire, 1671-72; M.P. thereof, 1685-87; *suc. to the Baronetcy* about 1669. He *m.* Sarah, da. and coheir of (—) BARKER, of Abrighlee, Salop. She was *bur.* 13 Feb. 1685, at Langford. He *d.* s.p. and was *bur.* there 15 Jan. 1687/8. Will pr. July 1689.

III. 1688, to 1727. SIR EDWARD COKE, Bart. [1641], of Langford aforesaid, br. and h., *bap.* 6 Oct. 1648, at Langford; matric. at Oxford (Lincoln Coll.), 13 July 1666, aged 17; Barrister (Middle Temple) 1675; *suc. to the Baronetcy*, 15 Jan. 1687/8. He *m.* in or before 1684, Catharine. She was *bur.* 13 Dec. 1688, at Langford. He *d.* s.p. 26 Aug. 1727, when the *Baronetcy* became *extinct*. Will pr. Dec. 1727.

Memorandum.—ALL BARONETCIES CONFERRED by Charles I, AFTER 4 JAN. 1641/2,(a) WERE (until the Restoration) DISALLOWED under the act of [the Rump] Parl. dated 4 Feb. 1651/2, whereby "all and every honours, titles, dignities and precedences whatsoever granted, confirmed and given by the late King since 4 Jan. 1641" were made "null and void"; no one, after 25 March 1652, being allowed to assume them; each Peer so doing to forfeit £100, each Baronet or Knight to forfeit £40; all such patents to be brought into the Court of Chancery so that they might be cancelled.

All Royalist Baronetcies conferred after 22 May 1642(a) had previously been so disallowed by Parl., 11 Nov. 1643, under the act which made void "all grants since 22 May 1642 of any honours, dignities, baronies, hereditaments or other thing whatsoever to any person or persons which have voluntarily contributed, or shall voluntarily contribute any aid or assistance to the maintenance of the unnatural war raised against the Parliament." The new Great Seal "already made and provided [*i.e.*, on 28 Sep. 1643] was then placed in the hands of six Commissioners for use. Thus, for nearly three years there were *two* (rival) Great Seals of England, until, on 11 Aug. 1646, the *King's* Great Seal (which was taken at Oxford) was broken to pieces with great solemnity in the presence of both houses of Parl. After that date this seal of 1643 would, presumably, be, even after the Restoration of the Monarchy, considered as the legitimate Great Seal of the realm, but it seems a moot point how far the Parliamentary Great Seal, when for nearly three years (1643—1646) it ran concurrently with, and often in opposition to, that of the King, would be thus acknowledged. On 9 Jan. 1648/9, a new Great Seal was ordered. [*Ex inform.* W. D. Pink].

(a) There is some reason for the selection of the date of 22 May 1642, but there is none for that of the earlier date of 4 Jan. 1641/2. "By no manner of reasoning could it be pretended that Grants and Patents which had passed the (one) Great Seal between Jan. and May 1642, when that Seal *was* in actual attendance upon Parl. could be illegal." The date of 4 Jan. 1641/2, however, appears to have been chosen as being that on which the King attempted the arrest of the five members of the House of Commons, and so to have been looked on as the *date of the commencement of the Civil War*, after which everything done by the King alone was considered illegal. The fixing of this early date (4 Jan. 1641/2) was an afterthought, enacted nine years after the later date, 22 May 1642, had been fixed upon on the much more intelligible ground, as being that on which the Great Seal was held to have deserted the Parl. on its having been delivered by Lord Keeper Lyttelton to the King at York. [*Ex inform.* W. D. Pink].

CUNNINGHAM, *or* CUNYNGHAME:

cr. 21 Jan. 1641/2(a).

I. 1642, to 1659. "DAVID CUNNINGHAM, of the city of London, Knt. and Bart. of Scotland," s. of Patrick CUNNINGHAM, of Kirkland, was Master of the Works to James VI [S.], whom he accompanied into England, being made Cofferer to Charles, Prince of Wales; bought Balgray in the parish of Irvine, 1630; had crown charter of Anchenharvie in the parish of Stewarton, co. Ayr, 19 Feb. 1631; had charter of the Barony of Auchenharvie in Cape Breton, 23 Dec. 1633; of Bolinshaw, 25 July 1634; and of Drumilling, Feb. 1636(b); was *cr. a Baronet* [S.] about 1626, though the patent, said to be one with rem. to heirs male whatsoever, was not sealed till 22 April 1634; and was *cr. a Baronet* [E.], as above, 21 Jan. 1641/2 (a) He appears to have *d.* unm.,(c) at all events s.p., and was *bur.* 7 Feb. 1658/9, at Charlton co. Kent, when the *Baronetcy* [E.] became *extinct* and the *Baronetcy* [S.] became *dormant*. Will as "of Covent Garden, Midx," dat. 15 Dec. 1647, to 18 Jan. 1658/9 (leaving his "honoured kinsman, Sir David Cuningham, of Robertland, Knt. and Bart.," his universal legatee), pr. 26 Aug. 1659, and 4 March 1674/5.

ASTLEY:

cr. 21 Jan. 1641/2;(a)

ex. 7 Dec. 1659.

I. 1642, to 1659. "ISAAC ASTLEY, of Melton Constable, co. Norfolk, Esq.," as also of Hill Morton, co. Warwick, 2d s. of Thomas ASTLEY, of the same, by Frances, da. and coheir of George DEANE, of Tilney, co. Norfolk, suc. his eldest br., Sir Frances Astley, in 1635, and was *cr. a Baronet*, as above, 21 Jan. 1641/2,(a) being *Knighted* the same day(d) at Whitehall. He was Sheriff of Warwickshire, 1641-42, and of Norfolk, 1645-46. He *m.* firstly, Rachael, da. of Augustine MESSENGER, of Hackford, Norfolk. He *m.* secondly, Bridget, widow of Edward DOYLEY, of Shottisham, Norfolk, da. of John COKE He *d.* s.p 7 Sep. 1659, and was *bur.* at Melton Constable, when the *Baronetcy* became *extinct.*(e) M.I. His widow *d.* Oct. 1700.

RAYNEY:

cr. 22 Jan. 1641/2(a);

ex. 1721.

I. 1642. "JOHN RAYNEY, of Wrotham, co. Kent, Baronet of Scotland," s. and h. of John RAYNEY, of the same, and of West Malling in that county (who was fined for declining the post of Alderman, and who was *bur.* at St. Benet's Gracechurch, London, 25 April 1633), by Susan, da. of Walter MANN, of Kingston, was *bap.* 5 April 1601, at St. Leonard's, Eastcheap; was *cr. a*

(a) Disallowed 4 Feb. 1651/2 by Parl. till the Restoration; see *Memorandum* as to creations after 4 Jan. 1641/2, on p. 152.

(b) *Ex inform.*, R. R. Stodart, Lyon Depute.

(c) There is a marriage licence 8 June 1637 (Bishop of London's office), for Sir David Cunynghame, Knt. and Bart., of St. Martin's in the Fields, bachelor, aged 29," with Elizabeth Harriott, of the same parish, widow of James Harriott, Esq., aged 28. This, presumably, must refer to Sir David Cuningham, Bart. [S. 1630], of Robertland, and in the *History of Heriots Hospital* it is so assigned. The age, unless grossly misstated, militates against its referring to this Sir David.

(d) The Isaac Astley who was Knighted 23 Feb. 1642/3 (afterwards the 2d Baron Astley of Reading), is, in Metcalfe's "List of Knights," called *rightly* "son of Sir Jacob," as also, but *wrongly*, is this one.

(e) His estates devolved on his nephew and h., Jacob Astley, who was *cr.* a Baronet 1660.

Baronet [S.], 13 Sep. 1636, with rem. to heirs male whatsoever, and was subsequently *cr. a Baronet* [E.], as above, 22 Jan. 1641/2(a), having been *Knighted* at Windsor, the day before, 21 Jan. 1641/2. He was Sheriff of Kent, 1644-45. He *m.* firstly, in or before 1627, Catherine, da. of Thomas STYLE, of St. Dionis Backchurch, London, by his 2d wife, Elizabeth, da. of John WOODWARD, of London. She, by whom he had seven children, was *bap.* 8 Sep. 1605, at St. Dionis Backchurch, and was *bur.* there 28 Sep. 1637. He *m.* secondly, 3 Oct. 1639, at Eltham, Kent, Frances, da. of Edward GIBBES, of Watergall, co. Warwick, by Margaret, da. of William WILKES. He *d.* at Wrotham, 3 and was *bur.* thence 9 March, 1660/1, at St. Benet's Gracechurch. Will dat. 22 Oct. 1660, pr. 2 April 1661. His widow *d.* in St. Bride's, London, and was *bur.* 28 Aug. 1690, at St. Benet's aforesaid. M.I. Admon. 21 Nov. 1690.

II. 1661. SIR JOHN RAYNEY, Bart. [E. 1642 and S. 1636], of Wrotham, and West Malling aforesaid, 1st s. and h., by 1st wife, was *b.* about 1627; *suc. to the Baronetcies*, 3 March 1660/1. He *m.* firstly, Susan, or Mary, da. of Jeremy BLACKMAN, of Southwark, Merchant, of London. He *m.* secondly, Ellen, da. of William SHORT, of co. Midx. He *d.* 1680, aged 53. Admon. 9 July 1680.

III. 1680. SIR JOHN RAYNEY, Bart. [E. 1642, and S. 1636], of Wrotham aforesaid, s. and h. by, apparently, his 1st wife, *b.* 1660; *suc. to the Baronetcies* in 1680, when a minor. He *m.* firstly, Vere, da. and coheir of Sir Thomas BEAUMONT, 3d Bart. [1627], of Grace Dieu, by Vere, da. of Sir William TUFTON, Bart. [I. 1622]. She *d.* 7 Dec. 1697, and was *bur.* at Wrotham. M.I. He *m.* secondly, 29 Dec. 1698, at St. Bride's, London, (Lic. Vic.-Gen., she about 30), Jane, 1st da. and coheir of Thomas MANLEY, of Rochester. She *d.* 14 Feb. 1700, and was *bur.* at Wrotham. M.I. Admon. 16 Feb. 1703/4. He *m.* thirdly, Jane, da. of Sir Demetrius JAMES, of Ightham, co. Kent, by Anne, da. of George BATE, M.D. He *d.* Feb. 1704/5, and was *bur.* at Wrotham. M.I. Will pr. 21 March 1704/5. His widow *d.* 27 Feb. 1714/5, aged 52, and was *bur.* at Wrotham. M.I. Will dat. 10 April 1711, pr. 9 March 1714/5.

IV. 1705. SIR JOHN BEAUMONT RAYNEY, Bart. [E. 1642 and S. 1636], of Wrotham aforesaid, s. and h., by 1st wife, *b.* about 1688; *suc. to the Baronetcies* in Feb. 1704/5, shortly after which he sold the estate of Wrotham Place, in Wrotham aforesaid. He was Lieut. Col. in the army. He *d.* in 1716. Admon. 7 Aug. 1716.

V. 1716, to 1721. SIR THOMAS RAYNEY, Bart. [E. 1642 and S. 1636], br. of the whole blood and h., *b.* 1690; *suc. to the Baronetcies* in 1716. He *d.* unm. 1721, aged 31, when the *Baronetcy* [E.] became *extinct*, and the *Baronetcy* [S.] *dormant*. Admon. 5 Oct. 1721, to Mary RAYNEY, his sister.

ELDRED:

cr. 29 Jan. 1641/2(a);

ex. 1652 or 1653.

I. 1642, to 1653? "REVETT ELDRED, of Great Saxham, co. Suffolk, Esq.," s. and h., of John ELDRED, of the same, by (—) da. of Reginald BROOKE, of Aspall, in that county, and of St. Michael's Bassishaw, London, was *cr. a Baronet*, as above, 29 Jan. 1641/2(a); was Sheriff of Suffolk, 20 Nov. 1645, but excused 6 Dec. He *m.*, before 4 June 1638, Anne, da. and coheir of John BLAKEY, or BLACKWELL, of co. Salop. He *d.* s.p. about 1653. Will dat. 21 May 1652, pr. 3 May 1653, when the *Baronetcy* became *extinct.* His widow *m.* (—) ARNOLD, of London, fined for declining the post of Alderman. Her will pr. June 1671.

(a) Disallowed 4 Feb. 1651/2 by Parl. till the Restoration; see *Memorandum* as to creations after 4 Jan. 1641/2, on p. 152.

GELL:

cr. 29 Jan. 1641/2(a);

ex. 14 July 1719.

I. 1642. "JOHN GELL, of Hopton, co. Derby, Esq.," s. and h. of Thomas(b) GELL, of the same, by Millicent, da. of Ralph SACHEVERELL, of Stanton-by-Bridge, in that county, was *b.* 22 June 1592, at Carsington, co. Derby; suc. his father in his infancy, before 1595, and was brought up at Kedleston, in the house of John Curzon, his step-father; matric. at Oxford (Mag. Coll.), 16 June 1610, aged 16; was Sheriff of Derbyshire, 1634-35, and was *cr. a Baronet*, as above, 29 Jan. 1641/2(a). He, however, in Oct. 1642, raised a regiment of Foot for the service of Parl., occupied Derby, and was appointed Gov. of that town by the Earl of Essex, 5 Jan. 1643, which he held against the King throughout the Civil War, in which he was one of the most active commanders, taking a share in the capture of Lichfield, the battle of Hopton Heath, etc.(c) He was, however, subsequently found guilty of plotting against the Commonwealth, 27 Sep. 1650, his estate sequestrated, March 1651, and himself imprisoned till April 1653, when he obtained a full pardon. On 4 June 1660, he claimed the benefit of the King's Act of Indemnity. He *m.* firstly, 22 Jan. 1609 (when only 16), Elizabeth, da. of Sir Perceval WILLOUGHBY, of Wollaton, Notts, by Bridget, da. and coheir of Francis WILLOUGHBY, of Wollaton aforesaid. He *m.* secondly, Mary, widow of Sir John STANHOPE, of Elvaston, da. of Sir Francis RADCLIFFE, of Ordsall, co. Lancaster, by Alice, da. of Sir John BYRON, of Newstead, Notts. She, by whom he had no issue, appears to have *d.* before him. He *d.* 26 Oct. 1671, at his house in St. Martin's Lane, London, aged 79 years, and was *bur.* at Wirksworth, co. Derby. M.I. Will dat. 24 May to 31 July, pr. 11 Nov. 1671.

II. 1671. SIR JOHN GELL, Bart. [1642], of Hopton aforesaid, s. and h., by 1st wife, *bap.* at Kedleston, Oct 1613; matric. at Oxford (Mag. Coll.), 23 Nov. 1632, aged 17; M.P. for Derbyshire (three Parls.), 1654-59, and Jan. to Feb. 1688/9; *suc. to the Baronetcy*, 26 Oct. 1671; Sheriff of Derbyshire, 1672-73. He *m.*, in or before 1648, Katharine, da. of John PACKER, of Donington Castle, Berks. She apparently *d.* before him. He *d.* 8 Feb. 1688/9, aged 75. Will dat. 18 Aug. 1687, pr. 14 May 1689.

III. 1689, to 1719. SIR PHILIP GELL, Bart. [1642], of Hopton aforesaid, 1st surv. s. and h.(d), *b.*, probably about 1655; was M.P. for Steyning, 1679-81, and for Derbyshire, 1689-90; *suc. to the Baronetcy*, 8 Feb. 1688/9. He *m.*, Elizabeth, one of the sixteen children of Sir John FAGG, 1st Bart. [1660], of Wiston, co. Sussex, by Mary, da. of Robert MORLE, of Glynd, in that county. He *d.* s.p. 14 July 1719, when the *Baronetcy* became *extinct*(e). Will pr. 1721.

(a) See p. 154, note "a."

(b) See *N. and Q.* 8th S., xii 401, correcting the article in the *Nat. Biogr.*, where (as elsewhere) the father's name is erroneously given as "John."

(c) He left a MS. account of his military services to vindicate certain charges brought against him by the Independents. Lord Clarendon says that the whole of Derbyshire was under the power of Sir John Gell, there being no visible party in it for the King.

(d) John Gell, the 1st s. and h. ap., said to be aged 15 in 1662 (Visit. of Derbyshire); matric. at Oxford (St. Edm. Hall), 26 July, 1666, when he is said to be aged 16; Barrister (Gray's Inn), 1674; *d.* s.p. and v.p.

(e) His nephew, John Eyre (2d s. of his sister Catharine, by William Eyre, of Highlow, co. Derby), inherited the Hopton estate, and took the name of Gell, being grandfather of the well-known classical antiquary, Sir William Gell, who *d.* 4 Feb. 1838, aged 59.

CORBET:

cr. 29 Jan. 1641/2(a);

ex. July or Aug. 1688.

I. 1642. "VINCENT CORBET, of Morton Corbet, co. Salop, Knt.," s. and h. of Sir Andrew CORBET, of the same, by Elizabeth, da. of William BOOTHBY, was *b.* 13 June and *bap.* there 13 July 1617; matric. at Oxford (Queen's Coll.), 24 Oct. 1634, aged 17; admitted to Lincoln's Inn, 11 Nov. 1637; *suc.* his father, 7 May 1637; was M.P. for Salop, April to May 1640; was *Knighted*, 29 June 1641, at Whitehall, and was *cr. a Baronet*, as above, 29 Jan. 1641/2(a). He was an active supporter of the Royal cause, and was fined £2,022 on 3 Dec. 1646, which was reduced to £433. He *m.*(b) Sarah, 4th da. and coheir of Sir Robert Monson, of North Carlton, co. Lincoln, which Robert was *bur.* there 15 Sep. 1638. He *d.* at St. Clement Danes, Midx., 28 Dec. 1656, aged 40. Admon. 1 June 1657, and 11 July 1676. His widow, on account of her husband's services on behalf of the late King, was *cr.* 23 Oct. 1679, a Peeress for life as VISCOUNTESS CORBET OF LINCHLADE, co. Buckingham. She *m.* (two months later), 18 Dec. 1679, at Stoke Newington, Midx., as his 4th and last wife (Lic. Vic. Gen., he aged 58), Sir Charles LEE, of Billesley, co. Warwick, and of Edmonton, Midx., who was *bur.* at Edmonton, 18 Dec. 1700. She *d.* 5 and was *bur.* there 10 June 1682, when the life *peerage* became *extinct.* Admon. 30 June and 11 July 1682, and 7 Nov. 1709.

II. 1656. SIR VINCENT CORBETT, Bart. [1642], of Moreton Corbet aforesaid and Acton Reynold, co. Salop, 2d but 1st surv. s. and h.,(c) *b.* about 1642; *suc. to the Baronetcy*, 28 Dec. 1656; was M.P. for Salop 1678/9 and 1679 till death. He *m.* in or before 1670, Elizabeth, da. and coheir of Francis THORNES, of Shelvock, Salop. He *d.* of the small pox, 4 Feb. 1680, aged about 37. Admon. 14 May 1681, and 8 March 1705/6. His widow, living Sep. 1688, *d.* about 1702. Will pr. Feb. 1702/3.

III. 1680, to 1688. SIR VINCENT CORBET, Bart. [1642], of Moreton Corbet and Acton Reynold aforesaid, only s. and h.; *b.* 22 May 1670; *suc. to the Baronetcy*, 4 Feb. 1680; matric. at Oxford (Ch. Ch.), 4 May 1686, aged 15. He *d.* unm., in College, 22 July or 6 Aug. 1688, when the *Baronetcy* became *extinct*(d). Admon. 5 Sep. 1688.

KAYE:

cr. 4 Feb. 1641/2(a);

ex. 25 Dec. 1809.

I. 1642. "JOHN KAYE, of Woodsome [in Almondbury], co York, Knt.," only s. and h. of Sir John KAYE, of the same (M.P. for Eye, 1610-11), by Anne, da. of Sir John FERNE, secretary to the Council of the North, was *bap.* 15 Aug. 1616, at Almondbury; suc. his father, 9 March 1640/1, was *Knighted* 24 May 1641, at Whitehall, and was *cr. a Baronet*, as above, 4 Feb. 1641/2(a). He was Colonel of a Regiment of Horse in the King's Service, and was a compounder 18 Feb.1644/5, and was on 22 March fined £500. He *m.* firstly, 27 April 1637, at Kirkby Wharf, Margaret, da. and coheir of Thomas MOSELEY, of Northcroft, sometime Mayor of York, by Elizabeth, da. and coheir of Thomas TRIGHT, *or* TRIGOTT, of South Kirkby, Yorkshire. He *m.* secondly, before 1649, Elizabeth, widow of Thomas

(a) Disallowed 4 Feb. 1651/2 by Parl. till the Restoration; see *Memorandum* as to creations after 4 Jan. 1641/2, on p. 152.

(b) The "Vincent Corbett, Esq., of the Inner Temple, Bachr., aged 26," on 15 July 1642, when he had lic. (London) to marry Jane Acton, Spinster, was, though exactly contemporary, probably the "Vincent Corbet" of Ynysmaengwyn, co. Merioneth (s. and h. of Robert Corbet)," who was admitted to Inner Temple in Nov. 1639.

(c) Andrew Corbet, the 1st son, was *bur.* 6 Sep. 1645, at Moreton Corbet.

(d) Beatrice, his only sister and h., *b.* 1669, *m.* before March 1705/6, John KYNASTON, by whom (besides a da., Beatrice, who *d.* unm.), she had a son, Corbet KYNASTON, sometime M.P. for Salop, who *d.* unm. 1741. The estate of Moreton Corbet, however, passed to his great uncle and h. male, Richard Corbet, ancestor of the Corbet, Baronets, so *cr.* 1808.

BURDETT, of Birthwaite, co. York, da. and h. of Sir Ferdinando LEIGH, of Middleton, near Leeds. She (by whom he had nine children, all of whom *d.* s.p.), was *bur.* 9 Sep. 1658, at Almondbury. He *m.* thirdly, 12 Feb. 1660, at Almondbury, Catharine, widow of Michael WENTWORTH, of Woolley, co. York, da. of Sir William ST. QUENTIN, 1st Bart. [1642], by Mary, da. and coheir of John LACY. By her he had no issue. He *d.* 25 and was *bur.* 26 July 1662, at Almondbury. His widow *m.* Henry SANDYS, of Down, co. Kent. She subsequently *m.* (for her 4th husband and his 2d wife), Alexander (MONTGOMERIE), 8th EARL OF EGLINTOUN [S.], who *d.* 1701. She was *bur.*, with her 3d husband, 6 Aug. 1700, at Down aforesaid. Admon. 4 Feb. 1700/1.

II. 1662. SIR JOHN KAYE, Bart. [1642], of Woodsome aforesaid, s. and h. by 1st wife, *b.* 1641; *suc. to the Baronetcy*, 25 July 1662, and was aged 25 at the Visit. of Yorkshire, 1665; M.P. for Yorkshire (four Parls.), 1685-98 and 1701, till death. He *m.*, in or before 1663, Ann, da. of William LISTER, of Thornton in Craven,(a) by Catherine, da. and h. of Sir Richard HAWKSWORTH, of Hawksworth. She was *bur.* June 1702, at Almondbury. He *d.* 8 and was *bur.* there 14 Aug. 1706, aged 65. Will dat. 21 June, pr. 26 Nov. 1706, at York.

III. 1706. SIR ARTHUR KAYE, Bart. [1642], of Woodsome aforesaid, s. and h., *b.* 1660; matric. at Oxford (Ch. Ch.), 2 March 1685/6, aged 15; *suc. to the Baronetcy*, 8 Aug. 1706; M.P. for Yorkshire (four Parls.), 1710 till his death. He *m.* (Lic. at York, 22 July 1690), Anne, 1st da. and coheir of Sir Samuel MAROW, Bart. [1679], of Berkswell, co. Warwick, by Mary, da. and h. of Sir Arthur CAYLY, of Newland, in that county. He *d.* s p.m. (b)in London 10 and was *bur.* 24 July 1726, at Almondbury. Will pr. 1726. His widow was *bur.* there 25 Aug. 1740. Will pr. 1740.

IV. 1726. SIR JOHN LISTER KAYE, Bart. [1642], of Denby Grange, in Kirkheaton, near Wakefield, co York, nephew and h. male, being s. and h. of George KAYE, of the same, by Dorothy, da. and h. of Robert SAVILE, of Bryan Royd, near Eland, co. York, which George (who was *bur.* 4 April 1710, at Almondbury) was 3d s. of the 2d Bart. He was *bap.* 4 Sep. 1697, at Almondbury; matric. at Oxford (Ch. Ch.), 24 May 1715, aged 18; *suc. to the Baronetcy*, 10 July 1726, and suc. to the Lister estates(a) in 1745, on the death of his paternal uncle, Thomas Lister, *formerly* Kaye. He was M.P. for the city of York, 1734-40; Alderman of that city, 1735, and Lord Mayor, 1737. He *m.* firstly, before 1745, at Huddersfield, Ellen, da. of John WILKINSON, of Greenhead, co. York. She *d.* 29 Jan. 1729. He *m.* secondly, 29 July 1730, at Wibsey, Dorothy, da. of Richard RICHARDSON, M.D., of North Bierley, in the West Riding of York, by Dorothy, da. of Henry CURRER, of Kildwick. He *d.* 5 April 1752, and was *bur.* at Flockton. Will dat. 8 Oct. 1751. His widow, who was *b.* 16 June 1712, *d.* 24 Aug. 1772, at Gainford.

V. 1752. SIR JOHN LISTER Kaye, Bart. [1642], of Denby Grange aforesaid, s. and h. by 1st wife, *b.* 26 June 1725, probably at Huddersfield; matric. at Oxford (Lincoln Coll.), 28 Feb. 1743/4, aged 18; *suc. to the Baronetcy*, 5 April 1752; Sheriff of Yorkshire, 1761-62. He *d.* unm., 27 Dec. 1789.(c)

VI. 1789, to 1809. SIR RICHARD KAYE, Bart. [1642], Dean of Lincoln, etc., *br.* of the half blood and h., being yst. s. of the 4th Bart., by his 2d wife, was *b.* 11 Aug. and *bap.* 8 Sep. 1736, at Kirkheaton; matric. at Oxford (Bras. Coll.), 27 March 1754, aged 17; Vinerian Scholar of Laws at Oxford, 1758, being the first so elected; B.C.L., 1761; D.C.L., 1770; was

(a) Christopher Lister, of Thornton aforesaid, only s. and h. of another Christopher Lister, of the same, *d.* unm. Nov. 1701, having devised his estates to his cousin Thomas Kaye, 2d surv. s. of the 2d Bart. He took the name of Lister, but *d.* unm. 1745, in his 70th year, when the estates devolved on his nephew, the 4th Bart., whose s. and h. the 5th Bart. devised them as in note "c" next below.

(b) Elizabeth, his only da. and h., who inherited the family estate of Woodsome, *m.* firstly, William LEGGE, *styled* VISCOUNT LEWISHAM, by whom she was mother of William, 2d EARL OF DARTMOUTH. She *m.* secondly, Francis (NORTH), 3d LORD GUILFORD (*cr.* in 1752, after her death, EARL OF GUILFORD), by whom she also had issue. She *d.* 21 April 1745.

(c) He devised his estates, being principally those inherited from the family of Lister, to his illegitimate son, John, who, as John LISTER-KAYE, was *cr. a Baronet*, 1812.

in Holy Orders; chaplain to the King, 1766; sometime Rector of Kirkby Clayworth, Notts; Preb. of York, 1768-83; of Southwell, 1774-80 and 1783—1809; of Durham, 1777-84; Archdeacon of Notts, 1780—1809; Preb. and Dean of Lincoln, 1783-1809; Rector of Marylebone, Midx., 1788-1809; F.R.S. and F.S.A.; *suc. to the Baronetcy*, 27 Dec. 1789. He *m.*, 29 Aug. 1791, Helen, widow of Thomas MAINWARING, of Goltho', co. Lincoln, da. of William FENTON, of Glasshouse, near Leeds, co. York. He *d.* s.p.m.(a) 25 Dec. 1809, aged 73, and was *bur.* in Lincoln Cathedral, when the *Baronetcy* became *extinct.* Will pr. 1810. His widow *d.* 14 July 1841, at Coleby, near Lincoln, aged 96. Will pr. 1842.

TROLLOPE, *or* TROLLOP:

cr. 5 Feb. 1641/2(b);

afterwards, BARONS KESTEVEN OF CASEWICK.

I. 1642. "THOMAS TROLLOP, of Casewicke, [in Uffington], co. Lincoln, Esq.," s. and h. of William TROLLOPE, of Casewicke, and of Bourne and Thurlby, in the said county, by Alice, da. of William SHARPE, of Bourne aforesaid, suc. his father, 8 June 1638; was Sheriff of Lincolnshire 1641-42, and was *cr. a Baronet*, as above, 5 Feb. 1641/2.(b) He *m.* firstly, in or before 1620, Hester, da. of Nicholas STREET, or STURT, of Hadley, Suffolk. He *m.* secondly, 16 Nov. 1635, Mary, da. of Sir Christopher CLITHEROE, Lord Mayor of London, 1635-36, by his 2d wife, Mary, da. of Sir Thomas CAMBELL, Lord Mayor of London, 1609-10. He *d.* about 1654. Will dat. 20 March 1651/2, pr. 7 March 1654/5. His widow, who was *b.* 10 Aug. 1608, was *bur.* 16 June 1688, at Uffington.

II. 1654? SIR WILLIAM TROLLOPE, Bart. [1642], of Casewick House, in Casewick aforesaid, s. and h. by 1st wife, *b.* 3 Jan. 1621; *suc. to the Baronetcy* about 1654; Sheriff of Lincolnshire, 1659-60. He *m.* Elizabeth, widow of William THOROLD, of Marston, co. Lincoln, da. of Sir Robert CARR, 3d Bart. [1611], Chancellor of the Exchequer. She was *bur.* 27 Feb. 1661, at Uffington. He *d.* s.p.m., 16 May 1678. Will dat. 21 Feb. 1669, pr. 1678.

III. 1678. SIR THOMAS TROLLOPE, Bart. [1642], of Casewick House, aforesaid, nephew, of the half blood, and h. male, being s. and h. of Thomas TROLLOPE, of Barham, co. Lincoln, by Anne, da. of Anthony COLLINS, of Whitton, Midx., which Thomas, last named, was s. by his 2d wife, of the 1st Bart., was *b.* about 1667; *suc. to the Baronetcy*, 16 May 1678; matric. at Oxford (Trin. Coll.), 31 March 1682, aged 15; was Sheriff of Lincolnshire, 1703-04. He *m.* in or before 1690, Susanna, 2d da. and coheir of Sir John CLOBERY(c), of Bradstone, Devon, by his 2d wife, Anne, sister and coheir of Sir William CRANMER, da. of George CRANMER(d), of Canterbury. She *d.* 2 and was *bur.* 5 June 1724/5, at Uffington. He *d.* at Casewick House, 22 and was *bur.* 25 Nov. 1729, at Uffington. Will pr. 1729.

IV. 1729. SIR THOMAS TROLLOPE, Bart. [1642], of Casewick House aforesaid, 1st surv. s. and h., *bap.* 21 Dec. 1691, at Uffington; admitted to Lincoln's Inn, 15 Nov. 1716; *suc. to the Baronetcy*, 22 Nov. 1729. He *m.*, in or before 1721, Diana, da. and coheir of Thomas MIDDLETON, of Stanstead, Essex, by Mary, da. of Sir Richard ONSLOW, 1st Bart. [1660]. He *d.* 7 Oct. 1784, aged 93. Will pr. Nov. 1784.

(a) Dorothy, *bap.* 31 March 1741, at Kirkheaton, wife of Robert Chaloner, of Bishop's Auckland, was the only child that married.

(b) Disallowed 4 Feb. 1651/2 by Parl. till the Restoration; see *Memorandum* as to creations after 4 Jan. 1641/2, on p. 152.

(c) A good account of the family of Clobery, and of the life of this Sir John, is given in Wotton's *Baronetage*. Edit. 1741.

(d) See full account of the family of Cranmer in R. E. Chester Waters' *History of the family of Chester, of Chicheley.*

V. 1784. SIR THOMAS-WILLIAM TROLLOPE, Bart. [1642], of Casewick House aforesaid, grandson and h., being s. and h. of Thomas-Middleton TROLLOPE (by Isabella, 1st da. of Sir John THOROLD, 8th Bart. [1642]. of Marston, which Thomas last named (who *d.* v.p. 27 April 1779, aged 58) was s. of the 4th Bart.(a) He was *b.* about 1762; was ed. at St. John's Coll. Cambridge; M.A., 1785, having *suc. to the Baronetcy*, 7 Oct. 1784. He *d.* unm., 13 May 1789, aged 27. Will pr. 1789.

VI. 1789. SIR JOHN TROLLOPE, Bart. [1642], of Casewick House aforesaid, br. and h., *b.* about 1766; *suc. to the Baronetcy*, 13 May 1789; Sheriff of Lincolnshire, 1811-12. He *m.* 24 March 1798, at St. Margaret's, Lincoln, Anne, da. of Henry THOROLD, of Cuxwold, co. Lincoln. He *d.* 28 April 1820, aged 54. Will pr. 1820. His widow *d.* 23 Dec. 1855, at Casewick. Will pr. Jan. 1856.

VII. 1820. SIR JOHN TROLLOPE, Bart. [1642], of Casewick House aforesaid. s. and h., *b.* there 5 May 1800; *suc. to the Baronetcy*, 28 April 1820; Sheriff of Lincolnshire, 1825-26; M.P. for South Lincolnshire, 1841-68; Chief Commissioner of the Poor Law Board, Feb. to Dec. 1852; P.C., 1852. He *m.* 26 Oct. 1847, at St. Marylebone, Julia Maria, 1st da. of Sir Robert SHEFFIELD, 4th Bart. [1756], by Julia Brigida, da. of Sir John NEWBOLD, Ch. Justice of Madras. She was living when, on 15 April 1868, he was *cr.* a Peer, as BARON KESTEVEN OF CASEWICK, co. Lincoln, in which peerage this *Baronetcy* became henceforth *merged.* See *Peerage.*

THOMAS:

cr. 3 March 1641/2(b);

ex. about 1690.

I. 1642. "EDWARD THOMAS, of Michael's Ville, *anglice* Michael's town, co. Glamorgan, Esq.," otherwise described as of Bettws in Tir-y-jarll, and of Llanvihangell, both in that county, s. and h. of Thomas AP GWILLIM Ap Howell GOCH, of Bettws aforesaid, Barrister, by Ann, da. and h. of entail of Robert THOMAS, of Llanvihangell aforesaid(c), was Sheriff of Glamorganshire, 1633-34, and was *cr. a Baronet*, as above, 3 March, 1641/2(b). He *m.* Susan, da. of Sir Thomas MORGAN, of Ruperra. In or about 1650, he sold his estates to Humphrey Edwin. He *d.* at Windsor, Berks, 1673. Will pr. 1673.

(a) "Middleton Trollope [*b.* 31 July 1721], eldest son of Sir Thomas Trollope, died at Devizes," see burial entry, 27 April 1779, at Uffington. The 5th and yst. son of the 4th Bart., the Rev. Anthony Trollope, Rector of Cotterel, Herts (*d.* 3 June 1806, aged 71), was father of Thomas Anthony Trollope, Barrister (*d.* 26 Oct. 1835, aged 61), who by Frances, da. of Rev. William Milton, Vicar of Heckfield, Hants (she, well-known as a writer of fiction, *d.* 6 Oct. 1863, aged 83), had two sons, viz: Thomas Adolphus Trollope, who *d.* 11 Nov. 1892, aged 82, and Anthony Trollope, who *d.* 6 Dec. 1882, aged 67, both of whom were also novelists, the younger being the most distinguished.

(b) Disallowed 4 Feb. 1651/2 by Parl. till the Restoration; see *Memorandum* as to creations after 4 Jan. 1641/2, on p. 152. The patent is not enrolled. The date here given is that in Dugdale's *Catalogue*. See *Memorandum* on p. 84. The date of the signet bill is 28 Feb. 1641/2.

(c) "Edward Thomas, s. and h. ap. of William [*sic*] Thomas, of Llanyhangell co. Glamorgan, Esq., Bencher," was admitted to Lincoln's Inn, 9 March 1619/20.

II. 1673, to 1690? SIR ROBERT THOMAS, BART. [1642], s. and h.; Gent. of the Privy Chamber, 1660; M.P. for Cardiff (three Parls.); 1661-81; *suc. to the Baronetcy* in 1673. He *m.*, in or before 1654, Mary, 2d da. of David JENKINS, of Hensol. He *d.* s.p.m.s.[a], at some date after 1681, when the *Baronetcy*, presumably became *extinct.*

COWPER:
cr. 4 March 1641/2;[b]
afterwards, since 1706, BARONS COWPER OF WINGHAM, *and subsequently*, since 1718, EARLS COWPER.

I. 1642. "WILLIAM COWPER, of Ratlinge Court [in Nonington], co. Kent, Baronet of Scotland," 2d s., but eventually h., of John COWPER, of St. Michael's Cornhill, Alderman of London, and sometime, 1551-52, Sheriff of that city, by Elizabeth, da. of John IRONSIDE, of co. Lincoln, was *b.* 7 March 1582; suc. his father, 3 June 1609, was Collector of the imposts in the port of London; was *cr. a Baronet* [S.], between 1625 and 1641, and was *cr. a Baronet* [E.], as above, 4 March 1641/2[b], being *Knighted* at Theobald's, 1 March following 1642/3. He and his eldest son, John COWPER, were, in Feb. 1642/3, imprisoned at Ely House, London, for their exertions on behalf of the King. On his release he resided at his Castle in Hertford. He was famed for his charity, hospitality, etc. He *m.*, 26 Sep. 1611, at Ospringe, Kent, Martha[c], sister of Sir Edward MASTER, da. of James MASTER, of East Langdon Court, in that county, by his 1st wife Martha, da. of (—) NORTON, of London. She was *bur.* 25 Nov. 1659, at St. Michael's, Cornhill. He *d.* 20, and was *bur.* there 23 Dec. 1664, aged 82. Will pr. 1664.

II. 1664. SIR WILLIAM COWPER, Bart. [E. 1642, S. 1640?], of Ratling Court and Hertford Castle aforesaid, grandson and h., being s. and h. of John Cowper, of Lincoln's Inn, London (adm. 20 Jan. 1631/2), by Martha, da. of George HEWKLEY, of London, merchant, which John was s. and h. ap. of the 1st Bart., but *d.* v.p. when in confinement at Ely house aforesaid, in Sep. 1643.[d] He *suc. to the Baronetcies*, 20 Dec. 1664. He was M.P. for Hertford in six Parls., 1679-1700; was an active Whig, and joined with the Earl of Shaftesbury, etc., in presenting, in 1680, an indictment against James, Duke of York, for non-attendance at church; was clerk of the Parliaments. He *m.* (Lic. Fac., 8 April 1663, she about 20, parents decd.) Sarah, da. of Samuel HOLLED, of St. Clement's, Eastcheap, London, merchant, by Anne his wife. He *d.* 26 Nov. and was *bur.* 2 Dec. 1706, at St. Michael's, Cornhill. Will pr. Jan. 1707. She *d.* 3 and was *bur.* 10 Feb. 1719, at Hertingfordbury, Herts, aged 76.

III. 1706. SIR WILLIAM COWPER, Bart. [E. 1642 and S. 1640?], of Ratling Court, and Hertford Castle aforesaid, s. and h.[e], is said to have been *b.* at Hertford Castle, about 1665; ed. at St. Albans' School; admitted to Middle Temple, 8 March 1681/2; Barrister, 25 May 1688; took an active part in assist-

[a] He is incorrectly called "Edward" in Burke's and in Courthope's *Extinct Baronetages.* His son, Robert Thomas, matric. at Oxford (Jesus Coll.), 14 Dec. 1671, aged 17; B.A. 1675; M.A. 1678, having been admitted to Lincoln's Inn, 1676, as 2d s. of Sir Robert Thomas, Bart. The last named Robert is presumed to have *d.* v.p. and s.p.m.. Susanna, said to have been the only surv. child of the 2d Bart., *m.* Robert SAVOURS, of Breach, and *d.* s.p. 2 Feb. 1747. Her portrait was at Llanvihangel in 1865.

[b] See p. 159, note "b."

[c] See a good account of the family of Master by Rev. George Streynsham Master, M.A., of which only 105 copies were privately printed, 1874; large 8vo, pages 104.

[d] This John was the "Mr. John Copper, out of Show lane," who was *bur.* 25 Sep. 1643, at St. Michael's, Cornhill.

[e] His next br., Spencer Cowper, one of the Justices of the Court of Common Pleas, 1727-28 (*d.* 10 Dec. 1728, aged 59), was father of the Rev. John Cowper, D.D., Rector of Berkhampstead, Herts (*d.* 10 July 1756, aged 62), who was father of William Cowper, the well-known Poet, *b.* 15 Nov. 1731; *d.* unm. 25 April 1800.

ing the Dutch invasion of England: King's Counsel 1694; Recorder of Colchester; M.P. for Hertford (two Parls.), 1695-1700, and for Beeralston 1901-02; was made P.C. and Lord Keeper of the Great Seal 11 Oct. 1705; a Commissioner for the treaty of the Union with Scotland 10 April 1706; *suc. to the Baronetcies*, 26 Nov. 1706, being a few weeks later *raised to the Peerage* as stated below. He *m.* firstly, about 1686, Judith, da and h. of Sir Robert BOOTH, of Wallbrook, London, merchant. She *d.* s.p. 2 April 1705. He *m.* secondly, "privately," bringing her home, 25 Feb. 1706/7,[a] Mary, da. of John CLAVERING, of Chopwell, co. Durham. She was living when he, being then L. KEEPER OF THE GREAT SEAL, was *cr.* a peer 9 Nov. or 14 Dec. 1706, as BARON COWPER OF WINGHAM, co. Kent, and, subsequently when (for the 2d time) L. Chancellor, he was *cr.* 18 March 1717/8, EARL COWPER, etc. In that peerage this *Baronetcy* then *merged* and still so continues. See *Peerage.*

STRUTT:
cr. 5 March 1641/2;[b]
ex. Sep. 1661.

I. 1642, to 1661. "DENNER STRUTT, of Little Warley Hall, co. Essex, Esq.," only s. of John STRUTT, of Toppesfield Hall in Hadley, co. Suffolk,[c] by Elizabeth, da. and h. of Edward DENNER, of Little Warley aforesaid, was admitted to Gray's Inn, 6 March 1627/8, and was *cr. a Baronet*, as above, 5 March 1641/2.[b] He adhered loyally to the Royal cause, was distinguished in the defence of Colchester, Aug. 1648, was a Compounder, 30 Nov. 1648, being, 11 Dec. 1648, fined £1,350. He *m.* firstly, Dorothy, da. of Francis STASMORE, of Forlesworth, co. Leicester, sometime M.P. She *d.* s.p. 17 Aug. 1641. He *m.* secondly, Elizabeth, 4th da. of Sir Thomas WODEHOUSE, 2d Bart. [1611], by Blanche, da. of John (CAREY), 3d BARON HUNSDON. He *m.* thirdly, Mary, da. and h. of Thomas CHAPMAN, of St. Leonard's, Foster Lane, citizen and leatherseller of London. She *d.* s.p. 4 Aug. 1658, aged 32. Will dat. 2 Jan. 1655/6, pr. 7 Sep. 1658. He *m.* fourthly, Elizabeth, da. of (—) CUSS, of co. Somerset. He *d.* s.p.m.s.[d] Sep. 1661, and was *bur.* at Little Warley, when the *Baronetcy* became *extnict.* M.I. Will dat. 6 and pr. 19 Sep. 1661. His widow *m.*, as his 3d wife, William WARD, of Little Houghton, co. Northampton, who was *bur.* 13 Jan. 1672/3, at St. Martin's in the Fields. She was *bur.* there 27 March 1675. Will dat. 18 Feb. 1674/5 pr. 1 Dec. 1675.

ST. QUINTIN:
cr. 8 March 1641/2[b];
ex. 22 July 1795.

I. 1642. "WILLIAM ST. QUINTIN, of Harpham, co. York, Esq.," s. and h. of George St. QUINTIN, of the same, by Agnes, da. of William CREYKE, of Cottingham, in that county, was *b.* 1579; and was *cr. a Baronet*, as above,

[a] Luttrell's *Diary.*

[b] Disallowed by Parl., 4 Feb. 1651/2 till the Restoration; see *Memorandum* on p. 152 as to creations after 4 Jan, 1641/2. No patent is enrolled. The date, as well as the description of the party, here given is that in Dugdale's *Catalogue.* See *Memorandum* on p. 84. It is to be observed that the creations of (1) Strutt; (2) St. Quintin; (3) Kemp; (4) Reade; (5) Enyon; (6) Williams; (7) Wintour; (8) Borlase; (9) Knollys, and (10) Ingilby, are omitted in the *List of Creations, 1483—1646*" (ap. 47th Rep. D. K. Pub. Records), in which the date of the warrant or Signet bill (failing that of the patent) for most of the Baronetcies down to Feb. 1644/5 is given.

[c] This John suc. his elder br., Nicholas Strutt, clothier, in that estate, both being sons of Nicholas Strutt, of the same, an opulent clothier, whose will dat. 23 Oct. 1601, is pr. 21 Feb. 1602. [*N. and Q.*, 4th S., vi, p. 180, and Essex *Arch. Assoc.*, Vol. v, p. 147.

[d] Thomas Strutt, his son (by 2d wife), was living 2 Jan. 1655/6.

X

8 March 1641/2[a]. He was Sheriff of Yorkshire 1648/49. He *m.*, in or before 1605, Mary, sister and coheir of John LACY, 1st da. of Robert LACY, both of Foulkton, co. York. She *d.* at St. Mary's, Beverley, 4 May 1649. He *d.* there a few months later, in his 70th year, and was *bur.* 8 Oct. 1649, at Harpham. M.I. to both of them at Harpham. Will pr. 1651.

II. 1649. SIR HENRY ST. QUINTIN, Bart. [1642], of Harpham aforesaid, s. and h. aged 7 in 1612, and aged 59 in 1665 [Visit. of Yorkshire]; *suc. to the Baronetcy* in Oct. 1649. He *m.* Mary, 2d da. of Henry STAPLETON, of Wighill, co. York, by Mary, illegit. da. of Sir John FORSTER, of Alnwicke. He *d.* in, or shortly after, Nov. 1695, at a great age.

III. 1695? SIR WILLIAM ST. QUINTIN, Bart. [1642], of Harpham, aforesaid, grandson and h., being 1st surv. s. and h.[b] of William ST. QUINTIN, by Elizabeth, da. of Sir William STRICKLAND, 1st Bart. [1641], which William St. Quintin, was s. and h. ap. of the 1st Bart., and *d.* v.p., being *bur.* at Harpham, 6 Nov. 1695, aged 63. He was aged 3 in 1665; *suc. to the Baronetcy* in, or shortly after, 1695; was M.P. for Hull (in eleven Parls.), 1695 till his death; a Commissioner of the Customs, 1698-1701; of the Revenue [I.], 1706-13; one of the Lords of the Treasury, 1714-17; and Vice Treasurer and Receiver General of Ireland, 1720 till his death. He *d.* unm., "universally lamented by all who knew him for his great abilities," 30 June, and was *bur.* 15 July 1723, at Harpham, in his 63d year. M.I. Will pr. 1723.

IV. 1723. SIR WILLIAM ST. QUINTIN, Bart. [1642], of Harpham aforesaid, and of Scampston, co. York, nephew and h., being s. and h. of Hugh ST. QUINTIN, by Catherine, 1st da. of Matthew CHITTY, which Hugh (who *d.* 6 Dec. 1702, aged 31), was yst. br. of the 3d Bart. He was *b.* about 1700; *suc. to the Baronetcy*, 30 June 1723; was M.P. for Thirsk, 1722-27; Sheriff of Yorkshire, 1729-30. He *m.* 11 June 1724, at Somerset House Chapel, Rebecca, da. and h. of Sir John THOMPSON, Lord Mayor of London, 1736-37, by his 1st wife. She *d.* Oct. 1757, and was *bur.* at Harpham. M.I. Admon. as "of Scampston, co. York," 20 Oct. 1757. He *d.* 9 May 1770, at Bath. Will pr. May 1770.

V. 1770, to 1795. SIR WILLIAM ST. QUINTIN, Bart. [1642], of Harpham and Scampston aforesaid, only surv. s. and h., *bap.* 4 July 1729, at Rillington, *suc. to the Baronetcy*, 9 May 1770; Sheriff of Yorkshire, 1772-73. He *m.* 14 May 1758, at St. James' Westm., Charlotte, da. of Henry FANE, of Wormsley, Oxon., M.D. (br. of Thomas, 8th EARL OF WESTMORLAND), and only child of his 1st wife, Charlotte, da. of Nicholas ROWE, the Poet. She *d.* 17 and was *bur.* 24 April 1762, at Harpham. M.I. He *d.* s.p. 22 and was *bur.* 31 July, 1795, at Harpham, when the *Baronetcy* became *extinct*[c]. M.I. Will pr. Dec. 1797.

KEMP, *or* KEMPE:
cr. 14 March, 1641/2[a].

I. 1642. "SIR ROBERT KEMPE, of Gissing[d], co. Norfolk, Knt.", s. and h. of Robert KEMPE, of the same, by Dorothy, da. and sole h. of Arthur HERRIS, of Crixeth Essex, was admitted to Gray's Inn, 26 Feb.

[a] See p. 161, note "b," *sub* Strutt.

[b] Henry, aged 11 at the Visit. of 1665, (being eight years his senior,) was the eldest son.

[c] The estate of Scampston, co. York, went to his Nephew, William Thomas DARBY, of Sunbury, Midx., s. of George DARBY, of Newton, Hants, by Mary, the only one of his sisters who had issue. He, in 1795, took the surname of ST. QUINTIN, and *d.* 18 Jan. 1805, aged 35, leaving issue.

[d] This manor came into the family as early as 1324, by the marriage of Alan *Kemp*, with Isabel, da. of Sir Philip HASTINGS, of Gissing aforesaid.

1604/5; *suc.* his father 24 April 1614, was Gentleman of the Bed Chamber to Charles I, in 1631, and, being distinguished for his loyalty to that King, was *Knighted*, 7 Aug. 1641, at Whitehall, and was *cr. a Baronet*, as above, 14 March 1641/2[a], all the fines and fees of passing the patent thereof being remitted. He *m.* Jane, da. of Sir Matthew BROWNE, of Beechworth Castle, Surrey, by Jane, da. of Sir Thomas VINCENT, of Stoke Dabernon. He *d.* 20 Aug. 1647. Will pr. in Consistory Court of Norwich, 1647.

II. 1647. SIR ROBERT KEMPE, *or* KEMP, Bart. [1642], of Gissing aforesaid, s. and h., *b.* 2 Feb. 1627, at Walsingham Abbey, Norfolk; *suc. to the Baronetcy*, 20 Aug. 1647; M.P. for Norfolk, May 1675 to 1679; for Dunwich. 1679-81 and 1681. He *m.* firstly, 15 July 1650, at St. Barth. the Less, London, Mary, da. of Thomas KERRIDGE, of Shelley Hall, Suffolk, by Susan, his wife. She was *b.* Feb. 1631, and *d.* s.p. June 1655. He *m.* secondly, 20 Nov. 1657, Mary, da. and sole h. of John SONE, of Ubberston, Suffolk, by Mary, da. of William DADE, of the same county. She, who was *b.* 6 April 1637, *d.* at Ubberston, 29 July, and was *bur.* 2 Aug. 1705, at Gissing. He *d.* 26 Sep. 1710, aged 83, and was *bur.* at Gissing. M.I. Will pr. 1710, in Archdeaconry of Suffolk.

III. 1710. SIR ROBERT KEMP, Bart. [1642], of Gissing and Ubberston aforesaid, s. and h. by 2d wife, *bap.* 25 June 1667, at Ubberston; *suc. to the Baronetcy*, 26 Sep. 1710; was several times M.P. for Dunwich, 1701-09 (four Parls.) and 1713-15; for Suffolk, Feb. 1732 to 1734, and 1734 till death. He *m.* firstly, Letitia, widow of Sir Robert KEMPE, of Finchingfield, Essex, da. of Robert KING, of Great Thurlow, by Elizabeth, da. of Thomas STEWARD, of Barton Mills. She *d.* s.p.m. He *m.* secondly, in or before 1699, Elizabeth, da. and h. of John BRAND, of Edwardston, Suffolk. She *d.* 1709. He *m.* thirdly, Martha, da of William BLACKWELL, of Mortlake, Surrey. She *d.* 1727. He *m.* fourthly, 9 July 1728, Amy, widow of John BURROUGH, of Ipswich, da. of Richard PHILLIPS, of Edwardston aforesaid, but by her had no issue. He *d.* 18 Dec. 1734, aged 68, at Ufford, Suffolk. Will pr. 1735. His widow *d.* 1745. Her will pr. 1746.

IV 1734. SIR ROBERT KEMP, Bart. [1642], of Gissing aforesaid, s. and h. by 2d wife, *b.* 9 Nov. 1699; *suc. to the Baronetcy*, 18 Dec. 1734; was M.P. for Orford, Feb. 1730 to 1734. He *d.* unm. 15 Feb. 1752.

V. 1752. SIR JOHN KEMP, Bart. [1642], of Gissing aforesaid, br., of the whole blood, and h., *b.* 19 Dec. 1700; was sometime a merchant in London; *suc. to the Baronetcy*, 15 Feb. 1752. He *m.* Elizabeth, widow of Isaac Brand COLT, of Brightlingsea, co. Essex, da. of Thomas MANN. He *d.* s.p. 25 Nov. 1761. Will pr. 1761. The will of his widow pr. March 1768.

VI. 1761. SIR JOHN KEMP, Bart. [1642], of Gissing aforesaid, nephew and h., being s. and h. of Rev. Thomas KEMP, Rector of Gissing and Flordon, Norfolk, afterwards of Penryn, Cornwall, by Priscilla (who, in May 1771, was wife of Andrew Merry), which Thomas (who *d.* 1761, aged 65) was br. of the whole blood to the 4th and 5th Baronets. He was *b.* 1754; *suc. to the Baronetcy*, 25 Nov. 1761; was ed. at Westminster School; but *d.*, a minor, and unm., 16 Jan. 1771. Admon. 16 May 1771.

VII. 1771. SIR BENJAMIN KEMP, Bart. [1642], of Gissing aforesaid, uncle and h., being br., of the whole blood, of the 4th and 5th Baronets; *b.* 29 Dec. 1708; ed. at Caius Coll., Cambridge, of which he was Fellow, 1733 till death; B.A., 1731; M.A., 1735; was a Physician; *suc. to the Baronetcy*, 16 Jan. 1771. He *m.* Elizabeth, widow of John COLT, of Tooting, co. Surrey. He *d.* s.p. 25 Jan. 1777, at Coln St. Denis, co. Glouc. M.I. there. Will pr. 1777. That of his widow (as of Tooting, Surrey) pr. 1790 in the Prerog. Court [I.].

[a] See p. 161, note "b" *sub* Strutt.

VIII. 1777. SIR WILLIAM KEMP, Bart. [1642], of Gissing aforesaid, cousin and h. male, being s. and h. of William KEMP, of Antingham, Norfolk, by Elizabeth, only da. and h. of Henry SHARDELOW, Alderman of Norwich, which William, last named, was younger s. of the 2d Baronet, by his 2d wife. He was *b.* 31 Dec. 1717; *suc. to the Baronetcy* 25 Jan. 1777. He *m.* Mary, da. of (—) IVES, of Colts Hall. She was *bur.* 22 Nov. 1751. He *d.* 5 Nov. 1799.

IX. 1799. SIR WILLIAM ROBERT KEMP, Bart. [1642], of Gissing aforesaid, s. and h., *bap.* 18 May 1744; *suc. to the Baronetcy* 5 Nov. 1799. He *m.*, 9 Dec. 1788, Sarah, da. and h. of Thomas ADCOCK, of Carleton, Norfolk. He *d.* 11 Oct. 1804. His wife survived him.

X. 1804. SIR WILLIAM ROBERT KEMP, Bart. [1642], of Gissing aforesaid, s. and h., *b.* 14 Nov. 1791; *suc. to the Baronetcy* 11 Oct. 1804; ed. at Christ's Coll., Cambridge; M.A. 1813; was in Holy Orders; Rector of Gissing and Flordon, co. Norfolk, 1816 till his death. He *m.*, 10 March 1859, Mary, 5th da. of Charles SAUNDERS, of Camberwell, Surrey, and of Gissing aforesaid. She *d.* Jan. 1866. He *d.* 29 May 1874, at Gissing Hall, in Gissing, in his 83d year.

XI. 1874, May. SIR THOMAS JOHN KEMP, Bart. [1642], of Gissing Hall, aforesaid, br. and h., *b.* 14 Oct. 1793; *suc. to the Baronetcy*, 29 May 1874, but *d.* unm., a few months later, 7 Aug. 1874, at Long Stratton, in his 81st year.

XII. 1874, Aug. SIR KENNETH HAGAR KEMP, Bart. [1642], of Gissing Hall aforesaid, cousin and h. male, being only surv. s. and h. of the Rev. Nunn Robert Pretyman KEMP, of Erpingham, Norfolk, by Mary Harriet, da. of Rev. Thomas HAGAR, of Lonmay, co. Aberdeen, which Nunn (who *d.* v.p. 25 Aug. 1859, aged 45,) was 1st s. of the Rev. Thomas Cooke KEMP, Vicar of East Meon, Hants (*d.* 17 Oct. 1867, aged 79), s. and h. of Thomas Benjamin KEMP, of Swafield, co. Norfolk (*d.* 24 June 1838), who was br. to the 9th and s. of the 8th Baronet. He was *b.* April 1853, at Erpingham aforesaid; ed. at Jesus Coll., Cambridge; B.A., 1874; *suc. to the Baronetcy*, 7 Aug. 1874. Barrister (Inner Temple), 1880; Major 3d Batt. Norfolk Reg. (Militia); partner in the banking firm of "Lacon, Youells and Kemp," at Yarmouth and Norwich. He *m.*, 30 Aug. 1876, at Chilham, co. Kent, Henrietta Maria Eva, 1st da. of Henry HAMILTON, of Chilham aforesaid, formerly of Blackrock, co Leitrim.

Family Estates.—These, in 1883, consisted of 2,133 acres in Norfolk, worth £3,163 a year. *Principal Residences.*—Gissing Hall, near Diss, and Mergate Hall, near Braconash, co. Norfolk.

READE:

cr. 16 March 1641/2;(a)

ex. 22 Feb. 1711/2;

but assumed since 1810.

I. 1642. "JOHN READE,(b) of Brockett Hall [in Hatfield], co. Herts, Esq.," 4th but 2d surv. s.(c) of Sir Thomas READE, of Dunstew, Oxon (*bur.* there 20 Dec. 1650), by Mary, 5th da. and coheir of Sir John BROCKET, of Brocket Hall aforesaid, was *b.* about 1616; admitted to Lincoln's Inn, 7 June 1632; was *Knighted* at Newmarket, 12 March 1641/2, and was, four days later (tho' apparently only under the designation of an "Esq.") *cr. a Baronet*, v.p., as above, 16 March 1641/2.(a) He was assessed at £600 for the war expenses, but was respited.(b) During the Usurpation he was Commissioner for Herts, Nov. 1650; Sheriff of Herts, 1655-56; and (the honours conferred on him by Charles I(a) not being recognised) was base enough to accept *a fresh Baronetcy*, dated 25 June 1656, *from the Protector* for himself and "his heirs," being the first hereditary honour granted by Cromwell. At the Restoration he obtained a pardon, 7 June 1660, for all offences during the Civil War and the Commonwealth. He was again Sheriff of Herts, 1673-74, and was also elected as such Nov. 1671, Nov. 1676, and Nov. 1677, but did not act. On 20 Jan. 1679, he purchased the estate of Calthorp, co. Oxon. He *m.* firstly, 2 Jan. 1640, Susanna, 2d da. of Sir Thomas STYLE, 1st Bart. [1627], of Wateringbury, by Elizabeth, da. and h. of Robert FOULKES. She was *bur.* 18 May 1657 in the Brocket chapel at Hatfield. M.I. He *m.* secondly, 15 Jan. 1662/3, at St. Nicholas Acons, London (Lic. Lond. 13, he aged 46, she of Hatton Garden, aged 40), "Lady Alisimon," widow of the Hon. Francis PIERREPONT. They were, however, separated in about three and a half years' time,(c) and she was living 6 May 1682. He was *bur.* 6 Feb. 1693/4 in the Brocket chapel aforesaid. Admon. 26 Feb. 1693/4, as also in the Prerog. Court of Dublin.

II. 1694. SIR JAMES READE, Bart. [1642], of Brocket Hall and Dunstew aforesaid, 4th but only surv. s. and h. by 1st wife, *bap.* 10 March 1654/5, at Hatfield; matric. at Oxford (Trin. Coll.), 14 May 1675, and then called 17; Sheriff of Herts, 1693-94; *suc. to the Baronetcy*, Feb. 1693/4; Sheriff of Oxon, 1700-01. He *m.* 26 Jan. 1689/90, at Mercers' chapel, Cornhill, London (Lic. Vic. Gen. 24, he about 30 and she about 25), Love, 2d da. and coheir of Robert DRING, of Isleworth, Midx., Alderman of London (*d.* about 1697), by Dorothy his wife. He *d.* of a fever 16 and was bur. 21 Oct. 1701, in the Brocket chapel aforesaid, aged 46 years, 7 months and 11 days. M.I. Admon. 19 Dec. 1701. His widow, whose dowry was £10,000, *d.* 9 and was *bur.*, with her husband, 18 Nov. 1731, aged 76. M.I. Will dat. 23 July 1729, pr. 26 Nov. 1731.

III. 1701, to 1712. SIR JOHN READE, Bart. [1642], of Brocket Hall and Dunstew aforesaid, only s. and h., *b.* 1691; *suc. to the Baronetcy*, 16 Oct. 1701; ed. at Eton; matric. at Oxford (Wadham Coll.), 7 Nov. 1705, aged 14; became a Jacobite,(d) and *d.* unm., of the small pox, at Rome, 22 Feb., being *bur.* 11 June 1712, in the Brocket chapel aforesaid, aged 21, when the *Baronetcy* became *extinct.*(e) Admon. 24 March 1711/2.

(a) See p. 161, note "b," *sub* "Strutt."

(b) See "A record of the Redes," by Compton Reade, 4to., 1899.

(c) He is called "second son" in his admittance to Linc. Inn in 1632, as also in a deed made by his father 2 Jan. 1639. Of his three elder brothers (1), Walter Reade, *d.* unm. v.p. and was *bur.* 9 Sep. 1625, at St. Nicholas', Abingdon, aged 24; (2) Thomas Reade, *b.* at Barton Court, and *bap.* 12 Feb. 1606/7, at St. Helen's, Abingdon, *m.* 8 Sep. 1624, without his father's consent, and *d.* v.p. Sep. 1634, leaving issue, of whom Compton Reade, of Shipton Court, Oxon, was *cr. a Baronet*, 4 March 1660/1, and (3) Richard Reade, *b.* 12 June 1610, living in 1623, sometimes thought to be ancestor of the family of Reade, of Rossenara in Ireland, but who more probably *d.* v.p. and s.p.

(a) See p. 161, note "b" *sub.* "Strutt."

(b) "Though a Baronet, he is a very poor one . . . has a poor stock and only a little money, which his father send [*sic*] him." See p. 164, note "b."

(c) "He kept a mistress in his house and encouraged her to insult his wife. He padlocked her into her room," etc. See p. 164, note "b."

(d) His uncle, Almericus (de Courcy) Baron Kingsale (I.), who had married his mother's sister, held a post in the court of the titular James III.

(e) Of his five sisters and coheirs, two *d.* unm. and two *d.* without issue, one of which last, Love, inherited the Brocket Hall estate, and *m.*, 6 Aug. 1719, Thomas Winnington, who by his will, pr. 2 May 1746, left it to his own collateral relations, by whom it was sold to Matthew Lambe, and became the seat of Viscount Melbourne [I.], Prime Minister, 1834 and 1835-39, and subsequently of Viscount Palmerston [I.], Prime Minister, 1855-58 and 1859-65. Dorothy, the eldest sister, and the only one who had issue, *m.* Robert Dashwood, and was mother of Sir James Dashwood, 2d Bart. [1684], who is called in the will (dat. 7 Aug. 1752, and pr. 7 Aug. 1754) of his maternal aunt, Mary Reade, spinster, "the only living branch of the coheirs of Sir John Reade, Bart." This Dorothy inherited the estate of Dunstew, as also that of Minsden (in Hitchin), Herts, which had been inherited by the Readee, thro' the families of Brocket and Lytton.

This Baronetcy was assumed in April 1810 by the Rev. William Reade, who at first alleged himself to be descended from a younger son of the 1st Bart., whom, at that date, he stated to be Major John Reade.(a) The name of this younger son he subsequently, however, altered to Matthew, and a statement was added that this Matthew, whose very existence is questionable, succeeded to the Baronetcy in 1712. As to the fact that Matthew, or any of the persons undermentioned, were, until 1810, ever known as "Baronets," it seems more than doubtful. The pedigree, as finally alleged, is as under.(b)

IV. 1712. "SIR MATTHEW READE, Bart." [1642], of Kiléavy, co. Clare, stated to have been uncle and h. male of the 3d, and younger s. of the 1st Bart., and to have *suc. to the Baronetcy*, 22 Feb. 1711/2. He *m.* Anne, da. of Sir Edward DOWDALL, of Drogheda, by Anne, da. of "the Right Hon. THE EARL OF DESMOND." He *d.* June 1721. The will of "Sir Matthew Reade, of Kileavy, co. Clare," dat. 15 June 1721 (in which, most aptly for proving the pedigree, he mentions his son John Reade, his father, Sir John Reade, Bart., deceased, and his brother, Sir James Reade, Bart., deceased) proved to be a forged one (written on modern paper), brought into the Prerog. Office [I.] for proof, by the claimant's son, 18 April 1710, about 90 years after the death of the alleged testator.

V. 1721. "SIR JOHN READE, Bart." [1641], of Kileavy aforesaid, only s. and h. He *m.* Anastacia, da. and h. of Michael NICHILL, of Glascongue, co. Clare, and of Pennywell (or Rennywell), co. Limerick. No date of death is given.(b)

VI. 1750? "SIR WILLIAM READE, Bart." [1641], of Ballymacranen, co. Clare, only s. and h. He was M.P. [I.] for Dublin till his death. He *m.* Sarah, da. and h. of Thomas LUCAS, of Ballingaddy, co. Clare, niece to Charles LUCAS, M.D. He *d.* 12 Aug. 1787.

VII. 1787. "SIR WILLIAM READE, Bart." [1641], of Moynoe House, co. Clare, 1st s. and h.(c) of six sons; *b.* 1762; was in Holy Orders, being sometime Rector and Preb. of Tomgraney, co. Clare; was a Magistrate for co. Clare in 1791, but not described as a Baronet, though that date was four years after his father's death. He took an active part against the Irish rebels of 1798. In 1810, however, he *assumed the style of a Baronet*(a) as above mentioned. He *m.*, in or before 1788, Alicia, da. of Anthony BRADY, of Kielty, co. Clare. He was living 1811, in his 50th year.

VIII. 1820? "SIR JOHN READE, BART." [1642], of Moynoe House aforesaid, only s. and h., *b.* 3 Aug. 1788. He, having presented himself for Knighthood as the eldest son of a Baronet,(d) at the Court of the Viceroy [I.] (the Duke of Richmond) was *Knighted* accordingly 18 June 1811. He was a Magistrate for co. Clare, 1814; took Holy Orders, and subsequently became blind. He *m.*, 4 Nov. 1810, Urania Maria, da. and coheir of Edward VERO,(a) of Dublin, and of Lough Raer, co. Galway, by Mary, da. and h. of Jervis HERIDE, of Annadonn, co. Galway. She *d.* in 1842.(b) He was *bur.* 14 Dec. 1842, at St. Anne's, Soho.

IX. 1842. "SIR JOHN CECIL READE, Bart." [1644], 1st surv. s. and h., was Governor of Darlinghurst gaol, Sydney, New South Wales. He *m.* 28 Nov. 1838, Ann, 1st da. of Michael EAGAN, of Dublin. He *d.* March 1899. His widow living 1900, at Arawa Bronte, Waverley, in New South Wales.(b)

X. 1899. "SIR WILLIAM VERO READE, Bart." [1644], 1st s. and h., *b.* 22 Sep. 1839; was, as early as 1855, in the employment of the Railway Department in New South Wales, and for many years chief traffic manager. He *m.*, in 1867, Emily Anne, 5th da. of William TINDALE, of Hornsey Wood, Penrith, New South Wales, and has issue, William John Cecil Read, being his eldest son.(b)

(a) In a "letter from Sir William Betham to George Nayler, Esq.," dat. 31 March 1814, the writer states that, in 1809, the Rev. William Read said he had a claim to an English Baronetcy, through his ancestor, Major John [*sic.*] Read, 2d son of the 1st Bart., but that sometime afterwards he produced a copy of the will of Sir Matthew Read, "making out a very different case to that originally stated to me." This was printed in 1832, as also were copies of all papers in the Heralds' College connected with this claim.

(b) The pedigree, as in the text, deducing the "Sir William," of 1810, from the "Sir Matthew," of 1712, is printed in (that most uncritical work) Playfair's *Baronetage*, 1811. It was doubtless furnished by Sir William himself, together with a laudatory account of his own exploits against the Irish rebels.

(c) Two *elder* brothers, the Rev. John Reade and Charles Reade, are, however, stated to have been living in 1810.

(d) This misrepresentation was apparently the cause of the omission of the clause enforcing such Knightage in the patents of Baronetage. It would have been a more desirable result had it lead to the granting such Knighthood, in the cases only where *proof* of the father's Baronetcy had been furnished.

ENYON:

cr. 9 April 1642(c);

ex. the same year.

I. 1642. "JAMES ENYÓN, of Flowre [*i.e.*, Flore], co. Northampton, Esq., only s. and h. of James Enyon, of the same, by Dorothy, da. of Thomas COXE, of Bishop's Itchington, co. Warwick (which James last named, was s. and h. of James Enyon, of Whitechapel, Brewer, who purchased the manor of Flore, and *d.* in 1623,) was *b.* about 1587; matric. at Oxford (Ch. Ch.), 30 March 1604, aged 17; adm. to Gray's Inn, 17 March 1602/3, being then of St. Mary's Whitechapel, late of Barnard's Inn, and was *cr. a Baronet*, as above, 9 April 1642.(c) He *m.* Jane, da. of Sir Adam NEWTON, 1st Bart. [1620], of Charlton, by Dorothy, da. of Sir John PUCKERING, sometime Lord Keeper of the Great Seal. He was killed in a duel at the quarters of the Royalist army at Gloucester, a few months after his creation, by his friend, Sir Nicholas Crispe, who ever afterwards wore mourning for him. He *d.* s.p.m.(d) when the *Baronetcy* became *extinct.* His admon. (as "Sir James Onion") 19 May 1648, to a creditor. The will of his widow was pr. 1664.

(a) A correspondent writes that "in the old Dublin almanacs, I find, 1798—1819, an Edward Vero, a tailor, but he may not be the father [of Urania] however *Si non e Vero, e ben trovato.*"

(b) The information as to this family, since 1811, is kindly furnished by C. M. Tenison, of Hobart, in Tasmania.

(c) See p. 161, note "b," *sub* "Strutt."

(d) The estate of Flore went to his three daughters and coheirs [Baker's *Northamptonshire*, vol. i, p. 153.]

WILLIAMS:

cr. 19 April 1642(a);

ex. 14 Nov. 1680.

I. 1642. "EDMUND WILLIAMS, of Marnhull, co. Dorset, Knt.," s. and h. of John WILLIAMS, of Marnhull aforesaid, and of St. Peter's, Eastcheap, London, citizen and goldsmith, by Joan, sister of Edward ALLEN, Alderman and sometime (1620-21) Sheriff of London, 3rd da. of Thomas ALLEN, citizen and haberdasher of London, by his 1st wife Joan, da. of Edward WOODGATE, of Kent; *suc.* his father, 14 Sep. 1637; was one of the Gentlemen of the Privy Chamber; was *Knighted*, as "of London," 8 Jan. 1638/9, at Whitehall, and was *cr. a Baronet*, as above, 19 April 1642.(a) He *m.* Mary, 4th da. of Sir John BEAUMONT, 1st Bart. [1627], of Gracedieu, by Elizabeth, da. of John FORTESCUE. He *d.* early in 1644. Will, in which he directs to be *bur.* with his father, at St. Peter's, in Cheapside, dat. 15 to 20 Dec. 1643, pr. 10 April 1644.(b) His widow, who was *b.* 7 July 1617, *m.* before 1647, John TASBURGH, and had issue. Her admon. 18 Jan. 1650/1, to her said husband.

II. 1644, to 1680. SIR JOHN WILLIAMS, Bart. [1642], only s. and h.; *bap.* 11 Sep. 1642, at St. Andrew's, Holborn; *suc. to the Baronetcy* (when an infant) in 1644; matric. at Oxford (St. John's Coll.), 26 Oct. 1660, and was *cr.* M.A., 9 Sep. 1661. He suc. to the estate of Minster Court, co. Kent, on the death, 26 March 1669, of his uncle, Sir John Williams, Bart. [so *cr.* 22 April 1642], of the same. He *m.*, 30 April 1673, at Westm. Abbey, Susan, da. of Sir Thomas SKIPWITH, 1st Bart. [1678], of Metheringham, by his 1st wife Elizabeth, da. and h. of Ralph LATHAM. He *d.* s.p.m.,(c) in St. Martin's in the Fields, and was *bur.* 14 Nov. 1680, in the Temple Church, London, when the *Baronetcy* became *extinct*. Admon. 22 Nov. 1680. His widow was *bur.* 26 Sep. 1689, at Westm. Abbey. Her will dat. 15 Sep. 1689, pr. 13 Jan. 1689/90, and Jan. 1692/3.

WILLIAMS:

cr. 22 April 1642(a);

ex. 26 March 1669.

I. 1642, to 1669. "JOHN WILLIAMS, of Minster in the Isle of Thanet, co. Kent,"(d) yr. br. of Sir Edmund WILLIAMS, 1st Bart. [1642], of Marnhull, Dorset, being 4th s. of John WILLIAMS, of Marnhull aforesaid, by Joan, da. of Thomas ALLEN, was *b.* about 1609; matric. at Oxford (Oriel Coll.), 8 July 1625, aged 16; Barrister (Inner Temple), 1637, and was *cr. a Baronet*, as above, 22 April 1642(a). He was Sheriff of Kent, 1667-68. He *d.* unm. in the Inner Temple, 27 Feb., and was *bur.* 26 March 1669, in the Temple church, when the *Baronetcy* became *extinct*. M.I. Admon. 26 March 1669, to his nephew and next of kin, Sir John WILLIAMS, 2d Bart. [1642] next above mentioned; again, 7 May 1681 and 16 Dec. 1689.

(a) See p. 161, note "b," *sub* "Strutt."

(b) He directed the estate of Marnhull to be sold, which was effected before 1657.

(c) Of his two daughters and coheirs (1) Mary *m.* (for her 2d. husband) Lieut. Gen. Henry CONYNGHAM, by whom she was ancestress of Henry, MARQUESS CONYNGHAM [I.], who was *cr.*, in 1821, BARON MINSTER of Minster Abbey, co. Kent, having inherited that estate. (2) Susanna, *m.* Henry CORNWALL, of Bradwardine Castle co. Hereford, and had issue.

(d) No description of the grantee (as "Knight, "Esq.," or "Gent.") is given in Dugdale's *List*.

WINTOUR:

cr. 29 April 1642(a);

ex. 4 June 1658.

I. 1642, to 1658. "GEORGE WINTOUR, of Huddington, co. Worcester, Esq.," was *cr. a Baronet*, as above, 29 April 1642.(a) He *m.* firstly, Frances, 1st da. of John (TALBOT), 10th EARL OF SHREWSBURY, by his 1st wife, Mary, da. of Sir Francis FORTESCUE. He *m.* secondly (Lic. Worcester, 4 July 1642), Mary, da. of Charles (SMITH), 1st VISCOUNT CARRINGTON OF BURFORD [I.], by Elizabeth, da. of Sir John CARYLL. He *m.* thirdly, Mary da. and coheir of Sir George KEMPE, Bart. [*cr.* 1627], of Pentlow, co. Essex, by Thomazine, da. of (—) BROOKE. He *d.* s.p. 4 June 1658, when the *Baronetcy* became *extinct*. He devised his estate to the Talbot family.

BORLASE:

cr. 4 May 1642(a);

ex. 1 Feb. 1688/9.

I. 1642. "JOHN BORLASE, of Bockmer [in Medmenham], co. Bucks, Esq.," and of Stratton Audley, co. Oxon, 1st s. and h. of Sir William BORLASE,(b) of the same (*d.* 10 Dec. 1629), by Amy, da. of Sir Francis POPHAM, of Littlecote, Wilts, was *b.* at Littlecote, 21 Aug. 1619 (reg. at Medmenham, Bucks); matric. at Oxford (Mag. Hall), 30 April 1625, aged 16; admitted to the Inner Temple, 27 Jan. 1636/7; was a staunch Royalist; was M.P. for Great Marlow, April to Nov. 1640, for Corfe Castle, from Jan. 1641 till disabled, 4 March 1643/4 (being one of 118 members who attended the King's summons to Oxford), and for Wycombe, 1661 till his death; and was *cr. a Baronet*, as above, 4 May 1642.(a) He was fined £6,800, on 10 Jan. 1645/6, as a delinquent, and was imprisoned by the Puritan party.(c) He *m.* 4 Dec. 1637, at St. Giles' in the Fields, Alice, 1st da. of Sir John BANCKS, Lord Chief Justice of the Common Pleas, 1641-44, by Mary,(d) da. of Ralph HAWTREY, of Riselip, Midx. He *d.* at Bockmer, 8 and was *bur.* 12 Aug. 1672, at Little Marlow, aged 53. Will dat. 7 and pr. 19 Aug. 1672. His widow, who, at the age of 57, adopted the Roman Catholic faith while staying at Bourbon in France, *d.* in Paris 16 Nov. 1683, and was *bur.* "among the poor, whose nurse she was, in the churchyard of St. Jaques, in this city." M.I.(e) Will dat. 8 Jan. 1679, pr. 31 Jan. 1683/4.(f)

II. 1672, to 1689. SIR JOHN BORLASE, Bart. [1642], of Bockmer and Stratton Audley, aforesaid, 1st s. and h., *b.* about 1640, at Bockmer; matric. at Oxford (Oriel Coll.), as "John Borlase, Esq.," 31 July 1658; *suc. to the Baronetcy*, 8 Aug. 1672; was M.P. for Wycombe

(a) See p. 161, note "b," *sub* "Strutt."

(b) See family of *Borlase, of Borlase*, by W. C. Copeland Borlase, 8vo., 1888.

(c) He is constantly confused with his cousin and contemporary, Sir John Borlase, "Knt.," master of the ordnance, and subsequently, 1643, one of the Chief Governors of Ireland, under the title of Lord Chief Justice. That John Borlase (*Knighted* at Greenwich, 13 July 1606), *m.* 1 Oct. 1610, at Stoke Newington, Midx., Alice, widow of Thomas Ravis, Bishop of London, 1607-1609, and *d.* 15 March 1647, in his 72d year, at St. Barth. the Great, London, leaving, among other issue, Sir John Borlase, junior (*Knighted* at Dublin, 1 Nov. 1641), who *d.* 15 Feb. 1675, and was *bur.* at St. Patrick's, Dublin.

(d) This Mary was the celebrated Lady Banks who so successfully defended Corfe Castle against the rebels.

(e) This curious inscription is printed in Borlase's "*Borlase Family*," p. 59. See note "b" above.

(f) Portraits by Vandyke of herself and her husband are at Kingston Lacy, Dorset, the seat, after the destruction of Corfe Castle, of the family of Banks.

(four Parls.) 1673-81, and for Marlow 1685 till death. He *d.* unm. 1 Feb. 1688/9, and was *bur.* at Stratton Audley, aged 48, when the *Baronetcy* became *extinct*. M.I. Will dat. 7 Jan. 1683, pr. 8 Nov. 1689.(a)

KNOLLYS:

cr. 6 May 1642;(b)

ex. July 1648.

I. 1642, to 1648. "HENRY KNOLLYS, of Grove Place, [in Nursling], co. Southampton, Esq.," 1st s. and h. of Sir Henry KNOLLYS,(c) of the same, Comptroller of the Household to Charles I, by Catherine, only da. of Sir Thomas CORNWALLIS, Groom Porter to James I, was *b.* about 1611, was, probably, the "Henry Knowles, Esq." admitted to Gray's Inn, 5 March 1630/1; was aged 22 in Jan. 1633/4; suc. his father, 9 Oct. 1638, and was *cr. a Baronet*, as above, 6 May 1642.(b) He was a Royalist, and was fined £1,250 on 7 March 1646. He *d.* unm. at Bowcombe, in the Isle of Wight, July 1648, when the *Baronetcy* became *extinct*. Will, directing his burial to be at Carisbrooke, dat. 22 May, and pr. 29 July 1648.(d)

HAMILTON:

cr. 11 May 1642;(e)

ex. probably about 1670.

I. 1642, to 1670? "JOHN HAMILTON, of London, Esq.," was *cr. a Baronet*, as above, 11 May 1642,(e) but nothing further has been ascertained about him. The *Baronetcy* became *extinct* presumably at his death, say about 1670, but certainly before 1727.(f)

(a) Of his six sisters (1) Amy or Ann, was *bap.* 11 and *bur.* 12 April 1640, at Little Marlow. (2) Mary, *m.* 1 March 1663/4, at Medmenham, Sir Humphrey Miller, 1st Bart. [1660], and had issue, but *d.* before 1683. (3) Frances, *bap.* 25 July 1647, at Medmenham, *m.* (Lic. Fac. 6 Feb. 1667/8), Joseph Langton, of Newton St. Loe, co. Somerset, and was living 1683. She had issue, of which, in 1900, Earl Temple is the representative. (4) Katherine, *m.* John Webb, of Mussenden, Bucks, Lieut. General in the army, and *d.* before 1683, leaving issue, her husband being then living. (5) Amie, who *d.* unm. Nov. or Dec. 1673. (6) Anne, *bap.* 12 March 1656/7, at Medmenham; *m.* 26 June 1676, at St. Barth. the Less, London, Arthur Warren, of Stapleford Hall, Notts, Sheriff of Notts, 1685. She, who *d.* a widow in Aug. 1703, inherited the whole of the estates of the Borlase family, which passed to her great grandson, Admiral Sir John Borlase Warren, Bart., so *cr.* 1 June 1775, and were (save as to the estate of Stratton Audley) alienated by him.

(b) See p. 161, note "b," *sub* "Strutt."

(c) See pedigree by B. W. Greenfield in "*the Hampshire Field Club Papers*," 1895.

(d) He was suc. in his estates by his brother, Thomas Knollys, M.P. for Southampton, 1659, Oct. 1670 to 1679, and March to July 1679, whose male issue became extinct 8 Dec. 1752, when they passed to the family of Mill, Baronets (a creation of 1619) till that title became extinct in Feb. 1835.

(e) Disallowed 17 Feb. 1651/2 by Parl., till the Restoration. See *Memorandum* as to creations after 4 Jan. 1641/2 on p. 152. No patent is enrolled. The date here given is that in Dugdale's *Catalogue*. See *Memorandum* on p. 84. The date of the signet bill is 3 May 1642.

(f) It is omitted accordingly in Wotton's [*existing*] Baronetage of England, published in 1727.

MORGAN:

cr. 12 May 1642;(a)

ex. between 1715 and 1727.

I. 1642. "EDWARD MORGAN, of Llanternam, co. Monmouth, Esq.," s. and h. of William MORGAN, of the same (admon. 24 March 1639), by Frances, da. of Edward (SOMERSET), 4th EARL OF WORCESTER, was *b.* about 1604; matric. at Oxford (Jesus Coll.), 3 May 1616, aged 14; B.A., July 1619; Sheriff of Monmouthshire, 1624-25 and 1640-41; and *cr. a Baronet*, as above, 12 May 1642.(a) He was a Royalist, and his estate was sequestrated in 1645, but discharged in 1653. He *m.* Mary, da. of Sir Francis ENGLEFIELD, 1st Bart. [1611], by Jane, sister of Anthony Mary, 2d VISCOUNT MONTAGU, da. of the Hon. Anthony BROWNE. He *d.* 24 June 1653, aged 48. Will dat. 20 July 1650, pr. 30 March 1654, by his widow and executrix.

II. 1653. SIR EDWARD MORGAN, Bart. [1642], of Llanternam aforesaid, s. and h.; *suc. to the Baronetcy*, 24 June 1653,(a) being then under age. He *m.* before 4 Nov. 1661, Frances, widow of (—) LEWIS, of Llandewy Court, co. Monmouth, da. of Thomas MORGAN,(b) of Maugham, in that county, by his 2d wife, Elizabeth, da. and h. of Francis WINDHAM. He was living 13 March 1664/5 and probably survived his wife, who was *bur.* Dec. 1669, at Llanternam.

III. 1675? SIR EDWARD MORGAN, Bart. [1642], of Llanternam aforesaid, s. and h.; *suc. to the Baronetcy* on the death of his father; was M.P. for Monmouthshire, Nov. 1680 to 1681, and 1681 till death. He *m.* Mary, da. and coheir of Humphrey BASKERVILLE, of Pontrilas, co. Hereford. He *d.* s.p.m.(c) at an early age, in 1682. Will dat. 22 Jan. 1680/1, pr. 4 July 1682. His widow *m.* John Grubham HOWE, of Stowell, co. Gloucester (who *d.* 1721), and was mother of the 1st BARON CHEDWORTH.

IV. 1682, to 1720? SIR JAMES MORGAN, Bart. [1642], of Abergavenny, uncle and h. male, being 3d s. of the 1st Bart.; *suc. to the Baronetcy* in 1682; was "an English Catholic nonjuror" in 1693 and 1715. Estate, co. Monmouth, valued at £158 rental. He *m.* Alice (a "Protestant"), widow of Nicholas JONES (whom she *m.* 17 April 1683), da. of Sir Edward HOPTON, of Canon Froome, by Deborah, da. of Robert HATTON. He *d.*, presumably s.p.m.s., between 1715 and 1727,(b) when the *Baronetcy* appears to have become *extinct*.(d)

KEMEYS, *or* KEMEYES:

cr. 13 May 1642;(a)

ex. 29 Jan. 1734/5.

I. 1642. "NICHOLAS KEMEYES, *or* KEMEYS, of Keven Mabley [Cefn Mabley], co. Glamorgan, Knt.," 2d s. of Rhys KEMEYS, of Llanfair Castle, co. Monmouth, by Wilsophet, da. of Rev. William AUBREY, D.C.L.,

(a) Disallowed 17 Feb. 1651/2 by Parl., till the Restoration. See *Memorandum* on p. 152. No patent is enrolled. The date here given is that in Dugdale's *Catalogue*. See *Memorandum* on p. 84. The date of the signet bill is 11 May 1642.

(b) He (in his will, dat. 4 Nov. 1661, pr. 2 Dec. 1664), and his widow (in her will, dat. 13 March 1664/5, pr. 11 May 1666) mention their da., "Dame Frances Morgan."

(c) Of his two daughters and coheirs (1) Anne *d.* unm.; (2) Frances *m.* Edmund Braye, being, by her da. Mary, who *m.* John Blewitt, ancestress of the family of Blewitt, who inherited the Llantarnam estate.

(d) An apparently groundless claim to this title was made through Robert Morgan, said to have been a yr. s. of the 1st Bart., and to have settled in Ireland. There appear, however, to have been but four sons, of whom Edward and James inherited the Baronetcy; Henry, the yst., *d.* before 1693, and William, the 2d son, before 1688, his admon. being dat. 7 Feb. 1687/8.

of Brecknock; was M.P. for Monmouthshire, 1628-29; inherited the estate of Cefn Mabley, on the death of his great niece, 31 June 1637; was Sheriff of Glamorganshire, 1638-39; was Colonel of a Regiment of Horse in the army of the King; was *Knighted*, 31 May 1641, at Whitehall, and was *cr. a Baronet*, as above, 13 May 1642.(a) He was imprisoned Jan. 1646 to Sep. 1647; was Governor of Chepstow Castle, which he held for a long time against Cromwell's forces, but, a breach having been effected, he was, with forty of his men, slain at its capture. His estate was valued at £1,800 a year. He was a man of gigantic stature and strength. He *m.* firstly, Jane, da. of Sir Rowland WILLIAMS, of Llangibby, co. Monmouth, by Jane, da. of Sir Edward MANSEL, of Margam, co. Glamorgan. He *m.* secondly, in 1644, Jane, widow of William HERBERT, of Cogan Pill, da. of Sir Raleigh BUSSEY. He *d.* as aforesaid, 25 May 1648. Admon. 3 July 1652(b) and 22 Feb. 1660/1.

II. 1648. SIR CHARLES KEMEYS, Bart. [1642], of Cefn Mabley aforesaid, s. and h., *b.* about 1614; matric. at Oxford (Jesus Coll.), 3 Feb. 1631/2, aged 17; admitted to Gray's Inn, 1634; *Knighted* at Oxford, 13 June 1643; served in the Royal forces, and was with his father during the siege of Chepstow Castle. Sheriff of Glamorganshire, 1643-45; *suc. to the Baronetcy*, 25 May 1648(a); was fined, for his father's delinquency, £5,262. He *m.* firstly, Blanche, da. of Sir Lewis MANSEL, 2d Bart. [1611], of Margam, by his 2d wife Katharine, da. of Sir Edward LEWIS, of Van, co. Glamorgan. She *d.* s.p. Admon. 30 April 1651. He *m.* secondly, in or before 1651, Margaret, da. of Sir George WHITMORE, sometime, 1631-32, Lord Mayor of London, by Mary, da. and h. of Reginald COPCOTT. He *d.* 1658. Will dat. 15 May, and pr. 2 July 1658, that of his widow, dat. 20 May 1682, pr. 25 June 1684.

III. 1658. SIR CHARLES KEMEYS, Bart. [1642], of Cefn Mabley aforesaid, s. and h. by 2d wife; *b.* at Balmes House, 18 and *bap.* 29 May 1651, at Hackney, Midx.; *suc. to the Baronetcy* in 1658; matric. at Oxford (Wad. Coll.), 26 May 1669, aged 18; *cr.* M.A. 9 July following; was M.P. for Monmouthshire, 1685-87; for Monmouth, 1690-95, and for Monmouthshire (again) 1695-98; elected Sheriff of Glamorganshire, 1689, but did not act. He *m.* firstly, in 1678, Mary, widow of Edward THOMAS, of Wenvoe, co. Glamorgan, sister of Thomas (WHARTON), 1st MARQUESS OF WHARTON, da. of Philip, 4th BARON WHARTON, by his 2d wife, Jane, da. and h. of Arthur GOODWIN. Her will (during coverture) dat. 27 March, and pr. 16 May 1699. He *m.* secondly, in 1701, Mary, widow of Sir John AUBREY, 2d Bart. [1660], and formerly, 1691, of William JEPHSON, 1st da. and coheir of William LEWIS, by Margaret, da. and h. of Laurence BANISTER, both of Boarstall, Bucks. He was *bur.* 22 Dec. 1702 (with his ancestors) at Michaelstown. Will dat. 8 June 1702, pr. 5 May 1703 and 7 July 1710. His widow *m.* 10 Aug. 1703, at Boarstall (for her 4th husband), William AUBREY, B.C.L. (Oxford), and *d.* s.p. 1717, being *bur.* at Boarstall.

IV. 1702, to 1735. SIR CHARLES KEMEYS, Bart. [1642], of Cefn Mabley aforesaid, only s. and h., *b.* 23 Nov. and *bap.* 8 Dec. 1688, at Ruperra; *suc. to the Baronetcy* in Dec. 1702; Sheriff of Glamorganshire, 1712-13; was M.P. for Monmouthshire (thirteen Parls.) 1713-15 and Feb. 1716 to 1734. He was a Jacobite and a staunch adherent to the exiled Royal Family. He *d.* unm. 29 Jan. 1734/5, when the *Baronetcy* became *extinct.*(c) Admon. 8 March 1734/5 to his sister, Dame Jane Tynte, widow.

(a) See p. 171, note "a," *sub* "Morgan."

(b) In this he is described as "Knight," and his eldest son, Charles, as "Esq.," the Baronetcy not being at that date recognised. See *Memorandum* on p. 152.

(c) The estates devolved on his nephew, Charles Kemeys TYNTE, youngest son of his only sister Jane, by Sir John Tynte, 2d Bart. [1673]. He, on the death of his two brothers, became, in 1740, the 5th Bart., but *d.* s.p. 1785, when that Baronetcy became extinct.

WILLIAMS:

cr. 14 May 1642;(a)

ex. Dec. 1758.

I. 1642. "TREVOR WILLIAMS, of Llangibbie, co. Monmouth, Esq.," s. and h. of Sir Charles WILLIAMS, of the same, (*d.* March 1641/2, aged 52), by his 2d wife, Anne, da. of Sir John TREVOR, of Plas Têg, co. Flint (which Charles was s. and h. of Sir Rowland WILLIAMS, also of the same, Sheriff of Monmouthshire, 1604-05), was *b.* about 1622; admitted to Gray's Inn, 3 March 1633/4, and, having suc. his father in March 1641/2, was, *cr. a Baronet*, as above, 14 May 1642.(a) He was Gov. of Monmouth, for the King, on its capture in Oct. 1645; was M.P. for Monmouth, 1660; for Monmouthshire, Nov. 1667 to 1679; for Monmouth (again), March to July 1679; and for Monmouthshire (again, in three Parls.), 1679-90. He *m.* Elizabeth, da. and h. of Thomas MORGAN, of Machen and Tredegar, co. Monmouth, by his 1st wife, Rachel, sister and coheir of Ralph (HOPTON), BARON HOPTON OF STRATTON, da. of Robert HOPTON, of Wytham, co. Somerset, by Jane, da. of Rowland KEMEYS. He *d.* Dec. 1692, aged 69.

II. 1692. SIR JOHN WILLIAMS, Bart. [1642], of Llangibby Castle aforesaid, and Pontrylas, co. Hereford, 1st surv. s. and h.,(b) *b.* about 1651; matric. at Oxford (Jesus Coll.), 28 May 1666, aged 15; admitted to Gray's Inn, 21 March 1667/8, being, presumably, Barrister thereof, 1680; was M.P. for Monmouth, Feb. 1688/9 to Feb. 1689/90; for Monmouthshire (four Parls.), 1698 till death; *suc. to the Baronetcy* in Dec. 1692; was Lord of the manors of Ewyas Lacy, Waterslow, and Trescaillon, co. Hereford, and of that of Cairwent, co. Monmouth, which last he sold, under an act of Parl., to pay debts contracted in the public service. He *m.* firstly, Anne, da. and coheir of Humphrey BASKERVILLE, of Pontrylas aforesaid. He *m.* secondly, Catharine (*b.* 9 and *bap.* 10 June 1654, at St. Bennets', Paul's Wharf, London), 2d da. of Philip (HERBERT), 5th EARL OF PEMBROKE, by his 2d wife, Catharine, da. of Sir William VILLIERS, 1st Bart. [1619]. He *d.* s.p. Nov. 1704. Will dat. 31 Oct. 1704, (his wife Catherine being then living), pr. Feb. 1704/5.

III. 1704. SIR HOPTON WILLIAMS, Bart. [1642], of Llangibby Castle aforesaid, br. and h.; aged 20 in 1683 [*Visit. of Monmouthshire*], *suc. to the Baronetcy* in Nov. 1704; was M.P. for Monmouthshire, 1705-08. He *m.* Mary, da. of [—].(c) He *d.* s.p.m.s., at Llangibby, 25 Nov. 1722, aged 60.

IV. 1722. SIR JOHN WILLIAMS, Bart. [1642], of Llangibby Castle, aforesaid, nephew and h., being s. and h. of Thomas WILLIAMS, by his 1st wife, Delariviere (relict of Thomas LEWIS, of St. Pierre), da. of Gen. Sir Thomas MORGAN, which Thomas Williams (aged 18 in 1683), was yst. s. of the 1st Bart. He *suc. to the Baronetcy*, 25 Nov. 1722; was Sheriff of Monmouthshire, 1725-26. He *m.* Temperance, widow of [—] WILLIAMS, of co. Monmouth, and da. of [—] RAMSEY. He *d.* s.p.m.,(d) 11 March 1738/9. Will dat. 13 Jan. 1735 to 14 Feb. 1738, pr. 18 June 1739. The will of his widow as "of Bristol," dat. 2 Sept. 1773, pr. 28 July 1774.

V. 1739, to 1758. SIR LEONARD WILLIAMS, Bart. [1642], br. of the half blood and h. male, being s. of Thomas WILLIAMS abovenamed (the yst. s. of the 1st Bart.), by [—], his 2d wife. He *d.* s.p. at Usk, co. Monmouth, Dec. 1758, when the *Baronetcy* became *extinct.*

(a) See p. 171, note "a," *sub* "Morgan."

(b) Trevor Williams, his eldest br. was aged 34, and married in 1683 [*Visit. of Monmouthshire*], but *d.* s.p. and v.p.

(c) She is said by Le Neve to have been "a servant maid." Le Neve assigns two sons to her, Thomas and John, both of whom presumably died s.p.m.s. and v.p.

(d) Ellen, his 1st da., *m.* William ADDAMS, and was mother of William ADDAMS-WILLIAMS, of Llangibby Castle aforesaid.

RERESBY:

cr. 16 May 1642;(a)

ex. 11 Aug. 1748.

I. 1642. "JOHN RERESBY, of Thribergh, co. York, Esq.," s. and h. of Sir George RERESBY, of the same, by Elizabeth, da. and coheir of John TAMWORTH, of Sherville Court, Hants, was *bap.* 11 April 1611, at Thribergh, suc. his father 3 Feb. 1628; took the Royalist side in the Civil War, though never accepting any command, and was *cr. a Baronet*, as above, 16 May 1642.(a) He *m.*, 21 April 1633, at Thribergh, Frances, da. of Edmund YARBURGH, of Balne Hall, near Snaith, co. York, by Sarah, da. and coheir of Thomas WORMELEY, of Hatfield, in that county. He *d.* April 1646, at Thribergh, where he had for two years been a prisoner. His widow *m.* 12 Jan. 1650, at Beverley, James MOYSER, of Beverley, where she *d.* She was *bur.* 7 Sep. 1669, at Thribergh.

II. 1646. SIR JOHN RERESBY, Bart. [1642], of Thribergh aforesaid, s. and h., *b.* there 14, and *bap.* 21 April 1634; *suc. to the Baronetcy* in April 1646(a); Sheriff of York, 1666-67; Governor of Bridlington, 1678; M.P. for Aldborough, Nov. 1673 to 1679, April 1679 till void, and 1681, and for York 1685-87; Governor of York, 1682; is the author of an interesting autobiography, the *Memoirs of Sir John Reresby*, 1634-89. He *m.* 9 March 1664/5, at St. Dunstan's in the West, London, (Lic. 4, at Vic. Gen., she 23, of St. Mary's Savoy, parents dead,) Frances, da. of William BROWNE, of York, Barrister. He *d.* 12 and was *bur.* 28 May 1689, at Thribergh. M.I. Will dat. 15 May 1688, pr. at York. His widow *d.* 11, and was *bur.* 16 May 1699, at Thribergh. Will, as "of Doncaster," dat. 17 July 1697 pr. at York 25 Oct. 1699.

III. 1689. SIR WILLIAM RERESBY, Bart. [1642], of Thirbergh aforesaid, s. and h., *bap.* 19 Jan. 1668/9, at Thriberg; *suc. to the Baronetcy*, 1689. He wasted all his estate by gambling and every other kind of debauchery, and is said to have staked and lost the estate of Dennaby on a single main. In 1705 he sold Thriberg to John SAVILE, of Methley, co. York, and was eventually reduced to great poverty, being, at one time, Tapster of the Fleet Prison.(b) He *d.* s.p.m.s. and presumably unm., between 1727 and 1741.(c).

IV. 1735? to 1748. SIR LEONARD RERESBY, Bart. [1642], br. and h., being 5th and yst. s. of the 2d Bart.; *bap.* 23 Oct. 1679, at Thriberg; *suc. to the Baronetcy* between 1727 and 1741.(d) He *d.* unm., at his chambers in the King's Bench Walk, Temple, London, 14 and was *bur.* 27 Aug. 1748, at Thriberg, aged 69, when the *Baronetcy* became *extinct.* M.I. Will dat. 27 Feb. 1745/6, to 23 Nov. 1746, in which he leaves the Foundling Hospital as his residuary legatee, pr. 17 Nov. 1748.

INGLEBY:

cr. 17 May 1642;(d)

ex. 14 July 1772.

I. 1642. "WILLIAM INGLEBY, of Ripley, co. York, Esq.," s. and h. of Sampson INGLEBY, of Spofforth manor, Steward to the Earl of Northumberland, by Jane, da. of [—] LAMBERT, of Killinghall, which Sampson (who

---

(a) The Baronetcy was disallowed, 4 Feb. 1651/2, by Parl. till the Restoration. See *Memorandum* as to creations after 4 Jan. 1641/2, on p. 152. No patent is enrolled. The date here given is that in Dugdale's *Catalogue*. See *Memorandum* on p. 84. The date of the signet bill is 14 May 1642.

(b) Thoresby, in his *History of Leeds*, says that though he had "an estate of £1,700 a year, and £4,000 in monies left him by his father," he has not £100 a year left.

(c) Wotton's [existing] *Baronetages* of those dates.

(d) See p. 161, note "b," *sub* "Strutt."

d. 18 July 1604) was 4th s. (his issue becoming heir male) of Sir William INGLEBY, of Ripley (*d.* Feb. 1578/9, aged 60); was *b.* about 1603, being nine years old in 1612; suc. his father, 18 July 1604; admitted to Gray's Inn, as "heir of Sir William Ingleby, of Ripley Knt.," 20 Nov. 1611, whom he suc. 5 Jan. 1617, and was *cr. a Baronet*, as above, 17 May 1642.(a) He served as a Volunteer, on behalf of the King, at the battle of Marston Moor in 1644, and was fined £718 for delinquency. He *m.* Ann, da. of Sir James BELLINGHAM, of Levens, Westmoreland. She *d.* 1640. He *d.* 22 Jan. 1652, and was *bur.* at Ripley.

II. 1658. SIR WILLIAM INGLEBY, Bart. [1642], of Ripley aforesaid, s. and h.; *bap.* 13 March 1620/1, at Ripley; matric. at Oxford (Mag. Coll.), 14 Sep. 1638, aged 16; admitted to Gray's Inn, 2 Nov. 1639; *suc. to the Baronetcy*, 22 Jan. 1652.(a) He *m.* Margaret, 1st da. of John SAVILE, of Methley, co. York, by his 2d wife, Margaret, da. of Sir Henry GARRAWAY, sometime (1639-40) Lord Mayor of London. He *d.* 6 Nov. 1682, aged 61. His widow *d.* 9 Nov. 1697, and was *bur.* at Ripley.

III. 1682. SIR JOHN INGLEBY, Bart. [1642], of Ripley aforesaid, only s. and h.; *bap.* 9 Oct. 1664, at Ripley; *suc. to the Baronetcy*, 6 Nov. 1682. He *m.* Mary, da. of (—) JOHNSON. She was *bur.* 14 July 1733, at Ripley, aged 64. He *d.* 21 Jan. and was *bur.* 6 Feb. 1741/2, at Ripley.

IV. 1742, to 1772. SIR JOHN INGLEBY, Bart. [1642], of Ripley aforesaid, only surv. s. and h., *b.* about 1705; *suc. to the Baronetcy*, 21 Jan. 1741/2. He *d.* s.p. 14 July, and was *bur.* 20 Aug. 1772, when the *Baronetcy* became *extinct.*(b) Will dat. 11 June 1770.

MOORE, *or* MORE:

cr. 18 May 1642;(c)

ex. 24 July 1684.

I. 1642. "POYNINGS MOORE [*or* MORE], of Loseley [near Guildford], co. Surrey, Esq.," s. and h. of Sir Robert MORE, of Loseley aforesaid, by Frances, da. of Sampson LENNARD and Margaret, *suo jure* BARONESS DACRE, was *b.* 13 Feb. 1605/6; suc. his father, 2 Feb. 1625/6, and his grandfather, Sir George MORE, 16 Oct. 1632; was M.P. for Haslemere, 1624-25, 1625 and 1626, and for Guildford, 1628-29, and for Haslemere (again), Nov. to Dec. 1640; and was *cr. a Baronet*, as above, 18 May 1642.(c) He *m.* in or before 1644, Elizabeth, widow of Christopher ROUS, of Henham, co. Suffolk, da. of Sir John FYTCHE, of Woodham Walter, co. Essex, by Dorothy, da. of Sir Charles CORNWALLIS. He *d.* at Loseley, 11 April 1649, and was *bur.* in the Loseley chapel, at St. Nicholas, Guildford, aged 43 years, 1 month, and 27 days. M.I. Admon. 23 April 1649. His widow *d.* at Loseley 13 Sep. 1666, and was *bur.* with him. Admon. 14 Nov. 1666.

II. 1649, to 1684. SIR WILLIAM MORE, Bart. [1642], of Loseley aforesaid, 2d but 1st s. and h.; *b.* 1644; *suc. to the Baronetcy*, 11 April 1649(a); was admitted to Gray's Inn, 3 July 1661; elected Sheriff of Surrey, 1668, but did not act; was M.P. for Haslemere, June 1675 to 1679, April to July 1679, Oct. 1679 till void in Nov., and 1681; Sheriff of Sussex, 1670.

(a) The Baronetcy was disallowed, 4 Feb. 1651/2, by Parl. till the Restoration. See *Memorandum* on p. 152.

(b) John INGILBY (*b.* 1757), his illegitimate son (by Mary Wright), inherited Ripley, and was *cr. a Baronet*, 6 June 1781. That Baronetcy, however, became extinct on the death of (the grantee's son), the 2d Bart., 14 May 1854, who devised the estates to his cousin, John Henry Ingleby, s. and h. of the Rev. Henry Ingleby (*d.* 4 Sep. 1833, aged 72), who was another illegit. son of the 4th Bart. [1642]. This John Henry Ingilby, being then of Ripley, was *cr. a Baronet*, 26 July 1866.

(c) Disallowed, 4 Feb. 1651/2, by Parl. till the Restoration. See *Memorandum* as to creations after 4 Jan. 1641/2, on p. 152. No patent is enrolled. The date here given is that in Dugdale's *Catalogue*. See *Memorandum* on p. 84. The date of the signet bill is 16 May 1642.

II

He *m.* 18 Feb. 1663, Mary, da. and h. of Sir Walter HENDLEY, Bart. [*cr.* 1661], by Frances, da. and coheir of Sir Thomas SPRINGETT, of Broyle Place, Sussex. He *d.* s.p. 24 July 1684, in his 41st year, when the *Baronetcy* became *extinct*.(a) Will pr. Feb. 1684/5. His widow *m.* in 1685, William CLARK, of Gray's Inn, Barrister, and was living in 1691, when she sold her father's estate at Cuckfield, co. Sussex.

A Baronetcy was assumed by William Moore, as early or earlier than 1701, but whether it was in right of any presumed claim for *this* Baronetcy, or for any other, is not known.

"SIR WILLIAM MOORE, Knt. and Bart., of St. Margaret's, Westm., Bachr., aged 27," had lic. (Bp. of London) 16 Sep. 1701, to marry "Abigail SNELLGROVE, of St. Mary, Whitechapel, spr., aged 16, with her parents consent." It appears from Peter Le Neve's notes [*Top. and Gen.*, iii. 47] that in 1703, she being then aged 17 (her father being described as "of Deptford, Kent") eloped from her husband "Sir William Moor, of York place, Surrey, Bart." The death of William Moore, of South Lambeth," occurs in 1732, and the will of "Sir William Moore, Midx.," is pr. July 1738.

DAWNAY, *or* DAWNEY:
cr. 19 May 1642 (b);
ex. probably in 1657.

I. 1642. "CHRISTOPHER DAWNEY, of Cowick, co. York, Esq.," 2d s. of John DAWNEY, *or* DAWNAY, of Wormsley in that county (*d.* v.p. 15 March 1629/30, aged 36), by Elizabeth, da. of Sir Richard HUTTON, of Goldesborough, one of the Justices of the Court of Common Pleas, was *b.* about 1620 ;(c) was admitted to Gray's Inn, 2 Nov. 1639 ; suc. his grandfather, Sir Thomas DAWNAY, of Sessay and Cowick aforesaid, in May 1642, and was, within a few days thereof, *cr. a Baronet*, as above, 19 May 1642(b). He *m.* Jane, da. and h. of John MOSELEY, of Uskelfe, co. York. He *d.* 13 and was *bur.* 25 July 1644, at Snaith. Inq. p.m. at York, 17 Oct. 1644. His widow was then living.

II. 1644, to 1657 ? SIR THOMAS DAWNAY, Bart. [1642], of Cowick aforesaid, only surv. s. and h. ; aged 3 months at his father's death, when he *suc. to the Baronetcy*,(b) 13 July 1644. He *d.* unm. and presumably in his infancy, though sometimes said to be aged 13.(d) [*Qy.* in 1644, or 1657] ; when *the Baronetcy* became *extinct*(e).

(a) The Loseley estate reverted to his uncle and h. male, the Rev. Nicholas More, Rector of Fetchham, who *d.* a few months later, 22 Dec. 1684, and was suc. by his son, Robert More, of Loseley, who *d.* s.p. 1689. His sister Margaret, wife of Sir Thomas Molyneux, became eventually his sole heir and on her death, 14 Sep. 1704, it passed to her son and heir, Sir More Molyneux.

(b) Disallowed 4 Feb. 1651/2 by Parl. till the Restoration. See *Memorandum* as to creations after 4 Jan. 1641/2, on p. 152. No patent is enrolled. The date here given is that in Dugdale's *Catalogue*; see *Memorandum* on p. 84. The date of the signet bill is as early as 3 May 1642.

(c) His eldest br. Thomas Dawnay, *d.* unm., and was *bur.* 19 April 1639, aged 22.

(d) The age of 13 is given in Foster's *Yorkshire pedigrees*, but the date of death there given is 1644, when it is certain he was only 3 months old.

(e) It has often been supposed that Sir John Dawnay, of Cowick, who suc. to the estates, being br. of the 1st and uncle of the last Bart., suc. also to the Baronetcy. There is, however, no evidence of any spec. rem. having been in the grant of that dignity, and this John Dawnay was, when returned M.P. in April 1660, designated an "Esq."; was *Knighted* 2 June following, and was, as a "Knight," not as a Baronet," *cr.* 19 Feb. 1680, VISCOUNT DOWNE [I.]

HAMPSON:
cr. 3 June 1642 ;(a)

I. 1642. "THOMAS HAMPSON, of Taplow, co. Bucks, Esq.," 2d s. of Sir Robert HAMPSON, Alderman and, sometime [1598-99], Sheriff of London (*d.* 2 May 1607, in his 70th year), by Katharine, da. of John Goore, Citizen and Merchant Tailor of London, was *b.* about 1589 ; matric. at Oxford (Oriel Coll.) 21 Nov. 1606, aged 17 ; admitted to Gray's Inn, 1609, becoming an Ancient thereof in 1632 ; was Master of the Statute office ; suc. his eldest br. Nicholas HAMPSON (who *d.* aged 59), 6 Oct. 1637, and was *cr. a Baronet*, as aforesaid, 3 June 1642(a). He, presumably, though possibly it was his son, is the "William Hampson, of Taplow, *Esq.*,"(a) who was Sheriff of Bucks, 1653-54. He *m.* Ann, 1st da. and coheir of William DUNCOMBE, of London, and of Ivinghoe, Bucks, by Anne, da. of Sir Thomas BENNET, sometime [1603-4], Lord Mayor of London. She *d.* 2 Feb. 1643, aged 47. He *d.* 14 Aug. 1655. Both were *bur.* at Taplow.

II. 1655. SIR THOMAS HAMPSON, Bart.(a) [1642], of Taplow aforesaid, s. and h., *b.* about 1626 ; matric. at Oxford (Oriel Coll.), 4 June 1641, aged 15 ; admitted to Middle Temple, 1644 ; *suc. to the Baronetcy*, 21 Aug. 1655.(a) He *m.* (Lic. Fac. 28 Dec. 1650, he aged 24), Mary, 1st da. and coheir of Sir Anthony DENNIS, of Buckland and Orleigh, Devon, by his 2d wife, Gertrude, da. of Sir Bernard GRANVILLE, of Stow, co. Cornwall. He *d.* at St. George's, Southwark, [*Qy.* in the King's Bench prison] 22 and was *bur.* 23 March 1670, at Taplow. Admon. 31 May 1671. His widow was *bur.* 7 July 1694, at Taplow, aforesaid. Will pr. 1694.

III. 1670. SIR DENNIS HAMPSON, Bart. [1642], of Taplow, aforesaid, s. and h., *suc. to Baronetcy*, 22 May 1670, being then under age. Sheriff of Bucks, 1680 (but did not act), and again, 1683-84 ; M.P. for Wycombe, 1685-87. He *d.* unm., and was *bur.* at St. Sepulchre's, London, 10 April 1719. Admon. 29 April 1719, to a creditor.

IV. 1719. SIR GEORGE HAMPSON, Bart. [1642], of St. Michael's, Gloucester, cousin and h male, being s. and h. of George HAMPSON, M.D., by Grace, da. of Edward HOLTE, and sister of Sir Robert HOLTE of Aston, 2d Bart. [1611] which George (who *d.* before Nov. 1677), was 4th s. of the 1st Bart. He who was a minor in 1677 and was subsequently a Physician at Gloucester, *suc. to the Baronetcy*, in April 1719. He *m.* Mary, da. of John COGHILL, of Blechington, Oxon. He *d.* 9 Sep. 1724 and was *bur.* at St. Michael's, Gloucester. Admon. 12 Nov. 1729, his widow being then living.

V. 1724. SIR GEORGE HAMPSON, Bart. [1642], of the island of Jamaica, s. and h., *suc. to the Baronetcy*, 9 Sep. 1724. He *m.* firstly Sarah, da. of Thomas SEBROCOLD, of London. She *d.* s.p. 1 Jan. 1737/8, at Hackney, Middlesex, aged 39. Admon. 3 Jan. 1737/8. He *m.* secondly, at Plobsheim, in Alsace, 16 Feb. 1738, Jane da. of (—) STILL, *or* SILL, of Halifax, co. York. He *d.* in 1754, in Jamaica.

VI. 1754. SIR GEORGE FRANCIS HAMPSON, Bart. [1642], of Jamaica, aforesaid, only surv. s. and h. by 2d wife,(b) *b.* 10 Nov. 1738, at Plobsheim aforesaid ; *suc. to the Baronetcy* in 1754. He *m.* in 1759, Mary, 1st da. of Thomas PINNOCK, of Pinnock, in St. Andrew's, Jamaica. She *d.* there Jan. 1772, aged 35. He *d.* 25 Dec. 1774. Will pr. Jan. 1776.

(a) The Baronetcy was disallowed 11 Nov. 1643, by Parl. till the Restoration. See *Memorandum* as to creations after 4 Jan. 1641/2, and 22 May 1642 (this being, apparently, the first Baronetcy created after the latter date), on p. 152. No patent is enrolled. The date here given is that in Dugdale's *Catalogue*; see *Memorandum* on p. 84. The date of the signet bill is 20 May 1642.

(b) Kimber, in his *Baronetage* of 1771, states this title to be *extinct*. He must either have been unaware of the birth of this Baronet, or have considered him to have been illegitimate.

VII. 1774. SIR THOMAS PHILIP HAMPSON, Bart. [1642], s. and h., *b.* Oct. 1765 ; *suc. to the Baronetcy*, 25 Dec. 1774 ; admitted to Lincoln's Inn, 23 Jan. 1783 ; matric. at Oxford (Univ. Coll.), 28 Feb. 1783, aged 18 ; B.A. 1787. He *m.* 25 June 1788, at St. Geo. Han. Sq., Jane, 1st da. and eventually coheir of Peter HODGSON, of London, and of Buck, co. Cumberland. She *d.* 6 May 1791. Admon. Nov. 1840. He *d.* in Manchester sq., Marylebone, 22 Feb. 1820. Will pr. 1820, and again, Oct. 1840.

VIII. 1820. SIR GEORGE FRANCIS HAMPSON, Bart. [1642], only surv. child and h., *b.* 22 Oct. 1788 ; ed. at Eton ; admitted to Lincoln's Inn, 1 Nov. 1806, aged 18 ; Barrister ; *suc. to the Baronetcy*, 22 Feb. 1820. He *m.* 25 Aug. 1822, Mary Foreman, 1st da. of Rear Admiral William BROWN. He *d.* 8 May 1833, in Bolton street, Piccadilly. Will pr. June 1833.

IX. 1833. SIR GEORGE FRANCIS HAMPSON, Bart. [1642], of Thurnham Court, near Hollingbourne, Kent, s. and h., *b.* 28 Sep. 1823, in Hertford street, Mayfair ; *suc. to the Baronetcy*, 8 May 1833 ; ed. at Eton ; Captain 2d Dragoons, 1847-58, and served in the Crimean campaign of 1855, at the battle of Tchernaya and at the fall of Sebastopol. He *m.* 12 July 1854, Ann, only child of Thomas Hastings ENGLAND, of Snitterfield, co. Warwick. She *d.* 4 May 1893. He *d.* s.p., 21 July 1896, at Thurnham Court, aged 73. Will pr. at £3,658 personalty.

X. 1896. SIR GEORGE FRANCIS HAMPSON, Bart. [1642], nephew and h. male, being s. and h. of the Rev. William Seymour HAMPSON, M.A., Rector of Stubton, co. Lincoln, by Julia Jane, da. of Charles FRANKS, which William (who *d.* 8 June 1868, aged 37), was 2d s. of the 9th Bart. He was *b.* 14 Jan. 1860 ; was ed. at Charterhouse School and Exeter College, Oxford ; matric , 13 Oct. 1877 ; B.A. 1880 ; *suc. to the Baronetcy*, 21 July 1896. He *m.* 1 June 1893, Minnie Francis, 1st da. of Col. Clark KENNEDY, C.B., of Knockgray, co. Kirkcudbright.

HARDRES:
cr. 3 June 1642(a) ;
ex. 31 Aug. 1764.

I. 1642. "RICHARD HARDRES, of Hardres Court [in Upper Hardres], co. Kent, Esq.," s. and h. of Sir Thomas HARDRES, of the same, by Eleanor, da. and h. of Henry THORESBY, of Thoresby, co. York, was *bap.* 23 April 1606, at Upper Hardres ; admitted to Gray's Inn, 3 Feb. 1625/6 ; suc. his father, 29 March 1628, and was *cr. a Baronet*, as above, 3 June 1642.(a) He was one of the Sequestration Committee for Kent, 1643. He *m.* Anne, sister of Sir Thomas GODFREY, da. of Thomas GODFREY, of Lydd, Kent, by Dorothy, da. of Thomas WILDE, of Canterbury. He was *bur.* 25 Oct. 1669, at Upper Hardres. Will dat. 12 Nov. 1668, but not pr. till 1 Feb. 1681/2. His widow *d.* at Hammersmith, Midx., and was *bur.* 3 Jan. 1679/80, at Upper Hardres. Admon. 24 Jan. 1679/80.

II. 1669. SIR PETER HARDRES, Bart. [1642], of Hardres Court aforesaid, s. and h., *bap.* 15 Feb. 1635, at St. Giles, Cripplegate, London, reg. at Upper Hardres ; admitted to Gray's Inn, 28 June 1651 ; *suc. to the Baronetcy*, in Oct. 1669. He *m.* Phœbe, da. of Edward BERRY, of Lydd, Kent. He was *bur.* 6 March 1673 at Upper Hardres. Admon. 22 July 1675. His widow was *bur.* there 30 Oct. 1724, aged 88.

(a) Disallowed by Parl. 11 Nov. 1643, till the Restoration. See *Memorandum* as to creations after 4 Jan. 1641/2 and 22 May 1642, on p. 152. No patent is enrolled. The date here given is that in Dugdale's *Catalogue*; see *Memorandum* on p. 84. The date of the signet bill is 22 May 1642.

III. 1673. SIR THOMAS HARDRES, Bart. [1642], of Hardres Court aforesaid, s. and h., *b.* 6 and *bap.* 21 Dec. 1660 at Hinxhill, registered at Upper Hardres ; *suc. to the Baronetcy*, 6 March 1673. He *m.* Ursula, da. of Sir William ROOKE, of Horton, co. Kent, by Jane, da. and coheir of Thomas FINCH, of Coptree He *d.* 23 and was *bur.* 26 Feb. 1688, aged 28, at Upper Hardres. His widow was *bur.* there 10 Jan. 1707.

IV. 1688. SIR WILLIAM HARDRES, Bart. [1642], of Hardres Court aforesaid, s. and h., *b.* 25 July and *bap.* 5 Aug. 1686, at St. Laurence, near Canterbury, registered at Great Hardres ; *suc. to the Baronetcy*, 23 Feb. 1688 ; M.P. for Kent, June 1711 to 1713 ; for Dover, 1713-15 ; for Canterbury, 1727-34 and 1734 till unseated, in April 1735. He *m.* Elizabeth, widow of William DISHER, of London, merchant, da. of Richard THOMAS, of Lamberhurst, Kent. He *d.* at Hardres Court, 8 July 1736, and was *bur.* at Upper Hardres. His widow was *bur.* there 22 June 1755. Her admon., as "of East Malling, Kent," 11 Nov. 1755.

V. 1736, to 1764. SIR WILLIAM HARDRES, Bart. [1642], of Hardres Court aforesaid, only s. and h., *bap.* 12 June 1718, at Great Hardres ; *suc. to the Baronetcy*, 8 July 1736. He *m.* Frances, da. of John CORBET, LL.D., of Bourne Place, Kent, by Elizabeth, da. of Sir Anthony AUCHER, 1st Bart. [1666]. He *d.* s.p., 31 Aug., and was *bur.* 7 Sep. 1764, at Upper Hardres, aged 46, when the *Baronetcy* became *extinct*. Will pr. 1764. His widow, to whom he had devised all his estates in fee, *d.* intestate,(a) 23 Feb. 1783, at Walmer, aged 66, and was *bur.* at Upper Hardres. Admon. April 1783.

WILLIAMSON:
cr. 3 June 1642.(b)

I. 1642. "THOMAS WILLIAMSON, of East Markham, co. Notts, Esq.," s. and h. of Robert WILLIAMSON, of the same, by Faith, 5th da. of Sir Edward AYSCOUGH, of South Kelsey, co. Lincoln, was *bap.* 14 May 1609, at East Markham ; suc. his father, 28 Jan. 1632/3 ; was Sheriff of Notts, 1639-40 ; and, for his fidelity to the King during the Civil Wars, was *cr. a Baronet*, as above, 3 June 1642.(b) He had to pay £3,400 to the sequestrators of estates, and lost £30,000 for the royal cause, thereby ruining his estate. He *m.* firstly, 27 Aug. 1633, at Honington, co. Lincoln, Jane, 1st surv. da. of Sir Edward HUSSEY, 1st Bart. [1611], by Elizabeth, da. of George ANTON. She, who was *bap.* 27 Jan. 1611/2 at Honington, was *bur.* 22 Aug. 1642/3 at East Markham. He *m.* secondly, 5 May 1647, at St. Barth. the Less, London, Dionysia(c) (*b.* 1611), da. of William HALE, of King's Walden, Herts, by Rose, da. of Sir George BOND, sometime (1587-88) Lord Mayor of London. He *d.* 14 and was *bur.* 16 Oct. 1657, at East Markham. Will pr. Nov. 1657. His widow, who was *b.* 17 and *bap.* 31 March 1611, at King's Walden, *d.* s.p. 1684. Will pr. Feb. 1685.

(a) The estates consequently devolved on her heirs, *i.e.*, her four sisters or their descendants. These are set forth in Burke's *Extinct Baronets* [edit. 1841, p. 243].

(b) Disallowed by Parl. 11 Nov. 1643, till the Restoration. See *Memorandum* as to creations after 4 Jan. 1641/2 and 22 May 1642, on p. 152. No patent is enrolled. The date here given is that in Dugdale's *Catalogue*; see *Memorandum* on p. 84. The date of the signet bill is 22 May 1642.

(c) She contributed £4,000 towards the rebuilding, after the great fire, of the church of St. Dustan's in the East, London, where there is a monument to her grandfather, Richard Hale, who *d.* 1620.

II. 1657. SIR THOMAS WILLIAMSON, Bart. [1642], of East Markham aforesaid, s. and h. by 1st wife, *bap.* there 10 May 1636; *suc. to the Baronetcy*, 14 Oct. 1657.(a) He *m.* Dorothy yst. da. and coheir of George FENWICK, of Brinkburne, Northumberland, and of Monk Wearmouth Hall,(b) near Sunderland, co. Durham, a Col. in the Parl. army, by Alice, sister and h. of Edward APSLEY, da. of Sir Edward APSLEY, of Thakeham, co. Sussex. She *d.* 4 Nov. 1699, being her birthday of 53. He *d.* s.p. 23 April 1703. Both *bur.* at Monk Wearmouth. M.I.

III. 1703. SIR ROBERT WILLIAMSON, Bart. [1642], of Monk Wearmouth Hall aforesaid, br. of the whole blood, and h. *suc. to the Baronetcy*, 23 April 1703. He *m.* in or before 1681, Rebecca, da. of John BURROWS, merchant of London. He was *bur.* 25 May 1707. Will pr. April 1708.

IV. 1707. SIR WILLIAM WILLIAMSON, Bart. [1642], of Monk Wearmouth Hall aforesaid, only surv. s. and h., *bap.* 9 Oct. 1681, *suc. to the Baronetcy* in 1708; Sheriff of co. Durham, 1723 till death. He *m.* firstly, 1703, Elizabeth, yst. da. and coheir of John HEDWORTH, of Harraton, co. Durham. She *d.* 1736, by her he had twelve children. He *m.* secondly, before 1741, Mary, widow of Thomas WILKINSON, of Durham, da. and eventually h. of William FEATHERSTONHAUGH, of Brancepath and Stanley, co. Durham. By her he had no issue. He *d.* April 1747. His widow *d.* s.p. 17 April 1752.

V. 1747. SIR HEDWORTH WILLIAMSON, Bart. [1642], of Monk Wearmouth Hall aforesaid, 2d but 1st surv. s. and h.,(c) by 1st wife, *b.* about 1710; *suc. to the Baronetcy* in April 1747; Sheriff of co. Durham, 1747 till death. He *m.* 1748, Elizabeth, 1st da. and coheir of William HUDLESTON, of Millom Castle, Cumberland, by Gertrude, da. of Sir William MEREDITH, of Henbury, in Cheshire. He *d.* 9 Jan. 1788. His widow *d.* 10 Oct. 1793.

VI. 1788. SIR HEDWORTH WILLIAMSON, Bart. [1642], of Whitburn Hall, co. Durham, and Millom Castle aforesaid, s. and h., *b.* 1751; matric. at Oxford (Linc. Coll.), 13 March 1769, aged 18; B.A. and M.A., 1778; *suc. to the Baronetcy*, 13 Jan. 1788; Sheriff of co. Durham, 1788 till death. He *m.* 23 Oct. 1794, Maria, da. of Sir James HAMILTON, of co. Monaghan. He *d.* 14 March 1810. Will pr. 1810. His widow *d.* 10 Jan. 1848. Will pr. March 1848.

VII. 1810. SIR HEDWORTH WILLIAMSON, Bart. [1642], of Whitburn Hall aforesaid, s. and h., *b.* there 1 Nov. 1797; *suc. to the Baronetcy*, 14 March 1810; ed. at St. John's Coll., Cambridge; M.A., 1819; M.P. for co. Durham, 1831-32; for North Durham, 1832-37, and for Sunderland, Dec. 1847 to 1852; Mayor of Sunderland, 1841-42, and 1847-48. He *m.* 18 April 1826, Anne Elizabeth, 3d da. of Thomas-Henry (LIDDELL), 1st BARON RAVENSWORTH, by Maria Susanna, da. of John SIMPSON. He *d.* 24 April 1861, at Whitburn Hall, aged 63. His widow *d.* 4 Nov. 1878, aged 77, at 32 Lower Belgrave street.

VIII. 1861. SIR HEDWORTH WILLIAMSON, Bart. [1642], of Whitburn Hall aforesaid, s. and h., *b.* 25 March 1827, at Florence; ed. at Eton and at Christ Church, Oxford; matric. 15 May 1845, aged 18; Attaché at St. Petersburgh, 1848, and at Paris, 1850 to 1854; *suc. to the Baronetcy*, 24 April 1861; M.P. in the Liberal interest for North Durham, 1864-74; Sheriff of co. Durham, 1877; Provincial Grand Master of the Durham Freemasons, 1885. He *m.* 3 Feb. 1863, his cousin, Elizabeth, 4th da. of Henry Thomas (LIDDELL), 1st EARL OF RAVENSWORTH, by Isabella Horatia, da. of Lord George SEYMOUR. He *d.* at Whitburn Hall, 26 and was *bur.* 30 Aug. 1900, at Whitburn, aged 73. Will pr. at £302,136, the net personalty being £250,626. His widow, who was *b.* 20 March 1831, living 1900.

(a) The Baronetcy was disallowed till the Restoration. See p. 179, note "b."

(b) This estate, which she left to her husband, became, subsequently, the principal seat of his family, their paternal estates in Notts having been much incumbered.

(c) His elder br., Fenwick Williamson, matric. at Oxford (Merton College), 5 March 1724/5, aged 17; was an Ensign in the Guards, and *d.* unm., v.p., in 1737.

IX. 1900. SIR HEDWORTH WILLIAMSON, Bart. [1642], of Whitburn Hall aforesaid, 1st s. and h., *b.* 23 May 1867; ed. at Eton and at Christ Church, Oxford; matric. 16 April 1886, aged 18; *suc. to the Baronetcy*, 26 Aug. 1900.

DENNY:

cr. 3 June 1642;(a)

ex. 19 June 1676.

I. 1642, to 1676. "WILLIAM DENNY, of Gillingham, co Norfolk, Esq.," said(b) to be s. of "Sir William DENNY, Serjeant at Law, by (—), da. of (—) KNEVITT" (being, presumably, the "William, son of William Denny, of Bockells, Suffolk, Esq.," who was admitted to Gray's Inn, 2 Nov. 1621); was *cr. a Baronet*, as of Gillingham abovenamed, 3 June 1642.(a) He *m.* Catharine, da. of (—) YOUNG. He *d.* s.p. of fever, in extreme indigence, and was *bur* 19 June 1676, at St. Giles', Cripplegate, London, when the *Baronetcy* became *extinct*. In the same register there is, 9 Dec. 1682, recorded the burial "at Tindalls," of "Jane, the relique of Sir William Denny, Kn^t, dec^d," possibly a second wife of this Baronet.

LOWTHER:

cr. 11 June 1642;(c)

ex. 2 Jan. 1755.

I. 1642. "CHRISTOPHER LOWTHER, of Whitehaven, co. Cumberland, Esq.," 2d s. of Sir John LOWTHER, of Lowther, co. Westmorland, by Eleanor, da. of William FLEMING, of Rydal in that county; was Sheriff of Cumberland, 1640, and was *cr. a Baronet*, as above, 11 June 1642.(c) He *m.* Frances, da. and h. of Christopher LANCASTER, of Stockbridge, Westmorland. He *d.* 1644, and was *bur.* at St. Bees, Cumberland. Admon. 14 March 1653/4. His widow *m.* John LAMPLUGH, of Lamplugh, co. Westmorland.

II. 1644. SIR JOHN LOWTHER, Bart. [1642], of Stockbridge, co. Westmorland, only s. and h., *bap.* 20 Nov. 1642, at St. Bees; *suc. to the Baronetcy*,(c) when an infant, in 1644; matric. at Oxford (Balliol Coll.), 29 Oct. 1657; was M.P. for Cumberland (nine Parls.), 1665-81, 1685-87, and 1689-1700; one of the Commissioners of the Admiralty, 1689-96. He *m.* Jane, da. of Woolley LEIGH, of Addington, co. Surrey, by Elizabeth, da. of Sir John HARE, of Stow Bardolph. She probably *d.* before Oct. 1705. He was *bur.* 17 Jan. 1705/6, at St. Bees aforesaid. Will dat. 8 Oct. to 26 Dec. 1705, pr. 22 April 1706.

(a) The Baronetcy was disallowed by Parl. 11 Nov. 1643, till the Restoration. See *Memorandum* as to creations after 4 Jan. 1641/2 and 22 May 1642, on p. 152. No patent is enrolled. The date here given is that in Dugdale's *Catalogue*; see *Memorandum* on p. 84. The date of the signet bill is 26 May 1642.

(b) Le Neve's *Baronetage*. William Denny, of Norwich, King's Councillor, was Knighted, at Norfolk, 31 Oct. 1627, and, when a widower and about 50, had lic. (Fac. office), 18 Feb. 1632/3, to marry Dorothy Kempe. He, possibly, was the William Denny, then of Thavies Inn, admitted to Lincoln's Inn, 8 Aug. 1612, as "son of Thomas Denny, of Thurlton, co. Norfolk, Gent."

(c) See note "a" above, save that, in this case, the date of the signet bill is 29 May 1642.

III. 1705. SIR CHRISTOPHER LOWTHER, Bart. [1642], 1st s. and h., *b.* about 1666; matric. at Oxford (Queen's Coll.), 3 Nov. 1685, aged 19; was a Barrister (Middle Temple), 1690; *suc. to the Baronetcy*, Jan. 1705/6, but was disinherited by his father save as to a weekly allowance. He *m.* firstly, Jane, da. of the Rev. P. NANSON, Rector of Newnham, Hants. He *m.* secondly, Hannah [*Qy.* Hannah TAYLOR, spinster]. He *d.* s.p., in Brook street, Holborn, 2 and was *bur.* 7 Oct. 1731, at St. Andrew's, Holborn. Admon. 2 Dec. 1731, to the widow. She *d.* in or before 1753. Her admon., as "Dame Hannah Lowther, *alias* Taylor, of St. James', Clerkenwell, widow," granted, 13 April 1753, to a creditor.

IV. 1731, to 1755. SIR JAMES LOWTHER, Bart. [1642], of Whitehaven aforesaid, br. and h., *b.* about 1673; matric. at Oxford (Queen's Coll.), 17 Dec. 1688, aged 15; Barrister (Middle Temple), 1712; Bencher, 1714; M.P. for Carlisle (five Parls.), 1694-1702; for Appleby, 1723-27; for Cumberland (nine Parls.), 1708-22, and 1727 till death; F.S.A., etc.; *suc. to the Baronetcy*, 2 Oct. 1731. He *d.* unm. 2 Jan. 1755, when the *Baronetcy* became *extinct*. Will pr. 1755. His fortune, said to be £2,000,000, devolved on his cousin, James Lowther, afterwards (1784), 1st Earl of Lonsdale.

ALSTON:

cr 13 June 1642(a);

ex. 29 June 1791;

but assumed till 1853.

I. 1642. "THOMAS ALSTON, of Odell, co. Bedford, Knt.," 2d s. of Thomas ALSTON(b), of Polstead and Asin, co. Suffolk, by Frances, da. of Simon BLUNDEVILL, *otherwise* BLOMFIELD, of Monks Illey in that county, was *b.* about 1609; matric. at Oxford (St. John's Coll.), 8 July 1625, aged 16; was of the Inner Temple before 1634 (Visit. of Beds, 1634); Barrister, 1639, having suc. his eldest br., William ALSTON, 16 March 1636/7; was Sheriff of Beds, 1641-42, and, having been *Knighted* before 1641, was *cr. a Baronet*, as above, 13 June 1642.(a) He was an Assessment Commissioner for Beds, 1643 and 1660. He was aged 60 in 1669, when he entered and signed his pedigree in the Visit. of Bedfordshire. He *m.* in or before 1650, Elizabeth, sister of Sir Oliver ST. JOHN, 1st Bart. [1660], da. of Sir Rowland ST. JOHN, K.B., by Sybella, da. of John VAUGHAN. She *d.* 8 and was *bur.* 10 Sep. 1677, at Odell, otherwise Woodhall. He was *bur.* there 11 July 1678. M.I. His will dat. 25 April, pr. 19 July 1678.

II. 1678. SIR ROWLAND ALSTON, Bart. [1642], of Odell aforesaid, 2d but 1st surv. s. and h.,(c) *b.* about 1654, being aged 17 in 1669; *suc. to the Baronetcy* in July 1678. He *m.* in or before 1676, Temperance, 2d da. and coheir of Thomas (CREWE), 2d BARON CREWE OF STENE, by his first wife, Mary, da. of Sir Roger TOWNSHEND, 1st Bart. [1617]. He was *bur.* 24 Sep. 1697, at Odell, in his 47th year. M.I. Will dat. 23 Dec. 1686, pr. 6 April 1698. His widow, who was *bap.* 8 May 1656, at Flore, co. Northampton, *m.* 7 Feb. 1699, at Allhallows, Bread street, London (as his second wife), Sir John WOLSTENHOLME, 3d Bart. [1665], who was *bur.* 6 Feb. 1708/9, at Enfield. She *d.* 18 Oct. 1728, and was *bur.* at Odell. M.I. Will pr. 1728.

(a) Disallowed by Parl. 11 Nov. 1643, till the Restoration. See *Memorandum* as to creations after 4 Jan. 1641/2 and 22 May 1642, on p. 152. No patent is enrolled. The date here given is that in Dugdale's *Catalogue*; see *Memorandum* on p. 84. There is also no signet bill, but the warrant for granting the receipt for money paid on creation (filed on the bundle of signet bills) is dated 28 May 1642.

(b) The editor is indebted to Lionel Cresswell, of Wood Hall, Calverley, Yorkshire, for much information as to this family.

(c) His eldest br., Thomas Alston, matric. at Oxford (St. Edm. Hall), 9 Nov. 1666, aged 18, and *d.* unm. and v.p. at Oxford, 2 June 1668.

III. 1697. SIR THOMAS ALSTON, Bart. [1642], of Odell aforesaid, s. and h., *b.* about 1676; *suc. to the Baronetcy*, Sep. 1697; M.P. for Bedford, 1698-1700. He is said(a) to have wasted his estate, and to have lived in the Fleet prison. He *d.* unm. Dec. 1714. Will dat. 9 Dec. 1714, pr. 3 March 1714/5.

IV. 1714. SIR ROWLAND ALSTON, Bart. [1642], of Odell aforesaid, br. and h.; *suc. to the Baronetcy*, Dec. 1714; M.P. for Bedfordshire (three Parls.), 1722-41. He *m.*, after 1714, Elizabeth, da. and h. of Capt. Thomas REYNES. She *d.* 12 Aug. 1742, aged 44, and was *bur.* at Odell. M.I. Admon. 1 Dec. 1742. He *d.* at St. Marylebone, Midx., 2 Jan. 1759, aged 80, and was *bur.* at Odell. M.I. Will dat. 27 May 1758, pr. 15 Jan. 1759, and again, 16 July 1766.

V. 1759. SIR THOMAS ALSTON, Bart. [1642], of Odell aforesaid, s. and h.; M.P. for Bedfordshire, 1747, and for Bedford in 1760; *suc. to the Baronetcy*, 2 Jan. 1759. He *m.* 30 Aug. 1750, at Longstow, co. Cambridge, Catharine DAVIS-BOVIE, spinster, da. of (—) DAVIS and heir of the Rev. (—) BOVEY, D.D., Rector of Longstow aforesaid. They were separated some two years after marriage by mutual consent. He *d.* s.p. leg.(b) and was *bur.* at Odell, 18 July 1774. Limited admon. 14 Feb. 1776, reciting that Dame Catharine, his relict, was surviving, as also his br., Sir Rowland Alston, Bart., and his sister, Ann, wife of Robert PYE, LL.D., they being his only next of kin. Will dat. 6 Sep. 1766, and pr. 21 Nov. 1776, by Margaret LEE, of Great James street, St. Margaret's, Westm., spinster, extrix. and universal legatee of all real and personal estate. His widow was *bur.* at Longstow.

VI. 1774, to 1791. SIR ROWLAND ALSTON, Bart. [1642], br. and h.; Colonel of the 1st Regiment of Foot Guards; *suc. to the Baronetcy*, 18 July 1774. Sheriff of Beds, 1779-80. He *m.* Gertrude, sister of Stillingfleet DURNFORD, of the Tower of London, da. of the Rev. (—) DURNFORD, DD. He *d.* s.p., 29 June 1791, when the *Baronetcy* became *extinct*. Will dat. 22 March 1790, pr. 13 July 1791 by his widow and universal legatee. She *d.* 13 March 1807, in Harley street, Midx., aged 76. Will dat. 10 Jan. 1792, pr. April 1807.

VII. 1791? "SIR JOHN ALSTON, Bart." [1642], *formerly* JOHN WASSE, s. of Catherine, the wife of the 5th Bart., by John WASSE, of Stafford (said to have been a Horse Dealer), was *b.* at Gayton, in 1763, some years after his mother's separation (1752) from her husband, and was *bap.* under the name of Wasse. He assumed ***the name of Alston***, and, many years after the death (1774) of his mother's husband, ***styled himself a Baronet***. He *m.* in or before 1789, Elizabeth, da. of Charles WASSE. He *d.* s.p.m.s. 20 Feb. 1807, in his 45th year. Will pr. 1807. The will of "DAME Elizabeth Alston," was pr. in 1808, and that of "Dame Elizabeth Alston, co. Huntingdon," in Sep. 1852.

VIII. 1807, to 1853. "SIR CHARLES ALSTON, Bart." [1642], formerly CHARLES WASSE, own br. of the above *b.* 17 Dec. 1769: ***assumed the title of Baronet*** at his brother's death. He *m.* 28 Sep. 1807, at Bath, Mary, widow of Col. Pigot, da. of John WILLIAMSON, and niece of General JOHNSON. He *d.* s.p.m.s.(c) 1853. Admon. April 1853, as "Sir Charles Alston, Bart., Midx."

(a) Le Neve's *Baronetage*

(b) His illeg. son (by Margaret Lee), Thomas Alston, inherited, under his will, the family estates, and was ancestor of the present (1900) owner, Sir Francis Beilby Alston, K.C.M.G.

(c) Charles Twisleton, student of Corpus Christi, who died 16 Jan. 1834, aged 22, "was his only son" [*Ex-inform* L. Cresswell; see p. 182, note "b."]

CORBET, *or* CORBETT:

cr. 20 June 1642(a);

ex. probably 25 Sep. 1774;

but assumed 1774 to 1808.

I. 1642. EDWARD CORBETT, of Leighton, co. Montgomery, Esq.," s. of Sir Thomas Corbet, of the same by (—), da. and coheir of (—) MORETON, was *cr. a Baronet*, as above, 20 June, 1642(a). He was Sheriff of Salop, 1650-51, and of Montgomeryshire, 1651-52. He *m.* Margaret, da. and h. of Edward WAITESS, of Leighton aforesaid, and of Burway, Salop. He was living in May 1653, but *d.* before July 1658.

II. 1655 ? SIR RICHARD CORBET, Bart. [1642], of Leighton, aforesaid, and of Longnor, Salop, grandson and h., being s. and h. of Edward Corbet, by Anne, da. of Richard (NEWPORT), 1st BARON NEWPORT OF HIGH ERCALL, which Edward (*b.* 1620, matric. at Oxford, 1638), was s. and h. ap. of the 1st Bart., but *d.* v.p., 30 May, 1653. He was *b.* 1640; matric. at Oxford (Ch. Ch.), 31 July 1658; having *suc. to the Baronetcy*,(a) on the death of his grandfather, before that date; was M.P. for Shrewsbury (four Parls.), 1677-81; Chairman of the Committee of Elections, *temp.* Charles II. He *m.* (Lic. Fac. 5 Jan. 1661/2, he 23 and she 21) Victoria, 1st da. and coheir of Sir William UVEDALE, of Wickham, Hants, by Victoria, then wife of Bartholomew PRICE, "Esq." She *d.* 1679. He *d.* 1 and was *bur.* 3 Aug. 1683, at St. Margaret's, Westm., in his 43d year. M.I. Will pr. Aug. 1683.

III. 1683. SIR UVEDALE CORBET, Bart. [1641], of Condover, co. Salop, and of Leighton and Longnor aforesaid, only s. and h., *b.* about 1668; *suc. to the Baronetcy*, 1 Aug. 1683; matric. at Oxford (Christ Church), 10 April 1685, aged 17. Sheriff of Montgomeryshire, 1699-1700. He *m.* (Lic. Fac. 14 Aug. 1693, he 21 and she 18) Mildred, 5th da. of James (CECIL), 3d EARL OF SALISBURY, by Margaret, da. of John (MANNERS), EARL OF RUTLAND. He *d.* 15 Oct. 1701. Will pr. March 1702. His widow *m.* after Oct. 1707 (as his 2d wife), Sir Charles HOTHAM, 4th Bart. [1622], who *d.* 8 Jan. 1722/3. She *d.* 18 and was *bur.* 26 Jan. 1726/7, at St. Margaret's, Westm. M.I.

IV. 1701, to 1774. SIR RICHARD CORBET, Bart. [1642], of Leighton and Longnor aforesaid, s. and h., *b.* 1696; *suc. to the Baronetcy*, 15 Oct. 1701; matric. at Oxford (New Coll.), 30 June 1713, aged 17; M.P. for Shrewsbury (four Parls.), 1723-27 and 1734-54. He *d.* unm., 25 Sep. 1774, aged 78, when the *Baronetcy* probably became *extinct*. Will dat. 19 Nov. 1764 to 7 June 1771, pr. Nov. 1774.

The *Baronetcy* was *assumed*, possibly rightfully, as under.

V. 1774. "SIR CHARLES CORBET, Bart." [1642], said to be cousin and h. male, being s. and h. of Charles CORBET, of London, bookseller, by Ann, da. of Nathan HORSEY, of Norfolk, which Charles (*b.* 16 Feb. 1709/10, at St. Mary's Hill, London, and *d.* 1752) was s. of Thomas CORBET, of St. Dunstan's in the West (*d.* 5 Aug. 1741, aged 58), who is stated to have been s. of Waitess CORBET, of Elton, co. Hereford, s. of (another) Waitess CORBET, by Margaret, da. of (—) WEAVER, of Elton aforesaid, which last named Waitess Corbet (*d.* 20 Feb. 1689) was yst. s. of the 1st Bart. He was *b.* 1734, at St. Clement Danes; was a clerk in a lottery office in London, and *assumed* the *Baronetcy* in Sep. 1774. He *m.* Elizabeth, da. of Thomas ROBBINS, of Barbadoes. She was *bur.* at Clerkenwell. He *d.* in much reduced circumstances, in Compton street, 15 and was *bur.* 26 May 1808, at St. Anne's, Soho, on the same day as his son, Thomas Corbet, who had married, but who *d.* s.p. seven days after his father, at the same place, and who, as well as his father, is styled "Baronet" in the burial register.

VI, or VII. 1808. RICHARD CORBET, last surv. s. of the abovenamed Charles, was *b.* at St. Dunstan's in the West, and appears never to have assumed the title. He was in the East India Company's service, and was living in 1811, but of him nothing further is known.

(a) The Baronetcy was disallowed by Parl. 11 Nov. 1643, till the Restoration. See *Memorandum* as to creations after 4 Jan. 1641/2, and 22 May 1642, on p. 152. No patent is enrolled. The date here given is that in Dugdale's *Catalogue*; see *Memorandum* on p. 84. The date of the signet bill is (—) June 1642.

MIDDLETON:

cr. 24 June 1642(a);

ex. 27 Feb. 1673.

I. 1642, to 1673. "GEORGE MIDDLETON, of Leighton, co. Lancaster, Knt.," s. and h. of Thomas MIDDLETON, of Leighton Hall, in Leighton aforesaid, by Katharine, sister of Sir Richard HOGHTON, 1st Bart. [1611], da. of Thomas HOGHTON, of Hoghton Tower, co. Lanc., was *b.* 1600, *Knighted* at York, 26 [16?] June 1642, and was *cr. a Baronet*, as above, 24 June 1642(a). He was a zealous adherent of the King, during the Civil War, in whose army he was Colonel, and was accordingly fined £855 on 9 Nov. 1648, subsequently increased to £1,015. He was Sheriff of Lancashire, 1660-62. He *m.* firstly, Frances, da. and h. of Richard RIGG, of Little Strickland. He *m.* secondly, Anne, da. of George PRESTON, of Holker Hall, co. Lancaster. He *d.* s.p.m.s., 27 Feb. 1673, aged 73, and was *bur.* at Warton, when *the Baronetcy became extinct*. His widow was *bur.* there 12 April 1705.

PAYLER:

cr. 28 June 1642;(b)

ex. 30 Sep. 1705.

I. 1642. "EDWARD PAYLER, of Thorraldby [*i.e.*, Thoroby] co. York, Esq." (whose parentage is not given in the Visit. of Yorkshire of 1666) was, probably, the "Edward Payler, of York, gent., son of William Payler, Esq.," admitted to Gray's Inn, 5 June 1592, and was *cr. a Baronet*, as above, 28 June 1642.(b) He *m* Anne, da. of William WATKINSON. He *d.* about 1642. Will pr. 1649.

(a) Disallowed by Parl. 11 Nov. 1643 till the Restoration. See *Memorandum* as to creations after 4 Jan. 1641/2 and 22 May 1642, on p. 152. No patent is enrolled. The date here given (24 June 1642) is that in Dugdale's *Catalogue*. See p. 84. The date of the signet bill is 10 June 1642. The date of *Knighthood* is said to have been *26* June 1642, but he is, however, styled a "Knight" when, on *24* June 1642, he was *cr. a Baronet*.

(b) Disallowed by Parl. 11 Nov. 1643 till the Restoration. See *Memorandum* as to creations after 4 Jan. 1641/2, and 22 May 1642, on p. 152. No patent is enrolled. The date here given is that in Dugdale's *Catalogue*, see *Memorandum* on p. 84. The date of the signet bill is 15 June 1642.

II. 1642 ? to 1705. SIR WATKINSON PAYLER, Bart. [1642], of Thoroby aforesaid, grandson and h., being s. and h. Watkinson PAYLER, by Margaret, da. of Thomas (FAIRFAX), 1st VISCOUNT FAIRFAX OF EMLEY [I.], which Watkinson (who was admitted to Gray's Inn, 10 Aug. 1616), was s. and h. ap. of the late Bart., but *d.* v.p. He *suc. to the Baronetcy*(a) on his grandfather's death; was admitted to Gray's Inn,(a) 23 March 1651/2, and entered his pedigree in the Visit. of Yorkshire, 1666; was M.P. for Malton, 1678/9, 1678-81 and 1681. He *m.* in or before 1664, Alathea, da. of Sir Thomas NORCLIFFE, of Langton, co. York, by his maternal aunt, Dorothy, da. of Thomas (FAIRFAX), 1st VISCOUNT FAIRFAX OF EMLEY [I.], abovenamed. He *d.*, s.p.m.s.(b), and was *bur.* 30 Sep. 1705, from St. Anne's, Soho, when the *Baronetcy* became *extinct*. Will pr. May 1707.

WIDDRINGTON:

cr. 9 July 1642(c);

afterwards, 2 Nov. 1643, BARONS WIDDRINGTON OF BLANKNEY,

forfeited 31 May 1716.

I. 1642. "WILLIAM WIDDRINGTON, of Widdrington, co. Northumberland, Knt.," s. and h. of Sir Henry WIDDRINGTON, of the same, by Mary, da. of Sir Henry CURWEN, of Workington, co. Cumberland, was aged 4 in 1615; suc. his father, 4 Sep. 1623; was *Knighted*, 18 March 1631/2; was Sheriff of Northumberland, 1636-37; M.P. for that County, April to May 1640, and Nov. 1640 till disabled in Aug. 1642; was one of the most zealous of the King's supporters, and was *cr. a Baronet*, as above, 9 July 1642.(c) He *m.*, in 1629, Mary, da. and h. of Sir Anthony THOROLD, of Blankney, co. Lincoln, by Elizabeth, da. of Thomas MOLYNEUX, of Haughton. She was living when he was *cr.*, 2 Nov. 1643, BARON WIDDRINGTON OF BLANKNEY, co. Lincoln. In that peerage this *Baronetcy* then *merged*, and so continued, till by the attainder, 31 May 1716, of the 4th Baron and Baronet, it and all other his honours became *forfeited*. See *Peerage*.

VALKENBURG, *or* VAN VALKENBURG:

cr. 20 July 1642(c);

ex., presumably, 1 Sep. 1679.

I. 1642. "MATTHEW VALKENBURG [*or* VAN VALKENBURG], of Middleing, co. York, Esq.," br. of "Mark VAN VALKENBURG,(d) Esq." (living May 1643), was apparently a member of the East India Company in Holland, and was *cr. a Baronet*, as above, 20 July 1642.(c) He *m.* Isabella, da. of (—). He *d.* in or before 1649. Will dat. 1 May 1643, pr. 3 Jan. 1649/50, and 7 July 1664. His widow, living 1649/50, *d.* before 1664.

(a) The admission to Gray's Inn, 23 March 1651/2, of "Watkinson Payler, of Thoraldby, co. York, Esq.," can only refer to him, and is to be accounted for by the non-recognition of the Baronetcy at that period, see *Memorandum* on p. 152.

(b) His son, Watkinson Payler, *b.* 1668, *d.* v.p. He had Lic. (Fac.) 30 May 1693 (being then 25), to marry Dame Mary Stoughton, widow, which he accordingly did on 1 June, following, at St. Mary Mag., Old Fish street, London.

(c) See p. 161, note "b," *sub* "Strutt."

(d) Cornelia, da. of Marcus Van Valkinburgh, of Valkinburgh in Holland, *m.* in or before 1656, Roger Tocketts, of Tocketts, co. York, and was living as mother of six children in 1666. [Visit. of Yorkshire, 1666].

II. 1649 ? to 1679. SIR JOHN ANTHONY VAN VALKENBURG, Bart. [1642], s. and h.; *suc. to the Baronetcy*, in or before 1649; was a minor in 1650, but of full age in July 1664. He *d.*, apparently, s.p.m.s., and was *bur.* 1 Sep. 1679, at St. Margaret's in the Close, Lincoln, when the *Baronetcy*, presumably, became *extinct*.

CONSTABLE:

cr. 20 July 1642(a);

ex. July 1746.

I. 1642. "PHILIP CONSTABLE, of Everingham, co. York, Esq.," s. and h. of Marmaduke CONSTABLE, of the same, by Jane, da. of Thomas METHAM, of Metham, co. York (which Marmaduke was s. and h. of Sir Robert CONSTABLE, of Everingham aforesaid), was *b.* about 1595, being aged 17 in 1612; suc. his father, 3 April 1632, and was *cr. a Baronet*, as above, 20 July 1642.(a) He was a great sufferer in the Royal cause, his estate being included in the bill for the sale of forfeited estates, 2 July 1652 and 28 Oct. 1655; but he apparently was let off with a fine of £758. He *m.*, in or before 1618, Anne (*b.* 28 April 1587), only da. of Sir William ROPER, of Well hall in Eltham, Kent, by his 1st wife, Katharine, da. and coheir of Sir Humphrey BROWNE, one of the Justices of the Court of Common Pleas. He *d.* 25 Feb. 1664, and was *bur.* at Steeple Barton, Oxon. M.I.

II. 1664. SIR MARMADUKE CONSTABLE, Bart. [1642], of Everingham aforesaid, s. and h., *b.* 22 April 1619, *suc. to the Baronetcy*, 25 Feb. 1664; aged 45 at the Visit. of Yorkshire in 1665. He *m.*, in or before 1650, Anne, da. of Richard SHERBORNE, of Stonyhurst, co. Lancaster, by his 2d wife, Elizabeth, da. of Thomas WALMESLEY, of Dunkenhalgh. She was *bur.* 5 June 1679, at St. Martin's, Coney street, York.

III. 1680 ? SIR PHILIP MARK CONSTABLE, Bart. [1642], of Everingham aforesaid, only s. and h., *b.* 25 April 1651; *suc. to the Baronetcy* on his father's death; was committed to the Tower 26 April 1696.(b) He *m.* Margaret, da. of Francis (RADCLIFFE), 1st EARL OF DERWENTWATER, by Katharine, da. and h. of Sir William FENWICK, of Meldon, co. Northumberland. She was *bur.* 19 Aug. 1688, at Everingham.

IV. 1710 ? to 1746. SIR MARMADUKE CONSTABLE, Bart. [1642], of Everingham aforesaid, s. and h., *bap.* 7 Aug. 1682, at Everingham; *suc. to the Baronetcy* on his father's death. He *d.* abroad and unm. July 1746, when the *Baronetcy* became *extinct*.(c) Will pr. 1747.

BLAKISTON, *or* BLACKSTONE:

cr. 30 July 1642(a);

ex. 8 Oct. 1713.

I. 1642. "RALPH BLACKSTONE [*or* BLAKISTON], of Gibside [in Whickham], in the Bishopric of Durham, Esq.," s. and h. of Sir William BLAKISTON, of the same (*Knighted*, 24 April 1617), by Jane, da. of Robert LAMBTON, of Lambton, was *b.* about 1589; admitted to Gray's Inn, 3 May 1608; aged 26 in 1615 [Visit. of Durham]; suc. his father, 18 Oct. 1641; and was *cr. a Baronet*, as above, 30 July 1642.(a) He *m.* firstly, Margaret, da. of Sir William

(a) See p. 161, note "b," *sub* "Strutt."

(b) Luttrell's *Diary*.

(c) The estates passed to his great nephew William HAGGERSTON, 2d s. of Sir Carnaby Haggerston, 3d Bart. [1643], who was s. and h. of William Haggerston, by Anne, sister of the said Sir Marmaduke CONSTABLE. He assumed the name of Constable in addition to his own, and was grandfather of William CONSTABLE-MAXWELL, who, in right of his grandmother, Lady Winifred Maxwell, was declared in 1858 to be LORD HERRIES [S.]

FENWICK, of Wallington, co. Northumberland. He *m.* secondly, Frances, da. of Sir Charles WREN, of Binchester, Durham, by whom he had no issue. He was *bur.* 20 Dec. 1650, at Whickham aforesaid. Admon. 14 Feb. 1650/1, to a creditor.

II. 1650. SIR WILLIAM BLAKISTON, Bart. [1642], of Gibside aforesaid, s. and h., by 1st wife; admitted to Gray's Inn, 10 Feb. 1640/1, and *suc. to the Baronetcy*, 20 Dec. 1650. He *m.* Mary, da. of Cecil (CALVERT), 2d BARON BALTIMORE [I.], by Anne, da. of Thomas (ARUNDELL), 1st BARON ARUNDELL OF WARDOUR. He *d.* s.p.s., and was *bur.* 26 Feb. 1692, at Whickham aforesaid.

III. 1692, to 1713. SIR FRANCIS BLAKISTON, Bart. [1642], of Gibside aforesaid, br. (of the whole blood) and h.; *suc. to the Baronetcy*, 26 Feb. 1692. He *m.* Anne, da. of Sir George BOWES, of Bradley, co. Durham. She was *bur.* 26 Jan. 1700/1, at Whickham. He *d.* s.p.m.(a) 8 and was *bur.* there 11 Oct. 1713, when the *Baronetcy* became *extinct.*

WIDDRINGTON:
cr. 8 Aug. 1642(b);
ex. 13 July 1671.

I. 1642, to 1671. "SIR EDWARD WIDDRINGTON, of Cartington, co. Northumberland, Baronet of Scotland," s. and h. of Roger WIDDRINGTON, of Cartington aforesaid, by Mary, da. of Francis RADCLYFFE, of Derwentwater, was aged 1 year in 1615; was *cr. a Baronet* [S.], 26 Sep. 1635 with rem. to "heirs male," and was *cr. a Baronet* [E.], as above, 8 Aug. 1642.(b) He was a devoted Royalist, and his estate was included in the bill of sale by the Treason trustees. He *m.* "Christiana STUART," grand-daughter [*neptem*] of the EARL OF BOTHWELL [S.], presumably, da. of the Hon. John STEWART, Commendator of Coldingham, 2d s. of Francis, 1st Earl.(c) He *d.* s.p.m.s.,(d) 13 July 1671, in his 57th year, and was *bur.* in the Convent of Capuchin Monks, at Bruges, when the *Baronetcy* [E.], became *extinct,* and the *Baronetcy* [S.], *dormant,* or *extinct.* M.I.(b)

MARKHAM:
cr. 15 Aug. 1642(b);
ex. 1779.

I. 1642. "ROBERT MARKHAM, of Sedgebrooke, co. Lincoln, Esq.," 2d s., but eventually h. of Sir Anthony MARKHAM, of the same (who *d.* Dec. 1604), by Bridget, da. of Sir James HARINGTON, 1st Bart. [1611], was *b.* 1597, admitted to Gray's Inn, 11 May 1621, and was *cr. a Baronet*, as above, 15 Aug. 1642.(b) He was a Royalist, and fought at the siege of Newark, 1644, and was fined £1,000 on 5 June 1646. He *m.* firstly, Barbara, da. of Edward EYRE, of Derby.(e)

(a) Elizabeth, his da. and h., *m.* Aug. 1693, Sir William Bowes, of Streatlam Castle. See Surtees' *Durham*, vol. ii, p. 255.
(b) See p. 161, note "b," *sub* "Strutt."
(c) *Top. and Gen.*, vol. ii, p. 491.
(d) Roger, his s. and h. ap., *b.* about 1641, was living 1652, but *d.* v.p. and s.p. Mary, his 1st da. and coheir, *m.* Sir Edward Charleton, Bart. [so. *cr.* 1645] of Hesleyside, who *d.* s.p.m.
(e) Wotton's *Baronetage*, and *Her. and Gen.*, vol. vii, p. 401, but see p. 189 of this work, note "a," as to his 1st wife being "a Nevill." In Markham's *Markham Family* [1854, 8vo] only one wife (Rebecca Hussey), is assigned to him.

She *d.* s.p. 1641. He *m.* secondly, 21 April 1642, at Honington, co. Lincoln, Rebecca, da. of Sir Edward HUSSEY, 1st Bart., by Elizabeth, da. of George AUTON. She, who was *bap.* there, 16 Oct. 1622, *d.* June 1664. He *d.* on Candlemas day [2 Feb.], 1667.(a)

II. 1667. SIR ROBERT MARKHAM, Bart. [1642], of Sedgebrooke aforesaid, s. and h. by 2d wife, *b.* 1644; matric. at Oxford (Wad. Coll.), 6 June 1660; *suc. to the Baronetcy*, 2 Feb. 1667; M.P. for Grantham, March 1678 to Jan. 1679; for Newark upon Trent (three Parls.) 1679-81. He *m.*, 31 Aug. 1665, at York, Mary, 3d da. and coheir of Sir Thomas WIDDRINGTON, of Chesbourne, co. Northumberland, and of Shirburne Grange, Durham, Serjeant at Law, by Frances, da. of Ferdinando (FAIRFAX), 2d LORD FAIRFAX OF CAMERON [S.]. She was *b.* 19 Jan. 1644, and *d.* in childbirth 7 and was *bur.* 13 April 1683 (in great state), at Sedgebrooke.(b) He *d.* 27 Oct. 1690, and was *bur.* at Sedgebrooke. Will, dat. 25 Aug. 1690, pr. 6 March 1690/1.

III. 1690. SIR GEORGE MARKHAM, Bart. [1642], of Sedgebrooke aforesaid, s. and h., *b.* 27 May 1666, at Sedgebrooke; *suc. to the Baronetcy*, 27 Oct. 1690; was F.R.S. He *d.* unm., at Bath, 9 June 1736, and was *bur.* at Sedgebrooke.(c) Will pr. 1736.

IV. 1736, to 1779. SIR JAMES JOHN MARKHAM, Bart. [1642], cousin and h. male, being s. and h. of Thomas MARKHAM, by Frances, da. of Andrew COVENANT, M.D., which Thomas was only s. of Anthony MARKHAM, Colonel in the Guards (*b.* March 1646), who was 2d s. of the 1st Bart. He was *b.* 1698, and *suc. to the Baronetcy* (but to none of the estates) 9 June 1736. He *m.* 29 Aug. 1755, Sarah, sister of Robert, 1st BARON CLIVE OF PLASSEY [I.], 2d da. of Richard CLIVE, of Styche, co. Salop, by Rebecca, da. of Nathaniel GASKELL. He *d.* s.p. 1779, aged 81, when the *Baronetcy* became *extinct.* Will pr. Jan. 1779. His widow, who was *b.* 20 April 1737, *d.* 2 Feb. 1828. Will pr. March 1828 and Nov. 1844.

HUNGATE:
cr. 15 Aug. 1642(d);
ex. 3 Dec. 1749.

I. 1642. "PHILIP HUNGATE, of Saxton, co. York, Esq.," 2d s. of William HUNGATE, of the same, by Margaret, da. and h. of Roger SOTHEBY, of Pocklington, co. York; suc. his elder br., Sir William HUNGATE, of Saxton aforesaid, Dec. 1634, and was *cr. a Baronet*, as above, 15 Aug. 1642.(d) He *m.* Dorothy, widow of Andrew YOUNG, of Bourne, in Brayton, co. York, da. of Roger LEIGH, *or* LEE, M.D., of York and Hatfield, in that county. He was *bur.* 20 Dec. 1655, at Hatfield.

(a) "MARKEHAM; at Sedgbrooke, neare Grantham, about £1,600 per ann. The present son is a hopefull yong man; is to marry the da. and h. of Sir Tho. Widdrington. They descend lineally from Judge Markham in Hen. VI. time, and possess the same estate. Sir Robert is the present chiefe; bred a soldier, being a second brother; married a Hussey, by whom he hath his children. His 1st wife was a Nevill. The Judge settled first at Sedgebrook. He was of Markham, Notts, which is nere Sir T. Williamson's." [Sir Joseph Williamson's *Lincolnshire Families, temp. Car II.* See *Her. and Gen.*, vol. ii, p. 123.]
(b) An account of her funeral is in *N. & Q.*, 2d S., xi, 263.
(c) He devised his estates to the Rev. Bernard WILSON, D.D., Prebendary of Worcester and Rector of Newark-upon-Trent.
(d) Disallowed, 11 Nov. 1643, by Parl. till the Restoration. See *Memorandum* as to creations after 4 Jan. 1641/2, and 22 May 1642, on p. 152. No patent is enrolled. The date here given is that in Dugdale's *Catalogue;* see *Memorandum* on p. 84. The date of the warrant for granting receipt for £1,095 on the creation is 10 August 1642.

II. 1655. SIR FRANCIS HUNGATE, Bart. [1642], of Saxton aforesaid, grandson and h., being 1st s. and h. of Francis HUNGATE, a Colonel in the Royalist army, by Joan, da. of Robert, and sister and coheir of Francis MIDDLETON, of Leighton, co. Lancaster, which Francis HUNGATE last named was only s. and h. ap. of the late Bart., but *d.* v.p., being slain at Chester, 1645. He was *b.* 1643; *suc. to the Baronetcy,*(a) 20 Dec. 1655, and was aged 23 at the Visit. of Yorkshire, 1666. He *m.*, in or before 1661, Margaret, 4th da. of Charles (SMITH), 1st VISCOUNT CARRINGTON OF BARREFORE [I.], by Anne, da. of Sir John CARYLL. She was *bur.* 28 Feb. 1674/5, at Saxton. M.I. He *d.* intestate, at St. Paul's, Covent Garden, Westm. Admon. 23 Oct. 1682, at York.

III. 1682? SIR PHILIP HUNGATE, Bart. [1642], of Saxton aforesaid, 1st s. and h., *b.* 1661, being aged 5 in 1666; *suc. to the Baronetcy*, on the death of his father. He *m.* Elizabeth, da. of William (MONSON), VISCOUNT MONSON OF CASTLEMAINE [I.], being the only child of his third wife, Elizabeth, da. of Sir George RERESBY. He *d.* 10 April 1690, and was *bur.* at Saxton. M.I. Will dat. 9 April, pr. May 1690. His widow *m.* Lewis SMITH, of Wotton Wawen, co. Warwick, both being living, 1712.

IV. 1690. SIR FRANCIS HUNGATE, Bart. [1642], of Saxton aforesaid, s. and h., *b.* 1683; *suc. to the Baronetcy*, 10 April 1690; cut off the entail of the estates. He *m.*, 22 Dec. 1707, Elizabeth, widow of Nicholas FAIRFAX, of Gilling, co. York, only da. of William WELD, of Lulworth Castle, Dorset, by Elizabeth, da. of Richard SHERBURNE, of Stonyhurst, co. Lancaster. He *d.* s.p.m., 26 July 1710,(b) at York, aged 27. Admon. there 29 July 1710. His widow *d.* 1 July 1740. Will dat. 10 June 1736, pr. 18 Dec. 1740, at York.

V. 1710. SIR PHILIP HUNGATE, Bart. [1642], br. and h. male, *b.* about 1685. He was in the army, and was, in Sept. 1707, Lieut. Col. of the Earl of Essex's Dragoons, having in 1706 conformed to the Church of England. He *suc. to the Baronetcy*, 26 July 1710. He *m.* Elizabeth, da. of (—) COTTON. He *d.* s.p.s, before 1741.(c)

VI. 1740? to 1749. SIR CHARLES CARRINGTON HUNGATE, Bart. [1642], br. and h. male; *b.* 1686; was a Capt. of Marines; *suc. to the Baronetcy*, on the death of his brother. He *d.* a lunatic 3 and was *bur.* 8 Nov. 1749, at Saxton, aged 63, when the *Baronetcy* became *extinct.* M.I.(d)

The Baronetcy was, however, subsequently assumed. It was before 1835, "the subject of claim by a Lieut. Hungate, who entirely failed in establishing his right to the dignity."(e) Admon. of the goods of "Sir William Anning Hungate, *Bart.*, co. York and Surrey," was granted Oct. 1852. He, possibly, was the "Lieut. Hungate," abovenamed. "William Anning Hungate" was (according to Foster's *Yorkshire Pedigrees*), son of William Hungate, son of John Hungate of London (*b.* 1712), who was a descendant of Robert Hungate, of Saxton, co. York, great uncle of the 1st Bart.

(a) The title was, however, disallowed by Parl. till the Restoration. See p. 189, note "d."
(b) Mary, his only surv. da. and h., *b.* 10 Aug. 1709; *m.* firstly, 26 Nov. 1726, at Saxton, Sir Edward Gascoigne, 5th Bart. [S. 1635], who *d.* at Cambray, in Flanders, May 1750. She *m.* secondly, 15 Nov. 1753, Gerard Strickland (who *d.* 1 Sep. 1791), and *d.* Jan. 1764.
(c) Wotton's *Baronetage*, 1741.
(d) He is there called "the last male heir of that ancient family," and was, doubtless, the last male descendant of the 1st Baronet.
(e) Courthope's *Extinct Baronetage*, 1835.

LENNARD:
cr. 15 Aug. 1642(a);
ex. 8 Oct. 1727.

I. 1642. "STEPHEN LENNARD, of West Wickham, co. Kent, Esq.," s. and h. of Sir Samuel LENNARD, of the same, by Elizabeth, da. of Sir Stephen SLANY, sometime [1595-96], L. Mayor of London (which Stephen, was 3d s. of John LENNARD, of Chevening, co. Kent), was *b.* about 1604; suc. his father, 16 April 1618; was admitted to Gray's Inn, 15 May 1622, and was *cr. a Baronet*, as above 15 Aug. 1642.(a) He *m.* firstly, in or before 1626, Catherine, da. of Richard HALE, of Clatry, co. Essex. She *d.* s.p.m. He *m.* secondly, 24 Nov. 1631, at St. Peter le Poor, London (Lic. Lond., he 27 and she 17), Anne, da. of Sir Multon LAMBARD, of Westcombe, Kent, by Jane, da. of Sir Thomas LOWE, sometime [1604-05], Lord Mayor of London. She, who was *b.* 13 Oct. 1614, *d.* 15 and was *bur.* 26 Feb. 1633, at West Wickham. He *m.* thirdly, in or before 1635, Anne, sister of Sir William OGLANDER, 1st Bart. [1665], 1st da. of Sir John OGLANDER, of Nunwell, Hants, by Frances, da. of Sir George MORE, of Loseley, Surrey. He was *bur.* "in woollen" 29 Jan. 1679/80, from Addington, at West Wickham.

II. 1680. SIR STEPHEN LENNARD, Bart. [1642], of West Wickham aforesaid, 3d but 1st surv. s. and h.,(b) by third wife, was *bap.* there 2 March 1636/7; *suc. to the Baronetcy*, 29 Jan. 1679/80; was M.P. for Winchilsea, 1681; for Kent, 1698-1700, and 1708 till death. He *m.* (settlement 30 Dec. 1671) Elizabeth, widow of John ROY, of Woodlands, da. and h. of Delalynd HUSSEY, of Tomson and Shapwick, by Elizabeth, da. of James HANHAM, of Holwell, all in co. Dorset. He *d.* 15 and was *bur.* 23 Dec. 1709, at West Wickham. Will dat. 5 Jan. 1705, pr. 23 May 1710. His widow was *bur.* there 14 June 1732. Will pr. 1732.

III. 1709, to 1727. SIR SAMUEL, *erroneously* SAMPSON(c) LENNARD, Bart. [1642], of West Wickham aforesaid, only s. and h., was *b.* there 2 and *bap.* 3 Oct. 1672; admitted to Middle Temple, 1689; matric. at Oxford (Trin. Coll.), 4 April 1690, aged 16; *suc. to the Baronetcy*, 15 Dec. 1709; was Lieut. Col. 2d troop of Horse Guards; M.P. for Hythe (three Parls.) 1715 till his death. He *d.* unm. and s.p. legit.(d) at St. Martin's in the Fields, 8, and was *bur.* 25 Oct. 1727, "in linnen," at West Wickham, when the *Baronetcy* became *extinct.* Will dat. 16 Dec. 1726, pr. 29 Oct. 1727, 7 June 1809, and 25 June 1734.

(a) See p. 161, note "b," *sub* "Strutt."
(b) His eldest br. (of the half blood) Samuel Lennard, was *b.* 15 and *bap.* 29 Jan. 1632, at West Wickham, and was *bur.* there 11 Aug. 1638; while another elder br. (of the whole blood) John Lennard, was *bap.* 23 Feb. 1635, and *bur.* 2 Dec. 1638, both at West Wickham.
(c) The will is that of Sir *Sampson* Lennard, but it is manifest that this must be a clerical error. In the pedigree entered at the College of Arms he is called "Samuel"; the baptism, the entrance to the Temple, the matric. at Oxford, the return to Parl., etc., all refer to "Samuel"; the will of "Sir *Sampson,*" directs his burial to be at West Wickham, where, accordingly (two days before its proof) "Sir *Samuel* Lennard, Bart.," is buried. The name of "*Sampson* Lennard" does not occur either among the burials or anywhere else, in the parish register of West Wickham. (See *Mis. Gen. et Her.*, 2d Series, vol. iv, p. 394), where, from 1672 to 1686, seven of the children of the 2d Bart. are baptized.
(d) He had two bastard sons by Mary Johnson; the elder of whom, Stephen Lennard, suc. to the estate of West Wickham, and was *bur.* there 15 March 1755, aged 31, leaving by Jane, his wife, a da. and h., Mary, *b.* 19 Jan. and *bap.* 14 Feb. 1750, at West Wickham, who *m.* Sir John Farnaby, 4th Bart. [1726], and had issue.

THOROLD:

cr. 24 Aug. 1642.(a)

I. 1642. "WILLIAM THOROLD, of Marston, co. Lincoln, Knt.," 2d s. of William THOROLD, by Frances, da. of Sir Robert TYRWHITT, of Kettleby, in that county, which William, who *d.* v.p., was yr. br. of Thomas THOROLD, who also *d.* v.p. and s.p.m., both being sons of Sir Anthony THOROLD, of Marston aforesaid (who *d.*, at a great age, 26 June 1594), was *b.* about 1591 (being in his 3d year at his grandfather's death), was admitted to Gray's Inn, 19 Aug. 1610; *Knighted*,(b) presumably 3 Aug. 1617; suc. his elder br., Anthony THOROLD (who was Sheriff of Lincolnshire, 1617-18, but who *d.* s.p.m.), as heir male; was Sheriff of Lincolnshire, 1632-33, and was *cr. a Baronet*, as above, 24 Aug. 1642.(a) He was a great sufferer for the Royal cause, his estate being sequestrated 15 March 1643 and himself fined £4,160, on 1 Dec. 1646. He was M.P. for Grantham 1661 till death.(c) He *m.* Anne, da. of John BLYTHE, of Stroxton, near Grantham, co. Lincoln. He *d.* 1677. The will of Dame Anne Thorold, co. Lincoln, is pr. Feb. 1683.

II. 1677. SIR WILLIAM THOROLD, Bart. [1642], of Marston aforesaid, and of Cranwell, near Sleaford, co. Lincoln, grandson and h., being s. and h. of Anthony THOROLD, by Grisel (*m.* 19 Dec. 1654, at Glentworth, co. Lincoln), da. of Sir John WRAY, 2d Bart. [1611], which Anthony, who was 2d s., but eventually h. ap. of the late Bart., *d.* v.p. He, who was *b.* about 1659, *suc. to the Baronetcy*, in 1677. He *m.* 11 March 1679/80, at St. Benet's Fink, London (Lic. Fac., he 20, Baronet, she 17), Rebecca, da. of (—) GARRETT, of St. Matthew, Friday street, London (then decd.), by Mary, his wife. He *d.* s.p. in or before 1681. Will pr. 1681.

III. 1681? SIR ANTHONY THOROLD, Bart. [1642], of Marston and Cranwell aforesaid, br. and h., *b.* about 1663; *suc. to the Baronetcy* in or before 1681. He *m.* 20 Aug. 1683, at St. Giles' in the Fields (Lic. Fac. on 17th, he about 20 and a Baronet, and she about 19), Anna Maria, only da. of Thomas HARRINGTON, of Boothby Pannell, co. Lincoln. He *d.* s.p., between April and Dec. 1685, in France. Admon. 19 Dec. 1685 to his relict. His widow *m.* John Lewis MORDAUNT. Her admon., as "of Boothby, co. Lincoln," granted 21 Nov. 1689 to him.

IV. 1685. SIR JOHN THOROLD, Bart. [1642], of Marston and Cranwell aforesaid, br. and h.; *suc. to the Baronetcy* in 1685. He was M.P. for Grantham 1685-87, and Dec. 1697 to 1700; for Lincolnshire, 1701-08, and for Grantham, again, Jan. 1711 to 1715; was one of the most accomplished gentlemen of his time. He *m.* 7 Aug. 1701, at Westm. Abbey, Margaret, widow of the Hon. Francis COVENTRY (who d. 16 Nov. 1699, aged 86), da. of (—) WATERER, and sometime, 9 Feb. 1687/8, a maidservant to her first husband's

(a) See p. 189, note "d," *sub* "Hungate."

(b) William Thorold, of "co. York," was *Knighted* 3 Aug. 1617, at Brougham Castle. This description can be explained by his not having as yet succeeded his brother Anthony in the *Lincolnshire* estates. It is hardly probable that the William Thorold of Lincolnshire, who was knighted 15 March 1603/4, can refer to him, as he was then but a younger son, aged about 13. This last-named William was probably of the Harmeston branch.

(c) He and his then eldest surv. s., Anthony, are thus mentioned in Sir Joseph Williamson's *Lincolnshire Families*, *temp. Car. II.*

"THOROLD. There are three familyes of them, all [descended] from an Atturney at Comon law by about 3 or 4 descents."

"Sir William, Bart., of Maston, neare £2,500 [a year], a Dep. Lieut. His eld. son is Mr Anthony, a hopefull young man, marryed Sir Jo. Wray's daughter. His elder son [William], dead, who *m.* Sir Robert Carre's daughter, ye now Lady Trollop."

"Sir Robert, Bart., at ye Heath House, near Grantham, a Papist, not more than £600 a year. In ye Fleet now."

"Sir William, Knt, of Hough on the Hill; a Papist about £800 [a year]; a very spreading family of this county. Many Papists and severall under branches of £300 and £400 per an." [*Her. and Gen.*, vol. ii, p. 125.]

first wife.(a) He *d.* s.p. 14 Jan. 1716/7, aged 54, and was *bur.* at Syston, co. Lincoln. M.I. Will dat. 12 Dec. 1712, pr. 15 Jan. 1716/7. His widow *d.* 23 and was *bur.* 29 Jan. 1732/3 with her first husband, at Mortlake, co. Surrey, aged about 81. Will dat. 23 July to 30 Oct. 1732, pr. 29 Jan. 1732/3.

V. 1717. SIR WILLIAM THOROLD, Bart. [1642], of Cranwell aforesaid, cousin and h. male, being s. and h. of John THOROLD, by Elizabeth,(b) his 1st wife, da. of Sir William TREDWAY, which John was 3d s. of the 1st Bart. He *suc. to the Baronetcy*, 14 Jan. 1716/7.

VI. 1720? SIR ANTHONY THOROLD, Bart. [1642], of Cranwell aforesaid, s. and h., *b.* about 1710; *suc. to the Baronetcy* on the death of his father. He *d.* at school, in his 12th year, 25 and was *bur.* 30 Aug. 1721, at Hough-on-the-hill, co. Lincoln.

VII. 1721. SIR JOHN THOROLD, Bart. [1642], of Cranwell aforesaid and of Syston Park, near Grantham, co. Lincoln, uncle of the half blood and h. male, being s. of John THOROLD abovenamed (3d s. of the 1st Bart.), by Elizabeth, his 2d wife,(c) relict of Thomas SAUNDERSON, M.D. He was *bap.* 8 Dec. 1675, at Grantham; *suc. to the Baronetcy* in Aug. 1721; Sheriff of Lincolnshire, 1722-23. He *m.* firstly, in or before 1703, Alice, only da. and h. of William SAMPSON, of Gainsborough. He *m.* secondly, Shortclift, da. of William LANGLEY. He *d.* Jan. 1748. His widow *d.* at Bath, 1789. Admon. May 1789.

VIII. 1748. SIR JOHN THOROLD, Bart. [1642], of Cranwell and of Syston Park aforesaid, s. and h., by 1st wife, *b.* 1703; matric. at Oxford (Lincoln Coll.), 10 Oct. 1721, aged 18; B.A., 1724; *suc. to the Baronetcy* in Jan. 1748. Sheriff of Lincolnshire, 1751-52. He *m.* 6 Aug. 1730, at Gray's Inn Chapel, Midx., Elizabeth, da. and coheir of Samuel AYTON, of West Herrington, co. Durham. He *d.* 5 June 1775, on his return journey from Bath, aged 72, and was *bur.* at Marston. M.I. Admon. 22 March 1775. Will pr. March 1776. The will of his widow pr. May 1779.

IX. 1775. SIR JOHN THOROLD, Bart. [1642], of Syston Park aforesaid, s. and h., *b.* 18 Dec. 1734, and *bap.* 5 Jan. 1734/5, at St. James', Westm.; matric. at Oxford (Hertford Coll.), 24 Nov. 1752, aged 18; *suc. to the Baronetcy*, 5 June, 1775; was Sheriff of Lincolnshire, 1751-52; M.P. thereof (four Parls.), Dec. 1779 to 1796. He *m.* 18 March 1771, at St. Marylebone, Jane, only da. and h. of Millington HAYFORD, of Oxton Hall, Notts and of Millington, co. Chester. She *d.* March 1807. Will pr. 1807. He *d.* 25 Feb. 1815, aged 81. Will pr. April 1815, and July 1842.

X. 1815. SIR JOHN-HAYFORD THOROLD, Bart. [1642], of Syston Park aforesaid, s. and h., *b.* 30 March 1773; *suc. to the Baronetcy*, 25 Feb. 1815. He *m.* firstly, 1 Oct. 1811, Mary, sister, whose issue (in 1848) became coheirs, to Sir Charles William EGLETON-KENT, 2d Bart. [1782], 1st da. of Sir Charles KENT, 1st Bart. [1782], by Mary, da. of Josias WORDSWORTH. She *d.* Dec. 1829. Will pr. Jan. 1830. He *m.* secondly, 12 July 1830, Mary-Anne, widow of John DALTON, of Turnham Hall, co. Lancaster, da. of George CARY, of Tor Abbey, Devon, by his 2d wife, Frances, da. of Thomas STONOR. He *d.* 7 July 1831. Will pr. Aug. 1831. His widow *m.* 10 April 1834, as his 3d wife, and her 3d husband, Admiral Sir Charles OGLE, 2d Bart. [1816], who *d.* 16 June, 1858, aged 83, at Tunbridge Wells. She *d.* s.p. in Belgium, 4 Feb. 1842.

(a) The conjecture in the note by Col. Chester to this marriage in his *Westm. Abbey Registers*, is confirmed by his subsequent MS. addition thereto, viz., that in the will of Dame Eliz. Hoskins (1st wife of the said Francis Coventry), dat. 9 Feb. 1687/8 and pr. 2 Oct. 1688 (in the Surrey Archdeaconry Court) legacies are left to her maid, "Margaret Waters" [*sic*], who, however, twice signs herself therein (as witness) "Margaret Waterer."

(b) They were *m.* 3 Aug. 1665, at Grantham, co. Lincoln.

(c) They were *m.* 8 Oct. 1674, at Grantham.

XI. 1831. SIR JOHN CHARLES THOROLD, Bart. [1642], of Syston Park aforesaid, s. and h. by 1st wife, *b.* 26 June 1816, at Gipple House, near Grantham; ed. at Eton; *suc. to the Baronetcy*, 7 July 1831; matric. at Oxford (Ch. Ch.), 15 May 1834, aged 16; Sheriff of Lincolnshire, 1841. He *m.*, 17 March 1841, Elizabeth Frances, da. of Col. Thomas Blackborne THOROTON-HILDYARD, of Flintham Hall, Notts. He *d.* 26 April 1866, in his 50th year, at Syston Park. Will pr. at Lincoln. His widow *d.* 3 April 1894, at 64 Rutland Gate.

XII. 1866. SIR JOHN-HENRY THOROLD, Bart. [1642], of Syston Park aforesaid, s. and h., *b.* 9 March 1842, in Eaton square; ed. at Eton; entered the army, 1859; Lieut. 17th Foot, 1862; M.P. for Grantham, 1865-68; *suc. to the Baronetcy*, 26 April 1866; Sheriff of Lincolnshire, 1876; LL.D. of Cambridge, 1894. He *m.* 3 Feb. 1869, at Wollaton, Notts, Henrietta-Alexandrina-Matilda, 1st da. of Henry (WILLOUGHBY), 8th BARON MIDDLETON, by Julia Louisa, da. of Alexander William Robert BOSVILLE. She was *b.* 6 Oct. 1845.

Family Estates.—These, in 1883, consisted of 12,533 acres in Lincolnshire, worth £17,652 a year. *Principal Seat.*—Syston Park, near Grantham, co. Lincoln.

RUDSTON:

cr. 29 Aug. 1642;(a)

ex., probably, about 1700.

I. 1642. "WALTER RUDSTON, of Hayton, co. York, Esq.," s. and h. of Walter RUDSTON, of the same, by Frances, sister of Sir Philip CONSTABLE, 1st Bart. [1642], da. of Marmaduke CONSTABLE, of Everingham, was *b.* about 1597, being aged 15 in 1612 [Visit. of Yorks.]; was *cr. a Baronet*, as aforesaid, 29 Aug. 1642.(a) He was a zealous Royalist, and entertained the King at Hayton when on his road to demand possession of Hull. His estates were accordingly confiscated. He *m.* firstly (—), da. of (—) RAMSDEN. She *d.* s.p. He *m.* secondly, at Snaith, co. York, 9 May 1631, Margaret (*bap.* at Snaith 11 Nov. 1595), da. of Sir Thomas DAWNAY, of Sessay and Cowick in that county, by Faith, da. of Richard LEGARD. He *d.* between 20 Sep. 1650 and 20 Feb. 1651.(b) Admon. 7 March 1654/5 to Margaret, his widow.

II. 1650? SIR THOMAS RUDSTON, Bart. [1642], of Hayton aforesaid, s. and h., *bap.* there 8 Aug. 1639; *suc. to the Baronetcy*, about 1650, and was fined £878, on behalf of his late father; matric. at Oxford (Ch. Ch.), 29 Oct. 1657. He *m.* Katharine, da. and h. of George MOUNTAYNE, of Westow, co. York, and was living 1682.

III. 1690? to 1700? SIR THOMAS RUDSTON, Bart. [1642], of Hayton aforesaid, s. and h.; *suc. to the Baronetcy* on the death of his father. He *d.* s.p., probably about 1700, when the *Baronetcy* became *extinct*.(c)

(a) Disallowed by Parl. 11 Nov. 1643 till the Restoration. See *Memorandum* as to creations after 4 Jan. 1641/2 and 22 May 1642 on p. 152. No patent is enrolled. The date here given is that in Dugdale's *Catalogue*. See *Memorandum* on p. 84. The date of the signet bill is 6 Aug. 1642.

(b) The respective dates of his own petition and that of his s. and h., Sir Thomas, to compound.

(c) The estates devolved on his sister Elizabeth, who *m.* Henry Cutler, and *d.* a widow and s.p., devising them to her heir at law Rudston Calverley, great grandson of William Calverley, by Hester, da. of William Rudston, yr. br. of the 1st Baronet. He, consequently, took the name of Rudston.

WROTTESLEY, WROTESLY, *or* DE WROTESLEY:

cr. 30 Aug. 1642(a);

afterwards, since 1838, BARONS WROTTESLEY.

I. 1642. "WALTER WROTESLY, *or* DE WROTESLEY [*or* Wrottesley], of Wrotesley [Wrottesley], co. Stafford, Esq.," s. and h. of Sir Hugh Wrottesley,(b) of Wrottesley aforesaid, by Mary, sister of Walter, 5th VISCOUNT HEREFORD, da. of the Hon. Sir Edward DEVEREUX, 1st Bart. [1611], was *bap.* 6 May 1606, at Castle Bromwich (registered at Aston, near Birmingham), was eight years old in 1614; suc. his father in 1633, and was *cr. a Baronet*, as above, 30 Aug. 1642.(a) He was a zealous Royalist, his house being converted into a garrison for the King's soldiers, and he himself fined £1,332. He *m.* in or before 1632, Mary or Margaret, da. of the Hon. Ambrose GREY, of Enville, co. Stafford, by his 1st wife, Margaret, da. of Richard PRINCE. He *d.* 6 Nov. 1659. The will of Dame Mary Wrottesley pr. 1665.

II. 1659. SIR WALTER WROTTESLEY, Bart. [1642], of Wrottesley aforesaid, s. and h., *b.* about 1632, being aged 32 at the Visit. of Staffordshire in April 1663: admitted to Lincoln's Inn, 11 May 1646; *suc. to the Baronetcy*, 6 Nov. 1659. Sheriff of Staffordshire, 1666-67. He *m.* in or before 1658, Elizabeth, da. of Sir Thomas WOLRYCH, 1st Bart. [1641], by Ursula, da. of Thomas OTELEY, of Pitchford, Salop. He *d.* in or before 1686. Will pr. June 1686.

III. 1686? SIR WALTER WROTTESLEY, Bart. [1642], of Wrottesley aforesaid, s. and h., aged 5 years in April 1663; matric. at Oxford (Mag. Hall), 18 March 1675/6, aged 17; *suc. to the Baronetcy* in or before 1686. Sheriff of Staffordshire, 1686-87. He pulled down the old mansion, and in 1696 erected the more stately one called Wrottesley Hall. He *m.* firstly (Lic. Vic. Gen., 27 June 1678, he aged 20 and she 18), Eleanor, da. of Sir John ARCHER, of Coopersale, in Theydon Garnon, Essex, Justice of the Common Pleas (1663-81), by Eleanor, da. of Sir John CURZON, Kedleston, co. Derby. He *m.* secondly, Anne, of da. of (—), BURTON, of Longnor, Salop. He *d.* 1712. Will pr. March 1713. The will of Dame Anne Wrottesley, pr. 1732.

IV. 1712. SIR JOHN WROTTESLEY, Bart. [1642], of Wrottesley Hall aforesaid, 1st surv. s. and h. by 1st wife; M.P. for Staffordshire, 1700-10; *suc. to the Baronetage* in 1712. He *m.* in or before 1708, Frances, sister of Harry, 3d EARL OF STAMFORD, da. of Hon. John GREY, of Enville aforesaid, 3d s. of Henry, 1st EARL OF STAMFORD, by his 2d wife, Katharine, da. of Edward (WARD), LORD DUDLEY and BARON WARD OF BIRMINGHAM. He *d.* Oct. 1726, and was *bur.* at Tetnal. Will dat. 12 March 1725, pr. 1 Feb. 1726/7 by his widow. Her will pr. 1769.

V. 1726. SIR HUGH WROTTESLEY, Bart. [1642], of Wrottesley Hall aforesaid, 1st surv. s. and h.; *suc. to the Baronetcy* in Oct. 1726. He *d.* a minor and unm., 1729. Admon. 18 Nov. 1729.

VI. 1729. SIR WALTER WROTTESLEY, Bart. [1642], of Wrottesley Hall aforesaid, br. and h.; *suc. to the Baronetcy* in 1729. He *d.* a minor and unm., Feb. 1731. Will pr. 1732.

(a) Disallowed by Parl. 11 Nov. 1643, till the Restoration. See *Memorandum* as to creations after 4 Jan. 1641/2, and 22 May 1642, on p. 152. The patent of this creation and of many others in the later months of 1642, as also in Feb. and March 1642/3, is enrolled, though those in the earlier months of that year (between 28 Feb. 1641/2, and 10 Aug. 1642) are not.

(b) This Hugh was 8th in descent and heir male of Sir Hugh de Wrottesley, one of the Founders of the most noble Order of the Garter.

VII. 1731. Sir Richard Wrottesley, Bart. [1642], of Wrottesley Hall aforesaid, br. and h., *b.* about 1721; *suc. to the Baronetcy* in Feb. 1731; ed. at Winchester School, 1736; matric. at Oxford (St. John's Coll.), 31 Aug. 1739, aged 18; was M.P. for Tavistock, Dec. 1747 to 1754; one of the principal Clerks of the Board of Green Cloth, June 1749. He afterwards took Holy Orders, and became Chaplain to the King, 1763; Dean of Worcester, 1765 till death. He *m.* in or before 1744, Mary, da. of John (Leveson-Gower), 1st Earl Gower, by his 1st wife, Evelyn, da. of Evelyn (Pierrepont) Duke of Kingston. He *d.* 29 July 1769. Will pr. 1769. His widow *d.* 30 April 1778.

VIII. 1769. Sir John Wrottesley, Bart. [1642], of Wrottesley Hall aforesaid, only s. and h., *b.* 1744; entered the Army, becoming eventually, in 1782, Major-Gen.; Col. of the 45th Foot; Master of the Horse to H.R.H. the Duke of York. M.P. for Newcastle under Lyne, March to June 1768, and for Staffordshire (fourteen Parls.), July 1768 till death, having *suc. to the Baronetcy*, 29 July 1769; cr. D.C.L. of Oxford, 8 July 1773. He *m.* 17 June 1770, at St. James', Westminster, Frances, 1st da. of William (Courtenay), 1st Viscount Courtenay of Powderham, by Frances, da. of Heneage (Finch), 2d Earl of Ailesford. He *d.* 23 April 1787. Will pr. June 1787. His widow, who was *b.* March 1746/7, and who was sometime Maid of Honour to Charlotte, the Queen Consort, *d.* 24 Feb. 1828. Will pr. March 1828.

IX. 1787. Sir John Wrottesley, Bart. [1642], of Wrottesley Hall aforesaid, s. and h., *b.* 24 Oct. 1771; *suc. to the Baronetcy*, 23 April 1787; sometime an officer in the 13th Lancers, serving in Holland and France; M.P. (in the whig interest) for Lichfield, March 1799 to 1806; for Staffordshire, 1823-32, and for South Staffordshire, 1832-37; F.S.A.; Lieut. Col. of the West Staffordshire Militia. He *m.* firstly, 23 June 1795, Caroline, 1st da. of Charles (Bennet), 4th Earl of Tankerville, by Emma, 2d da. and coheir of Sir James Colebrooke, Bart. [1759]. She, who was *b.* 22 Oct. 1722, *d.* 7 March 1818. Will pr. 1823. He *m.* secondly, 19 May 1819, Julia, widow of (his 1st wife's brother), Hon. John Astley Bennet, Capt. R.N., da. of John Conyers, of Copthall, Essex. She was living when he was *cr.*, 11 July 1838, BARON WROTTESLEY, of Wrottesley, co. Stafford. In that peerage *this Baronetcy* thenceforward *merged*, and so continues. See *Peerage*.

BLAND:

cr. 30 Aug. 1642;[a]

ex. 16 Oct. 1756.

I. 1642. "Thomas Bland, of Kippax Park [near Ferrybridge], co. York, Esq.," s. and h. ap. of Sir Thomas Bland,[b] of the same, by Katherine, sister of Thomas, 1st Earl of Sussex, da. of John (Savile), 1st Baron Savile of Pomfret, was *b.* about 1614; served in the Royal army, and was, in consideration of his father's and his own services to the King, *cr. a Baronet*, as above, 30 Aug. 1642.[a] He was fined £405, on 24 March 1648, and his estates sequestrated, though he obtained some relief by pleading that he had never been in Parl., was not a Popish recusant, was £1,500 in debt, had "a wife and five small children," etc. He *m.* in or before 1642, Rosamond, 2d da. of Francis Nevile, of Chevet, co. York, by his 1st wife, Rosamond, da. of Cyril Arthington. He was *bur.* 24 Oct. 1657, at Kippax. M.I. Admon. 10 Feb. 1657/8, to his widow. She, who was *b.* 1617, *m.* Walter Walsh, of Houghton, and was *bur.* 6 Oct. 1669, at Castleford.

II. 1657. Sir Francis Bland, Bart. [1642], of Kippax Park aforesaid, 1st s. and h., *b.* about 1642; *suc. to the Baronetcy*, Oct. 1657. He *m.* Jane, da. of Sir William Lowther, of Great Preston, co. York, by Jane, da. of William Busfield, of Leeds. He *d.* 14 Nov. 1663, aged 21, and was *bur.* at Kippax. M.I. His widow, who outlived him fifty years, *d.* 7 and was *bur.* 10 April 1713, at Norton, co. Durham, aged 72. M.I.

(a) See p. 161, note "b," under "Strutt."
(b) See Nicholas Carlisle's *History of the Family of Bland*. London, 4to, 1826.

III. 1663. Sir Thomas Bland, Bart. [1642], of Kippax Park aforesaid, 1st s. and h., *b.* 21 Dec. 1662; *suc. to the Baronetcy*, 14 Nov. 1663. He *d.* in childhood, 14 Dec. 1668, and was *bur.* at Kippax. M.I.

IV. 1668. Sir John Bland, Bart. [1642], of Kippax Park aforesaid, only br. and h., *b.* 2 Nov. 1663; *suc. to the Baronetcy*, 14 Dec. 1668; matric. at Oxford (Univ. Coll.), 14 Nov. 1670, aged 16; was M.P. for Appleby (when under age) 1681, and for Pontefract (eight Parls.), 1690—1713; was a Commissr. of the Revenue [I.], 1704-06. He *m.* 31 March 1685, at Chorlton Chapel, Manchester (Lic. Fac., he about 22 and she about 23), Anne, da. and h. of Sir Edward Moseley, of Hulme, in Manchester, by Jane Merial, da. of Richard Saltonstall. He *d.*, on his journey from Bath to Yorkshire, 25 and was *bur.* 29 Oct. 1715, at Didsbury, in Manchester, aged 52. M.I. Will dat 24 Dec. 1712, pr. 7 May 1716. His widow *d.* 26 July and was *bur.* 3 Aug. 1734, at Didsbury. Will dat. 20 June 1721.

V. 1716. Sir John Bland, Bart. [1642], of Kippax Park and Hulme aforesaid, only surv. s. and h., *b.* about 1691; matric. at Oxford (Ch. Ch.), 10 Oct. 1707, aged 16; M.P. for Lancashire (three Parls.), 1713-27; *suc. to the Baronetcy*, 25 Oct. 1715, in which year he was committed to custody on suspicion of high treason. He *m.* 16 Oct. 1716, Frances (£8,000 portion), 5th da. of Heneage (Finch), 1st Earl of Aylesford, by Elizabeth, da. and coheir of Sir John Banks, Bart. [*cr.* 1661]. He *d.* 9 April 1743, at Bath, and was *bur.* at Kippax. M.I. Will dat. 6 Jan. 1741, pr. 1744. His widow resided at St. Geo. Han. sq., Midx. Her will dat. 4 Aug. 1758, pr. 21 March 1759.

VI. 1743. Sir John Bland, Bart. [1642], of Kippax Park and Hulme aforesaid, 1st s. and h., *b.* about 1722; matric. at Oxford (St. John's Coll.), 28 Jan. 1739/40, aged 18; *suc. to the Baronetcy*, 14 April 1743; was M.P. for Ludgershall, 1754 till death. "By his wild dissipation and his unconquerable disposition to play, he squandered immense estates—the whole of Manchester and its environs—and left little more at his death than the family patrimony at Kippax."[a] He *d.* unm., near Calais in France, 3 Sep. 1735. Admon. 1 Oct. 1755 and 12 Jan. 1757.

VII. 1755, to 1756. Sir Hungerford Bland, Bart. [1642], of Kippax Park aforesaid, only br. and h., *b.* about 1726; Lieut. 3d Reg. of Foot Guards, 1753, and afterwards Capt. in the Horse Guards Blue; *suc. to the Baronetcy*, 3 Sep. 1755. He *d.* unm., 16 Oct. 1756, aged 30, at Kippax Park, and was *bur.* at Kippax, when the *Baronetcy* became *extinct*.[a] M.I. Admon. 12 Jan. 1757.

THROCKMORTON, *or* THROGMORTON:

cr. 1 Sep. 1642[b];

sometime, 1819-26, Courtenay-Throckmorton.

I. 1642. "Robert Throckmorton, of Coughton, co. Warwick, Esq." being also described[c] as "of Weston Underwood, Bucks, Knt.," s. and h. of John Throckmorton, by Agnes, da. of Thomas Wilford, of Newman Hall, in Quendon, Essex, which John was s. and h. ap. of Thomas Throckmorton, of Coughton and Weston aforesaid, *suc.* his said grandfather 13 March 1614, and was *cr. a Baronet*, as above, 1 Sep. 1642.[b] He kept a bountiful house at

(a) The Kippax estate passed firstly to his two sisters, Elizabeth and Anne, who both *d.* unm., the yst. and survivor on 20 Jan. 1786, when they went to her cousin, Thomas Davison, who thereupon took the name of Bland after his patronymic. He was s. and h. of Thomas Davison, of Blakiston manor, co. Durham (*d.* 5 April 1756, aged 43), who was s. and h. of Thomas Davison, of the same, by Anne, 1st da. of Sir John Bland, 4th Bart.
(b) See p. 161, note "b," under "Strutt."
(c) On the M.I. to his first wife who died in 1617.

Weston till his estates were sequestrated in the time of the Civil War, his house at Coughton being turned into a garrison for the parliament forces, and he himself obliged to retire to Worcester for security. He *m.* firstly, Dorothy, da. of Sir John Fortescue, **K.B.**, of Salden, Bucks. She *d.* s.p. 4 Nov. 1617, and was *bur.* at Coughton. M.I. He *m.* secondly, Mary, sister of Charles, 1st Viscount Carrington of Barrefore [I.], da. of Sir Francis Smith, of Ashby Folville, co. Leicester, by Anne, da. of Sir Thomas Markham. He *d.* 16 Jan. 1650, and was *bur.* at Coughton. M.I. The will of Dame Mary Throckmorton pr. 1663.

II. 1650. Sir Francis Throckmorton, Bart. [1642], of Coughton Court in Coughton and of Weston Underwood aforesaid, s. and h. by 2d wife, *suc. to the Baronetcy*, 16 Jan. 1650. He rebuilt the house at Coughton, where he exercised great hospitality after the Restoration. He *m.* Anne, da. and sole h. of John Monson, of Kinnersley, Surrey. He *d.* 7 Nov. 1680, aged 40, and was *bur.* at Weston. M.I. Will pr. 1681. The will of Dame Anne Throckmorton, pr. 1728.

III. 1680. Sir Robert Throckmorton, Bart. [1642], of Coughton Court and of Weston Underwood aforesaid, 1st surv. s. and h., *b.* 10 Jan. 1662, at Moorhall, co. Warwick; *suc. to the Baronetcy*, 7 Nov. 1680, and was admitted to Gray's Inn, 15 Jan. 1682/3. He partially re-built the mansion at Weston, and was a great benefactor to that parish and that of Coughton. He *m.* Mary, sister and h. (1690) of Sir John Yate, 4th Bart. [1622], da. of Sir Charles Yate, 3d Bart., by Frances, da. of Sir Thomas Gage, 2d Bart. [1622], of Firle, co. Sussex. By her he acquired the estate of Buckland, near Farringdon, Berks. He, who was one of the "Catholic nonjurors," *d.* 8 and was *bur.* 15 March 1720/1, aged 58, at Weston. Will pr. 1721. His widow was *bur.* there 12 May 1722.

IV. 1721. Sir Robert Throckmorton, Bart. [1642], of Coughton Court, Weston Underwood and Buckland aforesaid, only surv. s. and h., *b.* 21 and *bap.* 22 Aug. 1702, at Weston; *suc. to the Baronetcy*, 8 March 1720/1. He *m.* firstly, Theresa, 5th da. of William (Herbert), 2d Marquess of Powis, by Mary, da. and coheir of Sir Thomas Preston, 3d Bart. [1644]. She *d.* 17 and was *bur.* 22 June 1723, at Weston aforesaid. He *m.* secondly, Jan. 1737/8, Catharine, da. of George Collingwood, of Elsington, Northumberland. She *d.* s.p.m. He *m.* thirdly, in 1763, Lucy, da. of James Heywood, of Morriston, Devon, but by her had no issue. He *d.* 8 Dec. 1791, and was *bur.* at Coughton. Will pr. Feb. 1792. The will of his widow pr. Dec. 1795.

V. 1791. Sir John Courtenay Throckmorton, Bart. [1642], of Coughton Court, Weston Underwood and Buckland aforesaid, grandson and h., being s. and h. of George Throckmorton, by Anna Maria, only da. of William Paston, of Horton, co. Gloucester (by Mary, his wife, only child that had issue of John Courtenay, of Molland, Devon), which George was s. and h. ap. of the 4th Bart., but *d.* v.p. 30 Aug. 1767. He was *b.* 27 July 1753; *suc. to the Baronetcy*, 8 Dec. 1791, and was *cr.* D.C.L. of Oxford, 15 June 1796. He *m.* 19 Aug. 1782, Maria Catharine, da. of Thomas Giffard, of Chillington, co. Stafford,[a] by his 1st wife, Barbara, da. of Robert James (Petre), 8th Baron Petre of Writtle. He *d.* s.p., 3 Jan. 1819. Will pr. 1819. His widow *d.* 7 Jan. 1821, in her 59th year, at Hengrave Hall, Suffolk. Will pr. 1821.

VI. 1819. Sir George Courteney-Throckmorton, Bart. [1642], of Coughton Court, Weston Underwood, and Buckland aforesaid, and of Molland, co. Devon., br. and h., *b.* 15 Sep. 1754. In 1792 he took the name of Courtenay before that of Throckmorton, having inherited, through his mother, the estate of Molland, formerly that of the Courtenay family. He *suc. to the Baronetcy*, 3 Jan. 1819. He *m.* 29 June 1792, Catharine, only da. of Thomas Stapleton, of Carleton, co. York, by his 1st wife, Catherine, da. of Henry Witham, of Cliffe. He *d.* s.p., 16 July 1826, aged 72, at Weston; *bur.* there. M.I. Will pr. Sep. 1826. His widow *d.* 22 Jan. 1839. Will pr. March 1839.

(a) She was a friend of the poet Cowper.

VII. 1826. Sir Charles Throckmorton, Bart. [1642], of Coughton Court, Weston Underwood, and Buckland aforesaid, br. and h., *b.* 2 Nov. 1757, and *bap.* at Weston aforesaid; *suc. to the Baronetcy*, 16 July 1826. He *m.* 28 Dec. 1787, Mary Margaretta, da. of Edmund Plowden, of Plowden, Salop, by Elizabeth, da. and coheir of Sir Berkeley Lucy, 3d Bart. [1618]. He *d.* s.p., 3 Dec. 1840. Will pr. Feb. 1841.

VIII. 1840. Sir Robert-George Throckmorton, Bart. [1642], of Coughton Court, Weston Underwood, and Buckland aforesaid, nephew and h., being s. and h. of William Throckmorton, by Frances, only da. of Thomas Giffard, of Chillington, co. Stafford, which William was br. to the 5th, 6th and 7th Barts., and *d.* 31 March 1819, aged 56. He was *b.* 5 Dec. 1800, in Queen street, Mayfair, Middlesex; M.P. for Berks, 1831-1835; Sheriff of that county, 1843; *suc. to the Baronetcy*, 3 Dec. 1840. He *m.* 16 July 1829, Elizabeth, only da. of Sir John-Francis-Edward Acton, 6th Bart. [1644], by (his niece) Mary Anne, 1st da. of (his brother) Gen Joseph Edward Acton. She *d.* 4 April 1850. He *d.* 28 June 1862, in Hereford street, Park lane, aged 61.

IX. 1862. Sir Nicholas-William-George Throckmorton, Bart. [1642], of Coughton Court, Weston Underwood and Buckland aforesaid, 1st surv. s. and h., *b.* 26 April 1838, at Buckland aforesaid; *suc. to the Baronetcy*, 28 June 1862; Sheriff of Berks, 1872.

Family Estates.—These, in 1883, consisted of 7,618 acres in Warwickshire (worth £9,918 a year); 6,589 in Devon; 3,618 in Worcestershire; 3,008 in Berks, and 1,552 in Bucks. *Total*, 22,385 acres, worth £27,092 a year. *Principal Seat.*—Coughton Court, co. Warwick.

HALTON:

cr. 10 Sep. 1642[a];

ex. 9 Feb. 1823.

I. 1642. "William Halton, of Samford[b] [*or* Little Sandford], co. Essex, Esq.," 3d s. of Robert Halton, of Sawbridgeworth, Herts, by his 1st wife, Hesther, da. of William Booth, of co. Lincoln; was *b.* about 1620; was executor and testamentary heir of his uncle Sir William Halton, of Great Abington, Cambridgeshire (who *d.* 20 Nov. 1639, aged nearly 70), and was *cr. a Baronet*, as above, 10 Sep. 1642.[a] He *m.* firstly, Mary, da. of Sir Edward Altham, of Marks Hall, in Latton, Essex, by Joan, da. of Sir John Leventhorpe, 1st Bart. [1622]. She *d.* 29 Dec. 1644, aged 26, and was *bur.* at Little Saudford. He *m.* secondly, 12 June 1649, at St. James', Clerkenwell (Lic. Fac, 11th, he about 28), Ursula, da. (whose issue became heir), of Sir Thomas Fisher, 1st Bart. [1627], by Sarah, da. and coheir of Sir Thomas Fowler, Bart. (*cr.* 1628), of Islington, co. Midx. He was *bur.* 29 Oct. 1662, at St. Leonard's, Shoreditch. Admon. Oct. 1662. His widow *m.* Matthew Meriton, of London, merchant.

II. 1662. Sir William Halton, Bart. [1642], of Little Sandford aforesaid, s. and h. by 1st wife; *suc. to the Baronetcy*, Oct. 1662. He sold the estate of Little Sandford in 1670 to Edward Peck. He *d.* unm., 4 March 1675/6 at Salisbury, and was *bur.* at Latton, Essex. Admon. 12 June 1676. Will pr. Dec. following.

III. 1676. Sir Thomas Halton, Bart. [1642], of Barnsbury in Islington, co. Midx. (which he inherited from his mother's family), half br. and h., being s. of the 1st Bart. by his 2d wife; *suc. to the Baronetcy*,

(a) See p. 195, note "a," under "Wrottesley."
(b) He had recently purchased this estate from Sir Edward Green, Bart. [*cr.* 1660], paying his fine for ingress, in 1640.

4 March 1675/6. He *m.* Elizabeth, da. of John CRESSENER, of London. She *d.* 26 Aug. 1716. He *d.* 6 Sep. 1726; both were *bur.* at Islington. His admon. 26 Sep. 1726 and 7 July 1756.

IV. 1726. SIR WILLIAM HALTON, Bart. [1642], of Barnsbury aforesaid and of Turnham Green, Midx., only surv. s. and h.; *suc. to the Baronetcy*, 6 Sep. 1726. He *m.* Frances, widow of John JERMY, of Sturton, Suffolk, da. and h. of Sir George DALSTON (s. and h. ap. of Sir William DALSTON, 1st Bart. [1641]), by Brown, da. of Sir William RAMSDEN, of Byrom, co. York. He *d.* s.p., 12 Feb. 1754, having devised the valuable manor of Barnsbury to the family of TUFNELL. Will pr. 1754.

V. 1754. SIR THOMAS HALTON, Bart. [1642], cousin and h. male, being s. and h. of George HALTON, by Hannah, 1st da. of Fenwick LAMBERT, of London, which George (who *d.* 7 May 1729), was s. and h. of Richard HALTON (*d.* 1703), youngest s. of the 1st Bart. by his 2d wife; *suc. to the Baronetcy*, 12 Feb. 1754. He *m.* Mary, da. of (—) BURTON, of London. He went abroad about 1762, and *d.* 1766.

VI. 1766, to 1823. SIR WILLIAM HALTON, Bart. [1642], s. and h., *b.* about 1751; *suc. to the Baronetcy* in 1766. He *m.* in or before 1771, in which year he was about 20, Mary, da. of Michael GARNER, of Kings Ripon, co. Huntingdon. He *d.* s.p.m.,(a) 9 Feb. 1823, when the *Baronetcy* became *extinct*.

SPENCER:

cr. 26 Sep. 1642;(b)

ex. 16 Nov. 1712.

I. 1642. "BROCKETT SPENCER, of Offley, co. Hertford, Esq.," only br. and h. male of Sir John SPENCER of the same, Bart. (so *cr.* 1627), was *b.* about 1605; suc. his said brother in the family estate, Sep. 1633, and was *cr. a Baronet*, as above, 26 Sep. 1642.(b) He *m.* in or before 1646, Susan, da. of Sir Nicholas CAREW, formerly THROCKMORTON, of Beddington, Surrey, by his 2d wife, Susan, da. of (—) BRIGHT. He *d.* 3 and was *bur.* 5 July 1668, at Offley, aged 63. His widow, who was *bap.* 8 July 1619, at Beddington, *d.* 9 and was *bur.* 12 May 1692, at Offley, aged 72. Will pr. 1692.

II. 1668. SIR RICHARD SPENCER, Bart. [1642], of Offley aforesaid, s. and h., *b.* about 1647; *suc. to the Baronetcy*, 3 July 1668. He m. 23 July 1672, at Hornsey, Midx. (Lic. Lond. 18th, he 24 and she 19), Mary, da. of Sir John MUSTERS, of Colwick, Notts, by Anne, da. of Sir John MAYNARD. He *d.* 21 and was *bur.* 23 Feb. 1687/8, at Offley, aged 41. Will pr. 1688. His widow *m.* (settlement 22 April 1691), Sir Ralph RADCLIFFE, of Hitchin, Herts, whose will, dat. 3 Feb. 1713/4, was pr. 29 July 1720. Her will, dat. 19 May 1719 (in his lifetime), was pr. 18 Sep. following.

III. 1688. SIR JOHN SPENCER, Bart. [1642], of Offley aforesaid, only surv. s. and h., *bap.* 27 Feb. 1677/8, at Offley; *suc. to the Baronetcy*, 21 Feb. 1687/8. He *d.* unm. 6 and was *bur.* 12 Aug. 1699, at Offley. Admon. 21 Aug. 1699.

(a) Mary, his only da. and h., *m.* John Haughton JAMES, of Haughton Hall, in Jamaica, and had a numerous family.

(b) See p. 195, note "a," under "Wrottesley."

IV. 1699, to 1712. SIR JOHN SPENCER, Bart. [1642], of Offley aforesaid, uncle and h., *b.* about 1650; matric. at Oxford, 12 July 1667, aged 17; Barrister (Inner Temple), 1675; *suc. to the Baronetcy*, 6 Aug. 1699. He *d.* s.p., 16 Nov., and was *bur.* 1 Dec. 1712, at Offley, when the *Baronetcy* became *extinct*.(a) Will pr. 1712.

GOLDING:

cr. 27 Sep. 1642(b);

ex. Dec. 1715.

I. 1642. "EDWARD GOLDING, of Colston Bassett, co. Nottingham, Esq.," s. and h. of Edward GOLDING,(c) of Eye, co. Suffolk, by Mary, da. of Richard GODFREY, of Hendringham, co. Norfolk, was *cr. a Baronet*, as above, 27 Sep. 1642.(b) He *m.* in or before 1610, Ellinor, sister of Sir Robert THROCKMORTON, 1st Bart. [1642], da. of John THROCKMORTON, of Coughton, co. Warwick, by Agnes, da. of Thomas WILFORD. She was *bur.* 22 Sep. 1652, at Colston.(d) He was living Jan. 1655/6, and became eventually a Capuchin Friar. He *d.* at Rouen, in Normandy.

II. 1656? SIR CHARLES GOLDING, Bart. [1642], of Colston Bassett aforesaid, 2d s. and h.,(e) *b.* about 1624; *suc. to the Baronetcy*, on the death of his father, in or after 1656. He *m.* 9 Jan. 1655/6, at St. Paul's, Covent Garden, Mary, da. of James RAVENSCROFT, of Alkmondbury, co. Huntingdon. He *d.* 28 and was *bur.* 30 Sep. 1661, at Colston, aged 37. His widow was *bur.* there 15 Feb. 1688/9, aged 53.

III. 1661, to 1715. SIR EDWARD GOLDING, Bart. [1642], of Colston Bassett aforesaid, s. and h.; *suc. to the Baronetcy*, in 1667. He *m.* Winifred, da. and h. of John WYLDMAN, of co. Leicester. He *d.* s.p.m., and was *bur.* 8 Dec. 1715, at Colston, when the *Baronetcy* became *extinct*. Admon. 30 April 1716, to Winifred, the relict.

SMITH, *or* SMITHE:

cr. 27 Sep. 1642(b);

ex. in or before 1661.

I. 1642, to 1661? "WILLIAM SMITHE, of Crantock, co. Cornwall, Esq.," presumably a descendant of the family of SMITH, of Tregonnack, in that county, was a merchant in London, and was *cr. a Baronet*, as above, 27 Sep. 1642.(b) He *m.* (—), but *d.* s.p.m. in or before 1661, when the *Baronetcy* became *extinct*. Will pr. 1661.

(a) The Offley estate became vested in his four sisters, all of whom *d.* s.p. excepting Elizabeth, who *m.* 2 Nov. 1677, Sir Humphrey GORE, of Gilston, Herts. Their only da. and h., Elizabeth, *m.* 1714, Sir Henry PENRICE, LL.D., whose only da. and h., Anna Maria, *m.* Sir Thomas SALISBURY, LL.D., and conveyed the estate and manor to him. She *d.* s.p., 7 March 1759. See Clutterbuck's *Herts*, vol. iii, p. 97.

(b) See p. 195, note "a," under "Wrottesley."

(c) "Edward Golding, of Eye, co. Suffolk," was admitted, 16 Oct. 1588, to Gray's Inn.

(d) *Genealogist*, vol. ii., 99, where extracts from this parish register are given.

(e) John Golding, the 1st s., *b.* before 1614, became a Capuchin Friar at Rouen. It is possible that, though passed over as succeeding to the Baronetcy, he may have survived his father, in which case the burial, 15 April 1689, of "John, son of Sir Edward Golding, Baronet," may refer to him, and not to some (infant) son of the 3d Baronet.

HENN, *or* HENE:

cr. 1 Oct. 1642;(a)

ex. about 1710.

I. 1642. "HENRY HENN, of Wingfeild [*i.e.*, Winkfield], co. Berks, Esq.," 2d s. of William HENE, of Dorking, co. Surrey, by Anne (*m.* at Dorking, 2 Sep. 1565), da. of (—) BIRCH, of Birches in Coleshill, was *b.* about 1577, and, having acquired the manor of Folijohn, in Winkfield, Berks, in 1630, was *cr. a Baronet*, as above, 1 Oct. 1642.(a) He *m.* Dorothy, da. of Henry STAPLEFORD, of Pauls Walden, Herts. He was living 28 March 1665 (Visit. of Berks), aged 88, and *d.* in or before 1668. Will pr. 1668.

II. 1668? SIR HENRY HENE, Bart. [1642], of Winkfield aforesaid, s. and h., *b.* about 1632; matric. at Oxford (Christ Church), 17 May 1647; aged 31 in 1665; *suc. to the Baronetcy* in or before 1668. He *m.* in or before 1652,(b) Muriel, da. of Sir John CORBET, 1st Bart. [1627], of Stoke, by Ann, da. of Sir George MANWARING.

III. 1675? SIR HENRY HENE, Bart. [1642], of Winkfield aforesaid, 1st s. and h.; *bap.* 14 Oct. 1651; was aged 13 in 1665; *suc. to the Baronetcy* on the death of his father. He *m.* (—). He *d.* 16 Jan. 1705.

IV. 1705, to 1710? SIR RICHARD HENE, Bart. [1642], of Winkfield aforesaid, only surv. s. and h., *b.* about 1675; was an idiot in 1697; but was *m.* in or before 1702. He *suc. to the Baronetcy* between 1702 and 1708, but *d.* s.p.m.(c) about 1710, when the *Baronetcy* became *extinct*. The will of "Dame Ann Hene, Berks," was pr. Nov. 1716.

BLUNT, *or* BLOUNT:

cr. 6 Oct. 1642(a).

I. 1642. "WALTER BLUNT, of Sillingtone [*i.e.*, Sodington], co. Worcester, Esq.," s. and h. of Sir George BLOUNT, *or* BLUNT,(d), of the same, by Eleanor, da. of William NORWOOD, of Leckhampton, co. Gloucester, was *b.* about 1594; matric. at Oxford (Ball. Coll.), 12 Oct. 1610, aged 16; admitted to Inner Temple, 1611; Sheriff of Worcestershire, 1619-20; M.P. for Droitwich, 1624-25; and was *cr. a Baronet*, as above, 6 Oct. 1642.(a) He was taken prisoner at Hereford in December 1645; was a great sufferer for the King in the Civil War, and was imprisoned at Oxford and afterwards in the Tower of London.(e) His house at Sodington was burnt by Cromwell's soldiers, and his estates confiscated, 2 Nov. 1652, and sold in 1655. He *m.* (when very young) Elizabeth, da. of George WYLDE, of Droitwich, Serjeant at Law, by Frances, da. of Sir Edmond HUDLESTON, of Sawston, co. Cambridge. He *d.* at Blagdon, co. Devon, 27 and was *bur.* 29 Aug. 1654, at Paignton, in that county. M.I. His widow *d.* at Mawley Hall, 23 and was *bur.* 25 April 1656, at Mamble, co. Worcester. M.I.

II. 1654. SIR GEORGE BLOUNT, *or* BLUNT, Bart. [1642], of Sodington aforesaid, and of Mawley Hall, co. Worcester, s. and h.; *suc. to the Baronetcy*, 27 Aug. 1654. He *m.* Mary, d. and h. of Richard KIRKHAM (s. and h. of Sir

(a) See p. 195, note "a," under "Wrottesley."

(b) In the Visit. of Berks for 1665 he had six children, of whom the two sons were (1) Henry, aged 13, and Corbett. This Corbett Hene, who was a Col. in the Army, *m.* (Lic. Fac. 30 Sep. 1686, aged 32), Dame Mary Beckford, widow, and *d.* Sep. 1693, in Golden square. Will pr. 1693.

(c) Of his two daughters (1) Ann was *bap.* 17 Feb. 1702/3 (when he was Esq.), and (2) Arabella, 8 April 1708 (when he was a Baronet), at Clewer, Berks. According to Lysons' *Berks*, the estate of Folijohn was inherited by his two daughters.

(d) See "Croke family, originally named Le Blount," by Sir Alexander Croke, D.C.L. and F.S.A., 2 vols. 4to, Oxford, 1823.

(e) His four surviving sons, his three brothers, as also he himself, bore arms for the Royal cause.

William KIRKHAM), of Blagdon aforesaid, by his 2d wife, Mary, da. of Sir Henry TICHBORNE, 3d s. of the 1st Bart. [1611]. He *d.* 12 Nov. 1667, at Mawley Hall, and was *bur.* at Mamble aforesaid. M.I. Admon. 10 Feb. 1667/8, to his relict.

III. 1667. SIR WALTER KIRKHAM BLOUNT, Bart. [1642], of Sodington aforesaid, s. and h.; *suc. to the Baronetcy*, 12 Nov. 1667; was Sheriff of Worcestershire, 1687-88. He was an author, translating *The Office of the Holy Week*, printed at Paris in 1670. He *m.* firstly, Alicia, da. of Sir Thomas STRICKLAND, of Sizerg, co. Westmorland, by his 1st wife, Jane, da. of John MOSELEY. She *d.* 1 Dec. 1680. He *m.* secondly, Mary, da. of Sir Cæsar CRANMER, *otherwise* WOOD, of Astwoodbury, Bucks, by Lelis, da. of Charles PELLIOTT, Sieur de la Garde, of Paris. She was living 11 Nov. 1690.(a) He *d.* s.p., at Ghent, in Flanders, 12 May 1717. Will pr. 17 Oct. 1717.

IV. 1717. SIR EDWARD BLOUNT, Bart. [1642], of Sodington and Mawley Hall aforesaid, nephew and h., being s. and h. of George BLOUNT, of Mawley Hall aforesaid, by Constantia, his 2d wife, da. of Sir George CAREY, of Torr Abbey, Devon, which George BLOUNT was 2d s. of the 2d Bart., and *d.* 20 May 1702. He *suc. to the Baronetcy*, 12 May 1717. He *m.* (Lic. Worcester, 11 Aug. 1722, each above 21), Apollonia, da. of Sir Robert THROCKMORTON, 3d Bart. [1642], of Coughton, by Mary, da. of Sir Charles YATE, 3d Bart. [1622]. She *d.* at Mawley 19 Jan. 1749. He *d.* there 16 Feb. 1758. Both *bur.* at Mamble. M.I. His will pr. 1758.

V. 1758. SIR EDWARD BLOUNT, Bart. [1642], of Sodington and Mawley Hall aforesaid, s. and h., *b.* about 1724; *suc. to the Baronetcy*, 16 Feb. 1758. He *m.* 1752, Frances, da. and h. of William MOLYNEUX, of Mosborough, co. Lancaster. He *d.* at Bath, s.p.s., 19 Oct. 1765, aged 41, and was *bur.* at Mamble. M.I. Admon. 31 Dec. 1765. His widow *d.* 18 Dec. 1787. Will pr. 1788.

VI. 1765. SIR WALTER BLOUNT, Bart. [1642], of Sodington and Mawley Hall aforesaid, br. and h.; ed. at Douay College; *suc. to the Baronetcy*, 19 Oct. 1765. He *m.* 21 Sep. 1766, at Worksop Manor, Notts, Mary, 1st da. and coheir of James (ASTON), 5th LORD ASTON [S.], by Barbara, da. of George (TALBOT), EARL OF SHREWSBURY. He *d.* at Lisle, in Flanders, 5 Oct. 1785. Will pr. March 1806. His widow *d.* 31 Jan. 1805. Will pr. 1805.

VII. 1785. SIR WALTER BLOUNT, Bart. [1642], of Sodington, and Mawley Hall aforesaid, s. and h., *b.* 3 Sep. 1768; *suc. to the Baronetcy*, 5 Oct. 1785; was *cr.* D.C.L. of Oxford, 4 July 1793. He *m.* 25 Nov. 1792, Anne, yst. da. of Thomas RIDDELL, of Felton Park and Swinburne Castle, both co. Northumberland, by Elizabeth, da. and h. of Edward Horsley WIDDRINGTON, of Felton aforesaid. He *d.* at Laycock Abbey, Wilts, and was *bur.* 31 Oct. 1803, at Bath Abbey, aged 35. Admon. Nov. 1803. His widow *d.* 15 Feb. 1823. Will pr. 1823.

VIII. 1803. SIR EDWARD BLOUNT, Bart. [1642], of Sodington and Mawley Hall aforesaid, only surv. s. and h., *b.* 3 March 1795, at Mawley Hall; *suc. to the Baronetcy*, Oct. 1803; Sheriff of Worcestershire, 1835. He *m.* 14 Sep. 1830, at St. Mary's, Bryanstone square, Marylebone, Mary Frances, sister of Walter Aston Edward BLOUNT, Clarenceux King of Arms [*d.* 9 Feb. 1894, aged 87]. 1st da. of Edward BLOUNT, of Shablington, Bucks, sometime M P. for Steyning, by Frances, da. and coheir of Francis WRIGHT, which Edward was next br. of the late Baronet. He *d.* 28 May 1881, at Mawley Hall, and was *bur.* at Mamble aforesaid, aged 86. His widow, who was *b.* 28 April 1804, at Mapledurham, Oxon, *d.* at Mawley Hall, 26 May 1893, in her 90th year.

IX. 1881. SIR WALTER DE SODINGTON BLOUNT, Bart. [1642], of Sodington and Mawley Hall aforesaid, 1st s. and h., *b.* 19 Dec. 1833, in Great Cumberland street, and *bap.* at St. James' Catholic chapel, Spanish place;

(a) Will of that date of Thomas Wood, Bishop of Coventry and Lichfield.

ed. at Oscott College; sometime Capt. Worcester Yeomanry Cavalry; *suc. to the Baronetcy*, 28 April 1881. He *m.* in 1874, Elizabeth Anne Mould, da. of James Zacharies WILLIAMS, of Cader Idris.

Family Estates.—These, in 1883, consisted of 2,861 acres in Salop, and 2,622 in Worcestershire. Total, 5,483 acres, worth £5,069 a year. *Principal Seats.*—Sodington Court and Mawley Hall, near Bewdley, co. Worcester.

LITTLETON:
cr. 14 Oct. 1642;(a)
afterwards POYNTZ, *otherwise* LITTLETON;
ex. 1 Jan. 1709/10.

I. 1642. "ADAM LITTLETON, of Stoke Milburge, co. Salop, Esq.," s. and h. of Thomas LITTLETON,(b) of the same, by Frances, da. of Adam LUTLEY, of Bronscroft Castle, in that county; suc. his father, 1621, and was *cr. a Baronet*, as above, 14 Oct. 1642.(a) By the death of his wife's cousin, Richard POYNTZ, *otherwise* MAURICE, on 15 Aug. 1643, he suc. to the estates of that family at North Ockendon, co. Essex. He *m.* Etheldred, 1st da. and coheir, but eventually sole h., of Thomas POYNTZ, of North Ockendon aforesaid, by Jane, da. and coheir of Sir William PERIAM, Lord Chief Baron of the Exchequer. He was *bur.* 6 Sep. 1647, at North Ockendon. His widow *bur.* there 25 May 1648. Her will dat. 10 March 1647/8, pr. 27 Oct. 1648.

II. 1647. SIR THOMAS LITTLETON, *otherwise* POYNTZ, Bart. [1642], of North Ockendon and Stoke Milburgh aforesaid, s. and h., *b.* about 1622; matric. at Oxford (Jesus Coll.), 15 June, 1638, aged 16; Barrister (Inner Temple), 1642; *suc. to the Baronetcy*, Sep. 1647; was M.P. for Much Wenlock, April to May 1640, and Nov. 1640 till disabled, Feb. 1643/4; re-elected 1661-78; M.P. for East Grinstead, April to July 1679; and for Yarmouth (Isle of Wight), Feb. 1681 till death; was a Compounder "on his own discovery," 4 May 1649; fined £220 on 9 Aug. 1649, afterwards raised to £295; was a Lord of the Admiralty, Feb. 1679/80 till his death. He *m.* (Lic. Lond., 6 Oct. 1637, he stated to be 17 and she 12), his cousin Anne, da. and h. of Edward (LITTLETON), BARON LYTTELTON OF MOUNSLOW (so *cr.* 18 Feb. 1640/1), sometime Lord Keeper of the Great Seal, by Ann, da. of John LITTLETON, of Frankley, co. Worcester. He *d.* 12 and was *bur.* 16 April 1681, at North Ockendon, aged 57. Will dat. 2 Dec. 1665, to 11 April 1681, pr. 18 June 1681. His widow, who was *b.* 21 Aug. 1623, *d.* 27 Nov. and was *bur.* 4 Dec. 1705, at North Ockendon, aged 82. Admon. as "of St. Giles' in the Fields, Midx.," 8 Dec. 1705.

III. 1681, to 1710. SIR THOMAS LITTLETON, *otherwise* POYNTZ, Bart. [1642], of North Ockendon and Stoke Milburgh aforesaid, *b.* 3 April 1647; matric. at Oxford (St. Edm. Hall), 21 April 1665, aged 18; Barrister (Inner Temple), 1671; *suc. to the Baronetcy*, 12 April 1681; M.P. for New Woodstock (six Parls.), 1689—1702; for Castle Rising, 1702-05; for Chichester, 1705-08; and for Portsmouth, 1708 till death; was one of the Lords of the Treasury, 1696-99; Privy Councillor; SPEAKER OF THE HOUSE OF COMMONS, 6 Dec. 1698 to 1700; Treasurer of the Navy, 1699 till death. He *m.* Ann, da. of Benjamin BAUN, *or* BARON, of Weston, co. Gloucester. He *d.* s.p., 1 Jan. 1709/10, and was *bur.* at North Ockendon, M.I., when the *Baronetcy* became *extinct*. Will dat. 19 to 23 Sep. 1709, pr. 21 Jan. 1709/10. His widow *d.* 21 July 1714, and was *bur.* at North Ockendon. Will dat. 13 Feb. 1713, pr. 11 Aug. 1714.

(a) See p. 195, note "a," under "Wrottesley."
(b) This Thomas was descended, as also was Sir Edward LITTLETON, Lord Keeper of the Great Seal, 1640-1645 (*cr.* BARON LYTTELTON OF MOUNSLOW, in 1640), from Thomas LITTLETON, of Spechley, co. Worcester, 3d s. of Sir Thomas LITTLETON, K.B., of Frankley, in that county, the celebrated Judge.

LIDDELL:
cr. 2 Nov. 1642;(a)
sometime, 1747-84, BARON RAVENSWORTH;
subsequently, since 1821, BARONS RAVENSWORTH;
and, since 1874, EARLS OF RAVENSWORTH.

I. 1642. "THOMAS LIDDELL, of Ravensholme [*i.e.*, Ravensworth] Castle, co. pal. Durham, Esq.," s. and h. of Thomas LIDDELL, of the same, by Margaret, da. of John WATSON, suc. his father in 1615; was admitted to Gray's Inn, 15 March 1619/20, and was *cr. a Baronet*, as above, 2 Nov. 1642. He was a zealous Royalist, and gallantly defended Newcastle against the Scots. He was fined £4,000 as "a delinquent." He *m.* Isabel, da. of Henry ANDERSON, by (—), da. and coheir of (—) MORLAND. He *d.* 1650. Will pr. 1652.

II. 1650. SIR THOMAS LIDDELL, Bart. [1642], of Ravensworth Castle aforesaid, grandson and h., being s. and h. of Sir Thomas LIDDELL (by Bridget, da. of Edward WOODWARD, of Lee, Bucks), which Thomas was s. and h. ap. of the 1st Bart., and *d.* v.p. 1627. He *suc. to the Baronetcy*, 1650. He *m.* Anne, da. of Sir Henry VANE, of Raby Castle, Durham, by Frances, da. and coheir of Thomas DARCY, of Tolleshunt Darcy, Essex. He *d.* 1697.

III. 1697. SIR HENRY LIDDELL, Bart. [1642], of Ravensworth Castle aforesaid, s. and h.; M.P. for Durham city, 1689-98; for Newcastle, 1700-05 and Jan. 1706 to 1710; *suc. to the Baronetcy* in 1697. He *m.* in or before 1670, Catharine, only surv. da. and h. of Sir John BRIGHT, Bart. (so *cr.* 1660), of Badsworth, co. York, and Carbrook, co. Derby, by his 1st wife, Catharine, da. of Sir Richard HAWKSWORTH. She was *bur.* 24 Feb. 1703, at Kensington. He *d.* 1 Sep. 1723. Will dat. 17 July 1722 and 19 Aug. 1723, pr. 2 Nov. 1723.

IV. 1723. SIR HENRY LIDDELL, Bart. [1642], of Ravensworth Castle aforesaid, grandson and h., being s. and h. of Thomas LIDDELL, by Jane (*m.* 12 Oct. 1707), da. of James CLAVERING, of Greencroft, co. Durham, which Thomas (who *d.* v.p. 3 June 1715, aged 34), was s. and h. ap. of the late Baronet. He was *b.* 1708; *suc. to the Baronetcy*, 1 Sep. 1723; was M.P. for Morpeth, 1734-47, being, on 29 June 1747, *cr.* a Peer, as LORD RAVENSWORTH, BARON OF RAVENSWORTH, co. Durham. He *m.*, 27 April 1735, Ann, only da. of Sir Peter DELME,(b) Lord Mayor of London [1723-24], by his 1st wife Anne, da. of Cornelius MACHAM, of Southampton. He *d.* s.p.m.,(c) 30 Jan., and was *bur.* 8 Feb. 1784, at Lamersley, co. Durham, when the *Peerage* became *extinct*. Will pr. March 1784. His widow, who was *b.* 5 and *bap.* 11 June 1712, at St. Gabriel's Fenchurch, London, *d.* 12 June 1794, in St. James' square, aged 82. Will pr. June 1794.

V. 1784. SIR HENRY GEORGE LIDDELL, Bart. [1642], of Ravensworth Castle aforesaid, nephew and h. male, being s. and h. of Thomas LIDDELL, by Margaret, da. of Sir William BOWES, of Gibside, which Thomas was next br. to the 4th Bart. He was *b.* 25 Nov. 1749, and *suc. to the Baronetcy*, on the death of Lord Ravensworth, 30 Jan. 1784. He *m.* April 1773, Elizabeth, da. of Thomas STEELE, of Hampsnett, Sussex. He *d.* 26 Nov. 1791. Will pr. Feb. 1792.

(a) See p. 195, note "a," under "Wrottesley."
(b) An interesting account of the Delmé family, by the Rev. G. W. Minns, LL.B., is in the Hampshire Field Club Papers, 1895, with an engraving of the beautiful picture of "Lady Betty Delmé and two children," by Sir Joshua Reynolds, which picture, in 1895, sold for 11,000 guineas, the estate and mansion of Cams Hall, near Fareham, Hants (from whence it was taken), realising but £10,250!
(c) Anne, his only da. and h., became Duchess of Grafton, and, subsequently, having been divorced, in 1769, Countess of Upper Ossory [I.]
(d) He is said to have had "a warm, generous, but somewhat romantic disposition." His excursion in Lapland (for a wager) is described in Consett's "Tour through Sweden."

VI. 1791. SIR THOMAS HENRY LIDDELL, Bart. [1642], of Ravensworth Castle aforesaid, s. and h., *b.* 8 Feb. 1775, at Newton Hall, co. Durham; *suc. to the Baronetcy*, 26 Nov. 1791; ed. at Trin. Coll., Cambridge; M.A., 1795; was M.P. for co. Durham, 1806-07. He *m.* 26 March 1796, at her mother's house, in Upper Harley Street, Marylebone, Maria Susanna, da. of John SIMPSON, of Bradley, co. Durham, by Anne, da. of Thomas (LYON), EARL OF STRATHMORE AND KINGHORN [S.]. She was living when he was *cr.* 17 July 1821, BARON RAVENSWORTH of Ravensworth Castle, co. Durham. In that title this *Baronetcy* then *merged*, and still so continues, the 2d Baron being *cr.* 2 April 1874, EARL OF RAVENSWORTH. See *Peerage*.

LAWDAY, *or* LAWDEY:
cr. 9 Nov. 1642;(a)
ex. 1648.

I. 1642, to 1648. "RICHARD LAWDEY, of Exeter, co. Devon, Esq.," whose only connection with that county was through his marriage(b); was *cr. a Baronet*, as above, 9 Nov. 1642.(a) He was a Colonel in the King's service. He *m.* (—), widow of Nicholas MARTIN, of Exeter, da. of (—) SHEERS, with whom he had £3,000 or £4,000. He *d.*, s.p.m., being slain while in arms under the Earl of Worcester in Wales, in or shortly before Oct. 1648, when the *Baronetcy* presumably became *extinct*.(c) A sum of £800 together with his estate was sequestrated 1 Nov. 1648 for his delinquency. Will pr. 1648.

CHAMBERLAYNE, *or* CHAMBERLYNE:
cr. 4 Feb. 1642/3(a);
ex. 25 Jan. 1776.

I. 1643. "THOMAS CHAMBERLYNE, of Wickham, co. Oxford, Esq.," s. and h. of Sir Thomas CHAMBERLAYNE, one of the Justices of the Court of King's Bench, by his first wife Elizabeth, da. of Sir George FERMOR, of Easton Neston, Northants; suc. his father in Sep. 1625; was a Royalist, and was *cr. a Baronet*, as above, 4 Feb. 1642/3(a); Sheriff of Oxfordshire, 1643. He *m.* firstly, (—), da. of (—) ACLAND. He *m.* secondly, Anne, da. of Richard CHAMBERLAYNE, of Temple House, co. Warwick, and of the Court of Wards. He *d.* (during his Shrievalty and a few months after receiving his Baronetcy) 6 Oct. 1643.

II. 1643. SIR THOMAS CHAMBERLAYNE, Bart [1643], of Wickham aforesaid, and of Northbrooke, Oxon, 1st s. and h., *b.* probably about 1635; *suc. to the Baronetcy*, 6 Oct. 1643, but the title (one conferred after 4 Jan. 1641/2) being void under the Act of Parl. (4 Feb. 1651/2) then in force, he accepted another Baronetcy from "the Lord Protector," being by him *cr. a Baronet*, 6 Oct. 1657, under the designation of "Thomas Chamberlayne, of Wickham, *Esquire*." This creation became, of course, invalid after the Restoration. He *m.* (under the designation of "*Sir* Thomas,") 8 April 1657, at St. Dionis, Backchurch, London

(a) See p. 195, note "a," under "Wrottesley."
(b) Le Neve's MS. Baronetage.
(c) "Mr. William Lawday, sometime of Bath, in Somersetshire, living in 1822, claimed to be the immediate representative of the Baronet, but the title has lain dormant (if it did not then become extinct) since the decease of Sir Richard" [Burke's *Extinct Baronetage*.]

(Banns pub. at St. Dunstan's in the West), Margaret, da. of Edmund PRIDEAUX, of Ford Abbey, Devon, sometime (1649) Attorney General, by his second wife Margaret, da. of William IVERY, of Cotthay, Somerset. He *d.* s.p.m.(a) 1682. Will dat. 16 Sep. 1681, pr. 23 Nov. 1682.

III. 1682. SIR JAMES CHAMBERLAYNE, Bart. [1643], of Dunstew, Oxon, br. and h. male, *b.* probably about 1640; matric. at Oxford (Queen's Coll.), 15 June 1657; *suc. to the Baronetcy*, in 1682. He *m.* Margaret, da. of (—) GOODWIN, of Bodicote, Oxon. He *d.* Oct. 1694. Will pr. 1694.

IV. 1694. SIR JAMES CHAMBERLAYNE, Bart. [1643], of Dunstew aforesaid, s. and h.; *suc. to the Baronetcy*, in Oct. 1694; was sometime Lieut.-Col. in the Horse Guards. He *m.* 15 June 1725, at St. Paul's, Covent Garden, "Betty Clarke WALKER, of Little London, in Hillingdon, Midx., spinster," da. of (—) WALKER, Clerk to the House of Commons. She *d.* before him. He *d.* s.p.m., 23 Dec. 1767, and was *bur.* at Dunstew. Admon. 29 Jan. 1768, to his three daughters, and only issue.

V. 1767, to 1776. SIR HENRY CHAMBERLAYNE, Bart. [1643], br. and h. male; *suc. to the Baronetcy*, 23 Dec. 1767. He *d.* s.p. 25 Jan. 1776, and was *bur.* at Dunstew, when the *Baronetcy* became *extinct*.(b) Will pr. Feb. 1776.

HUNLOKE:
cr. 28 Feb. 1642/3;(c)
ex. 22 June 1856.

I. 1643. "HENRY HUNLOKE, of Wingerworth, co. Derby, Esq.," s. and h. of Henry HUNLOKE,(d) of the same, Sheriff of Derbyshire, 1624 (who *d.* when in office, 14 Aug. 1624), by his 2d wife, Anne, da. and h. of Richard ALVEY, of Corber, co. Derby, was *bap.* 28 Oct. 1618, at Wingerworth; admitted to Gray's Inn, 14 May 1636; suc. his father, 14 Aug. 1642; was in his 23d year, at the battle of Edgehill, 23 Oct. 1642, where he was severely wounded, and was *cr. a Baronet*, as above, 28 Feb. 1642/3,(c) being subsequently *Knighted* at Oxford, 2 March 1642/3.(e) He had levied a troop of horse for the King at his own expense whereof he was Colonel. His estates were sequestrated 18 Aug. 1646, and himself fined £1,458, and his house at Wingerworth was made into a garrison for the Parl. troops. He *m.* June 1644, at Worcester, Marina, sister of Thomas (WINDSOR, *formerly* HICKMAN), 1st EARL OF PLYMOUTH, da. of Dixie HICKMAN, of Kew, co. Surrey, by Elizabeth, da. of Henry (WINDSOR), LORD WINDSOR. He *d.* 13 and was *bur.* 14 Jan. 1647/8, at Wingerworth. Will pr. 15 Dec. 1648 and 30 May 1649. His widow *m.* 25 May 1653, at St. Andrew's Wardrobe, London, Col. William MICHELL, one of Cromwell's officers (through whose influence much of the Hunloke estate was spared from forfeiture), who was, in 1662, Dep. Gov. of Jamaica. She was *bur.* at Worcester, 7 Feb. 1669/70, aged 50. Will dat. 29 Jan. 1669, pr. 8 June, 1671.

(a) Of his two daughters and coheirs (1) Katharine, who inherited the estate of Wickham, became Viscountess Wenman [I.], and, subsequently, Countess of Abingdon; (2) Penelope, who inherited the estate of Northbrooke, *m.* Robert Dashwood, who was *cr. a Baronet*, in 1684, as "of Northbrooke."
(b) There was, however, a younger brother Thomas Chamberlayne, who is sometimes conjectured (though, apparently, in error), to have left male issue.
(c) See p. 195, note "a," under "Wrottesley."
(d) In J. J. Howard's *Catholic Families of England*, is a well worked up pedigree of Hunloke, from which this account is, mostly, compiled.
(e) The tradition that he was Knighted by the King on the battlefield of Edgehill, 22 Oct. 1642, seems groundless.

II. 1648. SIR HENRY HUNLOKE, Bart. [1643], of Wingerworth aforesaid (which estate he enjoyed 67 years), s. and h., *b.* 20 and *bap.* 21 Nov. 1645, at St. Michael's, Bedwardine, Worcester; *suc. to the Baronetcy*, when an infant, 13 Jan. 1647/8: admitted to Gray's Inn, 16 Dec. 1654, at 9 years of age; elected Sheriff of Derbyshire, Dec. 1687, but did not act. He *m.* 28 (settlement 27 Jan. 1673/4), Catharine, only da. and h. of Francis TYRWHITT, of Kettleby, co. Lincoln, by Elizabeth, da. and h. of Robert LLOYD, M.D. She was *b.* at Kettleby, 13 May 1657. He *d.* 3 and was *bur.* 5 Jan. 1714/5, at Wingerworth, in his 70th year. Will dat. 5 July 1711, pr. 8 Nov. 1715.

III. 1715. SIR THOMAS WINDSOR HUNLOKE, Bart. [1643], of Wingerworth aforesaid, only surv. s. and h., *b.* and *bap.* 10 Nov. 1684, at Wingerworth; *suc. to the Baronetcy*, 3 Jan. 1714/5. He pulled down the old mansion at Wingerworth, and erected a more stately one, on a hill adjoining, 1726-30. He *m.* 2 May (settlement 12 April) 1720, at Weston Underwood, Bucks, Charlotte, 5th da. of Sir Robert THROCKMORTON, 3d Bart. [1642], of Coughton, by Mary, da. of Sir Charles YATE, 3d Bart. [1622]. She *d.* at Wingerworth, 31 Dec. 1738, and was *bur.* there, 3 Jan. 1738/9, aged 38. He *d.* there 30 Jan. and was *bur.* 4 Feb. 1752, at Wingerworth, aged 68. Will dat. 13 March 1744, pr. 24 April 1752.

IV. 1752. SIR HENRY HUNLOKE, Bart. [1643], of Wingerworth aforesaid, s. and h., *b.* and *bap.* there, 25 March 1724; *suc. to the Baronetcy*, 30 Jan. 1752. He *m.* 21 Dec. 1769 (reg. at Holkham, co. Norfolk, and at Langford, co. Derby), Margaret, sister of Thomas William, 1st EARL OF LEICESTER, 1st da. of Wenman COKE, *formerly* ROBERTS, of Holkham and Langford aforesaid, by Elizabeth, da. and sole h. of George DENTON, *formerly* CHAMBERLAYNE, of Hillesden, Bucks, and of Wardington, Oxon. He *d.* 15 and was *bur.* 21 Nov. 1804, at Wingerworth, aged 81. Will dat. 6 Sep. 1799, pr. 28 July 1805. His widow *d.* 22 Jan. and was *bur.* 2 Feb. 1824, at Wingerworth, aged 69. Will pr. Nov. 1825.

V. 1804. SIR THOMAS WINDSOR HUNLOKE, Bart. [1643], of Wingerworth aforesaid, 1st s. and h., *b.* there 2 and *bap.* 3 March 1773; *suc. to the Baronetcy*, 15 Nov. 1804. He *m.* 18 Oct. 1807, Anne, sister and eventually coheir of Charles SCARISBRICK, *formerly* ECCLESTON, 1st da. of Thomas ECCLESTON, of Scarisbrick Hall, co. Lancaster, by Eleanor, da. of Thomas CLIFTON, of Lytham, in that county. He *d.* 19 Jan. 1816, of fever, at Paris, aged 42, and was *bur.* in the Eastern Cemetery there. Will dat. 16 Jan. 1816, pr. 18 July 1817. His widow, who was *b.* 15 March 1788, and who, by Royal lic. in 1860, took the name of *Scarisbrick* in lieu of *Hunloke*, *d.* at Scarisbrick Hall 6 and was *bur.* 13 March 1872, at Wingerworth, aged 83. Will dat. 4 June 1828.

VI. 1816. SIR HENRY JOHN JOSEPH HUNLOKE, Bart. [1643], of Wingerworth aforesaid, only s. and h., *b.* there 29 and *bap.* 30 Sep. 1812; *suc. to the Baronetcy*, 19 Jan. 1816. He *d.* unm.,(a) in Grafton street, 8 and was *bur.* 16 Feb. 1856, at Wingerworth, aged 43. Will pr. March 1856.

VII. 1856, Feb. to June. SIR JAMES HUNLOKE, Bart. [1643], of Birdholme, co. Derby, uncle and h. male, being 3d s. of the 4th Bart.; *b.* and *bap.* 5 July 1784, at Wingerworth; *suc. to the Baronetcy*, 8 Feb. 1856. He *d.* unm. a few months later, at Birdholme, 22 and was *bur.* 27 June 1856, at Wingerworth, aged 72, when the *Baronetcy* became *extinct.*(b) Will pr. Aug. 1856.

(a) Of his two sisters and coheirs (1) Charlotte *d.* unm. 16 May 1857, and (2) Eliza Margaret *m.* Leon Biodos, MARQUESS DE CASTEJA.

(b) The estates were inherited by the descendants of his sister Harriet, being the only one of the eight daughters of the 4th Baronet who left issue. She *m.* 29 April 1799, at Wingerworth, John Shelley-Sidney, and *d.* 5 Feb. 1811, aged 28, being mother of Philip Charles, 1st Baron De L'Isle and Dudley, so *cr.* 13 Jan. 1835.

BADD:

cr. 28 Feb. 1642/3;(a)

ex. 10 June 1683.

I. 1643, to 1683. "THOMAS BADD, of Cames Oyselle, co. Southampton, Esq.," son of "Emmanuel Bad, Esq.," who *d.* 18 Aug. 1632 and was *bur.* at Fareham, Hants, was *b.* about 1607, and was *cr. a Baronet*, as above, 28 Feb. 1642/3.(a) He was subsequently *Knighted* at Oxford, 5 March 1642/3; was a Royalist, and was fined £470 in Dec. 1647, being then styled "of Fareham." He *m.* in or before 1658 (—), possibly indeed he had previously married, before 1632, a wife, named Elizabeth (who was *bur.* at Fareham 11 Dec. 1634), and another wife before 1638.(b) He *d.* s.p.s., 10 June 1683, aged 76, and was *bur.* at Fareham, Hants, when the *Baronetcy* became *extinct.* His widow was *bur.* 2 June 1688, at Fareham aforesaid.

CRANE:

cr. 20 March 1642/3;(a)

ex. March 1644/5.

I. 1643, to 1645. "RICHARD CRANE, of Woodrising, co. Norfolk, Esq., one of the Gentlemen of the Privy Chamber," br. and h. of Sir Francis CRANE, Chancellor of the Order of the Garter, and Director of the Tapestry Works, at Mortlake, Surrey; suc. his said brother in the estate of Woodrising aforesaid, and in that of Stoke Nash, in Stoke Bruen, co. Northampton,(c) in June or July 1636, being then a Captain and a Gentleman of the Privy Chamber, and was *cr. a Baronet*, as above, 20 March 1642/3.(a) He *m.* firstly, Mary, da. of William (WIDDRINGTON), 1st BARON WIDDRINGTON OF BLANKNEY, by Mary, da. and h. of Sir Anthony THOROLD, of Blankney aforesaid. She *d.* s.p. He *m.* secondly, in 1639, Jane, widow of Jacob JAMES. He *d.* s.p. at Cardiff, March 1644/5, when the *Baronetcy* became *extinct.* Admon. 17 May 1648, and 10 March 1653/4, the will, dat. 20 Sep. 1643, being pr. 12 March 1655/6 (probably a mistake for 1654/5). The will of his widow, as "of Woodrising, Norfolk, dat. 9 March 1646/7, pr. 25 Feb. 1651/2.

DANVERS:

cr. 21 March 1642/3;(a)

ex. 20 Aug. 1776.

I. 1643. "SAMUEL DANVERS, of Culworth, co. Northampton, Esq.," 2d but 1st surv. s. and h. of Sir John DANVERS, of the same, by Dorothy, da. of Gabriel PULTENEY, of Misterton, co. Leicester, was *bap.* 29 Oct.

(a) See p. 195, note "a," under "Wrottesley."

(b) There are baptisms at Fareham, 8 April 1632, to 11 Aug. 1633, and again from 27 Dec. 1638, to 21 Aug. 1643, of children of "Mr. Thomas Badde," or "Thomas Badd, Esq.," and there is the burial, 11 Dec. 1634, of "Elizabeth, wife of Thomas Badde, Esq.," and, on 20 Oct. 1658, the baptism of Margaret, da. of "*Sir* Thomas Badd."

(c) See pedigree in Baker's *Northamptonshire*, vol ii, p. 243.

(d) There is a good pedigree of the Culworth branch of the Danvers family in Baker's *Northamptonshire*, vol. i, p. 605. See also F. N. Macnamara's *Danvers Family, of Dauntsey and Culworth.* London, 8vo, 1895.

1611, at Culworth; suc. his father (who *d.* aged 63), 17 Feb. 1641/2, and was *cr. a Baronet*, as above, 21 March 1642/3.(a) On 27 June 1644, the King slept at his house at Culworth, before the battle of Cropredy Bridge. He was Sheriff of Northamptonshire, 1648-49, the year the King was murdered, and appeared at the assizes with all his retinue clothed in black. He was a great sufferer during the Rebellion. He *m.* in 1634 (Lic. Oxford, she aged 18 and he 23), Anne, sister of Thomas, 2d EARL OF DOWNE [I.], da. of the Hon. Sir William POPE, of Wroxton, Oxon, by Elizabeth, da. of Sir Thomas WATSON, of Halstead, Kent. She was *bur.* 22 March 1677/8, at Culworth. He *d.* 27 and was *bur.* there 30 Jan. 1682/3, aged 73. M.I. Admon. 27 April 1683.

II. 1683. SIR POPE DANVERS, Bart. [1643], of Culworth aforesaid, 3d but only surv. s. and h., *bap.* 12 Dec. 1644, at Culworth; matric. at Oxford (Trin. Coll.), 12 Dec. 1661, aged 17; admitted to Middle Temple, 1664; *suc. to the Baronetcy*, 27 Jan. 1682/3. He *m.* Anne, da. and coheir of William BARKER, of Sunning, Berks, by Mary, da. of William BRIDEN, of Ipswich, merchant. He *d.* 4 and was *bur.* 6 May 1712, at Culworth, aged 68. M.I. Will pr. June 1712. His widow *d.* 16 and was *bur.* 18 May 1718, also at Culworth. Her will pr. 1718.

III. 1712. SIR JOHN DANVERS, Bart. [1643], of Culworth aforesaid, 3d but 1st surv. s. and h., *b.* at Sunning, Berks, 10 July 1673; birth reg. at Culworth; matric. at Oxford (St. John's Coll.), 23 Jan. 1691/2, aged 17; *suc. to the Baronetcy*, 4 May 1712. He *m.* firstly, Muriel, da. of Sir Robert LEYCESTER, 2d Bart. [1660] of Tabley, by Muriel, da. and h. of Francis WATSON, of Church Aston, Salop. She *d.* in childbirth, 22 Dec. 1701, aged 29, at Tabley aforesaid. He *m.* secondly, Susannah, eldest sister and coheir of Sir Edward NICHOLS, 3d Bart., da. of Sir Edward NICHOLS, 2d Bart. [1660], of Hardwick, by his 2d wife Jane, da. of Sir Stephen SOAME. This marriage was an unhappy one, and they were separated. She *d.* s.p. 17 June 1730, and was *bur.* at Faxton, co. Northampton. Will, leaving her estates to her nephew, John Nichols RAYNSFORD, pr. 1730. He *m.* thirdly, in or before 1731, Mary, da. of the Rev. John HUTCHINS, Rector of Eydon, co. Northampton (1692-1729). He *d.* 26 and was *bur.* 29 Sep. 1744, aged 71, at Culworth. M.I. Will dat. 1740, pr. 5 Oct. 1745, at Northampton, by the widow. She, who is said to have *m.* soon afterwards "a Villager of humble station," *d.* 4 Dec. 1784, aged 75, and was *bur.* at Culworth.

IV. 1744. SIR HENRY DANVERS, Bart. [1643], of Culworth aforesaid, s. and h. by 3d wife, *b.* 30 April and *bap.* 20 May 1731, at Culworth; ed. at Abingdon School; *suc. to the Baronetcy*, 26 Sep. 1744; matric. at Oxford (Linc. Coll.), 16 July 1748, aged 17. He *d.* unm. 10 and was *bur.* 13 Aug. 1753, at Culworth, aged 22. M.I.

V. 1753, to 1776. SIR MICHAEL DANVERS, Bart. [1643], of Culworth aforesaid, br. and h., *b.* 29 Sep. and *bap.* 22 Oct. 1738, at Culworth; ed. at Abingdon School; *suc. to the Baronetcy*, 10 Aug. 1753; matric. at Oxford (Linc. Coll.), 17 May 1757, aged 18; Sheriff of Northamptonshire, 1763-64. He *d.* unm. 20 and was *bur.* 26 Aug. 1776, at Culworth, when the *Baronetcy* became *extinct.* Will pr. 8 Feb. 1777.(b)

(a) See p. 195, note "a," under "Wrottesley."

(b) The estate passed to his sister, Meriel, who *d.* unm. 5 Nov. 1794, aged 60, having devised it to her two cousins, Martha and Frances, daughters and coheirs of Daniel RICH, by Martha, da. and coheir of her uncle Daniel Danvers, of Eydon. See Baker's *Northamptonshire*, vol. i, p. 605.

ANDERSON:

cr. 3 July 1643;(a)

ex. 16 Aug. 1699;

assumed from 1699 to 1741, or later.

I. 1643. "HENRY ANDERSON, of Penley [in the parish of Tring], co. Herts, Esq.," s. and h. of Sir Richard ANDERSON,(b) of the same, by Mary, da. of Robert (SPENCER), 1st BARON SPENCER OF WORMLEIGHTON, was *b.* about 1608; admitted to Lincoln's Inn, 18 Nov. 1628; suc. his father, 3 Aug. 1630, and was *cr. a Baronet*, as above, 3 July 1643.(a) He was a devoted Royalist,(c) and, as such, had to pay £2,810 to the sequestrators, besides other fines. He *m.* firstly (Lic. Fac. 18 Dec. 1632, he about 23), Jacomina, da. of Sir Charles CÆSAR, of Benington, Herts, Master of the Rolls, by his 1st wife, Anne, da. of Sir Peter VANLORE. She, who was *bap.* 10 Dec. 1615, at Benington, *d.* Oct. 1639, and was *bur.* at Tring. M.I. He *m.* secondly, Mary, said to be a da. of Sir William LYTTON. He *d.* 7 July 1653, aged 45, and was *bur.* at Tring. M.I. Will pr. 1659. His 2d wife survived him.

II. 1653, to 1699. SIR RICHARD ANDERSON, Bart. [1643], of Penley aforesaid, s. and h. by 1st wife, *b.* about 1635; *suc. to the Baronetcy*, 7 July 1653. He was a benefactor to the church of Tring. He *m.* firstly, Elizabeth, sister of the whole blood and coheir of George, VISCOUNT HEWETT OF GOWRAN [I.], da. of Sir William HEWETT, 1st Bart. [1660], of Pishiobury, Herts, by his 2d wife, Margaret, da. of Sir William LYTTON, of Knebworth. She *d.* 25 Dec. 1698, and was *bur.* at Albury, Herts. M.I. Will pr. 1698. He *m.* secondly, Mary, widow of Humphrey SIMPSON, da. of the Right Hon. John METHUEN, sometime Lord Chancellor of Ireland and Ambassador to Portugal, by Mary, da. of Seacole CHEVERS, of Comerford, Wilts. He *d.* s.p.m.s.,(d) 16 and was *bur.* 20 Aug. 1699, at Albury aforesaid, aged 64, when the *Baronetcy* became *extinct.* M.I. Admon. 1 Jan. 1699/700. Will dated 25 July 1699, pr. 5 March following. His widow *m.* Sir Brownlow SHERARD, 3d Bart. [1674], of Lopthorpe, co. Lincoln, who *d.* 30 Jan. 1736, aged 60.

III. 1699. "SIR RICHARD ANDERSON, Bart." [1643], of East Meon, Hants, calling himself "nephew to the said Sir Richard and grandson to Sir Henry, who was cr. a Baronet,"(e) is stated to have *suc. to* "*the title* but not to the estate."(e) His parentage is unknown. He *m.* Anne, da. of (—) ALDERSEY, of Faversham, Kent. He *d.* 1724.(e)

(a) Disallowed by Parl., 11 Nov. 1643, till the Restoration. See *Memorandum* as to creations after 4 Jan. 1641/2 and 22 May 1642, on p. 152. The patent is not enrolled. The date here given is that in Dugdale's *Catalogue.* See *Memorandum* on p. 84. The date of the "warrant for granting receipt for £1,095 to Henry Anderson, of Penley, co. Herts, Esq., on his creation, as Baronet" (Signet Bills) is 30 June 1643.

(b) This Richard was only surv. s. and h. of Sir Henry Anderson, of St. Olave's, Jewry, Alderman and sometime (1601-02), Sheriff of London, who *d.* 13 April 1605. See pedigree in Clutterbuck's *Herts*, vol. i, p. 285.

(c) On his monument it is tastefully said of him that he was "Regi dilectus, quem non, vel desertum, deseruit."

(d) Richard Anderson, his 2d s. but eventually (1677) h. ap., who was admitted to Lincoln's Inn, 10 Feb. 1675/6; was M.P. for Aylesbury, 1685-87; married, but *d.* v.p. and s.p., 1695. Elizabeth, his only da. by his 1st wife, *m.* (Lic. Fac. 3 Jan. 1677/8), Simon HARCOURT, Clerk of the Crown, by whom she had a son, Henry Harcourt, who inherited the Penley estate.

(e) See Wotton's *Baronetage* (1741), where the authority is given as "*Ex inform.* Dom. Ric. Anderson, Bar., 1724," to which, however, Wotton appends the following note:—"I don't yet find that Sir Richard [the 2d Baronet] above mentioned ever had a brother. Indeed, his father, Sir Henry [the 1st Baronet] had a brother

IV. 1724. "SIR KENDRICH ANDERSON, Bart." [1643], s. and h.,(a) *bap.* 5 July 1705, at Stifford, Essex. He *d.* unm. 10 Nov. 1735.(a)

V. 1735. "SIR RICHARD ANDERSON, Bart." [1643], br. and h. He d. s.p., "at the Black Horse Alehouse, Southwark,"(b) 18 Sep. 1738.(a) Will pr. 1739.

VI. 1738, to 1760? "SIR FRANCIS ANDERSON, Bart." [1643], called, in 1741, "the present Baronet,"(a) br. and h., who "was in foreign parts when his br. died."(b) After his death, at some date, presumably, before 1771, the *assumption of the Baronetcy* was, apparently, discontinued.(c)

VAVASOUR, *or* VAVASOR:

cr. 17 July 1643;(d)

ex. 18 Feb. 1659.

I. 1643, to 1659. "WILLIAM VAVASOR, of Yorkshire, Esq.," *i.e.*, of Copmanthorpe in that county, br. of Sir Charles VAVASOUR, Bart. (so *cr.* 22 June 1631), both being sons of Sir Thomas VAVASOUR, of Copmanthorpe aforesaid (*d.* Nov. 1620), by Mary, da. and h. of John DODGES, of Cope, co. York, was *cr. a Baronet*, as above, 17 July 1643.(d) He, who was a Royalist and banished from England in Dec. 1645, was a Major Gen. in the service of the King of Sweden. He *m.* firstly a Dutch lady. He *m.* secondly, in or before 1654, Olive, da. of Brian STAPLETON, *or* STAPYLTON, of Myton, co. York, by Frances, da. of Sir Henry SLINGSBY, of Scriven. He *d.* s.p.m.,(e) 18 Feb. 1658/9, when the *Baronetcy* became *extinct*. Admon. 11 March 1658/9, as "late of Medringham, co. Lincoln, but deceased at the siege of Copenhagen," to his widow. She, who was *b.* at Lacock Abbey, Wilts, 1620, *m.* Richard TOPHAM, of Westminster, and was *bur.* 26 Nov. 1714, at Chelsea.

Robert, of Chichester, from whence some have imagined *this* Sir Richard descended, but then he could not be a Baronet, unless [there was] a particular limitation in the patent," but as Sir Richard, of East Meon, and his sons have been deemed Baronets, and as I know nothing certain to the contrary, I have inserted the account of them." There is, however, no reason to suppose that there was any special limitation in this creation.

(a) See p. 211, note "e."

(b) MSS. additions [*Qy.* in Brooke's writing ?] to the copy of Wotton's *Baronetage*, in the Editor's possession.

(c) No mention is made of this Baronetcy in Kimber's *Baronetage* (1771).

(d) Disallowed by Parl., till the Restoration. See *Memorandum* as to creations after 4 Jan. 1641/2 and 22 May 1642 on p. 152. No patent is enrolled. The date of "July 1643" (between 3 and 25 July) is in Dugdale's *Catalogue*, and the date "17 July 1643" is that of the docquet in Black's *Docquets*. See *Memorandum* on p. 84.

(e) Frances, his only da. and h. (by 2d wife), *b.* 26 Oct. 1654 in Drury Lane, *m.* firstly, Sir Thomas Norcliffe, and secondly, Moses Goodyere, and was *bur.* at Chelsea, 16 Dec. 1731, leaving issue.

JONES:

cr. 25 July 1643;(a)

ex. in or before May 1644.

I. 1643, to 1644? "HENRY JONES, of Abermarles, co. Caermarthen, Knt.," only s. and h. of Sir Henry(b) JONES, of the same, by his 1st wife, Elizabeth, sister of Edward, 1st BARON HERBERT OF CHERBURY, da. of Richard HERBERT, of Montgomery, was Sheriff of Carmarthenshire, 1638-39; suc. his father in or shortly before 1641; was *Knighted* 7 Sep. 1642, at Caermarthen, and was *cr. a Baronet*, as above, 25 July 1643.(a) He *m.* Margaret, da. of Sir Henry WILLIAMS, of Gwernevet, co. Brecon, by Eleanor (living Aug. 1642), da. of Eustace WHITNEY. He *d.* s.p.m.,(c) in or before May 1644, when the *Baronetcy* became *extinct*. Will dat. 15 Aug. 1642, desiring to be *bur.* at Llansadorn, or at Aberllyney, co. Brecon: Inventory of goods dat. 31 May 1644. Probate renounced by the widow 29 July, and will pr. 6 Dec. 1644 at Carmarthen.

WALDEGRAVE:

cr. 1 Aug. 1643;(d)

afterwards, since 1686, BARONS WALDEGRAVE OF CHEWTON;

and subsequently, since 1729, EARLS WALDEGRAVE.

I. 1643. "EDWARD WALDEGRAVE, of Hever Castle, co. Kent, Knt.," being also of Staininghall, co. Norfolk, and of Chewton, co. Somerset, s. and h. of Charles WALDEGRAVE, of Staininghall and Chewton aforesaid, by Jeronyma, da. of Sir Henry JERNINGHAM, of Cossey Hall, co. Norfolk, was *b.* about 1568; was, possibly, M.P. for Sudbury, 1584-85; was *Knighted*, 19 July 1607, at Greenwich, and was *cr. a Baronet*, as above, 1 Aug. 1643.(d) Though aged above 70 at the breaking out of the Civil War, he commanded a Regiment of Horse, with which he did great service against the Parliamentary troops in Cornwall and elsewhere. He lost two sons in the Royal cause, is said to have lost £50,000 therein, and was, 7 Sep. 1647, named by the Parliamentary party among those to be removed from the King's Council and to be made incapable of any appointment. He *m.* in or before 1598, Eleanor, sister and heir of Sir Francis LOVELL, da. of Sir Thomas LOVELL, both of Harling, co. Norfolk. She *d.* 12 Dec. 1604. He survived her more than 43 years.

II. 1650? SIR HENRY WALDEGRAVE, Bart. [1643], of Staininghall and Chewton aforesaid, s. and h., *b.* 1598; *suc. to the Baronetcy*, on the death of his father. He *m.* firstly Anne, da. of Edward PASTON, of Appleton, and by her had eleven children. He *m.* secondly, Catharine, da. of Richard BACON, and by her had twelve more children. He *d.* 10 Oct. 1658, aged 60, and was *bur.* in Cossey church, co. Norfolk. M.I. The will of his widow pr. 1695.

(a) Disallowed by Parl. till the Restoration. See *Memorandum* as to creations after 4 Jan. 1641/2, and 22 May 1642, on p. 152. No patent is enrolled. The date here given is that in Dugdale's *Catalogue*. See *Memorandum*, on p. 84. The date of the signet bill is 24 July 1643.

(b) This Henry, who matric. at Oxford (Jesus Coll.), 28 April 1598, aged 16; was admitted to Lincoln's Inn, 28 Oct. 1599, became a Barrister in 1605, and whose will was proved at Carmarthen 1640-41, was s. and h. of Sir Thomas Jones, of Abermarles (*d.* 1604), by Jane, da. of Rowland PULESTON, of Carnarvon. [*Ex inform.* W. D. Pink, who has supplied many other particulars in the above account, correcting that generally received, as also the suggestion (*N. and Q.*, 1st S., xi, 38) that there were two Baronets, each named Henry.]

(c) Elizabeth, his 2d and yst. da., and eventually sole heir (a minor in 1642), *m.*, in 1665, Sir Francis Cornwallis, who thus became of Abermarles. He was *bur.* 4 Sep. 1675, at St. Giles' in the Fields, leaving issue.

(d) Disallowed by Parl., till the Restoration. See *Memorandum* as to creations after 4 Jan. 1641/2 and 22 May 1642 on p. 152. No patent is enrolled. The date here given for the patent is that in Dugdale's *Catalogue*, but (oddly enough) the *same* date is assigned to the docquet in Black's *Docquets*. See *Memorandum* on p. 84.

III. 1658. SIR CHARLES WALDEGRAVE, Bart. [1643], s. and h.; *suc. to the Baronetcy*, 10 Oct. 1658.(a). He *m.* Helen, da. of Sir Francis ENGLEFIELD, 2d Bart. [1611], by Winifred, da. and coheir of William BROOKSBY. He *d.*, in or before 1684. Will pr. 1684.

IV. 1684? SIR HENRY WALDEGRAVE, Bart. [1643], of Chewton, Navestock, and Staininghall aforesaid, 1st s. and h.; *suc. to the Baronetcy*, about 1684. Having *m.*, 29 Nov. 1683, Henrietta FITZJAMES, spinster, illegit. da. of **James II,** by Arabella CHURCHILL, spinster (sister of John, the famous DUKE OF MARLBOROUGH), he was, by that King (in his said wife's lifetime), *cr.* 20 Jan. 1685/6, BARON WALDEGRAVE OF CHEWTON, co. Somerset, in which peerage this *Baronetcy* then *merged* and so continues, the 2d Baron and 5th Baronet being *cr.*, 13 Sep. 1729, EARL WALDEGRAVE. See *Peerage*.

PATE:

cr. 28 Oct. 1643;(b)

ex. 5 Sep. 1659.

I. 1643, to 1659. "JOHN PATE, of Sysonby, co. Leicester, Esq.," 2d s. of Edward PATE, of Eye Kettleby, was Sheriff of Leicestershire, 1640-41, and was *cr. a Baronet*, as above, 28 Oct. 1643.(b) He was a zealous Royalist and was fined £523 in Oct. 1649; increased to £4,316 but reduced, in 1651, to £1,520. He *m.* firstly, Elizabeth, da. of Sir William SKIPWITH, of Cotes, co. Leicester. She *d.* 17 Aug. 1628, aged 37. He *m.* secondly, Lettice, widow of Francis BRADSHAW, of Derbyshire, 1st da. of Sir Thomas DILKE, of Maxstoke Castle, co. Warwick. She *d.* before him. Admon. as "of Ham, co. Surrey," 15 Jan. 1658/9. He *d.* s.p.m., and was *bur.* from St. Martin's in the Fields, at St. Giles' in the Fields, 5 Sep. 1659, when the *Baronetcy* became *extinct*. Admon., as of Ham aforesaid, 20 Sep. 1659, to his daughters Abigail Smyth and Frances Carrington, *alias* Smyth.

BALE:

cr. 9 Nov. 1643;(c)

ex. shortly before 1654.

I. 1643, to 1653? "JOHN BALE, of Carlton Curlieu, co. Leicester, Esq.," s. and h. ap. of Sir John BALE, of the same, and of Sadington in that county (Sheriff of Leicestershire, 1624, living 1652), by his 1st wife, Emma, da. of William HALFORD, of Welham, co. Leicester, was *b.* about 1617; was a stedfast Royalist, his house at Carlton being made a garrison for that cause; was one of the King's Commissioners of Array in June 1642, and was *cr. a Baronet*, as above, 9 Nov. 1643.(c) He is said to have been heavily fined. He *m.* in or shortly after 1651, Jane,(d) last surv. child of Sir Thomas PUCKERING, Bart.

(a) Imhoff (*Genealogy of Great Britain*, 1690, p. 234), speaking of the Peerage conferred on his son, writes, "Patre natus est Medico Primario Regis Jacobi II," etc. The person, however, here alluded to was not this Sir *Charles* Waldegrave, but Sir *William* Waldegrave, probably a son of Philip Waldegrave, of Borley, co. Essex. He was a doctor of medicine at Padua 12 March 1659, and was, by James II., constituted, in 1686, a Fellow of the Coll. of Physicians of London. His will was pr. June 1702.

(b) See p. 213, note "c," under "WALDEGRAVE."

(c) Disallowed by Parl. 11 Nov. 1643 (being only two days after its creation) till the Restoration. See *Memorandum* as to creations after 4 Jan. 1641/2, and 22 May 1642, on p. 152. No patent is enrolled. The date here given is that in Dugdale's *Catalogue*. See *Memorandum*, on p. 84. The date of the signet bill is 2 Nov. 1643.

(d) She had previously been abducted, 26 Sep. 1649, from Greenwich, and married under compulsion at Dunkirk, but this marriage was set aside in 1651. [Drake's *Hasted's Kent*, vol. i, p. 121].

[so. *cr.* 1611], by Elizabeth, da. of Sir John MORLEY. She *d.* in childbirth, 27 Jan. 1651/2, aged about 24. Admon., as of St. Martin's in the Fields, 10 Feb. 1651/2, to her husband. He *d.* shortly afterwards, before 1654,(a) when the *Baronetcy* became *extinct*.

O'NEILL, *or* O'NEALE:

cr.(b) 13 Nov. 1643;(c)

dormant, since 1799.

I. 1643. "BRIAN O'NEALE, of Dublin, Esq.," s. of Owen O'NEIL(d) (who was 5th in descent from Henry Caoch O'NEIL, 2d s. of Murtagh Ceanfadda, Chief of the Claneboys) served in Holland, under the Prince of Orange, serving afterwards in England on the Royalist side; was taken prisoner by the Scots at Newburn, and was, in consideration of his gallant services to the Royal side at the battle of Edgehill, *cr. a Baronet*,(b) as above, 13 Nov. 1643.(c) He *m.* firstly, Jane, da. of (—) FINCH. He *m.* secondly, Sarah, 1st da. of Patrick SAVAGE, of Portaferry, co. Down, by Jeane, da. of Hugh (MONTGOMERY), 1st VISCOUNT MONTGOMERY OF THE GREAT ARDS [I.] His will as "of Backerstown, co. Dublin, Knt. and Bart.," dat. 8 Oct. 1670, pr. the same year in Prerog. Court [I.]. His widow *m.* (Lic. Dublin, 1 Dec. 1671), Richard RICH.

II. 1670. SIR BRIAN O'NEALE, *or* O'NEILL, Bart. [1643], of Backerstown aforesaid, s. an h., by 1st wife; admitted to Gray's Inn, 30 June 1664; *suc. to the Baronetcy*, 1670; was one of the Justices of the Court of King's Bench in Ireland, 26 Jan. 1686/7, to 3 Nov. 1690. He was an adherent of James II, and, as such, suffered great loss of estate. He *m.*, in or before 1674, Mary, widow of James WOLVERSTON, of Stillorgan, co. Dublin, sister to Christopher, BARON DUNSANY [I.], da. of Hon. Edward PLUNKETT, by Catharine, da. of Randal (MCDONNELL), 1st EARL OF ANTRIM [I.]. He *d.* 1694. The will of his widow pr. 1699 in Prerog. Court [I.]

III. 1694. SIR HENRY O'NEILL, Bart. [1643], of Kellystown, near Drogheda, co. Meath, s. and h., *b.* about 1674; *suc. to the Baronetcy*, in 1694. He *m.* firstly, Mary, da. of Mark BAGOT, of Mount Arran, co. Carlow, by [presumably] Mary, relict of Sir Daniell O'NEILL, 3d Bart. [I. 1666], 1st da. of Sir Gregory BYRNE, 1st Bart. [I. 1671], by Margaret, da. and coheir of Col. Christopher COPLEY, of Wadworth, co. York. She *d.* intestate. Admon. 12 April 1715, in Prerog. Court [I.]. He *m.* secondly, Rose (*b.* 23 Aug. 1688), 2d da. of Capt. James BRABAZON,(e) by Mary, da. of Dudley COLLEY, of Castle Carbery, co. Kildare. He *d.* 1 Nov. 1759, "near Drogheda," aged 85, and was *bur.* in the old church at Mount Newton. Will dat. 22 Dec. 1755 (codicil unproved dat. 11 June 1756), pr. 31 Oct. 1760, in the diocese of Meath, by Rose O'Neill, the widow.

IV. 1759. SIR BRIAN O'NEILL, Bart. [1643], of Kellystown aforesaid, 1st surv. s. and h.,(f) by first wife; *suc. to the Baronetcy*, 1 Nov. 1759. He *d.* s.p.m.

(a) In 1654 his estates were purchased by Sir Geoffrey Palmer, 1st Bart. [1660].

(b) This creation is *subsequent* to the Act of Parl., 11 Nov. 1643, by which all creations conferred by the King after 22 May 1642 were disallowed. See *Memorandum* as to creations after 4 Jan. 1641/2, and 22 May 1642, on p. 152.

(c) No patent is enrolled. The date here given is that in Dugdale's *Catalogue* as to which see the *Memorandum* on p. 84. The date of the warrant is 9 Nov. 1643.

(d) The principal information as to this family has been kindly furnished by G. D. Burtchaell, of the Office of Arms, Dublin. In Burke's *Vicissitudes of Families* (1st series, pp. 149-161), is an account of these Baronets, brought down, presumably, to the date (1859) of that work. The exact date could, probably, be ascertained, as it is therein mentioned that Sergeant-Major Bryan O'Neill (youngest son of "Sir Francis O'Neill the 6th [*sic*] Baronet") was "now in his 75th year."

(e) This James was 6th s. of James Brabazon, 2d s. of the Hon. Sir Anthony Brabazon, the 3d s. of Edward, 1st Baron Brabazon of Ardee [I.]

(f) The sole authority for the existence and succession of this Brian is a pedigree in Ulster Office. No such son, however, is mentioned in the third Baronet's will, and it has been conjectured that, even if he ever existed, he *d.* v.p. and s.p.

V. 1765? Sir Randall O'Neill, Bart. [1643], of Kellystown aforesaid, br. of the whole blood and h.(a); *suc. to the Baronetcy*, about 1765; was a Surveyor of Excise at Rush, co. Dublin, and is called(b) "M.D." He *m.* about 1750, "Margaret Thompkims, a lady of English extraction."(a) He *d.* at Rush, June 1779.

VI. 1779. Sir William O'Neill, Bart. [1643], of Kellystown aforesaid, only s. and h ; *b.* about 1754 ;(a) *suc. to the Baronetcy*, in June 1779. He *d.* s.p.m. at Rush, March 1784.

VII. 1784, to 1799. Sir Francis O'Neill, Bart. [1643], of Kellystown aforesaid, uncle (of the half blood) and h. male, being 6th and yst. s. of the 3d Bart. by his 2d wife. He was *b.* probably about 1730, and *suc. to the Baronetcy* in March 1784. He was ejected from his property under the *Popery Acts*, and after renting two small farms near Kellystown, kept "a small huckster's shop and dairy" at Slane.(c) He *m.* (—), da. of (—) Fleming, of co. Louth, by whom he had fourteen or fifteen children. He was in possession of the patent of Baronetcy in 1798, but *d.* 1799, being *bur.* (with his father) at Mount Newton. His widow *d.* eighteen months later. Since his death the *Baronetcy* has remained *dormant*.(d)

HICKMAN:

cr. 16 Nov. 1643 ;(e)

ex. March 1781.

I. 1643. "Willoughby Hickman, of Gaynsborough, co. Lincoln, Esq.," s. and h. of Sir William Hickman, of the same, by his 2d wife Elizabeth, sister of William, 3d Baron Willoughby of Parham, da. of Hon. William Willoughby, by Elizabeth, da. and h. of Sir Christopher Hildyard, was *b.* 25 May and *bap.* 3 June 1604, at Gainsborough; suc. his father, 25 Sep. 1625. and, in consideration of his fidelity to Charles I, was *cr. a Baronet*, as above, 16 Nov. 1643.(e) He was fined £1,100 in March 1646. He *m.* in or before 1628, Bridget, 1st da. of Sir John Thornhaugh, of Fenton, Notts, by (—), da. of Francis Rodes, of Staveley Woodthorpe, Notts, Justice of the Common Pleas. He *d.* 28 May 1650. His widow *d.* 14 March 1682/3, in her 77th year. Both were *bur.* at Gainsborough. M.I.

II. 1650. Sir William Hickman, Bart. [1643], of Gainsborough aforesaid, only s. and h., *bap.* there 8 Jan. 1628/9; *suc. to the Baronetcy*, 28 May 1650. He was Sheriff of Notts, 1653-54; M.P. for East Retford (five Parls.), 1660-81. He *m.*, about 1652, Elizabeth, da. and h. of John Nevile, of Mattersly, Notts. He was *bur.* 10 Feb. 1681/2,(f) and his widow 24 Nov. 1691, at Gainsborough. His will pr. 1682.

(a) Kimber's *Baronetage* [1771].

(b) "The Freeman's Journal" [June 1779].

(c) The information about this Baronet and his issue is entirely from Burke's *Vicissitudes* [1859]. See p. 215, note "d."

(d) The eldest son, Henry, was last heard of in 1798, being then in a Spanish Regiment. Francis O'Neill, 1st s. of John, the second son, was [1859 ?] a working millwright in Drogheda. James, another son of Sir Francis, was a working baker in Dublin, and *d.* about 1800. Bryan, the yst. and only surv. son, was *b.* in Kellystown; was Sergeant-Major in the Army, 1813-1830, and Chief Officer of the Newgate Guards, Dublin, 1830-1836; was living [1859 ?] at the age of 75 in Dublin, with his eldest son, Francis O'Neill, a coffin maker. In Burke's *Extinct Baronetage* [1844], it is said that "One of the sons of Sir Francis was employed about twenty-five years ago at a small Inn near Duleek in the capacity of boots and ostler."

(e) See p. 215, note "b," under O'Neill. No patent is enrolled. The date here given is that in Dugdale's *Catalogue*, as to which see *Memorandum* on p. 84. The date of the warrant is 11 Nov. 1643.

(f) In Sir Joseph Williamson's *Lincolnshire Families, temp. Charles II*, he is thus noticed "Sir Wm. Hickman, of Gainsborough, ye best of his estate [is] in his dues upon ye faires kept there; about £800 per annum, not more; but a late family." [*Her. and Gen.*, vol. ii, p. 122].

III. 1682. Sir Willoughby Hickman, Bart. [1643], of Gainsborough aforesaid, 1st surv. s. and h., *bap.* there 29 Aug. 1659; was M.P. for Kingston-on-Hull, 1685-87; for East Retford (three Parls.), 1698-1705, and for Lincolnshire (two Parls.), 1713 till death; *suc. to the Baronetcy*, 10 Feb. 1681/2. He *m.* (Lic. Vic. Gen., 8 Sep. 1683, he 24 and she 17), Anne, da. of Sir Stephen Anderson, 1st Bart. [1664] of Eyworth, Beds, by his 1st wife Mary, da. of Sir John Glynne. She was *bur.* 15 May 1701, at Gainsborough. He *d.* 28 and was *bur.* 31 Oct. 1720, also at Gainsborough. Will pr. 1721.

IV. 1720. Sir Nevile Hickman, Bart. [1643], of Gainsborough aforesaid, 1st surv. s. and h., *bap.* there 13 May 1701; *suc. to the Baronetcy*, 31 Oct. 1720. He *m.* about 1722, Frances, da. of Edward Hall, said to be one of the family of Hall, of Gretfold, co. Lincoln. He *d.* June 1733. His widow *m.* Feb. 1737, as his 2d wife, Sir Francis Whichcote, 3d Bart. [1660], who *d.* at Grantham, 27 Oct. 1775.

V. 1733, to 1781. Sir Nevile George Hickman, Bart. [1643], of Thonock Grove, near Gainsborough, only surv. s. and h.; *suc. to the Baronetcy* when a minor, June 1733. He *m.* 13 Sep. 1746, Frances Elizabeth, da. of Christopher Tower, of co. Essex. Her admon. 17 Dec. 1772. He *d.* s.p.m., March 1781, when the *Baronetcy* became *extinct*. Will pr. May 1781.

BOTELER:

cr. 7 Dec. 1643 ;(a)

ex. 25 June 1657.

I. 1643, to 1657. "George Boteler, of Bromfeild [*i.e.*, Brantfield], co. Hertford, Esq.," yr. br. of the half blood to John, 1st Baron Boteler of Brantfield, being 5th s. of Sir Henry Boteler, of Hatfield Woodhall, Herts, and of Brantfield aforesaid, and 4th s. by the 2d wife, Alice, da. of Edward Pulter, was *b.* about 1583; and was *cr. a Baronet*, as above, 7 Dec. 1643(a); was a Royalist, and was fined £569 on 13 June 1648, being then "of Ellerton, co. York." He *m.* Jane, widow of Sir Hugh Bethell, of Ellerton aforesaid (*d.* 1611), da. of Thomas Young, Archbishop of York. He *d.* s.p. and was *bur.* 25 June 1657, at Tewin, Herts, aged 74, when the *Baronetcy* became *extinct*. Will pr. 1657.

ACTON:

cr. 17 Jan. 1643/4 ;(b)

afterwards, since 1833, Dalberg-Acton;

subsequently, since 1869, Barons Acton of Aldenham.

I. 1644. "Edward Acton, of Aldenham [*i.e.*, Aldenham Hall, in Morville], co. Salop, Esq.," being also of Acton Scott, in that county, s. and h. of Walter Acton, of Aldenham Hall aforesaid, by Frances, da. and h. of Edward Acton, of Acton Scott abovenamed, was *bap.* 20 July 1600; was M.P. for Bridgnorth, April to May 1640 and Nov. 1640 till disabled, 5 Feb. 1643/4; sat in the Oxford Parl., and, on account of his loyal service to his King, was *cr. a Baronet*, as above, 17 Jan. 1643/4.(b) He was fined £5,242 in Feb. 1647, reduced to £2,000 in

(a) See p. 215, note "b," under O'Neill. No patent is enrolled. The date here given is that in Dugdale's *Catalogue* (as to which, see *Memorandum* on p. 84), where, however, the grantee is erroneously called "John [*sic*] Butler." The date of the warrant is 30 Nov. 1643.

(b) See p. 215, note "b," under O'Neill. No patent is enrolled. The date (presumably that of the patent) here given is that in Dugdale's *Catalogue*, but the same date is assigned to the docquet in Black's *Docquets*. See *Memorandum* on p. 84.

July 1649. He *m.* Sarah, da. of Richard Mytton, of Halston, Salop, by Margaret, da. of Thomas Owen, one of the Justices of the King's Bench. He was *bur.* 29 June 1659, aged 59. Will dat. 20 March 1651, pr. 20 Dec. 1659, by his widow. She *d.* 13 Sep. 1677.

II. 1659. Sir Walter Acton, Bart. [1644], of Aldenham Hall and Acton Scott aforesaid, s. and h, *b* about 1620; *suc. to the Baronetcy*, 29 June 1659; M.P. for Bridgnorth, 1660. He *m.* Catharine, da. of Richard Cressett,(a) of Upton Cressett and Cound, Salop. He *d.* 1665, aged 44. The will of his widow pr. Dec. 1691.

III. 1665. Sir Edward Acton, Bart. [1644], of Aldenham Hall and Acton Scott aforesaid, s. and h., *b.* about 1650(b); *suc. to the Baronetcy*, 1665; matric. at Oxford (Queen's Coll.), 4 May 1666, aged 16; *cr.* M.A., 23 April 1667; Sheriff of Salop, 1684-85; M.P., for Bridgnorth (seven Parls.), 1698-1705; Recorder of Bridgnorth, 1701. He *m.* Mary, da. and h. of (—) Walter, of Somerset. He *d.* 28 Sep. 1716 aged 66, and was *bur.* (as was his wife) at Morville. Will dat. 28 Sep. 1714, pr. 31 Oct. 1716.

IV. 1716. Sir Whitmore Acton, Bart. [1644], of Aldenham Hall and Acton Scott aforesaid, s. and h., *b.* about 1674; matric. at Oxford (St. Edmund's Hall), 14 Feb. 1694/5, aged 17; admitted to Middle Temple, 1698; M.P. for Bridgnorth, v.p., 1710-13; *suc. to the Baronetcy*, 28 Sep. 1716; Sheriff of Salop, 1727-28. He *m.* Elizabeth, da. of Matthew Gibbon, of Westcliffe, Kent, and of Putney, Surrey, by Hester, his wife. He *d.* 8 Jan. 1731/2, aged 56, and was *bur.* at Morville. Will dat. 19 Dec. 1731, pr. 27 March 1732. His wife, who was *bap.* 2 Jan. 1680, at St. Andrew's Undershaft, London, survived him.

V. 1732. Sir Richard Acton, Bart. [1644], of Aldenham Hall and Acton aforesaid, s. and h., *b.* 1 Jan. 1711/2; *suc. to the Baronetcy*, 8 Jan. 1731/2; Sheriff of Salop, 1751-52. He *m.* 21 Sep. 1744, Anne, da. of Henry (Grey), 3d Earl of Stamford, by Dorothy, da. of Sir Nathan Wright, Lord Keeper of the Great Seal. She *d.* at Worcester, and was *bur.* at Acton. He *d.* at Aldenham, s.p.m.,(c) 20 Nov. 1791, and was *bur.* at Acton. Will pr. May 1792.

VI. 1791. Sir John-Francis-Edward Acton, Bart. [1644], cousin and h. male, being s. and h. of Edward Acton, of Besançon, in Burgundy, by Catharine, da. of Francis-Loijs de Grey, also of Burgundy, which Edward was s. and h. of Edward Acton, of Birchin lane, London, goldsmith and banker, s. and h. of Walter Acton, of London, goldsmith and mercer, who was 2d s. of the 2d Bart. He was *bap.* 3 June 1736, and served under the King of the Two Sicilies, being Commander-in-Chief of the Land and Sea Forces of Naples, and for several years Prime Minister there. He *suc. to the Baronetcy*, 20 Nov. 1791, and after the death of his cousin, Mrs. Langdale, the da. and h. of the late Baronet (under his will) to the whole of the family estates, of which (under the said will) he had obtained a portion in her lifetime. In 1796 or 1800, at the mature of age of 60

(a) Richard Crescett, aged 52 in the Visit. of co. Stafford in 1663, is there stated to have *m.* Jane, da. of John Huxley, and to have had two sons. No daughters, however, are mentioned.

(b) He and his six brothers averaged 6 feet 2 inches each in height. He rebuilt, with stone, the family mansion at Aldenham, which is said in Wotton's *Baronetage* (1741) to be "perhaps the best house in the county" [of Shropshire], and "with a fine park adjoining."

(c) He devised his estates after the death without issue of his only surv. child Elizabeth, wife of Philip Langdale, to his cousin and successor in the Baronetcy, in tail male, who inherited accordingly.

or 64, having procured a dispensation from the Pope, the marriage ceremony(a) was performed between him and one of his nieces, then aged 14 or 18, viz., Mary-Anne, 1st da. of his br. Joseph-Edward Acton, Lieut. Gen. in the service of the said King of the Two Sicilies, by Eleanora, Countess Berg de Trips of Dusseldorf, in Germany. He *d.* at Palermo, 12 Aug. 1811, aged 75. Will pr. 1811. His widow *d.* (sixty-two years afterwards) 18 March 1873.(b)

VII. 1811. Sir Ferdinand-Richard-Edward Acton, *afterwards*, (since 1833), Dalberg-Acton, Bart. [1644], of Aldenham Hall and Acton aforesaid, s. and h., *b.* 24 July 1801; and *suc. to the Baronetcy*, 12 Aug. 1811. He, having *m.* at Paris, 9 July 1832, Marie-Louise-Pelline, only da. and h. of Emeric-Joseph, Duke of Dalberg, in France, took by royal lic., 20 Dec. 1833, the surname of Dalberg before that of Acton. He *d.* 31 Jan. 1837. His widow *m.*, at the Spanish chapel and afterwards in Devonshire House, Piccadilly (as his first wife), 25 July 1840, George Granville (Leveson-Gower), 2d Earl Granville, who *d.* 31 March 1891, aged 75. She *d.* 14 March 1860, aged 48, at Brighton.

VIII. 1837. Sir John-Emerich-Edward Dalberg-Acton, Bart. [1644], of Aldenham Park and Acton aforesaid, only s. and h., *b.* 10 Jan. 1834, at Naples; *suc. to the Baronetcy*, 31 Jan. 1837; ed. at the Roman Catholic Coll. at Oscott; M.P. for Carlow, 1859-65, and for Bridgnorth, 1865-66. He *m.* 1 Aug. 1865, the Countess Marie Arco-Valley, da. of Maximilian Arco-Valley, of Austria and Bavaria, by Anne (*née*) Countess Marescalchi. She was living when he was *cr.*, 11 Dec. 1869, BARON ACTON OF ALDENHAM, co. Salop. In that title this *Baronetcy* then *merged*, and so continues. See *Peerage*.

HAWLEY:

cr. 14 March 1643/4 ;(c)

afterwards, 1645-1790, Barons Hawley of Donamore [I.];

ex. 19 Dec. 1790.

I. 1644. "Francis Hawley, of Buckland, co. Somerset, Knt.," 2d s. of Sir Henry Hawley, of Wiveliscombe, in that county, by Elizabeth, da. of Sir Anthony Paulett, was *b.* about 1608; distinguished himself in the Royal cause, for which he raised a troop of horse in 1642, and, having been *Knighted*,(d) was *cr. a Baronet*, as above, 14 March 1643/4.(c) He *m.* Jane, da. of Sir Ralph Gibbes, of Honington, co. Warwick, by Gertrude, da. of Sir Thomas Wroughton. She *d.* before him, possibly before he was *cr.* 8 July 1645, LORD HAWLEY, BARON OF DONAMORE, co. Meath [I.] In that peerage this *Baronetcy* then *merged*, till both became *extinct*, by the death of the 4th Baron and Baronet, 19 Dec. 1790. See *Peerage*.

(a) This marriage, which was "*voidable*," became eventually valid (having never been set aside by the Ecclesiastical Court of England, during the lifetime of both the parties), under (Lord Lyndhurst's) Act of Parliament, which confirmed all marriages, incestuous or otherwise, made before 31 Aug. 1835, where one, or both of the parties, were dead before that date. See "Hubback's Evidence of Succession," edit. 1844.

(b) Their 2d s., Charles-Januarius-Edward Acton, *b.* 6 March 1803, became a Cardinal, 24 Jan. 1842, and *d.* 27 June 1847.

(c) See p. 217, note "b," under "Acton."

(d) His Knighthood was recognised by Parl. when he "compounded" in 1645, and so was probably (not, however, certainly) conferred before the Civil War.

PRESTON:

cr. 1 April 1644;(a)

ex. 27 May 1709.

I. 1644. "JOHN PRESTON, of the manor of Furnese, co. Lancaster, Esq.," being also of Preston Patrick and Under Levins, co. Westmorland, 2d but only surv. s. and h. of John PRESTON, of the same (admitted to Gray's Inn, 2 Feb. 1590/1), by Elizabeth, da. and coheir of Richard HOLLAND, of Denton, co. Lancaster, was *b.* 1617; suc. his father in or shortly after Sep. 1642, and, having distinguished himself in the Royal cause, was *cr. a Baronet*, as above, 1 April 1644.(a) His estates were forfeited, as "a Papist in arms," and given to John Pym's children. He *m.* in or before 1640, Jane, da. and coheir of Thomas MORGAN, of Weston-sub-Weathley, co. Warwick, and of Heyford Hall, co. Northampton (slain at Newbury, 20 Sep. 1643), by Jane, da. of Sir Richard FERMOR, of Somerton, Oxon. He was mortally wounded, at Furness, in 1645 at the head of a regiment he had raised.

II. 1645. SIR JOHN PRESTON, Bart. [1644], of Furness Manor, Preston Patrick, Under Levins and Heyford aforesaid, s. and h.; *suc. to the Baronetcy* in 1645. He *d.* unm. April 1663. Will pr. 1663.

III. 1663, to 1709. SIR THOMAS PRESTON, Bart. [1644], of Furness Manor, Preston Patrick, Under Levins and Heyford aforesaid, br. and h., *b.* about 1641, being aged 21 in 1664, having *suc. to the Baronetcy*, in April 1663. He *m.* firstly, Elizabeth (a French lady), da. of Peter DE PLAUZE. She *d.* s.p. a few weeks later. He *m.* secondly, Mary, da. of Caryll (MOLYNEUX), 3d VISCOUNT MOLYNEUX OF MARYBOROUGH [I.], by Mary, da. of Sir Alexander BARLOW. She *d.* at Furness, 6 June 1673, and was *bur.* at Heversham, co. Westmorland. He entered the society of Jesuits, 28 June 1674 (aged 31), and *d.* s.p.m.s.,(b) at Watten, in France, 27 May 1709, when the *Baronetcy* became *extinct.*

WEBB:

cr. 2 April 1644;(c)

ex. 19 Aug. 1874.

I. 1644. "JOHN WEBB, of Odstock, *otherwise* Oadstock, co. Wilts, Esq.," s. and h. of Sir John WEBB, of the same, and of Great Canford, Dorset, by his 2d wife, Catharine, da. of Sir Thomas TRESHAM, of Rushton, co. Northampton, was admitted to Gray's Inn, 11 Aug. 1619, and (apparently), again, 10 Feb. 1622/3; suc. his father in or before Feb. 1626, and was, as a reward for the loyalty of his family, *cr. a Baronet*, as above, 2 April 1644.(c) In 1646, his lands in Wilts, worth £300 a year, were sequestrated. He *m.* Mary, da. of Sir John CARYL, of Harting, Sussex, by Mary, da. of Robert (DORMER), 1st BARON DORMER OF WING. She *d.* 1661. He *d.* 1680, and was *bur.* at Odstock. Will pr. 1681.

(a) See p. 217, note "b," under "ACTON." The original patent of this creation was at Ugbrook, Devon, in 1830, in the possession of Lord Clifford, of Chudleigh, a descendant of the grantee.

(b) Francis, his only son, *d.* young, 18 Sep. 1672. Of his two daughters and coheirs (1) Mary, Marchioness of Powis, inherited the Northamptonshire estates, and Anne, Baroness Clifford of Chudleigh, inherited those in Westmorland. The manor of Furness he devised to the society of the Jesuits, which devise, however, was declared to be illegal.

(c) See p. 215, note "b," under O'NEILL. The patent is enrolled, being the first that was so for the space of more than a year (viz. after that of Danvers, 21 March 1642/3), and being the penultimate one so enrolled of the Baronetcies [E.] conferred by Charles I; that of Vyvyan, 12 Feb. 1644/5, being the last.

II. 1680. SIR JOHN WEBB, Bart. [1644], of Odstock and Great Canford aforesaid, s. and h., *suc. to the Baronetcy* in 1680. He *m.* Mary, the childless widow of Richard DRAYCOT, only da. of William BLOMER, of Hatherop, co. Gloucester, by Frances, da. of Anthony (BROWNE), 2d VISCOUNT MONTAGU. He *d.* 29 Oct. 1700, and was *bur.* at Odstock. Will pr. Nov. 1700. His widow *d.* 29 March 1709, and was *bur.* at Hatherop. Will pr. June 1709.

III. 1700. SIR JOHN WEBB, Bart. [1644], of Odstock, Great Canford and Hatherop aforesaid, only s. and h., *suc. to the Baronetcy*, 29 Oct. 1700. He *m.* firstly, in or before 1700, Barbara, da. and coheir of John (BELASYSE), BARON BELASYSE OF WORLABY, by his 3d wife, Anne, da. of John (PAULET), 5th MARQUESS OF WINCHESTER. She *d.* 28 March 1740. Will pr. 1740. He *m.* secondly, Helen, da. of Sir Richard MOORE, 3d Bart. [1627], of Fawley, Herts, by Anastacia, da. of John AYLWARD. He *d.* at Aix la Chapelle, in France, Oct. 1745. Will pr. 1745.

IV. 1745. SIR THOMAS WEBB, Bart. [1644], of Odstock, Great Canford and Hatherop aforesaid, 1st surv. s. and h. male(a); *suc. to Baronetcy*, Oct. 1745. He *m.*, about 1738, Anne, da. and coheir of William GIBSON, of Welford, co. Northampton. He *d.* 29 June 1763, and was *bur.* at St. Pancras, Midx. Will pr. 1763. His widow *d.* 7 Oct. 1777, and was *bur.* at St. Pancras. Will pr. 1777.

V. 1763. SIR JOHN WEBB, Bart. [1644], of Odstock, Great Canford and Hatherop aforesaid, s. and h.; *suc. to the Baronetcy*, 29 June 1763. He *m.* in or before 1760, Mary, 1st da. of Thomas SALVIN, of Easingwold, co. York, by Mary TALBOT, his wife. She *d.* 1782, and was *bur.* at Louvaine. He *d.* s.p.m., April 1797, and was *bur.* at St. Pancras. Will pr. 1797.(b)

VI. 1797. SIR THOMAS WEBB, Bart. [1644], nephew and h. male, being s. and h. of Joseph WEBB, of Welford aforesaid, by Mary, da. of John WHITE, of Canford, which Joseph was 2d s. of the 4th Bart. He *suc. to the Baronetcy* in April 1797. He *m.* firstly, 14 March 1799, at St. Geo. Han. sq., Frances Charlotte, da. of Charles (DILLON), 12th VISCOUNT DILLON OF COSTELLO GALLEN [I.], by his 1st wife, Henrietta Maria, da. of Constantine (PHIPPS), 1st BARON MULGRAVE [I.] She, who was *b.* 17 Feb. 1780, *d.* 17 April 1819. He *m.* secondly, 11 July 1822, at the British Embassy, Paris, Martha Matilda, Dow. VISCOUNTESS BOYNE [I.], da. of Sir Quaile SOMERVILLE, 2d Bart. [I. 1748], by his 2d wife, Mary, da. of Thomas TOWERS. He *d.* 26 March 1823, at Grillon's Hotel, Albemarle street, aged 48. Will pr. 1823. His widow, by whom he had no issue, *d.* 16 Sep. 1826.

VII. 1823, to 1874. SIR HENRY WEBB, Bart. [1644], only s. and h. by 1st wife, *b.* 27 April 1806, at Lyons, in France; *suc. to the Baronetcy*, 26 March 1823. He *d.* unm. 19 Aug. 1874, at Esslingen, Würthemberg, when the *Baronetcy* became *extinct.* Will pr. 9 Nov. 1874.

(a) John Webb, his elder br., *m.* twice, but *d.* v.p. and s.p.m. 9 March 1744/5, aged 44, leaving an only da. Barbara, who *m.* Sir Edward Hales, 5th Bart. [1611].

(b) "He left the manor of Great Canford to Edmond Arrowsmith, Esq., upon certain trusts and uses, by a will almost as extraordinary as Mr. Thellusson's." [Hutchins's *Dorset.*] Barbara, Countess of Shaftesbury (*b.* 1762), his only surv. child and sole heir, left an only child, Barbara, who *m.* in 1814 the Hon. William Francis Ponsonby. He, in 1838, was *cr.* BARON DE MAULEY, his wife being (through her mother's mother, Mary Salvin, abovementioned) a coheir of the old Barony of De Mauley.

PRESTWICH:

cr. 25 April 1644;(a)

ex. Sep. 1676;

assumed 1787? to 1795.

I. 1644. "THOMAS PRESTWICH, of Holme [*i.e.*, Hulme, in Manchester], co. Lancaster, Esq.," 2d but 1st surv. s. and h. of Edmund PRESTWICH, of the same (who entered and signed his pedigree in the Visit. of Lancashire, 1613, and who was *bur.* 17 Feb. 1628/9, in the Coll. Church of Manchester), by Margaret, da. of Edward BRERETON, was *bap.* there 6 Dec. 1604(b); matric. at Oxford (Bras. Coll.), 2 Nov. 1621, aged 18; B.A., 1626; M.A., 1629, being incorporated at Cambridge, 1632; admitted to Gray's Inn, 15 June 1624; was found by the Court-leet to be heir to his father, 21 April 1629; was a Commissioner of Array, 1642; served in Cheshire in 1644, and elsewhere, on behalf of the King, and was *cr. a Baronet*, as above, 25 April 1644.(a) In the same year, after having been taken prisoner, 20 Aug. 1644, at the battle of Ormskirk, he was 1 Sep. 1644, *Knighted* on the field of battle, during the pursuit of Essex's army, whereby he is often considered a *Knight Banneret.* He was a compounder, and was, 30 March 1647, fined £925, reduced to £443, which was paid 2 Nov. 1649. In July 1648, he was a prisoner for being within the lines of communication. In 1660, he alienated the Hulme estate to Sir Edward Mosley, the sale being confirmed by Act of Parliament in 1673. He *m.* in or before 1625, Elizabeth. He was *bur.* in the church of St. Martin's in the Fields, Midx., 3 Jan. 1673/4.

II. 1674, to 1676. SIR THOMAS PRESTWICH, Bart. [1644], s. and h., *b.* about 1625, admitted 20 March 1649/50, to Gray's Inn; *suc. to the Baronetcy*, in Jan. 1673/4. He *m.* 29 Nov. 1649, at Mortlake, Surrey (Lic. Fac., same day, he 24 and she 13), Mary, da. of "Edward HUNT, Esq., deceased," and grandchild of Elizabeth CHILD, widow. He *d.* s.p.m.s., and was *bur.*, with his father, 20 Sep. 1676, when the *Baronetcy* became *extinct.* Admon. 4 June 1689, to a creditor, his daughters(c) having been cited.

From information kindly supplied by G. D. Burtchaell [Office of Arms, Dublin], it appears that in 1775 a pedigree of PRESTWICH, of Holme in Lancashire, was registered in Ulster's office, verified 10 Jan. 1775 (1) by the joint certificate of George Evans PARKER and of George Purdon DREW, one of the six clerks in Chancery [I.], the latter being s. of Francis DREW, of Drew's Court, co. Limerick, by the eldest da. of John RINGROSE, who was s. of Richard RINGROSE of Minoe, co. Clare, by Margaret, 3d da. of Sir Thomas PRESTWICH, of Holme in Lancashire, Bart., which Margaret "came over to Ireland to her brother Elias, the s. of Sir Thomas PRESTWICH, who resided at Balliculline in co. Limerick"; and (2) by the affidavit

(a) See p. 217, note "b," under "ACTON."

(b) This fact and many others in this article have been kindly supplied by Ernest Axon.

(c) In the admon. of 1689, they are called *Isabella* Prestwich and *Priscilla* Prestwich. Their real names appear to have been *Arabella*, who, 23 June 1692, was wife of Matthew Moreton, afterwards 1st Baron Ducie, and who *d.* 14 March 1749/50, aged 90, and *Penelope*, who was unm. at the said date of 23 June 1692. See a deed of that date in the *Mis. Gen. et Her.*, new series, vol. i, p. 14. In that deed they call themselves heirs to John Prestwich, late of All Souls' College, Oxford, the brother of Sir Thomas, their grandfather. The printed continuation of the pedigree in the Visit. of Lancashire, 1613 [*Chetham Soc.*, vol. 82, p. 41], accords therewith, and states that the said John (who *d.* 30 July 1672, aged 72), gave a legacy of £20 in his will, proved 1680, to his cousin Elias Prestwich, of Ballacullom, near Limerick, in Ireland. It appears also that Arms to be used at the funeral, at Mortlake, 6 July 1655, of another sister, Mary, were ordered [Harl. MS. 1372]. In Burke's *Extinct Baronetage* yet another sister is mentioned, who does not elsewhere appear, viz., Margaret, wife of Richard Ringrose, of Moynoe, co. Clare, Col. in the Army, whose issue is there set out, but the existence of this Margaret seems doubtful.

sworn 16 Feb. 1775, of "Elias PRESTWICH, of the city of Dublin, gent.," stating that he is the true and lawful son and heir of Richard PRESTWICH, who was the s. and h. of Elias PRESTWICH, who was the s. and h. of Thomas PRESTWICH, of Holme, in Lancashire, Bart.

In the following year (1776) there is registered the "Genealogy of John PRESTWICH, Esq., only s. of Sir Elias PRESTWICH, Bart." This second pedigree gives more details, but they are practically the same so far as the descent and marriages of the male line are concerned. John PRESTWICH was not married at the time the first pedigree was entered. According to the second pedigree, it was Margaret, yst. (not eldest) da. of John RINGROSE, who *m.* Francis DREW.

The daughters of Sir Thomas PRESTWICH are stated to be Arabella (eldest da.) *m.* Matthew DUCIE, Lord Morton; "Precelia, her name supposed to be, 2d da., *m.* (—), merchant of London, *d.* without issue," and Margaret, 3d da., *m.* Richard RINGROSE, of Barraboy, near Moynoe, co. Clare.

Elias PRESTWICH is mentioned as "brother-in-law" by Captain William GOUGH, of Dunass, co. Clare, who *m.* Mercy, da. of George PARKER, of Dunkip, in his will dat. 14 Sept. 1664; and also as "brother-in-law" by William CARPENTER, of Limerick, gent., in his will dat. 27 March 1684. He (Carpenter) presumably *m.* another da. of George PARKER, of Dunkip.

The Pedigrees registered in Ulster Office state that—

THOMAS PRESTWICH, of Holme, in Lancashire, Esq., *cr. a Baronet*, 25 April 1644, had two sons. John, the eldest, *d.* unm. in England, and

ELIAS PRESTWICH, 2d son, who was in the Army, and who came over to Ireland in the Army, under the command of Oliver Cromwell, settling at Ballaculine, co. Limerick. He *m.* Anne, da. of George PARKER, of Dunkip, co. Limerick, Esq., and had

RICHARD PRESTWICH, who was a minor about eight years old at his father's death. His house and effects were burned by the Irish, but he was preserved and secreted by his nurse (an Irish Roman Catholic), during the late wars in Ireland. He *m.* Elizabeth, eldest da. of John LOMBARD, of White Church, co. Cork, and had

ELIAS PRESTWICH, about sixteen years old at the death of his father. He *m.* Catherine, da. of John LANDER, of the City of Cork, merchant, and had an only son,

JOHN PRESTWICH, "now [*i.e.*, 1775] living in London," *b.* 29 Jan. 1744/5, or (according to second pedigree) "January the 30th 1744/5, O.S., at six o'clock in the evening." He *m.* in April 1776, at London, Margaret, da. of Joseph HALL, Alderman of Dublin, by Ruth, 2d da. of Francis DREW, of Drew's Court, co. Limerick.

These two pedigrees do not give the title of "Sir" or the style of "Baronet" to any of the above, and in some particulars differ from the one in the Visit. of Lancashire, as printed in the *Chetham Society.* They both ignore Thomas PRESTWICH, the 2d Baronet, who undoubtedly was the first surviving son [and successor] of Sir Thomas, the 1st Bart.

The title is stated by Courthope, in his *Extinct Baronetage* [1833] to have been "assumed and borne for several generations by the possessors of Holm." It certainly was assumed, late in the eighteenth century by the John PRESTWICH, last abovenamed, who signs himself as "Baronet" in his preface, dated "Bath, 5 April 1787," to his "*Respublica*," and whose arms, surmounted with the badge of Baronetcy, appear on the title page thereto. His descent (indicated on p. 152 therein) is set forth fully in a pedigree (apparently composed by himself), which is printed as an addition to the Visit of Lancashire, 1613 [*Chetham Society*, vol. lxxxii, p. 41]. This makes his father, "Sir Elias PRESTWICH, now [1787] living in London," to be s. of "Sir Richard PRESTWICH," who was s. of "Sir Elias PRESTWICH," s. of "Thomas PRESTWICH, of Hulme, co. Lancaster, Bart., cousin to Sir Thomas PRESTWICH, Banneret." He *d.* in Dublin, 15 Aug. 1795.

WILLIAMS:

cr. 4 May 1644 ;(a)

ex. in 1694 or 1695 ;

but assumed from about 1740, to 21 Jan. 1798.

I. 1644. "HENRY WILLIAMS, of Gwernevet, co. Brecon, Esq.," s. and h. of Sir Henry WILLIAMS,(b) of the same, by Eleanor, da. of Eustace WHITNEY, of Whitney, co. Hereford, was *b.* about 1607 ; matric. at Oxford (St. John's Coll.), 24 Oct. 1623, aged 16 ; admitted to the Middle Temple, 1621 ; was M.P. for Breconshire, 1628-29 ; suc. his father 21 Oct. 1636, and was *cr. a Baronet,* as above, 4 May 1644.(a) He was a Royalist, and entertained Charles I, at Gwernevet, after the defeat at Naseby, in June 1645, being in that year a Commissioner of Array for Breconshire. His estates were, apparently, confiscated and mostly sold. He *m.* (post nuptial settl. 25 Aug. 1631) Anne, da. of Sir Walter PYE, of the Mynde, co. Hereford, by his 1st wife, Joane, da. of William RUDHALL, of Rudhall, in that county. He was living 10 Feb. 1649, but *d.* in or before 1652. Admon. 8 May 1652, to a creditor, and, probably, again in April 1666. The will of his widow, then of "Hereford," dat. 4 March 1685, pr. 1 July 1689.

II. 1652? SIR HENRY WILLIAMS, Bart. [1644], of Gwernevet aforesaid, s. and h., *b.* about 1635 ; matric. at Oxford (Queen's Coll.), 10 Nov. 1651 ; *suc. to the Baronetcy* in or before 1652 ; was M.P. for Brecknock, 1660 and 1661 till void, 25 July 1661. He *m.* Jan. 1657/8, at St. Dunstans in the West, London, Abigail, da. of Samuel WIGHTWICK, of St. Margaret's, Westm., Prothonotary of the King's Bench. He *d.* s.p.m.(c) before 22 March 1665/6, when his widow was sued (Brecon Plea Rolls) as his executrix. Possibly it is his admon. that was granted (C.P.C) April 1666. His widow *m.* (Lic. Vic. Gen. 26 Aug. 1667, being then about 26) "Thomas Lane, Esq.," of Bentley, co. Stafford, who *d.* 1715. She was living 9 July 1675.

III. 1665? to 1695? SIR WALTER WILLIAMS, Bart. [1644], of Ludlow, co. Salop, br. and h. male, *b.* about 1636 ; matric. at Oxford (Ball. Coll.), 27 June 1652 ; admitted to Middle Temple, 1656 ; *suc. to the Baronetcy* before 22 March 1665/6. He *d.* s.p. in or before 1695, when the *Baronetcy* became *extinct.* Will, directing his burial to be at Ludlow, dat. 24 May 1694, pr. 11 Feb. 1694/5.(d)

(a) See p. 217, note "b," under "ACTON."

(b) This Sir Henry was eldest of the nine sons of Sir David Williams, of Gwernevet, one of the Justices of the King's Bench, 1604-13, who *d.* 22 Jan. 1612/3. He matric. at Oxford (St. John's Coll.), 16 April 1594, aged 15, and is often (erroneously) called the 1st Baronet, but was dead eight years before the creation of that dignity, as he *d.* at Gwernevet, 21 Oct. 1636, and was *bur.* at Aberllynfri, co. Brecon. Funeral certificate in Coll. of Arms. Will dat. 12 Sep. 1633, pr. 11 Feb. 1636/7.

(c) Elizabeth, the first of his three daughters and coheirs, was *bap.* 19 May 1662, at Glasbury, co. Brecon ; *m.* (Lic. Vic. Gen., 9 July 1675, she about 13, with consent of her mother, Abigail Lane), Sir Edward Williams, who (to the great confusion of the Williams pedigree) thus became of Gwernevet. She was *bur.* at Glasbury, 27 Jan. 1705, and he 28 July 1721. He was a younger son of Sir Thomas Williams, 1st Baronet [1674] of Elham, and was father of Sir David Williams, 3d Baronet [1674], who inherited the estate of Gwernevet.

(d) In this will he leaves the £1,000 charged on the Gwernevet estate to his nephew [*i.e.*, great nephew] Henry Williams, 1st s. of Sir Edward Williams and Elizabeth [*i.e.*, Elizabeth, da. of testator's brother ; see note "c" above]. He leaves his watch to his cousin "David Williams, of Herts, minister," but devises the bulk of his property to a family named Wigmore.

After a lapse of above forty years, the title was assumed by the Rev. Gilbert Williams, whose relation to the previous Baronets was as under.

I, or VIII?(a) *1740?* GILBERT WILLIAMS, *called* SIR GILBERT WILLIAMS, Bart. [1644], s. and h. of Matthew WILLIAMS, citizen and mercer of London, by Elizabeth, only child that had issue of Robert GILBERT, of Goldington in Sarratt, Herts, citizen and mercer of London, which Matthew (who *d.* 8 July 1737, aged 76) was br. and h. of Carew WILLIAMS (*d.* s.p. 1722, aged 59), br. and h. of David WILLIAMS, M.D. (*d.* s.p. 27 Nov. 1709, aged 58), all three being sons of David WILLIAMS, of Corneden in Winchcombe, co. Gloucester (*d.* 18 Jan. 1698, aged 85), s. and h. of Thomas WILLIAMS, of Corneden aforesaid (*d.* May 1636, aged 64), who was a yr. br. of Sir Henry WILLIAMS, of Gwernevet abovementioned, the father of the 1st Baronet, both being sons of Sir David WILLIAMS, the Judge.(b) He was *b.* about 1692 ; matric. at Oxford (Trin. Coll.), 22 Oct. 1709, aged 17 ; B.A., 1713 ; M.A., 1719 ; took Holy Orders ; was Vicar of Sarratt, Herts, 1725 ; Rector of Hinxworth, Herts, 1728-39 ; Vicar of Islington, Midx., 1740-68 ; suc. his father 8 July 1737, becoming then of Clifford's Court, co. Hereford, and of Goldington aforesaid, shortly after which date, certainly before 1741(c) he "under an erroneous impression as to his descent, some years after the death of Sir Walter WILLIAMS of Gwernevet, Bart., in 1698 [*sic*, but query 1695] assumed the title which was in error continued by his son and grandson"(d) He *m.* 5 Feb. 1724, Dorothy, widow of Thomas DAY, of Rickmansworth, Herts, da. of William WANKFORD, of the same. He was *bur.* at Sarrett 9 April 1768, aged 75. Will dat. 14 July 1763, pr. 31 May 1768. His widow was *bur.* 20 Sep. 1773 at Sarrett aforesaid.

II. or IX.(a) *1768.* DAVID WILLIAMS, *called* SIR DAVID WILLIAMS, Bart. [1644], of Clifford's Court and Coldington aforesaid, s. and h., *b.* 13 May and *bap.* 13 June 1726 at Sarratt ; matric. at Oxford (Trin. Coll.), 16 June 1742, aged 16 ; B.A., 1748 ; M.A., 1751 ;

(a) To the succession to the Baronetcy after the death of Sir Walter in 1695 there were at least four more persons entitled prior to himself, viz., his father, two of his father's elder brothers, and his grandfather. This, too, is exclusive of any issue male of the numerous *brothers* of the 1st Baronet, one of whom, Thomas Williams, of London (1653), had a son, David Williams, of Stapleford, Herts, whose will dat. 16 Jan. 1712/3 to 26 Oct. 1715, was pr. 3 Sep. 1717. [*Ex inform.* H. J. T. Wood.] The claimant's ancestor was but an *uncle* of the grantee.

(b) The pedigree in Clutterbuck's *Herts* (vol. iii., p. 224) is wrong in making David Williams, of Corneden, the grandfather of "Sir Gilbert" to be son of Henry Williams, of Gwernevet and Eleanor (Whitney), and in making the said Henry (instead of his son) to be the 1st Bart. The information supplied by "Sir Gilbert" to Wotton for his *Baronetage* of 1741 (who is careful to quote him as his sole authority) as to his descent from the 1st Baronet is false and must apparently have been known so to be by the informant, who speaks of himself as "successor to his cousin, Sir Walter" [who died in or before 1695], but styles his father, through whom he derived his claim, and who did not die till 1737 as "Matthew Williams, *Esq.*," and makes no mention of any of his uncles, the elder brothers (living long after Sir Walter's death) of the said Matthew, having either assumed or even laid claim to the title. The descent of "Sir Gilbert" from Sir David Williams, the Judge, as given in the text, is from the pedigree recorded in the College of Arms [*Norfolk*, vol. vii.] in 1836.

(c) Wotton's *Baronetage* of that date. The "Sir David Williams, Bart., Guerneyer [*sic*] and Langoyd Castle, Breconshire," who died 1740, and the "Sir Henry Williams, Bart., Guernevel [*sic*], Breconshire, aged 18," who died 1741, were of the family of Williams, Baronets (so cr. 1674). See p. 224, note "c."

(d) Pedigree registered in College of Arms. See note "b" above.

suc. his father in April 1768. He *m.* 19 Aug. 1762 at Aylesbury, Rebecca, da. of Thomas Harding ROWLAND, of that town, by Martha, sister and coheir of George ROWLAND, of the same. He *d.* 9 and was *bur* 15 Dec. 1792, at Sarratt. His widow *d.* 3 and was *bur.* 11 Jan. 1819 at Sarratt. Will, as of Aston Clinton, Bucks, dat. 8 Dec. 1818, pr. 1819.

III. or X.(a) *1792, to 1798.* DAVID WILLIAMS, *called* SIR DAVID WILLIAMS, Bart. [1644], of Clifford's Court and Goldington aforesaid, s. and h., *bap.* 27 April 1765, at Sarratt ; suc. his father in Dec. 1792. He *m.* 10 June 1794, at Chenies, Bucks, Sarah Sophia, 1st da. and coheir of the Rev. John Fleming STANLEY, Rector of Warehouse, Kent, by Elizabeth, his wife. He *d.* s.p.m.(b) 21 and was *bur.* 29 Jan. 1798 at Clifford, co. Hereford, when the male issue of his grandfather became extinct, and the *assumption of this Baronetcy* came to an end. Admon. 12 March 1798. His widow *m.* 7 Sep. 1798, Bigoe ARMSTRONG, who *d.* at Boulogne 24 March 1825. She *m.* thirdly, 27 July 1832, at Shoreditch, James Deacon GIBBON, and was living 1836.

LUCAS:

cr. 20 May 1644 ;(c)

ex. in or before 1668.

I. 1644, to 1668? "GERVASE LUCAS, of Ferton *alias* Fenton, co. Lincoln, Esq.," s. of Anthony LUCAS, of the same, was *bap.* there 28 July 1611, suc. his father, 25 May 1613, was a zealous Royalist, was Gov. of Belvoir Castle for the King, and was *cr. a Baronet,* as above, 20 May 1644.(c) He *d.* unm.(d) at Bombay, in the East Indies, in or before 1668, when the *Baronetcy* became *extinct.* Admon. 10 Feb 1668/9, and 29 April 1674.

THOROLD:

cr. 14 June 1644 ;(e)

ex. 30 Nov. 1706.

I. 1644. "ROBERT THOROLD, of Hawley [*i.e.*, the Haugh], co. Lincoln, Knt.," s. and h. of Anthony THOROLD, of the same, by Catharine, da. of Edward HASELWOOD, of Maidwell, co. Northampton, was admitted to Gray's Inn, 9 Feb. 1589/90 ; *Knighted* at Whitehall, 1 June 1641, and was *cr. a Baronet,* as above, 14 June 1644.(e) He was a Royalist, was fined £1,300 on 5 June 1646, being then of Harrowby, co. Lincoln, and was assessed at £800 in May 1650. He *m.* firstly, Anne, sister to Sir Henry CARVIL, of St. Mary's in Marshland,

(a) See p. 225, note "a."

(b) Sophia Charlotte, only da. and h. (*b.* 11 June 1795), who inherited the estate of Rose Hall in Sarratt, Herts. *m.* Thomas Tyringham Bernard, of Winchinden, Bucks, and *d.* 15 May 1837.

(c) See p. 215, note "a," under "O'NEILL." No patent is enrolled. The date here given as that of the patent (20 May 1644) is that in Dugdale's *Catalogue*, but a subsequent date, 14 June 1644, is given to the Docquet in Black's *Docquets*, being the same as that of Thorold. See *Memorandum* on p. 84. There is therefore some error.

(d) There is, however, a marriage lic. (London) 11 Feb. 1641/2, of "Jervas Lucas, of London, gent., aged 28, bachelor," with "Experientia White, aged 28, spinster."

(e) See p. 217, note "b," under "ACTON."

Norfolk, da. of Henry CARVIL. She *d.* s.p. He *m.* secondly, about 1630 (after 1622) Katharine, da. of Christopher (ROPER), 2d BARON TEYNHAM, by Katharine, da. of John SEBORNE. She was living (probably as a widow) 1662.

II. 1660? SIR ROBERT THOROLD, Bart. [1644], of the Haugh aforesaid, s. and h., by 2nd wife. He *suc. to the Baronetcy* on the death of his father, and is, presumably, the "Sir Robert Thorold, Baronet, at ye Heath House, near Grantham, a Papist ; not more than £600 per annum ; in the Fleet now,"(a) who was living temp. Car. II.(b) He was committed to the Tower for high treason in May 1692. He *m.* in or before 1653, Katharine (aged 5 in Jan. 1633/4), da. of Sir Henry KNOLLYS, of Grove Place, in Nursling, Hants, Comptroller of the Household to Charles I, by Katharine, da. of Sir Thomas CORNWALLIS, groom porter to James I. He *d.* in or before 1695. Will pr. 1695.

III. 1695? to 1706. SIR ROBERT THOROLD, Bart. [1644], s. and h., said to have been "a gentleman of very solid judgment much improved by learning ;" *suc. to the Baronetcy* in or before 1695. He *d.* s.p. at St. James' Place, 30 Nov. and was *bur.* 1 Dec. 1706, at St. James', Westminster, at night (being a "Papist,") when the *Baronetcy* became *extinct.* Will pr. Dec. 1706.

SCUDAMORE:

cr. 23 June 1644 ;(c)

ex. between 1718 and 1727.

I. 1644. "JOHN SCUDAMORE, of Ballingham, co Hereford, Esq.," 1st s. of William SCUDAMORE,(c) of the same, by Sarah, da. and h. of Anthony KYRLE, surveyor of York, was *b.* 2 Aug. 1600, and was *cr. a Baronet,* as above, 23 June 1644.(d) He *m.*, in 1625, Penelope, da. of Sir James SCUDAMORE, of Holme Lacy, co. Hereford. He *d.* before 1649. The will of his widow pr. 1658.

II. 1649? SIR JOHN SCUDAMORE, Bart. [1644], of Ballingham aforesaid, 1st s. and h. ; *b.* 30 July 1630 ; matric. at Oxford (Ch. Ch.), 17 May 1647, aged 17 ; admitted to Middle Temple, 1648 ; *suc. to the Baronetcy* before 1649, and was K.B., 23 April 1661, at the Coronation of Charles II. He *m.* Margaret, da. of Sir George GRYMES, *otherwise* CRIMES, of Peckham, Surrey, by Alice, da. and coheir of Charles LOVELL, of West Harling, Norfolk. He *d.* s.p.m., and was *bur.* 22 Aug. 1684. Admon. 24 Oct. 1684, to Margaret, the relict, and again 10 Feb. 1684/5, to Barnaby, the brother. His widow, who was *bap.* 1 May 1640, at Camberwell, was *bur.* 20 Dec. 1715.

III. 1684, to 1720? SIR BARNABY SCUDAMORE, Bart. [1644], br. and h. male ; *suc. to the Baronetcy*, 22 Aug. 1684 ; was a citizen and mercer of London (voting as such 1710), being also Collector of Customs at Liverpool. He *m.* Sarah, widow of William HARRIS, of London, da. of John ROW, merchant of Bristol. She was *bur.* 31 Dec. 1710. He *d.* s.p.s., between 1718 and 1727, when the *Baronetcy* became *extinct.*

(a) There is a burial at St. Bride's, Fleet Street, of a "William Thorold, aged, from the Fleet," 27 Oct. 1692.

(b) See p. 192, note "c," under "THOROLD," Baronetcy cr. 1642.

(c) See pedigree in J. C. Robinson's *Mansions of Herefordshire.*

(d) See p. 215, note "b," under "O'NEILL." No patent is enrolled, and no signet bill or docquet exists. The date and description, as above, is as given in Dugdale's *Catalogue.* See *Memorandum* on p. 84.

BARD:

cr. 8 Oct. 1644;(a)

afterwards, 1645—1660, VISCOUNT BELLOMONT [I.];

ex. 1660.

I. 1645, to 1660. "SIR HENRY BARD, of Staines, co. Midx., Knt., Commander in the King's army," 2d and yst. s. of the Rev. George BARD,(b) Vicar of Staines aforesaid (*d.* 1616), by Susan, da. of John DUDLEY; was ed. at Eton; admitted to King's Coll., Cambridge, 1631; distinguished himself as a linguist, and was a great traveller in the East and elsewhere; was a zealous Royalist; *cr.* D.C.L. of Oxford, 1643; *Knighted*, 22 Nov. 1643; lost his arm at the battle of Cheriton Down; was Governor of Campden House, co. Gloucester, and subsequently of Worcester, and was *cr. a Baronet*, as above, 8 Oct. 1644.(a) He was at the taking of Leicester in May 1645, and was in command at Naseby the month following. He was *cr.*, 18 July 1645, BARON BARD OF DROMBOY, co. Meath, and VISCOUNT BELLOMONT [I.]. He accompanied Charles II to the Hague, and was by him sent, in 1656, on an embassy to the Shah of Persia.(c) He *m.*, in 1645, Anne, da. of Sir William GARDINER, of Peckham, co. Surrey, by Frances, da. of Christopher GARDINER, of Bermondsey. He *d.* s.p.m.,(d) 1660, in Arabia (being choked by sand in a whirlwind in the desert), when *all his titles* became *extinct*. His widow, who applied for relief to King's Coll., Cambridge, *d.* in or before 1668, at St. Martin's in the Fields, Midx. Admon. as "Lady Ann Bard, widow," 13 July 1668.

VYVYAN *or* VIVIAN:

cr. 12 Feb. 1644/5.(e)

I. 1645. "RICHARD VYVYAN, of Trelewaren [*i.e.*, Trelowarren, near Helston], co. Cornwall, Knt.," s. and h. of Sir Francis VYVYAN, of the same (Sheriff of Cornwall, 1617-18), by Loveday, da. of John CONNOCK, of Treworgy, in St. Cleere, co. Cornwall, was *b.* about 1613; matric. at Oxford (Ex. Coll.) 20 June 1631, aged 18, being made B.A. the same day; admitted to the Middle Temple, 1631; suc. his father, 11 June 1635; was *Knighted*, 1 March 1635/6; was M.P. for Penhryn, April to May 1640; for Tregony, 1640 till disabled Jan. 1644; for St. Mawes, 1661 and March 1663 till death, having been *cr.* D.C.L. of Oxford, 19 Feb. 1643/4, and *cr. a Baronet*, as above, 12 Feb. 1643/4.(e) He was a zealous Royalist, and during the Civil Wars was Master of the Mint at Exeter. He sat in the Oxford Parl. Jan. 1644; was fined £600, in Oct. 1646, by the sequestrators of the estates,

(a) See p. 217, note "b," under "ACTON."

(b) A good pedigree of the family is in *Coll. Top. et Gen.*, vol. iv, pp. 59-61, and vol. iii, pp. 15 and 18. See also *Mis. Gen. et Top.*, 2d series, vol. v, pp. 64 and 80, but the statement therein "that the first Viscount Bellomont had a son, Charles, 2d Viscount, slain 1685" seems a confusion for the death of Charles, *Earl* of Bellomont, who died 1683, and who was of a totally different family.

(c) Anthony a Wood (*Fasti Oxon.*) describes him as "a compact body of vanity and ambition, yet robust and comely." He is also ill-spoken of in Clarendon's *Rebellion*.

(d) Of his daughters (1) Ann was living unm. in July 1668; (2) Frances was mistress to Prince Rupert, and mother by him of Dudley Bard, otherwise Rupert Dudley, who was slain at the siege of Buda, 1686, aged about 20, in her lifetime; (3) Persiana, *m.* her cousin, Nathaniel Bard, of Caversfield, and died 1739, leaving issue.

(e) See p. 215, note "b," under "O'NEILL." The patent is enrolled, and is the last patent of any Baronetcy created by Charles I that is so.

having previously lost nearly £1,000 in the King's service. He *m.* (Lic. Exeter, 24 Sep. 1636), Mary, da. of James BULTEEL, of Barnstaple, Devon. He *d.* 3 and was *bur.* 10 Oct. 1665, at Mawgan in Meneage. Will dat. 1 Aug. 1665, pr. 1 Nov. 1666. His widow living 1665.

II. 1665. SIR VYELL VYVIAN, BART. [1645], of Trelowarren aforesaid, 1st s. and h., *bap.* 20 May 1639 at Mawgan aforesaid; *suc. to the Baronetcy*, 3 Oct. 1665; was *Knighted* before 29 Oct. 1657, when he matric. at Oxford (St. John's Coll.); M.P. for St. Mawes, Dec. 1665 till void; for Helston, 1679-81; Sheriff of Cornwall, 1682-83. He *m.* firstly, 30 June 1671, at Constantine, Thomazine, da. and coheir of James ROBYNS, of Glasney and Penrhyn, co. Cornwall, Attorney at Law. She *d.* s.p. He *m.* secondly, 24 Feb. 1683/4, at Mawgan aforesaid, Jane, widow of Michael COADE, da. of Thomas MELHUISH, of Penrhyn. He *d.* s.p.s., 24 and was *bur.* 27 Feb. 1696/7, at Mawgan. Will dat. 5 Sep. 1696, pr. 23 April 1697. His 2d wife, Jane, survived him.

III. 1697. SIR RICHARD VYVIAN, Bart. [1645], of Trelowarren aforesaid, nephew and h., being 1st s. and h. of Charles VYVYAN, of Merthen, Cornwall, by Mary, 1st da. and coheir of Richard ERISYE, of Trevanna, in that county, which Charles (who was *bur.* 12 Nov. 1687, at Constantine) was 2d s. of the 1st Bart. He was *b.* about 1677; matric. at Oxford (Ex. Coll.), 7 July 1694, aged 17, being Fellow, 1696-97; admitted to Middle Temple, 1694; *suc. to the Baronetcy*, 24 Feb. 1696/7; was M.P. for St. Michael's, 1700/1, and 1701-02; for Cornwall, 1703-10 and 1712-13; was suspected of being a Jacobite, and, accordingly, imprisoned in the Tower, 1717. He *m.*, 9 Nov. 1697, at St. Eval, Mary, only da. and h. of Francis VIVIAN, of Cosworth, by Anne, da. and h. of Henry MAYNARD, of Cosworth, by Bridget, his wife, da. and h. of Sir Samuel COSWORTH, of Cosworth aforesaid. He *d.* 9 May or 12 Oct. 1724. Will dat. 27 Oct. 1712 to 28 Oct. 1721, pr. 1724, in Archdeaconry Court of Cornwall. His widow, who was *bap.* 28 Sep. 1681, at Colan, was *bur.* 3 Dec. 1736, at Mawgan.

IV. 1724. SIR FRANCIS VYVIAN, Bart. [1645], of Trelowarren aforesaid, 1st s. and h.; *bap.* 29 Sep. 1698, at Mawgan; matric. at Oxford (Ex. Coll.), 17 Dec. 1718, aged (it is said) 15; *suc. to the Baronetcy*, 12 Oct. 1724; Sheriff of Cornwall, 1739. He *m.* 30 May 1730, Grace, only da. and h. of Rev. Carew HOBLYN,(a) of Georgeham, Devon. She *d.* 3 and was *bur.* 11 Nov. 1740, at Mawgan. He was *bur.* there 29 Dec. 1745.

V. 1745. SIR RICHARD VYVIAN, Bart. [1645], of Trelowarren aforesaid, 1st s. and h., *b.* 11 and *bap.* 12 May 1731, at Mawgan; *suc. to the Baronetcy*, 29 Dec. 1745; matric. at Oxford (Oriel Coll.), 27 Nov. 1749, aged 17. He *m.* 6 Dec. 1754, Jane, da. of Christopher HAWKINS, of Trewinnard, Cornwall. He *d.* s.p. 13 or 20 Oct. 1781. Will pr. Dec. 1781. The will of his widow pr. Feb. 1787.

VI. 1781. SIR CAREW VYVIAN, Bart. [1645], of Trelowarren aforesaid, br. and h., *bap.* 11 Jan. 1736/7, at Mawgan; matric. at Oxford (Oriel Coll.), 4 April 1754, aged 17; B.A., 1757; M.A., 1762; was in Holy Orders; *suc. to the Baronetcy*, 20 Oct. 1781. He *d.* s.p., 4 Oct. 1814. Admon. Nov. 1814.

VII. 1814. SIR VYELL VYVYAN, Bart. [1645], of Trelowarren aforesaid and of Tresmarrow, Cornwall, cousin and h. male, being s. and h. of Philip VYVYAN, of Tresmarrow aforesaid, by Mary, da. and h. of Sheldon WALTER, of Tremeal, Cornwall, which Philip (who *d.* March 1791, aged 59), was s.

(a) He was s. of Robert Hoblyn, by Grace, 1st da. and coheir of John CAREW, of Penwharne, Cornwall.

and h. of Richard VYVYAN, of Tresmarrow,(a) Barrister, Recorder of Launceston (*d.* 14 Jan. 1771, aged 70), who was 2d s. of the 3d Bart. He was *b.* 12 July 1767; matric. at Oxford (Trin. Coll.), 10 Oct. 1785, aged 18; *suc. to the Baronetcy*, 4 Oct. 1814; Sheriff of Cornwall, 1815-16. He *m.* 14 Aug. 1799, Mary, only da. of Thomas-Hutton RAWLINSON, of Lancaster. She *d.* 5 Sep. 1812. He *d.* 27 Jan. 1820. Will pr. 1820.

VIII. 1820. SIR RICHARD-RAWLINSON VYVYAN, Bart. [1645], of Trelowarren aforesaid, s. and h., *b.* there 6 June 1800; educated at Harrow; matric. at Oxford (Ch. Ch.), 22 May 1818, aged 18; *suc. to the Baronetcy*, 27 Jan. 1820; was M.P. for Cornwall, 1825-31; for Okehampton, 1831-32; for Bristol, 1832-37, and for Helston, 1841-57. Sheriff of Cornwall, 1840. He *d.* unm., 15 Aug. 1879, at Trelowarren, aged 79.

IX. 1879. SIR VYELL-DONNITHORNE VYVYAN, Bart. [1645], of Trelowarren aforesaid, nephew and h., being s. and h. of Rev. Vyell-Francis VYVYAN, Rector of Withiel, co. Cornwall, by Anna, yst. da. of John-Vych-Rhys TAYLOR, of Southgate, Middlesex, which Vyell Francis (who *d.* 30 Jan. 1877, aged 75), was next br. of the late Baronet. He was *b.* 16 Aug. 1826, was ed. at St. Aidan's College, and at St. John's College, Cambridge; took Holy Orders, 1854; Rector of Winterbourne Monkton, Dorset, 1856-66; Vicar of Broad Hinton, Wilts, 1866-77; Rector of Withiel aforesaid, 1877-79; *suc. to the Baronetcy*, 15 Aug. 1879. He *m.* 16 April 1857, Louisa-Mary-Frederica, 3d da. of Richard BOURCHIER, of Brook Lodge, Dorset.

Family Estates.—These, in 1883, consisted of 9,738 acres in Cornwall, worth £18,147 a year. *Principal Seat.*—Trelowarren, near Helston, and Trewan, near St. Colomb, both co. Cornwall.

VAN COLSTER:

cr. 28 Feb. 1644/5;(b)

ex., apparently in or before 1665.

I. 1645, to 1665? "WILLIAM [but apparently should be JOSEPH] VAN COLSTER,(c) of Amsterdam, in Holland," was *cr. a Baronet*, as above, 28 Feb. 1644/5,(b) being apparently the first foreigner on whom that distinction was conferred. He *m.* (—). He *d.*, it is said, s.p.m.(d) in or before April 1665, when, apparently, the *Baronetcy* became *extinct*. The admon. of "Sir *Joseph* Van Coulster, of Fulham, co. Midx., Knt. and Bart.," granted 22 April 1665, to a creditor.(e)

(a) The wife of this Richard (*m.* 16 Jan. 1728) was Philippa, 1st da. and h. of Philip PYPER, of Tresmarrow aforesaid.

(b) See p. 217, note "b," under "ACTON."

(c) The Christian name is "William" in Black's *Docquets* and in Dugdale's *Catalogue*. [See *Memorandum* on p. 84], but it is given as "Joseph" in most accounts, which name is borne out by the admon. of 1665. See also note "d" next below.

(d) "Henrietta Maria, da. of Sir Joseph [*sic*] Van Colster, of Colster, in Germany, Bart.," was mother by "Henry Stanihurst, Esq., of Godoff, in Ireland," of Cecilia Stanihurst, one of the English Ladies of Pontoise, who died 1746, aged 73. [*Her. and Gen.*, vol. iii, p. 415].

(e) BARONETCIES CONFERRED ON FOREIGNERS.

The following account of these creations seems worth reproducing from Wotton's *Extinct Baronetage*, edit. 1741, vol. iv, p. 268:—

"A list of those Baronets who were foreigners at the time of creation, and still [1741] continue so if in being, whereof no certain information can be had to be depended on; with the dates of their several creations and the order they stood in.

BOREEL, *or* DE BOREEL:

cr. 21 March 1644/5.(a)

I. 1645. "WILLIAM DE BOREEL, of Amsterdam, in Holland,"(b) 2d s. of Sir James BOREEL,(c) of Middleburgh, Envoy from the States Gen. to England, by his 2d wife, Mary GRIMMINCK, was *b.* 24 March 1591; Envoy to England, where it is said he was *Knighted* by James I, about 1619; Pensionary of Amsterdam, 1628; Ambassador to Venice, 1636; to Sweden, 1640; to England (again) 1642, being *cr. a Baronet*, as above, 21 March 1644/5.(a) He was again, in 1648, Ambassador to Venice. He is said to have had a Royal warrant from Charles II in exile, 28 June 1653, to create him a Baron. He *m.* 22 Sep. 1626, Jacoba CARELS. She *d.* in Paris 17 June 1657. He *d.* there 29 Sep. 1668.

II. 1668. SIR JOHN BOREEL, *or* DE BOREEL, Bart. [1645], s. and h., *b.* 29 Oct. 1627, *suc. to the Baronetcy*, 29 Sep. 1668. He was Marshal at the Court of the Prince of Orange (afterwards William III), and a Lieut.-Col. in the Dutch Service. He *m.* 7 Nov. 1666, Amarantha VAN VREDENBURGH. He *d.* 29 March 1691. His widow *d.* 27 July 1715.

III. 1691. SIR WILLIAM BOREEL, Bart. [1645], s. and h., *b.* 4 Oct. 1672; *suc. to the Baronetcy*, 29 March 1691; was a Capt. in the Dutch Service. He *d.* unm. 23 Sep. 1710.

IV. 1710. SIR ADRIAN BOREEL, Bart. [1645], br. and h., *b.* 9 Dec. 1674; *suc. to the Baronetcy*, 23 Sep. 1710; Lieut.-Col. in the Dutch Army, and a Capt. in the Dutch Navy; Chief D'Escadra, and Contra Admiral in Portugal. He *m.* Margaret VAN-DEN-BOSCH. He *d.* s.p.m. 15 July 1723. His widow *d.* 14 April 1726.

[By] King Charles I.

1644 [*i.e.*, 1644/5] Feb. 28. VAN-COLSTER, of Amersterdam.
" " March 21. DE BOREEL, of Amsterdam.

[By] King Charles II.

1652 April 2. CURTIUS, Resident to the King of Sweden.
1658 Aug. [—]. CARPENTIER, of Brussels.
1660 April [—]. DE MERCES, of France.
" May 30. DE RAED, of Holland.
" Nov. 16. MOTTET, of Liege.
1661 Oct. 4. VAN-FREISENDORF, of Herdick, Sweden.
1674 March 25. TRUMP, Vice-Admiral of Holland.
1675 April 23. TULPE, of Amsterdam.
1680 Oct. 22. SAS-VAN-BOSCH, servant to the Prince of Orange, Holland.
1682 June 29. GANS, of the Netherlands.

[By] King James II.

1686 Sep. 9. SPEELMAN, of Holland.

[By] King William III.

1699 June 9. VANDERBRANDE.

[By] Queen Anne.

1709 [*i.e.*, 1708/9]. NEUFVILLE, of Franckfort, Germany."

(a) See p. 217, note "b," under "ACTON." Arms were granted to him by a docquet of the King, 22 Aug. following.

(b) See p. 230, note "e," as to Baronetcies conferred on Foreigners.

(c) Nearly all the particulars of this family are from Burke's *Baronetage*, 1875, nothing, apparently, having previously been known about them in this country, till Sir J. Bernard Burke, Ulster King of Arms, obtained an elaborate pedigree of Boreel from Amsterdam, which he printed in the above stated work.

V. 1723. SIR BALTHASAR BOREEL, Bart. [1645], cousin and h. male, being surv. s. and h. of James BOREEL, Ambassador from the United Provinces to France, by Isabella COYMANS, his wife, which James (who *d.* 21 Aug. 1697, aged 67), was 2d s. of the 1st Bart. He was *b.* 21 May 1673, was Counsellor Deputy of Holland, and *suc. to the Baronetcy*, 14 April 1723. He *m.* 17 Dec. 1720, Apollonia RENDORP. He *d.* s.p. 28 June 1744. His widow *d.* 28 Oct 1757.

VI. 1744. SIR WILLIAM BOREEL, Bart. [1645], nephew and h., being 1st surv. s. and h. of James BOREEL, Commissary of the Post, by Sarah SAMAER, his wife, which James (who *d.* 28 March 1736, aged 57) was br. to the 5th Bart. and grandson to the grantee. He was *b.* 1712, was Master of the Veudution [?] at Amsterdam, and *suc. to the Baronetcy*, 28 June 1744. He *d.* unm. 14 Feb. 1787. Will pr. Sep. 1787.

VII. 1787. SIR WILLIAM BOREEL, Bart. [1645], cousin and h., being surv. s. and h. of James BOREEL, Ambassador from the United Provinces to England, by Agnes Margarette MUNTER, his wife, which James (who *d.* 4 April 1778, aged 67) was s. and h. of John Hieronymus BOREEL, Echevin of Amsterdam (*d.* 9 Sep. 1738, aged 53), who was 5th s. of James BOREEL (father of the 5th and grandfather of the 6th Bart.) abvenamed, the 2d s. of the 1st Bart. He was *b.* 20 June 1744, was Echevin of Amsterdam, Deputy to the States General, and *suc. to the Baronetcy*, 14 Feb. 1787. He *m.* 30 Dec. 1766, Mary TRIP. He *d.* 31 July 1796. His widow *d.* 23 Jan. 1813.

VIII. 1796. SIR JAMES BOREEL, Bart. [1645], s. and h., *b.* 25 Oct. 1768; Member of the Equestrian Order of the States of Holland; *suc. to the Baronetcy*, 31 July 1796. He *m.* 21 Aug. 1791, Jane Margaret, da. of William MUNTER, Echevin of Amsterdam. He *d.* at the Hague, 12 April 1821. Will pr. Oct. 1821. His widow *d.* there 1 Nov. 1846.

IX. 1821. SIR WILLIAM BOREEL, Bart. [1645], s. and h., *b.* 23 March 1800, at Velsen; *suc. to the Baronetcy*, 12 April 1821; Member of the Upper House of the Netherlands; Minister of State, and several times Governor of North Holland. He *m.* 24 July 1833, Margaret Jaqueline Mary Pauline, da. of his paternal uncle, Lieut. Gen. William Francis BOREEL, by Catharine Anne, da. of Francis FAGEL, Greffier of the States General. She was sometime Dame-du-Palais to the Queen of Holland. He *d.* in 1883. His widow *d.* about 1893.

X. 1883. SIR JACOB WILLIAM GUSTAVUS BOREEL, Bart. [1645], of Meervliet, Velsen, in North Holland, s. and h., *b.* 10 Sep. 1852, at Velsen; ed. at Leyden Univ.; Gent. of the Privy Chamber to the King of the Netherlands, and *suc. to the Baronetcy* in 1883. He *m.* 14 March 1878, Maria Cornelia, da. of the BARON SCHIMMELPENNICK VANDEROYE, Grand Master of the Ceremonies to the King of the Netherlands. She *d.* Nov. 1891.

CARTERET, *or* DE CARTERETT:

cr. 9 May 1645;(a)

afterwards, 1681—1776, BARONS CARTERET OF HAWNES;

and subsequently, 1744—1776, EARLS GRANVILLE;

ex. 13 Feb. 1776.

I. 1645. "GEORGE DE CARTERETT, of Metesches, in Jersey, Esq.," s. and h. of Helier DE CARTERET, of the same, Deputy Governor of Jersey (who was 2d s. of Sir Philip DE CARTERET, Seignior of St. Owen in that island), by Elizabeth DUMASQUE (*m.* 1608), his wife, was *b.* between 1609 and 1617; entered the naval service and was Lieut. in 1632; Capt. in 1633, being second in command in the expedition, 1637, to Sallee, and being in 1639 Comptroller of the Navy; was Bailiff of Jersey, 1643, and an active supporter of the King, by whom

(a) See p. 217, note "b," under "ACTON."

he was made Lieut.-Gov. of that island. He is stated to have been *Knighted*(a) 21 Jan. 1644 [1644/5?] and was *cr. a Baronet*, as above, 9 May 1645.(b) In 1646 he received Prince Charles in Jersey, and again after that Prince was King, 17 Sep. 1649 to 13 Feb. 1650, when he received the grant of several Seigneuries, as also of the island of New Jersey, in America. He was, however, finally compelled to surrender Jersey, 12 Dec. 1651, to the Parliament, though when Castle Elizabeth lowered the Royal Standard, it was the last fortress in the kingdom that surrendered. He joined the exiles in France, but was expelled therefrom in 1657. After the Restoration he was made P.C., 11 July 1660; was Treasurer of the Navy (1660-67); Vice-Chamberlain of the Household (to which post he is said to have been appointed as early as 1647), 1660-70; Vice-Treasurer [I.], 1667-73; Commissioner of the Board of Trade, 1668-72, and a Lord of the Admiralty, 1673-79. He was M.P. for Portsmouth, 1661-79. He acquired an enormous fortune.(c) He *m.* Elizabeth, da. of his paternal uncle, Sir Philip CARTERET, of St. Owen in Jersey, by Anne, da. of Sir Francis DOWSE. He *d.* 14 Jan. 1679/80, aged about 70. Will pr. 1700. His widow is said to have been granted by warrant,(d) 14 Feb. 1680, the precedence of a peer's widow, in consequence of a peerage about to have been conferred on her husband. Her will pr. Feb. 1700.

II. 1680. SIR GEORGE CARTERET, Bart. [1645], grandson and h., being s. and h. of Sir Philip CARTERET, Governor of Mount Orgueil, by Jemima (mar. lic. 29 July 1665, Fac. Office), da. of Edward (MONTAGU), 1st EARL OF SANDWICH, which Philip *d.* v.p., being blown up at sea (together with the said Earl, his wife's father) in the fight off Solebay, 28 May 1672. He was *b.* about 1667, and was *m.* through his grandfather's influence (Lic. Fac., 15 March 1674/5) when but a boy, to Grace, yst. da. of John (GRANVILLE), 1st EARL OF BATH. He *suc. to the Baronetcy*, on his grandfather's death, 14 Jan. 1679/80, and shortly afterwards was *cr.*, 19 Oct. 1681, in his said wife's lifetime,(e) BARON CARTERET OF HAWNES, co. Bedford. In that Peerage this *Baronetcy* then *merged*, the 2d Baron succeeding his mother, 27 Oct. 1744, as EARL GRANVILLE. It continued thus merged till, on the death of Robert, EARL GRANVILLE, 3d BARON CARTERET OF HAWNES, and 4th Baronet, 13 Feb, 1776, it and all other his honours became *extinct*. See *Peerage*.

WINDEBANKE:

cr. 25 Nov. 1645;(b)

ex., presumably, 23 Sep. 1719.

I. 1645. "THOMAS WINDEBANKE, of Haynes Hill [in Hurst], co. Wilts [should be Berks], Esq.," 1st s. and h. ap. of Sir Francis WINDEBANKE, of the same, the well known Sec. of State to Charles I (*d.* 1 Sep. 1646, in Paris, aged 64), by (—) his wife, was *b.* about 1612; was a Gent. of the Privy Chamber, 1627; matric. at Oxford (St. John's Coll.), 13 Nov. 1629, aged 17; was admitted to Lincoln's Inn, 19 March 1632/3; was Clerk of the Signet about 1636; M.P. for Wootton Basset, April to May 1640; was a Royalist, and was *cr. a Baronet*, as above, 25 Nov. 1645.(b) He was a Compounder in Aug. 1646, being fined £810. He took out admon. to his father, 16 Oct. 1650. He *m.*, in or before 1646, Anne, da. of John GRYMES, of Bury St. Edmunds, by Susan, da. of Ambrose JERMYN, of Stanton, co. Suffolk.(f) He was living 1655, but *d.* before July 1669.(f)

(a) He was, however, apparently called "Esq." in his creation as a Baronet a few months later.

(b) See p. 217, note "b," under "ACTON."

(c) The *Flagellum Parl.* accuses him of having robbed the King of £300,000.

(d) *Dict. Nat. Biogr.*, where it is stated that this warrant is quoted by Chalmers.

(e) She, survived him, and was, after his death, *cr.*, 1 Jan. 1714/5, Countess Granville, with rem. of that Earldom to her issue male.

(f) *Coll. Top. et Gen.*, vol. iii, p. 157. It is presumed that he was the father of "Frances Windebanck of St. Paul's, Covent Garden, spinster, about 23, parents dead," 12 July 1669, when she had licence (Vic. Gen.) to marry Sir Edward Hales, 3d Bart. [1611]. The father of this lady, however, is usually called "Sir Francis [*sic*] Windebank, of Oxford," but if she was, as is possible, the da. of the Secretary of State, she must have been born the year of her father's death (1646), when he was 64. See, however, W. D. Pink's "Notes on the Windebank Family" in *N. & Q.*, 8th S., I, 23.

II. 1660? to 1719. SIR FRANCIS WINDEBANK, Bart. [1645], s. and h., *b.* about 1656, was apparently suspected as a Jacobite, being "taken into custody" 14 May 1692, and "committed to a messenger" 9 April 1696.(a) He *m.* 4 May 1686, at Lee, co. Kent (Lic. Fac., 28 April, he "of the Tower of London, Bart., aged 30, bachelor"), Elizabeth PARKHURST, about 20, spinster, da. of Frances Parkhurst, widow. He *d.* in Eagle street, apparently s.p.m., and was *bur.* 23 Sep. 1719 at St. Andrew's, Holborn, when the *Baronetcy* presumably became *extinct*. Will dat. 3 Feb. 1715/6, pr. 8 Oct. 1719, leaving all to his wife, Elizabeth. Her will pr. 1730.

WRIGHT:

cr. 7 Feb. 1645/6;(b)

but "*suspended* by the King's warrant";

ex. on death of grantee.

I. 1646, to 1670? "BENJAMIN WRIGHT, of Dennington, co. Suffolk, Esq.," yr. br. of Nathan Wright, of London, the father of Sir Benjamin Wright, 1st Bart. [1661], both being sons of the Rev. Robert WRIGHT, D.D., Rector of Dennington aforesaid (*d.* 1624), by Jane, sister of Sir Oliver and da. of John BUTLER, of Sheby, co. Essex, was a merchant of London, and was *cr. a Baronet*, as above, 7 Feb. 1645/6, the patent, however, being "suspended" by the King's warrant. He *m.* (—). He *d.* s.p.m. in Spain, when the *Baronetcy* became *extinct*.

CHARLTON, *or* CHARLETON:

cr. 6 March 1645/6;(c)

ex. on death of grantee.

I. 1646, to 1670? "EDWARD CHARLTON, of Hesleyside, co. Northumberland, Gent.," s. and h. of William CHARLTON, or CHARLETON, of the same, was *cr. a Baronet*, as above, 6 March 1645/6.(c) He *m.* Mary, da. and coheir of Sir Edward WIDDRINGTON, Bart. [1642], of Cartington, co. Northumberland, by Christiana STUART, his wife. He *d.* s.p.m.(d) when the *Baronetcy* became *extinct*.

WILLIS, *or* WILLYS:

cr. 11 June 1646;(e)

but *suspended*;

ex. 1701.

I. 1646. "RICHARD WILLYS, of Ditton, co. Cambridge, Knt.," next br. to Sir Richard WILLYS, 1st Bart. [1641], both being sons of Richard WILLYS, of Fen Ditton and Horningsey, co. Cambridge, by Jane, da. and h. of William HENMARSH, of Balls, in Ware, co. Herts, was *b.* about 1615; was a

(a) In 1692, however, he is called [erroneously] Sir *Thomas*, though [correctly] in 1696, Sir *Francis* Windebank. [Luttrell's *Diary*.]

(b) See p. 217, note "b," under "ACTON." In a marginal note to the docquet is written "Suspended per warrant Regis."

(c) See p. 217, note "b," under "ACTON"

(d) Of his three daughters and coheirs, one *m.* her first cousin, William Charleton, who, by purchase and otherwise, acquired the whole of the estate of Hesleyside, and is ancestor of the family there seated.

(e) See p. 217, note "b," under "ACTON." In a marginal note to the docquet is written "suspended," but whether by order of the King (as in the case of Wright, 7 Feb. 1645/6), or of Parl., is not stated.

Royalist, being, eventually, Colonel of a Regiment of Horse, Colonel General of the counties of Lincoln, Notts, and Rutland, and Governor of Newark for the King, by whom he was *Knighted*, 1 Oct. 1642, at Shrewsbury, and was *cr. a Baronet*, as above, 11 June 1646.(a) He *m.*, in or before 1659, Alice, da. and sole h. of Thomas FOX, M.D., of Warlies, in Waltham Holy Cross, Essex [*bur.* there 26 Nov. 1662], and of Shipton, Oxon, by Anne, da. of Robert HONYWOOD, of Pett, in Charing, Kent. Her will, dat. 27 Oct. 1684, pr. 28 March 1688. He was *bur.* 9 Dec. 1690, at Fen Ditton. His will dat. 16 to 20 May, and pr. 10 Dec. 1690.

II. 1690, to 1701. SIR THOMAS FOX WILLYS, Bart. [1646], of Warlies aforesaid, s. and h., *b.* 30 June 1661, and *bap.* at Waltham aforesaid; *suc. to the Baronetcy*, 9 Dec. 1690. He, who was "bereft of his wits," *d.* unm. 1701, aged 59, when the *Baronetcy* became *extinct*.(b) Will pr. Nov. 1701.

Memorandum.—On 11 Aug. 1646, the Great Seal of Charles I was broken to pieces in the presence of both houses of Parliament. See *Memorandum* on p. 152.

(a) See p. 234, note "e."

(b) Anne Fox Willys, *bap.* 21 Feb. 1659/60, at Waltham, his only surv. sister and heir, *m.* Christopher Davenport, and had issue, living 1690.

Baronetcies [E.] not on record,

1640—1648;

ARRANGED ALPHABETICALLY.

Memorandum.—There are some Baronetcies conferred shortly before or during the *Civil War*, of which not only the patents (which possibly in many cases had never passed the Seals), but not even the docquets or warrants were enrolled, and which are not mentioned in Dugdale's carefully compiled CATALOGUE OF THE BARONETS OF ENGLAND, as to which see *Memorandum* on p. 84. A complete, or even approximately complete, list of these is unattainable, but there seems reason to believe that the following persons obtained, or at all events had the Royal warrant for, Baronetcies. The unlawful assumption of titles, which was so common in the nineteenth and even in the eighteenth century, was not usual in the seventeenth; and it will be observed that the position of the parties who thus styled themselves, and were recognised as, Baronets, was such as to render it unlikely that they would expose themselves to the ridicule and contempt attending such assumption. At the same time it is evident that in the cases of some of them (*e.g.*, in those of Acland, Boothby, and Edwards, where a patent *de novo* was granted with a clause giving the precedency of the former creation), the grant of the dignity by Charles I was not held to be sufficient; while on the contrary, the sufficiency of the creation of others has been generally acknowledged. Each case therefore should be judged separately. The dates of these Baronetcies, not being in many cases ascertainable, the names are here given in alphabetical order.

ACLAND:

cr.(a) 24 June 1644;(b)

cr., *de novo*, 21 Jan. 1677/8.

I. 1644. JOHN ACLAND, of Columb-John, in Broadclyst, Devon, Esq., s. and h. of Sir Arthu rACLAND, of the same, by Elizabeth, da. and h. of Robert MALLET, of Woolley, Devon, was *b.* about 1591; suc. his father, 26 Dec. 1610; was aged 29 at the Visitation of Devon in 1620; Sheriff of Devon, 1641, and, having distinguished himself in the cause of his King, was *cr. a Baronet*,(a) 24 June 1644.(b) He maintained a garrison at Columb-John, which at one time was the only force for the King that remained in the county. The house was afterwards plundered, and he himself fined £1,800. He *m.* before 1635, Elizabeth, da. of Sir Francis VINCENT, 1st Bart., [1620], by his 1st wife, Sarah, da. of Sir Amyas PAULET. He *d.* 24 Aug. 1647, and was *bur.* at Stoke D'Abernon, Surrey. M.I. Will, in which he describes himself as "Baronet," dat. 1 Dec. 1646, pr. 30 Nov. 1648, 19 Feb. 1650, 25 June 1670, and 5 July 1671. His widow *d.* in or before 1650; her admon. 25 Jan. 1650/1, 25 June 1670, and 6 July 1671.

II. 1647. SIR FRANCIS ACLAND, Bart. [1644], of Columb-John and Killerton, in Broadclyst aforesaid, s. and h., *suc. to the Baronetcy*, 24 Aug. 1647. He *d.* unm. and a minor, 1649, and was *bur.* at Stoke D'Abernon.

(a) See p. 215, note "b," under "O'NEILL." No patent, docquet, or sign manual is enrolled; nor is the creation given in Dugdale's *Catalogue*; see *Memorandum* in text above.

(b) The date of the creation, as in the text, is that given in Wotton's *Baronetage* (edit. 1741).

III. 1649. SIR JOHN ACLAND, Bart. [1644], of Columb John and Killerton aforesaid, br. and h., *b.* about 1636, *suc. to the Baronetcy* in 1649. He *m.* about 1654, Margaret, da. and coheir of Dennis ROLLE, of Stevenstone, Devon, by Margaret, da. of John (POULETT), 1st BARON POULETT OF HINTON ST. GEORGE. He *d.*, under age, in 1655. His widow *m.* Henry AYSHFORD. She *d.* about 1673. Admon. 25 Nov. 1673, to her da. Margaret Acland.(a)

IV. 1655. SIR ARTHUR ACLAND, Bart. [1644], of Columb John and Killerton aforesaid, only s. and h., *b.* about 1655, *suc. to the Baronetcy* in his infancy, 1655; matric. at Oxford (Ex. Coll.), 27 July 1669, aged 14, subscribing himself as a Baronet. He *d.* a minor and unm., 1672.

V. 1672. SIR HUGH ACLAND, Bart. [1644], of Columb John and Killerton aforesaid, uncle and heir male, was *b.* about 1639; matric. at Oxford (Ex. Coll.), 27 Nov. 1652; B.A., 22 June 1655; *suc.*, by the death of his nephew in 1672, *to the Baronetcy* conferred, 24 June 1644, on his father, and, though styled "Baronet" in his marriage license (Vic. Gen.), 19 March 1673/4, was nevertheless *cr. a Baronet* [*de novo*] 21 Jan. 1677/8, it being stated(b) that "amidst the confusion of those Civil Wars, the letters patents [24 June 1644] were destroyed, and new letters patents not being granted till the year 1677 (by reason of a long minority in this family), there was in them inserted a special clause of precedency from the date of the first, *viz.*, 24 June 1644."(c) See "ACLAND" Baronetcy, *cr.* 21 Jan. 1677/8.

BATHURST:

cr. 15 Dec. 1643;(d)

ex., or *dormant*, about 1780;

but *assumed* subsequently.

I. 1643. EDWARD BATHURST, of Lechlade, co. Glouc., and of Farrington, co. Oxon, Esq., 2d s. of Robert BATHURST, of the same, by Elizabeth, relict of Sir John LAURENCE, da. of Ralph WALLER, was *b.* about 1603; suc. his elder br., Robert Bathurst, in 1628, being then aged 13; distinguished himself in the cause of the King in the Civil War, and was *cr. a Baronet*, 15 Dec. 1643,(d) being subsequently(e) *Knighted*. He was a Royalist, and was fined £720 by the

(a) This Margaret, who was h. to her br., the 4th Bart., *m.* John (Arundell), 2d Baron Arundell of Trerice. Under the will of her grandson, the 4th Baron, the Acland family inherited Trerice and other of the Arundell estates.

(b) Wotton's *Baronetage*, edit. 1741.

(c) The previous creation of Boothby, 13 July 1660, was practically a similar case, and that of Edwards, 22 April, 1678 (the next creation following this one) was precisely similar.

(d) See p. 236, notes "a" and "b." In this case, however, there is said to have been a warrant for its creation under the Privy Seal at Oxford, dat. 15 Dec. 1641. If the creation was before 4 Jan. 1641/2, it would not be affected by the disallowing acts of Parl. (see *Memorandum* on p. 152). Unlike many other unrecorded creations of this period, this particular one appears to have been considered fictitious by (Dugdale) Garter; as also by (St. George) Clarenceux, and four other Heralds, 3 Sep. 1679 and 19 May (1681), 33 Car. II. See "1 L. 2," (p. 156b, 145) in the College of Arms, London. It was, however, recognised in the Visitation of Gloucestershire in 1682, and is said [but *Query*] to have been exemplified under the Great Seal by Car. II, 18 Jan. (1682/3), 34 Car. II.

(e) In the Cal. Com. for advance of money, p. 824, it is stated, under 28 May 1647, "that he was made a Baronet by the King since the war began; gave £170 to Richard Lloyd to be a Baronet, and *afterwards* £20 to be made a Knight"; again, under 6 and 7 Sep. 1648, "Information that he is a delinquent, and was at Oxford when it was the King's garrison. Depositions to prove that when at Oxford he paid £160 for a blank warrant for a Baronetcy, which was filled in with his name." [*Ex inform.*, W. D. Pink.]

sequestrators. He *m.* firstly, in or before 1634, Anne, da. of Thomas MORRIS, of Great Coxwell, Berks. He *m.* secondly, in or before 1654, Susan, widow of Thomas COOK, da. of Thomas RICH, of North Cerney, co. Glouc. He *m.* thirdly, Dorothy, da. of (—) NASH, of Worcestershire. He *d.* 6 Aug. 1674, aged 61, at Lechlade. M.I. His widow, by whom he had no issue, *d.* 18 March 1683/4, and was *bur.* at Spelsbury, co. Oxford. M.I. Will pr. 1684.

II. 1674. SIR EDWARD BATHURST, Bart. [1643], of Lechlade aforesaid, grandson and h., being s. and h. of Laurence BATHURST, by Susan, da. of the abovenamed Thomas COOK, of Stanton, co. Worcester, which Laurence (who was admitted to Gray's Inn, 10 Feb. 1657/8), was s. and h. ap. of the late Baronet, by his 1st wife, but *d.* v.p., 15 Sep. 1671. He, who was *b.* about 1665, *suc. to the Baronetcy*, 6 Aug. 1674, and *d.* unm. 21 March 1677, aged 12.(a)

III. 1677. SIR EDWARD BATHURST, Bart., [1643], of Lechlade aforesaid, uncle and heir male, being 2d s. of the 1st Bart. by his 1st wife, and *b.* about 1635, *suc. to the Baronetcy*, 21 March 1677; entered his pedigree at the Heralds' Visitation of co. Glouc. in 1682, being then aged 47, in which his own, his nephew's, and his father's Baronetcy are all recognised. He *m.* in or before 1672, Mary, da. of Francis PEACOCK, of Chawley, Oxon; she was living 1682.

IV. 1688? SIR EDWARD BATHURST, Bart. [1643], s. and h., said to be aged about 10 in the Visitation of 1682, was a scholar at Winchester College, 1686 (then said to be 12) to 1688, when, apparently (1688) as "Dominus Bathurst" he became a commoner of that School,(b) having previously *suc. to the Baronetcy* on his father's death. He *d.* unm.

V. 1690? SIR FRANCIS BATHURST, Bart. [1643], br. and h., aged about 6 in 1682, *suc. to the Baronetcy* on his brother's death. He *m.* Frances, da. of the Rev. (—) PEACOCK. He, with his wife and part of his family, embarked (with Gen. Oglethorpe) for New Georgia, where his wife *d.* Jan. 1736/7, and he himself, shortly afterwards, about 1738.

VI. 1738? to 1780? SIR LAURENCE BATHURST, Bart. [1643], 1st and only surv. s. and h.;(c) *suc. to the Baronetcy* about 1738, and was residing in Georgia, 1741 and 1771.(d) He *d.* there s.p., probably about 1780, at whose decease the *Baronetcy* is said(e) to have become *extinct*, though it is stated(f) "by other accounts to be vested in a gentleman still(g) [1841] resident in America," possibly a descendant of Lancelot Bathurst, 5th s. of the 1st Bart., aged 36 in 1682, and then living in Virginia with issue.

(a) The manor of Lechlade devolved on his two sisters and coheirs, passing finally to Thomas Coxeter, s. and h. of one, and nephew and h. of the other.

(b) See *N. & Q.*, 1st S., iv, 345.

(c) Robert, his only br., was killed in Georgia by the Indians, before 1741.

(d) See note "b," p. 237.

(e) Courthope's *Extinct Baronetage*.

(f) Burke's *Extinct Baronetage* [1841].

(g) It seems extremely probable that there may be heirs to this Baronetcy among the issue of two of the 4 younger sons (by the 2d wife) of the 1st Baronet. Of these two (I), Robert Bathurst, of Lechlade, was living 1682, aged 38, having had several sons, of whom Robert (aged 14), Charles (aged 8), Edmond (aged 2), and Laurence (aged 9 months), were then alive; (II) Lancelot Bathurst, of Virginia, was living there, 1682, aged 36, with issue. In the additions made by Sir Thomas Phillipps to the Visitation of Gloucestershire of 1682 (printed by the Harleian Society), the abovenamed Robert Bathurst, s. of Robert, is said to have died 1726, aged 59, having had two sons (1), Robert, who *d.* 1765, aged 67, and (2), Edward, who *m.* Barbara Coxeter, and *d.* 1762, aged 57.

"H.H." [*Genealogist*, vol. iv, p. 58], states that he is "credibly informed that the title actually expired as under":—

VII. 1780? SIR ROBERT BATHURST, "7th and last Bart." [1643], who *suc. to the Baronetcy* about 1780, being s. of Robert Bathurst [aged 5 in 1682], yr. br. of the 4th and 5th Barts., all three being sons of the 3d Bart.

Besides the above-named Robert, there was also (see *N. & Q.*, 7th S., ix, 377, 1st S., xii, 379 and 357):—

CHARLES BATHURST, *b.* 15 and *bap.* 18 Nov. 1711, at St. Martin's in the Fields (being s. of John Bathurst, *bur.* there 11 Dec. 1719), who was "generally reputed a Baronet [Bathurst of Lechlade, *cr.* 15 Dec. 1643], though he did not choose to assert his title." It is not, indeed, by any means clear how (if, indeed, anyhow) he descended from the grantee. He was a Bookseller, opposite St. Dunstan's Church, in Fleet street, and suc. his partner (brother-in-law to his wife) therein, 12 March 1738. He *m.* firstly, a da. of the Rev. Thomas BRIAN, Head Master of Harrow School, by whom he had one son, Charles Bathurst, who *d.* v.p. and s.p. 1763, and was *bur.* at Harrow. He *m.* secondly, at Kelmscott, Oxon, Elizabeth CARTER, spinster, and *d.* s.p.m.s. 21 July 1786, aged 77.

BOOTHBY:

cr.(a) 5 Nov. 1644;(b)

cr., *de novo*, 13 July 1660.

I. 1644. HENRY BOOTHBY, of Clater Clote, co. Oxford, Esq., 3d s. but eventually (23 Aug. 1623) heir of William BOOTHBY, citizen and haberdasher of London, by Judith (afterwards wife of Sir Richard CORBET, K.B., of Moreton Corbet, Salop), da. of Thomas AUSTEN, of Oxley, co. Stafford, was *b.* about 1592, suc. his mother, 21 March 1637, in the estate of Clater Clote aforesaid, Croperdy, co. Oxford, Boddington, co. Northampton, Broadlow Ash, in Ashbourne, co. Derby, and others, which she had acquired since the death of her first husband, and was *cr. a Baronet*,(a) 5 Nov. 1644,(b) such Baronetcy being recognised in the Heraldic Visitations of Derbyshire, 1662, and of Staffordshire in 1663, as also on his monumental inscription.(c) He was a Royalist, and compounded in 1646 for £2,500, having, as early as Oct. 1643, been assessed at £1,000. He *m.*, in or before 1638, Mary, one of the twenty children of Sir Thomas HAYES, sometime, 1614-15, Lord Mayor of London, being, presumably, a da. by his [4th ?] wife, Mary (*m.* 26 Sep. 1609), da. of Humphrey MILWARD, of London, merchant. He *d.* 3 Sep. 1648, aged 56, and was *bur.* (with his eldest br. William Boothby, who *d.* 23 Aug. 1623) at Boddington aforesaid. M.I.(b) Will dat. 2 Sep. 1648, pr. 6 Jan. 1648/9. His widow, who was *bap.* 5 May 1613, at St. Mary Aldermanbury, London, was living 1649.

II. 1648. SIR WILLIAM BOOTHBY, Bart. [1644], of Broadlow Ash, Croperdy, etc., aforesaid, only s. and h., *b.* about 1638, and *suc. to the Baronetcy*, 3 Sep. 1648, but was, nevertheless, *cr. a Baronet* [*de novo*], 13 July 1660,

(a) See p. 236, note "a."

(b) "Created Baronet by letters patent, 5 Nov. 1644, signed by His Majesty's sign manual; but the Civil Wars prevented its passing the seals." [Wotton's *Baronetage*, 1741].

(c) "Sir Henry Boothby, Baronet, the first Baronet of that family, sonne to Dame Lady Judith Corbet," etc.

II

it being stated(a) ["*ex inform. dom. Will. Boothby, Bar.*"] that "at the Restoration, the King was pleased to renew his patent gratis(b) by the name of SIR WILLIAM BOOTHBY, OF BROADLOW ASH, the former patent being OF CLATER-CLOTE." See "BOOTHBY" Baronetcy, *cr.* 13 July 1660.

COKAYNE, *or* COKAINE:

cr. about 10 Jan. 1641/2 ;(c)

ex. 13 Feb. 1683/4.

I. 1642, to 1684. ASTON COKAYNE, or COKAINE, of Ashbourne Hall, co. Derby, and of Pooley, in Polesworth, co. Warwick, Esq., 1st s. and h. of Thomas COKAYNE (s. and h. of Sir Edward COKAYNE), of the same, by Anne, sister (of the half-blood) to Philip, 1st EARL OF CHESTERFIELD, da. (by 2d wife) of Sir John STANHOPE, of Shelford and Elvaston, co. Derby, was *b.* at Elvaston and *bap.* 20 Dec. 1608, at Ashbourne ; was ed. (as a Fellow Commoner) at Trin. Coll., Cambridge ; suc. his father, 26 Jan. 1638/9, and was *cr. a Baronet* about 10 Jan. 1641/2,(c) such Baronetcy being acknowledged in the Heralds' Visitation of Derbyshire, 1662, and in that of Hampshire, 1686 (under "LACY"), as also in his will, burial register, etc. He was *cr.* M.A. of Oxford, 21 Feb. 1642/3. A zealous Royalist and "a Popish delinquent," he was assessed (with his mother) 17 Dec. 1646, at £1,500, his estate being sequestrated for non-payment, 8 March 1648 ; was fined £356, and finally suffered such heavy losses that in 1671 he sold the long-inherited estate of Ashbourne, and in 1683 that of his "beloved Pooley."(d) He *m.* in or before 1635, Mary, da. of Sir Gilbert KNIVETON, 2d Bart. [1611], of Mercaston, co. Derby, by his 1st wife, Mary, da. of Andrew GREY. She *d.* shortly before him, and was *bur.* 14 May 1683, at Polesworth. He *d.* s.p.m.s.(e) at Derby, "at the breaking up of the great frost," and was *bur.* 18 Feb. 1683/4, at Polesworth, aged 75, when the *Baronetcy* became *extinct.* Will (signed "Aston Cokaine") dat. 6 Feb. 1683/4, pr. 24 March(f) following at Lichfield.

(a) Wotton's *Baronetage* [edit. 1741], where it is also said that he "was Knighted by King Charles II in the field," which, considering that he was but 13 at the battle of Worcester (which, presumably, is the "field" alluded to) seems improbable.

(b) The creations, *de novo*, of Acland, 21 Jan. 1677/8, and of Edwards, 22 April 1678, are, practically, similar cases.

(c) If the creation was *before* 4 Jan. 1641/2 it would not be affected, but if *later* it would have been disallowed by Parliament till the Restoration. See *Memorandum* as to creations after 4 Jan. 1641/2 and 22 May 1642, on p. 152. No patent, docquet, or sign manual is enrolled, nor is the creation given in Dugdale's *Catalogue*, (see *Memorandum* on p. 236), but its existence is acknowledged (as stated in the text) in the Heralds' Visitations and elsewhere. The date of creation is indicated in Lodge's *Peerage of Ireland* (edit. 1789, vol. iv, p. 328), as "created, after the King had by violence been compelled to leave the Parliament, about 10 Jan. 1641."

(d) See his Poems. Anthony a Wood says that he "was esteemed by many an ingenious gentleman, a good poet and a great lover of learning, yet by others a perfect boon fellow, by which means he wasted all he had." He was a friend and cousin of Charles Cotton (well known as an angler and poet), who, in his poems, praises him highly for his "Tragedy of Ovid."

(e) Thomas Cokayne, his only s., *b.* 8 May 1636, *m.*, 14 Jan. 1657/8, at St. Peter's, Paul's wharf, London, Rachel, da. and coheir of Carew STURRY, of Rossall, co. Salop, and *d.* v.p. and s.p. about 1680, his widow dying before 1 Dec. 1686, when admon. was granted to her sister, wife of Sir Thomas Kniveton, 4th Bart. [1611].

(f) This is the date on the endorsement. That in the body is "24 *April*, 1683," which, as the date of the will is 6 Feb, and the inventory 27 Feb. 1683 [*i.e.*, 1683/4], is clearly a clerical error. See a facsimile of his signature thereto and other particulars about him in the *Mis. Gen. et Her.*, 3d S., vol. iv.

CROKE, *or* CROOKE:

cr. in or soon after 1642 ;(a)

ex. 16 Jan. 1728.

I. 1642 ? JOHN CROKE, of Chilton, Bucks, Esq., s. and h. of Sir John CROKE of the same (*d.* 10 April 1640, aged 54), by Rachael, da. and h. of Sir. William WEBB, of Motcombe, Dorset, was *b.* probably about 1610, suc. his father, 10 April 1640, and having raised for the King in the Civil War a troop of horse, of which he was Colonel, was *cr. a Baronet* in or soon after 1642.(a) He was removed from his office of Justice for his conduct as to a charge of felony (1668) against the Incumbent of Chilton, whom he undertook to "hang at the next assizes." He *m.* firstly, Jane, da. of Moses TRYON, of Harringworth, co. Northampton. She *d.* s.p.m., in childbirth, 9 May 1636, aged 20, and was *bur.* at Chilton. M.I. He *m.* secondly, Sarah (—), in or before 1644. She was living 14 Jan. 1672 [MS. deed], but was dead in May 1676. He alienated the family estates, and *d.* a prisoner in the Fleet, being *bur.* 14 March 1678/9, at St. Bride's, Fleet street, London. Will, in which he makes no mention of his son, dat. 4 Oct. 1678, pr. 11 July 1682, by Mary HIDE, widow, da. and extrix.

II. 1679, to 1728. SIR DODSWORTH CROKE, Bart. [1642 ?], only s. and h., by 2d wife, *b.* about 1644, *suc. to the Baronetcy* in March 1678/9. He *d.* unm. and in obscurity,(b) 16 Jan. 1728, aged 84, and was *bur.* at Chilton, when the *Baronetcy* became *extinct.*

COURTENAY:

cr. Feb. 1644 ;(c)

afterwards, 1762—1835, VISCOUNTS COURTENAY ;

and, since 1831, EARLS OF DEVON.

I. 1644. WILLIAM COURTENAY, of Powderham Castle, co. Devon, Esq., s. and h. of Francis COURTENAY (s. and h. of Sir William COURTENAY), of the same, by his 2d wife, Elizabeth, da. of Sir Edward SEYMOUR, 3d Bart. [1611], was *bap.* 7 Sep. 1628 ; suc. his father, 5 June 1638, and was, at the age of 16, *cr. a Baronet*, by Privy Seal,(d) in Feb. 1644,(e) such Baronetcy being recognised in the pedigree recorded in the College of Arms. He was fined under the Oxford Articles, April 1649 ; was instrumental in promoting the Restoration, raising a troop in co. Devon for that purpose ; was nominated a Knight of the intended

---

(a) See p. 236, note "a." In a deed dat. 20 Jan. 1664, the grantee, as "Sir John Croke, *Bart.*, with "Dame Sarah, his wife," and "Dodsworth Croke, Esq.," his son, and others, conveyed Whitsand Leas, in Chilton, to Martha Lloyd. He is also described as a Baronet in the relation (entitled "The Perjured Phanatick," etc.") of the trial against him, in 1668; also on the margin of his will, etc. Neither he nor his son were apparently Knighted. See Lipscomb's *Bucks*, vol. i, pp. 132-148, for an account of this family, where (p. 140) is given in full and interesting account of the above mentioned trial.

(b) Nothing seems known of him save that in the trial of 1668 (see note "a" above), he swears that "the ring stolen had been *pawned* by himself" to the plaintiff.

(c) See p. 236, note "a." The date here given is that of the Privy Seal. See note "d" below.

(d) Notice of this Privy Seal is recorded in College of Arms (Norfolk, iv, 210), in which the grantee and his successors are styled Baronets. Le Neve (in his MS. Baronetage, vol. ii, 230) states that "Sir William Courtenay had a like patent [of Baronetcy] with Acland in 1644, but never passed the patent." In Collins' *Peerage* (vol. vi, 259, edit. 1779) it is said that "some time before the Restoration he was *cr. a Baronet*, but not affecting that title, as much greater he thought of right appertained to his family, never took out his patent, and therefore was not inserted

order of "The Royal Oak" (estate valued at £3,000 a year) ; was Sheriff of Devon, 1664-65 ; M.P. for Ashburton, 1668, and for Devon (three Parls.), 1677-81. He *m.* about 1643, Margaret, da. of Sir William WALLER, the well-known Parliamentary General, by his 1st wife, Jane (of whom she was only child), da. of Sir Richard REYNELL, of Wolborough, Devon, their united ages being, it is said, under 30, when their first child was born. She was *bur.* 9 Jan. 1693/4, at Wolborough. He *d.* of palsy, 4 Aug. 1702, and was *bur.* with her, aged 74. Will dat. 28 July 1702.

II. 1702. SIR WILLIAM COURTENAY, Bart. [1644], of Powderham Castle aforesaid, grandson and h., being s. and h. of Francis COURTENAY, by Mary (*m.* Nov. 1670), da. of William BOEVEY, of Flaxley Abbey, co. Glouc., and of St. Dunstan's in the East, London, merchant, which Francis, who *d.* v.p. and was *bur.* 12 May 1699, at Chelsea, aged 47, was 1st s. and h. ap. of the late Baronet. He was *b.* 11 March 1675/6 ; was M.P. for Devon (eleven Parls.), 1701-10, and June 1712 till death ; *suc. to the Baronetcy*, 4 Aug. 1702 ; was L.-Lieut. of Devon, 1715. He *m.* 20 July 1704, Anne, 2d da. of James (BERTIE), 1st EARL OF ABINGDON, by his 1st wife, Eleanor, da. and coheir of Sir Henry LEE, 3d Bart. [1611]. She *d.* 31 Oct. 1728, and was *bur.* at Powderham. Admon. 26 March 1734, granted to her husband, "Sir William Courtenay, *Baronet.*" He *d.* 6 and was *bur.* 11 Oct. 1735, at Powderham. Will dat. 19 Sep. 1734, as "Sir William Courtenay, Baronet," pr. 15 Jan. 1735/6, by "Sir William Courtenay, Baronet," the son.

III. 1735. SIR WILLIAM COURTENAY, Bart. [1644], of Powderham Castle aforesaid, 3d but 1st surv. s. and h., *b.* 11 and *bap.* 15 Feb. 1709/10, at St. Martin's in the fields, matric. at Oxford (Mag. Coll.), 4 June 1729 (as son of a Baronet), aged 19 ; *cr.* M.A. 28 Jan. 1730/1, and D.C.L. (as a "Baronet") 26 May 1739, having *suc. to the Baronetcy* 6 Oct. 1735. He was M.P. for Honiton, 1734-41, and for Devon, 1741-62, and was *cr.*, 6 May 1762, VISCOUNT COURTENAY OF POWDERHAM CASTLE, co. Devon.(a) He *m.* (Lic., 2 April 1741, to marry at Duke street Chapel, Westm.) Frances, 4th da. of Heneage (FINCH), 2d EARL OF AYLESFORD, by Mary, da. and h. of Sir Clement FISHER, 3d Bart. [1622]. She, who was *b.* 4 and *bap.* 21 Feb. 1720/1, *d.* at Bath, 19 and was *bur.* 31 Dec. 1761, at Powderham. He *d.* in London (ten days after his elevation to the peerage), 16 and was *bur.* 31 May 1762, at Powderham. Will pr. June 1762.

IV. 1762. WILLIAM (COURTENAY), 2d VISCOUNT COURTENAY OF POWDERHAM and 4th Baronet [1644], only s. and h., *b.* 30 and *bap.* 31 Oct. 1742, at St. James', Westm. ; matric. at Oxford (Mag. Coll.), 21 March 1761, aged 18 ; *suc. to his father's titles*, 16 May 1762. He *m.*, at Edinburgh, 7 May 1762, and, again subsequently, 19 Dec. 1763, at Powderham, Frances, da. of Thomas CLACK, of Wallingford, Berks. She *d.* in Grosvenor square 25 March, and was *bur.* 5 April 1782, at Powderham. He *d.* in Grosvenor square, 14 Dec. 1788, and was *bur.* at Powderham. Will pr. Dec. 1788.

V. 1788. WILLIAM (COURTENAY), 3d VISCOUNT COURTENAY OF POWDERHAM and 5th Baronet [1644], only s. and h., *b.* 30 July and *bap.* 30 Aug. 1768, at Powderham ; *suc. to his father's titles*, 14 Dec. 1788. He was by an extraordinary decision of the House of Lords, confirmed 15 May 1831, declared EARL OF DEVON, under the remainder in the creation of that dignity, 3 Sep. 1553, to the "heirs male" of the grantee, he being, indeed, collaterally heir male to the Earl thus created (who *d.* unm., 1556, three years after such creation), inasmuch as his grandfather's grandfather's grandfather, Sir William Courtenay, who *d.* 1557 (though he and his abovenamed descendants were all unconscious of any right to such Earldom), was, though a very distant cousin, collaterally heir male of the grantee of 1553, whose ancestor in the seventh degree (a man who *d.* in 1377),

---

in the list of Baronets ; but he was always styled Baronet in the Commissions sent him by the King." This, however (as also the motive thus strangely attributed to him) is incorrect, for both he and his two successors manifestly *did* "affect" the title till 1762, when it became merged in the Peerage. See also *Herald and Genealogist*, iv, 279.

(a) As "Sir William Courtenay, *Baronet*," he kissed the King's hand at St. James', 28 April 1762, on being created an English Peer [*Ann. Reg.*, 1762].

was the said Sir William's grandfather's grandfather's grandfather's grandfather. In the Earldom of Devon this *Baronetcy* then (1831) *merged*, and still so continues, though on the death of this Earl, 26 May 1835, the *Viscountcy of Courtenay* became *extinct.* See *Peerage.*

EDWARDS, *or* EDWARDES:

cr. 21 March 1644/5 ;(a)

cr., *de novo*, 22 April 1678 ;

ex. 24 Aug. 1900.

I. 1645. THOMAS EDWARDS, of Grete and of the College, Shrewsbury, co. Salop, Esq., 2d s. of Thomas EDWARDS of the same (who was Sheriff of Salop 1622, and *d.* 19 March 1634, aged 79, being *bur.* at St. Chad's, Shrewsbury), by Anne, relict of Stephen DUCKET, da. and coheir of Humphrey BASKERVILLE, Alderman and sometime (1561-62) Sheriff of London, was possibly the "Thomas Edwards of Salop, son of an Esq.," who matric. at Oxford (Ex. Coll.), 31 May 1616, aged 16, being B.A. 13 June 1616. He, who was probably the King's Sheriff of Salop 1644, was *cr. a Baronet*, 21 March 1644/5. He was assessed, 11 May 1647 at £500, as "Thomas, or Sir Thomas, Edwards, of Creet," but let off, in 1651, on the ground of having compounded. He is styled "Knt. and Bart." in the admission of his 2d son to Gray's Inn, 1 July 1665. He *m.*, after 1623,(b) Anne, da. of Bonham NORTON, of Stretton, Salop, the King's printer. She *d.* s.p.m. He *m.* secondly, before 1645, Cicely, da. of Edward BROOKES, of Stretton aforesaid. He *d.* and was *bur.* 27 April 1660, at Shrewsbury. Admon. 10 Aug. 1660. His widow was *bur.* there 28 Dec. 1677. Her will pr. 1678.

II. 1660. SIR FRANCIS EDWARDS, Bart. [1644], of Grete and of Shrewsbury aforesaid, 1st s. and h., being one of six sons by 2d wife ; *b.* probably about 1645 ; *suc. to the Baronetcy*, 27 April 1660, and matric., *as a Baronet*, at Oxford (Ball. Coll.), 26 Oct. 1660, but was, nevertheless, *cr. a Baronet*, *de novo*, 22 April 1678, it being stated(c) that "in the Civil Wars 'tis supposed the Baronet's patent [of 1644] was lost, for in April 1678, a new one was granted(d) to Francis (then Sir Francis) Edwards of Shrewsbury, and to the heirs male of his body, with remainder to [his brothers] Thomas, Benjamin, Herbert, and Jonathan, and the heirs male of their bodies, etc., with a special clause for precedency before all Baronets, created after the year 1644, viz., according to the former patent." See "EDWARDS" Baronetcy, *cr.* 22 April 1678.

GREAVES, *or* GRAVES:

cr. 4 May 1645 ;(e)

ex. 11 Nov. 1680.

I. 1645, to 1680. EDWARD GREAVES, or GRAVES, of St. Leonard's Forest, Sussex, Doctor of Medicine, yr. br. of John GREAVES, Savilian Professor of Astronomy at Oxford and Gresham Professor of Geometry, both being sons of the Rev. James GREAVES, Rector of Colemore, Hants, was *b.* at Croydon, 1608 ; ed. at Merton Coll., Oxford ; B.A., 23 Oct. 1633 ;

(a) See p. 236, note "a." The date of the *year* of the creation "1644," is given in Wotton's *Baronetage* (1741), but the exact date, 21 March 1644/5, is given in Burke's *Baronetage* (1900) and elsewhere.

(b) Visit. of Salop, 1623.

(c) Wotton's *Baronetage* (1741).

(d) The previous creation, that of the Baronetcy of Acland, 21 Jan. 1677/8, is a precisely similar case, as also practically was that of Boothby, 13 July 1660.

(e) See p. 236, note "a." This Baronetcy is omitted in all the printed lists of Baronets, except in the 5th edit. [1679] of Guillim's *Heraldry*, where it is placed

Fellow of All Souls' Coll., 1634; M.A., 13 July 1637; B. Med., 18 July 1640; D. Med., 8 July 1641; Senior Linacre Lecturer of Physic, 1643; travelling physician to Charles, Prince of Wales (afterwards Charles II), and was *cr. a Baronet*, 4 May 1645.(a) Admitted to Coll. of Physicians, 4 April 1653; Fellow, 1 Oct. 1657; Herveian Orator, 1661; one of the Physicians in Ordinary to Charles II, and for many years a resident in Bath. He *m.* firstly (Lic. Fac. 20 Jan. 1663/4), Hester, da. of Thomas TYTHER, of Northaw, Herts, citizen and draper, of London. She was living Dec. 1664, and was *bur.* at Northaw aforesaid. Admon. 21 March 1665/6, to her husband, "Sir Edward Greaves, Bart." He *m.* secondly, 27 Feb. 1667/8 (Lic. Fac., he said to be aged 45 and she 35), Alice, widow of Peter CALFE (*bur.* 5 Dec. 1667), of Tottenham, Midx. He *d.* s.p.m. in his house in Henrietta street, and was *bur.* 11 Nov. 1680, at St. Paul's, Covent Garden, when the *Baronetcy* became *extinct*.(b) Will, as a "Baronet," dat. 25 March 1679, pr. 23 Nov. 1680, by da., Mary Greaves. His widow was *bur.* (with her two husbands) 15 Jan. 1683/4. Will dat. 22 July 1683, pr. 3 Nov. 1684, by her son, "Peter Calfe, Esq."

HAGGERSTON:

cr. 15 Aug. 1642.(c)

I. 1642. THOMAS HAGGERSTON, of Haggerston Castle, co. Northumberland, Esq., s. and h. of William HAGGERSTON of the same, by Margaret, da. of Henry BUTLER, of Rowcliffe, co. Lancaster, having distinguished himself in the Civil Wars, where he was Colonel of a regiment on behalf of the King, was *cr. a Baronet*, 15 Aug. 1642.(c) He *m.* Alice, da. and h. of Henry BANASTER, of Bank, co. Lancaster, by (—), da. and h. of (—) CUERDON, of Cuerdon, in that county. She was *bur.* 10 April 1673. He *d.* at a great age, and was *bur.* 7 March 1673/4.

II. 1674. SIR THOMAS HAGGERSTON, Bart. [1642], of Haggerston Castle aforesaid, 2d but yst. surviving s. and h.;(d) *suc. to the Baronetcy*, 7 March 1673/4. He was Governor of Berwick Castle, his house there being burnt down 19 Feb. 1687 and the damage sustained being above £6,000. He *m.*

as the 450th, between Boreel and Carteret. Anthony a Wood indeed speaks (*more suo*) of Dr. Greaves as a "Pretended Baronet," but Dr. Munk, in his "Roll of the Royal College of Physicians," aptly remarks, "I am disposed to believe, despite Wood's sneer, that he was really entitled to that dignity. I find him so characterised in the *Annals*; he styles himself Baronet on the title page of his Herveian Oration . . . . Thomas Guidott, M.B., of Bath, writing of him in 1676 says, 'he is full of honour, wealth, and years, being a Baronet, a Fellow of the College of Physicians in London, and Physician in Ordinary to His Majesty," and in the official list of the Fellows of the College prefixed to the *Pharmacopœia Londinensis* of 1677, his Baronetcy is acknowledged, and he appears as *Edvardus Greaves, Baronettus*. The point is of some interest, as this is the first instance of an English Physician being honoured with an hereditary title." The original patent of creation is said to be "in the family of one Mr. Calfe, of St. Leonard's Forest, Sussex" [probably descendants of his 2d wife], and a letter of Le Neve, Norroy, says that "he was apt to think" that "as the patent was dated at Oxford, 4 May 1645, there was no enrollment thereof, which was the case of several persons of honour passed about that time, the Rolls being taken into the possession of Parliament."

(a) See p. 243, note "e."

(b) The burial at Christ Church, London, 19 Nov. 1669, of "Sir Thomas Graves, *Barronet*, from Newgate," may possibly, if not an erroneous designation, relate to this creation.

(c) See p. 236, note "a." Le Neve in his MS. *Baronetage* (vol. ii, p. 217) writes, "Sir Thomas Haggerton in his letter to me, dated 12 July 1696, saith his patent is dated 15 Oct. 1642," but the date usually [though apparently incorrectly] given to it is a year later, *viz*, 15 Oct. 1643, between Waldegrave (1 Aug. 1643) and Pate (28 Oct. 1643).

(d) John Haggerston, his elder br., *d.* s.p. and v.p., being slain Oct. 1644 at Ormskirk fight.

firstly, Margaret, da. of Sir Francis HOWARD, of Corby Castle, co. Cumberland, by his 2d wife Mary, da. of Sir Henry WIDDRINGTON. She, by whom he had nine sons, *d.* in childbirth. He *m.* secondly, Jane, da. and coheir of Sir William CARNABY, of Farnham, Northumberland, but by her had no issue.

III. 1710? SIR CARNABY HAGGERSTON, Bart. [1642], of Haggerston Castle aforesaid, grandson and h., being s. and h. of William HAGGERSTON, by Ann, da. of Sir Philip Mark CONSTABLE, 3d Bart. [1642], of Everingham, co. York, sister and h. of the 4th Bart., which William, who was 2d s. of the 2d Bart., by his 1st wife, *d.* v.p. He, who was probably *b.* about 1700, *suc. to the Baronetcy* on the death of his grandfather. He *m.*, 20 Nov. 1721, Elizabeth, sister and coheir of William MIDLETON, of Kilvington and Stockeld, co. York, da. of Peter MIDLETON, of Stockeld aforesaid. He was *bur.* 20 July 1756. His widow *d.* at York, Dec. 1769.

IV. 1756. SIR THOMAS HAGGERSTON, Bart. [1642], of Haggerston Castle aforesaid, s. and h., *bap.* 11 Sep. 1722, *suc. to the Baronetcy*, 20 July 1756. He *m.* 1754, Mary, da. of George SILVERTOP, of Minster Acres, co. Northumberland. She *d.* 22 May 1773, on her journey from Bath to London. He *d.* 1 Nov. 1777.

V. 1777. SIR CARNABY HAGGERSTON, Bart. [1642], of Haggerston Castle aforesaid, s. and h., *b.* May 1756, *suc. to the Baronetcy* 1 Nov. 1777. He *m.* Frances,(a) 2d da. of Walter SMYTHE (2d s. of Sir John SMYTHE, 3d Bart. [1661], of Eshe), by Mary, da. of John ERRINGTON. He *d.* s.p.m.(b) at Haggerston Castle, 3 Dec. 1831, aged 75. Will pr. May 1844. His widow *d.* 1836. Will pr. May 1844.

VI. 1831. SIR THOMAS HAGGERSTON, Bart. [1642], of Ellingham, co. Northumberland, nephew and h. male, being s. and h. of Thomas HAGGERSTON, of Sandoe, co. Northumberland, by Winifred, da of Edward CHARLTON, which Thomas was 2d s. of the 4th Bart., and *d.* 1829. He was *b.* 13 July 1785, and *suc. to the Baronetcy* 3 Dec. 1831. He *m.* 24 Jan. 1815, Margaret, only da. of William ROBERTSON, of Ladykirk, co. Berwick. She *d.* 26 Oct. 1823. He *d.* s.p.m., 11 Dec. 1842.

VII. 1842. SIR EDWARD HAGGERSTON, Bart. [1642], of Ellingham aforesaid, br. and h. male, *b.* about 1797, *suc. to the Baronetcy* 11 Dec. 1842. He *d.* s.p. 6 May 1857, at Ellingham, aged 59. Will pr. Sep. 1857.

VIII. 1857. SIR JOHN HAGGERSTON, Bart. [1642], of Ellingham aforesaid, br. and h. male, *b.* 18 Aug. 1798, sometime Captain in the 80th Foot, *suc. to the Baronetcy* 6 May 1857. He *m.* 5 Aug. 1851, Sarah Anne, da. of Henry KNIGHT, of Terrace Lodge, Axminster, Devon. He *d.* 8 March 1858, aged 59. His widow *d.* 24 March 1883, aged 65, at Cathcart House, South Kensington.

IX. 1858. SIR JOHN DE MARIE HAGGERSTON, Bart. [1642], of Ellingham aforesaid, s. and h., *b.* 27 Nov. 1852 at Furzebrooke House, Axminster, *suc. to the Baronetcy* 8 March 1858; ed. at Ushaw College, Durham. He *m.* 11 Jan. 1887, at the Servite Fathers' (Roman Catholic) Church, St. Mary's Priory, Fulham, his cousin, Marguerite, 2d da. of Lewis EYRE, of 78 Redcliffe Gardens, South Kensington.

Family Estates.—These, in 1883, consisted of 14,285 acres in Northumberland, worth £8,623 a year. *Principal Seat*.—Ellingham Hall, near Alnwick, co. Northumberland.

(a) Her sister, MRS. FITZHERBERT, who *d.* 27 March 1827, was well known for her connection with the Prince Regent, afterwards George IV.

(b) Mary, his only da. and h., *m.*, 1805, Sir Thomas STANLEY, 9th Bart. [1661], of Hooton, and *d.* 20 Aug. 1857, leaving issue.

I'ANSON:

Warrant for Baronetcy given by Charles I, probably between 1642 and 1644,(a) recognised to the grantee by Charles II. Baronetcy *cr.* (*de novo*) 28 Dec. 1651; See Creations of Baronetcies [E.] under that date.

LLOYD:

cr. 21 June 1647;(b)

ex. 1 April 1700.

I. 1647. EVAN LLOYD, of Yale, co. Denbigh, Esq., s. and h. of John LLOYD, of the same, by his 1st wife, Margaret, da. of Sir Bevis THELWALL, which John was s. and h. of Evan LLOYD, of Yale (*d.* 17 April 1637, being *bur.* at Llanarmon), was *b.* about 1622; matric. at Oxford (Ch. Ch.) 12 Sep. 1640, aged 18; was a Royalist; was fined £1,000 on 16 June 1646; and was *cr. a Baronet*, 21 June 1647.(b) He *m.* in or before 1654, Anne, sister of Sir Trevor WILLIAMS, 1st Bart. [1642], da. of Sir Charles WILLIAMS, of Llangibby, co. Monmouth, by Anne, da. of Sir John TREVOR. He *d.* Oct. 1663. Will pr. 1664.

II. 1663, to 1700. SIR EVAN LLOYD, Bart. [1646], of Yale aforesaid, s. and h., *b.* about 1654, *suc. to the Baronetcy*, Oct. 1663. He *m.* (Lic. Fac., 17 March 1674/5, he 20 [*sic*], and she 30 [*sic*], spinster, parents deceased) Mary, da. and coheir of Rice TANNAT, of Abertanat, Salop. He *d.* s.p.m.(c) 6 April 1700, when the *Baronetcy* became *extinct*.

NEALE:

cr. 26 Feb. 1645/6;(d)

ex., presumably, 28 March 1691.

I. 1646, to 1691. SIR WILLIAM NEALE, of Wollaston, co. Northampton, Knt., probably the 3d s. of John NEALE, of the same, by his 2nd wife, Elizabeth, da. of Sir Richard CONQUEST (which John entered his pedigree in the Visit. of Northamptonshire in 1618, having then three sons, Edward, aged 18, John, and William); was "Scout Master General" in the Civil Wars to the forces of the King, by whom he was

(a) The creations after 4 Jan. 1641/2 were disallowed till the Restoration, under an Act of Parl., 4 Feb. 1651/2, and those after 22 May 1642 were so disallowed, 11 Nov. 1643. See *Memorandum* on p. 152.

(b) See p. 236, note "a." No date is assigned to this creation in the list of Baronetcies in Kimber's *Baronetage* [1771], but the date of "21 June 1647" is given, both by Courthope and Burke, in their respective *Extinct Baronetages*. It is, however, to be observed that this date is after the King's Great Seal had been broken up, at Oxford, 11 Aug. 1646.

(c) Margaret, his da. and h., *m.* Richard VAUGHAN, of Corsygedol, and was mother of Catherine, who *m.* Rev. Hugh WYNN, D.D., Prebendary of Salisbury. Their da., Margaret, was h. to her uncle, William Vaughan, and *m.* Sir Roger MOSTYN, 5th Bart. [1660], of Mostyn.

(d) See p. 236, note "a."

Knighted at Oxford, 3 Feb. 1642/3, and was, by warrant,(a) dat. at Oxford, 26 Feb. 1645/6,(b) *cr. a Baronet*, as above. He, as "Sir William NEALE, Baronet," was Capt. of a troop of horse in Ireland, 1666.(c) He *d.* apparently s.p.m., and was *bur.* 28 March 1691, at St. Paul's, Covent Garden (from St. Andrew's, Holborn), when, presumably, the *Baronetcy* became *extinct*.(d)

PETRE:

cr., probably between 1642 and 1644;

ex., presumably, 22 Feb. 1722.

I. 1642? FRANCIS PETRE, of Cranham Hall, co. Essex, s. and h. of the Hon. Thomas PETRE, of the same, by Elizabeth, 2d da. and coheir of William BASKERVILLE, of Wanborough, Wilts (which Thomas, who was 3d s. of John, 1st BARON PETRE OF WRITTLE, *d.* 3 Oct. 1625, aged 40), was *b.* about 1605, and was, apparently, *cr. a Baronet* by Charles I, probably between 1642 and 1644. He sold the estate of Cranham. He *m.*, probably about 1628, Elizabeth, 2d da. of Sir John GAGE, 1st Bart. [1611] of Firle, by Penelope, da. of Thomas (DARCY), EARL RIVERS. She *d.* before 14 March 1655, and was *bur.* at Hengrave, Suffolk. His will, as a Baronet, dat. 14 March 1655, pr. 26 July 1660, 28 Nov. 1670, and 22 Feb. 1697.

II. 1660? SIR FRANCIS PETRE, Bart. [1642?] of London, s. and h., *b.* about 1630; *suc. to the Baronetcy* between 1655 and 1660; living 18 Nov. 1670, but *d.* unm. before 12 Jan. 1679. Will as "of St. Bride's, London," pr. 28 Nov. 1681, and 19 Nov. 1698.(f)

III. 1679? SIR EDWARD PETRE, Bart. [1642], br. and h., *b.* about 1632, in London; ed. at St. Omer's College, 1649, and at the Society of Jesuits at Watten, 1652; becoming "professed" in 1671; *suc. to the Baronetcy* in or before 1679; was Vice-Provincial of the Jesuits of England, 1680; Clerk of the Royal Closet; P.C. [11 Nov. 1687], and Chief Almoner to James II, on whose expulsion he also quitted England and became, in 1693, Rector of St. Omer's College. He, well known as "Father Petre" *d.* unm. at Watten, near Flanders, 15 May 1699, aged 68. Admon. as a "Baronet," 17 May 1699, to his sister Mary Petre.

IV. 1699. SIR THOMAS PETRE, Bart. [1642], next br. and h., *b.* 1640; ed. at St. Omer's College; *suc. to the Baronetcy*, 15 May 1699, but it is uncertain if he ever assumed it. He was living at Rome 1712, but is presumed to have *d.* unm. before 1722.

V. 1715? to 1722. SIR WILLIAM PETRE, Bart. [1642], br. and h., being yst. of six brothers, *b.* 1650. He joined the Society of the Jesuits in 1670, becoming "professed" in 1687, and, presumably, at some date after 1712, *suc. to the Baronetcy* on his brother's death. He *d.* unm., 22 Feb. 1722, at Ghent, when, unless the elder br. Thomas abovementioned was still surviving, the issue male of the grantee and the *Baronetcy* became *extinct*.

(a) Copy of this warrant is in *The Genealogist* [O.S.], vol. vi, p. 211, but the date of 3 Feb. 1642/3 is sometimes given [W. D. Pink].

(b) See p. 236, note "a."

(c) Hist. MSS. com., 14th Rep., Ormonde MSS., vol. i, p. 347.

(d) Of this family was "Edmund Neale, of Wollaston," who *d.* 21 Sep. 1671, aged 73, and was *bur.* there. M.I. [Bridges's *Northamptonshire*]. As also "Sir Charles Neale, of Woolaston, co. Northampton, Knt., aged 28, and a bachelor," 27 Feb. 1678/9, when he had lic. (Fac. Office) to marry Frances Clerke, spinster.

(e) See p. 246, note "a." It is possible, however, that the creation of the Baronetcy of Petre may have been by Charles II, during his exile, in which case it would, of course, not be recognised by Parl. till the *de facto* accession of that King in 1660.

(f) Statement in the elaborate pedigree in J. J. Howard's *Catholic Families*, from which this article is chiefly compiled.

II

WARD.

Humble Ward, of Himley, co. Stafford, whow as *cr.*, 23 March 1643/4, BARON WARD OF BIRMINGHAM, had previously [1643 ?] received the *promise of a Baronetcy*,(a) of which, however, no official record seems extant. For particulars of him see *Peerage*.

(a) Deposition, 15 May 1646, of William Ward, of Himley, co. Stafford, that he is the reputed owner of Himley, Dudley, and other manors, co. Stafford, which cost him £30,000; that he and his son [Humble Ward] lent the King £400 or £500, and that he *gave £500 to have his son made a Baronet*, and £1,500 to have him made a Peer of Parliament. [*Ex inform.*, W. D. Pink.]

Baronetcies of Ireland,(a)

1619—1800.

SECOND PART,

VIZ.:

CREATIONS BY CHARLES I,

27 March 1625 to 30 Jan. 1648/9.

BARRET:

"Sir James Barret, Knight and Baronet," is so described in a funeral entry, 1626, in the Office of Arms, Dublin. He was *Knighted* 7 Feb. 1621/2, in Dublin, but there is no record of his having been *cr. a Baronet*. He *m.* Janet, da. of Dominick (Sarsfield), 1st Viscount Sarsfield of Kilmallock [I.], in whose funeral entry, 1637, he is described only as a "Knight," so that the previous one is probably erroneous. He *d.* 30 June 1629. Inq. p.m., wherein, also, he is described as "Miles" [only]. His grandson, William Barret, was *cr.* a Baronet [I.], 4 June 1665.

MAC DONELL, *or* MACDONNELL:
cr. 30 Nov. 1627;(b)
forfeited 1690.

I. 1627. "Alexander Mac-Donell, Esq., of Moye [or Moyane], co. Antrim," "natural"(c) s. of Sir James Mac-Sorley-Boye-Macdonnel, of Dunluce, in said county (br. of Randal, Earl of Antrim [I.]), by Mary, da. of Hugh Mac Phelimy O'Neill, of Claneboye, was, by patent dat. at Dublin, 30 Nov. 1627 (Privy Seal dat. at Southwick 20 June previous), *cr. a Baronet* [I.] as above,(b) being subsequently *Knighted* in Ireland, 21 May 1628. He was Sheriff of co. Antrim, 1629. He *m.* Evelyn, da. of Arthur (Magennis), 1st Viscount Magennis of Iveagh [I.], by Sarah, da. of Hugh (O'Neill) Earl of Tyrone [I.]. He *d.* 10 May 1634, at Moyane, and was *bur.* in the abbey of Bonamargy. Funeral certificate.

(a) See vol. i, p. 223, note "a," for acknowledgment of the kind assistance of Sir Arthur Vicars, Ulster, and others, and more especially of the copious and invaluable information given by G. D. Burtchaell (of the Office of Arms, Dublin), as to the Irish Baronetcies.

(b) See vol. i, p. 223, note "b," as to the description and dates of these Irish Baronetcies.

(c) Funeral certificate in Ulster's Office.

II. 1634. Sir James Macdonnell, Baronet(a) [I. 1627], of Ballybannagh, co. Antrim, s. and h.; *suc. to the Baronetcy*, 10 May 1634. He *m.* Mary, da. of Donal O'Brien, of Dough, co. Clare, by Ellis, da. of Edmund FitzGerald, called the "Knight of Glyn." He was living 1678; *attainted*, after death, 10 July 1691.

III. 1680? to 1691? Sir Randal Macdonnell, Baronet [I. 1627], of Moye aforesaid, 2d and yst. but only surv. s. and h.;(b) *suc. to the Baronetcy* on the death of his father; was Captain of a ship of war to Charles II in the action of Mamora against the Moors, and, subsequently, served in the Army of James II, to whom he remained faithful, and whom he accompanied into exile, being, consequently, attainted, 10 July 1691, when the *Baronetcy* became *forfeited*, his estates being granted in 1696 in trust for his wife and children. He *m.*, Jan. 1686, Hannah, da. of Edward Roche, of Ballinard, co. Tipperary, by Joanna, da. of Richard Butler, of Kilenault, in that county. He *d.* about 1697. Will pr. 1697. His widow *d.* 26 Dec. 1628, and was *bur.* at St. James' Church, Dublin. Will pr. 1728 in the Prerog. Court [I.].

The right to the Baronetcy, subject to the attainder, appears to have been as under:—

IV. 1710. "Sir James Macdonnell, Baronet" [I. 1627], 1st s. and h. He *d.* unm. 24 May 1728, and was *bur.* in St. James Churchyard, Dublin.

V. 1728. "Sir Randal Macdonnell, Baronet" [I. 1627], of Cross, co. Antrim, br. and h., assumed the style and title of a Baronet on the death of his br. He was a Captain in the French service, and *d.* unm. 1740. Will pr. 1741, in the Prerog. Court [I.].

VI. 1740. John Richard Macdonnell, yst. and only surv. br. and h., of whom and whose successors, if any, nothing further is known.

(a) The words "Baronet" [in full] and "Bt." [when abbreviated], are henceforth used in this work instead of the word "Bart.," which familiar abbreviation appears to have recently [1900] become odious to several existing Baronets; indeed, in *The Athenæum* of 1 Sep. 1900, the reviewer of Pixley's *History of the Baronetage* speaks of this usage as being, in that work, indicated to be "one of the worst wrongs inflicted on the long-suffering degree." According to the statement of a certain Baronet (10 Sep. 1900), "the words *Bart.* and *Barts.* cannot be recognised as anything but very impure English," but, as he also states in the previous sentence that they "do not exist," his sense of impurity seems supernatural. The compiler of the present work is no philologist, and consequently is not deeply moved in the matter, but for the sake of courtesy he is willing to comply with the suggestion as under, made to him, 19 Sep. 1900, by the author of the abovenamed valuable work, "Francis W. Pixley, F.S.A., Registrar to the Honourable Society of the Baronetage":—"It would be gratifying to this Representative Society if you would instruct your printers and publishers to refrain throughout the work from printing the abbreviation *Bart.* for Baronet, and to substitute *Bt.* in cases where it is desired not to print the title at full length."

(b) The eldest son, Alexander Macdonell, was killed in a duel, 1677, having had an only son, Randal, who *d.* young. This Alexander is sometimes mistaken for his namesake, generally known as "Coll. Kittagh," who was killed at the battle of Knockranos, 13 Nov. 1647 [O'Donovan's *Annals of the Four Masters*.]

STAPLES:
cr. 18 July 1628.(a)

I. 1628. "Thomas Staples, Esq., of Lisson [*i.e.*, Lissane], co. Tyrone,"(a) and of Faughanvale, co. Londonderry, 5th s. of Alexander Staples, of Yate Court, co. Gloucester, was by patent dat. 18 July 1628, at Dublin (the Privy Seal being dat. 4 June previous, at Westm.). *cr. a Baronet* [I.], as above,(a) being *Knighted* 6 Aug. following; was of the Middle Temple; Sheriff of co. Tyrone, 1640. He *m.* before Sep. 1623, Charity, only da. and h. of Sir Baptist Jones, of Vintnerstown, co. Londonderry, by Elizabeth, da. of Robert Lee, of Dublin. He *d.* 31 May 1653. Inq. p.m.

II. 1653. Sir Baptist Staples, Baronet [I. 1628], of Lissane and Faughanvale aforesaid, s. and h., *suc. to the Baronetcy* in 1653. He *d.* s.p. (probably unm.), June 1672. Will dat. 30 May 1672, pr. 19 March 1673/4, at Derry.

III. 1672. Sir Alexander Staples, Baronet [I. 1628], of Lissane and Faughanvale aforesaid, br. and h.; Sheriff of co. Tyrone, 1661; M.P. [I.] for Strabane, 1661, till expelled, 14 Nov. 1665, for the plot against the Duke of Ormond, the then Viceroy [I.]. He *suc. to the Baronetcy*, June 1672, and enjoyed it only a few months. He *m.* Elizabeth. He *d.* s.p.m. Will dat. 26 May 1665, pr. 5 March 1672/3, in Prerog. Court [I.]; that of his widow was pr. there 1681.

IV. 1673? Sir Robert Staples, Baronet [I. 1628], of Lissane aforesaid, br. and h., *suc. to the Baronetcy* about 1673; M.P. [I.] for Dungannon, 1692-95, and for Clogher, 1695-99; Sheriff of co. Tyrone, 1703. He *m.*, in or before 1684, Mary, 1st da. of John Vesey, Archbishop of Tuam [1678—1716], by his 1st wife, Rebecca. He *d.* 21 Nov. 1714. Will pr. 1714, in Prerog. Court. [I.].

V. 1714. Sir John Staples, Baronet [I. 1628], of Lissane aforesaid, *b.* 22 Sep. 1684, ed. at Trin. Coll., Dublin; B.A., 1706; M.A., 1709; *suc. to the Baronetcy*, 21 Nov. 1714; in Holy Orders; Preb. of Cloneamery, in diocese of Ossory, 1728-30. He *m.* Mary, widow of Josias Haydock, of Kilkenny, da. of (—) Goslin. He *d.* s.p.m. in 1730. Admon., 1 Oct. 1730, in Prerog. Court [I.]. The will of his widow was pr. 1748, in the Prerog. Court [I.].

VI. 1730. Sir Alexander Staples, Baronet [I. 1628], of Dublin, next surv. br. and h. male, being 4th s. of the 4th Bt., *b.* 11 June 1693; ed. at Trin. Coll., Dublin; B.A., 1714; *suc. to the Baronetcy* in 1730. He *m.* (Lic., Dublin, Sep. 1735) Abigail, da. and h. of Thomas Townley, of co. Cavan. He *d.* 6 July 1741, and was *bur.* at St. Mary's, Dublin. His will pr. 1741, in Prerog. Court [I.]. That of his widow was pr. there 1748.

VII. 1741. Sir Robert Staples, Baronet [I. 1628], of Dunmore, Queens County, only s. and h., *b.* 1 Aug. 1740; *suc. to the Baronetcy* in his 1st year; was B.A., Dublin, 1761; was Sheriff of co. Tyrone, 1763, and of Queens County, 1776. He *m.* firstly (Lic. 6 Oct. 1761), Alicia, da. of Rev. Thomas Staples, of Lissane (3d s. of the 1st Baronet), by Grace, da. of John Houston, of Castle Stewart, co. Tyrone. She *d.* s.p.m. He *m.* secondly, in or before 1771, Mary, widow of Chambre Brabazon Ponsonby, 1st da. of Sir William Barker, 3d Baronet [1676], of Kilcooley Abbey, co. Tipperary, by Mary, da. of Valentine Quin. She *d.* in 1773. He *m.* thirdly, 29 Feb. 1776, Jane, 3d da. of John Denny (Vesey), 1st Baron Knapton [I.], by Elizabeth, da. of William Brownlow, of Lurgan. He *d.* 1816. His widow *d.* 1822.

(a) See p. 249, notes "a" and "b." G. D. Burtchaell (see vol. i, p. 223, note "a") supplies the succession of the 2d and 3d Baronets, (omitted in the Baronetages of Playfair, etc., and, till supplied as above in 1900, in that of Burke), and many other particulars as to this family.

VIII. 1816. Sir Robert Staples, Baronet [I. 1628], of Dunmore, aforesaid, 2d but only surv. s. and h.,(a) by 2d wife, *b.* 13 Feb. 1772, *suc. to the Baronetcy*, 1816; Sheriff of Queens County, 1819. He *d.* unm. 24 June 1832.

IX. 1832. Sir Thomas Staples, Baronet [I. 1628], of Lissane aforesaid, cousin and h. male, being 1st s. and h. of the Rt. Hon. John Staples (many years M.P. [I.] for co. Antrim), by his 2d wife, Henrietta, da. of Richard (Molesworth), 3d Viscount Molesworth of Swords [I.], which John (who *d.* 22 Dec. 1820, aged 86) was s. and h. of the Rev. Thomas Staples, Rector of Derryloran (*d.* Aug. 1762, aged 60), br. of the 5th and 6th Baronets, and 5th s. of the 4th Baronet. He was *b.* 31 July 1775, in Palace row, Rutland sq., Dublin; was ed. at Eton and Trin. Coll., Dublin; B.A., 1796; LL.B. and LL.D., 1807; M.P. [I.] for Knocktopher, co. Kilkenny, 1799-1800;(b) Barrister, Dublin, 1802; King's Counsel, 1822, and King's Advocate in the Admiralty Court [I.] till his death; *suc. to the Baronetcy*, 24 June 1832; Bencher of King's Inns, Dublin, 1833. He *m.* 27 Oct. 1813, Catherine, da. of Rev. John Hawkins, 1st s. of James Hawkins, Bishop of Raphoe, by Anne, sister of Sir Henry Conyngham Montgomery, 1st Baronet [1808], da. of Alexander Montgomery, of the Hall, co. Donegal. He *d.* s.p. 14 May 1865, at 11 Merrion square, Dublin, in his 90th year. His widow *d.* 20 Jan. 1872.

X. 1865. Sir Nathaniel Alexander Staples, Baronet [I. 1628], of Lissane aforesaid, nephew and h., being 2d but 1st surv. s. and h. of the Rev. John Molesworth Staples, Rector of Lissane and Upper Melville, by Annie, da. of Nathaniel Alexander, Bishop of Meath, which John (who *d.* 4 April 1859, aged 82), was next br. to the late Baronet. He was *b.* 1 May 1817, at Lissane; was ed. at Addiscombe College; was sometime 1834-54, in the Bengal Artillery, retiring as Captain; *suc. to the Baronetcy*, 14 May 1865. He *m.*, 27 Oct. 1844, Elizabeth Lindsay, only da. and h. of James Head, Capt. in East Indian Service, by Cecilia Maria, da. of the Hon. Robert Lindsay, 2d s. of James, 5th Earl of Balcarres [S.] He *d.* 12 March 1899, at Lissane aforesaid, in his 82d year.

XI. 1899. Sir John Molesworth Staples, Baronet [I. 1628], of Lissane aforesaid, 1st s. and h.; *b.* 29 Dec. 1848, at Dumdum, in the East Indies; *suc. to the Baronetcy*, 12 March 1899.

Family Estates.—These, in 1883, consisted of 3,078 acres in co. Tyrone, 1,457 in co. Dublin, and 990 in co. Londonderry. *Total*, 5,525 acres, worth £4,018 a year. *Principal Seat.*—Lissane, near Cookstown, co. Tyrone.

BOURKE, *or* BURKE:

cr. 2 Aug. 1628.(c)

I. 1628. "Ulick Bourke, Esq., of Glinsk, co. Galway," s. and h. of Edmund Bourke, of Imlaghvodagh, co. Roscommon, by Ellis, 1st da. of Iriel O'Ferrall-Boy, of Mornine, co. Longford, which Edmund was s. and h. ap. of Sir Hubert Bourke, of Glinsk aforesaid, suc. his said grandfather in 1598, when aged 4 years (though deprived of part of his estate by his uncle, Festus Bourke), and was *cr. a Baronet*, as above, by patent dat. at Dublin, 2 Aug. 1628, the Privy Seal being dat. at Westm. 27 June previous.(c) He was M.P. [I.] for co. Galway, 1639-48. He, in 1660, though apparently then dead, was restored to his estate as an "Ensignman" by the Act of Settlement. He *m.* firstly Katharine, 6th da. of Theobald (Dillon), 1st Viscount Dillon of Costello Gallen [I.], by Eleanor, da. of William Tuite, of Tuitestown, co. Westmeath. He *m.* secondly, Jennet, da. of (—) Browne. She, who survived him, *d.* s.p. Her Admon., 1 July 1679, in Prerog. Court [I.]

(a) William the 1st s., *b.* 1 Feb. 1771; *d.* 9 June 1773.
(b) At his death in 1865 he was the last surviving of the members of the last Irish Parliament.
(c) See p. 249, notes "a" and "b."

II. 1660? Sir Edmund Bourke, *or* Burke, Baronet [I. 1628], of Glinsk aforesaid, and of Garvagh, co. Galway, s. and h., *suc. to the Baronetcy* on the death of his father. He was restored to his estate as a "Nominee," by the Act of Explanation. He *m.* firstly (—), da. of (—) Fleming, of Slane. He *m.* secondly, Honora, da. of Col. John Kelly, of Skreen. He *m.* thirdly, April 1674, Mary, 2d da. of Nicholas Netterville, of Lecarrow, co. Galway, by Cecilia, da. of Sir Redmond Burke. His will dat. 20 Aug. 1676, pr. 5 Feb. 1686/7, in Prerog. Court [I.]. His widow *m.* Roger O'Shagnesby, of Castlegar, co. Galway.

III. 1686? Sir Ulick Burke, Baronet [I. 1628], of Glinsk aforesaid, only s. and h. by 1st wife, *suc. to the Baronetcy* on the death of his father. He was M.P. [I.] for co. Galway, in the Parl. of James II, in 1689 (whose cause he espoused), and was included in the articles of Limerick. He *m.* Ismay, 4th da. of the abovenamed Col. John Kelly, of Skreen, by Ismay, da. of Sir William Hill, of Allenstown, co. Meath. He *d.* s.p. 1708.

IV. 1708. Sir John Burke, Baronet [I. 1628], of Milford, co. Galway and of Glinsk aforesaid, br. of the half-blood and h., being only s. of the 2d Baronet by his 2d wife; *suc. to the Baronetcy* in 1708. He *m.* Jane, da. of Theobald (Dillon), 7th Viscount Dillon of Costello Gallen [I.], by Mary, da. of Sir Henry Talbot, of Templeoge, co. Dublin. His will dat. June 1721, pr. 1724, in the Prerog. Court [I.].

V. 1722? Sir Festus [Feiagh] Burke, Baronet [I. 1628], of Glinsk aforesaid, 1st s. and h., *suc. to the Baronetcy* between 1721 and 1724. He *m.* (settl. 23 Nov. 1708) Lætitia, 1st da. of John (de Burgh), 9th Earl of Clanricarde [I.], by Bridget, da. of James Talbot, of Temple Oge, co. Dublin. He *d.* s.p. His widow *d.* 29 June 1740. Will pr. 1743, in Prerog. Court [I.].

VI. 1730? Sir Theobald Burke, Baronet [I. 1628], of Glinsk aforesaid, br. and h., *suc. to the Baronetcy* on the death of his brother. He was found to be a lunatic. He *d.* unm.

VII. 1740? Sir Henry Burke, Baronet [I. 1628], of Glinsk aforesaid, br. and h., *suc. to the Baronetcy* on the death of his brother. He *m.* Cicely, 1st da. of Patrick Netterville, of Longford, co. Galway, by Margaret, sister of James Ferrall, of Kilmore, co. Roscommon. He *d.* 15 March 1747/8. Will dat. 25 May 1747, pr. 17 July 1756, in Prerog. Court [I.].

VIII. 1748. Sir Ulick Burke, Baronet [I. 1628], of Glinsk aforesaid, s. and h., *suc. to the Baronetcy*, 15 March 1747/8. He *m.*, May 1753, Elizabeth, da. of Remigius O'Carroll, of Ardagh, co. Galway, by Susanna, da. of Robert Carroll, of Emmett, co. Tipperary. He *d.* 11 April 1759. His widow *m.* her husband's first cousin, Sir John Burke,(a) afterwards of Glinsk, Knight of St. Jago in Spain (who *d.* 1781), by whom she was grandmother of the 10th and 11th Baronets.

IX. 1759. Sir Henry John Burke, Baronet [I. 1628], of Glinsk aforesaid, only s. and h., *suc. to the Baronetcy* on his father's death. He was declared an idiot, and his estate was settled by Act. of Parl. on the next heir male, viz., Sir John Burke, his stepfather, abovenamed. He *d.* unm. in April 1814.

X. 1814. Sir John Ignatius Burke, Baronet [I. 1628], of Glinsk aforesaid, cousin and h. male, being s. and h. of Rickard Burke, of Keelogues, co. Galway, and Glinsk, by Joanna Harriet, 1st da. of Joseph Blake, of Ardfry, co. Galway, which Rickard (who *d.* in or before Dec. 1791), was s. and h. of Sir John Burke,(a) of Glinsk, Knight of St. Jago in Spain, abovementioned (*d.* 1781), who was s. and h. of Rickard Burke, yr. br. of the 5th, 6th, and 7th Baronets, and 4th s. of the 4th Baronet. He was *b.* 19 March 1784, suc. his father in the Glinsk estate, when a minor, and *suc. to the Baronetcy* in 1814. He *m.* firstly, 26 Oct. 1816, at the British Embassy at Paris, Sydney, sister to Hughes Ball. She *d.* 1830. He *m.* secondly, April 1834, Sophia, 1st da. of William Dawson, of Settle, co. York, and of St. Leonard's Hill, Berks. He *d.* s.p.m., 1845. His widow *d.* s.p., 6 May 1862.

(a) This Sir John Burke appears to have considered his stepson, the 9th Baronet, as legally defunct, and to have accordingly assumed that Baronetcy. In his mar. lic. [I.], 1 Dec. 1780, he is called "Baronet," as also elsewhere.

XI. 1845. Sir Joseph Burke, Baronet [I. 1628], of Glinsk aforesaid, br. and h., *b.* 31 Jan. 1786, at Ardfry, *suc. to the Baronetcy* in 1845. He *m.*, 9 Aug. 1816, Louisa, 1st da. of Sir William Manners, *afterwards* Talmash, 1st Baronet [1793], *styled* Lord Huntingtower (s. and h. ap. of Louisa, *suo jure* Countess of Dysart [S.]), by Catherine Rebecca, da. of Francis Grey, of Lehena, co. Cork. She, who was *b.* 1791, *d.* 18 April 1830. He *d.* at Nice, 30 Oct. 1865.

XII. 1865. Sir John Lionel Burke, Baronet [I. 1628], of Glinsk aforesaid, only s. and h., *b.* 26 Nov. 1818 at Glinsk, *suc. to the Baronetcy*, 30 Oct. 1865. He *d.* unm., 21 July 1884, aged 65.

XIII. 1884. Sir Theobald Hubert Burke, Baronet [I. 1628], of Glinsk aforesaid, cousin and h. male, being the 4th but 1st surv. of the seven sons(a) of William Burke, of Knocknagur, co. Galway, by Fanny Xaveria, only da. of Thomas Tucker, of Brook Lodge, Sussex, which William (who *d.* 1877, aged 83) was s. and h. of Rickard Burke, of Keelogues, co. Galway (*d.* Aug. 1819), s. and h. of William Burke, of Keelogues aforesaid, the yst. br.(b) of Rickard Burke, abovementioned, of Glinsk, father of the 10th and 11th Baronets. He was *b.* 25 March 1833; was sometime an officer in the 18th Regiment, serving in the Crimean War and Indian Mutiny, retiring as Lieut. Col.; *suc. to the Baronetcy*, 21 July 1884.

COLCLOUGH, *or* COCKLEY:

cr. 21 July 1628;(c)

ex. 22 Sep. 1687;

but *assumed* from about 1790 to 1794.

I. 1628. "Adam Cockley [*i.e.*, Colclough], Esq., of Tinterne [Abbey], co. Wexford," s. and h. of Sir Thomas Colclough, of Tintern Abbey aforesaid, by his 1st wife, Martha, 4th da. of Adam Loftus, Archbishop of Dublin, was *b.* probably about 1590; suc. his father (who *d.*, aged 60) 23 Aug. 1624, and was *cr. a Baronet* [I.], as above, by Privy Seal dat. at Westm., 21 July 1628, no patent being enrolled.(c) He *m.*, in or before 1624, Alice, da. of Sir Robert Rich, a Master in Chancery, in London. He *d.* 4 April, and was *bur.* 1 June 1637 in the Church of Tintern. Funeral certif. [I.] Will dat. 4 April, pr. 3 May 1637 in Prerog. Court [I.].

II. 1637. Sir Cæsar Colclough, Baronet [I. 1628], of Tintern Abbey aforesaid, only s. and h., *b.* 1624, *suc. to the Baronetcy* in 1637, was M.P. for Newcastle under Lyne, 1661-79. He *m.*, 5 June 1647, at St. Bartholomew the Less, London, Frances, da. of Sir Francis Clerke, of Weston, and Tame, Oxon. She *d.* before him. He *d.* 22 June 1684, at Tintern and was *bur.* there. Will pr. 1684 in Prerog. Court [I.].

III. 1684, to 1687. Sir Cæsar Colclough, Baronet [I. 1628], of Tintern Abbey aforesaid, only s. and h., *b.* about 1650, matric. at Oxford (Ch. Ch.) 5 Aug. 1668, aged 18. He *d.* unm. 22 Sep. 1687 at Tintern, and was *bur.* there, when the *Baronetcy* became *extinct*.(d)

(a) The second of these sons, Thomas Henry Burke, Under Secretary of State for Ireland, was barbarously murdered in Phœnix Park, Dublin, 6 May 1882, aged 52, being at that date heir presumptive to this Baronetcy.
(b) There was, however, an intermediate brother, Michael Burke, who had two sons, James and William, whose issue male, if any, would come before that of this William.
(c) See p. 249, notes "a" and "b."
(d) The estates devolved on his sister, Margaret, who *m.* twice, but *d.* s.p. 1722, when they devolved on Col. Cæsar Colclough, descended from a br. of the 1st Baronet, whose grandson *assumed* the Baronetcy, as stated in the text.

1766? to 1794. "Sir Vesey Colclough, Baronet" [I. 1628], of Tintern Abbey aforesaid, *assumed this Baronetcy* (on a supposed right), probably on or soon after 15 April 1766, at which date he suc. his grandfather, Col. Cæsar Colclough, on whom that estate had devolved in 1722,(a) and who was great grandson and heir of Sir Dudley Colclough, a younger br. of the 1st Baronet. He was M.P. [I.] for co. Wexford, 1766-90, and is described as a "Baronet" in the Commons Journals [I.] 1783-90, but only as "Esquire" when M.P. [I.] for Enniscorthy, 1790-94. He *d.* 8 July 1794, aged 49. His will, as "Baronet," dat. 12 June 1794, pr. 3 March 1798, in Prerog. Court [I.]. After his death, however, though he left male issue (*extinct* 23 Aug. 1842), the assumption of this Baronetcy appears to have ceased.

ESMOND, *or* ESMONDE:

cr. 28 Jan. 1628/9.(b)

I. 1629. "Thomas Esmond, Esq., afterwards Knt., of Clonegall, co. Wexford," illegit. s.(c) of Laurence (Esmond), Baron Esmond of Limerick [I.], by (—), sister of (—) O'Flaherty, of Connaught, was *cr. a Baronet*, as above, by patent dat. at Dublin, 28 Jan. 1628/9, the Privy Seal being dat. 13 Aug. previous at Southwicke, Hants,(b) where (three days later), 16 Aug. 1628, he had been *Knighted*. He was M.P. [I.] for Enniscorthy 1641, till expelled, 22 June 1642. He was a Royalist and was General of Horse in the service of Charles I. On the death of his father, 26 March 1645, he is said to have succeeded to a considerable estate. He *m.* firstly (pardon, 19 March 1629), Ellice, Dowager Baroness Caher [I.], da. of Sir John FitzGerald, of Dromana, co. Waterford. She *d.* 16 Jan. 1644. Funeral entry [I.]. He *m.* secondly, Joane, widow of Theobald Purcell, of Loughmoe, co. Tipperary, formerly wife of George Bagenal, of Dunleckney, co. Carlow (who *d.* 17 Sep. 1625), 5th da. of Walter (Butler), Earl of Ormonde and Ossory [I.], by Helena, da. of Edmund (Butler), 2d Viscount Mountgarret [I.]. She was living when he, she, and his son, Laurence, were "transplanted," 22 Aug. 1656. He was restored to his estate, as a "Nominee," by the Act of Explanation, and was living, 1664, at Dunleckney aforesaid.

II. 1665? Sir Laurence Esmonde, Baronet [I. 1629], of Huntington Castle, co. Carlow (which he built), 1st s. and h. by 1st wife; *suc. to the Baronetcy* on the death of his father; was Sheriff of co. Carlow, 1687. He *m.* firstly Lucia, 1st da. of Col. Richard Butler, of Kilcash, co. Tipperary (br. of James, 1st Duke of Ormonde), by Frances, da. of Mervyn (Touchet), 1st Earl of Castlehaven [I.]. She *d.* at Clonegal 17 and was *bur.* 21 April 1685 at Limbrick. Funeral entry [I.]. He *m.* secondly, Lucy, da. of Charles Kavanagh, of Carrickduff, co. Carlow, by Mary, da. of Brian Kavanagh, of Borris, in the same county. He *d.* 1688. Admon. 22 Oct. 1688 to his widow. She *m.*, about 1691, Col. the Hon. Richard Butler, 2d s. of Edward, 2d Viscount Galmoy [I.].

(a) See p. 254, note "d."
(b) See p. 249, notes "a" and "b."
(c) As "Sir Thomas Esmonde, of Farralstown, co. Wexford, *Knt. and Baronet*, sonne to the said Lord Esmond," he signs the funeral certificate of the latter, whose wife is therein stated to have been Ellis, da. of Walter Butler, of Nodstone, co. Tipperary, by whom he had no issue [Original certificate in Ulster's office]. The contemporary author of "An Aphorismical Discovery of Treasonable Faction" refers to him as "a spurious son of Lord Esmond," whose widow also refers, 19 June 1645, to her late husband's "illegitimate son." The extinction of the peerage, as also the admon. to his father's estate which was granted to a nephew, 6 April 1646, militates against there having been a *lawful* son. [*Ex inform.* G. D. Burtchaell].

III. 1688. SIR LAURENCE ESMONDE, Baronet [I. 1629], of Huntington Castle aforesaid, 1st s. and h. by 1st wife; was a Privy Counciilor [I.] to James II; *suc. to the Baronetcy* in 1688. He *m.*, in 1703, Jane, da. of Matthew FORDE, of Coolgreany, co. Wexford, by Margaret, da. of Sir George HAMILTON, 1st Baronet [I. 1662], of Donalong, co. Tyrone. His admon. 20 June 1717 in Prerog. Court [I.].

IV. 1717? SIR LAURENCE ESMONDE, Baronet [I. 1629], of Huntington Castle aforesaid, only s. and h., *suc. to the Baronetcy* on the death of his father. He *d.* unm. 1738. Admon. 26 Feb. 1739, in Prerog. Court [I.].

V. 1738. SIR JOHN ESMONDE, Baronet [I. 1629], of Huntington Castle aforesaid, uncle and h., *suc. to the Baronetcy* in 1738. He *m.* (Lic. Cork, 22 Oct. 1742) Helen, da. of William GALWEY, of Lota, co. Cork, by Mary, da. of John BUTLER, of Westcourt, co. Kilkenny. He *d.* s.p.m., 30 June 1758. Will pr. 1760, in Prerog. Court [I.].

VI. 1758. SIR WALTER ESMONDE, Baronet [I. 1629], of Creggi, co. Tipperary, only surv. br. and h. male, *suc. to the Baronetcy*, 30 June 1758. He *m.*, after Jan. 1722, Joanna, widow of James BUTLER, of Caherbane, co. Clare, 2d da. of Theobald (BUTLER), 7th BARON CAHIR [I.], by his 1st wife, Mary, 1st da. of Sir Redmond EVERARD, 2d Baronet [I. 1622]. He *d.* s.p.m., Feb. 1766, at Creggi, and was *bur.* at Limbrick. Will pr. 1769, in Prerog. Court [I.].

VII. 1766. SIR JAMES ESMONDE, Baronet [I. 1629], of Ballynastragh, co. Wexford, cousin and h. male, being s. and h. of Laurence ESMONDE, of the same, by Elizabeth, da. of Henry BROWNRIGG, of Wingfield, co. Wexford, which Laurence (who *d.* from a fall, when out hunting, aged 84), was s. and h. of James ESMONDE, of Ballynastragh aforesaid, 4th s. of the 1st Baronet. He was *b.* 23 April 1701, and was, when young, an officer in the French service. He *m.* Ellice, da. and h. of Thomas WHITE, of Pembrokestown, co. Waterford, by Catharine, da. of Arthur DUIGNAN. He *suc. to the Baronetcy* in Feb. 1766, but *d.* two days afterwards, and was *bur.* the same day as his predecessor, at Limbrick. Admon., wherein he is styled "James Esmonde, *Esq.*," 22 July 1767, to his widow.

VIII. 1766. SIR THOMAS ESMONDE, Baronet [I. 1629], of Ballynastragh aforesaid, 1st s. and h., *suc. to the Baronetcy* in Feb. 1766. He *m.* firstly, in March 1776, at Arran Chapel, co. Dublin, Catherine Mary, da. and h. of Myles DOWDALL, of Clown, co. Meath. He *m.* secondly, Lætitia, da. of (—) HILL, niece and h. of Nicholas DEVEREUX, of Ringville, co. Kilkenny. He *d.* s.p., in London, 19 Dec. 1803. Will pr. 1805.

IX. 1803. SIR THOMAS ESMONDE, Baronet [I. 1629], of Ballynastragh, aforesaid, nephew and h., being s. and h. of John ESMONDE, by Helen, da. and coheir of Bartholomew CALLAN, or O'CALLAN, of Osberstown House, co. Kildare, which John, who was slain in the Irish Rebellion of 1798, was 2d s. of the 7th Baronet. He was *b.* 10 Dec. 1786; *suc. to the Baronetcy* in 1803; was M.P. for Wexford, 1841-47; P.C. [I.], 1847. He *m.* firstly, Mary, only da. of E. PAYNE. She *d.* 7 March 1840. He *m.* secondly, 16 April 1856, Sophia Maria, widow of Hamilton Knox Grogan MORGAN, of Johnstown Castle, co. Wexford, da. of Ebenezer Radford ROWE, of Ballyharty, co. Wexford. She *d.* 22 Nov. 1867, at Johnstown Castle, in her 62d year. He *d.* s.p. 31 Dec. 1868, at Johnstown Castle, aged 82, and was *bur.* 5 Jan. 1869 in the cemetery in Marlborough street, Dublin.

X. 1868. SIR JOHN ESMONDE, Baronet [I. 1629], of Ballynastragh, aforesaid, nephew and h., being s. and h. of James ESMONDE, of Pembrokestown, co. Waterford, Lieut. R.N., by Anna Maria, da. of James MURPHY, of Ringmahon castle, co. Cork, which James ESMONDE, who *d.* 4 Oct. 1842, was yr. br. of the late Baronet. He was *b.* 16 May 1826; ed. at Trin. Coll., Dublin; B.A., 1848; admitted to Lincoln's Inn, 6 May 1848, aged 22; Barrister (King's Inns, Dublin), 1850; was M.P. for co. Waterford, 1852-76; Sheriff of co. Wexford, 1866; one of the Lords of the Treasury for a few weeks (2 June to 12 July) in 1866; *suc. to the Baronetcy*, 31 Dec. 1868; was Sheriff of co. Wicklow, 1875; sometime Lieut. Col. of the Waterford Artillery Militia, 1875. He *m.* 11 April 1861, Louisa, 4th da. and coheir of Henry GRATTAN, of Tinnehinch, co. Wicklow (s. of the Rt. Hon. Henry GRATTAN), by Mary O'Kelly, da. and h. of Philip Whitfield HARVEY, of Grove House, co. Dublin. He *d.*, 9 Dec. 1876, at Ballynastragh. His widow *d.* 31 Jan. 1880, of bronchitis, at Kensington.

XI. 1876. SIR THOMAS HENRY GRATTAN ESMONDE, Baronet [I. 1629], of Ballynastragh aforesaid, 1st s. and h., *b.* 21 Sep. 1862, at Pau, in France; ed. at Oscott College; *suc. to the Baronetcy*, 9 Dec. 1876; M.P. for South div. of co. Dublin, 1885-92, and for West Kerry since 1892; Sheriff for co. Waterford, 1887, being, however, immediately superseded; Chairman of the co. Wexford County Council; Chamberlain to the Pope at Rome. He *m.*, 21 July 1891, Alice Barbara, da. of Patrick DONOVAN, of Frogmore, near Tralee, co. Kerry, br. of Sir Henry DONOVAN.

Family Estates.—These, in 1883, consisted of 3,533 acres in co. Wexford; 2,088 in co. Wicklow; 717 in co. Tipperary; 701 in co. Waterford; 629 in co. Kilkenny, and 389 in King's County. *Total*, 8,057 acres, worth £4,563 a year, besides a rental of £264 in co. Longford, shared into two others. *Principal Seats.*—Ballynastragh, near Gorey, co. Wexford, and Glenwood, near Rathdrum, co. Wicklow.

MAC MAHON:

cr. 15 Aug. 1628;(a)

ex., presumably, about 1680.

I. 1628. "TIEGE MAC-MAHON, Esq.," s. and h. of Terence, *otherwise* Tirlagh roe MAC MAHON, of Clondirrala, co. Clare (Sheriff of that county, 1609), by his 1st wife, Any, da. of Sir Donal O'BRIEN, of Duagh, co. Clare, had livery of his estate, 24 March 1629, for a fine of £72 10s. Irish; was *cr. a Baronet* [I.], as above,(a) by Privy Seal dat. at Southwick, Hants, 15 Aug. 1628,(a) no patent being enrolled,(b) and was *Knighted* 14 Dec. following.(c) He *m.* Mary, 3d da. of Dermot O'RYAN.

II. 1650? to 1680? SIR TURLOGH MAC-MAHON, Baronet [I. 1628], s. and h., *suc. to the Baronetcy* on the death of his father. He *m.* Elinor, 1st da. of Col. the Hon. Garret FITZMAURICE (2d s. of Thomas, LORD KERRY [I.]), by Lucia, relict of John ANKETILL, of Newmarket, co. Cork, da. of Mervyn (TOUCHET), 2d EARL OF CASTLEHAVEN [I.]. She *d.* s.p. On his death [*Qy.* about 1680?] the *Baronetcy* is presumed to have become *extinct*.

(a) See p. 249, notes "a" and "b."

(b) The patent of Esmond, of which the date of the Privy Seal was 13 Aug. 1628 (2 days before this date), was dated 28 Jan. 1628/9, and that of Magrath, of which the Privy Seal was 18 Aug. 1628 (3 days after this date), was 5 June 1629. The date of the Privy Seal for Mac-Mahon was, however, *25* (not 15) Aug. 1628, according to the Calendar of State Papers [I.], *temp* Car. I.

(c) The pedigree was, in 1625, registered in Ulster's office, at which date the father of the 1st Baronet was living.

BUTLER:

cr. 16 Aug. 1628.(a)

I. 1628. "THOMAS BUTLER, of Cloughgrenan, co. Carlow, Esq.," an illegit. s.(b) of Sir Edmund BUTLER, of Cloughgrenan aforesaid, and of Roscrea, co. Tipperary (who was 2d s. of James, 9th EARL OF ORMOND [I.]; was Sheriff of co. Carlow, 1612 and 1622, and was *cr. a Baronet* [I.], as above, the Privy Seal being dat. at Southwick, 16 Aug. 1628,(a) but the date of the patent, which was not enrolled, being unknown. He was M.P. [I.] for co. Carlow, 1634-35 and 1639 till his death. He *m.* (settlmt. 3 July 1618) Anne, widow of Nicholas BAGENAL, da. of Sir Thomas COLCLOUGH, of Tyntern Abbey, co. Wexford, by Martha, da. of Adam LOFTUS, Archbishop of Dublin. He was living 1639.

II. 1640? SIR EDMUND BUTLER, Baronet [I. 1628], of Cloughgrenan aforesaid, and of Ballybar, co. Carlow, s. and h., admitted to Lincoln's Inn, 5 June 1637, after which date he *suc. to the Baronetcy* on the death of his father. He *m.* Juliana, da. of Barnard HYDE, of Shinfield, Berks. He was *bur.* at Cloydagh.(c) Admon. 1653 to his widow. She *d.* at Ballybar 1 and was *bur.* 4 Jan. 1683, at Cloydagh aforesaid. Funeral certificate in Ulster's office. Will dat. 10 July 1683, pr. 10 Jan. 1683/4, at Leighlin.

III. 1650? SIR THOMAS BUTLER, Baronet [I. 1628], of Garryhunden, co. Carlow, s. and h., *suc. to the Baronetcy* on the death of his father. He was Sheriff of co. Carlow, 1670 and 1691; M.P. [I.] thereof, 1692-95, 1695-99, and 1703 till death. He *m.* firstly, Jane, da. of Richard BOYLE, Bishop of Ferns and Leighlin [1666-82], by Abigail, da. of (—) WORTH. He *m.* secondly, July 1700, Jane, widow of John REYNOLDS, da. of Capt. Edward POTTINGER. He *d.* Jan. or Feb. 1703. Admon., 21 July 1705 in Prerog. Court [I.], to his brother, James. His widow, by whom he had no issue, *m.* Agmondisham VESEY, of Lucan, co. Dublin.

IV. 1703. SIR PIERCE BUTLER, Baronet [I. 1628], of Garryhunden aforesaid, s. and h. by 1st wife; admitted to Lincoln's Inn, 14 Jan. 1691/2; *suc. to the Baronetcy* in Jan. or Feb. 1703. He was M.P. [I.] for co. Carlow (two Parls.), 1703-14; P.C. [I.], 7 June 1712. He *m.* (settl. 8 Dec. 1697). Anne, da. of Joshua GALLIARD, of Edmonton, co. Midx., by Anne, da. of William WAKEFIELD. His will dat. 10 Nov. 1731, pr. 1732, in Prerog. Court [I.].

V. 1732? SIR RICHARD BUTLER, Baronet [I. 1628], of Garryhunden aforesaid, nephew and h., being s. and h. of James BUTLER, by his 1st wife, Frances, relict of Sir John PARKER, of Fermoyle, co. Longford, da. of Sir Edward ABNEY, which James (whose will, dat. 23 Aug. 1720, was pr. 14 March 1723, in the Prerog. Court [I.]) was next br. of the late Baronet. He was *b.* 1699, and *suc. to the Baronetcy* about 1732. He was M.P. [I.] for co. Carlow, 1729-60. He *m.* in 1728, Henrietta, da. and coheir of Henry PERCY, of Seskin, co. Wicklow (s. of Sir Anthony PERCY, Lord Mayor of Dublin, 1699), by Eliza, da. and h. of William PAUL, of Moyle, co. Carlow. She *d.* a widow 14 Jan. 1794.

(a) See page 249, notes "a" and "b."

(b) Since the publication, in 1880, of the *Calendar of the State Papers*, Ireland, 1615-25, his parentage has ceased to be a matter of conjecture. There was considerable litigation between him and the representatives of his legitimate brother, Theobald, Viscount Butler of Tulleophelim [I.], who *d.* s.p. in Jan. 1613. Tulleophelim is part of the estate of these Baronets, and the bordure that surrounds their arms is an indication of their illegitimacy.

(c) He, probably, is not identical with Sir Edmund Butler, *Knight* (in no place called *Baronet*), who was killed, 4 Oct. 1649, at the taking of Wexford by Cromwell. That Edmund, who possibly was the "Sir (—) Butler, Irish," *Knighted* at Oxford, 15 July 1640, was a Roman Catholic, whereas the Cloughgrenan family, from the 1st to the present Baronet, have always been Protestants. [*Ex inform.* G. D. Burtchaell.]

VI. 1768? SIR THOMAS BUTLER, Baronet [I. 1628], of Garryhunden aforesaid, s. and h., *suc. to the Baronetcy* on the death of his father. He was M.P. [I.] for co. Carlow, 1761-68, and for Portarlington, 1771-72. He *m.* (settl. 19 June 1759), Dorothea, only child of Edward BAYLY, D.D., Archdeacon of Ardfert and Dean of St. Patrick's, Dublin (2d s. of Sir Edward BAYLY, 1st Baronet [I. 1730]), by Catharine, da. and coheir of James PRICE, of Hollymount, co. Down. He *d.* 7 Oct. 1772. Will pr. 1772 in Prerog. Court [I.]. She *d.* a widow, at Bath, 1824, aged 81, and was *bur.* at Walcot, Somerset. Will pr. 1824.

VII. 1772. SIR RICHARD BUTLER, Baronet [I. 1628], of Garryhunden aforesaid, s. and h., *b.* 14 July 1761; *suc. to the Baronetcy* on the death of his father. He was M.P. [I. and U.K.] for co. Carlow, 1783-90, 1796-97, 1798-1800, and 1801-02; Sheriff of that county, 1784. He *m.* 23 Aug. 1782, Sarah Maria, only da. of Thomas Worth NEWENHAM, of Coolmore, co. Cork, by Elizabeth da. of William DAWSON, of Castle Dawson, co. Londonderry. He *d.* 16 Jan. 1817.

VIII. 1817. SIR THOMAS BUTLER, Baronet [I. 1628], of Garryhunden and of Ballintemple, co. Carlow, s. and h., *b.* 23 Oct. 1783; sometime Capt. in 6th Dragoon Guards; *suc. to the Baronetcy*, 16 Jan. 1817; Sheriff of co. Carlow, 1818. He *m.* 30 Jan. 1812, Frances, 4th da. of John Graham CLARKE, of Fenham, co. Northumberland, and Sutton, co. York, by Arabella, da. and coheir of Roger ALTHAM, of Mark Hall, Essex. He *d.* 9 Nov. 1861, and was *bur.* at Clonmulsh, aged 78. M.I. His widow *d.* 30 Aug. 1868, at Westwood Park, aged 78.

IX. 1861. SIR RICHARD PIERCE BUTLER, Baronet [I. 1628], of Ballintemple and Garryhunden aforesaid, s. and h., *b.* 4 March 1813, *suc. to the Baronetcy*, 9 Nov. 1861; Sheriff of co. Carlow, 1836. He *m.* 28 May 1835, Matilda, 2d da. of Thomas COOKSON, of Hermitage, co. Durham, by Elizabeth, da. and eventually h. of Charles Edward SELBY, of Earle, co. Northumberland. He *d.* 21 Nov. 1862, in his 49th year, and was *bur.* at Clonmulsh. She *d.* 18 Sept. 1893, and was *bur.* at Clonmulsh.

X. 1862. SIR THOMAS PIERCE BUTLER, Baronet [I. 1628], of Ballintemple and Garryhundon aforesaid, s. and h., *b.* 16 Dec. 1836; ed. at Cheltenham Coll.; sometime an officer in the 24th Foot, and served as Lieut. in 56th Foot in the Crimean War, but resigned in 1858; *suc. to the Baronetcy*, 21 Nov. 1862; was Sheriff of co. Carlow, 1866. He *m.* 8 Sep. 1864, at Castle Bellingham church, Hester Elizabeth, 1st da. of Sir Alan Edward BELLINGHAM, 3d Baronet [1796], by Elizabeth, da. and h. of Henry CLARKE, of Boston, co. Lincoln.

Family Estates.—These, in 1883, consisted of 6,455 acres in co. Carlow, valued at £4,136 a year. *Principal Seat.*—Ballintemple, near Tullow, co. Carlow.

MAGRATH:

cr. 5 June 1629;(a)

ex., presumably, about 1670.

I. 1629. "JOHN MAGRATH, Esq., of Allevollan, co. Tipperary," s. and h. of Terence, *otherwise* Terlogh MAGRATH, of Allevolan (who was s. and h. of Meiler MAGRATH, Archbishop of Cashel, 1570—1622), suc. his father in 1627, and was by patent, dat. at Dublin, 5 June 1629, the Privy Seal being dat. at Southwick, 18 Aug. 1628, was *cr. a Baronet* [I.], as above.(a) He was Sheriff of co. Tipperary, 1641, and was excepted from pardon of life and estate, 1652. He *m.* Ellen, 1st da. of Sir Edward FITZHARRIS, 1st Baronet [I. 1622], by Gyles, da. and h. of John ROCHE.

(a) See p. 249, notes "a" and "b." The King, in consequence of a petition in 1628 of Sir Frederic Hamilton "of the Boyne family," granted to him by Privy Seal the creation of two Irish Baronets, and in consequence accepted his nomination, 20 May 1629, of Magrath and Wilson to that dignity.

II. 1652? SIR TERENCE *or* TERLOGH MAGRATH, Baronet [I. 1629], s. and h., *suc. to the Baronetcy* on the death of his father. He *m.* firstly, Catherine, 3d da. of Sir Valentine BROWNE, 1st Baronet [I. 1622], by his 1st wife, Ellis, da. of Gerald (FITZGERALD), EARL OF DESMOND [I.]. He *m.* secondly, Mary, da. of (—) MAC I BRIEN ARA. She *d.* s.p.

III. 1660? to 1670? SIR JOHN MAGRATH, Baronet [I. 1629],(a) s. and h. He *m.* Ellen, sister of Patrick and Almericus, successively BARONS KINGSALE [I.], da. of John (DE COURCY), BARON KINGSALE [I.], by Ellen, da. of Charles MAC CARTHY REAGH. He *d.* apparently s.p.m., when the *Baronetcy*, presumably, became *extinct*.

WILSON:

cr. 2 July 1629;(b)

ex. 16 April 1636.

I. 1629, to 1636. "JOHN WILSON, Esq. [Knight?], of Killenure, co. Donegal," s. and h. of William WILSON, of Aghagalla, in that county, was by patent, dat. at Dublin, 2 July 1629, the Privy Seal being dat. at Southwick, 18 Aug. 1628, *cr. a Baronet* [I.], as above,(b) having been *Knighted* in Ireland 28 June previous. His estates were, by patent dat. 24 Feb. 1629/30, erected into the manor of Wilson's Fort. He *m.* Martha, 1st da. of Sir Thomas BUTLER, 1st Baronet [I. 1628], of Cloughgrenan, by Ann, da. of Sir Thomas COLCLOUGH, of Tintern. She *d.* 28 Sep., and was *bur.* 5 Oct. 1634, at Claudy. Funeral Certif. [I.] He *d.* s.p.m.(c) at Lifford, 16 April 1636, and was *bur.* at the Cathedral of Raphoe, when the *Baronetcy* became *extinct*. Funeral Certif. [I.] Will as "of Wilson's Fort, co. Donegal," pr. 1636(d) in Prerog. Court [I.].

OSBORNE:

cr. 15 Oct. 1629.(e)

I. 1629. "RICHARD OSBORNE, Esq., of Ballintaylor, co. Tipperary" [should be "co. Waterford"], whose parentage is unknown,(f) was, together with Henry OSBORNE, appointed, 4 Oct. 1616, Joint Clerk of the King's Courts, Prothonotary, Clerk of the Crown and Clerk of the Assizes to the counties of Limerick and Tipperary, offices which they surrendered 26 Jan. 1628/9, the said Richard being shortly afterwards *cr. a Baronet* [I.], as above, by patent dat. at Dublin, 15 Oct. 1629, the Privy Seal bearing date, at Whitehall, 27 March 1628.(e) He was also of Ballymelon, co. Waterford. He, in the Civil Wars, took the side of Parl., but had to surrender his castle of Knockmoane, near Ballintaylor, after a long siege in 1645, and with difficulty obtained the benefit of the "Cessation." He was M.P. [I.] for co. Waterford, 1639-49 and 1661-66. He is said(g) to have

(a) There is a draft pedigree of these three Baronets in Ulster's Office.

(b) See p. 259, note "a," under "Magrath."

(c) Anne, his only da. and h., *d.* Aug. 1639, aged 5. Inq. p.m.

(d) See vol. i, p. 223, note "a."

(e) See p. 249, notes "a" and "b."

(f) "The origin of the family has been obscured by Betham having attributed to them the arms of a totally different family, that of Osborne of Dublin, which arms now appear in all the Baronetages. The arms, however, used by them on seals, certainly as old as the Baronetcy, are:—Quarterly, *Argent* and *azure* a cross, engrailed *or*; in the 1st and 4th quarters an ermine spot." [G. D. Burtchaell.]

(g) *N. & Q.*, 5th S. II, 494, where it is said, by "Y.S.M." (following Betham's unsupported statement), that the 1st Baronet died in 1638, and the 6th Baronet on 13 May (not 13 Jan.) 1718. The returns to Parl. [I.] of the father and son in 1639, in which the latter is called "Esq.," and the fact that both "Sir Richard Osborne" and "Mr. Richard Osborne" are named on a Committee, 28 July 1641, and the former on one, 1 Aug. 1642, disprove the first statement, and the careful and accurate Lodge gives 1667 and 13 *Jan.* 1718 as the date of the respective deaths.

m. "Mary, 2d da. of Sir George CAREW, Lord Deputy" [*Qy.* Sir George CAREY, L. Deputy of Ireland, 1603-04, but no such da. is attributed him]. He, presumably, *m.* (—), da. of Roger DALTON, of Knockmoan, co. Waterford.(a) He *d.* in or before 1667. Admon., at Waterford, 1667.

II. 1667? SIR RICHARD OSBORNE, Baronet [I. 1629], of Ballintaylor aforesaid, s. and h.; was M.P. [I.] for Dungarvan, 1639-48. He *suc. to the Baronetcy* about 1667; was Sheriff of co. Waterford, 1671. He *m.*, in or before 1645, Elizabeth (—), who survived him. He *d.* 2 March 1684/5. Will dat. 20 Nov. 1684, pr. at Waterford, 12 March 1684/5.

III. 1685. SIR JOHN OSBORNE, Baronet [I. 1629], of Taylorstown or Ballintaylor aforesaid, 1st s. and h., *b.* about 1645, *suc. to the Baronetcy*, 2 March 1685. He *m.* in 1669, Elizabeth, 4th da. of Col. Thomas WALSINGHAM (*d.* 22 Nov. 1691), of Scadbury, co. Kent, by Ann, da. of Theophilus (HOWARD), 2d EARL OF SUFFOLK. He *d.* s.p., 4 April 1713, in his 69th year. Will dat. 18 April 1695, pr. 17 Feb. 1713/4, in Prerog. Court [I.]. His widow *d.* 22 Feb. 1733, aged 86. M.I. at Saffron Walden.

IV. 1713. SIR RICHARD OSBORNE, Baronet [I. 1629], of Ballintaylor aforesaid, br. and h., *suc. to the Baronetcy* in April 1713. He, who was a lunatic, *d.* unm. probably a few months later, in or before 1714.

V. 1714? SIR THOMAS OSBORNE, Baronet [I. 1629], of Tickencor, co. Waterford, cousin and h. male, being s. and h. of Nicholas OSBORNE, of Cappagh, Clerk of the Crown, 2d s. of the 2d Baronet; was Sheriff of co. Waterford, 1672; was *Knighted*, v.p., 5 Nov. 1679, in the Presence Chamber, Dublin Castle. He, probably not long before his death, *suc. to the Baronetcy* about 1714. He *m.* firstly (—). He *m.* secondly, in 1704, his cousin, Anne, yst. da. of Beverley USHER, of Kilmeadon, by Grace, da. of Sir Richard OSBORNE, 1st Baronet [I. 1629]. Will, in which he is described as "Knight," dat. 16 Oct. 1713, pr. 1717 in Prerog. Court [I.]. He was living 25 Dec. 1714. His widow *m.* Aug. 1717, Francis SKIDDY, of Dublin.

VI. 1715? SIR NICHOLAS OSBORNE, Baronet [I. 1629], of Tickencor aforesaid, grandson and h., being s. and h. of Nicholas OSBORNE, by Anne, da. of Sir Laurence PARSONS, 1st Baronet [I. 1677], which Nicholas, last-named, was only s. and h. ap. of the late Baronet, but *d.* v.p. 25 Dec. 1714, his will being pr. at Waterford, 9 May 1715. He was *b.* in or soon after 1685, and *suc. to the Baronetcy*, probably about 1715. He *m.* in or before 1709, Mary, da. of Thomas SMITH, D.D., Bishop of Limerick (1695-1725), by Dorothea, da. of Ulysses BURGH, Bishop of Ardagh (1692). He *d.* s.p.m., 13 Jan. 1718/9. Will dat. 1 April 1718, pr. 17 Feb. 1718/9 in Prerog. Court [I.]. His widow *m.* Col. John RAMSAY, and *d.* at Clontarf, 9 Feb. 1762.

VII. 1719. SIR JOHN OSBORNE, Baronet [I. 1629], of Newtown, *otherwise* Newtown-Anner, co. Tipperary, br. and h. male, *b.* about 1697, *suc. to the Baronetcy*, 13 Jan. 1718/9; admitted to Trin. Coll., Dublin, 8 Oct. 1713, aged 16, and to the Middle Temple, London, 13 Jan. 1714, and to King's Inns, Dublin, 1726; Barrister-at-Law; was M.P. [I.] for Lismore, 1719-27, and for co. Waterford, 1727-43. He *m.* Editha, only da. of William PROBY, Gov. of Fort St. George, in India, by Henrietta, da. of Robert CORNWALL, of Berington, co. Hereford. He *d.* 11 April 1743. Admon., 20 June 1745, to a creditor. His widow *d.* 19 Jan. 1745.

(a) This Roger Dalton *d.* 25 Dec. 1620, leaving Richard his heir. The manor of Knockmoan was granted to Sir Richard Osborne, "Knt. and Bt.," 13 May 1639, who calls his 3d son "Roger," a name which bears out the suggested marriage. [*Ex inform.* G. D. Burtchaell.]

VIII. 1743. SIR WILLIAM OSBORNE, Baronet [I. 1629], of Newtown aforesaid, 1st s. and h., *suc. to the Baronetcy*, 11 April 1743; was Sheriff of co. Waterford, 1750; M.P. [I.] for Carysfort, 1761-68; for Dungarvan (two Parls.), 1768-83, and for Carysfort (again), Oct. 1783, till death; P.C. [I.], 7 May 1770. He *m.* (Lic. dat. 20 March 1749), Elizabeth, 1st da. of Thomas CHRISTMAS, of Whitfield, co. Waterford, by Elizabeth, da. of Robert MARSHALL. He *d.* Nov. 1783. Will pr. 1794, in Prerog. Court [I.]. The will of his widow pr. there 1793.

IX. 1783. SIR THOMAS OSBORNE, Baronet [I. 1629], of Newtown aforesaid, 1st s. and h., *b.* 1757; *suc. to the Baronetcy*, Nov. 1783; was M.P. [I.] for Carysfort (three Parls.), 1776-97; Sheriff of co. Waterford, 1795. He *m.* 6 April 1816, Catherine Rebecca, 1st da. of Robert SMITH, Major, Royal Engineers. He *d.* 3 June 1821. His widow *d.* 10 Oct. 1856, at Newtown aforesaid.

X. 1821. SIR WILLIAM OSBORNE, Baronet [I. 1629], of Newtown aforesaid, only s. and h., *b.* 1817; *suc. to the Baronetcy*, 3 June 1821, and *d.* in boyhood, 23 May 1824(a)

XI. 1824. SIR HENRY OSBORNE, Baronet [I. 1629], of Beechwood, co. Tipperary, uncle and h. male,(b) being 4th s. of the 8th Baronet, *suc. to the Baronetcy*, 23 May 1824. He was M.P. [I.] for Carysfort, 1798-99, and for Enniskillen, 1800; Sheriff of co. Tipperary, 1804. He *m.* firstly, in or before 1783, Harriet, 1st da. and coheir of Daniel TOLER, of Beechwood aforesaid (br. to John, 1st EARL OF NORBURY [I.]), by Rebecca, da. of Paul MINCHIN. He *m.* secondly,(c) 12 June 1813, Elizabeth, da. of William HARDING, of Ballyduff, co. Tipperary. He *d.* 27 Oct. 1837. His widow *d.* 9 Jan. 1864, at Walham Green, Fulham, Midx.

XII. 1837. SIR DANIEL TOLER OSBORNE, Baronet [I. 1629], of Beechwood, aforesaid, 1st s. and h., by 1st wife; *b.* 10 Dec. 1783, *suc. to the Baronetcy*, 27 Oct. 1837. He *m.* Jan. 1805, Harriet, da. of William Power Keating (LE POER TRENCH), 1st EARL OF CLANCARTY [I.], by Anne, da. of the Rt. Hon. Charles GARDINER. He *d.* 25 March 1853, at Rathmines, near Dublin, aged 70. His widow who was *b.* Sep. 1785, *d.* 17 Nov. 1855, at the house of her son-in-law (then) Lieut. Col. Wynne.

XIII. 1853. SIR WILLIAM OSBORNE, Baronet [I. 1629], of Beechwood, aforesaid, 1st s. and h., *b.* 16 Oct. 1805; *suc. to the Baronetcy*, 25 March 1853; was Sheriff of co. Tipperary, 1861. He *m.* 22 July 1842, Maria, only da. of William THOMPSON, of Clonfin, co. Longford, by Mary, da. of John GARNET, of Hollywoodrath, co. Dublin. He *d.* s.p., 2 July 1875, in his 70th year, at Dunleckney Manor, Bagnalstown. His widow *d.*, shortly afterwards, 25 Oct. 1875.

XIV. 1875. SIR CHARLES STANLEY OSBORNE, Baronet [I. 1629], of Beechwood, aforesaid, br. and h., being 5th and yst s. of the 12th Baronet; *b.* 30 June 1825; *suc. to the Baronetcy*, 2 July 1875. He *m.* firstly, 13 July 1846, Emilie, da. of Geantz DE REUILLY, of Ardennes, in France. She *d.* 20 Dec. 1869. He *m.* secondly, 8 July 1873, Emma, da. of Charles WEBB, of Clapham

(a) The estates, above 13,000 acres in the counties of Waterford and Tipperary, devolved on his only sister, Catherine Isabella, who *m.* 20 Aug. 1844, Ralph Bernal, afterwards Bernal-Osborne, of Newtown Anner aforesaid, and *d.* s.p.m. 21 June 1880.

(b) According to some pedigrees, the Rt. Hon. Charles Osborne (*d.* 5 Sep. 1817) was *older* than Henry, the 11th Baronet. This Charles left an only son, William Osborne, Major 71st Foot, who in the supposed case would, in 1824, have been entitled to the Baronetcy, but who *d.* s.p. 13 July 1867, aged 73. According, however, to the will of the 8th Baronet, the order of his sons was (1) Thomas, (2) John Proby, (3) William, (4) *Henry*, (5) *Charles*, and (6) Robert.

(c) In Foster's *Baronetage* (1883) "the evidences" of this marriage are cited in full as if there was some question of its validity, of which, however, the proofs seem conclusive.

Common, Surrey. He *d.* s.p., 16 July 1879, aged 54, at St. Stephen's Green, Dublin.(a) His widow living 1900.

XV. 1879. SIR FRANCIS OSBORNE, Baronet [I. 1629], of the Grange, Framfield, Sussex; cousin and h. male, being 1st s. and h. of Charles OSBORNE, of the Audit Office, Somerset House, by Ann, da. of Stephen GEARY, of Euston Place, Architect, which Charles (*b.* 14 July 1816, and *d.* 15 June 1871) was s. of Sir Henry, the 11th Baronet, being his 1st s. by his 2d wife. He was *b.* 1 Nov. 1856; ed. at Lancing College; *suc. to the Baronetcy*, 16 July 1879. He *m.* 1 July 1890, Kathleen Eliza, da. of George WHITFIELD, of Modreeny, co. Tipperary, and of Cornwall Gardens, London.

HERBERT, *or* HARBERTT:

cr. 4 Dec. 1630(b);

ex. Dec. 1712.

I. 1630. "SIR GEORGE HARBERTT [*i.e.*, Herbert] late Esq., now Knight, of Dorrowe [*i.e.* Durrow], King's County,"(b) s. and h. of Sir Edward HERBERT, of the same, by Elizabeth, da. of Patrick FINGLASS, of Westpalstown, co. Dublin; was Sheriff of King's county 1614, and 1624; suc. his father, 3 Oct. 1629, was *Knighted*, 21 March 1629/30, at Whitehall, and was *cr. a Baronet* [I.], as above, by patent dat. at Dublin, 4 Dec. 1630, the Privy Seal being dat. at Westm. 31 March 1630(b). He *m.*, in or before 1620, Frances, da. of Sir Edward FITZGERALD, of Tecroghan, co. Kildare, by Alison, da. of Sir Christopher BARNEWALL, of Turvey, co. Dublin.

II. 1650? SIR EDWARD HERBERT, Baronet [I. 1630], of Durrow, aforesaid, s. and h., *b.* about 1620; entered Trin. Coll., Dublin, 1 June 1638, aged 18; *suc. to the Baronetcy* on the death of his father. He *m.* 8 May 1662 Hester, da. of Charles (LAMBART), 1st EARL OF CAVAN [I.], by Jane, da. of Richard (ROBARTES), 1st BARON ROBARTES OF TRURO. He *d.* May 1677. Will dat. 3 May 1677, pr. 19 May 1713 in Prerog. Court [I.]. His widow *m.* 19 Nov. 1679, Lieut. Col. Simon FINCH, of Kilcolman, co. Tipperary.

III. 1677, to 1713. SIR GEORGE HERBERT, Baronet [I. 1630], of Durrow, aforesaid, only s. and h., *b.* about 1673; *suc. to the Baronetcy* in May 1677. He *m.* (Lic. Fac., 20 Oct. 1697, he about 24 and she about 22) Jane, da. and coheir of Sir John KNATCHBULL, 2d Baronet [1641], by Jane, da. and coheir of Sir Edward MONINS, 2d Baronet [1611]. He *d.* s.p., Dec. 1712, when *the Baronetcy* became *extinct*.(c) Admon 12 Sep. 1714, in Prerog. Court [I.]. His widow *m.* Richard WHITSHED, of Dublin.

(a) His estates in 1876, consisted of 940 acres, co. Tipperary, and 492 co. Westmeath. *Total*, 1,432 acres valued at £909 a year. His name was on the list of those returned to serve as Sheriff for co. Tipperary in 1878, and retained in 1879 and 1880 notwithstanding his death, and it is even stated that a warrant so appointing him was made out in Jan. 1881. [*Ex inform.* G. D. Burtchaell.]

(b) See p. 249, notes "a" and "b."

(c) The estates of Durrow passed to his sisters Rose, Frances, and Elizabeth, of whom two *d.* unm., but the other, Frances, *m.*, before Sep. 1714, Major Patrick Fox, and *d.* s.p. in 1740, being *bur.* at Durrow.

MORRES:

cr. 28 March, 1631;(a)

afterwards, since 1795, VISCOUNTS MOUNTMORRES [I.].

I. 1631. "JOHN MORRES, Esq., of Knockagh, co. Tipperary"(a), s. and h. of Redmond MORRES, of the same (*d.* 31 Aug. 1624, aged 72), by his 1st wife, Elinor, da. of (—) CANTWELL, of Lahagres, co. Tipperary, was *b.* probably about 1573, and, having suc. his father, 31 Aug. 1624, was *cr. a Baronet* [I.], as above, by patent dat. at Dublin, 28 March 1631, the Privy Seal being dat. at Westm. 30 April 1630.(a) He *m.* before 1601, Catherine, da. of Sir Edmond WALSHE, of Owney Abbey, *otherwise* Abington, co. Limerick, and of Grange, co. Kilkenny, by Ellis, da. of (—) GRACE. He *d.* 1647/8, aged 75. Will dat. 29 Jan. 1647/8, pr. at Prerog. Court [I.]

II. 1648. SIR REDMOND MORRES, Baronet [I. 1631], of Knockagh, aforesaid, 1st s. and h.; *b.* probably about 1595, *suc. to the Baronetcy*, 1647/8. He *m.* in or before 1620, Ellice, da. of Garret WALL, of Coolnamucky Castle, co. Waterford. He *d.* in or before 1656, in which year his widow was, on account of her great age, exempted by Cromwell's Commissioners from transplantation into Connaught.

III. 1655? SIR JOHN MORRES, Baronet [I. 1631], of Knockagh, aforesaid, 1st s. and h., *b.* 29 Aug. 1620; *suc. to the Baronetcy* in or before 1656, was known for his wit and eccentricities, and was also a poet. He *m.* probably about 1665, Ellin, (*b.* 11 Feb. 1638), da. of Thomas (BUTLER), 3d BARON CAHER [I.], by Elinor his wife. He *d.* 26 Oct. 1720, and was *bur.* at Lateragh, co. Tipperary, aged 100. M.I. Will dat. 11 July 1719, pr. in Prerog. Court [I.] 12 Dec. 1720. His widow *d.* 27 May 1721, aged 83.

IV. 1720. SIR JOHN MORRES, Baronet [I. 1631], of Knockagh and Lateragh, aforesaid, grandson and h., being 1st s. and h. of Redmond MORRES, a Colonel in the French service, by Mary da. of (—) TRACY, a Merchant in France, which Redmond, *d.* v.p. in London in 1704, being *bur.* at St. Mary's in that city, his heart being sent to Drom, near Knockagh. He was a minor at his father's death in 1704, and *suc. to the Baronetcy*, 26 Oct. 1720. He *m.*, in or before 1717, Margaret, da. of Edmund O'SHEE, of Cloran, co. Tipperary, by Catherine, da. of (—) O'DWYER. He *d.* 1723. Will dat. 4 Feb. 1723, pr. at Cashel.

V. 1723. SIR REDMOND MORRES, Baronet [I. 1631], of Knockagh and Lateragh, aforesaid, 1st s. and h.,(b) *b.* probably about 1717; *suc. to the Baronetcy* in 1723. He conformed to the established religion; enclosed the deer park at Lateragh with a wall, and, having quarrelled with his uncle, devised all the family estates to his cousin Hervey Morres, afterwards 1st Viscount Mountmorres of Castle Morres [I.].(c) He *d.* unm. of the small pox at Carlow, 11 Oct. 1740, and was *bur.* at Lateragh. Will pr. 1740 in Prerog. Court [I.]

VI. 1740. SIR SIMON MORRES, Baronet [I. 1631], uncle and h. male, *suc. to the Baronetcy*, but to none of the estates, 11 Oct. 1740. He *m.* Jane, da. of the Rev. (—) GREGORY. He was living 5 July 1747 when he took out admon. to his sister.

(a) See p. 249, notes "a" and "b."
(b) Edmond Morres his only br., who was living 25 Nov. 1725, *d.* unm. before him.
(c) He, according to Playfair's *Irish Baronetage*, "sold the Lordships and Castles of Knockagh, Lateragh, and Castle Lyny, which for upwards of 600 years [*sic*] had been in possession of the Montmorency-Morres [*sic*] family."

VII. 1750? SIR GEORGE MORRES, Baronet [I. 1631], of Maine, co. Louth, only s. and h., *suc. to the Baronetcy* on the death of his father. He *m.* (—), who *d.* 24 April 1758, only two days before him. He *d.* s.p. 26 April 1758, at Maine aforesaid. Admon. 7 Dec. 1758 at Prerog. Court [I.], to his sister Mary Cockhill, *otherwise* Morris, widow.

VIII. 1758. SIR RICHARD MORRES, Baronet [I. 1631], cousin and h. male, being 3d(a) but only surv. s. of Nicholas MORRES, of Seafield, near Malahide, co. Dublin, by Susanna, da. of Richard TALBOT, of Malahide aforesaid, which Nicholas (who *d.* 23 March 1742, aged 66, was 3d s. of Sir John MORRES, 3d Baronet [I.]. He was a Col. in the French Service. He *suc. to the Baronetcy*, 26 April 1758, though he does not appear to have assumed the title. He resided in France. He *d.* unm., being killed, 1774, by the fall of a scaffold at the coronation of Louis XVI of France.

IX. 1774. SIR NICHOLAS MORRES, Baronet [I. 1631], cousin and h. male, being 2d(b) but only surv. s. of James MORRES, of Rosetown, co. Tipperary, by Anne, da. of Edward MORRES, which James (who *d.* 1718) was 4th s. of Sir John MORRES, the 3d Baronet. He was *b.*, probably, about 1710; was a Col. in the French Service and a Knight of St. Louis of France. He *suc. to the Baronetcy* in 1774, though he does not appear to have assumed the title. He *m.* Isabel, 1st da. of Donald CAMERON, of Lochiel, by Anne, da. of Sir James CAMPBELL, 5th Baronet [S. 1628] of Auchinbreck in Scotland. He *d.* s.p. 1795.

X. 1795. HERVEY REDMOND (MORRES), VISCOUNT MOUNTMORRES OF CASTLE MORRES [I.], and 10th Baronet [I. 1631], cousin and h. male, being s. and h. of Hervey, 1st VISCOUNT MOUNTMORRES OF CASTLEMORRES [I.] (so *cr.* 29 June 1763), by his 1st wife, Letitia, da. of Brabazon (PONSONBY), 1st EARL OF BESSBOROUGH [I.], which Hervey, who *d.* 6 April 1766, was s. and h. of Francis MORRES, of Castle Morres, co. Kilkenny, who was s. and h. of Hervey MORRES, of the same (*d.* 1722/3), 2d s. of Sir John MORRES, 2d Baronet [I. 1731], abovenamed. He was *b.* about 1743; *suc. to the Peerage* [I.], as above, as second Viscount, on the death of his father, 6 April 1766, and *suc. to the Baronetcy*, on the death of his cousin, the 9th Baronet, in 1795. In that peerage this *Baronetcy* then *merged*, and still so continues. See *Peerage*.

BARRET:

cr. possibly in 1631.

"ANDREW BARRET, of Inniscarry, co. Cork," is given as the 14th Baronet [I.],(c) *cr.* by Charles I, in Beatson's *Political Index* [1806], but not, apparently, elsewhere. He was s. and h. of Sir James BARRET; was M.P. [I.] for co. Cork, 1613-15 (as "Esq."), and for Cork city (as a "Knight"), 1639-48, having been *Knighted*, 7 July 1639, at Dublin. He was father of William BARRET, *cr.* a Baronet [I.] by Privy Seal, 4 July 1665.

(a) The 1st s., John Morres, *d.* unm. Will pr. 1744 in Prerog Court [I.]. The 2d s., Nicholas Morres, who was a Brigadier Gen. in the French Service and a Knight of St. Louis of France, *m.* (—), da. of (—) Fraser, but *d.* 1745 s.p., at Amboise, in France. This Nicholas is, in Playfair's *Irish Baronetage*, erroneously made to succeed the 7th Baronet in the title (whereas he died thirteen years before him) and is confused with Nicholas, the 9th Baronet, who was also a Knight of St. Louis.
(b) John Morres, his elder br., *d.* unm.
(c) Of the 13 previous Baronetcies [I.] 11 (*viz.*, Macdonnel, Staples, Bourke, Butler, Colclough, Esmond, Magrath, Wilson, Osborne, Herbert and Morris are the same as in the text above (Mac Mahon being omitted); the 12th and 13th are "John Talbot, of Cartown, co. Kildare (Lord Tyrconnel), 1631," and "William Dungan, of Castletown, co. Kildare (Earl of Limerick), 1631," of which two, however, (1) Talbot, a creation of 4 Feb. 1622/3, and (2) Dungan, one of 23 Oct. 1623, belong to the previous reign.

FITZGERALD:(a)

cr. 8 Feb. 1643/4;(b)

attainted 1691;

assumed 1780 to 1894;

being from 1861 to 1894, DALTON-FITZGERALD.

I. 1644. "SIR EDMOND FITZGERALD, Knt., of Clenlish, co. Limerick," s. and h. of Thomas FITZGERALD, of the same, by Mary, da. of Cormac MacDermot MACCARTHY, of Muskerry, co. Cork, suc. his father (who *d.* in London), Dec. 1635, and was *cr. a Baronet* [I.], as above, by patent dat. at Dublin, 8 Feb. 1643/4, the Privy Seal being dat. at Oxford, 23 April 1643. He is said(c) to have raised a regiment of horse for the Royal cause during the great rebellion, and to have burnt his castle of Clenlish to prevent it falling into the enemy's hands. He suffered great losses, and was one of the persons named in 1662, by Charles II, in "the Act of Explanation," to be restored as far as possible to his former possession, but he *d.* before Feb. 1670, and before such restoration.(d)

II. 1665? to 1691. SIR JOHN FITZGERALD, Baronet [I. 1644], of Gortnatubbrid, co. Limerick, s. and h., *suc. to the Baronetcy* on his father's death; was restored to a portion of his father's estate (of which Gortnatubbrid was part) by decree enrolled in Chancery [I.], 16 Feb. 1670.(e); was M.P. [I.] for co. Limerick, 1689, in the Parl. of James II. He *m.* in 1674. Ellen, da. of (—), on which occasion he settles his estates with a remainder to his brothers, Maurice, Richard, Thomas and Edmund. Adhering to James II, he was attainted in 1691, when the *Baronetcy* became *forfeited*. He *d.* abroad, being, it is said,(f) killed at the battle of Oudenarde, 11 July 1708. His wife, or widow, was living 21 June 1703, when his estates, subject to her interest, were sold to the family of FitzMaurice.

For nearly 100 years no trace appears of this Baronetcy, but on 18 Nov. 1780, Sir William Hawkins, Ulster King of Arms, certified, at the end of a pedigree recorded by him in the College of Arms, Dublin, "that Sir Richard FitzGerald, of Castle Ishen, in the county of Cork, Baronet, is lawfully descended in a direct line from Sir Edmund FitzGerald, of Clinlish, in the

(a) Between the creations of Morres and FitzGerald the following creation is inserted in the *Liber Munerum Hiberniæ*:
"SIR PIERCE CROSBIE, Knt., of Queen's County. Neither King's letter nor patent is enrolled, but I suppose him, says Lodge, to have been created about this time. He is a Baronet of Nova Scotia." [He was so created in July 1630. See those creations.]
(b) Disallowed by Parl., 11 Nov. 1643, till the Restoration. See *Memorandum* on p. 152 as to all Baronetcies *cr.* after 4 Jan. 1641/2, and 22 May 1642. See p. 249, notes "a" and "b."
(c) Playfair's *Baronetage of Ireland*.
(d) This Edmond seems often confused with another Sir Edmond FitzGerald, of Cloyne, co. Cork, who *m.*, in or after 1589, Honora, widow of John FitzGerald, Seneschal of Imokilly, da. of James FitzGerald, of Desmond, and who *d.* 10 March 1611. By her (according to a pedigree entered 1684 in Ulster's office) he had four sons of whom the youngest, Maurice, was of Castlelisheen, sometimes (incorrectly) called Castle Ishen, co. Cork. This Honora FitzGerald, widow, in her will, pr. 1628 in Prerog. Court [I.], mentions her sons, John and Maurice. Of these two sons John, who was *b.* 1594, was *Knighted* 17 April 1617, and *d.* 2 Jan. 1640/1, leaving male issue, and mentioning in his will, dat. 1 Sep. 1640, his brother Maurice FitzGerald, of Castlelisheen. This, apparently, is the same Maurice who, in a pedigree certified, 19 Nov. 1780, by Hawkins, Ulster King of Arms, is (incorrectly) made to be a son of Sir Edmond FitzGerald, the *Baronet* (of Clenlish), and whose descendant, in right of such descent, assumed that Baronetcy, as stated in the text below.
(e) Deed "recited in a decree, dat. Dec. 1701" (No. 1564, Trustee Collection, P.R.O., Ireland).
(f) Dalton's *King James' Irish Army List* (vol. ii, p. 423), but see also O'Callaghan's *Irish Brigades*, pp. 116, 119, 120.

county of Limerick, Knt, who was *cr. a Baronet* the 8 Feb. 1644,"(a) a statement which (coupled with the title of "Baronet" having been given to the said Richard), presumably, implied that he was *heir male of the body* of the said grantee, and, as such, was *entitled to the Baronetcy of the abovenamed date*. The pedigree as given by Hawkins, the parts within brackets being however supplied from elsewhere, is below:—"SIR RICHARD FITZGERALD, of Castle Ishin, co. Cork, Baronet, son of MAURICE FITZGERALD, by Helen, da. of Walter BUTLER (1st son of Richard BUTLER, Esq., of Kilcash), which Maurice [who *d.*, presumably v.p., 16 Sep. 1726, being *bur.* at Buttevant Abbey, and called on the M.I. there 'of Castle Ishin, of the house of Desmond'] was s. [and h.] of JAMES FITZ-GERALD (living Jan. 1753), by [his 1st wife] Amy, da. of Thomas FITZGERALD, Knight of Kerry, which James was [a younger] son(b) of GARRET FITZGERALD, by [his 2d wife] Catherine, da. of Charles O'BRIEN, commonly called LORD VISCOUNT CLARE [I.], which Garret was son of MAURICE FITZGERALD, of Castle Ishin [will dat. 20 March 1678/9 as 'of Castlelisshyne, co. Cork, Esq.,' pr. 7 June 1679 in Prerog. Court of Ireland], by Lady Honora [MACCARTHY], da. of [Donogh], EARL OF CLANCARTY [I.], which Maurice was [according to this pedigree, see, however, p. 266, note "d"] son of SIR EDMUND FITZGERALD, of Clonlish, co. Limerick, Knt, who was *cr. a Baronet* [I.], 8 Feb. 1644."

VII?(c) 1780. "SIR RICHARD FITZGERALD, Baronet" [I. 1644], of Castle Ishen, co. Cork, whose parentage and alleged ancestry have been above stated. He apparently was *b.* between 1710 and 1721,(d) and having suc. his father, 16 Sep. 1726, obtained, 18 Nov. 1780, the certificate from Ulster King of Arms mentioned above, styling him a Baronet, and implying that he was entitled to the Baronetcy [I.] conferred 6 Feb. 1643/4.(e) He *m.* Joanna Maria, da. and h. of James TRANT, of Dingle, co. Kerry. He *d.* about 1787. Will pr. 1787 in Prerog. Court [I.].

(a) Foster's *Baronetage* for 1883, p. 698 (being in the part of that work called "Chaos"), where a full account of this assumption is given, from which the one in the text is mainly derived.
(b) An elder br. of this James is said to have been Maurice FitzGerald "of Castle Ishen," who *d.* s.p. Feb. 1750, but the date of the will of the said James, also of Castle Ishen, dat. 19 Jan. 1753, and pr. 27 Nov. 1768, is hardly consistent with his son and his son's wife (the continuators of the line), having *d.* in 1726 and 1721 respectively.
(c) This number is purely conjectural. "Sir Richard" is stated in Playfair's *Baronetage* to have been "the second of this family who bore that title, but the 6th in descent from the 1st Baronet." The *second* Baronet was, however, s. and h. of the first, and was not (even according to Hawkins' pedigree) one of "Sir Richard's" lineal ancestors. "Sir Richard's" grandfather had an elder brother, Maurice, who *d.* s.p. Feb. 1750 (see note "b" above), and who may, apparently, be reckoned, equally with himself, as entitled to this dignity, thereby rendering "Sir Richard" the 7th in succession.
(d) His sister Mary, who *m.* 29 Nov. 1731, the Earl of Fingall [I.], was probably *b.* about 1710; their mother *d.* in 1721.
(e) "There can be no doubt that the claim of the Castle Ishen (properly Castlelishen) family to the title was devoid of foundation. It was not acknowledged by Sir W. Betham, Ulster King of Arms. The fact that Maurice Fitzgerald, late of Castlelisheen, Esq., was 4th and yst. s. of Sir Edmund FitzGerald, of Cloyne (by Honora, widow of John FitzGerald, of Ballymarter, commonly called the Seneschal of Imokilly, da. of James FitzGerald, of Desmond) appears from a pedigree of the Desmond family in Ulster's office in the year 1684, as also that Katharine, 2d da. of Conor O'Bryen, 2d Lord Clare, married Gerrott FitzGerald, surv. s. of Maurice, of Castlelisheen" [G. D. Burtchaell].

VIII ?(a) 1787? "SIR JAMES TRANT FITZGERALD, Baronet" [I. 1644], of Castle Ishen aforesaid, only s. and h., suc. his father in 1787. He *m.* 1 Oct. 1786, Bridget Anne, da. of Robert DALTON, of Thurnham Hall, co. Lancaster, by his 3d wife, Bridget, da. (whose issue became eventually sole h.) of Thomas MORE, of Barnborough, co. York. He *d.* July 1824. Will pr. 1825. His widow *d.* abroad. Will pr. Aug. 1835.

IX ?(a) 1824. "SIR JAMES FITZGERALD, Baronet" [I. 1644], of Castle Ishen aforesaid, and of Wolseley Hall, co. Stafford, only s. and h., *b.* 22 Aug. 1791; suc. his father in July 1824. He *m.* 27 Sep. 1826, at Swanbourne, Bucks, Augusta Henrietta, sister of the 1st BARON COTTESLOE, 2d da. of Vice Admiral Sir Thomas Francis FREMANTLE, **G.C.B.**, by Elizabeth, da. of Richard WYNNE, of Falkingham, co. Lincoln. He *d.* 25 Sep. 1839, at Chalons-sur-Saone, near Nice. Will pr. Oct. 1839. His widow *d.* 11 June 1863, at the Convent, Roehampton, Surrey, aged 60.

X ?(a) 1839. "SIR JAMES GEORGE FITZGERALD, *afterwards* (1861) DALTON-FITZGERALD, Baronet" [I. 1644], of Castle Ishen aforesaid, 1st s. and h., *b.* 6 Jan. 1831; suc. his father, 25 Sep. 1839. He took, by royal lic. 31 May 1861, the name of *Dalton* before that of *Fitzgerald*, on succeeding to the estate of Thurnham Hall aforesaid, formerly the possession of the Dalton family. He *m.* 26 June 1856, Blanche Mary, 3d da. of the Hon. Philip Henry Joseph STOURTON, of Holme Hall, co. York (3d s. of Charles Philip, BARON STOURTON), by Catherine, da. of Henry HOWARD, of Corby. He *d.* s.p. 16 Jan. 1867, aged 36. His widow, who took the veil, *d.* 7 June 1875, at the Convent of the Sisters of Charity, Harold's Cross, Dublin.

XI ?(a) 1867, to 1894. "SIR GERALD RICHARD FITZGERALD, *afterwards* (March 1867) DALTON-FITZGERALD, Baronet" [I. 1644], of Castle Ishen and Thurnham Hall aforesaid, br. and h., *b.* 21 Aug. 1832; suc. his brother 16 Jan. 1867, and shortly afterwards took, by royal lic. 23 March 1867, the name of *Dalton* before that of *FitzGerald*. He *m.* 15 Jan. 1861, Agnes Georgiana, 2d da. of George WILDES, of Manchester. He *d.* s.p. at 36 Lowndes sq., 22 Feb. 1894, and was *bur.* at Thurnham aforesaid, aged 61, when *the issue male of Richard FitzGerald*, who in 1760 *assumed this Baronetcy*, became *extinct*. His widow living 1900.

BUTLER:

cr. 8 July 1645;(b)

ex. or *dormant*, 1762.

I. 1645. "WALTER BUTLER, Esq., of Poulstoun [Polestown], co. Kilkenny,"(b), s. and h. of Edmund BUTLER,(c) of the same (M.P. [I.] for co. Kilkenny, 1634-35), by Ellice (*d.* 1651), 6th da. of Nicholas SHORTALL, of Upper Claragh, co. Kilkenny, suc. his father, 21 April 1636, and was *cr. a Baronet* [I.], as above, by patent dat. at Dublin, 8 July 1645, the Privy Seal being dat. at

(a) See p. 267, note "c."
(b) See p. 266, note "b," under "FITZGERALD."
(c) This Edmund, was s. and h. of Sir Richard Butler (*Knighted* 21 April 1605), s. and h. of Walter Butler, s. and h. of Edmund Butler, s. and h. of Richard, s. and h. of (another) Walter Butler, 2d s. of (another) Edmund Butler, all of Polestown aforesaid, which Edmund last named, was 3d s. of James, 3d Earl of Ormonde [I.]. [Pedigree in Ulster's office, 23 July 1636.]

Oxford, 19 April 1643.(a) He was Gov. of Kilkenny, when it surrendered, 28 March 1650, to Cromwell.(b) He *m.* Elizabeth, 1st da. of Richard (BUTLER), 3d VISCOUNT MOUNTGARRET [I.] by his 1st wife, Margaret, da. of Hugh (O'NEILL), EARL OF TYRONE [I.]. He, having with his troop quitted Kilkenny after its surrender, *d.* soon afterwards at Polestown, about May 1650.(c) His widow was living 1683, as party to a Chancery suit on behalf of her grandson. She, presumably, *d.* 31 Aug. 1686.(d)

II. 1650. SIR RICHARD BUTLER, Baronet [I. 1645], of Polestown, aforesaid, only s. and h.; *suc. to the Baronetcy* about May 1650. He *m.* before 1675, Elizabeth.(e) He *d.* in Germany 1679 or 1680. Will dat. 16 Nov. 1678 ["now going into Germany"], pr. 20 Jan. 1680 in Ireland. His widow *m.* about 1684, Theobald DENN, of Grenan, co. Kilkenny.

III. 1679? SIR WALTER BUTLER, Baronet [I. 1645], of Polestown aforesaid, only s. and h.; *b.* about 1678, being directed in his father's will "to be called by the name of Edmond, and Walter when the Bishop shall confirm him"; *suc. to the Baronetcy* in 1679 or 1680; was a dissolute spendthrift and drunkard, and was, before 1706 "delirious and of non sane memory." He *m.* firstly, April 1697, Lucy, 3d da. of Walter BUTLER, of Garryricken, co. Kilkenny, by Mary, da. of Christopher (PLUNKETT), EARL OF FINGALL [I.]. She *d.* 1703. He *m.* secondly, in or before 1706 (—), "with whom he had no fortune," and who subsequently left him and went to live in London. He *d.* 8 Oct. 1723. Admon. 14 March 1723/4, in Ireland, to a creditor.

IV. 1723, to 1762. SIR EDMUND BUTLER, Baronet [I. 1645], 2d but only surv. s. and h., being only s. by 2d wife(f), *b.* about 1708; *suc. to the Baronetcy*, 8 Oct. 1723, and filed a bill in the Exchequer [I.] 29 March 1732 to recover the family estates, but no decree was made thereon. He was a Col. in the French Service. He *d.* presumably s.p.m. in Paris, in Sep. or Oct. 1762, aged 54(g) when *the Baronetcy* became *extinct* or *dormant*.

BORROWES, *or* BURROWES:

cr. 14 Feb. 1645/6.(a)

I. 1646. "ERASMUS BORROWES, Esq., of Grangemellon, co. Kildare," s. and h. of Henry BORROWES (who emigrated from Devonshire into Ireland) by (as stated in the registered pedigree) his 2d wife, Jane, da. of Sir Arthur SAVAGE, of Rheban, co. Kildare, but more probably by his 1st wife, Catharine,

(a) See p. 266, note "b," under "FITZGERALD."
(b) This and almost all the other particulars in this article are supplied by G. D. Burtchaell. See vol. i, p. 223, note "a."
(c) Petition to the Court of Claims by his daughter, who adds, that "he died in His Majesty's service in opposition to the late Usurper."
(d) Lodge [*Irish Peerage*, 1st edit., vol. ii, p. 14] says, "1636," presumably an error for 1686.
(e) "I suspect a sister of Edmond Blanchfield or Blanchville, who, with her, is made one of the Executors of Sir Richard's will. If so, she was da. of Capt. Garret Blanchville, who *d.* v.p. 21 Feb. 1646, being eldest s. and heir ap. of Sir Edmond Blanchville, of Blanchevillestown, co. Kilkenny, by Elizabeth, sister of Sir Edward Butler, *cr.* Viscount Galmoy [I.] in 1646. Lodge states that Sir Edmond Blanchville married Elizabeth, da. of Walter (Butler), 11th Earl of Ormond [I.], but this is utterly wrong; there is abundant proof that his wife was the lady stated above. She was living as his widow in 1664." [G. D. Burtchaell.]
(f) By the first wife were two children, viz., Richard, who *d.* v.p., and a daughter.
(g) "The Dublin newspapers of 2 Oct. 1762, contain notice of this death, viz., 'At the beginning of this month, at Paris, aged 54, Sir Edmund Butler, of Polestown, Baronet, Colonel of Horse in the French Service.'" [G. D. Burtchaell.]

da. of Alexander EUSTACE, of Grangemore, co. Kildare, suc. his father, 20 March 1614; was of Gilltown, co. Kildare; Sheriff for that county, 1641-42, at the breaking out of the Irish Rebellion, in the course of which he lost in goods, corn, and cattle, at his several houses of Grangemellon, Gilltown, and Corbally, £9,396; in debts, £11,932, besides an annual income of about £1,200, and, having suffered much in the Royal cause, was *cr. a Baronet* [I.], as above, by patent dat. at Dublin, 14 Feb. 1645/6, the Privy Seal being dat. at Ragland, 7 July 1644.(a) He *m.* firstly, about 1620, Sarah, 1st da. of Walter WELDON, of Athy, by Jane, da. of John RYDER, Bishop of Killaloe (1612-32). He *m.* secondly (Lic. 13 Dec. 1632), Martha, widow of Barnabas HANCOCK, afterwards TOTTENHAM, of Ballyduffe, co. Waterford, formerly widow of (—) HOUMAN, da. of John SALISBURY. He *m.* thirdly (Lic. 11 Jan. 1644), Rebecca, widow of Sir Nathaniel CATELYN, Speaker of the House of Commons [I. 1634-35], 3d da. of William THIMBLEBY, of Dublin, by Alice, da. of Richard CLARK, of Chimpton Hall, co. Suffolk. He *d.* probably about 1650. The will of his widow dat. 1 July 1681, pr. 1682 in the Prerog. Court [I.]

II. 1650? SIR WALTER BORROWES, Baronet [I. 1646], of Gilltown aforesaid, s. and h., *b.* about 1620;(b) *suc. to the Baronetcy* on the death of his father; Sheriff of co. Kildare, 1673. He *m.* firstly, 16 Feb. 1656, in great state, before the Lord Mayor of Dublin, Eleanor, 3d da. of George (FITZGERALD), EARL OF KILDARE [I.], by Joan, da. of Richard (BOYLE), 1st EARL OF CORK [I.]. She *d.* 3 Aug. 1681, and was *bur.* at Gilltown. He *m.* secondly, Margaret, 5th da. of the Rt. Hon. Sir Adam LOFTUS, of Rathfarnam, by Jane, da. of Walter VAUGHAN, of Golden Grove, King's County, but by her had no issue. He *d.* 1685, and was *bur.* at Gilltown. Will pr. 1691, in Prerog. Court [I.]. That of his widow pr. there 1698.

III. 1685. SIR KILDARE BORROWES [I. 1646], of Gilltown aforesaid, s. and h., by 1st wife, *b.* about 1660; *suc. to the Baronetcy* in 1685; was Sheriff of co. Kildare, 1697 and 1707; M.P. [I.] thereof, 1703, till death. He *m.* Elizabeth, sister and coheir of Robert DIXON, of Colverstown, co. Kildare, da. of Sir Richard DIXON, by Mary, da. of William EUSTACE, of Blackrath. He *d.* in or shortly before May 1709, and was *bur.* at Gilltown. Will pr. 1709, in Prerog. Court [I.]. His widow *d.* 11 March 1745.

IV. 1709. SIR WALTER DIXON BORROWES, Baronet [I. 1646], of Gilltown aforesaid, s. and h.; *suc. to the Baronetcy* in 1709. He was M.P. [I.] for Harristown, 1721-27, and for Athy, 1727-41. On 5 March 1725, he inherited the estate of Colverstown aforesaid, on the death of his maternal uncle Robert DIXON abovenamed. He *m.* 18 March 1720, Mary, da. and coheir of Capt. Edward POTTINGER, of Belfast. He *d.* 9 June 1741, at Colverstown. Admon. 19 Jan. 1742 in Prerog. Court [I.]. His widow *d.* 28 Sep. 1763. Her will, as "of Dublin," pr. 1764, in Prerog. Court [I.].

V. 1741. SIR KILDARE DIXON BORROWES, Baronet [I. 1646], of Gilltown and of Colverstown aforesaid, s. and h.; *suc. to the Baronetcy*, 9 June 1741; was M.P. [I.] for co. Kildare, 1745-76; Sheriff of that county, 1751. He *m.* firstly, Feb. 1759, Elizabeth, da. and h. of John SHORT, of Grange, in Queen's County, by Elizabeth, da. of Sir Kildare BURROWES, 3d Baronet [I. 1646]. She *d.* 23 Aug. 1766. He *m.* secondly, 10 May 1769, Jane, da. of Joseph HIGGINSON, of Mount Ophaley, co. Kildare, by Bridget, da. of James MOTTLEY, of Tullow, co. Carlow. He *d.* 22 June 1790, aged 69, and was *bur.* at Gilltown. Will pr. 1790, in Prerog. Court [I.]. His widow *d.* Sep. 1793.

(a) See p. 266, note "b," under "FITZGERALD."
(b) His yr. br. Wingfield Burrowes matric. at Oxford (Linc. Coll.), 12 Sep. 1640, aged 15.

VI. 1790. SIR ERASMUS DIXON BURROWES, Baronet [I. 1646], of Colverstown aforesaid, of Lauragh [near Portarlington], in Queen's County and of Barretstown, co. Kildare, s. and h., by 1st wife, *b.* 20 Dec. 1759; *suc. to the Baronetcy*, 22 June 1790; was Sheriff of Queen's County, 1800, and of co. Kildare, 1809. He *m.* 1783, Henrietta de Robillard (sister of the Countess of Uxbridge), yst. da. of the Very Rev. Arthur CHAMPAGNÉ, Dean of Clonmacnoise, by Marianne, da. of Col. Isaac HAMON. She *d.* 11 June 1807. He *d.* 19 Sep. 1814.

VII. 1814. SIR WALTER DIXON BORROWES, Baronet [I. 1646], of Lauragh and of Barretstown Castle aforesaid, s. and h., *b.* 21 Sep. 1789; *suc. to the Baronetcy*, 19 Sep. 1814; Sheriff of Queen's County, 1817, and of co. Kildare, 1829. He *d.* unm., 7 March 1834.

VIII. 1834. SIR ERASMUS DIXON BORROWES, Baronet [I. 1646], of Lauragh and of Barretstown Castle aforesaid, only surv. br. and h., *b.* 21 Sep. 1799, at Portarlington, Queen's County; *suc. to the Baronetcy*, 7 March 1834; was in Holy Orders; Rector of Ballyroan, in Queen's County. He *m.*, March 1825, Harriett, 4th da. of Henry HAMILTON, of Ballymacoll, co. Meath (niece of Hans HAMILTON, thirty years M.P. for co. Dublin), by Mary, da. of John WETHERALL, of Dublin. He *d.* 27 May 1866, at Lauragh aforesaid in his 67th year. His widow *d.* in or before 1880.

IX. 1866. SIR ERASMUS DIXON BORROWES, Baronet [I. 1646], of Barretstown Castle aforesaid, 2d but 1st surv. s. and h.; *b.* 19 Dec. 1831, in Dublin; ed. at Cheltenham College, Ensign 80th Foot, 1852; Capt. 1859; Major (13th Foot), 1867, had medal for service in the Burmese War, 1853, and in the Indian Mutiny where he was wounded; *suc. to the Baronetcy*, 27 May 1866; Sheriff for co. Kildare, 1873, and for Queen's County, 1880. He *m.* firstly, 14 Aug. 1851, Frederica Esten, 1st da. of Brig. Gen. George HUTCHESON, Col. 97th Foot. She *d.* 17 Aug. 1886, at Barretstown Castle aforesaid. He *m.* secondly, 5 Oct. 1887, Florence Elizabeth, da. of William RUXTON, of Ardee House, Ardee. He *d.* Oct. 1898. Will pr. at £4,179. His widow living 1900.

X. 1898. SIR KILDARE BORROWES, Baronet [I. 1646], of Barretstown Castle aforesaid, 1st s. and h., *b.* 21 Sep. 1852; ed. at Cheltenham College; sometime Capt. 11th Hussars, retiring as Lieut. Col.; was A.D.C. to the Viceroy of Ireland; *suc. to the Baronetcy* in Oct. 1898; served in the Imperial Yeomanry in the Transvaal War, 1900. He *m.* 31 March 1886, at St. Paul's, Knightsbridge, Julia Aline, yst. da. of William HOLDEN, of Palace House, co. Lancaster, by Blanche, da. of J. PAULET, of Seaforth House, in that county.

Family Estates.—These, in 1883, consisted of 5,065 acres in co. Kildare, Queen's County and co. Meath, worth £2,774 a year.

Baronetcies [I.] not on record,

1640—1648;

ARRANGED ALPHABETICALLY.

Memorandum.—As in England (see *Memorandum* on p. 236), so in Ireland there were apparently some Baronetcies conferred during the Civil Wars, of which no patent, nor even docquet or warrant was enrolled. A complete list of these is unattainable, but the following persons, herein arranged alphabetically, seem to have been among them.

BOURKE:

cr. about 1645;

ex. or *dormant* about 1700.

I. 1645. DAVID BOURKE, of Kilpeacon, co. Limerick, Esq., s. and h. of Oliver Bourke, of Limerick, merchant (Sheriff, 1585, and Mayor, 1591, of that city), was *b.* 1588; was in ward to Thomas Ashe, 10 May 1597; had livery, 12 June 1611, of the estate of his br., Edmund BOURKE; was one of the Sheriffs of the city of Limerick, 1613 and again 1614, and was *cr. a Baronet* [I.] by the Earl of Ormonde, according to the direction of the King, "during the time of the cessation after the beginning of the Rebellion"(a) [*i.e.*, the Ulster Civil War, which began Oct. 1641], but no patent or Privy Seal is enrolled. He was transplanted to Clare in 1653, being then aged 65, and was living at Monanoe in that county in 1661.(b) He *m.* in or before 1615, Catherine, widow of (—) BLAKE, da. of (—) COMYN, of Limerick. He *d.* 1661. Will dat. 8 July 1660, pr. 1661 in Prerog. Court [I.].

II. 1661. SIR OLIVER BOURKE, Baronet [I. 1645 ?], s. and h., *b.* about 1615; was (with his parents and brother) transplanted in 1653; *suc. to the Baronetcy* in 1661. He, with Mary his wife, formerly wife of Pierce CREAGH, claimed in 1676, lands set out to his father, "Sir David BOURKE, Baronet," and to the said Pierce CREAGH, both of whom being "transplanted Papists." In his will, dat. 29 April 1695, pr. at Killaloe 2 Feb. 1696, he mentions his nephew James, son of his br. David, as his heir.

III. 1696, to 1700 ? SIR JAMES BOURKE, Baronet [I. 1645 ?] nephew and h., being s. of David BOURKE, 4th s. of the 1st Baronet; *suc. to the Baronetcy.* An undated petition from him, "to be placed on the establishment," is among the Ormonde MSS. The *Baronetcy* at his death became *extinct* or *dormant.*(c)

(a) The name of "James Bourke, of co. Limerick," occurs, as the recipient of a Baronetcy, in a list in the Office of Arms [I.] of "all the honours granted by the Earl of Ormond by direction of the late King during the time of the cessation after the beginning of the Rebellion," but this seems to be a mistake for "David." [G. D. Burtchaell.]

(b) *Ex inform.* C. M. Tenison.

(c) Sir David Bourke, the 1st Baronet, had three younger sons, viz., Edmund, Patrick, and David. Of these, Edmund and Patrick appear to have died s.p.

HORSFALL:

possibly, 1642 ? to 1693.

"SIR CIPRIAN HORSFALL," only s. and h. of John HORSFALL, Bishop of Ossory, 1586-1609; was *Knighted* in Ireland, 6 Aug. 1628; Sheriff of co. Kilkenny, 1641, and is sometimes stated to have been *cr. a Baronet*(a) by Charles I [1642 ?]. He *m.* firstly, 15 July 1601, at Knockmoan, co. Waterford, Jane, da. of Roger DALTON, of Knockmoan aforesaid, and Kirkbynsperton, co. York. He *m.* secondly, before July 1606, Margaret, 1st da. of David CLERE, Dean of Ossory, 1582-1602. He *d.* s.p.m.(b) in or before 1693 when the *Baronetcy*, if indeed it ever existed, became *extinct.* His admon., in which, however, he is styled a "Knight," 31 Oct. 1693, in Prerog. Court [I.], to his next of kin.

HURLY:(c)

cr. about 1645;

attainted 1691;

assumed till 1714, or later.

I. 1645 ? THOMAS HURLY, of Knocklong, co. Limerick, s. and h. of Maurice HURLY, of the same (who *d.* 3 June 1637), by his 1st wife, Grania, da. of Ogan O'HOGAN, of Ardcrony, co. Tipperary; suc. his father in June 1637; was Sheriff of co. Limerick, 1639, and is said to have been *cr. a Baronet* [I.] by Charles I, presumably about 1645. He *m.*, before June 1637, Lettice, da. of Lucas SHEE, of Kilkenny,(d) by Ellen, da. of Edmund (BUTLER), 2d VISCOUNT MOUNTGARRET [I.]. He *d.* before 1653. His widow, Lettice, was transplanted, in 1653, to Connaught, being then aged 60.

II. 1647 ? SIR MAURICE HURLY, Baronet [I. 1645 ?] of Knocklong aforesaid, of Kilduff, co. Limerick, and afterwards of Doone, co. Galway, s. and h.; *suc. to the Baronetcy* on the death of his father, and was one of the supreme council at Kilkenny in 1647. He (with his mother) was transplanted, in 1653, into Connaught, and his estates forfeited. He *m.* Margaret, da. of (—) O'DWYER. His will, as of "Doone, co. Galway, Baronet," dat. 1683, pr. 1684, in Prerog. Court [I.].

(a) In three copies of lists of Baronets of Ireland in Ulster's office, in the handwriting of Thomas Preston, Ulster, the name of Horsfall, but with a query, is placed between those of MacMahon and Esmond; but in these lists the names of Bourke, Colclough, Butler, Wilson, Osborne, and Harbert are omitted, and those of Barnewall, MacBrian, Magrath, and Morres are (also) queried. In a revised list, dat. 7 March 1639, Horsfall is omitted, but so also are Colclough and Butler.

(b) Joan, his only child, *m.* Oliver Grace, of Courtstown, co. Kilkenny.

(c) Most of the particulars in this article have been supplied by G. D. Burtchaell and C. M. Tenison. See vol. i, p. 223, note "a." There is an account of this family, by Richard Caulfield and John D'Alton, in the *Top. and Gen.*, vol. iii, pp. 462-467.

(d) Lettice Shee, who survived him, is the only wife assigned to him, when he entered and signed his father's funeral certificate in June 1637. A previous wife (unsupported, however, by the O'Ryan pedigree) is sometimes given to him, *viz.*, Joanna, da. of John BROWN, of Camus, co. Tipperary, by Catherine, da. of Dermot O'RYAN, of Solloghod, in that county.

III. 1684 ? to 1691. SIR WILLIAM HURLY, Baronet [I. 1645 ?] s. and h., *suc. to the Baronetcy* on the death of his father, was M.P. [I.] for Kilmallock, 1689, in the Parl. of James II, for whom he was in command of a troop, near Cashel, in 1690, where he received wounds, of which he probably died. He *m.* Mary, da. of Col. BLOUNT, by (—), da. of Walter BOURKE, of the Devil's Bit, co. Tipperary. He *d.* 1691, and was attainted, whereby his estate and *Baronetcy* became *forfeited.* His widow *m.* Brian O'BRYAN.

IV. *1691.* "SIR JOHN HURLY, Baronet" [I. 1645 ?] s. and h., who, notwithstanding the attainder, assumed the title on his father's death. He was arrested in Dublin, about 1714, for trying to raise forces for the titular King James III.

V. *1720 ?* "SIR JOHN HURLY, Baronet" [I. 1645 ?], said to be s. and h. of the above, and to have also assumed the title. Of him, however, if he ever existed, nothing further is known, and there is no mention of him in the pedigree entered in Ulster's office.

WALSH:(a)

cr. July 1645;

ex. about 1690 ?

I. 1645. "JAMES WALSH, of Little Island, co. Waterford, Esq.," and of Ballygoner, co. Waterford, 1st s. and h. of Robert WALSH, of the same, sometime (1601 and 1602) Mayor of Waterford, by Beale, da. of James WHITE, of Kelis, co. Kilkenny: was *b.* about 1580; suc. his father, 3 Jan. 1603; was M.P. [I.] for co. Waterford, 1634-35, and was *cr. a Baronet* [I.], the Privy Seal being dat. at Oxford, 23 Jan. 1644/5, and "Fiant" at Dublin, 9 July [1645] 21 Car. I, no patent being enrolled. He *m.* firstly, Katherine, da. of (—) SHERLOCK. He *m.* secondly, in 1603, Katherine, da. of Piers BUTLER, of Callan, co. Kilkenny, by his 1st wife, Jenet, da. of Edward WHITE, of Ballinderry, co. Roscommon. He *d.* about 1650.

II. 1650 ? to 1690 ? SIR ROBERT WALSH, Baronet [I. 1645] of Ballygoner aforesaid, s. and h.,(b) by (—) wife. He was *Knighted*, v.p., 24 Oct. 1642, at Edgehill, by Charles I, and *suc. to the Baronetcy* about 1650. He *m.* before July 1629, Mary, 2d da. of Sir George SHERLOCK,(c) of Leitrim, co. Cork, by Anstace, da. of (—) WYSE, of Waterford. He and his son Pierce were living 1663, claiming as "Innocents," and again 22 Dec. 1680, as defendants in a Chancery suit. He *d.* s.p.m.s.,(d) probably about 1690, when the *Baronetcy* became *extinct.*

(a) See p. 248, note "a." "It is given to few mortals to comprehend even superficially the mysteries of the maze of Irish political movements, 1641-1651; but the Cessation, 15 Sep. 1643, and the Peace, 30 July 1646, are well marked points in connection with dealing out honours to the Catholic Loyalists who were against the Government. Several privy seals were issued, while these negotiations were proceeding, some of which were afterwards enrolled; some suggested titles appear never to have reached a privy seal, and so were not assumed, *e.g.*, the Earldom of Wexford for Viscount Mountgarret, and the Viscounty of Newry for Walter Bagenal, of Dunleckney. The privy seal for Walsh is set out in full in the *Fiant.* I think the same year may be assigned to Bourke and Hurly" [G. D. Burtchaell].

(b) He had two brothers, neither of whom left male issue.

(c) Knighted 28 Nov. 1606.

(d) His son, Pierce, who was living 1663 and 1666 [5th Rep. D.K.R. Ireland, p. 69, and 19th Report, p. 70], as well as in Dec. 1680, *m.* Henrietta Maria de Mouzan, of Lorraine, and *d.* v.p. and s.p.m.

Baronetcies of Scotland, or Nova Scotia,(a)

1625—1707.

Memorandum.—The province of Nova Scotia in North America was annexed to the Kingdom of Scotland, and granted, under the Great Seal, 10 [not 29] Sep. 1621, to Sir William Alexander, of Menstrie (subsequently EARL OF STIRLING [S.]) as a foreign plantation. "The personal influence of Sir William with the King [James I] caused him to approve of the scheme of creating in Scotland an hereditary dignity under the titles of Knights Baronets of Nova Scotia, by means of a scheme similar to that which had proved successful for colonising the districts in the province of Ulster."(b) He accordingly informed the Privy Council of Scotland of his design, 18 Oct. 1624, who, on 30 Nov. following, issued a proclamation announcing the King's intention of creating 100 such Baronets on 1 April next. Before that date was reached, viz. on 27 March 1625, King James died, but the grant of 1621 was confirmed in a *novodamus*, 12 July 1625, by Charles I, who, however (six weeks before), on 28 May 1625, had already nominated the premier Baronet, Gordon, as also, then, or a few days later, some others. Pixley [*History of Baronetage*, p. 160], states that *ten* Baronetcies had been created between 28 May and 19 July 1625, viz., Gordon, Strachan, Keith, Campbell, Innes, Wemyss, Livingston, Douglas, Macdonald, and Murray. This statement is probably correct, but it is added that, on the said 19 July, the King acquainted the Lords of the Privy Council [S.], "that he *had created the above* [*ten*] *Baronets*," whereas in his letter of that date, he makes no mention of the names or number of such his creations, but merely says that "we have preferred *some* to be Knight Baronettes." The Royal charter of 28 May 1625 (given in full in Pixley's work, pp. 59-89), "which was twice ratified and confirmed by acts of the Parl. of Scotland, viz., 31 July 1630 and 28 June 1633 . . . . was made, by subsequent instruments under the Great Seal, the regulating charter for the Baronets of Scotland and Nova Scotia."(b) Each Baronet received, on the resignation of Sir William Alexander, abovenamed "a grant of 16,000 [or more in some cases, as in that of Keith] acres of land in the Royal Province of Nova Scotia (which, as anciently bounded, comprehended Nova Scotia proper, Cape Breton, Anticosti, Gaspe, Prince Edward's Island and New Brunswick), to be incorporated into a full entire and free Barony and Regality for ever to be held of the Kingdom of Scotland(b) . . . . The number of persons when this order was instituted in 1625 was not to exceed 150, and Nova Scotia was nominally divided into so many Baronies. The sum payable by each was 3,000 merks (the equivalent to £166 „ 13s. 4d. sterling) of which one-third was to go into [Sir W.] Alexander's pocket, he engaging that the other two-thirds should be expended in setting forth the plantation. During the first four years the applicants who received patents were only about 60; during the next 10 years about 50 more, and thus the object remained unaccomplished during the reign of Charles although its original sphere was so enlarged as to render persons not connected with Scotland admissible to this dignity."(b) During the entire reign of Charles I "122 Baronets [S.] appear to have

(a) The Editor is deeply indebted to Sir James Balfour Paul, Lyon King of Arms, for numerous and most valuable additions (of which the most important only are specifically acknowledged) to the account here given of these dignities. The reader, however, must not imagine that (unless expressly so stated) this account has the official, or even the practical *imprimatur* of "Lyon," but must consider it merely as the one which seems to be the most correct, or at least the most probable, to the compiler. Robert Riddle Stodart, Lyon Clerk Depute (1863-86), kindly gave, from his own genealogical collection, much information as to some of these Baronetcies.

(b) *History of the Baronetage*, by Francis W. Pixley, 1900.

been created, of whom about 111 had grants of 16,000 acres each,"(a) but such grants ceased altogether after 1638.(b)

The somewhat complicated history of Nova Scotia as respects its alternate possession by England or France, and the sale, or alleged sale, in 1630, by Sir W. Alexander of all "his title to the whole of Nova Scotia, with the exception of Port Royal," are set forth in Laing's *New Scotland Tracts*.(c)

"It is no easy matter to prepare a very accurate or satisfactory LIST OF THESE KNIGHT BARONETS [S.]. The earliest list I have met with is contained in *A catalogue of the Dukes*, etc. *of England, Scotland, and Ireland*, etc., collected by T. W. [*i.e.*, Thomas Walkeley] London, 1640, 12mo. At p. 21 [pp. 117-120 of the edit. pub. in 1642] *the names of Knight Baronets of Scotland*, amounting in all to 95, including Sir Henry Gib (of St. Martin's) but the dates of the patents are not given. Of this catalogue by T. W., or Thomas Walkeley, Lowndes quotes several editions."(c) This catalogue ends about 1638, with the names of Sir John Lowther, Sir Gilbert Pickering, Sir Edward Longevile, Sir Thomas Perse [*i.e.*, Piers], Sir Edward Musgrave, and Sir William Witherington, all six stated to be English.

Another list (containing, however, but 70 Baronets) ending, about the same date, with the name of Sir Henry Bingham [*cr.* 30 June 1634], and signed "T. P., Ulster" [*i.e.*, Thomas Preston, Ulster King of arms, 1633-1642], is now remaining in Ulster's office. A copy of this has courteously been sent to the Editor by G. D. Burtchaell, with the kind permission of Sir Arthur Vicars, Ulster King of arms.

The "ROLL OF BARONETS OF NOVA SCOTIA who had territorial grants from Sir William Alexander, Earl of Stirling," is printed in Laing's *New Scotland Tracts*.(c) The grantees there given are 114 in number and it is stated that "the Precepts are entered" in a volume at the General Register House, Edinburgh, entitled "*Regist. Precep. Cart. pro Baronettis Nov. Scotiæ*, 1625-1630." The reference to the pages in that volume, which refers to 94 of these Baronetcies, are set out, it being (somewhat perplexingly) added, that as to the remaining 20, "the names having no references are given on the authority of former lists." The date, presumably that of the creation of the dignity is affixed to all but these three, viz.:—No. 41, "James Campbell of Aberuchill," placed between 13 Dec. 1627 and 1 Jan. following; No. 63, "Edward Barrett, Lord of Newburgh," placed between 2 Oct. 1628, and 26 June following, and No. 93 "Sir John Gascoigne" placed next, after 6 Jan. 1634/5, to whom however the date *in brackets* of "8 June" is affixed. At the end of this list, which concludes with No. 114, Sir Edward Longueville, 17 Dec. 1638, is added: "Two blank precepts, names and dates not supplied. Several of the above are included in the Register of the Great Seal, and also at great length in the *Register of Signatouris in the office of Comptrollerie*, but others, probably from not having paid the fees, seem not to have been registered."(c) This chronologically arranged list is the one chiefly followed, as to the placing of these Baronetcies, by the editor of this present work.

By far the most valuable list of these Baronets is that by Robert Milne, printed from a MS. in the Advocates' Library, Edinburgh, supposed to have been taken from a list or book of accounts in the Exchequer which was destroyed by a fire that occurred in that office. This list has been printed (with various additions) by Joseph Foster in his *Baronetage* for 1883, and (unlike the lists abovenamed) extends beyond the reign

(a) See p. 275. note "b."

(b) The following interesting and contemporary account of this institution is given by the first member thereof, Sir Robert Gordon, in his *History of the Earldom of Sutherland*. "This yeir of God 1625, King Charles created and instituted the order of *Knights-Baronets in Old Scotland*, for the furtherance of the plantation of *New Scotland* in America, being the true mean or honor betuein a Barone of Parlament and a Knight; a purpose intended by his father of worthie memorie, bot perfyted by his Majestie. Sir Robert Gordoun, tutor of Southerland, wes maid *the first Baronet of the Kingdome of Old Scotland* and called *Baronet Gordoun*, which dignitie wes by his Majestie's lettres patent under his Great Seale granted to him and to his heyrs-maill whatsoever. The Lairds of Cluny and Lesmoir, both of the surname of Gordoun, were also this yeir created Baronets. James Gourdoun, the Laird of Lesmoir's eldest sone, wes knighted, according to the tennor of his father's patent, wherby the Baronet's eldest sones are to be knighted at the aige of 21 years, iff ther fathers bee then alive."

(c) "Royal Letters, Charters and Tracts relating to the colonization of New Scotland, and the institution of the order of Knight-Baronets of Nova Scotia, 1621—1638," by David Laing, published by the Bannatyne Club, Edinburgh, 1867.

of Charles I, down to the end of these creations in 1707, being the date of the Union with Scotland.

Another list, extending also through the whole period (1625—1707), but in which no date save that of the year is given to the various creations, is in Beatson's *Political Index* (1806), vol. iii, pp. 70-77. In this work 141 creations are assigned to Charles I, 89 to Charles II, 17 to James II, 23 to William III and 27 to Queen Anne, in all 297 creations.

Besides the above, there is in Banks's *Baronia Anglica concentrata* (1843, 4to, vol. ii, pp. 210-248), an account of the institution and continuance of this degree. The author of that work styles himself "Sir T. C. Banks, Bart., N.S.," but though his claim to that dignity was very absurd, the work itself has considerable merit. In it is a "List of Baronets, who had sasine of their Baronies in Nova Scotia taken from the minute book of general register of sasines at Edinburgh." This list commences with Sir Alexander STRACHAN, July 1625, and ends with Sir Andrew KER, Dec. 1637, and Sir Robert CAMPBELL, Nov. 1640. It contains 73 names in all, out of which three seem to relate to the same Baronetcy. There is also another list, viz., of "The persons [who] obtained charters of lands in Nova Scotia, which do *not* appear to have been followed by seisin." The number of these is 41.

These lists, when referred to, will be styled *Milne's List, Laing's List, Walkeley's List, Ulster's List, Beatson's List*, and *Banks's Lists*, which last refer as well to the Baronets who *did*, as to those who *did not*, obtain seizin of the Nova Scotia territory.

"After the restoration of King Charles II, the description of *Nova Scotia* was omitted; so that the Baronets thus created cannot be considered as coming under the conditions of the original foundation of that order. The following patents *de titulo Militis Baronetti in Scotland* are given as a few examples [from the] Index to [the] Register of the Great Seal of Scotland: *Diploma* to Sir Andrew Gilmour, 16 Aug. 1661; to Sir John Foulis, of Ravelston, 15 Oct. 1661; to Sir George Ogilvy, of Barras, 5 March 1661/2; to Sir David Carnegy, 20 Feb. 1663; to Sir Thomas Hay, of Park, 23 Aug. 1663; to Sir George Mowat, of Ingliston, 2 June 1664; to Sir James Brown, of Barbadoes, 17 Feb. 1664; to Sir James Murray, of Stanhope, 13 Feb. 1664; to Sir John Henderson, of Fordel, 16 July 1664 [and] to Sir John Kircaldie, of Grange, 14 May 1664." [Banks's *Baronia Anglica concentrata* above mentioned.]

GORDON

(Premier Baronetcy of Scotland):
cr. 28 May and sealed 23 July 1625(a);
dormant, 1795—1806;
re-assumed, since 1806.

I. 1625. THE HONBLE. SIR ROBERT GORDON, Knt., 4th but 2d surv. s.(b) of Alexander (GORDON), EARL OF SUTHERLAND [S.], by his 2d wife, Jean, da. of George (GORDON), 4th EARL OF HUNTLY [S.], was *b.* 14 May 1580, at Dunrobin Castle, co. Sutherland; ed. at the Univ. of St. Andrew's and, 1598, at that of Edinburgh; was in 1606 a Gent. of the Privy Chamber to King James, and subsequently, 1625, to Charles I; was *cr.* M.A. of the Univ. of Cambridge, March 1614/5, and, having been *Knighted*, was *cr. a Baronet* "with precedence of all the rest by particular clause in his patent,"(a) 28 May 1625, "sealed 23 July 1625" with rem. to heirs male whatsoever(a) and with a grant of 16,000 acres in

(a) Milne's List and Laing's List. A copy *in extenso* of the lengthy patent of this Baronetcy is printed in Douglas' *Baronage of Scotland* [1798], pp. 2-13, under "Gordon, of Gordonstoun," as also (31 pages, close print, 4to) in Pixley's *History of the Baronage*, pp. 59-89.

(b) He was one of five brothers, of whom the 2d and 3d died in infancy; the issue male of the first brother, John, Earl of Sutherland [S.], became extinct, 16 June 1766, on the death of William, the 17th Earl. The 5th and yst. br., was the Hon. Sir Alexander Gordon, of Navidale. He was *b.* 5 March 1585, emigrated with his family to Ireland in 1631, and had five sons (born 1614 to 1627), all of whom apparently died without issue. Had any male issue been existing in 1795 the heir to the Baronetcy would, presumably, have been among such issue.

Nova Scotia, forming the Barony and Regality of Gordon, of which, however, no seizin appears to have followed.(a) He was Sheriff of Invernesshire 1629, and M.P. [S.] thereof 1630; was guardian to his nephew, the Earl of Sutherland [S.], 1615-30; Vice-Chamberlain of Scotland, 1630, and P.C. [S.], 1634. He was the author of the well-known *History of the Earldom of Sutherland*, which was, however, not printed (though written nearly 200 years before) till 1813. Having bought the estate of Plewlands, co. Moray, it and others were by charter, 20 June 1642, erected into *the Barony of Gordonstoun*. He *m.* 16 Feb. 1612/3, in London, Louisa, da. and h. of John GORDON, of Glenluce, co. Wigtoun and of Longormes in France, Dean of Salisbury, 1602-19 (son of Alexander Gordon, Bishop of Galloway, 1568-83), by his 2d wife Genevieve(b), da. of Gideon PÉTAU, Seigneur de Moylett, President of the Parl. of Brittany. He *d.* March 1656, aged 76. Will dat. 11 July 1654. His widow, who was *b.* 20 Dec. 1597, *d.* Sep. 1680, aged 83.

II. 1656. SIR LUDOVICK GORDON, Baronet [S. 1625], of Gordonstoun aforesaid, s. and h., *b.* 15 Oct. 1624, at Salisbury,(c) M.P. [S.] for Elgin and Forresshire, 1649; *suc. to the Baronetcy* in March 1656; suffered severely during the Civil War, his losses amounting to £10,000, and was fined £3,600 in 1667. In or about 1688 he registered in Lyon's office, his arms and supporters as *Premier Baronet of Scotland*. He *m.* firstly, 2 Jan. 1644, at Aberdeen, Elizabeth, da. and coheir of Sir Robert FARQUHAR, of Menie in Daviot, co. Aberdeen. She *d.* Nov. 1661, age 38. He *m.* secondly (contract 6 March 1669) Jean, da. of John STEWART, of Ladywell. He *d.* in or before 1688, possibly in Sep. 1685.

III. 1685? SIR ROBERT GORDON, Baronet, [S. 1625], of Gordonstoun aforesaid 1st s. and h. by 1st wife, *b.* 7 March 1647, at Gordonstoun; was M.P. [S.] for co. Sutherland, 1672-74, 1678, 1681-82 and 1685-86; for Elgin and Forresshire, 1696, till void 1 Oct. 1696; said to have been *Knighted* about 1683(d); *suc. to the Baronetcy* in or before 1688, possibly in Sep. 1685; F.R.S., 3 Feb. 1686, being a scientific mechanist and inventor of machinery; was served heir general to his father, 21 Sep. 1688; was a gent. of the household to James II. He executed an entail of the Gordonstoun estate in 1697, and obtained a "Novodamus" thereof, 27 June 1698. He *m.* firstly, 23 Feb. 1676, Margaret, Dow. BARONESS DUFFUS [S.], da. of William (FORBES), LORD FORBES [S.], by his 1st wife, Jean, da. of Sir John CAMPBELL. She *d.* s.p.m. 13 April 1677. He *m.* secondly, in 1691, Elizabeth, da. and h. of Sir William DUNBAR, 1st Baronet [S. 1700], of Hempriggs, by Margaret, da. of Alexander SINCLAIR, of Lathron. He *d.* 5 Sep. or Oct. 1704. M.I. at Ogston. His widow *m.* Hon. James SUTHERLAND, afterwards DUNBAR, who inherited the estate of Hempriggs, and was *cr.* a Baronet [S.] 10 Dec. 1706, whom see.

IV. 1704. SIR ROBERT GORDON, Baronet [S. 1625], of Gordonstoun aforesaid, s. and h. by 2nd wife, *b.* 1696; *suc. to the Baronetcy*, 5 Oct. 1704, served heir general of his father, 12 July 1705, was M.P. for Caithness, 1715-22; was out in the rising of 1715, but soon afterwards conformed to Government. In 1766 he claimed the EARLDOM OF SUTHERLAND [S.] as heir *male*, but without success, against the heir *general*. On 11 May 1767, he entailed various lands in Morayshire. He *m.* 26 May 1734, Agnes, 1st da. of Sir William MAXWELL, 3d Baronet [S. 1627] of Calderwood, by Christian, da. of Alexander STEWART, of Torrence. He *d.* 8 Jan. 1772. Will pr. Dec. 1773. His widow *d.* 11 March 1808, aged 89, at Lossiemouth.

V. 1772. SIR ROBERT GORDON, Baronet [S. 1625], of Gordonstoun aforesaid, s. and h., *b.* about 1738; *suc. to the Baronetcy*, 8 Jan. 1772, and was, on 30 April 1774, served h. of provision general to his father. He *d.* unm. 2 June 1776 in his 39th year.

(a) Banks' Lists.

(b) She *d.* at Gordonstoun, 6 Dec. 1643, in her 83d year.

(c) James, Duke of Lennox, and George, Lord Gordon, were his godfathers, and Frances, Duchess of Richmond and Lennox, was his godmother, by whose direction he was called Ludovick, after the late Duke.

(d) He is called a Knight in 1685, but not in 1682; possibly, however, the word "Knight" may be used for "Baronet."

VI. 1776, to 1795. SIR WILLIAM GORDON, Baronet [S. 1625], of Gordonstoun(a) aforesaid, only br. and h.; *suc. to the Baronetcy*, 2 June 1776, and was, on 20 Dec. 1776, served h. of provision general to his br. He *d.* unm. in the Canongate of Edinburgh (Thursday) 5 and was *bur.* 11 March 1795 in the Chapel Royal of Holyroodhouse, aged 56,(b) when the issue male of the grantee became, presumably, *extinct*.(c)

[The Baronetcy remained dormant for about 10 years after the death in 1795 of the 6th Baronet, at which date the collateral heir male of the grantee is supposed to have been among the descendants of one of the two younger brothers of his grandfather's grandfather, Adam Gordon, of Aboyne, *jure mariti* Earl of Sutherland [S.], the 2d son of George, 2d Earl of Huntly [S.]. Sir William Gordon, of Gight, co. Aberdeen (who was killed at Flodden 9 Sep. 1513) was the elder of these two, but his male issue is supposed to have become *extinct* on the death of Sir George Gordon, the 8th of Gight. The younger brother (4th and yst. s. of the said Earl of Huntly) was Sir James Gordon of Letterfourie, co. Banff, Admiral of the Fleet [S.], 1513, whose descendant assumed the Baronetcy in 1806, as below.]

VII. *1795.* ALEXANDER GORDON, of Letterfourie, co. Banff, was (according to the Scotch service, obtained in 1806 by his son) cousin and h. male of the late Baronet, and, as such, would have been, after 5 March 1795, *entitled to the Baronetcy*, which, however, he never assumed. He was 4th and yst. s. of James GORDON of Letterfourie aforesaid, by Glicerie, da. of Sir William DUNBAR, 1st Baronet [S. 1698], of Durn, which James (who *m.* 1695, and *d.* aged 87,) was s. and h. of John GORDON, of the same (*b.* 1627, and *d.* 1721), s. and h. of James GORDON of Letterfourie, 1633 and 1649, who, according to the service of 1806, was s. of another James GORDON,(d) the s. and h. of James GORDON, Admiral of the Fleet [S.] 1513, the first of Letterfourie, who was youngest br. of Adam (GORDON), EARL OF SUTHERLAND [S.], the great great grandfather of the 1st Baronet. He was *b.* 1715; was in the rising of 1745, soon after which he joined his br., James GORDON, a wine merchant in Madeira. On 12 July 1791 he was served heir general of his father and of his said br. He *m.*, 1778, Helen, da. of Alexander RUSSELL, of Moncoffer, co. Banff. He *d.* 16 Jan. 1797, in his 83d year.

VIII. *1797.* 1806. JAMES GORDON, *afterwards* (according to the service of 22 April 1806) SIR JAMES GORDON, Baronet [S. 1625], of Letterfourie aforesaid, s. and h., *b.* 1779. On 11 Nov. 1797 was served heir special of his father in estates at Durn, etc., co. Banff. On 3 May 1804 was served heir male and heir of line general to his great great great

(a) Gordonstoun is called in Douglas' *Baronage* [S.], 1798, "a noble house with fine gardens," and together with "Drainy and Dollas all in the county of Murray," is said to be among "the chief seats" of the family.

(b) He had an illegitimate son, William GORDON, of Halmyre, co. Peebles, who had issue. The estates, after a law suit between the descendants (heirs of line) of Lucy, wife of David SCOTT, of Scotstarvit, da. of the 3d Baronet, and Alexander Penrose CUMMING, of Altyre (great great grandson of Lucy, da. of the 2d Baronet by her 1st husband, Robert CUMMING, of Altyre), went to the latter (presumably under some entail), who took the name of GORDON, and was *cr.* a Baronet in 1804.

(c) The issue male of Robert Gordon, of Pulrossie, co. Sutherland, the only one of the younger sons of the 1st Baronet who had issue, had apparently failed. He bought the estate of Cluny, co. Aberdeen, from Sir John Gordon, 2d Baronet [S. 1625] of Cluny, and was ancestor of Robert Gordon, of Cluny, living in Oct. 1745 but "past the age of action in the field," who however had then a son described as "a very fine young gentleman and may be of great use," which son, however, presumably died s.p. before the death of the 6th Baronet in 1795.

(d) No evidence appears to exist for this part of the pedigree. It is to be noted that there are only 7 generations in more than 300 years. The 1st Laird of Letterfourie was *b.* probably about 1460, while Sir James GORDON, who assumed the Baronetcy in 1806, and who was 7th in descent from him, was *b.* 1779. There is evidence also of a William GORDON, of Letterfourie in 1572, and of a Patrick GORDON, of Letterfourie in 1592 and in 1625.

great grandfather, Sir James GORDON, the first of Letterfourie. On 22 April 1806 he was served heir male general to his cousin, Sir William GORDON, 6th Baronet [S. 1625] of Gordonstoun, after which date he *assumed the Baronetcy*. He *m*. in 1801 Mary, 1st da. and coheir of William GLENDONWYN, of Parton, co. Kircudbright. He *d*. 24 Dec. 1843 at Letterfourie. His widow *d*. 18 May 1845, aged 62.

IX. 1843. SIR WILLIAM GORDON, Baronet [S. 1625],(a) of Letterfourie aforesaid, s. and h., *b*. 26 Dec. 1803. Major, 66th Regiment; Lieut. Col. in the army; *suc. to the Baronetcy*,(a) 24 Dec. 1843. He *d*. unm. 5 Dec. 1861, aged 58, at Letterfourie.

X. 1861. SIR ROBERT GLENDONWYN GORDON, Baronet [S. 1625],(a) of Letterfourie aforesaid, youngest br. and h.; *b*. 1824. Deputy Lieut. for Banffshire; *suc. to the Baronetcy*,(a) 5 Dec. 1861.

Family estates.—These, in 1883, consisted of 2,331 acres, in the counties of Banff, Dumfries and Kirkcudbright. *Principal Seat*.—Letterfourie, near Buckie, co. Banff.

KEITH;

EARL MARISCHAL [S.]:
cr. 28 May 1625;
forfeited, 1716.

I. 1625. WILLIAM (KEITH), EARL MARISCHAL [S.], who had succeeded to that dignity on the death of his father, 2 April 1623, was *cr. a Baronet* [S.], 28 May 1625,(b) with rem. to heirs male whatsoever, and with a grant of no less than 48,000 acres (three times the usual amount) in Nova Scotia, of which however he appears never to have had seizin.(c) By another charter of the same date he gets the ratification of a grant by Sir William Alexander "de officio Admiralitatis" of the said lands, and of coining money in Nova Scotia, for nineteen years after the date of 23 May 1625, and the ratification of a contract made between them "apud Strand" on the date last named. The patent is not in the Great Seal Register [S.]. This Baronetcy devolved with the peerage, till *forfeited* therewith in 1716. See *Peerage*.

INNES:

cr. 28 May 1625, but not sealed till 2 April 1628;(d)
afterwards, 1769—1807, INNES-NORCLIFFE,
subsequently, since 1807, INNES-KER;
and, since 1812 (*de jure* since 1805), DUKES OF ROXBURGHE [S.].

I. 1625. SIR ROBERT INNES, of that ilk, in Urquhart, co. Elgin, s. and h. of Robert INNES, of the same (M.P. [S.] for Elgin, 1612), by Elizabeth, da. of Robert (ELPHINSTONE), 3d LORD ELPHINSTONE [S.], was *cr. a Baronet* [S.], 20 May 1625,(d) sealed 2 April 1628, but not recorded in the Great Seal Register, with rem. to heirs male whatsoever and with a grant of presumably 16,000

(a) According to the service of 22 April 1806, whereby his lineal ancestor was served heir male general to the 6th Baronet.
(b) Laing's List, not, however, in Milne's List, nor in the Great Seal Register.
(c) Banks's Lists.
(d) Milne's List, where the date is given as 28, and Laing's list, where it is given as 29 May 1625. This Baronetcy is called in Douglas' *Baronage* [S.] the second [*i.e.*, second according to order of *creation*, not of precedency] in the order of Baronets [then] existing in Scotland. Douglas apparently reckons this Baronetcy next to that of Gordon.

acres in Nova Scotia, of which he had seizin in May 1628.(a) Was M.P. [S.] for Elgin, 1639-41 and 1648; had charters of the lands and barony of Delny, 12 Feb. 1631, and of those of Newton, Banacoul, etc., 25 July 1636. He was made by the Parl. one of the committee of estates and a P.C. [S.], yet in 1649 appears to have been considered a Royalist. He *m*. Grizel, da. of James (STEWART), EARL OF MORAY [S.], by Elizabeth, 1st da. and heir of line of James (STEWART), EARL OF MORAY [S.], sometime Regent [S.]. He *d*. between 1649 and 1660.

II. 1655? SIR ROBERT INNES, Baronet [S. 1625], of that ilk, 1st s. and h.; *suc. to the Baronetcy* on his father's death, and had (being then a Baronet) charter of his lands, 15 July 1661; was M.P. [S.] for Elgin, 1661-63 and 1678. He *m*. Jean, da. of James (ROSS), 6th LORD ROSS OF HALKHEAD [S.], by Margaret, da. of Walter (SCOTT), 1st LORD SCOTT OF BUCCLEUCH [S.]. She was served, 6 Feb. 1649, coheir to her brother, and again 19 Oct. 1653, coheir to her mother.(b)

III. 1690? SIR JAMES INNES, Baronet [S. 1625], of that ilk, 1st s. and h.; *suc. to the Baronetcy* on his father's death. He *m*. (contract 18 July 1666) Margaret, 3d da. and coheir of Harry KER, *styled* LORD KER, by Margaret, da. of William (HAY), EARL OF ERROLL [S.], which Harry was only surv. s. and h. ap. of Robert (KER), 1st EARL OF ROXBURGH [S.], but *d*. v.p. and s.p.m. Feb. 1642/3. She *d*. before 25 Feb. 1691.

IV. 1700? SIR HARRY INNES, Baronet [S. 1625], of that ilk, 2d but 1st surv. s. and h.(c), *b*. about 1670; M.P. [S.] for Elgin and Forres-shire, 1704-07; *suc. to the Baronetcy* on his father's death, before 1704. He *m*. (contract 3 and 4 Sep. 1694) Jean, da. of Duncan FORBES, of Culloden. He *d*. 12 Nov. 1721.

V. 1721. SIR HARRY INNES, Baronet [S. 1625], of that ilk, 2d but 1st surv. s. and. h.(d); *suc. to the Baronetcy*, 12 Nov. 1721, and was served heir male to his father 29 June 1723; Inspector of Seizures [S.], March 1748. He *m*. (contract 9 Oct. 1727) Anne, 2d da. of Sir James GRANT, *formerly* COLQUHOUN, 6th Baronet [S. 1625], by Anne, da. and h. of Sir Humphrey COLQUHOUN, 5th Baronet [S. 1625]. He *d*. 31 Oct. 1762. His widow *d*. at Elgin 9 Feb. 1771.

VI. 1762. SIR JAMES INNES, *afterwards*, [1769-1807], INNES-NORCLIFFE, *and subsequently* INNES-KER, Baronet [S. 1625], sometime of Innes aforesaid, 2d but 1st surv. s. and h.(e); *b*. 10 Jan. 1736 at Innes House, in Innes; ed. at Leyden Univ.; Capt. 88th Foot 1759, 58th Foot 1779; *suc. to the Baronetcy*, 31 Oct. 1762, being served heir, 7 Feb. 1764; sold the ancient family estate of Innes in 1767 to James (Duff), Earl Fife [I.]. He *m*. firstly, 19 April 1769, at St. James' Westm., Mary, 1st sister and coheir (10 Jan. 1805) of Sir Cecil WRAY, 12th Baronet [1611], da. of Sir John WRAY, 11th Baronet, by Frances, da. and h. of Fairfax NORCLIFFE of Langton, in the East Riding of Yorkshire. She inherited her mother's estates, whereupon he, by royal lic., 31 May 1769, took the name of *Norcliffe* after that of *Innes*, but, on losing the Langton estate by her death, s.p., 20 July 1807, he dropped the name of Norcliffe and took that of *Ker* in addition to *Innes*. He *m*. secondly (8 days after his 1st wife's death) 28 July 1807, at Kensington, Harriet, da. of Benjamin CHARLEWOOD, of Windlesham, Surrey. She was living when, by a decision in the House of Lords, 11 May 1812, he was declared

(a) Banks's Lists.
(b) In the first of these services she is called "Domina Jeanna Ross, Domina Innes, sponsa Roberti Innes, Junioris, de eodem," and in the second one "Jean Ross, Lady Innes." It seems clear that her husband being called "*Junior*" in 1649 had not at that date succeeded to his father's title. It is just possible that the word "Domina" in 1649 (as also, perhaps, "Lady" in 1653) was applied to her as being the daughter of a Peer.
(c) Robert Innes, the 1st s., *d*. in France v.p. and unm.
(d) Robert Innes, the 1st son, capt. in the army, *d*. v.p. and unm.
(e) Harry Innes, the 1st son, *d*. v.p. and unm.

to have succeeded as DUKE AND EARL OF ROXBURGHE, etc. [S.], after the death of the late Duke, 22 Oct. 1805, and when, accordingly (not having done so before), he assumed that title(a) in which this *Baronetcy* then *merged* and so continues. See *Peerage*.

WEMYSS, *or* WEEMS:

cr. 29 May 1625, sealed 30 Sep. 1626(b);
afterwards, 1628-1679, LORD WEMYSS OF ELCHO [S.];
and subsequently, 1633-1679, EARLS OF WEMYSS [S.];
dormant, June 1679.

I. 1625. SIR JOHN WEEMS [*or* WEMYSS], of that ilk, co. Fife, 2d s. of Sir John WEMYSS, of the same, by his 2d wife, Mary [not Anne], sister of James, EARL OF MORAY [S.], da. of James (STEWART), 1st LORD DOUNE [S.], was served heir, 17 April 1610, to his elder br., David WEMYSS (who *d*. v.p. in Aug. 1608, having, however, been enfeft of the property), was M.P. [S.] for Fifeshire, 1617; suc. his father after Aug. 1620, and was *cr. a Baronet* [S.], 29 May 1625,(b) sealed 30 Sep. 1626, with rem. to heirs male whatsoever, and with a grant of, presumably, 16,000 acres in Nova Scotia, entitled the Regality of New Wemyss, of which he had seizin Nov. 1626.(c) He *m*., 1610, Jean, 1st da. of Patrick (GRAY) LORD GRAY [S.], by his 2d wife, Mary, da. of Robert (STEWART), 1st EARL OF ORKNEY [S.]. She was living when he was *cr*. 1 April 1628, LORD WEMYSS OF ELCHO [S.], and, subsequently, 25 June 1633, EARL OF WEMYSS [S.]. In those peerages this *Baronetcy* then *merged*, till on the death of his son, the 2d EARL OF WEMYSS [S.], s.p.m.s. June 1679, the peerage titles devolved in the female line (see *Peerage*), but the *Baronetcy*, to which the heir male of the grantee was entitled, became *dormant*, and so continues.

CAMPBELL:

cr. 29 May 1625, but not sealed till 30 June 1627;(b)
sometime, 1677-81, EARL OF CAITHNESS [S.];
afterwards, since 1681, EARLS OF BREADALBANE AND HOLLAND [S.];
and sometime, 1831-62, and since 1885, MARQUESSES OF BREADALBANE.

I. 1625. SIR DUNCAN CAMPBELL, of Glenurchie, *otherwise* Glenorchy, co. Perth, s. and h. of Sir Colin CAMPBELL, of the same, by Catherine, da. of William (RUTHVEN), 2d LORD RUTHVEN [S.], was *b*. about 1550; suc. his father, 11 April 1583; was one of the Barons to attend at the Coronation of Anne, Queen Consort of James VI [S.], 18 May 1590, when he was *Knighted*; was a minor Baron [S.], 1592 and again Dec. 1599; was M.P. [S.] for Argyllshire, 1593 and was *cr. a Baronet* [S.], 29 May 1625,(b) sealed 30 June 1627, but not recorded in the Great Seal Register, with rem. to heirs male whatsoever and with a grant of, presumably, 16,000 acres in Nova Scotia, of which both he (July 1627) as also his son (Sep. 1631) had seizin.(d) He was made, by Charles I, Hereditary Sheriff of Perthshire for life. He was known as "Black Duncan," and was a great planter

(a) This Dukedom had been conferred, 25 April 1707, on the 5th Earl of Roxburghe [S.], with the same remainder as that of the Earldom. Sir James was neither *heir male* nor even *heir of line* of the 1st Earl, though he was a descendant of him through his yst. grand-daughter. He, in fact, inherited the Peerage under a nomination in 1648 of the Roxburghe dignities.
(b) Milne's List and Laing's List.
(c) Banks's Lists.
(d) Banks's Lists. The seizin of Sir Colin in Sep. 1631 is spoken of as that "of the Barony of Glenurquhy Campbell in Nova Scotia and haill iron and gold mines within the same, and privilege of transporting all gold affecting mines thereto."

and builder, as well as a great traveller. He *m*. firstly, in 1574, Jean, 4th da. of John STEWART), 4th EARL OF ATHOLL [S.], Lord Chancellor [S.] 1577-79, being his 2d da. by his 2d wife, Margaret, da. of Malcolm (FLEMING), 3d LORD FLEMING [S.]. Her will confirmed 25 July 1595. He *m*. secondly, Elizabeth, da. of Henry (SINCLAIR), LORD SINCLAIR [S.], by his 2d wife, Elizabeth, da. of William (FORBES), 7th LORD FORBES [S.]. He *d*. 23 June 1631, aged 81, and was *bur*. at Finlarig, near Loch Tay.

II. 1631. SIR COLIN CAMPBELL, Baronet [S. 1625], of Glenorchy aforesaid, 1st s. and h., by 1st wife, *b*. about 1577; *suc. to the Baronetcy*, June 1631. He, in Sep. 1631, had seizin of the lands in Nova Scotia.(a) He *m*. about 1600, Juliana, 1st da. of Hugh (CAMPBELL), 1st LORD LOUDOUN [S.], by his 1st wife, Margaret, da. of Sir John GORDON, of Lochinvar. She, who was 52 in 1633, was living 1648. He *d*. s.p., 6 Sep. 1640, aged 63.

III. 1640. SIR ROBERT CAMPBELL, Baronet [S. 1625], of Glenorchy aforesaid, br. and h., *b*. about 1580; was sometime of Glenfalloch; *suc. to the Baronetcy*, 6 Sep. and was served heir to his brother, 27 Oct. 1640; M.P. [S.] for Argyllshire, 1639-41, 1643-44, and 1644-49. He *m*. about 1610 (before Nov. 1620), Isabel, da. of Lachlan MACINTOSH, of Torcastle, Captain of the clan Chattan. He was living 1647.

IV. 1650? SIR JOHN CAMPBELL, Baronet [S. 1625], of Glenorchy, 1st s. and h., *b*. about 1615; *suc. to the Baronetcy* after 1647. He was M.P. [S.] for Argyllshire, 1661-63. He *m*. firstly, in or before 1635, Mary, 1st da. of William (GRAHAM), EARL OF AIRTH AND MENTEITH [S.], by Agnes, da. of Patrick (GRAY), LORD GRAY [S.]. He *m*. secondly, Christian, da. of John MUSCHET, of Craighead, in Menteith. He *d*. before June 1677.

V. 1670? SIR JOHN CAMPBELL, Baronet [S. 1625], of Glenorchy aforesaid, only s. and h., by 1st wife, *b*. about 1635, took an active part in the rising [S.] for Charles II, which was suppressed in 1654. He, or his father, was M.P. [S.] for Argyllshire 1669-74. He *m*. firstly, 17 Dec. 1657, at St. Andrew's Wardrobe, London, Mary, da. of Henry (RICH), 1st EARL OF HOLLAND, by Isabel, da. and h. of Sir Walter COPE, of Kensington. She *d*. 8 Feb. 1666. He, before his 2d marriage (7 April 1678) with Mary, Dow. COUNTESS OF CAITHNESS, was, under the style of "Sir John Campbell, of Glenurchy, Baronet,"(b) *cr*. 28 June 1677, EARL OF CAITHNESS, etc. [S.], which dignity, however, he resigned in 1681, when he was *cr*., 13 Aug. 1681, EARL OF BREADALBANE AND HOLLAND [S.], with the precedency of 28 June 1677. In these Earldoms this *Baronetcy* then *merged*, and in the title of Breadalbane has so continued, save that on the death of the 1st Earl, 19 March 1717, it should, apparently, have passed to his 1st s. and h., Duncan, *styled* LORD ORMELIE, who, on account of his incapacity, was passed over in the succession to the Earldom, and who *d*. s.p. in 1727, aged 67, when the said Baronetcy vested in the next brother the 2d Earl, the heir male of the grantee. See *Peerage*.

DOUGLAS:

cr. 28 May,(c) and sealed 18 Aug. 1625:(c)
dormant since 28 Nov. 1812.

I. 1625. SIR WILLIAM DOUGLAS of Glenbervie, co. Kincardine, s. and h. of the Hon. Sir Robert DOUGLAS, of the same, by Elizabeth, da. of Sir George AUCHINLECK, of Balmanno, which Robert (living July 1592, was 2d

(a) See p. 282, note "d."
(b) Wood's *Douglas' Baronage* [S.], vol. ii, p. 688 [appendix].
(c) The date of 30 May 1625 is that assigned both in Milne's List and Laing's List, but it is stated (Macfarlane's *Genealogical Collections*, vol. ii, p. 272) that "the patent itself is of the date 28 May 1625." This Baronetcy is in Douglas' *Baronage* called

s. of William, 9th EARL OF ANGUS [S.], had charter of the Barony of Glenbervie 3 Dec. 1622, and was *cr. a Baronet* [S.] 28 May,(a) sealed 18 Aug. 1625, with rem. to heirs male whatsoever, and with a grant of, presumably, 16,000 acres of land called the Barony of Douglas in Nova Scotia, of which he had seizin in the said month of Aug.(b) Living 25 March 1653. He *m.* before 1624, Janet, 3d da. of Alexander IRVINE, of Drum.

II. 1660? SIR WILLIAM DOUGLAS, Baronet [S. 1625] of Glenbervie aforesaid, only s. and h., *suc. to the Baronetcy* on the death of his father. He *m.* in 1642, Anne, only da. and h. of James DOUGLAS, of Stoneypath and Ardit, with whom he had a great estate. He *d.* before 1688, probably before 1685. Will confirmed at Brechin, 11 Jan. 1688.

III. 1680? SIR ROBERT DOUGLAS, Baronet [S. 1625], of Glenbervie aforesaid, only s. and h., *suc. to the Baronetcy* on the death of his father. He was a general officer in the army, Col. of the Scotch Greys, which he commanded at the battle of Steinkirk, where he was slain. He *m.* Jane. He *d.* s.p.m. 24 July 1692.(c) Admon. 15 Dec. 1692 to a creditor. "Jane, relict of Sir Robert DOUGLAS of Glenberry," *i.e.* "Glenbervie," *d.* Dec. 1735. Will pr. 1735 in Prerog. Court [I.].

IV. 1692. SIR ROBERT DOUGLAS, Baronet [S. 1625], of Ardit, *afterwards* called Glenbervie, co. Fife, cousin and heir male collateral, being only s. and h. of William DOUGLAS, of the same, by Agnes, da. of Patrick and sister of Sir John SCOTT, 1st Baronet [S. 1671] of Ancrum, which William was s. and h. of the Rev. George DOUGLAS, D.D., Rector of Stepney, Midx. (1634-41), which George DOUGLAS was next br. to Sir William DOUGLAS, 1st Baronet. He was *b.* about 1662, and *suc. to the Baronetcy*, 24 July 1692. He *m.* firstly in or before 1690, Mary, 1st da. of Sir William RUTHVEN, of Dunglass, by Katharine, da. of William (DOUGLAS), MARQUESS OF DOUGLAS [S.]. He *m.* secondly in or before 1694, Janet PATERSON, heiress of Dunmure. He *d.* 27 Jan. 1748, in his 87th year.(d) His widow, who was *b.* 2 Feb. 1655, *d.* 9 Feb. 1750, aged 95, having had 60 descendants, of whom 41 were then living.

V. 1750. SIR WILLIAM DOUGLAS, Baronet [S. 1625], of Ardit, *otherwise* Glenbervie aforesaid, s. and h. by 1st wife ; *b.* about 1690 ; was an Advocate of some eminence, and from 1726 to 1745 was annually chosen as Provost of the city of St. Andrew's ; was Inspector of the Customs on Tobacco in Scotland. He *suc. to the Baronetcy*, Feb. 1748. He *m.*, about 1718, Elizabeth, da. of John DOUGLAS, of Garvald, by Elizabeth, da. of William and Isabel DOUGLAS. He *d.* s.p. 23 July 1764, in his 75th year. His widow *d.* 11 May 1777.

VI. 1764. SIR ROBERT DOUGLAS, Baronet [S. 1625] of Ardit, *otherwise* Glenbervie aforesaid, br. of the half-blood and h., being s. of the 4th Baronet by his 2d wife ; was *b.* 1694, and when, nearly 70, *suc. to the Baronetcy*, 23 July 1764. He was the author (1764) of the well known *Peerage of Scotland*,(e) as also of a posthumous work (1798) called *The Baronage of Scotland*, of which, however, but one vol. was published. Both these works have been the

"the third" of the order of Baronets or Knights of Nova Scotia now [1798] subsisting in Scotland according to the dates of their patents"; the Baronetcy of Innes being therein called the second, and that of Gordon the first.

(a) See p. 283, note "c."

(b) Banks's Lists.

(c) The standard of his regiment having been captured he "jumped over a hedge into the midst of the enemy, seized it from the officer in whose charge it was, threw it back to his own men and fell pierced with wounds, unmarried" [Wood's *Douglas' Peerage of Scotland*, vol. i, p. 440].

(d) Douglas' *Baronage* [S.] states "died *anno* 1750, in the 85th year of his age."

(e) A second edit., 2 vols., folio, ed. by J. P. Wood, was issued in 1813.

text for all succeeding genealogical writers on Scotch families. He *m.* firstly, Dorothea, da. and coheir of Anthony CHESTER, Attorney General of Barbadoes, said(a) to be "2d s. of Sir Anthony CHESTER, Baronet." She *d.* s.p. He *m.* secondly, before 1738, Margaret, 1st da. of Sir James MACDONALD, 6th Baronet [S. 1625] of Macdonald, by Janet, da. of Alexander MACLEOD, of Grisharnish. He *m.* thirdly, Anne, da. of Alexander HAY, of Huntingdon, Advocate. He *d.* at Edinburgh 24 April 1770, in his 77th year.

VII. 1770, to 1812. SIR ALEXANDER DOUGLAS, Baronet [S. 1625], of Ardit otherwise Glenbervie aforesaid, only surv. s. and h., by 2d wife ; *b.* 1738 ; studied medicine at Leyden 1759 ; M.D. of St. Andrew's College, 1760 ; *suc. to the Baronetcy*, 20 April 1770 ; Fellow of the Coll. of Physicians at Edinburgh, where he practised for more than 50 years, being founder, in 1781, of the Dispensary for the Poor there ; physician to the King's forces in Scotland, licentiate of the Royal College of London, 1796. He *m.*, 1778, Barbara, da. of James CARNEGIE, of Finhaven, "a lady of great beauty and accomplishments."(b) He *d.* s.p.m.s.(c) 28 Nov. 1812, since which time *the Baronetcy* has remained *dormant*. Will pr. 1813. The admon. of his widow granted Feb. 1816.

STRACHAN, *or* STRAQUHAN:

cr. 28 May, and sealed 24 June 1625(d);

dormant, since 1659;

but assumed till 1854.

I. 1625, to 1659. SIR ALEXANDER STRAQUHAN(e) *or* STRACHAN, of Thornton, co. Kincardine, s. and h. of Robert STRACHAN, by Sarah (*m.* 5 April 1586), 4th da. of William (Douglas) 9th EARL OF ANGUS [S.], the said Robert (who *d.* v.p., before March 1597) being s. and h. ap. of Alexander STRACHAN, of Thornton was *b.* about 1587, suc. his grandfather, the said Alexander STRACHAN in May 1601, being, 30 Sep. 1606, served his heir male ; was M.P. [S.] for Kincardineshire, 1617 and 1630, and possibly, 1650, and was *cr. a Baronet* [S.], 28 May 1625,(d) sealed 24 June following, with rem. to heirs male whatsoever, and with a grant of, presumably, 16,000 acres in Nova Scotia, of which seizin

(a) Douglas' *Baronage* [S.], but not according to Chester Waters's *Family of Chester of Chicheley*.

(b) Playfair's *Baronetage* [S.].

(c) His only son, Robert Douglas, *d.* 1780, in infancy.

(d) Milne's List as also Laing's List, in which last, however, the creation is stated to be "given on the authority of former lists." In Macfarlane's *Genealogical Collections* (vol. ii, p. 272) there is given "a demonstrative proof that the patent was the next immediately following [that of] Sir William Douglas, which from the patent itself is of the date 18 May 1626," and it is also stated, that this date is "marked" for it in the *minute book* of David Sibbald, Dep. Keeper of the Great Seal [S.], the writer adding that "I know none [that] has precedency of the heir male of the house of Thornton, but Sir William Gordon and Sir Robert Douglas." Playfair in his *Baronetage* [S.] states the grantee to have been "the third Baronet [S] created," and designates the then [1811] Baronet as "Premier Baronet" [S.], considering the Baronetcy of Gordon (which, however, he, subsequently, acknowledges in the appendix) as being then dormant, and placing "Strachan" above Innes, Leslie, Livingston, and Douglas, which last (at all events) should (as above stated) rightly precede it.

(e) See *Memorials of the families of Strachan and Wise*, by Rev. Charles Rogers, LL.D. [1873 ; 2d edit., 1877), and *Her. and Gen.*, viii, pp. 302-307 where it is (not very favourably) reviewed. See also Macfarlane's *Genealogical Collections*, vol. ii, pp. 270-273 ; also *N. & Q.* 8th iv, 242-243, and 323-325. The account here given, down to the date of 1686 has been kindly revised by Sir J. Balfour Paul (see p. 275, note "a") with the result of making it a very different one from any previously given.

was subsequently made in July following.(a) He was a Commissioner of the Exchequer in 1630, and, subsequently, of the Treasury, being allowed £3.000 in 1631 for the surrender of some of his offices. He *m.* firstly (contract 19 Jan. 1605), Margaret, 3d da. of John LINDSAY, of Balcarres, a Lord of Session [S.], under the style of Lord Menmuir, (s. of David, EARL OF CRAWFORD [S.]), by Margaret, da. of Alexander GUTHRIE, of Edinburgh. He *m.* secondly, after April 1623, Margaret, Dow. COUNTESS MARISCHAL [S.], da. of James (OGILVY) LORD OGILVY OF AIRLIE [S.] by Jean, da. of William (FORBES), LORD FORBES [S.]. He, and his then only son and h. ap. Alexander, were living 1 Aug. 1635, but he appears to have wasted his estates, "lived long in France" with his 2d wife and *d.* in exile at Bruges about 1659, s.p.m.s. Will dat. 15 May 1657, confirmed 24 Jan. 1662, at Edinburgh.(b)

[ALEXANDER STRACHAN, *b.* probably about 1608, yr. of the two sons of the 1st Baronet (both being by his 1st wife), is generally said to have *suc.* him *as 2d Baronet*, but there is no record of his having done so. His elder br. John is spoken of as "Fiar of Thornton" in Aug. 1626, but must have died before 1 Aug. 1635, when this Alexander is described as "only lawful son of Sir Alexander Strachan" and as being married to Elizabeth DOUGLAS. He, presumably (and not his father), was M.P. for Kincardineshire, 1650. There is no mention of him in his father's will, dat. 15 May 1657, and he probably was then dead without issue.]

The title was assumed as under by a descendant "from a remote ancestor of the 1st Baronet."(c) The relationship, however, is so distant, and the pedigree so uncertain that the right of such assumption seems extremely doubtful.

II. 1659. SIR JAMES STRACHAN, Baronet [S. 1625],(d) of Thornton aforesaid, of Inchtuthill, in the parish of Delvine, co. Perth, of Fettercairn and Monboddo, s. and h. of James Strachan, of Inchtuthill,(e) Fettercairn, and Monboddo, an opulent Burgess of Edinburgh, by Mary, da. of David RAMSAY, of Balmaine, which James (who *d.* 6 Jan. 1651), was s. and h. of (—) Strachan, the 1st s. and h. ap. of James Strachan, of Monboddo aforesaid (*d.* 10 July 1614) and was heir to the said James, his grandfather, who was the s. and h. of Sir William Strachan, of Monboddo, "third son of John Strachan, of Thornton, great great grand-uncle of the first Baronet."(c) He had acquired lands at Thornton, is called the "Laird of Thornton" as early as 1658. By him, also, Thornton Castle was subsequently enlarged. On the death of the 1st Baronet in 1659 he appears to have *assumed the Baronetcy*, and as "Sir James Strachan, of Thornton, Knight Baronet,"(f) sold the estate of Inchtuthill, 20 April 1661. He *m.* 24 Jan. 1654, at Ellon, his cousin, Elizabeth, 3d da. of Thomas FORBES, of Waterton, by Jean, da. of David RAMSAY, of Balmain. She *d.* 10 Jan. 1661, in her 25th year, and was *bur.* at Marykirk. M.I. After her death he "involved his estate and impoverished his fortune,"(c) and (with James his s. and h. ap.) sold the lands of Thornton, 28 March 1683, for £13,924. He *m.* secondly (—) by whom he had no male issue. He *d.* 1686.

[JAMES STRACHAN, only s. and h. ap. of the above, *b.* probably about 1656, entered King's College, Aberdeen, 1670. He *m.* when young (contract 9 June 1669, registered 16 Nov. 1670), Barbara, 3d da. of Robert FORBES,

(a) Banks's Lists.

(b) He, who was probably a Royalist, is often confused with Col. Archibald Strachan, a Parliamentarian, as to whom see *Her. and Gen.*, viii, 302.

(c) Rogers's *Strachan Family*, see p. 285, note "c."

(d) According to the assumption of that dignity.

(e) The estate of Inchtuthill was purchased by him 29 May 1650, and sold by his son, 20 April 1661. It has sometimes, in error, been attributed to Thomas Strachan, who was *cr. a Baronet* [S.], 8 May 1685.

(f) In the M.I. erected to his wife in 1661, he, however, describes himself (only) as "*Eques auratus*."

of Newtoun, with a dowry of 8,000 merks. They were both living 28 March 1683, but he *d.* v.p. before 1686, leaving a son James, who, according to one account, "died in infancy,"(a) but according to another account "was alive in 1710, probably then being about 40 years of age,"(b) but who apparently never assumed the Baronetcy.]

* * * * *

III. 1686. SIR JAMES STRACHAN, Baronet [S. 1625],(c) of Pittendreich (part of the Thornton estate), said to be "probably a nephew,"(a) but who more likely was a cousin of the late Baronet,(c) was *b.* about 1640 ; ed. at King's College, Aberdeen ; M.A., 28 March 1660 ; took Holy Orders and was Minister of Keith, 1665 till deprived in Nov. 1689 for nonconformity ; *assumed the Baronetcy* in 1686.(d) He *m.* about 1680, Katherine Ross. She, by whom he had six sons, *d.* 8 April 1689, and was *bur.* at Keith. M.I. He *d.* at Inverness, 1715, aged 75.

IV. 1715. SIR WILLIAM STRACHAN, Baronet [S. 1625],(c), 1st surv. s. and h. ; *suc. to the Baronetcy*(c) in 1715. He is named *Sir William Strachan of Thorntoun* in the parish register of Marykirk, where William, his natural son was baptized, 21 July 1715.

V. 1725? SIR FRANCIS STRACHAN, Baronet [S. 1625],(c) br. and h. male ; *suc. to the Baronetcy*(c) on the death of his brother. He lived at Paris, took Holy Orders in the Church of Rome, became a Jesuit, and was Rector of the College at Douay, 1734. He *d.* unm., having, it is said, previously resigned the title to the next presumptive heir, John STRACHAN, of Sweden.(e)

VI. 1753? SIR JOHN STRACHAN, Baronet [S. 1625],(c) cousin and h. male, stated to be grandson of a brother of the grandfather of the late Baronet.(e) He, presumably, is the "John Strachan, born in London and made [*sic*, but *query* if not tantamount to "inherited as"] a Baronet of Nova Scotia in 1753," being s. of "John STRACHAN, of Sweden, by Margaret, da. of Peter BOMGREEN, also of Sweden."(f) He having, presumably, inherited the Baronetcy(c) in 1753, *d.* s.p.m. in about 1765. Will of "Sir John Strachan, Midx.," pr. Aug. 1769.

* * * * *

VII. 1765? SIR JOHN STRACHAN, Baronet [S. 1625],(c) apparently nephew and h., being 1st surv. s. and h. of Patrick STRACHAN, Surgeon, and Elizabeth (*m.* in or before 1718), da. of Edward GREGORY, Capt.

(a) Rogers's *Strachan Family*, see p. 285, note "c."

(b) Statement of R. R. Stodart, Lyon Clerk Depute (1863-86) as furnished by Sir J. Balfour Paul, Lyon King of Arms.

(c) According to the assumption of that dignity.

(d) "In the records of the Synod of Moray in 1687, he is styled *Mr. James Strachan* ; and in the baptismal register of Keith, he is, on 6 Jan. 1687, described as "*Sir James Strachan*, of Thornton, Minister." See note "a" above. In his wife's M.I., erected in 1689 at Keith, he describes himself as "*D. Jac. Strachanus de Thornt. hujus ecclesiæ Pastor*.

(e) In Macfarlane's *Genealogical Collections* it is said that Francis (the 5th Baronet) "has now the matter, though perhaps not with all the formalitys requisite, resigned the title of the Baronetship of the family of Thornton to another gentleman, John Strachan, who resides in Sweden and designs himself by the title of Thornton, as the heir male of the family, and in one of his letters he acknowledges that his own grandfather and this gentleman's grandfather were two brothers."

(f) Burke's "*Commoners*" (1837), vol. ii, p. 405, foot note.

II

R.N., which Patrick(a) who was *bur.* at Greenwich, 10 Sep. 1749, was, presumably, yr. br. of the late Baronet. He was *bap.* 10 March 1728/9 at Greenwich; was Lieut. R.N. Jan. 1746/7; captured, when in command, 8 July 1757, of a French privateer of 20 guns off Alicante; was attached to the fleet under Hawke, 1759-69, and under Harland, to the East Indies, 1770-72, having *suc. to the Baronetcy*(b) about 1765. He *m.* Elizabeth, da. of Robert LOVELACE, of Battersea Rise, co. Surrey. He *d.* s.p.m., 26 Dec. 1777, at Bath. Will pr. 1778. His widow *m.* Lieut.-Col. Joseph WALTON. The will of "Dame Elizabeth Strachan, Midx.," was pr. April 1833.

VIII. 1777, to 1828. SIR RICHARD JOHN STRACHAN, Baronet(b) [S. 1625], nephew and h. male, being 1st s. and h.(c) of Patrick STRACHAN, Lieut. R.N., by Caroline (*m.* 1759), da. of John PITMAN, Capt. R.N., which Patrick (*bap.* 10 Sep. 1733, at Greenwich) was yst. br. of the late Baronet and *d.* in New York, 1776. He was *b.* 27 Oct. 1760, at Plymouth; *suc. to the Baronetcy*,(b) 26 Dec. 1777, when aged 17, and, having entered the navy in 1772, became Lieut. 1779; Capt. 1783; captured four French ships off Cape Finisterre, 4 Nov. 1805, that had escaped from Trafalgar, receiving the thanks of both houses, with an annual pension of £1,000; Rear-Admiral, 1805; **K.B.**, 29 Jan. 1806, becoming afterwards (1815) **G.C.B.** Had the naval command of the disastrous expedition against Walcheren in 1808, the Earl of Chatham being in command of the military(d); became Vice-Admiral, 1810; and Admiral, 1821. He *m.*, April 1812, Louisa DILLON, spinster. He *d.* s.p.m.s.(e) at his house in Bryanston sq.,

(a) This Patrick (called "Doctor Patrick Strachan" and "Patrick, M.D., Physician to Greenwich Hospital") is stated in the *second* edit. (differing entirely from the account of his descent given in the *first* edit.) of Rogers's "Families of Strachan," etc. [see p. 285 note "e"], to have been a yr. br. of Sir Thomas Strachan, who was *cr. a Baronet* [S.], 8 May 1685, and to have assumed that Baronetcy on the death, s.p., of his said brother. This statement is said to be, "according to a family pedigree deposited in the College of Arms, by Admiral Sir Richard Strachan," grandson of the said Patrick. No such pedigree, however, is recorded either in the College of Arms, London, or in the Lyon office, Edinburgh, and the statement is at variance with all other accounts of the family. The burial at Greenwich of the said Patrick Strachan (the Surgeon), 10 Sep. 1749 (64 years after the said Sir Thomas, his alleged brother, had been created a Baronet), does not describe him as a Baronet; there is no proof that the said Sir Thomas (whose parentage is unknown) ever had any brothers; and, finally, the creation of the Baronetcy of 8 May 1685 was to the heirs male *of the body* of the grantee, and consequently could not have passed, after his death without such issue, to a younger brother, but must have become *extinct*.

(b) According to the assumption of that dignity.

(c) His only br., Jervis Henry Strachan, an officer in the marines, *d.* unm. being slain in 1780, during a sea fight.

(d) The recriminations of the two commanders as to their respective dilatoriness gave rise to the well known epigram, quoted thus in the *Dict. Nat. Biogr.*, under "Pitt," John, 2d Earl of Chatham:—

"Great Chatham, with his sabre drawn,
Stood *waiting* for Sir Richard Strachan;
Sir Richard, longing to be at 'em,
Stood *waiting* for the Earl of Chatham.

According, however, to a writer in the *Athenæum* (27 April 1701), quoting "the late Mr. Carrick Moore, whose reminiscences, through his father, Dr. Moore, and his uncle, Sir John, reach back to the date of Walcheren," the first line was—

"Chatham, impatient for the dawn."

This seems the more appropriate version, as being in allusion "to the combined action by the land and sea forces *intended* to take place at daybreak." Another version, given in the *Morning Chronicle* of 6 Feb. 1810, is quoted in G.E.C.'s *Complete Peerage* (vol. ii, p. 213), under "Chatham."

(e) He left three daughters, all married to foreigners.

3 Feb. 1828, after a short illness, aged 67, when *the Baronetcy* became *dormant*. Will dat. 12 Feb. 1816 to 31 Jan. 1828, pr. Feb. 1828. His widow *m.* (—) PICALILLO, an Italian. She resided at Naples, and was by the King thereof *cr.* MARCHESA DI SALZA.(a) She *d.* there in 1868, at an advanced age.

* * * * *

[Notwithstanding the resignation of the Baronetcy to "the heir male" expectant, by Sir Francis STRACHAN, the 5th Baronet,(b) the title was, after his death, assumed as under.]

VI bis. 1753? SIR ALEXANDER STRACHAN, Baronet(b) [S. 1625], called "the 6th Baronet of Nova Scotia," conjectured to be grandson of the Rev. Sir James STRACHAN, Baronet abovenamed. He *m.* before 1736, "Jané BREMNER, of Atterbury."(c)

VII bis. 1760? SIR ALEXANDER STRACHAN, Baronet(b) [S. 1625], s. and h.; "*suc. to the title*, with its slender income, on the death of his father." He was a Jesuit Priest, and having travelled much, *d.* unm. in his old age, 3 Jan. 1793, at the English College at Liege.(c)

VIII bis. 1793, to 1826. ROBERT STRACHAN, *or* SIR ROBERT STRACHAN, Baronet(b) [S. 1625], br. and h., *b.* about 1737. He was a clerk in Gaudolfe's Bank, Exeter. He *suc. to the Baronetcy*, 3 Jan. 1793, but possibly never assumed the title. He *d.* unm. at Exeter, 3 April 1826, aged 89, and was *bur.* at St. Nicholas in that city.(c)

* * * * *

The title was also assumed as under.

"About 12 years after the death of Admiral Sir Richard Strachan, Mr. John Strachan, of Cliffden, Teignmouth, Devonshire, preferred a claim to the representation of the house of Thornton and passed through a form of service before the *Bailies of Canongate*. In his claim, or brief, Mr. Strachan sought to instruct his descent from Roger Strachan, of Glichno, brother of John Strachan, of Thornton, great grandfather of the 1st Baronet. Roger Strachan was set forth as father of Dr. Robert Strachan, Physician in Montrose [*d.* between 1656 and 1659], whose son, John was Minister of Strachan [and *d.* Feb. 1701]. George [said, in a sasine of 8 June 1696, to be] a son of the Minister, was represented as a Merchant in Montrose, and father of James Strachan, Lieut. R.N., father of the claimant. This statement of pedigrees, unsupported by evidence and in entire variance with chronological requirements, being accepted by a friendly jury and certified by the Canongate Bailies, formed the basis of a retour in Chancery, bearing date 8 Nov. 1841." [Rogers's *Memorials of the Strachans* as quoted in *Her. and Gen.*, viii, p. 306.]

IX. 1841. "SIR JOHN STRACHAN, Baronet,"(d) [S. 1625], of Cliffden, Teignmouth, Devon, only s. of James STRACHAN, Lieut. R.N. (*d.* 9 Sep. 1794, aged 93, *bur.* at Montrose), by Catherine, da. of James DONALDSON, of Montrose, was *b.* 22 March 1751, and *assumed the style of a Baronet* after the abovementioned retour of 8 Nov. 1841, as heir male collateral of the grantee. He was a magistrate for Stirlingshire. He *m.* Elizabeth, da. of David HUNTER, of Blackness, co. Forfar. He *d.* 9 June 1844, aged 93, at Cliffden aforesaid. Will pr. Aug. 1844.

(a) She is said to have purchased that title with a legacy left to her, in 1842, by the Marquess of Hertford.

(b) According to the assumption of that dignity.

(c) Rogers's *Strachan Family*, see p. 285, note "e."

(d) According to the assumption of the title, in consequence of the retour of 8 Nov. 1841.

X. 1844, to 1854. "SIR JOHN STRACHAN, Baronet"(a) [S. 1625], of Cliffden aforesaid, 1st and only surv. s. and h., *b.* at Montrose; was, presumably, ed. at Winchester School, 1799; *suc. to the Baronetcy*,(a) 9 June 1844. He *m.* Mary Anne, da. of Isaac ELTON, of Whitestanton, co. Somerset, and Stapleton House, co Gloucester. He *d.* s.p., 28 Jan. 1854, at Cliffden aforesaid, when the assumption of the Baronetcy ceased. He was *bur.* at East Teignmouth. M.I.(b) Will dat. 29 June 1848, pr. March 1854. His widow *m.* in 1855, John Chappell TOZER, of Teignmouth, and *d.* apparently in 1857.

LIVINGSTONE, *or* LIVINGSTOUN:
cr. 30 May 1625(c);
dormant, since about 1634.

I. 1625, to 1634? SIR DAVID LIVINGSTOUN, of Dunipace, co. Stirling, 2d s. of John Livingstoun, or LIVINGSTONE, who was s. and h. apparent of another John LIVINGSTONE, of the same, was served heir general of his said grandfather, as also of his elder br., John LIVINGSTONE, of Dunipace, 22 Jan. 1620, inheriting thereby an immense estate, and was *cr. a Baronet* [S.], 30 May, sealed 20 Aug. 1625,(c) with rem. to heirs male whatever and with a grant of, presumably, 16,000 acres in Nova Scotia, being the Barony of Livingstone-Dunipace of which he had seizin, July 1625.(d) He, being then "heir ap. of Dunipace," *m.* before 3 May 1609, Barbara FORRESTER, probably da. of Sir James FORRESTER, of Garden. He was living 1631, but *d.*, having apparently, dissipated all his property(e), before 25 Feb. 1634, leaving male issue, but after his death the *Baronetcy* appears to have become *dormant*.(f)

(a) See p. 289, note "d."

(b) See p. 289, note "c."

(c) Milne's List and Laing's List. The creation is between that of Strachan and Macdonald; see p. 291, line 8, and p. 285, note "d." A Baronetcy [S.] of this same date (30 May 1625) is sometimes said to have been conferred on Sir George Livingstone, of Ogleface, co. Linlithgow, a yr. br. of Alexander, 1st Earl of Linlithgow [S.], but this is an error. That creation is, however, indicated (though not actually asserted) in Playfair's Baronetage [S.], and has been adopted in some more modern Baronetages.

(d) Banks's Lists.

(e) Dunipace was in the hands of the Earl of Callender (S.) before 1646. In 1649 Margaret, da. of the Baronet, had a decree for £500 for parts of the land of Dunipace. The Livingstones of Balrounie, 1600 to 1729, descend from Patrick Livingstone, of the same, uncle of the Baronet; there appear also to have been other branches of the Dunipace family, all of whom would be within the limitation of the Baronetcy. Alexander Livingstone, the founder of the family of Dunipace (beheaded 1446), was a bastard br. of the 1st Lord Livingstone (S.). [*Ex inform.* R. R. Stodart, Lyon Clerk Depute, 1863-86.]

(f) His son, John Livingstone, living as "heir ap. of Dunipace," 9 Aug. 1630, 11 June and 9 July 1631, survived him, and was living 25 Feb. 1634, when he had protection from the creditors of his deceased father, but, having inherited nothing from him, he apparently *never assumed the Baronetcy*, and nothing more is known of him. There were two sisters of the first Baronet, one of whom *m.*, about 1590, James Arbuthnott, and was mother of Sir Robert Arbuthnott of that ilk, while the other, Jean, known as "Lady Warriston," *m.* John Kincaird, of Warriston, near Edinburgh, and was executed 5 July 1600 for his murder. See an interesting article thereon in the *Scottish Record*, for Oct. 1850.

MACDONALD:
cr. 14 July 1625(a);
afterwards, since 1776, BARONS MACDONALD OF SLATE [I.].

I. 1625. DONALD MACDONALD, *formerly* GORME, of Slate, in the Isle of Skye, co. Inverness, s. and h. of Archibald MACDONALD, of the same, by Margaret, *or* Mary, da. of Angus MACDONALD, of Duniveg and Glennis, suc. his uncle Donald MACDONALD, *otherwise* GORME, of Slate, in 1616 and was *cr. a Baronet* [S.], 14 July 1625, with rem. to heirs male whatever, and with precedency over Douglas, Strachan, and Livingstone, the three creations next above him,(a) and with the grant of, presumably, 16,000 acres in Nova Scotia, of which, however, he never had seizin.(b) The patent is not in the Great Seal Register, but "only in one old list."(a) He supported Charles I in the Civil Wars. He *m.* Janet, sister of Colin, 1st EARL OF SEAFORTH [S.], 2d da. of Kenneth (MACKENZIE), 1st LORD MACKENZIE OF KINTAIL [S.] by his 1st wife Anne, da. of George ROSS, of Balnagowan. He *d.* Oct. 1643.

II. 1643. SIR JAMES MACDONALD, Baronet [S. 1625], of Slate aforesaid, s. and h., *suc. to the Baronetcy* in Oct. 1643 and was served heir to his father, 20 Feb. 1644. He supported the Royal Cause in 1645, again in 1651, and quelled a disturbance in the Highlands in 1664. He *m.* firstly (contract 23 Feb. 1633), Margaret, aunt of George, 1st EARL OF CROMARTY [S.], da. of Sir Roderick MACKENZIE, of Lorgeach, by Margaret, da. and h. of Torquil MACLEOD, of Lewes. He *m.* secondly, Mary, da. of John MACLEOD, of Macleod, by Sybella, da. of Kenneth (MACKENZIE), 1st LORD MACKENZIE OF KINTAIL [S.]. He *d.* 8 Dec. 1678.

III. 1678. SIR DONALD MACDONALD, Baronet [S. 1625], of Slate aforesaid, s. and h. by 1st wife, *suc. to the Baronetcy*, 8 Dec. 1678. In 1684 he was "sued as unfaithful."(c) He *m.*, 24 July 1662, at Perth, Mary, 2d and yst. da. of Robert (DOUGLAS) EARL OF MORTON [S.], by Elizabeth, da. of Sir Edward VILLIERS. She, in 1681, became coheir to her br., Robert, EARL OF MORTON [S.]. He *d.* 5 Feb. 1695.

IV. 1695. SIR DONALD MACDONALD, Baronet [S. 1625], of Slate aforesaid, and of Duntulm, in the Isle of Skye, s. and h., *suc. to the Baronetcy*, 5 Feb. 1695. He engaged in the rebellion of 1715 and is said to have been attainted, but no forfeiture of the title, apparently, followed. He *m.* Mary, da. of Donald MACDONALD, of Castleton. He *d.* 1718.

V. 1718. SIR DONALD MACDONALD, Baronet [S. 1625], only s. and h., *b.* about 1697; mat. at Oxford (Ch. Ch.), 7 Nov. 1712, aged 15; *suc. to the Baronetcy*, in 1718. He *d.* unm. 1720.

VI. 1720. SIR JAMES MACDONALD, Baronet [S. 1625], of Slate aforesaid, and of Oransay, uncle and h. male; *suc. to the Baronetcy* in 1720. He *m.* firstly, Janet, widow of John MACLEOD, of Talisker, da. and h of Alexander MACLEOD of Grishernish, in Skye. He *m.* secondly, Margaret, da. of John MACDONALD, of Castleton, by whom he had no issue.(c) He *d.* 1723, at Forres.

VII. 1723. SIR ALEXANDER MACDONALD, Baronet [S. 1625], of Slate aforesaid, s. and h. by 1st wife, *b.* 1711; *suc. to the Baronetcy* in 1723. He was almost the only person of consideration in that district, who, in 1745, supported the Government, and was consequently in great favour with the Duke of Cumberland. He *m.* firstly, 5 April 1733, Anne, widow of James OGILVY, *styled* LORD OGILVY OF AIRLIE da. of David ERSKINE, of Dun, co. Forfar, a Lord of Session [S].

(a) Milne's List and Laing's List.

(b) Banks's Lists.

(c) Alexander Sinclair's *Macdonalds of the Isles*.

She *d.* at Edinburgh, 27 Nov. 1735, in her 27th year. He *m.* secondly, 24 April 1739, at St. Paul's, Edinburgh, Margaret, 9th da. of Alexander (MONTGOMERIE), 9th Earl of Eglington [S.], being his 4th da. by his 3d wife Susanna, da. of Sir Archibald KENNEDY, 1st Baronet [S. 1681], of Culzean. He *d.*, suddenly at Bernera (on his way to London) 23 Nov. 1746, aged 35. His widow, who was a distinguished partisan of the exiled house of Stuart, *d.* 30 March 1799 in Welbeck Street, Marylebone. Will pr. April 1799.

VIII. 1746. SIR JAMES MACDONALD, Baronet [S. 1625], of Slate aforesaid, s. and h. by 2d wife, *b.* at Edinburgh about 1742; matric. at Oxford (Ch. Ch.), 9 May 1759, aged 17; was an accomplished scholar and mathematician, being considered "The Marcellus of the North"; *suc. to the Baronetcy* in Nov. 1746. He *d.* unm., at Rome, 26 July 1766, aged 24, and, though a protestant, had, by leave of Pope Clement XIII, a public funeral. M.I. at Slate.

IX. 1766. SIR ALEXANDER MACDONALD, Baronet [S. 1625], of Slate aforesaid, br. and h.,(a) *b.* about 1745; was, sometime about 1761-66, an officer in the Coldstream Guards; *suc. to the Baronetcy*, 26 July 1766. He *m.* 3 May 1768, at St. Giles' in the Fields, Elizabeth Diana, 1st da. of (whose issue in 1813 became coheir to) Godfrey BOSVILLE, of Gunthwaite, co. York, by Diana, da. of Sir William WENTWORTH, 4th Baronet [1664], of Bretton. She, who was *bap.* 25 July 1748, was living when he was raised to the peerage, being *cr.* 17 July 1776, BARON MACDONALD OF SLATE, CO. ANTRIM [I.].(b) In that peerage this *Baronetcy* then merged and still so continues.

MURRAY:

cr. 19 July 1625(c);

subsequently, 1636-58, EARLS OF ANNANDALE [S.];

dormant, since 1658.

I. 1625. SIR RICHARD MURRAY, of Cockpool, 6th s. of Sir Charles MURRAY, of the same, by Margaret, da. of Hugh (SOMERVILLE) LORD SOMERVILLE [S.], suc., in 1620, his elder br. Sir James Murray in that estate, and was *cr. a Baronet* [S.], 19 July 1625, sealed 20 Oct. 1625,(c) with rem. to heirs male whatsoever, and a grant of, presumably, 16,000 acres in Nova Scotia, entitled the Barony of Cockpool, of which he had sasine in Oct. following.(d) In 1635 he had sasine of the lands of Lockerbie, Hutton, Hoddam, etc. He *d.* s.p., probably unm., in 1636.

II. 1636. JOHN (MURRAY) EARL OF ANNANDALE [S.] (so *cr.* 13 March 1624/5), only surv. br. and h. male, being 8th and yst. s. of Sir Charles MURRAY abovenamed, *suc. to the Baronetcy* as heir male collateral in 1636, when *the Baronetcy merged* in this peerage till its extinction (*See* "Peerage"), on the death of the 2d Earl, 28 Dec. 1658, on which date the *Baronetcy* became *dormant*, the issue male of the grantee as well as of his father being *extinct*.

(a) Archibald Macdonald, the 3d and yst br., was L. Ch. Baron of the Exchequer, 1793-1813, and was *cr. a Baronet*, 27 Nov. 1813.

(b) "Slate, *co. Antrim in Ireland*," is non-existent, the place referred to being Slate or Sleat in *the island of Skye, in Scotland*. Such fictions, however, were not unusual when Scotsmen were (after the union with Scotland) raised to the peerage. Such *e.g.*, was the elevation to the Irish peerage of William Duff, in 1735, as Baron Kilbryde, co *Cavan*, and in 1759 as Earl Fife, *in Ireland*.

(c) Milne's List and Laing's List.

(d) Banks's Lists, where it is added "Represented by the Earl of Mansfield," which representation, however, is only in right of female descent through the families of Scott and Grierson, from the 1st da. and heir of line to Sir James Murray, of Cockpool, elder br. of the first Baronet.

ALEXANDER:

cr., 12 July 1625(a);

afterwards, 1630—1739, VISCOUNTS STIRLING [S.];

and subsequently, 1633—1739, EARLS OF STIRLING [S.];

dormant, since 4 Dec. 1739.

I. 1625. SIR WILLIAM ALEXANDER, of Menstre, in Logie, co. Clackmannan, afterwards, 1630, VISCOUNT, and subsequently, in 1633, EARL OF STIRLING [S.] (for whom see fuller accounts in *Peerage*), was *b.* about 1567; Sec. of State and P.C. [S.], 1626; *Knighted* at Whitehall, 2 March 1626/7; had a grant from Charles, 10 Sep. 1621, of the vast territory of Nova Scotia, with permission (for the purpose of Colonization) to divide the same into 100 tracks of 16,000 acres and dispose of each, *together with the rank of Baronet*. This grant was, however, not acted upon, until it was confirmed by Charles I (the number of 100 being changed to 150), by Charter, 12 July 1625, sealed 9 Sep. following,(a) on which date the grantee himself is said(a) to have been *cr. a Baronet* [S.], with rem. to his heirs male whatever,(b) He had seizin "of one part of the continent of Nova Scotia" in the same month of Sep. 1625.(c) As late, however, as 30 Nov. 1629 he styles himself [only] "Knight."(d) On 2 Feb. 1628 he had charters of the Lordship of Canada. He was *cr.* 4 Sep. 1630, VISCOUNT STIRLING, etc. [S.], and subsequently, 14 June 1633, EARL OF STIRLING, VISCOUNT CANADA, etc. [S.], with rem. in both cases to his heirs male of the name of Alexander. In these peerages *this Baronetcy* then *merged*, and so continued till, on the death of his great grandson the 5th Earl, 4 Dec. 1739, it, and the said Peerage dignities became *dormant*. See *Peerage*.

COLQUHOUN;

cr. 30 Aug. 1625(e);

regranted, with a different remainder, 29 April 1704;

afterwards, 1719—1811, GRANT;

and finally, since 1811, EARLS OF SEAFIELD [S.].

This Baronetcy was (erroneously) assumed by the heir male, 1718—1838.

I. 1625. JOHN COLQUHOUN, of Luss and Tilliquhoun, co. Dumbarton, s. and h. of Alexander COLQUHOUN, of the same, by Helen, da. of Sir George BUCHANAN, of Buchanan, suc. his father, 23 May 1617, was M.P. [S.]

(a) Milne's List. This creation does not appear in Laing's List, nor is it registered in the great Seal Register, though apparently it is in the *Registrum Preceptorum Cartarum pro Baronettis Novæ Scotiæ, 1625-30*.

(b) It seems curious that, as he had all the land of which a grant of but 16,000 acres constituted a Baronetcy, he should not if he accepted of a Baronetcy have had one of the earliest date. In Beatson's list of these (edit. 1806) he is placed but 13th, those of Gordon of Gordonstoun, Wemyss, Innes, Strachan, Douglas, Colquhoun, Livingstone, Murray, Gordon of Cluny, Leslie, Campbell of Glenorchy, and Gordon of Lesmore, being placed above him. Most unquestionably the premier Baronetcy was Gordon of Gordonstoun, but it must be born in mind that by the charter of 1625 the said "Sir William Alexander and his Leirs male descending of his body as Lieutenants aforesaid [*i.e.*, of Nova Scotia] shall * * * take * * * precedence as well before all Esquires, Lairds, and Gentlemen of our said kingdom of Scotland as *before all the aforesaid Knight Baronets* of our said Kingdom." [Banks's *Baronia Anglica Concentrata*, vol. ii, p. 213.]

(c) Banks's List.

(d) The use, however, of the word "Knight" for "Baronet" was not uncommon in the early days of the Baronetcy.

(e) Milne's List and Laing's List.

for Dumbartonshire, 1621, and was *cr. a Baronet* [S.], 30 Aug. 1625, sealed 20 Oct. following,(a) with rem. to heirs male whatsoever, and with a grant of, apparently, 16,000 acres in Nova Scotia, afterwards called Tilliquhoun, of which seizin was made in the said month of October.(b) He was "fugitated and excommunicated," and deprived of the life rent of his estates, as the result of a criminal suit in 1632 for his seduction of his wife's sister, Lady Katherine Graham. He *m.* (contract 30 June and 6 July 1620) Lilias, 1st da. of John (GRAHAM), 4th EARL OF MONTROSE [S.], by Margaret, da. of William (RUTHVEN), 1st EARL OF GOWRIE [S.]. He *d.* about 1650.

II. 1650? SIR JOHN COLQUHOUN, Baronet [S. 1625], of Luss aforesaid, 1st s. and h., *b.* about 1622; suc. to the family estates in 1647 (which had been preserved to the family by his uncle, Sir Humphrey Colquhoun, of Balvie, who was M.P. [S.], for Dumbartonshire, 1643-49); *suc. to the Baronetcy* about 1650. He purchased the estate of Balloch in 1652, and acquired that of Lochend, co. Haddington (which, however, he sold in 1678) by marriage; was M.P. [S.] for Dumbartonshire 1650, 1661-63, 1665, 1667, and 1669-74. He *m.* (contract, 17 Feb. 1636) Margaret, da. and h. of Sir Gideon BAILLIE, Baronet [S. 1636], by Magdalen, da. and coheir of David CARNEGIE, *styled* LORD CARNEGIE. He *d.* 11 April 1676. Will pr. 27 Feb. 1677. His widow *m.* 1 April 1677, Archibald STIRLING, of Garden, and *d.* 20 July 1679.

III. 1676. SIR JAMES COLQUHOUN, Baronet [S. 1625], of Luss aforesaid, 2d but only surv. s. and h., *suc. to the Baronetcy*, 11 April 1676. He *d.* unm. 1680.(c)

IV. 1680. SIR JAMES COLQUHOUN, Baronet [S. 1625], of Luss aforesaid, uncle and h. male, formerly of Corcagh, co. Donegal; *suc. to the Baronetcy* in 1680. He *m.*, before Nov. 1669, being then of Corcagh aforesaid, Penuel, coheir of her brothers John and Robert Cunningham, of Ballyachen, co. Donegal, yst. da. of James(d) CUNNINGHAM of the same.(d) He *d.* 1688.

V. 1688. SIR HUMPHREY COLQUHOUN, Baronet [S. 1625], of Luss aforesaid, only s. and h., *suc. to the Baronetcy* in 1688; was M.P. [S.] for Dumbartonshire, 1703-07, voting on all occasions against the Scotch union; was a Commissioner of Supply; Lieut.-Col. of the Militia of the Counties of Argyll, Dumbarton, and Bute. He *m.* (contract 1 and 4 April 1684) Margaret, 1st da. of Sir Patrick HOUSTON, 1st Baronet [S. 1668] by Anne, da. of John (HAMILTON), 1st LORD BARGENY [S.] He, having no male issue, *resigned his Baronetcy*, 30 March 1704, into the hands of the Crown, and obtained a new grant (*novodamus*) thereof, with the former precedence, to himself and the heirs male of his body, whom failing, to (his son-in-law) JAMES GRANT, of Pluscardine, and the heirs male begotten between the said James, by Anne, his wife, only da. of the said Humphrey, with rem. to heirs male of the body of the said Anne, rem. to the other heirs of entail of the said Humphrey.(e)

(a) Milne's List and Laing's List.

(b) Banks's Lists.

(c) He had several sisters, who or whose issue became the heirs general of the 1st Baronet.

(d) Not "William" as stated in Fraser's *Chiefs of Colquhoun* (vol. i, p. 294). See will of James Cunningham, of "Ballyachen, co. Donegall, Esq.," dated 7 May 1664, and pr. 11 March 1667. Admon. of John Cunningham, 13 Nov. 1669 (to Robert Sanderson, Esq., and Katherine his wife, and James Colquhoun and Penuel his wife, sisters of the deceased) and of Robert Cunningham, 22 Dec. 1682. There are also several Chancery bills, concerning the Cunningham estate, to which *Sir James* was a party, further bearing out the connection [*Ex. inform.*, G. D. Burtchaell].

(e) By the Scotch law which prevailed before the union [S.] there is no doubt that this surrender and re-grant (unlike the law in England) was valid.

He also executed an entail of the Colquhoun estates, with a proviso that they should never be held with those of the family of Grant. He *d.* s.p.m., 1718, when, according to the *novodamus* of 1704, the Baronetcy of 1625 devolved as under.

VI. 1718. SIR JAMES COLQUHOUN, *subsequently* (after 1719) GRANT, Baronet [S. 1625], formerly JAMES GRANT, of Pluscardine, 2d s. of Ludovic GRANT, of Grant (*d.* 1717), by his 1st wife, Janet, da. and h. of Alexander BRODIE, of Lethen. He was *b.* 28 July 1679, and, having *m.*, 29 Jan. 1702, Anne (*b.* 1685), only child of Sir Humphrey COLQUHOUN, the last Baronet, by Margaret his wife, both abovenamed, *suc. to that Baronetcy* on the death of his said father-in-law, in 1718 (by virtue of the spec. rem. in the *novodamus* of that dignity), and to the estate of Luss, by virtue of the entail thereof, on which occasion he took the name of COLQUHOUN. The next year, however, he suc. on the death, in 1719, s.p.s., of his elder brother, Brig.-Gen. Alexander Grant, to the paternal estate of Grant, and re-assumed his patronymic of GRANT. He was M.P. for Inverness-shire (three Parls.), 1722-41, and for the Elgin burghs, 1741-47. His wife *d.* 25 June 1724, aged 39. He *d.* 16 Jan. 1746/7.

VII. 1747. SIR LUDOVIC GRANT, Baronet [S. 1645], of Grant, *formerly* (1719-32) LUDOVIC COLQUHOUN, of Luss, 2d but 1st surv. s. and h., *b.* 13 Jan. 1707; received from his father, in 1719, the Colquhoun estates, and accordingly continued to bear the name of Colquhoun. These he endeavoured, unsuccessfully, to retain(a) after the fee expectant of the Grant estates had, in 1735, been made over to him on the death of his elder brother, Humphry Grant, who *d.* v.p. and unm. in 1732. He thereupon took the name of GRANT; was M.P. for Elgin and Forres-shire (three Parls.), 1741-61, and *suc. to the Baronetcy*, 16 Jan. 1746/7. He *m.* firstly, Marion, 2d da. of the Hon. Sir Hew DALRYMPLE, 1st Baronet [S. 1698], by Marion, da. of Sir Robert HAMILTON. She, who was *b.* 6 July 1696, *d.* s.p.m. He *m.* secondly, Nov. 1735, Margaret, eldest of the two daughters of James (OGILVY), 5th EARL OF FINDLATER [S.], and 2d EARL OF SEAFIELD [S.], by Elizabeth, da. of Thomas (HAY), 6th EARL OF KINNOUL [S.]. She *d.* 20 Feb. 1757. He *d.* 18 March 1773.

VIII. 1773. SIR JAMES GRANT, Baronet [S. 1625], of Grant, only s. and h. by 2d wife, *b.* 19 May 1738; was M.P. for Elgin and Forres-shire, 1761-68, and for Banffshire, 1790; *suc. to the Baronetcy*, 18 March 1773; served heir to his father, 14 May 1773; raised the 1st Reg. of Fencible Infantry in 1793, and the 97th Reg. in 1794; was Receiver and Cashier [S.], 1790-95; Receiver of Excise [S.], 1795; L. Lieut. of Inverness-shire, 1794-1809. He *m.* 4 Jan. 1763, Jean, only da. of Alexander DUFF, of Hatton, co. Aberdeen, by Anne, 1st da. of William (DUFF), 1st EARL FIFE [I.]. She *d.* 15 Feb. 1805. He *d.* 18 Feb. 1811.

IX. 1811. SIR LEWIS-ALEXANDER GRANT, Baronet [S. 1625], of Grant aforesaid, s. and h., *b.* 22 March 1767; admitted to Lincoln's Inn, 1788; was an Advocate [S.], 1789; M.P. for Elginshire, 1790-96; *suc. to the Baronetcy*, 18 Feb. 1811, and, eight months later, suc., 5 Oct. 1811, as EARL OF SEAFIELD, etc. [S.], on the death of his father's 2d cousin, James (OGILVY), EARL OF FINDLATER and EARL OF SEAFIELD [S.], when he assumed the name of OGILVY after that of GRANT, and registered arms at the Lyon office, with the badge thereon of a Baronet of Nova Scotia. In the Earldom of Seafield this *Baronetcy* then *merged*, and still so continues. See *Peerage*.

(a) Luss and the other Colquhoun estates were confirmed by a legal decision in 1738, to his younger brother, James Grant, who accordingly took the name of Colquhoun, and was *cr. a Baronet*, as "Colquhoun of Luss," 27 June 1786.

The Baronetcy was (erroneously) assumed in 1710, as under, by the *heir male* (to whom it had, in the original patent, been limited), notwithstanding the surrender by the 5th Baronet, and the *novodamus* thereof, in 1704, which had altered the line of its descent.

VI. 1718. SIR JOHN COLQUHOUN, Baronet [S. 1625],(a) of Tillyquhoun, *otherwise* Tillychewan, co. Dumbarton, s. and h. of Alexander COLQUHOUN, of the same, by Annabella, da. of George STEWART, of Scotstoun, the said Alexander being 3d and yst. s. of the 1st Baronet and br. of the 2d and 4th Baronets; suc. his father before 1718, in which year he became heir male to his cousin, the 5th Baronet, and, as such, *assumed the Baronetcy*. He *m.* Elizabeth, da. of Andrew ANDERSON, King's Printer for Scotland.

VII. 1720? SIR HUMPHREY COLQUHOUN, Baronet [S. 1625],(a) only s. and h.; *suc. to the Baronetcy*(a) on his father's death, shortly after which he sold the estate of Tillyquhoun to the widow of his uncle, Captain James Colquhoun, hereafter mentioned. He *d.* unm. 19 Aug. 1722, "by cutting his own throat with a penknife at the 'Katherine Wheel,' without Bishopsgate."(b)

VIII. 1722. SIR GEORGE COLQUHOUN, Baronet [S. 1625],(a) of Tillyquhoun aforesaid, cousin and h. male, being s. and h. of Capt. James COLQUHOUN, 3d Foot Guards, by Elizabeth, da. of John COLQUHOUN, of Auchintarlie, which James was br. of the 6th Baronet.(a) He was *b.* 1708, and *suc. to the Baronetcy*(a) in 1722, and to the estate of Tillyquhoun on the death of his mother, who had purchased the same as abovestated. He was a Col. in the service of the States General. He *m.* firstly, 7 Jan. 1751, Rebecca, only da. of William JONES, Collector of the Stamp Duties [S.]. She *d.* s.p.m. He *m.* secondly, in 1777 (being then in his 70th year), Charlotte, da. of David BARCLAY. He *d.* at Edinburgh, 1785. Will pr. June 1787. His widow *d.* 10 Feb. 1816, also at Edinburgh.

IX. 1785. SIR JAMES COLQUHOUN, Baronet [S. 1625],(a) of Tillyquhoun aforesaid, 1st s. and h. by 2d wife; *suc. to the Baronetcy*,(a) when a child, in 1785. He was Lieut. in the 19th Foot, and *d.* unm., on the march to Seringapatam in the East Indies, 1799. Will pr. 1807.

X. 1799. SIR GEORGE WILLIAM ORANGE COLQUHOUN, Baronet [S. 1625],(a) of Tillyquhoun aforesaid, next br. and h., was Capt. in the 2d Royals; *suc. to the Baronetcy*,(a) in 1799. He *d.* unm., being slain at the battle of Salamanca, 22 July 1812. Admon. March 1813 and June 1816.

XI. 1812, to 1838. SIR ROBERT DAVID COLQUHOUN, Baronet [S. 1625](a) only surv. br. and h.; *b.* (posthumous) 1786; *suc. to the Baronetcy*,(a) 22 July 1812; was Brevet Major in the Bengal army. He *m.* Feb. 1822, at Calcutta, Anna Maria, 2d da. of James COLVIN, of Calcutta. He *d.* s.p. at sea, on his passage to India, 2 June 1838, aged 52, when the *issue male of the 1st Baronet* became *extinct*, and the *assumption of the Baronetcy* ceased.

(a) According to the assumption of the title by the heir male, notwithstanding the *novodamus* of 1704, whereby the right of such heir thereto was barred.
(b) Mawson's Obits.

GORDON:

cr. 31 Aug. and sealed 20 Oct. 1625;(a)
dormant, before 1668.

I. 1625. SIR ALEXANDER GORDON, of Cluny, co. Aberdeen,(b) s. and h. of Sir Thomas GORDON,(c) of the same, by Grizel, da. of James (STEWART) LORD INNERMEATH [S.], had spec. service to his father, 11 July 1607; was M.P. [S.] for Aberdeenshire, 1612-1617; *Knighted* (*Qy.* at Lanark?), May 1617, and was *cr. a Baronet* [S.], 31 Aug., sealed, 20 Oct. 1625, with rem. to heirs male whatsoever, and with a grant of, presumably, 16,000 acres in Nova Scotia, entitled the Barony of New Cluny, of which he had seizin in the same month of Oct.(d) His affairs soon became involved, and in 1630 he was a prisoner for debt in the Tolbooth in Edinburgh. In 1632 he sold his estate of Tillyfour, etc. In 1639 he was Lieut. of the North. in 1644 he was adjudged a prisoner till payment was made of 1,100 marks, due to Sir Thomas NICOLSON. He *m.* firstly, Elizabeth, da. of William (DOUGLAS), 9th EARL OF ANGUS [S.], by Egidia, da. of Sir Robert GRAHAM. He *m.* secondly, Violet, da. of John URQUHART, of Craigfintry, co. Aberdeen. He *m.* thirdly, 22 June 1641, a few months after her husband's death, Elspeth, widow of Sir John LESLIE, 1st Baronet [S. 1625], of Wardes, da. of John GORDON, of Newton. She had previously intrigued with him, and had caused her then husband to make over to him his heavily burdened estates in co. Aberdeen. She *d.* at Durham, 2 Dec. 1642. He *d.* before 1650.

II. 1648? to 1665? SIR JOHN GORDON, Baronet [S. 1625], of Cluny aforesaid, s. and h. He, who about 1622, had become a Roman Catholic, *suc. to the Baronetcy* before 1650. In 1650 he wadset the estate of Cluny to the abovenamed Sir Thomas Nicholson, from whom it passed by apprising sale to Robert GORDON, of Pulrossie. He *m.* Elizabeth, da. of the abovenamed Sir John LESLIE, 1st Baronet [S.], of Wardes, by his step mother Elspeth, da. of John GORDON, of Newton. He *d.* before 1668, when the *Baronetcy* became *dormant*.(e) His widow *m.* Colonel Sir George CURRIER.

LESLIE:

cr. 1 Sep. 1625; sealed 5 April 1626;(a)
dormant after about 1660;
but assumed since about 1800.

I. 1625. JOHN LESLIE, of Wardis, co. Aberdeen, 1st s. and h. of John LESLIE, of the same, by Jane, da. of Sir James CRICHTON, of Frendraught, suc. his father about 1620, and was *cr. a Baronet* [S.], 1 Sep. 1625, sealed 5 April 1626, with rem. to heirs male whatsoever, and with a grant of,

(a) Milne's List; Laing's List.
(b) The Editor is indebted to R. R. Stodart *Lyon Clerk Depute* (1863-86), for most of the information in this article.
(c) This Thomas was s. and h. of John Gordon, of Cluny aforesaid, who was s. and h. of the Hon. Alexander Gordon, of Strathdon, co. Aberdeen, 3d s. of Alexander, 3d Earl of Huntly [S.].
(d) Banks's Lists.
(e) His brother german, William Gordon, of Cotton, near Aberdeen, had, by Marion, da. of Patrick GORDON, of Gordonsmilne, two sons, of whom (1) John Gordon, a Capt. in the Swedish service, *d.* at Cracow, about 1664; and (2) William Gordon (then late Bailie of Old Aberdeen) had a birthbrief, 4 June 1668, to prove him heir to his said brother. All of these that survived the 2d Baronet would, in their turn, have been entitled to the Baronetcy. If the issue male of all the younger sons of the 3d Earl of Huntly [S.] has failed, the MARQUESS OF HUNTLY [S.] would be entitled to the Baronetcy, and to him, accordingly, it is assigned in Broun's *Baronetage*.

presumably, 16,000 acres in Nova Scotia, entitled the Barony of Wardes and Findrassie, of which he had seizin in June 1626.(a) He had charter, 30 July 1629, of lands of Balcomie, co. Fife. He *m.* Elspeth, da. of John GORDON, of Newton. He *d.* 1640. His widow *m.* (as his 3d wife), 24 June 1641, Sir Alexander GORDON, 1st Baronet [S. 1625] of Cluny, who *d.* before 1650. She *d.* at Durham 2 Dec. 1642.

II. 1640. SIR JOHN LESLIE, Baronet [S. 1625], of Wardis aforesaid, 1st but only surv. son,(b) *suc. to the Baronetcy*, in 1640, and *d.* unm. 1645.

III. 1645, to 1660? SIR WILLIAM LESLIE, Baronet [S. 1625], uncle and h. male, being next br. to the 1st Baronet and consequently *entitled to the Baronetcy* in 1645, under the rem. to heirs male whatsoever. He "is the last we find designed by this title"(c) and, not having inherited the family estates, it is doubtful whether he ever assumed it. He *m.* Helen, da. of George GORDON, of Newton, by whom he had four sons, John, William, Patrick, and Alexander, "but there is no male succession to any of them."(c)

WILLIAM LESLIE, of Aberdeen, s. and h. of Patrick LESLIE, of New Raine (who in 1700 sold that estate), s. and h. of John LESLIE, of New Raine, s. and h. of Norman LESLIE, yst. br. of the 1st Baronet, is said to have had "undoubtedly a title to the Baronetcy, as he appears to be the male representative of the family."(c) He is also said(d) to have had an only s. William, who *d.* s.p.

JOHN LESLIE, though not mentioned in Douglas' *Baronage*,(c) is said(d) to have been a brother of William Leslie, of Aberdeen, and a yr. s. of the said Patrick, and to have left issue, as under.

IV ?(e) 1800.(f) SIR JOHN LESLIE, Baronet [S. 1625],(g) of Findrassie, co. Moray, s. and h. of John LESLIE, next abovenamed, *b.* about 1750; was Writer to the Signet, 10 Nov. 1784; *assumed the Baronetcy*, probably about 1800.(f) He *m.*, 15 July 1794, Caroline Jemima, da. and h., of Abraham LESLIE, of Findrassie aforesaid. She *d.* 1810. He *d.* at Edinburgh, 30 Sep. 1825, aged 75.

V ?(e) 1825. SIR CHARLES ABRAHAM LESLIE, Baronet [S. 1625],(g) of Findrassie aforesaid, 1st s. and h., *b.* 4 July 1796; *suc. to the Baronetcy*,(g) 30 Sep. 1825. He *m.*, in or before 1822, Anne, da. of Adam WALKER. He, who is said to have dissipated all his fortune, *d.* 1 March 1847, in Edinburgh, aged 50. His widow *d.* 7 Oct. 1868, at Mellenden lodge, Wanstead, Essex.

(a) Banks's Lists.
(b) His younger brothers, Francis and Alexander, both *d.* unm., being killed in the German Wars.
(c) Douglas' *Baronage* [S.], 1798.
(d) Burke's *Baronetage* 1901 states him positively to be a yr. s. of Patrick. Playfair's *Baronetage* [S.], published in 1811, where this John first appears, states that Patrick "we have *reason to believe*, had two sons. William and John."
(e) This is the enumeration given in Burke's *Baronetage*, but it is evident that there must have been many who should have been reckoned as *entitled* to the Baronetage after the death of the 3d Baronet, before those who are here set out.
(f) "It is said that this Baronetcy was claimed and assumed without even the customary service of a Jury. No date given" [Foster's *Baronetage* 1883 in "Chaos"]. Playfair's *Baronetage* [S.], published in 1811, states that "within these few years only it has been claimed."
(g) According to the assumption of the Baronetcy in or about 1800.

VI ?(a) 1847. SIR NORMAN ROBERT LESLIE, Baronet(b) [S. 1625], 1st s. and h.; *b.* 10 Dec. 1822; *suc. to the Baronetcy*(b) 1 March 1847(c); was Lieut., 5th Irregular Bengal Cavalry. He *m.*, 17 Dec. 1846, Jessie Elizabeth, 3d da. of Robert Wood SMITH, Major 6th Bengal Light Cavalry. He was murdered at Rohnee, in India, 12 June 1857, during the Sepoy mutiny, aged 34. His widow *d.* 1 July 1876, at Lucknow.

VII ?(a) 1857. SIR CHARLES HENRY LESLIE, Baronet(b) [S. 1625], only s. and h., *b.* 27 Nov. 1848, at Lahore, in Bengal; *suc. to the Baronetcy*(b), 12 June 1857; ed. at Grange School, Edinburgh, and at Sandwich; an officer, 107th Foot, 1867; Major, 1887; Col., Bengal Staff Corps; served in the Chin Lushai, Manipur, Chitral, and Tirah campaigns, 1895-98. C.B., 1896. He *m.*, 7 Jan. 1879, Emma May, da. of R. M. EDWARDS, of the Bengal Civil Service.

Residence.—Rakloh, Punjab.

GORDON:

cr. 2 Sep. 1625; sealed 6 April 1626;(d)
dormant since 9 Nov. 1839.

I. 1625. JAMES GORDON,(e) of Lesmoir, co. Aberdeen, s. and h. of Alexander GORDON,(f) of the same, by Marion, da. of Alexander FORBES, of Pitsligo, co. Aberdeen, had, on 18 March 1592, a remission for his complicity in the slaughter of the Regent [S.], the Earl of MORAY [S.]; suc. his father in 1609, to whom, on 10 April 1610, he had spec. service in lands at Balmad, etc., and was *cr. a Baronet* [S.], 2 Sep. 1625, sealed 6 April 1626 with rem. to heirs male whatsoever,(d) and with a grant of, presumably, 16,000 acres in Nova Scotia, entitled the barony of New Lesmoir, of which he had seizin in June 1626.(g) He *m.* firstly, Anna MERCER, who was living 1605. He *m.* secondly, Rebecca, da. of William KEITH, of Ravenscraig, co. Aberdeen. He was alive 1637, but *d.* in or before 1641.

II. 1640? SIR JAMES GORDON, Baronet [S. 1625], of Lesmoir aforesaid, great grandson and h., being only s. and h. of James GORDON (by (—), da. of (—) MENZIES, of Pitfoddels, co. Kincardine), which James (who *d.* July 1634), was only s. and h. of James GORDON, M.P. [S.], for Aberdeenshire, 1625, who was 1st s. and h. ap. of the late Baronet, but who *d.* v.p. in France, 5 Sep. 1633. He suc. his father in July 1634, being served his heir general 15 Dec. 1637. He *suc. to the Baronetcy* in or before 1641, and on 9 June 1641, was served heir general of his said great grandfather, and, on 24 April 1642, his heir special in the Barony of Newton of Garioch with the privilege of Free Royalty. He *d.* s.p. before 1648.

(a) See p. 298 note "e."
(b) According to the assumption of the Baronetcy in or about 1800.
(c) The date of his succession to the title is given in Dod's *Baronetage* and elsewhere as 1833. The Hon. Sir Charles Leslie, 2d Baronet [1784], died 4 Feb. 1833, and it is probable that the two Baronets of the same name have been confounded.
(d) Milne's List; Laing's List.
(e) The Editor is indebted to R. R. Stodart (*Lyon Clerk Depute*, 1863-86) for most of the information in this article.
(f) This Alexander was s. and h. of George, the s. and h. ap. of James Gordon, the first owner of Lesmoir, and suc. his grandfather in that estate before 25 Sep. 1607. This family is one of the illegitimate branches of the race of Gordon.
(g) Banks's Lists.

III. 1647? SIR WILLIAM GORDON, Baronet [S. 1625], of Lesmoir aforesaid, great-uncle and h. male, being 2d and yst. s. of the 1st Baronet. He *suc. to the Baronetcy* about 1647, and had spec. service on 19 Jan. 1648, to his grandnephew in the Barony of Newton aforesaid, and also as heir male general of his said father. He *m.* Christian WALKER, whose father was probably of Peterhead. He is also said to have *m.* Isabella, da. of Sir Patrick LESLIE, of Iden, co. Aberdeen, Provost of Aberdeen. He *d.* before 1672.

IV. 1671? SIR WILLIAM GORDON, Baronet [1625], of Lesmoir aforesaid, s. and h. by Christian WALKER aforesaid; *suc. to the Baronetcy* about 1671, and on 9 Oct. 1672 was served heir general of his cousin german, James GORDON, "Fiar of Lesmoir," and heir spec. of his grandfather, the 1st Baronet, in lands at Essie, etc. He registered arms, about 1672, in the Lyon office. He *m.* Margaret, da. of Sir James LEARMONTH, of Balcomie, co. Fife, a Senator of the College of Justice [S.], 1627-57. He was alive 1683, but *d.* in or before 1685.

V. 1684? SIR JAMES GORDON, Baronet [S. 1625], of Lesmoir aforesaid, s. and h., who, in 1681, had, v.p., been enfeoffed in the said Barony of Newton; *suc. to the Baronetcy*, about 1684. He *m.*, about 1680, Jean, only child of Sir John GORDON, 2d Baronet [S. 1642], of Haddo, by Mary, da. of Alexander (FORBES), 1st LORD FORBES OF PITSLIGO [S.]. He was living 1696.

VI. 1710? SIR WILLIAM GORDON, Baronet [S. 1625], of Lesmoir aforesaid, grandson and h., being only s. and h. of William GORDON, by Margaret, da. of William DUFF, of Drummuir, co. Banff, which William GORDON last named was s. and h. ap. of the late Baronet, but *d.* v.p. He *suc. to the Baronetcy* about 1710. He *m.* Lilias, da. of James GORDON, of Carnousie, co. Banff. He *d.* s.p., 15 Sep. 1750, leaving very little property.

VII. 1758. SIR ALEXANDER GORDON, Baronet [S. 1625], of Lesmoir aforesaid, cousin and h., being s. and h. of Alexander GORDON, Collector of Customs at Aberdeen, by Isabel, da. of James GORDON, merchant of Holland, which Alexander was 3d s. of the 5th Baronet. He *suc. to the Baronetcy* 15 Sep. 1750. He *m.*, 5 April or 2 May 1759, Margaret, 1st da. of Robert SCOTT, of Duninald, co. Forfar, by Anne, da. of George MIDDLETON, of Seaton, co. Aberdeen. He *d.* 25 March 1782.

VIII. 1782, to 1839. SIR FRANCIS GORDON, Baronet [S. 1625], 3d but 1st surv. s. and h., *b.* about 1764; *suc. to the Baronetcy* in 1782. He was in the service of the Hon. East India Company; had a severe sunstroke when young, from which he never altogether rallied; returned home in 1800, and lived many years in Yorkshire. He *d.* s.p., presumably unm., 9 Nov. 1839, aged 75, when the *Baronetcy* became *dormant*.

(a) The cadets of this family were numerous and founded several families, which lasted for generations, so that it is unlikely that the title is extinct. A caveat was lodged, 23 Oct. 1871, by Hugh GORDON, then in India. John Gordon, of Kinneller, co. Aberdeen, 4th of the five sons of Sir James Gordon, the 5th Baronet, had four sons, whose male issue, if any, would probably be entitled. In Aug. 1887 Herbert Spence-Compton Gordon, Capt. of the Princess Louise's Argyll and Sutherland Highlanders, s. and h. of John Henry Gordon (by Amelia, da. of Sir Herbert Compton, Chief Justice of Bombay) and nephew and h. of Edward Gordon, who *d.* s.p., claimed the Baronetcy, on the ground that his said uncle, Edward Gordon, was, on the death of Sir Francis Gordon in 1839, the *de jure* Baronet, being s. and h. of Edward GORDON (*d.* 1832), who was s. and h. of Edward GORDON (*d.* 1802), who was the 1st s. that left male issue of John GORDON (*d.* 18 Nov. 1728), which last named John, who left Scotland for India, was supposed to be s. and h. of Alexander Gordon, of Gerry, the yr. s. of the 1st Baronet. This supposition, however, is, by a comparison of the dates, very unlikely.

RAMSAY:

cr. 3 Sep. and sealed 2 Nov. 1625;(a)

sometime, 1754—1806, RAMSAY-IRVINE;

dormant, 11 Feb. 1806;

but assumed, till 1830.

I. 1625. GILBERT RAMSAY, of Balmain, co. Kincardine, s. and h., ap. of David RAMSAY, of the same, sometime (1612, 1625, and 1630) M.P. [S.] for Kincardineshire (who *d.* 1636), by Margaret, da. of Sir Gilbert OGILVIE, of Ogilvie, was *cr. a Baronet* [S.] as "of Balmaine," 3 Sep., sealed 2 Nov. 1625,(a) with rem. to heirs male whatsoever, and with a grant of, presumably, 16,000 acres in Nova Scotia, of which he had seizin in the said month of Nov.(b) He took part with the Covenanters in 1636; was M.P. [S.] for Kincardineshire, 1639-41, 1645-46, and 1661-63; was one of the committee appointed by Parl. [S.] in 1641 to collect the English supply; one of the Committee of Parl. [S.], July 1644; a Commissioner of Excise, etc., 1646. He is said(c) to have *m.* Elizabeth, da. of George AUCHINLECK, of Balmanno. He undoubtedly(d) *m.* "Grizel DURHAM," *i.e.*, Grizel, widow of Sir Alexander FOTHERINGHAM, da. of James, and sister of Sir Alexander DURHAM, of Pitkerrow. He was living July 1639, and some years afterwards,(e) probably as late as 1663. His widow *m.*, as his 1st wife, John (MIDDLETON), 1st EARL OF MIDDLETON [S.], who *d.*, 1673, at Tangiers. She *d.* Sep. 1666, at Cranstoun.

II. 1663? SIR DAVID RAMSAY, Baronet [S. 1625], of Balmain aforesaid, only s. and h.; *suc. to the Baronetcy* on the death of his father. He had charter *de novo* of his lands and Barony, 12 Aug. 1670. He is said(c) to have *m.* firstly, Margaret, da. of Sir James CARNEGIE, of Balnamoon.(f) He was M.P. [S.] for Kincardineshire, 1672, till his death. He *m.* secondly, in or after 1663, Elizabeth, widow of Sir Alexander BURNETT, 2d Baronet [S. 1626], da. of (—) COUTTS, of Auchtercoull. He *d.* Sep. 1673, being killed by a fall from his horse.

III. 1673. SIR CHARLES RAMSAY, Baronet [S. 1625], of Balmain aforesaid, only s. and h. by 1st wife, *suc. to the Baronetcy* in 1673. He *m.* firstly, about 1673, Margaret, 1st da. of Sir John CARNEGIE, of Boysack. She *d.* s.p. He *m.* secondly, Elizabeth, only da. of Sir Alexander FALCONER, of Glenfarquhar. He *d.* 1695.

IV. 1695. SIR DAVID RAMSAY, Baronet [S. 1625], of Balmain aforesaid, 1st s. and h.; *suc. to the Baronetcy* in 1695; was M.P. [S.] for Kincardineshire 1705-07, and again [G.B.], 1707-08 and 1708-10. He *d.* s.p., probably unm., Sep. 1710.

V. 1710. SIR ALEXANDER RAMSAY, Baronet, [S. 1625], of Balmain aforesaid, next br. and h.; Advocate [S.] 1705; *suc. to the Baronetcy* in Sep. 1710; was M.P. for Kincardineshire 1710-13; when he retired to improve his estate by better methods of agriculture. He *d.* unm. 27 Jan. 1754.

VI. 1754, to 1806. SIR ALEXANDER RAMSAY-IRVINE, Baronet [S. 1625], of Balmain aforesaid, nephew and h., being only s. and h. of Charles RAMSAY, by Catherine, da. of James MILL, of Balweylo, sometime Provost of Montrose, which Charles, who *d.* in 1727, was br. of the late two baronets, being 3d and yst s. of the 3d Baronet. He, being then Alexander

(a) Milne's List; Laing's List.
(b) Banks's Lists.
(c) Playfair's *Baronetage* [S.].
(d) See a Charter, dat. 31 July 1632, in the Laing Charters, no. 2114.
(e) *Ex inform.*, Sir J. Balfour Paul, Lyon King of Arms.
(f) No such "Sir James" is mentioned, and no such alliance is given in Lord Southesk's *History of the Carnegie Family*.

RAMSAY, took the name of IRVINE after that of RAMSAY; *suc. to the Baronetcy*, 27 Jan. 1754; was M.P. for Kincardineshire, 1765-68. He *d.* unm. 11 Feb. 1806, when the issue male of the grantee was apparently extinct and the *Baronetcy* became *dormant*.(a)

The title was, however, assumed as under:—

VII. 1806. JAMES RAMSAY, sometime resident in Barbadoes, whose parentage and descent is unknown "in the year 1806, served himself [*sic*] heir to the 1st Baronet,"(b) becoming thus "SIR JAMES RAMSAY, Baronet" (b) [S. 1625]. He *d.* s.p. 1807. Will as "Baronet," pr. 1808.

VIII. 1807, to 1830. "SIR THOMAS RAMSAY, Baronet"(c) [S. 1625], only surv. br. and h., *b.* about 1765; was in the East India Company's service; *suc. to the Baronetcy*(c) in 1807, but returned to the East Indies in 1809 to resume his situation as Captain.(b) He, being then "of Edinburgh," *m.* firstly, 29 June 1809, at St. James', Westminster, "Anne STEELE," then of St. James's Street, spinster, da. of the Rev. Dr. STEELE, late of Jamaica, deceased. He *m.* secondly, in 1819, Elizabeth, widow of William CHISHOLM, of Chisholm, 2d da. of Duncan MACDONNELL, of Glengarry, by Margery, da. of Sir Ludovick GRANT, 6th Baronet [S. 1688], of Dalvey. He *d.*, abroad, s.p.m., in 1830, when the assumption of this Baronetcy ceased. Will pr. June 1832. His widow *d.* 7 Oct. 1859, at Thorn Faulcon, co. Somerset, aged 82.

GRAHAM, *or* GRÆME:

cr. 28 Sep. 1625, sealed 23 Jan. 1630;(d)

dormant, since, apparently, about 1700.

I. 1625. THE HON. SIR WILLIAM GRAHAM, of Braco, in the parish of Muthill, co. Perth, 2d s. of John (GRAHAM), 3d EARL OF MONTROSE (S.), by Jean, da. of David (DRUMMOND), LORD DRUMMOND (S.) had in 1614 a wadset from his wife's father of his whole estate redeemable on payment of 80,000 marks; had sasine of the Barony of Braco in Anti Costi, 28 Dec. 1625, and was *cr. a Baronet* [S.], as "Sir William Græme, of Bracco," 28 Sep. 1625, sealed 23 Jan. 1630,(d) but not recorded in the *Registrum Preceptorum Cartarum pro Baronettis Novæ Scotiæ*, with rem. to heirs male whatsoever, and with a grant of, presumably, 16,000 acres in Nova Scotia, called the Barony of New Braco, of which he had seizin in Jan. 1630.(e) He *m.* Mary, widow of John CUNNINGHAM, of Cunninghamhead, co. Ayr, da. of Sir James EDMONSTONE, of Duntreath, co. Stirling. He *d.* before 1636.

(a) He devised his estates to his nephew Alexander Burnett, 2d s. of his sister Catherine, by Sir Thomas Burnett, 6th Baronet [S. 1626], which Alexander accordingly took the name of Ramsay, and was *cr. a Baronet* as "of Balmain, co. Kincardine," 13 May 1806.
(b) Playfair's *Baronetage* [S.] where it is added that "Sir Thomas is also the representative collateral descendant of the family of Ramsay, of Abbotshall, in Fife, an old family in which there was also a Baronetage [*cr.* 1669], which is now extinct or dormant."
(c) According to the service of 1806 abovementioned.
(d) Milne's List; the date, however, of the creation in Laing's List is "28 *Dec.* 1625," and there placed between the creations of "Erskine" and "Hume," both of the same date, all three being after that of "Forrester," 17 Nov. 1625.
(e) Banks's Lists.

II. 1635? SIR JOHN GRAHAM, Baronet [S. 1625], of Braco aforesaid, s. and h., *suc. to the Baronetcy* about 1635 and was served heir gen. of his father, 23 Jan. 1636; was a Royalist and was imprisoned for aiding his cousin the gallant Marquis of Montrose [S.], but released 8 March 1645 on paying 2,000 merks, etc. He *m.* Margaret, da. of Sir Dugald CAMPBELL, 1st Baronet [S. 1628], of Auchinbreck, by his 1st wife, Mary, da. of Sir Alexander ERSKINE, of Gogar. He *d.* before 1647.

III. 1646? SIR WILLIAM GRAHAM, Baronet [S. 1625], of Braco aforesaid, s. and h., *suc. to the Baronetcy* about 1646 and was, on 9 Oct. 1647, served heir spec. in Braco, etc., co. Perth, and in the Barony of Aithray, co. Stirling. He registered arms about 1672 in the Lyon office. He *m.* Mary,(a) da. of John COWAN, of Tailzartoun, co. Stirling, by Katherine, da. of Patrick SMITH, of Braco, in the parish of Redgorton, co. Perth. He *d.* before 1685.

IV. 1684? to 1700? SIR JAMES GRAHAM, Baronet [S. 1625], of Braco aforesaid, s. and h.; *suc. to the Baronetcy* about 1684; under 25 years of age in 1685, being then next agnate, on the father's side, to James, 4th MARQUESS OF MONTROSE [S.]. He *d.* unm., but the date, however, is not given in his funeral escutcheon. At his death *the Baronetcy* became *dormant*, the issue male of the grantee and that of his only yr. br. (Sir Robert Graham, of Scotstoun, who *d.* s.p. in or before Oct. 1617), being, apparently, extinct. In that case the title would vest in the DUKES OF MONTROSE [S.], the heirs male of the body of the grantee's eldest brother, John, 4th Earl of Montrose [S.].

FORRESTER:

cr. 17 Nov. 1625;(b) sealed 4 Dec. 1630;(c)

afterwards, 1633-54, LORD FORRESTER OF CORSTORPHINE [S.];

dormant, since 1654.

I. 1625, to 1654. "SIR GEORGE FORRESTER, Knt.,"(b) of Corstophine, co. Edinburgh, s. and h. of Henry FORRESTER, of the same, by Helen, da. of (—) PRESTON, of the house of Craigmiller, was served heir to his uncle Sir James Forrester, of Corstorphine aforesaid (who *d.* s.p. June 1589) 17 May 1622, and was *cr. a Baronet* [S.] 17 Nov. 1624,(b) sealed 4 Dec. 1630,(c) but not registered in the Great Seal register, with rem. to heirs male whatsoever, and with a grant of, presumably, 16,000 acres, entitled the Barony of Corstorphine in Nova Scotia, of which he had seizin in Jan. 1630/1.(d) He was M.P. [S.] for Edinburghshire, 1625 and 1628-33. He *m.*, before 15 Nov. 1607, Christian, da. of Sir William LIVINGSTONE, of Kilsyth. He was *cr.*, 22 July 1633, LORD FORRESTER OF CORSTORPHINE [S.]. Having no male issue then living,(e) he resigned his peerage and obtained a regrant thereof 5 July 1651 with a spec. rem. in favour of James Bailie his son-in-law, etc. He *d.* s.p.m s.,(e) 1654, when the peerage devolved according to the spec. rem., and the *Baronetcy* became *dormant*. See *Peerage*.

(a) So called in her son's funeral escutcheon, though called "Katherine," in Douglas' *Peerage* [S.].
(b) Laing's List; the date of the creation in Milne's List (in which the Knighthood is not mentioned) is "17 *March* 1625."
(c) Milne's List.
(d) Banks's Lists.
(e) His s. and h., ap. "the master of Corstorphine," *m.* in 1634 the widow of Alexander Keith, but *d.* v.p. and s p.

II

NICOLSON:

creation, "sealed 17 Dec. 1625 ;"(a)

but nothing more is known.

I. 1625. "MR. JAMES NICOLSON, of Cockburnspeth," 1st s. of Thomas NICOLSON, Advocate [S.], Commissary of Aberdeenshire, by his wife, Margaret SCOTT, was *cr. a Baronet* [S.], as above, with rem. to heirs male whatsoever, such creation being "sealed 17 Dec. 1625,"(a) but not recorded in the Great Seal Register [S.]. Nothing more is known of this creation or of the grantee,(b) and no grant or seizin of lands in Nova Scotia is recorded.

ERSKINE:

cr., 28 Dec. 1625 ;(c)

but nothing more is known.

I. 1625. "[—] ERSKINE" is said(c) to have been *cr. a Baronet* [S.]. 28 Dec. 1625, but no particulars are known of him, and, though he, apparently, obtained a grant of, presumably, 16,000 acres in Nova Scotia, no seizin thereof is recorded.(d)

HUME, *or* HOME:

cr. 28 Dec. 1625 ;(e)

afterwards, 1690—1794, LORDS POLWARTH [S.];

and 1697—1794, EARLS OF MARCHMONT [S.];

dormant, since 10 Jan. 1794.

I. 1625. PATRICK HUME *or* HOME, of Polwarth, s. and h. of Sir Patrick HOME, of the same, by Janet (afterwards COUNTESS OF HADDINGTON [S.]), da. of Sir Thomas KERR, of Fernihirst, suc. his father, 10 June 1609 to whom he was returned heir special, 1 Feb. 1611, and was *cr. a Baronet* [S.] as "of Polwart," 28 Dec. 1625.(e) The usual grant of lands in Nova Scotia was, presumably, made to him, but no seizin is recorded thereof.(d) He was M.P. [S.] for Berwickshire, 1630. He *m.*, in or before 1640, Christian, da. of Sir Alexander HAMILTON, of Innerwick, by (—). He *d.* April 1648. His widow *m.* Robert (Kerr), 4th LORD JEDBURGH [S.], who *d.* s.p. 4 Aug. 1692.

II. 1648. SIR PATRICK HUME, *or* HOME, Baronet [S. 1625], of Polwarth aforesaid, 1st s. and h., *b.* 13 Jan. 1641 ; *suc. to the Baronetcy* in April 1648 ; was M.P. [S.] for Berwickshire, 1665, 1667, 1669-74, and 1689-90 ; took part against the Government and was imprisoned, 1675-79. He joined in Argyll's invasion of Scotland, 1685 ; was, accordingly, *attainted*, and fled to Utrecht ; but was, however, restored 1689, having come over with William, Prince of Orange,

(a) Milne's List ; no such creation, however, is in Laing's List, Walkley's List, etc.

(b) The estate of Lasswade was acquired by John Nicolson, Advocate [S.], Commissary of Edinburgh, who was an uncle of this James. Of this John's sons (1) John Nicolson was *cr. a Baronet* [S.], 27 July 1629, and (2) Thomas Nicolson was of Cockburnspath.

(c) Laing's List (though stated therein to be "given on the authority of former lists;") not, however, in Milne's List nor in the *Registrum Preceptorum Cartarum pro Baronettis Novæ Scotiæ*.

(d) Banks's Lists.

(e) Laing's List (though stated therein to be "given on the authority of former lists"), as also, though without any date, in Milne's List, where it is added—"In one old list, and so designed in his patent when nobilitate." It is not, however, in the *Registrum Preceptorum Cartarum pro Baronettis Novæ Scotiæ*.

afterwards **William III**, with whom he was in the greatest favour. He *m.*, in or before 1665, Grizel, da. of Sir Thomas KER, or CARRE, of Cavers. She was living when he was raised to the peerage, being *cr.* 26 Dec. 1690, LORD POLWARTH [S.] with a spec. rem., and subsequently, 23 April 1697, EARL OF MARCHMONT, etc. [S.], with rem. to heirs male whatsoever. In these peerages this *Baronetcy* then merged, and so continued till the death, s.p.m.s., of the 3d Earl and 4th Baronet, when, the issue male of the grantee apparently failed and both dignities became *dormant*. The Barony of Polwarth [S.], however, was in 1835 allowed to the grandson and heir general of the last Earl. See *Peerage*.

FORBES:

cr., 30 March, and sealed, 2 May 1626 ;(a)

sometime, 1864-66, HEPBURN-STUART-FORBES.

I. 1626. WILLIAM FORBES, of Monymusk, co. Aberdeen, s. and h. of William FORBES, of the same, by Margaret, da. of William (DOUGLAS), EARL OF ANGUS [S.], suc. his father between 1608 and 1618, and was *cr. a Baronet* [S.] as "of Monymusk," 30 March, sealed 2 May 1626,(a) with rem. to heirs male whatsoever, and with a grant of, presumably, 16,000 acres in Nova Scotia, called the Barony of Forbes, of which he had seizin in the said month of May 1626.(b) He *m.* Elizabeth, da. of (—) WISHART, of Pittarrow. He *d.* before July 1661.

II. 1650? SIR WILLIAM FORBES, Baronet [S. 1626], of Monymusk aforesaid, 1st s. and h. ; *suc. to the Baronetcy* before 22 July 1661, when he obtained a charter under the great seal. He *m.* Jane, da. of Sir Thomas BURNETT, 1st Baronet [S. 1626], of Leys, by his first wife, Margaret, da. of Sir Robert DOUGLAS, of Glenbervie.

III. 1680? SIR JOHN FORBES, Baronet [S. 1626], of Monymusk aforesaid, only s. and h. ; *suc. to the Baronetcy* on the death of his father. He *m.* firstly, Margaret, da. of Robert (ARBUTHNOTT), 1st VISCOUNT ARBUTHNOTT [S.], by his first wife, Marjory, da. of David (CARNEGIE) 1st EARL OF SOUTHESK [S.]. He *m.* secondly, 21 Feb. 1673, Barbara, da. of John DELMAHOY, by Rachel WILBRAHAM, his wife, which John was 2d. son of Sir John DALMAHOY, of Dalmahoy. He *d.* before 1713.

IV. 1700? SIR WILLIAM FORBES, Baronet [S. 1626], of Monymusk aforesaid, 1st s. and h. by first wife ; *suc. to the Baronetcy* before 1713, in which year he sold the estate of Monymusk to Sir Francis Grant, a Lord of Session [S.]. He *m.* Jean, 1st da. of John (KEITH), 1st EARL OF KINTORE [S.], by Margaret, da. of Thomas (HAMILTON), 2d EARL OF HADDINGTON [S.].

V. 1720? SIR WILLIAM FORBES, Baronet [S. 1626], of Edinburgh, grandson and h., being 1st s. and h. of John FORBES, by Mary, da. [whose issue, in 1781, became heir of line] of Alexander (FORBES), 3d LORD FORBES OF PITSLIGO [S.]. He was an Advocate [S.], 6 Jan. 1728. He *m.* in 1730 Christian, da. of John FORBES, of Boyndlie, by his 1st wife, Susan, da. of George MORISON, of Bognie, which John was a yr. s., by the 2nd wife, of the 3d Baronet. He *d.* 12 May 1743. His widow *d.* 1789.

VI. 1743. SIR WILLIAM FORBES, Baronet [S. 1626], of Edinburgh and afterwards of Pitsligo, co. Aberdeen, 2d but 1st surv. s. and h., *b.* in Edinburgh, 5 April 1739 ; *suc. to the Baronetcy* in 1743 ; was apprenticed to Messrs. Coutts & Co., Bankers, Edinburgh, in 1754, becoming a partner in 1760. That firm in 1773 was known as "Forbes, Hunter and Co.," and began to issue notes in 1783. He is said to have been frequently consulted in financial matters, and to have declined in 1799 an Irish Peerage. He was well known for his literary taste, was author of a life of the poet Beattie, etc. He acquired, both by purchase and by the devise of the attainted heir (who *d.* 1781), much of the estate of Pitsligo, co. Aberdeen

(a) Milne's List ; Laing's List. The date is given as 2 April 1626 in Douglas' *Baronage* [S.], followed by Playfair's *Baronetage* [S.].

(b) Banks's Lists.

2 Q

(the inheritance of the family of his paternal grandmother abovementioned), which he greatly improved.(a) He *m.* 20 Sep. 1770, Elizabeth [" the beautiful and truly amiable Miss Hay "(a)] 1st da. of Sir James HAY, 4th Baronet [S. 1635], of Haystoun, by Dorriel, da. and coheir of Daniel CAMPBELL, of Greenyards. She, who was *b.* 1 Feb. 1753, *d.* 1802. He *d.* 12 Nov. 1806. Will pr. 1808.

VII. 1806. SIR WILLIAM FORBES, Baronet [S. 1626], of Pitsligo, co. Aberdeen, 1st s. and h.,(b) *b.* 21 Dec. 1773 ; *suc. to the Baronetcy*, 12 Nov. 1806, and was head of the Banking house abovenamed : F.S.A. He *m.*, 19 Jan. 1797, Williamina, only child of Sir John STUART [previously (1777-97) Sir John BELSHES-WISHART, and before that, John BELSHES], 3d Baronet(c) [S. 1707], of Fettercairn, co. Kincardine, one of the Barons of the Exchequer [S.], by Jane, da. of David (LESLIE), 6th EARL OF LEVEN [S.]. She *d.* v.p., 5 Dec. 1810. He *d.* at Edinburgh, 24 Oct. 1828.

VIII. 1828. SIR JOHN STUART FORBES, *afterwards* (1864-66), HEPBURN-STUART-FORBES, Baronet [S. 1626], of Fettercairn and Pitsligo aforesaid, and *afterwards* (1864) of Invermay and Balmanno, both in co. Perth, 2d but 1st surv. s. and h.,(d) *b.* 25 Sep. 1804, at Dean House, near Edinburgh ; was an Advocate [S.] 8 July 1826 ; *suc. to the Baronetcy*, 24 Oct. 1828. On the death, in 1864, of his cousin, Alexander HEPBURN-MURRAY-BELSHES, he inherited the estate of Invermay as heir of entail, and that of Balmanno (both abovenamed) as heir at law when he assumed the additional surname of HEPBURN. He *m.*, 14 June 1834, Harriet Louisa Anne, 3d da. of William (KERR), 6th MARQUESS OF LOTHIAN [S.], by his second wife Harriet, da. of Henry (SCOTT), DUKE OF BUCCLEUCH [S.]. He *d.* s.p.m.,(e) 27 May 1866, in Wimpole Street, aged 61. His widow, who was *b.* 19 Oct. 1808, *d.* 26 April 1884, at 67 Princes Gate, Hyde Park.

IX. 1866. SIR WILLIAM FORBES, Baronet [S. 1626], nephew and h. male, being s. and h. of Charles FORBES, of Canaan park, co. Edinburgh, by Jemima Rebecca, da. of Alexander Ranaldson MACDONNELL, of Glengarry, which Charles, who *d.* 5 Nov. 1859, aged 53, was next br. to the late Baronet. He was *b.* 16 June 1835 and *suc. to the Baronetcy*, but presumably to none of the family estates, 27 May 1866. He *m.*, 1 July 1865, Marion, 3d. da. of J. WATTS, of Bridgend, Nelson, in New Zealand, Civil Engineer. She *d.* 1890.

Family Estates.—Those assigned to the 9th Baronet in Bateman's *Great Landowners* (1883), consist of 5,007 acres, co. Kincardine, valued at £4,056 a year, being, apparently, the Stuart property at Fettercairn. These 5,007 acres of the value of £4,056 a year, however, also in the same work as assigned to Lord Clinton, to whom (with the other estates) it is believed they went. At all events, in more recently dated Baronetages, no such property is attributed to the 9th Baronet, whose residence is given as "Carterton, Wellington, New Zealand," and whose estates, if any, are not mentioned.

(a) Playfair's *Baronetage* [S.], where there is a flaming account both of his improvements of the Pitsligo estate, and of other of his "patriotic labours."

(b) The second son John Hay Forbes, of Medwyn, co. Peebles, was a Lord of Session [S.], as Lord Medwyn (1825-54), and *d.* 25 July 1854, aged 77.

(c) In 1797 his right to the Baronetcy [S.], of Wishart, was confirmed by the Lyon Court. This Baronetcy was *cr.* 17 June 1706, with a spec. rem., failing heirs male of the body, to "heirs whomsoever and their heirs male for ever." The grantee *d.* s.p.m., between 1718 and 1722, and the title was assumed by his grandson William Stuart, of Colinton, co. Edinburgh, whose mother, Margaret, was 1st da. and heir of line of the grantee. He *d.* s.p. Dec. 1777. It was then assumed by the Grantee's great nephew, John Belshes (mentioned in the text), s. and h. of William Belshes, by Emilia Stuart, only child of her mother Mary, 1st surv. sister of the late Baronet. [*Ex inform.*, R. R. Stodart, Lyon Clerk Depute, 1863-86.]

(d) William Forbes, Capt. in the army, the eldest son, *d.* unm. and v.p., 16 Sep. 1826, at Malta.

(e) His estates (Invermay, Balmanno, Pitsligo, and, presumably, Fettercairn, or a part thereof) passed to his only child, Harriet Williamina, Baroness Clinton, first wife of Charles Henry Rolle (Trefusis, *afterwards* Hepburn-Stuart-Forbes-Trefusis) Lord Clinton. She died 4 July 1869, aged 34.

JOHNSTON:

cr. 31 March, and sealed 23 May 1626 ;(a)

I. 1626. GEORGE JOHNSTON, of Caskieben, co. Aberdeen, s. and h. of John JOHNSTON, of the same (who had sold the fee of Johnston in 1595, though retaining the superiority) by his 1st wife Janet, da. of (—) TURING, of Foveran, co. Aberdeen, suc. his father, 4 Feb. 1613/4, and had spec. service to him in the Barony of Johnston, etc., 3 May 1614, and was *cr. a Baronet* [S.] 31 March, sealed 23 May 1626, as "of Caskieben," with rem. to heirs male whatsoever, and with a grant of, presumably, 16,000 acres in Nova Scotia entitled the Barony of Johnston, of which he had seizin in the said month of May, and again in Nov. 1626,(b) was Sheriff of co. Aberdeen, 1630-31. In 1641 he and his son were cited before Parliament as incendiaries. He *m.* Elizabeth, da. of William FORBES, of Tolquhoun, co. Aberdeen.

II. 1650? SIR GEORGE JOHNSTON, Baronet [S. 1626], of Caskieben aforesaid, s. and h. ; *suc. to the Baronetcy* on the death of his father. In 1660 he sold Caskieben to Sir John Keith, who changed its name to Keith Hall. He *m.*, in or before 1648, (—), da. of Sir William LESLIE, 3d Baronet [S. 1625], of Wardes, by Helen, da. of George GORDON, of Newton. He *d.* before 10 June 1695.

III. 1680? SIR JOHN JOHNSTON, Baronet [S. 1626], only s. and h., *b.* about 1648 ; *suc. to the Baronetcy* on the death of his father ; was a Capt. in the army and served at the battle of the Boyne, on behalf of King William. In Nov. 1690, having aided in the abduction, by Capt. the Hon. James(c) CAMPBELL, of Mary Wharton, a rich heiress aged 13, he (though Campbell escaped) was hanged at Tyburn, 23 Dec. 1690, aged 42. He *d.* unm.

IV. 1690. SIR JOHN JOHNSTON, Baronet [S, 1626], of New Place, near Aberdeen, cousin and h. male, being s. and h. of John JOHNSTON, of New Place aforesaid, by his cousin, (—), da. of Thomas JOHNSTON, of Craig, in the parish of Dyce, which John last named was 2d and yst. s. of the first Baronet. He *suc. to the Baronetcy*, 23 Dec. 1690, but did not assume the title till 10 years later. He entailed the estate of Craig, 18 Dec. 1699 (which he had purchased), and bought part of the estate of Cordyce, changing its name to "Caskieben." He was in the rising in 1715, his only son, John, being slain (at his side) at Sheriffmuir, aged 25. He *m.*, April 1683, Janet, da. of Thomas MITCHELL, Baillie of Aberdeen. He *d.* s.p.m.s., at Edinburgh, Nov. 1724. His widow *d.* Sep. 1725.

V. 1724. SIR WILLIAM JOHNSTON, Baronet [S. 1626], of Craig aforesaid, cousin and h. male, being s. and h. of John JOHNSTON, of Bishopstown, by Margaret (*m.* Nov. 1672), da. and coheir of John ALEXANDER, which John JOHNSTON (who *d.* 1716, aged 67) was 3d s. of Thomas JOHNSTON, of Craig aforesaid (*d.* Aug. 1656), yr. br., of the half-blood, to the 1st Baronet, being s. of John JOHNSTON, of that ilk, by his 2d wife, Katherine, da. of William LUNDIE. He was *b.* about 1675 ; was an Advocate in Aberdeen ; *suc. to the Baronetcy* in Nov. 1724, but became insolvent in 1725, when his property was soon afterwards sold. He *m.* (contract 8 Jan. 1704) Jean, sister of Alexander SANDILANDS, M.D., 1st da. of James SANDILANDS, of Craibston, near Aberdeen, by his 2d wife, Elizabeth, da. of (—) DONALDSON, of Hilton. She *d.* June 1744. He *d.* 18 March 1750.

VI. 1750. SIR WILLIAM JOHNSTON, Baronet [S. 1626], of Hilton, in the parish of Old Machar, co. Aberdeen, s. and h., *b.* Nov. 1714 ; Lieut. R.N., 1741 ; Commander, 1750 ; *suc. to the Baronetcy* in March 1750. He purchased the estate of Hilton aforesaid with his prize money and entailed it, 21 Feb. 1784. He *m.* firstly, Sarah, da. of Thomas KIRBY, of London, merchant, a West Indian proprietor. She *d.* s.p.m.s. He *m.* secondly, March 1757, Elizabeth,

(a) Milne's List ; Laing's List.

(b) Banks's Lists.

(c) This Capt. James Campbell was yst. s. of Archibald, 9th Earl, and br. of Archibald, 1st Duke of Argyll [S.]. In Anderson's *Scottish Nation* the young lady's consent to the proposed marriage is alleged, and the hard fate of Johnston is attributed "to the bitter animosity then entertained by the English against the Scotch."

da. of William CLELAND, of that ilk, co. Lanark, Capt. R.N., by whom he had six sons and five daughters. She d. 25 Aug. 1772, aged 41. He m. thirdly, Amy, widow of John PUDSEY, da. of Newman FRENCH, of Belchamp, co. Essex. He d. at Brompton Row, Midx., 19 March 1794, in his 81st year. Admon. Oct. 1794.

VII. 1794. SIR WILLIAM JOHNSTON, Baronet [S. 1626], of Hilton aforesaid, s. and h., by 2d wife, b. Aug. 1760 at Hilton. He served against the French in India in seven actions on the coast of Malabar; *suc. to the Baronetcy*, 19 March 1794. In 1798 he raised a regiment of Fencibles, which was disbanded in 1802; was a Colonel in the army; was M.P. for New Windsor, 1801-02; was subsequently insolvent and consequently lived within the precincts of Holyrood Abbey. He m. firstly, 24 Feb. 1783 or 1784, Mary, da. of John BACON, of Shrubland Hall, Suffolk. She, who was 34 years older than her husband, d. s.p., July 1802, in Gloucester Place. He m. secondly, Dec. 1802, Maria, da. of John BACON, of Fryern House, Midx., and of the First Fruits Office. He d. at the Hague, 13 Jan. 1844. Will pr. June 1844. His widow d. at Ramsgate, 27 Oct. 1847. Admon. April 1849.

VIII. 1844. SIR WILLIAM BACON JOHNSTON, Baronet [S. 1626], of Hilton aforesaid, s. and h. by 2d wife, b. 17 March 1806, was an officer in the First Royals; *suc. to the Baronetcy*, 13 Jan. 1844. In July 1852 he disentailed the estate of Hilton (describing himself as unmarried), and paid his brother and cousins for their consent thereto. He m. at St. Pancras, Midx., 11 Sep. 1855,(a) Mary Ann, da. of William TYE, of Medlesham, Suffolk, shoemaker, by Susan HOWLETT, his wife. He d. 3 Aug. 1865, at Hilton House aforesaid, aged 59. His widow living 1901.

IX. 1865. SIR WILLIAM JOHNSTON, Baronet [S. 1626], only s. and h., b. 31 July 1849 at Hawley Road, Kentish town, before his parents' marriage, but legitimated thereby 11 Sep. 1855, according to the law of Scotland; *suc. to the Baronetcy*, 3 Aug. 1865, and was in 1867, during his absence in China, served h. gen. to his father by the Court of Chancery in Scotland; is Secretary to the Travancore plantation Tea Company.

Family Estates.—These appear to have been alienated by the late Baronet. The *Residence* of the present (1901) Baronet and of his mother is given as "The Ranche, Buckhurst Hill, Essex."

BURNET, *or* BURNETT:

cr. 21 April, and sealed 12 June 1626.(b)

I. 1626. SIR THOMAS BURNET, of Leys, co. Kincardine, 1st surv. s. and h. of Alexander BURNET, of the same, M.P. [S.] for Kincardineshire, 1621, by Katharine, da. of Alexander GORDON, of Lesmoir, co. Aberdeen, suc. his father in 1619; was *Knighted* before 6 Aug. 1621, and was *cr. a Baronet* [S.] as "of Leys," 21 April, sealed 12 June 1626, with rem. to heirs male whatsoever and a grant of, presumably, 16,000 acres in Nova Scotia, of which he had seizin in the said month of June.(c) He was, however, an active Covenanter. He endowed three Bursaries in the University of Aberdeen. He m. firstly, Margaret, da. of Sir Robert DOUGLAS, 1st Baronet [S. 1625], of Glenbervie, by Elizabeth, da. of Sir George AUCHINLECK. He m. secondly, 1621, Jane, widow of Sir Simon FRASER, of Inverallochy, da. of Sir John MONCREIFF, 1st Baronet [S. 1626], of Moncreiff, by Mary, da. of William (MURRAY), 2d EARL OF TULLIBARDINE [S.]. He d. 1653.(d)

(a) "We have heard there were two marriages, the first private, the second by special licence in England." [See *Doubtful Baronetcies* in the *Herald and Genealogist*, vol. v, pp. 89 and 186.]
(b) Milne's List; Laing's List.
(c) Banks's Lists.
(d) Gilbert Burnett, the celebrated Bishop of Salisbury (1689—1716), author of the *History of His own Time*, etc., was nephew of the 1st Baronet, being s. of his yr. br. Robert Burnett, who was a Lord of Session [S.] under the name of Lord Crimond.

II. 1653. SIR ALEXANDER BURNETT, Baronet [S. 1626], of Leys aforesaid, grandson and h., being s. and h. of Alexander BURNETT, by Jane (m. 1633), da. of Sir Robert ARBUTHNOTT, of Arbuthnott, which Alexander was s. and h. ap. of the 1st Baronet, by his 1st wife, but d. v.p. He *suc. to the Baronetcy* in 1653. He m. Elizabeth, da. of (—) COUTTS, of Auchtercoull. He d. 1663. His widow m. Sir David RAMSAY, 2d Baronet [S. 1625], of Balmain, who d. 1673.

III. 1663. SIR THOMAS BURNETT, Baronet [S. 1626], of Leys aforesaid, s. and h., *suc. to the Baronetcy* in 1663; M.P. [S.] for co. Kincardine, 1689—1707 (three Parls.), and [G.B.] 1707-08, being a zealous opponent of the Scotch Union. He m. in 1677, Margaret, da. of Robert (ARBUTHNOT), 2d VISCOUNT ARBUTHNOT [S.], by Elizabeth, da. of William (KEITH), 7th EARL MARISCHAL [S.]. He d. 1714.

IV. 1714. SIR ALEXANDER BURNETT, Baronet [S. 1626], of Leys aforesaid, s. and h., *suc. to the Baronetcy* in 1714. He m. Helen, 1st da. of Robert BURNETT, of Muchalls. He d. 1758.

V. 1758. SIR ROBERT BURNETT, Baronet [S. 1626], of Leys aforesaid, 3d and yst. but only surv. s. and h., *suc. to the Baronetcy* in 1758. He d. unm. 1759.

VI. 1759. SIR THOMAS BURNETT, Baronet [S. 1626], of Crathes Castle, co. Kincardine, cousin and h. male, being s. and h. of William BURNETT, of Criggie, by Jean, da. of Robert BURNETT, of Muchalls, which William (who d. 1747, aged 64) was 2d s. of the 3d Baronet. He *suc. to the Baronetcy* in 1759. He m. in or before 1755, Catherine, sister, whose issue became heir (11 Feb. 1806) to Sir Alexander RAMSAY, 6th Baronet [S. 1626], of Balmain, 4th da. of Charles RAMSAY, by Catherine, da. of James MILL, Provost of Montrose. He d. May 1783. His widow d. 10 Dec. 1798.

VII. 1783. SIR ROBERT BURNETT, Baronet [S. 1626], of Crathes Castle aforesaid, s. and h., b. 20 Dec. 1755, was an officer in the Royal Scots Fusileers, serving in the first American War, and being taken prisoner in 1777 at Saratoga; *suc. to the Baronetcy* in May 1783. He m. 16 Sep. 1785, Margaret, 4th da. of General Robert DALRYMPLE-HORN-ELPHINSTONE (*formerly* DALRYMPLE), of Logie Elphinstone, co. Aberdeen, by Mary, da. and h. of Sir James ELPHINSTONE, of Logie aforesaid. He d. 5 Jan. 1837. Will pr. April 1838. His widow d. 18 March 1849, at Logie Elphinstone, aged 84.

VIII. 1837. SIR THOMAS BURNETT, Baronet [S. 1626], of Crathes Castle aforesaid, s. and h., b. 22 Aug. 1778, *suc. to the Baronetcy*, 5 Jan. 1837; Lieut. and Sheriff Principal of Kincardineshire, 1847. He d. unm. 16 Feb. 1849, at Crathes aforesaid, aged 60.

IX. 1849. SIR ALEXANDER BURNETT, Baronet [S. 1626], of Crathes Castle aforesaid, br. and h., b. 1789 at Crathes aforesaid, was an officer in the East India Company's service; *suc. to the Baronetcy*, 16 Feb. 1849. He d. unm. 20 March 1856.

X. 1856. SIR JAMES HORN BURNETT, Baronet [S. 1626], of Crathes Castle aforesaid, br. and h., being 5th and yst s. of the 7th Baronet, b. 22 June 1801 at Crathes Castle; Writer to the Signet [S.], 1824; *suc. to the Baronetcy*, 20 March 1856; Lord Lieut. of Kincardineshire, 1863. He m. firstly, 3 Feb. 1831, Caroline Margaret, da. of Charles SPEARMAN, of Thornley Hall, co. Durham, by Sarah, da. and coheir of Samuel BROOKE, of Birchington, co. Kent. She d. 22 March 1836. He m. secondly, 12 July 1837, Lauderdale, widow of David DUNCAN, of Rosemount, co. Forfar, da. of Sir Alexander RAMSAY, 1st Baronet [1806], of Balmain (*formerly* Alexander BURNETT), by Elizabeth, da. and coheir of Sir Alexander BANNERMAN, 4th Baronet [S. 1682]. He d. 17 Sep. 1876, at Crathes Castle, aged 75. His widow d. 4 Nov. 1888, at 47 Heriot Row, Edinburgh.

XI. 1876. SIR ROBERT BURNETT, Baronet [S. 1626], of Crathes Castle aforesaid, s. and h., b. at Edinburgh, 28 Aug. 1833; matric. at Oxford (Ch. Ch.), 22 Oct. 1851, aged 18; B.A., 1856; *suc. to the Baronetcy* 17 Sep. 1876. He m. 23 May 1864, Matilda Josephine, da. of James MURPHY, of New York. She d. 25 April 1888. He d. s.p.m.s.(a) 15 Jan. 1894, at Crossburn House, East Wemyss, aged 60. Personalty sworn at £47,799.

XII. 1894. SIR THOMAS BURNETT, Baronet [S. 1626], of Crathes Castle aforesaid, br. of the half-blood and h., being 2d s., 1st by the 2d wife, of the 10th Baronet, b. 27 Nov. 1840; sometime in the Royal Horse Artillery; Lieut.-Col., 1885; Col., 1890; *suc. to the Baronetcy*, 15 Jan. 1894. He m., 2 June 1875, Mary, 1st da. of James CUMINE, of Rattray, co. Aberdeen.

Family Estates.—These, in 1883, consisted of 12,025 acres in Kincardineshire, and 84 in Aberdeenshire. *Total*, 12,109 acres, worth £5,114 a year. *Principal Seat.*—Crathes Castle, co. Kincardine.

MONCREIFF:

cr. 22 April and sealed 22 June 1626(b);
dormant in 1744, *but assumed* since about 1750;
afterwards, 1767—1827, MONCREIFF-WELLWOOD;
subsequently, 1827—1883, WELLWOOD-MONCREIFF;
and finally, since 1883, BARONS MONCREIFF.

I. 1626. JOHN MONCREIFF, of Moncreiff, co. Perth, 2d but 1st surv. s. and h. of William MONCREIFF, of the same (who sat as a minor Baron [S.] 1579), by Anne, da. of Robert MURRAY, of Abercairnie, sat (as "Laird of Easter Moncreiff") as a minor Baron [S.] 1605, and was *cr. a Baronet* [S.] as "of Moncreiff," 22 April, sealed 22 June 1626,(b) with rem. to heirs male whatsoever, and with a grant of, presumably, 16,000 acres in Nova Scotia, entitled the Barony of Moncreiff, of which he had seizin in the said month of June(c); was M.P. [S.] for Perthshire, 1639-41. He m. firstly, Anne, da. of David BEATON, of Creich. He m. secondly, in or before 1635, Mary,(d) da. of William (MURRAY), 2d EARL OF TULLIBARDINE [S.], by his 2d wife, Dorothea, da. of John (STEWART), 5th EARL OF ATHOLL [S.]. She d. Dec. 1650 "att Moncriefe in Stratherne," and he d. shortly afterwards.

II. 1651? SIR JOHN MONCREIFF, Baronet [S. 1626], of Moncreiff aforesaid, 2d but 1st surv. s. and h., being 1st s. by the 2d wife, b. 1635; *suc. to the Baronetcy* on the death of his father about 1651. His estates being greatly encumbered, he, in 1657, sold his lands of Carnbee, co. Fife, and in 1663 sold the Barony of Moncreiff to his cousin, Thomas Moncreiff, one of the Clerks of the Exchequer.(e) He d. unm. at Edinburgh, 1674.

III. 1674. SIR DAVID MONCREIFF, Baronet [S. 1626], next br. and h., *suc. to the Baronetcy* on the death of his brother. He d. unm.

IV. 1690? SIR JAMES MONCREIFF, Baronet [S. 1626], only surv. br. and h., was an officer in the army, becoming eventually a Colonel. He *suc. to the Baronetcy* on the death of his brother. He d. s.p. 1698, when the issue male of the 1st Baronet became *extinct*.

(a) James Lauderdale Burnett, his only s., d. in childhood, 1874.
(b) Milne's List; Laing's List.
(c) Banks's Lists.
(d) "By mistake called *Anne* in the peerage" (Douglas's *Baronage* [S.]).
(e) He accordingly was *cr. a Baronet* [S.] 30 Nov. 1685, as "of Moncreiff."

V. 1698. SIR JOHN MONCREIFF, Baronet [S. 1626], of Tippermalloch, or Tippermalach, cousin and h. male, being only s. and h. of Hugh MONCREIFF (living 12 Oct. 1666), by Isabel, da. of (—) HAY, of Megginch, co. Perth, which Hugh MONCREIFF was next br. to the 1st Baronet. He was b. about 1628; *suc. to the Baronetcy* in 1698. He was a physician. He m. about 1680, Nicholas, da. of (—) MONCREIFF, of Easter Moncreiff. Was living 1709, having then relinquished his estates to his son. He d. 27 April 1714, aged 86.

VI. 1714. SIR HUGH MONCREIFF, Baronet [S. 1626], only surv. s. and h., *suc. to the Baronetcy*, 27 April 1714, and d. unm. 1744.(a)

[The Baronetcy was apparently *dormant* for some years(b) but was assumed "after 1744, without service or proof of pedigree" as under.]

VII. *1744.* 1750? SIR WILLIAM MONCREIFF, Baronet(c) [S. 1626], cousin and h. male,(d) being s. and h. (one of sixteen children) of the Rev. Archibald MONCREIFF, Minister of Blackford [1697—1739], by Catherine, da. of John HALLIDAY, of Tullibole, or Tulliebole Castle,(e) co. Kinross, which Archibald (who d. 1739) was s. and h. of the Rev. William MONCREIFF, Minister of Moonzie, co. Fife (d. about 1711), who was s. and h. of the Rev. George MONCREIFF, Minister of Arngask (d. before 1665), who was 2d s. of the Rev. Archibald MONCREIFF, of Balgony (which he purchased before 1611), Minister of Abernethy (1580) and Commendator of the Monastery of Elcho (1601), who was yr. br. of William MONCREIFF (d. v.p. 26 Nov. 1570), the father of the 1st Baronet, both being sons of William MONCREIFF of that ilk, who d. between 1573 and 1575. He was in Holy Orders and was Minister of Blackford aforesaid. His right to the *Baronetcy* is supposed to have accrued on the death of the 6th Baronet, in 1744, and, some years later (1750?) he accordingly assumed that dignity. He m. in or before 1749, Catherine, niece of Henry WELLWOOD, of Garvock, co. Kinross, and of Tullibole Castle abovenamed, 1st da. of Robert WELLWOOD, of Garvock aforesaid. He d. 9 Dec. 1767.

VIII. 1767. SIR HENRY MONCREIFF-WELLWOOD, Baronet(c) [S. 1626], of Tullibole Castle aforesaid, formerly Henry MONCREIFF, 1st s. and

(a) The estate of Tippermalloch devolved on his nephew, John Moncrieff, s. and h. of his sister, Bethia, by the Rev. William Moncrieff, Minister of Methven.
(b) In Douglas' *Baronage* [S.] it is stated that "the Baronetcy appears to have devolved upon Sir William [Moncreiff, 4th Baronet of the creation of 1685], of Moncreiff, as next heir male, being lineally descended from John, the 3d son of Sir John Moncreiff," who was great great grandfather of the 1st Baronet. This Sir William Moncreiff is accordingly designated therein as "the 4th Baronet [1685] of this branch, the 6th [should be 7th] Baronet [1626] of the house of Moncreiff."
(c) According to the assumption of the Baronetcy, in, or about, 1750.
(d) Foster's *Baronetage* for 1883, under "Chaos," p. 703, where it is added that William Moncreiff, Minister of Blackford, who assumed the Baronetcy, "was 4th in descent from Archibald, Minister of Abernethy, Perthshire. * * * The pedigree in Douglas's *Baronage* [S.] only mentions William and David as brothers of [which two brothers] William [was] father of the 1st Baronet, though a note is appended that he [the said William] is said to have had another brother, Archibald, Minister of Abernethy. The pedigree in Playfair's *Baronetage* [S.] gives six brothers [*i.e.*, William, Archibald, Hugh, David, John, and James] and four sisters, but unaccompanied by any evidence to prove that Archibald was the *next* brother of William, father of the 1st Baronet."
(e) The estate of Tullibole (a picturesque though not large castle, erected about 1608) was sold in 1749 by the creditors of Robert Halliday, grandson of John Halliday, the *maternal* grandfather of Sir William Moncreiff. It was purchased by Henry Wellwood, of Garvock, who, three years later, conveyed it to Henry Moncreiff, afterwards the 8th Baronet, 1st s. and h. of his niece, Catharine (da. of his yr. br., Robert Wellwood), by her husband, Sir William Moncreiff, the 7th Baronet, on condition of his taking the name of Wellwood.

h., *b.* 7 Feb. 1750. at Blackford, inherited in infancy the Tullibole estate[a] from his maternal uncle, Henry Wellwood abovenamed, when he took accordingly the additional name of WELLWOOD; was ed. at Glasgow College; *suc. to the Baronetcy*[b] 9 Dec. 1767. He was in Holy Orders, and was in 1771 Minister of Blackford,[c] and of St. Cuthbert's, Edinburgh, 1775; Moderator of the Gen. Assembly of the Church of Scotland, Chaplain to the Prince of Wales, and D.D. of the Univ. of Glasgow, all in 1785. In 1772 he obtained a Crown charter for the Tullibole estate.[d] He *m.* 16 Nov. 1772, Susan Robertson, 1st da. of James Robertson BARCLAY, of Keavil, co. Fife. She *d.* 1826. He *d.* 9 Aug. 1827, in Edinburgh.

IX. 1827. SIR JAMES MONCREIFF, *otherwise* WELLWOOD-MONCREIFF, Baronet[b] [S. 1626] of Tullibole Castle aforesaid, 2d but 1st surv. s. and h.[e], *b.* about 1776; matric. at Oxford (Ball. Coll.), 30 Nov. 1793, aged 17; B.C.L., 1800; Advocate [S.], 1799; *suc. to the Baronetcy*[b] 9 Aug. 1827; was a Lord of Session [S.] 1829-51, with the courtesy title of *Lord Moncreiff*. He *m.* 19 June 1808, Anne, da. of George ROBERTSON, Lieut. R.N. She *d.* 28 May 1843, in Brompton Square, Midx. He *d.* 4 April 1851, at Moray Place, Edinburgh, in his 75th year.

X. 1851. SIR HENRY MONCREIFF, *otherwise* WELLWOOD-MONCREIFF, Baronet[b] [S. 1626], of Tullibole Castle aforesaid, 1st s. and h., *b.* in Edinburgh, 12 May 1809; ed. at the High School and at the Univ. there; matric. (as Gent. Commoner) at Oxford (New Coll.), 5 May 1827, aged 17; B.A., 1831; 3d class classics and math.; was in Holy Orders; Minister (in the Established Church) of Baldernock, co. Stirling, 1836-37; of East Kilbride, co. Lanark, 1837-43, and subsequently of the Free Church there, and after that, 1852-83, of St. Cuthbert's, Edinburgh; *suc. to the Baronetcy*.[b] 10 April 1851; D.D. (Edinburgh); Prin. Clerk of the Free Church General Assembly and Moderator, 1861. He *m.* firstly, 8 March 1838, Alexina Mary, da. of George BELL, of Edinburgh. She *d.* 12 April 1874, at 3, Bruntsfield Terrace, Edinburgh. He *m.* secondly, 19 Aug. 1875, at Stenton, co. Perth, Lucretia, yst. da. of Andrew MURRAY, of Murrayshall, co. Perth, sometime Sheriff of Aberdeenshire. He *d.* s.p., 3 Nov. 1883, at Morningside Crescent, Edinburgh, in the 75th year of his age and the 48th of his ministry. His widow *d.* 10 Sep. 1885, at 4, Lynedoch Place, Edinburgh.

XI. 1883. JAMES (MONCRIEFF), 1st BARON MONCRIEFF OF TULLIEBOLE, br. and h., *b.* 29 Nov. 1811 at Edinburgh. He, who had been *cr. a Baronet*, as "of Kilduff, co. Kinross," 23 May 1871, and raised to the peerage, as above, 9 Jan. 1874, *suc. to the Baronetcy*[b] [S. 1626], 3 Nov. 1883, which then became *merged* in that peerage, and still so remains. See *Peerage*.

(a) See p. 311, note "e."
(b) According to the assumption of the Baronetcy, in, or about, 1750.
(c) He was the 6th in lineal succession of a line of officiating Clergymen of the Church of Scotland.
(d) It was granted to him, as under. "Reverendo Domino Henrico Moncreiff Wellwood, Baronetto, de Denham Tulliebole, Ministro Evangelii apud Blackford, filio legitimo natu maximo demortuii Domini Gulielmi Moncreiff, Baronetti, nuper Ministri evangelii apud Blackford." The designation of the estate as "*Denham's* Tulliebole" was in compliance of the wish of Henry Wellwood (the Baronet's uncle), whose mother, Catherine, was 6th da. of John *Denham*, of Muirhouse and West Shields. As a matter of fact, however, this designation was never used.
(e) The eldest br. William Wellwood-Moncreiff, matric. at Oxford (Ball. Coll.) 20 March 1793, aged 17; B.A., 1797; M.A., 1799; B.C.L. and D.C.L., 1803; Barrister (Mid. Temple), 1800 Fellow of the Coll. of Advocates, London, 21 Nov. 1807; King's Advocate in the Admiralty Court, Isle of Malta; *d.* unm., 5 Sep. 1813, aged 38.

OGILVY, *or* OGILVIE:

cr. 24 April and sealed 22 June 1626;[a]

succession unknown till about 1800;

dormant since 20 Feb. 1861.

I. 1626. GEORGE OGILVIE, of Carnousie, co. Banff, s. and h. of George OGILVIE,[b] of the same, M.P. [S.] for Banffshire, 1621, by Margaret his wife, suc. his father, 1 Feb. 1625, being served heir to him 10 May following, and was *cr. a Baronet* [S.] 24 April, sealed 22 June 1626, as "of Carnousie," with rem. to heirs male whatsoever, and with a grant of, presumably, 16,000 acres in Nova Scotia, called the Barony of "New Carnousie," of which, however, he appears never to have had seizin.[c] He *m.* Jean, da. of Sir Thomas GORDON, of Cluny (*Reg. Mag. Sig.*).[d] He was alive in 1668, but there is no record of his having had any issue.[d]

* * * * * *

The succession to this Baronetcy is unknown, but it was borne early in the nineteenth century as below, by, presumably, the collateral heir male, possibly a descendant of a br. of the grantee.[e]

VIII. 1800? SIR WILLIAM OGILVIE, Baronet [S. 1625]. He *m.* Christian, da. of the Rev. John PATTISON, of Edinburgh. He *d.* 1824. Will pr. 1824.

IX. 1824, to 1861. SIR WILLIAM OGILVIE, Baronet [S. 1625], s. and h., *b.* 1810, *suc. to the Baronetcy*, 1824, is called "the 9th Baronet"; was a claimant of the Barony of Banff [S.] as heir male collateral. He *m.* 1838, Augusta Porter, da. of James GRANGE, of the Treasury. He *d.* s.p.m. at Christchurch, New Zealand, 20 Feb. 1861, when the *Baronetcy* became *dormant*. His widow was apparently living in 1893.[f]

(a) Milne's List, Laing's List.
(b) This George was yr. br. of Sir Walter Ogilvy, of Banff and Dunlugus, father of George, *cr.* 31 Aug. 1642, Lord Banff [S.].
(c) Banks's Lists.
(d) *Ex inform.*, Sir J. Balfour Paul, Lyon, who states that there is absolutely nothing to be found about the succeeding Baronets, and that there are no services of heirs in the family. It appears that "Capt. Gordon, son of Edinglassie, had a charter of Carnousie, in 1695, the lands having fallen under recognition, owing to alienation made thereof by the deceased Sir George" Ogilvy, but "the decreet of recognition which would no doubt give the names of Sir George's heir or heirs" cannot be found.
(e) George Ogilvy, the grantee's father, *m.* twice. By his 1st wife he had (besides two daughters, Elspeth and Helen) three sons, viz.: (1), George, the Baronet; (2), John Ogilvy, of Burns, of whose posterity, if any, nothing is known; (3), Thomas, of whom nothing is known. By his 2d wife, Barbara, da. of Sir Alexander Fraser, of Philorth, he appears to have had (4), Alexander. No Alexander is mentioned in Margaret Ogilvy's testament dative, *Ogilvie of Carnousie*, but John Ogilvy of Burns is called cousin german both of Sir George and of Alexander. Alexander Ogilvy was of Knock and had at least three sons, viz. (1), James, his s. and h., who *m.* Christian Stewart, and sold Knock in 1659; (2), Alexander; (3), Patrick. [*Ex inform.* J. Maitland Thomson, communicated by Sir J. Balfour Paul, Lyon.]
(f) She appears in Dod's *Baronetage* for 1893, but not in that for 1894.

GORDON:

cr. 1 May 1626 [a];

afterwards, 1633-1716 and 1824-47, VISCOUNTS KENMURE [S.];

attainted, 1716-1824;

dormant, since 1 Sep. 1847.

I. 1626. SIR ROBERT GORDON, of Lochinvar, co. Kirkcudbright, and of Stichill, co. Roxburgh, s. and h. of Sir John GORDON, of the same, by his 2d wife, Elizabeth, da. of John (MAXWELL) LORD HERRIES [S.], was *b.* about 1565; was one of the Gentlemen of the Bedchamber; suc. his father, 23 Aug. 1604; was M.P. [S.] for Kirkcudbright 1612; had a grant of the Barony of Galloway in Nova Scotia, 8 Nov. 1621, and a charter of the Barony and Lordship of Charles' island 1 May 1626, with, (as is sometimes, though, probably erroneously, conjectured) the *grant of a Baronetcy*[a] [S.]. He appears to have been Governor of Nova Scotia.[a] He *m.* Isabel, da. of William (RUTHVEN), 1st EARL OF GOWRIE [S.], by Dorothea, da. of Henry (STEWART), LORD METHVEN [S.]. She was divorced from him, and *m.*, as the second of his three wives, Hugh (CAMPBELL), 1st LORD CAMPBELL OF LOUDOUN [S.], who *d.* 15 Dec. 1622. He *d.* Nov. 1628.

II. 1628. SIR JOHN GORDON, Baronet [b] [S. 1626], of Lochinvar aforesaid, 1st s. and h.; *b.* about 1600; suc. his father Nov. 1628, and was served heir 20 March 1628-9, shortly after which date he sold the Barony of Stichill. He *m.* in 1628, Jean, 3d da. of Archibald (CAMPBELL), 7th EARL OF ARGYLL [S.], by his 1st wife, Anne, da. of William (DOUGLAS), 1st EARL OF MORTON [S.]. She was living when he (having attended the King's coronation in Scotland), was *cr.* (about 16 months before his death) 8 May 1633, VISCOUNT KENMURE and LORD LOCHINVAR [S.], with rem. to heirs male whatsoever. In that peerage this *Baronetcy* then *merged*, and followed the fortunes thereof. See *Peerage*.

MURRAY:[c]

cr. 1 June 1625; *sealed* 14 July following:[d]

dormant about 1700.

I. 1626. SIR WILLIAM MURRAY, of Clermont, co. Fife, 1st s. of Sir Mungo MURRAY of Feddalls, Dinoch and Clermont, by Margaret, relict of Sir Andrew MURRAY, of Balvaird, da. of (—) CRICHTON, was (having pre-

---

(a) Milne's List, where it is added "He was made Governour of Nova Scotia, but his patent does not invest him [in the] tytle [of] Baronet, bot he hes power to create Judges, Generals, Archbishops, Bishops, etc." The patent is not recorded in the "Registrum Preceptorum Cartarum pro Baronettis Novæ Scotiæ." The creation is in Laing's List, it being, however, stated that it is "given on the authority of former lists."
(b) According to the (probably erroneous) conjecture stated in the text above.
(c) Nearly all the information in this article has been furnished by Sir J. Balfour Paul, Lyon King of Arms.
(d) *Precept. cart. pro Baronnettis Novæ Scotiæ*, 1625, folio. 27. The date of the sealing is that given in Milne's List, where the date of creation is given as 1 *July* 1625. In Laing's List, however, the date is correctly given as 1 *June* 1626.

viously been knighted)[a] *cr. a Baronet* [S.], 1 June 1626, the patent being sealed 14 July following[b] with rem. to heirs male whatsoever, and with a grant of, presumably, 16,000 acres in Nova Scotia, called the Barony of Clermont of Hillhead,[c] of which he had seizin in the said month of July 1626.[c] He was served heir to his father 27 July 1630; and had seizin of the lands of Blebo, 31 Jan. 1634, on the ratification of John Traill, of Blebo. He *m.* Euphemia OGILVY. He *d.* between 1643 and 1648.

II. 1645? SIR MUNGO MURRAY, Baronet [S. 1626] of Blebo aforesaid, s. and h., *suc. to the Baronetcy*, 1643-48; had Crown charter of lands of Westertown of Airthrey to himself and "Lady Anne GRAHAM, his spouse," 24 May 1648; made a renunciation of Blebo to Sir William Bruce, of Balcaskie, 19 July 1666.

* * * * * *

III. 1670? to 1700? SIR MUNGO MURRAY, Baronet [S. 1626], of Blebo aforesaid, presumed to be s. and h. of the above and to have *suc. him to the Baronetcy*. He *m.* Christian HAMILTON. He appears to have died s.p.m., as, after his death, *the Baronetcy* became *dormant*. His widow *d.* Feb. 1709/10, her will being recorded 15 June 1710 in the Commissarial Court of Edinburgh.

BLACKADER *or* BLACCADER:

cr. 28 July 1626, sealed 3 Feb. 1627;[d]

dormant about 1670;

but assumed, wrongfully, 1734-36.

I. 1626, to 1670? JOHN BLACCADER [*i.e.*, BLACKADER], of Tulliallan, co. Perth, s. and h. of James BLACKADER, of the same, by Elizabeth, da. of (—) BRUCE (probably Archibald BRUCE of Powfoulis, *otherwise* Batfoullis), was *b.* the Sunday after Easter, 1596, and *bap.* June following[e]; *suc.* his father at the age of 14, in 1610, and was *cr. a Baronet* [S.], as "of Tulliallan," 28 July 1626, the patent being sealed 3 Feb. 1627, with rem. to heirs male whatsoever, and with a grant of, presumably, 16,000 acres in Nova Scotia, of which he had seizin in Feb. 1627.[f] He was one of the captains in the Scotch regiment levied for the King of France in 1642. He *m.* Christian, da. of John (GRAHAM), EARL OF MENTEITH [S.], by Mary, da. of Sir Colin CAMPBELL, of Glenorchy. "By his foolish generosity, whoredom, and every other unfortunate way, together with the prodigality and pride of his Lady he squandered away an honourable and ancient estate of 3,600 marks or £2,000 sterling yearly."[e] He was living 1666 and *d.* before 1675 leaving male issue, but after his death *the Baronetcy* became *dormant*.

(a) He is called a knight in Laing's List.
(b) See p. 314, note "d."
(c) Banks's Lists.
(d) Milne's List; Laing's List.
(e) MS. relating to the Blackader family belonging to R. R. Stodart, Lyon Clerk Depute [1863-86], to whom the Editor is indebted for most of the information in this article. The estate of Tulliallan was acquired in 1486 by the marriage of Cuthbert Blackader, of Blackader, co. Berwick, with Elizabeth, da. and h. of Sir James Edmonstone, of Tulliallan.
(f) Banks's Lists.

JAMES BLACKADER, 1st s., joined as heir ap. with his father, 20 Feb. 1644, in a deed of sale. He never assumed the title, and *d.* before 1675, possibly in his father's lifetime.

ARCHIBALD BLACKADER, s. and h. of the above James; was living in 1675 and 1676 as a merchant factor at Cadiz, and was at that time anxious to redeem the estate of Tulliallan, which had been sold to Col. John Erskine. He, however, never assumed the title.

JOHN BLACKADER, a tailor of Edinburgh, s. of John, who was s. of Patrick BLACKADER, a bastard uncle of the 1st Baronet, was served heir, 10 April 1734, to the 1st Baronet, who was stated in that service to be his grandfather. He, accordingly, *assumed the Baronetcy*, and for two years was called "SIR JOHN BLACKADER, Baronet," [S. 1626]. In Jan. 1736, however, his pedigree was disproved, and on 8 Jan. 1737 he was sentenced to have his ear nailed to the post for perjury.

OGILVY:

cr. 29 Sep. 1626; sealed 30 June 1627.(a)

I. 1626. JOHN OGILVY, of Inverquharity, in the parish of Kirriemuir, co. Forfar, s. and h. of Sir John OGILVY, of the same (*d.* about 1624), by Matilda, da. of Thomas FOTHERINGHAM, of Powrie, co. Forfar, was *b.* about 1587 and was *cr. a Baronet* [S.], 29 Sep. 1626, the patent being sealed 30 June 1627, but not recorded in the Great Seal register, with rem. to heirs male whatsoever, and with a grant of, presumably, 16,000 acres in Nova Scotia, of which he had sasine in July 1627.(b) He *m.*, covenant 16 Sep. 1622, Anne, da. of Sir Alexander IRVINE, of Drum, co. Aberdeen, by Marion, da. of Robert (DOUGLAS) EARL OF BUCHAN [S.]. He, who was a zealous royalist, was living in 1647, when he had a remission on payment of a fine, but *d.* before 1663.

II. 1660? SIR DAVID OGILVY, Baronet [S. 1626], of Inverquharity aforesaid, 3d but 1st surv. s. and h.,(c) *b.* about 1630, *suc. to the Baronetcy* on the death of his father; M.P. [S.] for co. Angus, 1665 and 1678. He *m.*, 1662, Margaret, da. of Sir John ERSKINE, of Dun, co. Forfar. He *d.* in or before 1679.

III. 1679? SIR JOHN OGILVY, Baronet [S. 1626], of Inverquharity aforesaid, s. and h., *suc. to the Baronetcy* on the death of his father. He *m.* 1697, Margaret, 1st da. of James OGILVY, of Cluny. He *d.* in or before 1735.

IV. 1735? SIR JOHN OGILVY, Baronet [S. 1626], of Inverquharity aforesaid, s. and h.; *suc. to the Baronetcy* before 23 June 1735, when he had general service to his father. He *m.* firstly, 1720, Helen, 2d da. and coheir of Sir Laurence MERCER, of Aldie, Melgins and Lethendy, co. Perth. He *m.* secondly, Anne, 1st da. and coheir of James CARNEGIE, of Finhaven, co. Forfar, by Margaret, da. of Sir William BENNETT, Baronet [S. 1670], of Grubbet. He *d.* at Kinnordy, Feb. 1748. His widow *d.* at Inverquharity, 1 Dec. 1750.

(a) Milne's List, Laing's List.
(b) Banks's Lists.
(c) Alexander Ogilvy, the 1st s., fought under Montrose, was taken prisoner at Philiphaugh, and executed, v.p., 23 Oct. 1646, aged 18.

V. 1748. SIR JOHN OGILVY, Baronet [S. 1626], of Inverquharity aforesaid, s. and h., by 1st wife, *b.* about 1732, *suc. to the Baronetcy* in Feb. 1748. In 1781 he was served h. gen. of his father and of his paternal great great grandfather, and in 1798 h. of his maternal uncles, Charles and Robert MERCER, in Lethendy, co. Perth, and other lands. About 1790 he sold the estate of Inverquharity.(a) He *m.*, 1754, Charlotte, 1st da. and coheir of Walter TULLIEDEPH, of Tulliedeph (formerly Bank), in Strathmartine, co. Forfar, sometime a physician in the island of Antigua. She (by whom he had nine sons) inherited this estate, and *d.* there aged 70, being *bur.* at Strathmartine. He *d.* 15 March 1802, and was *bur.* in St. Cuthbert's churchyard, Edinburgh. Will pr. 1802.

VI. 1802. SIR WALTER OGILVY, Baronet [S. 1626], of Baldovan, formerly Tulliedeph aforesaid, s. and h.; *suc. to the Baronetcy*, 1 March 1802; had spec. service on 2 May 1806, to his granduncle Robert MERCER in parts of Lethendy and Pittendreich; and on 27 March 1807, to his father, in Baldovan and Lethendy. He appears to have sold the estate of Lethendy. He *d.* unm. 21 Aug. 1808.

VII. 1808. SIR JOHN OGILVY, Baronet [S. 1626], of Baldovan aforesaid, br. and h.; *suc. to the Baronetcy* 21 Aug. 1808; on 16 Oct. 1809, had spec. service to his br. in the lands of Baldovan, etc. He *d.* unm. 1819.

VIII. 1819. SIR WILLIAM OGILVY, Baronet [S. 1626], of Baldovan aforesaid, br. and h., *b.* about 1765; served in the Royal Navy, becoming eventually Rear-Admiral; *suc. to the Baronetcy* in 1819. He *m.* in 1802, Sarah, da. of James MORLEY, of Kempshot, Hants, an officer in the Bombay civil service. He *d.* 1823. His widow *d.* 26 May 1854. Admon. Sep. 1854.

IX. 1823. SIR JOHN OGILVY, Baronet [S. 1626], of Baldovan, aforesaid, s. and h., *b.* in Edinburgh, 17 March 1803; matric. at Oxford (Ch. Ch.), 5 Nov. 1811, aged 18; *suc. to the Baronetcy*, 1823; Convener of co. Forfar, 1855; Hon. Col. of Dundee R.V., 1865; M.P. for Dundee (four Parls.) 1857-74; Major-Gen. of the "Royal Company of Archers," *i.e.*, the Royal Body Guard. He *m.* firstly, 7 July 1831, at St. Geo., Han. sq., Juliana Barbara, yst. da. of Lord Henry HOWARD-MOLYNEUX-HOWARD (br. to the Duke of Norfolk), by Elizabeth, da. of Edward LONG, Chief Judge of the Vice-Admiralty Court in Jamaica. She, who was *b.* 31 March 1812, *d.* 27 Dec. 1833. Will pr. Aug. 1835. He *m.* secondly, 5 April 1836, at Charlton, Wilts, Jane Elizabeth, 3d da. of Thomas (HOWARD), 16th EARL OF SUFFOLK, by Elizabeth Jane, da. of James (DUTTON), 1st BARON SHERBORNE. She, who was *b.* 25 July 1809, *d.* 28 July 1861 at Baldovan House. He *d.* 29 March 1890, in his 88th year, at Archerfield, East Lothian.

X. 1890. SIR REGINALD HOWARD ALEXANDER OGILVY, Baronet [S. 1626], of Baldovan aforesaid, 1st s. and h., being only s. by 1st wife; *b.* 29 May 1832 at Edinburgh; matric. at Oxford (Oriel Coll.), 5 Dec. 1850, aged 18; B.A., 1854; admitted to Inner Temple, 1860; Hon. Col. Forfar and Kincardine Artillery; Aide-de-camp to Queen Victoria; *suc. to the Baronetcy*, 29 March 1890. He *m.* 27 July 1859, Olivia Barbara, only da. and h. of George William Fox (KINNAIRD), 9th LORD KINNAIRD, by Frances Anne Georgiana, da. of William Francis (PONSONBY), 1st BARON DE MAULEY. She, who was *b.* 22 Jan. 1839, *d.* 6 Aug. 1871.

Family Estates.—These, in 1883, appear to have been under 2,000 acres. *Principal Residence.*—Baldovan House, near Strathmartine, Forfarshire.

(a) He reserved, however, the Castle (now a ruin) and a piece of land round it, but without any right of access. The estate is said to have been in the family for fourteen generations.

NAPIER:

cr. 2 March, or 2 May 1627, sealed 9 June 1627;(a)
sometime, 4 May 1627 to 1683, LORDS NAPIER OF MERCHISTOUN [S.];
dormant, 1683—1817;
assumed since 1817
being then named MILLIKEN-NAPIER.

I. 1627. SIR ARCHIBALD NAPIER, of Merchistoun, co. Midlothian, s. and h. of John NAPIER, of the same (distinguished for his learning and for the invention of logarithms), by his 1st wife, Elizabeth, da. of Sir James STIRLING, of Keir, was *b.* about 1575; matric. at Glasgow Univ., March 1593; was Gent. of the Privy Chamber to James VI [S.], whom he accompanied to England on his accession to that kingdom; P.C., 1615; was *Knighted* at Royston, 28 July 1616; suc. his father 3 April 1617; Treasurer Depute [S.], 1622-31; Lord Justice Clerk [S.], 1623-24; a Lord of Session [S.], 1623-25; extra Lord of Session 1616, and was *cr. a Baronet* [S.] 2 March or 2 May 1627(a), the patent being sealed 9 June 1627, but not entered in the Great Seal register, with rem. to heirs male whatsoever, and with a grant of, presumably, 16,000 acres in Nova Scotia, called the Barony of Nepar (being on the north side of Argulis bay), of which, however, he apparently never had seizin.(b) He *m.* (contract 15 April 1619) Margaret, 2d da. of John GRAHAM, 4th EARL OF MONTROSE [S.], by Margaret, da. of William (RUTHVEN), 1st EARL OF GOWRIE. She, who was living 15 Dec. 1626, was presumably alive when on 4 May 1627, he was *cr.* LORD NAPIER OF MERCHISTOUN [S.]. For particulars of his after career see *Peerage*. He *d.* Nov. 1645, aged about 70.

II. 1645. ARCHIBALD (NAPIER), LORD NAPIER OF MERCHISTOUN [S.], and a Baronet [S. 1627], 2d but only surv. s. and h., *b.* about 1625; *suc.* to his father's honours, Nov. 1645. He *d.* 1660.

III. 1660, to 1683. ARCHIBALD (NAPIER), LORD NAPIER OF MERCHISTOUN [S.], and a Baronet [S. 1627], s. and h.; *suc.* to his father's honours in 1660, when under age. He resigned his peerage, 20 Nov. 1676, and received a new grant thereof 17 Feb. 1677 in favour of his sisters and their issue. He *d.* unm., Aug. 1683, when the peerage devolved on his sister's son, but the *Baronetage* became *dormant*, and so continued for 134 years, not being noticed in Douglas' *Baronage* [S.] or in Playfair's *Baronetage* [S.], till assumed in 1817, as under.

For further particulars see *Peerage.*

* * * * * * *

VIII.(c) 1817. SIR WILLIAM JOHN MILLIKEN-NAPIER, Baronet(d) [S. 1627], of Milliken, co. Renfrew, heir male collateral of the grantee(d), being s. and h. of Col. Robert John MILLIKEN-NAPIER, *formerly* NAPIER, of Culcreuch, co. Stirling, and of Milliken aforesaid, by Anne, da. of Robert CAMPBELL, of Downie, co. Argyll, which Robert John (who was *b.* 1765; who was in command at the siege of Mangalore in the East Indies; and who assumed the additional name of MILLIKEN on inheriting the estates of his maternal grandfather, and who *d.* 1803, having previously sold the estate of Culcreuch), was only s. of William NAPIER, of Culcreuch, by Jean, 1st da. of James MILLIKEN, of Milliken aforesaid, the said William Napier (who was under age in 1735) being only s. of John NAPIER, of Culcreuch (*b.* 1686; *d.* 1735), s. and h. of Alexander NAPIER (*d.* 1702), of

(a) 2 March 1627 in Milne's List, but 2 May 1627 in Laing's List.
(b) Banks's Lists, and Banks's *Bar. Ang. Conc.*, vol. ii, p. 241.
(c) This is the numbering given in Burke's *Baronetage* of 1901, reckoning apparently Alexander, John, William, and Robert, the four immediate ancestors of the "8th Baronet" to have been the 4th, 5th, 6th, and 7th Baronets.
(d) According to the service of 17 March 1817.

Culcreuch (by purchase from his elder brother), who was 4th s. of Robert NAPIER, of Drumbony, 1628, and afterwards of Culcreuch aforesaid (*d.* before June 1655), who was younger br., of the half blood, of Archibald the 1st Baronet, and the 1st LORD NAPIER OF MERCHISTOUN [S.].(a) He was *b.* 1788 at Milliken House; suc. his father in 1808, and was, on 17 March 1817, served heir male general of Archibald (NAPIER), 3d LORD NAPIER OF MERCHISTOUN [S.], and 3d Baronet [S. 1627], when he consequently *assumed that Baronetcy*. He was Convener of co. Renfrew. He *m.*, 11 Nov. 1815, Eliza Christian, 5th and yst. da. of John STIRLING, of Kippendavie, co. Perth. He *d.* 4 Feb. 1852, at Milliken house aforesaid, aged 63. His widow *d.* 3 March 1860, at Pau in France.

IX.(b) 1852. SIR ROBERT JOHN MILLIKEN-NAPIER, Baronet(c) [S. 1627], of Milliken aforesaid, 1st s. and h., *b.* 7 Nov. 1818 at Milliken house; entered the army 1835; Capt. 79th Foot, 1844; *suc. to the Baronetcy*(c) 4 Feb. 1852; Lieut.-Col. Renfrewshire Militia, 1854; Convener of that County, 1859; Hon. Col. 4th Batt. Sutherland and Argyll Highlanders. He *m.*, 4 April 1850, at Pitfour Castle, co. Perth, Anne Salisbury Meliora, only surv. da. of John Ladeveze ADLERCRON, of Moyglare, co. Meath. He *d.* 4 Dec. 1884, at Edinburgh, aged 66. His widow living 1901.

X.(b) 1884. SIR ARCHIBALD LENNOX MILLIKEN-NAPIER, Baronet(c) [S. 1627], of Westfield, North Berwick, 1st s. and h.; *b.* in Moray place, Edinburgh, 2 Nov. 1855; sometime Lieut. Grenadier Guards; *suc. to the Baronetcy*(c) 4 Dec. 1884. He *m.*, 16 Dec. 1880, at St. Paul's, Knightsbridge, Mary Allison Dorothy, 4th and yst. da. of Sir Thomas FAIRBAIRN, 2d Baronet [1869], by Allison, da. of Thomas CALLAWAY, of Chiselhurst, Kent.

MACKAY:

cr. 28 March 1627; sealed 2 Nov. 1628;(d)
afterwards, since 1628, LORDS REAY [S.].

I. 1627. SIR DONALD MACKAY, of Far, Tongue, and Strathnaver, s. and h. of Hugh MACKAY, of the same, by his 2d wife, Jean, da. of Alexander (GORDON), 11th EARL OF SUTHERLAND [S.], was *b.* Feb. 1590/1; suc. his father 11 Sep. 1614; was Coroner of North Kintyre, 1615; *Knighted* about 1616; raised 3,000 men in 1626 to assist Count Mansfeld in Germany, and was *cr. a Baronet* [S.] 28 March 1627, as "of Stranaver," sealed 2 Nov. 1628,(d) but not recorded

(a) The pedigree, as above given, is that in Burke's *Baronetage* of 1901, where it is stated that the issue of the elder brothers [two of whom undoubtedly left issue] of Alexander Napier, who purchased Culcreuch, is now extinct. In Foster's *Baronetage* for 1883, p. 704, under "Chaos"] three different descents are given of this family from Robert Napier, the yr. br. of the 1st Baronet and Peer, viz. [1] "in Burke's *Peerage*, edit. 1837-41," wherein William John Millikin Napier (*b.* 1788, who obtained the service of 17 March 1817) "is said to be third in descent from this Robert, viz., son of Robert John, son of Alexander, son of Robert, of Culcreuch aforesaid; [2] In the editions of the same work, 1846-52, Robert, of Culcreuch, is said to be ancestor of William, father of Robert John aforesaid (Alexander being omitted), and [3] since 1853 the descent has been published in the same work as follows:—William Millikin, *b.* 1788, son of Robert John, *b.* 1765, son of William, *b.* 1712, son of John, *b.* 1665 [*sic*, but in the edit. of 1901 the date is 1686] son of Alexander, *b.* 1621, son of Robert, of Culcreuch aforesaid. It would be interesting to know which of these three descents was under consideration, when, after a lapse of 134 years, William Millikin Napier was served heir male general of Archibald, 3d Baron Napier, on 17 March 1817."
(b) See p. 318, note "c."
(c) See p. 318, note "d."
(d) Laing's List in which the creation is given as 18 March 1627, and Milne's List in which it is given as 28 March 1627.

in the Great Seal Register [S.], with rem. to heirs male whatsoever, and with a grant of, presumably, 16,000 acres in Nova Scotia, of which he had seizin in Nov. 1628.([a]) He *m.* firstly, Aug. 1610, Barbara, 1st da. of Kenneth (Mackenzie), 1st Lord Mackenzie of Kintail [S.], by Anne, da. of George Ross, of Balnagowan. She was living 9 Jan. 1617, but possibly was dead before he was *cr.*, 20 June 1628, LORD REAY [S.]. In that peerage this *Baronetcy* then *merged*, and still so continues. See *Peerage*.

MAXWELL :

cr. 18 or 28 March 1627 ; sealed 17 Sep. 1630 ;([b])

afterwards, since 1885, Barons Farnham [I.].

I. 1627. Sir James Maxwell, of Calderwood, co. Lanark, 2d but 1st surv. s. and h. of Sir James Maxwell, of the same, by his 2d wife, Isabel, da. of Sir Alexander Hamilton, of Innerwick, suc. his father in 1622, and was *cr. a Baronet* [S.], 18 or 28 March 1627, sealed 17 Sep. 1630,([b]) but not entered in the Great Seal Register [S.] till (as late as) 1830, as "of Calderwood," with rem. to heirs male whatsoever, and with a grant of, presumably, 16,000 acres in Nova Scotia, called the Barony of Mauldslie, of which he had seizin in April 1631.([c]) On the death, s.p., in 1647, of his cousin, Sir John Maxwell, of Pollock, he unsuccessfully claimed that estate under a deed, dat. 18 Dec. 1400, whereby two brothers, John Maxwell, of Pollock, and Robert Maxwell, of Calderwood, the respective lineal ancestors of the said John and of himself, had agreed that, failing male issue of the one, the male issue of the other should inherit both estates. He *m.* firstly, Jean, da. of Sir James Hamilton, of Evandale, by Margaret, da. of James (Conyngham), 7th Earl of Glencairn [S.]. She *d.* s.p.m. He *m.* secondly (contract, 1 July 1637), Mary, da. of James Couttes, of Edinburgh. He was living, "old and blind," 1670, but *d.* soon afterwards.

II. 1670? Sir William Maxwell, Baronet [S. 1627], of Calderwood aforesaid, only s. and h., by 2d wife, *b.* about 1640; *suc. to the Baronetcy* about 1670. He continued, but also unsuccessfully, in 1695, his father's claim to the Pollock estates. He *m.*, before 9 Nov. 1666, Jean, da. of his paternal uncle, Sir Alexander Maxwell, of Saughton Hall, by Janet, da. and h. of Thomas Moodie, of Saughton Hall aforesaid. He *d.* s.p.s.([d]), 30 April 1703.

III. 1703. Sir William Maxwell, Baronet [S. 1627], of Calderwood aforesaid, formerly of Abington, cousin and heir, being only s. and h. of Col. John Maxwell, by Elizabeth, da. of Sir James Elphinstone, of Blythswood, which John (who was slain on the King's side at the battle of Dunbar, 1650) was yr. br. (of the half blood) to the 1st Baronet, being s. of Sir James Maxwell, of Calderwood, by his 3d wife, Margaret, (*m.* 8 Sep. 1610, she being then the widow of Sir James Hamilton), da. of James (Conyngham), 7th Earl of Glencairn [S.], all abovenamed. He *suc. to the Baronetcy*, as h. male collateral of the grantee, 30 April 1703, but did not assume the title.([e]). He *m.* Margaret, da. of Capt. Wood, of Culter. He *d.* before 23 March 1716. His widow living 1729.

IV. 1715? Sir William Maxwell, Baronet [S. 1627], of Calderwood aforesaid, only surv. s. and h.; *suc. to the Baronetcy* on the death of his father. He *m.* Christian, da. of Alexander Stewart, of Torrance, by Isabel, da. of Sir Patrick Nisbet, of Deen. He d. 1750.

([a]) Banks's Lists.
([b]) Milne's List, in which the creation is given as 18, and Laing's List, in which it is given as 28 March 1627.
([c]) Banks's Lists.
([d]) His son, Alexander Maxwell, *m.* Margaret, da. of Sir George Maxwell, of Pollock, but *d.* s.p. and v.p.
([e]) *Ex inform.* Sir J. Balfour Paul, Lyon King of Arms, by whom many of the statements in this article have been supplied.

V. 1750. Sir William Maxwell, Baronet [S. 1627], of Calderwood aforesaid, 1st s. and h.; *suc. to the Baronetcy* in 1750. He *m.*, in or before 1747, Grizel, da. of James Peadie, of Roughill. He d. 2 Jan. 1789.

VI. 1789. Sir William Maxwell, Baronet [S. 1627], of Calderwood aforesaid, only surv. s. and h.; *b.* 7 Jan. 1748; *suc. to the Baronetcy* 2 June 1789. He *m.*, 5 May 1807, Hannah Leonora, yst. da. of Robert Pasley, of Mount Annan, co. Dumfries. He *d.* s.p. 12 Aug. 1829. Will pr. Nov. 1829.

VII. 1829. Sir William Maxwell, Baronet [S. 1627], of Calderwood aforesaid, cousin and h., being s. and h. of Alexander Maxwell, of Leith, merchant, by Mary, da. of Hugh Clerk, of Edinburgh, merchant, which Alexander was 3d and yst. s. of the 4th Baronet. He was *b.* 4 Dec. 1754; was an officer in the army; served in the American War; was taken prisoner at Saratoga, 1777, and at Yorktown, 1781, becoming a full General, 1812. He *suc. to the Baronetcy* 12 Aug. 1829. He *m.*, 2 July 1792, Isabella, da. and h. of Henry Wilson, of Newbottle, co. Durham. She *d.* 1 Oct. 1829. Admon. Nov. 1829. He *d.* 16 March 1837, at Edinburgh, aged 82. Will pr. June 1837.

VIII. 1837. Sir William Alexander Maxwell, Baronet [S. 1627], of Calderwood aforesaid, 1st s. and h.; *b.* in Edinburgh, 30 April 1793; sometime an officer in the 1st Dragoons, becoming Colonel in 1851, but retiring in 1853; *suc. to the Baronetcy* 16 March 1837. He *m.*, 15 June 1847, "at St. Mary's, Grosvenor Square," Catherine Cameron, widow of Henry Paget Gill, Capt. 50th Foot, 5th da. of Walter Logan, of Fingalton, co. Lanark. He *d.* s.p., 4 April 1865, at 27 Adelaide Crescent, Brighton. His widow *d.* there 13 Oct. 1866.

IX. 1865. Sir Hugh Bates Maxwell, Baronet [S. 1627], of Calderwood aforesaid, only surv. br. and h.; *b.* 14 Feb. 1797, at Parkhill, co. Stirling; admitted an Advocate [S.], 1818; *suc. to the Baronetcy* 4 April 1865. He *m.*, 1 May 1827, Mary Anne Barbara, only surv. da. of John Hunter, of Lisburne, co. Antrim. He *d.* 9 Feb. 1870, at Edinburgh. His widow *d.* 18 July 1875, at Gilsland, co. Cumberland.

X. 1870. Sir William Maxwell, Baronet [S. 1627], of Calderwood aforesaid, only s. and h., *b.* 11 Aug. 1828, *suc. to the Baronetcy*, 9 Feb. 1870. He *m.* 20 April 1880, at 20 Belhaven terrace, Glasgow, Jane, yst. da. of Frank Baird, of Glasgow. He *d.* s.p. 4 Dec. 1885, aged 56, at Calderwood Castle, co. Lanark, when the issue male of the father of the grantee is presumed to have become extinct. His widow *m.* in 1887, George Leader Owen, of Withybush, co. Pembroke, and was living 1901.

XI. 1885. James Pierce (Maxwell), 9th Baron Farnham [I. 1756], cousin and h. male collateral, *b.* 1813; *suc. to the Peerage* on the death of his brother, 4 June 1884, and *suc. to the Baronetcy* on the death of his distant cousin, the 10th Baronet, 4 Dec. 1885, proving his right thereto in the Lyon Court, in 1900. His lineal ancestor, Robert Maxwell, Dean of Armagh, was yr. br. of Sir James Maxwell, of Calderwood, the father of the 1st Baronet, both being sons of Sir John Maxwell, of Calderwood aforesaid. The said Dean of Armagh (who *d.* March 1625), was suc. by his eldest s., Robert Maxwell, Bishop of Kilmore and Ardagh (*d.* 7 Nov. 1672), whose s., Henry Maxwell, Rector of Derrynoose, co. Armagh (*d.* 1703), was father of John Maxwell, of Farnham, co. Cavan, who became in 1737 the representative of his great grandfather, and who was *cr.*, 6 May 1756, BARON FARNHAM [I.], being great grandfather of James Pierce (Maxwell), 9th Baron Farnham [I. 1756], and 11th Baronet [S. 1627] abovenamed. See *Peerage*.

HAMILTON :

cr. in 1627.

dormant or *extinct* about 1670.

I. 1627 to 1670? William Hamilton, called "3d brother to the Earl of Abercorn" [S.]([a]), was *cr. a Baronet* [S.], presumably "as of Westport," in 1627, apparently before 28 March 1627([a]), but no record is entered in the Great Seal Register, and no grant, or seizin of lands in Nova Scotia, is recorded. In Burke's *Extinct Baronetage*, however, "Sir James [*sic*] Hamilton, of Preston, sprung from Alexander, son to the Lord Hamilton" is said to have been thus created in 1627. The grantee was probably the Hon. William Hamilton, yr. br. of James, 2d Earl of Abercorn [S.], being 3d s. of James, the 1st Earl, by Marion, da. of Thomas (Boyd), Lord Boyd [S.]. He was *b.* about 1605; was Resident in Rome, about 1660, on behalf of the Queen Dow. of Charles I. He *m.*, after 1645, Jean, Dow. Baroness Cathcart [S.], widow of Sir Duncan Campbell, 2d Baronet [S. 1628], of Auchinbreck, who was slain in 1645. He *d.* s.p. (*Qy.* about 1670?) when the *Baronetcy* became *dormant* or *extinct.*

STEWART, *or* STUART :

cr. 28 March 1627; sealed 28 April 1632([b]);

afterwards, since 1703, Earls of Bute [S.];

and, since 1796, Marquesses of Bute.

I. 1627. James Stewart, of the isle of Bute, Hereditary Sheriff of Buteshire, s. and h. of Sir John Stewart, of the same (living Aug. 1615), by Elizabeth, 1st da. and coheir of Robert Hepburn, of Foord, co. Edinburgh, was *cr. a Baronet* [S.] as "of Bute" 28 March 1627, sealed 28 April 1632([b]), but not recorded in the Great Seal Register [S.], with rem. to heirs male whatsoever, but no grant, or seizin of lands in Nova Scotia, is recorded. He was retoured heir of all his ancestors, 1630; was M.P. [S.] for Buteshire, 1644-45; was a zealous Royalist, being the King's Lieutenant over the West of Scotland; was fined 5,000 marks by the Parl. of 1646, his estate being sequestrated. He *m.* Isabella, 1st da. of Sir Duncan Campbell, 2d Baronet [S. 1628], of Auchinbreck, by Mary, da. of Sir Alexander Erskine, of Gogar. He *d.* in London, 1662, and was *bur.* in Westm. Abbey.([c])

II. 1662. Sir Dugald Stewart, Baronet [S. 1627], of Bute aforesaid, Hereditary Sheriff of Buteshire, 1st s. and h.; *suc. to the Baronetcy* in 1662; was M.P. [S.] for Buteshire, 1661-63, 1665 and 1669-70; was made Baillie of the regality of Glasgow, 2 Sep. 1671. He *m.* Elizabeth, da. of Sir John Ruthven, of Dunglass, by Barbara, da. of Alexander (Leslie), 1st Earl of Leven [S.]. He *d.* 1672.

III. 1672. Sir James Stewart *or* Stuart, Baronet [S. 1627], of Bute aforesaid, Hereditary Sheriff of Buteshire, 1st s. and h.; *suc. to the Baronetcy* in 1672, at an early age; was Sheriff of Tarbet, 1684; of Argyllshire, 1685; admitted as an Advocate, 1685; was M.P. [S.] for co. Bute, 1685-86, 1689,

([a]) Milne's List, in which, however, no date is given. This Baronetcy is not given in Laing's or Walkeley's Lists, but in Beatson's List the creation of "Hamilton, of Westport," is placed between "Maxwell" and "Stuart," which indicates the date (given in Burke's *Extinct Baronetage*) of 1627. In Ulster's List [ending 1642] "Sir William Hamilton, br. of the Earl of Abercorn" occurs.
([b]) Milne's List; not, however, in Laing's List.
([c]) Douglas' *Peerage* [S.]. No such burial, however, is recorded in the Register of Westm. Abbey, edited by Col. Chester.

1689-93 (when unseated for not having taken the oath of allegiance) and 1702-03; P.C. to Queen Anne; a Commissioner for a proposed union with Scotland, 1702. He *m.*, firstly, Agnes, 1st da. of Sir George Mackenzie, of Rosehaugh, King's Advocate [S.], by his first wife, Elizabeth, da. of John Dickson, of Hartree, a Lord of Session [S.]. She, who was *b.* 2 Jan. 1663, was living 28 Nov. 1692. He *m.*, secondly, Christian, da. and coheir of William Duncan, of Kincavel, Advocate [S.]. She was living when he was *cr.* 14 April 1703, EARL OF BUTE, etc. [S.] In that peerage this *Baronetcy* then *merged* and still continues, the 4th Earl being *cr.*, 21 March 1796, MARQUESS OF BUTE.

STEWART :

cr. 18 April 1627([a]);

afterwards, since 1649, Earls of Galloway [S.].

I. 1627. The Hon. James Stewart, of Corsewall, 2d and yst s. of Alexander, 1st Earl of Galloway [S.], by Grizel, da. of Sir John Gordon, of Lochinvar, was *b.* about 1604, and was v.p. *cr. a Baronet* [S.], 18 April 1627([a]), as "of Corsewall," with rem. to heirs male, and with, presumably, a grant of 16,000 acres in Nova Scotia, of which, however, he never appears to have had seizin([b]). He was served heir, 5 Sep. 1643, to his elder br., Alexander Stewart, *styled* Lord Garlies, being, after, that date, himself *styled* LORD GARLIES. He was constant to the Royal cause, and was accordingly fined £4,000 under Cromwell's "Act of Grace," in 1654. He *m.* in 1642, Nicola,([c]) da. of Sir Robert Grierson, of Lag, co. Dumfries. She, presumably, was living when, in 1649, he suc. his father as EARL OF GALLOWAY [S.]. In that peerage this *Baronetcy* then *merged*, and still so continues.

LIVINGSTONE, *or* LEVINGSTON :

cr. 29 June and sealed 17 July 1627([d]);

afterwards, 1647-94, Viscounts Newburgh [S.];

and subsequently, 1660-94, Earls of Newburgh [S.];

dormant, since 6 April 1694.

I. 1627. Sir John Livingstone, of Kinnaird, in Gowrie, co. Perth, was Groom of the Bedchamber to James I before 1612; was *Knighted* before 1617; acquired the Barony of Kinnaird, from John Kinnaird, of that ilk, and had charter thereof, 26 March 1618, ratified by Crown charter 6 Dec. 1618, and by Parl. [S.], in 1621; was *cr. a Baronet* [S.] 29 June, sealed 17 July 1627([d]), but not entered in the Great Seal register, with rem. to heirs male whatsoever, and with a grant of, presumably, 16,000 acres at Anti Costi, in Nova Scotia, of which he had seizin in July 1627.([b]) He *m.* Janet, da. of (—) Thoxton. He *d.* March 1628. His widow *m.* 1645, as his 2d wife, Edward (Gorges), 1st Baron Gorges of Dundalk [I.], who *d.* before 16 April 1652. She was *bur.* from Lincoln's Inn Fields, 15 May 1666, at St. Margaret's, Westm. Admon. 11 July 1665, to her son James, Earl of Newburgh [S.].

([a]) Laing's List.
([b]) Banks's Lists.
([c]) As to his alleged marriage with Catherine, da. of Sir Robert Hoghton, 1st Baronet [1611], see *Northern Notes and Queries* (*Scottish Antiquary*), vol. iv, p. 42.
([d]) Milne's List. In Laing's List the creation is dated 25 June 1627.

II. 1628. SIR JAMES LIVINGSTONE, Baronet [S. 1627], of Kinnaird aforesaid, s. and h., *suc. to the Baronetcy* March 1628, being then under age, but obtaining his majority in 1640. His uncle, James Livingstone, was served tutor to him 22 Dec. 1628, and he was served heir to his father in the Barony of Kinnaird, &c., 19 March 1629. He was one of the Gentlemen of the Bedchamber to Charles I. He *m.* after 23 Oct. 1642, Catherine, widow of Lord George STUART, da. of Theophilus (HOWARD), 2d EARL OF SUFFOLK, by Elizabeth, da. of George (HOME), EARL OF DUNBAR [S.]. She was living, though possibly not then as his wife, 13 Sep. 1647, when he was *cr.* VISCOUNT NEWBURGH [S.], being subsequently *cr.*, 31 Dec. 1660, EARL OF NEWBURGH, &c. [S.]. In these peerages this *Baronetcy* then *merged*, and so continued, till on the death s.p.m., 6 April 1694, of his son, Charles, the 2d Earl, the issue male of the grantee became extinct, and the *Baronetcy* became *dormant*(a).

LIVINGSTONE, *or* LEVINGSTONE:
cr. 29 June 1627;(b)
sometime, 1696—1711, VISCOUNT TEVIOT [S.];
dormant since 1718.

I. 1627. THOMAS LIVINGSTONE, of Newbigging, co. Lanark, 2d s. of Mungo LIVINGSTONE,(c) of the same, by Jean, da. of John LINDSAY, of Covington in that county, was a Colonel in the service of the States General of Holland, and was *cr. a Baronet* [S.], 29 June 1627,(b) with a grant of, presumably, 16,000 acres in Nova Scotia, of which he had seizin in March 1629.(d) He acquired a large fortune by his marriage with (—), da. and h. of Col. EDMOND, an officer in the service of the said States, the son of a baker in Stirling.

II. 1660? SIR THOMAS LIVINGSTONE, Baronet [S. 1627], s. and h., *b.* about 1650 in Holland; *suc. to the Baronetcy* on his father's death; was a Colonel in the service of the States General; accompanied the Prince of Orange, afterwards William III, to England, serving in several of his campaigns; Col. 2d Reg. of Dragoons, 1688; Com. in chief of the forces in Scotland; Major General, 1696, and finally, 1704, Lieut. General. He *m.* Macktellina WALRAVE, a native of Nimeguen, who was living when he was *cr.* 4 Dec. 1696, VISCOUNT TEVIOT, etc. [S.] In that peerage this *Baronetcy* then *merged*, till on his death, s.p. 14 Jan. 1710/1, in his 60th year, his peerage honours became *extinct*. For fuller account of him after 1696, see *Peerage*.

III. 1711, to 1718. SIR ALEXANDER LIVINGSTONE, Baronet [S. 1627], only br. and h. He was a Col. of Foot in the service of the States General, and was afterwards, in the English service, Col. of the Scots Cameronian Regiment. He *suc. to the Baronetcy*, 14 Jan. 1710/1,

(a) The heir male to the Earldom (which was, however, limited to heirs *general*), and, consequently, to the Baronetcy was James Livingston, s. and h. of John Livingston, Capt. of Dragoons, by Eliz., da. of Sir Robert Hamilton, of Silverhill. Possibly he was a grandson of James Livingston (br. of the 1st Baronet), who was served tutor to his nephew, the 2d Baronet, 22 Dec. 1628, as above stated.

(b) Wood's *Douglas' Peerage*, vol. ii, p. 590. The date is the same as the creation of the Baronetcy of Livingstone of Kinnaird, and possibly is confused therewith. This creation is not mentioned in Milne's List or Laing's List, but it is stated in Banks's Lists that "Sir James [*sic*] Livingstoun, of Newbigging, represented by Viscount Teviot," had seizin of lands in Nova Scotia in March 1629, so that the date cannot be very far wrong.

(c) This Mungo was a yr. s. of William Livingstone, of Jerviswood, co. Lanark, whose grandson and heir sold that estate about 1644 to George Baillie, and died soon afterwards s.p. [*Ex inform.* R. R. Stodart, Lyon Clerk Depute, 1863-86, as also is much else in this article.]

(d) Banks's Lists.

and was served heir to his brother, 8 May 1711, in the estates of Waughton, co. Haddington, Abbotshall, co. Fife, etc. He *m.* Sarah TIELLEUS, da. of a Burgomaster of Amsterdam. He *d.* s.p.m.(a) in Holland in 1718, when the *Baronetcy* became *dormant*. Will pr. Dec. 1718.

CUNINGHAM, CUNINGHAME, *or* CONYNHAM;
cr. 4 July 1627, and sealed 26 July 1627(b);
sometime, April to Oct. 1722, RUTHVEN;
dormant, since Oct. 1732.

I. 1627. WILLIAM CUNINGHAM, of Cuninghamhead, in the parish of Dreghorn, co. Ayr, s. and h. of John CUNINGHAM, of the same, by Mary, 1st da. of Sir James EDMONSTONE, of Duntreath, co. Stirling, was *b.* 24 Nov. 1601; was heir general of his Father, 24 Oct. 1610; was heir general of his father, 24 Oct. 1610; was *cr. a Baronet* [S.] 4, sealed 26 July 1627,(b) but not recorded in the Great Seal register [S.], with rem. to heirs male whatsoever, and with a grant of, presumably, 16,000 acres, called the Barony of Cuningham in Anti Costi, Nova Scotia, of which he had seizin July 1627.(c) He was M.P. [S.] for co. Ayr, 1628-33 and 1639-40. He *m.* firstly, in 1619, Elizabeth, da. of Thomas NICOLSON, Commissary of Aberdeen. He *m.* secondly, Margaret, da. of Hugh (CAMPBELL), 1st LORD CAMPBELL OF LOUDOUN [S.], by Elizabeth, da. of William (RUTHVEN), 1st EARL OF GOWRIE [S.]. He *d.* June 1640.

II. 1640. SIR WILLIAM CUNINGHAME, Baronet [S. 1625], of Cuninghamhead aforesaid, only s. and h. by 1st wife; *suc. to the Baronetcy* June 1640, and had the gift, *gratis*, of his own ward and marriage, on account of his father's death in service of the State. On 12 May 1642, he had spec. service to his father; was Colonel and a member of the Committee of Estates, 1649. He was M.P. [S.] for Ayrshire, 1648-49 and 1650; was a great Anti-Episcopalian, and in 1661 was fined £4,800; committed to prison in Sep. 1662, and was not finally discharged till 1669. He *m.* in Aug. 1661, Anne, 1st da. of Thomas (RUTHVEN), 1st LORD RUTHVEN OF FREELAND [S.], by Isabel, da. of Robert (BALFOUR, *formerly* ARNOT), 2d LORD BALFOUR OF BURLEIGH [S.]. He *d.* 1670. His widow *m.* William CUNINGHAME, of Craigends, and *d.* about 1689, when her son was served her heir.

III. 1670, to 1722. SIR WILLIAM CUNINGHAME, *afterwards* (April to Oct. 1722) SIR WILLIAM RUTHVEN, Baronet [S. 1627], of Cuninghamhead(d) and of Freeland, co. Perth, only s. and h., was *b.* about 1665; *suc. to the Baronetcy* in 1670, and had spec. service to his father, 29 Aug. 1672; heir general of his mother, 21 May 1689. On the death, s.p., of his maternal uncle, David (RUTHVEN), 2d LORD RUTHVEN [S.], in April 1701, he became heir(e)

(a) Catherine Elizabeth, his da. and h., *m.* Matthew le Stevenson Van Barkenrode, Burgomaster of Amsterdam, and their son entered his pedigree in the Lyon office, Edinburgh, 20 Aug. 1764.

(b) Milne's List; Laing's List.

(c) Banks's Lists.

(d) The estate of Cuninghamhead was sold 28 Jan. 1728, for £23,309 to John Snodgrass.

(e) The Barony of Ruthven of Freeland [S.] was cr. about Jan. 1651, with a limitation (according to the Macfarlane MS. in the Advocates library) to heirs *male*. No patent, however, was ever enrolled, and since 1701 it has been irregularly assumed in right of *female* descent, and that too not always (even) by the heir of line.

of line to his maternal grandfather, Thomas (RUTHVEN), LORD RUTHVEN OF FREELAND [S.], but did not take that title which was arbitrarily assumed by his aunt Jean, the yst. of the three sisters and coheirs of the late Lord, on whose death the said Jean had, under a deed of entail, 26 April 1674, suc. to the family estate of Freeland. This, on her death unm. in April 1722, devolved on him (six months before his death) when he assumed the name of RUTHVEN. He *m.* Ann, da. of Sir Archibald STEWART, 1st Baronet [S. 1668] of Castlemilk, by Mary, da. of William CARMICHAEL, s. and h. ap. of James, 1st LORD CARMICHAEL [S.]. He *d.* s.p. Oct. 1722, when the *Baronetcy* became *dormant*. Will "given up" 28 March 1723.

CARMICHAEL:
cr. 17 July 1627(a);
subsequently, 1647—1817, LORD CARMICHAEL [S.];
and, 1701—1817, EARLS OF HYNDFORD [S.];
dormant since 18 April 1817.

I. 1627. SIR JAMES CARMICHAEL, of Westraw and Hyndford, both in co. Lanark, s. and h. of Walter CARMICHAEL, of Hyndford aforesaid, by Grizel, da. of Sir John CARMICHAEL, of Meadow Flat, in that county, Captain of the Castle of Crawfurd, suc. his Father in 1616; was Cupbearer, Carver and Chamberlain [S.] to James I., and was *cr.* a Baronet [S.], 17 July 1627,(a) as "of Westraw," being designed "the King's servant," with rem. to heirs male whatsoever, and with, presumably, a grant of 16,000 acres, called the Barony and Regality of Carmichael, in Nova Scotia, of which he had seizin in Jan. 1633, "with power to dig for searching of gold mines, and for that effect to transport thither all gold affecting mines."(b) Having, on the death of his cousin, Sir John Carmichael, of Carmichael, co. Lanark (living 9 Feb. 1619), suc. to that estate, he was thenceforth designated "of Carmichael;" was Sheriff of Lanarkshire, 1632; Lord Justice Clerk, 1634-36, and again 1649; Treasurer Depute 1636; P.C. [S.] for life (by Parl.), 1641. He *m.* Agnes, sister of John WILKIE of Foulden, co. Berwick, da. of William WILKIE. She, presumably, was living when, for his services to the King, he was cr., 27 Dec. 1647, LORD CARMICHAEL [S.], with rem. to heirs male whatsoever. He, however, did not assume that title till the patent was ratified, 3 Jan. 1651. Between these dates, 10 March 1649, he was deprived of all his offices for his part in "the engagement." In that peerage this *Baronetcy*, accordingly, *merged*, the 2d Baron being *cr.*, 25 July 1701, EARL OF HYNDFORD [S.], and so continued till, on the death, unm., 18 April 1817, of the 6th Earl, 7th Baron, and 7th Baronet, it became *dormant*.

MACGILL:
cr. 19 July and sealed 3 Dec. 1627(c);
afterwards, 1661-1706, VISCOUNTS OXFURD [S.];
dormant since 8 Dec. 1706.

I. 1627. JAMES MACGILL, of Cranston-Riddell, co. Midlothian, 2d s. of David MACGILL, of the same, by Mary, da. of Sir William SINCLAIR, of Herdmanstoun, suc. his elder br., David MACGILL, 15 May 1619, and was *cr. a Baronet* [S.] 19 July, sealed 3 Dec. 1627(c), but not recorded in the Great Seal register, with rem. to heirs male whatsoever, and with the grant of, presumably,

(a) Milne's List.

(b) Banks's Lists.

(c) Milne's List and Laing's List, in which last the grantee is called "Master James Makgill, of Cranstounriddell."

16,000 acres in Nova Scotia, of which he had seizin, Dec. 1627(a). He was a Lord of Session [S.], 3 Nov. 1629, and was again so appointed by Parl. 14 Nov. 1641, by which also he was made, 1 Feb. 1643, a Commissioner; was M.P. [S.] for co. Edinburgh, 1630. He *m.* firstly, before 1630, Catharine, da. of Sir John COCKBURN, of Ormeston. He *m.* secondly, about 1645, Christian, da. of Sir William LIVINGSTONE, of Kilsyth. She, presumably, was living when he was *cr.*, 19 April 1661, VISCOUNT OXFURD, &c. [S.]. In that peerage this *Baronetcy* then *merged*, and so continued till the death s.p.m.s. 8 Dec. 1706, of the 2d Viscount and Baronet, when both titles became *dormant*.

OGILVY:
cr. 30 July, sealed 4 Aug. 1627(b);
afterwards, 1642-1803, LORDS BANFF [S.];
dormant, since 4 June 1803.

I. 1627. SIR GEORGE OGILVY, of Banff, s. and h. of Sir Walter OGILVY, of Dunlugus, co. Banff, by Helen, da. of Walter URQUHART, of Cromarty, suc. his father soon after 1625, and was *cr. a Baronet* [S.], 30 July, the patent being sealed 4 Aug. 1627,(b) but not recorded in the Great Seal Register, with rem. to heirs male whatsoever, and with a grant of, presumably, 16,000 acres in Nova Scotia, of which apparently (though the name is given, probably, in error, as "Sir *James* Ogilvy, of Banff"), he had seizin in Aug. 1627.(a) He is styled "*Dominus Georgius Ogilvy, Baronettus*," in a charter to him, 28 Jan. 1628/9, of the Barony of Banff. He *m.* firstly, before 9 March 1610/1, Margaret, da. of Sir Alexander IRVINE, of Drum. She *d.* s.p.m. He *m.* secondly, Mary SUTHERLAND, of Duffus. She, presumably, was living as his wife, when (after having distinguished himself in an engagement against the Covenanters at the bridge of Dee, 19 June 1639), he was *cr.*, 31 Aug. 1642, LORD BANFF [S.] In that peerage, this *Baronetcy* then *merged* till on the death, 4 June 1803, of the 8th Lord and 8th Baronet, both became *dormant*.

COCKBURN:(c)
cr. 22 Nov. 1627, sealed 16 April 1629(d);
dormant, since 20 Nov. 1880.

I. 1627. WILLIAM COCKBURN, of Langton, co. Berwick, Heretable Usher [S.], s. and h. of William COCKBURN,(e) of Langton aforesaid, by Janet, da. of (—) HOME, of Wedderburn; suc. his father 15 Feb. 1587; was M.P. [S.] for Berwickshire, 1612, and was *cr. a Baronet* [S.], 22 Nov. 1627; the

(a) Banks's Lists.

(b) Milne's List, in which, however, the Christian name is left blank; in Laing's List the date is 20 July 1627; in Beatson's List the creation is called "Ogilvie, of Forglen, now Lord Banff."

(c) The pedigrees of Cockburn are most contradictory. (1) The most reliable, and the one that is here followed, appears to be a tabular one in MS. compiled by Sir Edward Cludde Cockburn, and lent by him, in July 1901, to Sir James Balfour Paul, Lyon King of Arms. (2) An extensive pedigree, compiled by Sir William Betham, Ulster King of Arms [1820-53] for "Sir William Cockburn, Baronet" [see the 7th Baronet under "Cockburn" Baronetcy [S.] said to have been *cr.* in 1628], which pedigree is now among the Betham MSS. in Ulster's Office. (3) The very confused account given in Playfair's *Baronetage* [S.], published in 1811; and (4) *The House of Cockburn of that ilk*, by T. H. C. Hood, Edinburgh, published in 1888.

(d) Milne's List; Laing's List, where, however, the date is given as 21 Nov. 1627.

(e) This William was s. of James and grandson of Alexander, both of Langton aforesaid, the said Alexander, who was slain with his father at the battle of Flodden, 9 Sep. 1513, being one of the three sons of Sir William Cockburn, of that ilk, by Anne, da. of Alexander (Home) Lord Home [S.] Of the two other sons (1) William Cockburn, was father of William, father of Alexander, father of William, father of

III. 1680? SIR JOHN NICOLSON, Baronet [S. 1629], of Lasswade aforesaid, s. and h.; *suc. to the Baronetcy* on the death of his father. He *d.* s.p., May 1681, probably unm.

IV. 1681. SIR WILLIAM NICOLSON, Baronet [S. 1629], of Lasswade aforesaid, br. and h.; *suc. to the Baronetcy* on the death of his brother, to whom he was served heir 21 Sep. 1681. He *m.* Elizabeth, da. of John TROTTER, of Mortonhall. He was *bur.* 29 Jan. 1687, at Lasswade. His widow *d.* 28 March 1723.

V. 1687. SIR JOHN NICOLSON, Baronet [S. 1629], of Lasswade aforesaid, s. and h.; *suc. to the Baronetcy*, Jan. 1687. He *d.* s.p.m., presumably unm., and was *bur.* in Greyfriars churchyard, 30 Oct. 1689.

VI. 1689. SIR THOMAS NICOLSON, Baronet [S. 1629], br. and h.; *suc. to the Baronetcy*, 30 Oct. 1689; *d.* s.p.m., presumably unm., and was *bur.* in Greyfriars churchyard, 8 April 1693.

VII. 1693, to 1743. SIR JAMES NICOLSON, Baronet [S. 1629], br. and h.; *suc. to the Baronetcy* in April 1693. He *m.* firstly, 16 Dec. 1721, Isabel, da. of Henry SIMPSON, factor, at Eishington, co. Northumberland. He *m.* secondly, Elizabeth, daughter of James CARNEGIE, of Craigs. He *d.* s.p. May 1743, after which the *Baronetcy* appears to have remained *dormant* for some 80 years. His widow was living 1764.(a)

* * * * * * * *

The title was assumed in 1826 as under.

VIII.(b) 1826. SIR ARTHUR NICOLSON, Baronet(c) [S. 1629], of Brough Lodge, Fetlar, in Shetland, cousin and h. male,(c) being s. and h. of Arthur NICOLSON, of Lochend, in Shetland aforesaid, by Mary, da. of Alexander INNES, Commissary Clerk of Aberdeen, which Arthur last named (who *d.* May 1796, aged 39, was s. and h. of another Arthur NICOLSON, also of Lochend (*d.* 1793), s. of John NICOLSON, of Gilsbreck (*d.* 1728), 2d s. of Rev. James NICOLSON, Minister of Tingwall in Shetland, 1660 (*d.* before 1675), s. of James NICOLSON, Advocate [S.] and Commissary of Brechin (*d.* before 1685), s. of James NICOLSON, Bishop of Dunkeld, 1606-07, who was yr. br.(d) to John NICOLSON, of Lasswade, the father of the 1st Baronet. He was *b.* 1794, and was *in 1826* served heir male to the 1st Baronet, and thereupon *assumed the Baronetcy*. He *m.* 27 April 1821, Eliza Jane, da. of the Rev. William JACK, D.D., Principal of King's College, Aberdeen. He *d.* s.p. 16 Sep. 1863 at Norwood, co. Surrey, aged 69. His widow *d.* 26 March 1891, at Hayden Court, Cheltenham, aged 91.

(a) The information respecting him and the earlier Baronets has been kindly supplied by Sir J. Balfour Paul, Lyon King of Arms.
(b) This numbering is exclusive of any Baronets who may have succeeded, or have been entitled, to that dignity, between the death of his 7th Baronet in 1743 and the date of the service in 1826.
(c) According to the service in 1826.
(d) If, as is believed to be the case, Thomas Nicolson of Carnock, *cr. a Baronet* [S.], 16 Jan. 1636/7, was *brother* of the grantee of 1629, the heir to the Baronetcy of 1629 would be the (now existing) Baronet of 1637 in preference to the descendant of an *uncle*. See p. 304, note "b," and the *corrigenda* thereto.

IX.(a) 1863. SIR ARTHUR BOLT NICOLSON, Baronet(b) [S. 1629], of Melbourne, in Australia, cousin and h. male, being 1st surv. s. of James NICOLSON, of Aith, Capt. R.N., by Katharine Anne, sister of Alexander Maxwell BENNETT, Major in the army, da. of Thomas BENNETT, which James, who *d.* 1827, was uncle of the late Baronet. He was *b.* 6 March 1811; served as an officer in the 4th Foot, in New South Wales, in 1831; was again in New South Wales, in 1853, being sometime Sub-Commissioner of Goldfields in Victoria; *suc. to the Baronetcy*,(b) 16 Sep. 1863, and was served heir male to his cousin in Nov. 1866. He *m.* in 1839, Margaret, da. of the Rev. George BISSET, of Udny, co. Aberdeen. She *d.* at Melbourne aforesaid, in 1869. He *d.* 14 July 1879, in Portland street, Richmond, Melbourne.

X.(a) 1879. SIR ARTHUR THOMAS BENNETT ROBERT NICOLSON, Baronet(b) [S. 1629], of Melbourne aforesaid, only s. and h.; *b.* at Morphett Vale, Adelaide, South Australia, 1842; ed. at Melbourne College; *suc. to the Baronetcy*,(b) 14 July 1879. He *m.* 14 July 1881, at St. Peter, Windermere, Annie, 1st da. of John RUTHERFORD, of Bruntsfield place, Edinburgh, formerly of Illilawa, New South Wales.

ARNOT, or ARNOTT:

cr. 27 July 1629, sealed 3 July 1630;(c)
succession doubtful after 1711;
assumed till 1782 or possibly till about 1840.

I. 1629. MICHAEL ARNOT, "fiar of Arnot,"(d) co. Fife, s. and h. ap. of Walter ARNOT, of the same, by Mary, sister of Michael, 1st LORD BALFOUR OF BURLEIGH [S.], da. of Sir James BALFOUR, was *cr. a Baronet* [S.], 27 July 1629, the patent being sealed 3 July 1630,(c) but not recorded in the Great Seal Register [S.], with rem. to heirs male whatsoever, and with a grant of, presumably, 16,000 acres in Nova Scotia, of which he had seizin in July 1630.(e) He *m.* April 1612, Anne, eldest of the three das. and coheirs of Robert BROWNE, of Balquharne, co. Clackmannan, Finderlie, co. Kinross, and of Auchingownie, co. Perth, Gentleman of the Wine Cellar to King James, by Katharine DOUGLAS, his wife. He was alive in 1670, but *d.* before 1685.

II. 1680? to 1711. SIR DAVID ARNOT, Baronet [S. 1629], of Arnot aforesaid, grandson and h., being s. and h. of Col. Charles ARNOT, by Helen, da. of James REID, of Pitlethie (by Margaret BRUCE, his wife), which Charles was 1st s. of the 1st Baronet, but *d.* v.p. before 1652. He was served h. to his father, 1670; *suc. to the Baronetcy* on his grandfather's death and was served heir to him, 1685; was M.P. [S.] for Kinross, 1689-1702. He, who appears to have sold the estate of Arnot, *d.* s.p. 1 Jan. 1711.(f)

(a) See p. 364, note "b."
(b) According to the service in 1826.
(c) Milne's List and Laing's List.
(d) Laing's List.
(e) Banks's Lists.
(f) Helen, his sister, widow of James LIVINGSTONE, was in 1729 served his heir special in lands of Balrownie, Balliehill, etc., co. Forfar. In Playfair's *Baronetage* [S.] he is said to be father of two sons, John and William, of whom the eldest is said to have been the 3d Baronet, who *d.* July 1782 and who is conjectured to be father of John, the 4th Baronet, father of William, the 5th Baronet, father of William, the 6th and then (1811) existing Baronet. Thus the Sir William, who *d.* July 1782, is made the 3d, instead of the 7th Baronet, as in the text above.

III. 1711? SIR JOHN ARNOTT, Baronet(a) [S. 1629], of Abbotshall (near Kircaldy), co. Fife, the name of which he changed to "Arnott," and afterwards of York, whose relationship to the grantee is unknown; *assumed the Baronetcy*, probably in or about 1711. He was Adj. Gen. of Scotland, 1727; Brig. Gen., 1735; Major Gen. 1739, and afterwards Lieut. Gen. in the army. By deed, dat. 16 Feb. 1749/50, he disponed his Barony of Arnot in trust for his two sons and three daughters. He *m.* Mary, da. of (—). She was *bur.* 11 Oct. 1745 at Trinity in Micklegate, York. He *d.* 4 and was *bur.* there 6 June 1750. Will dat. 17 Feb. 1749/50, pr. 20 June 1750.

IV. 1750. SIR JOHN ARNOTT, Baronet(a) [S. 1629], 1st s. and h., sometime Capt. in Col. La Torrey's regiment of marines; *suc. to the Baronetcy*,(a) 4 June 1750. He *m.* Eleanor, da. of (—). He *d.* s.p.m., about 1762. Will (in which he leaves all to his wife for life, with rem. to his da., Anne Arnot) dat. 17 March 1762, but not proved till 19 March 1774, his widow (the extrix.) being then living.

* * * * * * * *

V. 1762? SIR JOHN ARNOTT, Baronet(a) [S. 1629], of the island of Jersey, whose relationship to the grantee is unknown(b); was sometime (1750 a Capt. in Foulis' regiment; and *assumed the Baronetcy* probably about 1762. He *d.* a widower and s.p. probably about 1765, although the admon. to his effects was dated as late as 10 Aug. 1781, when it was granted to "Matthew Robert ARNOTT, Esq.," a creditor, Mary ARNOTT, spinster, sister and only next of kin, having renounced.

* * * * * * * *

VI. 1765? SIR ROBERT ARNOT, Baronet(a) [S. 1629], of Dalginch, co. Fife, s. and h. of Major William ARNOT, of the same, and formerly of Auchmuir, but whose relationship to the grantee is unknown; suc. his father 6 Oct. 1735, being served his heir special, 1736; and *assumed the Baronetcy* probably about 1765. He *d.* s.p. at Dalginch aforesaid 3 June 1767.

VII. 1767, to 1782. SIR WILLIAM ARNOT, Baronet(a) [S. 1629], of Dalginch aforesaid, br. and h.; Lieut. Col. of the 2d (Queen's) Dragoon Guards; entered the army 1735, and sold out in 1779. He *suc. to the Baronetcy*,(a) 5 June 1767. He *m.* Mary, 3d da. of Richard NASH, of St. Peter's, Droitwich, co. Worcester, by Elizabeth, da. of George TREADWAY, Turkey merchant (sister to Dr. Treadway NASH, the Historian of Worcestershire). He *d.* s.p. 19 July 1782, at Powick, co. Worcester, and was *bur* there. Will dat. 25 Feb. 1780, proved 28 Sep. 1782. His widow, who was *b.* 19 Feb. 1716/7, *d.* 6 March 1783, and was *bur.* at Powick aforesaid. By her will, dat. 13 July 1782, in her husband's lifetime, she left her estate of Orleton, co. Worcester, to her brother, Dr. NASH abovenamed.

* * * * * * * *

(a) According to the assumption of that dignity.
(b) He, certainly, was not a son of William Arnot, Col. of the 53d Regt., only br. of the last Baronet, as that William *d.* s.p. before 1762, when his sisters were served his coheirs of provision general.

VIII. 1782? MATTHEW ROBERT ARNOTT,(a) Clerk of the Private Committees of the House of Commons, Usher of the Green Rod, etc., was (according to a statement said to be in the "Scottish Nation") a *de jure* Baronet, presumably as succeeding to this Baronetcy [S. 1629] in July 1782. He was s. and h. of the Rev. George ARNOT, Vicar of Wakefield, co. York, 1728 to 1750, but his relationship to the grantee is unknown. He *d.* s.p. 1801, his sister's son, George ROBINSON, Capt. R.N., being, it is believed, his heir.

* * * * * * * *

IX. 1801? to 1840? SIR WILLIAM ARNOT, Baronet(e) [S. 1629], is given in Playfair's *Baronetage* [S.], 1811, and in Burke's *Baronetage*, 1837 to 1840, as the then existing Baronet of this creation, but of him (if, indeed, he ever existed) nothing is known.

OLIPHANT:

cr. 28 July, and sealed 24 Aug. 1629;(b)
dormant probably soon after 1691.

I. 1629. SIR JAMES OLIPHANT, of Newtoun, formerly of Muirhouse, a Lord of Session [S.], s. and h.(c) of Sir William OLIPHANT(d) of Newtoun aforesaid, Lord Advocate [S.] by Katherine BLAIR, his wife, suc. his father (who *d.* aged 77) 13 April 1623 and was *cr. a Baronet* [S.] 28 July, the patent being sealed 24 Aug. 1629, but not recorded in the Great Seal Register [S.], with rem. to heirs male whatsoever and with a grant of, presumably, 16,000 acres in Nova Scotia, of which he had seizin in Aug. 1629.(e) He resigned his seat as a Lord of Session [S.] before 27 July 1632.(f) He *m.* firstly, Marjory, da. of Patrick GRAEME, of Inchbrackie. He *m.* secondly, Geilis, apparently widow of the Rev. James BENNET, Minister of Auchtermuchtie (in which case the date must have been after 1640), da. of (—) MONCRIEFF. He *d.* 1648.

(a) Doubtless the person who, as creditor, was the administrator to "Sir John Arnott, Baronet," 10 Aug. 1781.
(b) Milne's List, where, however, the word *Ogilvie* is by error put for *Oliphant*. The same date of creation is given in Laing's List, but the grantee is there called "Master *John* Oliphant of Newtoun."
(c) He had three yr. brothers: [i], William Oliphant, of Kirkhill, Advocate [S.], who *m.* Janet, da. of William Maule, Burgess of Edinburgh, and had two sons, of whom the yr., William Oliphant, *d.* s.p. before 1652, when his br. Patrick was served his heir. This Patrick Oliphant, *bap.* 2 Aug. 1618, Advocate [S.] 1649, was for many years the possessor of the Newtoun estate in virtue of a royal gift of the escheat of the 2d Baronet. He *m.* Isobel, widow of Sir William Douglas, da. of (—) Hay, and *d.* s.p.m., leaving two daughters; [ii], John Oliphant, portioner of Broughton, Advocate [S.] and King's Solicitor [S.], who *m.* Elizabeth Winram; [iii], Laurence Oliphant, of Fordun, Advocate [S.].
(d) This William was yr. br. to Laurence Oliphant, of Williamston, afterwards of Forgandenny, who was ancestor of the Oliphants of Bachilton, and whose male line failed in 1770, the heir of line being Lord Elibank [S.]. They were sons of Thomas Oliphant, of Freeland, afterwards of Williamston aforesaid [1546-77], by Isabel Gibb, which Thomas is the first on record of the family, being traditionally said to have been descended from Lawrence, Abbot of Inchaffray, who fell at Flodden.
(e) Banks's Lists.
(f) The cause, according to the *Staggering State* (p. 139), by Scot of Scotstarvet, was that he had "shot his gardener dead with a hagbut."

II. 1648. SIR JAMES OLIPHANT, Baronet [S. 1629], s. and h. by 1st wife, who, having stabbed his mother, fled the country, and when by his father's death he *suc. to the Baronetcy*, probably never assumed that dignity.(a) He *d.* s.p. 1659.

III. 1659, to 1695? SIR GEORGE OLIPHANT, Baronet [S. 1629], of Newtoun aforesaid, br. and h., *suc. to the Baronetcy* in 1659, on the death of his br., to whom he was served h. in 1674.(b) He, in 1691, sold the estate of Newtoun. He *m.* firstly, Margaret, da. of (—) DRUMMOND, of Invermay. He *m.* secondly, Margaret, 1st da. of James (ROLLO), 1st LORD ROLLO [S.], by his 2d wife, Mary, da. of Archibald (CAMPBELL), 7th EARL OF ARGYLL [S.]. He *d.* s.p., probably not long after 1691, when the *Baronetcy* became *dormant*.(c)

AGNEW(d):

cr. 28 July 1629;

sealed 22 *Feb.* 1630(e).

I. 1629. SIR PATRICK AGNEW, of Lochnaw, co. Wigtown, 8th Hereditary Sheriff of Galloway, s. and h. of Sir Andrew AGNEW, of the same, 7th Hereditary Sheriff as aforesaid, by Agnes, da. of Sir Alexander STEWART, of Garlies, was *b.* about 1578; suc. his father in 1616, being served h. to him 17 Jan. 1617, and, having been *Knighted*, was *cr. a Baronet* [S.] 28 Feb. 1629, the patent being sealed 22 Feb. 1630(e) with rem. to heirs male whatsoever, and with a grant of, presumably, 16,000 acres in Nova Scotia, which were erected into the Barony of Agnew, of which he actually got enfeoffment on the Castle Hill, Edinburgh(f) He was M.P. [S.] for Wigtownshire, 1628-33, 1643, 1644, and 1645-47. He acted as Sheriff of Galloway for thirty-three years, but resigned that office in 1649 to his son. He *m.* about 1598, Margaret, 1st da. of the Hon. Sir Thomas KENNEDY, of Culzean (s. of Gilbert, 3d EARL OF CASSILIS [S.]) by Elizabeth, da. of David MCGILL, of Cranstoun Riddel. He *d.* at Lochnaw, at a good old age, in the autumn of 1661, and was *bur.* with his wife, in the old church of Leswalt, M.I.

II. 1661. SIR ANDREW AGNEW, Baronet [S. 1629], of Lochnaw aforesaid, 9th Hereditary Sheriff of Galloway, s. and h., *suc. to the Baronetcy* in 1661, and was served h. to his father, 29 Oct. 1661. He had been previously *Knighted*; was five times M.P. [S.] for Wigtownshire, 1644, 1648-49, 1665, 1667, and 1669-72; was one of the Commissioners for Scotland, during the interregnum after the execution of Charles I. In 1656 he was *appointed* Sheriff of *all* Galloway, which included Kircudbrightshire. In 1661 he was *restored* to his ancient *Hereditary* Shrievalty. He *m.* (contract 22 March 1625) Anne, da. of Alexander STEWART, 1st EARL OF GALLOWAY [S.], by Grisel, da. of Sir John GORDON, of Lochinvar. He *d.* 1671. Will dat. at Lochnaw, 15 Feb. 1668.

(a) He was, apparently, landless, the estate of Newtoun had been granted to his cousin, Patrick Oliphant. See p. 367, note "c."

(b) Neither he nor his elder brother are styled Baronets in this retour, but in the disposition of 1691 he is styled "Sir George."

(c) He had two yr. brothers, viz.: [i], William Oliphant, mentioned in 1641, and [ii], John Oliphant, *bap.* 13 Oct. 1626. No heir male, however, of the family is now [1901] known to exist. [*Ex inform.*, Sir J. Balfour Paul, Lyon King of Arms, chiefly from notes supplied by J. Maitland Thomson, Curator of the Scottish Historical dept., from which source, also, almost all the information in this article is taken.]

(d) See "The Agnews of Lochnaw, Hereditary Sheriffs of Galloway" by Sir Andrew Agnew, Baronet, M.P., Edinburgh, 1st edit., 1864; 2d edit. (2 vols.) 1893.

(e) Milne's List; Laing's List.

(f) See note "d" above, but, according to Banks's *List*, no seisin appears to have followed the grant.

III. 1671. SIR ANDREW AGNEW, Baronet [S. 1629], of Lochnaw aforesaid, 10th Hereditary Sheriff of Galloway, s. and h., *suc. to the Baronetcy* in 1671, and was enfeoffed in his father's estates, 2 Oct. 1671. In 1682 he was superseded as Sheriff(a) for refusing to take the test act, but was restored, 25 April 1689, by the Grand Convention of Estates, of which he was a member. He was M.P. [S.] for Wigtownshire, 1685, and 1689 till his death. He *m.* (covenant dat. 24 Oct. 1656) Jane, da. of Sir Thomas HAY, of Park, 1st Baronet [S. 1663], by Marion HAMILTON, an illegit. da. of James, DUKE OF HAMILTON [S.]. He was *bur.* 9 June 1702.

IV. 1702. SIR JAMES AGNEW, Baronet [S. 1629], of Lochnaw aforesaid, 11th Hereditary Sheriff of Galloway, s. and h., *suc. to the Baronetcy* in June 1702. In 1708 he sold the Irish estates of the family (which had been long in their possession) to his agent, Patrick Agnew. In 1724 he resigned the Sheriffdom to his son. He *m.* (covenant dat. 22 June 1683) Mary da. of Alexander MONTGOMERIE, 8th EARL OF EGLINTON [S.] by his 1st wife, Elizabeth, 1st da. of William (CRICHTON), 2d EARL OF DUMFRIES [S.] By her he had a large family. He *d.* aged 75 and upwards, at Edinburgh, 9 March 1735. His widow *d.* April 1742, aged 90. Both *bur.* in the Abbey of Holyrood.

V. 1735. SIR ANDREW AGNEW, Baronet [S. 1629], of Lochnaw aforesaid, 12th Hereditary Sheriff of Galloway, s. and h., *b.* 21 Dec. 1687. *suc. to the Baronetcy*, 9 March 1735. Having entered the army, he was in command of the Government troops at Blair Castle in 1745 against the young Chevalier. He was made Governor of Tinmouth Castle, becoming finally, 1759, Lieut.-Gen. in the Army. In 1747, on the final abolition of all Hereditary jurisdictions in Scotland, he received £4,000 as compensation for his Hereditary Shrievalty of Galloway, or the county of Wigtown(b). He *m.* 12 May 1714, at St. Benet's Paul's wharf, London, his cousin, Eleanor, only da., and eventually sole h. of Thomas AGNEW, of Creoch and of Richmond, co. Surrey, sometime a Captain in the Scotch Greys by (—), da. of John DUNBAR of Mochrum. It was a runaway match, the bride being only 15, and the post-nuptial settlement was dated 22 April 1719. By her he had 7 sons and 11 daughters. He *d.* 14 or 21 Aug. 1771, aged 84. His widow *d.* 29 May 1785.

VI. 1771. SIR STAIR AGNEW, Baronet [S. 1629] of Lochnaw aforesaid, 15th child and 5th but 1st surv. s. and h., *b.* 9 Oct. 1734; sometime a merchant, and, as such, had been to Virginia; *suc. to the Baronetcy* in Aug. 1771. He *m.* firstly, Marie, da. of Thomas BAILLIE, of Polkemmet. She *d.* Nov. 1769. He *m.* secondly, 11 April 1775, Margaret, da. of Thomas NAESMYTH, of Dunblair. He *d.* 28 June 1809. His widow *d.* 30 May 1811.

VII. 1809. SIR ANDREW AGNEW, Baronet [S. 1629], of Lochnaw aforesaid, grandson and h., being posthumous s. and h. of Andrew AGNEW, an officer in the army, by Martha, da. of John (DE COURCY) LORD KINGSALE [I.], which Andrew was 1st s. and h. ap. of the late Baronet, but *d.* v.p. 11 Sep. 1792. He was *b.* 21 March 1793; *suc. to the Baronetcy*, 28 June 1809; M.P. for Wigtownshire, 1830-37; and was well-known for his endeavours to enforce a stricter observance of Sunday. He *m.* 11 June 1816 Madeline, yst. da. of Sir David CARNEGIE, of Southesk, 5th Baronet [S. 1663], by Agnes-Murray, da. of Andrew ELLIOT. He *d.* 12 April 1849 at his house, Rutland sq., Edinburgh, aged 56. His widow *d.* 21 Jan. 1858, at Edinburgh, aged 62.

(a) John Graham, of Claverhouse, was appointed in his room.

(b) In only four families was, after 1567, the Shrievalty of their respective counties continuous, viz. (1) the Campbells, Earls and afterwards Dukes of Argyll [S.], for co. Argyll and co. Tarbert; (2) the Leslies, Earls of Rothes [S.], for co. Fife, the Murrays of Philiphaugh for co. Selkirk, and (4) the Agnews for Galloway.

VIII. 1849. SIR ANDREW AGNEW, Baronet [S. 1629], of Lochnaw aforesaid, s. and h., *b.* 2 Jan. 1818 at Edinburgh, ed. at Harrow, entered the army, 1835, sometime an officer of the 93rd Foot, serving during the rebellion in Canada, 1838, but retired when Captain in the 4th Light Dragoons, *suc. to the Baronetcy* 12 April 1849; was M.P. for Wigtownshire, 1856-68; Vice-Lieut., 1852. He *m.* 20 Aug. 1846, Mary Arabella Louisa, 1st da. of Charles (NOEL), 1st EARL OF GAINSBOROUGH, by his 3d wife, Arabella, da. of Sir James WILLIAMS, *formerly* HAMLYN, 2d Baronet [1795]. She who was *b.* 16 March 1822, *d.* 27 June 1883, aged 61, at Lochnaw Castle. He *d.* there 25 March 1892, aged 74.

IX. 1892. SIR ANDREW NOEL AGNEW, Baronet [S. 1629], of Lochnaw aforesaid, 1st s. and h., *b.* 14 Aug. 1850 at Exton Park, co. Rutland; ed. at Harrow and at Trin. Coll., Cambridge; LL.B., 1871; Barrister (Inner Temple), 1874; M.P. for South Edinburgh since 1900; *suc. to the Baronetcy*, 25 March 1892. He *m.*, 15 Oct. 1889, at St. Peter's, Eaton sq., Pimlico, Gertrude, 3d and yst. da. and coheir of the Hon. Gowran Charles VERNON (yr. s. of the 1st BARON LYVEDEN), by Caroline, da. of John Nicholas FAZAKERLEY, of Burwood, Surrey. She was *b.* 16 June 1860.

Family Estates.—These, in 1883, consisted of 6,777 acres in Wigtownshire, worth £11,100 a year. *Principal Seat.*—Lochnaw Castle, near Stranraer, co. Wigtown.

KEITH:

cr. 28 July 1629;

sealed 8 May 1630(a);

dormant, apparently, after 14 Feb. 1771.

I. 1628. SIR WILLIAM KEITH, of Ludquhairn, only s and h. of Sir William KEITH, of the same, by Margaret, sister of George, 5th EARL MARISCHAL [S.], da. of William KEITH, *styled* LORD KEITH, suc. his father before 1625 and was *cr. a Baronet* [S.] 28 July 1629, the patent being sealed 8 May 1630(a) with rem. to heirs male whatsoever, no grant or seizin of lands in Nova Scotia however being recorded. He was a Royalist and was Col. of horse in Hamilton's "engagement." He *m.* (—). He *d.* before 1660.

II. 1655? SIR ALEXANDER KEITH, Baronet [S. 1629], of Ludquhairn aforesaid, 2d but only surv. s. and h.(c) *suc. to the Baronetcy* on the death of his father. He *m.* Margaret, da. of Alexander BANNERMAN, of Elsick, co. Kincardine.

III. 1680? SIR WILLIAM KEITH, Baronet [S. 1629], of Ludquhairn aforesaid, s. and h., *suc. to the Baronetcy* on the death of his father. He *m.* (—), da. and coheir of George SMITH, of Rapness in the Orkneys, by Anne, da. of Patrick GRAHAM, of Inchbraikie. He *d.* before her. His widow *m.* Sir Robert MURRAY, of Abercairny.

IV. 1700? SIR WILLIAM KEITH, Baronet [S. 1629], of Ludquhairn aforesaid, s. and h., *b.* about 1669. *suc. to the Baronetcy* on the death of his father; was, from 1716 to 1726, Governor of Pennsylvania in North America. He *m.* (—), da. of (—) NEWBERRY. He *d.* 18 Nov. 1749, aged 80.

(a) Milne's List; and Laing's List, in which last he is called "Knight." The creation is sometimes given as 28 *June*.

(b) This William was 6th in descent from John Keith, of Innerugy, 2d son of Sir Edward Keith, Marischal of Scotland.

(c) His eldest son, Sir William Keith, was much in favour with Charles I, by whom he was, though a young man, made Knight Marischal [S.]. He *d.* s.p. and v.p.

V. 1749, to 1771. SIR ROBERT KEITH, Baronet [S. 1629], s. and h., *suc. to the Baronetcy*, 18 Nov. 1749. He served in the Prussian service, under his cousin, the well-known Field-Marshal Keith, in Russia, Poland, Germany, Turkey, and Sweden, becoming a Lieut.-Colonel, and was subsequently (after the Marshal's death in 1758) in the Danish service, in which he became Major-General, and Commandant of Hamburg. He *m.* in or before 1751, Margaret Albertina Conradina, only da. of Ulrich Frederich VON SUCHIN, Envoy from the King of Poland (Elector of Saxony) to the court of Russia, by Elizabeth, da. of Peter VON LITH, Envoy from the Czar of Russia to the Court of Prussia. He *d.* 14 Feb. 1771, when the *Baronetcy* became *dormant*.(a)

SAINT ETIENNE, *or* DE LA TOUR:

cr. 30 Nov. 1629 (b)

dormant or *extinct* probably about 1660.

I. 1629. "SIR CLAUDE SAINT ETIENNE, Knight, Seigneur de la Tour and Uuarse" sometimes spoken of as "CLAUDE DE LA TOUR," a native of France, who had rendered Sir William Alexander, great assistance in the settlement of the colony of Nova Scotia, was *cr. a Baronet* [S.] by patent, dat. at Whitehall, 30 Nov. 1629, with rem. to the heirs male of his body(b), the said patent, however, not being recorded in the *Registrum Preceptorum cartarum pro Baronettis Novæ Scotiæ*, or in the Great Seal Register [S.]. He, together with his son Charles (who was similarly created 12 May 1630) received, 30 April 1630, a grant of lands, presumably 16,000 acres each, in Nova Scotia, entitled respectively the Barony of St. Etienne and the Barony of De la Tour(c), on condition that they, their heirs and successors should be "good and faithful vassals" of the King of Scotland. This condition he ceased to fulfil (thereby apparently, forfeiting the said grant) when he took part with the French, on their entry into Nova Scotia after the treaty of St. Germain (29 March 1632) by whom he was made Gov.-Gen. of the province, another Frenchman, named D'Aulney, being subsequently added as a co-partner with him. He apparently was dead before 13 May 1649, when Charles, his son and successor (see next below) is called "Lord of De la Tour in France."

II. 1645? to 1660? SIR CHARLES SAINT ETIENNE, Baronet [S. 1629], s. and h., who, v.p., as "CHARLES SAINT ETIENNE, Esquire, Seigneur de St. Denniscourt and Baigneux" had already been *cr. a Baronet* [S.] by patent dat. at Whitehall, 12 May 1630,(b) in like manner as his father, with whom he received grant of lands in Nova Scotia, as above stated(c). He *suc. to the Baronetcy* conferred on his father, apparently before 13 May 1649, when as "Lord of De la Tour in France and Knight Baronet of Scotland" he, for £2,084 to be redeemed 20 Feb. 1652, mortgages the Fort La Tour and plantation near the mouth of the St. John's river, as the same was purchased, 30 April 1630, by Sir Claude St. Etienne, of Sir William Alexander. This fort he had held for many years against the French, when they, according to their construction [or misconstruction] of the treaty of St. Germain (29 March 1632) invaded Nova Scotia. He made good his title to these premises when in England in 1656. On his death, *both of his Baronetcies* appear to have become *dormant* or *extinct*.

(a) He had two sons: (1), Frederick William Keith, *b.* 7 Oct. 1751, Lieut. in the Danish Guards; (2), Robert George Keith, *b.* 6 Oct. 1752. Of these, however, nothing more is known. They possibly *d.* unm. and before their father.

(b) The patent of 30 Nov. 1629; an abstract of that of the Baronetcy [S.], 12 May 1630 and the grant of lands, dat. 30 April 1630 are given in Banks's account of Nova Scotia Baronets [*Baronia Anglica concentrata*, vol. ii, pp. 210-248] from which work the description of these grantees and the particulars of their career are also taken. The same dates of creation are given in Laing's List, "on the authority of former lists."

(c) No Seizin of these lands is recorded in Banks's Lists.

HANNAY, *or* AHANNAY:

cr. 31 March 1630;(a)

dormant, 1689—1783, and again since 1842.

I. 1630. ROBERT HANNAY, *or* AHANNAY, of Mochrum, co. Kirkcudbright, "Knight,"(a) whose parentage is unknown, was appointed Clerk of the Nichells [I.] by Privy Seal, 19 Oct. 1629 (patent 11 Dec. 1631), which office he surrendered 30 May 1639, and was *cr. a Baronet* [S.] 31 March 1630,(a) the patent, however, not being in the Great Seal Register, [S.] with rem. to heirs male whatsoever, and with a grant of, presumably, 16,000 acres in Nova Scotia, of which he does not appears to have had seizin.(b) He *m.* (—), da. of (—) STEWART. He *d.* 8 and was *bur.* 24 Jan. 1657/8 in Dublin. Funeral entry [I.]. Admon. 29 Nov. 1658 [I.] to his s., Sir Robert Hannay. His widow *d.* 22 March and was *bur.* 27 March 1662 in Christ Church, Dublin. Funeral entry [I.].

II. 1658 to 1689. SIR ROBERT HANNAY, Baronet [S. 1630], s. and h., *suc. to the Baronetcy* 8 Jan. 1657/8; was a Captain of Foot [I.] 1661. He *d.* s.p.,(c) presumably unm.,(d) and was *bur.* at St. Michan's, Dublin, 30 April 1689,(e) when the *Baronetcy* appears to have remained *dormant* for nearly 100 years.

* * * * * * * *

III. 1783. SIR SAMUEL HANNAY, Baronet(f) [S. 1630] of Kirkdale, co. Galloway, was served and retoured heir male of the 1st Baronet, 26 Sep. 1783, and *assumed the Baronetcy* accordingly. He was s. and h. of William HANNAY, of Kirkdale aforesaid, by Margaret da. of the Rev. Patrick JOHNSTON, of Girthon, which William is said to have been(g) s. of Samuel, s. of William, s. of Patrick, s. of another Patrick, s. of John, s. of Alexander HANNAY, who purchased Kirkdale, in 1532, and who was uncle to Patrick HANNAY, of Sorbie, ancestor of the first Baronet. He *m.* in 1768, Mary, da. of Robert MEAD. He *d.* 11 Dec. 1790. Admon. Jan. 1791. Admon. of his widow, March 1800.

IV. 1790 to 1842. SIR SAMUEL HANNAY, Baronet(f) [S. 1630], s. and h., *b.* 12 Aug. 1772, *suc. to the Baronetcy*,(f) 11 Dec. 1790; was in the service of the Emperor of Austria, holding an official post at Vienna, where he *d.* s.p.m. (presumably unm.) 1 Jan. 1842, when the *Baronetcy* became *dormant*.

(a) Laing's List, in which he is called "Knight," though in Milne's List, where no date of creation is given, he is called "Esquire of the body."

(b) Banks's Lists.

(c) Of his two sisters and coheirs one *m.*, as his 1st wife, Sir George Acheson, 3d Baronet [S. 1628], who *d.* 1685, aged 55; while the other, Jane, *m.* firstly, before May 1645, Charles (Coote), 1st Earl of Mountrath [I.], secondly, Sir Robert Reading, Baronet [I.], and *d.* Nov. 1684.

(d) "The Lady Elinor Hanna" *bur.* 4 Jan. 1673 at St. Mary's, Reading, may possibly have been his wife.

(e) G. D. Burtchaell, of Ulster's office, Dublin, has kindly supplied most of the information in this article.

(f) According to the retour of 1783.

(g) Playfair's *Baronetage* [S.] but the number of generations in 200 years [1581-1783] seems excessive.

STEWART:

cr. 18 April 1630(a)

cancelled 7 June 1632.

I. 1630, to 1632. JAMES (STEWART), LORD STEWART OF OCHILTREE [S.], who had been so *cr.* 9 June 1615 was *cr. a Baronet* [S.] 18 April 1630,(a) but being shortly afterwards "under a criminal processe" (b) the patent was cancelled, 7 June 1632, before it passed the Great Seal Register [S.]. There is no record of any grant or seizin of lands in Nova Scotia. For further particulars of him, see *Peerage*.

FORBES:

cr. 20 April 1630.(c)

I. 1630. WILLIAM FORBES, of Craigievar and Fintray, co. Aberdeen, 1st s. and h. of William FORBES, of the same, Merchant, (who had purchased Craigievar in 1610, and who finished building the Castle there), by Margaret, da. of Nicol UDWARD, Provost of Edinburgh, suc. his father in Dec. 1627, and was *cr. a Baronet* [S.] 20 April 1630,(c) the patent, however, not being recorded in the Great Seal Register [S.], with rem. to heirs male whatsoever, and with a grant of, presumably, 16,000 acres in Nova Scotia, of which he does not appear to have had seizin(d). He was M.P. [S.] for Aberdeenshire, 1639-41; 1644, and 1645-46; was Sheriff of Aberdeen, 1647; commanded a troop of horse in the Parliamentary service and held various public offices for that party during the Civil War. He *m.*, in or before 1636, Bethia, 2d da. of Sir Archibald MURRAY, 1st Baronet [S. 1628], by Margaret, da. of (—) MAULE. He *d.* 1648. His widow *m.* Sir Alexander FORBES, of Tolquhoun.

II. 1648. SIR JOHN FORBES, Baronet [S. 1630], of Craigievar and Fintray aforesaid, 1st s. and h., *b.* 1636, *suc. to the Baronetcy* in 1648; was known as "Red Sir John" and as a man of great energy. He was M.P. [S.] for Aberdeenshire, 1689, and 1689-1702. He *m.* in or before 1659, Margaret, da. of (—) YOUNG, of Auldbar. He *d.* 1703.

III. 1703. SIR WILLIAM FORBES, Baronet [S. 1630], of Craigievar and Fintray aforesaid, 1st s. and h., *b.* 1660, *suc. to the Baronetcy* in 1703. He *m.* 16 Oct. 1684, Margaret, 1st da. of Hugh ROSE, of Kilravock, by Margaret, da. of Sir Robert INNES, of Innes.

IV. 1730? SIR ARTHUR FORBES, Baronet [S. 1630], of Craigievar and Fintray aforesaid, 6th but 1st surv. s. and h.(e); *b.* 1709, *suc. to the Baronetcy* on the death of his father; was M.P. for Aberdeenshire, 1732-47. He *m.* firstly, in 1729, Christian, 1st da. of (—) ROSS, of Arnage, Provost of Aberdeen. She *d.* s.p. He *m.* secondly, in 1750, Margaret, widow of John BURNETT, of Elrick, co. Aberdeen, da. of (—) STRACHAN, of Balgall. He *d.* 1 Jan. 1773.

(a) Laing's List, where it is stated to be "given on the authority of former lists."

(b) Laing's List, as in note "a" above. In 1631 he was imprisoned for having made, but failed to establish, a charge of high treason against the Marquess of Hamilton [S.].

(c) Laing's List; Milne's List, in which last these words are added: "No document before bot ane old list."

(d) Banks's Lists.

(e) One of his elder brothers, Hugh Forbes, the 2d s. and for a long time the heir ap. of his father, *m.* Jane, da. of James (Ogilvy), Earl of Finlater [S.], but *d.* s.p. and v.p. before 1722.

V. 1773. SIR WILLIAM FORBES, Baronet [S. 1630], of Craigievar and Fintray aforesaid, 2d but 1st surv. s. and h., by 2d wife, *b.* 1755, *suc. to the Baronetcy* 1 Jan. 1773. He *m.* 7 June 1780, at Sempill house, Sarah, 1st da. of John (SEMPILL), 13th LORD SEMPILL [S.], by Janet, da. of Hugh DUNLOP, of Bishoptoun. She *d.* 8 Dec. 1799 at Fintray House. He *d.* 15 Feb. 1816 in his 68th year.

VI. 1816. SIR ARTHUR FORBES, Baronet [S. 1630], of Craigievar and Fintray 1st s. and h., *b.* 1784; sometime an officer in the 7th Hussars; *suc. to the Baronetcy*, 15 Feb. 1816. He *d.* unm. 1823.

VII. 1823. SIR JOHN FORBES, Baronet [S. 1630], of Craigievar and Fintray aforesaid, br. and h., *b.* 2 July 1785; was sometime a Judge in the East India Company's service; *suc. to the Baronetcy*, 1823. He *m.* 24 May 1824, Charlotte Elizabeth, 3d da. of James Ochoncar (FORBES), 17th LORD FORBES [S.], by Elizabeth, da. and h. of Walter HUNTER, of Polmood. He *d.* 16 Feb. 1846 at Fintray House, aged 60. His widow *d.* 5 Feb. 1883, in her 83d year, at 26 Albyn place, Aberdeen.

VIII. 1846. SIR WILLIAM FORBES, Baronet [S. 1620], of Craigievar and Fintray aforesaid, 1st s. and h., *b.* at Fintray House, 20 May 1836, *suc. to the Baronetcy*, 16 Feb. 1846; ed. at Eton; sometime, 1854-57, Lieut. Coldstream Guards, serving in the Crimean campaign; Capt. 9th Aberdeenshire Rifle Volunteers, 1859-61 and subsequently Hon. Col. thereof. He *m.* firstly, 23 June 1858, at Clapham, Surrey, Caroline Louisa, only da. of Sir Charles FORBES, 3d Baronet [1873] of Newe, by Caroline, da. of George BATTYE. She was divorced in Dec. 1861(a). He *m.* secondly, 18 Nov. 1862, at St. James' Westm., Frances Emily, 7th and yst. da. of Sir Robert John ABERCROMBY, 5th Baronet [S. 1636], by Elizabeth Stephenson, da. of Samuel DOUGLAS, of Netherlaw. She was living when he *suc. to the Peerage* as LORD SEMPILL [S.] on the death, 5 Sep. 1884, of his cousin, Mary Jane, *suo jure* BARONESS SEMPILL [S.]. In that Peerage this *Baronetcy* then *merged* and still so continues; see *Peerage*.

MURRAY:

cr. 20 April or 2 Oct., and sealed 4 Dec. 1630;(b)

sometimes, 1794—1811, MURRAY-PULTENEY.

I. 1630. WILLIAM MURRAY, of Dalrene, *i.e.*, Dunerne, co. Fife, s. and h. ap. of William MURRAY, of Dunerne aforesaid, by his 1st wife, Marjorie SCHAW (which William, last named, was 4th and yst. s. of Andrew MURRAY, of Blackbarony) was *cr. a Baronet* [S.], 20 April or 2 Oct., the patent being sealed 4 Dec. 1630(b), but not recorded in the Great Seal Register [S.], with a grant of, presumably, 16,000 acres in Nova Scotia, called the Barony of New Dunearn, of which he had seizin in the said month of Dec. 1630.(c) He, who had suc. his father, 25 Dec. 1628, purchased the lands and Barony of Newton, in Midlothian. He *m.* 27 July 1620 at Kensington, Mary, 2d da. of William (ALEXANDER), 1st EARL OF STIRLING [S.], by Janet, da. and coheir of Sir William ERSKINE. He *d.* in or before 1641. Will conf. 4 March 1641.

(a) She *m.* 19 June 1862, Septimus E. Carlisle, and *d.* 11 Dec. 1872.

(b) "No charter of this Baronetcy is known to be on record, except in an instrument of sasine, where a charter of creation is narrated, the date of which is 20 April 1630" [Burke's *Baronetage*, 1901]. The date of the creation is 2 Oct. and that of the sealing, 4 Dec. 1630, in Milne's List. In Laing's List the date is also 2 Oct. 1630, it being there stated to be given "on the authority of former lists."

(c) Banks's Lists.

II. 1641? SIR WILLIAM MURRAY, Baronet [S. 1630], of Newton aforesaid, 1st s. and h., *suc. to the Baronetcy* on the death of his father. He *m.* (contract 3 Feb. 1644) Jane, da. of Patrick (MURRAY), 1st LORD ELIBANK [S.], by his 4th wife, Helen, da. of Sir James LINDSAY.

III. 1670? SIR WILLIAM MURRAY, Baronet [S. 1630], of Newton aforesaid, 1st s. and h., *suc. to the Baronetcy* on the death of his father. He *m.* (—) Marion CRICHTON.

IV. 1700? SIR WILLIAM MURRAY, Baronet [S. 1630], of Newton aforesaid, only s. and h., *suc. to the Baronetcy* on the death of his father. He *d.* s.p.s.

V. 1730? SIR JAMES MURRAY, Baronet [S. 1630], of Hilhead, cousin and h. male, being 2d s. of James MURRAY, of Outerston, by Magdalen, da. and h. of John JOHNSTON, of Polton, which James last named was 4th and yst. s. of the 1st Baronet. He, who was Receiver General of the Customs [S.], *suc. to the Baronetcy* on the death of his cousin. He *m.* Marian, da. of James NAIRN. He *d.* s.p. at Edinburgh, 14 Feb. 1769.

VI. 1769. SIR ROBERT MURRAY, Baronet [S. 1630], nephew and h. male, being only s. of Colonel William MURRAY, by Anne, da. of Hosea NEWMAN, which William was yr. br. of the late Baronet, being 3d and yst. s. of James MURRAY, of Polton abovenamed. He was Receiver Gen. of the Customs [S.], by resignation of his uncle, on whose death in 1769 he *suc. to the Baronetcy*. He is said to to have *m.* firstly, 22 June 1750, Janet, 4th da. of Alexander (MURRAY), 4th LORD ELIBANK [S.], by Elizabeth, da. of George STIRLING, of Edinburgh. She *d.* 9 Aug. 1759. He *m.* secondly, Susan, da. of John RENTON, of Lamerton, by Susan, da. of Alexander (MONTGOMERIE), EARL OF EGLINGTON [S.]. He *d.* 21 Sep. 1771.

VII. 1771. SIR JAMES MURRAY, *afterwards* (1794-1811) MURRAY-PULTENEY, Baronet [S. 1630], 1st s. and h. by 1st wife, *b.* about 1755; *suc. to the Baronetcy* 21 Sep. 1771, having entered the army that year; served in America, 1775; was at the capture of St. Lucia, 1778; Adjutant-General to the troops in Flanders, 1793-94; Col. of the 18th Foot, 1794; becoming finally Lieut.-General, 1799. He was M.P. for Weymouth, 1790 till his death; was P.C., 30 March, 1807, and Secretary at War, 1807-09. Having *m.*, 23 July 1794, Henrietta Laura, *suo jure* BARONESS BATH, *afterwards* COUNTESS OF BATH, only da. and h. of Sir William JOHNSTONE, *afterwards* PULTENEY, 5th Baronet [S. 1700], by his 1st wife, Frances, da. and eventually sole heir of Daniel PULTENEY, he assumed the name of PULTENEY, his wife having inherited the vast estates, formerly belonging to William (PULTENEY) EARL OF BATH. She, who was *b.* 6 Dec. 1766, and who was *cr.* a Baroness 23 July 1792, and a Countess 26 Oct. 1803, *d.* at Brighton 14 and was *bur.* 23 July 1808 (with her parents) from Bath House, Picadilly, in Westm. Abbey, aged 41. Will pr. Aug. 1808. He *d.* s.p., 26 April 1811, from the bursting of a powder flask at Buckenham, co. Norfolk. Will pr. 1811, and again May 1825.(a)

VIII. 1811. SIR JOHN MURRAY, Baronet [S. 1630], br. of the half-blood and h., being s. of the 6th Baronet, by his 2d wife. He was *b.* about 1768; entered the army, 1788; served in Flanders, 1793-94; was in command in India, 1800-05; was tried, Jan. 1815, by court-martial for his conduct at Tarragona, in May 1813, but acquitted of all but "error in judgment," and

(a) He is said to have left £600,000 to his brother of the half-blood, John Murray, afterwards the 8th Baronet, and £200,000 to William Murray, another such brother, afterwards the 9th Baronet. The Pulteney estates which he enjoyed seventeen years (for he held them for life after his wife's death) were valued at £40,000 a year.

became Col. of the 56th Foot in 1818, and a full General in 1825. He was M.P. for Wootton Bassett, 1807-11, and for Weymouth, 1811-18. He *suc. to the Baronetcy*, and to a fortune of above half-a-million, on the death of his br., 26 April 1811; was **G.C.H.**, and had the orders of the Red Eagle of Prussia and of St. Januarius of Naples. He *m.* 25 Aug. 1807, Anne Elizabeth, only da. and h. of Constantine John (PHIPPS), 2d BARON MULGRAVE [I.], by Anne Elizabeth, da. and coheir of Nathaniel CHOLMLEY, of Whitby Abbey and Howsham, co. York. He *d.* s.p. 15 Oct. 1827, at Frankfort-on-Maine. Will pr. Jan. 1828. His widow *d.* at Turin, 10 April 1848, aged 50. Will pr. Oct. 1848.

IX. 1827. SIR WILLIAM MURRAY, Baronet [S. 1630], next br. and h., *b.* in Edinburgh about 1769; ed. at Westminster; matric. at Oxford (Ch. Ch.) 14 June 1786, aged 17; B.A., 1790; M.A., 1793; was in Holy Orders; Rector of Lavington, Wilts, 1795; Rector of Lofthouse, co. York, 1802-42; *suc. to the Baronetcy*, 15 Oct. 1827. He *m.* in 1809, Esther Jane, da. of (—) GAYTON. He *d.* 14 May 1842. Will pr. Sep. 1842. His widow *d.* 6 Feb. 1875, at 52 Elgin terrace, Notting Hill, Midx., aged 83.

X. 1842. SIR JAMES PULTENEY MURRAY, Baronet [S. 1630], of Englefield Green, Berks, 1st s. and h., *b.* about 1814; *suc. to the Baronetcy*, 14 May 1842. He *d.* unm., 20 Feb. 1843, in his 30th year. Will pr. July 1843.

XI. 1843. SIR ROBERT MURRAY, Baronet [S. 1630], br. and h., *b.* 1 Feb. 1815, in London, *suc. to the Baronetcy*, 20 Feb. 1843. He *m.* firstly, 21 Aug. 1839, at St. Geo. Han. sq., Susan Catherine Saunders, widow of Adolphus COTTIN-MURRAY, 2d da. and coheir of John MURRAY, of Ardeley Bury, Herts, Commissary Gen. in the Peninsular War. She *d.* 31 April 1860. He *m.* secondly, 1 Dec. 1868, at Walcot, near Bath, Laura, widow of the Rev. William Henry CRAWFORD, of Haughley park, Suffolk, yst. da. of the Rev. Charles TAYLOR, Rector of Biddesham, Somerset. She *d.* 5 March 1893. He *d.*, at 21 Brunswick sq., Brighton, 15 April 1894, aged 79. Both were *bur.* at Brighton. His will pr. 28 Nov. 1894, at £5,156.

XII. 1894. SIR WILLIAM ROBERT MURRAY, Baronet [S. 1630], of Ashenden Lodge, in Buntingford, Herts, only s. and h., by 1st wife, *b.* 19 Oct. 1840, at Ardeley Bury aforesaid; *suc. to the Baronetcy*, 15 April 1894. He *m.* firstly, in 1868, Lastania, da. of J. FONTANILLA, of La Plata. She *d.* s.p.m. in 1873. He *m.* secondly, in 1874, Esther Elizabeth, widow of John RICKARD, of London, da. of P. BODY, of co. Sussex. She *d.* 1884. He *m.* thirdly, 22 Sep. 1885, Magdalene Agnes, da. of Gerard GANDY, of Oaklands, Windermere.

CROSBIE, *or* CROSBY:

cr. 24 April 1630;(a)

dormant in 1646 or 1647.

I. 1630, to 1646? "SIR PIERS CROSBIE, Knt., Privy Councellor of Ireland"(a), of Maryborough, in Queen's County, only s. and h. of Patrick CROSBIE, *or* CROSBY,(b) of Maryborough aforesaid, (who *d.* 22 March 1610, being elder br. of John CROSBIE, Bishop of Ardfert, 1600-21) by (—) da. of (—),(c) was *Knighted* at Theobalds, 17 July 1616; served

(a) Laing's List.

(b) Most of the information in this and the following article has been supplied by G. D. Burtchaell, of Ulster's office, Dublin.

(c) This Patrick, in his will, calls Sir Thomas Roper (afterwards, 1627, 1st Viscount Baltinglass [I.]), his brother, so possibly he *m.* Roper's sister. Roper's wife, Ann, was a da. of Sir Henry Harington.

at the relief of Rochelle, 1627, and also, as Colonel, under Gustavus Adolphus, King of Sweden; was a Gent. of the Privy Chamber to Charles I; P.C. [I.] and was *cr. a Baronet* [S.] 24 April 1630(a) (being the same date as the creation of his cousin, Walter CROSBIE), the patent, however, not being recorded in the Great Seal Register [S.], with rem. to heirs male and with a grant of, presumably, 16,000 acres in Nova Scotia, of which he appears never to have had seizin.(b) He was M.P. [I.] for Queen's County, 1634-35, and for Gowran, 1641-46, opposing the Irish policy of the Earl of Strafford, for which conduct he was condemned by the Star Chamber and confined in the Fleet prison. By patent 4 April 1637, his lands in Queen's County were erected into the Manor of Ballyfin, and those in co. Kerry into the Manor of Odorney. He *m.* firstly, after 1610, Sarah, 3d da. of Sir Patrick BARNEWALL, of Gracedieu and Turvey, co. Dublin, by Mary, da. of Sir Nicholas BAGENALL, Marshall of the Army [I.]. She *d.* s.p.m.,(c) 10 March 1617/8. Funeral certificate [I.]. He *m.* secondly, 6 March 1618/9, at St. Bride's, London, Elizabeth, Dow. COUNTESS OF CASTLEHAVEN [I.], sister of Edward, 2d VISCOUNT CAMPDEN, da. of Sir Andrew NOEL, of Dalby, co. Leicester, by Mabel, da. of Sir James HARINGTON. She was living 8 Dec. 1644. He *d.* s.p.s. between Nov. 1646 and Nov. 1647, when *the Baronetcy* became *dormant*. Will in which he directs his burial to be at St. Patrick's, Dublin, or in the Franciscan Monastery of Kildare, and in which he devises all his estate to "his lawful heir," Sir John CROSBIE, Baronet [S. 1630] dat. 17 Nov. 1646, pr. by the said Sir John, 12 Nov. 1647 at Leighlin and again in the Prerog. Court [I.] 28 Oct. 1663.

CROSBIE, *or* CROSBY:

cr. 24 April 1630(a)

I. 1630. WALTER CROSBIE, of Maryborough, 1st s. and h.(d) of John CROSBIE, Bishop of Aldfert, 1600-21, suc. his father in Sept. 1621, was Sheriff of Queen's County, 1626-27, and was *cr. a Baronet* [S.] 24 April 1630(a) (being the same date as the creation of his cousin, Piers CROSBIE), the patent, however, not being recorded in the Great Seal Register [S.], with rem. to heirs male and with a grant of, presumably, 16,000 acres in Nova Scotia, of which he appears never to have had seizin.(b) He was M.P. [I.] for Maryborough 1634-35. He *m.* firstly, Mabel, sister of Sir Valentine BROWNE, 1st Baronet [I. 1622], 4th da. of Sir Nicholas BROWNE, of Molahiffe, co. Kerry, by Sheela, da. of O'Sullivan BEARE. He *m.* secondly Anne, widow of Capt. Richard CHRISTY, da. of John TENDALL, of Dickleborough, Norfolk. He *d.* at Ballybrittas, Queen's county, 4 and was *bur.* 6 Aug. 1638, in Maryborough Church. Funeral certificate [I.]. Will dat. 21 April 1630, pr. 1 Sept. 1638 [I.]. *Inq. p.m.* 17 Jan. 1668. His widow *m.* in 1662, Walter FURLONG. Will dat. 31 Dec. 1662, pr. 4 Jan. 1662/3 [I.].

(a) Laing's List.

(b) Banks's Lists.

(c) Elizabeth, her only da., *d.* unm. 11 Jan. 1625. Funeral certificate.

(d) The 2d son, David Crosbie, of Ardfert, was ancestor of the Barons Brandon [I.] 1758-1832, who were Earls of Glandore [I.] from 1776 to 1815; the 3d son (who is often ignored and who is not to be confounded with his nephew, Sir John Crosbie, the 2d Baronet) was Sir John Crosbie, *or* Crosby, of Tullyglass, co. Down, *Knighted* at Southwick, 16 Aug. 1628, who *m.* 23 July 1638, at St. Werburgh's, Dublin, Mary, widow of Richard Fowler, of Bedfordshire, sister of Elizabeth, Countess of Devonshire, both being daughters of Edward Boughton, of Causton, co. Warwick. He *d.* s.p. 14 and was *bur.* 16 Jan. 1639/40, in Dromore Cathedral. Funeral Certificate [I.]. The will of his widow was pr. 1658 in Prerog. Court [I.] The 4th son of the Bishop was Patrick Crosbie, admitted to Gray's Inn, 7 May 1619, who is also generally ignored. [See p. 376, note "b"].

II. 1638. SIR JOHN CROSBY, *or* CROSBIE, Baronet [S. 1630], of Ballyfin, Queen's County and of Waterstown, co. Kildare, 3d but 1st surv. s. and h.,(a) by 1st wife, *suc. to the Baronetcy* 4 Aug. 1638; was indicted for high treason, 1642, and his estates forfeited during the Commonwealth. He *m.* after Oct. 1638, Elizabeth FITZGERALD.(b) He was living 1688.

III. 1695? SIR WARREN CROSBIE, Baronet [S. 1630], of Crosbie Park, co. Wicklow, grandson and h., being s. and h. of Maurice CROSBIE, of Knockmoy, Queen's County, by Dorothea, da. of John ANNESLEY, of Ballysonan, co. Kildare, which Maurice was attainted in 1688 and *d.* v.p.(c) He *suc. to the Baronetcy* on the death of his grandfather. He was Capt. in Gen. Sutton's Reg. of foot. He *m.* Dorothy, da. of Charles HOWARD, of Haverares, co. Northumberland. She *d.* 29 Oct. 1748, being drowned in the Slaney, while passing the ford, co. Carlow. He *d.* at Crosbie park 30 Jan. 1759. Will dat. 3 June 1757, pr. 21 Feb. 1759 [I.].

IV. 1759. SIR PAUL CROSBIE, Baronet [S. 1630], of Crosbie Park aforesaid, s. and h., *suc. to the Baronetcy* 30 Jan. 1759. He *m.* Mary, da. of Edward DANIEL, of Freadsom, Cheshire. He *d.* in Jarvis street, Dublin, Nov. 1773. Admon. [I.] 7 Dec. 1773 to his brother, Edward CROSBIE.

V. 1773. SIR EDWARD WILLIAM CROSBIE, Baronet [S. 1630], of Crosbie Park aforesaid, and of Viewmount, co. Carlow, s. and h.; *suc. to the Baronetcy* in Nov. 1773; was B.A. (Trin. Coll.) Dublin, 1774. He registered his pedigree in Ulster's office, 14 Feb. 1776. He *m.* by spec. lic. 14 Dec. 1790 in Granby Row, Dublin, Castiliana, widow of Capt. Henry DODD, of the 14th Dragoons, 1st da. of Warner WESTENRA, of Rossmore park, co. Monaghan, by Hester, da. of Richard (LAMBART), 4th EARL OF CAVAN [I.]. He *d.* 5 June 1798, being executed at Carlow for alleged complicity with the Irish rebels. Will pr. [I.] 1804; that of his widow pr. [I.] 1806.

VI. 1798. SIR WILLIAM CROSBIE, Baronet [S. 1630], of Bray, co. Wicklow, only s. and h., *b.* 18 May 1794 at Viewmount aforesaid; *suc. to the Baronetcy* 5 June 1798. He *m.* 30 March 1830, his cousin, Dorothea Alicia, da. of John WALSH, of Dublin, by Henrietta, 3d da. of Sir Paul CROSBIE, 4th Baronet abovenamed. He *d.* s.p., 3 Oct. 1860, at Bray. Will pr. [I.] 25 April 1861, by his widow. She *d.* 11 Feb. 1880. Her will pr. [I.] 7 April 1880.

VII. 1860. SIR WILLIAM RICHARD CROSBIE, Baronet [S. 1638], of Bedford, Beds., cousin and h. male, being only s. and h. of Edward CROSBIE, by Jane, yst. da. of James HENRY, of co. Kildare, which Edward (who *d.* 25 June 1834) was only s. and h. of Richard CROSBIE (*m.* 1780), who was 2d son of Sir Paul CROSBIE, 4th Baronet abovenamed. He was *b.* 30 Sep. 1820, and *s. to the Baronetcy* 3 Oct. 1860. He *m.* 11 April 1854, Catherine, only da. of the Rev. Samuel MADDEN, of Kells Grange, co. Kilkenny, by Thomasine, only child of Thomas DUCKET, of Graignasmutton, Queen's County. He *d.* 6 May 1877, at Bedford, aged 56. His widow *d.* 5 Dec. 1882.

(a) Of his elder brothers (1) John *d.* an infant, and (2) Maurice *d.* 18 and was *bur.* 20 April 1633 at St. Audoen's, Dublin, being then the heir apparent. Funeral certificate [I.]. [See p. 376, note "b"].

(b) She is said (by James McCullagh, Ulster King of Arms, 1759-65) to have been a da. of Thomas, Earl of Kildare [I.], but this is impossible. Possibly she may have been sister to George, 16th Earl of Kildare [I.], and yst. da. of Thomas Fitzgerald, by Frances, da. of Thomas Randolph. She is *not*, however, named in the pedigree registered in Ulster's office. [See p. 376, note "b"].

(c) Admon. [I.] 16 Jan. 1716/7, to his son.

VIII. 1877. SIR WILLIAM EDWARD DOUGLAS CROSBIE, Baronet [S. 1630], 1st s. and h., *b.* 13 Oct. 1855; sometime Lieut. in the Bedfordshire Militia; *suc. to the Baronetcy* 6 May 1877. He *m.*, 21 June, 1893, Georgina Mary, yst. da. of Thomas Edward Milles MARSH, of 34 Grosvenor Place, Bath.

SAINT ETIENNE:

cr. 12 May 1630;

dormant, or *extinct*, probably about 1660.

I. 1630, to 1660? "CHARLES SAINT ETIENNE, Esquire, Seigneur de St. Denniscourt and Baigneux," s. and h. ap. of Sir Claude SAINT ETIENNE, Baronet [S.], so cr. 30 Nov. 1629, with rem. to the heirs male of his body, was himself *cr. a Baronet* [S.] 12 May 1630, with like remainder, receiving, 30 April 1630, a grant of land in Nova Scotia, together with his father, *to whose Baronetcy he succeeded* apparently before 13 May 1649. See fuller particulars, p. 371, under the creation of 30 Nov. 1629. On his death [*Qy.* about 1660?] *both these Baronetcies* appear to have become *dormant* or *extinct*.

SIBBALD:

cr. 24 July 1630;(a) sealed 31 Dec. 1630;

dormant 1680? to 1833, and since 1846.

I. 1630. JAMES SIBBALD, of Rankeillour, in the parish of Monimail, co. Fife, 1st s. and h.(b) of Andrew SIBBALD, of the same, by Margaret, da. of George LEARMOUTH, of Balcomie, co. Fife, was *cr. a Baronet* [S.] 24 July 1630(a) the patent being sealed 30 Dec. following (but not entered in the *Reg. Precept. Cart. pro. Baronettis Novæ Scotiæ*) with rem. to heirs male whatsoever, with a grant of, presumably, 16,000 acres in Nova Scotia, entitled the Barony of Rankeillour-Sibbald in Anti Costi, having on the 28th, a Crown Charter of the same as a Regality, and having seizin thereof 3 Feb. 1631.(c) He *m.* in 1606, Margaret, 1st da. of David BARCLAY, of Cullerny. He *d.* at his house at Cupar, 21 May 1650, and was *bur.* at Cupar.(d)

II. 1650, to 1680? SIR DAVID SIBBALD, Baronet [S. 1630], of Rankeillour aforesaid, s. and h. *Knighted*, 22 June 1633, at Holyrood; *suc. to the Baronetcy*, 21 May 1650. He sold Rankeillour to Sir Archibald HOPE. On 9 Dec. 1673 he was served heir to his uncle, George SIBBALD, M.D., of Giblistoun, co. Fife. He *m.* (contract 12 Nov. 1625) Anna, da. of Sir Henry WARDLAW, of Pitreavie, by whom he had several sons,(e) who all *d.* s.p. and possibly v.p.(d); on his death the *Baronetcy* became *dormant* and remained so more than one hundred and fifty years.

* * * * * * *

(a) Laing's List.

(b) His yst. br., David Sibbald, was father of Sir Robert Sibbald, M.D., author of several antiquarian works, who died Aug. 1722, aged 81.

(c) Banks's Lists; see also Banks's *Bar. Angl. Conc.*, vol ii, p. 241.

(d) *Ex inform.* R. R. Stodart, Lyon clerk depute (1863-86).

(e) James, probably the 1st son, was *b.* 4 Nov. 1627; the 2d son, Henry Sibbald, of Giblistoun abovenamed, was living 1674 and soon afterwards sold that estate. The youngest son, George *d.* s.p., his brother, John Sibbald, being served, 27 May 1678 his heir general.

III. 1833, to 1846. SIR WILLIAM SIBBALD, Baronet([a]) [S. 1630], of Edinburgh, sometime a sailor at South Shields, was only s. of James SIBBALD, master mariner at South Shields, 2d s. of James SIBBALD, desk and trunk maker at South Shields, 3d s. of David SIBBALD, a sailor, Portioner of Canongate (who, on 28 July 1694, was served heir general of his grandfather), s. of George SIBBALD, of Canongate, only s. of George SIBBALD, of the same, formerly of Uthrogall, near Rankeillour aforesaid, who was 2d of the 1st Baronet. He, on 31 May 1831, was served heir male of Henry SIBBALD, 2d s. of the 2d Baronet, and on 18 Nov. 1833 was served heir male special to the 1st Baronet in the Barony and Regality of Rankeillour-Sibbald in Nova Scotia, whereupon he *assumed the Baronetcy*. He, on 13 May 1834 (as a Baronet) was served heir to his great grandfather,([b]) David SIBBALD. In 1846, however, these services were reduced before the Court of Session at the instance of the Lord Advocate, though it has been remarked thereon (by Maidment) that the evidence in *Sir* William's case was better than that produced by many wealthy persons left to enjoy their assumed honours without challenge.([c])

RICHARDSON:

cr. 13 Nov. 1630; sealed 31 Jan. 1631([d]);

dormant 1640, or 1642, to 1678?; 1752 to 1783? and 1821 to 1837.

I. 1630. ROBERT RICHARDSON, of Pencaitland, co. Haddington, younger s. of James RICHARDSON, of Smeaton in that county and of Pencaitland aforesaid, by Elizabeth DOUGLAS, his wife; was M.P. [S.] for co. Haddington 1630, and was *cr. a Baronet* [S.] 13 Nov. 1630, the patent being sealed 13 Jan. 1631,([a]) but not recorded in the Great Seal Register [S.], with apparently rem. to heirs male whatsoever, and with a grant of, presumably, 16,000 acres in Nova Scotia, entitled the Barony of Pencaitland in New Brunswick, of which he had seizin in Feb. 1631.([e]) He *m.* 4 Jan. 1610, Euphan, da. of Sir John SKENE, of Currichill, Lord Clerk Register [S.] 1594-1612. In 1634 he was old and in bad health, and, being offended with his eldest son, sold his estate to John SINCLAIR, but *d.* April 1635, within a year of this transaction, when his son reduced the sale([f]).

II. 1635, to 1640? SIR ROBERT RICHARDSON, Baronet [S. 1630], of Pencaitland aforesaid, 1st s. and h., *b.* 24 Jan. 1613, *suc. to the Baronetcy* in April 1635, and was on 30 of that month served heir general of his father, and on 30 Sep. following, heir special. He sold his estate of Pencaitland to James MACGILL, of Cranstoun Riddell. He *d.* s.p.,([g])

([a]) According to the service of 18 Nov. 1833.

([b]) In both cases it was before a respectable jury. In 1833 one of the jury was a writer to the Signet and the trial was held before George Tait, Sheriff Substitute of Edinburgh. In 1834, one of the jurors was John Melville, afterwards Knighted and sometime Lord Provost of Edinburgh.

([c]) See p. 379, note "d."

([d]) Laing's List; as also in Milne's List, where the date of the sealing is added, and the description given as "of Eister Pentland."

([e]) Banks's Lists.

([f]) *Ex inform.* R. R. Stodart, Lyon clerk depute (1863-86), as also is much else contained in this article.

([g]) His only br., Alexander Richardson had *d.* the year before him, presumably, s.p.m.

being then an "indweller in Smeaton" in 1640, or 1642, when the *Baronetcy* became *dormant* and remained so for nearly forty years.

* * * * * * * *

III. 1678? SIR JAMES RICHARDSON, Baronet [S. 1630,] of Smeaton aforesaid, cousin and h. male, being s. and h. of James RICHARDSON, of the same (*d.* 11 June 1634), by Rachel WARDLAW, which James, was s. and h. of Sir James RICHARDSON, of Smeaton aforesaid (*d.* 25 Dec. 16**), elder br. of the 1st Baronet. He, however, did not assume the Baronetcy till long after the death of the 2d Baronet, though they both were actually residents in the same parish. He was *Knighted* by Charles II, at Scone, 2 Jan. 1651, and was served heir general of his grandfather, 20 June 1656. On 25 May 1672 the testament of his 1st wife is recorded as "spouse of Sir James Richardson of Smeaton, *Knight*." Before the end of 1678, however, he *assumed the Baronetcy*, and recorded his arms as "*Knight Baronet*," though (oddly enough) the badge of Nova Scotia was omitted. He *m.* firstly, before 1649, Anne MCGILL, whose will is recorded 25 May 1672. He *m.* secondly, Helen, widow of Sir John HAMILTON, of Redhouse, co. Haddington, formerly Helen RICHARDSON, spinster, probably one of the two sisters and coheirs of the 2d Baronet.([a]) He *d.* 1680. His widow *d.* 1688.

IV. 1680. SIR JAMES RICHARDSON, Baronet [S. 1630,] of Smeaton aforesaid, s. and h. by 1st wife, *suc. to the Baronetcy*, 1680. In 1707 he petitioned Parliament for protection from arrest. In 1708 he sold the estate of Smeaton. He *m.* in 1666, Margaret, 6th da. of William (KERR), EARL OF LOTHIAN [S.], by Ann, *suo jure* COUNTESS OF LOTHIAN [S.]. He *d.* 28 May 1717, at Holyrood. His widow was confirmed as his sole executrix on 29 Nov. following.

V. 1717. SIR JAMES RICHARDSON, Baronet [S. 1630], s. and h.; sometime Captain in the Scots Foot Guards, *suc. to the Baronetcy*, 28 May 1717. He *d.* s.p. 13 April 1731. Will pr. 1731.

VI. 1731. SIR WILLIAM RICHARDSON, Baronet [S. 1630], br. and h.; sometime Lieut. in Col. Kerr's Dragoons, *suc. to the Baronetcy*, 13 April 1731. He *m.* Eleanor, 1st da. of Robert HILTON, of Bishop's Auckland, by Elizabeth, da. of George CROZIER, of Newbiggin. He *d.* in England, 4 April 1747.([b])

VII. 1747, to 1752. SIR ROBERT RICHARDSON, Baronet [S. 1640], s. and h.; sometime Captain in the Royal Artillery, *suc. to the Baronetcy*, 4 April 1747. He *d.* s.p., 1752,([c]) when the *Baronetcy* again became *dormant*, and so remained for about thirty years.

* * * * * * * *

VIII. 1783? SIR JAMES RICHARDSON, Baronet([d]) [S. 1630,] having assumed the title without a service, registered arms in the Lyon office [S.], 8 Feb. 1783, as "*Sir James Richardson*, of Bellmount, in Hanover parish, Jamaica, *Baronet*, heir male of the families of Smeaton and Pencaitland." In 1768, however, no such Baronetcy is mentioned in the registration of arms (10 May 1768) to his yr. br. George RICHARDSON, who is merely described as "descended of a younger son of the family of Richardson of Smeaton." He was

([a]) This match may have been the cause of his (tardy) assumption of the Baronetcy, but it is, however, *just possible* that the heir male from 1640 to 1678 might be a son or grandson of Alexander Richardson, next elder br. of the 1st Baronet, though no such descendant can be found in any of the family pedigrees.

([b]) The will of "Sir William Richardson" is proved 1769, being, however, apparently that of a "Knight," who died at Bermondsey, 16 March 1769.

([c]) His uncle, George Richardson, Captain in Col. Handysides' Reg. of Foot, had *d.* s.p. 1748.

([d]) According to the registration of 8 Feb. 1783.

s. and h. of George RICHARDSON,([a]) Writer [S.], by Jean, da. of James WATSON, of Woodend, co. Stirling, which George was s. and h. of James RICHARDSON, Burgh Clerk of Perth (*d.* 1723), s. of James RICHARDSON, said to have been Notary Public at Forgandenny,([b]) co. Perth (but more probably at Forgan, co. Fife), who is said to have been a legitimate s. of Robert RICHARDSON, who was (undoubtedly) 2d s. of Sir James RICHARDSON, of Smeaton, Knt., br. of the 1st Baronet. He *d.* unm., 24 Nov. 1788, at Paradise, Savannah-le-Mar, Jamaica.

IX. 1788. SIR GEORGE RICHARDSON, Baronet([c]) [S. 1630], of Abingdon street, Westminster, br. and h.; sometime a naval officer in the East India Company's service, and Capt. of the ship "Pigott," when he registered arms, 10 May 1768, in the Lyon office [S.]. Was Commander of the "Ganges"; *suc. to the Baronetcy*,([c]) 24 Nov. 1788. He *m.* at Freeland, co. Perth (at some date subsequent to the birth of their sons, who, of course were legitimated [S.] thereby), Mary, da. of David COOPER, R.N. He *d.* 11 and was *bur.* 20 Dec. 1791, at St. Margaret's Westm. Will pr. Jan. 1792. His widow was *bur.* there (from Marylebone) 15 Jan. 1828, aged 76. Will pr. Feb. 1828.

IX. *bis.* 1791, to 1801. SIR JOHN RICHARDSON, Baronet([d]) [S. 1630], br.; who, denying the legitimacy of his nephews, *assumed* the *Baronetcy*([c]) in 1791. He was a Barrister at Law of the Middle Temple, London. He *d.* s.p. at Calcutta, 1801. Will pr. 1804.

X. 1791. SIR GEORGE PRESTON RICHARDSON, Baronet([c]) [S. 1630], s. and h. of Sir George abovenamed, *suc. to the Baronetcy*,([c]) 11 Dec. 1791; was a Major in the 64th Foot. He was mortally wounded at the taking of St. Lucia, 22 June 1803 and *d.* unm. 21 Oct. following in his 26th year at Barbadoes. Admon. Jan. 1805.

XI. 1803. SIR JAMES RICHARDSON, Baronet([c]) [S, 1630], br. and h.; Lieut. 17th Native Infantry. He *suc. to the Baronetcy*,([c]) 22 June 1803. He *d.* unm. in India, 8 Nov. 1804, of wounds received in Lord Lake's action. Admon. March 1808.

XII. 1804, to 1821. SIR JOHN CHARLES RICHARDSON, Baronet([c]) [S. 1630], br. and h.; *b.* about 1785; sometime Commander in the Royal Navy; *suc. to the Baronetcy*,([c]) 8 Nov. 1804, and entered and signed his pedigree at the Heralds' College, London, 15 June 1807. He *d.* s.p., in Marylebone, 12 and was *bur.* 19 April 1821, at St. Margaret's Westm., aged 36, when the *Baronetcy* became again *dormant*, and so remained for sixteen years. Will pr. 1823.

* * * * * * * *

([a]) This George is styled "Sir George Richardson, Baronet" in the service of 9 Jan. 1837, mentioned in the text below, but if he had been a Baronet, or had even so styled himself, surely his son George would not (as abovestated) have been described in 1768 as "descended of a *younger* son, etc."

([b]) In a service dated 26 Jan. 1693, of James Richardson, the Burgh Clerk of Perth to (his maternal grandmother) Janet JOHNSTON, (mother of his mother, Margaret MILLER) of Forgan, he is stated to be son of James Richardson, Notary Public in *Forgan*, not *Forganderry*, which last is a small village in Perthshire.

([c]) According to the registration of 8 Feb. 1783.

([d]) According to his own view of his heirship to the person registered as a Baronet in 1783.

XIII. 1837. SIR JOHN STEWART-RICHARDSON, Baronet([a]) [S. 1630], of Pitfour, co. Perth, cousin and h. male, being s. and h. of James RICHARDSON, of Pitfour aforesaid, by Elizabeth, 1st da. and coheir of James STEWART, of Urrard, co. Perth, which James RICHARDSON (who *d.* 26 July 1823, having assumed the supporters granted to the Baronetcy, though, apparently, not the Baronetcy itself, on the death, 12 April 1821, of the 12th Baronet), was s. and h. of John RICHARDSON, of Pitfour (who purchased that estate and *d.* 1821), who was s. of Thomas RICHARDSON, of Perth, a Baker, and "Deacon of the Bakers" of that burgh,([b]) who was s. of William RICHARDSON, of Forgandenny, co. Perth, who is stated (in the service of 1837) to have been younger s. of James RICHARDSON,([c]) Notary Public (see p. 382, line 3), to have been a legitimate s. of Robert RICHARDSON, who was (undoubtedly) 2d s. of Sir James RICHARDSON, of Smeaton, Knt., br. of the 1st Baronet. He was *b.* 1 Sep. 1797; was an Advocate [S.] 1 July 1820. He, on inheriting one-third of the estate of Urrard, being that of his maternal grandfather, assumed the name of *Stewart* before that of *Richardson*. He was served 9 Jan. 1837 heir male of Sir John Charles RICHARDSON, the 12th Baronet and of that Baronet's father, Sir George, the 10th Baronet, and on the 27 May 1837 *was entered* in Lyon's office [S.] *as a Baronet*; was Secretary to the order of the Thistle, 1843-75; was Major-Gen. of "the Royal Company of Archers" [S.] *i.e.* the Queen's body-guard. He *m.* 20 Dec. 1826, Mary da. of James HAY, of Colliepriest, Devon. He *d.* 1 Dec. 1881, at Edinburgh, aged 84. His widow *d.* there 21 July 1886 in her 79th year.

XIV. 1881. SIR JAMES THOMAS STEWART-RICHARDSON, Baronet([a]) [S. 1630], of Pitfour aforesaid, 1st s. and h., *b.* 24 Dec. 1840; sometime Captain in the 78th Highlanders; Hon. Colonel 3d Vol. Batt. of the Black Watch; Secretary to the Order of the Thistle (on the resignation of his father) 1875-95; *suc. to the Baronetcy*,([a]) 1 Dec. 1881. He *m.* 20 Oct. 1868, Harriett Georgina Alice, 2d surv. da. of Rupert John COCHRANE, of Halifax, Nova Scotia. He *d.* 14 Feb. 1895, at Pitfour Castle, aged 54. His widow living 1901.

XV. 1895. SIR EDWARD AUSTIN STEWART-RICHARDSON, Baronet([a]) [S. 1630], 1st s. and h.; *b.* 24 July 1872; Lieut. 3d Batt. Black Watch; *suc. to the Baronetcy*([a]), 14 Feb. 1895; aide-de-camp to the Gov.-Gen. of Queensland.

Seat.—Pitfour Castle, co. Perth.

MAXWELL:

cr. 25 Nov. 1630;([d])

ex. or *dormant* 1 Nov. 1647.

I. 1630, to 1647. SIR JOHN MAXWELL, of Pollok, co. Renfrew, only s. and h. of Sir John MAXWELL, of Pollok aforesaid, by his 1st wife, Margaret (*m.* 1569), da. of William CUNNINGHAM, of Caprington, was *b.* about 1583; suc. his father (who was killed at the battle of Lockerby), 7 Dec. 1593, and was *cr. a Baronet* [S.], 25 Nov. 1630,([d]) there

([a]) According to the entry in the Lyon office [S.] of 27 May 1837. As to this entry, R. R. Stodart (see p. 380, note "f") remarks:—"On which assumption [*i.e.*, that of the Baronetcy of Richardson] much has been and is said, but Sir John is as safe as anyone in such a false position can be, having had every sort of recognition."

([b]) Thomas, s. of William Richardson bap. at Forgandenny, 23 Feb. 1696, was probably this Thomas. It is difficult to see how any satisfactory proof was afforded of the parentage of the said William. There are other Richardsons in these Registers, all of them apparently obscure people.

([c]) In the pedigree lodged with his petition, this James, the "notary," is left out, and James Richardson, the town clerk (ancestor of the 8th and 9th Baronets), and William Richardson, of Forgandenny, are put as *sons* (not as grandsons) of Robert, the 2d s. of Sir James.

([d]) Laing's List, where however it is stated to be "given on the authority of former lists.

being however no record of the same in the *Reg. Precept. Cart. pro Baronettis Novæ Scotiæ*, with rem. apparently to the heirs male of his body(a) and with a grant of presumably, 16,000 acres in Nova Scotia, of which, however, he appears never to have had sasine.(b) He *m.* firstly, before he was twelve years of age(c) (contract 21 Aug. 1593), Isobel, 2d da. of Hugh (CAMPBELL), 1st LORD CAMPBELL OF LOUDOUN [S.], by his 1st wife, Margaret, da. of Sir John GORDON, of Lochinvar. She *d.* 1612. He *m.* secondly, before 1615, Grizel, widow of David BLAIR, of Adamton, da. of John BLAIR, of Blair, by Grizel, da. of Robert (SEMPILL), LORD SEMPILL [S.]. He *d.* s.p.m. 1 Nov. 1647, when the *Baronetcy* became *extinct*(a) or *dormant*.(d)

CUNINGHAM:

cr. 25 Nov. 1630; sealed 8 June 1631(e);

sometime, 1811-81, CUNINGHAM-FAIRLIE;

and, since 1881, FAIRLIE-CUNINGHAME.

I. 1630. DAVID CUNINGHAM, of Robertland, in the parish of Stewarton, co. Ayr, s. and h. of David CUNINGHAM,(f) of the same, by Margaret, da. of Patrick FLEMING, of Barochan, co. Renfrew, suc. his father in April 1619, being in Nov. following served his heir general and, in Oct. 1628, his heir special in Robertland, and was *cr. a Baronet* [S.], 25 Nov. 1630, sealed 8 June 1631,(e) but not recorded in the Great Seal Register [S], with rem. to heirs male whatsoever, and with a grant of, presumably, 16,000 acres in Nova Scotia, entitled the Barony of New Robertland, of which, however, he appears never to have had seizin.(g) He was, as "my honoured kinsman, Sir David Cuningham, of Robertland, Knt. and Baronet," appointed universal legatee and executor in the will, dated 15 Dec. 1647, of "Sir David Cuningham, of Covent Garden, co. Midx, Knt. and Baronet,"(h) which he accordingly proved 26 Aug. 1659. He was a Commissioner of Supply [S.] in 1661. He, apparently, is the "SIR DAVID CUNYNGHAME, KNT. AND BARONET. of St. Martin's in the Fields, Bachelor, aged 29," who had lic. (London), 8 June 1637, to marry at St. Faith's, "Elizabeth HARRIOTT, of the same parish, widow, aged 28, widow of James HARRIOTT, Esq.," *i.e.*, widow of James HERIOT, Jeweller to the King, da. of Robert JOYCE, Keeper of the Robes.(i) He, possibly (though more probably it was his son) *m.*, as a 2d wife, Eva,(k) sister of James, 1st EARL OF KILMARNOCK [S.], da. of James (BOYD), 8th LORD BOYD [S.], by Catharine, da. of Robert CREYKE. He *d.* between Oct. 1661 and Nov. 1671. His will, unless, indeed, it is that of his son and successor, styling himself as "of

(a) In the petition for the grant of the Baronetcy [S.] of Maxwell, of Pollok, *cr.* 25 May 1682, it was asked (though not granted) that "the title might be revived and a patent granted bearing precedence from the date of the former."
(b) Banks's Lists.
(c) Fraser's *Maxwell of Pollok*, vol. i, p. 44.
(d) He left his estate to his distant cousin, possibly his heir male, George Maxwell, of Auldhouse, a descendant of Thomas Maxwell, of Pollok, living 1440, from whom testator was 6th in descent. This George was father of John Maxwell, of Pollok *cr. a Baronet* [S.], 25 May 1682.
(e) Laing's List; Milne's List.
(f) This David, who *d.* in April 1619, was s. and h. of Sir David Cuningham (living 1597, being ancestor of the 5th and succeeding Baronets), s. of David, s. of another David, who was the 1st of Robertland, 1530, and who is said to have been a yr. s. of William Cuningham, of Craigends.
(g) Banks's Lists.
(h) See page 153, *sub.* "Cuningham."
(i) See the *History of Heriots hospital*, where this Baronet is assigned as husband to this lady.
(k) As her father was *b.* about 1600 (his elder brother, the 6th Lord was *b.* Nov. 1595), the marriage is more likely to belong to the 2d than the 1st Baronet.

Scotland, Knt. and Baronet," is dat. 8 Oct. 1661. In it he directs his burial to be at Kilmauris, with his predecessors, stating his "great debts, burthens, etc., and not mentioning any wife or child other than his "son and heir" David, who is said (possibly by mistake),(a) to have pr. the same 2 Nov. 1671.

II. 1665? SIR DAVID CUNINGHAM, Baronet [S. 1630], of Robertland aforesaid, only s. and h.; *suc. to the Baronetcy* on the death of his father. He presumably (and not his father), *m.* Eva,(b) sister of James, 1st EARL OF KILMARNOCK [S.], da. of James (BOYD), 8th LORD BOYD [S.], by Catharine, da. of Robert CREYKE. She *d.* 6 May 1665.(c) Will confirmed 20 May 1667 in the Glasgow Com. Court. He *d.* s.p.(d) before 2 Nov. 1671, when admon. was granted, he being therein styled as "Knight and Baronet of Robertland in Scotland" to "Sir James Cunningham, Knight and Baronet [*sic.*](e) uncle by the father's side and next of kin."

III. 1671? SIR ALEXANDER CUNINGHAM, Baronet [S. 1630], of Robertland aforesaid, uncle and h. male *suc. to the Baronetcy* in or before 1671. Had spec. service, in Kirkland of Kilmaurs, to his nephew David, 29 Feb. 1672, and to his brother, David, in Robertland, 21 July 1692. He was much in debt and disponed Robertland to Sir David Cuningham, 1st Baronet [S. 1702] of Milncraig. He *m.* Elizabeth, da. and coheir of the Hon. John CUNINGHAM, of Cambuskeith, a yr. s. of James, 7th EARL OF GLENCAIRN [S.]. He was dead in 1696.

IV. 1690? to 1708? SIR DAVID CUNINGHAM, Baronet [S. 1630], s. and h. *suc. to the Baronetcy* on the death of his father. He was insolvent and was a prisoner in the Tolbooth of Ayr. In 1696 was released by Parliament and had authority to dispose of all his estates for his creditors. Was accused of many frauds, as also of an endeavour to murder his father. He *m.* Elizabeth, widow of James CUNINGHAM, *styled* LORD KILMAURS, 2d da. and coheir of William (HAMILTON), 2d DUKE OF HAMILTON [S.], by Elizabeth, da. and coheir of James (MAXWELL), EARL OF DIRLETON [S.]. He was living, Aug. 1705, but *d.* s.p.m.,(f) probably soon afterwards when *the Baronetcy* became *dormant* for about 70 years.

* * * * * * *

V. 1778. SIR WILLIAM CUNINGHAM, Baronet(g) [S. 1630], of Auchinskeith in Riccarton, cousin and h. male, being s. and h. of William CUNINGHAM, of Auchinskeith aforesaid, by (—), da. of (—) MACILVEIN, of Grimmet, co. Ayr, which William, who *d.* June 1727, was s. and h. of John

(a) This date of probate (2 Nov. 1671) is also that of the admon. of "Sir David Cunningham, Baronet, of Robertland," *i.e.* (presumably) the *second* Baronet [S.] The admon. *de bonis non* to the will of Sir David Cuningham, the English Baronet [1642], pr. 26 Aug. 1659 by Sir David Cuningham, the 1st Baronet [S.] of Robertland, is granted 4 March 1674/5, "to Sir James Cuningham, Knight, administrator of Sir David Cuningham, of Robertland in Scotland, Knight and Baronet deceased, son of David Cuningham, of Robertland aforesaid, who was exor. and principal legatee of Sir David Cuningham, of Auchinharvey." The administration thus mentioned can apparently be no other than that of 2 Nov. 1671, *i.e.*, that of the 2d Baronet, as assigned to him in the text.
(b) See p. 384, note "k."
(c) Burke's Baronetage for 1901.
(d) Euphemia, his only sister *m.* James (Livingstone), 1st Viscount Kilsyth [S.], who *d.* 7 Sep. 1661.
(e) The word "Baronet" is probably a mistake, and he is not so designated, 4 March 1674/5, see note "a" above. This James was a yr. br. of Alexander, who (as in the text) suc. their nephew as the 3d Baronet.
(f) Diana, his da. and h. *m.* Thomas Cochrane, of Polkelly, co. Ayr, who *d.* s.p. 1694.
(g) According to the service of 3 Aug. 1778.

CUNINGHAM, of Wattieston, who was s. and h. of Christierne CUNINGHAM, yr. br. to Sir David CUNINGHAM, of Robertland, father of the 1st Baronet, to whom and to whose brothers the said Christierne, in 1619, was "Tutor." He suc. his father in June 1727, to whom he was served h. general, 19 March 1734; had sasine of Inchbean and other lands, 12 Oct. 1764, and was served heir male of his great great grandfather, Sir David CUNINGHAM, of Robertland, 3 Aug. 1778, when he *assumed the Baronetcy*, as cousin and h. male of the 1st Baronet, grandson of Sir David last named. He *m.* in 1741, Margaret, da. of William FAIRLIE, of Fairlie, co. Ayr. He *d.* 25 Oct. 1781. His widow subsequently, in 1803, suc. her br., Alexander FAIRLIE, in the family estates, and became heir-of-line of the family of MURE, of Rowallan. She *d.* 1811.

VI. 1781. SIR WILLIAM CUNINGHAM, afterwards (on his mother's death), CUNINGHAM-FAIRLIE, Baronet(a) [S. 1630], of Fairlie aforesaid, s. and h. *suc. to the Baronetcy*,(a) 25 Oct. 1781. He *m.* firstly, Anne, da. of Robert COLQUHOUN, of the Island of St. Christopher's. He *m.* secondly, Marianne, da. of Sir James CAMPBELL, 3d Baronet [S. 1668], of Aberuchill, by his 2d wife, Mary Anne, da. of Joseph BURN. He *d.* at Fairlie House, 15 Oct. 1811. His widow *m.* James HATHORN and *d.* s.p.

VII. 1811. SIR WILLIAM CUNINGHAM-FAIRLIE, Baronet(a) [S. 1630], of Fairlie House aforesaid, s. and h., *suc. to the Baronetcy*,(a) 15 Oct. 1811. He *m.* 21 May 1818, Anne, da. of Robert COOPER, of Woodbridge. co. Suffolk. He *d.* s.p., 1 Feb. 1837. His widow *d.* 21 Dec. 1873.

VIII. 1837. SIR JOHN CUNINGHAM-FAIRLIE, Baronet(a) [S. 1630], of Fairlie House aforesaid, br. and h. *b.* 29 July 1779. He *suc. to the Baronetcy*,(a) 1 Feb. 1837, and registered arms as a Baronet in the Lyon office, 13 Dec. 1837. He *m.* 8 Aug. 1808, Janet Lucretia, da. of John WALLACE, of Cessnock and Kelly, co. Renfrew. He *d.* s.p. 28 Feb. 1852, at Fairlie House, in his 73d year. His widow, who, after his death, resumed her patronymic of WALLACE, *d.* 25 June 1877, at Mabie House, co. Kirkcudbright, aged 95.

IX. 1852. SIR CHARLES CUNINGHAM-FAIRLIE, Baronet(a) [S. 1630], of Fairlie House aforesaid, br. and h., *b.* 22 Sep. 1780 in Scotland; sometime in the East India Company's service. He *suc. to the Baronetcy* 28 Feb. 1852.(a) He *m.* 10 June 1806, Frances, 3d da. of Sir John CALL, 1st Baronet [1791], by Philadelphia, 3d da. and coheir of William BATTY, M.D. She *d.* at Pisa, 12 May 1848. He *d.* 1 June 1859, at 34, Thurloe Square, Brompton, Midx., aged 78.

X. 1859. SIR ARTHUR PERCY CUNINGHAM-FAIRLIE, Baronet(a) [S. 1630], of Fairlie House aforesaid, s. and h., *b.* 22 Oct. 1815, at Forston House, Dorset, *suc. to the Baronetcy*,(a) 1 June 1859. About 1870 he sold the estate of Fairlie. He *m.* 5 Feb. 1839, Maria Antonia, 6th da. of William Bowman FELTON, of Sherbrook, Canada East, a member of Parliament in Quebec. He *d.* at Monaco, in the Riviera, 21 Sep. 1881, aged 65. His widow, who was *b.* 23 March 1820, *d.* 9 Jan. 1897, aged 76, at 8 Grosvenor street.

XI. 1881. SIR CHARLES ARTHUR FAIRLIE-CUNINGHAME, Baronet(a) [S. 1630], of Garnock House, Ryde, in the Isle of Wight, 1st s. and h., *b.* 2 Jan. 1846, at Dieppe, educated at Cheltenham College and Trinity College, Cambridge; Lieutenant in the Ayrshire Yeomanry, 1865-75; *suc. to the Baronetcy*,(a) 21 Sep. 1881, when (the estate of Fairlie having been sold) he assumed the name of FAIRLIE-CUNINGHAME in lieu of that of CUNINGHAM-FAIRLIE. He *m.* 7 Nov. 1867, Caroline Madelina, 2d da. of William Fordyce BLAIR, of Blair Dalry, co. Ayr, Capt. R.N., by Caroline Isabella, da. of John SPROT. He *d.* s.p.m. 27 Dec. 1897 in his 52d year, at the Hotel Victoria, Northumberland Avenue, Strand. His widow living 1901.

(a) See p. 385, note "g."

XII. 1897. SIR ALFRED EDWARD FAIRLIE-CUNINGHAME, Baronet(a) [S. 1630], of Dawlish, co. Devon, br. and h., *b.* 20 April 1852, at Dieppe, assumed (like his brother) in 1881, the name of FAIRLIE-CUNINGHAME in lieu of that CUNINGHAM-FAIRLIE; *suc. to the Baronetcy*,(a) 27 Dec. 1897. He *m.* 12 Nov. 1885, Arabella Annie, only da. of Frederick CHURCH, an officer R.N., by Emma, da. of the Rev. Theobald WALSH, of Grimblethorpe Hall, co. Lincoln, and of Bridge House, Dawlish, co. Devon.

CUNINGHAM:

supposed to have been cr. about 1630;

ex. or *dormant* about 1670.

I. 1630? to 1670? "SIR WILLIAM CUNINGHAM, of Capringtoun" [*i.e.*, Caprington in the parish of Riccarton, co. Ayr], appears in Milne's List of Scotch Baronets without any date and with the remark that the creation is "only in ane old list."(b) No record thereof is in the Great Seal Register [S.], and no grant of lands in Nova Scotia is known, and the probability is it never existed. The person indicated was, doubtless, SIR WILLIAM CUNINGHAM, of Capringtoun, or Caprington, s. and h. of William CUNINGHAM, of the same, by Agnes, da. of Sir Hugh CAMPBELL, of Loudoun. He suc. his father, between 1602 and 1618; was *Knighted* before 31 July 1618. He had several charters of lands under the Great Seal, 1619-37, and was, according to the above account *cr. a Baronet* [S.] probably about 1630. He was at first on the side of the Parliament and was one of their Commissioners in 1640 and 1641, but subsequently joined Montrose; was fined £1,500 and imprisoned in Edinburgh Castle in 1646 to 1647. By these fines and by his own extravagance he ruined his estate, from which he was finally evicted by his creditors, who sold the same. He *m.* Margaret, 2d da. of James (HAMILTON), 1st EARL OF ABERCORN [S.] by Marion, da. of Thomas (BOYD), 5th LORD BOYD [S.]. Her will as that of "Dame Isabel Hamilton, spouse to Sir William Cuningham, Knight," pr. at Edinburgh, 4 May 1642. He *d.* s.p.m. and probably s.p., when the *Baronetcy* (if indeed it ever existed) became *extinct* or *dormant*.

WARDLAW:

cr. 5 March 1630/1; sealed 14 April 1631(c).

I. 1631. SIR HENRY WARDLAW, of Pitreavie, co. Fife, s. and h. of Cuthbert WARDLAW, of Balmule, was *b.* 1565; suc. his father in or before 1596; was Chamberlain to Anne, the Queen Consort [S.], acquired the estate of Pitreavie in 1606, which was erected into a Barony in 1627; was *Knighted* 23 Oct. 1613, at Royston and was *cr. a Baronet* [S.], 5 March 1630/1; sealed 14 April 1631(c), but not recorded in the Great Seal Register [S.], with rem. to heirs male whatsover and with a grant of, presumably, 16,000 acres in

(a) See p. 385, note "g."
(b) No such creation is mentioned in Laing's List where there are very many creations given "on the Authority of former lists."
(c) Milne's List; Laing's List,

Nova Scotia, called the Barony of Wardlaw, of which he had seizin in April 1631.(a) He *m.* Elizabeth, da. of (—) HUTTON.(b) He *d.* 5 April 1637. Will pr. at Edinburgh Commissariat, 8 Feb. 1638.

II. 1637. SIR HENRY WARDLAW, Baronet [S. 1631], of Pitreavie aforesaid, s. and h., *suc. to the Baronetcy*, 5 April 1637, and in July 1637 had seizin of the lands in Nova Scotia.(a) He *m.* Margaret, da. of DAVID BETHUNE of Balfour.(c) He *d.* 2 March 1653. Will at St. Andrew's Commissariat, 26 April 1653.

III. 1653. SIR HENRY WARDLAW, Baronet [S. 1631], of Pitreavie aforesaid, s. and h., *bap.* 24 March 1618, at Edinburgh; *suc. to the Baronetcy*, 2 March 1653; was M.P. [S.] for Fifeshire, 1661-63. He *m.* 24 April 1672, Elizabeth, da. of John SKENE, of Hallyards. Will at St. Andrew's Commissariat, 16 May 1683.

IV. 1683? SIR HENRY WARDLAW, Baronet [S. 1631], of Pitreavie aforesaid, 1st s. and h., *b.* 1674, *suc. to the Baronetcy* on the death of his father. He *m.* 13 June 1696, at Edinburgh, Elizabeth,(d) 2d da. of Sir Charles HALKETT, 1st Baronet [S. 1662], of Pitfirrane, by Janet, da. of Sir Patrick MURRAY, of Pitdennis. Will pr. at St. Andrew's Commissariat, 5 Oct. 1709; at Edinburgh, 19 March 1714.

V. 1709? SIR HENRY WARDLAW, Baronet [S. 1631], of Pitreavie aforesaid, only s. and h., *b.* 1705, *suc. to the Baronetcy* on the death of his father. He *d.* s.p.

VI. 1720? SIR GEORGE WARDLAW, Baronet [S. 1631], uncle and h. male, being 2d s. of the 3d Baronet; *b.* 1675, *suc. to the Baronetcy* on the death of his nephew. He *m.* (—) da. of (—) OLIPHANT.

VII. 1730? SIR HENRY WARDLAW, Baronet [S. 1631], only s. and h. *suc. to the Baronetcy* on the death of his father. He was "a private soldier in the 3d Reg. of the 2d Foot Guards," and, as such, made his will, 20 June, proved at St. Andrew's, 15 July 1739. He *d.* unm. between those dates.

VIII. 1739. SIR DAVID WARDLAW, Baronet [S. 1631], of Craighouse, uncle and h. male, being 4th s. of the 3d Baronet; *b.* 1678, *suc. to the Baronetcy* in 1739. He *m.* firstly, Jean, da. and h. of (—) ROLLAND, of Craighouse aforesaid, and of Drumcaple, by Christian, da. of (—) HUTTON. He *m.* secondly, Jean, da. of (—) MERCER, of Aldie, but by her had no issue.

IX. 1750? SIR HENRY WARDLAW, Baronet [S. 1631], of Craighouse aforesaid, only s. and h. by 1st wife, *suc. to the Baronetcy* on the death of his father. He *m.* Janet, da. of (—) TAYLOR. He *d.* Feb. 1782.

(a) Banks's Lists.
(b) Chalmers' *History of Dunfermline*. Her father was possibly of Edinburgh, merchant, as she is elsewhere called "da. of (—) Wilson [*sic*], of Edinburgh, merchant."
(c) Sir Henry Wardlaw, Baronet, is sometimes said to have *m.* in 1653, as a 2d wife, Margaret, da. of Sir John Henderson, of Fordell, by whom he had a da., Elizabeth. This said Margaret is also said to have secondly married (—) Hay, of Naughton.
(d) She was a Poetess and the author of the well known Scotch poem called *Hardy Knute*.

X. 1782. SIR DAVID WARDLAW, Baronet [S. 1631], s. and h., *suc. to the Baronetcy* in Feb. 1782. He *m.* Margaret, da. of Andrew SYMSON, of Broomhead, Town Clerk of Dunfermline. He *d.* 13 April 1793.

XI. 1793. SIR JOHN WARDLAW, Baronet [S. 1631], 5th and yst. but only surv. s. and h.,(a) *suc. to the Baronetcy*, 13 April 1793. He was an officer in the army, becoming finally Lieut. Col. in the 64th Reg. He *m.* Jean, sister of Admiral Sir Andrew MITCHELL, 2d da. of Charles MITCHELL, of Piteadie and Baldridge, by Margaret, da. of William FORBES, writer to the Signet. She *d.* at his house in Gayfield place, Edinburgh, 16 Feb. 1800, and was *bur.* in the family vault at Dunfermline. He *d.* s.p.m.s., 1 Jan. 1823.

XII. 1823. SIR WILLIAM WARDLAW, Baronet [S. 1631], cousin and h. male, being 1st s. and h. of Alexander WARDLAW, an officer of Excise, by Margaret, da. of (—) CAMPBELL, of Burnside, which Alexander was s. of William WARDLAW(b) (*b.* 1680), yr. br. of the 4th, 6th, and 8th Baronets, and 5th s. of the 3d Baronet. He was *b.* 1794, and *suc. to the Baronetcy*, 1 Jan. 1823. He *m.* 12 July 1782, Elizabeth, da. of George ANDERSON, in Carlungie, Angus. He was living 1823.

XIII. 1830? SIR ALEXANDER WARDLAW, Baronet [S. 1631], 3d but 1st surv. s. and h., *b.* about 1790; *suc to the Baronetcy* on the death of his father. He *d.* unm. 1833.

XIV. 1833. SIR WILLIAM WARDLAW, Baronet [S. 1631], of Chessels Court, Canongate, Edinburgh, br. and h., *b.* about 1791, at Alloa, co. Clackmannan; *suc. to the Baronetcy* in 1833. He *d.* unm. 23 Dec. 1863.

XV. 1863. SIR ARCHIBALD WARDLAW, Baronet [S. 1631], br. and h., *b.* 23 Jan. 1793, at Alloa aforesaid; *suc. to the Baronetcy* 23 Dec. 1863. He *d.* s.p. 29 Jan. 1874.

XVI. 1874. SIR HENRY WARDLAW, Baronet [S. 1631], of Balmule, near Tillicoultry, cousin and h. male, being s. and h. of James WARDLAW, of the same, by his 1st wife, Margaret, da. of John MONRO, of Dollar, which James (who *d.* 5 March 1867, aged 80) was s. of Henry WARDLAW, an officer of Excise (*d.* 21 July 1820, aged 74), who was yr. br. of William, the 12th Baronet. He was *b.* 22 March 1822; *suc. to the Baronetcy*, 29 Jan 1874. He *m.* 24 July 1845, Christina, 3d da. of James PATON. He *d.* in 1897.

XVII. 1897. SIR HENRY WARDLAW, Baronet [S. 1631], of Balmule aforesaid, 2d but only surv. s. and h., *b.* 8 Feb. 1867; *suc. to the Baronetcy* in 1897. He *m.* in 1892, Janet Montgomerie, da. of James WYLIE.

Residence.—Glendevon, Honor Oak Park, Forest Hill, co. Kent.

(a) Of his four elder brothers (1) Henry, was an officer in the army; (2) Andrew, a midshipman R.N.; (3) David, an officer in the Dragoons.
(b) The descent of the 12th and the succeeding Baronets from this William as here given, agrees with that in Foster's *Baronetage* for 1883, wherein it is stated to have been "very courteously supplied by Messrs. Duncan and Archibald, of Edinburgh, solicitors to Sir Henry Wardlaw," it being, however, added that "the information is unfortunately most meagre, and this is clearly a case for investigation prior to the title being officially acknowledged."

SINCLAIR:

cr. 2 June 1631, and sealed 18 June 1631(a);

afterwards, since 1789, EARLS OF CAITHNESS [S.].

I. 1631. JAMES SINCLAIR, of Canisbay, co. Caithness, s. and h. ap. of Sir William SINCLAIR,(b) of Canisbay aforesaid, of Mey in the said county, and of Cadboll, co. Ross, by Catherine, da. of Sir David Ross, of Balnagowan, co. Ross, was *cr. a Baronet* [S.] 2, the patent being sealed 18 June 1631, but not recorded in the Great Seal register [S.] with rem. to heirs male whatsoever, and with a grant of, presumably, 16,000 acres in Nova Scotia, called the Barony of Cannisby Sinclair, of which he had seizin with "haill gold mines within the said Barony," in July 1631.(c) He suc. his father in 1643 and had, 18 July 1643, special service to his grandfather, the Hon. George SINCLAIR, of Mey aforesaid (yr. s. of George, EARL OF CAITHNESS [S.]), in the lands afterwards erected into the Barony of Cadboll. He *m.* Elizabeth, 3d da. of Sir Patrick LESLIE, of Lindores, by Jean, da. of Robert (STEWART), EARL OF ORKNEY [S.]. He *d.* 1662.

II. 1662. SIR WILLIAM SINCLAIR, Baronet [S. 1631], of Mey and Canisbay aforesaid, s. and h.; *suc. to the Baronetcy* in 1662. He had special service, 15 April 1657 to his great uncle, Sir John(d) SINCLAIR, of Dunbeath, co. Caithness, who *d.* Sep. 1651. He *m.* (contract 4 Oct. 1648) Margaret, 2d da. of George (Mackenzie), 2d EARL OF SEAFORTH [S.], by Barbara, da. of Arthur (FORBES), 9th LORD FORBES [S.]. He was living 1670, but dead in 1685.

III. 1677? SIR JAMES SINCLAIR, Baronet [S. 1631], of Mey and Canisbay aforesaid, s. and h.; *suc. to the Baronetcy* on the death of his father. He *m.* Jane,(e) sister and (in 1698) heir of George, EARL OF CAITHNESS [S.], da. of the Hon. Francis SINCLAIR, of Keiss, Tister, and Northfield. He was unjustly ejected from the Keiss and other of his wife's estates, by the Earl of Breadalbane [S.], who claimed them under a disposition made in 1672, by George, the then Earl of Caithness [S.]. He was living 1704.

IV. 1710? SIR JAMES SINCLAIR, Baronet [S. 1631], of Mey and Canisbay aforesaid, s. and h.; *suc. to the Baronetcy* on the death of his father. He *m.* Mary, da. of James (SUTHERLAND), 2d LORD DUFFUS [S.],(f) by Margaret, da. of Kenneth (MACKENZIE), 3d EARL OF SEAFORTH [S.].

V. 1730? SIR JAMES SINCLAIR, Baronet [S. 1631], of Mey and Canisbay aforesaid, s. and h.; *suc. to the Baronetcy* in or before 1736 and was, on 11 Aug. 1736, served heir male of entail and of provision general to his father. He *m.* Margaret, da. of John SINCLAIR, of Barrack, by his 1st wife, Anne, d. of Robert SINCLAIR, of Durran. He *d.* 4 Oct. 1760.

(a) Milne's List; Laing's List.
(b) Erroneously called a Baronet by Sir Robert Gordon in his history of the Sutherland family [*Ex inform.* R. R. Stodart, Lyon Clerk Depute, 1863-86, by whom much else in this article was supplied.]
(c) Banks's Lists.
(d) This John is often, erroneously, supposed to have been *cr. a Baronet*. See note to Sir James Sinclair, 1st Baronet [S. 1704], of Dunbeath, nephew and h. male of the said John.
(e) In Douglas's *Baronage* [S.], his wife is given as "Frances, da. of Sir John Towers, of that ilk." There never was such a family. Probably it is a confusion with Jean, da. and h. of Sir John Towers, of Innerleith, who, about 1680, *m.* Sir John Sinclair, 2d Baronet [S. 1664], of Longformacus.
(f) See Fraser's *Sutherland*, contradicting the account in Wood's *Douglas' Peerage* [S.], which makes her da. of Alexander, the 1st Lord.

VI. 1760. SIR JOHN SINCLAIR, Baronet [S. 1631], of Mey and Canisbay aforesaid, s. and h., *suc. to the Baronetcy*, 4 Oct. 1760, and was, on 1 May 1765, served heir male of entail and provision special of his father in Mey, Canisbay, etc. He *m.* Charlotte, 2d da. of the Hon. Eric SUTHERLAND (who, but for his father's attainder, would have been 4th LORD DUFFUS [S.]), by Elizabeth, 3d da. of Sir James Dunbar, 1st Baronet [S. 1706], of Hempriggs. He *d.* April 1774, at Barrogill Castle, co. Caithness.

VII. 1774. SIR JAMES SINCLAIR, Baronet [S. 1631], of Mey aforesaid, s. and h., *b.* 31 Oct. 1766, at Barrogill Castle; *suc. to the Baronetcy* in April 1774, and had, on 5 Dec. 1785, special service to his father. He *m.* 2 Jan. 1784, at Thurso Castle, Jean, 2d da. of General Alexander CAMPBELL, of Barcaldine, by Helen, da. of George SINCLAIR, of Ulbster, co. Caithness. She was living, when by the death, 8 April 1789, of his distant cousin John, the 11th Earl, he became EARL OF CAITHNESS [S.]; his right, as such, being allowed 4 May 1793. In that peerage this *Baronetcy* then *merged* and still so continues.

SINCLAIR:

cr. (as alleged) 3 Jan. 1631(a);

ex. soon after 1650.

I. 1631 to 1652? SIR JOHN SINCLAIR, of Dunbeath, co. Caithness, 2d s. of the Hon. George SINCLAIR, of Mey, by Margaret, da. of William (FORBES) LORD FORBES [S.], which George was younger s. of George, EARL OF CAITHNESS [S.], is said to have been *cr. a Baronet* [S.] 3 Jan. 1631, with rem. to the heirs male of his body.(a) He was M.P. [S.] for Caithness-shire 1649-50. He *m.* firstly, before 31 July 1634 (when she was living as his wife) Christian, da. of Magnus MOWAT, of Bucholie. He *m.* secondly, Catherine (*b.* 1619), da. of Hugh (FRASER) LORD LOVAT [S.], by Isabel, da. of Sir John WEMYSS. He was living May 1650 (Act Parl.) but *d.* s.p.m.(b) probably shortly afterwards, when the *Baronetcy became extinct*.(c) His widow *m.*, as his second wife, Robert (ARBUTHNOTT) 1st VISCOUNT ARBUTHNOTT [S.], who *d.* 10 Oct. 1655. She *m.* thirdly, in 1663, Andrew (FRASER) 3d LORD FRASER [S.], who *d.* 22 May 1674.

(a) There is, however, no mention of any such creation in Milne's, Laing's, Banks's or any other List. Neither, apparently, is the supposed grantee called a Baronet in any Act of Parl. or other record. The limited remainder is an unusual one, at that date, for Nova Scotia Baronetcies, though so stated in Douglas's *Baronage* [S.], p. 252, and Playfair's *Baronetage* [S.], p. cclxviii, in which last the date of "2 Jan." is supplied.
(b) Margaret, his da. (by his 1st wife), *m.* Hugh Rose, of Kilravock, and her eldest son, Hugh Rose, inherited £10,000 from his grandfather, Sir John Sinclair; her second son, John Rose, 5,000 merks and lands of the value of 50,000 merks; and her daughter Margaret 5,000 merks.
(c) The estate of Dunbeath was inherited by his nephew and h. male, William Sinclair, s. of his brother, Alexander Sinclair, of Latheron, co. Caithness, who *d.* before 1638. This William was a Royalist, and is incorrectly spoken of as the *second* Baronet (Burke's *Baronetage*, 1841-71, and Foster's, 1883, in the "Chaos"), but never assumed that title. He was suc. in the estate of Latheron by John Sinclair, his 2d but 1st surv. s. and h., who was suc. therein by James Sinclair, his s. and h. (*d.* 1775), who was suc. therein by another James Sinclair, who *d.* unm. 1788. The estate of Dunbeath, however, was inherited by James Sinclair, *fourth* s. of William Sinclair abovenamed, who in 1704, which James was *cr. a Baronet* [S.] 12 Oct. 1704. This creation, of 1704, is unnoticed in Playfair's *Baronetage* [S.], in which it is, misleadingly, said that he "appears to have claimed and used the title of Baronet under his grand-uncle's patent" of 2 Jan. 1631.

MACLELLAN :

cr.(a) about 1631 ;

afterwards, 1633-1832, LORDS KIRKCUDBRIGHT [S.] ;

dormant 19 April 1832.

I. 1631 ? SIR ROBERT MACLELLAN, of Bombie in Galloway, s. and h. of Sir Thomas MACLELLAN of the same, by Grizell, da. of John (Maxwell), LORD HERRIES [S.], suc. his father July 1597; was Gentleman of the Bedchamber to James VI [S.], before and after his accession to the English throne, as also to Charles I; was M.P. [S.] for Wigtonshire, 1621, and was *cr. a Baronet* [S.](a) about 1631, being subsequently *cr.*, 25 June 1633, LORD KIRKCUDBRIGHT [S.], in which Peerage this *Baronetcy* then *merged*, and so continued till, on the death of the 10th holder, 19 April 1832, it became *dormant*. He *m.* three wives, as to whom, and as to other particulars about him and his successors, see *Peerage*.

GORDON :

cr. 18 and sealed 29 June 1631(b).

I. 1631. JOHN GORDON, of Embo, co. Sutherland, s. and h. of John GORDON, of the same, who, though of illegitimate descent, had acquired a great estate in that county, suc. his father 23 Nov. 1628, and was *cr. a Baronet* [S.] 18, the patent being sealed 29 June 1631,(b) but not recorded in the Great Seal Register [S.], with rem. to heirs male whatsoever, and with a grant of, presumably, 16,000 acres in Nova Scotia, entitled the Barony of New Embo, of which he had seizin in the said month of June 1631(c). In 1634 he bought the estate of Achrinnes. On 25 May 1648 he was served heir general of his father. He *m.* Margaret, da. of Hon. Robert LESLIE, of Findrassie, co. Moray, by Margaret, da. of Alexander DUNBAR, of Grange, Dean of Moray and one of the Lords of Session, which Robert was son of George, EARL OF ROTHES [S.]. He *d.* 1649, his estate being "much decayed."

II. 1649. SIR ROBERT GORDON, Baronet [S. 1631], of Embo aforesaid, s. and h.; *suc. to the Baronetcy* in 1649, and was, on 5 June 1649, served heir general. His liabilities amounted to £10,862 2s. 4d., and he was adjudged in 1649 to be imprisoned till that sum was paid. He was M.P. [S.] for Sutherlandshire, 1649-50 and 1661, being in 1663 excused from attendance, as in the King's service. He *m.* Jean,(d) da. of Robert LESLIE, of Findrassie, co. Moray, by Isabel, da. of Abraham FORBES, of Blackford. He *d.* 16 Oct. 1697.

III. 1697. SIR JOHN GORDON, Baronet [S. 1631], of Embo aforesaid, s. and h., was (v.p.) M.P. [S.] for Sutherlandshire, 1681-82, 1689 and 1689-1700, being in 1689 excused, as absent on the King's service, and being in 1693, ordered to sign the Assurance, on pain of forfeiting his seat. He *suc. to the Baronetcy*, 16 Oct. 1697. He *d.* shortly before 10 May 1701.

IV. 1701. SIR WILLIAM GORDON, Baronet [S. 1631], of Embo aforesaid, s. and h.; *suc. to the Baronetcy*, 10 May 1701, and on 10 Jan. 1721, had special service to his grandfather, in Embo, etc.(e) He *d.* 14 April 1760.

(a) The creation, without any date, is in Milne's List, being therein stated to be "in ane old list," and that "his armes as Baronet is in the Lyon's book."
(b) The date of creation in Laing's List, and that of the sealing in Milne's List.
(c) Banks's Lists.
(d) She is often, though erroneously, called a sister of Lord Duffus.
(e) He is often (erroneously) called M.P. [S.] for Cromarty and Nairn, 1741-42, but this relates to his namesake the 1st Baronet [S. 1704] of Dalpholly and Invergordon.

V. 1760. SIR JOHN GORDON, Baronet [S. 1631], of Embo aforesaid, s. and h.; *suc. to the Baronetcy*, 14 April 1760, and had, 19 Feb. 1761, special service to his father in Embo aforesaid, etc. He is said(a) to have *m.* firstly Charlotte, da. of Kenneth (SUTHERLAND) 3d LORD DUFFUS [S.]; and secondly, in 1727, Margaret, widow of James SUTHERLAND, of Pronsy, da. of William SUTHERLAND. He *d.* 24 Jan. 1779 at Embo.

VI. 1779. SIR JAMES GORDON, Baronet [S. 1631], of Embo aforesaid, 1st s. and h.; *suc. to the Baronetcy*, 24 Jan. 1779. He was a Colonel in the service of the States of Holland. He *d.* unm. at Zutphen, in Guelderland, 1786.

VII. 1786. SIR WILLIAM GORDON, Baronet [S. 1631], of Embo aforesaid, br. and h.; *b.* 1736, entered the army 1755, becoming Captain in the 19th Foot, and subsequently in the Norfolk Militia; *suc. to the Baronetcy* in 1786. He *m.* 15 June 1760, Sarah, only da. of Crosby WESTFIELD, an officer R.N.; by whom he had 14 children. He *d.* at Colchester, 7 Jan. 1804. Will proved 1804. Will of "Dame Sarah Gordon" proved 1819.

VIII. 1804, Jan. SIR JOHN GORDON, Baronet [S. 1631], of Embo aforesaid, 6th, but 1st surv. s. and h.(b) Lieut. of Engineers in the East India service, *suc. to the Baronetcy*, 7 Jan. 1804, and *d.* unm. a few months later, 12 Nov. 1804, in Prince of Wales' Island.

IX. 1804. Nov. SIR ORFORD GORDON, Baronet [S. 1631], of Embo aforesaid, only surv. br. and h., being 8th and yst. s. of the 7th Baronet; *b.* at Norwich; Capt. 78th Reg. of Foot; *suc. to the Baronetcy*, 12 Nov. 1804. He *m.* 20 Dec. 1813, Frances, da. of General Gore BROWNE, Col. 44th Reg. He *d.* 19 June 1857, at Brighton. Will proved July 1857. His widow *d.* there (24 Brunswick Square), 11 Aug. 1866, aged 72.

X. 1857 SIR WILLIAM HOME GORDON, Baronet [S. 1631], of Embo aforesaid, only s. and h., *b.* at Devonport in 1818; educated at Trinity College, Cambridge; B.A., 1839; D.L. for Sutherlandshire; *suc. to the Baronetcy*, 19 June 1857. He *m.* 26 March 1844 at Speldurst, co. Kent, Ellen Harriet, yst. da. of Bartholomew BARNEWALL, of Weymouth Street, Marylebone, by Mary, da. of John Charles LUCENA, Consul General for Portugal in London. He *d.* 18 Sep. 1876, at (the residence of his sister) 64 Upper Brunswick Place, Brighton. His widow living 1901.

XI. 1876. SIR HOME SETON GORDON, Baronet [S. 1631], of Embo aforesaid, only s. and h.; *b.* 21 March 1845; educated at Eton and at the Royal Military College of Sandhurst; Ensign 76th Foot, 1864, and subsequently in the 44th Foot, with which he served in India; retired 1869; Captain in the Glamorgan Light Infantry Militia till 1875; *suc. to the Baronetcy*, 18 Sep. 1876. He *m.* 25 Nov. 1870, at Crawley, co. Sussex, Mabel Montagu, only child of Montagu David SCOTT, of Hove in that county, by Margaret, da. of James BRIGGS, of Oaklands, Herts.

(a) Burke's *Baronetage* for 1901.
(b) Of his five elder brothers, two died in infancy, but (1) William Gordon, Major 41st Foot, *d.* 30 June 1794 in his 30th year, at St. Domingo; (2) Paulus Æmilius Gordon, Lieut. 47th Foot, *d.* in the Bahama Islands; and (3) Robert Crosby Gordon, Major 85th Foot, *d.* at Derby in 1797. A younger brother (the 7th son), Walter Gordon, Midshipman R.N., *d.* in the West Indies; all six being unm.

MACLEAN :

cr. 3 Sep. 1631, or 13 Feb. 1632 ; sealed 12 Jan. 1632.(a)

I. 1632. SIR LAUCHLAN MACLEAN, of Morvaren, or Morven, s and h. of Hector Og MACLEAN, of Duart, by his 1st wife, Jeannette, da. of Colin MACKENZIE, of Kintail; suc. his father in 1618; was M.P. [S.] for Tarbert Sheriffdom, 1628-33, and was *cr. a Baronet* [S.] 3 Sep. 1631, or 13 Feb. 1632, the patent being sealed 12 Jan. 1632,(a) but not recorded in the Great Seal Register [S.], with rem. to heirs male whatsoever, and with a grant of, presumably, 16,000 acres in Nova Scotia, entitled the Barony of New Morvaren, of which he had seizin in Feb. 1632.(b) He was a Royalist, and, as such, was at the battles of Inverlochy and (Aug. 1645) of Kilsyth. He *m.* Mary, 2d da. of Roderick MACLEOD, of Macleod, by Isabel, da. of Donald MACDONALD, of Glengarry. He *d.* 18 April 1649.

II. 1649. SIR HECTOR MACLEAN, Baronet [S. 1632], of Morven aforesaid, 1st s. and h., *b.* about 1625; *suc. to the Baronetcy*, 18 April 1649; raised 700 men of his clan for the Royal cause, with whom he was defeated and slain at the battle of Innerkeithing in 1651. He *d.* unm.

III. SIR ALLAN MACLEAN, Baronet [S. 1632], of Morven aforesaid, br. and h., *b.* about 1637; *suc. to the Baronetcy* in 1651. He *m.* Giles, 3d da. of John MACLEOD, of Macleod, by Sybilla, da. of Kenneth (MACKENZIE), 1st LORD MACKENZIE OF KINTAIL [S.]. He *d.* 1674 in his 38th year. His widow *m.* (—) CAMPBELL, of Glendaroul.

IV. 1674. SIR JOHN MACLEAN, Baronet [S. 1632], of Morven aforesaid, only surv. s. and h.; *suc. to the Baronetcy* in 1674; fought (with his clan) on behalf of the House of Stuart, at the battle of Killiecrankie (1689), and at that of Sheriffmuir in the rising of 1715. He *m.* in or before 1704, Mary, da. of Sir Æneas MACPHERSON, of Invereshie. She *d.* before him. He *d.* in or before 1719. Admon. 7 Oct. 1719, as "of Gordon Castle, Scotland," granted to a creditor.

V. 1719 ? SIR HECTOR MACLEAN, Baronet [S. 1632], of Morven aforesaid, only s. and h.; *b.* about 1704; *suc. to the Baronetcy* in or before 1719. He was arrested in Edinburgh in 1745 on suspicion of treason and imprisoned two years in London. He *d.* unm. at Paris, Jan. or Feb. 1751, aged 47,(c) when the issue male of the grantee became extinct.

VI. 1751. SIR ALLAN MACLEAN, Baronet [S. 1632], of Brolas in Mull, 3d cousin and h. male, being only surv. s. and h. of Donald MACLEAN, of Brolas aforesaid, by Isabella, da. of Allan MACLEAN, of Ardgour, which Donald (who *d.* 1750) was s. and h. of Lauchlan MACLEAN, of Brolas, by Isabella, da. of Hector MACLEAN, of Torloish, which Laughlan (*b.* 1650; M.P. [S.] for Argyleshire, 1685-86, who *d.* 1687), was s. and h. of Donald MACLEAN, also of Brolas, who was yr. br. (of the half blood) to the 1st Baronet, being s. of Hector Og MACLEAN abovenamed, by his 2d wife, Isabella, da. of Sir Archibald ACHESON. He *suc. to the Baronetcy* in 1781; was sometime Captain in the Dutch service, but afterwards served in the American war, and was finally Major in the 119th regiment. He *m.* Una, da. of Hector MACLEAN, of Coll. He *d.* s.p.m. 10 Dec. 1783. Admon. March and Aug. 1798.

(a) Milne's List for the date of sealing. The date of creation is given in Laing's List as 3 Sep. 1631, but in Douglas's *Baronage* [S.] as 13 Feb. 1632, it being there added that the charter, one to heirs male whatsoever, was in the public archives.
(b) Banks's Lists.
(c) Macfarlane's *Genealogical Collections*. In Douglas's *Baronage* [S.] he is said to have died at Rome, in Oct. 1750.

VII. 1783. SIR HECTOR MACLEAN, Baronet [S. 1632], 2d cousin and h. male, being s. and h. of Donald MACLEAN, Collector of Customs at Montego Bay, Jamaica, by his 1st wife, Mary, da. of John Dickson, of Glasgow, which Donald, was s. of John MACLEAN,(a) by Florence, da. of (—) MACLEAN, the said John being s. of Hector Og MACLEAN, yr. br. of Lauchlan MACLEAN, of Brolas, abovementioned, the grandfather of the 6th Baronet. He was an officer in the army; *suc. to the Baronetcy* 10 Dec. 1783. He *d.* s.p., probably unm., 2 Nov. 1818, at Hatfield, co. York.

VIII. 1818. SIR FITZROY JEFFREYS GRAFTON MACLEAN, Baronet [S. 1632], br. of the half blood and h., being s. of Donald MACLEAN abovenamed by his 2d wife, Margaret, da. of James WALL, of Clonea Castle, co. Waterford; entered the army 1787; served in the West Indies at the capture of Tobago, the attack on Martinique, Guadaloupe, etc., as also at the capture (1808) of the islands of St. Thomas and St. John, of which he was made Governor in 1808; became a full General in 1837 and Col. of the 54th Foot in 1841. He *suc. to the Baronetcy* 2 Nov. 1818. He *m.* firstly, Elizabeth, widow of John BISHOP, of Barbadoes, only child of Charles KIDD. She *d.* 1832. He *m.* secondly, 17 Sept. 1838, Frances, widow of Henry CAMPION, of Malling Deanery, co. Sussex, 3d da. of the Rev. Henry WATKINS, of Conisbrough. She *d.* 12 June 1843. Admon. June 1843. He *d.* 5 July 1847, at 53 Cadogan Place, Pimlico. Will pr. Aug. 1847.

IX. 1847. SIR CHARLES FITZROY MACLEAN, Baronet [S. 1632], 1st s. and h., by 1st wife; *b.* 14 Oct. 1798; ed. at Eton and at Woolwich; entered the Scots Fusileer Guards, 1816; sometime, 1832-39, Lieut.-Col. 81st Foot, and, subsequently, Military Sec. at Gibraltar; Col. in the army, 1846; *suc. to the Baronetcy*, 5 July 1847. He *m.* 10 May 1831, at Wateringbury, Kent, Emily Eleanor, 4th da. of the Hon. Jacob MARSHAM, D.D., Canon of Windsor (yr. s. of Robert, 2d Baron ROMNEY), by Amelia Frances, da. and h. of Joseph BULLOCK, of Caversfield, Oxon. She, who was *b.* 10 Feb. 1803, *d.* 12 April 1838. He *d.* 27 Jan. 1883, at West Cliff House, Folkestone, Kent, in his 85th year.

X. 1883. SIR FITZROY DONALD MACLEAN, Baronet [S. 1632], of Overblow, near Shorne, co. Kent, only s. and h., *b.* 18 May 1835; served in the Crimean war, 1854-55, being present at Alma and Sebastopol; sometime Lieut.-Col. of the 13th Hussars, and Col. of the West Kent Yeomanry Cavalry; *suc. to the Baronetcy* 27 Jan. 1883. He *m.* 17 Jan. 1872, at St. James', Piccadilly, Constance Marianne, 2d and yst. da. and coheir of George Holland ACKERS,(b) of Moreton Hall, Cheshire, by Harriett Susan, da. of Henry William HUTTON, of Beverley, co. York.

BALFOUR :

cr. 22 Dec. 1633(c),

dormant since 1793.

I. 1633. SIR JAMES BALFOUR, of Denmiln and Kinnaird, co. Fife, Lyon King of Arms [1630-54], 1st s. and h. ap. of Sir Michael BALFOUR, of Denmiln aforesaid, who was M.P. [S.] for Fifeshire, 1643-44,

(a) *Account of the Clan Maclean.*
(b) He died but three days afterwards, viz. 20 Jan. 1872, aged 59, at 15 Hyde Park terrace.
(c) Laing's List and Milne's List.

and Comptroller of the Household [S.] to Charles I., by Joanna, da. of James DURHAM, of Pitkerro, co. Forfar,(a) was *b.* 1603-04, probably at Denmiln; was *cr.* 20 April 1630, LYON KING OF ARMS [S.]; *Knighted* 2 May, and crowned 15 June following, being subsequently *cr. a Baronet* [S.] 22 Dec. 1633,(b) with rem. to heirs male whatsoever, and with a grant of, presumably, 16,000 acres in Nova Scotia, of which, however, he appears never to have had seizin.(c) He suc. his father (who *d.* aged 72) 14 Feb. 1652, and was deprived of his office of "Lyon" in 1654. He *m.* firstly Anne, da. of Sir John AYTON, of Ayton. She *d.* 1644. He *m.* secondly, early in 1645, Jean, widow of James SINCLAIR, of Stevenson, da. of Sir James DURHAM, of Pitkerro, co Forfar. She *d.*, a few months later, 19 July 1645. He *m.* thirdly, Margaret, da. of Sir James ARNOT, of Ferney, co. Fife. She *d.* 15 Dec. 1653, aged 25. He *m.* fourthly, in June 1654, Janet, da. of Sir William AUCHINLECK, of Balmanno. He, who was not only an author of several antiquarian works, but a most diligent collector of MSS., *d.* 14 Feb. 1657,(d) aged 57, and was *bur.* in the church of Abdie, co. Fife.

II. 1657. SIR ROBERT BALFOUR, Baronet [S. 1633], of Denmiln aforesaid, only surv. s. and h. by 3d wife; *b.* 1652; *suc. to the Baronetcy* 14 Feb. 1657. He *d.* s.p., probably unm., being killed in a duel, 1673, by Sir James MACKGILL, of Rankeillour.

III. 1673. SIR ALEXANDER BALFOUR, Baronet [S. 1633], of Denmiln aforesaid, uncle and h. male, being next yr. br. of the 1st Baronet. He was a graduate of St. Andrew's University 1626, and was minister of Abdie, co. Fife, 1634. He *suc. to the Baronetcy* in 1673. He *m.* Euphemia, da. of (—) CARSTAIRS. She *d.* Aug. 1634. He is sometimes said to have subsequently *m.* Janet, da. of Peter HAY, of Leys.

IV. 1680? SIR MICHAEL BALFOUR, Baronet [S. 1633], of Denmiln aforesaid, 1st s. and h.; *suc. to the Baronetcy* on the death of his father. He *m.* (—), da. of (—) AYTON, of Ayton. He *d.* Feb. 1698.

V. 1698. SIR MICHAEL BALFOUR, Baronet [S. 1633], of Denmiln aforesaid, only s. and h.; *suc. to the Baronetcy* in Feb. 1698. He *m.*, in 1698, Marjory, da. of George MONCRIEFF, of Reidie. He *d.* 1709, being probably murdered, having left his house on horseback and being never again seen. His widow *d.* 22 or 29 Aug. 1762, aged 86.

VI. 1709. SIR MICHAEL BALFOUR, Baronet [S. 1633], of Denmiln aforesaid, only s. and h.; *suc. to the Baronetcy* in 1709. He sold the estate of Denmiln in 1750, a few months before his death. He *m.* Jane, da. of (—) ROSS, of Invernethie. He d. 1750.

VII. 1750. SIR JOHN BALFOUR, Baronet [S. 1633], 1st s. and h. *suc. to the Baronetcy* in 1750. He *d.* unm. 1773.

(a) Several particulars in this article have been kindly supplied by Sir J. Balfour Paul, Lyon King of Arms, from memoranda by R. R. Stodart, Lyon Clerk Depute [1863—86], and other sources.
(b) See p. 395, note "c."
(c) Banks's Lists.
(d) So stated by R. R. Stodart (see note "a" above), but it is to be noted that the date of "14 Feb." is the same as that of the death of his father.

VIII 1773, to 1793. SIR PATRICK BALFOUR, Baronet [S. 1633], only br. and h.; *suc. to the Baronetcy* 1773, and was served heir to his brother 20 Oct. 1779. He *d.* unm. in 1793, when the *Baronetcy* became *dormant*.(a)

CUNNINGHAM, *or* CUNYNHAME;
cr. 23 Dec. 1633, sealed 22 April 1634;(b)
dormant since Feb. 1658/9.

I. 1633, to 1659. DAVID CUNNINGHAM, of Auchinharvie, in the parish of Stewarton, co. Ayr, *was cr. a Baronet* [S.] 23 Dec. 1633, the patent being sealed 22 April 1634,(b) but not entered in the Great Seal Register [S.], with remainder to heirs male whatsoever, and with a grant, presumably, of 16,000 acres in Nova Scotia, entitled the Barony of Auchinharvie, in Cape Breton, of which he had seizin in June 1634.(c) He, as "*David Cunningham of the City of London, Knight and Baronet of Scotland*," was, subsequently, *cr. a Baronet* [E.], 21 Jan. 1641/2, which dignity became *extinct* at his death, s.p.m. in Feb. 1658/9, when the *Baronetcy* [S. 1633], became *dormant*.(d) For fuller particulars of him see page 153 above, under his English creation.

VERNATE, *or* VERNATTI:
cr. 7, and sealed 30 June 1634(b);
dormant in, or shortly after, 1678.

I. 1634. SIR PHILIBERT VERNATTI,(e) of Carleton [near Snaith], co. York, br. of Sir Gabriel VERNATTI, of Hatfield in that county (*d.* 1 Oct. 1655), of Maximilian VERNATTI and Peter VERNATTI, all of them being sons of (—) VERNATTI, of Holland. received the degree of LL.D. from the Univ. of Leyden, and was incorp. as such at Oxford, 18 March 1612/3; took, with many others of his countrymen, an active part in the drainage of Hatfield Level in 1626 (of which, in 1635, he was one of the proprietors), and was *cr. a Baronet* [S.] 7, sealed 30 June 1634,(b) though not recorded in the Great Seal Register [S.], with rem. to heirs male whatsoever, and with a grant of, presumably, 16,000

(a) The heir male of the grantee must, after 1793, be sought for further back than among the descendants of his 4 brothers, Alexander (afterwards 3d Baronet), Michael, Andrew, and David. The Rev. William Balfour, 2d and yst. s. of Alexander, *d.* s.p.m. So also did Michael Balfour, of Randerston, the next br. to Alexander. The next br., Sir David Balfour, of Forret, had two sons, but the line of each ended in daughters. The yst. br., Sir Andrew Balfour, Physician and Botanist (nearly 30 years younger than the grantee), *m.* Anne Napier, but *d.* s.p.m., 10 Jan. 1692, aged 62. Colonel James William Balfour, of Trenabie, co. Orkney, in a letter, dat. 23 Oct. 1897, to the Sec. of State for Home affairs, claimed the representation of the family, as the descendant of Michael Balfour, of Garth, "all the senior branches" having (according to his statement) "died out."
(b) The date of creation is given in Laing's list; that of the sealing is in Milne's list.
(c) Banks's lists, where it is added, "Represented, as considered, by Robert Cunninghame, of Seabank."
(d) Robert Conynham, of Auchinharvie aforesaid, Physician [S.] to Charles II (whose relationship to the grantee of 1633 is unknown), was *cr. a Baronet* [S.], 3 Aug. 1673; see under that date.
(e) See *Her. & Gen.*, vol. v, pp. 146-155, for an account of this family by "Q.F.V.F.," from which the above is compiled.

acres in Nova Scotia, of which, however, he appears never to have had seizin.(a) In 1637 he was employed in the King's service. He *m.* Elizabeth, da. of Henry DENTON, of Warnell Denton, co. Cumberland, by Elizabeth, da. of William OGLETHORPE. He *d.* in Scotland between 2 May and 14 June 1643. Admon. 9 March 1648/9 and 11 Dec. 1650 to a creditor. His widow's will, as of Caversham, Oxon (directing her burial to be at Bardsey, co. York, near her mother, Elizabeth Thorpe, widow), dat. 22 Aug., pr. 4 Oct. 1666.

II. 1643, to 1680? SIR PHILIBERT VERNATTI, Baronet [S. 1684], s. and h., *suc. to the Baronetcy* in May or June 1643; was a student at the Univ. of Leyden in 1649, having been "grieved to the very heart" by the "murther of his Sacred Majesty"; was living in Batavia in 1658, and contributed a paper to the Royal Society, London, in Jan. 1677/8. He *m.* before July 1664, (—), da. of Isaac VIGNY, a Frenchman. After Jan. 1677/8 all trace of him is lost, and on his death the *Baronetcy* is presumed to have become *dormant*.

BINGHAM:
cr. 7 and sealed 30 June 1634;(b)
afterwards, since 1776, BARONS LUCAN OF CASTLEBAR [I.];
and subsequently, since 1795, EARLS OF LUCAN [I.].

I. 1634. HENRY BINGHAM, of Castlebar, Co. Mayo, 1st s. and h. of Sir George BINGHAM,(c) Governor of Sligo, by Cicely, da. of Robert MARTIN, of Athelhampton, Dorset, was *bap.* 1573 at Milton Abbas in that county; suc. his father (—); was serving in Ireland, as a Captain, in 1634; M.P. [I.] for Castlebar, 1634-35, and 1639-48, and was *cr. a Baronet* [S.], 7, sealed 30 June 1634,(b) but not recorded in the Great Seal office [S.], with rem. to heirs male whatsoever, and with a grant of, presumably, 16,000 acres in Nova Scotia, of which, however, he never appears to have had seizin.(a) He *m.* before 1625 (—), da. of John BYRNE, of Ballinclough, co. Wicklow.

II. 1640? SIR GEORGE BINGHAM, Baronet [S. 1634], of Castlebar aforesaid, s. and h., *b.* about 1625; *suc. to the Baronetcy* on the death of his father; was M.P. [I.] for Castlebar, 1661-66. He *m.* firstly (—). He *m.* secondly 1 June 1661, at St. Benet's, Paul's Wharf, London (Lic. Vic. Gen. 31 May 1661, he about 35, widower) Anne PARGITER, of St. Andrew's Holborn, widow, about 30. She *d.* a few months later. Her admon. as "of Hayes, co. Midx.," 11 Sep. 1661. He (very quickly) *m.* thirdly (Lic. Vic. Gen. 5 Dec. 1661) Rebecca (aged 24, parents deceased), 2d da. of Sir William MIDDLETON, 2d Baronet [1622], by Eleanor, da. of Sir Thomas HARRIS, 1st Baronet [1622], of Boreatton.

(a) Banks's Lists.
(b) The date of creation is given in Laing's List; that of the sealing is in Milne's List. The reason for conferring a Scotch, instead of an Irish, Baronetcy on him is (as is often the case elsewhere) not obvious.
(c) This Sir George and his br., Sir Richard Bingham, the well known Marshal of Ireland (*d.* 19 Jan. 1598, aged 70), were younger sons of Robert Bingham, of Melcombe Bingham, Dorset, who *d.* 1561, being ancestor of the family still (1900) of that place. He is confounded in Lodge's *Irish Peerage* [1789] with his cousin, Capt. George Bingham, who was murdered in Sligo Castle in 1595 [*ex inform.* G. D. Burchaell, Office of Arms, Dublin].

III. 1690? SIR HENRY BINGHAM Baronet [S. 1634], of Castlebar, aforesaid, 1st s. and h. by 1st wife; admitted to Middle Temple, London, 13 Sep. 1673; *suc. to the Baronetcy* on the death of his father; was M.P. [I.] for co. Mayo (4 Parls.) 1692-99 and 1703-14. He *m.* 4 Sep. 1677, Jane, da. of James CUFFE, of Pakenham Hall, co. Longford. He *m.* secondly, Lettice, da. of (—). He *d.* s.p.m., in or shortly before 1714. Will pr. [I.] 1714. That of his widow pr. [I.] 1728.

IV. 1714? SIR GEORGE BINGHAM Baronet [S. 1634], of Castlebar aforesaid, br. of the half blood and h. male, being son of the 2d Baronet by his 3d wife. He was an officer in the army of James II, whom, however, he deserted at the battle of Aughrim, in 1691. He *suc. to the Baronetcy* about 1714. He *m.* firstly, about 1688, Mary, da. of (—) SCOTT. He *m.* secondly, Phœbe, da. of (—) HAWKINS. He was living in 1727.(a)

V. 1730? SIR JOHN BINGHAM, Baronet [S. 1634], of Castlebar aforesaid, s. and h. by first wife; *b.* about 1690; admitted to the Middle Temple, London, 27 July 1717; *suc. to the Baronetcy* on the death of his father(a); was M.P. [I.] for co. Mayo, 1727 till his death, and Governor of that Shire. He *m.* in or before 1730, Anne, 1st da. and coheir of Agmondesham VESEY, of Lucan, co. Dublin, by Charlotte, only da. of William SARSFIELD, of Lucan aforesaid, br. to the well known General, Patrick SARSFIELD, who was *cr.* EARL OF LUCAN [I.] in 1691, by James II after his deposition. He *d.* 21 Sep. 1749, aged 60, and was *bur.* at Castlebar. His widow *d.* 1762.

VI. 1749. SIR JOHN BINGHAM, Baronet [S. 1634], of Castlebar aforesaid, 1st s. and h., *b.* 1730; *suc. to the Baronetcy* 21 Sep. 1749. He *d.* unm. 10 Oct. 1752, aged 22, and was *bur.* at Castlebar.

VII. 1752. SIR CHARLES BINGHAM, Baronet [S. 1634], of Castlebar aforesaid, br. and h., *b.* 22 Sep. 1735; *suc. to the Baronetcy* 10 Oct. 1752; was M.P. [I.] for co. Mayo, 1761-76. He *m.* 25 Aug 1760, at Bath, Margaret, da. and coheir of James SMITH, of St. Audries, co. Somerset, and Canons Leigh, co. Devon, by Grace, his wife. She was living when he was *cr.*, 24 July 1776, BARON LUCAN OF CASTLEBAR, co. Mayo [I.], being subsequently *cr.*, 1 Oct. 1795, EARL OF LUCAN [I.]. In that Barony this *Baronetcy* then *merged*, and still so continues. See *Peerage*.

MONRO, *or* MUNRO:
cr. 7 June(b) and sealed 3 July 1634.(c)

I. 1634. "Colonel HECTOR MONRO, of Foullis,"(b) co. Ross, br. and h. male of Colonel Robert MONRO, or MUNRO, of the same (who served in the Swedish service in the German wars, and *d.* s.p.m., at Ulm, in Germany, 1633), both being sons of Hector MUNRO, of Foulis (*d.* 14 Nov. 1603), by his 1st wife, Anne, da. of Hugh (FRASER), LORD LOVAT [S.], served, like his brother, in the Swedish service in the German wars, and attained the rank of Colonel, and, having suc. in 1634 to the family estates, was *cr. a Baronet* [S.] 7 June,(b) sealed 3 July 1634,(c) with rem. to heirs male whatsoever, and with a grant of, presumably, 16,000 acres in Nova Scotia, entitled the Barony of New Foulis, of which he had seizin in Aug. 1634.(d) He *m.* in 1619, Mary, sister of Donald, 1st LORD REAY [S.], da. of Hugh MACKAY, of Strathnaver, by his 2d wife, Jean, da. of Alexander (GORDON), EARL OF SUTHERLAND [S.]. He *d.* April 1635, at Hamburgh, and was *bur.* at Buckstehood, on the Elbe.

(a) John Bingham, afterwards 5th Baronet, is called "Esq." when, in 1727, elected M.P. [I.] for the Parl. which lasted the whole reign of George II.
(b) Laing's List.
(c) Milne's List.
(d) Banks's Lists.

II

II. 1635. SIR HECTOR MUNRO, Baronet [S. 1634], of Foulis aforesaid, only s. and h.; b. about 1635, and *suc. to the Baronetcy* in April of that year. He married,(a) but d. s.p. Dec. 1651, at the house of his cousin, John MACKAY, afterwards 2d Lord REAY [S.], at Durness in Strathnaver,(a) in his seventeenth year.

III. 1651. SIR ROBERT MUNRO, Baronet [S. 1634], of Foulis aforesaid, and formerly of Obsdaill, 2d cousin and h. male, being 2d but 1st surv. s. and h. of Col. John MUNRO, of Obsdaill (who served in the German wars and d. in Germany, March 1633), s. and h. of George MUNRO, of Obsdaill afsd. (d. 1589), who was br. of the half-blood, to Hector MUNRO, of Foulis abovenamed (d. 14 Nov. 1603), the father of the 1st Baronet, both being sons of Robert-More MUNRO, of Foulis, who d. 4 Nov. 1588. He was M.P. [S.] for Inverness-shire, 1649, and for Ross-shire, 1649-50. He *suc. to the Baronetcy*, and to the family estates in 1651. He m. Jean, sister and coheir of his predecessor, 1st da. of Sir Hector MUNRO, 1st Baronet [S. 1634], by Mary, da. of Hugh MACKAY, abovementioned. He d. 14 Jan. 1668.(b)

IV. 1668.(b) SIR JOHN MUNRO, Baronet [S. 1634], of Foulis aforesaid, s. and h., *suc. to the Baronetcy*, 14 Jan. 1668(b); was M.P. [S.], for Ross-shire, 1689-97, and a zealous supporter of the Revolution. He m. Agnes, 2d da. of Sir Kenneth MACKENZIE, 1st Baronet [S. 1673], of Coull, by his first wife, Jean, da. of Alexander CHISHOLM, of Comar. He d. shortly before 29 Sep. 1697.

V. 1697. SIR ROBERT MUNRO, Baronet [S. 1634], of Foulis aforesaid, s. and h., *suc. to the Baronetcy* in 1697; was M.P. [S.] for Ross-shire, 1697-1701, and a firm Presbyterian and supporter of the Protestant Succession. Sheriff of the counties of Ross and Cromarty, 1725. He m. in or before 1684, Jean, da. of John FORBES, of Culloden, by Anne, da of Alexander DUNBAR, of Grange. He d. 11 Sep. 1729. Admon. as "of Foulis," 16 Oct. 1729.

VI. 1729. SIR ROBERT MUNRO, Baronet [S. 1634], of Foulis aforesaid, s. and h., b. about 1684; served with the army in Flanders, 1705-12, as Cornet of Dragoons, and Capt. of the Royal Scots, and greatly distinguished himself as Lieut. Col. of a Highland regiment at the battle of Fontenoy in April 1745; was M.P. for the Wick Burghs (six Parls.), 1710-41; Gov. of Inverness Castle, 1715; a Commissioner for forfeited estates, 1716; *suc. to the Baronetcy* in 1729. He m. Mary, da. of Henry SEYMOUR, of Woodlands, Dorset. She d. 24 May or 11 June 1732. Admon. as "of Kilterne, co. Ross," 19 Jan. 1732/3. He d. 17 Jan. 1745/6, being slain at the battle of Falkirk, at the head of his regiment, by the insurgents. M.I. at Falkirk. Admon. as "of Foulis," 26 March 1747.

VII. 1746. SIR HARRY MUNRO, Baronet [S. 1634], of Foulis aforesaid, s. and h.; ed. at Westm. School and at the Univ. of Leyden; *suc. to the Baronetcy* 17 Jan. 1745/6; was M.P. for Ross-shire, 1746-47, and for the Wick Burghs (two Parls.), 1747-61. He m., in or before 1762, Anne, da. of Hugh ROSE, of Kilravock, co. Nairn, by his 2d wife Jean, da. of Hugh ROSE, of Broadley. He d. 12 June 1781, at Edinburgh.

VIII. 1781. SIR HUGH MUNRO, Baronet [S. 1634], of Foulis aforesaid, s. and h., b. 1763; *suc. to the Baronetcy*, 12 June 1781. He m.(c) Jane, da. of Alexander LAW, of London. She was drowned 1 Aug. 1803, while bathing in Cromarty Firth, near Foulis. He d. s.p.m., 2 May 1848, at 22 Manchester square, Marylebone, aged 85. Will pr. May 1848.

(a) Macfarlane's *Genealogical Collections*.
(b) This is the date given by Macfarlane (see note "a" above), but in Mackenzie's account of the Munro family it is said to be 1666.
(c) The legality of this marriage was questioned; but the da. and only child thereof was found by the House of Lords to be legitimate.

IX. 1848. SIR CHARLES MUNRO, Baronet [S. 1634], of Foulis aforesaid, and formerly of Culrain, co. Ross, 5th cousin and h. male, being s. and h. of George MUNRO, of Culrain aforesaid, by Margaret, da. of John MONTGOMERY, of Milmount house, co. Ross, which George (who d. 19 Dec. 1845, at Edinburgh) was s. and h. of James MUNRO, br. and h. of Gustavus MUNRO, both being sons of George MUNRO (d. 1724), s. and h. of Sir George MUNRO, Commander in Chief of the Royalist army in Ireland, all of Culrain aforesaid, which Sir George (who d. 1690), was yr. br. of Robert, the 3d Baronet, both being sons of Col. John MUNRO, of Obsdaill abovementioned, who d. in Germany, March 1633. He was b. 20 May 1795, at Culrain aforesaid; ed. at the High School and at the Univ. of Edinburgh; entered the army, 1810; Lieut. 45th Foot, 1812, receiving a medal and six clasps for his conduct (1812-14) at Rodrigo, Badajoz (where he was wounded), Salamanca, the Nive, Orthes, and Toulouse; fought in the war of Independence in South America, and was in command of a division of the Columbian army (under Bolivar) at the victory of Agnotmar. He *suc. to the Baronetcy*, 2 May 1848. He m. firstly, 20 June 1817, Amelia, da. of Frederick BROWNE, of Dublin, sometime an officer in the 14th Dragoons. She d. 14 Sep. 1849. He m. secondly, 14 Jan. 1853, Harriette, da. of Robert MIDGLEY, of Essington, co. York. She d. 17 July 1886, aged 78. He d. (five days afterwards), 22 July 1886, aged 91.

X. 1886. SIR CHARLES MUNRO, Baronet [S. 1634] of Foulis aforesaid, s. and h. by 1st wife; b. 20 Oct. 1824; sometime Capt. in the Ross-shire Militia; *suc. to the Baronetcy*, 22 July 1886. He m. 19 March 1847, Mary Anne, da. of John NICHOLSON, of Camberwell, co. Surrey. He d. 29 Feb. 1888, at Edinburgh, aged 63. His widow living there 1901.

XI. 1888. SIR HECTOR MUNRO, Baronet [S. 1634], of Foulis aforesaid, s. and h.; b. 13 Sep. 1849; Lieut. Col. Com. 3rd Seaforth Highlanders Militia; *suc. to the Baronetcy*, 29 Feb. 1888: Lord Lieut. of the counties of Ross and Cromarty. He m. 7 April 1880, Margaret Violet, 1st da. of John STIRLING, of Fairburn, co. Ross.

Family Estates.—These, in 1883, consisted of 4,458 acres in Ross-shire, worth £3,780 a year. *Principal Seats.*—Foulis Castle, near Evanton, and Ardullie Lodge, both in co. Ross.

FOULIS:

cr. 7 June, and sealed 22 July 1634;(a)

afterwards, since 1843, LISTON-FOULIS.

I. 1634. ALEXANDER FOULIS, "*fear of Colinton*," co. Edinburgh, only s. and h. ap. of Sir James FOULIS, of Colinton, Advocate [S.] 1576, and sometime [1612] M.P. [S.] for Edinburgh, by Mary, da. of Sir John LAUDER, of Hatton, was *cr. a Baronet* [S.] 7 June, sealed 22 July 1634,(a) but not recorded in the Great Seal Register [S.], with rem. to heirs male whatsoever,(b) and with a grant of, presumably, 16,000 acres in Nova Scotia, of which he had seizin in Aug. 1634.(c) He m. v.p. (settlement 30 March 1619) Elizabeth, widow of Sir John STEWART, of Bute, 1st da. and coheir of Robert HEPBURN, of Foord, co. Edinburgh. He was living 7 Aug. 1643, and probably in 1663, but was dead in 1672.(d)

(a) The date of the creation is given in Laing's List, but that of the sealing in Milne's List, in which, however, the Baronetcy is assigned [not to Alexander, but] to "Sir *James*, of Collingtoun."
(b) Douglas's *Baronage* [S.].
(c) Banks's Lists.
(d) The 2d Baronet is styled "knight" in the Parl. of 1661-63, being first called "Baronet" in the Convention of 1672.

II. 1670? SIR JAMES FOULIS, Baronet [S. 1634], of Colinton aforesaid, s. and h.; was *Knighted* v.p. 14 Nov. 1641; took part in the Civil Wars on the side of the King; was a member of the Committee of Estates 1646; was M.P. [S.] for co. Edinburgh (in ten Parls. or conventions) 1645 to 1684; was taken prisoner by Monk's forces at Alyth, 28 Sep. 1651, and carried to London; was made a Senator of the College of Justice [S.] 14 Feb. 1661, being then entitled LORD COLINTON; *suc. to the Baronetcy* on his father's death, probably about 1670(a); was a Lord of the Articles and a Lord of Justiciary [S.] 1671; P.C. [S.] 1674; Lord Justice Clerk [S.] 22 Feb. 1684. He m. firstly, Barbara, da. of Andrew AYNSLEY, a magistrate of Edinburgh. He m. secondly (contract 1 June 1661) Margaret, widow of Sir John MACKENZIE, 1st Baronet [S. 1628], of Tarbat (who d. 10 Sep. 1654), da. and coheir of Sir George ERSKINE, of Innerteil, a Lord of Session [S.]. He d. in Edinburgh, 19 Jan. 1688. His widow living 1693.

III 1688. SIR JAMES FOULIS, Baronet [S. 1634], of Colinton aforesaid s. and h. by 1st wife; was Advocate [S], 8 June 1669, and was (v.p.) a Senator of the College of Justice [S.], 10 Nov. 1674, being then entitled LORD REIDFORD; M.P. [S.] for co. Edinburgh, 1685-86, 1689 and 1689-93, when his seat was declared vacant as he had not taken the allegiance oath. He *suc. to the Baronetcy*, 19 Jan. 1688. P.C. [S.], 1702. He m. 4 Sep. 1670, Margaret da. of John BOYD, Dean of Guild, of Edinburgh. He d. 1711.

IV. 1711. SIR JAMES FOULIS, Baronet [S. 1634], of Colinton aforesaid s. and h.; was *Knighted* v.p. before 1704; M.P. [S.] for co. Edinburgh, 1704-07; *suc. to the Baronetcy* in 1711. He d. unm., July 1742.

V. 1742. SIR JAMES FOULIS, Baronet [S. 1634], of Colinton aforesaid nephew and h., being 1st s. and h. of Henry FOULIS, by Jean, da. of Adam FOULIS, of Edinburgh, Merchant, which Henry was 2d and yst. s. of the 3d Baronet. He was an Antiquary of some note, and as early as 1701, wrote a treatise on the Celtic origin of the Scots. He *suc. to the Baronetcy* in July 1742. He m. Mary, da. of Archibald WIGHTMAN, of Edinburgh, Writer to the Signet [S.]. He d. 3 Jan. 1791.

VI. 1791. SIR JAMES FOULIS, aforesaid Baronet [S. 1634], of Colinton 1st and only surv. s. and h.; *suc. to the Baronetcy*, 3 Jan. 1791, and, shortly afterwards, m., 17 June 1791, Margaret, da. of William DALLAS. He sold the estate of Colinton. He d. s.p. 1825, when the issue male of the grantee and of the grantee's father became extinct.

VII. 1825. SIR JAMES FOULIS, Baronet [S. 1634], of Woodhall, co. Edinburgh, 6th cousin and h. male. being yst. s. of William FOULIS, of Woodhall aforesaid by (—), da. of (—) CAMPBELL, of Carsebank, co. Forfar, which William (b. 6 Nov. 1732, d. June 1796), was only s. of John FOULIS of Woodhall (b. 25 Feb. 1709, d. Dec. 1732), s. of William FOULIS, also of Woodhall, Advocate [S.], 1700 (b. 20 May 1674, d. June 1737), who was yst. s.(b) of Sir John FOULIS, 1st Baronet [S. 1661], of Ravelstoun (the purchaser, in 1701, of the estate of Woodhall where he d. 5 Aug. 1707, in his 70th year), who was s. and h. of George FOULIS of Ravelstoun (b. 6 April 1606), s. and h. of George FOULIS, Master of the Mint [S.], the purchaser of the estate of Ravelstoun (d. 28 May 1633, aged 64), who was yr. br. of Sir James FOULIS of Colinton abovenamed, the father of the 1st Baronet [S. 1634], both being sons of James FOULIS of Colinton, by Agnes, da. and h. of Robert HERIOT, of Lumphoy. He was b. 9 Sep. 1770, and, having first suc. to his paternal estate of Woodhall, subsequently *suc. to the Baronetcy* in 1825. He m. 29 Aug. 1810, Agnes, 1st da. of John GRIEVE, of Edinburgh. He d. 2 May 1842, aged 71, at Woodhall house. His widow is said to have d. in 1870.(c)

(a) See p. 401, note "d."
(b) The male issue of the eldest son became extinct, 28 Jan. 1747, on the death of the only son of the 2d Baronet (grandson of the 1st Baronet), who had been executed, 15 Nov. 1746, for high treason, whereby the Baronetcy became attainted, which otherwise would have passed to the family of Foulis, of Woodhall.
(c) Foster's *Baronetage* for 1883. If 1870 was the date of her death she must have survived her marriage some sixty years.

VIII. 1842. SIR WILLIAM FOULIS, *afterwards* LISTON-FOULIS, Baronet [S. 1634], of Woodhall aforesaid s. and h., b. 27 July 1812, at Shenstone, co. Stafford; *suc. to the Baronetcy* 22 May 1842. He m. firstly, 20 June 1843, Henrietta Ramage LISTON, of Millburn Tower, co. Edinburgh, spinster, 1st da. of Ramage LISTON, Capt. R.N., great niece and testamentary heir of the Right Hon. Sir Robert LISTON, G.C.B. He thereupon assumed the name of *Liston* before that of *Foulis*. She d. 1850. He m. secondly, 7 April 1852, Mary Anne, 1st da. of Robert CADELL, of Ratho. He d. 22 Feb. 1858. His widow living 1901, at Edinburgh.

IX. 1858. SIR JAMES LISTON-FOULIS, Baronet [S. 1634], of Woodhall and Millburn Tower aforesaid, s. and h. by 1st wife; b. 3 July 1847, at Millburn Tower; *suc. to the Baronetcy* in 1858; ed. at the Royal Mil. Coll. at Woolwich; Ensign 16th Foot, 1865-66: Capt. Edinburgh Militia, 1870-76. He m. 8 Dec. 1868, Sarah Helen, 1st da. of Sir Charles Metcalfe OCHTERLONY, 2d Baronet [1823], by Sarah, da. of William P. TRIBE of Liverpool. He d. at Millburn Tower, 29 Dec. 1895, aged 48. His widow, who was b. 29 Sept. 1846, living 1901.

X. 1895. SIR WILLIAM LISTON-FOULIS Baronet [S. 1634], of Woodhall and Millburn Tower aforesaid, s. and h., b. 27 Oct. 1869; *suc. to the Baronetcy*, 29 Dec. 1895.

Family Estates.—These, in 1883, consisted of 2,804 acres in Midlothian, valued at £2,163 a year. *Principal Residences.*—Woodhall, and Millburn Tower, near Corstorphine, both in co. Edinburgh.

GIBB:

cr. 4 July 1634;(a)

dormant, probably, 8 April 1650;

but possibly assumed, 1650-1734,

and certainly assumed 1867-76.

I. 1634, to 1650. HENRY GIBB, of Falkland, but formerly of Caribber, co. Linlithgow, Groom of the Bedchamber, 2d s. of Sir John GIBB,(b) of Knock, near Dunfermline, and of Caribber aforesaid, Groom of the Bedchamber to James VI. [S.], by Isabel LINDSAY, his wife, accompanied that King to England in 1603; was naturalised 1610; obtained the estate of Caribber, 22 June 1615, from his father, but disponed it,

(a) Milne's List. There is no mention whatever of this creation in Laing's List, neither is it in Ulster's List. It is, however, in Walkley's List and in Beatson's List, being placed in each case between the creations of Munro (sealed 3 July) and Foulis (sealed 22 July), which, as it was sealed between these dates, seems to be the proper place.
(b) The whole of the information, as to the collateral relatives of the grantee, is taken from a work entitled *The Life and Times of Robert Gib, Lord of Caribber*, by "Sir George Duncan Gibb, Baronet, of Falkland and Caribber," pub. 1874, in 2 vols, 8vo, by Longman & Co., London. Its author claimed to be heir male of the grantee, but the absence of dates and of the marriages of many of the parties concerned, constitute a great defect in the pedigree, which appears mainly to rest on the following statement, said to be a copy of an entry (now lost), which, it is stated, was written (in a volume of sermons) by Thomas Gibb (who, in the text, is set forth as 4th in succession to the Baronetcy), the great grandfather of the said George Duncan Gibb. It is dated "July 24, 1744," and is as under:—"Robert Gib, of Carieber, had two sons, John and Patrick. Patrick was a Burgess of Linlithgow, and left a son, Robert, named after his grandfather. Robert had a twin son and daughter; the son was named after his grand-uncle, John Gib. John was a zealous supporter of the blessed Covenant; he was at

24 Oct. 1629, to his elder br., James GIBB,(a) of Knock; was sometime Clerk of the Signet; was Groom of the Bedchamber to Henry, Prince of Wales, and subsequently to James I and Charles I, and was *cr. a Baronet* [S.], the patent being sealed 4 July 1634(b), though not recorded in the Great Seal Register [S.], with rem. to heirs male whatsoever, but apparently without any grant of territory in Nova Scotia.(c) He acquired property at Jarrow, co. Durham. In 1645 he was on the Committee for Estates [S.], but, nevertheless, his own were sequestrated by Parl. 28 Aug. 1648. He *m.* firstly, 15 Feb. 1598, Katharine GRAY, said(d) to be a da. of the Hon. James GRAY, 2d s. of Patrick, LORD GRAY [S.] He *m.* secondly, in or before 1622 (a post nuptial settlement dat. 3 Aug. 1631), Anne, 3d da. of Sir Ralph GIBBS, of Honiton, co. Warwick, by Gertrude, da. of Sir Thomas WROUGHTON, of Broad Hinton, Wilts. He *d.* s.p.m.(e) 8 April 1650 at Falkland, and was buried at Kilgour. Admon. as "of St. Martin's in the Fields, Midx.," 18 Nov. 1650, and again 24 Nov. 1676. His widow *d.* 30 May and was *bur.* 1 June 1658, at St. Botolph's, Bishopsgate, London, in her 54th year. Will dat. 25 Feb. 1655, pr. 21 June 1658.

The assumption of the title and the right thereto, after 1650, is said(f) to be as below.

II. 1660? SIR JOHN GIBB, Baronet(f) [S. 1634], of Linlithgow, cousin and h. male, being s. and h. of Robert GIBB, of Kersiebank in Linlithgow, Burgess of that town, by (—), his wife, which Robert was s. and h. of Patrick GIBB, of Bearcrofts, co. Stirling, also a Burgess of Linlithgow, next br. to Sir John GIBB, of Knock, the father of the 1st Baronet. He was *bap.* 13 Aug. 1618, at Linlithgow, and *assumed the Baronetcy*,(f) after the Restoration, but is said to have "abandoned it when he got into trouble."(f) He fought on the side of the Covenant at Bothwell Muir, 22 June 1679. He *m.*, late in life, (—). He *d.* 1703, aged 84, at Dairsie or Cupar Fife, and was *bur.* there.

Bothwell Muir in 1679; settled at Cupar Fife; married late, and had children named John and Christian. His grandson, Thomas, married Euphem Brydie, of Leven." It is to be observed that the writer of the memorandum makes no mention of any Baronetcy, though, according to Sir G. D. Gibb's abovementioned work, he himself was entitled to it, and his father, possibly, and grandfather, certainly, assumed it.

(a) This James is called the last Gibb of Caribber, which estate he disponed 7 March 1640, to James Menteith. He died s.p.m. at Dunfermline, presumably before his brother, Henry, whom else he would have succeeded in the Baronetcy. Janet, his da. and h., *m.* in 1633, Adam French, of Thorndikes.

(b) See page 403, note "a."

(c) No such grant appears in Banks's Lists.

(d) *Query* if legitimate. Her father's marriage is ignored in Wood's *Douglas Peerage* [S.].

(e) Of his two surviving daughters and coheirs by his second wife, (1) Elizabeth, *b.* 1622, *m.* before 1653, as his 1st wife, Sir Richard Everard, 2d Baronet [1629], and *d.* before 1676; (2) Frances, *b.* 1626, *m.* firstly, about 1654, William Glanville, of Broad Hinton, Wilts (who *d.* 11 Oct. 1680, aged 78), and secondly, John Stone, of Baldwin Brightwell, Oxon, who *d.* 30 Oct. 1704, aged 78. She *d.* 6 March 1714/5, aged 89, and was *bur.* at Broad Hinton. There was a son, Charles, *bap.* 19 Dec. 1624, and *bur.* 19 Feb. 1630.

(f) The assumption or non-assumption of this Baronetcy, after the death of the grantee, is, in all cases, given on the sole authority of Sir G. D. Gibb's work [see note "b" above]. It is to be observed, however, that the proceedings taken to establish the right to the dignity at the court of Lyon King of Arms in 1868 were unsuccessful. In a letter dated 27 May 1867, signed "George Duncan Gibb, Bart.," that gentleman writes to R. R. Stodart, the then Lyon Clerk Depute, "I have established my claim to the Baronetcy as the nearest lawful heir male whatsoever and on 30 April by the advice of my Council, including the

II

III. 1703. JOHN GIBB, of Dairsie aforesaid, s. and h.; possibly, for some short period, *assumed the Baronetcy*(a). He *m.* (—). He *d.* near Dairsie 1734.

IV. 1734. THOMAS GIBB, s. and h., suc. his father in 1734, but *did not assume the Baronetcy*.(a) He, being then of Wickham, in England, *m.* 4 Oct. 1740, at Leven, Euphemia, da. of James BRYDIE, of Scoome, co. Fife. He *d.* in London, 1777 or 1778. His widow *d.* there 1782.

V. 1777? BENAIAH GIBB, of Montreal, in Canada, 1st surv. s. and h., *b.* 1756; emigrated to Montreal, 27 May 1774; suc. his father in 1777 or 1778, but *did not assume the Baronetcy*.(a) He was a "Knight of Portugal." He *m.* firstly, in or before 1793, Catharine, 4th da. of Moses CAMPBELL, 42d Highlanders, by Elizabeth COOMBS, of Albany, in North America. She *d.* Jan. 1804. He *m.* secondly, Eleanor Leech, da. of Abraham Leech PASTORIUS. She *d.* Dec. 1821. He *d.* at Montreal 18 March 1826, aged 70.

VI. 1826. THOMAS GIBB, s. and h. by 1st wife, *b.* Aug. 1793; a Captain in the Army; suc. his father 18 March 1826, but *did not assume the Baronetcy*.(a) He *m.* (his 2d cousin) Magdalen, da. of James Ellice CAMPBELL, of Hochelaga, in Canada, by Elizabeth, da. of Capt. Joseph THURBER. He *d.* of cholera, 7 Aug. 1832, aged 39. His widow, who was *b.* July 1799, *d.* March 1845.

VII. 1832, or 1867, to 1876. SIR GEORGE DUNCAN GIBB, Baronet(a) [S. 1634], s. and h., *b.* 25 Dec. 1821, at Montreal; suc. his father 7 Aug. 1832, but *did not assume the Baronetcy*(a) till thirty-five years later; was ed. at MacGill College; M.D. there 1846; L.R.C.S., Dublin, 1848; practised as a Physician at Montreal, 1849-53; and was President of the Pathological Society there, 1853; settled in London, 1853; M.R.C.P., London, 1859, and Assistant Physician to Westminster Hospital. On 30 April 1867 he *assumed* the *Baronetcy*(a), and in June 1874 (in a roll pedigree of the Gibb family, compiled by himself) he styles himself "7th Baronet, of

Solicitor Gen., Sir J. B. Karslake, I assumed the title, a record of which with my genealogy is recorded in the Court of Chancery, London. I shall be obliged if you will kindly inform me what steps must be taken to record my succession as the 3d Baronet in the Lyon office. The last Baronet died 1703." It must be observed, however, that the writer does not say where this claim was "established." The Sheriff of the county where the grantee was domiciled, or the Sheriff Court of Chancery at Edinburgh, were the two processes substituted by the Act 10 and 11 Vict. (1847-48) for the old "brieve," with its attendant "retour" by a jury. See *N. & Q.*, 3d S., vol. xii (*passim*), and 4th S., vol. i, p. 37, where Sir Duncan's "agent" mentions the *quantity* of "the evidence on which Sir Duncan relies" as "filling several volumes," but says nothing as to the *quality* thereof. In a subsequent letter, dat. 5 Dec. 1867, Sir Duncan writes "My petition for service in the Sheriff's Court is in abeyance" owing to "the destruction of a large part of the ancient borough records of Linlithgow." He adds also "with regard to the 2d Baronet, Sir John Gibb, my direct ancestor, no proof from the public records has been found that the title was recognised by the Crown. It was therefore left out in my petition for service. He assumed the title and abandoned it when he got into trouble."

(a) See page 404, note "f."

Falkland, 12th Lord of Caribber,(a) M.A., M.D., and LL.D." He *m.* Mary Elizabeth, da. of William RUMLEY, of Ayrfield house, co. Kildare. She *d.* Dec. 1861. He *d.* 16 Feb. 1876, at 1 Bryanston street, Portman square, Marylebone, aged 54, when it is believed the *assumption* of this *Baronetcy* ceased.(b)

HAMILTON:

cr. 6 Jan. 1635;(c)

afterwards, 1647-79, LORD BELHAVEN AND STENTON, [S.].

dormant, or *extinct*, 17 June 1679.

I. 1635. JAMES HAMILTON, of Broomhill, s. and h. of Claud HAMILTON(d), of the same, by Margaret, da. of James HAMILTON, of Kilbrackmont; suc. his father in 1605; was Sheriff of co. Perth; and was *cr. a Baronet* [S.], 5 Jan. 1635(c), the patent however, not being entered in the Great Seal Register [S.], with probably (at that date) rem. to heirs male whatsoever, and with a grant of, presumably, 16,000 acres in Nova Scotia, of which he never had seizin(e). He *m.* Margaret, 1st da. of William HAMILTON, of Udston, by Margaret, da. of (—) HAMILTON, of Longhermiston. He *m.* secondly Jean HAMILTON, spinster, heiress of Parkhead. He *d.* apparently before 1647.

II. 1645? to 1679. SIR JOHN HAMILTON, Baronet [S. 1635], of Broomhill aforesaid and afterwards, of Biel, s. and h. by 1st wife; *suc. to the Baronetcy*, on the death of his father, in or before 1647, and was in that year *cr.* 15 Dec. 1647, LORD BELHAVEN AND STENTON, receiving subsequently, 10 Feb. 1675 (having no male issue) a *novodamus* of that Peerage, with a spec. rem. in favour of the husband of one of his grand-daughters. He *m.* Margaret HAMILTON, spinster, illegit. da. of James (HAMILTON), 2d MARQUESS OF HAMILTON [S.], by Anne, widow (for such she remained) of John (ABERNETHY), LORD SALTOUN [S.], da. of Walter (STEWART), 1st LORD BLANTYRE [S.]. She was living 24 Oct. 1666. He *d.* s.p.m. 17 and was *bur.* 20 June 1679, in Holyrood Abbey Church, when his peerage devolved according to the spec. rem. in the *novodamus* thereof but the *Baronetcy* became *dormant* or *extinct*. For fuller particulars of him see "Peerage."

(a) The "last Gibb of Caribber" had, however, apparently died before 1650. See p. 404, note "a."

(b) In Foster's *Baronetage* for 1883, this Baronetcy is (in the "*Chaos*" of that work) assigned to the eldest s. and h. of Sir G. D. Gibb, the late holder, *viz*: "SIR JAMES CAMPBELL GIBB, formerly in the Crown lands department, Canada, and late Capt. Federal army, U.S.," of whom however no further particulars are known.

(c) Laing's List. In Milne's List, where, however, no date is given, it is said that "Sir John Hamilton, of Beill, is designed Barronet in his title of honor who was made Lord 15 Dec. 1647."

(d) This Claud was grandson of John Hamilton, of Broomhill, legitimated under the Great Seal [S.], 20 Jan. 1512/3, being one of the many illegit. brothers of James, 1st Earl of Arran [S.].

(e) Banks's Lists.

GASCOIGNE:

cr. 8 June 1635;(a)

dormant, or *extinct*, 11 Feb. 1810.

I. 1635. JOHN GASCOIGNE, of Barnbow, Lasingcroft and Parlington, co. York(b), s. and h. of John GASCOIGNE, of Parlington, (living 1584,) by Maud, da. of William ARTHINGTON, of Ardwick-in-the-street, co. York, suc. his father (or possibly in 1592 his uncle Richard GASCOIGNE) in the family estates and was *cr. a Baronet* [S.], 8 June 1635(b), the patent not being entered in the Great Seal Register [S.], with probably (at that date) rem. to heirs male whatsoever and with a grant of, presumably, 16,000 acres in Nova Scotia, of which he had seizin in Aug. 1685.(c) He *m.* in or before 1596, Anne, da. of John INGLEBY, of Lawkland, by his 2d wife Anne, da. of William CLAPHAM, of Beamsey, both in co. York. He *d.* 3 May 1637, and his widow *d.* a few weeks later, 2 or 20 June 1637.

II. 1637. SIR THOMAS GASCOIGNE, Baronet [S. 1635,] of Barnbow, etc. aforesaid 1st s. and h., *b.* about 1596; *suc. to the Baronetcy*, 3 May 1637. He entered his pedigree in the Heralds' Visitation of Yorkshire, 1666, being then aged 70. He was tried for high treason, but acquitted 24 Jan. 1679/80, (being then in his 85th year) by the court of King's Bench. He *m.* in or before 1620, Ann, da. of George SYMONDS, of Brightwell park, Oxon. She *d.* before him. He *d.* at "Lambspring," beyond the seas in or before 1686; admon. 4 Jan. 1686/7 and again 15 Jan. 1699/1700.

III. 1686? SIR THOMAS GASCOIGNE, Baronet [S. 1635], of Barnbow, etc., aforesaid, 3d but 1st surv. s. and h.; *b.* about 1623, being aged 43 in 1666, *suc. to the Baronetcy* about 1686. He *m.*, before that date, Elizabeth, da. and coheir of William SHELDON, of Beoley, co. Worcester. He *d.* s.p. 1698. Will dat. 26 Feb. 1697, pr. 4 Feb. 1699.

IV. 1698. SIR THOMAS GASCOIGNE, Baronet [S. 1635], of Barnbow, etc., aforesaid, nephew and h., being 1st s. and h. of George GASCOIGNE, of Parlington, by Anne, da. and coheir of Ellis WOODROWE, of Helperley, which George was 2d surv. s. of the 2d Baronet, but *d.* v.p. before Dec. 1682. He was *b.* about 1659, being aged 7 in 1666. He *suc. to the Baronetcy* in

(a) Laing's List only, where the date "8 June" is put within brackets.

(b) This appears to be the first of a series of *English* gentry, not connected with Scotland, on whom a Baronetcy of that kingdom was conferred. In Wotton's *Baronetage*, 1741, is "an account of such Nova Scotia Baronets as are of English families and resident in England: numbered according, to their order as Nova Scotia Baronets." These are as follow:—"71, Gascoigne, of Barnbow, Yorkshire, [1635]; 73, Pilkington, of Stainley, Yorkshire, 1635; 87, Slingsby, of Scriven, Yorkshire, [1638]; 91, Pickering, of Titchmarsh, Northamptonshire, [1638]; 92, Longueville, of Wolverton, Buckinghamshire, 1638; 95, Musgrave, of Hayton Castle, Cumberland, 1638; 96, Meredith, of Ashley Castle, Cheshire, 1639." To these may be added (1) Norton, of Cheston, co. Suffolk, 1635; (2) Widdrington, of Cairtington, co. Northumberland, 1635; (3) Bolles, of Osberton, Notts, 1635; (4) Rayney, of Wrotham, co. Kent, 1635; (5) Fortescue, of Salden, Bucks, 1635; (6) Moir, or More, of Longford, Notts, 1636; (7) Curzon, of Kedleston, co. Derby, 1636; and (8) Piers, of Stonepit, in Sele, co. Kent, 1638. The grantee of the Baronetcy [S.], of Thomson, *cr.* 20 Feb. 1635/6, is erroneously said, in Walkley's List, to have been "English." Certain *Irish* Gentry, not apparently in any way connected with Scotland, were likewise so honoured, as, for instance, the two Baronetcies granted in 1630 to the name of Crosby; in 1634, the Baronetcy of Bingham; in 1636, that of Browne of the Neale; also the three granted to the name of Bourke, the one to Macarthy, etc.

(c) Banks's Lists.

1698. He *m.* Magdalen, da. of Patricius CURWEN, of Workington, co. Cumberland. He, who was living 1712, *d.* s.p.s. in or before 1718. Admon. 3 Nov. 1718, at York. Admon. of his widow, then of St. Anne's, Westminster, 22 Feb. 1721/2, to Henry Curwen, of Workington, br. and next of kin.

V. 1718? SIR JOHN GASCOIGNE, Baronet [S. 1635], of Parlington, aforesaid, br. and h., *b.* about 1662, being aged 4 and more in 1666; admitted to Gray's Inn, 4 Dec. 1682; *suc. to the Baronetcy* about 1718. He *m.* Mary, da. and coheir of Roger WIDDINGTON, of Harbottle. He *d.* at Bath, 11 June, 1723. Will dat. 30 March 1720/1, pr. 15 Aug. 1723. at York.

VI. 1723. SIR EDWARD GASCOIGNE, Baronet [S. 1635], of Parlington aforesaid, s. and h.; *suc. to the Baronetcy*, 11 June 1723. He *m.* Mary (then a minor, whose wardship was granted to him as her husband, 23 Aug. 1728), da. and h. of Sir Francis HUNGATE, 4th Baronet [1642], of Hudleston, co. York, by Elizabeth, da. of William WELD, of Lulworth, Dorset. He *d.* at Cambray in Flanders, 31 May 1750. Will dat. 16 Sep. 1742, pr. 24 March 1750/1, at York. His widow *m.* 15 Nov. 1753, Gerard STRICKLAND, of Sizergh, co. Westmorland, who *d.* 1 Sep. 1791, aged 87. She *d.* 14 Jan. 1764.

VII. 1750. SIR EDWARD GASCOIGNE, Baronet [S. 1635], of Parlington and Hudleston aforesaid, 1st s. and h.; *suc. to the Baronetcy*, 31 May 1750. He gave, from his quarry at Hudleston, the stone for repaving York Minster. He *d.* unm. at Paris, 16 Jan. 1762. Will dat. 31 March 1758 to 11 May 1760, pr. 12 Aug. 1762.

VIII. 1762, to 1810. SIR THOMAS GASCOIGNE, Baronet [S. 1635], of Parlington aforesaid, br. and h., *b.* Feb. 1743; *suc. to the Baronetcy*, 10 Jan. 1762. He renounced the Roman Catholic faith, and read a recantation of its tenets before the Archbishop of Canterbury; was M.P. for Thirsk, 1780-84; for Malton, April to Aug. 1784; and for Arundel, Feb. 1795 to 1796. He *m.* firstly, in 1772 (—), da. of (—) Montgomery. He *m.* secondly, 4 Nov. 1784, at Aston upon Trent, Mary, widow of Sir Charles TURNER, 1st Baronet [1782], of Kirkleatham, co. York, da. of James SHUTTLEWORTH, of Gawthorp, co. Lancaster, by Mary, da. of Robert HOLDEN, of Aston Hall, co. Derby. She *d.* in childbirth at Parlington, 1 Feb. 1786. Admon. 4 April 1786, at York. He *d.* s.p.s.,(a) 11 Feb. 1810, when the *Baronetcy* became *dormant* or *extinct*. Will pr. 1810.(b)

NORTON:

cr. 18 June 1635;(c)

dormant or *extinct* in or before 1673.

I. 1635. WALTER NORTON, of Cheston, co. Suffolk,(d) and afterwards of Sibsey, co. Lincoln, Sheriff of that county, 1635-36 (being then styled, possibly erroneously, "knight"); was *cr. a Baronet* [S.], 18 June 1635,(c) the patent not being entered in the Great Seal Register [S.], with probably (at that date), rem. to heirs male whatsoever, and with a grant of, presumably, 16,000

(a) His only child, Thomas Gascoigne, *b.* 7 Jan. 1786, *d.* unm. and v.p. 20 Oct. 1809 from a fall out hunting, aged 24.

(b) Under his will the Parlington and other Gascoigne estates, went to Richard Oliver, of Castle Oliver, Ireland, the husband of Mary, eldest da. of his late wife, by her 1st husband, Sir Charles Turner abovenamed. He took the name of Gascoigne; was Sheriff for co. York 1816, and *d.* 14 April 1843, s.p.m.s. leaving two daughters and coheirs.

(c) Laing's List, but not in Milne's List.

(d) One of the Nova Scotia Baronetcies conferred on Englishmen not connected with Scotland, as to which see p. 407, note "b," under "Gascoigne."

acres in Nova Scotia, of which he had seizin in Sep. 1635.(a) He *m.* Mary, da. of Edward (STOURTON), BARON STOURTON, by Frances, da. of Sir Thomas TRESHAM, of Rushton, co. Northampton. She *d.* at Drury lane, in childbirth. 23, and was *bur.* 24 May 1633, at St. Giles' in the Fields. He *d.* in or before 1656. Admon. 22 Feb. 1655/6, as of Brackenboro', co. Lincoln.

II. 1656? to 1673? SIR EDWARD NORTON, Baronet [S. 1635], s. and h. *suc. to the Baronetcy* on the death of his father. He *d.* s.p., probably unm., in or before 1673, when the *Baronetcy* became *dormant*. Will, as of St. Dunstan's in the West, London, dat. 29 Nov. 1669, in which he devises all to his good friend, Daniel Norton, of London, merchant, pr. 4 June 1673.

PILKINGTON:

cr. 29 June 1635;(b)

sometime, 1854 and 1856, MILBORNE-SWINNERTON,

subsequently MILBORNE-SWINNERTON-PILKINGTON.

I. 1635. ARTHUR PILKINGTON, of Stanley (near Wakefield), and of Nether Bradley, co. York(c), s. and h. of Frederick PILKINGTON, by Frances, da. of Sir Francis RODES, of Barlborough, co. Derby, Justice of the Common Pleas, (which Frederick was 2d s., but the only one whose male issue continued more than one generation, of Thomas PILKINGTON, of Bradley, Bow Bearer to Queen Elizabeth), having suc. to the family estates, was *cr. a Baronet* [S.], 29 June 1635(b), the patent not being entered in the Great Seal Register [S.], with, probably (at that date) rem. to heirs male whatsoever, and with a grant of, presumably, 16,000 acres in Nova Scotia, of which he had seizin in Sep. 1635(d). He *m.* in or before 1613, Ellen, da. of Henry LYON, of Roxby, co. Lincoln, and Twyford in Willesden, co. Midx., merchant. She was *bur.* at Wakefield, 5 Feb. 1646/7. He was *bur.* 5 Sep. 1650, at St. Mary's, Castlegate, York.

II. 1650. SIR LYON PILKINGTON, Baronet [S. 1635], of Stanley and Bradley aforesaid, s. and h., *bap.* 14 Nov. 1613, at Wakefield: admitted to Gray's Inn, 2 March 1631/2: *suc. to the Baronetcy* in Sep. 1650. He *m.* firstly(e), (—) da. of Sir Thomas NEWTON. She *d.* s.p. He, being then of St. Andrew, Holborn, "Esq., aged 26, widower," had lic. (London,) June 1639, to marry Jane ONSLOW, aged 21, spinster. He *m.* subsequently (Lic. Fac., 15 Aug. 1650, Phœbe, (then aged 30), 2d da. of Capt. Robert MOYLE, of Buckwell, in Boughton Aluph, co. Kent, by Priscilla, da. of Charles FOTHERBY, Dean of Canterbury. He was *bur.* 5 Nov. 1684, at St. John's, Hackney, co. Midx. His widow *d.* 20 and was *bur.* 25 June 1686, in York Minster. Will pr. 7 Jan. 1686/7.

(a) Banks's Lists, the entry therein being, "Sir Walter Norton, of one Barony of land in New Scotland, represented by the Editor of this work [who styles himself on the title page thereof "Sir T. C. Banks, Bart., N.S."]; confirmed into another charter of lands erected into the Barony of St. Maur in New Scotland."

(b) Laing's List, this also being the date given in the pedigree recorded in the College of Arms. In Foster's copy of Milne's List the date is given as 29 *Jan.* 1635, but it is partially enclosed by *one* bracket and so may not be in Milne's original List, as those that are "within brackets" are not in that list.

(c) See p. 408, note "d" under "Norton."

(d) Banks's Lists.

(e) This marriage is said in Foster's YORKSHIRE PEDIGREES to have taken place 31 Dec. 1639, at St Benets' Pauls wharf, London, but *query*.

III. 1684. SIR LYON PILKINGTON, Baronet [S. 1635], of Stanley and Bradley aforesaid, 1st s. and h. by last wife; *b.* about 1660; *suc. to the Baronetcy* in Nov. 1684. He *m.* firstly in or before 1683, Amy, only da. of Thomas EGGLETON, of Grove in Ellesborough, Bucks, by Amy, da. of Nicholas DENTON, of Barton, Beds. She, who was *bap.* 8 March 1660/1, at Elleslow, *d.* 4 and was *bur.* 6 April 1695, at Wakefield, aged 36. He *m.* secondly (settlement 18 March 1698), Lennox, (aged 6 in 1665), widow of George SMITH, of Osgodby, co. York, da. and h. of Cuthbert HARRISON, of Acaster Selby, co. York, by Lennox, da. of Marmaduke (Langdale), 1st BARON LANGDALE OF HOLME. He was *bur.* 7 Aug. 1714, at Wakefield, aged 54. M.I. Will pr. at York, 15 Jan. 1714/5.

IV. 1714. SIR LYON PILKINGTON, Baronet [S. 1635], of Stanley and Bradley aforesaid, sometime of Hickleton, co. York, 1st s. and h. by 1st wife; *bap.* 5 June 1683, at Ellesborough; *suc. to the Baronetcy* in Aug. 1714. He *m.* 3 Feb. 1705, at Hickleton, co. York, Anne, 4th da. of Sir Michael WENTWORTH, of Wolley, co. York, by Dorothy, da. of Sir Godfrey COPLEY, 1st Baronet [1611], of Sprotborough. He was *bur.* (less than two years after his father), 26 June 1716, at Wakefield, in his 34th year. M.I. Will pr. at York 8 Aug. 1716. His widow, who was *b.* 16 and *bap.* 20 March 1683, at Woolley, *m.* secondly (as his 2d wife), Sir Charles DALSTON, 3d Baronet [1641], who *d.* 8 March 1723, aged 83. M.I. She *m.* (for her 3d husband) 1 Dec. 1730, at Horbury, John MAUDE, of Alverthorpe Hall and of Wakefield. She *d.* at Chevet, in Royston, co. York, 5. and was *bur.* 9 Aug. 1764, at Wakefield.

V. 1716. SIR LIONEL PILKINGTON, Baronet [S. 1635], of Stanley aforesaid, afterwards of Chevet in Royston, co. York; *bap.* at Hickleton, 20 Jan. 1706/7; *suc. to the Baronetcy* in June 1716; matric. at Oxford (Ch. Ch.) 14 May 1725, aged 18; was Sheriff of Yorkshire, 1740-41; M.P. for Horsham (three Parls.), 1748-68. He purchased the estate of Chevet, co. York (formerly belonging to the family of Neville) 4 July 1765. He *d.* unm. at Chevet 11, and was *bur.* 17 Aug. 1778, at Wakefield. Will pr. 5 Oct. 1778.

VI. 1778. SIR MICHAEL PILKINGTON, Baronet [S. 1635], of Lupset in Wakefield, co. York, br. and h., *bap.* at All Saints', Wakefield, 25 May 1715; *suc. to the Baronetcy*, 11 Aug. 1778. He *m.* firstly, 7 Dec. 1738, at West Ardsley, Judith, da. and coheir of the Rev. Charles NETTLETON, of Earls Heaton, co. York, Rector of Bulwick, co. Northampton. She *d.* s.p. at Wakefield, and was *bur.* there 29 Jan. 1772. He *m.* secondly, 11 Nov. 1772, at Badsworth Isabella, da. of the Rev. William RAWSTORNE, Vicar of Badsworth, by Elizabeth, only child of Samuel WALKER, of Stapleton park, co. York. He *d.* at Lupset, 6 and was *bur.* 18 Feb. 1788, at Wakefield. Will pr. 20 March 1788. His widow *m.*, April 1791, at St. James', Westm., Thomas HEWETSON, Major in the army. She *d.* at Doncaster, 25 Feb. 1823, and was *bur.* at Wakefield, aged 75.

VII. 1788. SIR THOMAS PILKINGTON, Baronet [S. 1635], of Chevet aforesaid, 1st s. and h., by 2d wife, *b.* 7 Dec. 1773 and *bap.* at Badsworth 10 Jan. 1774; *suc. to the Baronetcy*, 6 Feb. 1788; matric. at Oxford (Merton Coll.) 1 Aug. 1791, aged 17; *cr.* M.A. 5 July 1793; Sheriff of Yorkshire, 1798-99. He *m.*, 1 Aug. 1797, at Great Waltham, Essex, Elizabeth Anne, 1st da. of William TUFNELL, of Langley, co. Essex, by Anne, da. of John CLOSE, of Easby House, co. York. He *d.* s.p.m. 9 and was *bur.* 15 July 1811, at Wakefield, aged 37. Will, in which he devised all his estates to his daughters, pr. Feb. 1839. His widow *m.* William MULES, and *d.* Nov. 1842, being *bur.* at Dedham, Essex.

VIII. 1811. SIR WILLIAM PILKINGTON, Baronet [S. 1635], of Chevet aforesaid, br. and h. male, *bap.* 14 Nov. 1775, at Wakefield, *suc. to the Baronetcy*, 9 July 1811, and purchased the estate of Chevet from his nieces soon

afterwards. He *m.*, 25 June 1825, at St. Marylebone, Mary, 2d da. and coheir of Thomas SWINNERTON, of Butterton Hall, in Trentham, co. Stafford, by Mary, da. and h. of Charles MILBORNE, of Wonastow, co. Monmouth, and of the Priory, Abergavenny. He *d.* at Chevet Hall, 30 Sep. 1850, and was *bur.* at Sandal Magna, in his 75th year. Will pr. Jan. 1851. His widow, who by Act of Parl., 1836-37, took the name of *Milborne-Swinnerton* before that of *Pilkington*, *d.* 11 and was *bur.* 20 Dec. 1854, at Butterton. aged 61. Will pr. Feb. 1855.

IX. 1850. SIR THOMAS EDWARD PILKINGTON, Baronet [S. 1635], of Chevet aforesaid, 1st s. and h., *b.* 19 March and *bap.* 9 April 1829, at Chevet Hall. and was reg. at Sandal Magna; matric. at Oxford (Univ. Coll.) 16 Oct. 1847, aged 18; *suc. to the Baronetcy* 30 Sep. 1850; Capt. in the West Riding Yeomanry Militia, 1852-53. He *d.* unm. at Funchal, in Madeira, 7 Jan. 1854, aged 24, and was *bur.* in the English cemetery there.

X. 1854. SIR WILLIAM MILBORNE-SWINNERTON, *afterwards* MILBORNE-SWINNERTON-PILKINGTON, Baronet [S. 1635], of Chevet aforesaid, br. and h., *b.* 8 and *bap.* 28 June 1831 at Chevet Hall, reg. at Sandal Magna. He, in infancy, took the name of *Milborne-Swinnerton* in lieu of that of *Pilkington*, by Act of Parl., 1836-37, but by another Act of Parl., 1854, resumed the final name of *Pilkington*, having *suc. to the Baronetcy* 7 Feb. 1854; Lieut. Staffordshire Yeomanry, 1854. He *d.* unm., 12 Nov. 1855, aged 24, at Hillingdon, and was *bur.* at Butterton. Admon. Jan. 1856.

XI. 1855. SIR LIONEL PILKINGTON, *afterwards* MILBORNE-SWINNERTON and MILBORNE-SWINNERTON-PILKINGTON, Baronet [S. 1635], of Chevet aforesaid, br. and h., *b.* 7 July 1835, at Chevet Hall, and *bap.* at Sandal Magna, 4 Aug. following; ed. at Charterhouse school; Cornet 1st West York Yeomanry Cavalry, 1854; *suc. to the Baronetcy*, 12 Nov. 1855, and took by royal lic., 15 Feb. 1856, the name of *Milborne-Swinnerton* only, but subsequently resumed the final name of *Pilkington*; Sheriff of Yorkshire, 1859. He *m.* 3 Feb. 1857, at St. Geo., Hanover sq., Isabella Elizabeth, da. and h. of the Rev. Charles KINLESIDE, Rector of Polling, co. Sussex. He *d.* at Chevet Park, 25 June 1901. Will pr. at £73,017. His widow living 1902.

XII. 1901. SIR THOMAS EDWARD MILBORNE-SWINNERTON-PILKINGTON, Baronet [S. 1635], of Chevet aforesaid, 1st s. and h., *b.* 9 Dec. 1857, at Chevet; matric. at Oxford (Ch. Ch.) 13 Oct. 1876, aged 18; B.A., 1879; M.A., 1883; sometime Major King's Royal Rifle Corps; *suc. to the Baronetcy* 25 June 1901. He *m.* 23 July 1895, at St. Mark's, North Audley street, Kathleen Mary Alexina, da. and h. of William Ulick O'Connor (CUFFE), 4th EARL OF DESART [I.] by his 1st wife, Maria Emma Georgiana, da. of Thomas Henry PRESTON, of Moreby, co. York. She was *b.* 17 May 1872.

Family Estates.—These, in 1883, consisted of 4,808 acres in the West Riding of Yorkshire; 2,195 in Staffordshire; 1,457 in Monmouthshire; 149 in Herefordshire, and 135 in Kent. *Total.*—8,744 acres, worth £13,597 a year. *Principal Seats.*—Chevet Park, near Wakefield, co. York; Butterton Hall, near Newcastle-under-Lyme, co. Stafford, and Wonastow Court, co. Monmouth.

HAY :

cr. 20 July 1635 ;(a)

dormant 1683 ? to 1805 ;

but assumed since 1805.

I. 1635. JAMES HAY, of Smithfield, co. Peebles, only surv. s. and h. of John HAY, of the same (called "Dumb John"), was made "Esquire of the Body," 1624; suc. his father in 1628; was M.P. [S.] for Peebles-shire, 1628-33, and again 1643, and was *cr. a Baronet* [S.], 20 July 1635, by patent dat. at Oatlands,(a) but not recorded in the *Registrum Preceptorum Cartarum pro Baronettis Novæ Scotiæ*, with probably (at that date) rem. to heirs male whatsoever, and with a grant of, presumably, 16,000 acres in Nova Scotia, "extending 3 miles along the river Grand Solbison in Capricorne and Stretchbury and from thence northwards for 6 miles to be thenceforth called the Barony and Regality of Smithfield,"(a) of which he had seizin in [Dec. ?] 1635.(b) He *m.*(c) Sidney MASSEY, an English or Irish lady, who survived him.(d) He *d.* 1654. Admon. (in C.P.C., London), 21 June 1655, to a creditor. Will dat. 19 Feb. 1654, pr. 6 April 1659, in Prerog. Court [I.].

II. 1654. SIR JOHN HAY, Baronet [S. 1635], who *suc. to the Baronetcy* in 1654, but to none of his father's estate save £1,000, all else being left to his yr. br., William. He *m.* before 1652. He *d.* about 1659, in Scotland. Admon. as "of Peebles," 24 Aug. 1668, to "Sir James Douglas, Knight," principal creditor.

III. 1659 ? to 1683 ? SIR JAMES HAY, Baronet [S. 1635], only s. and h., *b.* at Peebles, 1652, *suc. to the Baronetcy* about 1659, and subsequently became h. to his uncle, William HAY, of Smithfield, but the estates had been wasted. He *m.* 23 July 1678, Grace, yst. da. of the Rev. Thomas CLAVERING, Rector of Piddlehinton, Dorset. He *d.* s.p.m. in or soon after 1683. His widow *d.* 1753, aged 96. After his death the *Baronetcy* became *dormant*, and so remained for above 120 years.

* * * * * *

IV.(e) 1805. SIR JAMES HAY, Baronet(e) [S. 1635], of Haystoun, co. Peebles, cousin and h. male,(f) being 2d but 1st surv. s. and h. of John HAY, of the same, by Grizel THOMPSON (*m.* 7 March 1712), which John (who *d.* 1762) was s. of John HAY, of Haystoun (living 1689), s. of [another] John HAY, of Haystoun, one of the Principal Clerks of Session [S.] (*d.* 27 Oct. 1679), 1st s. and h. of Andrew HAY, of Haystoun (which estate he purchased in 1635), Writer to the Signet [S.], who *d.* 1655, being 1st s. of John HAY, of Kingsmeadows (an estate he purchased in 1570), yr. br. of Thomas HAY, of Smithfield aforesaid (who *d.* 1570, being father of "Dumb John Hay," the father of the 1st Baronet), the said John HAY, of Kingsmeadows, and Thomas, his elder brother, both abovenamed, who were sons of John HAY, of Smithfield, living 1525. He suc. his father in 1762 in the estate of Haystoun. He was a Physician at Edinburgh. On 9 Nov. 1805, he was "served heir at Peebles to John HAY, of Kingsmeadows, his great-great [apparently great-great-great] grandfather and *assumed the title* [*of Baronet*] as heir male of the 3d Baronet."(a) He *m.* 13 Dec. 1751, Dorriel, yst da. and coheir of Daniel CAMPBELL, of Greenyards, Sec. to the Bank of Scotland, by Elizabeth, da. of Thomas TULLOCH, Writer. She *d.* 28 March 1770. He *d.* 21 Oct. 1810.

(a) Playfair's *Baronetage* [S.], 1811. The date of creation as in Laing's List (said therein to be given "on the authority of former lists") is *10 Dec.* 1635. It is omitted in Milne's List.

(b) Banks's Lists.

(c) According to a note of R. R. Stodart (Lyon Clerk Depute, 1863-86) the mother of his only da. Anne (who *m.* 10 Feb. 1649 Sir James Douglas, afterwards Earl of Morton [S.]), was "a da. of Lord Beaumont, by (—) Wilford, of Worcestershire," as stated in the "birthbrief" (date or history not mentioned) of the said Anne. [*Ex inform.* Sir J. Balfour Paul, Lyon King of Arms.]

(d) The funeral entry in Ulster's Office of "Lady Hay," who *d.* 30 March and was *bur.* 2 April 1677 in St. Bride's Church, London, may refer to her, but as it is added that "she was married to Sir James Hay, Baronet of Scotland," it looks as if her husband was then living, in which case she might be a *1st* wife of Sir James, the 3d Baronet, who a year after this date *m.* Grace Clavering. The arms entered for her are those of LAXTON, impaled with HAY. [*Ex inform.* G. D. Burtchaell, Office of Arms, Ireland.]

(e) According to the service at Peebles, 9 Nov. 1805. The numbering, however, (as given after the 3d holder) does not include those persons who, according to such service, would have been entitled to the Baronetcy.

(f) The want of any reliable proof of heirship in this somewhat dateless descent is discussed, and the existence of other sons of this family is shewn, in the *Her. and Gen.*, vol. iv, p. 372

V.(b) 1810. SIR JOHN HAY, Baronet(b) [S. 1635], of Haystoun aforesaid, 1st s. and h., *b.* 15 Jan. 1755; was a Banker in Edinburgh; *suc. to the Baronetcy.*(b) 21 Oct. 1810. He *m.*, 9 July 1785, Mary Elizabeth, yst. da. of James (FORBES), 16th LORD FORBES [S.], by Catherine, only child of Sir Robert INNES, 6th Baronet [S. 1628], of Balvenie. She, by whom he had eight sons and seven daughters, *d.* 2 Nov. 1803. He *d.* 23 May 1830. Will pr. Oct. 1830.

VI.(b) 1830. SIR JOHN HAY, Baronet(b) [S. 1635], of Haystoun aforesaid, 3d but 1st surv. s. and h., *b.* 3 Aug. 1788; Advocate [S.], 28 June 1811; M.P. for Peebles (three Parls.), 1831-37; *suc. to the Baronetcy*,(b) 23 May 1830. He *m.* 6 Oct. 1821, Anne, da. and h. of George PRESTON, Capt. in the Royal Marines (*d.* 1798, aged 60), 4th s. of Sir George PRESTON, 4th Baronet [S. 1637], of Valleyfield, co. Perth. He *d.* s.p. 1 Nov. 1838, at Rome, aged 50. His widow, who in April 1855, inherited the estate of Valleyfield aforesaid, *d.* 2 Sep. 1862, in Devonshire-place house, New road, Marylebone.

VII.(b) 1838. SIR ADAM HAY, Baronet(b) [S. 1635], of Haystoun aforesaid, br. and h., being the 7th s. of the 5th Baronet(b); *b.* 14 Dec. 1795, in St. Andrew's parish, Edinburgh; was a banker at Edinburgh; M.P. for Linlithgowshire, 1826-30; *suc. to the Baronetcy*,(b) 1 Nov. 1838; Vice Lieut. of co. Peebles, 1839-67. He *m.*, 23 March 1823, Henrietta Callender, 1st da. of William GRANT, of Congalton, co. Haddington. She *d.* at Edinburgh, 6 June 1849. He *d.* 18 Jan. 1867, at Cannes, in France, aged 71.

VIII.(b) 1867. SIR ROBERT HAY, Baronet (b), [S. 1635], of Haystoun aforesaid, 2d but 1st surv. s. and h., *b.* 8 May 1825; *suc. to the Baronetcy*,(b) 18 Jan. 1867. He *m.*, 3 Aug. 1853, at Castle Menzies, co. Perth, Sally, da. of Alexander DUNCAN, of Providence, Rhode Island, U.S.A.. and of Knossington Grange, co. Leicester. He *d.* suddenly, 29 May 1885, at Lyons, in France, aged 60. Will pr. 19 Aug. 1885, over £90,000. His widow living 1902.

IX. 1885.(b) SIR JOHN ADAM HAY, Baronet(b) [S. 1635], of Haystoun aforesaid, 1st s. and h., *b.* 5 May 1854; ed. at Eton; sometime Lieut. in the Scots Guards; Major 3d Vol. Batt. Lothian Regt.; *suc. to the Baronetcy*,(b) 29 May 1885. He *m.* 10 March 1885, at All Saints, Ennismore Gardens, Anne Salisbury Mary Meliora, 1st da. of Sir Robert John MILLIKEN-NAPIER, 9th Baronet [S. 1627], by Anne Salisbury Meliora, da. of John Ladeveze ADLERCRON. He *d.* 4 May 1895, at his mother's residence, North House, Putney hill, co. Surrey, in his 41st year. His widow living 1902.

(a) Burke's *Baronetage* for 1901.

(b) See page 412, note "e."

X.(a) 1895. SIR DUNCAN EDWARD HAY, Baronet(a) [S. 1633], of Haystoun aforesaid, only s. and h., *b.* 25 Sep. 1882; *suc. to the Baronetcy*,(a) 4 May 1895.

Family Estates.—These, in 1883, consisted of 9,155 acres in co. Peebles, and 600 in co. Selkirk. *Total*, 9,755 acres, worth £4,514 a year. *Principal Seats.*—King's meadows and Haystoun, co. Peebles.

WIDDRINGTON :

cr. 26 Sep. 1635 ;(b)

dormant, or *extinct*, 13 July 1671.

I. 1635, to 1671. EDWARD WIDDRINGTON, of Cartington, co. Northumberland,(c) was *cr. a Baronet* [S.], 26 Sep. 1635,(b) the patent not being entered in the Great Seal Register [S.], with probably (at that date) rem. to heirs male whatsoever, and with a grant of, presumably, 16,000 acres in Nova Scotia, of which he had seizin in Dec. 1635.(d) He was subsequently *cr. a Baronet of England*, 8 Aug. 1642, but *d.* s.p.m.s., 13 July 1671, when that Baronetcy became extinct and the *Baronetcy* [S. 1635], became *dormant* or *extinct*. See fuller account of him on page 188.

BOLLES :

cr. 19 Dec. 1635 ;(e)

subsequently, after 1662, JOPSON.

dormant, or *extinct*, about 1670.

I. 1635. MARY BOLLES,(f) of Osberton,(g) in Worksop, co. Nottingham,(c) widow, was *cr. a Baronetess* [S.],(h) 19 Dec. 1635,(e) the patent however not being entered in the Great Seal Register [S.], with rem. of the dignity of a Baronet [S.], "to her heirs male and assignees,"(i) with a grant of, presumably, 16,000 acres in Nova Scotia, of which she never had seizin.(j) She, who was *bap.* 30 June 1879, at Ledsham, co. York, was da. of William WYTHAM, of Ledsham aforesaid, by Eleanor, da. of John NEALE, of co. Northampton. She *m.* firstly Thomas JOPSON, of Cudworth, in Royston, co. York. She *m.* secondly (Lic. at York, 1611), as his 2d wife, Thomas BOLLES, of Osberton aforesaid, and by him had two daughters but no son. He, who entered his pedigree in the Visit. of Notts, 1614, *d.* 19 March 1634/5, and was *bur.* at Worksop. Funeral certificate "testified by the *Lady Mary Bolles, Barronettes*, late wife and executrix." Will dat. 15 March 1634/5. Within nine months of his death she was *cr. a Baronetess* [S.], as above mentioned. She resided at Heath Hall, near Wakefield, co. York, and *d.* 5 May, being *bur.* 16 June 1662, at Ledsham aforesaid, aged about 81.

(a) See page 412, note "e."

(b) Laing's List, but not in Milne's List. In Walkley's List the 95th and last creation therein given is "Sir William [*sic*] Witherington, English," but as there is no Sir *Edward* Widdrington in that List, the christian name of *William* is probably a mistake.

(c) See p. 408, note "d" under "Norton."

(d) Banks's Lists, in which however "Sir Edward" is [incorrectly] said to have been "afterwards Lord Widdrington."

(e) Laing's List, but not in that of Milne.

(f) This is the only case of a Baronetcy having been conferred on a female, or even enjoyed *suo jure*, by one. The rank of the *widow of a Baronet* has occasionally been conferred, as was the case in the Baronetcy of Speelman, 9 Sep. 1686, where the mother of the grantee was so honoured.

(g) In Walkley's List the grantee is described as "Dame Mary Bolles, of Ardworth, English." She is sometimes called "of Cudworth, co. York," the residence of her 1st husband.

(h) J. C. Brooke (Somerset Herald, 1778-94), states in his Yorkshire collections ("I.C.B. vol. 1, p. 408, Coll. of Arms) that she purchased her title. He adds that there is a tradition, that, after her death "she haunted her house at Heath and parts adjacent till such time as she was conjured into a certain deep place in the river Calder, near that town [*i.e.* Wakefield], called from thence *Lady Bolles's Pit.*"

(i) Foster's List of Nova Scotia Baronets, in his *Baronetage* for 1883.

(j) Banks's Lists.

II. 1662, to 1670 ? SIR WILLIAM JOPSON, Baronet [S. 1635], of Cudworth and of Heath Hall aforesaid, grandson and h., being 4th but only surv. s. and h. of Thomas JOPSON, of Cudworth, by his 1st wife, Anne (*m.* 31 July 1626, at Worksop), da. of Nicholas STRINGER, of Sutton-upon-Lound, co. Notts, which Thomas (who *d.* before his mother, 26 Aug. 1653, was only s. and h. ap. of DAME MARY BOLLES, *suo jure* Baronetess [S.], by her 1st husband, Thomas JOPSON, both abovenamed. He was *b.* probably about 1635 and *suc. to the Baronetcy* on the death of his said grandmother, 5 May 1662. He *m.* Lucy, da. of Henry TINDALL, of Brotherton, co. York. He *d.* s.p.m.(a) in or before 1673 (leaving a will), when the *Baronetcy* became *dormant*. His widow *m.* between 1667 and 1673, as his 2d wife, Sir John JACKSON, 1st Baronet [1660], of Hickleton, co. York, who *d.* in or before 1678.

RAYNEY :

cr. 19 Dec. 1635 and (again) 13 Sep. 1636 ;(b)

cr. a Baronet [E.] 22 Jan. 1641/2 ;

dormant, 1721.

I. 1635, and 1636. JOHN RAYNEY, of Wrotham, co. Kent,(c) was *cr. a Baronet* [S.] 19 Dec. 1635, as also again (possibly owing to some defect in the former creation) on 13 Sep. 1636,(b) with rem. to heirs male whatsoever, and with a grant of, presumably, 16,000 acres in Nova Scotia, of which he never had seizin.(d) He was, a few years later, *cr. a Baronet of England*, 22 Jan. 1641/2; see that creation which became *extinct* on the death of the 5th Baronet in 1721, when the *Baronetcy* [S.] became *dormant*.

FORTESCUE :

cr. 17 Feb. 1635/6 ;(e)

dormant, 9 Nov. 1729.

I. 1636. JOHN FORTESCUE, of Salden, in Mursley, Bucks,(c) s. and h. of Sir Francis FORTESCUE, K.B., of the same, by Grace (*m.* before 1590), da. of the Hon. Sir John MANNERS, of Haddon, co. Derby (which Francis was son of Sir John FORTESCUE, Chancellor of the Exchequer, who purchased the estate of Salden in 1590 and *d.* 23 Dec. 1607, aged 76), was *bap.* at Mursley, 1592; matric. at Oxford (Merton Coll.) 11 July 1606, aged 12; admitted to Inner Temple, 1612; suc. his father in Jan. 1623/4 and was *cr. a Baronet* [S.] 17 Feb. 1635/6,(e) the

(a) Lucy, his da. and eventually sole heir, who inherited the estate of Cudworth, *m.* in 1686, Robert (Ridgeway), 4th Earl of Londonderry [I.], who *d.*, s.p.m.s., 7 March 1713/4. She *d.* 4 Sep. 1724, leaving a da. Frances (only child who left issue) wife of Thomas (Pitt), 1st Baron and Earl of Londonderry [I.], being so created respectively in 1719 and 1726, who in her right inherited the estate of Cudworth

(b) Laing's List for both dates and Milne's List for the latter.

(c) See p. 408, note "d," under "Norton."

(d) Banks's Lists.

(e) Laing's List.

II

patent not being entered in the Great Seal Register [S.], with rem. to heirs male whatsoever, and with a grant of, presumably, 16,000 acres in Nova Scotia, of which he never had seizin.(a) In the Civil War, he was in arms on the King's side and was taken prisoner, May 1644, near Islip, Oxon. He *m.* Frances, da. of Sir Edward STANLEY, K.B., of Ensham, Oxon. He *d.* Sep. 1656, and was *bur.* at Mursley. Admon. 6 Nov. 1656.

II. 1656. SIR JOHN FORTESCUE, Baronet [S. 1636], of Salden aforesaid, 1st s. and h., *bap.* 13 July 1614, at Mursley; reverted to the ancient religion of his family; *suc. to the Baronetcy* in Sep. 1656. He *m.* firstly, Margaret, da. of Thomas (ARUNDELL), 1st BARON ARUNDELL OF WARDOUR, by his 2d wife, Ann, da. of Miles PHILIPSON. She *d.* s.p.m. 1638. He *m.* secondly, in or before 1644, Mary, da. of Sir William STONOR, of Stonor, Oxon, by Elizabeth, da. of Sir Thomas LAKE, Secretary of State to James I. She was *bap.* 11 Nov. 1622. He *m.* thirdly, Elizabeth, 2d da. of Sir John WINTOUR, of Lydney, co. Gloucester, by Mary, da. of Lord William HOWARD. She *d.* s.p.s. 1674. He was *bur.* 14 June 1683 at Mursley.

III. 1683. SIR JOHN FORTESCUE, Baronet [S. 1636], of Salden aforesaid, 1st and only surv. s., by 2d wife, *b.* 1644; *suc. to the Baronetcy* in June 1683; *d.* s.p. 1717, aged 73.

IV. 1717, to 1729. SIR FRANCIS FORTESCUE, Baronet [S. 1636], of Salden aforesaid, cousin and h. male, being s. of Francis FORTESCUE, the only surv. s. of Sir Edward FORTESCUE,(b) (*bur.* at Mursley, 14 Feb. 1662), yr. s. of the 1st Baronet. He was *b.* about 1662, *suc. to the Baronetcy* in 1717. He *m.* before 7 May 1713, Mary, da. of Henry HUDDLESTON, of Sawston, co. Cambridge (who *d.* 1714/5), by Mary, da. of Richard BASTOCK, of Wixhall, Salop. He *d.* s.p. at Bath, 9 and was *bur.* 11 Nov. 1729, at Salden, aged 67, when the *Baronetcy* became *dormant*, he being "the last male descendant of Queen Elizabeth's minister and so far as we know of Sir Adrian Fortescue also."(c) M.I. Will dat. 18 Sep. 1724, pr. 8 Jan. 1729/30. The will of his widow, dat. 26 Jan. 1743, pr. 8 Feb. 1744/5.

THOMSON:

cr. 20 Feb. 1635/6;(d)

dormant since Jan. 1691.

I. 1636. SIR THOMAS THOMSON, of Duddingston, co. Edinburgh,(e) br. and h. of John THOMSON, of the same, both being sons of Alexander THOMSON, of Easter and Wester Duddingston, Advocate (who *d.* in or

(a) Banks's Lists.

(b) There is an admon., 18 June 1651, of *Dame Frances Fortescue*, wife of Sir Edward Fortescue, of Salden, Bucks (who renounces), da. of "Robert Brooke, Esq.," and Joan his wife, both deceased, granted to "Robert Slingsby, Esq.," uncle of Catherine Fortescue, minor, da. of deceased. A subsequent admon. was granted, 11 May 1680, to Wm. Waller, the said minor having died. This Frances was Sir Edward's 1st wife; the 2d wife was Mary, da. of Gilbert Reresby, by whom he had two sons and four daughters [Napier's *Swyncombe, Oxon*].

(c) Lord Clermont's *Fortescue Family*.

(d) Laing's List and Milne's List. "The Baronetcy is recorded in the *Reg. Mag. Scot.*, 20 Feb. 1636; grant of lands to Thomas Thomson, of Duddingston, *Miles*, and his heirs male and assigns whomsoever (next the lands and Barony of Salden, Nova Scotia, belonging to Sir John Fortescue, of Salden, Baronet), and creating him a Baronet [S.], with rem. to heirs male." [Sir J. Balfour Paul, Lyon King of Arms.]

(e) In Walkley's Catalogue this creation stands as being that of "Sir Thomas Tompsone of Dudingstone, English," but the word *English* has doubtless been inserted in error. See p. 407, note "b," under "Gascoigne."

shortly before May 1603), by Margaret, sister of Sir John PRESTON, L. President of the Court of Session, da. of Alexander PRESTON, of Edinburgh, Baker;(a) was *Knighted* before 23 Feb. 1633, and was *cr. a Baronet* [S], 20 Feb. 1635/6,(b) with rem. to heirs male whatsoever and with a grant of, presumably, 16,000 acres in Nova Scotia, of which he never had seizin.(c) He *m.*, in or before 1627,(d) Margaret, da. of John SCRIMGEOUR, Constable of Dundee. She was living 1654, on which date she and the heirs of her body had an annuity of £120 settled on them, her husband having been exempted from the Act of Pardon in that year. He *d.* between 1654 and March 1666.

II. 1666? SIR PATRICK THOMSON, Baronet [S. 1636], of Duddingston aforesaid, 1st surv. s. and h., *b.* 24 Dec. 1637; *suc. to the Baronetcy* on the death of his father, to whom he was served heir, 13 March 1666, shortly after which date he alienated the family estates. He apparently *d.* s.p. His will confirmed 15 April 1674, in the Commissariat of Edinburgh.

III. 1674? to 1691. SIR JAMES THOMSON, Baronet [S. 1636], heir male, presumably brother,(e) but possibly son, of the above; *suc. to the Baronetcy*, in or before April 1674. He *d.*, apparently s.p.m., in or before Jan. 1691, when the *Baronetcy* became *dormant*. Will confirmed, as above, 28 Jan. 1691.

ABERCROMBY:

cr. 20 Feb. 1635/6.(f)

I. 1636. ALEXANDER ABERCROMBY, of Birkenbog, co. Banff, s. and h. ap. of Alexander ABERCROMBY, of the same, Grand Falconer in Scotland to Charles I, by Elizabeth, da. of (—) BETHUNE, *or* BEATON, of Balfour, was *b.* about 1603; obtained, 21 April 1636 (with others) a monopoly of trading from Scotland to Africa for 15 years, and was *cr. a Baronet* [S.] 20 Feb. 1635/6,(f) with remainder to heirs male and with a grant of, presumably, 16,000 acres in Nova Scotia, of which, however, he never had seizin(c). He suc. his father between 1641 and 1648; was M.P. [S.] for Banffshire, 1640-41, 1643, 1646-47, 1648, and 1661-63. He took an active part against the King, being considered "A Main Covenanter," and in May 1645, joined the forces of Major Urry, and was present at the battle of Auldearn. He *m.* firstly, Jane, 2d da. of Sir Thomas URQUHART, senior, of Cromarty, by Christian, 4th da. of Alexander (ELPHINSTONE), 4th LORD ELPHINSTONE [S.]. She *d.* s.p. He *m.* secondly, Jane, da. of (—) SUTHERLAND, of the family of Kilminity. She also *d.* s.p. He *m.* thirdly,(g) Elizabeth, da. of Sir James BAIRD, of Auchmedden. His widow *m.* Col. Patrick OGILVIE, of Inchmartin.

(a) For the whole of the information as to this family the Editor is indebted to Sir J. Balfour Paul, Lyon King of Arms. The grandfather of the grantee was Alexander Thomson, of Duddingston, who *m.* Catharine, da. of Sir William Lawson, of Boghall, and who was s. of Thomas Thomson, also of Duddingston, by Catherine, da. of John Towers, of Innerleith, co. Edinburgh.

(b) See p. 416, notes "d" and "e."

(c) Banks's Lists.

(d) A son, Thomas, was *bap.* 9 Dec. 1627.

(e) The 2d Baronet had a younger br. James, born 15 July 1641.

(f) The Abercromby Charter is on the same terms and of the same date as that of Thomson. [*Ex inform.* Sir J. Balfour Paul, Lyon King of Arms.] No date is given in Milne's List, but in Laing's List it is stated to be 18 June 1636, and to be "given on the authority of former lists."

(g) The date of this marriage is given as "22 Aug. 1668" in Burke's *Baronetage* (1901).

II. 1670? SIR JAMES ABERCROMBY, Baronet [S. 1636], of Birkenbog aforesaid, s. and h.,(a) by 3d wife; *suc. to the Baronetcy* on the death of his father; was M.P. [S.] for co. Banff, 1693—1702. He *m.* 1645, Mary, da. of Arthur GORDON, of Straloch. He *d.* 20 Sep. 1734.(b).

III. 1734. SIR ROBERT ABERCROMBY, Baronet [S. 1636], of Birkenbog aforesaid, 3d but 1st surv. s. and h.; *suc. to the Baronetcy*, 20 Sep. 1734. He *m.* 1739, Helen, da. of his paternal uncle, Alexander ABERCROMBY, of Tullibody, co. Clackmannan. He *d.* 11 March 1787.

IV. 1787. SIR GEORGE ABERCROMBY, Baronet [S. 1636], of Birkenbog aforesaid, and subsequently [after 1803] of Forglen House, co. Banff, s. and h., *b.* 1750; Advocate [S.] 4 Dec. 1773; Sheriff for co. Elgin and co. Nairn, 1783; *suc. to the Baronetcy*, 11 March 1787; Clerk for the admission of Notars, 1807. He *m.* 1778, Jane, da. of Alexander (OGILVIE), 7th LORD BANFF [S.], by Jean, da. of William NISBET, of Dirleton, co. Haddington. She was eldest sister and coheir of William, the 8th Lord, on whose death, unm., 4 June 1803, his estate of Forglen passed to this family. Sir George *d.* 18 July 1831.

V. 1831. SIR ROBERT ABERCROMBY, Baronet [S. 1636], of Birkenbog and Forglen House aforesaid, s. and h., *b.* 4 Feb. 1784; M.P. for Banffshire, 1812-18; *suc. to the Baronetcy*, 18 July 1831. He *m.* 22 Oct. 1816, Elizabeth-Stephenson, da. and sole h. of Samuel DOUGLAS, of Netherlaw. He *d.* 6 July 1855. His widow *d.* 28 Dec. 1863.

VI. 1855. SIR GEORGE-SAMUEL ABERCROMBY, Baronet [S. 1636], of Birkenbog and Forglen House aforesaid, s. and h., *b.* 22 May 1824; *suc. to the Baronetcy*, 8 July 1835. He *m.* 12 June 1849, Agnes Georgiana, 2d da. of John Cavendish (BROWNE), 3d BARON KILMAINE [I.], by his 1st wife, Eliza, da. of David LYON. He *d.* 14 Nov. 1872.

VII. 1872. SIR ROBERT JOHN ABERCROMBY, Baronet [S. 1636], of Birkenbog and Forglen House aforesaid, s. and h., *b.* 14 June 1850 in Chester Square, Middlesex; ed. at Eton; *suc. to the Baronetcy* 14 Nov. 1872; Vice-Lieut. of co. Banff. He *m.* 26 June 1883, at Apsley Guise, Beds., Florence Anita Eyre, only da. of Eyre COOTE, of West Park, Rockburne, Hants, by Jessie Mary, da. of Major-Gen. Henry Lechmere WORRALL. He *d.* at Forglen House 24 July 1895, aged 45. Will pr. at £127,653. His widow, who was *b.* 23 Dec. 1860, at Florence, and *bap.* in the English Church there, *m.* 10 June 1899, at St. Saviour's, Walton Place, as his 2d wife, Francis George BARING, *styled* VISCOUNT BARING, s. and h. ap. of Thomas George, 2d EARL OF NORTHBROOK.

VIII. 1895. SIR GEORGE WILLIAM ABERCROMBY, Baronet [S. 1636], of Birkenbog and Forglen House aforesaid, 1st s. and h., *b.* 18 March 1886; *suc. to the Baronetcy* 24 July 1895.

Family Estates.—These, in 1883, consisted of 8,053 acres in Banffshire; 1,942 in Aberdeenshire; 1,339 in Kirkcudbrightshire; and 434 (worth £2,579 a year) in co. Cork. *Total.*—11,768 acres, worth £12,395 a year. *Principal Seats.*—Forglen House (near Turriff), and Birkenbog, both in Banffshire; Castle Douglas, in Scotland, and Fermoy, co. Cork, in Ireland.

(a) His next br., Alexander Abercromby, who in 1699 became of Tullibody, co. Clackmannan, was grandfather of the celebrated General SIR RALPH ABERCROMBY, whose widow, for her late husband's services, was *cr.* BARONESS ABERCROMBY in 1801. Her 3d s., JAMES ABERCROMBY, was Speaker of the House of Commons 1835 to 1839, and was *cr.* BARON DUNFERMLINE in 1839, which last peerage became *extinct* 12 July 1868.

(b) *Query* as to his identy with "The Lord James Abercrombie," who *d.* at a chateau in Westphalia, 1726, aged 98, and was *bur.* there.

BROWNE:

cr. 21 June 1636;(a)

afterwards, since 1789, BARONS KILMAINE [I.]

I. 1636. JOHN BROWNE, of the Neale, near Ballinrobe, co. Mayo,(b) s. and h. ap. of Josias BROWNE, of the same, by Joan, da. of Edward BIRMINGHAM, of Carrick, co. Kildare, was *cr. a Baronet* [S.], 21 June 1636,(a) the patent not being recorded in the *Registrum Preceptorum Cartarum pro Baronettis Novæ Scotiæ*, and the limitation being unknown, but, probably (at that date), being to heirs male whatsoever, and with a grant of, presumably, 16,000 acres in Nova Scotia,(c) but no record of such grant, nor any seizin of such lands is known.(d) Possibly owing to this cause it may have been considered that the grant of the Baronetcy was not valid,(e) as he did not assume the title, neither did any of his descendants, till about the year 1762. He suc. his father, in Dec. 1634 (who was *bur.* at Kilmaine, aged 55); was excepted from pardon for life and estate by Ordinance, 1652, but restored to his estate at the Restoration. He *m.*, in 1626, Mary, da. of Sir Dominick BROWNE, of Carra Browne, co. Galway and Castle Margarett, co. Mayo, by Anastacia, da. of James DARCY. He *d.* Whitsunday 1670, and was *bur.* in Ross Abbey, co. Galway. Funeral certif.

II. 1670. GEORGE BROWNE, of the Neale aforesaid, 1st s. and h.;(f) suc. his father in 1670, but *never assumed the Baronetcy*. He, in Nov. 1684, had a regrant of the Neale; was Sheriff of co. Mayo, 1690; had pardon for himself and son in June 1693, reciting that he himself had served as Sheriff, and that neither had ever been indicted or outlawed. He *m.* Alicia, only da. of Sir Henry BINGHAM, 1st Baronet [S. 1634] of Castlebar, co. Mayo, by Catherine, da. of John BYRNE, of Ballinclough. He *d.* May 1698. His wife survived him.

III. 1698. JOHN BROWNE, of the Neale aforesaid, s and h. He was sometime Captain in the Irish Army of James II, and was taken prisoner, 6 May 1689, at the siege of Derry. He suc. his father in May 1698, but *never assumed the Baronetcy*. He *m.* firstly (settl. 27 and 28 May 1680), Anne, 1st da. of George (HAMILTON), 3d BARON STRABANE [I.], by Elizabeth, da. of Christopher FAGAN. She *d.* s.p. 14 and was *bur.* 17 Aug. 1680, "in the country." Funeral certif. He *m.* secondly, Juliana, 3d da. of Sir Patrick BELLEW, 1st Baronet [I. 1688] of Barmeath, by Elizabeth, 4th da. of Sir Richard BARNEWALL, 2d Baronet [I. 1622]. His will dat. 11 Sep. 1700, pr. 21 Nov. 1712 in the Prerog. Court [I.]. The will of his widow dat. 15 Nov. 1728, pr. there 10 May 1729.

(a) This creation is not in Milne's, Walkley's or Ulster's Lists, but it is in that of Laing, under the date of 17 [*sic*] June 1636, and is there stated to be given "on the authority of former Lists." There is a letter, dated 19 Dec. 1776, from the then Baronet, Sir John Browne, to Lord Charlemont, in which he writes "The date of my patent is June 21 1632 [*sic*], so I shall be pretty forward on the bench of Baronets, if any there be." See, however, the correct date, 21 June 1636, in the copy of the patent in Lodge's Irish Peerage, [1789], vol. iii, p. 271.

(b) See p. 407, note "b," *circa finem*, *sub.* Gascoigne.

(c) About this date "the French, by the construction of the treaty of St. Germain [made 29 March 1632] between them and King Charles, entered upon Nova Scotia as included therein" [Banks's *Baronia Anglica Concentrata*, vol. ii, p. 218, and app. 45]. After the year 1637 no seizin took place of lands granted in Nova Scotia, save one in Nov. 1640, *viz.*, that of "Sir Robert Campbell."

(d) No mention of such occurs in Banks's Lists.

(e) Such, however, was not the case with the kindred family of Bingham, who were similarly situated, and who certainly assumed the Baronetcy [S.] granted to them.

(f) His next br., John Browne, Col. in the Irish Army of James II, and one of the capitulators of Limerick, was grandfather of John Browne, *cr.* Baron Monteagle [I.], 1760; Viscount Westport [I.], 1768; and Earl of Altamont [I.], 1771, whose grandson, the 3d Earl, was *cr.* Marquess of Sligo [I.] in 1800.

IV. 1712? GEORGE BROWNE, of the Neale aforesaid, s. and h., suc. his father about 1712, but *never assumed the Baronetcy*; was M.P. [I.] for Castlebar, 1713-14. He *m.*, in 1709, his cousin Bridget, da. of Edward (BERMINGHAM), LORD ATHENRY [I.], by his 2d wife, Bridget, da. of Col. John BROWNE, of Westport, co. Sligo, 2d s. of the 1st Baronet. He *d.* s.p. 8 May 1737, at the Neale. Will dat. 6 April 1737, pr. 4 March 1737/8 at the Prerog. Court [I.]. His widow *d.* 25 Sep. 1747.

V. 1737. JOHN BROWNE, of the Neale aforesaid, and formerly of Rahins, co. Mayo, br. and h.; Sheriff of co. Mayo, 1731; suc. his brother 8 May 1737, but *never assumed the Baronetcy*; was M.P. [I.] for Castlebar (*vice* Henry Bingham) from, probably, about 1740 to 1760. He *m.* firstly, 30 June 1722, Margaret, 1st da. and coheir of Henry DODWELL, of Athlone, by his 2d wife Catharine, da. of Arthur ORMSBY, of Ballyvenose, co. Limerick. She *d.* 23 April 1739, and was *bur.* in Kildare cathedral. Admon. 11 June 1741, in Prerog. Court [I.] He *m.* secondly, Catherine, widow of Denis DALY, of Carrownakelly, da. of Sir Walter BLAKE, 6th Baronet [I. 1622], of Menlo, by his 2d wife, Agnes, da. of John BLAKE. He *d.* 2 Oct. 1762. His 2d wife, by whom he had no issue, survived him.

VI. 1762. SIR GEORGE BROWNE, Baronet [S. 1636], of the Neale aforesaid, 1st s. and h. by 1st wife, *b.* in or before 1725; Sheriff of co. Mayo, 1747; suc. his father 2 Oct. 1762, and *assumed the Baronetcy* at that date, being the *first* of his family who did so. He *m.* Oct. 1761, Anastacia, 1st da. of Denis DALY, of Raford, co. Galway, by Anne, da. of Michael (DE BURGH), EARL OF CLANRICARDE [I.] He *d.* s.p. 9 Sep. 1765.

VII. 1765. SIR JOHN BROWNE, Baronet [S. 1636], of the Neale aforesaid, br. of the whole blood and h; *b.* 20 May 1726; *suc. to the Baronetcy*, 9 Sep. 1765, and registered his pedigree in Ulster's office, Ireland, as such 28 Feb. 1777, and in the Lyon office, Scotland, 7 April 1777; was M.P. [I.], for Newtown, 1777-83, and for Carlow, 1783-89; Sheriff of. co. Mayo, 1778 and 1788; purchased the estate of Gaulston, co. Westmeath. He *m.* 30 March 1764, (Lords' entries, in Ulster's office), Alice, only da. of James (CAULFEILD), 3d VISCOUNT CHARLEMONT [I.], by Elizabeth, da. of Francis BERNARD, 3d Justice of the Common Pleas [I.]. She was living when he was *cr.* 21 Sep. 1789, BARON KILMAINE([a]) [I.], in which dignity this *Baronetage then merged* and so continues See "*Peerage*."

MOIR, *or* MOORE:

cr. 18 June 1636;([b])

dormant, or *extinct*, Aug. 1644.

I. 1636, to 1644. EDWARD MOIR, or MOORE, of Langford, Notts,([c]) s. and h. of William MOORE, of Thelwell, Cheshire, by Elizabeth, da. of Alexander VAUDREY, of the Bank, co. Chester, was *b.* about 1610; suc. his father about 1632, and was *cr. a Baronet* [S.], 18 June 1636([b]), the patent not being in the Great Seal Register [S.], with, it is supposed, rem. to heirs male whatsoever, and with a grant of, presumably, 16,000

([a]) "The peerages of Kilmaine, Cloncurry and Glentworth, were sold for hard cash and the proceeds laid out in the purchase of members" [Fitzpatrick's *Secret Service under Pitt*, p. 254].

([b]) Laing's List. In the copy of Milne's List in Foster's *Baronetage* for 1883, the date is given as 18 *Feb.* 1636, but it is there marked as being in Laing's List only, where the date is 18 *June* 1636.

([c]) See p. 408, note "d," under "Norton."

acres in Nova Scotia, of which, however, he never had seizin.([a]) He, who fought on the Royal side in the Civil Wars, *d.* at Newark-upon-Trent of wounds received at the battle (2 July 1644) of Marston Moor, and was *bur.* 1 Aug. 1644 at Newark. He *d.* s.p.m.,([b]) when the *Baronetcy* became *dormant* or *extinct*. Admon. as "of Kirtlington, Notts," 26 Feb. 1657/8, to the guardian of Elizabeth Moore, da. of deceased, then a minor.

SINCLAIR:

afterwards, since 1899, SINCLAIR-LOCKHART;

cr. 18 June 1636.([c])

I. 1636. JOHN SINCLAIR, of Stevenston, co. Haddington, s. and h. of George SINCLAIR([d]) (who *d.* about 1670), having acquired a considerable fortune as a merchant at Edinburgh, purchased in 1624 the Barony of Stevenston and lands at Wester Pencaithland, Easter Winsheills, etc., in the counties of Edinburgh, Haddington, and Berwick, and was *cr. a Baronet* [S.] 18 June 1636, the patent, not, however, being recorded in the Great Seal Register [S.] with rem. to heirs male whatsoever, and with a grant of, presumably, 16,000 acres in Nova Scotia, called the Barony of Stevenston and Murkle, of which he had seizin in July 1636.([a]) He *m.* Margaret, da. of (—) MACMATH, probably of Newbyres, but sometimes called a da. of Sir John MACMATH, "of that ilk." He *d.* 1648/9.

II. 1649. SIR JOHN SINCLAIR, Baronet [S. 1636], of Stevenston aforesaid, grandson and h., being 1st s. and h. of John SINCLAIR, by Isabel, da. of Robert (BOYD), 6th LORD BOYD [S.], which John was only s. and h. ap. of the 1st Baronet, but *d.* v.p. in 1643. He was *b.* 26 July 1642, and *suc. to the Baronetcy* on the death of his grandfather, to whom he was served heir 24 May 1650. He *d.* unm. before July 1652.

III. 1652. SIR ROBERT SINCLAIR, Baronet [S. 1636], of Stevenston, or Stevenson aforesaid, br. and h., *b.* 15 Oct. 1643 (posthumous), *suc. to the Baronetcy* on the death of his brother, to whom he was served heir, 5 July 1652; was Sheriff of co. Haddington, 1689; M.P. [S.] for Haddington Constabulary, 1689-1702; P.C. and a Lord of the Exchequer [S.] 1690; nominated a Lord of Session [S.], but declined to act; P.C. [S.] again, 1703. He *m.* firstly, 10 Sep. 1663, at the Chapel of Holyrood, Helen, da. of John (LINDSAY), EARL OF CRAWFORD [S.], by Margaret, da. of James (HAMILTON), 2d MARQUESS OF HAMILTON [S.] He *m.* secondly, Anne, widow of Sir Daniel CARMICHAEL, of Hyndford, da. of Sir William SCOTT, of Ardross. He *d.* July 1713.

([a]) Banks's Lists.

([b]) John Moore of Kirtlington, Notts, aged 47 in the Visit. of 1662, was his next br. and h. male, but appears never to have assumed the Baronetcy.

([c]) Laing's List; as also, but with the Christian name given (erroneously) as "James," in Milne's List.

([d]) It seems hardly likely that the family are descended, as is often alleged, in the male line from the old race of Sinclair of Longformacus, and the arms (a saltire charged with bezants) assigned to them in 1672, were thought by R. R. Stodart (Lyon Clerk Depute, 1863-86), to indicate an unknown origin. In the funeral escutcheon in 1713 of the 3d Baronet, his grandfather the 1st Baronet, is, however, called a son of Sir Matthew Sinclair, of Longformacus, but on the other hand, in that of the 4th Baronet in 1726, it is the *mother* (not father) of the 1st Baronet who is said to be of the family of Longformacus. Father Hay, a well-known genealogist (*b.* about 1650) says that the grandfather of the 1st Baronet was "a famous brewer of Leith," where "Sinclair's Society is yet extant," and that upon him the song of the "Clouting of the Caldron" was written. [*Ex inform.* Sir J. Balfour Paul, Lyon King of Arms.]

IV. 1713. SIR JOHN SINCLAIR, Baronet [S. 1636], of Stevenson aforesaid, s. and h., by 1st wife; M.P. [S.] for Lanarkshire, 1702-07, and an opposer of the Scotch Union; *suc. to the Baronetcy*, July 1713; was a staunch supporter of the Hanoverian Succession. He *m.* in 1698, Martha, widow of Cromwell LOCKHART, of Lee, co. Lanark, da. and eventually sole heir (on the death of her brother) of Sir John LOCKHART, of Castlehill, in that county, a Lord of Session [S.], under the title of LORD CASTLEHILL, He *d.* 1726. His widow *d.* at Stevenson, 15 May 1752.

V. 1726. SIR ROBERT SINCLAIR, Baronet [S. 1636], of Stevenson aforesaid, 1st s. and h.; *suc. to the Baronetcy* in 1726. He *m.* Sep. 1733, Isabella, only da. of da. of James KERR, Col. 3rd Foot Guards. He *d.* 25 Oct. 1754.

VI. 1754. SIR JOHN SINCLAIR, Baronet [S. 1636], of Stevenson, aforesaid, 1st s. and h.; *suc. to the Baronetcy*, 25 Oct. 1754. He, on the death, 9 Dec. 1765, of Alexander (SINCLAIR), EARL OF CAITHNESS [S.], suc. to the estate of Murchill or Murkley, co. Caithness, and other lands, under a deed executed in 1761 by that Earl. He *m.* 12 Feb. 1760, at Edinburgh, Mary, yst. da. of William BLAIR, *formerly* SCOT, of Blair, Advocate [S.], by his 2d wife, Catharine, da. of Alexander TAIT, of Edinburgh, Merchant. He *d.* 13 Feb. 1789.

VII. 1789. SIR ROBERT SINCLAIR, Baronet [S. 1636], of Stevenson and Murkley aforesaid, 1st s. and h.; *suc. to the Baronetcy*, 13 Feb. 1789; was Gov. of Fort St. George in Scotland. He *m.*, 2 April 1789, in the house of the Earl of Bristol, St. James' square, Madelina (then a minor), 2d da. of Alexander (GORDON), 4th DUKE OF GORDON [S.], by Jane, da. of Sir William MAXWELL, 3d Baronet [S. 1681], of Monreith. He *d.* 4 Aug. 1795, at Fort St. George. His widow *m.*, 25 Nov. 1805, at Kimbolton Castle, Charles Fysche PALMER, of Luckley Park, Berks, who *d.* Jan. 1843. She, who, on 28 May 1836, became coheir to her brother George, 5th DUKE OF GORDON [S.], *d.* 1 June 1847, in Chapel street, Grosvenor place, aged 75.

VIII. 1795. SIR JOHN GORDON SINCLAIR, Baronet [S. 1636], of Stevenson and Murkley aforesaid, only s. and h., *b.* 31 July 1790 in Edinburgh; *suc. to the Baronetcy*, 4 Aug. 1795, when aged 5; entered the Royal Navy, 1800, and served in "The Victory" under Nelson; was in command of "The Redwing" at Morjean and Cassis (1813) in the Mediterranean; Capt. 1814; Rear Admiral, 1849; Vice Admiral of the blue, 1856; Admiral, 1861; was sometime Capt. of the port at Gibraltar. He *m.* 15 June 1812, at Stonehouse, Devon, Anne, da. of Admiral the Hon. Michael DE COURCY (yr. s. of John, LORD KINGSALE [I.]), by Anne, da. of Conway BLENNERHASSETT. She *d.* 23 Sep. 1857, at Stevenson. He *d.* there 12 Nov. 1863, aged 73.

IX. 1863. SIR ROBERT CHARLES SINCLAIR, Baronet [S. 1636], of Stevenson and Murkley aforesaid, 1st s. and h., *b.* 25 Aug. 1820, in Paris, Capt. 38th Foot, 1849; *suc. to the Baronetcy*, 12 Nov. 1863; Lieut.-Col. Caithness and Sutherland Vols., 1864-80: Colonel, 1880. He *m.* firstly, in 1851, Charlotte Anne, da. of Lieut. John COOTE, 71st Foot. She *d.* 7 July 1874. He *m.* secondly, 5 Dec. 1876, at St. Andrew's Cathedral, Inverness, Louisa, 1st da. of Roderick HUGONIN, of Kinmylies House, co. Inverness. He *d.* s.p., 5 May 1899, at Stevenson aforesaid, in his 79th year. His widow living 1902.

X. 1899. SIR GRÆME ALEXANDER SINCLAIR-LOCKHART, Baronet [S. 1636], of Castlehill and Cambusnethan, co. Lanark, cousin and h. male, being 5th but 1st surv. s. of Robert LOCKHART, of Castlehill and Cambusnethan aforesaid, *i.e.*, his 2d s. by his 2d wife Charlotte Simpson, da. of Capt. William MERCER, of Potterhill, which Robert (who *d.* 2 Nov. 1850), was s. and h. of James LOCKHART, *formerly* SINCLAIR, of Castlehill aforesaid (an estate he inherited on the death, 5 May 1764, of his paternal uncle, George LOCKHART,

formerly SINCLAIR), which James was next br. to the 6th, being the 2d s. of the 5th Baronet. Major-Gen. LOCKHART (to call him by the name under which in 1899 he was known), was *b.* 23 Jan. 1820; entered the army, 1837; Capt., 1850; Major, 1858; Lieut.-Col., 1859; Col., 1866; retiring as Major-General, 1867. He served with 78th Highlanders in the Persian war, 1857, and in Indian Mutiny Campaign, 1857-58 (medal with clasp in both cases), C.B., 1861; suc. to the Lanarkshire estates on the death of his brother in 1873; *suc. to the Baronetcy*, 5 May 1899 and thereupon assumed the name SINCLAIR before that of LOCKHART. He *m.* in 1861, Emily Udny, da. of James BREMBER of Aberdeen, Advocate [S.]

Family Estates.—Those in 1883 attributed to the then Baronet, were 18,874 acres in Caithness and 473 in Haddingtonshire. *Total*, 19,374 acres, worth £6,326 a year. These, however, appear to be now (1901) enjoyed by his widow or descendants. The estates in 1883 attributed to Gen. Lockhart (who, in 1899, suc. to the Baronetcy), were 4,422 acres in Lanarkshire, worth £5,250 a year. *Principal Residence*, Cambusnethan House, near Wishaw co. Lanark.

CURZON:

cr. 18 June 1636;([a])

cr. a Baronet [E.] 11 Aug. 1641;

subsequently, since 1761, BARONS SCARSDALE.

I. 1636. JOHN CURZON, of Kedleston, co. Derby,([b]) was *cr. a Baronet* [S.] 18 June 1636,([a]) the patent not being recorded in the Great Seal Register [S.], with, it is supposed, rem. to heirs male whatsoever and with a grant of, presumably, 16,000 acres in Nova Scotia, of which, however, he never had seizin.(c) He was subsequently, 11 Aug. 1641, *cr. a Baronet of England*; see that dignity, pp. 132-133, the 5th Baronet being *cr.* 9 April 1761, BARON SCARSDALE, co. Derby, in which peerage these Baronetcies then *merged* and still so continue, see *Peerage*.

RAYNEY:

cr. 13 Sep. 1636;

and previously 19 Dec. 1635.

See that creation, p. 415.

BAILLIE:

cr. 21 Nov. 1636;([d])

dormant in or shortly before 1648.

I. 1636. GIDEON BAILLIE, of Lochend co. Haddington, s. and h. of Sir James BAILLIE,([e]) of the same, one of the Receivers of the Crown [S.] (who in 1614 had for 1,700 marks purchased that estate), by

([a]) Laing's List.

([b]) See p. 408, note "d," under "NORTON."

([c]) Banks's List.

([d]) Laing's List and Milne's List.

([e]) It is said by Lord Napier that this James was basely borne, and was educated by a butcher. [*Ex inform*, R. R. Stodart, Lyon Clerk Depute, 1863-86]. There appears, however, to be no foundation for this statement.

II

Jean NISBET, his wife, was *b.* 29 Feb. 1616, and was *cr. a Baronet* [S.], 21 Nov. 1636(a), with rem. to heirs male whatsoever, and with a grant of, presumably, 16,000 acres, called the Barony of Lochend, in Nova Scotia, of which, however, he never had seizin.(b) He *m.* (contract 17 Feb. 1636) Margaret, da. and coheir of David CARNEGIE, *styled* LORD CARNEGIE (s. and h. ap. of David, 1st EARL OF SOUTHESK [S.]), by Margaret, da. of Thomas (HAMILTON), 1st EARL OF HADDINGTON [S.]. He *d.* 30 Aug. 1640, being killed at the blowing up of Douglas Castle. His widow *m.* Sir John CRAWFORD, of Kilbirnie.

II. 1640, to 1648? SIR JAMES BAILLIE, Baronet [S. 1636], of Lochend aforesaid, only s. and h.; *suc. to the Baronetcy*, 30 Aug. 1640, and was, by Act of Parl. 11 Aug. 1641, allowed to enter without composition on the lands of his father, who had fallen in his country's service. He *d.* s.p. in or shortly before 1648(c), when the *Baronetcy* became *dormant*.(d)

NICOLSON:

cr. 16 Jan. 1636/7.(e)

I. 1637. "Master THOMAS NICOLSON, of Carnock" co. Stirling, 2d s. of John NICOLSON, of Lasswade,(f) by Elizabeth, da. of Dr. Edward HENDERSON, Advocate [S.], was an Advocate [S.] 1612, and was *cr. a Baronet* [S.] 16 Jan. 1636/7,(e) with rem. to heirs male whatsoever and with a grant of, presumably, 16,000 acres in Nova Scotia, of which he had seizin in Feb. 1637.(g) He was M.P. [S.] for Stirlingshire, 1644. He *m.* Isabel, da. of Walter HENDERSON, of Granton. He *d.* 8 Jan. 1646.

II. 1646. SIR THOMAS NICOLSON, Baronet [S. 1637], of Carnock aforesaid, s. and h.; *b.* 10 June 1628; *suc. to the Baronetcy*, 8 Jan. 1646.(h) He *m.* Margaret, da. of Alexander (LIVINGSTONE), 2d EARL OF LINLITHGOW [S.], by his 2d wife, Mary, da. of William (DOUGLAS), EARL OF ANGUS [S.]. He *d.* 24 July 1664. His widow *m.* in 1666, as his 4th wife, Sir George STIRLING, of Keir, who *d.* s.p., 1667. She *m.* thirdly, in 1668, as his 1st wife, Sir John STIRLING, of Keir and Cawder, who *d.* 1684. She *d.* 1674.

III. 1664. SIR THOMAS NICOLSON, Baronet [S. 1637], of Carnock aforesaid, s. and h.; *b.* 15 Sep. 1649; *suc. to the Baronetcy*, 24 July 1664. He *m.*, in or before 1668, Jean, 1st da. of Archibald (NAPIER), 3d LORD NAPIER OF MERCHISTOUN [S.], by Elizabeth, da. of John (ERSKINE), EARL OF MAR [S.]. He *d.* 20 Jan. 1670. His wife, who probably survived him, *d.* before Aug. 1683.

(a) See p. 423, note "d."
(b) Banks's Lists.
(c) Margaret, his only surv. sister and heir, *m.* (contract 17 Feb. 1636), as her 1st husband, Sir John Colquhoun, 2d Baronet [S. 1625], of Luss, who, in 1678, sold the estate of Lochend.
(d) A certain "William Baillie, of Letham," acts in some deeds with the family.
(e) Laing's List and Milne's List, in which last mention is made, without, however, any date, that "Sir John [*sic*] Nicolson of that ilk hes taken out his armes as Baronet."
(f) See p. 304, note "b" and the *corrigenda* thereto.
(g) Banks's Lists, where the Baronetcy is stated to be "represented by Sir Michael Shaw-Stewart, of Blackhall," a descendant of Eleanor, sister of the 3d and 1st da. of the 2d Baronet, by her husband, Sir John Shaw, 2d Baronet [S. 1687] of Greenock.
(h) He is not to be confused with another Sir Thomas Nicolson, who was Lord Advocate [S.] 1649.

IV. 1670. SIR THOMAS NICOLSON, Baronet [S. 1637], of Carnock aforesaid, only s. and h., *b.* 14 Jan. 1669; *suc. to the Baronetcy*, 20 Jan. 1670, and was served heir of his father in Carnock 3 Oct. 1671. He became, in Aug. 1683, LORD NAPIER OF MERCHISTOUN [S.], by the death, in Aug. 1683, of his maternal uncle, the 3d Lord. He *d.* unm., 9 June 1686, in France, in his 18th year, when the *peerage devolved on his maternal aunt*, and the estate of Carnock, etc., on his three paternal aunts and coheirs.

V. 1686. SIR THOMAS NICOLSON, Baronet [S. 1637], of Tillicoultrie, cousin and h. male, being 1st s. and h. of Sir John NICOLSON, also of Tillicoultrie, by Sabina (sometimes called Martha), da. of Col. Walter ROBERTSON, *otherwise* COLYEAR, which John, who *d.* 1683, was 2d s. of the 1st Baronet. He *suc. to the Baronetcy*, 9 June 1686, and, his affairs having become embarrassed, sold the estate of Tillicoultrie in 1697. He *d.* 2 Jan. 1699.

VI. 1699. SIR GEORGE NICOLSON, Baronet [S. 1637] only s. and h., *suc. to the Baronetcy*, 2 Jan. 1699; served in a Scotch Regiment in the service of the States of Holland, retiring in 1746 as a Major, and residing at the Hague. He *m.* Charlotte, 2d daughter of Edward HALKETT. He *d.*, at the Hague, Oct. 1771.

VII. 1771. SIR WALTER PHILIP NICOLSON, Baronet [S. 1637], 1st s. and h.; *suc. to the Baronetcy* in Oct. 1771; was an officer in a Scotch Regiment in the Dutch service. He *m.* Helen Frances Carpenter. He. *d.* s.p. legit, 1786. Will pr. in 1786.

VIII. 1786. SIR DAVID NICOLSON, Baronet [S. 1637], br. and h.; *suc. to the Baronetcy* in 1786; was an officer in a Scotch Regiment in the Dutch service. He *d.* unm. at Breda, 19 Oct. 1808. Will pr. 1809.

IX. 1808. SIR WILLIAM NICOLSON, Baronet [S. 1637], cousin and h. male, being only s. and h. of George NICOLSON, of Tarviston co. Lanark, by Catharine EDMONDSTONE, which George (who *d.* 1769), was 1st s. of William NICOLSON, Lieut.-Col. in the service of the states of Holland (*d.* at Ypres, 1720), yr. br. of the 5th Baronet, both being sons of Sir John NICOLSON, of Tillicoultrie abovenamed. He was *b.* 1758; entered the army, 1778; served in America, India, Ireland, and the Mauritius, becoming, finally, 1804, Major-Gen.; *suc. to the Baronetcy*, 19 Oct. 1808. He *m.*, 5 July 1804, Mary, da. of John RUSSELL, Writer to the Signet [S.], by Eleanor, da. of William ROBERTSON, D.D., of Edinburgh, the well known historian. He *d.* 5 Aug. 1820. Will pr. 1821. His widow *d.* 20 Feb. 1853, aged 73, in Eaton terrace. Admon. March 1853.

X. 1820. SIR FREDERICK WILLIAM ERSKINE NICOLSON, Baronet [S. 1637], only s. and h., *b.* 22 April 1815, at Ham Common; *suc. to the Baronetcy*, 5 Aug. 1820; entered the navy, 1827; Capt., 1846; C.B., 1859; Commodore Superintendent of Woolwich Dockyard, 1861-64; Rear Admiral of the Blue, 1863; Vice-Admiral, 1870-73; Admiral (retired), 1877; sometime Chairman of the Thames Conservatory Board. He *m.* firstly, 26 May 1847, at St. Geo., Han. sq., Clementina Maria Marion, 2d da. of James LOCH, of Drylaw, co. Edinburgh, by Ann, da. of Patrick ORR, of Bridgeton. She *d.* 17 July 1851, at 15 William street, Knightsbridge, aged 27. He *m.* secondly, in 1855, Augusta Sarah, widow of Capt. HAY, only da. of Robert CULLINGTON, of Old Lakenham. She *d.* 19 April 1861, at 15 William street, aforesaid. He *m.* thirdly, 16 Aug. 1867, at Lydeard Saint Lawrence, Somerset, Anne, only child of R. CROSSE, niece of Rev. James CROSSE, M.A., Rector of that parish. She *d.* 8 Jan. 1896, at 26, Ladbrooke square, Notting Hill. He *d.* 29 Dec. 1899, aged 84, at 39, Egerton gardens. Will pr. at £22,058.

XI. 1899. SIR ARTHUR NICOLSON, Baronet [S. 1637], only s. and h. by 1st wife; *b.* 19 Sep. 1849; entered Foreign Office, 1870; acting Chargé d'Affaires at Athens, 1882-85; Sec. of Legation, 1885; C.M.G.,

1886; Sec. of Legation at Teheran and acting Chargé d'Affaires in Persia, 1885-88; Consul Gen. for Hungary, at Buda-Pest, 1888-93; K.C.I.E., 1888; Sec. of Embassy at Constantinople, 1893-94; Consul Gen. at Sofia, in Bulgaria, 1894-95; Minister at Tangier since 1895. He *m.*, 20 April 1881, Mary Katharine, 3d and yst. da. of Archibald Rowan HAMILTON, of Killyleagh Castle, co. Down, sometime Capt. 5th Dragoon Guards, by Anne, da. of the Rev. George CALDWELL.

PRESTON:

cr. 13 March 1636/7;(a)

dormant since 25 Nov. 1873.

I. 1637. "Master GEORGE PRESTON, fear of Valafield" [*i.e.*, Valleyfield], co. Perth, *i.e.*, s. and h., ap. of Sir John PRESTON, of Valleyfield aforesaid, by Grizel, da. of Alexander COLVILLE, Commendator of Culross, was *cr. a Baronet* [S.], 13 March 1636/7,(a) the patent, however, not being entered in the Great Seal Register [S.] with rem. to heirs male, whatsoever, and with a grant of, presumably, 16,000 acres in Nova Scotia "with the haill gold mines therein, and power to transport thereto all gold affecting mines," of which Barony he had seizin in the same month.(b) He obtained £1,000 from Parl., 6 May 1646, for payment of four Perthshire troops and was in 1649 made Colonel of them. He *m.*, in 1634, Marian, 1st da. of Hugh (SEMPILL), 5th LORD SEMPILL [S.], being the only child of his 1st wife, Anne, da. of James (HAMILTON), 1st EARL OF ABERCORN [S.]. He *d.* 26 Nov. 1679.

II. 1679. SIR WILLIAM PRESTON, Baronet [S. 1637], of Valleyfield aforesaid, 1st s. and h.(c), to whom his father made over certain lands there, 10 May 1663. He *suc. to the Baronetcy*, 26 Nov. 1679. He *m.* Anne, da. of Sir James LUMSDEN, of Innergelly. He *d.* between 1702 and 1705.

III. 1703? SIR GEORGE PRESTON, Baronet [S. 1637], of Valleyfield aforesaid, 1st s. and h., *b.* about 1670; *suc. to the Baronetcy* about 1703. He *m.* Agnes (well known for her beauty), da. of Patrick MUIRHEAD, of Rashyhill. He *d.* Sep. 1741, aged 70.

IV. 1741. SIR GEORGE PRESTON, Baronet [S. 1637], of Valleyfield aforesaid, 1st s. and h., *suc. to the Baronetcy* in 1741. He *m.*, about 1730, Anne, sister of Thomas, 8th EARL OF DUNDONALD [S.], 4th and yst. da. of William COCHRANE, of Ochiltree (grandson of the 1st Earl), by Mary, da. of Alexander (BRUCE), EARL OF KINCARDINE [S.]. He *d.* 2 March 1779, at Valleyfield. His widow *d.* a few months later, 7 Nov. 1779.

V. 1779. SIR CHARLES PRESTON, Baronet [S. 1637], of Valleyfield aforesaid, 3d(d) but 1st surv. s. and h. male; *b.* probably about 1735, was Capt. in the 26th Foot and distinguished himself early in 1775,

(a) Laing's List, but not in Milne's List.
(b) Banks's Lists.
(c) George Preston the 2d son (*b.* 1660) was Capt. in the service of the States General in 1688; served in the wars under Marlborough; was Gov. of Edinburgh Castle in 1715 and Commander-in-Chief [S.] soon afterwards. He *d.* at Valleyfield, 7 July 1748, in his 89th year.
(d) His eldest br., Patrick Preston, Major in the British service, and Brig.-General in that of Portugal, *d.* v.p., 25 April 1776, leaving two daughters, who successively inherited the family estate of Valleyfield. On the death of the survivor, 6 April 1855, it was inherited by her cousin, Ann, da. and h. of George Preston, widow of Sir John Hay, 6th Baronet [S. 1635], on whose death, s.p., 2 Sep. 1862, it passed to the descendants of Mary, wife of Robert Wellwood, sister of the 5th and 6th, da. of the 4th Baronet.

being then a Major, in his defence of Fort St. John against the Americans. He *suc. to the Baronetcy*, 2 March 1779. He was M.P. for Kirkcaldy Burghs, 1784-90, and was a Commissioner of Customs [S.], 1798-1800. He *d.* unm. 23 March 1800.

VI. 1800. SIR ROBERT PRESTON, Baronet [S. 1637], of Valleyfield aforesaid, yst. br. and h. male, being 5th s. of the 4th Baronet, was *b.* 21 April 1740; was some time in the sea service of the East India Company and was in command of the "Asia" frigate, becoming eventually an elder brother of the Trinity House. He *suc. to the Baronetcy*, 23 March 1800. He *m.* Elizabeth, da. of George BROWN, of Stockton. He *d.* s.p., 7 May 1834, at Valleyfield aforesaid, aged 94. His will, as also that of his wife or widow, pr. July 1834. On his death the issue male of the 1st Baronet became *extinct*.

VII. 1834. SIR ROBERT PRESTON, Baronet(a) [S. 1637], of Lutton, co. Lincoln, and of Sydney Place, Bath, cousin and h. male, being only s. and h. of George PRESTON, Gen. in the Army, and Col. of the Scots Greys, by Lucy, da. of James JOHNSTONE, which George (who *d.* 7 Feb. 1785) was 2d and yst. s. of William PRESTON, of Gorton, a Major in the Army (*d.* 1733), who was 5th of the six sons of Robert PRESTON, a Lord of Session [S.] (*d.* 1674), yr. br. of the 1st Baronet. He was *b.* 3 Jan. 1757, *assumed the Baronetcy*, 7 May 1834, and was, in 1835, served heir male general of the 6th Baronet at the Sheriff's Court at Edinburgh. He *m.* about 1780 his cousin, Euphemia, da. of John PRESTON, of Gorton aforesaid. He *d.* 30 Aug. 1846, at Blackadder, aged 90. Will pr. Nov. 1846.

VIII. 1846. SIR ROBERT PRESTON, Baronet(a) [S. 1637], of Lutton and of Sydney Place, both aforesaid, 1st s. and h., *b.* about 1780, sometime a Col. in the Army; *suc. to the Baronetcy*,(a) 30 Aug. 1846. He *m.* in 1826 (—), widow of (—) WILLIAMS, Major E.I.C.S., da. of Charles DEANE, of Hendon, co. Midx. He *d.* s.p. 23 Oct. 1858, at Sydney Place aforesaid. His widow *d.* at Bath 15 Dec. 1867, in her 89th year.

IX. 1858, to 1873. SIR HENRY LINDSAY PRESTON, Baronet(a) [S. 1637], of Lutton and of Sydney Place aforesaid, only br. and h.; *b.* 18 Feb. 1789; entered the Navy, 1801; Commander, 1830; Capt. on the retired list, 1856; *suc. to the Baronetcy*,(a) 23 Oct. 1858. He *d.* unm. at Bath, 25 Nov. 1873, aged 84, when the *Baronetcy* became *dormant*.

KERR, *afterwards* [1776-91] CARR:

cr. 31 July 1637(b);

dormant (rightfully) *since* 16 Aug. 1776;

but assumed, in 1776, as CARR;

till 6 March 1791.

I. 1637. ANDREW KERR, of Greenhead, co. Roxburgh, 1st of the seven sons of Sir Andrew KERR, of Greenhead, Hietoun and Prymsideloch in that county (*d.* between Nov. 1612 and March 1617), by Alison, da. of Gilbert WAUCHOPE, of Niddrie Marischal, co. Edinburgh,(c) was served heir special to his father, 18 March 1617, and was *cr. a Baronet* [S.] 31 July 1637,(b) with rem. to heirs male whatsoever, and with a grant of, presumably,

(a) According to the service in 1835.
(b) Laing's List and Milne's List.
(c) See an article by "S" [R. R. Stodart] in the *Her. and Gen.*, vol. vi, pp. 231-240, as to this family. See, also, *Genealogist*, orig. series, vol. iii, p. 66.

16,000 acres, entitled the Barony of Greenhead, in Nova Scotia, of which he had seizin in Dec. following.(a) He was on the Committee of War, co. Roxburgh, 1643-49; was M.P. [S.] for that county 1645 and 1648-49, and [E.] for the Sheriffdom of Roxburgh, 1659; was on the Committee of Estates, 1649; was styled "Colonel" in 1650, and was an active supporter of the Covenant, being consequently imprisoned at Edinburgh in 1660, and fined £6,000 in 1662. He *m.* firstly, in 1634, Elizabeth, 1st da. of Sir William SCOTT, of Harden, co. Roxburgh, by his 1st wife, Agnes, da. of Sir Gideon MURRAY, of Elibank. He *m.* secondly,(b) 16 Aug. 1664, at Edinburgh, Katherine, widow of David CARNEGIE, of Craig, 5th and yst. da. of John (WEMYSS), 1st EARL OF WEMYSS [S.], by Jean, da. of Patrick (GRAY), LORD GRAY [S.]. He *d.* May 1665. His widow *d.* 24 Feb. 1668 at Dysart.

II. 1665. SIR ANDREW KERR, Baronet [S. 1637], of Greenhead aforesaid, 1st s. and h.; was M.P. for Roxburghshire [S.], 1669-74; *suc. to the Baronetcy* in May 1665. He *m.*, 4 Dec. 1664, Jean, da. of Sir Alexander DON, 1st Baronet [S. 1667], of Newton, by Isabel SMITH his wife. He *d.* s.p.m., in or before June 1676. His widow(c) *m.* in 1685, Sir Roger HAY, of Harcarse, Senator of the College of Justice [S.].

III. 1676? SIR WILLIAM KERR, Baronet [S. 1637], of Greenhead aforesaid, br. and h. male; *suc. to the Baronetcy* on the death of his brother, to whom he was served heir special 15 June 1676; was a Commisr. of Supply, 1685-1704; Col. of Militia, 1689, and was M.P. [S.] for Roxburghshire, 1685-86 and 1702-07, and [G.B.] 1707-08. He *m.* Jean COCKBURN.(c) He *d.* in or before March 1718.

IV. 1718? SIR WILLIAM KERR, Baronet [S. 1637], of Greenhead aforesaid, grandson and h., being only s. and h. of Andrew KERR, a Commis. of Supply, 1698-1704, by Helen HAY, his wife, which Andrew was 1st s. and h. ap. of the late Baronet, but *d.* v.p. before March 1718. His house at Bridgend, Kelso, with all its contents, was destroyed by fire in Aug. 1741. He *suc. to the Baronetcy* on the death of his grandfather, being served heir to his father, his grandfather, and great uncle 30 March 1721. He *d.* s.p.,(d) Aug. 1741.

V. 1741. SIR ROBERT KERR, Baronet [S. 1637], of Greenhead aforesaid, uncle and h. male; *suc. to the Baronetcy* in Aug. 1741 and was served heir of provision to his nephew, 27 Aug. 1745. He sold the estate of Greenhead and most of the other estates. He *m.* (—), da. of Gilbert KERR, of Bamfmiln in Sprouston. He *d.* April 1746.

VI. 1746. SIR WILLIAM KERR, Baronet [S. 1637], of Softlaw and of Bridgend aforesaid, 1st s. and h.; *suc. to the Baronetcy* in April 1746, and was served heir special to his father, 9 Oct. 1750. He sold the last of the family estates, and *d.* s.p. at Boulogne, 8 Dec. 1755.

(a) Banks's Lists, it being the last entry therein of the seizins, save the somewhat unintelligible one, in Nov. 1640, of "Sir Robert Campbell, of one part of Nova Scotia." who, possibly, may have been the *successor* of a grantee, and not a grantee himself.

(b) See Lamont's *Diary* as to this match.

(c) The widow of the 2d Baronet is, probably, the "Lady Greenhead" who was fined 16,000 Scots, 4 Sep. 1684, for her adherence to the Covenant, but possibly the reference is to Jean, wife of the 3d Baronet. This "Jean Cockburn" was not improbably a daughter of Sir James Cockburn, of Ryslaw, by his 2d wife, Jean, daughter of Andrew Kerr, of Lintoun.

(d) His two sisters, both of whom *d.* unm., were served heirs portioners general to their cousin, the 7th Baronet, 26 Jan. 1779, but seem to have inherited no landed property. Agnes, the survivor, *d.* 1 March 1785, at a great age.

VII. 1755, to 1776. SIR ROBERT KERR, Baronet [S. 1637], only br. and h., *suc. to the Baronetcy*, but to none of the estates, 8 Dec. 1755. He was served heir general to Gilbert KERR, his maternal grandfather, 27 Sep. 1768. He resided in the town of Kelso. He *d.* s.p. 16 Aug. 1776, when the male issue of the grantee became *extinct*, and when the *Baronetcy* (no one having proved any descent in the male line from a common ancestor of the grantee) became (rightfully) *dormant*.

VIII. 1776. SIR WILLIAM CARR, Baronet(a) [S. 1637], of Etall, co. Northumberland, calling himself cousin and h. male, but whose pedigree as such is unknown.(b) He was s. of (—) by (—). He, who was *b.* about 1705,(c) *assumed the Baronetcy* 16 April 1776. He *m.* in or before 1742 (—). He *d.* s.p.m.(d) 11 April 1777. Will dat. 19 Oct. 1776 to 20 Jan. 1777.

IX. 1777, to 1791. SIR ROBERT CARR, Baronet(a) [S. 1637], br. and h. male, *b.* about 1707; was sometime a Mercer on Ludgate Hill, London, and was subsequently of Hampton, co. Midx.; *suc. to the Baronetcy*(a) but not to the family estates, 11 April 1777. He *m.* firstly, Grace, da. of Thomas BIGGE, of Newcastle-on-Tyne, by Elizabeth, da. of Edward HINDMARSH. He *m.* secondly, Mary, da. of (—) LITTLE. He *d.* s.p.m.(e) 6 March 1791, in his 85th year, and was *bur.* at Hampton aforesaid. M.I. Will pr. March 1790. After his death *the assumption of this Baronetcy ceased.*

(a) According to the assumption of the Baronetcy in 1776.

(b) He was descended from Col. Sir Robert Carr, of Etal aforesaid (presumably of Scottish descent), who obtained in 1647 two warrants of Baronetcies, of which, owing to the Civil War, he was unable to make any use. On 8 Aug. 1661, however, Charles II, on his petition, allowed their renewal, provided "he nominate two meete persons to His Majestie capable for their extraction and estates of the dignity and honour of a Knight Baronett." Whether he ever did nominate anyone is unknown, but he "certainly seems not to have thought of appropriating one of the titles at his disposal to himself as he always styles himself, and was styled by others, *Knight.*" [See R. R. Stodart's "Notes on the traffic in Baronetcies," in *The Genealogist*, O.S., vol. iii, pp. 65-68.] One of the six yr. brothers of the 1st Baronet is there "*said*" to have been "ancestor of the Carrs of Etall" in Stodart's article on the family, as on p. 427, note "c."

(c) As to this assumption he shewed "a scrupulousness worthy of all praise," inasmuch as though in his will, dat. 19 Oct. 1776, he designs himself "Sir William Carr, of Etal, Baronet," he explains in a codicil of 20 Jan. following, as under:—"I did apprehend I was warranted in taking the title of Baronet, but as I do not find that I can, by indisputable evidence, satisfie myself that I have undoubted right to, and [*sic*] therefore I have declined that title." [See p. 427, note "c."]

(d) Of his two daughters and coheirs, Isabel, the eldest (*b.* 31 March 1742), and the only one that left issue (inheritors of the estate of Etall), *m.* 3 Aug. 1762, at Ford, co. Northumberland, James (Hay, *formerly* Boyd), EARL OF ERROLL [S.], and *d.* 3 Nov. 1808.

(e) Of his two daughters and coheirs, Elizabeth, only child of the 1st wife, *m.* in March 1754, Sir Richard Glyn, 1st Baronet [1759], of Ewell.

Memorandum.—In and after 1638 no seizin of any land in Nova Scotia is recorded, though, apparently, five Baronets (Slingsby, Piers, Musgrave, Longueville, and Meredith, who were created from March 1637/8 to Jan. 1638/9) had *grants* of land there.(a) After Jan. 1638/9, however, no such grants seem to have been made.

SLINGSBY:

cr. 2 March 1637/8;(b)

dormant since 4 Feb. 1869.

I. 1638. HENRY SLINGSBY, of Scriven, near Knaresborough, co. York, 2d but 1st surv. s. and h. of Sir Henry SLINGSBY, of Scriven aforesaid, and of the Red House, near Marston Moor, in that county (*d.* 17 Dec. 1634, aged 74), by Frances, da. of William VAVASOUR, of Weston, co. York, was *b.* 14 Jan. 1601/2; sometime (1619-21) of Queen's Coll., Cambridge, and was *cr. a Baronet* [S.] by patent dat. at Stirling, 2 March 1637/8,(b) not, however, recorded in the Great Seal Register [S.] with rem. to "heirs male," and with presumably a grant of land in Nova Scotia, of which, however, he appears to have never had seizin.(a) He had shortly before entertained the King at Red House, in whose service he was a Colonel, and to whose cause he stedfastly adhered. He was M.P. or Knaresborough, 1625, April to May 1640, and again 1640 (Long Parliament), till disabled in Dec. 1642, and was one of the fifty-nine members who opposed the attainder of the Earl of Strafford. He refused to compound, and in 1651 his estate was ordered to be sold. In 1655, being implicated in a Royalist rising, he was imprisoned at Hull. He *m.* 7 July 1631, at Kensington, Barbara, 1st da. of Thomas (BELASYSE), 1st VISCOUNT FAUCONBERG, by Barbara, da. of Sir Henry CHOLMLEY, of Roxby, co. York. She, who was *bap.* 11 Oct. 1609, at Coxwold, in that county, *d.* in London, 31 Dec. 1641, and was *bur.* at St. Martin's in the Fields. He, having entered into a scheme for the landing of Charles II. at Hull, was executed by the then Government, 8 June 1658, on Tower Hill, being, however, *bur.* with his ancestors, at Knaresborough.(c)

II. 1658. SIR THOMAS SLINGSBY, Baronet [S. 1638], of Scriven and Red House aforesaid, 1st s. and h., *b.* 15 June 1636; *suc. to the Baronetcy*, 8 June 1658. Sheriff of Yorkshire, 1660-61; Governor of Scarborough Castle, 1670; M.P. for co. York, Nov. 1670 to 1678; for Knaresborough (three Parls.), 1679-81; for Scarborough, 1685-87. He *m.* 29 July 1658, at St. Gregory's, London, Dorothy, da. and coheir of George CRADOCK, of Caverswall Castle, co. Stafford. She *d.* 24 Jan. and was *bur.* 2 Feb. 1673, at Knaresborough. M.I. He *d.* at St. Martin's in the Fields, and was *bur.* 1 March 1687/8, at Knaresborough. Admon. 10 April 1688 and 26 March 1692. Admon. at York 15 June 1692.

III. 1688. SIR HENRY SLINGSBY, Baronet [S. 1638], of Scriven and Red House aforesaid, 1st s. and h., *b.* about 1660, being aged 4 years and 6 months at the Visit. of Yorkshire, 23 March 1665; was M.P. for Knaresborough 1685-87, and 1690 till void same year; *suc. to the Baronetcy* in Feb. 1687/8. He *d.* unm. and was *bur.* 15 Sep. 1691, at Knaresborough. Admon. 19 March 1691/2.

(a) Banks's Lists. The creations of Slingsby, Piers, Musgrave, Longueville, and Meredith are the last in the list of those Baronets [S.], who are said to have "obtained charters of land in Nova Scotia, which do not appear to have been followed by seisins."

(b) Laing's List, but not in that of Milne.

(c) His *diary* is a most valuable account of the Civil War, 1638-1648, as far as it concerned Yorkshire.

IV. 1691. SIR THOMAS SLINGSBY, Baronet [S. 1638], of Scriven and Red House aforesaid, br. and h., *b.* probably about 1668; *suc. to the Baronetcy* in Sep. 1691. He *m.* 12 April 1692, at Methley, co. York, Sarah (*bap.* there 22 June 1669), da. of John SAVILE, of Methley, by Sarah, da. of Peter TRYON. He was *bur.* 15 Nov. 1726, at Knaresborough.

V. 1726. SIR HENRY SLINGSBY, Baronet [S. 1638], of Scriven and Red House aforesaid, 1st s. and h., *b.* about 1693; matric. at Oxford (Univ. Coll.), 13 Oct. 1710, aged 17; M.P. for Knaresborough, 1714 to Jan. 1715, and (seven Parls.) 1722-63. He *m.* in or before 1729, Mary, da. of John AISLABIE, of Studley, Chancellor of the Exchequer. She *d.* at Beaconsfield, 31 May and was *bur.* 7 June 1736, at Knaresborough. He *d.*, s.p.s. legit., 18 Jan. 1763. Will pr. 1769.

VI. 1763. SIR THOMAS SLINGSBY, Baronet [S. 1638], of Scriven and Red House aforesaid, br. and h., *b.* about 1695; was, for many years, blind; *suc. to the Baronetcy*, 18 Jan. 1763. He *d.* unm. 18 Jan. 1765.

VII. 1765. SIR SAVILE SLINGSBY, Baronet [S. 1638], of Scriven and Red House aforesaid, br. and h., *b.* about 1698; *suc. to the Baronetcy*, 18 Jan. 1765. He *d.* unm. Nov. 1780, aged 82. Will pr. Dec. 1780.

VIII. 1780. SIR THOMAS TURNER SLINGSBY, Baronet [S. 1638], of Scriven and Red House aforesaid, nephew and h., being only s. and h. of Charles SLINGSBY, of Lofthouse hill, co. York, Barrister, by Catherine, 1st da. of John TURNER, of Stainsby, in that county, which Charles (who *d.* Aug. 1772), was yst. s. of the 4th Baronet. He was *b.* about 1741; matric. at Oxford (Queen's Coll.), 26 April 1759, aged 18; *suc. to the Baronetcy*, Nov. 1780; was Sheriff of Yorkshire, 1785. He *m.* firstly, 28 Oct. 1773, at Kippax, his maternal cousin, Catherine, yst. da. of George BUCKLEY, of Thurnscoe, co. York, by Anne, yst. da. of John TURNER abovenamed. She *d.* 16 Jan. 1778. He *m.* secondly, 25 Oct. 1781, at Moor Monckton, Mary Fletcher SLINGSBY, spinster, illegit. da. of his paternal uncle, Sir Henry SLINGSBY, the 5th Baronet. He *d.* 14 April 1806. Will pr. 1806. His widow *d.* s.p. 18 Feb. 1815. Will pr. 1816.

IX. 1806. SIR THOMAS SLINGSBY, Baronet [S. 1638], of Scriven and Red House aforesaid, 1st s. and h., by 1st wife; *b.* 10 Jan. and *bap.* 10 June 1775, at Knaresborough; matric. at Oxford (Queen's Coll.) 11 April 1793, aged 18; *suc. to the Baronetcy*, 14 April 1806. Sheriff of Yorkshire, 1812. He *d.* unm. at Brighton, 26 Feb. 1835, and was *bur.* at Knaresborough, aged 60. Will pr. July 1835.

X. 1835, to 1869. SIR CHARLES SLINGSBY, Baronet [S. 1638], of Scriven and Red House aforesaid, nephew and h., being only s. and h. of Charles SLINGSBY, of Lofthouse hill aforesaid, by Emma Margaret, da. of Thomas ATKINSON, of Ripley, co York, which Charles (who was *b.* 17 March 1777 and *d.* 20 May 1832), was 2d and yst. s. of the 8th Baronet, by his 1st wife. He was *b.* at Lofthouse hill, 22 and *bap.* 23 Aug. 1824 at Staveley; *suc. to the Baronetcy*, 26 Feb. 1835; entered the Royal Horse Guards 1843, retiring as a Lieut. 1847. He *d.* unm., being drowned (with four other members of the York and Ainsty hunt) while crossing the river Ure, near Ripon, 4 and was *bur.* 11 Feb. 1869, at Knaresborough, aged 44.(a) At his death, the issue male of the grantee being apparently extinct, the *Baronetcy* became *dormant*.

(a) His only sister and sole heir, Emma Louisa Catherine, *m.* 19 July 1860, Capt. Thomas Leslie, who by Royal license, in 1869, took the name of Slingsby, and was Sheriff of Yorkshire in 1886. She *d.* s.p., at Scriven park, 29 June 1899, aged 70, when the estates descended to her maternal cousin Charles Atkinson, who accordingly took the name of Slingsby.

PIERS, *or* PEIRS:

cr. 24 March 1637/8;(a)

dormant since 7 May 1720.

I. 1638. THOMAS PIERS, or PEIRS,(b) of Stonepit, in the parish of Seale, co. Kent, s. and h. of Laurence PIERS, of Westfield, co. Sussex, by Catherine, da. of John THEOBALD, of Stonepit aforesaid, was *b.* about 1616 and was *cr. a Baronet* [S.], 24 March 1637/8,(a) with rem. to heirs male whatsoever,(b) and with, presumably, a grant of land in Nova Scotia, of which he apparently never had seizin.(c) He *m.* firstly, in or before 1643, Jane, sister of Sir Henry OXENDEN, 1st Baronet [1678], da. of Sir James OXENDEN, of Dene, co. Kent, by Mary, da. of Thomas NEVINSON. He *m.* secondly, 21 May 1649, at St. Bartholomew the Less, London (Lic. Fac. 19 May, he 33, widower, and she 23 spinster), Audrey, da. of Sir Edward MASTER, of Ospringe, co. Kent. by Audrey, da. and coheir of Robert STREYNSHAM. She *d.* 6 and was *bur.* 9 Jan. 1656/7, at Seal. M.I. He *d.* at Stonepit 7 and was *bur.* 10 April 1680, at Seale, aged 64. Will dat. 16 to 17 April 1679, pr. 24 May 1680.

II. 1680. SIR THOMAS PIERS, Baronet [S. 1638], of Stonepit aforesaid, 1st s. and h., being only s. and h. by 1st wife, *b.* about 1643; admitted to Gray's Inn, 6 April 1657; *suc. to the Baronetcy*, 7 April 1680. He *m.*, 9 Sep. 1669, at St. Bartholomew the Great, London (Lic. Fac. 5 July, he 26, bachelor, and she 23, spinster), Elizabeth, da. of Sir George COURTHOPE, of Whiligh, co. Sussex, by Elizabeth, da. and h. of Edward HAWES, of London. He was *bur.* 26 Aug. 1693, at Seal aforesaid. Admon. 3 Feb. 1693/4, his widow being then living.

III. 1693, to 1720. SIR GEORGE PIERS, Baronet [S. 1638], of Stonepit aforesaid, 1st s. and h., *bap.* 25 Oct. 1670, at Seal; matric. at Oxford (Mag. Hall). 4 July 1689, and then said to be aged 16; *suc. to the Baronetcy* in Aug. 1693. He *d.* s.p., probably unm., 7 and was *bur.* 20 May 1720, at Seal, aged 50, when the issue male of the grantee was apparently extinct,(d) and the *Baronetcy* became *dormant*. Will pr. 1720.

PICKERING:

cr. 5 June 1638;(e)

descent uncertain after July 1749;

assumed till April 1803.

I. 1638. "GILBERT PICKERING, of Tichmersh, co. Northampton, Esq.," s. and h. of Sir John PICKERING, of the same (*d.* 29 Jan. 1627/8, aged 43) by Susan, da. of Sir Erasmus DRYDEN, of Canons Ashby in that county, was *b.* about March 1610/1 (being 16 years, 10 months and 18 days old at his father's death), and was *cr. a Baronet* [S.], 5 June 1638,(a) with possibly(b) (like other creations in that year) a grant of lands in Nova Scotia, of which, however, no record is known; admitted to Gray's Inn 16 Nov. 1629; was a Col. in the Army; M.P. for Northamptonshire (five parls.) 1640-58; a zealous Parliamentarian, serving on numerous committees, 1640-51, and on each of the five Councils of State of the Commonwealth; was one of Cromwell's *House of Lords*, Dec. 1657, and was Chamberlain to him and to his son Richard. He, though one of the Regicide Judges (not, however, one who signed the death warrant) obtained pardon at the Restoration. He *m.* in or before 1640, Sidney, sister of Edward, 1st EARL OF SANDWICH, only da. of Sir Sidney MONTAGU, of Hinchinbroke, co. Huntingdon, by his 1st wife Paulina, da. of John PEPYS, of Cottenham. By her he had twelve children. He *m.* secondly, Elizabeth, da. of John PEPYS, of Cottenham, by Edith, da. and h. of Sir Edmund TALBOT. He *d.* about Michaelmas 1668, aged 57. Admon. 5 May 1669 to Elizabeth his relict, who subsequently proved his will 4 Dec. 1672. She *d.* about 1679.

(a) Laing's List, but not in that of Milne.

(b) In the Privy Seal Register [S.] he is styled "Thomas Peiris, of Stenypites, Kent," and the rem. is to "heirs male whatsoever."

(c) See p. 430, note "a," under "Slingsby."

(d) The only br. of the the last Baronet, John Piers, was *bap.* at Seal 12 Oct. 1673, and *bur.* there 9 April 1692. Of their three uncles of the half blood, sons of the 1st Baronet by the 2d wife (1), Edward, *b.* about 1652, was living 5 May 1681; (2), Richard, *bap.* 1 Jan. 1655/6, was a Factor at Aleppo, and *d.* unm. between Sep. 1678 and May 1680; (3), Streynsham, *bap.* 22 Dec. 1656. *d.* unm. and was *bur.* at Seal, 5 April 1681. Will pr. 5 May 1681.

(e) This is the date of the Royal warrant, given at Dalkeith, for affixing the Great Seal. The diploma of this Baronetcy is among the MS. collection entitled the "H. MSS." [vol. xxi, 84], in the College of Arms, London. The creation is not in Laing's or in Milne's List, but is in that of Walkley (1641), and the Baronetcy is recognised in the Visitation of Northamptonshire made in 1681.

II. 1668. SIR JOHN PICKERING, Baronet [S. 1638], of Tichmersh aforesaid, 1st s. and h. of eight sons by 1st wife; *b.* about 1640; matric. at Oxford (Ch. Ch.) 18 March 1656/7; *suc. to the Baronetcy* in 1668; entered his pedigree in the Visit. of Northamptonshire 1681, being then aged 41. He *m.* in or before 1670, Frances, 1st da. of Sir Thomas ALSTON, 1st Baronet [1642], of Odell, Beds, by Elizabeth, da. of Sir Rowland ST. JOHN. She was living 1681, and was *bur.* at Tichmersh. He was *bur.* there 3 April 1703. Will pr. April 1704.

III. 1703. SIR GILBERT PICKERING, Baronet [S. 1638], of Tichmersh aforesaid, and of West Langton, co. Leicester, 1st and only surv. s. and h.; aged 11 years in 1681; *suc. to the Baronetcy* in April, 1703. Sheriff of Leicestershire, 1704-05; M.P., 1708-10. He *m.* in or before April 1691, Elizabeth (then aged about 14), da. and h. of Stavely STAUNTON, of Birchmore, in Woburn, Beds, by Elizabeth, da. of Sir Thomas ALSTON, 1st Baronet abovenamed. He *d.* March 1735/6, in Cavendish square, Midx. Will pr. 1736. His widow, who was *b.* 24 and *bap.* 26 Aug. 1677, at Woburn aforesaid, and who brought him a large fortune, *d.* July 1741.

IV. 1736, to 1749. SIR EDWARD PICKERING, Baronet [S. 1638], of Tichmersh aforesaid, only s. and h.; *b.* about 1716; matric. at Oxford (Ch. Ch.), 25 May 1732, aged 16; *cr.* M.A. 9 June 1736, having *suc. to the Baronetcy* in March 1735/6; M.P., for St. Michael, Nov. 1745 to 1747. He *d.* unm. July 1749 when the issue male of the 2d Baronet became *extinct*. Admon. 17 Aug. 1749, and again 13 March 1773.

V. 1749? SIR GILBERT PICKERING, Baronet(c) [S. 1638], *assumed the Baronetcy*, presumably in 1749 but certainly before Oct. 1762, as heir male of the grantee. He is said(d) to have been s. of John PICKERING, which John is said(d) to have been s. of Gilbert PICKERING (by Elizabeth PINCHON, his wife), the 2d s. of the 1st Baronet.(e) It is, however, much more likely that the 5th Baronet(c) was identical with the Gilbert PICKERING, *b.* after 1681 and before 1697, when he was living as son of the abovenamed Gilbert, the 2d s. of the 1st Baronet. He *m.* Anne, da. of Franks BERNARD, of Castlebar, King's County,(a) and of Clonmush, co. Carlow. She *d.* in New Ross, co. Wexford, 16 Oct. 1762, when, apparently, he was alive.(b)

(a) See p. 432, note "e."

(b) See *Memorandum* on p. 430.

(c) According to the assumption of the Baronetcy, 1749-62.

(d) Atkins Davis' MSS. in Ulster's office, kindly inspected by G. D. Burtchaell.

(e) The Visitation of Northamptonshire in 1681 sets out the male issue of the 1st Baronet, moreover a very full account of such of his descendants as were living 30 March 1697, is given in the will of that date (proved 21 Oct. 1699) of his brother, Edward Pickering. From these and other sources it can be gathered that of the six younger sons of the 1st Baronet who survived infancy (1), Gilbert, *m.* 30 Sep. 1666, at St. Leonard's, Shoreditch (he 21 and she 26, Lic. Vic. Gen.), Elizabeth Pinchon, widow, both of whom were living in 1681, with a da., Elizabeth, aged 12. Gilbert, however, had subsequently a son, Gilbert, living 1697, who presumably is the Gilbert who, 1749-62, assumed the Baronetcy. (2), Sydney, *b.* about 1647, *m.* (Lic. Vic. Gen., 19 Nov. 1673) his cousin, Honor Pickering, of Whaddon. He had a son, Sydney, living 1697. (3), Oliver, *d.* unm. before 1681. (4), Montagu, of Birchmore, Beds, *m.* 18 May 1679, at Campton, Beds, the "widow Stanton," and had a son Edward, *bap.* 31 March 1681, at Woburn in that county, who was living 1697. He himself was *bur.* at Woburn, 1 April 1694. (5), Francis, a merchant of Oporto, unm. 1681, but living 1697 with two sons, Francis and Edward. (6), Theophilus Pickering, D.D., *b.* at Tichmarsh, who *d.* unm. 20 March 1710, aged 48. M.I. there. It will thus be seen that there is no lack of persons who themselves or whose issue male were in remainder to this Baronetcy. In Burke's *Commoners* (edit. 1837, vol. ii, p. 194) is a pedigree of Pickering, of Clapham, Surrey, deducing that family in the male line from Edward Pickering, said to be a son of Gilbert, the 2d s. of the 1st Baronet, and to have had for a mother Mary, da. of John Creed, of Tichmarsh. The existence of such Mary, however, is doubtful (see M.I. to John Creed in Bridges's *Northamptonshire*, vol. ii, p. 386), and that of such Edward as son of the said Gilbert, is still more so. If the pedigree there given could be established the Baronetcy of Pickering would presumably be in that family.

VI. 1765? to 1803. SIR EDWARD PICKERING, Baronet(c) [S. 1638], 1st s. and h.(a); *suc. to the Baronetcy*(c) on the death of his father. He was sometime Cornet in a Cavalry Regiment, but afterwards held a staff appointment at Duncannon Fort, co. Wexford.(b) He *m.* 6 July 1770, at St. Mary's, New Ross aforesaid, Elizabeth, 3d da. of George GLASCOTT, of Aldertoun, by Anne, da. of William GIFFORD, of Polemalse, co. Wexford. She, who was *b.* 1745, *d.* 5 and *bur.* 20 Sep. 1791, at Whitechurch, co. Wexford. He *d.* s.p. and was *bur.* there 29 April 1803, when *the Baronetcy* became *dormant*.(d)

MUSGRAVE:

cr. 20 Oct. 1638;(e)

sometime, 1746-55, HYLTON;

dormant or *extinct* since 30 Sep. 1875.

I. 1638. EDWARD MUSGRAVE, of Scaleby and of Hayton Castle in Aspatria, co. Cumberland, s. and h. of William MUSGRAVE, (which William was s. and h. ap. of Sir Edward MUSGRAVE, of the same), by Catharine, da. and coheir of (—) SHERBURNE, of Lancashire, was *b.* about 1621; suc. his father (who *d.* v.p.), 27 Jan. 1633/4; matric. at Oxford (Queen's Coll.), 27 May 1636, aged 15; entered Gray's Inn, 19 June 1638, and was *cr. a Baronet* [S.], 20 Oct. 1638,(a) with, presumably, a grant of lands in Nova Scotia, of which, apparently, he never had seizin;(b) was a zealous Royalist, raising a regiment for Charles I., for whose cause he was, 18 April 1646, fined £960, and had to sell his estate of Scaleby and other lands, said to be worth, in all, £2,000 a year. At the battle of Worcester, 3 Sep. 1651, he surrendered his horse to the young King, and escaped into Scotland and thence to the Isle of Man. He *m.* Mary, 2d da. of Sir Richard GRAHAM, 1st Baronet [1629], of Esk, by Catharine, da. and coheir of Thomas MUSGRAVE, of Cumcatch. He was *bur.* 22 Nov. 1673 at Aspatria.

(a) See p. 433, note "d."

(b) An article by "Y. S. M." in *Notes and Queries* [4th S., vi, p. 47] gives many particulars as to the Baronets of this race in Ireland, among others that of the death of "the Lady of Sir Gilbert Pickering," 16 Oct. 1762, a description which implies that her husband was then living.

(c) See p. 433, note "c."

(d) His only br., Townsend Edward Pickering, *m.* Martha, 2d da. and coheir of Kennedy Cavanagh, of New Ross, and, it is presumed, *d.* s.p.m. before him. He had five sisters, of whom Frances, or Elizabeth, *m.* John Bernard, Capt. R.N.; Anne *m.* (—) Maddocks; Mary *m.*, in 1773, Henry Rudkin; and Dorothy *m.*, in 1779, Richard Baldwin Thomas.

(e) The creation is not in Laing's List, nor in that of Milne, but it is the penultimate entry in the (dateless) List of Walkley, pub. in 1641, being placed there next to that of Piers. The date, 20 Oct. 1638, is assigned to it in Wotton's *Baronetage* [1741], vol. iv, p. 354.

II. 1673. SIR RICHARD MUSGRAVE, Baronet [S. 1638], of Hayton Castle aforesaid, s. and h., *b.* probably about 1650; matric. at Oxford (Queen's Coll.) 25 May 1666; *suc. to the Baronetcy* in Nov. 1673; Sheriff of Cumberland, 1684-85; rebuilt Hayton Castle and Chapel about 1691; was Vice-Admiral of Cumberland and Westmorland in the reign of Queen Anne. He *m.*, 18 Jan. 1670, at Washington, co. Durham, Dorothy, da. and coheir of William JAMES,(c) of Washington, by Dorothy da. of Leonard WASTELL, of Scorton, co. York. He *d.* 8 and was *bur.* 11 May 1710, at Aspatria. Will dat. 23 March 1709, pr. at York, 25 July 1710. His widow, who was *bap.* 30 Dec. 1649 at Washington, and whose "great fortune and prudence" are said to have "redeemed the family estate," *d.* 12 and was *bur.* 15 Dec. 1718, at Aspatria, aged 69. M.I. Will dat. 11 Oct. 1717, pr. at York.

III. 1710. SIR RICHARD MUSGRAVE, Baronet [S. 1638], of Hayton Castle aforesaid, s. and h., *b.* about 1675; matric. at Oxford (Queen's Coll.), 8 Dec. 1697, aged 17; entered Gray's Inn, 17 July 1693; was M.A. of Edinburgh Univ., 9 March 1697/8, being, apparently, incorp. at Oxford (St. Edmund Hall) as B.A., 18 July 1698. He was in attendance at the treaty of Ryswick, 1697; was M.P. for Cumberland 1700-02 and 1705-08, and *suc. to the Baronetcy*, 8 May 1710. He *m.*, in or before 1701, Elizabeth, widow of Thomas RAMSDEN, of Croston in Halifax, co. York, da. and coheir of Joseph FINCH, of Leeds, by Judith, da. of William HORTON, of Barkisland, co. York. He was *bur.* 11 Oct. 1711, at Aspatria. Will dat. 17 Sep. 1711, pr. March 1712. His widow *d.* 1713. Her will dat. 17 Feb. 1713.

IV. 1711. SIR RICHARD MUSGRAVE, Baronet [S. 1638], of Hayton Castle aforesaid, s. and h., *b.* about 1701; *suc. to the Baronetcy* in Oct. 1711; matric. at Oxford (Queen's Coll.) 31 May 1721, aged 18, and was *cr.* M.A., 18 June 1723; Sheriff of Cumberland, 1730-31. He *m.* 13 Jan. 1723/4, at Monkwearmouth, Anne, sister and coheir [1746] of John HYLTON, of Hylton Castle, co. Durham, 2d da. of John HYLTON, of the same, by Dorothy, da. of Sir Richard MUSGRAVE, 2d Baronet [S.] abovementioned. He *d.* intestate 5 and was *bur.* 8 Oct. 1739, at Aspatria, aged 38. M.I. His widow, who was *b.* 26 Jan. 1697, and *bap.* at Washington aforesaid, *d.* in London 1 and was *bur.* 16 Feb. 1766 at Aspatria. Will pr. 1766.

V. 1739. SIR RICHARD MUSGRAVE, *afterwards*, 1746-55, HYLTON, of Hayton Castle aforesaid, 1st s. and h., *bap.*, at Aspatria, 13 Oct. 1724; *suc. to the Baronetcy*, 5 Oct. 1739; matric. at Oxford (Oriel Coll.), 16 Feb. 1742/3, aged 18. In compliance with the will of his maternal uncle, John HYLTON abovenamed (who *d.* unm. 25 Sep. 1746, aged 47), he, in 1746, took the name of *Hylton* in lieu of that of *Musgrave*, on inheriting Hylton Castle and the other

(a) See p. 434, note "e."

(b) See p. 430, note "a," under "Slingsby."

(c) This William was s. of Francis James, the yst. s. of William James, Bishop of Durham, 1606-17. See Surtees' *Durham*, vol. i, p. 216.

estates of that family. He *m.* 17 Nov. 1746, at Chester-le-Street, Eleanor, da. and coheir of John HEDWORTH, of that place, being only child of his 1st wife, Susanna Sophia, da. of William PELSANT, of London. He *d.* intestate and s.p.m.s.(a) 16 and was *bur.* 24 June 1755, at St. Martin's in the Fields. His widow *d.* 1 and was *bur.* there 5 June 1764. Her will dat. 11 Nov. 1760.

VI. 1755. SIR WILLIAM MUSGRAVE, Baronet [S. 1638], br. and h. male; *b.* at Hayton Castle aforesaid 8 Oct. 1735; ed. at Houghton-le-Spring school; entered Middle Temple, 7 April 1753; Barrister, 5 May 1758, being Bencher, 2 May 1789, Reader, and subsequently (1795) Treasurer; *suc. to the Baronetcy*, but not, apparently, to the family estates, 16 June 1765; was a Commissioner of Customs, 15 March 1763; F.R.S., 14 March 1774, becoming V.P. thereof in 1780; F.S.A., 12 Nov. 1778, becoming V.P. thereof 1786; a trustee of the British Museum, 1783; a Commissioner of Accounts, July 1785. He *m.* 10 Dec. 1759, by spec. lic. at Whitehall, St. Margaret's, Westm., Isabella Dow. COUNTESS OF CARLISLE, da. of William (BYRON), 4th BARON BYRON OF ROCHDALE, by his 3d wife Frances, da. of William (BERKELEY), 4th BARON BERKELEY OF STRATTON. She, who was *b.* 10 Nov. 1721, *d.* 22 Jan. 1795. He *d.* s.p. 3 and was *bur.* 16 Jan. 1800, at St. James', Westm., aged 65.(b) M.I.(c)

VII. 1800. SIR THOMAS MUSGRAVE, Baronet [S. 1638], only surv. br. and h. male, *b.* 1737; was an officer in the army, becoming eventually (1802) full General, and being at his death, Colonel of the 76th foot and Governor of Gravesend and Tilbury forts. He *suc. to the Baronetcy*, 3 Jan. 1800. He *d.* unm 31 Dec. 1812.

VIII. 1812. SIR JAMES MUSGRAVE, Baronet [S. 1638], of Barnsley park, near Cirencester, co. Gloucester, cousin and h. male, being s. and h. of the Rev. James MUSGRAVE, D.C.L., Rector of Chinnor, Oxon (1750-80), by (—), da. of (—) HUGGINS, which James last named (who *d.* 7 Nov. 1780, aged 70) was s. of the Rev. James MUSGRAVE, M.A., Vicar of Kirkby Moorside, co. York (1707), and Rector of Little Gransden, co. Huntingdon (1714), who was *b.* about 1681, and was yr. s. of the 2d Baronet. He was *b.* about 1752; matric. at Oxford (St. John's Coll.), 30 June 1769, aged 17; B.A. 1773; M.A. 1777; Sheriff of Gloucestershire, 1802-03; *suc. to the Baronetcy*, 31 Dec. 1812. He *m.* in 1781, Clarissa, da. of Thomas BLACKHALL, of Great Haseley, Oxon. He *d.* 27 April 1814. Will pr. 1814. The will of his widow was pr. 1823.

IX. 1814. SIR JAMES MUSGRAVE, Baronet [S. 1638], of Barnsley park aforesaid, 1st s. and h.; *b.* 24 May 1785 in London; ed. at Eton; matric. at Oxford (Ch. Ch.), 21 Oct. 1803, aged 18; B.A., 1807; *suc. to the Baronetcy*, 27 April 1814; Sheriff of Gloucestershire, 1825-26. He *d.* unm. 6 Dec. 1858.

X. 1858, to 1875. SIR WILLIAM AUGUSTUS MUSGRAVE, Baronet [S. 1638], br. and h.; *b.* 1792, at St. Marylebone; ed. at Westm. School; matric. at Oxford (Ch. Ch.), 17 May 1809, aged 17; B.A., 1813; M.A., 1815; in Holy Orders; Rector of Chinnor aforesaid, 1816-75; Rector of Emmington, Oxon, 1827-72. He *d.* unm. at Chinnor Rectory, 30 Sep. 1875, when *the Baronetcy* became *dormant* or *extinct*.

(a) Eleanor, his only surv. da. and h., *bap.* 27 June 1752, *m.* 28 Aug. 1769, at St. Margaret's, Westm., William Jolliffe, whose grandson, the Right Hon. Sir William George Hylton-Jolliffe, Baronet (so *cr.* 20 Aug. 1821), was raised to the peerage, 19 July 1866, as Baron Hylton.

(b) His laborious compilation, generally known as *Musgrave's Obituary*, is comprised in twenty-three vols. in the British Museum (Addit. MSS. 5727-5749), and gives (as its compiler states) "reference to the books where the persons are mentioned," as also date and place of death. This most useful *Obituary* (which, however, of course ends *prior* to 1800) has, *as far as relates to England, Scotland, and Ireland*, been pub. (1899-1901) by the Harleian Society in six vols.

(c) Printed in full in Malcolm's *Londinium Redivivum*, vol. iv, p. 227.

LONGUEVILLE:

cr. 17 Dec. 1638;(a)

extinct, or *dormant*, 1759.

I. 1638. EDWARD LONGUEVILLE, Esq., of Wolverton, Bucks, and of Little Billing, co. Northampton, 1st s. and h. of Sir Henry LONGUEVILLE,(b) of the same, by Katharine, sister of Henry, 1st VISCOUNT FALKLAND [S.], da. of Sir Edward CAREY, of Aldenham, Herts, was *bap.* there 23 April 1604; suc. his father (who was *bur.* at Wolverton) 17 May 1621, and, having carried great sums to the King when at Edinburgh, was *cr. a Baronet* [S.] 17 Dec. 1638,(a) with rem. to heirs male and with presumably a grant of lands in Nova Scotia, of which he, apparently, never had seizin.(c) The patent, however, is not recorded in the Great Seal Register [S.]. He *m.*, in or before 1631, Hester, 8th da. of Sir Thomas TEMPLE, 1st Baronet [1611], of Stowe, by (the prolific) Hester, da. of Miles SANDYS, of Latimers, in that county. He was *bur.* 6 Aug. 1661, at Wolverton.(d) Admon. 15 Feb. 1664/5. His widow *d.* at Buckingham, and was *bur.* at Wolverton, 18 Aug. 1665. Admon. 5 Oct. 1669.

II. 1661. SIR THOMAS LONGUEVILLE, Baronet [S. 1638], of Wolverton and Little Billing aforesaid, s. and h.; aged 3 years in 1634 (Visit. of Bucks); *suc. to the Baronetcy*, in Aug. 1661. He *m.* firstly, in or before 1662, Mary, da. and coheir of Sir William FENWICK, of co. Northumberland, by Elizabeth, sister of Francis, 1st EARL OF DERWENTWATER, da. of Sir Edward RADCLYFFE, 2d Baronet [1620]. She was *bur.* 17 Nov. 1683 at Wolverton. He *m.* secondly, 7 May 1685 at Monken Hadley, co. Middx., Katharine, 2d da. and coheir of Sir Thomas PEYTON, 2d Baronet (1611), of Knowlton, co. Kent, by his 1st wife, Elizabeth, da. of Sir Peter OSBORNE. He *d.*, breaking his neck, near Wolverton, by a fall from his horse, 25 and was *bur.* there 29 June 1685 (only a week after his second marriage, aged 54. M.I. Will dat. 25 June, and pr. 4 Aug. 1685. His widow, who probably was *bap.* 10 July 1641, at St. Margaret's, Westm., *d.* s.p. 30 Dec. 1715 and was *bur.* 7 Jan. following in Westm. Abbey, aged, it is said, 70. M.I.

III. 1685. SIR EDWARD LONGUEVILLE, Baronet [S. 1638], of Wolverton and Little Billing aforesaid, only s. and h. by 1st wife; *bap.* 27 July 1662, at Wolverton;(d) *suc. to the Baronetcy*, 25 June 1685; was Sheriff of Bucks, 1687-88, in which year he sold the estate of Little Billing, selling subsequently, about 1712, that of Wolverton, with lands at Stony Stratford, for about £50,000 and lands at North Seaton, co. Northumberland and elsewhere. He was a zealous Roman Catholic,(e) and a firm supporter of the cause of James II. He *m.* Mary, 1st da. of his paternal uncle, Edward LONGUEVILLE, by Mary, da. of (—), SYLVESTER, of Iver, Bucks. He *d.* s.p. 19 or 28 Aug. 1718, having, like his father, broken his neck by a fall from his horse, at Bicester races, and was *bur.* at Fretwell, Oxon, aged 46. Will dat. 7 Jan. 1717/8, pr. 11 Dec. 1719 and 13 Oct. 1727. His widow *m.*, as his 2d wife, John LAWTON, of Lawton, Cheshire, who *d.* 10 June 1736, aged 80. She apparently *d.* about 1766.

(a) Laing's List, this being the last creation recorded in that most valuable catalogue, in which, after this entry, is added, "Two blank precepts, names and dates not supplied."

(b) The printed pedigrees and references to this family are very numerous (see *N. & Q.*, 8th S., iv, 215), the fullest are those in Baker's *Northamptonshire*, vol. i, p. 27, vol. ii, p. 131, and in the *Her. & Gen.*, vol. vi, pp. 49-53.

(c) See p. 430, note "a," under "Slingsby."

(d) No such entry, however, is among the extracts from those registers in *Mis. Gen. et Her.*, O.S., vol. i, pp. 64-65, which, presumably, contain all therein of the name of Longueville.

(e) Although the religion of the 1st Baronet is doubtful, many of the family were of the old faith. See an interesting account of some of these in Gillow's *Bibl. Dict. of the English Catholics.*

IV. 1718, to 1759. SIR THOMAS LONGUEVILLE, Baronet [S. 1638], of Prestatin, co. Flint, and Esclusham. co. Denbigh, cousin and h. male, as also br. in law to the late Baronet, being only s. and h. of Edward LONGUEVILLE and Mary, da. of (—) SYLVESTER, all three abovenamed, which Edward was 2d and yst. s. of the 1st Baronet. He entered the naval service, becoming Lieut. in 1709. He *suc. to the Baronetcy* in Aug. 1718; was Sheriff of Flintshire, 1746-47. He *m.* firstly, in or before 1722, his cousin, Mary Margaretta, 1st da. and coheir of Sir John CONWAY, 2d Baronet [1660] of Bodrythan, by his 1st wife Margaretta Maria, 1st da. and coheir of John DIGBY, of Gayhurst, Bucks, and Margaret, his wife, da. of Sir Edward LONGUEVILLE, 1st Baronet [S. 1638] abovenamed. She, by whom he acquired the North Wales estates, *d.* s.p.m. Aug. 1731, and was *bur.* at Rhyddlan. He *m.* secondly, Elizabeth, da. of Sir Robert OWEN, of Porkington, Salop, by whom he had no issue. He *d.* s.p.m.(a) at Wrexham, co. Denbigh, 1759, and was *bur.* there, when the *Baronetcy* became *extinct* or *dormant*.

MEREDITH, *or* AMEREDETH:

cr. 2 Jan. 1638/9, *or* 2 June 1639(b);

dormant 2 Jan. 1790.

I. 1639. AMOS AMEREDETH, *otherwise* MEREDITH, of Marston in Tamerton Folliott, co. Devon, and subsequently (in right of his 2d marriage) of Ashley, co. Chester, s. and h. of Edward AMEREDETH,(c) of Marston aforesaid, by Margaret, relict of Gamaliel SLANNING, da. of Edward MARTEN, of London, was *cr. a Baronet* [S.] 2 Jan. 1638/9, or 2 June 1639,(b) with rem. to heirs male whatsoever and with, presumably, a grant of land in Nova Scotia, of which, however, he apparently never had seizin.(d) During the Civil War he was Col. of a troop of Horse and Gov. of Exmouth for the King, in whose cause he is said to have expended £20,000. At the Restoration he was made a Gent. of the Privy Chamber. He was M.P. [I.] for Ballynakill, 1661-66, and was a Commissioner of Excise and Custom [I.]. He *m.* firstly, Elizabeth, widow of Francis COURTENAY, of Powderham (*d.* 5 June 1638), da. of Sir Edward SEYMOUR, 2d Baronet [1611], by Dorothy, da. of Sir Henry KILLIGREW. By her he had no male issue. He *m.* secondly, 6 Feb. 1664, at Bowdon, co. Chester, Anne, 2d da. of Robert TATTON, of Whithenshaw, by Jane, da. of William, and sister and coheir of Thomas BRERETON, of Ashley aforesaid. He *d.* 5 and was *bur.* 8 Dec. 1669 in the burial place of Sir Charles MEREDITH(e) at St. Patrick's,

(a) Of his three daughters and coheirs, Maria Margaretta, *b.* 1722, *m.* 1739 for her 1st husband John Jones, who *d.* 29 Sep. 1747, from whom descends the family of Longueville-Jones, of Prestatin.

(b) The date, 2 Jan. 1639 [*i.e.*, 1638/9], is given in Wotton's *Baronetage* (1741, vol. iv, 358), but that of 2 *June* 1639, as also the limitation is in the pedigree (2 D xiv, 127) recorded in the College of Arms. The creation is not in Laing's, Milne's, or Banks's Lists, nor is it in that of Walkley, published in 1641, or of Ulster, compiled 1633-43.

(c) In Ormerod's *Cheshire*, under "Henbury," is a well worked up pedigree of this family, which is the last of the "Nova Scotia Baronets of English families and resident in England" (*viz.* Gascoigne, Pilkington, Slingsby, Pickering, Longueville, Musgrave and Meredith) of which an account is given in Wotton's *Baronetage* (1741) and in that of Kimber (1771).

(d) See p. 430, note "a," under "Slingsby."

(e) This Charles, who had recently, 14 Sep. 1664, been *knighted*, was a yr. br. of Sir William Meredith, *cr. a Baronet* [I.] 20 Nov. 1660. His will was pr. in England 1700. In Playfair's *Irish Baronetage* (p. 100) a common, though *very distant*, male descent of the two families is set forth.

Dublin. Funeral entry in Ulster's Office. Will as "of Ballynekil, in Queen's County," dat. 5 Dec. 1669, pr. in Prerog. Court [I.] 1669. His widow, living 2 June 1685, *m.*, as his 1st wife, Sir Samuel DANIELL, of Over Tabley, co. Chester, who *d.* s.p.s. 24 Dec. 1726.

II. 1669. SIR WILLIAM MEREDITH, Baronet [S. 1639], of Ashley aforesaid, and afterwards of Henbury, co. Chester, 1st s. and h.(a) by 2d wife, *b.* 6 Dec. 1665; *suc. to the Baronetcy*, 5 Dec. 1669; sold the estate of Ashley and, in 1693, purchased that of Henbury. He *m.*, 2 June 1685, at St. Bride's, London (Lic. Vic. Gen. 31 May, both stated to be about 19),(b) Mary, da. and h. of Henry ROBINSON, of Whaplode, co. Lincoln, by Elizabeth, da. of Christ. THURSBY, of Dorwood's hall, Essex. He was *bur.* 19 Jan. 1752, at Prestbury. Will pr. 1753.

III. 1752, to 1790. SIR WILLIAM MEREDITH, Baronet [S. 1639], of Henbury aforesaid, grandson and h., being 1st s. and h.(c) of Amos MEREDITH, by Joanna (*m.* 27 May 1718), da. of Thomas CHOLMONDELEY, of Vale Royal, co. Chester, which Amos was only s. and h. ap. of the late Baronet, but *d.* v.p. at Bath, 6 May 1744, aged 57. He was *b.* about 1725; matric. at Oxford (Christ Church), 24 March 1742/3, aged 18, and was *cr.* D.C.L., 14 April 1749; *suc. to the Baronetcy*, 19 Jan. 1752; was M.P. for Wigan, 1754-61, and for Liverpool, 1761-80; a Lord of the Admiralty, 1765-66; Comptroller of the Household, 1774-77; P.C. 9 March 1774. He sold the estate of Henbury in 1779, and *d.* unm. at Lyons, in France, 2 Jan. 1790, when the *Baronetcy* became *dormant*.

COWPER, *or* COOPER:

cr. 24 March 1638;(e)

afterwards, from 1642 Baronets [E.];

from 1706, BARONS COWPER OF WINGHAM;

and from 1718, EARLS COWPER.

I. 1638. WILLIAM COWPER, of Ratling Court, in Nonington, co. Kent, was *cr. a Baronet* [S.] shortly before 1641,(d) and was subsequently *cr.*, 4 March 1641/2, *a Baronet* [E.]. See p. 160 for fuller particulars of him and for the devolution of the title.

(a) George Meredith, of Oldfield Hall, Altrincham, *b.* 7 June 1667, who was his only brother, apparently *d.* s.p.m.

(b) In his case this statement is probably an error for 29.

(c) The 2d and only other brother, the Rev. Theophilus Meredith, matric. at Oxford (Christ Church), 2 June 1707, aged 16; B.A. (St. Edmund Hall), 1761; M.A. 1762; Vicar of Linton, co. Hereford, 1769; Rector of Ross, 1771-75; *d.* s.p.m., at Bristol, 26 Sep. 1776, aged 45.

(d) See an article by "W. S. Cooper, Advocate," on "Cooper of Gogar," in *The Genealogist* [O.S., vol. i, p. 334].

LOWTHER :

cr. about 1638 ; (a)

sometime 1696-1751, VISCOUNTS LONSDALE ;

afterwards, 1784-1802, EARL OF LONSDALE ;

extinct or *dormant*, 24 May 1802.

I. 1638 ? JOHN LOWTHER, of Lowther, co. Westmorland, 1st s. and h.(b) of Sir John LOWTHER, of the same, by Eleanor, da. of William FLEMING, of Rydal in that county, was *b.* 20 Feb. 1605 : was M.P. for Westmorland, 1628-29 (together with his father), and subsequently (as a Baronet), 1660. He suc. his father 15 Sep. 1637 ; was a great sufferer in the Royal cause ; was, 18 Aug. 1646, a Compounder for £1,500, with £50 a year settled, being, in the documents relating to such composition, styled a Baronet, having been *cr. a Baronet* [S.] about 1638.(a) He was Sheriff of Cumberland, 1661-62. He *m.* firstly, in or before 1655, Mary, 3d da. of Sir Richard FLETCHER, of Hutton, co. Cumberland, by his 2d wife, Barbara, da. of (—) CRAKENTHORP, of Newbiggin, in that county. He *m.* secondly, Elizabeth, widow of Woolley LEIGH, of Addington and Thorpe, co. Surrey (*d.* 23 Dec. 1644), sister of Sir Ralph HARE, 1st Baronet [1641], da. of Sir John HARE, of Stow Bardolph, co. Norfolk. He *d.* 30 Nov., and was *bur.* 4 Dec. 1675, at St. Michael's, Lowther. M.I. Will pr. 1676. That of his widow dat. 14 July 1692, pr. 21 Oct. 1699.

II. 1675. SIR JOHN LOWTHER, Baronet [S. 1638 ?], of Lowther aforesaid, grandson and h., being s. and h. of Col. John LOWTHER, of Hackthorpe and Mauds Meaburn, by his 1st wife, Elizabeth (*m.* in or before 1655), da. and [1650] coheir of Sir Henry BELLINGHAM, 1st Baronet [1620] of Hilsington, co. Westmorland, which John (who was M.P. for Appleby, 1661, till his death in or shortly before March 1867/8), *d. v.p.* He was *b.* 25 April 1655, at Hackthorpe Hall, in Lowther; was ed. at Kendal and Jedburgh; matric. at Oxford (Queen's Coll.), 12 Nov. 1670; *suc. to the Baronetcy*, on the death of his grandfather, 30 Nov. 1675; Barrister (Inner Temple), 1677; M.P. for Westmorland (seven Parls.), 1677-96, and was a zealous promoter of the Revolution; P.C., 19 Feb. 1688/9; Vice Chamberlain of the Household, 1689-90; L. Lieut. of Cumberland and Westmorland, 1689-94; First Lord of the Treasury, March to Nov. 1690; Second Lord, Nov. 1690 to Nov. 1691. He *m.* 3 Dec. 1674 at Westm. Abbey, Katherine, 2d and yst. da. of Sir Henry Frederick THYNNE, 1st Baronet [1641], by Mary, da. of Thomas (COVENTRY), 1st BARON COVENTRY OF AYLESBOROUGH. She was living when he was *cr.*, 28 May 1676, BARON LOWTHER of Lowther, co. Westmorland, and VISCOUNT LONSDALE, co. Westmorland. See fuller particulars in *Peerage*. He *d.* 10 July 1700.

III. 1700. RICHARD (LOWTHER), VISCOUNT LONSDALE AND BARON LOWTHER, also a Baronet [S. 1638 ?], s. and h. ; *b.* 1692 ; *suc. to the titles* 10 July 1700 ; *d.* unm. 1 Dec. 1713.

IV. 1713. HENRY (LOWTHER), VISCOUNT LONSDALE AND BARON LOWTHER, also a Baronet [S. 1638 ?], br. and h. ; *b.* 1694; *suc. to the titles* 1 Dec. 1713 ; L. Privy Seal, 1732-35 ; *d.* unm. 12 March 1750/1, when the *peerage dignities* became *extinct*.

(See fuller particulars in *Peerage*.)

(a) The limitation is not known. The creation is not in Milne's or Laing's List, but is in that of Walkley, being among the last entries therein. That most useful list, published in 1642, and containing, in all, ninety-five Baronetcies [S.], has (with this article) been now exhausted, though (no dates being therein given) the order of it has not in this work been strictly followed, the last ten entries therein being Slingsby, Cowper, Sinclair, Lowther, Pickering, Longueville, Piers, Musgrave, and Witherington.

(b) The second son, Christopher Lowther, of Whitehaven, was *cr. a Baronet* [E.] 11 June 1642, a dignity which became *extinct* 2 Jan. 1755.

V. 1751. SIR JAMES LOWTHER, Baronet [S. 1638 ?], of Lowther aforesaid, cousin and h. male, being 2d but 1st surv. s. and h. of Robert LOWTHER, of Mauds Meaburn, co. Westmorland, Gov. of Barbadoes, by Catharine, da. of Sir Joseph PENNINGTON, 2d Baronet [1676], of Muncaster, and Margaret his wife, sister to Henry (LOWTHER), 3d Viscount LONSDALE abovenamed, which Robert (who *d.* Sep. 1745, aged 63) was s. and h. of Richard LOWTHER, of Mauds Meaburn aforesaid (*b.* 1638), who was 2d surv. s. of the 1st Baronet. He was *b.* 5 Aug. and *bap.* 6 Sep. 1736, at St. George's Bloomsbury ; *suc. to the Baronetcy*, 12 March 1750/1, on the death of his 2d cousin and great uncle, Henry, Viscount LONSDALE, abovenamed, whose vast estates he also inherited, as subsequently, 2 Jan. 1755, he did the valuable estate of Whitehaven and about £2,000,000 on the death of his cousin, Sir James LOWTHER, 4th and last Baronet [1642], of Whitehaven. He was ed. at Cambridge; was M.P. for Cumberland, 1757-61 ; for Westmorland, 1761-63 ; for Cumberland (again), 1763-68 ; for Cockermouth, 1769-74 ; and for Cumberland (the 3d term), 1774-84. He *m.* 7 Sep. 1761, at St. Geo. Han. sq., Mary, 1st da. of John (STUART), 3d EARL OF BUTE [S.], by Mary, da. of Edward WORTLEY-MONTAGU. She, who was *b.* 20 Jan. 1738, was living when he was *cr.*, 24 May 1784, EARL OF LONSDALE, etc. He was subsequently *cr.*, 26 Oct. 1797, VISCOUNT LOWTHER OF WHITEHAVEN, with a spec. rem. in favour of his distant kinsman, Sir William LOWTHER, of Swillington. In these peerages *this Baronetcy* then *merged* till on his death s.p., 24 May 1806, aged 65, the peerage of 1797 devolved according to the spec. remainder, but that of 1784 became *extinct*, and the issue male of the grantee of this Baronetcy having failed, the *Baronetcy* became either *extinct* or *dormant*.

MACCARTY :

cr. about 1638 ; (a)

afterwards, 1640-91, VISCOUNTS MUSKERRY [I.] ;

and subsequently, 1658-91, EARLS of CLANCARTY [I.] ;

forfeited 11 May 1691.

I. 1638 ? DONOGH MACCARTY, 2d but 1st surv. s. and h. ap. of Cormac *Oge* (MACCARTY), 1st VISCOUNT MUSKERRY [I.], by his 1st wife, Margaret, da. of Donogh (O'BRIEN), was *b.* 1594, was *Knighted* before 1634, being (as a Knight) M.P. [I.] for co. Cork 1634-35 and 1639-40, and was *cr. a Baronet* [S.] probably about 1638,(a) but there is no record thereof in the Great Seal Register [S.], and the limitation is unknown ; suc. his father, 20 Feb. 1640, as VISCOUNT MUSKERRY [I.], and was *cr.* 27 Nov. 1658, EARL OF CLANCARTY [I.], in which peerages this *Baronetcy* consequently *merged*, till it and the peerage honours became *forfeited*, 11 May 1691, on the attainder of the 4th Earl. See *Peerage*.

WALLACE :

cr. about 1638(b) ;

resigned 1659.

I. 1638 ? to 1659. SIR HUGH WALLACE, of Craigie Wallace and Newton, both in co. Ayr, s. and h. of John WALLACE, of the same, by Margaret, da. of John (MAXWELL), LORD MAXWELL [S.], and at one time EARL OF MORTON [S.], was *b.* about 1600; suc. his father before July 1614 ; sold the office of Heritable Baillie of Kyle in 1626, for

(a) Milne's List, but without the date of creation ; not, however, in the lists of Laing or Walkley, but in that of Ulster, shewing thereby the date of creation to be previous to 1643, the date of the death of its compiler, Thomas Preston, Ulster King of Arms, 1633-43.

(b) This creation is not in the List of Laing or Walkley, nor in that of Milne,

£10,000 ; is styled "Sir Hugh" in 1631, having possibly been, at or before that date, *cr. a Baronet* [S.], as certainly he was before 1642, and as he is styled in 1649 in certain pleadings before Parliament. He was taken prisoner, fighting in the Royal cause, 1645. He *m.* Hester, da. of John KER, of Littledean, co. Roxburgh. She was an Anabaptist, and was, in 1653, "dipped" by the English in the Leith. In 1649 he accused his two sons, Hugh(a) and William, of robbing and endeavouring to murder him. He accordingly disinherited his children in favour of his cousin, Thomas Wallace, and executed a *resignation of the Baronetcy* in his favour.(b) He was alive 1659, but *d.* before 8 March 1660.(c)

HOME, *or* HUME :

cr. about 1638 ;(d)

forfeited about 1716.

I. 1638 ? SIR DAVID(e) HOME, *or* HUME, of Wedderburn, only s. and h. of SIR George HOME, of the same, by Jean, da. of John HALDANE, of Gleneagles ; suc. his father in Nov. 1616, being retoured heir special 10 April 1617, and was, presumably, *cr. a Baronet* [S.] apparently about 1638,(d) but there is no entry in the Great Seal Register [S.], and no particulars of the creation are known. He was M.P. [S.] for Berwickshire, 1639, 1640-41, 1645-46 and 1649-50, being, however, always styled "Knight." He *m.* Margaret, widow of Sir Mark KER, of Dolphinston, da. of Sir John HOME, of Coldingknows. He, with his eldest son, George, was slain fighting for the Royal cause, 3 Sep. 1650, at the battle of Dunbar.

II. 1650, to 1716 ? GEORGE HOME, *or* HUME, of Wedderburn aforesaid, grandson and h., being s. and h. of George HOME, *or* HUME, by Katharine (mar. lic. 16 Aug. 1635), da. of Alexander MORISON, of Preston Grange, a Lord of Session [S.] 1626-32, which George (who was M.P. [S.] for North Berwick, three Parls., 1639-45) was s. and h. of Sir David HOME abovenamed, and was slain with him 3 Sep. 1650, as above stated. He was *b.* 1641, and *suc.*, presumably, *to the Baronetcy*, 3 Sep. 1650, but does not appear to have ever assumed the same. He *m.* Isobel, da. of Sir Francis LIDDELL, of Ravensworth. He *d.* about 1716, when *the Baronetcy* or the right thereto, devolved on George HOME,(f) his 1st s. and h., who had been convicted of high treason for taking part in the rising of 1715, and became consequently *forfeited*.

save that, under the patent, 8 March 1670, to Sir Thomas Wallace, it is there incidentally mentioned that "He seems to have a former patent disponed to him by the last Sir Hewgh Wallace, which is ratifyed, 8 March 1670, but maketh him not to take place conforme to date of the said patent." The name, of "Sir Hugh Wallace of Cragie Wallace" appears 7th in Ulster's List of Scotch Baronets, made before 1643.

(a) This Hugh mentions that, owing to his father's treatment, he had for a time become deranged and had fled with his wife to Ireland, where he was in such a state of poverty as to be unable to maintain his children. It is not known what became of him or of his brothers William and John.

(b) The creation of 1670, as it did not convey the precedence of this one (see p. 441, note "b") must be considered as a new one, and is accordingly dealt with under the date of 1670, being that of its grant.

(c) Much of the information in this article was supplied by R. R. Stodart, Lyon Clerk Depute (1863-86).

(d) See p. 441, note "a."

(e) He is, however, called "Sir *James* Home, of Wedderburn," in Ulster's List, apparently by mistake.

(f) This George *d.* at Wedderburn 1720, leaving issue. Some account of this family is in Wood's *Douglas' Peerage* [S.], vol. ii, pp. 175-176, under "Marchmont," but there is no mention therein of the grant or assumption of any Baronetcy.

HOME, *or* HUME :

cr. about 1638 ;(a)

extinct or *dormant* April 1747.

I. 1638 ? GEORGE HOME, *or* HUME, of North Berwick, in Scotland, s. and h. ap. of Sir John HOME, of North Berwick aforesaid (which estate he sold in 1633), and of Ardgorte, co. Fermanagh. M.P. [I.] for that county,(b) was *cr. a Baronet* [S.], apparently about 1638 (possibly, however, before 1633, the date of the sale of the North Berwick estate), but there is no entry of such creation in the Great Seal Register [S.], and no particulars of it are known. He suc. his father (who was *bur.* at St. Michan's, Dublin) 26 Sep. 1639, in whose *inq. p. mortem*, 23 March 1639/40, he is styled "Baronet" and to whom he was served heir, 10 Feb. 1642. He obtained in 1641 a grant of the manor of Tully, co. Fermanagh, and is consequently spoken of as being of Castle Tully. He *m.* Mary, 1st da. of Sir William MAYNARD, of Curriglasse, co. Cork, by Mary, da. of Samuel NEWCE, of Brickendbury, Serj.-at-arms of the province of Munster. He *d.* in Edinburgh intestate in or about 1657, before 15 June 1657. The will of his widow, dat. 30 Aug. 1699, pr. 12 July 1705 [I.].

II. 1657 ? SIR JOHN HUME, Baronet [S. 1638 ?], of Castle Hume, presumably the same as Castle Tully aforesaid, s. and h., *suc. to the Baronetcy* on the death of his father ; was Sheriff of co Fermanagh 1662, and Governor thereof during the wars of 1689, and, being a zealous partizan of King William, was attainted in the Irish parl. of James II. He *m.* Sidney, yr. da. and coheir of James HAMILTON, of Manor Hamilton, co Leitrim, by Catharine, da. of Claud (HAMILTON), 1st BARON STRABANE [I.]. She, by whom he had ten children, *d.* 10 and was *bur.* 23 Jan. 1685 in St. Michael's [*sic.*, but probably St. Michan's], Dublin. Funeral certificate [I.]. He *d.* Midsummer eve 1695. Will dat. 12 June 1690, pr. 1695 [I.].

III. 1695. SIR GUSTAVUS HUME, Baronet [S. 1638 ?], of Castle Hume aforesaid, 3d but only surv. s. and h.,(c) *b.* about 1670 ; *suc. to the Baronetcy*, 23 June 1695 ; was Sheriff for co. Fermanagh, 1701 ; M.P. [I.] thereof 1713-14, 1715-27 and 1727 till his death ; P.C. [I.] to George I, 1714. He *m.* 11 Sep. 1697, at St. Michan's, Dublin (Lic. dat. 10 Sep. 1697), Alice, 1st da. of Henry (MOORE) 3d EARL OF DROGHEDA [I.], by Mary, da. of Sir John COLE, 1st Baronet [I. 1660], of Newland, co. Dublin. He *d.* s.p.m.s.(d) 25 Oct. 1731. Will dat. 18 Aug. 1729, pr. 21 Feb. 1731/2 [I.], and 1732 [E.] His widow, who was *bap.* 29 Dec. 1679, *d.* at Dublin 13 April 1750. Will dat. 18 April 1740, pr. 20 April 1750 [I.].

IV. 1731, to 1747. SIR CHARLES HUME, Baronet [S. 1638 ?], cousin and h. male, being only surv. s. of the Rev. George HUME, of Tully, co. Fermanagh, by Dorothy, his wife, which George (whose admon. [I.] was dated 6 May 1699) was 2d son of the 1st Baronet. He *suc. to the Baronetcy*, 25 Oct. 1731. He *d.* s.p. April 1747 (Pue's *Occurrences*), when the *Baronetcy* became *extinct* or *dormant*.

(a) See p. 441, note "a."

(b) G. W. Burtchaell, of the Office of Arms, Dublin, has kindly supplied most of the information in this article. The estate of North Berwick devolved on the Baronet's father, Sir John Home, on the death of Alexander Home, uncle of the said John, in or before Sep. 1608. See Wood's *Douglas Peerage* [S.], vol. ii, p. 178.

(c) Of his two brothers, James *d.* 1689, and John, who ent. Trin. Coll., Dublin, 30 May 1685, aged 18, *d.* 1690.

(d) An account of his six children, his three brothers (who all *d.* unm.), and six sisters is given in Archall's *Lodge's Peerage* [I.], vol. ii, p. 112, under "Drogheda." To this it may be added that Moore, the 1st son, ent. Trin Coll., Dublin, 28 Oct. 1721, aged 17.

(e) Of his two brothers, John, ent. Trin. Coll., Dublin, 27 Oct. 1708, aged 18, and James, 14 Dec. 1711, aged 15.

BOURKE, Viscount Mayo [I.]:

cr. about 1638; (a)

extinct or *dormant* 12 Jan. 1767.

I. 1638? MILES (BOURKE), VISCOUNT MAYO [I.], who succeeded to that title (*cr.* 21 June 1627) as 2d Viscount 13 June 1629, was (*apparently* on the same date as was his s. and h. ap.) *cr. a Baronet* [S.], probably about 1630,(a) but there is no record of such creation in the Great Seal Register [S.], and the limitation is unknown. In the abovenamed peerage this *Baronetcy* continued *merged*, till on the death of the 8th Viscount and 7th Baronet, 12 Jan. 1767, both became *extinct* or *dormant*. See *Peerage*.

BOURKE:

cr. about 1638; (a)

afterwards, 1649-1767, VISCOUNTS MAYO [I.];

extinct or *dormant* 12 Jan. 1767.

I. 1638? THE HON. THEOBALD BOURKE, s. and h. ap. of Miles (BOURKE) 2d VISCOUNT MAYO [I.] next abovenamed, by his 2d wife Elizabeth, da. of (—) FREKE, was v.p. (apparently on the same date as was his said father), *cr. a Baronet* [S], probably about 1638,(a) but there is no record of such creation in the Great Seal Register [S.], and the limitation is unknown. The date was certainly before 1639 when, as "Knt. and Baronet," he was M.P. [I.] for co. Mayo. He *m.* firstly, Elizabeth (*b.* 1613), widow of Thomas LEWIS, of Marr, co. York, da. and coheir of Thomas TALBOT, of Bashall, in that county, by Anne, sister of John Rushworth. She *d.* s.p. He *m.* secondly, Eleanor, da. of Sir Luke FITZ-GERALD, of Tecroghan, co. Meath. This marriage was presumably before 1649, when he suc. to his father's honours becoming thus the 3d VISCOUNT MAYO [I.]. In that peerage this *Baronetcy* then *merged*, and so continued till on the death of the 8th Viscount, 12 Jan. 1767, both became *extinct* or *dormant*. See *Peerage*.

Memorandum.—Each successive eldest son and heir ap. of these Viscounts appears to have been, anomalously, considered as entitled to the style of a Baronet in his father's lifetime; on the ground, apparently, of such son of the 2d Viscount having been created a Baronet in the lifetime of *his* father.(b) In some instances it probably was, for various reasons, not assumed, but it is as well to set out each of the five cases in which it was or might have been so assumed.

(1) Theobald Bourke, a minor when he suc. his father, 12 Jan. 1652/3, as 4th Viscount Mayo [I.].

(a) See p. 441, note "a."

(b) The fact that the father having (though a Viscount) been *cr. a Baronet* (as well as, and probably at the same time as the son) may possibly have somewhat contributed to this extraordinary opinion. In Archdall's *Lodge's Peerage* [I.], vol. iv, 236, note, it is stated that "Mr. Lodge" (after stating that the creation by Charles I. of this Baronetcy must have been after that of the Viscountcy) says "certain it is that the eldest son of the Viscount Mayo enjoys the title of Baronet, and is stiled *Sir*, during his father's lifetime." The notion that the son and heir ap. of a Peer, who was also a Baronet, was entitled v.p. to his father's Baronetcy, was apparently held by Francis Holles, who was *cr. a Baronet*, 27 June 1660, and who subsequently, 17 Feb. 1679/80, suc. his father as the 2d Baron Holles of Ifield. He, in his will, dat. 3 Sep. 1680, speaks of his only surv. son (who, subsequently, 1 March 1689/90, succeeded to his titles) as being "called Sir Denzell Holles, *Baronet*." See *Complete Peerage*, by G. E. C., vol. iv, p. 245, note "c."

(2) Miles Bourke, br. and h. to the above, who, having been in his brother's lifetime heir *presumptive* (not *apparent*), is not likely to have assumed the Baronetcy before he suc. to the peerage, as 5th Viscount, 5 June 1676.

(3) Theobald Bourke, only s. and h. of the above; *b.* 6 Jan. 1681, who but three months later, in March 1681, suc. to his father's dignities as 6th Viscount.

(4) Theobald Bourke, 1st s. of the above; *b.* probably in or shortly after 1703. He was unquestionably *styled Baronet*(a) in his father's lifetime, to which title as also to the peerage he suc. 25 June 1741, as 7th Viscount.

(5) John Bourke, br. and h. to the above, to whom the same remark applies as to Miles, the 5th Viscount. He suc. to his brother's titles 7 Jan. 1741/2, but *d.* s.p.m.s., 12 Jan. 1767, when they became *extinct* or *dormant*.

BOURKE:

cr. about 1638: (b)

subsequently BARONS BOURKE OF BRITTAS [I]:

forfeited 1691.

I. 1638? THE HON. JOHN BOURKE, s. and h. ap. of Theobald (BOURKE), 1st BARON BOURKE OF BRITTAS [I.], by Margaret, da. of Richard (BOURKE) 2d EARL OF CLANRICARDE [I.]; was v.p. *cr. a Baronet* [S.], probably about 1638,(b) but there is no record of such creation in the Great Seal Register [S.], and the limitation is unknown. He *m.* in or after 1638, Margaret, widow of Walter BERMINGHAM (who *d.* 13 June 1638), da. of Thomas (FITZ-MAURICE), LORD KERRY [I.], by his 2d wife, Gillies, da. of Richard (POWER) BARON POWER OF CURRAGHMORE. He suc. his father in 1654 as the 2d BARON BOURKE OF BRITTAS [I.], in which peerage this *Baronetcy* then *merged*, and became forfeited therewith in 1691, on the attainder of his successor, the 3d Baron. See *Peerage*.

COOPER, *or* COUPER:

stated to be a Baronetcy [S.]; (c)

created about 1638, or 1646.(d)

I. 1638? JOHN COOPER, *or* COUPER, of Gogar, co. Midlothian, only s. and h. of Adam COOPER, Clerk of Session [S.], by Katharine DENNISTOUN, his wife, suc. his father (who had purchased the estate of Gogar in or shortly before 1601) in 1608, and is said to have been *cr. a Baronet* [S.],(c) probably about 1638,(d) but "no patent is entered in the Great Seal Register, and it does not seem anywhere to be asserted that the original exists."(c) He *m.* in or before 1620, Helen SKENE, said to have been da. of Robert SKENE, of Halyards. He *d.* 30 Aug. 1640, at the blowing up of Dunglas Castle. His testament (Comm. Reg. Edinburgh) describes him as "John Coupar, of Gogar," the cautioner for the widow being "David Gray, Tailor, Burgess of Edinburgh." His widow, "Helen Skene, widow of John Coupar, of Gogar," was *bur.* 21 July 1667, at the Greyfriars, Edinburgh.

(a) "There is among the Prerog. [Marriage] Licences [I.] one, 29 Nov. 1723, for Theobald Bourke, of the parish of St. Andrew, Dublin, *Baronet*, and Sibilla Blake of same parish, spinster. But on examining the grant book, I find he is there designated *Honblem* as well as *Baronettum*, so I conclude that this refers to

(b) (c) (d) See these notes on p. 446.

II. 1640, to 1686? JOHN, *afterwards* (1643) SIR JOHN COOPER, *or* COUPER, of Gogar aforesaid, s. and h., *bap.* 18 March 1621; served heir to his father, 27 Oct. 1640, and then styled "John Couper, of Nether Gogar;" was *Knighted* before 26 Aug. 1643, and appears as *Knight*, but never as *Baronet*, in various commissions; was M.P. [S.] for co. Edinburgh, 1681-82; He *m.* 15 March 1661, Margaret INGLIS, of the family of Inglis of Otterston. He *d.* s.p.m.,(e) in or shortly after 1686, when the estate of Gogar was sold to pay his debts.

* * * * * * *

[Nothing was heard of this (supposed) Baronetcy for upwards of one hundred and thirty years, when it was assumed as under].

III.(f) *1775.* SIR GREY COOPER, Baronet [S. 1638?],(g) claiming to be cousin and h. male. He was s. and h. of William GREY, M.D., who practised as a physician at Newcastle-upon-Tyne, by Mary (*m.* in or before 1726), da. of Edward GREY, of Alnwick, which William(h) (who *d.* 5 May 1758), was only s. of another William COOPER,(h) M.D., who practised as a Physician at Berwick-upon-Tweed, who was s. of the Rev. James COOPER,(h) Minister of Wigton, 1664; of Mochrum, 1666; and of Humbie 1681, till deprived as a non juror in 1695, when he became Curate of Holyisland, near Berwick (where he died early in 1701), which James (though not licensed as a minister(i) till 16 Feb. 1663) is stated(g) to be identical with James (seemingly(i) born 1622), 2d s. of the 1st Baronet.(k) He was *b.* about 1726 at Newcastle-upon-Tyne; was admitted

Theobald [afterwards 7th Viscount], 1st s. and h. of Theobald, 6th Viscount Mayo. This marriage licence, however, has never been noticed in any peerage. Certain it is that [the future 7th Viscount] Theobald Bourke, of Ballintubber, co. Mayo, *Baronet*, is so described in his mar. lic. with Ellis Agar, of Gowran, co. Kilkenny, spinster, 18 March 1726." [G. D. Burtchaell, Ulster's office].

(b) See p. 441, note "a."

(c) An article on "Cooper of Gogar," by "S***," in *The Genealogist* [O.S., vol i, pp. 257-266 and 334], supplementing one in the *Her. and Gen.* [vol. viii, p. 193], deals fully with this family, and "furnishes a negative reply" to the two questions—(1), "Was a Baronetcy ever conferred on a Cooper, of Gogar?" and (2), "Is Mr. [William] Cooper, of Failford [in 1876], the heir male of the Gogar family?"

(d) The date of 1638 and the remainder to heirs male, are given in Playfair's *Baronetage* [S.]. In Paterson's *Ayrshire*, it is stated that the first Baronet "does not appear to have assumed the title. It is, however, sometimes alleged that the Baronetcy was not created till 1646 in the person of the son.". This date, "1646," is the one given in Edmondson's List of Scotch Baronetcies.

(e) He left two daughters and coheirs, viz., (1), Mary, who *m.* Thomas Chalmers, and had issue; and (2), Margaret, *m.* 28 Oct. 1680, Archibald Graham, Bishop of the Isles, by whom she had two daughters and coheirs.

(f) This numbering is exclusive of any who might have had a right to the (supposed) Baronetcy, after the death, about 1686, of Sir John Cooper, the s. and h. of John, the presumed grantee.

(g) According to the service of 1 Aug. 1775.

(h) None of these three persons assumed the Baronetcy, which, in the case of James, who for many years survived the 2d Baronet (said to be his brother), is (to say the least of it) very remarkable.

(i) See note "c" above.

(k) "One would expect to find the son of a gentleman, who had a residence in the town of Edinburgh, and whose estate was only at a distance of five miles, a graduate of the University there, but the name of this James is not on the list. Then he was not licensed till 16 Feb. 1663, when James, the son of Gogar, would have been over 40 years. It is not impossible that [James] the clergyman, was the James, yr. br. of Sir John, but it seems unlikely, and one would like to see the proofs that satisfied the jury." [See note "c" above].

to the Temple, and became a Barrister; was M.P. for Rochester, 1765-68; for Grampound, 1768-74; for Saltash, 1774-84; and for Richmond, 1786-90; was a zealous supporter of the Rockingham Ministry [1765-66], and was Joint Sec. of the Treasury (under three Ministries), 1765-82; was a Lord of the Treasury, April to Dec. 1783; P.C., 29 April 1796. Having suc. his father 5 May 1758, he was, 1 Aug. 1775, served heir male to Sir John COOPER, of Gogar, called the 2d Baronet and stated to have been brother of his great grandfather, James COOPER, by a service before the Sheriff of Edinburgh, which was, however, "never retoured to Chancery, and [even] if it had been, could have conveyed no right to a title which had no existence."(a) He accordingly after that date *assumed the Baronetcy*, that was ascribed in that service to the family of COOPER, of Gogar. He *m.* firstly, 5 Oct. 1753, Margaret, sister of Charles, 1ST EARL GREY, da. of Sir Henry GREY, 1st Baronet [1746] of Howick, by Hannah, da. of Thomas WOOD, of Falloden, co. Northumberland. She, who was *bap.* 8 Dec. 1726, *d.* s.p. in 1755. He *m.* secondly, 19 July 1762, Elizabeth, da. of (—) KENNEDY, of Newcastle-upon-Tyne. He *d.*, suddenly, 30 July 1801 at his seat at Worlington, co. Suffolk, aged 75, and was *bur.* in the church there. M.I. Will pr. 1801. His widow *d.* there, 3 Nov. 1809, aged (also) 75.

IV.(b) *1801.* SIR WILLIAM HENRY COOPER, Baronet [S. 1638?],(c) 1st s. and h. by 2d wife; *b.* 29 May 1766; took Holy Orders; was a Prebend of Rochester Cathedral, 1793-97; *suc. to the Baronetcy*,(c) 30 July 1801, was sometime detained prisoner in France by Napoleon. He *m.*, 21 May 1787, Isabella Ball, only da. of Moses FRANKS, of Teddington, co. Midx. He *d.* about 1834. Will pr. Jan. 1835. His widow *d.* 27 Jan. 1855, at Isleworth House, co. Midx., aged 85. Will pr. Feb. 1855.

V.(b) *1834?* SIR WILLIAM HENRY COOPER, Baronet [S. 1638?],(c) only s. and h., *b.* 28 March 1788; *suc. to the Baronetcy*,(c) about 1834. He *m.* 10 April 1827, at St. Geo., Han. sq., Anne, 1st da. of Charles KEMEYS-TYNTE, of Kevenmably, co. Glamorgan, by Anne, da. of the Rev. Thomas LEYSON, Vicar of Bossaleg, co. Monmouth. He *d.*, s.p.s., 14 Jan. 1836, at Chilton Lodge (near Andover), Berks, aged 47. Will pr. Feb. 1836. His widow *d.* 17 Sep. 1880, at Leversdown, Bridgwater.

VI.(b) *1836.* SIR FREDERICK GREY COOPER, Baronet [S. 1638?],(c) uncle and h.; *b.* 19 March 1769; was a "Colonel" before 1805; *suc. to the Baronetcy*,(c) 14 Jan. 1836. He *m.* 7 Jan. 1805, at St. Geo., Han. sq., Charlotte Dorothea (then a minor), 2d da. of Sir John HONYWOOD, 4th Baronet [1660], by Frances, da. of William (COURTENAY), 2d VISCOUNT COURTENAY OF POWDERHAM. She *d.* July 1811. He *d.* 23 Feb. 1840, at Barton Grange, Somerset, aged 71. Will pr. April 1840.

VII.(b) *1840, to 1850.* SIR FREDERICK COOPER, Baronet [S. 1638?],(c) only s. and h., *b.* probably about 1808; *suc. to the Baronetcy*,(e) 23 Feb. 1840. He *d.* unm. 1850, when the issue male of his grandfather, Grey COOPER, became extinct, and the *assumption of the Baronetcy*(c) (commenced by his said grandfather in 1775) *ceased*.(d)

(a) See p. 446, note "c."

(b) See p. 446, note "f."

(c) See p. 446, note "g."

(d) The notice in Debrett's *Baronetage* for 1870, that William Cooper, of Failford, co. Ayr, claims this Baronetcy "as representative of the 3d son of the 1st Baronet," is not correct as far as such claim goes, though apparently the pedigree is correct. The matter is very fully discussed in *The Genealogist* [O.S., vol. i, pp. 257-266, corrected by p. 334], and in the *Her. and Gen.* [vol. viii, pp. 193-196], where is a quotation that the Rev. John Cooper, formerly Couper (who

DICK :

stated to be a Baronetcy [S.] ; (a)

created about 1638, 1642, or 1646.

I. *1638 ?* SIR WILLIAM DICK, of Braid, co. Edinburgh,(b) s. of John DICK, Merchant Burgess of Edinburgh, by Margaret, da. of William STEWART, of Edinburgh, Writer, was *b.* 1580, and acquired a considerable fortune (estimated in 1642, at £222,166) as a merchant and Banker in that city; was Provost thereof, 1638-39; was a zealous Covenanter, advancing enormous sums for that cause, as, on the other hand, did he, in 1641, for Charles I, and subsequently, in 1650 (to the extent of £20,000), for Charles II. He was *Knighted* between 10 Aug. and 17 Nov. 1641, and is (apparently in error) *supposed* to have been *cr. a Baronet* [S.] about 1638, 1642 or 1646.(a) He was a member of the Committee of Estates, 1644-51, but, having incurred the displeasure of the then Government, was fined £64,934, and reduced to poverty. He *m.* Elizabeth, da. of John MORISON, of Preston Grange. He *d.* at his lodgings (according to some, in the debtor's prison) in Westminster, 19 Dec. 1655, aged 75.

II. *1655.* WILLIAM DICK, of Braid aforesaid, grandson and h., being s. and h. of John DICK, "fiar of Braid" and (1628), Sheriff-Depute of Orkney, by Nicholas, da. of Sir George BRUCE, of Carnock, which John was s. and h., ap. of Sir William abovenamed, but *d.*, v.p., 1642. He suc. his grandfather, 19 Dec. 1655, but *never styled himself a Baronet*, which he undoubtedly would have done, after the Restoration, had such title ever been conferred. He, who was *bap.* 10 Aug. 1631, sold the estate of Braid in 1676, and, in a petition, dated 1681, states he had sacrificed £8,000, for payment of his grandfather's creditors. He *m.*, in 1678, Elizabeth DUNCAN. He *d.* in or before 1695, when his widow was living. Her will (as Elizabeth Duncan, widow of Mr. William Dick, of Braid) pr. 24 April 1697, in the Edinburgh Commissariat Court.

III. *1695 ?* WILLIAM DICK, s. and h., aged 16 in 1695, being the son of "a poor widow"; was in 1707 an Ensign in the Foot Guards; was at the battle of Almanza; but afterwards settled in America, and was styled "Captain in the independant army of the State of New York." He is stated, as heir male of his great grandfather, to have *assumed the title of Baronet*, but such "is *not the case*."(b) He *m.* (—), widow of Capt. FOULIS, but *d.* s.p.m., in 1733, his only child, Agnes, being served his heir general.

died s.p. 1789, aged 80), "considered himself entitled to the Baronetcy of Gogar, and was proceeding to claim it, but desisted therefrom on the appearance of Sir Grey Cooper, claiming descent from an elder branch." This John was elder brother to William Cooper, formerly Couper, of Curries' Close, High Street, Glasgow, merchant, who, in 1786, purchased the estate of Failford, which his descendants still hold.

(a) In Milne's List it is given without any date, and as "only in ane old list." In Beatson's List the date is 1638; in Debrett's *Baronetage* (1873) it is 1642; and in Dod's (1876) it is 1646.

(b) An accurate and very full account of this family and of "the pretensions to a Baronetcy" by the descendants of Sir William Dick, of Braid, is given by "S***," [*i.e.*, R. R. Stodart, Lyon Clerk Depute, 1863-86], in the *Her. and Gen.*, vol. viii, pp. 257-269. The singular career of this Sir William is mentioned in Scott's *Heart of Mid-Lothian*. See also *The Grange of St. Giles*, by Mrs. J. Stewart Smith [Edinburgh, 1898].

IV. *1733.* ROBERT DICK, of Frackafield, near Lerwick in Shetland, cousin and h. male. He was s. and h. of William DICK, of Frackafield aforesaid (*bap.* 5 Nov. 1679, at Kirkwall) who was s. of Capt. Andrew DICK, M.P. [S.], for the Orkney and Zetland Stewartry, 1678 (*bap.* 12 Dec. 1637, and living 1700), who was yr. br. to William DICK, of Braid. He became the "head of the family"(a) in 1733, but *never assumed the title of Baronet*. He *m.*, in or before 1738, Jane DICKSON. He *d.* a bankrupt in 1743.

V. 1743. CHARLES DICK, of Frackafield aforesaid, s. and h., *bap.* 13 Oct. 1736. He never made up any title to the estate (which was sold by the creditors in 1770), and *never assumed the title of Baronet*, though in consequence of the assumption thereof in 1768 by his cousin (as below mentioned), he took steps to prove his position as heir male to Sir William DICK, of Braid, his grandfather's grandfather's father. He *m.* 11 Oct. 1760, Martha MONTGOMERIE. He was living in London 1805.

* * * * * * * *

V *bis.* 1768, to 1804. SIR JOHN DICK, Baronet [S. 1638 ?],(b) after having been served, 14 or 21 March 1768, by a Jury in Edinburgh, heir male to Sir William DICK, of Braid, abovenamed, *assumed the style of a Baronet*,(c) on the supposition that such dignity had been granted to the abovenamed William, and that he himself was the heir male of the said grantee's body. He was 2d but 1st surv. s. and h. of Andrew DICK, of West Newton, co. Northumberland, by Janet, da. of Roger DURHAM, of Newcastle-upon-Tyne, which Andrew (who *d.* 1744, in his 68th year) was s. of Andrew DICK, of Newton aforesaid, s. of Louis DICK, 5th and yst. s. of Sir William DICK abovenamed. He was *b.* 1720; was a merchant residing in Holland in or soon after 1739; was British Consul at Leghorn, 1754 to 1771 and probably later, when for his services there to the Russian fleet, the Empress Catherine made him a Knight of the Russian Order of St. Alexander Newski.(d) He finally obtained the lucrative post of Head Auditor and Comptroller of the Army Accounts in London. He *m.* Anne, sister of General BRAGG, and da. of Joseph BRAGG, of Somerset. She, who was *b.* 13 Oct. 1720, *d.* 31 Jan. 1781. He *d.* s.p. 3 Dec. 1804, at Mount Clare, Roehampton, co. Surrey, in his 85th year. M.I. at Eastham, Essex. He left no portion of his fortune (above £70,000) to any of his relatives.(e) Will pr. Dec. 1804.

* * * * * * * *

(a) See p. 448, note "b."

(b) According to the service of 14 March 1768.

(c) He was a descendant, but certainly not the heir male of Sir William Dick, of Braid. See p. 448, note "b."

(d) This, presumably, is the reason why he is stated in Playfair's *Baronetage* [S]. (appendix ccxviii) to have obtained from George III "the distinguished honour of Knight of the Bath," an honour which he certainly did *not* obtain.

(e) *Annual Register*, 1804, where the residuary legatees, in four equal divisions, are stated to be (1), Mr. Carr; (2), Mr. Simons, of Carlisle street, Soho, testator's apothecary; (3), the Rev. Mr. Cleaver; and (4), Dr. Vaughan, testator's physician. Playfair (as in note "d" above) writes that "Sir John's nearest relations and heirs were the Prestonfield family [*i.e.*, the descendants of Sir James Dick, 1st Baronet (S. 1677) of Prestonfield, son of Alexander, 4th s. of Sir William Dick, of Braid], who would have succeeded to a large fortune, but Sir John was induced in his old age to leave almost the whole to a stranger and three of that stranger's friends."

VI. *1810 ?* to 1821. SIR WILLIAM DICK Baronet [S. 1638 ?],(a) 1st s. and h. of Charles DICK, of Frackafield and Martha his wife, both abovenamed; *b.* 8 Dec. 1765; was sometime a Major in the East India Company's Service; suc. his father between 1805 and 1820; and was 15 Jan. 1821, served heir male of his lineal ancestor, Sir William DICK, of Braid, abovenamed, when he *assumed the Baronetcy*,(a) supposed to have been conferred on the said Sir William. He *m.*, 27 April 1821, Caroline, widow of Lieut.-Col. Alexander FRASER (76th Regiment), da. of John KINGSTON, of Rickmansworth, Herts. He *d.*, s.p.m., 17 Dec. 1840. The will of his widow (who *d.* at Bath), pr. Jan. 1843.

VII. 1840. SIR PAGE KEBLE DICK, Baronet [S. 1638],(a) br. and h. male; *b.* 29 Sep. 1769; suc. his brother, 17 Dec. 1840, and *assumed the presumed Baronetcy*.(a) He was of Port Hall, near Brighton. He *m.*, 1795, Nancy, da. of Richard PARTRIDGE, of Birmingham. She *d.* 1850. He *d.* in London, 27 July 1851, aged 81. Admon., Jan. 1852.

VIII. 1851. SIR CHARLES WILLIAM HOCKADAY DICK, Baronet [S. 1638 ?],(a) only s. and h., *b.*, 1802; suc. his father, 27 July 1851, and *assumed the presumed Baronetcy*.(a) He *m.*, in 1835, Elizabeth, da. of George CHASSERAU, of Brighton. He *d.*, in straightened circumstances,(b) 3 Dec. 1876, at his residence, 42 Elm Grove, Brighton, aged 74. His widow *d.*, apparently, in 1880.

IX. 1876. SIR HENRY PAGE DICK, Baronet [S. 1638 ?],(a) only s. and h., *b.* 1853; suc. his father 3 Dec 1876, and *assumed the presumed Baronetcy*(a); was sometime in the London and County Bank. He *m.* in 1880, Eliza, da. of J. HYLDEN, of Brighton.(c)

SETON :

cr. 1638 ?

"SETON OF TOUGH [*i.e.*, Touch], now of Culbeg," is said in Beatson's List of Scotch Baronets to have been *cr. a Baronet* [S.] in 1638. No such creation, however, is known.(d)

(a) According to the service of 15 Jan. 1821, "The evidence in support of *descent* is satisfactory" [see p. 448, note "b"], but, of course, it could not convey the right to a title that had no existence.

(b) It is stated that "in extreme old age" he was "so entirely destitute" as to be "unable to do more than keep the sticks and umbrellas of visitors" at the Brighton Museum. Two pamphlets were published at Brighton in 1864, on "the claims of Sir Charles W. H. Dick, Baronet" (as to £52,418, £83,988, etc.), on Government, and it is remarked thereon (see p. 448, note "b"), that "surely Government could not be blamed if some provision were made, even at this date, for the descendant of one [Sir William Dick, of Braid], who was ruined by his trust in the good faith of the authorities of his time."

(c) On 30 March 1881 was born "a son and heir" of "Sir Henry Dick, Baronet," at Islip street, Kentish Town. He received the name of Charles Henry Chasserau.

(d) Walter Seton, of Abercorn, was *cr. a Baronet* [S.], 3 June 1663. His grandson, the 3d Baronet, on the death of James Seton, of *Touch*, became the representative of that family, whose son, the 4th Baronet, was of *Culbeg*.

PRETYMAN :

often (erroneously) considered as *cr.* about 1638;

see under 1660.

GUTHRIE :

date unknown. Qy. about 1638.

"SIR HARIE GUTHRIE, of Kingsward" [*Qy.* King Edward, co. Banff], appears without date, in Milne's List of Scotch Baronets, but nothing is known of this creation.

GORDON :

cr. 13 Aug. 1642 ; (a)

afterwards, since 1682, EARLS OF ABERDEEN [S.].

I. 1642. SIR JOHN GORDON, of Haddo, only s. and h. of George GORDON, by Margaret, da. of Sir Alexander BANNERMAN, of Elsick, which George (who *d.* v.p. Oct. 1610) was 1st s. and h. ap. of James GORDON, of Methlic and Haddo, was *b.* early in 1610; suc. his grandfather in Nov. 1624; was next in command of the Royal forces to oppose the Covenanters, and was in the action at Turreff in 1639. He joined the King at Newark, and was by him *cr. a Baronet* [S.], 13 Aug. 1642,(a) with remainder to the heirs male of his body. In Oct. 1643 he protested against the Covenant; was besieged in his house at Kelly, and taken prisoner at its surrender, 8 May 1644; was found guilty of treason, and accordingly beheaded at Edinburgh, 19 July following, aged 34. He *m.*, in 1630, Mary, da. of William FORBES, of Tolquhoun. She survived him.

II. 1644. SIR JOHN GORDON, Baronet, [S. 1642], of Haddo aforesaid, 1st s. and h., *b.* about 1632; *suc. to the Baronetcy*, 19 July 1644, which was, however, owing to his father's attainder, under forfeiture till the Restoration in 1660. He *m.* Mary, only da. of Alexander (FORBES), 1st LORD FORBES OF PITSLIGO [S.], by Jean, da. of William (KEITH), 5th EARL MARISCHAL [S.]. He *d.* s.p.m. 1665.

III. 1665. SIR GEORGE GORDON, Baronet [S. 1642], of Haddo aforesaid, br. and h. male; *b.* 3 Oct. 1637; *suc. to the Baronetcy* in 1665. Advocate, 7 Feb. 1668; M.P. [S.] for co. Aberdeen, 1669-74, 1678 and 1681-82. P.C., 1678; one of the Lords of Session, 1 June 1680; President, 1 Nov. 1681. High Chancellor [S.], 1 May 1682. He *m.*, Anne, 1st da. of George LOCKHART, of Torbrecks, by Anne, da. of Sir James LOCKHART, of Lee. She, who became, in 1672, heir to her br., William LOCKHART, was living when her husband, six months after having been made High Chancellor [S.], was *cr.*, 30 Nov. 1682, EARL OF ABERDEEN, etc. [S.] In that peerage *this Baronetcy* then *merged*, and still so continues. See *Peerage*.

TURING :

cr. about 1642.

I. 1642 ? SIR JOHN TURING, of Foveran, co. Aberdeen, s. of James TURING,(b) of the same, was *b.* about 1595; espoused the royal cause, and, having previously been *Knighted*, obtained in, or shortly before, 1641

(a) Milne's List.

(b) "The Lay of the Turings," by H. McK. [*i.e.*, Mackenzie], pub. in 1849, which besides a tabular pedigree, contains notes illustrative thereof.

a warrant for the creation of a Baronet [S.], which warrant he on 7 Aug. 1641 held, "to bestow to the best advantage,"(a) though it is *presumed* that he not long afterwards *nominated himself as such Baronet* [S.].(b) He was taken prisoner by the Covenanters, 27 May 1639, by whom his house of Foveran was subsequently sacked. He fought on behalf of the young King at the battle of Worcester, 3 Sep. 1651. He *m.* about 1620, Barbara, da. of George GORDON, of Gight. She *d.* Feb. 1639. He *d.* 1662.

II. 1662. JOHN TURING, of Foveran aforesaid, grandson and h., being s. and h. of George TURING, by Margaret (marr. contract, 18 June 1652), da. of John FORBES, of Leslie, which George was only s. and h. ap., of Sir John Turing abovenamed, but *d.*, v.p., between 1652 and 14 Feb. 1657. He suc. his grandfather in 1662, but *never assumed the Baronetcy*, to which he was heir, presuming the said Sir John Turing to have nominated himself as a Baronet. He sold the estate of Foveran, and *d.* unm. in the Canongate of Edinburgh, Feb. 1682, when *the Baronetcy* remained dormant for about 100 years.

* * * * * * * *

III. 1682. JOHN TURING, 2d cousin and h. male, being s. of John TURING, by JANET SEATON, his wife, which John (*b.* 1650) was s. of Henry TURING, next br. to Sir John TURING (who *d.* 1662) first abovenamed, to whose male representation he succeeded in 1682, when possibly, though not probably, he *assumed the Baronetcy*.(c) He was *b.* 1680, was in Holy Orders, and was sometime, 1703-33, Minister of Drumblade. He *m.*, Dec. 1700, Jean, da. of Rev. John DUNBAR, of Forglen. He *d.* 1733.

IV. 1733. ALEXANDER TURING, 1st s. and h., *bap.* 9 Aug. 1702; was in Holy Orders, and was sometime, 1729-82, Minister of Oyne; suc. his father in 1733, when possibly, but not probably, he *assumed the Baronetcy*.(c) He *m.*, in 1740, Anna BROWN. He *d.* 1782, aged 80.

V. 1782. SIR INGLIS TURING, Baronet(c) [S. 1642?] 1st surv. s. and h.; *bap.* 4 Dec. 1743; suc. his father in 1782, when probably (as certainly he did subsequently) he *assumed the Baronetcy*.(c) He, also, was in Holy Orders, and was Rector of St. Thomas-in-the-Vale, Jamaica, where he *d.* unm. in 1791.

(a) See *Genealogist* (O.S., vol. iii., pp. 65-68), in an article by "S * * * *" (*i.e.*, R. R. Stodart, Lyon Clerk Depute, 1863-86), on the "Traffic in Baronetcies in the seventeenth century," where it is stated that Sir John Turing, of Foverne, for £180 paid him by John Turing, of Covent Garden, Midx., agrees on 7 Aug. 1641, to give half of any money that should be paid for the Baronetcy by his nominee, to the said John, with whom for security he "leaveth the patent for ye said Knight Barronett until we both jointly can find a seasonable opportunity to bestow it to the best advantage." This is conclusive evidence that, as late as Aug. 1641, he had not nominated *himself* as a Baronet, though the date of 1638 is positively assigned to the creation in Mackenzie's "Lay of the Turings."

(b) In like manner Sir Robert Carr, of Etal, co. Northumb., had, in 1647, two warrants of Baronetcy [S.], which he still held in 1661, when he asks for and obtains their renewal. What however, was their ultimate fate is unknown. A like warrant was obtained for John Bannatine, Minister of Lanark, who sold it (1676?) to his parishioner, Carmichael of Bonnington, who and whose issue male, held the title without dispute, till their extinction in July 1738; see *Genealogist*, as in note "a" above.

(c) This is on the supposition that the grant of the Baronetcy was to heirs male whatsoever.

VI. 1791. SIR ROBERT TURING, Baronet(a) [S. 1642?], of Banff Castle, co. Banff, br. and h.; *bap.* 25 Dec. 1745; *suc. to the Baronetcy*(a) in 1791, as to which "a service was expede at Banff" 9 July 1792.(b) He, who had acquired a fortune in India, returned thence in 1792 and settled at Banff Castle. He *m.* 12 Oct. 1797, at Edinburgh, Anne, da. of Col. Donald CAMPBELL, of Glensaddel. She *d.* 7 Dec. 1809. He *d.* s.p.m. 21 Oct. 1831.(c) Will pr. June 1832 and Nov. 1851.

VII. 1831. SIR JAMES HENRY TURING, Baronet(a) [S. 1642?], cousin and h. male, being s. and h. of John TURING, of Campvere in Zealand, Factor, by Margaret, da. of Smart TENNENT, of Musselburgh, Scotland, which John (who *d.*, 1798, aged 48), was s. of James TURING, also of Campvere, Factor, which James (who *d.*, 1788, aged 74), was s. of the Rev. Walter TURING, Minister of Rayne, co. Aberdeen, yr. br. of John TURING (*d.*, 1738, aged 58), numbered (above) as the 3d Baronet. He was *b.* 10 Dec. 1791; *suc. to the Baronetcy*,(a) 21 Oct. 1831; was British Consul at Rotterdam, 1845-60, having previously been Vice-Consul there. He *m.* in 1821, Antoinette, 3d da. of Sir Alexander FERRIER, K.H. British Consul for the Hague,(d) by Antoinette JONES his wife. He *d.* at Rotterdam, 13 Feb. 1860, aged 68. His widow *d.*, 9 April 1884, at Rotterdam, aged 80.

VIII. 1860. SIR ROBERT FRASER TURING, Baronet,(a) [S. 1642?], 3d but 1st surv. s. and h., *b.* 29 Aug. 1827; British Vice-Consul at Rotterdam, 1852-60; Consul, 1860-74; having *suc. to the Baronetcy*,(a) 13 Feb. 1860, his claim thereto being admitted by the Lyon office in 1882. He *m.*, 29 June 1853, at the British Legation, at the Hague, Catherine Georgiana, da. of Walter S. DAVIDSON, of Saxonbury, Kent and of Lowndes square.

HAMILTON:

cr. about 1646 (e)

I. 1646? ROBERT HAMILTON, of Silvertonhill, co. Lanark, s. and h. ap. of Edward HAMILTON, formerly of Balgray, but subsequently of Silvertonhill aforesaid, by Marion, da. of James MURE, of Caldwell, was a steady Loyalist, and is said to have been *cr. a Baronet* [S.], by Charles I about

(a) See p. 452, note "c."

(b) See *Genealogist* as on p. 452, note "a"; it being there added as to the statement that this Robert had been "served heir in 1792," that "no such service was retoured to Chancery, and no record of it exists in the Sheriff Court books of Banffshire where *Sir* Robert resided." This Robert appears as the "present [1811] Baronet" in Playfair's *Baronetage* [S.], where, however, its Editor adds that "we are totally unable to trace any of the intermediate generations" from the 1st Baronet to him.

(c) The title was claimed in 1831 by John Turing, who, however, gave up his claim to James Henry Turing. [*Pall Mall Budget*, 13 July 1878].

(d) He died at Rotterdam in 1845, aged 72.

(e) The date of 1646 is usually assigned for this creation, though 1642 is a more probable one. There is no entry thereof in the Great Seal Register, or, apparently, elsewhere; neither is it in Milne's List, or even in that of Beatson. The grantee, Robert Hamilton, in his service to his uncle, William, in 1655, is not given any title at all, and in his service to his father, Edward, in 1666, is simply called *Dominus*, with no addition of *Miles* or *Miles Baronettus*, which last is usual in the case of a Baronet. On the other hand, Sir Frederic Hamilton recorded arms in the Lyon office in 1790, being styled in the entry in the Register, grandson and heir of Sir Robert Hamilton, 4th Baronet, who was great grandson and representative of Sir Robert Hamilton, *cr.* a Baronet of Nova Scotia, by patent, *anno* 1646, under the great seal of Charles I. [*ex inform.*, Sir J. Balfour Paul, Lyon King of arms]. The Baronetcy is omitted by Playfair in his existing *Baronetage* [S.] of 1811.

1646.(a) He suc. his father in 1649; sold the estate of Provan,(b) and burdened his other estates. He was M.P. [S.] for Lanarkshire, 1661-63, as (possibly) also 1678. He *m.* Anne, 2d da. of John (HAMILTON), 1st LORD BELHAVEN [S.] (who *d.* s.p.m., 17 June 1679) by Margaret, illegit. da. of James (HAMILTON), 2d MARQUESS OF HAMILTON [S.].

II. 1670? SIR ROBERT HAMILTON, Baronet(c) [S. 1646?], of Silverstonhill aforesaid, s. and h.; *suc. to the Baronetcy*(c) on the death of his father. He (or, possibly his father) was M.P. [S.] for Lanarkshire, 1678;(d) served in the army of Holland, under the Prince of Orange; was subsequently Capt. (1688) and Major (1700), in the Earl of Leven's Foot. He *m.* firstly in Holland, Aurelia Katharine VAN HETTINGEN, of Friesland. He *m.* secondly, Isabel, da. of John HAMILTON, of Boggs, in Scotland. He *d.* at Fort William, 1708.

III. 1708. SIR JOHN HAMILTON, Baronet(c) [S. 1646?], s. and h. by 1st wife; *suc. to the Baronetcy* in 1708.(c) He *m.* firstly, Mary, da. of (—) LEWERS. He *m.* secondly, Rachael, da. of (—) LEMPRIERE. He *d.* in Jersey in 1748. Admon., 21 Jan., 1748/9, to a creditor. His 2d wife survived him. Her will pr. 1751.

IV. 1748. SIR ROBERT HAMILTON, Baronet(c) [S. 1646?], s. and h. by 1st wife; *suc. to the Baronetcy*(c) in 1748; was an officer in the army, becoming eventually, 1777, Lieut.-Gen.; was sometime Col. of the 108th and subsequently, 1770, of the 40th Foot. He *m.* firstly, Louisa,(e) sister of Sir Hutchins WILLIAMS, 1st Baronet [1747], da. of William Peere WILLIAMS, Barrister, by Anne, da. of Sir George HUTCHINS. She *d.* 15 Jan. 1777. He *m.* secondly, 6 Feb. 1778, Anne, da. of Sir John HEATHCOTE, 2d Baronet [1733], of Normanton, by Bridget, da. of Thomas WHITE. He *d.* in Grosvenor street, 10 Aug. 1786. Will pr. Aug. 1786. The will of Dame Anne HAMILTON was pr. 1816.

V. 1786. SIR FREDERIC HAMILTON, Baronet(c) [S. 1646], grandson and h, being only s. and h. of John William HAMILTON, Capt. 54th Regiment, by Mary Anne, da. of Richard ST. GEORGE, of Kilrush, co. Kilkenny, which John William was 1st s. and h. ap., by his 1st wife, of the late Baronet, but *d.* v.p. He was *b.* 14 Dec. 1777, in Dublin; *suc. to the Baronetcy*,(c) 10 Aug, 1786, and was in the East India Company service, 1792-1833, being sometime Collector of Revenues for the district of Benares. He *m.*, 20 Aug. 1800, Eliza Ducarel, yst. da. of John COLLIE, M.D., of Calcutta. She *d.* 11 Feb. 1841. He *d.* 14 Aug. 1853, aged 76. Will pr. Nov. 1853.

VI. 1853. SIR ROBERT NORTH COLLIE HAMILTON, Baronet [S. 1646?], 1st s. and h., *b.* at Benares aforesaid, 7 April 1802; was in the Bengal Civil Service, 1819-1860; Magistrate and Collector of Meerut, 1834; Civil and Session Judge of Delhi, 1837; Sec. to the Lieut. Gov. of the N.W. Provinces, 1841; *suc. to the Baronetcy*, 14 Aug. 1853; Agent to the Gov. Gen. in Central India, 1854; was thanked by Parl. for his services during the Indian mutiny, and made provisional member of the Council of the Gov. Gen. in 1859; K.C.B., 1860; Sheriff of Warwickshire, 1866. He *m.* 9 Oct. 1831, at St. Marylebone, his cousin, Constantia, 3d da. of Gen. Sir George ANSON, G.C.B., by Frances, sister of Sir Frederic HAMILTON, 5th Baronet [S.] abovenamed. She *d.* 28 Nov. 1842. He *d.* at Avoncliffe, near Stratford-on-Avon, co Warwick, 30 May 1887, in his 86th year. Will pr. 26 Sep. 1887, above £18,000.

VII. 1887. SIR FREDERIC HARDING ANSON HAMILTON, Baronet [S. 1646?], 2d but 1st. surv. s. and h., *b.* 24 Sep. 1836; ed. at Eton; sometime Major 60th Rifles; *suc. to the Baronetcy*, 30 May 1887. He *m.* 18 Sep. 1865, Mary Jane, da. of H. WILLAN.

(a) See p. 453, note "e."

(b) His grandmother, Elizabeth, wife of Sir Robert Hamilton, was da. and heir of Sir William Baillie, of Provan, President of the Court of Session.

(c) According to the entry in the Lyon office. See p. 453, note "e."

(d) Both in 1661 and 1678 the M.P. is styled "Knight" only.

(e) In Anderson's *House of Hamilton* she is called "Mary."

Supplemental Creations by Charles I.

A search, kindly made by J. Horace Round through the Signet office Docquet Books (vols. 12 and 13) from the beginning of the year 1642, discloses some creations of Baronetcies by Charles I, which are not in the list given in the "appendix to the 47th report of the Deputy Keeper of the Public Records" or in the extracts from *Black's Docquets*(a) printed at the end thereof.(b) The date of the month is not given in these books.

These creations are eight in number, *viz.*,

1643, Oct. "EDWARD BATHURST, of Lechlade, co. Gloucester, Esq." [See this creation set out on page 237.]

1643/4, Feb. "ROBERT DALLISON, of Greetwell, co. Lincoln, Esq." [As to this creation, which, apparently, is nowhere else noticed, see p. 456 below].

1644, April. "SIR JOHN AWBREY [AUBREY], of Llantrithed, co. Glamorgan, Knt." [See under 1660, in which year the grantee(b) obtained a *patent* of Baronetcy.]

1644, April. "FRANCIS GAMULL, of Chester, co. Cheshire, Esq." [As to this creation, which, apparently, is nowhere else noticed, see p. 456 below.]

1644, April. "EVAN LLOYD, of Yale, co. Denbigh, Esq." [See this creation set out on page 246].

1644/5, Feb. "WILLIAM COURTNAY [COURTENAY], of Powderham, co. Devon, Esq." [See this creation set out on page 241, where, however, the date is given as "Feb. 1644," instead of "Feb. 1644/5."]

1644/5, March. "WOLSTAN DIXIE, of Market Bosworth, co Leicester." [See under 1660, in which year the grantee(b) obtained a *patent* of Baronetcy.]

1645, July. "JOHN KNIGHTLEY, of Offchurch, co. Warwick, Esq." [See under 1660, in which year the grantee(b) obtained a *patent* of Baronetcy.]

"These creations are described as *By warrant under His Majesties signe Manuall. procured by Mr. Secretary Nicholas, Lord Digby*, or some other."

It may be noted that the creation of JOHN PRESTON [of Furness co. Lancaster], given as 1 April 1644 in *Black's Docquets* occurs as early as May 1643 in the Signet Office Docquet Book, this being an earlier stage in the process of creation" [J. Horace Round].

(a) "The Ashmolean MS. from which *Black's Docquets* are printed has now been ascertained to be only the draft. The fair copy of it has been found in the *Crown Office* at the House of Lords" [J. Horace Round].

(b) Three Baronetcies, of which no patents exist, were conferred, as under, *viz.*, 24 Nov. 1644, on JOHN ACLAND, of Columb John, Devon; 5 Nov. 1644, on HENRY BOOTHBY, of Clattercote, Oxon: and 21 March 1644/5, on THOMAS EDWARDS, of Grete, Salop; but though these grants were followed by patents from Charles II, such patent in each case was *not to the* original *grantee*, who had died before that event, but to his son. Those persons, therefore, that held that dignity before the patentee of Charles II (in the case of Acland these were as many as four) are dealt with in this Volume, pp. 236, 239, and 243.

DALLISON:

cr. Feb. 1643/4.

existing as late as April 1714.

I. 1644. ROBERT DALLISON, of Greetwell, co. Lincoln, s. and h. of William DALLISON, of the same, by Hester, da. and h. of George BLESBY, of Blesby in that county, was admitted to Gray's Inn. 17 Aug. 1632, and, again, 23 June 1637; was aged 17 in 1634 (*Visit. of Lincolnshire*); matric. at Oxford (Christ Church), 20 May 1636, aged 18; raised a regiment of horse(a) at his own charge for the King, and was *cr. a Baronet*, the docquet being dated Feb. 1643/4 (see p. 455). He, with his father, was at the siege of Newark in March 1644, and both were living 1650, when discharged of their amercement. He was living after the Restoration.

II. 1670? SIR ROBERT DALLISON, Baronet [1644], apparently s. and h., presumed to be identical with the "Sir Robert Dallyson, Baronet, of Greetwell,(b) co. Lincoln," who had lic. (Vic. Gen.) 17 April 1677 to marry at Swinderly, co. Lincoln, Mrs. Alice ANDREWES, of Lincoln, widow.

III. 1680? SIR THOMAS DALLISON, Baronet [1644], apparently s. and h., presumed to be identical with "Sir Thomas Dallison, Baronet, of St. Paul's, Covent Garden, Midx., Bachelor," administration of whose goods was granted 25 June 1713, to a creditor, "Dame Alice Dallison," the mother of deceased, having renounced.

IV. 1713, to 1720? SIR JAMES DALLISON, Baronet [1644], possibly br. and h. male, supposed to be identical with "Sir James Dalyson, Baronet, of Chelsea, Midx., about 25 and a Bachelor" 13 April 1714, when he had lic. (Vic. Gen.) to marry Anne SYMONDS, of the same, aged 18, spinster, with consent of her mother, Anne, wife of John SYMONDS, then at Barbadoes.

GAMULL:

cr. April 1644;

ex. or dormant Nov. 1654.

I. 1644, to 1654. FRANCIS GAMULL, of Chester, s and h. of Thomas GAMULL, Recorder of that city, by Alice, da. of Richard BAVAND, was *bap.* at St. Oswald's, Chester, 25 Nov. 1606; suc. his father 11 Aug. 1613; was *Knighted* at Oxford, 25 April 1644, and was *cr. a Baronet*, the docquet bearing date that same month (see p. 455). He was Alderman of Chester; Mayor, 1634-35; and M.P. thereof 1640, till disabled 22 Jan. 1643/4. He was a Royalist delinquent, and fled the kingdom, his estate being sequestrated in July 1649. He *m.* firstly, Oct. 1624, at Eccleston, Christiana, da. of Sir Richard GROSVENOR, 1st Baronet [1622] by his 2d wife, Lettice, da. of Sir Hugh CHOLMONDELEY. She was *bur.* 11 June 1640, at St. Mary's, Chester. He *m.* secondly, Elizabeth, widow of Robert RAVENSCROFT, da. of Sir Randle

(a) See *Mis. Her. & Gen.*, 2d S., Vol. ii, p. 289, in a petition (without date) to the King from "Sir Robert Dalyson, Baronet." At p. 259 thereof is an extract from "*Lloyd's Memories*," stating that besides "Sir Thomas Dallison, a Lancashire [*Qy.* Lincolnshire] gentleman . . . . whose loyalty cost him his life at Nazeby and £12,000 in his estate . . . . there were in the King's army three Colonels more of that name, viz., Sir Charles, *Sir Robert*, and Sir William, who spent £130,000 therein."

(b) The parish registers of Greetwell do not begin till 1723, after which date there are no Dallison entries in them.

MAINWARING, of Over Peover, by Jane, da. of Sir Thomas SMITH, of Hough, co. Chester. By her he had no issue. He *d.* 27 Nov. 1654, and was *bur.* at St. Mary's aforesaid, *when the Baronetcy* presumably became *extinct*, and certainly was never subsequently assumed.(a) Admon. 12 Dec. 1660 to his da., Sidney BRERFWOOD, *otherwise* GAMULL. His widow *d.* at Chester, 13 Aug. 1661, and was *bur.* at Harden with her first husband.

(a) According to the pedigree in Ormerod's *Cheshire* (edit. 1882, vol. iii, p. 475), he had three sons, viz. (1), Thomas Gamull, slain in the Civil Wars, v.p., and *bur.* 12 June 1644 at St. Mary's, Chester; (2), Edward Gamull; and (3), Edmund, who died s.p. It is there stated that Edward, the 2d son, was *bur.* 16 Feb. 1663/4, at St. Mary's, in which case he would have been entitled to his father's Baronetcy during the ten years that he survived him. It is, however, not unlikely that the Edmund who died in 1664 was only a relation, not a son, of Sir Francis. See particulars as to the career and estates of this Francis in the Royalist Composition papers, where it is to be noted he is occasionally styled "Baronet."

CORRIGENDA ET ADDENDA.

p. 8; note (o), *for* "Sir John Winter," *read* "(as his 2d wife) Sir George Wintour, Baronet [1642], and *d.* s.p."

p. 17; line 4, *after* "Goodwyns," *add* "[in Hoo]"; line 7, *for* "about 1585," *read* "6 and *bap.* 27 March 1607, at Letheringham"; *for* "1609," *read* "1609/10"; line 10, *for* "aged 53," *read* "was *bur.* 31, at Letheringham, in his 33d year. M.I."; line 11, *after* "1642," *add* "She was *bur.* 6 April 1642, at Letheringham"; line 15, *after* "HALLIDAY," *add* "She was *bur.* 22 June 1652, at Letheringham"; line 18, *after* "1657," *add* "She was *bur.* 13 Nov. 1656, at St. Giles' in the Fields."

p. 25; 3d and 2d lines from bottom; *for* "*d.* s.p., being killed," *read* "who was a Jesuit Priest (though he obtained a dispensation to marry), *d.* s.p., being killed near Dartford."

p. 26; line 23, *after* "was," *read* "*b.* 10 March 1606, being."

p. 31; line 26, *after* "Chichester," *add* "She was *bur.* 18 June 1623, at North Mundham"; line 27, *for* "before 1634," *read* "4 June 1624, at St. Mary le Strand, Midx."; line 30, *for* "1650," *read* "1649/50"; line 37, after "1648," *add* "Her admon. 13 March 1655"; line 38, *dele* "(a)"; line 39, *after* "widow," *add* "She was *bur.* 31 July 1687, at North Mundham." Note (e), *for* "136," *read* "137."

p. 32; line 17, *for* "William," *read* "Robert"; line 18, *for* "1655," *read* "1657."

p. 36; line 31, *for* "William ATHERTON, of Skelton, co. York," *read* "John ATHERTON, by Anne, da. of Sir John BYRON (Visit. of Lanc. 1665)"; line 33, *after* "widow," *add* "who was *b.* at Newstead, Notts"; line 37, *for* "pr. Feb. 1645," *read* "dat. 8 July 1644, pr. 26 Feb. 1644/5."

p. 37; note (a), line 1; *after* "adjudged," *add* "in 1678"; line 3, *before* "invalid," *insert* "apparently."

p. 49; line 37, *after* "London," *add* "He *d.* 1 Jan. 1691/2"; line 44, *after* "by," *add* "apparently."

p. 56; line 43, *for* "about 1730," *read* "presumably 4 May 1761."

p. 66; in margin, *for* "1669," *read* "1670"; line 13, *after* "*m.*," *add* "7 May 1663"; lines 17 and 20, *for* "1669," *read* "1669/70"; line 22, *after* "*m.*," *add* "in or shortly before June 1689."

p. 67; in margin, *for* "1630," *read* "1629"; *for* "1700?" *read* "1706"; line 12, *for* "1629/30," *read* "1628/9"; line 13, *for* "presumably about 1700," *read* "Sep. 1706"; line 18, *after* "1602," *add* "suc. his father 18 Sep. 1629"; *dele* "1615-16, and"; line 19, *for* "Margaret," *read* "Catharine"; line 21, *after* "Hooton," *add* "She was *bur.* 12 Sep. 1639, at St. Mary's, Chester"; line 23, *for* "1630," *read* "1629"; line 27, *for* "father," *read* "grandfather"; line 28, *dele* "in or" *to* "Mary," *and insert* "8 May 1649, Mary (*b.* 26 June 1626)"; line 29, *for* "Carnarvon," *read* "Flint. She was living 9 Jan. 1652/3"; *for* "Jane," *read* "in or before 1657, Jane, widow of Col. John MARRON (*d.* Aug. 1644) and previously of Henry HARDWARE, of Peel, co. Lanc."; line 30, *after* "Flint," *add* "She was *bur.* at Gresford, 17 Feb. 1684/5"; lines 31 and 32, *dele* "it is" *to end* and *insert* "and was *bur.* at Gresford 28 Sep. 1706, when the *Baronetcy* became *extinct.*(d) Will dat. 11 Feb. 1705/6." Note (b), *dele* the whole of this note. Note (c), lines 3 and 6, *dele* "before 1694" *to the end, and insert* "and was *bur.* at Gresford, 16 April 1689, aged 39, leaving four surviving children, viz., two daughters by his 1st wife, and one son and one daughter by his 2d. The son, Samuel, *bap.* at Gresford 18 July 1682, was living 11 Feb. 1705/6, but *d.* s.p. a few months later, as, had he survived to Sep. 1706, he would have inherited the Baronetcy, whereas Winifred (the heiress of Horsley) then wife of "Edward Lloyd, Esq.," is spoken of, 19 Sep. 1707, at a Court Baron of Horsley, as sister and next heir of Samuel Powell, *Esquire*, decd." [*Mem.*—These valuable corrections to the Powell family were furnished by H. R. Hughes, of Kinmel Park, co. Denbigh].

p. 69; line 39, *dele* "of Eske, co. Cumberland [E.]."

p. 72; note (c), *conclude* "In Oct. following, Alderman Sir Robert Ducie (who had been Sheriff, 1620-21, and Lord Mayor, 1630-31) was similarly honoured; as, in Dec. 1641, was Sir Richard Gurney, the then Lord Mayor, he being the first person who received a Baronetcy during his Mayoralty. [See W. D. Pink's *Citizen Baronets* in *N. & Q.*, 9th S., ix, 61.].

p. 73; line 13, *after* "firstly," *add* "1 April 1656, at Holkham."

p. 77; lines 2 and 12, *for* "1629," *read* "1629(a)." Note (a), *conclude* "As to these Citizen Baronetcies, see p. 72, note "c," and the *addenda* thereto."

p. 79; lines 2 and 8, *for* "9," *read* "19."

p. 81; line 43, *for* "1663," *read* "1683."

p. 89; line 31, *for* "Besilden Lee," *read* "Besselsleigh"; line 32, *after* "there," *add* "before him, who *d.* 9 Nov. 1581."

p. 93; note (a), *conclude* "He petitions in Dec. 1696, to surrender his Baronetcy for one to be granted to himself for life, with rem. to his kinsman, John Thornicroft, of Gray's Inn, stating that he is in years and unmarried, and is anxious to prevent its descent to any person not qualified to support the dignity [*Rawlinson's MSS.*]. A Baronetcy in 1701 was conferred on this John Thornicroft."

p. 96; line 28, *for* "Telton," *read* "Teston."

p. 98; line 29, *for* "29 July 1811," *read* "26 June 1811, aged 52, at Ballogie, of which he was tenant (under the designation of Mr. Brown, an Irish gentleman, his real name being unknown till after his death), and was *bur.* at Birse, co. Aberdeen. M.I."; line 32, *for* "29 July," *read* "26 June."

p. 120; line 8, *after* "1875-76," *add* "He *m.* 18 March 1902, at Christ Church, Folkestone, Margaret Elizabeth, widow of John Dillon BROWNE, 100th Regiment"; line 18, *after* "firstly," *add* "28 Jan. 1646/7, at Wrotham, Kent"; line 20, *after* "She," *add* "who was *bap.* 27 April 1626, at St. Dionis Backchurch, London"; line 26, *for* "of the," *read* "of Stidulfe's Place, *i.e.*, the."

p. 126; line 23, *for* "*b.* about," *read* "*bap.* at Werrington aforesaid, 24 Jan."

p. 147; line 30, *for* "*Baronet*," *read* "Baronet(d)," *and insert as note* (d) "He was the first Lord Mayor *cr.* a Baronet during his term of office."

p. 148; line 8, *after* "1628," *add* "admitted to Gray's Inn (with his brother Richard) 2 Feb. 1630/1, as of St. John's, Herts"; line 10, *after* "1665-66," *add* "named, in 1660, as a Knight of the intended order of the Royal Oak, his estate being then valued at £1,000 a year." Note (a), *conclude* "It is sometimes said that about 1658, he received a Baronetcy from Oliver Cromwell, but this presumably is an error. It would, in any case, have been unnecessary, as his creation in 1641 was previous to the date (4 Jan 1641/2) on and after which the King's creations were disallowed, and his fidelity to the Royal cause seems evidenced by his being nominated in 1660 among the projected Knights of the Royal Oak."

p. 153; lines 9 and 10, *for* "about 1626," *read* "23 Dec. 1633"; *dele* "said to be."

p. 154; line 1, *after* "[S.]," *add* "19 Dec. 1635 and again"; *for* "was," *read* "and with a grant, presumably, of 16,000 acres in Nova Scotia (of which, however, he never had seizin), being"; lines 3 and 4, *for* "in or before 1627," *read* "21 Dec. 1624, at St. Dionis Backchurch, London"; *for* "Backchurch. London," *read* "aforesaid"; lines 14, 15, and 16, *for* "*b.* about," *read* "*bap*, at St. Dionis aforesaid, 28 Aug."; *after* "firstly," *add* "in or before 1670"; *dele* "or Mary"; *after* "London," *add* "She was *bur.* 27 Aug. 1663, at

Wrotham"; *after* "secondly," *add* "in or before 1666"; line 20, *after* "firstly," *add* "in or about 1683"; line 31, *for* "s. and h.," *read* "2d but 1st surv. s. and h."; *for* "*b.* about 1688," *read* "*bap.* 12 March 1685/6, at Wrotham"; line 36, *for* "*b.*," *read* "*bap.* at Wrotham, 10 June."

p. 156; line 13, *after* "at," *add* "Exeter House"; *after* "40," *add* "and was *bur.* 21 Jan. 1656/7, at Moreton Corbet"; line 24, *for* "1670," *read* "1668"; line 25, *after* "*d.*," *add* "in London"; *after* "4," *add* "and was *bur.* at Moreton Corbet, 24"; line 26, *for* "living Sep. 1688, *d.* about," *read* "was *bur.* at Moreton Corbet, 16 Nov."; line 28, *for* "*b.*," *read* "*bap.* at Moreton Corbet." Note (b), line 3, *dele* "the"; note (d), line 1, *for* "*b.* 1669," *read* "*bap.* 4 Dec. 1668, at Moreton Corbet."

p. 166; note (d), line 1, *after* "omission," *add* "(made 19 Dec. 1827)."

p. 168; line 26, *after* "1680," *add* "16 Dec. 1689 and 31 Oct. 1699." Note (c), line 4, *for* "Bradwardine," *read* "Bredwardine."

p. 186; line 8, *for* "in or before 1664," *read* "5 July 1662, at Langton"; line 10, *after* "abovenamed," *add* "She was *bur.* 18 Jan. 1670/1, at Bugthorpe"; line 15, *for* "2 Nov. 1643," *read* "1643—1716."

p. 187; in margin, *for* "1680?" *read* "1680"; line 25, *conclude* thus "He was *bur.* 20 Aug. 1680 in the church of the Augustine Convent, Louvain"; line 28, *for* "on his father's death," *read* "Aug. 1680."

p. 194; line 33, *for* "Katharine, da. and h.," *read* "1679/80, at Westow, co. York, Katharine, 2d da. and coheir"; *for* "co. York and" *read* "aforesaid, by Mary, da. of Sir Thomas GOWER, of Stittenham. She was aged 14, in 1666. He."

p. 196; line 39, *for* "*b.* about 1614," *read* "*bap.* 2 Jan. 1616/7, at Kippax"; line 47, *for* "1617, *m.* Walter WALSH, of Houghton and," *read* "1617(c)." *Add* as note (c) "The marriage at Kippax, 25 Jan. 1654/5, of 'Walter Walsh and Dame Katherine Bland,' refers presumably to the Baronet's mother, who, however, must then have been about sixty years old"; line 49, *for* "*b.* about," *read* "*bap.* at Kippax, 6 June."

p. 197; in margin, *for* "1668," *read* "1667"; line 2, *for* "1662," *read* "1661 and *bap.* at Kippax 2 Jan. 1661/2"; line 3, *for* "1668," *read* "1667"; line 5, *after* "2," *add* "and *bap.* at Kippax, 8"; line 15, *for* "*b.* about," *read* "*bap.* at Kippax, 10 Sep."; line 24, *for* "*b.* about 1722," *read* "*bap.* at Kippax, 13 Jan. 1721/2"; line 32, *for* "*b.* about," *read* "*bap.* at Kippax, 7 Sep."

p. 207; line 2, *after* "Devon," *add* "one of the Baronets created by Oliver Cromwell."

p. 220; note (a), *conclude* "The docquet is dated as early as May 1643. See p. 455 below."

p. 227; line 6, *for* "ye," *read* "the"; line 20, *for* "1644( )," *read* "1644(d)"; line 25, *after* "Penelope," *add* "sister of John, 1st VISCOUNT SCUDAMORE [I.]"; line 26, *after* "Hereford," *add* "by Ann, da. of Sir Thomas THROGMORTON"; *after* "1649," *add* "at Ballingham"; lines 31 and 32, *for* "George," *read* "Thomas"; *dele* "by Alice" *as far as* "Norfolk," *and insert* "2d Baronet [1652?], by Mary, da. of Thomas BOND(e)," *and add as note* (e) "Dame Margaret Scudamore is generally said to have been Margaret, *bap.* 1 May 1640, at Camberwell, Surrey, *sister* of Sir Thomas, the 2d Baronet, but the will (dat. 1 Sep. 1708, pr. 16 Nov. 1709) of her brother Edmund, shews her to be da. of the 2d and sister of the 3d Baronet"; last line, *for* "*extinct*," *read* "extinct(f)," *and add as note* (f) "Robert Scudamore, who as *Baronetti filius*, matric. at Oxford (Trin. Coll.), 7 May 1695; B.A., 4 Feb. 1698/9; M.A., 23 March 1701/2; Vicar of West Malling, Kent, 1704-17; was presumably a son of this Sir Barnabas. He *m.* Martha, da. of Sir Felix Wild, 2d Baronet [1660], and was living 1709, s.p., but presumably must have *d.* v.p."

p. 233; line 14, *for* "Owen," *read* "Ouen"; line 15, *after* "DOWSE," *add* "of Wallop, Hants"; *after* "70," *add* "and was *bur.* 12 Feb. at Hawnes, Beds"; line 18, *after* "husband," *add* "She was *bur.* 19 March 1696, at Hawnes."

p. 234; line 36, *for* "Sir Richard," *read* "Sir Thomas"; last line, *after* "1615," *add* "was (with his said br. Thomas) admitted to Gray's Inn, 2 Feb. 1630/1, being then of St. John's, Herts."

p. 237; note (d), line 1, *for* "notes a and b," *read* "note (b), and p. 215, note (b); see also p. 455 as to the date of the docquet being in Oct. 1643."

p. 239; line 3, *for* "Bart.," *read* "Bart.(d)," and *add*, as note (d) "He is said to have had a da. who *m.* (—) Woodman, and was mother of Charles Bathurst Woodman [*ex inform.* H. Gough]; line 23, *for* "Clote," *read* "Cote."

p. 241; in margin, *for* "1644," *read* "1645"; lines 23 and 30, *for* "1644," *read* "1644/5." Note (c), *for* "236, note 'a,'" *read* "215, note 'b'"; note (d), *commence* "See p. 455 as to the date of the docquet being in Feb. 1644/5."

p. 242; lines 8, 21, 34, and 41, *for* "1644," *read* "1645."

p. 245; line 11, *after* "MIDLETON," *add* "or MIDDLETON"; line 12, *after* "aforesaid," *add* "by his 2d wife, Elizabeth, da, of Marmaduke (LANGDALE), 3d BARON LANGDALE"; line 13, *for* "Dec. 1769," *read* "1 and was *bur.* 4 Jan. 1770, at Spofforth."

p. 246; note (b), line 1, *for* "236, note (a)," *read* "215, note (b), and p. 455, as to the date in the Signet office docquet book being in April 1644."

p. 257; line 39, *after* "Elinor," *add* "(*b.* about 1640)"; line 42, *after* "Cork," *add* "(who *d.* 12 April 1638)"; *after* "s.p.," *add* "He also (or possibly a successor of the same name) *m.* Joan, da. of Theobald ROCHE (a minor in 1642), of Ballamagooly, in the Barony of Fermoy, by Ann, da. of John BOYLE."

p. 259: lines 4 and 5, *for* "Archdeacon of Ardfert and Dean," *read* "Dean of Ardfert and Archdeacon."

p. 261; line 6, *after* "s. and h.," *add* "admitted to Gray's Inn. 23 June 1628 as, s. and h. of Richard Osborn, of Capagh, co. Waterford, Esq."

p. 262; note (b), *conclude* "The said Charles, moreover, is described as the *fifth son* when admitted to Lincoln's Inn, 16 Dec. 1780."

p. 272: line 28, *dele* "of whom"; line 29, *after* "Papists," *add* "He was one of the Aldermen of Limerick, appointed 1687 by James II."

p. 278: line 19, *for* "1644," *read* "1643/4"; line 24, *for* "1647," *read* "1646/7."

p. 280; line 2 from bottom, *for* "20," *read* "28." Note (d), lines 4 and 5, *dele from* "Douglas" *to end.*

p. 286; note (b), line 2, *for* "as to whom see," *read* "the great champion of the Kirk, who was *bur.* 13 Nov. 1652, at Leith, 'excommunicate because he came into the English.' See *N. & Q.*, 9th s., vii, 446 and."

p. 294; line 16, *dele* "and h."; *after* "1636]," *add* "of Lochend aforesaid"; line 18, *after* "widow," *add* "(who was h. to her br. the 2d Baronet)."

p. 304; note (b), line 3, *for* "was of," *read* "who inherited"; line 4, *conclude* "and who was *cr. a Baronet* [S.] 16 Jan. 1636/7, as of Carnock, co. Stirling."

p. 305; line 6, *after* "death," *add* "10 Jan. 1794."

p. 314; line 3 from bottom, *after* "Fife," *add* "and afterwards of Blebo."

p. 319; line 18, *for* "living 1901," *read* "*d.* 5 Jan. 1902, at Penicuik House, Penicuik, Scotland."

p. 325; line 8, *for* "1732," *read* "1722."

p. 336; note (f), *for* "5th," *read* "6th."

p. 341; line 27, *conclude* "He *d.* s.p.m., 25 Dec. 1900, at Waipukuran, Hawkes Bay, New Zealand."

p. 349; in margin, *for* "1638," *read* "1628."

p. 355; between lines 10 and 11, *insert* "*Forfeited* 14 Sep. 1763."

p. 374; line 32, *for* "scmetimes," *read* "sometime."

INDEX

TO THE SURNAMES OF THE SEVERAL HOLDERS OF THE BARONETCIES CREATED BY CHARLES I.

including not only those of the grantees themselves but of their successors; to which is added the local or, failing that, personal description of each grantee. The name of any Peerage dignity held with such Baronetcy is not included in the alphabetical arrangement, neither is the surname of the holder of any such peerage, when different(a) from that of any Baronet who was a Commoner.

(a) See vol. i, p. 263, note "a."

II

3 N

PROSPECTUS

OF THE

Complete Baronetage,

EXTANT, EXTINCT, OR DORMANT.

EDITED BY

G. E. C.

EDITOR OF THE

"Complete Peerage."

Vol. I. BARONETCIES (English and Irish) created by JAMES I., 1611 to 1625; issued at 14s. to Subscribers, June 1900; price, after publication, £1 1s. net.

Vol. II., BARONETCIES (English, Irish, and Scotch) created by CHARLES I., 1625 to 1649; issued at £1 1s. to Subscribers, May 1902; price, after publication, £1 11s. 6d. net.

Vols. III. and IV. will contain BARONETCIES (English, Irish, and Scotch), created 1649 to 1 May 1707 (the date of the Union with Scotland), each Vol. to be issued on the same terms as Vol. ii.

Vols. V. and VI. will contain the BARONETCIES of Great Britain and those of Ireland, 1707 to 1 Jan. 1801 (the date of the Union with Ireland), while the remaining Vols. will deal with those of the United Kingdom, viz., from 1801 to the date of publication.

All applications to be made to

Messrs. W. POLLARD & CO. Ltd.,
Publishers,
North Street,
EXETER.

[MAY 1902].

Complete Baronetage

VOLUME THREE
1649–1664

Complete Baronetage.

EDITED BY

G. E. C.

EDITOR OF THE

"Complete Peerage."

VOLUME III

1649—1664.

EXETER:
WILLIAM POLLARD & Co. Ltd., 39 & 40, NORTH STREET.
1903.

CONTENTS.

III

LIST OF SUBSCRIBERS.

Adams, Rev. H. W., Normanhurst, Eton Avenue, Hampstead, N.W.
Aldenham, Lord, St. Dunstan's, Regent's Park, N.W.
Amherst of Hackney, Lord, F.S.A., per Sotheran & Co., 140, Strand W.C.
Anderson, J. R., 84, Albert Drive, Crosshill, Glasgow.
Annesley, Lieut.-Gen. A. Lyttelton, Ter[illegible]emere, Weybridge, Surrey.
Anstruther, Sir R., Bt., Balcaskie, Pillenweena, Scotland.
Antrobus, Rev. Frederick, The Oratory, South Kensington, S.W.
Armytage, Sir George, Bt., F.S.A., Kirklees Park, Brighouse.
Arnold, Charles T., Stamford House, West Side, Wimbledon.
Assheton, Ralph, Downham Hall, Clitheroe.
Astley, John, Moseley Terrace, Coundon Road, Coventry.
Athenæum Club, per Jones, Yarrell & Poulter, 8, Bury Street, S.W.
Athill, Charles H., F.S.A., Richmond Herald, College of Arms, E.C.
Attwood, T. A. C., 7, Hyde Park Mansions, W.

Bain, J., Bookseller, 1, Haymarket, S.W. (4).
Baronetage, The Hon. Society of the, per Sotheran & Co., 140, Strand, W.C.
Batten, H. B., Aldon, Yeovil.
Beaven, Rev. A. B., Greyfriars, Leamington.
Bedford, Duke of, per Sotheran & Co., 140, Strand, W.C.
Bell & Sons, York Street, Covent Garden, W.C.
Boase, F., 28, Buckingham Gate, S.W.
Boyle, Colonel the Hon. R. E., 6, Summer Terrace, S.W.
Brigg, W., Cowthorpe Hall, Wetherley.
British Museum, Department of MSS., per Sotheran & Co., 140, Strand, W.C.
Brooking-Rowe, J., Castle Barbican, Plympton.
Bruce Bannerman, W., F.S.A., The Lindens, Sydenham Road, Croydon, Surrey.
Bullock, J. M., 118, Pall Mall, S.W.
Burke, Ashworth P., per Harrison & Sons, 59, Pall Mall, S.W.
Burke, Henry Farnham, C.V.O., F.S.A., Somerset Herald, College of Arms, E.C.
Burnard, Robert, 3, Hillsborough, Plymouth.

Carington, R. Smith, F.S.A., Ashby Folville Manor, Melton Mowbray.
Carlton Club, Pall Mall, per Harrison & Sons, 59, Pall Mall, S.W.
Carmichael, Sir Thomas D. Gibson, Bt., Castlecraig, Dolphinton, N.B.
Cazenove & Son, C. D., 26, Henrietta Street, Covent Garden, W.C.
Chadwyck-Healey, C. E. H., F.S.A., per Sotheran & Co., 140, Strand, W.C.
Clarke, C. L., Homewood, Stevenage, Herts.
Clements, H. J. B., Killadoon, Cellridge, co. Kildare, Ireland.
Codrington Library, All Souls College, Oxford.
Colyer-Fergusson, T. C., Ightham Mote, Ivy Hatch, near Sevenoaks.
Comber, John, Myddleton Hall, near Warrington.
Conder, Edward, F.S.A., The Conigree, Newent, Gloucester.
Cooper, Samuel J., Mount Vernon, near Barnsley.
Craigie, Edmund, The Grange, Lytton Grove, Putney Hill, S.W.
Crawford and Balcarres, Earl of, per Sotheran & Co., 140, Strand, W.C.
Crawley-Boevey, A. W., 24, Sloane Court, S.W.
Cresswell, L., Wood Hall, Calverley, Leeds.
Crisp, F. A., F.S.A., Grove Park, Denmark Hill, S.E.
Croft-Lyons, Lieut.-Colonel G. B., 3, Hertford Street, Mayfair, W.
Culleton, Leo., 92, Piccadilly, W.
Cullum, G. M. G., 4, Sterling Street, Montpelier Square, S.W.
Cust, Lady Elizabeth, 13, Eccleston Square, S.W.

Dalrymple, Hon. Hew., Oxenfoord Castle, Dalkeith.
Davies, Seymour G. P., English, Scottish, and Australian Bank Ltd., Melbourne, Australia.
Davison, R. M., Grammar School, Ilminster.
Denny, A. & F., 32, Charing Cross, S.W.
Douglas-Crompton, S., per Sotheran & Co., 140, Strand, W.C.
Douglas, David, 10, Castle Street, Edinburgh.
Douglas & Foulis, 9, Castle Street, Edinburgh (6).
Duleep Singh, His Highness Prince, per Sotheran & Co., 140, Strand, W.C.
Dunkin, E. H. W., Rosewyn, 70, Herne Hill, S.E.

Edwardes, Sir Henry H., Bt., per Harrison & Sons, 59, Pall Mall, S.W.
Eland, H. S., High Street, Exeter.
Exeter Royal Albert Memorial Museum, Exeter.

Foley, P., F.S.A., Prestwood, Stourbridge, per A. & F. Denny, 304, Strand, W.C.
Foster, Joseph, 21, Boundary Road, N.W.
Fox, Charles Henry, M.D., 35, Heriot Row, Edinburgh.
Fox, Francis F., Yate House, Chipping Sodbury, Gloucester, per W. George's Sons, Bristol.
Fry, E. A., 172, Edmond Street, Birmingham.

George, William Edwards, Downside, Stoke Bishop, near Bristol, per W. George's Sons, Bristol.
George's Sons, William, Top Corner, Park Street, Bristol (6).
Gibbs, Antony, Tyntesfield, near Bristol.
Gibbs, H. Martin, Barrow Court, Somerset, per W. George's Sons, Bristol.
Gibbs, Rev. John Lomax, Speen House, near Newbury, Berks.
Gibbs, Hon. Vicary, M.P., St. Dunstan's, Regent's Park, N.W.
Glencross, R. M., Lavethan, Bodmin, Cornwall.
Gough, Henry, Sandcroft, Redhill, Surrey.
Graves, Robert Edmund, Lyndhurst, Grange Park, Ealing, W. (2).
Greaves-Bagshawe, W. H., Ford Hall, Chapel en le Frith.
Green & Sons, W., Law Booksellers, Edinburgh (2).
Guildhall Library (per C. Welch), E.C.
Gurney, Mrs. R., 15, Mansfield Street, W.

Hanson, Sir Reginald, Bt., 4, Bryanston Square, W.
Harben, H. A., 107, Westbourne Terrace, Hyde Park, W.
Hardy & Page, 21, Old Buildings, Lincoln's Inn, W.C.
Harrison & Sons, 59, Pall Mall, S.W. (7).
Haslewood, Rev. F. G., Chislet Vicarage, Canterbury.
Hatchards, 187, Piccadilly, W. (6).
Hawkesbury, Lord, per Sotheran & Co., 140, Strand, W.C. (2).
Head, Christopher, 6, Clarence Terrace, Regent's Park, N.W.
Hesilrige, Arthur G. M., 160A, Fleet Street, E.C.
Hodges, Figgis & Co., 104, Grafton Street, Dublin (3).
Hofman, Charles, 16, Grovenor Street, W.
Hoskyns, H. W. P., 26, St. Leonard's Terrace, Chelsea, S.W.
Hovenden, R., F.S.A., Heathcote, Park Hill Road, Croydon.
Hughes of Kimmell, H. R., Kimmel Park, Abergele, North Wales, per Sotheran & Co., 140, Strand, London, W.C.
Hull Subscription Library (William Andrews, Librarian), Royal Institution, Hull.

Incorporated Law Society (F. Boase, Librarian), 103, Chancery Lane, W.C.
Inner Temple Library, per Sotheran & Co., 140, Strand, W.C.
Iveagh, Lord, F.S.A., per Sotheran & Co., 140, Strand, W.C.

Johnston, G. Harvey, 22, Garscube Terrace, Murrayfield, Edinburgh, per W. & A. K. Johnston, 5, White Hart Street, Warwick Lane, E.C.
Johnston, H. A., Markethill, co. Armagh.
Johnston, Col. W., C.B., Newton Dee, Murtle, Aberdeen.

Kildare Street Club, Dublin.
King's Inns Library, Dublin, per Hodges, Figgis & Co., Dublin.

Larpent, Frederic de H., 11, Queen Victoria Street. E.C.
Lawton, William F., Librarian, Public Libraries, Hull.
Lea, J. Henry, 18, Somerset Street, Boston, Mass., U.S.A.
Lee, W. D., Seend, Melksham.
Leeds Library (Charles W. Thonger, Librarian), Commercial Street, Leeds.
Lefroy, Edward Heathcote, 65, Belgrave Road, S.W.
Lincoln's Inn Library (A. F. Etheridge, Librarian), W.C.
Lindsay, Leonard C. C., 87, Cadogan Gardens, S.W.
Lindsay, W. A., K.C., F.S.A., Windsor Herald, College of Arms, E.C.
Littledale, Willoughby A., F.S.A., 26, Cranley Gardens, S.W.
Loraine, Sir Lambton, Bt., 7, Montagu Square, W.

Macdonald, W. R., Carrick Pursuivant, Midpath, Weston Coates Avenue, Edinburgh.
MacGregor, J., 57, Grange Loans, Edinburgh.
Mackenzie, Sir E. M., Bt., Naval & Military Club, Melbourne, Australia.
MacLehose & Sons, J., 61, St. Vincent Street, Glasgow.
Macmillan & Bowes, Cambridge.
Maddison, Rev. Canon, F.S.A., Vicars' Court, Lincoln.
Magrath, Rev. John Richard, D.D., Queen's College, Oxford.
Malcolm, Sir J. W., Bt., Hoveton Hall, Norwich.
Manchester Free Library, per J. E. Cornish, 16, St. Ann's Square, Manchester.
Marshall, George W., LL.D., F.S.A., Sarnesfield Court, Weobley, R.S.O.
Marshall, Julian, 13, Belsize Avenue, N.W.
Marsham-Townshend, Hon. Robert, F.S.A., Frognal, Foot's Cray, Kent.
Maskelyne, Anthony Story, Public Record Office, Chancery Lane, W.C.
Mitchell Library, (F. T. Barrett, Librarian), 21, Miller Street, Glasgow.
Montagu, Col. H., 123, Pall Mall, S.W.
Mosley, Sir O., Bt., Rolleston Hall, Burton-on-Trent.
Murray, Keith W., F.S.A., 37, Cheniston Gardens, Kensington, W.
Myddelton, W. M., Spencer House, St. Albans.

National Library of Ireland, Dublin, per Hodges, Figgis & Co., Dublin.
National Portrait Gallery, per Eyre & Spottiswoode, 5, Middle New Street, E.C.
Newberry Library, Chicago, per H. Grevel & Co., 33, King Street, Covent Garden, W.C.
Nudd, W. A., Bookseller, 2, The Haymarket, Norwich.

O'Connell, Sir Ross., Bt., Killarney, per Bickers & Son, 1, Leicester Square, W.C.
Office of Arms, Dublin Castle, Ireland, per Hodges, Figgis & Co., Dublin.
Oxford & Cambridge Club, Pall Mall, per Harrison & Sons, 59, Pall Mall, S.W.

Parker & Co., J., 27, Broad Street, Oxford.
Paul, Sir James Balfour, Lyon King of Arms, per W. Green & Sons, Edinburgh.
Penfold, Hugh, Rustington, Worthing.
Phillimore, W. P. W., 124, Chancery Lane, W.C.
Pixley, F. W., F.S.A., per Sotheran & Co., 140, Strand, W.C.
Pollard, W. & Co. Ltd., Exeter.
Public Record Office, per Eyre and Spottiswoode, 5, Middle New Street, E.C.

Ramden, J. C., Willinghurst, Guildford, Surrey.
Ramsay, Sir James H., Bt., Bamff, Alyth, N.B.
Reform Club, Pall Mall, per Jones, Yarrell & Poulter, 8, Bury Street, S.W.
Rich, Sir Charles H. Stuart, Bt., F.S.A., Devizes Castle.
Richardson, W. H., F.S.A., 2, Lansdown Place, Russell Square, W.C.
Rimell & Son, J., 91, Oxford Street, W. (2).
Rye, Walter, St. Leonard's Priory, Norwich.
Rylands, J. Paul, F.S.A., 2, Charlesville, Birkenhead.
Rylands Library, The John, Manchester, per Sotheran & Co., 140, Strand, W.C.
Rylands, W. H., F.S.A., 37, Great Russell Street, Bloomsbury, W.C.

Schomberg, Arthur, Seend, Melksham.
Scott-Gatty, A. S., F.S.A., York Herald and Acting Registrar, College of Arms, E.C.
Seton, Sir Bruce Maxwell, Bt., Durham House, Chelsea, S.W.
Shadwell, Walter H. L., F.S.A., Trewollack, Bodmin.
Shaw, W. A., Hillcrest, Mountfield Road, Finchley, N.
Sherborne, Lord, 9, St. James's Square, S.W.

Simpkin, Marshall, Hamilton, Kent, & Co., Ltd., 4, Stationers' Hall Court, E.C.
Smith, J. Challoner, F.S.A., Whitchurch, Oxon. (2).
Sotheran & Co., 140, Strand, W.C. (26).
Stevens, Son, & Stiles, 39, Great Russell Street, W.C.
Stewart, C. P., Chesfield Park, Stevenage.
Strange, Hamon le, Hunstanton Hall, Norfolk.
Stoddart, A. R., Fishergate Villa, York.
St. Leger, James, White's Club, St. James's Street, S.W.

Tempest, Mrs., Broughton H[illegible], Skipton, Yorks.
Tempest, Sir Tristram, Bt., Tong Hall, Drighlington, Bradford, Yorks.
Tenison, C. M., Hobart, Tasmania.
Thompson, W. N., St. Bees, Cumberland.
Toynbee, Paget, Dorney Wood, Burnham, Bucks.
Turnbull, Alex H., per Sotheran & Co., 140, Strand, W.C.

United University Club, per Major H. C. Giblings, 1, Suffolk Street, Pall Mall East, S.W.

Wedderburn, Alexander, K.C., 47, Cadogan Place, S.W.
Weldon, William H., C.V.O., F.S.A., Norroy King of Arms, London, E.C.
Were, Francis, Gratwicke Hall, Flax Bourton, Somerset, per George's Sons, Bristol.
Wilson, Sir S. Maryon-, Bt., Fitzjohn, near Rugby.
Wood, F. A., Highfields, Chew Magna, Somerset, per George's Sons, Bristol.
Wood, H. J. T., Fingest Cottage, near High Wycombe, Bucks.
Woods, Sir Albert W., G.C.V.O., K.C.B., K.C.M.G., F.S.A., Garter King of Arms, 69, St. George's Road, S.W.

Yarborough, Countess of, per H. Sotheran & Co., 140, Strand, W.C.

ABBREVIATIONS

USED IN THIS WORK.

Besides those in ordinary use the following may require explanation.

admon., administration of the goods of an intestate.
ap., apparent.
b., born.
bap., baptised.
bur., buried.
cr., created.
d., died.
da., daughter.
h., heir.
m., married.
M.I., Monumental Inscription.
pr., proved.
s., son.
s.p., sine prole.
s.p.m., sine prole masculo.
s.p.m.s., sine prole masculo superstite.
s.p.s., sine prole superstite.
suc., succeeded.

III

Baronetcies of England.

1611—1707.

THIRD PART.

VIZ.,

CREATIONS,

30 Jan. 1648/9 to 31 Dec. 1664.(a)

[*Memorandum.* The valuable list of the "Creations of Peers and Baronets compiled from original documents in the Public Record Office, 1483—1646," by R. Douglas Trimmer (issued in the appendix to the Forty-seventh Report of the Deputy Keeper of the Public Records), having come to an end with the creations of Charles I, the most reliable list for the *subsequent* creations of English Baronetcies appears to be the *Catalogue of the Baronets of this Kingdom of England, etc., until 6 Dec. 1681*, compiled by the well known Sir William Dugdale, Garter King of Arms, 1677-86. From this *Catalogue*, therefore, the descriptions, when placed within inverted commas, of the grantees of Charles II, from 1 Sep. 1649 to 6 Dec. 1681, are taken, as, likewise, from *the continuation* (hereafter mentioned) of this Catalogue are those of Cromwell's grantees as well as those of the grantees of Baronetcies of England, Great Britain, or the United Kingdom from 20 Jan. 1681/2 to 29 Sep. 1809, the conclusion of this *continuation*. "The preface," by Dugdale, to the abovenamed *Catalogue* is as follows:—

"Whereas in the year 1667 a Catalogue of the Baronets of England was by authority published, to the end that such as had obtained patents for that Honour, which were not enrolled, should, by descerning an omission of their names therein, take care to supply that defect, so that upon a second impression thereof they might be inserted; Now whereas, after twelve years and more, no enrolments are yet to be found for sundry persons who have assumed this Title, which causeth some to doubt whether they can make any justifiable claims thereto.

"Whereas therefore no person whatsoever ought to take upon them this Title of dignity but such as have been really advanced thereto by Letters patent under the Great Seal of England, it is thought fit by the Right Hon. Robert, Earl of Aylesbury,(b) who now exerciseth the office of Earl Marshall of England, that this present Catalogue of such touching whom the docquet books, remaining with the Clerk of the Crown in Chancery, do take notice, shall be published, to the end that those, of whom no memorial upon Record is to be found to justifie their right to

(a) The date of 31 Dec. 1664 has been arbitrarily selected as comprising (notwithstanding the chronological disparity of the division) an approximate half of the number of Baronetcies of the three Realms created between 30 Jan. 1648/9 (the death of Charles I) and 1 May 1707, the date of the Scotch Union, after which epoch the creation of *Scotch* Baronetcies ceased. The remaining portion (1 Jan. 1664/5 to 1 May 1707) will be contained in the next volume.

(b) Appointed Joint Commissioner for the office of Earl Marshal, 20 June 1673.

B

this title, may be known; and care henceforth taken in commissions of the peace and otherwise that it be not given unto them until they shall manifest the same unto the Lord Chancellor of England and have special order from his Lordship to enroll such patents, whereby they pretend Title to that dignity.

"As also that regard he had of giving credit to any other Catalogues of the Baronets which are already publisht, or that shall be publisht, than what is taken from the authority of those docquet books above mentioned or the enrollment of their Patents."

An extract from a letter of Dugdale [*Hist. MSS.*, Twelfth Report, App. vii, p. 187], which supplements this matter, is kindly supplied by J. Horace Round. It is written from the Heralds' College, 3 June 1682:—"We have also a note of a greater number, which do take upon them the title of Baronets from the late King to pass patents for that title but did not proceed any further therein."

Dugdale's *Catalogue of English Baronets*, which (as above stated) ends 6 Dec. 1681, has been continued by "T. C. Banks, Esq.," in his edition [folio 1812] of Dugdale's *Ancient usage in bearing Arms*, down to the end of those creations, 27 June 1706. To this is appended a list of the Baronetcies of Great Britain, 1707-1800, of those of the United Kingdom, from 20 March 1801 to 29 Sep. 1809, as also of those conferred by the Lord Protector Cromwell, 1657-1658.

During the interval that elapsed between the death of Charles I, 30 Jan. 1648/9, and the Restoration of Charles II to the Crown, 29 May 1660, *Baronetcies were created by two parties*—(1) by the young King during his exile (which Baronetcies though not recognised on their creation became valid after the Restoration), and (2) by the *actual* Ruler (in possession) of the Realm. For the first eight years however of the [so called] Commonwealth, no Baronetcies or other hereditary honours(a) were created by the existing Powers. It was not till after the date, 25 May 1657, of the *Petition and Advice* and the commencement of what is termed the *Second Protectorate* (the first being 12 Dec. 1653) that Oliver Cromwell (who had previously conferred the *life* honour of Knighthood) took on himself to confer *hereditary* honours. There is nothing in the *Petition and Advice* which specially gives such authority to the Protector, unless indeed the fact that thereby a House of Lords was created implies that *hereditary* dignities were to be revived. Anyhow, the Viscountcy of Howard of Morpeth (conferred on Charles Howard, 20 July 1657) and the Baronetcies of Read and Claypole (25 June and 20 July 1657) may be looked upon as somewhat in the light of the Protector's *Coronation honours*.

The best authority for the Cromwellian creations appears to be Masson's *Life of Milton*(b) in which 11 Baronetcies are stated to have been thus created, *viz.*, Read, Cleypole, Chamberlayne (25 June, 20 July, and 6 Oct. 1657), Beaumont (5 March 1657/8), Ingoldsby, Twisleton, Wright, Williams, Prideaux, Ellis and Wyndham (10 April [*ter*] 28 May, 13 Aug. [*bis*] and 28 Aug. 1658). Of these eleven, the Baronetcy of Wyndham is omitted in Noble's *Cromwell* (vol. i, pp. 439-442, edit. 1787), while Baronetcies ascribed to Dunch and Willis (certainly in error) and to Lenthal (presumably in error) are therein inserted.(c) All the Cromwellian Baronetcies became, of course, invalid on the Restoration of Monarchy, 29 May 1660. The date of their creation (1657-1658) is *later* than that of many Baronetcies which were conferred by the young King during his exile, but, for the sake of convenience, they will here be dealt with first.]

(a) Several *Knighthoods* however had been conferred by the Speaker of the House of Commons, after the death of Charles I and before the Accession, 12 Dec. 1653, of Oliver Cromwell to the Protectorship, who after such succession himself conferred that honour.

(b) Masson, who is eminently painstaking and careful, states that the list is the best he has been able to put together. It is mostly the same as that in the [old] *Parl. History* (vol. xxi, p. 220), where these creations stand thus: 1656 [*sic*] June 25, Read; 1657, July 16, Cleypole; Oct. 6, Chamberlain; Nov. 5, Beaumont; Nov. 24, Twisleton; 1658, March 31, Ingoldsby and Wright; May 28, Williams; Aug. 13, Prideaux and Ellis: Aug. 28, Wyndham. The first date herein (1656) is clearly wrong.

(c) The editor is indebted to W. D. Pink for much information as to the Cromwellian creations.

CREATIONS

By Oliver Cromwell, Lord Protector,

1657—1658.

READE, *or* READ.

I. 1657 to 1660.

"JOHN READ, of Brocket Hall, Herts, Esq.," who had been *cr. a Baronet* by Charles I, 16 March 1641/2, which creation (as were all others after 4 Jan. 1641/2) was disallowed by Act of Parl., 4 Feb. 1651/2,(a) was again *cr. a Baronet* by the Lord Protector Cromwell, 25 June 1657.(b) The *dignity* so created was however, of course, *disallowed* after the Restoration in May 1660, but, on the other hand, the disallowance of the former Baronetcy of 1642 then ceased, and the Grantee obtained the Royal Pardon in June 1660. See fuller particulars in vol. ii, p. 164, under "READE," *cr.* 16 March 1641/2; *ex.* 22 Feb. 1711/2.

CLAYPOLE, *or* CLEYPOLE.

I. 1657, to 1660.

"JOHN CLEYPOLE, Esq., son in law to Oliver, Lord Protector" was *cr. a Baronet*, by the said Lord Protector Cromwell, 20 July 1657. He was of Norborough, near Peterborough, co. Northampton, being s. and h. of John CLEYPOLE(c), of the same, by Mary (*m.* 1622) da. of William ANGELL, of London; was *b.* there 21 Aug. 1625; *m.* 13 Feb. 1645/6, at Trinity Church, Ely, as his 1st wife, Elizabeth, 2d da. of Oliver CROMWELL, afterwards (1653-58) **Lord Protector of England,** by Elizabeth, da. of Sir James BOUCHIER, of Felstead, Essex; was admitted to Gray's Inn, 30 June 1651, in which year he was head of a troop of Horse to oppose the march of Charles II into England; was M.P. for Carmarthenshire, 1654-55, and for Northamptonshire, 1656-58; was a Lord of the Bedchamber to the Protector, Master of the Horse, Ranger of Whittlebury Forest, taking a leading part in the ceremonials during the Protectorate; was *Knighted* 16 July 1657 and four days afterwards was *cr. a Baronet*, as abovestated, 20 July 1657. He, five months later, by writ of 10 Dec. 1657, became a member [1657-58] of Cromwell's "other House or *House of Lords*," but all his honours were, of course, *disallowed*, after the Restoration. His said wife, who was *b.* and *bap.* 2 July 1629 at St. John's,

(a) See *Memorandum* in vol. ii, p. 152 as to the creations of Charles I after 4 Jan. 1641/2 and 22 May 1642.

(b) The date is erroneously given in Noble's *Cromwell* as "25 June *1656*," but no hereditary dignity was conferred by the Protector till *after* the date (25 May 1657) of the *Petition and Advice*. See *Memorandum*, pp. 1-2. Why this renegade Royalist was honoured by receiving the first hereditary dignity bestowed by the Protector is difficult to conjecture. He was not even a M.P.

(c) According to Noble's *Cromwell* this John and not his son was the person who was *cr. a Baronet* in 1657. He was *bap.* at Maxey, 13 April 1595; admitted to Gray's Inn 7 May 1619; was prosecuted for non-payment of the Ship money in 1637; M.P. for Northamptonshire 1654-55; became a widower 10 April 1661, his wife being *bur.* at Norborough. He was living 1664 (having then given up the estate of Norborough to his son John) and is supposed to have died in London and to have been *bur.* there not long afterwards. It is perhaps some confirmation of Noble's view that "the son is spoken of as Lord Cleypole" all through the Commons Journal and also in the Acts and Ordnances. Inasmuch as "the other House" only began in 1657 it is not clear why he is thus early spoken of as "Lord," but several of Cromwell's chief officers (Lambert, Desborough, etc.) are so styled before the creation of "the other House." [*Ex. inform.* W. D. Pink].

Huntingdon, and who *m.* (as abovestated) at the age of 16, *d.* at her father's residence, Hampton Court, Middlesex, 6 and was *bur.* 10 Aug. 1658, with great state from Whitehall, in the Chapel of Henry VII in Westm. Abbey,(a) aged 29. He retained his offices during the short Protectorate of his brother Richard Cromwell, and, save for the forfeiture of his honours, was unmolested at the Restoration in May 1660. He signed a declaration of allegiance to the King, 5 June 1660. To his wife's mother, the Protector's widow, he gave an asylum at his house at Norborough where she died 19 Nov. 1665. He was, in June 1678, imprisoned on suspicion, but was shortly released.(b) He appears however to have fallen into debt and to have alienated his estates. He *m.* secondly, 21 March 1670, Blanche (the rich), widow of Launcelot STAVELEY, of London, Merchant. He *d.* 26 June 1688, being then of the Middle Temple, London, having survived his children (all of whom died unm.) by his 1st wife,(c) and leaving by his last wife one da., then aged 14.(d) In his will dat. 26 June and pr. 14 Nov. 1688 he styles himself "John Claypoole, of London, Esq.," and leaves 10s. each to his wife Blanche(e) and his da. Bridget, and the residue to his "loving friend, Mrs. Anne OTTEY, wife or widdowe of Edmund OTTEY."(f)

CHAMBERLAYNE, *or* CHAMBERLYNE.

I. 1657, to 1660. "THOMAS CHAMBERLAYNE, of Wickham [Oxon], Esq.," was s. and h. of Sir Thomas CHAMBERLAYNE, 1st Baronet [1643], of Wickham, aforesaid, who had been *cr. a Baronet* by Charles I, 4 Feb. 1642/3. He, a few months later, by his father's death, 6 Oct. 1643, *suc. to the Baronetcy*, which title, however (as was the case with all creations after 22 May 1642) was disallowed by Act of Parl., 11 Nov. 1643,(g) and he accordingly was *cr. a Baronet*, 6 Oct. 1657, by the Lord Protector Cromwell, to whose Attorney-General, Edmond PRIDEAUX, he was son-in-law. That dignity, however, was, of course, *disallowed* after the Restoration in May 1660, but on the other hand the disallowment of the former Baronetcy of 1643 then ceased. See fuller particulars in vol. ii, p. 206, under CHAMBERLAYNE, *cr.* 4 Feb. 1642/3; *ex.* 25 Jan. 1776.

BEAUMONT.

I. 1658, to 1660. "THOMAS BEAUMONT, of Stoughton Grange, co. Leicester, Esq.," was *cr. a Baronet* by the Lord Protector Cromwell, 5 March 1657/8. That dignity, however, was of course *disallowed* after the Restoration in May 1660, but he was shortly afterwards *cr. a Baronet* by Charles II. See fuller particulars, further on, under "BEAUMONT," *cr.* 21 Feb. 1660/1.

(a) Kennet's statement that she was exhumed at the Restoration is false. Her coffin was seen in 1725 in its place in the Abbey. *See N. & Q.*, 7th S. xi, 172.

(b) As to the supposed plot which led to his arrest *see N. & Q.*, 7th S. xi, 172.

(c) Of these children, Cromwell Claypoole, to whom his father had resigned the manor of Norborough, was the eldest son and the survivor. He *d.* v.p. and was *bur.* 28 May 1678 at Norborough.

(d) Bridget, who *m.* Charles Price, Col. in the Guards, and *d.* his widow in Oct. 1738.

(e) "Mrs. Claypole" was *bur.* 26 Feb. 1709/10, at North Luffenham, Rutland. Possibly she was widow of this "Lord Cleypole."

(f) *See N. & Q.*, 7th S. xi, 172.

(g) See p. 3, note "a," under "Reade."

INGOLDSBY.

I. 1658 to 1660. "HENRY INGOLDSBY, ESQ," a Colonel in the Army, was *cr. a Baronet* by the Lord Protector Cromwell, 10 April 1658, which dignity, however, was, of course, *disallowed* after the Restoration in May 1660, but he was shortly afterwards *cr. a Baronet* by Charles II. See fuller particulars further on, under "INGOLDSBY," *cr.* 30 Aug. 1661; *ex.* 25 April 1726.

TWISLETON.

I. 1658, to 1660. "JOHN TWISLETON, of Horsman's in Dartford, co. Kent, Esq.," was *cr. a Baronet* by the Lord Protector Cromwell, 10 April 1658, "with rem. in default of issue male of his own body, to Sir Philip TWISLETON, Knt., 2d brother of the said John, and his issue male, and, for default to George Twisleton(a), third brother of the said John Twisleton and his heirs male for ever."(b) This dignity was, however, of course, *disallowed* after the Restoration in May 1660. The grantee was s. and h. of John TWISLETON, of Drax and Barley, co. York, and of Horsmans Place in Dartford, aforesaid, by Margaret, da. of William CONSTABLE; was *b.* about 1614; was admitted to Gray's Inn, 3 Aug. 1629, and was *cr. a Baronet* 24 March 1656/7, as above, and was so designated till May 1660. Sheriff of Kent, 1671-72. He *m.* firstly (Lic. Lond. 27 April 1636, he 22 and she 19), Elizabeth, da. and h. of Augustine SKINNER, of Tolsham, or Tattsham Hall, co. Kent. He *m.* secondly, Lucy, 5th da. of Samuel DUNCH, of Baddesley, Berks. She was *bur.* at Dartford. He *m.* thirdly (Lic. Fac. 12 May 1649, she 18), Elizabeth, elder da. and coheir (whose issue, in 1715, became sole heir) of James (Fiennes), 2d VISCOUNT SAYE AND SELE [1624], LORD SAYE AND SELE [1447], by Frances, da. and coheir of Edward (CECIL), VISCOUNT WIMBLEDON. She *d.* 28 March 1674, and was *bur.* in Bunhill fields. He *m.* fourthly, Anne, da. and h. of John Christopher MEYERN, a German. He *d.* s.p.m.s.(c) 4 Dec. 1682, in his 69th year, and was *bur.* (as "John Twisleton, Esq.") at Dartford. M.I. His widow *m.* Sir John PLATT.

WRIGHT.

I. 1658, to 1660. "HENRY WRIGHT, of Dagenham, co. Essex, Esq.," was, at the age of about 21, *cr. a Baronet*(d) by the Lord Protector Cromwell, 10 April 1658. That dignity, however, was of course *disallowed* after the Restoration in May 1660, but he was shortly afterwards *cr. a Baronet* by Charles II. See fuller particulars under "WRIGHT," *cr.* 11 June 1660; *ex.* 1688.

(a) Presumably Col. George Twisleton, M.P. for Anglesey, 1654-55, 1656-58, and 1659.

(b) Banks's continuation to Dugdale's *Catalogue*. It seems probable that the words "his heirs male" are a mistake for "the heirs male of his body." The orig. patent is said [*Parl. Hist.*, vol. xxi, p. 220] to be in the hands of his descendants at Rawcliffe, co. York.

(c) Cecil, his only surv. da. and sole heir, was sole heir also to her mother, and in that capacity was in 1715 *entitled* to the Barony of Say and Sele (the abeyance of which had at that date terminated), which Barony was accordingly, though not till 1781, *allowed* to her grandson and heir, Thomas Twisleton.

(d) The reason of this creation was, presumably, because the grantee's father (then lately deceased) was Physician to the Lord Protector.

WILLIAMS.

I. 1658, to 1660. "GRIFFITH WILLIAMS, of co. Carnarvon, Esq.," who was a Commissioner of Assessment for Carnarvonshire in 1656, was *cr. a Baronet* by the Lord Protector Cromwell, 28 May 1658. That dignity, however, was of course *disallowed* after the Restoration in May 1660, but he was shortly afterwards *cr. a Baronet*, as "of Penrhyn, co. Carnarvon," by Charles II. See fuller particulars under "WILLIAMS," *cr.* 17 June 1661.

PRIDEAUX.(a)

I. 1658. EDMOND PRIDEAUX, Attorney General, was *cr. a Baronet*(a) by the Lord Protector, 13 Aug. 1658, for "his voluntary offer for the mainteyning of 34 Foot souldiers in his Highnes' army in Ireland."(b) He was 2d surv. s. of Sir Edmund PRIDEAUX, 1st Baronet [1622] of Netherton, co. Devon, by his 2d wife Katharine, da. of Piers EDGCOMBE, of Mount Edgcombe, and was *bap.* 27 Feb. 1601 at Farway; ed. at Sydney Sussex Coll., Cambridge, and was incorp. at Oxford, as M.A., 6 July 1625; Barrister (Inner Temple) 23 Nov. 1623 and subsequently (1642) Bencher. Recorder of Exeter, and subsequently (1649) of Bristol; was M.P. for Lyme Regis (five Parls.) 1640-59, being throughout a staunch Presbyterian; was one of the Lay members of the Westm. Assembly, 1643; Master of the Posts and Couriers, 7 Sep. 1644; was a Commissioner of the Great Seal, 1643-46; Solicitor General, 12 Oct. 1648, but resigned office shortly afterwards when the King's trial was imminent; was Attorney General, April 1649, till his death in 1659, being *cr. a Baronet*(b) as abovestated, 31 May 1658. He was on the Council of State Feb. to Nov. 1651, and, again, Dec. 1652 to April 1653. He acquired a large fortune and bought the estate of Ford Abbey, at Thornecombe, Devon. He *m.* firstly, 23 Aug. 1627, Jane, da. and h. of Henry COLLINS, of Salston in Ottery St. Mary, Devon, by Joan, da. and h. of Humphrey FARANT. She, who was aged 10 in 1620, *d.* s.p.m. and was *bur.* 16 Nov. 1629, at Ottery aforesaid. He *m.* secondly, shortly afterwards, Margaret, da. and coheir of William IVERY, of Cotthay, Somerset. He *d.* 19 Aug. 1659 aged 57, and was *bur.* in the Chapel at Ford Abbey. Will dat. 1 April, pr. 7 Dec. 1659. His widow *d.* 25 April 1683 and was *bur.* with her husband. Will dat. 23 April, pr. 5 July, 1683

II. 1659, to 1660. SIR EDMUND PRIDEAUX, Baronet(c) [1658], 1st and only surv. s. and h. by 2d wife; bap. 4 Dec. 1634, at Ottery St. Mary aforesaid; matric. at Oxford (Exeter Coll.) 12 Nov. 1650, and said to be aged 18; *suc. to the Baronetcy*(c) 19 Aug. 1659, which dignity, however, was shortly afterwards, viz., after the Restoration, in May 1660, of course, *disallowed*. He was M.P. for Taunton, Dec. 1680 to 1681; took part in the Duke of Monmouth's rebellion and is said to have escaped the consequences thereof by a heavy bribe to the Lord Chief Justice Jeffreys. He *m.*, 19 March 1655/6, at Combe Flory, co. Somerset, Amy, da. and coheir of John FRAUNCEIS, of Combe Flory. He *d.* s.p.m.s.(d) 16 Oct. 1702. Admon. 7 Dec. 1702. His widow *d.* 8 Jan. 1703/4 Both *bur.* in the Chapel at Ford Abbey. By his death the male issue of the grantee became *extinct*.

(a) The undoubted Baronetcies of Prideaux, Ellis, and Wyndham are not in Banks's continuation of Dugdale's *Catalogue*; the Cromwellian creations given therein (eight in all) being Read, Beaumont, Twisleton, Cleypole, Chamberlayne, Ingoldsby, Wright and Williams. Dunch, Willis and Lenthal (for all three of which Noble's *Cromwell* seems the only authority) are also (apparently rightly) omitted.

(b) *Public Records*, 5th Rep., App., p. 273, as quoted in Foss's *Judges*, under "Prideaux."

(c) According to the Lord Protector Cromwell's Creation, which of course remained valid till the Restoration in May 1660.

(d) Francis Prideaux, his only son, matric. at Oxford (Wadham Coll.), 11 May 1676, aged 17; admitted to the Inner Temple, 1677; *d.* unm. and v.p. See Vivian's *Visitations of Devon* as to the female issue of the grantee and his son.

ELLIS.(a)

I. 1658, to 1660. WILLIAM ELLIS, Solicitor General, was *cr. a Baronet*,(a) by the Lord Proctor Cromwell, 13 Aug. 1658. He was presumably identical with William ELLIS, a post-Restoration Judge. That Judge was yr. br. of Thomas ELLIS, the father of Sir Thomas ELLIS, 1st Baronet [1660], of Wyham, co. Lincoln, both being sons of Sir Thomas ELLIS, of Grantham, co. Lincoln (*bur.* there 7 Sep. 1627), by Jane, da. of (—) ARMSTRONG, of Wissall, Notts. In that case he was *bap.* at Grantham, 19 July 1607, and admitted to Gray's Inn, 6 Nov. 1627,(b) becoming a Barrister 9 Feb. 1634 and an Ancient in 1659 and Reader in 1664.(c) William ELLIS was M.P. for Boston, April to May 1640, and 1640 till excluded, 1648; re-admitted June 1649 to 1653; re-elected 1654-55; M.P. for Grantham, 1656-58, 1659, and 1660, till void 18 May. William ELLIS was made Solicitor General 24 May 1654 which office he continued to hold under Richard Cromwell and was *cr. a Baronet*,(a) as abovestated on or soon after 31 May 1658, but the dignity, however, was, of course, *disallowed* after the Restoration in May 1660. William Ellis was Serjeant at Law, 26 Aug. 1669; King's Serjeant, 10 April 1671, and was *Knighted* 30 April 1671; made a Justice of the Common Pleas, 18 Dec. 1672; was removed 1676, being M.P. for Boston, Feb. 1678/9, till re-instated as a Judge, 5 May 1679. He *d.* unm. at his chambers in Serjeant's Inn, Fleet street, 11, and was *bur.* 17 Dec. 1680 at Nocton, co. Lincoln. Will, in which he leaves his estate to his nephew [*i.e.* great nephew] Sir William Ellis, 2d Baronet [1640], pr. 1680. Funeral Certificate in Coll. of Arms.

WYNDHAM.(d)

I. 1658, to 1660. WILLIAM WYNDHAM, Esq., of Orchard Wyndham, Somerset, having been M.P. 1656-58, was *cr. a Baronet* by the Lord Protector Cromwell, 28 Aug. 1658, which dignity, of course, was *disallowed* after the Restoration in May 1660. He was, however, shortly afterwards (before the Parl. of 1661) *Knighted* by Charles II, and *cr. a Baronet* by him. See fuller particulars under "WYNDHAM," *cr.* 9 Dec. 1661; *ex.* (together with the Earldom of Egremont) 2 April 1845.

DUNCH.

1658 to 1660.

There is an apparently erroneous statement in Noble's *Cromwell* [vol. i, pp. 438-442, edit. 1787] that "EDMUND DUNCH, of Little Wittenham, in Berkshire, Esq. [was] *created a Baronet*, April 26, 1657-8" [*sic*] by the Lord Protector Cromwell. The date, 26 April 1658 [presumably the one above indicated], is that on which he was created *a Peer* by the Lord Protector, as BARON BURNELL OF EAST WITTENHAM, Berks. See *Peerage*.

(a) See p. 6, note "a."

(b) There was, however, another William Ellis admitted to Gray's Inn, 5 March 1628/9 as "son and heir of George Ellis, of Wiham, co. Lincoln, Gent., and though this William was, apparently, not the Judge who *d.* in 1680 (whose will shews him to be uncle [*i.e.* great uncle] of the then Baronet) it is by no means certain that he was not the Solicitor General to the Protector who, in that case would not be identical (as suggested in the text) with the said Judge.

(c) The Solicitor General (made identical with the Judge) is erroneously said, in the Dict. Nat. Biogr. and elsewhere, to have been ed. at Gonville and Caius College, Cambridge, but the William Ellis, who was scholar, fellow and (1639-40) Greek Lecturer there (B.A. 1632; M.A. 1636), was a totally different person, and was (son of John Ellis, Cook of King's Coll.) *bap.* at Cambridge, 14 April 1611. See Venn's *History of Gonville and Caius College*.

(d) See p. 6, note "a." This Baronetcy of Wyndham is also omitted in Noble's *Cromwell*, but there seems no doubt that it was one of Cromwell's creations. See *Memorandum*, pp. 1-2.

WILLIS.

1658 ? to 1660.

Another apparently erroneous statement in Noble's *Cromwell* abovementioned is that

"THOMAS WILLIS, of Cambridgeshire, Esq., [was] *created a Baronet* by Oliver [Cromwell, the Lord Protector], was returned to represent that county in Richard's parliament, and was so well received by King Charles II that he was set down for a Knight of the Royal Oak. His estate was then valued at £1,000 per annum." The person thus indicated was doubtless SIR THOMAS WILLIS, of Fen Ditton, co. Cambridge, who had been *cr. a Baronet* by Charles I on 15 Dec. 1641, who had an estate of £1,000 a year in Cambridgshire, and who was nominated in 1661 as a Knight of the Royal Oak. See full particulars of him in Vol. ii, p. 148. It is to be observed that no date is assigned to this alleged Cromwellian creation, and that, inasmuch as the creation by Charles I (being *before* 4 Jan. 1641/2) was of a date when all the creations of that King were held valid by the succeeding Government, there would be no necessity for a fresh creation.(a) His name as "Sir Thomas Willows [*sic*], Baronet," appears in an act passed in the Session of 1656, among forty-seven Assessment Commissioners for the county of Cambridge. [Scobell's *Acts and Ordinances*.](b) This date of 1656 is previous to any Cromwellian Baronetcies, and shews clearly that the Baronetcy conferred on him, in 1641, by Charles I was never disallowed. He also appears as a Baronet in Richard Cromwell's parl. of 1659,(b) and the next thing that is heard of him is his nomination in 1661, by the King, as a Knight of the Royal Oak.

LENTHAL.(c)

1658 ? to 1660.

Another statement, presumably also erroneous(d), in Noble's *Cromwell* abovementioned, is that a Baronetcy(c) was conferred by the Lord Protector on

"JOHN LENTHALL, Esq., only son of Will. Lenthall, one of Oliver's Lords." No date is assigned to this alleged Cromwellian creation, but, if it ever was conferred, it would probably have been in 1658. He was the only s. of William LENTHAL, the well known Speaker of the House of Commons (1641-54) and afterwards one of Cromwell's "House of Lords," (who *d.* 3 Sep. 1662, aged 71) by Elizabeth, da. of Ambrose EVANS, of Loddington, co. Northampton. He was *b.* about 1625; matric. at Oxford (Corpus Coll.) 12 Sep. 1640, aged 14; admitted to Linc. Inn 1640; was M.P. for Gloucester, 1645-53; for Abingdon, 1659 and 1660 till void; was one of the Judges appointed for the trial of Charles I, but did not sit thereon; one of the Six Clerks in Chancery, 9 March 1657; was *Knighted* by Cromwell, 9 March 1657/8, and (as abovementioned) is said, probably, however, in error,(a) to have been *cr. a Baronet*(b) by him, presumably in 1658. He, who was Col. of a Reg. of Foot, and who, 18 Jan. 1659/60 was Gov. of Windsor Castle, resided at Burford, Oxon, and, after his father's death, 3 Sep. 1662, at Besselsleigh, Berks.; was Sheriff of Oxon, 1672-73, and was [again] *Knighted* 13 March 1677/8, by Charles II, at Whitehall. He *m.* firstly, a wife who *d.* s.p. and who is said(c) to have been "Rebecca, da. of Thomas BENNETT, Alderman of London." He *m.* secondly, between May 1654 and 1659, Mary, widow of Sir James STONEHOUSE, 2d Baronet [1641], of Amerden Hall, Essex, da. of (—) BLEWITT, of Holcombe, Devon She, who was living June 1669 was *bur.* in the church of Besselsleigh. He *m.* thirdly, Catharine, da. of Eusebius ANDREWS, of Edmonton, Midx., by whom he had no issue. He *d.* 9 Nov. 1681 in his 57th year and was *bur.* at Besselsleigh aforesaid. M.I. Admon. 3 March 1681/2 to his widow, and again 14 May 1694.(d) The will of his widow was pr. 1692.

(a) The Cromwellian creations of the Baronetcies of Read and Chamberlayne were also conferred on persons who had received that dignity from Charles I, but both those Baronetcies had been conferred by that King *after* the date of 4 Jan. 1641/2, the date after which none of his creations were allowed.
(b) *Ex inform.*, W. D. Pink.
(c) See p. 6, note "a," *sub* "Prideaux."
(d) No less than twenty-seven times his name is mentioned from May 1659 to April 1660, but he never once occurs as a Baronet [*ex inform.*, W. D. Pink].

Besides the above creations (which refer to England) there was a

BARONETCY OF IRELAND(e)

Conferred by the Lord Protector Cromwell,

viz.

FENTON.

I. 1658. to 1668. SIR MAURICE FENTON, who had been *Knighted* at Dublin (during the Usurpation) 7 June 1658, was *cr. a Baronet* [I.] by the Lord Protector Cromwell, by patent 14 July 1658, privy seal dat. 25 May last past. Both these honours were, of course disallowed after the Restoration in May 1660, but the grantee was, however, shortly afterwards again *cr. a Baronet* [I.], 22 July 1661. See fuller particulars further on, under that date.

(a) See p. 8, note "d."
(b) See p. 6, note "a," *sub* "Prideaux."
(c) Berry's *Berkshire Pedigrees*. If Rebecca, da. of Sir Thomas Bennett, Lord Mayor of London [1613-14], is meant, she *m.* 22 June 1620 at Morden, Surrey, as his first wife Sir Bulstrode Whitlock, and *d.* before him.
(d) By his second wife he had issue, William Lenthall (to whom Gen. Monk stood Sponsor) who died Sep. 1686, aged 27, and is ancestor in the male line of the family of Lenthall, still (1902) seated at Besselsleigh.
(e) This apparently is the only *Irish* Baronetcy created by the Protector, who does not appear to have ever created a *Scotch* one.

C

CREATIONS BY CHARLES II.

1649—1685.

FIRST PART.

30 Jan. 1648/9 to 31 Dec. 1664.(a)

[*Memorandum*. The honours conferred by Charles II during the time (11 years and 4 months) that elapsed between the death of his father (30 Jan. 1648/9) and his own recognition (29 May 1660) as King, were, of course, not recognised by the Powers that then ruled the land. On and after the Restoration, 29 May 1660, these grants, however, which he began within a few months of his (theretofore unrecognised) accession to the Crown, became valid].

BROWNE:

cr. 1 Sept. 1649;

ex. 12 Feb 1682/3.

I. 1649, to 1683. "RICHARD BROWNE, of [Sayes Court, in] Deptford [co. Kent], Esq., for several years resident for King Charles I and his now Majesty with the French Kings Lewis XIII and the present King Lewis XIV, and one of the Clerks of His Majesty's Most Hon. Privy Council," was only s. and h. of Christopher BROWNE, of Sayes Court, aforesaid, by Thomazine, da. of Benjamin GONSON, of Much Badow, Essex, Treasurer to the Navy, the said Christopher being s. and h. of Sir Richard BROWNE, also of Sayes Court, Clerk of the Green Cloth(b); was *b.* about 1605; matric. at Oxford (Ch. Ch.) 26 June 1623, aged 18; B.A. (from St. Alban's Hall) 1623; Fellow of Merton Coll., 1624; M.A., 28 July 1628; admitted to Gray's Inn, 23 Feb. 1626/7; Esquire of the Bedchamber, and, 27 Jan. 1640/1, Clerk of the Council to Charles I; Resident Minister at the Court of France for 19 years, 1641 to 1660, within which period he suc. his father in 1645 and was *cr. a Baronet*, 1 Sep. 1649(c), by letters patent, dat. at St. Germain's, in France, being *Knighted*, 19 Sep., a few days later. He was the first Baronet created by the young King, then an exile, to whom (as formerly to his father) he was Clerk of the Council till Jan. 1671/2. He *m.* Elizabeth, da. of Sir John PRETYMAN, of Dryfield, co. Gloucester, by Mary, da. of William BOURCHIER, of Barnesley, in that county. She *d.* 6 Oct. 1652, aged 42. He *d.* s.p.m.s.(d), 12 Feb. 1682/3, aged 78, when the *Baronetcy* became *extinct*. Both were *bur.* at St. Nicholas, Deptford. M.I. Will dat. 22 May 1678, pr. 20 March 1682/3.

(a) See p. 1, note "a."
(b) A pedigree of the family, with coats of arms containing many quarterings, etc., is in the *Mis. Gen. et Her.*, 2d series, vol. i, pp. 123-125.
(c) This, according to the *Dict. Nat. Biog.*, was "in virtue of a dormant warrant sent to him by Charles I in Feb. 1643."
(d) Mary, his only surv. da. and heir, *m.* 27 June 1647, presumably at Paris, when about 12 years of age, the celebrated John Evelyn, of Wotton, Surrey, and died his widow, 9 Feb. 1708/9, in her 74th year, leaving issue.

DE VIC:

cr. 3 Sep. 1649;

ex. shortly after 1672.

I. 1649. "HENRY DE VIC, of the Isle of Garnsay [*i.e.*, Guernsey], Resident for his late Majesty near twenty years in Bruxells, afterwards Chancellor of the most noble order of the Garter;" *b.* about 1599; was presumably the "Henry Derick" elected to Oxford from Westm. School in 1616; matric. at Oxford (Ch. Ch.), 12 Nov. 1619 (as 1st s. of an Esquire), aged 20; B.A., 17 Dec. following; was Sec. of the French tongue; as also Resident at Brussels and Chancellor of the Order of the Garter (as abovestated) and was *cr. a Baronet*, 3 Sep. 1649, by letters patent dat. at St. Germain en Laye, in France. He *m.*, Margaret, da. of Sir Philip CARTERET, of St. Ouens in Jersey. She *d.* before him. He *d.* 20 Nov. 1671, and was *bur.* at St. George's Chapel, Windsor. Will dat. (—), 1669, then aged 71 and upwards, pr. 15 Feb. 1671/2.

II. 1671, to 1680 ? SIR CHARLES DE VIC, Baronet [1649], only surv. s. and h.; *suc. to the Baronetcy*, 20 Nov. 1671, and proved his father's will in Feb. 1671/2. He apparently must have married before 1672, but appears to have *d.* s.p.m.(a) shortly afterwards when the *Baronetcy* became *extinct*.

FORSTER:

cr. 18 Sep. 1649;

ex. before 1714.

I. 1649. "RICHARD FORSTER, of Stokesley, co. York, Esq.," s. and h. of William FORSTER, of Erdeswycke in that county, by (—), da. of (—) LONGLEY, of the Bishopric of Durham, was Treasurer to the Queen Dowager and to Charles II during their exile, and was *cr. a Baronet*, 18 Sep. 1649, by letters patent dat. at St. Germain en Laye. He *m.*, in or before 1622, Joan, da. of (—) MIDDLETON, of Leighton, co. Lancaster. He *d.* in Paris, 17 Jan. 1661.

II. 1661. SIR RICHARD FORSTER, Baronet [1649], of Stokesley aforesaid, 1st s. and h., *b.* about 1623,(b) being aged 42 when he entered his pedigree, 25 Aug. 1665, in the Visit. of Yorkshire. He *suc. to the Baronetcy*, 17 Jan. 1661. He *m.*, in or before 1658, Clare, 2d da. of Anthony METYNILL, of North Kilvington, co. York, by Mary, da. of James THWAYTES, of Marston, co. York.

III. 1680 ? to 1710 ? SIR RICHARD FORSTER, Baronet [1649], of Stokesley aforesaid, s. and h., aged 12 years in Aug. 1665. He *d.* unm. before 1714, when the *Baronetcy* became *extinct*.

(a) Elizabeth his da. and h., *m.*, 31 May 1698, at St. Sepulchre's, London (being there, in error, called Anne), as his 2nd wife, Sir Edward Hussey, 3d Baronet [1611], of Honington, co. Lincoln. In the Mar. Lic. (Vic. Gen.) she is called "about 22," but was apparently 26, according to the M.I. in Caythorpe, in which she is called 78 at her death, 20 Jan. 1750, being there described as "da. of Sir Charles de Vic, Baronet, brother [*sic*] of Sir Henry de Vic, Baronet."
(b) Charles Forster, s. and h. [*qy.* heir ap.] of Sir Richard Forster, Baronet, of Stokesley, *m.* Martha, 5th da. of George Anne, of Frickley (living 1585; *d.* 1620) by Martha, da. of Richard Fenton. As her nephew, Michael Anne, was aged 40 in 1666 (Visit. of Yorkshire), this Charles was presumably the son of the 1st Baronet.

FANSHAWE:
cr. 2 Sep. 1650;
ex. July 1694.

I. 1650. "RICHARD FANSHAWE, a younger brother to Thomas, LORD VISCOUNT FANSHAWE OF DROMORE in Ireland, Sec. of State to His Majesty at Worcester battle [1651] where he was taken prisoner, Master of the Requests since His Majesty's restoration, and Ambassador Extraordinary in Spain and Portugal," was 4th and yst. s. of Sir Henry FANSHAWE, of Ware Park, Herts, Remembrancer of the Exchequer (*d.* March 1615/6, aged 48), by Elizabeth, da. of Thomas SMYTHE, of Ostenhanger, Kent; was *bap.* 12 June 1608, at Ware; admitted to Jesus Coll., Cambridge (Fellow Commoner), Nov. 1623; admitted to Inner Temple, 22 Jan. 1626; Secretary to the Embassy at the Court of Spain, 1635; and afterwards, 1638, Chargé d' Affaires there; Sec. of War to the Prince of Wales, 1644; had "credentials for Spain," 1648; was Treasurer of the Navy (under Prince Rupert), 1648-50 and was *cr. a Baronet*, 2 Sep. 1650, being, soon afterwards, Sec. of State in Scotland to the young King; was taken prisoner at the battle of Worcester, 3 Sep. 1651; was (though already a Baronet) *Knighted* at Breda by the young King, April 1660, and made Sec. of the Latin tongue and Master of the Requests; M.P. for the Univ. of Cambridge, 1661, till his death; represented the Duke of Normandy at the Coronation, 23 April 1661; P.C. [I.], 1661; P.C. [E.], 1663; Ambassador to Portugal, 1662-63, and to Spain and Portugal, 1664 to May 1666. He *m.*, 18 May 1644, at Wolvercot, Oxon, Anne, 1st da. of Sir John HARRISON, of Ball's park in Ware aforesaid, by Margaret, da. of Robert FANSHAWE, of Fanshawe Gate in Dronfield, co. Derby. He *d.* at his house in the Siete Chimineosi, Madrid, 16 June 1666, aged 59, three weeks after the arrival of his successor, and was *bur.* 26, at Allhallows, Hertford, and thence removed to Ware.(a) M.I. His widow, who was *b.*, 25 March 1625, at St. Olave's, Hart Street, London, *d.*, 30 Jan. 1679/80, aged 55, and was *bur.* at Ware.(b) Will dat. 3 Oct. 1679, pr. 6 Feb. 1679/80.

II. 1666, to 1694. SIR RICHARD FANSHAWE, Baronet [1650], 6th and yst. but only surv. s. and h., *b.* at Madrid, 6 Aug. 1665; was deaf and dumb. He *suc. to the Baronetcy*, 16 June 1666. He *d.* unm., and was *bur.* (from Clerkenwell, Midx.), 12 July 1694, at Ware, when *the Baronetcy* became *extinct*.

CURTIUS:
cr. 2 April 1652;
ex. or *dormant* about 1690.

I. 1652, to 1690? "WILLIAM CURTIUS, then resident for his Majesty with Gustavus, King of Sweden and the Princes of Germany," was *cr. a Baronet*, 2 April 1652, but nothing further is known of him or of his descendants, if any, and the *Baronetcy* is presumed to have become *extinct* or *dormant* on his death.

(a) He was a skilled classic and the translator of several Latin, Italian, Spanish and Portuguese works, being also an English poet of some merit.
(b) Her interesting "*Memoir*" of her husband was first printed in 1829.

I'ANSON:
cr. 6 May 1652;(a)
ex. about 1800.

I. 1652. SIR BRIAN I'ANSON, Knt., of Ashby Ledgers, co. Northampton and of London, 2d s. of Brian I'ANSON (aged 74 in 1633) of the same, and of Bassettsbury, Bucks, by Anne, da. of Robert LEE, of Beaconsfield, in that county; was *b.* about 1590; matric. at Oxford (Mag. Coll.), 15 March 1604/5, aged 15; admitted to Inner Temple, Nov. 1605; was Groom of the Bedchamber to Charles I; was *Knighted* (possibly by James I) before 1633 (*Visit. of London*, and was *cr. a Baronet*, 6 May 1652, by a confirmation of Charles II, dat. 6 May 1652, at the Louvre in Paris, of a warrant granted by the late King. He *m.*, in or before 1616, Mary, da. of Henry BRYARS, Alderman of Coventry. She by whom he had sixteen children was living 1633, but *d.* before him. He was living 1663, but *d.* before 23 March 1665/6, when admon. of his goods (he being described as "Sir Brian I'Anson, Knight, of Allhallows on the wall, London") was granted to his son "Henry I'Anson, Dr. of Law," who, however, is not therein described as a Baronet.

II. 1665? SIR HENRY I'ANSON, Baronet [1652], 1st s. and h., *b.* about 1617; matric. at Oxford (Balliol Coll.), 15 June 1632, aged 15; B.A., 15 Jan. 1634/5; B.C.L., 18 June 1636; Fellow of All Souls College, 1638; D.C.L., 2 July 1641; was an officer in the Royalist Army; *suc. to the Baronetcy* about 1665, but seems not to have assumed the title; was in attendance on Charles II in France, during his exile. He *m.*, in or before 1647, Mary, da. of (—) ELMES, of Bowney, Oxon. He, who became a Roman Catholic, *d.* abroad about 1684, in poor circumstances.

III. 1684? SIR THOMAS I'ANSON, Baronet [1652], only s. and h., *b.* at the Louvre in Paris about 1648; is said to have been M.A. (King's College) of Cambridge(b); *suc. to the Baronetcy* about 1684; purchased the estate of New Bounds, in Tunbridge, Kent, in 1701. He *m.* about 1696, at Oulston, co. Lincoln, Dorothy, 5th da. of William ROKEBY, of Ackworth Park and Skellow Hall, co. York, by Emma, da. of Sir William BURY, of Grantham. He *d.* 28 Dec. 1707 and was *bur.* at Tunbridge. M.I. Admon. 27 June 1709. His widow, who was *b.* 2 March 1674 at Ackworth, *d.* in London 27 July 1744, and was *bur.* with him. M.I.

IV. 1707. SIR THOMAS I'ANSON, Baronet [1652], 2d but 1st surv. s. and h., *b.* at Skellow Hall aforesaid, about 1701; *suc. to the Baronetcy* 28 Dec. 1707; appointed Gent. Porter of the Tower of London, 22 June 1741 (by the name of "Sir Thomas I'Anson") and was 3d Lieut. of the Tower Hamlets. He *m.*, in or before 1724, Mary, only surv. da. of John BANKES, of Kingston Hall, Dorset, by Margaret, da. of Sir Henry Parker, 2d Baronet [1681]. He *d.* 10 June 1764, aged 62, and was *bur.* at Tunbridge. M.I. His widow *d.* Jan. 1774.

(a) There is no mention of this creation in Dugdale's *Catalogue*. The sign manual for it is mentioned by Wotton in his *Baronetage* of 1741. (See p. 24, note "b" under "Bunce"). See, however, *Herald and Genealogist* (vol. iv, p. 281) as also Hutchins' *Dorset* (edit. 1861, vol. i, p. 546, where there is a good pedigree of the family) for grant and confirmation by Charles II, 6 May 1652, "of the special warrant" given by his father, "for the expediting" unto Sir Brian I'anson, Knt., of Ashby Ledgers, co. Northampton; "letters patents for the dignity of a Baronett." See also Baker's *Northamptonshire*, vol. i, p. 245.
(b) No such degree is given in the *Cambridge Graduates*, 1659—1823.

V. 1764. SIR THOMAS BANKES I'ANSON, Baronet [1652], 1st s. and h., *b.* at Montpelier in France, 30 March 1724; matric. at Oxford (Univ. Coll.), 15 Dec. 1741, aged 17; B.C.L., 1 July 1748; was in Holy Orders; Rector of Corfe Castle, Dorset, 1748-1799; Prebendary of Wells, 1760-99, Sub-Dean, 1766-73, and Precentor, 1773-99. He *m.*, 24 May 1753, at Kingston Chapel, Corfe Castle, Dorset, Mary, da. of Edmund HAYTER, of Creech, in the Isle of Purbeck, by his 2d wife, Mary, only da. of Seth JERMY, Capt. R.N. She *d.* 1782. He *d.* 25 Jan. 1799, aged 75. Admon. June 1799, and June 1803.

VI. 1799. SIR JOHN BANKES I'ANSON, Baronet [1652], 1st s. and h., *b.* 13 Sep. and *bap.* 14 Oct. 1759 at Corfe Castle aforesaid; is possibly the same as "Henry [*sic*] Bankes I'Anson" who was LL.B. (Emman. Coll., Cambridge) 1784. He was in Holy Orders, and was for 7 months (July to Oct. 1799) Rector of Corfe Castle aforesaid. He *d.* unm., and was *bur.* there, 4 Nov. 1799, aged 40. Will pr. 1803.

VII. 1799? to 1800? SIR JOHN I'ANSON, Baronet [1657], of Epsom, Surrey, uncle and (if then surviving) h. male, *b.* 1 Sep. 1733 at New Bounds, aforesaid, and *bap.* at Tunbridge; was "bred to the law"; lived sometime at Channel Row, St. Margaret's, Westm. He, presumably, *suc. to the Baronetcy*(a) in Nov. 1799. He *m.* firstly, 16 March 1762, at St. Geo., Han. sq., Mary, da. and coheir of John FYLER, of London, by Mary, da. and coheir of John HOBBS, of Stoke Courcy, Somerset. She *d.* s.p.m.(b) 30 June 1765, aged 27, and was *bur.* at Tunbridge. M.I. He *m.* secondly, 16 Aug. 1766, at St. Margaret's aforesaid, Mary HARPUR, spinster, probably da. or other relative of "H. Harpur, Vicar of Tunbridge," who performed the ceremony.(c) On his death, s.p.m., presumably shortly *after* 1799, or possibly on the death of his predecessor *in* 1799, the *Baronetcy* became *extinct*.

SCOTT:
cr. 9 Aug. 1653(d);
dormant, or *possibly ex*, about 1775.

I. 1653. WILLIAM SCOTT, afterwards of Kew Green, Surrey, 3d s. of James SCOTT, of Middleburgh in Zealand (living 1600), by Hester BACQUIER, his wife, was sometime President of the Council, Governor and Admiral to the States General, but settled at Rouen in France in 1641, whence he raised two Scotch regiments (each of 1,500 men) for the service of Charles I; received the young King Charles II at his house after the defeat at Worcester (3 Sep. 1651), and supplied him with money, and was by him *cr. a Baronet*, 9 Aug. 1653.(d) He was naturalised in France, and bought (for 80,000 livres) the important post of *Secretaire du Roi*, as also the Lordships of Mezangere, Bosheville and Gaillon in Normandy, and "was admitted into the order of the

(a) He is called "Baronet" in the elaborate pedigree of Fyler in Hutchins's *Dorset* (edit. 1841), vol. i, p. 419.
(b) Mary, her only child, *b.* in Channel Row, 2 Feb. and *bap.* 6 March 1761, at St. Margaret's, Westm., *m.* there, 6 Jan. 1785, her 1st cousin, Samuel Fyler, of Twickenham, Midx., and *d.* May 1794, leaving issue.
(c) The following burials at St. Margaret's, Westm., possibly relate to this family—*viz.*, 1770 July 15 "Mrs. J'Anson, removed;" 1744 Feb. 1 "Lady J'Anson, removed;" and 1777 April 12, "Elizabeth J'Anson."
(d) There is no mention of this creation in Dugdale's *Catalogue*, but it appears in Wotton's *Baronetage* (1741), where is given a full account of the family (stated to have been originally Scotch, but settled in the Low Countries after 1519), as also of their coat of arms.

Nobility by the King of France."(a) [*Qy.* as Marquis de la Mezangere, which title was borne by the 3d and 4th Baronets]. He *m.* Catharine, da. of Samuel FORTREY, of London, merchant, and of Kew aforesaid, by Catharine, 1st da. of John DE LATFLEUR, of Hainault. He, who was "a Protestant,"(a) *d.* 1681. His widow *d.* 1684.

II. 1681. SIR WILLIAM SCOTT, Baronet [1653], only s. and h.; *suc. to the Baronetcy* in 1681, and was "Lord of Mezangere and was Councellor of the Parl. in Normandy"(a) in 1683. He *m.* Margaret DE RAMBOUILLET DE LA SABLIEVE.

III. 1700? SIR WILLIAM SCOTT, Baronet [1653], "Marquis de la Mezangere"(a) in France, 1st s. and h.; *suc. to the Baronetcy* on the death of his father; was "of the King's Council and President of accounts, aids and finances in Normandy" in France. He *m.* Mary Leveze de Pais DE BOIS L'ABBE, one of the Maids of Honour to the Queen of France. He *d.* 1723.

IV. 1723, to 1775? SIR WILLIAM SCOTT, Baronet [1653], "Marquis de la Mezangere"(a) in France, 1st s. and h.; *suc. to the Baronetcy* in 1733, living unm. 1741,(a) and probably 1771.(b) He probably *d.* s.p.m.(b); at all events, after his death *the Baronetcy* appears to have become *dormant* or possibly *extinct*.(c)

CRYMES, CRIMES, GRYMES, *or* GRIMES:
cr. about 1654;(d)
ex. or *dormant* probably about 1770.

I. 1654? SIR GEORGE GRYMES, *or* CRYMES, of Peckham in Camberwell, Surrey, s. and h., ap. of Sir Thomas CRYMES, *or* GRYMES, of the same (*bur.* 7 May, 1664, at Camberwell), by Margaret, da. of Sir George MORE, of Loseley, in that county, was *bap.* 10 Feb. 1604/5, at Camberwell; matric. at Oxford (Brasenose Coll.) 6 Dec. 1622, aged 14; was M.P. for Haslemere 1628-29; was *Knighted*, 19 Dec. 1628, at Theobalds, and was *cr. a Baronet* v.p. probably about 1654.(d) He *m.*, 25 May 1637, at St. Margaret's, Lothbury, London, Alice, da. and coheir of Charles LOVELL, of East Harling, Norfolk. He *d.* v.p. and was *bur.* 15 Oct. 1657, at Camberwell. Admon. 16 March 1657/8, to Alice, his widow.

II. 1657. SIR THOMAS GRYMES, *or* CRYMES, Baronet [1654?], of Peckham aforesaid, 1st s. and h., *bap.* 10 May 1638 at Camberwell; *suc. to the Baronetcy* in Oct. 1657, and was restored to his lands, by Act of Parl., 29 Dec. 1660, the estate of Peckham (which he shortly afterwards sold to his

(a) Wotton's *Baronetage* (1741) to the 1st edit. (1727) to which work the 4th Baronet supplied the information therein contained.
(b) In Kimber's *Baronetage* (1771) it is remarked after the succession of the 4th Baronet in 1723 "We can say nothing further with any tolerable degree of certainty concerning this family who have constantly resided in France."
(c) He had, however, no less than three brothers, John Anthony, Edward Francis Peter, and Anthony. His uncle, also, Sir Anthony Scott (the 2d and yst. s. of the 2d Baronet), *m.* Elizabeth de Bourrer and had issue.
(d) There is no mention of the creation of this Baronetcy in Dugdale's *Catalogue*, but the grantee (who *d.* Oct. 1657) is spoken of as "Knt. and Baronet," in the Visit. of Surrey, 1662, signed by his son and heir who is also so described, which son moreover was, as a *Baronet*, restored to his lands, 29 Dec. 1660. See as to this family, *Coll. Top. et Gen.* vol. iii, pp. 155-157.

brother-in-law, Sir Thomas Bond) being worth £1,500 a year.(a) He entered and signed (as "Tho. Crymes"), his pedigree in the Visit. of Surrey, 1662.(b) He *m.*, in or before 1660, Mary, sister of SIR THOMAS BOND, 1st Baronet [1658], da. of Thomas BOND, M.D., of Hoxton, Midx., by Catherine, da. of John OSBALDESTON. He *d.* before 1694.

III. 1690? SIR THOMAS GRYMES, Baronet [1654?], 2d but 1st surv. s. and h.(c) *b.* probably about 1664; *suc. to the Baronetcy* on the death of his father, before 1694, when he was living but without children in "Yorkshire or in Gloucester."(a) Was also living 15 Nov. 1709, when he was executor to the will of his brother Edmund GRYMES.

IV 1720? SIR GEORGE GRYMES, Baronet [1654?], of Naas, co Kildare, nephew and h. male, being s. and h.(d) of Edmund GRYMES, of Dublin and of Tipperkevin, co. Kildare, by Lydia TITCHBORNE (mar. lic. Dublin, 3 Oct. 1683), which Edmund (whose will dat. 1 Sep. 1708, was pr. 15 Nov. 1709 [I.], was 4th and yst. s. of the 2d Baronet.(e) He who was *b.* probably about 1685, was a surgeon and *suc. to the Baronetcy* on the death (after 1709) of his uncle. He *m.* probably about 1720, Anne who survived him. His will dat. 6 Feb. 1740, pr. 1 May 1745 [I.]. The admon. [I.] of his widow was subsequent thereto.

V. 1745? to 1770? SIR EDMUND GRYMES, Baronet [1654?], of Dublin, only s. and h., was a minor in Feb. 1740; *suc. to the Baronetcy* in or before 1745. He *m.* March 1761 (—), da. of the Rev. Michaell CAHILL, of Rathernon, co. Kildare. At his death *the Baronetcy* is presumed to have become *extinct* or *dormant*.

BENNINGTON(f):

cr. possibly about 1657?;

No particulars known.

"SIR ROGER BENNINGTON, Knt. and Baronet," obtained a licence at York, 20 Aug. 1660, to marry "Ann Robinson, Spinster," but of him or of this Baronetcy, if indeed it ever existed, nothing further is known.

(a) Le Neve's *Baronets*.
(b) See p. 15, note "d."
(c) Edward, 1st s. and h. ap., aged three in 1662, was *bap.* 6 Sep. 1660 and *bur.* 19 April 1664, at Camberwell, these two entries being apparently the last relating to this family in those registers.
(d) His brothers Henry and Edmund were living at the date of their father's will, 1 Sep. 1708, who devised to them the reversion of his estates in tail male In that will also Margaret, Lady Scudamore is mentioned as a sister then living. The information as to this family, after their settlement in Ireland, has been kindly supplied by G. D. Burtchaell, of the Office of Arms, Dublin.
(e) His next elder brother, the 3d son, William Grymes, was living in Virginia in 1694, having issue, a daughter [Le Neve's *Baronets*].
(f) There is no mention of this creation in Dugdale's *Catalogue*.

PALMER:(a)

cr. about 1657?

Not assumed after 1681.

I. 1657? to 1681. SIR PHILIP PALMER, of Dorney Court, Bucks, 1st s. and h. of Sir James PALMER, of the same, Chancellor of the Order of the Garter, by his 1st wife, Martha, da. of Sir William GARRARD, of Dorney Court aforesaid (which James was 3d s. of Sir Thomas PALMER, 1st Baronet [1621] of Wingham, co. Kent), was *b.* 1615, was Col. in the King's service during the Civil War; suc. his father 15 March 1657, and was possibly soon after that date *cr. a Baronet*,(a) though such creation seems doubtful. He is, however, sometimes called "Baronet," as in his mar. lic., 15 Nov. 1669, and in his admon., 28 Nov. 1681. He *m.* firstly, Phœbe, da. of Sir Henry PALMER, of Howletts, Kent, and by her had seven children. He *m.* secondly (Lic. Vic. Gen., 15 Nov. 1669), Anne, widow of Sir Henry PALMER, Junior, of Howletts aforesaid, da. of Isaac BARGRAVE, D.D., Dean of Canterbury. He *d.* at Dorney, 1683, in his 68th year, and was *bur.* there. Admon. 28 Nov. 1681, to his son "Henry Palmer, Esq." After his death the *Baronetcy was never assumed*, though his grandson, Charles PALMER, of Dorney Court, suc. in Nov. 1723, as 5th Baronet, to the Baronetcy of Palmer, *cr.* 29 June 1621, as of Wingham abovenamed. See vol. i, p. 166.

SLINGSBY:

cr. 19 Oct. 1657;

dorm. or *extinct* about 1700.

I. 1657. "SIR ARTHUR SLINGSBY, of [Bifrons in Patrixbourne] "near Canterbury,". yr. br. of Sir Robert SLINGSBY, Baronet [1661], being 7th s. of Sir Guilford SLINGSBY, Comptroller of the Navy, by Margaret (*m.* 1609), da. of William WATERS, Alderman of York (which Guilford, who *d.* 1631, aged 66, was 8th s. of Thomas SLINGSBY, of Scriven, co. York), was *b.* about 1623, being aged 4 in 1627; *Knighted* at Brussels 24 June 1657, and was a few months later "*cr. a Baronet*, by letters patent, dated 19 Oct. 1657, at Bruges, in Flanders." He *m.* a Flemish lady. He was *bur.* 12 Feb. 1665/6, at Patrixbourne, in his 42d year. His widow living 26 April 1666.(b)

II. 1666, to 1700? SIR CHARLES SLINGSBY, Baronet [1657], of Bifrons aforesaid, 1st s. and h.; was a minor in 1664; *suc. to the Baronetcy* in Feb. 1665/6; was (as was his br. Peter) living abroad in 1669.(c) He sold the estate of Bifrons in 1677, after which nothing is known of him, and the *Baronetcy* at his death became *dormant* or *extinct*.(d)

(a) There is no mention of this creation in Dugdale's *Catalogue*.
(b) On this date Mary, a posthumous child, was *bap.* at Patrixbourne.
(c) Will of his uncle, Francis Slingsby, pr. 1670.
(d) It is conjectured that he may have been the husband of "Dame Mary Slingsby," who was *bur.* 1 March 1693/4, at St. Pancras, Midx., "from St. James'." See the *Dict. Nat. Biogr.* as to the career of this lady, "Mrs. Aldridge, afterwards Mrs. Lee, afterwards Lady Slingsby," who, as "Mrs. Lee," from 1660 to 1680, and as "Lady Slingsby," from 1681 to 1685, was a well-known actress.

D

WOOD:

cr. probably about 1657;(a)

ex. 25 May 1671.

I. 1657? to 1671. SIR HENRY WOOD, of Hackney, Midx., eldest br. to Thomas, Bishop of Lichfield (1671-92), being s. and h. of Thomas WOOD, of Hackney aforesaid, Sergeant of the Pastry (*d.* 18 May 1649), by Susanna, da. of (—) CRANMER, Merchant of London, was *bap.* at Hackney, 17 Oct. 1597; was Clerk of the Spicery in the Royal Household; attended the Court at Oxford in 1643; was *Knighted* there, 16 April 1644, and in that year accompanied the Queen, Henrietta Maria, to France, as Treasurer to her Household, an office he retained till his death; was a Compounder 31 May, being fined £273 on 15 June 1649; M.P. for Hythe, 1661 till his death. He was *cr. a Baronet*, presumably about 1657(a) by Charles II, when in exile. He purchased the estate of Loudham Park in Ufford, and other lands in Suffolk, producing "a rental of nearly £4,500 a year." At the Restoration he was made a Clerk of the Board of Green Cloth; was in 1661 in attendance on Queen Catharine on her voyage from Lisbon, and was subsequently a member of her Council. He *m.* firstly, about 1630, Anne WEBB, presumably sister of Anthony Webb, Warden of the Merchant Taylors' Company, 1658-60. She *d.* s.p.s. and was *bur.* at Charenton, near Paris, 9 June 1648. He *m.* secondly, at Paris, Nov. 1651, Mary (MAID OF HONOUR to Queen Henrietta Maria), 4th da. of Sir Thomas GARDINER, of Cuddesdon, Oxon, sometime (1643) Solicitor General, by Rebecca, da. of (—) CHILDE, of London, merchant. She, who was *bap.* 26 Feb. 1626/7, at Greenford Magna, Midx., was one of the four Dressers to Queen Catharine, and *d.* of the smallpox 17 March, being *bur.* 1 April 1665, in Westm. Abbey, aged 38. He *d.* s.p.m.s.(b) 25 and was *bur.* 31 May 1671, at Ufford, when the *Baronetcy* became *extinct*. M.I. at Ufford. Will, in which he describes himself as "Knight and Baronet," dat. 24 and pr. 29 May 1671.

PRICE:

cr. presumably about 1658;(c)

ex. apparently in or before 1689.

I. 1658? HERBERT PRICE, of the Priory, Brecon, s. of Thomas PRICE, of Herefordshire, by Anne, sister and h. of John RUDHALL, of Rudhall, was M.P. for Brecknock, April to May 1640, and 1640 (Long. Parl.)

(a) There is no mention of this creation in Dugdale's *Catalogue*, but it is stated in the *Family of Chester, of Chicheley*, by R. E. Chester Waters (where there is a good account of the family of Wood), that "Charles II created him a Baronet at the time when he had nothing but titles of honour to bestow. The date of his creation is unknown for his patent was never enrolled, but Sir Thomas Bond, the Comptroller of Queen Henrietta's Household, was made a Baronet 9 Oct. 1658, and it is not likely that the Queen's Treasurer, who had precedence of the Comptroller, would be passed over in the distribution of honours. Sir Henry's name does not occur in any list of Baronets which I have seen, but there is no doubt about his creation, for he is constantly styled Baronet in Royal Warrants after 1660, and is so described on his father's monument, and in his own will."
(b) Mary, his only surv. child and sole heir, *m.*, as his 1st wife, Charles (Fitzroy), Duke of Southampton, but *d.* s.p., aged 27, and was *bur.* 16 Nov. 1680, in Westm. Abbey, with her mother.
(c) There is no mention of this creation in Dugdale's *Catalogue*, but as (Sir Thomas Bond) the Comptroller of the household of Queen Henrietta Maria, was certainly *cr.* a Baronet, 9 Oct. 1658, as also was (Sir Henry Wood) the Treasurer (probably shortly before), it seems not unlikely that the date of the creation of the Master of that household was about the same time. He is styled "Baronet" in the marriage licence of his son, dat. 16 June 1675, and in his own admon., 1 Nov. 1679, while his son is also so styled in the admon. to his (the son's) estate, 23 Dec. 1689.

till disabled, 8 May 1643, as also 1661 till his death, was *Knighted* when he entertained Charles I, at the Priory House, Aug. 1645; was a Colonel in the Royalist Army, holding Hereford till its surrender 25 April 1643; was Master of the Household to Queen Henrietta Maria, and subsequently to Charles II, by whom, during exile, he was, apparently, *cr. a Baronet* about 1658.(a) He *m.*, in or before 1641, Goditha, 2d da. and coheir of Sir Henry ARDEN, of Park Hall, co. Warwick, by Dorothea, da. of Basil FEILDING, of Newnham in that county. He was *bur.* 3 Feb. 1677/8, in Westm. Abbey. Admon. 6 Nov. 1679. His wife, who was a Lady of the Privy Chamber to the Queen mother (the said Henrietta Maria) survived him.

II. 1678, to 1689? SIR THOMAS ARDEN PRICE, Baronet [1654?], of Park Hall aforesaid, s. and h., *bap.* 13 March 1641/2, at St. Martins-in-the-Fields; *suc. to the Baronetcy* in Feb. 1677/8. He *m.* (Lic. Vic. Gen., 16 June 1675, she being then of Whittington, co. Glouc., about twenty-one, her parents deceased), Elizabeth, da. and coheir of Sir John DENHAM, K.B. (the poet), by his 1st wife, Anne, da. of Daniel COTTON, of Whittington aforesaid. He *d.* s.p. in or before 1689, when the *Baronetcy*, presumably, became *extinct*. Admon. 23 Dec. 1689 to Elizabeth, his widow. She *d.*, in or before 1701. Her admon. (as of St. Martin's-in-the-Fields), 21 March, 1701/2, to Mary Morley and Cecilia Morley, nieces, by the sister and next of kin.

ORBY:

cr. 9 Oct. 1658;

ex. 7 Feb. 1723/4.

I. 1658. "THOMAS ORBY, Esq., of [—], Servant to the Queen mother," 2d but only surv. s. and h. of Peter ORBY, *otherwise* ARPE,(b) of Burton Pedwardine, co. Lincoln, and Chertsey Abbey, co. Surrey, by Elizabeth, da. of Robert and sister and h. (2 April 1631) of Thomas HORSEMAN, both of Burton aforesaid, suc. his father 21 Sep. 1633; was in the household of the Dowager Queen, Henrietta Maria, during her exile, and was *cr. a Baronet*, by letters patent dat. 9 Oct, 1658, at Brussels. He had a grant of Croyland Abbey with the manor of Croyland, 15 Sep. 1671. He *m.* (after Oct. 1633) Katharine, da. of (—) GUERNIER, of France. He *d.* at his house in St. Paul's, Covent Garden. Admon. 23 March 1691/2. His widow *d.* at St. Martin's-in-the-Fields, and was carried thence for burial, 1 Feb. 1705/6. Admon. 6 July 1717.

II. 1691? SIR CHARLES ORBY, Baronet [1658], of Croyland Abbey, aforesaid, 1st s. and h., *b.*, probably, about 1640; *suc. to the Baronetcy* about 1691. He sold the Chertsey Abbey estate in 1710. He *m.* firstly, Anne, widow of Thomas WINTER, Gov. of Messalapatam in the East Indies (*bur.* at Fulham, Midx., Jan. 1681/2, aged 66), da. of Richard SWINGLEHURST, of London. She *d.* s.p., 15 March 1689/90, aged 54. He *m.* secondly (Lic. Lond. 9 July 1707), Anne, widow of Sir William BEESTON, Gov. of Jamaica (*d.* 4 Nov. 1702), da. of (—) HOPEGOOD, *or* HOWGOOD. He *d.* s.p., at St. Martin's-in-the-Fields. Admon. 11 May 1716 and 5 March 1735/6. His widow *d.* 1721, and was *bur.* with her 1st husband at Titchfield, Hants. Will pr. 1721.

III. 1716? to 1724. SIR THOMAS ORBY, Baronet [1658], of Croyland Abbey aforesaid, only br. and h., *b.* about 1658, in Paris; matric. at Oxford (Wadham Coll.), 22 July 1676, aged 18; B.A., 1680; *suc. to the Baronetcy* about 1716. He *m.*, in or before 1692, Charlotte, widow of Thomas MAINWARING, da. of Charles (GERARD), 1st EARL

(a) See p. 18, note "c."
(b) An elaborate pedigree of this family, by "Everard Green, F.S.A.," is in the *Genealogist*, Orig. Ser., vol. iii, pp. 271—273.

OF MACCLESFIELD, by Jane, da. of Pierre DE CIVELLE. He *d.* s.p.s. in St. Martin's-in-the-Fields, and was *bur.* 11 Feb. 1724/5, in the Chapel of the Savoy, when the *Baronetcy* became *extinct.*(a) Will dat. 13 Sep. 1723, pr. 12 Feb. 1723/4 and 2 April 1730. His widow *m.* Edward MANBY, who was living April 1730. She *d.* about 1727, in St. Geo., Han. sq., aged 76. Admon. 7 March 1728/9.

BOND:

cr. 9 Oct. 1658;

ex. or *dormant* 22 June 1716.

I. 1658. "THOMAS BOND, Esq., Servant to the Queen Mother," 1st s. of Thomas BOND,(b) M.D., of Hoxton, Midx., by Catharine, da. and h. of John OSBALDESTON, of Harbens, co. Warwick, was Comptroller of the Household to the Dowager Queen, Henrietta Maria, and was *cr. a Baronet* by letters patent, dat. at Brussels, 9 Oct. 1658. He purchased from his brother-in-law, Sir Thomas CRYMES, *or* GRYMES, a considerable estate at Peckham, in Camberwell, Surrey, where he built a splendid mansion. He *m.* Marie DE LA GARDE, da. of Charles PELIOT, of Paris, SIEUR DE LA GARDE.(c) He was *bur.* at Camberwell 8 June 1685, being described as "Knight and Papist." Will dat. 27 June 1676 to 11 Jan. 1682, pr. 25 June 1685. His widow who is said to have *d.* in the house of her da., Mary GAGE, at Hengrave, Suffolk, was *bur.*, 12 Aug. 1696, in Westm. Abbey. Will dat. 9 Aug. 1695, pr. 20 Aug. 1696.

II. 1685. SIR HENRY BOND, Baronet [1658], of Peckham aforesaid, and afterwards of St. Martin's-in-the-Fields, 1st s. and h., *suc. to the Baronetcy,* 8 June 1685; was M.P. [I.] for Portarlington, 1689; Receiver General in Ireland for James II, whom he accompanied to France, thereby incurring attainder and forfeiting his lands, which were, however, restored to him in 1707. He was a Non-Juror. He sold the estate of Peckham to the Trevor family. He *m.* (—), da. of (—) NOIR, of France. He, who resided chiefly abroad, *d.* 1721. Will dat. 22 Aug. 1721, pr. 1721.

III. 1721. SIR THOMAS BOND, Baronet [1658], s. and h., *suc. to the Baronetcy* in 1721, and resided chiefly in Wales. He *m.* Dorothea, da. of Stafford WYNNE, of Wales, his guardian under his father's will. He *d.* Aug. 1734, aged 25. Will pr. 1735.

IV. 1734, to 1767. SIR CHARLES BOND, Baronet [1658], posthumous s. and h., *b.* Dec. 1734, and *suc. to the Baronetcy* at his birth. He *d.* s.p., presumably unm., 22 June 1767, at Beaumaris, co. Anglesey, when the *Baronetcy* became *extinct* or *dormant.*(d)

(a) Croyland Abbey and the other family estates devolved on his nephew, only son of his sister Elizabeth, by her 2nd husband, Major-Gen. Robert Hunter.

(b) This Thomas was s. of Sir William Bond, of Highgate, and matric. at Oxford (Corpus Christi) 23 July 1596, aged 16, as "*Eq. fil.,*" being living 12 Feb. 1630/1, when he renounced administration to his father's estates.

(c) Her sister, Mlle. de la Garde, was one of the Maids of Honour to Catherine, Queen Consort to Charles II.

(d) It seems possible that issue male may have then existed of Thomas Bond, the 2d son of the grantee. His son, Henry Jermyn Bond, of Bury St. Edmunds, had 3 sons, of whom the youngest, James Bond (*b.* 1724), married and had issue.

CARPENTIER:

cr. 9 Oct. 1658;

Nothing further known.

I. 1658. "ARTHUR MARIGNI CARPENTIER,(a) a Frenchman," who, not improbably, held (like the two persons who were created Baronets at the same date) some post in the Royal Household, was *cr. a Baronet* by patent dat. at Brussels 9 Oct. 1658. He, apparently, never resided in England, and nothing more is known of him, or of his issue, if any.

BROWNE:

cr. 1 July 1659;

ex. 20 June 1754.

I. 1659. "HENRY BROWNE, of Kiddington [co. Oxford], Esq., son [and heir] of Sir Peter Browne,(b) Knt., slain in the service of King Charles I" (he having *d.* at Oxford, aged 30, of wounds received at the battle, 14 June 1645, of Naseby), by Margaret, da. of Sir Henry KNOLLYS, of Grove Place, Hants, was *b.* about 1639; was *cr. a Baronet* by letters patent dat. at Brussels, 1 July 1658, with rem. in "default of issue male to Francis, his brother,(c) etc." Sheriff of Oxon, 1687-88. He *m.* before 1662, Frances, 3d da. and coheir of the Hon. Sir Charles SOMERSET, K.B. (6th s. of Edward, 4th EARL OF WORCESTER), by Elizabeth, da. and h. of Sir William POWEL, of Llanpylt, co. Monmouth. He *d.* early in 1689, and was *bur.* at Kiddington, aged 50. M.I. Will dat. 16 July 1688, pr. 6 Feb. 1688/9, by Frances, the relict.

II. 1689. SIR CHARLES BROWNE, Baronet [1659], of Kiddington aforesaid, 1st s. and h., *b.* about 1663—1671; was a non-Juror; *suc. to the Baronetcy* early in 1689. He *m.*, in or before 1694, Mary, 1st da. of George PITT, of Strathfield Saye, Hants, by Jane, DOWAGER BARONESS CHANDOS, da. of John (SAVAGE), EARL RIVERS. She *d.* Aug. 1739. He *d.* in Clarges Street, 20 and was *bur.* 24 Dec. 1751, at Kiddington, aged 80, or 88. M.I. Will pr. Dec. 1751.

III. 1751, to 1754. SIR GEORGE BROWNE, Baronet [1659], of Kiddington aforesaid, only s. and h., *b.* about 1694; *suc. to the Baronetcy,* 20 Dec. 1751. He *m.* firstly, May 1725, Barbara, widow of (—) LEE, Col. in the army, 4th da. of Edward Henry (LEE), 1st EARL OF LICHFIELD, by Charlotte, formerly Lady Charlotte FITZROY, illegit. da. of Charles II. She was *b.* 3 March 1694, in St. James' Street. He *m.* secondly, (—), widow of (—) HOLMAN, of Warkworth. He *m.* thirdly, Frances, widow of Henry FERMOR, of Tusmore, Oxon (*d.* 17 Jan. 1746/7, aged 32), da. of Edward SHELDON, of Beoley,

---

(a) A branch of this family is said to have left Cambray in the time of Philip II of Spain, for Amsterdam, and to have existed about two centuries in Holland. In 1860 a work (4to) was published at Nancy, entitled "Famille de Carpentier, Seigneurs de Guvigny, par Jean Cayon."

(b) This Peter was s. and h. of the Hon. Sir Henry Browne, also of Kiddington (*bur.* there 6 Feb. 1628), who was a yr. s. (by his second wife, Magdalen Dacre) of Anthony (Browne), 1st Viscount Montagu.

(c) This, apparently, is the first special remainder of a Baronetcy, inasmuch as the remainder to heirs male whatsoever, which was the *usual* one in the Baronetcies of Scotland, cannot (though a most extensive one) be called *special* in Scotch cases.

co. Worcester, by Elizabeth, da. of Sir John SHELLEY, 3d Baronet [1611]. He *d.* s.p.m.(a) 20 June 1754, aged 60, when the *Baronetcy* became *extinct.* He was *bur.* at Kiddington. M.I. Will pr. July 1754.(b) His widow *d.* 20 March 1790.

WHICHCOTE:

cr. 2 April 1660.

I. 1660. "JEREMY WHICHCOT, of the Inner Temple, London," Barrister at Law and Solicitor General to the Prince Elector Palatine, 7th s.(c) of Christopher WHICHCOTE, of Stanton Lacy and of Stoke, both of co. Salop, by Elizabeth, da. of Edward Fox, of Greet, in that county, was *b.* about 1614; admitted to Inner Temple, Nov. 1638; purchased the Wardenship of the Fleet prison at the request of Charles II (during his exile), and, inasmuch as he occasionally officiated there in person, and by that means sheltered the agents of that King, was *cr. a Baronet* by letters patent dat. at Brussels, 2 April 1660. He was subsequently of Hendon, Midx. He *m.*, 5 Oct. 1641, Anne, 1st da. and coheir of Joseph GRAVE, by Anne,(d) da. of John BRERETON, of Nantwich, Cheshire. He *d.* 22 June 1677, æt. 63, and was *bur.* at Hendon. M.I. Will pr. 1677. His widow was also *bur.* there. Her will dat. 16 March 1701, pr. 29 March 1715.

II. 1677. SIR PAUL WHICHCOTE, Baronet [1660], of Quy Hall, co. Cambridge, 1st s. and h., *b.* 5 March 1643; *suc. to the Baronetcy,* 22 June 1677; was *cr.* M.A. of Cambridge 1701. He *m.*, 14 June 1677, at Guildhall Chapel, St. Lawrence Jewry, London (Lic. Vic. Gen., he said to be about 26, she about 14, with her mother's consent) Jane, da. and coheir of Sir Nicholas GOULD, Baronet (so *cr.* 1660), by Elizabeth, da. of Sir John GARRARD, 2d Baronet [1622], of Lamer. She, who was *bap.* 23 June 1661, at St. Peter le Poor, London, *d.* in 1698. He *d.* Dec. 1721. Admon. 4 May 1727 to Francis Tregagle, grandson, his daughters, Anna Maria Adamson and "Dame Frances Whichcote," being cited but not appearing.

III. 1721. SIR FRANCIS WHICHCOTE, Baronet [1660], of Grantham and Aswarby, co. Lincoln, and of Chesham, Bucks, only surv. s. and h., *b.* about 1686; *suc. to the Baronetcy,* Dec. 1721; M.P. for Cambridgeshire, Nov. 1718 to 1722. He *m.* firstly, Mary, only da. of Joseph BANKS, of Revesby Abbey, co. Lincoln, by Mary, da. of Rev. Rowland HANDCOCK, of Shirecliffe Hall, in Ecclesfield, co. York. She *d.* s.p., 19 Sep. 1726, and was bur. at Chesham. He *m.* secondly, Feb. 1737, Frances, widow of Sir Nevile HICKMAN, 4th Baronet [1643], da. of Edward HALL, said to be of the family of Hall, of Gretfold, co. Lincoln. She *d.* 20 July 1772, aged 75. He *d.* at Grantham, 27 Oct. 1775, aged 89. Both *bur.* at Aswarby. M.I. Will dat. 28 Aug. 1772, pr. 7 Nov. 1775.

(a) Barbara, his da. and sole h., by his first wife, *b.* 1729, *m.* firstly, Sir Edward Mostyn, 5th Baronet [1670] of Talacre, who was *bur.* at Kiddington 13 March 1755. She *m.* secondly, in or before 1760, Edward Gore, of Barrow Court, Somerset (who was *bur.* 11 April 1801, at Barrow Gurney), and had issue by both husbands. Charles Mostyn, her 2d son, inherited the estate of Kiddington, and took the surname of Browne.

(b) He is said to be the "*Sir Plume*" mentioned in Pope's *Rape of the Lock.*

(c) His next eldest br. was the well known Benjamin Whichcote, Vicar of St. Laurence Jury, London, and Provost of King's College, Cambridge, where he *d.*, May 1683, aged 74.

(d) The mother of this Anne Brereton was Amy, sister of Sir Paul Pindar.

IV. 1755. SIR CHRISTOPHER WHICHCOTE, Baronet [1660], of Aswarby aforesaid, s. and h. by 2d wife, *bap.* 15 March 1737/8, at St. Peter's, Eastgate, Lincoln; *suc. to the Baronetcy,* 27 Oct. 1775. Sheriff of Lincolnshire, 1777-78. He *m.*, in or before 1762, Jane, da. of Thomas WHICHCOTE, of Harpswell,(a) co. Lincoln (M.P. for that county), by (—), da. of John TREGALE. He *d.* 9 March 1786. Will pr. March 1786. His widow *d.* 30 Jan. 1812. Will pr. 1812.

V. 1786. SIR THOMAS WHICHCOTE, Baronet [1660], of Aswarby aforesaid, only s. and h., *b.* 5 March 1763; *suc. to the Baronetcy,* 9 March 1786; Sheriff of Lincolnshire, 1790-91. He *m.*, 24 June 1785, Diana, 3d da. of Edmund TURNOR, of Panton, and Stoke Rochford, co. Lincoln. She *d.* 4 Feb. 1826, aged 63. He *d.* at Aswarby 22 Sep. or 4 Oct. 1828, aged 66, both *bur.* at Aswarby. M.I. Will pr. Dec. 1828.

VI. 1828. SIR THOMAS WHICHCOTE, Baronet [1660], of Aswarby aforesaid, s. and h., *b.* 10 Aug. 1787; *suc. to the Baronetcy* in Sep. or Oct. 1828. He *m.*, 9 April 1812, Sophia, sister and coheir of Robert (SHERARD), 6th and last EARL OF HARBOROUGH, 3d da. of Philip, 5th Earl, by Eleanor, da. of Col. the Hon. John MONCKTON. He *d.* 23 Aug. 1829. Will pr. March 1830. His widow, who was *b.* 16 Nov. 1795, *m.*, as his 1st wife, 23 April 1840, at Leamington, the Hon. William Charles EVANS FREKE, who, after her death, suc., 25 Nov. 1889, as 8th BARON CARBERY [I.], and who *d.* 7 Nov. 1894, aged 72. She *d.* 23 Sep. 1851, aged 55.

VII. 1829. SIR THOMAS WHICHCOTE, Baronet [1660], of Aswarby aforesaid, s. and h., *b.* 23 May 1813, at Stapleford Park, co. Leic.; ed. at Eton; *suc. to the Baronetcy,* 23 Aug. 1829; sometime an officer in the Grenadier Guards; Major in the South Lincoln Militia, 1852—1854. He *m.* firstly, 10 July 1839, at St. Geo., Han. sq., Marianne, only da. of Henry BECKETT, by Mary, da. of James LYLE, of Philadelphia, U.S., merchant, which Henry was 7th s. of Sir John BECKETT, 1st Baronet [1813]. She *d.* s.p., being accidentally killed at Aswarby, 10 May 1849, by a fall from her carriage. He *m.* secondly, 25 May 1856, Isabella Elizabeth, da. of Sir Henry Conyngham MONTGOMERY, 1st Baronet [1808], by Sarah Mercer, da. of Leslie GROVE, of Grove Hall, co. Donegal. He *d.* s.p.m.s. 17 Jan. 1892, at Bournemouth, aged 78, and was *bur.* in the church of Aswardby. His widow *d.* a few months later, 29 Aug. 1892, after a long illness, aged 70, and was *bur.* at Aswardby.

VIII. 1892. SIR GEORGE WHICHCOTE, Baronet [1660], of Aswarby and Calverton House, near Stony Stratford, Bucks, br. and h. male, *b.* 31 May 1817 at Stapleford park, aforesaid; sometime Capt. in the Northamptonshire Militia; *suc. to the Baronetcy* 17 Jan. 1892. He *m.*, 10 April 1866, Louisa Day, 3d da. of Thomas William CLAGETT, of Fetcham, Surrey. He *d.* 14 April 1893, at Calverton House, aforesaid, aged 75. Will pr. at £11,215. His widow living 1902.

IX. 1893. SIR GEORGE WHICHCOTE, Baronet [1660], of Aswarby aforesaid, 1st s. and h., *b.* 3 Sep. 1870; ed. at Mag. Coll., Cambridge; *suc. to the Baronetcy* 14 April 1893; Sheriff of Lincolnshire, 1900.

Family Estates.—These in 1883 consisted of 11,213 acres in Lincolnshire, 4 in Rutland, and 1 in Northamptonshire. Total, 11,218 acres, worth £16,922 a year. *Principal Seat.*—Aswarby Park, near Folkingham, co. Lincoln.

(a) According to Wotton's *Baronetage* [1741], Harpswell had then been for upwards of 300 years the seat of the family of Whichcote, from a cadet whereof descended the 1st Baronet.

III

MERCES :

cr. April or May 1660 ;(a)

ex. or *dorm.* about 1690.

I. 1660, to 1690? "SIR ANTHONY DE MERCES, a Frenchman," was *cr. a Baronet*, between 2 April and 2 May 1660(a), but of him or his issue, if any, nothing more is known, and the *Baronetcy*, apparently, became *extinct* or *dormant* at his death.

BUNCE :

cr. May 1660 ? (b)

ex., apparently, 15 Aug. 1741.

I. 1660. SIR JAMES BUNCE, of Otterden, Kent, sometime Alderman of London, 1st s. and h. of James BUNCE, of St. Benet's, Gracechurch, Citizen and Leatherseller of London, by Mary (*m.* 13 Jan. 1595/6, at St. Benet's Gracechurch), da. of George HOLMEDON, of Brookhouse, Kent, was *b.* about 1600; admitted to Linc. Inn, 6 Aug. 1631; suc. his father, 26 Jan. 1631/2; was (like him) a Linendraper by trade, in Gracechurch street, and free of the Leathersellers' company; Alderman of London (Bread Street ward), 20 Aug. 1642, till discharged 7 April 1649; Capt. in the Trained Bands, 1640; Sheriff, 1643-44, being at the same time [1643-44] Master of his company; was trustee and treasurer in the Act for abolishing Bishops, 5 Oct. 1646; was one of five Aldermen(c) who were imprisoned, 24 Sept. 1647 till 8 June 1648, as Royalists; was fined an enormous sum by the Sequestrators, his estates being sold under an Act of Parl., July 1650. These were restored at the Restoration, and he was *Knighted* at the Hague by Charles II in May 1660, and is said to have been *cr. a Baronet*(b) by warrant dat. the same month. He was restored as Alderman, 4 Sep. 1660, and was then styled "Knight and Baronet." He *m.*, in or before, 1628, Sarah, da. of Thomas GIPPS, of London and Bury St. Edmund's, by Mary, da. of Richard SHERWOOD, of Ludlow. She was living July 1645, but, apparently, *d.* before him. He *d.* 13 Dec. 1670, at the house of "Fabian Phillips, Esq., co. Midx.," whom he calls "Father" in his nunc. will (in which he himself is styled "Knt. and Baronet") dat. 12 Dec. 1670, pr. 19 March 1673/4.

II. 1670. SIR JOHN BUNCE, Baronet [1660?], of Otterden aforesaid, 1st surv. s. and h., *bap.* 24 Jan. 1629/30, at St. Benet's, Gracechurch; adm. to Gray's Inn, 1 June. 1647; *suc. to the Baronetcy*, 13 Dec. 1670; sold the estate of Bunce's Court, otherwise Pollards, in Otterden abovenamed. He *m.*, in or before 1658, Amy, da. of (—). He *d.* 1683, and was *bur.* at Otterden. His widow was *bur.* there, from Greenwich, 1686.

(a) This creation is placed in Dugdale's *Catalogue* between 2 April and 29 May 1660.

(b) Wotton in his *Baronetage* (1741), vol, i, p. v, states that he omits any account of "Sir Thomas I'Anson, Sir James Bunce, Sir William Courtenay, and some others, whose ancestors procured a sign manual for this title but never took out their patents for it, and still labour under this defect." This Sir James Bunce is, however, described in many deeds as "of East Greenwich, co. Kent, Knt. and Baronet."

(c) The then [1646-47] Lord Mayor Gayer (who *d.* 12 April 1649), Aldermen Adams, Langham, Bunce, and Cullum (the four last named being all of them subsequently created Baronets) were committed to the Tower on 24 and impeached for high treason 27 Sept. 1647. These last named four, also, were, together with the then [1648-49] Lord Mayor Reynardson, "disabled," 7 April 1649, for refusing to proclaim the Act abolishing the office of King.

III. 1683. SIR JOHN BUNCE, Baronet [1660], 1st s. and h., *b.* about 1659; *suc. to the Baronetcy* in 1683. He m., 6 April 1686, at St. Christopher Le Stocks, London (Lic. Vic. Gen., he about 27, bachelor and a Baronet, she about 24. widow), Frances COTTON, of St. Margaret's, Westm., London. He *d.* s.p.m., 1687, and was *bur.* at Otterden. Will, in which he styles himself "Baronet," dat. 27 Jan. 1686/7, and pr. 2 June 1687.

IV. 1687. SIR JAMES BUNCE, Baronet [1660?], br. and h. ; *suc. to the Baronetcy* in 1687; [living unm. in 1696, and then "commonly called Sir James Bunce."(a) He *d.* unm.

V. 1710? SIR JOHN BUNCE, Baronet [1660?], of Kemsing, Kent, cousin and h. male, being 3d but 1st surv. s. of James BUNCE, of Kemsing aforesaid, by Dorothy (mar. lic. 4 Dec. 1661), da. of Sir William HUGESON, of Linstead, Kent, which James (*bap.* 30 Nov. 1632, at St. Benet's, Gracechurch), was 2d s. of the 1st Baronet. He *suc. to the Baronetcy* on the death of his cousin. He *m.*, in 1699, Alans, da. of James BERNARD, of Playhatch, Oxon.

VI. 1720? to 1741. SIR JAMES BUNCE, Baronet [1660?] of Kemsing aforesaid, s. and h. ; *suc. to the Baronetcy* on the death of his father. He *d.* s.p.m.s.(b), 15 Aug. 1741, at Kemsing, when the *Baronetcy* became *extinct* or *dorm.* Will pr. 1741.

EVELYN *or* EVELIN :

cr. 29 May 1660 ;

ex. 10 Aug. 1671.

I. 1660 to 1671. "SIR JOHN EVELIN," *or* EVELYN, of Godstone and Marden, Surrey, 2d but 1st surv. s. and h. of Sir John EVELYN, of the same, by Thomazine, da. and coheir of William HEYNES, of Chesington, Surrey, was *b.* 12 March 1632/3; was presumably (though possibly it was his aged father) M.P. for Blechingley, 1660; suc. his father 18 Jan. 1663/4 and was *cr. a Baronet* by letters patent dat. at the Hague in Holland, 29 May 1660. He was Sheriff of Surrey, 1665-66. He *m.* firstly, 7 Feb. 1653/4, at St. Peter's, Paul's Wharf, London. Mary, da. of George FARMER, one of the Prothonotaries of the Court of Common Pleas. She *d.* s.p., and was *bur.* at Godstone, 18 Feb. 1663/4. He *m.* secondly (Lic. Fac. 23 Nov. 1664, she being about 20, spinster), Anne, da. of Sir John GLYNNE, of Henley park, in Ash, co. Surrey, Serjeant-at-Law, and sometime (1655-60) Lord Chief Justice of the King's Bench, by his first wife, Frances, da. of Arthur SQUIB. By great extravagance he wasted his estate, and *d.* s.p.m.(c) 10, being *bur.* 17 Aug. 1671 at Godstone, when the *Baronetcy* became *extinct*.(d) Will pr. 14 Nov. 1671. His widow was *bur.* (with her father) 29 April 1690 or 1691, at St. Margaret's, Westm. Will dat. 14 June 1681, pr. April 1691.

(a) Le Neve's ***Knights***, where, however, his elder br. John is omitted.

(b) "Mary Anne, da. of Sir James Bunce, Baronet, of Kemsing, Kent," *d.* unm. 6 Jan. 1776, and was *bur.* at Kemsing. She is called elsewhere "only da. and h."

(c) Frances, his only da. and h. (by the second wife) *d.* unm., and was *bur.* 21 June 1681 at St. Margaret's, Westm.

(d) The estate of Marden was sold to Sir Robert Clayton. That of Godstone devolved on his br. and h. male, George Evelyn, of Nutfield, Surrey, whose great granddaughter and h. *m.* Sir George Shuckburgh, 6th Baronet [1660], and had female issue.

E

DE RAED, *or* DE RAEDT :

cr. 30 May 1660 ;

existing Oct. 1754.

I. 1660. "SIR GUALTER DE RAED, of [The Hague] in Holland," was *cr. a Baronet* 30 May 1660. but no further particulars are known of him. He appears, however, to have left issue.

* * * * *

III? 1700? to 1759? The will of "SIR DIRCK DE RAET, Baronet [1660], and Burgomaster of Leyden(a), presumably a grandson or other descendant of the above, is dat. at the Hague 15 Oct. 1754, and proved in respect of English property in the C.P.C., London, 26 Nov. 1759, by the widow "Lady Anna HULSHOUT."(a) It, however, furnishes no further information.

WEBSTER :

cr. 31 May 1660(b) ;

ex. April 1675.

I. 1660, to 1675. JOHN WEBSTER, of Kirby, Norfolk, a Merchant of London, residing in Holland in or before 1644, where he was "Lord of Wolluenhorst, Cromwick, Linschoterhaar, etc., etc., and Commissary for the Emperor of all Russia and Muskovia,"(c) was *cr. a Baronet* "31 May 1660, at Igravenhaag." He was residing at the Hague in 1667. He *d.* s.p., probably unm., in Durham yard, and was *bur.* 14 April 1675 in Westm. Abbey, when the *Baronetcy* became *extinct*. Will dat. 18 Feb. 1674/5, pr. 16 April 1675.

BRIDGEMAN :

cr. 7 June 1660(d) ;

afterwards, since 1794, BARONS BRADFORD ;

and subsequently, since 1815, EARLS OF BRADFORD.

I. 1660. "SIR ORLANDO BRIDGEMAN, of Great Lever, co. Lancaster, Knt., Chief Baron of the Exchequer,(e) then [*i.e.*, subsequently, in Oct. 1660] Lord Chief Justice of the Common Pleas, and afterwards

(a) *Notes and Queries*, 6th s., vol. 267.

(b) There is no mention of this creation in Dugdale's *Catalogue*.

(c) See inscription, under his engraved portrait, supplied by "Capt. P. C. G. Webster Lichfield" to the *Mis. Gen. et Her.* (N. S. ii, 456), where, also, there is some little information about him and his relatives. Of this there is more (from a private MS.) in an article by J. Horace Round, entitled *The Webster Papers*, which appeared in 1881 in *The Antiquary*, vol. iv, pp. 259-261.

(d) The three first Baronetcies conferred by the King after his landing in England, on his "Restoration," were (1) on the Chief Baron of the Exchequer ; (2), on the Attorney-General ; and (3), on the Solicitor-General. The only other recipient of that honour on that day (7 June 1660) was the loyal Alderman Langham. All four Baronetcies, oddly enough, are still (1902) extant.

(e) The posts of (1) Chief Justice of the King's or Upper Bench, (2) Chief Justice of the Common Pleas, and (3) Chief Baron of the Exchequer, were all three vacant at the Restoration (the respective appointments *by the Parl.* thereto of Oliver St. John to the first, in 1648, of Richard Newdegate to the second, and of John Wilde to the third, both in Jan. 1659/60, being, of course, invalid), but in the two former cases these posts were not filled up *by the King* till October 1660.

[1667-74] Lord Keeper of the Great Seal of England," s. and h. of John BRIDGEMAN, Bishop of Chester 1619 (who *d.* 11 Nov. 1652, aged 75), by Elizabeth, da. of the Rev. William HELYAR, D.D., Archdeacon of Barnstaple, was *b.* 30 Jan. 1608/9, at Exeter(a) ; admitted to Queen's Coll., Cambridge, July 1619 ; B.A., Jan. 1624 ; Fellow of Mag. Coll., Cambridge, July 1624 ; admitted to Inner Temple, Nov. 1624 ; Barrister, Feb. 1632 ; Vice-Chamberlain of Chester, 1638 ; Attorney of the Court of Wards and Solicitor-General to the Prince of Wales, 1640 ; M.P. for Wigan, April to May 1640, and 1640 (Long Parl.) till disabled in April 1642, voting against the attainder of Strafford ; sat in the Parl. at Oxford, and was *Knighted* there 17 Nov. 1643. He was one of the King's Commissioners at the treaty of Uxbridge, 1645 ; was a compounder Aug. 1646, and was fined £2,246. At the Restoration he was made, 30 May 1660, Serjeant at Law, and 1 June 1660, Chief Baron of the Exchequer, being six days later *cr. a Baronet*(b), 7 June 1660, and a few months afterwards, 22 Oct. 1660, being made Chief Justice of the Common Pleas. He presided at the trials of the Regicides. He retained the office of Chief Justice till May 1668, conjointly, for nine months, with that of Lord Keeper of the Great Seal, which high office he held from 30 Aug. 1667 to 17 Nov. 1672.(c) He *m.* firstly, 30 Jan. 1627/8, Judith, 1st da. and eventually sole heir of John KYNASTON, of Morton, Salop. She *d.* at Oxford, 12 and was *bur.* 13 July 1644, at St. Mary's there. He *m.* secondly, in or before 1648, Dorothy, widow of George CRADOCK, of Cavershall Castle, co. Stafford, da. of John SAUNDERS, M.D., Provost of Oriel College, Oxford [1644-53]. He *d.* at Teddington, Midx., 25 June 1674, aged 66, and was *bur.* there. Will pr. 1674. His widow was *bur.* 12 Jan. 1696/7 at Teddington aforesaid. Will pr. 1697.

II. 1674. SIR JOHN BRIDGEMAN, Baronet [1640], of Castle Bromwich, co. Warwick, 1st s. and h., by 1st wife, *b.* 16 Aug. 1631 ; admitted to the Inner Temple, Nov. 1646 ; *suc. to the Baronetcy*, 25 June 1674. He *m.* in or before 1663, Mary, 3d and yst da. and coheir of the abovenamed George CRADOCK, by Dorothy, da. of John SAUNDERS, M.D., both also abovenamed. He *d.* at Castle Bromwich, 24 Aug. 1710, aged 80, and was *bur.* at Aston, near Birmingham. Will pr. Nov. 1710. His widow *d.* 30 Dec. 1713, and was *bur.* at Aston. Will pr. March 1714.

III. 1710. SIR JOHN BRIDGEMAN, Baronet [1660], of Castle Bromwich aforesaid, 2d but 1st surv. s. and h., *b.* 9 Aug. 1667 ; matric. at Oxford (Oriel Coll.) 25 Aug. 1685, aged 18 ; admitted to Inner Temple, 1689 ; *suc to the Baronetcy*, 24 Aug. 1710. He *m.* 19 June 1694, Ursula, da. and h. of Roger MATTHEWS, of Blodwell, Salop. She *d.* 31 Jan. 1719/20 and was *bur.* at Blodwell. He *d.* 21 July 1747 and was *bur.* there. Will pr. 1748.

IV. 1747. SIR ORLANDO BRIDGEMAN, Baronet [1660], of Castle Bromwich aforesaid, 1st s. and h., *b.* 2 July 1695, at Blodwell aforesaid; matric. at Oxford (New Coll.), 28 May 1712, aged 17 ; admitted to Inner Temple, 1713 ; M.P. for Shrewsbury, April 1723 to 1727 ; *suc. to the Baronetcy*, 21 July 1747. He *m.*, 9 April 1719, Anne, 2d da. (only child whose issue lasted beyond the first generation) of Richard (NEWPORT), 2d EARL OF BRADFORD, by Mary, sister and coheir [1692], of Sir Thomas WILBRAHAM, 3d Baronet, da. of Sir Thomas WILBRAHAM, 2d Baronet [1621], of Weston-under-Lizard, co. Stafford, by Elizabeth, da. and coheir of Sir Roger WILBRAHAM. She *d.* 19 Aug. 1752, and was *bur.* at Weston aforesaid. He *d.* 25 July 1764, and was *bur.* there. Will pr. July 1764.

V. 1764. SIR HENRY BRIDGEMAN, Baronet [1660], of Castle Bromwich and Weston-under-Lizard aforesaid, 2d but 1st surv. s. and h., *b.* 7 Sep. 1725 ; was M.P. for Ludlow (three Parls.), Dec. 1748 to 1768, and for Wenlock (five Parls.), 1768-94 ; inherited the estate

(a) His birthplace is thus given in Foss's *Judges*.

(b) See p. 26, note "d."

(c) "The profundity of his learning and the extent of his industry," as also his honest principles and his moderation, were undoubted, but he is said to have had little knowledge of equity, and to have been, more especially in his old age, "timorous to an impotence." [See Foss's *Judges*.]

of Weston aforesaid on the death, 18 April 1762, of his maternal uncle, Thomas (NEWPORT), 4th and last EARL OF BRADFORD; *suc. to the Baronetcy* and the paternal estate, 25 July 1764; *cr.* LL.D. of Cambridge, 3 July 1769, and D.C.L. of Oxford, 4 July 1793. He *m.* 12 July 1755, Elizabeth, da. and h. of the Rev. John SIMPSON, of Stoke Hall, co. Derby, and Stamford, co. York, by (—), da. of (—) STRINGER (s. of Francis STRINGER), of Sutton-upon-Lound. She was living when he was *cr.*, 13 Aug. 1794, BARON BRADFORD of Bradford, Salop, the 2d Baron being *cr.* 30 Nov. 1815, EARL OF BRADFORD, in which peerages *this Baronetcy merged* and still (1902) so continues. See *Peerage*.

PALMER:

cr. 7 June 1660.(a)

I. 1660. "SIR GEOFFREY PALMER, of Carleton [*i.e.* East Carlton], co. Northampton [and of Carlton Carlieu, co. Leicester], Knt., Attorney General to His Majesty," s. and h. of Thomas PALMER, of East Carlton aforesaid, by Catharine, sister of Lewis, 1st BARON ROCKINGHAM, da. of Sir Edward WATSON, of Rockingham, co. Northampton, was *b.* 1598; admitted to Middle Temple, 14 June 1616; Barrister, 1623; Treasurer, 1661; was M.P. for Stamford, Nov. 1640, till disabled, 7 Sep. 1642; and, though appointed one of the managers to conduct the trial of the Earl of Strafford, declared afterwards against "The Grand Remonstrance"; sat in the King's Parl. at Oxford, was *cr.* D.C.L., 16 June 1643, and was one of the Commissioners appointed by the King at the treaty of Uxbridge. He was a compounder in Aug. 1646, and was fined £580; was imprisoned in the Tower of London in May 1655, on pretence of having plotted against the Protector. In 1654 he purchased the estate of Carlton Curlieu, co. Leicester. At the Restoration he was, 31 May 1660, made Attorney General (which office he retained till his death, ten years later), and soon after (having previously been *Knighted*) was *cr. a Baronet*, 7 June 1660, Chief Justice of Chester, 1661-62. He *m.*, about 1625, Margaret, sister of Sir Henry MOORE, 1st Baronet [1627], 1st da. of Sir Francis MOORE, of Fawley, Berks, Serjeant at Law, by Ann, da. of William TWITTY, of Boreham, Essex. She *d.* 16 May 1665, aged 47, and was *bur.* at East Carlton. M.I. He *d.* at Hampstead, Midx., 5 May 1670, aged 72, and having lain in state in the Middle Temple Hall, was *bur.* at East Carlton aforesaid. M.I. Will dat. 20 Sep. 1669 (in which he mentions having by deed, of Jan. 1667/8, made provision for payment of the debts, not exceeding £3,000, of his son Lewis), pr. 8 June 1670.

II. 1670. SIR LEWIS PALMER, Baronet [1660], of East Carlton and Carlton Curlieu, both aforesaid, 2d but 1st surv. s. and h., *b.* about 1630; was M.P. for Higham Ferrers 1661-79, and *suc. to the Baronetcy*, 5 May 1670. He *m.* firstly in or before 1654, Jane, da. and coheir of Robert PALMER, of Carlton Scroop, co. Lincoln. She was *bap.* at Carlton Scroop, 8 Nov. 1632, and was living 1656 and probably much later.(b) He *m.* secondly, Frances. She *d.* at Wellingborough in or before 1703. Admon. 31 Aug. 1703, to her husband. He *d.* in or before 1714. Will pr. July 1714.

III. 1714? SIR GEOFFREY PALMER, Baronet, [1660], of East Carlton and Carlton Curlieu, both aforesaid, s. and h.; *b.* at Carlton Scroop, co. Lincoln, 12 and *bap.* 26 June 1655. M.P. for Leicestershire in four Parls., 1708-13 (being then "Esq."), and Aug. 1714 (then a "Baronet") to 1722; *suc. to the Baronetcy* in or shortly before 1714. He *m.* Elizabeth, da. and coheir of Thomas GRANTHAM, of Goltho, co. Lincoln, by Frances, da. and coheir of Sir George WENTWORTH, of Wolley, co. York. He *d.* s.p. 29 Dec. 1732. Will pr. 1733. The will of his widow pr. 1741.

(a) See p. 26, note "d," *sub* "Bridgeman."

(b) Not improbably she may be the "Lady Palmer" who died 11 Feb. 1700, at St. Mary Magdalen, Lincoln.

IV. 1732. SIR THOMAS PALMER, Baronet [1660], of East Carlton and Carlton Curlieu, both aforesaid, nephew and h., being s. and h. of Robert PALMER, by Hester, da. of Sir Francis LAWLEY, 2d Baronet [1641], which Robert (who was *b.* 8 and *bap.* 18 Dec. 1656 at Carlton Scroop aforesaid, and who *d.* 1724) was 2d s. of Sir Lewis, the 2d Baronet. He *suc. to the Baronetcy* 29 Dec. 1732; was Sheriff of Northamptonshire, 1740-41; M.P. for Leicestershire, 1754 till his death. He *m.* in or before 1735, Jemima, 1st da. of Sir John HARPUR, 4th Baronet [1626], by Catherine, da. and coheir of Thomas (CREWE), 2d BARON CREWE OF STEYNE. She *d.* 22 June 1763. He *d.* 14 June 1765. Will pr. June 1765.

V. 1765. SIR JOHN PALMER, Baronet [1660], of Carlton Park, in East Carlton, and Carlton Curlieu, both aforesaid, only surv. s. and h., *b.* about 1735; *suc. to the Baronetcy*, 14 June 1765; M.P. for Leicestershire (three Parls.), Dec. 1765 to 1780. He *m.* 23 July 1768, Charlotte, da. of Sir Henry GOUGH, 1st Baronet [1728], by his 2d wife, Barbara, da. of Reynolds CALTHORPE, of Elvetham, Hants. She *d.* 7 Aug. 1783. He *d.* 11 Feb. 1817, aged 82. Will pr. 1817.

VI. 1817, Feb. SIR THOMAS PALMER, Baronet [1660], of Carlton Park and Carlton Curlieu, both aforesaid, grandson and h., being only s. and h. of Thomas PALMER, by Sophia, da. of Sir Justinian ISHAM, 7th Baronet [1627], which Thomas, who *d.* v.p. 4 June 1810, aged 39, was 2d but 1st surv. s. and h. ap. of the 5th Baronet. He *suc. to the Baronetcy* 11 Feb. 1817, but *d.* unm. 16 April 1817, aged 21, a few months afterwards(a). Admon. June 1817.

VII. 1817, April. SIR JOHN HENRY PALMER, Baronet [1660], of Carlton Park and Carlton Curlieu, both aforesaid, uncle and h. male, being 2d. s. of 5th Baronet. He was *b.* 11 April, 1775 at East Carlton; matric. at Oxford (Mag. Coll.,) 11 July 1795, aged 20; B.A., 1799. He *suc. to the Baronetcy*, 16 April 1817; was Sheriff of Northamptonshire, 1819-20. He *m.* 3 May 1808, Grace, 1st da. of Lewis Thomas (WATSON), 2d BARON SONDES OF LEES COURT, by Mary Elizabeth, only da. and h. of Richard MILLES, of North Elmham, Norfolk. She, who was *b.* 29 Dec. 1786, *d.* 26 Nov. 1853, in London. Will pr. Dec. 1853, and Feb. 1854. He *d.* at Carlton Park, 26 Aug. 1865, aged 90.

VIII. 1865. SIR GEOFFRY PALMER, Baronet [1660], of Carlton Park and Carlton Curlieu, both aforesaid, 1st s. and h., *b.* 9 June 1809, at Skeffington Hall, co. Leicester. Educated at Eton; matric. at Oxford (Ch. Ch.), 12 Dec. 1827, aged 18; B.A., 1830; Barrister (Inner Temple) 1838; sometime Capt. in the Leicestershire Yeomanry; Sheriff of Northamptonshire, 1871; *suc. to the Baronetcy*, 26 Aug. 1865. He rebuilt the Mansion at Carlton Park, where he *d.* unm. 10 Feb. 1892, aged 82.

IX. 1892. SIR LEWIS HENRY PALMER, Baronet [1660], of Carlton Park and Carlton Curlieu, both aforesaid, next br. and h., *b.* 16 Aug. 1818; matric. at Oxford (Ch. Ch.), 20 Oct. 1836, aged 18; B.A., 1840; M.A., 1844; in Holy Orders; Rector of East Carlton aforesaid, 1843-78; *suc. to the Baronetcy*, 10 Feb. 1892.

Family Estates.—These, in 1883, consisted of 2,428 acres in Northamptonshire, and 1,692 in Leicestershire. *Total*—4,120 acres, worth £7,529 a year. *Principal Seat.*—Carlton Park, near Rockingham, co. Northampton.

(a) Caroline Sophia, his only sister and h., *m.* 21 July 1827, Robert CLOSE, Major in the Army, and had issue.

FINCH:

cr. 7 June 1660(a)

afterwards, since 1673, BARONS FINCH OF DAVENTRY,

since 1681, EARLS OF NOTTINGHAM,

and since 1729, EARLS OF WINCHILSEA.

I. 1660. "SIR HENEAGE FINCH, of Raunston, Bucks, Knt., Solicitor-General to His Majesty, then [*i.e.*, afterwards, 1670-73] Attorney-General, now [*i.e.*, after 1675] Lord Chancellor of England and English Earl, *viz.* EARL OF NOTTINGHAM," was s. and h. of the Hon. Sir Heneage FINCH, of Kensington, sometime Recorder of London, and Speaker of the House of Commons, by his 1st wife Frances, da. of Sir Edmund BELL, of Beaupré Hall, Norfolk, which Heneage, last named, was 3d s. of Elizabeth, *suo jure* COUNTESS OF WINCHILSEA. He was *b.* 23 Dec. 1621, in Kent, probably at Eastwell; ed. at Westminster School; matric. at Oxford (Ch. Ch.), 18 Feb. 1635/6, aged 14; Barrister (Inner Temple), 1645; Treasurer, 1661-72. At the Restoration he was, 31 May 1660, made Solicitor General and soon after (having previously been *Knighted*) was *cr. a Baronet*, 7 June 1660.(a) He was M.P. for Canterbury in the Convention Parl. of 1660, and for Oxford University, 1661-73, being *cr.* a D.C.L. of Oxford, 7 Nov. 1665. He was Attorney General, 1670-73; P.C. and Keeper of the Great Seal, 1673, and Lord Chancellor, 1675, which office he held till his death. He *m.* 30 July 1646, at Allhallows'-in-the-Walls, London, Elizabeth, 1st da. of Daniel HARVEY, of Folkestone, Kent, Citizen and Grocer, and Turkey Merchant, of London, by Elizabeth, da. of Henry KYNNERSLEY, also of London, Merchant. She was living when he was *cr.*, 10 Jan. 1673, BARON FINCH OF DAVENTRY, co. Northampton. In that peerage and subsequently in those of Nottingham and Winchilsea this *Baronetcy* then *merged* and still so continues, the grantee being *cr.* 12 May 1681, EARL OF NOTTINGHAM, and his son the 2d Earl, becoming, 9 Sep. 1729, EARL OF WINCHILSEA, inheriting at the same time the Baronetcy conferred, 29 June 1611, on his paternal ancestor, Sir Moyle FINCH.

LANGHAM:

cr. 7 June 1660.(a)

I. 1660. "SIR JOHN LANGHAM, of Cottesbrooke, co. Northampton, Knt., Alderman of London," s. and h. of Edward LANGHAM, of Guilsborough in that county, by Anne, da. of John WEST, of Cotton End, co. Northampton, was *b.* at Northampton, 1584; acquired a large fortune as a Turkey Merchant in London; was Alderman of Portsoken ward, 11 Jan. 1641/2, being committed to Newgate, 1 Feb. for refusing to act, but discharged, on taking the oath, 12 May 1642: Alderman of Bishopsgate, 29 Aug. 1648, but discharged by Parl. 7 April 1649, and, though replaced at the Restoration, was again discharged, at his own request, 18 Sep. 1660; was Sheriff of London, 1642-43; was one of five Aldermen committed to the Tower in 1647 as Royalists, and disabled in 1649;(b) was M.P. for London, 1654; for Southwark 1660 and 1661 till void 26 June following; was, in 1660, one of the citizens deputed to meet the King at the Hague, where he was *Knighted* 25 May 1660, being shortly afterwards *cr. a Baronet*, 7 June 1660.(a) His charitable foundations both in Northamptonshire and London are numerous. He *m.* before 1620, Mary, sister to the loyal Alderman Sir James BUNCE, 1st Baronet [1660], only da. of James BUNCE, of London. By her he had fifteen children. She *d.* 8 April 1652, aged 52. He *d.* at Crosby House, Bishopsgate, London, 13 May 1671, in his 88th year. Both were *bur.* at Cottesbrooke aforesaid. M.I. His will pr. June 1671.

(a) See p. 26, note "d," under "Bridgeman."

(b) See p. 24, note "c," under "Bunce."

II. 1671. SIR JAMES LANGHAM, Baronet [1660], of Cottesbrooke aforesaid, 1st s. and h., *b.* about 1620; admitted to Lincoln's Inn, 3 Dec. 1640; *Knighted*, at the Hague, May 1660; M.P. for Northamptonshire, 1656-58, and for Northampton, 1659 and 1661, till unseated in April 1662; Sheriff of Northamptonshire, 1664-65; *suc. to the Baronetcy*, 13 May 1671. Fellow of the Royal Society, 1677. He *m.* firstly (Lic. Lond. 8 Dec. 1647, he 26 and she 20), Mary, da. and coheir of Sir Edward ALSTON, M.D., President of the College of Physicians, by Susan, da. of Christopher HUDSON, of Norwich. She was *bur.* 11 Sep. 1660 at St. Helen's, Bishopsgate.(c) He *m.* secondly, (Lic. Vic. Gen. 18 Nov. 1662, he 32 [42?] and she 22) Elizabeth, da. of Ferdinando (HASTINGS), EARL OF HUNTINGDON, by his 1st wife Lucy, da. of Sir John DAVYS. She *d.* 28 March 1664.(a) He *m.* thirdly (Lic Vic. Gen. 13 April 1667, he about 40 [48?] and she 24), Penelope, da. of John (HOLLES), 2d EARL OF CLARE, by Elizabeth, da. and coheir of Horatio (VERE), BARON VERE OF TILBURY. She *d.* s.p. He *m.* fourthly, Dorothy, da. of (—) POMEROY. He *d.*, s.p.m.,(b) Aug. 1699. Will dat. 12 July and pr. 15 Sep. 1799 by his widow, Dorothy. Her will pr. 1713.

III. 1699. SIR WILLIAM LANGHAM, Baronet [1660], of Cottesbrooke aforesaid, formerly of Walgrave, co. Northampton, br. and h. male, being 4th s. of the 1st Baronet; *b.* in or before 1631;(c) is said to have been "a person of great learning and generosity;" was a Doctor of Physic; was *Knighted* 14 Dec. 1671; was Sheriff of Northamptonshire, 1671-72; M.P. for Northampton (four Parls.) 1679-81, and 1689-95, and *suc. to the Baronetcy* Aug. 1699. He *m.* firstly, in 1657, Elizabeth, 2d da. of Sir Anthony HASLEWOOD, of Maidwell, co. Northampton, by Elizabeth, da. of Sir William WILMER, of Sywell. She *d.* s.p. within the space of two years afterwards. He *m.* secondly, banns published June 1659, at St. Helen's, Bishopsgate, Alice ROLL, of St. Giles, Cripplegate, widow, sister of Sir George CHUDLEIGH, 1st Baronet [1622], da. of John CHUDLEIGH, of Ashton, Devon, by Elizabeth, da. of George SPEKE, of White Lackington, Somerset. She *d.* s.p.m. and was *bur.* 17 Feb. 1663/4 at St. Helen's aforesaid. He *m.* thirdly, 10 July 1666, at St. Helen's, Bishopsgate, Martha POLHILL, of Kent, then aged about 26, widow, (Lic. Vic. Gen. 3 July 1666, he being of Wallgrave, co. Northampton, about 40, widower), da. of Herbert HAY, of Glinebourne, by Frances, da. of John COLEPEPER, of Wigsell, both in Sussex. His will pr. Feb. 1701.

IV. 1701? SIR JOHN LANGHAM, Baronet [1660], of Cottesbrooke aforesaid, s. and h. by 3d wife; *b.* about 1670; *suc. to the Baronetcy* in or shortly before 1701; Sheriff of Northamptonshire, 1703-04. He *m.* firstly, in or before 1697, Elizabeth, da. of Sir Thomas SAMWELL, 1st Baronet [1675], by his 1st wife Elizabeth, da. and h. of George GOODAY, of Bower Hall, Essex. Hd *m*, secondly, Maria, widow of Rev. Richard WEST, D.D., sister and coheir of Richard, 1st VISCOUNT COBHAM, da. of Sir Richard TEMPLE, 3d Baronet [1611] of Stow, Bucks, by Mary, da. and coheir of Henry KNAPP. He *d.* May 1747. Will pr. 1747. His widow *d.* 16 Nov. 1673, in Northampton, and was *bur.* at Cottesbrooke. Her will dat. 15 Nov. and pr. 3 Dec. 1763.

V. 1747. SIR JAMES LANGHAM, Baronet [1660], of Cottesbrooke aforesaid, s. and h. by 1st wife, *b.* about 1696; *suc. to the Baronetcy* in May 1747. He *d.* s.p. 12 Aug. 1749.(d) Will pr. 1749.

(a) In Wilford's *Memorials* (folio, 1741) the characters of Mary, Lady Langham and of the Lady Elizabeth Langham are given at some length.

(b) Mary, his only surv. child and heir (by his 1st wife), was *bap.* 10 March 1652/3, and *m.* 7 July 1670, both at St. Helen's, Bishopsgate, Henry (Booth), 1st Earl of Warrington. She died 23 March 1690/1 in the lifetime of her husband and of her father, leaving issue.

(c) He was living with two *younger* brothers at the date of the Visitation of London, 1633-34.

(d) The following cutting from a Glasgow newspaper, in April or May 1901, relates apparently (if indeed it relates to *any* member of this family) to the 5th or 6th Baronet. "HUSSEY FAMILY (April 17, 24, 1901).—Although in no way an answer to Inquirer's query, the following may be an item of some interest. Elizabeth, daughter of William Hussey, of Harlescott, and Mary his wife, was baptised at St.

III

VI. 1749. SIR JOHN LANGHAM, Baronet [1660], of Cottesbrooke aforesaid, br. (of the whole blood) and h.; *b.* at Gayton, co. Northampton, about 1698; ed. at Rugby School, 1715, and matric. at Oxford (Ball. Coll.), 19 Aug. 1717, aged 19; *suc. to the Baronetcy*, 12 Aug. 1749. He *d.* s.p. Sep. 1766.(a) Will pr. 1766.(b)

VII. 1766. SIR JAMES LANGHAM, Baronet [1660], of Cottesbrooke aforesaid, nephew and h., being s. and h. of William LANGHAM, of Rance, co. Northampton, by Mary, da. of Anthony DROUGHT, Merchant, which William was 3d s. (by 1st wife), of the 4th Baronet, and *d.* v.p. He was *b.* 31 Jan. 1736; matric. at Oxford (Linc. Coll.), 26 Oct. 1753, aged 17; *suc. to the Baronetcy*, Sep. 1766; was Sheriff of Northamptonshire, 1767-68; M.P. for that county, 1784-90. He *m.* 2 June 1767, Juliana, sister and sole h. of Thomas MUSGRAVE, of Old Cleeve, Somerset. He *d.* 7 Feb. 1795. Will pr. March 1795. His widow *d.* 21 March 1810. Will pr. 1810.

VIII. 1795. SIR WILLIAM LANGHAM, Baronet [1660], of Cottesbrooke aforesaid, 2d but 1st surv. s. and h., *b.* 10 Feb. 1771; *suc. to the Baronetcy*, 7 Feb. 1795; Sheriff of Northamptonshire, 1797-98. He *m.*, firstly, 20 Aug. 1795, Henrietta Elizabeth Frederica, only da. and h. of the Hon. Charles VANE, of Mount Ida, Norfolk (6th s. of Gilbert, 2d BARON BARNARD), by (—), da. of Richard WOOD. She *d.* 11 Nov. 1809, aged 29. He *m.* secondly, 19 May 1810, Augusta Priscillia, only da. of Hon. William Henry IRBY (2d s. of William, 1st BARON BOSTON), by Mary, da. and coheir of Rowland BLACKMAN, of Antigua. He *d.* 8 March 1812. Will pr. 1812. His widow, who was *b.* 28 Sep. 1785, *d.* 17 Sep. 1849, at Tunbridge Wells. Will pr. Dec. 1849.

IX. 1812, March. SIR WILLIAM HENRY LANGHAM, Baronet [1660], of Cottesbrooke aforesaid, only s. and h., by 1st wife; *b.* about 1796; *suc. to the Baronetcy*, 8 March 1812. He *d.* unm. (two months after his father), at Penzance, Cornwall,(c) 12 May 1812, aged 16. Admon. Aug. 1812.

X. 1812, May. SIR JAMES LANGHAM, Baronet [1660], of Cottesbrooke aforesaid, uncle and h. male, being 2d s. of the 7th Baronet; *b.* 21 Aug. 1776, at Marylebone; ed. at Eton; matric. at Oxford (Ch. Ch.) 27 Oct. 1794, aged 18; B.A. 1798; M.A. 1801; Barrister (Linc. Inn) 1802; M.P. for St. Germans, 1802-06; *suc. to the Baronetcy*, 12 May 1812: Sheriff of Northamptonshire, 1816-17. He *m.* 26 May 1800, Elizabeth, sister of Sir Francis BURDETT, 5th Baronet [1619], of Bramcote, 2d da. of Francis BURDETT, by Mary Eleanor, da. and coheir of William JONES, of Ramsbury, Wilts. He *d.* 14 April 1833, in Langham Place, Marylebone, aged 56. Will pr. 1833. His widow *d.* 30 Nov. 1855, at Twickenham, Midx., aged 78. Will pr. Dec. 1855.

XI. 1833. SIR JAMES HAY LANGHAM, Baronet [1660], of Cottesbrooke aforesaid, s. and h., *b.* 13 Nov. 1802, in Bedford Square, Middlesex; ed. at Eton; matric. at Oxford (Ch. Ch.); 20 Feb. 1821, aged 18; *suc. to the Baronetcy*, 13 April 1833. He *m.* 8 June 1828, Margaret Emma, 1st da. of George (KENYON), 2d BARON KENYON OF GREDINGTON, by Margaret Emma, only da. of Sir Thomas HANMER, 2d Baronet [1774]. She was *b.* 5 Nov. 1803, and *d.* 3 Feb. 1829, of consumption, aged 25. He *d.*, s.p., 13 Dec. 1893, in his 92d year at 25, Palmyra square, Hove, Sussex.

Mary's, Shrewsbury, on 7 August, 1680. When grown up she left home, and entered the service of a baronet, named LANGHAM, whom she nursed assiduously through a virulent attack of small pox, which alarmed the other servants so much that they were afraid of attending to him. He recovered, and proved his gratitude by marrying her. On his death, without issue, she returned to her native country and lived in the house now No. 85 Castle Foregate. She died there, and was buried at St. Mary's, 19 April 1762."

(a) See p. 31, note "d."

(b) The 6th Baronet is said to have left £6,000 to the Corporation of London for the relief of poor soldiers and sailors and their wives.

(c) Henrietta, his only sister and h., *m.* in 1817, Edward Ayshford SANDFORD, of Nynehead, Somerset.

XII. 1893. SIR HERBERT HAY LANGHAM, Baronet [1660], of Cottesbrooke aforesaid, nephew and h. male, being 1st s. and h. of Herbert LANGHAM, by Laura Charlotte, da. of Nathaniel MICKLETHWAIT, of Taverham Hall, Suffolk, which Herbert (who *d.* 27 Feb. 1874, at Westfield House, Brighton, aged 80), was next br. to the late Baronet. He was *b.* 28 April 1840, was sometime Lieut. 1st Life Guards; *suc. to the Baronetcy*, 13 Dec. 1893. He *m.* 25 Aug. 1868, Anna Maria Frances, 2d da. of Arthur Marcus Cecil (SANDYS), BARON SANDYS OF OMBERSLEY, by Louisa, da. of Joseph BLAKE. She who was *b.* 21 Oct. 1841, *d.* 27 May 1876.

Family Estates.—These, in 1883, consisted of 9,118 acres in Northamptonshire, 532 in Oxon, and 19 in Huntingdonshire. *Total.*—9,669 acres, worth £14,803 a year. *Principal Seat.*—Cottesbrooke Park, near Northampton, Northamptonshire.

WINCH:

cr. 9 June 1660;
ex. Dec. 1703;
assumed 1703 to 1717.

I. 1660, to 1703. "HUMPHREY WINCH, of Hawnes, co. Bedford, Esq., now [1679-84] one of the Commissioners of the Admiralty," s. and h. of Onslow WINCH, of Everton, Beds (admitted to Lincoln's Inn, 29 Oct. 1606) by Judith, da. of Roger BURGOYNE, of Sutton, Beds (which Onslow was the only child that survived infancy of Sir Humphrey WINCH, Justice of the Common Pleas, 1611-25), was *bap.* 3 Jan. 1621/2, at Sutton aforesaid; purchased in 1654 the estate of Hawnes, *otherwise* Haynes, abovenamed, which he sold in 1667, having in the interval been *cr. a Baronet*, 9 June 1660. He was M.P. for Bedford, 1660 and 1661-79; for Great Marlow, 1679-81 and 1685-87, being then of Harleyford, Bucks, and was, 1678-84, a Commissioner of the Admiralty. He *m.* in or before 1653, Rebecca, da. of Martin BROWNE, Alderman of London. He *d.* s.p.m.(a) Dec. 1703, at St. Giles'-in-the-Fields, being carried thence 3 Jan. 1703/4 for burial, when *the Baronetcy became extinct*. Will dat. 27 May 1701, pr. Dec. 1703, by his brother, "*Sir Richard Winch, Baronet*" [*sic*], and again 18 Aug. 1825, and 18 Dec. 1834. His widow *d.* 3 March 1712/3, at St. Giles', aforesaid, and was carried thence for burial, aged 79. Will dat. 4 June 1709, pr. 20 March 1712/3, by her da. Dame Judith Forster.

II. 1703. SIR RICHARD WINCH, Baronet(b) [1660], of Branston, co. Lincoln, sometime of Tewin, Herts, and at one time [1661] of Hawnes, Beds, br. and h. male, *b.* about 1635; admitted to Lincoln's Inn, 17 June 1651, becoming afterwards a Barrister; *assumed the Baronetcy* in Dec. 1703, apparently on the grounds of it having been granted with a spec. rem. to heirs male of the grantee, to whose estate of Branston he succeeded. He *m.* 15 Oct. 1661, at Arlesey, Beds. (Lic. Fac., 30 Sep. 1661, he about 26 and she about 27), Dorothy, da. of Sir Samuel BROWNE, sometime, 1660-68, Judge of the Common Pleas, by Elizabeth, da. of John MEADE, of Finchingfield, Essex. He *d.* a widower at Branston aforesaid, probably about 1710. Limited admon. 11 May 1743.

(a) Of his two daughters and coheirs (1) Judith, *b.* about 1654, *m.* 26 Nov. 1672, Sir Humphrey Forster, 2d Baronet [1621], of Aldermaston; (2), Rebecca, *bap.* 8 Sep. 1660, at Hawnes, *m.*, April 1681, Sir Thomas Lawley, 3d Baronet [1641], of Spoonhill.

(b) According to the assumption of the Baronetcy in 1703.

F

III. 1710? to 1717. SIR HUMPHREY WINCH, Baronet(a) [1660], of Branston aforesaid, 2d but only surv. s. and h.(b); *bap.* 30 Nov. 1665, at Arlesey, Beds.; admitted to Lincoln's Inn, 14 Jan. 1683/4; *assumed the Baronetcy* on the death of his father. He *d.* unm. 15 Feb. 1716/7, when the *assumption of this Baronetcy ceased*. Will pr. July 1717.

ABDY:

cr. 9 June 1660;
ex. 1 April 1759.

I. 1660. "SIR ROBERT ABDY, of Albyns [in Stapleford Abbots], Essex, Knt.," was younger br. of Sir Thomas ABDY, Baronet, 1st Baronet [1641] of Felix Hall, Essex, and elder br. of Sir John ABDY [so *cr.* 22 June 1660], all three being sons of Sir Anthony ABDY, of St. Andrew Undershaft, London, Alderman and sometime [1630-31] Sheriff of London (who *d.* 10 Sep. 1640), by Abigail (*m.* 14 Aug. 1610 at St. Mary Aldermary), da. of Sir Thomas CAMBELL, sometime [1609-10] Lord Mayor of London; was *b.* about 1615, and, having been *Knighted*, 4 June, was *cr. a Baronet*, 9 June 1660. He *m.*, in or before 1643, Catharine, 1st da. of Sir John GAYER, sometime [1646-47] Lord Mayor of London, by Catharine, da. of Sampson HOPKINS, of Coventry. She *d.* 6 and was *bur.* 25 Sep. 1662, at Stapleford Abbots. Funeral certificate. He *d.* 1670, and was also *bur.* there. Will dat. 28 May 1670, pr. 12 Nov. 1670 and 9 Mar. 1691.

II. 1670. SIR JOHN ABDY, Baronet [1660], of Albyns aforesaid, s. and h., *b.* about 1643, being aged 21 in 1664 [Visit. of Essex]; *suc. to the Baronetcy* in 1670. He *m.* 10 May 1687, at Westminster Abbey, Jane, only da. of George NICHOLAS (youngest s. to Sir Edward NICHOLAS, Secretary of State), by Anne, da. and h. of William DENTON, M.D., Physician to Charles I. and Charles II. He *d.* 1691, and was *bur.* at Stapleford. Admon. 9 March 1691/2, and again 7 July 1721. His widow, who was *bap.* 26 March 1666, at St. Paul's Covent Garden, *d.* 1721, and was also *bur.* at Stapleford. M.I.

III. 1691. SIR ROBERT ABDY, Baronet [1660], of Albyns aforesaid, only s. and h.; *bap.* 8 April 1688, at St. Paul's Covent Garden; *suc. to the Baronetcy* in 1691; matric. at Oxford (Trinity Coll.), 4 Aug., 1705, and then said to be 15; M.P. for Essex (four Parls.), 1727 to 1748. Described [Morant's *Essex*] as "a Great Antiquarian and a true Patriot." F.S.A. He *m.* 5 July, 1711, at St. Christopher le Stocks, London, Theodosia, only surv. da. and h. of George BRAMSTONE, LL.D., Master of Trinity Hall, Cambridge, by Rebecca, da. of (—) WOOD. She was *b.* 1 and *bap.* 3 March, 1696, at St. Bennet's, Paul's Wharf, London, and *d.* 8 Aug. 1732. He *d.* 27 Aug. 1748, and was *bur.* at Stapleford. M.I.

IV. 1748, to 1759. SIR JOHN ABDY, Baronet [1660], of Albyns aforesaid, only surv. s. and h., *b.* about 1714; matric. (with his yr. br. Robert) at Oxford (Trinity Coll.), 11 July, 1732, aged 18; *suc. to the Baronetcy*, 27 Aug. 1748; M.P. for Essex, 1748-59. He *d.* unm. 1 April 1759, and was *bur.* at Stapleford, when *the Baronetcy became extinct*(c). Will dated 31 Dec. 1757 to 16 April 1758, pr. 19 April 1759.

(a) According to the assumption of the Baronetcy in 1703.

(b) His elder br. Samuel was *bap.* 1 Sep. 1664, at Arlesey, and was living 27 May 1701, and, apparently, in 1703.

(c) His only br. Robert *d.* unm., aged 20 in 1735. His sister and sole heir Theodocia *m.* in 1752, Rev. Stotherd Abdy, Rector of Theydon Gernon, and *d.* s.p. 1758.

DRAPER:

cr 9 June 1660;
ex Dec. 1703.

I. 1660, to 1703. "THOMAS DRAPER, Esq. of Sunninghill Park, Berks." and of Eastham, Essex, s. of (—) DRAPER,(a) by a lady who survived him(b) was Sheriff of Berks, 1660-61, and was *cr. a Baronet*, 8 June 1660. He *m.* before 1656, Mary, da. and h. of (—) CAREY, of Sunninghill, aforesaid, with whom he acquired that estate. He *d.* s.p.m., Dec. 1703, when the *Baronetcy* became *extinct*.(c) Will dat. 2 April 1702, and proved 3 Dec. 1703. His widow *d.* 1717. Her will dat. 17 Jan. 1711, and 17 May 1714, pr. 10 Dec. 1717.

WRIGHT:

cr. 11 June 1660;
ex. 1681.

I. 1660. "HENRY WRIGHT, of Dagenham [in Romford], Essex, Esq.," only surv. s. and h. of Laurence WRIGHT, M.D., of London, and of Dagenham, aforesaid (*d.* 3 Oct. 1657, aged 67), by Mary, da. of John DUKE, M.D., of Toulton Hall, in Ramsey and of Colchester, Essex, was *b.* about 1637; suc. his father, 3 Oct. 1657, for whose services, presumably(d), he was *cr. a Baronet* by the Lord Protector Cromwell, 10 April 1658, a dignity which, of course, was disallowed after the Restoration in May 1660, though a few weeks later he was, notwithstanding his recent recognition of the late Government, again *cr. a Baronet*, 11 June 1660, the grantor on this occasion being the King. It is not easy to conjecture what service he had rendered to be thus highly favoured. He was M.P. for Harwich, 1660 and 1661 till his death. He *m.*, 23 March 1658, at St. Giles'-in-the-Fields, Anne, da. of John (CREWE), 1st BARON CREWE OF STEYNE, by Jemima, da. and coheir of Edward WALDEGRAVE. He *d.* 5 Feb. 1663/4, aged 27, and was *bur.* at South Weald, Essex. M.I. Will dat. 24 Oct. 1663, pr. June 1664. His widow *d.* 27 Sep. 1708, aged 71, and was also *bur.* at South Weald. M.I. Will pr. March 1709.

II. 1664, to 1681. SIR HENRY WRIGHT, Baronet [1660], of DAGENHAM aforesaid, only s. and h., *bap.* 1 July 1662 at St. Giles'-in-the-Fields; *suc. to the Baronetcy* 5 Feb. 1663/4. He *d.* unm. in 1681, aged 19, and was *bur.* at South Weald, when the *Baronetcy* became *extinct*.(e) Will pr. 1681.

(a) "Thomas Draper, s. and h. of Robert Draper, late of Islington, Midx., Esq., dec." was admitted to Lincoln's Inn, 18 Nov. 1644. The Baronet had two brothers, one a "Stockjobber in London," the other, Robert Draper, of Remenham, Berks. The name of their father is not given in Le Neve's *Baronets*.

(b) She, who purchased the Manor of Eastham from (—) Allington, *m.* for her 2d husband, Sir Nicholas Kempe, who *d.* 1624.

(c) Of his two daughters and coheirs (1) Mary, *b.* 1656, *m.* John Baber, and had a s. and h., John Draper Baber, who having sold the Manor of Eastham to John Henniker, *d.* 30 March 1765, aged 80, leaving a s. and h., who in 1769 sold Sunninghill Park, to Jeremiah Crutchley; (2), Mary *m.* Sir Henry Ashurst, 2d Baronet [1688], who *d.* s.p., 17 May 1732.

(d) See p. 5, note "d," under "Wright."

(e) Anne, his only sister and h, *m.* firstly, 4 March 1678/9, at St. Giles'-in-the-Fields, Edmund Pye, M.D., of Faringdon, Berks, s. and h. of Sir Robert Pye, of the same. She *m.* secondly William Ryder, and was living July 1720.

KEATE:

cr. 12 June 1660;

extinct 6 March 1757.

I. 1660. "JONATHAN KEATE, of the Hoo [in the parish of Kimpton], Herts, Esq.," 2d s. of Gilbert KEATE, of London, by his 2d wife, Elizabeth, da. of Gilbert ARMSTRONG, of Remston, Notts, was *b.* about 1633 and was *cr. a Baronet*, 12 June 1660. He, who was a Merchant of London, was Sheriff of Herts, 1665-66, and M.P. for that county, 1679-81. He re-built the fine mansion of the Hoo. He *m.* firstly, 1 May 1655, at St. Dunstan's in the East, London, Susanna, sister and h. of Thomas Hoo, of the Hoo aforesaid, only da. of William Hoo, of the same, and of St. Paul's Walden, Herts, by Mary, da. of Sir Francis BICKLEY, 1st Baronet [1661]. She, who was *bap.* 26 Dec. 1639, at St. Paul's Walden, *d.* 11 and was *bur.* 19 June 1673, at Kimpton,(a) aged 34. M.I. He *m.* secondly (Lic. Vic. Gen. 17 March 1674/5, each party said to be about 30), Susanna, da. of John ORLEBAR, of London, Citizen and Woollen Draper, yst. s. of John ORLEBAR, of Harold, Beds. He *d.* 17 Sep. 1700, aged 67. Will pr. Oct. 1700. His widow *d.* s.p. 13 Jan. 1719, aged 90. Will pr. 1720. Both *bur.* at Kimpton. M.I.

II. 1700. SIR GILBERT HOO KEATE, Baronet [1660], of the Hoo aforesaid, s. and h. by 1st wife, *b.* about 1661; *suc. to the Baronetcy*, 17 Sep. 1700. He *m.* Elizabeth. He *d.* 13 and was *bur.* 16 April 1705, at Kimpton, aged 44. M.I. Will pr. Dec. 1705.

III. 1705. SIR HENRY HOO KEATE, Baronet [1660], of the Hoo, aforesaid, s. and h., *b.* about 1696 at Hatfield, Herts.; *suc. to the Baronetcy*, 13 April 1705; matric. at Oxford (Worcester Coll.), 6 Sep. 1714, aged 18; *cr.* M.A., 9 July 1717 and D.C.L., 4 July 1741. In 1732, he sold the whole of his estates to Margaret BRAND, widow.(b) He resided chiefly at Walcot, near Bath, and *d.* unm. 8 Aug. 1744. Will as "Henry Hoo Keate" [nothing about his being a Baronet], leaving all to Mrs. Elizabeth Vaughan, spinster, pr. 1744.

IV. 1744, to 1757. SIR WILLIAM KEATE, Baronet [1660], yst. br. and h. *b.* about 1700; matric. at Oxford (Worcester Coll.), 13 July 1717, aged 17; B.A. 1721; B.C.L. 1724; D.C.L. 1731. In Holy Orders; Vicar of Kimpton aforesaid, 1725-57, and Rector of Digswell, Herts., 1729-57; *suc. to the Baronetcy*, Aug. 1744. He *d.* unm. 6 and was *bur.* 17 March 1757, at Digswell, aged 57, when the *Baronetcy* became *extinct*. Will pr. 1757.

SPEKE:

cr. 12 June 1660;

ex. 14 Jan. 1682/3.

I. 1660. "SIR HUGH SPEKE, of Hasilbury, Wilts, Knt.," s. and h. of George SPEKE, of the same (aged 34 in the Visit. of Wilts, 1626), by Margaret, da. of William TEMPEST, of Soudton, Oxon, was having previously been *Knighted*, *cr. a Baronet*, 12 June 1660. He *m.*, in or before 1653, Anne, the divorced wife of (—) CROKE, da. and h. of John MAYNE, *or* MAYNEY, of Staplehurst, Kent. He was M.P. for Chippenham, 1661 till his death in that year. He *d.* 5 July 1661, and was *bur.* in Box Church, Wilts. M.I. Admon., 11 Oct. 1661, to Anne, the widow. Her will pr. Dec. 1686.

(a) Her character is given in Wilford's *Memorials*.
(b) Her great grandson, Thomas Brand, *b.* at the Hoo, 15 March 1774 became Lord Dacre, on the death of his mother, Gertrude, *suo jure* Baroness Dacre, 3 Oct. 1719.

II. 1661, to 1683. SIR GEORGE SPEKE, Baronet [1660], of Hasilbury aforesaid, s. and h., *b.* 1 Oct. 1653, *suc. to the Baronetcy*, 15 July 1661. He *m.* Rachael, 1st da. of Sir William WYNDHAM, 1st Baronet [1661], by Frances, da. of Anthony HUNGERFORD. He *d.* s.p. 14 Jan. 1682/3, and was *bur.* in Box Church aforesaid, when the *Baronetcy* became *extinct*. M.I. Will pr. April 1683. His widow *m.* Richard MUSGRAVE, and *d.* in or before Dec. 1711. Will pr. Dec. 1711.

GOULD:

cr. 13 June 1660;

ex. Jan. 1663/4.

I. 1660, to 1664. "NICHOLAS GOULD, of the City of London, Esq.," 5th s. of Edward GOULD(a), of Staverton, Devon (*d.* 18 March 1607/8), by Elizabeth, da. of William MAN, of Broad Hempston, Devon, was executor to the will of his mother, 27 May 1633; was on several Parl. Committees, 1648-50, and appears to have been a consistent "Rumper"; M.P. for Fowey, 1648-53 and 1659-60, and was *cr. a Baronet*, 13 June 1660. He *m.*, in or before 1660, Elizabeth (*b.* probably about 1640), 1st da. of Sir John GARRARD, 2d Baronet [1622], of Lamer, by Jane, da. of Sir Moulton LAMBARDE. He *d.* s.p.m.(b) and was *bur.* 23 Jan. 1663/4, at St. Peter le Poor, London. Admon. 28 Jan. 1663/4, to his widow. She *m.* there (6 months later), 13 June 1664, Thomas NEALE, Groom Porter, and was *bur.* 24 Feb. 1682/3, at St. Peter's aforesaid. Will pr. Oct. 1685.

ADAMS:

cr. 13 June 1660;

ex. or *dormant* 12 April 1770.

I. 1660. "SIR THOMAS ADAMS, Knt., Alderman [and sometime (1645-46) Lord Mayor] of London," s. of Thomas ADAMS, of Wemm, Salop, by Margaret, da. of John ERPE, of Shrewsbury, was *b.* about 1586; was Citizen and Draper of London, of which Company he was sometime Master; was Alderman of Portsoken ward, 1639-41; of Billingsgate, 1641-46; of Cornhill, 16 Sep. 1646, till "discharged" by Parl. as a suspected Royalist, 7 April 1647, but restored 4 Sep. 1660; was Sheriff, 1639-40; President of St. Thomas' Hospital, 1643-49, and again, 1660-68; was Treasurer of War to the "New Model," 1645; trustee for the sale of the Bishops' lands, 5 Oct. 1646, till discharged by Parl. 5 March 1646/7; was Lord Mayor, 1645-46; was one of five Aldermen who, in 1647, were committed to the Tower as Royalists, and disabled in 1649;(c) was M.P. for London, 1654-55 and 1656-58. He purchased Sprowston Hall, in Norfolk, and other estates there; was a great sufferer in the Royal cause, and is said to have remitted as much as £10,000 to Charles II. when in exile; was deputed by the City to meet that King at Breda, where he was *Knighted* in May 1660, and shortly afterwards was, at the age of about 74, *cr. a Baronet*, 13 June 1660. He founded a Grammar School at Wemm, and endowed a lectureship at Cambridge with £40 a year.(d) He *m.*, in or before 1616, Anne, da. of Humphrey MAPSTED, of Trenton, Essex.

(a) See Vivian's *Visitations of Devon* for an extensive pedigree of the family of Gould.
(b) Of his two daughters and coheirs (1) Elizabeth *bap.* 25 June 1661, at St. Peter le Poor, *m.* 14 June 1677, Sir Paul Whichcote, 2d Baronet [1660]; (2) Jane, *bap.* there 4 July 1663, *m.*, firstly, in or before 1678, Sir John Boteler, of Watton Woodhall, Herts, who d. in March 1672, and secondly John Gage.
(c) See p. 241, note "c," under "Bunce."
(d) His character is in Wilford's *Memorials*, and elsewhere.

She *d.* 16 Jan. 1641/2, and was *bur.* at St. Leonard's, Eastcheap, London. He *d.*, of the stone (being at that time the "Father of the City"), 24 Feb. 1667/8, aged 81, at his house in Ironmonger lane, Fenchurch street. His body after lying in state in St. Katherine-Cree Church, was *bur.* at Sprowston. M.I. Burial registered at Allhallows', Staining. Funeral Certificate at College of Arms. Will pr. April 1668.

II. 1668. SIR WILLIAM ADAMS, Baronet [1660], of Sprowston Hall, aforesaid, 3d and yst. but only surv. s. and h., *b.* 8 and *bap.* 15 June 1634, at St. Leonard's, Eastcheap; was not improbably the "William Adams, Esq.," who matric. at Oxford (Univ. College) 2 April 1653; *suc. to the Baronetcy* 24 Feb. 1667/8; was Sheriff of Norfolk, 1672-73; Sheriff of Essex, 1678-79. He *m.* firstly, in or before 1658, Anne, sister of Sir James RUSHOUT, 1st Baronet, da. of John RUSHOUT, of Northwick, co. Worcester, Merchant of London, by Anne, da. of Joas GODSCHALCH. He *m.* secondly (Lic. Vic. Gen. 25 Aug. 1679, he about 42, widower, she about 35), Jane, widow of William ALINGTON, of Bury, Suffolk, and of London (*d.* 20 May 1678, in 60th year), da. of (—) BURNETT, of Yarmouth. He *d.* 1687. Admon. 21 May 1690, and again 21 June 1691. His widow *d.* in Bedford Row, 10 and was *bur.* 26 Jan. 1726/7, at St. Andrew's, Holborn. Will dat. 26 July 1726, pr. 26 Jan. 1726/7, and again 12 Nov. 1730.

III. 1687. SIR THOMAS ADAMS, Baronet [1660], of Sprowston Hall, aforesaid, 2d but 1st surv. s. and h. male,(a) by 1st wife; *bap.* 16 Aug. 1659 at St. Dionis, Backchurch; said to be 6 years old at the Heralds' Visitation of Norfolk in 1667; *suc. to the Baronetcy* in 1687. He *d.* unm., Aug. 1690, and was *bur.* at Sprowston.

IV. 1690. SIR CHARLES ADAMS, Baronet [1660], sometime of Sprowston Hall, aforesaid, br. and h. male, being 6th s. of the 2d Baronet, by his 1st wife.(a) He was *b.* about 1665, at Isleham, co. Cambridge, being 2 years old in 1667; ed. at Norwich School for six years; admitted to Gonville and Caius College, Cambridge, Michaelmas 1683, and then aged 17; Scholar, 1683-90; B.A., 1686/7; M.A., 1690; *suc. to the Baronetcy* Aug. 1690; Sheriff of Norfolk, 1693-94. He *m.*, 10 June 1693, at St. James', Westm. (Lic. Vic. Gen., 3 June, he 25, she 18) Frances, da. of Sir Francis ROLLE, of Shapwick, Somerset, by Priscilla, da. of Sir Thomas FOOTE, 1st Baronet [1660]. She *d.* in or before 1724. Her will pr. March 1724. He *d.* s.p. 12 Aug. 1726, and was *bur.* at Ealing, Midx. Will, as of Old Brentford, in Ealing, leaving all (but a few unimportant legacies) to his br. Robert ADAMS, dat. 12 Aug. 1726, and pr. 14 July 1729.

V. 1726. SIR ROBERT ADAMS, Baronet [1660], only surv. br. and h. male, being 8th s. of the 2d Baronet by his 1st wife. In 1699 he had been clerk to an attorney in London, and for nine years had practised there as a Solicitor. He *suc. to the Baronetcy*, 12 Aug. 1726. He *m.* firstly, Dorothea, da. and coheir of Piercy WISEMAN, by (—), da. of Col. (—) CLAGGETT. She *d.* s.p. Feb. 1725/6. He *m.* secondly, before 1741, Diana, da. of (—), of co. Northampton. He *d.* about 1754. Will pr. 1754. His widow *d.* at Wandsworth, 10 Jan. 1765.

(a) His eldest br., William Adams, *bap.* 12 March 1660/1, at St. Dionis, Backchurch, *m.* (Lic. Lond. 13 June 1682), Mary, widow of Francis Buller, da. of Sir John Maynard, of Isleham, co. Cambridge. He d. v.p. and s.p.m., leaving an only da. and h., Jane, who eventually established her right, as heir *general*, to Sprowston and the other family estates, as against that of her uncle, Charles, the 4th Baronet and heir *male*.

VI. 1754? to 1770. SIR THOMAS ADAMS, Baronet [1660], 1st s. and h., by 2d wife, *suc. to the Baronetcy* about 1754; Capt. R.N., 17 Aug. 1760; Commander of His Majesty's frigate, "The Boston," on the Virginian station, 1770. He presumably *m.* (Lic. Dublin 1764, for "Sir Thomas Adams, Baronet") the "Honble. Frances Anne WARTER WILSON," doubtless widow of Ralph WARTER WILSON, of Bilboa, co. Limerick, who *d.* 1756. He *d.* s.p. in Virginia, 12 April 1770, when the *Baronetcy* presumably became *extinct*.(a) Will pr. Nov. 1770.

ATKINS;

cr. 13 June 1660;

ex. 10 June 1756.

I. 1660. "RICHARD ATKINS, of Clapham, Surrey, Esq.," 1st surv. s. and h. of Sir Henry ATKINS, of the same, by Arabella, da. and sole h. of John HAWKINS, of Chiddingstone, Kent, which Henry was s. and h. of Henry ATKINS, M.D., Physician to James I., was probably the Richard ATKINS, of Balliol Coll., Oxford, and who was aged 14 in 1629; suc. his father, 3 July 1638, was Sheriff of Bucks, 1649-50, being of Newport Pagnell in that county, and was *cr. a Baronet*, 13 June 1660. He *m.* in or before 1655, Rebecca, da. and coheir of Sir Edmund WRIGHT, *otherwise* BUNCKLEY, of Swakeleys in Ickenham, Middlesex,, sometime [1640-41] Lord Mayor of London, by his 2d wife, Jane, da. of William MILLS. He *d.* 19 and was *bur.* 24 Aug. 1689, at Clapham. M.I. Admon. 19 Sep. 1689. His widow who was *bap.* 5 June 1634, at St. Olave's Jewry, London, was *bur.* 13 June 1711, at Clapham. Will pr. June 1711.

II. 1689. SIR RICHARD ATKINS, Baronet [1660], of Clapham and of Newport Pagnell aforesaid, only surv. s. and h., *b.* about 1655; Col. of a Regiment of Foot; *suc. to the Baronetcy*, 19 Aug. 1689; was M.P. for Bucks, 1695-96. He *m.*, in or before 1684, Elizabeth, da. of Sir Thomas BYDE, of Ware Park, Herts, by his 1st wife Mary, da. and h. of John SKINNER, of Hitchin. He *d.* 26 Nov. 1696, in his 42d year, and was *bur.* at Newport Pagnell. M.I. The will of a "Dame Elizabeth Atkins" was pr. Nov. 1711.

III. 1696. SIR HENRY ATKINS, Baronet [1660], of Clapham aforesaid, s. and h., *b.* at Hanwell, Midx., about 1684; *suc. to the Baronetcy*, 26 Nov. 1696; matric. at Oxford (Corpus Coll.), 23 April 1700, aged 16. He *m.*, in or before 1707, his 1st cousin, Rebecca Maria, 1st da. of Sir Wolstan DIXIE, 3d Baronet [1660] of Market Bosworth, co. Leicester, by Rebecca, da. of Sir Richard ATKINS, 1st Baronet abovenamed. He was *bur.* 6 Aug. 1712, at Clapham. Will pr. Dec. 1714. His widow *d.* 17 and was *bur.* 24 Aug. 1731, at Clapham.

IV. 1712. SIR HENRY ATKINS, Baronet [1660], of Clapham aforesaid, only s. and h., *b.* at Market Bosworth about 1707; *suc. to the Baronetcy*, Aug. 1712; matric. at Oxford (Mag. Coll.), 8 June 1722, aged 15. He *m.* 31 Oct. 1723 at St. Andrew's Holborn, Penelope, da. of Sir John STONHOUSE, 7th Baronet [1628], of Radley, by his 2d wife, Penelope, da. of Sir Robert DASHWOOD, 1st Baronet [1684]. He *d.* of consumption, in France, 29 March, and was *bur.* 27 April 1728 at Clapham. Will pr. 1728. His widow *m.*, at St. George's,

(a) He had, however, a br. William Adams, probably living in 1741, and perhaps later.

Queen square, Midx., 31 Oct. 1733 (as the 2d of his three wives), John (LEVESON-GOWER), 2d BARON GOWER OF STITTENHAM, who, after her death, was *cr.*, 8 July 1746, EARL GOWER, and who *d.* 25 Dec. 1754, aged 60. She *d.* at Trentham, co. Stafford, 19 Aug. 1734 and was *bur.* there.

V. 1728. SIR HENRY ATKINS, Baronet [1660], of Clapham aforesaid, s. and h., *b.* about 1726; *suc. to the Baronetcy*, 29 March 1728; ed. at Abingdon Grammar School 1732. He *d.* unm. 1 and was *bur.* 9 Sep. 1742, at Clapham, aged 16. Will pr. Sep. 1742.

VI. 1742, to 1756. SIR RICHARD ATKINS, Baronet [1660], of Clapham aforesaid, only br. and h., *b.* about 1728; *suc. to the Baronetcy*, 1 Sep. 1742; Sheriff of Bucks, 1750-51. He *d.* unm. 10 and was *bur.* 17 June 1756 at Clapham, aged 28 when the *Baronetcy* became *extinct.*(a) Will dat. 1 Jan. to 29 May 1756, pr. 1756.

ALLEN, *or* ALEYN;

cr. 14 June 1660;

ex. 10 June 1730.

I. 1660. [SIR] "THOMAS ALLEN, then [*i.e.*, 1659-60], Lord Mayor of London," was(d) 2d of the three sons (living in 1634) of William ALEYN, of London, Druggist (yr. s. of Thomas ALLEN, of Hatfield Peverill, Essex), by Elizabeth, da. of William COMPTON, *or* CROMPTON,(d) also of London (Visit. of London, 1634); was a citizen, and grocer of London, residing in Leadenhall street; Alderman of Cheap Ward, 1652-60; of Aldgate, 1660-79; and of Bridge Without, 25 Nov. 1679 till superseded 4 Oct. 1683, but restored 15 Oct. 1689 till his death; Sheriff, 1654-55; Lord Mayor, 1659-60, conducting Charles II. in great state to London, 29 May 1660,(b) when he was *Knighted* at St. George's, Southwark, being, a few days later, *cr. a Baronet*, 14 June 1660. On 5 July following he entertained the King and both Houses of Parliament at Guildhall. He was at the head of the Commission in 1660 for trying the Regicides; was nominated as a Knight of the intended Order of the Royal Oak in 1660, his estate in London and Midx. being then estimated at £2,000 a year; was M.P. for Midx. 1661-79. He, in 1664, purchased the estate of Pointer Grove, in Totteridge, Midx. Admitted to Gray's Inn, 12 March 1673/4. He *m.* in or before 1648, Elizabeth, da. of (—) BIRCH, of London, Vintner. He *d.* "poor, not above £300 a year,"(d) 15 Dec. 1690, and was *bur.* at Totteridge.

II. 1690, to 1730. SIR THOMAS ALLEN Baronet [1660], of Totteridge, aforesaid, s. and h., *b.* about 1648; *suc. to the Baronetcy*, 15 Dec. 1690. He *m.* Elizabeth, da. of (—) ANGELL, "Serjeant of the [—] at Whitehall."(d) He *d.* s.p.s., 10 June 1730, aged 82, and was *bur.* at Totteridge, when the *Baronetcy* became *extinct.*(c) Will pr. 1730.

(a) On a loose sheet in vol. 3 of the Parish Registers of Clapham along with a small pedigree of the Atkins family (remaining in 1873) is this note.—"Sir Richard Atkins, ob. 1756, resided at Lovelace's house; kept Fanny Murray, died unmarried and young." On his death the estates went to his only sister and h., Penelope, who *m.*, 4 Jan. 1745/61, George (PITT), 1st Baron Rivers and *d.* 8 Feb. 1795, leaving issue.

(b) His Pageant was entitled (as were many others) "*London's Triumph*," celebrated 29 Oct. 1659, and was by John Tatham. It is so scarce that Fairholt (author of the history of these Pageants) was not able to see a copy.

(c) It is so reckoned in Wotton's *Baronetage*, pub. (ten years later) in 1741.

(d) Le Neve's *Baronets*.

NORTH:

cr. 14 June 1660;

ex. 5 July 1695.

I. 1660. "HENRY NORTH, of Mildenhall, Suffolk, Esq.," s. and h. of Sir Roger NORTH, of the same, and of Great Finborough in the said county, by his 1st wife, Elizabeth, da. and coheir of Sir John GILBERT, of Finborough aforesaid (which Roger was s. and h. of the Hon. Sir Henry NORTH, of Mildenhall, aforesaid, yr. s. of Roger, LORD NORTH DE KIRTLING), was admitted to Gray's Inn, 1 Nov. 1624; was M.P. for Suffolk, 1656-58, 1660 and 1661 till death, and was *cr. a Baronet*, 14 June 1660. He *m.* firstly, Sarah, da. of John RAYNE, *or* RAYNEY, of West Malling, Kent, Citizen of London. She *d.* 1 July 1670. He *m.* secondly (—) da. of (—) ONSLOW. He *d.* 29 Aug. 1671, and was *bur.* at Mildenhall.

II. 1671, to 1695. SIR HENRY NORTH, Baronet [1660], of Mildenhall aforesaid, only s. and h. by 1st wife; admitted to Gray's Inn, 6 Nov. 1647; *suc. to the Baronetcy*, 29 Aug. 1671; was M.P. for Suffolk, 1685-87. He *d.* unm., 5 July 1695, when the *Baronetcy* became *extinct*. Will dat. 10 June, pr. 12 Sep. 1695.

WISEMAN:

cr. 15 June 1660;

ex. 14 June 1688.

I. 1660, to 1688. "SIR WILIAM WISEMAN, of Rivenhall, Essex, Knt.," s. and h. of Sir Thomas WISEMAN, of the same, by Elizabeth(a) (*m.* 3 Dec. 1616, at St. Bartholomew the Great), da. of Sir Isaac SEDLEY, 1st Baronet [1621], of Great Chart, was aged 5 years in 1634; suc. his father about 1659, and, having been *Knighted*, was *cr. a Baronet*, 15 June 1660; was M.P. for Malden, Feb. 1677 to 1679 and 1679-80. He *m.*, before 1664, Elizabeth, da. of Sir Lewis MANSEL, 2d Baronet [1611], of Margam, by his 3d wife, Elizabeth, da. of Henry (MONTAGU), EARL OF MANCHESTER. He *d.* s.p.m.(a), in London, and was *bur.* there 14 June 1688, when the *Baronetcy* became *extinct*. Burial reg. at Rivenhall. Admon. 2 July 1688 to relict, Elizabeth. Her will pr. Jan. 1708.

CULLUM:

cr. 18 June 1660;

ex. 28 Jan. 1855.

I. 1660. "THOMAS CULLUM of Hawsted, co. Suffolk, Esq.," s. of John CULLUM(b) of Stanhill in Thorndon, in that county (*bur.* there 27 Feb. 1609), by Rebecca, da. of Thomas SMYTHE, of Bacton, Suffolk, was *b.* about 1587; was citizen and draper of London; Alderman of Cordwainer Ward, 3 Aug. 1643, till discharged 23 Dec. 1652; Sheriff 1646—47, when he was one of the five Aldermen who were in that year committed to the Tower as Royalists, and disabled in 1649.(c) He in 1656 purchased the estates of

(a) Elizabeth, his only da. and h., living 1664, *m.* firstly John Lamotte Honywood, of Markshall, Essex, and secondly Sir Isaac Rebow. The estate of Rivenhall was sold to Thomas Western.

(b) He was s. of John Cullum, of the same place, citizen of London, a successful draper in Gracechurch street.

(c) See p. 24, note "c," under "Bunce."

Hawstead and Hardwicke, co. Suffolk(a), and was, subsequently when about 70 years old, *cr. a Baronet*, 18 June 1660. He *m.* 18 Feb. 1622/3, at Allhallows', Lombard street, Mary, 2d. da. and coheir of Nicholas CRISPE, of London, Merchant, by Rebecca, da. of John PAKE of Broomfield, Essex. She who was *bap.* at Allhallows' aforesaid, 18 April 1602, *d.* 22 and was *bur.* there 28 July 1637, aged 36. M.I. at St. Benet's Gracechurch, London. He *d.* 6 and was *bur.* 9 April 1664, at Hawstead aforesaid, aged 77. M.I.(b) Will dat. 2 May 1662, pr. 20 May 1664.

II. 1664. SIR THOMAS CULLUM, Baronet [1660], of Hawstead Place in Hawstead, and Hardwick House in Hardwick aforesaid, 1st s. and h.; *bap.* 26 Dec. 1628, at Allhallows' aforesaid; *suc. to the Baronetcy*, 6 April 1664. He *m.* 27 May 1656, at Wickhambrook, Suffolk, Dudleia, 3d sister and coheir of Sir Henry NORTH, 2d Baronet [1660], of Mildenhall, Suffolk, da. of Sir Henry NORTH, 1st Baronet, by Sarah, da. of John RAYNEY. They both *d.* within six weeks of each other. She, who was *bap.* at Wickambrook, 13 Jan. 1637, was *bur.* 10 Sep., and he was *bur.* 16 Oct. 1680, both at Hawstead aforesaid. His will dat. 13 Sep. 1679, pr. 1 Feb. 1680/1.

III. 1680. SIR DUDLEY CULLUM, Baronet [1660], of Hawstead Place and Hardwick House aforesaid, 1st s. and h., *bap.* at Wickambrook, 17 Sep. 1657; ed. at Bury School and at St. John's College, Cambridge (1675); *suc. to the Baronetcy*, 16 Oct. 1680; Sheriff of Suffolk, 1689, but did not act; and M.P. for that county, 1702-05. He *m.* firstly, 3 Sep. 1681, at Berkeley [afterwards Devonshire] House, St. Martin's-in-the-Fields, Anne, da. of John (BERKELEY), 1st BARON BERKELEY OF STRATTON, by Christian, da. and h. of Sir Andrew RICCARD. She *d.* s.p. aged 44 and was *bur.* 2 June 1709, at Hawstead. M.I. He *m.* secondly, 12 June 1710, at Hawstead, Anne, da. of James WICKS, of Bury St. Edmunds, by Dorothy his wife. He *d.* s.p. 16 and was *bur.* 27 Sep. 1720, at Hawstead, aged 63. M.I. Will dat. 20 March 1715 to 16 April 1716, pr. 17 Feb. 1720/1. His widow *m.* Rev. John FULHAM, Rector of Compton, Surrey, Vicar of Isleworth, Middlesex, Archdeacon of Llandaff, and Canon of Windsor, who *d.* at Compton aforesaid, July 1777, aged 80. She *d.* 22 Jan. and was *bur.* 3 Feb. 1737, at Hawstead, aged 55. M.I.

IV. 1720. SIR JASPER CULLUM, Baronet [1660], of Hawstead Place and Hardwick House aforesaid, cousin and h. male, being 4th s. and h. male, of John Cullum, of London, by Anna (*m.* April 1662), da. of Thomas LAWRENCE, of Woodborough, Wilts, which John (who *d.* Jan. 1710/1, aged 75), was 2d s. of the 1st Baronet. He was *bap.* 6 Aug. 1674, at Allhallows', Lombard street, and *suc to the Baronetcy*, 16 Sep. 1720; was Sheriff of Suffolk, 1721-22. He *m.* 27 Jan. 1697/8, at Allhallows' aforesaid, Anne, da. and h. of William WYATT,(c) of Bursledon, Hants., by Anne, his wife. She *d.* 9 and was *bur.* 17 Feb. 1735/6, at Hawstead, aged 56. He *d.* 4 and was *bur.* there 8 Nov. 1754, aged 84. M.I.

V. 1754. SIR JOHN CULLUM, Baronet [1660], of Hawstead Place and Hardwick House aforesaid, only s. and h.; *bap.* 7 May 1699 at St. Benet's, Gracechurch street; was, in 1725, a Barrister of the Inner Temple, London; *suc. to the Baronetcy*, 4 Nov. 1754. He *m.* firstly (Lic. 6 July 1728), Jane, da. and h. of Thomas DEANE, Esq., of Freefolk, Hants. She *d.* s.p.m., and was *bur.* 14 Dec. 1729, at Whitchurch, Hants. He *m.* secondly, 30 Nov. 1731, at Ely Chapel, St. Andrew's, Holborn, Susanna, 2d da. and coheir of Sir Thomas

(a) See "*History of Hawstead*," etc., by the Rev. Sir John Cullum, the 7th Baronet, pub. in 1784 and 1813. See also J. J. Muskett's "*Suffolk Manorial Families*."

(b) His town house stood on the site of Cullum street.

(c) He *d.* June 1693, aged 39. His widow *m.* Michael BRIXEY, who was *bur.* 6 Dec. 1729, at Hawstead. She *d.*, aged 98, and was *bur.* there 16 Jan. 1757.

GERY, one of the Masters in Chancery, by Elizabeth, da. of James WITTEWRONGE, of Rothamstead, Herts. He *d.* 16 and was *bur.* 22 Jan. 1774 at Hawstead in his 75th year. M.I. Will dat. 20 July 1773, pr. 17 March 1774. His widow *d.* at Bury 12 and was *bur.* 18 Nov. 1783, at Hawstead, aged 72. M.I.

VI. 1774. SIR JOHN CULLUM, Baronet [1660], of Hawstead Place and Hardwick House aforesaid, s. and h. by 2d wife, *b.* 21 June 1733, and *bap.* 19 July following in the chapel at Hawstead Place; ed. at Bury School and at Catharine Hall, Cambridge; B.A., 1756; Fellow, 1759; in Holy Orders; Rector of Hawstead, 1762; Rector of Great Thurlow, Suffolk, 1774; *suc. to the Baronetcy*, 16 Jan. 1774; F.S.A., 1774; F.R.S., 1775; author of the *History of Hawstead and Hardwick*. He *m.*, 10 July 1765, at Westham, Essex, Peggy, only da. of Daniel BISSON, of Westham aforesaid. He *d.* s.p., at Hardwick House, 9 and was *bur.* 15 Oct. 1785 at Hawstead, aged 52. M.I. Will dat. 1 Dec. 1784 to 2 Oct. 1785, pr. 7 Nov. 1785. His widow, who was *bap.* 15 Feb. 1731/2, at St. Leonard's, Bromley, *d.* at Hardwick House, 2 Aug. 1810, aged 78, and was *bur.* with her husband. M.I. Will dat. 15 March 1807, pr. 22 Aug. 1810.

VII. 1785. SIR THOMAS GERY CULLUM, Baronet [1660], of Hawstead Place and Hardwick House aforesaid, br. and h., *b.* 30 Nov. 1741, at Hardwick, and *bap.* in the chapel there, 5 Jan. 1742; ed. at Corpus Coll., Cambridge, appointed Bath and Gloucester King of Arms, 14 Dec. 1771, which office he resigned in March 1801.(a) He was F.R.S., F.S.A., and F.L.S. He *suc. to the Baronetcy*, 9 Oct, 1785. He *m.* 1 Sep. 1774, at St. Mary's, Bury, Mary, sister and coheir of SIR Levett HANSON, Chamberlain to the Duke of Modena, da. of Robert HANSON, of Bury aforesaid, and of Normanton, co. York, by Elizabeth, da. of Edward Isaac Jackson, of Bury. She who was *b.* 28 Jan. 1745, *d.* 13 and was *bur.*, 18 Sep. 1830, at Hawstead in her 86th year. He *d.* in Northgate street, Bury, 8 and was *bur.*, 13 Sep. 1831, at Hawstead, aged 89. Will pr. Dec. 1831.

VIII. 1831, to 1855. SIR THOMAS GERY CULLUM, Baronet [1660], of Hawstead Place, and Hardwick House aforsaid, 1st s. and h., *b.* at Bury, 23 Oct. and *bap.* 19 Dec. 1777, at St. Mary's in that town; ed. at Pemb. Coll., Cambridge; B.A., 1799; M.A., 1802; took Holy Orders; was sometime Rector of Knoddishall, Suffolk, which he resigned when he *suc. to the Baronetcy*, 8 Sep. 1831; was Chaplain to H.R.H. the Duke of Sussex. He *m.* firstly, 27 Aug. 1805, at Woodford, Essex, Mary Anne, da. and h. of Thomas EGGERS, of Woodford aforesaid. She *d.* at Rue D'Augoulême, Paris, 29 Jan., and was *bur.* 20 Feb. 1830, at Hawstead, aged 47. He *m.* secondly, 30 April 1832, at St. Marylebone, "Miss LLOYD, of Kingston, Dublin," *viz.* Anne LLOYD, sister of William HANFORD-FLOOD, of Flood Hall, co. Kilkenny. He *d.* s.p.m.(b) at Hardwick, 26 Jan. and was *bur.* 3 Feb. 1855, at Hawstead, aged 67, when the *Baronetcy* became *extinct*. Will pr. March 1855. His widow *d.* at Hardwick House aforesaid, and was *bur.* 23 Feb. 1875, at Hawstead.

(a) This resignation was in favour of his 2d and yst. son, John Palmer Cullum, *b.* 18 May 1783, who was consequently appointed, in his 18th year, Bath King of Arms, 3 April 1801, and, a few days later, 21 April 1801, Gloucester King of Arms. He was also an Attorney and an Alderman of Bury, where he *d.* s.p., somewhat suddenly, 20 Aug. 1829.

(b) Arethusa Susanna his only da. and h. (by 1st wife) *b.* 11 Jan. 1814, *m.* 23 Feb. 1832, the Rt. Hon. Thomas Milner-Gibson, of Theberton House, Suffolk, (who *d.* 25 Feb. 1884), and left at her death, 22 Feb. 1885, issue, of whom the 2d son took by Royal Lic., 13 Dec. 1878, the name of Cullum on succeeding to the estates of that family.

DIXWELL:

cr. 19 June 1660;([a])

ex. 25 March 1750.

I. 1660. "BASIL DIXWELL, of Bromehouse [in Barham], co. Kent, Esq." s. and h. of Mark DIXWELL,([b]) of the same, by Elizabeth, sister and h. of William READ, of Folkestone, Kent, da. of Matthew READ, was *b.* 22 June 1640; suc. his father, 1643, and was *cr. a Baronet,* 19 June 1660.([a]) He *m.* 15 March 1659/60, at Chelsea, Midx., Dorothy, 1st da. and coheir of Sir Thomas PEYTON, 2d Baronet [1611], of Knowlton, by his 1st wife, Elizabeth, da. of Sir Peter OSBORNE. He *d.* 7 May 1668 in London. Will pr. 1668.

II. 1668, to 1750. SIR BASIL DIXWELL, Baronet [1660], of Brome House aforesaid, only s. and h., *b.* 11 Dec. 1665; *suc. to the Baronetcy,* 7 May 1668; matric. at Oxford (Ch. Ch.), 15 Nov. 1682, aged 16. M.P. for Dover (three Parls.), 1689-90 and 1698-1700; Governor of Dover Castle; Auditor of Excise, being dismissed by Queen Anne, but restored by George I. He *m.* firstly, Dorothy, said to have been da. of John TEMPLE of East Sheen, Surrey, Paymaster General. She *d.* about 1718. He *m.* secondly, 25 April 1720, at St. Martin's-in-the-Fields, his cousin, Catharine, da. of William LONGUEVILLE, of the Inner Temple, London, by Elizabeth, da. and coheir of Sir Thomas PEYTON, 2d Baronet [1611], abovenamed. He *d.*, s.p., 25 March 1750, when the *Baronetcy* became *extinct.*([c]) Will pr. 1750.

DARCY:

cr. 19([d]) June 1660;

ex. Oct. 1698.

I. 1660. "THOMAS DARCY, of St. Clere's Hall, in St. Osyths, Essex, Esq.," and of Tiptree, in that county, posthumous s. and h. of Thomas DARCY, of the same, by Mary, da. of Sir Andrew ASTLEY, of Writtle, Essex, was *b.* 1632, and *cr. a Baronet,* 19 June 1660; M.P. for Malden (five Parls.), 1679 till death. He *m.* firstly, Cicely, da. of Sir Symonds D'EWES, 1st Baronet [1641], by his 1st wife, Anne, da. and h. of Sir William CLOPTON. By her he had no surv. issue. She was *bur.* 1 June 1661, in the Clopton aisle, at Long Melford, Suffolk. M.I. He *m.* secondly (Lic. Vic. Gen., 12 Feb. 1662/3), Jane, da. and h. of Robert COLE, of the Temple, London. He *d.* 1693. His will, as well as that of his wife, proved in 1693.

([a]) The date of 19 June 1660, is that ascribed to this creation in Wotton's *Baronetage* and elsewhere. It is, however, sometimes given as *18* June 1640, and placed next before "Cullum," while in Dugdale's "*Catalogue*" it is given as 19 *July* 1660, and placed between "Honywood" and "Browne."

([b]) This Mark Dixwell, son of William Dixwell, of Coton Hall, co. Warwick, was nephew of Sir Basil Dixwell, Baronet (so *cr.* 18 Feb. 1627/8), of Tirlingham, co. Kent, whose estates he inherited 28 Dec. 1642.

([c]) He left his estates to his great nephew, George Oxenden (grandson of his sister, Elizabeth, wife of George Oxenden, LL.D.), who took the name of Dixwell, but *d.*, s.p., 20 Oct. 1753, being suc. by his elder br., Sir Henry Oxenden, 6th Baronet [1678].

([d]) The date in Dugdale's *Catalogue* is given as *20* June 1660.

II. 1693, to 1698. SIR GEORGE([a]) DARCY, Baronet [1660], of St. Osyths and Tiptree, aforesaid, and of Braxted, Essex, 1st s. and h. by 2d wife, *b.* about 1677; *suc. to the Baronetcy* in 1693; matric. at Oxford, 10 Dec. 1695, aged 18. He *d.* unm., Oct. 1698, at Chelsea, when the *Baronetcy* became *extinct.*([b]) Admon. 6 Dec. 1698.

HOWE:

cr. 20([c]) June 1660;

ex. 19 Jan. 1735/6.

I. 1660. "GEORGE GRUBHAM HOWE, of Cold Barwick, Wilts., Esq.," s. and h. of Sir George HOWE,([d]) of the same, by Dorothy, da. of Humphrey CLARKE, *otherwise* WOODCHURCH, of Woodchurch, Kent, was admitted to Lincoln's Inn, 19 April 1646, was M.P. for Hindon, 1660 and 1661 till death, and was *cr. a Baronet,* 20 June([c]) 1660. He *m.* 1650, Elizabeth, da. of Sir Harbottle GRIMSTON, 2d Baronet [1611], of Bradfield, Master of the Rolls, by his 1st wife, Mary, da. of Sir George CROKE, Justice of the Common Pleas. He *d.* 26 Sep. 1676. Will pr. 1676. The will of his widow pr. May 1709.

II. 1676, to 1736. SIR JAMES HOWE, Baronet [1660], of Cold Barwick, aforesaid, s. and h., *b.* about 1670, *suc. to the Baronetcy,* 26 Sep. 1676; was M.P. for Hindon, 1693-1700, 1701, 1702-05, and 1708 till void the same year. He *m.* firstly Elizabeth, da. of Edward NUTT, of Nackington, Kent. She *d.* 8 Sep. 1694. He *m.* secondly Elizabeth, da. and coheir of (—) STRATFORD, of Halling, co. Gloucester. He *d.*, s.p., 19 Jan. 1735/6, aged 66, when the *Baronetcy* became *extinct.* Will pr. 1736.

CUTTS:

cr. 21 June 1660;

ex. 1670.

I. 1660, to 1670. "JOHN CUTTS, of Childerley, co. Cambridge, Esq.," s. and h. of Sir John CUTTS of the same, and of Thaxted, Essex, by his 2d wife, Anne (*m.* Dec. 1632), da. of Sir John WELD, of Arnolds, Midx., was *b.* about 1634, being aged 5 years in 1639; suc. his father in 1646; was *cr. a Baronet,* 21 June 1660. He *d.* unm. 1670, at Salisbury, when the *Baronetcy* became *extinct.*([e]) Will pr. June 1670.

([a]) Often, erroneously, called Thomas.

([b]) Frances, his sister and h., *m.*, Nov. 1692, Sir William Dawes, 3d Baronet [1663], afterwards Archbishop of Canterbury.

([c]) The date in Dugdale's *Catalogue* is given as *21* June 1660.

([d]) He was younger br. to Sir John Howe, 1st Baronet [1660], of Compton, co. Gloucester, both being sons of John Howe, by Jane, sister and heir of Richard Grubham, of Wishford, and Cold Barwick, Wilts, and of Compton, co. Gloucester.

([e]) The estate of Childerley passed to his distant cousin, John Cutts, of Woodhall, Essex, whose 2d s. but eventually h., John Cutts, a most distinguished officer, was in 1690 *cr.* Baron Cutts of Gowran [I.], and *d.* s.p. 1707, having previously, in 1686, sold Childerley to Felix Calvert.

SWALE:

cr. 21 June 1660;

ex. apparently about 1760;

assumed since 1877.

I. 1660. "SOLOMON SWALE, of Swale Hall [in South Stainley], co. York, Esq.," eldest of the thirteen sons([a]) of Francis SWALE, of South Stainley aforesaid, by Anne, da. of Sampson INGLEBY, of Ripley, was *b.* about 1609, being aged 3 in 1612, and aged 55 in 1665 (Visits. of Yorkshire); suc. his father 26 Dec. 1629; admitted to Gray's Inn (being then of Staple Inn) 2 Feb. 1629/30; was M.P. for Aldborough, 1660 (in which Parl. he is said to have proposed the Restoration of the King), as also 1661 to 1678, and was *cr. a Baronet,* 21 June 1660. He was Sheriff of Yorkshire, 1670-71. He *m.* firstly, in or before 1637, Mary, da. of Robert POREY, of Poreys, Norfolk, by whom he had seven children. She was *bur.* at Paddington, Middx., in 1654. M.I. He *m.* secondly, before 1665, Anne (*bap.* 28 May 1609, at Aldborough), widow of Sir William ALLENSON, twice Lord Mayor of York (*d.* 6 Dec. 1656), 4th da. of Charles TANKARD, of Whixley, in that county, by Barbara, da. of William WYVELL. He *d.* 4 and was *bur.* 7 Nov. 1678 at St. Martin's-in-the-Fields, aged 70. Will pr. 1679.

II. 1678. SIR HENRY SWALE, Baronet, of Swale Hall aforesaid, 3d but 1st surv. s. and h., *b.* about 1639; admitted to Gray's Inn 29 Nov. 1648; matric. at Oxford (Balliol Coll.) 23 July 1656; was aged 26 in 1665; *suc. to the Baronetcy,* 4 Nov. 1678. He *m.* before Aug. 1665, Dorothy, da. of Thomas CRATHORNE, of Crathorne, co. York, by his 2d wife, Margaret, da. of Robert THORNETON, of Newton, in that county. He *d.* 19 Jan. 1682/3 and was *bur.* at South Stainley, aged 43.

III. 1683. SIR SOLOMON SWALE, Baronet [1660], of Swale Hall aforesaid, 1st s. and h., *b.* about 1665; *suc. to the Baronetcy,* 19 Jan. 1682/3. He, by action of the Crown, lost a great part of his estate, which had been held by a lease from the same. He *d.* unm. 30 Dec. 1733 and was *bur.* (near his grandmother) 3 Jan. 1733/4, in Paddington Church, aged 68. Will dat. 23 Nov. 1733, pr. 11 Feb. 1733/4 in the Commissary Court of London.

IV. 1733, to 1760? SIR SEBASTIAN FABIAN ENRIQUE SWALE, Baronet [1660], nephew and h., being 1st s. and h. of Henry SWALE, of Malaga, in Spain, merchant, by Elizabeth, da. of Rose Lunetia, da. of (—) COLOMO, also of Malaga, Merchant, which Henry was 2d s. of the 2d Baronet. He *suc. to the Baronetcy,* 30 Dec. 1733. He *m.* in or before 1738, Elizabeth, da. of (—) SMITH, of Poole, Dorset. He *d.*, apparently s.p.m.,([b]) at a date between 1741 and 1771,([c]) when the male issue of the 2d Baronet came to an end, and the *Baronetcy,* which is presumed then to have become *extinct,* was certainly *dormant* for above a century.

([a]) Of these sons, three were officers in the Royal cause, viz., (1) John, Captain of a Company of Foot, who was living, with issue, in 1665; (2) Charles, a Major in the army, who was in the garrison at Oxford and who *d.* s.p. in France before 1665, and (3) Robert, the 13th son, who was a Captain in the army of Charles I., as well as that of Charles II., and who was living, with issue, in 1665.

([b]) According to information supplied by himself to the editor of Wotton's *Baronetage* in 1741, three daughters were then living.

([c]) In Kimber's *Baronetage,* published in 1771, the title is given as "extinct."

V.([a]) 1877. SIR JOHN SWALE, Baronet([b]) [1660], of Birtley, co. Durham, assumed that title 8 March 1877, according to a notice of that date([c]) stating that he was heir male of the body of the grantee, as being "s. and h. male of William SWALE, s. and h. of William SWALE, s. and h. of William SWALE, s. and h. of William SWALE,([d]) s. and h. of Robert SWALE, 2d s. of Sir Solomon SWALE [the 1st] Baronet." He was 1st s. of William SWALE, of Rudfarlington, near Knaresborough,

([a]) These numbers take no account of any who may have had, or may have supposed themselves to have had, a right to the Baronetcy after the death of the 4th Baronet, and before the assumption in 1877.

([b]) According to the assumption of the Baronetcy in 1877.

([c]) The following is a copy of this notice as given in Foster's *Baronetage* for 1883, under "Chaos":—

"SWALE OF SWALE HALL,

County of York.—*Times,* 28 Jan. [*sic,* but the date of the document itself is 8 March] 1877.

"Whereas King Charles II, by his letters patent bearing date the 21st day of June 1660, conferred the rank, style and title of a Baronet upon SOLOMON SWALE, of Swale Hall and South Stainley, in the county of York, Esq., M.P. (in consideration for his great sufferings for his loyalty to King Charles I, and having in his place in Parliament proposed the Restoration of the said King Charles II), to hold to the said Solomon Swale and the heirs male lawfully begotten of his body for ever. And Whereas the said Solomon Swale, Baronet, had, amongst other children lawfully begotten of his body, two sons namely HENRY SWALE and ROBERT SWALE. And Whereas upon the death of SIR SEBASTIAN SWALE, the 4th Baronet, all the issue male lawfully begotten of the body of the said Henry Swale, eldest son of the said Sir Solomon Swale, Baronet, aforesaid, became and was entirely extinct and ended. And whereas I, who have hitherto been known as the Reverend JOHN SWALE, O.S.B., of Birtley in the county of Durham, am the son and heir male of WILLIAM SWALE, son and heir of WILLIAM SWALE, son and heir of WILLIAM SWALE, son and heir of WILLIAM SWALE, son and heir of the said ROBERT SWALE, second [surviving] son of the said Sir Solomon Swale, Baronet, as aforesaid; and by virtue of my said lineage as aforesaid I am the heir male lawfully begotten of the body of the said Sir Solomon Swale, so created a Baronet as aforesaid, and as such I am lawfully entitled to the said rank style and title of a Baronet under the said limitations of the same letters patent by which the said title was created as aforesaid, and which is fully set forth in a pedigree compiled by the celebrated genealogist, James Philippe, and enrolled in Her Majesty's High Court of Chancery on the 2d day of March 1877. And Whereas I consider it a sacred duty which I owe to the memory of my ancestors, and for the future benefit and welfare of my family to assume and take unto myself and the heirs male of the body of the said Sir Solomon Swale, Baronet lawfully begotten of his body, the title of a Baronet, Now be it known to all whom these presents may concern that I the said John Swale, have assumed the said Baronetcy and will hereafter be known only as the *Reverend Sir John Swale, Baronet,* O.S.B., at present of Birtley aforesaid. Dated this 8th day of March 1877. [*Signed*] JOHN SWALE. WITNESS, John Johnson, Birtley, near Chester-le-street, Agent. Vouched by me, G. H. de S. N. Plantagenet Harrison.—'*Times,*' 10 March 1877."

([d]) The descent of the four persons named William Swale from Robert, 2d surv. s. of the 1st Baronet, is unsupported by any evidence. The information given by the 4th Baronet in 1741 (see p. 46, note "b") respecting this Robert, his father's uncle, is that he was a doctor of physic, and left (by Isabel, da. of Thomas Mitchell, of London) two sons, Robert and William, both, apparently, living 1741. According to a pedigree, contributed (for the sake of acquiring evidence either in support of or against its validity) to the *Mis. Gen. et Her.* (N.S. vol. ii, p. 44) by "J. H. Chapman, M.A.," this Dr. Robert Swale was born 1635 and died 1690. As, however, Sir Henry, the 2d Baronet, his *elder* brother, was aged 26 in

III

co. York, by Helen, da. of Richard BLACKBURNE, of Scriven, in that county; was *b.* 1808; ed. at the College of Douay, in France; took Holy Orders, and was a Priest of the Order of St. Benedict in the Church of Rome; was for many years proprietor and landlord of the Royal Oak Hotel, Knaresborough; *assumed the Baronetcy*, 8 March 1877, as above stated. He *d.* unm. suddenly of cardial syncope, at the Royal Oak Hotel aforesaid, 23 July 1888, aged 80.

VI.(a) 1888. SIR BENJAMIN SWALE, Baronet(b) [1660], of Knaresborough aforesaid, next surv. br. and h. male, *b.* 1816; *suc. to the Baronetcy*,(b) 23 July 1888. He *m.* in 1840, Jane, da. of Samuel WADDINGTON. She *d.* 1862. He *d.* s.p. Oct. 1889, aged 73, at Scalabers, near Plumpton, the house of his nephew, James SWALE.

VII.(a) 1889. SIR JAMES SWALE, Baronet(b) [1660], of Rudfarlington aforesaid, br. and h., *b.* 1818; *suc. to the Baronetcy*,(b) in Oct. 1889. He *m.* in 1855, Sarah, da. of Samuel BISHOP, of Sheffield. He *d.* at Rudfarlington in Oct. 1901, aged 83.

VIII.(a) 1901. SIR JAMES BISHOP SWALE, Baronet(b) [1660], of Rudfarlington aforesaid, 1st s. and h., *b.* 1867; *suc. to the Baronetcy*,(b) Oct. 1901.

HUMBLE:

cr. 21 June 1660;

ex. 6 Feb. 1745.

I 1660. "WILLIAM HUMBLE, Citizen of London," 1st s. of George HUMBLE, citizen and stationer of London, sometime (1633) deputy of Langbourne Ward (when he entered his pedigree in the Visit. of London), by Agnes, da. of John MOODY, was *b.* 1612; is said to have furnished £20,000 to Charles II. when in exile,(c) and was *cr. a Baronet* 21 June 1660. He was Sheriff of Surrey, 1664-65, and of Lincolnshire, 1672-73. He *m.*, apparently about 1650, Eliza, da. of John ALLANSON. He *d.* 26 Dec. 1686. Will pr. 3 Jan. 1686/7.

II. 1686. SIR WILLIAM HUMBLE, Baronet [1660], of Stratford Langthorne, Essex, grandson and h., being 1st s. and h. of George HUMBLE, of Stratford aforesaid, by Mary, da. of Sir John NULLS, of London, which George, who *d.* v.p., was 1st s. and h. ap. of the late Baronet. He was *b.* about 1667; *suc. to the Baronetcy*, 26 Dec. 1686, and *d.* unm. two months afterwards, Feb. 1686/7, aged 20. Admon. 19 March 1686/7.

III. 1687. SIR GEORGE HUMBLE, Baronet [1660], br. and h., *b.* about 1670; *suc. to the Baronetcy* in Feb. 1686/7. He *d.* unm., being killed in quarrel at the Blue Posts tavern in March 1702/3.

1665, the birth of Robert could not have been before 1640. Of the two sons, Robert and William, therein assigned to him, William, the younger son, is credited with having left issue, while the elder son, Robert, is said to have been born 1662, and to have died 1710, leaving (by Mary, da. of J. Lumley, of North Allerton) a son, John, born 1700, who (by "a da. or niece of Sir Rowland Winn, of Nostell Priory") left issue.

(a) See p. 47, note "a."

(b) According to the assumption of the Baronetcy in 1877.

(c) His only br., Thomas Humble, merchant, is said to have "run the hazard of his life by carrying money" to that King during his banishment.

IV. 1703. SIR JOHN HUMBLE, Baronet [1660], of Thorpe Underwood, in Rothwell, co. Northampton, br. and h., *b.* 1680; *suc. to the Baronetcy*, in March 1702/3; was Paymaster to the Lottery. He *m.* (Lic. Fac. 10 July 1705) Sarah, 3d and yst da. and coheir of Andrew LANT (*d.* 17 Jan. 1694/5, in his 57th year), of Thorpe Underwood aforesaid,(a) by Judith (*m.* Oct. 1662), da. of William VANNAM, of St. Pancras, Soper Lane, London. He *d.* 7 Feb. 1723/4, at Chelsea, in his 44th year, and was *bur.* at Rothwell. Will dat. 3 Sep. 1721, pr. 4 March 1723/4. His widow *d.* Oct. 1739, and was *bur.* at Rothwell. Will pr. 15 Jan. 1739/40.

V. 1724. SIR WILLIAM HUMBLE, Baronet [1660], of Thorpe Underwood aforesaid, 4th but only surv. s. and h.; *suc. to the Baronetcy*, 7 Feb. 1723/4. He *m.* Oct. 1732, Elizabeth,(b) sister of Henry, 1st EARL OF DARLINGTON, 2d da. of Gilbert (VANE), 2d BARON BARNARD, by Mary, da. and h. of Morgan RANDYLL. He *d.* Oct. 1742, and was *bur.* at Rothwell. Will pr. 11 Feb. 1742/3. His widow *d.* 22 Feb. 1770, aged 57, and was *bur.* at Rothwell. M.I. Her will dat. 1 Aug. 1758, pr. 1 March 1770.

VI. 1742, to 1745. SIR JOHN HUMBLE, Baronet [1660], of Thorpe Underwood aforesaid, 2d and yst. but only surv. s. and h.,(c) *b.* about 1739; *suc. to the Baronetcy* in Oct. 1742. He *d.* at school at Felstead, in Essex, 6 Feb. 1745, aged 6 years, and was *bur.* at Rothwell, when *the Baronetcy* became *extinct.*

STAPLETON, *or* STAPYLTON:

cr. 22 June 1660;

ex. 2 Jan. 1817.

I. 1660. "HENRY STAPLETON, of Myton (near Boroughbridge), co. York, Esq.," 1st s. and h. of Bryan STAPYLTON, *or* STAPLETON, of the same, by Frances, da. of Sir Henry SLINGSBY, of Scriven, in that county, was *b.* about 1617; matric. at Oxford (St. Alban Hall) 13 June 1635, aged 19; admitted to the Inner Temple, Nov. 1636; M.P. for Boroughbridge, Nov. 1647 (taking the covenant 23 Feb. 1647/8), till secluded Dec. 1648, being re-elected 1660; suc. his father in or shortly before 1658, and was *cr. a Baronet*, 22 June 1660. He *m.* 18 Oct. 1650, at Hornby, Elizabeth, 2d da. of Conyers (DARCY), 1st EARL OF HOLDERNESS, by Grace, da. of Thomas ROKEBY. She was *bap.* 8 Dec. 1624, at Hornby. He *d.* 1679, and was *bur.* at Myton. Will pr. 1679.

II. 1679. SIR BRYAN STAPYLTON, Baronet [1660], of Myton aforesaid, 1st s. and h., *b.* about 1657; matric. at Oxford (Ch. Ch.) 3 Nov. 1674, aged 17; B.A., 16 June 1677; *suc. to the Baronetcy* in 1679; M.P. for Aldborough, 1679-81, and for Boroughbridge (eight Parls.) Nov. 1690 to 1695, 1698-1705, and 1708-15; Sheriff of Yorkshire, 1683-84. He *m.* 15 April 1680, at

(a) This Andrew was s. and h. of Robert Lant, of London, merchant, by Elizabeth, da. and h. of Richard Andrews, of Thorpe Underwood aforesaid.

(b) Her elder sister, the Hon. Anne Vane, who, though one of the Maids of Honour, was the mother, 4 June 1732, of a son by Frederick, Prince of Wales, is referred to by Dr. Johnson in his *Vanity of Human Wishes*, in the line "Yet VANE can tell what ills from *beauty* spring." She *d.* at Bath unm. 11 March 1735/6.

(c) His elder br., Robert, who was *bap.* 14 Jan. 1734, at Kingsthorpe, co. Northampton, *d.* v.p. in childhood, being *bur.* at Rothwell.

H

Almondbury, Anne, only da. of Sir John KAYE, 2d Baronet [1642] of Woodsome, co. York, by Anne, da. of William LISTER, of Thornton in Craven. He *d.* 23 Nov. 1727. Will pr. 1728. His widow, who was *bap.* 19 Jan. 1663/4, at Kirkheaton, *d.* 1 March 1729/30. Her will pr. 1730.

III. 1727. SIR JOHN STAPYLTON, Baronet [1660], of Myton aforesaid, only surv. s. and h., *b.* about 1684; matric. at Oxford (St. Edmund Hall), 12 June 1702, aged 18; was M.P. for Boroughbridge, 1705-08; *suc. to the Baronetcy*, 23 Nov. 1727. He *m.* in or before 1706, Mary (by whom he had eight sons and five daughters), da. and h. of Francis SANDYS, of Scroby, Notts. He *d.*, being killed by a fall from his horse, 24 Oct. 1733. Will pr. at York, 1734. The death of "Lady Stapylton, of Yorkshire," 3 Feb. 1743, is presumably that of his widow.

IV. 1733. SIR MILES STAPYLTON, Baronet [1660], of Myton aforesaid, 1st s. and h., *b* about 1706; matric. at Oxford (Univ. Coll.), 16 Nov. 1726, aged 18; *suc. to the Baronetcy*, 24 Oct. 1733; M.P. for Yorkshire, 1734-50; Commissioner of the Customs. He *m.* in May 1738 Anne ("£12,000 fortune"), da. of Edmund WALLER, of Hall Barn in Beaconsfield, Bucks, by (—), da. of (—) AISLABIE. He *d.* s.p.m.,(a) 14 and was *bur.* 18 May 1752, in Bath Abbey. Will pr. June 1752. His widow *d.* 13 Nov. 1791, in her 73d year, in Wimpole street, Marylebone. Will pr. Dec. 1791.

V. 1752. SIR BRYAN STAPYLTON, Baronet [1660], of Myton aforesaid, br. and h. male; *b.* probably about 1712; *suc. to the Baronetcy*, 14 May 1752. He *d.* unm., 27 June 1772, at Baldwin Brightwell Rectory, Oxon.

VI. 1772. SIR JOHN STAPYLTON, Baronet [1660], of Myton aforesaid, br. and h., *b.* probably about 1718; was an officer in the Royal Navy, served under Admiral Keppel, distinguishing himself at the capture of Havannah in Aug. 1762; *suc. to the Baronetcy*, 27 June 1772. He *d.* unm. of paralysis, after a long illness, 10 Feb. 1785.

VII. 1785. SIR MARTIN STAPYLTON, Baronet [1660], of Myton aforesaid, br. and h., *b.* about 1723; matric. at Oxford (Univ. Coll.), 17 Dec. 1747, aged 24; was sometime an officer in the army, but subsequently took Holy Orders; Rector of Baldwin Brightwell, Oxon, and one of the Fellows of St. Katharine's College, London Docks, 1750-1801; *suc. to the Baronetcy*, 10 Feb. 1785. He *m.* 29 April 1742, Leckie, da. of John LOVE, of Bristol, merchant. She *d.* in or before 1797. Admon. July 1797. He *d.* 21 Jan. 1801. Will pr. 1801.

VIII. 1801, to 1817, SIR MARTIN STAPYLTON, Baronet [1660], of Myton aforesaid, 3d and yst. but only surv. s. and h., *b.* 14 Sep. and *bap.* (with his twin elder br. Henry) 13 Oct. 1751, at Baldwin Brightwell;(b) *suc. to the Baronetcy*, 21 Jan. 1801. He *d.* unm. 2 Jan. 1817, when the *Baronetcy* became *extinct.* Will pr. 1817.

(a) Anne, his only da. and h., *d* unm., 9 June 1770.

(b) His eldest brother, Samuel Francis Stapylton, matric. at Oxford (Linc. Coll.), 14 Jan. 1761, aged 16; was a Capt. in the Army, and was slain at the battle of Bunker's Hill, 17 June 1775, leaving one son, Luke, who *d.* unm. before his grandfather. The other brother, Henry, matric. at Oxford (Linc. Coll.), 14 July 1769, aged 17, and *d.* unm. before his father. Anne, the only sister, *m.* the Rev. John Bree, M.A. [1759], of Ball. Coll., Oxford, who was *b.* about 1734. Their son, Martin Bree, inherited the estate of Myton, in 1817, on the death of his maternal uncle, the 8th Baronet, and took the name of Stapylton accordingly

ELWES:

cr. 22 June 1660;

ex. or *dormant* Jan. 1787.

I. 1660. "GERVASE ELWES, of Stoke juxta Clare, co. Suffolk." s. and h. of Sir Gervase ELWES, of Woodford, Essex (who fined for Alderman of London), by Frances, da. of Sir Robert LEE, of Billesley, co. Warwick, was *bap.* 21 Aug. 1628, at St. Mary's Bothaw, London; suc. his father in April 1653, and was *cr. a Baronet*, 22 June 1660. He was M.P. for Sudbury, May 1677 to 1679; for Suffolk, 1679; for Sudbury, again (two Parls.) 1679-81; for Suffolk, again (two Parls.) 1690-98, and for Sudbury, again (four Parls.) 1700, till death; was sometime Lieut. of the Tower of London. He *m.* Amy, da. of William TRIGGE, M.D., of Highworth, Wilts. He *d.* May 1706, and was *bur.* at Stoke. Will pr. Oct. 1706.

II. 1706. SIR HERVEY ELWES, Baronet [1660], of Stoke aforesaid, grandson and h., being s. and h. of Gervase ELWES, by Isabella, sister of John, 1st EARL OF BRISTOL, da. of Sir Thomas HERVEY, of Ickworth, Suffolk, which Gervase (who was M.P. for Sudbury, 1679-81), was 2d but 1st surv. s. and h. ap. of the 1st Baronet, but *d.* v.p. He *suc. to the Baronetcy*, May 1706. He was M.P. for Sudbury, Dec. 1706, and 1708-10. He was of most parsimonious habits. He *d.* unm., at Stoke, 18 Sep. 1763.(a) Will pr. 1763.

III. 1763. SIR WILLIAM ELWES, Baronet [1660], cousin and h. male, being s. of a yr. s.(b) of the 1st Baronet. He *suc. to the Baronetcy*, 18 Sep. 1763, but to none of the family estate, living in very reduced circumstances. He *m.* (or is said to have *m.*) Johanna BOBULIA. He *d.* s.p.m. legit.(c) in Sion Lane, and was *bur.* 26 Nov. 1778, at Isleworth Midx. Will pr. July 1779. His widow *d.* in or before 1787. Admon. Aug. 1787.

IV. 1779, to 1787. SIR HENRY ELWES, Baronet [1660], br. and h. male,(d) *suc. to the Baronetcy* in Nov. 1776. He *d.* s.p.m., probably unm., and was *bur.* (as a Baronet) 19 Jan. 1787, at St. Nicholas, Newcastle, when *the Baronetcy* became *extinct* or *dormant.*

(a) He left his large estates to his nephew, John Elwes (formerly John Meggot) of Marcham, Berks, who in 1751 had assumed the name of Elwes, being s. and h. of his only sister, Amy, by Robert Meggot, of Southwark, an eminent brewer. This was the notorious "Elwes the miser," sometime (1772-84) M.P. for Berks, who *d.* unm., 26 Nov. 1789, aged above 80, and whose two illegitimate sons inherited his vast personal property. The real estate went, on the miser's death, to his great nephew John Timms, who assumed the name of Elwes, and *d.* at Stoke, 29 Feb. 1824.

(b) Courthope's *Extinct Baronetage.* There were, according to Wotton's *Baronetage* [1741], three younger sons of the 1st Baronet, viz. (1) Richard Elwes, (2) John Elwes, and (3) Capt. William Elwes, all [before 1741] deceased.

(c) He appears to have left three sons (1), Henry, who, if legitimate, would have been the 4th Baronet; (2) William and (3) Thomas, which two last named proved their father's will in 1779.

(d) *Notes and Queries*, 5th S., iv, 520, where it is said that "Sir William had a younger brother, Sir Henry, who certainly succeeded him in the Baronetcy, as a trial in Chancery * * * proves." It is also there stated (among other interesting particulars of these descendants) that Henry Elwes, the illegit. son of Sir William, the 3d Baronet [see note "c" above] became a Colonel, and had a son William Henry Elwes, born 1785 at Newcastle, who left issue.

CORDELL:
cr. 22 June 1660;
ex. May 1704.

I. 1660. "ROBERT CORDELL, of Melford, co. Suffolk, Esq.," s. and h. of Sir John CORDELL, of St. Lawrence Old Jewry, London,(a) (who fined for Alderman of London, and who *d.* 5 March 1648/9), to whom he took out admon. 4 May 1649, by Sarah, da. of of Robert BANKWORTH, *or* BARROW, of London, having repurchased from the family of Savage,(b) the estate of Melford (formerly belonging to Sir William CORDELL, Master of the Rolls, 1557-81) before 1643, when he was residing there, was Sheriff of Suffolk, 1653-54, and was *cr. a Baronet*, 22 June 1660. He was M.P. for Sudbury, 1660 till void in May, as also (2 Parls.) March 1662 to 1679. He *m.* in or before 1643, Margaret, da. of Sir Edmund WRIGHT, of Swakeleys, in Ickenham, Midx., sometime (1640-41) Lord Mayor of London, by his 1st wife, Martha, da. of Edward BARON, of London. He was *bur.* 3 Jan. 1679/80, at St. Lawrence Jewry, London. Will dat. 18 Dec. 1679, pr. 12 Jan. 1679/80. His widow was *bur.* 24 March 1680/1 (with her father and husband) at St. Lawrence aforesaid. Her will pr. 1681.

II. 1680. SIR JOHN CORDELL, Baronet [1660], of Melford Hall, in Melford aforesaid, 1st s. and h., *b.* there 10 Nov. 1646; *suc. to the Baronetcy*, in Jan. 1679/80; Sheriff of Suffolk, 1684, but did not act; M.P. for Sudbury, 1685-87, and for Suffolk, 1689-90. He *m.*, in or before 1674, Elizabeth, da. of Thomas WALDEGRAVE, of Smalbridge, Suffolk.(c) He was *bur.* 9 Sept. 1690, at Melford. Will dat. 26 Aug. and pr. 1 Dec. 1690. His widow (living 17 July 1704) was *bur.* there 26 April 1709.

III. 1690, to 1704. SIR JOHN CORDELL, Baronet [1660], of Melford Hall aforesaid, only s. and h.; *bap.* at Melford, 11 Nov. 1677; *suc. to the Baronetcy* in Sep. 1690; M.P. for Sudbury, 1701. He *m.*, 24 Dec. 1701, at Allhallows' Staining, London (Lic. Fac., he about 23 and she about 22), Eleanor, da. and coheir of Joseph Haskin STYLES, of London, merchant, by Sarah, da. of Sir John EYLES, of South Broom Hall, Wilts.(d) He *d.* s.p., being killed by a fall from his horse 8 and was *bur.* 12 May 1704, at Melford, aged 26, when *the Baronetcy* became *extinct*. Admon. 17 July 1704, to a creditor, the widow, the mother, and the two sisters(e) renouncing. His widow was *bur.* 21 May 1705, at Melford.

ROBINSON:
cr. 22 June 1660.

I. 1660. "SIR JOHN ROBINSON, Knt., Lord Mayor [1662-63], Lieutenant of the Tower of London," 3d s. of the Rev. William Robinson, D.D., Archdeacon of Notts, Rector of Bingham in that County, and

(a) In that church was buried 28 Dec. 1646, "Lady Cordwell," doubtless wife of this Sir John, and probably mother of the Baronet, whose parentage is not given in Dr. J. J. Howard's pedigree of him and his descendants and of various members of the Cordell family, enlarged from the Visitation of Suffolk and other sources.

(b) See Candler's Suffolk MSS.

(c) "Thomas Waldegrave died 1 June 1727, aged 56." See Howard's pedigree of Cordell, as in note "a" above.

(d) Courthope, in his *Extinct Baronetage*, following Le Neve's *Baronets*, states [apparently in error] that he married "(—), da. of (—) Adams, of London."

(e) Of these, Margaret the younger da., *bap.* at Melford, 8 Feb. 1675, who *m.* Sir Charles Firebrace, 2d Baronet [1698], appears to have inherited the Melford estate.

of Long Whatton, co. Leicester,(a) by Sarah, da. of William BAINBRIGGE, of Lockington, co. Leicester, was *b.* probably about 1625; was a Citizen and Clothworker, of London, being Master of that Company, 1656; Alderman of Dowgate, 18 Dec. 1655; of Cripplegate, 7 Dec. 1658, and of the Tower, 22 April 1663 till his death; Sheriff of London, 1657-58; Col. of the Green Regt. of London Militia, 1659, and President of the Royal Artillery Company, 1660 till his death; was, in May 1660, one of the Commissioners from the City of London to the King at Breda; M.P. for London, 1660, and for Rye (two Parls.) Nov. 1661 to 1679; a Member of the East India Company, 1660, 1667, 1668, 1670, 1675, and 1677; was *Knighted* at Canterbury, 26 May 1660, and was, a month later, *cr. a Baronet*, 22 June 1660.(b) Lieutenant of the Tower of London, 25 June 1660 till his death; Lord Mayor of London, 1662-63,(c) during which period he entertained, at the Clothworkers' Hall, 23 June 1663, the King, the Queen, the Queen dowager, etc.; admitted to Gray's Inn, 29 Feb. 1669/70. He *m.* in Dec. 1654, at Hackney, Midx., Anne, da. of Sir George WHITMORE, of Balmes, in that parish, sometime [1631-32] Lord Mayor of London, by Mary, da. and h. of Reginald COPCOTT. He *d.* in or shortly before Feb. 1679/80, and was *bur.* at Nuneham Courtenay. Will pr. 24 Feb. 1679/80 and 25 Oct. 1683.(d) His widow, who was *bap.* 13 Oct. 1636, at Hackney, *m.* (Lic. Fac. 25 Sep. 1680, he about 30 [*sic*] and a Bachelor) William SHENTON, of the Tower of London, who *d.* 1692. Her will, dat. 16 Jan., pr. 10 Feb. 1699/700, by her son, Sir James Robinson, Baronet.

II. 1680? SIR JOHN ROBINSON, Baronet [1660], of Farming Woods, co. Northampton, eldest surv. s. and h.,(e) *b* about 1660; *suc. to the Baronetcy* about Feb. 1679/80. He *m.*, in or before 1686, Mary, da. of Sir William DUDLEY, 1st Baronet [1660], of Clapton, co. Northampton, by his third wife, Mary, da. and h. of Sir Paul PINDAR, of London. He *d.* s.p.m.(f) in or shortly before 1693. Will dat. 13 Oct. 1692, pr. 3 Feb. 1692/3.

III. 1693? SIR JAMES ROBINSON, Baronet [1660], of Cranford, co. Northampton, br. and h. male, *b.* about 1669; *suc. to the Baronetcy* about 1693. He in 1715 purchased the manor of Cranford St. Andrew, in Cranford aforesaid, where he had resided before 1699. He *m.* (Lic. Fac. 29 April 1699, he about 30 and she about 22) Anne, 2d da. and coheir of Sir William JESSON, of Newhouse, co. Warwick, by Penelope, da. (whose issue became heir) of Sir George VILLIERS, 2d Baronet [1619] of Brooksby. She *d.* in or before 1728. He *d.* 28 Aug. 1731. Will dat. 22 Feb. 1727/8, pr. 15 Nov. 1731.

(a) This Dr. Robinson was uterine brother of the celebrated Archbishop Laud, their mother, Lucy (sister of Sir William Webb, sometime Lord Mayor of London), having *m.* firstly, John Robinson, and secondly, William Laud, both of Reading, Berks.

(b) An augmentation to his Arms was granted, 20 Oct. 1663, in consequence of a Royal Warrant of the 13th instant. It is given in full in *The Genealogist* [Orig. Series] vol. i, p. 153.

(c) His Pageant was (like several others) called "London's Triumph."

(d) His portrait is at Clothworkers' Hall, to which he was a Benefactor. Pepys speaks of his wife as "proud and cunning," and of himself as a "talking, bragging, buffle-headed fellow" but attentive to the wants of the city. See also *Gent. Mag.* for Nov. 1769 as to his character.

(e) His elder brother, William, born 16 and bap. 31 Dec. 1655 [not 1654 as on his M.I.] at St. Mary Mag., Milk Street, London, travelled abroad for five years, was Knighted, 24 Nov. 1678, but *d.* unm. and v.p., 14 Feb. 1678-9, and was *bur.* at Nuneham aforesaid. M.I. Will pr. 1682.

(f) Of his two daughters and coheirs, who inherited the estate of Farming Woods, (1) Mary, *m.* as his second wife (then aged 22), 5 Jan. 1708/9, David (Wemyss) Earl of Wemyss [S.], but *d.* s.p. before 1712 (2) Anne, who eventually suc. to her father's estates, *m.*, in 1718, Richard (Fitzpatrick) 1st Baron Gowran [I.], and had issue John, 1st Earl of Upper Ossory [I.].

IV. 1731. SIR JOHN ROBINSON, Baronet [1660], of Cranford aforesaid, 1st s. and h., *b.* about 1705; *suc. to the Baronetcy*, 28 Aug. 1731; Sheriff of Northamptonshire, 1737-38. He *m.* firstly, 5 May 1726, at St. Benet's, Paul's wharf, London, Mary, only da. and h. of John MORGAN, of Kingsthorpe, co. Northampton, by Tryphena, the only child that had issue of Robert SHEFFIELD,(a) grandson of Edmund, 1st EARL OF MULGRAVE. She *d.* 12 Feb. 1733/4, aged 24, and was *bur.* at Kingsthorpe. M.I. Will pr. Dec. 1735. He *m.* secondly, 7 June 1736, at St. Paul's Cathedral, London, Elizabeth PERKINS, of Cransley, co. Northampton, spinster, da. of (—) PERKINS, of Marston, co. Warwick. He *d.* 31 Aug. 1765. Will pr. Sep. 1765.

V. 1765. SIR GEORGE ROBINSON, Baronet [1660], of Cranford aforesaid, 2d but 1st surv. s. and h. by first wife, *b.* about 1730; ed. at Trin. Coll., Cambridge, of which he was several years Fellow; B.A., 1753; M.A., 1756; *suc. to the Baronetcy*, 31 Aug. 1765; Sheriff of Northamptonshire, 1766-67; M.P. for Northampton, 1774-80. He *m.* 2 Dec. 1764, Dorothea, only child of John CHESTER, of St. Paul's, Covent Garden, by Elizabeth, da. and coheir of Sir William CHESTER, 5th Baronet [1620] and his wife Penelope, da. of George HEWETT, of Stretton Hall and Great Glen, co. Leicester. She, who was *bap.* 15 Oct. 1739, at St. Paul's aforesaid, inherited, through her said (maternal) grandmother, the Hewett estates above mentioned, and *d.* at Cranford Hall, 27 Jan. 1815, aged 75, being the last survivor of the ancient family of Chester, of Chicheley Bucks. He *d.* (a few months later) 10 Oct. 1815. Will pr. 1815.

VI. 1815. SIR GEORGE ROBINSON, Baronet [1660], of Cranford and Stretton Hall aforesaid, 1st s. and h., b. 1765; *suc. to the Baronetcy*, 10 Oct. 1815; M.P. for Northampton (four Parls.) 1820-32. He *d.* unm. 23 Nov. 1833, aged 68, at his residence in South Street, Midx. Will pr. March 1834.

VII. 1833. SIR GEORGE STAMP ROBINSON, Baronet [1660], of Cranford aforesaid, nephew and h., being 1st s. and h. of the Rev. William Villiers ROBINSON, M.A., Rector of Grafton Underwood and of Irchester cum Wollaston, co. Northampton [1794-1829], by Anne, da. of Stamp BROOKSBANK, of Lower Grosvenor street, which William, who *d.* 14 Jan. 1829, aged 63, was next br. to the late Baronet. He was *b.* 29 Aug. 1797, at Grafton Underwood; matric. at Oxford (New Coll.), 5 Dec. 1815, aged 18; Fellow, to 1827; B.A., 1819; M.A., 1824; in Holy Orders; Rector of Cranford, 1822-33; *suc. to the Baronetcy*, 23 Nov. 1833; Hon. Canon of Peterborough, 1853-73. He *m.* 24 May 1827, his cousin, Emma, 6th da. of Robert Willis BLENCOWE, of Hayes, Midx., by Penelope, da. of Sir George ROBINSON, 5th Baronet [1660] abovenamed. He *d.* 9 Oct. 1873, of serous apoplexy, aged 76. His widow *d.* 20 Jan. 1874, at Cranford Hall, in her 72d year.

VIII. 1873. SIR JOHN BLENCOWE ROBINSON, Baronet [1660], of Cranford aforesaid, 2d but 1st surv. s. and h., *b.* 20 May 1830, at Cranford; ed. at Eton; matric. at Oxford (Ch. Ch.), 15 June 1848, aged 18; *suc. to the Baronetcy*, 9 Oct. 1873. He *m.*, 5 Dec. 1861, Winifred, 1st da. of the Rev. Edward STUART, Vicar of Sparsholt, Hants, by Louisa Anne, da. of Charles John HERBERT, of Muckross, co. Kerry. He *d.* s.p. 10 Aug. 1877, at Moulton Park, co. Northampton, aged 47. His widow, who was *b.* 1839, living 1902.

IX. 1877. SIR FREDERICK LAUD ROBINSON, Baronet [1660], of Cranford aforesaid, br. and h., *b.* 28 June 1843; ed. at Rugby; matric. at Oxford (Trin. Coll.), 5 June 1862, aged 18; in Holy Orders; Rector of

(a) This Robert Sheffield was for many years heir presumptive (on the death of the Duke of Buckingham) to the Earldom of Mulgrave. He *d.* at Kingsthorpe, 21 April 1725, in his 84th year, leaving this grand-daughter, but having survived all his children and his two sons-in-law.

Cranford aforesaid, 1870-93; *suc. to the Baronetcy*, 10 Aug. 1877. He *m.*, 14 Dec. 1870, Madeleine Caroline, 1st da. of Frederick SARTORIS, of Rushden Hall, co. Northampton, by Mary, da. of the Rev. Joseph PRATT, Rector of Paston in that county. He *d.* 6 Feb. 1893, at Weldon Rectory. His widow living 1902.

X. 1893. SIR FREDERICK VILLIERS LAUD ROBINSON, Baronet [1660] of Cranford aforesaid, only s. and h., *b.* 4 Dec. 1880; *suc*, *to the Baronetcy* 6 Feb. 1893; Lieut. 3rd Batt. Northants Reg.

Family Estates.—These, in 1883, consisted of 2,087 acres in Northamptonshire, worth £4,737 a year. *Principal Seat.*—Cranford Hall, near Kettering, Northamptonshire.

ABDY:
cr. 22 June 1660;
ex. about 1662.

I. 1660, to 1662? "SIR JOHN ABDY, of Moores [in Salcot Virley], co. Essex, Knt.," was yst. br. of Sir Thomas ABDY, Baronet [so *cr.* 14 July 1641] and of Sir Robert ABDY, Baronet [so *cr.* 9 June 1660] all being sons of Anthony ABDY, of St. Andrew's Undershaft, Alderman and sometime [1630-31] Sheriff of London, by Abigail, da. of Sir Thomas CAMBELL, sometime [1609-10] Lord Mayor of London. He was *b.* probably about 1620, and was *cr. a Baronet*, 22 June 1660, having been previously *Knighted.* He *d.* unm. about 1662 when the *Baronetcy became extinct* and his estates devolved on his brother Sir Robert Abdy, 1st Baronet [1660] of Albyns.

HILDYARD, *or* HILLIARD:
cr. 25 June, 1660;
ex. 6 Nov. 1814.(a)

I 1660. "SIR ROBERT HILLIARD [HILDYARD], of Partington [*i.e.* Patrington], co. York, Knt.," 3d but 2d surv. s. of Sir Christopher HILDYARD, of Winestead in Holderness in that county (*d.* Nov. 1634), by Elizabeth, da. and h. of Henry WELBY, of Goxhill, co. Lincoln, was *b.* 22 May 1612, at Winestead; was Gent. of the Privy Chamber in 1641 to Charles I, and afterwards in 1660 to Charles II; greatly distinguished himself as a Royalist during the Civil Wars, particularly at Marston Moor, 2 July 1644; was Colonel of a Regt. of Foot, and in command of a Brigade of Horse, and finally was Major-General of all the Horse in England and Wales; was fined £610, on 15 Jan. 1647/8. He was *Knighted*(b) by Charles I, by whose successor he was *cr. a Baronet*, 25 June

(a) In the *Mis. Gen. et Her.* (new series, vol. ii, pp. 40-42) is a pedigree of the numerous descendants of Robert Hilliard, a Capt. in 1649, in the Parl. Army in Ireland, who settled at Baltygarron, co. Kerry, and whose father, it is suggested may have been Robert (aged 23 in 1665) the second son of the 1st Baronet. The compiler (J. F. Fuller, F.S.A.) adds that he is of opinion that this Baronetcy is not extinct. The last named Robert, however, appears to have *m.* 11 Nov. 1669, at St. Mary's, Hull, and to have been *bur.* 9 June 1685, in Beverley Minster, having had an only son Robert, *bap.* 26 April 1671, and *bur.* 1 May 1683, at St. Mary's, Hull, and an only surv. da. Jane, who *m.* John Legard.

(b) According to the account given by the 3d Baronet in 1741 to Wotton, for the *Baronetage* of that date, "he was made in the field a Knight-Banneret for having slain a Scotchman, who had "sent a challenge to any gentleman in the King's Army that would accept it."

1660. He entered his pedigree in the Visit. of Yorkshire, 1665, being then of Beverley. He *m.* firstly, Jane, widow of John LISTER, of Linton (s. and h. of Sir John LISTER), d. and h. of Christopher CONSTABLE, of Hatfield, co. York. She *d.* s.p. He *m.* secondly, 3 Sep. 1634, at St. Mary's Hull,(a) Anne, widow first of Thomas FERRIES, sometime [1620] Mayor of Hull (who *d.* 1631), and subsequently of Sir Edward MOUNTFORD, of Bescote, co Stafford (who *d.* Dec. 1632), da. and coheir of Thomas THACKRAY, Merchant, Alderman and twice Mayor of Hull, by Elizabeth his wife. She was presumably dead before 14 Sep. 1648, the date of her mother's will.(b) He *m.* thirdly, after 1665, Helen, who *d.* s.p. and was *bur.* 20 Aug. 1679, in Beverley minster. He *d.* at Winestead, 7 March 1684/5.

II. 1685. SIR ROBERT HILDYARD, Baronet [1660], of Winestead aforesaid,(c) grandson and heir, being 1st s. and h. of Christopher HILDYARD, by Frances, da. and coheir of William DOBSON, Alderman and sometime Mayor of Hull, which Christopher, who *d.* three months before his father, 7 Jan. 1684/5, aged 44, was 1st s. and h. ap. of the late Baronet. He *suc. to the Baronetcy* 7 March 1684/5; was M.P. for Hedon, 1701-02; rebuilt the hall at Winestead, and *d.* unm. 30 Nov. 1729. Admon. 2 April 1730.

III 1729. SIR ROBERT HILDYARD, Baronet [1660], of Winestead aforesaid and Bishop's Burton, nephew and h., being posthumous s. and h. of the Rev. William HILDYARD, M.A., Rector of Rowley St. Peter, co. York, by Nancy, da. of Thomas CROFT, of Stillington, co. York, which William, who *d.* Nov. 1715, aged 36, was yr. br. of the late Baronet. He was *bap.* at York, 15 July 1716; *suc. to the Baronetcy*, 30 Nov. 1729; was M.P. for Great Bedwyn, 1754-61. He *m.* in May 1738, Maria Catherine, da. and h. of Henry DARCY, of Sedbury, co. York. She *d.* 21 Aug. 1747. He *d.* at Gilling, co. York, 1 Feb. 1781. Will pr. Feb. 1781.

IV. 1781, to 1814. SIR ROBERT DARCY HILDYARD, Baronet [1660], of Winestead aforesaid, 1st and only surv. s. and h., *b.* 1743; *suc. to the Baronetcy*, 1 Feb. 1781; Sheriff of Yorkshire, 1783-84. He *m.*, 23 Sep. 1769, Mary, da. of Sir Edward DERING, 5th Baronet [1627] by his 2d wife, Mary, da. of Charles FOTHERBY, of Barham, Kent. He *d.* s.p.s. 6 Nov. 1814, aged 71, when the *Baronetcy* became *extinct*.(d) Will pr. 1815. His widow *d.* 3 Nov. 1816, in her 75th year. Will pr. 1816.

ASTLEY:

cr. 26 June 1660;

afterwards, since 1841, LORDS HASTINGS.

I. 1660. "JACOB ASTLEY, of Hill Morton, co. Warwick, Esq.," s. and h. of Edward ASTLEY, by Elizabeth, da. of Jacob (ASTLEY), 1st BARON ASTLEY OF READING, was *b.* about 1639; suc. his father 15 March

(a) Foster's *Yorkshire Families.*

(b) In that will her parentage (though she herself is not mentioned) is proved, inasmuch as testatrix mentions "my son in law," Sir Robert Hildiard and "my grandsons," Christopher and Robert, his sons. This Anne is usually, though erroneously, called da. of Alderman *Herries* of Hull.

(c) The estate of Patrington had been granted to the 1st Baronet only for his own life, and those of his two sons, and was consequently, after their death, given by William III to the Earl of Portland.

(d) The estate of Winestead devolved on his niece, Anne Catherine, the only surv. child of his only married sister Catherine, 2nd wife of James Whyte, of Denbies, Surrey. She *m.* in May 1815, Thomas Blackborne Thoroton, of Flintham, Notts, who by Royal Lic. took the name of Hildyard, and *d.* July 1830, leaving issue.

1653; matric. at Oxford (Christ Church), 19 July 1659; suc. to the estate of Hill Morton aforesaid and to that of Melton Constable, co. Norfolk, 7 Sep. 1659, on the death of his paternal uncle, Sir Isaac ASTLEY, Baronet, (so *cr.*, 21 Jan. 1641/2), and was himself *cr. a Baronet*, 26 June 1660. He was Sheriff of Norfolk, 1663-64, and M.P. (38 years) for that county, 1685-87, 1689-90, 1695-1701, 1702-05, and 1710-22, being a Commissioner of Trade, 1714-17. On the death, in 1688, of his maternal cousin, Jacob, 3d Baron Astley of Reading, he suc. to the representation and estates of his undermentioned maternal grandfather, the 1st Baron. He *m.* 6 Feb. 1661, at Kimberley, co. Norfolk, Blanche, 1st da. of Sir Philip WODEHOUSE, 3d Baronet [1611], of Kimberley aforesaid, by Lucy, da. of Sir Thomas COTTON, 2d Baronet [1611], of Connington. He *d.* 17 and was *bur.* 21 Aug. 1729, at Melton Constable, aged 90. Will dat. 3 June 1729, pr. 1 April 1730.

II. 1729. SIR PHILIP ASTLEY, Baronet [1660], of Melton Constable and Hill Morton aforesaid, 2d but 1st surv. s. and h.(a), *b.* 20 and *bap.* 30 July 1667, at Melton Constable; *suc. to the Baronetcy* 17 Aug. 1729. He *m.* 2 Dec. 1690, at Westminster Abbey (Lic. Fac., she about 18, parents deceased), Elizabeth, da. and h. of Thomas BRANSBY, of Caistor, Norfolk, by Elizabeth his wife. She *d.* 30 March, and was *bur.* 7 April 1738, aged 67, at Melton Constable. He *d.* 7 July, and was *bur.* there, 12 Aug. 1739, aged 72. Will dated 19 March 1738, pr. 4 Aug 1739.

III. 1739. SIR JACOB ASTLEY, Baronet [1660], of Melton Constable and Hill Morton aforesaid, s. and h., *b.* 3 and *bap.* 23 Jan. 1691/2, at Melton Constable; *suc. to the Baronetcy*, 7 July 1739. He *m.*, firstly, 1721, Lucy, second and youngest of the two sisters and coheirs of Sir Henry L'Estrange, 6th and last Baronet, da. of Sir Nicholas L'ESTRANGE, 4th Baronet [1629], of Hunstanton, Norfolk, by Ann, da. of Sir Thomas WODEHOUSE, of Kimberley in that county. She was *bap.* 23 Jan. 1699, at Hunstanton, and *d.* 25, and was *bur.* 13 July 1739, aged 39, at Melton Constable. He *m.*, secondly, 1 May 1740, at Finchingfield, Essex, Judith, widow of Gresham PAGE, of Saxthorpe, Norfolk, da. of Isaac WATLINGTON, sometime M.P. for Cambridge. She *d.*, s.p., 7 and was *bur.* 9 March 1742/3, at Melton Constable. He *m.*, thirdly, (sett. dat. 14 July 1744), Sarah, 1st da. and coheir of Christopher BEDINGFELD, of Wighton, Norfolk, by Elizabeth, da. of Arthur KING, of Tilney St. Lawrence. He *d.* 5 and was *bur.* 11 Jan. 1760, at Melton Constable. M.I. Will dat. 19 Dec. 1751, pr. 26 Jan. 1760. His widow *d.* s.p., at Bath, and was *bur.* 9 Aug. 1764, at Melton Constable. Will pr. Aug. 1764.

IV. 1760. SIR EDWARD ASTLEY, Baronet [1660], of Melton Constable aforesaid, s. and h. by 1st wife; *bap.* 26 Dec. 1729, at Hindolveston, Norfolk; M.P. for Norfolk (24 years), 1768-90; *suc. to the Baronetcy*, 5 Jan. 1760. He *m.*, firstly, 1751, Rhoda, sister of John Hussey, 1ST BARON DELAVAL, 1st surv. da. of Francis Blake DELAVAL, of Seaton Delaval, Northumberland, by Rhoda, da. of Robert APREECE, of Washingley, co. Huntingdon. She *d.* at Bath, and was *bur.* at Widcombe, Somerset, 27 Oct. 1757, aged 31. He *m.* secondly, 24 Feb. 1759, at St. Margaret's, Westm., Anne, yst. da. of Christopher MILLES, of Nackington, Kent. She *d.* 11 and was *bur.* 23 July 1792, at Melton Constable. He *m.* thirdly, 30 July 1793, at St. Marylebone, Elizabeth BULLEN. He *d.* 27 March, and was *bur.* 2 April 1802, at Melton Constable. M.I. Will dat. 1 March 1800, pr. 7 June 1803. His widow *d.* s.p. at New Walsingham, Norfolk, and was *bur.* there. Will dat. 5 Oct. 1810, pr. 8 Dec. following.

V. 1802. SIR JACOB HENRY ASTLEY, Baronet [1660], of Melton Constable and Seaton Delaval aforesaid, s. and h. by 1st wife; *b.* 12 Sep. 1756, M.P. for Norfolk (20 years), Nov. 1797 till death; *suc. to the*

(a) Jacob Astley, the eldest son, matric. at Oxford (Ch. Ch.), 15 June 1680, aged 15, and *d.* there 9 June 1681, being *bur.* at Melton Constable, where is a long and most flattering monumental inscription to him.

Baronetcy, 27 March 1702. He *m.* 14 Jan. 1789, at St. Margaret's, Lynn, Norfolk, Hester, yst. da. and coheir of Samuel BROWNE, of King's Lynn. He *d.* 28 April and was *bur.* 10 May 1817, aged 61, at Melton Constable. Will pr. 1817. His widow, who was *b.* 27 Nov. 1767, and *bap.* 8 Aug. 1768, at St. Margaret's, Lynn aforesaid, *d.* 13 Jan. 1855, at Burgh Hall, Norfolk, aged 87. Will pr. April 1855.

VI. 1817. SIR JACOB ASTLEY, Baronet [1660], of Melton Constable and Seaton Delaval aforesaid, 1st s. and h., *b.* at Burgh Hall aforesaid, 13 Nov. 1797, and *bap.* the same day at Melton Constable; Matric. at Oxford (Mag. Coll.), 18 Feb. 1817, aged 19; *suc. to the Baronetcy*, 28 April following, and was *cr.* D.C.L. of Oxford, 14 June in the same year. He was M.P. for West Norfolk (2 Parls.), 1832-37. He *m.* 22 March 1819, at St. Geo., Han. sq., Georgiana Caroline (*b.* 16 March 1796), 3d. da. of Sir Henry Watkin DASHWOOD, 3d. Baronet [1684] of Kirklington, Oxon, by Mary Helen, da. of John GRAHAM, Member of Council in Bengal. She was living when he was sum. to the House of Lords by writ, 18 May 1841(a) as LORD HASTINGS, having proved that he was the junior coheir of the junior coheiress of that ancient Barony, to which the precedence of 1290 is allowed, but which for above 450 years, previous to the determination of its abeyance in 1841, had been unheard of! (b)

BOWYER:

cr. 25 June 1660.

I. 1660. "SIR WILLIAM BOWYER, of Denham, Bucks, Knt.," was s. and h. of Sir Henry BOWYER, by Anne, da. of Sir Nicholas SALTER, of London, which Henry was s. and h. ap. of Sir William BOWYER (one of the Tellers of the Court of Exchequer, who purchased the estate of Denham aforesaid), but *d.* v.p., 27 Dec. 1613, aged 23; was *bap.* 29 June 1612 at St. Olave's, Hart Street, London; suc. his said grandfather, Aug. 1616; was admitted to Lincoln's Inn, 14 April 1630; and, having been *Knighted* at some date after April 1660, was *cr. a Baronet*, 25 June 1660; was Sheriff of Bucks, 1646-47 and M.P. for that county (three Parls.), 1659-60 and 1661-79. He *m.* 29 May 1634, at St. Olave's, Old Jewry, Margaret, da. of Sir John WELD, of Arnolds in Edmonton, Midx., by Frances, da. of William WHITMORE, of London. She *d.* 8 Jan. 1678. He *d.* 2 Oct. 1679(c), both being *bur.* at Denham. M.I. Limited admon. to him, 23 July 1683.

(a) This (as is stated in the *Complete Peerage, by G. E. C.*, vol. iv, p. 179) "is one of a series of Baronies which, having been unheard of for *centuries*, were claimed in the earlier years of Queen Victoria's reign by any coheir who possessed sufficient interest to make success probable. In the short space of four years, 1838-1841, the abeyance of no less than five such Baronies (Vaux, Camoys, Braye, Beaumont, and Hastings), of which the average time of their *disappearance* was above 300 years, has terminated in favour of some distant descendant who seldom possessed even a particle of the ancient *Baronial* estate."

(b) His great grandfather the 3d Baronet, had *m.* Lucy, 2d and yst. sister and coheir of Sir Henry Lestrange, 6th Baronet [1629], whose ancestor in the 6th degree, Hamon Le Strange, had *m.* Elizabeth, 2d and yst. sister and coheir of John Hastings (*d.* 1542) who, according to the decision of the House of Lords in 1840, was *de jure* Lord Hastings, in right of his descent from another John Hastings, who also, after 1389, was thereby held to be such *de jure* Lord, as being cousin and heir, tho' of the *half* blood (which at that period would almost certainly have been held a fatal bar to such succession) of John, Earl of Pembroke and Lord Hastings, on whose death, in 1389, that Barony became dormant or in abeyance for 452 years, till its revival in 1841.

(c) He had considerable literary knowledge, and is said to have assisted Dryden (who frequently stayed at Denham) in his translation of Virgil.

II. 1679. SIR WILLIAM BOWYER, Baronet [1660], of Denham Court, in Denham aforesaid, s. and h., *b.* about 1639; admitted to Inner Temple, Nov. 1654; *suc. to the Baronetcy*, 2 Oct. 1679. He *m.* (Lic. Vic. Gen., 24 Dec., 1679, he about 42, she about 26), Frances, da. of Charles CECIL, *styled* VISCOUNT CRANBOURNE (s. and h. ap. of William, 2d EARL OF SALISBURY), by Jane, da. and coheir of James (MAXWELL) EARL OF DIRLETOUN [S.]. He *d.* 13 Feb. 1721/2, and was *bur.* at Denham, in his 83d year. Will pr. March 1722. His widow *d.* 15 June 1723, in her 75th year. Both *bur.* at Denham. M.I.

III. 1722. SIR WILLIAM BOWYER, Baronet [1660], of Denham Court aforesaid, grandson and h., being s. and h. of Cecil BOWYER, by Juliana (*m.* 22 July 1707, at St. Paul's, London), da. of Richard PARKER, of Hedsor, Bucks, which Cecil, who *d.* v.p., 5 Dec. 1720, aged 36, was s. and h. ap. of the late Baronet. He was *b.* about 1710; *suc. to the Baronetcy*, 13 Feb. 1721/2; matric. at Oxford (Mag. Coll.), 13 July, 1728, aged 18; was *cr.* M.A., 17 Oct. 1730. He *m.* 21 Aug. 1733, Anne, da. (whose issue became coheir) of Sir John STONEHOUSE, 7th and 4th Baronet [1628 and 1670], of Radley, Berks, by Penelope, da. of Sir Robert DASHWOOD, 1st Baronet [1684], of Northbrooke. He *d.* 12 July 1767, in his 57th year. Will pr. July 1767. His widow *d.* 22 May 1785, in her 76th year. Will pr. May 1785. Both *bur.* at Denham. M.I.

IV. 1767. SIR WILLIAM BOWYER, Baronet [1660], of Denham Court aforesaid, s. and h., *b.* about 1736; matric. at Oxford (Mag. Coll.), 1 Feb. 1754, aged 18; sometime a Capt. in the Guards; *suc. to the Baronetcy*, 12 July 1767. He *m.* 26 Aug. 1776, at St. Marylebone, Anne, widow of James BAKER, Capt. R.N., da. of (—) CAREY. He *d.* s.p., April 1799. Will pr. May 1799. His widow *d.* 25 Dec. 1802. Will pr. 1803.

V. 1799, April. SIR GEORGE BOWYER, Baronet [1660 and 1794], of Radley House, in Radley, Berks, and, possibly, of Denham Court aforesaid, Admiral in the Royal Navy, next surv. br. and h.; *b.* 1739; Lieut. in the Royal Navy, 1758; Commander, 1761; Post Capt., 1762, serving in North America and the West Indies, 1778-81; Commodore, 1781. He was M.P. for Queenborough, 1784-90. In 1790 he was made Rear Admiral of the White, and on 1 June 1794, he distinguished himself in Lord Howe's naval victory over the French, in which he lost a leg. He was rewarded with an annual pension of £1,000, and was *cr. a Baronet*, 8 Sep. 1794, as "of Radley, Berks," an estate to which he was entitled (under the will of his maternal uncle Sir James STONHOUSE, 9th and 6th Baronet [1628 and 1670] of Radley aforesaid), on the death, 1 Jan. 1795, of his cousin Penelope, Baroness RIVERS. He *suc. to the paternal Baronetcy* of 1660, in April 1799, in which thenceforth *the Baronetcy of 1794 merged* within five years of its creation. He became Rear Admiral of the Red, in April, and Vice-Admiral of the Blue in July 1794; Vice-Admiral of the Red 1795, and Admiral of the Blue Feb. 1799. He *m.* firstly, 11 Nov. 1768, at Putney, Surrey, Margaret, widow of Sir Jacob Garrard DOWNING, 4th Baronet [1663], da. of the Rev. (—) PRICE, Curate of Barrington, co. Gloucester. She, by whom he had no issue, *d.* 18 Sep. 1778, at Mount Pleasant, Putney, and was *bur.* at Croyden, co. Cambridge. Her admon. 22 Feb. 1781. He *m.* secondly, 4 June 1782, Henrietta, da. and h. of Admiral Sir Piercy BRETT, of Beckenham, Kent, by Henrietta, da. of Thomas COLBY, clerk of the Cheque at Chatham. He *d.* 6 Dec. 1799, at Radley House, aged 60, within eight months of inheriting the Baronetcy of 1660. Will pr. Dec. 1800. His widow *d.* abroad, Nov. 1845. Will pr. Feb. 1846.

VI *and* II. 1799. Dec. SIR GEORGE BOWYER, Baronet [1660 and 1794], of Radley House and, possibly, of Denham Court aforesaid, 1st s. and h. by 2d wife; *b.* at Radley House, 3 March 1783; *suc. to the Baronetcies*, 6 Dec. 1799; matric. at Oxford (Ch. Ch.), 17 Jan. 1801, aged 17; B.A., 1804; M.A., 1807; M.P. for Malmesbury, 1807-10, and for Abingdon,

June 1811 to 1818.(a) He *m.* 19 Nov. 1808, Anne Hammond, 1st daughter of Sir Andrew Snape DOUGLAS, Capt. R.N. (Capt. of the Fleet in Admiral Howe's action, 1 June 1794), by Anne, da. of (—) BURGESS, of New York. She *d.* 1844. He *d.* 1 July 1860, at Dresden, aged 77.

VII. *and* III. 1860. SIR GEORGE BOWYER, Baronet [1660 and 1794], 1st s. and h., *b.* at Radley House aforesaid, 8 Oct. 1811; admitted to Middle Temple, 1 June 1836; Barrister, 7 June 1839, being admitted *ad eundem* to Lincoln's Inn, 11 Jan. 1845; was Hon. M.A. Oxford, 12 June 1839; Hon. D.C.L., 20 June 1844; author of *Commentaries on Modern Civil Law*, 1848, and other legal works; was M.P. (Liberal) for Dundalk, 1852-68, and for Wexford, 1874-80,(b) having in 1849 unsuccessfully stood for Reading, and having *suc. to the Baronetcies*, 1 July 1860. He joined the Church of Rome, 1850, and built for that communion the Church of St. John of Jerusalem, in Great Ormond Street, Midx; was made Chamberlain to Pope Pius IX.; Knight of Justice of the Order of Malta, Knight Grand Cross of the Order of St. Gregory, and Grand Collar of the Constantian Order of St. George. He *d.* unm. (being found dead in his bed) at his Chambers, 13 King's Bench Walk, Temple, and was *bur.* at Radley, 7 June 1883, aged 71. Will pr. 24 Aug. 1883, under £9,000.

VIII. *and* IV. 1883. SIR WILLIAM BOWYER, Baronet [1660 and 1794], br. and h., *b.* Oct. 1812; Barrister (Middle Temple), 1851; *suc. to the Baronetcies* in June 1883. He *m.* 16 June 1857, Ellen Sarah, da. of Shirley Foster WOOLMER, Barrister. He *d.* s.p., 30 May 1893, at 25 Park Crescent, Brighton, in his 81st year. His widow *d.* there, 7 Dec. 1899. Both *bur.* in Brighton Cemetery.

IX. *and* V. 1893. SIR GEORGE HENRY BOWYER, Baronet [1660 and 1794], nephew and h., being only s. and h. of Henry George BOWYER, Inspector of Schools, by Katherine Emma, only child of the Rev. George SANDBY, of Denton, Norfolk, which Henry George (who *d.* 25 Sep. 1883, aged 70) was 3d and yst. s. of the 6th and 2d Baronet. He was *b.* 9 Sep. 1870; was sometime Lieut. 4th Batt. Cheshire Militia, and *suc. to the Baronetcy*, 30 May 1893. He *m.*, 4 May 1899, at St. James' Westm., Ethel, da. of Francis HAWKINS, "a man not in the same walk of life" as the Baronet.(c) From her he obtained a divorce,(d) 7 Nov. 1900.

Family Estates.—These, 1876-83, consisted of 4,451 acres in Berks, valued at £9,412 a year. *Principal Seat*—Radley House, near Abingdon, Berks.

STANLEY:

cr. 25 June 1660;

afterwards, since 1839, BARONS STANLEY OF ALDERLEY.

I. 1660. "THOMAS STANLEY, of ALDERLEY, co. Chester, Esq.," only surv. s. and h. of Sir Thomas STANLEY, of Alderley and Wever, in that County, by Elizabeth, da. and h. of Sir Peter WARBURTON, of Grafton

(a) He disposed of Radley House, probably by long lease, to the trustees of the school called St. Peter's College, Radley, opened 6 March 1847. The Denham estate was alienated before (probably long before) 1876.

(b) He was, however, expelled from the Reform Club, 23 June 1876, for frequently voting against the Liberal party.

(c) Judge Jeune's remark in the divorce proceedings.

(d) The cause was *crim. con.* with Carey Johnstone, an American hotel proprietor.

Hall, in Tilston, co. Chester, sometime, 1600-21, a Judge of the Common Pleas, was *b.* 31 May 1597; *suc.* his father, 21 Nov. 1605; "subscribed" at Oxford, 1 July 1613; admitted to Lincoln's Inn, 25 April 1616; Sheriff of Cheshire, 1630-31, and was *cr. a Baronet*, 25 June 1660. He *m.*, in or before 1625, Elizabeth, da. of Sir Thomas PITT, of Kyrewyard, co. Worcester, by Mary, da. of Sir Arthur HEVENINGHAM. He was *bur.* 31 Aug. 1672, at Alderley, aged 75. Will pr. at Chester, 2 Sep. 1672. His widow, who was *b.* 1602, was living 1672.

II. 1672. SIR PETER STANLEY, Baronet [1660], of Alderley and Wever aforesaid, 2d but 1st surv. s. and h., *b.* at Alderley 29 May 1626; admitted to Gray's Inn, 2 Aug. 1647; *suc. to the Baronetcy* in Aug. 1672; Sheriff of Cheshire, 1677-78. He *m.*, 1650, in London, Elizabeth, da. of Sir John LEIGH, of Northcourt, in the Isle of Wight. She *d.* before him. He was *bur.* at St. Margaret's, Westm., 4 Oct. 1683, aged 57. Will dat. 27 Sep. 1683, pr. 17 Jan. 1683/4.

III. 1683. SIR THOMAS STANLEY, Baronet [1660], of Alderley and Wever, 1st s. and h., *b.* 25 March 1652; admitted to Gray's Inn, 13 June 1673; *suc. to the Baronetcy*, 1683; sold the estate of Wever, about 1710, which had been above 200 years in the family. He *m.*, before 1682, Christian, da. of Sir Stephen LENNARD, 1st Baronet [1642], of West Wickham, by his 3d wife, Anne, da. of Sir John OGLANDER. She was *bur.* 16 Feb. 1711/2, at Alderley. He *d.* at West Wickham, 1721.

IV. 1721. SIR JAMES STANLEY, Baronet [1660], of Alderley 1st s. and h.; *suc. to the Baronetcy* in 1721. He *m.*, Nov. 1740, Frances, da. of George BUTLER, of Ballyragget, co. Kilkenny, by Catherine, da. of John (KING) 3d BARON KINGSTON [I.]. He *d.* s.p. and was *bur.* 17 March 1746/7, at Alderley. Will dat. 13 Dec. 1745, pr. 20 May 1747, at Chester. His widow *d.* in London, March 1786. Will dat. 4 July 1785, pr. 28 March 1786.

V. 1747. SIR EDWARD STANLEY, Baronet [1660] of Alderley, aforesaid, br. and h.; *suc. to the Baronetcy* in March 1746/7. He *m.* in or before 1726, Mary, only da. of Thomas WARD, of London, Banker. He *d.* "suddenly in his coach," 28 Aug., and was *bur.* 5 Sep. 1755, at Alderley. Will pr. March 1756. His widow *d.* at Bath, 1771.

VI. 1755. SIR JOHN THOMAS STANLEY, Baronet [1660] of Alderley aforesaid, 2d but only surv. s. and h., *b.* 26 March 1735; *suc. to the Baronetcy* in Sep. 1755; was a Gent. of the Privy Chamber to George III. He *m.* 20 April 1763, Margaret, da. and h. of Hugh OWEN, of Peurhos, co. Anglesey. He *d.* in London, 29 Nov. 1807, and was *bur.* in South Audley Street Chapel. Will pr. 1808. His widow *d.* 1 Feb. 1816. Will pr. 1816.

VII. 1807. SIR JOHN THOMAS STANLEY, Baronet [1660], of Alderley aforesaid, 1st s. and h., *b.*, 26 Nov. 1766, and *bap.*, 1 Jan. 1767, at Alderley; ed. at Brunswick, Turin, Neufchatel, and at Edinburgh Universities. M.P. for Wotton Basset, 1790-96; *suc. to the Baronetcy*, 29 Nov. 1807; was upwards of twenty years Chairman of the Quarter Sessions in Cheshire. He *m.*, 11 Oct. 1796, at Fletching, Sussex, Maria Josepha, 1st da. of John (HOLROYD), 1st EARL OF SHEFFIELD [I.] by his 1st wife, Abigail, da. of Lewis WAY. She, who was *b.* 3 Jan. 1771, was living when he was *cr.*, 9 May 1839, BARON STANLEY OF ALDERLEY, co. Chester. In that peerage this *Baronetcy* then *merged* and still so continues.

SHUCKBURGH, *or* SHUCKBOROUGH:

cr. 25 June 1660;

sometime, 1793—1804, SHUCKBURGH-EVELYN.

I. 1660. "JOHN SHUCKBOROUGH, of Shuckborough, co. Warwick, Esq.," 1st s. and h. of Sir Richard SHUCKBURGH, of Shuckburgh aforesaid (who suffered severely in the cause of Charles I.), by his 3d wife, Grace,(a) da. of Sir Thomas HOLTE, 1st Baronet [1611], of Aston, was *b.* 1635; matric. at Oxford (Ch. Ch.), 8 May 1652; admitted to the Middle Temple, 1654; suc. his father (who *d.* aged 60), 13 June 1656; and was, for his father's services, *cr. a Baronet*, 25 June 1660. He *m.*, 18 Dec. 1656, at All Saints', Northampton, Catherine, yst. da. of Sir Hatton FERMOR, of Easton Neston, co. Northampton, by Anne, sister of Charles, 1st VISCOUNT CULLEN [I.], da. of Sir William COKAYNE, of Rushton in that county. He *d.* 1661, aged 26. Will pr. 1661. His widow *m.* 12 May 1663, at Easton Neston (reg. at Brampton), Sir Roger NORWICH, 2d Baronet [1641], of Brampton, co. Northampton, who was *bur.* there 4 Sep. 1691. She *d.* at St. Paul's, Covent Garden, 19 and was *bur.*, 28 May 1681 at Brampton. Admon. 16 March 1681/2.

II. 1661. SIR CHARLES SHUCKBURGH, Baronet [1660], of Shuckburgh aforesaid, only s. and h., *b.* Nov. 1659; *suc. to the Baronetcy* in 1661; matric. at Oxford (Ch. Ch.) 4 June 1675, aged 15; Sheriff of Warwickshire, 1685-86; M.P. for that county (four Parls.) 1698 till his death; Master of the Buckhounds to Queen Anne. He *m.* (Lic. Vic. Gen., 19 Sep. 1679, each aged about 20) Catherine, da. of Sir Hugh STEWKLEY, 2d Baronet [1627] of Hinton Ampney, Hants, by his 1st wife Catharine, da and h. of Sir John TROTT, Baronet [so *cr.* 1660] of Laverstoke, in that county. She *d.* between Aug. 1683 and Oct. 1684. He *m.* secondly (Lic. at Worcester, 26 Oct. 1684) Diana, da. of Richard (VERNEY), LORD WILLOUGHBY DE BROKE, by his 2d wife, Frances, da. of Thomas DOVE, of Upton, co. Northampton. He *d.* suddenly at Winchester, 2 Sep. 1705, aged 45. Will pr. Dec. 1705. His widow *d.* at Highwood Hill, Midx., 28 Sep. 1725. Will pr. 1749.

III. 1705. SIR JOHN SHUCKBURGH, Baronet [1660], of Shuckburgh aforesaid, 1st s. and h., being only s. by 1st wife, *b.* 18 Aug. 1683; entered Rugby school, 20 June 1690; matric. at Oxford (New. Coll.) 13 May 1700, aged 16; *suc. to the Baronetcy*, 2 Sep. 1705. He *m.* in or before 1705, Abigail, da. of George [or John] GOODWIN, of Latchford, Oxon. He *d.* 19 June 1724, aged 41. Will pr. 1726. His widow's will pr. 1759.

IV. 1724. SIR STEWKLEY SHUCKBURGH, Baronet [1660], of Shuckburgh aforesaid, only s. and h.(b), *b.* 9 March 1711; matric. at Oxford (Mag. Coll.), 8 April 1730, aged 18; *suc. to the Baronetcy*, 19 June 1724. He *d.*, unm., at Bath, 10 March 1759, and was *bur.* at Shuckburgh, aged 48. Will pr. 1759.

V. 1759. SIR CHARLES SHUCKBURGH, Baronet [1660], of Shuckburgh aforesaid, cousin and h. male, being 3d but 1st surv. s. of Charles SHUCKBURGH, of Longborough, co. Gloucester, and of Farthingstone, co. Northampton, by Sarah, da. of Col. Henry HUNT, of Blockley, co. Worcester, which Charles, who *d.* in 1752, was 2d s. of the 2d Baronet, being 1st

(a) This Grace *m.* secondly, 27 Oct. 1659, John Keating, Lord Chief Justice of the Common Pleas [I.], at whose house in Dublin, she *d.* 12 April 1677, and was *bur.* at Palmerston, near there. M.I. at Shuckburgh.

(b) He had, however, no less than ten sisters, of whom nine were married, three of them having two husbands and one of them having three.

s. by the 2d wife. He was *bap.* 17 March 1721/2, at Longborough(a); matric. at Oxford (Balliol Coll.), 2 March 1742/3, aged 20; B.A., 1746; M.A. (from All Souls' Coll., of which he was then a Fellow), 1749; B. Med. (from Balliol Coll.), 1753; practiced sometime as a medical man at Warwick; *suc. to the Baronetcy*, 10 March 1759; was Sheriff of Warwickshire, 1770-71. He *m.* 5 May 1749, Anne, widow of Campbell PRICE, of Westbury, Bucks, da. of (—) ROBINSON, of Covent Garden, Midx. He *d.* s.p., at Warwick, 10 Aug. 1773, in his 52d year, and was *bur.* at St. Mary's, Warwick. M.I.(b) Will pr. Sep. 1773. His widow *d.* 8 Oct. 1776, aged 57, and was *bur.* there.

VI. 1773. SIR GEORGE AUGUSTUS WILLIAM SHUCKBURGH *afterwards* [1793-1804], SHUCKBURGH-EVELYN, Baronet [1660], of Shuckburgh aforesaid, nephew and h., being 1st s. and h. of Lieut.-Col. Richard SHUCKBURGH, 1st Reg. of Guards, by Sarah, relict of Edward BATE, da. of (—) HAYWARD, of Plumstead, Kent, Capt. R.N., which Richard, who *d.*, 3 Sep. 1772, aged 45, was only br. of the late Baronet. He was *b.* about 1752, probably at Limerick; was ed. at Rugby school; matric. at Oxford (Balliol Coll.), 22 April 1768, aged 16; B.A. 1772; *suc. to the Baronetcy*, 10 Aug. 1773; F.R.S. 1774; F.S.R.; M.P. for Warwickshire (six Parls.), 1780, till his death in 1804; *assumed the additional name of Evelyn* on the death of his father-in-law, in July 1793, which was confirmed by Act of Parl. 1794. He *m.* firstly, in 1782, Sarah Johanna, da. of John DARKER, of Gayton, co. Northampton, many years M.P. for Leicester. She *d.*, s.p., at Bristol 10 and was *bur.*, 18 April 1783, at Shuckburgh. M.I. He *m.* secondly, 6 Oct. 1785, Julia Annabella, da. and sole heir of John EVELYN, of Felbridge, co. Surrey, by his 1st wife, Annabella, da. and (June 1796) sole heir of Thomas MEDLEY, of Buxted and Friston, Sussex. She was *bur.*, 23 Sep. 1797, at Shuckburgh. He *d.* s.p.m.(c) 11 and was *bur.* 20 Aug. 1804, at Shuckburgh.

VII. 1804. SIR STEWKLEY SHUCKBURGH, Baronet [1660], of Shuckburgh aforesaid, br. and h., male, *b.* about 1760; ed. at Rugby School, 1771; *suc. to the Baronetcy*, 11 Aug. 1804. He *m.*, 5 Sep. 1786, Charlotte Catherine, da. of Thomas TYDD, of Curdworth, co. Worcester, and Elizabeth, his wife. He *d.* 21 and was *bur.* 23 July 1809, at Shuckburgh. His widow *d.*, at Bath, 8 and was *bur.* 18 Feb. 1837 at Shuckburgh, aged 72.

VIII. 1809. SIR FRANCIS SHUCKBURGH, Baronet [1660], of Shuckburgh aforesaid, 1st s. and h., *b.* 12 March 1789; *suc. to the Baronetcy*, 21 July 1809; Sheriff of Warwickshire, 1804; F.R.S. He *m.*, 27 Oct. 1825, at Chelsea, Anne Maria DRAYCOTT, sister of Sir George William DENYS, 1st Baronet [1813], only da. of Peter DENYS, of the Pavilion, Hans Place, Chelsea, by Charlotte, da. of George (FERMOR), 2d EARL OF POMFRET. She *d.* 8 Nov. 1846. Will pr. July 1847. He *d.* 29 Oct., and was *bur.* 4 Nov. 1876, at Shuckburgh, aged 88.

IX. 1876. SIR GEORGE THOMAS FRANCIS SHUCKBURGH, Baronet [1660], of Shuckburgh aforesaid, only s. and h., *b.* 23 July 1829; Captain Scots Fusilier Guards, 1850; Major in the Army, 1854, serving that year in the Crimean Campaign; *suc. to the Baronetcy*, 29 Oct. 1876. He *m.*, 24 June

(a) The following extracts from the Longborough registers [*Mis. Gen. et Her.* 2d Series, vol. iii., p. 310] seem to relate to his elder brothers. *Baptism*, 1721 March 17, "Charles the (second), third son of Charles Shuckberg, Esq." *Burials*, 1719 Dec. 27, Charles ye sone of Charles Shuckberg, Esq." 1721 March 21, Charles ye second sone of Charles Shuckberg, Esq."

(b) See Playfair's *Baronetage* for his character.—"An excellent classical scholar; a brilliant companion," etc.

(c) Julia Evelyn Medley, his only da. and h., *b.* 5 Oct. 1790, who inherited Buxted and other family estates, *m.* 19 July 1810, at St. Geo., Han. sq., Charles Cecil Cope (Jenkinson), 3d and last Earl of Liverpool, who *d.* 3 Oct. 1851, s.p.m., at Buxted Park, leaving three daughters and coheirs.

1879, at Chelsea, his cousin, Ida Florence Geraldine, only da. of the Rev. Frederick William ROBERTSON, by Helen, da. of the abovenamed Sir George William DENYS, 1st Baronet [1813]. He *d.* at Shuckburgh, 12 and was *bur.* there 18 Jan. 1884, aged 54. His widow *m.* there, 25 Nov. 1886, Henry James SHUCKBURGH, Major, Norfolk Regiment, who *d.* 9 Feb. 1895. She was living 1902.

X. 1884. SIR STEWKLEY FREDERICK DRAYCOTT SHUCKBURGH, Baronet [1660], of Shuckburgh aforesaid, 1st s. and h., *b.* there 20 June 1880; *suc. to the Baronetcy*, 12 Jan. 1884.

Family Estates.—These, in 1883, consisted of 3,368 acres in Warwickshire and 134 in Northamptonshire. *Total*, 3,502 acres, worth £6,290 a year. *Principal Seat.*—Shuckburgh Park, near Daventry.

WRAY:

cr. 27 June 1660;
ex. in or shortly before 1687.

I. 1660. "WILLIAM WRAY, of Ashby, co. Lincoln, Esq.," s. and h. of Sir Christopher WRAY, of the same, by Albinia, 2d. da. and coheir of Edward (CECIL), VISCOUNT WIMBLEDON, which Christopher was a yr. s. (by his 2d wife) of Sir William WRAY, 1st Baronet [1611] of Glentworth, co. Lincoln, was *b.* about 1625; admitted to Lincoln's Inn, 5 Nov. 1638, suc. his father, the said Christopher, 6 Feb. 1644/5, was Capt. in the Parliamentary Army; Deputy-Governor of Beaumaris Castle, 1654; M.P. for Grimsby, Oct. 1645 till secluded Dec. 1648, re-elected 1654-55, 1656-58, 1659 and 1660; had an estate worth £3,000 a year,(a) was *Knighted*, 6, and was *cr. a Baronet*, 27 June 1660. He *m.* in or before 1652, Olympia, da. (whose issue in 1685 became heir) of Sir Humphrey TUFTON, 1st Baronet [1641], of the Mote, near Maidstone, by Margaret, 1st da. and coheir of Herbert Morley, of Glynd, co. Sussex. He *d.* 17 Oct. 1669, aged 43, and was *bur.* at Ashby. Will dat. 15 Oct. 1669, pr. 1 Feb. 1669/70, 15 June 1684, and 6 Nov. 1687. His widow *d.* at the Mote aforesaid, Sep. 1680. Nunc. will dat. 11 Sep., and pr. 2 Dec. 1680, and 8 Nov. 1687.

II. 1669. SIR CHRISTOPHER WRAY, Baronet [1660], of Ashby aforesaid, 1st s. and h., *b.* about 1652; matric. at Oxford (Univ. Coll.), 19 May 1668, aged 16; *suc. to the Baronetcy* [1660] on the death of his father, 17 Oct. 1669, and *suc. to the older Baronetcy* [*cr.* 25 Nov. 1611] on the death, 19 Feb. 1671/2, of his cousin, Sir Bethel WRAY, 5th Baronet [1611]. He *d.* unm., and was *bur.* 31 Aug. 1679, at St. Giles-in-the-Fields, Midx. Admon. 14 Dec. 1682, in the Court of Delegates, and again 28 March 1695.

III. 1679, to 1687? SIR WILLIAM WRAY, Baronet [1611 and 1660], of Ashby aforesaid, and of Louth, co. Lincoln, br. and h.; *suc. to the Baronetcies* in Aug. 1679. He *d.* unm., between 9 March 1685/6 and 8 Nov. 1687, when the *Baronetcy* [1660] *became extinct*, but the older Baronetcy [1611] devolved on his cousin and h. male. Will as "of Louth," dat. 9 March 1685/6, pr. 8 Nov. 1687, 9 Feb. 1694/5, and 30 June 1711.

See "WRAY," *Baronetcy, cr.* 1611.

(a) Sir Joseph Williamson's notes on Lincolnshire proprietors [*Her. and Gen.*, vol. ii, p. 126].

STEWARD, STEWART, *or* STUART:

cr. 27 June 1660.

I. 1660. "NICHOLAS STEWARD, of Hartley Mauduit, Hants, Esq.," s. and h. of Simeon STEWART, of the same, by Dorothy, relict of Sir Christopher Pigott, da. of Sir Richard INGOLDSBY, of Lethenborough, Bucks., was *b.* about 1616; suc. his father before 16 Nov. 1636, when he was admitted to Lincoln's Inn; was fined £1,400, as a Royalist, 16 Dec. 1647, and was *cr. a Baronet*, 27 June 1660, being Chamberlain of the Exchequer, 1660 till death; M.P. for Lymington, March 1663 to 1679. He *m.* about 1640, Mary, only da. of Sir Miles SANDYS, of Miserden, co. Glouc., by Mary, da. of Sir John HANBURY, of Kelmarsh, co. Northampton. He *d.* 15 Feb. 1709/10, aged 93. Will pr. May 1710.

II. 1710. SIR SIMEON STUART, Baronet [1660], of Hartley Mauduit aforesaid, grandson and h., being only s. and h. of Charles STUART, by Clemence(a) (Mar. Lic. Fac., 12 Aug. 1678, she 17) da. and coheir of Sir William HOVELL, of Hillingdon, Norfolk, which Charles (aged 21 in Aug. 1678) was 3d and yst. s.(b) of the 1st Baronet, but *d.*, v.p., before May 1709. He *suc. to the Baronetcy*, 15 Feb. 1709/10; was M.P. for Southampton, 1708-10, and for Hants, 1710-13; was Chamberlain of the Exchequer, 1712 till death. He *m.* Elizabeth, only da. and (after Jan. 1738/9), heir of Sir Richard DEREHAM, 3d Baronet [1661], by Frances, da. of Robert WRIGHT, *afterwards* VILLIERS and *finally* DANVERS, reputed son of John (VILLIERS) VISCOUNT PURBECK. She *d.* before 28 March 1750. Admon. of that date. He *d.* 11 Aug. 1761. Will pr. 1761.

III. 1761. SIR SIMEON STUART, Baronet [1660], of Hartley Mauduit aforesaid, only surv. s. and h.; *suc. to the Baronetcy*, 11 Aug. 1761, and was Chamberlain of the Exchequer, 1761 till death. He *m.* (—), da. of Lieut. Col. (—) HOOKE, Gov. of Minorca. He, who was a bankrupt at the Bath Court, Oct. 1775, *d.* 19 Nov. 1779. Will pr. Dec. 1782.

IV. 1779. SIR SIMEON STUART, Baronet [1660], of Hartley Mauduit aforesaid, only s. and h.; *suc. to the Baronetcy*, 19 Nov. 1779. He *m.* about 1784, Mary Anne Stowe.(c) He subsequently *m.* 20 May 1789, at Woodford, Essex, Frances Maria, 1st da. and coheir of John (LUTTRELL-OLMIUS) 3d. and last EARL OF CARHAMPTON, by his 1st wife (to whom she was sole heir), Elizabeth, da. of John (OLMIUS) 1st BARON WALTHAM OF PHILIPSTOWN [I.]. He *d.* 14 Jan. 1816. His widow, *d.* at Southampton, 4 Jan. 1848, aged 79. Admon. 15 March 1848, under £1,000.

V. 1816. SIR SIMEON HENRY STUART, Baronet [1660], 1st s. and h., by 2d wife, *b.* 23 Oct. 1790; sometime Captain in the 10th Hussars; served through the Peninsular war [medal and four clasps]; *suc. to the Baronetcy*, 14 June 1816; was Comptroller of the Household to George IV. He *m.* 25 Oct. 1815, Georgiana Frances, 6th and yst. da. of George GUN-CUNINGHAME, of Mount Kennedy, co. Wicklow. She *d.* 16 Jan. 1840. He *d.* 23 Oct. 1868, on his 78th birthday, at Hayward's Heath, Sussex.

VI. 1868. SIR SIMEON HENRY STUART, Baronet [1660], 1st s. and h., *b.* 15 June 1823, at Farnham, Dorset; sometime Lieut. in the Royal Canadian Rifles; Capt. of the 7th Lancashire Militia, 1855; *suc. to the Baronetcy*, 23 Oct. 1868. He *m.* firstly, 15 April 1846, Julia Maria, yst. da. of James CUTHBERT, of Bertheir Manor, Canada East, sometime 60th Regt. of Foot. She *d.* s.p., 10 Jan. 1848. He *m.*, secondly, 15 Oct. 1850, Catherine Henrietta, da.

(a) She who was unfaithful to her husband, *m.* 11 Feb. 1713/4, at St. Bride's, London, Sir Thomas Montgomerie.
(b) His eldest br. Nicholas, *b.* 26 March 1642, matric. at Oxford (Oriel Coll.), 31 July 1658; was admitted to Lincoln's Inn, 17 Nov. 1662, and *d.* unm., v.p., Nov. 1664.
(c) Betham's *Baronetage*, 1802.

of Henry Lechmere WORRALL, Lieut.-Gen., Bengal Cavalry. He *d.* in London, 21 Aug. 1891, aged 68. His widow *d.* 14 Dec. 1897.

VII. 1891. SIR SIMEON LECHMERE STUART, Baronet [1660], of Broomfield Manor, Essex, only s. and h., *b.* 15 May 1864, at [apparently] Dublin; matric. at Oxford (Mag. Coll.), 16 Oct. 1882, aged 18; admitted to Inner Temple, 1884; sometime Lieut. 5th Dragoon Guards; *suc. to the Baronetcy*, 21 Aug. 1891; Marshal of the City of London, 1893-99; served as Major in the Imperial Yeomanry in the South African war, 1900-1 [medal with three clasps]. He *m.* 31 March 1891, Florence Louise, only da. of Henry Harmond GUDGE, Sec. to the Austrian Legation.

WARBURTON:

cr. 27 June 1660;
ex. 13 May 1813.

I. 1660. "GEORGE WARBURTON, of Arley, co. Chester, Esq.," 2d s. of Peter WARBURTON, of the Lodge in Crowley, in that county (*d.* 1 Jan. 1625), by his 2d wife Elizabeth, da. of Sir Richard EGERTON, of Ridley, was *b.* about 1622; suc. his elder br. Peter Warburton, in the estate of Arley and Warburton, co. Chester, 1 Aug. 1641, and was *cr. a Baronet*, 27 June 1660. He *m.* firstly, 16 May 1649,(a) Elizabeth, sister of Sir Thomas MIDDLETON, 1st Baronet [1660] da. of Sir Thomas MIDDLETON, of Chirk, co. Denbigh, by his 2d wife, Mary, da. of Sir Robert NAPIER, 1st Baronet [1611] of Luton. She was living 1654. He *m.* secondly in 1655, Diana, da. of Sir Edward BISHOPP, 3d Baronet [1620] of Parham, by Mary, da. of Nicholas (TUFTON), 1st EARL OF THANET. He *d.* 18 May 1676, aged 55, and was *bur.* at Great Budworth. M.I. His widow *d.* 15 March 1693, and was *bur.* at St. John's, Chester. Will pr. 1694.

II. 1676. SIR PETER WARBURTON, Baronet [1660], of Warburton and Arley aforesaid, 1st s. and h. by 1st wife; *suc. to the Baronetcy*, 18 May 1676. Sheriff of Cheshire, 1689, but did not act. He *m.* (settl. 1 July 1673) Martha, da. and h. of Thomas DOCWRA, of Putteridgebury in Lilley, Herts, by Margaret, da. of Robert CHERRY. He *d.* at Offley, Herts, between 1697 and Sep. 1698. Admon. 9 Sep. 1698. His widow *d.* 21 Dec. 1707, and was *bur.* at Lilley aforesaid. Will pr. Jan. 1708.

III. 1698? SIR GEORGE WARBURTON, Baronet [1660], of Warburton and Arley aforesaid, 1st s. and h., *bap.* 1 June 1675, at Offley aforesaid; *suc. to the Baronetcy* between 1697 and Sep. 1698; was M.P. for Cheshire (four Parls.), 1702-05 and 1713-22. He *m.*, 18 June 1700, at Fulham, Midx. (Lic. Fac., he 25 and she 21), Diana, sister and coheir of Giles (ALINGTON), 4th BARON ALINGTON OF KILLARD [I.] and 2d BARON ALINGTON OF WYMONDLEY, being da. of William, the 3d and 1st Baron by his 3d wife, Diana, da. of William (RUSSELL), 1st DUKE OF BEDFORD. She who was *b.* 1676, *d.* 17 June 1705 and was *bur.* at Lilley aforesaid, aged 28. M.I. He *d.* s.p.s.(b) 29 June 1743, in his 69th year, and was *bur.* there. M.I. Will pr. 1743.

IV. 1743. SIR PETER WARBURTON, Baronet [1660], of Warburton and Arley aforesaid, nephew and h., being only s. and h. of Thomas WARBURTON, of Turner's Hall, Herts, by his 2d wife, Anne, da. of William DOCWRA, of London, which Thomas, who was *bap.*, 19 Sep. 1676, at Offley and who *d.* before July 1739, was next br. to the late Baronet. He was *b.* about

(a) Date as given in Ormerod's *Cheshire*, where, however it is also stated that Peter, the son of this marriage was living 1696, aged 53, and consequently born in 1643.
(b) Diana, the only child that survived infancy, *m.* 1724, as his 2d wife Sir Richard Grosvenor, 4th Baronet [1622], who *d.* 12 July 1732, and *d.* s.p. and v.p., 18 Feb. 1729/30, aged 27.

1708; *suc. to the Baronetcy*, 29 June 1743; was Sheriff of Cheshire, 1744-45. He *m.*, 1 March 1745/6, Elizabeth, 1st da. of Edward (STANLEY), 11th EARL OF DERBY, by Elizabeth, da. and h. of Robert HESKETH. He *d.*, 18 Nov. 1774, in his 67th year. His widow *d.*, 25 Aug. 1780, at Knutsford, aged 64.

V. 1774, to 1813. SIR PETER WARBURTON, Baronet [1660], of Warburton and Arley aforesaid, only s. and h., *b.* 27 Oct. 1754; matric. at Oxford (Ch. Ch.), 7 July 1772, aged 17; *suc. to the Baronetcy*, 18 Nov. 1774; was Sheriff of Cheshire, 1782-83. He *m.* 15 Aug. 1781, Alice, da. of the Rev. John PARKER, of Astle, co. Chester and Breightmett, co. Lanc. He *d.* s.p. 14 May 1813, and was *bur.* at Great Budworth, when the *Baronetcy* became *extinct*. Will pr. 1813.(a) His widow *d.* 9 Sep. 1837, aged 75. Will pr. Dec. 1837.

HOLLES:

cr. 27 June 1660;
afterwards, 1680-94, BARONS HOLLES OF IFIELD;
ex. 24 Jan. 1693/4.

I. 1660. "FRANCIS HOLLES, of Winterbourn, Dorset, Esq., son and heir [ap.] to Denzill, LORD HOLLES, English Baron," *i.e.*, BARON HOLLES OF IFIELD, co. Sussex (who, however, was not so *cr.* till 20 April 1661), by his 1st wife, Dorothy, da. and h. of Sir Francis ASHLEY, of Dorchester, Dorset, Serjeant at Law, was *b.* at Dorchester, 19 Aug. 1627; was M.P. for Lostwithiel, Jan. 1647 till secluded in Dec. 1648; for Wilts, 1654-55; for Northallerton, July 1660 till void, and for Dorchester, March to July 1679 and Oct. 1679 to Feb. 1679/80, having been v.p., *cr. a Baronet*, 27 June 1660. He *m.* firstly, 22 Aug. 1661, in Westm. Abbey (Lic. Fac.), Lucy, 3d and yst. dau. of Sir Robert CARR, 2d Baronet [1611] of Sleaford, by Mary, dau. and coheir of Sir Richard GARGRAVE. She (who is styled "*Baronettess*" in the directions as to her monument given in the will of her husband) *d.* s.p.m., 15 and was *bur.* 25 Sep. 1667, at Ifield, Sussex, in her 32d year. He *m.* secondly, 9 June 1670, at Kensington (Lic. Fac.), Anne, 1st dau. and coheir of Sir Francis PILE, 2d Baronet [1628] of Compton Beauchamp, by his 2d wife, presumably Margery, da. of John HUNTBACH, of Sewall, co. Stafford. She was living when, by the death of his father, 17 Feb. 1679/80, he became BARON HOLLES OF IFIELD, in which peerage this *Baronetcy then merged* till both became extinct by the death of his son, the 2d Baronet and 3d Baron, 24 Jan. 1693/4. See *Peerage*.

["SIR DENZELL HOLLES, Baronet," only surv. s. of the above by his 2d wife, was so styled, 1680 to 1690, by his father(b) (after his said father's accession to the Peerage, 17 Feb. 1679/80), to whom he was heir ap., on the theory, apparently, that the s. and h. ap. of a Baron, who was also a Baronet, was entitled by courtesy to his father's Baronetcy.(c) To this Baronetcy, as also to the Barony of Holles, of Ifield, he became unquestionably entitled on his father's death, 1 March 1689/90, but both became, shortly afterwards, *extinct* on his death unm., 24 Jan. 1693/4, in his 18th year. See *Peerage*.]

(a) The estates of Warburton and Arley devolved under his will on his great nephew, Rowland Eyles Egerton, who accordingly took the additional surname of Warburton, he being son of the Rev. Rowland Egerton, by Emma, da. of James Croxton and Emma his wife, sister to the testator.
(b) In Lord Holles' will, dat. 3 Sep. 1680, he mentions his son as "called Sir Denzell Holles, Baronet." On a wooden tablet in Aldenham Church, Herts, over the Holles pew was inscribed "the Honourable Sir Denzil Holles, Baronet, the only sonne and heyre apparent, of Francis, Lord Holles, of Ifield, aged eleaven yeares."
(c) See vol. ii, p. 444, note "b," as to this extraordinary opinion which was undoubtedly that of the Viscounts Mayo [I.] (*cr.* 1627; *ex.* 1767) who held in addition to their Viscountcy an Irish Baronetcy *cr.* 1638.

SAINT JOHN:

cr. 28 June 1660;

afterwards, since 1711, BARONS SAINT JOHN OF BLETSHO.

I. 1660. "OLIVER SAINT JOHN, of Woodford, co. Northampton, Esq.," only s. and h. of the Hon. Sir Rowland SAINT JOHN, K.B., by Sybilla, da. of John VAUGHAN, of Hargast, co. Hereford, which Rowland (who *d.* Aug. 1645) was yr. br. to Oliver, 1st EARL OF BOLINGBROKE, both being sons of Oliver, 3d BARON SAINT JOHN OF BLETSHO (a title *cr.* 13 Jan. 1558/9), was *b.* about 1624; suc. his father, Aug. 1645, and was *cr. a Baronet*, 28 June 1660. He *m.* about 1648, Barbara, 3d and yst. da. and coheir of John ST. ANDREW, of Gotham, Notts, and of East Haddon, co. Northampton, by Elizabeth, da. of John BAINBRIDGE, of Lockington, co. Leicester. He *d.* 3 Jan. 1661/2, aged 37. Will pr. 1662.

II. 1662. SIR ST. ANDREW SAINT JOHN, Baronet [1660], of Woodford and East Haddon(a) aforesaid, 1st s. and h., *b.* about 1650; *suc. to the Baronetcy*, 3 Jan. 1661/2. He *m.* 10 March 1680/1, at St. Leonard's, Shoreditch (Lic. Vic. Gen., he 22, she 14, with consent of mother), Jane, da. of Sir William BLOIS, of Cockfield Hall, in Culpho, Suffolk, by his 2d wife, Jane, da. of Sir Nathaniel BARNADISTON, of Ketton, in that county. He *d.* 1708. Will pr. Feb. 1710. The will of his widow, dat. 23 Jan. 1710/1, as of Woodford, pr. 1711, in the Court of Delegates.

III. 1708. SIR OLIVER SAINT JOHN, Baronet [1660], of Woodford and East Haddon aforesaid, 1st s. and h., *b.* about 1683; *suc. to the Baronetcy* 1708, and *d.* soon afterwards unm.

IV. 1710? SIR ST. ANDREW SAINT JOHN, Baronet [1660], of Wood ford and East Haddon aforesaid, br. and h., *b.* about 1685; *suc. to the Baronetcy* about 1710. He *m.*(b) Anne, da. of Sir William JAMES, of Korlings, Suffolk, and of Kensington. He *d.* at Kensington early in 1711. Admon. 7 Nov. 1711, to his widow. She *d.* 10 Jan. 1739. Will pr. 1739.

V. 1711. SIR PAULET ST. ANDREW SAINT JOHN, Baronet [1660], of Woodford and East Haddon aforesaid, posthumous s. and h., *b.* 1711, and *suc. to the Baronetcy* at his birth. Very shortly afterwards, by the death, 5 Oct. 1711, of his cousin, Paulet, 4th Earl of Bolingbroke and 7th Baron Saint John of Bletsho, he became BARON SAINT JOHN OF BLETSHO, in which peerage this *Baronetcy* then *merged*, and still so continues.

DELAVAL:

cr. 29 June 1660;

ex. or *dormant*, 10 June 1729.

I. 1660. "RALPH DELAVAL, of Seton [*i.e.* Seaton Delaval] Northumberland, Esq.," s. and h. of Robert DELAVAL, of the same, by Barbara, da. of Sir George SELBY, of Whitehouse, co. Durham, which George (who *d.*, v.p., 4 March 1622/3) was s. and h. ap. of Sir Ralph DELAVAL, of Seaton Delaval, was *bap.*, 27 Oct. 1622, at Earsdon; suc. his said grandfather, 24 Nov. 1628; matric. at Oxford (Queen's Coll.), 15 June 1638, aged 16; admitted to Lincoln's

(a) The estate of East Haddon continued in the family, till alienated in 1807 by Andrew, 13th Baron Saint John of Bletsho.

(b) To this marriage in Collins's *Peerage* [edit. 1811] is put "ex regist. eccles. St. Peter, Cornhill," but no such marriage is in the extracts from that register pub. by the *Harleian Society*.

Inn, 28 Nov. 1639; M.P. for Northumberland (six Parls.), 1659, 1660 and March 1676/7 to 1682, and was *cr. a Baronet*, 29 June 1660. He entered his pedigree in the Visit. of Northumberland in Aug. 1666, being then aged 43. He *m.*, 2 April 1646, at St. Nicholas', Newcastle (regd. at Earsdon), Anne, widow of Hugh FRASER, Master of Lovat (who *d.*, v.p., May 1643), 3d da. of Alexander (LESLIE), 1st EARL OF LEVEN [S.], by Agnes, da. of David RENTON. He *d.* 29 Aug. and was *bur.* 1 Sep. 1691, at Earsdon. His widow was *bur.* there 26 Nov. 1696.

II. 1691. SIR RALPH DELAVAL, Baronet [1660], of Seaton Delaval aforesaid, 3d but 1st surv. s. and h.(a); *bap.*, 26 Nov. 1649, at Earsdon; *suc. to the Baronetcy*, in Aug. 1691. He *m.* (settlement, 2 Nov. 1684), Diana, sister of Henry, 1st EARL OF WARRINGTON, da. of George (BOOTH), 1st BARON DELAMERE, by his 2d wife, Elizabeth, da. of Henry (GREY), 1st EARL OF STAMFORD. He *d.* s.p.m.,(b) and was *bur.* 30 Aug. 1696, at Earsdon. His widow *m.* 21 Oct. 1699, at St. Mary-le-bow, Durham (as his 3d and last wife), Sir Edward BLACKETT, 2d Baronet [1673], who *d.* 23 April 1718, aged 69. She *d.* 7 Oct. 1713. M.I. at Ripon.

III. 1696. SIR JOHN DELAVAL, Baronet [1660], br. and h. male, being 5th s. of the 1st Baronet; *bap.* 7 Nov. 1654, at Earsdon aforesaid; *suc. to the Baronetcy* in Aug. 1696. He *m.* (—). He was *bur.*, 8 June 1727, at Earsdon.

IV. 1727. SIR THOMAS DELAVAL, Baronet [1660], s. and h., *suc. to the Baronetage* in June 1727.(c) He is mentioned in Wotton's *Baronetage* [edit. 1727], as being father of "Sir (—) DELAVAL the present Baronet."

V. 1728? to 1729. SIR JOHN DELAVAL, Baronet [1660], "of the Lodge, co. Northumberland," who, being presumably s. and h. of the above, *suc. to the Baronetage* about 1728. He *d.* s.p.m.(d) 10 June 1729, after which date the *Baronetcy* became either *extinct* or *dormant*.

HENLEY:

cr. 20 June 1660.

ex. in 1740.

I. 1660. "ANDREW HENLEY, of Henley, co. Somerset, Esq.," 2d s. of Robert HENLEY, of Crewkerne in that county, and of the Grange in Mitcheldever, Hants, one of the six Clerks in Chancery and Master of

(a) Robert the eldest son, bap. 2 July 1647, at Earsdon, and living unm. Aug. 1666, aged 19, *m.*, Elizabeth, only da. of James (Livingstone), 1st Earl of Newburgh [S.], but *d.* s.p. and v.p., 1 Aug. 1682, in his 36th year and was *bur.* in St. George's Chapel, Windsor.

(b) His da., Diana, appears to have inherited most of the estates. She *d.* 10 Jan. 1710, having *m.*, before 1703, William Blackett, 1st s. and h. ap. (by his 2d wife) of Sir Edward Blackett, 2d Baronet [1673] abovenamed, which William *d.* v.p. 23 Feb. 1713. They had an only da. and heir, Diana (heir to her mother's estates), who *m.* firstly, 26 July 1725, Henry Mainwaring, of Over Peover, co. Chester, and secondly the Rev. Thomas Wetenhall. She *d.* 2 May 1738, aged 34.

(c) So stated, both by Courthope and Burke (in their *Extinct Baronetages*), but he was clearly dead in, or before, 1727 [Wotton's *Baronetage* of that date], and the 3d Baronet did not die till June 1727. It would seem more probable that he was brother to the 3d Baronet (whom he probably predeceased) and father of John, the Baronet living in 1727. The only issue ascribed to Sir John, the 3d Baronet, in Le Neve's MS. *Baronetage* [1704] is a daughter.

(d) He is said to have had a da., who *m.* John Rogers, of Denton [*ex inform.* W. D. Pink].

the King's Bench (*bur.* 29 Feb. 1655/6, in the Temple Church), being 1st s. by his 2d wife, Anne, da. of John ELDRED, of Saxmundham, Suffolk, was *b.* about 1622; matric. at Oxford (Exeter Coll.), 22 March 1638/9, aged 16; Barrister (Middle Temple), 1646; was of Bramshill Park, in Eversley, Hants; Sheriff of that county, 1653-54; was M.P. for Portsmouth, May to Dec. 1660, and was *cr. a Baronet*, 20 June 1660, being *Knighted* 21 July following. He *m.* firstly, Mary, 3d da. of Sir John GAYER, sometime, 1646-47, Lord Mayor of London, by Catherine, da. of Sampson HOPKINS, of Coventry. She *d.* 30 July 1666, and was *bur.* at Eversley. M.I. He *m.* secondly, 20 May 1672, at St. Marylebone, Constance, widow of Thomas MIDDLETON, of Stansted Montfichet, Essex (who *d.* 21 Aug. 1668), da. of Thomas BROMFIELD, Merchant, Alderman of London. She *d.* at Bramshill soon afterwards. Admon. 4 Nov. 1672. He *d.* in or shortly before 1675. Will pr. 1675.

II. 1675? SIR ROBERT HENLEY, Baronet [1660], of Bramshill, aforesaid, 1st s. and h. by 1st wife; *suc. to the Baronetcy* in or shortly before 1675. He was M.P. for Bridport, 1679-81. He mortgaged his estates for £20,000, and *d.* unm. about 1689. Will pr. 1690.

III. 1689. SIR ANDREW HENLEY, Baronet [1660], of Bramshill aforesaid, br. and h., *suc. to the Baronetcy* about 1689. In 1695 he "killed a man and fled for it,"(a) and, probably about that time, alienated the estate of Bramshill to the family of COPE. He *m.* Sarah, da. of (—) BULL, of Yateley, Hants. He was *bur.*, 14 Sep. 1703, at St. James', Westm. His widow was *bur.* there 3 Sep. 1725. Will dat. 6 May 1723, pr. 4 Sep. 1725, by her son Sir Robert HENLEY, Baronet.

IV. 1703, to 1740. SIR ROBERT HENLEY, Baronet [1660], only s. and h., *suc. to the Baronetcy* in Sep. 1703; went "with the Queen's letter" to sea; was sometime a Customer in the port of Sandwich, and subsequently Capt. of H.M.'s fireship "Eleanor." He *m.* firstly, (—) CRADOCK, of Salisbury, who *d.* s.p.(b) He *m.* secondly, Rebecca BOWLES, of Camberwell, Surrey, sister of Brig. Gen. BOWLES. He *d.* s.p. at St. Martins-in-the-Fields, 1740, when the *Baronetcy* became *extinct*. Will pr. 1740 by a creditor. His widow *d.* April 1743.

ELLIS, *or* ELLYS:

cr. 30 June 1660;

ex. 14 Feb. 1741/2.

I. 1660. "THOMAS ELLIS, of Wyham, co. Lincoln, Esq.," was s. and h. of Thomas ELLIS, or ELLYS, by Elizabeth (*m.* 8 Nov. 1627, at Northill, Beds), da. of (—) HARDING, which Thomas (who was elder br. of Sir William Ellis, sometime [1672-80] Justice of the Common Pleas, presumed to be the person *cr. a Baronet* in 1658, by the Protector Cromwell) was s. and h. of Sir Thomas ELLYS, of Grantham, who was *bur.* there 7 Sep. 1627. He was *bap.* 8 Oct. 1627, at Northill aforesaid, suc. his father at some date after 1631; was admitted to Inner Temple, Nov. 1646, and was *cr. a Baronet*, 30 June 1660.(c) He

(a) Le Neve's MS., *Baronetage*.

(b) See for this marriage Hutchins' *Dorset* (3d Edit., vol. iii, p. 742). At St. James', Westm., there is a baptism, 7 Oct. 1727, of "Andrew Henley, son of Robert and Ann, born 3," which possibly may refer to some child (who died v.p.) of this marriage, if indeed Miss Cradock's christian name was Ann.

(c) In Sir Joseph Williamson's "Lincolnshire Families," temp. Charles II (*Her. and Gen.*, vol. ii, p. 121), he is thus noticed, "Sir Tho. Ellis, of Wyham, near Louth, a late Baronet, ancient family here: nephew to ye Lawyer and his heire: between them make £3,000 [*i.e.*, yearly income]: marryed a fair Lady, Sir John Stanhop's daughter, of Derbyshire: a drunken sott: ye Lawyer had £1,500 per ann. at Grantham."

m., in or shortly before 1653, Anne, da. of Sir John STANHOPE, of Elvaston, co. Derby, by his 2d wife, Mary, da. of Sir John RADCLIFFE, of Ordsall, co. Lancaster. She, possibly, is the "Ladie ELLIS," who was *bur.*, 25 Nov. 1661, at Grantham. He *d.* before Nov. 1670.

II. 1668? SIR WILLIAM ELLYS, Baronet [1660], of Wyham aforesaid and afterwards of Nocton, co. Lincoln, 1st s. and h., *b.* about 1654; *suc. to the Baronetcy* on the death of his father about 1668; matric. at Oxford (Linc. Coll.), 4 Nov. 1670, aged 16, being then a Baronet; *cr.* M.A., 21 March 1670/1; was M.P. for Grantham (thirteen Parls.), 1679-81 and 1689-1713. By the death, 11 Dec. 1680, of his great uncle, Sir William Ellis abovenamed, he suc. to the estate of Nocton. He *m.*, Isabella, only da. of the Rt. Hon. Richard HAMPDEN, of Great Hampden, Bucks, sometime chancellor of the Exchequer, by Lætitia, da. of William (PAGET), LORD PAGET. He *d.*, 6 Oct. 1727, aged 74. Will pr. 1728.

III. 1727, to 1742. SIR RICHARD ELLYS, Baronet [1660], of Nocton aforesaid, s. and h., *b.* about 1674(a); M.P. for Grantham, 1701-02, and for Boston (three Parls.), Dec. 1719 to 1734; *suc. to the Baronetcy*, 6 Oct. 1727. He *m.* firstly (Lic. 21 May 1714, he 30 [*Qy.* 40] and she 26), Elizabeth, da. and coheir of Sir Thomas HUSSEY, 2d Baronet [1611], of Honington and Doddington, co. Lincoln, by Sarah, da. of Sir John LANGHAM, 1st Baronet [1660]. She *d.* 11 and was *bur.* 27 Aug. 1724, at Honington. M.I. Will dat. 12 Sep. 1722, pr. 3 Dec. 1724.(b) He *m.* secondly, Sarah, da. and coheir of Thomas GOULD, of Iver, Bucks. He *d.* s.p., 14 Feb. 1741/2, when the *Baronetcy* became *extinct*. Will dat. 8 May 1740, pr. 23 Feb. 1741/2.(c) His widow *m.*, 19 Dec. 1745 at St. Geo., Han. sq., Francis (DASHWOOD), LORD LE DESPENCER, who *d.* s.p. legit., 11 Dec. 1781, aged 73. She *d.* 19 Jan. 1769, at West Wycombe, Bucks. M.I.

COVERT:

cr. 2 July 1660;

ex. 11 March 1678/9.

I. 1660, to 1679. "JOHN COVERT, of Slaugham, co. Sussex, Esq.," s. and h. of Sir Walter COVERT, of Maidstone, Kent, by Anne, da. and h. of John COVERT, of Slaugham aforesaid, was *b.* 6 June 1620; suc. his mother (who *d.* a widow), 22 Sep. 1632 in the estate of Slaugham; was a compounder, 23 Oct. 1644; fined £500 but reduced to £300, and was *cr. a Baronet*, 2 July 1660; was M.P. for Horsham, 1661-79. He *m.* Isabella, widow of Gervase WARMSTREY, of Worcester, da. of Sir William LEIGH, of Longborow, co. Gloucester. He *d.* s.p.m.(d) 11 and was *bur.* 20 March 1678/9, at Slaugham, when the *Baronetcy* became *extinct*. Admon. 21 May 1679, and again (to a creditor) 8 Nov. 1680. His widow *d.* Sep. 1680, in St. Martin's-in-the-Fields or St. Mary's Savoy. Her Admon. 23 Oct. 1680.

(a) He was second of three brothers living in 1680, of whom William, the eldest, was then aged 7.

(b) See R. E. G. Cole's *Doddington, co. Lincoln.*

(c) In it he leaves Nocton and other estates (valued at £4,000 a year), after the death of his widow, to his distant relative John (Hobart) 1st Baron Hobart of Blickling, afterwards (1746) Earl of Buckinghamshire, whose grandmother, Mary, was yst. sister of Richard Hampden, testator's maternal grandfather. It was not, however, till after a protracted law suit against the heir at law, that the Hobart family obtained possession of them.

(d) Walter, the only son, *d.* Sep. 1672. Of the two surviving daughters and coheirs (1), Mary *m.* firstly, as his 2d wife, 2 Feb. 1675/6, Henry Goring (who *d.* v.p. 1687), and was mother of Sir Harry Goring, 4th Baronet [1678]. She *m.* secondly, Nicholas Best, of Horsham; (2). Anne, who inherited the estate of Slaugham, *m.* 26 Dec. 1671, Sir James Morton, whose second son, James Morton sold it to Charles Sergison.

LEAR:

cr. 2 July 1660;

ex. in 1683.

I. 1660, to 1683. "PETER LEAR, of London, Gent.," sometime a Planter in Barbadoes, having acquired there a considerable fortune, was *cr. a Baronet* 2 July 1660. He was of Lindridge in Bishops Teignton, Devon,(a) and was Sheriff of that county, 1673-74. He *m.* Susan, da. of Richard LANT, of London. He *d.* s.p. in 1683, when the *Baronetcy* became *extinct*. M.I. at Bishops Teignton. Will pr. 1684 His widow *m.* Dennis ROLLE. Her will pr. Jan. 1713.

BERKELEY:

cr. 2 July 1660;

afterwards, June 1668, VISCOUNT FITZHARDINGE [I.];

ex. 13 June 1690.

I. 1660, to 1690. "MAURICE BERKELEY, of Bruton, co. Somerset, Esq., Irish Viscount, *viz.*, VISCOUNT FITZHARDING," was elder br. of Charles (BERKELEY) EARL OF FALMOUTH, who had been *cr.*, 14 July 1663, VISCOUNT FITZHARDINGE OF BEREHAVEN, co. Kerry [I.] (with a spec. rem.), both being sons of Sir Charles BERKELEY, of Bruton aforesaid, afterwards (3 June 1665) 2d VISCOUNT FITZHARDINGE OF BEREHAVEN [I.], by Penelope, da. of Sir William GODOLPHIN. He was v.p. *cr. a Baronet* 2 July 1660; was M.P. for Wells, 1661-79; and for Bath, 1681, 1685-87, 1689-90, and 1690 till death, having, on the death of his father in June 1668, *suc. to the* [Irish] *peerage* as 3d VISCOUNT FITZHARDINGE OF BEREHAVEN [I.], in which title *this Baronetcy* then *merged*. He *m.*, before Dec 1666, Anne, da. of Sir Henry LEE, 1st Baronet [1611] of Quarendon, by Eleanor, da. of Sir Richard WORSLEY. He *d.* s.p.m. legit. 13 June 1690, and was *bur.* at Bruton, when *the Baronetcy* became *extinct*, but the peerage devolved on his brother and heir male. Will dat. 22 April to 3 May, and pr. 27 June 1690. His wife, who was *bap.* 8 July 1623, at Spelsbury, Oxon, survived him.

HUDSON:(b)

cr. 3 July 1660;

ex. in or shortly before 1781.

I. 1660. "HENRY HUDSON, of Melton Mowbray, co. Leicester, Esq.," 2d but 1st surv. s. and h. of Robert HUDSON of the same and of Leadenhall street, London, by his 2d wife, Jane, da. of Thomas BILTON, of London, was *b.* about 1609; admitted to Gray's Inn. 10 Oct. 1634; suc. his father about 1641, and was *cr. a Baronet*, 3 July 1660. During the coronation time in 1661 he kept open house for all the county of Leicester, entertaining the Archbishop of Dublin, Lord de Ros, etc., with great splendour. He *m.* firstly, before 1634, Margaret, sister of Sir John BROMFIELD, 1st Baronet [1661], da. of Sir Edward BROMFIELD, sometime, 1636-37, Lord Mayor of London, by his 3d wife, Margaret, da. and coheir of John PAYNE, of London. She was living 1652. He *m.* secondly, 24 April 1654, at Melton Mowbray, Mary, only da. of Thomas NEVINSON, 1st s. of Sir Roger NEVINSON. He was *bur.* at Melton Mowbray, 27 Aug. 1690, aged about 81. Will pr. 1690. His widow was *bur.* at Hammersmith, Midx., 29 Sep. 1715. Will pr. Feb. 1716.

(a) His nephew, "Thomas Lear of Lindridge, co. Devon, Esq.," was *cr. a Baronet*, 2 Aug. 1683, and suc. to his estates.

(b) There is no account given of this Baronetage in Wotton's *Baronetage* for 1741, where, indeed, it is placed among those that were then extinct. In Kimber's *Baronetage* for 1771 it is inserted in the appendix to the last volume.

II. 1690. SIR EDWARD HUDSON, Baronet [1660], of Melton Mowbray aforesaid, 1st s. and h., by 1st wife, *b.* about 1637; being aged 45 in 1681, *suc. to the Baronetcy* in Aug. 1690. He *m.* firstly (Lic. Fac. 26 June 1661, he 24, she 21, parents deceased), Frances, da. of Nathaniel WRIGHT, of London, merchant. He *m.* secondly, in or before 1683, Eleanor, da. of Peter SERJEANT, of Melton Mowbray. He was *bur.* there 9 June 1702. His widow *d.* 1723. Will, as of Old Ford in Stratford Bow, dat. 27 Dec. 1722, pr. 23 July 1723.

III. 1702. SIR BENJAMIN HUDSON, Baronet [1660], of Melton Mowbray aforesaid, 2d but 1st surv. s. and h., by first wife; *b.* about 1665, being aged 14 in 1681; *suc. to the Baronetcy* in June 1702. He *m.* (—). The date, or even approximate date, of his death is unknown.

IV. 1730? SIR CHARLES HUDSON, Baronet [1660], only s. and h; *suc. to the Baronetcy* on his father's death. He *d.* s.p. 1 April 1752, and was *bur.* at Midhurst, Sussex.

V. 1752. SIR SKEFFINGTON HUDSON, Baronet [1660], uncle of the half blood and h. male, being 4th s. of the 2d Baronet, 1st s. by 2d wife; *bap.* 11 May 1683 at Melton Mowbray; *suc. to the Baronetcy*, 1 April 1752. He *m.* Elizabeth, da. of (—) PASSMORE. He *d.* 26 Feb. 1760, at Poplar, Midx., and was *bur.* there.

VI. 1760. SIR CHARLES HUDSON, Baronet [1660], 1st s. and h., *b.* at Poplar; Captain of a trading ship in the service of the East India Company; *suc. to the Baronetcy*, 26 Feb. 1760. He *m.* 19 Dec. 1748, at Charterhouse chapel, London, Deborah, da. of the Rev. Peter VALLAVINE, LL.B., Vicar [1743-67] of Preston, near Wingham, Kent. He *d.* 18 Oct. 1773 at Eltham, Kent. Admon. 23 Dec. 1774, to a creditor. His widow *d.* 1 and was *bur.* 8 Jan. 1780, at Eltham aforesaid.

VII. 1773, to 1781? SIR CHARLES VALLAVINE HUDSON, Baronet [1660], only s. and h., *b.* 14 Sep. 1755, at Preston aforesaid; *suc. to the Baronetcy*, 18 Oct. 1773; was a minor in Dec. 1774; was second mate of the East India merchant ship "The Duke of Kingston." He *d.* unm., in or shortly before 1781,(a) when *the Baronetcy* became *extinct*. Admon. 15 Dec. 1781 to a creditor.

HERBERT:

cr. 3 July 1660.

ex. April 1740.

I. 1660. "THOMAS HERBERT,(b) of [Little] Tinterne [near Colebrooke], co. Monmouth, Esq.," as also of The Pavement, in the parish of St. Crux, in the City of York, s. and h. of Christopher HERBERT, of

(a) He appears in most of the *Baronetages* long after that date, viz., in Betham's 1802, in Playfair's 1811, in Debrett's 1840, in Burke's 1841, and probably later (being, in the two lastnamed, credited with having "Wanlop [*sic*] Hall, Leicestershire" for his "seat," alluding, apparently, to "Wanlip," which belongs to the family of Hudson-Palmer), also in Dod's, as late as 1854 (when he would have been in his 100th year), being in the last three styled "Sir Charles Villavince Hudson, F.R.S." According to Betham's *Baronetage*, his father had five younger brothers, "Robert, who *m.* and had one da., Penelope; James, William, Henry and Edward, all deceased." This Penelope, then the wife of John Buck, as cousin german and one of the next of kin, and Jane Eleanor Hudson, spinster, a minor (by her mother, Mary Hudson, widow), also cousin german and next of kin to deceased, renounce administration to Sir Charles Hudson, [7th] Baronet, 15 Dec. 1781.

(b) See a full account of this family, "by Robert Davies, F.S.A., York," in the *Yorkshire Archæological Journal* [1870], vol. i, p. 182-214.

Otterington, in the North Riding of Yorkshire (*d.* 3 March 1624/5), by Jane, da. of John AKROYD of Foggathorpe, in the East Riding, was *b.* at The Pavement, and *bap.*, 4 Nov. 1606, at St. Crux; is said to have entered Jesus College, Oxford, 1621, and to have subsequently migrated to Trinity College, Cambridge. Early in 1627 he accompanied the English Embassy to Persia. He was one of the gentlemen appointed by the Parliament to attend Charles I. from Newcastle to Holdenby, in whose service he remained to the last, being with him on the scaffold.(a) At the Restoration, accordingly, he was *cr. a Baronet*, 3 July 1660, "as a badge of the fair esteem the King had of him for faithfully serving his Royal father during the two last years of his life." He was aged 58 at the Visit. of Yorkshire in 1666. He *m.* firstly, in 16 April 1632, at Knightsbridge Chapel, Midx. (Lic. Lond., he 24 and she 20), Lucy, da. of Sir Walter ALEXANDER, one of the Gentlemen of the King's Bedchamber, by Anne, da. of Alphonso FOWLES, of Westminster. She *d.* 19 Dec. 1671 and was *bur.* at St. Crux. He *m.* secondly, 11 Nov. 1672, at St. Michael-le-Belfry, York (Lic. York), Elizabeth, da. of Sir Gervase CUTLER of Stainbrough, co. York, by his 2d wife, Magdalen, da. of John (EGERTON), 1st EARL OF BRIDGEWATER. He *d.* at Petergate, York, 1 and was *bur.* 3 March 1681/2, at St. Crux, aged 76. M.I. Will dat. 20 Dec. 1679, pr. 31 March 1682, at York. His widow, who was *bap.* at Silkstone, 19 Oct. 1637, *m.* 20 Oct. 1684, at York Minster, Henry EDMUNDS, of Worsboro', co. York, who *d.* 22 and was *bur.* 26 March 1709, there. She *d.* 13 and was *bur.* 16 May 1696 at Worsboro'. M.I.

II. 1682. SIR HENRY HERBERT, Baronet [1660], of Middleton-Quernhow in Wath, in the North Riding (2d, but apparently the only surv.) s. and h. by 1st wife; *bap.* 19 March 1638/9, at St. Margaret's Westminster, being aged 25 at the Visit. of Yorkshire, 1665; *suc. to the Baronetcy*, 1 March 1681/2. He *m.* firstly, in July 1659, at York Minster, Ann, da. of Sir Thomas HARRISON, of Copgrave, co. York, by Margaret, da. of Conyers (DARCY), LORD DARCY AND CONYERS. She *d.* s.p.m.s., and was *bur.* 19 July 1670, at St. Saviour's, York. He *m.* secondly, 28 March 1671, at Long Newton, Durham, Anne, 2d da. of Sir George VANE, of Long Newton, by Elizabeth, da. and sole h. of Sir Lyonel MADDISON. He was *bur.* 13 Aug. 1687, at Wath. Admon. 12 Oct. 1687, at York, to his widow. She, who was *bap.* at Stanhope, Durham, 29 Aug. 1653, was living at Newcastle, March 1700/1.

III. 1687. SIR HUMPHREY HERBERT, Baronet [1660], of Middleton-Quernhow aforesaid, 1st surv. s. and h., being 2d s. by 2d wife, *b.* about 1674; *suc. to the Baronetcy* in Aug. 1687. He *m.* in 1700 Mary, widow of Thomas WARD, of York, da. of (—) DEWTRESS, a tradesman of that city. He was *bur.*, 28 June 1701, at St. Crux. Will dat. 20 March 1700/1, proved 3 Oct. 1701 at York, by his creditors. His widow, who was of St. James' Westminster, was *bur.* there 7 Feb. 1707/8. Admon. 21 Feb. 1707/8, in trust for Mary Ward, a minor, her daughter.

IV. 1701. SIR THOMAS HERBERT, BARONET [1660], only s. and h., *b.* 1700 or 1701; *suc. to the Baronetcy* in his infancy, June 1701. In June 1723 he sold the house at Petergate, York, having probably dissipated the remainder of the property. He *d.* unm., and was *bur.* 13 March 1723/4, at St. James' Westminster. Will dat. 10 Aug. 1722, pr. 20 March 1723/4 by Margaret DEWTRESS, spinster, aunt and extrix.

(a) His *Threnodia Carolina*, an account of the last two years of Charles I, is well known. He also published *Travels in Africa and Asia*, which went through four editions (1638 to 1677) in his lifetime.

V. 1724. SIR HENRY HERBERT, Baronet [1660], uncle and h., *b.* about 1675; *suc. to the Baronetcy* in March 1723/4. He *d.* s.p., probably unm., at Mr. Bright's house at Badsworth, near Doncaster, and was *bur.* 23 Jan. 1732/3, at Badsworth, aged about 59.(a)

VI 1733, to 1740. SIR CHARLES HERBERT, Baronet [1660], of Newcastle, only surv. br. and h., *bap.* 7 Jan. 1680 at Wath, co. York; *suc. to the Baronetcy* in Jan. 1732/3.(b) He *d.* s.p.m. in April 1740, aged 60, when the *Baronetcy* became *extinct*.

MIDDLETON, *or* MYDDLETON:

cr. 4 July 1660;

ex. 5 Jan. 1717/8.

I. 1660. "THOMAS MIDDLETON, of Chirk, co. Denbigh, Esq.," 2d but 1st surv. s. and h. ap. of Sir Thomas MIDDLETON, of Chirk Castle, the famous Parliamentary General (who *d.* 1666 in his 79th year), by his 2d wife, Mary, da. of Sir Robert NAPIER, 1st Baronet [1611] of Luton-Hoo, was *b.* about 1625; matric. at Oxford (Oriel Coll.), 20 March 1639/40, aged 15; was M.P. for Flint, 1646 till secluded in Dec. 1648; for Montgomery in 1660; and for Denbighshire, 1661 till his death; was Governor of Chirk Castle on behalf of the united Royalist and Presbyterian party (to which his father then belonged), 1646 till its surrender in 1659 to General Lambert, and was, in consideration of his own and (of late years) his father's services towards the Restoration, *cr. a Baronet*, 4 July 1660. He *m.* firstly, in or before 1650, Mary, 1st da. of Thomas CHOLMONDELEY, of Vale Royal, co. Chester, by Elizabeth, da. and h. of John MINSHULL, of Minshull. She was *b.* at Vale Royal, and *bap.* 11 Jan. 1628/9 at Whitegate, and was living 1654. He *m.* secondly, Jane, da. of Sir John TREVOR, of Brynkinalt, co. Denbigh, by Mary, da. of John JEFFREYS, of Helon in that county. He *d.* v.p. in London, July 1663, aged 39. Admon. 22 Oct. 1664 to his father, and again 9 Jan. 1666/7 to his mother (his principal creditor), Dame Mary MIDDLETON, widow. His widow *d.* very shortly after him. Admon. 4 Feb. 1664/5, on behalf of her son Thomas MIDDLETON, a minor.

II. 1663. SIR THOMAS MIDDLETON, Baronet [1660], of Chirk aforesaid, 1st. s. and h. by 1st wife, *b.* about 1651; *suc. to the Baronetcy* in July 1663, and to the family estates (on the death of his grandfather) in 1666; matric. at Oxford (Ch. Ch.) 24 June 1668, aged 16; *cr.* M.A. 2 July 1669; M.P. for Denbighshire, 1679-81. He *m.* firstly, Elizabeth, 1st da. and coheir of Sir Thomas WILBRAHAM, 3d and last Baronet [1621] of Woodhey, Cheshire, by Elizabeth, da. and h. of Edward MYTTON, of Weston. She *d.* s.p.s. about a year afterwards. M.I. at Chirk. He *m.* secondly, in 1677, Charlotte, da. of Sir Orlando BRIDGEMAN, 1st Baronet [1660], sometime Lord Keeper of the Great Seal, by his 2d wife Dorothy, da. of the Rev. John SAUNDERS. He *d.* s.p.m.,(c) 5 Feb. 1683/4 in his 33d year. Will pr. 1684. The will of his widow, desiring to be *bur.* at Chirk, dat. 7 Oct. 1690, pr. 24 April 1694.

(a) Drake (author of the *Eboracum*) states that the "title, without estate, descended to another brother, a low tradesman at Newcastle." Only two of the late Baronet's brothers were alive in March 1700/1, viz., Rice, *bap.* 5 Dec. 1676 at Wath, who, presumably, *d.* s.p.m. before his elder brother, and Charles.

(b) In the *London Mag.* for 1740 it is expressly stated that he was a descendant of the grantee of 1660 and that the title became extinct on his death.

(c) Charlotte, his only surv. child, and heir ("worth £20,000"), da. by the 2d wife, *m.* firstly, Feb. 1696/7, Edward (Rich) 6 Earl of Warwick, and secondly, 9 Aug. 1716, the Right Hon. Joseph Addison, the well known author.

III. 1684. SIR RICHARD MIDDLETON, *or* MYDDLETON, Baronet [1660], of Chirk aforesaid, next surv. br. of the whole blood and h. male; *b.* 23 March 1654/5; matric. at Oxford (Bras. Coll.), 21 Oct. 1670, aged 15(a); was M.P. for Denbighshire (thirteen Parls.), 1685-87, and 1689 till his death in 1716; *suc. to the Baronetcy*, 5 Feb. 1683/4; and purchased the Lordship of Ruthin. Sheriff of Denbighshire June to Nov. 1688. He *m.* 19 April 1686, at Twickenham, Midx. (Lic. Vic. Gen. 17 April, "he about 28, bachelor," she about 20, widow, with consent of her mother), Frances, widow of William WHITMORE, of Hackney, 1st da. and coheir of Sir Thomas WHITMORE, **K.B.**, of Buidwas, Salop, by Frances, da. and coheir of Sir William BROOKE, *otherwise* COBHAM, **K.B**. She *d.* 24 June 1694, aged 28. He *d.* 9 April 1716, aged 62. Both were *bur.* at Chirk. M.I. His will dat. 18 Feb. 1711, pr. 17 Aug. 1716.

IV. 1716, to 1718. SIR WILLIAM MYDDELTON, Baronet [1660], of Chirk aforesaid, only s. and h., *b.* 26 Feb. 1693/4; *suc. to the Baronetcy*, 9 April 1716; but *d.* unm. not long afterwards, 5 Jan. 1717/8, aged 24, and was *bur.* at Chirk, when *the Baronetcy* became *extinct.*(b) M.I. Will dat. 14 Sep. 1717, pr. 27 Feb. 1717/8.

NOEL, *or* NOELL:

cr. 6 July 1660;

afterwards, 1745-1815, LORDS WENTWORTH:

and subsequently, 1762-1815,

VISCOUNTS WENTWORTH OF WELLESBOROUGH;

extinct 17 April 1815.

I. 1660. "VERNEY NOELL, of Kirkby [Mallory], co. Leicester, Esq.," 2d s. of William NOEL, of the same, sometime Sheriff of Leicestershire, by Frances, 1st da. and coheir of John FULLWOOD, of Frerehall, co. Warwick, was aged 11 in the Visit. of Leicester, 1619; suc. his elder br., William NOEL, in the family estates in 1645. He *m.*, in or before 1641, Elizabeth, sister of Sir Wolstan DIXIE, 1st Baronet [1660], 2d da. of Sir Wolstan DIXIE, of Market Bosworth, co. Leicester, by Frances, da. of Sir Thomas BEAUMONT, of Stoughton, in that county. He *d.* 1670, and was *bur.* at Kirkby. Will pr. March 1671.

II. 1670. SIR WILLIAM NOEL, Baronet [1660], of Kirkby Mallory aforesaid, only s. and h., *b.* 1642; matric. at Oxford (Wadham Coll.), 28 April 1659; *suc. to the Baronetcy* in 1670. He *m.* firstly, in 1660, Margaret, 3d da. of John (LOVELACE), 2d BARON LOVELACE OF HURLEY, by Anne, da. of Thomas (WENTWORTH) EARL OF CLEVELAND, which Anne became, 23 July 1686, *suo jure* BARONESS WENTWORTH. She *d.* 14 April 1671, aged 27, and was *bur.* in Westm. Abbey. He *m.* secondly, 9 July 1672, at Himley, co, Worcester, Frances, 3d da. of Humble (WARD), 1st BARON WARD OF BIRMINGHAM, by Frances, *suo jure* BARONESS DUDLEY, da. and h. of the Hon. Sir Ferdinando SUTTON, *otherwise* DUDLEY, **K.B.** He *d.* 13 April 1675, aged 33, and was *bur.* at Kirkby. M.I.

III. 1675. SIR THOMAS NOEL, Baronet [1660], of Kirkby Mallory aforesaid, 1st s. and h. by 1st wife; *b.* about 1662: matric. at Oxford (Ex. Coll.), 27 Feb. 1679/80, aged 17; *suc. to the Baronetcy*, 13 April 1675. He *m.* Anne, 1st da. of Sir William WHITLOCK, of Phillis Court in Henley, Oxon,

(a) At the same date as his elder brother, William, then aged 16.

(b) Mary, his only sister and heir, *d.* unm. 8 April 1747. The Chirk estates, however, devolved at his death on the heir male, a descendant of Richard Myddelton, of Lysrasy, a brother of the 1st Baronet.

by Mary, da. of Sir Thomas OVERBURY. He *d.* s.p. 1688, and was *bur.* at Hurley aforesaid. Admon. 7 Dec. 1688 to his brother, and again 2 April 1701. His widow *d.* 8 Jan. 1737, aged 75. Will pr. 1737.

IV. 1688. SIR JOHN NOEL, Baronet [1660], of Kirkby Mallory aforesaid, br. and h.; *b.* about 1668; matric. at Oxford (Jesus Coll.), 26 March 1686, aged 18; adm. to Inner Temple, 1688; *suc. to the Baronetcy*, 1688. He *m.* between 1687 and 1695, Mary, da. and coheir of Sir John CLOBERY, of Bradstone, Devon, by Anne, da. of William CRANMER, of London and Rotterdam, merchant. He *d.* 1 July 1697, aged 30, and was *bur.* at Kirkby. Admon. 5 March 1697/8 to his widow. She was living 2 April 1701.

V. 1697. SIR CLOBERY NOEL, Baronet [1660], of Kirkby Mallory aforesaid, 1st s. and h., *b.* about 1695; *suc. to the Baronetcy*, 1 July 1697; matric. at Oxford (Mag. Coll.), 30 Dec. 1710, aged 15; Sheriff of Leicestershire, 1717-18; and M.P. for that county, 1727, till his death in 1733. He *m.* 24 Aug. 1714, at St. John's College chapel, Oxford, Elizabeth, da. of Thomas ROWNEY, of Oxford, sometime M.P. for that city. He *d.* 30 July 1733, aged 39. Will pr. 1733. His widow *d.* in St. Giles', Oxford, 25 June 1743, aged 49. Admon. 14 Nov. 1743. Both were *bur.* at Kirkby.

VI. 1733. SIR EDWARD NOEL, Baronet [1660], of Kirkby Mallory aforesaid, 1st s. and h.; *b.* 30 Aug. and *bap.* there 11 Sep. 1715; matric. at Oxford (New Coll.), 23 July 1733, aged 17; *suc. to the Baronetcy*, 30 July 1733; was *cr.* M.A., 19 July 1736, and D.C.L., 23 Aug. 1744. He *m.* 20 July 1744, at Wilbye, co. Northampton, Judith, da. and h. of William LAMB, of Wellesborough, co. Leicester, and of Farndish, Beds. She was living, when, by the death, 18 July 1745, of his father's first cousin, Martha, *suo jure* BARONESS WENTWORTH, he became LORD WENTWORTH. He was subsequently *cr.*, 5 May 1762, VISCOUNT WENTWORTH OF WELLESBOROUGH, co. Leicester. In those peerages *this Baronetcy* then *merged* till, on the death of his son, the 2d Viscount, 17 April 1815, it, as also the Viscountcy, became *extinct*, while the Barony of Wentworth fell into abeyance.

BUSWELL:

cr. 7 July 1660;

ex. 6 March 1667/8.

I. 1660, to 1668. "GEORGE BUSWELL, of Clipston, co. Northampton, Esq.," s. and h. of George BUSWELL, of the same, sometime Alderman of London (*d.* 5 May 1632, aged 77), by Elizabeth, 1st da. of Harold KYNNESMAN, of Broughton, co. Northampton, was *b.* about 1625, being 7 years old at the death of his father in 1632, and was *cr. a Baronet*, 7 July 1660. Sheriff of Northamptonshire, 1662-63. He *m.*, probably about 1665, Catherine, 3d and yst. da. and coheir of Sir James ENYON, Baronet [1642], of Flore, co. Northampton, by Jane, da. of Sir Adam NEWTON, 1st Baronet [1620], of Newton. He d. s.p.s. 6 March 1667/8, aged 41 years, 9 months, and 18 days, and was *bur.* at Clipston, when the *Baronetcy* became *extinct*. M.I. Will wherein he founds a free school at Clipston, dat. 18 March 1667, pr. 1668.(a) His widow *m.* (Lic. Vic. Gen. 6 May 1669, he 25 and she 23, *Qy.* 27) Sir John GARRARD, 3d Baronet [1622], of Lamer, who *d.* s.p.m. 13 Jan. 1700/1, aged 62. She *d.* 16 April 1702, and was *bur.* at Clipston, aged 60. M.I. Will pr. June 1702.

(a) Anne, his only surv. sister and h., *m.*, as his 2d wife, Sir Eusebius Pelsant, by whom she had Eusebius Pelsant, who took the name of Buswell, on inheriting the estate of Clipston, and who was father of Eusebius Buswell, *cr. a Baronet* 5 March 1713/4.

AUSTEN:

cr. 10 July 1660;

ex. 13 Feb. 1772.

I. 1660. "ROBERT AUSTEN of [Hall Place, in] Bexley, co. Kent, Esq.," as also of Heronden in Tenterden in that county, and of London, merchant, 3d s. of William AUSTEN, of Heronden aforesaid, by Elizabeth, da. of Edward HALES, of Tenterden, was *b.* about 1580, and was *cr. a Baronet*, 10 July 1660. He was Sheriff of Kent, 1660-61. He *m.* firstly, Margaret, da. of William WILLIAMSON, Citizen and Vintner of London. She *d.* s.p.m. He *m.* secondly, Anne, da. of Thomas MUNS, of Otteridge in Bersted, Kent, and of London. He *d.* 30 Oct. and was *bur.* 5 Nov. 1666, at Bexley, aged 79. M.I. Will pr. 1666. His widow *d.* 28 Oct. and was *bur.* there 3 Nov. 1687, aged 74. M.I. Her will pr. Dec. 1687.

II. 1666. SIR JOHN AUSTEN, Baronet [1660], of Hall Place in Bexley aforesaid, and of Stagenhoe, Herts, s. and h. by 2d wife, living 1634; admitted to Gray's Inn, 23 Oct. 1657; *suc. to the Baronetcy*, 30 Oct. 1666; was M.P. for Rye (five Parls.), Oct. 1669 to 1679; 1689-90, and 1695 till death; one of the Commissioners of the Customs, 1697-98. He *m.* (Lic. Fac. 6 Dec. 1661, he 21 [*Qy.* 26], and she 16) Rose, da. and h. of Sir John HALE, of Stagenhoe aforesaid, by Elizabeth, da. of Edmond BALE, of Saddington, co. Leicester. She *d.* May or Nov. 1695, and was *bur.* at Stagenhoe. He *d.* in Red Lion Square, London, 1698. Will dat. 27 March 1687/8, pr. 27 Sep. 1699.

III. 1698. SIR ROBERT AUSTEN, Baronet [1660], of Hall Place, in Bexley aforesaid, s. and h., *bap.* 19 March 1663, at Bexley; *suc. to the Baronetcy* in 1698. M.P. for Rye Jan. 1699 to 1701. He *m.*, about 1696, his cousin Elizabeth, da. and coheir of George STAWELL, of Cotheston, Somerset, by Ursula, da. of Sir Robert AUSTEN, 1st Baronet, and Anne, his 2d wife. He was *bur.* 5 July 1706 at Bexley. Will dat. 28 May 1706, proved 15 Aug. following. His widow *m.* (Lic. Vic. Gen. 26 April 1716, both 35, Bachr. and Widow) William WYND, of Norfolk (Chamberlain to the Princess Sophia), who survived her and *d.* 1742. Her will, in which she styles herself of Hall Place and directs to be *bur.* at Bexley, dat. 7 April 1716, and pr. 2 Dec. 1725.

IV. 1706. SIR ROBERT AUSTEN, Baronet [1660], of Hall Place, in Bexley aforesaid, s. and h., *b.* 6 Oct. 1697; *suc. to the Baronetcy* in July 1706; matric. at Oxford (Oriel Coll.), 10 Nov. 1715, aged 18; Sheriff of Kent, Jan. to Dec. 1724; M.P. for New Romney April 1728 to 1734. He *m.*, Nov. 1738, Rachael, sister of Francis, LORD LE DESPENCER, da. of Sir Francis DASHWOOD, 1st Baronet [1707] of West Wycombe, by his 2d wife, Mary, da. of Vere (FANE), 4th EARL OF WESTMORLAND. He *d.* s.p. 7 Oct. 1743, and was *bur.* at Churchdown, co. Gloucester. Will pr. 1743. His widow, on the death s.p. legit., 11 Dec. 1781, of her abovenamed brother, assumed the title of BARONESS LE DESPENCER, under the (erroneous) impression that the termination of the abeyance of that ancient Barony (19 April 1763) in favour of her brother was tantamount to its having been in favour of her mother, one of the coheirs thereto. She *d.* s.p. 16 May 1788, aged 82, when the abeyance of that Barony terminated in favour of Sir Thomas STAPLETON, 6th Baronet [1679]. Her will, in which she styles herself "Baroness Le Despencer," pr. 1788.

V. 1743. SIR SHEFFIELD AUSTEN, Baronet [1660], of Hall Place, in Bexley aforesaid, br. and h., *b.* about 1700; *suc. to the Baronetcy*, 7 Oct. 1743. He *m.* Susanna, da. of [—]. He *d.* s.p. in or shortly before 1758. Will dat. 28 Oct. 1743, pr. 17 Nov. 1758 by his widow. Her will pr. Jan. 1773 and May 1774, as also again, in Dublin, 1780.

VI. 1758? SIR EDWARD AUSTEN, Baronet [1660], of Boxley Abbey, co. Kent, cousin and h. male, being 2d s. of Robert AUSTEN, of Heronden in Tenterden aforesaid, by Jane, da. of William STRODE, of Barrington, Somerset, which Robert was s. and h. of Robert AUSTEN, also of Heronden,

who was 2d s. of the 1st Baronet by his 2d wife. He was *b.* about 1705, and *suc. to the Baronetcy* in or shortly before 1758. He *d.* unm. 16 and was *bur.* 28 Dec. 1760, at Allington, Kent, aged 55. M.I. Will pr. 1761.

VII. 1760, to 1772. SIR ROBERT AUSTEN, Baronet [1660], of Haslemere, Surrey, br. and h., *b.* about 1708; matric. at Oxford (Merton Coll.), 11 Dec. 1725, aged 17; *suc. to the Baronetcy*, 16 Dec. 1760.(a) He *m.*, but *d.* s.p. 13 Feb. 1772, when the *Baronetcy* became *extinct.* He was *bur.* at Godalming, Surrey. Will pr. Feb. 1772.

HALES:

cr. 12 July 1660:

ex. 12 April 1824.

I. 1660. "ROBERT HALES, of Beaksbourne, co. Kent, Esq.," s. and h. of Thomas HALES,(b) of the same, by Mary, da. of Sir Thomas PEYTON, of Knowlton, Kent, was *b.* about 1610; adm. to Inner Temple, Nov. 1628; Barrister, 1637; was M.P. for Hythe, 1659, being then described as "Knight and Baronet,"(c) but was *cr. a Baronet* (by Charles II), 12 July 1660. He *m.* Catharine, da. and coheir of Sir William ASHCOMB, of Alvescot, Oxon. She *d.* presumably before Dec. 1693. He *d.* about 1695. Will dat. 20 Dec. 1693, pr. 27 Feb. 1695/6 by "Robert(d) Hales, Esq.," grandson and residuary legatee.

II. 1695? SIR THOMAS HALES, Baronet [1660], of Beakesbourne aforesaid, and afterwards of Brymore, Somerset, grandson and h., being 1st surv. s. and h. of Thomas HALES, by Mary (Mar. Lic. Fac. 9 June 1662, aged about 14), da. and h. of Richard WOOD, of Abbots Langley, Herts, which Thomas (who was *b.* about 1640, adm. to the Inner Temple, Nov. 1654, and, who presumably, matric. at Oxford from Mag. Coll., 23 July 1656) was s. and h. ap. of the 1st Baronet, but *d.* v.p. He was *b.* about 1662; admitted to Inner Temple before 1688; *suc. to the Baronetcy* about 1695; was M.P. (eight Parls. in all) for Kent, 1701-05, for Canterbury, 1715-41 and Jan. 1746 to 1747. He *m.* (Lic. Fac. 4 Nov. 1688, he about 23 and she 22) Mary, sister and (1687/8) heir of Sir Charles PYM, 2d Baronet [1663], da. of Sir Charles PYM, 1st Baronet, of Brymore aforesaid, by Katharine, da. of Sir Gilbert GERARD, 1st Baronet [1611]. She *d.* 24 Nov. 1729. He *d.* at Holcliffe, near Canterbury, 7 Jan. 1748, aged about 87. Will pr. 1748.

III. 1748. SIR THOMAS HALES, Baronet [1660], of Beaksbourne aforesaid, 1st surv. s. and h., *b.* about 1694; matric. at Oxford (Oriel Coll.), 15 Dec. 1711, aged 17; admitted to Inner Temple; M.P. for Minehead, 1722-27; for Camelford, 1727-34; for Grampound, 1734-41; for Hythe, Dec. 1744 to 1761; and for East Grinstead, Dec. 1761 till his death; *suc. to the Baronetcy*, 7 Jan. 1748; Clerk of the Board of Green Cloth, and Deputy Warden of the Cinque Ports. He *m.*, 22 June 1723, at St. Martin's-in-the-Fields, Mary, sister of Robert, 1st BARON ROMNEY, da. of Sir Robert MARSHAM, 4th Baronet

(a) "Sir William Austen, Baronet, who *d.* s.p.," is sometimes inserted as br. and h. of Sir Edward, and consequently the predecessor of Robert, the last Baronet.

(b) This Thomas was s. and h. of Sir Charles Hales, of Thanington, Kent, by Anne, da. of Robert and the prolific Mary Honywood, of Charing, in that county, which Charles was grandson of Thomas Hales, Baron of the Exchequer, *temp.* Hen. VIII, ancestor of the family of HALES, of Woodchurch, co. Kent, Baronets 1611—1829.

(c) This description, if not a mistake, points to a Baronetcy of Cromwell's creation. Robert Hales, of Kent, "Esq.," was one of the Model Commissioners for Kent, and was also a Commissioner in Feb. 1645, and again 1656-7, so he was clearly a Parliamentarian.

(d) This Robert was the 3d (2d surv.) s. of the Baronet's eldest son, Thomas. He was Clerk to the Privy Council. To him and the heirs male of his body the Baronet devises all his land, with rem. to the *younger* children of the testator's son Thomas, thereby excluding the 2d Baronet, Thomas, who was the *elder* brother of Robert.

[1663], by Margaret, da. and h. of Thomas Bosvile. He *d.* 6 and was *bur.* 11 Oct. 1762, at Beakesbourne, aged 68. Will pr. 1762. His widow, who was *b.* 18 and *bap.* 20 May 1698, at St. Margaret's, Westm., *d.* 4 and was *bur.* 11 Aug. 1769, at Beakesbourne.

IV. 1762. Sir Thomas-Pym Hales, Baronet [1660], of Beakesbourne aforesaid, s. and h., *b.* at The Mote, near Maidstone, about 1726; matric. at Oxford (Wadham Coll.), 13 June 1743, aged 17; *suc. to the Baronetcy*, 6 Oct. 1762; was M.P. for Downton, Feb. 1762 to 1768, and for Dover, Jan. 1770 till death. He *m.* 11 Oct. 1764, Mary, widow of George Coussmaker, of Staple, co. Kent, da. of Gervase Heyward, of Sandwich. He *d.* s.p.m., 18 March 1773. Will pr. March 1773.

V. 1773, to 1824. Sir Philip Hales, Baronet [1660], of Brymore, Somerset, only surv. br. and h. male, being 6th and yst. s. of the 3d Baronet, was sometime Groom of the Bedchamber; *suc. to the Baronetcy*, 18 March 1773. He *m.*, 1795, Elizabeth, da. and h. of Thomas Smith, of Keyworth, Notts. He *d.* s.p.m. 12 April 1824, in Somersetshire, when the *Baronetcy* became *extinct.* Will dat. 4 Feb. 1820, pr. 16 Nov. 1824, by his relict, Dame Elizabeth; and again 28 Nov. 1834, after her death, by Elizabeth Hales spinster, the da., and again 21 Dec. 1836.

CLERKE:

cr. 13 July 1660 [a]

I. 1660. John Clerke, of Hitcham, Bucks, Esq., and afterwards of North Weston, near Tame, Oxon, 2d but 1st surv. s. and h. of Sir Francis Clerke,[b] of Hitcham aforesaid, by Grisel, da. of Sir David Woodroffe, of Poyle, Surrey, was *b.* about 1622; matric. at Oxford (Ch. Ch.), 28 June 1639, aged 17; *suc.* his father, 18 March 1631; and was *cr. a Baronet*, 13 July 1660.[a] He *m.* Philadelphia, 1st da. and coh. of Sir Edward Carr, of Hillingdon, Middx., by Jane, da. of Sir Edward Onslow, of Knoll, Surrey. He *d.* 7, and was *bur.* 10 Oct. 1667, at Tame aforesaid, aged 45. M.I. Admon. 19 Dec. 1667. His widow, who was *bap.* 14 Sep. 1626, *d.* 9. and was *bur.* 12 Aug. 1698, with her husband. Her will dat. 15 Aug. 1695, pr. 4 May 1699.

II. 1667. Sir William Clerke, Baronet [1660], of Shabbington, Bucks, s. and h., *b.* 9 July 1643; presumably matric. at Oxford (Trin. Coll.), 31 July 1658; *suc. to the Baronetcy*, 7 Oct. 1667. He *m.*, in or before 1662, Elizabeth, da. of William Muschamp, of Row Barnes, Surrey. He *d.* at Stoke, Surrey, 6 Sep. 1678, aged 35, and was *bur.* at Shabbington. Will dat. 16 May, proved 14 Sep. 1678. His widow was living in 1695. The will of "Dame Elizabeth Clerke, Midx.," pr. June 1708, possibly refers to her.

III. 1678. Sir William Clerke, Baronet [1660], of Shabbington, aforesaid, s. and h., *b.* in or before 1662; *suc. to the Baronetcy*, 6 Sep. 1678. He *m.*, 11 July 1683, at Allhallows Barking, London (Lic. Vic. Gen., he above 21, she about 20), Catherine, sister of Richard, 1st Baron Onslow, da. of Sir Arthur Onslow, 2d Baronet [1660], by his second wife, Mary, da. and coheir of

(a) This creation is omitted in Dugdale's *Catalogue*. A note thereto by its editor, T. C. Banks [edit. 1812], states that "John Clerk, of North Weston, Oxon, created 11 July 1660, should come in between Austen and Hales," but the date of the creation is apparently 13 (not 11) July, and its place therefore would be between Hales and Boothby. It is altogether omitted in Wotton's *Baronetage* [1741], not being even placed in the list of the extinct titles. It is, however, included (as a creation of 13 July 1660) in Kimber's *Baronetage* [1771] and in those following.

(b) This Francis was great-grandson of Sir John Clerke, of North Weston, Oxon, who in the wars with France took captive Louis D'Orleans, Duc de Longueville, 14 Aug. 1513, at Borny, near Theronenne, and who consequently received an augmentation to his coat of arms. Sir John died in 1539.

Sir Thomas Foote, Baronet [so *cr.* 1660], sometime, 1649-50, Lord Mayor of London. He *d.* 1699, and was *bur.* at North Weston, Oxon. Will dat. 14 July and pr. 1 Dec 1699. His widow *d.* 14 March 1741, aged 85, and was *bur.* in Hanwell Church, Midx.

IV. 1699. Sir John Clerke, Baronet [1660], of Shabbington, aforesaid, s. and h.; *suc. to the Baronetcy* in 1699. He *d.* s.p., 27 and was *bur.* 29 Feb. 1726/7, in Hanwell church, aged 31. Will pr. Feb. 1726/7.

V. 1727. Sir William Clerke, Baronet [1660], of Shabbington aforesaid, only br. and h.; *suc. to the Baronetcy*, 27 Feb. 1726/7. He joined with his mother in alienating the Shabbington estate. He *m.* (—), da. of (—) Bunsrow, of Fetter lane, London. He *d.* abroad, s.p. The will of "Sir Wm. Clerke, Midx.," pr. Nov. 1738, may possibly refer to him.

VI. 1738? Sir Francis Clerke, Baronet [1660], 1st cousin and h., being only s. and h. of John Clerke, of North Weston aforesaid, by Catherine, da. of Henry Jennings, of Devonshire, which John (who *d.* 1708) was 2d s. of the 2d Baronet. He was *b.* 12 July 1682, and *suc. to the Baronetcy* on the death of his cousin. He *d.* unm. 12 Feb. 1769, and was *bur.* in the chapel in South Audley street, Midx. Will pr. 1769.

VII. 1769. Sir Francis Carr Clerke, Baronet [1660], of North Weston, Oxon, aforesaid, and of Heath House, in Aston on Clun, Salop, cousin and h. male, being s. and h. of Francis Clerke, of North Weston, by Susanna Elizabeth (*m.* 1747), da. of Thomas Henry Ashurst, of Waterstock, Oxon, which Francis (*b.* 23 Sep. 1724 and *d.* 30 April 1760) was only s. and h. of Francis Carr Clerke, of Weston aforesaid (*d.* 27 May 1730, aged 36), who was 2d s. of Richard Clerke, of Horspath, Oxon (*b.* 4 March 1659; *m.* 13 March 1675), 6th and yst. s. of the 1st Baronet. He was *b.* 24 Oct. 1748 in St. George's Han. sq.; ed. at Abingdon Grammar School; admitted to the Inner Temple, London, but was afterwards Lieut. in the 3d Reg. of Foot Guards, being aide-de-camp to Gen. Burgoyne. He *suc. to the Baronetcy*, 12 Feb. 1769. He *d.* unm., being slain by a musket shot at Saratoga, 15 Oct. 1778, but brought thence to England for burial. Will pr. May 1779.

VIII. 1778. Sir William Henry Clerke, Baronet [1660], of Heath House aforesaid, Rector of Bury, co. Lancaster, only br. and h., *b.* 25 Nov. 1751 and *bap.* at North Weston aforesaid; ed. at Abingdon Grammar School; matric. at Oxford (Ch. Ch.), 15 Dec. 1769, aged 17; Fellow of All Souls' Coll.; B.C.L. 1778. In Holy Orders. Rector of Bury, co. Lanc.; *suc. to the Baronetcy*, 15 Oct. 1778. He *m.*, 5 May 1792, at St. Geo. Han. sq., Byzantia, 1st da. of Thomas Cartwright, of Aynhoe, co. Northampton, by Byzantia, da. of Ralph Lane, of Woodbury, co. Chester. She *d.* 30 April 1815. He *d.* 10 April 1818, aged 66.

IX. 1818. Sir William Henry Clerke, Baronet [1660], of Heath House aforesaid, s. and h.; *b.* 13 Sep. 1793 in London; entered the Army 1811, served with the 52d Regiment in the Peninsular War and at Waterloo (war medal and four clasps); retired in 1858 as Brevet Major; *suc. to the Baronetcy*, 10 April 1818. He *m.*, 2 May 1820, Mary Elizabeth, 1st da. of George Watkin Kenrick, of Mertyn Hall, co. Flint, by his 1st wife [—], da. of [—] Foulkes, of Mertyn Hall aforesaid. He *d.* 16 Feb. 1861 at the Heath aforesaid, aged 67. His widow *d.* there 12 June 1873, aged 74.

X. 1861. Sir William Henry Clerke, Baronet [1660], of Mertyn Hall aforesaid, s. and.; *b.* 17 Nov. 1822 at Clonmel; sometime Principal Clerk in the Treasury; *suc. to the Baronetcy*, 16 Feb. 1861. He *m.* 28 Nov. 1849, at Lyne church, in Chertsey, Surrey, Georgina, 1st da. of Robert Gosling, of Botleys Park in Chertsey and of Fleet street, London, Banker, by Vere, da. of the Right Hon. John Sullivan, of Richings, Bucks. He *d.* 8 Feb. 1882, at 10 Eaton Place South, in his 60th year. His widow living 1902.

XI. 1882. Sir William Francis Clerke, Baronet [1660], of Mertyn Hall aforesaid, 1st s. and h., *b.* 16 Jan. 1856; ed. at Eton; matric. at Oxford (Ch. Ch.) 28 May 1874, aged 18; B.A., 1878; Barrister (Inner Temple) 29 June 1881; *suc. to the Baronetcy*, 8 Feb. 1882. He *m.*, 21 June 1884 Beatrice, da. of Graham Menzies, of Hallyburton and Pitcur, co. Forfar.

Family Estates.—These, in 1873, were under 3,000 acres.

BOOTHBY:

cr. 13 July 1660.

I. 1660. "Sir William Boothby, of Bradley [*i.e.*, Broadlow] Ashe [in Ashbourne], co. Derby, Knt.," and of Croperdy, Oxon, only s. and h. of Sir Henry Boothby, Baronet (who was so nominated 5 Nov. 1644,[a] but whose patent, owing to the Civil Wars, never passed the Great Seal), by Mary, da. of Sir Thomas Hayes, sometime, 1614-15, Lord Mayor of London, was *b.* about 1638; *suc. to the Baronetcy* thus conferred, on his father's death, 3 Sep. 1648, but was, nevertheless, *cr. a Baronet* [*de novo*] 13 July 1660, it being stated[b] ["*ex inform.* Dom. Will. Boothby, Bar."] that "at the Restoration the King was pleased to renew[c] his patent gratis, by the name of Sir William Boothby, of Broadlow Ash, the former patent being of Clater Cote." He entered his pedigree at the Visit. of Derbyshire in 1662, and was Sheriff for that county, 1661-62. In 1671 he purchased Ashbourne Hall and the manor of Ashbourne.[d] He *m.* firstly (settl. before marriage, 13 Aug. 1653) Frances, 2d da. and coheir of Col. John Milward, of Snitterton in North Darley, co. Derby. She was *bur.* 11 Sep. 1654, at Darley. He *m.* secondly, 6 April 1657, at Chiswick, Midx. (publication 27 Dec. [*sic*] 1657, at St. Bride's, London), Hill, da. and coheir of Sir William Brooke, K.B., by his 2d wife, Penelope, da. of Sir Moyses Hill, Marshal of Ulster. By royal warrant, 19 May 1665, she (as also her two sisters of the whole blood) was granted the precedence of the daughter of a Baron, her said father being nephew and heir to Henry (Brooke), Lord Cobham, who had, however, been attainted in 1603. She *d.* at Offcote 14 and was *bur.* 17 May 1704 at Ashbourne, aged 68. M.I. He *d.* at Ashbourne Hall 24 and was *bur.* 27 March 1707 at Ashbourne. Will dat. 27 Oct. 1706, pr. 14 May 1707.

II. 1707. Sir Henry Boothby, Baronet [1660], of Broadlow Ash aforesaid, grandson and h., being only s. and h. of Francis Boothby, of Peterborough (aged 8 in the Visit. of Derbyshire, 1662), by Anne (Marr. Lic. Fac., 25 Sep. 1678), da. and coheir of Thomas Child, of Dogsthorpe, co. Northampton, which Francis, who was s. and h. ap. of the 1st Baronet [1660], being only child by his 1st wife, *d.* v.p. 1684, aged 30. He was *b.* about 1682; matric. at Oxford (Trin. Coll.), 19 Nov. 1607, aged 15; adm. to the Inner Temple, 1700; *suc. to the Baronetcy*, 24 March 1706/7; was of Newport, Isle of Wight, and

(a) See vol. ii, p. 239.

(b) Wotton's *Baronetage*, edit. 1741, where also it is said that he "was Knighted by King Charles II in the field," which, considering that he was but 13 years old at the battle of Worcester (presumably the "field" alluded to) seems improbable. He apparently assumed the prefix of "Sir" and the style of a Baronet, on his father's death in 1648.

(c) The creations *de novo* of Acland, 21 Jan. 1677/8, and of Edwards, 22 Sep. 1678, are practically similar cases.

(d) The vendor was the spendthrift, Sir Aston Cokayne, Baronet [1641], whose ancestors had possessed that estate above 500 years. It was bought with money acquired from the Brooke family, and was settled accordingly on the descendants thereof, of whom was Brooke Boothby, yst. s. of the 1st Baronet, by Hill, da. of Sir William Brooke, his 2d wife, which Brooke Boothby, who died at Ashbourne Hall, Oct. 1737, was father of the 5th Baronet of the creation of 1660 and ancestor of the succeeding ones.

about to embark with the troops in July 1708. He *d. unm.* in London, and was *bur.* 25 Nov. 1710, at Ashbourne. Will dat. 16 July 1708, pr. 10 Nov. 1710 by Anne Boothby, spinster, the sister.[a]

III. 1710. Sir William Boothby, Baronet [1660], of St. Mary's, Nottingham, uncle of the half blood and h. male, being 1st surv. s., by the 2d wife, of the 1st Baronet [1660], was *bap.* 1 Jan. 1663/4 at Tamworth, co. Warwick. He *suc. to the Baronetcy* in Nov. 1710. He *m.*, in or before 1695, Frances, 4th da. of Sir Trevor Williams, 1st Baronet [1642], of Langibby, co. Monmouth, by Elizabeth, da. of Thomas Morgan. She was living July 1698. He was living in Aug. 1730,[b] when he would have been 66 years old.

IV. 1740? Sir William Boothby, Baronet [1660], of Mansfield Woodhouse, Notts, grandson and h., being only s. and h. of Gore Boothby, by Elizabeth, da. of John Bury, of Nottingham, which Gore was s. and h. ap. of the late Baronet, but *d.* v.p., and was *bur.* at Ashbourne 19 Aug. 1730, aged 32. He was *bap.*, 4 May 1721, at St. Mary's, Nottingham; *suc. to the Baronetcy* on the death, probably about 1740, of his grandfather; was Capt. in the Army, Feb. 1741, becoming finally, 1783, Major-General in the Army; and being Col. of the 63d Foot, 1760; of the 50th Foot, 1764; and of the 6th Foot, 1773. He *d.* unm. 15, and was *bur.*, 23 April 1787, in Bath Abbey. Will dat. 24 Feb., and pr. 7 May 1787 by William Boothby, of Edwinstowe, Notts, cousin and residuary legatee.

V. 1787. Sir Brooke Boothby, Baronet [1660], of Ashbourne Hall aforesaid, cousin and h. male, being only s. and h. of Brooke Boothby, of the same, by his 2d wife, Elizabeth, da. of John Fitzherbert, of Somersall Herbert, co. Derby, which Brooke, who was *bur.*, 10 Oct. 1727, at Ashbourne, was yr. br. of the late Baronet. He was *b.* and *bap.* 8 Nov. 1710, at Ashbourne, and *suc. to the Baronetcy*, 15 April 1787. He *m.* firstly, 13 Oct. 1737, Anne, da. of (—) Byard, of Derby. She, who was *b.* 29 Jan. 1720, *d.* s.p.m. 4 and was *bur.* 5 Oct. 1739, at Ashbourne. He *m.* secondly, in 1742, Phœbe, da. and h. of William Hollins, of Mosely, co. Stafford. She, who was *b.* 4 Oct. 1716, *d.* at Lichfield 5 and was *bur.* 11 May 1788, at Ashbourne, aged 71. He *d.* 9 and was *bur.* 16 April 1789, at Ashbourne, aged 78

VI. 1789. Sir Brooke Boothby, Baronet [1666], of Ashbourne Hall aforesaid, s. and h. by 2d wife, *b.* 3 and *bap.* 4 June 1744, at Ashbourne; *suc. to the Baronetcy*, 9 April 1789; was a writer on political and other subjects, as also of poetry.[c] He *m.*, in or before 1785, Susanna, da. of Robert Bristow, of Mitcheldever, Hants, by Susanna, da. and h. of John Philipson, one of the Lords of the Treasury. She *d.* in or before 1823. Will pr. 5 June 1823. He *d.* at Boulogne, in France, 23 Jan. and was *bur.* 13 Feb. 1824, at Ashbourne, in his 80th year.

(a) To her he left the estate of Broadlow Ash, with rem. to his cousin, George Boothby, which thus passed away from the title.

(b) The death, 6 June 1751, is recorded in the *Gent. Mag.*, 1751, of "Sir Wm. Boothby, Bart., of Tooley Hall, co. Leicester," where, also, it is stated that "his father, Sir Thomas, died 29 May last." The Boothbys of Tooley Hall were cousins to the Baronets, but did not themselves ever possess or, apparently, ever assume a Baronetcy, and this attributing of one to them seems to be a mistake.

(c) In 1796 he published a collection of sonnets entitled "*Sorrows sacred to the memory of Penelope.*" This Penelope was his only child, *b.* 11 April 1785; *d.* 19 March 1791, and "was in form and intellect most exquisite." See inscription (in Latin, Italian, French and English) on her justly celebrated monument in Ashbourne church, executed by T. Banks, R.A. The recumbent figure of the sleeping girl thereon, which is a masterpiece, is supposed to have suggested to Chantrey the design of the two children, on the well-known monument in Lichfield Cathedral.

VII. 1824, Jan. SIR WILLIAM BOOTHBY, Baronet [1660], of Ashbourne Hall aforesaid, and of Edwinstowe, Notts, br. and h., *b.* 4 and *bap.* 16 March 1745/6, at Ashbourne; sometime Major in the 51st Foot; *suc. to the Baronetcy*, 23 Jan. 1824. He *m.* 14 May 1781, "the Baroness" Rafela, da. of Don. Miguel DEL GARDO, of Mahon, in the isle of Minorca. He *d.* (a few months after succeeding to the title) at Edwinstowe 17 and was *bur.* 24 March 1824, at Ashbourne, aged 78. Will pr. 9 May 1825. His widow *d.* at Edwinstowe, and was *bur.* 30 March 1829, at Ashbourne, aged 72.

VIII. 1824, March. SIR WILLIAM BOOTHBY, Baronet [1660], of Ashbourne Hall aforesaid, 1st s. and h., *b.* 25 March 1782; sometime Captain 15th Light Dragoons and Aide-de-camp to H.R.H. the Duke of Cumberland; Receiver-General of Customs at the Port of London, and Paymaster to the Corps of the Gentlemen at Arms; *suc. to the Baronetcy* 17 March 1824. He *m.* firstly, 29 Jan. 1805, Fanny, niece to Charles, 1st EARL OF LIVERPOOL, sister to Sir Charles JENKINSON, 10th Baronet [1661], only da. of Col. John JENKINSON, of Winchester, by Frances, da. of Admiral John PARKER. She *d.* at Ashbourne Hall, 2, and was *bur.* 9 Jan. 1838 at Ashbourne. M.I. He *m.* secondly, 15 Oct. 1844, at St. Mary's, Fulham, Midx., Louisa Cranstoun (the celebrated actress), widow of John Alexander NISBETT, of Brettenham Halle, Suffolk, an officer in the 1st Life Guards, 1st da. of Frederick Hayes MACNAMARA, an officer in the 52d Foot, by (—), da. of (—) WILLIAMS. He *d.* at Ashbourne Hall, 21, and was *bur.* 27 April 1846 at Ashbourne, aged 64, having directed by will the sale of that property which accordingly was effected. Will pr. June 1846. His widow, who was *b.* 1 April 1812, at Balls Pond, Islington, *d.* at Rose Mount, St. Leonards on Sea, 16 Jan. 1858, aged 45.(a)

IX. 1846. SIR BROOKE WILLIAM ROBERT BOOTHBY, Baronet [1660], 1st s. and h. by 1st wife, *b.* 29 Jan. 1809, in Winchester; ed. at Charterhouse school; matric. at Oxford (Ch. Ch.), 17 Dec. 1825, aged 16; B.A. and Fellow of All Souls' Coll., 1829; M.A., 1833; in Holy Orders, Rector of Elmley, Kent, 1846-52; Rector of Welwyn, Herts, 1852-65; *suc. to the Baronetcy*, 21 April 1846. He *m.*, 7 Sep. 1852, at Hawkesbury, co. Gloucester, Martha Serena, 1st da. of his paternal uncle, the Rev. Charles BOOTHBY, Vicar of Sutterton and Rector of Barnoldby, both co. Lincoln, by Marianne Catherine, da. of the Rev. Basil BERIDGE, of Algarkirk in that county. He *d.* 21 Sep. 1865 at Tunbridge Wells, aged 56. His widow living 1902.

X. 1865. SIR BROOKE BOOTHBY, Baronet [1660], 1st s. and h., *b.* 13 Nov. 1856, at Welwyn Rectory, Herts; ed. at Harrow; *suc. to the Baronetcy*, 21 Sep. 1865; entered the Diplomatic Service, 1881; 2d Sec. at Vienna; Sec. of Legation at Rio de Janeiro; Sec. of Legation at Tokio, since 1901.

Family Estates.—These, in 1876, were under 3,000 acres.

(a) The short but brilliant career of this accomplished and most popular actress was a very sad one. Owing to the extravagance of her father (an officer who had served at Corunna) she, under the name of "Louisa Mordaunt," went, at an early age, on the provincial stage, appearing when 17, at Drury lane, 16 Oct. 1829, and at the Haymarket in 1830. In Jan. 1831 she *m.* her first husband, who, seven months afterwards, was killed, at the age of 22, by a fall from his gig, 2 Oct., 1831, leaving her ill-provided for. She returned to the stage in Oct. 1832, as "Mrs. Nesbitt," taking the part of Constance in the *Love Chase* for nearly 100 nights, 1837-38, and that of Lady Gay Spanker in *London Assurance*, 1841, "in both of which parts she was unequalled" [Boase's *Modern English Biography*]. Her second marriage, in 1844, lasted but eighteen months, and she again returned to the stage as "Lady Boothby," her last appearance being 8 May 1851, at Drury Lane, in the part of Lady Teazle in Sheridan's *School for Scandal*. The death of her mother, brother, and sister, all within eighteen months of her own, is supposed to have hastened that event.

DIXIE, *or* DIXEY:

cr. 14 July 1660.

I. 1660. "WOLSTAN DIXEY, of Market Bosworth, co. Leicester, Esq.," s. and h. of Sir Wolstan DIXIE, *or* DIXEY, of the same,(a) by Frances, da. of Sir Thomas BEAUMONT, of Stoughton, in that county (which Sir Wolstan, was early on the King's side in the rebellion of 1641, contributed nearly £2,000 out of the £25,643 raised by the Leicestershire gentry, and *d.* 25 July 1650, aged 74), was aged 16 at the Heralds' Visitation of co. Leicester in 1619; had a warrant of Baronetcy, dat. March 1644/5(b), from Charles I, and was *cr. a Baronet*, 14 July 1660. He was Sheriff of Leicestershire, 1661-62, and was presumably (though called "Esq." in the return) M.P. [I.] for Dundalk, 1661-66. He *m.* firstly, about 1629, Barbara, widow of John HARPUR, of Swarkeston, co. Derby, da. and h. of Sir Henry BEAUMONT, of Gracedieu, co. Leicester, by Barbara, da. of Anthony FAUNT. She was *bur.* 31 Dec. 1666, at St. Giles' in the Fields. He *m.* secondly, 1 Sep. 1670, at Swepston, co. Leicester, Frances, widow of Walter CHETWYND, of Grendon, co. Warwick, da. of Edward HESILRIGG, of Theddingworth, co. Leicester, by Frances, da. and coheir of William BROCAS, of the same. He *d.* at Grendon aforesaid 13 Feb. 1681/2, and was *bur.* 24 April 1682 at Bosworth, aged 80. Funeral certificate at Coll. of Arms. His 2d wife, by whom he had no issue, survived him.

II. 1682. SIR BEAUMONT DIXIE, Baronet [1660], of Bosworth Park in Market Bosworth aforesaid, 1st s. and h. by 1st wife, *b.* about 1630; *suc. to the Baronetcy*, 13 Feb. 1681/2. He *m.* Jan. 1652, Mary, sister and h. of Sir William WILLOUGHBY, Baronet [so *cr.* 1660], da. of William WILLOUGHBY, of Selston, Notts, by Elizabeth, da. and coheir of Timothy PUSEY, of Selston aforesaid. He *d.* May 1692, and was *bur.* at Bosworth. Will dat. 23 Feb. 1688/9, pr. 23 June 1692. His widow *d.* at Selston, and was *bur.* 2 Dec. 1710, at Bosworth.

III. 1692. SIR WOLSTAN DIXIE, Baronet [1660], of Bosworth Park aforesaid, 1st s. and h.; *bap.* 25 March 1657, at Bosworth; Lieut. Col. of the Leic. Militia, 1681; *suc. to the Baronetcy* in May 1692. He *m.* (Lic. Vic. Gen. 10 Dec. 1685), Rebecca, da. of Sir Richard ATKINS, 1st Baronet [1660], of Clapham, Surrey, by Rebecca, da. of Sir Edmund WRIGHT. He *d.* 10 Dec. 1713, and was *bur.* at Bosworth. His widow was *bur.* 22 Dec. 1744, at Clapham aforesaid. Will pr. 1747.

IV. 1713. SIR WOLSTAN DIXIE, Baronet [1660], of Bosworth Park aforesaid, 1st s. and h., *b.* about 1701; *suc. to the Baronetcy*, 10 Dec. 1713; Sheriff of Leicestershire, 1726-27. He *m.* firstly, 1 May 1735, Anna ("£20,000 portion"), da. of Tobias FRERE, Gov. of Barbadoes. She *d.* July 1739. He *m.* secondly, 24 Dec. 1741, Theodosia, da. of Henry WRIGHT, of Mobberley, Cheshire, by Purefoy, da. of Sir Willoughby ASTON, 2d Baronet [1628], of Aston, in that county. She *d.* 14 July 1751. He *m.* thirdly, 17 Sep. 1753, Margaret, da. of William CROSS, of Scarboro', co. York. He *d.* 29 Jan. 1767, and was *bur.* at Bosworth, aged 66. M.I. Will pr. Feb. 1767. His widow, by whom he had no issue, *d.* 1797. Will pr. Nov. 1797.

(a) This Wolstan inherited this estate of Bosworth from his great uncle, Sir Wolstan Dixie, one of the most eminent members of the Skinners Company, London, sometime, 1585-86, Lord Mayor of London; founder of a Grammar School at Market Bosworth, and of various Fellowships and Scholarships at Emmanuel College, Cambridge, etc.; who *d.* s.p. 8 Jan. 1593/4, and was *bur.* at St. Michael's, Bassishaw, London, aged 69.

(b) See vol. ii, p. 455. It is, however, not improbable that it was the father (who would then have been about 70), and not the son, to whom the warrant was issued.

V. 1767. SIR WOLSTAN DIXIE, Baronet [1660], of Bosworth Park aforesaid, 1st s. and h., being only s. by 1st wife; *b.* 9 March 1737; *suc. to the Baronetcy*, 29 Jan. 1767. He *d.* unm. 14 Jan. 1806, aged 68. Admon. Feb. 1806.

VI. 1806. SIR BEAUMONT JOSEPH DIXIE, Baronet [1660], of Bosworth Park aforesaid, cousin and h. male, being s. and h. of the Rev. Beaumont Joseph DIXIE, M.A., Rector of Newton Blossomville, Bucks, [1763-73], and Vicar of St. Peter's, Derby, by Margaret, da. of Joseph or Richard SHEWIN *or* SNEWEN, of Strady, co. Carmarthen, which Beaumont Joseph (who *d.* about 1785) was only s. and h. of the Rev. Beaumont DIXIE, Rector of Bosworth (*d.* at Bath, 22 Feb. 1739/40), who was 2d s. of the 3d Baronet. He was *b.* 6 July 1769 at Newton Blossomville; was an officer in the Royal Navy; *suc. to the Baronetcy*, 14 Jan. 1806; was taken prisoner in France in 1802, and detained there at Verdun, Bitche, and Saar Louis till 1814. He *d.* unm. 14 July 1814, at Bosworth, only six days after his return home.

VII. 1814. SIR WILLOUGHBY WOLSTAN DIXIE, Baronet [1660], of Bosworth Park aforesaid, br. and h., *b.* about 1775; *suc. to the Baronetcy*, 14 July 1814; was subject to fits of derangement.(a) He *m.* 21 Nov. 1815, Bella Anna, da. of the Rev. Thomas ADNUTT, Rector of Croft, co. Lincoln. She *d.* 28 Dec. 1830. Admon. Nov. 1848. He *d.* 26 Oct. or 23 Nov. 1827, at Bosworth. Admon. May 1828 and Nov. 1848.

VIII 1827. SIR WILLOUGHBY WOLSTAN DIXIE, Baronet [1660], of Bosworth Park aforesaid, 1st s. and h., *b.* 16 Oct. 1816, at Humberston, co. Leicester; ed. at Eton; matric. at Oxford (Ch. Ch.), 23 Oct. 1834, aged 18; *suc. to the Baronetcy* in Oct. or Nov. 1827; Sheriff of Leicestershire, 1843-44. He *m.* 16 March 1841, at St. Geo. Han. sq., Louisa Anne, yst. da. of Lieut. Gen. Sir Evan LLOYD, **K.C.B.**, of Ferney Hall, Salop, by Alice, Dow. BARONESS TRIMLESTOWN [I.], da. of Lieut. Gen. Charles EUSTACE. He *d.* s.p.m., at Bosworth, 23 July 1850, aged 33. Will pr. 1851. His widow *d.* 25 Jan. 1864, at Springfield, co. Warwick.

IX. 1850. SIR ALEXANDER DIXIE, Baronet [1660], of Bosworth Park aforesaid, uncle and h. male, being yr. br. of the 6th and 7th Baronets; *b.* 1780, in London; entered the Royal Navy, 1795, served at the victory of Trafalgar, was twice wounded in battle, and became Capt. R.N., 1 July 1851; *suc. to the Baronetcy*, 23 July 1850. He *m.* firstly, in 1818, Rosamond Mary, da. of the Rev. Joseph Dixie CHURCHILL, Rector of Blickling, Norfolk. She *d.* 1831. He *m.* secondly, Rebecca, da. of Thomas BARNHAM. He *d.* 29 Dec. 1857, at Bosworth, aged 77. His widow *d.* 8 June 1887, at 18 Malvern Villas, Hounslow, aged 94.

X. 1857. SIR ALEXANDER BEAUMONT CHURCHILL DIXIE, Baronet [1660], of Bosworth Park aforesaid, 1st s. and h. by 1st wife, *b.* 24 Dec. 1819, at Orton on the Hill, co. Leicester; took the degree of M.D.; *suc. to the Baronetcy*, 29 Dec. 1857. He *m.* 29 June 1843, Maria Catherine, yst. da. of the Rev. Charles WALTERS, M.A., Rector [1831] of Bramdean, Hants. He *d.* suddenly, 8 Jan. 1872, at Bosworth, in his 53d year. His widow *d.* 18 April 1902, at Stanton House, Stony Stanton, co. Leicester, and was *bur.* at Bosworth.

(a) In one of these he fired at a clergyman in 1825, being accordingly imprisoned in Leicester gaol. See *Gent. Mag.* for 1828, p. 81.

XI. 1872. SIR ALEXANDER BEAUMONT CHURCHILL DIXIE, Baronet [1660], of Bosworth Park aforesaid, only s. and h., *b.* 22 Dec. 1851, at Manor Lodge, Bognor, Sussex; ed. at Harrow; *suc. to the Baronetcy*, 8 Jan. 1872; Sheriff of Leicestershire, 1876-77, shortly after which time he sold the family estate of Market Bosworth. He *m.*, 3 April 1875, at St. Peter's Eaton square, Pimlico, Florence Caroline, 2d and yst. da. of Archibald William (DOUGLAS), 7th MARQUESS OF QUEENSBURY [S.], by Caroline Margaret, da. of Lieut. Gen. Sir William Robert CLAYTON, 5th Baronet [1732], She was *b.* 25 May 1855.

Family Estates.—These, in 1883, consisted of 5,379 acres in Leicestershire (worth £10,405 a year); 523 in Notts and 31 in Derbyshire. *Total*, 5,933 acres, worth £11,115 a year. *Principal Seat*, Bosworth Park, near Hinkley, co. Leicester, but this, with the Leicestershire estate (which had been above 300 years in the family) was sold by the 11th Baronet, 1880-90.

BRIGHT:

cr. 16 July 1660;

ex. 13 Oct. 1688.

I. 1660, to 1688. "JOHN BRIGHT, of Badsworth, co. York, Esq," 3d but 1st surv. s. and h. of Stephen BRIGHT, of Carbroke, in that county (*d.* 6 June 1642, aged 58), by his 1st wife Jane, da. of George WESTBYE, of Elmley, was *bap.* 14 Oct. 1619, at Sheffield; admitted to Gray's Inn, 18 June 1639; suc. his father, 6 June 1642; took an active part in the Civil War against the King; was Col. in the Parl. Army; Gov. of Sheffield, of York and of Hull; Sheriff of Yorkshire (two years), 1654-56; and was one of the six M.P.'s for that county 1664-65. Having supported the Restoration he was *cr. a Baronet*, 16 July 1660. He entered his ped. at the Visit. of Yorkshire, 1665-66, being then aged 46. He *m.* firstly, in or before 1657, Catharine, widow of William LISTER, of Thornton in Craven (slain at Tadcaster, 1642), da. of Sir Richard HAWKSWORTH, of Hawksworth, co. York, by his 1st wife Anne, da. of Thomas WENTWORTH, of Emsall in that county. She *d.* before 1665, at or before which date he *m.* secondly, Elizabeth, 3d da. of Sir Thomas NORCLIFFE, of Langton, co. York, by Dorothy, da. of Thomas (FAIRFAX), 1st VISCOUNT FAIRFAX OF EMLEY [I.]. She *d.* 26 June 1674, aged 50. He *m.* thirdly (Lic. Lond. 11 July 1682), Frances (then aged 23), widow of Thomas VANE, of Raby Castle, da. of Sir Thomas LIDDELL, 2d Baronet [1642], by Anne, da. of Sir Henry VANE, of Raby aforesaid. She *d.* suddenly, a few months later, on her journey from London, Nov. 1682. He *m.* fourthly, 7 June 1683, at St. Mary's, Beverley, Susanna, sister and coheir of Sir Michael WHARTON, da. of Michael WHARTON, of Beverley. He *d.* s.p.m.s.(a) at Badworth 13, and was *bur.* there 21 Oct. 1688, when *the Baronetcy* became *extinct*. His widow *m.*, 23 March 1690/1, at St. Giles' in the Fields, as his 2d wife, Sir John NEWTON, 3d Baronet [1660], who *d.* 12 Feb. 1734, aged 85. She *d.* 19 April 1737, aged 86, and was *bur.* at Haydon, co. Lincoln. M.I. Will pr. 1737.

(a) John Bright, only surv. s. and h. ap., by 1st wife, was aged 8 in 1666. He *m.* Lucy, yst. da. of Edward (Montagu), 2d Earl of Manchester, but *d.* v.p. and s.p. Catherine, the only surv. da. and h., also by the 1st wife, *m.* in or before 1670, Sir Henry Liddell, 3d Baronet [1642], by whom she had three sons. (1) Thomas Liddell, ancestor of the Barons Ravensworth; (2) John Liddell, who took the name of Bright, having inherited Badsworth and the chief estates of his maternal grandfather. These, afterwards, devolved on his grand-daughter, Mary, Marchioness of Rockingham, and on her death on the Earls of Fitzwilliam. (3) Henry Liddell, who inherited the estate of Carbrook, but *d.* s.p.

WARNER:

cr. 16 July 1660;

ex. 21 March 1705.

I. 1660, to 1705. "JOHN WARNER, of Parham [co. Suffolk], Esq.," s. and h. of Francis WARNER, of the same (admitted to Inner Temple, Nov. 1621), by Elizabeth, da. of Sir John ROUS, of Henham, co. Suffolk, was *b.* about 1640; was, presumably, the "John Warner, Gent.," who matric. at Oxford (Queen's Coll.), 6 Aug. 1658, and was *cr. a Baronet*, 16 July 1660. He *m.*, 7 June 1659, Trevor, da. of Sir Thomas HANMER, 2d Baronet [1620], of Hanmer, co. Flint, by his 1st wife, Elizabeth, da. of Sir Thomas BAKER. Both became converts to the Roman Catholic faith in 1664, and agreed to separate. She, who took the habit of the English nuns called Sepulchrines, at Liège (with her sister in law, Elizabeth Warner), 30 April 1665, and who was called "Sister Clare of Jesus," *d.* 26 Jan. 1670, aged 33.(a) He became a Jesuit early in 1665; was ordained Priest, 1671; was subsequently, 1685, Rector of Watten, in Flanders, Confessor at Watten, Consultor of the Province, and Spiritual Father. In Oct. 1664, he made over his estates to his br., Francis Warner, on whose death 3 April 1667, he resettled them on his only surv. br., Edward Warner, of London, merchant. He *d.* s.p.m.,(b) 21 March 1705, aged 65, when the *Baronetcy* became *extinct*.

HARBY:

cr. 17 July 1660;

ex July 1674.

I. 1660. "SIR JOB HARBY, of Aldenham, Herts, Knt.," 3d s. of Thomas HARBY, of Adston, co. Northampton (*d.* 3 May 1594), by his 3d wife, Catherine, da. of Clement THROCKMORTON, of Haseley, co. Warwick, was *b.* probably about 1590(c); was a merchant in London, and one of the Farmers of the Customs; was *Knighted* 4 Dec. 1637; purchased the manor, advowson and estate of Aldenham aforesaid, 25 June 1642, of Lucius (CAREY), 2d VISCOUNT FALKLAND [S.], and was *cr. a Baronet* 17 July 1660. He *m.*, in or before 1617,(d) Elizabeth, sister to Sir Peter WYCHE, Ambassador to Constantinople, da. of Richard WYCHE, of St. Dunstan's in the East, London, merchant, by Elizabeth, da. of Sir Richard SALTINGSTALL, sometime (1597-98) Lord Mayor of London. He was *bur.*, 9 April 1663, at Aldenham. Will dat. 28 May 1662, pr. 1663. His widow was *bur.* 8 Nov. 1673, at St. Dunstan's in the East. Will pr. 1674.

II. 1663, to 1674. SIR ERASMUS HARBY, Baronet [1660], of Aldenham aforesaid, 3d but only surv. s. and h., *bap.* at St. Dunstan's in the East, 15 Feb. 1627/8; admitted to the Inner Temple, Nov. 1648; Barrister, 1658; *suc. to the Baronetcy* in April 1663, soon after which date he sold the Aldenham estate to the Holles family. He *m.* firstly, Frances, da. of Mildmay (FANE), 2d EARL OF WESTMORLAND, by his 1st wife, Grace, da. of Sir William THORNIHURST. She *d.* before him. He *d.* s.p., and was *bur.* 29 July 1674 at Aldenham, when *the Baronetcy* became *extinct*. Will dat. 2 April 1674, pr. 15 Dec. 1675.

(a) A life of this Lady Warner, by Edward Scarisbrick, with portrait, was published in 1690 and 1692, but the information in this article is mostly from Foley's invaluable *Records of the Society of Jesus*.

(b) Of his daughters, Anne *d.* 1689, Catherine in 1696, and Susan in 1711, all three being nuns.

(c) His eldest br., Francis, matric. at Oxford (Ex. Coll.) 10 Dec. 1591, aged 15, and their father *d.* in May 1594. There is a good pedigree of the family in the Visitation of Northamptonshire, 1681.

(d) "Susanna, da. of Job Harby," was *bap.* 30 Nov. 1617 at St. Dunstan's in the East."

MORLAND, *or* MORLEY:

cr. 18 July 1660;

ex. Nov. 1716.

I. 1660. "SAMUEL MORLAND, *alias* MORLEY, of Sulhamstede Banister, Berks, Esq., one of the Gentlemen of His Majesty's Privy Chamber in ordinary and Master of the Mechanicks," was a yr. s. of the Rev. Thomas MORLAND, B.A., Rector (1615) of Bright Waltham, Berks, and subsequently (1625) of Sulhampstead aforesaid; was *b.* at Sulhampstead 1625; admitted to Winchester, 1638; was a Sizar at Mag. Coll., Cambridge, in May 1644, becoming a Fellow, Nov. 1649 to 1653, and Tutor in 1650, but never took a degree; was a zealous supporter of the Parl. party from 1647; was on the embassy to Sweden in 1653, and was sent by Cromwell, in May 1655, to remonstrate with the Duke of Savoy on the persecution of the Waldenses or Vaudois. He was publicly thanked, 18 Dec. 1656, for his conduct in this mission,(a) and became assistant to Secretary Thurloe. He, however, promoted the Restoration; was *Knighted*, 20 May 1660, at Breda, by the young King, and was, two months later, *cr. a Baronet*, 18 July 1660, made a Gent. of the Privy Chamber, and obtained a pension of £500 on the Post Office. His knowledge of mathematics led him to try various experiments in hydrostatics and hydraulics, which, though ingenious, were not very practical, and which gave no profit to their inventor. In 1681 he was made *Magister Mechanicorum* to the King. He *m.* firstly, in 1657, Susanne, da. of Daniel DE MILLEVILLE, Baron of Boissay in Normandy, by Catherine, his wife. She was living 1660. He *m.* secondly, 26 Oct. 1670, in Westm. Abbey, Carola, da. of Sir Roger HARSNETT, Serjeant at Arms to the House of Lords (*d.* Oct. 1692), by Carola, da. of Robert BARNE, of Great Grimsby, co. Lincoln. She *d.* 10 and was *bur.* 14 Oct. 1674, in Westm. Abbey, aged 22. He *m.* thirdly, 16 Nov. 1676, in Westm. Abbey, Anne, 3d da. of George FEILDING, of Solihull, co. Warwick, by Mary, da. of Sir Thomas SHIRLEY, of Wiston, Sussex. She *d.* 20 and was *bur.* 24 Feb. 1679/80, in Westm. Abbey, in her 19th year. He *m.* fourthly, 1 Feb. 1686/7, at Knightsbridge chapel, Midx., Mary AYLIF (da. of a coachman), a person of bad character, who had represented herself as an heiress of £20,000. From her he obtained a divorce 16 July following.(b) He, who had been blind some three years, *d.* 26 Dec. 1695, and was *bur.* 9 Jan. 1695/6, at Hammersmith, Midx., aged 70. Will, by which he disinherited his only son and successor, leaving all to "Mrs. Zenobia Hough, of St. James' Westm.," dat. 25 and pr. 30 Dec. 1695.

II. 1695, to 1716. SIR SAMUEL MORLAND, Baronet [1660], of St. James', Westminster, only s. and h., by 1st or 2d wife, *suc. to the Baronetcy*, 26 Dec. 1695. He *m.* Martha. He *d.* s.p. Nov. 1716, when the *Baronetcy* became *extinct*. Will dat. 20 July 1708, pr. 8 May 1717. The admon. of his widow, as of St. Dunstan's in the West, London, 5 Feb. 1727/8 and 17 July 1729.

HEWETT, *or* HEWIT:

cr. 19 July 1660;

afterwards, April to Dec. 1689, VISCOUNT HEWETT OF GOWRAN [I.];

ex. 2 Dec. 1689.

I. 1660. "SIR THOMAS HEWIT, of Pishobury [in Sawbridgeworth], Herts, Knt.," s. and h. of Sir William HEWETT, of Brightwell, Sussex, and of St. Martin's in the Fields, Midx. (who purchased the estate

(a) He published, in 1658, a "History of the Evangelical Churches of the Valleys of Piemont, together with a most naked and punctual relation of the late Bloody Massacre, 1655," etc. The dedication of this work to Cromwell is "couched in a strain of extreme adulation," and was withdrawn, after the Restoration, from all copies he could lay hold of.

(b) She *m.*, after April 1693, as his 2d wife, Sir Gilbert Cosins Gerard, 2d Baronet [1666] of Fiskerton, co. Lanc., who *d.* before July 1695.

of Pishobury, 22 Aug. 1635, and was *bur.* 19 Oct. 1637), by Elizabeth, da. of Richard WISEMAN, was *b.* about 1605; admitted to the Inner Temple, Nov. 1617; suc. his father in Oct. 1637; was M.P. for New Windsor, 1628-29; Sheriff of Herts, 1638-39, and, again, 1660-61, and having been *Knighted*, 10 July 1641, was *cr. a Baronet*, 19 July 1660. He *m.* firstly, 14 May 1629, at St. Barth. the Great, London, Frances, yst. da. of Sir Henry HOBART, 1st Bart. [1611], Lord Chief Justice of the Common Pleas [1613-25], by Dorothy, da. of Sir Robert BELL, Lord Ch. Baron of the Exchequer. She *d.* s.p.m. 21 May 1632, and was *bur.* at Highgate, Midx. He *m.* secondly, in or shortly before 1634, Margaret, widow of Thomas HILLERSDON, of Elnestone, Beds, 1st da. of Sir William LYTTON, of Knebworth, Herts, by his 1st wife, Ann, da. and h. of Stephen SLANEY, of Norton, Salop. He *d.* 4 and was *bur.* 19 Aug. 1662 at Sawbridgeworth, aged 57. His widow, who was *b.* 14 Sep. 1613, *d.* 1 Aug. 1689, and was *bur.* at Sawbridgeworth. Will pr. 1689.

II. 1662, to 1689. SIR GEORGE HEWETT, Baronet [1660], of Pishobury aforesaid, 4th but only surv. s. and h. by the 2d wife, *b.* 1652; *suc. to the Baronetcy*, 4 Aug. 1662. He was *cr.*, 9 April 1689,(a) VISCOUNT HEWETT OF GOWRAN, co. Kilkenny, etc. [I.], in which peerage *this Baronetcy* then *merged*. He, however, *d.* unm. a few months later, at Chester, 2 and was *bur.* 15 Dec. 1689 at Sawbridgeworth, aged 37, when *all his honours* became *extinct*.(b) Will pr. Dec. 1689.

HONYWOOD:

cr. 19 July 1660.

I. 1660. "EDWARD HONYWOOD, of Evington [in Elmsted], co. Kent, Esq.," s. and h. of Sir John HONYWOOD, of the same, sometime Sheriff of Kent, by Mary, da. of Thomas GODFREY, of Lid, in that county, was *b.* about 1628; admitted to Gray's Inn, 6 May 1647; suc. his father (who *d.* aged 68), 16 Nov. 1652, and (having remitted £3,000(c) to Charles II when in exile, was *cr. a Baronet*, 19 July 1660. He *m.*, in or before 1654, Elizabeth, da. of Sir John MAYNARD, K.B., of Tooting, Graveney, Surrey, and of Iselham, co. Cambridge, by Mary, da. of Sir Thomas MIDDLETON, of Chirk Castle, co. Denbigh. He *d.* 1670, aged 42. His widow *m.* Charles MELVIN, and was *bur.* 26 Oct. 1680 at St. Martin's in the Fields. Admon. 4 Nov. 1680 to her husband, Charles MELVIN, "Esq."

II. 1670. SIR WILLIAM HONYWOOD, Baronet [1660], of Evington aforesaid, 1st s. and h., *b.* about 1654; matric. at Oxford (Jesus Coll.), 29 March 1672, aged 17; *suc. to the Baronetcy* in 1670; M.P. for Canterbury, 1685-87 and 1689-98. He *m.*, 15 July 1675, at Westm. Abbey (Lic. Dean and Chap. of Westm.) Anna-Christiana, da. of Richard NEWMAN, of Fifehead Magdalen, Dorset, by Anne, 1st da. of Sir Charles HARBORD. She *d.* 26 Oct. 1736, aged 79. He *d.* 1 June 1748, aged 94. Both *bur.* at Elmsted. M.I. His will dat. 14 April 1746, pr. 29 July 1748.

III. 1748. SIR JOHN HONYWOOD, Baronet [1660], of Evington aforesaid, grandson and h., being 1st s. and h. of William HONYWOOD, of Cherdon, by Frances, da. of William RALEIGH, which William, who *d.* v.p. in 1719, was s. and h. ap. of the late Baronet. He was *b.* about 1710; matric. at

(a) A "Coronation peerage" (the only Irish one) made at the accession of William and Mary.

(b) He is said to be the "Sir Fopling Flutter" in Etheredge's comedy of *The Man of the Mode*. See Clutterbuck's *Herts*, vol. iii, p. 202, for a full account of his numerous sisters and coheirs and the subsequent devolution of the estate.

(c) Wotton's *Baronetage*, edit. 1741.

Oxford (Corpus Christi Coll.), 21 Sep. 1726, aged 16; *suc. to the Baronetcy*, 1 June 1748; was Sheriff of Kent, 1752-53. In 1754 he suc. to Malling Abbey, Kent, and other estates of his kinsman, Frazer HONYWOOD, of London, banker. He *m.* firstly, Annabella, da. of William GOODENOUGH, of Langford, Berks. She *d.* 22 July 1737, aged 33. M.I. at Elmsted. He *m.* secondly, Dorothy, da. of Sir Edward FILMER, 3d Baronet [1674], of East Sutton, Kent, by Mary, da. of John WALLIS, of Soundness, Oxon. He *d.* 26 June 1781, aged 71. Will pr. July 1781. His widow d. 8 Oct. 1781, aged 70. Will pr. 1781. Both *bur.* at Elmsted. M.I.

IV. 1781. SIR JOHN HONYWOOD, Baronet [1660], of Evington aforesaid, grandson and h., being 1st. s. and h. of William HONYWOOD, of Malling Abbey aforesaid, by Elizabeth, da. of Thomas CLACK, of Wallingford, Berks, which William was 1st s. and h. ap. of the 3d Baronet, but *d.* v.p. 23 Oct. 1764, aged 33. He was *b.* about 1757; matric. at Oxford (Corpus Christi Coll.), 11 Feb. 1775, aged 18; *suc. to the Baronetcy*, 26 June 1781; was M.P. for Steyning, 1784-85; and 1788-90; for Canterbury (two Parls.), 1790-1802, and for Honiton 1802, till his death. He *m.*, 13 Dec. 1788 or 1789, his cousin Frances (*b.* Jan. 1763), 1st sister and coheir of William (COURTENAY), EARL OF DEVON (who established his claim to that Earldom [*cr.* in 1553] in 1831), da. of William, 2d VISCOUNT COURTENAY, *de jure* (according to the startling decision of 1831) EARL OF DEVON, by Frances, da. of Thomas CLACK, abovenamed. He *d.* 29 March 1806. Will pr. 1806.

V. 1806. SIR JOHN-COURTENAY HONYWOOD, Baronet [1660], of Evington aforesaid, only s. and h., *b.* 1787; *suc. to the Baronetcy*, 29 March 1806; Sheriff of Kent, 1811-12. He *m.* 27 July 1808, Mary-Anne, 1st da. of Rev. "Sir" William-Henry COOPER, "Baronet [S. 1638?], of Gogar,"(a) Prebendary of Rochester, by Isabella Ball, da. of Moses FRANKS, of Teddington, Midx. He *d.* 12 Sep. 1832, at Evington. Will pr. Dec. 1832. The will of his widow was pr. April 1841.

VI. 1832. SIR JOHN-EDWARD HONYWOOD, Baronet [1660], of Evington aforesaid, 1st s. and h., *b.* 16 March 1812; *suc. to the Baronetcy*, 12 Sep. 1832. He *m.*, 17 April 1834, at Patrixbourne, Mary, 2d da. of Rev. Charles-Hughes HALLETT, of Higham, Kent. He *d.* 17 July 1845 in his 33d year. Will pr. Aug. 1845. His widow *m.* 11 July 1848, at Tor, Devon, William CLARK, of Oswald's, Torquay, Devon, who *d.* 20 Feb. 1849. She *d.* 27 May 1884, at 43 Manor Road, Folkestone, aged 68.

VII. 1845. SIR COURTENAY HONYWOOD, Baronet [1660], of Evington aforesaid, only s. and h., *b.* 5 March 1835; *suc. to the Baronetcy*, 17 July 1845; Sheriff of Kent, 1860. He *m.*, 23 Aug. 1855, Annie-Maria, 2d da. of William PAYNTER, of Cambourne House, Richmond, Surrey, and of Belgrave square. He *d.* 17 April 1878, at 19 Sackville street, Piccadilly. His widow living 1902.

VIII. 1878. SIR JOHN-WILLIAM HONYWOOD, of Evington aforesaid, 1st s. and h., *b.* 15 April 1857, at Evington Place; an officer in the East Kent Yeomanry; *suc. to the Baronetcy*, 17 April 1878. He *m.*, 22 Aug. 1877, Zaidée-Emily-Iseulte, 1st da. of John-Bodychan SPARROW, of Bodychan and Gwyn-du, co. Anglesey. She, who was *b.* 12 May 1857, *d.* at Evington Place, 15 Oct. 1893.

Family Estates.—These, in 1883, consisted of 5,601 acres in Kent, worth £5,871 a year. *Principal Seat.*—Evington Place, near Ashford, co. Kent.

(a) According to a Scotch service, 1 Aug. 1775.

BROWNE:

cr. 22 July 1660;([a])

ex. or *dorm.* June or July 1739.

I. 1660. "RICHARD BROWNE, Lord Mayor of London" [1660-61], s. of John BROWNE, *otherwise* MOSES,([b]) of Wokingham, Berks, and of London, by Anne, da. of John BEARD, of Wokingham aforesaid, was a "Woodmonger" of London, 1634, when he entered his ped. in the Visit. of London; was free of the Merchant Taylors, as also apparently of the Cloth-workers' Company, and appears to have been a "Coal merchant"; was one of the Parl. Commissioners to receive the King from the Scots, Jan. 1647; Sheriff of London, 1648-49; Alderman of Langbourne Ward, 29 June 1648, but discharged 11 Dec. 1649, though restored in 1660; Alderman of Bridge without, 16 Nov. 1663, till discharged 1 March 1663/4, he being at that date Senior Alderman; was one of the most active officers in command of the trained bands of London on behalf of the Parl., and was, in June 1644, Major Gen. of Oxon, Bucks, and Berks; Gov. of Abingdon, 1645; one of the Parl. Commissrs. to Newport, 1648; was M.P. for Wycombe, Oct. 1645, till secluded, 12 Dec. 1648, and imprisoned; M.P. for London, 1656-58, 1659, and 1660, and for Ludgershall, 1661-69. He headed the procession when the King entered London in May 1660, was *Knighted* (with his eldest son) 29 May 1660 at Whitehall, and *cr. a Baronet*, a few weeks later, 22 July 1660; was Lord Mayor, 1660-61, keeping his Mayoralty at his residence near Goldsmiths' Hall.([c]) Major-Gen. of the City of London, 1661. He purchased the manor and estate of Debden, co. Essex, before May 1662. He *m.*, in or before 1631, Bridget, da. of Robert BRYAN, of Henley on Thames, Oxon. She probably *d.* before him. He *d.* 24 Sep., and was *bur.* 12 Oct. 1669 at Debden. Admon. as of St. Andrew's, Holborn, 28 Jan. 1670/1, to his son Richard.

II. 1669. SIR RICHARD BROWNE, Baronet [1660], of Depden aforesaid, 1st s. and h., *b.* before 1634; admitted to Lincoln's Inn, 24 Nov. 1646; was *Knighted* (with his father) 29 May 1660, at Whitehall; *suc. to the Baronetcy*, 24 Sep. 1669. He *m.*, before 1656, Frances, da. of Sir Edward ATKINS, of Hensington, Oxon, one of the Judges of the Court of Common Pleas, by Ursula, da. of Sir Thomas DACRES, of Cheshunt, Herts. He *d.* at St. Martin's-in-the-Fields, a widower, but both he and his wife were *bur.* on the same day, 23 Sep. 1684, at Depden. His admon. 31 July 1685.

III. 1684. SIR RICHARD BROWNE, Baronet [1660], of Depden aforesaid, s. and h., *b.* about 1656; admitted to Lincoln's Inn, 12 May 1670; was sometime a Capt. in the Guards; *suc. to the Baronetcy* in Sep. 1684. He *m.* 13 Sep. 1688, at St. James' Westm. (Lic. Lond., he 32 and she 27), Dorothy, widow of Michael BLACKETT, of Newcastle, da. of William BARNES, of Sadberg and Darlington, co. Durham. He *d.* s.p., being slain in Flanders, 1689, by Col. Billingsley. Will, "as of Whitehall, Midx," dat. 13 Oct. 1688, pr. 9 Jan. 1689/90 by the widow. She *m.*, as his 2d wife, John MOORE, D.D., Bishop of Ely [1707-14], who *d.* 31 Aug. 1714, aged 68.

IV. 1689. SIR JOHN BROWNE, Baronet [1660], uncle, or possibly br., and h. male, Citizen and Woodmonger of London, sometime of of White Friars in that City; *suc. to the Baronetcy* in 1689; was nominated one of the Poor Brothers of the Charter House, London, 24 Feb. 1695/6, receiving his last payment therefrom on Christmas, 1700. He *m.* (—), da. of (—) HUSSEY, Alderman of London. She was *bur.* 1 June 1681, at Debden. He *d.* 1701, leaving numerous issue.

([a]) In Dugdale's *Catalogue*, between the creations of Honywood, on 19 July, and of Browne, on 22 July 1660, is inserted that of "Basil Dixwell, of Bromehouse, co. Kent, Esq., 19 July 1660," but this creation appears to have been on 19 *June* [not July] 1660, and is consequently dealt with under that date.

([b]) There is a good account of this family in *The Genealogist* (O.S., vol. iii, p. 377; vol. iv, p. 128, and vol. v, p. 185). See also an account of the 1st Baronet, by W. Duncombe Pink, in *N. and Q.*, 8th S., viii, 54.

([c]) His Pageant, by John Tatham, was entitled *The Royal Oak*.

V. 1701, to 1739. SIR THOMAS BROWNE, Baronet [1660], s. and h., *b.* before 1680; *suc. to the Baronetcy* in 1701; was living unm. 1727. He *d.* s.p. in June or July 1739, at Dorchester, Dorset, when the *Baronetcy* became *extinct*, or, possibly, only *dormant*. Will dat. 16 June, and pr. 6 July 1739.

VERNON:

cr. 23 July 1660;

ex. 1 Oct. 1725.

I. 1660. "HENRY VERNON, of Hodnet, Salop, Esq.," s. and h. of Sir Robert VERNON, of the same, K.B., Comptroller of the Household to Queen Elizabeth, by Mary, sister of Robert, 1st VISCOUNT KILMOREY [I.], da. of Robert NEEDHAM, of Shavington, Salop, was *b.* about 1605, being aged 16 in the Visit. of Salop 1623; suc. his father in 1625, and, having distinguished himself in the Royal cause during the Civil War, was *cr. a Baronet*, 23 July 1660. He was M.P. for Salop, 1660; and for West Looe, 1661 till his death. He *m*, in 1636, Elizabeth, da. and h. of Sir Richard WHITE, of The Friars, Anglesey. She *d.* at Bloomsbury (St. Giles' in the fields) 8 and was *bur.* 15 May 1675, at Hodnet. He *d.* April 1676. Will pr. 1677.

II. 1676. SIR THOMAS VERNON, Baronet [1660], only s. and h.; *suc. to the Baronetcy* in April 1676. He was one of the Tellers of the Exchequer. He *m.* firstly, 9 Sep. 1675, at Whitegate, co. Chester, Elizabeth, da. of Thomas CHOLMONDELEY, of Vale Royal, Cheshire, by his 1st wife, Jane, da. of Lionel TOLLEMACHE. She, who was *b.* at Vale Royal, and *bap.* 9 March 1652/3, at Whitegate, *d.* s.p. and was *bur.* at Hodnet, 19 June 1676. He *m.* secondly, 30 June 1677, at St. Peter-le-poor, London, Mary (sister of Diana, COUNTESS OF OXFORD), da. of George KIRKE, one of the Grooms of the Bedchamber, by his 2d wife, Mary (*m.* 26 Feb. 1645/6), da. of Aurelian TOWNSHEND, composer of Masques for the Court. He *d.* 5 Feb. 1682/3. His widow, who was sometime Maid of Honour to Katherine, the Queen Consort, *d.* at Greenwich, whence she was carried away for burial, 17 Aug. 1711.

III. 1683, to 1725. SIR RICHARD VERNON, Baronet [1660], of Hodnet aforesaid, only s. and h. by 2d wife; *b.* 22 June 1678, probably at Shrewsbury; *suc. to the Baronetcy*, 5 Feb. 1682/3; matric. at Oxford (Ch. Ch.) 24 Oct. 1692, aged 14. He, who alienated a large portion of the family estates, was sometime Envoy to Augustus, King of Poland. He *d.* unm. in France, 1 Oct. 1725, when the *Baronetcy* became *extinct*.([a]) Will dat. 22 Jan. 1723, pr. 1725.

AUBREY:

cr. 23 July 1660;

ex. 5 Sep. 1856.

I. 1660. "SIR JOHN AUBREY, of Llantrithyd, co. Glamorgan, Knt.," s. and h. of Sir Thomas AUBREY,([b]) of the same, by Mary, da. and h. of Anthony MANSELL of Llantrithyd aforesaid, was *b.* about 1606; matric. at Oxford (Wadham Coll.), 3 Nov. 1626, aged 20; admitted to Gray's Inn,

([a]) The estate of Hodnet devolved on his two sisters, Diana and Henrietta, and after their death unm., on the family of Heber, of Marton, co. York, through the families of Atherton and Cholmondeley in right of the marriage (1675) of Elizabeth, da. of the 1st Baronet, with Robert Cholmondeley.

([b]) This Thomas was 2d s. of William Aubrey, D.C.L., Regius Professor of Law at Oxford, one of the Queen's Council in the Marches of Wales, and one of the Masters of the Requests, who *d.* 25 June, 1595, aged 66, and was *bur.* at St. Paul's Cathedral, London, 23 July following, leaving three sons, all of whom had issue.

1626; had a warrant of Baronetcy, dat. April 1644, from Charles I.,([a]) and was (apparently as *Sir* John Aubrey, though there is no evidence of his having been Knighted) *cr. a Baronet*, 23 July 1660. He *m.* in or before 1650, Mary, da. and h. of Sir Richard SOUTH, of Cheapside, London, Goldsmith, by Elizabeth, da. of Richard GOSSON, Citizen and Grocer of London. He was *bur.* 25 March 1679, at Llantrithyd. Will pr. 1679. His widow *d.* shortly afterwards. Her admon. 5 July 1680.

II. 1679. SIR JOHN AUBREY, Baronet [1660], of Llantrithyd aforesaid, 2d and yst. but only surv. s. and h., *b.* about 1650; matric. at Oxford (Jesus Coll.), 29 Oct. 1668, aged 18; *suc. to the Baronetcy* in March 1679; was Sheriff of Glamorganshire, 1685-86; M.P. for Brackley, 1698 till his death in 1700. He *m.* firstly, 1 March 1678/9, at St. James', Clerkenwell (Lic. Vic. Gen. 27 Feb., he 27 and she 19), Margaret, 15th child of Sir John LOWTHER, 1st Baronet [S. 1638?] of Lowther, co. Westmorland, being yst. da. by his 2d wife, Elizabeth, da. of Sir John HARE, of Stow Bardolph, Norfolk. She, who was *b.* 27 April 1658, was living in June 1680. He *m.* secondly Mary, widow of William JEPHSON (who *d.* in 1691), 1st da. and coheir of William LEWIS, of The Van, co. Glamorgan, and of Boarstall and Brill, Bucks, by Margaret, da. and h. of Laurence BANASTER, of Boarstall and Brill aforesaid. By her he had no issue. He *d.* at Boarstall, from injuries received by a fall from his horse, Sep. 1700, and was *bur.* at Llantrithyd. His widow *m.* in 1701 (as his 2d wife) Sir Charles KEMEYS, 3d Baronet [1642], who was *bur.* 22 Dec. 1702, at Michaelstown, co. Glamorgan. She afterwards *m.*, 10 Aug. 1703, at Boarstall (for her 4th husband), William AUBREY, of New College, Oxford, B.C.L. (1698), 2d cousin of her 2d husband. She *d.* s.p., 1717, and was *bur.* at Boarstall.

III. 1700. SIR JOHN AUBREY, Baronet [1660], of Llantrithyd, and afterwards of Boarstall([b]) aforesaid, only s. and h., by 1st wife, *b.* 20 June 1680; matric. at Oxford (Jesus Coll.), 7 April 1698, aged 17; *suc. to the Baronetcy* in Sep. 1700; was M.P. for Cardiff, Feb. 1706 to 1710; Sheriff of Glamorganshire, 1710-11. He *m.* firstly, as soon as he was of age, 20 June 1701, at St. James's, Westminster (Lic. Fac.), Mary STEALY, of that parish, then about 30, spinster, "waiting-maid to Mary, Lady Aubrey."([c]) He *m.* secondly, Frances, da. of William JEPHSON, of Boarstall aforesaid, by, presumably, Mary (afterwards wife of the 2d Baronet), da. of William LEWIS, all abovenamed. She *d.* s.p.m. He *m.* thirdly, 1 Feb. 1724/5, at St. Benet's, Paul's Wharf, London, Jane THOMAS, of Boarstall, spinster, but by her had no issue. She *d.* before 1741. He *d.* 16 and was *bur.* 23 April 1743, at Boarstall. Will pr. 1743.

IV. 1743. SIR JOHN AUBREY, Baronet [1660], of Llantrithyd and of Boarstall aforesaid, s. and h. by 1st wife; *b.* about 1707; matric. at Oxford (Jesus Coll.), 17 Dec. 1722, aged 15; *suc. to the Baronetcy*, 16 April 1743. He *d.* unm. 14 Oct. 1767.

V. 1767. SIR THOMAS AUBREY, Baronet [1660], of Llantrithyd and Boarstall aforesaid, br. and h., being 2d s. of the 3d Baronet by his 1st wife; *suc. to the Baronetcy*, 14 Oct. 1767. He *m.* 18 July, 1738, Martha, 1st da. of Richard CARTER, of Chilton, Bucks, by Martha, da. of the Rev. (—) CORNISH, Vicar of Watlington, Oxon. He *d.* 4 and was *bur.* 13 Sep. 1786 at Llantrithyd, aged 79. Will pr. Feb. 1789. His widow *d.* at Bath 5, and was *bur.* 14 Dec. 1788, at Llantrithyd, aged 76. Admon. Feb. 1789.

([a]) See vol. ii, p. 455.

([b]) This estate he inherited on the death s.p., in 1717, of his stepmother, Dame Mary Kemeys abovenamed, under the settlement made on her marriage with his father. It is said that Boarstall had never been sold from the time of Edward the Confessor, when it was possessed by one Nigel the Huntsman (the reputed owner of the famous Boarstall horn), from whom it passed by descent through the families of Handlo, De la Pole, James, Rede, Dynham, and Banaster to that of Lewis, and thence, by settlement, to the Aubrey family. See Lipscomb's *Bucks*, vol. i, p. 72.

([c]) Le Neve's *Baronets*, vol. ii, p. 295.

VI. 1786. SIR JOHN AUBREY, Baronet [1660], of Llantrithyd and Boarstall aforesaid, and of Dorton, Bucks, s. and h., *b.* 4 June and *bap.* 2 July 1739, at Boarstall; ed. at Westminster School; matric. at Oxford (Ch. Ch.), 24 May 1758, aged 18; *cr.* D.C.L., 8 July 1763; M.P. for Wallingford, 1768 to 1774; for Aylesbury, 1774-80; for Wallingford, again, 1780-84, for Bucks, 1784-90; for Clitheroe, 1790-96; for Aldborough, 1796-1812; for Steyning, 1812-20; for Horsham, 1820 till decease; having *suc. to the Baronetcy*, 4 Sep. 1786; was a Lord Commissioner of the Admiralty 1782; one of the Lords of the Treasury, 1783 to 1789. In 1783, he purchased the estate of Dorton, Bucks, where thenceforth he chiefly resided. He *m.* firstly, 9 March 1771, Mary, sister of Emma, COUNTESS OF TANKERVILLE, 1st da. and coheir of Sir James COLEBROOKE, 1st Baronet [1759] of Gatton, by Mary, da. and coheir of Stephen SKYNNER. She, who was *b.* 10 March 1750, *d.* s.p.s.,([a]) 14 and was *bur.* 20 June 1781 at Boarstall. He *m.* secondly, 26 May 1783, Martha Catherine, da. and h. of his maternal uncle, George Richard CARTER, of Chilton Bucks, by Julia Augusta, da. and sole h. of James SPILMAN, of Warlies, Essex. She *d.* s.p. at Bath, Somerset, 3 Sep. 1815. Admon. June 1817. He *d.* 14 March 1826, s.p. legit([b]), at Dorton House, aged 86. Will pr. April 1826. Both were *bur.* at Boarstall.

VII. 1826, to 1856. SIR THOMAS DIGBY AUBREY, Baronet [1660], of Llantrithyd and Boarstall aforesaid, nephew and h. male, being s. and h. of Richard AUBREY, Lieut.-Col. of the Glamorganshire Militia, by Frances, da. of the Hon. Wriothesley DIGBY, which Richard was 3d s. of the 5th Baronet, but *d.* April 1808, aged 63. He was *b.* 2 Dec. 1782; ed. at St. John's College, Cambridge; B.A., 1803; M.A., 1809; Sheriff of Bucks, 1815-16; *suc. to the Baronetcy* and to the entailed (and some other) estates, 14 March 1826. He *m.* 9 Dec. 1813, Mary, da. of Thomas WRIGHT, of London, niece of the Rev. Robert VERNEY, *formerly* WRIGHT,([c]) of Middle Claydon, Bucks. She *d.* 27 Nov. 1817, and was *bur.* at Middle Claydon. He *d.* s.p. at Oving House, near Aylesbury, Bucks (where he chiefly resided), 5 Sep. 1856, aged 73, when the *Baronetcy* became *extinct*.([d]) Will pr. Sep. 1856, under £160,000.

THOMAS:

cr. 23 July 1660;

ex. 18 Nov. 1706.

I. 1660, to 1706. "WILLIAM THOMAS, of Folkington, co. Sussex, Esq.," s. and h. of William THOMAS, by Katharine, da. of George ROSE, of Estergate, near Chichester, (which William, who *d.* v.p., was s. and h. ap. of William THOMAS, of West Deane, co. Sussex), was *b.* about 1641, was probably the "William THOMAS, Gent.," who matric. at Oxford (Oriel

([a]) Her only s. John Aubrey, *b.* 6 Dec. 1771, was accidentally poisoned, and *d.* 2 Jan. 1777, and was *bur.* at Boarstall. In Lipscomb's *Bucks* (vol. i, p. 244) it is stated that "a picture of this interesting child, playing with a lamb," is [1847] at Dorton House, Bucks.

([b]) Mary, his illegitimate da., *m.* 7 May 1792, at Dorton, Bucks, Samuel WHITCOMBE, of Hempstead Court, co. Gloucester. Elizabeth Sophia, his niece, da. of his next br., Thomas Aubrey (who *d.* s.p.m. 15 Jan. 1814), and wife of Charles Spencer RICKETTS, was his heir at law, and inherited, under his will, a large part of his unentailed estates.

([c]) This Robert, in 1811, took the name of *Verney*, instead of that of *Wright*, his wife (Catherine, da. of Richard Calvert), having inherited, in 1810, the Verney estates at Middle Claydon, devised to her by her uterine sister Mary, *suo jure* Baroness Fermanagh [I.].

([d]) The greater part of his property went to his wife's distant connection, Sir Harry Verney, formerly Calvert, 2d Baronet [1818], grandson of Peter Calvert, 1st cousin of Catherine Calvert, the childless wife of Dame Mary Aubrey's uncle, Robert Verney, formerly Wright. See note "c" above.

III

Coll.), 21 March 1658/9, and was *cr. a Baronet*, 23 July 1660. He was M.P. for Seaford (three parls.), 1661-81; for Sussex, 1681; for Seaford, again, 1685-87; for Sussex, again (four parls.), 1689-1700; for Seaford, again, 1701; for Sussex, again, 1701-02, and for Seaford, again, 1702 till decease. He *m.* Barbara, da. and h. of Sir Herbert SPRINGETT, Baronet [so *cr.* 1661], of The Broyle, co. Sussex, by Barbara, da. of Sir William CAMPION. She *d.* at St. Paul's, Covent Garden, 25 and was *bur.* 28 Oct. 1697, at Folkington, aged 57. M.I. He *d.* s.p. 18 and was *bur.* 22 Nov. 1706, at Folkington, aged 65, when the *Baronetcy* became *extinct*. M.I.

SCLATER:

cr. 25 July 1660;

ex. 10 Dec. 1684.

I. 1660, to 1684. "THOMAS SCLATER, of Cambridge, co. Cambridge, Esq.," s. of William SCLATER, of Halifax, co. York, was *b.* and *bap.*, 9 July 1615, at Halifax; is said to have been sometime Fellow of Trinity College, Cambridge; was incorp. B.A. at Oxford therefrom, 1635-36; M.A., 1639; *cr.* Doc. Med., 13 June 1649; incorp. at Cambridge, 1649; M.P. for the University of Cambridge, 1659; and was *cr. a Baronet*, 25 July 1660. He purchased Catley park and other estates in Cambridgeshire, and entered his pedigree in the Visit. of that county 1683, of which he was Sheriff, 1683-84. He *m.* 25 Feb. 1653, Susan, widow of Thomas COMBER, D.D., Dean of Carlisle and Master of Trin. Coll. aforesaid, formerly widow of (—) COTTON, of London, da. of (—) FRESTON, of Norwich. He *d.* s.p.m.s.(a) 10 Dec. 1684, aged 69, when the *Baronetcy* became *extinct*. Will dat. 6 Feb. 1656/7, pr. Jan 1684/5. The will of his widow, dat. 21 Jan. 1684/5, was pr. 1688.

CONWAY:

cr. 25 July, 1660;

ex. 27 April 1721.

I. 1660. "HENRY CONWAY, of Bodrythan, co. Flint, Esq.," s. and h. of William CONWAY, of the same, by Lucy, da. of Thomas MOSTYN, of Rhyd (2d s. of Sir Thomas MOSTYN), was *b.* 1630; was Sheriff of Flintshire, 1656-57, and was *cr. a Baronet*, 25 July 1660. He was M.P. for Flintshire, 1661 till decease in 1669. He *m.* in 1661, Mary, da. and h. of Richard LLOYD, of Esclusham, co. Denbigh. He *d.* in 1669. Will pr. 1676. The will of Dame Mary Conway pr. 1687.

II. 1669, to 1721. SIR JOHN CONWAY, Baronet [1660], of Bodrythan, *or* Bodryddan, aforesaid, s. and h., *b.* about 1663(b); *suc. to the Baronetcy* in 1669; matric. at Oxford (Ch. Ch.), 10 June 1679, aged 16; *cr.* D.C.L., 22 May 1683; M.P. for Flintshire, 1685-87, 1695-1701, and 1705-08; for Flint, 1701-02 and 1708 till death. He *m.* firstly, Margaretta Maria, da. and coheir of John DIGBY, by his 2d wife, Margaret, da. of Sir Edward LONGUEVILLE. He *m.* secondly, Penelope, da. of Richard GRENVILLE, of Wotton Underwood, Bucks, by Eleanor, da. of Sir Peter TEMPLE, of Stanton Barry. He *d.*, s.p.m.s.,(c) 27 April 1721, when the *Baronetcy* became *extinct*. Will pr. 1721. His widow, who was *b.* 6 and *bap.* 21 April 1674, *d.* 1745.

(a) His only s., William, *d.* unm. before 1683, at which date his da., Elizabeth, had *m.* firstly (—) Voice, and secondly John Pitchford, of Ely, and had had issue by both husbands.

(b) His br., Henry Conway, was admitted to Gray's Inn, 16 May, 1680.

(c) His s., Henry Conway, matric. at Oxford (Ch. Ch.) 16 March 1705/6, aged 17, but *d.* s.p. and v.p. The da. and heir *m.* James Russell Stapleton, and was ancestor to the family of Shipley, who took the name of Conway, on inheriting the Bodryddan estate.

GREEN:

cr. 26 July 1660;

ex. Dec. 1676.

I. 1660, to 1676. "EDWARD GREEN, of [Little] Sampford, co. Essex, Esq.," s. and h. of John GREEN, by Frances, or Margaret, da. of Sir John RUSSELL, of Streynsham, co. Worcester, which John GREEN (who *d.* v.p.) was s. and h. ap. of William GREEN, of Little Sampford aforesaid, suc. his grandfather in that estate, 11 July 1621, and was *cr. a Baronet*, 26 July 1660. By extravagance and gambling he entirely ruined himself, and sold the estate of Sampford and others. He *m.* firstly, about 1635, Ann, da. of Sir George SIMEON, of Baldwin Brightwell, Oxon, by Mary, da. of the Hon. George VAUX. She *d.* s.p.m.(a). He *m.* secondly, Jeronyma, da. and coheir of William EVERARD, of Linsted, by whom he had six daughters. He *m.* thirdly, Mary, da. of (—) TASBURGH. He *m.* fourthly, Katharine, sometime [1657-60?] mistress of Charles II, da. of Thomas PEGGE, of Yeldersley, co. Derby, by Katharine, da. of Sir Gilbert KNIVETON, 1st Baronet [1611]. He *d.* s.p.m.(a) in Flanders, Dec. 1676, when the *Baronetcy* became *extinct*. His widow *d.* 1678.

STAPLEY, *or* STAPELEY:

cr. 28 July 1660;

ex. 22 Aug. 1701;

assumed since 1887.

I. 1660, to 1701. "JOHN STAPELEY, of Patcham, co. Sussex, Esq.," 2d but 1st surv. s. and h. of Col. Anthony STAPLEY,(b) or STAPELEY, of the same, one of the Regicides (*bap.* at Framfield, co. Sussex, 30 Aug. 1590, and *d.* 31 Jan. 1654/5), by his 1st wife, Anne, sister of George, EARL OF NORWICH, da. of George GORING, of Danny, co. Sussex, was *bap.* 29 June 1628, at Patcham; was M.P. for Sussex, 1654-55 and 1656-58; and for Lewes, 1660 and 1661-79. He in June 1657 entered into a Royalist plot, which he basely betrayed to Cromwell in 1658, causing the arrest of Dr. John Hewit and others. He was, however, *cr. a Baronet*, 28 July 1660,(c) and *Knighted* 6 Aug. following. He also obtained a post, said to be worth £1,000 a year, in the Customs. He *m.* in or about 1658, Mary, 1st da. and coheir of Sir Herbert SPRINGETT, Baronet (so *cr.* 1661), of Broyle Place in Ringmer, co. Sussex, by Barbara, da. of Sir William CAMPION, of Combwell, co. Kent. In 1700, having sold the Patcham estate, he removed to Broyle Place,

(a) Eugenia, a da. by his 1st wife, and Justinia, a da. by his last wife, were among the English ladies at Pontoise. The eldest *d.* there 1709, aged 73, and the youngest 1717, aged 50. See *Her. & Gen.*, vol. iii, p. 413. Of other daughters (1), Anne, *m.* William Gossip, of Thorpach; (2), Mary, m. Joshua Field, of Heaton; and (3), Gertrude, *m.* William Peck, of Brampton.

(b) See a very interesting account of this family, by H. W. Forsyth Harwood, in *The Genealogist*, N.S., vol. xviii (Jan. 1902), from which this account is compiled.

(c) He is styled "Esquire" in the patent of his Baronetcy, which is one with the ordinary limitation to heirs male *of the body*, and not (as sometimes erroneously stated) to heirs male *general*. See note "b" above.

O

and *d.* s.p.m.s.(a) 22, being *bur.* 24 Aug. 1701, in his 74th year at Ringmer, when the *Baronetcy* became *extinct*. M.I. Will dat. 20 and pr. 28 Aug. 1701, in the Peculiar Court of South Malling, Lewes. His widow *d.* 20 and was *bur.* 25 March 1709, at Ringmer aforesaid. M.I. Will, as "of Street, co. Sussex," dat. 21 Nov. 1706, pr. 27 May 1709, at the Archdeaconry Court of Lewes.

In 1887, after the lapse of nearly 200 years, the Baronetcy was assumed as under.

II.(b) 1887. "SIR HARRY STAPLEY, Baronet,"(b) [1660], 1st s. and h. of John STAPLEY (*d.* 1881), by Mary, da. of Thomas HOLDON, of Glynde, co. Sussex, which John was s. of Robert STAPLEY, of Framfield, in that county, said to be grandson of John STAPLEY, said to be son of Herbert STAPLEY,(c) the s. and h. ap. of the 1st Baronet. He was *b.* 28 Aug. 1856; was sometime Lieut. 2d Batn. Vol. Royal Fusiliers (City of London Regt.); and *assumed the Baronetcy* in 1887,(d) on the ground of his father (whom, however, he had succeeded as early as 1881) having been *de jure* a Baronet.(d) He *m.* firstly, in 1878, Sarah, da. of John SHELDEN. She *d.* 1886. He *m.* secondly, Anne Bromley GUY, spinster, niece and adopted da. of Anne, BARONESS MONTFORT. She *d.* 19 Jan. 1890, in her 30th year, at Albert Mansions, 93 Victoria street, Westminster.

ROBINSON:

cr. 30 July 1660;

ex. 6 Feb. 1689.

I. 1660, to 1689. "METCALFE ROBINSON, of Newby [on Swale, in Richmondshire], co. York, Esq.," 2d but 1st surv. s. of Sir William ROBINSON, Sheriff of Yorkshire [1639], a zealous loyalist, being 1st s. by his 2d wife Frances, da. of Sir Thomas METCALFE, of

(a) Of his two sons, only one survived infancy, *viz.*, Herbert Stapley, *b.* 3 and *bap.* 6 Nov. 1655, at Patcham; matric. at Oxford (Trin. Coll.), 3 July 1672, and was M.P. for Seaford, 1679-81. He *m.* in or before 1675, Alicia, only da. and eventually (18 May 1723) h. of Sir Richard Colepeper, 2d Baronet [1627], of Prestonhall in Aylesford. He was living May 1686, but *d.* in or before 1693, leaving issue, all of whom died young or unm. before their grandfather. See note "c" below.

(b) According to the assumption of the Baronetcy in 1887.

(c) This Herbert Stapley had no doubt four sons, of whom William, the eldest, *bap.* 26 Feb. 1676/7, was *bur.* 4 Oct. 1678, at Ringmer. Herbert the 4th son, *bap.* 1 March 1684/5, was *bur.* 28 May 1687. Thomas, the only son mentioned in the family wills, *d.* unm. (shortly before his grandfather, the Baronet), and was *bur.* at Aylesford, 16 Feb. 1699. Another son might not improbably have been named John, but he must apparently have died young, and was, possibly, the John Stapley who was *bur.* at Aylesford, 22 Sep. 1682. At all events, the will of their mother, Dame Alicia Taylor, pr. 2 Nov. 1734 (254 Ockham), shows conclusively that she had no surviving issue at the date, 6 Jan. 1727/8, of the making thereof. See p. 97, note "b."

(d) Debrett's *Baronetage* for 1900. In a former edition of that work, it is said that "the Baronetcy was conferred on *heirs male whatsoever*," which statement, however (an erroneous one, see p. 97, note "c"), was subsequently omitted, the descent of "Sir Harry" being then given as "grandson of Robert Stapley, of Framfield, who was grandson of Sir John, *de jure* 2d Baronet (son of Herbert), who being under age and in consequence of his pecuniary resources, did not assume the title." The existence, however, of this John, or "Sir John" is more than doubtful. See note "c" above.

Nappa, was *b.* about 1630; suc. his father in 1658, and was *cr. a Baronet*, 30 July 1660. He was M.P. for York (three Parls.), 1660, 1661-79 and 1685-87. He *m.* Margaret, da. of Sir William DARCY, of Witton, co. Durham. He *d.* s.p. 6 Feb. 1689, in his 59th year, and was *bur.* at Topcliffe, co. York, when the *Baronetcy* became *extinct*.(a) M.I.

GRESHAM(b):

cr. 31 July 1660;

ex. 20 Sep. 1801.

I. 1660. "MARMADUKE GRESHAM, of Limpsfield, co. Surrey, Esq.," 2d and yst. s. of Sir Edward GRESHAM, of Limpsfield aforesaid and of Titsey, co. Surrey, being the only s. of his 2d wife, Mary, da. of Edward CAMPION, of Putney, in that county, was *bap.* 24 Jan. 1627, at Betchworth; suc. his father in the family estates,(c) 2 Jan. 1647; was M.P. for East Grinstead, 1660; for Bletchingley, 1685-87, being *cr. a Baronet*, as above, 31 July 1660. He *m.* at Godstone (Lic. Fac. 18 Dec. 1647, he about 21 and she about 22, parents deceased), Alice, only da. of Richard CORBET, Bishop of Norwich [1632-35], by Alice, da. of the Rev. Leonard HUTTON, D.D. She *d.* at Titsey 1 and was *bur.* there 3 Sep. 1682.(d) He *d.* at Gresham College, London, 14 and was *bur.* 20 April 1696, at Titsey, aged 68. Will dat. 14 Jan. 1695, pr. 3 Jan. 1697.

II. 1696. SIR EDWARD GRESHAM, Baronet [1660], of Titsey aforesaid, 1st s. and h., *b.* 30 Jan. and *bap.* 2 Feb. 1648/9, at St. Bride's, London; *suc. to the Baronetcy*, 14 April 1696; M.P. for Bletchingley (two parls.), 1701-02. He sold the advowson of Westerham and divers lands there and elsewhere. He *m.* 23 Feb. 1671/2 (Lic. Fac. 16 Feb., he 23 and she 21), at St. Clement Danes, Martha, 1st da. of Sir John MAYNARD, Serjeant at Law, by his 1st wife, Elizabeth, da. of Andrew HENLEY. He *d.* s.p.m.s.(e) 23, and was *bur.* 30 April 1709, at Titsey, aged 60 years and 12 weeks. Admon. 7 June 1709. His widow *d.* 14 and was *bur.* 18 Jan. 1711/2, at Limpsfield. M.I.

III. 1709. SIR CHARLES GRESHAM, Baronet [1660], of Titsey aforesaid, next surv. br. and h. male, being 6th s. of the 1st Baronet, *b.* at New Hall, Limpsfield, 30 May 1660; matric. at Oxford (Trin. Coll.), 31 May 1677, aged 17; B.A., 1 Feb. 1680; M.A. (Hart. Hall), 7 Dec. 1683); Professor of Rhetoric in Gresham Coll., 1686-96; F.R.S., 1688-99; *suc. to the Baronetcy*, 23 April 1709. He *m.* 1696, Mary, da. of William GODFREY, M.D., of Ongar, co. Essex.(f) He *d.* at Titsey 28 March, and was *bur.* there 1 April 1718. Will dat. 24 June 1715, pr. 2 May 1718. His widow was *bur.* at Titsey, 4 March 1749, aged 88.

(a) The estates passed to his nephew, William Robinson, who was *cr. a Baronet*, as "of Newby, co. York," 13 Feb. 1689/90.

(b) Compiled from the elaborate and profusely illustrated "Genealogy of the Family of Gresham, by Granville Leveson Gower, Esq., F.S.A.," (*d.* 30 May 1895, aged 68), printed privately 1883; much of which appeared in Howard's *Mis. Gen. et Her.*

(c) Thomas Gresham, his eldest br. (by his father's 1st wife), who matric. at Oxford (Queen's Coll.), 9 Nov. 1632, aged 17, was disinherited. He *d.* s.p.m. in the Fleet prison, and was *bur.* 6 Jan. 1654/5, at St. Faith's, London, leaving an only da. and h., Jane, who *m.* John Lloyd and had issue.

(d) "A religious, loyal, wise and virtuous Lady."

(e) Elizabeth, his only surv. child and h., *bap.* 2 March 1691/2, at St. Andrew's Holborn, *d.* unm. Will dat. 21 June 1718. pr. 8 March 1727.

(f) Dr. Godfrey's will was pr. 1679, in the Archdeaconry Court of Essex.

IV. 1718. SIR MARMADUKE GRESHAM, Baronet [1660], of Titsey aforesaid, 1st s. and h., *bap.* 14 July 1700, at Mortlake, co. Surrey; *suc. to the Baronetcy*, 28 March 1718. He *m.* 27 Nov. 1724,(a) at the Fleet, London, Anne, 1st da. of William HOSKINS, of Barrow Green in Oxted, co. Surrey, by Martha his wife. He *d.* at Bath 2 and was was *bur.* 21 Jan. 1741/2, at Titsey, aged 41. Will dat. 4 June 1741, pr. 5 Feb. 1744/5. His widow, who was *bap.* 24 Dec. 1696, at Westerham, was appointed Housekeeper at the General Post office in 1765, and *d.* at her house in Bolton street, being *bur.* 31 Aug. 1769, at Titsey. Will dat. 8 Feb. 1768, pr. 13 Sep. 1769.

V. 1742. SIR CHARLES GRESHAM, Baronet [1660], of Titsey aforesaid, 1st s. and h., *suc. to the Baronetcy*, 2 Jan. 1741/2. He *d.* unm. and under age, being lost in the East India ship "The Mumford," between Jan. and March 1749/50. Admon. 26 Feb. 1751.

VI. 1750, to 1801. SIR JOHN GRESHAM, Baronet [1660], of Titsey aforesaid, 2d and only br. and h., *bap.* there 9 Oct. 1735; *suc. to the Baronetcy* in 1749/50;(b) educated at Cambridge; sometime an officer in the army; a Commissioner of Salt Duties, 1765-85. He pulled down the old manor house at Titsey 1767-75, and the old church there in 1775. He *m.* 2 June 1765, at St. George's, Hanover square, Henrietta Maria, 1st da. of Sir Kenrick CLAYTON, 2d Baronet [1732], of Marden, co. Surrey, by Henrietta Maria, da. of Henry HERRING. He *d.* s.p.m.,(c) at Brompton Villa, after a long and painful illness, 20 and was *bur* 30 Sep. 1801, at Titsey, aged 65, when the *Baronetcy* became *extinct*. Will dat. 27 May 1796 to 17 Sep. 1799, pr. 3 Oct. 1801. His widow *d.* at her house in Hill street, 26 Jan. and was *bur.* 3 Feb. 1804, at Titsey, aged 66. Will dat. 5 April to 15 Nov. 1802, pr. 18 Feb. 1804.

DUDLEY:

cr. 1 Aug. 1660;

ex. 15 June 1764.

I. 1660. "WILLIAM DUDLEY, of Clopton, [*otherwise* Clapton], co. Northampton, Esq.,"(d) 2d s. of Edward DUDLEY, of the same (*d.* 6 May 1632, aged 62) by Elizabeth, da. of Robert WOOD, of Lamley, Notts, suc. his elder br., Edward DUDLEY, who *d.* s.p.m., 13 Nov. 1641, and was *cr. a Baronet*, 1 Aug. 1660. He was Sheriff of Northamptonshire, 1660-61, and was M.P. for Northampton, March 1663 till void 9 April following. He *m.* three times, viz., firstly, (—), da. of Monsieur DE PLEURE. She *d.* s.p. He *m.* secondly, Jane, da. of Sir Roger SMITH, of Edmondthorpe, co. Leicester, by his 2d wife, Anne, da. of Thomas GOODMAN, of London. She also *d.* s.p. He *m.* thirdly, Mary, da. and h. of Paul PINDAR, of London, by Susan, da. of John FLAMSTED, of Leicester, which Paul was nephew of

(a) The tradition is that "on his wedding day he drove from London to Titsey Place in a coach and four, his horses shod with silver."

(b) "A short man in person, but considered to be a very excellent horseman . . . . . succeeded to the estate of that very respectable family after a considerable diminution of it." *Gent. Mag.* 1801.

(c) Catherine, his only da. and h., *m.* 20 Aug. 1804, William Leveson-Gower (grandson of John, 1st Earl Gower), and is ancestress of the family of that name now of Titsey aforesaid.

(d) The manor of Clapton was held by the Dudley family from 1395, when Richard Dudley held it in right of his wife, Joan, da. and h. of Robert Hotot, descended from Alfred de Grauntkort, who was said to have possessed it about 1090.

Sir Paul PINDAR, sometime Ambassador to Constantinople. He *d.* 18 Sep. 1670, aged 73, was and *bur.* at Clapton. M.I. Admon. 10 Dec. 1670, to the widow, who was living 12 Oct. 1672.

II. 1670. SIR MATTHEW DUDLEY, Baronet [1660], of Clapton aforesaid, 1st s. and h. by 3d wife; *suc. to the Baronetcy*, 18 Sep. 1670; was Sheriff of Northamptonshire, 1683-84; M.P. for Northampton, 1703-05, and for Huntingdonshire, 1713-15; a Commissioner of the Customs in 1706, but was deprived of office in 1711, though reinstated by George I. in 1714; F.R.S. He *m.* Mary, 3d and yst. da. of Henry (O'BRIEN), 7th EARL OF THOMOND [I.], by Sarah, da. of Sir Francis RUSSELL, 2d Baronet [1629], of Chippenham. He *d.* in office, 13 April 1721. Will pr. 1721. His widow *d.* 9 Nov. 1735. Will pr. 1735.

III. 1721, to 1764. SIR WILLIAM DUDLEY, Baronet [1660], of Clapton aforesaid, only s. and h., *b.* there 2 March 1696; *suc. to the Baronetcy*, 13 April 1721. He *m.* 12 Dec. 1719, in London, Elizabeth, da. and h. of Sir Richard KENNEDY, 4th Baronet [I. 1660?], of Mount Kennedy, co. Wicklow,(a) by Katharine, da. of Sir Francis BLAKE. Her will dat. 9 July 1747, pr. 9 Feb. 1749/50. He *d.* s.p.s.,(b) at York, 15 June 1764, aged 68, when the *Baronetcy* became *extinct*. Will pr. 1764.

SMITHSON:

cr. 2 Aug. 1660;

afterwards, since 1750, EARLS OF NORTHUMBERLAND;

and, since 1766, DUKES OF NORTHUMBERLAND.

I. 1660. "HUGH SMITHSON, of Stanwick, co. York, Esq.," 2d s. of Anthony SMITHSON, of Newsome in Kirby-on-the-Mount, co. York, by Eleanor, da. and h. of George CATTERICK, of Stanwick aforesaid, was *b.* about 1598; suc. to his mother's estate of Stanwick; was a Loyalist in the Civil War; was fined as a Recusant, and was *cr. a Baronet*, 2 Aug. 1660. He *m.* firstly, Dorothy, da. of Jerome RAWSTHORNE, of Plaistow, Essex. He *d.* 21 Oct. 1670, aged 72, and was *bur.* at Stanwick St. John's. M.I. The will of his widow pr. 1692.

II. 1670. SIR JEROME SMITHSON, Baronet [1660], of Stanwick aforesaid, 1st s. and h., *b.* probably about 1630(c); *suc. to the Baronetcy*, 21 Oct. 1670. He *m.*, in or before 1657, Mary, da. of Edward WINGATE, of Lockley Hall in Welwyn, Herts, by Mary, da. and coheir of Ralph ALLWAY, of Canons in Shenley, in that county. She was *bap.* at Welwyn, 30 Aug. 1636. He *d.* 1684.

III. 1684. SIR HUGH SMITHSON, Baronet [1660], of Stanwick aforesaid, only s. and h., *b.* 1657; *suc. to the Baronetcy* in 1684. He conformed to the established religion,(d) and is said [erroneously?] to have been M.P. for Notts. He *m.* Elizabeth, 2d da. of Marmaduke (LANGDALE), 2d BARON LANGDALE OF HOLME, by Elizabeth, da. of the Hon. Thomas SAVAGE, of Beeston. He *d.* 2 March 1733.

(a) The entail of this estate had been barred by her father, but inasmuch as the remainder man (under the entail to heirs *male*) was then under forfeiture, there was a lawsuit to decide as to whether the reversion had not been previously forfeited.

(b) Of his four children, three (O'Brien, William, and Elizabeth) died in infancy, while one, John, *d.* v.p. and unm.

(c) His next br., Hugh Smithson, of St. Augustine's, London, haberdasher, was aged "about 31" and a widower, 9 May 1663, when he had licence (Vic. Gen.) to marry Alice Yeend, spinster.

(d) His four daughters, however, all took the veil in Flanders.

IV. 1733. SIR HUGH SMITHSON, Baronet [1660], of Stanwick aforesaid, and, after 1740, of Tottenham, Midx., grandson and heir, being only s. and h. of Langdale SMITHSON, by Philadelphia,(a) da. of William REVELY, of Newby Wisk, co. York, which Langdale was 2d and yst. but only surv. s. and h. ap. of the late Baronet, and *d.* v.p. He was *b.* about 1714; matric. at Oxford (Christ Church), 15 Oct. 1730, aged fifteen; *suc. to the Baronetcy*, 2 March 1733; was F.R.S., 1736; Sheriff of Yorkshire, 1738-39. By the death, s.p.s., of his grandfather's 1st cousin, Hugh Smithson, of Tottenham aforesaid and of Armine in the West Riding of Yorkshire, 4 Sep. 1740, aged 79, he inherited those estates, residing chiefly at Tottenham; was M.P. for Midx., 1740-50. He *m.* 16 July 1740 (Lic. Vic. Gen.), at Percy Lodge, in Iver, Bucks, Elizabeth, only da. and h. of Algernon (SEYMOUR), 7th DUKE OF SOMERSET, by Frances, da. and coheir of the Hon. Henry THYNNE, which Duke, being s. and h. of Charles, 6th DUKE OF SOMERSET, by his 1st wife, Elizabeth, da. and h. of Joceline (PERCY), EARL OF NORTHUMBERLAND, was himself *cr.*, 2 Oct. 1749, EARL OF NORTHUMBERLAND, etc., with a spec. rem. in favour of his son in law, the abovenamed Sir Hugh Smithson, and his issue male by the said Elizabeth, the said Duke's only surv. child. He accordingly, on the death s.p.m., 7 Feb. 1749/50, of his father in law, the said Duke of Somerset, became, under the spec. rem. abovestated, EARL OF NORTHUMBERLAND, etc., his said wife being then living. A few month's later, he, by Act of Parl., 12 April 1750, took the name of PERCY (being that of his wife's grandmother, whose principal estates he had then inherited) in lieu of that of SMITHSON. He was subsequently *cr.*, 22 Oct. 1766, DUKE OF NORTHUMBERLAND, etc. In these peerages this *Baronetcy* then *merged*, and still so continues. See *Peerage*.

MOSTYN, *or* MOSTIN:

cr. 3 August 1660;

ex. 17 April 1831.

I. 1660. "SIR ROGER MOSTIN, of Mostin, co. Flint, Knt.," 1st s. and h. of Sir Thomas MOSTYN, *or* MOSTIN, of Kilken, by Elizabeth, da. of Sir James WHITELOCKE, Justice of the King's Bench [1624-32], which Thomas (who was admitted to Linc. Inn, 3 May 1620) was 1st s. and h. ap. of Sir Roger MOSTYN, of Mostyn aforesaid, but *d.* v.p., was *b.* probably about 1620; was admitted to the Inner Temple, Nov. 1637; Barrister, 1656; suc. to the family estates on the death, 18 Aug. 1642, of his said grandfather; distinguished himself as a Royalist during the Civil War, raising 1,500 men for the King's service; took the Castle of Hawarden; was Governor of Flint in 1643, where he stood a long siege; was fined £852 on 17 Jan. 1647/8, and is said to have expended £60,000 in the Royal cause; was *Knighted*, 5 June, and was *cr. a Baronet*, 3 Aug. 1660. He was named in 1660 a Knight of the intended order of the Royal Oak, his estates being then valued at £4,000 a year; was Sheriff of Montgomeryshire, 1660-61; of Flintshire, 1665-66; and of Carnarvonshire, 1666-67; was *cr.* M.A. (from Ch. Ch.), 14 July 1696. He *m.* firstly, Prudence, 1st da. of Sir Martin LUMLEY, 1st Baronet [1641], being only child of his first wife, Jane (*m.* 15 Jan. 1620/1), da. of John MEREDYTH. She, who was *b.* between 1621 and 1627, *d.* s.p.m.s., having had four children. He *m.* secondly, in or before 1651, Mary, da. of Thomas (BULKELEY), 1st VISCOUNT BULKELEY OF CASHEL [I.], by his 1st wife, Blanche, da. of Robert COYTMORE. She, by whom he had eight children, *d.* 16 Oct. 1662. He *m.* thirdly, Lumley, da. of (—) COYTMORE, of Coytmore, co. Carnarvon, by whom he had no issue. He *d.* between 1689 and 1691.

II. 1690? SIR THOMAS MOSTYN, Baronet [1660], of Mostyn aforesaid, 3rd but 1st surv. s. and h., being 1st s. by the 2d wife; *b.* about 1651; matric. at Oxford (Christ Church), 15 May 1667, aged 16; was

(a) This Mrs. Smithson, "the mother of the [then] Earl of Northumberland," died 15 May 1764, aged 75.

M.P. for Carnarvon (three Parls.), 1679-81; *suc. to the Baronetcy* on the death of his father; was elected Sheriff for Carnarvonshire (as "Esq."), 1689, but did not act; and was (as "Baronet") Sheriff for Anglesey, 1691-92. He *m.* Bridget, da. and h. of Darcy SAVAGE, of Leighton and Beeston, co. Chester, by (—), da. of (—), which Darcy was son of the Hon. Thomas SAVAGE and grandson of Elizabeth, *suo jure* COUNTESS RIVERS. By this great heiress he had eleven children. He *d.* in or shortly before 1700.

III. 1700? SIR ROGER MOSTYN, Baronet [1660], of Mostyn and Leighton aforesaid, 1st surv. s. and h., *b.* about 1675; matric. at Oxford (Jesus Coll.), 10 Feb. 1689/90, aged 15; *suc. to the Baronetcy* on the death of his father; was (as "Baronet") Sheriff of Carnarvonshire, 1700-01; M.P. for Flintshire, 1701-02; for Cheshire, 1702-05; for Flint, 1705-08, and for Flintshire again (six Parls.), 1708-34; Paymaster of the Marines to Queen Anne, and, in 1715, a Teller of the Exchequer to George I. He *m.* 20 July 1703, at St. James', Westm. (Lic. Fac. 9 July, he 27 and she 15), Essex, da. of Daniel (FINCH), EARL OF WINCHILSEA AND NOTTINGHAM, by his 2d wife, Anne, da. of Christopher (HATTON), 1st VISCOUNT HATTON OF GRETTON. She *d.* of the small pox, 23 May 1721. He *d.* 5 May 1739. Will pr. 1739.

IV. 1739. SIR THOMAS MOSTYN, Baronet [1660], of Mostyn and Leighton aforesaid, 1st s. and h., *b.* about 1704; matric. at Oxford (Christ Church), 13 Oct. 1720, aged 16; M.P. for Flintshire, 1734-41 and 1747 till death, having *suc. to the Baronetcy* 5 May 1739. He *m.*, in or before 1735, Sarah, da. and coheir of Robert WESTERN, of St. Peter's, Cornhill, London, and of Rivenhall, Essex, by Anne, sister and coheir of Sir Richard SHIRLEY, 3d Baronet [1665], 1st da. of Sir Richard SHIRLEY, 2d Baronet [1665], of Preston, Sussex. She *d.* 28 May 1740.(a) He *d.* 24 March 1758. Will dat. 9 May 1752, pr. 2 Aug. 1758. The will of "Dame Sarah Mostyn, Flint," is proved March 1783 in the C.P.C.

V. 1758. SIR ROGER MOSTYN, Baronet [1660], of Mostyn and Leighton aforesaid, 1st s. and h., *b.* about 1735; *suc. to the Baronetcy*, 24 March 1758; matric. at Oxford (Ch. Ch.), 19 June 1751, aged 16; was M.P. for Flintshire (eight Parls.), 1758 till his death in 1796; Lord Lieut. of that county. He *m.* 19 May 1776, at St. Geo. Han. sq. (Lic. Lond., both above 21), Margaret, da. and h. of the Rev. Hugh WYNNE, LL.D., Prebendary of Salisbury, by "Catharine, sister of William VAUGHAN, of Corsygedol, in Merionethshire, and heiress of Robert WYNNE, of Bodygallen, in Caernarvonshire."(a) She *d.* 14 Oct. 1792. Admon. March 1793, Nov. 1798, and July 1833. He *d.* at Mostyn Hall, 26 July 1796. Will pr. Oct. 1796 and Aug. 1846.

VI. 1796, to 1831. SIR THOMAS MOSTYN, Baronet [1660], of Mostyn and Leighton aforesaid, only s. and h., *b.* about 1776, probably at Chrisleton, co. Chester; matric. at Oxford (Ch. Ch.), 23 Oct. 1793, aged 17; *suc. to the Baronetcy*, 26 July 1796; M.P. for Flintshire, 8 Nov. 1796, but disqualified as a minor; again elected 1799 till his death in 1831; Sheriff of Carnarvonshire, 1798-99; of Merionethshire, 1799-1800. He *d.* unm. 17 April 1831, at Park Place, St. James', Midx., in his 55th year, when the *Baronetcy* became *extinct*.(b) Will pr. July 1831.

(a) Betham's *Baronetage*.

(b) The Mostyn estates passed chiefly to his nephew, Edward Lloyd, who took the name of Lloyd-Mostyn by royal licence in 1831, and suc. 3 April 1834 as 2d Baron Mostyn, on the death of his father, who had been so *cr.* 10 Sep. 1831, within five months of the death of his brother-in-law, the last Baronet.

WILLOUGHBY :

cr. 4 Aug. 1660 ;

ex. 10 Feb. 1670/1.

I. 1660, to 1671. "WILLIAM WILLOUGHBY, of Willoughby [*Qy.* if not "of Selston"], Notts, Esq.," s. and h. of William WILLOUGHBY (*d.* 12 Nov. 1630 in his 22d year), by Elizabeth, da. and coheir of Timothy PUSEY, of Selston, Notts, was *b.* in or shortly before 1630; suc. to the estate of Selston on the death of his mother, 3 Oct. 1659, and was *cr. a Baronet*, 4 Aug. 1660. He *m.* 24 Dec. 1657, at St. Paul's, Covent Garden, Midx. (Banns pub. at St. Dunstan's in the West), Margaret, da. and h. of George ABBOTT, of Easton, Hants, by Mary, da. and coheir of Sir Hugh WINDHAM, Baronet [so *cr.* 1641], which George was s. and h. of Sir Maurice ABBOTT, and nephew of George, sometime, 1611-33, Archbishop of Canterbury. He d. s.p.s. legit,(a) 10 Feb. 1670/1, at Selston, and was *bur.* there, when the *Baronetcy* became *extinct.*(b) Funeral certificate at College of Arms. Will dat. 1 Feb. 1670/1 pr. in Court of Delegates.(c)

OLDFIELD :

cr. 6 Aug. 1660 ;

ex. Aug. 1705 ;

I. 1660. "ANTHONY OLDFIELD, of Spalding, co. Lincoln, Esq.," 1st s. and h. of John OLDFIELD, of the same (who entered his ped. in the Visit. of Lincolnshire, 1634, was a zealous Royalist, a Compounder for £1,390, and who was *bur.* at Spalding, 24 Nov. 1659, aged 61), by Mary, da. of John BLYTHE, of Denton in that county,(d) was *bap.* 27 July 1626, at Spalding; was an Attorney at Law, and sometime Steward at Northumberland House, Strand, to the Duchess of Somerset, and was *cr. a Baronet*, 6 Aug. 1660. He is said to have been Sheriff of Lincolnshire, 1661. He *m.* firstly, (—), da. of (—) PARK, of Fleet, co. Lincoln, by whom he had four children, who *d.* young or unm. He *m.* secondly, 19 June 1658, at St. Bride's, London (banns pub. at St. Andrew's, Holborn), Elizabeth, sister of Sir Marmaduke GRESHAM, 1st Baronet [1660], da. of Sir Edward GRESHAM, of Titsey, Surrey, by his 2d wife, Mary, da. of Edward CAMPION, of Putney in that county. He *d.*, from injuries inflicted by the Spalding watermen, 4, and was *bur.* 5 Sep. 1668, at Spalding, aged 42.(e) M.I. Will pr. 6 Oct. 1668. His widow, who was *bap.* 15 June 1626, at Bletchworth, Surrey, *d.* 22 and was *bur.* 24 Jan. 1687/8, at Spalding. M.I. Will dat. 6 May 1681, pr. 5 Dec. 1685.

(a) William Willoughby, an infant son, *d.* 26 Aug. 1668.

(b) Mary, his sister and sole h., *m.*, Jan. 1652, Sir Beaumont Dixie, 2d Baronet [1660], and *d.* Dec. 1710, leaving issue.

(c) He devised the estate of South Muskham, Notts, to his very distant cousin Francis Willoughby, of Wollaton, in that county.

(d) See a good ped. of this family by Everard Green [Rouge Dragon Pursuivant, 1893] in the *Genealogist* [O.S.], vol i, pp. 242-247.

(e) He is thus mentioned in Sir Joseph Williamson's "Lincolnshire Families, temp. Charles II" [*Her. & Gen.*, ii, 124], "Sir Anthony Oldfield, of Spalding, late created Baronet; his grandfather, an Attorney, Deputy Lieut. Not more than £800 a year." The Baronet himself as well as his grandfather [Anthony, born at Bingley, co. York, in 1609] was an attorney at Spalding, though his father, John, was not one.

II. 1668, to 1705. SIR JOHN OLDFIELD, Baronet [1660], of Spalding, aforesaid, 1st s. and h.; *b.* 29 Oct. and *bap.* 3 Nov. 1659 at St. Giles'-in-the-Fields, Midx.; *suc. to the Baronetcy*, 4 Sep. 1668; admitted as Fellow Commoner at St. John's Coll., Cambridge, 27 June 1676, aged 16. He *m.*, in or before 1681, Margaret, da. of Sir Simon DEGGE, of Derby, and of Blythebridge, co. Stafford, Bencher of the Inner Temple, London, by Alice, da. of Anthony OLDFIELD, of Spalding, grandfather of the 1st Baronet. He *d.* s.p.m.s. Aug. and was *bur.* 2 Sep. 1705, at Spalding, aged 46, when the *Baronetcy* became *extinct.*(a) Will pr. Feb. 1706. His widow *d.* March 1738/9 aged 30, and was *bur.* at Spalding. M.I. Will pr. 1739.

LEICESTER, *or* LEYCESTER :

cr. 10 Aug. 1660 ;

ex. 5 Aug. 1742.

I. 1660. "PETER LEICESTER, of Tabley, co. Chester, Esq.," 1st s. and h. of Peter LEICESTER, *or* LEYCESTER, of the same (*d.* 7 March 1647, aged 59), by Elizabeth, da. of Sir Randle MAINWARING, of Over Pever, in that county, was *b.* 3 March 1613/4, at Nether Tabley; matric. at Oxford (as Gen. Commoner of Bras. Coll.), 13 Oct. 1629; entered Gray's Inn, 20 Aug. 1632; was a Royalist, and compounded for £747; was imprisoned in 1655, at Chester Castle, on suspicion, and was *cr. a Baronet*, 10 Aug. 1660. He was a writer of great research, and author of the history of Bucklow Hundred in Cheshire.(b) He *m.* 6 Nov. 1642, at Dutton, co. Chester, Elizabeth, 3d and yst. da. of Gilbert (GERARD), 2d BARON GERARD OF GERARD'S BROMLEY, by Eleanor, da. and h. of Thomas DUTTON, of Dutton aforesaid. He *d.* 11 Oct. 1678, in his 65th year. His widow *d.* 26 Jan. 1678/9, in her 59th year. Both were *bur.* at Budworth, in Cheshire. M.I.

II. 1678. SIR ROBERT LEICESTER, *or* LEYCESTER, Baronet [1660], of Tabley aforesaid, 1st s. and h.; *b.* 11 Sep. 1643, at Chester; matric. at Oxford (Bras. Coll.), 13 July 1660; B.A., 12 March 1662/3; *suc. to the Baronetcy*, 11 Oct. 1678. He *m.* 6 June 1667 (Lic. Fac. 25 May, and Lic. Westm. 5 June 1667, each aged about 23, she with consent of her mother, Elizabeth, now wife of "Francis Pigot, of Marcham, Berks Esq."), Meriell, da. and h. of Francis WATSON, of Church Aston, Salop, and Elizabeth, his wife. He *d.* 7 July 1684. His widow *d.* 29 Sep. 1707.

III. 1684, to 1742. SIR FRANCIS LEICESTER, *or* LEYCESTER, Baronet [1660], of Tabley aforesaid, 2d but 1st surv. s. and h.,(c) *b.* 30 July 1674; *suc. to the Baronetcy*, 7 July 1684; was ed. at Eton; admitted 6 April 1692 as a Fellow Commoner at St. John's Coll. Cambridge, aged 17; was Sheriff of Cheshire, 1705-06; M.P. for Newton, co. Lanc. (two Parls.), 1715-27. He *m.*, between July 1701 and 1705, Frances, widow of Byrom THORNHILL, of Fixby, co. York (*d.* July 1701), da. and h. of Joshua WILKINSON, of Pontefract and of Colton, co. York. She *d.* 23 April 1716 aged 33. He *d.* s.p.m.(d) 5 Aug. 1742, aged 68, when the *Baronetcy* became *extinct*. Will pr. 1743 [I.].

(a) There appears to have been a subsequent assumption of this dignity. See Debrett's *Baronetage* for 1826.

(b) A considerable controversy was carried on between him and Sir Thomas Mainwaring, respecting the legitimacy of Amicia, wife of Ralph Mainwaring, da. of Hugh Kevelloc, Earl of Chester.

(c) Robert, the 1st s., was *b.* 16 April, 1669, at Marcham, Berks, and was *bur.* there at the age of 7 years.

(d) Meriel, his only da. and h., *d.* 25 Nov. 1705, had by her 2d husband, Sir John Byrne, 3d Baronet [I. 1671], a s. and h., Sir Peter Byrne, 4th Baronet [I. 1671], who by act of Parl., 1744, took the name of Leicester on inheriting the Tabley estate.

WHELER :(a)

cr. 11 Aug. 1660.

I. 1660. "SIR WILLIAM WHEELER [*rectius* WHELER] of the city of Westminster, Knt.," presumably a yr. s.(b) of John WHELER, of London, goldsmith,(c) by Martha (*bap.* 1 June 1585; *m.* 6 Oct. 1606), da. of Robert HERRICK, of St. Martin's, Leicester (br. to Sir William HERRICK, of Beaumanor) was "a 4th son, born in Holland"(d) probably in 1611(b); was a Lay Member of the Westm. Assembly in 1643, and active as M.P. for Westbury (Long Parl.) 1640 till secluded in 1648; re-elected Feb. to April 1659; was M.P. for Queenborough, 1660; was sometime of the First Fruits office(e); was *Knighted* at Hampton Court, 26 Aug. 1657, by the Protector Cromwell, and presumably again by Charles II, by whom he was *cr. a Baronet*, 11 Aug. 1660, with a spec. rem.(f) failing the heirs male of his body, "to Charles WHEELER [*rectius* WHELER], cosin to the said Sir William and the heires males of the body of the said Sir Charles." He *m.* Elizabeth, da. and h. of Michael COLE, of Kensington, Midx. She was laundress to Charles I.(g) He *d.* s.p. at Derby (where he had removed in 1665 from London to escape the plague), 6 Aug. 1666, and was *bur.* at All Saints there, in [it is stated] his 66th [*Qy.* 56th] year.(h) M.I. Will pr. 6 July 1667. His widow *d.* in the country, but was *bur.* 20 Sep. 1670, at St. Margaret's, Westm.

(a) Much of the information in this article is given by Edward Galton Wheler, great grandson of the 7th Baronet, and the editor of a very interesting *Autobiography of the Rev. Sir George Wheler, Prebendary of Durham* [*Genealogist*, N.S., vol. ii, 202, and vol. iii, 41 and 216], who, though no relation to the 1st Baronet, succeeded under his will, on the death of the widow, to his estates in Hampshire and Wiltshire, and to a house in Canon Row, Westminster.

(b) Of the children of John and Martha Wheler, John, *bap.* 23 Aug. 1607, at St. Martin's, Leicester [Registers of Martin Husingtree, co. Worcester], is mentioned as *eldest* son in his father's will, pr. 13 Feb. 1621. Mary was *bap.* 20 Nov. 1608, at St. Vedast's, Foster Lane, London, and George was *bap.* 20 Sep. 1610, at Eton, near Windsor. The assertion that the 1st Baronet (if the son of parents, who did not marry till 1606) died in his 66th year (in Sep. 1666) must be erroneous, being probably a mistake for his 56th year. The lastnamed John, who entered (and signed as "John Wheeler") his pedigree in the Visit. of London, 1633-34 (having then one da.), *d.* s.p.m. in 1643, before the Baronet.

(c) The parentage of the 1st Baronet has, in the more recent Baronetages, been attributed to Sir Edmund Wheler, of Datchet, Bucks, who was in truth his great uncle. That affiliation, however, is conclusively disproved in the *Autobiography* mentioned in note "a" above, where it is stated that "Sir William Wheler was *related* to Sir Edmund, seeing he calls him [Sir Edmund] and his son, William, cozen"; and again, "William, son to Sir Edmund, left Sir William most of his land in the country, and Sir William purchased of him that part I possess in Spittlefields." The daughters of William Wheler, late of Datchet, are mentioned in the will of the 1st Baronet. William, son of Sir Edmund, *bap.* at Datchet, 28 July 1605, and living at the date of his father's will, 16 Dec. 1633, was apparently buried at Datchet, 13 Nov. 1672, as "William Wheeler, Esq.," though possibly a grandson of Sir Edmund may be thus indicated. Anyhow, it is stated in the Visit. of Warwickshire, 1682, that no male issue of Sir Edmund was then existing.

(d) Le Neve's MS. *Baronetage*, where, however, no parentage is given.

(e) *Autobiography*, as in note "a" above, where the writer adds concerning Sir William, "I remember him to be a comely old gentleman, with a round plump face, a rudy cheerfull countenance adorned with curled grey hair. His Study of bookes he left shew he was a man of study and learning, curious and inquisitive, for they consisted of Greek and Latine, French and Spanish, and some divinity. I found a case where medales had been."

(f) Apparently the second of such special remainders. See p. 21, note "c."

(g) In Echard's *England* (vol. ii, p. 639, edit. 1718) it is stated that early in the rebellion the King confided to her a casket, which she restored to him the night before his execution.

(h) See as to his age at death, note "b" above.

II. 1666. SIR CHARLES WHELER, Baronet [1660], of Birdingbury, co. Warwick, cousin, and h. to the title under the spec. rem. thereof, being s. of William WHELER, of Martin Husingtree, co. Worcester, and Nantwich, co. Chester, by Eleanor (*d.* 1 June 1678, aged 85), da. of Edward PULESTON, of Allington, co. Denbigh, by Winifred, only sister of Sir Thomas TREVOR, sometime [1625-49] one of the Barons of the Exchequer, which William was younger br. of John WHELER, of London, goldsmith, father of the 1st Baronet. He was *b.* about 1620; was a student at Cambridge, 1638; sometime Fellow of Trin. Coll., Cambridge, being ejected thence 18 April 1644.; he was M.A. of that Univ., and was entrusted with others to carry the plate thereof to Charles I, for his assistance against the rebels; was a Gent. of the Privy Chamber, 1660, and apparently then a Knight; was Colonel of the 7th Regt. of Foot; was M.P. for the Univ. of Cambridge, 1667-79; and Governor of the Leeward Islands. He *suc. to the Baronetcy*, 6 Aug. 1666, under the special clause of remainder, but to none of the grantee's estates.(a) On the death s.p., 5 Feb. 1676, of his mother's 1st cousin, Sir Thomas TREVOR, Baronet [so *cr.* 1641] (only s. of Sir Thomas Trevor abovenamed), he suc. under his will to the estate of Leamington Hastings, co. Warwick. He, who was sometime Lieut. Colonel of the Guards to Charles II, entered and signed his pedigree in the Visitation of Warwickshire, 1682, being then aged 62. He *m.* (Lic. Lond. 7 Aug. 1648, he of St. Mildred Poultry, aged about 28, and she aged about 22) Dorothy, sister of Sir Robert BINDLOSSE, Baronet [1641], da. of Sir Francis BINDLOSSE, of Borwick Hall, co. Lanc., by his 2d wife, Cecilia, da. of Thomas (WEST), LORD DELAWARR. He *d.* 26 Aug. 1683, and was *bur.* at Leamington Hastings, aged 64. M.I. Will dated 7 to 12 March 1682/3, pr. 8 Sep. 1683.(b) His widow *d.* 16 Aug. 1684, and was *bur.* there, aged 60. M.I. Will pr. Sep. 1687.

III. 1683. SIR WILLIAM WHELER, Baronet [1660], of Leamington Hastings aforesaid, 2d but 1st surv. s. and h.,(c) *b.* 1654; being aged 28 and unm. in 1682; *suc. to the Baronetcy*, 6 Aug. 1683. He *m.* 15 Jan. 1695/6 (the Chaplain to the Portuguese Envoy officiating), at St. Martin's-in-the-Fields, Teresa, da. of the Hon. Edward WIDDRINGTON, of Horsley,(d) 2d s. of the 1st BARON WIDDRINGTON OF BLANCKNEY. He *d.* 23 Feb. 1708/9, in his 55th year, and was *bur.* at Leamington aforesaid. M.I. Will pr. April 1709. His widow was *bur.* there 7 May 1718. Her will pr. Jan. 1719.

(a) See as to these estates p. 106, note "a." In the *Autobiography* there mentioned, it is said that "Sir Charles, imprudently pressing Sir William to settle the estate upon him before he died, disobliged Sir William to that degree that he refused to do it, whereupon Sir Charles began to sue Sir William," etc. The 2d Baronet actually brought a suit (unsuccessfully, however) after Lady Wheler's death, to get possession, alleging that "King Charles wd witness that he gave Sir Wm the Barronett Patent upon Sir W's promise to settle his estate on him." There was, however, a charge on the Spitalfields estate, which was devised by Sir William to go with the Baronetcy.

(b) In this will a bequest is left "in gratitude to Mr. Warren, Apothecary, who did hospitably receive me into his house when I was in disgrace with the King [Charles II], and when none of my relatives in blood did offer or show me the least kindness."

(c) The eldest s., Trevor Wheler, Major in his father's regiment of foot, *d.* unm. v.p., 12 Oct. 1678. The 3d and yst. s., Admiral Sir Francis Wheler, Governor of Deal Castle (aged 24 in 1682), *m.* 12 Nov. 1685, at St. Bride's, London (Lic. Lon.), Arabella Clifton, and was drowned off Gibraltar, 1693, being grandfather of Francis Wheler, of Whitley, co. Warwick, whose only da. and h., Jane, *m.* 10 Sep. 1772, Henry (Hood), 2d Viscount Hood of Whitley, being, through her 1st s., ancestor of the succeeding Viscounts, and by her 2d s., (Samuel Hood, afterwards 2d Baron Bridport [I.],) of the Viscounts Bridport. Dorothy Elizabeth, afterwards Countess of Nassau, da. of the 2d Baronet, was Maid of Honour to the Queen of Charles II.

(d) Not of his son Edward Widdington as generally stated. "This point has just been worked out by the editor of the Northumberland county history, for the next volume." [*Ex inform.* E. G. Wheler.]

IV. 1709. **Sir Trevor Wheler**, Baronet [1660], of Leamington Hastings aforesaid, 1st s. and h., *bap.* there 25 Nov. 1697; entered Rugby School, 6 June 1706; *suc. to the Baronetcy*, 23 Feb. 1708/9. He *d.* unm. at Bath, a month before his age of 21, and was *bur.* 17 Oct. 1718, at Leamington aforesaid. Admon. 5 Dec. 1718.

V. 1718. **Sir William Wheler**, Baronet [1660], of Leamington Hastings aforesaid, br. and h., *b.* about 1704;(a) entered Rugby School, 7 Feb. 1711/2; *suc. to the Baronetcy* in 1718; matric. at Oxford (Mag. Coll.), 5 May 1720, aged 15. He *m.* in or before 1726, Penelope, 2d da. of Sir Stephen Glynne, 3d Baronet [1661], of Ambrosden, Oxon, by Sophia, yst. da. and coheir of Sir Edward Evelyn, Baronet [so *cr.* 1683] of Long Ditton, Surrey. She was *bur.* 23 Jan. 1739/40, at Leamington Hastings.(b) He *d.* in Hampshire, and was *bur.* 4 June 1763, at Leamington aforesaid. Will pr. 1763.

VI. 1763. **Sir William Wheler**, Baronet [1660], of Leamington Hastings aforesaid, 1st s. and h., *b.* there 16 July, and *bap.* 4 Aug. 1726; matric. at Oxford (Trin. Coll.) 13 Nov. 1744, aged 18; *suc. to the Baronetcy*, June 1763; was Sheriff of Warwickshire, 1771-72. He *m.*, in or before 1754, Lucy, da. and h. of Giles Knightley, of Woodford, co. Northampton, by Angel, da. of (—) Stanley, of Ashenhurst, co. Stafford. She was *bur.* 27 March 1791, at Leamington Hastings, aged 58. Her will pr. 1801. He *d.* s.p.m.s.,(c) and was *bur.* 16 April 1799, at Leamington aforesaid. Will pr. Sep. 1799.

VII. 1799. **Sir Charles Wheler**, Baronet [1660], of Leamington Hastings(d) aforesaid, br. and h.; *b.* 22 Dec. 1730, at Paris; ed. at Clare Coll. Camb.; B.A., 1753; M.A., 1756; in Holy Orders; Vicar of Leamington Hastings, 1757-1821, and Prebendary of York, 1779-1821; *suc. to the Baronetcy* in April 1799. He *m.* 20 Jan. 1762, at King's Walden, Herts, Lucy, da. and eventually coheir of the Right Hon. Sir John Strange, Master of the Rolls [1750-54], by Susan, da. and coheir of Edward Strong, of Greenwich. She was *bur.* 26 Dec. 1800, at Leamington aforesaid. Will pr. 1801. He *d.* at Bath, 12 July 1821, aged 91, and was *bur.* at Walcot Cemetery, Somerset. Will pr. 1821.

VIII. 1821. **Sir Trevor Wheler**, Baronet [1660], of Leamington Hastings aforesaid,(d) 1st s. and h., *bap.* there 23 June 1763; entered Rugby School, 16 July 1771: *suc. to the Baronetcy*, 12 July 1821. He *m.* 20 March 1792, at Ashbourne, co. Derby, Harriet, 3d da. of Richard Beresford, of Fenny Bentley, in that county, by Alice, da. of Richard Garle, of Leicester. She was *bap.*, at Ashbourne, 5 Feb. 1771, and *d.* 9 Aug. 1806, aged 35. He *d.* 4 Feb. 1830, at Woodseat, in Rocester, co. Stafford, and was *bur.* at Rocester. Will pr. March 1830. M.I. to both at Leamington aforesaid.

IX. 1830. **Sir Trevor Wheler**, Baronet [1660], of Leamington Hastings aforesaid,(d) 1st s. and h., *b.* 20 Dec. 1792, at Wantage house, Berks; entered Rugby School, 1801; an officer in the 16th Light Dragoons, 1808; Capt., 1817, having served in the Peninsular Wars, 1810-14, and being present at Waterloo; Capt. 5th Dragoon Guards, 1822; Major, 1829, retiring in 1830; *suc. to the Baronetcy*, 4 Feb. 1830; Lieut. Col. Commanding North Devon Yeomanry, 1851-62. He *m.* firstly, 15 Oct. 1817, Lucy, only da. of George Dandridge, of the Commandery, Worcester. She *d.* 25 April 1859, and was *bur.* at Leamington Hastings aforesaid. He *m.* secondly, 14 Dec. 1865, at St. Geo. Han. sq., Frances, widow of the Rev. Jocelyn Willey, of Camblesforth Hall, co. York, 3d da. of the Rev. William Carus-Wilson, of Casterton Hall, Westmorland,

(a) His next yr. br., Charles, was *bap.* 30 May 1705.

(b) Her "most excellent character" fills nine lines of Wotton's *Baronetage*.

(c) Knightley Wheler, the only s. that survived infancy, *b.* 1754; entered Rugby, 31 Aug. 1763; matric. at Oxford (Trin. Coll.), 16 July 1772, aged 18; was *cr.* M.A., 24 Jan. 1777, and *d.* unm. and v.p. in 1798. Lucy, the only surv. da. and sole h., to whom passed the manor house and greater part [some 2,000 acres] of the Leamington Hastings estate (the remainder [about 700] being still in the possession of the present Baronet), *m.* in 1777 Edward Sacheverell Wilmot Sitwell, and is ancestress of the present [1902] owner thereof.

(d) See note "c" above as to the devolution of the greater part of that estate.

by Anne, da. of Gen. Ne[illegible]e. He *d.* s.p.m. 6 Sep. 1869, at Limerick House, Leamington Priors, co. Warwick, aged 76, and was *bur.* at Leamington Hastings. His widow *d.* 6 Oct. 1872, at Leamington Priors aforesaid, aged 55, and was *bur.* at Old Milverton.

X. 1869. **Sir Francis Wheler**, Baronet [1660], of Leamington Hastings aforesaid,(a) br. and h. male, *b.* 9 Nov. 1801, at Crakemarsh Hall, co. Stafford; entered Rugby School, 1810; entered the Bengal Army, 1818; served in Bundelkund, 1821-22; in Afghanistan, 1839-49; in the Punjab, 1848-49, and in the Indian Mutiny, 1858; Major Bengal Light Cavalry, 1851-54; Lieut. Col. 1854-61; Brig. Commander of the Saugor District, 1857-61; Commander of the Meerut District, 1861-65; Lieut. Gen., 1870; C.B., 28 Jan. 1862; *suc. to the Baronetcy*, 6 Sep. 1869. He *m.* firstly, Feb. 1827, at Nuserabad, Caroline, da. of the Rev. [—] Palmer. She *d.* Jan. 1833. He *m.* secondly, 18 Nov. 1841, at Lucknow, Elizabeth, da. of William Bishop, of Greyswood, Surrey, and North Bank, St. John's Wood, Midx. He *d.* at the Roccles, in Sydenham, Kent, 4 April 1878, and was *bur.* at Leamington Hastings. His widow *d.* 16 March 1900, at South Lawn, Southport, co. Lancaster, aged 78. Will pr. at £17,884.

XI. 1878. **Sir Trevor Wheler**, Baronet [1660], of Leamington Hastings aforesaid,(a) 1st s. and h. by 1st wife, *b.* 12 March 1828, at Muttra, in India; entered Bengal Army, 1844; served in Sutlej campaign, 1846; in in Burmese War, in Indian Mutiny campaign, 1858-59; in Central India with Eusofzai field force (severely wounded) 1863, and in the Bhootan War, 1865-66, retiring as Colonel in 1870; *suc. to the Baronetcy*, 4 April 1878. He *m.* 21 June 1852, at Simla, Cordelia Mary Jane, da. of John A. Scott, Major in the Bengal Cavalry. She *d.* 15 May 1893, at Ealing, Midx. He *d.* 10 Jan. 1900, at "Charlecote," Lansdown, Bath, aged 71, and was *bur.* at Leamington Hastings.

XII. 1900. **Sir Edward Wheler**, Baronet [1660], of Leamington Hastings aforesaid,(a) 2d and yst. but only surv. s. and h., *b.* 5 Dec. 1857; Major Royal Sussex Reg.; *suc. to the Baronetcy*, 10 Jan. 1900. He *m.* 4 July 1883, at St. James', Picadilly, Mary Leontine, da. of Sir Richard Wood, G.C.M.G., by Christina, da. of Sir William Duncan Godfrey, 3d Baronet [I. 1785].

NEWTON:

cr. 16 Aug. 1660;

ex. 6 April 1743.

I. 1660. "**John Newton**, of Barscote [*i.e.*, Barrscourt in Bitton], co. Gloucester, Esq.," s. and h. of Sir Theodore Newton(b), of the same, by Penelope, da. of Sir John Rodney, of Rodneys Stoke, co. Somerset, was aged 12 in 1623; suc. his father in or before Nov. 1632, and was *cr. a Baronet*, 16 Aug. 1660, for life (no mention being made of the heirs male of his own body) with a special remainder to John Newton,(c) of Haydor, co. Lincoln, Esq., and the heirs male of his body. He *m.* Grace, da. of (—) Stone. He *d.* s.p. 14 Feb. 1661, and was *bur.* in Bristol Cathedral. M.I.(d) Admon. (now lost) June 1662. His widow was living at Hannam, in Bitton, 1672.(b)

(a) See p. 108, note "d."

(b) See an account of this family in H. T. Ellacombe's *History of Bitton* (correcting Atkyns' *Gloucestershire*,) where the direct descent, generally attributed to this family, from Joan, da. and heir of Sir John Barr, of Barrscourt, is disproved.

(c) Lord Monson (*N. & Q.* 3d S., i, 190-191) states "There was no relationship whatever between the Newtons of Gloucestershire and the Newtons of Lincolnshire; no, not the most distant," and adds that he "can supply more minute details of what was certainly a curious transaction," viz., one done for money.

(d) See *Her. and Gen.*, vol. iv, p. 299 and 444. "He was a man of great courage and the greatest loyalty to his Prince," etc.

II. 1661. **Sir John Newton**, Baronet [1660], of Barrscourt and of Haydor abovenamed and of Barkston, co. Lincoln, s. and h. of Thomas Newton,(a) of Gunby and Haydor, co. Lincoln, by Elizabeth, da. of Thomas Parker, of Kibworth, co. Leicester, was *b.* 9 June 1626; suc. his father in April 1640; was one of the persons named in 1660 a Knight of the intended order of the Royal Oak, his estate being then given as £3,000 a year; *suc. to the Baronetcy* (as also to the estate of Barrscourt), 14 Feb. 1661 under the spec. rem. in the patent thereof; was M.P. for Grantham (five Parls.), 1660-81.(b) He *m.* in or before 1645, Mary, da. of Sir Gervase Eyre, of Rampton, Notts, by Elizabeth,(c) 1st da. and coheir of John Babington, of Rampton aforesaid. He *d.* 31 May 1699, and was *bur.* at Bitton aforesaid. M.I. Will dat. 29 Nov. 1686 to 11 March 1698/9, pr. 22 Feb. 1699/700. His widow, by whom he had seventeen children, *d.* 23 Nov. 1712 in her 85th year, and was *bur.* at Bitton. M.I. Will pr. June 1713.

III. 1699. **Sir John Newton**, Baronet [1660], of Barrscourt and of Culverthorpe, in Haydor aforesaid, and Thorpe, co. Lincoln, 1st surv. s. and h.(d), *b.* about 1651; admitted to Gray's Inn, 8 May 1672; *suc. to the Baronetcy*, 31 May 1699. He *m.*, firstly, 22 June 1676, at Westm. Abbey (Lic. Dean and Chapter), Abigail, da. of William Heveringham, of Heveringham, co. Suffolk (the Regicide), by Mary, only surv. da. and h. of John (Carey), 2d Earl of Dover. She *d.* s.p.m.s.,(e), 11 and was *bur.* 29 May 1686, at Haydor, in her 26th year. He *m.*, secondly, 23 March 1690/1, at St. Giles'-in-the-Fields (Lic. Fac. 21 March), Susanna, widow of Sir John Bright, Baronet [so *cr.* 1660], of Badsworth, co. York, sister and coheir of Sir Michael Wharton, and da. of Michael Wharton, of Beverley, by Susanna, da. of John (Poulett), 1st Baron Poulett of Hinton St. George. He *d.* 12 Feb. 1733/4, aged 83, and was *bur.* at Haydor. M.I. Will dat. 15 April 1714 to 28 March 1718, pr. 1 March 1733/4. His widow *d.* 19 April 1737, in her 86th year. M.I. at Haydor.

IV. 1734, to 1743. **Sir Michael Newton**, Baronet [1660], **K.B.**, of Barrscourt and Culverthorpe aforesaid, only s. and h. by second wife, *b.* about 1695; was M.P. for Beverley, 1722-27, and for Grantham (three Parls.), 1727, till death; suc., 25 March 1725, to a large estate on the death of his maternal uncle, Sir Michael Wharton; was installed **K.B**. 1725; *suc. to the Baronetcy*, 12 Feb. 1733/4. He pulled down the old house at Barrscourt. He *m.* 14 April 1730, at St. Anne's, Soho, Margaret, *suo jure* Countess of Coningsby, da. of Thomas (Coningsby), 1st Earl of

(a) See elaborate pedigree in *Mis. Gen. et Her.*, N.S., vol. i, p. 170, from John Newton, of Westby in Basingthorp, co. Lincoln, living 1541 (grandfather and the first known ancestor of the said Thomas), whose eldest son, John Newton of Westby (*d.* Dec. 1563), was great great grandfather of the celebrated Sir Isaac Newton, as therein is fully set forth.

(b) He is thus spoken of in Sir Joseph Williamson's *Lincolnshire Families temp. Charles II* [*Her. and Gen.*, vol. ii, 124], "Newton, Sir John, son to a chief constable at Hatherthorp, £3,000 [a year]; severall children; Dep. Lieut. and Col. of a Foot Regiment; an heir to Hixon, an usurer, who lived at Mr. T. Newton's this Sir John's father and left him great part of his estate." Lord Monson adds [*N. & Q.*, 3d S., i, 190] "Hickson, I suspect, a scrivener and money lender (temp. Charles I), accumulated large property round Grantham, and leaving no kindred of his own, left it to those of his wife, and thus it came to the Newtons."

(c) This Dame Eliz. Eyre was *bur.* at Haydor, 2 Aug. 1671.

(d) His elder br. Richard Newton was admitted to Gray's Inn, 8 Nov. 1666, as "s. and h. ap.," but was dead before he himself was admitted, 8 May 1672, under the like designation.

(e) Carey Newton, a da., her only surv. child was made heir by Lady Mary Heveringham (grandmother of the said Carey) to the estates of the Earl of Dover, to the exclusion of Sir William Heveringham, son of the said Mary. She, who was *b.* in Pall Mall, 9 June 1680, *m.*, 4 June 1695, Edward Coke, of Holkham, co. Norfolk, and was mother of Thomas Coke, *cr.* Earl of Leicester in 1744.

Coningsby, by his 2d wife, Frances, da. of Richard (Jones), Earl of Ranelagh [I.]. He *d.* s.p.s.(a) at St. James' Westm., 6 and was *bur.* 21 April 1743, at Haydor, when *the Baronetcy* became *extinct*(b). Admon. 9 May 1743. His widow, who was *b.* about 1709, and who had, v.p., been *cr.* Viscountess Coningsby of Hampton Court, co. Hereford, and had suc., 1 May 1729, as Countess Coningsby, on the death of her father, *d.* in Hill Street, Midx. 12, and was *bur.* 24 June 1761, at Haydor, aged 52, when all her honours became extinct. M.I. Will pr. 3 July 1761.

LEE:

cr. 16 Aug. 1660;

ex. 27 Sep. 1827.

I. 1660. "**Thomas Lee**, of Hartwell, Bucks, Esq.," s. and h. of Thomas Lee, by his 2d wife Elizabeth, da. of Sir George Croke, of Waterstock, Oxon, one of the Justices of the Court of King's Bench, was *bap.* at Hartwell, 26 May 1635, suc. his grandfather, Sir Thomas Lee, of Hartwell, 23 March 1641(c); joined his stepfather, Sir Richard Ingoldsby,(d) in endeavouring to persuade Sir Bulstrode Whitelock to go over to the King with the Great Seal, and was *cr. a Baronet*, 16 Aug. 1660. He was M.P. for Aylesbury (five Parls.) 1660-81, for Bucks 1689-90, and for Aylesbury, again, 1690 till death; was one of the Lords Commissioners of the Admiralty, 1689-91. He *m.* in or before 1660, Anne, da. of Sir John Davis,(e) of Bere Court, Pangbourne, Berks, by his 1st wife, Anne, da. of Sir John Suckling. He *d.* and was *bur.* 24 Feb. 1690/1, at Hartwell. Will dat. the day of his death, pr. 28 March 1691. His widow *d.* 23 and was *bur.* 27 Sep. 1708, at Hartwell, aged 77. Will dat. 20 May 1707, pr. 24 Sep. 1708.

II. 1691. **Sir Thomas Lee**, Baronet [1660], of Hartwell aforesaid, s. and h., *b.* there 1661; was M.P. for Aylesbury (six Parls. 1689-99 and 1701-2; *suc. to the Baronetcy*, 24 Feb. 1690/1. He *m.*, in or before 1686, Anne, da. and coheir of Thomas Hopkins, Citizen of London. He was *bur.* 13 Aug. 1702, at Hartwell. His widow was *bur.* there 17 Jan. 1728/9. Will dat. 20 March 1724.

III. 1702. **Sir Thomas Lee**, Baronet [1660], of Hartwell aforesaid, 1st s. and h.,(f) *b.* 31 March 1687; *suc. to the Baronetcy*, Aug. 1702; was M.P. for Wycombe 1710-22, and for Bucks. 1722-27 and 1729-41. He *m.*, 13 Sep. 1720, at Allhallows' Stayning, London, Elizabeth, da. of Thomas Sandys, Citizen of London, by (—), da. of (—) Congreve. She *d.* 10 and was *bur.* 20 Dec. 1728, at Hartwell. Will dat. 25 Feb. 1725, pr. 14 Feb. 1728/9. He *d.* 17 Dec. 1749 and was *bur.* at Hartwell, 4 Jan. 1749/50. Admon. 23 Jan. 1749/50.

(a) The only son John Newton, *styled* Viscount Coningsby, *b.* 16 Oct. 1732, *d.* in London 4 and was *bur.* 8 Jan. 1732/3.

(b) Susanna, his only sister, wife of William Archer (formerly Eyre) survived him, and was mother of Michael Newton, who on succeeding to the Barrscourt and Culverthorpe estates, took the name of Newton, by Act of Parl., 1761. The Barrscourt estate (350 acres) was for sale in 1867.

(c) See pedigree in Lipscomb's *Bucks*, vol. ii, pp. 307-308.

(d) Among the burials at Hartwell are those of the mother and stepfather of the 1st Baronet as under:—"1675, May 7, Elizabeth, wife of Sir Richard Ingoldesby, Knight of the Bath; 1685, Sep. 16. Sir Richard Ingoldesby, Knight of the Bath, was buried in linnen; one of King Charles ye first's Judges."

( ) This Sir John Davis was *bur.* at Hartwell, 2 July 1674.

( ) Of his younger brothers, (1) the Right Hon. Sir William Lee (*b.* 2 Aug. 1688), Lord Chief Justice of England, 1737, *d.* 8 April 1754, leaving issue; (2) the Rt. Hon. Sir George Lee, Dean of the Arches, etc., *d.* s.p. 18 Dec. 1758, aged 58.

III

IV. 1749. SIR WILLIAM LEE, Baronet [1660], of Hartwell aforesaid, 2d but only surv. s. and h.,(a) b. 12 Sep. 1726; *suc. to the Baronetcy*, 17 Dec. 1749. Sheriff of Bucks, 1772-73. He *m.* 20 June 1763, Elizabeth, da. of Simon (HARCOURT), 1st EARL HARCOURT, by Rebecca, da. and h. of Charles LE BASS. He *d.* 6 and was *bur.* 13 July 1799, at Hartwell, aged 72. Will pr. Aug. 1799. His widow, who was *b.* 18 June 1739, *d.* 21 and was *bur.* 30 Jan. 1811, at Hartwell. Will pr. 1811.

V. 1799. SIR WILLIAM LEE, Baronet [1660], of Hartwell aforesaid, 1st s. and h., *b.* June 1764; Lieut. Col. 16th Light Dragoons and afterwards of the 25th Light Dragoons; *suc. to the Baronetcy*, 6 July 1799. He *d.* unm. 7 Feb. 1801, at Madras. Will pr. 1807.

VI. 1801, to 1827. SIR GEORGE LEE, Baronet [1660], of Hartwell aforesaid, br. and h., *b.* 8 July and *bap.* 3 Aug. 1767, at St. James', Westm.: matric. at Oxford (St. John's Coll.), 7 Dec. 1784, aged 17: B.A., 1788; M.A., 1791; in Holy Orders; Vicar of Stone, Bucks, 1792-1803; Rector of Hartwell aforesaid, 1793-1803; Vicar of South Repps, Norfolk, 1803; Vicar of Bishop's Langham in that county, 1804; Rector of Grendon Underwood, Bucks, 1804-08; Rector of Water Stratford in that county, 1804-15; Rector of Beachampton in that county, 1815-27, having *suc. to the Baronetcy*, 7 Feb. 1801.(b) F.S.A. He *d.* unm. at Beachampton Rectory, 27 Sep. 1827, aged 60, and was *bur.* at Beachampton, when *the Baronetcy* became *extinct*.(c) Cenotaph at Hartwell.

SMITH:
cr. 16 Aug. 1660;
ex. [May?] 1706.

I. 1660. "THOMAS SMITH, of Hatherton, co. Chester, Esq.," 1st s. and h. ap. (being one of the twenty-two children) of Sir Thomas SMITH, of the same, Mayor of Chester, 1622, and Sheriff of Cheshire, 1622-23 (living 1666), by Mary, da. of Sir Hugh SMITH, of Long Ashton, Somerset, was *b.* in that county about 1622; matric. at Oxford (Mag. Coll.), 9 June 1638, aged 16, and was *cr. a Baronet*, 16 Aug. 1660, with a spec. rem., in default of male issue, to his brother Laurence Smith in tail male, and his brother Francis Smith in like manner, respectively. He was M.P. for Cheshire, 1661 till his death in 1675. He *m.*, in or before 1659, Abigail, 1st da. and coheir of Sir John PATE, Baronet [so *cr.* 1643], of Sysonby, co. Lincoln, by his 1st wife, Elizabeth, da. of Sir William SKIPWITH, of Cotes. He *d.* s.p.m. 22 and was *bur.* from Pall Mall, 31 May 1675, at St. Paul's Covent Garden. Admon. 22 Dec. 1675, to Abigail his widow. She *d.* 25 Oct. 1691, aged 67. Will pr. 1692.

II. 1675, to 1706. SIR THOMAS SMITH, Baronet [1660], of Hatherton aforesaid, nephew and heir male, being s. and h. of Sir Laurence SMITH, of Stratford Bow, Midx. (*Knighted* 27 Oct. 1660 and *d.* 19 Feb. 1664/5), by Jane his wife, *suc. to the Baronetcy*, 22 May 1675, according to the spec. rem. in the limitation thereof. He sold the Hatherton estate. He *d.* s.p.m., probably unm., in 1706, when the *Baronetcy* became *extinct*.(d). Will pr. May 1706.

(a) Thomas Lee, the eldest son, was *b.* at St. Andrew's Holborn, 16 Feb. 1722/3; *d.* unm. and v.p. 26 July and was *bur.* 1 Aug. 1740, at Hartwell.

(b) During his tenure of the estates, Hartwell House was occupied, 1809-14, by Louis XVIII, King of France (during exile), whose Queen died there 13 Nov. 1812, aged 57.

(c) He left his estates to John Lee, LL.D., said to have been the heir male.

(d) Francis Smith (also in the *spec.* rem.), the yst. br. of the grantee, had *d.* s.p.m. in 1663. The second Baronet had two brothers, of whom (1) Laurence Smith *d.* unm. and was *bur.* 11 April 1677, at Stratford Bow; (2) Lionel Smith, living 30 June 1679, when he proved his brother's will, *d.* s.p.m. before 1707. The pedigree in Ormerod's *Cheshire* is singularly defective.

ASSHETON *or* ASHTON:
cr. 17 Aug. 1660;
ex. 31 Dec. 1765.

I. 1660. "SIR RALPH ASHTON, of Middleton, co. Lancaster, Knt.," 2d but 1st surviving s. and h.(a) of Ralph ASHTON *or* ASSHETON of the same, Commander-in-Chief of the Parl. army in Lancashire (sometime M.P. for Clitheroe), by Elizabeth, da. of John KAYE, of Woodsome, co. York, was *b.* 9 July 1626, at Denby Grange, co. York; admitted to Gray's Inn, 13 Aug. 1639; *suc.* his father, 17 Feb. 1650/1; was *Knighted*, 16 July, and was *cr. a Baronet*, 17 Aug. 1660. He *m.*, about 1647, Anne, 1st da. (whose issue became coheir) of Sir Ralph ASSHETON, 1st Baronet (1620) of Lever and of Whalley Abbey, by his first wife Dorothy, da. of Sir James BELLINGHAM. He *d.* 23 April 1665, in his 39th year, and was *bur.* at Middleton. M.I. Admon. in Consistory Court of Chester. His widow *d.* 27 Oct. 1684, in her 60th year, and was *bur.* at Middleton. M.I. Admon. 4 Dec. 1684 in Consistory Court of Chester.

II. 1665. SIR RALPH ASSHETON, Baronet [1660], of Middleton aforesaid, and afterwards of Whalley Abbey, co. Lancaster, 1st s. and h., *b.* 11 and *bap.* 19 Feb. 1651, at Middleton; *suc. to the Baronetcy*, 23 April 1665; matric. at Oxford (Brasenose), 16 July 1668, being then aged 16; M.P. for Liverpool, March 1677 to 1679, and for Lancashire (two Parls.) Feb. 1694 to 1698. He, on the death, 11 June 1697, of his maternal uncle Sir John ASSHETON, 4th and last Baronet [1620], inherited Whalley Abbey and other estates of that family. He *m.*, firstly, Mary, da. and h. of Thomas VAVASOUR, of Spaldington, co. York, by Dorothy, da. of Sir Ferdinando LEIGH. She *d.* 11 Nov. 1694, and was *bur.* at Middleton. M.I. He *m.*, secondly, Mary, only surv. da. and h. of Robert HYDE(b), of Denton, co. Lancaster. He *d.* s.p.m.s., 3 May 1716, aged 63, and was *bur.* at Middleton. M.I. Will dat. 8 July 1709 to 6 April 1716, pr. 13 Feb. 1716/17.(c) His widow *d.* s.p. in London, 16 June, and was *bur.* 6 July 1721 in the chapel of Denton. M.I. Her will, dat. 4 March 1720, pr. 27 June 1721.

III. 1716, to 1765. SIR RALPH ASSHETON, Baronet [1660], of Middleton aforesaid, nephew and heir, being s. and h. of Richard Assheton, of Allerton Gledhow, co. York, by Mary, da. of John PARKER, of Extwistle, co. Lancaster (sometime wife of Benjamin WADDINGTON, of Allerton Gledhow aforesaid), which Richard, who *d.* Sep. 1705, was 2d s. of the 1st Baronet. He *suc. to the Baronetcy* and to the estate of Middleton, 3 May 1716; was Sheriff of Lancashire, 1738-39. He *m.* firstly, 3 Oct. 1734, Mary, 1st da. of Sir Holland EGERTON, 4th Baronet [1617], by Eleanor, da. of Sir Roger CAVE, 2d Baronet [1641]. She *d.* s.p. 11 Jan. 1735/6. Will pr. 26 June 1746. He *m.* secondly, 28 May 1739, at Thornhill, co. York, Eleanor, widow of John HULTON, of Hulton, co. Lancaster, da. of the Rev. John COPLEY, Rector of Thornhill aforesaid, by

(a) His eldest br. Richard Assheton *d.* young in 1630, "being supposed to be bewitched to death by one Utley, who, for this, was executed at Lancaster Assizes." See Whitaker's *Whalley*, 3d edit. (1818), p. 528.

(b) See a pedigree of Hyde in the Rev. J. Booker's *Denton Chapel*.

(c) All his large estates (excepting the maternal one of Middleton) devolved on his three surviving daughters (by his first wife) and coheirs, of whom (1) Anne, *m.* Humphrey TRAFFORD, and, inheriting the (Vavasour) estate of Spaldington, was ancestress of the family of VAVASOUR, of Spaldington, *cr.* Baronets in 1801; (2) Catharine, *m.* Thomas LISTER, of Gisburne Park, co. York, inherited the (Hyde) estate of Denton (which belonged to her step-mother), and was ancestress of the BARONS RIBBLESDALE; (3) Mary, *m.* Sir Nathaniel CURZON, 4th Baronet [1641], inherited the (Assheton) estate of Whalley Abbey, and was ancestress of the BARONS SCARSDALE and the EARLS HOWE.

Ellen, da. of (—) DIGGLES. He *d.* s.p.m.,(a) 31 Dec. 1765, and was *bur.* at Middleton, when *the Baronetcy* became *extinct*. M.I. His widow *d.* 25 March 1793, aged 76, at her house in Manchester, and was *bur.* at Middleton aforesaid M.I.

ROUS:
cr. 17 Aug. 1660;
afterwards, since 1796, BARONS ROUS OF DENNINGTON;
and subsequently, since 1821, EARLS OF STRADBROKE.

I. 1660. "JOHN ROUS, of Henham, co. Suffolk, Esq., 2d but 1st s. and h.,(b) of Sir John ROUS, of the same (*bur.* there 10 Sep. 1652) by Elizabeth, da. of Sir Christopher YELVERTON, sometime (1602-12) one of the Justices of the Court of King's Bench, was *b.* about 1608; admitted to Gray's Inn, 10 Aug. 1627; was Sheriff of Suffolk, 1635-36; was a Royalist and a Compounder, 13 Jan. 1645/6, for £144, and was *cr. a Baronet* 17 Aug. 1660; was M.P. for Dunwich, 1660 and 1661, and for Eye, 1665. He *m.* firstly, 23 June 1636, Anne, only da. of Nicholas BACON, of Gillingham, Norfolk, by his first wife, Anne, da. and h. of Sir James WESTON, one of the Barons of the Exchequer. She *d.* s.p. He *m.* secondly, in or before 1656, Elizabeth, sister of Sir John KNYVETT, K.B., da. of Thomas KNYVETT, of Ashwelthorpe, Norfolk, by Catharine, da. of Thomas (BURGH), LORD BURGH DE GAYNESBORO. She *d.* in London 7 and was *bur.* 17 July 1670, at Wangford, Suffolk. He *d.* 27 and was *bur.* 29 Nov. 1670 there. M.I. Will dat. 12 Oct. 1670 and pr. 31 May 1671.

II. 1670. SIR JOHN ROUS, Baronet [1660], of Henham Hall, in Henham aforesaid, s. and h., by second wife, *b.* about 1656, being aged 8 in 1664; *suc. to the Baronetcy*, 27 Nov. 1670; *cr.* M.A. of Cambridge, 1673; Sheriff of Suffolk, 1678-79; M.P. for Eye, 1685-87, and for Suffolk, 1689-90. He *m.* firstly, in or before 1676, Philippa, da. and eventually coheir of Thomas BEDINGFELD, of Darsham Hall, Suffolk, by Hannah, da. and h. of Philip BACON, of Wolverston. He *m.* secondly (Lic. 8 Sep. 1686), Anne, da. and h. of Robert WOOD, of Kingston upon Thames, Surrey, and of Islington, Midx. He *d.* 8 April 1730 in his 74th year. Will dat. 16 April 1729, pr. 3 June 1730. His widow was *bur.* 25 Feb. 1735/6, at Wangford.

III. 1730. SIR JOHN ROUS, Baronet [1660], of Henham Hall aforesaid, 1st s. and h. by 1st wife, *b.* about 1676; M.P. for Dunwich 1705-08; *suc. to the Baronetcy* 8 April 1730, but *d.* soon afterwards unm. 1 and was *bur.* 10 Feb. 1730/1 in his 56th year, at Wangford. M.I.

IV. 1731. SIR ROBERT ROUS, Baronet [1660], of Henham Hall aforesaid, br. of the half blood and h., being 3d s. of the 2d Baronet, the 1st s. by 2d wife; *suc. to the Baronetcy*, 1 Feb. 1730/1. He *m.*, in or before 1726, Lydia, da. of John SMITH, of Holton, Suffolk. He *d.* at Bristol 8 and was *bur.* 18 June 1735, at Wangford, in his 49th year. Will dat. 9 May and pr. 14 June 1735. His widow *d.* 13 Oct. 1769, and was *bur.* there. M.I.

(a) Of his two daughters and coheirs, by his second wife, (1) Mary, *m.*, 7 Oct. 1760, Sir Harbord HARBORD, 2d Baronet [1745], *cr.* in 1786 BARON SUFFIELD. She inherited the estate of Middleton; (2) Eleanor, *m.*, 12 Sep. 1769, Sir Thomas EGERTON, 7th Baronet [1617], *cr.* in 1801, EARL OF WILTON. Their only da. and h. *m.* Robert GROSVENOR, 1st MARQUESS OF WESTMINSTER, by whom she is ancestress, in the male line, of the DUKES OF WESTMINSTER, EARLS OF WILTON, BARONS EBURY and BARONS STALBRIDGE.

(b) Christopher Rous, the eldest son, *m.* (Lic. London, 5 May 1630, he about 33 and she about 18) Elizabeth, da. of Sir William Fytche, of Ramsden, Essex, and *d.* v.p. and s.p.s., 23 March 1635, aged 30 years and 4 months, and was *bur.* at Henham. M.I.

V. 1735. SIR JOHN ROUS, Baronet [1660], of Henham Hall aforesaid, 2d and yst. but only surv. s. and h., *b.* about 1727; *suc. to the Baronetcy* 8 June 1735; Sheriff of Suffolk, 1759-60; M.P. for that county, 1768. He *m.* at St. Geo. Han. sq., 5 June 1749, Judith, 1st da. and coheir of John BEDINGFELD, of Beeston St. Andrew and Caistor, co. Norfolk, by his 1st wife Judith, da. of (—) KENDALL. He *d.* in Upper Grosvenor street, 31 Oct., and was *bur.* 8 Nov. 1771, at Wangford, in his 44th year. Will dat. 8 Dec. 1769, pr. 14 Dec. 1771 and 27 Oct. 1810. His widow *m.* (as his third wife) the Rev. Edward LOCKWOOD, of Stapleton, co. Gloucester, and of Dews Hall, in Lambourne, Essex, and *d.* in his life time. 10 Sep. 1794, in Portman square, being *bur.* at Lambourne aforesaid. Admon. 24 Sep. 1794.

VI. 1771. SIR JOHN ROUS, Baronet [1660], of Henham Hall aforesaid, only s. and h., *b.* in Upper Grosvenor Street, 10 and *bap.* 21 June 1750, at St. Geo., Han. sq.; ed. at Westm. School; matric. at Oxford (Mag. Coll.), 17 May 1768, aged 17; *cr.* M.A., 8 Feb. 1771; *suc. to the Baronetcy*, 31 Oct. 1771; M.P. for Suffolk (13 Parls.), 1780-96; Capt. of the Suffolk Yeomanry, 1794. He *m.* firstly, Jan. 1788, at Yoxford, Suffolk, Frances Juliana, da. and h. of Edward WARTER-WILSON, of Bilboa, co. Limerick, by Frances Anne Freke, da. of George (EVANS), 2d BARON CARBERY [I.]. She *d.* s.p.m., 20 June 1790. He *m.* secondly, 23 Feb. 1792, at St. Marylebone, Charlotte Maria, da. of Abraham WHITAKER, of Stratford, co. Essex, and Lyster House, co. Hereford.(a) She, who was *b.* in 1769, was living when he was *cr.*, 14 June 1796, BARON ROUS OF DENNINGTON, co. Suffolk, being *cr.* (25 years later) 18 July 1821, VISCOUNT DUNWICH and EARL OF STRADBROKE, both co. Suffolk. In these titles this *Baronetage* then *merged*, and still so continues. See "Peerage."

MASSINGBERD, *or* MASSINGBEARD:
cr. 22 Aug. 1660;
ex. 1 Dec. 1723.

I. 1660. "HENRY MASSINGBEARD, of Bratoft Hall, co. Lincoln, Esq.," 1st s. and h. of Thomas MASSINBERD *or* MASSINGBEARD, of Bratoft Hall and Gunby in that county, Barrister (*d.* 5 Nov. 1636, aged 74), by Frances, da. of Robert HALTON, of Clee, co. Lincoln, Sergeant at Law, was *b.* 26 and *bap.* 27 Aug. 1609, at Gunby; admitted 18 Nov. 1627 (as a Fellow Commoner) to Christ's College, Cambridge; admitted 17 June 1629 to the Inner Temple; was *cr. a Baronet* in 1658 by the Lord Protector Cromwell, to whom he had "good affection"(b) (his brother, Sir Drayner Massingberd, being also a Parliamentarian), which dignity was, of course, *forfeited* at the Restoration, shortly after which he was *cr. a Baronet*, by the King, 22 Aug. 1660. He was Sheriff of Bedfordshire, 1667-68.(c) He *m.* firstly, 18 Dec. 1632, at Colby, co. Lincoln, Elizabeth, da. of William LYSTER, of Colby aforesaid and of Rippingale, co. Lincoln, sometime Sheriff of that county. By her he had no male issue who survived him. He *m.* secondly, in or before 1649, Anne, widow of Nicholas STOUGHTON, of Stoke, da. and finally heir of William EVANS, of London, by

(a) The names of his "wife, father and mother" are asked for by "Harflete" in N. & Q. (8th S. xii, 329), where he is stated to have been a "Drysalter," and to have had three daughters (1) "Charlotte, Countess of Stradbroke, (2) Diana, Lady Hamlyn-Williams, and (3) Marianne, Lady Gooch."

(b) This creation has unfortunately been omitted among Cromwell's Creations of Baronetcies, pp. 3-9 of this Vol. The preamble is set out in Burke's *Extinct Baronetcies* reciting "his faithfulness and good affection to us and his country." The patent "with a good likeness" of Cromwell "in a robe of ermine" was then [1844] "in possession of Thomas Massingberd, Esq., of Candlesby House."

(c) Sir Joseph Williamson, in his *Lincolnshire Families, temp. Charles II* [*Her. and Gen.*, vol. ii], says he had "£1,800 [a year] in the Fore Marsh," and "his brother [Drayner Massingberd, of Ormsby] hath £1,500 [a year] in ye Marsh."

Margaret, da. of Robert WAKE, of that city. She possibly is the "Lady Ann Massinbrook," who was *bur.* at St. Giles'-in-the-fields, 18 Jan. 1671/2.(a) He *m.* thirdly, Elizabeth, da. of [—] RAYNER, of co. York. He *d.* Sep. 1680, aged 71. Will pr. 1680.

II. 1680. SIR WILLIAM MASSINBERD, Baronet [1660], of Bratoft Hall and Gunby aforesaid, 1st surv. s. and h., being 1st s. by 2d wife, *b.* in Lincoln's Inn fields, 23, and *bap.* 31 Jan. 1649/50 at St. Giles'-in-the-fields; matric. at Oxford (Wadham Coll.), 13 March 1667/8, aged 18; admitted to Inner Temple, 1668; *suc. to the Baronetcy*, Sep. 1680; was Sheriff of Beds., 1694-95. He *m.* 11 July 1673, at St. James', Clerkenwell (Lic. Vic. Gen. 9 July) Elizabeth (aged 18), da. of Richard WYNN, of Cateaton street, London. She was *bur.* 30 July 1714, at Gunby. He *d.* 1719, in his 70th year. Will pr. Aug. 1719.

III. 1719, to 1723. SIR WILLIAM MASSINGBERD, Baronet [1660], of Bratoft Hall and Gunby aforesaid, only s. and h., *bap.* 25 Sep. 1677, at Bratoft; *suc. to the Baronetcy* in 1719; was M.P. for Lincolnshire Jan. 1720/1 till death. He *d.* unm. 1 Dec. 1723, in Golden square, St. Anne's, Soho, aged 46, when the *Baronetcy* became *extinct*.(b) Will dat. 22 Nov. and pr. 9 Dec. 1723.

HALES:

cr. 28 Aug. 1660;

ex 16 Jan. 1806.

I. 1660. "JOHN HALES, of [Hales Place, otherwise White friars, in] Coventry, co. Warwick, Esq.," s. of Christopher HALES, of the same (who matric. at Oxford from Mag. Coll., 18 March 1635/6, aged 17), and grandson of John HALES, of the same, by Frideswide, da. of Anthony FAUNT, of Foston, co. Leicester,(c) was *b.* about 1646, and was *cr. a Baronet*, 28 Aug. 1660. He matric. at Oxford (Ch. Ch.) as a Baronet, 3 July 1663, aged 16, and was *cr.* M.A., 28 Sep. 1663. He *m.* (Lic. Vic. Gen., 22 March 1668/9, each being about 22 years old, and at own disposal), Anne, da. of [—] JOHNSON, of Ilford, co. Essex, Citizen (fined for the Aldermancy) of London.(d) He *d.* in St. Dunstan's in the West, London, and was *bur.* at St. Michael's, Coventry, in or shortly before 1677. Admon. 11 Nov. 1677 and 13 May 1713. The will of his widow, dat. 14 June 1710, pr. 16 April 1713.

II. 1677? SIR CHRISTOPHER HALES,(e) Baronet [1660], of White-friars aforesaid, 1st or 1st surv. s. and h., *b.* about 1670; *suc. to the Baronetcy* in or shortly before 1677, matric. at Oxford (Ch. Ch.) as a Baronet, 28 Feb. 1688/9, aged 18; was M.P. for Coventry (seven Parls.) 1698, tlil unseated in Feb. 1706/7, and again April 1711 till 1715. He *d.* unm. 7 Jan. 1716/7. Will dat. 21 Sep. 1716, pr. 3 Dec. 1717.

(a) Sir Drayner Massingberd's wife, was, however, also named Ann, and a child of theirs (Elizabeth) was *bap.* at St. Giles'-in-the-fields, 25 July 1680.

(b) His estates devolved on his sister Elizabeth, wife of Thomas Meux, whose 1st son, William Meux, took the name of Massingberd.

(c) See Pedigree in *Mis. Gen. et Her.*, New Series, Vol. i, pp. 69-71.

(d) The marriage, 23 March 1668/9, of "John Halles and Ane Colinsone" [*sic*], at St. James', Clerkenwell (one of the two places specified in the license) is apparently the one in question, "Colinsone" being a misreading of "Johnson."

(e) In Wotton's *Baronetage* [1741] is this note, "I find a Sir Thomas Hales, of Coventry, Bart., who *m.* Jane, da. of George Purefoy, of Drayton, co. Leicester, Esq., and was *bur.* at Coventry, 17 Aug. 1676. MSS. P. Le Neve. *Qy.* if this Sir Thomas was not successor to Sir John and father of Sir Christopher and Sir Edward which makes a descent more than mentioned by the Editor of Dugdale" [*i.e.*, of Dugdale's *Warwickshire*]. If this Thomas was a son of the 1st Baronet he would be but 7 years old or under at his death in 1676, and too young for marriage.

III. 1717. SIR EDWARD HALES, Baronet [1660], of Whitefriars aforesaid, br. and h., *suc. to the Baronetcy* 7 Jan. 1716/7. He, by Act of Parliament, sold the Warwickshire estates about 1718 to pay off the encumbrances thereon as also his brother's debts. He *m.* Elizabeth, da. of(—) THORPE, of St. Martin's-in-the-fields, Midx. He *d.* 7 Sep. 1720, and is said to have been *bur.* at St. Martin's aforesaid. Will dat. 6 and pr. 19 Sep. 1720. His widow *d.* at Lincoln and was *bur.* at St. Margaret's, in that city, 24 April 1766, aged 90.

IV. 1720. SIR CHRISTOPHER HALES, Baronet [1660], of Lincoln and afterwards of Fulham, co. Midx., 1st s. and h., *suc. to the Baronetcy* 7 Sep. 1720. He *m.* in Sep. 1736, Harrison, da. of Col. Benjamin COLUMBINE, of Morley, co. Antrim, by Mary, da. of Edward HARRISON, of Morley aforesaid, by Joanna his wife, da. of Jeremy TAYLOR, Bishop of Dromore. She was *bur.* 3 June 1762, at Hammersmith, Midx. Admon. 29 Nov. 1763. He *d.* 8 and was *bur.* 15 May 1766, at Hammersmith.

V. 1766. SIR JOHN HALES, Baronet [1660], 2d but only surv. s.,(a) *b.* about 1743 at Hackthorn, co. Lincoln; *suc. to the Baronetcy*, 8 May 1766. He *m.* 13 May 1777, at St. Geo., Han. sq., Anne, da. and h. of John SCOTT, of North End in Fulham, Midx. She *d.* 25 Sep. 1799, and was *bur.* at Fulham. He *d.*, in his 60th year, 15 Feb. 1802, and was also *bur.* there.

VI. 1802. SIR JOHN SCOTT HALES, Baronet [1660], 1st s. and h., *b.* 17 Nov. 1779, at Hammersmith, and *bap.* there; was an Officer in the 90th Regiment of Foot; *suc. to the Baronetcy*, 15 Feb. 1802, but *d.* unm. a year later at Lisbon, 22 Feb. 1803, and was *bur.* there, aged 23. Will pr. 1812.

VII. 1803. SIR SAMUEL HALES, Baronet [1660], br. and h., *b.* 10 Oct. 1782, at Hammersmith, and *bap.* there; Lieut. Royal Navy; *suc. to the Baronetcy*, 22 Feb. 1803. He *d.* unm. at Hammersmith, 22 Jan. 1805, and was *bur.* at Fulham, aged 22. Admon. Feb. 1805.

VIII. 1805, to 1806. SIR CHRISTOPHER HALES, Baronet [1660], of Lincoln, only surv. br. and h., *b.* 24 Aug. 1785, at Fulham; *suc. to the Baronetcy*, 22 Jan. 1805. He *d.* unm. at Lisbon 16 Jan. 1806, when the *Baronetcy* became *extinct*.

BOVEY:

cr. 30 Aug. 1660;

ex. Oct. 1679.

I. 1660, to 1679. "RALPH BOVEY, of Hillfields, co. Warwick, Esq.," was presumably admitted to Gray's Inn, 3 Aug. 1633, as "s. and h. of Ralph BOVEY, Esq.,(b) deceased"; was an attorney of the Court of Common Pleas, was Sheriff of Warwickshire (being then "of Solyhull"), 1652-53, and was *cr. a Baronet*, 30 Aug. 1660. He was subsequently of Long Stow, co. Cambridge; and was Sheriff of Beds., Nov. 1668 and 1669-70. He *m.* Mary, da. of William (MAYNARD), 1st BARON MAYNARD OF ESTAINES, by

(a) His elder br. Christopher Hales, *bap.* 28 Dec. 1737, at St. Margaret's, Lincoln, was a Capt. in the Army, and *d.* unm. v.p. in the Highlands of Scotland, and was *bur.* there.

(b) This Ralph was presumably the Ralph Bovey, of St. Alban's, Wood street, London, 1619, whose will was proved 8 July 1630, by Ursula (sister of Richard Aldworth, of Reading), his widow, and whose father, William Bovy, of London, was 1st cousin of William Bovy, of Alcester, co. Warwick. See Visit. of Warwickshire, 1619.

his 2nd wife, Anne, da. of Sir Anthony EVERARD. She gave £300 to the Vicarage of Warden, Beds. He *d.* s.p. legit.,(a) and was *bur.* (in linen) 11 Oct. 1679, at Stow aforesaid, when the *Baronetcy* became *extinct*. Will pr. 15 Sep. 1679, by Elizabeth Symonds, widow.

KNIGHTLEY:

cr. 30 Aug. 1660;

ex. in 1689.

I. 1660. "JOHN KNIGHTLEY, of Offchurch, co. Warwick, Esq.," 1st s. and h. of Robert KNIGHTLEY,(b) of the same, by Ann, da. of Sir John PETTUS, of Norwich, was *b.* about 1611, being aged 8 at the Visit. of Warwickshire, 1629; had a warrant of Baronetcy, dated July 1645,(c) from Charles I, and was *cr. a Baronet*, 30 Aug. 1660. He (or possibly his son) was Sheriff of Warwickshire 1664-65. He *m.* Bridget, da. of Sir Lewis LEWKNOR, of Selsey, co. Sussex, Master of the Ceremonies to James I.

II. 1670? to 1689. SIR JOHN KNIGHTLEY, Baronet [1660], of Offchurch aforesaid, s. and h.; *suc. to the Baronetcy* on his father's death; was Dep. Lieut. of co. Warwick. He *d.* s.p.m.,(d) in 1689, when the *Baronetcy* became *extinct*. Will dat. 13 July 1688, pr. 25 June 1689, by Mary WASTENEYS, his sister.

DRAKE:

cr. 31 Aug. 1660;

ex. 21 Oct. 1733.

I. 1660. "SIR JOHN DRAKE, of Ashe [in the parish of Musbury] co. Devon, Knt.," 1st s. and h. of Sir John DRAKE, of the same, by Eleanor, da. and h. of John (BOTELER), 1st BARON BOTELER OF BRAMFIELD, was *b.* about 1619; suc. his father, 25 Aug. 1636; admitted to the Inner Temple, Nov. 1644; was M.P. for Bridport, 1660; Knighted 5 June 1660. at Whitehall, and was *cr. a Baronet*, two months later, 31 Aug. 1660. He *m.* firstly, in or before 1646, Jane, 1st da. of Sir John YONGE, 1st Baronet [1661] of Culleton, co. Devon, by Elizabeth, da. of Sir William STRODE, of Newnham. She *d.* July 1652. M.I. at Musbury. He *m.* secondly, Dionysia, 8th da. of Sir Richard STRODE, of Newnham aforesaid, 6th da. by his 2d wife, Elizabeth, da. of Thomas (SACKVILLE), EARL OF DORSET. He was *bur.* 7 July 1669, at Axminster.(e) Will pr. 30 Dec. 1669. His widow was *bur.* 25 Nov. 1679, at Axminster.

II. 1669. SIR JOHN DRAKE, Baronet [1660], of Ashe aforesaid and of Mount Drake in the same parish, 1st s. and h. by 1st wife, *b.* 13 Jan. 1646/7, at Lyme, co. Dorset; matric. at Oxford (Ex. Coll.), 16 March

(a) Charles Bovy, of Warden Abbey, Beds. was his illegit. son, by his executrix abovenamed. He, who was aged about 21 in 1697, inherited the estates and was living 1713, but *d.* s.p.m. "Charles Bovey, of Longhow, co. Cambridge, gent.," was admitted to Lincoln's Inn, 24 July 1701.

(b) This Robert (living 1619) was 4th son of Sir Valentine Knightley, of Fawsley, co. Northampton (who *d.* 8th March 1566), the ancestor of the family still (1902) of that place.

(c) See Vol. ii, p. 455.

(d) He devised his estate to John Wightwick (whom he calls his grandson) when 21. He took the name of Knightley, and had lic. (Fac. off.) 13 Dec. 1699, being then aged 19, to marry Mary Marowe, of Berkswell, co. Warwick, spinster.

(e) His sister, Elizabeth, *m.* Sir Winston Churchill, and was by him mother of the famous Duke of Marlborough, who was *b.* in the family mansion of Ashe.

1664/5, aged 17; admitted to the Inner Temple, 1667; *suc. to the Baronetcy* in July 1669. He rebuilt the manor house of Mount Drake, which had been destroyed by the rebels during the Civil Wars. He *d.* unm., 13 March 1683/4, and was *bur.* at Musbury. Admon. 31 May 1684 to his sister, Elizabeth DRAKE, spinster.(a)

III. 1684. SIR BERNARD DRAKE, Baronet [1660], of Ferrybere in Bickington, Devon, br. of the half blood and h. male, being s. of the 1st Baronet by his 2nd wife; *suc. to the Baronetcy*, 13 March 1683/4. He *m.* Elizabeth, widow of Hugh STOWELL, of Ferrybere aforesaid, da. of George PRESTWOOD, of Butterford, Devon. He *d.* s.p.m., having killed himself, 1687. His widow was *bur.* 6 Sep. 1715, at Ilsington.

IV. 1687. SIR WILLIAM DRAKE, Baronet [1660], of Ashe and Mount Drake aforesaid, br. and h. male, *b.* about 1659; matric. at Oxford (Oriel Coll.), 4 June 1675, aged 16; B.A. (from Corpus Christi Coll.), 1679; M.A., 6 March 1682/3; *Knighted*, 13 March 1684/5, at Whitehall; *suc. to the Baronetcy* in 1687, and to the family estates of Ashe and Mount Drake, on the death of his sister, Dame Elizabeth Briscoe, 9 Nov. 1694.(b) He was M.P. for Honiton (ten Parls.), 1690-1715, being also elected for Dartmouth, 1713. He was one of the Lords of the Admiralty, 1710-14. He *m.* firstly, 5 April 1687, Judith, da. and coheir of William EVELEIGH, of Olcomb, in Ottery St. Mary, Devon. She *d.* 8 and was *bur.* 14 May 1701, at Musbury. M.I. He *m.* secondly, 16 April 1705, at Farway, Devon, Mary, 4th da. of Sir Peter PRIDEAUX, 3d Baronet [1622], by Elizabeth, da. of Sir Bevill GRANVILLE, of Stow, co. Cornwall. He *d.* 28 Feb. 1715/6, and was *bur.* at Musbury. M.I. Will dat. 14 Jan. 1714, pr. 16 May 1716. His widow, by whom he had no children, was *b.* 30 July 1658, and *d.* 20 Nov. 1729. Her will, as of St. Geo. the Martyr, Midx., dat. 30 April 1729, pr. 3 June 1730.

V. 1716. SIR JOHN DRAKE, Baronet [1660], of Ashe and Mount Drake aforesaid, 1st s. and h. by 1st wife; *b.* about 1689; matric. at Oxford (Corpus Christi Coll.), 30 Oct. 1707, aged 18; *suc. to the Baronetcy*, 28 Feb. 1715/6. He *d.* unm., at Ashe, 4 Sep. 1724, and was *bur.* at Musbury. M.I. Will dat. 2 Sep., pr. 6 Oct. 1724.

VI. 1724, to 1733. SIR WILLIAM DRAKE, Baronet [1660], of Ashe and Mount Drake aforesaid, br. and h., *b.* about 1695: *suc. to the Baronetcy*, 4 Sep. 1724. He *m.* 18 June 1726, at St. George's, Queen square, Midx., Anne, sister of Sir Hutchins WILLIAMS, 1st Baronet [1747], 1st da. of William Peere WILLIAMS, Barrister, by Anne, da. and coheir of Sir George HUTCHINS. He *d.* s.p., 21 Oct., 1733, aged 38, and was *bur.* at Axminster, when the *Baronetcy* became *extinct*. Will dat. 12 Oct. 1732, pr. 25 Jan. 1733/4, at Exeter. His widow *m.* (as his 3d wife), George SPEKE, of Whitelackington, Somerset, and *d.* s.p.m.,(c) 31 May 1782. Will pr. June 1782.

(a) The estates devolved on this Elizabeth, his only sister of the whole blood, who subsequently *m.* Sir John Briscoe, of Boughton, co. Northampton, and *d.* s.p., 9 Nov. 1694, aged 46, being *bur.* at Musbury. M.I.

(b) See note "a" above.

(c) Anne, her only surv. child by her 2d husband (a fortune of £4,000 a year), *m.* 20 May 1756, at St. James', Picadilly, Frederick (North), 2d Earl of Guilford, well known as Lord North.

SAINT GEORGE:

cr. 5 Sep. 1660;

afterwards, 1715-35,

BARON SAINT-GEORGE OF HATLEY SAINT GEORGE [I.];

ex. 4 Aug. 1735.

I. 1660. "OLIVER SAINT-GEORGE, of Carrickermick [*i.e.* Carrickdrumrusk], co. Trim [*i.e.* Leitrim], Ireland, Esq.," s. and h. of Sir George SAINT-GEORGE,(a) of the same, Vice Admiral of Connaught (who was *b.* 13 Jan. 1583, at Hatley St. George, and who *d.* at Headford, co. Galway, 5 Aug. 1660), by Catharine, da. of Capt. Richard GIFFORD, of Ballymagarrett, co. Roscommon,(b) was *Knighted* at Dublin Castle, 23 Feb. 1658/9, by Henry Cromwell, Lord Deputy [I.], and again *Knighted*, 11 July 1660, by Charles II, at Whitehall; was, at the Restoration, appointed a Commissioner for Irish affairs; suc. his father, 5 Aug. 1660, and, a month later, was *cr. a Baronet*, 5 Sep. 1660.(c) He was M.P. [I.] for Galway 1661-65, and 1692-93. He *m.* in or before 1651, Olivia, widow of George THORNTON, da. of Michael BERESFORD of COLERAINE, by Mary, da. of Sir John LEAKE. He *d.* Oct. 1695. Will dat. 20 May 1695, pr. 3 Jan. 1695/6, at Dublin.

II. 1695 to 1735. SIR GEORGE SAINT-GEORGE, Baronet, of Carrickdrumrusk aforesaid, s. and h.; *b.* about 1650; entered Trin. Coll., Dublin, 9 July 1675, in his 16th year; LL.D. (honoris causâ), 1709, having *suc. to the Baronetcy* in Oct. 1695; was Sheriff of co. Galway, 1700, and of co. Leitrim, 1702 and 1703; M.P. [I.] for co. Roscommon, 1692-93, 1695-99, and 1703 to 1715, in which year he was, 18 April 1715, *cr.* BARON SAINT GEORGE OF HATLEY SAINT GEORGE in the counties of Roscommon and Leitrim [I.], with a spec. rem., failing heirs male of his body, to those of his father. He *m.* 29 Nov. 1681, Margaret, da. of John (SKEFFINGTON), 2d VISCOUNT MASSEREENE [I.], by Mary, only da. and h. of John (CLOTWORTHY), 1st VISCOUNT MASSEREENE [I.]. She *d.* 1711. He *d.* s.p.m. 4 Aug. 1735, aged 84, when *all his honours* became *extinct*.(d)

BOWYER:

cr. 11 Sep. 1660;

ex. Feb. 1701/2.

I. 1660. "SIR JOHN BOWYER, of Knipersley, co. Stafford, Knt.," 6th but 1st surv. s. and h. of Sir William BOWYER, of the same, by Hester, da. of Sir William SKEFFINGTON, of Fisherwick in that county, was *bap.* 21 Sep. 1623, at Biddulph; suc. his father in March 1640/1; was Colonel in the army and Governor of Leek for the Parl., but subsequently became a Royalist; was M.P. for Staffordshire, Aug. 1646 till secluded Dec. 1648; for Newcastle-under-Lyme, 1656-58 and 1660. He was *Knighted*, 30 May, and was *cr. a Baronet*, 11 Sep. 1660; was Sheriff of Staffordshire, 1662-63. He *m.*, 4 April 1648, at Snitterton, co. Derby, Mary, da. and h. of Robert MILWARD, of Broadlow Ash, in that county. She was *bur.* 6 June 1665, at Leek, aged 35. He *m.* secondly, 11 Sep. 1665, Elizabeth, or Anne, da. of Sir Ralph EGERTON, of Betley, co. Stafford, by whom he had no issue. He was *bur.* 18 July 1666, at Biddulph.

(a) This George was 4th s. of Sir Richard Saint-George, Clarenceux King of Arms, 1623 to 1635, one of five Kings of Arms made from this family in the short space of eighty years, 1623 to 1703. See *Complete Peerage*, by G.E.C., vol. vii, p. 11, note "b."

(b) Most of the information in this article has been kindly fu nished by G. D. Burtchaell, of the office of Arms, Dublin.

(c) Possibly also at the same date, created a Baronet of Ireland. He appears in the list of Irish Baronets in Ulster's office. See creations of Lane, 9 Feb. 1660/1, and of Gifford, 4 March 1660/1, for somewhat similar cases.

(d) His yr. br., Oliver St. George, Captain of Dragoons, 1685, M.P. [I.] for Carrick, 1703-13, and for Dungannon, 1715-31, had *d.* unm. 18 April 1731, aged 70.

II. 1666. SIR JOHN BOWYER, Baronet [1660], of Knipersley aforesaid, 1st s. and h., *b.* 25 April 1653, presumably at Biddulph; *suc. to the Baronetcy* in July 1666, matric. at Oxford (Ch. Ch.), 11 July 1668, aged 15; *cr.* M.A., 9 July 1699; Sheriff of Staffordshire, 1677-78; M.P. for Warwick, Feb. 1677/8 to Jan. 1678/9; for Staffordshire, 1679, 1679-81, and 1681. He *m.* (Lic. Vic. Gen., 10 July 1672, to marry at St. Mary's, Warwick) Jane, da. and coheir of Henry MURRAY, Groom of the Bedchamber, by Anne, *suo jure* VISCOUNTESS BAYNING OF FOXLEY. He was *bur.* at Biddulph, 18 July 1691, aged 38. Will dat. 16 Feb. 1687/8, pr. 20 April 1695. His widow *d.* 19 Oct. 1727, at the Priory, Warwick, and was *bur.* at Biddulph. Will dat. 27 Sep. 1720, pr. 29 Dec. 1727.

III. 1691. SIR JOHN BOWYER, Baronet [1660], of Knipersley aforesaid, only s. and h.; *suc. to the Baronetcy* in July 1691. He *d.* unm. at the Priory, Warwick, and was *bur.* at Biddulph, 10 May 1701, aged 28. Admon. 19 May 1701 to his mother.

IV. 1701, to 1702. SIR WILLIAM BOWYER, Baronet [1660], of Knipersley aforesaid, uncle and h.; *b.* 23 July 1654, presumably at Biddulph; *suc. to the Baronetcy* in May 1702. He *m.*, in or before 1672, Anne, da. of George DALE, of Flagg in Chelmorton, co. Derby, by Millicent, da. of Robert DAKEYNE, of Priestcliff, in that county. He *d.* s.p.m.s.,(a) and was *bur.* at Biddulph, 17 Feb. 1701/2, aged 47, when the *Baronetcy* became *extinct*. Will dat. 20 June 1701, pr. 30 April 1702 at Lichfield. His widow *d.* in her 60th year, and was *bur.* 8 June 1709, at Biddulph.

WILDE:

cr. 13 Sep. 1660;

ex. (probably soon) after Nov. 1721.

I. 1660. "SIR WILLIAM WILDE, Knt., Recorder of the City of London, afterwards [1673] one of the Justices of the King's Bench," sometime of the parish of St. Barth. the Great, London, was s. of William WILD, of Bread Street, London, Vintner (who *d.* 25 March 1650); was *b.* about 1611; admitted to the Inner Temple, 19 Feb. 1629/30, being then of Clifford's Inn; Barrister, 21 May 1637; Bencher, 1652; Recorder of London, 3 Nov. 1659 to 18 April 1668, having been continued in that office after the Restoration; M.P. for London, April 1660; *Knighted* at the Hague in May following, and was *cr. a Baronet*, 13 Sep. 1660; Serjeant-at-Law, 5 Oct. 1661; King's Serjeant-at-Law, 10 Nov. 1661; one of the Justices of the Court of Common Pleas, 1668-73, and of the King's Bench, 1673 till dismissed (seven months before his death), 29 April 1679.(b) He purchased the manor of Goldston in Ash, co. Kent. He *m.* firstly (—). He *m.* secondly, in or before 1652, Jane, da. of Felix WILSON, of Stanwell, Midx. She *d.* 23 Aug. and was *bur.* 5 Sep. 1661, at St. Barth. aforesaid. Funeral Certificate. He *m.* thirdly (Lic. Lond. 30 Oct. 1662, Frances (then aged 32), da. of

(a) Of his five sons, four *d.* in infancy, and the eldest, John, *d.* unm. in 1693, aged 21. Of his four daughters and coheirs (1), Mary, *b.* about 1674, inherited the estate of Norton-le-Moors, *m.* 8 April 1702, Charles Adderley, and was *bur.* 31 Oct. 1723, being ancestress of the Barons Norton; (2), Jane, *bap.* 31 Oct. 1676, *m.* 26 June 1702, at Astbury, Leftwich Oldfield, of Leftwich, Cheshire, and *d.* 17 Oct. 1749; (3), Anne, *bap.* 15 Dec. 1687, *m.* twice, but *d.* s.p. 26 July 1754, leaving her share of the Bowyer estates to her nephew, Sir Nigel Gresley, 6th Baronet [1611]; and (4), Dorothy, *b.* 29 Oct. 1691, who inherited the estate of Knipersley, and who *m.*, 5 April 1719, Sir Thomas Gresley, 4th Baronet [1611].

(b) "Burnet says that Sir William Wilde, '*a worthy and ancient judge*,' was turned out for his plain freedom in telling Bedlow, one of the witnesses of the Popish Plot, that he was a perjured man." [Foss's *Judges*].

Thomas BARCROFT, of St. Michael Bassishaw, London. He *d.* 23 Nov. 1679, and was *bur.* in the Temple church, London, aged 68. M.I.(a) Will dat. 4 Dec. 1678, pr. 7 Oct. 1679.

II. 1679, to 1722? SIR FELIX WILDE, Baronet [1660], of East Malling, co. Kent, s. and h. by 2d wife, aged 7 in 1661, having already been admitted to the Inner Temple (as the son of a Bencher), Nov. 1657; *suc. to the Baronetcy*, 23 Nov. 1679. He *m.* firstly, 23 Feb. 1674/5, at St. Andrew's, Holborn (Lic. Vic. Gen., each aged about 20), Eleanor, da. of Sir Thomas TWISDEN, 1st Baronet [1666], of Bradbourn, co. Kent, by Jane, sister of Matthew TOMLINSON, the Regicide. He *m.* secondly (Lic. Vic. Gen., 10 April 1690), Mary (then about 26, spinster), da. of Sir Thomas STYLE, 2d Baronet [1627], of Wateringbury, co. Kent, by his 1st wife, Elizabeth, da. of Sir William AIRMYNE, 1st Baronet [1619]. He was living 3 Nov. 1721(b), but *d.*, probably soon afterwards, s.p.m., when the *Baronetcy* became *extinct*.

ASHE:

cr. 19 Sep. 1660;

ex. 8 Nov. 1733.

I. 1660. "JOSEPH ASHE, of Tittenham [*i.e.*, Twickenham], co. Middlesex, Esq.," 3d s. of James ASHE, of Westcombe in Batcombe, co. Somerset, by Grace, da. of Richard PITT, of Melcombe Regis, Dorset, was *b.* 1618, and was, "in consideration of the services he had rendered to the Crown,"(c) *cr. a Baronet*, 19 Sep. 1660. He was M.P. for Heytesbury, 1661 till void in May; for Downton (four Parls.) Dec. 1670 to 1681. He *m.* in or before 1658, Mary, da. of Robert WILSON, of London, merchant (who fined for Alderman), by Katharine, da. of Richard RUDD, Merchant of London. He *d.* 15 and was *bur.* 21 April 1686, at Twickenham, in his 69th year. M.I. Will dat. 17 March 1685, pr. 21 April 1686. His widow *d.* 27 Nov. and was *bur.* there 8 Dec. 1705. Will dat. 19 Oct. 1702, pr. 4 Jan. 1705/6.

II. 1686, to 1733. SIR JAMES ASHE, Baronet [1660], of Twickenham aforesaid, only s. and h., *bap.* there 27 July 1674; *suc. to the Baronetcy*, 15 April 1686; was M.P. for Downton, 1701-02 and 1702-05; Sheriff of Wilts, 1706-07. He *m.* in 1698, Catharine, da. and co-heir of Sir Edmund BOWYER, of Camberwell, Surrey, by his 2d wife, Martha (relict of Sir Edward CROPLEY), 3d da. of Robert WILSON. She, who had been separated from him for many years, *d.* (of St. Anthony's fire) May and was *bur.* 5 June 1717 at Camberwell. Admon. 1 June 1719, to her sister, Frances BOWYER, spinster. He *d.* s.p.m.s., 8 Nov. 1733, in his 60th year, and was *bur.* at Halstead, co. Kent, when the *Baronetcy* became *extinct*. M.I. Admon. 22 Nov. 1733 to his da., Martha,(d) wife of Joseph WINDHAM.

(a) There is also at the Temple church an inscription to "George Wylde of the Inner Temple, Esq., ob. 31 July 1679, aged 81 years," who possibly was his eldest brother. At St. Barth. the Great is one to Gilbert Wyld, his 3d son (by "Dame Frances, his wife"), who died 23 Nov. 1671.

(b) On that date he settled his estates on his only surv. child, Margaret, then wife of John Cockman, M.D. She, who was *bur.* 11 Nov. 1723 at Maidstone, had an only child, Eleanor, who *m.*, 23 June 1735, Nicholas Toke, of Godenton, co. Kent. Eleanor, the yst. da., was *bur.* 19 March 1709, at West Malling.

(c) Burke's *Extinct Baronetage*.

(d) She (who *m.* in 1715) was his only surviving child (out of six) and sole heir. Her husband who was one of the Gentlemen of the Privy Chamber, took the name of Ashe after that of Windham, and enlarged the house at Twickenham, which, in 1751, was sold to Richard Owen Cambridge, and from him called Cambridge House. Anne, their granddaughter, *m.* 22 March 1779, Sir William Smyth, 7th Baronet [1661], of Hill Hall, Essex.

HOWE, *or* HOW:

cr. 22 Sep. 1660;

afterwards 1730-99, VISCOUNTS HOWE [I.];

and sometime, 1788-99, EARL HOWE.

I. 1660. "JOHN HOW, of [Little] Compton [in Withington], co. Gloucester, Esq.," and also of Wishford, Wilts, s. and h. of John How, *or* HOWE, of Huntspill, Somerset, by Jane, sister and heir of Sir Richard GRUBHAM, of Wishford and Little Compton aforesaid, da. of Nicholas GRUBHAM, of Bishop's Lydiard, Somerset, was, conceivably, the "John Howe, Gent.," admitted to Lincoln's Inn, 13 Aug. 1638; was Sheriff of Gloucestershire, 1650-51; M.P. for that County, 1654-55, and 1656-58, and was *cr. a Baronet*, 22 Sep. 1660. He *m.* 23 July 1620, Bridget, da. of Thomas RICH, of North Cerney, co. Gloucester, a Master of the Court of Chancery, by Anne, da. and coheir of Thomas BOURCHIER, of Barnsley in that county. She *d.* 15 June 1642, aged 46, and was *bur.* at Withington. M.I. He was living 13 Oct. 1661,(a) but *d.* before May 1675.

II. 1670? SIR RICHARD GRUBHAM HOWE, Baronet [1660], of Wishford and Little Compton aforesaid, 1st s. and h., *b.* 28 Aug. 1621; matric at Oxford (Hart Hall), 27 March 1640, aged 18; admitted to Lincoln's Inn, 24 Feb. 1640/1; was M.P. for Wilts, 1656-58; for Wilton, 1659 and 1660; for Wilts (again), May 1675 to 1681 (four Parls.), and 1690-95, having *suc. to the Baronetcy* before May 1675, and having been (as "Knight," but *query* if not "Baronet") Sheriff of Wilts, 1668-69. He *m.* firstly v.p., probably before 1642, Lucy, 2d da. of Sir John ST. JOHN, 1st Baronet [1611], of Lydiard Tregoz, Wilts, by his 1st wife, Anne, da. of Sir Thomas LEIGHTON. She *d.* s.p. He *m.* secondly, shortly before 1651, Anne, widow of John DUTTON, of Sherborne, Dorset (who *d.* 14 Jan. 1646/7), 4th da. of John KING, Bishop of London [1611-21], by Joan, da. of Henry FREEMAN, of co. Stafford. His will pr. Aug. 1703.

III. 1703? SIR RICHARD GRUBHAM HOWE, Baronet [1660], of Wishford and Compton aforesaid, only s. and h., by 2d wife; *b.* about 1651; matric. at Oxford (Ch. Ch.), 13 July 1667, aged 16; was M.P. for Hindon, 1678-81; for Tamworth, 1685-87; for Cirencester, 1690-98; and for Wilts, 1700-27, sitting in thirteen Parls. He *suc. to the Baronetcy*, in or before 1703. He *m.* 12 Aug. 1673, at Westm. Abbey (Lic. Vic. Gen.), Mary [*not* Elizabeth], then aged 18, sister of Thomas, 1st VISCOUNT WEYMOUTH, 1st da. of Sir Henry Frederick THYNNE, 1st Baronet [1641], by Mary, da. of Thomas (COVENTRY), 1st BARON COVENTRY OF AYLESBOROUGH. He *d.* s.p., 3 July 1730. Will dat. 3 June 1728/9, pr. 11 July 1730. His widow *d.* 5 Sep. 1735, and was *bur.* at Wishford. Her will dat. 3 April 1732 to 19 Jan. 1732/3, pr. 22 Nov. 1735.

IV. 1730. EMANUEL SCROPE (HOWE), 2d VISCOUNT HOWE and BARON OF CLENAWLY [I.], and 4th Baronet [E. 1660], cousin and h. male, being 1st surv. s. and h. of Scrope (HOWE), 1st s. and h. of John Grubham HOWE, of Langar, Notts (*b.* 25 Jan. 1624) the 2d son of the 1st Baronet. He was *b.* about 1700; *suc. to the Peerage* [I.] on the death of his father, 26 Jan. 1712/3, and *suc. to the Baronetcy* on the death of his cousin, 3 July 1730. He *d.* 29 March 1735.

V. 1735. GEORGE AUGUSTUS (HOWE), 3d VISCOUNT HOWE, etc. [I.], and 5th Baronet [E. 1660], 1st surv. s. and h., *b.* about 1724; *d.* unm. 6 July 1758.

VI. 1758. RICHARD (HOWE), 4th VISCOUNT HOWE, etc. [I.], and 6th Baronet [E. 1660], br. and h.; *b.* 19 March 1725/6. He was the celebrated "Admiral Howe," whose victory, 1 June 1794, over the French Navy, occurring at a time of great depression, was so highly appreciated. He had, however, before that victory, been *cr.* VISCOUNT HOWE OF LANGAR, Notts, 20 April 1782, and BARON HOWE OF LANGAR, Notts, and EARL HOWE, 19 April 1788, with a spec. rem. of the said

See fuller particulars in Peerage.

(a) *Wilts Notes and Queries*, vol. ii, p. 175.

Barony; K.G., 2 June 1797. He *d.* s.p.m., 5 Aug. 1797, aged 73, when the *Earldom* and *Viscountcy* became *extinct*.(a)

VII. 1799, to 1814. WILLIAM (HOWE), 5th VISCOUNT HOWE, etc. [I.], and 7th Baronet [E. 1660], br. and h. male; *b.* 10 Aug. 1729; was a General in the Army. He *d.* s.p., 12 July 1814, in his 85th year, when *all his honours* became *extinct*. (See fuller particulars in *Peerage*.)

SWINBURNE:

cr. 26 Sep. 1660.

I. 1660. "JOHN SWINBURNE, of Chap Heton [*i.e.*, Capheaton], co. Northumberland, Esq.," s. and h. of John SWINBURNE, of the same (said to have had the promise of a Baronetcy from Charles I.), by his 2d wife, Isabella, da. of Sir Thomas TEMPEST, 2d Baronet [1622], of Stella, suc. his father, Feb. 1652, and was *cr. a Baronet*, 26 Sep. 1660. He pulled down the old Castle of Capheaton and built a stately mansion on its site. He *m.* Isabel, da. and h. of Henry LAWSON, of Brough, co. York, by Catherine, da. and coh. of Sir William FENWICK, of Meldon, co. Northumberland. By her he had twenty-four children. He *d.* 19 June 1706.

II. 1706. SIR WILLIAM SWINBURNE, Baronet [1660], of Capheaton aforesaid, 2d but 1st surv. s. and h., *suc. to the Baronetcy*, 19 June 1706. He *m.*, in 1697, Mary, da. of Anthony ENGLEFIELD, of White Knights, near Reading, Berks, by Alice, da. of Thomas STOKES, of London. He *d.* 17 April 1716.

III. 1716. SIR JOHN SWINBURNE, Baronet [1660], of Capheaton aforesaid, s. and h., *b.* 8 July 1698; *suc. to the Baronetcy*, 17 April 1716. He *m.* 1721, Mary, only da. and eventually h. of Edward BEDINGFELD, Barrister (yr. s. of Sir Henry BEDINGFELD, 1st Baronet [1661]), by Mary, sister of Sir Clement FISHER, 3d Baronet [1622], da. of Thomas FISHER. He *d.* 8 Jan 1744/5, in his 47th year, at Bath. M.I. at Bath Abbey. His widow *d.* 7 Feb. 1761.

IV. 1745. SIR JOHN SWINBURNE, Baronet [1660], of Capheaton aforesaid, 2d but 1st surv. s. and h., *b.* 2 July 1724;(b) *suc. to the Baronetcy*, 8 Jan. 1744/5. He d. unm., 1 Feb. 1763, at Paris, and was *bur.* there.

V. 1763. SIR EDWARD SWINBURNE, Baronet [1660], of Capheaton aforesaid, br. and h., *b.* 24 Jan. 1733; *suc. to the Baronetcy*, 1 Feb. 1763. He *m.*, 1761, Christiana, only child of Robert DILLON, by Martha, his 1st wife, da. of William NEWLAND. She *d.* 13 Aug. 1768, and was *bur.* at Newcastle. He d. 2 Nov. 1786.

VI. 1786. SIR JOHN EDWARD SWINBURNE, Baronet [1660], of Capheaton aforesaid, 1st s. and h., *b.* 6 March 1762, at Bordeaux in France; *suc. to the Baronetcy*, 2 Nov. 1786; M.P. for Launceston, 1788-90; Sheriff of Northumberland, 1799; F.R.S. and F.S.A. He *m.*, 12 July 1787, Emilie Elizabeth, da. of Richard Henry Alexander BENNETT, of Beckenham, co. Kent, by Elizabeth Amelia, da. of Peter BURRELL, of Beckenham aforesaid. She *d.* 28 March 1839, aged 72. Admon. Dec. 1841. He *d.* 26 Sep. 1860, aged 98, at Capheaton.

(a) Sophia Charlotte, his 1st da. and coheir, inherited, on his death, the Barony of Howe of Langar, and by her husband, the Hon. Penn Assheton Curzon was mother of Richard William Curzon, created, 15 July 1821, Earl Howe, who, on her death, 3 Dec. 1835, inherited the abovenamed Barony.

(b) As he appears to have become a Baronet in Jan. 1744/5, he apparently is not "John Swinburn, of Newcastle-upon-Tyne, Esq.," who was admitted to Lincoln's Inn, 24 Feb. 1744/5, a month *after* that date.

VII. 1860. SIR JOHN SWINBURNE, Baronet [1660], of Capheaton aforesaid, grandson and h., being 1st. s. and h. of Edward SWINBURNE,(a) of Calgarth, near Windermere, by his 1st wife Anna Antonia, da. of Robert Nassau SUTTON, which Edward was s. and h. ap. of the late Baronet, but *d.* v.p., 14 Nov. 1855, aged 67. He was *b.* 1831; was in the Royal Navy, serving in the Burmese War in 1852, the China War, and in the Baltic, 1854; Lieut., 1854; Commander, 1865, retiring 1871; retired Captain in 1880, having *suc. to the Baronetcy*, 26 Sep. 1860; Sheriff of Northumberland, 1866; M.P. for Lichfield Division of Staffordshire, 1885-92. He *m.* firstly, Jan. 1863, at St. George's, Hanover Square, Emily Elizabeth, only da. and eventually h. of Rear Admiral Henry BROADHEAD, by Mary Anne, da. of George Bernard EGAN, of Stanmore, Herts. She *d.* 23 July 1881. He *m.* secondly, 10 Sep. 1895, at St. James's, Westm., Mary Eleanor, da. and h. of JOHN CORBETT. She *d.* s.p., 16 May 1900, at Capheaton.

Family Estates.—These, in 1883, consisted of 28,902 acres in Northumberland, worth £13,131 a year. *Seat.*—Capheaton, near Newcastle, co. Northumberland.

TROTT, *or* TROT:

cr. 12 Oct. 1660;

ex. 14 July 1672.

I. 1660, to 1672. "JHON [*i.e.*, JOHN] TROT [*or* TROTT], of Laverstoke, co. Southampton, Esq.," s. of John TROTT, of St. Peter-le-Poor, London, merchant, by Katharine, da. of Daniel HILLS, of London, was aged 19 in 1634 (when his father entered his pedigree in the Visitation of London); was Sheriff of Hampshire, 1651-52, and was *cr. a Baronet*, 12 Oct. 1660; was M.P. for Andover, 1660 and 1661 till his death. He *m.*, 6 Feb. 1637/8 (Lic. London, 5, she aged 16), at St. Olave's, Old Jury, London, Elizabeth, da. and coheir of Sir Edmund WRIGHT, sometime (1640-41) Lord Mayor of London, by his 1st wife, Martha, da. of Edward BARON, of London. He *d.* s.p.m.,(b) 14 July 1672, when the *Baronetcy* became *extinct*. Will pr. 1672. His widow *m.* (Lic. Fac., 5 July 1682), as his 1st wife, the Hon. (afterwards LORD) JAMES RUSSELL (then aged 34), of Maidwell, co. Northampton, 6th s. of William, 1st DUKE OF BEDFORD (so *cr.* 1694), which James *d.*, s.p.m., 22 June 1712. She *d.* before Aug. 1698.

MILLER:

cr. 13 Oct. 1660;

ex. 1714.

I 1660. "HUMPHREY MILLER, of Oxenheath [*i.e.*, Oxenhoath in West Peckham], co. Kent, Esq.," s. and h. of Sir Nicholas MILLER, of the same, by Anne, da. of William STYLE, of Langley in Beckenham, co. Kent, was admitted to Inner Temple, Nov. 1654; suc. his father (who *d.* aged 66), 20 Feb. 1658; and was *cr. a Baronet*, 13 Oct. 1660. He was Sheriff of Kent 1665-66. He *m.* firstly, 1 March 1663/4, at Medmenham, Bucks (Lic. Fac. 15 Feb., he 28, and she 18), Mary, sister and coheir of Sir John BORLASE, 2d Baronet [1642], 1st da. of Sir John BORLASE, 1st Baronet, by Alice, da. of Sir John BANKS, Lord Chief Justice of the Common Pleas. He *m.* secondly, Frances, da. of [—] PILKINGTON, of co. Warwick. He *d.* Aug. 1709. Will pr. March 1712.

(a) This Edward was elder br. of Admiral Charles Henry Swinburne (*d.* 4 March 1877, in his 80th year), the father of Algernon Charles Swinburne, *b.* 5 April 1837, the well known Poet.

(b) Catherine, his only surv. child and h., *m.*, as his 1st wife, Sir Hugh Stewkeley, 2d Baronet [1627], of Hinton, co. Southampton, and *d.* before May 1679. Of two sons, who *d.* v.p. and unm., John and Edmund, both matric. at Oxford (Oriel Coll.), 7 Dec. 1660, one aged 18 and the other 17; both also entered the Inner Temple, London, one in 1661, and the other in 1664.

II. 1709, to 1714. SIR BORLASE MILLER, Baronet [1660], of Oxenhoath aforesaid, s. and h. by 1st wife; *suc. to the Baronetcy*, Aug. 1709. He *m.* in 1714, Susanna (£10,000 portion), da. of Thomas MEDLEY, of Buxted, co. Sussex. He *d.* shortly afterwards, s.p., 1714, when the *Baronetcy* became *extinct*.(a) Admon. 15 Dec. 1714 to the widow. She *d.* 2 March 1753, in Argyll buildings, aged 80. Will pr. 1753.

LEWIS, *or* LEWES:

cr. 15 Oct. 1660;

ex. 14 Aug. 1671.

I. 1660, to 1671. "SIR JOHN LEWES [*i.e.*, LEWIS], of Ledston, co. York, Knt.," 2d but 1st surv. s. and h. of Richard LEWIS, of Selston, Notts, by Jane, 1st da. and coheir of Gervase BRINSLEY, of Brinsley in that county, was *b.* about 1615; acquired a large fortune by trading in India and Persia, wherewith he bought the estate of Ledstone; was *Knighted* at the Hague, 1660, and was *cr. a Baronet*, 15 Oct. 1660. He was aged 50 at the Heralds' Visitation of Yorkshire, 13 Sep. 1665. He *m.* in or before 1644, Sarah, 2d da. and coheir of Sir Thomas FOOTE, Baronet [so *cr.* 1660], sometime (1649-50) Lord Mayor of London, by Elizabeth, da. of William MOTT, of Plaistow, co. Essex. He *d.* s.p.m.s.,(b) 14 Aug. 1671, and was *bur.* at Ledston, when the *Baronetcy* became *extinct*. Will dat. 21 June 1670 to 1 Aug. 1671, pr. 1 Dec. 1671, and pr. in Ireland 1678. His widow *m.* Denzil ONSLOW, of Pirford, Surrey, one of the Commissioners of the Navy, 1706-21, who *d.* s.p. 1721.

FRANCKLYN, *or* FRANKLIN:

cr. 16 Oct. 1660;

ex. 5 Oct. 1728.

I. 1660. "SIR RICHARD FRANKLIN, of Moore Park [in Rickmansworth], co. Hertford, Knt.," 1st s. and h. of Sir John FRANKLIN, *or* FRANCKLIN, of Willesden, Middlesex, sometime M.P. for that county (who *d.* 24 March 1647, aged 48), by Elizabeth, da. of George PUREFOY, of Wadley, Berks, was *bap.* 20 July 1630, at Willesden; admitted to Gray's Inn, 23 June 1648; matric. at Oxford (Balliol Coll.), 19 March 1648/9; purchased the Moore Park estate in May 1652 (which he subsequently sold in July 1663); was *Knighted*, 14 July 1660, at Whitehall, and was, three months later, *cr. a Baronet*, 16 Oct. 1660; was M.P. for Herts, 1661-79. He *m.* firstly, in or before 1655, Elizabeth, da. and coheir of Sir Thomas CHEEKE, of Pirgo, Essex, by his 2d wife, Essex, da. of Robert (RICH), 1st EARL OF WARWICK. She was *bur.* 21 Nov. 1660, at Willesden aforesaid. He *m.* secondly, 30 April 1661, at St. James's, Clerkenwell (Lic. Vic. Gen., 20), Mary (then aged 18), da. of Sir Samuel TRYON, 1st Baronet [1620], by his 1st wife, Eleanor, da. of Sir Henry LEE, of Quarendon, Bucks. He *d.* at St. Martin's-in-the-Fields, and was *bur.* 16 Sep. 1685, at Willesden, aged 55. Admon. 22 May 1686. His widow *d.* s.p.m. Her will pr. Aug. 1703.

II. 1685. SIR RICHARD FRANKLIN, *or* FRANCKLYN, Baronet [1660], 1st s. and h. by 1st wife, *b.* about 1655; matric. at Oxford (Ch. Ch.), 19 July 1672, aged 17; admitted to Gray's Inn, 17 Nov. 1671; *suc. to the Baronetcy*, Sep. 1685. He *m.* Anne, widow of Thomas BARRINGTON (who *d.* v.p. 31 Jan. 1681/2, aged 38), da. and coheir of Robert (RICH), 3d EARL OF WARWICK, by his 2d wife, Anne, da. of Sir Thomas CHEEKE, of Pirgo, Essex. He *d.* s.p.m., 1695.

(a) The estate of Oxenhoath devolved on his nephew Philip Bartholomew, whose da., Mary, *m.* Admiral Sir Francis Geary, Baronet [so *cr.* 1782], whose son, afterwards the 2d Baronet, inherited the same, 26 April 1757.

(b) Of his two daughters and coheirs (1), Elizabeth, aged 11 in 1665, *m.* Theophilus (Hastings), 7th Earl of Huntingdon, and (2), Mary, aged 7 in 1665, *m.* Robert (Leke), 3d Earl of Scarsdale.

III. 1695, to 1728. SIR THOMAS FRANKLIN, *or* FRANCKLYN, Baronet [1660], of Dean, co. Middlesex, br. of the whole blood and h. male; *b.* about 1656; admitted to Gray's Inn, 26 May 1677, having been two years of Staple Inn; *suc. to the Baronetcy* in 1695. He *m.* Mary, widow of Christopher CLITHEROW, of Pinner, Middx., da. of Ralph HAWTREY, of Riselip in that county, by Barbara, da. of Sir Robert DE GREY, of Merton, co. Norfolk. He *d.* s.p., 5 Oct. 1728, aged 72, when the *Baronetcy* became *extinct*. Will pr. 1728. His widow *d.* 19 March 1736/7. Will pr. 1737.

BEALE:

cr. 19 Oct. 1660;

ex. 3 Oct. 1684.

I. 1660, to 1684. "JOHN BEALE, of Maidstone, co. Kent, Esq.," s. of John BEALE, of the same, Merchant, of London (living 1633), by Anne, da. of Allan DUCKET, was *b.* about 1621, and was *cr. a Baronet*, 19 Oct. 1660. Sheriff of Kent, 1664-65, being then of Farningham Court in that county. He *m.* firstly, in 1655, Anne, da. of Sir William COLEPEPER, 1st Baronet [1627], of Prestonhall in Aylesford, by Helen, da. of Sir Richard SPENCER. She *d.* s.p. 1657. He *m.* secondly (Lic. Fac. 9 May 1662), Jane (then 17), da. of Richard DUKE, of Maidstone. He *d.* s.p.m., 3 Oct. 1684, when the *Baronetcy* became *extinct*. Will pr. 1684.

RUSSELL:

cr. 8 Nov. 1660;

ex. about 1714.

I. 1660, to 1714? "WILLIAM RUSSELL, of Langhorn [*i.e.*, Laugharne], co. Carmarthen, Esq.," 9th and yst. s. of Sir William RUSSELL, 1st Baronet [1629], of Chippenham, co. Cambridge, being 2d s. by his 3d wife, Elizabeth, da. and coheir of Michael SMALLPAGE, of Chichester, was *cr. a Baronet*, 8 Nov. 1660. He was usually called "the white Sir William."(a) He *m.* Hester, da. of Sir Thomas ROUSE, 1st Baronet [1641], of Rouse Lench, co. Worcester, by his 1st wife, Jane, da. of Sir John FERRERS. He *d.* s.p.m.. in or shortly before 1714. Will pr. Jan. 1713/4. His widow *d.* at Poston Court, in Vowchurch, co. Hereford. Admon. 3 Sep. 1717 to her da. Mary, wife of Lord Arthur SOMERSET.

BOOTHBY:

cr. 9 Nov. 1660;

ex. 6 Dec. 1669.

I. 1660. "THOMAS BOOTHBY, of Friday Hill, in the parish of Chingford, co. Essex, Esq.," 1st s. and h. of Robert BOOTHBY, of the same, by Mary (*m.* Aug. 1621), da. and h. of George HYER, of Weston, in Sheer and Albury, co. Surrey, was *b.* probably about 1622; suc. his father (who was *bap.* at St. Antholin's, London, 22 Dec. 1591), in Dec. 1641, and was *cr. a Baronet*, 9 Nov. 1660. He *m.* in or before 1645, Elizabeth, da. of (—) STYLES, of Westerham, co. Kent. He was *bur.* 20 Aug. 1661, at St. Antholin's aforesaid. Will dat. 4 June, and pr. 27 Aug. 1664. The will of his widow, in which she directs her burial to be at Chingford, dat. 23 Feb., and pr. 6 May 1674.

(a) To distinguish him from his elder brother of the half blood, called "the black Sir William" (*b.* 1617), who was of Bury St. Edmunds, being, for his loyalty, styled "the cream of the Russells," and who *d.* s.p., before 18 May 1663, when admon. was granted to his widow, Anne.

II. 1661, to 1669. SIR THOMAS BOOTHBY, Baronet [1660], of Friday Hill aforesaid, only s. and h., b. about 1645; *suc. to the Baronetcy* in Aug. 1661. He *d.* unm.,(a) 1 Dec. 1669, aged 24, and was *bur.* at Chingford, when the *Baronetcy* became *extinct*.

BACKHOUSE:
cr. 9 Nov. 1660;
ex. 22 Aug. 1669.

I. 1660, to 1669. "WILLIAM BACKHOUSE, Esq., grandchild to Rowland BACKHOUSE, late Alderman of London," being only s. and h. of Nicholas BACKHOUSE, of London, by Christian, da. of William WILLIAMS, of London, merchant, which Nicholas (who *d.* 1650), was s. and h. of Rowland BACKHOUSE abovenamed (who *d.* 1648, aged 93), was *b.* about 1641, and was, when aged about 19, *cr. a Baronet*, 9 Nov. 1660. He was aged 23 at the Heralds' Visitation of Berks, 2 Feb. 1664, and was Sheriff of Berks, 1664-65, being then of Swallowfield in that county. He *m.* 23 Nov. 1662, at St. Andrew's, Holborn (Lic. Vic. Gen., 12), Flower, widow of William BISHOP, of South Wanborough, Hants, da. and (after Sep. 1660) h. of Sir John BACKHOUSE, K.B., of Swallowfield aforesaid (who *d.* 2 Oct. 1649, aged 65), by Flower, da. of Benjamin HENSHAW, of London. He *d.* s.p. 22 Aug. 1669, aged 28, and was *bur.* at Swallowfield, when the *Baronetcy* became *extinct*. Funeral certificate in Coll. of Arms. Admon. 14 Oct. 1669. His widow *m.* (as his 2d wife), before 1676, Henry (HYDE), 2d EARL OF CLARENDON, who *d.* 31 Oct. 1709, aged 71. She *d.* 17 July 1700.

CUTLER:
cr 12 Nov. 1660;
ex. 15 April 1693.

I. 1660, to 1693. "SIR JOHN CUTLER, of the city of London, Knt.," s. of Thomas CUTLER, Citizen and Grocer of London, was *b.* about 1608; was Free of the Grocers' Company and a Merchant of London; *Knighted*, 17 June 1660, at the Lord Mayor's house, and was *cr. a Baronet*, 12 Nov. 1660. He, who was fined both for Sheriff and Alderman of London, was Sheriff of Kent, 1675-76; M.P. for Taunton, 1679 till void in Dec. 1680, and for Bodmin (two Parls.) till death. He purchased an estate at Wimpole, co. Cambridge; was F.R.S., etc. He *m.* firstly (in or before 1648) Elizabeth, da. and coheir of Sir Thomas FOOTE, Baronet [so *cr.* 1660], sometime (1649-50) Lord Mayor of London, by Elizabeth, da. of William MOTT, of Plaistow, co. Essex. She, who was *bap.* 9 Jan. 1626/7, at St. Benet's, Gracechurch, was *bur.* there 28 May 1650. He *m.* secondly (Lic. Fac. 26 July 1669, he a widower, she about 30, spinster), Elisha, *or* Elicia, da. of Sir Thomas TIPPING, of Wheatfield, Oxon. She was *bur.* 10 May 1685 at St. Margaret's, Westm. He *d.* s.p.m.s.(b) 15, and was *bur.* there 28 April 1693, aged 85, worth £300,000, or £600,000,(c) when the *Baronetcy* became *extinct*. Will dat. 27 June 1690, pr. 29 April 1693.

(a) His only sister and heir, Elizabeth, *m.* twice, and had issue, but the estate of Friday hill passed to Robert Boothby (nephew of the 1st Baronet), who *d.* 1 Dec. 1733, aged 73, and whose grandson, Robert Boothby, died possessed of it 11 Oct. 1774.

(b) Of his two daughters and coheirs (1), Elizabeth, *m.* before 4 June 1689, Charles Bodvile (Robartes), 2d Earl of Radnor, and *d.* s.p. 13 Jan. 1696/7; (2) (—), *m.*, as his 1st wife, Sir William Portman, 6th Baronet [1611], who *d.* s.p. 1690.

(c) Luttrell's diary, where both sums are given. It is there stated that his estates in Yorkshire, Cambridgeshire and elsewhere go, to the amount of £6,000 a year, to the Countess of Radnor and her issue, with rem. to his nephew, Mr. Boulter, a grocer, who accordingly inherited them in Jan. 1696/7, and *d.* s.p. Feb. 1708/9, "worth £150,000."

MOTTET:
cr. 16 Nov. 1660;
ex. or *dormant* probably soon afterwards.

I. 1660. "GILES MOTTET, of Leige [*i.e.*, Liege, in Flanders]. Esq.," was *cr. a Baronet*, as above, 16 Nov. 1660, but of him and his issue (if he had any) nothing more is known.

GIFFORD:
cr. 21 Nov. 1660;
ex. 6 June 1736

I. 1660. "HENRY GIFFORD, of Burstall. co. Leicester, Esq.," 1st s. and h. of Thomas GIFFORD, of the same, by Anne, d. and h. of Gregory BROOKSBY; was *cr. a Baronet*, as above, 21 Nov. 1660. He *m.* (settl. 18 May 1654), Mary, da. of Baynham VAUGHAN, of Ruerden, co. Gloucester. He *d.* in 1664, or 1665. Will dat. 22 June 1664, pr. 3 April 1665.

II. 1665? to 1736. SIR JOHN GIFFORD, Baronet [1660], of Burstall aforesaid, only s. and h.; under age, 1664; *suc. to the Baronetcy* about 1665. He was a Roman Catholic, and was living in France, 1695. He *m.* Frances, da. of [—]. He *d.* s.p., probably unm., in Golden square, Midx., 6 June 1736, when the *Baronetcy* became *extinct*. Will dat. 28 Aug. 1734, pr. 18 June 1737 by Dame Frances GIFFORD, the widow.

FOOTE:
cr. 21 Nov. 1660;
ex 12 Oct. 1688,
though the precedency thereof was granted
to a creation of ONSLOW,
8 May 1674.

I. 1660, to 1688. "SIR THOMAS FOOTE, Knt., Citizen of London," s. of John FOOTE, of Royston, co. Cambridge, by Margaret, da. of (—) BROOKE, of London, was *b.* about 1572; Free of the Company of Grocers, London; Sheriff of London, 1645-46; Alderman of Broad street, 16 May 1643, and of Coleman street, 1648 till displaced, 2 Aug. 1660; Lord Mayor, 1649-50; M.P. for London, 1654-55, and 1656-58; was *Knighted*, by the Protector Cromwell, 5 Dec. 1657; Member of the Council of State, 1 Jan. to 1 April 1660, and having, presumably, been again *Knighted* by the King, was *cr. a Baronet*, as above, 21 Nov. 1660. On 8 May 1674, his son-in-law, ARTHUR ONSLOW, then "of West Clandon, co. Surrey, Esq.," obtained the reversion of a Baronetcy on his death, with a clause granting the precedency of this creation. He *m.* 20 Dec. 1625, at St. Benet's, Gracechurch, Elizabeth BODDICOTT, of Stepney, widow, da. of William MOTT, of London, and of Plaistow, co. Essex. She *d.* 10 and was *bur.* 31 Oct. 1666, at West Ham, co. Essex. M.I. He *d.* s.p.m., 12 Oct. 1688, aged 96, and was *bur.* there, when the *Baronetcy* of 1660 became *extinct*, but the one conferred in 1674 on Arthur ONSLOW took effect. M.I. Will dat. 26 Oct. 1680, pr. 17 Nov. 1688.

MAINWARING:
cr. 22 Nov. 1660;
ex 6 April 1797.

I. 1660. "THOMAS MAINWARING, of Over Pever, co. Chester, Esq.," 3d but 1st surv. s. and h. of Philip MAINWARING, of the same, by Ellen (*m.* 1622), da. of Edward MINSHULL, of Stoke, near Nantwich; was

S

b. 7 April 1623; matric. at Oxford (Bras. Coll.), 28 April 1637, aged 13; admitted to Gray's Inn (with his elder br. Randolph), 15 Feb. 1637/8; suc. his father 10 Dec. 1647; was Sheriff of Cheshire, 1657; M.P. for that county, 1660, and was *cr. a Baronet*, 22 Nov. 1660. He *m.*, 26 May 1642, Mary, da. of Sir Henry DELVES, 2d Baronet [1621], of Dodington, co. Chester, by his 1st wife, Catherine, da. and coheir of Sir Roger WILBRAHAM. She *d.* at Baddiley, 1 March 1670, and he *d.* 28 June 1689, aged 66, both being *bur.* at Over Peover. M.I.

II. 1689. SIR JOHN MAINWARING, Baronet [1660], of Over Peover aforesaid, 4th but 1st surv. s. and h.; *b.* 8 May 1656; matric. at Oxford (Bras. Coll.), 2 June 1671, aged 15; *suc. to the Baronetcy*, 28 June 1689; was M.P. for Cheshire (six Parls.), 1689, till death in 1702; Captain of Light Horse. He *m.*, 28 Sep. 1676, Elizabeth, 1st da. of Col. Roger WHITLEY, of Peel, co. Chester. He *d.* 4 Nov. 1702, aged 46, and was *bur.* at Over Peover. His widow *d.* 7 Nov. 1719, and was *bur.* there.

III. 1702. SIR THOMAS MAINWARING, Baronet [1660], of Baddiley and Over Peover aforesaid, 1st surv. s. and h., *b.* at Peel, 7 Aug. 1681; matric. at Oxford (Bras. Coll.), 29 Nov. 1697, aged 16; *suc. to the Baronetcy*, 4 Nov. 1702, and sold the estate of Over Peover to his brother Henry. He *m.* 20 March 1724/5, Martha, 1st da. and coheir of William LLOYD, of Halghton, co. Flint. He *d.* s.p., 21 Sep. 1726, aged 45, and was *bur.* at Baddiley. His widow *m.* Edward MAINWARING, of Whitmore.

IV. 1726, to 1797. SIR HENRY MAINWARING, Baronet [1660], of Over Peover aforesaid, nephew and h., being posthumous s. and h. of Henry MAINWARING, of the same, by Diana, da. of William BLACKETT, of Newby, co. York, which Henry (who *d.* 1 July 1726, aged 39) was yst. br. of the late Baronet. He was *b.* 7 and *bap.* 20 Nov. 1726, and *suc. to the Baronetcy* at his birth; matric. at Oxford (Corpus Ch. Coll.), 28 Feb. 1743/4, aged 17; *cr.* M.A., 23 May 1747; Sheriff of Cheshire, 1772-73. He *d.* unm. 6 April 1797, aged 70, when the *Baronetcy* became *extinct*. His will pr. July 1797.(a)

BENNET:
cr. 22 Nov. 1660;
ex. 23 May 1701.

I. 1660. "THOMAS BENNET, of Baberham [*i.e.*, Babraham], co. Cambridge, Esq.," 2d s. of Thomas BENNET, Alderman(b) and sometime [1613-14] Sheriff of London (who purchased the Babraham estate, and *d.* 19 April 1620), by Dorothy, da. of Richard MAY, of London, and of Rawmers, Sussex, was *b.* about 1597; admitted (with his elder br. Richard) Nov. 1615 to the Inner Temple, and was *cr. a Baronet*, as above, 22 Nov. 1660. He *m.*, about 1630, Mary, da. and coheir of Levinus MONKE, one of the Clerks to the Signet. He was *bur.* 30 June 1667, at Babraham, aged 70. Will pr. 1667. His widow was *bur.* there 20 May 1684. Will pr. 1684.

II. 1667. SIR LEVINUS BENNET, Baronet [1660], of Babraham aforesaid, s. and h., *b.* about 1631; admitted to Gray's Inn, 3 Feb. 1643/4; was Sheriff of Cambridgeshire, 1652-53; *suc. to the Baronetcy* in June 1667; was M.P. for Cambridgeshire (five Parls.), 1679 till death; was aged 53 at the Heralds' Visitation of Cambridgeshire, 1684. He *m.* 6 July 1653, at Allhallows', London Wall, Judith, da. of William BOEVEY, of Flaxley Abbey, co.

(a) He devised his estates to his uterine brother Thomas Wetenhall (*b.* 26 Nov. 1736), who assumed the name of Mainwaring, and *d.* 4 July 1798, leaving a son Henry Mainwaring, who was *cr. a Baronet*, as of Over Peover, 26 May 1804.

(b) Alderman Thomas Bennet was yr. br. to Sir John Bennet, of Dawley in Harlington, Midx. (ancestor of the Earl of Arlington, the Barons Ossulston, and Earls of Tankerville), both being sons of Richard Bennet, br. of Sir Thomas Bennet, Lord Mayor of London, 1603-04.

Gloucester, Merchant of London, by Anne, da. of John LUCIE, of London and Antwerp, Merchant. He *d.* in London, 5 and was *bur.* 14 Dec. 1693, at Babraham. Will dat. 3 Dec. 1690, pr. Jan. 1693/4. His widow was *bur.* there 22 Jan. 1702/3. Will dat. 6 Aug. 1701, pr. 4 Feb. 1702/3.

III. 1693, to 1701. SIR RICHARD BENNET, Baronet [1660], of Babraham aforesaid, only surv. s. and h., *bap.* 15 July, 1673, at Babraham; *suc. to the Baronetcy*, 5 Dec. 1693. He *m.* 27 June 1695, at Ely Chapel, St. Andrew's, Holborn (Lic. Lond., 22), Elizabeth (then aged 16), da. of Sir Charles CÆSAR, *otherwise* ADELMARE, of Bennington, Herts, by Susanna, da. and h. of Sir Thomas BONFOY, Alderman of London. He *d.* s.p.m.,(a) of small-pox, at St. Giles'-in-the-Fields, 23, and was *bur.* 29 May 1701, at Babraham, in his 28th year, when the *Baronetcy* became *extinct*. Admon, 23 June 1701. His widow *m.*, 31 Jan. 1704, James BUTLER, of Worminghurst, Sussex, who *d.* 17, and was *bur.* there 20 May 1741, aged 61. She *d.* 1, and was *bur.* 5 July 1727, in her 48th year, at Worminghurst.

WROTH:
cr. 29 Nov. 1660;
ex. 27 June 1721.

I. 1660. "JOHN WROTH, of Blendenhall [in Bexley], co. Kent, Esq.," was apparently 1st s. and h. of Sir Peter WROTH,(b) of the same (*bur.* 13 May 1644 at Bexley), by Margaret, da. of Sir Anthony DERING, of Pluckley, co. Kent (which Peter was s. of Thomas WROTH, of Bledenhall aforesaid, Bencher of the Inner Temple, who *d.* 1610), was aged 7 in the Heralds' Visitation of London 1634, and was *cr. a Baronet*, as above, 29 Nov. 1660. He was M.P. for Bridgwater, 1659. He *m.*, in or before 1651,(c) Dame Anne HARRIS, widow of Sir Paul HARRIS, and formerly of Sir Ralph GORE, 2d Baronet [I. 1622], da. of Toby (CAULFEILD), 2d BARON CAULFEILD OF CHARLEMONT [I.], by Mary, da. of Sir John KING. He *d.* about 1664.(d) at South Petherton, Somerset. Admon. of his goods was granted to a creditor, 16 April 1672. His widow *d.* 1682. Will as of Wells, co. Somerset, directing her burial to be at Newton Placey in North Petherton, dat. 27 Sep. 1682, pr. 17 Feb. 1682/3.

II. 1664? SIR JOHN WROTH, Baronet [1660], of Bledenhall and South Petherton aforesaid, 1st surv. s. and h.; *bap.* 16 Nov. 1653, at Bexley; matric. at Oxford (St. John's Coll.), 3 Feb. 1670/1; *suc. to the Baronetcy* about 1664. He *m.* Elizabeth, da. (whose issue became sole heir) of Colonel Peregrine PALMER, of Fairfield, in Stogursey, co. Somerset, by Anne, da. of Nathaniel STEPHENS, of Gloucestershire. He *d.* about 1674.(d) No mention is made of his wife in his will, dat. 1 Oct. 1672, pr. Nov. 1677 and 31 Jan. 1677/8.

III. 1674? to 1721. SIR THOMAS WROTH, Baronet [1660], of South Petherton aforesaid, only surv. s. and h.,(e) *b.* about 1674, in which year, apparently, he *suc. to the Baronetcy*; admitted to Winchester School 1686; was M.P. for Bridgwater, 1701-08; for Somerset, 1710-13, and for Wells, 1713-15; Sheriff of Somerset, 1708-09. He *m.* Mary, da.

(a) Judith, his only child, *d.* 6 July 1713, in her 13th year, leaving her eight aunts as coheirs to an estate of about £2,000 a year.

(b) In the will of Sir Thomas Wroth of Petherton Park, Somerset, dat. 1 Feb. 1671, pr. 24 Aug. 1672, Sir John Wroth, Baronet, is called "son of Sir John [*sic*] Wroth, my brother" [Brown's *Somersetshire Wills*].

(c) "Thomas, s. of John Wroth and Lady Harris, his wife," was *bap.* 31 Oct. 1651, at Bexley.

(d) *Ex inform.* W. D. Pink.

(e) An elder brother, John, is sometimes said to have suc. as the 3d Baronet, and to have *d.* unm. shortly afterwards, but there seems no authentic record of such fact.

of Thomas OSBALDESTON, of Aldersbrook, Essex, by Cicely, da. of Sir John MORLEY, of Halnaker, Sussex. She apparently *d.* before him. He *d.* s.p.m. at Killerton, 27 June 1721, aged 46, when *the Baronetcy* became *extinct*.(a) Will without date, pr. 31 March 1722.

WYNNE, *or* WINN :

cr. 3 Dec. 1660;

afterwards, since 1 June 1833,

LORDS HEADLEY, BARONS ALLANSON AND WINN OF AGHADOE [I.].

I. 1660. "GEORGE WYNNE, of Nostell, co. York, Esq.," 1st s. and h. of Edmund WINN, of Thornton Curtis, co. Lincoln (*d.* about 1645), by Mary, da. of Rowland BERKELEY, of Worcester, was *b.* about 1607; was, with his brother Rowland WINN, Alderman of London, a liberal contributor to the Royal cause; purchased the estate of Nostell Priory, in 1655, from his said brother; was Sheriff of Lincolnshire, 1657-58; and was *cr. a Baronet*, as above, 3 Dec. 1660. He was aged 59 at the Visitation of Yorkshire, 9 April 1666. He *m.* firstly, Rachel, da. of John TURNER, of Ham, co. Surrey. She *d.* s.p. in or before 1643. He *m.* secondly, about 1643, Elizabeth, da. of Robert JEFFREYS, Alderman of London [presumably a da. of Sir Robert JEFFREYS, sometime (1685-86) Lord Mayor of London, by Priscilla, da. of Luke CROSSLEY]. By her he had five sons. He *m.* thirdly, 16 April 1654, at Thornton Curtis aforesaid, Anne, da. of Sir William PELHAM, of Brocklesby, co. Lincoln, by Frances, da. of Edward (CONWAY), 1st VISCOUNT CONWAY. He *d.* 18 July 1667, and was *bur.* at Wragby. Admon. 1 Oct. 1667. His widow was *bur.* at Wragby 18 Jan. 1701/2.

II. 1667. SIR EDMUND WINN, Baronet [1660], of Nostell and Thornton Curtis aforesaid, and of Huntwick, co. York, 1st s. and h. by his 2d wife, *b.* about 1644, being aged 22 at the Visitation of Yorkshire, 9 April 1666; *suc. to the Baronetcy*, 18 July 1667; was Sheriff of Lincolnshire, 1671-72. He *m.* firstly (Lic. Vic. Gen., 11 Dec. 1668), Elizabeth (then aged 25), sister of the above-mentioned Anne, being a yr. da. of Sir William PELHAM and Frances his wife, both abovenamed. He *m.* secondly, in or before 1674, Catharine, da. of (—). He was *bur.* at Wragby, 30 Aug. 1694. Admon. 20 Nov. 1694. His widow *bur.* there 15 Nov. 1704. Will pr. 5 Feb. 1707, at York.

III. 1694. SIR ROWLAND WINN, Baronet [1660], of Nostell, etc., 1st s. and h. by 2d wife, *bap.* 1 July 1675 at Wragby; *suc. to the Baronetcy* in Aug. 1694. He *m.* (Lic. Fac. 18 April 1702) Lætitia, 4th da. and coheir of William HARBORD, of Grafton park, co. Northampton, Ambassador to Turkey, being only child of his 2d wife, Catharine, sister of Edward, EARL OF ORFORD, da. of Edward RUSSELL. She *d.* of smallpox, at Bath, in Feb., and he *d.* there "of a diabetes" shortly afterwards, aged 46, both being *bur.* 6 March 1721/2, at Wragby. Admon. 7 May 1722 on behalf of his seven minor children.

IV. 1722. SIR ROWLAND WINN, Baronet [1660], of Nostell, etc., 1st s. and h., *b.* about 1706; *suc. to the Baronetcy* in March 1721/2; Sheriff of Yorkshire, 1731-32, and candidate, 1733, in a very severe contest, for the representation of that county. He *m.* 29 Aug. 1729, Susanna, da. and coheir of Charles HENSHAW, of Wellhall in Eltham, co. Kent, and of Fenchurch street, London, merchant, by Elizabeth, only surv. da. and h. of Edward ROPER, of Wellhall aforesaid, well known as a veteran sportsman. She was *bur.* at Wragby 24 March 1741/2. He *d.* 23 Aug., and was *bur.* 3 Sep. 1765 at Wragby, in his 59th year. M.I. Will pr. 1766.

(a) Of his two daughters and coheirs, (1) Elizabeth *m.* firstly Sir Hugh Acland, 1st Baronet [1678], who *d.* 29 July 1728, leaving issue; (2) Elizabeth *m.* her cousin, Thomas Palmer, the antiquary, and *d.* 1737, s.p.

V. 1765. SIR ROWLAND WINN, Baronet [1660], of Nostell, etc., 1st s. and h., *bap.* 24 Feb. 1739, at Wragby; *suc. to the Baronetcy*, 23 Aug. 1765; M.P. for Pontefract, 1768, till unseated in Nov. of that year. He *m.*, in or before 1768, Sabine Louise, da. and h. of Jacques Philippe, BARON D'HERVERT, Governor of Vevay, in Switzerland. He *d.* 20 Feb. 1785, aged 46. Will pr. Aug. 1787. His widow was *bur.* at Wragby, 21 Sep. 1798, aged 60. Will pr. March 1799.

VI. 1785. SIR ROWLAND WINN, Baronet [1660], of Nostell, and Thornton Curtis aforesaid, only s. and h., *b.* 13 June 1775; *suc. to the Baronetcy*, 20 Feb. 1785; Sheriff of Yorkshire, 1799-1800. He *d.* unm. at Nostell Park 14, and was *bur.*, with great state, 21 Oct. 1805, at Wragby, aged 30.(a) Admon. Dec. 1805.

VII. 1805. SIR EDMUND MARK WINN, Baronet [1660], of Ackton in Featherstone, co. York, cousin and h. male, being only s. and h. of Thomas WINN, of Ackton aforesaid, by Mary (*m.* 11 Dec. 1753), da. of Humphrey DUNCALF, of Highgate, Midx., which Thomas (who *d.* 7 May 1780, aged 66) was s. of Edmund WINN, of Ackton aforesaid (*d.* Feb. 1743, aged 64), next br. to the 3d Baronet. He was *bap.* 16 Sep. 1762, at Featherstone; *suc. to the Baronetcy* (but to none of the family estates), 14 Oct. 1805. He *d.* unm. 1 June 1833, and was *bur.* at Featherstone, aged 43. M.I.

VIII. 1833. CHARLES (WINN-ALLANSON) LORD HEADLEY, BARON ALLANSON AND WINN OF AGHADOE [I.], Baronet [1660 and 1776], cousin and h. male, being s. and h. of George (WINN), LORD HEADLEY, etc. [I.], who was *cr. a Baronet*, 14 Sep. 1776, being subsequently, 14 Nov. 1797, *cr. a Peer* [I.], as above, which George was only s. and h. of Pelham WINN, of South Ferriby, co. Lincoln, an officer in the Army, only s. and h. of George WINN, of South Ferriby aforesaid (aged 21 in 1666), who was yr. br. of the 2d, and 2d s. of the 1st Baronet. He was *b.* 25 June 1784, and *suc. to the Irish Peerage and the Baronetcy of 1776*, on the death of his father, 9 April 1798. He *suc. to the Baronetcy of 1660*, on the death of his cousin, as above, 1 June 1833, which *Baronetcy* became henceforth *merged in the Barony of Headley* [I.]. See *Peerage*.

FETHERSTON :

cr. 4 Dec. 1660;

ex. 17 Oct. 1746.

I. 1660. "HENEAGE FETHERSTON, of Blakesware [in Ware], co. Hertford," Esq., only s. and h. of Henry FETHERSTON, of Blackfriars, London, and of Hassenbrooke manor in Stanford le Hope, co. Essex, by his 2nd wife, Katharine, da. of Michael HENEAGE, Keeper of the Records in the Tower of London; was *b.* about 1628, being 7 years old at the Heralds' Visitation of London 1635; suc. his father May 1647; was admitted to Gray's Inn, 6 July 1650, and, having distinguished himself for his loyalty during the Cromwellian usurpation,(b) was *cr. a Baronet*, as above, 4 Dec. 1660; was Sheriff of Essex, 1665-66, and sold the estate of Blakesware aforesaid. He *m.* in 1660, Mary, da. of Sir Thomas BENNET, 1st Baronet [1660], of Babraham, co. Cambridge, by Mary, da. of Levinus MONKE. She *d.* 12 and was *bur.* 24 Jan. 1710, at Stanford le Hope, aged 77. He *d.* 23 Oct. and was *bur.* there 2 Nov. 1711, aged 84. M.I. Will pr. Dec. 1711.

(a) His estates passed to his nephew, John Williamson (then aged 11), 1st son of his only sister, Esther Sabina, by her 1st husband, John Williamson. He took the name of Winn, and was suc., 17 Nov. 1817, by his brother, Charles Winn, of Nostell, whose son Rowland was *cr.*, 6 July 1885, BARON ST. OSWALD OF NOSTELL.

(b) Lloyd's *Memoirs*, where it is stated that he "put as fair for Martyrdom" as [his namesake] Sir Timothy Fetherstonhaugh, who was beheaded, 22 Oct. 1651, after the battle of Wigan.

II. 1711, to 1746. SIR HENRY FETHERSTON, Baronet [1660], of Hassenbrooke Manor aforesaid, 1st s. and h.,(a) *b.* about 1654; *suc. to the Baronetcy*, 23 Oct. 1711; Sheriff of Essex, 1713-14. He *m.* Anna Maria, da. and h. of James WILLIAMSON, of London, merchant, by Anne, his wife. She *d.* 12 and was *bur.* 21 March 1689/90, at Stanford le Hope, aged 20. M.I. He *d.* s.p. 17 and was *bur.* there 24 Oct. 1746,(b) when the *Baronetcy* became *extinct*.(c) Will pr. 1746.

MONOUX, MONNOUX, *or* MONNOX :

cr. 4 Dec. 1660;

ex. 3 Feb. 1814.

I. 1660. "HUMPHREY MONNOX, of Wotton [*i.e.*, Wootton], co. Bedford, Esq.," 1st s. and h. of Lewis MONNOX, MONNOUX, *or* MONOUX, of the same, by his 1st wife, Elizabeth (*bur.* 14 Nov. 1611, at Leighton Buzzard), da. and coheir of Thomas WALSHE, of Waldern, co. Sussex, was admitted to Gray's Inn, 1 Nov. 1621; suc. his father, 10 Nov. 1628; recorded his pedigree at the Visit. of Beds, 1634, and was *cr. a Baronet*, as above, 4 Dec. 1660. He *m.*, in or before 1636, Mary, da. of Sir Thomas WODEHOUSE, 1st Baronet [1611], by Blanche, sister of Henry, 1st EARL OF DOVER, da. of John (CAREY), 3d BARON HUNSDON. He was *bur.* 4 Feb. 1675/6, at Wootton. Will pr. 1676.

II. 1676. SIR HUMPHREY MONOUX, Baronet [1660], of Wootton aforesaid, 2d but 1st surv. s. and h., *bap.* 10 Dec. 1640, at Wootton; admitted to Gray's Inn, 12 Oct. 1660; Sheriff of Notts, 1663-64; *suc. to the Baronetcy* in Feb. 1675/6; M.P. for Beds, 1678-79, 1679-81, and 1681. He *m.* 10 July 1666, at St. Margaret's, Westm. (Lic. Vic. Gen. 6) Alice (then aged 17), da. of Sir Thomas COTTON, 2d Baronet [1611], of Connington, co. Huntingdon, by his 2d wife, Alice, da. and h. of Sir John CONSTABLE. She was living May 1684. He was *bur.* 2 Aug. 1685, at Wotton aforesaid, aged 44. Will pr. Dec. 1685. "Lady MONAX" was carried away from St. Giles'-in-the-Fields for burial 18 Jan. 1719/20.

III. 1685. SIR PHILIP MONOUX, Baronet [1660], of Wootton aforesaid, 2d but only surv. s. and h.; *bap.* 25 Jan. 1678/9, at Wootton; *suc. to the Baronetcy* in Aug. 1685; matric. at Oxford (Hart. Hall), 12 Nov. 1696, said to be aged 15; was M.P. for Bedford, 1705 till death. He *m.*, in or before 1702, Dorothy, 1st da. of William HARVEY, of Chigwell, co. Essex, by Dorothy, da. and h. of Sir Robert DYCER, 2d Baronet [1661]. He *d.* s.p. 25 [Nov.?](d) 1707, in his 29th year, and was *bur.* at Wootton. M.I. His widow *d.* 15 May 1758.

IV. 1707. SIR HUMPHREY MONOUX, Baronet [1660], of Wootton aforesaid, only s. and h., *b.* about 1703; *suc. to the Baronetcy*, in 1707; matric. at Oxford (Trin. Coll.), 19 Feb. 1719/20, aged 17; *cr.* M.A., 3 May 1723, and D.C.L., 11 July 1733; was M.P. for Tavistock, Feb. 1728 to 1734, and for Stockbridge, 1734-41. He *m.*, Dec. 1742, Elizabeth, widow of [—] JONES, of Waltham Abbey, Essex. He *d.* s.p., 3 Dec. 1757. Will pr. 1758. His widow *d.* at Wootton, 12 Sep. 1770. Will pr. June 1771.

(a) His br. Heneage (then aged 40 and unm.) had lic. (London), 18 July 1699, to marry Frances, da. of Thomas Western of Rivenhall, Essex. He *d.* v.p. and was *bur.* 19 March 1710/1, at Stanford le Hope.

(b) He survived his two brothers and six sisters, all of whom *d.* s.p. He left his estates, said to be worth £400,000, to Matthew Fetherstonhaugh, who was *cr. a Baronet*, 3 Jan. 1746/7, and who *d.* 1774, having a monument at Stanford le Hope.

(c) In Mawson's *Obits* mention is made of the death, 24 Dec. 1724, of Sir Henry Fetherston, Baronet, at his house in Southampton street, Bloomsbury.

(d) Wotton's *Baronetage* gives 25 *Dec.* 1707, but the writ for the election in his place, as deceased, was ordered 4 Dec. 1707.

V. 1757. SIR PHILIP MONOUX, Baronet [1660], of Sandy Place, in Sandy, co. Bedford, cousin and h. male, being s. and h. of Humphrey MONOUX, one of the Benchers of Gray's Inn, by Mary, da. of Thomas SAVAGE, of Elmley Castle, co. Worcester, which Humphrey was 1st s. and h. of Lewis MONOUX, of Sandy aforesaid, also one of the Benchers of Gray's Inn, who was 2d s. of the 1st Baronet. He was *b.* about 1739; was admitted to Gray's Inn, 18 July 1754; *suc. to the Baronetcy*, 3 Dec. 1757; was Major in the Beds Militia, 1760, and Sheriff of Beds, 1763-64. He *m.*, 22 June 1762, Elizabeth, da. of Ambrose RIDDELL, of Eversholt, Beds. She *d.* at Wootton 12 Sep. 1770. Will pr. June 1771. He *d.* 17 April 1805, at the Salisbury Arms, Hatfield (on his way to London), aged 66. Will pr. 1805. The will of his widow pr. 1814.

VI. 1805. SIR PHILIP MONOUX, Baronet [1660], of Sandy Place aforesaid, only s. and h.; ed. at Trinity Hall, Cambridge; B.A., 1793; *suc. to the Baronetcy*, 17 April 1805; Sheriff of Beds, 1807-08. He *d.* unm. 27 Feb. 1809. Admon. April 1809.

VII. 1809, to 1814. SIR PHILIP MONOUX, Baronet [1660], Rector of Sandy aforesaid, cousin and h. male, being s. and h. of the Rev. Lewis MONOUX, M.A. (1727, Christ's Coll. Cambridge), Rector of Sandy aforesaid, by (—), sister of William EDWARDS, of Bedford, which Lewis was next br. to Humphrey MONOUX abovenamed, father of the 5th Baronet, both being grandsons of the 1st Baronet. He was ed. at Christ's Coll., Cambridge; B.A., 1756; M.A., 1759; was in Holy Orders; Rector of Sandy aforesaid; *suc. to the Baronetcy*, 27 Feb. 1809. He *d.* s.p., probably unm., 3 Feb. 1814, when the *Baronetcy* became *extinct*. Will pr. 1814.

PEYTON :

cr. 10 Dec. 1660;

ex. 25 Dec. 1661.

I. 1660, to 1661. "JOHN PEYTON, of Dodington within the isle of Ely, co. Cambridge, Esq.," 1st s. and h. of the Rev. Algernon PEYTON, D.D. [1661, Cambridge], Rector of Dodington aforesaid, by Elizabeth, da. of John COOK, of Chissel, co. Essex (which Algernon was br. and h., in 1658, of Robert PEYTON, of Dodington, both being sons of Sir John PEYTON, of the same, who *d.* 1635), was admitted to Gray's Inn, 5 Feb. 1657/8, and was *cr. a Baronet*, as above, 10 Dec. 1660. He *d.* unm., 25 Dec. 1661, when the *Baronetcy* became *extinct*.(a)

ANDERSON :

cr. 11 Dec. 1660;

ex. 8 Oct. 1891.

I. 1660. "EDMUND ANDERSON, of Broughton, co. Lincoln, Esq.," only s. and h. of William ANDERSON,(b) of Broughton aforesaid and of Lea in that county, by his 1st wife, Joan, sister and h. of Sir William ESSEX, Baronet [so cr. 1611], only da. of Thomas ESSEX, of Lambourne,

(a) Algernon Peyton, his br. and h., was *cr. a Baronet*, 21 March 1667/8, which dignity became *extinct* 29 June 1771; shortly after which date Henry Dashwood, nephew and h. of the last Baronet, took the name of Peyton, and was *cr. a Baronet*, as "of Doddington, co. Cambridge," 18 Sep. 1776.

(b) This William was 3d but 2d surviving s. of Sir Edmund Anderson, Lord Chief Justice of the Common Pleas, 1582 to 1605, being br. of Sir Francis Anderson, of Eyworth, Beds., ancestor of the Earls of Yarborough.

Berks, was *b.* 10 Aug. 1605, at Redbourne, Herts; admitted to Gray's Inn, 29 Jan. 1622/3; was said to be aged 26 at the Heralds' Visitation of Lincolnshire in 1634, and was *cr. a Baronet*, as above, 11 Dec. 1660. He *m.* firstly, 3 Dec. 1623, at St. Margaret's, Westm. (Lic. 28 Nov., Dean and Chapter), Mary, sole heir of Barnay WOOD, of Kilnwick Percy, in the East Riding, co. York, being da. of Thomas WOOD, of Oldfield, co. York, by Mary, da. of George BOTELER, of Stotfold, Beds. She, who was mother of ten children, *d.* in childbed 30 Jan. 1636/7, before her age of 30, and was *bur.* at Malton, co. York. M.I. at Lea, co. Lincoln. He *m.* secondly, 11 Sep. 1649, Sybilla (then aged 44), widow of Edward BELLOT, of Morton, co. Chester, da. of Sir Rowland EGERTON, 1st Baronet [1617], by Bridget, da. of Arthur (GREY), LORD GREY DE WILTON. He was *bur.* 19 Jan. 1660/1 at Broughton, aged 55. Will dat. 2 Sep. 1660, proved 12 Feb. 1660/1. His widow, by whom he had no issue, *d.* 1661, and was *bur.* at Broughton. Her will, dat. 27 Aug., proved 23 Nov. 1661.

II. 1661. SIR JOHN ANDERSON, Baronet [1660], of Broughton(a) and of Kilnwick Percy aforesaid, 3d but 1st surv. s. and h. by 1st wife, *b.* 23 Dec. 1628, at Broughton, and *bap.* there 6 Jan. 1628/9; *suc. to the Baronetcy* in Jan. 1660/1. He *m.*, in or before 1661, Elizabeth, da. and eventually h. of Hugh SNAWSELL, of Bilton, in the Anesty of the city of York, by Isabel, da. of Sir Thomas BEAUMONT, of Stoughton, co. Leicester. He *d.* 18 March 1670, and was *bur.* at Broughton, aged 41. His widow was *bur.* there 16 July 1698. Her will dat. 9 Dec. 1697, pr. 26 July 1698.

III. 1670 SIR EDMUND ANDERSON, Baronet [1660], of Broughton aforesaid, etc., only s. and h., aged 8 at the Visitation of Lincolnshire in 1669; *suc. to the Baronetcy*, 18 March 1670. He *d.* unm. at the University [of Cambridge?] 17 and was *bur.* 30 Dec. 1676, at Broughton. Admon. as "of St. Martin's-in-the-Fields," 1 Oct. 1689, to Dame Elizabeth Anderson, the mother.

IV. 1676. SIR EDMUND ANDERSON, Baronet [1660], of Broughton aforesaid, etc., and of Porters in the parish of Shenley, Herts, uncle and h., being 4th s. of the 1st Baronet by his 1st wife, was *bap.* 7 Jan. 1629, at at Broughton; admitted to Gray's Inn, 1 March 1646/7; *suc. to the Baronetcy* in Dec. 1676. He *m.* firstly (Lic. Fac. 31 May 1662), Mary (then aged 21), da. and coheir of William COX, of Porters aforesaid. He *m.* secondly, 26 March 1686, at St. Martin's, Outwich, London (Lic. Fac. 24), Elizabeth (then aged 26), da. of Sir Anthony DEANE, of Allhallows' Staining, London, one of the Commissioners of the Mint. His will (as of "Bedford Walk, in St. Andrew's, Holborn," in which he directs to be *bur.* at Shenley), dat. 16 Feb. 1701/2, pr. by his widow, 12 March 1702/3. Her admon., as of St. Andrew's, Holborn, dat. 18 Jan. 1715/6.

V. 1703? SIR EDMUND ANDERSON, Baronet [1660], of Lea, co. Lincoln, and Kilnwick Percy aforesaid, 3d but only surv. s. and h., being only s. by 2d wife;(b) *bap.* 4 Nov. 1687 at St. Giles' in the Fields; *suc. to the Baronetcy* in 1702, or 1703. He *m.* firstly, in or before 1721, Mary, da. of William HARVEY, of Rolls, in Chigwell, Essex, by Dorothy, da. and h. of Sir Robert DYCER, 2d Baronet [1661]. She *d.* 16 and was *bur.* 22 Aug. 1748 at Kilnwick aforesaid. He *m.* secondly, 11 Feb. 1754, at the Savoy Chapel, Midx., Frances, da. of J. BATTY, of Tadcaster, co. York. He *d.* 3 and was *bur.* 10 May 1765 at Kilnwick, aged 77. M.I. Will pr. Oct. 1765. His widow *d.* 11 Sep. 1801, and was *bur.* at Kilnwick, aged 72. Will pr. Oct. 1801.

VI. 1765. SIR WILLIAM ANDERSON, Baronet [1660], of Lea and Kilnwick Percy aforesaid, only s. and h., by 1st wife, *bap.* 31 March 1721/2, at St. Giles' in the Fields; ed. at Trin. Coll., Cambridge; B.A. 1741; M.A. 1745; in Holy Orders; Rector of Lea aforesaid, 1743-85; Rector of

(a) His estate "at Broughton near Gainsborough" is given as "near £2,000" a year in Sir Joseph Williamson's *Lincolnshire Families, temp. Car. II* [*Her. and Gen.*, vol. ii, p. 119].

(b) His elder br. Edmund, admitted to Gray's Inn 4 May 1683, *d.* v.p. and s.p. 17 Sep. 1684, aged 21.

Epworth, co. Lincoln, 1757-84; *suc. to the Baronetcy*, 3 May 1765. He *m.*, 7 Aug. 1747, at Little Grimsby, Anne, da. of John MADDISON, of Stainton-le-Vale, co. Lincoln. She *d.* 31 Aug., and was *bur.* 5 Sep. 1783 at Lea, aged 56. He *d.* at Bell Hall, near York, 9, and was *bur.* 15 March 1785, at Lea, aged 63. M.I.

VII. 1785. SIR EDMUND ANDERSON, Baronet [1660], of Lea Hall in Lea aforesaid, etc., s. and h., *b.* 11 Sep., and *bap.* 18 Oct. 1758 at Lea; *suc. to the Baronetcy*, 9 March 1785. He *m.* Catharine, 2d da. of Thomas PLUMER. She *d.* 2, and was *bur.* 8 Dec. 1798, aged 39, at Lea. He *d.* 30 May, and was *bur.* 7 June 1799, aged 40, at Lea. M.I. Will pr. Sep. 1799.

VIII. 1799. SIR CHARLES JOHN ANDERSON, Baronet [1660], of Lea Hall aforesaid, etc., br. and h., *b.* 5 Oct. 1767; matric. at Oxford (Univ. Coll.), 3 May 1787, aged 19; B.A. 1791; M.A. 1797; in Holy Orders; Rector of Lea aforesaid, 1795-1846; *suc. to the Baronetcy*, 30 May 1799; Prebendary of Lincoln, 1812. He *m.*, 13 Dec. 1802, at Scawby, Frances Mary, 2d da. of Sir John NELTHORPE, 6th Baronet [1666], of Scawby, by Anne Maria Charlotte, da. of Andrew WILLOUGHBY. She *d.* at Neuhausen, near the falls of the Rhine, 18 Aug., and was *bur.* 7 Sep. 1836, at Lea, aged 60. M.I. Admon. Nov. 1836. He *d.* at Lea Rectory, 24 March 1846, in his 78th year. Will pr. May 1846.

IX. 1846, to 1891. SIR CHARLES HENRY JOHN ANDERSON, Baronet [1660], of Lea Hall aforesaid, etc., only s. and h., *b.* 24 Nov. 1804 at Lea Hall; matric. at Oxford (Oriel Coll.), 28 Feb. 1823, aged 18; B.A. 1826; M.A. 1829; admitted *ad eundem* at Cambridge, 1854; *suc. to the Baronetcy*, 24 March 1846; Sheriff of Lincolnshire, 1851. He *m.*, 11 Sep. 1832, Emma, youngest da. of John Savile FOLJAMBE, of Aldwarke, co. York, and Osberton, Notts, by Elizabeth, da. of Rev. the Hon. James WILLOUGHBY, br. to Henry, 5th BARON MIDDLETON. She *d.* 8 Aug. 1870 in Onslow Square, Middx. He *d.* s.p.m.s.(a) at Lea Hall, 8 Oct. 1891, in his 87th year, when the *Baronetcy* became *extinct*.

Family Estates.—These, in 1883, consisted of 2,647 acres in the East Riding of Yorkshire, 2,153 in Lincolnshire, and 293 in Notts. *Total*—5,093 acres, worth £6,994 a year. *Principal Residence*—Lea Hall, near Gainsborough, Lincolnshire.

FAGG:

cr. 11 Dec. 1660.

I. 1660. "JOHN FAGG, of Wiston,(b) co. Sussex, Esq.," s. and h. of John FAGG, of Rye, in that county, and Brensett, co. Kent (admitted to Gray's Inn 1 Nov. 1619), by Elizabeth, da. of [—] HUDSON, was admitted to Gray's Inn, 1 July 1644; purchased the estate of Wiston(a) from Dr. Thomas SHIRLEY, and that of Mystole in Chartham, near Canterbury; was M.P. for Rye, Oct. 1645 to 1653; for Sussex (three Parls.), 1654-59; for Steyning (four Parls.), 1660-81; for Sussex again, 1681, and for Steyning again (six Parls.), 1685 till death; was Col. in the Parl. Army; a Commissioner for the trial of the King; one of the [Rump] Council of State, 1659, receiving the thanks of that Parl. for his services, 29 Dec. 1659, but was, nevertheless, a year later, *cr. a Baronet*, as above, 11 Dec. 1660.(c) He *m.* firstly, 19 March 1645, at Glynde, co. Sussex, Mary, da. of Robert MORLEY, of Glynde aforesaid, by Susan, da. and h. of Thomas HODGSON, of Framfield. She, who was *bap.* 25 Sep. 1626, and by whom he had sixteen children, *d.* 20 and was *bur.* 23 Nov.

(a) Of his three sons, the eldest *d.* young; the youngest, Charles Whichcott Anderson, *d.* unm. 7 Sep. 1877, aged 32; and the 2d son, Francis Foljambe Anderson, *d.* 15 Sep. 1881, aged 40, leaving three daughters and coheirs.

(b) See *State Trials* (vol. vii, p. 453) for proceedings as to this estate on a claim of this Dr. Shirley, who, for a breach of privilege, was ordered into custody.

(c) In Wotton's *Baronetage*, edit. 1741, is a mendacious recitement as to his "refusing to act" against Charles I, which, on the contrary, he consistently did; indeed, as early as 1643, he offered to lend £1,000 to the Party to support the cause against him. [*Ex inform.* W. D. Pink.]

1687. He *m.* secondly Anne, widow of (—) HENSHAW, da. of Philip WESTON, of Newbury. She, by whom he had no issue, *d.* 11 May 1694. Admon. 5 March 1696/7, on behalf of her infant son, Philip HENSHAW, and again, 7 April 1705, to him when of full age. He *d.* 18 and was *bur.* 19 Jan. 1700/1. Will, in which he devises the estate of Mystole to his son, Charles, pr. July 1701.

II. 1701 SIR ROBERT FAGG, Baronet [1660], of Wiston aforesaid, 1st surv. s. and h., *b.* about 1649; was M.P. for Shoreham, 1679 and 1681, and for Steyning, 1690-95 and 1701-02; *suc. to the Baronetcy*, 18 Jan. 1700/1. He *m.* 21 Sep. 1671, at Wiston (Lic. Fac. 11), Elizabeth (then 16, an orphan, with consent of Mary BEARD, her aunt), da. of Benjamin CULPEPER, of Lindfield, co. Sussex. He *d.* 26 Aug. 1715 and was *bur.* at Albourne, co. Sussex. M.I. Will pr. Sep. 1715.

III. 1715. SIR ROBERT FAGG, Baronet [1660], of Wiston aforesaid, 2d but only surv. s. and h., *bap.* 9 Aug. 1673; *suc. to the Baronetcy*, 26 Aug. 1715. He *m.*, in or before 1698, Christian, da. of Sir Cecil BISHOPP, 3d Baronet [1611], by Anne, da. and h. of George BERRY. He *d.* at Horley Heath, near Reigate, Surrey, 22 and was *bur.* 29 June 1736, at Albourne. Admon. 4 Dec. 1736, 26 April 1753, and 9 Nov. 1758. His widow *d.* at Reigate, 30 Aug., and was *bur.* 4 Sep. 1765, at Albourne, aged 96. Will pr. 1765.

IV. 1736. SIR ROBERT FAGG, Baronet [1660], of Wiston aforesaid, 3d but only surv. s. and h., *bap.* 20 Sep. 1704; was M.P. for Steyning, 1734 till death; *suc. to the Baronetcy*, 22 June 1736. He *m.* in 1729, Sarah, da. of William WARD, M.D., of York. He *d.* s.p.s., 14 and was *bur.* 22 Sep. 1740, at Albourne.(a) Admon. 6 Nov. 1740. His widow *m.*, before 26 April 1753, Roger TALBOT, of Woodend, co. York, and *d.* 4 Dec. 1791.

V. 1740. SIR WILLIAM FAGG, Baronet [1600], of Mystole above named, cousin and h. male, being 1st surv. s. and h. of Charles FAGG, of the same, by Elizabeth (*m.* Feb. 1723), da. of William TURNER, of Whitefriars, Canterbury, which Charles (who *d.* 8 April 1739), was s. and h. of Charles FAGG, of Mystole aforesaid (*bap.* 1 Jan. 1661 and *d.* 10 March 1714), 2d s. of the 1st Baronet by his 1st wife. He was *b.* about 1726; *suc. to the Baronetcy* (but not to the family estates), 14 Sep. 1740. He *m.* Elizabeth, da. of Abraham LE GRAND, of Canterbury. She *d.* 27 Feb. 1785, aged 59. He *d.* 14 Nov. 1791, aged 65. Will pr. Jan. 1792.

VI. 1791. SIR JOHN FAGG, Baronet [1660], of Mystole aforesaid, only s. and h., *b.* about 1760; ed. at Clare Coll., Cambridge, B.A., 1781; M.A., 1784; in Holy Orders; Vicar of Chislet, co. Kent, and Vicar of St. Nicholas in Thanet, 1785-1803; Rector of Chartham in that county, 1803-22, having *suc. to the Baronetcy*, 14 Nov. 1791. He *m.* 27 Aug. 1789, Anne, da. and h. of Daniel NEWMAN, of Canterbury, Barrister, Recorder of Maidstone and Faversham. He *d.* 23 Sep. 1822. Will pr. 1822. His widow *d.* 16 June 1857, at the Royal Dockyard, Chatham, aged 88. Will pr. Feb. 1857.

VII. 1822. SIR JOHN FAGG, Baronet [1660], of Mystole aforesaid 1st s. and h., *b.* there 8 Sep. 1798; matric. at Oxford (Ch. Ch.), 5 Oct. 1816, aged 18; *suc. to the Baronetcy*, 23 Sep. 1822. He, who was well known in the sporting world, *d.* unm. 16 April 1873, in his 75th year, at Mystole aforesaid.

VIII. 1873. SIR JOHN WILLIAM CHARLES FAGG, Baronet [1660], of Wincheap, near Canterbury, nephew and h. male, being 1st s. and h. of John William Thomas FAGG, of Westbere House, near Canterbury, by Frances, yst. da. of William CARTER, M.D., of Canterbury, which John last named (who *d.* 1 Oct. 1840) was next br. to the late Baronet. He was *b.* at Westbere House aforesaid, 10 Oct. 1830; was sometime Lieut. 21st Foot; *suc. to the Baronetcy*, 16 April 1873. He *m.* 1 Sep. 1864, Anne Elizabeth, only da. of Thomas Holttum, of Sturry, co. Kent. She *d.* there 17 Sep. 1877.

(a) He left his estates to his sister Elizabeth, *bap.* 5 May 1703, who *m.* (as his 2d wife) 20 April 1743, Sir Charles Goring, 5th Baronet [1678], of Highden, Sussex, whose issue, by her, inherited the Wiston estate.

HERBERT:

cr. 18 Dec. 1660;

ex. Oct. 1668.

I. 1660, to 1668. "MATTHEW HERBERT, of Broomfield, co. Salop, Esq.," 1st s. and h. of Francis HERBERT,(a) of Dolgiog, co. Montgomery, by Margaret, sister of Francis FOXE, of Bromfield aforesaid, was admitted to the Inner Temple, Nov. 1648; Sheriff of Shropshire, 1654-55; and was *cr. a Baronet*, as above, 18 Dec. 1660. He *m.* Mary, da. of Sir Thomas LUCY, of Charlecote, co. Warwick, by Alice, da. and h. of Thomas SPENCER, of Claverdon, in that county. He *d.* s.p. in the Fleet prison, and was *bur.* 30 Oct. 1668, at St. Margaret's, Westm., when the *Baronetcy* became *extinct*. Admon. 27 Feb. 1668/9, and 16 May 1670. His widow *d.* at St. Martin's-in-the-Fields, 14, and was *bur.* 17 Feb. 1669/70, at St. Margaret's, Westm. Nunc. will pr. 10 March 1669/70.

WARD:

cr. 19 Dec. 1660;

ex. about 1770.

I. 1660. "EDWARD WARD, of Bexley [*i.e.*, Bixley], co. Norfolk, Esq.,"(b) s. and h. of Thomas WARD,(c) of the same (*bur.* there 17 Sep. 1632), by Anne, da. of William PERT, of co. Essex, was *b.* about 1618; admitted to Gray's Inn, 1 Nov. 1635; was Sheriff of Norfolk, 1655-56 and 1656-57; was *Knighted*, during office, by the Lord Protector Cromwell, at Whitehall, 2 Nov. 1657, and was (by the King) *cr. a Baronet*, as above, 19 Dec. 1660. He *m.* firstly Mary, da. of Richard CATELYNE, of Kirby Cane. She *d.* s.p., and was, apparently, *bur.* at Postwick, co. Norfolk. He *m.* secondly Elizabeth, da. and h. of John HARBOURNE, of Mundham, co. Norfolk, who was s. of William HARBOURNE, Ambassador [1582] to Turkey. He was *bur.* 2 Sep. 1684, at Bixley.

II. 1684. SIR EDWARD WARD, Baronet [1660], of Bixley and Mundham aforesaid, 1st s. and h. by 2d wife; admitted to Gray's Inn, 24 Nov. 1660; *suc. to the Baronetcy* in Sep. 1684. He *m.* (Lic. Vic. Gen. 3 Dec. 1662, each aged about 21), Jane, da. of William RANT, M.D., of Thorpe Market, Norfolk, by Jane, da. of Sir John DINGLEY, of Wolverton, in the isle of Wight. He was *bur.* 18 March 1686, at Postwick. His widow was *bur.* there 10 Feb. 1713.

III. 1686. SIR THOMAS WARD, Baronet [1660], of Bixley and Mundham aforesaid, 1st s. and h.; *suc. to the Baronetcy* in March 1686. He *d.* unm., and was *bur.* 20 Jan. 1692, at Postwick.

IV. 1692. SIR EDWARD WARD, Baronet [1660], of Bixley and Mundham aforesaid, br. and h.; *suc. to the Baronetcy* in Jan. 1692. He *m.* Barbara, da. and coheir of Leonard GOOCH, of Earsham, Norfolk. He was *bur.* 2 Aug. 1719, at Bixley. His widow *d.* 25 May 1755, aged 91. Will pr. 1756.

V. 1719. SIR EDWARD WARD, Baronet [1660], of Bixley and Mundham aforesaid, 1st s. and h.; *suc. to the Baronetcy* in Aug. 1719. He *m.* 5 July 1720, at St. Barth. the Great, London, Susan, da. and h. of William RANDALL, of Yarmouth, merchant. He *d.* 2 and was *bur.* 7 March 1736/7, at Bixley. Will pr. 1737. His widow *d.* 4 June 1759. Will pr. 1765.

(a) This Francis was s. of Matthew Herbert, of Dolgiog aforesaid, M.P. for Montgomery, 1586-87, uncle to the well known Edward Herbert, 1st Baron Herbert of Cherbury.

(b) The Knighthood, conferred by Cromwell, was, of course, ignored.

(c) This Thomas was s. and h. of another Thomas Ward (*d.* Feb. 1610), the s. of Edward Ward, who first settled at Bixley (*d.* 1583, aged 41), whose 5th s., William Ward, Citizen and Goldsmith, of London, was father of Humble, 1st Baron Ward of Birmingham.

VI. 1737. SIR EDWARD WARD, Baronet [1660], of Bixley and Mundham aforesaid, 1st s. and h.; *b.* 1721; *suc. to the Baronetcy,* 2 March 1736/7. He *d.* unm., 7 April 1742, aged 21.

VII. 1742. SIR RANDALL WARD, Baronet [1660], of Bixley and Mundham aforesaid, br. and h.; *suc. to the Baronetcy,* 7 April 1742. He *m.* (—) da. of (—) RANDALL. He *d.* 8 and was *bur.* 17 May 1762, at Bixley. Will pr. 1762. His widow *d.* at Blackheath, 12 July 1765.

VIII. 1762, to 1770? SIR EDWARD WARD, Baronet [1660], s and h.; *suc. to the Baronetcy,* 8 May 1762. He *d.* s.p., about 1770, when the *Baronetcy* became *extinct.*(a)

KEYT:
cr. 22 Dec. 1660;
ex. 6 July 1784.

I. 1660. "JOHN KEYT, of Ebrington, co. Gloucester, Esq.," 1st s. and h. of John KEYT, of the same ("a true son of the Church of England," Sheriff of Worcestershire and afterwards of Gloucestershire, who *d.* 25 April 1660, aged 76), by his 1st wife, Jane, da. of Thomas PORTER, of Mickleton, co. Gloucester, was *b.* at Beauchamps Lodge in Alcester, co. Warwick, 6 July 1616; raised a troop of Horse for Charles I during the Rebellion; and, having suc. his father 25 April 1660, was *cr. a Baronet,* as above (in the same year), 22 Dec. 1660. He *m.* in or before 1638, Margaret, da. and h. of William TAYLOR, of Brixworth, co. Northampton. He *d.* 26 Aug. 1662, aged 56. His widow *d.* 28 June 1660, both being *bur.* at Ebrington. M.I. Her will pr. July 1669.

II. 1662. SIR WILLIAM KEYT, Baronet [1660], of Ebrington aforesaid, 1st s. and h., *b.* at Ragley, co. Warwick, 1638; admitted to the Inner Temple, Nov. 1654; *suc. to the Baronetcy,* 26 Aug. 1662. He *m.* (Lic. Vic. Gen., 5 June 1662) Elizabeth (then aged 22), da. and coheir of the Hon. Francis COVENTRY, by his third wife, Elizabeth, da. and coheir of John MANNING, of London, which Francis was 3d s. of Thomas, 1st BARON COVENTRY OF AYLESBOROUGH, sometime L. Keeper of the Great Seal. He, having survived his four sons, *d.* 30 Nov. 1702, and was *bur.* at Ebrington, aged 66. M.I. Will pr. June 1703.

III. 1702. SIR WILLIAM KEYT, Baronet [1660], of Ebrington aforesaid, of Old Stratford-on-Avon, co. Warwick, and of Norton, in Mickleton, co. Gloucester, grandson and h., being 1st s. and h. of William KEYT, by Agnes(b) (*m.* 19 Oct. 1687), 1st da. of Sir John CLOPTON, of Clopton, co. Warwick, which William (who *d.* 31 Oct. 1702, only thirty-five days before his father, aged 34), was 3d, but last surv. s. of the late Baronet. He was *b.*

(a) This *Baronetcy* was, however, assumed by Mr. Charles S. G. Green, M.R.C.V.S. (London), of 54 Edbrooke road, St. Peter's Park, Paddington, who claims both title and estates on the ground of direct descent from Sir Edward, the 5th Baronet, through his da., Susan, who *m.* the 3d Earl of Rosebery [S.], and *d.* (reputedly without issue) in 1774." [Dod's *Peerage,* etc., for 1902]. This descent, even if established, being through a female, would not, however, entitle him to a Baronetcy granted, presumably, to the heirs *male* of the body of the grantee.

(b) This Agnes and her five younger children were by Royal Warrant, 5 June 1704, raised to the rank of the widow and children of a Baronet, as if the said William had survived his father, the 2d Baronet, and suc. to the Baronetcy. A similar case occurred in 1686 (see vol. ii, p. 19, note "b") when Frances, widow of Francis Moore, s. and h. ap. of Sir Henry Moore, Baronet [1627], had a grant of the like precedence. The admon. of this "*Dame Agnes Keyt,*" of Stratford on Avon, co. Warwick, widow, was granted 21 Feb. 1725/6 to her son, Sir William Keyt, Baronet. One of the younger sons, John, *b.* 24 Sep. 1695, matric. at Oxford (Univ. Coll.), 8 May 1712, aged 16, as "son of William, of Stratford, co. Warwick, *Baronet,*" and became B.A. 1715, and M.A. 1718.

8 July 1688; *suc. to the Baronetcy,* 30 Nov. 1702; was M.P. for Warwick (three Parls.), Nov. 1722 till void, Feb. 1735. He *m.* 23 Nov. 1710, at Toddington, co. Gloucester, Anne, da. of William (TRACY), 4th VISCOUNT TRACY OF RATHCOOLE [I.], by his 2d wife Jane, da. of Sir Thomas LEIGH. He was burned to death in his house at Norton (being supposed to have been a lunatic and to have set fire thereto) in Sep. 1741. Admon. 3 Dec. 1741, and 6 May 1761. His widow living 6 May 1761.

IV. 1741. SIR THOMAS CHARLES KEYT, Baronet [1660], of Ebrington, Norton and Old Stratford aforesaid, 1st s. and h., *b.* 1713; matric. at Oxford (University Coll.), 3 July 1729, aged 16; *suc. to the Baronetcy* in Sep. 1741, and shortly afterwards sold the Ebrington estate. He *d.* unm. 18 or 24 July 1755.

V. 1755, to 1784. SIR ROBERT KEYT, Baronet [1660], of Mickleham, co. York, yst. and only surv. br. and h.; *bap.* 24 Dec. 1724; *suc. to the Baronetcy,* 18 or 24 July 1755. He *d.* s.p. (probably unm.), 6 July 1784, when the *Baronetcy* became *extinct.* Will pr. Oct. 1784.

KILLEGREW, *or* KILLIGREW:
cr. 22 Dec. 1660;
ex. 8 Jan. 1704/5.

I. 1660. "WILLIAM KILLEGREW, of Arwynike [*i.e.,* Arwenick], co. Cornwall, Esq.," 6th s. of John KILLIGREW, of the same (*d.* 12 Aug. 1605), by Dorothy, da. of Thomas MONK, of Potheridge, co. Devon, was aged 22 in the Visit. of Cornwall 1622; was a distinguished soldier, and Colonel of a Regiment in Holland; served sometime under the King of Denmark, and was *cr. a Baronet,* as above, 22 Dec. 1660, with a spec. rem., failing heirs male of his body, "to Peter KILLEGREW, of Arwynike, aforesaid, Esq., son of Sir Peter KILLEGREW, Knight," and the heirs male of his body. He *d.* unm. in Pall Mall, and was *bur.* 17 July 1665, in Westm. Abbey. Will dat. 15 to 24 June 1665, pr. 4 Sep. 1668.

II. 1665, to 1705. SIR PETER KILLEGREW, Baronet [1660], of Arwenick aforesaid, nephew, being only surv. s. and h. of Sir Peter KILLIGREW (*d.* July 1668, aged 74), of the same (well known as "Sir Peter the Post"), by Mary, da. of Sir Thomas LUCAS, of Colchester, was *b.* about 1634; matric. at Oxford (Queen's Coll.), 16 Nov. 1650; was M.P. for Camelford, 1660 till void in May; was a Gent. of the Privy Chamber, 1660; *suc. to the Baronetcy,* on the death of his uncle, in July 1665, under the spec. rem. in the creation thereof, and suc. his father three years later. He *m.* (Lic. Fac., 24 Dec. 1662), Frances (then aged 19), da. of Sir Roger TWISDEN, 2d Baronet [1611], of East Peckham, by Isabella, da. and coheir of Sir Nicholas SAUNDERS. He *d.* s.p.m.s.,(a) at Ludlow, 8 Jan. 1704/5, aged 71, and was *bur.* at Falmouth, when the *Baronetcy* became *extinct.* Will dat. 15 Feb. 1691/2, pr. 7 Feb. 1704/5. His widow *d.* April 1711, and was *bur.* there. Will dat. 22 Sep. 1709, pr. 9 April 1711.

BUCK, *or* BUCKE:
cr. 22 Dec. 1660;
ex. 7 June 1782.

I. 1660. "JOHN BUCK, of Lamby [*i.e.,* Hamby] Grange [in Leverton], co. Lincoln, Esq.," s. and h. of Sir John BUCK, of the same; Sheriff of Lincolnshire, 1619-20 and, of Yorkshire, 1640-41, by Elizabeth,

(a) George Killigrew, his only surv. s. and h. ap., was killed v.p. in a duel, 20 March 1687, s.p.m., leaving a da., who *m.* John Dunbar, and who was living 1743.

da. and h. of William GREEN, of Filey, co. York; was admitted to the Inner Temple, Nov. 1612; suc. his father in 1648, and was *cr. a Baronet,* as above, 22 Dec. 1660.(a) He was Sheriff of Lincolnshire, 1663-64. He *m.* firstly, Anne, da. of Sir John STYLE, 1st Baronet [1627], of Wateringbury, Kent, by Elizabeth, da. and h. of Robert FOULKES. She *d.* s.p.s. He *m.* secondly (settlement 21 Aug. 1652), Mary (aged 4 at the Visit. of Herts in 1634), da. and h. of William ASHTON, of Tingrey, Beds, and of The Grove, in the parish of Watford, Herts, by Mary, da. and h. of Henry EWER, of South Mimms, Midx. He *d.* in 1668 *or* 1669. Will dat. 31 July 1668, pr. 21 June 1669, directing his burial to be at Osbournby, co. Lincoln. His widow *d.* at Hamby Grange, in or before July 1679. Admon. 2 July 1679.(b)

II. 1669? SIR WILLIAM BUCKE, Baronet [1660], of Hamby Grange and the Grove aforesaid, 1st s. and h., by 2d wife; *b.* about 1655; *suc. to the Baronetcy* in 1668 or 1669; admitted to Lincoln's Inn, 1 Dec. 1674; Sheriff of Lincolnshire, 1689-90. He *m.,* in or before 1684, Frances, da. of Daniel SKINNER, of London, merchant. She was *bur.* 5 Nov. 1711, aged 51, at Osbournby. M.I. He *d.* 15 Aug. 1717, aged 62, and was *bur.* at Watford, Herts. Admon. 10 Sep. 1717.

III. 1717. SIR CHARLES BUCK, Baronet [1660], of Hamby Grange and the Grove aforesaid, 3d but only surv. s. and h.; *b.* about 1692; Fellow Commoner of Trin. Coll., Cambridge, 29 March 1712, aged 20; *suc. to the Baronetcy,* 15 Aug. 1717. He sold the Grove estate, 4 Feb. 1728, to the Greville family.(c) He *m.,* in or before 1721, Anne, da. of Sir Edward SEBRIGHT, 3d Baronet [1626], by Anne, da. and h. of Thomas SAUNDERS, of Beechwood, Herts. He *d.* 20 June 1729, aged 37. Admon. 24 May 1733. His widow *d.* 18 Sep 1764, aged 63, and was *bur.* in Bath Abbey. M.I.

IV. 1729, to 1782. SIR CHARLES LOUIS BUCK, Baronet [1660], of Hamby Grange aforesaid, only s. and h., *b.* 31 Jan. 1721/2; *suc. to the Baronetcy,* 20 June 1729; Sheriff of Lincolnshire, 1780-81. He *m.* 10 April 1758, Mary, sister and coheir of William CARTWRIGHT, da. of George CARTWRIGHT, of Ossington, Notts, by Mary, da. and coheir of John DIGBY, of Mansfield Woodhouse in that county. She *d.* at Bath, 21 July 1764. He *d.* s.p.s.(d) in London, 7 June 1782, aged 60, when the *Baronetcy* became *extinct.* M.I. at Osbournby aforesaid. Will pr. July 1782. The will of Dame Mary Buck was pr. 1813.

FRANKLAND:
cr. 24 Dec. 1660;
sometime, 1837-49, FRANKLAND-RUSSELL.

I. 1660. "WILLIAM FRANKLAND, of Thirkelby, co. York, Esq.," only s. and h. ap. of Sir Henry FRANKLAND, of the same (aged 56 at the Visit. of Yorkshire, 23 Aug. 1665), by Anne, da. of Sir Arthur HARRIS, of Cricksey, Essex, was *b.* about 1640 (being aged 25 at the abovenamed visitation

(a) Sir John Buck had £500 a year "at Hanby Grange, in Kesteven in this county," ond £1,500 a year in Yorkshire, according to Sir Joseph Williamson's *Lincolnshire Families, temp. Car. II.* [*Her. and Gen.,* vol. ii, p. 120].

(b) She is sometimes said to have *m.,* as his 2d wife, Sir Edward Turnour, Lord Chief Baron of the Exchequer, who *d.* 4 March 1676. There is no indication, however, thereof in her admon., wherein she is styled "Dame Mary Buck, widow."

(c) This was afterwards purchased, in 1753, by the Hon. Thomas Villiers, who in 1786 was *cr.* Earl of Clarendon.

(d) Of his two sisters and coheirs, (1) Anne *m.* Ambrose Isted, of Ecton, co. Northampton, and had issue; (2) Catherine m., in 1751, Sir Henry Englefield, 6th Baronet [1611], and *d.* 31 May 1805, in her 80th year. William, his only son, is said [Kimber's *Baronetage,* 1771] to have *d.* in his 15th year, at Westm. School.

in 1665), and was v.p. *cr. a Baronet,* as above, 24 Dec. 1660, and suc. his father more than six years later, about 1667, was M.P. for Thirsk (four Parls.), 1671-81. He *m.,* in or before 1662, Arabella, da. of the Hon. Henry BELASYSE (s. and h. ap. of Thomas, 1st VISCOUNT FAUCONBERG OF HENKNOWLE), by Grace, da. and h. of Sir Thomas BARTON. She *d.* 26 Feb. 1687, in her 50th year. He *d.* 2 Aug. 1697, both being *bur.* at Thirkelby. M.I.

II. 1697. SIR THOMAS FRANKLAND, Baronet [1660], of Thirkelby aforesaid, 1st s. and h., *b.* in or shortly after 1665; admitted to Lincoln's Inn, 2 April 1683; *suc. to the Baronetcy,* 2 Aug. 1697; was M.P. for Thirsk (three Parls.), 1685-95; for Hedon, 1695-98; and for Thirsk again (seven Parls.), 1698-1711; a Commissioner of the Exchequer, 1689; Joint Postmaster Gen., 1690-1715, and a Commissioner of the Customs, 1715-18. He inherited a considerable estate at Chiswick, Midx., from his uncle, Thomas (BELASYSE), EARL OF FAUCONBERG. He *m.* (Lic. Vic. Gen., 14 Feb. 1682/3, he 18 and she 17) Elizabeth (*b.* 4 May 1664), da. (whose issue in 1836 became coheir) of Sir John RUSSELL, 4th Baronet [1629], of Chippenham, by Frances, relict of Robert RICH, yst. da. of Oliver CROMWELL, "**Lord Protector.**" He *d.* 30 Oct. 1726 in his 62d year. His widow *d.* 20 July 1733, both being *bur.* at Thirkelby. M.I. His will pr. 1726, and hers in 1733.

III. 1726. SIR THOMAS FRANKLAND, Baronet [1660], of Thirkelby aforesaid, 1st s. and h.; M.P. for Harwich, 1708-13, and for Thirsk (five Parls.), 1715 till death; Clerk of the Deliveries, Sec. to the Muster Master Gen., and a Commissioner of the Revenue [I.]; *suc. to the Baronetcy,* 30 Oct. 1726; was on the Board of Trade [E.], 1728-30; one of the Lords of the Admiralty, 1730-41. He was M.P. for Thirsk. He *m.* firstly, Dinah, da. and coheir of Francis TOPHAM, of Aglethorpe, co. York. She *d.* s.p.m., 2 Feb. 1740/1. He *m.* secondly, shortly before 29 July 1743,(a) Sarah, da. of (—) MOSELEY, of co. Worcester. He *d.* s.p.m.,(b) 17 April 1747. Will proved 1747. His widow enjoyed the Thirkelby estate for her life. She, who lived in Holles street, Marylebone, *d.* 1783. Will pr. Oct. 1783.(c)

IV. 1747. SIR CHARLES HENRY FRANKLAND, Baronet [1660], nephew and h. male, being 1st s. and h. of Henry FRANKLAND, sometime of Mattersey, Notts, but afterwards Governor of Bengal, by Mary,(d) da. of Alexander CROSS, Merchant, which Henry (who *d.* 23 Aug. 1728, in India), was yr. br. to the late, and 4th s. of the 2d Baronet. He was *b.* about 1716,(e) and was (when 23) Collector of the Port of Boston, in America, 1741 to 1757; *suc. to the Baronetcy,* but not to the estates, 17 April 1747; was Consul General at Lisbon, July 1757 till July 1767, six months before his death, having also been at Lisbon when the great earthquake occurred, 1 Nov. 1755, from which, though buried in the ruins, he "miraculously escaped." He *m.,* before April 1756,(f)

(a) She is then spoken of as "a young lady of 18, a very pretty woman," and on 21 Aug. 1744, a contemporary writes: "Lady Frankland has bedevilled Sir Thomas, and he is an old superannuated fool."

(b) Of his two daughters and coheirs (1), Elizabeth, *m.* John Morley Trevor, of Glynd, co. Sussex; (2), Dinah, *m.* Jan. 1744/5, George Henry (Lee), 3d Earl of Lichfield.

(c) In Musgrave's *Obituary* is, however, the following notice:—"Lady Frankland, relict of Sir Thomas F., Baronet," *d.* 18 Jan. 1761."

(d) This Mary *d.* 14 Oct. 1783, having survived her husband 56 years.

(e) The particulars about his romantic career and marriage are from the *Her. and Gen.* (vol. vii, pp. 258-270, and 383), being a review of Elias Nason's account of him, published 1865 at Albany, New York.

(f) He mentions his *wife* in a mem. of that date. The tradition is that, shortly after the earthquake of 1755, he *m.* this Agnes firstly at Belem (a "Romish priest" officiating), and secondly on board ship soon afterwards. He is said to have brought her, in 1742, from Marblehead to Boston for education, and "subsequently to have made her his mistress." See note "e" above.

Agnes (*bap.* at Marblehead, New England, 17 April 1726), yr. da. of Edward and Mary Surriage. He quitted Lisbon in Aug. 1762, and, after a long illness, *d.* s.p. legit.,[a] at Bath, 11 Jan. 1768, in his 52d year, and was *bur.* at Weston, near there. M.I. Will pr. Jan. 1768. His widow *m.*, Nov. 1781, John Drew, of Chichester, Banker, and *d.* there, 23 April 1783, being *bur.* at St. Pancras, Chichester. M.I., wherein her age is stated to be "about 55."

V. 1768. Sir Thomas Frankland, Baronet [1660], Admiral R.N., afterwards of Thirkelby aforesaid, br. and h., *b.* about 1718; Capt. in the Royal Navy, 1740; captured a French ship, off Havannah, in Dec. 1744; Vice-Admiral of the Red, 1747, and finally Admiral of the White, 1775; was M.P. for Thirsk (seven Parls.), 1747-80 and 1784 till death, having *suc. to the Baronetcy*, 11 Jan. 1768. He, who inherited the Thirkelby estate, sold, 4 Oct. 1779, the estate of Mattersey, Notts (formerly belonging to his grandfather), for £22,000.[b] He *m.* in May 1743, at South Carolina, America, Sarah Rhett (then aged 18), da. or grand da. of Chief Justice Rhett. He *d.* 21 Nov. 1784 at Bath, in his 66th year. M.I. at Thirkelby. Will pr. Dec. 1784, March 1809, and Feb. 1833. His widow, by whom he had nineteen children, *d.* 20 Sep. 1808, aged 84. Will pr. 1808.

VI. 1784. Sir Thomas Frankland, Baronet [1660], of Thirkelby aforesaid, 2d but 1st surv. s. and h.; *b.* in Old Bond Street, Sep. 1750; ed. at Eton, 1761; matric. at Oxford (Merton Coll.), 28 June 1768, and then said to be 17; *cr.* M.A., 4 July 1771; admitted to Lincoln's Inn, 22 Jan. 1772; M.P. for Thirsk, 1774-80, and 1796 to Oct. 1801, having *suc. to the Baronetcy* 21 Nov. 1784; Sheriff of Yorkshire, 1792; F.R.S., F.L.S., and F.H.S., being a distinguished man of science. He *m.* in March 1773, Dorothy, da. of William Smelt, br. to Leonard Smelt, Sub. Gov. to George, Prince of Wales, afterwards George IV. She *d.* 19 May 1820. He *d.* 4 Jan. 1831 at Thirkelby, aged 80. M.I.

VII. 1831. Sir Robert Frankland, *afterwards* (1837-49) Frankland-Russell, Baronet [1660], of Thirkelby aforesaid, 2d but only surv. s. and h., *b.* July 1784; was M.P. for Thirsk (seven Parls.), 1815 to March 1834; *suc. to the Baronetcy* and to the Frankland estates, 4 Jan. 1831, and subsequently, on the death, 14 Dec. 1836, of his cousin, Sir Robert Greenhill-Russell, Baronet [so *cr.* 1831], suc. to the estate of Checquers Court in Ellesborough, Bucks (being that of his ancestor, Sir John Russell, 4th Baronet [1629], whose da. Elizabeth *m.*, in 1683, Sir Thomas Frankland, 2d Baronet), and took by Royal Lic., Feb. 1837, the name of Russell after that of Frankland. He *m.*, 30 Nov. 1815, Louisa Anne, 3d da. of Lord George Murray, Bishop of St. Davids (2d s. of John, 3d Duke of Atholl [S.]), by Anne Charlotte, da. of Lieut.-Gen. Francis Grant. He *d.* s.p.m.[c] 11 March 1849, in his 65th year, at Thirkelby Hall. Will pr. May 1849. His widow, who was *b.* 29 May 1790, *d.* 21 Feb. 1871. at Checquers Court aforesaid, aged 80.

(a) He had an illegitimate son, named Harry Cromwell (to commemorate his descent from Oliver Cromwell), who, according to the inscription on his monument, was *b.* 1 March 1745, but who, according to a mem. of his father (23 Oct. 1756), was *b.* Feb. 1741. He entered the Royal Navy, Oct. 1756, and became Vice-Admiral of the Red. He took the name of Frankland by Royal licence, 1 Jan. 1806, and *d.* 31 Jan. 1814. M.I. at Chichester Cathedral.

(b) *Her. and Gen.*, vol. vii, p. 383.

(c) His estates (of which Thirkelby had been held above 200 years by the Frankland family in the male line) devolved, after the death of his widow, on his daughters and coheirs, of whom (1) Emily Anne, Lady Payne-Gallwey, inherited Thirkelby, and took by Royal lic., 2 Oct. 1882, the name of Payne-Frankland. See Payne, Baronet, *cr.* 1812, under the 2d Baronet. (2) Rosalind Alicia, *m.* 7 Sep.. 1854, Lieut.-Col. Francis L'Estrange Astley (who *d.* 9 April 1866), and, having inherited the estate of Checquers, took, in 1872, the name of Frankland-Russell-Astley.

VIII. 1849. Sir Frederick William Frankland, Baronet [1660], cousin and h. male, being 1st s. and h. of the Rev. Roger Frankland, Canon of Wells and Rector of Yarlington, co. Somerset, by Catharine (*m.* June 1792), da. of John (Colville), Lord Colville of Culross [S.], which Roger, who *d.* 23 March 1826, was yr. br. of the 6th and 5th s. of the 5th Baronet. He was *b.* 11 May 1793, at Yarlington; ed. at the Military Coll. of Marlow and at Woolwich; joined the army in Portugal, Dec. 1812, serving in the campaigns of 1813, 1814, and 1815, in the battles of the Pyrenees, Nivelle, Nive, Bidassoa, Toulouse, and Waterloo, receiving Peninsula and Waterloo medals; served afterwards in the West and East Indies till 1825; *suc. to the Baronetcy* (but to none of the family estates), 11 March 1849. He *m.*, 22 Aug. 1821, at Paris, Katharine Margaret, only da. of Isaac Scarth, of Stakesby, co. York, Capt. in Royal Durham Rangers, by Elizabeth, sister of William Johnston, of Annandale, in the island of Grenada. She *d.* 1 Nov. 1871, at her son's house at Cheltenham. He *d.* 11 March 1878, at Hilldrop Villa, Torquay, Devon, in his 85th year.

IX. 1878 Sir William Adolphus Frankland, Baronet [1660], 4th but 1st surv. s. and h.; *b.* at Muntham Park, co. Sussex, 12 Aug. 1837; ed. at Woolwich; Lieut. Royal Engineers, 1855; Capt. 1862; Major, 1872: Lieut. Col., 1881, when he retired, having *suc. to the Baronetcy* 11 March 1878. He *m.* 25 Feb. 1864, Lucy Ducarel, 1st da. of Francis Adams, of Cotswold Grange, co. Gloucester, by Maria, da. of the Rev. John Frederick Doveton, of Everdon Hall, co. Northampton, Rector of Mells and Burnet, co. Somerset. He *d.* at Sunbury on Thames, 29 Nov. 1883, aged 46. His widow. living 1902.

X. 1883. Sir Frederick William Francis George Frankland, Baronet [1660], 1st s. and h., *b.* 2 Sep. 1868, at Manchester; *suc. to the Baronetcy*, 29 Nov. 1883; ed. at Cheltenham College; sometime Lieut. Royal Dublin Fusileers; served in the Transvaal War; was, in 1894, Inspector of Mines at Matabele; Capt. Beds. Militia. He *m.* firstly, 10 Dec. 1890, at the church of the Incarnation, Maddison Avenue, New York, Charlotte, only da. of John Augustus de Zerega, of Island Hall, West Chester, New York. She *d.* s.p., 24 March 1892, at the Hotel D'Albion, Hyeres, in South France, and was *bur.* 12 April, from Woodlawn, at New York. He *m.* secondly, 12 Nov. 1901, at Trinity Church. Chelsea, Mary Cecil, only child of Col. George Augustus Curzon (grandson of Harriett Anne, *suo jure* Baroness de la Zouche), by his 2d wife, Mary, da. of William Ince Anderton.

STYDOLPH, *or* STIDDOLPH:

cr. 24 Dec. 1660;

ex. 13 Feb. 1676/7.

I. 1660, to 1677. "Richard Stiddolph [*or* Stydolph] of Norbury [in Mickleham], co. Surrey, Esq.," only surv. s. and h. of Sir Francis Stydolph, of the same (*d.* 12 March 1655, aged 75), by Mary, da. of Sir James Altham, one of the Barons of the Exchequer, was *b.* probably about 1630,[a] and, having suc. his father in March 1655, was *cr. a Baronet*, as above, 24 Dec. 1660; Sheriff of Surrey, 1667-68. He *m.* Elizabeth, da. of Sir George Stonhouse, 3d Baronet [1628], of Radley, by Martha, da. of Richard (Lovelace), 1st Baron Lovelace of Hurley. He *d.* s.p.m.,[b] 13 Feb. 1676/7, and was *bur.* at Mickleham, when the *Baronetcy* became *extinct*. Will dat. 10 April 1676, pr. 1677. His widow *m.*, 25 June 1685, at Westm. Abbey (Lic. Fac.), as his 2d wife, William (Byron), 2d Baron Byron of Rochdale, who *d.* 13 Nov. 1695. She *d.* in London, 28 Dec. 1703, in her 77th year, and was *bur.* with her 1st husband. Will dat. 8 Jan. 1702/3, pr. 1 Jan. 1703/4.

(a) His elder br., Thomas, *d.* unm., v.p., 21 June 1652, aged 25.

(b) Of his two daughters and coheirs (1), Frances, Baroness Astley of Reading, *d.* s.p. 11 July 1692; (2), Margaret, *m.* Thomas Tryon, of Bullwick, co. Northampton, and had issue.

GARDINER, *or* GARDNER:

cr. 24 Dec. 1660;

ex. 20 Dec. 1779.

I. 1660. "William Gardner [*or* Gardiner], Citizen of London," and of St. Michael's, Bassishaw, in that city, s. of Robert Gardiner, of Wigan, co. Lanc., by Mary, sister to Sir William Palmer, of Hill, co. Bedford, was *b.* probably about 1618; was a Burgess of Wigan, 1639; a Barrister [*Qy.* Middle Temple]; M.P. for Wigan, 1660, till unseated in June, and was *cr. a Baronet*, as above, 24 Dec. 1660. He was subsequently made **K.B.** at the coronation of Charles II, in April 1661. He *m.*, 28 May 1661, at St. Pancras, Midx. (Lic. Fac. 27), Jane (then aged 18), sister and h. of Bernard Brocas, of Beaurepaire, Hants (*d.* unm. 1650, aged 21), only da. of Robert Brocas, of the same, by Jane, da. of Sir John Bodley. With her he acquired the estate of Roche Court, in Fareham, Hants. He was *bur.*, 23 June 1691, at Fareham. Admon., 6 July 1691, to a creditor. His widow *m.*, in 1691, David Morris, of Lambeth.

II. 1691. Sir Brocas Gardiner, Baronet [1660], of Roche Court aforesaid, 1st s. and h., *b.* about 1664[a]; admitted to the Inner Temple; *suc. to the Baronetcy* in June 1691; was one of the Commissioners of the Stamp office, 1713-29. He *m.*, in or before 1697, Alicia, 4th da. of Sir John Kelinge, Serjeant at Law (s. and h. of Lord Ch. Justice Kelinge), by Philippa, da. of Amerigo Salvetti Antellminelli, Resident for the Duke of Tuscany. She *d.* 3 Jan. 1734, aged 66. He *d.* 13 Jan. 1739/40, and was *bur.* at St. George the Martyr, Midx., aged 76.

III. 1740, to 1779. Sir William Gardiner, Baronet [1660], of Roche Court aforesaid, only surv. s. and h.,[b] *b.* probably about 1700; *suc. to the Baronetcy*, 13 Jan. 1739/40; was Sheriff of Hants, 1751; held a post in the Pay Office. He *m.* Elizabeth Cole. She *d.* 4, and was *bur.* 10 July 1747, at Fareham. He *d.* s.p.[c] 20, and was *bur.* 25 Oct. 1779, at Fareham, aged about 80, when the *Baronetcy* became *extinct*. Will pr. Nov. 1779.

JUXON:

cr. 28 Dec. 1660;

ex. 3 Feb. 1739/40.

I. 1660 "William Juxon, of Albourne, co. Sussex, Esq.," only s. and h. of John Juxon, of St. Bennets, Paul's Wharf, London (*bur.* there 12 Jan. 1654/5), by his 2d wife, Anne (*m.* Nov. 1635), da. of William Michelborne, of Westmeston, co. Sussex, was *b.* in 1637, and was, presumably in consideration of the services of his uncle, William Juxon, Archbishop of Canterbury (who, when Bishop of London, had attended Charles I. at his Execution in Jan. 1648/9), *cr. a Baronet*, as above, 28 Dec. 1660. By the death of the said Archbishop, 4 June 1663 (in his 81st year) he inherited the estate of Little Compton, co. Gloucester. He was Sheriff of that county, 1676-77, and recorded his pedigree at the Heralds' Visitation thereof 1682, being then aged 45. He *m.* 7 April 1659, at Saresden, Oxon (publication at St. Paul's, Covent Garden), Eliza-

---

(a) His yr. br. Bernard, *bap.* 25 Sep. 1668, at Fareham, was Warden of All Souls' College, Oxford, 1702, till his death, 22 April 1726.

(b) His br., Brocas Gardiner, matric. at Oxford (Mag. Coll.) 4 June 1712, aged 15; B.A. (New Coll.), 1719.

(c) The estates devolved on John Whalley, of Tackley, Oxon, whose mother, Grace, was da. of the Rev. Bernard Gardiner, D.D., Warden of All Souls', Oxford, yr. s. of the 1st Baronet. This John took the name of Gardiner after that of Whalley, and was *cr. a Baronet* 14 Jan. 1783, which dignity became *extinct* 6 Oct. 1868.

beth, da. of Sir William Walter, 1st Baronet [1641], of Saresden aforesaid, by Elizabeth, da. of Thomas Lucas, of Colchester. She was *bur.* 22 Aug. 1709, at Little Compton aforesaid. He was *bur.* there 11 Sep. 1719. Limited admon. (wherein he is called "of Seasoncote, co. Glouc.") 9 Dec. 1736.

II. 1719, to 1740. Sir William Juxon, Baronet [1660], of Little Compton, aforesaid, 1st s. and h., *b.* 8 and *bap.* 24 June 1660, at Saresden aforesaid; matric. at Oxford (St. John's Coll.), 19 Jan. 1676/7, aged 16; *suc. to the Baronetcy* in Sep. 1719. He *m.* 2 Dec. 1726, at St. Bennet's, Paul's Wharf aforesaid, Susanna, yst. da. of John Marriott, of Sturton Hall, Suffolk, and of Sonning, Berks. He *d.* s.p. 3, and was *bur.* 12 Feb. 1739/40, at Little Compton, when the *Baronetcy* became *extinct*.[a] M.I. Will dat. 18 Sep. 1738 to 25 Sep. 1739, pr. 27 March 1742. His widow *m.* 7 June 1749, at St. Bennet's aforesaid, Charles (Fane), 2d Viscount Fane [I.], who *d.* s.p., 24 Jan. 1766. She *d.* in Curzon street, Mayfair, 10 April 1792, aged 86. M.I. at Little Compton. Will pr. April 1792.

LEGARD:

cr. 29 Dec. 1660.

I. 1660. "John Legard, of Ganton, co. York, Esq.," only s. and h. of John Legard, (aged 6 in 1612, who *d.* v.p. before 1643), by Mary, da. and h. of John Dawnay, of Potter Brompton, co. York, was *b.* about 1631; suc. his grandfather, John Legard, in the family estates, in 1643; took part in the taking of the city of York to facilitate the King's Restoration, and was *cr. a Baronet*, as above, 29 Dec. 1660. He was M.P. for Scarborough, 1660, and was aged 34 at the Visit. of Yorkshire in 1665. He *m.* firstly, 18 Oct. 1655, at Hornby, co. York, Grace, 3d da. of Conyers (Darcy), 1st Earl of Holdernesse, by Grace, da. and h. of Thomas Rokeby. She *d.* s.p.m., in or before 1658. He *m.* secondly, 12 Aug. 1658, at St. Andrew's, Holborn, Frances, 1st da. and coheir of Sir Thomas Widdrington, of Chesbourne Grange, co. Northumberland, by Frances, 1st da. and coheir of Ferdinando (Fairfax), 2d Lord Fairfax of Cameron [S.],[b] He *d.* 1678, and was *bur.* at Ganton.

II. 1678. Sir John Legard, Baronet [1660], of Ganton aforesaid, 1st s. and h., by 2d wife; *bap.* 16 June, 1659, at Coney street; aged 6 at the Visit. of Yorkshire, 1665; having, apparently, been already admitted to Gray's Inn, 2 Feb. 1662/3.[c] He *suc. to the Baronetcy* in 1678, and was Mayor of Scarborough, 1685. He *m.* firstly, probably about 1682, Elizabeth (aged 3 in 1665), 1st da. of Leonard Wastell, of Scorton, co. York, by Elizabeth, da. of John Savile, of Methley. She, by whom he had nine children, *d.* in or before 1695.

(a) His eight brothers (six of whom were living 1682) all *d.* unm., and before him. Of his four sisters, three did so likewise, but Elizabeth, *bap.* 31 Jan. 1663/4, at St. Paul's, Covent Garden, *m.* James St. Amand, of that parish, and had an only child, Martha, *bap.* there 15 March 1704/5, who *m.* firstly Thomas Hesketh, of Rufford, co. Lancaster, and secondly, before Sep. 1738, (—) Chetwynd. By her first husband she had Robert Hesketh, *b.* 23 April 1729, who in 1792 *took the name of Juxon*, and who, on 4 March 1778, by the death of his elder br., Sir Thomas Hesketh, Baronet (so. *cr.* 5 May 1761), became *Sir Robert Juxon* Baronet [1761], and *d.* 30 Dec. 1796.

(b) In right of this match the 5th Baronet claimed part of the Sheffield estates, the mother of the said Frances Fairfax, being Mary, da. of Edmund (Sheffield), 1st Earl of Mulgrave, whose male issue expired on the death of Edmund, 4th Earl of Mulgrave and 2d Duke of Buckingham, in 1735.

(c) The admission of that date is, "John Legard, son and h. of John Legard, of Ganton, co. York, Baronet," and though he was not then 4 years, it is hardly possible to doubt the identity.

He *m.* secondly, in 1695, Dorothy, 1st da. of Sir William CAYLEY, 2d Baronet [1661], of Brompton, co. York, by Mary, da. and h. of Barnabas HOLBECH. He *d.* 5 May 1715, and was *bur.* at Ganton. His widow *d.* 11 July 1739.

III. 1715. SIR JOHN LEGARD, Baronet, [1660], of Ganton aforesaid, 2d but 1st surv. s. and h., by 1st wife; *b.* about 1685; *suc. to the Baronetcy*, 5 May 1715. He *d.* unm. 14 April 1719.

IV. 1719. SIR THOMAS LEGARD, Baronet [1660], of Ganton aforesaid, next br. (of the whole blood) and h.; *b.* about 1686; *suc. to the Baronetcy*, 14 April 1719. He *m.*, 1726/7, Frances, 1st sister and coheir of John DIGBY, of Mansfield Woodhouse, Notts, one of the seven daughters of John DIGBY, of the same. He *d.* 1735. His widow was *bur.* at Coney street, 4 May 1736.

V. 1735. SIR DIGBY LEGARD, Baronet [1660], of Ganton aforesaid, only s. and h., *b.* probably about 1730; *suc. to the Baronetcy* in 1735. He was well known as an experimental agriculturalist. He *m.* in Aug. 1755, Jane, sister and coheir of William CARTWRIGHT, of Ossington, Notts, 3d da. of George CARTWRIGHT, of the same, by (—), one of the seven daughters of the abovenamed John DIGBY, of Mansfield Woodhouse. He *d.* 4 Feb. 1773, at Ganton. Will pr. 29 March 1773. His widow *d.* 15 Sep. 1811, in Yorkshire, aged 75. Will pr. Dec. 1811.

VI. 1773. SIR JOHN LEGARD, Baronet [1660], of Ganton aforesaid, 1st s. and h., *b.* about 1758; *suc. to the Baronetcy*, 4 Feb. 1773. He *m.* 22 June 1782, Jane, da. of Henry ASTON, of Aston, co. Chester. He *d.* s.p., 16 July 1807. Will pr. 1807. His widow *d.* 19 Dec. 1833, at Chester.

VII. 1807. SIR THOMAS LEGARD, Baronet [1660], of Ganton aforesaid, next br. and h., *bap.* 5 Dec. 1762 at the Belfry church, York; was a Commander in the Royal Navy; *suc. to the Baronetcy*, 16 July 1807. He *m.* 26 Dec. 1802, Sarah BISHOPP, Spinster, sometimes said to be a da. of Sir Cecil BISHOPP, Baronet [1620]. She *d.* 26 Jan. or 30 April 1814, aged 33. He *d.* 5 July 1830, aged 67.

VIII. 1830. SIR THOMAS DIGBY LEGARD, Baronet [1660], of Ganton aforesaid, 1st s. and h., *b.* 30 May 1803, at Falsgrave, near Scarborough; matric. at Oxford (Mag. Coll.), 27 June 1821, aged 18; B.A., 1824; admitted to Lincoln's Inn, 30 April 1825; *suc. to the Baronetcy*, 5 July 1830. He *m.* 31 May 1822, Frances, 2d da. of Charles (DUNCOMBE), 1st BARON FEVERSHAM, by Charlotte, da. of William (LEGGE), 2d EARL OF DARTMOUTH. He *d.* at Ganton 10 Dec. 1860, aged 57. His widow, who was *b.* 5 June 1802, *d.* at Scarborough 15 June 1881, in her 80th year.

IX. 1860. SIR FRANCIS DIGBY LEGARD, Baronet [1660], of Ganton aforesaid, 1st s. and h., *b.* 8 May 1833 in Arlington street, Midx.; ed. at Winchester; matric. at Oxford (St. John's Coll.), 10 Dec. 1851, aged 18; *suc. to the Baronetcy*, 10 Dec. 1860. He *d.* unm. at Madeira, 5 Jan. 1865, aged 31.

X. 1865 SIR DARCY WIDDRINGTON LEGARD, Baronet [1660], of Ganton aforesaid, next br. and h.; *b.* 10 Dec. 1843, at Ganton; matric. at Oxford (Oriel Coll.), 23 Jan. 1863, aged 19; *suc. to the Baronetcy*, 5 Jan. 1865. He *d.* unm. at Rome, of a fever, 12 April 1866, aged 22.

XI. 1866. SIR CHARLES LEGARD, Baronet [1660], of Ganton aforesaid, only surv. br. and h.; *b.* 2 April 1846, at Ganton; sometime an officer in the 43d Foot; *suc. to the Baronetcy*, 22 April 1866; was M.P. for Scarborough, 1874-80; Chairman of the East Riding County Council; was an "all round" sportsman. He *m.* 30 April 1878, at Finchley, co. Midx., Frances Emily, yr. da. of Francis Alexander HAMILTON, of Brent Lodge, Finchley. He *d.* s.p. at Scarborough, 7 Dec. 1901, aged 55, and was *bur.* at Ganton. His widow living 1902.

XII. 1901. SIR ALGERNON WILLOUGHBY LEGARD, Baronet [1660], cousin and h. male, being 1st s. and h. of Henry Willoughby LEGARD, an officer in the 9th Lancers, by Charlotte Henrietta, sister of Henry, 8th BARON MIDDLETON, da. of Henry WILLOUGHBY, of Birdsall, co. York, which Henry W. LEGARD (who *d.* 21 Nov. 1845) was br. to the 8th and s. of the 7th Baronet. He was *b.* 14 Oct. 1842; ed. at Marlborough School and Trin. Coll., Cambridge; was sometime Conservative agent for East Derbyshire; *suc. to the Baronetcy*, 7 Dec. 1901. He *m.* 27 July 1872, Alicia Egerton, yst da. of the Rev. George William BROOKS, M.A. [Oxford], Rector of Great Hampden, Bucks.

Family Estates.—These, in 1883, consisted of 6,407 acres in the North and East Ridings of Yorkshire, worth £7,751 a year. *Principal Seat.*—Ganton Hall, near York.

MARWOOD:

cr. 31 Dec. 1660;

ex. 23 Feb. 1739/40.

I. 1660. "GEORGE MARWOOD, of Little Buskby, co. York, Esq.," 1st s. and h. of Henry MARWOOD, of the same (*d.* about 1639),(a) by Anne, da. of John CONSTABLE, of Dromonby, co. York, was *bap.* 28 April 1601, at Stokesley; matric. at Oxford (Lincoln Coll.), 21 March 1616/7, aged 16; was Sheriff of Yorkshire, 1651-52; M.P. for Malton, 1659, and for Northallerton, 1660, and was *cr. a Baronet*, as above, 31 Dec. 1660; was aged 64 at the Visitation of Yorkshire, 1665. He *m.* 3 April 1625, at Alne, co. York, Frances, da. of Sir Walter BETHELL, of Alne aforesaid, by Mary, da. of Sir Henry SLINGSBY, of Scriven. He *d.* 19 Feb. 1679/80, and was *bur.* at St. Michael le Belfry, York, aged 78. Will dat. 26 Aug. 1679, pr. 16 March 1679/80, at York. His widow was *bur.* 6 Jan. 1683/4 at St. Michael's aforesaid. Admon. 7 July 1684, at York.

II. 1680. SIR HENRY MARWOOD, Baronet [1660], of Little Buskby aforesaid, 1st s. and h.; *b.* about 1635; matric. at Oxford (Lincoln Coll.), 2 Oct. 1652; admitted to Gray's Inn, 23 June 1653; was aged 30 at the Visit. of Yorkshire, 1665; Sheriff of Yorkshire, 1674-75; *suc. to the Baronetcy*, 19 Feb. 1679/80; M.P. for Northallerton, 1685-87. He *m.* firstly, 19 May 1658, at Hornby, Margaret, 4th da. of Conyers (DARCY), 1st EARL OF HOLDERNESS, by Grace, da. and h. of Thomas ROKEBY. She *d.* s.p.m., and was *bur.* 18 June 1660, at Stokesley. He *m.* secondly, 6 July 1663, at Heversham, Dorothy, da. of Alan BELLINGHAM, of Levins, co. Westmorland. She was living 1668. He *m.* thirdly, before 1679, Martha, widow of Thomas WOMBWELL, of Wombwell (who *d.* 7 Aug. 1665), da. of Sir Thomas WENTWORTH, of Elmsall, co. York, by his 2d wife, Martha, da. of Sir Thomas HAYES. She, by whom he had no issue, was *bur.* at St. Anne's, Soho, 28 Sep. 1704. Admon. 6 Nov. 1704, at York. He *d.* s.p.m.s., 1, and was *bur.*, 6 Nov. 1725, at Stokesley, aged 89.(b) Will pr. 1728.

III. 1725. SIR SAMUEL MARWOOD, Baronet [1660], nephew and h. male, being 1st s. and h. of George MARWOOD, Hamburg merchant [1665], by Mary, da. of Sir Samuel SWINNOCK, of London, merchant;

(a) "Mr. Henry Marwood, *bur.* 1655 at St. Martin's, Coney street, York," is (if that date is correct) presumably another person, as the date of death given by his son in the Visitation of Yorkshire is "about 1639," viz., sixteen years earlier.

(b) His only s., George Marwood, *bap.* at Stokesley, 27 July 1665, *m.* twice, but *d.* s.p.m. and v.p., being *bur.* at Stokesley, 12 Nov. 1700, leaving an only da. and h., Jane, who *m.* 9 June 1709, Cholmley Turner. She *d.* 10 April 1764, and left the Buskby estate (which she had inherited in 1725) to her cousin John Medcalfe, great grandson of William Medcalfe, of Northallerton, by Anne, da. of Sir George Marwood, the 1st Baronet. He accordingly took the name of Marwood by Act of Parl. in 1765.

was *b.* about 1672, being aged 21 in 1693; and *suc. to the Baronetcy*, but not to the estates, 1 Nov. 1725. He *m.* 8 May 1735, Mary ("£10,000 portion"), da. of [—] PIERSON, of Stokesley. He *d.* s.p., and was *bur.* 31 Oct. 1739 at Stokesley, aged 67.

IV. 1739, to 1740. SIR WILLIAM MARWOOD, Baronet [1660], br. and h., *b.* about 1681, being aged 13 in 1693; *suc. to the Baronetcy* in Oct. 1739. He *m.* Margaret, da. of [—] WOODESON. He *d.* s.p., in Leicester Fields, Midx., 23, and was *bur.* 29 Feb. 1739/40 at Paddington, when the *Baronetcy* became *extinct*. Will, dat. 20 Nov. 1732, pr. 4 June 1740. His widow *d.* a few months after him in St. James', Westm., and was *bur.* 16 Nov. 1740, at Paddington. Admon. 6 Nov. 1740, to Victoria WOODESON, spinster, sister and next of kin.

JACKSON:

cr. 31 Dec. 1660;

ex. about 1730

I. 1660. "JOHN JACKSON, of Hickleton, co. York, Esq.," 1st s. and h. of Sir John JACKSON, of Edderthorpe in that county (*d.* 2 July 1637) by his 2d wife, Fiennes, da. of Sir Thomas WALLER, Governor of Dover Castle, was *b.* about 1631, and was *cr. a Baronet*, as above, 31 Dec. 1660. He was aged 34 at the Visit. of Yorkshire in 1665. He *m.* firstly, in or before 1653, Katharine, sister of George, 1st BARON DELAMERE, da. of William BOOTH, of Dunham, co. Chester, by Vere, da. and coheir of Thomas (EGERTON), 1st VISCOUNT BRACKLEY. She, who was *b.* 11 May 1624, *d.* 1667. He *m.* secondly, Lucy, widow of Sir William JOPSON, 2d Baronet [S. 1635], of Cudworth in Royston, co. York, da. of Henry TINDALL, of Brotherton in that county. He *d.* in or before 1670. Will pr. 1670. The will of his widow dat. 30 June, was pr. 22 Dec. 1693.

II. 1670? SIR JOHN JACKSON, Baronet [1660], of Hickleton aforesaid, 1st s. and h. by 1st wife, *b.* 15 and *bap.* 31 March 1653 at Womersley, co. York; aged 11 in the Visit. of Yorkshire, 1665; matric. at Oxford (Univ. Coll.), 19 May 1670, aged 16; *suc. to the Baronetcy* in or before 1670. He, by his extravagance, ruined the family, and sold or mortgaged most of the estates. He *d.* unm., 6 Feb. 1679/80, and was *bur.* at Hickleton, aged 27. M.I. Will dat. 19 Jan. 1679, pr. at York, 23 April 1680.

III. 1680, to 1730? SIR BRADWARDINE JACKSON, Baronet [1660], br. of the half blood and h. male, being yst. s. of the 1st Baronet by his 2d wife, was *b.* probably about 1670; *suc. to the Baronetcy*, 6 Feb. 1679/80; admitted to Gray's Inn, 9 May 1689. He, who was a Commissioner of land tax, temp. Queen Anne, disposed of what remained of the family estate, 16 Nov. 1704, for an annuity of £40 to himself and to [his uterine sister] Lucy, Countess of Londonderry [I.]. He was in prison for debt in 1706; "still under a cloud" in 1712, and was living unm. in 1727. On his death s.p.m.,(a) the *Baronetcy* became *extinct*.(b)

(a) He had three sisters of the half blood, *viz.* (1) Frances, who *m.* Nicholas Mauleverer, and *d.* May 1712; (2) Vere, who *m.* John Adams, of Owston, co. York; and (3) Katharine.

(b) An article by "C.J.," in the *Her. and Gen.* (vol. v., p. 270), disposes of the theory (Betham's *Baronetage*, vol. v, p. 33, and elsewhere) that George Jackson, of Thirsk (whose great grandson, George Duckett, *formerly* Jackson, was *cr. a Baronet*, 21 June 1791) was a yr. br. of Sir Bradwardine Jackson, of whom, also, some particulars, not elsewhere given, are therein related.

PICKERING:

cr. 2 Jan. 1660/1;

ex. April to Oct. 1705.

I. 1661. "SIR HENRY PICKERING, of Whaddon, co. Cambridge, Knt.," only s. of the Rev. Henry PICKERING, D.D., Rector of Aldwinckle, co. Northampton (*d.* Sep. 1657, aged 73), purchased the estate of WHADDON in 1648; was Col. of Foot in the "New Model," 1645; Sheriff for Cambridgeshire and Huntingdonshire, 1648-49; M.P. for Cambridgeshire, 1654, 1656, and 1658/9; was *Knighted* by the Protector Cromwell, 1 Feb. 1657/8, at Whitehall, and having been, presumably, again *Knighted* by the King, was *cr. a Baronet*, as above, 2 Jan. 1660/1. He *m.* 19 July 1647, at Hackney, Elizabeth, da. of Sir Thomas VINER, 1st Baronet [1661], by his 1st wife, Anne, da. of Richard PARSONS, of London. He *d.* at Whaddon, 4 March 1667/8. Will dat. 1 Nov. 1666, pr. 21 April 1668. His widow was carried away for burial from St. Giles'-in-the-Fields, 24 May 1694. Will dat. 28 April 1693, pr. 21 May 1694.

II. 1668, to 1705. SIR HENRY PICKERING, Baronet [1661], of Whaddon aforesaid, 2d but only surv. s. and h., *b.* about 1653, being under 14, in Nov. 1666; *suc. to the Baronetcy*, 4 March 1667/8; was Sheriff for Cambridgeshire and Huntingdonshire, 1683-84; M.P. for Morpeth, 1685-87, and for Cambridge (four Parls.) 1698-1705. He *m.* firstly, 8 March 1676/7, (Lic. Vic. Gen., 1) Philadelphia (then aged 17), da. of Sir George DOWNING, 1st Baronet [1663], by Frances, sister of Charles, 1st EARL OF CARLISLE, da. of Sir William HOWARD, of Naworth Castle. She probably *d.* at Barbadoes, in or shortly before 1693. He *m.* secondly, before 28 April 1693, Grace, da. of (—) SYLVESTER, of Barbadoes. He *d.* at Barbadoes, s.p.s.,(a) between April and Oct. 1705, and was *bur.* at Whaddon, when the *Baronetcy* became *extinct*. Will dat. 15 April and pr. 27 Oct. 1705. His widow sold the estate of Whaddon in 1716. Her will dat. 17 Aug. 1730, pr. 20 April 1733.

BEDINGFIELD, *or* BEDINGFELD:

cr. 2 Jan. 1660/1;

afterwards, since 1830, PASTON-BEDINGFELD.

I. 1661. "HENRY BEDINGFIELD, of Oxbrough [*i.e.*, Oxburgh], co. Norfolk, Esq.," s. of Sir Henry BEDINGFIELD, of the same (a zealous Royalist, who *d.* 22 Nov. 1657, aged 70), by his 2d wife, Elizabeth, da. and coheir of Peter HOUGHTON, of Houghton Tower, co. Lancaster, was *b.* Sep. 1614; was a Capt. in the King's Army, and was, for the losses sustained by his family in the Royal cause (estimated at £47,000), *cr. a Baronet*, as above, 2 Jan. 1660/1. He suc. to the family estates on the death s.p., 26 April 1665, of his elder br. (of the half blood) Col. Thomas BEDINGFELD, of Oxburgh. He *m.*, in April 1635, Margaret, da. and h. of Edward PASTON, of Appleton, co. Norfolk, and of Horton, co. Glouc., by Frances, da. of Sir John SYDENHAM, of Brimpton, co. Somerset. He *d.* 24 Feb. 1684/5, aged 70 years and 5 months, and was *bur.* at Oxburgh. M.I. Will dat. 30 June 1684, pr. 9 March 1684/5 in the Consistory Court of Norwich. His widow *d.* 14 Jan. 1702, aged 84, and was *bur.* at Oxburgh.(b) M.I. Will pr. May 1703.

(a) Of his children by his 1st wife (1), Elizabeth was *bap.* 27 Nov. 1679, at St. Margaret's, Westm., and was living 28 April 1693; (2), Anne, *d.* unm.; and (3), Mary, "heir expectant," *m.* (as his 2d wife), Jan. 1696/7, John (Cutts), Baron Cutts of Gowran [I.], and *d.* in childbed s.p., Nov. 1697, before him, who *d.* s.p., 26 Jan. 1707. His only sister, Honour, *b.* 9 and *bap.* 23 Sep. 1652, *m.* (Lic. Vic. Gen., 19 Nov. 1673) Sidney Pickering, of London, Merchant, and *d.* before 1681, in his lifetime.

(b) See an account of her merits in Wotton's *Baronetage* [1740], vol. iii, p. 215.

II. 1685. SIR HENRY BEDINGFIELD, or BEDINGFELD, Baronet [1661], of Oxburgh aforesaid, s. and h., b. 1636; accompanied H.R.H. the Duke of Gloucester to England in 1660 and was *Knighted* v.p., probably soon afterwards, but certainly before 1682; *suc. to the Baronetcy*, 24 Feb. 1684/5. He *m.* firstly, Anne, da. and h. of Charles (HOWARD), 2d EARL OF BERKSHIRE, by Dorothy, da. of Thomas (SAVAGE), VISCOUNT SAVAGE. She *d.* s.p., 19 Sep. 1682, aged 32, and was *bur.* at Oxburgh. M.I. He *m.* secondly, about 1685, Elizabeth, yst. da. and coheir of Sir John ARUNDELL, of Lanherne, co. Cornwall, by his 1st wife, Elizabeth, da. of John (ROPER), BARON TEYNHAM. She *d.* 13 April 1690, in her 35th year, and was *bur.* at Oxburgh. M.I. He *d.* 14 Sep. 1704, aged 68, and was *bur.* there. M.I. Will pr. May 1705.

III. 1704. SIR HENRY ARUNDELL BEDINGFELD, Baronet [1661], of Oxburgh aforesaid, s. and h. by 2d wife, *b.* between 1683 and 1690, *suc. to the Baronetcy*, 14 Sep. 1704. He *m.* in Aug. 1719, Elizabeth, 1st da. of Charles (BOYLE), 2d EARL OF BURLINGTON, by Juliana, da. and h. of Henry NOEL, of North Luffenham. She *d.* 25 Nov. 1751. He *d.* 15 July 1760, both being *bur.* at Oxburgh. M.I. Will dat. 17 June 1760, pr. 1760.

IV. 1760. SIR RICHARD HENRY BEDINGFELD, Baronet [1661], of Oxburgh aforesaid, 5th but 1st surv. s. and h., *b.* 14 Sep. 1720, *suc. to the Baronetcy* 15 July 1760. He *m.* 30 March or Sep. 1761, Mary, da. of Anthony (BROWNE), 6th VISCOUNT MONTAGU, by Barbara, da. of Sir John WEBB, 3d Baronet [1644]. She, who was *b.* 27 May 1733, *d.* in childbirth, 17 and was *bur.* 23 Sep. 1767, in Bath Abbey. M.I. He *d.* 27 March 1795, at Oxburgh. Admon. April 1795.

V. 1795. SIR RICHARD BEDINGFELD, Baronet [1661], of Oxburgh aforesaid, only s. and h., *b.* 23 Aug. 1767 at Bath, *suc. to the Baronetcy* 27 March 1795. He *m.* 16 June 1795, at St. Geo., Han. sq., Charlotte Georgiana, sister of George, LORD STAFFORD, da. of Sir William JERNINGHAM, 6th Baronet [1621], by Frances, da. of Henry (DILLON), 11th VISCOUNT DILLON OF COSTELLO GALLEN [I.]. He *d.* 22 Nov. 1829. Will pr. Feb. 1830 and June 1852. His widow, who by royal warrant in Oct. 1831, was granted the precedence of the da. of a Baron, and who was Woman of the Bedchamber to Adelaide, the Queen Consort, *d.* in London 29 July 1854. Will pr. Sep. 1854.

VI. 1829. SIR RICHARD HENRY BEDINGFELD, *afterwards* [1830-62] PASTON-BEDINGFELD, Baronet [1661], of Oxburgh aforesaid, 1st s. and h., *b.* there 10 May 1800; *suc. to the Baronetcy*, 22 Nov. 1829. Having *m.*, 30 Aug. 1826, at Bath, Margaret, only da. and h. of Edward PASTON, of Appleton, co. Norfolk, he took by royal lic., 11 April 1830, the name of *Paston* before that of *Bedingfeld*. He was, in 1858, declared by the Committee for Privileges to be one of the coheirs(a) of the Barony of Grandison, which was *cr.* by writ, 6 Feb. 1298/9, but had been in abeyance for about five centuries. He *d.* 4 Feb. 1862. His widow, who in his lifetime had by royal lic., 26 March 1841, taken the name of *Bisshopp* before that of *Bedingfeld* (on inheriting the estate of George BISSHOPP, M.D., of Brailesford, co. Warwick), *d.* 31 Jan. 1887, at 4, The Circus, Bath, in her 80th year.

VII. 1862. SIR HENRY GEORGE PASTON-BEDINGFELD, Baronet, [1661], of Oxburgh, 1st s. and h., *b.* 21 June 1830, at Norwich; ed. at Stonyhurst Coll.; Captain in West Norfolk Militia; served in the Austrian cavalry; *suc. to the Baronetcy*, 4 Feb. 1862. He *m.* 27 Oct. 1859, Augusta, only child of Edward CLAVERING, of Callaby Castle, co. Northumberland. He *d.* 18 Jan. 1902, at 45 Cromwell Houses, Cromwell Road, London, in his 72d year. His widow living 1903.

(a) He was, through the families of Paston, Tuddenham, Patteshull, and Grandison, heir to Dame Katherine Tuddenham, in whom *one-fourth of a third* of the representation of the Barony of Grandison had vested.

VIII. 1902. SIR HENRY EDWARD BEDINGFELD, Baronet [1661], of Oxburgh aforesaid, 1st s. and h. *b.* 29 Aug. 1860; Captain 3d Liverpool Reg. (Militia), *suc. to the Baronetcy*, 18 Jan. 1902.

Family Estates.—These, in 1883, consisted of 4,800 acres in Norfolk, and 838 in Warwickshire. *Total*, 5,638 acres, worth £5,844 a year. *Principal Seat*, Oxburgh Hall, near Stoke Ferry, co. Norfolk.

PLOMER, *or* PLUMER:

cr., 4 Jan. 1660/1;

ex., 26 April 1697.

I. 1661 to 1697. "WALTER PLOMER, of the Inner Temple, London, Esq.," s. of Thomas PLOMER, *or* PLUMER, of Mitcham, Surrey, (*d.* 1639), by Mary (*bap.* 27 Nov. 1586, at St. Mary Bothaw, London), da. of Geoffrey ELWES, Alderman and sometime (1607-08) Sheriff of London, was *b.* about 1621; matric. at Oxford (Queen's Coll.), 24 Nov. 1637, aged 16; admitted to Inner Temple, Nov. 1640, and was *cr. a Baronet*, as above, 4 Jan. 1660/1; Sheriff of Surrey, 1663-64. He *d.* unm., 26 April 1697, aged 77, and was *bur.* at St. Swithin's, London, when the *Baronetcy* became *extinct.*(a) Will, as of Mitcham, dat. 21 July 1692, pr. 29 April 1697, by John Plumer, of Blakesware, Herts, the universal legatee.

SPRINGET:

cr. 8 Jan. 1660/1;

ex. 5 Jan. 1661/2.

I. 1661, to 1662. "HERBERT SPRINGET, of Broyle [Place, in Ringmer], co. Sussex, Esq.," 1st s. and h. of Sir Thomas SPRINGET, of the same (*d.* 17 Sep. 1639, aged 51), by Mary, da. of John BELLINGHAM, of Erringham, was *b.* about 1615; was M.P. for New Shoreham, 1646 till secluded in 1648; for Sussex, 1654-55, and for New Shoreham (again), 1660 and 1661 till his death; and was *cr. a Baronet*, as above, 8 Jan. 1660/1. He *m.* in or before 1635, Barbara, 1st da. of Sir William CAMPION, of Combwell, co. Kent, by Elizabeth, da. and coheir of Sir William STONE, of London. He *d.* s.p.m.(b) 5 and was *bur.* 14 Jan. 1661/2, at Ringmer, when the *Baronetcy* became *extinct*. Will dat. 2 Jan. 1661/2, pr. 20 Oct. 1662. His widow was *bur.* 6 March 1696/7, at Ringmer. Will dat. 15 June 1694, pr. 12 April 1697.

(a) In Aug. 1885, "John Bagwell Plumer, of Allerton, near Totness, landowner and landholder [son of John Plumer, of the Stock Exchange, and] grandson and lineal heir male of Richard Plumer, of the South Sea House, Esq., deceased," petitioned the Queen "that the Baronetcy conferred on Walter Plumer, in the year 1660, may be conferred on the heirs male of the body of the said Richard Plumer." Richard Plumer (mentioned as his son in the will of Robert Plumer, of Monmouth, pewterer, in 1686) was, by the petitioner, assumed to have been (in reality) a son of the 1st Baronet, to have *m.* at Ludlow in 1663, and to have had two children living in 1686, viz., Richard (presumably ancestor to the petitioner) and Christian.

(b) Of his three daughters and coheirs (1), Mary, *m.* Sir John Stapley, Baronet [so *cr.* 1660], and *d.* 1708, aged 74; (2), Elizabeth, *m.* John Whalley, of Ringmer, and (3), Charity, *d.* unm.

POWELL, *otherwise* HINSON:

cr. 23 Jan. 1660/1;

ex. 11 Dec. 1680.

I. 1661, to 1680. "WILLIAM POWELL, *alias* HINSON, of Pengethley, co. Hereford, Esq.," 2d s.(a) of Thomas HINSON, of Dublin, and afterwards of Fulham, co. Midx. (*d.* 1669) by Anne, sister of Sir Edward POWELL, Baronet [so *cr.* 18 Jan. 1621/2], of Pengethly in Sellack, co. Hereford, da. of Edmund POWELL, of the same, and of Mustow in Fulham aforesaid, was *b.* probably about 1620; admitted to the Middle Temple, 4 Dec. 1646; Barrister, 11 Feb. 1647; suc. to the estates of his said uncle in 1653; assumed the name of *Powell*; was Sheriff of Herefordshire, 1657-58, and M.P. for that county, 1660, and was *cr. a Baronet*, as above, 23 Jan. 1660/1. He *m.* firstly, 22 May 1649, at St. Barth. the Less, London, Katharine, da. of Richard ZOUCH, D.C.L., Judge of the Admiralty Court [1641], by Sarah, da. of [—]. She *d.*, v.p., before Oct. 1660. He *m.* secondly Mary, widow of Sir John BRYDGES, 2d Baronet [1627] of Wilton (who *d.* 21 Feb. 1651/2) only da. and h. of James PEARLE, of Dewsal and Aconbury, co. Hereford. She was *bur.* at Aconbury. He *d.* s.p.m.,(b) 11 Dec. 1680, and was *bur.* at Sellack, when the *Baronetcy* became *extinct*. M.I. Will pr. 1681.

NEWTON:

cr. 25 Jan. 1660/1;

ex. Nov. 1670.

I. 1661, to 1670. "ROBERT NEWTON, of the city of London, Esq.," citizen thereof, was *cr. a Baronet*, as above, 25 Jan. 1660/1. He *m.* Elizabeth, da. and coheir of Francis LANGSTONE, *or* LONGSTON, of London and Shropshire. She was *bur.* 6 Feb. 1661/2, at St. Benet's, Gracechurch, London. Funeral certif. at the Coll. of Arms. He *d.* s.p.m.(c) and was *bur.* there 3 Nov. 1670, when the *Baronetcy* became *extinct*. Will pr. Oct. 1670.

STOUGHTON, *or* STAUGHTON:

cr. 29 Jan. 1660/1;

ex. Jan. 1691/2.

I. 1661. "NICHOLAS STAUGHTON [*rectius* Stoughton], of Staughton [*i.e.*, Stoughton, in Stoke, by Guildford], co. Surrey, Esq." 2d but only surv. s. and h. of Anthony STOUGHTON, of the same, by Agnes, da. of Robert PEARSE (which Anthony, who *d.* 14 Jan. 1643/4, aged 46, was s. and h. of Sir Laurence STOUGHTON), was *bap.* 8 Feb. 1634/5, at Stoke; admitted to Inner

(a) His elder br., Thomas Hinson, Registrar-General for the Province of Munster, was *cr.* a B.C.L. of Oxford, 31 Jan. 1643/4. He was *bur.* at Fulham, 29 Nov. 1685.

(b) Of his eight children (four by each wife), the yst. da. Mary, *bap.* 27 Jan. 1662/3, alone survived him. She *m.* Sir John Williams, 2d Baronet [1674] of Eltham, and was *bur.* 6 May 1723, at Sellack. Her 4th da. and coheir, Penelope, *m.* Thomas Symonds, of Sugwass, co. Hereford, whose great-grandson, Thomas Powell Symonds (*b.* Dec. 1788), inherited the Pengethley estate.

(c) Elizabeth, his da. and h., *m.* firstly Sir John Baker, 3d Baronet [1611], of Sissinghurst, who *d.* 28 March 1661. She *m.* secondly, 23 March 1668, Sir Philip Howard (who was *bur.* 15 April 1686 at Westm. Abbey), and was *bur.* 29 Nov. 1693, with her first husband, at Cranbrook.

Temple (being then of St. John's, Warwick), Nov. 1648; matric. at Oxford (Ex. Coll.) 21 July 1653; B.C.L. 12 March 1656/7; D.C.L. 18 May 1659; incorp. at Cambridge, 1659, and was *cr. a Baronet*, as above, 29 Jan. 1660/1; was sheriff of Surrey, 1662-63. He *m.* 2 June 1662 (Lic. Lond., 30 May, to marry at Chipping Barnet, Herts), Elizabeth (then aged 20), 2d da. of Sir Henry MASSINGBERD, 1st Baronet [1660], by his first wife, Elizabeth, da. of William LYSTER. She *d.* 6 Sep. 1682. He *d.* 30 June 1686. Will pr. May 1691.

II. 1686, to 1692. SIR LAURENCE STOUGHTON, Baronet [1661] of Stoughton aforesaid, only s. and h., *b.* 17 Sep. 1668; *suc. to the Baronetcy*, 30 June 1686; matric. at Oxford (Corpus Christi Coll.), 9 Nov. 1686, aged 18; adm. to Inner Temple, 6 May 1686, and to Gray's Inn, 26 April 1689. He *m.* 18 Dec. 1691, at St. Mary Mag., Old Fish street, London (Lic. Fac., 17), Mary (then about 16), da. of John BURNABY, of St. Martin's-in-the-Fields, co. Midx., Brewer. He *d.* s.p.(a) (a few weeks subsequently) at St. Martin's aforesaid, Jan. 1691/2, when the Baronetcy became *extinct.*(b) Admon. 19 July and will pr. Dec. 1692. His widow *m.* 1 June 1693, at St. Mary Mag. aforesaid (Lic. Fac., 30 May) Watkinson PAYLER (s. and h. ap. of Sir Watkinson PAYLER, 3d Baronet [1642], who *d.* v.p. before 1705. She *m.* (as her 3d husband), Thomas TURNER, Barrister, and *d.* in Lincoln's Inn Fields, March, 1732. Admon. 27 April 1732, to her said husband "Thomas Turner, Esq.," and again Aug. 1821.

ROKEBY:

cr. 29 Jan. 1660/1;

ex. 6 July 1678.

I. 1661. "WILLIAM ROKEBY, of Syers [*i.e.*, Skiers], co. York, Esq.," s. and h. of William ROKEBY, of Hotham in that county (aged 28, in 1584), by Dorothy, da. of William ROKEBY, of Skiers aforesaid, was *b.* about 1601, purchased the estate of Skiers from the heirs of his maternal grandfather, and was *cr. a Baronet*, as above, 29 Jan. 1660/1; was aged 64 at the Visit. of Yorkshire, in 1665. He *m.* in or before 1628, Frances, sister of Sir Willoughby HICKMAN, 1st Baronet [1643], da. of Sir William HICKMAN, of Gainsboro', by his second wife, Elizabeth, sister of William, 3d BARON WILLOUGHBY OF PARHAM, da. of the Hon. William WILLOUGHBY. He, who was living 1665, *d.* in or before 1676 and, as was his wife, was *bur.* at Wentworth. Monuments erected there in 1676.

II. 1676? SIR WILLIAM ROKEBY, Baronet [1661] of Skyres aforesaid, grandson and h., being only s. and h. of Alexander ROKEBY, by Margaret (*m.* 25 April 1653, at Holkham, co. Norfolk, da. of John COKE, of Holkham aforesaid, which Alexander, who *d.* v.p. 1667, aged 37, and was *bur.* at Welton, was 2d s. of the late Baronet. He was *b.* about 1656, being aged 9 at the Visit. of Yorkshire, 1665; *suc. to the Baronetcy* on the death of his grandfather. He *m.*, about 1676, Dorothy, da. and h. of Edward DARCY.(c) He *d.* s.p.m.,(d) April 1678, aged about 22. Admon. 2 July 1678. His widow, who lived at Whitehall, *m.* Col. the Hon. Thomas PASTON, who *d.* at sea in 1691. She was *bur.* 6 Dec. 1729, at St. James', Westm. Will pr. 1730.

(a) In Feb. 1695/6, an Act was passed for the sale of his estates to pay his debts and raise portions for his sisters and coheirs.

(b) In Gibson's *Camden* he is called "a young gentleman of great hope."

(c) According to Hunter's *Familiæ Minorum Gentium*, she was "da. of [—] Stanhope," but it is added that "Wilson's MS., Leeds, says that Sir Wil. d. s.p., and that his sister and h., Dorothy, m. [—] Stanhope."

(d) Elizabeth, his da., is mentioned in the will of her uncle, the 3d Baronet, who leaves her £1,000. She is not to be confused with the "da. of Lady Rookeby (her fortune said to be about £10,000)," who *m.* in Oct. 1708 (as his 2d wife), Sir Stafford Fairborn, for that person (*m.* 20 Oct. 1708, at St. Giles'-in-the-Fields) was *Rebecca Paston*, her ladyship's da. *by her second husband*, Colonel Paston.

III. 1678, April to July. SIR WILLOUGHBY ROKEBY, Baronet [1661], uncle and h. male, being 3d and yst. s. of the 1st Baronet, was *b.* about 1632; admitted to St. John's Coll., Cambridge, 18 June 1646; admitted to Lincoln's Inn, 22 Dec. 1649; aged 33 at the Visit. of Yorkshire, 1665; *suc. to the Baronetcy* in April 1678, but *d.* unm. three months afterwards, 6 July 1678, aged 46, when the *Baronetcy* became *extinct*. Will dat. 6 July 1678.

ERNLE, *or* ERNLEY:
cr. 2 Feb. 1660/1;
ex. 30 March 1734,
or 26 Dec. 1787.

I. 1661. "WALTER ERNLEY [*or* ERNLE], of New Sarum, Wilts, Esq.," s. and h. of Edward ERNLEY, of Etchilhampton in that county (*d.* 30 Nov. 1656, in his 70th year), by Gertrude, da. of John ST. LOWE, of Knighton, Wilts, was *cr. a Baronet*, as above, 2 Feb. 1660/1, with, possibly, a spec. rem. in favour of his br. Michael and the heirs male of his body; Sheriff of Wilts, 1661-62; M.P. for Devizes, 1679 and 1681. He *m.* in or shortly before 1649, Martha, 1st sister and coheir of Sir Giles TOOKER, Baronet [so *cr.* 1664], da. of Edward TOOKER, of Maddington, Wilts, by Mary, da. of Sir John HUNGERFORD. He *d.* 25 July 1682, and was *bur.* (with his father) at Bishops Canning, Wilts. Will pr. 1682. His widow was *bur.* 24 May 1688, at Maddington. Her will dat. 12 March 1684 to 17 May 1688, pr. 8 July 1688.

II. 1682. SIR WALTER ERNLE, Baronet [1661], of Etchilhampton aforesaid, grandson and h., being s. and h. of Edward ERNLE, by Anne, da. of Edward ASHE, of Heytesbury, which Edward (*b.* 17 Oct. 1649), was 1st s. and h. ap. of the late Baronet, but *d.*, v.p., 21 June 1675. He *suc. to the Baronetcy* 25 July 1682; matric. at Oxford (Wadham Coll.) 3 June 1690, aged 18, and *d.* a minor and unm. the same year.

III. 1690. SIR EDWARD ERNLE, Baronet [1661], of Brimslade Park, co. Wilts, and Etchilhampton aforesaid, br. and h., *suc. to the Baronetcy* in 1690; was M.P. for Wilts, 1695-1700; for Wareham, 1701; for Heytesbury, 1701-02; for Wareham (again), 1704-06 and 1710-13; for Portsmouth, 1715-22, and for Wareham (third time), 1722-27. He *m.* Frances, da. and h. of Lieut.-General the Right Hon. Thomas ERLE, of Charborough park, Dorset, by Elizabeth, da. of Sir William WYNDHAM, 1st Baronet [1661]. She *d.* 14 May 1728. Admon. 11 March 1728/9 to her "da. and only child Elizabeth,(a) wife of Henry Drax, Esq." He *d.* s.p.m. 31 Jan. 1728/9. Will dat. 10 May 1727, pr. 10 March 1728/9.

IV. 1729. SIR WALTER ERNLE, Baronet [1661], of Conock Manor, Wilts, cousin and h. male, being s. and h. of Walter ERNLE, of the same, by Mary, sister and coheir of Anthony HUNGERFORD, of the Leigh, near Cricklade, Wilts, which Walter, who was Sheriff of Wilts, 1708-09, and who *d.* 27 Jan. 1720/1, was 2d s. of the 1st Baronet. He was *b.* in 1676, and *suc. to the Baronetcy*, 31 Jan. 1728/9. He *d.* s.p. 16 July 1732, aged 56.

V. 1732. SIR JOHN ERNLE, Baronet [1661], of Conock Manor aforesaid, br. and h., *b.* about 1681, matric. at Oxford (Hart Hall), 17 May 1698, aged 17; B.A., 21 July 1701; M.A., 2 May 1704(b); in Holy Orders;

(a) She inherited her mother's estate of Charborough, and is ancestress of the family of Erle-Drax of that place.

(b) According to the "Oxford Graduates" [1851]: "Ernle, John, Oriel, B.A. Oct. 25 1726—Sir John, Bart.—[was] *cr.* M.A. July 11 1729."—It is, of course, conceivable that though Sir John was already M.A. (1704) he was granted an honorary degree of M.A. in 1729, but it is quite certain that the Oriel B.A. was son of Nathan Ernle of Shaftesbury, Gent., and matric. 3 April 1723, aged 17, and was *not* the son of Walter Ernle, of Conock, as was the 5th Baronet, who graduated from Hart Hall.

Vicar of Shrewton, Wilts, 1708; Rector of All Cannings in that county, 1709-34. He *m.* in or before 1718, Elizabeth, da. of John SMITH, of Alton, Wilts. He *d.* s.p.m.s.(a) 30 March 1734, when the heirs male of the body of the 1st Baronet and *probably the Baronetcy* itself became *extinct*. Will pr. 1734.

VI. 1734. SIR MICHAEL ERNLE, Baronet [1661],(b) of Brimslade Park, Wilts, cousin and h. male, being s. and h. of Edward ERNLE, of the same, by Eleanor, da. of Alexander DISMORE, which Edward (who *d.* 27 Feb. 1733/4, aged 63) was s. of Michael ERNLE, of the same, next br. of the 1st Baronet.(c) He was *b.* about 1704; matric. at Oxford (Balliol Coll.) 13 July 1722, aged 17; admitted to the Middle Temple, 24 March 1724/5; to Gray's Inn 22 June 1728; suc. his father, 27 Feb. 1733/4, and *suc. to the Baronetcy*(b) 30 March 1734. He *d.* unm. 16 Feb. 1771, aged 67. Will pr. March 1771.

VII. 1771, to 1787. SIR EDWARD ERNLE, Baronet [1661],(b) of Brimslade park aforesaid, br. and h., *b.* about 1713; matric. at Oxford (Trin. Coll.), 7 June 1729, aged 16; Fellow of All Souls Coll.; B.C.L., 1737; D.C.L., 1742; in Holy Orders; Rector of Avington; *suc. to the Baronetcy*(b) 16 Feb. 1771. He *d.* unm. 26 Dec. 1787, aged 75, when the *Baronetcy* became *extinct*, if it had not already, 30 March 1734, done so.

HUBAND:
cr. 2 Feb. 1660/1;
ex. 10 Nov. 1730.

I. 1661. "JOHN HUBAND, of Ipsley, co. Warwick, Esq.," s. and h. of Ralph HUBAND, of the same, by Anne, da. of Gervase TEVERY, of Stapleford, Notts, was *b.* about 1649, and having suc. his father, 29 Oct. 1651, was in his 12th year, *cr. a Baronet*, as above, 2 Feb. 1660/1. He, as a Baronet, matric. at Oxford (Queen's Coll.), 10 Dec. 1664, aged 15, and was *cr.* M.A. 28 March 1667. He is said to have *m.* Jane, "da. [*Qy.* illegit.] of Lord Charles POWLETT, of Dowles, Hants," presumably 5th s. of William, 4th MARQUESS OF WINCHESTER. He *d.* 1710. Will pr. March 1711.

(a) Walter, his only son, matric. at Oxford (St. Mary's Hall) 10 Dec. 1729, aged 16, and *d.* v.p. unm. Elizabeth, his da. and h., *b.* 30 April 1718, inherited the estate of Conock manor. She *m.* Gifford Warriner, and *d.* 12 Nov. 1737, leaving issue.

(b) On the presumption that there was a spec. rem. in the patent in favour of the grantee's brother, Michael.

(c) It is suggested in Wotton's *Baronetage* [1741] (who inserts the succession of Michael in 1734) "Ex inform. Ed. Ernle, de Omn. Anim. Coll: Oxon: Soc." (*i.e.*, of Edward, the next br. of the said Michael) that Michael Ernle of Brimslade was a yr. *son* (and not a brother) of the grantee—in which case his male issue would be entitled under the ordinary limitation. The *eldest* son, however, of the grantee was *b.* 17 Oct. 1649; the second, Walter (ancestor of the 3d, 4th, and 5th Baronets), could not have been born till 1650, so that any yr. son cannot have been born before 1651, and is not likely to have been father of Edward, *b.* in 1670, the father of Sir Michael and the informant.

II. 1710. SIR JOHN HUBAND, Baronet [1661], of Ipsley aforesaid, s. and h., *suc. to the Baronetcy* in 1710. He *m.* in or before 1713, Rhoda, 1st da. of Sir Thomas BROUGHTON, 2d Baronet [1661], by Rhoda, da. of John AMCOATS. He *d.* 24 Jan. 1716/7. Admon. 22 May 1717. His widow *d.* at St. Andrew's, Holborn. Admon. 3 Oct. 1745 to da. Jane,(a) wife of "Robert Henley, Esq."

III. 1717, to 1730. SIR JOHN HUBAND, Baronet [1661], of Ipsley aforesaid, only s. and h., *b.* about 1713, *suc. to the Baronetcy* 24 Jan. 1716/7. He *d.* a schoolboy, at Eton, 10 Nov. 1730, aged 17, when the *Baronetcy* became *extinct*.

MORGAN:
cr. 7 Feb. 1660/1;
ex. 29 April 1767.

I. 1661. "THOMAS MORGAN,(b) of Langattock, co. Monmouth," s. and h. of Lewis MORGAN, of the same, was *b.* about 1607(c); served in the Low Countries and in the Thirty years' war [1618-48]; was Col. of Dragoons in 1645, and Com.-in-Chief of Gloucestershire on behalf of the Parl.; was Major Gen. in Scotland, capturing Dunottar Castle, 26 May 1652; took a leading part at the battle of the Dunes, 4 June 1658, and was *Knighted* by the Protector, Richard CROMWELL, 25 Nov. 1658(d); accompanied Gen. MONK in his march, from Scotland to England, to effect the Restoration, and was *cr. a Baronet*, as above, 7 Feb. 1660/1. In 1665 he was made Gov. of Jersey, where he repaired the forts and reorganised the militia.(e) He, who was, sometime, of Chenstone, co. Hereford, *m.* about 1650, Delariviere, da. of Richard CHOLMONDELEY, of Brame Hall, in Spowford, co. York. He *d.* 13 April 1679, aged 73. Will pr. 1679. His widow *d.* about 1683. Will pr. 1683.

II. 1679. SIR JOHN MORGAN, Baronet [1661], of Kinnersley Castle, co. Hereford, 1st surv. s. and h. (out of nine sons), *b.* about 1650(f); *suc. to the Baronetcy*, 13 April 1679; was Gov. of Chester; M.P. for New Radnor, 1681; for Herefordshire, 1685-87 and 1689 till death. He, apparently, was attainted in Ireland by James II in 1689. He *m.* Hester, da. and coheir of James PRICE, of Pilleth, co. Radnor. He *d.* in or before Feb. 1692/3. Will dat. 4 Aug. 1692, pr. 8 Feb. 1692/3.

III. 1693? SIR THOMAS MORGAN, Baronet [1661], of Kinnersley Castle aforesaid, only s. and h.; *suc. to the Baronetcy* in 1692 or 1693; was M.P. for Herefordshire (three Parls.), 1712 till death. He *m.*, in or before 1711, Anne, only child of John ROYDHOUSE, of St. Martin's-in-the-Fields. He *d.* 14 Dec. 1716. Will pr. Jan. 1717/8. The will of Dame Anne Morgan pr. 1764.

(a) She was one of the three sisters and coheirs of the last Baronet. Her husband was *cr.* Earl of Northington. Of the other two (1), Rhoda *m.* Sir Thomas Delves, 4th Baronet [1621], and (2), Mary, *m.* Thomas Wright, of Warwick, and *d.* 8 Oct. 1768.

(b) No description is given of his rank. His Knighthood, by Richard Cromwell, would of course, be ignored.

(c) He is said, in the *Dict. Nat. Biog.* to be "second son of Robert Morgan, of Llahrymny," whose eldest son, Sir Henry Morgan (the "Buccaneer"), was born about 1635. As, however, he served in the "thirty years war," which *ended* in 1648 (when Henry, therein called his eldest brother, was but thirteen) it is evident that this affiliation (which contradicts the account in Wotton's *Baronetage*) is a mistake.

(d) The person so *Knighted* is, however, called *John* Morgan (presumably in error) in Noble's list of the Cromwellian Knights.

(e) In Falle's "*Jersey*" is a most laudatory account of his diligent government of that island.

(f) His yr. br. Cholmley Morgan, matric. at Oxford (Linc. Coll.), 27 July 1672, aged 17.

IV. 1716, to 1767. SIR JOHN MORGAN, Baronet [1661], of Kinnersley aforesaid, only s. and h., *b.* 11 and *bap.* 14 July 1710, at St. Martin's-in-the-Fields; *suc. to the Baronetcy*, 14 Dec. 1716; matric. at Oxford (Queen's Coll.), 20 June 1726, aged 15; *cr.* M.A., 29 July 1729. He was M.P. for Hereford, 1734-41, and for Herefordshire (two Parls.), 1755 till death. He *m.*, 17 Dec. 1750 [—], da. of Sir Jacob JACOBSON. She *d.* 18 Sep. 1764. He *d.* s.p., 29 April 1767, when the *Baronetcy* became *extinct*. Will pr. May 1767.

LANE:
cr. 9 Feb. 1660/1;
afterwards, 1676-1724, VISCOUNTS LANESBOROUGH [I.];
ex. 2 Aug. 1724.

I. 1661. "GEORGE [*rectius* RICHARD] LANE, of Tulske, co. Roscommon, Ireland," s. and h. of Capt. George LANE, of the same, by Amy, da. of Cormac O'FERRALL, of Coillincrubach, co. Longford, suc. his father, 22 Feb. 1614/5; was Sheriff of co. Roscommon, 1644-45; was *cr. a Baronet*, as above, 9 Feb. 1660/1 [possibly(a) both of England and Ireland], and was *Knighted* by the Lords Justices [I.] on the 22nd of the same month. He *m.* firstly Mabel, da. and h. of Gerald FITZGERALD, of Donore, Clonbolg and Rathaman, co. Kildare, by Grace, da. of [—] MANNING, of [—], in Wales. She *d.* 19 Nov. 1631. Funeral Certificate.(b) He *m.* secondly Mary, da. of Thomas LEICESTER. He (Sir *Richard* LANE), *d.* 5 Oct. 1668.

II. 1668. SIR GEORGE LANE, Baronet [I.], of Tulske aforesaid, 1st s. and h. by 1st wife, *b.* Christmas 1620; admitted to Trin. Coll., Dublin, 5 June 1638, "æt. 17 annos a festo nativitatis domini"; was *Knighted* at Bruges, 27 March 1657; admitted to Lincoln's Inn, 1 Nov. 1660; was M.P. [I.] for co. Roscommon, 1662-65; *suc. to the Baronetcy*, 5 Oct. 1668; was Sec. of War, Clerk of the Star Chamber, Keeper of the Records, P.C., and Sec. of State in Ireland. He *m.*, probably as his 1st wife, Susan,(c) da. of Sir Edward NICHOLAS, Sec. of State [*d.* 1669], by Jane, da. of Henry JAY. She, apparently, *d.* s.p. He *m.*, 21 March 1644, Dorcas, da. of Sir Anthony BRABAZON, of Tallaghstown, co. Louth (br. to William, 1st EARL OF MEATH [I.]), by Margaret, da. of Christopher HOVENDEN, of Chisnor, Oxon. She *d.* 7 and was *bur.* 16 July 1671, at St. Catharine's, Dublin. Funeral entry. Admon. [I.], 25 Sep. 1671. He *m.* subsequently, 11 Dec. 1673, at St. Giles'-in-the-Fields, Frances, da. of Richard (SACKVILLE), 5th EARL OF DORSET, by Frances, da. of Lionel (CRANFIELD), 1st EARL OF MIDDLESEX. She, who was *b.* 6 Feb. 1655, was living when he was *cr.* 31 July 1676, VISCOUNT LANESBOROUGH of Longford [I.]. In that peerage this *Baronetcy* then *merged*, till both became *extinct* on the death of the 2d Viscount and 3d Baronet, 2 Aug. 1724.(d) See *Peerage*.

(a) The patent of the same date is included (probably in error) in the list of Irish Baronetcies given in the *Liber Munerum Hiberniæ* [pub. by Government in 1828], where, however, the place from which it was dated is given as "*Westminster*," not (as in other cases) *Dublin*.

(b) This and most of the other information in this article has been kindly furnished by G. D. Burtchaell, of the Office of Arms, Dublin.

(c) "George Lane, who after 1657, was *Sir* George Lane, married most certainly Susan Nicholas, sister of Sir John Nicholas and da. of Sir Edward Nicholas" [G. F. Warner].

(d) The second Baronet had three younger brothers, Bartholomew, Henry and John, of whom nothing is known. The third Baronet (2d Viscount) was the fourth son of eight, of whom seven (Thomas, Richard, Brabazon, Anthony, Ormond, Edward, and [another] Ormond) *d.* unm. and v.p.

OSBORN:

cr. 11 Feb. 1660/1.

The date of "11 Feb. 1660," *i.e.*, 1660/1 (instead of that of 11 Feb. 1661/2) is given in Wotton's *Baronetage* [1741] to this creation, with the note that it is "From the patent in the family as sent for the edition, 1727." It is placed there accordingly between MORGAN, *cr.* 7 Feb. 1660/1, and COLLETON, *cr.* 18 Feb. 1660/1. The date of 11 Feb. 1661/2 (being that given in Dugdale's *list*, and the one usually acknowledged) is, however, the one under which it is treated in this work.

WAKEMAN:

cr. 13 Feb. 1660/1;

ex. about 1690.

I. 1661, to 1690? "GEORGE WAKEMAN, of Beckford, co. Gloucester, Esq.," 2d s. of Edward WAKEMAN, of the same, Barrister (*d.* 9 Sep. 1659, aged 67), by Mary, da. of Richard COTTON, of Warblington, Sussex, was (as was his elder br., Richard WAKEMAN, who raised a troop of horse for the King) a zealous Royalist, and being involved in a plot against the Lord PROTECTOR, was imprisoned till the Restoration, after which he was *cr. a Baronet*, as above, 13 Feb. 1660/1, of which Baronetcy, however, "the patent was engrossed but never sealed." Having probably graduated in medicine at Paris, he was practising as a physician in London in Aug. 1668, and was, about 1670, made Physician in Ordinary to the Queen Consort. He was accused by Titus Oates and Bedloe of being in "the Popish Plot"; was tried for high treason, 18 July 1679, and, though acquitted, left the country. He was, however, back before 8 May 1685, when he gave evidence in a trial for perjury against his accusers. He *d.* s.p., at Paris, probably about 1690 when the *Baronetcy* became *extinct*.

WRIGHT:

cr. 15 Feb. 1660/1;

ex. 10 Jan. 1737/8.

I. 1661. "BENJAMIN WRIGHT, of Cranham Hall, co. Essex,"(a) s. and h. of Nathan WRIGHT(b), of the same, merchant, Alderman of London (*d.* 1657), by Anne, da. of Giles FLEMING, of Warley place, Essex, was v.p. admitted to Lincoln's Inn, 29 Jan. 1656/7, and was *cr. a Baronet*, as above, 15 Feb. 1660/1; Sheriff of Essex, 1661-62. He *m.*, in or before 1661, Jane, da. of William WILLIAMS, merchant. He *d.* Oct. 1706.

II. 1706. SIR NATHAN WRIGHT, Baronet [1661], of Cranham Hall aforesaid and of Dagnams, in Romford, Essex, s. and h., *b.* 21 Aug. 1661; *suc. to the Baronetcy* in Oct. 1706. He *m.* firstly, in or before 1684, Anne, da. of John MERRICK, of London, merchant. He *m.* secondly, Elizabeth, da. of Francis BRAGG, of Hatfield Peverell, Essex. He *m.* thirdly, 14 Dec. 1704, at St. Matthew's, Friday street, London, Elizabeth, da. of John BOWATER, of Coventry. He *m.* fourthly, 21 July 1709, at the Temple Church,

(a) No description is given of his rank.

(b) This Nathan was uncle to Sir Nathan Wright, L. Keeper of the Great Seal, who *d.* 4 Aug. 1728.

London, Abigail, da. of Samuel TRIST, of Culworth, co. Northampton. He *d.* 16 Oct. 1727, aged 66, and was *bur.* at Cranham. M.I. Will pr. 8 Nov. 1727. His widow *m.* Herbert TRIST, and *d.* 7 Dec. 1741, aged 62, being *bur.* at Cranham. M.I.

III. 1727. SIR NATHAN WRIGHT, Baronet [1661], of Cranham Hall aforesaid, of Lofts in Malden, Essex, and of Southall, Midx., s. and h. by 1st wife, *b.* 1684; *suc. to the Baronetcy*, 16 Oct. 1727. He *m.* Margaret, widow of Leonard POWELL, 3d da. of Sir Francis LAWLEY, 2d Baronet [1641], by Anne, da. of Sir Thomas WHITMORE, 1st Baronet [1641]. He *d.* s.p.m.s.(a) and was *bur.* at Bath Abbey, 27 March 1737. Will pr. 25 June 1737. His widow *d.* Jan. 1747/8. Will pr. 13 Feb. 1747/8.

IV. 1737, to 1738. SIR SAMUEL WRIGHT, Baronet [1661], of Cranham Hall aforesaid, br. of the half blood and h. male, being s. of the 2d Baronet by his 3d wife; *suc. to the Baronetcy* in March 1737. He *d.* unm. at Lisbon, 10 Jan. 1737/8, when the *Baronetcy* became *extinct*.(b) Will pr. 25 Feb. 1737/8.

COLLETON:

cr. 18 Feb. 1660/1.

I. 1661. "JOHN COLLETON, of the City of London, Esq.," sometime of Exeter and of Lamsworthy, Cornwall,(c) 2d but only son that had issue of Peter COLLETON, Sheriff of Exeter, 1618 (*bur.* 8 Aug. 1622, at St. Olave's, Exeter), by Ursula (*d.* 1647), da. of Henry HALL, of that city; was *b.* about 1608, being aged 12 at the Heralds' Visit. of Devon, 1620; suc. his elder br., Peter (who *d.* unm., aged 18), in 1623; was Captain of Foot for the King, and had the commission of Colonel from Sir John Berkeley; raised a regiment of 1,100, and is said to have expended above £60,000(d) in the Royal cause; was fined £244 by the Sequestrators, said to be a tenth of his estate; migrated to Barbadoes (where he acquired a large property), till the Restoration, soon after which he was *cr. a Baronet*, as above, 18 Feb. 1660/1. By charter, 1663, he was made one of the eight Lord Proprietors of Georgia and North and South Carolina in America. He *m.*, 19 Nov. 1634, at St. Mary Arches', Exeter, Katherine, da. of William AMY, of that city. She was living 1 Feb. 1646/7.(e) He *d.* 1666. Will, dat. 23 April 1666, pr. 8 July 1667.

II. 1666. SIR PETER COLLETON, Baronet [1661], of Exmouth, Devon, s. and h., *bap.* 17 Sep. 1635, at St. Mary Olave's, Exeter; *suc. to the Baronetcy* and to the joint Proprietorship of the Carolinas(f) in 1666, and had, with five other such Proprietors, a charter in 1667 of the whole of the

(a) Of his two daughters and coheirs, (1) Anne *m.* Thomas Lewis, of Harpton Court, co. Radnor, and *d.*, his widow and s.p. devising her estate of Lofts to her nephew, Sir Thomas Hussey Apreece, 1st Baronet [1782]; and (2) Dorothy *m.* Thomas Hussey Apreece, by whom she was mother of the abovementioned Baronet.

(b) Elizabeth, his only sister of the whole blood (*b.* 1708), *m.* Gen. James Edward Oglethorpe, founder of the colony of Georgia, who *d.* 1 July 1785. She *d.* 26 Oct. 1787, aged 79, both being *bur.* at Cranham. M.I.

(c) "The pedigree and memoir of the Colleton family," by David Ross [30 pp., 1844], has been consulted, as also Col. Vivian's "Visitations of Devon."

(d) Letter to the King, 12 Dec. 1660 [Wotton's *Baronetage*, 1741], from the said John Berkeley (then Baron Berkeley of Stratton), presumably written for the sake of obtaining a Baronetcy or some other favour for him.

(e) Will of her mother-in-law, Ursula Colleton, widow, pr. 15 Sep. 1647.

(f) He introduced therefrom into England the plant, called *Magnolia grandiflora*.

X

Bahama Islands, as Sovereign Proprietors, being Gov. of Barbadoes, 1673-74; was M.P. for Bossiney, 1681 and 1689 till his death in 1694, and many years a Commissioner of the Public Accounts; F.R.S. He *m.*, in or before 1669, Elizabeth, widow of William JOHNSTON, sister of Col. John LESLIE, of Barbadoes. She probably is the "Lady Elizabeth COLLYDON" *bur.* 17 July 1683, at St. Martin's-in-the-Fields. He *d.* in Golden square 24, and was *bur.* (as "Sir Peter COLLINGTON") 26 March 1694, at St. James', Westm. Will, dat. 12 Jan. 1693/4, pr. 19 Nov. 1697 and 31 Jan. 1700.

III. 1694. SIR JOHN COLLETON, Baronet [1661], of Westham, co. Essex, and of the Friars, Exeter, and Wythycombe Raleigh, co. Devon, only surv. s. and h., *b.* Aug. 1669; *suc. to the Baronetcy* and the joint Proprietorship of the Carolinas, etc., 24 March 1693/4. He and six other of his co-proprietors, by act of Parl. 1728, sold their Sovereign rights and some portion of the soil in the Carolinas to the Crown. He *m.*, 10 Dec. 1700, at St. Pancras', Exeter, his cousin, Elizabeth, da. of John SNELL, of Exeter, sometime M.P. for that city, by Elizabeth,(a) da. of John BUTLER. She was living May 1739. He *d.* Sep. 1754, aged 85, and was *bur.* at Withycombe aforesaid. Will dat. 22 April 1751, pr. 13 Nov. 1754.

IV. 1754. SIR JOHN COLLETON, Baronet [1661], of Withycombe Raleigh aforesaid and of Fairlawn, near Charleston, St. John's parish, Berkeley county, South Carolina, in America, grandson and h., being 2d but only surv. s. of John COLLETON, of Fairlawn aforesaid, by Susanna, da. of his maternal uncle, Rev. John SNELL, Canon of Exeter, which John COLLETON, who *d.* v.p. 1751, aged 50, was 1st s. and h. ap. of the late Baronet. He was *b.* 1738, and *suc. to the Baronetcy* in Sep. 1754. He *m.* firstly, 9 Feb. 1759, at St. Stephen's, Exeter, Anne, da. of Francis FULFORD, of Great Fulford, Devon, by Anne, da. of Sir Arthur CHICHESTER, 2d Baronet [1641], of Raleigh. She, by whom he had no male issue, was *divorced* by act of Parl. 1772.(b) He *m.* secondly, 21 April 1774, at Bovey Tracey, Devon, Jane MUTTER. He *d.* 1778, and was *bur.* at Monks Corner, in St. John's parish, Charleston abovenamed. Will, in which he disinherited his son and left all to his da., Louisa Caroline (only child by his 1st wife), dat. 13 July 1776, pr. 3 Dec. 1779, *d.* 9 April 1785. His widow remarried, and was "most barbarously treated during the sacking of Fairlawn by the [American] troops, and *d.* in consequence, leaving her second husband in possession for the heiress (Mrs. Graves as she became afterwards), then an infant."(c)

V. 1778. SIR JOHN SNELL COLLETON, Baronet [1661], only s. and h., by 2d wife; *bap.* 27 Jan. 1775 at Withycombe Raleigh aforesaid; was a Lieut. R.N., and sometimes Commander of the "Swift" sloop; *suc. to the Baronetcy*, but to none of his father's estates, in 1778. He *m.* in 1801, a few months before his death, Martha, da. of [—]. He *d.* s.p. July 1801, aged 26, at Melcombe Regis, Dorset. Will pr. Sep. 1801 by his widow, who was living 1832.

(a) The mother of this Elizabeth Butler was Elizabeth, da. of Sir Hugh Crocker, by Elizabeth (*m.* July 1651), da. of Peter Colleton, and sister of the 1st Baronet.

(b) It appears from the printed case of "Colleton *v.* Colleton" [26 pp., small 8vo.] that the Libel, dated 26 Feb. 1770, shewed that in Sep. 1759 (seven months after their marriage) Sir John Colleton and Dame Anne, his wife, left England for South Carolina. That in Oct. 1767 the said Dame Anne returned to England, but that Sir John continued to reside in South Carolina till 15 Aug. 1769, and landed at Dover on 24 Sep. following. That while in England the said Dame Anne had *crim. con.* with one or more persons, and was delivered of a male child in lodgings in Church lane, Kensington, on 21 Feb. 1769, which on the 17 of March following was *bap.* at Hammersmith, in Fulham, Midx., as "*John Fulford.*" Sentence given for the divorce.

(c) See "Pedigree of Colleton," mentioned on p. 161, note "c."

VI. 1801. SIR JAMES NASSAU COLLETON, Baronet [1661], of Ash Park, Herts, cousin and h. male, being 2d but only son that had issue of Robert COLLETON, Capt. 1st Reg. of Foot Guards, by Anne, da. and h. of James COLLETON, of South Carolina aforesaid, which Robert, who *d.* March 1755, aged 42, was 3d son of the 3d Baronet. He was *b.* 23 March, and *bap.* 10 April 1752, at Battersea, Surrey; was, upwards of twenty years, clerk in the Home Office; *suc. to the Baronetcy* in July 1801. He *m.* 3 Dec. 1778, at St. Pancras, Midx., Susanna, da. of William NIXON, of Lincoln, by Elizabeth, da. and h. of William SMALLEY, of Lincolnshire. He *d.* intestate in the Old Bailey 16, and was *bur.* 28 Jan. 1815 at St. James, Westm., aged 63. His widow *d.* 31 Jan. 1830, and is said to have been *bur.* with him.

VII. 1815. SIR JAMES ROUPELL COLLETON, Baronet [1661], of Colleton Hill in Witheridge, North Devon, 1st s. and h., *b.* 22 Dec. 1783, and *bap.* March 1784, at St. Michael's, Charleston, North America; entered the army in 1802; was Adj. Quarter Master Gen. in the Peninsular war, and Col. in the Staff Corps; *suc. to the Baronetcy*, 16 Jan. 1815. He *m.*, 12 Dec. 1819, at the British Embassy at the Hague, and subsequently, 6 Jan. and again 19 Feb. 1820, at St. James', Westm., Septima Sexta Colleton, 6th but 3d surv. da. of Admiral Richard GRAVES, of Henbury Fort, Devon, by Louisa Caroline, only da. of Sir John COLLETON, 4th Baronet, by his 1st wife. She *d.* at New York, 14 Dec. 1831, and was *bur.* 4 April 1832 from Camera street, King's road, Chelsea, at St. James', Westm. He *d.* in London 28 July, and was *bur.* 4 Aug. 1848 at St. James' aforesaid, aged 64. Will pr. June 1849.

VIII. 1848. SIR ROBERT AUGUSTUS FULFORD GRAVES COLLETON, Baronet [1661], 3d and yst., but only surv. s. and h., *b.* 19 Sep. 1824, at Hythe, and *bap.* at Eltham, co. Kent; Lieut. 45th Foot, 1845, and subsequently Barrack Master at Buttevant, co. Cork, which post he retained till his death; *suc. to the Baronetcy*, 28 July 1848. He *m.*, 1 Oct. 1853, at Tiverton, Devon, Mary, yst. da. of William COMINS, of Witheridge aforesaid. He *d.* 28 Oct. 1866, at Fermoy, co. Cork, aged 42. His widow *m.*, 5 April 1875, Lieut. Col. William Edward WALLACE (sometime Major 18th Royal Irish), who *d.* 1892; and *d.*, 17 Oct. 1900, at 15 Robertson terrace, Hastings.

IX. 1866. SIR ROBERT AUGUSTUS WILLIAM COLLETON, Baronet [1661], 1st s. and h., *b.* 31 Aug. 1854, at King William's town, Cape of Good Hope; *suc. to the Baronetcy*, 28 Oct. 1866; ed. at Christ's Coll., Finchley; Lieut. 96th Foot, 1874, and in the Welsh Fusiliers, 1875; Capt., 1885; Major, 1892; Lieut. Col. commanding, 1900; Dep. Assistant Adj. Gen. for Musketry, at Calcutta, 1887-91; served in the Hazara expedition, 1891, and in the S. African war (despatches), 1900-01; C.B., 1901. He *m.*, 7 Aug. 1880, at St. Saviour's, Croydon, Edith, 3d da. of Thomas Robert ABRAHAM, of Eversley, in Croydon.

MODYFORD:

cr. 16 Feb. 1660/1;

ex. Nov. 1678.

I. 1661. "SIR JAMES MODYFORD, of the City of London, Knt.," br. of Sir Thomas MODYFORD, Baronet [so *cr.* 1 March 1663/4], being a yr. s. of John MODYFORD, Mayor of Exeter, 1622 (*d.* before 1632), by Maria, da. of Thomas WALKER, Alderman of Exeter, was *b.* probably about 1625; was, when young, at Constantinople, in the service of the Turkey Company, was a Merchant of London, residing sometime at Chiswick; Clerk of the First-Fruits in Ireland, 18 Oct. 1660, when probably he was *Knighted*, and was *cr. a Baronet*, as above, 16 Feb. 1660/1. In 1663 was on the Royal African Company; was Lieut.-Gen., Dep. Gov. and Chief Judge of the Admiralty Court at Jamaica, 1667-71, of which his said brother, Thomas, was then Governor. He *m.*, in or before 1660, Elizabeth (*b.* 1634), da. of Sir Nicholas SLANNING, of Maristow, Devon (slain 26 July 1643, in the Royalist assault on Bristol), by Gertrude, da. of Sir James BAGGE, of Saltram. He *d.* in Jamaica and was *bur.*, 13 Jan. 1672/3, at St. Andrew's there. Admon. 26 July 1673. His widow, who was *bap.* 11 Jan. 1634/5, at Plympton St. Mary, Devon, and who, on the extinction (Dec. 1700) of the issue of her br. Sir Nicholas SLANNING, 1st Baronet [1663], became the heiress of the estate of Maristow, *d.* 30 March 1724 in her 90th year, and was *bur.* at Bickleigh, Devon.(a) M.I.

II. 1673, to 1678. SIR THOMAS MODYFORD, Baronet [1661], only s. and h. *suc. to the Baronetcy* in Jan. 1672/3, but *d.* "a youth" and unm. soon afterwards, and was *bur.* 5 Nov. 1678 in Westm. Abbey, when *the Baronetcy* became *extinct.*

BEAUMONT:

cr. 21 Feb. 1660/1.

I. 1661. "THOMAS BEAUMONT, of Stoughton Grange,(b), co. Leicester, Esq.," s. and h. of Sir Henry BEAUMONT, of the same, by Frances, da. of Sir George TURPIN, of Knaptoft, co. Leicester, and Elizabeth, da. of Richard (FIENNES), LORD SAY AND SELE, suc. his father in April 1648; was on the Committee for the New Model 15 Feb. 1644/5; was M.P. for Leicestershire, 1654-55, 1656-58, and 1659, being described as a *Baronet*, having been *cr. a Baronet* 5 March 1657/8 by the Lord Protector Cromwell, and was (this dignity being of course disallowed after the Restoration) *cr. a Baronet*, as above, by the King, 21 Feb. 1660/1. Sheriff of Leicestershire, 1668-69. He *m.* before 1638, Elizabeth, da. and coheir of Sir Nicholas TROTT, of Quickswood, Herts, by Mary, da. and h. of Sir George PERIENT. She *d.* before him. He *d.* 11 Aug. 1676, and was *bur.* at Stoughton. M.I.(c). Admon. 15 Aug. 1676 to his son William.

II. 1676. SIR HENRY BEAUMONT, Baronet [1661], of Stoughton Grange aforesaid, 1st s. and h., *bap.* 2 April 1638, at Stoughton, was possibly the "Henry BEAUMONT, Gent.," who matric. at Oxford (St. John's Coll.) 5 April 1655; *suc. to the Baronetcy*, 11 Aug. 1676; was M.P. for Leicestershire (four Parls.) 1679-87. He *m.*, 2 April 1662, at St. Andrew's, Holborn, Elizabeth, sister of Sir Edward FARMER, da. of George FARMER, of Holbeach, co. Lincoln, one of the Prothonotaries of the Court of Common Pleas, by his 1st wife, Elizabeth, da. of Anthony OLDFIELD. He *d.* 27 and was *bur.* 30 Jan. 1688/9, at Stoughton. Will dat. 9 April 1682, pr. 18 May 1689. His widow (by whom he had 14 sons and 7 daughters), *d.* 30 Sep. and was *bur.* 2 Oct. 1727, at Stoughton, aged 80. Her Admon. 18 Nov. 1727 in the Bishop's Court at Lincoln.

(a) Of her two daughters and coheirs (1) Mary, *m.* John Deane and *d.* s.p. 27 Oct. 1734, aged 74, and was *bur.* at Bickleigh. M.I. (2) Grace, *m.* firstly Edward Drake, who *d.* 5 Oct. 1680 in Jamaica, and secondly Peter Heywood, by whom she was grandmother of James Modyford Heywood, Sheriff of Devon, 1759.

(b) Catharine, da. and h. of Thomas Farnham, of Stoughton Grange, *m.* Sir Thomas Beaumont (yr. br. of Sir Henry Beaumont, of Cole Orton, father of Thomas, 1st Viscount Beaumont of Swords [I.]) and was mother of Sir Henry Beaumont, of Stoughton Grange aforesaid, the father of the 1st Baronet.

(c) The Admon., 8 May 1677, of "Dame Jane Beaumont, *alias* Watts, late of Stoughton Grange, co. Leicester, but decd in Drury Lane, Midx." (granted to her da. "Jane Watts") presumably refers to a second wife *of his father*. It may, however, refer to a second wife *of his own*, who in that case must have died before him as he is stated in his Admon. (15 Oct. 1676) to be then a widower.

III. 1689. SIR THOMAS BEAUMONT, Baronet [1661], of Stoughton Grange aforesaid, 1st s. and h., *b.* about 1664, *suc. to the Baronetcy*, 27 Jan. 1688/9; was an officer in the Horse Guards to James II, whom, however, he deserted, and was made by William III, Lieut.-Col. of Dragoons and Standard Bearer to the first troop of Guards. He *d.*, of the flux, unm., when serving in Ireland, 5 Dec. 1690, aged 25, and was *bur.* at Stoughton. Will pr. March 1691.

IV. 1690. SIR GEORGE BEAUMONT, Baronet [1661], of Stoughton Grange aforesaid, br. and h., *b.* about 1665, matric. at Oxford (New Coll.) 9 Feb. 1682/3, aged 18; B.C.L., 1690; D.C.L. by diploma, 7 Dec. 1713, having *suc. to the Baronetcy*, 5 Dec. 1690. By the death, 11 June 1702, of his father's third cousin, Thomas (BEAUMONT), 3d VISCOUNT BEAUMONT OF SWORDS [I.], to whom he was heir male, he inherited, under his will, his estates, including the ancestral one of Cole Orton, co. Leicester. He was M.P. for Leicester (nine Parls.) 1702 till his death, 1737; was a Commissioner of the Privy Seal, 1711-12, and one of the Lords of the Admiralty, April to Oct. 1714. He *d.* unm. 9 April 1737, aged 73, and was *bur.* at Stoughton. M.I. Will, in which he devised the Stoughton Grange estate to his sisters,(a) and their issue, pr. 9 May 1737.

V. 1737. SIR LEWIS BEAUMONT, Baronet [1661], of Cole Orton aforesaid, only surv. br. and h., *b.* about 1675; matric. at Oxford (New Coll.), 24 Aug. 1694, aged 19. B.A., 1698. M.A., 16 Jan. 1701/2; in Holy Orders, Rector of Pyecombe, Sussex, 1702, and Preb. of Chichester, 1719 till death. He *m.* Elizabeth, widow of the Rev. [—] TEMPLE, da. of [—] COURTENAY. He *d.* s.p. 23 Dec. 1738. Will dat. 19 Jan. 1737/8, pr. 23 Jan. 1738/9.

VI. 1738. SIR GEORGE BEAUMONT, Baronet [1661], of Cole Orton aforesaid, and of Great Dunmow, co. Essex, cousin and h. male, being s. and h. of William BEAUMONT, of Great Dunmow aforesaid, by Elizabeth, sister and h. of Thomas, da. of William JORDAIN, both of Buckland in Reigate, Surrey, which William Beaumont was s. and h. of William BEAUMONT, of Great Dunmow aforesaid, and of Hackney, co. Midx. (*d.* 1719), 3d and yst. s. of the 1st Baronet. He was *bap.* 16 March 1726, at Great Dunmow, ed. at Winchester, 1735; *suc. to the Baronetcy*, 23 Dec. 1738; matric. at Oxford (New Coll.) 27 Nov. 1745, aged 19; was Sheriff of Leicestershire, 1761-62. He *m.* 26 March 1751, at St. John's, Clerkenwell, Rachel, da. of Matthew HOWLAND, of Stonehall, in Great Dunmow aforesaid, by Hannah, da. of George COLDHAM, of Haverhill, co. Suffolk. He *d.* at Dunmow, 4 Feb. 1762, and was *bur.* there, aged 36. M.I. Will dat. 13 Jan. 1762, pr. 10 Feb. 1763. His widow *d.* 5 May 1814 and was *bur.* with him. M.I. Will dat. 17 Feb. 1812, pr. 16 June 1814.

VII. 1762. SIR GEORGE HOWLAND BEAUMONT, Baronet [1661], of Cole Orton and Great Dunmow aforesaid, only surv. s. and h., *b.* 6 Nov. and *bap.* 17 Dec. 1753, at Dunmow; *suc. to the Baronetcy*, 4 Feb. 1762; ed. at Eton; matric. at Oxford (New Coll.) 4 May 1772, aged 18; M.P. for Beeralston, 1790-96; F.S.A., F.R.S.; Trustee of the British Museum; was a munificent patron of English Painters, being himself a painter of landscapes and a collector of pictures, many of the best of which, in 1826, he presented to the National Gallery, then but newly established. He *m.*, 6 May 1778 (Spec. Lic.), Margaret, 1st da. of John WILLES, of Astrop, co. Northampton, Flazer of the Court of Common Pleas (s. and h. of Sir John WILLES, Lord Ch. Justice thereof), by Frances, da. of Thomas FREKE, of Bristol. He *d.* s.p. 7 Feb. 1827, aged 73, at Cole Orton Hall. Will dat. 26 Aug. 1824, pr. 24 March 1827. His widow *d.* there 14 July 1829, aged (also) 73. Will pr. Oct. 1829.

(a) Of these, Catherine (the fifth da.) *m.* William Busby, of Loughborough, who *d.* 2 April 1726 leaving an only surv. son William Busby, who suc. to the Stoughton Grange estate. He, with his three surv. aunts (Anne, Arabella, and Christiana) erected the monument at Stoughton to the 4th Baronet.

VIII. 1827. SIR GEORGE HOWLAND WILLOUGHBY BEAUMONT, Baronet [1661], of Cole Orton aforesaid, cousin and h. male, being s. and h. of Thomas BEAUMONT, of Buckland aforesaid, by Bridget, yst. da. and coheir of the Rev. William DAVIE, Vicar of Axminster and Preb. of Exeter, which Thomas (who *d.* Feb. 1818) was 1st surv. s. of another Thomas BEAUMONT, of Buckland aforesaid, yr. br. of Sir George BEAUMONT, the 6th Baronet. He was *b.* 16 Dec. 1799; matric. at Oxford (Ch. Ch.), 14 Oct. 1819, aged 19 *suc. to the Baronetcy*, 7 Feb. 1827. He *m.* 16 June 1825, at St. Geo., Han. sq., Mary Anne, 1st da. and coheir of William HOWLEY, Archbishop of Canterbury [1828-48], by Mary Frances, da. of John BELLI, East India Company Service, of Southampton. She *d.* 15 Feb. 1834. He *d.* 7 June 1845 at Cole Orton Hall, aged 45. Will pr. July 1845.

IX. 1845. SIR GEORGE HOWLAND BEAUMONT, Baronet [1661] of Cole Orton aforesaid, 1st s. and h., *b.* 12 Sep. 1828 at Addington Park, Surrey, the residence of his maternal grandfather; ed. at Winchester; *suc. to the Baronetcy*, 7 June 1845; matric. at Oxford (Ch. Ch.), 4 June 1846, aged 17; Sheriff of Leicestershire, 1852; Capt. Leicestershire Yeomanry Cavalry, 1856. He *m.* firstly, 4 June 1850, at St. Peter's, Eaton sq., his cousin, Pauline Menzies, 1st da. of William Hallows BELLI, East India Company Civil Service. She *d.* 9 Dec. 1870, at Cole Orton Hall. He *m.* secondly, 4 April 1872, at St. Paul's, Knightsbridge, Octavia Willoughby, widow of John Richard Smyth WALLIS, of Drishane Castle, co. Cork, Major 4th Dragoon Guards, illegit. da. of Digby (WILLOUGHBY), 7th BARON MIDDLETON. He *d.* 8 June 1882, at Cole Orton Hall, aged 53. His widow *d.* 19 June 1901, at 66 Cromwell Road, London, and was *bur.* at Cole Orton. Will pr. at £12,196.

X. 1882. SIR GEORGE HOWLAND WILLIAM BEAUMONT, Baronet, [1661], of Cole Orton aforesaid, *b.* 10 March 1851, in Eaton sq., Midx.; ed. at Eton; sometime Capt. Royal Horse Artillery; *suc. to the Baronetcy*, 8 June 1882. He *m.* 24 Feb. 1880, at St. George's church, Agra, Lillie, 2d da. of George Ayton CRASTER, Major-Gen. Royal Engineers.

Family Estates.—These, in 1883, consisted of 2,977 acres in Leicestershire, 378 in Essex, and 201 in Suffolk. *Total.*—3,556 acres, worth £4,660 a year. *Seat.*—Cole Orton Hall, near Ashby-de-la-Zouch.

SMITH, *or* SMYTHE:

cr. 23 Feb. 1660/1.

I. 1661. "EDWARD SMITH, of Eshe, co. Durham, Esq.," yst. s. of John SMITH, *or* SMYTHE, by Margaret, da. of Sir Bertram BULMER, was *cr. a Baronet*, as above, 23 Feb. 1660/1, at, presumably, an early age. He *m.* Mary, 2d da. and coheir of Sir Richard LEE, 2d Baronet [1620], of Langley, Salop, by Elizabeth, da. of Edward ALLEN, Alderman of London. By her he acquired the estates of Langley and Acton Burnell, Salop. He *d.* 12 Oct. 1714. Will pr. Dec. 1714.

II. 1714. SIR RICHARD SMYTHE, Baronet [1661], of Eshe, and of Langley and Acton Burnell aforesaid, 1st s. and h., *suc. to the Baronetcy*, 12 Oct. 1714. He *m.* in 1688, Grace, da. and h. of the Hon. Carrill CARRINGTON, *otherwise* SMITH, of Ashby Folville, co. Leicester, by Grace (living, a widow, 31 Oct. 1670), da. of Henry TURVILLE. She *d.* before him. He *d.* s.p.m.(a) in Dec. 1736. Admon., as of Wenlock, co. Salop, 3 May 1737, and 17 Dec. 1746.

(a) Clare, his only child, was *b.* deaf and dumb, and *d.* unm. 29 March 1751.

III. 1736. SIR JOHN SMYTHE, Baronet [1661], of Eshe, and of Acton Burnell aforesaid, only surv. br. and h. male, *suc. to the Baronetcy* in Dec. 1736. He *m.* in or before 1719, Constantia, sister of Sir Edward BLOUNT, 4th Baronet [1642], da. of George BLOUNT, of Sodington, co. Worcester, by his 2d wife, Constantia, da. of Sir George CARY, of Tor Abbey, co. Devon. He *d.* 17 Sep. 1737. Will pr. 1737, and, at York, Dec. 1738.

IV. 1737. SIR EDWARD SMYTHE, Baronet [1661], of Eshe, and of Acton Burnell aforesaid, 1st s. and h., *b.* 21 Oct. 1719, *suc. to the Baronetcy*, 17 Sep. 1737. He *m.* firstly, 25 July 1743, Maria, da. of Peter GIFFARD, of Chillington, co. Stafford, by his 2d wife, Barbara, da. of Sir Robert THROCKMORTON, 3d Baronet [1642]. She *d.* 30 May 1764. He *m.* secondly, 14 April 1766, at St. Geo., Han. sq., Mary, 2d and yst. da. of Hugh (CLIFFORD), BARON CLIFFORD OF CHUDLEIGH, by Elizabeth, da. of Edward BLOUNT, of Blagdon, co. Devon. He *d.* 2 Nov. 1784, aged 65. Will pr. Dec. 1784. His widow, who was *b.* 27 April 1731, *d.* at Bath. Will pr. April 1797.

V. 1784. SIR EDWARD SMYTHE, Baronet [1661], of Eshe and of Acton Burnell aforesaid, 1st s. and h., being only s. by 1st wife; *b.* 21 May 1758; *suc. to the Baronetcy*, 2 Nov. 1784. He *m.*, 15 Oct. 1781, Catherine Maria, da. and h. of Peter HOLFORD, of Wootton Hall, in Wootton Wawen, co. Warwick, by Constantia, da. and coheir of Francis CARRINGTON, *otherwise* SMITH, of the same, and of Aston Hall, Salop. He *d.* 11 April 1811, at Wootton Hall aforesaid. Admon. Dec. 1811. His widow *d.* there in 1831. Admon. July 1831.

VI. 1811. SIR EDWARD JOSEPH SMYTHE, Baronet [1661], of Eshe, Acton Burnell and Wootton Hall aforesaid, only s. and h., *b.* 3 Aug. 1787; *suc. to the Baronetcy*, 11 April 1811; was Sheriff of Shropshire, 1831-32. He *m.* 23 Oct. 1809, Frances, sister of Patrick, 1st BARON BELLEW OF BARMEATH [I.], da. of Sir Edward BELLEW, 6th Baronet [I. 1688], by Mary Anne, da. of Richard STRANGE, of Rockwell Castle, co. Kilkenny. He *d.* at Acton Burnell Hall, 11 March 1856, in his 69th year. Will pr. May 1856. His widow *d.* 17 Aug. 1860 at Wootton Hall aforesaid, aged 70.

VII. 1856. SIR CHARLES FREDERICK JOSEPH SMYTHE, Baronet [1661], of Eshe, Acton Burnell, and Wootton Hall aforesaid, 3d but 1st surv. s. and h., *b.* 16 March 1819; ed. at St. Gregory's College, Downside; *suc. to the Baronetcy*, 11 March 1856; Sheriff of Shropshire, 1867-68. He *m.* 17 Oct. 1855, at Stonor Park, Oxon, Maria, 4th da. of Thomas (STONOR), LORD CAMOYS, by Frances, da. of Peregrine Edward TOWNELEY. He *d.* s.p.m.s., 14 Nov. 1897, aged 78, at Elmley Lodge, Leamington, co. Warwick. His widow, who was *b.* 23 April 1832, living 1903.

VIII. 1897. SIR JOHN WALTER SMYTHE, Baronet [1661], of Eshe, and of Acton Burnell aforesaid, br. and h. male, being 4th and yst. s. of the 6th Baronet, *b.* 7 Nov. 1827: sometime Capt. Louth Rifles; *suc. to the Baronetcy*, 14 Nov. 1897. He *m.* 13 Feb. 1864, Marie Louise, 2d and yst. da. of William HERBERT, of Clytha Park, co. Monmouth, by Frances, da. of Edward HUDDLESTON, of Sawston Hall, co. Cambridge.

Family Estates.—These, in 1883, consisted of 5,313 acres in Shropshire, 3,501 in Warwickshire, and 70 in the county of Durham. *Principal Seat.*—Acton Burnell Hall, near Shrewsbury, Salop.

NAPIER, *otherwise* SANDY:

cr. 4 March 1660/1;

merged April 1675;

ex. 2 Jan. 1747/8.

I. 1661. "JOHN NAPIER, *alias* SANDY, Esq.," 2d s. of Sir Robert NAPIER, 2d Baronet [1611], being the elder of his two sons (John and Alexander) by his 2d wife, Penelope, da. of John (EGERTON), 1st EARL OF BRIDGWATER, was *bap.* 5 July 1636, at Luton, Beds; suc. his father (who was *bur.* 7 March 1660/1, at Luton) in the family estates, and was (apparently between his father's death and burial) *cr. a Baronet*, as above, 4 March 1660/1, with a spec. rem. failing issue male of his body to his yr. br., Alexander NAPIER, and the heirs male of his body, "with rem. to the heirs male of Sir Robert NAPIER, Knight [*rectius* Baronet], grandfather to the said John, and with precedency before all Baronets made since 24 Sep. [1611], 10 Jac., at which time the said Sir Robert was created a Baronet: which letters patent so granted to the said Sir Robert NAPIER, were surrendered by Sir Robert NAPIER (father of the said John and Alexander) lately deceased, to the intent that the said degree of Baronet should be granted to himself with rem. to the said John and Alexander." This surrender of the Baronetcy of 1611 by the 2d Baronet was presumably invalid, in which case, on his death in March 1660/1, it devolved on his grandson and heir male, Robert NAPIER, who however (having been disinherited) seems not to have assumed it. On his death, however, unm., and under age in April 1675, that Baronetcy undoubtedly devolved on his uncle and heir male, the said Sir John NAPIER, Baronet (so *cr.* 4 March 1660/1), whose *Baronetcy* of 1661 became accordingly *merged* in that of 1611 till *both* became *extinct*, 2 Jan. 1747/8. See vol. i, pp. 80-81, under "NAPIER."

GIFFORD,(a) *or* GIFFARD:

cr. 4 March 1660/1;

ex. 4 May 1662;

but assumed July 1747 to Sep. 1823.

I. 1661, to 1662. "THOMAS GIFFORD, of Castle Jordan, co. Meath, Ireland,"(b) 1st s. and h. of Sir John GIFFORD, *or* GIFFARD, of the same,(c) M.P. [I.] for Jamestown, 1639-49, by Elizabeth, da. of Sir John JEPHSON, of Mallow, co. Cork, suc. his father 24 April 1657, and was *cr. a Baronet*, as above, possibly both of England and Ireland,(d) 4 March 1660/1. He was M.P. [I.] for Trim, 1661, till his death next year. He *m.* 21 April 1662, at St. Werburgh's, Dublin, Martha, sister of Sir William TEMPLE, Baronet [so *cr.* 31 Jan. 1665/6], 1st da. of Sir John TEMPLE, Master of the Rolls [I.], by Mary, da. of John HAMMOND, M.D., of Chertsey, Surrey, Physician to Henry, Prince of Wales. He *d. s.p.* (a few days later) 4, and was *bur.* 9 May 1662, at St. Audoen's, Dublin, when the *Baronetcy* became *extinct*. Funeral entry in Ulster's Office, Dublin. His widow who was *b.* 1638, *d.* in Dover street, 31 Dec. 1722, and was *bur.* as "Martha, Lady Giffard," 5 Jan. 1722/3, in Westm. Abbey, aged 84.(a) Will dat. 22 Dec. 1722, pr. 2 Jan. 1722/3.

(a) Most of the information in this article has been kindly supplied by G. D. Burtchaell, Office of Arms, Dublin.

(b) No description of his rank is given in Dugdale's *Catalogue*.

(c) He inherited that estate from his mother. Mary, da. and h. of Sir Henry Duke, of Castle Jordan aforesaid, whose 1st husband (his father), Capt. Richard Gifford, of Ballymagrett, co. Roscommon, was murdered by rebels in 1595. Her 2d husband, Sir Francis Ruish, *d.* 18 June 1623, and her 3d husband, Sir John Jephson, *d.* 16 May 1638. She was living Sep. 1645, but *d.* in or before 1655.

(d) See p. 159, note "a," under "LANE," *cr.* 9 Feb. 1660/1.

After the lapse of 85 years, this Baronetcy was assumed in July 1747 (unless, indeed, it can be held that a Baronetcy of that date(b) was then *created*) as under—

II.(c) 1747. SIR THOMAS GIFFORD, *or* GIFFARD, Baronet,(c) of Castle Jordan aforesaid, was 1st s. and h. of Duke GIFFORD, *or* GIFFARD, of the same, M.P. [I.] for Philipstown, by Elizabeth, da. of William HANDCOCK, of Twyford, co. Westmeath, which Duke (whose will dat. 9 June 1707 was pr. [I.] 31 Oct. 1713) was 1st s. and h. of John GIFFORD, *or* GIFFARD, of Castle Jordan aforesaid (*d.* 22 July 1676), who was the br. and h. of the 1st Baronet. He was *b.* about 1695; admitted to Trin. Coll., Dublin (as Fell. Comm.), 17 May 1712, aged 17; suc. his father in or shortly before 1713, and *assumed the style of a Baronet* in July 1747, presumably on the supposition that the heir male collateral of the grantee of 4 March 1660/1 was entitled to the dignity,(d) but possibly in right of a new creation.(b) He *m.* Nov. 1716, Eleanor, da. of Robert EDGEWORTH, of Longwood, co. Meath, by Catherine, only child of Sir Edward TYRRELL, Baronet [I. 1686], of Lynn, co. Westmeath. She *d.* at Castle Jordan, May 1761. He *d.* there, 3 months later, 18 Aug. 1761. Admon. 26 Aug. 1761, and 26 May 1800 [I.].

III.(c) 1761. SIR DUKE GIFFORD, *or* GIFFARD, Baronet,(c) of Castle Jordan aforesaid, only s. and h., *suc. to the Baronetcy*(c) 18 Aug. 1761; Sheriff of King's County, 1765. He *m.* Mary, elder da. and coheir of Richard EUSTACE, of Cradockstown, co. Kildare, by Jane, da. of Patrick LATTIN, of Morristown, in that county. She *d.* Sep. 1784. He *d.* Feb. 1798. Admon. 19 May 1798 [I.].

IV.(c) 1798. SIR DUKE GIFFORD, *or* GIFFARD, Baronet,(c) of Castle Jordan aforesaid, 1st s. and h., *suc. to the Baronetcy*(c) in Feb. 1798. He *m.* 28 Jan. 1781, Mary Arabella, *or* Anna Maria, da. of the Rev. Hinton MADDOCK, of Darland, Wales. He *d.* 28 Oct. 1801. His widow *m.*, 20 May 1805 (spec. lic.), in the house of Messrs. Le Neufrille and Tavernier, 33 Mount street, St. Geo., Han. sq., John Henry (PETTY), 2d MARQUESS OF LANSDOWNE, who had suc. his father as such on the 7th inst., and who *d. s.p.* 15 Nov. 1809, in his 44th year. She *d.* 24 April 1833, at Wycombe Lodge, Kensington. Will pr. June 1833.

V.(c) 1801. SIR THOMAS RICHARD WALTER GIFFORD, *or* GIFFARD, Baronet,(c) of Castle Jordan aforesaid, only s. and h., *suc. to the Baronetcy*,(c) 28 Oct. 1801. He *d.* unm., and under age, 22 April 1802.

VI.(c) 1802, to 1823. SIR JOHN ALEXANDER GIFFORD, *or* GIFFARD, Baronet,(c) uncle and h. male, *suc. to the Baronetcy*,(c) 22 April 1802. He *d.* unm. Sep. 1823, when the *assumption* of the *Baronetcy ceased*. Will of "Sir John GIFFORD, Baronet," pr. 1824.

(a) Though said to have been "maid, wife, and widow in one day" it will be seen that her husband lived 13 days after their marriage.

(b) In the *Gent. Mag.* for 1747 it is stated that "Sir Thomas Gifford, of Castle Jordan, co. Meath, was created a Baronet, July 1747."

(c) According to the assumption of the Baronetcy in July 1747.

(d) In that case, however, both his father and grandfather would have been entitled to the Baronetcy, neither of whom ever assumed it.

CLIFTON:

cr. 4 March 1660/1;

ex. Nov. 1694.

I. 1661, to 1694. "THOMAS CLIFTON, of Clifton, co. Lancaster, Esq.," 1st surv. s. and h. of Thomas CLIFTON, of Clifton, Lytham, and Westby, in that county, by Anne, da. and coheir of Sir Cuthbert HALSALL, of Halsall, and Clifton(a) aforesaid, was *b.* 7 July 1628; suc. his father 15 Dec. 1657, and was *cr. a Baronet*, as above, 4 March 1660/1. He, with other Lancashire gentlemen of the old faith, was accused of high treason in May 1690, but was acquitted. He *m.* firstly, Bridget, da. of Sir George HENEAGE, of Hainton, co. Lincoln. She was *bur.* 11 Dec. 1662, at Kirkham. He *m.* secondly (settlmt. 7 July 1664), Bridget (*bap.* 1 Nov. 1626, at Honington, co. Lincoln), 4th da. of Sir Edward HUSSEY, 1st Baronet [1611], by Elizabeth, da. of George AUTON. He *d.* s.p.m.s.,(b) and was *bur.* 13 Nov. 1694 at Kirkham, when the *Baronetcy* became *extinct*.(c) Will dat. 8 June 1694. His widow living at St. Andrew's, Holborn, in 1710, and then aged 87.

WILSON:

cr. 4 March 1660/1;

afterwards, since 1899, MARYON-WILSON.

I. 1661. "WILLIAM WILSON, of Eastborne, co. Sussex, Esq.," 3d but 1st surv. s.(d) of John WILSON, of Sheffield House, in Fletching, co. Sussex, formerly of Akeham, co. York (*d.* 1640), by Mary (*m.* 25 June 1601), da. of Thomas GARDENER, of London, Master of the Fine office, was *b.* about 1608; was in the King's army in 1639 against the Scots; purchased the estate of Eastbourne in April 1644; was, though apparently a consistent Royalist,(e) Sheriff of Sussex, 1652-53, and was *cr. a Baronet*, as above, 4 March 1660/1. He *m.* in or before 1644, Mary, da. of Francis HADDON, of London, merchant, by Judith, da. of (—) CARTER. She was *bur.* at Eastbourne, 3 Oct. 1661. He *d.* 9 Dec. 1685, and was *bur.* there, aged 77. M.I. Will pr. Jan. 1686.

II. 1685. SIR WILLIAM WILSON, Baronet [1661], of Eastbourne aforesaid, 1st s. and h., *b.* about 1644, *suc. to the Baronetcy*, 9 Dec. 1685. He *m.* in or before 1680, Ricarda, 2d da. and coheir of Richard PEACOCK, of North End, in Finchley, co. Midx. She was *bur.* 1 March 1686, at Eastbourne. M.I. He *d.* 26 Dec. 1718, aged 74, and was *bur.* there.

(a) This Cuthbert Halsall inherited the estate of Clifton through his grandmother, Anne (wife of Henry Halsall, of Halsall), da. of Sir William Molyneux, of Sefton (*d.* 1548), and heiress of her mother (his 2d or 3d wife), Elizabeth, da. and h. of Cuthbert Clifton (*d.* s.p.m., 1512), of Clifton aforesaid.

(b) Thomas Clifton, his last surv. s., *b.* 1668, was admitted to Gray's Inn, 7 Nov. 1683, but *d.* five days afterwards, and was *bur.* at Kirkham. Mary, da. by 1st wife, *m.* Thomas (Petre), 6th Baron Petre of Writtle, and *d.* a widow, 4 Feb. 1729/30, at Ghent. Bridget, da. by the 2d wife, *m.* Sir Francis Andrews, 4th Baronet [1641], of Denton, who *d.* 3 April 1759.

(c) The estates devolved on his nephew and heir male, Thomas Clifton (*d.* Dec. 1720), whose male descendants still [1903] possess them.

(d) The eldest son, Charles, *d.* of the smallpox unm. and a minor, July 1621. The 2d son, the Rev. John Wilson, M.A. (Trin. Coll.), Cambridge, *m.* but *d.* s.p. 1649.

(e) See Wotton's *Baronetage* [1740], where a very full account is given of his doings, as also of his frequent presents to the King, of "those rare birds called Wheat-Ears," often found on his estate.

III. 1718. SIR WILLIAM WILSON, Baronet [1661], of Eastbourne aforesaid, grandson and h., being only s. and h. of William WILSON, by Jane, da. of Nicholas TOWNLEY, of the Inner Temple, London, Barrister, which William was only s. and h. ap. of the late Baronet, but *d.* v.p. 15 July 1718, in his 32d year. He was *b.* about 1704, and *suc. to the Baronetcy*, 26 Dec. 1718. He, "who was designed for the army," *d.* unm. "at Major Foubert's academy," 23, and was *bur.* 27 Jan. 1723/4, at St. James', Westm., aged 19, being afterwards re-interred at Eastbourne.

IV. 1724. SIR THOMAS WILSON, Baronet [1661], of Eastbourne aforesaid, cousin and h. male, being only s. and h. of Thomas WILSON, by Anne, da. of George COURTHOPE, of Wadhurst, co. Sussex, which Thomas, who *d.* v.p. 23 June 1684, was 4th s. of the 1st Baronet. He was *b.* about 1682, and *suc. to the Baronetcy*, 27 Jan. 1723/4. He *m.* in or before 1724, Elizabeth, da. of William HUTCHINSON, of Uckfield, co. Sussex. He *d.* 6 Oct. 1759, aged 77. Will pr. 1759. His widow *d.* 4 July 1768, aged 77.

V. 1759. SIR EDWARD WILSON, Baronet [1661], of Uckfield aforesaid, 1st s. and h., *b.* in or before 1725; "well versed in the history and antiquities of the Kingdom"; F.S.A.; *suc. to the Baronetcy*, 6 Oct. 1759. He *d.* unm., 24 June 1760, at Uckfield.

VI. 1760. SIR THOMAS SPENCER WILSON,(a) Baronet [1661], General in the army, br. and h., *b.* 25 Jan. 1726, at Uckfield; entered the army; was wounded at the battle of La Val and La Feldt in Flanders, and thanked for his conduct at the battle of Minden; Lieut.-Col. 2d Reg. of Foot Guards; Col. of the 50th Foot, becoming, finally, 1796, full General in the army. He *suc. to the Baronetcy*, 24 June 1760. He *m.* 25 June 1767, in the chapel of Charlton House, near Greenwich, Jane, da. and h. of John Badger WELLER, of Hornchurch, in Romford, co. Essex, by Margaretta Maria (*d.* 19 June 1777, aged 64), da. (but not h. or coheir) of William PEERS, of Bocking, and devisee, under the will of her maternal uncle, the Rev. John MARYON,(b) Rector of White Roding, co. Essex (*d.* 17 Nov. 1760, aged 68), of the manor of Charlton, co. Kent. He *d.* 29 Aug. 1798, aged 73, and was *bur.* at Charlton. M.I. Will pr. Nov. 1798, as also [I.] in 1803. His widow *d.* 17 Aug. 1818, aged 71. Will pr. 1818.

VII. 1798. SIR THOMAS MARYON WILSON, Baronet [1661], of Charlton aforesaid, only s. and h., *b.* about 1773, *suc. to the Baronetcy*, 29 Aug. 1798. He *m.*, 1799, in the chapel of Charlton House, Elizabeth, da. of James SMITH, Capt. R.N. She *d.* 5 Nov. 1818, and was *bur.* at Charlton, aged 48. M.I. He *d.* 22 July 1821, aged (also) 48.(c) Will pr. 1821.

VIII. 1821. SIR THOMAS MARYON WILSON, Baronet [1661], of Charlton aforesaid, 1st s. and h., *b.* 14 April 1800, at Southend, co. Essex; *suc. to the Baronetcy*, 22 July 1821, and, having been ed. at St. John's Coll., Cambridge, was M.A. 1822-29; Sheriff of Kent, 1828-29; Col. of the West Kent Militia, 1853. He *d.* unm. 4 May 1869, at Folkestone, and was *bur.* at Charlton.

(a) He received these names from his godfathers, *Thomas* (Pelham-Holles), Duke of Newcastle, and *Spencer* (Compton), Earl of Wilmington.

(b) In Drake's *Hasted's Kent* (Hundred of Blackheath) is a good pedigree of the Maryon family, shewing the descent of this John Maryon from (his great grandfather), John Maryon, of Braintree, Essex, clothier (will dat. 18 June 1664), and that his mother, Margaret, was one of the twelve children of Charles Crouch, by Frances, da. and h. of Benjamin Langhorn, of Hipolite, Herts, which Benjamin was presumably a relative of Sir William Langhorn, Baronet [so *cr.* 1668], who purchased Charlton Manor in 1680, and *d.* s.p. 16 Feb. 1714, aged 85.

(c) He was owner of a private menagerie of wild animals, some of which were allowed to run loose about his house at Charlton.

IX. 1869. Sir John Maryon Wilson, Baronet [1661], of Charlton aforesaid, br. and h., b. 12 Dec. 1802, at Lewisham, and *bap.* 11 Jan. 1803; Lieut. 11th Essex Rifle Volunteers, 1860; *suc. to the Baronetcy,* 4 May 1869.(a) He *m.* 22 Dec. 1825, Charlotte Julia, da. of George Wade, of Dunmow, Essex. He *d.* 11 May 1876, at Charlton House, aged 74. His widow *d.* 8 March 1895.

X. 1876. Sir Spencer Maryon Wilson, Baronet [1661], of Charlton aforesaid, and of Searles, in Fletching, co. Sussex, 2d but 1st surv. s. and h.,(b) *b.* 4 Dec. 1829, at FitzJohns, near Dunmow, co. Essex; Lieut. R.N., April 1855; retired 1870; *suc. to the Baronetcy,* 11 May 1876; Sheriff of Sussex, 1889. He *m.* 29 July 1856, Rose Emily, da. of the Rev. Henry Sharp Pocklington, of Stebbing, co. Essex. He *d.* 31 Dec. 1897, at 6 Prince's gardens, London, and was *bur.* at Fletching, aged 68. His widow living 1902.

XI. 1897. Sir Spencer-Pocklington-Maryon Wilson, *afterwards* (since 1899) Maryon-Wilson, Baronet [1661], of Charlton and Searles aforesaid, 1st s. and h., *b.* 19 July 1859 at Bembridge, Isle of Wight; ed. at Eton; matric. at Oxford (Mag. Coll.) 23 April 1879, aged 19; sometime Capt. West Kent Yeomanry Cavalry; *suc. to the Baronetcy,* 31 Dec. 1897, and by royal lic., in 1899, took the name of *Maryon* before that of *Wilson.* He *m.* 29 Oct. 1887, at All Saints, Ascot, Berks, Minnie Elizabeth, only child of Gen. Anthony Robert Thornhill, of Lavender farm, in Ascot aforesaid.

Family Estates.—These, in 1883, consisted of 1,644 acres in Sussex, 1,529 in Essex, 650 in Kent, and 550 in Middlesex. *Total.*—4,373 acres. The value of the 3,173 acres in Sussex and Kent was £3,418 a year, but that of the valuable estates of 1,200 acres in Kent and Middlesex, being wholly within the Metropolitan area, is unreturned. *Principal Seats.*—Charlton House, near Greenwich, co. Kent, and Searles, in Fletching, co. Sussex.

READ, *or* READE:

cr. 4 March 1660/1.

I. 1661. "Compton Read,(c) of Barton, co. Berks, Esq.," 1st s. of Thomas Read, *or* Reade,(d) of Ipsden, Oxon, and of Barton aforesaid, by Mary (*m.* 8 Sep. 1624), da. of Sir Thomas Cornwall, of Burford, Salop, was *bap.* 24 Jan. 1624/5, at Burford; matric. at Oxford (Mag. Coll.) 1 July 1642, aged 16; suc. his father 14 Sep. 1634; suc. his grandfather, Sir Thomas Reade, 20 Dec. 1650, and, having been a faithful adherent of the King, was *cr. a Baronet,* as above, 4 March 1660/1. He was nominated one of the Knights of the intended Order of the Royal Oak, his income being then valued at £2,000 a year; was Sheriff of Berks, 1663-64, with lic. to reside out of the county, he "having no fit

(a) Under an Act of Parl., 29 June 1871, he sold the Lordship of the Manor of Hampstead, for £55,045, to the Metropolitan Board of Works, thus preserving Hampstead Heath from being built upon, which his brother, the late Baronet, had frequently endeavoured to do.

(b) His elder br., John Maryon Wilson, *bap.* 18 Aug. 1829, at Charlton House chapel, Lieut. 33d West India Reg., *d.* v.p. and s.p.m. 12 Aug. 1853, at Kingston, in Jamaica, leaving an only da. and h., Eliza Eily Dora, who *m.* 21 Nov. 1876, Col. Charles Greenlaw Leggett, and has issue.

(c) See an account of this family in "*A Record of the Redes, of Barton Court, Berks,*" by Compton Reade, 4to, Hereford, 1899.

(d) This Thomas (who *d.* v.p.) was elder br. of John Reade, who survived their father, Sir Thomas Reade, and inherited, on his death in 1650, the estate of Brocket, Herts (their mother having been Mary, da. and h. of Sir John Brocket, of Brocket aforesaid), and who was *cr. a Baronet,* 16 March 1641/2, a dignity which became *extinct,* 22 Feb. 1711/2.

residence in it."(a) He purchased the estate of Shipton Court, in Shipton-under-Wychwood, Oxon, 17 Nov. 1663. He *m.*, in 1650, at Dunstew, Oxon, his cousin, Mary, 1st da. of Sir Gilbert Cornewall, of Burford aforesaid, by Elizabeth, da. of Sir Thomas Reade abovenamed. He *d.* 29 Sep. 1679, and was *bur.* at Shipton. Will dat. 9 Sep. and pr. 6 Nov. 1679. His widow *d.* 26 April 1703, aged 73, and was *bur.* there. Will dat. 16 Nov. 1702, pr. 9 Dec. 1703.

II. 1679. Sir Edward Reade, Baronet [1661], of Shipton Court aforesaid, 2d but only surv. s. and h., *b.* 30 June and *bap.* 6 July 1659, at Burford aforesaid; matric. at Oxford (St. Mary's Hall), 27 Feb. 1673/4, aged 14; *suc. to the Baronetcy,* 29 Sep. 1679; Sheriff of Oxon, 1685-86. He *m.* 9 June 1684 Elizabeth, da. of Edward Harby, of Adston, co. Northampton, by Frances, da. of John Elmes, of Greens Norton, in that county. He *d.* 4 Sep. 1691, and was *bur.* at Shipton, aged 32 years and 2 months. M.I. His widow *m.*, 3 Feb. 1701/2, at Allhallows, Staining, London, Henry Fermor, then of St. Margaret's, Westm., "Esq." She *d.* 13 Sep. 1730, aged 69, and was *bur.* at Shipton. M.I. Will dat. 15 July 1729, pr. 22 Sep. 1731.

III. 1691. Sir Winwood Reade, Baronet [1661], of Shipton Court aforesaid, 1st s. and h., *bap.* 25 July 1682, at Canons Ashby, co. Northampton; *suc. to the Baronetcy,* 4 Sep. 1691, but *d.* nine months afterwards, 30 June 1692, in his tenth year, and was *bur.* at Shipton. Admon. 4 July 1692.

IV. 1692. Sir Thomas Reade, Baronet [1661], of Shipton Court aforesaid, br. and h., *b.* about 1683; *suc. to the Baronetcy,* 30 June 1692; was M.P. for Cricklade (six Parls.), 1715 to 1747, and a supporter of Walpole's Ministry; Gent. of the Privy Chamber to George I, and Clerk of the Household to George II; Founder of the "Reade Lecture" at the Univ. of Cambridge. He *m.* 29 Oct. 1719, at Sherborne, co. Glouc., Jane Mary, da. of Sir Ralph Dutton, 1st Baronet [1678], by his 1st wife, Mary, da. of Peter Berwick, M.D. She *d.* 28 June 1721, and was *bur.* at Sherborne. He *d.* 25 Sep. 1752, aged 69, and was *bur.* at Shipton. Will dat. 21 Sep. 1748, to 6 Sep. 1750, pr. 3 Nov. 1752.

V. 1752. Sir John Reade, Baronet [1661], of Shipton Court aforesaid, only s. and h., *b.* in Golden sq., 21, and *bap.* 27 June 1721, at St. James', Westm.; *suc. to the Baronetcy,* 25 Sep. 1752. He *m.* 18 Oct. 1759, at Ely Chapel, Holborn, Harriet, da. and h. of William Barker, of Sonning, Berks, by Olivia, da. of John Marriott, of Stunton Hall, Norfolk. He *d.* 9 Nov. 1773, in Golden sq., aforesaid, and was *bur.* at Shipton.(b) Will dat. 6 Jan. to 11 March, and pr. 25 Nov. 1773. His widow *d.* 23 Dec. 1811, and was *bur.* at Shipton. Will dat. 1810 to 1811, pr. 1812.

VI. 1773. Sir John Reade, Baronet [1661], of Shipton Court aforesaid, 1st s. and h. (one of twin sons), *b.* 8 March 1762, in Han. sq., and *bap.* at St. Geo., Han. sq.; *suc. to the Baronetcy,* 9 Nov. 1773; matric. at Oxford (Mag. Coll.) 18 Jan. 1780, as a Gent. Commoner, aged 18; *cr.* M.A. 2 July 1783. In 1787 he alienated the manor of Barton and the ruins of Barton Court (which had been in the family since 1547), and purchased an estate at Oddington, co. Glouc. He *m.* 13 Jan. 1784, at St. Marylebone, Jane, 2d da. of Sir Chandos Hoskyns, 5th Baronet [1676], by Rebecca, da. of Joseph May, merchant. He *d.* 7 Nov. 1789, and was *bur.* at Shipton, aged 27. Will dat. 16 Jan., and pr. 28 Nov. 1789. His widow, who survived him 58 years, resided at Oddington, and *d.* there 17 Dec. 1846, aged 91, being *bur.* at Shipton. Will pr. March 1847.

(a) Barton Court, as well as another family residence at Beadon, near Newbury, both in Berks, had been destroyed in the Civil War.

(b) He had been "early in life, a man upon town," and the father of several bastards by various persons. The legitimacy of his twin boys was doubted "by the lower orders of West Oxon." See *Rede Family* as on p. 172, note "c."

VII. 1789. Sir John Chandos Reade, Baronet [1661], of Shipton Court and of Oddington aforesaid, 1st s. and h., *b.* 13 Jan. 1785 in Harley street, and *bap.* at St. Marylebone; *suc. to the Baronetcy,* 7 Nov. 1789; ed. at Harrow; matric. at Oxford (Ch. Ch.) 27 April 1804, as a Gent. Commoner, aged 19; Sheriff of Oxon, 1811-12. He *m.* 6 Jan. 1814, at St. James', Westm., Louisa, yst. da. of the Hon. David Murray (br. of Alexander, 7th Lord Elibank [S.]), by Elizabeth, da. and coheir of the Hon. Thomas Harley, sometime [1767-68] Lord Mayor of London. She *d.* 6 Feb. 1821, and was *bur.* at Shipton. He *d.* there, s.p.m.s., 14 Jan. 1868, and was *bur.* at Little Rollright, Oxon, aged 83. His will is dat. 20 Dec. 1856, before which date four of his five children had *d.* s.p.,(a) the survivor, Emily (who *d.* unm., 23 Nov. 1897, aged 78) being imbecile. In it he makes no mention of any relative, but (to the exclusion of his heir at law) devises the Shipton Court estate and (with trifling exception) all his real and personal estate to Joseph Wakefield, apparently his servant, whom he directs to take his name. The will was declared valid, and pr. 24 June 1868, when the devise took effect.

VIII. 1868. Sir Chandos Stanhope Reade, Baronet [1661], great nephew and h. male, being only s. and h. of George Reade, Lieut. in the Madras Army, by Jane Anne, da. of J. Norton, which George (who *d.* v.p., 20 Oct. 1863, aged 51) was s. and h. of George Compton Reade, of Elvaston, near Budleigh Salterton, Devon, sometime an officer in the Grenadier Guards (*d.* 24 Dec. 1866, aged 78), who was 2d s. of the 6th Baronet. He was *b.* 5 Sep. 1851, at Madras, was in the Madras Civil Service, and *suc. to the Baronetcy* (though to none of the family estates), 14 Jan. 1868; is said to have been sometime Sheriff of Anglesey. He *m.*, 11 March 1880, at St. Geo. Han. sq., Maria Emma Elizabeth Conway, da. and h. of Richard Trygarn Griffith, of Carreglwyd and Berw, co. Anglesey.(b) He *d.* s.p. 28 Jan. 1890 at Meldreth, St. Leonards-on-Sea, aged 38. M.I. His widow living 1903.

IX. 1890. Sir George Compton Reade, Baronet [1661], of Howell, Livingstone county, Michigan, in the United States of America, cousin and h. male, being 1st s. and h. of John Stanhope Reade, by Louisa (*m.* 1836) da. of (—) Walton, of Dexter, in Michigan aforesaid, which John, who *d.* 1883, was 2d s. of George Compton Reade abovenamed, the grandfather of the 8th, and the 2d s. of the 6th Baronet. He was *b.* 17 Dec. 1845, and *suc. to the Baronetcy,* 28 Jan. 1890. He *m.*, 4 June 1868, Melissa, da. of Isaac Ray, of Michigan aforesaid.

BROUGHTON:

cr. 10 March 1660/1;

sometime, 1727-66, Broughton-Delves.

I. 1661. "Sir Brian Broughton, of Broughton, co. Stafford, Knt.," s. and h. of Thomas Broughton, of the same (who for his loyalty to Charles I suffered a fine amounting to £3,200), by Frances, da. of Walter Bagot, of Blithfield, co. Stafford, was *b.* 23 May 1618; suc. his father

(a) The eldest s., Compton Reade, *b.* 17 Oct. 1814, matric. at Oxford (Trin. Coll.) 14 Feb. 1833, aged 18, and *d.* unm. 31 July 1851. The 2d s., John Chandos Reade, *b.* 1816, *d.* in infancy. The eldest da., Louisa Jane, *b.* 20 July 1817, *d.* unm. 9 Feb. 1837, and the 3d and yst. da., Clara Louisa, *b.* 25 Jan. 1821, *m.* 13 Oct. 1846, as his 1st wife, the Hon. John Talbot Rice, but *d.* s.p. and v.p. 11 Aug. 1853, her husband inheriting the estate at Oddington, which had been her marriage portion.

(b) These estates, in 1883, consisted of 3,764 acres in Anglesey, worth £3,273 a year.

25 July 1648; was *Knighted,* at Whitehall, 13 June 1660; Sheriff of Staffordshire, 1660-61, and was *cr. a Baronet,* as above, 10 March 1660/1. He *m.*, in or before 1648, Bridget, da. of Sir Thomas Lucy, of Charlecote, co. Warwick, by Alicia, da. of Thomas Spencer, of Claverdon, in that county. She *d.* 1 Sep. 1692, aged 71, and was *bur.* at Broughton. He *d.* 30 July 1708, in his 91st year, and was *bur.* there. M.I.

II. 1708. Sir Thomas Broughton, Baronet [1661], of Broughton aforesaid, 1st s. and h.; *b.* about 1648; matric. at Oxford (Trin. Coll.) 8 March 1666/7, aged 18; *suc. to the Baronetcy,* 30 July 1708. He *m.* 10 July 1672, at St. Paul's, Covent Garden, Midx. (Lic. Vic. Gen., 6, he aged 24 and she 19), Rhoda, da. and h. of John Amcotts, of Aystrop, co. Lincoln, by Rhoda, da. of Thomas Hussey, of Caythorpe in that county. She, who was *bap.* 2 Dec. 1653, at Great Corringham, *d.* before him. He *d.* soon after his father, in or before 1710, in St. Anne's, Soho,(a) Midx. Admon. 23 May 1710.

III. 1710? Sir Brian Broughton, Baronet [1661], of Broughton and Aystrop aforesaid, 2d but 1st surv. s. and h.; *b.* probably about 1678; was, presumably, B.A. (Christ's Coll.) Cambridge, 1699; *suc. to the Baronetcy* in or shortly before 1710; was M.P. for Newcastle-under-line 1715 till death in 1724, and one of the Gentlemen of the Bedchamber. He *m.*, in or before 1714, Elizabeth, da. and h. of Sir Thomas Delves, 4th and last Baronet [1621], of Doddington, Salop, by his 1st wife, Jane, da. of Sir Richard Knightley, K.B. He *d.*, "of yellow jaundice and dropsy," 12 Sep. 1724, at Broughton. Will pr. 16 Oct. 1724. His widow *d.* 2 Jan. 1746. Her will pr. 3 March 1746.

IV. 1724. Sir Brian Broughton, *afterwards* (1727-44) Broughton-Delves, Baronet [1661], of Broughton and Aystrop aforesaid, only s. and h., *b.* 6 Jan. 1717/8; *suc. to the Baronetcy,* 12 Sep. 1724, and by the death, 12 Sep. 1727, of his maternal grandfather, Sir Thomas Delves, 4th and last Baronet [1621], suc. to the considerable estate of Doddington, co. Chester, and took the name of *Delves,* after that of *Broughton*; ed. at Winchester 1734; matric. at Oxford (Queen's Coll.), 7 July 1735, aged 16; M.P. for Wenlock, 1741 till death and Dep. Ranger of Needwood forest. He *m.*, 21 May 1738, by Spec. Lic. at her father's house, John's Square, St. James', Clerkenwell, Mary, da. of William Forrester, of Watling Street, Salop. He *d.* 11 Aug. 1744, in his 27th year. Will pr. 1744. His widow *m.*, in 1746, Humphrey Mackworth Praed, and *d.* 26 Sep. 1779.

V. 1744. Sir Brian Broughton-Delves, Baronet [1661], of Doddington, Broughton and Aystrop aforesaid, 1st s. and h., *b.* April 1740; *suc. to the Baronetcy,* 11 Aug. 1744; matric. at Oxford (Mag. Coll.), 2 June 1757, aged 17; *cr.* M.A. 5 July 1759. He *m.* Mary, da. of Thomas Hill, of Tern, co. Salop. He *d.* s.p. 16 Jan. 1766, near Andover, Hants, aged 25. Will pr. 25 Feb. 1766.

VI. 1766. Sir Thomas Broughton, Baronet [1661], of Doddington and Broughton aforesaid, *formerly* Broughton-Delves, only br. and h., *b.* about 1744; matric. at Oxford (Mag. Coll.), 25 Oct. 1762, aged 17; *suc. to the Baronetcy,* 16 Jan. 1766, when he assumed the name of *Broughton* only; was Sheriff of Staffordshire, 1772-73. He *m.* firstly, 31 March 1766, Mary, da. and h. of John Wicker, of Horsham, Sussex, by Charlotte, da. of James Colebrune, of Chilham Castle, Kent. She *d.* 7 June 1785, and was *bur.* at Broughton. He *m.* secondly, 6 June 1787, Anne, 3d da. of Other Lewis (Windsor), 4th Earl of Plymouth, by Catharine, da. of Thomas (Archer), 1st Baron Archer of Umberslade. She, who was *bap.* 20 Jan. 1761, at Hewell, co. Worc., *d.* s.p. 10 Aug. 1793, and was *bur.* at Broughton. He *m.* thirdly, 2 July 1794, Mary, widow of Thomas Scott Jackson, a Director of the Bank of England, da. of Michael Keating, of Cork. He *d.* 23 July 1813, at Doddington Hall. Will pr. 1814. His widow *d.* a few months later, 17 Nov. 1813, in her 61st year. Her will pr. 1814.

(a) In that parish was *bur.* his eldest son Amcotts Broughton, who *d.* v.p. 14 Sep. 1700, aged 25.

VII. 1813. Sir John Delves Broughton, Baronet [1661], of Doddington and Broughton aforesaid, 2d but 1st surv. s. and h., *bap.* 17 Aug. 1769, at Eccleshall, co. Stafford; was an officer in the army, becoming in 1830 full General; *suc. to the Baronetcy*, 23 July 1813. He *m.* 5 June 1792, Elizabeth, sister of Sir John Egerton, *afterwards* Grey-Egerton, 3d Baronet [1617], da. of Philip Egerton, of Oulton, co. Chester, by Mary, da. of Sir Francis Haskyn Eyles-Styles, 3d Baronet [1714]. He *d.* s.p. 9 Aug. 1847, at Bank farm, near Kingston, Surrey, aged 78. Will pr. Oct. and Dec. 1847. His widow *d.* 27 Jan. 1857, at Hoole House, Cheshire, aged 86. Will pr. April 1857.

VIII. 1847. Sir Henry Delves Broughton, Baronet [1661], of Doddington and Broughton aforesaid, br. of the whole blood and h.; *b.* 10 Jan. and *bap.* 21 April 1777, at Eccleshall aforesaid; *ed.* at Rugby, Jan. 1787, and at Eton; matric. at Oxford (Oriel Coll.), 29 Oct. 1794, aged 17, and was afterwards of Jesus Coll. Cambridge, being B.A. 1801 and M.A. 1805 of that Univ.; in Holy Orders; Incumbent of Broughton, 1803, and of Haslington, co. Chester, 1829; *suc. to the Baronetcy*, 9 Aug. 1847. He *m.* 15 June 1807, at Cheltenham, Mary, da. of John Pigott, of Bevere, co. Worcester, and of Capard in Queen's County, Ireland. He *d.* 3 Nov. 1851 at Broughton Hall aforesaid. Will pr. Dec. 1851. His widow *d.* 26 Dec. 1863 at Rhyll, North Wales.

IX. 1851. Sir Henry Delves Broughton, Baronet [1661], of Doddington and Broughton aforesaid, 1st s. and h., *b.* 22 June 1808, and *bap.* at Cheadle, co. Chester; matric. at Oxford (Wadham Coll.), 1 June 1825; *suc. to the Baronetcy*, 3 Nov. 1847; Sheriff of Staffordshire, 1859, and of Cheshire, 1871. He *m.* 24 Feb. 1857, at the Registry Office, Lambeth, Surrey, Eliza Florence Alexandrina Rosenzweig, then of Tillotson Place, Waterloo Road, Lambeth, aged 19, spinster, da. of Louis Rosenzweig, "Gentleman." She *d.* there 14 Nov. 1882, aged 45. He *d.* 26 Feb. 1899, and, after cremation, was *bur.* at Eccleshall aforesaid. Will pr. at £766,746 gross, and £167,871 net personalty.

X. 1899. Sir Delves Louis Broughton, Baronet [1661], of Doddington and Broughton aforesaid, 1st s. and h., *b.* 1 June 1857, at Tillotson Place aforesaid; sometime Lieut. North Staff. Reg.; *suc. to the Baronetcy*, 26 Feb. 1899. He *m.* firstly, 26 April 1881, at Yazor, co. Hereford, Rosamond, da. of John Lambart Broughton, of Almington Hall, co. Stafford, by Anne Selina, da. of Ralph Adderley, of Coton in that county. She *d.* 11 Oct. 1885, aged 24. He *m.* secondly, 21 Dec. 1887, Mary Evelyn, 2d da. of Rowland Hugh Cotton, of Etwall Hall, co. Derby, by Mary Louisa, da. of John Bill, of Farley Hall, co. Stafford.

Family Estates.—These, in 1883, consisted of 13,832 acres in Cheshire, 1,320 in Staffordshire, and 2 in Shropshire. *Total.*—15,154 acres worth £21,744 a year. *Seats.*—Doddington Park, near Nantwich, co. Chester, and Broughton Hall, near Eccleshall, co. Stafford.

SLINGSBY:

cr. 16 March 1660/1;

ex. 26 Oct. 1661.

I 1661, March to Oct. "Robert Slingsby,(a) of Newcells, co. Hertford, Esq." elder br. of Sir Arthur Slingsby, Baronet [so *cr.* 19 Oct. 1657], being 2d of the eight sons of Sir Guilford Slingsby, Comptroller of the Navy, by Margaret (*m.* 1609), da. of William Waters, Alderman of York (which Guilford, who *d.* at sea 1631, aged 66, was 8th son of Thomas Slingsby, of Scriven, co. York), was *b.* about 1611 and

(a) He was author of a *Discourse upon the past and present state of His Majesty's Navy*, printed in 1801 and again in 1896.

was, when 22, in command of a pinnace; conveyed troops to Edinburgh in 1642 for the King; was declared a delinquent and fined £140; retired abroad after the siege of Bristol; was, at the Restoration, made Comptroller of the Navy and was *cr. a Baronet*, as above, 16 March 1660/1. He *m.* firstly Elizabeth, da. of Robert Brooke, of Newcells aforesaid, with whom he acquired that estate. He *m.* secondly Elizabeth, widow of Sir William Fenwick, of Meldon, co. Northumberland, da. of Sir Edward Radclyffe, of Dilston, in that county. He *d.* s.p., 26 Oct. 1661 (a few months after his creation) at St. Mary's Axe, Lime Street, London, when the *Baronetcy became extinct*. Admon. 23 Dec. 1661, to Elizabeth the relict and others. The will of Dame Elizabeth Slingsby was pr. Aug. 1704.

CROFTS:

cr. 16 March 1660/1;

ex. Dec. 1664.

I. 1661, to 1664. "John Crofts, of Stow [*i.e.* West Stow], co. Suffolk, Esq.," s. and h. of Anthony Crofts of the same, by Mary, relict of Sir John Smyth, of Leeds Castle, Kent, da. of Richard Franklin, of Willesden, Midx.(a) (which Anthony, who *d.* 1 Oct. 1657 in his 64th year, was 2d s. of Sir John Crofts, of Little Saxham, co. Suffolk), was *b.* 1635; suc. his father in Oct. 1657, and was *cr. a Baronet*, as above, 16 March 1660/1. He *m.* Bryers, only da. and h. of George Wharton, by Anne Bryers,(b) his wife. He *d.* s.p.s., and was *bur.* at West Stow, Dec. 1664, aged 29 years and 5 months, when *the Baronetcy* became *extinct*. Will dat. 21 Nov. 1664, pr. 6 Jan. 1664/5. His widow *d.* 13, and was *bur.* 14 Jan. 1669/70 at West Stow. Will dat. 13 Nov. 1669, pr. 1 Feb. 1669/70, in which she devises all her estates to "Edward Progers, of St. Martin's-in-the-Fields, co. Midx., Esq.," who proved the same.

VERNEY:

cr. 16 March 1660/1;

afterwards, 1703-91, Viscounts Fermanagh [I.];

and subsequently, 1743-91, Earls Verney [I.];

ex. 31 March 1791.

I. 1661. "Ralph Verney, of Middle Claydon, co. Buckingham, Esq.," [but should be "Knight"], s. and h. of Sir Edmund Verney, of the same, Knight Marshal and Standard Bearer to Charles I, by Margaret, da. of Sir Thomas Denton, of Hillesden, Bucks, was *b.* 12 and *bap.* 18 Nov. 1613, at Hillesden; *Knighted* v.p. 8 March 1640/1, at Whitehall; suc. his father (who was slain at the battle of Edgehill) 22 Oct. 1642; was at first on the side of the Parl. but went into exile in 1643 rather than sign the Covenant; his estate sequestrated in 1646; returned and was imprisoned in 1653, and was *cr. a Baronet*, as above, 16 March 1660/1. He was M.P. for Aylesbury April to May 1640, and Nov. 1640 till disabled 22 Sep. 1645; for Great Bedwyn 1660 till void 17 May, and for Buckingham 1681, 1685-87, and 1689-90. He *m.* (in his 16th year) 31 May 1629, at Hillesden, Mary (then apparently about 13), da. and h. of John Blacknall, of Wasing and Abingdon, Berks. She *d.* at Blois, in France, 10 May, and was *bur.* 19 Nov. 1650, at Middle Claydon, aged about 34. M.I. He *d.* 24 Sep., and was *bur.* there 9 Oct. 1696, aged 84. M.I.

(a) This Dame Mary Smyth *d.* 11 and was *bur.* 15 May 1678 in her 80th year, at West Stow. M.I. *See* Rev. Sydenham H. A. Hervey's valuable history of *West Stow, Suffolk*, containing the parish registers, M.I.'s, etc.

(b) This Anne Bryers *m.* secondly, John George Steiner, "Esq.," who *d.* 26 Sep. 1672. She *d.* 14 Oct. 1673, aged 52, both being *bur.* at West Stow. M.I. *See* Hervey's *West Stow* as in note "a" above.

Z

II. 1696. Sir John Verney, Baronet [1661], of Middle Claydon aforesaid, 2d but 1st surv. s. and h. male,(a) *b.* 5 Nov. 1640, and *suc. to the Baronetcy* 24 Sep. 1696. He *m.*, firstly, 27 May 1680, at Westm. Abbey (Lic. Vic. Gen., he of London, Merchant, about 35, bachelor, and she about 16, spinster), Elizabeth, 1st da. of Ralph Palmer, of Little Chelsea, Midx., by Alice, da. of (—) White. She *d.* 20 and was *bur.* 28 May 1696, at Middle Claydon. He *m.*, secondly, 16 July 1692, also at Westm. Abbey, Mary, 1st da. of Sir Francis Lawley, 2d Baronet [1641], by Anne, da. of Sir Thomas Whitmore, 1st Baronet [1641]. She *d.* 24 Aug. and was *bur.* 5 Sep. 1694, at Middle Claydon. He *m.*, thirdly, 8 April 1696, at Kensington, Elizabeth, da. of Daniel Baker, of Penn House, Bucks, Alderman of London, by Barbara, his wife. She was living when he was *cr.*, 16 June 1703, VISCOUNT FERMANAGH, etc. [I.], being as such M.P. for Bucks, 1710-13, and for Amersham, 1713-17. In this title this *Baronetcy* then merged, the 2d Viscount being *cr.*, 22 March 1742/3, EARL VERNEY [I.], till all these dignities became *extinct*(b) on the death of the 2d Earl, 3d Viscount, and 4th Baronet, 31 March 1791. See *Peerage*.

STANLEY:

"William Stanley, of Hooton, co. Chester, Esq.," was *cr. a Baronet*, as above, according to some accounts on 20 March 1660/1, but the usually received date is 17 June 1661, and it is here dealt with accordingly.

DYCER, *or* DICER:

cr. 18 March 1660/1;

ex. 1676.

I. 1661. "Robert Dicer, of Uphall, co. Hertford, Esq.," s. of Robert Dicer or Dycer, of Wrentham, co. Suffolk, by Elizabeth, da. of (—) Maddocks, of Ipswich, was *b.* about 1595; was, presumably, a merchant of London, and was *cr. a Baronet*, as above, 18 March 1660/1. He entered (and signed as "Robert Dicer") his pedigree in the Vist. of Midx., 1664, being then of Hackney in that County. He *m.*, before 1644, Dorothy, da. of William Styles, of Emingston, co. Suffolk. He *d.* at Hackney 26 Aug. and was *bur.* 10 Sep. 1667 from Leathersellers Hall, St. Helen's, Bishopsgate, at Braughing, Herts, aged 72. Funeral Certificate. Will pr. 1667. His widow *m.* 4 March 1668/9, at Hackney (Lic. Vic. Gen. 23 Feb., he about 53, wid.) Robert Huntington, of Stanton Harcourt, Oxon.

(a) The eldest s., Edmund Verney, *bap.* at Middle Claydon, 29 Dec. 1636, *d.* v.p., and was *bur.* there, 6 Sep. 1688, leaving issue, of which one da., Mary (*bap.* there 23 Jan. 1674) survived her grandfather. She *m.* John Kelyng, and *d.* 19 Feb. 1695/6, leaving one da., Mary, who was *bur.* at Claydon 14 May following.

(b) In *The Times* newspaper for 15 May 1880, is a letter from Lord Braye, contradicting a statement (apparently well founded) "that the 2d Earl Verney was the last *male* of the old family" of Verney, and stating that he (Lord Braye) is "the only male representative of the race [of Verney], being the only male descendant of Sarah Cave, Baroness Braye" [his grandmother]. The noble Lord's descent from the family of Verney is through his *mother's mother's* great grand*mother*, and that he should consider that such descent constitutes him the "*male* representative of the race," argues an ignorance of the well known rule in grammar, which teaches us that a woman is of the feminine gender, and that consequently any representation derived through her must be in the *female* (not in the male) line.

II. 1667. Sir Robert Dycer, Baronet [1661], of Hackney aforesaid, 1st s. and h., *b.* about 1644; admitted to Gray's Inn, 24 Jan. 1664/5; *suc. to the Baronetcy*, 26 Aug. 1667; Sheriff of Suffolk, 1669-70. He *m.* (Lic. Vic. Gen. 2 May 1666, he about 22 and she about 21) Judith, da. of Richard Goulston, *or* Gulston, of Widdiall, Herts. Will pr. 1675.

III. 1675? to 1676. Sir Robert Dycer, Baronet [1661], of Braughing aforesaid, only s. and h., *b.* 1667; *suc. to the Baronetcy* in or shortly before 1675. He *d.* in boyhood at Widdiall, Herts, in 1676 before July, when the *Baronetcy* became *extinct*.(a) Admon. 5 July 1676 to "Richard Gulston, Esq.," grandfather and next of kin.

BROMFIELD:

cr. 20 March 1660/1;

ex. or *dormant* 6 Sep. 1733.

I. 1661. "John Bromfield, of Southwark, co. Surrey, Esq.," 1st s. and h. of Sir Edward Bromfield, Citizen and Fishmonger, sometime [1636-37] Lord Mayor of London, by Margaret, da. and coheir of John Payne, of Southwark, was *b.* probably about 1610; admitted to the Inner Temple, Nov. 1626, becoming a Barrister 1637, and was *cr. a Baronet*, as above, 20 March 1660/1. He *m.* firstly, in or before 1630, Joyce, da. of William Austen, of Cheversall, Essex. She was living 1634.(b) He *m.* secondly Elizabeth, da. and coheir of William Michelborne, of Westmeston, Sussex. He *m.* thirdly, Anne (*b.* before 1623), da. of Christopher Woodward, of Lambeth, Surrey, by Catherine, da. of Thomas Audley, of London. He entered and signed his pedigree in the Her. Visit. of Surrey 1663, but *d.* in or before 1666. Will pr. 1666. The will of Dame Ann Bromfield, pr. 1696.

II. 1666? Sir Edward Bromfield, Baronet [1661], of Suffolk Place in Southwark aforesaid, 1st s. and h., by 1st wife, aged 2 years or more 1634(b); *suc. to the Baronetcy* in or before 1666; Sheriff of Surrey, 1677, but did not act, and again 1689. He *m.* (Lic. at Oxford, 14 April 1666) Susan Bowell, of Cockthorp, in Ducklington, Oxon. He *d.* suddenly, s.p.m.,(c) 17 Feb. 1703/4.

III. 1704, to 1733. Sir Charles Bromfield, Baronet [1661], nephew and h. male, being s. and h. of Charles Bromfield, who was living 1663 as 2d son of the 1st Baronet,(d) being 1st son by the 2d wife. He was *b.* about 1672, and was, possibly, the "Charles Bromfield, Gent.," who matric. at Oxford (Wadham Coll.) 1 June 1693. He *suc. to the Baronetcy* 17 Feb. 1703/4. He *m.* Theodosia, sister and coheir of Samuel Steele, da. of John Steele, both of Orton on the Hill, co. Leicester. He *d.* s.p.m. 6 Sep. 1733, at Barton under Needwood, co. Stafford, aged 61, when *the Baronetcy* became *extinct* or *dormant*. The will of his widow was pr. 1737.

(a) Dorothy, his sister, *m.* 1 Sep. 1681 at St. Martin's, Outwich, London, William Harvey, and had issue.

(b) Visit. of London, 1634.

(c) Joyce, his da. and h., *m.* Thomas Lant.

(d) He presumably is the Charles Bromfield, of St. George's, Southwark, aged about 25 on 31 Jan 1667/8, when he obtained Lic. (Vic. Gen.) to marry Mary (then aged 21), da. of Nicholas Salter, of London.

"The title, on the decease of Sir Charles, is said to have vested in Philip BROMFIELD, a teaman in Lombard Street, and on his death s.p. in William BROMFIELD, Esq., Surgeon to the Princess Dow. of Wales, but neither of these gentlemen chose to assume it" [Courthope's *Extinct Baronetcies*]. The last mentioned person was presumably William Bromfield, a surgeon, in Conduit Street, St. Geo. Han. sq., who died 24 Nov. 1792, aged 80.

RICH :

cr. 20 March 1660/1 ;

ex. 6 April 1803.

I. 1661. "THOMAS RICH, of Sunning [or Sonning], co. Berks, Esq.," s. and h. of Thomas RICH, of Astwood Court, co. Worcester, Alderman of Gloucester [1600], by Anne, da. of Thomas MACHYN, of that city, was *b.* about 1601 in Gloucester; ed. in London; was, presumably, the Thomas RICH who matric. at Oxford (Wadham Coll.), 8 May 1618, aged 17; was Citizen and Vintner, and a Turkey merchant of London; elected Alderman of Bridge within, 11, but discharged by fine 24 Sep. 1650 (being, however, recommended 5 May 1662 by the King, whom, during exile, he had largely assisted, to be replaced); was Sheriff of Berks, 1657-58; M.P. for Reading, 1660; and was *cr. a Baronet*, as above, 20 March 1660/1. He *m.* firstly Barbara, da. of Gilbert MOREWOOD, of Seale, co. Leicester, by whom he had no issue that survived him. He *m.* secondly, in or before 1647, Elizabeth, 3d and yst. da. of William COKAYNE, Merchant, Citizen and Skinner of London, by his 1st wife Ellen, sister of John FLUD, *otherwise* LLOYD. He, who is said to have left £16,000 to various charities, *d.* 15 Oct. 1667 and was *bur.* at Sonning, aged 60. M.I. Will dat. 16 May 1666 to 14 Oct. 1667, pr. 20 Nov. 1667. His widow, who was *bap.* 11 Oct. 1618, at St. Peter le Poor, London, *d.* 1675 and was *bur.* at Sonning. Will dat. 6 June 1674, pr. July 1675.

II. 1667. SIR WILLIAM RICH, Baronet [1661], of Sonning aforesaid, only surv. s. and h., by 2d wife; *b.* about 1654; *suc. to the Baronetcy*, 15 Oct. 1667. He was M.P. for Reading, 1689-98; for Gloucester, 1698—1700; and for Reading, again, 1705-08. He *m.* (Lic. Fac. 28 May 1672, he about 18 and she about 12) Anne, one of the 17 children of Robert (BRUCE), 2d EARL OF ELGIN [S.], and 1st EARL OF AILESBURY, by Diana, da. of Henry (GREY), 1st EARL OF STAMFORD. He *d.* 1711. Will dat. 26 Feb. 1709, pr. 29 April 1712. The will of Lady Ann RICH pr. 1716.

III. 1711. SIR ROBERT RICH, Baronet [1661], of Sonning aforesaid, only s. and h.; *bap.* 29 March 1673 at Sonning; matric. at Oxford (New Coll.), 26 June 1688, aged 15; *suc. to the Baronetcy* in 1711. He *m.* 7 May 1698, at St. Antholin's, London, Mary, da. of Sir William WALTER, 2d Baronet [1641], by his 1st wife, Mary, da. of John (TUFTON), 2d EARL OF THANET. He *d.* 9 Nov. 1724. Will pr. Sep. 1725. His widow was living at Sonning 1741.

IV. 1724. SIR WILLIAM RICH, Baronet [1661], of Sonning aforesaid, 1st s. and h.; *suc. to the Baronetcy*, 9 Nov. 1724; living unm. in 1741. He *m.* Elizabeth, da. of William ROYALL, of Minstead, Hants. He *d.* 17 July 1762, aged probably about 60.(a) His widow *d.* in St. Margaret's, Westm., 27 April 1771. Admon. 9 Dec. 1771 to her son, Sir Thomas RICH, Baronet.

(a) His age is given as "70" in various obituaries, but as it is certain that his parents did not marry till 1698, "70" is probably a mistake for "60."

V. 1762, to 1803. SIR THOMAS RICH, Baronet [1661], of Sonning aforesaid, Admiral of the Royal Navy, s. and h., *b.* about 1733; *suc. to the Baronetcy*, 17 July 1762; entered the Royal Navy, becoming in 1794 Rear-Admiral of the Red; in 1795 Vice-Admiral of the Blue; in 1799 Vice-Admiral of the Red, and, finally, in 1801 Admiral of the Blue. He was M.P. for Great Marlow, 1784-90. He *m.* Ann, da. and coheir of Richard WILLIS, of Digswell, Herts. He *d.* s.p. legit. 6 April 1803, at his house at Sonning, aged about 70, when the *Baronetcy* became *extinct*. Will pr. May 1803. His widow *d.* 13 Sep. 1808 in Beaumont Street, Devonshire Place, Marylebone. Will pr. 1808.

SMITH *or* SMYTH :

cr. 20 March 1660/1 ;

ex. 15 Feb. 1720/1.

I. 1661. "EDWARD SMITH, of Edmundthorpe, co. Leicester, Esq.," s. and h. of Edward SMITH, of Cressy Hall, co. Lincoln (who *d.* v.p. 1632, aged 32) by Elizabeth, da. of Sir Edward HERON, K.B., was *b.* probably about 1630; was admitted to Linc. Inn, 8 Feb. 1648/9; was M.P. for Leicestershire, 1653; suc. his grandfather, Sir Roger SMITH (who *d.* aged 84), in 1655 in the family estates and was *cr. a Baronet*, as above, 20 March 1660/1. He was Sheriff of Leicestershire, 1665-66. He *m.* firstly Constance, da. of Sir William SPENCER, 2d Baronet [1611] of Yarnton, Oxon, by Constance, da. of Sir Thomas LUCY, of Charlecote. He *m.* secondly (Lic. Lond. 4 May 1682, he about 50 and she about 40) Frances, widow of Sir Richard WESTON, 2d da. of Sir George MARWOOD, 1st Baronet [1660], of Little Buskeby, co. York, by Frances, da. of Sir Walter BETHELL. By her he had no issue. He *m.* thirdly Bridget, widow of Richard BAYLIS, of Woodford, co. Essex, da. of [—], of Andover, Hants. He *d.* 6 Sep. 1707. Admon. 3 Oct. 1707 to his son Sir Edward, and again (limited) 5 July 1751.

II. 1707, to 1721. SIR EDWARD SMITH, Baronet [1661], of Edmundthorpe aforesaid, 1st s. and h. by first wife; *b.* about 1655; admitted 8 Aug. 1671 to Linc. Inn; *suc. to the Baronetcy*, 6 Sep. 1707. He *m.* (Lic. Fac., 14 June 1683, he 28 and she 18) Olivia, da. and h. of Thomas PEPYS, of Merton Abbey, Surrey, by Ursula his wife. He *d.*, s.p.s., 15 Feb. 1720/1, when *the Baronetcy* became *extinct*.(a) Will pr. 1721. His widow *d.* Jan. 1736.

LONG :

cr. 26 March 1661 ;

ex. 21 May 1710.

I. 1661. "WALTER LONG, of Whaddon, co. Wilts, Esq.," 2d but 1st surv. s. and h. of Henry LONG, of the same, by Rebecca, da. of Christopher BAILEY, was admitted to Lincoln's Inn, 30 April 1611: suc. his father in 1612; M.P. for Salisbury, 1625; for Wilts, 1626; for Bath, 1628-29; and for Ludgershall, Jan. 1642, till secluded in Dec. 1648; Sheriff of Wilts, 1627-28; a Puritan and a zealous Parliamentarian, being one of the seven members sent to the Tower in 1628 by Charles I, and one of the eleven members expelled by the army in Jan. 1647; raised a troop of Horse with which he fought at Edgehill, 23 Oct. 1642, against the King, being there wounded; Registrar of Chancery, 1643-47; took the Covenant, 25 Sep. 1643; was one of the most active members of the House between 1642 and 1647, being awarded £5,000 in Jan. 1647, but having, subsequently, incurred the displeasure of his Party, joined Charles II,

(a) He left the estate of Edmundthorpe to his distant cousin and h. male, Edward Smith, descended from an uncle of the 1st Baronet. This Edward was, sometime, M.P. for Leicestershire and *d.* s.p. 1762, being the last of his race there settled.

when in exile, and was *cr. a Baronet*, as above, 26 March 1661. He *m.* firstly, in or before 1627, Mary, da. of Joseph COCKS, *or* COXE. He *m.*, secondly, 2 Jan. 1665/6, at Ludlow, Elizabeth, da. of John COTES, of Woodcote, Salop, but by her had no issue. He *d.* 1672. Will pr. 1672. The will of Dame Elizabeth LONG was pr. Nov. 1688.

II. 1672, to 1710. SIR WALTER LONG, Baronet [1661], of Whaddon aforesaid, 1st s. and h., by 1st wife, *bap.* there 1627; admitted to Lincoln's Inn, 25 Nov. 1644; *suc. to the Baronetcy* in 1672; was Sheriff of Wilts, 1671-72; and M.P. for Bath, 1679-81. He *d.* unm., 21 May 1710, in his 84th year, when the *Baronetcy* became *extinct*.(a) Will pr. July 1710.

FETTIPLACE :

cr. 30 March 1661 ;

ex. 8 April 1743.

I. 1661. "JOHN FETTIPLACE, of Chilrey [*i.e.* Childrey], co. Berks, Esq.," s. and h. of Edward FETTIPLACE (*d.* 1656), Barrister at Law (Lincoln's Inn), by Anne, da. of (—) COX, of London, Wine cooper; was admitted to Lincoln's Inn, 31 May 1647; suc. to the estates of Childrey and Swinbrook, co. Oxon, on the death in 1657 (aged 76) of his uncle, John Fettiplace, of the same, many years M.P. for Berks and a zealous Royalist, and was, "in consideration of services and sufferings for King Charles I," *cr. a Baronet*, as above, 30 March 1661; Sheriff of Berks, 1667-68. He *m.* firstly, in or before 1654, Anne, sister of Sir Francis WENMAN, 1st Baronet [1662], da. of Sir Francis WENMAN, of Caswell, Oxon, by Anne, da. of Sir Samuel SANDYS. She was *bur.* 1668 (in or after Oct.) at Swinbrook aforesaid. He *m.* secondly, Susan, widow of Lawrence BATHURST, of Lechlade, co. Glouc., da. of Thomas COOK, of Staunton, co. Worc. He *d.* 26 Sep. 1672. Admon. 5 Sep. 1673 on behalf of his 10 minor children (the relict Susanna renouncing), and again 27 Nov. 1680 to his son, Sir Edmund, then of full age. His widow, by whom he had no issue, *m.* (for her 3d husband) Sir Thomas CUTLER, of Lechlade aforesaid (who *d.* in or before 1711), and *d.* at Oxford in or before 1687. Admon. 23 Nov. 1687 to her said husband.

II. 1672. SIR EDMUND FETTIPLACE, Baronet [1661], of Childrey and Swinbrook aforesaid, 1st s. and h.; *b.* about 1654; matric. at Oxford (Queen's Coll.) 19 Dec. 1668, aged 14; *suc. to the Baronetcy* in 1672; Sheriff of Oxon, 1675-76. He *d.* unm. in 1707. Will pr. March 1707.

III. 1707. SIR CHARLES FETTIPLACE, Baronet [1661], of Childrey and Swinbrook aforesaid, next surv. br. (of the whole blood) and h.; *suc. to the Baronetcy* in 1707; Sheriff of Oxon, Nov. to Dec. 1713. He *d.* unm. in Dec. 1713. Will pr. April 1714.

IV. 1713. SIR LORENZO FETTIPLACE, Baronet [1661], of Childrey and Swinbrook aforesaid, next br. (of the whole blood) and h.; *b.* about 1662; matric. at Oxford (Oriel Coll.), 28 Feb. 1678/9, aged 16; *suc. to the Baronetcy* in Dec. 1713; Sheriff of Oxon, Dec. 1713 to 1714. He *d.* unm. and was *bur.* 4 Sep. 1725, at Swinbrook. Admon. 5 March 1725/6.

(a) He devised Whaddon to his nephew, Calthorpe Parker, a yr. s. of his sister, Rebecca, by Sir Philip Parker, 1st Baronet [1661], of Arwarton, Suffolk. This Calthorpe took the name of Long, but *d.* s.p. in 1729, aged 72, being suc. in this estate by his nephew, Sir Philip Parker-a-Morley-Long, 3d and last Baronet [1661], on whose death, s.p.m., 20 Jan. 1740/1, aged 58, it passed to a distant cousin, Thomas Long, of Rowden.

V. 1725, to 1743. SIR GEORGE FETTIPLACE, Baronet [1661], of Childrey and Swinbrook aforesaid, next and yst. br. (of the whole blood) and h.; *bap.* 13 Oct. 1668 at Swinbrook, *suc. to the Baronetcy* in Sep. 1725. He, who was one of the Governors of Christ's Hospital, London, *d.* unm. in Red Lion Street, Clerkenwell, 8, and was *bur.* 21 April 1743, at Swinbrook, when *the Baronetcy* became *extinct*.(a) Will pr. 1743.

COCKS :

In Courthope's *Extinct Baronetcies* the creation of "COCKS, of DUMBLETON, Gloucester," is given as on 7 April 1661 (between those of Fettiplace and Hendley), as well as on 7 Feb. 1661/2, which last is, apparently, the right date, and is that under which it is here treated.

HENDLEY :

cr. 8 April 1661 ;

ex. July 1675.

I. 1661, to 1675. "WALTER HENDLEY, of Louchfield [*i.e.* Cuckfield], co. Sussex, Esq.," 3d but 1st surv. s. and h. of Sir Thomas HENDLEY, of the same, and of Cranbourn, co. Kent, somtime Sheriff of that county, by Elizabeth (*m.* 28 Feb. 1597), da. of John WILFORD, of Enfield, was *b.* about 1612; matric. at Oxford (Wadham Coll.) 28 Jan. 1630/1, aged 18; admitted to the Middle Temple, 1631; suc. his father Feb. 1655, and was *cr. a Baronet*, as above, 8 April 1661. He was Sheriff of Sussex 1661-62. He *m.* about 1646, Frances, sister of Sir Herbert SPRINGETT, Baronet (so cr. 8 Jan. 1660/1), da. of Sir Thomas SPRINGETT, of Broyle Place, Sussex, by Mary, da. of John BELLINGHAM. He *d.* s.p.m.,(b) and was *bur.* 17 July 1675, at Cuckfield, when *the Baronetcy* became *extinct*. Will pr. 1675. His widow *d.* 25, and was *bur.* there 27 Dec. 1680. Her will, without date, pr. 22 March 1680/1.

PARSONS :

cr. 9 April 1661 ;

ex. 1812.

I. 1661. "WILLIAM PARSONS, of Langley, co Buckingham, Esq.," 2d but 1st surv. s. and h. of Sir John PARSONS, of Boveney, in that county, and of Langley aforesaid, by Elizabeth, da. and h. of Sir John KIDDERMINSTER, of Langley, was *b.* probably about 1636(c); matric. at Oxford (Queen's Coll.), 10 Nov. 1651; admitted to the Inner Temple, Nov. 1651; suc. his father

(a) He is said to have had an estate of £5,000 a year and £100,000 in money. Of his 5 sisters, Diana *m.* Robert Bushel, of Cleve Pryer, co. Worcester, and was mother of Charles Bushel, who in 1743 inherited the estate of Childrey and took the name of Fettiplace, and *d.* 17 Oct. 1767, leaving two sons, who both *d.* s.p. (Richard, in 1799, and Charles, on 16 Dec. 1805), when the estates passed to his grandson, Richard Gorges, who took the name of Fettiplace, but *d.* s.p. 21 May 1806 in his 48th year, the estates passing to his seven sisters.

(b) Mary, his da. and h., *m.* firstly, 18 Feb. 1663, Sir William More, of Loseley, co. Surrey, who *d.* s.p. 1684. She *m.* secondly, in 1685, William Clark, and sold the Cuckfield estate in 1691.

(c) His elder br., Charles, was aged 9 at the Heralds' Visit. of Bucks in 1634.

in 1653, and was *cr. a Baronet*, as above, 9 April 1661. He *m.*, in or before 1656, Dorothy, da. of William PARSONS, of Birr, in King's County, Ireland, by Dorothy, da. of Sir Thomas PHILIPS, of Newtown Limavady, co. Londonderry.(a) He *d.* at Oxford in 1662, or late in 1661. Inventory of his goods as "late of Jesus College, Oxford," taken 21 and exhibited 30 May 1662, by Thomas Ellis, Administrator. Will pr. 1664. His widow *d.* 20 and was *bur.* 24 Feb. 1668, in Dublin. Funeral entry in the Coll. of Arms [I.].(a) Will pr. Feb. 1670.

II. 1662? SIR JOHN PARSONS, Baronet [1661], of Langley aforesaid (which, however, was, soon afterwards, sold in 1669, under the directions in his father's will), 1st s. and h., *b.* about 1656; *suc. to the Baronetcy* in 1662 or 1661; matric. at Oxford (Ch. Ch.) 1 June 1674, aged 17; admitted to the Inner Temple, 1676. He *m.*, in or before 1686, Catherine, sister and coheir of Sir William CLIFTON, 3d Baronet [1611], of Clifton, Notts, da. of Sir Clifford CLIFTON, by Frances, da. of Sir Heneage FINCH. He *d.* 17 Jan. 1704, at Stanton le Wolds, Notts, aged 48, and was *bur.* there. M.I.

III. 1704. SIR WILLIAM PARSONS, Baronet [1661], of Stanton le Wolds aforesaid and [1746] of Kew, co. Surrey, only s. and h., *bap.* 2 May 1686, at St. Mary's, Nottingham; *suc. to the Baronetcy*, 17 Jan. 1704. He *m.* firstly, in or before 1716, Frances, sister of Mary, Duchess of Northumberland (*d.* 11 Sep. 1738) and of Capt. Mark DUTTON, da. of Henry DUTTON. She *d.* 28 May 1735. He *m.* secondly Isabella, widow of Delaval DUTTON, 5th da. and coheir of James HOLTE, of Castleton, co. Lancaster. She *d.* in or before 1746. Will pr. 1746. He *d.* 1760 and was *bur.* at Arnold, Notts, of which place his eldest son John (who *d.* v.p. and unm.) had been Vicar.

IV. 1760, to 1812. SIR MARK PARSONS, Baronet [1661], of Epsom, co. Surrey, grandson and h., being only s. and h. of William PARSONS, Lieut. in Cholmondeley's Foot, by Mary, (*m.* before 1741), da. of John FRAMPTON, of the Exchequer, which William (who was *b.* in Red Lion Square and *bap.* 1 Jan. 1717/8 at St. Andrew's, Holborn, and who in 1751 was hung at Tyburn, having returned from transportation after a conviction for highway robbery and forgery),(b) was 2d and yst. s. of the late Baronet. He was *b.* about 1741; *suc. to the Baronetcy* in 1760; matric. at Oxford (Ch. Ch.) 22 Dec. 1760, aged 19; *cr.* M.A. (then of Oriel Coll.) 22 Nov. 1765. He *d.* unm., "in great retirement," 1812, when *the Baronetcy* became *extinct*. Will pr. 1812.

CAMBELL:

cr. 9 April 1661;

ex. 23 May 1662.

I. 1661, to 1662. "JOHN CAMBELL, of Woodford, co. Essex, Esq.," br. and h. of James CAMBELL, of the same, both being sons of James CAMBELL, of Woodford aforesaid, by Theophila (*m.* 8 Nov. 1638), da. of John (MOHUN), 1st BARON MOHUN OF OAKHAMPTON (which lastnamed James (who *d.* 1659, aged 44), was 1st br. of Sir Thomas CAMBELL,

(a) *Ex inform.* G. D. Burtchaell. It will be seen that the name and parentage of this lady differs from the account in Wotton's *Baronetage*. See Lodge's *Irish Peerage* (edit. 1754), vol. ii, p. 64.

(b) Godfrey's notes on the parish register of St. Mary's, Nottingham. In this the conviction for "highway robbery" is mentioned, but that for "forgery" is in Musgrave's *Obituary*.

1st Baronet [1664]), suc. his said brother in Aug. 1660, and was *cr. a Baronet* as above, 9 April 1661. He *d.* s.p.,(a) and was *bur.* 21 May 1662 at Barking co. Essex, when *the Baronetcy* became *extinct*.

MORICE, *or* MORRICE:

cr. 20 April 1661;

ex. 24 Jan. 1749/50.

I. 1661. "WILLIAM MORRICE, of Werrington, co. Devon, Esq., eldest son [and h. ap.] to William MORRICE, Knt., one of His Majesties' Principal Secretaries of State," by Elizabeth, da. of Humphrey PRIDEAUX, of Souldon in Holsworthy, in that county, was *b.* about 1628, at Churston Ferrers, Devon; matric. at Oxford (Ex. Coll.), 21 May 1647, aged 19, and was, "in consideration of his father's well known services," *cr. a Baronet*, as above, v.p., 20 April 1661. He suc. his father (who was *b.* 6 Nov. 1602 at St. Martin's, Exeter, and who resigned his office of Secretary in 1668) 12 Dec. 1676, and was M.P. for Newport, co. Cornwall, 1689-90. He *m.* firstly, Gertrude, 2d da. of Sir John BAMPFYLDE, 1st Baronet [1641], by Gertrude, da. of Amias COPLESTONE, of Warleigh. She was living Nov. 1657. He *m.* secondly (Lic. Exeter, 5 Sep. 1676), Elizabeth, 4th da. of Richard REYNELL, of Ogwell, Devon, by his 1st wife, Mary, da. of John BENNETT, of London. She was *bur.* 3 April 1684 at Werrington. He was *bur.* there 7 Feb. 1689/90. Will pr. March 1690.

II. 1690. SIR NICHOLAS MORICE, Baronet [1661], of Werrington aforesaid, 2d but only surv. s. and h., being 1st s. by the 2nd wife(b); *b.* about 1681; *suc. to the Baronetcy* in Feb. 1689/90; matric. at Oxford (Ex. Coll.), 14 April 1698, aged 17; M.P. for Newport aforesaid (seven Parls.) 1702 till death. He *m.* 21 March 1703/4, at St. James', Westm., Catherine, 1st da. of Thomas (HERBERT), 8th EARL OF PEMBROKE, by his 1st wife, Margaret, da. of Sir Robert SAWYER. She was *bur.* 18 Sep. 1716, at Werrington. He *d.* 27 Jan., and was *bur.* there 7 Feb. 1725/6. Will pr. 1726.

III. 1726, to 1750. SIR WILLIAM MORICE, Baronet [1661], of Werrington aforesaid, only s. and h., *b.* about 1707; *suc. to the Baronetcy*, 27 Jan. 1725/6; matric. at Oxford (Corpus Ch. Coll.), 24 Aug. 1724, aged 17; M.P. for Newport aforesaid, 1727, and for Launceston, 1734 till death. He *m.* firstly, Sep. 1731, Lucy, da. of Thomas (WHARTON), 1st MARQUESS OF WHARTON, by his 2d wife Lucy, da. of Adam (LOFTUS), VISCOUNT LISBURNE [I.]. She, who appears to have been divorced from him, *d.* at Bath 2 Feb. 1738/9. Admon. as "Lady Lucy WHARTON, formerly Lady Lucy MORIS" of Chelsea, Midx., 2 March 1738/9, to her sister and only next of kin, Lady Jane COKE. He *m.* secondly, before 1741, Anne, da. of Thomas BERRY, of Berrynarbor, co. Devon. He *d.* s.p. 24 Jan. 1749/50, when *the Baronetcy* became *extinct*. Will pr. 1750. "Lady MORRIS of Leicester Square," possibly his widow, *d.* 15 Feb. 1754.

(a) Of his sisters and coheirs, (1) Theophila *m.*, 28 Nov. 1658, at Woodford (as his 1st wife), Sir John Corbet, 3d Baronet [1627], of Stoke, and *d.* in or before 1672; (2) Philadelphia *m.* Sir William Bassett, of Claverton, co. Somerset, whose will, dat. 21 Sep. 1693, was pr. 20 March 1693/4; (3) Isabel *m.* (—) Owen.

(b) His elder br. (of the half blood), William Morice, M.P. for Newport, 1681 and 1685-87, *m.* Anne, da. and coheir of Richard Lower, M.D., but *d.* v.p. and s.p., being *bur.* at Werrington, 24 June 1688.

GAWDY, *or* GAWDEY:

cr. 20 April 1661;

ex., probably, about 1720.

I. 1661. "SIR CHARLES GAWDEY, of Crowshall [in Debenham], co. Suffolk, Knt.," s. and h. of Sir Charles GAWDEY, *or* GAWDY,(a) of the same, by Vere (*bap.* 4 July 1612, at Romford, and *m.* before 1636), da. and coheir of Sir Edward COOK, of Gidea Hall, in Romford (*bur.* there 20 July 1625), was *b.* probably about 1635; suc. his father (who *d.* aged 38, and was *bur.* at Debenham) 10 Nov. 1650, and, having previously been *Knighted*, was *cr. a Baronet*, as above, 20 April 1661. He *m.* firstly, Mary, da. of George (FEILDING), EARL OF DESMOND [I.], by Bridget, da. and coheir of Sir Michael STANHOPE. She was *bur.* 8 Sep. 1691, at Debenham. He *m.* secondly, Elizabeth. He, having sold the estate of Crowshall, was *bur.* 15 Sep. 1707, at Romford, with his mother's family. Will dat. 15 April 1699, mentioning his wife, Elizabeth, as being then in Holland, pr. 10 Jan. 1710/1.

II. 1707 to 1720? SIR FRAMLINGHAM GAWDY, Baronet [1661], only s. and h.; *suc. to the Baronetcy* in Sep. 1707. He was of infirm mind and *d.* unm. at Havering, co. Essex, when the *Baronetcy* became *extinct*.

CAYLEY, *or* CALEY:

cr. 26 April 1661.

I. 1661. "WILLIAM CALEY, of Brumpton [*i.e.*, Brompton in Pickering lithe], co. York, Esq.," 1st s. and h. of Edward CALEY *or* CAYLEY, of the same, by Anne (*m.* in 1604) da. of William WATTERS, of Cundall, co. York, was *bap.* 5 Dec. 1610, at Brompton; admitted to Gray's Inn, 10 Aug. 1627; was *Knighted*, 2 March 1640/1, at Theobalds; suc. his father, 7 Dec. 1642; and was *cr. a Baronet*, as above, 26 April 1661. He entered his pedigree in the Visit. of Yorkshire, 1665, being then aged 55. He *m.*, in 1633, Dorothy, 1st da. of Sir William ST. QUINTIN, 1st Baronet [1642], by Mary, sister and coheir of John LACY. He d. 2 May 1681 in his 71st year and was *bur.* at Brompton. Will dat. 22 Jan. 1677; pr. 21 July 1681 in the Exchequer Court of York. His widow was *bur.* 24 Nov. 1684 at Brompton.

II. 1681. SIR WILLIAM CAYLEY, Baronet [1661], of Brompton aforesaid, 2d but 1st surv. s. and h., *bap.* 23 June 1635 at Brompton, being aged 30 in 1665; *suc. to the Baronetcy*, 2 May 1681. He *m.*, in or before 1653, Mary, da. and h. of Barnaby HOLBECH, of Birchley Hall, in Fillongley, co. Warwick, by Mary, da. of Anthony OLDFIELD, of Spalding, co. Lincoln, Attorney at Law. He *d.* in or shortly before 1708. Will dat. 13 Sep. 1706, pr. 16 March 1708 in the Exchequer Court of York. His widow was *bur.* 25 Sep. 1709, at Brompton.

(a) The admon. of this Sir Charles Gawdy was granted 16 June 1651 to Dame Vere Gawdy, his relict, whose will was pr. July 1689. He was s. and h. of another Sir Charles Gawdy, also of Crowshall (whose will was pr. 6 Feb. 1629), and who was 2d s. of Sir Bassingborne Gawdy, of West Harling, co. Norfolk, by his 1st wife, Ann, da. and h. of Sir Charles Framlingham, of Crowshall aforesaid, being made heir to that estate by his abovenamed maternal grandfather. The elder br. of the last-named Charles was Framlingham Gawdy, who was father of William Gawdy, *cr. a Baronet* 13 July 1663. The three persons of the name of Charles, who successively were of Crowshall, cause much confusion.

III. 1708? SIR ARTHUR CAYLEY, Baronet [1661], of Brompton aforesaid, 2d but 1st surv. s. and h.; *b.* about 1654, being aged 10 in 1665; was admitted to Grays Inn, 12 June 1674; *suc. to the Baronetcy* in or before 1708. He *m.*, 28 May 1699, Everilda, 1st da. of George THORNHILL, of Fixby, co. York, by Mary, da. and coheir of Thomas WYVILL, of Bellerby. He *d.* 19 May 1727 in his 74th year. His widow, who was *bap.* 22 June 1680, at Elland, *d.* 12 Sep. 1753. Will pr. 1753.

IV. 1727. SIR GEORGE CAYLEY, Baronet [1661], of Brompton aforesaid, 3d and yst. but only surv. s. and h.,(a) *b.* about 1707, *suc. to the Baronetcy* 19 May 1727. He *m.* 31 May 1730, Philadelphia, one of the seven sisters and coheirs of John DIGBY, of Mansfield Woodhouse, Notts, da. of John DIGBY, of the same, by Jane, da. of Sir Thomas WHARTON, K.B. She *d.* 14 Jan. 1765, at Brompton. He *d.* there Sep. 1791, aged 84. Will pr. Jan. 1799.

V. 1791. SIR THOMAS CAYLEY, Baronet [1661], of Brompton aforesaid, 1st s. and h., *b.* Aug. 1732; *suc. to the Baronetcy*, Sep. 1791. He *m.* in 1763, Isabella, da. of John SETON, of Parbroath. He *d.* 15 March 1792, at Brompton, in his 60th year. His widow *d.* 30 July 1828.

VI. 1792. SIR GEORGE CAYLEY, Baronet [1661], of Brompton aforesaid, only s. and h., *b.* 27 Dec. 1773, *suc. to the Baronetcy* 15 March 1792; was distinguished for scientific pursuits; F.R.S., etc.; Chairman of the Polytechnic institution, London, as also of the Whig Club in York; M.P. for Scarborough, 1832-34. He *m.* 9 July 1795, Sarah, da. of the Rev. George WALKER, of Nottingham, also F.R.S. She *d.* 8 Dec. 1854, at Brompton, aged 81. He *d.* 15 Dec. 1857, in his 84th year.

VII. 1857. SIR DIGBY CAYLEY, Baronet [1661], of Brompton aforesaid, only s. and h., *b.* 13 March 1807, at York; ed. at Trin. Coll., Cambridge; *suc. to the Baronetcy* 15 Dec. 1857. He *m.*, 8 July 1830, Dorothy, 2d da. and coheir of the Rev. George ALLANSON, Preb. of Ripon, and Rector of Hodnet, by Anne Elizabeth, sister and h. of the Rev. Whitehall WHITEHALL-DAVIES, of Llannerch Park, co. Denbigh, da. of Peter DAVIES, of Broughton, co. Flint. She *d.* 4 April 1881, at Brompton, aged 79. He *d.* 21 Dec. 1883, aged 76.

VIII. 1883. SIR GEORGE ALLANSON CAYLEY, Baronet [1661], of Brompton and of Llannerch Park aforesaid, 1st s. and h., *b.* 31 Dec. 1831; ed. at Eton; sometime Registrar of Deeds for the North Riding of Yorkshire, and Lieut. in the Yorkshire Hussars; Sheriff of Denbighshire, 1883; *suc. to the Baronetcy*, 21 Dec. 1883. He *m.*, 5 July 1859, at St. James', Westm., his 1st cousin, Catherine Louisa, 1st. da. of Sir William WORSLEY, 1st Baronet [1838], of Hovingham, co. York, by Sarah Philadelphia, da. of Sir George CAYLEY, 6th Baronet [1661], abovenamed. He *d.* 10 Oct. 1895 at Port Said, aged 63, and was *bur.* at Brompton aforesaid. Estate duty paid on £54,522 net, the gross value being £62,274. His widow living 1903.

IX. 1895. SIR GEORGE EVERARD ARTHUR CAYLEY, Baronet [1661], of Brompton and of Llannerch Park aforesaid, 1st s. and h., *b.* 8 July 1861; somtime Capt. Royal Welsh Fusileers; *suc. to the Baronetcy*, 10 Oct. 1895; Sheriff of Denbighshire, 1898. He *m.*, 17 Sep. 1884, Mary Susan, sister of Francis John, 2d EARL OF WHARNCLIFFE, da. of the Hon. Francis Dudley MONTAGU-STUART-WORTLEY, by Maria Elizabeth, da. of William Bennet MARTIN. She, who was *b.* 15 Dec. 1861, received, by royal warrant, 25 April 1900, the precedence of the da. of an Earl.

Family Estates.—These in 1883 consisted of 8,459 acres in the North and West Ridings of Yorkshire, worth £9,126 a year, of which £1,284 was returned as Lady Cayley's. The Welsh estate is not given in that return. *Principal residences* in 1903.—High Hall in Brompton, near Scarboro', co. York, and Llannerch Park, near St. Asaph, co. Denbigh.

(a) His 1st br., William, *d.* 1719, at Saffron Walden, Essex, aged 19.

GODOLPHIN :

cr. 29 April 1661 ;

ex. 27 Aug. 1710.

I. 1661, to 1710. "WILLIAM GODOLPHIN, of Godolphin, co. Cornwall, Esq.," 1st s. and h. of Sir Francis GODOLPHIN, of the same, K.B., by Dorothy (*m.* before 1635), da. of Sia Henry BERKELEY, of Yarlington, co. Somerset, was *b.* probably about 1640 and was *v.p.* *cr. a Baronet*, as above, 29 April 1661. presumably on account of the loyal services of his father to the late King. He was M.P. for Helston, Oct. 1665 to 1679 and March to June 1679. He *suc.* his said father in 1666 or 1667.(a) He *d.* unm. 17 Aug. and was *bur.* 3 Sep. 1710 in Westm. Abbey, when the *Baronetcy* became *extinct*. Will dat. 13 Sep. 1707, pr. 6 Sep. 1710 by his brother and residuary legatee, Sidney, 1st Earl of Godolphin.

CURSON :

cr. 30 April 1661 ;

ex. 25 Feb. 1765.

I. 1661. "THOMAS CURSON,(b) of Waterperry, co. Oxon, Esq.," 3d but only surv. s. and h. of Sir John CURSON, of Waterperry aforesaid and of Addington, Bucks, by his 1st wife, Magdalen, da. of Robert (DORMER), 1st BARON DORMER OF WING was *bap.* 3 April 1611, at Waterperry, suc. his father (who *d.* in his 79th year) 15 Jan. 1655, and was *cr. a Baronet*, as above, 30 April 1661 ; recorded his pedigree in the Visit. of Oxon, 1668. Sheriff of Oxon, 1678. He *m.*, 14 Sep. 1654 (reg. at Waterperry), Elizabeth, da. of William BURROUGH, of Burrough, co. Leicester. He was *bur.* 25 Jan. 1681/2, at Waterperry. M.I. Admon. 8 Feb. 1681/2. His widow was *bur.* there 27 July 1690. Her admon. 22 July 1690.

II. 1682. SIR JOHN CURSON, Baronet [1661], of Waterperry aforesaid, only s. and h.; aged 11 years in 1668; matric. at Oxford (Oriel Coll.) 11 Nov. 1671, aged 14; *suc. to the Baronetcy* in Jan. 1681/2. He *m.* firstly, before 1680, Penelope, da. and coheir of William CHILD, of co. Worcester. She, by whom he had six sons and two daughters, was *bur.* 1 Oct. 1697, at Waterperry. He *m.* secondly, Anne, widow of Edmond POWELL, of Sandford, Oxon, sister and coheir of Rowland, 4th BARON DORMER OF WING, da. of Robert DORMER, of Grove Park, co. Warwick, by Anne, da. of Rowland EYRE, of Hassop, co. Derby. He *d.* 17 Dec. 1727, aged 71, and was *bur.* 2 Jan. 1727/8, at Waterperry. M.I. Will dat. 3 Feb. 1724, pr. 8 Feb. 1727/8. His widow, by whom he had no issue, *d.* s.p., 12 Oct. 1746, at Grove Park aforesaid, and was *bur.* at Budbrooke, co. Warwick. Admon. 7 April 1747.

III. 1727. SIR FRANCIS CURSON, Baronet [1661], of Waterperry aforesaid, 2d but 1st surv. s. and h.(c) by 1st wife, *b.* about 1678; was "apprenticed to a merchant in London, in 1693"(d); *suc. to the Baronetcy*, 17 Dec. 1727. He *m.* firstly (settl. 7 Nov. 1700) Elizabeth, da. of Francis KNOLLYS, of Winchendon, Bucks, by Anna, da. and coheir of (—) BATEMAN. She

(a) The will of Sir Francis Godolphin is dat. (—) June 1665 to (—) Feb. 1665/6, and is pr. 31 May 1667.

(b) See pedigree in *Mis. Gen. et Her.*, 3d series, vol. i, pp. 209-217 ; vol. ii, p. 80; and vol. iii, 127.

(c) His elder br. Thomas, with whom he was a twin, *d.* "at a month old," according to Wotton's *Baronetage*, but more probably "aged about 17," as stated by Le Neve. See note "d" below.

(d) Le Neve's MS. Baronetage.

d. 15 and was *bur.* 19 Nov. 1723 at Waterperry, aged 43. M.I. He *m.* secondly (settl. 12 July 1729), Winifred, 1st da. and coheir of John POWELL, of Sandford, co. Oxford, by Ann, da. of Thomas WINDHAM, of Tale, co. Devon. He *d.* s.p.s. 29 May and was *bur.* 7 June 1750, at Waterperry. M.I. Will dat. 8 Aug. 1749, pr. 2 Aug. 1750. His widow, who was *b.* 10 May 1705, at Sandford aforesaid, and who enjoyed the estate of Waterperry for her life,(a) sold her family estate of Sandford in 1760, and *d.* 2 being *bur.* 8 April 1764, at Waterperry, aged 50. M.I. Will dat. 30 March and pr. 5 May 1764.

IV. 1750, to 1765. SIR PETER CURSON, Baronet [1661], only surv. br. and h.; being 6th and yst. s. of the 2d Baronet by his 1st wife ; *b.* 31 July 1687 ; admitted to the Society of the Jesuits, 1706 ; Chaplain of Brambridge, Hants ; *suc. to the Baronetcy*, but to none of the family estates, 29 May 1750. He *d.* unm. at Winchester, 25 Feb. 1765, aged 77, and was *bur.* in the Jesuit Cemetery, at Brambridge, when the *Baronetcy* became *extinct*. M.I. there as "Sir Peter Curson."(b)

FOWELL :

cr. 1 May 1661 ;

ex. Nov. 1692.

I. 1661. "EDMUND FOWELL, of Fowell [*i.e.*, Fowellscombe in Ugborough], co. Devon. Esq." [but should apparently be "Knight"], 3d s. of Arthur FOWELL, of the same (*d.* in or before 1606), by Mary (*m.* 13 Sep. 1574, at Ugborough), da. of Richard REYNELL, of East Ogwell, Devon, was *bap.* 15 Aug. 1593, at Ugborough ; suc. to the family estates, June 1612, on the death, in his 20th year, of his elder br. Arthur Fowell ; was *Knighted* at Greenwich, 3 Nov. 1619 ; M.P. for Ashburton in the Long Parl., 1640 till secluded in Dec. 1648 ; was a Parliamentarian, took the Covenant in Sep. 1643, and was President of the Devon Committee for sequestration, but took no part in politics after the "Purge" of 1648. He was *cr. a Baronet*, as above, 1 May 1661. He *m.*, in 1614, Margaret, sister of John, 1st BARON POULETT OF HINTON ST. GEORGE, da. of Sir Anthony POULETT, of Hinton aforesaid, Governor of Jersey, by Catherine, da. of Henry (NORRIS), LORD NORRIS DE RYCOTE. She was living Oct. 1638. He was *bur.* 9 Oct. 1674, at Ugborough, aged 81. Will pr. in the principal Reg. at Exeter, 9 Oct. 1675.

(a) At her death the Waterperry estate devolved, under her husband's will, on his niece Catherine Brinckhurst, da. of John Brinckhurst, of Great Marlow, Bucks, by his 1st wife Mary, da. of Sir John Curson, 2d Baronet. She took the name of *Curson* after her patronymic and *d.* unm. 3 Aug. 1776, aged 76. It then passed to her nephew, John Barnewall, son of Frances, her sister of the whole blood, by her 1st husband, the Hon. Thomas Barnewall. He also took the name of *Curson* after his patronymic, and *d.* s.p. legit. in 1787, under whose will (dat. 2 Oct. 1780 and pr. 29 Aug. 1787) it passed to his cousin, Henry Francis Roper, s. of the Hon. Francis Roper, by Mary, 1st da. and coheir of Lancelot Lyttleton, and Charlotte, sister of the half blood to Catherine Brinckhurst-Curson, spinster, and to the Hon. Frances Barnewall both abovenamed, being da. of the said John Brinckhurst by a second wife. He, by Royal Lic., 22 Feb. 1788, took the name of *Curson* in lieu of that of Roper, in compliance with his cousin's will, but by another Royal Lic., 22 June 1813 (having shortly before barred the entail of the estate), took the name of *Roper-Curzon* in lieu of his then name. On 6 Sep. 1824 he suc. to the peerage as Baron Teynham, and about 1830 sold the estate of Waterperry, which had been in the Curson family upwards of 300 years.

(b) Oliver's *Scotch, English and Irish Members of the Society of Jesus* [Dolman, 1845].

II. 1674. SIR JOHN FOWELL, Baronet [1661], of Fowellscombe aforesaid, 1st s. and h., *bap.* 14 Aug. 1623, at Ugborough ; was Col. of a Reg. of Foot in the service of Parl. ; Gov. of Totnes, and distinguished himself at the taking of Dartmouth ; M.P. for Ashburton, 1659, 1660, and 1661 till death, in 1677 ; *suc. to the Baronetcy* in Oct. 1674. He *m.*, in or before 1665, Elizabeth, da. of Sir John CHICHESTER, of Hall, Devon, by his 2nd wife, Elizabeth, da. of Sir Lewis POLLARD. He was *bur.* 17 Jan. 1676/7, at Ugborough. Will dat. 2 June 1676 to 7 Jan. 1676/7, pr. 9 Jan. 1677/8 and 9 Sep. 1681. His widow, who was *bap.* 2 Feb. 1637/8, at Bishop's Tawton, was *bur.* 31 Oct. 1677, at Ugborough. Will dat. 26 Oct. 1677, pr. 9 Jan. 1677/8.

III. 1677, to 1692. SIR JOHN FOWELL, Baronet [1661], of Fowellscombe aforesaid, only surv. s. and h., *bap.* 12 Dec. 1665, at Ashprington ; *suc. to the Baronetcy* in Jan. 1676/7 ; was M.P. for Totnes, 1689 till death, in 1692, being one of the 151 members who voted against the Prince of Orange (afterwards William III) being made King of England. He *d.* unm. and was *bur.* 26 Nov. 1692, at Ugborough, when the *Baronetcy* became *extinct*. Will dat. 4 Nov. 1691, pr. 2 Jan. 1692/3.(a)

CROPLEY :

cr. 7 May 1661 ;

ex. 22 Oct. 1713.

I. 1661. "JOHN CROPLEY, of Clerkenwell, co. Middx., Esq.," 1st s. and h. of Edward CROPLEY, of Soham, co. Cambridge, and of St. Michael le Quern, London, Mercer (living 1634),(b) by Priscilla, da. of Thomas MORE, of London, was admitted to Gray's Inn, 30 Oct. 1629, and was *cr. a Baronet*, as above, 7 May 1661. He entered his pedigree in the Visitation of Midx., 1664. He *m.*, in or before 1634,(b) Elizabeth, da. and h. of Daniel HOLLINGWORTH, of St. James', Clerkenwell, which Daniel was *bur.* there 5 Feb. 1661/2. He was *bur.* 5 Nov. 1676, at St. James', Clerkenwell. Will pr. 1696. His widow was *bur.* there 17 Dec. 1680. Her will pr. 1680.

II. 1676, to 1713. SIR JOHN CROPLEY, Baronet [1661], of Friern Baronet, co. Midx., grandson and h., being only s. and h. of Sir Edward CROPLEY, of St. James', Clerkenwell, by Martha,(c) da. of Robert WILSON, of London, Merchant, which Edward, who was *b.* about 1637 and matric. at Oxford (Queen's Coll.), 27 Feb. 1650/1, being *Knighted* 7 May 1661, was 1st s. of the 1st Baronet, but *d.* v.p. and was *bur.* 10 March 1664/5, at St. James' aforesaid). He was *b.* 15 and *bap.* 23 July 1663, at St. James' aforesaid; *suc. to the Baronetcy* in Nov. 1676. He *d.* unm. 22 Oct. 1713, when the *Baronetcy* became *extinct*.(d)

(a) He devised the Fowellscombe estate to the heir male, in compliance with the wish both of his grandfather and father, failing heirs male of the body of the former. The devise, however, was invalid, not having been signed before three witnesses, and the estates devolved on his two sisters and coheirs (the heirs at law), Elizabeth, wife of George Parker, of Burrington, and Margaret, wife of Arthur Champernowne, of Dartington. Fowellscombe was sold by the Champernowne family in 1759. See a very full account of this matter in Burke's *Extinct Baronetcies*.

(b) Visit. of London, 1634.

(c) This Martha *m.* subsequently, 17 Jan. 1670/1 (Lic. Vic. Gen.), Sir Edmund Bowyer, of Camberwell.

(d) His sister *m.* Thomas Marsh, of Coulfoot, but he left the greater part of his estate to Thomas Micklethwait.

SMITH, *or* SMYTH :

cr. 10 May 1661 ;

ex. 20 June 1732.

I. 1661. "WILLIAM SMITH, of Redcliff, co. Buckingham, Esq.," 1st s. of Robert SMITH,(a) or SMYTH, of Buckingham and Akeley in that county, Principal of New Inn, London, by Martha, his wife, which Robert (aged 16 when he matric. at Oxford, 15 June 1610), was slain in 1645 fighting for the King's cause, was *b.* about 1616; matric. at Oxford (Trin. Coll.), 13 March 1634/5 as a Gent. commoner, aged 18, but "left it without the ceremony of a degree" ; *cr.* D.C.L. 10 Nov. 1642 ; Barrister (Middle Temple), 1641 ; M.P. for Winchelsea, 1640, till disabled in 1644 ; Gov. of Chepstow Castle for the King, and was *cr. a Baronet*, as above, 10 May 1661. He was M.P. for Buckingham, 1661-79. He *m.* firstly, Margaret, *bap.* 6 Nov. 1625, at Hillesden, Bucks), da. of Sir Alexander DENTON, of Hillesden, by Mary, da. and coheir of Edmund HAMPDEN, of Hartwell. He *m.* secondly (—), da. of Sir Nathaniel HOBART, one of the Masters in Chancery. He *d.* at Stepney, co. Midx., 1696, aged about 80. Will directing his burial to be at Akeley, dat. 18 Aug. 1694, pr. 10 Feb. 1696/7.

II. 1697, to 1732. SIR THOMAS SMYTH, Baronet [1661], 2d and yst. but only surv. s. and h. by 2d wife ; *suc. to the Baronetcy*, in 1696 ; was Ranger of the Park, Dublin. He *d.* there unm., 20 June 1732, when the *Baronetcy* became *extinct*.(b)

COOKE :

cr. 10 May 1661.

I. 1661. "GEORGE COOKE, of Wheateley, co. York, Esq.," 3d s. of Brian COOKE, of Sandall, in that county, Mayor of Doncaster, 1630 (*d.* 26 Dec. 1653, aged 83), by Sarah, da. and h. of Henry RYLEY, of Doncaster, was *bap.* 8 July 1628, at Doncaster ; admitted to the Inner Temple, Nov. 1653 ; suc. his elder br. Bryan COOKE, of Wheatley aforesaid, a Barrister of the Inner Temple (who *d.* 5 Jan. 1660/1, aged 40) and was, "in consideration of the great sufferings of his father(c) for his loyalty to Charles I," *cr. a Baronet*, as above, 10 May 1661, with a spec. rem., failing heirs male of his body, to his br. Henry COOKE, in like manner. He recorded his pedigree in the Visit. of Yorkshire in 1666, being then aged about 36. He *d.* unm., 16 Oct. 1683. Will dat. 1683.

(a) This Robert was s. of William Smith, of Great Brickhill and Akeley, Bucks, who was *b.* at Worlaby, co. Lincoln, 1542 ; admitted to Winchester College, 1555, aged 13 ; Fellow of New Coll., Oxford, 1558-71 ; B.C.L., 1565 ; D.C.L., 1573 ; Incorp. at Cambridge, 1583 ; Surrogate for the county of Bucks and Berks ; Advocate in Doctors Commons, London, 4 May 1577 ; being possibly the same as William Smith in Holy Orders, a Preb. of Lincoln, 1581-1614, and Rector of Mursley, Bucks, 1580 till death, in 1621.

(b) He is said in Wotton's *Baronetage* (1741) to have been "succeeded by his cousin, SIR WILLIAM SMYTH, of Warden, in Bedfordshire, who is unmarried," but though the "seat" of the family is there given as "At Warden, near Biggleswade, Bedfordshire," there is no indication given as to how this cousinship existed, or as to there having been a spec. rem. in the creation to extend the Baronetcy beyond the heirs male of the body of the grantee.

(c) He had been "fined by the Sequestrators (besides what he was obliged to settle on their teachers) £1,460."

II. 1683. SIR HENRY COOKE, Baronet [1661], of Wheatley aforesaid, and Adwick, co. York, formerly of Carlinghow, near Batley, br. and h., *bap.* 29 Oct. 1633, at Doncaster; admitted to the Inner Temple, Nov. 1653; *suc. to the Baronetcy*, 16 Oct. 1683, according to the spec. limitation thereof, and rebuilt Wheatley Hall. He *m.* firstly, 29 Aug. 1659, at Coates, co. Lincoln, Diana, only da. of Anthony BUTLER, of Coates aforesaid, by Jane, da. of William COUPER, of Thurgerton, Notts. She *d.* 5 Jan. 1668/9 and was *bur.* at Doncaster. He *m.* secondly, Anne, da. of William STANHOPE, of Linby, Notts (yr. br. of the half-blood, to Philip, 1st EARL OF CHESTERFIELD), by Anne, da. of (—) GAWDY. She *d.* s.p. and was *bur.* 16 Jan. 1685/6. He was *bur.* 16 July 1689. Will pr. 1693.

III. 1689. SIR GEORGE COOKE, Baronet [1661], of Wheatley and Adwick aforesaid, 2d but 1st surv. s. and h. by 1st wife(a); *bap.* 16 May 1662; *suc. to the Baronetcy* in July 1689; was M.P. for Aldborough, 1698 to 1700. He *m.* 19 June 1683, Catherine, da. of Sir Godfrey COPLEY, 1st Baronet [1661], of Sprotborough, by his 2d wife, Elizabeth, da. of William STANHOPE abovenamed. She, who was *bap.* 14 Feb. 1665, was *bur.* 9 April 1703, at Arksey. He *d.* 18 Oct. 1732, aged 70. Will pr. 1733.

IV. 1732. SIR BRYAN COOKE, Baronet [1661], of Wheatley and Adwick aforesaid, 1st s. and h., *bap.* 17 Dec. 1684; M.P. for Retford, Notts, 1711-13; *suc. to the Baronetcy*, 18 Oct. 1732. He *m.*, in or before 1713, Priscilla, da. and coheir of Robert SQUIRE, sometime M.P. for Scarborough, by Priscilla, da. and h. of Edward BOWER, of Bridlington, co. York. She, who was *bap.* 13 April 1685, at St. Michael's le Belfry, York, was *bur.* 22 June 1731, at Arksey, co. York. He *d.* at the Hotwells, near Bristol, 25 Oct. 1734, in his 50th year.

V. 1734. SIR GEORGE COOKE, Baronet [1661], of Wheatley and Adwick aforesaid, 1st s. and h., *b.* 14 and *bap.* 31 March 1714, at St. James', Westm.; matric. at Oxford (Ch. Ch.) 12 June 1733, aged 19; *suc. to the Baronetcy*, 25 Oct. 1734; Sheriff of Yorkshire, 1739. He *m.*, in or before 1739, Catharine, da. and coheir of John SUNDERLAND, of Doncaster. He *d.* s.p.m.(b) 16 Aug. 1756, aged 42. Admon. 14 Jan. 1757, to his widow. She *d.* 11 April 1792.

VI. 1756. SIR BRYAN COOKE, Baronet [1661], of Wheatley aforesaid, br. and h. male; *b.* 11 and *bap.* 29 Aug. 1717, at St. James', Westm.; *suc. to the Baronetcy*, 16 Aug. 1756. He *m.*, about 1780, Mary, da. of Col. Samuel FOLEY (s. of Samuel FOLEY, Bishop of Downe and Connor), by Mary, da. and coheir of John SUNDERLAND, abovenamed. He *d.* 4 March 1766, at Wheatley.

VII. 1766. SIR GEORGE COOKE, Baronet [1661], of Wheatley aforesaid, only s. and h., *b.* probably about 1745; admitted to Linc. Inn 23 Jan., 1759; sometime an officer in the Horse Guards; *suc. to the Baronetcy*, 4 March 1766; Col. of the 3d Batt. of the West Yorkshire Militia. He *m.* firstly, 20 June 1770, Frances Jory, da. of Sir John Lambert MIDDLETON, 4th Baronet [1662], of Belsay, by Anne, da. of Sir Nathaniel HODGES. She *d.* 1796. He *m.* secondly, 1798, Harriet, widow of Thomas HEWETT, of Bilham, da. of James FARRER, of Barnborough Grange. She, by whom he had no issue, *d.* 1814. He *d.* 2 June 1823. Will pr. Aug. 1825.

(a) His elder br. Bryan (who *d.* aged 15 months) was *bap.* at Coates, co. Lincoln, 31 March 1661, but he himself was, probably, *bap.* at Doncaster.

(b) Of his two daughters and coheirs, Priscilla, *d.* unm. 20 Jan. 1800, aged 59, but her elder sister, Catherine, *m.* John Cooke (who was not a member of this family, being a grandson of Sir Thomas Cooke, of Hackney) and left issue.

VIII. 1823. SIR WILLIAM BRYAN COOKE, Baronet [1661], of Wheatley aforesaid, 2d and yst. but only surv. s. and h.(a) by 1st wife; *b.* 3 March 1782; matric. at Oxford (Ch. Ch.), 23 Oct. 1799, aged 17; B.A., 1803; M.A., 1806; sometime an officer in the Foot Guards; *suc. to the Baronetcy*, 2 June 1823; Mayor of Doncaster, 1836; Sheriff of Yorkshire, 1845; Lieut. Col. West Yorkshire Militia. He *m.* 8 April 1823, Isabella Cecilia Viviana, yst. da. of his maternal uncle, Sir William MIDDLETON, 5th Baronet [1662], of Belsay, by Jane, da. and h. of Laurence MONCK. He *d.* 24 Dec. 1851, at Wheatley Hall, in his 70th year. Will pr. Nov. 1854. His widow *d.* 25 Nov. 1869, at Swansfield House, in Alnwick, co. Northumberland.

IX. 1851. SIR WILLIAM RIDLEY CHARLES COOKE, Baronet [1661], of Wheatley Hall aforesaid, 1st s. and h., *b.* there 5 Oct. 1827; ed. at Eton; sometime Capt. 7th Hussars; *suc. to the Baronetcy*, 24 Dec. 1851; Capt. West Yorkshire Yeomanry, 1853. He *m.* firstly, 17 April 1855, his cousin, Harriet Eloise, da. of the Rev. Jonathan TREBECK, Vicar of Melbourne, co. Cambridge, by Charlotte, da. and coheir of John COOKE, of Maltby,(b) by Harriet, da. of Sir George COOKE, 7th Baronet. She was divorced in 1862.(c) He *m.* secondly, 27 April 1871, at St. Martin's, Scarborough, Harriet Blanche Juanetta Georgiana, yst. da. of Sir William Henry FEILDEN, 2d Baronet [1846], by Mary Elizabeth, da. of Col. James Balfour WEMYSS. He *d.* of pneumonia at Wheatley Hall, 27 Sep. 1894, aged 66, and was *bur.* at Arksey aforesaid. His widow, who was *b.* 29 Oct. 1843, at Cambo House, co. Fife, living 1903.

X. 1894. SIR WILLIAM HENRY CHARLES WEMYSS COOKE, Baronet [1661], of Wheatley Hall aforesaid, 1st s. and h. by 2d wife, *b.* 21 June 1872; ed. at Eton; sometime Lieut. in the Yorkshire Imperial Yeomanry; *suc. to the Baronetcy*, 27 Sep. 1894. He *m.*, 15 July 1902, at St. Andrew's, Wells street, Marylebone, Mildred Adelaide Cecilia, 5th and yst. da. of William Henry Forester (DENISON), 1st EARL OF LONDESBOROUGH, by Edith Frances Wilhelmine, da. of Henry (SOMERSET), 7th DUKE OF BEAUFORT. She was *b.* 8 March 1872.

Family Estates.—These, in 1883, consisted of 3,638 acres in the West Riding of Yorkshire, worth £6,228 a year. *Seat.*—Wheatley Hall, near Doncaster, co. York.

LLOYD:

cr. 10 May 1661;

ex. Nov. 1743.

I. 1661. "CHARLES LLHOYD [*rectius* LLOYD], of Garth, co. Montgomery, Esq.," one of the sons of David LLOYD, of Moyle-y-Garth, by Elizabeth, da. of Owen VAUGHAN, of Llwydyarth (possibly the "Charles Lloyd, of London," admitted to the Inner Temple in Nov. 1657), was M.P. for Montgomeryshire, 1654-55 and 1656-58; for Montgomery (town), 1659, and was *cr. a Baronet*, as above, 10 May 1661. He was Sheriff of Montgomeryshire, 1669-70. He *m.* Elizabeth, da. of John BOWATER, of Whitley, co. Warwick. He *d.* at Shrewsbury, in or before 1678. Admon. 22 March 1677/8, to Elizabeth, his widow. She *d.* April or May 1691. Her will was pr. May 1691.

II. 1678? SIR CHARLES LLOYD, Baronet [1661], of Garth aforesaid, 1st s. and h.; *suc. to the Baronetcy* about 1678. He *m.* Catherine, da. of John HUXLEY, of Wirehall, in Edmonton, co. Midx. He *d.* in 1691 or 1692. Will as of St. Mary's, Whitechapel, London, dat. 4 April 1691, pr. 12 Feb. 1691/2. His widow living 1692.

(a) His elder br., George Augustus Cooke, *m.* but *d.* s.p. and v.p. 1808, aged 28.

(b) This John Cooke was himself a grandson, through his *mother* (see p. 192, note "b") of the 5th Baronet.

(c) She *m.*, 20 June 1863, Mansfeldt de Cardonnell Elmsall-Greaves, of Pwllpiran, co. Cardigan, who *d.* 30 Dec. 1864.

III. 1691? to 1743. SIR CHARLES LLOYD, Baronet [1661], of Garth aforesaid, only s. and h.; *suc. to the Baronetcy* 1691, or 1692, and was Sheriff of Montgomeryshire, 1706-7. He *m.* firstly, at St. Chad's, Shrewsbury, Victoria, da. of Sir Richard CORBET, 2d Baronet [1642], of Leighton, by Victoria, da. and coheir of Sir William UVEDALE. She *d.* 26 Nov. 1705. Admon. 4 March 1708/9. He *m.* secondly, Jane, widow of Thomas JONES, of Shrewsbury, da. of Sir Edward LEIGHTON, 1st Baronet [1693], by his 2d wife Jane, da. of Daniel NICHOLL. She *d.* June 1734. He *d.* s.p.m.s.(a) Nov. 1743, when the *Baronetcy* became *extinct*. Will pr. 1743.

POWELL:

cr. 10 May 1661;

ex. 5 July 1742.

I. 1661. "NATHANIEL POWELL, of Ewhurst, co. Essex [*rectius* Sussex], Esq." [presumably should be "Knight"(a)], s. and h. of Meredith POWELL, of Brampton Ralf, co. Somerset, by Alice, da. of John SAFFIN, of Culhampton, co. Devon, having purchased the manor of Kingsnorth, co. Kent, *temp.* Car. I, and acquired lands at Ewhurst, co. Sussex, was presumably *Knighted* 30 July 1660,(b) and was *cr. a Baronet*, as above, 10 May 1661. He *m.*, before 1640, Sarah, da. of William MUDDLE, of Ewhurst aforesaid. He *d.* March 1674/5. Will pr. 1675.

II. 1675. SIR NATHANIEL POWELL, Baronet [1661], of Ewhurst aforesaid, 1st s. and h., b. about 1640; was admitted to Inner Temple, Nov. 1656; was *Knighted* v.p. before Jan. 1667/8; *suc. to the Baronetcy* in March 1674/5. He *m.* firstly, Elizabeth, da. of Sir Robert BARNHAM, 1st Baronet [1663], of Boughton Monchelsey, co. Kent. He *m.* secondly, 26 Jan. 1667/8, at St. Martin's-in-the-Fields (Lic. Vic. Gen., 24, he a Knight and a widower, about 28, and she about 24), Frances, da. of Philip STAPLETON, of Wartre, co. York, by his 2d wife, Barbara, da. of Henry (LENNARD), LORD DACRE. He *d.* in or before 1707. Will pr. July 1707. The will of his widow pr. May 1719.

III. 1707? SIR NATHANIEL POWELL, Baronet [1661], of Wyerton Place, in Boughton Monchelsey aforesaid, grandson and h., being 1st s. and h. of Barnham POWELL, by Elizabeth, da. of James CLITHEROW, of Boston House in Brentford, co. Midx., which Barnham, who was 1st s. and h. ap. of the late Baronet by his 1st wife, *d.* v.p. He was *b.* about 1688; matric. at Oxford (Queen's Coll.), 13 June 1705, aged 17, and *suc. to the Baronetcy* about 1707. He *d.* unm. 1708. Will pr. 21 July 1709.

IV. 1708, to 1742. SIR CHRISTOPHER POWELL, Baronet [1661], of Wyerton Place aforesaid, br. of the whole blood and h., *b.* about 1690, at Boston House aforesaid; *suc. to the Baronetcy* in 1708; matric. at Oxford (Queen's Coll.), 15 July 1709, aged 19; was M.P. for Kent, Feb. 1735 to 1741. He *m.* in 1728 (—), da. of (—) NEWINGTON. He *d.* s.p. 5 July 1742, when the *Baronetcy* became *extinct*. Will pr. July 1742.

(a) His only surv. child (one by his 2d wife) in 1741 was Victoria, who, presumably, became his heir.

(b) It is, however, possible that the Knighthood may refer to his son, afterwards the 2d Baronet.

ASHBURNHAM:

cr. 15 May 1661;

afterwards, since 1899, ASHBURNHAM-CLEMENT.

I. 1661. "DENNEY ASHBURNHAM, of Bromham [in Guestling], Sussex, Esq.," s. and h. of Laurence ASHBURNHAM(a), of the same, by Bridget, sister of James FLEETWOOD, Bishop of Worcester, da. of Sir George FLEETWOOD, of Chalfont St. Giles, Bucks, "being a person of known loyalty"; was *cr. a Baronet*, as above, 15 May 1661; was M.P. for Hastings, 1660, 1661-79, and 1685-87; a Commissioner of the Excise, 1678-89; and Victualler of the Navy. He *m.* firstly, his distant cousin, Frances (*b.* 1632), da. of John ASHBURNHAM, of Ashburnham, Sussex, the well known Groom of the Bedchamber to Charles I, by his 1st wife, Frances, da. of William HOLLAND, of Westburton in that county. He *m.* secondly (Lic. Fac. 14 Sep. 1675), Anne (aged about 30), da. of Sir David WATKINS, of Gloucestershire, and Honora his wife. He was *bur.* 11 Dec. 1697, at Guestling. Will dat. 10 April 1695, pr. 13 Dec. 1697. His widow was *bur.* there 21 Dec. 1729.

II. 1697. SIR WILLIAM ASHBURNHAM, Baronet [1661], of Bromham aforesaid, 4th but 1st surv. s. and h., being 1st s. by 2d wife, *b.* probably about 1677; *suc. to the Baronetcy* in Dec. 1697; M.P. for Hastings, 1710-13; for Seaford, 1715-17, and for Hastings, again, 1722-41; a Commissioner of the Alienation office and one of the Chamberlains of the Exchequer, 1710-55. He *m.* Margaret, da. of Sir Nicholas PELHAM, of Catsfield, Sussex, by Jane, da. of James HUXLEY, of Oxon. She was *bur.* 26 March 1742, at Guestling. He *d.* s.p. 7 and was *bur.* there 8 Nov. 1755.

III. 1755. SIR CHARLES ASHBURNHAM, Baronet [1661], br. of the whole blood and h., being the yst. s. of the 1st Baronet; *b.* probably about 1680; *suc. to the Baronetcy*, but to none of the family estates, 7 Nov. 1755.(b) He *m.*, in or before 1710, (—). He *d.* 3 Oct. 1762, and was *bur.* in Chichester Cathedral.

IV. 1762. SIR WILLIAM ASHBURNHAM, Baronet [1661], Bishop of Chichester (1754-97); 1st s. and h., *b.* 16 Jan. 1710; ed. at Cambridge, being Fellow of Corpus Christi College; B.A., 1731; M.A. (per lit. regias), 1734; D.D., 1749; sometime Vicar of Bexhill, Sussex, and Chaplain to Chelsea Hospital; Dean of Chichester, 1741; Bishop of Chichester, 1754 till his death in 1797, being at that time "Father of the Bench." He suc. to the family estate of Bromham, etc., on the death, 7 Nov. 1755, of his uncle, the 2d Baronet, and *suc. to the Baronetcy* on the death of his father, 3 Oct. 1762. He *m.* 9 Nov. 1736, at Guestling, Margaret, da. of Thomas PELHAM, of Lewes, Sussex, by Elizabeth, da. of Henry PELHAM, of Stanmer, Clerk of the Pells. She, who was *b.* 14 April 1712, *d.* 29 Aug. and was *bur.* 6 Sep. 1780, at Guestling. He *d.* 4 and was *bur.* there 14 Sep. 1797, aged 87. Will dat. 8 Oct. 1796, pr. 5 Oct. 1797.

V. 1797. SIR WILLIAM ASHBURNHAM, Baronet [1661], of Bromham aforesaid, 1st s. and h., *b.* 5 and *bap.* 29 March 1739, at St. Anne's, Soho; M.P. for Hastings, 1761-74; *suc. to the Baronetcy*, 4 Sep. 1797; Sheriff of Sussex, 1802-03. He *m.*, in April 1766, at St. Clement Danes, Midx., Alicia, 3d da. of the Rev. Francis WOODGATE, Rector of Mountfield, Sussex. She *d.* 10 and was *bur.* 18 Jan. 1777, at Guestling. He *d.* at Bromham, 21 Aug. 1823, in his 85th year. Will pr. 1824.

(a) This Laurence was great grandson of Thomas Ashburnham, s. and h. of Richard Ashburnham, of Bromham, who acquired that estate by his marriage with (—), da. and h. of Sir John Stoneling, of Bromham. The abovenamed Richard was yr. br. of John, ancestor of the Earls of Ashburnham, both being sons of Thomas Ashburnham, of Ashburnham, co. Sussex, *temp.* Hen. VI.

(b) His obscure marriage was not improbably the reason for his being thus passed over.

VI. 1823. SIR WILLIAM ASHBURNHAM, Baronet [1661], of Bromham aforesaid, 1st s. and h.; *b.*, 21 June 1769, in Scotland Yard, Westm.; *suc. to the Baronetcy*, 21 Aug. 1823. He *m.* 7 July 1825, Juliana, 3d da. of the Rev. William HUMPHREY, Rector of Sele and Vicar of Kemsing, co. Kent. He *d.* s.p. at Bromham, 23 March 1843. Will pr. March 1844. His widow *d.* there 22 Feb. 1865.

VII. 1843. SIR JOHN ASHBURNHAM, Baronet [1661], of Bromham aforesaid, br. and h., *b.* 26 Dec. 1770, in Scotland Yard aforesaid; in Holy Orders; Rector of Guestling; Preb. and Chancellor of Chichester, 1795-1854, and Vicar of Pevensey, 1816-54; was, presumably, B.D. 1815 (Clare Hall), Cambridge; *suc. to the Baronetcy*, 23 March 1843. He *m.* firstly, 4 July 1804, at Hollington, Sussex, Fanny, 7th da. of William FOSTER, of Hollington aforesaid. She, who was *b.* 29 Aug. 1787, *d.* 11 April 1838, aged 50. He *m.* secondly, Anne, da. of Thomas HARMAN. He *d.* at Guestling Rectory, 1 Sep. 1854, in his 84th year. Admon. Sep. 1854. His widow, by whom he had no issue, *d.* 1873.

VIII. 1854. SIR ANCHITEL ASHBURNHAM, Baronet [1661], of Bromham aforesaid, 2d but 1st surv. s. and h.,(a) by 1st wife; *b.* 8 Feb. 1828 at Guestling Rectory; *suc. to the Baronetcy*, 1 Sep. 1854; was found by the House of Lords, 26 June 1858, to be coheir to the Barony of Grandison, *cr.* 1299;(b) was land agent to the Battle Abbey and Normanhurst estates in Sussex. He *m.*, 7 June 1859, at East Bridgford, Notts, Isabella, 1st da. of George Bohun MARTIN, C.B., Capt. R.N., and of Crabbs Abbey, Norfolk. He *d.*, 2 Dec. 1899, at Bromham park. Will pr. at £2,057. His widow living 1903.

IX. 1899. SIR ANCHITEL PIERS ASHBURNHAM-CLEMENT, Baronet [1661], of Bromham aforesaid, 1st s. and h.; *b.* 22 Aug. 1861; *suc. to the Baronetcy*, 2 Dec. 1899, having, early in that year, taken, by Royal Lic., the name of *Clement* after his patronymic. He *m.*, 4 Dec. 1895, Elizabeth Ellen, da. of George Burry CLEMENT, of Silverhill House, Silverhill, in St. Leonards-on-Sea, Sussex.

Family Estates.—These, in 1883, did not amount to 3,000 acres.

SMITH:

cr. 16 May 1661;

ex. July 1741.

I. 1661. "HUGH SMITH, of Long Ashton, co. Somerset, Esq." [*rectius*, "Knight"], s. and h. of Thomas SMITH, of the same, by Florence, da. of John (POULETT), 1st BARON POULETT OF HINTON ST. GEORGE, was made K.B. at the coronation of Charles II, 23 April 1661, and was *cr. a Baronet*, as above, 16 May following. He *m.* Elizabeth, da. of John ASHBURNHAM, of Ashburnham, Sussex, the well known Groom of the Bedchamber to Charles I, by his 1st wife, Frances, da. of William HOLLAND, of Westburton in that county. He was M.P. for Somerset, 1660, and March to July 1679; Sheriff thereof 1665-66. He *d.* 28 July 1680. Will pr. 1681. His widow (then aged 40) had lic. (Vic. Gen.) 3 Aug. 1681 to marry Col. John ROMSEY, of Bristol, then about 42 and a Bachelor.

(a) His elder br., John Piers Ashburnham, *b.* 28 March 1821; *d.* 8 June 1839.

(b) He represented a third part thereof in right of descent from Agnes, wife of Sir John Northwode, 3d and yst. da. of the 1st Baron, of which Agnes he was found to be heir. See *N. & Q.*, 1st S., x, 442, as to the Northwode descent from Grandison. Sir Henry Richard Paston-Bedingfield, 6th Baronet [1661], on whose petition (for the termination of the abeyance of that Barony in his favour) the matter was brought forward, represented but a *fourth* of a third part thereof.

II. 1680. SIR JOHN SMITH, Baronet [1661], of Long Ashton aforesaid, s. and h.; *suc. to the Baronetcy*, 28 July 1680; Sheriff of Somerset, 1689-90. He *m.* (—), da. and coheir of Sir Samuel ASTREY, of Henbury, co. Gloucester, Clerk of the Crown in the King's Bench, by Elizabeth, da. and h. of George MORSE, of Henbury aforesaid. He *d.* 26 May 1726. Will pr. 1726.

III. 1726, to 1741. SIR JOHN SMITH, Baronet [1661], of Long Ashton aforesaid, 1st s. and h., *suc. to the Baronetcy*, 26 May 1726; Sheriff of Somerset, 1732-33. He *m.* 26 Nov. 1728, at St. Benet's, Paul's wharf, London, Anne, da. of (—) PYM, of St. Olave's, Oxford. She *d.* Sep. 1733. He *d.* s.p. July 1741,(a) when the *Baronetcy* became *extinct*. Will pr. 1741.

JENKINSON:

cr. 18 May 1661;

sometime, 1789-1851, BARONS HAWKESBURY;

and (afterwards) sometime, 1796-1851, EARLS OF LIVERPOOL.

I. 1661. "ROBERT JENKINSON,(b) of Walcot [in Charlbury], co. Oxford, Esq.," as also of Hawkesbury,(c) co. Gloucester, 1st s. and h. of Sir Robert JENKINSON, of the same, by Anne Maria, da. of Sir Robert LEE, of Billesley, co. Warwick, was *b.* about 1621, being aged 12 in 1634; matric. at Oxford (Trin. Coll.), 16 Dec. 1636, aged 16; admitted to the Inner Temple, Nov. 1638; Barrister, 1649, having suc. his father in 1645; is said to have been "a friend of Lord HALE and Robert BOYLE"; was Sheriff of Oxon, 1649-50; M.P. for Oxon, 1654-5, 1656-8, and 1659, till void 6 April, and was *cr. a Baronet*, as above, 18 May 1661. He *m.*, in or before 1653, Mary, 2d da. of Sir John BANCKS, of Corfe Castle, and Kingston Lacy, co. Dorset, Ch. Justice of the Court of Common Pleas (1640-44), by Mary,(d) da. of Ralph HAWTREY, of Riselip, Midx. He *d.* 30 March and was *bur.* 10 April 1677, at Charlbury. M.I. Will pr. 1677. His widow *d.* 13 June 1691 and was *bur.* there. Will pr. 1692.

II. 1677. SIR ROBERT JENKINSON, Baronet [1661], of Walcot and Hawkesbury aforesaid, only s. and h.; *b.* about 1655; matric. at Oxford (Bras. Coll.), 11 Nov. 1671, aged 17; admitted to the Inner Temple, 1672; *suc. to the Baronetcy*, 30 March 1677; M.P. for Oxon (nine Parls.), 1689 till death in 1710. He *m.*, in or before 1685, Sarah, sister and h. of Thomas TOMLINS, da. of Thomas TOMLINS, of Bromley, co. Midx., by Susanna, sister of Sir William CRANMER, who *d.* unm. 1697. She *d.* 8 and was *bur.* 15 Aug. 1709, at Charlbury. M.I. He *d.* 30 Jan. and was *bur.* there 4 Feb. 1709/10. M.I. Will pr. March 1710.

III. 1710. SIR ROBERT JENKINSON, Baronet [1661], of Walcot and Hawkesbury aforesaid, 1st s. and h.; *bap.* 23 Nov. 1685, at Charlbury; matric. at Oxford (Trin. Coll.), 18 Feb. 1702/3, aged 15; admitted to Lincoln's Inn, 22 Oct. 1705; Barrister, 1713, having *suc. to the Baronetcy*, 30 Jan. 1709/10. He was M.P. for Oxon. (four Parls.), Feb. 1709/10, till his death. He *m.* (Lic. Fac. 4 Feb. 1711/2), Henrietta Maria, da. of Charles SCARBOROUGH, of St. James' Westm., one of the Clerks of the Board of Green Cloth. He *d.* s.p. 29 Oct. and was *bur.* 5 Nov. 1717, at Charlbury, in his 32d year. M.I. Admon.

(a) The estate of Long Ashton devolved on Florence, one of his sisters and coheirs, whose 2d husband, Jarret Smyth, of Bristol (M.P. for that city 1756 and 1761), was *cr. a Baronet*, as "of Long Ashton, co. Somerset," 27 Jan. 1763, a dignity which became *extinct* 19 May 1849, on the death of the 4th Baronet.

(b) See *Mis. Gen. et Her.*, 2d S., vol. v, pp. 7-14, 27-30, 33-36, 61-63, etc., for a good pedigree of this family and its connections.

(c) This estate was purchased by the father of the 1st Baronet about 1620, from the executors of Arthur Crewe, of Alderley.

(d) This Lady Bancks distinguished herself by her resolute holding of Corfe Castle against the King's enemies, and *d.* 11 April 1661.

12 Nov. 1717. His widow *m.* 9 Aug. 1731, at Westm. Abbey, as his 2d wife (Lic. Fac.), Charles EVERSFIELD, of Denne, co. Sussex (who *d.* 17 Jan. 1748/9), and was *bur.*, with him, at Horsham 16 Aug. 1760. Will pr. 1761.

IV. 1717. SIR BANKS ROBERT JENKINSON,(a) Baronet [1661], of Walcot and Hawkesbury aforesaid, next br. and h., bap. 24 Jan. 1686/7, at Charlbury; matric. at Oxford (Trin. Coll.), 18 Feb. 1702/3, aged 14, and admitted to Lincoln's Inn, 22 Oct. 1705, in each case on the same day as his elder br.; *suc. to the Baronetcy*, 29 Oct. 1717; M.P. for Oxon (two Parls.), 4 Dec. 1717 to 1727. He *m.* 12 June 1718, at Kirtlington, Oxon (Lic. 7 at Archdeaconry of Oxford), Catharine, 3d da. of Sir Robert DASHWOOD, 1st Baronet [1684], of Northbrook, by Penelope, da. and coheir of Sir Thomas CHAMBERLAYNE, 2d Baronet [1643], of Wickham. He *d.* 2 and was *bur.* 6 July 1738, at Charlbury. Will pr. 1738. His widow was *bur.* 24 March 1780, at Hawkesbury. Will pr. May 1780.

V. 1738. SIR ROBERT JENKINSON, Baronet [1661], of Walcot and Hawkesbury aforesaid, 1st s. and h., *bap.* 13 Aug. 1720, at Charlbury; matric. at Oxford (St. John's Coll.), 31 May 1738, aged 17; *suc. to the Baronetcy*, 2 July following; *cr.* M.A., 17 Nov. 1742, and D.C.L., 14 April 1749. He *m.* his 1st cousin, Mary, 3d da. of Sir Jonathan COPE, 1st Baronet [1713], of Brewerne, by Mary, da. of Sir Robert JENKINSON, 2d Baronet abovenamed. She *d.* 30 July 1765, at North End, Fulham, Midx. He *d.* s.p. 8 and was *bur.* 12 Aug. 1766, at Hawkesbury, in his 46th year. M.I. Will pr. 1766.

VI. 1766. SIR BANKS JENKINSON, Baronet [1661], of Walcot and Hawkesbury aforesaid, only br. and h., *bap.* 20 Nov. 1721, at Charlbury; matric. at Oxford (St. John's Coll.), 29 June 1739, aged 17; Fellow of All Souls' Coll.; B.A., 1745; M.A., 1749; *suc. to the Baronetcy*, 8 Aug. 1766. He *d.* unm. at Headington, Oxon, 22 and was *bur.* 29 July 1790, at Hawkesbury. Will pr. Aug. 1790.

VII. 1790. CHARLES (JENKINSON), BARON HAWKESBURY [1786] and 7th *Baronet* [1661], 1st cousin and h. male, being 1st s. and h. of Charles JENKINSON, Col. in the Army, by Amarantha, da. of Wolfran CORNEWALL, Capt. R.N., which Charles (*bap.* 13 June 1693, at Charlbury, and *bur.* 23 June 1750, at Shipton-under-Whichwood) was br. to the 4th and 3d, being 5th s. of the 2d Baronet. He was *b.* 26 April 1727, and having served several high offices, was *cr.*, 21 Aug. 1786, BARON HAWKESBURY, co. Gloucester. He *suc. to the Baronetcy* and to the family estates, 22 July 1790, and was, subsequently, *cr.* 28 May 1796, EARL OF LIVERPOOL. He *d.* 17 Dec. 1808, aged 81.

VIII. 1808. ROBERT (JENKINSON), 2d EARL OF LIVERPOOL [1796], BARON HAWKESBURY [1786], and 8th *Baronet* [1661], 1st s. and h.; *b.* 7 June 1770; *styled* LORD HAWKESBURY, 1796-1808; *suc.*, as above, 17 Dec. 1808; well known as a Statesman, being fifteen years PRIME MINISTER, 1812-27. He *d.* s.p. 4 Dec. 1828, aged 58.

IX. 1828. CHARLES CECIL COPE (JENKINSON), 3d EARL OF LIVERPOOL [1796], BARON HAWKESBURY [1786], and 9th *Baronet* [1661] br. (of the half blood) and h., *b.* 29 May 1784; *suc.*, as above, 4 Dec. 1828. He *d.* s.p.m.(b) 3 Oct. 1851, aged 67, when the *Peerage* honours became *extinct*.

See fuller account in *Peerage*.

(a) In his burial register he is called "Robert Banks," but in the baptismal register "Banks Robert."

(b) Of his three daughters and coheirs the eldest *d.* s.p. 5 Dec. 1877, aged 66, but the second, Selina Charlotte, widow of William Charles Fitzwilliam, *styled* Viscount Milton, *m.* for her second husband (and as his second wife) George Savile Foljambe, of Osberton, Notts and Aldwark, co. York (who *d.* 18 Dec. 1869, aged 69), and *d.* 24 Sep. 1883, aged 71, leaving a son and heir, Cecil George Savile Foljambe (*b.* 7 Nov. 1846), who was *cr.*, 24 June 1893, Baron Hawkesbury of Haselbech, co. Northampton, and of Ollerton, co. Nottingham.

X. 1851. SIR CHARLES JENKINSON, Baronet [1661], of Eastwood Park, in Falfield, co. Gloucester, and of Hawkesbury aforesaid, 1st cousin and h. male, being 1st s. and h. of John JENKINSON, Col. in the Army, and sometime (1768-80) M.P. for Corfe Castle, by Frances, da. of Rear-Admiral John PARKER, which John JENKINSON was next br. to Charles, 1st Earl of Liverpool, the 7th Baronet. He was *b.* 23 Feb. 1779; was sometime an officer in the Foot Guards; M.P. for Dover, 1806-18; *suc. to the Baronetcy* and to some of the family estates, 3 Oct. 1851. He *m.* 4 Feb. 1803, Catherine, 5th da. of Walter CAMPBELL, of Shawfield, co. Lanark and of Islay, co. Argyll. She *d.* in Paris, and was *bur.* 14 Feb. 1855, at Hawkesbury, aged 75. He *d.* s.p.m. at Paris (a few days later) 6 and was *bur.* 15 March 1855, at Hawkesbury, aged 76.

XI. 1855. SIR GEORGE SAMUEL JENKINSON, Baronet [1661], of Eastwood Park and Hawkesbury aforesaid, nephew and h. male, being 2d but 1st surv. s. and h. of John Banks JENKINSON, Bishop of St. David's (1825-40), by Frances Augusta, da. of Augustus PECHELL, of Berkhampstead, Herts, which Bishop (who *d.* 6 July 1840, aged 58) was next br. to the late Baronet. He was *b.* 27 Sep. 1817, at Worcester; ed. at Winchester; was sometime Lieut. in the Rifle Brigade, in the 11th Hussars, and the 8th Hussars; *suc. to the Baronetcy*, 6 March 1855; Sheriff of Gloucestershire, 1862; M.P. for North Wilts, 1868-80. He *m.* 31 July 1845, Emily Sophia, 1st da. of Anthony LYSTER, of Stillorgan Park, co. Dublin. He *d.* of influenza, at Eastwood Park 19 and was *bur.* 28 Jan. 1892, at Falfield, aged 75. Will pr. at £89,796. His widow *d.* there (a few days later) 23 Feb. 1892, aged 65.

XII. 1892. SIR GEORGE BANKS JENKINSON, Baronet [1661], of Eastwood Park and Hawkesbury aforesaid, 1st s. and h., *b.* 10 May 1851; ed. at Harrow; sometime Capt. Glouc. Militia; *suc. to the Baronetcy*, 19 Jan. 1892. He *m.* 10 Aug. 1880, at Berkeley, co. Glouc., Madeline Holme, da. of Arthur Holme SUMNER, of Hatchlands, in East Clandon, Surrey, by Georgiana Emily, da. of Thomas Henry KINGSCOTE, of Kingscote, co. Gloucester.

Family Estates.—These, in 1883, consisted of 3,047 acres in Gloucestershire and 577 in Wilts. *Total.*—3,624 acres, worth £5,517 a year. *Principal Seat.*—Eastwood Park, near Gloucester.

GLINNE, *or* GLYNNE:

cr. 20 May 1661;

ex. 17 June 1874.

I. 1661. "WILLIAM GLINNE, of Bisseter, *alias* Burncester [*i.e.*, Bicester], co. Oxford, Esq.," 1st s. and h., ap. of Sir John GLINNE or GLYNNE, sometime (1655-57) Ch. Justice of the Upper Bench, during the Commonwealth, and subsequently, 8 Nov. 1660, King's Sergeant at Law (*b.* 1602 at Glenllivon, in Llandinog, co. Cardigan, and *d.* 15 Nov. 1666) by his 1st wife, Frances, da. of Arthur SQUIBB, one of the Tellers of the Exchequer, was *b.* probably about 1638; admitted to Lincoln's Inn 15 Nov. 1652; matric. at Oxford (Jesus Coll.) 20 July 1654; B.A., 25 March 1656; M.P. for Carnarvon, 1660, and was v.p. *cr. a Baronet*, as above, 20 May 1661; suc. his father 15 Nov. 1666. Sheriff of Oxon, 1668-69; of Flintshire, 1672-73, and of Oxon (again) 1688-89. He *m.*, 12 July 1659, at St. Giles'-in-the-Fields, Midx., Penelope, sister of Sir Stephen ANDERSON, 1st Baronet [1664], 1st da. of Stephen ANDERSON, of Eyworth, Beds., by Catharine, da. of Sir Edwyn SANDYS, of Ombersley. He, who resided at Ambrosden, Oxon., *d.* at St. Giles'-in-the-Fields, Midx., and was carried thence, 8 Sep. 1690, for burial, probably at Bicester. Admon. 9 Dec. 1690 and 17 June 1692. His widow was *bur.* at Bicester, 24 Feb. 1691/2. Admon. 17 June 1692.

II. 1690. SIR WILLIAM GLYNNE, Baronet [1661], of Bicester and Ambrosden aforesaid, 2d but 1st surv. s. and h.; b. 17 May and bap. 8 June 1663, at Eyworth aforesaid; matric. at Oxford (St. Edm. Hall), 5 Dec. 1679, aged 16; cr. D.C.L., 26 April 1706, having suc. to the Baronetcy in Sep. 1690; M.P. for the Univ. of Oxford, 1698-1700, and for Woodstock, 1702-05; Sheriff of Oxon, 1706-07. He m., 6 July 1688, at St. Giles'-in-the-Fields, Midx., Mary, 2d da. and coheir of Sir Edward EVELYN, Baronet [so cr. 16 Feb. 1682/3] of Long Ditton, Surrey, by Mary, da. and coheir of Charles BALAM, of Sawston, co. Cambridge. She, who was b. 1662, was bur. 18 April 1694, at Bicester. He d. s.p.m.s.(a) 3 and was bur. there 9 Sep. 1721. Will pr. 1722.

III. 1721. SIR STEPHEN GLYNNE, Baronet [1661], of Bicester and Ambrosden aforesaid, br. and h. male, b. 7 and bap. 27 Feb. 1665, at Eyworth aforesaid; suc. to the Baronetcy, 3 Sep. 1721; Sheriff of Flintshire, Jan. to Dec. 1724. He m., in or before 1696, Sophia (sister of his brother's wife abovenamed) yst. da. and coheir of Sir Edward EVELYN, Baronet, by Mary, da. and coheir of Charles BALAM, all abovenamed. He was bur. 29 April 1729 at Bicester. Will pr. 1729. His widow d. 5 and was bur. 18 Jan. 1738/9, at Long Ditton, Surrey.

IV. 1729, April. SIR STEPHEN GLYNNE, Baronet [1661], of Bicester aforesaid, 1st s. and h.; b. at Long Ditton aforesaid about 1696; matric. at Oxford (Univ. Coll.) 18 Nov. 1710, aged 14; suc. to the Baronetcy in April 1729, but d. unm., a few months later, Sep. 1729. Will pr. 1730.

V. 1729, Sep. SIR WILLIAM GLYNNE, Baronet [1661], of Bicester aforesaid, next surv. br. and h.(b); b. about 1710; matric. at Oxford (Queen's Coll.), 8 July 1726, aged 16(c); suc. to the Baronetcy in Sep. 1729, but d. unm. at Aix-la-Chapelle in Aug. 1730. Will pr. 1730.

VI. 1730. SIR JOHN GLYNNE, Baronet [1661], of Bicester aforesaid, and afterwards of Hawarden, co. Flint, yst. and only surv. br. and h.; b. about 1713; suc. to the Baronetcy in Aug. 1730; matric. at Oxford (Queen's Coll.), 13 Nov. 1730, aged 17.(c) He m. firstly, Aug. 1731, Honora, posthumous da. and h. of Henry CONWAY, of Bodrhyddan, co. Flint, by Honora (m. 30 Sep. 1716, at Wrexham), da. and coheir of Thomas RAVENSCROFT, of Broadlane House, in Hawarden,(d) co. Flint (by Honora, da. of Ralph SNEYD, of Keel, co. Stafford), which Henry, was only s. and h. ap. of Sir John CONWAY, 2d and last Baronet [1661], of Bodrhyddan, but d. v.p. 23 July 1717, aged 28. She, who was b. in London, 28 Oct. 1717, d. 10 Feb. 1769. He m. secondly, in 1772, Augusta BEAUMONT, spinster. He d. 1 June 1777. Will pr. 1777. His widow m., in 1780, Peregrine COURTENAY, who d. at Bath, 2 Dec. 1785, aged 65. She d. s.p. in Portland Place, Marylebone, 2 July 1790. Admon. July 1790.

(a) His s. and h. ap., William, b. at Long Ditton, matric. at Oxford (Queen's Coll.) 16 June 1704, aged 15, was Fellow of All Souls' College; cr. M.A., 16 July 1713, and was bur. 25 June 1719, at Bicester, being "a Gentleman of great hopes."

(b) Francis Glynne, the intermediate br., was b. about 1701; matric. at Oxford (Queen's Coll.), 12 July 1720, aged 19; B.A., 19 Feb. 1724/5; took Holy Orders and was Vicar of Hawarden, co. Flint, but d. before 1729.

(c) He (as also his br. Francis) is described in his matric. as "son of Stephen, of Martin, Oxford," presumably, "St. Martin's [i.e. Carfax Church], Oxford."

(d) This house, when rebuilt by the Glynne family, was called Hawarden Castle. The old Castle (formerly belonging to the Earls of Derby) had been purchased by Serjeant Glynne, in the time of the Commonwealth, and was, presumably, owned by the 1st and succeeding Baronets, who, however, never resided there till the middle of the 18th Century.

VII. 1777. SIR STEPHEN GLYNNE, Baronet [1661], of Hawarden aforesaid, 3d and yst., but only surv. s. and h.,(a) b. about 1744; matric. at Oxford (Queen's Coll.), 14 Dec. 1762, aged 18; B.A., 1766; M.A., 1769; in Holy Orders; Rector of Hawarden aforesaid; suc. to the Baronetcy, 1 June 1777. He m., in Aug. 1779, Mary, da. and h. of Richard BENNETT, of Farmcot, Salop. He d 1 April 1780. Admon. 1 Aug. 1780. His widow d. 1 June 1812. Will pr. 1812.

VIII. 1780. SIR STEPHEN RICHARD GLYNNE, Baronet [1661], of Hawarden aforesaid, posthumous s. and h., b. May 1780, at Claverley, Salop, and suc. to the Baronetcy on his birth; ed. at Eton.; matric. at Oxford (Ch. Ch.), 27 April 1798, aged 17; Sheriff of Flintshire, 1802-03; was cr. D.C.L. of Oxford, 5 July 1810. He m., 11 April 1806, at St. Geo., Han. sq., Mary, 2d da. of Richard (ALDWORTH-NEVILLE-GRIFFIN), 2d BARON BRAYBROOKE, by Catherine, da. of the Rt. Hon. George GRENVILLE. He d. at Nice, 5 March 1815, in his 35th year. Will pr. 1816. His widow, who was b. 5 Aug. 1786, d. 13 May 1854, aged 68. Will pr. May 1854.

IX. 1815, to 1874. SIR STEPHEN RICHARD GLYNNE, Baronet [1661], of Hawarden aforesaid, 1st s. and h., b. 22 Sep. 1807, at Hawarden Castle; suc. to the Baronetcy 5 March 1815; ed. at Eton; matric. at Oxford (Ch. Ch.), 1 June 1825, aged 17; B.A. and 3d class Classics, 1828; M.A., 1831. He was Sheriff of Flintshire, 1831-32; M.P. for the Flint burghs, Feb. 1832 to 1837, and for Flintshire (two Parls.), 1837-47; L. Lieut. of that county, 1845 till death. Was an Antiquary of some note.(b) He d. unm. 17 June 1874, at Dr. Flack's Surgery, 56 High street, Shoreditch, having been taken ill in the street with affection of the heart and was bur. at Hawarden, aged 66, when the Baronetcy became extinct.(c)

Family Estates.—These, in 1878 (being then held by Mrs. Gladstone, sister of the late Baronet), consisted of 6,908 acres in Flintshire and 59 in Staffordshire. *Total.*—6,966 acres, worth £18,195 a year. *Seat.*—Hawarden Castle, co. Flint.

CHERNOCK, *or* CHARNOK:

cr. 21 May 1661;

ex. 1779.

I. 1661. "JOHN [*rectius* "St. John"] CHARNOK, of Holcot [i.e., Hulcote], co. Bedford, Esq.," s. and h. ap. of Sir Robert CHARNOK, or CHERNOCK, of the same, and of Aspley Guise in that county, by Anne (sometimes called Agnes), sister of Oliver, 1st EARL OF BOLINGBROKE, da. of Oliver (ST. JOHN), 3d BARON ST. JOHN OF BLETSO, was b. about 1619 (being aged about 15 at the Visit. of Beds, 1634), was, apparently when an infant,

(a) The eldest son d. young, before 1741; John Conway Glynne, the 2d s., matric. at Oxford (Queen's Coll.), 14 Dec. 1762, aged 20, and was a Lieut. of Dragoons in Ireland. He m. Sarah, da. of Charles Crewe, but d. s.p. and v.p., May 1774.

(b) He made notes of the architectural details of 5,530 English Churches, of which those relating to some 300, in Kent, were published in 1877.

(c) He left his estates to Catherine, the elder of his two sisters, who was b. 6 Jan. 1812; m. 25 July 1839, the Right Hon. William Ewart Gladstone (the well known Prime Minister [1868-74, 1880-85, 1886, Feb. to Aug., and 1892-94], who d. 19 May 1898, aged 88), and d. his widow, 11 June 1900, aged also 88, both being bur. in Westm. Abbey. This devise was to the exclusion of his nieces and heirs at law, the two surv. daughters of his brother the Rev. Henry Gladstone, Rector of Hawarden, who d. 30 July 1872, shortly before him. Of these (1) Mary, was living unm. in 1875, and (2) Gertrude, m. (as his second wife), 21 Oct. 1875, George Sholto Gordon (Douglas-Pennant), 2d Baron Penrhyn of Llandegai, and had issue.

admitted to Gray's Inn, 5 Aug. 1620,(a) and was cr. a Baronet, as above, 21 May 1661. He is described as of Salford, Beds, 1669, in the Visit. of Beds held that year. He suc. his father, 26 July 1670. He m. firstly, in or before 1640, Audrey, da. of Sir William VILLIERS, 1st Baronet [1619], of Brokesby, co. Leicester, by his 2d wife, Anne, da. of Richard (FIENNES), LORD SAY AND SELE. She d. in childbirth with twins (her 4th and 5th sons), who d. with her. He m. secondly, 21 Feb. 1665, at Hulcote, Margaret HARRIS. He, who is said to have d. March 1680, aged 61,(b) was bur. at Hulcote 27 Nov. 1681. His widow was bur. there, 5 Nov. 1690.

II. 1680? SIR VILLIERS CHERNOCK, Baronet [1660], of Hulcote aforesaid, 3d but only surv. s. and h. by 1st wife,(c), b. about 1641; suc. to the Baronetcy in 1680 or 1681; was Sheriff of Beds, 1680-81; M.P. for that county, 1685-87. He m., in or before 1677, Anne, 3d da. and coheir of John PYNSENT, of Carleton Curlieu, co. Leicester, and of Combe in Croydon, co. Surrey, one of the Prothonotaries of the Court of Common Pleas, by Mary, da. of Simon CLIFFORD, of Boscombe, Wilts. She was bur. 19 Sep. 1684, at Hulcote. Admon. 13 Nov. 1684. He was bur. there 27 Nov. 1694, aged 53. Will pr. 1695.

III. 1694. SIR PYNSENT CHERNOCK, Baronet [1661], 1st surv. s. and h.,(d) b. in or after 1670; suc. to the Baronetcy in Nov. 1694; was Sheriff of Beds, 1703, and M.P. for that county 1705-08 and 1713-15. He sold the estate of Tingriffe, Beds, having involved himself in great expense in contesting the county elections with the family of RUSSELL. He m., 9 June 1691, at Biddenham, Beds, Helen (bap. there 9 Jan. 1672), da. and coheir of William BOTELER, of BIDDENHAM. He d. 2 Sep. 1734. Admon. 17 May 1736, 14 April 1744 and Sep. 1806. His widow d. Nov. 1741.

IV. 1734. SIR BOTELER CHERNOCK, Baronet [1661], of Hulcote aforesaid, 1st s. and h., bap. there 30 April 1696; matric. at Oxford (Merton Coll.), 5 Feb. 1713/4, aged 17; suc. to the Baronetcy, 2 Sep. 1734; was M.P. for Bedford (two Parls.), 1740 to 1747. He d. unm. in or before 1756. Will pr. 1756.

V. 1756? to 1779. SIR VILLIERS CHERNOCK, Baronet [1661], of Hulcote aforesaid and of Twyford, co. Southampton, yst. but only surv. br. and h., suc. to the Baronetcy in or before 1756. He m. 24 May 1746, at Winchester Cathedral, Anne, da. of Roger HARRIS, of Silkstead. He d. s.p., at Winchester, and was bur. 10 June 1779, in the Cathedral there, when the Baronetcy became extinct. Will pr. June 1779. His widow was bur. there 27 Aug. 1789. Her will pr. 1789.

BROKE, *or* BROOKE:

cr. 21 May 1661;

ex. 25 Feb. 1693/4.

I. 1661, to 1694. "ROBERT BROOKE [*rectius* BROKE], of Netton [*i.e.*, Cowhall, in Nacton], co. Suffolk, Esq.," s. and h. of Sir Richard BROKE, of the same, by Mary, da. of Sir John PAKINGTON, of Hampton Lovett, co. Worcester, was b. about 1630; suc. his father, 23 March 1639/40 and was cr. a Baronet, as above, 21 May 1661. He was Sheriff

(a) "Saint John Chernock, s. and h. of Robert Chernock, of Holkett, Beds, Knt."

(b) Wotton's *Baronetage* for date of death and age, and Hulcote registers [Blaydes's *Gen. Bedford.*] for the burial.

(c) John, or Saint John, Chernock, the 1st son, was bap. 17 Dec. 1640, at Ampthill, Beds; matric. at Oxford (Pembroke Coll.), 13 Dec. 1658; admitted to the Inner Temple, 1660, but d., as did his next eldest br., v.p. and unm., at about the age of 20.

(d) His elder br. Vincent Chernock was aged two in the Visit of Beds, 1669.

of Suffolk, 1679-80; M.P. for that county, 1685-87. He m. firstly, Anne, 3d da. of Sir Lionel TOLLEMACHE, 2d Baronet [1611], by Elizabeth, da. of John (STANHOPE), BARON STANHOPE OF HARRINGTON. He m. secondly, 26 May 1685 at St. Sepulchres, London (Lic. Vic. Gen., 20, he about 55, wid.), Martha THOMLINSON, then of St. Mary le Savoy, about 33, widow. He d. s.p.m.(a) 25 Feb. 1693/4, when the Baronetcy became extinct. Will dat. 16 Dec. 1693, pr. 3 May 1694. His widow d. in St. Andrew's, Holborn, in or before 1700. Admon. 6 June 1700, to her da. Grace, wife of "Edward HART, Esq."

NEVILL:

cr. 25 May 1661;

ex. 25 Feb. 1711/2.

I. 1661, to 1712. "THOMAS NEVILL, of Holt, co. Leicester, Esq.," s. of Henry NEVILL, otherwise SMITH, of Holt aforesaid, and of Cressing Temple, co. Essex (d. 1665), by his 1st wife, Alice, da. of Sir John DACOMBE, was b. about 1625, and was cr. a Baronet, as above, 25 May 1661. He was Gent. of the Bedchamber to Charles II and James II. He m., probably about 1675, Sarah (—). She d. 17 and was bur. 19 Oct. 1710, in Westm. Abbey, in her 60th year. M.I. He d. s.p.m.(b) 25 and was bur. there, 28 Feb. 1711/2, in his 87th year, when the Baronetcy became extinct. M.I.

ANDREWS:

cr. 27 May 1661;

ex. Aug. 1696.

I. 1661, to 1696. "HENRY ANDREWS, of Lathbury, co. Buckingham, Esq.," 1st s. and h. of Sir William ANDREWS, of the same, Sheriff of Bucks, 1620, by Anne, da. of Sir Thomas TEMPLE, 1st Baronet [1611], of Stowe, was b. about 1629; adm. to Gray's Inn, 30 April 1638; suc. his father in Aug. 1657 and was cr. a Baronet, as above, 27 May 1661. He m. firstly, in or before 1650, (—), da. of (—) Browne, of co. Kent. He m. secondly, 27 Feb. 1662/3, at St. Gregory's, London (Lic. Fac. 26, he about 34, widower), Elizabeth DREW, of South Broom, Wilts, widow of John DREW, late of Devizes, Wilts, then about 28.(c) The will of "Dame Elizabeth ANDREWS, Bucks," was pr. Nov. 1686. He d. s.p.s. and was bur. 27 Aug. 1696, at Lathbury, when the Baronetcy became extinct.(d)

(a) Of his three daughters and coheirs by his first wife, the yst. m. his nephew and heir male, Robert Broke, of Nacton, but d. s.p.m., though her husband (by a second wife) was great grandfather of Admiral Philip Bowes Vere Broke, cr. a Baronet in 1813, a dignity which became extinct in 1887.

(b) Anne, his only da. and h., m. Jonathan Elford, of Bickham, Devon, M.P. for Saltash (who d. s.p. Dec. 1755, aged 60), and d. 4, being bur. 9 May 1728, in Westm. Abbey.

(c) Their da. Margaret, d. 4 May 1680, in her 14th year and was bur. at Lathbury. M.I.

(d) The Lathbury estate devolved on his nephew Henry, son of his yr. br., Edward. This Henry Andrews, who resided there, was Sheriff of Bucks, 1704 and d. s.p.m., 1744, leaving four daughters and coheirs.

CRAVEN:

cr. 4 June 1661;

ex. 1712, *or* 1713.

I. 1661, to 1713? "ANTHONY CRAVEN, of Spersholt [*i.e.*, Sparsholt], co. Berks. Esq.," s. and h. of Thomas CRAVEN, of Appletreewick, co. York (*d.* 1636. aged 51), by Margaret, da. of Robert CRAVEN (2d s. of Henry, br. to Sir William CRAVEN, sometime, 1610-11, L. Mayor of London), was *bap.* 5 March 1625/6, at Burnsall, co. York, is described in 1660 as "of Appletreewick. co. York. gent.," but was *cr. a Baronet*, as above [*i.e.*, as "of Sparsholt, Berks"], 4 June 1661, being *Knighted* 14 of same month; was subsequently of Benham in Speen in that county, of Caversham, Oxon (1665-72), and, finally, of Lenchwick, co. Worcester.(a) He contributed towards the rebuilding of the College of Arms, and his pedigree is recorded in 1673, accordingly, in the book called "*Benefactors*."(b) He *m.* (Lic. Fac. 7 April 1662, he about 30 and she about 23) Theodosia, da. of Sir Thomas WISEMAN, 1st Baronet [1628] of Canfield, by Elizabeth, da. of Sir Henry CAPELL. He *d.* s.p.m.s.,(c) at Lenchwick aforesaid, between April 1712 and May 1713, when the *Baronetcy* became *extinct*. Will dat. 1 April 1712, pr. 12 May 1713. His widow *d.* 2 Oct. 1717, in her 74th year, and was *bur.* at Speen, co. Berks. M.I. Will dat. 23 May and pr. 14 Oct. 1717.

CLAVERING:

cr. 5 June 1661;

ex. 9 Nov. 1893.

I. 1661. "John [*but should be* "JAMES"] CLAVERING, of Axwell, co. Durham, Esq.," s. and h. of John CLAVERING, of the same (aged 23 and unm. in the Visit. of Northumberland, 1615), by Anne, da. of Robert SHAFTO, of Newcastle-upon-Tyne, was *bap.* 3 Feb. 1619/20, at St. Nicholas, in Newcastle aforesaid; admitted to Gray's Inn, 30 April 1638; suc. his father in May 1648; was Sheriff of the County of Durham, 1649-50 and again 1673-74, being M.P. thereof, 1656-58; and (tho' he had served on several Parl. Committees, 1645-46), was, "in consideration of his loyalty and sufferings for King Charles I and II," *cr. a Baronet*, as above, 5 June 1661. He entered his ped. in the Her. Visit. of Durham in Aug. 1666, stating himself to be aged 40. He *m.* 23 April 1640, at Newcastle, Jane, da. of Henry MADISON, of Newcastle aforesaid. She was *bur.* 1 July 1688, at Whickham. He was *bur.* there, 24 March 1701/2, aged 81.

(a) See an accurate account of this family (correcting numerous errors in all previous ones) in the Rev. W. J. Stavert, M.A., in "Notes on the pedigree of the Cravens of Appletreewick, published in the *Yorkshire Archæological Journal*, vol. xiii [1895].

(b) At that date he had six children, viz., William, 1st son, aged eight; John, 2d son, aged 4, Elizabeth, Mary, Ann, and Flower.

(c) Of his two sons (1) William, *b.* and *bap.* 27 June 1665 at Caversham, appears to have lived till full age and to have made a will; (2) John, *b.* 7 July and *bap.* 2 Aug. 1669 as aforesaid. matric. at Oxford (Wadham Coll.), Jan. 1687/8; B.A., 1691; M.A., 1694, having been admitted to the Middle Temple, 1691. Of the daughters, Mary, *b.* 30 Sep. and *bap.* 5 Oct. 1666 at Caversham, is mentioned in his will (1 April 1712, as wife of "Edward Broughton, Esq.," with issue, but the estate of Sparsholt is left therein (after the death of testator's widow) to Samuel Palmer, his grandson, *i.e.*, son of his da. Elizabeth, by Samuel Palmer (*m.* 1692), of Allhallows', Lombard Street. See also *N. & Q.*, 8th Series, iv, 333. This Baronet is continually confused with his maternal uncle, Sir Anthony Craven, *Knight*, who *m.* Elizabeth, da. of Baron Polnitz, of Mark, in Germany, and *d.* s.p. in 1670.

II. 1702. SIR JAMES CLAVERING, Baronet [1661], of Axwell aforesaid, grandson and h., being 1st surv. s. and h. of John CLAVERING, of Whitehouse, co. Durham, by Dorothy (*m.* in or before 1666), da. of Henry SAVILE, of Methley, co. York, which John (who was aged 25 in Aug. 1666), was 1st s. and h. ap. of the late Baronet, but *d.* v.p., 26 Feb. 1687/8. He was *bap.* 8 April 1668, at Ryton, matric. at Oxford (St. Edm. Hall), 17 June 1687, aged 18, and *suc. to the Baronetcy*, in March 1701/2. He *m.* Elizabeth, da. of Sir William MIDDLETON, 1st Baronet [1662], of Belsay, by his 2d wife, Elizabeth, da. of John MUNDY. He *d.* s.p.m.s. and was *bur.* 8 July 1707, at Whickham. His widow *bur.* there 6 May 1708.

III. 1707. SIR JOHN CLAVERING, Baronet [1661], of Axwell aforesaid, next surv. br. and h. male; *bap.* 9 April 1672 at Ryton; was sometime of Newcastle; *suc. to the Baronetcy* in July 1707. He *m.*, 17 Dec. 1702, at St. Nicholas', Newcastle, Jane, da. of Robert MALLABAR, of that town, Merchant, by Alice (*m.* 11 June 1667), formerly Alice PROCTOR, widow, da. of William SWINBORNE, of Newcastle, Merchant. He was *bur.* 13 May 1714, at Whickham. His widow, who was *bap.* at St. Nicholas' aforesaid, 7 Feb. 1668/9, *d.* 22 Feb. 1734/5 in her 66th year, and was *bur.* at St. Nicholas,' Newcastle. M.I. Will dat. 11 Dec. 1734.

IV. 1714. SIR JAMES CLAVERING, Baronet [1661], of Axwell aforesaid, 2d but only surv. s. and h., *bap.* 3 Aug. 1708, at All Saints, Newcastle; *suc. to the Baronetcy* in May 1714; matric. at Oxford (Queen's Coll.), 6 Nov. 1724, aged 15. He *d.* unm. on his travels abroad, 18 May 1726, aged 18.

V. 1726. SIR FRANCIS CLAVERING, Baronet [1661], of Axwell aforesaid, uncle and h. male; *bap.* 9 Sep. 1673, at Ryton; *suc. to the Baronetcy* in May 1726. He *m.* Susan, da. of [—] SELLS. He *d.* s.p. 31 Dec. 1738, and was *bur.* 16 Jan. 1738/9, aged 66. Will dat. 23 May 1734, pr. 1739. His widow *m.* [—] RICHARDSON. She *d.* 28 March 1759, at Kensington, aged 72. Will pr. 1760.

VI. 1738. SIR JAMES CLAVERING, Baronet [1601], of Axwell aforesaid and of Greencroft. co. Durham, cousin and h. male, being only s. and h. of James CLAVERING, of Greencroft aforesaid, by Jane, da. and coheir of Benjamin ELLISON, of Newcastle aforesaid, Merchant, which James (who was aged 20 in 1666 and *d.* Jan. 1721/2) was 2d s. of the 1st Baronet. He was *bap.* 19 Aug. 1680, at All Saints', Newcastle, and *suc. to the Baronetcy*, 31 Dec. 1738. He *m.* firstly, in or before 1714, Catharine, da. of Thomas YORKE, of Richmond, co. York, by whom he had seven sons. She *d.* 29 Nov. 1723. M.I. at Lanchester. He *m.* secondly, before 1740, Elizabeth, da. of Lionel VANE, of Long Newton, co. Durham. She, by whom he had no issue, was *bur.* 26 Feb. 1747, at Lanchester. He *d.* 12 and was *bur.* 18 May 1748, at Lanchester.

VII. 1748. SIR THOMAS CLAVERING, Baronet [1661], of Axwell aforesaid, 4th but 1st surv. s. and h., *bap.* 19 June 1719; matric. at Oxford (Corpus Christi Coll.), 20 Jan. 1736/7, aged 18; *suc. to the Baronetcy*, 18 May 1748; was M.P. for St. Mawes, Jan. 1753 to 1754; for Shaftesbury, 1754-61, and for Durham (four Parls.), 1768-90. He was *cr.*, 17 June 1782, D.C.L. of Oxford. He *m.*, May 1746, at Gosforth, Martha, da. of Joshua DOUGLAS, of Newcastle aforesaid. She *d.* 16 Aug. 1792, aged 66. M.I., at Whickham. He *d.* s.p. 14 Oct. 1794. M.I. at Whickham. Will pr. 1817.

VIII. 1794. SIR THOMAS JOHN CLAVERING, Baronet [1661], of Axwell and Greencroft aforesaid, nephew and h., being only s. of George CLAVERING, of Greencroft aforesaid, by his second wife, Dame Mary POLE, relict of Sir John POLE, 5th Baronet [1628], of Shute, da. of the Rev. [—] PALMER, of Combe Raleigh, Devon, which George, who *d.* 23 May 1794, aged 74, was 5th, but 2d surv. s. of the 6th Baronet. He was *b.* 6 April 1771; *suc. to the Baronetcy*, 14 Oct. 1794; raised a troop of Yeomanry at his own expense in 1796, and was

Sheriff of Northumberland, 1817. He *m.*, 21 Aug. 1791, Clare, da. of John de Callais de la Bernadine, COUNT DE LA SABLE, of Anjou, in France, by Petronella, his wife. He *d.* 1853. Will pr. June 1854. His widow *d.* abroad. Her admon. Sep. 1854.

IX. 1853. SIR WILLIAM ALOYSIUS CLAVERING, Baronet [1661], of Axwell and Greencroft aforesaid 4th but only surv. s. and h.; *b.* 21 Jan. 1800; ed. at Trin. Coll. Cambridge; B.A., 1821; M.A., 1825; *suc. to the Baronetcy* in 1853. Sheriff of Durham, 1859. He *d.* unm. (of apoplexy) at St. George's Hospital, London, 8 Oct. 1872, aged 72.

X. 1872, to 1893. SIR HENRY AUGUSTUS CLAVERING, Baronet [1661], of Axwell aforesaid, cousin and h. male, being 2d and yst. but last surv. s. of Rawdon Forbes CLAVERING, Major in the Royal Engineers, by Jane, da. of Sir Archibald DUNBAR, 5th Baronet [S. 1698], which Rawdon (who *d.* 1831), was s. of Brig.-Gen. Henry CLAVERING, by Augusta, da. of John (CAMPBELL), 5th DUKE OF ARGYLL [S.], the said Henry being s. of Lieut.-Gen. Sir John CLAVERING, K.B., com.-in-chief of the Forces in Bengal (*d.* at Calcutta, 30 Aug. 1777), who was uncle to the 8th, yr. br. to the 7th, being the 7th and yst. s. of the 6th Baronet. He was *b.* 30 Aug. 1824; ed. at the Royal Naval College; Lieut. R.N., 1847; Commander, 1865; Capt. (retired list), 1880, having, at the age of 34, been admitted to Lincoln's Inn, 28 April 1858, and having *suc. to the Baronetcy*, 8 Oct. 1872. He *m.*, 12 Jan. 1853, Christina, 2d da. of Andrew ALEXANDER, LL.D., Professor of Greek at the Univ. of St. Andrew's, Scotland. He *d.* s.p.m.(a) suddenly at Axwell Park, 9 Nov. 1893, in his 70th year, when the *Baronetcy* became *extinct*. His widow *d.* 17 Nov. 1898, at Greencroft house, Victoria avenue, Harrogate, aged 65. Will pr. at £27,521.

Family Estates.—These in 1883 consisted of 8,334 acres in Northumberland (worth but £3,551 a year); 5,179 in Durham, and 173 in the North Riding of Yorkshire. *Total*, 13,686 acres, worth £10,498 a year. *Seat*—Axwell Park, near Blaydon-on-Tyne, Durham.

DEREHAM, *or* DERHAM:

cr. 8 June 1661;

ex. 16 Jan. 1738/9

I. 1661. "THOMAS DERHAM, of West Dereham, co. Norfolk, Esq.," s. and h. of Sir Thomas DERHAM, *or* DEREHAM, of Dereham Grange in West Dereham aforesaid, by his 1st wife, Catharine, da. of Sir Henry ANDERSON, of St. Olave's Jury, London, Alderman and sometime [1601-02] Sheriff of London, was *b.* probably about 1600; was admitted to the Inner Temple, Nov. 1618; suc. his father, 20 April 1645, and was *cr. a Baronet*, as above, 8 June 1661. He *m.* firstly, in or before 1625, Elizabeth, da. and h. of Richard SCOTT, of Scott's Hall, co. Kent, by Catharine, da. of Sir Rowland HEYWARD, sometime [1570-71] L. Mayor of London. She, who was *b.* 1603 and who "fell mad in childbed," was *bur.* 24 Jan. 1640/1, at West Dereham. He *m.* secondly, in or before 1643, Elizabeth, 1st da. and coheir of Sir Richard GARGRAVE, of Kingsley Park and Nostell, co. York, by Catharine, sister to Henry, EARL OF DANBY, da. of Sir John DANVERS. He was *bur.* 30 March 1668, at St. Giles-in-the-Fields, Midx. Will pr. 1668. His widow was *bur.* 12 Nov. 1677, at West Dereham. Admon. 7 Dec. 1677.

(a) Of his four daughters, one *d.* unm. before 1902, when two others (the 1st and 4th) were living unm., but the 3d da., Ivy Valerie, *m.*, 5 July 1876, Henry Alexander Campbell, Lieut. Royal Horse Artillery (3d s. of Colin Campbell, of Colgrain, co. Dumbarton), and *d.* 29 June 1898, leaving issue.

II. 1668. SIR HENRY DEREHAM, Baronet [1661], of Dereham Grange aforesaid, s. and h. by 2d wife, *b.* about 1643; *suc. to the Baronetcy* in March 1668. He *m.* (Lic. Vic. Gen. 23 Jan. 1678/9, he about 35, bachelor), Dorothy MAYNARD, of St. Giles-in-the-Fields, about 31, spinster, and at her own disposal,(a) possibly da. of Sir John MAYNARD the elder, of Tooting Gravening, Surrey. He *d.* s.p. and was *bur.* 27 May 1682, at West Dereham. Admon. 1 Aug. 1682 to his br., Sir Richard Dereham, Baronet.

III. 1682. SIR RICHARD DEREHAM, Baronet [1661], of Dereham Grange aforesaid, only surv. br. and h., *bap.* 10 April 1644, at West Dereham; adm. to Lincoln's Inn, 28 Nov. 1661; *suc. to the Baronetcy* in May 1682. He *m.*, in or before 1678, Frances, 1st da. of Robert WRIGHT, *otherwise* VILLIER, *otherwise* DANVERS, *often styled* VISCOUNT PURBECK(b) by Elizabeth, da. of Sir John DANVERS, of Chelsea, one of the Regicide Judges. Having wasted his property and alienated the family estates, he *d.* in Jamaica. His widow was *bur.* 27 Dec. 1720, at West Dereham. Will dat. 5 Aug. 1720, pr. 2 March 1720/1.

IV. 1710? to 1739. SIR THOMAS DEREHAM, Baronet [1661], of Dereham Grange aforesaid, 1st s. and h., *b.* about 1678, being aged 15 in 1693; suc. to the Dereham estate on the death, s.p., in Oct. 1697, of his father's first cousin, Sir Thomas Dereham, Envoy to the Court of Tuscany, where he himself "had been brought up(c)," (which Thomas had purchased the same from his father) and *suc. to the Baronetcy* on the death of his said father; F.R.S., in 1720. He *d.* unm. at Rome, 16 Jan. 1738/9, when the *Baronetcy* became *extinct*.(d) Will pr. 1741.

STANLEY:

cr. 17 June 1661(e);

afterwards, 1792-1863, STANLEY-MASSEY-STANLEY;

subsequently, 1863-93, ERRINGTON;

ex. 19 March 1893.

I. 1661. "WILLIAM STANLEY, of Houton [*i.e.*, Hooton(f)] in the hundred of Whitehall], co. Chester. Esq.," 1st s. and h. of William STANLEY, of Hooton aforesaid and of Storeton in that county, by Mary, da. of John DRAYCOTT, of Painsley, co. Stafford, was *b.* Sep. 1628 (being aged 17 at the death of his father, who was *bap.* 26 April 1606, at Eastham, co. Chester, and who *d.* 20 Feb. 1643/4), and was *cr. a Baronet*, as above, 17 June 1661.(e) He *m.*, in or before 1651, Charlotte, da. of Richard (MOLYNEUX) 1st VISCOUNT MOLYNEUX OF MARYBOROUGH [I.], by Mary, da. of Sir Thomas CARYLL. She *d.* 31 July 1662, and was *bur.* at Eastham. M.I. He was *bur.* there 30 Sep. 1673. Admon. at Chester, 1675.

(a) She is often called da. of Sir John Maynard, the celebrated Serjeant-at-Law, who did not die till Oct. 1690, some twelve years after the marriage, and who does not appear to have had such a daughter. Her own parents were, presumably, dead before 1679.

(b) He was the son of Frances, wife of John (Villiers), Viscount Purbeck who eloped from her said husband in 1621 and took the name of Wright, but who gave birth to this child in her husband's lifetime. His illegitimacy, however, was legally pronounced in 1678 (four years after his death) when his son claimed the Earldom of Buckingham.

(c) Courthope's *extinct Baronetage*.

(d) Elizabeth his only sister and h., *m.* Sir Simeon Stuart, 2d Baronet [1660], of Hartley Mauduit, Hants, who *d.* 11 Aug. 1761 leaving issue.

(e) The date of creation is sometimes given as 17 March (1660/1), 13 Charles II.

(f) Sir William Stanley of Storeton and Stanley, co. Chester, who *d.* 1428, and from whom the 1st Baronet was 10th in descent, acquired the estate of Hooton by marriage with Margaret, da. and h. of Sir William Hooton, of Hooton.

II. 1673. SIR ROWLAND STANLEY, Baronet [1661], of Hooton and Storeton aforesaid, 2d but 1st surv. s. and h., *bap.* June 1653, at Eastham; *suc. to the Baronetcy* in Sep. 1673. He *m.*, in or before 1654, Anne, da. of Clement PASTON, of Bernigham, co. Norfolk. She was *bur.* 13 March 1693, at Eastham. He *d.* at Hooton, 5 June 1737, aged 84.

III. 1737. SIR WILLIAM STANLEY, Baronet [1661], of Hooton and Storeton aforesaid, 1st s. and h., *bap.* 11 Nov. 1679, at Eastham; *suc. to the Baronetcy*, 5 June 1737; was "a gentleman of strict honour, generosity and hospitality." He *m.*, in or before 1707, Catharine (living Nov. 1719), da. of Rowland EYRE, of Hassop, co. Derby. He *d.* July 1740.

IV. 1740. SIR ROWLAND STANLEY, Baronet [1661], of Hooton and Storeton aforesaid, 1st s. and h., *bap.* 23 Aug. 1707, at Eastham; *suc. to the Baronetcy* in July 1740. He *m.* (articles dat. 4 April 1743) Elizabeth, da. of Thomas PARRY, of Perthymael, co. Flint. She *d.* at Bath, 12 May 1761, and was *bur.* at Eastham aforesaid. He *d.* 9 April 1771, and was *bur.* there.

V. 1771. SIR WILLIAM STANLEY, Baronet [1661], of Hooton and Storeton aforesaid, only surv. s. and h., *b.* in or after 1753; *suc. to the Baronetcy*, 9 April 1771. He *m.* (being then a Baronet), 5 Aug. 1785, at Chiswick, co. Midx. (articles dat. 30 July 1785), Barbara, only da. of John TOWNELEY, of Towneley, co. Lanc., by Barbara, da. of Edward DICCONSON, of Wrightington in that county. He *d.* s.p. 29 May 1792. His widow *d.* 5 Aug. 1836, in her 79th year, at Towneley aforesaid. Will pr. Aug. 1836.

VI. 1792. SIR JOHN STANLEY-MASSEY-STANLEY, Baronet [1661], of Hooton and Storeton aforesaid, and of Puddington in Burton, co. Chester, uncle and h. male, being 3d son of the 3d Baronet. He was *bap.* 28 Feb. 1711, at Eastham; took the name of *Massey* after that of *Stanley* on inheriting the estate of Puddington,(a) and, subsequently, *suc. to the Baronetcy* and to the family estates of Stanley, 29 May 1792, when he took the name of *Stanley* after that of *Stanley-Massey*. He *m.* Mary, da. of Thomas CLIFTON, of Lytham, co. Lanc., by Mary, da. of Richard (MOLYNEUX), 5th VISCOUNT MOLYNEUX OF MARYBOROUGH [I]. She *d.* 21 May 1770, in her 40th year. He *d.* at Hooton 24 Nov. 1794, in his 84th year, both being *bur.* at Burton aforesaid. M.I.

VII. 1794. SIR THOMAS STANLEY-MASSEY-STANLEY, Baronet [1661], of Hooton, Storeton and Puddington aforesaid, 2d but 1st surv. s. and h., *b.* about 1755; *suc. to the Baronetcy*, 24 Nov. 1794. He *m.*, in or before 1780, Catherine, da. of William SALVIN, of Croxdale, co. Durham. He *d.* at York, 19 Feb. 1795, aged 40, and was *bur.* at Eastham. M.I. at Burton aforesaid. His widow was *bur.* 5 Nov. 1798, at Eastham. Will pr. Feb. 1799.

VIII. 1795. SIR WILLIAM STANLEY-MASSEY-STANLEY, Baronet [1661], of Hooton, Storeton and Puddington aforesaid, 1st. s. and h., *b.* about 1780; *suc. to the Baronetcy*, 19 Feb. 1795. He *d.* a minor and unm., 14 June 1800.

IX. 1800. SIR THOMAS STANLEY-MASSEY-STANLEY, Baronet [1661], of Hooton, Storeton and Puddington aforesaid, next br. and h., *b.* 23 Jan. 1782; *suc. to the Baronetcy*, 14 June 1800; Sheriff of Cheshire, 1831-32. He *m.*, Jan. 1805, Mary, da. and h. of Sir Carnaby HAGGERSTON, 5th Baronet [1642], of Haggerston, by Frances, da. of Walter SMYTHE, of Brambridge House, Hants, and Mary his wife, sister of Henry ERRINGTON, of Sandhoe, co. Northumberland. He *d.* at Hooton Hall, 20 Aug. 1841. M.I. at Eastham. Will pr. Dec. 1841. His widow *d.* 20 Aug. 1857, at Haggerston Castle.

(a) This estate passed under the will of William Massey, of Puddington, the last heir male of that family (who *d.* Feb. 1715/6, a prisoner in Chester Castle for high treason), to his infant godson (not apparently a relation) Thomas Stanley, 4th s. of 3d Baronet. He accordingly took the name of Massey, and on his death, s.p., they passed to his next elder br., John, afterwards the 6th Baronet.

X. 1841. SIR WILLIAM THOMAS STANLEY-MASSEY-STANLEY, Baronet [1661], of Hooton, Storeton and Puddington aforesaid, 1st s. and h., *bap.* 24 Nov. 1806, at Eastham; was M.P. for Pontefract, 1837-41; *suc. to the Baronetcy*, 20 Aug. 1841; Sheriff of Cheshire, 1845. About 1850 he sold the Hooton and Storeton estates (which had been in the family for above four centuries) to Christopher Naylor of Liverpool. He *d.* unm., at Paris, 29 June 1863.

XI. 1863. SIR ROWLAND ERRINGTON, Baronet [1661], of Sandhoe, co. Northumberland and of Puddington aforesaid, br. and h.; *bap.* 4 April 1809, at Eastham; took by Royal lic., 26 June 1820, the name of ERRINGTON only, on inheriting the estates of his mother's mother's maternal uncle, Henry ERRINGTON abovenamed, at Sandhoe aforesaid and Red Rice, Hants. He *suc. to the Baronetcy* and to the Puddington estate, 29 June 1863. He *m.*, 7 Jan. 1839, at St. James', Westm., Julia, 1st da. of Lieut.-Gen. Sir John MACDONALD, K.C.B., Adj.-Gen. of the Forces. She *d.* Aug. 1859. He *d.* s.p.m.(a) 31 March 1875, in Curzon street, Mayfair, aged 65.

XII. 1875, to 1893. SIR JOHN STANLEY-MASSEY-STANLEY, *afterwards*, 1877-93, ERRINGTON, Baronet [1661], of Sandhoe and Puddington aforesaid, only surv. br. and h. male; *bap.* 30 April 1810, at Eastham aforesaid; *suc. to the Baronetcy* and the Puddington estate, 31 March 1875, as also to those of the Errington family, at Sandhoe, and consequently by Royal lic., 7 Aug. 1877, took the name of *Errington* only, in lieu of that of Stanley-Massey-Stanley. He *m.*, 21 Aug. 1841, Maria, only da. of the BARON DE TALLEYRAND. He *d.* s.p. 19 March 1893, at the Villa L'Estrel, Cannes, in South France, and was *bur.* at Eastham, aged 82, when the *Baronetcy* became *extinct*. His widow living 1903.

Family Estates.—These, in 1883, consisted of 10,563 acres in Northumberland, worth £8,487 a year, and 3,147 in Cheshire, worth £4,894 a year. *Total.*—13,710 acres, worth £13,381 a year. *Principal Seats.*—Sandhoe, co. Northumberland, and Puddington College, near Neston, co. Chester.

CULLEN:

cr. 17 June 1661;

ex. 15 Oct. 1730.

I. 1661. "ABRAHAM CULLEN,(b) of East Sheen [in Mortlake], co. Surrey, Esq.," s. and h. of Abraham CULLEN,(c) by Abigail, da. of (—) MOONE, "of a noble house in Brabant," was a merchant of London, residing at St. Andrew's, Undershaft, and was *cr.* a *Baronet*, as above, 17 June 1661. He was, also, of Upton, co. Warwick, and was M.P. for Evesham, 1661, till his death in 1668. He *m.* 10 Dec. 1650, at St. Dionis Backchurch, London (Lic. Fac. 2, he about 26 and she about 17), Abigail, sister of Sir James RUSHOUT,

(a) Of his two surv. daughters and coheirs (1) Ethel Stanley, *m.* 28 June 1876, the celebrated Sir Evelyn Baring, who was *cr.* in 1892, Baron Cromer, and in 1899 (after her death), Viscount Cromer, and subsequently 1901, Earl of Cromer and VISCOUNT ERRINGTON of Hexham. She *d.* 16 Oct. 1898, leaving an only child, Rowland Thomas Baring (*b.* 29 Nov. 1877), *styled Viscount Errington*; (2) Venetia Stanley, *m.* 24 April 1867, John Horatio (SAVILE), 5th Earl Mexborough of Lifford [I.], and *d.* s.p.s. 13 Nov. 1900.

(b) An elaborate pedigree of this family, originally Van Ceulen, of Breda in the Duchy of Brabant, in Flanders, is recorded in the College of Arms.

(c) Possibly the "Abraham Cullen, merchant," who *m.* [as his 2d wife], 13 Oct. 1656 at St. Helen's, Bishopsgate, "Mrs. Susan Lodowick, of St. Andrew's Hubbard, widow."

1st Baronet [1661], da. of John RUSHOUT, of St. Andrew's-aforesaid, merchant, by his 1st wife Anne, da. of Joas GODSCHALK, of London. He *d.* 28 Aug. and was *bur.* 2 Sep. 1668, at Mortlake. Admon. 3 Nov. 1668, 26 Sep. 1678, and 6 Oct. 1713. His widow was *bur.* there, April 1678, leaving a will of which her said br. Sir James RUSHOUT was executor.

II. 1668. SIR JOHN CULLEN, Baronet [1661], of Upton aforesaid, 1st s. and h., *bap.* 22 Oct. 1652 at St. Dionis Backchurch; admitted to Middle Temple, 1668; matric. at Oxford (Ch. Ch.), 3 Dec. 1669, aged 17; *suc. to the Baronetcy*, 28 Aug. 1668. He *d.* unm., 1677. Will pr. 1678.

III. 1677, to 1730. SIR RUSHOUT CULLEN, Baronet [1661], of Upton aforesaid, next surv. br. and h.,(a) *b.* 12 and *bap.* 12 Aug. 1661, at Mortlake; *suc. to the Baronetcy* in 1677; was M.P. for Cambridgeshire (seven Parls.), 1697—1710. He *m.* firstly, his cousin, Mary, widow of William ADAMS, of Sprowston, co. Norfolk (*d.* 1683-85), and formerly wife of Francis BULLER, only da. and eventually h. of Sir John MAYNARD, of Tooting Graveney, Surrey, and of Iselham, co. Cambridge, by Katherine, da. of John RUSHOUT, merchant, abovenamed. She *d.* s.p.m. Will pr. 1694. He *m.* secondly, 19 June 1696, at St. Dionis Backchurch aforesaid (Lic. Fac. 17, he about 40 widower and she 25 spinster), Eleanor, da. of William JARRET, of that parish, merchant. He *d.* s.p.m.(b) 15 Oct. 1730 in Warwickshire, when *the Baronetcy* became *extinct*. Will pr. Nov. 1730. The will of his widow pr. 1756.

RUSHOUT, *or* ROUSHOUT:

cr. 17 June 1661;

afterwards, 1797—1887, BARONS NORTHWICK;

ex. 11 Nov. 1887.

I. 1661. "JAMES ROUSHOUT [*rectius* RUSHOUT], of Milnst-Maylers [*i.e.* Maylards in Havering], co. Essex, Esq.," only surv. s. and h. of John RUSHOUT, of the same and of St. Andrew's, Undershaft, London, merchant (who came from Flanders(c) to England, was naturalised, 1635, and *d.* 28 Oct. 1653, aged 60), by his 1st wife, Anne, da. of Joas GODSCHALK, of London, was *b.* about 1644; matric. at Oxford (Ch. Ch.), 5 Dec. 1660, aged 16; *cr.* M.A., 12 Sep. 1661, and was *cr. a Baronet*, as above, 17 June 1661. He was M.P. for Evesham (four Parls.), Feb. 1670 to 1681; for Worcestershire, 1689-90; and for Evesham, again, 1690 till his death, 1698. He purchased the estate of Northwick Park, in Blockley, co. Worcester, about 1665. He was appointed Ambassador to Constantinople, in May 1697, but *d.* before setting out. He *m.*, in or before 1672, Alice, the childless widow of Edward PALMER, da. and h. of Edmund PITT, of Harrow on the Hill, Midx., with whom he acquired a considerable estate there. He *d.* Feb. 1697/8, and was *bur.* from Northwick. Will pr. 1698. His widow, "a zealous Protestant," *d.* 1698. M.I. to both at Blockley.

(a) Another Rushout Cullen, his elder br., was *bap.* 28 Oct. 1656, and *bur.* 13 Sep. 1658 at Mortlake.

(b) Mary, his only da. and h. (by 1st wife), *m.* (as his 1st wife) Sir John Dutton, 2d Baronet [1678], and *d.* s.p.

(c) He is said, "on the authority of the Baronetages" (Brydges' *Collins' Peerage*), to be descended "in a direct male line, after several generations," from Jean Rushaut, yst. s. of Joachim, Sieur de Boismenart, etc., living 1439. A pedigree is mentioned in Foster's *Peerage* [1883], "certified 1632, by Henry, Prevost de la Val, Artois King of Arms," in France, deducing his descent "from Thibaut Rushaut, *noble Chevalier Anglois*, who settled in France [!] at the commencement of the 14th century." In this it is presumed the grandfather of the grantee is indicated.

II. 1698. SIR JAMES RUSHOUT, Baronet [1661], of Northwick Park and Harrow aforesaid, 2d but 1st surv. s. and h., *b.* 1676; *suc. to the Baronetcy* in Feb. 1697/8; was M.P. for Evesham, 1700-02. He *m.*, 17 Feb. 1699/700, at Teddington, Midx., Arabella (*b.* 1670), da. of Thomas VERNON, of Twickenham Park, Midx., and of London, Merchant. Both of them *d.* 1705. M.I. at Blockley. His will pr. June 1706.

III. 1705. SIR JAMES RUSHOUT, Baronet [1661], of Northwick Park and Harrow aforesaid, only s. and h., *b.* 1701; *suc. to the Baronetcy* in 1705. He *d.* in boyhood at Twickenham Park, near Isleworth, 21 Sep. 1711. M.I. at Blockley. Admon. 20 Nov. 1711, to "Thomas Vernon, Esq.," and again, 15 Feb. 1724/5, to Elizabeth RUSHOUT, spinster, the sister.(a)

IV. 1711. SIR JOHN RUSHOUT, Baronet [1661], of Northwick Park aforesaid, uncle and h. male, *b.* 1685; *suc. to the Baronetcy*, 21 Sep. 1711; was M.P. (three Parls.), April 1713 to 1722, for Malmesbury, and for Evesham (seven Parls.), 1722-68, being an opponent of Walpole's ministry, and of the Excise bill; was a Lord of the Treasury, Feb. 1742 to Aug. 1743; Treasurer of the Navy, 1743-44, and P.C., 19 Jan. 1744. He *m.* 16 Oct. 1729, Anne, 4th da. of George (COMPTON), 4th EARL OF NORTHAMPTON, by his 1st wife, Jane, da. of Sir Stephen Fox. She, who was *b.* 1695, and who was "one of the best of women," *d.* 20 Dec. 1766, in her 72d year, at Northwick, and was *bur.* at Blockley. M.I. Admon. 7 June 1768. He *d.* 2 Feb. 1775, in his 92d year, "his memory, good humour, and politeness" being "then in their full bloom." Will pr. March 1775.

V. 1775. SIR JOHN RUSHOUT, Baronet [1661], of Northwick Park aforesaid, only s. and h., *b.* 23 and *bap.* 30 July 1738, at St. George's, Bloomsbury; matric. at Oxford (Ch. Ch.), 20 Oct. 1756; was M.P. for Evesham (six Parls.), 1761-96; *suc. to the Baronetcy*, 2 Feb. 1775. He *m.* 2 June 1766, at Wanstead, co. Essex, Rebecca, da. of Humphrey BOWLES, of Wanstead. She was living when he was *cr.* 26 Oct. 1797, BARON NORTHWICK of Northwick Park, co. Worcester. In that Peerage *this Baronetcy* then merged, and so continued till both became *extinct*, 11 Nov. 1887, on the death of the 4th Baron and 7th Baronet.(b)

COPLEY:

cr. 17 June 1661;

ex. 9 April 1709.

I. 1661. "GODFREY COPLEY, of Sprotborough, co. York, Esq.," 1st s. and h. of William COPLEY, of the same, by Dorothy, da. of William ROOTH, of Romley, co. Derby, was *b.* 21 Feb. and *bap.* 23 March 1623, at Sprotborough; suc. his father in 1644, and was *cr. a Baronet*, as above, 17 June 1661. He was aged 40 and upwards at the Heralds' Visit. of Yorkshire in 1666. He *m.* firstly, in or before 1653, Eleanor, da. of Sir Thomas WALMESLEY, of Dunkenhalgh, co. Lancaster, by Johana, da. of Sir Richard MOLYNEUX, 1st Baronet [1611] of Sefton. She is said(c) to have been *bur.* 18 Nov. 1649 [*Qy.* 1659], at Sprotborough. He *m.* secondly, in or before 1663,

(a) She *m.*, 9 Aug. 1731, as his 1st wife, Paulett St. John, but *d.* s.p. 21 Dec. 1733. Her husband was, subsequently, *cr. a Baronet*, 9 Oct. 1772, as "of Farley, co. Southampton."

(b) Harriet, aunt of the last, and da. of the 1st Baron, *m.* 13 Feb. 1808, Sir Charles Cockerell, 1st Baronet [1809], whose s., the 2d Baronet, took by royal lic., 4 June 1849, the name of *Rushout* in lieu of that of *Cockerell*.

(c) Clay's Dugdale's Visit. of Yorkshire, 1666 [*Genealogist* N.S., vol. xvi., p. 112], based on extracts from the register by Dr. Sykes and on Hunter's *South Yorkshire*, which date of burial, however [1649], if, as stated in the Visitation, she was mother of Godfrey, aged 13 in 1666, is impossible.

Elizabeth, da. of William STANHOPE, of Linby, co. Notts. She was *bur.* at Sprotborough, 22 Sep. 1682. He was *bur.* there, 21 Feb. 1677. Admon. 6 Nov. 1684.

II. 1677, to 1709. SIR GODFREY COPLEY, Baronet [1661], of Sprotborough aforesaid, s. and h., being only child by 1st wife; said to have been aged 13 at the Heralds' Visitation of Yorkshire, 1666; admitted to Lincoln's Inn, 17 Nov. 1674; *suc. to the Baronetcy* in Feb. 1677; Sheriff of Yorkshire, 1676-77 and 1677-78; M.P. for Aldborough (three Parls.), May 1679 to 1681, and for Thirsk (seven Parls.), 1695—1709; F.R.S. 1691, and Founder of the Copley prize awarded by that Society yearly since 1731; a Commissioner of Public Accounts and Controller of the Army Accounts in 1691. He *m.* firstly (lic. fac. 16 Oct. 1681, he about 27 and she about 24), Katharine, da. and coheir of John PURCELL, of Nantriba, co. Montgomery. She was living March 1686. He *m.* secondly, about 1700, Gertrude, da. of Sir John CAREW, 3d Baronet [1641], of Antony, co. Cornwall, by his 3d wife, Mary, da. of Sir William MORICE, 1st Baronet [1661], of Werrington. He *d.* s.p.m.s.(a) of quinsy, in Red Lion Square, Midx., 9 and was *bur.* 23 April 1709 at Sprotborough, when *the Baronetcy* became *extinct.* Will dat. 14 Oct. 1704, pr. 11 April 1709. His widow (by whom he had no issue, and who was *bap.* at Antony aforesaid, 26 May 1682) *m.*, in or before 1618, Sir Coplestone Warwick BAMFYLDE, 3d Baronet [1641] of Poltimore, Devon, who *d.* 7 Oct. 1727, and *d.* his widow 14, being *bur.* 23 April 1736 at Poltimore. Will pr. 1736.

WILLIAMS:

cr. 17 June 1661;

afterwards, since 1827, WILLIAMS-BULKELEY.

I. 1661. "GRIFFITH WILLIAMS, of Penrhin [Penrhyn], co. Carnarvon, Esq.," only s. and h. of Robert WILLIAMS, of Penryallt, near Conway, by Elizabeth (*d.* 26 April 1608, *bur.* at Conway), da. of Griffith John GRIFFITH, of Cefnamwlch (which Robert, who *d.* before Feb. 1623/4, was elder br. of the well known John WILLIAMS, sometime [1621-25] when Bishop of Lincoln, Lord Keeper of the Great Seal, and afterwards [1641-50] Archbishop of York), was admitted to Lincoln's Inn, 21 Feb. 1623/4; was Sheriff of Carnarvonshire, 1650-51; a Commissioner of Assessment there in 1656, and was *cr. a Baronet* by the Lord Protector Cromwell, 28 May 1658, a dignity, which, of course, was disallowed after the Restoration in May 1660, though about a year later he was (presumably on account of the loyal services of his late uncle, Archbishop Williams, abovementioned) *cr. a Baronet*, as above, 17 June 1661, by the King. He *m.*, in or before 1627, Gwen, da. of Hugh BODWRDA, of Bodwrda, co. Carnarvon. He *d.* 1663. Will dat. 3 Sep. and pr. 3 Dec. 1663. The will of his widow (by whom he had nineteen children) pr. 1676.

(a) Catherine, his only surv. da. and h. (by 1st wife), *m.* Joseph Moyle, and left a son Joseph Moyle, who, on inheriting the Sprotborough estates in Nov. 1766, took the name of *Copley* and was *cr. a Baronet*, 28 Aug. 1778, a dignity which became *extinct*, 4 Jan. 1882, on the death of the 4th Baronet. The Sprotborough estates, however, had devolved in 1709, to the exclusion of the said Catherine, on Lionel Copley, of Wadworth, co. York, great great grandson of Christopher Copley, of the same, a younger son of Sir William Copley, of Sprotborough (who *d.* 1556), the great great grandfather of Sir Godfrey Copley, 1st Baronet [1661], as in the text. This Lionel Copley (who *d.* Feb. 1720) entailed these estates on his two sons Godfrey and Lionel, and, failing their issue, on the descendants of the said Catherine Moyle, she being the da. and h. of the person from whom he had received them. On the death s.p., 20 Nov. 1766, of Lionel Copley, last named (who on the death, in April 1761, of his elder br., Godfrey, had inherited the same) this devise took effect.

II. 1663. SIR ROBERT WILLIAMS, Baronet [1661], of Penrhyn aforesaid, 1st surv. s. and h., *b.* about 1627; was M.P. for Carnarvonshire, 1656-58, and for Carnarvon, 1659; *suc. to the Baronetcy* in 1663; Sheriff of Carnarvonshire, 1669-70. He *m.* firstly, Frances, sister (of the whole blood) to Sir William GLYNNE, 1st Baronet [1661], da. of Sir John GLYNNE, sometime [1655-60] Chief Justice of the Upper Bench, by his 1st wife, Frances, da. of Arthur SQUIB. By her he had five children. He *m.* secondly, at St. Andrew's, Holborn, 12 June 1671 (Lic. Vic. Gen., 8, he about 44, widower), Frances WHITE (then of St. Bride's, London, about 38, widow), relict of Col. WHITE, of the Fryars, co. Anglesey, da. of Sir Edward BARKHAM, 1st Baronet [1623], of Southacre, co. Norfolk, by Frances, da. of Sir Thomas BERNEY, of Redham, in that county. He *d.* in 1678. Will pr. 1681.

III. 1678. SIR JOHN WILLIAMS, Baronet [1661], of Penrhyn aforesaid, s. and h. by 1st wife; *suc. to the Baronetcy* in 1678, but *d.* a minor and unm. about 1682. Admon. 27 Feb. 1682/3 to his sister, Frances LLOYD, widow.

IV. 1682? SIR GRIFFITH WILLIAMS, Baronet [1661], of Penrhyn aforesaid, br. (of the full blood) and h.; *suc. to the Baronetcy* about 1682. He also *d.* a minor and unm.(a)

V. 1685? SIR HUGH WILLIAMS, Baronet [1661], of Marle, co. Carnarvon, uncle and h. male, being 2d surv. s. of the 1st Baronet; was admitted to Lincoln's Inn, 26 Oct. 1650; *suc. to the Baronetcy* on the death of his nephew; was Sheriff of Carnarvonshire. He *m.* Jane, da. and coheir of Henry VAUGHAN, of Pantglas, co. Carnarvon. He *d.* in or before 1706. The admon. of his widow granted 3 Feb. 1706/7, to her son Griffith, the then Baronet.

VI. 1706? SIR GRIFFITH WILLIAMS, Baronet [1661], of Marle and Pantglas aforesaid, only s. and h.; *suc. to the Baronetcy* in or before 1706; Sheriff of Carnarvonshire, Dec. 1707 to Nov. 1708. He *m.* Catherine, 1st da. and coheir of Owen ANWYL, of Penrhyn-dau-draeth and of Park, co. Merioneth. She *d.* 1726. He *d.* at Marle, July 1734. Admon. 4 Oct. 1734, and Sep. 1790.

VII. 1734. SIR ROBERT WILLIAMS, Baronet [1661], of Marle, Pantglas and Park aforesaid, only s. and h.; *suc. to the Baronetcy*, July 1734, being then a minor. He *d.* unm. Nov. 1745. Admon. 9 Jan. 1745/6 to his sister and next of kin, Anne, wife of the Rt. Hon. Sir Thomas PRENDERGAST, 2d Baronet [I. 1698](b).

(a) On his death the Penrhyn estate devolved, under his will, on his three sisters and coheirs, viz., (1), Frances, who *m.* firstly Robert Lloyd, of Esclusham, co. Denbigh, and secondly Lord Edward Russell; (2), Ann, *m.* Thomas Warburton, of Winnington, co. Chester, and (3), Gwen, who *m.* Sir Walter Yonge, 3d Baronet [1661]. Of these coheirs, Lady Edward Russell *d.* s.p.s., so that Anne Susanna Warburton (da. and h. of Lieut.-Gen. Hugh Warburton, s. and h. of Thomas Warburton and Ann his wife, abovenamed) possessed a moiety of the whole. She *m.*, 6 Dec. 1765, Richard Pennant, *cr.*, 19 Nov. 1783, Baron Penrhyn, co. Louth [I.], whose father, John Pennant, had purchased the other moiety from Sir George Yonge, 5th Baronet [1661], grandson and h. of Sir Walter Yonge and Gwen his wife, abovenamed. Thus the whole of the valuable estate of Penrhyn came into the possession of the Pennant family. [See Playfair's *Baronetage.*]

(b) This Anne, who was "at one time Maid of Honour to Queen Caroline, *m.*, 11 Jan. 1739, the Rt. Hon. Sir Thomas Prendergast, Baronet, Postmaster-Gen. of Ireland, who *d.* s.p. 23 Sep. 1760. She *m.* secondly, his distant kinsman, Captain Terence -Prendergast, whereupon they assumed the surname of Williams, in addition to that of Prendergast. Shortly afterwards they were separated by a Deed, dated 28 Dec. 1762. She, the greatest heiress in Wales, *d.* s.p. in the greatest poverty, in Dec. 1770, at Nant Gwilym, parish of Bodfari, near Denbigh, and was *bur.* in the family vault at Eglwys Rhos, co. Carnarvon. Her husband *d.* at Marle and was *bur.* at Eglwys Rhos aforesaid, 30 Oct. 1776." [*Ex inform.*, H. R. Hughes, of Kinmel.]

VIII. 1745. SIR HUGH WILLIAMS, Baronet [1661], of Nant, co. Carnarvon, and Caerau, co. Anglesey, cousin and h. male, being s. and h. of Griffith WILLIAMS, of Ariannws in that county, by Margaret, da. of Robert WILLIAMS, of Roe, which Griffith was s. and h. of Edmund WILLIAMS, of Ariannws aforesaid (by Mary, da. of William WOOD, of Dalyllyn, co. Anglesey), the 3d surv. s. of the 1st Baronet. He was *b.* about 1718, and *suc. to the Baronetcy* Nov. 1745; was M.P. for Beaumaris, 1768-80, and was a Lieut.-Col. in the Army (53d Foot), 1761. He *m.* 28 June 1760, at St. Geo., Han. sq., Emma, Dow. VISCOUNTESS BULKELEY OF CASHEL [I.], da. and h. of Thomas ROWLANDS, of Nant and Caerau aforesaid. She *d.* 13 Aug. 1770, at Baron hill, co. Anglesey, and was *bur.* at Llanfairynghornwy in that county. He *d.* 19 Aug. 1794, aged 76. Will pr. March 1795.

IX. 1794. SIR ROBERT WILLIAMS, Baronet [1661], of Nant and Caerau aforesaid, 1st s. and h., *b.* 20 July 1764; was sometime in the 1st Regiment of (Grenadier) Guards, and was present, 1793, at the siege of Valenciennes; *suc. to the Baronetcy*, 19 Aug. 1794; was M.P. (seventeen Parls.) for Carnarvonshire, 1790-1826, and for Beaumaris, 1826 till death in 1830. He *m.* 11 June 1799, in the drawing room of her father's house, Anne, sister of William LEWIS, 1st BARON DINORBEN, 2d da. of the Rev. Edward HUGHES, of Kinmel Park, co. Denbigh, by Mary, da. and coheir of Robert LEWIS, of Llysdulas, co. Anglesey. He *d.* 1 Dec. 1830, at Nice, aged 66, and was *bur.* at Llanfairynghornwy, co. Anglesey. Will pr. July 1831. His widow, who was *b.* 26 Oct. 1775, *d.* 11 Sep. 1837, and was *bur.* at Llanfairynghornwy aforesaid.

X. 1830. SIR RICHARD BULKELEY WILLIAMS-BULKELEY, Baronet [1661], of Baron hill, co. Anglesey and of Nant and Caerau aforesaid, 1st s. and h., *b.* 23 Sep. 1801, in St. Marylebone, Midx.; matric. at Oxford (Ch. Ch.), 24 Nov. 1820, aged 19; suc. to the Baron hill and other Bulkeley estates in co. Anglesey, on the death, 23 Feb. 1826, of the widow of Thomas James (WARREN-BULKELEY), 7th and last VISCOUNT BULKELEY OF CASHEL [I.], who was uterine brother to his father, and who *d.* s.p. 3 June 1822, aged 69. He, in consequence, took by royal lic., 3 June 1826, the name of *Bulkeley* after that of *Williams.* He *suc. to the Baronetcy*, 1 Dec. 1830; was M.P. for Beaumaris, Feb. 1831 to 1833; for Anglesey, 1832-37; for Flint boroughs, 1841-47, and for Anglesey (again), 1847-68; was L. Lieut. of Carnarvonshire, 1851-66; Sheriff of Anglesey, 1870. He *m.* firstly, 27 May 1828, at St. Geo., Han. sq., Charlotte Mary, 1st da. of his maternal uncle, William Lewis (HUGHES), 1st BARON DINORBEN, by his 1st wife, Charlotte Margaret, da. of Ralph William GREY, of Backworth, co. Northumberland. She, who was *b.* 23 June 1805, *d.* s.p. 11 May 1829, at her father's house in South Audley street. He *m.* secondly, 30 Aug. 1832, at St. Geo. Han. sq. (the marriage having previously been performed by a Roman Catholic Priest), Maria Frances, only da. of Sir Thomas STANLEY-MASSEY-STANLEY, 9th Baronet [1661], by Mary, da. and h. of Sir Carnaby HAGGERSTON, 5th Baronet [1642]. He, who was well known in the sporting world, *d.* 28 Aug. 1875, at Baron hill aforesaid, in his 74th year. His widow *d.* 4 March 1889, at Pelling place, Old Windsor. Will pr. 13 May 1889.

XI. 1875. SIR RICHARD MOSTYN LEWIS WILLIAMS-BULKELEY, Baronet [1661], of Baron hill aforesaid, 1st s. and h., by 2d wife; *b.* 20 May 1833, in Arlington street, Midx.; ed. at Eton; sometime, 1857-65, Capt. Royal Horse Guards; Constable of Conway Castle, 1874; *suc. to the Baronetcy*, 28 Aug. 1875; Sheriff of Anglesey, 1877. He *m.* firstly, 18 May 1857, at the British Embassy, Paris, Mary Emily, 1st da. of Henry Bingham BARING, sometime M.P. for Marlborough, by Augusta, da. of Robert (BRUDENELL), 6th EARL OF CARDIGAN. She was divorced in Nov. 1864.(a) He *m.* secondly, 12 Aug. 1866, Margaret Elizabeth, 1st da. of Lieut.-Col. Peers WILLIAMS, of Temple

---

(a) She *m.*, 27 July 1867, John Oakley Maund, Lieut., R.M.A.

House, in Great Marlow, and of Craig-y-don, co. Anglesey, by Emily, da. of Anthony BACON, of Elcott, Berks. He *d.* 28 Jan. 1884, at Baron hill aforesaid, aged 50. Will pr. June 1884, over £77,000. His widow living 1903.

XII. 1884. SIR RICHARD HENRY WILLIAMS-BULKELEY, Baronet [1661], of Baron hill aforesaid, only s. and h., by 1st wife; *b.* 4 Dec. 1862, in Eaton square, Midx.; *suc. to the Baronetcy*, 28 Jan. 1884; was Mayor of Beaumaris, 1885-87, 1889-90 and 1892-93; Sheriff of Anglesey, 1887; L. Lieut. of that County; Lieut.-Col. Royal Anglesey Engineers. He *m.*, 10 Dec. 1885, at the Savoy Chapel, Midx., Magdalen, 2d and yst. da. of Charles Philip (YORKE), 5th EARL OF HARDWICKE, by Sophie Georgiana Robertine, da. of Henry Richard Charles (WELLESLEY), 1st EARL COWLEY.

Family Estates.—These, in 1883, consisted of 16,516 acres in Anglesea (worth £17,997 a year) and 13,362 in Carnarvonshire (worth but £3,141 a year). *Total.*—29,878 acres, worth £21,138 a year. *Chief Seat.*—Baron hill, near Beaumaris, co. Anglesey.

WINCHCOMBE, *or* WINCHECUMBE:

cr. 18 June 1661;

ex. 5 Nov. 1703.

I. 1661. "HENRY WINCHECUMBE [*rectius* WINCHCOMBE], of Buckdebury [*i.e.*, Bucklebury in Reading Hundred], co. Berks, Esq.," s. and h. of Henry WINCHCOMBE,(a) of the same, by Elizabeth, da. of George MILLER, of Swallowfield, Berks, was *b.* probably about 1631; suc. his father in April 1642, and was *cr. a Baronet*, as above, 18 June 1661. He recorded his pedigree in the Heralds' Visit. of Berks, 1665. He *m.* in or before 1659, Frances, da. and h. of Thomas (HOWARD) 3d EARL OF BERKSHIRE, by his 1st wife Frances, da. of Sir Richard HARRISON, of Hurst, Berks. He *d.* 2, and was *bur.* 19 Dec. 1667, at Bucklebury, aged [36?]. M.I. Admon. 21 April 1668. His widow *d.* 22, and was *bur.* there 27 Dec. 1707, aged 66. M.I. Will pr. Dec. 1707.

II. 1667, to 1703. SIR HENRY WINCHCOMBE, Baronet [1661], of Bucklebury aforesaid, s. and h., *b.* 16 June 1659; aged 5 at the Heralds' Visit. of Berks., 1665; *suc. to the Baronetcy*, 2 Dec. 1667; was M.P. for Berks, 1689-90, and 1690-95. He *m.* firstly, in or before 1680, Elizabeth, da. of (—) HUNGERFORD. She *d.* 5 Aug. 1685, and was *bur.* at Bucklebury. M.I. He *m.* secondly, Elizabeth, da. of (—) ROLLE. He *d.* s.p.m.,(b) 5 and was *bur.* 16 Nov. 1703, at Bucklebury, when the *Baronetcy* became *extinct.* M.I. Will pr. Feb. 1704. His widow *m.* in 1710, Thomas SKERRAT.

(a) This Henry was s. and h. of another Henry Winchcombe, Lord of the Manors of Thatcham and Bucklebury, whose burial, in April 1629, is recorded in the register of both these parishes. In Thatcham are several baptisms, from 1578 to 1608, of children of John Winchcombe, the younger, as also the burial, 3 June 1610, of "John Winchcombe, the elder, Gent."

(b) He had one da., Henrietta, by his 2d wife, and three daughters by the 1st, of which the 2d da., Elizabeth, *d.* unm. 7 Sep. 1705, aged 23, and was *bur.* at Bucklebury. M.I. The 1st da., Frances, *m.* 22 May 1701, at St. Dunstan's-in-the-East, London (as his 1st wife), Henry (St. John), 1st Viscount Bolingbroke (the well known statesman), and *d.* s.p. 24 Oct. 1718, aged 38, being *bur.* at Bucklebury. M.I. The 3d da., Mary, *m.* Robert Packer, of Shillingford, Berks, whose issue inherited the Bucklebury estate, and transmitted it to the family of Hartley.

CLERKE, *or* CLARKE:

cr. 18 June 1661;

ex. 10 July 1759.

I. 1661. "CLEMENT CLARKE, of Laude [*i.e.*, Launde] Abbey, co. Leicester, Esq.," 3d s. of Sir George CLARKE, or CLERKE, of Watford, co. Northampton, Alderman and sometime, 1641-42, Sheriff of London (who *d.* 30 Jan. 1648/9), by Barbara, da. of Robert PALMER, of Hill, Beds. was made Gent. of the Privy Chamber in 1661, and was *cr. a Baronet*, as above, 18 June 1661. He *m.* Sarah, often called Catharine, da. and h. of George TALBOT, of Ridge, Salop. She is *bur.* (as "Sarah") 13 Nov. 1693, in Westm. Abbey, and he is *bur.* there 1C Dec. following.

II. 1693. SIR TALBOT CLERKE, *or* CLARKE, Baronet [1661], of Launde Abbey aforesaid, s. and h., *suc. to the Baronetcy* in Dec. 1693. He *m.*, 17 March 1688/9, at the Savoy chapel, Midx., Hannah TILECOTE. He, who was sometime of St. Martin's-in-the-Fields, Midx., d. at Mitcham, Surrey, in or shortly before 1708. Admon. 19 April 1708, to a creditor. His widow living April 1708.

III. 1708? SIR CLEMENT CLERKE, *or* CLARKE, Baronet [1661], of Launde aforesaid, 1st s. and h., *suc. to the Baronetcy* in or shortly before 1708. He *d.* unm. at Durrant Hall, in Chesterfield, co. Derby, in or shortly before 1715. Admon. 17 June 1715.

IV. 1715? SIR TALBOT CLERKE, *or* CLARKE, Baronet [1661], of Launde Abbey aforesaid, br. and h.; *suc. to the Baronetcy* in or shortly before 1715. He *m.*, in or before 1719, Barbara, da. and coheir of Thomas GLADIN, of Durrant Hall aforesaid, where he *d.* 16 Feb. 1723/4. Admon. 13 Dec. 1725 to his relict "Dame Barbara CLARKE, now wife of John Moncke MORGAN, Esq., of Monmouthshire."

V. 1724. SIR TALBOT CLERKE *or* CLARKE, Baronet [1661], of Launde Abbey aforesaid, only s. and h., *b.* about 1719; *suc. to the Baronetcy* in his infancy, 16 Feb. 1723/4. He *d.* while at Westm. School, 21, and was *bur.* 25 Nov. 1732, at Westm. Abbey, aged about 13.

VI. 1732, to 1759. SIR TALBOT CLERKE, *or* CLARKE, Baronet [1661], cousin and h. male, being only s. and h. of George CLERKE, *or* CLARKE, by Dorothy, da. of [—] PEARSE, of Oakfield, Berks, which George was 3d s. of the 1st Baronet. He *suc. to the Baronetcy*, 21 Nov. 1732. He *m.* Lucy, da. of the Rev. [—] ROGERS, of Painswick, co. Gloucester. He *d.* s.p.,(a) 10 July 1759, when *the Baronetcy* became *extinct*. Will pr. 1759.

VYNER, *or* VINER:

cr. 18 June 1661;

ex. May 1683.

I. 1661. "THOMAS VINER [late], Alderman of London," yst. s. of Thomas VINER, *or* VYNER, of North Cerney, co. Glouc., by his 2d wife, Anne, da. of Daniel ELLYS, was *bap.* there 15 Dec. 1588; became free of the Goldsmiths' Company; entered his pedigree in the Heralds' Visit. of London, 1634; was Alderman of Billingsgate, 1646-51, and of Langbourne, 1651 till discharged in 1660, having been Sheriff of London, 1648-49 (being sometimes said to have been present as Sheriff at the execution of Charles I.), and Lord Mayor, 1653-54, being *Knighted*, as such, by the Lord Protector Cromwell, at Grocers' Hall, 8 Feb. 1653/54. After the Restoration he was again *Knighted*,

(a) Dorothy, his sister, *m.* Philip Jennings, of Duddleston, Salop, and was ancestress of Philip Jennings Clerke, of Duddleston, *cr. a Baronet*, 26 Oct. 1774; a dignity which became *extinct*, 22 April 1788.

1 Aug. 1660, at Whitehall, by the King, and was *cr. a Baronet*, as above, 18 June 1661. He *m.* firstly, in or before 1630, Anne, da. of Richard PARSONS, of London, merchant. She *d.* s.p.m., and was *bur.* 7 Oct. 1636, at St. Mary's, Wolnoth, London. He *m.* secondly, in or before 1639, Honor, sister of Sir William HUMBLE, 1st Baronet [1660], da. of George HUMBLE, Citizen and Stationer of London, by Agnes, da. of John MOODY. She *d.* 26 June and was *bur.* 10 July 1656, at St. Mary's, Wolnoth, aforesaid. He *m.* thirdly (settlmt. 25 May 1668), Alice, widow of John PERRIN, Alderman of London, da. of [—] ROBINSON. He, who resided at Hackney, Midx., *d.* at "the Black and White House," near the Church there, 11 May and was *bur.* 1 June 1665, at St. Mary's, Wolnoth aforesaid, aged 77.(a) M.I. Will dat. 16 March 1664, pr. 19 May 1665. His widow, by whom he had no issue, was *bur.* (with her 1st husband) at East Acton, Midx. Will dat. 24 Feb. 1676/7, pr. 9 June 1682.

II. 1665. SIR GEORGE VYNER, Baronet [1661], of Hackney aforesaid, s. and h. by 2d wife, *b.* about 1639; *Knighted*, v.p., at Whitehall, 24 June 1663; admitted to Lincoln's Inn, 24 April 1656, and, subsequently, 29 April 1659, to Gray's Inn; *suc. to the Baronetcy*, 11 May 1665. He *m.* 18 Aug. 1663, at St. Alphage's, London (Lic. Fac. 15, he above 24, and she about 18), Abigail, da. of Sir John LAWRENCE, of Putney, co. Surrey, Alderman and sometime [1664-65], Lord Mayor of London, by his 1st wife, Abigail, sister to Sir Abraham CULLEN, 1st Baronet [1661], da. of Abraham CULLEN, Merchant, of London. She was *bap.* 15 June 1643, at St. Helen's, Bishopsgate, and was "of great beauty." He *d.* at Hackney, 5 and his widow *d.* 24 July 1673, both being *bur.* on 18 Aug. (their wedding day), at St. Mary's, Wolnoth aforesaid. His admon. 21 July 1673, 29 Aug. following, 20 Sep. 1686, and 7 March 1705/6.

III. 1673, to 1683. SIR THOMAS VYNER, Baronet [1661], of Hackney aforesaid, only surv. s. and h.; *bap.* there 21 June 1664; *suc. to the Baronetcy*, 5 July 1673. He *d.* a minor and unm., and was *bur.* 3 May 1683, with his maternal grandmother, Dame Abigail Laurence (who *d.* June 1681), in the Tryon vault at St. Helen's, in Bishopsgate, when the *Baronetcy* became *extinct*. Will dat. 29 July 1681, pr. 28 April 1683 by Charles CHAMBERLAINE, exor. and residuary legatee.(b)

SEYLIARD, SYLYARD, *or* SULIARD:

cr. 18 June 1661;

ex. Sep. 1701.

I. 1661. "JOHN SYLYARD, of Delawarre [in Brasted], co. Kent, Esq.," as also of Chiddingstone in that county, 1st s. and h. of Thomas SEYLIARD,(c) of the same, by Elizabeth, da. of Francis BEAUMONT, of Grace Dieu, co. Leicester, one of the Justices of the Court of Common Pleas, was *b.* about 1613, being aged 7 at the Heralds' Visit. of Kent

(a) There is a good three-quarter portrait of him in his robes as Lord Mayor at the Goldsmiths' hall; of which a copy, greatly inferior, is at Christ's Hospital, Newgate street.

(b) His coheirs were apparently the daughters of the 1st Baronet by the 1st wife, or their issue, viz.: (1) Mary, who *m.* 3 Jan. 1644/5, at Hackney (as his 1st wife), Sir Richard Napier, of Great Linford, Bucks, and *d.* before 1649, leaving issue; (2) Elizabeth, who *m.*, 19 July 1647, at Hackney, Sir Henry Pickering, 1st Baronet [1661] of Whaddon; and (3) Rebecca, who *m.*, 22 April 1652, at Hackney, Sir Richard Pigot, of London.

(c) See an extensive pedigree of the family, down to the date of 1597, in *Mis. Gen. et Her.*, 2d Series, vol. i, pp. 7-20, and see also Howard and Hovenden's *Pedigrees in the Visit. of Kent, 1663-68*, pp. 62-91.

in 1620; was admitted to the Inner Temple (as "John Sulyard, of Brasted, Kent"), Nov. 1633; suc. his father, Feb. 1649/50; was M.P. for Kent, 1654-59, and was *cr. a Baronet*, as above, 18 June 1661. He *m.*, in or before 1648, Mary, da. of (—) GLOVER. He was *bur.* 19 Dec. 1667, at Edenbridge, co. Kent. Will dat. 10 Dec. 1667, pr. 2 March 1667/8. His widow was *bur.* there 25 Oct. 1685.

II. 1667. SIR THOMAS SEYLIARD, *or* SULIARD, Baronet [1661], of Delawarre and Chiddingstone aforesaid, s. and h., *b.* about 1648; *suc. to the Baronetcy* in Dec. 1667. He *m.* firstly (Lic. Vic. Gen. 2 Dec. 1670, he above 21 and she about 19), Frances, da. and h. of Henry WYATT, of Boxley Abbey, Kent (then deceased), by Jane, da. of Sir Edward DUKE, of Copington in that county, which Henry was 1st s. of Sir Francis WYATT, of Boxley aforesaid. She was *bur.* 12 June 1686, at Edenbridge. He *m.* secondly, in or before 1690, Margaret, widow of Major DUNCH, of Pusey, Berks (*d.* 27 Sep. 1679, aged 28), da. of Philip (WHARTON), 4th BARON WHARTON, by his 2d wife, Jane, da. and h. of Arthur GOODWIN. He was *bur.* 4 May 1692, at Edenbridge. Will dat. 13 June 1689, pr. 12 May 1692. His widow *m.* William Ross.

III. 1692. SIR THOMAS SEYLIARD, Baronet [1661], of Delawarre and Boxley aforesaid, s. and h. by first wife; *b.* at Boxley about 1673; matric. at Oxford (Trin. Coll.), 7 June 1689, aged 16; *suc. to the Baronetcy* in May 1692; sold the estate of Delawarre about 1700. He *m.* in or before 1696, Elizabeth, da. and h. of Sir Sandys FORTESCUE, 2d Baronet [1664], of Fallapit, co. Devon, by Elizabeth (*m.* May 1680), da. of Sir John LENTHALL. He was *bur.* 11 Jan. 1700/1, at Edenbridge. His widow was *bur.* 28 Dec. 1732, at Boxley.

IV. 1701, Jan. to Sep. SIR JOHN SEYLIARD, Baronet [1661], of Boxley aforesaid, only s. and h., *bap.* 25 July 1700, at Boxley; *suc. to the Baronetcy* in Jan. 1700/1, but *d.* in infancy the same year, and was *bur.* at Boxley, 23 Sep. 1701, when the *Baronetcy* became *extinct*.

GUISE:

cr. 10 July 1661;

ex. 6 April 1783.

I. 1661. "CHRISTOPHER GUISE, of Elsmore [*i.e.*, Elmore], co. Gloucester, Esq.," as also of Brockworth and Rendcombe in that county, 1st s. and h. of William GUISE, of the same, Sheriff of Gloucestershire, 1647, and M.P. thereof, 1654-55 (the s. and h. of Sir William GUISE, who *d.* 19 Sep. 1642), by Cecilia (*m.* 20 Feb. 1616/7), da. of John DENNIS, of Pucklechurch, was *b.* about 1620, suc. his father 26 Aug. 1653 and was *cr. a Baronet*, as above, 10 July 1661. He *m.* firstly, Elizabeth, da. of Sir Laurence WASHINGTON, of Garsdon, Wilts. She *d.* s.p. He *m.* secondly, in or before 1654, Rachel, da. of Nicholas CORSELLIS, of London, Merchant, by [—], da. of Sir Thomas CAMBELL, 1st Baronet [1664], of Clay Hall. She *d.* before him. He *d.* in 1670, aged 53, and was *bur.* at Brockworth aforesaid. M.I. Will pr. 1671.

II. 1670. SIR JOHN GUISE, Baronet [1661], of Elmore, Brockworth and Rendcombe aforesaid, only s. and h., by second wife, *b.* about 1654; matric. at Oxford (Ch. Ch.) 3 Dec. 1669, aged 15; *suc. to the Baronetcy* in 1670; was M.P. for Gloucestershire (six Parls.), 1679, till his death in 1695. He was Col. of Foot, 12 Nov. 1688, and Mayor of Gloucester, 1690. He *m.*, in or before 1678, Elizabeth, da. of John GRUBHAM-HOWE, of Compton in the Hole, co. Glouc., and of Langar, Notts, by Arabella (raised to the rank of an Earl's da., 1 June 1663), illegit. da. of Emmanuel (SCROPE) EARL OF SUNDERLAND, and

heiress of Langar aforesaid. He *d.* of the small-pox, 19 and was *bur.* 22 Nov. 1695, at Elmore. His widow was living June 1696. The will of Dame Eliz. Guise was pr. April 1704, as also Nov. 1720.

III. 1695. SIR JOHN GUISE, Baronet [1661], of Elmore and Rendcombe aforesaid, *b.* about 1678; *suc. to the Baronetcy*, 19 Nov. 1695; was M.P. for Gloucestershire (two Parls.), 1705-10, and for Great Marlow, 1722-27. He *m.* firstly (Lic. Fac. 4 June 1696, he 18 and upwards and she 22), Elizabeth, da. of Sir Nathaniel NAPIER, 2d Baronet [1641] of Critchell, Dorset, by his 1st wife Blanche, da. of Sir Hugh WYNDHAM. She *d.* in or before 1701. Admon. 11 Feb. 1700/1. He *m.* secondly (mar. lic. at Worcester, 2 Jan. 1710/1, he about 35 and she about 38), Anne, widow of Sir Henry EVERY, 3d Baronet [1641], who *d.* Sep. 1709, formerly widow of Richard LYGON, 1st da. and coheir of Sir Francis RUSSELL, 3d Baronet [1627] of Strensham, by Anne, da. of Sir Rowland LYTTON. He *d.* 16, and was *bur.* 22 Nov. 1732, at Elmore. Will pr. 1734. His widow, by whom he had no issue, *d.* 22 Feb. 1734/5.

IV. 1732. SIR JOHN GUISE, Baronet [1661], of Elmore and Rendcombe aforesaid, only s. and h. by 1st wife; *b.* about 1701; matric. at Oxford (New Coll.), 27 June 1720, aged 19; M.P. for Aylesbury, 1722-27; sometime Col. in the Guards; *suc. to the Baronetcy*, 16 Nov. 1732. He *m.*, about 1731, Jane, sister and h. of John SAUNDERS, of Mongewell, Oxon (*d.* 1731), da. of John SAUNDERS, of the same, by Anne, da. of Edmund MADOCK, of Tidenham, co. Gloucester. He *d.* in or before 1769, and was *bur.* at Rendcombe.(a) Will pr. 1769.

V. 1769? to 1783. SIR WILLIAM GUISE, Baronet [1661], of Elmore and Rendcombe aforesaid, 2d but only surv. s. and h., *bap.* 26 July 1737, at Elmore; matric. at Oxford (Queen's Coll.), 5 July 1754, aged 16; *cr.* M.A. 29 Oct. 1759, having been admitted to Lincoln's Inn, 6 June 1755; *suc. to the Baronetcy* in or before 1769; was M.P. for Gloucestershire, Aug. 1770, till his death in 1783. He *d.* unm. 6 April 1783, when the *Baronetcy* became *extinct*.(b) Will pr. 1783.

FORSTER:

cr. 11 July 1661;

ex. 11 Aug. 1705.

I. 1661. "REGINALD FORSTER, of East Greenewiche, co. Kent, Esq.," and formerly of Watling Street, co. Salop, s. and h. of John FORSTER, of Rodington, co. Salop, by Blanche, da. of Reginald WILLIAMS, of Willaston, in that county, was *b.* about 1618; admitted to the Inner Temple, Nov. 1627; Barrister, 1635; lived in Old Street, Cripplegate; was a Justice of the Peace, and was *cr. a Boronet*, as above, 11 July 1661. He is said to have expended a large fortune in the service of Charles I.; and to have once

(a) There is no memorial to him or to any of his name there, excepting so far as they are included in the following curious inscription set up in the church: "Sacred to the family of Guise, distinguished during six centuries, by hereditary worth, by active virtue and by the parliamentary confidence of the county of Gloucester."

(b) His cousin and h. male, John Guise, of Highnam, co. Gloucester (great grandson of Henry Guise, a yr. br. of the 1st Baronet), inherited the family estates after the death of the only sister of the last Baronet, Jane, who *m.*, as his 2d wife, 20 June 1770, the Hon. Shute Barrington, Bishop of Durham [1791-1820]. Her death occurred, 8 Aug. 1807, aged 74, and his 25 March 1826, aged 91. This John Guise was himself *cr. a Baronet*, 9 Dec. 1783, only eight months after the death of his cousin, the late Baronet.

"had £3,000 a year" though latterly to have had "not 3d. left."(a) He *m.* firstly, 19 April 1631, at St. Mary's, Wolnoth, London, Blandina, da. of John ACTON, of London, Goldsmith, by his 2d wife, Blandina, da. of John PENUEN, of Badgeworth, co. Somerset. "The Lady Foster, from E[ast] Lane," was *bur.* 9 Nov. 1665, at Greenwich. He had lic. to marry, 25 Jan. 1667/8 (Fac. Office), Alice HAYWARD, of St. Giles'-in-the-Fields, about 50, widow. He *m.* 24 Nov. 1668, at St. Giles', Cripplegate (Lic. Vic. Gen., 2, he about 60, widower), Anne BRIGGS, of Bow, Midx., about 45, widow. She *d.* in or before 1674. Admon. 13 May 1674, 4 June and 24 Oct. 1685. He *d.* of fever, and was *bur.* 27 June 1684, at St. Giles', Cripplegate. Will pr. 1684.

II. 1684, to 1705. SIR REGINALD FORSTER, Baronet [1641], of East Greenwich aforesaid, s. and h., by 1st wife; *b.* probably about 1640; *suc. to the Baronetcy* in June 1684; Sheriff of Warwickshire, 1688-89. He *m.* firstly, in or before 1675,(b) Mary, da. and h. of Capt. Edward NASH, of Greenwich. "Mrs. Foster" was *bur.* there, 17 June 1677. He *m.* secondly an heiress from co. Warwick, with about £600 a year.(a) He *d.* s.p.m.,(c) 11 Aug. 1705, at Greenwich, and was carried thence for burial, presumably at Stratford-on-Avon, when the *Baronetcy* became *extinct.*

PARKER:

cr. 16 July 1661;

afterwards, 1729-41, PARKER-A-MORLEY-LONG;

ex. 20 Jan. 1740/1.

I. 1661. "PHILIP PARKER, of Erwarton [co. Suffolk], Esq.," s. and h. ap. of Sir Philip PARKER, of the same, M.P. for Suffolk in the Long Parl. (*d.* 22 June 1675), by Dorothy, da. and h. of Sir Robert GAWDY, of Claxton, co. Norfolk; was *b.* about 1625; admitted to Gray's Inn, 2 Feb. 1640/1, and was *cr. a Baronet*, as above, 16 July 1661. He suc. his father 22 June 1675; was M.P. for Harwich, 1679-81, and for Sandwich, 1685-87. He *m.* firstly, about 1640, Rebecca, sister (whose issue became heir, 21 May 1711) of Sir Walter LONG, 2d Baronet [1661], only da. of Sir Walter LONG, 1st Baronet [1661], of Whaddon, co. Wilts, by his 1st wife, Mary, da. of Joseph COCKS. By her he had six children. He *m.* secondly, 7 Nov. 1661, at St. Martin's-in-the-Fields (Lic. Vic. Gen. 4, he about 36, widower), Hannah, widow of Thomas BEDINGFELD, of Darsham, d. and h. of Philip BACON, of Wolverston, by Anne, da. of Robert BROKE, of Nacton, all in co. Suffolk. He *d.* about 1690. Will pr. March 1690.

II. 1690? SIR PHILIP PARKER, Baronet [1661], of Erwarton aforesaid, 1st s. and h., by 1st wife, *b.* about 1650; *suc. to the Baronetcy* on the death of his father. He *m.*, 13 March 1680/1, at St. Barth.-the-Less, London (Lic. Fac., 12, he 30 and she 28), Mary, da. of Samuel FORTREY, of Kew, co. Surrey, of the Tower of London, and of Byall Fenn, co. Cambridge, by Theodora, da. of Torrell JOSCELINE, of Torrell's Hall, co. Essex. He *d.* in or before 1698. Will pr. July 1700.

III. 1698? to 1741. SIR PHILIP PARKER, *afterwards* PARKER-A-MORLEY-LONG, Baronet [1661], of Erwarton aforesaid, only s. and h., *b.* 23 March 1681/2, in London; *suc. to the Baronetcy* on the death of his father, and matric. at Oxford (Corpus Ch. Coll.), 5 Nov. 1698, aged 16, as a Baronet; was M.P. for Harwich (three Parls.), 1715-34. He, on the death, s.p., in May 1729, of his uncle, Calthorpe LONG, *formerly* PARKER, of Whaddon, co. Wilts, inherited that estate under the will of Sir Walter LONG, 2d Baronet [1661], of Whaddon, and assumed the surname of

(a) Le Neve's MS. *Baronetage.*

(b) "Edward Foster, Capt. Nash's grandchild," was *bur.* 11 April 1675, at Greenwich. "Capt. Edward Nash, Esq.," was *bur.* there 28 March 1679.

(c) Jane, da. and h., by his 1st wife, *m.* Franclyn Miller, and had four children living in 1696, of whom one, Jane, *m.* William Norcliffe, of the Temple, London.

PARKER-A-MORLEY(a)-LONG instead of that of PARKER. He *m.*, 11 July 1715, at St. Martin's-in-the-Fields, Martha, da. of William EAST, of the Middle Temple, London. He *d.* s.p.m. 20 Jan. 1740/1, when the *Baronetcy* became *extinct.*(b) Will pr. 1741. The will of his widow pr. 1755.

DUKE:

cr. 16 July 1661;

ex. 25 Aug. 1732.

I. 1661. "SIR EDWARD DUKE, of Denhall [*i.e.*, Benhall], co. Suffolk, Knt.," as also of Brampton and Worlingham, in that county, s. and h. of Ambrose DUKE, of the same (*d.* 1610), by Elizabeth, da. and coheir of Bartholomew CALTHORPE, of co. Suffolk, was *b.* about 1604; admitted to Gray's Inn, 25 Nov. 1622; was Sheriff of Suffolk, 1637-38; M.P. for Orford, April to May 1640; was *Knighted*, at Whitehall, 4 July 1641, and was *cr. a Baronet*, as above, 16 July 1661. He *m.*, in or after 1618 (when she was aged 18 and unm.), Ellenor, yst. da. of John PANTON, of Brunslip, co. Denbigh (*bur.* 13 March 1618/9, in Westm. Abbey), by Eleanor, da. of Sir William BOOTH, of Dunham Massey. By her he had twenty-nine children. He *d.* 1671, aged 67. Will pr. June 1671.

II. 1671. SIR JOHN DUKE, Baronet [1661], of Benhall, etc., aforesaid, 1st surv. s. and h.; *suc. to the Baronetcy* in 1671; was M.P. for Orford, 1679-90, and March 1697 to 1698. He *m.*, in or before 1694, Elizabeth, da. of his distant cousin, Edward DUKE, M.D., Hon. Fellow of the College of Physicians, by Elizabeth, da. of Robert TOLLEMACHE, of Helmingham, Suffolk. He *d.* 1705. Will pr. Nov. 1705 and Jan. 1705/6. The will of Dame Elizabeth DUKE, pr. 1725.

III. 1705, to 1732. SIR EDWARD DUKE, Baronet [1661], of Benhall, etc., aforesaid, only s. and h., *b.* about 1694; *suc. to the Baronetcy* in 1705. He was M.P. for Orford, Dec. 1721 to March 1722. He *m.* 1 Dec. 1715, at Kensington (Lic. Lond. 28 Nov. he 21), Mary (then aged 17), da. of Thomas RUDGE, of Staffordshire, and of Bromley-by-Bow, co. Midx., by Mary, his wife. He *d.* s.p.m.s., 25 Aug. 1732, when the *Baronetcy* became *extinct.* Will dat. 9 to 15 Aug., and pr. 23 Oct. 1732. The will of his widow, as "of Sackville street," Midx., dat. 27 Dec. 1741, pr. 16 March 1741/2.

HUSSEY:

cr. 21 July 1661;

merged 19 Dec. 1706:

ex. 14 Feb. 1729/30, *or*, possibly 1 April 1734.

I. 1661. "CHARLES HUSSEY, of Caythorpe, co. Lincoln, Esq.," 3d s. of Sir Edward HUSSEY, 1st Baronet [1611], of Honington, in that county, by Elizabeth, da. of George ANTON, sometime M.P. for Lincoln, was

(a) The name of Morley was to shew his descent from the Lords Morley, whose heiress *m.* Sir Henry Parker, sum. as Lord Morley, 1523-55, their eldest grandson being ancestor of the succeeding Lords, and their youngest grandson being Sir Philip Parker, of Erwarton (whose mother, Elizabeth Calthorpe, was heiress of the Erwarton estate), the great grandfather of the 1st Baronet.

(b) The Whaddon estate passed, on his death, to Thomas Long, of Rowdon, but the Suffolk estates devolved on his daughters, both of whom, however (Martha, Baroness Chedworth, who *d.* 30 Nov. 1775, and Elizabeth, wife of James Plunkett), *d.* s.p., when the representation of the family vested in the children of his two aunts, of whom the eldest was Catherine, Countess of Egmont [I.].

bap. 30 Oct. 1626, at Honington; admitted to Gray's Inn, 31 Oct. 1646; was M.P. for Lincolnshire, 1656-58 and 1661 till his death in 1664, and was *cr. a Baronet*, as above, 21 July 1661. He was one of the Gentlemen of the Privy Chamber to Charles II. He *m.* (Lic. Fac. 10 April 1649, he of Somerton, co. Lincoln, "Esq.," about 22, and she about 17) Elizabeth, 1st da. of Sir William BROWNLOW, 1st Baronet [1641] of Humby, co. Lincoln, by Elizabeth, da. and coheir of William DUNCOMBE. He *d.* in London, 11 Dec. 1664, in his 39th year. Will dat. 3 Dec. 1664, pr. 1664. His widow, who was *b.* 9 Dec. 1630, *d.* also in London, 25 Dec. 1698. Both were *bur.* at Caythorpe. M.I.

II. 1664. SIR CHARLES HUSSEY, Baronet [1661], of Caythorpe aforesaid, s. and h., *suc. to the Baronetcy*, when under age, 11 Dec. 1664. He *d.* unm. in or shortly before 1680. Admon. 22 May 1680, to his mother.

III. 1680? SIR EDWARD HUSSEY, Baronet [1661], of Caythorpe aforesaid, br. and h.; *suc. to the Baronetcy* conferred, as above, in or shortly before 1680. He was M.P. for Lincoln, 1689-95 and 1698-1705. Having already been a Baronet for about 26 years, he, on the death, 19 Dec. 1706, of his cousin, Sir Thomas HUSSEY, 2d Baronet [1611], *suc. to the* (more ancient) *Baronetcy*, conferred 29 June 1611 on his grandfather, in which dignity this *Baronetage* of 1661 then *merged*, and so continued till both became *extinct*, probably 14 Feb. 1729/30, but possibly 1 April 1734. See vol. i, p. 61.

BARKHAM:

cr. 21 July 1661;

ex. 13 Feb. 1710/1.

I. 1661. "EDWARD BARKHAM, of Waynflete, co Lincoln, Esq.," s. and h. of Sir Robert BARKHAM, of Wainflete St. Mary aforesaid and of Tottenham, co. Midx., by Mary, da. of Richard WILCOX, of London, which Robert (who *d.* 27 Feb. 1660/1, aged 62) was a yr. br. of Sir Edward BARKHAM, 1st Baronet [1623], both being sons of Sir Edward BARKHAM, sometime, 1621-22, Lord Mayor of London, was *b.* 20 and *bap.* 24 March 1630/1, at St. Barth. the Great, London, and was *cr. a Baronet*, as above, 21 July 1661. He was Sheriff of Lincolnshire, 1664-65. He *m.* (banns pub. at Tottenham, Sep. 1656), Anne, da. and h. of Sir Robert LEE, of Billesley, co. Warwick, by Frances, da. of Sir William COPE, 2d Baronet [1611]. He *d.* 14 Sep. 1669, and was *bur.* at Wainflete.(a) His widow *m.* (Lic. Vic. Gen. 21 Dec. 1671, she described therein as "Mrs. Anne BARKHAM, of Sharsted, co. Kent, widow, about 28") John HODGES, of the Inner Temple (then about 30 and unm.), Recorder of Ipswich. She was living 1682.

II. 1669. SIR ROBERT BARKHAM, Baronet [1661], of Wainfleet aforesaid, s. and h., *suc. to the Baronetcy*, 14 Sep. 1669, being then under age. He *m.* 20 May 1679, at Westm. Abbey, Hester, da. of Thomas JEFFREY, of Wigtoft, co. Lincoln, and Earlscombe, co. Worcester. She *d.* 1 May 1691. He *d.* in or before 1701. Admon. 23 June 1701.

III. 1701? to 1711. SIR EDWARD BARKHAM, Baronet [1661], of Wainfleet aforesaid, 1st s. and h., *b.* about 1680; matric. at Oxford (Bras. Coll), 14 Dec. 1695, aged 15; *suc. to the Baronetcy* in or before 1701. He *m.* 11 March 1704/5, at Louth, co. Lincoln, Mary, da. and coheir of John WOLLEY, of Alford in that county, by Anne, da. and coheir of John BOSWELL, of South Thoresby. She was *bur.* 19 Dec. 1709, at South Thoresby. He d. s.p., in London, 13, and was *bur.* 15 Feb. 1710/1, at Tottenham, when the *Baronetcy* became *extinct.* Will dat. 19 Jan. 1709 [1709/10], pr. June 1711.

(a) In Sir Joseph Williamson's *Lincolnshire Families, temp. Car. II.*, his estate is reckoned at £1,600 a year, and he himself is spoken of as "a drinker" [*Her. and Gen.*, vol. ii, p. 120].

NORTON:

cr. 23 July 1661;

ex. 1691.

I. 1661, to 1691. "THOMAS NORTON, of the city of Coventry, co. Warwick, Esq.," yr. br. of John NORTON, of Allesley in that county, being 5th but the 1st s. that had issue of Simon NORTON, of Coventry (*d.* 1641), by Prudence, da. of (—) JESSON, of Coventry, was *b.* about 1616, and was *cr. a Baronet*, as above, 23 July 1661. He was aged 67 in 1683.(a) He *m.* Anne, da. of John JERMY, of Stutton Hall, co. Suffolk. He *d.* s.p.m., 1691, when the *Baronetcy* became *extinct.* Will pr. Nov. 1691. The will of his widow, dat. 23 Oct. 1691, pr. 7 Feb. 1693/4.

DORMER:

cr. 23 July 1661;

ex. 9 March 1725/6.

I. 1661. "JOHN DORMER, of the Grange [*i.e.*, Lee Grange in Quainton], co. Buckingham, Esq." [*rectius* "Knight"], as also of Purston, co. Northampton, 1st s. and h. ap. of John DORMER, of the same, Barrister-at-law (*d.* 22 May 1679, aged 68), by Katharine, da. and h. of Thomas WOODWARD, of Ripple, co. Worcester, was *b.* about 1640; matric. at Oxford (Ch. Ch.), 23 July 1656, being *cr.* M.A. 28 Sep. 1663; admitted to Linc. Inn, 26 May 1658; *Knighted* 10, and was *cr. a Baronet*, as above, 23 July 1661. He *m.* (Lic. Vic. Gen. 9 Aug. 1662, he about 22 and she about 18, with consent of her mother), Susanna, da. and coheir of Sir Richard BRAWNE, of Allscott in Preston on Avon, co. Gloucester, by Theodosia, his wife. She *d.* at Richmond, co. Surrey, 24 Feb., and was *bur.* 13 March 1672/3, at Quainton, aged 35. He *d.* at Leghorn, in Italy, 7 Nov. 1675, and was *bur.* 23 Feb. 1675/6, at Quainton. M.I.

II. 1675, to 1726. SIR WILLIAM DORMER, Baronet [1661], of Lee Grange and Purston aforesaid, 2d but only surv. s. and h., *bap.* 28 Sep. 1669; *suc. to the Baronetcy*, 7 Nov. 1675; matric. at Oxford (Trin. Coll.), 23 April 1686, aged 16. He *d.* insane, and unm., 9 March 1725/6, and was *bur.* at Quainton, aged 57, when the *Baronetcy* became *extinct.* M.I. Admon. 13 May 1726, to "Dormer Sheldon, Esq.," nephew by the sister, and next-of-kin.(c)

CAREW:

cr. 2 Aug. 1661.

I. 1661. "THOMAS CAREW, of Haccombe, co. Devon, Esq.," 1st s. and h. of Thomas CAREW,(d) of the same (aged 19 at the Heralds' Visit. of Devon, 1620), by Anna, da. of the Rev. John CLIFFORD, D.D., of Ugbrook, was *bap.* 21 June 1632, at Chudleigh; admitted to Middle Temple, 1649; matric. at Oxford (Exeter Coll.), 12 Nov. 1650; was, presumably, B.A., 11 Feb. 1652/3, and M.A., 28 June 1655; suc. his father, 6 Dec. 1656, and was *cr. a Baronet*,

(a) Le Neve's MS. *Baronetage.*

(b) See pedigree in Baker's *Northamptonshire*, vol. i, p. 668.

(c) His only sister, Susanna, who had *m.* Francis Sheldon, of Abberton, co. Worcester, had *d.* his widow, 22 Nov. 1719, aged 50.

(d) This Thomas was 5th in descent from Sir Nicholas Carew, of Haccombe, who was 2d s. of Sir Nicholas Carew, of Carew, by Joan, da. of Sir Hugh Courtenay, of Haccombe (br. to Edward, Earl of Devon), which Joan brought that estate to the Carew family.

as above, 2 Aug. 1661; was M.P. for Tiverton, 1661 till death in 1674. He *m.* firstly, in or before 1653, Elizabeth, 1st da. and coheir of Sir Henry CAREW, of Bickleigh, near Tiverton, co. Devon (living 1640), by Dorothy, da. of Sir Reginald MOHUN, of Cornwall. By her he had six children. He *m.* secondly (Lic. Vic. Gen. 20 June 1672, he about 40, to marry at St. Leonard's, Devon), Martha, widow of Nicholas DUCK, of Mount Radford, in Heavitree (*bur.* there 25 Aug. 1667), and formerly widow of William DUCK, 1st da. and coheir of Arthur DUCK, D.C.L., Fellow of the College of Advocates, Doctors' Commons, by Margaret, da. of Henry SOUTHWORTH, of Wells, co. Somerset, Merchant of London. He *d.* in Sep. 1673. Nunc. will dat. 13 Sep. 1673, pr. 2 Jan. 1673/4. His widow was *bur.* 10 Jan. 1673/4, with her 2d husband, at Heavitree. M.I.

II. 1673. SIR HENRY CAREW, Baronet [1661], of Haccombe and Bickleigh aforesaid, 3d but only surv. s. and h., by 1st wife; *b.* about 1654; matric. at Oxford (Exeter Coll.), 17 March 1670/1, aged 16; *suc. to the Baronetcy* in Sep. 1673. He *m.* firstly (Lic. Vic. Gen. 8 April 1673, he about 19 and she about 17), Elizabeth, 2d da. of Thomas (CLIFFORD), 1st BARON CLIFFORD OF CHUDLEIGH, by Elizabeth, da. of William MARTIN, of Lindridge. She, who was *b.* 12 June 1655, at Chudleigh, *d.* s.p. He *m.* secondly, 3 Jan. 1683/4, at Highweek, Katharine, da. of John TOWNES, of Whitleigh. She also *d.* s.p. He. *m.* thirdly, in or before 1687, Gratiana, da. of Thomas DARRELL, of Treworgan, co. Cornwall. He *d.* in 1695. Will dat. 15 Sep., pr. 2 Dec. 1695. His widow living July 1708.

III. 1695. SIR HENRY DARRELL CAREW, Baronet [1661], of Haccombe and Bickleigh aforesaid, 1st s. and h. by 3d wife, *b.* about 1687; *suc. to the Baronetcy* in 1695; matric. at Oxford (Exeter Coll.), 2 Dec. 1706, aged 19. He *d.* unm. soon afterwards, in or near London. Admon. 7 July 1708, to his mother.

IV. 1707? SIR THOMAS CAREW, Baronet [1661], of Haccombe and Bickleigh aforesaid, next br. and h., *b.* about 1692; *suc. to the Baronetcy* in 1707 or 1708; matric. at Oxford (Exeter Coll.), 7 April 1709, aged 17. He was Sheriff of Devon, 1731-32. He *m.*, probably about 1725,(a) Dorothy, da. and coheir of Peter WEST, of Tiverton Castle, by, presumably, his paternal aunt, Dorothy, da. of Sir Thomas CAREW, 1st Baronet [1661]. The will of "Sir Thomas CAREW" is pr. 1746. That of "Dame Dorothy CAREW, Devon," pr. April 1776.

V. 1746? SIR JOHN CAREW, Baronet [1661], of Haccombe and Bickleigh aforesaid, 1st s. and h., *b.* presumably about 1726; *suc. to the Baronetcy* on the death of his father. He *m.*, in or before 1755, Elizabeth, da. and coheir of the Rev. Henry HOLDSWORTH, Vicar of Townstall, in Dartmouth. He was living 1757, and probably long afterwards,(b) though dead before Feb. 1773. His widow *d.* 8 Feb. 1817, in her 89th year. Will pr. 1817.

VI. 1770? SIR THOMAS CAREW, Baronet [1661], of Haccombe, Bickleigh, and Tiverton Castle aforesaid, 1st s. and h., *b.* about 1755, at Thorverton, Devon; *suc. to the Baronetcy* before 1773, and matric. (as a Baronet) at Oxford (Merton Coll.), 18 Feb. 1773, aged 18. He *m.* 19 June 1777, Jane, 1st da. of the Rev. Charles SMALLWOOD, Vicar of Kirkoswald, co. Cumberland. He *d.* April 1805. Will pr. July 1805 and Feb. 1839. His widow *d.* 4 May 1838. Will pr. June 1838.

(a) Thomas Carew, a *younger* son of this (the 4th) Baronet, matric. at Oxford (Queen's Coll.), 22 May 1749, aged 19, and was B.A. 1753.
(b) "John Carew, *Esq.*, of a large estate in Devonshire," died 4 Jan. 1751 [*London Mag.*], but as the eldest of the three sons of this (the 5th) Baronet was *b.* in 1755, this death (besides being that of an "Esq.") is too early to apply to him.

VII. 1805. SIR HENRY CAREW, Baronet [1661], of Haccombe, Bickleigh, and Tiverton Castle aforesaid, and of Newton Abbot, co. Devon, 1st s. and h., *b.* 10 Jan. 1779; ed. at Eton; matric. at Oxford (Trin. Coll.) 13 Feb. 1797, aged 18; *suc. to the Baronetcy* in April 1805. He *m.* 3 Oct. 1806, Elizabeth, only da. and h. of Walter PALK, of Marley and Rattery, co. Devon. He *d.* 31 Oct. 1830, at Exeter. Will pr. May 1831. His widow *d.* 7 March 1862.

VIII. 1830. SIR WALTER PALK CAREW, Baronet [1661], of Haccombe, etc., aforesaid, 1st s. and h., *b.* 9 July 1807 at Rattery aforesaid; matric. at Oxford (Ch. Ch.) 14 Dec. 1825, aged 18; *suc. to the Baronetcy* 31 Oct. 1830; was Sheriff of Devon 1846. He *m.*, 24 Jan. 1837, at Richmond, co. Surrey, Anne Frances, 1st da. of Major-Gen. Thomas William TAYLOR, C.B., of Ogwell House, Devon, by Anne Harvey, da. of John PETRIE, of Gatton, co. Surrey. She *d.* 8 June 1861 at Haccombe, aged 44. He *d.* s.p.m.s.(a) at Marley aforesaid, 27 Jan. 1874, aged 66.

IX. 1874. SIR HENRY PALK CAREW, Baronet [1661], of Woolhanger Manor, near Barnstaple, Devon, nephew and h. male, being only s. and h. of Henry CAREW, of Marley aforesaid, by Susan, da. of John SYMES, which Henry (who *d.* 24 Oct. 1871, aged 63) was next br. to the late Baronet. He was *b.* 26 Feb. 1870, and *suc. to the Baronetcy*, though not to the family estates, 27 Jan. 1874. He *m.* 9 Dec. 1889, Frances Gertrude, yst. da. of Robert Lock ROE, of Lynmouth Manor, North Devon.

Family Estates.—These, in 1883 (being then the property of "the Misses E. A. and B. Carew, of Haccombe and Buckfastleigh, Devon") consisted of 10,889 acres in Devon, worth £15,148 a year.

MILBANKE:

cr. 7 Aug. 1661;

sometime, 1815-25, NOEL,

and from 1866-68, MILBANKE-HUSKISSON.

I. 1661. "MARKE MILBANKE, of Halnaby, co. York,"(b) 2d but 1st surv. s. and h. ap.(c) of Mark MILBANKE, of Newcastle-upon-Tyne, Merchant, sometime, 1658 and 1672, Mayor of that city, by Dorothy (*m.* 14 July 1629), da. and h. of Ralph COOKE, Alderman of Newcastle, was *b.* probably about 1630; admitted to Gray's Inn, 22 April 1659, and was, for the services of his father (who is said to have sent vast sums to Charles II., when in exile), *cr. a Baronet*, as above, 7 Aug. 1661. He suc. his father in May 1677, inheriting besides the estates in Yorkshire, that of Dalden Tower, co. Durham. Sheriff of Northumberland, 1678-79. He *m.* firstly, probably before 1660, Elizabeth, da. and h. of John ACCLOME, of Moreby, co. York. She, by whom he had five children, and who was living 1669, was *bur.* at Croft, co. York. He *m.* secondly, his 1st wife's cousin, Faith, da. of Thomas ACCLOME, of Bonwick, co. York. He *d.* in 1680, and was *bur.* at Croft aforesaid. Will dat. 28 June, and pr. 25 Sep. 1680, at York. His widow, by whom he had no issue, *m.* Thomas METCALFE, and *d.* 31 April 1689. Her M.I. at St. Olave's, York.

(a) The estates (Haccombe, Newton Abbot, Marley House, Tiverton Castle, etc.) devolved on his 2 daughters and coheirs, Elizabeth Anne and Beatrice. His only s., Walter Palk Carew, Capt. in the Royal Horse Guards, *m.* in April 1872, but *d.* s.p. and v.p. 14 June 1873, aged 35.
(b) No designation is given him in Dugdale's *List.*
(c) His elder br. Ralph was admitted to Gray's Inn, 10 Dec. 1650.

II. 1680. SIR MARK MILBANKE, Baronet [1691], of Halnaby and Dalden Tower aforesaid, 1st s. and h. by 1st wife, *b.* probably shortly before 1660; *suc. to the Baronetcy* in 1680; Sheriff of Northumberland, 1685-86; M.P. for Richmond, 1690-95. He *m.* 3 Feb. 1680, at Houghton-le-Spring, Jane, da. of Sir Ralph CARR, of Cocken, co. Durham, only surv. child of her mother, Jane, da. of Sir Francis ANDERSON, of Bradley. He *d.* May 1698, and was *bur.* at Croft. Will dat. 17 Sep. 1697, pr. 10 June 1698. His widow *d.* in London and was *bur.* 14 May 1704, at St. Andrew's, Holborn.

III. 1698. SIR MARK MILBANKE, Baronet [1661], of Halnaby, etc., aforesaid, 1st s. and h., *b.* about 1685; ed. at Eton; *suc. to the Baronetcy* in May 1698; went, at the age of 18, to travel two years on the Continent, returning April 1705, but *d.* unm. the May following at Halnaby, aged about 20.

IV. 1705. SIR RALPH MILBANKE, Baronet [1661], of Halnaby, etc., aforesaid, br. and h., *b.* about 1688; *suc. to the Baronetcy* in May 1705; Sheriff of Yorkshire, 1721-22. He *m.* firstly, in May 1708, Elizabeth, sister of Robert (DARCY), 3d EARL OF HOLDERNESSE, da. of John DARCY (who *d.* before his grandfather, the 1st Earl), by Bridget, da. of Robert (SUTTON), 1st BARON LEXINGTON OF ARAM. She, who was *b.* 17 and *bap.* 27 Oct. 1686, at St. James', Westm., *d.* s.p.m., Oct. 1720. He *m.* secondly, Anne, da. of Edward DELAVAL, of South Dissington, co. Northumberland. He *d.* 9 May 1748, and was *bur.* at Croft aforesaid. Will pr. 1748. His widow *d.* 21 March 1765. Will pr. April 1765.

V. 1748. SIR RALPH MILBANKE, Baronet [1661], of Halnaby, etc., aforesaid, 1st s. and h. by 2d wife, *b.* probably about 1725; *suc. to the Baronetcy*, 9 May 1748; was Sheriff of Yorkshire, 1753-54; M.P. for Scarborough, 1754-61, and for Richmond, 1761-68. He *m.*, in or before 1748, Elizabeth, da. and coheir of John HEDWORTH, of Chester-le-Street, co. Durham, sometime M.P. for that county. She *d.* 6 July 1767, at Bath. He *d.* 8 Jan. 1798,(a) and was *bur.* at Croft.

VI. 1798. SIR RALPH MILBANKE, *afterwards*, 1815-25, NOEL, Baronet [1661], of Halnaby, etc., aforesaid, of Seaham, co. Durham, and afterwards [1815-25], of Kirkby Mallory, co. Leicester, 1st s. and h., *b.* about 1748; *suc. to the Baronetcy*, 8 Jan. 1798(a); was M.P. for co. Durham (five Parls.), 1790-1812, declining to be nominated in 1812, having spent a large fortune in contested elections. He by Royal lic., 1815, took the name of *Noel* only, in compliance with the will of his wife's brother, Thomas (NOEL), 2d VISCOUNT WENTWORTH, whose estates in Leicestershire (worth about £7,000 a year) he and his wife had inherited. He *m.* 7 Jan. 1777, Judith, 1st sister and coheir of VISCOUNT WENTWORTH abovenamed, da. of Edward (NOEL), 1st VISCOUNT WENTWORTH, by Judith, da. and h. of William LAMB, of Farndish. She, who was *b.* 3 Nov. 1751, *d.* 28 Jan. 1822. Will pr. 1822. He *d.* s.p.m.,(b) 19 March 1825. Will pr. April 1825.

VII. 1825. SIR JOHN PENISTON(c) MILBANKE, Baronet [1661], of Halnaby aforesaid, nephew and h. male, being 1st s. and h. of John MILBANKE, by Cornelia, da. of Sir William CHAMBERS, which John (who *d.* 12 March 1800) was next br. to the late Baronet. He was *b.* 20 Aug. 1776; and *suc. to the Baronetcy*, 19 March 1825. He *m.* firstly, 29 Sep. 1799, Eleanor,

(a) *Ann. Reg.* of 1798. The death of the 5th Baronet is elsewhere given as 1793.
(b) Anna Isabella, his only da. and h., who, in 1825, inherited most of the family estates, was *b.* May 1793, *m.*, 2 Jan. 1815, the celebrated poet, George Gordon (Byron) 6th Baron Byron of Rochdale (who *d.* 19 April 1824), became, 19 Nov. 1856, *suo jure* Baroness Wentworth, and *d.* 26 May 1860, being ancestress of the succeeding Lords Wentworth.
(c) His name of Peniston was doubtless taken from that of Peniston (Lamb), 1st Viscount Melbourne [I.], who had *m.*, 13 April 1769, his aunt, Elizabeth, da. of the 5th Baronet.

yst. da. of Julines HERRING, of Heybridge Hall, co. Essex, and of the island of Jamaica. She *d.* 30 July 1819. He *m.* secondly, 3 Jan. 1821, Elizabeth, widow of Thomas GREY, M.D., da. of Captain James FENWICK. He *d.* 27 July 1850, at Halnaby aforesaid, in his 75th year. His widow, by whom he had no issue, *d.* 6 Nov. 1873, at St. Mary's, York, in her 91st year.

VIII. 1850. SIR JOHN RALPH MILBANKE, *afterwards*, 1866-68, MILBANKE-HUSKISSON, Baronet [1661], of Halnaby aforesaid, and afterwards, of Eartham House, near Chichester, co. Sussex, only s. and h. by 1st wife; *b.* 5 Nov. 1800; admitted to Gray's Inn, 1 May 1820; was a clerk in the Foreign Office, Oct. 1823; Sec. of Legation at Frankfort, Sep. 1826; Sec. of Embassy at St. Petersburg, Nov. 1835, and at Vienna, Oct. 1838; Envoy at Munich, Nov. 1843; at Vienna, Oct. 1862, and afterwards at the Hague and at Berne, but resigned 1867, having *suc. to the Baronetcy*, 27 July 1850. By royal lic., 5 Jan. 1866, he took the name of *Husskisson*, after that of *Milbanke*, under the will of his father's 1st cousin, Elizabeth Emily, da. of Admiral Mark MILBANKE (3d s. of the 4th Baronet) and widow of the Rt. Hon. William HUSKISSON, the well known Statesman (*d.* s.p. 15 Sep. 1830, aged 60), to whose estate at Eartham, co. Sussex, he then succeeded. He *m.* 13 July 1843, at St. Geo., Han. sq., Emily, sister of William ROSE, 1st BARON SANDHURST, 3d da. of John MANSFIELD, of Diggeswell House, Herts, by Mary Buchanan, da. of Gen. Samuel SMITH, of Baltimore, U.S.A. He *d.* 30 Dec. 1868, at Eartham House, aged 68. His widow living 1903.

IX. 1868. SIR PENISTON MILBANKE, Baronet [1661], of Eartham House aforesaid, 1st s. and h., *b.* at Munich, 14 Feb. 1847; matric. at Oxford (Ch. Ch.), 7 June 1875, aged 18; *suc. to the Baronetcy*, 30 Dec. 1868; was a member of the Banking firm of "Milbanke and Co.," at Chichester. He *m.* 20 Jan. 1870, at Singleton, co. Sussex, Elizabeth Margaret, 2d da. of the Hon. Richard DENMAN, of Westergate in that county (3d s. of Thomas, 1st BARON DENMAN OF DOVEDALE), by Emma, da. of Hugh JONES, of Lark Hill, co. Lancaster. He *d.* suddenly (while shooting on Lord Leconfield's preserves), 30 Nov. 1899, aged 52, and was *bur.* at Eartham. Will pr. at £31,586; the net personalty £19,992. His widow, who was *b.* 28 April 1847, living 1903.

X. 1899. SIR JOHN PENISTON MILBANKE, Baronet [1661], of Eartham House aforesaid, 2d but 1st surv. s. and h., *b.* 9 Oct. 1872; ed. at Harrow; *suc. to the Baronetcy*, 30 Nov. 1899; sometime Capt. 10th Hussars, serving in the Transvaal War as aide-de-camp to Gen. FRENCH, and receiving the *Victoria Cross*. He *m.* 6 Dec. 1900, at St. Peter's, Eaton sq., Amelia, only da. of Lieut. Col. the Hon. Charles Frederick CRICHTON (2d s. of the 3d EARL ERNE [I.]), by Madeline, da. of Thomas (TAYLOUR), 3d MARQUESS OF HEADFORT [I.]. She was *b.* 20 Jan. 1876.

Family Estates.—These, in 1883, were under 3,000 acres.

ROTHWELL:

cr. 16 Aug. 1661;

ex. 1693.

I. 1661 to 1693. "RICHARD ROTHWELL, of Ewerby and Stapleford, co. Lincoln, Esq.(a), 2d but 1st surv. s. and h. of William ROTHWELL, of the same, by Alice, da. and h. of George STOW, of Stapleford aforesaid, was *b.* about 1628, and was *cr. a Baronet*, as above, 16 Aug. 1661. He recorded and signed his pedigree in the Visit. of Lincolnshire, 1666; was M.P. for Newark (three Parls.), April 1677 to 1681; was nominated Sheriff of Lincolnshire, 1692, but did not act. He

(a) In Sir Joseph Williamson's *Lincolnshire Families temp. Charles II.* (*Her. and Gen.* ii, 124), his estate "at Stappleford" is valued at £1,500 a year, and he is said to be the son of "a Chief Constable."

m. (Lic. Vic. Gen., 12 Feb. 1672/3, he about 45, bachelor) Elizabeth ROTHWELL, of Haverholme, co. Lincoln, about 35, widow. He *d.* s.p.m.(a) 1693, when *the Baronetcy* became *extinct.* Will pr. 1694. His widow living 14 Feb. 1693/4.

BANKS, *or* BANKES:

cr. 22 Aug. 1661;

ex. 18 Oct. 1699.

I. 1661 to 1699. "JOHN BANKES, of the city of London, now [1681] of Alesford, in Kent,"(b) s. and h. of Caleb BANKS, of Maidstone in that county, Woollen Draper, by Martha, da. of Stephen DANN, of Feversham, co. Kent, was *b.* about 1627; was M.P. for Maidstone (three Parls.), 1654-59; for Winchilsea, Feb. till void, 7 March 1677/8; for Rochester (five Parls.), 1679-90; for Queenborough, 1690-95, and for Maidstone, again, 1695-98, and was *cr. a Baronet,* as above, 22 Aug. 1661. He was of Lincoln's Inn Fields, Midx., and of Aylesford, co. Kent, which estate he purchased. He *m.*, in or before 1657, Elizabeth, da. of Sir John DETHICK, sometime, 1655-56, Lord Mayor of London (*b.* at West Newton, co. Norfolk, and *d.* 31 March 1671), by his 2d wife, Martha, da. of Edmund TRAVERS, of Tottenham, co. Midx., Merchant. She was *bur.* 2 Nov. 1696, at Aylesford. He *d.* s.p.m.s.(c) 18 and was *bur.* 31 Oct. 1699, at Aylesford, in his 72d year, when the *Baronetcy* became *extinct.* M.I. Will dat. 22 Nov. 1697, to 7 Oct. 1699, pr. 11 Dec. 1699.

INGOLDSBY:

cr. 30 Aug. 1661;

ex. 25 April 1726.

I. 1661. "HENRY INGOLDSBY,(d) of Lethenborow, co. Buckingham, Esq.," being also of Waldridge, in that county, and of Beggstown, *otherwise* Ballybeg, co. Meath, yr. br. to the celebrated Parl. General, Sir Richard INGOLDSBY, K.B., being 5th s. of Sir Richard INGOLDSBY, of Lethenborow aforesaid (*bur.* at Buckingham, 20 Dec. 1656), by Elizabeth, da. of Sir Oliver Cromwell, K.G., of Hinchinbrooke, co. Huntingdon, was *bap.* 16 Jan. 1622/3, at Buckingham; was an officer in the army of Charles I, whom, however, he soon deserted, becoming eventually a Col. in the Parl. service in Ireland; was M.P. for the counties of Kerry, Limerick, and Clare, 1654, 1656, and 1659; Mayor of Limerick, 1656, and was *cr. a Baronet,* by the Lord Protector Cromwell, 10 April (or 31 March) 1658, a dignity which, of course, was *disallowed* after the Restoration, in May 1660, but, within 15 months thereof,

(a) Of his daughters and coheirs (1) Elizabeth *m.*, about 1690, Thomas (Willoughby), 1st Baron Middleton, and (2) Anne *m.* (Lic. Fac. 14 Feb. 1693/4, she aged 19, with consent of her mother) Sir Thomas Barnardiston, 3d Baronet [1663], and *d.* 21 Feb. 1701/2, leaving issue.

(b) No description of his rank is given in Dugdale's *List.*

(c) Of his two daughters and coheirs (1) Elizabeth, who inherited the Aylesford estate, *m.*, about 1677, Heneage Finch, who, in 1713, was *cr.* Earl of Aylesford; (2) Mary, *m.* John Savile, of Methley, co. York, and *d.* Nov. 1740, aged 82, leaving issue. Their brother, Caleb Bankes, admitted to Gray's Inn, 2 Feb. 1674/5; was M.P. for Queenborough, 1685-87; for Maidstone, 1689-90; for Rochester, Oct. 1691 to 1695, and for Queenborough (again), 1665 till his death. He *m.* Elizabeth, da. of Samuel Fortney, of Chatteris, co. Cambridge, but *d.* s.p. and v.p., 13 Sep. 1696, aged 37, and was *bur.* at Aylesford, as also was "John Bankes," presumably an elder brother, 31 May 1669.

(d) G. D. Burtchaell, of the Office of Arms, Dublin, kindly supplied most of the information in this article, which differs in many respects from the hitherto received account of these Baronets.

he was, by the King, *cr. a Baronet,* as above (possibly of Ireland as well as of England), 30 Aug. 1661. He was M.P. [I.] for co. Clare, 1661-66 and 1695-99; had large grants under the act of settlement in the counties of Clare, Meath, and Limerick, and was P.C. [I.]. He *m.* before April 1658,(a) Anne, da. of Sir Hardress WALLER (the Regicide), by Elizabeth, da. and coheir of Sir John DOWDALL, of Kilfinny, co. Limerick. He *d.* in March 1701, and was *bur.* at St. Bride's, Dublin. Will dat. 19 March 1700/1, and pr. 28 March 1701 [I.], and June 1701. The will of "Dame Anne Ingoldsby, Midx.," was pr. Jan. 1708/9.

II. 1701, to 1726. SIR WILLIAM INGOLDSBY, Baronet [1661], of Ballybeg aforesaid, 2d but 1st surv. s. and h.,(b) *b.* 1670; *suc. to the Baronetcy* in March 1701. He *m.*, 27 Oct. 1691, at Westm. Abbey (Lic. Vic. Gen., 26, he about 20), Theophila, da. of Sir Kingsmill LUCY, 2d Baronet [1618], by Theophila, da. of George (BERKELEY), 1ST EARL OF BERKELEY. She, who was *b.* and *bap.* 24 Jan. 1670/1, at St. Martin's-in-the-Fields, Midx., *d.* 30 July and was *bur.* 4 Aug. 1721 (with her mother), at Cranford, co. Midx. He *d.* s.p.m.s., in York Buildings, 25 and was *bur.* 28 April 1726, at St. Martin's-in-the-Fields aforesaid, when the *Baronetcy* became *extinct.*(c) Admon. 10 May 1726, to his da. Elizabeth, wife of the "Hon. Col. Thomas FOWKES, Esq."

BICKLEY:

cr. 3 Sep. 1661;

ex., probably, 18 Sep. 1754;

but assumed till 29 July 1773.

I. 1661. "FRANCIS BICKLEY, of Attilborough, co. Norfolk, Esq.,"(d) 3d s. of Francis BICKLEY, of Lolworth, co. Cambridge, by Amy, da. of [—] MAJOR, of co. Huntingdon, was *b.* about 1582; was a citizen and draper of London, living at Budge Row and at Dalston in Hackney, co. Midx.; entered his pedigree in the Visit. of London, 1634, and, having acquired considerable wealth, purchased Attleborough Hall, co. Norfolk, in 1653, and was *cr. a Baronet* as above, 3 Sep. 1661. He *m.*, presumably before 1615,(e) Mary, da. of Richard PARSONS, of London, "who came out of Gloucestershire." She was living 1634. He *d.* 11 Aug. 1670, aged nearly 90, and was *bur.* at Attleborough. M.I. Will pr. Nov. 1670.

II. 1670. SIR FRANCIS BICKLEY, Baronet [1661], of Attleborough aforesaid, 1st s. and h., *b.* about 1623, matric. at Oxford (Univ. Coll.), 24 March 1636/7, aged 14; admitted to Gray's Inn, 14 Aug. 1640. He *m.* in or before 1644, Mary, da. of [—] MAN, Alderman of Norwich; *suc. to the Baronetcy,* 11 Aug. 1670. He *d.* 1681. His widow *d.* 1694. Will dat. 18 July and pr. 14 Aug. 1694.

(a) At that date she was chief mourner at her mother's funeral.

(b) George Ingoldsby, the eldest son (sometimes, erroneously, said to have suc. his father as 2d Baronet, and often confused with his uncle, Sir George Ingoldsby, Sheriff of co. Limerick 1667 and 1668), *m.* Mary, da. of Sir Peter Stanley, 2d Baronet [1660], of Alderley, and *d.* v.p. and s.p. Admon. 16 Jan. 1688/9 [I.] to his widow.

(c) His yr. br., Charles Ingoldsby, of Clondirralaghe, co. Clare, *m.* Frances, da. of Sir Robert Gore, of Newtown, co. Leitrim, and *d.* 1 Sep. 1704, leaving (besides a da., Angel, Countess of Roscommon [I.]), an only son, Henry Ingoldsby, of Dublin, who *d.* s.p., leaving (by will, dat. 12 Oct. 1719, which, after considerable litigation, was pr. 20 June 1720 [I.]) all his property to his wife, Elizabeth.

(d) See J. J. Barrett's *History of Attleborough, co. Norfolk,* London, 1848.

(e) Ann, their 1st da., *m.* 11 June 1633, at Hackney, Richard Edisbury.

III. 1681. SIR FRANCIS BICKLEY, Baronet [1661], of Attleborough aforesaid, 1st s. and h., *bap.* 19 April 1644, at Hackney; matric. at Oxford (Mag. Coll.), 14 Dec. 1660, aged 16; *suc. to the Baronetcy* in 1681. He, it is presumed, sold the Attleborough estate.(a) He *m.* firstly, in or before 1667, Deborah, da. of Sir Cornelius VERMUYDEN (*Knighted* 6 Jan. 1628/9), by whom he had 3 children. She *d.* in childbirth, 6 March 1669, and was *bur.* at Attleborough. M.I. He *m.* secondly, Mary, da. and coheir of Sir Humphrey WINCH, Baronet [so *cr.* 9 June 1660], of Braunston, co. Lincoln, by Rebecca, da. of Martin BROUNE, Alderman of London. He *m.*, thirdly, "Mrs. Poynter,(b) but by her had no issue." He *d.* 1687. Will pr. at the Consistory Court of Norwich, 1687/8.

IV. 1687. SIR FRANCIS BICKLEY, Baronet [1661], 1st s. and h., by 1st wife, *bap.* 28 Jan. 1667, at Attleborough; was sometime Capt. in the Duke of Norfolk's Reg. in Ireland; *suc. to the Baronetcy* in 1687. He *m.* (Lic. Vic. Gen. 5 May 1691, he aged 23) Alathea (then aged 16), 1st da. and coheir of Jacob GARRARD, of Langford, co. Norfolk (s. and h. ap. of Sir Jacob GARRARD, 1st Baronet [1662]), by Ursula [*Qy.* Abigail], da. of Sir John HOLLAND, 1st Baronet [1629], of Quiddenham. She *d.* Feb. 1739/40. Will pr. 1740. He *d.* s.p.s. 4 July 1746. Will pr. 1746.

V. 1746 to 1754. SIR HUMPHREY BICKLEY, Baronet [1661], br. of the half blood and h. male, being next surv. s. of the 3d Baronet by his 2d wife. He took Holy Orders, and was Rector of Attleborough before 1739 till his death; *suc. to the Baronetcy* 4 July 1746. He *d.* unm., 18 Sep. 1754, when *the Baronetcy,* presumably, became *extinct.*

VI. 1754 to 1773. SIR SAMUEL BICKLEY, Baronet(c) [1661], possibly nephew or cousin and h. male, but whose relationship to the late Baronet is not known(d), is (in Kimber's *Baronetage,* 1771) called "the present Baronet and a Bachelor"; *assumed the Baronetage* in 1754; was in Holy Orders, Vicar of Bapchild, co. Kent, 1759-64. He "dishonoured a respectable family by crimes which involved him in distress and infamy," and for which he suffered "a disgraceful punishment" at Lincoln.(e) He *d.* s.p. in great poverty, at the King's Head Inn, Enfield, Midx., 27 and was *bur.* 29 July 1773, as "a Baronet," at Enfield.

JASON:

cr. 5 Sep. 1661;

ex. 5 May 1738.

I. 1661. "ROBERT JASON, of Broad Somerford, co. Wilts, Esq.," s. and h. of Robert JASON, of Enfield, co. Midx., by Susan, da. of John LYON, of Holand; was nominated Sheriff of Hants,

(a) It was sold before 1692; there is, under that date, a note in Le Neve's MS. *Baronetage* to the then Baronet, "no child yet living; the estate sold; he not worth anything; my Lady works plain work for her living." The 4th Baronet is, however, called "of Attleborough" in his marriage licence of 1691, but probably that was his residence, not his property.

(b) Wotton's *Baronetage* [1741].

(c) According to the assumption of that title in 1754.

(d) There were two younger brothers of the 5th Baronet, either of whom could possibly have been father of this Samuel, viz. (1), John Bickley, Capt. in the army, living (probably unm.) in 1741, and (2), Joseph Bickley, of Virginia, who *m.* there, and was living 1741 with issue.

(e) Lysons's *Environs of London* (1st edit., 1795, vol. ii, p. 326). See also *Gent. Mag.* for 1773, p. 413.

1648, but declined to act, and was *cr. a Baronet,* as above, 5 Sep. 1661. He purchased the manor and advowson of Hinton-on-the-Green, co. Glouc. He *m.* firstly, in or before 1640, Cecilia, da. of Sir Henry ROWE, of Shackleford, in Hackney, co. Midx. She *d.* 3 and was *bur.* 16 Feb. 1654/5, in the Rowe vault at Hackney. He *m.* secondly (Lic. Vic. Gen., 29 April 1674), Anne RAVES, of Dunsten, co. Oxon, spinster, then about 30. He *d.* within a year thereof. Admon. as "of Enfield, co. Midx.," 4 May 1675. His widow, who was *b.* July 1644, and who held the estate of Hinton in jointure till her death, *m.*, as his 2d wife (Lic. Fac., 22 Sep. 1675), Sir Christopher EYRE, of Northall, co. Midx., whose will was pr. June 1686. She *m.* for her 3d husband, David WARREN, of Greet, co. Glouc. (who *d.* 28 Sep. 1708, aged 56), and *d.* 29 Jan. 1713, being *bur.* at Hinton. M.I.

II. 1675? SIR ROBERT JASON, Baronet [1661], of Broad Somerford aforesaid, 1st s. and h., by 1st wife, *bap.* 27 Nov. 1640, at Hackney; admitted to Gray's Inn, 18 March 1655/6; *suc. to the Baronetcy* in 1674 or 1675. He *m.* Anne, da. of George DACRES, of Cheshunt, co. Herts. He *d.* in or before 1687. Will pr. Dec. 1687. His widow *m.* Samuel BRETTON, who survived her, and *d.* in or before 1697. Admon. as "of St. Bride's, London," 3 March 1697/8, to her da. Anne, wife of Thomas PARTINGTON.

III. 1687? SIR GEORGE JASON, Baronet [1661], of Broad Somerford aforesaid, s. and h.; *suc. to the Baronetcy* in or before 1687. He *d.* unm. in or before 1697. Admon. as "of St. Bride's, London," to his sister, Ann PARTINGTON, above-named.

IV. 1697? SIR ROBERT JASON, Baronet [1661], cousin and h. male, being s. and h. of Henry JASON (*bap.* 10 July 1643, at Hackney, and admitted to Gray's Inn, 18 March 1655/6), 2d s. of the 1st Baronet; *suc. to the Baronetcy* in or before 1697, succeeding after 1713 to the Hinton estate. He *m.*, in or before 1705, Anne, da. of Capt. David WARREN, said sometimes to be the David Warren above-named, 3d husband of his grandfather's widow. He *d.* about 1723.

V. 1723. SIR WARREN JASON, Baronet [1661], of Hinton aforesaid, 1st s. and h., *b.* about 1705; *suc. to the Baronetcy* about 1723. He *d.* unm., at Hinton, 12 Nov. 1728, aged 23. Admon. 28 Nov. 1728, 23 Dec. 1732, and (with will annexed) July 1798.

VI. 1728, to 1738. SIR ROBERT JASON, Baronet [1661], of Hinton aforesaid, br. and h., *b.* probably about 1708; *suc. to the Baronetcy* 12 Nov. 1728. He *m.* (—), da. of (—) COLLINS. He *d.* s.p. at Worcester, 5 May 1738, when the *Baronetcy* became *extinct.* His widow *m.* in 1738, Joseph SWAYNE, of Bristol, who, having become possessed of the Hinton estate, sold it shortly afterwards (before 1750) to the family of STEPHENS.

YONGE, *or* YOUNG:

cr. 26 Sep. 1661;

ex. 25 Sep. 1812.

I. 1661. "SIR JOHN YOUNG, of Culliton [*i.e.,* Colyton], co. Devon, Knt.," 1st s. and h. of Walter YOUNG, *or* YONGE, of the same, and of Upton Hylyons in that county (*bur.* 26 Dec. 1649, at Colyton), by Jane, da. and coheir of Sir John PERIAM, of Exeter, was *bap.* 2 Oct. 1603, at Colyton; matric. at Oxford (Exeter Coll.), 17 Dec. 1619, being then called 18; B.A. 14 June 1621; M.A. 22 June 1625; admitted to Middle Temple 1619; is called 16 in the Heralds' Visit. of Devon in 1620(a); *Knighted* 15 Sep. 1625, at

(a) This is signed "Wa. Younge" by his father.

Ford, co. Devon; was one of the Committee of Compounders; was M.P. for Plymouth April 1642, till secluded in Dec. 1648; for Honiton, 1654-55; for Devon, 1656-58, and for Honiton again, 1660, and was *cr. a Baronet*, as above, 26 Sep. 1661. He *m.*, in or before 1623, Elizabeth, *or* Margaret, da. of Sir William STRODE, of Newnham, Devon, by his 1st wife, Mary, da. of Thomas SOUTHCOTT, of Bovey Tracey. He was *bur.* 26 Aug. 1663, at Colyton. Will dat. 27 April 1661, pr. 17 Sep. 1663.

II. 1663. SIR WALTER YONGE, Baronet [1661], of Colyton aforesaid, 2d but 1st surv. s. and h., *b.* about 1625; admitted to the Inner Temple, Nov. 1645; was M.P. for Honiton, 1659; for Lyme Regis, 1660, and for Dartmouth, 1666 till his death in 1672; *suc. to the Baronetcy* in Aug. 1663. He *m.* 30 March 1649, at Sandford, Devon, Isabel, da. of Sir John DAVIE, 1st Baronet [1641], of Creedy, only child of his 2d wife, Isabel, da. of (—) HELE, of Greaton, Devon. He *d.* 21 Nov. and was *bur.* 3 Dec. 1670, at Colyton. His widow, who was *bap.* 7 Oct. 1631, at Sandford, was *bur.* there 15 Jan. 1672/3.

III. 1672. SIR WALTER YONGE, Baronet [1661], of Colyton aforesaid, 2d but 1st surv. s. and h., *bap.* 8 Sep. 1653, at Sandford aforesaid; matric. at Oxford (Ex. Coll.), 25 Feb. 1669/70, aged 16; *suc. to the Baronetcy*, 21 Nov. 1670; was M.P. for Honiton (three Parls.), 1679-81; for Ashburton, 1689-90, and for Honiton again (nine Parls.), 1690 till unseated, Feb. 1711; Commissioner of Customs, 1694-1701, and, again, 1714 till his death. He purchased in 1680 an estate at Escott, in Tallaton, co. Devon, and began the building there of Escott House. He *m.* firstly (Lic. at Exeter, 19 April 1677), Gertrude, da. of Sir William MORRICE, 1st Baronet [1661], of Werrington, Devon, by Gertrude, da. of Sir John BAMPFYLDE, 1st Baronet [1641]. She was *bur.*, with her only child, 13 Jan. 1678/9, at Colyton. He *m.* secondly, 18 June 1691, at St. James', Clerkenwell (Lic. Vic. Gen. 15, he above 30, widower, and she above 21, spinster), Gwen, da. of Sir Robert WILLIAMS, 2d Baronet [1661], of Penrhyn by his 1st wife, Jane, da. of Sir John GLYNNE, sometime [1655-60], Chief Justice of the Upper Bench, the said Gwen being sister of the 3d and 4th Baronets and coheir of the latter. He *d.* in Red Lion square, Midx., 18 and was *bur.* 29 July 1731, at Colyton. Will dat, 25 July 1728, pr. 20 July 1731 by his widow. She was *bur.* at Colyton. 19 Nov. [1739?] at Colyton.

IV. 1731. SIR WILLIAM YONGE, Baronet [1661], of Colyton and Escott aforesaid, only s. and h., by second wife; *b.* probably about 1693; M.P. for Honiton (six Parls.), 1714-54, and for Tiverton, 1754 till his death in 1755; a Commissioner of Army Accounts, 1717; a Lord of the Treasury, 1724-27, and again, 1730-35, having been a Lord of the Admiralty, 1728-30; **K.B.** (one of the Knight Founders), 1725; *suc. to the Baronetcy*, 18 July 1731. P.C., 6 Nov. 1735; Secretary of War, 1735-41; Cofferer of the Household, 1741-43, and Joint Vice-Treasurer [I.], 1746-54. He *m.* firstly, 30 July 1716, at Ely Chapel, Holborn (Hackney par. reg.), Mary, sister of Sir William HEATHCOTE, 1st Baronet [1733], da. of Samuel HEATHCOTE, of Hackney, by Mary, da. of William DAWSONNE, of Hackney aforesaid. She who was *b.* 18 June and *bap.* there 2 July 1696, was divorced by Act of Parl. 1724.(a) He *m.* secondly, 14 Sep. 1729, at Colyton, Anne, da. and coheir of Thomas (HOWARD), 7th BARON HOWARD OF EFFINGHAM, by his 1st wife, Mary, da. and h. of Ruishe WENTWORTH. He *d.* 10 and was *bur.* 14 Aug. 1755, at Colyton. Will dat. 15 Dec. 1737, pr. 23 Dec. 1755. His widow *d.* at Waltham House, Essex, 12 Sep. 1775, and was *bur.* at Colyton. Will pr. 1775.

V. 1755, to 1812. SIR GEORGE YONGE, Baronet [1661], of Colyton and Escott aforesaid, only s. and h., *b.* 1731; ed. at Eton and at Leipsic; was M.P. for Honiton (seven Parls.), 1754-61, and Nov. 1763 to 1796; *suc. to the Baronetcy* 10 Aug. 1755; was a Lord of the Admiralty, 1766-70; P.C., 10 April 1782; Joint Vice Treasurer [I.] April to September, 1782; Secretary of War, 1782-83 and 1783-94;

(a) She (as "Mrs. Mary Heathcote") *m.* Dec. 1724, "Patrick Macmahon, Esq., co. Tipperary."

K.B., 1788; Master of the Mint, 1794-99; Gov. of the Cape of Good Hope, 1799, till dismissed in Jan. 1801. He sold "the large house at Colyton which had been sometime a seat of the family,"(a) residing chiefly at Escott House (where on 14 Aug. 1789 he had entertained George III, the Queen Consort, and three of the Princesses), which, however, in 1794, he also sold.(b) He *m.* 10 July 1765, Anne, only da. and the rich heiress of Bourchier CLEEVE, of Footscray Place, Kent, and Spring Gardens, Midx., citizen and pewterer of London (*d.* 1 March 1760, aged 44), by Mary, da. of (—) HAYDON, of London, timber merchant.(c) On their return from the Cape they (being, apparently, no longer in affluent circumstances), were granted apartments at Hampton Court Palace. He *d.* there s.p., 25 Sep. 1812, aged 81, when the *Baronetcy* became *extinct*. His widow *d.* there 7 Jan. 1833.

VAN-FREISENDORF:

cr. 4 Oct. 1661;

Succession, if any, *unknown*.

I. 1661. "JOHN FREDERICK VAN FREISENDORF, of Herdick, Lord of Kymp, of Councill to the King of Sweden, and Embassadour Extraordinary to His Majesty King Charles the II," for the purpose of congratulating him on his accession, was *cr. a Baronet*, as above, 4 Oct. 1661. He returned to Sweden, soon after 23 of the same month, but of him nothing more is known.

ROBERTS:

cr 4 Oct. 1661;

ex. May 1698.

I. 1661. "WILLIAM ROBERTS(d) of Willesden, co. Middlesex, Esq.," 1st s. and h. ap. of Sir William ROBERTS, of the same, one of the Commissioners appointed for the trial of Charles I, and in 1655 an active member of Cromwell's "Upper House," by Eleanor, only surv. child of Robert ATY, of Kilburn Priory, co. Midx., was *b.* 21, *bap.* 28 June 1638, at Willesden aforesaid, and was *cr. a Baronet*, as above, 8 Nov. 1661. He suc. his father (who *d.* aged 58), 19 Sep. 1662, and was M.P. for Middlesex (three Parls.), 1679-81. He *m.* 7 April 1658, at Hackney, co. Midx., Sarah, da. of Robert HOLTE, Citizen of London. She *d.* 2 and was *bur.* 5 Sep. 1686, at Willesden. M.I. He *d.* 14 and was *bur.* there 18 March 1687/8, in his 50th year. M.I. Will dat. and pr. 21 March 1687/8.

II. 1688, to 1698. SIR WILLIAM ROBERTS, Baronet [1661], of Willesden aforesaid, only s. and h., *b.* and *bap.* there, 17 Jan. 1658/9; *suc. to the Baronetcy*, 14 March 1687/8. He *d.* unm. and was *bur*, there 18 May 1698, when the *Baronetcy* became *extinct*.(e) Will dat. 22 June 1694, pr. 24 May 1698.

(a) Lysons's *Devonshire*. The chief estate in Colyton never belonged to the Yonge family.
(b) It was burnt to the ground, 28 Dec. 1808.
(c) See *N. & Q.*, 8th series, v, 184.
(d) See pedigree by Francis Grigson in the *Genealogist*, O.S., vol. v, pp. 300-07.
(e) It is often ascribed to his cousin and h. male, William Roberts, of Willesden, s. of Thomas Roberts of the same (*bur.* there 8 March 1634/5, in his 40th year), a yr. br. of the 1st Baronet. He, however, had no right thereto, and, apparently, never assumed it, but *d.* s.p.s., 11 Dec. 1700, aged 27, and was *bur.* at Willesden. M.I. Will dat. 2 and pr. 17 Dec. 1700.

LUCKYN:

cr. 15 Nov. 1661:

ex. in or before 1700.

I. 1661. "WILLIAM LUCKYN, of [Little] Waltham, co. Essex,"(a) 2d s. of Sir William LUCKYN, 1st Baronet [1629], of Waltham aforesaid, by Mildred, da. of Sir Gamaliel CAPELL, of Rookwood Hall in that county, was *b.* about 1633; admitted Nov. 1657 to the Inner Temple, and was *cr. a Baronet*, as above, 15 Nov. 1661; was Sheriff of Essex, 1664-65. He *m.* (Lic. Fac. 4 Oct. 1661, he about 26 and she 19), Winifred, da. of Sir Richard EVERARD, 1st Baronet [1629], of Much Waltham in that county, by his 1st wife, Joan, da. of Sir Francis BARRINGTON, 1st Baronet [1611]. He *d.* in or before 1678. Will pr. 1678.

II. 1678? to 1690? SIR WILLIAM LUCKYN, Baronet [1661], of Waltham aforesaid, only s. and h.; *suc. to the Baronetcy* in or before 1678. He *d.* unm. in or before 1700, when the *Baronetcy* became *extinct*.(b)

SMITH, *or* SMYTH:

cr. 28 Nov. 1661;

afterwards, since 1788, *or* 1799, SMIJTH;

subsequently, since 1839, BOWYER-SMIJTH.

I. 1661. "THOMAS SMITH, of Hill Hall [in Theydon Mount], co. Essex,"(a) 3d and yst. s. of Sir William SMITH,(c) of the same, Sheriff of Essex, 1615-16 (*d.* Dec. 1626, aged 76), by Bridget, da. of Thomas FLEETWOOD, of the Vache, co. Buckingham,(d) was *b.* about 1602; admitted to Gray's Inn, 5 Feb. 1619/20; suc. his nephew, Edward SMITH (who *d.* unm. aged 22), in the estate of Hill Hall aforesaid; was Lord of the manor of Thaxted and owner of Horham Hall in that parish, and was *cr. a Baronet*, as above, 28 Nov. 1661. He was Sheriff of Essex, 1663-64. He *m.* firstly, in or before 1633, Joan, da. of Sir Edward ALTHAM, of Mark Hall, in Latton, co. Essex, by Joan, da. of Sir John LEVENTHORPE. She, by whom he had eleven children, *d.* 14 July 1658, and was *bur.* at Theydon Mount. M.I. He *m.* secondly, in or after 1664, Beatrice, widow of Sir John LLOYD, 1st Baronet [1662], of Woking (who *d.* 1 Jan. 1663/4), and formerly widow of James ZOUCHE, of Woking (who *d.* 1643), 3d da. of Francis (ANNESLEY), VISCOUNT VALENTIA [I.], by his 1st wife, Dorothy, da. of Sir John PHILIPPS, 1st Baronet [1621], of Picton. She, by whom he had no issue, was *b.* 27 March 1619, at Fishamble street, in St. John's parish, Dublin, and *d.* 26 March 1668, being *bur.* at Theydon Mount. He *d.* (five weeks afterwards) 5 and was *bur.* 14 May 1668 there. M.I. Will dat. 30 April, pr. 11 June 1668.

(a) His rank is not stated in Dugdale's *List*.
(b) Ann, only da. of the 1st Baronet, *m.* Sir Henry Palmer, 3d Baronet [1611] of Wingham, who *d.* s.p. 19 Sep. 1706.
(c) The name is spelt "Smith" on the monument, 1577, of Sir Thomas Smith, of Hill Hall, Chancellor of the order of the Garter, as also on that, 1626, of Sir William Smith (father of the 1st Baronet), and on that, 1631, of Sir William Smith, s. and h. of the same; but on that of the 1st Baronet, in 1668, and of his son, Sir Edward, the 2d Baronet, in 1713, it is spelt "Smyth."
(d) See pedigree in *Mis. Gen. et Her.*, 2d Series, vol. iv, p. 241-246.

II. 1668. SIR EDWARD SMYTH, Baronet [1661], of Hill Hall, etc., aforesaid, 2d but 1st surv. s. and h., by 1st wife, *bap.* 28 Sep. 1637, at Thaxted; admitted to Gray's Inn, 4 Feb. 1656/7; *suc. to the Baronetcy*, 5 May 1668; was Sheriff of Essex, 1680-81. He *m.* 6 May 1674, at St. Olave's, Hart street, London (Lic. Vic. Gen. 4), Jane, sister of Sir Peter VANDEPUT, Alderman of London, da. of Peter VANDEPUT, of St. Margaret's Pattens, London, merchant (*d.* 10 Feb. 1668, aged 57), by Jane, da. of Dietrich HOSTE, also of London, merchant. He *d.* 24 June and was *bur.* 1 July 1713, at Theydon Mount, in his 76th year. M.I. Will dat. 24 July 1712, pr. 1 July 1713. His widow *d.* 28 July 1720, aged 67, and was *bur.* there. Will dat. 5 to 9 July 1720, pr. 14 Feb. 1720/1.

III. 1713. SIR EDWARD SMYTH, Baronet [1661], of Hill Hall, etc. aforesaid, only surv. s. and h., *b.* 1686; *suc. to the Baronetcy*, 24 June 1713. He *m.* firstly, 16 Jan. 1709/10, at St. Geo. the Martyr, Queen square, Midx., Anne, only da. of the Rt. Hon. Sir Charles HEDGES, of Compton Basset, Wilts, Judge of the Prerogative Court of Canterbury [1710-14], and sometime Sec. of State, by Eleanor, da. of George SMITH, a Proctor in Doctors Commons London. She *d.* 18 Oct. 1719 and was *bur.* at Theydon Mount. He *m.* secondly, Elizabeth, da. of John WOOD, of London. He *d.* 16 and was *bur.* 28 Aug. 1744, at Theydon Mount, in his 59th year. Will dat. 26 Nov. 1741, pr. 30 Aug. 1744. His widow, by whom he had no issue, *d.* 23 and was *bur.* 31 May 1748, in her 57th year, at Theydon Mount. Will dat. 23 July 1745, pr. 7 June 1748.

IV. 1744. SIR EDWARD SMYTH, Baronet [1661], of Hill Hall, etc., aforesaid, 1st. s. and h., by 1st wife; *b.* in St. James' Court 12 and *bap.* 16 Nov. 1710, at St. James', Westm.; *suc. to the Baronetcy*, 16 Aug. 1744. He *m.* 11 June 1747, at Milton Bryan, Beds, Elizabeth MAYSE, of that parish, spinster (said to have been *bap.* there 19 Aug. 1716), presumably illegit. da. of Joseph JOHNSON, of Milton Bryan.(a) He *d.* s.p. 4 and was *bur.* 8 March 1760, at Theydon Mount, in his 50th year. His widow *d.* 22 and was *bur.* there, 30 June 1770, in her 54th year. Will dat. 23 April 1763, pr. 26 June 1770.

V. 1760. SIR CHARLES SMYTH, Baronet [1661], of Hill Hall, etc., aforesaid, next br. and h., *bap.* 12 Oct. 1711, at St. James', Westm., *suc. to the Baronetcy*, 4 March 1760; Sheriff of Essex, 1760-61. He *m.* 11 Aug. 1760, Elizabeth, da. of John BURGESS, of London. He *d.* s.p.m. 24 March and was *bur.* 1 April 1773, at Theydon Mount, aged 61. Will dat. 24 May 1769, pr. 3 April 1773. His widow *d.* 2 Feb. 1776, at Bromley, co. Kent, and was *bur.* at Theydon Mount. Admon. 13 March 1776, to Thomas BURGES, a creditor, Ann SMYTH, spinster, the only child, renouncing.

VI. 1773. SIR WILLIAM SMYTH, Baronet [1661], of Hill Hall, etc., aforesaid, br. and h. male, being 5th and yst. s. of the 3d Baronet, by his 1st wife, *b.* about 1719; ed. at Trin. Hall, Cambridge; LL.B., 1754; took Holy Orders and was Rector of Stapleford Tawney and Theydon Mount, 1754/5, presumably, till his death; *suc. to the Baronetcy*, 24 March 1773. He *m.* in or before 1746, Abigail, sister and h. of Richard WOOD, da. of Andrew WOOD, of Shrewsbury. He *d.* 25 Jan. and was *bur.* 8 Feb. 1777, at Theydon Mount, aged 57. Will pr. 1777. His widow *d.* 28 Feb., and was *bur.* there 8 March 1787, aged 71. Will dat. 14 Feb. 1786, pr. 9 March 1787.

(a) This Joseph *d.* unm. 4 Feb. 1742/3, aged 61, and his will was pr. that month by "*Elizabeth Mayse, commonly called Miss Johnson.*" See pedigree of Johnson in *Mis. Gen. et Her.*, N.S., ii, 122.

VII. 1777. Sir William Smyth, afterwards, 1796? to 1823, Smijth,(a) Baronet [1661], of Hill Hall and Horham Hall aforesaid, and of Attleborough Hall, co. Norfolk, 1st s. and h., b. 23 April 1746, at Shrewsbury; *suc. to the Baronetcy*, 25 Jan. 1777; Col. of the West Essex Militia, and a Verderer of Waltham Forest, 1799. He *m.*, 22 March 1779 (as "*Sir William Smyth*"), at St. Geo., Han. sq., Anne, sister and h. of Joseph Windham, of Woodmansterne and Camberwell, co. Surrey, only da. of John Windham, *afterwards* Windham-Bowyer, of the same, and of Wawn, near Beverley, co. York, by Mary,(b) da. and eventually sole h. of Joseph Windham, *afterwards* Ashe, of Twickenham, co. Midx. She (who was b. in St. Geo., Han. sq.) d. 20 Dec. 1815, and was *bur.* at Theydon Mount. Admon. 22 April 1818. He *d.* 1 May 1823, aged 78, and was *bur.* there. Will dat. 26 March 1816 to 4 May 1821, pr. 6 June 1823.

VIII. 1823. Sir Thomas Smijth, Baronet [1661], of Hill Hall, etc., aforesaid, *formerly* Thomas Smyth, 2d but 1st surv. s and h.,(c) b. 6 Feb. 1781 in Upper Grosvenor street, Midx.; ed. at Eton (as "Smyth") 1793-96; *suc. to the Baronetcy*, 1 May 1823. He *d.* unm. at Hill Hall, 5 Oct. 1833, in his 53d year, and was *bur.* at Theydon Mount. Admon. Oct. 1833.

IX. 1833. Sir John Smijth, Baronet [1661], of Hill Hall, etc., aforesaid, br. and h., b. 8 June 1782, in Upper Grosvenor street; Commander in the Royal Navy; *suc. to the Baronetcy*, 5 Oct. 1833. He *d.* unm. at Woodmansterne aforesaid, 9 Dec. 1838, and was *bur.* at Theydon Mount in his 57th year. Will pr. Dec. 1838 and Aug. 1853.

X. 1838. Sir Edward Smijth, *afterwards*, 1839-50, Bowyer-Smijth, Baronet [1661], of Hill Hall, etc., aforesaid, *formerly* Edward Smyth, br. and h., b. 1 March 1785, in Margaret street, Marylebone; ed. at Eton (entered there as "Smyth") 1796-1802, and at Trin. Coll., Cambridge; B.A., 1807; M.A., 1811; in Holy Orders; Vicar of Camberwell, co. Surrey, 1809; sometime Chaplain to George IV; Rector of Stapleford Tawney and Theydon Mount, 1837-38; *suc. to the Baronetcy*, 9 Dec. 1838. By royal lic., 10 June 1839, he took the name of Bowyer-Smijth in lieu of that of Smijth. He *m.* 29 May 1813, at St. Geo., Han. sq., Lætitia Cecily, yst. da. of John Weyland, of Woodrising, co. Norfolk, and Woodeaton, co. Oxford, by Elizabeth, da. and coheir of John Nourse, of Woodeaton aforesaid. He *d.* 15 Aug. 1850, at Hill Hall aforesaid. Will pr. Oct. 1850. His widow *d.* 3 March 1868, in her 82d year, at Thorpe Lee, co. Surrey.

XI. 1850. Sir William Bowyer-Smijth, Baronet [1661], of Hill Hall, Horham Hall, and Attleborough Hall aforesaid, 1st s. and h., b. 22 April 1814; ed. at Eton and at Trin. Coll., Cambridge; *suc. to the Baronetcy*, 15 Aug. 1850; was M.P. for South Essex, 1852-57; Lieut. 19th Essex

(a) The unmeaning and fantastic name of "Smijth" was assumed between March 1779 and April 1799 by Sir William Smyth, who, on 29 April 1799, signed as "Smijth" a pedigree then entered in the College of Arms, in continuation of one that had been entered as recently as 1778, under the old name. It is to be regretted that a member of a family of respectable antiquity should have yielded to the false taste and the affectation of singularity that prevailed at that period by adopting a fantastic and ludicrous name, which disguised and rendered ridiculous the one borne by his ancestors for nearly three centuries, being that, also, of one of its most distinguished members, Sir Thomas Smith, the Sec. of State to Queen Elizabeth.

(b) The mother of this Mary was Martha, da. and coheir of Sir James Ashe, 2d Baronet [1660], of Twickenham, by Catharine, da. and coheir of Sir Edmund Bowyer, of Camberwell.

(c) The eldest s., William Smijth, *or* Smyth, Capt. in the West Essex Militia, *d.* unm. and v.p. in 1802, and was *bur.* at Theydon Mount, aged 22.

Rifle Volunteers, 1860-61. He sold the estate of Horham Hall to Francis George West. He *m.* firstly, 2 April 1839, at Cheshunt, Herts, Marianne Frances, 2d da. of Sir Henry Meux, 1st Baronet [1831], of Theobalds Park, by Elizabeth Mary, da. of Thomas Smith, of Castlebar House, co. Midx. She *d.* at 24 Chesham place, 11 March 1875, and was *bur.* in Brompton Cemetery. He *m.* secondly, 19 March 1875, at Cheltenham, Eliza Fechnie, only da. of David Baird Malcolm, of Crieff, co. Perth. He *d.* 20 Nov. 1883, at Twineham Court, co. Sussex, in his 69th year. His widow *m.* 2 Sep. 1890, in London, William Herbert Edward Stanford, and was living at Twineham Court aforesaid 1903.

XII. 1883. Sir William Bowyer-Smijth, Baronet [1661], of Hill Hall aforesaid, 1st s. and h. by 1st wife, b. 1 and privately *bap.* 21 Sep. 1840, at 13 Lower Grosvenor street, being received into the Church, 11 Jan. 1841; ed. at Eton; entered the Diplomatic Service, 1858; was Attaché at Florence, Munich, and Paris; 3d Secretary, 1863; 2d Sec. at Constantinople, 1874-81; Sec. of Legation at Yeddo, 1881-83; *suc. to the Baronetcy*, 20 Nov. 1883; Sheriff of Essex, 1889.

Family Estates.—These, in 1883, consisted of 4,418 acres in Norfolk, and 2,819 in Essex. *Total.*—7,237 acres, worth £9,100 a year. *Principal Seats.*—Hill Hall, near Epping, co. Essex, and Attleborough Hall, near Norwich, co. Norfolk.

SADLEIR, *or* SADLER:
cr. 3 Dec. 1661;
ex. 14 July 1719.

I. 1661. "Edwyn Sadler, of Temple Donesley [*i.e.*, Temple Dinsley, in Hitchin], co. Hertford, Esq.," 2d but 1st surv. s. and h. of Thomas Leigh Sadler, *or* Sadleir(a), of the same, and of Aspley Guise, co. Bedford, by Frances (*m.* 15 March 1612), da. of Francis Berry, of Beckening Park, Beds, was b. about 1620(b); admitted to the Inner Temple, Nov. 1640; suc. his father in 1658, and was *cr. a Baronet*, as above, 3 Dec. 1661. He *m.* (articles 8 and 9 Aug. 1654), Elizabeth, sister of Sir George Walker, 1st Baronet [1680], of Bushey, Herts, da. of Sir Walter Walker, Doctor of Law and sometime Judge of the Prerog. Court of Canterbury, by Mary, da. of [—] Lynne, of Southwick, co. Northampton. He *d.* July 1672. His widow living Aug. 1686.

II. 1672 to 1719. Sir Edwin Sadleir, Baronet [1661], of Temple Dinsley aforesaid, 3d but 1st surv. s. and h., b. in or before 1656, *suc. to the Baronetcy* in July 1672. He sold the estate of Temple Dinsley in 1712 for £3,922, to Benedict Ithell. He *m.* 9 Dec. 1686 (articles 30 and 31 Aug. previous), at St. Martin's-in-the-Fields (Lic. London, 4, he aged 28), Mary Crone (then of St. Peter le Poor, aged 30, widow), relict of William Crone, M.D., da. and coheir of John Lorymer, Citizen and Apothecary of London. Her will pr. Nov. 1706. He *d.* s.p. 14 July 1719, said to be in his 58th [*Qy.* 64th] year, when the *Baronetcy* became *extinct*. Will, as "of London," dat. 20 Sep. 1717, directing his burial to be at Aspley Guise. Beds, among his ancestors, pr. 23 July 1719, by his kinsman, "George Sadleir, of London, Gent.," the universal legatee.

(a) This Thomas (who *d.* 1658, in his 70th year) was s. and h. of Lee Sadleir (*d.* 5 Jan. 1587/8), who was s. and h. of Edward Sadleir, of Temple Dinsley (*d.* 4 April 1584), the 2d son (legitimated by Act of Parl.) of Sir Ralph Sadleir, of Standon, Herts, the well-known Statesman.

(b) His elder br. Thomas was aged 15 at the Her. Visit. of Beds, 1634.

WYNDHAM, *or* WINDHAM:
cr. 9 Dec. 1661;
afterwards, 1750—1845, Earls of Egremont:
ex. 2 April 1845.

I. 1661. "Sir William Windham, of Orchard Windham [in St. Decumans], co. Somerset, Knt.," s. and h. of John Windham, of the same, by Catharine, sister and coheir of Ralph, Baron Hopton of Stratton, da. of Robert Hopton, of Witham, co. Somerset, which John (who *d.* before May 1649) was the eldest of the nine sons of Sir John Windham, of Orchard Windham, and of Felbrigg, co. Norfolk (*d.* 1 April 1645, in his 87th year), was b. about 1633; admitted to Lincoln's Inn, 7 May 1649; was M.P. for Somerset, 1656-58; was *cr. a Baronet* by the Lord Protector Cromwell, 28 Aug. 1658, and sat as such in Parl. in 1659, but, that dignity being, of course, disallowed after the Restoration, he sat as an "Esq." in the Convention Parl. of 1660, though having been *Knighted*, by the King, between April 1660 and April 1661, he was elected as a "Knight" to the Parl. 1661-79, in all three cases being M.P. for Taunton. He was (possibly for "important services,")(a) *cr. a Baronet*, as above, 9 Dec. 1661. He *m.* (settlement 21 April 1656) Frances, da. of Anthony Hungerford, of Farley Castle, Wilts. He *d.* 29 Oct. 1683, in his 51st year, and was *bur.* at St. Decumans. M.I. Will dat. 22 Oct. 1683, pr. 3 Nov. 1684. The will of his widow dat. 19 Nov. 1696 [1686?], directing her burial to be at St. Decumans, pr. 4 May 1697.

II. 1683. Sir Edward Wyndham, Baronet [1661], of Orchard Windham aforesaid, only surv. s. and h., b. about 1667; *suc. to the Baronetcy*, 29 Oct. 1683; was M.P. for Ilchester, 1685-87, 1689-90, and 1690-95. He *m.* 16 May [*sic*, but *Qy.* if not June] 1687, at St. Peter's, Cornhill, London (Lic. Vic. Gen. 14 June [*sic*] 1687, he above 20 and she 17), Catharine, sister of John, 1st Baron Gower of Stittenham, da. of Sir William Leveson Gower, 4th Baronet [1620], by Jane, da. of John (Granville), Earl of Bath. He *d.* in St. James', Westm., and was *bur.* [*Qy.* at St. Decuman's?] 29 June 1695. Admon. 1 July 1695. His widow *d.* 14 March 1704. Will dat. 11 March 1704, pr. 27 July 1705, and 4 July 1710.

III. 1695. Sir William Wyndham, Baronet [1661], of Orchard Windham aforesaid, only s. and h., b. about 1688, at Trentham, co. Stafford; *suc. to the Baronetcy* in June 1695; matric. at Oxford (Ch. Ch.), 1 June 1704, aged 15; M.P. for Somerset (seven Parls.), April 1710 till death in 1740, being a Tory and a supporter of the party of Lord Bolingbroke; was Master of the Buckhounds, 1710; Sec. at War, 1712-13; P.C., 1713; Chancellor of the Exchequer, 1713-14. He abetted in Somersetshire the Rising of 1715, and was, accordingly, committed to the Tower in Sep. 1715, but released on bail, July 1716, and (owing to the interest of the Duke of Somerset, his father in law) was never brought to trial. He was an opposer of Walpole's Ministry, and supported Frederick, Prince of Wales in his quarrel with the King.(b) He *m.* firstly, 15 (21) July 1708, at Isleworth, co. Midx., Catharine, 2d da. of Charles (Seymour), 6th Duke of Somerset ("the proud Duke"), by his 1st wife, Elizabeth,

(a) His merits, little heeded apparently by his contemporaries, are set forth on his monument at St. Decumans, where he is said to be "most worthy of immortal memory," "Chief of the antient, great and noble family of Wyndham, of Felbrig, co. Norfolk, who, having heroically trod in the steps of his ancestors, in their faithfull and important services to the Crown, and, in particular, having with blessed success, *like another Curtius*, devoted himself and his very weighty interest to the closing the dreadful breach of the late monstrous division, betook himself . . . to the enjoyment of his most glorious immortality," etc.

(b) His fame is, perhaps, chiefly preserved by the lines of Pope, who describes him as—

"Wyndham, just to freedom and the throne,
The master of our passions and his own."

This throne, however, was, apparently, that of the House of Stuart.

da. and h. of Josceline (Percy), Earl of Northumberland. She *d.* 9 April 1731. He *m.* secondly, 1 June 1734, at Harlington, co. Midx., Maria Catherina, widow of William Godolphin, styled Marquess of Blandford, da. of Peter de Jonge, of Utrecht in Holland. He *d.* at Wells, co. Somerset, 17 July 1740, in his 53d year. Will pr. 1741. His widow, by whom he had no issue, *d.* 1 and was *bur.* 15 Sep. 1779, at Mortlake, co. Surrey, aged 96. Will pr. Sep. 1779.

IV. 1740. Sir Charles Wyndham, Baronet [1661], of Orchard Windham aforesaid, 1st s. and h.,(a) was b. 19 and *bap.* 30 Aug. 1710, at St. Martin's-in-the-Fields; matric. at Oxford (Ch. Ch.), 4 May 1725, aged 14; *suc. to the Baronetcy*, 17 June 1740; was M.P. for Bridgwater, 1735-41, for Appleby, 1741-47, and for Taunton, 1747-50. He (being at that date unm.) suc. as EARL OF EGREMONT and Baron Cockermouth (as also to the Cockermouth and other estates, co. Cumberland), on the death, s.p.m.s., 7 Feb. 1750, of his maternal uncle, Algernon (Seymour), 7th Duke of Somerset, who had been thus *cr.*, 3 Oct. 1749, with a spec. rem. in his favour.(b) In that peerage this *Baronetcy* then *merged* till both became *extinct*, 2 April 1845, on the death of the 4th Earl and 7th Baronet. See *Peerage*.

SOUTHCOTE, *or* SOUTHCOTT:
cr. 24 Jan. 1661/2;
ex. in or before 1691.

I. 1662. "George Southcote, of Bliborough, co. Lincoln, Esq.," s. and h. of Thomas Southcott, of the same (*d.* 10 April 1639), by Anne, da. of Sir Thomas Carey, of Stanton, co. Devon; was *cr. a Baronet*, as above, 24 Jan. 1661/2. He *m.* Katharine, da. and h. of John Elliot, of Essex. He *d.* Dec. 1663. Will pr. 1654. His widow *m.* the Hon. Nicholas Fairfax (s. of Thomas Viscount Fairfax), who *d.* before her. She *d.* at Tumby, co. Lincoln, in or before 1691. Admon. 6 July 1691.

II. 1664, to 1680? Sir George Southcote, Baronet [1662], of Bliborough aforesaid, posthumous s. and h., b. 1664, *suc. to the Baronetcy* on his birth. He *d.* s.p., probably unm., before (probably long before) July 1691.

TREVELYAN, *or* TREVILIAN:
cr. 24 Jan. 1661/2.

I. 1662. "George Trevilian, of Nettlecombe, co. Somerset, Esq.," s. and h. of George Trevilian, *or* Trevelyan, of the same, by Margaret, da. of Sir Robert Strode, of Parnham, co. Dorset, was b. probably about 1635; matric. at Oxford (Wadham Coll.), 22 March 1650/1; suc. his father (who had suffered much for his loyalty in the late Rebellion), in 1653, and

(a) His yr. br., Percy Wyndham, took the name of O'Brien, in 1741, on inheriting the estates of Henry (O'Brien) 8th Earl of Thomond [I.], the husband of his maternal aunt, formerly Lady Elizabeth Seymour. This Percy O'Brien was himself *cr.* 11 Dec. 1756, Earl of Thomond, [I.] but *d.* unm. 21 July 1774, when that Earldom became extinct.

(b) This Duke had also been *cr.* on the previous day (2 Oct. 1749), Earl of Northumberland and Baron Warkworth, with a spec. rem. to his son-in-law, Sir Hugh Smithson, 4th Baronet [1660], by Elizabeth, da. of the grantee, which Hugh (afterwards Duke of Northumberland) and his posterity inherited these honours accordingly.

was *cr. a Baronet*, as above, 29 Jan. 1661/2. He *m.* 8 Jan. 1655, Margaret, da. and h. of John WILLOUGHBY, of Ley Hill, near Honiton, co. Devon. He *d.* in 1671. Will dat. 2 March 1663, pr. 1 March 1672/3. The will of his widow dat. 3 June 1688, pr. 28 Nov. 1689.

II. 1671. SIR JOHN TREVELYAN, Baronet [1662], of Nettlecombe aforesaid, only s. and h., *b.* about 1670; *suc. to the Baronetcy* in 1671; matric. at Oxford (Wadham Coll.), 25 Oct. 1687, aged 17; was M.P. for Somerset, 1695-98, and 1700-01; for Minehead 1708, till unseated in 1716, and again, 1718-22. Sheriff of Somerset, 1704-05. He *m.* firstly, in 1693, Urith, da. of Sir John POLE, 3d Baronet [1628], of Shute, by Anne, da. of Sir William MORRICE. She *d.* s.p.s. in 1697. He *m.* secondly, in 1700, Susanna, da. and h. of William WARREN, of Stallensthorn, co. Devon. She *d.* 1718. He *d.* 25 Sep. 1755, aged 85. Will pr. 1756.

III. 1755. SIR GEORGE TREVELYAN, Baronet [1662], of Nettlecombe aforesaid, 3d but only surv. s. and h., *bap.* 18 Nov. 1707; *suc. to the Baronetcy*, 25 Sep. 1755. He *m.* in 1733, Julia, sister and h. (in 1777) of Sir Walter CALVERLEY-BLACKETT, 2d Baronet [1711], only da. of Sir Walter CALVERLEY, 1st Baronet [1711], of Calverley, by Julia, 1st da. of Sir William BLACKETT, 1st Baronet [1685] of Newcastle. He *d.* 11 Sep. 1768. Will pr. Oct. 1768. His widow *d.* 28 Dec. 1787, aged 73.

IV. 1768. SIR JOHN TREVELYAN, Baronet [1662], of Nettlecombe aforesaid and of Wallington, co. Northumberland, 1st s. and h., *b.* 6 Feb. 1734/5, at Escholt in Guiseley, co. York; matric. at Oxford (New Coll.), 26 May 1753, aged 18; *cr.* M.A., 6 July 1757; *suc. to the Baronetcy*, 11 Sep. 1768; M.P. for Newcastle-upon-Tyne, 1777-80, and for Somerset, 1780-96. He *m.* 20 May 1757, Louisa Marianna, da. and coheir(a) of Peter SIMOND, of Winchester street, London, merchant. She *d.* 29 Feb. 1772. He *d.* 18 April 1828, in Great Pulteney street, Bath, aged 93. Will pr. Jan. 1829.

V. 1828. SIR JOHN TREVELYAN, Baronet [1662], of Nettlecombe and Wallington aforesaid, 1st s. and h., *b.* 1 Jan. 1761; ed. at Winchester, 1773; *suc. to the Baronetcy*, 18 April 1828. He *m.* Aug. 1792, Maria, da. of Sir Thomas Spencer WILSON, 6th Baronet [1661], by Jane, da. of John Bridger WELLER. He *d.* 23 May 1846, at Nettlecombe, aged 85. Will pr. Dec. 1846. His widow *d.* at Hertford, 9 April 1851. Will pr. May 1851.

VI. 1846. SIR WALTER CALVERLEY TREVELYAN, Baronet [1662], of Nettlecomb and Wallington aforesaid, 1st s. and h., *b.* 31 March 1797, at Wallington; ed. at Harrow; matric. at Oxford (Univ. Coll.), 26 April 1816, aged 18; B.A., 1820; M.A., 1822; *suc. to the Baronetcy*, 23 May 1846; Sheriff of Northumberland, 1850; F.S.A., 1855. He *m.* 21 May 1835, at Swaffham Prior, Paulina, 1st da. of the Rev. W. JERMYN, D.D. She *d.* 13 May 1866, at Neuchâtel, in Switzerland. He *m.* secondly, 11 July 1867, at Pakenham, co. Suffolk, Laura Capel, da. of Capel LOFT, of Troston Hall in that county. He *d.* s.p. 23 March 1879, at Wallington, aged 81.(b) His widow *d.* there a few days later, 2 April 1879, in her 74th year.

VII. 1879. SIR ALFRED WILSON TREVELYAN, Baronet [1662], of Nettlecombe and Wallington aforesaid, nephew and h., being posthumous s. and h. of Alfred Wilson TREVELYAN, by Matilda Margaret, da. of John BOYCE, of Limerick, which Alfred (who *d.* 1830, aged 23) was yr. br. of the late and 4th and yst. s. of the 5th Baronet. He was *b.* 26 April 1831, and *suc. to the Baronetcy*, 23 March 1879. He *m.* 15 Feb. 1860, Fanny, da. of the Rt. Hon. James Henry MONAHAN, Chief Justice of the Common Pleas in Ireland, 1850-76. He *d.* s.p.m., at 74 Harley street, Marylebone, 18 April 1891, aged 59. His widow living 1903.

(a) Susanna Louisa, her sister, the other coheir ("a fortune of £200,000"), *m.* in 1755 John (ST. JOHN), 12th Baron Saint John of Bletso.
(b) He was a naturalist and a good antiquary.

VIII. 1891. SIR WALTER JOHN TREVELYAN, Baronet [1662], of Nettlecombe aforesaid and Piran Uthnoe, co. Cornwall, cousin and h. male, being only s. and h. of Willoughby John TREVELYAN, of Uthnoe aforesaid, by Eliza, da. of the Rev. Charles Saunders Skelton DUPUIS, Rector of Binton, co. Warwick, which Willoughby John (who *d.* 25 Aug. 1867, aged 27) was s. and h. of John TREVELYAN (*d.* 20 July 1852), s. and h. of the Rev. Walter TREVELYAN, Vicar of Henbury and Nettlecombe (*d.* 3 Nov. 1830, aged 67), who was yr. br. to the 5th and 2d s. of Sir John TREVELYAN, 4th Baronet. He was *b.* 28 Jan. 1866, at Goldsithney, co. Cornwall; matric. at Oxford (Exeter Coll.), 21 Oct. 1886, aged 20, and *suc. to the Baronetcy*, 18 April 1891. He *m.* 16 July 1901, at St. Paul's, Knightsbridge, Alice Edith, yst. da. of William James MONEY, C.S.I. (of Harrington Road, Queen's Gate), by Emily Harriet, da. of Gen. J. C. C. GRAY.

Family Estates.—Those belonging to the 6th Baronet [1846-79] and presumably to the 7th Baronet [1879-91] consisted of 22,058 acres in Northumberland (worth £15,448 a year), 6,361 in Somerset, 565 in Devon, and 126 in Cornwall. *Total.*—29,110 acres, worth £24,463 a year.

DUNCOMBE:

cr. 4 Feb. 1661/2;

ex. July 1706.

I. 1662. "FRANCIS DUNCOMBE, of Tangley [in Wonersh], co. Surrey, Esq.," 2d s. of George DUNCOMBE, of Shalford in that county (*d.* 29 Oct. 1674), by Charity, da. of John MUSCOTT, Alderman of London, was admitted to the Inner Temple, Nov. 1646; Barrister, 1653, and was *cr. a Baronet*, as above, 4 Feb. 1661/2. He *m.*, in or before 1658, Hester, widow of John CARYLL, of Tangley aforesaid (*d.* 30 May 1656), da. and coheir of John STYNT, Alderman of London. He *d.* 4 Nov. 1670. Admon. 19 Nov. 1670. His widow *d.* 1675.

II. 1670, to 1706. SIR WILLIAM DUNCOMBE, Baronet [1662], of Tangley aforesaid, only s. and h., *b.* 1658, being aged 4 in 1662; *suc. to the Baronetcy*, 4 Nov. 1670. He *m.* Anne, da. of Sir Ralph BAESH, K.B., of Stansteadbury, Herts, by Anne, da. of Edward SKIPWITH, of Gosberton, co. Lincoln. She *d.* before him. He *d.* s.p. and was *bur.* 21 July 1706, at St. Martin's-in-the-Fields, when the *Baronetcy* became *extinct*. Admon. 16 Oct. 1706, to his sister, Diana DUNCOMBE.

BACON:

cr. 7 Feb. 1661/2;

ex. Oct. 1685.

I. 1662. "NICHOLAS BACON, of Gillingham [St. Mary], co. Norfolk, Esq.," s. and h. of Nicholas BACON, of the same, by his 2d wife, Margaret (*m.* 26 Oct. 1622, at Fornham, co. Suffolk), da. of Eustace DARCY, of Bury St. Edmunds (which Nicholas was 4th s. of Sir Nicholas BACON, 1st Baronet [1611], of Redgrave), was *bap.* 31 Oct. 1623; admitted to Gray's Inn, 18 June 1639; suc. his father, Aug. 1641, and was *cr. a Baronet*, as above, 7 Feb. 1661/2. He *m.* (Lic. Fac. 31 May 1647, he 23 and she 20) Elizabeth, da. of Richard FRESTON, of Mendham, co. Norfolk. He *d.* 3 and was *bur.* 4 Aug. 1666, at Gillingham. Will pr. 1666. His widow *m.*, 14 April 1670 (Lic. Vic. Gen., 5 Feb. 1669/70, she about 38, he about 45, and a widower), Sir William GODBOLD, of Mendham, co. Norfolk, whose will was pr. Nov. 1687.

II. 1666. SIR EDMUND BACON, Baronet [1662], of Gillingham aforesaid, 1st s. and h., *b.* about 1660; *suc. to the Baronetcy*, 3 Aug. 1666; admitted to Lincoln's Inn, 6 Nov. 1669; aged 14 at the Her. Visit. of Norfolk, 1674. He *d.* unm. and was *bur.* 5 Nov. 1683, at Gillingham. Admon. 25 June 1684.

III. 1683, to 1685. SIR RICHARD BACON, Baronet [1662], of Gillingham aforesaid, br. and h., *b.* probably about 1663; *suc. to the Baronetcy*, Nov. 1683. He *m.* his cousin, Anne, da. of Sir Henry BACON, 2d Baronet [1627], of Mildenhall, by Barbara, da. of William GOOCH. He *d.* s.p. and was *bur.* 8 Oct. 1685, at Gillingham, when the *Baronetcy* became *extinct*.(a) Will pr. May 1686.

COCKS, *or* COX:

cr. 7 Feb. 1661/2;

ex. 4 April 1765.

I. 1662. "RICHARD COX [*rectius* COCKS], of Dumbleton, co. Gloucester,"(b) 2d s. of Richard COCKS, of Castleditch, co. Hereford, by Judith, da. and coheir of John ELLIOTT, of London, merchant, was *b.* about 1602; accompanied his uncle, Christopher COCKS, to Muscovy; is said to have been "a great sufferer for his love to the Royal Family"(c); inherited the estate of Dumbleton, 15 Aug. 1654, on the death of his uncle, Charles COCKS,(d) of the same, one of the Masters in Chancery, and was *cr. a Baronet*, as above, 7 Feb. 1661/2. He was Sheriff of Gloucestershire, 1665-66. He *m.*, probably about 1630, Susanna, da. of Ambrose ELTON, of the Hasle, co. Hereford, by Anne, da. of Sir Edward ASTON, of Tixall, co. Stafford. He *d.* 16 Sep. 1684, aged 82, and was *bur.* at Dumbleton. M.I. Will pr. 4 July 1688. His widow *d.* 10 March 1689, aged 84, and was *bur.* there. M.I.

II. 1684. SIR RICHARD COCKS, Baronet [1662], of Dumbleton aforesaid, grandson and h., being 1st s. and h. of Richard COCKS, Barrister at Law (Middle Temple), by Mary, da. of Sir Robert COOKE, of Highnam, co. Gloucester, which Richard was s. and h. ap. of the late Baronet, but *d. v.p.*, 1670; was *b.* about 1658, and *suc. to the Baronetcy*, 16 Sep. 1684; M.P. for Gloucestershire (three Parls.), 1698-1702; Sheriff of that county, 1692-93. He *m.* firstly (Lic. Vic. Gen., 6 Oct. 1688, he 30 and she 24, to marry at Waltham, Berks), Frances, 5th and yst. da. of Col. Richard NEVILLE, of Billingbeare, Berks, by Anne, da. of Sir Christopher HEYDON, of Bocansthrop, co. Norfolk. She *d.* 1 Feb. 1723, in her 60th year, and was *bur.* at Dumbleton. M.I. He *m.* secondly, Mary (*b.* 21 Aug. 1691), da. of William BETHELL, of Swindon, and Ellerton, co. York, by Elizabeth, da. of Sir John BROOKE. He *d.* s.p., 21 Oct. 1726.

III. 1726. SIR ROBERT COCKS, Baronet [1662], of Dumbleton aforesaid, br. and h., *b.* about 1660; matric. at Oxford (Oriel Coll.), 26 Feb. 1674/5, aged 15; B.A., 1678; Fellow of Brasenose Coll. and M.A., 1681; in Holy Orders; B.D. and D.D., 1695; Rector of Great Rollright, Oxon,

(a) The estate of Gillingham went to his wife's brother, Sir Henry Bacon, 3d Baronet [1627], of Mildenhall, who and whose successors resided there for above 50 years. See vol. ii, p. 32.
(b) His rank is not stated in Dugdale's *List*.
(c) See his M.I.
(d) This Charles Cocks had inherited Dumbleton, 28 June 1646, on the death of his sister, Dame Dorothy Percy, widow of the Hon. Sir Charles Percy (*d.* 9 July 1628), and formerly wife of Edmund Hutchens, of Dumbleton (*d.* 1602), who had devised that estate to her.

1695; Rector of Bladon with Woodstock in that county, 1715; sometime Chancellor of the Diocese of Gloucester; Chaplain to the 1st (King's) regiment of Guards till 1730 having *suc. to the Baronetcy*, 21 Oct. 1726. He *m.* "Mrs. Anne FULKS, of Oxford." She *d.* 5 Nov. 1712, aged 43, and was *bur.* at Great Rollright. M.I. He *d.* 9 Feb. 1735/6, at Woodstock. Will pr. 1737.

IV. 1736, to 1765. SIR ROBERT COCKS, Baronet [1662], of Dumbleton aforesaid, 4th but 1st surv. s. and h.; Sheriff of Gloucestershire, 1727-28; *suc. to the Baronetcy*, 9 Feb. 1735/6. He *m.* 12 Aug. 1727, at St. Paul's Cathedral, London, Elizabeth, da. of James CHOLMELEY, of Easton, co. Lincoln, by Katharine, da. of [—] WOODFINE. She *d.* 30 Jan. 1749, aged 39 (three of her children dying of the same distemper within a few days), and was *bur.* at Dumbleton. M.I. He *d.* s.p.m.s., through a fall from his horse, 4 April 1765, and was *bur.* there, when the *Baronetcy* became *extinct*.(a) Will dat. 28 Oct. 1762, pr. 5 June 1765.

OSBORN, *or* OSBURNE:

cr. 11 Feb. 1661/2.(b)

I. 1662. "JOHN OSBURNE [*rectius* OSBORN], of Chicksand [*i.e.*, the extra-parochial estate of Chicksands Priory], co. Bedford, Esq.," 1st s. and h. of Sir Peter OSBORN, of the same, Remembrancer to the Treasury, and (28 years) Gov. of Guernsey, by Dorothy, sister of Henry, EARL OF DANBY, da. of Sir John DANVERS, of Dauntsey, co. Wilts, was *b.* about 1615; suc. his father in March 1656; was a Gent. of the Privy Chamber, and was *cr. a Baronet*, as above, 11 Feb. 1661/2; had a grant of the Office of Remembrancer to the Treasury in 1674. He *m.* (Lic. Lond. 22 Dec. 1647, he of St. Peter's, Westcheap, about 25 [32 ?], and she of St. Mary, Aldermanbury, about 24) Eleanor, da. of Charles DANVERS, of Baynton, Wilts. She *d.* 16 Nov. 1677, and was *bur.* at Hawnes, co. Bedford. M.I. He *d.* 5 and was *bur.* there 14 Feb. 1698/9, aged 83. M.I. Will dat. 20 May 1691, pr. 4 March 1698/9.

II. 1699. SIR JOHN OSBORN, Baronet [1662], of Chicksands Priory aforesaid, only s. and h., *b.* about 1650; *suc. to the Baronetcy*, 5 Feb. 1698/9. He *m.* firstly, in or before 1682, Elizabeth, da. of William STRODE, of Street, co. Somerset, by (—), da. and coheir of (—) RIVITT, of King's Somborne, Hants. She *d.* 27 and was *bur.* 28 March 1683, at Hawnes, in her 22d year. M.I. He *m.* secondly, in or before 1688, Martha, da. of Sir John KELYNG, Serjeant at Law, by Philippa, da. of Amerigo Salvetti ANTELLMINELLI, Resident for the Duke of Tuscany. She was *bur.* 12 Nov. 1713, at Campton, Beds. He *d.* 28 April 1720, aged 70, and was *bur.* at Hawnes. M.I. Will pr. 1720.

III. 1720. SIR DANVERS OSBORN, Baronet [1662], of Chicksands Priory aforesaid, grandson and h., being only s. and h. of John OSBORN, by Sarah, da. of George (BYNG), 1st VISCOUNT TORRINGTON, which John (who was *bap.* 1 April 1683, at Campton, and matric. at Oxford [Univ. Coll.] 13 Oct. 1701) was 1st s. and h. ap. of the late Baronet, being only child of his 1st wife, but *d.* v.p. and was *bur.* 14 Jan. 1718/9 at Campton.(c) He was *b.* 17 Nov. 1715; *suc. to the Baronetcy* 28 April 1720; was M.P. for Beds, 1747-53; Governor of New York, for a few months in 1753, till his death. He *m.* 25 Sep. 1740,

(a) John Cocks, his 2d cousin once removed (being grandson of Thomas Cocks, of Castleditch, the elder br. of the 1st Baronet), suc. to the Dumbleton estate, and *d.* 24 Jan. 1771, leaving a son and heir, Charles Cocks (*b.* 29 June 1725), who was *cr. a Baronet*, as "of Dumbleton," 7 Oct. 1772, and who subsequently was *cr.*, 17 May 1784, Baron Sommers of Evesham.
(b) See p. 160, as to the date of this creation being on 11 Feb. 1660/1 (13 Car. II) instead of (as in the text) 11 Feb. 1661/2 (14 Car. II).
(c) His widow survived him 56 years! and was *bur.* 22 Nov. 1775, at Campton.

Mary, da. of George (MONTAGU), 1st EARL OF HALIFAX, by his 2d wife, Mary, da. of Richard (LUMLEY), EARL OF SCARBROUGH. She *d.* at Chicksands, 23 and was *bur.* 30 July 1743, at Campton aforesaid. He *d.* in his garden at New York, shortly after his arrival there, 27 Dec. 1753, and was *bur.* 7 Aug. 1754, at Campton. Will pr. 1754.

IV. 1753. SIR GEORGE OSBORN, Baronet [1662], of Chicksands Priory aforesaid, 1st s. and h., *b.* 10 May 1742; *suc. to the Baronetcy,* 27 Dec. 1753; was an officer in the army, becoming, eventually, 26 Jan. 1797, General; was Colonel of the 40th Regiment; many years Groom of the Bedchamber; M.P. for Northampton, 1768, till void in Feb. 1769; for Bossiney, April 1769 to 1774; for Penrhyn, 1774-80, and for Horsham, 1780-84. He acted as Proxy for H.R.H. the Duke of York, on his installation as a Knight of the Bath in 1772. He *m.* firstly, in 1771, Elizabeth, 1st da. and coheir of John BANNISTER and Elizabeth his wife. She was *bur.* 16 March 1773, at Campton.(a) He *m.* secondly, 22 Aug. 1778, Heneage, da. of Daniel (FINCH), EARL OF WINCHILSEA AND NOTTINGHAM, by his 2d wife, Mary, da. and coheir of Sir Thomas PALMER, 4th Baronet [1621], of Wingham. He *d.* at Chicksands Priory, 29 June 1818, in his 77th year. Will pr. 1818. His widow, who was *b.* Dec. 1741, and by whom he had no children, *d.* 4 May 1820.

V. 1818. SIR JOHN OSBORN, Baronet [1662], of Chicksands Priory aforesaid, only s. and h. by 1st wife; *b.* 3 Dec. 1772; ed. at Westm. School; matric. at Oxford (Ch. Ch.), 22 April 1790; B.A., 1793; M.A., 1814, being *cr.* D.C.L., 13 June 1834; M.P. for Beds, 1794-1807; for Cockermouth, 1807-08; for Queenborough, 1812-18; for Wigton Burghs, 1821-24; and for Beds, again, 1818-20; a Lord of the Admiralty, 1812-24, having *suc. to the Baronetcy,* 29 June 1818; a Commissioner for Auditing Public Accounts, 1829, till his death; Colonel of the Beds Militia. He *m.* 14 Sep. 1809, Frederica Louisa, illegit. da. of Sir Charles DAVERS, 6th and last Baronet [1682], of Rougham. He *d.* 28 Aug. 1848, at 44 Porchester terrace, Bayswater, aged 75. Will pr. Sep. 1848. His widow *d.* 23 July 1870, at Campton House, Beds, in her 80th year.

VI. 1848. SIR GEORGE ROBERT OSBORN, Baronet [1662], of Chicksands Priory aforesaid, 1st s. and h., *b.* 29 Oct. 1813, at the Admiralty, Whitehall; ed. at Westm. School; matric. at Oxford (Ch. Ch.), 10 Nov. 1831, aged 18; served in the army, 85th Foot, till 1835; *suc. to the Baronetcy* 28 Aug. 1848; Sheriff of Bedfordshire, 1857. He *m.* firstly, 22 Aug. 1835, Charlotte Elizabeth, 4th da. of Vice-Admiral Lord Robert Mark KERR (3d s. of William John, 5th MARQUESS OF LOTHIAN [S.]), by Charlotte (formerly Charlotte MACDONNELL), *suo jure* COUNTESS OF ANTRIM [I.]. She, who was *b.* 31 May 1811, *d.* 17 Jan. 1866, at Chicksands Priory, aged 54. He *m.* secondly, 20 May 1871, at Christ Church, Folkestone, Mary Elizabeth, 2d da. of Sir George SITWELL, 2d Baronet [1808], by Sarah, da. of Craufurd TAIT, of Harvieston, co. Clackmannan. He *d.* 11 Jan. 1892, at Chicksands Priory, aged 78. Will pr. at £65,130. His widow living 1903.

VII. 1892. SIR ALGERNON KERR BUTLER OSBORN, Baronet [1662], of Chicksands Priory aforesaid, grandson and h., being only s. and h. of Henry John Robert OSBORN, Lieut. 1st Life Guards, by Emily, (*m.* 28 April 1866, at Hatley St. George), 3d da. of Thomas ST. QUENTIN, of Hatley Park, co. Cambridge, which Henry John Robert (*b.* 12 Sep. 1839, at Carlsruhe, in the Duchy of Baden) was 1st s. and h. ap. of the late Baronet, but *d.* v.p., being drowned, 29 March 1889. He was *b.* 8 Aug. 1870, and *suc. to the Baronetcy,* 11 Jan. 1892.

Family Estates.—These, in 1883, consisted of 3,049 acres in Bedfordshire, worth £4,695 a year. *Seat.*—Chicksands Priory, near Biggleswade, co. Bedford.

(a) Her mother, "Elizabeth, relict of John Bannister, Esq.," was subsequently *bur.* there, 14 May 1789.

CORYTON, *or* CORITON:
cr. 27 Feb. 1661/2;
ex. 22 May 1739.

I. 1662. "JOHN CORITON, of Newton (*i.e.*, West Newton Ferrers, in St. Mellion], co. Cornwall, Esq.," 3d but only surv. s. and h. of William CORITON, *or* CORYTON, of the same, Vice-Warden of the Stanneries, 1603-30, Sheriff of Cornwall, 1613-14, and many years [1624-41] M.P.,(a) (*d.* 30 April 1651, aged above 70), by Elizabeth, da. of John CHICHESTER, of Raleigh, co. Devon, was *bap.* 29 July 1621, at St. Mellions; was fined £297, in 1651; was M.P. for Callington, 1660; for Cornwall, 1661-79; for Callington, again, 1679, and for Launceston, 1679, till his death, having been *cr. a Baronet*, as above, 27 Feb. 1661/2. He *m.* firstly, 27 Dec. 1643 (Mar. Lic. at Exeter, 13), at Colebrooke, co. Devon, Elizabeth, only da. and h. of John MILLS, of Colebrooke aforesaid. She, who was *bap.* 29 Nov. 1629, at Colebrooke, *d.* 27 Sep. 1677, and was *bur.* there. He *m.* secondly (Lic. Fac., 24 May 1680), Anne WAYTE, widow,(b) of Acton, co. Midx. He *d.* a few months later, and was *bur.* 23 Aug. 1680, at St. Mellions. Will dat. 15 Aug. 1680. His widow was *bur.* 8 May 1707, at Acton aforesaid. Will pr. April [?] 1707.

II. 1680. SIR JOHN CORYTON, Baronet [1662], of Newton aforesaid, 1st s. and h., by 1st wife, *bap.* 21 Jan. 1648, at St. Mellions; matric. at Oxford (Exeter Coll.), 23 Nov. 1666, aged 17; *suc. to the Baronetcy* in Aug. 1680; M.P. for Newport, 1679, and for Callington, 1685, till unseated the same year, and again 1689, till death; Sheriff of Cornwall, 1683-84. He *m.* 22 Feb. 1671/2, at St. James', Clerkenwell (Lic. Vic. Gen., 13, he about 23 and she about 18), Elizabeth, da. and coheir of Sir Richard CHIVERTON, sometime 1657-58, Lord Mayor of London, by (—). He *d.* s.p.m.s., and was *bur.* 30 July 1690, at St. Mellions. Admon. 4 Aug. 1690, to his widow.

III. 1690. SIR WILLIAM CORYTON, Baronet [1662], of Newton aforesaid, br. of the whole blood and h. male, *bap.* 24 May 1650 at St. Mellions; matric. at Oxford (Exeter Coll.), with his elder br., 23 Nov. 1666, aged 16; Barrister (Middle Temple), 1675; was M.P. for Bossiney, 1679; for Newport, 1679-81; for Callington, 1681 and 1685-87; for St. Michael, Sep. 1689 to Feb. 1690; for Callington, again, 1695-1701, and Nov. 1703, till his death, having *suc. to the Baronetcy* in July 1690. He *m.* firstly, 11 Dec. 1688, at Lee, co. Kent, Susanna, sister of Sir Edward LITTLETON, 3d Baronet [1627], da. of Edward LITTLETON, of Pillaton, co. Stafford, by Susanna, da. of Sir Theophilus BIDDULPH, 1st Baronet [1664]. She *d.* 6 Aug. 1695, and was *bur.* at St. Mellions, aged 24. He *m.* secondly, Sarah, widow of Thomas WILLIAMS, of London, Banker. He *d.* 6 Dec. 1711, and was *bur.* at St. Mellions. M.I. Will pr. Oct. 1712. His widow *m.* (as the 2d of his three wives), 29 Oct. 1716, at St. Stephen's-by-Saltash, Sir Nicholas TREVANNION, Commissioner of Portsmouth Dockyard (who *d.* 16 Nov. 1737), and *d.* 27, being *bur.* 30 Sep. 1719, at St. Germans. M.I.

IV. 1711, to 1739. SIR JOHN CORYTON, Baronet [1662], of Newton aforesaid, only s. and h., by 1st wife, *b.* at Greenwich about 1690; admitted to Rugby School, 10 Aug. 1698; matric. at Oxford (Ch. Ch.), 14 Oct. 1708, aged 18; *suc. to the Baronetcy,* 6 Dec. 1711; was M.P. for Callington, 1713-22 and 1727-34. He *m.* 31 Oct. 1715, at East Coker, co. Somerset, Rachel, da. of William HELYAR, of East Coker, by Joanna, da. and coheir of [—] HOLE, of South Tawton, Devon. He *d.* s.p. 22 May and was *bur.* 9 June 1739, at St. Mellions aforesaid, when the *Baronetcy* became *extinct.*(c) Will pr. 1740.

(a) This William Coryton, who was formerly one of the so-called Patriots, became in 1640 a Royalist, and was accordingly fined £1,244, which was, however, reduced to £828, and allowed to his da. Philippa, for her services in the Parl. cause.

(b) Presumably widow of "Mr. D. Wayte," who was *bur.* "in the church" at Acton, 29 March 1677.

(c) He had a sister, Susanna, *m.* to Edward Eliot, but the estates apparently devolved on his cousin, Peter Goodall (whose grandfather, William Goodall, of Fowey, had *m.* Elizabeth, da. of the 1st Baronet), who took the name of Coryton, and *d.* 1756, leaving issue.

LLOYD, *or* LLHOYD:
cr. 28 Feb. 1661/2;
ex. 1674.

I. 1662. "JOHN LLHOYD [*rectius* LLOYD], of Woking, co. Surrey, Esq.," being also of the Forest, co. Carmarthen, s. of Griffith LLOYD, of the Forest aforesaid, by Janet, da. of William WOGAN, of Pembrokeshire, took the Covenant, 9 Dec. 1646; was Col. in the Parl. Army; M.P. for Carmarthenshire April 1646, till secluded Dec. 1648; and again 1660, and was *cr. a Baronet,* 28 Feb. 1661/2. He *m.* in or after 1643, Beatrix, widow of James ZOUCHE, of Woking aforesaid (who *d.* 1643), 3d da. of Francis (ANNESLEY), VISCOUNT VALENTIA [I.], by his 1st wife Dorothy, da. of Sir John PHILIPPS, 1st Baronet [1621], of Picton. He *d.* 1 Jan. 1663/4, and was *bur.* at Woking. M.I. Admon. 8 Feb. 1663/4, 16 July 1668, 16 Feb. 1675/6, and finally 2 Dec. 1676, to his da. Anne, wife of Gawen TURNER.(a) His widow, who was *b.* 27 March 1619, at Fishamble street, St. John's parish, Dublin, *m.* (as her 3d husband and his 2d wife), Sir Thomas SMITH, 1st Baronet [1661], and *d.* (five weeks before him), 26 March 1668, being *bur.* at Theydon Mount, co. Essex.

II. 1664, to 1674. SIR JOHN LLOYD, Baronet [1662], of the Forest, co. Carmarthen aforesaid, only s. and h., *b.* about 1651; *suc. to the Baronetcy,* 1 Jan. 1663/4; matric. at Oxford (Jesus Coll.), 29 Oct. 1668, aged 17; *cr.* M.A. 9 July 1669; admitted to Lincoln's Inn (as "FLOYD"), 27 Nov. 1671. He *m.* Mary, da. of the Rev. Matthew SMALLWOOD, LL.D., Dean of Lichfield, she being a minor at the time of his death. He *d.* s.p.m. 1674. Admon. 4 March 1674/5, and 3 March 1678/9. His widow *m.* (Lic. Vic. Gen., 19 June 1675, she about 20 and he about 24), Charles HUTCHINSON, of Pinner, co. Midx., both being living March 1678/9.

MORE, *or* MOORE:

"EDWARD MOORE, of Moore Hall, co. Lancaster, Esq.," is placed under the date of 1 March 1661/2 in Dugdale's *List* of creations of Baronetcies, with the note that "though at this time the Receipt was made, the patent did not pass the seal until 22 Nov. 1675." Under the latter date, accordingly, it is here dealt with.

PROBY:
cr. 7 March 1661/2;
ex. 1689.

I. 1662. to 1689. "THOMAS PROBY, of Elton Hall, co. Huntingdon, Esq.," as also of Raines, in Amersham, Bucks, 2d but 1st s. and h. ap. of Sir Heneage PROBY, of the same (who was s. and h. of Sir Peter PROBY, Lord Mayor of London, 1622-23), by Helen, da. of Edward ALLEN, of Finchley, Midx., was *b.* about 1634; was M.P. for Agmondesham 1660, and 1666 to 1679, and subsequently, 1679-81, for Huntingdonshire, and was *cr. a Baronet,* as above, 7 March 1661/2. He suc. his father, 10 Feb. 1662/3. He *m.* in or before 1673, Frances, da. of Sir Thomas COTTON, 2d Baronet [1611], of Connington, by his 2d wife, Alice, da. and h. of Sir John CONSTABLE. He *d.* s.p.m.s.(b) 1689, when the *Baronetcy* became *extinct.*

(a) Another da. Beatrice, *m.* Sir John Barlow, 1st Baronet [1677], of Slebech, co. Pembroke. These daughters or their issue, on the death, s.p., between 1676 and 1698, of Anne, wife of John Tredenham, and only child of the 2d Baronet, became coheirs of the family.

(b) Thomas Proby, his only s., *d.* unm. on his travels. Alice, *b.* 1673 (the only da. that married), *m.* Hon. Thomas Watson-Wentworth, and was mother of the 1st Marquess of Rockingham.

STAPLETON, *or* STAPYLTON:
cr. 20 March 1661/2;
ex. Feb. 1706/7.

I. 1662, to 1707. "MILES STAPLETON, of Carleton, co. York, Esq.," 3d s.(a) of Gilbert STAPLETON, *or* STAPYLTON, of the same (*d.* about 1636), by his 2d wife, Eleanor, da. of Sir John GASCOIGNE, 1st Baronet [S. 1635], was *bap.* 19 Oct. 1626, at Carleton, and, being in possession of the family estates, was *cr. a Baronet,* as above, 20 March 1661/2. He recorded his pedigree at the Heralds' Visit. of Yorkshire, 1666, calling himself then 38. He *m.* firstly, in or before 1661, Elizabeth, 2d da. of Robert (BERTIE), 1st EARL OF LINDSEY, by Elizabeth, da. of Edward (MONTAGU), 1st BARON MONTAGU OF BOUGHTON. She *d.* 28 Feb. and was *bur.* 3 March 1683/4, at Snaith. M.I. He *m.* secondly, Elizabeth, da. of Sir Thomas LONGUEVILLE, 2d Baronet [S. 1638], by his 1st wife, Mary, da. and coheir of Sir William FENWICK. He *d.* s.p.s. and was *bur.* 19 Feb. 1706/7, at Snaith, when the *Baronetcy* became *extinct.* Will dat. 27 Jan. 1693, pr. at York, 25 Nov. 1707.

BRAHAM:
cr. 16 April 1662;
ex. 1675-77.

I. 1662, to 1676? "SIR RICHARD BRAHAM, of New Windsor, Berks, Knt.," 1st s. and h. of Richard BRAHAM, *or* BREAME, of the same, and of Wandsworth, co. Surrey (*d.* 2 March 1618, aged 33), by Elizabeth, da. of Nathaniel GILES, Mus. Doc., was *b.* about 1613; admitted to Gray's Inn, 7 March 1633/4; M.P. for Windsor, July 1645, till void, and again, 1661 till death. *Knighted* at Oxford, 21 March 1644/5, was a Compounder in May 1646, being fined £364, and was *cr. a Baronet,* as above, 16 April 1662. He entered his pedigree in the Heralds' Visit. of Berks, 1667. He *m.* firstly, Susan, da. of Sir George SOUTHCOTE, Governor of Dartmouth Castle, Devon. She *d.* s.p. 5 May 1642, aged 22, and was *bur.* at New Windsor. M.I. He *m.* secondly, Susan, da. of Sir Robert GAWSELL, of Watlington, co. Norfolk. She also *d.* s.p. He *m.* thirdly (Lic. Vic. Gen., 6 May 1663, he of St. Margaret's, Westm., about 50, widower), Jane SCOBELL, of St. Margaret's, Westm., about 40, widow, da. of Thomas DEVENISH, of Langham, co. Dorset. She *d.* s.p.s. 1667. He appears to have *m.* fourthly (Lic. Fac.), 29 Nov. 1671, Dorothy BRANDLING, of Carmarthen, widow. He *d.* s.p.m., between 22 Nov. 1675 and 16 Feb. 1676/7, when the *Baronetcy* became *extinct.*

WITTEWRONG, *or* WITERONG:
cr. 2 May 1662;
ex. 13 Jan. 1771.

I. 1662. "SIR JOHN WITERONG [*rectius* WITTEWRONG], of Stantonbury [*or* Stanton-Barry], co. Buckingham, Knt.," only s. and h. of Jacob, *or* James WITTEWRONG, *or* WITTEWRONGLE, of Westham, co. Essex, and of London, brewer (*b.* at Ghent, in Flanders, 15 Jan. 1558, and *d.* 5 July 1622), by his 2d wife, Ann,(b) yst. da. and coheir of Gerard VANACKER, of Antwerp, merchant, was *b.* in Grantham lane, Allhallows, London, Oct., and *bap.* 1 Nov. 1618, in the

(a) Of his elder brothers (1) Richard, *b.* 23 Feb. 1620/1, was found a lunatic, 17 April 1650, and (2) Gregory, a monk at Douay, *d.* 4 Aug. 1680.

(b) She *m.* (as his 4th wife) 18 Dec. 1623, at St. Mary's, Aldermary, London, Sir Thomas Middleton, sometime, 1613-14, Lord Mayor of London (who *d.* 12 Aug. 1631, aged about 81), and *d.* 7 Jan. 1646/7, being *bur.* at Harpenden, Herts.

III

Dutch church(a); was brought up [1622-31] in the house of his step-father, Sir Thomas MIDDLETON, Alderman of London; matric. at Oxford (Trin. Coll.), 17 Oct. 1634, aged 16; purchased the estate of Rothampstead, in Harpenden, Herts, and subsequently that of Stanton Barry aforesaid; was *Knighted*, 16 Feb. 1640/1, at Whitehall; was Sheriff of Herts, 1646-47, and again 1658-59; having been M.P. for that county, 1654-58, and was *cr. a Baronet*, as above, 2 May 1662. Sheriff of Montgomeryshire, 1664-65. He *m.* firstly, 30 Dec. 1638, in the chapel of Chirk Castle, co. Denbigh, Mary, sister of Sir Thomas MIDDLETON, 1st Baronet [1660], da. of Sir Thomas MIDDLETON, of Chirk Castle aforesaid, by his 2d wife, Mary, da. of Sir Robert NAPIER, 1st Baronet [1611], of Luton Hoo. She *d.* of smallpox, 4 April 1640, and was *bur.* (with her husband's father) at Westham. He *m.* secondly, "Wed. 23 June 1642,"(a) at Stansted Montfichet, co. Essex (Lic. London, 17 June 1641 [*sic*], both aged 23), Elizabeth, 2d da. of Timothy MIDDLETON, of that place, by Martha, da. and h. of Robert JOHNSON, Alderman of London. She *d.* of fever at Rothamsted 6, and was *bur.* 18 Oct. 1649, at Harpenden. He *m.* thirdly, 4 July 1650, at her father's house in Stepney, Catharine, sister of John, 1st BARON HAVERSHAM, da. of Maurice THOMPSON, of Haversham, Bucks, by Dorothy (or Ellen), da. of John VAUX, of Pembrokeshire. She *d.* 10 and was *bur.* 28 April 1659, at Harpenden. He *d.* at Rothamsted and was *bur.* 23 June 1693, at Harpenden, in his 75th year. Will dat. 7 June 1688, pr. 3 July 1693.

II. 1693. SIR JOHN WITTEWRONG, Baronet [1662], of Stanton Barry aforesaid, 1st s. and h., being only child by 1st wife,(b) *b.* in London, 18 Feb. 1639/40; matric. at Oxford (Mag. Coll.) 29 Oct. 1657; admitted to Inner Temple, 1 Nov. 1658; *suc. to the Baronetcy* in June 1693. He *m.* firstly (Lic. Lond., 4 Oct. 1664, he "of Rothamsted, Herts, Esq., aged 24") Clare (then aged 19), 1st da. of Sir Joseph ALSTON, 1st Baronet [1682], by Mary, da. and coheir of (—) VAN CROOKENBERG. She *d.*, s.p.m.s., 12 Oct. 1669 and was *bur.* at Stanton Barry. M.I. He *m.* secondly (Lic. Vic. Gen., 29 Oct. 1670) Martha (then of Mark lane, London, about 19, spinster), da. of (—) SEABROOKE, and niece of Edward BACKWELL, Alderman of London. He *d.* 30 Jan. and was *bur.* 4 Feb. 1697, at Stanton Barry. Will dat. 11 Jan. 1697, pr. 19 July 1703. His widow was *bur.* there 2 June 1698.

III. 1697. SIR JOHN WITTEWRONG, Baronet [1662], of Stanton Barry aforesaid, 1st surv. s. and h., by 2d wife; *bap.* there 11 July 1673; *suc. to the Baronetcy* 30 Jan. 1697, was M.P. for Aylesbury 1705-13, and for Wycombe 1713 till death. He served in the wars in Flanders, and was Col. of a Foot Reg. on the Irish establishment, called "Wittewrong's," which was disbanded in 1717. He *m.* in or before 1695, Mary, da. of Samuel WHITE, niece of Richard PERRY, both of London, Merchants. She was *bur.* 15 May 1716, at Isleworth, co. Midx. He *d.* 30 Jan. 1721/2 and was *bur.* at Stanton Barry. Will dat. 2 Dec. 1721, pr. Feb. 1721/2, and in Ireland 1731.(c)

IV. 1722. SIR JOHN WITTEWRONG, Baronet [1662], of Stanton Barry aforesaid, 1st surv. s. and h., *bap.* there 21 Dec. 1695; admitted to Rugby School, 13 Jan. 1706/7; was a Capt. in Col. Maurice Nassau's regiment; fled abroad for the murder, 2 May 1721, of Joseph Griffith, at Newport Pagnell, but returned after some years; *suc. to the Baronetcy*, 30 Jan. 1721/2, and sold the Stanton Barry estate about 1727 to Sarah, Duchess of Marlborough. He *d.* unm., in the Fleet prison, of wounds received in a drunken brawl, 27 March, and was *bur.* 7 April 1743, at St. Pancras, Midx.

(a) See a most interesting account of himself and his relatives, written by the 1st Baronet in 1659, when (for the 3d time) a widower, printed in Clutterbuck's *Hertfordshire*, vol. i, pp. 407-10.

(b) James Wittewrong, of Rothamsted aforesaid (who inherited that estate), Barrister at Law and Recorder of St. Albans, his yr. br. of the half blood (*b.* 13 June 1647 in Covent Garden), was *bur.* 5 March 1721, at Harpenden, leaving male issue, which, apparently, became extinct on the death of his great grandson, James Wittewronge, who was *bur.* there 28 Sep. 1748, aged 28.

(c) In it he leaves a legacy to the well known actress, Mrs. Anne Bracegirdle, and £2,000 each to his two sons, Wittewrong Beaumont and John Beaumont, by his mistress Margaret Beaumont [*N. & Q.*, 8th S., i, 476.]

V. 1743. SIR WILLIAM WITTEWRONG, Baronet [1662], br. and h., *bap.* 19 Dec. 1697, at Stanton Barry; admitted to Rugby School (together with his elder br.), 13 Jan. 1706/7; *suc. to the Baronetcy*, but not to any estate, 27 March 1743; was Gov. of the Poor Knights of Windsor, Aug. 1760. He *m.* Sybilla, da. of (—). He *d.* at St. Mary's, Lambeth, Surrey, 20 Jan. 1761. Admon. 18 Dec. 1765, "to his son and only child, Sir John WITTEWRONG, Baronet, the relict, Dame Sybilla, having renounced." She was living Dec. 1771.

VI. 1761, to 1771. SIR JOHN WITTEWRONG, Baronet [1662], only s. and h., *suc. to the Baronetcy* 20 Jan. 1761; sometime Lieut. 36th Foot. He *d.* unm., 13 Jan. 1771, "near the Asylum, Westminster," when the *Baronetcy* became *extinct*. Will dat. 25 March 1761, pr. 11 Dec. 1771, by his mother, the sole legatee.

MATTHEWS:

cr. 13 June 1662;

ex. 11 July 1708.

I. 1662. "PHILIP MATTHEWS, of Great Gobions in Collyer-Row Ward [Havering], co. Essex, Esq.," s. and h. of Joachim MATTHEWS,(a) of the same, Col. in the Parl. army; D.C.L. [1651] of Oxford, and sometime [1653-59] M.P. for Essex (*bur.* at Romford, 5 May 1659), by Philippa (Mar. Lic., Lond., 31 Aug. 1637), da. and h. of [—] CREW, of London, merchant, was *b.* about 1642; admitted to Lincoln's Inn, 15 March 1655/6; suc. his father in May 1659, and was *cr. a Baronet*, as above, 13 June 1662. He was F.R.S., 1670. He *m.* (Lic. Lond., 7 April 1668, he 26 and she 19), Anne, da. of Sir Thomas WOLSTENHOLME, 2d Baronet [1665], by Elizabeth, da. of Phineas ANDREWS, of Denton Court, Kent. He, who sold the estate of Great Gobions, was *bur.* 7 Dec. 1685, at Edmonton, co. Midx. Admon. 23 Feb. 1680/1. His widow, who survived him 50 years, *d.* 30 March 1735, aged 89. Will pr. 1736.

II. 1685, to 1708. SIR JOHN MATTHEWS, Baronet [1662], s. and h., *suc. to the Baronetcy* in Dec. 1685; was a Col. in the army. He *d.* unm., being slain at the battle of Oudenarde, 11 July 1708, when the *Baronetcy* became *extinct*. Will pr. July 1708.

BERNARD:

cr. 1 July 1662;

ex. 2 Jan. 1789.

I. 1662. "ROBERT BERNARD, of Huntingdon, Hunts, Esq., Serjeant-at-Law," s. and h. of Francis BERNARD, of Kingsthorpe, co. Northampton, by (—), which Francis was 2d s. of Francis BERNARD, of Abington, co. Northampton, was *b.* 1601 at Kingsthorpe aforesaid; was a Barrister [*Qy.*, Middle Temple]; was M.P. for Huntingdon April to May 1640, being then Recorder of that town; was in Oct. 1648 and again in 1660, Serjeant at Law, and, having been Steward and Judge of the Court of the Isle of Ely, 1649, was *cr. a Baronet*, as above, 1 July 1682. He *m.* firstly, in or before 1630, Elizabeth, da. of Sir John TALLAKERNE, by whom he had a large family. He *m.* secondly,

(a) According to Symonds [Morant's *Essex*, vol. i, p. 63] this Joachim was "a forward lad" who got to be under Clerk to Sir Thomas Meautys, Clerk of the Privy Council, in which employment he got to his wife the heiress of a citizen worth £4,000, and that set him up in the world." His father, Joachim Matthews, was, however, a London merchant, who *m.* Sarah, da. of John Gibson, of London, merchant, and who himself was s. of a Burgomaster of Helven, in the Duchy of Brabant.

2 I

Elizabeth, widow of Robert (DIGBY), 1st BARON DIGBY OF GEASHILL [I.] (who *d.* 6 June 1642), formerly wife of Sir Francis ASTLEY, da. of Sir James ALTHAM, of Oxney, Herts, by his 2d wife, Mary, da. of Richard STAPERS, of London, merchant. She, who was aged 1 in 1602, *d.* 3 and was *bur.* 7 Jan. 1662/3, at St. Paul's, Covent Garden. Admon. 17 Nov. 1664 to a creditor. He *d.* 1666 in his 66th year, and was *bur.* at Abington aforesaid. M.I. Will pr. 1666.

II. 1666. SIR JOHN BERNARD, Baronet [1662], of Brampton, co. Huntingdon, 1st s. and h. by 1st wife, *b.* Nov. 1630; M.P. for Huntingdon, 1654-55, 1656-58, 1659 and 1660; *suc. to the Baronetcy* in 1666. He *m.* firstly, Elizabeth, da. of Sir Oliver ST. JOHN, sometime, 1648-60, Lord Chief Justice of the Common Pleas, by his 2d wife, Elizabeth, da. of Henry CROMWELL, of Upwood. By her he had nine children. He *m.* secondly (Lic. Fac., 30 Aug. 1670), Grace (then aged 30), da. of Sir Richard SHUCKBURGH, of Shuckburgh, co. Warwick, by his 3d wife, Grace, da. of Sir Thomas HOLTE, 1st Baronet [1611], of Aston. He *d.* June 1679, and was *bur.* at Brampton. M.I. Will pr. 1680. His widow, who was *b.* in Kenilworth Castle, and by whom he had no issue, *m.* [—] MARRETT. Her will pr. 1721.

III. 1679. SIR ROBERT BERNARD, Baronet [1662], of Brampton aforesaid, only s. and h., by 1st wife, *b.* before 1670; *suc. to the Baronetcy*, June 1679; was Sheriff of Cambridgeshire and Huntingdonshire 1688 (but did not act), and 1691-92; M.P. for Huntingdon, 1689-90. He *m.* 26 May 1692, at St. Margaret's, Westm. (Lic. Vic. Gen. 25, he above 21 and she about 20), Anne, da. of Robert WELDON, of St. Laurence Jewry, London. He *d.* in or before 1703. Will pr. 1703. His widow *m.*, as his 2d wife, 25 Sep. 1704, at Brampton (Lic. Fac. 13), Thomas (TREVOR), 1st BARON TREVOR OF BROMHAM (*d.* 19 June 1730, aged 72), and *d.* 5, being *bur.* 13 Dec. 1746, at Bromham, Beds. Will pr. 1746.

IV. 1703? SIR JOHN BERNARD, Baronet [1662], of Brampton aforesaid, only s. and h., *b.* probably about 1695; *suc. to the Baronetcy* in or shortly before 1703. He *m.* Jan. 1736/7, Mary, yst. da. and coheir of Sir Francis ST. JOHN, Baronet [so *cr.* 1715], of Longthorpe, co. Northampton, by Mary, da. of Sir Nathaniel GOULD. He *d.* 15 Dec. 1766. His widow *d.* 21 Sep. 1793, at a great age, apparently over 90.(a) Will pr. Oct. 1793.

V. 1766, to 1789. SIR ROBERT BERNARD, Baronet [1662], of Brampton aforesaid, only s. and h., *b.* about 1740; matric. at Oxford (Ch. Ch.) 10 May 1758, aged 18; *suc. to the Baronetcy*, 15 Dec. 1766; was M.P. for Huntingdon, Dec. 1765 to 1768, and, subsequently, April 1770 to 1773, for Westminster. He *d.* unm. 2 Jan. 1789, when the *Baronetcy* became *extinct*. Will pr. Jan. 1789.

LORT:

cr. 15 July 1662;

ex. 19 Sep. 1698.

I. 1662. "ROGER LORT, of Stockpoole [*i.e.*, Stackpole Court in St. Petrox], co. Pembroke, Esq.," s. and h. of Henry LORT, of the same, sometime Sheriff of that county (living 1630), by Judith, da. of Henry WHITE, of Henllam, co. Pembroke, was *b.* about 1608; matric. at Oxford (Wadham Coll.) 3 Nov. 1626, aged 18; B.A., 11 June 1627; admitted to the Middle Temple, 1627; was at first a supporter of the royal cause in Pembrokeshire, being sequestrated in 1643, and, though he afterwards served on several Parliamentary Committees, was *cr. a Baronet*, as above, 15 July 1662. He *m.* firstly, 10 May 1632, at St. Giles' in the Fields, Midx. (Lic. Lond. 3, he 23 and she 18), Hester, sister of Arthur, 1st EARL OF ANGLESEY, 2d da. of Francis (ANNESLEY),

(a) Two of the children of her parents were *bap.* as early as 1689/90 and 1696/7 respectively.

VISCOUNT VALENTIA [I.], by his 1st wife, Dorothy, da. of Sir John PHILIPPS, 1st Baronet [1611], of Picton. She, who was *b.* in Fishamble street 3 and *bap.* 20 April 1613 at St. John's, Dublin, was living 1637, and probably much later. He *m.* secondly, Anne, da. of Humphrey WYNDHAM, of Dunraven Castle, co. Glamorgan. He *d.* 1663, before July, and was *bur.* at St. Petrox's.(a) Will pr. 4 May 1664. His widow, by whom he had three children, *m.* Sir Edward MANSEL.

II. 1663. SIR JOHN LORT, Baronet [1662], of Stackpole Court aforesaid, 1st s. and h. by 1st wife, *b.* in or before 1637; admitted to Lincoln's Inn, 27 June 1660; *Knighted*, v.p., 17 Jan. 1661/2; *suc. to the Baronetcy* in 1663, before July, when he *m.*(b) (Lic. Vic. Gen., 12 July 1663, he a bachelor about 26, Baronet, and she about 22) Susanna, da. of John (HOLLES), 2d EARL OF CLARE, by Elizabeth, da. and coheir of Horatio (VERE), BARON VERE OF TILBURY. He *d.* in or before 1673. Will pr. 1673. The will of his widow pr. May 1710.

III. 1673? to 1698. SIR GILBERT LORT, Baronet [1662], of Stackpole Court aforesaid, only s. and h., *b.* about 1670; *suc. to the Baronetcy* in or before 1673. He *d.* unm. 19 and was *bur.* 27 Sep. 1698, at Westm. Abbey, in his 28th year, when the *Baronetcy* became *extinct*.(c) Will dat. 9 Aug. and pr. 3 Dec. 1698.

GAGE:

cr. 15 July 1662;

afterwards, 1843-72, ROKEWODE-GAGE;

ex. 3 Jan. 1872.

I. 1662. "EDWARD GAGE, of Hargrave [*i.e.*, Hengrave], co. Suffolk, Esq.," 3d s. of Sir John GAGE, 1st Baronet [1622], of Firle, co. Sussex, by Penelope, da. and coheir of Thomas (DARCY), EARL RIVERS, and Mary his wife, da. and coheir of Sir Thomas KITSON, of Hengrave aforesaid, was *b.* about 1626; inherited the Hengrave estate from his mother on her death in 1661, and was *cr. a Baronet*, as above, 15 July 1662. He *m.* firstly (settlement 1 July, Lic. Lond., 25 July 1648, he 22 and she 20), Mary, da. of Sir William HERVEY, of Ickworth, co. Suffolk, by Susan, da. of Sir Robert JERMYN, of Rushbrooke. She *d.* 13 July 1654. He *m.* secondly, Frances, 2d da. of Walter (ASTON), 2d LORD ASTON OF FORFAR [S.], by Mary, da. of Richard (WESTON), EARL OF PORTLAND. She was living 1665. He *m.* thirdly, Anne, da. of [—] WATKINS. He *m.* fourthly (settlement 1675) Frances, sister of William, 3d EARL OF DENBIGH, 2d da. of George (FEILDING), 1st EARL OF DESMOND [I.], by Bridget, da. and coheir of Sir Michael STANHOPE. She *d.* 1680, and was *bur.* at Hengrave. He *m.* fifthly, Bridget, widow of SLAUGHTER, da. of (—) FEILDING. She *d.* s.p., at St. Giles' in the Fields, Midx., and was *bur.* 7 Sep. 1704, at Hengrave. Admon. 27 June 1705. He was *bur.* there 8 Jan. 1706/7. Will dat. 8 June 1706, pr. 23 Jan. 1707.

(a) He is author of an extremely rare work, published in 1646, entitled *Epigrammatum liber primus*, of which, it is said (*Dict. Nat. Biog.*) that "the epigrams are not destitute of point."

(b) He had had a previous lic. (Fac. Office, 31 Jan. 1661/2), as "Sir John Lort, of Lincoln's Inn, Bach., aged 23," to marry "Lady Mary Stanhope, of St. Paul's, Covent Garden, Sp., 22, and at own disposal," but as in the mar. lic. of 12 July 1663 he is called "Bachelor," this marriage can never have taken place.

(c) His estates passed to his sister Elizabeth (*b.* 1666), wife of Sir Alexander Campbell, s. of Sir Hugh Campbell, of Cawdor Castle, co. Nairn. She *d.* his widow, 28 Sep., and was *bur.* 6 Oct. 1714 in Westm. Abbey in her 49th year, being ancestress of the Earls Cawdor, the present [1903] owners of Stackpole Court. These estates, being in the counties of Pembroke and Carmarthen with 21 acres in Cardiganshire, amounted in 1883 to 51,538 acres, worth £35,042 a year.

II. 1704. Sir William Gage, Baronet [1662], of Hengrave aforesaid, 1st s. and h. by 1st wife, *b.* about 1651; *suc. to the Baronetcy*, Sep. 1704. He *m.* firstly (settlement 19 and 20 Oct. 1675, and Lic. Vic. Gen. 11 Feb. 1675/6, he 24 and she 20), Mary, da. of Sir Thomas Bond, 1st Baronet [1658], of Peckham, by Marie, da. of Charles Peliott, Sieur de la Gard. She, who was a lady of the Court of Henrietta, Duchess of Orleans, was *bur.* 18 April 1708, at Hengrave. He *m.* secondly, Merelina, widow of Sir Thomas Spring, 3d Baronet [1641], 5th da. and coheir of Thomas (Jermyn), 2d Baron Jermyn of St. Edmundsbury, by Mary, da. of Henry Merry. He *d.* 8 and was *bur.* 15 Feb. 1727, at Hengrave. Will dat. 2 May 1715, pr. 23 June 1727. His widow, by whom he had no issue, *d.* at Hengrave, but was *bur.* 5 Sep. 1727, at Pakenham, co. Suffolk, with her 1st husband. Admon. 28 Nov. 1727.

III. 1727. Sir Thomas Gage, Baronet [1662], of Hengrave aforesaid, grandson and h., being 1st s. and h. of Thomas Gage, by Delariviere, sister and coheir of Sir Jermyn D'Ewes, 4th Baronet [1641], da. of Sir Symonds D'Ewes, 3d Baronet, both of Stowlangtoft, co. Suffolk, which Thomas was s. and h. ap. of the late Baronet, but *d.* v.p. 1 March 1716, aged 32. He was *b.* probably about 1710, and *suc. to the Baronetcy*, 8 Feb. 1727. He *d.* unm. 1 and was *bur.* 9 Sep. 1741, at Hengrave. Will dat. 31 Aug. 1741, pr. 10 Jan. 1741/2.

IV. 1741. Sir William Gage, Baronet [1662], of Hengrave aforesaid, br. and h., *b.* probably about 1712; *suc. to the Baronetcy* 1 Sep. 1741. He *m.* (settlement 2 June 1741) Frances, widow of John Ellis, of Cotton, co. Suffolk, sister of Sir Robert Harland, 1st Baronet [1771], da. of Capt. Robert Harland, R.N., of Sproughton, co. Suffolk, by Frances, da. of [—] Clyatt. She, who was *bap.* 5 Nov. 1711, at Highgate, Midx., *d.* 19 July 1763, at Bury St. Edmunds. Will dat. 8 July and pr. 22 Aug. 1763. He *d.* s.p. 17 and was *bur.* 24 May 1767, at Hengrave. Will dat. 14 and pr. 22 May 1767.

V. 1767. Sir Thomas Rookwood Gage, Baronet [1662], of Hengrave aforesaid and of Coldham Hall in Stanningfield, co. Suffolk, cousin and h. male, being 1st s. and h. of John Gage, by Elizabeth (*m.* 7 Jan. 1717), da. and h. of Thomas Rookwood, of Coldham Hall aforesaid, which John, who *d.* 20 July 1728, aged 40, was 3d s. of the 2d Baronet. He, who was *b.* probably about 1720, *suc. to the Baronetcy*, 17 May 1767. He *m.* firstly (settlement 28 Feb. 1746), Lucy, sister and h. of Richard Knight, da. of William Knight, of Kingerby, co. Lincoln. She *d.* 3 and was *bur.* 10 Sep. 1781, at Hengrave, aged 59. He *m.* secondly, 20 July 1783, at Stanningfield aforesaid, Mary, da. of Patrick Fergus, of the island of Montserrat. He *d.* 21 March, and was *bur.* 5 April 1796, at Hengrave. Will dat. 22 Dec. 1795, pr. 8 July 1796. His widow, by whom he had no issue, *d.* 11 and was *bur.* 15 April 1820, at Hengrave, aged 84.

VI. 1796. Sir Thomas Gage, Baronet [1662], of Hengrave and of Coldham Hall aforesaid, only s. and h. by 1st wife, *b.* about 1752; *suc. to the Baronetcy*, 21 March 1796. He *m.* firstly, 22 Nov. 1779, at Spetchley, co. Worcester, Charlotte, da. of Thomas Fitzherbert, of Swinnerton, co. Stafford, by Mary Theresa, da. of Sir Robert Throckmorton, 4th Baronet [1642]. She *d.* 29 Aug. and was *bur.* 7 Sep. 1790, at Hengrave, aged 34. He *m.* secondly, 22 Sep. 1796, at Preston, co. Lancaster, Charlotte, da. of John Hooke Campbell, *afterwards* Campbell-Hooke, of Bangeston, co. Pembroke, Lyon King of Arms (1754), by Eustachia, da. of Francis Basset, of Heanton, Devon. He *d.* 1 and was *bur.* 6 Dec. 1798, at Hengrave, in his 47th year. His widow *d.* s.p.m., at Tunbridge Wells, 8 Jan. 1849, aged 80. Will pr. Jan. 1849.

VII. 1798. Sir Thomas Gage, Baronet [1662], of Hengrave aforesaid, 1st s. and h.[a] by 1st wife, *b.* 2 March 1781; *suc. to the Baronetcy*, 1 Dec. 1798. He *m.* 9 Jan. 1809, in Montagu sq., Marylebone (spec. lic.), Mary Anne, da. of Valentine (Browne), 1st Earl of Kenmare [I.], by his 2d wife, Mary, da. of Michael Aylmer. He *d.* 27 Dec. 1820, at Rome, and was *bur.* "at the Gesù" in that city. Will dat. 1820, pr. June 1844. His widow, who was *b.* 15 Dec. 1786, *m.*, as his 2d wife, 22 April 1835, at Rome, William Vaughan, of Courtfield, co. Hereford, and *d.* in Montagu sq. aforesaid, 13 June 1840.

VIII. 1820. Sir Thomas Gage, *afterwards* [1842-66] Rokewode-Gage, Baronet [1662], of Hengrave aforesaid, 1st s. and h., *b.* 5 Sep. 1810, at Castlerosse, co. Kerry; *suc. to the Baronetcy*, 27 Dec. 1820; suc. to the estate of Coldham Hall abovenamed on the death, 14 Oct. 1842, of his uncle, John Gage-Rokewode, and accordingly took, by royal lic., 1843, the additional name of *Rokewode*. He was Sheriff of Suffolk, 1850. He *m.* 16 Sep. 1850, at the Spanish Chapel and at St. Peter's, Eaton sq., Adelaide, yst. da. and coheir of Henry Drummond, of Albury Park, co. Surrey, by Harriet, da. of Robert (Hay-Drummond), Earl of Kinnoull [S.]. He *d.* s.p., 7 June 1866, at Paris, aged 55. His widow *d.* 8 Jan. 1883, at Weston House, Albury, aged 64.

IX. 1866, to 1872. Sir Edward Rokewode-Gage, Baronet [1662], of Hengrave and of Coldham Hall aforesaid, br. and h., *b.* 20 March 1812, at Hengrave Hall; Major Scots Fusileer Guards. 1833; *suc. to the Baronetcy*, 7 June 1866, and took, by royal lic., the additional name of *Rokewode*. He *m.* 2 Aug. 1842, at St. Geo., Han. sq., Henrietta Mary, 2d and yst. da. of the Rev. Lord Frederick Beauclerk (s. of Aubrey, 5th Duke of St. Albans), by Charlotte, da. of Charles (Dillon), 12th Viscount Dillon of Costello [I.]. He *d.* s.p., at his house, Seymour street, Marylebone, 3 Jan. 1872, aged 59, when the *Baronetcy* became *extinct*. His widow, who was *b.* 1 July 1818, *d.* 6 Jan. 1887, at Marlborough buildings, Bath.

HOOKE:

cr. 22 July 1662;

ex. July 1712.

I. 1662. "Thomas Hooke, of Flanchford [in Reigate], co. Surrey, Esq.," yr. br. of Sir Humphrey Hooke, M.P. for Bristol 1661-77, being 2d s. of Thomas[b] Hooke (*bur.* at St. Stephen's, Bristol, 3 March 1658/9), by Mary, da. of Nicholas Hele, the only sister that had issue of John Hele, of Franchford aforesaid (which he purchased in 1656), was *b.* 8 July 1641; admitted to Linc. Inn, 29 Oct. 1659, and was (14 days after coming of age) *cr. a Baronet*, as above, 22 July 1662. Shortly afterwards, however, in 1666, he sold the Flanchford estate (which he had inherited) for £8,400, and settled at Tangier Park in Wootton, co. Southampton. He *m.* 4 May 1664, at St. Anne's, Blackfriars, Elizabeth, da. of Sir William Thompson. He *d.* in 1678. Will pr. 1678. His widow *d.* at Tangier park in or before 1708. Admon. 6 Oct. 1708.

(a) Robert Joseph Gage, the 2d son of the 6th Baronet by his 1st wife, inherited the [Rookwood] estate of Coldham Hall, and by Royal licence, 12 April 1799, took the name of Rookwood. He, however, *d.* s.p.s. 31 July 1838, aged 55, and was suc. in that estate by his yst. br. John Gage, who accordingly took the name of Rokewode [*sic*] 29 Nov. 1838. He, who was a Barrister and a good Antiquary (the author of the *History of Hengrave*, and subsequently of the *History of Thingoe Hundred*, Suffolk), *d.* unm., 14 Oct. 1842, aged 56, when the Coldham estate devolved on the 8th Baronet.

(b) This Thomas was son of Sir Humphrey Hooke, of King's Weston, three times Mayor, and sometime M.P. for that city, till expelled as a Royalist in 1642. This Sir Humphrey (often confused with his grandson, who was not knighted till 21 Feb. 1660/1) was *bur.* at St. Stephen's, Bristol, 31 March 1659.

II. 1678, to 1712. Sir Hele Hooke, Baronet [1662], of Tangier Park aforesaid, s. and h., *b.* in or before 1665; *suc. to the Baronetcy* in 1678; Sheriff of Hants, 1687-88; of Gloucestershire, 1688-89. He *m.* 3 July 1683, at Knightsbridge chapel (Lic. Vic. Gen. 2, he "about 21," with consent of his mother and guardian, she "about 20," with consent of her father), Esther, da. of [—] Underhill, of St. Matthew, Friday street, London. He *d.* s.p.s., July 1712, at Kensington, when the *Baronetcy* became *extinct*. Will pr. Sep. 1712. His widow *m.* Richard Lilly, and *d.* 15 May 1733, in Kensington sq., Midx. Admon. 10 July 1733 to her said husband.

SAVILE:

cr. 24 July 1662;

ex. 1689.

I. 1662, to 1689. "John Savile, of Copley, co. York, Esq.," only s. and h. of John Savile, of the same, by Anne, da. of Sir George Palmes, of Naburn, co. York, was *b.* about 1640; suc. his father about 1644, and was *cr. a Baronet*, as above, 24 July 1662. He was aged 26, at the Heralds' Visit. of Yorkshire, 1666. He *m.* in or before 1663, Mary, da. of Clement Paston, of Barningham, co. Norfolk. He *d.* s.p.m.[a] 1689, when the *Baronetcy* became *extinct*.

WANDESFORD:

cr. 5 Aug. 1662;

afterwards, 1706-84, Viscounts Castlecomer [I.];

ex. 12 Jan. 1784.

I. 1662. "Christopher Wandesford, of Kirklington, co. York, Esq.," 3d s. of Christopher Wandesford, Master of the Rolls [I.], 1633-40 (*d.* 3 Dec. 1640, aged 47), by Alice (*m.* 22 Sep. 1614, at Staveley), da. of Sir Hewet Osborne, of Kiveton, co. York, was *bap.* 14 Feb. 1627/8, at Kirklington; suc. his elder br., George Wandesford (who *d.* unm. 31 March 1651, aged 27) in that estate in 1651, and was *cr. a Baronet*, as above, 5 Aug. 1662. He was Sheriff of co. Kilkenny, 1675.[b] He *m.* 30 Sep. 1651, at Lowther, co. Westmorland, Eleanor, da. of Sir John Lowther, 1st Baronet [S. 1640], by Mary, da. of Sir Richard Fletcher. He *d.* Feb. and was *bur.* 12 March 1686/7, at Kirklington. M.I. Will dat. 18 Dec. 1686, pr. April 1687, as also in Ireland. His widow was *bur.* at Kirklington 20 Dec. 1714. Will dat. 28 Sep. 1713, pr. at York 23 Dec. 1714.

II. 1687. Sir Christopher Wandesford, Baronet [1662], of Wandesford aforesaid, 1st s. and h., *b.* 19 Aug. 1656; was M.P. for Ripon, 1679 and 1680-81; *suc. to the Baronetcy*, in Feb. 1686/7; Sheriff of Yorkshire, 1689-90; was attainted by the Parl. [I.] of James II in 1689; was M.P. [I.] for St. Canice, 1692-93, 1695-99, and 1703-07; P.C. [I.]. He *m.* in 1683, Elizabeth, da. of the Hon. George Montagu, of Horton, co. Northampton (yr. s. of Henry, 1st Earl of Manchester), by Elizabeth, da. of Sir Anthony Irby, of Boston. She was living when he was *cr.*, 15 March 1706/7, BARON WANDESFORD and VISCOUNT CASTLECOMER, co. Kilkenny [I.]. In that peerage this *Baronetcy* then *merged*, the 5th Viscount being *cr.*, in 1758, EARL WANDESFORD [I.], till both became *extinct*, on the death of the 6th Baronet, 5th Viscount, and 1st Earl, 12 Jan. 1784. See *Peerage*.

(a) Mary Elizabeth, his only da. and h., aged 3 in 1666, *m.* Lord Thomas Howard, and was mother of Thomas, who, in 1701, became Duke of Norfolk, and sold Copley Hall to Mr. Walker, of Huddersfield.

(b) He is often said to have been M.P. for Ripon, 1675-85, but this was not the case.

ASTLEY:

cr. 13 Aug. 1662;

ex. 29 Jan. 1772.

I. 1662. "Richard Astley, of Patshull, co. Stafford, Esq.," s. and h. of Walter Astley, of the same, by Grace, da. of Francis Trentham, of Rocester Priory, in that county, was *b.* about 1625; raised a troop of Horse for the King, in the Civil War; suc. his father (who *d.* aged 66), 18 Feb. 1658, and was *cr. a Baronet*, as above, 13 Aug. 1662; entered his pedigree at the Heralds' Visit. of Staffordshire in 1663, then aged 38. He *m.* firstly, in or before 1657, Elizabeth, da. of John Philipps, of Morleston, co. Pembroke.[a] He *m.* secondly, probably about 1680, Henrietta (*bap.* 4 Sep. 1660, at Great Marlow, Bucks), 4th da. and coheir of William Borlase, sometime (1659, 1660 and 1661-65) M.P. for Marlow, by Joanna, da. of Sir John Bancks, Lord Chief Justice of the Common Pleas. He *d.* 24 Feb. 1687/8, aged 63, and was *bur.* at Patshull.[b] M.I. His widow *m.*, as his 1st wife (Mar. Lic., Vic. Gen., 3 Feb. 1689/90, he of Radborn, Wilts, "Esq.," about 22, bachelor, and she about 27, widow), Major-Gen. John Richmond Webb, sometime M.P. for Ludgershall (who *d.* Sep. 1724), and *d.* 27, being *bur.* 29 June 1711, at Ludgershall, aged 50.

II. 1688, to 1772. Sir John Astley, Baronet [1662], of Patshull aforesaid, and of Eversley, co. Wilts, 2d but 1st surv. s. and h., being only s. by 2d wife; *bap.* 24 Jan. 1687, at Patshull; *suc. to the Baronetcy* 24 Feb. 1687/8; was M.P. for Shrewsbury, 1727-34, and subsequently (six Parls.) 1734 till death in 1772, for Salop. About 1750 he pulled down the church and the family residence at Patshull, and after re-erecting the latter at a great expense, sold it and the estate for £100,000. He *m.* 27 May 1711, at Tibberton, co. Salop, Mary, da. and h. of Francis Prynce, of Shrewsbury, by Mary, da. and h. of Samuel Gilly, of High Hall, co. Dorset. She *d.* 1764. He *d.* s.p.m.s.[c] 29 Jan. 1772, aged 84, when the *Baronetcy* became *extinct*. Will dat. 18 May 1771, pr. 18 Feb. 1772 and March 1840.

GARRARD, *or* GERARD:

cr. 16 Aug. 1662;

ex. 12 March 1727/8.

I. 1662. "Sir Jacob Gerard [*rectius* Garrard], of Langford, co. Norfolk, Knt.," s. of Thomas Garrard, of St. Benet, Gracechurch, London, Linendraper, Citizen and Salter, who, fined for the Shrievalty of London (*bur.* 13 Dec. 1632, at St. Benet's), was *bap.* 30 Nov. 1586, at St. Benet's aforesaid; was a member of the Salters Company, and (like his father) a Linendraper in Gracechurch street; was Alderman of Bishopsgate, London, 7 Feb. 1636/7; of Candlewick 1640, till discharged, as a Royalist, in 1648; Sheriff, 1636-37; was a merchant of great wealth and zealously attached to the Royal cause, being one of five Aldermen who were *Knighted* at Hampton Court, 3 Dec. 1641; was fined as a "delinquent," tried for his life in 1650, but acquitted

(a) So described in the Visit. of Staffordshire, 1662, but on her husband's monument called "da. of John Philipps, of Picton Castle, co. Pembroke, *Esq.*" The 1st *Baronet*, Sir John Philipps [1611] had a da., Elizabeth.

(b) Richard, aged 6 in 1662, his s. and h. ap. by 1st wife, *d.* v.p. and s.p. He had also an illegit. da. (by a Miss Reynell), who *m.* about 1686, Walter Stubbs, of Harrington, co. Stafford (*d.* Sep. 1697), and who received from her father, Beckbury Hall, Salop (near Patshull), where she *d.* in March 1729.

(c) Richard Prynce Astley, his only s., *d.* v.p. and s.p., Aug. 1756. Of his six surv. daughters and coheirs, two *d.* unm., but (1) Henrietta, *m.* Edward Daniel; (2) Alicia, *m.* 23 Sep. 1742, Charles (Bennet), 3d Earl of Tankerville; (3) Arabella, *m.* firstly, Anthony Langley Swimmer, and secondly, as his 3d and last wife, Sir Francis Vincent, 7th Baronet [1620], and *d.*, as his widow, 20 June 1785; (4) Frances, *m.* James o'Donnell.

for want of evidence, and was *cr. a Baronet*, as above, 16 Aug. 1662. He *m.*, in or before 1622, Mary, da. of Ambrose JENNINGS, Citizen of London. She was *bur.* 3 March 1663/4, at St. Benet's aforesaid. Funeral certificate at Coll. of Arms. He *d.* in or shortly before 1666. Will pr. 1666.

II. 1666? SIR THOMAS GARRARD, Baronet [1662], of Langford aforesaid and of Greenstreet in East Ham, co. Essex, 2d but 1st surv. s. and h., *bap.* 25 April 1627, at St. Benet's Gracechurch aforesaid, and *suc. to the Baronetcy* in or before 1666. He was Sheriff of Essex, 1668, but did not act, and again 1669-70. He *m.*, in or before 1658, Sarah, da. and h. of Nicholas BEAUMONT, of Peasenhall, co. Suffolk. He *d.* in or shortly before 1690, and was *bur.* at Langford. Will dat. 7 July 1684, pr. March 1690. The will of his widow, directing her burial to be at Langford, dat. 4 May 1690, pr. 18 Nov. 1710.

III. 1690? to 1728. SIR NICHOLAS GARRARD, Baronet [1662], of Greenstreet aforesaid, 2d but only surv. s. and h. male,(a) *b.* probably about 1655; admitted to Gray's Inn, 10 June 1675; *suc. to the Baronetcy* in or shortly before 1690. He *m.* Cecilia, only da. of Sir Edwyn STEDE, of Stede's Hill in Harrietsham, co. Kent, by Cecilia, da. of Sir Edward CLARK, of Ford in Wrotham, in that county. He *d.* s.p. 12 March 1727/8, and was *bur.* at Langford, when the *Baronetcy* became *extinct*. Will pr. 1728. His widow *d.* 8 and was *bur.* 14 July 1753, at East Ham.(b) M.I. Will pr. 1753.

FUST:

cr. 21 Aug. 1662;

ex. 16 April 1779.

I. 1662. "EDWARD FUST, of Hill [near Berkeley], co. Gloucester, Esq.," s. and h. of Richard FUST, of the same (who was *b.* 10 Oct. 1568, and purchased that estate about 1600) by his 1st wife, Anne (*m.* 14 Feb. 1602), da. and h. of Robert John HIDE, of Ingatestone, co. Essex and of Adisham, co. Kent, was *b.* 16 April 1606; suc. his father 11 Dec. 1613; was admitted to Gray's Inn, 17 March 1621/2, and "having upon several occasions signalized his loyalty," was *cr. a Baronet*, as above, 21 Aug. 1662. He was Lieut.-Col. of a Reg. of Militia. He *m.* in or before 1630, Bridget, da. of Sir Thomas DENTON, of Hillesden, Bucks (*bur.* there 28 Sep. 1633), by Susan, da. of John TEMPLE, of Stow in that county. She was *bap.* 20 Feb. 1607, at Stow. He *d.* 6 and was *bur.* 10 April 1674, at Hill. Will pr. 1674. His widow *d.* a few months later, 18, and was *bur.* 21 Dec. 1674, at St. Paul's, Covent Garden, Midx., but subsequently removed to Hill. Her will pr. 1675.

II. 1674. SIR JOHN FUST, Baronet [1662], of Hill Court in Hill aforesaid, 4th but 1st surv. s. and h., *b.* at Holt, co. Somerset, 5 Dec. 1637; matric. at Oxford (Oriel Coll.), 31 March 1658; *suc. to the Baronetcy* 6 April 1674; was Sheriff of Gloucestershire, 1675-76; entered his pedigree at the Heralds' Visit. of that county in 1682, being then "about 42." He *m.* 14 Aug. 1666, at Dumbleton, co. Gloucester, Elizabeth, da. of Sir Richard COCKS, 1st Baronet [1661], of Dumbleton, by Susanna, da. of Ambrose ELTON. He *d.* 12 Feb. 1698/9, and was *bur.* at Hill. His widow *d.* 7 Feb. 1716/7, and was *bur.* there. The will of Dame Elizabeth FUST was pr. 1733.

(a) Jacob Garrard, the 1st s. and h. ap., *m.* (Lic. Vic. Gen. 9 March 1673/4, each aged about 23) Abigail, da. of Sir John Holland, 1st Baronet [1629], and *d.* v.p. and s.p.m., leaving two daughters and coheirs, (1) Alathea, who *m.* Sir Francis Bickley, 4th Baronet [1661], who *d.* 4 July 1746, and (2) Sarah, who *m.* Charles Downing and *d.* 20 Oct. 1742, aged 63, being mother of Sir Jacob Garrard Downing, 4th Baronet [1663].

(b) In the *Hist. Reg.* of 1736, under the date of March 1735/6, is, however, recorded the death of "The Lady Garrard, relict of Sir Nicholas Garrard of the county of Norfolk, Bart."

III. 1699. SIR EDWARD COCKS FUST, Baronet [1662], of Hill Court aforesaid, only surv. s. and h., *b.* about 1668, being aged 14 in 1682; matric. at Oxford (Oriel Coll.), 15 Oct. 1685, aged 18; *suc. to the Baronetcy* 12 Feb. 1698/9; Sheriff of Gloucestershire, 1702-03. He *m.* firstly, Anne Mary (aged 18 and unm. in 1682), da. of Thomas STEPHENS, of Lypiat, co. Gloucester, by Anne, da. of Thomas CHILD, of Northwick, co. Worcester. She *d.* s.p.m.s., 3 March 1689/90. He *m.* secondly, in or before 1693, Elizabeth, da. and h. of William MOHUN, of Portishead, co. Somerset. She was *bur.* at Portishead, 18 Oct. 1701. He *m.* thirdly, in or before 1703, Catharine, da. of Francis MOHUN, of Fleet, co. Dorset, by Ellen, da. of Ralph SHELDON, of Stanton, co. Derby, which Francis was br. to William MOHUN, abovenamed. She *d.* at Hill, 1705. He *m.* fourthly, in or before 1710, Susan, widow of Roger THOMPSON, of London, merchant, sister of Sir Richard and Sir Robert COCKS, the 2d and 3d Baronets [1661], da. of Richard COCKS, by Mary, da. of Sir Robert COOKE, of Highnam. He *d.* 13 and was *bur.* 28 Aug. 1713, at Hill aforesaid. Admon. 20 Aug. 1717, to Dame Susanna, the relict. She *d.* s.p.s.

IV. 1713. SIR EDWARD FUST, Baronet [1662], of Hill Court aforesaid, 1st surv. s. and h., by 2d wife, *b.* 17 Oct. 1693, at Portishead aforesaid; *suc. to the Baronetcy*, 13 Aug. 1713; Sheriff of Gloucestershire, 1717-18. He *m.* 17 Sep. 1713, at Hill, Dorothy, da. of Roger THOMPSON, by Susan, da. of Richard COCKS, all three abovenamed. He *d.* s.p.s. 27 Feb. 1727/8, and was *bur.*, with his mother, at Portishead aforesaid, aged 34. Will pr. 1728. His widow *m.* Gilbert Maximilian MOHUN, of Fleet, co. Dorset. She *d.* at Fleet, 1734, and was *bur.* there.

V. 1728. SIR FRANCIS FUST, Baronet [1662], of Hill Court aforesaid, br. of the half-blood, and h., being s. of the 3d Baronet, by his 3d wife; *b.* 17 March 1704/5; *suc. to the Baronetcy*, 27 Feb. 1727/8. He, in 1750, built the great sewer in the parish of Hill, and remodelled the church and the family residence in that parish. He *m.* 28 Sep. 1724, at Gloucester Cathedral, Fanny, da. of Nicholas TOOKER, of Bristol, merchant, by Frances, da. of Richard OCKOLD, of Upton St. Leonard's, co. Gloucester. He *d.* 26 June 1769, and was *bur.* at Hill, aged 64. Admon. 18 July 1769 to his son, the bond being £10,000. Will pr. Aug. 1774. His widow living July 1769.

VI. 1769, to 1779. SIR JOHN FUST, Baronet [1662], of Hill Court aforesaid, 1st s. and h., *b.* 26 Aug. 1726, at Tocknells, in Painswick, co. Glouc.; Capt. in the Army in 1745, serving against the Jacobite rising; *suc. to the Baronetcy*, 26 June 1769. He *m.* 20 April 1773, at Bath, Philippa, then "of Hampton Court Palace," sister of Sir John HAMILTON, 1st Baronet [1776], da. of John HAMILTON, of Chilston Park, co. Kent, by Mary, da. of John WRIGHT, M.D. He *d.* s.p. 16 April 1779, aged 53, and was *bur.* at Hill, when the *Baronetcy* became *extinct*. M.I. Will, in which he left the estate to his widow, pr. May 1779. She *d.* in or before 1804. Will pr. 1804.

LONG:

cr. 1 Sep. 1662;

afterwards, 1767–1805, TYLNEY-LONG;

ex. 14 Sep. 1805.

I. 1662. "ROBERT LONG,(a) of the City of Westminster, Esq., Auditor General of the Exchequer and one of His Majesties most Honourable Privy Councell," 8th and yst. s. of Sir Walter LONG, of Wraxall and Draycot Cerne, co. Wilts (*d.* in or before 1610), being his 6th son by, his 2d wife,

(a) A tabular pedigree of this family down to 1878 is in the *Mis. Gen. et Her.*, new series, vol. iii, p. 58.

Catherine, da. of Sir John THYNNE, of Longleat in that county, was admitted to Lincoln's Inn, 14 Oct. 1619; Barrister, 6 June 1627; was M.P. for Devizes, 1626 and 1628-29; for Midhurst, April to May 1640; for Tewkesbury, 1659, and for Boroughbridge, 1661 till death in 1673; Surveyor of the lands of the Queen Consort, 1643; Sec. of Council to the Prince of Wales, 1644, and P.C. to him when Charles II, 14 May 1649, till dismissed in 1653, though pardoned in 1654; had his estate sequestrated by Parl. and ordered to be sold, under the Act of July 1650; was, on 8 Sep. 1660, made a Lord of the Treasury and was Chancellor of the Exchequer,(a) for one year, 1660-61, being, 21 May 1662, made Auditor of the Exchequer (an office he retained till his death), and was *cr. a Baronet*, as above, 1 Sep. 1662, with a spec. rem., "for lack of issue male, upon [his nephew] John [*rectius* James] LONG, of Draycot Cerne, co. Wilts, and the heirs male of his body." He was also again made P.C., 3 July 1672. He *d.* unm. 13 and was *bur.* 28 July 1673 in Westm. Abbey. Will dat. 27 March to 30 May, pr. 20 Dec. 1673.

II. 1673. SIR JAMES LONG, Baronet [1662], of Draycot Cerne, co. Wilts, nephew and testamentary h., being 1st s. and h. of Sir Walter LONG, of the same, and his only child by, his 1st wife, Anne, da. of James (LEY), 1st EARL OF MARLBOROUGH, which Walter (who *d.* 1637) was elder br. of the late Baronet, being 3d s.(b) (though 1st by the 2d wife) of Sir Walter LONG, of Wraxall abovenamed; was *bap.* 1617, at Bradford-on-Avon; ed. in France(c); admitted to Linc. Inn, 5 June 1634; suc. to the Draycot estate on the death of his father in 1637; was in the Royal army; Colonel of Horse in 1644; was defeated at Devizes in March 1645, but captured Chippenham five months later; Sheriff of Wilts for the King, 1644; a Royalist Compounder, Dec. 1646, for £714; *suc. to the Baronetcy*, according to the spec. rem. in the patent thereof, on the death of his uncle, 13 July 1673; M.P. for Malmesbury, 1678-81, and 1690 till death in 1692. He *m.* Dorothy, da. of Sir Edward LEACH, of Shipley, co. Derby. He *d.* suddenly, in London, 22 Jan. 1691/2, and was *bur.* at Draycot. Will pr. 1692. His widow *d.* 1710, and was *bur.* there. Will pr. March 1711.

III. 1692. SIR ROBERT LONG, Baronet [1662], of Draycot aforesaid, grandson and h., being 1st s. and h. of James LONG, by his 1st wife, Susan, da. of Col. Giles STRANGWAYS, of Melbury, co. Dorset, which James, who *d.* v.p. about 1690, was only s. of the late Baronet. He was *b.* 1673; *suc. to the Baronetcy*, 22 Jan. 1691/2, but *d.* of the smallpox only four days later, a minor and unm.

IV. 1692. SIR GILES LONG, Baronet [1662], of Draycot aforesaid, br. of the whole blood and h., *b.* 1675; *suc. to the Baronetcy*, 26 Jan. 1691/2. He *d.* unm. 1697. Will dat. 24 April 1694, at his age of 18 and upwards, pr. 12 March 1697/8, by Dame Dorothy LONG, the grandmother.

(a) It seems in the twentieth century an anomaly that, having held the (now reputed) high office of "*Chancellor*," he should subsequently have been made "*Auditor* of the Exchequer." Moreover, in the account of him supplied in 1727 by Sir James Long, 5th Baronet, to Wotton's *Baronetage*, no mention is made of his ever having been Chancellor of the Exchequer, though it is stated that he was Auditor. There can, however, be no doubt of the fact. The following appointments occur in Ockerby's Haydn's *Dignities*: (1) "Lord Treasurer, 8 Sep. 1660, Thomas, Earl of Southampton; Sir Rob. Long, Ch. Ex.," the next appointment being 24 May 1667; (2) "Chancellor of the Exchequer, 8 Sep. 1660, Sir Robt. Long," the next appointment being that of Anthony, Lord Ashley, in May 1667, which last date, however, is a mistake for May 1661.

(b) Of the two elder sons (by the 1st wife), the younger, Thomas, *d.* unm., but the eldest, John Long, suc. to the Wraxall estate, and *d.* 1736, being ancestor of the family there settled.

(c) "Not as Aubrey affirms, at Westm. School and Magdalen College, Oxford" [*Dict. Nat. Biogr.*]

V. 1697. SIR JAMES LONG, Baronet [1662], of Draycot aforesaid, br. of the full blood and h., *b.* about 1682; *suc. to the Baronetcy* in 1697; matric. at Oxford (Ball. Coll.), 1 Feb. 1698/9, aged 17; was M.P. for Chippenham, 1705-13; for Wootton Basset, 1715-22; and for Wiltshire, 1727 till death in 1729. He *m.* 9 June 1702, at St. Martin's in the Fields (Lic. Fac. 6, he about 20, and she 17), Henrietta, da. of Fulke (GREVILLE), 5th BARON BROOKE OF BEAUCHAMPS COURT, by Sarah, da. of Francis DASHWOOD. He *d.* 16 March 1728/9, aged 47, and was *bur.* at Draycot. Will pr. 1729. His widow *d.* at Bath, 18 May 1765. Will pr. June 1765.

VI. 1729. SIR ROBERT LONG, Baronet [1662], of Draycot aforesaid, only surv. s. and h., *b.* 1705 at St. James' Westm.; matric. at Oxford (Ball. Coll.), 17 March 1721/2, aged 16; *suc. to the Baronetcy* 16 March 1728/9; M.P. for Wootton Bassett, 1734-41, and for Wilts, 1741, till death in 1767. He *m.* 29 May 1735, at Woodford, co. Essex, Emma, only da. of Richard (CHILD), 1st EARL TYLNEY OF CASTLEMAINE [I.], by Dorothy, da. and eventually h. of John GLYNNE, of Henley Park, Surrey, and Dorothy, his wife, da. of Francis TYLNEY, of Tylney Hall, in Rotherwick, Hants. She *d.* 8 March 1758, and was *bur.* at Draycot. He *d.* 10 Feb. 1767, aged 62, and was *bur.* there. Will pr. 1767.

VII. 1767. SIR JAMES LONG, *afterwards*, 1784-94, TYLNEY-LONG, Baronet [1662], of Draycot aforesaid, 1st s. and h., *b.* 1736 in St. Geo. Han. sq.; matric. at Oxford (Oriel Coll.), 2 Nov. 1756, aged 19; M.P. for Marlborough, May 1762 to 1780; for Devizes, 1780-88, and for Wilts, 1788-94; having *suc. to the Baronetcy* 10 Feb. 1767 and to the estates of the Tylney and Child families at Rotherwick aforesaid and at Wanstead, co. Essex, on the death, 17 Sep. 1784, of his maternal uncle, John (CHILD), 2d EARL TYLNEY OF CASTLEMAINE [I.], when he took the name of *Tylney* before that of *Long*. He *m.* firstly, 10 July 1775, Harriet, sister of William, 1st EARL OF RADNOR, 4th da. of Jacob (BOUVERIE), 1st VISCOUNT FOLKESTONE, by his 1st wife, Mary, da. and h. of Bartholomew CLARKE. She, who was *b.* 17 Oct. 1736, *d.* s.p. 12 Nov. 1777, aged 41, and was *bur.* at Draycot. He *m.* secondly, 26 July 1785, Catherine Sidney, 1st da. of Other Lewis (WINDSOR), 4th EARL OF PLYMOUTH, by Catherine, da. of Thomas (ARCHER), 1st BARON ARCHER OF UMBERSLADE. He *d.* 28 Nov. 1794, aged 58, and was *bur.* at Draycot. Will pr. Dec. 1794. His widow *d.* 5 Jan. 1823, at Draycot, aged 68, and was *bur.* there. Will pr. 1823.

VIII. 1794, to 1805. SIR JAMES TYLNEY-LONG, Baronet [1662], of Draycot, Rotherwick, and Wanstead aforesaid, only s. and h. by 2d wife, *b.* early in 1794, and *suc. to the Baronetcy*, when a few months old, 28 Nov. 1794. He *d.* 14 Sep. 1805, after a short illness, aged 11, and was *bur.* at Draycot, when the *Baronetcy* became *extinct*.(a) Admon. Dec. 1805.

(a) He left three sisters of the whole blood and coheirs, of whom the two younger had no part of the family estates. These were Dorothy, who *d.* unm. 29 Nov. 1872, aged 81, and Emma, who also *d.* unm. 16 July 1879, aged 87, *viz.*, seventy-four years after her said brother. The whole of the estates (derived from the families of Long, Child and Tylney), valued at £25,000 a year, as also about £300,000 personalty, devolved on the eldest sister Catherine, *b.* 2 Oct. 1789. She *m.* 14 March 1812, at St. James', Westm., as his 1st wife, William Wellesley-Pole, who accordingly took the name of *Pole-Tylney-Long-Wellesley* in lieu of that of Wellesley-Pole, and who, 20 years after her death, became, 22 Feb. 1845, 4th Earl of Mornington [I.]. She *d.* at Richmond, co. Surrey, 12 Sep. 1825, aged 35, and was *bur.* at Draycot, leaving issue, which became extinct on the death, unm., of her only da., Victoria Catherine Mary, 29 March 1897, aged 78. Her eldest and only surv. son, the 5th Earl of Mornington [I.], had previously *d.* unm., 25 July 1863, in his 50th year, and had devised the Draycot estate (which came to him *maternally*, and which alone, through his father's extravagance, he had inherited) to his *paternal* cousin, Henry Richard (Wellesley), 1st Earl Cowley.

CANN, *or* CAN:

cr. 13 Sep. 1662;

ex. 20 July 1765.

I. 1662. "SIR ROBERT CAN, of Compton Greenfield, co. Gloucester, Knt.," 1st s. and h. of William CAN, *or* CANN, of Compton aforesaid, Mayor of Bristol, 1648, by Margaret, sister of Robert YEAMANS,[a] Sheriff of Bristol, 1642, was *b.* about 1630,[b] suc. his father in or before July 1662; was Mayor of Bristol, 1662, being *Knighted* 22 April 1662, and *cr. a Baronet*, as above, 13 Sep. 1662; Sheriff of Gloucestershire, 1670-71. He was again Mayor of Bristol, 1675, and M.P. for that city, 1678 and 1679 till expelled 28 Oct. 1681. He was also of Brean, co. Somerset, and of Elverton and Olston, co. Glouc. He *m.* firstly, Cecilia, da. of Humphrey HOOKE, Alderman of Bristol. He *m.* secondly, Anne, da. of W. POPLEY. He *d.* Nov. 1685, and was *bur.* at St. Walburgh's, Bristol. Will dat. 9 Aug. 1681, pr. 16 Nov. 1685. His widow *d.* Jan. 1688/9. Her will, dat. 31 Dec. 1688, directing her burial to be with her husband, pr. 1 Feb. 1688/9.

II. 1685. SIR WILLIAM CANN, Baronet [1662], of Brislington, co. Somerset, 1st s. and h. by 1st wife; was an Alderman of Bristol; *Knighted* v.p., 5 Sep. 1663; *suc. to the Baronetcy* in Nov. 1685. He *m.*, in or before 1694, Elizabeth, da. of Sir Thomas LANGTON, Mayor of Bristol [1666], by his 2d wife, Elizabeth, da. of (—) GONING, of Cold Ashton, co. Glouc. He *d.* 16 July 1698. Will dat. 24 July 1697 to 20 June 1698, directing his burial to be at St. Werburgh's abovenamed, pr. 21 Oct. 1698, and again Nov. 1834.

III. 1698. SIR WILLIAM CANN, Baronet [1662], of Brislington aforesaid, *b.* about 1694; *suc. to the Baronetcy*, 16 July 1698; matric. at Oxford (Oriel Coll.), 30 May 1711, aged 17. He *m.* Elizabeth, da. of Thomas CHESTER, of Knole Park in Almondsbury, co. Glouc. (*d.* 26 Feb. 1703), and sister of Thomas CHESTER of the same (*d.* s.p. 1 Oct. 1763), sometime M.P. for that county. She *d.* 6 Jan. 1724, aged 30. He *d.* s.p.m. 27 April 1726, aged 32, both being *bur.* at Almondsbury. M.I. His admon. 6 July 1726, and her admon. (her husband not having administered to her estate) 20 June 1727, were both granted to Thomas MASTER, uncle and guardian of their only child, Elizabeth Chester CANN, then a minor. Further admon. 29 March 1743 to said da., then of full age, and wife of Thomas MASTER "Esq.," Junior.[c]

IV. 1726. SIR ROBERT CANN, Baronet [1662], of Compton Greenfield aforesaid, cousin and h. male, being 1st s. and h. of Sir Thomas CANN, of Westbury and Stoke Bishop, co. Glouc., Alderman of Bristol (*Knighted* 18 April 1680), by (—), da. of Sir Thomas EARLE, which Thomas CANN was yr. s. of the 1st Baronet by his 2d wife. He was *b.* about 1683; matric. at Oxford (Ch. Ch.), 27 June 1700, aged 17; *suc. to the Baronetcy*, 27 April 1726; was Sheriff of Gloucestershire, 1726-27. He *d.* unm. Jan. 1748.

V. 1748. SIR WILLIAM CANN, Baronet [1662], of Compton Greenfield aforesaid, br. and h., *b.* about 1689; matric. at Oxford (Hart Hall), 22 April 1706, aged 17; admitted to Middle Temple, 1707; was Town

[a] This Robert Yeamans was executed 30 May 1643, in Wine street, Bristol, by command of Col. Fiennes, the then Governor of that city on part of the Insurgents, for having aided the scheme of admitting Prince Rupert and the King's troops into Bristol.

[b] Richard, his 3d and yst. br., was *b.* about 1637, and *d.* 29 Sep. 1696, aged 59, being *bur.* at Compton. M.I.

[c] The beautiful estate of Knole Park was eventually inherited by their grandson, William Chester Master, Lieut. Col. 3d Fusileer Guards, who *d.* 20 Nov. 1868, aged 83, leaving issue.

Clerk of Bristol before 1741; *suc. to the Baronetcy*, Jan. 1748. He *m.* firstly, in or before 1740, (—). He *m.* secondly, Frances, da. of Richard JEFFERIES, merchant. He *d.* 29 March 1753. Will pr. 1753. His widow *d.* 3 Nov. 1767. Her will pr. March 1768.

VI. 1753, to 1765. SIR ROBERT CANN, Baronet [1662], of Compton Greenfield aforesaid, only s. and h. by 1st wife, *b.* before 1741; *suc. to the Baronetcy*, 29 March 1753. He *m.* Anne, da. of Henry CHURCHMAN, of Aust, co. Glouc., and formerly of Bristol. He *d.* s.p., 20 July 1765, when the *Baronetcy* became *extinct*.[a] His widow *d.* 10 April 1771, aged 62, and was *bur.* (with her father) at Aust aforesaid. M.I. Will pr. June 1771.

MIDDLETON:

cr. 24 Oct. 1662;

sometime, 1799-1876, MONCK.

I. 1662. "WILLIAM MIDDLETON, of Belsey [*i e.*, Belsay] Castle [in Bolam], co. Northumberland, Esq.," 3d but only surv. s. and h. of Ralph MIDDLETON, of Trewick, and formerly (1615) of Eddington, both in that county (*d.* about 1652), by Isabel, da. of Ambrose FENWICK, of West Matfen in the same county, was *b.* about 1625; suc. to the family estate of Belsay Castle, on the death, in April 1656, of his cousin, Robert Middleton,[b] of the same, and was *cr. a Baronet*, as above, 24 Oct. 1662; Sheriff of Northumberland, 1666-67; entered his pedigree in the Her. Visit. of that county in 1666, being then aged 41. He *m.* firstly, in or before 1662, Mary, 2d da. of Sir Thomas WENTWORTH, of Elmsall, co. York, by his 2d wife, Martha, da. of Sir Thomas HAYES, sometime Lord Mayor of London. She *d.* s.p.s., 11 Sep. 1667, and was *bur.* at Rawmarsh, co. York. M.I. He *m.* secondly, Elizabeth, da. of John MUNDY, of Markeaton, co. Derby, by Anne, da. of Sir Francis COKE, of Trusley in that county. She was *bur.* 23 Feb. 1680, at Bolam. He was *bur.* there 22 March 1690.

II. 1690. SIR JOHN MIDDLETON, Baronet [1662], of Belsay Castle aforesaid, yst. but only surv. s. and h. by 2d wife, *bap.* 17 March 1678, at Bolam; *suc. to the Baronetcy* in March 1690; Sheriff of Northumberland, Feb. to Dec. 1711. He *m.* 15 June 1699, at Kirkby Malghdale, Frances (*bap.* there 26 May 1675), da. and h. of John LAMBERT, of Carlton in Craven, co. York (*d.* s.p.m. 14 March 1701/2), by Barbara, da. of Thomas LISTER, of Arnoldsbiggin, co. York, which John was s. and h. of John LAMBERT, of the same (*d.* 1683, aged 64), the celebrated Major Gen. in the Civil War. She was *bur.* 2 June 1712, at Bolam. He *d.* 17 Oct. 1717, aged 39, and was *bur.* there.

III. 1717. SIR WILLIAM MIDDLETON, Baronet [1662], of Belsay Castle aforesaid, 1st s. and h., *b.* about 1700; *suc. to the Baronetcy*, 17 Oct. 1717; was M.P. for Northumberland (six Parls.), 1722 till death in 1757. He *m.* Anne, da. and coheir of William ETTRICKE, of Silksworth, co. Durham, by Elizabeth, sister and coheir of Thomas and da. of George MIDDLETON, of Silksworth aforesaid. He *d.* s.p.m.[c] 29 Sep. 1757, and was *bur.* at Bolam. His widow *d.* 12 Dec. 1763, at Silksworth.

[a] His niece Catherine, da. and h. of his only sister Elizabeth, by Charles Jeffries, of Bristol, inherited the estates of Compton Greenfield and Stoke Bishop. She, "an heiress of £3,000 a year," *m.* 10 Feb. 1774, at Westbury on Trim, Henry Lippincott, who was *cr. a Baronet* 7 Sep. 1778, as "of Stoke Bishop," a dignity which became extinct 23 Aug. 1829.

[b] This Robert was only s. and h. of Charles Middleton (*d.* v.p. May 1628, and *bur.* in Bolam church), who was the only s. and h. of Thomas Middleton (*d.* about 1651), elder br. of Ralph Middleton, the father of the 1st Baronet.

[c] Catharine, his only da. and h., was a Lady of the Bedchamber to H.R.H. the Princess Amelia, at whose house in Cavendish Square she *d.* unm. in March 1784.

IV. 1757. SIR JOHN LAMBERT MIDDLETON, Baronet [1662], of Belsay Castle aforesaid, br. and h. male, *b.* there 14 June 1705; *suc. to the Baronetcy*, 29 Sep. 1757. He *m.*, in Gould square, Minories, about 1737, Anne, widow of Warner PERKINS, 1st da. of Col. Sir Nathaniel HODGES, of London. She, who was *b.* 14 April 1709, *d.* 1762. He *d.* 2 March 1768, at Belsay Castle, aged 62. Both were *bur.* at Charlton, co. Kent. Admon. 17 March 1768.

V. 1768. SIR WILLIAM MIDDLETON, Baronet [1662], of Belsay Castle aforesaid, 1st s. and h., *b.* 6 June 1738, in Gould square aforesaid; was a Capt. in the Royal Horse Guards Blue, and was wounded at the battle of Minden, 1 Aug. 1759; *suc. to the Baronetcy*, 2 March 1768; was M.P. for Northumberland (four Parls.) in the Liberal interest, 1774 till his death in 1795, having contested the election of 1774, at a great expense, against the Duke of Northumberland's interest. He *m.* 20 April 1774, at St. Geo. Han. sq., Jane, only surv. da. and h. of Laurence MONCK, of Caenby, co. Lincoln (*d.* 31 Dec. 1798, aged 86), by Jane, 1st da. and coheir of the Rev. Thomas CONINGTON, Vicar of Glentham, co. Lincoln, and Jane his wife, 2d da. and eventually heir of Anthony TOURNAY, of Caenby aforesaid. She *d.* June 1794, and was *bur.* at Charlton. He *d.* 7 July 1795, aged 57, and was *bur.* at Charlton.

VI. 1795. SIR CHARLES-MILES-LAMBERT MIDDLETON, *afterwards* (1799-1867) MONCK, Baronet [1662], of Belsay Castle aforesaid, only s. and h., *b.* in Golden square, Midx., 7 April, and *bap.* 14 May 1779, at St. James', Westm.; ed. at Rugby School, 1787; *suc. to the Baronetcy*, 7 July 1795; took by royal lic., 11 Feb. 1799, the name of *Monck* in lieu of that of *Middleton* in accordance with the will of his maternal grandfather abovenamed; was Sheriff of Northumberland, 1801-02, and M.P. for that county, 1812-20. He *m.* firstly, 11 Sep. 1804, at Doncaster, his cousin, Louisa Lucy, 2d da. of Sir George COOKE, 7th Baronet [1661] of Wheatley, co. York, by Frances Jory, da. of Sir John Lambert MIDDLETON, 4th Baronet abovenamed. She *d.* 5 Dec. 1824, at Belsay Castle, and was *bur.* at Bolam. He *m.* secondly, 26 July 1831, Mary Elizabeth, da. of Charles (BENNET), 4th EARL OF TANKERVILLE, by Emma, da. and h. of Sir James COLEBROOKE, 1st Baronet [1759]. She *d.* s.p. 27 Feb. 1864, at Belsay Castle. He *d.* there 20 July 1867, aged 88.

VII. 1867. SIR ARTHUR-EDWARD MONCK, *afterwards*, since 1876, MIDDLETON, Baronet [1662], of Belsay Castle aforesaid, grandson and h., being 1st s. and h. of Charles Atticus MONCK, sometime an officer in the Coldstream Guards, by Laura, da. of Sir Matthew WHITE-RIDLEY, 3rd Baronet [1756], which Charles (who was *b.* at Athens, 18 July 1805, was 1st s. and h. ap. of the late Baronet, but *d.* v.p. 1 Dec. 1856, aged 51. He was *b.* 12 Jan. 1838, at Humshaugh, Simonburn; was ed. at Rugby and at Trin. Coll., Cambridge; *suc. to the Baronetcy*, 20 July 1867; was M.P. for Durham, 1874-80; re-assumed his patronymic of *Middleton* in lieu of that of *Monck*, 12 Feb. 1876; Sheriff of Northumberland, 1884. He *m.* 8 Nov. 1871, at Riverhead, co. Kent, Constance Harriett, 3d da. of William Pitt (AMHERST), 3d EARL AMHERST OF ARRACAN, by Gertrude, da. of the Hon. Hugh PERCY, Bishop of Carlisle. She, who was *b.* 28 Feb. 1843, *d.* 7 Oct. 1879, at Belsay Castle.

Family Estates.—These, in 1883, consisted of 9,079 acres in Northumberland, worth £9,712 a year. *Seat.*—Belsay Castle, near Newcastle-upon-Tyne, co. Northumberland.

GRAHAM:

cr. 17 Nov. 1662.

I. 1662. "RICHARD GRAHAM, of Norton-Coniers, co. York, Esq.," 2d s. of Sir Richard GRAHAM, 1st Baronet [1629], of Esk, co. Cumberland (*bur.* at Wath, co. York, 11 Feb. 1653), by Catharine, da. and

coheir of Thomas MUSGRAVE, of Grimcatch in that county,[a] was *bap.* 11 March 1635/6, at Wath; admitted to Gray's Inn, 12 Feb. 1651/2, and to the Inner Temple, Nov. 1654, and was, for his father's services to the Royal cause, *cr. a Baronet*, as above, 17 Nov. 1662. He entered his pedigree in the Her. Visit. of Yorkshire, 1665, being then about 28. He *m.*, in or before 1660, Elizabeth, da. and h. of Col. Chichester FORTESCUE, of Dromiskin in Ireland, by Elizabeth (afterwards VISCOUNTESS PURBECK), da. of Sir William SLINGSBY, of Kippax. She was *bur.* 25 June 1705, at Wath. He was *bur.* there 21 Dec. 1711, aged 75.

II. 1711. SIR REGINALD GRAHAM, Baronet [1662], of Norton Conyers aforesaid, 3d but 1st surv. s. and h.,[b] *bap.* 30 July 1670, at Wath; was sometime Page of Honour to James II.; *suc. to the Baronetcy* in Dec. 1711. He *m.* firstly, in or before 1702, Frances, da. and h. of Henry BELLINGHAM, of Whitwell, co. York. She was living Aug. 1709. He *m.* secondly, 9 April 1724, at York Minster, Anne, da. of Sir David FOULIS, 3d Baronet [1620] of Ingleby, co. York, by Catherine, da. of Sir David WATKINS. He *d.* 20 and was *bur.* 23 May 1728, at Wath, aged 58. His widow, who was *bap.* 16 Sep. 1669, at Ingleby, *d.* s.p. and was *bur.* 11 May 1751, at St. Martin's, Coney street, York. Will dat. 11 Sep. 1742, pr. 17 May 1751.

III. 1728. SIR BELLINGHAM GRAHAM, Baronet [1662], of Norton Conyers aforesaid, 1st s. and h. by 1st wife, *bap.* 20 Aug. 1702 at Wath; *suc. to the Baronetcy*, 20 May 1728. He *d.* unm., and was *bur.* there 1 April 1730.

IV. 1730. SIR REGINALD GRAHAM, Baronet [1662], of Norton Conyers aforesaid, br. of the whole blood and h., *b.* 16 and *bap.* 17 May 1704, at Wath; *suc. to the Baronetcy* in April 1730. He *m.* 5 June 1727, at Pickhill, co. York, Jacoba Catherina, da. of Col. Metcalfe GRAHAM (*d.* 14 Jan. 1758, aged 78), sometime aide-de-camp to the great DUKE OF MARLBOROUGH, by Isabella Jacoba DE BONS, of Breda, his wife. He *d.* 29 and was *bur.* 31 Oct. 1755, at Wath, aged 51. His widow *m.* Col. (—) BROWN, whom she survived, and *d.* at St. George's the Martyr, Midx., being *bur.* 1 Dec. 1763 (with her parents), at Pickhill. Admon. 14 Dec. 1764.

V. 1755. SIR BELLINGHAM GRAHAM, Baronet [1662], of Norton Conyers aforesaid, *bap.* 14 June 1729, at Pickhill aforesaid; *suc. to the Baronetcy*, 29 Oct. 1755; Sheriff of Yorkshire, 1770-71. He *m.* 24 June 1763, Elizabeth, da. of Benjamin HUDSON, of Bridlington, co. York, by Elizabeth, da. and h. of Thomas WILSON, of Bridlington aforesaid. She *d.* 6 and was *bur.* 16 May 1767, in her 29th year, at Wath. M.I. He *d.* suddenly 3 and was *bur.* there 9 Oct. 1790, aged 61.

VI. 1790. SIR BELLINGHAM GRAHAM, Baronet [1662], of Norton Conyers aforesaid, 1st s. and h., *b.* about 1764; *suc. to the Baronetcy*, 3 Oct. 1790. He *m.* 31 Oct. 1785, Priscilla, sister of Charles, 1st EARL WHITWORTH, da. of Sir Charles WHITWORTH, of Leybourne, co. Kent, by Martha, da. of Richard SHELLEY. He *d.* at Whitwell, co. York, 13 and was *bur.* 21 April 1796, at Wath, aged 32. His widow *m.*, as his 1st wife, 1 Jan. 1800, at St. Geo. Han. sq., Francis Gerard (LAKE), 2d VISCOUNT LAKE, of Delhi (who *d.* s.p. 12 May 1836, aged 64), and *d.* at Bath, 8 May 1833, in her 75th year. Will pr. June 1833.

[a] The annotated extracts from the Parish Register of Wath, near Ripon, by the Rev. John Ward [*Top. and Gen.*. iii, 414-36] greatly illustrate this article.

[b] Of his two elder brothers, (1) "Richard Grahme, Esq.," aged four in 1665, a member of Christ's College, Cambridge, *d.* 3 and was *bur.* 4 March 1680, *æt.* 20, at Wath. M.I.; and (2) "Chichester Graham, Esq.," *bap.* at Wath 23 March 1662, *m.* but *d.* s.p. and v.p., and was *bur.* there 2 June 1694.

III

VII. 1796. SIR BELLINGHAM REGINALD GRAHAM, Baronet [1662], of Norton Conyers aforesaid, only s. and h., *b.* 4 Nov. and *bap.* 22 Dec. 1789, at Wath; *suc. to the Baronetcy*, 13 April 1796; ed. at Harrow. He *m.* firstly, 10 Nov. 1810, Henrietta, 3d da. of George CLARK, of West Hatch, co. Essex. She *d.* 9 Oct. 1830, in Paris. He *m.* secondly, 28 June 1831, at Bath, Harriet, 3d da. of the Rev. Robert COTTAM, M.A. [1809], Oxford. He *d.* at his house, 131 Park Lane, co. Midx., 15 June 1866, aged 76. His widow *d.* 17 Jan. 1903, at 60, Curzon street, Mayfair, in her 94th year.

VIII. 1866. SIR REGINALD HENRY GRAHAM, Baronet [1662], of Norton Conyers aforesaid, 4th but 1st surv. s. and h., being 1st s. by the 2d wife, *b.* 22 and *bap.* 23 April 1835, at Wath; ed. at Sandhurst; entered the 14th Foot, 1852; Capt. Rifle Brigade, 1856; served in the Crimea, and was at the taking of Sebastopol (medal and clasp and Turkish medal), retiring from the Army in 1863; *suc. to the Baronetcy*, 15 June 1866. He *m.* 24 July 1876, at St. Mark's, North Audley street, Annie Mary, 2d and yst. da. and coheir of Thomas SHIFFNER, of Westergate, co. Sussex (4th s. of Sir George SHIFFNER, 1st Baronet [1818]), by Mary, da. of James BROWN, of Harehill's Grove, near Leeds.

Family Estates.—These, apparently the same, or nearly so, as those of the 1st Baronet, were in 1883 under 3,000 acres. *Seat.*—Norton Conyers Hall, in Wath, near Ripon, co. York.

TANCRED, *or* TANKARD:

cr. 17 Nov. 1662.

I. 1652. "THOMAS TANKARD [*otherwise* TANCRED], of Burrow brigg [*i.e.*, Burroughbridge], co. York, Esq.," 2d s. but heir(a) of Thomas TANKARD, *otherwise* TANCRED, of the same and of Brampton in Aldborough in that county, by Anne, da. of Sir Edward FITTON, of Cheshire, suc. his father in Feb. 1626/7, and was *cr. a Baronet*, as above, 17 Nov. 1662. He *m.* Frances,(b) da. and coheir of Christopher MALTBY, of Cottingham, co. York, s. and h. of Christopher MALTBY, Alderman of York. She was *bur.* 27 April 1655, at Aldborough. He was *bur.* there 19 Aug. 1663.

II. 1663. SIR WILLIAM TANCRED, Baronet [1662], of Boroughbridge and Brampton aforesaid, only s. and h.; *suc. to the Baronetcy* in Aug. 1663. He *m.* firstly, Dorothy, da. and coheir of Robert WILDE, of Hunton. She *d.* s.p. and was *bur.* 30 July 1660, at Aldborough. He *m.* secondly, in or before 1663, Elizabeth, da. of Charles WALDEGRAVE, of Staininghall, co. Norfolk. She was *bur.* 9 Sep. 1681, at Aldborough. He was *bur.* there 22 Aug. 1703.

III. 1703. SIR THOMAS TANCRED, Baronet [1662], of Brampton aforesaid, 2d but 1st surv. s. and h. by 2d wife; *bap.* Aug. 1665, at Kirby; *suc. to the Baronetcy* in Aug. 1703; was a Non-juror in 1715. He *m.* before 1712, Elizabeth, da. of William MESSENGER, of Fountains Abbey, co. York. He was *bur.* 27 Aug. 1744, at Aldborough, aged 79. His widow, who was *b.* 22 Jan. 1672, was *bur.* there 21 Dec. 1753.

(a) He is said, in Foster's *Yorkshire Pedigrees* (but not in Clay's valuable additions to *Dugdale's Visitation of Yorkshire*, 1663) to have had an elder brother, Hugh Tankard, who was disinherited by his father.

(b) A previous wife, Margaret, "excommunicated 1634," is attributed to him by Foster, as in note "a" next above.

IV. 1744. SIR THOMAS TANCRED, Baronet [1662], of Brampton aforesaid, 3d but only surv. s. and h.; *suc. to the Baronetcy* in Aug. 1744. He *m.*, in or before 1740, Judith,(a) da. of Peter DALTON, of Greenanstown, co. Tipperary. He *d.* 30 May and was *bur.* 2 June 1759, at Aldborough. Will dat. 25 May, pr. 2 June 1759. His widow *d.* 1781. Will, as "of Fulford," dat. 22 Feb. 1779, pr. Nov. 1781.

V. 1759. SIR THOMAS TANCRED, Baronet [1662], of Brampton aforesaid, 1st s. and h.; *suc. to the Baronetcy*, 30 May 1759; was "on his travels in Italy" in 1771; admitted to Gray's Inn, 24 Jan. 1772; Barrister, 1775; *cr.* D.C.L. of Oxford, 7 July 1773. He *m.*, 7 Oct. 1776 (spec. lic., 28 Sep.), Penelope, da. of Thomas ASSHETON-SMITH, of Bowdon, co. Chester. He *d.* at his house in Mayfair, 3 Aug. 1784. Admon. Oct. 1784. His widow d. 21 April 1837, at 121 Park street, Midx. Will dat. 3 Aug. 1835, pr. May 1837.

VI. 1784. SIR THOMAS TANCRED, Baronet [1662], of Brampton aforesaid, 1st s. and h., *b.* 24 July 1780; *suc. to the Baronetcy*, 3 Aug. 1784. He *m.*, 25 April 1805, at Mucklestone, Salop (settlement dat. 1805), his cousin, Harriet Lucy, da. of the Rev. Offley CREWE, of Muxton, co. Stafford, by Harriet, da. of Thomas ASSHETON-SMITH abovenamed. He *d.* at Spa, in Belgium, 29 Aug. 1844, aged 64. Will pr. Sep. 1844. His widow *d.* 16 June 1864, at 13, Montague street, Russell sq., Bloomsbury.

VII. 1844. SIR THOMAS TANCRED, Baronet [1662], of Brampton aforesaid, 1st s. and h., *b.* 16 Aug. 1808, at Chessell Cottage, Southampton; matric. at Oxford [Ch. Ch.], 7 June 1827, aged 18; B.A. 1830; Fellow of Merton Coll., Oxford, 1832-40; M.A. 1834; admitted to Lincoln's Inn, 8 Nov. 1834; *suc. to the Baronetcy*, 29 Aug. 1844, was afterwards of New Zealand. He *m.*, 16 April 1839, at Bamborough, co. Northumberland, Jane, 3d da. of Prideaux John SELBY, of Twisell House, in that county. He *d.* Oct. 1880. His widow was, apparently, living 1902,(b) at Taralahi, Clareville, co. Wiararapa, New Zealand.

VIII. 1880. SIR THOMAS SELBY TANCRED, Baronet [1662], sometime of Rankapuka, near Canterbury, in New Zealand, 1st s. and h., *b.* 1 Oct. 1840; ed. at Radley School and Bradfield College, Berks; was a mining and railway engineer; *suc. to the Baronetcy*, Oct. 1880; a contractor for building the Forth bridge, 1883-89; constructed the Delagoa Bay railway, 1887. He *m.*, 1 May 1866, at St. Margaret's, Westm., Mary Harriet, 2d da. of Col. George Willoughby HEMANS, of Queen's sq., Westm.

HERON:

cr. 20 Nov. 1662;

sometime, 1770? to 1801, MYDDLETON;

ex. 27 May 1801;

but assumed to 1817 or later.

I. 1662. "CUTHBERT HERON, of Chipchase, co. Northumberland, Esq.," surv. s. and h.(c) of Cuthbert HERON, of the same (living 1639), by Dorothy, da. of (—), was *b.* probably about 1618, is said to have been

(a) "The amiable Judith" [Kimber's *Baronetage*, 1771].

(b) Dod's *Peerage*, etc., for 1902, but in that for 1903 she is omitted.

(c) Two brothers, John aged 18 and George aged 16, the 1st and 2d sons of Cuthbert Heron, of Chipchase, "Esq.," matric. together at Oxford (Ch. Ch.) 22 June 1632, of whom George was admitted to Gray's Inn, 29 Nov. 1634.

"a great sufferer in the wars for King Charles I.," and was *cr. a Baronet*, as above, 20 Nov. 1662; Sheriff of Northumberland (two years), 1667-69. He *m.* firstly, in or before 1652, Elizabeth, 3d da. of Sir Richard GRAHAM, 1st Baronet [1629], of Esk, by Katharine, da. and coheir of Thomas MUSGRAVE. He *m.* secondly, in or before 1686 (—), da. of George THOMPSON, of co. York. He *d.* 1688 and was *bur.* at Chollerford, co. Northumberland.

II. 1688. SIR JOHN HERON, Baronet [1662], of Chipchase aforesaid, 2d but 1st surv. s. and h. male,(a) by 1st wife, *b.* probably about 1654; *suc. to the Baronetcy* in 1688; Sheriff of Northumberland, 1689-90. He *m.*, probably about 1675, Anne, da. of John HERON, of Brampton, co. Huntingdon. He *d.* s.p.m.(b) in or before 1693. Will pr. March 1693. His widow *m.* George SAFFIN, of St. Margaret's, Westm. She *d.* 29 Oct. 1713, aged 45, and was *bur.* in Bath Abbey. M.I. Admon. 8 April 1715.

III. 1693? SIR CHARLES HERON, Baronet [1662], of Chipchase aforesaid, br. of the whole blood and h.; *suc. to the Baronetcy* in or before 1693. He *m.*, 15 May 1694, at Westm. Abbey, Catherine, 1st da. of Sir William PULTENEY, of Misterton, co. Leic., by Grace, da. of Sir John CORBET, 1st Baronet [1627] of Stoke, co. Salop. He *d.* in the Fleet prison between 1694 and 1711. Will dat. 24 July 1694, pr. 30 Oct. 1711. His widow was *bur.* 18 Oct. 1720, at St. Martin's-in-the-Fields. Will dat. 20 Sep., pr. 26 Oct. 1720.

IV. 1705? SIR HARRY HERON, Baronet [1662], of Chipchase aforesaid, only s. and h., *b.* probably about 1696; *suc. to the Baronetcy* before 1711; was a Lieut. in the 2d Reg. of Guards. In 1737 he mortgaged the Chipchase estate, which shortly afterwards was altogether alienated. He *m.* 18 March 1724/5, at St. Bennet's, Paul's Wharf, London, Elizabeth JUMP,(c) of Enfield, co. Midx., Spinster. She *d.* about 1734. He *m.* secondly, in or before 1748, Sarah. He was *bur.* 26 Feb. 1748/9, at Acton, co. Midx. Admon. 5 June 1751 to his cousin Sir Thomas HERON, Baronet, his sister Catherine Panton, widow, having renounced.

V. 1749. SIR CHARLES HERON, Baronet [1662], only s. and h., by 2d wife; *b.* 15 March and *bap.* 8 April 1748 at Acton aforesaid; *suc. to the Baronetcy* in Feb. 1748/9, but *d.* in infancy and was *bur.* 19 Jan. 1749/50 at Acton.(d)

VI. 1750, to 1801. SIR THOMAS HERON, *afterwards* [1770? to 1801] MYDDLETON, Baronet [1662], of Bowlby, near Whitby, co. York, cousin and h. male, being s. and h. of Cuthbert HERON, by Catharine, da. of Richard MYDDLETON, of Offerton, co. Durham, which Cuthbert (who *d.* 1738) was yst. s. of the 1st Baronet, and only s. of his 2d wife. He was *b.* 1723 at Durham; *suc. to the Baronetcy* in Jan. 1749/50, and having subsequently [*Qy.* about 1770] suc. to the estates at Mainsforth and elsewhere, co. Durham, of his maternal uncle, took the name of MYDDLETON. He *m.* firstly, in 1749, at Carrickfergus, in Ireland, Mary, da. of the Rev. [—] FINLAY, of Carrickfergus. She *d.* s.p.m., 1753, and was *bur.* at Ballinrobe, in Ireland. He *m.* secondly, in Aug.

(a) Cuthbert the 1st son, matric. at Oxford (Queen's Coll.), 2 Aug. 1669, aged 17; *m.* Elizabeth da. of Sir John Mallory, of Studley, co. York, and *d.* v.p. and s.p.m., leaving a da. and h., Elizabeth, living 1693. She *m.* Ralph Jennison, of Walworth.

(b) Henrietta Maria his only da. and h., *m.* George Huxley, of London, both being living in April 1715.

(c) She, however, is called "Elizabeth Coventry" in the pedigree entered at the College of Arms.

(d) He is, however, not called "Baronet" in the Burial Register, but only "Charles, son of the late Sir Henry Heron."

1758, Elizabeth, da. of Alexander ARBUTHNOT, of Fortree, in Scotland. He *d.* s.p.m.(a) 27 May 1801, when the *Baronetcy* became *extinct*. Will pr. 1801. The will of his widow pr. 1803.

> The Baronetcy was, however, assumed by CUTHBERT HERON, of Newcastle-upon-Tyne, whose "Lady" died 27 Nov. 1812 at South Shields. The burial at St. James', Westm., 28 June 1817, of "Capt. SIR HARRY HERON, R.N., from St. Pancras, aged 74," not improbably relates to a son of the said Cuthbert.

WENMAN:

cr. 29 Nov. 1662;

afterwards, 1686—1800, VISCOUNTS WENMAN OF TUAM [I.];

ex. 26 March 1800.

I. 1662. "SIR FRANCIS WENMAN, of Casswell [in Witney], co. Oxford, Knt.," 2d s. of Sir Francis WENMAN, of the same [*d.* 26 June 1640, aged 40], by Anne, da. of Sir Samuel SANDYS, of Ombersley, suc. his elder br. Samuel WENMAN, in 1645, and was *cr. a Baronet*, as above, 29 Nov. 1662; M.P. for Oxon, Nov. 1664 to 1679. He *m.* firstly, 4 July 1651, Mary, 6th and yst. da. and coheir of Thomas (WENMAN), 2d VISCOUNT WENMAN OF TUAM [I. 1628], by Margaret, da. and h. of Edmund HAMPDEN, of Hartwell. She, by whom he had five children, *d.* 13 Nov. 1657, in her 24th year and was *bur.* at Whitney. M.I. He *m.* secondly, Elizabeth, da. of Edward FETTIPLACE, of Swinbrook, Oxon. She *d.* 17 Sep. 1679, and he *d.* 2 Sep. 1680, both being *bur.* at Whitney. M.I. His will pr. 1680.

II. 1680. SIR RICHARD WENMAN, Baronet [1662], of Casswell aforesaid, 4th but only surv. s. and h. by 1st wife, was *b.* about 1657; matric. at Oxford (Oriel Coll.) 27 June 1673, aged 15; was M.P. for Brackley [four Parls.] 1679-90; *suc. to the Baronetcy*, 2 Sep. 1680. He *m.* 17 April 1682, at Kirtlington, Oxon, Catharine ("a fortune of £15,000") 1st da. and coheir of Sir Thomas CHAMBERLAINE, 2d Baronet [1643], of Wickham, by Margaret, da. of Edmund PRIDEAUX. She was living, when, on 20 April 1686, he became VISCOUNT WENMAN OF TUAM, etc. [I.], by the death s.p.m. of his maternal uncle Philip (WENMAN) 3d and last VISCOUNT WENMAN OF TUAM, etc. [I.] (of the creation of 30 July 1628) who had had a regrant of his peerage, 30 June 1683, with a spec. rem., failing heirs male of his body, to the said Richard. In that peerage this *Baronetcy* then merged till both became *extinct* on the death of the 4th Viscount and 5th Baronet, 26 March 1800. See *Peerage*.

PUREFOY, *or* PUREFEY:

cr. 4 Dec. 1662;

ex. 19 Aug. 1686.

I. 1662, to 1686. "HENRY PUREFEY [*rectius* PUREFOY], son and heir [apparent] to George PUREFEY [*rectius* PUREFOY], of Wadley, co. Berks, Esq.," by Catharine, relict of Sir James BELLINGHAM, 2d Baronet [1620], 4th da. and coheir of Sir Henry WILLOUGHBY, Baronet [so *cr.* 1611], of Risley, co. Derby, was *bap.* 14 Aug. 1656 and was *cr. a*

(a) Mary, his only da. and h., by the 1st wife, *b.* 1750; *m.* 1768 at Bishop Middleham, Robert Baron, of Alnwick and was living 1784 with issue.

Baronet, as above, 4 Dec. 1662. He (as a Baronet) matric. at Oxford (Oriel Coll.) 13 Nov. 1671, aged 17. He suc. his father about 1679 in the estates of Wadley and Shalleston, both in Bucks; elected Sheriff of Derbyshire, 1680, but did not act. He *d.* s.p., probably unm., 19 Aug. 1686, when the *Baronetcy became extinct.* Admon. 16 Nov. 1686. Will pr. May 1687.

COBB:
cr. 9 Dec. 1662;
ex. 29 March 1762.

I. 1662. "THOMAS COBB, of Adderbury, co. Oxford, Esq.," 1st surv. s. and h. (out of twenty-one children) of Sir William COBB, of the same, by Susan, da. and coheir of Noah FLOYD, of Gloucestershire, was *bap.* 28 Aug. 1627, at Adderbury; suc. his father 16 March 1658, and was *cr. a Baronet*, as above, 9 Dec. 1662. He was *cr.* M.A. of the Univ. of Oxford, 28 Sep. 1663. He *m.* firstly, Catherine, 2d da. of Sir Richard ONSLOW, of West Clandon, co. Surrey, by Elizabeth, da. and h. of Arthur STRANGEWAYS. She *d.* s.p.m., in childbirth, and was *bur.* 16 June 1659, at Adderbury. He *m.* secondly (Lic. Lond., 29 Oct. 1666), Christian (then aged 27), da. of Sir Edward BISHOPP, 2d Baronet [1620], of Parham, by Mary, da. of Nicholas (TUFTON), 1st EARL OF THANET. She was *bur.* 26 March 1697, at Adderbury. He was *bur.* there 6 Feb. 1699/700, aged 72. Will pr. May 1700.

II. 1700. SIR EDWARD COBB, Baronet [1662], of Adderbury aforesaid, 4th but 1st surv. s. and h. by 2d wife, *b.* about 1676; matric. at Oxford (Trin. Coll.), 15 Dec. 1693, aged 17; B.A., 28 Jan. 1697/8; *suc. to the Baronetcy* in Feb. 1699/700; Sheriff of Oxon, 1735-36. He *d.* unm. in 1744. Will pr. 1744.

III. 1744, to 1762. SIR GEORGE COBB, Baronet [1662], of Adderbury aforesaid and of Newton Park in Newton St. Loe, co. Somerset, br. and h., being 6th and yst. s. of the 1st Baronet,(a) *b.* probably about 1670; *suc. to the Baronetcy* in 1744. He *m.*, in or after 1708, Anne, widow of Robert LANGTON, of Brislington, co. Somerset, da. and coheir of Joseph LANGTON, of Newton Park aforesaid, by Frances sister and coheir of Sir John BORLASE, 2d Baronet [1642]. She *d.* 1749, aged 70. Will pr. 1750. He *d.* s.p.m.s.(b) (being accidentally drowned while staying with John Blagrave, near Reading) 29 March 1762, aged 90 and upwards, when the *Baronetcy* became *extinct*.

BROOKE, or BROOK:
cr. 12 Dec. 1662.

I. 1662. "HENRY BROOK, of Norton, co. Chester, Esq.," s. and h. of Sir Richard BROOK, of the same, by his 2d wife, Katharine, da. of Sir Henry NEVILL, of Billingbere, co. Berks, was *b.* about 1611; suc. his father 10 April 1632, being then aged 21 years and 2 months(c); was a Col. in the Parliamentary Army, 1643; Sheriff of Cheshire for the Parl. for four consecutive years, 1644-47(a); was afterwards, 1654-56, M.P. for that county, and was *cr. a Baronet*, as above, 12 Dec. 1662. He *m.*, probably about 1635, Mary, da. of Timothy PUSEY, of Selston, Notts. He *d.* 1664.

(a) John Cobb, D.D., the 5th son, Warden of New College, Oxford, 1712-20, and subsequently Warden of Winchester College, 1724-25. *d.* s.p. in 1725.

(b) Of his two daughters and coheirs, (1) Anne (unm. in 1741) *m.* firstly John Besey, and secondly, 6 Aug. 1745, John Blagrave, of Bulnash Court in Sonning, Berks, and *d.* 19 Dec. 1789, at Calcott House, Berks, leaving issue; (2) Christian, *m.* 25 June 1749, at St. Laurence Jewry, London, Paul Methuen, of Corsham, Wilts, and was grandmother of the 1st Baron Methuen of Corsham.

(c) *Inq. p. mortem*, 8 Car. I.

II. 1664. SIR RICHARD BROOKE, Baronet [1662], of Norton aforesaid, 1st s. and h., *b.* probably about 1635; matric. at Oxford (St. Mary Hall), together with his yr. br. Henry, 3 May 1652; *suc. to the Baronetcy* in 1664; Sheriff of Cheshire, 1667-68. He *m.* in April 1656, at Frodsham, Francisca Posthuma, sister of Richard LEGH, of Lyme, co. Chester, da. of Thomas LEGH, D.D., Rector of Sephton and of Walton-on-the-Hill, co. Lancaster, by Lettice, da. and h. of Sir George CALVELEY, of Lea. He *d.* Feb. 1709/10.

III. 1710. SIR THOMAS BROOKE, Baronet [1662], of Norton aforesaid, 1st s. and h., *b.* about 1664; matric. at Oxford (Ch. Ch.), 25 June 1685; *suc. to the Baronetcy* in Feb. 1709/10; was sometime Governor of Chester Castle; Sheriff of Cheshire, 1719-20. He *m.* 12 July 1688, Grace, 5th da. of Roger WILLBRAHAM, of Nantwich, by Alice, da. of Roger WILLBRAHAM, of Dorfold, both co. Chester. He *d.* 1737, aged 73, and was *bur.* at Runcorn, co. Chester. His widow *d.* 1739, aged 72, and was *bur.* there.

IV. 1737. SIR RICHARD BROOKE, Baronet [1662], of Norton aforesaid, grandson and h., being only s. and h. of Richard BROOKE, by Margaret, da. of John HILL, of Hawkstone, Salop, which Richard [who matric. at Oxford (Bras. Coll.), 11 Oct. 1708, aged 16], was 1st s. and h. ap. of the late Baronet, but *d.* v.p. in 1720. He was *b.* about 1719; *suc. to the Baronetcy* in 1737; matric. at Oxford (Bras. Coll.) 15 March 1737/8, aged 18; was Sheriff of Cheshire, 1752-53. He *m.*, in or before 1752, Frances, da. of Thomas PATTEN, of Winmarleigh, co. Lancaster, by Lettice, da. and coheir of the Rev. James PEAKE, of Bowdell, co. Chester. She *d.* 12 April 1778, aged 47, and was *bur.* at Runcorn. He *d.* 6 July 1781, aged 63, and was *bur.* there.

V. 1781. SIR RICHARD BROOKE, Baronet [1662], of Norton aforesaid, 1st s. and h.; *b.* about 1753; matric. at Oxford (Bras. Coll.), 15 Nov. 1771, aged 18; *cr.* M.A. 29 Oct. 1774; *suc. to the Baronetcy*, 6 July 1781; Sheriff of Cheshire, 1787-88. He *m.* 4 May 1780, at Chester, Mary, 2d da. of Sir Robert CUNLIFFE, 2d Baronet [1759], by Mary, da. of Ichabod WRIGHT, of Nottingham, Banker. He *d.* 6 March 1795, aged 42, and was *bur.* at Runcorn. His widow, who was *b.* at Liverpool 4 Aug. 1761, is probably the "Dame Mary Brooke, of Chester," whose will was proved Nov. 1852, when, however, she would have been 91.

VI. 1795. SIR RICHARD BROOKE, Baronet [1662], of Norton aforesaid, 1st s. and h., *b.* 18 Aug. 1785, at Norton Priory; *suc. to the Baronetcy*, 6 March 1795; matric. at Oxford (Ch. Ch.), 24 Oct. 1804, aged 18; *cr.* D.C.L., 5 July 1810; Sheriff of Cheshire, 1817-18. He *m.*, 4 Dec. 1809, at Gresford, Harriet, 2d da. of his maternal uncle, Sir Foster CUNLIFFE, 3d Baronet [1759], by Harriet, da. of Sir David KINLOCH, 6th Baronet [S. 1686]. She *d.* 13 April 1825. He *d.* 11 Nov. 1865, at Norton Priory, and was *bur.* at Runcorn, aged 80.

VII. 1865. SIR RICHARD BROOKE, Baronet [1662], of Norton aforesaid, 1st s. and h., *b.* 13 Dec. 1814, at Norton Priory; ed. at Eton; sometime Lieut. in the 1st Life Guards; Lieut. Col. 2d Batt. Cheshire Royal Volunteers; *suc. to the Baronetcy*, 11 Nov. 1865; Sheriff of Cheshire, 1869-70. He *m.* firstly, 12 Dec. 1848, at St. Peter's, Pimlico, Louisa Tollemache, sister of James (DUFF), 5th EARL FIFE [I.], 2d da. of Gen. the Hon. Sir Alexander DUFF, **G.C.H.**, by Anne, da. of James STEIN, of Kilbogie. She, who was granted by royal warrant, 2 June 1857, the rank of the da. of an Earl, *d.* 23 Sep. 1864. He *m.* secondly, 21 Dec. 1871, at Over Peover, co. Chester, Henrietta Elizabeth, 2d da. of Sir Harry MAINWARING, 2d Baronet [1804], by Emma, da. of Thomas William TATTON, of Withenshaw. He *d.* suddenly, 3 March 1888, aged 74, and was *bur.* at Halton, co. Chester. His widow living 1903.

(a) Sir Richard Grosvenor, 2d Baronet [1622], was Sheriff thereof *for the King*, 1643-44.

VIII. 1888. SIR RICHARD MARCUS BROOKE, Baronet [1662], of Norton aforesaid, 1st s. and h., *b.* 26 Oct. 1850; sometime Lieut. 1st Life Guards; *suc. to the Baronetcy*, 3 March 1888. He *m.* 16 Jan. 1888, at St. Mary's, Luton, Beds., Alice, da. of John Sambrooke CRAWLEY, of Stockwood Park, in that county, by Sarah Bridget, da. of Henry Octavius WELLS, Bengal Civil Service.

Family Estates.—These, in 1883, consisted of 4,898 acres in Cheshire; 1,400 in Lancashire and 99 in Flintshire. *Total.*—6,397 acres, worth £13,367 a year. *Principal Seat.*—Norton Priory, near Runcorn, co. Chester.

PINDAR:
cr. 22 Dec. 1662;
ex. in or before 1704/5.

I. 1662. "PETER PINDAR, of EDINSHAW [*i.e.*, Idenshaw], co. Chester, Esq.," s. of Reginald PINDAR, of Southwell, Notts (*d.* about 1644), by Frances, da. of John STEERE, of Farley, was Collector of the Customs at Chester, and having purchased the estate and manor of Idenshaw from his wife's brother, John HURLESTON, was *cr. a Baronet*, as above, 22 Dec. 1662. He *m.* firstly, Judith, da. and coheir of Jeffrey WALKENDEN, of the Inner Temple. He *m.* secondly, Dorothy, da. of John HURLESTON, of Pickton, co. Chester. He was living 8 Sep. 1687, but *d.* in or before 1693. Will pr. 1693.

II. 1693? SIR THOMAS PINDAR, Baronet [1662], of Idenshaw aforesaid, s. and h.; *suc. to the Baronetcy* in or before 1693. He *m.*, in or before 1680, Anne, da. and h. of Robert WYNNE, of Nequis, co. Flint. He *d.* in or before 1694.

III. 1694? to 1705? SIR PAUL PINDAR, Baronet [1662], of Idenshaw aforesaid, s. and h., *b.* at Chester about 1680, being an Act of Parl., 1694, for his education and maintenance, being a ward in Chancery, Feb. 1694/5; matric. at Oxford (Jesus Coll.), 6 July 1695, aged 15; *suc. to the Baronetcy* on the death of his father. He *d.* unm. in or before 1704/5, when the *Baronetcy* became *extinct*.(a) Will pr. 1705.

SLANNING, or SLANING:
cr. 19 Jan. 1662/3;
ex. 21 Nov. 1700.

I. 1663. "SIR NICHOLAS SLANING, of Maristow, co. Devon, Knight of the Bath and Standard Bearer to the Band of Gentlemen Pensioners," 2d but only surv. s. and h. of Sir Nicholas SLANNING, or SLANING, of Maristow aforesaid, and of Bickleigh, co. Devon, Gov. of Pendennis Castle (aged 9 in the Her. Visit. of Devon, 1620), by Gertrude (*m.* 25 Sep. 1625, at St. Andrew's, Plymouth), da. of Sir James BAGGE, of Saltram, was *b.* June 1643, being three months old at the death of his father (who *d.* from wounds received at the assault of Bristol, 26 July 1643) in Sep. 1643; was M.P. for Plympton, May 1669 to 1679, and for Penryn (three Parls.), 1679-87; Cupbearer to the Queen Dowager, 1660; was made **K.B.**, presumably at the Coronation of Charles II, 23 April 1661, and was *cr. a Baronet*, as above, 19 Jan. 1662/3. He *m.* firstly, Anne, 1st da. of Sir George CARTERET, 1st Baronet [1645], by Elizabeth, da. of Sir Philip CARTERET, of St. Owens, in Jersey. She *d.* s.p. He *m.* secondly, 22 June 1670, at St. Columb Major, co. Cornwall (Lic. 25 April, at Exeter), Mary, da. of James JENKYN, of Trekenning in that parish. She also *d.* s.p. in or before 1670. Admon. 9 July 1672. He *m.* thirdly, 4 Dec. 1673, at Eversley, Hants, Mary, da. of Sir Andrew HENLEY, 1st Baronet [1660], by Mary, da. of Sir John GAYER. He *m.* fourthly, 16 Nov. 1679, at Upton Hellion, Dame Amy DAVIE (*bap.* 8 Feb. 1648/9, at Plympton), widow of Sir John DAVIE, 2d Baronet [1641], of Creedy (who *d.* July 1678), and formerly widow of Walter HELE, of Newton Ferrers, da. of Edmund PARKER, of Boringdon in Plympton, by his 1st wife, Alice, da. of (—). He *d.* in or shortly before April 1691. Will pr. 24 Nov. 1692, Feb. 1696, and Feb. 1700. His widow *m.*, as his 3d wife and her 4th husband, 26 Dec. 1693, at Upton Pyne, Devon, Hugh STAFFORD, of Pynes, who *d.* April 1703. She was *bur.* 24 Oct. 1697, at Upton Pynes.

(a) Dorothy, his sister and heir, was living unm. 1708, aged about 22.

II. 1691? to 1700. SIR ANDREW SLANNING, Baronet [1663], of Maristow and Bickleigh aforesaid, only s. and h. by 3d wife, *b.* about 1674, being aged 20 in 1694; *suc. to the Baronetcy* in or shortly before 1691. He *m* 27 April 1692, at South Tawton, Devon, Elizabeth, da. and coheir of (—) HELE, a lime burner of that place. She was *bur.* 27 May 1700, at Bickleigh. Admon. 30 Dec. 1700 to her sister Joane, wife of William HELYAR. He *d.* s.p. 21 Nov. 1700, from wounds received three days before in a scuffle at the Rose Tavern, Covent Garden, and was *bur.* 16 Dec. following at Bickleigh, when the *Baronetcy* became *extinct*.(a) Admon. 6 Feb. 1700/1 to Dame Elizabeth Modyford, widow, his paternal aunt.

REEVE, or REVE:
cr. 22 Jan. 1662/3;
ex. in or before 1688.

I. 1633. "SIR GEORGE REEVE, of Thwayte, co. Suffolk, Knt.," 2d but 1st surv. s. and h. of Robert REEVE, or REVE(b), of the same, by Mary, sister of Sir Everard DIGBY, was admitted to Gray's Inn, 13 May 1637; *Knighted*, 20 May 1660, at Rochester, was M.P. for Eye, 1660 and 1661 till death, and was *cr. a Baronet*, as above, 22 Jan. 1662/3. He *m.* firstly, Anne(c), sister of Sir Edmund BACON, 4th Baronet [1611], da. of Robert BACON, by Catherine, da. of Grave VIOLETT, of Tatterford. He *m.* secondly, in 1660, Anne, widow of Stephen SOAME, formerly wife of Isaak CREAME, da. of Rev. Ambrose COPINGER, D.D., Rector of Laneham, by Judith, da. of (—) KERINGTON. He *d.* in, or shortly before, Oct. 1678. Will pr. 1679.

II. 1678? to 1688?. SIR ROBERT REEVE, Baronet [1663], of Thwayte aforesaid, only s. and h., by 1st wife; M.P. for Eye, Nov. 1675 to 1679, 1679 and 1681; *suc. to the Baronetcy* in or shortly before Oct. 1678. He *m.* Mary, sister of Richard, 1st BARON ONSLOW, da. of Sir Arthur ONSLOW, 1st Baronet [1674, with the precedency of 21 Nov. 1660], by Mary, da. and coheir of Sir Thomas FOOTE, Baronet [so *cr.* 21 Nov. 1660]. He *d.* s.p.m.(d) in or before 1688, when the *Baronetcy* became *extinct*. Will pr. Oct. 1668. His widow *m.* (Lic. Fac., 28 March 1690, she about

(a) His assailant, a Mr. Cowland, was executed for murder, 21 Dec. following.

(b) Sir Henry Reeve, his brother, Pensioner to James I and Charles I, was at his death (Will pr. Dec. 1642) the oldest of such Pensioners.

(c) See Bury St. Edmunds' Wills (p. 223, and note on p. 267 thereof), as also Chandler's *Suffolk Pedigrees*. The wife often (though erroneously) assigned to him, *viz.*, a da. and coheir of Sir Robert Crane, Baronet (so *cr.* 1627), is a confusion for that of his wife's brother, Sir Edmund Bacon, 4th Baronet abovenamed.

(d) Of his two daughters and coheirs (1) Anne, *m.* Philip (Sydney), 5th Earl of Leicester, and (2) Mary, *m.* the Hon. Thomas Sydney (brother of the said Earl), and was living Jan. 1710/1.

33, widow), Thomas VINCENT, of Fetcham, Surrey, then aged 33, widower. She *d.* a widow at Finingham, Suffolk. Will, in which she directs to be *bur.* at Thwayte, dat. 30 May 1699, and pr. 3 Jan. 1710/1.

BROGRAVE:

cr. 18 March 1662/3;

ex. 6 July 1707.

I. 1663. "THOMAS BROGRAVE, of Hammels [in Braughing], co. Hertford, Esq.," only s. and h., ap. of John BROGRAVE, of the same, and of Albury in that county, by Hannah, da. of Sir Thomas BARNARDISTON, of Ketton, co. Suffolk, was admitted to Gray's Inn, 24 Jan. 1652/3, and was *cr. a Baronet*, as above, 18 March 1662/3, Sheriff of Herts, 1664-65; suc. his father (who *d.* aged 74), in Feb. 1670/1; was "learned in the Greek tongue and in Hebrew."(a) He *m.* (Lic. Vic.-Gen., 9 Feb. 1662/3, he about 25) Grace (then about 23), 2d da. of Sir John HEWET, 1st Baronet [1621], of Waresley, co. Huntingdon, by Catherine, da. of Sir Robert BEVILL, K.B. He was *bur.* 4 June 1670, at Braughing.(b) His widow *m.* Giles DENT, of Shortgrave, in Newport, co. Essex (who *d.* 5 Feb. 1711/2, aged 78), and *d.* 20 Sep. 1704, aged 68, being *bur.* at Newport aforesaid. M.I.

II. 1670. SIR JOHN BROGRAVE, Baronet [1663], of Hammels aforesaid, 1st s. and h., *bap.* 31 March 1664, at Braughing; *suc. to the Baronetcy* in June 1670; ed. at St. Catharine's Hall, Cambridge.(a) He *d.* unm. of the smallpox in London, and was *bur.* 11 July 1691, at Braughing, aged 27. Will pr. Dec. 1691.

III. 1691, to 1707. SIR THOMAS BROGRAVE, Baronet [1663], of Hammels aforesaid, br. and h., *bap.* 25 March 1670 at Braughing, admitted to Gray's Inn, 22 Jan. 1689/90; was "a poor silly man."(a) He *m.* 26 Jan. 1691/2, at the Chapel Royal, Whitehall, Elizabeth, da. of William (MAYNARD) 2d BARON MAYNARD OF ESTAINES, by his 2d wife, Margaret, da. of William (MURRAY), 1st EARL OF DYSART [S.]. He *d.* s.p. 6 and was *bur.* 8 July 1707 at Braughing, aged 37, when the *Baronetcy* became *extinct*. Will pr. July 1707. His widow, who "spent all her fortune, and lived miserably,"(a) *m.* (—).

BARNARDISTON, *or* BERNARDESTON(c):

cr. 7 April 1663;

ex. Sep. 1745.

I. 1663. "SIR THOMAS BERNARDESTON [*rectius* BARNARDISTON], of Ketton, *alias* Keddington, co. Suffolk, Knt.," elder br. of Sir Samuel BARNARDISTON, 1st Baronet (so *cr.* 11 May 1663),(d) being 1st s. and h. of Sir

(a) Le Neve's MS. *Baronetage.*
(b) A very favourable character of him is given in Chauncy's "*Herts.*"
(c) An account of the family of Barnardiston, by Richard Almack, F.S.A. (60 pages, 8vo.), was reprinted about 1870 from the Proceedings of the Suffolk Institute of Archæology.
(d) These grantees were great grandsons of Sir Thomas Barnardiston, of Ketton, the 22d and last of the 22 Baronets *designate* at the first institution of that order, 22 May 1611. He was, however, one of four (the others were Trenchard, Strangways and Walsingham) whose patents were stayed [See vol. i, p. 1, note "c"]. Sir Thomas *d.* 23 Dec. 1619, having had a son Sir Thomas who *d.* v.p. 29 July 1610, being father of Sir Nathaniel, the father of the grantees of 1663.

Nathaniel BARNARDISTON, of Ketton aforesaid, three times M.P. for Suffolk,(a) by Jane, da. of Sir Stephen SOAME, sometime, 1598-99, Lord Mayor of London, was *b.* probably about 1618; admitted to Gray's Inn, 1 May 1635; was *Knighted*, 4 July 1641, at Whitehall; was M.P. for Bury St. Edmunds, Oct. 1645 till secluded, Dec. 1648; for Suffolk, 1654-55, 1656-58, and 1659, and for Ipswich 1661 till void in Feb. 1662; was a noted Parliamentarian; was in command of a Reg. of Foot in 1648 against the King's forces at Colchester; suc. his father 25 July 1653, and, having favoured the Restoration, was *cr. a Baronet*, as above, 7 April 1661. He *m.*, in or before 1643, Anne, 2d da. of Sir William ARMYNE, 1st Baronet [1619], by his 1st wife, Elizabeth, da. of Sir Michael HICKS. He *d.* 4 and was *bur.* 14 Oct. 1669, at Ketton. Admon. 6 Nov. 1669. His widow, who was *b.* at Osgodby, co. Lincoln, 6 and *bap.* 8 Aug. 1624, at Lavington, was *bur.* 25 Aug. 1671, at Ketton.

II. 1669. SIR THOMAS BARNARDISTON, Baronet [1662], of Ketton aforesaid and of Silk Willoughby, co. Lincoln, 2d but 1st surv. s. and h., *b.* about 1646; admitted to Gray's Inn, 19 June 1667; *suc. to the Baronetcy*, 4 Oct. 1669; was M.P. for Grimsby, 1685-87 and 1689-90; for Sudbury (three Parls.), 1695 till death in 1698. He *m.* (Lic. Fac. 26 July 1670) Elizabeth (then about 18), da. and only surv. issue of Sir Robert KING, of Boyle, co. Roscommon, by his 2d wife, Sophia, Dow. VISCOUNTESS WIMBLEDON, da. of Sir Edward ZOUCHE, of Woking, co. Surrey. He *d.* 7 and was *bur.* 15 Oct. 1698, at Ketton, aged 52. Will dat. 17 Aug. 1696, pr. 4 Jan. 1698/9. His widow was *bur.* there 21 Oct. 1707, aged 56. Will pr. Nov. 1707.

III. 1698. SIR THOMAS BARNARDISTON, Baronet [1662], of Ketton and of Silk Willoughby aforesaid, 1st s. and h., *b.* 7 Aug. 1674; *suc. to the Baronetcy*, 7 Oct. 1698. He *m.* (Lic. Fac. 14 Feb. 1693/4), Anne (then aged 19), da. and coheir of Sir Richard ROTHWELL, Baronet (so *cr.* 16 Aug. 1661), and Elizabeth, then his widow. He *d.* s.p.m.(b) 12 and was *bur.*, 21 Nov. 1700, in great state, at Ketton aged 26. M.I. Will pr. Feb. 1701/2. His widow *d.* 14 and was *bur.* there 21 Feb. 1701/2. Will pr. July 1702.

IV. 1700. SIR ROBERT BARNARDISTON, Baronet [1663], of Ketton aforesaid, br. and h. male; *b.* about 1676; *suc. to the Baronetcy*, 12 Nov. 1700. He was nearly ruined by law suits respecting his right of succession to the estates of the Armyne family. He *m.*, in or after 1706, Elizabeth, da. of (—) CHEEKE? He *d.* s.p., 16 and was *bur.* 24 July 1728, at Ketton. Will dat. 23 Feb. 1726, being then of Hatch Lodge, co. Somerset, pr. 20 Jan. 1728/9. His widow *d.* 16 and was *bur.* 20 Feb. 1737/8, at Long Melford, co. Suffolk. Will dat. 12 June 1732 (at Melford), and pr. 16 March 1737/8.

V. 1728. SIR SAMUEL BARNARDISTON, Baronet [1663], of Ketton aforesaid and of Lyston Hall, co. Essex, br. and h. male; *bap.* 20 Jan. 1680/1, at Ketton; *suc. to the Baronetcy*, 16 July 1728. He *m.* in Aug. 1730, Catharine, 1st da. of Sir Rowland WINN, 3d Baronet [1660], of Nostell, by

(a) This Nathaniel, a zealous republican, who was imprisoned for refusing to collect the "ship money," is quaintly styled by Fairclough [Clark's *Lives*] "one of the most eminent patriots of his time *and the 23d Knight of his family*." His *Insignia* placed upon a tree, shewing also the names of his ten children, form the frontispiece to the 4th book of Sylvanus Morgan's well known *Sphere of Gentry*, folio 1681. He *d.* 25 July 1653, aged 65, having been one of the so-called PATRIOTS whose resistance to authority (by them styled *arbitrary power*) contributed to bring on the horrors of Civil War, and to establish the *power* (which, though better than utter anarchy, was indeed *most arbitrary*) of a Usurper.
(b) Of his three daughters and coheirs (1) Elizabeth, *b.* 23 Jan. 1694/5; *d.* unm. and was *bur.* 7 May 1711, at Ketton; (2) Anna Maria, *bap.* 1 July 1697; *m.* 27 Sep. 1716, Sir John Shaw, 3d Baronet [1665], of Eltham, co. Kent; *d.* 3 and was *bur.* there 12 Feb 1750/1; (3) Charlotte *m.* 1729, as 2d wife, Sir Anthony Thomas Abdy, 3d Baronet [1641], and *d.* 19 Feb. 1731/2.

Lætitia, da. of Edward HARBORD. He *d.* s.p. at Ketton Hall, 4 and was *bur.* 13 Feb. 1735/6, at Ketton, aged 55. M.I. His widow, who was *bap.* at Wragby, co. York, 9 April 1708, and who enjoyed the estate of Ketton during her widowhood, was *bur.* there 3 Dec. 1757.(a) Will pr. 1757.

VI. 1736. to 1745. SIR JOHN BARNARDISTON, Baronet [1663], of Long Melford, co. Suffolk, nephew and h. male, being only s. and h. of John BARNARDISTON, by Sophia, relict of William GREY, and da. of [—] RICH, of Scotland, which John, who was *bur.* 11 Dec. 1731, at Ketton, was yr. br. of the 3d, 4th and 5th Baronets, being 5th and yst. s. of the 2d Baronet. He *suc. to the Baronetcy* 4 Feb. 1735/6. He *m.* before July 1737, Elizabeth, da. of William BLAKEWAY, of Stepney, Sailmaker, whose will dat. 11 July 1737, was pr. 9 June 1749. He *d.* s.p. and was *bur.* 29 Sep. 1745, at Ketton,(b) when the *Baronetcy* became *extinct*.(c) His widow was living June 1749.

BARNARDISTON, *or* BERNARDESTON:

cr. 11 May 1663;

ex. 21 Sep. 1712.

I. 1663. "SAMUEL BERNARDESTON [*rectius* BARNARDISTON], of Bright Hall [*i.e.*, Brightwell], co. Suffolk, Esq.," yr. br. of Sir Thomas BARNARDISTON, 1st Baronet (so *cr.* 7 April 1663), being a yr. s. of Sir Nathaniel BARNARDISTON, of Ketton, co. Suffolk, three times M.P. for Suffolk, by Jane, da. of Sir Stephen SOAME, sometime, 1598-99, Lord Mayor of London, was *b.* 23 June 1620, became a Turkey or Levant merchant of London; was a strenuous supporter of the Puritan party(d) but, joining in promoting the Restoration, was *cr. a Baronet*, as above, 11 May 1663, with a spec. rem., failing heirs male of his body "to Nathaniel Bernardeston, of Hackney, Esq." [one of his brothers], with rem. to "Pelitiah Bernardeston of London, Esq." [another such brother], in like manner. He was Sheriff of Suffolk, 1666-67; M.P. for that county (two Parls.), Feb. 1673 to 1681, and (five Parls.), 1690-1702; admitted (as a Baronet), 10 March 1673/4, to Gray's Inn; Dep. Gov. of the East India Company; was fined £10,000 for high misdemeanour, by Judge Jefferies, and was attainted by the Irish Parl. of James II, in 1689. He *m.* firstly, Thomazine, da. of Joseph BRAND, of Edwardston, co. Suffolk, by Thomazine, da. of (—) TROTTER, Merchant of London. She *d.* 1654. He *m.* secondly, Mary, da. of Sir Abraham REYNARDSON, sometime, 1648-49, Lord Mayor of London, by his 2d wife, Eleanor, da. of Richard WYNNE, of Shrewsbury. He *d.* s.p. 8 and was *bur.* 28 Nov. 1707, at Brightwell, aged 88. M.I. Will pr. Dec. 1707 and Dec. 1710. His widow was *bur.* with her parents, 13 Feb. 1729/30, at St. Martin's Outwich, London. Will pr. Feb. 1729/30.

II. 1707. SIR SAMUEL BARNARDISTON, Baronet [1663], of Brightwell aforesaid, nephew and heir of entail, being 4th but 1st surv. s. and h. of Nathaniel, BARNARDISTON, of Hackney, co. Midx., by Elizabeth (*m.* 24 May 1648), da. of Nathaniel BACON, of Friston, co. Suffolk, which Nathaniel was

(a) The estate, which was in the hands of mortgages, was sold 1780 and the Hall pulled down.
(b) There is a burial at Bath Abbey, 10 Oct. 1744, of "Sr Barnadiston."
(c) Had the Baronetcy promised in 1611 been legally carried out (see p. 272, note "d") it would have devolved in 1745 on the family of Barnardiston, settled at Bury St. Edmunds, descended from Thomas Barnardiston, Comptroller of the Mint (*d.* 14 March 1681/2, aged 88), the yst. s. of Sir Thomas Barnardiston, junior, the s. and h. ap. of the Sir Thomas Barnardiston to whom the Baronetcy was promised.
(d) His close cropped hair gave use to the party term of *Roundhead*, he himself having been so called by the Queen Consort in Dec. 1641, on the occasion of presenting a city address at Whitehall.

next elder br. of the late Baronet and was in rem. to the said dignity, but *d.* before him. He was *b.* 28 Jan. and *bap.* 9 Feb. 1659/60, at Hackney; admitted to Gray's Inn, 10 Feb. 1679/80; was M.P. for Ipswich, 1698-1700; *suc. to the Baronetcy*, 8 Nov. 1707, under the spec. rem. thereof. He *m.* 13 Aug. 1709, Martha ("£6,000 portion(a)"), da. and coheir of Thomas RICHMOND, of London, Apothecary. He *d.* s.p. a few months later in Charter House yard, Midx., 3 and was *bur.* 11 Jan. 1709/10 at Ketton, aged nearly 50. M.I. Admon. 20 Jan. 1709/10. Will pr. Dec. 1711. His widow *m.* 2 Oct. 1712, at Gray's Inn chapel, Charles EDWIN, "Esq.," of Lincoln's Inn, who survived her. She *d.* at St. Andrew's, Holborn, in or before 1718. Admon. 20 June 1718.

III. 1710. SIR PELETIAH BARNARDISTON, Baronet [1663], of Brightwell aforesaid, br. and h.; *bap.* 9 Sep. 1663 at Hackney, *suc. to the Baronetcy*, 3 Jan. 1709/10. He *d.* unm. 4 and was *bur.* 13 May 1712 at Ketton, aged 48. M.I. Will pr. June 1712.

IV. 1712, May to Sep. SIR NATHANIEL BARNARDISTON, Baronet [1663], of Brightwell aforesaid, cousin and heir of entail, being only s. and h. of Peletiah BARNARDISTON, of Hackney aforesaid, Merchant, by Martha, da. of Richard TURNER, which Peletiah was next surv. yr. br. of the 1st Baronet, and was in rem. to the said dignity, but *d.* before him and was *bur.* at Ketton, 23 July 1679. He was *bap.* 5 Sep. 1672, at Hackney, and *suc. to the Baronetcy*, 4 May 1712, under the spec. rem. thereof. He, however, *d.* unm. four months later, at Brightwell Hall,(b) on Sunday, 21 Sep., and was *bur.* 3 Oct. 1712, at Brightwell, when the *Baronetcy* became *extinct*. M.I. Will pr. Oct. 1712.

MALET.

1663. "SIR THOMAS MALET, one of the Justices of the Court of King's Bench had a *fiat for a Baronet's Patent*, bearing date 17 May 1663, with a remission of all duties and services, but neither he nor his descendants have taken out the Patent. The fiat is now [*i.e.*, 1771] in the possession of the Rev. Alexander MALET, of Coombe Flory, co. Somerset, his immediate descendant" [Kimber's *Baronetage*, 1771, vol. iii, p. 322]. Charles Warre MALET, the s. of this Alexander, who himself was great grandson of the Judge, was *cr. a Baronet*, 24 Feb. 1791. It is supposed that the reason why the Judge took no steps to have the patent passed was the great losses he had sustained owing to his resolute loyalty. He was admitted to the Middle Temple, 29 March 1600; Barrister, 7 Nov. 1601; M.P. for Tregony, 1614 and 1621-22; for Newtown, 1624, 1625 and 1626; was made a Justice of the Court of King's Bench and *Knighted* in July 1641, disabled Nov. 1645, and imprisoned in 1646, restored 1660 (being then in his 78th year), holding office till 1663. He *d.* 19 Dec. 1665, and was *bur.* at Pointington, co. Somerset.

DAWES:

cr. 1 June 1663;

ex. 28 May 1741.

I. 1663. "SIR JOHN DAWES, of [Roehampton, in] Putney, co. Middx. [but should be "Surrey"], Knt.," 3d but only surv. s. and h. of Sir Thomas DAWES, of the same, by Judith, da. of Sir Cuthbert HACKET,

(a) Le Neve's MS. *Baronetage.*
(b) This mansion, which was built by the 1st Baronet, devolved in 1717 on Sir John Shaw, 3d Baronet [1661], in right of his wife, da. and coheir of Sir Thomas Barnardiston, 3d Baronet [1663] of Ketton.

sometime, 1626-27, Lord Mayor of London, which Thomas was s. and h. of Sir Abraham DAWES, one of the Farmers of the Customs and one of the richest men of his period (*d.* in or shortly before 1640), was *bap.* 1 Feb. 1643/4, at Putney; suc. his father, 5 Dec. 1655; was a Gent. of the Privy Chamber, 1660; was *Knighted*, and was, "in memory of many services conferred and hardships undergone by the family in the civil confusion, and in acknowledgement of several sums of money transmitted to the Royal family in exile,"(a) *cr. a Baronet*, as above, 1 June 1663. He *m.* in or before 1668, Christian, da. and h. of William LYONS, of Lyons in Bocking, co. Essex, by (—), da. of John HAWKINS, of Braintree in that county. He was *bur.* 5 Dec. 1671, with his parents, at Putney, aged 27. Admon., as "of Bocking, co. Essex," 31 Jan. 1671/2. His widow *m.*, 25 July 1678, at St. Martin's Outwich, London (Lic. Vic. Gen. 22, both being about 40, widower and widow), Sir Anthony DEANE, of London, whose will was pr. June 1721.

II. 1671. SIR ROBERT DAWES, Baronet [1663], of Lyons aforesaid, 1st s. and h.; *suc. to the Baronetcy* in Dec. 1671; was a Fellow Commoner of St. Catharine's Hall, Cambridge, and made LL.D. (*comitiis Regiis*) 1690, but *d.* that year at Cambridge of a fever. Admon. 29 July 1690 to his sister Elizabeth, wife of Peter FISHER.

III. 1690. SIR WILLIAM DAWES, Baronet [1663], of Lyons aforesaid, *afterwards*, 1714-24, ARCHBISHOP OF YORK, only surv. br. and h.,(b) being 3d s. of the 1st Baronet, was *b.* 12 Sep. 1671, at Lyons aforesaid; admitted to Merchant Taylors' School, 1680; matric. at Oxford (St. John's Coll.), 1 July 1687, aged 18; *suc. to the Baronetcy* in 1690, when he migrated to St. Catharine's Hall, Cambridge; took Holy Orders and became Fellow of his College and M.A., 1695; D.D. (*per lit. regias*) 1696; Master of St. Catharine's Hall, 1696; Vice-Chancellor of the Univ. of Cambridge, 1698; Chaplain to William III, 1697, and to Queen Anne, 1702; Canon of Worcester, 1698; Rector and Dean of Bocking, co. Essex, 1699; Bishop of Chester, 1708-14; and finally, 1714, Archbishop of York, and P.C. He was one of the Lords Justices Regent, on Queen Anne's demise, in 1714. He *m.*, 1 Dec. 1692, at St. Edmund's the King, London (Lic. Fac. 26 Nov., he 22 and she 16), Frances, sister and coheir of Sir George DARCY, 2d Baronet [1660], of St. Osith's, co. Essex, da. of Sir Thomas DARCY, 1st Baronet, by his 2d wife Jane, da. and h. of Robert COLE. She *d.* 22 Dec. 1705, aged 29, and was *bur.* in the chapel of St. Catharine's Hall aforesaid. M.I. He *d.* in Cecil street, Strand, co. Midx., 30 April 1724, aged 53, and was *bur.* with his wife. Will pr. 1724.

IV. 1724. SIR DARCY DAWES, Baronet [1663], of Lyons aforesaid, only surv. s. and h.; ed. at St. Catharine's Hall, Cambridge; M.A., 1722; *suc. to the Baronetcy*, 30 April 1724. He *m.* in 1723, Janet, da. and coheir of Richard ROUNDELL, of Hutton Wandsley, co. York, by his 1st wife, Frances, sister of Sir William ST. QUINTIN, 3d Baronet [1642], da. of William ST. QUINTIN. He *d.* 16 Aug. 1732. Will pr. 1734. His widow *m.*, in or before 1742, as his 2d wife, Beilby THOMPSON, of Escrick, co. York (who *d.* 27 July 1750, aged 51) and *d.* 12 March 1773, aged 64.

V. 1732, to 1741. SIR WILLIAM DAWES, Baronet [1663], of Lyons aforesaid, only s. and h., *b.* 19 Aug. 1729; *suc. to the Baronetcy*, 16 Aug. 1732. He *d.* a minor and unm., 28 May 1741, aged 12, when the *Baronetcy* became *extinct*.

(a) *Dict. Nat. Biog.* and Wotton's *Baronetage*, quoting the preface by the Rev. Mr. Stackhouse, to Archbishop Dawes's works.
(b) John Dawes, Lieut. R.N., the next elder br., *d.* unm. very shortly before the 2d Baronet, being drowned at sea.

HOLMAN:
cr. 1 June 1663;
ex. in or before 1700.

I. 1663, to 1700? "SIR JOHN HOLMAN, of Banbury, co. Oxford, Knt.," as also of Weston Favell, co. Northampton, 2d s. of Philip HOLMAN (*d.* July 1669, aged 76), of Warkworth, in the county last named, and of London, Scrivener, by Mary, da. of (—) BARTA, of London, Merchant, was *b.* about 1633(a); was M.P. for Banbury, 1661-79, March to July 1679, 1679-81 and 1681, and having been *Knighted* (after April 1661), was *cr. a Baronet*, as above, 1 June 1663. He *m.* about 1660 Jane, da. and coheir of Jacob DE LA FORTERIE, *or* FORTREY, of London, Merchant. He *d.* s.p.m.(b) in or shortly before May 1700, when the *Baronetcy* became *extinct*. Will pr. 4 July 1700, by his widow. Her will pr. 10 July 1705, by William BOUVERIE.

BETENSON, *or* BETTENSON:
cr. 7 June, 1663(c);
ex. 15 June 1786.

I. 1663(c). "SIR RICHARD BETTENSON, of Wimbledon, co Surrey, Knt.," as also of Scadbury in Chislehurst, co. Kent, and of Layer Delahay, co. Essex, s. and h. of Richard BETENSON, *or* BETTENSON, of Layer Delahay aforesaid, was *b.* about 1602; admitted to Lincoln's Inn, 21 Nov. 1621; *Knighted*, 28 Feb. 1624/5; was Sheriff of Surrey, 1645-46 and was *cr. a Baronet*, as above, 7 June 1663(c); Sheriff of Kent, 1678-79, being so at the time of his death. He *m.* in or before 1627, Anne, da. of Sir William MONINS, 1st Baronet [1611], by his 2d wife, Jane, da. of Roger TWISDEN. He *d.* 29 Aug. 1679, aged 78, and was *bur.* at Chislehurst. M.I. Will pr. 23 Sep. 1679. His widow *d.* at a great age, 19 Feb. 1681, and was *bur.* there. M.I. Her will, dat. 28 Dec. 1680, pr. 3 March 1680/1.

II. 1679. SIR EDWARD BETENSON, Baronet [1663], of Scadbury, etc., aforesaid, grandson and h., being only s. and h. of Richard BETENSON, by Albinia, da. of Sir Christopher WRAY, of Ashby, co. Lincoln, and Albinia his wife, 2d da. and coheir of Edward (CECIL), VISCOUNT WIMBLEDON, which Richard (*b.* before 1631 and admitted to Gray's Inn, 31 Dec. 1650) was 1st s. and h. ap. of the late Baronet, but *d.* v.p. at Montpelier in France in 1677, and was *bur.* at Wimbledon. He was *b.* about 1675, and *suc. to the Baronetcy*, 29 Aug. 1679; Sheriff of Kent, 1704-05. He *d.* unm. 17 Oct. 1733, aged 58, and was *bur.* at Chislehurst. M.I. Admon. 5 Dec. 1733 to his three sisters(d).

III. 1733. SIR EDWARD BETENSON, Baronet [1663], of Bradburn Place, near Sevenoaks, co. Kent., cousin and h. male, being only s. and h. of Edward BETENSON, of Lincoln's Inn, by Catharine, da. and only child that had issue of Sir John RAYNEY, 3d Baronet [1642], of Wrotham, co. Kent, which Edward (who was admitted to Lincoln's Inn, 2 Nov. 1654) was 2d s. of the

(a) His elder br., George, *d.* 1698, aged 67. M.I. at Weston Favell.
(b) Mary his only child *m.*, 19 April 1682, at Weston Favell, as his 3d wife, Sir William Portman, 6th and last Baronet [1611], who *d.* s.p., 1690.
(c) This, however, is not the date given in Dugdale's *List* and elsewhere which is, "7 Feb. 1666/7," but is in Kimber's *Baronetage*, 1771 (vol. iii, p. 322), with the following notice:—"The date of this patent has till this time [*i.e.*, 1771] been wrong printed in all the lists of the Baronets. *Ex inform. Dom. Richard Betenson.*"
(d) These were "Albinia Selwyn, widow" (relict of Col. William Selwyn, Governor of Jamaica), "Theodosia Farrington, widow (relict of Major-Gen. William Farrington, and mother of Albinia, Duchess of Ancaster), and "Dame Frances Hewett, widow" (relict of Sir Thomas Hewett, of Shire Oaks, Notts). These three inherited the family estates.

1st Baronet, and *d.* 1700. He was *b.* about 1688; *suc. to the Baronetcy*, but not to the family estates, 12 Oct. 1733. He *m.* Ursula, da. of John NICKS, of Fort St. George, in India, Merchant. He *d.* 24 Nov. 1762, aged 74, and was *bur.* at Wrotham. M.I. Will pr. 13 Dec. 1762. His widow *d.* 11 June 1763, aged 67, and was *bur.* there.

IV. 1762, to 1786. SIR RICHARD BETENSON, Baronet [1663], of Bradburn Place aforesaid, only s. and h.; *suc. to the Baronetcy* 24 Nov. 1762. Sheriff of Kent, 17 He *m.* Lucretia, yst. da. and coheir of Martin FOLKES, of Hillingdon, co. Norfolk. She *d.* before 1771 about two years after marriage and was *bur.* at Wrotham. He *d.* s.p. 15 June 1786, when the *Baronetcy* became *extinct*. Admon. June 1786.

COOK:
cr. 29 June 1663;
ex. Jan. 1707/8.

I. 1663. "WILLIAM COOK, of Brome Hall, co. Norfolk, Esq.," s. and h. of William COOK, of Linsted, co. Suffolk, by Mary, da. and coheir of Ralph SHELTON, of Brome aforesaid, was *b.* probably about 1600, and was *cr. a Baronet*, as above, 29 June 1663. He *m.* firstly, in or before 1630, Mary, da. of Thomas ASTLEY, of Melton Constable, co. Norfolk. He *m.* secondly (—), widow of William STEWARD, of Barton mills, co. Suffolk. He *d.* in or before 1682. Will pr. 1682 in the Consistory Court of Norwich.

II. 1682? to 1708. SIR WILLIAM COOK, Baronet [1663], of Brome Hall, aforesaid, s. and h., by 1st wife, *b.* about 1630; admitted to Gray's Inn, 24 Nov. 1648; *suc. to the Baronetcy* in or before 1682; was M.P. for Great Yarmouth, 1685-87; for Norfolk, 1689-90, 1690-95 and 1698-1700. He *m.* Jane, da. and coheir of William STEWARD abovenamed. He *d.* s.p.m.(a), Jan. 1707/8, aged 78, at Letton, and was *bur.* at Cranworth cum Letton, when the *Baronetcy* became *extinct*. M.I. Will, describing him as "of Mendham," pr. 1708 in Consistory Court of Norwich.

BELLOT:
cr. 30 June 1663;
ex. presumably, 8 Feb. 1713/4.

I. 1663. "JOHN BELLOT, of Moreton, co. Chester, Esq.," 1st s. and h. of John BELLOT, of the same, Sheriff of that county, 1640, by Ursula, da. and h. of John BENTLEY, of the Ashes, in Leeke, co. Stafford, was *b.* about 1619; suc. his father in Nov. 1659; was Sheriff of Staffordshire, 1661-62, and of Cheshire, 1662-63, and was *cr. a Baronet*, as above, 30 June 1663. He recorded his pedigree in the Her. Visit. of Cheshire, 1664, being then aged 45. He *m.* in or before 1651, Anne, da of Roger WILBRAHAM, of Dorfold, co. Chester, by Mary, da. of Thomas RAVENSCROFT, of Bretton, co. Flint. He *d.* 14 July 1674 and was *bur.* at Astbury. His widow *d.* 27 Dec. 1711 and was *bur.* there, 1 Jan. 1711/2, aged 84.

II. 1674. SIR THOMAS BELLOT, Baronet [1663], of Moreton aforesaid, 1st s. and h., *b.* 22 Oct. 1651; matric. at Oxford (Ch. Ch.), 11 July 1668, aged 16; admitted to Lincoln's Inn (under the name of "Bellard") 20 March 1670/1; *suc. to the Baronetcy*, 14 July 1674; was M.P. for Newcastle-

(a) He left seven daughters, of whom the three elder *d.* s.p., but Elizabeth, the 4th da., *m.* Thornagh Gurdon, of Letton, co. Norfolk, and had issue.

under-Lyme (five Parls.), 1679-81, 1690-95, and 1698 till his death in 1699. He *m.* (spec. lic., Feb. 1674/5), Susanna, da. of Christopher PACKE, of Cotes, co. Leicester, sometime (1654-55), Lord Mayor of London, by his 1st wife, Anne, da. of Simon EDWARDS. He *d.* in or shortly before Feb. 1708/9.

III. 1709? to 1714. SIR JOHN BELLOT, Baronet [1663], of Moreton aforesaid, 1st s. and h., *b.* 30 Nov. and *bap.* 14 Dec. 1676; *suc. to the Baronetcy* in Jan. 1699. He was *bur.* 8 Feb. 1713/4, aged 37, when, as he is supposed to have *d.* s.p.m.(a) the *Baronetcy*, presumably, became *extinct*.

DOWNING(b):
cr. 1 July 1663;
ex. 7 Feb. 1764.

I. 1663. "SIR GEORGE DOWNING, of East Hatley, co. Cambridge, Knt., Embassador in Holland, and now [1681], one of his Majesty's Commissioners of the Customs," 2d s. of Emmanuel DOWNING, of the Inner Temple, London, afterwards one of the most active men in the colony of Massachusetts (*bap.* 12 Aug. 1585, at St. Laurence, Ipswich and *d.* at Edinburgh about 1660), being 1st s. by the 2d wife, Lucy, sister of John WINTHROP, Gov. of Massachusetts, and da. of Adam WINTHROP, was *b.* in Dublin, probably in Aug. 1623; ed. at the School at Massachusetts and at Harvard College, of which he was the second graduate; B.A., 1644, and previously (1643) a tutor; appears to have been a Preacher soon afterwards, but was, in 1650, Scout-Master-General of Cromwell's Army in Scotland, and was in 1656 made one of the Tellers of the Exchequer, being continued in that post by Charles II till his death in 1684. He was M.P. for Edinburgh, 1654-55, for Carlisle, 1656-58, and for Morpeth, 1660-81 (five Parls.); was sent by Cromwell, in 1655, to France to remonstrate on the Vaudois massacre; was appointed Resident in Holland in Dec. 1657, and was continued as such by Charles II, by whom, having been *Knighted*, May 1660, he was *cr. a Baronet*, as above, 1 July 1663. He was Sec. to the Treasury Commissioners, May 1667; admitted to Lincoln's Inn, 5 Aug. 1669; in 1670 he was again on an Embassy to Holland, but left suddenly before the war broke out; was a Commissioner of Customs, 1671, till his death in 1684. He received also the valuable grant of a strip of land abutting on St. James' Park, afterwards known as Downing street. He *m.*, in or before 1656, Frances ("a distinguished beauty"), sister of Charles, 1st EARL OF CARLISLE, 4th da. of Sir William HOWARD, of Naworth Castle, by Mary, da. of William (EURE), LORD EURE. She *d.* 10 July 1683 and was *bur.* at Croyden, co. Cambridge. He *d.* July 1684 and was *bur.* there. Will dat. 24 Aug. 1683 to 7 July 1684 as "of East Hatley, co. Cambridge," pr. 19 July 1684.

II. 1684. SIR GEORGE DOWNING, Baronet [1663], of Gamlingay Park, co. Cambridge, 1st s. and h., *b.* about 1656; was one of the Tellers of the Exchequer, 1680, till he resigned in 1689; *suc. to the Baronetcy* in July 1684; Sheriff of Cambridgeshire and Hunts, 1686-87. He *m.* (Lic. Vic. Gen., 12 July 1683, he 27 and she 19) Katharine, 1st da. of James CECIL, 3d EARL OF SALISBURY, by Margaret, da. of John (MANNERS), 8th EARL OF RUTLAND. She *d.* 13 Aug. 1688, and was *bur.* at Croyden aforesaid. He *d.* June 1711. Admon. 17 Jan. 1711/2.

(a) His yr. br., Thomas Bellot, *bap.* 18 July 1679, is presumed to have *d.* s.p.m. before him.
(b) See Muskett's *Suffolk Manorial Families*, vol. i, p. 99. His parentage is wrongly given by Anthony à Wood, who calls him son of Calybut Downing, Rector of Hackney, co. Midx.

III. 1711. Sir George Downing, Baronet [1663], of Gamlingay Park aforesaid, only s. and h., *b.* about 1685, being aged 8 in 1693; was M.P. for Dunwich (seven Parls.), 1710-15 and 1722 till death in 1749; *suc. to the Baronetcy* in June 1711; was made **K.B.**, 12 Jan. 1732. He *m.* Mary, da. of Sir William Forrester, of Watling Street, Salop, and of the Board of Green Cloth, Westminster. She, who was separated from him by Act of Parl., was *bur.* 3 Aug. 1734, at Hampton. Will pr. 1734. He *d.* s.p., suddenly, at Gamlingay Park, 10 June 1749. Will dat. as far back as 20 Dec. 1717 (in which he makes no mention of any wife), pr. 13 June 1749. In it he devises his estates to his cousin and h. at law (afterwards the 4th Baronet) for life and his issue in tail male, with other remainders in like manner, and finally, failing such nominees, in trust to purchase land at Cambridge and erect thereon a College called *Downing College.* This last remainder came into effect on the death of the 4th Baronet in 1764, but it was not till some years later, and after considerable litigation, that the said College was founded.

IV. 1749, to 1764. Sir Jacob Garrard Downing, Baronet [1663], of Gamlingay park aforesaid, and of Mount Prospect in Putney, co. Surrey, cousin and h., being only s. and h. of Charles Downing, of Bury St. Edmunds, Comptroller of Customs at Salem, in New England, by Sarah (*m.* before 1696), 2d da. and coheir of Jacob Garrard, 1st s. and h. ap. of Sir Thomas Garrard, 2d Baronet [1662], of Langford, co. Norfolk, which Charles, who *d.* 15 April 1740, aged about 80, was 3d and yst. s. of the 1st Baronet. He was probably *b.* about 1700; was M.P. for Dunwich, June 1749 to 1761, and April 1763 till death in 1764, and *suc. to the Baronetcy*, 10 June 1749. He *m.* 17 May 1750, Margaret, da. of the Rev. (—) Price, Curate of Barrington, co. Glouc. He *d.* s.p.m., in Hill street, Berkeley sq., co. Midx., 6 Feb. 1764, when the *Baronetcy* became *extinct.* Will dat. 23 Aug. 1763, pr. Feb. 1764. His widow *m.* 11 Nov. 1768, at Putney, as his 1st wife, George Bowyer, who, after her death, was *cr. a Baronet*, 8 Sep. 1794, becoming, subsequently, in April 1799, 5th Baronet [1660], and who *d.* 6 Dec. 1799, aged 60. She *d.* 18 Sep. 1778, at Mount Pleasant aforesaid, and was *bur.* at Croyden, co. Cambridge. Admon. 22 Feb. 1781.

GAWDY, *or* GAWDEY:

cr. 13 July 1663;

ex. 10 Oct. 1723.

I. 1663. "William Gawdey, of West Herting [*i.e.*, Harling], co. Norfolk, Esq.," 1st s. and h. of Framlingham Gawdey, *or* Gawdy, of the same, by Lettice, da. and coheir of Sir Robert Knowles (which Framlingham was s. and h. of Sir Bassingbourne Gawdy, of West Harling), was *b.* Sep. 1612; admitted to the Inner Temple, Nov. 1633; suc. his father, 25 Feb. 1654/5, and was *cr. a Baronet*, as above, 13 July 1663. He was M.P. for Thetford, 1661-69. He *m.* 1 Sep. 1636, Elizabeth, da. and h. of John Duffield, of East Wretham, co. Norfolk. She *d.* 1653. He *d.* Aug. 1669. Will pr. Feb. 1670.

II. 1669. Sir John Gawdy, Baronet [1663], of West Harling aforesaid, 2d but 1st surv. s. and h.[a]; *b.* 25 Sep. and *bap.* 9 Oct. 1639; was a deaf mute; a pupil of Sir Peter Lely and was himself a painter of considerable merit; *suc. to the Baronetcy* in Aug. 1669. He *m.* Anne, 2d and yst. da. and coheir of Sir Robert De Grey, of Merton, co. Norfolk (*d.* 20 Oct. 1644), by Elizabeth, da. and coheir of William Bridon, of Ipswich. He *d.* Jan. 1708/9.

(a) His elder br. Bassingbourne Gawdy, *b.* 17 July and *bap.* 2 Aug. 1637, *d.* unm. in London 23 Feb. 1660/1, as also did his yr. br. William, on the 21st of that month and his cousin Framlingham Gawdy, on the 26th, all three dying of the smallpox within six days of each other, and being *bur.* in the Temple Church. See M.I. there to Mary, his only sister, who *d.* 11 Oct. 1671, aged 22.

III. 1709, to 1723. Sir Bassingbourne Gawdy, Baronet [1663], of West Harling aforesaid, only s. and h., *suc. to the Baronetcy* in Jan. 1708/9. He *d.* unm. 23 Oct. 1724, when the *Baronetcy* became *extinct.* Admon. 8 Jan. 1723/4, to his nieces (by the sister) and next of kin.[a]

PYM:

cr. 14 July 1663;

ex. 4 May 1688.

I. 1663. "Sir Charles Pym, of Brymmore, co. Somerset, Knt.," 2nd but eventually 1st surv. s. and h. of John Pym, of the same, the notorious Republican (*d.* 8 Dec. 1643, aged 59), by Anne, da. of John Hook, of Bramshot, was *b.* probably about 1620; admitted to Lincoln's Inn, 10 Nov. 1635; was M.P. for Beeralston about Jan. 1642, till secluded, Dec. 1648, and for Minehead, 1660; took the covenant, 16 Oct. 1643, and was Capt. of Horse in Ireland, being, like his father and brother, a Parliamentarian; is said[b] to have been *cr. a Baronet* by Richard Cromwell, when Lord Protector; suc. his elder br., Col. Alexander Pym, about 1660; was *Knighted* by Charles II, 14 Feb. 1662/3, and by him shortly afterwards *cr. a Baronet*, as above, 14 July 1663. He *m.*, 26 Feb. 1662/3, at St. Nicholas Acons, London (Lic. Lond., 24 Feb. 1662/3, he 35 and she about 20), Katharine, da. of Sir Gilbert Gerard, 1st Baronet [1620], of Flamberds, by Mary, da. of Sir Francis Barrington, 1st Baronet [1611]. He *d.* in 1671. Will dat. 8 March 1670/1, pr. 8 Jan. 1671/2. His widow, who was *bap.* 6 July 1631, at Harrow, co. Midx., living June 1688.

II. 1671, to 1688. Sir Charles Pym, Baronet [1663], of Brymmore aforesaid, only s. and h., *b.* at Hatton Garden, 12 and *bap.* 23 Feb. 1663/4, at St. Andrew's, Holborn; admitted to Lincoln's Inn, 3 Aug. 1670; *suc. to the Baronetcy* in 1671. He *d.* unm., being "basely killed by one Waters, a Lifeguard-man, at the Swan Tavern in Fish street"[c], London, aged 24, when the *Baronetcy* became *extinct*[d]. Admon., as "of St. Andrew's, Holborn," 13 June 1688.

DOYLY, *or* DOYLEY:

cr. 29 July 1663.

I. 1663. "Sir William Doyley, of Shottesham, co. Norfolk, Knt.," s. and h. of William Doyley, *or* Doyly, of Hadleigh, co. Suffolk, by Elizabeth, da. of the Rev. Richard Stokes, Archdeacon of Norwich (which William was 2d s. of Edmund Doyly, of Shottisham aforesaid), was *b.* about 1614, being aged 23 at the death of his father in 1637; suc. to the family estate of Shottisham in 1648, on the failure of the issue of his great uncle Sir Henry Doyly, of the same; served in the wars under Gustavus Adolphus; was *Knighted* 2 July 1641, at Whitehall; retired to Rotterdam during the Civil Wars, when his estate was sequestrated; was M.P. for Norfolk, 1654-55, 1656-58, and 1659, and, subsequently, 1660 and 1661 till his death, for Yarmouth, being one of the members of the Convention Parl., who were most zealous for the Restoration,

(a) These were "Henrietta, wife of Edward Le Neve, Isabella Le Neve, Spinster, and Anne, wife of John Rogers, "being the 3 daughters and coheirs of Oliver Le Neve, of Great Wichingham, by Anne, sister of the deceased. These ladies sold the estate of West Harling to Joshua Draper.

(b) *Dict. Nat. Biog.*, under "John Pym."

(c) Luttrell's *Diary*, where it is added that "since, the Coroner's inquest have found it wilfull murder."

(d) Mary, his only sister, then unm., *m.*, a few months later, Sir Thomas Hales, 2d Baronet [1660], of Beaksbourne, co. Kent.

and was *cr. a Baronet*, as above, 29 July 1663. He rebuilt Blackford Hall, in Stoke Holy Cross, co. Norfolk, but became deeply involved in debt in or before 1675. He *m.* about 1637, Margaret, da. and h. of (—) Randall, of Pulham and Denton, co. Norfolk.[a] He *d.* Nov. 1677 and was *bur.* at Hadleigh aforesaid, aged 64. Will dat. 2 June 1677, but never proved. His widow *d.* May 1679.

II. 1677. Sir William Doyly, Baronet [1663], of Shottisham, etc., aforesaid, 1st s. and h., *b.* about 1637; admitted to Gray's Inn, 23 Jan. 1652/3; was *Knighted* v.p., 30 April 1664, and was one of the four Tellers of the Exchequer, 1666-77; *suc. to the Baronetcy* in Nov. 1677. He *m.* about 1666, Mary[b] da. of John Hadley, of Southgate, in East Barnet, co. Midx., citizen and grocer of London, by Anne, da. of Gilbert Harrison, Chamberlain of London. He *d.* in or before 1680. Admon. 23 July 1680, to a creditor, his widow being then living.

III. 1680? Sir Edmund Doyly, Baronet [1663], of Shottisham, etc., aforesaid, 1st. s. and h., *b.* probably about 1666; *suc. to the Baronetcy*, in or before 1680, being then a minor. He *m.* 13 Nov. 1684, at Ditchingham, co. Norfolk, Dorothy, 1st. da. of Philip Bedingfeld, of Ditchingham, by Ursula, da. of Sir John Potts, 1st Baronet [1641], of Mannington. He was *bur.* 24 Oct. 1700, at Shottisham. His widow *d.* Dec. 1718.

IV. 1700. Sir Edmund Doyly, Baronet [1663], of Shottisham, etc., aforesaid, 1st s. and h.[c]; *suc. to the Baronetcy* in Oct. 1700. In his lifetime the estate of Shottisham was sold and he retired to Cossey, co. Norfolk. He *d.* unm. 1763.

V. 1763. Sir Hadley Doyly, Baronet [1663], Rector of Wotton and Felixstow, co. Suffolk, cousin and h. male, being 3d but 1st. surv. s. and h. male of Hadley Doyly, of Castle Yard, Holborn, by Elizabeth, da. of Charles Yallop (s. of Sir Robert Yallop, of Beauthorpe, near Norwich), was *b.* about 1709; matric. at Oxford (Queen's Coll.), 4 April 1723, aged 14; B.A., 10 March 1726/7; M.A., 1729; in Holy Orders; Rector of Wotton and Felixstowe aforesaid, and *suc. to the Baronetcy* in 1763. He *m.*, in or before 1753, Henrietta Maynard, da. of the Rev. Henry Osborne, of Nailsworth, co. Wilts, Vicar of Thaxted, co. Essex. He *d.* 30 July 1764, and was *bur.* at St. Helen's, Ipswich. His widow *d.* at Lymington, co. Southampton, Aug. 1793. Will pr. May 1794.

VI. 1764. Sir John Hadley Doyly, Baronet [1663], 1st s. and h., *b.* Jan. 1754; *suc. to the Baronetcy*, 30 July 1764; was Collector of Customs at Calcutta, being one of the twenty-four "Pergunnahs;" was an intimate friend of Warren Hastings, Gov. Gen. of India (1771-85), and was finally senior Merchant in the Bengal establishment; was M.P. for Ipswich, 1790-96. He *m.*, March 1780, at Calcutta, Diana, widow of William Cotes, of Calcutta, da. of William Rochfort, of Clontarf (br. of Robert, 1st Earl of Belvedere [I.]), by Henrietta, da. of Col. John Ramsay. She *d.* 6 Sep. 1803. He *d.*, at Calcutta, Jan. 1818. Will pr. Dec. 1827.

VII. 1818. Sir Charles Doyly, Baronet [1663], 1st s. and h., *b.* 18 Sep. 1781; was in the Civil Service of the East India Company, becoming, finally, senior merchant and senior member of the Board of Customs at Calcutta; was distinguished as an amateur artist; *suc. to the Baronetcy* in Jan. 1818. He *m.* firstly, his cousin, Marian, 3d da. and coheir of William Greer, of Keyhaven, Hants, by Harriett, da. of his grandfather, Sir Hadley Doyly, 5th Baronet abovenamed. She *d.* s.p. 1814, at Calcutta. He *m.* secondly, Elizabeth

(a) She is said in Burke's *Baronetage* for 1902, to have been "stepdaughter of Sir Robert Bacon, Baronet," possibly being a da. of Katherine, the second wife [in 1650], of Sir Robert Bacon, 3d Baronet [1611], who *d.* Dec. 1655.

(b) Her sister Anne, *m.* Nov. 1672, as first wife, the notorious Admiral, Arthur (Herbert) Earl of Torrington, who *d.* s.p., 14 April 1716.

(c) His only br. William *d.* unm. in 1737.

Jane, 1st da. of Major Thomas Ross, Royal Artillery, by Isabella, da. of John Macleod, of Rasay, co. Inverness. He *d.* s.p. abroad 21 Sep. 1845. Will pr. Oct. 1845. His widow *d.* 1 June 1873.

VIII. 1845. Sir John Hadley Doyly, Baronet [1663], of Stepleton Park, near Blandford, co. Dorset, only br. and h., *b.* 29 Sep. 1794, was for more than 30 years in the East India Company's Service, which he entered, as writer, in April 1812; 2d assistant in public department 1813; head assistant to Collector of Customs, at Calcutta, 1817; 2d deputy opium agent at Behar, 1821; salt agent in North division of Cuttack, 1823; Collector of Customs there, 1825; Collector of Land Revenue at Midnapore and Puttaspore, 1828; Official Magistrate at Midnapore, 1831; Magistrate and Collector there, 1832; Civil and Session Judge at Beerboom, 1836, retiring in 1843; *suc. to the Baronetcy* 21 Sep. 1845. He *m.* firstly, 1 Dec. 1819, Charlotte, da. of George Nesbitt Thompson, of Penton Lodge, Hants (Secretary to Warren Hastings when Gov. Gen. of India, 1771-85), by Catherine Maria, relict of Henry Vansittart, da. of Thomas Powney, of Windsor. This marriage was dissolved in 1828. He *m.* secondly, in 1830, Mary, 1st da. of John Fendall, Member of the Supreme Council at Calcutta. He *d.* 21 March 1869 at Stepleton, aged 74. His widow, who was *b.* 1794, *d.* at Charlton Cottage, Blandford, co. Dorset, 26 May 1885, in her 92d year.

IX. 1869. Sir Charles Walters Doyly, Baronet [1663], of Newlands, near Blandford, co. Dorset, 1st s. and h., by 1st wife, *b.* 21 Dec. 1822; entered the Bengal Army, 1842; A.D.C. to the Gov. Gen. Dalhousie, 1851-56; Capt., 58th Reg., 1855; served in the Gwalior Campaign and Indian Mutiny (2 medals) 1857; transferred to Bengal Staff Corps, 1861; Col., 1873; Major Gen., retired, 1875, having *suc. to the Baronetcy*, 21 March 1869. He *m.* firstly, 25 Sep. 1855, at Bengalore, Emily Jane, 2d da. of Major Gen. George Nott, Madras Army. She *d.* 12 May 1857. He *m.* secondly, 5 June 1867, Elinor, 3d da. of James Winter Scott, of Rotherfield Park, Hants. He *d.* s.p.m. at Newlands aforesaid, 11 July 1900, aged 77. Will pr. at £52,298. His widow living 1903.

X. 1900. Sir Warren Hastings Doyly, Baronet [1663], br. of the half blood and h. male, being only s. of the 8th Baronet by his 2d wife; *b.* 6 April 1838; was in the Bengal Civil Service; *suc. to the Baronetcy* 11 July 1900. He *m.* in March 1859, Henrietta, da. of Sir Frederick James Halliday, **K.C.B.**, Lieut.-Gov. of Bengal [1856-59], by Eliza, da. of Gen. Macgregor, E.I.C.S.

MARSHAM:

cr. 12 or 16 Aug. 1663;

afterwards, since 1716, Barons Romney;

and, since 1801, Earls of Romney.

I. 1663. "Sir John Marsham, of [Whorn's Place, in] Cuckston [*i.e.*, Cuxton], co. Kent, Knt.," 2d s. of Thomas Marsham, Alderman of London (*bur.* 12 March 1624, at Islington), by Magdalen, da. of Richard Springham, Merchant of London, was *b.* at St. Bartholomew's the Great, London, 23 and *bap.* 29 Aug. 1692, at St. Michael-le-Quern; ed. at Westm. School; matric. at Oxford (St. John's Coll.), 22 Oct. 1619, aged 16; B.A., 17 Feb. 1622/3; M.A., 3 July 1625; admitted to Middle Temple, 1627; one of the six Clerks in Chancery, 17 Feb. 1637/8, till ejected by Parl. in 1641, but restored in 1660 till his resignation to his son Robert in 1680; attended the King and the Great Seal at Oxford; was a Compounder for £356: M.P. for Rochester, April to Dec. 1660; *Knighted*, 1 July 1660, and was *cr. a Baronet*, as above, 12 or 16 Aug. 1660, having previously purchased Whorn's Place abovenamed. He *m.*, 13 Jan. 1630/1, at St. Dunstan's Stepney, Elizabeth, da. of Sir William Hammond, of St. Alban's Court in Nonington, co. Kent, by Elizabeth, da. of Sir Anthony Aucher, of Bishopsbourne. He *d.* at Bushey Hall, Herts, 25 May, and was *bur.* 3 June 1685, at Cuxton.(a) M.I. Will pr. May 1685. His widow, who was *bap.* 12 March 1611/2, at Nonington, *d.* 24 and was *bur.* 29 Sep. 1689, at Cuxton. M.I.

II. 1685. SIR JOHN MARSHAM, Baronet [1663], of Whorn's Place, in Cuxton aforesaid, and of the Mote in Maidstone, co. Kent, 1st s. and h., *b.* and *bap.* 15 Sep. 1637, at St. Barth. the Great; matric. at Oxford (Queen's Coll.), 7 Nov. 1655; admitted to the Mid. Temple, 1658; *suc. to the Baronetcy*, 25 May, 1685; Sheriff of Kent, 1691-92. He *m.* firstly, 11 Jan. 1664/5, at St. Martins-in-the-Fields (Lic. Fac. 2, he 27 and she 20), Anne, da. of Sir Samuel DANVERS, 1st Baronet [1643], of Culworth, co. Northampton, by Anne, da. of Sir William POPE. She, who was *bap.* 10 Feb. 1641/2, at Culworth, *d.* s.p., 8 April 1672, and was *bur.* at Cuxton, aged 30. M.I. He *m.* secondly, 10 March 1674/5, at St. Andrew's, Undershaft (Lic. Fac. 13), Hester (then aged 22), posthumous da. and h. of Sir George SAYER, of Bourchier's Hall, in Aldham, co. Essex, by Jane, da. of John VAN DEN KERCKHOVE, Lord of Heenvhat in Zealand, He *d.* at the Mote aforesaid, 31 Dec. 1692, aged 55, and was *bur.* 5 Jan. 1692/3, at Cuxton. M.I. Will (without date), pr. 2 Jan. 1692/3. His widow, who was *b.* Sep. and *bap.* 8 Oct. 1650, at Aldham, *d.* at Chelsea, and was *bur.* 27 Oct. 1716, at Aldham aforesaid. Admon. 25 Feb. 1716/7 to James, Earl of Derby, cousin german and next of kin.

III. 1692. SIR JOHN MARSHAM, Baronet, of Whorn's Place and of the Mote aforesaid, only s. and h. by 2d wife, *b.* 12 Oct. 1679, in London; *suc. to the Baronetcy*, 31 Dec. 1692. He *d.* unm. 13 and was *bur.* 18 May 1696, aged 16, at Cuxton. M.I. Admon. 16 Sep. 1703, to the Guardian of his mother, she being then a lunatic.

IV. 1696. SIR ROBERT MARSHAM, Baronet [1663], of Whorn's Place and of the Mote aforesaid, and of Bushey Hall, Herts, uncle and h., being 2d and yst. s. of the 1st Baronet, *b.* 16 Dec. 1650, and bap. 2 Jan. 1650/1, at Blackfriars, London; matric. at Oxford (St. John's Coll.) 19 Oct. 1666, aged 18; admitted to the Middle Temple, 1669; was one of the six clerks in Chancery, 1680, on the resignation of his father, and was *Knighted*, 12 Dec. 1681; *suc. to the Baronetcy*, 13 May 1696; was M.P. for Maidstone (four Parls.), 1698 till unseated 24 Oct. 1702. He *m.*, 12 Dec. 1681, at St. Edmund's, Lombard street (Lic. Fac. 7, he about 30 and she about 20), Margaretta, da. and h. of Thomas BOSVILLE, of the Little Mote in Eynsford, co. Kent, by Elizabeth, da. of Sir Francis WYATT, of Boxley Abbey in that county, sometime Gov. of Virginia. He *d.* 26 and was *bur.* 30 July 1703, aged 53, at Cuxton. M.I. Will, without date, pr. 4 Nov. 1703. His widow, who was *b.* and *bap.* 9 Aug. at Horton Kirby, co. Kent, *d.* at Maidstone, and was *bur.* at Cuxton, 5 May 1710. Admon. 17 March 1711/2.

V. 1703. SIR ROBERT MARSHAM, Baronet [1663], of Cuxton and of the Mote aforesaid, etc., 1st s. and h., *b.* 17 and *bap.* 19 Sep. 1685 at Bushey, Herts.; matric. at Oxford (St. John's Coll.) 9 Aug. 1701; *suc. to the Baronetcy*, 26 July 1703, and was M.P. for Maidstone (four Parls.), 1708-16, being a great supporter of the Hanoverian succession. He *m.*, 19 Aug. 1708, at the Chapel Royal, Whitehall (Lic. Fac. 17), Elizabeth ("dowry £15,000 and £20,000 more at her mother's death"), 1st da. and coheir of Admiral Sir Cloudesley SHOVEL, by Elizabeth, (sometime wife of Sir John NARBOROUGH), da. of John HILL, a Commissioner in the Navy. She, who was *b.* 2 and *bap.* 22 Nov. 1692, at St. Mary's, Whitechapel, was living when he was *cr.*, 25 June 1716, BARON ROMNEY, co. Kent. In that Peerage this *Baronetcy* then *merged* and still [1903] so continues, the 3d Baron and 7th Baronet being *cr.*, 22 June 1801, EARL OF ROMNEY, etc. See *Peerage.*

(a) "He was an accomplished gentleman and excellent historian" and "acknowledged to be one of the greatest antiquaries and most accurate and learned writer [*Qy.* writers] of the time." [Brydges's *Collins' Peerage.*]

BARNHAM:

cr. 15 Aug. 1663;

ex. 1685;

but, apparently, *assumed*, 1685 to 1728.

I. 1663, to 1685? "ROBERT BARNHAM, of Boughton Munchensye, [*i.e.*, Monchelsea], co. Kent, Esq.," 2d but 1st surv. s. and h. of Sir Francis BARNHAM, of the same, and of Hollington, in that county (will pr. 1646), by Elizabeth, (*m.* 3 Jan. 1598/9, at Sevenoaks), sister of Henry, LORD DACRE, da. of Sampson LENNARD, of Chevening co. Kent, was *b.* probably about 1606(a); was M.P. for Maidstone, 1660 and 1661-79, and was *cr. a Baronet*, as above, 15 Aug. 1663. He recorded his pedigree in the Visit. of Kent, 1664. He *m.* firstly, in or before 1636, Eliz. or Anne, da. of Robert HENLEY, of Henley, co. Somerset, and of the Middle Temple, London. He *m.* secondly (Lic. Fac. 18 Aug. 1663, he about 47 [*Query* 57?], widower), Hannah LOWFIELD, of St. Dionis, Backchurch, aged 38, widow, da. of [—] NICHOLS, of London. He *d.* s.p.m.s. in May or June 1685, when probably the *Baronetcy* became *extinct.*(b) Will dat. 27 April and pr. 11 June 1685, by his widow.(c) Her will pr. Jan. 1685/6.

II. 1685? to 1728? SIR ROBERT BARNHAM, Baronet [1663], whose existence is, however, doubtful, is said to be grandson and h., as being only s. and h. of Francis BARNHAM, of Boughton Monchelsea, by Anne (mar. lic. Vic. Gen. 12 Sep. 1667), relict. of John SHIRLEY and da. of Sir Thomas PARKER, of Rotton, which Francis (aged 30 in Sep. 1667) was undoubtedly only s. and h. ap. of the late Baronet, by his 1st wife, but *d.* v.p., and possibly s.p.m., in 1668. A son, however, of this Francis, named Robert (as above stated), is sometimes supposed to have *suc. to the Baronetcy* in 1685, and to have *d.* s.p. (probably unm.) in 1728, when, if not before, the *Baronetcy* became *extinct.*

LEKE, *or* LEEKE:

cr. 15 Dec. 1663;

ex. June 1681.

I. 1663. "FRANCIS LEEKE,(d) of [the Chauntry, in] Newarke-upon-Trent, co. Nottingham, Esq., Governor of Gravesend," being also Lord of the Manor of Sandiacre, co. Derby, s. and h. of William LEEKE, *or*

(a) His eldest br., Dacre Barnham, was aged 15 in 1619.

(b) It is stated to be so by Courthope, but by Burke [*Extinct Baronetages*], is continued till 1728. The Visitation of Kent in 1664, shews Francis (only s. of the grantee), as then unm., with three sisters of the whole blood; (1) Mary, wife of Sir Nathaniel Powell (afterwards 2d Baronet [1661]), and then mother of three children; (2) Elizabeth, and (3), Anne, besides (4) another sister (Philadelphia), of the half blood. In Le Neve's MS. *Baronetage*, however, Francis is credited with three wives, the first being unnamed, the second being "the widow of Lowfield" [presumably a mistake for his father's second wife], by whom he is given a da. and h. who *m.* Thomas Ryder (the father of Sir Barnham Rider), the 3d wife being Anne Shirley, widow, da. of Sir Thomas Parker, who is said to have survived him thirty-six years and to have died, 16 April 1704, at Isleworth. This account is, apparently, very inaccurate, and the conjecture made in note "c" below, seems more probable.

(c) In this will occurs this strange bequest—"If I can dispose of it I give my honour of being a Baronet to my son, Thomas Rider." This Thomas was the husband of Philadelphia (*b.* 1664), his da. by the 2d wife and she *presumably* (to the exclusion of her elder sisters of the half blood, and of her nephew, the 2d Baronet, supposing that he existed), inherited the Boughton Monchelsea estate.

(d) See *Her. & Gen.*, vol. vii, pp. 495-499, for pedigree and account of this family.

LEKE, of Newark aforesaid (*d.* 1651, aged 46, being a yr. br. of the half blood of Francis, 1st EARL OF SCARSDALE), by Elizabeth, his 1st wife, da. of Sir Guy PALMES, was *bap.* 1 Nov. 1627, at Newark; was Sheriff of Notts, 1660-61; Governor of the Block house in Gravesend, and was (for having apprehended Col. HUTCHINSON, the Regicide), *cr. a Baronet*, as above, 15 Dec. 1663. He was M.P. for Notts, Oct. 1666 to 1679. He *m.* Frances, 4th da. of Sir William THOROLD, 1st Baronet [1642] of Marston, co. Lincoln, by Anne, da. of John BLYTHE. He *d.* in 1679. Will, dat. at Milton by Gravesend, 2 Oct., pr. 10 Nov. 1679. His widow *d.* in Park Place, St. James', and was *bur.* at St. Paul's, Covent Garden, 4 Jan. 1693/4.(a) Will dat. 23 Sep. 1690, pr. 13 Jan. 1693/4 by her da., Anne VYNER.

II. 1679. to 1681. SIR FRANCIS LEEKE, Baronet [1663], of the Chauntry aforesaid, Gov. of the Forts of Gravesend and Tilbury, only s. and h.; *suc. to the Baronetcy* in Oct. or Nov. 1679, but *d.* within two years, unm., and was *bur.* 19 June 1681, at St. Paul's, Covent Garden, when the *Baronetcy* became *extinct.* Will dat. 15 June 1681, pr. 10 May 1682 by his uncle, "Clifton LEEKE, Esq.," the residuary legatee, and again 13 June 1688.

SAINT-BARBE:

cr. 30 Dec. 1663;

ex. 7 Sep. 1723.

I. 1663, to 1723. "JOHN SAINT-BARBE, of Broadlands [in Romsey], co. Southampton, Esq.," and of Ashington, co. Somerset, 2d s. of John SAINTE-BARBE, of the same (*d.* 1658, aged. 42), by Grizel, da. and h. of John PYNSENT, Prothonotary of the Court of Common Pleas, was *b.* about 1655; suc. his elder br. Henry in 1661 at the age of six, and, when about eight years old, was *cr. a Baronet*, as above, 30 Dec. 1663. He was M.P. for Ilchester, 1681, and Sheriff of Hants, 1703-4. He *m.* firstly (Lic. Lond., 2 Dec. 1682, he aged 27), Honor (then aged 23), da. of Richard NORTON, of Southwick, Hants. She *d.* 1710, and was *bur.* at Ashington. He *m.* secondly, Alice, widow of John Horn, of Winchester, da. of the Hon. Richard FIENNES (4th s. of William, 1st VISCOUNT SAY AND SELE), by his 1st wife, Margaret, da. and h. of Andrew BURRELL, of Wisbech. He *d.* s.p. at Broadlands, 17 Sep. 1723, aged 67, and was *bur.* at Ashington, when the *Baronetcy* became *extinct*(b). M.I. Will pr. Sep. 1723. His widow *d.* 1734.

CAMBELL:

cr. 12 Feb. 1663/4;

ex. 23 May 1699.

I. 1664. "THOMAS CAMBELL, of Clay Hall [in Barking], co. Essex, Esq.," uncle of Sir John CAMBELL, Baronet [so *cr.* 9 April 1661], being 2d s. of Robert CAMBELL, of St. Olave's Old Jury, London, Alderman of that city (who was 2d s. of Sir Thomas CAMBELL, Lord Mayor of London, 1609-10), by Alice, da. of William WILLINGTON, of Clehonger, co. Hereford, was *b.* probably about 1620; suc. his father, 10 Nov. 1638, and was *cr. a Baronet*, as above, 12 Feb. 1663/4. He *m.* firstly, 6 July 1641, at St. Peter's le Poor, London, Hester, da. of Nicholas CORSELLIS, of London, Merchant. She *d.* s.p.m.s., and was *bur.* 28 Oct. 1659, at Barking. He *m.* secondly, in or before 1662, Mary, da. of

(a) The burial entry calls her (by mistake) "Lady *Dorothy* Leeke." The will, however, is that of "Dame *Frances* Leke."

(b) He devised his estates to his great grand-nephew, Humphrey Sydenham, grandson of Edward Sydenham, by Jane, da. of Sir William Pole, of Shute, and Catharine his wife, testator's sister.

Thomas (FANSHAWE), 1st VISCOUNT FANSHAWE OF DROMORE [I.], by his 2d wife, Elizabeth, da. of Sir William COKAYNE, Lord Mayor of London, 1619-20. He was *bur.* 2 Sep. 1665, at Barking. Will dat. 31 Aug. 1665, pr. Jan. 1665/6. His widow, who was *bap.* 7 Nov. 1635, at Ware, Herts, *m.*, before June 1668, her cousin, Robert SHEFFIELD(a), of Kensington, Midx., who *d.* s.p.m.s., 21 April 1725, in his 84th year, at Kingsthorpe, co. Northampton. She was *bur.* as "the Hon. Lady Cambell," 1 Dec. 1701, at Barking.

II. 1665. SIR THOMAS CAMBELL, Baronet [1664], of Clay Hall aforesaid, 1st s. and h. by second wife, *b.* probably in or shortly before 1662; *suc. to the Baronetcy* in Sep. 1665. He *d.* unm. and was *bur.* 27 May 1668, at Barking. Admon. 10 June 1668, to his mother, then wife of Robert Sheffield.

III. 1668, to 1699. SIR HENRY CAMBELL, Baronet [1664], of Clay Hall aforesaid, br. of the whole blood and heir; *b.* 14 and *bap.* 24 Nov. 1663, at S. Andrew's, Holborn, but registered at Barking; *suc. to the Baronetcy* in May 1668; matric. at Oxford (Ch. Ch.), 15 June 1680, aged 16; admitted to the Middle Temple, 1680. He *m.* firstly, in 1688 (portion £1,000), Katharine, 5th da. of Sir Anthony CHESTER, 3d Baronet [1620], of Chicheley, by Mary, da. of Samuel CRAMNER, Alderman of London. She who was *b.* 11 and *bap.* 12 Oct. 1662, at Chicheley, *d.* 18 and was *bur.* 21 Jan. 1691/2, at Barking. He *m.* secondly, Katharine, widow of Col. Anthony MARKHAM, of Sedgebrooke, co. Lincoln, da. of Sir William WHORWOOD, of Stourton Castle, co. Stafford, by Katharine, da. of Sir Sutton CONEY. He *d.* s.p.m.(b) at Kensington, 23 and was *bur.* 26 May 1699, at Barking, aged 35, when the *Baronetcy* became *extinct.* Will dat. 6 May and pr. 2 June 1699, by his widow.(c)

PENNYMAN:

cr. 22 Feb. 1663/4;

sometime, 1768-70, PENNYMAN-WARTON;

ex. 1852.

I. 1664. "JAMES PENNYMAN, of Ormesby in Cleveland, co. York, Esq.," 1st s. and h. of Sir James(d) PENNYMAN, of the same, by his first wife, Catharine (*m.* 18 Oct. 1603), da. of the Rev. William KINGSLEY, D.D., Archdeacon of Canterbury, was *b.* 6 March 1607/8; was (as well as his father, who *d.* 18 Oct. 1655, aged 75), a great sufferer in the Royal cause, raising a troop of horse at his own expense, and was *cr. a Baronet*, as above, 22 Feb. 1663/4. He entered his pedigree at the Her. Visit. of Yorkshire in 1665, stating his age as 58. He *m.* 26 Dec. 1632, at Castlegate, Elizabeth, 1st da. and coheir of Stephen

(a) He was s. and h. of the Hon. James Sheffield (7th s. of Edmund, 1st Earl of Mulgrave), by Jane, another da. of Sir William Cokayne abovenamed.

(b) Mary his only da. and h., by his first wife, was *bap.* 2 June 1689, at Chicheley, Bucks; inherited her father's estates at the age of ten; was in ward to her grandmother, Dame Mary Chester; *m.* in 1709, Thomas Price, of Westbury, Bucks (who *d.* 25 March 1733) and *d.* in childbirth, being *bur.* at Barking, 30 March 1713, leaving an only son, Cambell Price.

(c) She is said, in (a very reliable work) R. S. Chester Waters' *Family of Chester of Chicheley*, to have survived her husband "about 15 years," and to have "died in London in the parish of St. Giles'-in-the-Fields" being "buried at Barking, 6 Oct. 1714." There is, however, no such entry of burial at Barking, but among those at St. Giles' occurs, under 6 Oct. 1714, "Lady Cambwell, carried away." This, however, presumably refers to Dame *Elizabeth* Campbell, of Stackhole, co. Pembroke, widow, whose will is pr. that same month.

(d) *Qy.* if Thomas [*sic*] Pennyman, *Knighted* at York 24 April 1642, is not a mistake for James?

Norcliffe, of Langton, co. York, Barrister, by (—), da. of (—) Udal. She who was *bap.* 21 Oct. 1612, was *bur.* 8 April 1678. He *d.* 24 April 1679, aged 71.(a) Admon. at York 1679.

II. 1677. Sir Thomas Pennyman, Baronet [1664], of Ormesby aforesaid, 3d but only surv. s. and h., *bap.* 29 Aug. 1642, at South Bailey, Durham; *suc. to the Baronetcy*, 24 April 1679. Sheriff of Yorkshire, 1702-03. He *m.*, in or before 1661, Frances, da. of Sir John Lowther, 1st Baronet [S. 1640], of Lowther, co. Westmorland, by his 1st wife, Mary, da. of Sir Richard Fletcher. He *d.* at Ormesby, 3 Aug. 1708, aged 66. Will dat. 6 Dec. 1700, pr. Oct. 1708, at York.

III. 1708. Sir James Pennyman, Baronet [1664], of Ormesby aforesaid, and of Thornton in Cleveland, 1st s. and h.(b), *b.* about 1661, being aged 4 in 1665; *suc. to the Baronetcy*, 3 Aug. 1708. He *m.*, 7 Nov. 1692, at St. Giles' in the Fields (Lic. Fac. 24 Oct., he stated to be 25 and she 24, her parents dead), Mary, sister and coheir of Sir Michael Wharton (who *d.* 1725, aged 73), da. of Michael Wharton, of Beverley, co. York, by Susanna, da. of John (Poulett), 1st Baron Poulett of Hinton St. George. He *d.* 17 Nov. 1745, aged 84. Will pr. at York 1745.

IV. 1745. Sir William Pennyman, Baronet [1664], of Ormesby, 2d but 1st surv. s. and h.,(c) *b.* 1695; *suc. to the Baronetcy*, 17 Nov. 1745. Sheriff of Yorkshire, Jan. to Dec. 1750. He *d.* unm. 16 April 1768, aged 73. Will pr. May 1768.

V. 1768. Sir Warton Pennyman-Warton, Baronet [1664], of Ormesby aforesaid and of Beverley, co. York, br. and h., *b.* about 1701; assumed the name of *Warton* after that of *Pennyman*, in or before 1741; *suc. to the Baronetcy* 16 April 1768. He *m.*, 31 March 1725, Charlotte, da. of Sir Charles Hotham, 4th Baronet [1622], by his first wife, Bridget, da. of William Gee, of Bishop Burton. He *d.* s.p.m.s. 14 Jan. 1770, aged 69, and was *bur.* at Beverley. M.I. Will pr. Jan. 1770. His widow *d.* 7 and was *bur.*, 14 June 1771, at Trinity, Micklegate, York. Will pr. March 1771.

VI. 1770. Sir James Pennyman, Baronet [1664], of Ormesby aforesaid, nephew and h. male, being s. and h. of Ralph Pennyman, of Beverley, by Bridget, da. of Thomas Gee, of Bishop Burton, which Ralph (who *d.* 23 Aug. 1768 and was *bur.* at Beverley), was br. of the 4th and 5th and yst. s. of the 3d Baronet. He was *bap.* at Beverley, 6 Dec. 1736; matric. at Oxford (Ch. Ch.) 20 May 1756, aged 29; *suc. to the Baronetcy* 14 Jan. 1770; was

(a) He is said to have sold a portion of the Ormesby estates for £3,500, which was repurchased in 1770 for £47,500, by the then Baronet.

(b) He had five younger brothers, viz.: (1) John, aged 2 in 1665; (2) Thomas; (3) William; (4) Charles and (5) Henry. Of these it is stated that John, William, and Charles (the 3d son, admitted to Lincoln's Inn, 20 Oct. 1674) were dead (presumably s.p.) before 1771 [Kimber's *Baronetage*, 1771]. Thomas appears to have been living in 1694, and was possibly the "Thomas Pennyman of Lincoln's Inn, Esq.," who *m.* Margaret Aungier, of Northaw, Herts. at St. Martin's-in-the-Fields, 18 June 1703 (Lic. Lond. 17, he 34, bachelor, and she 21, spinster.) This lady was unquestionably the authoress of *Miscellanies in Prose and Verse, by the Hon. Lady Margaret Pennyman*, pub. in 1740, whose parentage and marriage, as stated in the preface to this work, agree with the above. It is, however, also there stated that her husband's "elder brother dying, he succeeded to the title [of a Baronet] and estates" but this apparently is incorrect. They appear "in less than three months' time" after their marriage, to have been "obliged to a separation by law" and she is said to have died, 16 June 1733, in her 46th year, and to have been *bur.* at St. Margaret's, Westm.

(c) James, the 1st. s. *bap.* 17 Jan. 1693/4, at Coney street, York, *m.* Dorothy, da. of William Wake, Archbishop of Canterbury and *d.* s.p. and v.p., Dec. 1743, aged 50. His widow *d.* 2 Dec. 1754, aged 55.

M.P. for Scarborough, 1770-74, and for Beverley (four Parls.), 1774-96. He *m.*, in or before 1763, Elizabeth, da. of Sir Henry Grey, 1st Baronet [1746], of Howick, by Hannah, da. of Thomas Wood. She, apparently, was living in 1776.(a) He *m.*, subsequently, 14 May 1801, at St. John's the Evangelist, Westm., Mary Maleham (*Qy.* Matcham) of that parish, Spinster. He *d.* 27 March 1808. Will pr. June 1808. His widow *d.* 19 Sep. 1815. Admon. July 1817.

VII. 1808, to 1852. Sir William Henry Pennyman, Baronet [1664], of Ormesby aforesaid, 1st but only surv. s. and h. by 1st wife, *bap.* 21 Jan. 1764 at St. Mary's, Beverley; matric. at Oxford (Mag. Coll.), 24 May 1781, aged 18; *suc. to the Baronetcy*, 27 March 1808. He *m.*, before 1802, Charlotte, da. of Bethell Robinson, of Calwick, in Holderness, co. York. She *d.* 3 May 1848, at Beverley, aged 82. He *d.* s.p. 1852, aged 88, when the *Baronetcy* became *extinct*.(b)

MODYFORD, *or* MUDDIFORD:

cr. 1 March 1663/4;

ex. 30 July 1702.

I. 1664. "Thomas Muddiford [*rectius* Modyford], of Lincoln's Inn, co. Middx., Esq.," br. of Sir James Modyford, Baronet [so *cr.* 18 Feb. 1660/1], being 1st s. of John Modyford, Mayor of Exeter, 1622 (*d.* before 1632), by Maria, da. of Thomas Walker, Alderman of Exeter, was *b.* probably about 1618; admitted to Lincoln's Inn, 11 Jan. 1631/2, becoming, afterwards, a Barrister; served in the King's army, during the Civil War, but in 1647, sailed for Jamaica and invested £7,000 in the purchase of an estate there. He, as Col. Modyford, signed the Royalist declaration there in 1651, but afterwards took the other side. He was made Speaker of the Assembly at Barbadoes in 1661; is sometimes said to have been *Knighted*, 18 Feb. 1660/1, and was *cr. a Baronet*, as above, 1 March 1663/4. He was Governor of Jamaica, Feb. 1664 till Dec. 1670, when he was recalled and imprisoned (as being implicated in buccaneering) till 1674 or later, in the Tower of London. He *m.* in 1640 Elizabeth, da. of Lewin Palmer, by Anne, da. of (—) Finch. She *d.* 12 Nov. 1668, of the plague, and was *bur.* at St. Catharine's, Jamaica. M.I. He *d.* 2 Sep. 1679 and was *bur.* in Spanish Town, Jamaica. M.I. Admon. 17 Jan. 1679/80, to his son, Sir Charles Modyford, Baronet.

II. 1679, Sep. Sir Thomas Modyford, Baronet [1664], of Jamaica, 1st s. and h.; was a Member of the Council at Jamaica; *suc. to the Baronetcy*, 2 Sep. 1679. He *m.*, in or before 1664, [—], da. of John Hethersall, of Gidea Hall, in Romford, co. Essex, Merchant of London. He, however, *d.* s.p.m.,(c) but six weeks after his father, 19 Oct. 1679 and was *bur.* with his father. M.I.

(a) Eight, or possibly ten, children were born between 1764 and 1776, of which two, possibly four, were born between 1770 and 1776. These last may have been by another wife if the statement in Musgrave's *Obituary* is true that the date of the death of the 1st wife was in 1770. The only authority, however, given for that statement is a "MS." In Playfair's *Baronetage* [1811] all ten children are credited to the 1st wife.

(b) The Ormesby estate passed (under his will) to his cousin James White Worsley (*b.* 5 Nov. 1792), 1st s. and h. of Col. James Worsley (*d.* 1807, aged 43), who was s. and h. of the Rev. James Worsley, Rector of Stonegrave, by Dorothy (*d.* 1811, aged 71) sister of Sir James Pennyman, the 6th Baronet and aunt to the testator. He took the name of *Pennyman* instead of that of *Worsley* and *d.* 1 Feb. 1870, aged 77, leaving issue.

(c) Elizabeth, his only da. and h., *m.* firstly, 25 Dec. 1676, Col. Thomas Barry, a Member of the Jamaica Council; and secondly (as the 3d of his five wives) Sir Nicholas Lawes, Gov. of Jamaica, 1718, who *d.* 18 June 1731, aged 79. She *d.* 11 Nov. 1694 in her 30th year and was *bur.* at Spanish Town in that island.

III. 1679, Oct. Sir Charles Modyford, Baronet [1664], of Jamaica, only surv. br. and h., sometime a Merchant in Mincing lane, London, and afterwards a Member of the Council in Jamaica, *suc. to the Baronetcy*, 19 Oct. 1679. He *m.*, in or before 1672, Mary, 1st da. and coheir of Sir Thomas Norton, Baronet [so *cr.* 23 July 1661], of Coventry, by Anna, da. of John Jermy. She *d.* between 1680 and 1684. He was *bur.* 22 July 1687, at St. Catherine's, Jamaica. Will dat. at London 18 Jan. 1679/80, and at "Angells in Jamaica," 3 March 1683/4, pr. 20 Dec. 1689.

IV. 1687. Sir Norton Modyford, Baronet [1664], of Jamaica, 1st s. and h., *b.* 25 Jan. 1673/4; *suc. to the Baronetcy*, in July 1687. He *m.*, when but a boy, Mary, da. of (—) Guy, *or* Gay, of Barbadoes.(a) He *d.* s.p., a widower, in Jamaica, and was *bur.* 14 Oct. 1690, at St. Catherine's there in his 17th year. Admon. 9 Aug. 1700 to a creditor.

V. 1690, to 1702. Sir Thomas Modyford, Baronet [1664], of "St. Jago de la Vega," Jamaica, br. and h., *b.* 10 March 1678/9; *suc. to the Baronetcy* in Oct. 1690. He *m.*, when under age, 12 June 1698, Jane da. and heir of Sir William Beeston, Governor of Jamaica (*d.* 3 Nov. 1702, aged 65), by Anne, da. of (—) Hopegood, *or* Goodhope. He *d.* s.p.m.(b), 30 July 1702, aged 23, and was *bur.* at St. Catherine's, Jamaica, when the *Baronetcy* became *extinct*. M.I. Will dat. 27 July 1702, pr. 13 Dec. 1703, and 7 June 1722. His widow *m.*, 27 May 1703, Charles Long, of Longville in Jamaica, and of Saxmundham, co. Suffolk (who *d.* 8 May 1723), and *d.* 29 June 1724, being *bur.* with him at St. Andrew's, Holborn, London. Her will pr. 1724.

SELBY:

cr. 3 March 1663/4;

ex. Sep. 1668.

I. 1664. "George Selby, of Whitehouse, co. Durham, Esq.," 2d but 1st surv. s. and h.(c) of Sir William Selby, of the same, and of Bolam, co. Northumberland, by Elizabeth, da. and h. of William Widdrington, suc. his father in 1649, and was *cr. a Baronet*, as above, 3 March 1663/4. He *m.* Mary, 2d and yst. da. of Richard (Molyneux), 1st Viscount Molyneux of Maryborough [I.], by Mary, da. of Sir Thomas Caryll. He *d.* Sep. 1668. His widow *m.* (as his third and last wife), Sir Edward Mostyn, 1st Baronet [1670], of Talacre, and was *bur.* 28 Jan. 1697/8, at St.-Giles-in-the-Fields. Admon. 27 June 1698, to her said husband.

II. 1668. Sir George Selby, Baronet [1664], of Whitehouse aforesaid, only s. and h., *suc. to the Baronetcy* in Sep. 1668, but *d.* in infancy the same day, an hour after his father, when the *Baronetcy* became *extinct*.

(a) In 1687/8 a caveat was lodged at the Vicar General's Office, London, against granting a licence to Sir Norton Modyford to marry Mary Gay without first consulting Mr. Chapman, Proctor.

(b) His two daughters, Annie Beeston and Mary, *d.* young and unm.

(c) His elder br. William Selby, *d.* v.p. and s.p., being slain in a duel, 4 Dec. 1636.

FORTESCUE:

cr. 31 March 1664;

ex. 27 Oct. 1683.

I. 1664. "Sir Edmund Fortescue, of Fallowpit [in East Allington], co. Devon, Knt.," 2d s. of Sir Edmund Fortescue, of the same [aged 10 at the Visit. of Devon, 1620], a well known Royalist Commander (*d.* v.p. before 1 March 1647/8, and *bur.* at Delft, in Holland), by Jane, da. of Thomas Southcott, of Mohun's Ottery, in that county, was *bap.* 22 Sep. 1642, at East Allington; suc. his grandfather, or, possibly, his elder br. John, in Feb. 1649/50; matric. at Oxford (Balliol Coll.), 9 Aug. 1658, and was *Knighted* and *cr. a Baronet*, as above, 31 March 1663/4. He was M.P. for Plympton, Oct. 1666, till his death three months later. He *m.*, in or before 1661, Margaret, 5th and yst. da. of Henry (Sandys), 5th Lord Sandys of the Vine, by Jane, da. of Sir William Sandys, of Missenden. He *d.* 20 Dec. 1666, aged 24, and was *bur.* at East Allington. M.I. Will dat. 14 Jan. 1664/5, pr. 10 Feb. 1667/8, and 2 June 1683. His widow *d.* May 1687. Will dat. 7, pr. 12 May 1687 and 14 Oct. 1709.

II. 1666, to 1683. Sir Sandys Fortescue, Baronet [1664], of Fallowpit aforesaid, only s. and h. *bap.* 6 July 1661, at East Allington; *suc. to the Baronetcy*, 20 Dec. 1666; matric. at Oxford (Exeter Coll.), 13 July 1677, aged 16. He *m.* (Lic. Fac. 23 May 1680, he 20 and she 18), Elizabeth, da. of Sir John Lenthall, of Besilsleigh, Berks. She was *bur.* 16 Jan. 1682/3, at East Allington, M.I. Admon. 2 June 1683, 23 Feb. 1683/4, and 28 May 1687. He *d.* s.p.m.(a) 27 Oct. and was *bur.* 2 Nov. 1683, at East Allington, in his 23d year, when the *Baronetcy* became *extinct*. M.I. Will pr. 23 Feb. 1683/4, and 20 Dec. 1709.

TUKE:

cr. 31 March 1664;

ex. 10 Aug. 1690.

I. 1664. "Samuel Tuke, of Cressing Temple, co. Essex, Esq.," [should be "Knight"], was presumably(b) a son of Thomas Tuke, of Layer Marney, co. Essex, and of Aldersgate street, London (grandson of Sir Brian Tuke), by his 2d wife, Judith (*m.* in or before 1612), da. of Edward North, of Walkeringham, Notts, and was probably *b.* about 1615; was in command on the Royalist side in 1644, being the eldest Colonel of Horse in 1645; was at the siege of Colchester, 1648; *Knighted*, 3 March 1663/4, and was *cr. a Baronet*, as above, 31 March 1664. He was a play writer and a minor poet. He *m.* firstly, in 1664, Mary, da. of Edward Guldeford, of Hemstead, co. Kent, "a kinswoman to my Lord Arundel of Wardour"(c). She *d.* 1666(c). He *m.* secondly, in 1668(c), Mary, "one of the dressers belonging to Queen Catherine"(d), da. of Edward Sheldon, of Ditchford, co. Warwick. He *d.*

(a) Elizabeth, his only da. and h. *m.* in or before 1696, Sir Thomas Seyliard, 3d Baronet [1661], and was *bur.* as his widow, 28 Dec. 1732, at Boxley, co. Kent. The Fallowpit estate, however, devolved on Edmund Fortescue (son of the late Baronet's great uncle, Peter), who *d.* s.p.m.s., 9 Jan. 1733/4, aged 74, leaving five daughters and coheirs.

(b) He is however identified in the *Dict. Nat. Biog.* with "Samuel Tuke, 3d son of George Tuke, of Frayting, Essex, Esq.," who (with his elder br. George, "s. and h." of the above George) entered Gray's Inn, 14 Aug. 1635.

(c) Evelyn's *Diary*, as quoted in the *Mis. Her. et Gen.* N.S., vol. i, 196.

(d) Wood's *Athenæ*, vol. ii, p. 802.

26 Jan, 1673/4, at Somerset House, Strand, Midx., and was *bur.* in the Chapel there. Will dat. 8 Jan. 1672/3, pr. 25 June 1674. His widow, who was accused in 1679 of complicity with the "Popish plot," went with the Queen Dowager to Portugal and *d.* there, 15 Jan. 1705, being *bur.* at Lisbon.

II. 1674, to 1690. SIR CHARLES TUKE, Baronet [1664], s. and h.(a) by 2d wife; *bap.* 19 Aug. 1671; *suc. to the Baronetcy,* 26 Jan. 1673/4. He was an officer in Tyrconnel's Regiment, fighting for James II in Ireland, where he *d.* unm. from wounds received at the battle of the Boyne, 10 Aug. 1690, aged 19, and was *bur.* at Drogheda, when the *Baronetcy* became *extinct.*

TEMPEST:

cr. 25 May 1664;

ex. 29 Jan. 1819.

I. 1664. "JOHN TEMPEST, of Tonge, co. York, Esq.," 3d but 1st surv. s. and h. of Henry TEMPEST, of the same, by Mary, da. of Nicholas BUSHEL, of Bagdell, in that county, was *b.* 1645; suc. his father in 1657, and was *cr. a Baronet,* as above, 25 May 1664. He entered his pedigree in the Her. Visit. of Yorkshire, 1666, being then aged 21. He *m.*, in or before Jan. 1664/5, Henrietta, da. of Sir Henry CHOLMELEY, of West Newton Grange, co. York, by Catharine, da. of Henry STAPLETON, of Wighill in that county. She, who was *b.* at Cumberland house, Clerkenwell Green, co. Midx., 24 and *bap.* 31 May 1645, at St. James', Clerkenwell, *d.* in London, 25 June 1680, and was *bur.*, with her parents, at West Newton. He *d.* 23 and was *bur.* 26 June 1693, at Tonge.

II. 1693. SIR GEORGE TEMPEST, Baronet [1664], of Tonge aforesaid, 4th but 1st surv. s. and h.(b), *bap.* 22 May 1672, at St. Michael's Belfry, York; matric. at Oxford (Univ. Coll.), 3 June 1690, aged 16; *suc. to the Baronetcy,* 23 June 1693. He rebuilt Tonge Hall in 1702. He *m.*, 19 Oct. 1694, at Campsall, co. York, Anne, da. and h. of Edward FRANK, *otherwise* ASHTON, of Campsall aforesaid. He was *bur.* 11 Oct. 1745, at Tonge, aged 73. Will (in which he passes over his eldest son, Henry) dat. 15 Aug. 1744, pr. 7 June 1755.(c) His widow, who was *bap.* 2 Dec. 1676, at Campsall, was *bur.* 13 Jan. 1745/6, at Tonge. Will dat. 6 Nov. 1745, pr. 29 Jan. 1745/6.

(a) According to a pedigree entered in the College of Arms and sworn to by Sir John Evelyn, Baronet, of Wotton, co. Surrey, 8 April 1742, who states that he is well acquainted with Teresa, widow of Charles Trinder, of Bourton on the Water, co. Glouc., only surv. sister and coheir of the last Baronet (and then residing at Ligny in the Duchy of Bar), there were two Baronets named Samuel, of whom the 2d *m.* Mary Sheldon, being *son* of the 1st Baronet by Mary Guldeford. No dates, however, are given, and the facts seem to have been as in the text.

(b) Of his elder brothers, John, *bap.* at Wath, co. York, 7 Jan. 1669/70, and George, *bap.* there 28 Nov. 1668, both died young, but Henry, the eldest son, *b.* at Newton, 22 Aug. 1666; matric. at Oxford (Univ. Coll.), 5 May 1682, aged 15; *m.*, in or before 1684, Alethea, da. of Sir Henry Thompson, and *d.* v.p. and s.p.m., 17 Nov. 1685, being *bur.* at St. Clements Danes, leaving two daughters, who inherited the estate of Newton Grange.

(c) He was suc. in the Tonge estates by his 2d son, Nicholas Tempest, *bap.* 12 May 1698, at Campsall, who *d.* s.p. and was *bur.* at Tonge, 18 Aug. 1755. To him suc. his nephew John Tempest, Major in the Royal Horse Guards, only s. of John Tempest, of Nottingham, who *d.* Oct. 1752. He also *d.* s.p. in Jan. 1786, when they devolved on his sister's son, John Plumbe, who took the name of Tempest.

III. 1745. SIR HENRY TEMPEST, Baronet [1664], of Campsall aforesaid, 1st s. and h., *bap.* there 1 Sep. 1696; matric. at Oxford (Univ. Coll.), 31 May 1714, aged 17; *suc. to the Baronetcy* in Oct. 1745. He *m.* 31 Aug. 1749, at St. Martin's, Oxtwich, London, Maria, da. of Francis HOLMES, of Wigston, co. Leicester. He *d.* 9 Nov. 1753, and was *bur.* at St. Pancras, Midx., aged 57. His widow *d.* 5 Feb. 1795. Admon. Feb. 1795.

IV. 1753, to 1819. SIR HENRY TEMPEST, Baronet [1664], of Campsall aforesaid, *afterwards* of Hope End, co. Hereford and of Thorpe Lee, co. Surrey, only s. and h., *b.* 13 Jan. 1753, *suc. to the Baronetcy* a few months later, 9 Nov. 1753; admitted to Lincoln's Inn, 28 Nov. 1775; Sheriff of Herefordshire, 1779. He *m.* 24 Jan. 1791, at St. Marylebone, Susanna Pritchard, da. and h. of Henry LAMBERT, of Hope End aforesaid, by (—) da. and h. of George PRITCHARD, of the same. He *d.* s.p. at Thorpe Lee, 29 Jan. 1819, in his 67th year, and was *bur.* at Thorpe, co. Surrey, when the *Baronetcy* became *extinct.* M.I. at Thorpe. Will dat. 10 Feb. 1815, pr. 27 Feb. 1819. The will of his widow was pr. Feb. 1825, and again Aug. 1833.

OSBALDESTON, *or* OSBOLDESTON:

cr. 25 June 1664;

ex. 7 April 1749.

I. 1664. "LITTLETON OSBOLDESTON [*rectius* OSBALDESTON] of Chadlington, co. Oxford, Esq.," 1st s. and h. ap. of John OSBALDESTON, of the same (living 1668, and then aged 66, but *d.* in or before 1688), by Joan, da. of SIR EDWARD LITTLETON, of Henley, co. Salop, was ed. at Mag. Coll. Oxford, being a Demy thereof, 1647, till ejected by the Parl. Visitors in 1648; was admitted to the Inner Temple, and was v.p. *cr. a Baronet,* as above, 25 June 1664. He entered his pedigree at the Her. Visit. of Oxon, 1668, and was M.P. for Woodstock (three Parls.), 1679-87. He *m.*, in or before 1658, Katharine, da. of Thomas BROWKER, of Sundridge, co. Kent, by Mary, da. of Thomas HAMON, of Brasted, in that county. He was *bur.* 30 Dec. 1691, at Chadlington. Will pr. 1692. His widow was *bur.* there 1 April 1695. Admon., as of "New Woodstock, Oxon," 5 April 1695.

II. 1691. SIR LACY OSBALDESTON, Baronet [1664], of Chadington aforesaid, 1st s. and h., *b.* about 1659, being aged 10 in 1668; matric. at Oxford (New Inn Hall), 10 Dec. 1678, and then called 17; *suc. to the Baronetcy* in Dec. 1691. He *m.*, in or before 1681, Elizabeth, da. and h. of William BLAGRAVE, of Whitehill, Oxon. He *d.* in or before 1699. Admon. 27 March 1699 to his widow. Her admon., as of "the city of Oxford," 3 Feb. 1701/2.

III. 1699? SIR RICHARD OSBALDESTON, Baronet [1664], of Chadlington aforesaid, 3d but 1st surv. s. and h.; *bap.* 14 Sep. 1684, at St. Ebb's, Oxford; *suc. to the Baronetcy* in or before 1699. He *d.* young and unm. in or before 1701. Admon. 15 July 1701 to his mother.

IV. 1701? SIR WILLIAM OSBALDESTON, Baronet [1664], of Chadlington aforesaid, br. and h., *b.* about 1687; *suc. to the Baronetcy,* in or before 1701; matric. at Oxford (Mag. Coll.) 23 May 1704, aged 17; *cr.* M.A. 13 Feb. 1707/8; admitted to the Inner Temple, 1705. He *m.*, in or after 1710, Catharine, widow of the Hon. Robert BERTIE (*d.* s.p. 16 Aug. 1710, aged 34), da. of Richard (WENMAN), VISCOUNT WENMAN OF TUAM [I.], by Catharine, da. and coheir of Sir Thomas CHAMBERLAINE, 2d Baronet [1643]. She *d.* 18 Sep. 1736. Admon. 7 Sep. 1737 to her said husband. He *d.* s.p.m.s., in or before 1739. Will pr. 1740.

V. 1739? to 1749. SIR CHARLES OSBALDESTON, Baronet [1664], of Chadlington aforesaid, br. and h. male; *b.* probably about 1690; *suc. to the Baronetcy* in or before 1739. He *m.* firstly (—). She was *bur.* 2 Aug. 1739, at St. Ebb's, Oxford. He *m.* secondly, Sophia, da. of (—) MOORE. He *d.* s.p. 16 April 1749, and was *bur.* at St. Ebb's aforesaid, when the *Baronetcy* became *extinct.* His widow was *bur.* 29 April 1750, as "Lady Osbalson, Sophia More," at St. Pancras, co. Midx.

TOOKER:

cr. 1 July 1664;

ex. 17 March 1675/6.

I. 1664, to 1676. "GILES TOOKER, of Maddington, co. Wilts, Esq.," only s. and h. ap. of Edward TOOKER, of the same (*d.* 1688, aged 86), by Mary, da. of Sir John HUNGERFORD, of Down Ampney, co. Wilts., was *b.* about 1625; admitted to Linc. Inn ("at the request of William EYRE, now Reader"), 16 Aug. 1633; matric. at Oxford (Exeter Coll)., 1 April 1642, aged 17, and was *cr. a Baronet,* as above, 1 July 1664. He *m.* Mary, da. of Sir Edmund PRIDEAUX, Attorney General, 1649-59 (*cr. a Baronet* by the Lord Protector Cromwell, 13 Aug. 1658), by his 2d wife Margaret, da. and coheir of William IVERY, of Cotthay, co. Somerset. He *d.* s.p. and v.p., 17 March 1675/6, when the *Baronetcy* became *extinct.* Will pr. 1678. The will of his widow (who was *bap.* 19 Jan. 1628/9, at Ottery St. Mary, Devon) pr. Nov. 1690.

ANDERSON:

cr. 13 July 1664;

ex. 17 Feb. 1773.

I. 1664. "STEPHEN ANDERSON, of Eyworth, co. Bedford, Esq.," 1st s. and h. ap. of Stephen ANDERSON(a), of the same (living June 1664), by Catharine, da. of Sir Edwyn SANDYS, of Ombersley, co. Worcester, was *b.* about 1644 and was *cr. a Baronet,* as above, 13 July 1664. Sheriff of Beds, 6 to 20 Dec. 1694. He *m.* firstly, 2 June 1664, at St. Giles'-in-the-Fields (Lic. Fac. 1, he aged 20, and she 15), Mary, sister of Sir William GLYNNE, 1st Baronet [1661], da. of Sir John GLYNNE, sometime (1655) Lord Chief Justice of the Upper Bench, by his 2d wife, Anne, relict of Sir Thomas LAWLEY, 1st Baronet [1641], da. and coheir of John MANNING, of Hackney, co. Midx. She *d.* 25 and was *bur.* 27 Feb. 1667/8, at Eyworth. M.I. He *m.* secondly, 8 April 1673, at Hackney, (Lic. Vic. Gen. 5, he about 28 and she about 23), Judith, da. of Sir John LAURENCE, sometime (1665-66) Lord Mayor of London, by his 1st wife Abigail, sister of Sir Abraham CULLEN, 1st Baronet [1661], da. of Abraham CULLEN, of London, Merchant. She, who was *bap.* 4 May 1648, at St. Helen's, Bishopsgate, London, was *bur.* there 10 May 1688. He *d.* at St. Andrew's Holborn, 19 and was *bur.* 28 Jan. 1706/7, at Eyworth. M.I. Admon. 2 April 1707.

II. 1707. SIR STEPHEN ANDERSON, Baronet [1664], of Eyworth aforesaid, only s. and h. by 2d wife; *bap.* 1 Oct. 1678, at St. Helen's aforesaid; matric. at Oxford (Univ. Coll.), 27 April 1696, aged 17; *suc. to the Baronetcy,* 19 Jan. 1706/7. He *m.* in or before 1707, Anne, da. of Sir Martin

---

(a) This Stephen was 2d s. but h. male of Sir Francis Anderson, of Eyworth (*d.* 22 Dec. 1616), who was s. of Sir Edmund Anderson, of the same and of Broughton, co. Lincoln, Lord Chief Justice of the Common Pleas, 1582-1605, ancestor of Sir John Anderson, Baronet [1629], of St. Ives, and of Sir Edmund Anderson, of Broughton, Baronet [1660].

LUMLEY, 3d Baronet [1641], by his 1st wife, Elizabeth, da. of Sir Jonathan DAWES, Alderman and sometime (1671-72), Sheriff of London. She who was *bap.* 6 Sep. 1684, at Great Bardfield, co. Essex, *d.* at St. Andrew's, Holborn, 27 Oct. and was *bur.* 12 Nov. 1719, at Eyworth. Admon. 9 Sep. 1720. He *d.* 21 and was *bur.* 30 Oct. 1741, at Eyworth, aged 63. Will, as of "St. George's, Bloomsbury," dat. 7 May and pr. 3 Nov. 1741.

III. 1741, to 1773. SIR STEPHEN ANDERSON, Baronet [1664], of Eyworth aforesaid, 1st s. and h., *bap.* 15 Nov. 1708, at St. Andrew's, Holborn; *suc. to the Baronetcy,* 21 Oct. 1741. He *m.* firstly, 27 Jan. 1731/2, Elizabeth, only da. of Miles BARNE, of London, Merchant. She *d.* 9 and was *bur.* 26 April 1769, at Eyworth. He *m.* secondly, 2 April 1771, at Haddington, in Scotland, Mary, da. of William ELSEGOOD, of Norwich. He *d.* s.p.s.(a) 19 and was *bur.* 28 Feb. 1773, at Eyworth, aged 64, when the *Baronetcy* became *extinct.*(b) Will dat. 24 Feb. 1772, pr. 25 Feb. 1773, and 28 July 1787. His widow, *m.* 30 March 1773, as his 1st wife, Rear Admiral the Hon. Thomas SHIRLEY, of Horkston Hall, co. Lincoln (yr. br. of the 6th EARL FERRERS), who *d.* s.p. 7 April 1814, aged 81. She *d.* 1808. Will pr. 1808.

BATEMAN:

cr. 31 Aug. 1664;

ex. Oct. 1685.

I. 1664, to 1685. "THOMAS BATEMAN, of How [*i.e.*, Hoo] Hall, co. Norfolk, Esq.," 5th and yst. s. of Robert BATEMAN [*bap.* 8 Sep. 1561, at Hartington, co. Derby], of Mincing lane, St. Dunstan's in the East, London (*bur.* there 31 Dec. 1644), Alderman, and sometime Chamberlain of London, being his 4th s. by his 2d wife, Elizabeth, da. and coheir of John WESTROW, of London, was *bap.* 29 Sep. 1622, at St. Dunstan's aforesaid; was a Merchant of London, residing in Coleman street, was Alderman of Walbrook in that city, 17 April 1662 till dismissed in 1664; was Sheriff of Cambridgeshire and Hunts, 1657-58, and, having purchased estates in Norfolk, was *cr. a Baronet,* as above, 31 Aug. 1664. He, with his two brothers, Sir William BATEMAN and Sir Anthony BATEMAN, sometime [1664] Lord Mayor of London, suffered severe loss from the great fire of London, in 1666. He *m.* Elizabeth, da. and h. of (—) MIDDLETON, sometimes (but apparently in error) said to have been Sheriff of Cambridgeshire and Hunts. She was *bur.* 19 May 1679, at St. Margaret's, Lothbury. He *d.* s.p.m.s. and was *bur.* there 13 Oct. 1685, when the *Baronetcy* became *extinct.*

LORAINE, *or* LORRAINE(c):

cr. 26 Sep. 1664.

I. 1664. "THOMAS LORRAINE [*rectius* LORAINE], of Kirkhall [*i.e.*, Kirkharle Tower, in Kirkharle], co. Northumberland, Esq.,"(d) only s. and h. of Thomas LORAINE, of the same, by Elizabeth, relict of William BEWICKE, in that county, da. of Henry MADDISON, of Newcastle-upon-Tyne, was

---

(a) Stephen, his only child, by his 1st wife, *d.* young.

(b) The Eyworth estate reverted to the heirs male of the body of Francis Anderson, of Manby, co. Lincoln (*d.* 15 April 1706, aged 63), yr. br. of the 1st Baronet, and ancestor of the Earls of Yarborough.

(c) The present [1903] Baronet has kindly supplied much of the information contained in this article.

(d) The patent, from which this description (rendered in English) is taken, is in the possession of the present [1903] Baronet. "Kirkhall" is manifestly an error for "Kirkharle," which in a deed, dated 1333, is spelt "Kyrke*herle*," being at that date a Lordship in possession of Chief Justice de *Herle*, but which in 1425 (as computed from a deed affecting it, dated 1456) belonged to the family of Loraine. As to the spelling of the name of that family, the present (1903)

b. 1638(a); suc. his father (who *d.* aged 35), 24 Oct. 1649; admitted to Christ's Coll., Cambridge, 11 June 1655, and to Gray's Inn, 10 Feb. 1656/7; was a strong loyalist and Churchman, and was *cr. a Baronet*, as above, 26 Sep. 1664. He refused assent to the repeal of the Penal laws and Test Act, as proposed by James II. He *m.*, 4 June 1657, at Hexham Abbey (before "Wm. Fenwicke, Esq.," J.P.), Grace, 1st da. of Sir William Fenwick, 2d Baronet [1628], by Jane, da. of Henry Stapleton, of Wighill, co. York. By the death, s.p.s., of her br., Sir John Fenwick, 3d Baronet (who was executed for high treason, 27 Jan. 1696/7), she became his heir. She *d.* 2 Dec. 1706. He *d.* 10 Jan. 1717/8, both being *bur.* at Kirkharle. M.I. His will dat. 29 Aug. 1717, was pr. at Durham.

II. 1718. Sir William Loraine, Baronet [1664], of Kirkharle aforesaid, s. and h., *b.* shortly before Sep. 1658; admitted to Lincoln's Inn, 18 June 1678; Barrister, 19 May 1692; was M.P. for Northumberland, 1701-02; *suc. to the Baronetcy*, 10 Jan. 1717/8, when aged 60. He added to and much improved the estate, built a new mansion "of his own plan and contrivance," remodelled the gardens(b), restored the church, etc. He *m.* firstly, about 1687, Elizabeth, da. of Sir John Lawrence, of St. Helen's, London, sometime (1664-65) Lord Mayor of London, by Abigail, sister of Sir Abraham Cullen, 1st Baronet [1661]. She, who was *b.* 23 Oct. and *bap.* 14 Nov. 1654, at St. Helen's aforesaid, *d.* s.p. 1690. He *m.* secondly, in 1692, Anne, sister of Richard Smith, of Enderby, co. Leic. (a follower of Charles II in his exile), only da. of Richard Smith, of Preston, Bucks. He *d.* 22 and was *bur.* 25 Jan. 1743/4, aged 84. Will dat. 11 Jan. 1734/5 to 19 Feb. 1740/1, pr. at Durham. His widow *d.* 24 Sep. 1756, aged 88. Her will dat. 17 Sep. 1753, pr., at Durham, 27 Sep. 1755. Both were *bur.* at Kirkharle. M.I.

III. 1744. Sir Charles Loraine, Baronet [1664], of Kirkharle aforesaid, 5th but only surv. s. and h.,(c) by the 2d wife; *b.* 1701; admitted to Christ's Coll., Cambridge, 4 July 1723; Scholar, 1727; LL.B., 1728; *suc. to the Baronetcy*, 22 Jan. 1743/4; Sheriff of Northumberland 1744. He *m.* firstly (settlement dat. 7 and bond(d) dat. 19 Feb. 1733), Margaret, da. of Ralph Lambton, of Lambton Hall, co. Durham, by Dorothy, da. and coheir of John Hedworth. She *d.* s.p.m. 30 June 1746, aged 42, and was *bur.* at Kirkharle. M.I. He *m.* secondly, at Ebchester, 22 Aug. 1748, Dorothy, da. and eventually h. of Ralph Mylott, *or* Millott, of Whitehill, co. Durham, by Isabell, da. of (—) Hixon. He *d.* 29 April and was *bur.* 4 May 1755, at Kirkharle. M.I. Will dat. 4 June 1754, pr. 3 Jan. 1757, at Durham. His widow *d.* 17 March 1787, aged 85, and was *bur.* at Kirkharle. M.I.

Baronet writes that "the early immigrants from the Duchy of Lorraine [Lotharii regnum, Lotharregne, Loharregne, Lorregne, Lorreyne or Lorraine] were styled *de Lorraine*, spelt anyhow [Lohereng, Lorens, Loreyn, de Loreyn, Loreyns, Loran, Loren, Deloraine, Lorayne, de la Reyne, Lorraigne, Lorreyne, Lorrane, Lorran, and even Lawrans]. The double R is chiefly met with in English deeds at the end of the sixteenth and in the seventeenth century. The 1st Baronet's father, in a conveyance (now [1903] at Belsay Castle), is styled therein *Thomas Lorran*, but signs it as *Thomas Loreyne*. The signature of the 1st Baronet as 'Tho. Loraine,' exists in the Visitation entry of his pedigree, 1666; in a letter to the Lord Lieut. of the County about the Test Act, 1688, and in his will, 1717."

(a) John Cosin, afterwards (1660-72) the well known Bishop of Durham, was his godfather.

(b) Lancelot Brown ("Capability Brown,") the well known Landscape Gardener and Architect, a native of Kirkharle (*b.* 1715, *d.* 6 Feb. 1783), had his first employment as gardener under him, till 1739, when he left for Stowe.

(c) Thomas, the 1st s. was *bur.* 1695 at St. Clement Danes', Midx., aged three weeks. William, the 2d s. was *bur.* 1705, at Mitford, Northumberland. John, the 3d s. was *bur.* there 1703/4, and Richard, the 4th s., who, after 1705, was the heir ap., *d.* 1738, at Newington, and was *bur.* at Kirkharle. M.I.

(d) The bond mentions either Chester le Street or the chapel of Harrowton [Harraton] as the place for the prospective marriage, but in neither place is there any registration thereof.

IV. 1755. Sir William Loraine, Baronet [1664], of Kirkharle aforesaid, s. and h. by 2d wife, *b.* 17 June 1749; *suc. to the Baronetcy* (when five years old), 29 April 1755; ed. at Eton; admitted to Christ's Coll., Cambridge, 16 Dec. 1767; Sheriff of Northumberland, 1774-75, and for some time Vice-Lieut. thereof. During the financial crisis of 1793 (consequent on the French Revolution), when the chief landowners of the vicinity combined together to support the credit of the Newcastle banks, he for that purpose joined one of them, and rendered his estate liable to the losses sustained. He pulled down the village of Kirkharle and rebuilt it. He *m.* firstly, 19 Oct. 1776 at Simonburn, Hannah, da. of Sir Lancelot Allgood, of Nunwick, co. Northumberland, by Jane, da. and h. of Robert Allgood, of Nunwick aforesaid. She *d.* 5 and was *bur.* 11 June 1797, at Kirkharle. M.I. He *m.* secondly, 5 Nov. 1799, at St. Margaret's, Westm., Frances, only surv. da. and h. of Francis (or François) Campart, of Kensington, Midx.(a) He *d.* 19 and was *bur.* 26 Dec. 1809, at Kirkharle, aged 60. M.I. Will dat. 13 June 1808, pr. 12 May 1810, at Durham. His widow *d.* at Newcastle, 21 Oct. 1811, aged 39, and was *bur.* at Kirkharle aforesaid. M.I.

V. 1809. Sir Charles Loraine, Baronet [1664], of Kirkharle aforesaid, s. and h., by 1st wife; *b.* 19 April 1779; ed. at Rugby (1791), and at Durham College; was for five years an officer in the Horse Guards (Blues); *suc. to the Baronetcy*, 19 Dec. 1809, as also to his father's partnership in the Tyne Bank, at Newcastle, which, after the crisis of 1815, closed its doors in 1816, though all liabilities were ultimately paid. He was Sheriff of Northumberland, 1814-15. He *m.* 26 June 1800, at Chiswick, Midx., Elizabeth, only da. of Vincent Campart, of Chiswick. She *d.* at Tynemouth, 5 Aug. 1829, aged 53. Will pr. Dec. 1829. He *d.* 18 Jan. 1833, aged also 53. Both were *bur.* at Kirkharle. M.I. His will dat. 9 Jan. was pr. 13 March 1833, at Durham.

VI. 1833. Sir William Loraine, Baronet [1664], of Kirkharle aforesaid, s. and h., *b.* 9 April 1801; ed. at Richmond School, Yorkshire, and at Edinburgh; admitted to Christ's Coll., Cambridge, 12 June 1820; was seven and half years an officer in the 39th Foot; *suc. to the Baronetcy*, 18 Jan. 1833. In consequence of the debts of the Newcastle Bank abovenamed, he was obliged, in 1834, to sell the estate of Kirkharle, which had been more than 400 years in the family.(b) He *d.* unm. at Elsinore, in Denmark, 29 May, and was *bur.* 2 June 1849, in the cemetery there, aged 48. M.I. Will, written in Danish, dat. 11 Sep. 1844, at Elsinore, pr. at York 18 Sep. 1849.

VII. 1849. Sir Charles Vincent Loraine, Baronet [1664], br. and h., *b.* 20 July 1807, at Kirkharle; sometime, after 1831, Capt. in the Northumberland Militia, residing at Kirkharle till 1834, but later on in France; *suc. to the Baronetcy*, 29 May 1849. He *m.* about 1842 Mary, da. of (—), who survived him. He *d.* s.p.s. at Lambeth, co. Surrey, 19 Aug. 1850, aged 43. Will dat. 24 Oct. 1849, pr. 15 May 1851 at Durham, by his widow.

VIII. 1850. Sir Henry Claude Loraine, Baronet [1664], br. and h., *b.* 4 April 1812 at Kirkharle where he resided till 1834; *suc. to the Baronetcy*, 19 Aug. 1850. He *d.* unm. 4 Jan. 1851, aged 38, in the Isle of Man, and was *bur.* at Ballure, near Ramsey in that Island. M.I. Will dat. 17 Feb. 1844, pr. 3 Feb. 1851, at Durham, by Sir William Loraine, 9th Baronet.

(a) The wife of this Francis Campart (mother of Lady Loraine) was sister of the *wife* of James Vere, of Kensington Gore, Banker, a lady well known in London society. [*Ex inform.* Sir L. Loraine, Baronet.]

(b) See p. 295, note "d."

IX. 1851, Jan. Sir William Loraine, Baronet [1664], uncle and h. male, being 2d s. of the 4th Baronet; *b.* 10 Oct. 1780, and *bap.* at Kirkharle; ed. at Rugby (1791) and at Durham Coll. He was associated with his father and eldest br. in the Newcastle Bank till 1816; *suc. to the Baronetcy*, 4 Jan. 1851. He *d.* unm. 1 March 1851, aged 70, at Newcastle, and was *bur.* in the cemetery at Jesmond, near there. M.I.

X. 1851, March. Sir John Lambton Loraine, Baronet [1664], br. and h., *b.* 30 July 1784, at Newcastle; resided on the Kirkharle estate during the tenure of his eldest br., the 5th Baronet (1809-33); was sometime an officer in the Northumberland Yeomanry, and subsequently resided at Fawdon Lodge, Northumberland; *suc. to the Baronetcy*, 1 March 1851. He *m.* 24 Feb. 1835, at Morpeth, Caroline Isabella, 1st da. of the Rev. Frederick Ekins, Rector of Morpeth and Ulgham, by Jane Ogle, da. and coheir of James Tyler, of Whalton, Northumberland. She *d.* 28 Feb. 1847, aged 42, and was *bur.* in the cemetery of Jesmond aforesaid. M.I. He *d.* in Jersey 11 and was *bur.* 19 July 1852, at St. Saviour's in that island, in his 68th year.

XI. 1852. Sir Lambton Loraine, Baronet [1664], of Bramford Hall, in Bramford, co. Suffolk, 1st s. and h., *b.* 17 Nov. 1838, at Fawdon Lodge aforesaid; ed. at Burlington House School, Fulham; *suc. to the Baronetcy*, 11 July 1852(a); entered the Royal Navy, 1852, receiving the freedom of the city of New York for services at Santiago de Cuba in the "Virginius" affair in 1873, and becoming Rear Admiral, 29 Nov. 1889. Chairman of Committee of the Society styled "*the Hon. Society of the Baronetage.*" He *m.* 22 Oct. 1878, at St. Peter's, Eaton square, Frederica Mary Horatia, yr. da. and coheir of Charles Acton Broke, Capt. R.E., by Anna Maria, da. of John Hamilton, of Sundrum, co. Ayr, which Charles was yr. s. of Admiral Sir Philip Bowes Vere Broke, 1st Baronet [1813].

Family Estates.—These, from about 1425 to 1834, consisted of between 2,000 and 3,000 acres in Northumberland and Durham, being the Kirkharle estate, of about 2,000 acres and other lands. In 1903 they consisted of 287 acres (with colliery) in Northumberland, 177 in Northamptonshire, and 2,000 in Suffolk, besides about 1,550 acres in the Colony of Natal. *Principal Residence.*—Bramford Hall, Suffolk.

WENTWORTH:

cr. 27 Sep. 1664;

afterwards, 1777 ? to 1792, Blackett;

ex. 10 July 1792.

I. 1664. "Thomas Wentworth, of Bretton, co. York, Esq.," 2d s. of George Wentworth, of West Bretton aforesaid (*bur.* at Silkstone 7 June 1638, in his 63d year), by Mary, da. of John Ashburnham, of Ashburnham, co. Sussex, was *b.* about 1615; suc. his elder br., William Wentworth, 22 Oct. 1642; was Col. of Foot and Lieut.-Col. of Horse in the service of Charles I., during the Civil War; compounded, as a Royalist; was fined £350, and was *cr. a Baronet*, as above, 27 Sep. 1664, with a spec. rem., failing his own male issue, to his brother Matthew Wentworth and the heirs male of his body. He entered his pedigree in the Her. Visit. of Yorkshire 1665, being then as alleged "aged 56," and Capt. of Horse in the trained bands for the West Riding. He *m.* Grace, da. and h. of Francis Popeley, of Morehouse, co. York, by Elizabeth, da. and h. of John Gomersal, of Gomersal. He *d.* s.p. 5 and was *bur.* 8 Dec. 1675, at Silkstone, "aged 60." M.I. His widow *m.* 2 Feb. 1678/9, as the 2d of his three wives, Alexander (Montgomerie) 8th Earl of Eglintoun [S.] and *d.* 30 March being *bur.* 2 April 1698, at Silkstone. Will dat. 18 April 1698.

(a) He is the 5th of five successive Baronets who inherited that dignity in the space of about three years, *viz.*, from May 1849, to July 1852.

II. 1675. Sir Matthew Wentworth, Baronet [1664], of Bretton aforesaid, br. and h. male; *suc. to the Baronetcy*, 5 Dec. 1675, according to the spec. limitation of that dignity. He *m.* firstly, 23 Sep. 1641, at Leeds, Judith, da. of Cotton Horn. She *d.* s.p. and was *bur.* 10 March 1643, at St. Michael's le Belfrey, York. He *m.* secondly, before 1663, Judith, widow of Samuel Thorpe, of Hopton, da. of Thomas Rhodes, of Flockton. She was living 1663. He *m.* thirdly, 18 Sep. 1676, at Hunmanby, Anne, 1st da. of William Osbaldeston, of Hunmanby, co. York, by Anne, 1st da. and coheir of Sir George Wentworth, of Wolley in that county. He *d.* 1 Aug. 1678 and was *bur.* at Silkstone. M.I. His widow, who was *bap.* 19 March 1656, at Hunmanby, *m.* 8 July 1680, Sir William Hustler, of Acklam.

III. 1678. Sir Mathew Wentworth, Baronet [1664], of Bretton aforesaid, only s. and h., by 2d wife, *b.* after 1663, probably about 1665; *suc. to the Baronetcy*, 1 Aug. 1678. He *m.*, 22 May 1677, at Hunmanby, Elizabeth (sister of his step mother), 2d da. of William Osbaldeston by Anne, da. of Sir George Wentworth, all three abovenamed. She, who was *bap.* 13 April 1658, at Hunmanby, was *bur.* 22 Jan. 1693/4, at Silkstone. He *d.* Feb. and was *bur.* there, 1 March 1705/6. Will dat. 22 Feb. 1703/4, pr. 23 July 1706, at York.

IV. 1706. Sir William Wentworth, Baronet [1664], of Bretton aforesaid, 2d but 1st surv. s. and h., *bap.* 29 Oct. 1686, at York Minster; *suc. to the Baronetcy* in Feb. 1705/6; was M.P. for Malton, 1731-41. He *m.*, 23 June 1720, at St. Paul's Cathedral, London, Diana, sister and coheir (Sep. 1728) of Sir William Blackett, 2d Baronet [1685], of Wallington and Hexham, co. Northumberland, 7th da. of Sir William Blackett, 1st Baronet [1685], of Newcastle, by Julia, da. of Sir Christopher Conyers, 1st Baronet [1628]. She, by whom he had nine children, was *bur.* 14 April 1742, at St. Martin's, Coney street, York. He *d.* 1 March 1763, and was *bur.* at Bretton, aged 76. M.I.

V. 1763, to 1792. Sir Thomas Wentworth, *afterwards*, 1777 ? to 1792, Blackett, Baronet [1664], of Bretton aforesaid, 3d but only surv. s. and h., *bap.* 12 April 1726, at St. Martin's aforesaid; *suc. to the Baronetcy*, 1 March 1763; Sheriff of Yorkshire, 1765-66. Having suc. to the estates at Hexham, etc., of his mother's family, presumably on the death, in 1777, of Sir Walter Calverley-Blackett, *formerly* Calverley, 2d Baronet [1711], he assumed the name of *Blackett* instead of that of *Wentworth*. He *d.* unm., 10 July 1792, in his 67th year, and was *bur.* at Bretton, when the *Baronetcy* became *extinct*. M.I. Will dat 29 May 1792(a).

BIDDULPH:

cr. 2 Nov. 1664.

I. 1664. "Sir Theophilus Biddulph, of Westcombe [Manor, in Greenwich], co. Kent, Knt.," as also of Elmhurst, in St. Chad's, *otherwise* Stow Church, in Lichfield, 3d s. of Michael Biddulph, of Elmhurst, afore-

---

(a) In it he devises the chief part of his Yorkshire and Northumberland estates (valued at more than £40,000 a year), viz., that of Bretton and of Hexham to the eldest of his three illegit. daughters, Diana, wife of Thomas Richard Beaumont, whose son, Thomas Wentworth Beamount, died possessed of them in 1849, leaving issue. There was a remainder to two other of his illegit. daughters, Sophia, who *m.* William Lee, of Grove Hall, co. York, and Louisa (then unm.), who *m.* William Stackpoole, of Instowe, co. Devon. These two enjoyed a rent charge on the estate of £3,000 a year. The estate of Gunneston, however, devolved on his nephew, William Bosville, of Gunthewaite, co. York (only son of his eldest sister Diana), who *d.* s.p. in 1813, devising his estates to the children of his sister, Elizabeth Diana, Baroness Macdonald [I.]

said (*d.* 20 Jan. 1657), by Elizabeth, da. of Sir William Skeffington, 1st Baronet [1627], was *b.* probably about 1615(a); was Citizen and Mercer of London, and a Silkman in Cheapside; M.P. for London, 1656-58 and 1659; for Lichfield, 1661-79; *Knighted* in 1660, and was *cr. a Baronet*, as above, 2 Nov. 1664. He *m.* 10 May 1641, at Morden, co. Surrey, Susanna, 1st da. of Zachary Highlord, Alderman of London, by Frances, da. of George Garth, of Morden aforesaid. He *d.* at Greenwich and was *bur.* thence 11 April 1683, at Stow Church aforesaid. Will dat. 30 April 1681, pr. 8 May 1683. His widow was *bur.* from Greenwich, 17 Nov. 1702, at Stow Church. Will pr. Nov. 1702.

II. 1683. Sir Michael Biddulph, Baronet [1664], of Elmhurst and Westcombe aforesaid, *b.* about 1652, being aged 11 in 1663; *suc. to the Baronetcy* in April 1683; was M.P. for Lichfield, 1679-81, 1689-90, 1695-1705, and 1708-10. He *m.* firstly, 31 Dec. 1673, in Westm. Abbey (Lic. Fac. 30, he of Greenwich, aged 24 and she aged 20), Henrietta Maria, da. of Richard Witley, then of St. Helen's, London, Colonel in the Army, afterwards of Peel, co. Chester, by Charlotte, da. of Sir Charles Gerard, of Halsall, co. Lancaster. She ("a fortune of £8,000"), was *bur.* 15 Sep. [*rectius* 15 Oct.] 1689, in Westm. Abbey. He *m.* secondly, 7 March 1697/8, at Battersea, co. Surrey (Lic. Vic. Gen.), Elizabeth, da. of William D'Oyly, of St. Martin's-in-the-Fields, Milliner, by Elizabeth Rudyard. He *d.* 20 April and was *bur.* 1 May 1718, at Greenwich. Will dat. 22 June 1706 to 6 June 1709, pr. 26 May 1719, devising the manor of Westcombe to his widow, by whom it was sold. She *d.* s.p.m., April 1740, at Sonning, Berks. Will dat. 28 July 1738, pr. May 1740.

III. 1718. Sir Theophilus Biddulph, Baronet [1664], of Elmhurst aforesaid, only s. and h., by 1st wife; *b.* probably about 1685; *suc. to the Baronetcy* 20 April 1718. He *m.* Cary, 5th and yst. da. of Sir Charles Lyttelton, 3d Baronet [1618], of Frankley, by his 2d wife, Anne, da. and coheir of Thomas Temple, of Frankton, co. Warwick. She *d.* at Elmhurst 18 April 1741. He *d.* there s.p., 16 May 1743.

IV. 1743. Sir Theophilus Biddulph, Baronet [1664], of Birdingbury, co. Warwick, cousin and h. male, being s. and h. of Edward Biddulph, of the same, by Anne, da. of Edward Birch, of Leacroft, which Edward Biddulph was s. and h. of Simon Biddulph, also of Birdingbury, the 4th s. of the 1st Baronet. He was *b.* about 1720; matric. at Oxford (Univ. Coll.), 26 June 1736, aged 16, and *suc. to the Baronetcy*, 16 May 1743. He *m.* about 1748, Jane, da. and h. of his uncle, the Rev. Michael Biddulph, M.A., Preb. of Lichfield [1727], Rector of Ripple, and Vicar of Blockley, co. Worcester, by (—) da. of (—). He *d.* in or before 1798. Will pr. 1798. His widow *d.* at Southampton, 14 Aug. 1818, aged 93. Will pr. Oct. 1818.

V. 1798? Sir Theophilus Biddulph, Baronet [1664], of Birdingbury aforesaid, 1st s. and h., *b.* 28 March 1757; admitted to Rugby School, 16 April 1765; matric. at Oxford (Univ. Coll.), 30 March 1775, aged 18; *suc. to the Baronetcy* in or shortly before 1798. He *m.* in 1784, Hannah, da. of Edward Prestridge. She *d.* 1824. He *d.* 30 July 1841, at Ryde in the Isle of Wight, aged 84. Will pr. Sep. 1841.

VI. 1841. Sir Theophilus Biddulph, Baronet [1664], of Birdingbury aforesaid, 1st s. and h., *b.* 28 and *bap.* 31 March 1785, at East Barnet, Herts; admitted to Rugby School, 1798; matric. at Oxford (Oriel Coll.), 9 March 1803, aged 17; was Lieut. in the 6th Enniskillen Dragoons, being present at the battle of Waterloo, 1815; *suc. to the Baronetcy*, 30 July 1841; Sheriff of Warwickshire, 1849. He *m.* 12 April 1825, at Wappenbury, co.

(a) His elder br., Michael, who was *bap.* 6 Nov. 1610, at Elford, entered his ped. at the Her. Visit. of Staffordshire, in 1663, being then aged 52. He *d.* s.p. and was *bur.* at Stowe Church, 3 Nov. 1666. The next br., George Biddulph, Merchant of London, was living, apparently, unm. in 1663.

Warwick, Jane Rebecca, da. of Robert Vyner, of Eathorpe in that county, Barrister, by Laura, only child of Philips Glover, of Wispington, co. Lincoln. She, who was *b.* 2 Oct. 1802, *d.* 19 March 1843, at Birdingbury Hall. He *d.* 15 July 1854, aged 68. Will pr. Sep. 1854.

VII. 1854. Sir Theophilus William Biddulph, Baronet [1664], of Birdingbury aforesaid, only s. and h., *b.* 18 Jan. 1830, at Nursling, Hants.; ed. at Eton; matric. at Oxford (Trin. Coll.), 1 Dec. 1847, aged 17; B.A., 1850; *suc. to the Baronetcy*, 15 July 1854; Major 2d Warwick Militia, 1855-58; Lieut. in Warwick Yeomanry, 1861-70. He *m.*, 18 June 1872, at St. Mary's, Bryanston square, Marylebone, Mary Agnes, sister and coheir of Hugh (Somerville), 18th Lord Somerville [S.], 3d da. of Kenelm, the 17th Lord, by Frances Louisa, da. of John Hayman. He *d.* 1 March 1883, at Mentone, and was *bur.* at Birdingbury. His widow, who was *b.* 19 Dec. 1837, *d.* 16 June 1889, at South Parade, Southsea, Hants.

VIII. 1883. Sir Theophilus George Biddulph, Baronet [1664], of Birdingbury aforesaid, *b.* 3 April 1874, at Mentone aforesaid; *suc. to the Baronetcy*, 1 March 1883.

Family Estates.—These, in 1883, were under 2,000 acres.

GREENE:

cr. 2 Nov. 1664;

ex. Oct. 1671.

I. 1664. "William Greene, of Micham [*i.e.*, Mitcham], co. Surrey, Esq.," who fined for Alderman and Sheriff of London, being possibly the "William Greene of the city of London, Esq.," who was admitted to Gray's Inn, 12 Feb. 1637/8, was *cr. a Baronet*, as above, 2 Nov. 1664; was Sheriff of Surrey, 1667-68. He *m.* (—), but *d.* s.p.m.(a) and was *bur.* 12 Oct. 1671, at Mitcham, when the *Baronetcy* become *extinct*. Will pr. Dec. 1671.

COOKES:

cr. 24 Dec. 1664;

ex. 8 June 1701.

I. 1664. "William Cookes, of Norgrave [*i.e.*, Norgrove, in Feckenham], co. Worcester, Esq.," and of Bentley Pauncefote, in Tardebig, in the same county, s. and h. of Edward Cookes, of the same,(b) by Mary, da. of Nicholas Cotton, of Hornchurch, co. Essex, Barrister, was *b.* probably about 1618; suc. his father 7 April 1637, and "for his zeal in support of the Royal cause," was *cr. a Baronet*, as above, 24 Dec. 1664; was Sheriff of co. Worcester, 1665-66. He *m.* firstly, Anne, da. and coheir of his uncle, John Cookes, of Tookeys farm, in Feckenham aforesaid, by Alice, da. of William Edmonds, of Wibheath, in Tardebig. She *d.* s.p. He *m.* secondly, in or before 1648, Mercy, da. of Edward Dineley, of Charlton in Cropthorn, co. Worcester, by Joyce, da. of Sir Samuel Sandys, of Ombersley. He *d.* in or before 1672, aged about 56. Will pr. 1672. His widow *m.* his 1st cousin, Mark Dineley of Norborow, co. Worcester (who *d.* s.p. at Evesham, 10 Sep. 1682), and was living 1683.

(a) Gertrude, his da. and h., *m.* William Peck, of Sanford Hall, co. Essex, and of Melharle, co. York.

(b) He had acquired the Norgrove property from his mother, Anne, da. and coheir of Humphrey Jennetts, of Norgrove.

II. 1672? to 1701. Sir Thomas Cookes, Baronet [1664], of Norgrove and Bentley Pauncefote aforesaid, only surv. s. and h., *b.* about 1649; matric. at Oxford (Pembroke Coll.) 7 June 1667, aged 17; admitted to Lincoln's Inn, 26 June 1669; *suc. to the Baronetcy* about 1672, entered his pedigree at the Her. Visit. of Worcestershire, in 1683, being then aged 35; was Sheriff of co. Worcester, 1605-06; augmented the endowment of the School at Bronsgrove and endowed that at Feckenham, and was, after his death, **Founder of Worcester College, Oxford**.(a) He *m.* in 1672, Mary, 1st da. of Thomas (Windsor), 1st Earl of Plymouth, by his 1st wife, Anne, sister of George, Marquess of Halifax, da. of Sir William Savile, 3d Baronet [1611]. She *d.* 3 Jan. 1694, in her 36th year (the 22d year of her marriage), and was *bur.* at Tardebig. M.I. He *d.* s.p. 8 June 1701, when the *Baronetcy* became *extinct*. Will dat. 19 Feb. 1696, pr. 9 July 1701.

BROUGHTON(b):

cr. or *assumed*, 1664 *or* 1665(c);

ex. 11 June 1718.

I. 1664? "Sir Edward Broughton, of Marchwiell, co. Denbigh, Knt.,"(d) s. and h. of Sir Edward Broughton, of the same (*d.* between 23 March 1648/9 and 20 Feb. 1649/50), by Frances, da. of Sir Edward Tyrell, of Thornton, Bucks, was *b.* probably about 1610(e); was a Captain in the Guards and a supporter of the Royal cause, being consequently, just before the Restoration, confined in the Gate House Prison, Westminster(f), of which place he subsequently, after his marriage with the widow of the late Keeper thereof, became Keeper. At some date between 24 Oct. 1664 and his death in June 1665 he apparently was either *cr. a Baronet*, or more probably had only a promise of such creation(g). He *m.* firstly, Alice, 6th da. of Sir Robert Honywood, of Charing, co. Kent, by Alice, da. of Sir Martin Barnham. She, who was *b.* 10 and *bap.* 19 Jan. 1612/3, at Charing, *d.* s.p. He *m.* secondly (settlement, in which he is styled "Esq.," dat. 6, coupled with a curious bond of "*Imprecation*,"(g) dat. 12 April 1660), Mary, widow of Aquila Wyke, Keeper of the Gate House Prison aforesaid (*d.* April 1659, aged 34), da. of William Knightley, of Kingston-on-Thames, co. Surrey (*d.* 1648), by Susan, da. of John Price, of the same. He was mortally wounded in a sea fight with the Dutch, 3 June 1665, but reached home and died there, being *bur.* 26 of that month in Westm. Abbey. Admon., in which he is described as "Knt. and *Baronet*," 28 July 1665. Will, in which he is described as "Knt." [only], dat. 21 Oct. 1664, but not pr. till 16 Dec. 1669. His widow, who was *bap.* 13 April 1630, at Kingston, was *bur.* 19 March 1694/5, in Westm. Abbey. Will dat. 20 Jan. 1680/1, pr. 21 March 1694/5.

(a) The sum of £10,000, which he left for the benefit of Oxford University, was, after some controversy, applied, 14 July 1714, for converting "Gloucester Hall" into "Worcester College."

(b) H. R. Hughes, of Kinmel Park, North Wales, has kindly supplied most of the information contained in this article.

(c) There is no notice of this creation in Dugdale's *List*.

(d) He describes himself in his will, dat. 24 Oct. 1664, merely as "Knt.," though in the admon., 28 July 1665 (granted more than four years before the *proof* of the said will), he is described as "Knight and *Baronet*."

(e) His 1st wife (probably his junior) was *b.* in 1612/3.

(f) Pennant's *Tour in Wales*, as quoted in an interesting note by Col. Chester in his *Westm. Abbey Registers*, p. 236.

(g) See note "d" above. It is conjectured by H. R. Hughes (see note "b" above) that he may have been promised a Baronetcy after the fight of 3 June 1665, which his untimely death (occurring so soon afterwards) prevented from being carried into effect.

II. 1665, to 1718. Sir Edward Broughton, Baronet(a) [1664?], of Marchwiel aforesaid, 1st and only surv. s. and h., *bap.* 30 Jan. 1660/1, at St. Margaret's, Westm.; *suc. to the Baronetcy*(a) in June 1665, his right to which, he "in 169[-]" was sum. to the Earl Marshal's Court to prove(b). He, on 21 March 1694/5, is, as executor of his mother's will, styled "Baronet," as also was he when Sheriff of Denbighshire, 1697-98. He *d.* unm. 11 and was *bur.* 14 June 1718, at Marchwiel (being, also, styled "Baronet" in the parish register), when the *Baronetcy*(a) became *extinct*. Admon. (in which he is styled "Baronet, *alias* Esquire"), 5 May 1738, to "Aquila Wyke, Esq., nephew by the brother on the mother's side and next of kin."

(a) Assuming the creation of a Baronetcy.

(b) The erasure in the patent or warrant over which the words "Edward Broughton" had been inserted "appeared plainly." The case, however, was dismissed as being "a matter of Record," and accordingly belonging to the Common Law. [Le Neve's MS. *Baronetage*.]

Baronetcies of Ireland.(a)

1619—1800.

THIRD PART.

VIZ.,

CREATIONS,

30 Jan. 1648/9 to 31 Dec. 1664.(b)

COGAN [I.]:

cr. 20 Sep. 1657 ;(c)

ex. Oct. 1660.

I. 1657, to 1660. SIR ANDREW COGAN, sometime of Crowley House, Greenwich, and formerly (1633) of London, merchant, 1st s. of Richard COGAN, of Dorset, by Mary, da. of Andrew HOUNSLOW, entered his pedigree in the Her. Visit. of London, 1633; purchased Crowley house aforesaid, and was *Knighted* between Aug. 1645 and 27 Sep. 1650. His estates were sequestrated for having served in the Kentish rising, and by Act of Parl. 1651 ordered to be sold. He was, by Charles II., made Admiral, 24 May 1649, and, subsequently, General, with power to raise 1,000 foot in Kent; was, 11 April 1654, made Ambassador to China, to the Mogul, to Japan, and to East India, and was by patent, dat. at Bruges, 20 Sep. 1657, *cr. a "Baronet of Ulster."*(d) He *m.* before 1633, Mary, da. of Sir Hugh HAMERSLEY, Lord Mayor of London, 1627-28, by Mary, da. of Baldwin DERHAM. She *d.* 29 June 1660. He *d.* s.p.m.(e) in October following, and was *bur.* 2 Nov. 1660, in the Hamersley vault at St. Andrew's Undershaft, when the *Baronetcy* became *extinct*.

(a) See vol. i, p. 223, note "a," for acknowledgment of the kind assistance of Sir Arthur Vicars, Ulster King of Arms, and others, and more especially of the copious and invaluable information given by G. D. Burtchaell (of the College of Arms, Dublin), as to the Irish Baronetcies.

(b) See page 1, note "a," as to the date of 31 Dec. 1664.

(c) The description (as well as the dates) of the grantees of these Irish Baronetcies is in most cases (not, however, in this one) placed within inverted commas, as being taken from the *Liber Munerum Publicorum Hiberniæ* [See vol. i, p. 223, note "b"]. In the instance of Cogan, however, almost all the particulars have been kindly furnished by W. Duncombe Pink, as there is no notice of the creation in the work abovementioned.

(d) Apparently equivalent to a Baronet of Ireland.

(e) Of his two daughters and coheirs (1), Mary *m.*, 31 May 1660, as his 1st wife, Sir Christopher MUSGRAVE, 4th Baronet [1611], and *d.* 8 July 1664, in her 28th year, being *bur.* at Edenhall, leaving issue; (2), Martha *m.* Charles Chipp, of of Westminster, and *d.* s.p.

HAMILTON:

cr. probably about 1660;

afterwards, since 1701, EARLS OF ABERCORN [S.];

since 1790, MARQUESSES OF ABERCORN [G.B.];

and, since 1868, DUKES OF ABERCORN [I.].

I. 1660? THE HON. GEORGE HAMILTON, of Donalong, co. Tyrone, and of Nenagh, co. Tipperary, 4th s. of James (HAMILTON), 1st EARL OF ABERCORN [S.], by Marion, da. of Thomas (BOYD) 5th LORD BOYD [S.], was *b.* probably about 1607; had a company in the Army in 1627; did good service, in Ireland, for Charles I, as also, in 1649, for Charles II, at which date he was Col. of Foot and Gov. of Nenagh Castle, but retired to France in 1651 till the Restoration, about which period [1660?] he is said(a) to have been *cr. a Baronet* [I.], being also rewarded with some small patent places. He *m.* in 1629 Mary, sister of James, 1st DUKE OF ORMONDE [I. and E.], 3d. da. of Thomas BUTLER, *styled* VISCOUNT THURLES, by Elizabeth, da. of Sir John POYNTZ. He *d.* 1679. His widow *d.* Aug. 1680.

II. 1679. JAMES HAMILTON, of Donalong aforesaid, grandson and h., being 1st s. and h. of Col. James HAMILTON, Groom of the Bedchamber, by Elizabeth, da. of John (COLEPEPER) 1st BARON COLEPEPER OF THORESWAY, which James (who *d.* v.p. of wounds received in an action against the Dutch, 6 and was *bur.* 7 June 1673, in Westm. Abbey) was 1st s. and h. ap. of the late Baronet.(b) He was *b.* about 1661 and was at the age of 17, in 1678, Groom of the Bedchamber. On the death of his grandfather, in 1679, he *suc. to the Baronetcy*, but appears never to have assumed it.(c) He was Col. of a Regiment and P.C. to James II, but, deserting him at the Revolution, took part in the defence of Londonderry in 1689. He was M.P. [I.] for co. Tyrone, 1692-93 and 1695-99. He *m.* (Lic. Fac. 24 Jan. 1683/4) Elizabeth (then aged 15), only child of Sir Robert READING, Baronet [I., so *cr.* 1675], by Jane, DOWAGER COUNTESS OF MOUNTRATH [I.], da. of Sir Robert HANNAY, Baronet [S. 1630]. She was living when in June 1701 he suc. to the Peerage as EARL OF ABERCORN [S.]. In that peerage this *Baronetcy* then merged, the 9th Earl being *cr.* 15 Oct. 1790 MARQUESS OF ABERCORN [G.B.] and the 2d Marquess being *cr.* 10 Aug. 1868 DUKE OF ABERCORN [I.]. See *Peerage*.

SAINT GEORGE:

cr. 5 Sep. 1660;

afterwards, 1715-35,

BARON SAINT GEORGE OF HATLEY SAINT GEORGE [I.];

ex. 4 Aug. 1735.

I. 1660. SIR OLIVER SAINT GEORGE, of Carrick Drumrusk, co. Leitrim, Knt., was *cr. a Baronet* [E.], 5 Sep. 1660, and possibly also at the same date a Baronet of Ireland, as he appears in the list of Irish Baronets in Ulster's office.(d) See an account of this Baronetcy on p. 120.

(a) Beatson's List, where the date is given as 1660; so also in Wood's *Douglas' Peerage* [S.]. He was "certainly a Baronet in 1662, probably much earlier" [G. D. Burtchaell]. In Lodge's *Irish Peerage* (edit. 1789, vol. v, p. 3) the Baronetcy is said to have been one of Nova Scotia.

(b) He and his younger brother Sir George Hamilton, Count Hamilton in France, play a conspicuous part in the *Memoires de Grammont* (compiled by their brother Anthony, Count Hamilton), their sister Elizabeth "La belle Hamilton" having *m.* Philibert Count de Grammont, thus commemorated.

(c) This non-assumption of the dignity throws some little doubt on its creation.

(d) See creations of "Lane," 9 Feb. 1660/1, and of "Gifford," 4 March 1660/1, for somewhat similar cases.

MEREDYTH, *or* MEREDITH;

cr. 20 Nov. 1660.

I. 1660. "WILLIAM MEREDITH, Esq., of Greenehill, co. Kildare,"(a) 1st s. and h. ap. of the Rt. Hon. Sir Robert MEREDYTH, of the same, and of Shrowland in that county, Chancellor of the Exchequer [I.], by Anne (*m.* in 1618) da. of Sir William USHER, Clerk of the Council [I.], was *b.* probably about 1620; was sometime a Major in the Parl. army; was M.P. [E.] for the counties of Kildare and Wicklow, 1654-55, and was *cr. a Baronet* [I.], as above, Patent at Dublin, 20 Nov. 1660. He was in command of a troop of Horse in Feb. 1662, and suc. his father 17 Oct. 1668. He *m.*, Nov. 1655, Mary, sister of John, 1st BARON KINGSTON [I.], da. of Sir Robert KING, of Boyle Abbey, co. Roscommon, Muster Master General [I.], by his 1st wife, Frances, da. of Henry (FOLLIOTT), 1st BARON FOLLIOTT OF BALLYSHANNON [I.]. He *d.* v.p. at Kilcullen, co. Kildare, and was *bur.* at St. Patrick's Cathedral, Dublin, 14 Feb. 1664/5. Will, in which he does not mention any children, but leaves all to his wife, dat. 2 June 1664, sworn to in Chancery [I.] 11 April 1665. His widow *m.* (as his 1st wife) William (FEILDING), 2d EARL OF DESMOND [I.], *afterwards*, in 1675, 3d EARL OF DENBIGH, who *d.* 23 Aug. 1685. She was *bur.* 12 Sep. 1669, at St. Michan's, Dublin.

II. 1665. RICHARD MEREDYTH, Baronet [I. 1660],(b) of Shrowland aforesaid, 1st s. and h., *b.* 1657; *suc. to the Baronetcy*(b) when seven years old, in Feb. 1664/5, but never assumed it; lived abroad many years, but was M.P. [I.] for Athy, 1703-13. He *m.*, 9 Jan. 1702/3, at Castledermot, co. Kildare, Sarah, sister and coheir of Col. Joshua PAUL, of the Footguards, da. of Jeffery PAUL, of Bough, co. Carlow, by (—), da. of Thomas VINCENT. He was *bur.* at St. Patrick's, Dublin, 8 Oct. 1743. His will, as of Dublin, "Esq.," dat. 19 Sep. and pr. [I.] 17 Oct. 1743. His widow was *bur.* 15 March 1769 at St. Patrick's aforesaid. Her will dat. 14 Dec. 1765, as of Dublin, pr. [I.] 23 March 1769.

III. 1743. ROBERT MEREDYTH, Baronet [I. 1660],(b) of Shrowland aforesaid, 1st s. and h., *b.* probably about 1704; *suc. to the Baronetcy*(b) in 1743, but never assumed it. He *m.*, in 1732, Sarah, da. of Lieut.-Col. Dudley COSBY, of Stradbally, in Queen's County, by his 2d wife, Sarah, da. of Periam POLE, of Ballyfin in that county. He was *bur.* at St. Patrick's aforesaid, 18 Feb. 1746/7. Will, as "Esq.," dat. 23 Jan. 1746/7, pr. [I.] 1747. His widow was *bur.* there 9 Sep. 1755.

IV. 1747. RICHARD MEREDYTH, Baronet [I. 1660],(b) of Shrowland aforesaid, only s. and h., *b.* Jan. 1733; *suc. to the Baronetcy*(b) in Feb. 1746/7, but never assumed it. He, as "Esq.," *m.* 20 June 1754, at

(a) This is the first creation by Charles II recorded in the *Liber Munerum Hiberniæ* (see p. 304 note "c"), and follows immediately that of Borrowes, *cr.* by Charles I, 11 Feb. 1645/6.

(b) According to a pedigree recorded in Ulster's Office, April 1808, supported by the affidavit of Richard Colles, Barrister, stating that "Richard Meredith, as appears from attested copies of wills, was legitimate son of Sir William Meredith, Baronet." If so, however, this Richard ignores (as do his successors for more than a century) any right to his father's title; moreover, on 30 Aug. 1666, Charles Meredith, who obtained 3,746 acres in co. Kildare, from the Commissioners of the Act of Settlement, is styled "son of Sir Robert Meredith, Knt., and brother *and heir* of Sir William Meredith, Baronet." This Charles (who was *knighted* between June 1669 and 1675) is styled (probably by inadvertence) in the Commons' Journal [I.] 1692-3 "Miles *et Baronettus*," and is bur. at St. Anne's, Soho, 11 Nov. 1700, as "*Baronet*." He apparently *d.* unm. The succeeding Baronets not improbably descend from Robert, who is mentioned in his father's (Sir Robert's) will, dated 10 Sep. 1664, he being a brother of the said Charles, as also of William, the 1st Baronet. The Baronetcy is omitted in the Catalogue of Baronets of Ireland, 1688, in Ulster's Office [*Ex inform.* G. D. Burtchaell].

Kilkenny, Martha, da. of Major Samuel MATTHEWS, of Bonnettstown, co. Kilkenny, by Elizabeth, da. and h. of William ROGERSON. He *d.* s.p., 1777, in Kilkenny, and was *bur.* there. Will, as "Esq.," dat. 5 June 1770, pr. [I.] 2 April 1778.

V. 1777. PAUL MEREDYTH, Baronet [I. 1660],(a) uncle and h. male, being 2d s. of the 2d Baronet, *b.* probably about 1720; *suc. to the Baronetcy*(a) in 1777, but never assumed it. He *d.* unm. 1783, and is said to have been *bur.* at St. Patrick's aforesaid.

VI. 1783. MOORE MEREDYTH, Baronet [I. 1660],(a) br. and h. male, *b.* probably about 1722; ed. at Trin. Coll., Cambridge; B.A., 1736; M.A. 1740; B.D. 1761; was in Holy Orders; Fellow and Vice-Master (latterly Senior Fellow) of his College; *suc. to the Baronetcy*(a) in 1783, but, apparently, never assumed it. He *d.* unm., 8 Nov. 1789, and was *bur.* at Cambridge.

VII. 1789. SIR BARRY COLLES MEREDYTH, Baronet [I. 1660],(a) nephew and h. male, being 1st s. and h. of Joshua MEREDYTH, of Clonegown, in Queen's County (will pr. [I.] 23 Jan. 1783), by Susanna (*m.* 1743), da. and h. of Barry COLLES, of Kilcollan, co. Kilkenny, which Joshua (who *d.* 1787) was br. of the 3d, 5th, and 6th Baronets,(a) being 4th s. of the 2d Baronet.(a) He was *b.* about 1749, and *suc. to the Baronetcy*,(a) 8 Nov. 1789, and then, or at a later period, assumed the dignity. He *m.*, 14 July 1770, Elizabeth, 1st da. of John EASTWOOD, of Castletown, co. Louth, by Letitia, da. of Samuel TURNER. He *d.* in Dublin, 14 Oct. 1813, aged 64.

VIII. 1813. SIR JOSHUA COLLES, *sometimes called* Joshua Paul, MEREDYTH, Baronet [I. 1660],(a) of Pelletstown, co. Dublin, 1st s. and h., *b.* 1 June 1771; Sheriff of co. Dublin, 1793; was *Knighted* (as the 1st son of a Baronet), 16 May 1793, at Dublin Castle, being then Capt. in the 89th Foot; received the Order of Military Merit from Louis XVIII of France, and that of "Louis of Hesse" from the Grand Duke of Hesse; *suc. to the Baronetcy*,(a) 14 Oct. 1813. He *m.* firstly, 16 Sep. 1795, Maria, da. and h. of Laurence Coyne NUGENT, of Finae, co. Cavan, by Barbara, da. and coheir of Christopher CHEVERS, of Dama, co. Kilkenny. She *d.* s.p.m. at Cheltenham, 15 Oct. 1813 (the day after her husband had suc. to the Baronetcy) aged 35. He *m.* secondly in 1822, DolignY, 2d da. and coheir of Col. EDWARDS, by Sarah, "heiress of Admiral Robinson." He *d.* s.p.m. 27 July 1850 in his 80th year at Dover. His widow *d.* s.p. 25 Jan. 1864, in Grosvenor street, Midx.

IX. 1850. SIR EDWARD NEWENHAM MEREDYTH, Baronet [I. 1660](a) of Madaleen, co. Kilkenny, br. and h. male, being 3d s. of the 7th Baronet, *b.* 1 May 1776 in Anglesea, *suc. to the Baronetcy*,(a) 27 July 1850. He *m.* firstly, 29 Aug. 1819, Lucretia, da. of Samuel HOLMES, of Keady, co. Armagh. She *d.* 20 Jan. 1837. He *m.* secondly, 10 Aug. 1839, Elizabeth, da. of James CREED, of Kilmallock, co. Limerick. He *d.* 23 March 1865, aged 87. His widow *d.* s.p., 5 July 1867.

X. 1865. SIR EDWARD HENRY JOHN MEREDYTH, Baronet [I. 1660],(a) of Madaleen aforesaid, only s. and h. by 1st wife, *b.* 29 May 1828 in Dublin; entered the Army, 1849; sometime Capt. 87th Foot; *suc. to the Baronetcy*,(a) 23 March 1865; one of the Military Knights of Windsor, 1886. He *m.* 15 Aug. 1861, at Youghal, co. Cork, Agnes Margaret Naylor, da. of the Rev. Pierce William DREW, of Heathfield Towers in that county, sometime Rector of Youghal aforesaid, by Elizabeth, da. and h. of Thomas OLIVER, of Cork.

(a) Assuming the succession to the 1st Baronet to be as given in the registered pedigree. See p. 306, note "b."

COLE:

cr. 23 Jan. 1660/1;

afterwards, 1715-54, BARON RANELAGH [I.];

ex. 12 Oct. 1754.

I. 1661. "JOHN COLE,(a) Esq., of Newland, co. Dublin," yr. br. of Michael COLE, (*b.* 1616), ancestor of the EARLS OF ENNISKILLEN [I.], both being sons of Sir William COLE, of Enniskillen Castle (*d.* 1653), by Susanna, da. and h. of John CROFT, of Lancashire, was *b.* probably about 1620; distinguished himself in the Civil War, in the relief of Enniskillen, on behalf of the King; was M.P. [E.] for the counties of Cavan, Fermanagh, and Monaghan, 1654-55, and was *cr. a Baronet* [I.], as above, 23 Jan. 1660/1, the Privy Seal being dat. at Whitehall, 4 Aug. 1660. He was M.P. [I.] for co. Fermanagh, 1661-66; Custos Rot. of that county, 2 April 1661; Sheriff thereof, 1666, and Commissioner for the forty-nine officers, 26 Oct. 1675. He *m.*, before 1660, Elizabeth, da. of the Hon. John CHICHESTER, of Dungannon, by Mary, da. of Roger (JONES), 1st VISCOUNT RANELAGH [I.]. He *d.* in or before 1691. Will dat. 1 Aug. 1688, pr. 3 Oct. 1691 [I.]. The will of his widow dat. 7 Nov. 1703, pr. 26 July 1711 [I.].

II. 1691? to 1754. SIR ARTHUR COLE, Baronet [I. 1660], of Newland aforesaid, 1st s. and h., *b.* about 1668; was attainted by James II, but restored by William III; *suc. to the Baronetcy* in or shortly before 1691; was M.P. [I.] for Enniskillen, 1692-93, and for Roscommon borough, 1695-99. He *m.* firstly (Lic. Vic. Gen., 8 Sep. 1692, he about 23), Catharine, da. of William (BYRON), 3d BARON BYRON OF ROCHDALE, by his 1st wife, Elizabeth, da. of John (CHAWORTH), VISCOUNT CHAWORTH [I.]. She was living when he, shortly after the death, s.p.m., 5 Jan. 1711/2, of his mother's first cousin, Richard (JONES), 3d VISCOUNT and 1st EARL OF RANELAGH [I.], was *cr.*, 18 April 1715, BARON RANELAGH [I.]. In that peerage this *Baronetcy* then *merged*, till both became *extinct*, on his death s.p., 12 Sep. 1754. See *Peerage*.

LANE:

cr. 9 Feb. 1660/1;

afterwards, 1676—1724, VISCOUNTS LANESBOROUGH [I.];

ex. 2 Aug. 1724.

I. 1661. "RICHARD LANE, Esq., of Tulske, co. Roscommon," was *cr. a Baronet* [E.], as above, 9 Feb. 1660/1, and possibly also a Baronet of Ireland, as his name appears in the list of such creations, under the same date, in the *Liber Munerum Hiberniæ*, though the patent is there stated to be (not at Dublin, but) at Westminster.(b) He was M.P. [I.] for Tuam, 1665-66. See an account of this Baronetcy on p. 159.

PIERS, *or* PIERCE:

cr. 18 Feb. 1660/1.

I. 1661. "HENRY PIERCE [PIERS], of Tristernagh, co. Westmeath," 1st and only surv. s. of Sir William PIERS, of the same (*d.* 1638, aged about 40), by Martha, da. of Sir James WARE, the elder, which

(a) See *Mis. Gen. et Her.*, 1st series, vol. ii, pp. 234-250, for an elaborate pedigree of this family.

(b) See creations of "Saint George," 5 Sep. 1660, and of "Gifford," 4 March 1660/1, for somewhat similar cases.

William was s. and h. of Henry PIERS, of Tristernagh aforesaid, a well known traveller (*d.* 16 Sep. 1623), by Jane, sister of Roger (JONES), 1st VISCOUNT RANELAGH [I.], da. of Thomas JONES, Archbishop of Dublin (1605-19), was *b.* about 1628; suc. his father in 1638; was *Knighted* at Dublin Castle, 30 Nov. 1658, by the Lord Deputy, Henry Cromwell; was Sheriff of co. Longford and Westmeath, 1657 and 1658; M.P. for the same counties and for King's County, 1659, and was *cr. a Baronet* [I.], as above, by patent 18 Feb. 1660/1, at Dublin, the Privy Seal being dat. 18 Jan. previous at Whitehall. He was subsequently M.P. [I.] for St. Johnstown, co. Longford, 1661-66, and Sheriff for co. Westmeath, 1663. He *m.*, in or before 1653, Mary, da. of Henry JONES, Bishop of Meath, by his 1st wife, Jane, da. of Sir Hugh CULLUM, of Cloghouter, co. Cavan.(a). He *d.* 19 Sep. 1691, aged 63.(b) Will pr. [I.] 1691.

II. 1691. SIR WILLIAM PIERS, Baronet [I. 1661], of Tristernagh aforesaid, 1st s. and h., *b.* about 1653; *suc. to the Baronetcy*, 19 Sep. 1691. He *m.* in or before 1678, Honora, sister of Thomas, 1st Earl of KERRY [I.], da. of William (FITZMAURICE), LORD KERRY [I.], by Constance, da. of William LONG, of London. He *d.* 2 June 1693, aged about 40. His widow *d.* at Dublin. Her will pr. [I.] 1710.

III. 1693. SIR HENRY PIERS, Baronet [I. 1661], of Tristernagh aforesaid, 1st s. and h., *b.* 1678; *suc. to the Baronetcy*, 2 June 1693. Sheriff of co. Westmeath, 1702. He *m.* firstly, Jane, da. of John PIGOTT, of Kilfinny, co. Limerick, by Garthrude, da. of Sir Thomas SOUTHWELL, 1st Baronet [I. 1661]. By her he had eight children. He *m.* secondly, as her 3d husband, 8 Dec. 1729 (Lic. 25 Nov.), Katharine, Dow. COUNTESS OF BARRYMORE [I.], widow of Francis GASH, one of the Revenue collectors [I.], da. of Richard (BARRY), 2d BARON BARRY OF SANTRY, by Elizabeth, da. of Henry JENERY. He *d.*, of an overdose of opium, 14 March 1733, and was *bur.* at St. Mary's, Dublin, aged 56 years and 8 months. Will pr. [I.] 1734. His widow, by whom he had no issue, *d.* 8 and was *bur.* 10 June 1737, at St. Mary's aforesaid. Will pr. [I.] 1744.

IV. 1733. SIR JOHN PIERS, Baronet [I. 1661], of Tristernagh aforesaid, 2d but 1st surv. s. and h. by 1st wife; *suc. to the Baronetcy*, 14 March 1733. He *m.* (Lic. 17 May 1739), Cornelia Gertrude, 1st da. of his maternal uncle, Southwell PIGOTT, of Capard, in Queen's County, by Henrietta Wynanda, da. of [—] VANDERGEAFF. He *d.*, after a long illness, 14, and was *bur.* 18 Feb. 1746/7, at St. Anne's, Dublin. Will pr. [I.] 1747. His widow *d.* 14 Jan. 1777. Her will pr. 1777.

V. 1747. SIR PIGOTT WILLIAM PIERS, Baronet [I. 1661], of Tristernagh aforesaid, only s. and h., *b.* probably about 1742; *suc. to the Baronetcy*, 14 Feb. 1746/7; ed. at Trin. Coll., Dublin; B.A., 1762; Sheriff of co. Westmeath, 1774. He *m.* (Lic. 17 April 1771), Elizabeth, da. and h. of John SMYTH, of Dublin. He *d.* 1798. Will pr. [I.] 1798.

VI. 1798. SIR JOHN BENNET PIERS, Baronet [I. 1661], of Tristernagh aforesaid, 1st s. and h., *b.* probably about 1775; *suc. to the Baronetcy* in 1798. He *m.* firstly, in Aug. 1796, Mary, da. of the Rev. Joseph PRATT, of Cabra Castle, co. Cavan, by Sarah, da. of Hervey (MORRES), 1st

(a) The Bishop's 2d wife, Mary, *m.* 31 Dec. 1646, was sister of the said Sir Henry Piers, the 1st Baronet.

(b) He was author of the chorographical description of the county of Westmeath, 1682, pub. in 1770, as No. 1 of *Collectanea de rebus Hibernicis*, by Col. Charles Vallancey.

VISCOUNT MOUNTMORRES [I.]. She *d.* s.p. 1798. He *m.* secondly, in 1815, Elizabeth KING, spinster. He *d.* s.p.m. legit.(a) 22 July 1845.(b). His widow *d.* 17 Feb. 1862, at Lucca, in Italy.

VII. 1845. SIR HENRY SAMUEL PIERS, Baronet [I. 1661], of Tristernagh aforesaid, nephew and h. male, being 2d but 1st surv. s. and h. of Frederick PIERS, by Phœbe,(c) da. of Samuel HARTNEY, of Pallas, co. Limerick, which Frederick, who *d.* 28 Oct. 1844, aged 66, was yr. br. of the late Baronet. He was *b.* 6 May 1811, and *suc. to the Baronetcy*, 22 July 1845. He *m.* 24 Nov. 1838, Alice, yst. da. of John Thomas GLINDON, *formerly* LINDON, sometime in the Royal Navy. He *d.* 15 April 1850, at Tristernagh Abbey, aged 39. His widow living 1903.

VIII. 1850. SIR EUSTACE FITZ MAURICE PIERS, Baronet [I. 1661], 1st s. and h., *b.* 28 Oct. 1840, at Clapham, co. Surrey; *suc. to the Baronetcy*, 15 April 1850; sometime Partner in the firm of "Ormerod, Grierson and Co.," St. George's iron works, Manchester; Captain 4th Batt. Manchester Reg. (Militia), 1868-81; Major, 1881-82. He *m.*, 29 July 1869, at St. Ann's church, Aigburth, Rose, yst. da. of Charles SAUNDERS, of Fulwood park, near Liverpool, co. Lanc. She *d.* 11 Nov. 1891, at St. Leonards on Sea.

GIFFORD, *or* GIFFARD:

cr. 4 March 1660/1;

ex. 4 May 1662;

but assumed July 1747 to Sep. 1823.

I. 1661. "THOMAS GIFFARD [*otherwise* GIFFORD], Esq., of Castle Jordan, co. Meath," was *cr. a Baronet* [E.], as above, 4 March 1660/1, and possibly also a Baronet of Ireland, as his name appears in the list of creations, under the same date, in the *Liber Munerum Hiberniæ*, though the patent is there stated to be [not at Dublin, but] at Westminster.(d) See an account of the Baronetcy on p. 168.

CROFTON:

cr. 1 July 1661;

ex. 9 Nov. 1780;

but assumed 1780 to 1838.

I. 1661. "EDWARD CROFTON,(e) Esq., of the Mote, co. Roscommon," 1st s. and h. of George CROFTON, of Ballymurray in that county, M.P. [I.] for Askeaton, co. Limerick, 1639 (the builder of the Castle at the Mote), by Elizabeth, da. of Sir Francis BERKELEY, of Askeaton

(a) He had, beside daughters, two illegit. sons by the person who was afterwards his 2d wife, *viz.*, William Stapleton Piers and John Piers.

(b) His trial for crim. con. with Elizabeth Georgiana, Baroness Cloncurry [I.], wife of the 2d Baron, damages £20,000, was pub. in 1807 [8vo Dublin]. That lady's marriage was dissolved 26 June 1811, and she *m.*, June 1819, the Rev. John Sandford, of Nynehead, co. Somerset.

(c) A note by Sir William Betham, Ulster, states that she and her husband were "married by a couple-beggar, named Harris."

(d) See creations of "Saint George," 5 Sep. 1660, and of "Lane," 9 Feb. 1660/1, for somewhat similar cases.

(e) In Beatson's *List of Irish Baronetcies* the creation of "Crofton" in 1661 is (erroneously) assigned to "Malby Crofton, Sligo."

aforesaid, and Katharine, his wife, da. of Adam LOFTUS, Archbishop of Dublin (1567-1605), was *b.* in Dublin, 1624; admitted to Trin. Coll. Dublin (as Fellow Commoner), 15 Feb. 1639/40; Sheriff of co. Roscommon, 1658, and was, "for his services during the Civil War,"(a) *cr. a Baronet*, as above, by patent dat. at Dublin, 1 July 1661, the Privy Seal being dat. 30 March previous at Whitehall. He was M.P. [I.] for Lanesborough, 1665-66. He *m.* firstly, at St. Werburgh's, Dublin (Lic. Dublin, 20 Oct. 1647), Mary, 1st da. of Sir James WARE, the well known Antiquary, Auditor Gen. [I.], by his 1st wife, Elizabeth, da. of Jacob NEWMAN, of Dublin, Clerk to the Master of the Rolls [I.]. She, who was *b.* 21 March 1625, *d.* 1651. He *m.* secondly, being then of St. Martins-in-the-Fields, Midx., aged 37 (Lic. Fac. 11 Jan. 1661/2), Susanna CLIFFORD, of St. Paul's, Covent Garden, aged 29, spinster, da. of Thomas CLIFFORD, of Devon, her parents being then dead. He *d.* 1675. His widow *m.* (Lic. Dublin, 24 Feb. 1676/7), Gerald DILLON, Recorder of Dublin, Prime Serjeant to James II (whom he followed to France) and eventually a Colonel in the French service.

II. 1675. SIR EDWARD CROFTON, Baronet [I. 1661], of the Mote aforesaid, 2d but only surv. s. and h., being only s. by the 2d wife,(b) *b.* in or after 1662, and *suc. to the Baronetcy* in 1675. He was attainted 7 May 1688 by the Parl. [I.] of James II, but restored soon afterwards; was M.P. [I.] for Boyle 1695-99, and for co. Roscommon, 1703 till death in 1729; Sheriff of co. Roscommon, 1700; P.C. [I.], 9 Oct. 1714. He *m.*, 2 Feb. 1684, Catherine, sister of George, 1st BARON ST. GEORGE OF HATLEY [I.], da. of Sir Oliver ST. GEORGE, 1st Baronet [1660], by Olivia, da. of Michael BERESFORD. He *d.* 24 Nov. 1729. Will dat. 17 May 1714, pr. [I.] 1733.

III. 1729. SIR EDWARD CROFTON, Baronet [I. 1661], of the Mote aforesaid, 1st s. and h., *b.* 25 May 1687; *suc. to the Baronetcy*, 24 Nov. 1729; was M.P. [I.] for Roscommon borough, 1713, till death in 1739. He *m.* (Lic. 4 March 1711) Mary, sister of David and da. of Anthony NIXON, both of Dublin, by Catharine, da. of Sir Edward CROFTON, 1st Baronet [I. 1661]. He *d.* 11 Nov. 1739, at Lyons in France, and was *bur.* in the church of Kilmain, co. Roscommon. Will, dat. 5 Jan. 1736, pr. [I.] 1740. His widow *d.* 10 Feb. 1758, in Mary street, Dublin.

IV. 1739. SIR EDWARD CROFTON, Baronet [I. 1661], of the Mote aforesaid, only s. and h., *b.* 12 April 1713; *suc. to the Baronetcy*, 11 Nov. 1739; was Sheriff for co. Roscommon, 1734, and M.P. [I.] thereof, 1735 till death in 1745. He *m.*, 17 June 1741 (Lic. Dublin 13), Martha, sister of Joseph, 1st EARL OF DORCHESTER, 2d da. of Joseph DAMER, of Came, co. Dorset, by Mary, da. of John CHURCHILL, of Henbury in that county. He *d.* s.p. 26 March 1745. His widow, who was *b.* 23 April 1719, *m.* Ezekiel NESBITT, M.D., of Bath, co. Somerset (whose will was pr. [I.] 1798), and *d.* there July 1777.

V. 1745, to 1780. SIR OLIVER CROFTON, Baronet [I. 1661], of Lissanard, co. Limerick, cousin and h. male, being posthumous s. and h. of Oliver CROFTON, of Lisnagrove, in that county, by Catharine ARMSTRONG his wife, which Oliver, who was drowned at Quebec in 1709, aged 21, was s. of the 2d and only br. of the 3d Baronet. He was *b.* 1710, and *suc. to the Baronetcy*, but not to the estates, 26 March 1745. He *m.*, at St. Audoen's, Dublin, 6 Dec. 1737, Abigail Jackson, da. of [—] BUCKLEY, heiress of estates in Cumberland, Yorkshire, Lancashire and Dublin. She *d.* Dec. 1763, at St. Stephen's Green, Dublin, aged 80. He *d.* s.p. legit.,(c) 9 Nov. 1780, aged 70, when *the Baronetcy* became *extinct*. Will pr. [I.] 1781.

(a) Playfair's *Irish Baronetage*, 1811.

(b) James Crofton, son by the 1st wife, *d.* young.

(c) He had four illegit. sons, viz., (1) James Crofton, of Roebuck Castle, co. Dublin, Clerk in the Treasury [I.]; (2) Edward Crofton; (3) John Crofton; and (4) Oliver Crofton.

III

The Baronetcy was, however, assumed as under:

VI. 1780. Sir Malby Crofton, Baronet [I. 1661],(a) of Longford House, co. Sligo, 4th but eventually only surv. s. of James Crofton, of the same, by Elizabeth, da. of Capt. Edward Robinson, which James (who *d.* 1755) was s. of Edward Crofton, s. of Henry Crofton (Sheriff of co. Sligo, 1687), s. of Thomas Crofton, all three of Longford House aforesaid, the said Thomas being yr. br. of Sir Edward Crofton, 1st Baronet [I. 1661], abovenamed. He was *b.* 1741; entered the Army when 14; was at the siege of Quebec, 1759, and served during the whole period of the American war; suc. his elder br. at some date after 1765; was Sheriff of co. Sligo, 1770, and "*assumed the title of Sir Malby Crofton*"(b) on the death, 29 Nov. 1780, of his distant cousin, Sir Oliver Crofton, 5th and last Baronet [I. 1661], presumably on the grounds of being heir male collateral of the grantee. He *m.* (settlement 9 July 1772) Elizabeth, 2d da. of Ignatius Kelly, of Cargins, co. Roscommon, by Catherine, da. of Daniel Kelly, of Turrock in that county. He *d.* 29 Jan. 1808. Admon. of "Sir Malby Crofton, Lieut. 90th Foot, Ireland," granted Dec. 1810.

VII. 1808, to 1838. Sir James Crofton, Baronet [I. 1661],(a) of Longford House aforesaid, only s. and h., *b.* 8 Aug. 1776; Sheriff of co. Sligo, 1802; suc. his father, 29 Jan. 1808, when he, also, *assumed the Baronetcy*, but as, however, he himself was *cr. a Baronet*, 18 Aug. 1838, such assumption came at that date to an end. See under Crofton, Baronetcy, *cr.* 18 Aug. 1838.

(a) By assumption; see note "b" below.

(b) Playfair's *Irish Baronetage* (1811), p. 113, *note*. In the *text* thereof (p. 117) this Baronetage is said to have "expired," 29 Nov. 1780. The history of the assumption is best illustrated by the memorial [undated] presented to the Lord Lieutenant [I.] by "James Crofton, Major of the Sligo Regiment of Militia," in which he states that on the death [9 Nov. 1780] of Sir Oliver Crofton, Baronet, "a notification of his succession to the title was made from the office of the late Ulster King of Arms to Malby Crofton, Esq., the then representative of the original Crofton family in Ireland, and father of your Excellency's Memorialist, and his name published by authority in the list of Irish Baronets uninterruptedly for 30 years." He then states that on the death of his said father, he assumed the title, but found to his "utter astonishment" his name had been struck off the list of Baronets, being then, for the first time informed at the office of Ulster King of Arms that he had no right to the title. He further states that since his father's death he had been uniformly addressed in all communications from the Castle of Dublin as a Baronet, while serving as a Captain of Yeomanry, that his commission as Major of the Sligo Militia was signed as "Sir James Crofton" by the Lord Lieutenant [I.], and that as a Grand Juror he has been invariably empanelled as a Baronet. That he is now placed "in a most humiliating and mortifying situation," etc. He then recites the military service of his late father, and that he had four uncles in the Army or Navy, all of whom lost their lives in the service of their country, and winds up by presuming to hope that he "may be relieved from the disappointing dilemma" in which he stands, by his Excellency's graciously having him honoured by a new creation.

The report, 20 March 1823, of Sir William Betham, Ulster King of Arms (to whom, 27 Dec. 1822, this memorial had been referred), was as under:—"I find nothing in the Records of this office to shew that any of my Predecessors, Kings of Arms, notified to Malby Crofton, Esq., the succession to the title," adding that he could not discover by what authority the name of the Memorialist was inserted in the annual list of Baronets, but he thought it his duty "to cause it to be

LAKE:

cr. 10 July 1661;

ex. 18 April 1674.

I. 1661, to 1674. "Edward Lake, LL.D., of Carnow, co. Wicklow," s. and h. of Richard Lake, of Irby, co. Lincoln, by his 1st wife, Anne, yst. da. and coheir of Edward Wardall, of Keilby, in that county, was *b.* about 1598 or 1600 (being called 77, at his death in 1674, but 66 in the Visit. of Lincolnshire in 1666); was ed. at St. Cath. Hall, Cambridge, and St. Alban Hall, Oxford; B.A. (Cambridge), 1626; incorp. at Oxford, 15 Dec. 1627; B.C.L. (Oxford), 24 Jan. 1627/8; M.A. (Cambridge), 1629; incorp. as LL.B. at Cambridge, 1636, being LL.D. thereof, 1637; was M.P. [I.] for Cavan, 1639 till expelled 9 Nov. 1640; was a zealous adherent of Charles I, in whose cause he received no less than sixteen wounds at the battle of Edgehill, 23 Oct. 1642, and from whom he received a warrant, dat. at Oxford, 30 Dec. 1643, for a patent (which, however, never passed the Seal) granting him a Baronetcy, with rem., failing heirs male of his body, to his "heirs male," as also the power of nominating a Baronet.(a) He was Chancellor of the diocese of Lincoln and King's Advocate Gen. for the Kingdom of Ireland, and was *cr. a Baronet* [I.] by pat. dat. at Dublin 10 July 1661, the Privy Seal being dat. 18 June previous, at Whitehall. He *m.* Anne, 1st da. and coheir of Symon Bibye, of Bugden, co. Huntingdon. She was living April 1665, but *d.* before Oct. 1670, and was *bur.* in Lincoln Cathedral. He *d.* s.p.s.(b), 18 April 1674, and was *bur.* in Lincoln Cathedral, when the *Baronetcy* became *extinct*.(c) M.I. there. Burial registered 20 July 1674, at St. Margaret's, Lincoln. Will dat. 8 April 1665, 6 Oct. 1670, 18 Jan. 1671/2, and, finally, 8 June 1674 (when he is described as of Bishop's Norton, co. Lincoln), pr. 13 July 1675,(d) by his nephew, Thomas Lake.

FENTON:

cr. 22 July 1661;

ex. March 1670/1.

I. 1661. "Sir Maurice Fenton, Knt., of Mitchelstowne, co. Cork," 2d but 1st surv. s. and h. ap. of Sir William Fenton,(e) of the same (who *d.* Oct. 1667), by Margaret, da. of Maurice FitzEdmund Fitzgibbon and

struck out of the list, together with the names of several other individuals who were not entitled to that honour." He says he believes that the allegations are correct, but begs leave to observe "that no length of usage of a title of Honour will establish a right to the same. It must originate from the Crown; nor will the reception at Court, or the designation of an individual by the Crown in any commission, warrant, or patent (except such as may be issued for that especial purpose) establish a right to a dignity" [*Ex inform.* G. D. Burtchaell, see p. 304, note "a"].

(a) A copy of this warrant is in Betham's *Baronetage* [1803], vol. iii, p. 154.

(b) Edward Lake, his only child, *d.* before 1666.

(c) His great nephew, Bibye Lake, who was *bap.* 10 April 1684, was *cr. a Baronet*, 17 Oct. 1711, having, it is said, represented to Queen Anne the warrant of Charles I of 1643, whereby, if it had been carried into effect, he would have succeeded to a Baronetcy of that date.

(d) In this interesting will testator leaves to his executor "my patent of Baronet," also "the picture of the late blessed King and Martyr, my most dear Master, King Charles the 1st, as it is in a frame in the shape of a Martyr in a white robe, with a palm in his right hand and a Crown of Stars upon his head, with an inscription in a table hanging under it," also the picture of "my most noble Lord Thomas, late Earl of Strafford, Lord Lieutenant of Ireland." There are, also, many directions about preserving the names of Bibye, Seaman, Wardall, and Caley as Christian names in the family.

(e) This William was s. of Sir Geoffrey Fenton, Sec. of State [I.] (who *d.* 19 Oct. 1608), by Alice, relict of Hugh Brady, Bishop of Meath, da. of Richard Weston, LL.D., Lord Chancellor [I.]. He *d.* 1667, three years after his son, Maurice.

heir of her brother Maurice (she being also cousin and heir of Edmund Fitzgibbon, called the "White Knight"), was *b.* in or after 1622; *knighted* at Cork House, Dublin, 7 June 1658, by Henry Cromwell, the Lord Deputy [I.], and was *cr. a Baronet* [I.] by the Lord Protector(a) by patent 14 July 1658, the Privy Seal being dat. at Whitehall 25 May last past. After the Restoration *these honours* were, of course, *forfeited*, but having again been *knighted* in consequence of King's Letters, 6 Dec. 1660, he was, by the King, again *cr. a Baronet* [I.], as above, by patent 22 July 1661 at Dublin, the Privy Seal being dat. at Whitehall the 6th inst. He (as a Baronet) was M.P. [E.] for co. Cork in Richard Cromwell's Parl. of 1659, and subsequently (having been elected as an Esquire) was M.P. [I.] for Fethard, co. Tipperary, 1661 till his death in 1664. He *m.* 23 Oct. 1653, Elizabeth, da. of Sir Hardress Waller, of Castletown, co. Limerick (the Regicide), by Elizabeth, da. and coheir of Sir John Dowdall, of Kilfinny, co. Limerick. He *d.* v.p. in 1664. His will dat. 18 Feb. 1663/4, pr. 23 June 1664 [I.]. His widow *m.*, in 1667, the well known Sir William Petty, Surveyor General of Ireland, who *d.* 16 Dec. 1687, and was *bur.* at Romsey, Hants, aged 64. She, for his services, was *cr.*, 31 Dec. 1688, BARONESS SHELBURNE, co. Wexford [I.], and *d.* Feb. 1708.(b) Will pr. 1711 [I.].

II. 1664, to 1671. Sir William Fenton, Baronet [I. 1661], only s. and h., *b.* probably about 1655; *suc. to the Baronetcy* in 1664, and to the family estates in 1667. He *d.* unm. and under age, 17, and was *bur.* 18 March 1670/1, at St. Brides, Dublin, when the *Baronetcy* bécame *extinct*.(c) Will dat. 28 Jan. 1669/70, pr. 7 Oct. 1671 [I.].

PERCEVAL, *or* PERCIVALL:

cr. 9 Sep. 1661;

afterwards, since 1715, Barons Perceval of Burton [I.],

since 1723, Viscounts Perceval of Kanturk [I.],

and since 1733, Earls of Egmont [I.].

I. 1661. "John Percivall [*rectius* Perceval], Esq., son and heir of Sir Philip Percivall [*rectius* Perceval], Knt., deceased, of Burton, co. Cork," by Catherine, da. of Arthur Usher (s. of Sir William Usher, Clerk of the Council [I.]), was *b.* in Dublin, 7 Sep. 1629; ed. at the Univ. of Cambridge; suc. his father, 10 Nov. 1647; admitted to Lincoln's Inn, 26 Nov. 1649; was concerned, in 1653, in the transplanting of the Papists into Connaught, and received, accordingly, remission of the sequestration on his estates; was *knighted* in Ireland, 22 July 1658, by the Lord Deputy, Henry Cromwell; was

(a) This apparently is the only *Irish* Baronetcy created by the Protector; no *Scotch* Baronetcy appears to have ever been so created. The preamble to this patent of 1658 is as under. "Whereas we, having taken into our consideration the faithful services performed unto us by our trusty and well beloved Maurice Fenton, Esq., we are now pleased to confer some such especial mark of our favour upon him for the same, as shall not only be an honour to him during his own life, but, descending by course of inheritance to his posterity, may give them cause seriously to imitate him in those virtuous courses for which he has found so gracious an acceptance in our sight."

(b) In Luttrell's *Diary*, 25 Feb. 1692/3, it is stated that "Lady Shelburn, widow to Sir Wm. Petty, worth £30,000 is married to Sir George Crofton, of Ireland," but there is no confirmatory evidence of this match, neither is there any trace of a *Sir* George Crofton in Ireland at that date. By her 2d husband, Sir William Petty, she was ancestress of the Earls of Shelburne [I.], Marquesses of Lansdowne.

(c) Catherine, his aunt, only surv. sister of the 1st Baronet, *m.*, before 1660, John (King), 1st Baron Kingston [I.], and *d.* 1669, leaving issue, who inherited the Mitchelstown estate, now (1902) belonging to her descendant, the Earl of Kingston [I.].

appointed, 7 May 1660, Clerk of the Crown, Prothonotary of the Common Pleas and Keeper of the Public Accounts [I.], and soon after the Restoration P.C. [I.], was *cr. a Baronet* [I.], as above, by patent, 9 Sep. 1661, at Dublin, the Privy Seal being dated 12 Aug. previous at Whitehall.(a) He was M.P. [I.] for co. Cork, 1661, till death in 1665; was Register of the Court of Claims, and (a short time before its abolition) of the Court of Wards, besides holding several other important offices. He *m.*, 14 Feb. 1655, Catharine, da of Robert Southwell, of Kingsale, by Helena, da. and h. of Robert Gore, of Sherston, Wilts. He *d.* 5 and was *bur.* 12 Nov. 1665 at St. Audoen's, Dublin, in his 37th year. Funeral entry. His widow, who was *b.* 1 Sep. 1637, at Kingsale, *d.* 17 Aug. 1679, and was *bur.* there. M.I. Will p. 1686 [I.].

II. 1665. Sir Philip Perceval, Baronet [I. 1661], of Burton aforesaid, 1st s. and h., *b.* 12 Jan. 1656, at Kingsale; *suc. to the Baronetcy*, 1 Nov. 1665; is said (in his M.I.) to have been ed. at Christ Church, Oxford(b); admitted to Lincoln's Inn, 6 Feb. 1674/5; travelled in France and Italy. He *d.* unm., of fever, 11 Sep. 1680, in his 24th year, and was *bur.* at Burton. M.I.

III. 1680. Sir John Perceval, Baronet [I. 1661], of Burton aforesaid, next surv. br. and h., being 3d s. of the 1st Baronet,(c) *b.* 22 Aug. 1660, at Egmont, "an old family seat"(b); matric. at Oxford (Christ Church), 26 June 1676, aged 16; admitted to Lincoln's Inn, 2 May 1678; *suc. to the Baronetcy*, 11 Sep. 1680, and received a grant (for three lives) of the offices of Clerk of the Crown, Prothonotary and Chief Clerk of the Common Pleas and Keeper of the writs and other records of the Court of King's Bench [I.]. He *m.* in Feb. 1680, Catharine, 4th da. of Sir Edward Dering, 2d Baronet [1627], of Surrenden, co. Kent, by Mary, da. of Daniel Harvey, of Folkestone. He *d.* of a distemper, caught at the assizes at Cork, 29 April 1686, aged 25, and was *bur.* at Burton, but was removed thence in 1730, to Bruhenny, *otherwise* Churchtown. Will made 24 Jan. 1685/6, pr. 1686 [I.]. His widow is said(b) to have *m.* in Aug. 1690, Col. Butler. She *d.* 2 and was *bur.* 5 Feb. 1690/1 (as "the Lady Katharine Persivall"), at Chelsea. Will dat. 8 Jan. 1686/7.(d).

IV. 1686. Sir Edward Perceval, Baronet [I. 1661], of Burton aforesaid, 1st s. and h., *b.* there 30 July 1682; *suc. to the Baronetcy*, 29 April 1686; was removed to England during the Irish troubles by his great uncle and guardian, Sir Robert Southwell, but was (as was his mother) attainted 7 May 1689, and is said(b) to have lost above £40,000. He *d.* unm. in London, of a polypus in the heart, 9 Nov. 1691, and was *bur.* at Henbury, co. Glouc., the burial place of the family of Southwell.

(a) In the patent is this remarkable clause of precedency, *viz.*, "That the eldest son or heir app. of every Baronet of this family, should at the age of 21 years, upon notice given thereof to the Lord Deputy, Chamberlain or Vice-Chamberlain of the Household, or in the absence of them to any other officer or minister attendant upon the person of the King, to [*sic*, but query if "to" should not be omitted] receive the order of Knighthood from the King, his heirs and successors, or the said deputy for the time being, of the King, his heirs, and successors, *to have, hold and enjoy* (although in the lifetime of his father or ancestor existing a Baronet by virtue of this patent) by virtue of the said Knighthood, the *same state, degree, dignity, style, title, name, place and precedency, with all and every other concessions made to said Sir John Perceval* and his heirs for ever." See note "b" below.

(b) Lodge's *Irish Peerage* [1789], under "Egmont."

(c) Robert Perceval, his next elder br., was *b.* 18 Feb. 1657, at Kingsale; ed. at the Univ. of Cambridge; admitted to Lincoln's Inn, 5 Feb. 1676/7; *d.* unm., being murdered in the Strand, 5 June 1677, and was *bur.* in Lincoln's Inn chapel.

(d) An abstract of it is given in Lodge's *Irish Peerage*, as in note "b" above. It does not, however, seem to have been proved, and if indeed she married (as is stated) some four years afterwards, would have been thereby made null.

V. 1691. Sir John Percival, Baronet [I. 1661], of Burton aforesaid, next br. and h., *b.* there 22 July 1683; *suc. to the Baronetcy*, 9 Nov. 1691; matric. at Oxford (Mag. Coll.), 18 Nov. 1699; F.R.S. (at the age of 19), 1702; M.P. [I.] for co. Cork (when under age), 1703-15; P.C. [I.], 1704 till his death; accomplished "the grand tour of Europe,"(a) 1705-07. He *m.* 10 June 1710, at St. Giles'-in-the-Fields, Midx., Catharine, 1st da. (whose issue, in 1775, became coheir) of Sir Philip Parker, 2d Baronet [1661] of Arwarton, co. Suffolk, by Mary, da. of Samuel Fortrey. She was living when he was *cr.*, 21 April 1715, BARON PERCEVAL OF BURTON, co. Cork [I.], and subsequently, 25 Feb. 1722/3, VISCOUNT PERCEVAL OF KANTURK, co. Cork [I.], and finally, 6 Nov. 1733, EARL OF EGMONT, co. Cork [I.]. In these Peerages this *Baronetcy* then *merged*, and still (1903) so continues. See *Peerage*, under "Egmont."

HAMILTON:

cr. 6 April 1662;

ex. 14 Feb. 1681/2.

I. 1662, to 1682. "Hans Hamilton, Esq., of Monella, co. Armagh," as also of Hamilton's Bawn in that county, 1st s. and h. of John Hamilton, of Coronary, co. Cavan, and of Monella aforesaid (who *d.* at Killyleagh, co. Down, 4 and was *bur.* 10 Dec. 1639, at Mallaghbrack, co. Armagh), by Sarah, da. of Anthony Brabazon, of Ballynasloe, co. Roscommon, (which John was br. to James, 1st Viscount Claneboye [I.], both being sons of the Rev. Hans Hamilton, Vicar of Dunlop, co. Ayr), suc. his father, 4 Dec. 1639; was M.P. [I.] for co. Armagh, 1661-66; and was *cr. a Baronet* [I.], as above, by pat. dat. at Dublin, 6 April 1662, the Privy Seal bearing date at Whitehall, 29 March previous. He was Sheriff of co. Armagh, 1669; P.C. [I.]. He *m.* Magdalen, sister to Marcus, 1st Viscount Dungannon [I.], yst. da. of Sir Edward Trevor, of Rose Trevor, co. Down, by his 2d wife Rose, da. of Henry Usher, Archbishop of Armagh, 1595—1613. He *d.* s.p.m.(b) 14 Feb. 1681/2, and was *bur.* at Mullaghbrack when the *Baronetcy* became *extinct*. Funeral entry [I.].

GORE:

cr. 10 April 1662;

afterwards, since 1758, Viscounts Sudley [I.];

and, since 1760, Earls of Arran [I.].

I. 1662. "Colonel Arthur Gore, of Newtown [*afterwards* Castle Gore], co. Mayo," 2d s. of Sir Paul Gore, 1st Baronet [I. 1622], by Isabella, da. of Francis Wickliffe, was Sheriff of co. Mayo and co. Galway, 1656; Constable for life of Fort Falkland, 20 Aug. 1660; was Capt. (afterwards Major) of a company of Foot in Dec. 1660; M.P. [I.] for co. Mayo, 1661-66, and was *cr. a Baronet* [I.], as above, by pat. dat. at Dublin 10 April 1662, the Privy Seal being dat. at Whitehall, 26 Nov. 1661; Sheriff for co. Mayo, 1670, and for co. Leitrim, 1677. He *m.* Eleanor, sister of Sir Oliver St. George, 1st Baronet [I. 1660], da. of Sir George St. George, of Carrickdrumrusk, co. Leitrim, by Catharine, da. of Richard Gifford. He *d.* 20 Dec. 1697, and was *bur.* in Killala Cathedral. M.I. His widow *d.* 1713. Will dat. 13 March 1712, pr. 28 Aug. 1713 [I.].

(a) Lodge's *Irish Peerage* [1789], under "Egmont."

(b) Sarah, his only child (who *d.* v.p.), *m.* Robert Hamilton, of Mount Hamilton, co. Armagh, who was *cr. a Baronet* [I.] 19 Feb. 1682/3, a dignity which became *extinct* on the death of his son about 1730.

II. 1697. Sir Arthur Gore, Baronet [I. 1662], of Castle Gore aforesaid, grandson and h., being 1st s. and h. of Paul Gore, by Anne, da. of Sir John Gore, of Sacombe, Herts, which Paul (who was a Fellow Commoner of Trin. Coll., Dublin, 2 July 1677, and then aged 19, and who *d.* v.p. 20 Oct. 1689), was 1st s. and h. ap. of the late Baronet. He was *b.* in or shortly after 1685; *suc. to the Baronetcy*, 20 Dec. 1697; was Sheriff of co. Mayo, 1711; M.P. [I.] for Donegal borough, 1713-14; for co. Mayo, 1715-27 and 1727 till his death in 1741. He *m.* Elizabeth, 1st da. of Maurice Annesley, of Little Rath, co. Kildare (grandson of Francis, Viscount Valentia [I.], by Sarah, da. of Richard (Blayney), 4th Baron Blayney of Monaghan [I.]. He *d.* at Newtown, 10 Feb. 1741, and was *bur.* at Killala. Will pr. 1742 [I.].

III. 1741. Sir Arthur Gore, Baronet [I. 1662], of Castle Gore aforesaid, 1st s. and h.; *b.* about 1713; Fellow Comm. of Trin. Coll., Dublin, 5 Nov. 1718, and then aged 15; B.A., 1722; M.P. [I.] for Donegal borough, 1727 till raised to the peerage [I.] in 1758(a); Sheriff of co. Wexford, 1738; *suc. to the Baronetcy*, 10 Feb. 1741; P.C. [I.], May 1748. He *m.*, 16 March 1730/2, at St. Mary's, Dublin, Jane, widow of William Worth, of Rathfarnham, only da. and h. of Richard Saunders, of Saunders Court, co. Wexford. She, who was *bap.* 20 Dec. 1704, *d.* 20 March 1747. He was, after her death, *cr.*, 15 Aug. 1758, BARON SAUNDERS OF DEEPS, co. Wexford, and VISCOUNT SUDLEY OF CASTLE GORE, co. Mayo [I.], being subsequently *cr.*, 12 April 1762, EARL OF ARRAN of the Arran Islands, co. Galway [I.]. In these peerages this *Baronetcy* then *merged*, and still [1903] so continues. See *Peerage*, under "Arran."

BRAMHALL:

cr. 31 May 1662;

ex. 1667.

I. 1662, to 1667. "Thomas Bramhall, Esq., of Bramhall Hall [in Rathmullyan], co. Meath, s. and h. [apparent] of John [Bramhall], Archbishop of Armagh" [1661-63], (who, as Bishop of Derry [1634-60], had suffered much for his active loyalty), by Elinor (*d.* 26 Nov. 1661), da. of William Halley,(b) of York, was M.P. [I.] for Dungannon, 1661-66, and was v.p. *cr. a Baronet* [I.], as above, by pat. dat. at Dublin, 31 May 1662, the Privy Seal being dat. 2 April previous at Whitehall. He suc. his father, 25 June 1663, and was Sheriff of co. Louth, 1664. He *m.* (Lic. 5 Jan. 1663/4) Elizabeth, 1st da. of Sir Paul Davis, of Kill, co. Kildare, Sec. of State [I.], by his 2d wife, Anne, da. of Sir William Parsons, 1st Baronet

(a) He was one of the nine Gores who are said to have been at the same time members of the Irish House of Commons between 1751 and 1758, being himself a member from 1727 to 1758. The others appear to have been (2) William Gore, of Woodford, M.P. for co. Leitrim, 1727-60; (3) Arthur Gore, of Tenelick, M.P. for co. Longford, 1739-58; (4) Sir Ralph Gore, 5th Baronet [I. 1622], M.P. for co. Donegal, 1745-64, afterwards Baron Gore, Viscount Bellisle and Earl of Ross [I.]; (5) Ralph Gore, of Barrowmount, M.P. for Kilkenny, 1747-60; (6) John Gore, M.P. for Jamestown, 1747-60, afterwards (1766) Baron Annaly [I.]; (7) Frederick Gore, of Limerick, M.P. for Tulske, 1747-60; (8) Capt. Henry Gore, br. of the above Frederick, M.P. for Killybegs, 1749-60, and (9) Paul Annesley Gore, of Elm Hall, M.P. for co. Mayo, 1751-60.

(b) She is sometimes (erroneously) called the "widow of (—) Halley." Her arms, as Halley, are impaled with those of Bramhall in the Funeral Entry of the Archbishop. See also Betham's *Baronetage*, vol. iv, p. 43, note under "Coghill."

[I. 1620]. He *d.* s.p.(a) in Dublin, 1667, when the *Baronetcy* became *extinct*. Will dat. 14 June 1667, pr. 1667 [I.]. His widow *m.* (Lic. Dublin, 16 Feb. 1668/9) John Topham, LL.D., Judge Advocate Gen. [I.] and Vicar Gen. of Dublin, who was *Knighted* in 1678, and who *d.* 3 April 1698 being *bur.* at St. Audoens, Dublin, his will being pr. [I.] in 1700. By him she had issue.

SOUTHWELL:

cr. 4 Aug. 1662;

afterwards, since 1717,

Barons Southwell of Castle Mattress [I.];

and, since 1776,

Viscounts Southwell of Castle Mattress [I.].

I. 1662. "Thomas Southwell, Esq., of Castle Mattress, co. Limerick," as also of Barham Hall, co. Suffolk, 5th but last surv. s. of Edmond Southwell, of the same, by Catharine, da. and h. of Garrett Herbert, of Rathkeale, was a Commissioner, 21 Nov. 1653, for the precinct of Limerick, to examine the delinquency of the Irish; was Sheriff in 1654 and 1655 of the counties of Clare, Cork, Kerry and Limerick, and was *cr. a Baronet* [I.], as above, by pat. dat. at Dublin, 4 Aug. 1662, the Privy Seal being dat. at Whitehall, 10 March 1661/2. He *m.* Elizabeth, da. of William Starkey, of Dromoland, co. Clare. He *d.* 1680, and was *bur.* at Rathkeale. M.I. Will dat. 7 Dec. 1680, pr. 1681 [I.]. His widow *d.* at a great age 19 Sep. 1705, and was *bur.* with him.

II. 1680. Sir Thomas Southwell, Baronet [I. 1662] of Castle Mattress aforesaid, grandson and h., being only surv. s. and h. of Richard Southwell, of Callow, by Elizabeth, da. of Murrough (O'Brien), 1st Earl of Inchiquin, which Richard, who was M.P. [I.] for Askeaton, 1661-66, was only s. and h. ap. of the late Baronet, but *d.* v.p. He *suc. to the Baronetcy* in 1680; distinguished himself against the army of James II in Ireland, by which, however, he was taken prisoner in March 1688/9,(b) but was pardoned by that King, 1 April 1690; was M.P. [I.] for co. Limerick, 1695-99, 1703-13, and 1715 till raised to the Peerage [I.] in 1717; a Commissioner of the Revenue [I.], 1697-1712 and 1714-20, as also for the building of Barracks, etc., 1710; P.C. [I.] to Queen Anne, 1710, and to Geo. I, 1714. He *m.* in April 1696, Meliora, 1st da. of Thomas (Coningsby), 1st Earl Coningsby, by his 1st wife, Barbara, da. of Ferdinando Gorges, of Eye, co. Hereford. She was living when he was *cr.*, 4 Sep. 1717, BARON SOUTHWELL OF CASTLE MATTRESS, co. Limerick [I.], in which Peerage this *Baronetcy* then *merged*, and still [1903] so continues, the 3d Baron and 4th Baronet being *cr.* 18 July 1776, VISCOUNT SOUTHWELL OF CASTLE MATTRESS, co. Limerick [I.]. See *Peerage*.

(a) Of his three sisters and coheirs, (1) Isabella, *m.* Sir James Graham (s. of William, Earl of Menteith [S.]), by whom she had an only da. and h., Helena, who *m.* Sir Arthur Rawdon, 2d Baronet [1666]; (2) Jane, *m.* William Toxteth, Alderman of Drogheda; (3) Anne, *m.* Standish Hartstonge, one of the Barons of the Exchequer, who was *cr.* a Baronet [I.], 20 April 1681.

(b) There is a very long account of this matter in Lodge's *Irish Peerage* (edit. 1789), vol. vi, pp. 20-23.

DANCER(a):

cr. 12 Aug. 1662.

I. 1662. "Thomas Dancer, Esq., of Waterford," whose parentage is apparently unknown, was admitted to King's Inns, Dublin, 28 Jan. 1656/7; Sheriff of co. Wexford, 1657; Mayor of Waterford, 1660; M.P. [I.] for New Ross, 1661-66, and was *cr. a Baronet* [I.], as above, by pat. dat. at Dublin, 12 Aug. 1662, the Privy Seal being dat. at Whitehall, 20 Nov. 1661. He was Mayor of Carrickfergus, 1669, and was Sheriff of King's County, 1677. He *m.* firstly, Sarah, widow of John Itchingham, of Dunbrody, co. Wexford, 9th da. of Sir Adam Loftus, of Rathfarnham, co. Dublin, Joint Keeper of the Great Seal [I.], by Jane, da. of Walter Vaughan, of Golden Grove, co. Carmarthen. He *m.* secondly, Bridget, widow of Philip Bigoe, of Newton in King's County, formerly widow of Garret Talbot, da. of Sir George Herbert, 1st Baronet [I. 1630] of Durrow, by Frances, da. of Sir Edward FitzGerald. By her he had no issue. He *d.* Aug. 1689.

II. 1689. Sir Thomas Dancer, Baronet [I. 1662], of Modreeny, co. Tipperary, 1st s. and h.; *suc. to the Baronetcy* in Aug. 1689; was a Major in the Regiment of Arthur, Earl of Donegall [I.], and *d.* unm., in Jamaica, about 15 Jan. 1702/3. Admon. [I.] 17 Sep. 1703 and [E.] 14 Oct. 1706, to "John Echingham Chichester, Esq.," nephew by sister and next of kin.

III. 1703. Sir Loftus Dancer, Baronet [I. 1662], of Modreeny aforesaid, br. and h.; *suc. to the Baronetcy* in 1703. He *m.*, in or before 1690, Catharine, da. of [—] Amyrald? He *d.* 27 March 1734, at Modreeny.

IV. 1734. Sir Thomas Dancer, Baronet [I. 1662], of Modreeny aforesaid, 1st s. and h., *b.* about 1699; admitted Fellow Commoner of Trin. Coll., Dublin, 21 Jan. 1714/5, aged 15; *suc. to the Baronetcy*, 27 March 1734; Sheriff of co. Tipperary, 1741; Mayor of Cashel, 1749. He *m.* (settl. 17 June 1718), Anchorita, da. of Daniel Rogers, of Ballynaven, co. Tipperary, by Charity, da. of (—) Freeman. He *d.* s.p.m.,(b) suddenly, at Thomastown, co. Tipperary, Nov. 1776, aged 76. Will dat. 3 March 1776, pr. 8 Feb. 1777 [I.].

V. 1776. Sir Amyrald Dancer, Baronet [I. 1662], of Modreeny aforesaid, grandnephew and h. male, being s. of Capt. Thomas Dancer, by Honora, da. of Thomas Jones, which Thomas Dancer was s. of Richard Dancer, br. of the late and yr. s. of the 3d Baronet. He was *b.* 14 Nov. 1768, and *suc. to the Baronetcy*, Nov. 1776. He *m.* 12 April 1804, Jemima Matilda, 3d da. and coheir of Philip Going, of Monaquil, co. Tipperary, by Grace, da. of Thomas Bernard. She *d.* 8 June 1824. He *d.* 22 Nov. 1843.

VI. 1843. Sir Thomas Bernard Going Dancer, Baronet [I. 1662], of Modreeny aforesaid, 1st s. and h., *b.* 9 Feb. 1806; *suc. to the Baronetcy*, 22 Nov. 1843; was Sheriff of co. Tipperary, 1852. He *m.* 7 Aug. 1845, at Leamington, co. Warwick, Helen Jane, only child of John Johnston, of Markyate, Herts, of Ballee, co. Down, and of York Terrace, Leamington. He *d.* 8 May 1872, aged 66, at 15 Queen's square, Bath. His widow *d.* there, 15 Nov. 1885, aged 60.

(a) Most of the information in this article has been kindly supplied by G. D. Burtchaell. See p. 304, note "a."

(b) His only da. and h., *m.* Samuel Eyre, and had, with female issue, two sons, (1) Thomas Dancer Eyre and (2) Chichester Eyre.

VII. 1872. SIR THOMAS JOHNSTON DANCER, Baronet [I. 1662], of Modreeny aforesaid, only s. and h., *b.* 3 Jan. 1852, at Kingstown in Ireland; ed. at Eton; *suc. to the Baronetcy*, 8 May 1872; sometime Lieut. 2d Somerset Militia. He *m.* 18 April 1877, at Goring, Oxon, Isabella Laura Elizabeth, only da. of Samuel Weare GARDINER, of Coombe Lodge in Whitchurch, Oxon, by Isabella, da. of Sir Laurence Vaughan PALK, 3d Baronet [1782]. She *d.* s.p.m., 23 July 1886, at Upton Grove, near Telbury, aged 31.

BOURKE(a):

fiat dated 1662.

It is stated in the Genealogy of "Theobald BOURKE, of St. Croix, Esq.," certified by William HAWKINS, Ulster King of Arms, 9 Nov. 1778 [Ulster's office, Dublin], under the family of "BOURKE, OF NEWCASTLE, co. LIMERICK" that "to the heir of which [*i.e.*, this] house, in 1662, King Charles II gave the *fiat of a Baronetage*, yet preserved, which was never taken out or registered."

AYLMER:

cr. about 1662, before 6 Nov. 1622(b);

afterwards, since 1776,

BARONS AYLMER OF BALRATH [I.].

I. 1662? CHRISTOPHER AYLMER, of Balrath, co. Meath, 1st s. and h. of Gerald AYLMER,(c) of the same (*d.* between July and Nov. 1662, his will being pr. [I.] in that year), by [—], his 1st wife,(d) was *b.* probably about 1620, and was, presumably, soon after his father's death in July 1662 and certainly before 6 Nov. in that year(b) *cr. a Baronet* [I.], as above. He was restored to his estate by decree of the Court of Claims, 8 May 1667. He *m.* shortly before 11 Aug. 1639 (settlement that year), Margaret, 3d da. of Matthew (PLUNKETT), 5th BARON LOUTH [I.], by Mary, da. of Sir Richard FITZWILLIAM, of Meryon, co. Dublin. He *d.* Sep. 1671. His widow *d.* 4 Dec. 1683. Admon. [I.] 1673 to her son, Sir Gerald.

(a) The information in this article has been kindly supplied by G. D. Burtchaell. See p. 304, note "a."

(b) There is no entry of this creation in the *Liber Munerum Hiberniæ*, but the date of 1662 is assigned to it in Beatson's *List*, and the petition of the son of the 1st Baronet to the Court of Claims shews it to have been before 6 Nov. 1662 [*Ex inform.* G. D. Burtchaell, see p. 304, note "a"].

(c) This Gerald was great grandson of Sir Gerald Aylmer, L. Ch. Justice of the King's Bench [I.], 1535-39, who was 2d son of Bartholomew Aylmer, of Lyons, co. Kildare.

(d) He *m.* for his 2d wife, at some date after 1629, Mary, Dow. Baroness Louth [I.], whose da. (by her 1st husband) *m.* his son, the 1st Baronet.

II. 1671. SIR GERALD AYLMER, Baronet [I. 1662?], of Balrath aforesaid, 1st s. and h.(a), *b.* about 1640; was adjudged "an innocent Papist," 17 Aug. 1663, by the Court of Claims; *suc. to the Baronetcy* in Sep. 1671, and was confirmed in his estate by patent, 5 Jan. 1679/80, having a further grant under the Act of Grace, 13 Nov. 1684. He *m.* Jan. 1664/5, Mary, sister of Sir Patrick BELLEW, 1st Baronet [I. 1688], da. of John BELLEW, of Willystown, co. Louth, by Mary, da. of Robert DILLON, of Clonbrock. He *d.* June 1702. Admon. [I.] 16 June 1702 to his widow.

III. 1702. SIR JOHN AYLMER, Baronet [I. 1662?], of Balrath aforesaid, 1st s. and h.; *suc. to the Baronetcy* in June 1702. He *m.* Alice, sister of George BROWNE. He *d.* s.p. 2 April 1714. Will dat. 6 Jan. 1713/4, pr. [I.] 28 April 1714. His widow *m.* Dominick MEADE, of Tullyheady, co. Tipperary, who *d.* s.p. Nov. 1717. She *m.* 7 March 1718/9 (as her 3d husband and his 2d wife), Thomas LYSTER, of Athleague, co. Roscommon, who *d.* 28 Aug. 1726. She *m.* finally (as her 4th husband) the Rev. Oliver CARTER, of Killala, co. Mayo, whose will was pr. [I.] 1768. Her will, dat. 20 Oct. 1743, was pr. [I.] 14 Jan. 1748/9.

IV. 1714. SIR ANDREW AYLMER, Baronet [I. 1662?], of Balrath aforesaid, br. and h., *suc. to the Baronetcy*, 2 April 1714. He *m.* Catharine, yr. da. of Edward HUSSEY, of Westown, co. Dublin, by Mabel, da. of (—) BARNEWALL. He *d.* 5 Nov. 1740, in King street, Oxmantown, Dublin. Will dat. 31 Oct. 1740, pr. [I.] 4 March 1755. His widow *d.* March 1746/7. Will dat. 1 March 1746/7, pr. 29 March 1747.

V. 1740. SIR GERALD AYLMER, Baronet [I. 1662?], of Balrath aforesaid, only s. and h.; *suc. to the Baronetcy*, 5 Nov. 1740. He *d.* unm. 12 July 1745. Will dat. 28 Jan. 1744/5, pr. [I.] 18 Jan. 1745/6.

VI. 1745. SIR MATTHEW AYLMER, Baronet [I. 1662?], of Dublin, cousin and h. male, being only s. and h. of Patrick AYLMER, of Mayfield, co. Kildare, Surveyor Gen. of Excise, by Williamsa, "an English heiress," which Patrick, who had become a Protestant, and who *d.* in 1739 (will dat. 3 March 1737/8, pr. [I.] 2 July 1739), was 4th son of the 2d Baronet. He was *b.* 10 April 1724, and *suc. to the Baronetcy*, 12 July 1745. He *m.* Dorothea, da. of [—] LORD. He *d.* s.p. in London, April 1776. Will dat. 10 April 1773, pr. [I.] 1 May 1776. His widow *d.* in Charlemont street, Dublin. Her will dat. 30 May 1789, was pr. [I.], 6 Aug. 1791.

VII. 1776. HENRY (AYLMER), BARON AYLMER OF BALRATH [I.], and Baronet [I. 1662?], cousin and h. male, being 2d but only surv. s. and h. of Henry, 3d Baron, by Anne, da. of William PIERCE, of Virginia, which Henry (who *d.* 7 Oct. 1766, aged 48) was 2d but 1st surv. s. and h. of Henry, 2d Baron (who *d.* 26 June 1754), only s. of Matthew, 1st Baron (so *cr.* 1 May 1718, who *d.* 18 Aug. 1720), 2d s. of the 1st Baronet. On the death of his father, 7 Oct. 1766, he *suc. to the Peerage* [I.], and ten years later, on the death of his cousin, *suc. to the Baronetcy*, 11 May 1776, which thenceforth became *merged in that peerage*. See *Peerage*.

(a) Matthew Aylmer, the 2d son, M.P. for Dover, 1697 till death in 1720, having distinguished himself in the Naval Service, was *cr.*, 1 May 1718, BARON AYLMER OF BALRATH, co. Meath [I.], and was great grandfather of Henry, the 4th Baron, who in 1776 *suc. to the Baronetcy*.

2 S

SHERIDAN(a):

cr., as alleged, in 1662(b);

assumed till 22 April 1836.

1662, to 1775. [—] SHERIDAN, of co. Wicklow and of Belturbet, co. Cavan, is stated to have been *cr. a Baronet* [I.] in 1662,(b) and to have been a relative of Sir THOMAS SHERIDAN, "a conspicuous character."(b)

1775. [—] SHERIDAN, Baronet(c) [I. 1662], presumably h. male of the body of the alleged grantee, *suc. to the Baronetcy*(c) in 1775,(d) and *d.* 1790.

1790. SIR HENRY WILLIAM SHERIDAN, Baronet(c) [I. 1662], of Elford House, co. Kent, s. and h.; *suc. to the Baronetcy*(c) in 1790. He *d.* 27 Jan. 1802. Will pr. 1802. The will of dame Anne SHERIDAN pr. 1808.

1802, to 1836. SIR WILLIAM HENRY SHERIDAN, Baronet(c) [I. 1662], s. and h.; *suc. to the Baronetcy*(c) in 1802, and was presented at Court on the occasion. He was, as early as 1808, Lieut. Col. in the Coldstream Guards, being, 22 July 1830, Lieut. General. In 1832 he was, as "Lieut. Gen. William SHERIDAN," made **K.C.H.** He *d.* abroad 22 April 1835, when the *assumption of this Baronetcy ceased*. Will as "Sir William SHERIDAN, *alias* William WEBB," pr. Dec. 1836 and Dec. 1838.

(a) The whole of the information in this article is kindly supplied by G. D. Burtchaell (see p. 304, note "a"), who remarks that the family of Sheridan was *not* connected with the county of Wicklow, and that no member of it was in 1662 of a sufficiently "conspicuous character" to make it likely that he should obtain a Baronetcy.

(b) In a letter from William H. Sheridan, Lieut. Col. Coldstream Guards, 3 March 1808 [Betham's Collections, now in possession of Sir Arthur Vicars, Ulster King of Arms], the writer states that "*the first creation* in my family of Baronet *took place in the year 1662*, county Wicklow and Belturbet, co. Cavan." He goes on to state that "Sir Thomas Sheridan, my original [*sic*] ancestor, was a conspicuous character, and many members of my family have filled the highest situations in the Irish government. I succeeded my father in 1800 [*Qy.*, Jan. 1802], since which period I find that my name has been omitted in the list." The above-named Sir Thomas (*b.* 1647; *d.* in or shortly before 1712) was s. of the Rev. Denis Sheridan, and was, in March, 1686/7, P.C. and Principal Sec. of State [I.] to James II. His son Thomas was *cr. a Baronet* [I.] in 1726 by the titular King, James III, and *d.* s.p. in Rome 25 Nov. 1746.

(c) Assuming a Baronetcy [I.] of Sheridan to have been created in 1662.

(d) "Sir" W. H. Sheridan (see note "b" above) writes as under:—"My grandfather assumed the Baronetcy in 1775, his claim being duly authorised by His Majesty. My father succeeded in 1790, and his claim was never disputed. In 1801 [*Qy.* Jan. 1802?] my father died, consequently I succeeded to the Baronetcy and was presented to the King on the occasion."

On this G. D. Burtchaell (see p. 304, note "b") remarks:—"I have not succeeded in identifying the grandfather who assumed the title in 1775. In O'Callaghan's *Irish Brigades* there is an account of a Sir Michael Sheridan, who was no doubt the Michael Sheridan, a Col. in the French service in 1765, one of the grandnephews of Sir Thomas, who registered their pedigree.

SHAEN:

cr. 7 Feb. 1662/3;

ex. 24 June 1725.

I. 1663. "SIR JAMES SHAEN, Knt., of Kilmore, co. Roscommon," as also of Bishopstone, co. Westmeath, 1st s. and h. of Patrick SHAEN,(a) was Sheriff of the counties of Longford and Westmeath, 1655; Cessor, Collector, and Receiver Gen. of the province of Leinster for life, 4 Oct., 1660; *Knighted*, 22 Dec. 1660; Register of the Court of Claims [I.], 30 March 1661; was M.P. [I.] for Clonmel, 1661-66; for Baltinglas, 1692-93, and 1695 till his death in that year, and was *cr. a Baronet* [I.], as above, by patent dat. at Dublin, 7 Feb., 1662/3, the Privy Seal being dat. at Hampton Court, 27 July 1662. He was made Surveyor Gen. [I.] for life, 13 Feb. 1667, and a Farmer of the Revenue and Commissioner of Excise [I.], 1692.(b) He *m.* 28 July 1650 (before a Justice of the Peace), Frances, 5th da. of George (FITZGERALD), 16th EARL OF KILDARE [I.], by Joan, da. of Richard (BOYLE), 1ST EARL OF CORK [I.]. He *d.* 13 Dec. 1695. Will pr. Commissary Court, 1696.

II. 1695, to 1725. SIR ARTHUR SHAEN, Baronet [I. 1663], of Kilmore aforesaid, only s. and h.; was M.P. [I.] for Lismore, 1692-93, 1695-99, and 1713 till his death in 1725; *suc. to the Baronetcy*, 13 Dec. 1695; was Sheriff of co. Mayo, 1708, and of co. Roscommon, 1709 and 1718. He *m.* firstly, Jane, da. and h. of Sir SAMUEL HELE, 2d Baronet [1627], of Flete, co. Devon, by Mary, da. of Anthony HUNGERFORD, of Farley, Wilts. She *d.* s.p. Her will pr. May 1719. He *m.* secondly Susanna, da. of Morgan MAGAN, of Togherstown, co. Westmeath. He *d.* s.p.m., 24 June, 1725,(c) at Kilmore, when the *Baronetcy became extinct*. Will pr. [I.] 1725. His widow *m.* Feb. 1725/6, Robert DILLON, of Clonbrook, co. Galway (*d.* 11 June 1746), and was grandmother of Robert, 1st BARON CLONBROOK [I].

(a) This Patrick was s. of John Shaen, cousin and h. of Sir Francis Shaen, Knt., who *d.* s.p. 24 Nov. 1614.

(b) See Lodge's *Irish Peerage* (edit. 1789), vol. i., p. 104, under "Leinster," where, however, the Baronet's parentage is incorrectly given.

(c) Of his three daughters and coheirs by his 2d wife (1) Frances, *m.* 1 June 1738, John Bingham, of Newbrook, co. Mayo, and had issue. (2) Elizabeth, *d.* unm. in 1727. (3) Susanna, *m.* firstly, in 1739, James Wynne, of Hazlewood, co. Sligo, who *d.* s.p. 25 Dec. 1748. She *m.* secondly, 23 Feb. 1750, Capt. Henry Boyle Carter, of Castlemartin, co. Kildare, and had issue, of which, as also of the earlier members of the Carter family, a copious account is given in Lodge's *Irish Peerage*, as in note "b" above.

Baronetcies of Scotland.(a)

1625—1707

SECOND PART.

VIZ.,

CREATIONS,

30 Jan. 1648/9 to 31 Dec. 1664.(b)

["After the Restoration of King Charles II [29 May 1660] the description of *Nova Scotia* was omitted, so that the Baronets thus created cannot be considered as coming under the conditions of the original foundation of that order." See vol. ii, p. 277.]

MACLEAN, *or* MACLEARE :(c)

1650 to 1667 or later.

1650. "JOHN [*otherwise* HANS] MACLEAN," an officer in the English fleet, settled in Sweden at some date after 1620; became a merchant at Gottenburgh, 1639; was ennobled in Sweden, under the name of MAKELEER, 1649, and "having rendered some service to the house of Stuart was *created an English* [*sic*. but query if not Scotch] *Baronet*, as "of Dowart," in 1650 by Charles II, during his exile" [Marryat's *One Year in Sweden*, 1862, p. 483; Stodart's *Scottish Arms*, vol. ii, p. 284; and Otto Downer's *Scottish Families in Finland and Sweden*, Helsingfors, 1884]. No patent, however, of such creation is recorded. Administration of the goods of "SIR JOHN MACKLEARE, Knt., who died at Gottenbourgh in the Kingdom of Sweden, was granted 15 Feb. 1666/7, to his son SIR JOHN MACKLEARE, Baronet."

PRIMROSE:

cr. 1 or 5 Aug. 1651;

subsequently, 1703-41, VISCOUNTS PRIMROSE [S.],

and since 1741, EARLS OF ROSEBERY [S.].

I. 1651. "SIR ARCHIBALD PRIMROSE, of Carringham"(d) [*i.e.*, Carrington], yr. s. of James PRIMROSE, Clerk of the Privy Council [S.], 1602 till his death in 1641, being his 1st s. by his 2d wife, Catherine,

(a) See vol. ii, p. 275, note "a," for acknowledgment of the kind assistance of Sir James Balfour Paul, Lyon King of Arms, as to these Scotch Baronetcies, to which must be added that of James R. Anderson, of Glasgow, who has compiled a valuable list of the Baronetcies [S.] made by Charles II.

(b) See p. 1, note "a," as to the date of 31 Dec. 1664.

(c) This and other alleged or obscure creations about this period have been kindly furnished by J. R. Anderson. See note "a" above.

(d) Milne's *List*, though sometimes described as "of Chester."

da. of Richard LAWSON, Bookseller, Burgess of Edinburgh, was *b.* 16 May 1616; was Clerk of the Privy Council [S.] on his father's death, 2 Sep. 1651; joined the army of Montrose, was taken prisoner at Philiphaugh, 13 Sep. 1645, and sentenced to death; took part in the "engagement" of 1648; was deprived of his office, 1649, though reinstated in 1652, and, having previously been *Knighted*, was *cr. a Baronet*, [S.], as above, by Charles II, by patent, dat. at Woodhouse, in Scotland, 1 Aug. 1651, but no record thereof is in the Great Seal Register. He, however, after the battle of Worcester, a month later, fled abroad, when his estates were sequestrated. On 7 Aug. 1660 he was made Lord Clerk Register of Scotland, and on 13 Feb. 1660/1 one of the Lords of Session [S.], taking the *designation of Lord Carrington* from an estate he had purchased. He was, however, forced to resign these offices 11 June 1676, though given the less lucrative post of Lord Justice General [S.], from which he was also removed, 16 Oct. 1678. He bought the Barony of Barnbougle, in Dalmeny, co. Linlithgow, in 1662, for 160,000 merks. He *m.* firstly, in or before 1641, Elizabeth, 1st da. and coheir of the Hon. Sir James KEITH, of Benholme (2d s. of George, 5th EARL MARISCHAL [S.]), by Margaret, da. of Sir David LINDSAY, of EDZELL. He *m.* secondly, Agnes, widow of Sir James DUNDAS, of Newliston, co. Linlithgow, da. of Sir William GRAY, of Pittendrum. He *d.* 27 Nov. 1679, in his 64th year, and was *bur.* at Dalmeny. M.I.

II. 1679. SIR WILLIAM PRIMROSE, Baronet [S. 1651], of Carrington aforesaid, 2d but 1st surv. s. and h.(a) by 1st wife, *b.* 14 Jan. 1649, at Edinburgh; Clerk of Notaries, 1 Nov. 1660; *suc. to the Baronetcy*, 27 Nov. 1679. He *m.*, in or before 1677, Mary, 3d da. of Patrick SCOTT, of Thirlestane, co. Selkirk. He *d.* 23 Sep. 1687, in his 39th year.

III. 1687. SIR JAMES PRIMROSE, Baronet [S. 1651], of Carrington aforesaid, 2d but 1st surv. s. and h., *b.* about 1680(b); *suc. to the Baronetcy*, 23 Sep. 1687, and was served heir to his father 4 Nov. following; was M.P. for co. Edinburgh, 1703. He *m.* Eleanor, 4th and yst. da. of James (CAMPBELL), 2d EARL OF LOUDOUN [S.], by Margaret, da. of Hugh (MONTGOMERY), EARL OF EGLINTON [S.]. She was living when he was *cr.*, 30 Nov. 1703, VISCOUNT PRIMROSE, etc. [S.]. In that Peerage this *Baronetcy* then *merged* till, on the death of the 3d Viscount, on 8 May 1741, the Peerage honours became, presumably, extinct, but the Baronetcy devolved on the EARL OF ROSEBERY [S.], who had been so *cr.* 10 April 1703, and who was yst. s. (only s. by the 2d wife) of the 1st Baronet. In this Peerage it still [1903] continues. See *Peerage*.

MARSHALL(c):

1658, to [—].

1658. "SIR WILLIAM MARSHALL," is said to have been *cr. a Baronet* [S.?] "by patent dat. at Brussels," 21 May 1658 [Stodart's *Scottish Arms*, vol. ii, p. 384], but no record thereof is in the Great Seal Register.

(a) His elder br., Sir James Primrose, of Barnbougle, *b.* 5 Feb. 1645, *m.* in or before 1669, Elizabeth, da. of Sir Robert Sinclair, of Longformacus, but *d.* s.p.m. and v.p. in or after 1671, leaving female issue.

(b) His elder br., Archibald, who *d.* young, was *b.* 12 Oct. 1678.

(c) See p. 324, note "c," under "Maclean."

ROLLO(a):

1658? to 1666.

1658? "SIR JOHN ROLLO, of Bannockburn," 2d s. of Andrew (ROLLO), 1st LORD ROLLO OF DUNCRUB [S.], by Catherine, da. of James (DRUMMOND), 1st LORD MADERTY [S.], had a charter of the lands of Bannockburn and Skeoch, united into the Barony of Bannockburn, 25 July 1636. He "is styled *Knight Baronet* in [the] service of his nephew, Lord Rollo [S.] as [his] heir male special of conquest, 1672: no patent of creation [of any Baronetcy] is recorded, but as he is styled *Sir* in 1658, the honour may have been conferred by Charles II abroad." [Stodart's *Scottish Arms*, vol. ii, p. 297.] He *d.* unm. in 1666.

MERCER:

1660 to [—].

1660. SIR JAMES MERCER, of Aldie is mentioned in the Great Seal Register [S.] as *Knight Baronet*. [Additions to Milne's *List* as given in Foster's *Baronetage*, 1883, p. xxiii, where the date of 1660 is assigned to the creation]. He was s. and h. of Sir Lawrence MERCER, of Aldie, by Cecily, da. of John (COLVILLE), LORD COLVILLE OF CULROSS [S.]; suc. his father in 1645; was M.P. [S.] for Perthshire, 1645-49, being then a Knight and "Laird of Aldie." He *m.*, in 1648, Jean, 1st da. of Sir Thomas STEWART, of Grandtully, and had issue. Admon. of the goods of "Sir James MERCER, *Knt.*, of St. Martin's-in-the-Fields, Midx.," was granted, 14 April 1671, to his relict, Dame Jane MERCER.

DRUMMOND :(a)

1660? *d.* 1713.

1660? "SIR WILLIAM DRUMMOND, of Hawthornden," co. Edinburgh, 2d but 1st surv. s. and h. of William DRUMMOND, of the same, the well known poet (*d.* 4 Dec. 1649, aged 64), by Elizabeth, sister to James LOGAN, of Mountlothian, was *b.* April 1636; and was *Knighted* by Charles II, by whom, also, he is sometimes said(b) to have been *cr. a Baronet* [S.], but no record exists of such creation. He, who inherited the estate of Carnock, *d.* in 1713, leaving a son, William, who *d.* 1735, aged 71, leaving one son, William, who *d.* s.p. in 1760, but neither of these assumed the style of a Baronet, so that probably the Baronetage is a confusion for the undoubted Knighthood. [See Douglas' *Baronage* [S.] for an account of this family.]

(a) See p. 324, note "c," under "Maclean."

(b) *Scottish Antiquary*, vol. xi, p. 129.

PRETYMAN [S.] :(a)

cr. about 1660 ;(b)

ex. or *dormant* in or shortly after 1749,

but assumed, 1823-27, as PRETYMAN-TOMLINE.

I. 1660? JOHN PRETYMAN, of Lodington and Horninghold, co. Leicester, formerly of Driffield, co. Gloucester, s. and h. of Sir John PRETYMAN, of Driffield aforesaid (which he had purchased in or before 1623), and of Bacton, co. Suffolk, by his 2d wife, Mary (*m.* 29 Nov. 1607, at St. Barth.-the-Great, London), da. of William BOURCHIER, of Barnesley, co. Gloucester, was *b.* about 1612; admitted to Lincoln's Inn, 3 Feb. 1628/9; suc. his father, 22 Dec. 1638, being then aged 26; was in the commission for subsidies and garrisons for that county, 1641-42; incurred great losses in the Royal cause and was obliged, in 1651, to sell the Driffield estate, but retained that of Horninghold, co. Leicester, 1643 (in right of his wife), and purchased, in 1649, the estate of Lodington, in that county, as also that of Greensfarm, in Willoughby, co. Lincoln; was engaged in Sir George BOOTH'S rising, 3 Aug. 1659, on behalf of the exiled King; was Sheriff of Leicestershire, 1653-54, after which date, probably, but certainly before 29 Aug. 1660 (when, being one of the commissioners for Leicestershire, he is styled in an Act of Parl., "Sir John PRETYMAN, Baronet"); he was *cr. a Baronet* [S.],(c) though no record exists of such creation. He was M.P. for Leicester, 1661 till his death. He *m.* firstly, in or shortly before 1631(d) (settlement 10 May 1634, after marriage), Elizabeth (heiress of Horninghold), da. and h. of George TURPIN, of Knaptoft, co. Leicester and Horninghold aforesaid, by Anne, da. of John QUARLES, of London. She, who was living 1643, *d.* in London about March 1663. He *m.* secondly, in or before 1664, Theodosia, widow of Lionel KNIVETT, sister of Henry and da. of Thomas ADAMS, of London, Merchant (*d.* 1651, aged 68), by Elizabeth, da. of Thomas CRESWELL, of Prior's Hall, co. Hereford. His estates were vested in trustees by Act of Parl., 1670, for payment of £19,864, debt to the Crown, etc. He *d.*, in involved circumstances, between 22 Nov. 1675 and 16 Feb. 1676/7, the date of the new writ, when the death of "Sir John Pretyman, Knight and Baronet," is mentioned in the Journals of the House of Commons. His widow(e), by whom he had no issue, *d.* at Cheshunt, Herts. Her will dat. 3 Aug. 1687, pr. 26 Nov. 1692.

(a) William Pretyman (Richmond Lodge, Bournemouth) has kindly furnished many of the particulars contained in this article relating to the pedigree of the grantee and his descendants. A full account thereof (now [1903] in the press) is in Muskett's *Suffolk Manorial Families*.

(b) Though this creation is generally ascribed to Charles I there does not seem any ground to suppose it to have been earlier than 1660, on and after which date it is repeatedly recognised. The grantee is indeed spoken of as "Sir John Pretyman, Baronet" on the monument to his son-in-law, Sir Thomas Burton, 2d Baronet [1662], who *d.* 3 April 1659, but that inscription was probably not put up till the following year, and he appears as an "Esq." at a later date, viz., 9 June to 13 Oct. 1659, in the Chancery Proceedings of "Pretyman *v.* Pretyman." The creation anyhow seems to have been later than 1645, up to which date the Great Seal Records [I.] are perfect, those of the Privy Seal being so for more than four years later. No mention is made of it in Milne's *List*, nor in that by Beatson. It is suggested by Mr. Pretyman (see note "a" above) that the grant of the Baronetcy was "possibly not unconnected with George Pretyman's [afterwards the 2d Baronet] audience with the King at Breda in the autumn of 1659 (he being then a Royalist fugitive), or in the spring of 1660."

(c) See note "b" above.

(d) The 1st child, Mary, was *bap.* 22 Aug. 1631 at Driffield. She *m.* (settlement, 29 Nov. 1651) as his 1st wife, Richard (Verney), Lord Willoughby de Broke.

(e) See her petition, 4 Dec. 1669, in a law suit against her husband.

II. 1676? SIR GEORGE PRETYMAN, Baronet [S. 1660?], of Lodington aforesaid, 2d but 1st surv. s. and h.([a]), *bap.* 17 Dec. 1638 at Driffield, co. Glouc.; admitted to Lincoln's Inn, 14 May 1655; joined (with his father) in Sir George BOOTH's rising, 3 Aug. 1659, on behalf of the exiled King, with whom he had had audience at Breda late in that year; was *Knighted* v.p. 29 Sep. 1660, being then of Lodington aforesaid; *suc. to the Baronetcy* on the death of his father about 1676.([b]) He *m.*, 22 Aug. 1661 (Lic. Fac., 17), at St. Clere's chapel (registered at Addington, co. Kent), Elizabeth (then aged 20), widow of Sir Robert HOUGHTON, of Shelton, co. Norfolk, da. and eventually coheir of Sir Isaac SEDLEY, 3d Baronet [1621], of St. Clere's, aforesaid, only da. by (—), his 1st wife. He was "living in London and goes a begging 1712,"(c) his wife being then "living in Staffordshire."([c]) He *d.* s.p.m.s.([d]), and was *bur.*, 14 April 1715, at St. James', Westm.

III. 1715. SIR WILLIAM PRETYMAN, Baronet [S. 1660?], of Greenwich, co. Kent, br. and h. male; *bap.*, 3 Feb. 1640/1, at Driffield aforesaid; *suc. to the Baronetcy*, on the death of his brother, in April 1715. He *m.* [—]. She, presumably, was the "Mrs. PRETTYMAN" who was *bur.* at Greenwich, 20 Sep. 1694. He *d.* s.p.m.,([e]) and was *bur.* as "Sir William PRITYMAN, Bart.," 8 Nov. 1719, at Greenwich aforesaid.([f])

IV. 1719, to 1749? SIR THOMAS PRETYMAN, Baronet [S. 1660?], of Greensfarm aforesaid, and of Hackney, co. Midx., nephew and h. male, being only s. and h. of Thomas PRETYMAN, of Greensfarm and Hackney aforesaid, Citizen and Draper of London, by Mary (*m.* 16 Jan. 1667/8), da. of Hugh NORRIS, of Hackney aforesaid, which Thomas, last named (*bap.* 9 Feb. 1642/3 at Driffield) was 4th and yst. s. of the 1st Baronet. He was *b.* about 1670; was a Merchant of London; *suc. to the Baronetcy* in Nov. 1719; was admitted in Aug. 1722 (as "Sir Thomas Pretyman Baronet, a poor merchant"), a Pensioner to Morden College, Kent, though it is doubtful if he ever became a Resident therein. He *m.*, 28 July 1698, being aged 28, at North Cray, co. Kent, Elizabeth, da. of John BUGGIN, of that place. She was *bur.* 11 April 1719 at North Cray. He was living 25 Dec. 1749,([g]) but *d.* s.p.m.([h]) shortly afterwards, when the *Baronetcy* became *extinct* or *dormant*.

([a]) John Pretyman, the 1st son, *bap.* 22 Dec. 1632 at Driffield, *m.*, in 1649, Margaret (*b.* 1635), da. and h. of Sir Matthew MENNES, K.B., by Margaret, da. and h. of John (STEWART, EARL OF CARRICK [S.]. He, who, in 1654, sold Sandwich Priory,. which he had obtained from his wife, *d.* v.p. 30 Aug. 1658, leaving (besides a son, Mathew, who was *bur.* 9 July 1656, at Lodington) a son and h. John, *b.* 1654, living June 1659, aged 5, who *d.* young "in Aug. or Sep. 1664" [Chancery Proceedings], being the "Mr. Esquire Pretyman" who was *bur.* at Greenwich, 29 Aug. 1664.

([b]) He is, however, presumably by mistake, called "Knt. and *Baronet*" in his marr. lic. 17 Aug. 1661. It is certain, however, that (though he was then a *Knight*) *his father* (the *Baronet*) was then alive, as appears by an Act of Parl. of 1670.

([c]) Le Neve's *Knights*.

([d]) He had two sons, (1) George, *bap.* 12 Nov. 1662, at Stockerston, co. Leic.; (2) Shirley, who had a da., Elizabeth, living 1712. See note "c" above. These sons *died* v.p. and s.p.m. before 1715.

([e]) Elizabeth, his da. and h., *m.*, about 1700, Digby Berkeley, of Ardusan, co. Carlow, and had issue.

([f]) His uncle, another William Pretyman, Remembrancer of the First Fruits, *died* 4, and was *bur.* 8 March 1687/8 also at Greenwich, leaving a widow (who *d.* 26 Sep. 1702) and an only son, also named William Pretyman, who was *bap.* there 29 Aug. 1665, was Capt. of a Company of Foot, but who *d.* unm. 7 Feb. 1707. See Le Neve's *Knights*.

([g]) The last payment to him from Morden College is 25 Dec. 1749. He is not buried in the burial ground of that College, and probably did not die there.

([h]) His three daughters all *died* unm., viz., Elizabeth, the survivor, in 1781; Mary in 1749; and Grace in her infancy. The estate of Greenfarms went in 1781 to their maternal relatives.

[The Baronetcy was, however, assumed as under].

V. 1823, to 1827. SIR GEORGE PRETYMAN-TOMLINE, Baronet [S. 1660?]([a]), BISHOP OF WINCHESTER, was served 22 March 1823, by a Jury at Haddington([b]), as heir male general to Sir Thomas PRETYMAN, Baronet [S. 1660?], (who *d.* in 1749), and, in consequence of such service, *assumed the Baronetcy*,([c]) formerly enjoyed by the said Thomas.([d]) According to a pedigree recorded by him in 1824 in Lyon's office (one without a single date therein) he was 10th in descent from William PRETYMAN, of Bacton, co. Suffolk, from whom the abovenamed Baronet was said to be 7th.([e]) He was 1st s. of George PRETYMAN, of Bacton, co. Suffolk, sometime a tradesman([f]) in Bury St. Edmunds, Suffolk (*d.* 1810, aged 88), by Susan, da.

([a]) According to the assumption of that title after the service of 22 March 1823, and after the registration of the pedigree in the Lyon office.

([b]) It is to be observed that there were no lands held at any time by the family in Haddingtonshire, or, indeed, anywhere else in Scotland, but the locality of "Greens farm in Habertoft" (which was in *Lincolnshire*), not being specified, the Haddington jury apparently dealt with it as having been in *Haddingtonshire*. Mr. Pretyman (see p. 327, note "a") kindly furnishes the Bishop's own views, in his own words, on the subject, as under:—"Farnham Castle, 29 Dec. 1823. Regarding my connection with Scotland, John Pretyman, eldest son of John Pretyman, Baronet of Nova Scotia, married Margaret, the eldest da. of Sir Matthew Mennes, and heiress of [*Query* through] her mother Lady Margaret Stuart, only da. of John (Stuart), Earl of Carrick, an illegitimate descendant of James V, to large estates in Haddingtonshire, and in whose family was the hereditary office of Lord Lieutenant of that county. This son and his issue died before his father. His widow married Sir John Heath, and their only child married George (Verney), 5th Lord Willoughby de Broke, and thus [arose] Lord Willoughby's claim to the Earldom of Carrick. Had John Pretyman left any descendants his [issue] would have had prior claim."

(c) He was received at a Court held at St. James', 20 May 1824, by George IV "*on coming to the title*," together with Lady Tomline, who had been presented, on the same event, by Lady Bolton.

([d]) In the Advocates' Library at Edinburgh, among the MSS. of the well known John Riddell is a printed copy of this case and evidence of the service, it being noted in the Catalogue that it is extremely rare. It has a *Genealogical table* at the end, which is the same (slightly enlarged) as that in Lyon's Office, mentioned in note "e" below, but it has the addition of a few year dates, *e.g.*, the words "living 1490, died circa 1518" being added to the common ancestor William Pretyman, of Bacton [*Ex inform.* Sir James Balfour Paul, Lyon King of Arms, by whom most of the information as to the Bishop's claim to this Baronetcy has been kindly supplied].

([e]) The "Rt. Rev. Sir George Pretyman Tomline, Bp. of Winchester," is there stated to be son of "George Pretyman, Esq., of Bury St. Edmunds," s. of "Peter Pretyman, Esq.," s. of George Pretyman of Bacton, s. of Peter Pretyman of Bacton and Cotton Beresworth, s. of George Pretyman of the same, s. of Peter Pretyman of the same, s. of William Pretyman of the same, son of Peter Pretyman of Bacton, s. of Thomas Pretyman "of Bacton or portioner of Bacton and Old Newton," s. of William Pretyman of Bacton, who (besides Thomas) had another son, William Pretyman of Bacton, father of Thomas Pretyman of Cotton, father of William Pretyman of Bacton, father of Sir John Pretyman of Bacton and Driffield, father of Sir John Pretyman, the 1st Baronet. "William Pretyman of Bacton is stated to be *abavi tritavus* of the Bishop, which would hardly stretch over the ten generations required" [*Ex inform.* Sir James Balfour Paul, Lyon, as in note "d" above].

([f]) See *Her. & Gen.*, vol. iv, p. 373, where some account of the Bishop's claim is given under the article entitled "Doubtful Baronetcies."

of John HUBBARD, and was *b.* 9 Oct. 1750, being *bap.* 7 Jan. 1751, at St. James', in that town, was ed. at the school there and at Pembroke Coll., Cambridge (B.A. 1772, Senior Wrangler and first Smith's Prizeman, 1773; M.A. 1775, D.D. 1784), where he was tutor to William Pitt (afterwards Prime Minister), to whom (when Chancellor of the Exchequer in 1782), he was Private Secretary, 1782-87; was Canon of Westminster, 1784-87; Bishop of Lincoln, 1787-1820; and Bishop of Winchester, 1820-27. Under the will of Marmaduke Tomline, of Riby, co. Lincoln (to whom, however, he was no relation), he inherited the Riby estate in June 1803, and *took the name of Tomline*, after that of *Pretyman*, and *assumed* in 1823 *the Baronetcy* [S. 1660] as above stated. He *m.*, in 1784, Elizabeth, 1st da. and coheir of Thomas MALTBY, of Germans, Bucks. She *d.* in Great George street, and was *bur.* as "Lady Elizabeth Pretyman-Tomline," 13 June 1826, at St. Margaret's, Westm., aged 68. He *d.* 14 Nov. 1827, at Kingston Hall, Dorset, aged 77, and was *bur.* in Winchester Cathedral. Will pr. Nov. 1827. At his death, though he left three sons([a]), the *assumption of the Baronetcy ceased*.

BAIRD:

cr. 1660([b]):

ex. Sep. 1745.

I. 1660. "JOHN BAIRD, of Newbyth," co. Haddington, 1st s. and h. of James BAIRD,(c) of Byth, co. Aberdeen, Commissary of Edinburgh, by Bethia, da. of John DEMSTER, of Pitliver, co. Fife, was *bap.* 10 Sep. 1620; admitted an Advocate [S.], June 1647; joined the party of the Covenanters, but is "said to have been *cr. a Baronet* [S.] on the restoration of Charles II"([b]), *i.e.*, in 1660. He was made LYON DEPUTE, 15 Aug. 1663, and was (as a "Knight") M.P. for co. Aberdeen, 1665 and 1667; was a Lord of Session [S.] *under the style of Lord Newbyth*, 1664-81 and 1689 till his death in 1698, having been one of the Lords Justiciary [S.], 1661; was a zealous Protestant, and a great promoter of the Revolution of 1688. He sold the Aberdeenshire estate of Byth, and purchased lands in the counties of Haddington and Edinburgh, which were erected into a Barony under the name of Newbyth. He *m.* before 1648, Margaret, da. of the Hon. Sir William HAY, of Linplum (br. to John 1st EARL OF TWEEDDALE [S.]), by Anna, da. of William MURRAY, of Dunearn. He *d.* 27 April 1698, at Edinburgh, in his 78th year.

([a]) The eldest son, William Edward Tomline, M.P. for Truro, died 28May 1836, having never assumed the Baronetcy. The two younger ones (the Rev. George Thomas Pretyman, Chancellor of Lincoln, and the Rev. Richard Pretyman, Precentor of Lincoln) retained the name of Pretyman.

([b]) See "Genealogical Collections concerning the sirname of Baird," reprinted from the MS. of William Baird (*b.* 1701, *d.* 1777) of the house of Auchmeddan, London, 4to, 1870. The creation is, however, very doubtful. In the patent of the Baronetcy of 4 Feb. 1679/80, the grantee's father is called Sir John Baird, of Newbyth, *Knight*.

(c) This James was 4th son of Gilbert Baird of Auchmeddan, the head of the house of Baird. He purchased the lands of Byth, co. Aberdeen, near the waters of Devern, and is said to have had a warrant from Charles I to be *cr.* a Peer as Lord Devern [S.]. See note "b" above.

I. 1680. II.([a]) 1698.([a]) SIR WILLIAM BAIRD, Baronet [S. 1660 and 1680], of Newbyth aforesaid, only surv. s. and h., *bap.* 12 Nov. 1654; was sent by the Scotch Parl. to London on a deputation to Charles II, and was, in his father's lifetime, as "WILLIAM BAIRD, son to LORD NEWBYTH" *cr. a Baronet* [S.], 4 Feb. 1679/80, with rem. to heirs male of his body. He was admitted an Advocate [S.], 31 July 1680, and *suc. to the Baronetcy*([a]) [S. 1660] on the death of his father, 27 April 1698. He *m.* firstly, Helen, da. of Sir John GILMOUR, of Craigmillar, President of the Court of Session [S.]. She *d.* 22 and was *bur.* 25 April 1701, at Libberton, co. Edinburgh. He *m.* secondly, Margaret, 3d da. of Henry (ST. CLAIR), LORD SINCLAIR [S.], by Grizel, da. of Sir James COCKBURN. He *d.* at Edinburgh 17 and was *bur.* 22 Feb. 1737, at Libberton, aged 82. His widow, who was *b.* about 1686, *d.* s.p. 23 Dec. 1756.

III. and II.([a]) 1737, to 1745. SIR JOHN BAIRD, Baronet [S. 1660 and 1680], of Newbyth aforesaid, 1st s. and h.; *suc. to the Baronetcies*,([a]) 17 Feb. 1737; was M.P. for co. Edinburgh, 1715-22. He *m.* Janet, only da. of the Hon. Sir David DALRYMPLE, 1st Baronet [S. 1700], Lord Advocate [S.], by Janet, da. of Sir James ROCHEAD. He *d.* s.p. at Berwick, Sep. 1745, when the *Baronetcies* [1660([a]) and 1680] became *extinct*.([b]) His widow, who was *b.* 31 March 1698, *m.* Gen. the Hon. James ST. CLAIR, of Dysart, who *d.* 30 Nov. 1762, and *d.* s.p. in London, 8 Jan. 1766, aged 68.

GILMOUR:([c])

cr. 16 Aug. 1661;

ex. 14 March 1662/3.

I. 1661, to 1663. "SIR ANDREW GILMOUR," of Edinburgh, yst. of the three sons of John GILMOUR, Writer to the Signet and Notary Public, probably by Elizabeth EDMOND, but possibly by a later wife, Margaret WINTON, was admitted to the Univ. of Edinburgh, 22 July 1637; became, subsequently, an Advocate [S.], and was *cr. a Baronet* [S.], as above, 16 Aug. 1661, with rem. to heirs male of his body. He *m.*, 15 Feb. 1652, Margaret FOULIS. He *d.* s.p.m.s., 14 March 1662/3, of a fever, at his house at Edinburgh, when the *Baronetcy* became *extinct*. His widow *d.* 1679.

FLEMING, *or* FLYMING:([d])

cr. 21, 23, or 25 Sep. 1661;

dormant or *extinct* 17 April 1764.

I. 1661. "ARCHIBALD FLEMING [*or* FLYMING], Commissary of Glasgow" [1637] (an office of which he had been deprived during the Protectorate, though restored at the Restoration), was of Farme, in Ruther-

([a]) Presuming a Baronetcy [S.] to have been created (as above) in 1660.

([b]) By entail, dat. 4 Aug. 1737, he had settled his estates on his 2d cousin, William Baird, s. and h. of William Baird, of Edinburgh, Merchant (*d.* Sep. 1737), who was 2d son of Sir Robert Baird, 1st Baronet [S. 1696], of Saughton, which Robert was yr. br. to Sir John Baird, 1st Baronet [S. 1660], of Newbyth abovementioned, both being sons of James Baird, of Byth. This William, who thus became of Newbyth, *d.* 5 Jan. 1765, being father of Gen. Sir David Baird, Baronet, so *cr.* 13 April 1809, with a spec. rem. to the issue of his elder br., now [1903] Baronets, of Newbyth.

([c]) See p. 324, note "c," under "Maclean."

([d]) See *N. & Q.*, 7th S., I, 116, for an article by "Sigma" [M. Shaw-Stewart]. Many of the particulars in this article were kindly furnished by James R. Anderson (see p. 324, note "c"), but some are from R. R. Stodart, many years Lyon Clerk Depute.

glen, co. Glasgow, being only s. and h. of William FLEMING, Clerk to the Commissariot of Glasgow (to whom he was served heir 20 Nov. 1636), by Margaret, da. of (—) BRODIE; was admitted an Advocate 14 Feb. 1644; acquired the lands of Calzill, Peile, Farme, etc., in co. Lanark, and was *cr. a Baronet* [S.], as above, 21, 23, or 25 Sep. 1661, with rem. to heirs male of his body, but is said to have died before the patent was sealed, though it was, in his son's life, recorded in the Great Seal Register [S.]. He is said(a) to have *m.* (contract 22 June 1637) Agnes, only child of David GIBSON, Notary in Glasgow, by Janet ADAIR, his wife. Another account(b) makes her da. of Henry GIBSON, Town Clerk, and afterwards Commissary of Glasgow, by Annabella, da. of David FORSYTH, of Blackill, while a third(c) makes her da. of Sir Alexander GIBSON, of Durie. He *d.* Jan. 1661/2.

II. 1662. SIR WILLIAM FLEMING, Baronet [S. 1661], of Farme aforesaid, only s. and h., *b.* 2 June 1639, *suc. to the Baronetcy* in Jan. 1661/2, and was, 17 April 1662, served heir to his father, being (like he had been) Commissary of Glasgow. He registered his arms in the Lyon office about 1672. He *m.* 29 Dec. 1663, Margaret, da. of Archibald STEWART, of Scotstown. He *d.* at Farme, 6 Feb. 1707. His widow, who was a Covenanter (causing thereby her husband to be fined 4,000 marks), was *bur.* 13 Oct. 1718 in the High Churchyard, Glasgow.

III. 1707. SIR ARCHIBALD FLEMING, Baronet [S. 1661], of Farme aforesaid, only s. and h., who by his improvidence and by becoming surety for the debts of his wife's father, ruined the family estate, *suc. to the Baronetcy* in Feb. 1707. He *m.* (contract 3 Aug. 1692) Elizabeth, 1st da. of Sir George HAMILTON, Baronet [S. 1692], of Barntoun, co. Edinburgh. He *d.* at Farme, 14, and was *bur.* in the High Churchyard, Glasgow, 21 April 1714.

[The pedigree after this period is unreliable. The much-encumbered estates were in 1711 in the hands of the Earl of Selkirk [S.] as heritable creditor. The descent of the title, was, apparently, as below.]

IV. 1714. SIR ARCHIBALD FLEMING, Baronet [S. 1661], of Farme aforesaid, presumably s. and h., *suc.* apparently *to the Baronetcy* in 1714, and appears to have sold the last remains of the estate in 1722.(d) He *d.* s.p.m. in Aug. 1738, his da., Janet, wife of William BOGLE, Writer, in Hamilton, being appointed his executrix dative.(e)

V. 1738. SIR GILBERT FLEMING, Baronet [S. 1661], presumably br. and h. male; *suc.* apparently *to the Baronetcy* in 1738. He *d.* s.p.m.(f)

VI. 1740? SIR WILLIAM FLEMING, Baronet [S. 1661], presumably br. and h. male, being apparently identical with "William, son of Sir Archibald, *bap.* 28 Dec. 1699"; was Lieut. in Gen. Handasyde's Horse; *suc. to the Baronetcy* apparently on the death of his brother Gilbert. He *m.* Jane, da. of [—] LENNOX, of Woodhead. He *d.* s.p. at Elgin, 25 Nov. 1746. Admon., 21 April 1748, to a creditor, his widow being then living.

(a) R. R. Stodart, see p. 331, note "d."
(b) *Memoirs of Robert Baillie* in the Bannatyne-Club edition of his letters, p. cxiv. [*Ex inform.* J. R. Anderson.]
(c) *Nisbet's Heraldry.*
(d) The date of 1722 is furnished by R. R. Stodart (see p. 331, note "d"), who, however, attributes the sale thereof to Sir *William*.
(e) *Ex inform.*, J. R. Anderson, from information furnished by Dr. Murray.
(f) His da. and h., Margery, *m.* John ELPHINSTONE, Master of Elphinstone, who *d.* v.p. 1753, leaving her in very poor circumstances. She *d.* s.p. at Edinburgh, 5 Aug. 1784.

VII. 1746, to 1764. SIR COLLINGWOOD FLEMING, Baronet [S. 1661], who, presumably, as s. and h., *suc. to the Baronetcy* on his father's death, and is mentioned as a Baronet, 21 April 1748. He *d.* 17 April 1764, in Virginia, since which time nothing more is known of the Baronetcy.(a)

FOULIS:(b)

cr. 15 Sep. or 15 Oct. 1661;

afterwards, 1707-46, PRIMROSE;

forfeited 15 Nov. 1746.

I. 1661. "SIR JOHN FOULIS, of Ravelston," s. and h. of George FOULIS, of the same, by his 2d wife, Jane, da. of Sir John SINCLAIR, of Stevenson, which George (who was living 1638, aged 32) was s. and h. of another George FOULIS, of Ravelston, Master of the Mint [S.], 28 May 1633, who was yr. br. of Sir James FOULIS, of Colinton (father of Alexander FOULIS, *cr. a Baronet* [S.], 7 June 1634, with rem. to heirs male whatsoever) was *b.* 20 Feb. 1638, and was *cr. a Baronet* [S.], as above, 15 Sep. or 15 Oct. 1661, with rem. to the heirs male of his body. He, in 1701, acquired the estate of Woodhall, co. Edinburgh.(c) He *m.* firstly, 5 Sep. 1661, Margaret, 1st da. of Archibald PRIMROSE, 1st Baronet [S. 1651], by his 1st wife, Elizabeth, da. and coheir of the Hon. Sir James KEITH, of Benholm. She, on whose issue her said father settled his estate of Dunipace, co. Stirling, was *b.* 31 Dec. 1641, and *d.* 15 April 1690. He *m.* secondly, 28 Aug. 1690, Anne, da. of Walter DUNDAS, of that ilk. She *d.* 10 Jan. 1696. He *m.* thirdly, 29 March 1697, Mary, widow of John CUNNINGHAME, of Enterkin, da. of John MURRAY, of Polmaise. She *d.* 27 Dec. 1702. He *m.* fourthly, 7 Sep. 1705, Agnes SCOTT, widow of Andrew BRUCE, Baillie of Edinburgh. He *d.* 5 Aug. 1707, aged 69. His widow was *bur.* 26 June 1720, aged 80.

II. 1707, to 1746. SIR ARCHIBALD PRIMROSE, Baronet [S. 1661], of Ravelston and Dunipace aforesaid, grandson and h., being s. and h. of George PRIMROSE, *formerly* FOULIS, by Janet, da. of Sir William CUNNINGHAM, of Caprington, co. Ayr, which George, (*b.* 10 May 1667) was 2d but eventually 1st s. and h. ap. of the 1st Baronet; took the name of *Primrose* on inheriting the estate of Dunipace, at the death of his elder br., Archibald, 15 April 1685, and *d.* in 1707, a few months before his father. He

(a) The succession given in *Sigma's* article [see p. 331, note "d"] is different, William, son of Sir Archibald, the 3d Baronet, being made to succeed him as 4th Baronet, in 1714 (Archibald and Gilbert, the 4th and 5th Baronets, as given in the text, being omitted), and to be himself succeeded 25 *Oct. 1745* [not Nov. 1746] by his son Collingwood, the 5th Baronet, whose death in Virginia is stated to have been on 17 April *1763* [not 1764], and who is stated to have been succeeded by his brother, James, the 6th Baronet, after whose death, *1 Oct. 1763*, "the title seems to have been considered as extinct." The Rev. Francis Patrick Fleming, LL.D., of Glenfeulan, co. Dumbarton (*b.* 1823, living 1877), s. of Patrick Fleming, the s. of another Patrick Fleming, s. of William Fleming, the s. of James Fleming, which James is said to have been s. of Malcolm Fleming, of Castle Collops, a Merchant in Glasgow, would, if such descent be correct, have some claim to the dignity, provided the creation could be shewn to have been to heirs male whatsoever.
(b) Most of the particulars in this article have been kindly supplied by Sir James Balfour Paul, Lyon King of Arms. "The Account Book of Sir John Foulis, of Ravelston," compiled principally by himself, contains many interesting genealogical references.
(c) Still (1903) in possession of his heir male, the 10th Baronet [S.] of the creation of 1634.

was *b.* in or after 1692; *suc. to the Baronetcy*, 5 Aug. 1707, and sold the estate of Ravelston. He *m.* firstly, Margaret, da. of John (FLEMING), 6th EARL OF WIGTOUN [S.], being his only child by his 1st wife, Margaret, da. of Colin (LINDSAY), 3d EARL OF BALCARRES [S.]. She *d.* s.p. He *m.* secondly, 19 Nov. 1724, Mary, 4th da. of Archibald (PRIMROSE), 1st EARL OF ROSEBERY [S.], by Dorothea, da. and h. of Everingham CRESSY. He took part in the Rising of 1745, was convicted of high treason and executed at Carlisle, 15 Nov. 1746, when the *Baronetcy* was *forfeited*, and his estates in the counties of Edinburgh, Linlithgow, and Stirling escheated to the Crown.(a) His widow, who had remained with him during his imprisonment, *d.* a month after him, at Dunipace, 17 Dec. 1746.

DAVIDSON(b) [S. *or* E.]:

cr. 1661;

extinct or *dormant* in or before 1685.

I. 1661, to 1685? "SIR WILLIAM DAVIDSON, of Curriehill," co. Edinburgh (an estate which he had purchased), Conservator of the Scots' Privileges at Campvere, was *cr. a Baronet* [S. *or* E.], as above, in 1661. His arms (with the badge of *Ulster*) are registered in the Lyon office, *Scotland*, as "Baronet of *England*." In 1668 he was served heir general of his br., James DAVIDSON, merchant, Burgess of Edinburgh. He *m.* [—], but *d.* s.p.m.s. in or before 1685,(c) when the *Baronetcy* became *extinct* or *dormant*.

HALKETT *or* HACKET:

cr. 25 Jan. 1661/2(d);

ex. March 1705.

I. 1662. "CHARLES HALKETT [*or* HACKET], of Pitfirrane," co. Fife, only s. and h. of Sir James HALKETT, of the same, a Col. of Horse in the Covenanters' army, by Margaret, da. of Sir Robert MONTGOMERY, of Skelmorlie, got charter of the lands of Knockhouse, etc., co. Fife, 17 Feb. 1660/1, and was *cr. a Baronet* [S.], as above, 25 Jan. 1661/2(d), with rem. to the heirs male of his body. He was M.P. [S.] for Fifeshire, 1682-83, and for Dumfermline, 1689, till his death in 1697, and was a member of the Committee which resolved, in 1689, that King James had forfeited the crown. He *m.* Janet, da. of Sir Patrick MURRAY, of Pitdennis. He *d.* 1697.

(a) Archibald Primrose, his only surv. s. (out of eleven children), *d.* unm., at Edinburgh, 28 Jan. 1747, leaving seven sisters, to whom a pension of £200 a year was granted. John Foulis, his [the 2d Baronet's] br., claimed the Dunipace estate as heir of entail, but his claim thereto was dismissed in 1751 by the Court of Session. The right to this Baronetcy, barring the forfeiture, would be now [1903] vested in the heir male of the body of William Foulis, of Woodhall, viz., Sir William Liston-Foulis, 10th Baronet [S. 1634], whose great grandfather su... in 1825, to the last-named (more ancient) Baronetcy as heir male collateral of the grantee.
(b) Most of the particulars in this article were kindly furnished by R. R. Stodart, many years Lyon Clerk Depute.
(c) Of his children (1) Peter Davidson *d.* s.p., v.p.; (2) Elizabeth *d.* unm. between 1685 and 1696, while (3) Anna, who inherited Curriehill, *m.*, after 1685, Franciscus Vanderburgh, rotulator, of Dort in the Netherlands, and was living as his widow in 1696.
(d) This is the date given in Douglas' *Baronage* [S.], where the patent is set out, but the date of 25 Jan. 1670/1 is assigned to it in Milne's *List*, as also in those of Miege, Chamberlayne and Beatson.

II. 1697 to 1705. SIR JAMES HALKETT, Baronet [S.] of Pitfirrane aforesaid, only s. and h.; *suc. to the Baronetcy* on the death of his father in 1697. He *d.* unm., March 1705, when the *Baronetcy* became *extinct*.(a)

OGILVIE:

cr. 5 March 1661/2, or 5 July 1662;

extinct or *dormant* about 1840.

I. 1664. "GEORGE OGILVIE, of Barras," in Dunottar, co. Kincardine, only s. of William OGILVIE, of the Mearns, was Governor of Dunottar Castle at the time of the Rebellion, and contrived to remove therefrom the Regalia of Scotland previous to its surrender in 1652, and having acquired the estate of Barras from his wife's brother was *cr. a Baronet* [S.], as above, 5 March 1661/2 or 5 July 1662, with rem. to the heirs male of his body. He *m.* (contract 31 Jan. 1634) Elizabeth, da. of the Hon. John DOUGLAS, of Barras aforesaid (yr. s. of William, EARL OF ANGUS [S.]), by Jean, da. of [—] FRASER, of Durris. He was living 11 Aug. 1679.

II. 1680? SIR WILLIAM OGILVIE, Baronet [S. 1662], of Barras aforesaid, only s. and h., *suc. to the Baronetcy* on the death of his father. He *m.* firstly, Margaret, widow of George TURING, the younger, of Foveran, da. of John FORBES, of Leslie. He *m.* secondly, Margery, da. of [—] RAIT, of Halgreen. He *m.* thirdly, Helen, only da. of Sir John OGILVIE, 1st Baronet [S. 1626], of Innerquharity, by Anne, da. of Sir Alexander IRVINE, of Drum. He was *bur.* 25 July 1707 in his own burial place. Funeral Certificate in Lyon Office.

III. 1707. SIR DAVID OGILVIE, Baronet [S. 1662], of Barras aforesaid, 1st s. and h.; *suc. to the Baronetcy* in July 1707. He *m.* firstly, Susanna, da. of [—], SCOTT, of Benholm. He *m.* secondly, Jean, da. of George Ross, of Aberdour, co. Aberdeen, Merchant. She *d.* s.p.m. He *m.* thirdly, Anne, da. and coheir of John GUTHRIE, of Westhall.

IV. 1740? SIR WILLIAM OGILVIE, Baronet [S. 1662], of Barras aforesaid, 1st s. and h., being only s. by 1st wife; *suc. to the Baronetcy* on the death of his father. He *m.* firstly, in or before 1729, Elizabeth, da. of Robert BARCLAY, of Urie. He *m.* secondly, Anne, da. of Isaac FULLARTON, Advocate [S.]. She *d.* 30 Jan. 1786. He *d.* Nov. 1791.

V. 1791. SIR DAVID OGILVIE, Baronet [S. 1662], of Barras aforesaid, 1st s. and h. by 1st wife, *b.* 1729; *suc. to the Baronetcy* in 1791. He was a Major in the Marines, from which he retired on full pay. He *m.*, about 1770, Jane, da. of John BENGER, of Devizes. He *d.* 5 Dec. 1799. His widow *d.* 20 Dec. 1800.

VI. 1799. SIR GEORGE MULGRAVE OGILVIE, Baronet [S. 1662], of Barras aforesaid, 1st s. and h., *b.* 10 Aug. 1779; sometime a Capt. in the Army; *suc. to the Baronetcy*, 1799. He *d.* unm. 9 March 1837, aged 57, at Newton Mill, co. Forfar.

(a) The estate devolved on his eldest sister and coheir, who *m.* Sir Peter Wedderburn, 1st Baronet [S. 1694], who afterwards took the name of Halkett, and is ancestor of the present (1903) Baronets of that name.

VII. 1837, to 1840? **Sir William Ogilvie**, Baronet [S. 1662], br. and h., *b.* about 1785; *suc. to the Baronetcy* 9 March 1837. He *d.* unm., apparently in or about 1840(a), when the *Baronetcy* became *extinct* or *dormant*.

MURE, *or* MUIR:

cr. 4 May 1662;

extinct or *dormant* about 1700.

I. 1662, to 1700? "Patrick Mure [*or* Muir], of Rowallan,"(b) yst. s. of Sir William Mure, of the same, the well-known poet (*d.* 1657), by his 1st wife Anne, da. of (—) Dundas, of Newliston, was *cr. a Baronet* [S.], as above, by patent said to be dated 4 May 1662(c), but "not recordit"(c) in the Great Seal Register. The *Baronetcy* became *extinct* or *dormant*,(d) apparently, on his death.

TEMPLE:

cr. 7 July 1662(e);

ex. 27 March 1674.

I. 1662, to 1674. "Sir Thomas Temple," 2d s. of Sir John Temple, of Stanton Barry, Bucks (*d.* 23 Sep. 1632), by Dorothy, da. and coheir of Edmund Lee, of Stanton aforesaid (which John was 2d s. of Sir Thomas Temple, 1st Baronet [1611] of Stowe), was *b.* at Stowe and *bap.* there 10 Jan. 1614; admitted to Lincoln's Inn, 21 Feb. 1621/2; was a moderate Parliamentarian; Col. of Horse, 1642; a Sequestration Commissioner for Hunts, 1643; acquired (jointly with William Crowne) 20 Sep. 1656, the interest of Sir Charles St. Etienne, 2d Baronet [S. 1629] in Nova Scotia, which was confirmed by the Lord Protector Cromwell, who appointed him, in 1657, as "Col. Thomas Temple, Esq.," Governor of Acadia. He was, however, by the King, *cr. a Baronet* [S.], 7 July 1662,(e) receiving three days later a fresh commission as Governor. After the cession of that province to France, by the treaty of Breda, in July 1667, he had to surrender his rights to that nation (which surrender, however, was not completed till 1680), he being promised £16,200 as an indemnity. He retired to Boston, in New England, but *d.* unm. in London, 27 and was *bur.* 28 March 1674, at Ealing, co. Midx., when the *Baronetcy* became *extinct*. Will (nuncupative) dat. 27 March and pr. 27 July 1674.

(a) He is given as alive in Oliver and Boyd's *Edinburgh Almanack* of 1840, but omitted in that of 1841.

(b) The "Historie and descent of the house of Rowallane, by Sir W. Mure, Knt." was pub. at Glasgow, 12 mo., 1825.

(c) Milne's *List*.

(d) His elder br., Sir William Mure, of Rowallan, a well-known Covenanter, *d.* 1686, leaving a son and h. William, who *d.* s.p.m. in 1700, leaving three daughters, Anne and Margaret, who d. unm., and Jean, who *m.* firstly, William Fairlie, the younger, and secondly (contract 16 June 1697), as his 2d wife, David (Boyle), 1st Earl of Glasgow [S.], and *d.* s.p.m. 3 Sept. 1724, leaving by her last husband a da., Jane, the heiress of Rowallan, who *m.* Sir James Campbell, and was mother of John, 5th Earl of Loudoun [S.].

(e) There is no entry of this creation in the Great Seal Register [S], and it is not noticed in Milne's *List*, etc. There is, however, no doubt of the fact. The debt due from "Sir Thomas Temple, *Baronet of Nova Scotia*," is mentioned in the will of his brother, Sir Purbeck Temple, dat. 14 July 1693, and pr. 27 Nov. 1695. See *Her. & Gen.*, vol. iii, p. 538, etc. The date of the creation is mentioned in the *Dict. Nat. Biog.*

CARNEGIE:

cr. 20 Feb. 1662/3, sealed 27 May 1663;

afterwards, since 1855, Earls of Southesk [S.].

I. 1663. "David Carnegie, fiar of Pittarrow," co. Kincardine 1st s. and h. ap. of the Hon. Sir Alexander Carnegie, of the same (*d.* March 1681/2), by Margaret, sister of Robert, 1st Viscount Arbuthnott [S.], da. of Sir Robert Arbuthnott, of Arbuthnott, co. Kincardine, which Alexander was 4th s. of David (Carnegie), 1st Earl of Southesk [S.] (so *cr.* 22 June 1633), was, on account of services rendered by him and his father to the Crown, *cr. a Baronet* [S.], 20 Feb. 1662/3, the patent being sealed 27 May 1663, "provydit to aires male."(a) He was M.P. [S.] for Kincardineshire, 1667 and 1669-74. He *m.* firstly (contract 29 Oct. 1673), Catherine, sister of the half-blood to Archibald, 1st Earl of Rosebery [S.], being 2d da. of Sir Archibald Primrose, 1st Baronet [S. 1651], by his 1st wife, Mary, da. of John (Fleming), 6th Earl of Wigtoun [S.]. She *d.* Oct. 1677. He *m.* secondly (contract 29 Oct. 1684), Catharine, Dowager Viscountess Arbuthnott [S.], da. of Robert Gordon, of Pitlurg and Straloch. She *d.* 23 April 1693. He *m.* thirdly, Jean da. of James Burnett, of Lagaron and Kair, by whom he had six children, having had in all nine sons and eight daughters. He *d.* Nov. 1708. His widow *d.* May 1740.

II. 1708. Sir John Carnegie, Baronet [S. 1663], of Pittarrow aforesaid, 4th but 1st surv. s. and h. by 1st wife, *bap.* 27 Jan. 1673; *suc. to the Baronetcy* in Nov. 1708. He *m.* in 1712, Mary, 2d da. of Sir Thomas Burnett, 3d Baronet [S. 1626], by Margaret, da. of Robert (Arbuthnott), 2d Viscount Arbuthnott [S.]. He *d.* 3 April 1729, aged 56. His widow *d.* June 1754.

III. 1729. Sir James Carnegie, Baronet [S. 1663], of Pittarrow aforesaid, 1st s. and h., *b.* about 1715; *suc. to the Baronetcy*, 3 April 1729. He, on the death of his cousin James, 5th Earl of Southesk [S.], in 1729, would have succeeded to that title, but for the attainder thereof in 1716. He was a Captain in the army, and fought at Fontenoy, in 1745, and at Culloden, in 1746; was M.P. for co. Kincardine (four Parls.), 1741 till his death in 1765. In 1764 he, for £36,870, purchased Kinnaird and other family estates in Forfarshire which had been forfeited by the Earl his cousin abovementioned, directing the estate of Pittarrow to be sold. He *m.*, 5 July 1752, Christian, 1st da. of David Doig, of Cookstoun, by Magdalen Symmers, heiress of Balyordie. He *d.* 30 April and was *bur.* 4 May 1765. His widow *d.* 4 Nov. 1820, aged 91.

IV. 1765. Sir David Carnegie, Baronet [S. 1663], of Pittarrow and Kinnaird aforesaid, 1st s. and h., *b.* 22 Nov. 1753; *suc. to the Baronetcy*, 30 April 1765; sold the estate of Pittarrow in 1767 to his uncle, George Carnegie; greatly improved that of Kinnaird, where he built an "elegant mansion,"(b) now called Kinnaird Castle; purchased Leuchars and other family lands co. Fife, which had been forfeited in 1716, as above stated; was M.P. for the Montrose Burghs, 1784-90, and for Forfarshire, 1796 (two Parls.) till his death, in 1805. He *m.*, 30 April 1783, Agnes Murray, da. of Andrew Elliot, of Greenwells, co. Roxburgh, Lieut.-Gov. of New York, 2d s. of Sir Gilbert Elliot, 2d Baronet [S. 1700]. He *d.* at his house in Gloucester Place, Marylebone, 25 May 1805, aged 51. Will pr. 1806. His widow *d.* at Leamington, co. Warwick, 9 June 1860, aged 96.

(a) Milne's *List*.

(b) Playfair's *Baronetage* [S.], 1811. Kinnaird Castle was rebuilt in 1862 by the then Earl.

V. 1805. Sir James Carnegie, Baronet [S. 1663], of Kinnaird aforesaid, 1st s. and h., *b.* 1799; *suc. to the Baronetcy*, 25 May 1805; was M.P. for the Aberdeen Burghs, 1830-31. He *m.*, 14 Nov. 1825, at Naples, Charlotte, da. of the Rev. Daniel Lysons, of Hempstead Court, co. Gloucester (one of the authors of the *Magna Britannia*, etc., a well known antiquary), by his 1st wife, Sarah, da. of Lieut.-Col. Thomas Carteret Hardy, York Fusileers. She *d.* 10 April 1848. He *d.* 30 Jan. 1849, at Kinnaird Castle, aged 49. Admon., April 1849.

VI. 1849. Sir James Carnegie, Baronet [S. 1663], of Kinnaird aforesaid, 1st s. and h., *b.* 16 Nov. 1827 in Edinburgh; ed. at Sandhurst; joined the army (92d Foot), 1845; was in the Grenadier Guards, 1846-49; *suc. to the Baronetcy*, 30 Jan. 1849; Lord-Lieut. of Kincardineshire, 1849-56. He *m.* firstly, 19 June 1849, at Exton Park, co. Rutland, Catherine Hamilton, da. of Charles Noel (Noel), 1st Earl of Gainsborough, by his 3d wife, Arabella, da. of Sir James Hamlyn Williams, 2d Baronet [1795]. She, who was *b.* 29 Sept. 1829, *d.* 9 March 1855, in Cavendish square, aged 25. A few months later, by the reversal, 2 July 1855, of the attainder of the Earldom of Southesk, etc. [S.], he became EARL OF SOUTHESK, etc. [S.], having that title confirmed to him by the House of Lords on the 24th of the same month. In that peerage this *Baronetcy* then *merged* and still (1903) so continues. See *Peerage*.

SETON:

cr. 3 June 1663.(a)

I. 1663. "Walter Seton, of Abercorn," co. Linlithgow, s. and h. of Alexander Seton,(b) of Kilcreuch (M.P. [S.] for Stirlingshire, 1612, and living 1636), by Margaret, da. of Walter Cornwall, of Bonhard, co. Linlithgow, was one of the principal "Customers" of the King; acquired the great Barony of Abercorn, of which he had charter in 1662 (but which about ten years later, he sold to the family of Hope, being thenceforth designated as of Northbank), and was *cr. a Baronet* [S.], as above, 3 June 1663,(a) though the patent (supposed to have been to heirs male whatsoever) is not recorded in the Great Seal Register [S.]. He, however, registered his arms (as a Baronet) about 1672 in the Lyon Office. He was M.P. [S.] for Linlithgowshire, 1665, 1667, and 1669-74. He *m.* Christian, da. of George Dundas, of that ilk, P.C. [S.], by Elizabeth, da. of Sir Alexander Hamilton, of Innerwick. He *d.* "20 Feb. 1692, about 8 a clock."(c)

II. 1692. Sir Walter Seton, Baronet [S. 1663], of Northbank aforesaid, 1st s. and h.; admitted an advocate [S.] 29 Jan. 1635; Commissary Clerk of Edinburgh; *suc. to the Baronetcy*, 20 Feb. 1692. He *m.* (contract, 6 Sep. 1702) Euphemia, da. of Sir Robert Murray, of Prestfield and Melgum. He *d.* at Preston, co. Haddington, 3 Jan. 1708.

(a) The dates of 1646 or 1648 are sometimes assigned to this creation. See also vol. ii., p. 430, as to an alleged creation granted to "Seton of Tough [*i.e.*, Touch], now of Culbeg."

(b) This Alexander was s. and h. of Sir Alexander Seton, of Gargunnock, co. Stirling (living 1612), yr. br. of John Seton, of Touch, in that county (whose male issue failed in 1742), both being sons of James Seton, of Touch, who was great-great-grandson and heir of Sir Alexander Seton, of Touch, *first* son of Alexander Seton, afterwards Gordon, 1st Earl of Huntly [S.], whom, however, he did not succeed in that dignity, which devolved on the *second* son, George, ancestor to the succeeding Earls, afterwards Marquesses of Huntly [S.]. The right, however, to the Barony of Gordon [S.] conferred about 1435 on the said 1st Earl, not improbably vested in the said Sir Alexander Seton, the first son and the heirs of his body, who after 1742, were the Baronets of this creation. See *Complete Peerage*, by G. E. C., vol. iv, p. 50, note "d."

(c) Foulis' *Account Book*, p. 145. [*Ex inform.* J. R. Anderson].

III. 1708. Sir Henry Seton, Baronet [S. 1663], of Northbank aforesaid, 1st s. and h.; *suc. to the Baronetcy*, 3 Jan. 1708. He became, by the death, 25 March 1742, of his cousin, James Seton, of Touch, the representative of the 1st Earl of Huntly [S.], as being descended from Alexander his first son.(a) He *m.* Barbara, sister and h. of Sir James Wemyss, 3d Baronet [S. 1704], only da. of Sir John Wemyss, 2d Baronet [S. 1704], by Anne, da. of Sir William Lockhart, Advocate [S.]. He *d.* 1751.

IV. 1751. Sir Henry Seton, Baronet [S. 1663], of Culbeg, co. Stirling, 1st s. and h.; Captain 17th Foot; Collector of Customs at Bowness; *suc. to the Baronetcy*, in 1751. He was, 8 Aug. 1761, served heir male general of John [*Qy.* James] Seton, of Touch. He *m.*, about 1770, Margaret, 2d da. of Alexander Hay, of Drumelzier, co. Peebles (grandson of John, 1st Earl of Tweeddale [S.]) by his 1st wife Anne, da. of Alexander (Stuart), 5th Lord Blantyre [S.]. He *d.* 29 June 1788, at Bridgeness. His widow *d.* 2 March 1809.

V. 1788. Sir Alexander Seton, Baronet [S. 1663], of Culbeg aforesaid, 1st surv. s. and h., *b.* 4 May 1772; *suc. to the Baronetcy*, 29 June 1788; was an officer in the East India (Bengal) Service. He *m.*, 20 May 1795, at the house of the Gov. Gen. of India, at Bengal, Lydia, 5th da. of Sir Charles William Blunt, 3d Baronet [1720], by Elizabeth, da. of Richard Peers. He *d.* at Calcutta ("at the house of the Hon. C. A. Bruce") 4 Feb. 1810, aged 37. Will pr. 1812. His widow, who was *b.* 25 Sep. 1773, at Odiham, Hants, *d.* 23 Feb. 1851, at Bath. Will pr. March 1851.

VI. 1810. Sir Henry John Seton, Baronet [S. 1663], 1st s. and h., *b.* 4 April 1796; *suc. to the Baronetcy*, 4 Feb. 1810; sometime Capt. in the Army, serving in the Peninsular war with the 52d Foot and the 5th Dragoon Guards; was one of the Grooms in waiting to Queen Victoria. He *d.* unm. 21 July 1868, at 14 King Street, St. James', from injuries received by having been run over by a cab, aged 72.

VII. 1868. Sir Charles Hay Seton, Baronet [S. 1663], br. and h., *b.* 14 Nov. 1797; sometime Capt. 5th Dragoon Guards; *suc. to the Baronetcy*, 11 July, 1868. He *m.* 19 May 1829, Caroline, da. of Walter Parry Hodges, Receiver Gen. for the County of Dorset. She *d.*, after a long illness, 17 Nov. 1868, at 9a Upper Brook Street. He *d.* there 11 June 1869, aged 71.

VIII. 1869. Sir Bruce Maxwell Seton, Baronet [S. 1663], only s. and h., *b.* 31 Jan. 1836, at Dorchester, Dorset; *suc. to the Baronetcy*, 11 June, 1869; was a Clerk in the War Office till 1882; Private Sec. to the L. President of the Council, 1867-74; to the Sec. of State for War, 1882. He *m.*, 30 Jan. 1886, Helen, da. of Gen. Richard Hamilton, C.B., Madras Army.

KEITH:

cr. 4 June 1663;

ex. or *dormant* on death of grantee.

I. 1663, to 1690? "James, *or* George Keith, of Powburn," co. Kincardine, s. and h. of Robert Keith, of the same, merchant, sometime Provost of Montrose (living 1633), 2nd s. of James Keith, of Craig (living 1570), who was great-great-grandson of William, 2nd Earl Marischal [S.], was a staunch loyalist and was, "in reward of his

(a) See p. 338, note "b."

constant loyalty and faithful services"(a) *cr. a Baronet* [S.], as above, 4 June 1663, the patent, however, being not recorded in the Great Seal Register [S.]. He *m.* Grizel GRAHAM, by whom he had a son, James, *bap.* at Edinburgh, 15 July 1663. He is also said to have *m.* [—], da. of [—] LAMMY, of Dunkennie.(a) He *d.* s.p.s., when the *Baronetcy* became *extinct* or *dormant.*

MAXWELL(b):
cr. 30 June 1663;
apparently, *ex.* or *dormant* 1693,
but assumed till 21 Sep. 1786

I. 1663. "ROBERT MAXWELL, of Orchardtoun," co. Kirkcudbright, as also of Ballycastle, co. Londonderry, s. of [Robert?] MAXWELL ("who maintained a company of Foot, brought over at his own expense, in Ireland and also a troop of horse")(c) acquired Ballycastle from his wife's father (who held it from the Haberdashers' Company), but was obliged, in 1649, to surrender it to the Parl. forces; acted as Lieut.-Col. under the Duke of Hamilton [S.](d) and was *cr. a Baronet* [S.] as above, 30 June 1663, the patent not being, however, recorded in the Great Seal Register [S.]. He *m.*, before Feb. 1639/40,(c) Anne or Marion, only da. and h. of Robert (MACLELLAN) 1st LORD KIRKCUDBRIGHT [S.] (who *d.* 13 Jan. 1638/9) by his first wife Anne, da. of Sir Matthew CAMPBELL. She *d.* 1650.(e) He was living 1669 but *d.* before 1673, probably about 1670.

II. 1670? to 1693. SIR ROBERT MAXWELL, Baronet [S. 1663], of Orchardtoun and Ballycastle aforesaid, as also of Waringstown and Killyleagh, co. Down, s. and h.; was *Knighted* before 1655; was M.P. [S.] for the Stewartry of Kirkcudbright (being then styled "the Younger of Orchardtown"), 1669-74, and again (as Baronet), 1681-82; *suc. to the Baronetcy* about 1670, and was (as Baronet) Sheriff for co. Down, 1673; Magistrate for the counties of Down and Londonderry, 13 Dec. 1683. He *m.* firstly, in 1668, Anne, widow of James (HAMILTON), 1st EARL OF CLANBRASSILL [I.] (who *d.* 20 June, 1659), 1st da. of Henry (CAREY), 2nd EARL OF MONMOUTH, by Martha, da. of Lionel (CRANFIELD), EARL OF MIDDLESEX. She *d.* Oct. 1688. He *m.* secondly(f) Margaret, 2d da. and coheir of Henry MAXWELL, of Mullaghatoney, co. Armagh, by Margaret, da. of Robert MAXWELL, D.D., Bishop of Kilmore, 1643-72. He *d.* s.p, 1693 [Ulster's Office], when the *Baronetcy* became, apparently, *extinct* or *dormant.*(g) His widow *m.* Capt. James BUTLER, of Bramblestown, co. Kilkenny, whose will dat. 12 Sep. 1713, was pr. 4 July 1715. Her will dat. 25 March 1754, was pr. 24 June, 1758.

(a) Douglas' *Baronage* [S.], where he is called George, and his creation is said to be "by the style of Sir George Keith, of Powburn." He is, however, called "James" in Milne's *List* and elsewhere.

(b) The information in this article has been kindly supplied by G. D. Burtchaell. See p. 304, note "a."

(c) Petition of "Robert Maxwell, Esq., who married the daughter of Lord Kirkcudbright," to the King, Feb. 1639/40 [Cal. of State Papers, Ireland, 1633-47, p. 234], This Robert is generally called "Sir Robert Maxwell, of Spottis, 2d s. of John, Lord Herries" [S.].

(d) Chancery petition, 20 July 1655 and answer of Col. Tristram Beresford [Chancery Decrees [I.].

(e) Chancery petition, 20 July 1655,

(f) It is conjectured by G. D. Burtchaell (see p. 304, note "a") that this marriage might be that of a *third* Baronet also named Robert (a s. and h. of the 2d Baronet) *b.* about 1669 [or even 1661, if the marriage of his parents took place, as well it might, in 1660 instead of (as stated) in 1668], the difference in age between the *second* Baronet and this Margaret being very great.

(g) It was, however, assumed subsequently, and the deaths occur of (1) "Sir George Maxwell, of Orchardton, 28 Dec. 1746," and (2) of "Sir Robert Maxwell, Baronet, of Orchardtown, 21 Sep. 1786," who is said to have been the 7th and last Baronet.

HAY:
cr. 25 or 26 Aug. 1663.

I. 1663. "SIR THOMAS HAY [the younger, Knt.] of Park" [part of the Abbey lands of Glenluce], co. Wigtown, s. and h. ap. of Sir Thomas HAY, of the same, by Margaret, da. of (—) KENNEDY, was, in his father's lifetime *cr. a Baronet* [S.] as above, 25 or 26 Aug. 1663 with rem. to the heirs male of his body. He *m.* in 1661, Marion HAMILTON, illegit. da. of James, DUKE OF HAMILTON [S.]. He *d.* v.p.

II. 1680? SIR CHARLES HAY, Baronet [S. 1663], of Park, aforesaid, s. and h., *b.* 1662; *suc. to the Baronetcy* on the death of his father. He *m.*, probably about 1685, his cousin, Grisel, da. of Sir Andrew AGNEW. 3d Baronet [S. 1629], by Jean, da. of Sir Thomas HAY, of Park abovenamed, sister to the 1st Baronet. He *d.* 1737.

III. 1737. SIR THOMAS HAY, Baronet [S. 1663], of Park aforesaid, grandson and h., being s. and h. of Thomas HAY, by Mary, da. of Sir William MAXWELL, of Monreith, which Thomas, who *d.* v.p. [also in] 1737, was 1st s. and h. ap. of the late Baronet. He was *b.* about 1730, and *suc. to the Baronetcy* in 1737. He distinguished himself against the Insurgents in 1745, at the battle of Preston Pans, where he was severely wounded in the defence of Col. James GARDINER. He *m.*, in 1747, Jean, da. of John BLAIR, of Dunskey. He *d.* 1777.

IV. 1777. SIR THOMAS HAY, Baronet [S. 1663], of Park aforesaid, only surv. s. and h., *suc. to the Baronetcy* in 1777. He *d.* unm. 30 April 1794,(a) and was *bur.* in the abbey of Old Luce, co. Wigtown.

V. 1794. SIR JAMES HAY, Baronet [S. 1663], cousin and h. male, being s. and h. of William HAY, of Crawfordton, by Mary, da. of Ludovick CANT, of Thurstone, which William was s. of James HAY, of Dumfries, Physician, who was br. to Thomas HAY, abovenamed (father of the 3d Baronet, and), 2d s. of the 2d Baronet. He was *b.* probably about 1775, and *suc. to the Baronetcy*, 30 April 1794. He *m.* [—]. He *d.* in Jamaica, in 1794, in or after May.

VI. 1794. SIR WILLIAM HAY, Baronet [S. 1663], s. and h., *b.* 1793, *suc. to the Baronetcy* on the death of his father. He *d.* unm. 7 Oct. 1801.

VII. 1801. SIR JOHN HAY, Baronet [S. 1663], of Stirling, cousin and h. male, being 1st s. and h. of Lieut.-Col. Lewis HAY, by Barbara, da. of John CRAIGIE, of Glendoick, co. Perth, which Lewis (who was killed at the landing of the British troops at the Helder, 27 Aug. 1799) was yr. br. of the 5th Baronet, both being great-grandsons of the 2d Baronet. He was *b.* 29 Aug. 1799, at Glendoick aforesaid, and *suc. to the Baronetcy*, 7 Oct. 1801; was an Advocate [S.], 9 March 1821, and for above twenty-five years Sheriff Substitute of Stirlingshire. He *m.*, 29 June, 1836, Sarah Beresford, da. of John COSSINS, of Weymouth, by Susanna Elizabeth, da. of George (TOUCHET), LORD AUDLEY. He *d.* 15 June 1862, in his 62d year.

VIII. 1862. SIR ARTHUR GRAHAM HAY, Baronet [S. 1663], of Redbarns House, Dundalk, co. Louth, 2d but 1st surv. s. and h., *b.* 5 June 1839; *suc. to the Baronetcy*, 15 June 1862. He *m.*, 29 June 1864

(a) The estate of Park devolved on his sister and h., Susanna, who *m.*, 14 July 1775, Col. John Dalrymple, who thereupon assumed the final name of Hay, and was *cr.* a Baronet, 7 April 1798.

(spec. lic.), at Ballykilbeg House, co. Down, Thomasine Isabella, yst. da. of John Brett JOHNSTON, late of the same, deceased. He *d.* 18 Nov. 1889, aged 50. His widow living 1903.

IX. 1889. SIR LEWIS JOHN ERROLL HAY, Baronet [S. 1663], of Dooriah, Tirhoot, in the province of Bengal, in India, 1st s. and h., *b.* 17 Nov. 1866; ed. at Fettes College, Edinburgh; *suc. to the Baronetcy*, 18 Nov. 1889. He *m.*, 25 Sep. 1895, at St. Columb's, Portree, Isle of Skye, Elizabeth Anne, da. of Lachlan MACDONALD, of Skeabost, in that island.

MURRAY(a):
cr. 12 or 13 Feb. 1663/4;
attainted 1746, *but assumed* notwithstanding;
ex. or dormant, 23 Aug. 1848;
but again assumed till 1878.

I. 1664. "WILLIAM(b) MURRAY, of Stanhope," co. Peebles, 2d but 1st surv. s. and h. of Sir David MURRAY, of the same (living 17 Dec. 1645), by Lilias, da. of John (FLEMING), 1st EARL OF WIGTOUN [S.], was served, 28 April 1654, heir general of his father and heir special of his brother, John MURRAY, in the Baronies of Broughton, Stobo, etc.; was a fervent Loyalist, and was, in 1654, fined £2,000, subsequently reduced to one third, and was *cr. a Baronet* [S.], as above, 12 or 13 Feb. 1663/4, with rem. to the heirs male of his body, the patent being registered in the Great Seal [S.]. He was M.P. [S.] for Peeblesshire, 1661-63, 1665, and 1667; had, 24 May 1671, a crown charter of the Barony of Broughton; registered arms in the Lyon Office about 1673, and held the heritable Bailliery of Stobo from the See of Glasgow in 1682. He *m.* Janet, 2d da. of James (JOHNSTONE), 1st EARL OF HARTFELL [S.], by his 1st wife, Margaret, da. of William (DOUGLAS), 1st EARL OF QUEENSBERRY [S.]. He was living 1689, but *d.* in or before 1690.

II. 1690? SIR DAVID MURRAY, Baronet [S. 1664], of Stanhope and Broughton aforesaid, 1st s. and h.; M.P. [S.] for Peeblesshire, 1681-82 and 1689, till declared void, in 1693, for not having taken the oaths. He appears to have favoured the Rising of 1715(c). In 1726 he purchased the estate of Ardnamurchan and the lead mines of Strontian. He *m.* firstly, 16 April 1684, Anne, da. of Alexander (BRUCE), 2d EARL OF KINCARDINE [S.], by Veronica, da. of Corneille VAN SOMMELSDYCK. He *m.* secondly in or before 1714, Margaret, widow of Thomas SCOTT, of Whitslaid, da. of Sir John SCOTT, 1st Baronet [1671], of Ancrum, by his 2d wife, Elizabeth, da. of Sir William BENNET, of Grubbet. He *d.* 14 and was *bur.* 17 Feb. 1729, in the Canongate churchyard, Edinburgh. His widow *d.* 5 Sep. 1761.

III. 1729. SIR ALEXANDER MURRAY, Baronet [S. 1664], of Stanhope and Broughton aforesaid, 2d but 1st surv. s. and h.; was M.P. for Peeblesshire, 1710-12 and in 1734; *suc. to the Baronetcy*, 14 Feb. 1729; sold

(a) See *Genealogist*, N.S., vol. xv, p. 193—202, for a good account of the "MURRAYS OF ROMANNO, BROUGHTON, and STANHOPE," by Sir J. Balfour Paul, Lyon. The account in Chalmers' *Peeblesshire*, and still more so that in Douglas' *Baronage* [S.] and Playfair's *Baronetage* [S.] is very inaccurate.

(b) Said in J. R. Anderson's *List* (see p. 323, note "a") to be "called *Sir James* in Banks' *Baronia*," but there can be no doubt of his christian name having been William.

(c) *Dict. Nat. Biogr.*, under "Murray, Sir John, 1718—1777," where, however, the 2d Baronet (who *d.* 1729, and whose son, the 3d Baronet, died in 1743) is confused with his grandson (the 4th Baronet) inasmuch as he is said to have taken part (twenty-six years after his death) in the Rising of 1745.

the estate of Broughton, about 1738, to his younger br., John MURRAY. He *m.* (contract, 16 June 1710) Grizel,(a) da. of George BAILLIE, of Jerviswood, co. Lanark, and of Mellerstaine, co. Berwick (one of the Lords of the Treasury), by Grizel, da. of Patrick (HOME), 1st EARL OF MARCHMONT [S.]. He *d.* s.p. 18 May 1743, when part of his estate remained in the hands of his creditors. His widow *d.* 6 June 1759, in her 68th year.

IV. 1743, to 1745. SIR DAVID MURRAY, Baronet [S. 1664], of Stanhope aforesaid, nephew and h., being s. and h. of David MURRAY, Merchant, at Leith, by "an English lady," probably Frances MACCLESFIELD,(b) or possibly "a daughter of SOMERVILLE, of Corsehouse,"(b) which David, whose will was confirmed 15 Sep. 1742, was 3d s. of the 2d Baronet. He *suc. to the Baronetcy*, 18 May 1743; was Capt. of a Hussar Regiment. He was active in the Jacobite Rising of 1745; was taken prisoner, and sentenced to death at York, when, having been attainted, the *Baronetcy* was *forfeited.* The estate of Stanhope was sold in 1767 for £40,500, and that of Strontian, co. Argyll, for £43,700. He joined the young Chevalier in France, and was in Paris in 1749, and *d.* s.p., probably unm., abroad about 1769.(c)

The Baronetcy, subject to the attainder, would have devolved as under, and was, apparently, assumed in reliance of such attainder having been made void, by the act of indemnity.

V. 1769? SIR CHARLES MURRAY, Baronet(d) [S. 1644], a Collector of Customs at Bo'ness, co. Linlithgow, uncle of the whole blood and h. male, being 5th s. of the 2d Baronet by his first wife, *suc. to the Baronetcy*(d) on the death of his nephew, but it is doubtful whether he ever assumed the title. He *m.* firstly, in 1733, "a lady with £16,000."(b) He *m.* secondly Isabella, widow of Hugh Dalrymple MURRAY, of Melgund and Kynynmond, da. and coheir of Hugh SOMERVILLE, of Invertie, co. Fife. She *d.* 8 Dec. 1760. He *d.* 1770.

VI. 1770. SIR DAVID MURRAY, Baronet(d) [S. 1664], only s. and h., by (—) wife; an officer in the Army; *suc. to the Baronetcy*(g) in 1770, but *d.* unm. in the same year, at Leghorn, 19 Oct. 1770.

VII. 1770, Oct. SIR JOHN MURRAY, Baronet(d) [S. 1664], sometime of Broughton(e) aforesaid (which he purchased of his eldest br. about 1738, as above stated, and sold soon after 1764), uncle of the half blood and heir male, being 7th s. of the 2d Baronet, viz., 2d but 1st surv. s. by the 2d wife. He was *b.* 1715; ed. at the Univ. of Edinburgh; was on a mission in Feb. 1741/2 to Rome to the titular James III., and to Prince Charles Edward 1743-45 at Paris, to whom he was Secretary during the campaign of 1745 in Scotland, his wife (a great beauty) taking a conspicuous part in the proclamation of

(a) She "was the subject of a very unpleasant adventure with one of her footmen, Arthur Gray, an episode on which Lady Mary Wortley Montagu wrote a ballad." See p. 342, note "a."

(b) See p. 342, note "a."

(c) Anne, his only sister, *m.* 22 May 1744, Capt. the Hon. William Henry Cranstoun, who tried to set aside the marriage, so that he might marry Miss Blandy, the Parricide.

(d) Subject, however, to the attainder, of 1745.

(e) This estate must not be confused with the more considerable one of Broughton, in co. Galloway, belonging to the family of "Murray of Broughton," to which family this infamous "John Murray, of Broughton," is consequently (though erroneously) often supposed to have belonged.

III

James, as King, at Edinburgh. He was taken prisoner, 28 June 1746, after the battle of Culloden, but, having had the meanness to turn "King's Evidence," was pardoned in May 1748, and had an annual pension of £200. In 1749 he was committed to Newgate for challenging the Earl of Traquair [S.], and had to find bail for £8,000. He was served heir to his mother, 21 April 1764, and *suc. to the Baronetcy*(a) in Oct. 1770. He was taken from his house in Denmark street, Soho, in July 1771, and placed by his sons in a lunatic asylum.(b) He *m.* soon after 1738, Margaret, da. of Col. Robert FERGUSON, of Creagh Darragh, co. Stirling, by Mabel, da. of John CALLENDAR, of Craigforth,(c) but deserted her before 1754.(d) He *d.* at Cheshunt, Herts, 6 and was *bur.* 10 Dec. 1777, in the new burial ground,(c) at St. Marylebone, aged about 62. Will pr. 1777. His widow was *bur.* there 20 Sep. 1779.(c) Her will pr. Sep. 1779.

VIII. 1777. SIR DAVID MURRAY, Baronet(a) [S. 1664], 1st s. and h., *b.* at Edinburgh, 12 Dec. 1743(c); Lieut. in the Royal Navy; *suc. to the Baronetcy.*(a) 6 Dec. 1777; was served heir gen. of his grandaunt Margaret FERGUSON, 15 Sep. 1781, and heir gen. of his father, 26 April 1786. He *d.* unm. at Hampstead, 23. and was *bur.* 29 June 1791, at St. Marylebone,(c) aged 47. Will pr. June 1791.

IX. 1791. SIR ROBERT MURRAY, Baronet(a) [S. 1664], of Darland, co. Chester, br. and h., *b.* at Edinburgh(c); 4 March, 1745, Student of Laws in the Univ. of Edinburgh; admitted to Lincoln's Inn, 3 Oct. 1763; Barrister at Law; *suc. to the Baronetcy*(a), 23 June 1791. He *m.*, probably about 1780, at Chester, Elizabeth, da. of Vice Admiral Francis PICKMORE, Gov. of Newfoundland. He *d.*, March 1793, at Keynsham, and was *bur.* there,(c) aged 48. His widow was living 1803.(c)

X. 1793. SIR DAVID MURRAY, Baronet(a) [S. 1664], 1st s. and h.; *suc. to the Baronetcy*(a) in March 1793. He *d.* unm. and a minor at the Cape of Good Hope before Feb. 1803.(c)

XI. 1800? to 1848. SIR JOHN MURRAY, Baronet(a) [S. 1664], br. and h., *b.* probably about 1783, *suc. to the Baronetcy*(a) about 1800, certainly before Feb. 1803, when he was a minor;(c) was an officer in the army. He *m.*, 17 Oct. 1801(c), Catherine, da. of Adam CALLENDER, of the family of Craigforth. She *d.* in 1831. He *d.* s.p.m.s.(e), 23 Aug. 1848, at Fecamp, in Normandy, when *the Baronetcy* (which had, apparently, been under attainder since 1746) became *extinct* or *dormant.*(f)

(a) Subject, however, to the attainder of 1745.

(b) *Ex inform.* R. R. Stodart, many years Lyon Clerk Depute, by whom several particulars in this article were supplied.

(c) Pedigree registered Feb. 1803, in the Coll. of Arms, London (6 D. xiv. 246) in which, however, the burial of Sep. 1779 is (by a mistake) said to have been at "St. Margaret's" instead of at St. Marylebone.

(d) He eloped with a Miss Webb, a young Quakeress, from a boarding school, by whom he had six children, the eldest Charles Murray (actor and dramatist, 1754-1821) being born at Cheshunt, Herts, in 1754.

(e) Besides two sons, Robert and Wellington, who *d.* young, he had an only surviving son, John Francis Murray, *b.* 24 April 1804, who *m.* Elizabeth, da. of James Fletcher, and *d.* v.p. and s.p. 13 July 1826. Of his daughters and coheirs, (1) Catherine Emily, *m.* in 1828, Samuel Hervey Howell, of London; (2) Frances Caroline, *m.* 30 Sep. 1835, Hamilton Gyll, of Shenley Lodge, Herts.

(f) His yst. br., Thomas Murray, Major 48th Reg., *m.* Nov. 1788, "at St. James'," [as is stated], Mrs. Hopkins," but *d.* s.p.m. before his brother.

The title, however, was subsequently assumed as under.

XII. 1848, to 1878. "SIR MURRAY HOWELL-MURRAY, Baronet"(a) [S. 1664], only s. and h. of Samuel Hervey HOWELL, of London, by Catherine Emily, 1st da. and coheir of the late Baronet, *b.* about 1838; assumed the Baronetcy(a) on the ground apparently of his mother being a coheir of the last holder, but *d.* of gastric fever, 1 Aug. 1878, aged 40, when, apparently, such assumption ceased.

BROUN, *or* BROWN:

cr. 17 Feb. 1663/4;

ex. about 1670.

I. 1664, to 1670? "JAMES BROUN [or BROWN] in the island of Barbadoes, Esq.," was *cr. a Baronet* [S.], as above, 17 Feb. 1663/4, with rem. to the heirs male of his body, but the *Baronetcy* is supposed to have become *extinct* on his death not long afterward.

KIRKALDY:

cr. 14 May 1664;

ex. presumably on death of grantee;

I. 1664, to 1680? "JOHN KIRKALDY, of Grange," presumably a relative of the well known Sir William KIRKALDY, of Grange (executed 3 Aug. 1573), was *cr. a Baronet* [S.], as above, 14 May 1664, with rem. to the heirs male of his body, but it is presumed that the *Baronetcy* became *extinct* on his death.

MOWAT:(b)

cr. 2 June 1664;

existing, presumably, till 1829.

I. 1664. "SIR GEORGE MOWAT, of Inglistoun," s. of Roger MOUATT or MOWAT, of Dumbruch, Advocate [S.], by Margaret MAJORIBANKS, was *cr. a Baronet* [S.], as above, 2 June 1664, with rem. to the heirs male of his body. He *m.* Elizabeth, da. of Sir John HOPE, 2d Baronet [S. 1628], of Craighall, by Margaret, da. of Sir Archibald MURRAY, 1st Baronet [S. 1628]. He *d.* Sep. 1666.

II. 1666. SIR ROGER MOWAT, Baronet [S. 1664], of Inglistoun aforesaid, s. and h., *suc. to the Baronetcy* in Sep. 1666. He *d.* in or before Feb. 1683.

III. 1683? SIR WILLIAM MOWAT, Baronet [S. 1664], of Inglistoun aforesaid, br. and h., *suc. to the Baronetcy*, on the death of his brother, to whom he was served heir in Feb. 1683.

(a) Subject, however, to the attainder, of 1745.

(b) The information in this article has been kindly supplied by Francis James Grant, Rothesay Herald and Lyon Clerk.

IV. 1690? SIR ALEXANDER MOWAT, Baronet [S. 1664], whose relationship to the former Baronets is unknown, *suc. to the Baronetcy*, and registered arms in the Lyon Office.

The further devolution of the dignity is unknown, but in—

1829, May 9. "Col. SIR JAMES MOWAT, Baronet, Bengal Engineers," *d.* at sea on board the E.I.C. ship "Prince Regent," aged about 63. M.I. in South Park Street Burial Ground, Calcutta. He was br. of George, who reg. arms in 1811 as representative of the house of MOWATT, of Balquhally, both being sons of George, s. of James, s. of another George, who was a yr. s. of Patrick MOWATT, of Balquhally, killed at the battle of Alford, 1645. The two houses (*viz.*, those of Inglistoun and of Balquhally) appear, however, to be entirely distinct.

DALRYMPLE:

cr. 2 June 1664;

afterwards, since 1690, VISCOUNTS STAIR [S.];

and subsequently, since 1703, EARLS OF STAIR [S.].

I. 1664. "SIR JAMES DALRYMPLE, of Stair," in Kyle, co. Ayr, only s. and h. of James DALRYMPLE, of the same (who *d.* 1625), by Janet, da. of Fergus KENNEDY, of Knockdaw, was *b.* May 1619, at his father's farm of Drummurchie, co. Carrick; ed. at Mauchline School and at the Univ. of Glasgow; M.A. and first Graduate in Arts, 1637; served in the army, 1637-41, and was for six years, 1641-47, Regent of Glasgow Univ.; was an Advocate [S.], 17 Feb. 1647/8; a Lord of Session, 1657-60 and 1661-70, and was *cr. a Baronet* [S.], as above, 2 June 1664, with rem. to the heirs male of his body; President of the Court of Session, 1670-81, and again, 1689-94. He was M.P. [S.] for Wigtonshire, 1672-74, 1678, and 1681-82, and for Ayrshire, 1689-90. Being in disfavour with the Court he quitted Scotland for Holland in 1682, but returned in 1688 with William III., who replaced him in his former post. He *m.*, 21 Sep. 1643 (contract dat. 20 at Balcail), Margaret, widow of Fergus KENNEDY, of Knoxdaw, 1st da. and heir of line of James Ross, of Balneil, co. Wigton, by Sarah, da. of Alexander SYME, Advocate. She was living when he was *cr.*, 21 April 1690, VISCOUNT STAIR, etc. [S.], his s. and h., the 2d Viscount, being *cr.*, 8 April 1703, EARL OF STAIR, etc., [S.], in which peerages this *Baronetcy* then *merged* and still [1903] so continues. See "PEERAGE."

HENDERSON:

cr. 15 *or* 16 July 1664;

ex. 3 Aug. 1833.

I. 1664. "JOHN HENDERSON, of Fordell," 1st s. and h. of Sir John HENDERSON, of the same, a steady loyalist (sometime in command on the coast of Africa), by Margaret, da. of [—] MENTEITH, was *cr. a Baronet* [S.], as above, 15 or 16 July 1664 with rem. to the heirs male of his body. He had a charter, 11 July 1670, of the Barony of Fordell. He *m.* Margaret, da. of Sir John HAMILTON, of Orbieston, Lord Justice Clerk [S.]. He *d.* 1683.

II. 1683. SIR WILLIAM HENDERSON, Baronet [S. 1664], of Fordell aforesaid; 2d but 1st surv. s. and h (a); *suc. to the Baronetcy* in 1683. He *m.* firstly, Jean, da. of John HAMILTON, of Mountain Hall. His 2d wife seems to have been Helen, widow of Charles MACKIE (Chamberlain to Sir Charles HALKITT, of Pitfirrane), da. of Andrew DONALDSON, Minister of Dalgety, co. Fife.(b) He *d.* in 1709.

III. 1709. SIR JOHN HENDERSON, Baronet [S. 1664], of Fordell aforesaid, 1st s. and h., *b.* 28 Dec. 1686 [Edinburgh Reg.], *suc. to the Baronetcy* in 1709. He *m.* Christian, 1st da. of Sir Robert ANSTRUTHER, 1st Baronet [S. 1694], of Balcaskie, co. Fife, by his 2d wife, Jean, da. and h. of William MONTEITH.

IV. 1730? SIR ROBERT HENDERSON, Baronet [S. 1664], of Fordell aforesaid, 2d but 1st surv. s. and h.; *suc. to the Baronetcy* on the death of his father; was elected Provost of Inverkeithen in 1744. He *m.* 3 Oct. 1748, Isabella, widow of George MACKENZIE, of Fairnie, da. of Archibald STUART, of Torrence. He *d.* at Fordell House, 19 Oct. 1781. His widow *d.* 16 Aug. 1796.

V. 1781. SIR JOHN HENDERSON, Baronet [S. 1664], of Fordell aforesaid, 1st s. and h., *b.* Jan. 1762; admitted an Advocate [S.], 1774; M.P. for Fifeshire, July 1779 to 1780; for Kirkaldy burghs, 1780-84; for Seaford, March 1785 till void in 1786; for Stirling burghs, 1802 till void in Feb. 1803, and again 1806-07; *suc. to the Baronetcy*, 19 Oct. 1781; director of the Chamber of Commerce, July 1789; Provost of the borough of Inverkeithen, Oct. 1802. He *m.*, in May 1781, (—) da. of General ROBERTSON, of Newbigging, Governor of New York; she *d.* 6 Feb. 1782. He *d.* s.p.m. 12 Dec. 1817, at Edinburgh.

VI. 1817, to 1833. SIR ROBERT BRUCE HENDERSON, Baronet [S. 1664], of Fordell aforesaid, br. and h. male, *b.* probably about 1760; admitted an Advocate [S.], 1783; *suc. to the Baronetcy*, 12 Dec. 1817. He *d.* s.p., unm., 3 Aug. 1833, when the *Baronetcy* became *extinct*. Will pr. May 1834.

MACCULLOCH:

cr. 10 Aug. 1664;

ex. 26 March 1697.

I. 1664. "SIR ALEXANDER MACCULLOCH, of Myrtoun," was *cr. a Baronet* [S.], 10 Aug. 1664, but the patent is not recorded in the Great Seal Register. He *m.* (—), who survived him, but *d.* before 1678.

II. 1675. SIR GODFREY MACCULLOCH, Baronet [S. 1664], of Myrtoun aforesaid, grandson and h., being s. and h. of John MACCULLOCH, who was 1st s. and h. ap. of the late Baronet, but who *d.* v.p. He *suc. to the Baronetcy* before 1678, when, as "Knight Baronet," he was M.P. [S.] for Wigtonshire. He *d.* s.p. legit., being executed at the Cross of Edinburgh,(c) 26 March 1697, for the murder of William GOURDON, when the *Baronetcy* became *extinct.*

(a) John, the 1st son, "a youth of great hopes," *d.* v.p. and unm. in his 18th year.

(b) See "*Glimpses of Pastoral Work in the Covenanting Times,*" by William Ross, LL.D. [London, 1878, pp. 226-227], where the authority for the statement is given as the "MS. inventory of writs, belonging to the Fordell family."

(c) See Pitcairn's *Criminal Trials*, where his speech and his letter to his wife and [illegit.] children are set out.

DUNBAR:

cr. 13 Oct. 1664;

dormant, apparently, since death of grantee.

I. 1664, to 1680? "DAVID DUNBAR, of Baldoon," co. Wigton, was *cr. a Baronet* [S.], as above, 13 Oct. 1664, with rem. "provydit to his heirs male and tailzie." This *Baronetcy*, however, appears to have become *dormant* on the death s.p.m.s. of the grantee.(a)

CHALMERS:(b)

cr. 24 Nov. 1664;

ex., presumably, after the death of the grantee,

but, apparently, *assumed* to 1 Oct. 1834.

I. 1664. "SIR JAMES CHALMERS, son to Cults"(c) [*i.e.*, of Gilbert CHALMERS,(d) Laird of Cults in the parish of Tarland, co. Aberdeen, Burgess of Aberdeen, by Christian, da. of Patrick CON, of Auchry], was *cr. a Baronet* [S.], as above, 24 Nov. 1664, with rem. to heirs male of his body. His "birth brief" is said to have been "dated 19 Jan. 1671 [*Qy.* 1641?], being then in Silesia."(e)

The succession to this Baronetcy is difficult to conjecture, unless indeed it is as under.

II? 1700? SIR CHARLES CHALMERS, Baronet [S. 1664?], *b.* 24 April 1717, is said(f) to have been "grandson of the first grantee," but, apparently, was s. and h. of Roderick CHALMERS,(g) Ross Herald (so appointed in 1724), by Mary, only child of George WILSON. He was, however, *recognised* at the Lyon Office (probably about

(a) Mary Dunbar, his granddaughter and heir, only child of his son, David Dunbar (who *d.* v.p.), was *b.* 1677, *m.* Lord Basil Hamilton (who *d.* 1701, in his 30th year), inherited the estate of Baldoon, and *d.* 15 May 1760, in her 84th year, being ancestress of the Earls of Selkirk [S.].

(b) Much of the information in this article was supplied by R. R. Stodart, many years Lyon Clerk Depute.

(c) In the "diploma" from Whitehall (24 Nov. 1664) the grantee is called "Dominus Jacobus Chalmers, filius Comarchi de Cultes." Patent recorded in the Great Seal Register, Book 63, No. 148.

(d) This Gilbert Chalmers appears to have sold Cults in 1612 to Sir James Gordon. He appears to have had another son (besides the future Baronet), viz., Gilbert Chalmers, whose birth brief was dated 23 Feb. 1650, and (according to Nisbet's *Heraldry*) yet another son, viz., Alexander Chalmers, of Cults.

(e) Believed to be communicated by R. R. Stodart (see note "b" above) but the date seems unintelligible. The "birth brief" of his brother, Gilbert, was in 1650; see note "d," above.

(f) Playfair's *Scotch Baronetage*, 1811.

(g) This Roderick was s. and h. of Capt. Charles Chalmers, Writer to the Signet, who was 2d s. of the Rev. James Chalmers, Minister of Paisley (Bishop designate of Orkney), who was 2d s. of the Rev. William Chalmers, Minister of Boyndie, co. Banff, the 2d. s. of Alexander Chalmers, of Cults, who was father of Gilbert Chalmers, of the same, the father of the 1st Baronet.

1745) *as a Baronet* of Nova Scotia [though *possibly* such recognition was not in respect of *this* Baronetcy of 24 Nov. 1664], and as the heir male of CULTS.(a) He, who had been a Captain in the Royal Reg. of Artillery, *d.* unm. at Pondicherry in the East Indies, Nov. 1760. Admon., 24 Sep. 1762, to his brother James CHALMERS. Will pr. [I.] 1765.

III? 1760. SIR GEORGE CHALMERS, Baronet [S. 1664?], br. and h.; long resident in India; *suc. to the Baronetcy*, Nov. 1760. He *d.*, about 1764, in India.

IV? 1764. SIR GEORGE CHALMERS, Baronet [S. 1664?], presumed to be s. and h., and to have *suc. to the Baronetcy* in 1764; was *b.* at Edinburgh; was a portrait painter of some note, exhibiting in the Royal Academy, 1775-90. He *m.*, 4 June 1768, at Edinburgh, Isabella, da. of John ALEXANDER, historical and portrait painter, of that city, being sister and heir of Cosmo ALEXANDER. She was *bur.*, 16 April 1784, at St. Pancras, Midx. He *d.* s.p.m.s. at Marylebone, and was *bur.*, 15 Nov. 1791, at St. Pancras aforesaid. Admon. (under £300) 14 May 1792.(b)

V? 1791. SIR ROBERT CHALMERS, Baronet [S. 1664?], cousin and h. male, but whether as such entitled to the Baronetcy is doubtful. He was s. and h. of John CHALMERS, by Lætitia, da. and eventually heir of Robert HALL, which John was yr. s. of Capt. Charles CHALMERS and brother to Roderick, father of Sir Charles CHALMERS, who was *recognised*, about 1745, by the Lyon Office *as a Baronet* [S.], as above mentioned. He was *b.* 1749; was a Captain in the Marines and Commander of the Alexander Lazaretto stationed at the Motherbank, and *assumed the Baronetcy* in Nov. 1791. He *m.* firstly, in or before 1779, at Portsmouth, Mary, da. of William BOON, M.D., of that town. She *d.* and was *bur.* there. He *m.* secondly, Elizabeth, da. of John GARDINER, of Maidstone. He *d.* at Portsmouth, 1807, aged 58, and was *bur.* at Portsea.

VI? 1807, to 1834. SIR CHARLES WILLIAM CHALMERS, Baronet [S. 1664?], only surv. s. and h., by 1st wife; *b.* 1779, at Portsmouth; *suc. to the Baronetcy* (as borne by his father) in 1807; was Capt. in the Royal Navy in or before 1815. He *m.*, July 1815, Isabella, widow of Capt. T. SCOTT, of the East India Service, da. of (—) HENDERSON, of Edinburgh. He *d.* 1 Oct. 1834, aged 54, at Appledore in Northam, when the *assumption of the Baronetcy ceased.* His widow *d.* 4 Oct. 1840, aged 60. M.I. at Northam aforesaid.

(a) "On what grounds he was so recognised does not appear, unless indeed he was heir male *of the body* of the 1st Baronet, but if the pedigree as given above is correct (which, having been furnished by *Ross Herald*, it doubtless is), there could be no right to the Baronetcy of 1664, which was to heirs male of the body; still it is possible that this Charles might be heir male of Cults (supposing the failure of the issue of the 1st Baronet) and *also* entitled to a Nova Scotia Baronetcy, as there are several such which, unfortunately, were never recorded. Possibly his father the Herald might have been the grantee" [R. R. Stodart, see p. 348, note "b."]

(b) Granted to Isabella Chalmers, of York, spinster, only child of deceased. She became a nun at York, in 1796.

SETON:(a)

cr. 9 Dec. 1664;

forfeited 1718-20;

but assumed till 1769;

and possibly till Aug. 1796.

I. 1664. The Hon. "JOHN SETON, of Garletoun," formerly Garmiltoun, co. Haddington, 10th s. of George (SETON), 3d EARL OF WINTOUN [S.] (*d.* 17 Dec. 1650, aged 65), being 5th s. by his 2d wife, Elizabeth, da. of John (MAXWELL), LORD HERRIES [S.], was *b.* 29 Sep. 1639, and was *cr. a Baronet* [S.], as above, 19 Dec. 1664, with rem. to the heirs male of his body. He was served heir, 20 Feb. 1672, to his yst. br., Sir Robert SETON, Baronet [S. 1671], of Windygoul. He *m.* Christian (or Isabel), da. of Sir John HOME, of Renton. He *d.* Feb. 1685/6, aged 47.

II. 1686, to 1719? SIR GEORGE SETON, Baronet [S. 1664], of Garletoun aforesaid, s. and h.; *suc. to the Baronetcy* in Feb. 1685/6, and was served heir general of his father, 7 Aug. 1686, and heir special in Garletoun, etc., united with the Barony of Athelstaneford, 13 Oct. following. He *m.*, in or shortly before 1685, Barbara, da. of Andrew WAUCHOPE, of Niddrie Mareschal, co. Edinburgh, by Margaret, da. of Sir John GILMOUR, of Craigmillar. She, who was *b.* 23 May 1667, obtained in 1705, a divorce from him (whom she survived), and was living 1731. He *d.* between June 1718 and May 1720, when the *Baronetcy*, the right to which devolved on his s. and h., was *forfeited* in consequence of the attainder of that son. [See below].

The right to the Baronetcy (which was sometimes assumed, notwithstanding the attainder) appears to have been as under.

III. 1719? SIR GEORGE SETON, Baronet [S. 1664],(b) of Garletoun aforesaid, s. and h., *b.* in 1685; joined the Jacobite Rising of 1715, was taken prisoner at Preston 13 Oct. of that year, and was attainted in 1716; *suc. to the right to the Baronetcy*(b) on the death of his father in 1718, 1719 or 1720, and on the death, 19 Dec. 1749, of his cousin, George, 5th EARL OF WINTOUN [S.], (who, however, by attainder in 1716, had forfeited his peerage dignities), became, apparently, heir to that Earldom, and is sometimes said to have assumed the same. He *d.* unm. at Versailles, in France, 9 March 1769, in his 84th year.(c)

IV. 1769. RALPH SETON, cousin and h., being s. and h. of John SETON, of Durham, by Frances, da. of Sir Richard NEALE, of Pleny (which John, who *d.* in Germany in 1715, was yr. s. of the 1st Baronet), was *b.* 27 June 1702 at Durham, and *suc. to the right to the Earldom, as well as to the Baronetcy*(b), 9 March 1769, but appears never to have assumed either dignity, though he is spoken of as "LORD SETON," and is so styled in the registry of his burial. He *d.* unm., and was *bur.*, 31 Dec. 1782, at Newcastle-on-Tyne.

(a) Much of the information contained in this article was kindly supplied by R. R. Stodart, many years Lyon Clerk Depute.

(b) Subject to the forfeiture thereof by the attainder of 1716.

(c) His only surv. sister, Mary, who in 1733 had *m.* John Arrot, of Fogarty, co. Forfar, was, 1 Dec. 1769, served his heir general.

V. 1782, to 1796. JOHN SETON, nephew and h., being s. and h. of John SETON, of St. Pancras, co. Midx., upholsterer, by Mary, da. of Francis NEWTON, of Irnham, co. Lincoln, which John, who *d.* Jan. 1775, was br. to Ralph SETON last named. He was *b.* Dec. 1755; *suc. to the right to the Earldom as well as to the Baronetcy*(a) in Dec. 1782, but appears never to have assumed either dignity. He *m.*, 16 Feb. 1786, Mary, da. of John HUGHES, of Berryhall, co. Warwick. He *d.* s.p.m.(b) 3 Aug. 1796, and was *bur.* at St. Pancras aforesaid, when *the Baronetcy* became *extinct.*(c)

SINCLAIR(d):

cr. 10 Dec. 1664;

ex. or *dormant* in or before 1843.

I. 1664. "SIR ROBERT SINCLAIR, of Longformacus," co. Berwick, s. and h. of James SINCLAIR, of the same, by Helen, da. of Patrick HEPBURN, of Nunraw, co. Haddington, suc. his father before Sep. 1632, to whom he was served heir in Longformacus, 4 Nov. 1647; was a steady Royalist; an Advocate [S.], 9 July 1647, and was *cr. a Baronet* [S.], as above, 10 Dec. 1664, with rem. to the heirs male of his body. He was M.P. [S.] for co. Berwick 1665-67 and 1669-74; acquired the Barony of Lochend, co. Haddington, lands at Ellem, Hairhead, etc., co. Berwick, and obtained the creation of Longformacus into a free Barony. He *m.* firstly, Elizabeth, da. and h. of Robert DOUGLAS, of Blackerston, co. Berwick. He *m.* secondly, in 1672, Margaret, sister and h. of William (ALEXANDER), 2d EARL OF STIRLING [S.], da. of William ALEXANDER, *styled* VISCOUNT CANADA, by Margaret, da. of William (DOUGLAS), 1st MARQUESS OF DOUGLAS [S.]. By her he had no male issue. He *d.* 1678.(e)

II. 1678. SIR JOHN SINCLAIR, Baronet [S. 1664], of Longformacus, Lochend, Ellem, etc., 1st s. and h. by 1st wife; *suc. to the Baronetcy* in 1678, was served heir general, 22 Dec. 1679, and heir special in the above Baronies, 8 April 1680. He *m.* Jean, da. and h. of Sir John TOWERS, of Inverleith, co. Edinburgh. He was living 1696.

III. 1698? SIR ROBERT SINCLAIR, Baronet [S. 1664], of Longformacus, etc., *suc. to the Baronetcy* on his father's death, about 1698, and had general service, 31 Oct. 1698; was M.P. [S.] for Berwickshire,

(a) Subject to the forfeiture thereof by the attainder of 1716.

(b) Mary Catherine, his only surv. child, was a milliner in London. She *m.*, 26 Jan. 1816, John Broadbent, of Kirkbarrow House, Kendal, co. Westmorland.

(c) As to the Earldom of Wintoun [S.] the issue male of the 3d Earl appears to have become extinct at his death in 1766. Some forty-four years later (the 2d Earl having died without issue in 1609), on 22 Dec. 1840, the Earl of Eglintoun [S.], who was heir male of the body of Alexander Seton (afterwards Earl of Eglintoun [S.]), 3d son of the 1st Earl of Wintoun [S.], was served heir male to the 4th Earl (father of the 5th and attainted Earl) and assumed the Earldom, without, however, having obtained the judgment of the House of Lords on his claim, which was not specifically acknowledged, though, perhaps, *practically* it was so, when, some twenty years later, he was *cr.* 23 June 1859, EARL OF WINTON [U.K.].

(d) See p. 350, note "a," under Seton.

(e) Sir Archibald Sinclair his 3d and yst. son was M.P. [S.] for Wick, 1690-96; was admitted an Advocate [S.], 1695; was Judge of Admiralty, etc. *Knighted* about 1697; *bur.* 20 Aug. 1719, at Holyrood. He *m.* Elizabeth, da. of Patrick Cockburn, of Borthlewick, and had issue.

1703-07; sold the estate of Lochend and other lands. He *m.* Christian, da. of the Rt. Hon. Adam COCKBURN, of Ormiston, Lord Justice Clerk [S.]. He *d.* 28 Sep. 1727.

IV. 1727. SIR JOHN SINCLAIR, Baronet [S. 1664], of Longformacus aforesaid, s. and h.; *suc. to the Baronetcy*, 28 Sep. 1727; and had general service in Longformacus, Newbank, etc., 27 Feb. and 1 March 1731. He *m.* Sydney, da. of Robert JOHNSTONE, of Hilton, co. Berwick. He *d.* s.p.m.(a) 5 Dec. 1764, at Newton, near Dalkeith. His widow *d.* 25 May 1777.

V. 1764. SIR HARRY SINCLAIR, Baronet [S. 1664], of Longformacus aforesaid, br. and h. male. He, in Aug. 1719, inherited, under a special entail, the estate of Carlowrie, co. Linlithgow, on the death of Henry SINCLAIR, of the same, but sold the same in 1745. He *suc. to the Baronetcy*, 5 Dec. 1764, and *d.* s.p. 25 June 1768, at Leith.

VI. 1768. SIR JOHN SINCLAIR, Baronet [S. 1664], cousin and h. male, being s. and h. of Robert SINCLAIR, by Lilias, da. of (—) ANDERSON, which Robert was s. and h. of George SINCLAIR, 2d s. of the 1st Baronet. He *suc. to the Baronetcy*, 25 June 1768, and was served heir general, 7 April 1771. He *m.* Elizabeth, da. of Charles ALLEN, of Edinburgh, surgeon. He *d.* 7 Jan. 1798. His widow received an annual pension of £100.

VII. 1798, to 1843? SIR JOHN SINCLAIR, Baronet [S. 1664], s. and h., *suc. to the Baronetcy*, 7 Jan. 1798. He, it is supposed, *d.* s.p.m. in or before 1843,(b) when *the Baronetcy* is presumed to have become *extinct*.

(a) Sydney, his da. and h., *m.* Sir William Dalrymple, and had issue.

(b) He appears for the last time in Oliver and Boyd's Edinburgh almanac for 1844, with the word "*extinct*" placed after his name, as also it had been in the previous year for 1843.

CORRIGENDA ET ADDENDA.

p. 2; line 5 from end, *after* "inserted," *add* "There was also another creation in 1658, viz., that of Massingberd."

p. 5; line 3, *after* "April," *add* "or 31 March."

p. 7; line 4, *for* "post Restoration," *read* "post—Restoration"; line 12, *for* "1666," *read* "1656;" between lines 30 and 31, *insert*

"MASSINGBERD *or* MASSINBEARD.

HENRY MASSINGBERD, *or* MASSINGBEARD, of Bratoft Hall, co. Lincoln, *b.* 26 Aug. 1609 was *cr. a Baronet* in 1658 by the Lord Protector, Cromwell, to whom he had 'good affection' (his brother, Sir Drayner Massingberd, being also a Parliamentarian) which dignity, was of course, disallowed after the Restoration in May 1660. He was, however, shortly afterwards *cr. a Baronet*, by the King, 22 Aug. 1660. See fuller particulars under that date.

p. 9; in margin, *for* "1668," *read* "1660"; line 22, *after* "MAURICE FENTON," *add* "of Mitchelstown, co. Cork."

p. 10; note (a), *conclude* "As to the Baronetcies created by the Lord Protector Cromwell, during some part of this period (1657-58), see pages 3 to 9."

p. 20; line 24, *for* "Receiver," *read* "Joint Receiver"; line 25, *after* "James II," *add* "July 1688, in whose Irish parl. of 1689 he was M.P. [I.] for Portarlington, and."

p. 22; line 5 from bottom, *after* "buried," *add* "3 Oct., in great state, from her house in Boswell Court."

p. 33 to **40**; head line, *for* "1666," *read* "1664."

p. 33; line 23, *after* "Hawnes," *add* "otherwise Haynes"; note (a), line 1, *dele* "two"; line 4, *add* at end "(3) Mary, *m.* Sir Francis Bickley, 3d Baronet [1661]."

p. 36; line 13, *for* "11," *read* "14."

p. 56; line 4, *for* "3," *read* "8"; line 35, *for* "26," *read* "25."

p. 57; line 4, *for* "26," *read* "25."

p. 59; line 25, *after* "BAKER," *add* "*or* BARKER."

p. 61; line 5, for "Thomas PITT, of Kyrewyard." *read* "James PYTTS, of Kyre"; last line, *conclude* "See PEERAGE."

p. 70; line 6, from bottom, *after* "HARDING," *add* "of Northill aforesaid"; line 2 from bottom, *for* "1627," read "1629"; *for* "at some date after 1631," *read* "6 April 1640, being then 10½ years old."

p. 71; line 14, *for* "pr. 1728," *read* "dat. 13 Sep. 1727, pr. 12 March 1727/8"; note (a), line 1, *for* "1680," *read* "Feb. 1680/1."

p. 72; line 13; *for* "June 1668," *read* 1668-90"; line 22, *after* "1661-79," *add* "for Lanesborough [I.], 1665-66."

p. 76; line 28, *after* "1645," *add* "and was *cr. a Baronet*, as above, 6 July 1660."

p. 77; line 7, *for* "between 1687 and 1695," *read* "4 July 1692, at Winchester cathedral."

p. 78; lines 31 and 32, *dele* "Her will" *to* "Bexley" and *insert* "She *d.* in London and was *bur.* 2 Dec. 1725, at Bexley. Will"; line 48, *for* "SHEFFIELD" *read* "SHEFFIELD(a)" and *insert* as note (a) "This Sir Sheffield Austen is altogether omitted in the pedigree [*Baronets* ii, 534] in the Heralds' College, and his cousin Edward is made to succeed to the title in 1743 as 5th 'Baronet.'"

p. 79; note (a), line 1, *after* "inserted" *add* "(as in the pedigree mentioned on p. 78, note 'a')".

p. 87; line 38, *for* "WHARTON," *read* (in two places) "WARTON"; line 39, *after* "Beverley," *add* "by Susanna, da. of John (POULETT), 1st BARON POULETT OF HINTON ST. GEORGE."

p. 89; note (b), line 1, *after* "*m.*," *add* "presumably"; *for* "Cosins," *read* "Cosin"; line 2, *erase* "Lanc." to end, *insert* "Lincoln."

p 92; line 29, *after* "Whitehall," *add* "M.P. for Wycombe, 1660."

p. 96; line 25, *for* "CONWAY," *read* "CONWAY,(b)" and *add* as note (b) "Much information as to the Conway family has been kindly supplied by H. R. Hughes, of Kinmel." *For* note "b," *read* note "c," *dele* note (c); line 28 [in text], *after* "Bodrythan," *add* "[*i.e.* Bodrhyddan]"; *for* "s.," *read* "3d but 1st surv. s. and h."; line 30, *after* "Rhyd," *add* "in that county," *for* "*b.* 1630," *read* "*bap.* 22 Feb. 1634"; line 32, *for* "in," *read* "7 April," *for* "h. of," *read* "coheir of Sir"; line 33, *for* "He *d.* in," *read* "by Margaret, da. of Ralph SNEYD, of Keele, co. Stafford. He *d.* June"; line 36, *for* "Bodryddan," *read* "Bodrhyddan"; *for* "1663(b)" *read* "1663(c)"; line 39, *after* "firstly," *add* "in or before 1689"; line 40, *for* "by his 2d wife," *read* "of Goathurst, Bucks, by his 2d wife, or reputed wife(d)"; line 41, *after* "LONGUEVILLE," *add* "1st Baronet [S. 1638]"; line 43, *for* (c), 27," *read* "(e), 28." *Add* as notes (d) and (e) as under: (d) "Of this John Digby it is stated that Margaret Longueville 'cohabited with him, but 'tis said, at his death [Sep. 1673], he owned his marriage with her.' [*Topographer*, edit. 1790, vol. ii, p. 212.]"; note (e), "His s. and h. ap., Henry Conway, *b.* 26 March and *bap.* 23 April 1689, matric. at Oxford (Ch. Ch.), 16 March 1705/6, aged 17, but *d.* s.p.m. and v.p., and was *bur.* 28 July 1717, at Rhuddlan, co. Flint, leaving by Honora, da. and coheir of Thomas Ravenscroft, of Hawarden, co. Flint, a posthumous da. and h., Honora, heir to her mother's estate, who *m.* Sir John Glynne, 2d Baronet [1661]. Margaretta Maria, sister of the whole blood of the said Henry Conway, *m.*, 30 May 1721, at Rhuddlan, Sir Thomas Longueville, 4th Baronet [S. 1638], and had issue, 3 daughters and coheirs. Penelope, sister of the half blood of the said Henry Conway (da. of the 2d Baronet by his 2d wife), *bap.* 21 Aug. 1705, at Wooton, *m.* James Russell Stapleton, and was ancestress to the family of Shipley, who took the name of Conway on inheriting the Bodrhyddan estate."

p. 103; line 18, *after* "1721," *add* "and was *bur.* at Gladwyth, co. Carnarvon."

p. 106; note (c), *conclude as under*, "That the name of the father of the 1st Baronet was John (not Edmund) is proved by the burial, 22 May 1663, at Allhallows, Staining, London, of *Anne Winne*, widow of Tobyah Winne, of London, Haberdasher, *da. of John Wheeler, Esq., and sister to Sir William Wheeler, Knt. and Baronet.*"

p. 108; line 9, *for* "in or about 1706," *read* "1 Nov. 1724, at Ambrosden, Oxon."

p. 109; line 38, *for* "Rodneys," *read* "Rodney"; line 41, *after* "Haydor," *add* "or Hather."

p. 110; line 2, *for* "and," *read* "Lord of the Manor"; line 9, *for* "or before 1645," *read* "1644"; line 16, *after* "of," *add* "Thorpe, *otherwise*;" *dele* "and Thorpe, co. Lincoln"; lines 24, 25 and 33, *for* "WHARTON," *read* "WARTON;" note (b), *commence*, "Viz., 1660, 1661-79, March to July 1679, 1679-81 and (the seven days Parl. in) 1681;" note (e), *commence*, "John Newton, her son, *b.* 26 Oct. 1677, *d.* 18 July 1681;" last line, *for* "and was," *read* "(being;" *for* "1744," *read* "1744) and *d.* 4 Aug. 1707."

p. 111; note (a), line 2, *after* "*bur.*," *add* "at Haydor;" note (b), lines 3 and 4, *dele* "1761. The Barrscourt estate (350 acres) was," and *insert* "1751, and *d.* 4 Nov. 1803, when the Gloucestershire property of the Newton family (described in Atkyns' *Gloucestershire* [1712] as a 'very great estate') was sold, a small portion whereof (350 acres), including the site of the house at Barrscourt, being again offered."

p. 118; line 7, *for* "*ex.* in 1689," *read* "*ex.* 13 July 1688"; *dele* lines 8 to 19, as also notes "b," "c," and "d" referring to the same, and *insert* as under.

I. 1660, to 1688, "JOHN KNIGHTLEY(b), of Offchurch, co. Warwick, Esq.," 1st s. and h. of Sir John KNIGHTLEY(c), of the same, who *had a warrant of Baronetcy* from Charles I. in July 1645 [see vol. ii. p. 455] by Bridget (*bur.* at Offchurch 26 June 1678), da. of Sir Lewis LEWKNOR, of Selsey, co. Sussex, Master of the Ceremonies to James I. (which John, aged 4½ years in 1615, *d.* v.p. and was *bur.* as a Baronet, 19 April 1650, at Offchurch), was *b.* probably about 1630, and apparently *styled himself a Baronet*, on the death of his father in April 1650, as he undoubtedly did in his bill in Chancery [Collins, 136] 22 June 1657; suc. to the family estates on the death of his grandfather Robert KNIGHTLEY, of Offchurch, in or soon after 1654, and was *cr. a Baronet*, as above (notwithstanding his previous assumption of that dignity), 30 Aug. 1660. He, who had conformed to the Church of England, was Sheriff of Warwickshire, 1664-65. He *m.* before 6 Sep. 1660 (when they were parties to a bill in Chancery against her late husband's executors) Mary, widow of Thomas WIGHTWICK, of Coventry, Serjeant at Law (*d.* 1 March 1655/6), da. of William SANDYS, of Askham, Notts. She, who was *b.* 1626, *d.* 26 Jan. 1686/7, aged 60, and was *bur.* at Offchurch. M.I. He *d.* s.p.s. 13 and was *bur.* 14 July 1688 there, when the *Baronetcy* became *extinct*. M.I. Will dat. 13 July 1688, pr. 25 June 1689, by his wife's sister, Mary, wife of Hardolph WASTENEYS.

Note "(b) The particulars of this Baronetcy have kindly been contributed by Oswald Barron, F.S.A."; *note* "(c) This John was s. and h. ap. of Robert Knightley, of Offchurch (a Roman Catholic recusant), by his 1st wife, Anne, da. of Sir John Pettus, of Norwich, which Robert (will dat. 1654) was s. of Edward Knightley, of Offchurch (will dat. 1613), who was 4th s. of Sir Valentine Knightley, of Fawsley, co. Northampton (*d.* March 1566), the ancestor of the family still (1903) of that place"; *note* "(d) Besides a brother, Lewis Knightley, living 1654, said to have been killed at the siege of Tangier, he had two sisters (1), Mary, wife of John Adams, and (2), Anne, wife of George Ayloffe, of Gritnam, Wilts. He, however, devised the Offchurch estate to his wife's grandson, John Wightwick, who took the name of Knightley, and was ancestor of John Wightwick Knightley, who *d.* s.p.m. in 1830, leaving a da. and h., Jane, Countess of Aylesford."

p. 121; line 18, *for* "1702," *read* "1701."

p. 122; line 14, *dele* "(b)."

p. 123; line, 3, *for* "1730-99," *read* "1730-1814"; *insert* between lines 4 and 5, "*ex.* 12 July 1814."

p. 124; line 2, *after* "*Earldom*," *add* "of 1788"; *after* "*Viscountcy*," *add* "of 1782."

p. 131; *note* (e), line 2, *for* "seems," *read* "is not only"; line 3, *for* "fact.," *read* "fact, but a petition, 19 Jan. 1692/3, of Sir Thomas, by which he obtained an act to make provision for his sister, expressly states that they were *the only* children living at their father's death."

p. 135; lines 28, 30 and 32, *for* "Dodington," *read* "Doddington"; line 29, *after* "h.," *add* "app."; line 31, *for* "Chissel," *read* "Chiswell"; line 32, *after* "Algernon," *add* "(who *d.* Feb. 1677/8)"; line 34, *after* "Baronet," *add* "v.p."; *after* "unm.," *add* "and v.p."

p. 143; line 2, *dele* "more" *to* "1667," and *insert* "27 Feb. 1665/6"; line 3, *for* "1662," *read* "1661"; line 8, *dele* "1st" *to* "after," and *insert* "3d but 1st surv. s. and h.; *bap.* at Thirkelby, 6 Oct."; line 18, *after* "1733," *add* "in her 68th year"; line 25, *dele* "He was M.P. for Thirsk"; lines 25 and 26, *for* "Feb. 1740/1," *read* "and was *bur.*, 13 Feb. 1740/1, at Thirkelby" line 26, *for* "shortly before 29 July 1743," *read* "July 1741, at St. Olave's, York"; line 27, *for* "17 April," *read* "and was *bur*. at Thirkelby, 8 May"; line 29, *for* "*d*.," *read* "was *bur*. at Stanmore Parva, Midx., 23 Oct."; note (a), line 1, *for* "then," *read* "in July 1743"; note (b), line 1, *after* "*m*.," *add* "in 1740."

p. 144; line 30, *after* "July," *add* "and *bap*. at York Minster, 5 Oct."; line 36, *after* "FRANKLAND," *add* "Sheriff of Yorkshire, 1838-39"; last line, *conclude* "and was *bur*. at Thirkelby."

p. 155; line 15, *after* "1691/2," *add* "of the small pox."

p. 159; line 17, *after* "month." *add* "He was M.P. [I.] for Tuam, 1665-66"; line 20, *for* "Thomas LEICESTER," *read* "Capt. Thomas LYSTER, by Cisley, da. of Jonac BURKE, of Tullyrey, co. Galway [O'Ferrall's *Linea Antiqua*]."

p. 163; lines 42 and 51, *for* "16," *read* "18."

p. 182; line 19, *for* "(aged 76)," *read* "or 1658 (aged about 76)"; line 21, *after* "Royalist," *add* "(will dat. 9 July 1656, pr. 20 May 1658)."

p. 185; line 1, *after* "brother," *add* "James."

p. 197; line 3 from bottom, *after* "da.," *add* "and coheir"; line 2 from bottom, *after* "Cloth," *add* "by Catharine, da. of Sir Alexander FRASER, 1st Baronet [S. 1673]."

p. 200; line 3 from bottom, *after* "1769," *add* "and was *bur*. at Hawarden(e)"; *add* as note "(e)," Her husband said of her, 'Her father died before she was born; she lost her mother at a month old, and her guardians defrauded her of at least £10,000.' [*Ex. inform*. H. R. Hughes, of Kinmel]."

p. 224; line 20, *for* "in or about 1687, Gratiana," *read* "24 Nov. 1686, at St. Minver, Cornwall, Graciana."

p. 233; line 21, *for* "4 Oct.," *read* "8 Nov."

p. 236; note (a), *conclude* "It is well observed by Oswald Barron, F.S.A., as to these Baronets that 'a grotesque misapprehension of the ancient written character [of their name] has urged them to write [it] of late years as SMIJTH' [*The Ancestor*, vol. iv, p. 34]."

p. 237; line 26, *for* "BERRY," *read* "BURY"; line 38, *for* "CRONE," *read* (bis) "CROWNE"; line 39, *after* "London," *add* "She *d*. in Throgmorton street, 29 Sep. 1706, and was *bur*. at St. Mildred's, Poultry, London"; line 41, *for* "*extinct*," *read* "*extinct*(c)"; last line, *conclude*, "M.I. at Aspley Guise"; *add as note* "(c)," "In the M.I., at St. Mary's, Southampton, to Richard Vernon Sadleir, who *d*. s.p. in 1810, it is stated that he '*was a Baronet by descent*, though he never assumed that title, and [that he was] lineally descended from Sir Ralph Sadleir, Knight Banneret,' etc. This descent was through William Sadleir, a brother of the 1st Baronet."

p. 243; line 22, *for* "1656," *read* "1653/4."

p. 244; line 12, *for* "as a," *read* "as the first and principal"; line 13, *after* "1772," *add* "for which service he received, 12 Aug. 1772, a grant of Supporters to his coat of arms, for his life"; line 3 from bottom, *conclude* "He *m*. 3 June 1903, at St. James', Paddington, Beatrice, da. of William Bunce GREENFIELD, of Haynes Park, Beds."

p. 282; line 10, *for* "1666," *read* "1663"; line 15, *for* "1666," *read* "1664"; line 16, *after* "minor," *add* "ed. at St. Paul's School, London; admitted (Fellow Commoner) 7 March 1681/2, to St. John's Coll., Cambridge, aged 17."

p. 305; line 1, "HAMILTON." The creation of this Baronetcy was apparently in or before 1634, and the probability seems that it was a *Scotch* (and not an *Irish*) dignity. G. D. Burtchaell (see p. 304, note "a") writes: "In the calendar of State Papers, Ireland, there is a King's Letter, dat. *5 June 1634*, to the Lord Deputy for a grant of lands (the Abercorn or rather Strabane estate) to Claude Hamilton, Esq., and *Sir George Hamilton, Knt. and Baronet*. This grant seems to have hung fire, but there is enrolled a grant

of these lands (the manor of Strabane, etc.), *23 May 1639*, to *Sir George Hamilton, of Donelong, Knt. and Baronet*, Sir George Hamilton, of Greenlaw, Knt., Sir William Stewart, of New Stuarton, Knt., and Sir William Semple, of Letterkenny, Knt., to hold to the uses, trusts, etc., appointed in an order made by the Commissioners for remedy of defective titles, 22 Feb. 1638/9. There is also a grant of *25 June 1639* to *Sir George Hamilton, Knt. and Baronet*, of the manor, etc., of Donnalonge, and he is *described as Knt. and Baronet invariably* after this date. That he is named in the grant of 23 May 1639, *before* his uncle, Sir George Hamilton, of Greenlaw, seems to emphasize the fact that he was a Baronet. I am, therefore, of opinion that *the date should be 1634*, and that *the title was of Nova Scotia*, as these titles seem to have been conferred in a very loose manner. Lodge [*Irish Peerage*] implies that he was created a Baronet after following the King to France in 1651. Wood, in his edition [1813] of Douglas' *Peerage* [of Scotland] seems to be the first to state that he was *created a Baronet of Ireland* in 1660."

p. 320; line 17, *for* "1622," *read* "1662."

p. 323; line 16, *for* "Dec. 1695," *read* "and was *bur*. 15 Dec. 1695, at St. Martin's in the Fields. His widow was *bur*. there, 27 Jan. 1706/7."

p. 332; line 1, *dele* "co."

INDEX

TO THE SURNAMES OF THE SEVERAL HOLDERS OF THE

BARONETCIES CREATED 30 JAN. 1648/9 TO 31 DEC. 1664;

including not only those of the grantees themselves but of their successors; to which is added the local or, failing that, personal description of each grantee. The name of any Peerage dignity held with such Baronetcy is not included in the alphabetical arrangement, neither is the surname of the holder of any such peerage, when different(a) from that of any Baronet who was a Commoner.

(a) See vol. i, p. 263, note "a."

Malet, Justice of the King's Bench, 17 May 1663 [*fiat only*] ... 275
Marshall [S.], 21 May 1658; devolution unknown ... 325
Marsham, of Cuxton, Kent, 12 or 16 Aug. 1663; *afterwards*, since 1716, Barons Romney, and since 1801, Earls of Romney ... 283
Marwood, of Little Buskby, co. York, 31 Dec. 1660; *ex.* 23 Feb. 1739/40 ... 149
Massey, *i.e.* Stanley-Massey-Stanley, *see* Stanley, 17 June 1661.
Maryon, *i.e.* Maryon-Wilson, *see* Wilson, 4 March 1660/1.
[Massingberd, *or* Massingbeard, of Bratoft Hall, co. Lincoln, 1658, by the Protector Cromwell; *forfeited* May 1660] } 7 as in the corrigenda.
Massingberd, *or* Massingbeard, of Bratoft Hall, co. Lincoln, 22 Aug. 1660; *ex.* 1 Dec. 1723 ... 115
Matthews, of Great Gobious [in Havering], Essex, 13 June 1662; *ex.* 11 July 1708 ... 249
Maxwell [S.], of Orchartoun, co. Kirkcudbright, 30 June 1663; apparently *ex.* or *dormant* 1693, though assumed till 21 Sep. 1786 ... 340
Mercer [S.], of Aldie, 1660? ; *Qy. ex.* or *dormant*, 1672 ... 326
Merces, "a Frenchman," April or May 1660; *ex.* or *dormant* about 1690 ... 24
Meredith, *or* Meredyth [I.], of Greenhill, co. Kildare, 20 Nov. 1660 ... 306
Middleton, *see* Myddleton
Middleton, *or* Myddleton, of Chirke, co. Denbigh, 4 July 1660; *ex.* 5 Jan. 1717/8 ... 75
Middleton, of Belsay [in Bolam], Northumberland, 24 Oct. 1662; *sometime* 1799-1876, Monck ... 261
Milbanke, of Halnaby, co. York, 7 Aug. 1661; *sometime* 1815-25, Noel; and, 1866-68, Milbanke-Huskisson ... 225
Miller, of Oxenhoath, Kent, 13 Oct. 1660; *ex.* 1714 ... 125
Modyford, of London, 18 Feb. 1660/1; *ex.* Nov. 1678 ... 163
Modyford, *or* Muddiford, of Lincoln's Inn, Midx., 1 March 1663/4; *ex.* 30 July 1702 ... 289
Monck, *see* Middleton, 24 Oct. 1662.
Monoux, Monnoux, *or* Monnox, of Wotton, Beds, 4 Dec. 1660; *ex.* 3 Feb. 1814 134
Moore, *or* More, of Moore or More Hall, co. Lancaster, 1 March 1661/2; but patent not till 22 Nov. 1675. See under that date ... 246
More, *see* Moore.
Moreland, *see* Morland.
Morgan, of Llangattock, co. Monmouth, 7 Feb. 1660/1; *ex.* 29 April 1767 ... 158
Morice, *or* Morrice, of Werrington, Devon, 20 April 1661; *ex.* 24 Jan. 1749/50 ... 185
Morland, Moreland, *or* Morley, of Sulhampstead, Berks, 18 July 1660; *ex.* Nov. 1716 ... 89
Morley, *see* Morland.
Morrice, *see* Morice.
Mostyn, of Mostyn, co. Flint, 3 Aug. 1660; *ex.* 17 April 1831 ... 102
Mottet, of Liege, in Flanders, 16 Nov. 1660; *ex.* or *dormant* probably soon afterwards ... 129
Mowat [S.], of Inglistoun, 2 June 1664; existing, presumably, till 1829 ... 345
Muddiford, *see* Modiford, 1 March 1663/4.
Muir [S.], *see* Mure.
Mure, *or* Muir [S.], of Rowallan, 4 May 1662; *ex.* or *dormant* about 1700 ... 336
Murray [S.], of Stanhope, co. Peebles, 12 or 13 Feb. 1663/4; *forfeited* 1746, *but assumed* notwithstanding; *ex.* or *dormant*, 23 Aug. 1848, but *again assumed*, as Howell-Murray, from 1848 to 1878 ... 342
Myddleton, *see* Middleton; *see also* Heron, 20 Nov. 1662.

Napier, *or* Sandy, of Luton Hoo, Beds, 4 March 1660/1; *merged* April 1675; *ex.* 2 Jan. 1747/8 ... 168
Nevill (*formerly* Smith), of Holt, co. Leicester, 25 May 1661; *ex.* 25 Feb. 1711/2 ... 203
Newton, of Barrs Court [in Bitton], co. Gloucester, 16 Aug. 1660; *ex.* 6 April 1743 ... 109
Newton, of London, 25 Jan. 1660/1; *ex.* Nov. 1670 ... 154

Noel, of Kirkby Mallory, co. Leicester, 6 July 1660; *afterwards*, 1745-1815, Lords Wentworth, *and* 1762-1815, Viscounts Wentworth of Wellesborough; *ex.* 17 April 1825 ... 76
Noel, *see* Milbanke, 7 Aug. 1661.
North, of Mildenhall, Suffolk, 14 June 1660; *ex.* 5 July 1695 ... 41
Norton, of Coventry, co. Warwick, 23 July 1661; *ex.* 1691 ... 223

Ogilvie [S.], of Barras [in Dunottar, co. Kincardine], 5 March 1661/2, or 5 July 1662; *ex.* or *dorm.* about 1840 ... 335
Oldfield, of Spalding, co. Lincoln, 6 Aug. 1660; *ex.* Aug. 1705 ... 104
Orby, "servant to the Queen mother," 9 Oct. 1658; *ex.* Feb. 1723/4 ... 19
Osbaldeston, of Chadlington, Oxon., 25 June 1664; *ex.* 7 April 1749 ... 293
Osborn, *or* Osburne, of Chicksand, Beds., 11 Feb. 1660/1 or (*rectius*) 11 Feb. 1661/2 ... 160 and 243

Palmer, of Dorney Court, Bucks, 1657? *not assumed* after 1681 ... 27
Palmer, of Carlton, co. Northampton, 7 June 1660 ... 28
Parker, of Erwarton, Suffolk, 16 July 1661; *afterwards* Parker-a-Morley-Long; *ex.* 20 Jan. 1740/1 ... 220
Parsons, of Langley, Bucks, 9 April 1661; *ex.* 1812 ... 183
Paston, see Bedingfeld, 2 Jan. 1660/1.
Pennyman, of Ormesby, in Cleveland, co. York, 22 Feb. 1663/4; *sometime*, 1768-70, Pennyman-Warton; *ex.* 1852 ... 287
Perceval, *or* Percivall [I.], of Burton, co. Cork, 9 Sep. 1661; *afterwards* since 1715, Barons Perceval of Burton [I.]; since 1713, Viscounts Perceval of Kanturk [I.], and since 1733, Earls of Egmont [I.] ... 314
Peyton, of Doddington, co. Cambridge, 10 Dec. 1660; *ex.* 25 Dec. 1661 ... 135
Pickering, of Whaddon, co. Cambridge, 2 Jan. 1660/1; *ex.* 1705 ... 151
Pierce, *see* Piers.
Piers, *or* Pierce [I.], of Tristernagh, co. Westmeath, 18 Feb. 1660/1 ... 308
Pindar, of Idinshaw, co. Chester, 22 Dec. 1662; *ex.* in or before 1704/5 ... 270
Plomer, *or* Plumer, of the Inner Temple, London, 4 Jan. 1660/1; *ex.* 26 April 1697 ... 153
Plumer, *see* Plomer.
Powell, *or* Hinson, of Pengethly, co. Hereford, 23 Jan. 1660/1; *ex.* 11 Dec. 1680 ... 154
Powell, of Ewhurst, Sussex, 10 May 1661; *ex.* 5 July 1742... ... 194
Pretyman [S.], about 1660; *ex.* or *dormant*, in or shortly after 1749, *but assumed*, 1823-27, as Pretyman-Tomline ... 327
Price, of the Priory, Brecon, 1658? ; *ex.* apparently in or before 1689 ... 18
[Prideaux, "Attorney-General," 13 Aug. 1658 by the Protector Cromwell; *forfeited* May 1660 ... 6
Primrose [S.], of Carrington, 1 or 5 Aug. 1651; *subsequently*, 1703-41, Viscounts Primrose [S.], *and since* 1741, Earls of Rosebery [S.] ... 324
Primrose, *see* Foulis [S.], Sep. or Oct. 1661.
Proby, of Elton Hall, Hunts, 7 March 1661/2; *ex.* 1689 ... 246
Purefoy, of Wadley, Berks, 4 Dec. 1662; *ex.* 19 Aug. 1686 ... 267
Pym, of Brymmore, Somerset, 14 July 1663; *ex.* 4 May 1688 ... 281

[Read, *or* Reade, of Brocket Hall, Herts, 25 June 1657 by the Protector Cromwell; *forfeited* May 1660] ... 3
Read, *or* Reade, of Barton, Berks, 4 March 1660/1 ... 172
Reeve, *or* Reve, of Thwaite, Suffolk, 22 Jan. 1662/3; *ex.* in or before 1688 ... 271
Rich, of Sonning, Berks, 20 March 1660/1; *ex.* 6 April 1803 ... 180
Roberts, of Willesdon, Midx., 8 Nov. 1661; *ex.* May 1698 ... 233
Robinson, of London, 22 June 1660 ... 52
Robinson, of Newby [on Swale], co. York, 30 July 1660; *ex.* 6 Feb. 1689 ... 98
Rokeby, of Skyers, co. York, 29 Jan. 1660/1; *ex.* 6 July 1678 ... 155
Rokewode-Gage, *see* Gage, 15 July 1662.

Rollo [S.], of Bannockburn, 1658? ; *ex.* or *dormant* 1666 ... 326
Rothwell, of Ewerby and Stapleford, co. Lincoln, 16 Aug. 1661; *ex.* 1693 ... 227
Rous, of Henham, Suffolk, 17 Aug. 1660; *afterwards*, since 1796, Barons Rous of Dennington, and since 1821, Earls of Stradbroke ... 114
Rushout, of Maylands [in Havering], Essex, 17 June 1661; *afterwards*, 1797-1887, Barons Northwick; *ex.* 11 Nov. 1887 ... 210
Russell, of Laugharne, co. Carmarthen, 8 Nov. 1660; *ex.* about 1714 ... 127
Russell, *i.e.*, Frankland-Russell, *see* Frankland, 24 Dec. 1660.

Sadleir, *or* Sadler, of Temple Dinsley [in Hitchin], Herts, 3 Dec. 1661; *ex.* 14 July 1719 ... 237
Saint Barbe, of Broadlands [in Romsey], Hants, 30 Dec. 1663; *ex.* 7 Sep. 1723 ... 286
Saint George [E. and possibly I.], of Carrickdrumrusk, co. Leitrim, 5 Sep. 1660; *afterwards*, 1715-35, Baron Saint George of Hatley Saint George [I.]; *ex.* 4 Aug. 1735 ... 120 and 305
Saint John, of Woodford, co. Northampton, 28 June 1660; *afterwards*, since 1711, Barons Saint John of Bletsho ... 68
Sandy, *otherwise* Napier, *see* Napier, 4 March 1670/1.
Savile, of Copley, co. York, 24 July 1662; *ex.* 1689 ... 254
Schlater, of Cambridge, co. Cambridge, 25 July 1660; *ex.* 10 Dec. 1684 ... 96
Scott, of Kew Green, Surrey, 9 Aug. 1653; *dormant* or possibly *ex.* about 1775 ... 14
Selby, of Whitehouse, co. Durham, 3 March 1663/4; *ex.* Sep. 1668 ... 290
Seton [S.], of Abercorn, co. Linlithgow, 3 June 1663 ... 338
Seton [S.], of Garletoun, co. Haddington, 9 Dec. 1664; *forfeited* 1718-20, but *assumed* till 1769, and possibly till Aug. 1796 ... 350
Seyliard, Sylyard, *or* Suliard, of Delawarre [in Brasted], Kent, 18 June 1661; *ex.* Sep. 1701 ... 217
Shaen [I], of Kilmore, co. Roscommon, 7 Feb. 1662/3; *ex.* 24 June 1725 ... 323
Sheridan [I.], of co. Wicklow, and of Belturbet, co. Cavan, 1662? ; *assumed* till 22 April 1836 ... 322
Shuckburgh, of Shuckburgh, co. Warwick, 26 June 1660; *sometime*, 1793-1804, Shuckburgh-Evelyn ... 62
Silyard, *see* Sylyard.
Sinclair [S.], of Longformacus, co. Berwick, 10 Dec. 1664; *ex.* or *dormant*, apparently, in or before 1843 ... 351
Slanning, *or* Slaning, of Marristow, Devon, 19 Jan. 1662/3; *ex.* 21 Nov. 1700 ... 270
Slingsby, of [Bifrons in Patrixbourne], Kent, 19 Oct. 1657; *dormant* or *ex.* about 1700 ... 17
Slingsby, of Newcells, Herts, 16 March 1660/1; *ex.* 26 Oct. 1661 ... 176
Smijth, *see* Smith, *cr.* 28 Nov. 1661.
Smith, of Hatherston, co. Chester, 16 Aug. 1660; *ex.* [May?] 1706 ... 112
Smith, *or* Smythe, of Eshe, co. Durham, 23 Feb. 1660/1 ... 166
Smith, *or* Smyth, of Edmundthorpe, co. Leicester, 20 March 1660/1; *ex.* 15 Feb. 1720/1 ... 181
Smith, *or* Smyth, of Redcliffe, Bucks, 10 May 1661; *ex.* 20 June 1732 ... 191
Smith, of Long Ashton, Somerset, 16 May 1661; *ex.* July 1742 ... 196
Smith, *or* Smyth, of Hill Hall [in Theydon Mount], Essex, 28 Nov. 1661; *afterwards*, since 1788 or 1799, Smijth, and since 1839, Bowyer-Smijth 234
Smithson, of Stanwick, co. York, 2 Aug. 1660; *afterwards*, since 1750, Earls of Northumberland, and since 1766, Dukes of Northumberland ... 101
Southcote, *or* Southcott, of Bliborough, co. Lincoln, 24 Jan. 1661/2; *ex.* in or before 1691 ... 239
Southwell [I.], of Castle Mattress, co. Limerick, 4 Aug. 1662; *afterwards*, since 1717, Barons Southwell of Castle Mattress [I.], and since 1776, Viscounts Southwell of Castle Mattress [I.] ... 318
Speek, *see* Speke.

Speke, *or* Speeke, of Haslbury, Wilts, 12 June 1660; *ex.* 24 Jan. 1682/3 ... 36
Springet, of Broyle [in Ringmer], Sussex, 8 Jan. 1660/1; *ex.* 5 Jan. 1661/2 153
Stanley, of Alderley, co. Chester, 25 June 1660; *afterwards*, since 1839, Barons Stanley of Alderley ... 60
Stanley, of Hooton, co. Chester, 20 March 1660/1, or (*rectius*) 17 June 1661; *afterwards*, 1792-1863, Stanley-Massey-Stanley; *subsequently*, 1863-93, Errington; *ex.* 19 March 1893 ... 178 and 207
Stapleton, *or* Stapylton, of Myton, co. York, 22 June 1660; *ex.* 2 Jan. 1817 49
Stapleton, *or* Stapylton, of Carleton, co. York, 20 March 1661/2; *ex.* Feb. 1706/7 ... 247
Stapley, *or* Stapeley, of Patcham, Sussex, 28 July 1660; *ex.* 22 Aug. 1701; *assumed* since 1887 ... 97
Stapylton, *see* Stapleton.
Staughton, *see* Stoughton.
Steward, *see* Stewart.
Stewart, Steward, *or* Stuart, of Hartley Manduit, Hants, 27 June 1660 ... 65
Stoughton, *or* Staughton, of Stoughton [in Stoke by Guildford], Surrey, 29 Jan. 1660/1; *ex.* Jan. 1691/2 ... 154
Stuart, *see* Stewart.
Stydolph, *or* Stiddolph, of Norbury, Surrey, 24 Dec. 1660; *ex.* 13 Feb. 1676/7 ... 145
Suliard, *see* Seyliard.
Swale, of Swale, co. York, 21 June 1660; *ex.* apparently about 1760; *assumed* since 1877 ... 46
Swinburne, of Capheaton, co. Northumberland, 26 Sep. 1660 ... 124
Sylyard, *see* Seyliard.

Tancred, *or* Tankard, of Burroughbridge, co. York, 17 Nov. 1662 ... 264
Tankard, *see* Tancred.
Tempest, of Tong, co. York, 25 May 1664; *ex.* 29 Jan. 1819... ... 292
Temple [S.], 7 July 1662; *ex.* 27 March 1674 ... 336
Thomas, of Folkington, Sussex, 23 July 1660; *ex.* 18 Nov. 1706 ... 95
Tomline, *i.e.*, Pretyman-Tomline, *see* Pretyman [S.], 1660?
Tooker, of Maddington, Wilts, 1 July 1664; *ex.* 17 March 1675/6 ... 294
Trevelyan, *or* Trevilian, of Nettlecombe, Somerset, 24 Jan. 1661/2 ... 239
Trott, *or* Trot, of Laverstoke, Hants, 12 Oct. 1660; *ex.* 14 July 1672 ... 125
Tuke, of Cressing Temple, Essex, 31 March 1664; *ex.* 10 Aug. 1690 ... 291
[Twisleton, of Horsmans, in Dartford, Kent, 10 April 1658, by the Lord Protector Cromwell; *forfeited* May 1660] ... 5

Van Freisendorf, of Herdick, in Sweden, 4 Oct. 1661; succession, if any, unknown ... 233
Verney, of Middle Claydon, Bucks, 16 March 1660/1; *afterwards*, 1703-91, Viscounts Fermanagh [I.], and *subsequently*, 1743-91, Earls Verney [I.]; *ex.* 31 March 1791 ... 177
Vernon, of Hodnet, Salop, 22 July 1660; *ex.* 1 Oct. 1725 ... 93
Viner, *see* Vyner.
Vyner, *or* Viner, of London, 18 June 1661; *ex.* May 1683 ... 216

Wakeman, of Beckford, co. Gloucester, 13 Feb. 1660/1; *ex.* about 1690 ... 160
Wandesford, of Kirklington, co. York, 5 Aug. 1662; *afterwards*, 1706-84, Viscounts Castleford [I.]; *ex.* 12 Jan. 1784 ... 254
Warburton, of Arley, co. Chester, 27 June 1660; *ex.* 13 May 1813 ... 66
Ward, of Bixley, Norfolk, 29 Dec. 1660; *ex.* about 1770 ... 139
Warner, of Parham, Suffolk, 16 July 1660; *ex.* 21 March 1705 ... 88
Warton, *i.e.*, Pennyman-Warton, *see* Warton, 22 Feb. 1663/4.
Webster, of Kirby, Norfolk, 31 May 1660; *ex.* April 1675 ... 26
Wenman, of Caswell [in Witney], Oxon, 29 Nov. 1662; *afterwards*, 1686-1800, Viscounts Wenman of Tuam [I.]; *ex.* 26 March 1800 ... 267

Complete Baronetage

VOLUME FOUR
1665–1707

Complete Baronetage.

EDITED BY

G. E. C.

EDITOR OF THE

"Complete Peerage."

VOLUME IV.

1665—1707.

EXETER:
WILLIAM POLLARD & Co. Ltd., 39 & 40, NORTH STREET.
1904.

CONTENTS.

LIST OF SUBSCRIBERS.

Adams, Rev. H. W., 40, Eton Avenue, Hampstead, N.W.
Aldenham, Lord, St. Dunstan's Regent's Park, N.W.
Amherst of Hackney, Lord, F.S.A., per Sotheran & Co., 140, Strand, W.C.
Anderson, J. R., 84, Albert Drive, Crosshill, Glasgow.
Annesley, Lieut.-Gen. A. Lyttelton, Templemere, Weybridge, Surrey.
Anstruther, Sir R., Bt., Balcaskie, Pillenweena, Scotland.
Armytage, Sir George, Bt., F.S.A., Kirklees Park, Brighouse.
Arnold, Charles T., Stamford House, West Side, Wimbledon.
Ashmore-Mitchell, Mrs. Charles, The Lodge, St. Kilda, Melbourne.
Assheton, Ralph, Downham Hall, Clitheroe.
Athill, Charles H., F.S.A., Richmond Herald, College of Arms, E.C.
Attwood, T. A. C., 7, Hyde Park Mansions, W.

Bacon, Sir Hickman, Bt., per Sotheran & Co., 140, Strand, W.C.
Bain, J., Bookseller, 1, Haymarket, S.W. (4).
Batten, H. B., Aldon, Yeovil.
Beaven, Rev. A. B., Greyfriars, Leamington.
Bedford, Duke of, per Sotheran & Co., 140, Strand, W.C.
Bell & Sons, York Street, Covent Garden, W.C.
Boase, F., 21, Boscobel Road, St. Leonards-on-Sea.
Boyle, Colonel the Hon. R. E., 95, Onslow Square, S.W.
Brigg, W., Milton Lodge, Harpenden, Herts.
Brooking-Rowe, J., Castle Barbican, Plympton.
Bruce Bannerman, W., F.S.A., The Lindens, Sydenham Road, Croydon, Surrey.
Bulloch, J. M., 118, Pall Mall, S.W.
Burke, Ashworth P., per Harrison & Sons, 59, Pall Mall, S.W.
Burke, Henry Farnham, C.V.O., F.S.A., Somerset Herald, College of Arms, E.C.
Burnard, Robert, 3, Hillsborough, Plymouth.

Carington, H. H. Smith, F.S.A., Ashby Folville Manor, Melton Mowbray.
Carmichael, Sir Thomas D. Gibson, Bt., Castlecraig, Dolphinton, N.B.
Carr, William, per Sotheran & Co., 140, Strand, W.C.

Chadwyck-Healey, C. E. H., F.S.A., per Sotheran & Co., 140, Strand, W.C.
Clements, H. J. B., Killadoon, Cellridge, co. Kildare, Ireland.
Clubs, *see under* Libraries.
Colyer-Fergusson, T. C., Ightham Mote, Ivy Hatch, near Sevenoaks.
Comber, John, High Steep, Jarvis Brook, Sussex.
Conder, Edward, F.S.A., The Conigree, Newent, Gloucester.
Cooper, Samuel J., Mount Vernon, near Barnsley.
Craig, Major A. Tudor, 96, York Mansions, Battersea Park, S.W.
Craigie, Edmund, The Grange, Lytton Grove, Putney Hill, S.W.
Crawford and Balcarres, Earl of, per Sotheran & Co., 140, Strand, W.C.
Crawley-Boevey, A. W., 24, Sloane Court, S.W.
Cresswell, L., Wood Hall, Calverley, Leeds.
Crisp, F. A., F.S.A., Grove Park, Denmark Hill, S.E.
Croft-Lyons, Lieut.-Colonel G. B., 3, Hertford Street, Mayfair, W.
Culleton, Leo., 92, Piccadilly, W.
Cullum, G. M. G., 4, Sterling Street, Montpelier Square, S.W.
Cust, Lady Elizabeth, 13, Eccleston Square. S.W.

Dalrymple, Hon. Hew., Oxenfoord Castle, Dalkeith.
Davies, Seymour G. P., English, Scottish, and Australian Bank, Ltd., Melbourne, Australia.
Davison, R. M., Grammar School, Ilminster.
Denny, A. & F., 147, Strand, W.C. (2).
Douglas-Crompton, S., per Sotheran & Co., 140, Strand, W.C.
Douglas, David, 10, Castle Street, Edinburgh.
Douglas & Foulis, 9, Castle Street, Edinburgh (6).
Duke, Rev. R. E. H., Maltby Rectory, Alford, Lincolnshire.
Duleep Singh, His Highness Prince, per Sotheran & Co., 140, Strand, W.C.
Dunkin, E. H. W., Rosewyn, 70, Herne Hill, S.E.

Edwardes, Sir Henry H., Bt., per Harrison & Sons, 59, Pall Mall, S.W.
Eland, H. S., High Street, Exeter.
Ellis & Elvey, 29, New Bond Street, W.

FitzGerald, Hon. J. D., K.C., per Sotheran & Co., 140, Strand, W.C.
Foley, P., F.S.A., Prestwood, Stourbridge, per A. & F. Denny, 147, Strand, W.C.
Foster, Joseph, 21, Boundary Road, N.W.

Fox, Charles Henry, M.D., 35, Heriot Row, Edinburgh.
Fox, Francis F., Yate House, Chipping Sodbury, Gloucester, per W. George's Sons, Bristol.
Fry, E. A., 172, Edmond Street, Birmingham.

George, William Edwards, Downside, Stoke Bishop, near Bristol, per W. George's Sons, Bristol.
George's Sons, William, Top Corner Park Street, Bristol (6).
Gibbs, Antony, Tyntesfield, near Bristol.
Gibbs, H. Martin, Barrow Court, Somerset, per W. George's Sons, Bristol.
Gibbs, Rev. John Lomax, Speen House, near Newbury, Berks.
Gibbs, Hon. Vicary, M.P., St. Dunstan's, Regent's Park, N.W.
Glencross, R. M., Colquites, Washaway, R.S.O., Cornwall.
Gough, Henry, Sandcroft, Redhill, Surrey.
Graves, Robert Edmund, Lyndhurst, Grange Park, Ealing, W. (2).
Greaves-Bagshawe, W. H., Ford Hall, Chapel en le Frith.
Green & Sons, W., Law Booksellers, Edinburgh (2).
Gregory, G., 5 and 5A, Argyle Street, Bath.
Gurney, Mrs. R., Gurney's Bank, Norwich.

Hanson, Sir Reginald, Bt., 4. Bryanston Square, W.
Harben, H. A., 107, Westbourne Terrace, Hyde Park, W.
Hardy & Page, 21, Old Buildings, Lincoln's Inn, W.C.
Harrison & Sons, 59, Pall Mall, S.W. (7).
Haslewood, Rev. F. G., Chislet Vicarage, Canterbury.
Hatchards, 187, Piccadilly, W. (6).
Hawkesbury, Lord, per Sotheran & Co., 140, Strand, W.C. (2).
Head, Christopher, 6, Clarence Terrace, Regent's Park, N.W.
Hesilrige, Arthur G. M., 160A, Fleet Street, E.C.
Hodges, Figgis & Co., Ltd., 104, Grafton Street, Dublin (3).
Hofman, Charles, 16, Grosvenor Street, W.
Hoskyns, H. W. P., North Perrott Manor, Crewkerne.
Hovenden, R., F.S.A., Heathcote, Park Hill Road, Croydon.
Hughes of Kinmel, H. R., Kinmel Park, Abergele, North Wales, per Sotheran & Co., 140, Strand, London, W.C.

Inns of Court, *see under* Libraries.
Iveagh, Lord, F.S.A., per Sotheran & Co., 140, Strand, W.C.

Johnston, G. Harvey, 22, Garscube Terrace, Murrayfield, Edinburgh, per W. & A. K. Johnston, Ltd., 7, Paternoster Square, E.C.

Johnston, Henry Augustus, Markethill, co. Armagh.
Johnston, Col. W., C.B., Newton Dee, Murtle, Aberdeen.

Larpent, Frederic de H., 11, Queen Victoria Street, E.C.
Lawton, William F., Librarian, Public Libraries, Hull.
Lea, J. Henry, 18, Somerset Street, Boston, Mass., U.S.A.
Lee, W. B., Seend, Melksham.
Lefroy, Edward Heathcote, 65, Belgrave Road, S.W.
Lennard, Thos. Barrett, Horsford Manor, Norwich.
LIBRARIES, CLUBS, PUBLIC OFFICES, INNS OF COURT, ETC.:—
Athenæum Club, per Jones, Yarrell & Poulter, 8, Bury Street, S.W.
Baronetage, The Standing Council of the, per Sotheran & Co., 140, Strand, W.C.
British Museum, Department of MSS., per Sotheran & Co., 140, Strand, W.C.
Carlton Club, per Harrison & Sons, 59, Pall Mall, S.W.
Chicago; The Newberry Library, per H. Grevel & Co., 33, King Street, Covent Garden, W.C.
Constitutional Club, per Sotheran & Co., 140, Strand, W.C.
Exeter; The Exeter Royal Albert Memorial Museum.
Guildhall Library E.C., per C. Welch.
Hull; The Hull Subscription Library, Royal Institution, Hull; William Andrews, Librarian.
Incorporated Law Society, 103, Chancery Lane, W.C.; F. Boase, Librarian.
Inner Temple Library, per Sotheran & Co., 140, Strand, W.C.
Ireland; Office of Arms, Dublin Castle, per Hodges, Figgis & Co., Ltd., Dublin.
„ King's Inns Library, per Hodges, Figgis & Co., Ltd., Dublin.
„ National Library of Ireland, per Hodges, Figgis & Co., Ltd., Dublin.
„ Kildare Street Club, Dublin.
Leeds; The Leeds Library, Commercial Street, Leeds; D. A. Cruse, Librarian.
Lincoln's Inn Library, W.C.; A. F. Etheridge, Librarian.
Manchester; The Manchester Free Library, per J. E. Cornish, 16, St. Ann's Square, Manchester.
„ Rylands Library, Manchester, per Sotheran & Co., 140, Strand, W.C.
National Portrait Gallery, per Eyre & Spottiswoode, 5, Middle New Street, E.C.

Oxford; Codrington Library, All Souls College.
Oxford & Cambridge Club, per Harrison & Sons, 59, Pall Mall, S.W.
Public Record Office, per Eyre and Spottiswoode, 5, Middle New Street, E.C.
Reform Club, Pall Mall, per Jones, Yarrell & Poulter, 8, Bury Street, S.W.
Scotland; Mitchell Library, 21, Miller Street, Glasgow; F. T. Barrett, Librarian.
Temple, *see* Inner Temple.
United University Club, per Major H. C. Gibbings, 1, Suffolk Street, Pall Mall East, S.W.
Wigan; The Wigan Public Library, per Sotheran & Co., 140, Strand, W.C.
Lindsay, Leonard C. C., F.S.A., 23, Belgrave Road, S.W.
Lindsay, W. A., K.C., F.S.A., Windsor Herald, College of Arms, E.C.
Littledale, Willoughby A., F.S.A., 26, Cranley Gardens, S.W.
Loraine, Sir Lambton, Bt., 7, Montagu Square, W.

Macdonald, W. R., Carrick Pursuivant, Neidpath, Wester Coates Avenue, Edinburgh.
MacGregor, J., 57, Grange Loan, Edinburgh.
Mackenzie, Sir E. Mackenzie, Bt., Naval & Military Club, Melbourne, Australia.
MacLehose & Sons, J., 61, St. Vincent Street, Glasgow (2).
Macmillan & Bowes, Cambridge.
Maddison, Rev. Canon, F.S.A., Vicars' Court, Lincoln.
Magrath, Rev. John Richard, D.D., Queen's College, Oxford.
Malcolm, Sir J. W., Bt., Hoveton Hall, Norwich.
Marshall, George W., LL.D., F.S.A., York Herald, Sarnesfield Court, Weobley, R S.O.
Marshall, Julian (deceased), 13, Belsize Avenue, N.W.
Marsham-Townshend, Hon. Robert, F.S.A., Frognal, Foot's Cray, Kent.
Maskelyne, Anthony Story, Public Record Office, Chancery Lane, W.C.
Mocatta, A. C., per H. Sotheran & Co., 140, Strand, W.C.
Montagu, Col. H., 123, Pall Mall, S.W.
Mosley, Sir O., Bt., Rolleston Hall, Burton-on-Trent.
Murray, Keith W., F.S.A., 37, Cheniston Gardens, Kensington, W.
Myddelton, W. M., Spencer House, St. Albans.

Nudd, W. A., Bookseller, 2, The Haymarket, Norwich.

O'Connell, Sir Ross., Bt., Killarney, per Bickers & Son, 1, Leicester Square, W.C.
Offices, Public, *see under* Libraries.

Parker & Co., J., 27, Broad Street, Oxford.
Paul, Sir James Balfour, Lyon King of Arms, per W. Green & Sons, Edinburgh.
Penfold, Hugh, Rustington, Worthing.
Phillimore, W. P. W., 124, Chancery Lane, W.C.
Pixley, F. W., F.S.A., per Sotheran & Co., 140, Strand, W.C.
Pollard, W. & Co., Ltd., Exeter.
Price, Major E., 17, Penywern Road, Earl's Court, S.W.
Public Offices, *see under* Libraries.

Ramsden, J. C., Willinghurst, Guildford, Surrey.
Ramsay, Sir James H., Bt., Bamff, Alyth, N.B.
Rich, Sir Charles H. Stuart, Bt., F.S.A., Devizes Castle.
Richardson, W. H., F.S.A., 2, Lansdown Place, Russell Square, W.C.
Rimell & Son, J., 91, Oxford Street, W. (2).
Rye, Walter, St. Leonard's Priory, Norwich.
Rylands, J. Paul, F.S.A., 2, Charlesville, Birkenhead.
Rylands, W. H., F.S.A., South Bank Lodge, 1, Campden Hill Place, W.

Schomberg, Arthur, Seend, Melksham.
Scott-Gatty, Sir Alfred S., F.S.A., Garter King of Arms, College of Arms, E.C.
Seton, Sir Bruce Maxwell, Bt., Durham House, Chelsea, S.W.
Shadwell, Walter H. L, F.S.A., Trewollack, Bodmin.
Shaw, W. A., Hillcrest, Mountfield Road, Finchley, N.
Sherborne, Lord, 9, St. James's Square, S.W.
Simpkin, Marshall, Hamilton, Kent, & Co., Ltd., 4, Stationers' Hall Court, E.C.
Smith, J. Challoner, F.S.A., c/o Mr. R. Reedman, 80, Oxford Terrace, London, W. (2).
Sinclair Wemyss, Miss, of Southdon, per Harrison & Sons, 59, Pall Mall, S.W.
Sotheran & Co., 140, Strand, W.C. (26).
Stevens, Son, & Stiles, 39, Great Russell Street, W.C.
Stewart, C. P., Chesfield Park, Stevenage.
Strange, Hamon le, Hunstanton Hall, Norfolk.
Stoddart, A. R., Fishergate Villa, York.
St. Leger, James, White's Club, St. James's Street, S.W.

Tempest, Mrs., Broughton Hall, Skipton, Yorks.
Tempest, Sir Tristram, Bt., Tong Hall, Drighlington, Bradford, Yorks.
Tenison, C. M., Hobart, Tasmania.
Thompson, W. N., St. Bees, Cumberland.
Toynbee, Paget, Dorney Wood, Burnham, Bucks.
Turnbull, Alex H., per Sotheran & Co., 140, Strand, W.C.

Vaughan, Capt. Wilmot, per Sotheran & Co., 140, Strand, W.C.

Wedderburn, Alexander, K.C., 47, Cadogan Place, S.W.
Weldon, William H., C.V.O., F.S.A., Norroy King of Arms, College of Arms, E.C.
Were, Francis, Gratwicke Hall, Flax Bourton, Somerset, per George's Sons, Bristol.
Wheler, E. G., Claverdon Leys, Warwick.
Wilson, Sir S. Maryon-, Bt., Fitzjohn, near Rugby.
Wood, F. A., Highfields, Chew Magna, Somerset, per George's Son's, Bristol.
Wood, H. J. T., Fingest Cottage, near High Wycombe, Bucks.
Woods, Sir Albert W., G.C.V.O., K.C.B., K.C.M.G., F.S.A., late Garter King of Arms (deceased), 69, St. George's Road, S.W.

Yarborough, Countess of, per H. Sotheran & Co., 140, Strand, W.C.

ABBREVIATIONS

USED IN THIS WORK.

Besides those in ordinary use the following may require explanation.

admon., administration of the goods of an intestate.
ap., apparent.
b., born.
bap., baptised.
bur., buried.
cr., created.
d., died.
da., daughter.
h., heir.
m., married.
M.I., Monumental Inscription.
pr., proved.
s., son.
s.p., sine prole.
s.p.m., sine prole masculo.
s.p.m.s., sine prole masculo superstite.
s.p.s., sine prole superstite.
suc., succeeded.

Baronetcies of England.

1611—1707.

FOURTH PART.

VIZ.,

CREATIONS,

1 Jan. 1664/5([a]) to 1 May 1707.

[See "*Memorandum*" in volume iii, part i, as to the authority from which the description of the grantees are taken between 1649 and 1809].

CREATIONS BY CHARLES II,

1 Jan. 1664/5([a]) to 6 Feb. 1684/5.

WOLSTENHOLME:

cr. 10 Jan. 1664/5;

ex. May 1762.

I. 1665. "SIR JOHN WOLSTENHOLME, of London, Knt., one of the farmers of His Majesty's Customs," 1st s. and h. of Sir John WOLSTENHOLME, of Nostell Priory, co. York, and of Stanmore, co. Midx., also a farmer of the said Customs (*d.* 25 Nov. 1639, aged 77), by his 2d wife, Catharine, "cousen and heire of Richard WANTON, of London, Esq.,"([b]) da. of (—), was *b.* about 1596; was admitted to Gray's Inn (together with his father), 13 Aug. 1611; was a partner with his father in farming the Customs; M.P. for West Looe, 1625 and 1626; for Newport, 1628 till void 14 April 1628, and for Queenboro', April to May 1640; was *Knighted* v.p. at Whitehall, 8 May 1633; was of Nostell, co. York, 1640, but was heavily fined and his estates sequestrated in Sep. 1643, (many being sold during the Civil Wars,) suffering a loss of above £100,000; was restored to his office at the Restoration, and made Collector "outward" of the port of London, and was *cr. a Baronet*, as above, 10 Jan. 1664/5. He *m.*, in or

([a]) The date of 1 Jan. 1664/5 has been arbitrarily selected as comprising (notwithstanding the chronological disparity of the division) the approximate half of the number of Baronetcies of the three realms, created between 30 Jan. 1648/9 (the death of Charles I.), and 1 May 1707, the date of the Union with Scotland, after which last named epoch the creation of *Scotch* Baronetcies ceased. The previous portion (30 Jan. 1648/9 to 31 Dec. 1664) of that period is contained in vol. iii.
([b]) See Funeral certificate of the 1st Baronet in *Mis. Gen. et Her.*, 2d s., vol. ii, p. 119.

before 1621, Anne, sister and [1645] h. of Sir Thomas DALLISON, Baronet (so *cr.* 27 Oct. 1624), of Laughton, co. Lincoln, da. of Sir Roger DALLISON, by his 2d wife, Elizabeth, da. of Marmaduke TYRWHIT, of Scotter. She *d.* in Fenchurch street, Allhallows' Staining, London, 25 Nov., and was *bur.* 5 Dec. 1661 at Stanmore. Funeral certificate. He *d.* in Fenchurch street aforesaid, 4 and was *bur.* 15 July 1670, at Stanmore.([a]) Funeral certificate. Will pr. July 1670.

II. 1670. SIR THOMAS WOLSTENHOLME, Baronet [1665], of Minchinden, in Edmonton, Midx., 2d but 1st surv. s. and h., *b.* probably about 1622([b]); *suc. to the Baronetcy*, 4 July 1670. He *m.* (Lic. Lond., 31 Jan. 1645/6, he of the Middle Temple, London, about 24, bachelor, she about 17, spinster) Elizabeth, da. of Phineas ANDREWS, of St Olave's, Hart street, London, and of Denton Court, co. Kent, by Mildred, sister of Thomas FANSHAWE, of Ashford, co. Kent. He was *bur.* 16 Nov. 1691, at St. Margaret's, Westm. Admon. 5 June 1716 to Sir Nicholas WOLSTENHOLME, Baronet. His widow was *bur.* there 20 Jan. 1696/7.

III. 1691. SIR JOHN WOLSTENHOLME, Baronet [1665], 1st s. and h., *b.* about 1650; *suc. to the Baronetcy* in Nov. 1691. Was M.P. for Middlesex (four Parls.), 1695—1700 and 1705 till death in 1709. He *m.* firstly, 27 May 1675, at Enfield, Midx. (Lic. Vic. Gen., 19 March 1674/5, he of Edmonton, Midx., about 25, bachelor, and she about 14, spinster) Mary, da. and h. of Nicholas RAYNTON, of Forty Hall in Enfield aforesaid, by Mary, da. of Michael HARVEY, of London. She, by whom he had eight children, was *bur.* at Enfield, 2 April 1691. He *m.* secondly, 7 Feb. 1699 (both being then of St. Anne's, Westm.), Temperance, widow of Sir Rowland ALSTON, 2d Baronet [1642], 2d da. and coheir of Thomas (CREWE), 2d BARON CREWE OF STENE, by his 1st wife, Mary, da. of Sir Roger TOWNSHEND, 1st Baronet [1617]. He was *bur.* 12 Feb. 1708/9, at Enfield. Will pr. Feb. 1709. His widow, by whom he had no issue, *d.* 18 Oct. 1728, and was *bur.* with her 1st husband, at Odell, Beds. Will pr. 1728.

IV. 1709. SIR NICHOLAS WOLSTENHOLME, Baronet [1665], of Forty Hall aforesaid, 1st s. and h., *bap.* 6 March 1675/6, at Enfield; *suc. to the Baronetcy* in Feb. 1708/9. He *m.* (Lic. Fac., 1 Nov. 1698, he about 22 and she about 17) Grace, da. and coheir of Sir Edward WALDO, of Pinner, Midx., Merchant of London, by his 3d wife, Elizabeth, da. of Sir Richard SHUCKBURGH. He *d.* s.p., 19 and was *bur.* 20 Feb. 1716/7, at Enfield. Will pr. Feb. 1717. His widow *m.* 11 Jan. 1717/8, at St. James', Westm., William Ferdinand (CAREY), 8th BARON HUNSDON (who *d.* s.p. 12 June 1765, in his 81st year) and *d.* 9 May 1729, in her 46th year, being *bur.* at Hutton Rudby, co. York. Will pr. 1729.

V. 1717. SIR WILLIAM WOLSTENHOLME, Baronet [1665], of Forty Hall aforesaid, next surv. br. and h., being 4th s. of the 3d Baronet, was *bap.* 12 Dec. 1689, at Enfield; *suc. to the Baronetcy*, 19 Feb. 1716/7. He *m.*, about 1718, Elizabeth, da. of Benjamin WHEELER. He *d.* s.p.m.s.([c]), 31 Jan., and was *bur.* 7 Feb. 1723/4, at Enfield. Admon. 1 April 1724. His widow *d.* 10 May 1739, and was *bur.* there, aged 40. Admon. 2 June 1739.

([a]) At the same date and in the same place was buried his niece, Dame Lætitia Corbet, widow of Sir John Corbet, 2d Baronet [1627], da. of Joan, his sister of the half blood by Sir Robert Knollys. See also p. 1, note "b."
([b]) Of his brothers and sisters, John Wolstenholme, the 1st s., was *bap* at St. Olave's, Hart street, 27 Feb. 1620/1; matric. at Oxford (Exeter Coll.) 2 Dec. 1636, aged 15; admitted to Gray's Inn, 13 May 1640; *m.* Dorothy Vere, but *d.* s.p. and v.p., 12 and was *bur.* at Great Stanmore, 21 Sep. 1669. M.I. His widow was *bur.* there 15 May 1688; Henry Wolstenholme, *bap.* as aforesaid, 22 May 1623, *d.* unm. and v.p., being slain *ex parte Regis*, at the battle of Marston Moor, 2 July 1644; Katharine, their sister, *bap.* as aforesaid, 8 July 1624; Edward, *bap.* 7 June 1627, etc.
([c]) Mary, the surv. child *d.* unm. in 1763. Elizabeth, the only married da., *m.*, in 1739, Eliab Breton, of Oldbury Hall, co. Warwick, who thus became, eventually, the sole owner of Forty Hall, which, on his death in 1785, aged 76, was sold for £80,000.

VI. 1724. SIR THOMAS WOLSTENHOLME, Baronet [1665], of Hurley, Berks, uncle and h. male, being 2d s. of the 2d Baronet, was *b.* probably about 1660; *suc. to the Baronetcy*, 31 Jan. 1723/4. He *m.* Mary, da. of (—) Hutton, an officer of the Revenue in Ireland. She *d.* before him, and is possibly the "*Lady Wolsthom*" who is *bur.*, 2 March 1724/5, at St. Margaret's, Westm. He *d.* Sep. 1738, and was *bur.* at Hurley. Admon. 7 Nov. 1738.

VII. 1738, to 1762. SIR FRANCIS WOLSTENHOLME, Baronet [1665], of Hurley aforesaid, 3d but only surv. s. and h.; *suc. to the Baronetcy* in Sep. 1738. He *d.* unm. and was *bur.* 6 May 1762 at Hurley, when the *Baronetcy* became *extinct*.

JACOB:

cr. 11 Jan. 1664/5;

ex. 4 Nov. 1790;

but assumed till 1804 or later.

I. 1665. "SIR JOHN JACOB, of Bromley [by Bow], co. Midx. [and of Woodbury, in Gamlingay, co. Cambridge], Knt., another of the Farmers of His Majesties Customs," 2d but 1st surv. s. and h. of Abraham JACOB, of Gamlingay and Bromley aforesaid (*d.* 6 May 1629, aged 56), by Mary (mar. lic. 27 Jan. 1591/2), da. of Francis ROGERS, of Dartford, co. Kent, was *b.* about 1598 at Gamlingay; matric. at Oxford (Merton Coll.) 17 Jan. 1616/7, aged 19; B.A. 1616/7; was one of the Farmers of the Customs of London to Charles I, by whom he was *Knighted* at Whitehall, 8 May 1633, being then of Stanstead, co. Essex; had an estate of £3,000 a year; was M.P. for Harwich, April to May 1640; for Rye 1640, till expelled 21 Jan. 1641; was a zealous adherent of Charles I, suffering great loss on his behalf, his lands being sequestered, etc., was restored to his office at the Restoration; made a Commissioner of the Customs, and was *cr. a Baronet*, as above, 11 Jan. 1664/3. He *m.* firstly, Elizabeth (aged 3 in 1611) only da. of John HALLYDAY, or HOLLIDAY, by Alice, da. of William FERRERS, of London, Mercer. By her he had three children. He *m.* secondly, 14 June 1632, at Stepney, Midx., Alice, widow of John EAGLESFIELD, of London, merchant, da. of Thomas CLOWES, of the same. He *m.* thirdly Elizabeth, 1st da. and coheir of Sir John ASHBURNHAM. He was *bur.* 13 March 1665/6, at Bromley aforesaid, aged about 68. Will pr. 1666. His widow *m.* (Lic. Fac. 30 June 1688) William WOGAN (then aged 30 and unm.), Serjeant at Law, and *d.* April 1697.

II. 1666. SIR JOHN JACOB, Baronet [1665], of Bromley and Woodbury aforesaid, 3d but 1st surv. s. and h., being 1st s. by the 2d wife; *b.* at Bromley aforesaid probably about 1633; matric. at Oxford (Mag. Hall.), 24 June 1653; admitted to Middle Temple 1654; *suc. to the Baronetcy* in March 1665/6. He *m.* 26 May 1664, at St. James', Clerkenwell, Catharine, da. of William (ALINGTON), 1st BARON ALINGTON OF KILLARD [I.], by Elizabeth, da. of Sir Lionel TOLLEMACHE, 2d Baronet [1611]. He *d.* 1674, and was *bur.* at St. Mary's, Savoy, Midx. Admon. as of St. Martin's in the Fields, 2 June 1674. His widow *d.* in St. Giles' in the Fields, and was carried thence for burial 11 May 1675. Admon. 12 June 1675.

III. 1674. SIR JOHN JACOB, Baronet [1665], of West Wratting, co. Cambridge, only surv. s. and h., *b.* probably about 1665; *suc. to the Baronetcy* in 1674; was an officer in the Army, serving under William III, in whose cause he was wounded at the battle of Killiecrankie in July 1689, being, in 1694, Col. of a Reg. of Foot. He is said to have suffered great loss by the seizure of his estates for Crown debts incurred by his grandfather for raising money in the cause of Charles I. He *m.* in or before 1692([a]) Dorothy, da. of Richard (BARRY), 3d EARL OF BARRYMORE [I.], by his 3d wife, Dorothy, da. and h. of John FERRER, of Dromore. He *d.* 31 March 1740. Will dat. 12 Feb. 1738, pr. 19 April 1740. His widow *d.* 27 Jan. 1748/9, aged 86, and was *bur.* at Wratting.

IV. 1740, to 1790. SIR HILDEBRAND JACOB, Baronet [1665], of Overswell, co. Glouc., grandson and heir, being only s. and h. of Hildebrand JACOB, by Meriel (*m.* 1717), da. of Sir John BLAND, 4th Baronet [1642], which Hildebrand was only surv. s. and h. ap. of the late Baronet, but *d.* v.p. in Clarges street, Midx., 3 and was *bur.* 5 June 1739, at St. Anne's, Soho, aged 46. He was *b.* about 1718; matric. at Oxford (Univ. Coll.), 25 May 1736, aged 18; *suc. to the Baronetcy*, 31 March 1740; was a Hebrew scholar of some note, and was *cr.* D.C.L. by the Univ. of Oxford, 8 July 1756. He *d.* unm., at Malvern Wells, co. Worcester, 4 and was *bur.* 21 Nov. 1790, at St. Anne's, Soho, aged 72, when the *Baronetcy* became *extinct*.([b]) Will dat. 5 Dec. 1788, pr. 4 Dec. 1790.

The Baronetcy was however assumed as below.([c])

V. 1790. SIR CLEMENT BRYDGES JACOB, Baronet([d]) [1665], 4th cousin and presumably heir male, being 1st s. and h. of the Rev. Alexander JACOB, Chaplain to the King, by Mary (*m.* 1756), da. of Robert CLEMENT, of Bletchingley, co. Surrey, which Alexander, who was author of *Jacob's Peerage* (*b.* 26 Dec. 1731, *d.* 9 and *bur.* 18 April 1785, in the Chandos vault at Whitchurch, Midx.), was only s. and h. of Lieut.-Col. Alexander JACOB (*d.* 13 April 1746, aged 54), who was 1st s. and h. of Alexander JACOB, of London, Turkey Merchant [by Elizabeth (*m.* 26 Dec. 1691) sister of James, 1st DUKE OF CHANDOS, da. of James (BRYDGES), 8th BARON CHANDOS OF SUDELEY], which Alexander was s. of Robert JACOB, yr. br. of the 1st Baronet. He was *b.* 1 Nov. 1758, and, on the death, 4 Nov. 1790, of his distant cousin, the 4th Baronet, *assumed the Baronetcy*, on the ground, apparently, of being heir male collateral of the grantee. He, who was unm. in 1802, *d.* s.p.m. 30 March 1804, in his 46th year.

VI. 1804, to 1820? SIR CHARLES JACOB, Baronet([d]) [1665], only br. and h., *b.* 26 April 1761; *suc. to the Baronetcy*([d]), 30 March 1804. He was unm. in 1802, and *d.* presumably s.p.m., when the *assumption of the Baronetcy* ceased.

([a]) "John, s. of Sir John Jacob, Baronet, and Lady Dorothy," was *bap.* 12 May 1692, at Kensington. This child presumably *d.* in infancy.

([b]) His only sister, Anne, *m.* firstly, in Oct. 1743, Dr. Peters, Physician to the King, and secondly, in March 1753, Capt. Hughes.

([c]) See Betham's *Baronetage* [1802], vol. ii., p. 367, for an account of the eccentricity of the 4th Baronet, as also of the assumption of that dignity after his death, in 1790, by his cousin.

([d]) According to the assumption of the Baronetcy in 1790.

YEAMANS, *or* YEOMANS:

cr. 12 Jan. 1664/5;

ex. 19 Feb. 1788.

I. 1665. "JOHN YEOMANS [*or* YEAMANS], of the city of Bristol, co. Somerset, Esq.," supposed([a]) to have been 1st s. and h. of Robert YEAMANS, Alderman, and sometime, 1642, Sheriff of Bristol (who was executed there, 30 May 1643, by the then Governor, for having planned the delivery of that city to the King's army), by Anne (afterwards, before 1646, wife of Robert SPEED, Quaker), was, probably in reward for that alderman's loyalty, *cr. a Baronet*, as above, 12 Jan. 1664/5. He afterwards settled in Barbadoes, and finally in South Carolina, where he was Gov. till 1680, having received a grant of four Baronies (48,000 acres), being at the same time created a Landgrave of that province, 5 April 1671, by John Berkeley, the "Palatinus Carolinæ." He *m.* firstly, in Barbadoes, (—), da. of (—) LIMP. He *m.* secondly there, Margaret, da. of the Rev. John FOSTER, of Barbadoes. He *d.* between 1680 and 1686.

II. 1680? SIR WILLIAM YEAMANS, Baronet [1665], of Barbadoes aforesaid, 1st s. and h., being only s. by the 1st wife; *suc. to the Baronetcy* on the death of his father. He *m.*, in Barbadoes, Willoughby, da. of Sir James BROWNE. She was living 1676-80.

III. 1685? SIR JOHN YEAMANS, Baronet [1665], of Barbadoes aforesaid, s. and h.; *suc. to the Baronetcy* on the death of his father. He *m.* Margaret, 3d da. of Philip GIBBES, of St. James', Barbadoes (*d.* July 1697), by (—), his 1st wife. He *d.* apparently([b]) before 1691. His widow *m.* William FOSTER and, subsequently, Major John BUTLER, who was living as her widower in Dec. 1691.

IV. 1690? SIR JOHN YEAMANS, Baronet [1665], of Barbadoes aforesaid, s. and h., *b.* about 1689, being aged 26 in 1715; *suc. to the Baronetcy* on the death of his father; was, possibly, the "John Yeamans, Gent.," admitted to Lincoln's Inn, 29 May 1713. He *m.* in Barbadoes, in or before 1715, Anne, apparently,([b]) widow of Col. Thomas HELMS, da. of (—) SCANTLEBURY, of Barbadoes. He *d.* before 1740.

V. 1730? SIR JOHN YEAMANS, Baronet [1665], of Barbadoes aforesaid, only s. and h., *b.* there about 1720; matric. at Oxford (Queen's Coll.), 15 July 1738, aged 18; *suc. to the Baronetcy* on the death of his father. He *m.* in or before 1742, (—). He was living in Barbadoes, 1771.

VI. 1780? to 1788. SIR ROBERT YEAMANS, Baronet [1665], s. and h., *b.* about 1742; matric. at Oxford (Merton Coll.), 17 Jan. 1759, aged 17; B.A., 1763; was in Holy Orders; Vicar of Fittleworth and Incumbent of Cold Waltham, Sussex, 1776-88. He *d.* s.p., presumably, unm., 19 Feb. 1788, aged about 46, when the *Baronetcy* became *extinct*.

([a]) In Le Neve's Baronetage this is put hypothetically, but in V. L. Oliver's *Antigua* as a certainty. There was, however, a John Yeamans, of St. Mary's Redcliffe, Bristol, Brewer (whose will was dat. 1645) and who not improbably was a brother or near relation of the alderman, and who certainly had three children, all *bap.* at St. Mary's aforesaid, viz., (1) John, *bap.* 28 Feb. 1611, possibly the Baronet of the creation of 1666; (2) Robert, *bap.* 19 April 1317, possibly the Baronet of the creation of 1668, who in his will, dated 1686, mentions the children of his brother John and of his brother Joseph; and (3) Joseph, *bap.* 27 Sep. 1617, who had three children, John, Robert and George.

([b]) "I have some old letters of Chester of Barbadoes which I cannot reconcile with Burke [*i.e.*, Burke's *Extinct Baronetage*.] They say that Dorothy Chester married in Dec. 1691, Major John Butler, then 35 years old, who was widower of Lady Yeamans, whose son, Sir John Yeamans, Baronet, married the widow of Col. Thomas Helms." [Letter, 15 July 1884, from Edmond Chester Waters].

PYE:

cr. 13 Jan. 1664/5;

ex. 23 May 1734.

I. 1665. "JOHN PYE, of Hone [in Marston on Dove], co. Derby, Esq.," 2d s. of Sir Robert PYE, of Faringdon, Berks,([a]) Auditor of the Exchequer, a zealous Royalist (*d.* 1662), by Mary, da. and coheir of John CROKER, of Battisford, co. Glouc., was *b.* about 1626, and was *cr. a Baronet*, as above, 13 Jan. 1664/5; el. Sheriff of Derbyshire, 1678, but did not act. He *m.* 27 Feb. 1648/9, at St. Mary's Aldermanbury, London (Lic. Fac. 24, he of Westminster, aged 23, and unm., and she aged 17, spinster), Rebecca, da. of Nicholas RAYNTON, of Enfield, Midx., by Rebecca, da. of John MOULSON, of Nantwich, co. Chester, which Nicholas was nephew of Sir Nicholas RAYNTON, Lord Mayor of London, 1622-23. He *d.* about 1697. His widow *d.* Sep. 1707. Will pr. Oct. 1707.

II. 1697? SIR CHARLES PYE, Baronet [1665], of Hone aforesaid, only s. and h., *b.* about 1661, at Mortlake, Surrey; matric. at Oxford (Wadham Coll.) 26 May 1669, aged 18; *suc. to the Baronetcy* about 1697; was M.P. for Derby, 1700-01; purchased the estates of Clifton Camvile and Houghton, co. Stafford. He *m.* firstly (Lic. Fac. 28 April 1680, he of Turnham Green, Chiswick, aged 28, unm., and she aged 19), Philippa, 1st da. of Sir John HOBART, 3d Baronet [1611], by his 1st wife Mary, da. of John HAMPDEN. She, who was living 23 April 1683, *d.* s.p.s. He *m.* secondly (Lic. Fac. 23 Feb. 1684/5; Anne (then 22, spinster) da. of Richard STEVENS, of Eastington, co. Glouc., by Anne, da. of Sir Hugh CHOLMLEY, 1st Baronet [1641], of Whitby. He *d.* at Clifton Camville 12 Feb. 1720/1. Admon. 5 April 1721, and 7 May 1729. His widow *d.* 12 July 1722.

III. 1721. SIR RICHARD PYE, Baronet [1655], of Hone and Clifton Camvile aforesaid, 1st s. and h., by 2d wife, *b.* probably about 1690; *suc. to the Baronetcy*, 12 Feb. 1720/1. He *d.* unm. 22 Nov. 1724, at Derby. Admon. 1 July 1725.

IV. 1724, to 1734. SIR ROBERT PYE, Baronet [1665], of Hone and Clifton Camvile aforesaid, br. and h., *b.* about 1696; matric. at Oxford (Wadham Coll.), 16 Feb. 1713/4, aged 18; B.A. 1717; M.A. 1720; in Holy Orders; *suc. to the Baronetcy*, 22 Nov. 1724; was F.R.S. He *d.* unm. 23 May 1734, when the *Baronetcy* became *extinct*. Will pr. June 1734.([b])

TAYLOR:

cr. 18 Jan. 1664/5;

ex. Jan. 1719/20.

I. 1665. "THOMAS TAYLOR, of the Parke house in the parish of Maidstone, co. Kent, Esq.," as also of Shadockhurst in that county, only s. and h. of Thomas TAYLOR, of Shadockhurst aforesaid, and of Newhall in Linstead, in that county, by his 2d wife, Anne, da. of Sir Thomas HENDLEY, of Corshorne, co. Kent, was *b.* in 1630, a year before his father's death, was admitted to Gray's Inn, 5 Nov. 1643, and was *cr. a Baronet*, as above, 18 Jan. 1664/5. He *m.* in or before 1657, Elizabeth, da. and h. of George HALL, of Maidstone. He is said to have *d.* in or soon after 1665; admon. not

---

([a]) "Sir Robert Pye, of Berkshire," had obtained a warrant of Baronetcy 22 Dec. 1662. See *Calendar of State Papers*, 1660-70.

([b]) Mary, his only surv. sister, suc. to the estates, but *d.* unm. in 1774, devising them, in tail, to her cousins, descendants of the daughters of the 1st Baronet. On their extinction, they passed to the heir male of the family of Pye, viz., Henry John Pye, of Farringdon, Berks, s. and h. of Henry James Pye, the Poet Laureate, a descendant of Sir Robert Pye, the eldest br. of Sir John Pye, the 1st Baronet.

till 20 Aug. 1688. His widow *m.* (Lic. Fac., 23 April 1667), Percy GORING, then of London, "Esq.," widower. Her admon. (the same date as that of her former husband), 20 Aug. 1688.([a])

II. 1665? SIR THOMAS TAYLOR, Baronet [1665], of Park house, etc., aforesaid, only s. and h., *b.* 19 Aug. 1657; matric. at Oxford (St. John's Coll.), 2 July 1675, aged 16; *suc. to the Baronetcy* on the death of his father; was M.P. for Maidstone (three Parls.), 1689 till death, in 1696. He *m.* in or before 1693, Alice, widow of Herbert STAPLEY, sister and, in 1723, h. of Sir Thomas COLEPEPER, 3d Baronet [1627], only da. of Sir Thomas COLEPEPER, 2d Baronet [1627], of Preston Hall, co. Kent, by Margaret, da. of (—) REYNOLDS. He *d.* 6 Feb. 1695/6. Will dat. 29 April 1693, pr. 14 July 1698. His widow *m.* before 20 Aug. 1701 Thomas COLEPEPER, of the Middle Temple, who *d.* 1704. She *m.* for her 4th husband, Oct. 1723, John MILNER, M.D., on whom and whose relations she settled the Preston Hall estates.([b]) He *d.* Feb. 1723/4. Admon. 21 Feb. 1723/4. She was *bur.* at Aylesford 3 April 1734. Will dat. 6 Jan. 1727/8, pr. 2 Nov. 1734.

III. 1696 to 1720. SIR THOMAS TAYLOR, Baronet [1665], only s. and h., *bap.* 11 Nov. 1693, at Boxley, co. Kent; *suc. to the Baronetcy* on 6 Feb. 1695/6. He *d.* unm. in his mother's lifetime, in Jan. 1719/20 when the *Baronetcy* became *extinct*. Will dat. 21 Dec. 1719, pr. 1 Feb. 1719/20.

LEMAN:

cr. 3 March 1664/5;

ex. presumably in 1762;

but assumed till 1842, or later.

I. 1665. "WILLIAM LEMAN, of [Nin Hall in] Northaw, *alias* Northall, co. Hertford, Esq.," as also of Warboys, co. Huntingdon, and of Cheapside, London, woollen draper, citizen, and Fishmonger of that city, 5th s. of William LEMAN, Portreeve of Beccles, co. Suffolk, by Alice, da. of [—] BOURNE, of Norwich, was nephew and principal testamentary heir of Sir John LEMAN, sometime (1616-17) Lord Mayor of London (who *d.* unm. 26 March 1632), from whom he inherited in 1632 the estate of Warboys, co. Huntingdon, in which year also he purchased the abovenamed estate at Northaw; was Sheriff of Herts, 1635-36, and of Hunts, 1640-41; M.P. for Hertford, Sep. 1645 to 1653, and 1659-60, taking the Covenant 29 Oct. 1645, serving on several Committees and being a member of the Council of State, Feb. to Nov. 1651. He, though not a *Cromwellian*, was a most active *Rumper*. He was Alderman of Bread street ward, April to Aug. 1649, and of Billingsgate, July to Sep. 1653; and was *cr. a Baronet*, as above, 3 March 1664/5. He *m.* in or before 1637, Rebecca, da. and coheir of Edward PRESCOTT, of Thoby, co. Essex, citizen and sadler, of London. He was *bur.* 3 Sep. 1667, at Northaw. Will dat. 2 July and pr. 1 Nov. 1667. His widow was *bur.* 22 Jan. 1675, at Northaw.

II. 1667. SIR WILLIAM LEMAN, Baronet [1665], of Nin Hall, in Northall, and of Warboys aforesaid, 1st s. and h., *bap.* 19 Dec. 1637, at Northall; *suc. to the Baronetcy* in Sep. 1667; Sheriff of Herts, 1676-77; M.P. for Hertford, 1690-95. He *m.*, 16 Aug. 1655, at Northaw (settlmt. 15 June 1655) Mary, da. of Sir Lewis MANSEL, 2d Baronet [1611], of Margam, by his 3d wife, Elizabeth, da. of Henry (MONTAGU), EARL OF MANCHESTER. He *d.* 18 and was *bur.* 28 July 1701, at Northaw. Will dat. 17 Nov. 1692, pr. 8 Sep. 1701. His widow *d.* 21 April 1722, in Great Russell street, Bloomsbury. Will dat. 25 Nov. 1721, pr. 2 May 1722.

([a]) In it she is described as "Dame Elizabeth Taylor, of Park House, in Maidstone, widow," no mention being made of her last husband, who presumably died before her.

([b]) These devolved at her death on Dr. Charles Milner, the brother of her fourth and last husband.

III. 1701. SIR WILLIAM LEMAN, Baronet [1665], of Nin Hall, in Northall, and of Warboys aforesaid, grandson and h., being only s. and h. of Mansell LEMAN, by Lucy (*m.* 20 May 1636, at Whitechapel), da. of Richard ALEY,(a) Alderman of London, which Mansel, who *d.* v.p. 13 March 1637, was 1st. s. and h. ap. of the late Baronet. He was *b.* 1685, and *suc. to the Baronetcy* 18 July 1701. He *m.*, shortly after 1727, Anna Margaretta BRETT, spinster, sometime mistress to **George I**, da. of Col. Henry BRETT, of Dowdeswell, co. Glouc., by Anne, divorced wife of Charles (GERARD), EARL OF MACCLESFIELD, da. of Sir Richard MASON, of Salop. He *d.* s.p.(b) 22 Dec. 1741, and was *bur.* 2 Jan. 1741/2, at Northaw. Will pr. 2 April 1742. His widow was *bur.* 24 Dec. 1745 at Northaw, aged 39. Will dat. 4 Dec. 1744, pr. 14 Dec. 1745.

IV. 1741, to 1762. SIR TANFIELD LEMAN, Baronet [1665], of St. George's, Southwark, co. Surrey, cousin and h. male, being only s. and h. of Philip LEMAN, of Snow Hill, London, apothecary, by Frances, his wife, which Philip (who *d.* 10 Nov. 1732) was s. of the Rev. Philip LEMAN, Rector of Warboys, co. Huntingdon (*bap.* 19 June 1640, at St. Barth. the Great, London, and *bur.* 24 Feb. 1693, at Warboys), who was 6th s. of the 1st Baronet. He was *bap.* 13 April 1714, at St. Margaret's Lothbury, London, and *suc. to the Baronetcy*, 22 Dec. 1741. He *m.* Catherine, da. of [—]. He *d.* s.p. at Southwark in 1762, when the *Baronetcy*, apparently, became *extinct*. Admon. 2 Aug. 1762, to the relict Dame Catherine.

The title has frequently been assumed.

V. 1762. JOHN LEMAN, of St Mary's, Nottingham,(c) stated to have been cousin and heir male, being s. and h. of John LEMAN, of St. Mary's aforesaid, by Sarah (*m.* there 26 Jan. 1718), da. of (—) GODFREY, which John, who *d.* July 1759, is stated to have been identical with John LEMAN, *bap.* at Warboys, co. Huntingdon, 28 July 1689,(d) s. of the Rev. Philip LEMAN, Rector of Warboys abovenamed, the 6th s. of the 1st Baronet. He was *bap.* 6 Oct. 1724 at St. Mary's, Nottingham, and on the death of the 4th Baronet in 1762 is stated to have *suc. to the Baronetcy*, but "being a soldier and abroad" never to have assumed the same. He *m.* 23 May 1745 at St. Mary's aforesaid, Mary, da. of (—) SMITHAM. He was *bur.* 13 May 1792, at St. Mary's, Nottingham.

VI. 1792. GODFREY LEMAN, of St. Mary's, Nottingham, s. and h., *bap.* there 13 Sep. 1753; stated to have *suc. to the Baronetcy* on his father's death in May 1792, but "from poverty, sickness

(a) See a very full account of the family of Aley or Alie, in the *Her. and Gen.*, vol. vi, pp. 223-231.

(b) The estate of Northaw was inherited by his only sister Lucy, who *d.* unm., and was *bur.* there, 3 Oct. 1745, when it passed to her cousin, Richard Aley (whose mother, Elizabeth, wife of Henry Aley, was dau. of Sir William Leman, the 2d Baronet), who took the name of Leman, and *d.* 6, being *bur.* 17 July 1749 at Northaw, aged 59. His sister Lucy succeeded him, but *d.* unm., being *bur.* 6 Oct. 1753 at Northaw, aged 63. She devised the estate to John Granger, who took the surname of Leman, and *d.* s.p. at Bath 29 Sep., being *bur.* 4 Oct. 1761 at Warboys, leaving his estate to his wife. In Oct. 1810 it was sold by auction under a decree of Chancery.

(c) As regards the claim to and subsequent assumption of the Baronetcy, by the family of Leman, of St. Mary's, Nottingham, see a small pamphlet called "The Leman Case," printed at Nottingham, 1840, being a reprint from *The Nottingham Review*, of 17 April 1840, with additions, signed "W. H. A. Fitz-Strathern."

(d) It is, however, almost certain that the John Leman who was *bap.* in July 1689, died in infancy before Feb. 1693, the date of his father's death.

and subsequent imbecility," never to have assumed the same. He *m.* 16 Feb. 1777, at St. Mary's aforesaid, Anne, da. of (—) WHITTAKER. He *d.* 1827.

VII. 1827. "SIR JOHN LEMAN, Baronet"(a) [1665], only surv. s. and h., *bap.* 28 Aug. 1781 at St. Mary's, Nottingham, was sometime a frame-work knitter in that town. He *assumed the Baronetcy* on the death of his father in 1827, and is said to have taken proceedings in the Scottish Court of Chancery to establish his right thereto and to estates estimated at £400,000 a year, in Goodman's Fields, Midx., and the Counties of Hertford, Huntingdon, and Cambridge. He *d.* s.p., 5 June 1839, aged 58 at Cliffe House, near Wakefield, and was *bur.* at Sandall, co. York.

VIII. 1839. "SIR EDWARD GODFREY LEMAN, Baronet,"(a) [1665], of Willoughby Row, Castle Gate, Nottingham, Bricklayer, cousin and h. male, being only s. and h. of Edward LEMAN, a soldier, by Elizabeth (*m.* 8 Oct. 1765), da. of (—) BATES, which Edward (*bap.* 5 June 1733 at St. Mary's Nottingham, and *d.* about 1790 in the West Indies) was yr. br. to JOHN LEMAN (*bap.* 6 Oct. 1724 at St. Mary's aforesaid), the grandfather of the "Sir John LEMAN" last named. He was *bap.* 28 April 1766, and *assumed the Baronetcy* on the death of his cousin, 5 June 1839. He *m.*, 1 April 1793, Mary, da. of (—) BURTON. He was living at Nottingham in 1840, aged 74, as also was Edward LEMAN (*b.* in Nottingham, 1804), his only son.

In 1842, "SIR JOSEPH LEMAN, Baronet," of North Cadbury, co. Somerset, *advertised his right to this Baronetcy* [1665], as against that of JOHN ASHALL LEMAN, of Lambeth, Surrey, *styling* himself "Baronet."

SMITH, *or* SMYTH:
cr. 30 March 1665;
ex. 11 July 1852.

I. 1665. "SIR ROBERT SMITH [*or* SMYTH], of Upton [in Westham], co. Essex, Knt.," s. of Robert SMYTH, citizen and draper of London, by Mary, da. of (—) BAINES, of London, merchant, was *b.* about 1594; was sometime a silkman of London; purchased the estate of Upton; was *Knighted* 25 Aug. 1660; entered his pedigree at the Heralds' Visitation of Essex in 1664, signing it as "*Robt. Smyth*," and was *cr. a Baronet*, as above, 30 March 1665. He *m.* firstly, about 1630, Judith, da. of Nicholas WALMESLEY, merchant of London (br. of Sir Thomas WALMESLEY, of Dunkenhalghe, co. Lancaster, Justice of the Common Pleas), by Sarah, da. of Thomas KEMBLE, of London. She *d.* 1653, M.I. at Westham. He *m.* secondly, Rebecca, widow of (—) SPURSTOW, da. of William ROMNEY, of London. He *d.* 12, and was *bur.* 23 June 1669, at Westham, aged 75. M.I. there, in which his name is spelled "*Smyth*." Will pr. 1669. The admon. of his widow, then "of Bassingborne, co. Cambridge," granted 18 Aug. 1690, to her da. Rebecca, wife of William ROBINSON.

II. 1669. SIR ROBERT SMYTH, Baronet [1665], of Upton aforesaid, 1st s. and h. by first wife(b); *b.* probably about 1630; *suc. to*

(a) According to the assumption of that dignity.

(b) Sir James Smyth, the second son was Lord Mayor of London, 1684-85, and *d.* 9 Dec. 1706, aged 73, being father of James Smyth, of Isfield, co. Sussex, who was *cr. a Baronet*, 2 Dec. 1714, a dignity which became extinct 2 Oct. 1811.

the Baronetcy, 12 June 1669. He *m.* in or before 1658, Jane, da. of John TRAFFORD, of Dunton Hall, co. Lincoln, and of Low Leyton, co. Essex. She, presumably, was "the Lady Smith, from Upton," who was *bur.* 8 May 1712, at Walthamstow, the burial place of the Trafford family of Low Leyton. He was living Feb. 1683/4.

III. 1700? SIR ROBERT SMYTH, Baronet [1665], of Upton aforesaid, 1st s. and h., *b.* about 1659, being aged 6 in the Heralds' Visitation of Essex, 1664; admitted to Middle Temple 1676; matric. at Oxford (St. Alban Hall) 30 March 1677, aged 17; was M.P. for Andover, 1695-98; *suc. to the Baronetcy* on the death of his father. He *m.* (Lic. Fac. 6 Feb. 1683/4, being then "of the Middle Temple, Esq., aged 28, Bachelor") Anne BUTTON, of Libbington, Hants, widow of John BUTTON, of Buckland, da. of Henry WHITEHEAD, of Titherley, Hants, by Sarah, da. of Richard NORTON, of Southwick, in that county. He *d.* 27 Jan. 1744/5, aged 86, and was *bur.* at Westham aforesaid. M.I. there. Will pr. 1745.

IV. 1745. SIR TRAFFORD SMYTH, Baronet [1665], of Upton aforesaid, and of Berechurch Hall in Berechurch, co. Essex, grandson and h., being s. and h. of Trafford SMYTH, Barrister at Law, by his 1st wife, Conway, da. and h. of Thomas HACKETT, D.D., Bishop of Down and Connor, which Trafford was 1st s. and h. ap. of the late Baronet, but *d.* v.p. Jan. 1731/2. He, who was *b.* probably about 1720, *suc. to the Baronetcy* 27 Jan. 1744/5. He *d.* unm. 8 Dec. 1765. Will pr. Feb. 1766.

V. 1765. SIR ROBERT SMYTH, Baronet [1665], of Berechurch Hall aforesaid, cousin and h. male, being s. and h. of the Rev. Robert SMYTH, B.A. [Oxford], Vicar of Woolavington, Sussex [1730-74], by Dorothy, da. of Thomas LLOYD, of Doleglunnen, co. Merioneth, which Robert (*b.* 1690), was 2d s. of the 3d Baronet. He was *b.* 10 Jan. 1744; *suc. to the Baronetcy*, 8 Dec. 1765; was sometime in business at Paris, where he was a Banker(a); was M.P. for Cardigan, 1774 till unseated 7 Dec. 1775, and for Colchester 1780-90. He *m.*, 10 Sep. 1776, "Miss BLAKE, of Hanover square," *i.e.*, Charlotte Sophia Delaval, da. of (—) BLAKE. He *d.* 12 April 1802, at Paris, aged 58, and was *bur.* at Berechurch. Will dated at Weston, near Bath, 1797, pr. 1802. His widow(b) *d.* 4 Feb. 1823, and was *bur.* at Versailles, near Paris.

VI. 1802, to 1852. SIR GEORGE HENRY SMYTH, Baronet [1665], of Berechurch Hall aforesaid, only s. and h., *b.* 30 Jan. 1784, ed. at Trin. Coll., Cambridge; *suc. to the Baronetcy*, 12 April 1802; was Sheriff of Essex, 1822-23; M.P. for Colchester, 1826-30, and 1835-50, and was a consistent Conservative. He *m.*, 28 July 1815, Eva, da. of George ELMORE, of Penton, Hants. He *d.* s.p. legit.,(c) 11 July 1852, at Berechurch Hall in his 68th year, when the *Baronetcy* became *extinct*. Will pr. Aug. 1852. His widow *d.*, apparently, in 1866.(d)

(a) He had the folly to "renounce his title of Baronet" at the notorious British dinner held in Paris, 18 Nov. 1792, during the French Revolution, when Thomas Paine and Lord Edward Fitzgerald were present [*N. & Q.*, 9th S., I. 252], a renunciation, however, which did not, apparently, last any length of time.

(b) There is a coloured engraving, 1789, by F. Bartolozzi, R.A., of the well known portrait by Sir Joshua Reynolds, of this Lady Smyth, with two girls and a boy.

(c) The estates went to the children of his illegit. da. Charlotte, *b.* 26 July 1813, and *bap.* at Berechurch, who *m.*, 26 July 1832, Thomas White, of Dobbins, in Wethersfield, co. Essex, and who *d.*, v.p., 17 Oct. 1845, leaving issue.

(d) She is mentioned as living in Dod's Baronetage for 1866, but is omitted in that for 1867.

CRISPE:
cr. 14 April 1665;
ex. 9 July 1740.

I. 1665. "SIR NICHOLAS CRISPE, of Hammersmith, co. Middlesex, Knt.," s. and h. of Ellis CRISPE,(a) Salter, Alderman and sometime (1625) Sheriff of London (*bap.* 23 May 1562 at Marshfield, co. Glouc., and *d.* 3 Nov. 1625, while in office), by Hester,(b) da. of John IRELAND, of Notts, was *b.* about 1598; was one of the principal merchants of London; settled the trade of gold from Guinea, where he built the Castle of Cormantine; was also the builder, about 1630, at the cost of £23,000, of a magnificent house at Hammersmith(c); was M.P. for Winchelsea, April to May 1640, and Nov. 1640 till expelled 2 Feb. 1640/1; again 1661 till death in 1666; was *Knighted* 1 Jan. 1640/1; was a Farmer of the Customs; a zealous Royalist, supplying the King during the Civil War with "thousands of gold"(d); raised and commanded a regiment in his service, and on his murder retired to France, his estates being sequestrated and himself heavily fined; re-embarked in trade after the Restoration, and was *cr. a Baronet*, as above, 14 April 1665, only ten months before his death. He *m.* firstly, in or before 1619, Anne, da. and h. of Edward PRESCOTT, Citizen and Salter of London. He *m.* secondly (Lic. Lon. 30 June 1628, he 29 and she 17), Sara, da. of Richard SPENCER, citizen and Haberdasher of London, and Sara, his wife; *d.* 26 Feb. 1665/6, aged 67, and was *bur.* at St. Mildred's, Bread street, London, his remains being removed to Hammersmith, and there *bur.* 18 June 1898. M.I.(e) The will of his widow, dat. 31 May 1669, pr. 6 Oct. 1699.

II. 1666. SIR NICHOLAS CRISPE, Baronet [1665], of Hammersmith aforesaid, and of Squeries, in Westerham, co. Kent, grandson and h., being s. and h. of Ellis CRISPE, by Anne(f) (Mar. Lic. Vic. Gen. 25 Jan. 1641/2), da. of Sir George STRODE, of Squeries aforesaid, which Ellis (aged 5½ in 1625) *d.* v.p. Aug. 1663. He was *b.* about 1643; matric. at Oxford (St. John's Coll.), 22 Aug. 1661, aged 18; *suc. to the Baronetcy*, 26 Feb. 1665/6, and sold the estate at Hammersmith in 1683. He *m.*, 30 April 1674, at Islington, Midx., registered also, at Newington (Lic. Vic. Gen., he, of Middle Temple, 30 and she 20), Judith, da. and h. of John ADRIAN, of London, merchant. He *d.* Nov. 1698, and was *bur.* at St. Mildred's aforesaid. Will dat. 11 Dec. 1693, pr. 9 Dec. 1698. His widow was *bur.* with him. Her will dat. 8 Feb. 1699, pr. 2 May 1700.

III. 1698. SIR JOHN CRISPE, Baronet [1665], of Squeries aforesaid, and afterwards of Salisbury, Wilts, 1st s. and h.; *b.* about 1676; *suc. to the Baronetcy* in Nov. 1698, and sold the estate of Squeries in 1700. He *m.*, 5 Nov. 1716, Elizabeth, da. of George SAYER, one of the Proctors of

(a) A good account of the family of Crisp, by F. A. Crisp, was privately printed in 1882, in three vols., small folio.

(b) This Hester, who *m.* secondly Sir Walter Pye, of the Mynde, co. Hereford, Attorney Gen. to the Court of Wards, was sister of John Ireland, sometime Prime Master of the Salters' Company.

(c) This was built of brick, the art of making which, as now practised, he is said to have invented. It was sold in 1683 to Prince Rupert, and was sometime the residence of Caroline, Queen Consort of George IV, being then known as Brandenburgh House. Hence Hook's sarcastic verses—

"What saw you at Brandenburgh, hey mam, ho mam;
What saw you at Brandenburgh, ho?
I saw a great dame.
With a face red as flame,
And a character spotless as snow, mam, ho mam,
A character spotless as snow."

(d) Lloyd's *Memoirs*, p. 627.

(e) The Rev. Tobias Crispe, B.D., a well known Puritan divine, who died 27 Feb. 1642/3, was his younger brother.

(f) This Anne was cousin to her husband, her mother, Rebecca, being da. of Nicholas Crispe, of London, merchant, uncle to the 1st Baronet.

Doctors Commons, London. He *d.* 18 Jan. 1727/8. Will pr. 4 March 1727/8. His widow *m.* John ELLIOT, of St. Mary's, Islington, and *d.* before him in or before Oct. 1741. Admon. 26 Oct. 1741.

IV. 1728. SIR NICHOLAS CRISPE, Baronet [1665], of Salisbury aforesaid, only s. and h., *b.* about 1718; *suc. to the Baronetcy*, 18 Jan. 1727/8. He *d.* unm., 1 June 1730, aged 12.(a)

V. 1730, to 1740. SIR CHARLES CRISPE, Baronet [1665], of Dornford in Wootton, co. Oxford, uncle and h. male, aged about 13 in 1693,(b) *suc. to the Baronetcy*, 1 June 1730; was Sheriff of Oxon, 1715-16. He *m.* his cousin, Anne, sole surv. child and h. of Sir Thomas CRISPE,(c) of Dornford aforesaid, by his 2d wife Dorothy, da. of the well-known Sir Harry VANE, who was beheaded, 1662. She *d.* 2 June 1718, in her 33d year. Admon. 19 Jan. 1718/9. He *d.* s.p., 9 July 1740, when the *Baronetcy* became *extinct*. Will dat. 16 June 1731, pr. 1 Aug. 1740. Both were *bur.* at Wootton aforesaid. M.I.

SHAW:

cr. 15 April 1665.

I. 1665. "SIR JOHN SHAW, of the City of London, Knt., one of the Farmers of His Majesty's Customs," 2d s. of Robert SHAW, of Southwark, Surrey, Citizen and Vintner of London, by Elizabeth, da. of John DOMILOWE, also of London, was *b.* about 1615, and, having made a good fortune in business, assisted Charles II during exile with considerable sums of money, by whom, shortly after 1660, he was made one of the Farmers of the Customs of London, and was *Knighted*, 28 July 1660; M.P. for Lyme Regis, 1661-79, obtaining in 1663 a Crown lease of the manors of Eltham and Woolwich, co. Kent, and being *cr. a Baronet*, as above, 15 April 1665. He resided in the Lodge (which he rebuilt) in the Great Park at Eltham, and rebuilt in 1667 the north aisle of Eltham Church. He *m.* firstly, in or before 1660, Sarah, da. of Joseph ASHE, of Beshford, co. Somerset. She *d.* Dec. 1662, and was *bur.* at St. Mildred's Bread street. He *m.* secondly, 24 June 1663, at Eltham (Lic. Fac. 22), Bridget, DOWAGER VISCOUNTESS KILMOREY [I.], 1st da. and coheir of Sir William DRURY, of Besthorpe, co. Norfolk, by Mary, da. of William COKAYNE, Merchant, of London. He *d.* in Great Southampton *otherwise* Bloomsbury square, St. Giles' in the Fields, Midx., 1 and was *bur.* 6 March 1679/80 at Eltham, aged 64. Will dat. 28 Feb., pr. 8 March 1679/80. His widow *m.* (for her 3d husband) 15 Feb 1680/1, at St. Brides' London (Lic. Fac.), Sir John BABER, widower, who *d.* 1704. She was *bur.* 11 July 1699, at Eltham.

II. 1680. SIR JOHN SHAW, Baronet [1665], of Eltham Lodge aforesaid, 1st s. and h., being only s. by the 1st wife, *b.* about 1660; *suc. to the Baronetcy*, 1 March 1679/80, as also to the Collectorship of the Customs of London. He in 1694 purchased an estate at Cheshunt, Herts. He *m.* firstly (Lic. London, 12 May 1684, he 25 and she 16) Margaret, da. and h. of Sir John PEAKE, of St. Benet's Gracechurch, citizen and mercer of London, sometime, 1686-87, Lord Mayor of London, by Judith, da. of Richard HALE, of

(a) Mary Theresa, his only sister, *m.* (Lic. 16 June 1731, she under 21), Rev. George Stonehouse, Minister of the Methodist church, Islington (1738-40), and was *bur.* 1751, in the Moravian church, Chelsea.

(b) Le Neve's MS. "*Baronetage.*"

(c) This Thomas, *bap.* 18 Jan. 1640/1, at St. Dionis, Backchurch, was a yr. s. of the 1st Baronet, and *d.* 29 July 1714, being *bur.* at St. Mildred's, Bread street.

Beckenham, co. Kent. She *d.* 23 and was *bur.* 29 Aug. 1690, at Eltham. Admon. 7 Nov. 1690. He *m.* secondly in or before 1695, Sarah, da. and coheir of William PAGGEN, of London, merchant. He *d.* 11 and was *bur.* 21 Dec. 1721, at Eltham. Will pr. 1722. His widow was *bur.* there 12 Jan. 1742/3.

III. 1721. SIR JOHN SHAW, Baronet [1665], of Eltham Lodge aforesaid, 1st s. and h., being only surv. s. by 1st wife, *b.* at Eltham 1687; matric. at Oxford (Trin. Coll.), 23 June 1702, aged 15; M.A., by decree, 3 April 1707; *suc. to the Baronetcy*, 11 Dec. 1721. He *m.*, Sep. 1716, Anna Maria, 1st surv. da. and coheir of Sir Thomas BARNARDISTON, 3d Baronet [1663], of Ketton, co. Suffolk, by Anne, da. and coheir of Sir Richard ROTHWELL, Baronet [1661]. He *d.* 4, and was *bur.* 13 March 1738/9, at Eltham. Admon. 26 March 1739. His widow, who was *bap.* 1 July 1697, at Ketton aforesaid, *d.* 30 Nov., and was *bur.* 10 Dec. 1755 at Eltham. Will pr. 1755.

IV. 1739. SIR JOHN SHAW, Baronet [1665], of Eltham Lodge aforesaid, and Coltshall, co. Suffolk, 2d but 1st surv. s. and h., *b.* 22 Nov., and *bap.* 19 Dec. 1728, at Eltham; *suc. to the Baronetcy*, 4 March 1738/9; matric. at Oxford (Trin. Coll.), 29 June 1745, aged 16: *cr.* M.A. 28 June 1748, and D.C.L. 12 June 1749; was Sheriff of Kent, 1753-54. He *m.* firstly, 4 or 26 Feb. 1749/50, Elizabeth, da. of William HEDGES, of Alderton, Wilts. She *d.* 3 and was *bur.* 12 Feb. 1750/1 at Eltham. He *m.* secondly, 17 Feb. 1752, Martha, da. and h. of John KENWARD, of Kenward park, in the parish of Yalding, co. Kent. He *d.* 18, and was *bur.* 26 June 1779, at Eltham, aged 51. Will pr. July 1779. His widow was *bur.* there 28 Oct. 1794, aged 64. Will pr. Nov. 1794.

V. 1779. SIR JOHN GREGORY SHAW, Baronet [1655], of Eltham lodge and of Kenward park aforesaid, 2d but 1st surv. s. and h., being 1st s. by the 2d wife, *b.* at Eltham, 25 July 1756; matric. at Oxford (Trin. Coll.), 26 Jan. 1774, aged 17; *cr.* M.A., 31 Oct. 1776; *suc. to the Baronetcy*, 18 June 1779. He *m.*, 9 March 1782, at St. Marylebone, Theodosia Margaret, yst. da. of John (MONSON), 2d BARON MONSON OF BURTON, by Theodosia, da. of John MADDISON. He *d.*, 28 Oct, 1831, at Kenward park aforesaid, aged 75. Will pr. Jan. 1832. His widow, who was *b.* 20 Sep. 1762, *d.* 24 Oct. 1847. Will pr. Nov. 1847.

VI. 1831. SIR JOHN KENWARD SHAW, Baronet [1665], of Kenward park aforesaid, 1st s. and h., *b.* 15 March 1783; ed. at Eton; matric. at Oxford (Trin. Coll.), 23 Oct. 1801, aged 18; *suc. to the Baronetcy*, 28 Oct. 1831; was Col. of the West Kent Militia, 1832-53. He *m.*, in 1809, Charlotte, 2d da. of William LLOYD, of Betchworth, Surrey. He *d.* s.p., 17 March 1857, at Paris, aged 74. His widow *d.* 12 Feb. 1870, in her 87th year, at her residence in Boulogne-sur-mer.

VII. 1857. SIR JOHN CHARLES KENWARD SHAW, Baronet [1665], of Kenward, near Tonbridge, co. Kent, nephew and h., being 1st s. and h. of Charles SHAW, Capt. R.N., by Frances Anne, da. of Sir Henry HAWLEY, 1st Baronet [1795], which Charles, who *d.* 2 May 1829, aged 43, was 2d s. of the 5th Baronet. He was *b.* posthumously, 8 June 1829, at Pembury, co. Kent (being twin with a younger brother); was ed. at Eton; matric. at Oxford (Merton Coll.), 15 March 1849, aged 19, and *suc. to the Baronetcy*, 17 March 1857. He *m.* firstly, 19 June 1860, at Pembury aforesaid, Maria, da. of Henry SPARKES, of Summerberry, in Shalford, co. Surrey. She *d.* 4 Sep. 1863, at Kenward aforesaid. He *m.* secondly, 15 Oct. 1868, at Pembury, Sophia Emma Anna Maria, 1st da. of John William FINCH, Capt. R.N., of Knights Place, in Pembury.

BROWNE:(a)

cr. 10 May 1665;

ex. 21 Jan. 1775.

I. 1665. "JOHN BROWNE, of Caversham, co. Oxford, Esq.," yr. s.,(b) being one of the nineteen children of George BROWNE,(c) of Caversham aforesaid (*bur.* 9 Feb. 1663/4, at St. Giles' in the Fields), by his 1st wife Ellinor, da. of Sir Richard BLOUNT, of Mapledurham, Berks, was *b.* about 1631, and was *cr. a Baronet*, as above, 10 May 1665. He *m.* (Lic. Fac. 10 May 1666, he aged 35 and unm.) Elizabeth VANDERSTECK, of Staines, co. Midx., widow, relict of William VANDERSTECK, formerly [1663] Elizabeth BRADLEY.

II. 1680? SIR ANTHONY BROWNE, Baronet [1665], of Caversham aforesaid, 1st s. and h., *suc. to the Baronetcy* on the death of his father, but *d.* unm., and was *bur.* 23 Dec. 1688, at St. Giles' in the Fields. Will dat. Dec. 1688.

III. 1688. SIR JOHN BROWNE, Baronet [1665], of Caversham aforesaid, br. and h., *suc. to the Baronetcy* in Dec. 1688. He *d.* s.p., probably unm. in or about 1692, before Dec. 1692.

IV. 1692? SIR GEORGE BROWNE, Baronet [1665], of Caversham aforesaid, br. and h., *suc. to the Baronetcy* in or about 1692; was an officer in the Austrian service. He *m.*, firstly, 2 May 1699, at Charter House Chapel, Midx, Gertrude MORLEY, of St. James', Westm., spinster. Her admon. as of St. Giles' in the Fields 2 July 1720 and 12 Jnne 1730. He *m.* secondly, 5 Feb. 1721/2, at Gray's Inn Chapel, Midx., Prudence, sister of Sir George THOROLD, 1st Baronet [1709], da. of Charles THOROLD, of Harmeston, co. Lincoln, by his 2d wife, Anne, da. of George CLARKE, of London. She, by whom he had no issue, *d.* 19 Dec. 1725, in Covent Garden, and was *bur.* at St. Andrew's, Undershaft, London. Will pr. 3 March 1725/6. He *d.* 20 and was *bur.* 24 Feb. 1729/30, at St. Paul's, Covent Garden. Will dat. 25 March 1715, pr. 16 March 1729/30.

V. 1730, to 1775. SIR JOHN BROWNE, Baronet [1665], of Sunning, Berks, 1st s. and h.; *suc. to the Baronetcy*, 20 Feb. 1729/30. He *d.* s.p., probably unm., 21 Jan. 1775, at Sunning aforesaid, when the *Baronetcy* became *extinct*. Will, in which he leaves all to his servant, Mary SMYTH, dat. 7 Jan., and pr. 2 March 1775.

RAWDON:

cr. 20 May 1665,

afterwards 1750-1868, BARONS RAWDON OF MOIRA [I.],

and 1761-1868, EARLS OF MOIRA [I.],

subsequently, 1816-1868, MARQUESSES OF HASTINGS;

ex. 10 Nov. 1868.

I. 1665. "GEORGE RAWDON,(d) of Moira, co. Down, in Ireland, Esq.," only s. and h. ap. of Francis RAWDON, of Rawdon in the parish of Guiseley, co. York (*bur.* there April 1668, aged 86), by Dorothy, da. of William

(a) A well worked pedigree of this nobly descended, but somewhat obscure family, is in the Rev. F. Brown's *Somersetshire Wills*, 3d series, p. 67.

(b) His elder br., Sir George Browne, K.B. [1661], who was *bur.* at Shefford, Berks, 7 Dec. 1678, left two daughters and coheirs (1) Winifred, *m.* Basil Brooke, of Madeley, Salop, and (2) Helen, who *m.* Henry Fermor, of Tusmore, Oxon, and was mother of Arabella Fermor, the *Belinda* in Pope's *Rape of the Lock*.

(c) He was s. and h. of the Hon. Sir George Browne, of Wickham, co. Kent, and Shefford, Berks, yr. s. of Anthony (Browne), 1st Viscount Montagu.

(d) Much of the information in this article has been kindly furnished by G. D. Burtchaell, of the office of arms, Dublin.

ALDBOROUGH, of Aldborough, was *b.* 1604, at Rawdon; ed. at Bradford and York; was Sec. to Edward, Lord Conway, Prin. Sec. of State in 1625, and was employed in the treaty at the Hague; emigrated to Ireland, and settled at Moira, co. Down; was M.P. [I.], for Belfast, 1639-49; M.P. [E.] for Down, Antrim and Armagh, 1659, and [I.] for Carlingford, 1661-66; distinguished himself in defeating Sir Phelim O'Neil and 8,000 rebels, at Lisburn, in Nov. 1641; was Governor of Carrickfergus, and P.C. [I.], 1660, and was *cr. a Baronet*, as above, 20 May 1665, possibly, both of England and Ireland.(a) He *m.* firstly (at his age of 35), in 1639, Ursula (or Anne), widow of Francis HILL, of Castle Eagle, co. Down, da. of Sir Francis STAFFORD, of Portglenore, co. Antrim, by his 2d wife Anne, da. of Farroll GROGAN. She *d.* s.p.s., at Brook hill, of consumption, aged 30. He *m.* secondly (at his age of 50), in Sep. 1654, Dorothy, 1st da. of Edward (CONWAY), 2d VISCOUNT CONWAY, by Frances, da. of Sir Francis POPHAM. She *d.* 1676. He *d.* 18, and was *bur.* 28 Aug. 1684, in the church of Lisburn. Admon., 16 April 1685 [I.]. Will dat. 19 Oct. 1683, to 31 July 1684, pr. 22 June 1722 [I.].

II. 1684. SIR ARTHUR RAWDON, Baronet [1665], of Moira aforesaid, 3d but only surv. s. and h.(b); *b.* 17 Oct. 1662; *suc. to the Baronetcy*, 18 Aug. 1684; was a zealous Protestant, and was attainted by the Irish Parl. of James II. in 1689; was Sheriff of co. Down, 1692, and M.P. [I.] for that county, 1692-93, and 1695 till his death. He *m.* (Lic. [I.], 15 Feb. 1681/2), Ellen, da. and h. of the Hon. Sir James GRAHAM, Gov. of Drogheda, by Isabella, 1st da. of John BRAMHALL, Archbishop of Armagh [1660-63], which James was 2d s. of William (GRAHAM), EARL OF MENTEITH AND STRATHERN [S.].(c) He *d.* 17 Oct. 1695, aged 33. His widow *d.* 17 March 1709/10, aged 47, and was *bur.* at St. Andrew's, Dublin. Admon. [I.], 20 Dec. 1710.

III. 1695. SIR JOHN RAWDON, Baronet [1665], of Moira aforesaid, only surv. s. and h., *b.* 1690; *suc. to the Baronetcy*, 17 Oct. 1695; was M.P. [I.] for co. Down, 1715 till his death in 1724. He *m.* 3 March 1716/7 (Lic. [I.] 1 March), Dorothy, 2d da. of Sir Richard LEVINGE, 1st Baronet [I. 1704], Chief Justice of the Common Pleas [I.], by his 1st wife, Mary, da. and coheir of Sir Gawen CORBYN, of London. He *d.* 2 Feb. 1723/4, aged 34, and was *bur.* at Moira. Will pr. [I.] 8 May 1724. His widow *m.* Charles COBBE, D.D., successively Bishop of Killala, 1720-26, Bishop of Dromore, 1726-32; Bishop of Kildare, 1732-43, and Archbishop of Dublin, 1742-65. She *d.* 12 Sep. 1733. Admon. [I.] 10 Nov. 1733.

IV. 1724. SIR JOHN RAWDON, Baronet [1665], of Moira aforesaid, 2d but 1st surv. s. and h., *b.* 17 March 1719/20; *suc. to the Baronetcy*, 2 Feb. 1723/4; ed. at Trin. Coll., Dublin; Sheriff of co. Down, 1749; LL.D. of Dublin, *honoris causa*, 1753; F.R.S., London. He *m.* firstly, 10 Nov. 1741, Helena, yst. da. of John (PERCEVAL), 1st EARL OF EGMONT [I.], by Catharine, da. of Sir Philip PARKER, 2d Baronet [1661]. She *d.* s.p.m. at the Hot Wells, Bristol, 11 June 1746. He *m.* secondly, 23 Dec. 1746, Anne, sister of Wills, 1st MARQUESS OF DOWNSHIRE [I.], da. of Trevor (HILL), 1st VISCOUNT HILLSBOROUGH [I.], by Mary, da. and coheir of Anthony ROWE. She was living when he was *cr.*, 9 April 1750, BARON RAWDON OF MOIRA, co. Down [I.], being subsequently *cr.* 30 Jan. 1762, EARL OF MOIRA [I.]. In these peerages

(a) The patent of the same date is included (probably in error), in the last of Irish Baronetcies given in the *Liber Munerum Hiberniæ* [pub. by Government in 1828], where, however, the place from which it was dated is given as *Westminster*, not (as in almost all other Irish cases), *Dublin*. See also vol. iii, p. 159, note "a," under "LANE." A warrant, dated 17 March 1664/5, to create George Rawdon "a Baronet of Ireland" exists among the *Calendars of State Papers* [E.], 1660-70.

(b) Of his two elder brothers (1) Edward, *b.* 1655; *d.* 1676; (2) John, *b.* 1656; *d.* 1677, both being killed in France.

(c) See an interesting article on the *Earls of Menteith*, by F. A. Blaydes, in *The Ancestor*, vol. iv, pp. 81-87 [1903], respecting a [groundless] claim of the Rawdon family to that Earldom.

this *Baronetcy* then *merged*, the 2d Earl (son and heir of the 1st Earl by his 3d wife, the heiress of the family of HASTINGS) being *cr.*, 13 Feb. 1817, MARQUESS OF HASTINGS; see *Peerage*. The *Baronetcy*, however, together with all the above named Dignities, became *extinct* on the death, 10 Nov. 1868, of the 4th Marquess, 5th Earl and Baron, and 8th Baronet.

JOCELYN:

cr. 8 June 1665;

afterwards, since 1778, EARLS OF RODEN [I.].

I. 1665. "ROBERT JOCELYN, of Hyde Hall [in Sawbridgeworth], co. Hertford, Esq.," 3d but 1st surv. s. and h. of Sir Robert JOCELYN, of the same, Sheriff of Herts, 1645-47 (*bur.* 3 May 1664 aged 64, at Sawbridgeworth), by Bridget, dau. of Sir William SMITH, of Hill Hall, co. Essex, was *bap.* 14 Jan. 1622/3, at Sawbridgeworth; suc. his father in May 1664, and was *cr. a Baronet*, as above, 8 June 1665; Sheriff of Herts, 1677-78. He *m.* in or before 1650, Jane, da. and coheir of Robert STRANGE, of Somerford, Wilts. She, by whom he had fourteen children, was *bur.* 29 March 1706 at Sawbridgeworth. He was *bur.* there 12 June 1712 in his 90th year. Will dat. 20 Feb. 1699, pr. 10 Feb. 1713/4.

II. 1712. SIR STRANGE JOCELYN, Baronet [1665], of Hyde Hall aforesaid, 1st surv. s. and h., *b.* in or before 1651; ed. at Queens' Coll., Cambridge; B.A., 1673; *suc. to the Baronetcy*, in June 1712. He *m.* in or before 1686, Mary, da. of Tristram CONYERS, of Copped Hall, in Epping, co. Essex, by Winifred, da. of Sir Gilbert GERARD, 1st Baronet [1620], of Flamberds. She *d.* at Hyde Hall, 19 and was *bur.* 24 May 1731, at Sawbridgeworth. He *d.* 3 and was *bur.* there 16 Sep. 1734. Will pr. 1734.

III. 1734. SIR JOHN JOCELYN, Baronet [1665], of Hyde Hall aforesaid, 2d but 1st surv. s. and h., *bap.* 4 Oct. 1689 at Sawbridgeworth; Barrister-at-Law; *suc. to the Baronetcy*, 3 Sep. 1734. He *d.* unm. at Hyde Hall, 1 Nov. 1741, aged 52. Will pr. 1741.

IV. 1741. SIR CONYERS JOCELYN, Baronet [1665], of Hyde Hall aforesaid, only surv. br. and h., being 6th s. of the 2d Baronet, *bap.* 19 July 1703 at Sawbridgeworth; is said to have taken the degree of M.D.; *suc. to the Baronetcy*, 1 Nov. 1741; Sheriff of Herts, 1745-46. He *d.* unm. 24 and was *bur.* 30 May 1778, at Sawbridgeworth. Will pr. 1778.

V. 1778. ROBERT (JOCELYN), 1st EARL OF RODEN [I.], 2d VISCOUNT JOCELYN AND BARON NEWPORT [I.], and 5th Baronet, cousin and h. male, being only s. and h. of Robert (JOCELYN), 1st VISCOUNT JOCELYN AND BARON NEWPORT [I.], sometime Lord Chancellor of Ireland, by his 1st wife, Charlotte, da. and coheir of (—) ANDERSON, of Worcester, which Robert was only s. and h. of Thomas JOCELYN, of Sawbridgeworth, 5th son of the 1st Baronet. He was *bap.* 31 July 1731; was M.P. [I.] for Old Leighlin, 1745-56; Auditor Gen. [I.] 1750; suc. to the peerage [I.] on the death of his father, 3 Dec. 1756; was *cr.* EARL OF RODEN [I.], 1 Dec. 1771, and *suc. to the Baronetcy*, 24 May 1778. See *Peerage*.

DUKINFIELD, *or* DUCKENFIELD:

cr. 16 June, 1665;

sometime, 1746-1758, DUKINFIELD-DANIEL;

ex. 24 Jan. 1858.

I. 1665. "ROBERT DUCKENFIELD, Junior, of Duckenfield Hall, co. Chester, Esq.," 1st s. and h. ap. of Robert DUCKINFIELD, *or* DUKINFIELD, of the same, a Colonel in the Parl. army, Governor of Chester, 1650, and one of the Council of the Lord Protector Cromwell (*d.* 18 Sep. 1689, in his 70th year), by his 1st wife, Martha, da. of Sir Miles FLEETWOOD, Receiver of the Court of Wards, was *b.* about 1642, being aged 21 in the Her. Visit. of Cheshire, 1663, and was v.p. *cr. a Baronet*, as above, 16 June 1665. He was Sheriff of Cheshire, 1674-75, and suc. to the family estates on the death of his father, 18 Sep. 1689. He *m.* firstly (Lic. Fac. 14 June 1665, he 23 and she about 18), Jane, da. of Sir Thomas ESTCOURT, of Chenston Pinkney, Wilts. She, by whom he had ten children, *d.* 19 Aug. 1678. He *m.* secondly, 7 Aug. 1683, at St. Leonard's, Shoreditch, Midx., Susanna, da. of Robert THOMPSON, of Culpho, co. Suffolk, and of London, Merchant, one of the Governors of the East India Company, br. of John, 1st BARON HAVERSHAM. He *d.* 6 Nov. 1729, in his 88th year, and was *bur.* in the Presbyterian chapel at Dukinfield. M.I. Will dat. 6 Sep. 1725. His widow, by whom he had fourteen more children, *d.* July 1742, aged 83, and was *bur.* in the Presbyterian Chapel in Cross street, Manchester.

II. 1729. SIR CHARLES DUKINFIELD, Baronet [1665], of Dukinfield aforesaid, 2d but 1st surv. s. and h. by 1st wife, *b.* 18 and *bap.* 29 Nov. 1670 at Ashton; admitted to Gray's Inn, 14 May 1692; *suc. to the Baronetcy*, 6 Nov. 1729. He *m.* firstly, 29 Sep. 1698, Mary, da. and coheir of John HOLYNSHED, of Macclesfield, by Joan, da. of [—] MOTTERSHED. She was *bur.* 21 March 1717/8, at Macclesfield. He *m.* secondly, 18 Dec. 1718, at Mobberley, co. Chester (settlmt. Oct. 1718), Sarah, only child of Hewit PARKER, of Mobberley aforesaid, by Sarah, sister of Sir Samuel DANIELL (who *d.* s.p. 24 Dec. 1726), only da. of Thomas DANIELL, both of Over Tabley. He *d.* 23 Feb. 1741/2, aged 71. His widow *d.* March 1745.

III. 1742. SIR WILLIAM DUKINFIELD, afterwards [1746-58] DUKINFIELD-DANIELL, Baronet [1665], of Dukinfield and Over Tabley aforesaid, 3d but 1st surv. s. and h.,(a) being 1st s. by the 2d wife; *b.* about 1725; *suc. to the Baronetcy*, 23 Feb. 1741/2: *took the additional name of Daniell*, by Act of Parl. 1746, on attaining his majority and succeeding to the estates of that family; Sheriff of Cheshire, 1750. He *m.*, in 1749, Penelope, 1st da. of Henry VERNON, of Hilton, co. Stafford, by Penelope, da. and coheir of Robert PHILIPS, of Newton, co. Warwick. He *d.* s.p.m.,(b) 12 Jan. 1758. Will dat. 8 Dec. 1756. His widow to whom, subject to the life interest of his daughter, he had devised the Dukinfield estates, *m.*, 7 Dec. 1759, as the second of his three wives, John ASTLEY, of Wem, Salop (a celebrated portrait painter), to whom she appointed the said estates. She, who had no issue by him (who survived her and *d.* at Dukinfield lodge, 14 Nov. 1787, aged 67), *d.* 31 Jan. 1762.

IV. 1758. SIR SAMUEL DUKINFIELD, Baronet [1665], of Bloomsbury, co. Midx., cousin and h. male, being 6th and yst. but only surv. s. of John DUKINFIELD, of Bristol, merchant, by Anne, da. of (—) ANDREWS, a sea captain and merchant of that city, which John (*b.* 12 Aug. 1677, and *d.* 1741), was 3d s. of the 1st Baronet, by his 1st wife. He was *b.* about 1716, and *suc. to the Baronetcy* (but to none of the estates), 12 Jan. 1758. He *m.*, 14 June 1759, Elizabeth, da. of Poulett WARNER, of Badmonsfield Hall, in Wickhambrook, co. Suffolk. He *d.* 15 May 1768, and was *bur.* in Bunhill fields, Midx., aged 52. Will dat. 14 Nov. 1767, pr. 21 July 1768. His widow *d.* 26 May 1803, in Bloomsbury square, aged 88. Will pr. 1803.

V. 1768. SIR NATHANIEL DUKINFIELD, Baronet [1665], of Sulham, Berks, cousin and h. male, being 1st surv. s. of Nathaniel DUKENFIELD, of London, merchant, sometime of Utkington, co. Chester, by his 2d wife, Margaret, da. of Thomas JOLLY, of Wigan, co. Lancaster, which Nathaniel (*b.* 1 and *bap.* 12 Jan. 1690, at Stockport, *d.* 2 May 1749, and *bur.* at Bunhill fields), was a yr. s. of the 1st Baronet, by his 2d wife. He was *b.* 13 June 1746; *suc. to the Baronetcy*, 15 May 1768; was Capt. in the 7th Dragoons, exchanging into the 32d Foot. He *m.*, 27 Feb. 1782, at Westerham, co. Kent, Katharine, only da. of John WARDE, of Squerries, in Westerham aforesaid, by his 2d wife, Kitty Anne, da. and h. of Charles HOSKYNS, of Croydon, Surrey. She *d.* 29 Sep. 1823, aged 67. He *d.* 20 Oct. 1824, aged 78. Will pr. 1824.

(a) Robert Dukinfield, 1st s. and h. ap., by the 1st wife, was *b.* 9 July 1707, but *d.* unm. v.p. 31 Dec. 1726.

(b) Henrietta, his only da., who had been insane for many years, *d.* unm. 29 Jan. and was *bur.* 3 Feb. 1771, at Rostherne, when (her mother being dead) the Dukinfield estates devolved on her step-father, John Astley, abovenamed, who, accordingly, was Sheriff of Cheshire, 1776-77, after whose death in 1787 they passed to his issue by his 3d and last wife.

VI. 1824. SIR JOHN LLOYD DUKINFIELD, Baronet [1665], of Sulham aforesaid, 2d but 1st surv. s. and h.,(a) *b.* 3 Feb. 1785, at Sulham; entered Rugby School, 1797; was an officer in the Grenadier Guards, served at Corunna, and was wounded, 1814, at Bergen-op-Zoom. He *d.* unm. 7 Dec. 1836, at Hyde Park Corner, aged 51. Will pr. Jan. 1837.

VII. 1836, to 1858. SIR HENRY ROBERT DUKINFIELD, Baronet [1665], of Mortimer, Berks, br. and h., *b.* 1 Jan. 1791, at Sulham aforesaid; ed. at Musselburgh, at Rugby, 1800 and at Eton; matric. at Oxford (Ch. Ch.), 26 Jan. 1809, aged 18; Student of Ch. Ch., 1809-16; B.A., 1813; M.A., 1816; in Holy Orders; Incumbent of Ruscombe, Berks, 1814-16; Vicar of Waltham St. Laurence and of St. Giles', Reading, 1816-34; Preb. of Salisbury, 1832-56; Vicar of St. Martin's in the Fields, Midx., 1834-48; *suc. to the Baronetcy*, 7 Dec. 1836. He *m.* 29 Aug. 1836, Jane, widow of Gen. Tilson CHOWNE, only da. of Sir James CRAUFURD, *afterwards* GREGAN-CRAUFURD, 2d Baronet [1781], by Maria Theresa, da. of Gen. the Hon. Thomas GAGE. He *d.* s.p. 24 Jan. 1858, at 33 Eaton Place, Pimlico, and was *bur.* at Kensal Green, Midx., aged 67, when the *Baronetcy* became *extinct*. His widow *d.* there 25 May 1884, in her 89th year.

LAWSON:

cr. 6 July 1665;

ex. Jan. 1834;

but *assumed* since Jan. 1877 as DE BURGH-LAWSON.

I. 1665. "JOHN LAWSON, of Brough [in Catterick], co. York, Esq.," 3d s. but h. male of Henry LAWSON, of the same (*d.* 1636), by Anne, da. of Robert HODGSON, of Hebburne, co. Durham, was *b.* about 1627, being aged 38 at the Her. Visit. of Yorkshire in 1665; was Capt. of Horse in the service of Charles I; suc. to the family estate on the death of his elder br. Henry LAWSON, of Brough, about 1644 (which was soon afterwards sequestrated, and in 1653 sold by the then Government, though subsequently, partially, recovered), and was *cr. a Baronet*, as above, 6 July 1665. He *m.* in or before 1660, Katharine, sister of Charles, 1st EARL OF CARLISLE, 3d da. of Sir William HOWARD, of Naworth, co. Cumberland, by Mary, da. of William (EURE), 4th BARON EURE OF WITTON. She *d.* 4 July 1668 and was *bur.* at Catterick. He *d.* 26 Oct. 1698 and was *bur.* there.

II. 1698. SIR HENRY LAWSON, Baronet [1665], of Brough aforesaid, 2d but 1st surv. s. and h., *b.* probably about 1663(b); *suc. to the Baronetcy*, 26 Oct. 1698. He *m.* in or before 1688, Elizabeth, da. of Robert KNIGHTLEY, of Offchurch, co. Warwick, by Anne, da. of Sir John PETTUS. He *d.* 9 May 1726. The will of Dame Elizabeth LAWSON is pr. 1735.

III. 1726. SIR JOHN LAWSON, Baronet [1665], of Brough aforesaid, 1st s. and h., *b.* about 1689; *suc. to the Baronetcy*, 9 May 1726. He *m.* in or before 1712, Mary, da. of Sir John SHELLEY, 3d Baronet, [1611], of Michelgrove, Sussex, by his 2d wife Mary, da. of Sir John GAGE, 4th Baronet [1622]. He *d.* at York 19 Oct. 1739, aged 50, and was *bur.* at Catterick.

(a) His elder br., Samuel George Dukinfield; *b.* at Sulham, Feb. 1784; entered Rugby School, 1797; Capt. 7th Light Dragoons; *d.* unm. and v.p., being drowned off the coast of Cornwall, 22 Jan. 1809.

(b) His eldest br. John Lawson, aged 14 in Aug. 1665, *d.* v.p. and unm. at Calais.

IV. 1739. SIR HENRY LAWSON, Baronet [1665], of Brough aforesaid, 1st s. and h., *b.* about 1712; *suc. to the Baronetcy*, 19 Oct. 1739. He *m.*, in or before 1742,(a) Anastasia, yst. da. of Thomas MAIRE, of Lartington, co. York, and of Hardwick, co. Durham, by Mary, da. of Richard FERMOR, of Tusmore, Oxon. She *d.* 5 Nov. 1764, and was *bur.* at Catterick. He *d.* 1 Oct. 1781, aged 69, and was *bur.* there. M.I. Will pr. March 1782.

V. 1781. SIR JOHN LAWSON, Baronet [1665], of Brough aforesaid, 1st s. and h., *b.* 2 (*i.e.* 13) Sep. 1744; *suc. to the Baronetcy*, 1 Oct. 1781. He was commander of a volunteer corps of infantry, which he raised in 1798. He *m.* firstly, 1 Aug. 1768, at St. Michael's le Belfry, York, Elizabeth, yst. da. and coheir of William SCARISBRICK, of Scarisbrick, co. Lancaster. She *d.* 10 June 1801, aged 52, and was *bur.* at Catterick. He *m.* secondly, 8 Feb. 1803, at St. Martin's, Covey street, York, Monica (*b.* 11 Aug. 1774), 1st da. of Miles STAPLETON, of Drax and Clint's, co. York, by his 2d wife, Mary, da. of Willoughby (BERTIE), 3d EARL OF ABINGDON. He *d.* s.p.m.s.,(b) 27 June 1811, at Brough Hall, aged nearly 67.

VI. 1811, to 1834. SIR HENRY LAWSON, Baronet [1665], of Brough Hall aforesaid, *formerly* HENRY MAIRE, of Lartington, co. York, br. and h.; *b.* 25 Dec. 1750; took the name of MAIRE, by royal licence in 1771, on inheriting the Lartington estate under the will of his maternal uncle, John MAIRE, but resumed that of LAWSON, on *inheriting the Baronetcy* and the Brough estate 27 June 1811.(c) He *m.* firstly, 2 Sep. 1773, Monica, 3d and yst. da. of Nicholas STAPLETON, *otherwise* ERRINGTON, of Carleton, co. York, by his 3d wife, Winifred, da. of John WHITE, of London. She, who was *b.* 1 May 1750, *d.* 8 Jan. 1800. He *m.* secondly, 18 May 1801, Catherine, da. of Henry FERMOR, of Worcester. He *d.* s.p. at Brough Hall, Jan. 1834, aged 83, when the *Baronetcy* became *extinct*. Will pr. June 1834.

The title was, however, assumed as under, in and after 1877.

VII, or VIII. 1877. "SIR HENRY DE-BURGH-LAWSON, Baronet [1665], of Gatherley Castle, co. York," according to his assumption of that dignity, in his notice, 16 Jan. 1877, "given at my castle of Gatherley aforesaid," wherein he states that he has "assumed the name of *De Burgh in addition* to my former name of *Lawson*," and that the issue male of Henry, 2d s. of the 1st Baronet, having become extinct by the death [in 1834], of the late Baronet, he himself is heir male of the body of

(a) Mary, the 1st da., was *b.* 26 July 1742. She was, as was all the family, of the old faith, and after being a nun at Bruges, *d.* unm. 1813, at Taunton, Somerset.

(b) Of his two daughters and coheirs, (1) Anastasia Maria, *b.* 25 May 1769; *m.* Thomas Strickland, *afterwards* Standish, of Sizergh, co. Westmorland, and *d.* 22 June 1807, leaving issue. (2) Elizabeth, *b.* 2 Nov. 1770; *m.*, 8 Jan. 1789, John Wright, of Kelvedon Hall, Essex, and *d.* 7 July 1812, leaving issue, of whom, William Wright, her 2d son, *b.* 8 May 1796, suc. to the Lawson estates in 1834, when he took the name of Lawson, and was *cr. a Baronet*, 8 Sep. 1841, as "Lawson, of Brough Hall, co. York."

(c) The estate of Lartington, which had formerly belonged to the family of Maire, then passed to his sister, Catharine, widow of John Silvertop, and was subsequently inherited by her 2d son, Henry Thomas Maire Silvertop, afterwards Witham.

she 1st Baronet, being "s. and h. of Henry Lawson, s. and h. of George Lawson, s. and h. of William Lawson, s. and h. of William Lawson, s. and h. of [the said] William Lawson,(a) 3d s. of the Sir John Lawson, who was created a Baronet,"(b) and that, consequently, he has assumed and hereby does assume the said Baronetcy. He, as above stated, was s. and h. of Henry LAWSON, who, according to the above pedigree, was heir to the Baronetcy in Jan. 1834, as 7th Baronet, but who did not assume the title, and who *d.* in 1854. He was *b.* 1817; suc. his father in 1854, and, about twenty-three years later, *assumed the Baronetcy* (as stated above), 16 Jan. 1877. He was a naval architect, and the inventor of several improvements in ironclad ships, etc. He *m.* firstly, in 1840, Mary, da. of A. STODDART, of Durham. She *d.* 1880. He *m.* secondly, in 1883, Fanny, widow of the Rev. George HERIOT, of Fellow Hills, co. Berwick. He *d.* of apoplexy, 1 Oct. 1892, at Gatherley Castle, aged 75. His widow living 1903.

(a) The 1st Baronet, John, appears to have had no less than seven sons, all of whom, excepting Henry, the 2d Baronet, appear to have *d. s.p.* William Lawson, the 4th son, from whom the claimant alleges himself to be derived, is said to have been a Priest. Five of these sons were living when the father entered his pedigree in the Visit. of Yorkshire, 1665, *viz.:* (1) John, aged 14; (2) Henry; (3) Charles; (4) William, and (5) Philip. The other sons (6) Ralph, and (7) Thomas, were born afterwards.

(b) In the "Chaos" to Foster's *Baronetage* [1883], this remarkable document is given in full, as under:—

"Know all whom this may concern that I, Henry Lawson, hitherto known as Henry Lawson, of Gatherley Castle, in the county of York, Esq., have taken and assumed the name of De Burgh in addition to my former surname of Lawson, and that I shall henceforth be known and sign myself by the name and designation of Henry De Burgh Lawson. And whereas His Majesty King Charles II, by his letters patent, bearing date 6 July 1665, conferred the rank, style, and title of a Baronet upon John Lawson, of Burgh Hall, near Catteryck, co. York, and the heirs male lawfully begotten of his body, and whereas the said Sir John Lawson, so created a Baronet as aforesaid, had issue by Catherine Howard, his lawful wife, three sons, namely, John Lawson, the eldest son, Henry Lawson, the 2d son, and William Lawson, the 3d son. That the said John Lawson, eldest son of the said Sir John Lawson died in the lifetime of his said father without heirs lawfully begotten of his body; that the said Henry Lawson, 2d son aforesaid succeeded his father in the said Baronetcy aforesaid. And whereas upon the death of the late Sir Henry Lawson of Burgh Hall aforesaid, Baronet, who died without heirs lawfully begotten of his body, all the heirs male lawfully begotten of the body of the said Henry Lawson, 2d son of the said Sir John Lawson, who was created a Baronet as aforesaid, became entirely extinct and ended. And whereas, I, the said Henry De Burgh Lawson, being the son and heir of Henry Lawson, son and heir of George Lawson, son and heir of William Lawson, son and heir of William Lawson, son and heir of the said William Lawson, 3d son of the said Sir John Lawson, who was created a Baronet as aforesaid, am now and stand the heir male lawfully begotten of the body of the said Sir John Lawson aforesaid, and am accordingly, by right of blood and inheritance, lawfully entitled to the said Baronetcy under the special [*sic*] limitations of the said original letters patent aforesaid, whereby the said Baronetcy was so created as aforesaid, as is fully set forth in my pedigree enrolled in Her Majestys High Court of Chancery on 11 Jan. in the present year of our Lord, 1877. And whereas in right of my said lineage aforesaid, as the heir male of the said Sir John Lawson, the 1st Baronet as aforesaid, lawfully begotten of his body and by virtue of the said limitations contained and set forth in the said original letters patent by which the said title was created as aforesaid, I the said Henry De Burgh-Lawson have assumed and hereby do assume as my lawful right to myself and the heirs male lawfully begotten of my body, the said Baronetcy, and I hereby make known that I shall hereafter from

VIII, or IX. 1892. SIR HENRY ALFRED STODDART DE-BURGH-LAWSON, Baronet(a) [1665], of Fond du Lac, in North America, 1st s. and h. by 1st wife; *b.* 1851; *suc. to the Baronetcy,*(a) 1 Oct. 1892.

TIRRELL, *or* TYRRELL:

cr. 20 July 1665;

ex. May 1714.

I. 1665. "PHILIP [but should be PETER] TYRRELL,(b) of Hanslape and [by grant from the King in 1663] Castlethorpe, Bucks, Esq.," 2d s. but eventually h. male of Sir Thomas TYRRELL, of Hanslape aforesaid, Colonel in the Parl. army, sometime (1659) a Commissioner of the Great Seal, but afterwards (1660) Justice of the Common Pleas (*d.* 8 March 1671/2, aged 78), by his 1st wife, Frances, da. of [—] SAUNDERS, was admitted to the Inner Temple, 1644, and was v.p. *cr. a Baronet,* as above, 20 July 1665. He *m.* firstly, Bridget, da. of Sir Edward ALTHAM, of Markhall in Latton, Essex, by Joan, da. of Sir John LEVENTHORPE, 1st Baronet [1622]. She *d.* s.p. He *m.* secondly (Lic. Dean of Westm. 28 Feb. 1664/5), Anne, da. of Carew RALEIGH, Gent. of the Privy Chamber (s. of the celebrated Sir Walter RALEIGH), by Philippa, relict of Sir Anthony ASHLEY, Baronet (so *cr.* 1622), da. of [—] WESTON. She was *bur.* 24 Jan. 1708, at Castlethorpe. He was *bur.* there 11 March 1710/1.

II. 1711, to 1714. SIR THOMAS TYRRELL, Baronet [1665], of Castlethorpe aforesaid, only s. and h., *b.* probably about 1670; admitted to the Inner Temple, 1686; matric. at Oxford (Queen's Coll.), 16 July 1687; *suc. to the Baronetcy* in March 1710/1. He *m.* in or before 1694, Dorothy, da. of Sir Giles EYRE, of Brickworth in Whiteparish, Wilts, one of the Justices of the Court of King's Bench (1689-95) by (presumably) his 1st wife, Dorothy (*d.* 1677) da. of John RYVES of Ranston, Dorset. He *d.* in Ireland, s.p.m.s., May 1714, and was *bur.* at Castlethorpe, when the *Baronetcy* became *extinct.* His widow *m.* Richard FREWEN, M.D. of Oxford, who *d.* 29 May 1761, aged 80.

BURDETT, *or* BURDET:

cr. 25 July 1665.

I. 1665. "FRANCIS BURDET, of Birthwaite, co. York, Esq.," only s. and h. of Francis BURDET, of the same, by Elizabeth, da. of Sir Ferdinando LEIGH, of Middleton, in that county, was *bap.* at Darton, co. York, 29 Sep. 1642; suc. his father in Feb. 1643/4; entered his pedigree in the Her. Visit. of Yorkshire in 1665, being then aged 22, and was *cr. a Baronet,* as above, 25 July 1665. He *m.* 21 Oct. 1669, at Darton, Frances, da. of (—) STEPHENSON, of Lincolnshire. She was *bur.* 11 June 1679, at Darton. He *d.* about 1719, aged about 77, having sold Birthwaite and other family estates.

---

the date of these presents be known by the name, rank, style and title of Sir Henry De-Burgh-Lawson, of Gatherley Castle, in the County of York, Baronet. Given at my Castle of Gatherley aforesaid on this 16 Jan. 1877.

HENRY DE BURGH-LAWSON.

Witness, John Bolton, Gentleman,
Waterford Lodge, Scarborough."

(a) According to the assumption of that dignity in 1877.

(b) See pedigree in Lipscomb's *Bucks,* vol. iv, p. 175.

II. 1719? SIR FRANCIS BURDET, *or* BURDETT, Baronet [1665], of York, 1st s. and h., *b.* 2 and *bap.* 21 Aug. 1675, at Darton; *suc. to the Baronetcy* about 1719. He *m.* firstly, 31 July 1710, at Charter House Chapel, Midx., Elizabeth, widow of William BARNHAM, da. and coheir of Charles WYNDHAM, of Stokesby, co. Norfolk. By her he had thirteen children. He *m.* secondly, before 1741, at York, where he then resided,(a) (—) da. of (—). He *d.* at Middleton, and was *bur.* 11 Sep. 1747, at Rothwell, near Leeds, aged 72. His widow *d.* 18 Nov. 1757, and was *bur.* at St. Mary's Castlegate, York.

III. 1747. SIR HUGH BURDETT, Baronet [1665], 2d but 1st surv. s. and h.(b) by 1st wife, was *b.* at Fulham Green, 18 Nov. 1715, and *bap.* at Fulham, Midx.; ed. at Charterhouse School; admitted Pensioner at Caius Coll., Cambridge, 1734, aged 18; Scholar, 1734-38; B.A., 1738; in Holy Orders; Incumbent of Wotton Underwood, Bucks, 1740-42; Rector of Newington, by Sittingbourne, Kent, 1742, till death in 1760; *suc. to the Baronetcy* in Sep. 1747. He *m.* Mary, da. of (—). He *d.* s.p. 8 Sep. 1760, aged nearly 45. Admon. 9 Oct. 1760 to his widow. Her will pr. May 1792.

IV. 1760. SIR CHARLES BURDETT, Baronet [1665], br. of the whole blood and h., *b.* 22 May and *bap.* 10 June 1728, at Chelsea, Midx.; Collector of Customs at the port of St. Augustine in East Florida, and one of the Privy Council there; *suc. to the Baronetcy,* 8 Sep. 1760, and was sometime (1777) of Acomb, co. York. He *m.* firstly, 29 Nov. 1756, Jane, da. of John HARRISON, a Pewterer, at York. She, by whom he had five children, *d.* there 3 Sep. 1764, aged 21. He *m.* secondly, 26 Sep. 1770, at Portsmouth in New Hampshire, America, Sarah, widow of (—) PHILLIPS, of Boston, in New England, da. of Joseph HALSEY, of Boston aforesaid. He *d.* 19 and was *bur.* 24 July 1803, at Paddington, Midx., aged 75. Will pr. 1803. His widow *d.* at Brighton, April 1812, and was *bur.* at Paddington, aged 77.

V. 1803. SIR CHARLES WYNDHAM BURDETT, Baronet [1665], 1st surv. s. and h. by 2d wife, *b.* 19 July and *bap.* 17 Aug. 1771, at St. Augustine's in East Florida aforesaid; sometime Major 56th Foot, and Lieut.-Col. in the Army; *suc. to the Baronetcy,* 19 July 1803; C.B. He *d.* unm. at Colombo, in the Isle of Ceylon, Dec. 1839, aged 68. Admon. June 1840.

VI. 1839. SIR CHARLES WENTWORTH BURDETT, Baronet [1665], nephew and h., being only s. and h. of Jerome BURDETT, Captain in the Army, by Elizabeth, da. of (—) BULLEYN, of Ireland, which Jerome (who was *b.* at York, 27 Sep. 1778, and *d.* in Jersey, March 1817) was yst. br. of the late and 4th s. of the 4th Baronet. He was *b.* 26 Sep. 1806; was Captain 41st Madras Native Infantry; *suc. to the Baronetcy* in Dec. 1839. He *m.* 31 Dec. 1834, at Buckland, co. Kent, his cousin, Harriet, da. of William Hugh BURGESS, of Birchin lane, London, Banker, by Elizabeth, da. of Sir Charles BURDETT, 4th Baronet [1665]. He *d.* 25 Aug. 1848, on his passage from India to England on sick leave, and was *bur.* at sea, aged nearly 42. His widow, who was *b.* 25 Nov. 1807, and *bap.* 28 Jan. 1808, at St. Edmund the King, London, *d.* at Kentish Town, St. Pancras, Midx., 21 July 1851. Admon. April 1852.

VII. 1848. SIR CHARLES WENTWORTH BURDETT, Baronet [1665], 1st s. and h., *b.* 4 Nov. 1835, at Seconderabad, in India; *suc. to the Baronetcy,* 25 Aug. 1848; sometime (1855-62) an officer in the 52d Foot, retiring as a Lieutenant. He *m.* in or before 1875, Grace, da. of the Rev. A. GRANT, of Napier in New Zealand. He *d.* there March 1890, aged 54. His widow living 1903.

(a) Wotton's *Baronetage,* 1741.

(b) His elder br., Francis Burdett, Capt. of Marines at the siege of Carthagena, 1741, was *b.* 19 April and *bap.* 13 May 1712, at St. Andrew's, Holborn; and *d.* v.p. and s.p. at Kingston in Jamaica.

VIII. 1890. SIR CHARLES GRANT BURDETT, Baronet [1665], of Dunedin, New Zealand, only s. and h., *b.* 1875; *suc. to the Baronetcy* in March 1890; ed. at Dunedin, passing the medical course there.

MOOR, MOORE, *or* MORE:

cr. 26 July 1665;

ex. 1678.

I. 1665, to 1678. "GEORGE MOORE, of Maids Morton, Bucks, Esq.," was "son of a Cutler in Fleet street, others say a Grocer, who got a great estate near Henley"(a); was *b.* about 1636, and was *cr. a Baronet,* as above, 26 July 1665. He sold, soon afterwards, the estate of Maids Morton. He *m.* firstly (Lic. Lond. 2 Jan. 1663/4, being then of St. Mildred's Poultry, aged 27, bach.), Elizabeth (then aged 23), sister of Sir George, and da. of Edward HUNGERFORD, of Cadenham, Wilts. He *m.* secondly (Lic. Vic. Gen. 22 April 1671), Frances (then aged 21), da. and coheir of Henry SANDFORD, of Bobbing Court, Kent, by Elizabeth his wife. He *d.* s.p.m. in 1678, and was *bur.* at Bobbing, Kent, when the *Baronetcy* became *extinct.* The will of "Sir George MORE, Baronet," was pr. in 1684. His widow *m.* Col. DIGBY, and subsequently as her 3d husband, Robert CRAWFORD, Gov. of Sheerness. She *d.* 18 Dec. 1693, and was *bur.* at Bobbing.

BARKER:

cr. 9 Sep. 1665;

ex. March 1706/7.

I. 1665. "ABEL BARKER, of Hambleton, *alias* Hambledon, Rutland, Esq.," s. and h. of Abel BARKER, of the same, by Elizabeth, da. of (—) WRIGHT, was *b.* about 1618; Sheriff of Rutland, 1646-47; M.P. thereof 1656-58, and 1679 till death in that year; purchased the estate of Lyndon, in that county, about 1661, where he erected a large mansion (completed in 1675), and was *cr. a Baronet,* as above, 9 Sep. 1665. He *m.* firstly, in or before 1648, Anne, da. of Sir Thomas BURTON, 1st Baronet [1622], of Stokeston, by Philippa, da. of the Hon. Henry BROOKE, s. of George, LORD COBHAM. He *m.* secondly, Mary, da. of Alexander NOEL, of Whitwell, Rutland, by whom he had no issue. He was *bur.* at Lyndon, 2 Sep. 1679, aged 63.

II. 1679, to 1707. SIR THOMAS BARKER, Baronet [1665], of Lyndon and Hambledon aforesaid, s. and h., by 1st wife, *b.* about 1648; was Sheriff of Rutland, 1670-71 and 1680-81; *suc. to the Baronetcy* in Sep. 1679, entered his pedigree in the Visit. of Rutland, 1681, being then aged 33 and unm. He *d.* s.p.m. (presumably unm.), and was *bur.* at Lyndon, 22 March 1706/7, when the *Baronetcy* became *extinct.*(b) Will pr. Nov. 1708.

(a) Le Neve's, MS. *Baronetage.*

(b) The Lyndon and other estates devolved on the descendants of his grand uncle, Samuel Barker, of North Luffenham.

OGLANDER:

cr. 12 Dec. 1665;

ex. 8 April 1874.

I. 1665. "SIR WILLIAM OGLANDER, of Nunwell, in the Isle of Wight, Hants, Knt.," 2d but 1st surv. s. and h.[a] of Sir John OGLANDER, of the same, Dep. Gov. of the Isle of Wight, a great sufferer for the Royal cause, by Frances, da. of Sir George MORE, of Loseley, Surrey, was *b.* about 1611[a]; admitted to Gray's Inn, 1 Nov. 1633; suc. his father 28 Nov. 1655; was M.P. for Yarmouth, April 1640 till void; for Newport, Isle of Wight, 1660 and 1661 till death in 1670; Dep. Gov. of that island; was *Knighted* 4 July 1665, and was, a few months later, in consideration of his own and his father's loyalty, *cr. a Baronet*, as above, 12 Dec. 1665. Sheriff of Hants, 1667, but did not act. He *m.* Dorothy, da. of Sir Francis CLARKE, of Hitcham, Bucks, by Grizell, da. of Sir David WOODROFFE, of Poyle, Surrey. He *d.* in 1670, before Nov. Will pr. Feb. 1670/1. The will of his widow pr. Dec. 1702.

II. 1670. SIR JOHN OGLANDER, Baronet [1665], of Nunwell aforesaid, 2d but 1st surv. s. and h., *b.* probably about 1642; matric. at Oxford (Wadham Coll.), 8 Dec. 1658; admitted to the Middle Temple, 1660; *suc. to the Baronetcy* in 1670. He *m.* (Lic. Vic. Gen., 6 May 1668, he being then of Brading, Hants, about 26, bachelor), Mary (then about 20), da. and coheir of William WEBB, of Totteridge, Herts, Alderman of London. He *d.* in or before 1683. Will pr. June 1683. The will of his widow pr. Jan. 1688/9.

III. 1683? SIR WILLIAM OGLANDER, Baronet [1665], of Nunwell aforesaid, only s. and h., *b.* about 1680; matric. at Oxford (St. Edm. Hall) 11 April 1695, aged 15; *suc. to the Baronetcy* in or before 1683. He *m.* in 1699, Elizabeth, da. of Sir John STRODE, of Parnham in Beminster, Dorset, by his 2d wife, Anne, DOW. BARONESS POULETT OF HINTON, 2d da. and coheir of Sir Thomas BROWNE, 2d Baronet [1621], of Walcot. She *d.* 1721. He *d.* 10 Aug. 1734. Will pr. 1734.

IV. 1734. SIR JOHN OGLANDER, Baronet [1665], of Nunwell aforesaid, only s. and h., *b.* about 1704; matric. at Oxford (St. John's Coll.), 20 Oct. 1721, aged 17; *suc. to the Baronetcy*, 10 Aug. 1734. By the death s.p. of his cousin (—) STRODE, of Parnham, he became heir to his maternal grandfather, Sir John STRODE, and inherited the estates of that family in Dorset and Somerset. He *m.*, in 1729, Margaret, da. of John COXE, of Stoneaston, Somerset. He *d.* 11 May 1767. Will pr. June 1767.

V. 1767. SIR WILLIAM OGLANDER, Baronet [1665], of Nunwell and Parnham aforesaid, 1st s. and h., *b.* 8 July 1733; matric. at Oxford (New Coll.), 19 Sep. 1751, aged 18; B.A. 1754; Fellow of All Souls', Oxford; B.C.L., 1760; *suc. to the Baronetcy*, 11 May 1767; was Sheriff of Hants, 1782-83. He *m.*, 21 Dec. 1765, Sukey, da. of Peter SEALE, of Testwood, Hants, by his 2d wife, Susanna, da. of Sir John STONHOUSE, 7th Baronet [1628]. She *d.* 18 July 1804 and was *bur.* at Beminster aforesaid. He *d.* 5 Jan. 1806, and was *bur.* there in his 73d year. Will pr. 1806.

VI. 1806. SIR WILLIAM OGLANDER, Baronet [1665], of Nunwell and Parnham aforesaid, 2d but 1st surv. s. and h., *b.* 13 Sep. 1769, at Parnham; matric. at Oxford (New Coll.), 3 March 1787, aged 17; B.A., 1790; *suc. to the Baronetcy*, 5 Jan. 1806; was M.P. for Bodmin, 1807-12. Sheriff of Dorset, 1817-18. He *m.* 24 May 1810, at St. Geo. Han. sq., Maria Anne, 1st da. of George Henry (FITZROY), 4th DUKE OF GRAFTON, by Charlotte Maria, da. of James (WALDEGRAVE), 2d EARL WALDEGRAVE. He *d.* 17 Jan. 1852, aged 82, at Parnham aforesaid. Will pr. March 1852. His widow, who was *b.* 3 Nov. 1785, *d.* 12 May 1855, at Parnham. Admon. March 1856.

(a) George Oglander, the 1st son, *d.* unm. and v.p. of the small-pox at Caen, in Normandy, 11 July 1632, aged 22; John Oglander, the 3d son, matric. at Oxford (New Coll.), 28 June 1633, aged 21.

VII. 1852, to 1874. SIR HENRY OGLANDER, Baronet [1665], of Nunwell and Parnham aforesaid, 1st s. and h., *b.* 24 June 1811, at Marylebone, Midx.; ed. at Winchester; matric. at Oxford (Ch. Ch.), 29 May 1829, aged 17; *suc. to the Baronetcy*, 17 Jan. 1852; Sheriff of Dorset, 1854; Captain of the 4th Isle of Wight Rifle Volunteers, 1860. He *m.*, 27 Nov. 1845, Louisa, 6th da. of Sir George William LEEDS, 1st Baronet [1812], of Croxton Park, co. Cambridge, only da. by his 2d wife, Eleanor, da of Owsley ROWLEY. He *d.* s.p. 8 April 1874 at Nunwell aforesaid, in his 63d year, when the *Baronetcy* became *extinct*. His widow *d.* 22 April 1894.

Family Estates.—These, in 1876, consisted of 3,867 acres in Hants [*Qy.* Isle of Wight], 3,059 in Dorset, and 953 in Somerset. *Total.*—7,879 acres, valued at £9,485 a year.

TEMPLE:

cr. 31 Jan. 1665/6;

ex. 27 Jan. 1698/9.

I. 1666, to 1699. "WILLIAM TEMPLE, of Sheene, co. Surrey, Esq., President for His Majesty at Bruxells, afterwards Embassador to the States General of the United Provinces, and one of His Majesty's Plenipotentiaries at the treaty of Nimmegen," [*i.e.* Nimeguen] 1st s. and h.[a] of Sir John TEMPLE, Master of the Rolls [I.] (*d.* 14 Nov. 1677), by Mary, da. of John HAMMOND, of Chertsey, Surrey, physician, was *bap.* 30 April 1628, at St. Anne's, Blackfriars, London; ed. at Bishops Stortford school; admitted to Emmanuel Coll., Cambridge (as Fellow Commoner), 13 Aug. 1644, but left, without any degree, 1648; was, possibly, the "(—) Temple," son of a Knight, who matric. at Oxford (Balliol Coll.), 19 March 1648/9; M.P. [I.] for Carlow, 1660, and for co. Carlow, 1661-63; settled at East Sheen, near Richmond, in 1663, in which year he went on an unsuccessful mission to the Prince Bishop of Munster; was made Envoy to Brussels in 1665, and *cr. a Baronet*, as above, 31 Jan. 1665/6. The triple alliance between England, Holland and Sweden was effected mainly by him, and he was soon afterwards, 1668, made Ambassador to the Hague, but was recalled in 1670, though again sent there in 1674, when he brought about the marriage, in 1677, of William of Orange with Mary, afterwards [1689], King and Queen of England. He was M.P. for Northampton, Oct. till void in Nov. 1678; and for Cambridge Univ., 1679-81. He took part in, but disapproved of the treaty of Nimeguen in 1679, in which year he returned to England. Was a member of the Privy Council, which body had been revived under his auspices, 21 April 1679, but was struck off the list 24 Jan. 1680/1, after which date he took no part in politics, but devoted himself to his "*Memoirs*" and other writings. By the death of his father, 23 Nov. 1677, he suc. him as Master of the Rolls [I.], but obtained licence for absence, appointing a deputy, and finally resigning the post, 29 May 1696. He removed from Sheen to Moor Park, in Farnham, Surrey, in 1680, where in 1689 he had, as his *amanuensis*, Jonathan Swift (then aged 22), the well-known author. He *m.*, 31 Jan. 1654/5,[b] Dorothy, sister of Sir John OSBORN, 1st Baronet [1662], da. of Sir Peter OSBORN, of Chicksands, Beds. (who defended Guernsey for Charles I), by Dorothy, da. of Sir John DANVERS, of Dauntsey, Wilts. She,[c] who was *b.* at Chicksands in 1627, *d.* at Moor park, and was *bur.*

(a) The 2d son, Sir John Temple, was father of Henry, 1st Viscount Palmerston [I.], a title which became extinct, 18 Oct. 1865.

(b) This date is given in the *Dict. Nat. Biogr.* The register of St. Giles' in the fields shew that the intention of marriage of "William Temple, Esq. and Miss Dorothy Osborne," was dated 9, and the certificate of publication, 14 Dec. 1654, but there is, apparently, no entry of the marriage itself, which, presumably, took place elsewhere.

(c) The original "Love letters of Dorothy Osborn to Sir William Temple," 1652-54 (first brought into notice by Macaulay's *Essay on Sir William Temple*), have been deposited, since 1891, in the British Museum. They were first published in 1888.

7 Feb. 1694/5, in Westm. Abbey, in her 66th year, according to her M.I. He *d.* at Moor Park, s.p.m.s.,[a] 27 Jan., and was *bur.* with his wife, 1 Feb. 1698/9, aged 70, when the *Baronetcy* became *extinct*. Will dat. 8 March 1694/5, pr. 29 March 1699.

SWAN:

cr. 1 March 1665/6;

ex. 7 April 1712.

I. 1666. "SIR WILLIAM SWAN,[b] of [Hook Place, in] Southfleet, co. Kent, Knt.," and of Denton, in that county, 1st s. and h. of Sir Thomas SWAN, of the same (*d.* 1639), by Cecilia (*m.* 22 Dec. 1630), da. of Sir John CLERKE, of Forde, in Wrotham, Kent, was *bap.* 6 Dec. 1631, at Southfleet; *Knighted* at Rochester, 28 May 1660;[c] and was *cr. a Baronet*, as above, 1 March 1665/6. He *m.*, in or before 1657, Utricia, *otherwise* Hester, sister of Sir Thomas OGLE, Gov. of Chelsea Hospital, da. of John OGLE, of Pinchbeck, co. Lincoln, by Elizabeth, da. of Cornelius DE VRIES, of Dordrecht, in Holland. He was *bur.* 9 Oct. 1680, at Southfleet, in his 49th year. Will dat. 5 Oct. 1680, pr. 3 Feb 1680/1, by William SWAN, uncle and executor. His widow *d.* 26 and was *bur.* 28 Feb. 1712, at Southfleet. M.I.

II. 1680, to 1712. SIR WILLIAM SWAN, Baronet [1666], of Southfleet aforesaid, and subsequently of Greenhithe in Swanscombe, co. Kent, only s. and h., *bap.* 17 March 1666/7, at Southfleet; *suc. to the Baronetcy* in Oct. 1680. He *m.* 30 July 1696, at St. James', Duke's place, London, Judith HOWE, of St. Andrew's, Holborn, spinster. He *d.* s.p. 7 and was *bur.* 12 April 1712, at Southfleet, aged 45, when the *Baronetcy* became *extinct*.[d] Will dat. 28 Nov. 1702, pr. 5 May 1712, by the widow and universal legatee. She *d.* at Dorfield in Greenhithe aforesaid, 19 and was *bur.* 24 April 1722, at Southfleet. Will pr. 1722.

(a) His last surv. son, John Temple, who, in 1684, when in Paris, received a curious "Diploma" of Nobility under the Common Seal of the College of Arms, London (see *Her. and Gen.* iii, 406), was made Paymaster Gen., and 12 April 1689, Sec. of State for War. He, however, committed suicide a few days later, leaving two daughters, viz.: (1) Elizabeth, *m.* her first cousin, John Temple, of Roundwood, co. Wicklow, and Moor Park abovenamed, (*bap.* 28 March 1680), who *d.* s.p.m.s., Feb. 1742, leaving four daughters and coheirs; (2) Dorothy, *m.* Nicholas Bacon, of Shrubland, Suffolk.

(b) Most of the information in this article has been kindly given by Thomas Collyer-Fergusson, of Wombwell Hall, near Gravesend and Ightham Mote, Ivy Hatch, near Sevenoaks, the present owner of Hook Place, in Southfleet.

(c) He is spoken of as "Esq." in the baptisms in the Southfleet registers in 1657, and is not to be confounded with Sir William Swan, *Knighted* at Breda by Charles II in 1649, a Capt. in Holland, and afterwards Envoy to Hamburgh, whose will was pr. Nov. 1678.

(d) John Swan, of Cambridge, upholsterer, who *d.* s.p. 1900, was "reputed to be a Baronet, but whether under the patent of 1 March 1665/6, or otherwise, does not appear. His father, of the same name, had the same business before him. Several of the family dwelt in Madingley, and are buried there." [*Ex inform.* H. Gough].

SHIRLEY:

cr. 6 March 1665/6;

ex. 1705.

I. 1666. "ANTHONY SHIRLEY,[a] of Preston [near Brighton], co. Sussex, Esq.," 1st s. and h. of Thomas SHIRLEY, of the same (*bur.* there 20 May 1654), by Elizabeth, da. and h. of Drew STAPLEY, of London, was *b.* 5 and *bap.* 8 July 1624, at Preston; matric. at Oxford (Mag. Hall), 14 July 1642, aged 14; was in the commission of peace for the Commonwealth, being styled in 1655, "a very honest gentleman"; was M.P. for Arundel, 1654-55; for Sussex, 1656-58; for Steyning, 1659, and was *cr. a Baronet*, as above, 6 March 1665/6; was Sheriff of Sussex (but did not act), 1667. He *m.* in or before 1651, Anne, 1st da. of Sir Richard ONSLOW, of West Clandon, Surrey, by Elizabeth, da. and h. of Arthur STRANGWAYS, of Durham. He was *bur.* 22 June 1683, at Preston, in his 59th year.

II. 1683. SIR RICHARD SHIRLEY, Baronet [1666], of Preston aforesaid, only s. and h.; *b.* probably about 1655: *suc. to the Baronetcy*, in June 1683. He *m.*, 13 March 1676/7, at St. Leonard's, Shoreditch, (Lic. Vic. Gen. 10), Judith (then about 17), sister of Sir James BATEMAN, da. of Joas BATEMAN, of London, merchant, by Judith his wife. He was *bur.* 30 March 1692 at Preston. Admon. 25 April 1692 in the Archdeaconry Court at Lewes. His widow *m.* Sir Henry HATSELL, one of the Barons of the Exchequer, 1697—1702 (who *d.* April 1714, aged 73), and was herself *bur.*, with her 1st husband, 4 June 1729 at Preston. Will dat. 10 Jan. 1728, pr. 9 June 1729.

III. 1692, to 1705. SIR RICHARD SHIRLEY, Baronet [1666], of Preston aforesaid, 1st s. and h., *b.* about 1680; *suc. to the Baronetcy*, in March 1692. He *d.* unm. in 1705,[b] when the *Baronetcy* became *extinct*. Will dat. 21 July 1703, pr. 28 July 1705.

DIGGS:

cr. 6 March 1665/6;

ex. 1672.

I. 1666, to 1672. "MAURICE DIGGS, of Chilham Castle, co. Kent, Esq.," 1st s. and h. ap. of Thomas DIGGS,[c] of the same (who survived him and *d.* in 1687), by Mary (*m.* 17 Nov. 1631), da. of Sir Maurice ABBOT, sometime (1638-39) Lord Mayor of London (br. to George ABBOT, Archbishop of Canterbury), was *b.* probably about 1633; matric. at Oxford (Wadham Coll.), 14 Nov. 1650; admitted to Gray's Inn, 21 Oct. 1652, and was v.p. *cr. a Baronet*, as above, 6 March 1665/6. He *m.* firstly, Bennet, sister of Sir Basil DIXWELL, 1st Baronet [1660], da. of Mark

(a) See Shirley's *Stemmata Shirleiana*.

(b) His only br. Anthony Shirley, *bap.* 10 May 1683, *d.* when at school at Eton 1694. Of his surv. sisters and coheirs (1) Anne, *m.* (Lic. 26 Dec. 1698) Robert Western, of Seaber Hall, Essex, and of London, merchant (who *d.* June 1728), and *d.* s.p.m. in 1712; (2) Judith, *d.* unm.; (3) Mary, *m.* firstly, Thomas Western, of Rivenhall, Essex (who *d.* 1 April 1733), by whom she had issue, who inherited the estate of Preston, which was sold in 1793 by her great grandson, Charles Callis (Western), Baron Western of Rivenhall. She *m.* secondly, John Brydges, of Cobham (who *d.* 14 Feb. 1763), and *d.* 1747.

(c) This Thomas was s. and h. of Sir Dudley Diggs, of Chilham Castle aforesaid, sometime, 1636-39, Master of the Rolls.

DIXWELL, of Broome, co. Kent, by Elizabeth, da. of Matthew READ, of Folkestone. He *m.* secondly, 1 July 1661, at St. Barth. the Great, London, Judith, da. and coheir of George ROSE, of Eastergate, Sussex. He *d.* s.p. and v.p. in 1672, when the *Baronetcy* became *extinct*. Will, in which he directs to be *bur.* by his 1st wife, dat. April 1667, pr. April 1672. His widow *m.*, before 1674, Daniel SHELDON, of Ham Court, Surrey, and was *bur.* 26 July 1689, at St. Paul's, Covent Garden.

GLEANE:

cr. 6 March 1665/6;

ex. 10 June 1745.

I. 1666. "PETER GLEANE, of Hardwick, co. Norfolk, Esq.," 1st s. and h. of Thomas GLEANE,(a) of the same (*d.* 27 Jan. 1660, aged about 70), by Elizabeth, da. and coheir of Thomas BREWSE, was *cr. a Baronet*, as above, 6 March 1665/6. He was M.P. for Norfolk, 1679-81. He is said to have "ruined his fortune by his fidelity."(a) He *m.*, about 1650, Penelope, 3d da. and coheir of Sir Edward RODNEY, of Rodney Stoke, Somerset, by Frances, da. of Sir Robert SOUTHWELL, of Woodrising, Norfolk. She was *bur.* 20 Feb. 1689, at Hardwick He was *bur.* there 7 Feb. 1694/5.

II. 1695. SIR THOMAS GLEANE, Baronet [1666], of Hardwick aforesaid, 1st s. and h.; *b.* probably about 1650(b); *suc. to the Baronetcy* in Feb. 1694/5; appears to have completed the ruin of the family, and was a prisoner "in very great poverty" in the Fleet Prison, 21 Dec. 1698.(c) He *m.* firstly, in or about 1672 (—), da. of Captain MAPES, of Rollesby, Norfolk. He *m.* secondly (—), da. of (—) CHAMBERLAYNE, but by her had no issue. He was living Dec. 1698.

III. 1700? SIR PETER GLEANE, Baronet [1666], s. and h. by 1st wife, *b.* about 1672; ed. at Wymondham School, Norfolk; admitted 12 Feb. 1688/9, aged 16, to Caius Coll., Cambridge, as Pensioner; Scholar, 1689-96; B.A., 1693; *suc. to the Baronetcy* on the death of his father; was a Proctor in the Prerog. Court of Canterbury. He *m.* firstly, in or before 1696, (—), da. of Dr. PETERS, of Canterbury. He *m.* secondly (—), widow of (—) MANGER, but by her had no issue. He *d.* before 1741.(d).

IV. 1735? to 1745. SIR PETER GLEANE, Baronet [1666], 1st s. and h., *b.* about 1696; *suc. to the Baronetcy* on the death of his father, before 1741. He *m.* Johanna SKINNER. He *d.* s.p. 10 June 1745, aged 49, when the *Baronetcy* became *extinct*.

(a) See *East Anglian N. & Q.*, vol. iii, p. 24, for an account of this family. This Thomas was s. and h. of Sir Peter Gleane, an eminent merchant of Norwich, Mayor of that city in 1615, whose will was pr. Feb. 1633/4. See also *N. & Q.*, 2d s, vols. viii and ix.

(b) His brother, Rodney Glean, was born at Pilton, Somerset, in 1652, being admitted, 10 Feb. 1668/9, to Caius College, Cambridge, when aged 16. He *d.* unm., and was *bur.* at Hardwick.

(c) See a letter of his in *East Anglian N. & Q.*, vol. iv, p. 18.

(d) Wotton's *Baronetage*, edit. 1741.

PACKE:

said to have been *cr.* 29 March 1666;

but, apparently, not a valid creation.

I. 1666. CHRISTOPHER PACKE, of Prestwold, co. Leicester, s. and h. ap. of Sir Christopher PACKE, of the same, some time, 1654-55, Lord Mayor of London and a member of Cromwell's *House of Lords* (*d.* 17 May 1682, aged about 84), by his 2d wife, Anne, da. of Simon EDMONDS, of Howell, co. Lincoln, was *b.* about 1642, and received, it is said, a *Baronetcy*, 29 March 1666, which, however, was apparently not a valid creation. He *m.* (Lic. Vic. Gen., 19 April 1665, he about 23 and she 18) Jane, da. of Sir Gervase CLIFTON, 1st Baronet [1611], by his 6th wife, Jane, da. of Anthony EYRE, of Rampton. He *d.* 8 Sep. 1699, leaving male issue, but neither he nor they ever assumed the style of a Baronet.

NELTHORPE:

cr. 10 May 1666;

ex 22 Nov. 1865.

I. 1666. "JOHN NELTHORPE, of Gray's Inn, co. Middlesex, Esq.," 2d and yst. s. of Richard NELTHORPE, of Scawby and Glamford Briggs, co. Lincoln, by Ursula, da. of Martin GROSVENOR, of Messingham, was *b.* 1614; admitted, 30 April 1631, to St. John's Coll., Cambridge, aged 16, and on 19 Nov. 1634, to Gray's Inn,(a) where, in the study of the Law, he spent the greater part of his future life, and was *cr. a Baronet*, as above, 10 May 1666, with a spec. rem., failing issue male of his body, to his nephew, Goddard NELTHORPE. He, who founded a grammar school at Scawby and at Glamford Briggs, *d.* unm. in Sep. or Oct. 1669, aged 55, and has a monument in the church of St. James', Clerkenwell.(b) Will dat. 11 to 19 Sep., pr. 5 Oct. 1669.(c)

II. 1669. SIR GODDARD NELTHORPE, Baronet [1666], of Clerkenwell, co. Midx., nephew of the above, being 2d s. of his elder br., Edward NELTHORPE, of Scawby aforesaid and Barton-on-Humber (aged 80 in 1684, *d.* between Dec. 1684 and Oct. 1686), by Magdalen, da. of Henry SANDWITH, of Barrow, was *b.* probably about 1630,(d) and *suc. to the Baronetcy*, according to the spec. rem. in the creation thereof, on his uncle's death in Sep. or Oct. 1669. He *m.* in or before 1659, Dorothy, widow of Nicholas POULTENEY, of Misterton, co. Leicester, da. of Hugh HENNE, of Rooksnest, in Dorking, Surrey, by Catherine, da. and h. of (—) BICKERSTAFF. He *d.* 22 and was *bur.* 28 Jan. 1703/4, at St. James', Clerkenwell. Will dat. 11 July 1693, pr. May 1704. His widow was *bur.* there 19 Oct. 1715. Will pr. Jan. 1715/6.

(a) His admission is as "John Nelthorpe, 2d son of Richard N., of Glanfordbridge, co. Lincoln, Esq.," while on the same date was admitted "John Nelthorpe, of Beverley, co. York, Esq."

(b) There appears, however, to be no record of his burial in the parish register.

(c) In it he gives "to my very dear friend, Mrs. Mary Langham, da. of Sir James Langham," a jewel of £500 and several other bequests, "in memory of him who truly loved her," as also "31 angels given me by my father to be presented to her, if she became my wife."

(d) His eldest br. Richard Nelthorpe (who suc. to the Scawby estate, and who was *bur.* there 1 March 1705/6), was *bap.* at Scawby 19 Nov. 1628, while a yr. br., John, was *bap.* there 26 May 1633.

III. 1704. SIR MONTAGU NELTHORPE, Baronet [1666], of Saxby, co. Lincoln, grandson and h., being 1st s. and h. of Henry NELTHORPE, by Anne, da. and h. of Nathaniel HOBSON, of Syston, co. Lincoln, which Henry (*b.* 30 July, and *bap.* 18 Aug. 1661, at St. James's, Clerkenwell, *bur.* there 26 Nov. 1698) was 1st surv. s. and h. ap. of the late Baronet, but *d.* v.p. He *suc. to the Baronetcy* on the death of his grandfather, 22 Jan. 1703/4. He *m.*, 7 Feb. 1716/7, at St. Paul's Cathedral, London (Lic. Fac.), Elizabeth, da. and h. of Henry COXWELL, of Turks Dean., co. Gloucester, by Leana, sister and h. of Sir William DODWELL. She *d.* in 1718. He *d.* at his lodgings at Hampstead, 21 Feb., and was *bur.* 1 March 1721/2, at St. James's, Clerkenwell.(a) Will dat. 23 Dec. 1721, pr. 1723.

IV 1722. SIR HENRY NELTHORPE, Baronet [1666], of Turvile Heath in Turvile, Bucks, only s. and h., *b.* about 1717; *suc. to the Baronetcy*, 21 Feb. 1721/2. He *d.* 16, and was *bur.* "from Rackett Court, Fleet street," 25 March 1729, at St. James's, Clerkenwell, aged 11. Admon. 2 April 1729, and again 14 Jan. 1748/9.

V. 1729. SIR HENRY NELTHORPE, Baronet [1666], of Barton-on-Humber, co. Lincoln, uncle and h., being yr. br. of the 3d Baronet; *suc. to the Baronetcy*, 16 March 1728/9; Sheriff of Lincolnshire, 1741. He *m.* firstly, Joan, sister of Thomas SEAMAN, of St. Andrew's, Suffolk. She *d.* s.p.m., and was *bur.* 17 July 1740, at St. James's, Clerkenwell. He *m.* secondly (settlement, 7 Nov. 1740), Elizabeth, widow of Joseph Woolmer, of Castlethorpe, co. Lincoln, da. of the Rev. Richard BRANSTON, of Gainsborough. He *d.* 28 June 1746. Admon. 18 Aug. 1746 and 13 Feb. 1768. His widow *d.* in or before 1768. Admon. 8 Feb. 1768.

VI. 1746. SIR JOHN NELTHORPE, Baronet [1666], of Barton aforesaid, and afterwards of Scawby, co. Lincoln, only s. and h. by 2d wife, *b.* 5 March 1745/6; *suc. to the Baronetcy* 28 June 1746; matric. at Oxford (Trin. Coll.), 20 Feb. 1764, aged 18; *cr.* M.A., 10 March 1768; Sheriff of Lincolnshire, 1767-68. He *m.* in 1772, Anna Maria Charlotte, da. of Andrew WILLOUGHBY (said to have been sent by the Jacobite party on an embassy to Prince Charles Edward), by Susanna, da. of Thomas CARTER, of Redbourne, co. Lincoln. He *d.* 24 June 1799, in his 53d year. M.I. at Barton. Will pr. July 1799. His widow *d.* 3 Feb. 1829, aged 80. M.I. at Lea, co. Lincoln.

VII. 1799. SIR HENRY NELTHORPE, Baronet [1666], of Scawby aforesaid, 1st s. and h., *b.* 25 Dec. 1773; admitted to Rugby School, 29 Aug. 1786; *suc. to the Baronetcy*, 14 June 1799; Sheriff of Lincolnshire, 1803. He *m.* 9 Dec. 1806, at St. Geo., Han. sq., Margaret, da. of James DUTHIE, of co. Stirling. He *d.* s.p. 12 May 1830, at Scawby, aged 56. Will pr. June 1830. His widow *d.* 29 Sep. 1851, at Blackheath, aged 71. Will pr. Oct. 1851.

VIII. 1830, to 1865. SIR JOHN NELTHORPE, Baronet [1666], of Scawby aforesaid, nephew and h., being 1st s. and h. of John NELTHORPE, of South Ferriby, co. Lincoln, by his 2d wife, Christian, da. of John BROWN, of London, which John Nelthorpe last named (who *d.* 1824, aged 48) was br. of the late and s. of the 6th Baronet. He was *b.* 1814, at South Ferriby; *suc. to the Baronetcy*, 12 May 1830; was Sheriff of Lincolnshire, 1842. He *m.*, 24 May 1838, his cousin, Frances Maria, 1st da. of the Rev. Sir Charles John ANDERSON, 8th Baronet [1660], of Lea Hall, co. Lincoln, by Frances Mary, da. of Sir John NELTHORPE, 6th Baronet [1666]. He *d.* s.p. at Scawby Hall, 22 Nov. 1865, aged 51, when the *Baronetcy* became *extinct*. His widow, who was *b.* 1809, *d.*, probably, in 1885.(b)

(a) He is spoken of as "a Yorkshire gentleman of great estate."

(b) She is given as living in Dod's *Baronetage* for 1885, but is absent in that for 1886.

VINER, *or* VYNER:

cr. 10 May 1666;

ex. 2 Sep. 1688.

I. 1666, to 1688. "SIR ROBERT VINER, Knt., Lord Mayor of London," Citizen and Goldsmith, being of Lombard street, in that city, and of Swakeleys, in Ickenham, co. Midx., yr. s. of William VYNER, of Eathorpe, co. Warwick, by his 2d wife, Susanna, da. of Francis FULWOOD, of Middleton, co. Derby, was *b.* 1631, at Warwick; apprenticed in the Goldsmiths' Company to his uncle, Sir Thomas Vyner; nominated, in 1660, one of the Knights of the intended "Order of the Royal Oak," his estates being then computed at £3,500 a year; was one of the Masters of the Mint, 1660-70, and made the Regalia(a) for the Coronation (23 April 1661), of Charles II. (the former ones having been destroyed), for £31,978 9s. 11d.; obtained, 8 Aug. 1661, a grant of the office of "King's Goldsmith," was *Knighted*, at Whitehall, 24 June 1665; was Alderman of Broad Street, 1666-79, and of Langbourne, 1679, till discharged in 1686; Sheriff of London, 1666-67; Lord Mayor, 1674-75, his pageant being one of more than usual magnificence.(b) He *m.*, 14 June 1665 (Lic. Vic. Gen. 13, he about 34, bachelor), Mary (aged about 34), widow of Sir Thomas HYDE, 2d Baronet (1621), of Albury, Herts (who had *d.* less than a month before), da. of John WHITCHURCH, of Walton, near Aylesbury, Bucks. She (who brought him £100,000), *d.* in Lombard street, 31 Dec. 1674, and was *bur.* (as Lady Mayoress), 19 Jan. 1674/5, at St. Mary's, Wolnoth. Admon. 12 Jan. 1674/5, and 31 July 1689. He *d.* s.p.s., at Windsor Castle, 2, and was *bur.* 16 Sep. 1688, at St. Mary's aforesaid, aged 57, when the *Baronetcy* became *extinct*. Will dat. 20 Aug., pr. Oct. 1688, and [I.], 1691.

TWISDEN, *or* TWYSDEN:

cr. 13 June 1666;

ex. 1 Jan. 1841.

I. 1666. "SIR THOMAS TWYSDEN, of Bradburne juxta East Malling, Kent, Knt., one of the Justices of the King's Bench," 2d s. of Sir William TWYSDEN, 1st Baronet [1611], of Roydon in East Peckham in that county, by Anne, da. of Sir Moyle FINCH, 1st Baronet [1611], and Elizabeth, *suo jure* COUNTESS OF WINCHILSEA, was *b.* at Roydon aforesaid, 8 Jan. 1601/2; ed. (as Fellow Commoner) at Emman. Coll., Cambridge; admitted to Inner Temple, 1618; Barrister, 1625; Bencher, 1646; M.P. for Maidstone, Jan. 1647, till secluded, Dec. 1648, being re-elected in 1660; Serjeant-at-Law, 1654, in which office he was confirmed, 1660, being King's Serjeant, 1660, and *Knighted* 2 July 1660, and, on 22 July 1660, made one of the Justices of the Court of King's Bench, an office he retained till his death in 1683, though excused from the duties thereof in Oct. 1678. He was *cr. a Baronet*, as above, 13 June 1666. He *m.*, in or before 1640, Jane, sister of the well known Col. Matthew THOMLINSON, the Regicide, 1st da. of John THOMLINSON, of St. Michael's le Belfry, York, by Eleanor, da. of Matthew DODSWORTH, Chancellor of the diocese of York. He *d.* 2 Jan. 1682/3, in his 81st year, and was *bur.* at East Malling. M.I. there, and at East Peckham. Will pr. June 1683. His widow *d.* 1702.

II. 1683. SIR ROGER TWISDEN, *or* TWYSDEN, Baronet [1666], of Bradbourne aforesaid, 1st s. and h., *b.* about 1640; *suc. to the Baronetcy*, 2 Jan. 1682/3; was M.P. for Rochester, 1689-90. He *m.* (Lic. Fac. 7 Dec. 1667, he 27 and she 20), Margaret, da. of Sir John MARSHAM, 1st Baronet [1663], by Elizabeth, da. of Sir William HAMMOND. He *d.* suddenly, 28 Feb. 1702/3. Will pr. June 1703.

(a) These regalia are still (1903) in use.

(b) According to Orridge's *Citizens and their Rulers*, he is "said to have invited Charles II (presumably when entertaining him as Lord Mayor), to come into the house again and finish the other bottle." His character (as are those of all the Aldermen in 1671-72), is given in the *Gent. Mag.* (Nov. 1769), vol. xxxix, p. 515.

IV

III. 1703. SIR THOMAS TWISDEN, Baronet [1666], of Bradbourne aforesaid, 1st s. and h., *b.*, probably, about 1670; *suc. to the Baronetcy* 28 Feb. 1702/3; was M.P. for Kent, 1722-27. He *m.* (Lic., Fac. 14 July 1701, he 39 and she above 21) Anne, da. of John MUSTERS, of Colwik Hall, Notts, by Millicent, da. and coheir of Adrian MUNDY, of Quordon, co. Derby. He *d.* 12 Sep. 1728, aged about 60. Will pr. 1728. His widow *d.* 20 Oct. 1729. Admon. 21 April 1792, to Dame Rebecca TWISDEN, widow.

IV. 1728. SIR THOMAS TWISDEN, Baronet [1666], of Bradbourne aforesaid, 1st s. and h., *b.* about 1704; matric. at Oxford (Univ. Coll.) 26 May 1721, aged 17; *cr.* M.A. 27 Jan. 1728/9, having *suc. to the Baronetcy*, 12 Sep. 1728. He went abroad early in 1730, and *d.* unm. at Grenada, in Spain, 24 Aug. 1737. Will pr. 1738.

V. 1737. SIR ROGER TWISDEN, Baronet [1666], of Bradbourne aforesaid, br. and h., *b.* about 1705; matric. at Oxford (Trin. Coll.), 23 May 1722, aged 17; *suc. to the Baronetcy*, 24 Aug. 1737; was *cr.* D.C.L. of Oxford, 3 July 1759; was M.P. for Kent (two Parls.), 1741-54. He *m.*, in or before 1740, Elizabeth, widow of Leonard BARTHOLOMEW, da. of Edmund WATTON, of Addington, Kent. He *d.* 7 March 1772. Will pr. April 1772. His widow *d.* 4 March 1775. Will pr. May 1775.

VI. 1772. SIR ROGER TWISDEN, Baronet [1666], of Bradbourne aforesaid, 1st s. and h., *b.* before 1741; was *cr.* M.A. of Oxford, 5 July 1759, the same day that his father was *cr.* D.C.L.; *suc. to the Baronetcy*, 7 March, 1772. He *m.* 25 Jan. 1779, Rebecca, da. of (—) WALDASH. He *d.* s.p.m.(a) 5 Oct. 1779. Admon. Oct. 1779, June 1834 and Aug. 1849. His widow, *d.* 3 Feb. 1833, "at Jennings," aged 74. Will pr. May 1833.

VII. 1779. SIR JOHN PAPILLON TWISDEN, Baronet [1666], br. and h. male, *b.* probably about 1745; *suc. to the Baronetcy*, 5 Oct. 1779. He *m.* 8 April 1782, Elizabeth, yst. da. of Sir Francis GEARY, 1st Baronet [1782], by Mary, da. of Philip BARTHOLOMEW. He *d.* 10 Feb. 1810. Will pr. 1810. His widow, who was *b.* 1754, *d.* Jan. 1816.

VIII. 1810 to 1841. SIR JOHN TWISDEN, Baronet [1666], only s. and h., *b.* June 1785; *suc. to the Baronetcy*, 10 Feb. 1810. He *m.* 25 Feb. 1811, Catharine Judith, da. of the Rev. William COPPARD, Rector of Graveley, co. Cambridge. She *d.* 29 April 1819, aged 29. He *d.* s.p.s. 1 Jan. 1841, aged 56, when the *Baronetcy* became *extinct*. Admon. Feb. 1841.

AUCHER:

cr. 4 July 1666;

ex. 26 May 1726.

I. 1666. "SIR ANTHONY AUCHER(b), of Bishopsbourne, co. Kent, Knt.," 1st s. and h. of Sir Anthony AUCHER of the same, Sheriff of Kent (1613-14), by Hester, da. and coheir of Peter COLLETT, of London, was *b.* 1614; suc. his father in July 1637; was *Knighted* at Whitehall, 4 July 1641; was imprisoned for nine months in 1643, in Winchester house, in connection with the Kentish petition; and having been "an ardent Royalist"(c) and frequently in arms for the King, was M.P. for Canterbury 1660, and was *cr. a Baronet*, as above, 4 July 1666. He *m.* firstly, probably about 1635, Elizabeth, da. of Sir Robert HATTON. She, by whom he had seven sons,(a) *d.* in exile at Calais, and was *bur.* 19 Sep. 1648, at Bourne aforesaid. He *m.* secondly, 13 Oct. 1681, at St. Bride's, London (Lic. Vic. Gen., 8, he widower, she aged 29, spinster), Elizabeth, da. of "Robert Hewytt, Esq., of St. Martin's in the Fields, who consents." He was *bur.* 31 May 1692, at Bourne. His widow *m.* Thomas HART, of Canterbury.

(a) Elizabeth, his posthumous da. and h. (*b.* 1780), inherited the family estates and *m.* Thomas Law Hodges, of Hempsted Place, Kent.

(b) Many of the particulars of this family have been kindly supplied by G. Bruce Angier.

(c) See Furley's *Weald of Kent*.

II. 1692. SIR ANTHONY AUCHER, Baronet [1666], of Bishopsbourne aforesaid, 8th but 1st surv. s. and h., being 1st s. by the 2d wife, *b.* about 1685; *suc. to the Baronetcy* in May 1692. He *d.* in his 10th year, and was *bur.* at Bourne, 14 March 1694/5.

III. 1695, to 1726. SIR HEWITT AUCHER, Baronet [1666], of Bishopsbourne aforesaid, only surv. br. and h., *b.* about 1687, at Canterbury; *suc. to the Baronetcy* in March 1694/5; admitted to St. John's Coll. Cambridge (as Fellow Commoner) 9 May 1700, aged 13. He *d.* unm. 26 May and was *bur.* 4 June 1726, at Bourne, when the *Baronetcy* became *extinct*. Will pr. 1726.(b)

D'OYLY, *or* D'OYLIE:

cr. 7 July 1666;

ex. 24 Nov. 1773;

but assumed till 1781 and later.

I. 1666. "JOHN D'OYLIE,(c) of Chiselhampton, Oxon., Esq.," as also of Wantage, Berks, 1st s. and h. of John D'OYLIE, *or* D'OYLY,(d) of the same, M.P. for Oxfordshire and one of the Parl. Commissioners for visiting the Univ. of Oxford (*d.* about 1660), by Mary, 6th da. and coheir of Sir John SHIRLEY, of Isfield, Sussex, was *bap.* Nov. 1640, at Stadhampton, Oxon; was presumably the "John Doyley, Esq.," who matric. at Oxford (Wadham Coll.), 15 June 1657; suc. his father about 1660, and was *cr. a Baronet*, as above, 7 July 1666. He was Sheriff of Oxon, 1684-85; was Capt. of the Oxon Militia, being one of the few who were faithful to their King (James II), in 1688; was M.P. for Woodstock, 1689-90. He *m.* (Lic. Fac. 11 July 1666) Margaret, da. and coheir of Sir Richard CHOLMELEY, of Grosmont, co. York, by Margaret, da. of John (POULETT), 1st BARON POULETT OF HINTON ST. GEORGE. She, by whom he had seven sons, *d.* Jan. 1704. He *d.* 13 April 1709, aged 68. Both *bur.* at Stadhampton.

(a) These were: (1) Anthony Aucher, *b.* 19 and *bap.* 24 April 1639, at Bourne; matric. at Oxford (Wadham Coll.) 10 March 1656/7; *m.* in 1665, Elizabeth, da. of Thomas Biggs, of Fordwich, but *d.* s.p. and v.p., and was *bur.* 12 Sep. 1673, at Bourne. (2) Hatton Aucher, admitted 18 May 1658, to Gray's Inn, as "2d son"; *bur.* 4 Sep. 1691 (a few months before his father) at Bourne. (3) Robert Aucher, *bap.* 22 Jan. 1643/4, at Bourne; matric. (as 3d son) at Oxford (Queen's Coll.) 10 June 1664, aged (it is said) 18; B.A., 1668; M.A., 23 Feb. 1670/1; in Holy Orders; Rector of Kingston, Kent, 1672, till his death in 1681. (4) George, *bap.* 11 July 1645, at Bourne. (5) Collett, *bap.* there 29 Nov. 1646. (6) Edwin, *d.* 1657; and (7) James, *d.* 1660.

(b) His two sisters of the whole blood became his coheirs, *viz.*, (1) Elizabeth, who *m.* John Corbett, LL.D., and had five daughters and coheirs, and (2) Hester, who *m.* Ralph Blomer, D.D., Preb. of Canterbury, and had issue.

(c) See, as to the family, the *Account of the House of D'Oyly*, by William D'Oyly Bayley, London, 1845, 8vo.

(d) This John was 1st s. and h. of Sir Cope D'Oyly, of Hambledon, Bucks (*d.* 4 Aug. 1633), only s. and h. of John D'Oyly, of Stedham, br. and heir (1577) of Sir Robert D'Oyly, both being sons of John D'Oyly, of Chiselhampton, which John, who *d.* 1569, was elder br. of Robert D'Oyly of Greenland House, Bucks, whose descendant, in 1773, assumed the Baronetcy.

F

II. 1709. SIR JOHN D'OYLY, Baronet [1666], of Chiselhampton aforesaid, 2d but 1st surv. s. and h.,(a) *b.* probably about 1670; *suc. to the Baronetcy*, 13 April 1709. He *m.* firstly (Lic. Vic. Gen., Jan. 1694/5), his cousin, Susanna, da. of Sir Thomas PUTT, 1st Baronet [1666], of Combe, Devon, by Ursula, da. and coheir of Sir Richard CHOLMELEY abovenamed. She *d.* Aug. 1722, and was *bur.* at Stadhampton. He *m.* secondly, before 1727, Rebecca, da. and coheir of Goddard CARTER, of Alverscot, Oxon. He *d.* 1746. Will pr. 1746. The will of his widow, by whom he had no issue, pr. 1746.

III. 1746. SIR THOMAS D'OYLY, Baronet [1666], of Chiselhampton aforesaid, 3d but 1st surv. s. and h., by 1st wife, *b.* about 1701; matric. at Oxford (Queen's Coll.), 12 Feb. 1717/8, aged 16; *suc. to the Baronetcy* in 1746, but, within two years' time, through reckless extravagance, was compelled to sell the Chiselhampton estate.(b) He *m.*, in or before 1737, his cousin, Mary, da. of Samuel WOTTON, of Englebourne, Devon, by Mary, da. of Sir John D'OYLY, 1st Baronet [1666]. He *d.* s.p.m.(c) at Cuxham Rectory, Oxon, 6 and was *bur.* 14 Feb. 1759 at Stadhampton. Will pr. 1759. His widow *d.* at Henley-on-Thames. Will, in which she directs to be *bur.* at Cuxham, dat. 7 June and pr. Aug. 1780.

IV. 1759, to 1773. SIR JOHN D'OYLY, Baronet [1666], br. and h., *b.* about 1702, matric. at Oxford (Merton Coll.), 15 Dec. 1720, and then aged 18; B.A. and Fellow, 1724; M.A., 1728; in Holy Orders. Rector of Cuxham, Oxon, and subsequently of Heston; *suc. to the Baronetcy* 6 Feb. 1759. He *d.* unm. 24 Nov. 1773, aged about 70, when the *Baronetcy* became *extinct*.(d) Will dat. March 1772 to Feb. 1773, pr. 28 Feb. 1774.

> The title was, however, assumed, apparently as under—
>
> *V. 1773, to 1781.* "SIR JOHN D'OYLY, Baronet" [1666], who presumably adopted that title on the death of the late Baronet, 24 Nov. 1773, but whose relationship to him is unknown, is said(e) to have *d.* 2 June 1781, at Little Milton, Oxon, aged 71, "whose title devolves upon Mr. D'OYLY, of Adderbury West."

(a) His elder br., Cholmeley D'Oyly, *m.* Elizabeth, da. and coheir of Richard Cabell, of Brook, Devon, but *d.* v.p. and s.p.

(b) The old Hall was pulled down by (—) Peers, the purchaser.

(c) Susanna, his only surv. da. and h., *b.* 1737 and *bap.* June 1739 at Stadhampton, *m.* 1767, as his 1st wife, William Newcombe, sometime (1766-77), Bishop of Dromore, and finally (1795-1800) Archbishop of Armagh (who *d.* 11 Jan. 1800, in his 81st year), and *d.* in or soon after 1768, leaving issue.

(d) William D'Oyly, his br., the 4th and yst. s. of the 2d Baronet, who *m.* a da. of (—) Monk by whom (who was dead before 1771) he had a son, James Monk D'Oyly (living 1771), who *d.* s.p.s. before March 1772, the date of his brother's will. He is often (though erroneously) said to have suc., in 1773, as the 5th Baronet.

(e) *Annual Register*, 1781.

> *VI. 1781 ?* WILLIAM D'OYLY, of Adderbury West, Oxon, s. and h. of William D'OYLY,(a) of the same (*d.* Jan. 1772), by Kezia, da. of Thomas WRIGHT, of Cropredy, Oxon, was *bap.* Sep. 1751, at Adderbury, and is said to have *assumed the Baronetcy* [1666] in right of a descent from a common ancestor of the 1st Baronet. He *m.* his cousin, Joanna, 3d da. of Benjamin APLIN, of Bodicote House, Oxon, and of Banbury, Solicitor, by Susanna, 2d da. and coheir of Christopher D'OYLY, of Twickenham, Midx.(b)

HOBY:

cr. 12 July 1666;

ex. 29 June 1766.

I. 1666. "EDWARD HOBY, of Bisham, Berks, Esq.," s. and h. ap. of Peregrine HOBY(c), of the same, sometime M.P. for Great Marlow (*d.* May 1679), by Katharine (*m.* 14 April 1631), da. of Sir William DODINGTON, of Breamor, Hants, was *bap.* at Bisham, 27 March 1634; matric. at Oxford (Balliol Coll.), 3 June 1652; admitted to the Middle Temple, 1654 and was *cr. a Baronet*, as above, 12 July 1666, with a spec. rem., failing issue male of his body, to his brothers. He *m.*, in or before 1667, Elizabeth, da. and coheir of Francis STYLES, of Little Missenden, Berks. She was *bur.* 21 Oct. 1670, at Bisham. He *d.* s.p.m. and v.p. in London, 12 and was *bur.* 16 Sep. 1675, at Bisham, aged 41.(d) Admon. 10 Dec. 1675, and 14 April 1681.

II. 1675. SIR JOHN HOBY, Baronet [1666], of Bisham aforesaid, and of Somerly, Hants, next br. and h., *bap.* 21 March 1635, at Bisham; *suc. to the Baronetcy*, by virtue of the spec. rem. in its creation, 12 Sep. 1675, and, subsequently, suc. to the estate of Bisham Abbey on death of his father, in May 1679. He *m.*, before 1667, Mary, da. and h. of Thomas LONG, of Wilts. She was *bur.* 16 Oct. 1685, at Bisham. He was *bur.* there 15 May 1702, aged 77. Will dat. 19 May 1697, pr. 19 May 1702.

III. 1702. SIR THOMAS HOBY, Baronet [1666], of Bisham and Somerly aforesaid, 2d but 1st surv. s. and h.,(e) *b.* 2 and *bap.* 10 Oct. 1685, at Bisham; matric. at Oxford (Balliol Coll.), 2 Sep. 1702, aged (it is said) 15; *suc. to the Baronetcy* in May 1702; was Sheriff of Hants, 1714-5. He *m.*,

(a) This William was br. and h. of Christopher D'Oyly, both being sons of Christopher, 2d s. (whose issue became heir male) of another Christopher, 5th s. of Robert D'Oyly, all of Adderbury aforesaid. The abovenamed Robert was a yr. s. of Robert D'Oyly, of Merton, Oxon, a yr. s. of Robert D'Oyly, of Greenland House, Bucks, who was yr. br. of John D'Oyly, of Chiselhampton (*d.* 1569), the great-great-grandfather of the 1st Baronet. See p. 33, note "d."

(b) Christopher D'Oyly, of Bodicot, near Banbury, *bap.* 30 Dec. 1780 at Adderbury, his only surv. s. and h., was living unm. in 1840.

(c) This Peregrine was the illegit. s. (though constituted the heir) of Sir Edward Hoby, of Bisham, by Katherine Pinkney, spinster. He entered his pedigree at the *Visitation of Berks*, 1 Sep. 1667, being then aged 65, and *d.* May 1678.

(d) Of his two daughters; (1) Elizabeth was *b.* 4 and *bap.* 13 Aug. 1667; (2) Catherine *b.* 15, *bap.* 22 Oct. 1669 and *bur.* 17 Aug. 1670, all at Bisham.

(e) His elder br. "John Hoby, Esq., aged about 18, son of Sir John Hoby, Baronet, of Bisham Abbey, Berks," had licence (Fac. office), 31 Dec. 1686, to marry "Elizabeth Hoby, of the same, spinster, about 19, her parents dead," she being presumably da. and h. of the 1st Baronet; see note "d" above. He, who was M.P. for Great Marlow, from Feb. to his death in Dec. 1689, *d.* v.p.

28 June 1706, at Winchester, Elizabeth, da. of Sir John MILL, 3d Baronet [1619], by Margaret, da. and h. of Thomas GREY, of Woolbeding, Sussex. Her will pr. 1731. He *d.*, a widower, 25 July 1730. Admon. 3 Nov. 1730, and 28 June 1744.

IV. 1730. SIR THOMAS HOBY, Baronet [1666], of Bisham and Somerly aforesaid, 1st s. and h., *b.* probably about 1714; *suc. to the Baronetcy*, 25 July 1730; was M.P. for Great Marlow (three Parls.), 1732 till death in 1744. He *d.* unm. 1 June 1744. Will pr. 1744.

V. 1744, to 1766. SIR PHILIP HOBY, Baronet [1666], of Bisham and Somerly aforesaid, br. and h., *b.* about 1716; matric. at Oxford (Balliol Coll.), 7 Nov. 1732, aged 16; B.A., 1736; M.A., 1739; in Holy Orders; *suc. to the Baronetcy*, 1 June 1744; Chancellor of St. Patrick's, Dublin, and Dean of Ardfert, 1748 till death in 1766; was *cr.* D.C.L. of Oxford, 14 April 1749. He *d.* unm. 29 June, and was *bur.* 4 July 1766, at Bisham, when the *Baronetcy* became *extinct*. Will dat. 16 May 1763 to 7 Dec. 1765, pr. 1766(a) as also in Ireland.

PUTT, *or* PUT:
cr. 20 July 1666;
ex. 5 May 1721.

I. 1666. "THOMAS PUTT, of Combe [in Gittisham], co. Devon, Esq.," s. of William PUTT, of Combe aforesaid, clothier, by Jane, da. of (—) IVORY, of Cothay, Somerset, which William was s. of Nicholas PUTT, who in 1615 had purchased the Comb estate, was *cr. a Baronet*, as above, 20 July 1666. Sheriff of Devon, 1672-73; M.P. for Honiton (four Parls.), 1679 till death in 1686. He *m.*, probably about 1675, Ursula, da. and coheir of Sir Richard CHOLMELEY, of Grosmont, co. York, by Margaret, da. of John (POULETT), 1st BARON POULETT OF HINTON ST. GEORGE. She *d.* 1674. He *d.* 1686. M.I. to both at Gittisham. His will pr. Feb. 1687.

II. 1686, to 1721. SIR THOMAS PUTT, Baronet [1666], of Combe aforesaid, only s. and h., *b.* probably about 1675; admitted to Winchester School (as a Commoner), 1686; *suc. to the Baronetcy* in that year. He *m.* Margaret, da. of Sir George TREVELYAN, 1st Baronet [1662], by Mary, da. and h. of John WILLOUGHBY. He *d.* s.p., 5 May 1721, when the *Baronetcy* became *extinct*.(b) Will pr. 1722.

(a) In it he leaves the Bisham Abbey estate to his maternal first cousin John Mill, 2d s. of Sir Richard Mill, 5th Baronet [1619], on condition of his taking the name of Hoby. He, who in 1770 became the 7th Baronet [1619], *d.* s.p. in 1790, leaving that estate to his widow, who sold it to George Vansittart.

(b) Of his 3 sisters (1) Margaret, *m.* Robert (Dillon), 6th Earl of Roscommon [I.], who *d.* 14 May 1715, and had issue; (2) [—] *m.* Charles Gorsuch; and (3) Susanna, *m.* in 1695, as his 1st wife, Sir John Doyly, 2d Baronet [1666], of Chiselhampton, and *d.* Aug. 1722, leaving issue. The estates, however, passed to Raimond Putt, cousin and h. male of the late Baronet.

TYRRELL, *or* TIRELL:
cr. 22 Oct. 1666;
ex. 5 Jan. 1766.

I. 1666. "JOHN TIRELL, of Springfield [Barney], co. Essex, Esq. [2d but 1st surv.] s. and h. ap. of Sir John TYRRELL, of Heron,(a) in East Horndon, co. Essex, Knt.," a staunch Royalist and M.P. for Malden 1661, till his death (*d.* 30 April 1675,(b) aged 82), by his 2d wife, Martha, da. of Sir Laurence WASHINGTON, of Garesden, Wilts, was *b.*, probably, about 1636; admitted to Gray's Inn, 24 June 1650, and was v.p., *cr. a Baronet*, as above, 22 Oct. 1666. He *m.* firstly, in or before 1660, Lettice, da. of Thomas COPPIN, of Mercatsal, Herts. He *m.* secondly (Lic. Vic. Gen. 30 May 1663, he about 27, widower), Anna YEANE, of St. Gabriel Fenchurch, London, about 25, spinster, da. of Richard YEANE, of London, merchant, by Anna, living as his widow in May 1663. She *d.* s.p., 24 April 1664, and was *bur.* at Springfield. He *m.* thirdly, Elizabeth, da. of John ALLEN, of co. Northampton, Alderman of London. He *d.* v.p., 30 March 1673. His widow, by whom he had no issue, *m.* Sir Thomas STAMPE, sometime, 1691-92, Lord Mayor of London, who *d.* 25 July 1711, at Springfield Hall.

II. 1673. SIR CHARLES TYRRELL, Baronet [1666], of Springfield and afterwards (1675) of Heron aforesaid, only s. and h. by 1st wife, *b.* about 1660; *suc. to the Baronetcy* 30 March 1673, and to the family estates (on the death of his grandfather) 30 April 1675; was Sheriff of Essex, 1695-96. He *m.*, probably about 1685, Martha, da. and h. of Charles MILDMAY, of Woodham-Mortimer, co. Essex, by Martha, da. and h. of Sir Cranmer HARRIS. She *d.* 27 March 1690, aged 27. He *d.* 3 Feb. 1714/5, aged 54; both *bur.* at East Horndon. M.I. Will pr. 1714/5.

III. 1715. SIR JOHN TYRRELL, Baronet [1666], of Heron and Woodham Mortimer aforesaid, only s. and h., *b.* probably about 1685; *suc. to the Baronetcy*, 3 Feb. 1714/5. He *m.* firstly, Mary, da. of Sir James DOLLIFFE, of Mitcham, Surrey, one of the Directors of the South Sea Company. She, by whom he had four daughters, *d.* s.p.m. He *m.* secondly, in or before 1725, Elizabeth, 1st da. of John COTTON, of East Barnet, and of the Middle Temple, London. He *d.* 21 June 1729. Will pr. 1730. His widow *d.* 28 March 1757.

IV. 1729. SIR CHARLES TYRRELL, Baronet [1666], of Heron and Woodham Mortimer aforesaid, 1st s. and h., by 2d wife, *b.* about 1725; *suc. to the Baronetcy*, 21 June 1729. He *d.* 27 July 1735, in his 11th year, at Felsted School, Essex. Admon. 21 April 1738, to his mother.

V. 1729, to 1766. SIR JOHN TYRRELL, Baronet [1666], of Heron and Woodham Mortimer aforesaid, br. and h., *b.* about 1728; *suc. to the Baronetcy*, 27 July 1735; was Sheriff of Essex, Jan. to Dec. 1750. He *m.*, 26 June 1762, Mary, da. and h. of Thomas CRISPE, of Perbold, co. Lancaster, and Mary his wife. He *d.* s.p.m.,(c) 5 Jan. 1766, when the *Baronetcy* became *extinct*. Admon. 20 Aug. 1766, 12 June 1767, and 26 June 1771. His widow *d.* 23 Sep. 1766. Will pr. 1766.

(a) Heron had been the principal seat of the family since the time of Richard II, when Sir James Tyrell *m.* Margaret, da. and h. of Sir William Heron, of Heron.

(b) The following quaint inscription is on his monument at East Horndon:—
"Semel decimatus, bis carceratus, ter sequestratus,
Tacet quoties spoliatus, hic jacet inhumatus
Johannes Tyrrel, Eques Auratus
Obiit die Martis, Aprilis XXX, A.D. MDCLXXV, ætat. lxxxij."

(c) Of his two daughters and coheirs (1) Mary, *m.* 29 Dec. 1787, at St. Geo., Han. sq., Arthur Saunders (Gore), 3d Earl of Arran [I.], and *d.* s.p., 31 Aug. 1832; (2) Elizabeth, unm. in 1784.

GERARD:
cr. 17 Nov. 1666;
afterwards, 1687, COSIN-GERARD;
ex. probably about 1730.

I. 1666. "GILBERT GERARD, of Fiskerton, co. Lincoln," as also of Brafferton, co. York, s. and h. of Col. Ratcliffe GERARD, of Halsall, co. Lancaster (will dat. 7 March 1660/1, pr. 29 Jan. 1669/70), by Jennet, da. of Edward BARRETT, of co. Pembroke, was, presumably, M.P. for Northallerton, 1661-81, and was *cr. a Baronet*, as above, 17 Nov. 1666, with a spec. rem. "entayling the same title upon his issue male, by Mary, his 2d wife. da. to Dr. John COZENS, Lord Bishop of Durham."(a) He was one of the "Benefactors" towards the re-building, in 1666, of the College of Arms, and was, presumably, Sheriff of co. Durham, 1672-73 and 1674-75, and admitted to Gray's Inn, 10 March 1673/4. He *m.* firstly, in 1643 or 1644, Mary, widow of Sir Michael HUTCHINSON (*d.* March 1642), sister of William, 2d BARON BRERETON OF LEIGHLIN [I.], 1st da. of the Hon. Sir John BRERETON, by Anne, da. of Sir Edward FITTON. By her he had four children, of whom the two sons(b) were passed over in the limitation of the Baronetcy. He *m.* secondly, before 7 March 1660/1, Mary, 1st da. of John COSYN, D.D., Bishop of Durham, 1660-72, by Frances, da. of Marmaduke BLAKISTON. She was *bur.* 5 Dec. 1680, at St. Paul's, Covent Garden. Admon. 7 June 1682. He *d.* "on his travels, at York," and was *bur.* 24 Sep. 1687, in York Minster. Nunc. will dat. 17, pr. 26 Sep. 1687, at York.

II. 1687, to 1730? SIR GILBERT COSIN-GERARD, Baronet [1666], of Brafferton aforesaid, 4th son, being 2d but 1st surv. s.(c) of the 2d wife, was aged 4 at the Visit. of Durham in 1666; *suc. to the Baronetcy*, according to the spec. rem. in its creation, in Sep. 1687. He took, v.p., the name of *Cosin*, in addition to that of *Gerrard*, having probably inherited some of the estates of his mother's family, and was admitted to Gray's Inn, 25 April 1684, as "Gilbert Cossein Gerard." He *m.* firstly, 2 May 1681, at Westm. Abbey (Lic. Vic. Gen., same date, he above 19 and she about 18), Mary, da. and h. of Charles (BERKELEY), EARL OF FALMOUTH, by Mary, da. of Col. Hervey BAGOT. She, who is said to have been divorced in 1684, *d.* 18, and was *bur.* 23 April 1693 at Bexley, Kent, in her 28th year. M.I. He *m.* secondly, Mary, sometime 4th wife of Sir Samuel MORLAND, *otherwise* MORLEY, 1st Baronet [1660] (from whom she was divorced, 16 July 1687), da. of (—) AYLIFF, a coachman.(d) He *m.* thirdly, 6 April 1712, at St. James's, Duke's place,

(a) A warrant, dat. 17 March 1663/4, and a docquet. dat. 31 May 1664, exist among the *Calendars of State Papers* [E.], 1660-70, for this creation, with the like remainder.

(b) These were (1) Gilbert Gerard, *b.* 1645; admitted to Lincoln's Inn, 21 March 1670/1; living 6 April 1675; (2) Charles Gerard, living 6 April 1675; *d.* unm. and v.p. at Neuport in Flanders. Admon. 2 Jan. 1679/80 to his father. Their sisters were (1) Anne, 1st wife of William Owen, of Henllys, co. Pembroke, by whom she had a son William, who *d.* s.p.; (2) Elizabeth, living unm. 6 April 1675. In the will of Vere Gerard, spinster, dat. 6 April 1675, pr. 28 Feb. 1675/6, she being da. of Charles Gerard, br. to the 1st Baronet, by Francis, sister to his 2d wife (see Visit. of Durham, 1666, under the pedigree of "Cosyn"), she mentions as living "my uncle Sir Gilbert Gerard and his wife, my cousin Gilbert Gerard, *their* son and my cousin Christian Gerard, my cousins Elizabeth Gerard and Mr. Gilbert Gerard, da. and son of the said Sir Gilbert *by his first lady*," and leaves the residue of her property to her cousin Charles Gerard.

(c) The burial in the Church of St. Paul's, Covent Gardens, 27 June 1661, of "John, son of Sir Gilbert Gerrard," presumably refers to an infant son by the 2d wife.

(d) See Col Chester's note, on p. 20 of his *Westm. Abbey Registers*.

London, Mary WHEELER, spinster, then aged 26, both being then of St. George's, Southwark (a) He apparently *d.* s.p.m., when the *Baronetcy* became *extinct*, probably about 1730.(b)

YEAMANS, *or* YEOMANS:
cr. 31 Dec. 1666;
ex. Feb. 1686/7.

I. 1666, to 1687. "SIR ROBERT YEOMANS [*or* YEAMANS], of Redlands [near Bristol], co Gloucester, Knt.," yr. br. of Sir John YEAMANS, 1st Baronet [1665], both supposed(c) to have been sons of Robert YEAMANS, Alderman, and sometime, 1642, Sheriff of Bristol (who, for his loyalty, was executed there, 30 May 1643, by the then Governor), by Anne, his wife, appears to have himself suffered imprisonment for the Royal Cause during the Commonwealth, received a letter of thanks from Charles II, dated Brussels, 13 Jan. 1660; was *Knighted* 7 Sep. 1663, and was *cr. a Baronet*, as above, 31 Dec. 1666. He was Mayor of Bristol 1669. He *m.* firstly, (—), who was *bur.* at St. Mary's, Redcliffe, Bristol. He *m.* secondly, Abigail, one of these two wives being possibly da. of Sir Edward STAFFORD, of Bradfield, Berks. He *d.* s.p. and was *bur.* 7 Feb. 1686/7, at St. Mary's aforesaid, when the *Baronetcy* became *extinct*. Will dat. 24 Jan. 1686, pr. 11 May 1687. His widow living 1716.

SCROOPE, *or* SCROPE:
cr. 16 Jan. 1666/7;
ex. in 1680.

I. 1667, to 1680. "CARR SCROOPE, of Cockerington, co. Lincoln, Esq.," 1st s. and h. ap. of Sir Adrian SCROPE, *or* SCROOPE, of the same, K.B. (*d.* 1667), by Mary, da. of Sir Robert CARR, 2d Baronet [1611], was *b.* in Lincoln, and *bap.* at Aswarby, 20 Sep. 1649; matric. at Oxford (Wadham Coll.) 26 Aug. 1664, aged 15, and was, v.p., *cr. a Baronet*, as above, 16 Jan. 1666/7, being *cr.* M.A. of Oxford, 4 Feb. following. He who was a wit and a poet at the Court of Charles II, *d.* unm. in 1680 (before Dec.) at St. Martin's in the Fields, Midx., when the *Baronetcy* became *extinct*. Admon. 11 Dec. 1680, 24 Oct. 1683, and 8 Sep. 1696.

FORTESCUE:
cr. 29 Jan. 1666/7;
ex. Aug. 1685.

I. 1667, to 1685. "PETER FORTESCUE, of Wood [in Woodleigh], co. Devon, Esq.,"(d) 3d but 1st surv. s. and h. of Francis FORTESCUE, of Preston, in that county (*d.* April 1649, aged 59), by Elizabeth, da. of Sir John SPECKOTT, of Thornborough, Devon, was six months old at the Visit. of Devon in 1620; matric. at Oxford (Exeter Coll.), 2 March

(a) There can be little doubt that the entry there of that date refers to him, viz., "Sir Gilbert Gerard, w., and Mary Wheeler, sp., both of St. George's, Southwark," in which parish the King's Bench prison, of which he not improbably was an inmate, is situated. It is, however to be noticed that the marriage licence of the same date (Bishop of London's office) omits, probably by mistake, the word "Sir."

(b) His brother, Sir Samuel Gerard, aged 2 at the Visit. of Durham in 1666, who was afterwards *Knighted*, was of Brafferton, co. Durham. He *m.* twice, but *d.* s.p., July 1695. Will dat. 22 and pr. 26 July 1695. In Le Neve's MS. *Baronetage* he is stated (erroneously) to have *suc. to the Baronetcy*.

(c) See p. 5, note "a," under "YEAMANS", Baronetcy, *cr.* 1665.

(d) See Vivian's *Visitations of Devon*, p. 357.

1637/8, aged 17; B.A. 9 Dec. 1641, and was *cr. a Baronet*, as above, 29 Jan. 1666/7. He *m.* firstly, 12 Jan. 1645/6, at Churchstowe, Devon, Bridget, da. of Sir John ELIOT, of Port Eliot, Cornwall, by Radigund, da. and h. of Richard GEDIE, of Treburscy. She, who was *bap.* 26 April 1620, at St. Germans, was *bur.* 16 June 1663, at Ermington, Devon. He *m.* secondly, 21 Nov. 1669, at Burian, Cornwall, Amy, widow of Sir Peter COURTENAY, of Trethurfe, da. of Peter COURTENAY, of St. Michael, Penkivel. He *d.* s.p.m.s.,(a) and was *bur.* 14 Aug. 1685, at Ermington, when the *Baronetcy* became *extinct*. Will dat. 29 June 1685, pr. 11 March 1685/6. His widow was *bur.* at Ermington, 4 Dec. 1700. Will dat. 19 Feb. 1697/8, pr. 10 July 1701.

BETENSON, *or* BETTENSON:

cr. 7 Feb. 1666/7;

see 7 June 1663.

I. 1667. "SIR RICHARD BETTENSON, of Wimbledon, co. Surrey, Knt.," is frequently said to have been *cr. a Baronet*, as above, 7 Feb. 1666/7, but the true date appears to have been 7 June 1663, under which accordingly it has here been placed. See vol. iii, p. 277.

PEYTON:

cr. 21 March 1666/7;

ex. 29 June 1771.

I. 1667. "ALGERNON PEYTON,(b) of Doddington, in the Isle of Ely, co. Cambridge," 2d but, after 1661, 1st surv. s. and h. ap. of the Rev. Algernon PEYTON, Rector of Doddington, by Elizabeth, da. of John COOK, of Chiswell, co. Essex (which Algernon suc. to the Doddington estate on the death, 26 April 1659, of his elder br., Robert), was *b.* probably about 1645, and was *cr. a Baronet*, v.p., 21 March 1666/7, as above, with, apparently, a spec. rem., failing his issue male, to that of his 2d br., Thomas, and of his 3d br., Henry, respectively,(c) their elder br., Sir Robert PEYTON, Baronet (who had been *cr. a Baronet* 10 Dec. 1660), having *d.* s.p. and v.p. 25 Dec. 1661. He *m.* 19 Nov. 1667, at St. James', Bury St. Edmund's, Frances, da. and h. of Sir Robert SEWSTER, of Raveley, Hunts. He *d.* v.p., on or soon after 17 May 1671, and was *bur.* at Doddington. Will of that date. His widow *m.* 18 Jan. 1673, Col. John SKELTON, whom she survived. Her will dat. 23 May 1680, pr. 26 May 1685.

(a) Among his sons were, by his 1st wife, (1) John, who matric. at Oxford (Exeter Coll.), 22 June 1666, aged 18; (2) Peter, *d.* young, *bur.* 9 Feb. 1664/5, at Ermington; (3), by the 2d wife, another Peter, *bap.* 14 and *bur.* 15 Oct. at Woodleigh. Of his daughters, Elizabeth, the only da. by the 1st wife, *m.* (Lic. at Exeter, 26 May 1667) John Turberville, of Golden, Somerset, and had a son and h., Fortescue Turberville, living 1701, who *m.*, before 1701, his mother's sister, by the half blood, viz., Bridget, da. and coheir of the said Sir Peter Fortescue, Baronet [1667], by Amy, his 2d wife, both abovenamed, and had issue.

(b) See pedigree in J. J. Howard's *Visitation of Suffolk*, vol. ii, p. 126.

(c) A warrant with this spec. rem., dated 15 Aug. 1663, exists among the *Calendars of State Papers* [E.] 1660-70.

II. 1671? SIR SEWSTER PEYTON, Baronet [1667], of Doddington aforesaid, only s. and h., *suc. to the Baronetcy* in early childhood, on the death of his father about 1671, and suc. to the family estate on the death of his grandfather in Feb. 1677/8. He was joint Master of the Buckhounds to Queen Anne. He *m.* 17 July 1701, at Westm. Abbey, Anne, sister of Sir Robert DASHWOOD, 1st Baronet [1684], 2d da. of George DASHWOOD, Alderman of London, by Margaret, da. of William PERRY, of Thorpe, co. Surrey. He *d.* 28 Dec. 1717, and was *bur.* at Doddington, being said to be in his 45th year.(a) Will dat. 10 Sep. 1706, pr. 23 June 1718, by his widow. She *d.* 4 April 1751. Will pr. May 1751.

III. 1717, to 1771. SIR THOMAS PEYTON, Baronet [1667] of Hagbeach Hall in Enneth, Norfolk, and of Doddington aforesaid, 1st s. and h., *b.* 1702; *suc. to the Baronetcy*, 28 Dec. 1717; Sheriff of Cambridgeshire, 1743. He *m.* in St. John's Chapel, All Saints', Cambridge, in 1738, Bridget, sister and h. of Thomas SKEFFINGTON, only da. and heir of Thomas SKEFFINGTON, of Skeffington, co. Leicester, by Elizabeth, da. of Sir John DUGDALE, of Blyth Hall, co. Warwick. She was *bur.* 29 Dec. 1762 at Doddington. He *d.* s.p. 29 June, and was *bur.* there 13 July 1771, in his 70th year, when the *Baronetcy* became *extinct*.(b) Will pr. Aug. 1771.

MARTIN:

cr. 28 March 1667;

ex. 16 Dec. 1854.

I. 1667. "ROGER MARTIN (c) of Long Melford, co. Suffolk, Esq.," 5th but 1st surv. s. and h. of Richard MARTIN, of the same (*d.* 1673, aged 62), by his 1st wife, Jane, da. of Sir Henry BEDINGFELD, of Oxburgh, Norfolk (which Richard was s. and h. of Sir Roger Martin, of Long Melford, who *d.* Oct. 1657, aged 71), was *b.* 1639, and was *cr. a Baronet*, as above, 28 March 1667. He *m.* in 1663, Tamworth, only da. of Edward HORNER(d) of Mells, co. Somerset, by Elizabeth, afterwards VISCOUNTESS MONSON OF CASTLEMAINE [I.], da. of Sir George RERESBY. She *d.* 15 and was *bur.* 20 Aug. 1698, at Long Melford. He *d.* 8 and was *bur.* there 12 July 1712, aged 73. Will dat. 29 April 1710, pr. 10 July 1713.

II. 1712. SIR ROGER MARTIN, Baronet [1667], of Long Melford aforesaid, 2d but 1st surv. s. and h., *b.* 1667; *suc. to the Baronetcy* 8 July 1712. He *m.* in or before 1689, Anna Maria HARVEY. She *d.* at Canterbury, 15 May 1739, and was, presumably, *bur.* there. Admon. 15 July 1742. He *d.* 3 and was *bur.* 30 March 1742, at Long Melford. Will pr. April 1742.

III. 1742. SIR ROGER MARTIN, Baronet [1667], of Long Melford aforesaid, s. and h., *b.* 1689; *suc. to the Baronetcy* 3 March 1741/2. He *m.* firstly, 6 June 1739, Sophia, da. and coheir of Brig.-Gen. the Hon. Lewis MORDAUNT (br. of Charles, 3d EARL OF PETERBOROUGH and 1st EARL OF MONMOUTH),

(a) He is, however, mentioned as alive in the will of his father, dated 17 May 1667, and the posthumous child, with which his mother was then *enceinte*, was a da. named Algerina.

(b) The estates devolved on his nephew, Henry Dashwood, son of his sister Margaret, who *m.* 9 June 1739, her cousin, George Dashwood (*d.* March 1762), son of George Dashwood, of Boxford (*d.* 1705), by Algerina, da. of Sir Algernon Peyton, 1st Baronet (1667). He took the name of Peyton, and was *cr. a Baronet*, as of Doddington, co. Cambridge," 18 Sep. 1776.

(c) See pedigree in J. J. Howard's *Visitation of Suffolk*, vol. i, pp. 207-230.

(d) See Horner pedigree in *Mis. Gen. et Her.*, N.S., vol. iv, p. 164.

by his 2d wife, Mary, da. of Lieut. Col. COLLYER, Lieut. Gov. of Jersey. She *d.* 22 Dec. 1752. He *m.* secondly, Lucy, widow da. of [—]. He *d.* 4 and was *bur.* 9 June 1762, at Long Melford. Will pr. 1763. His widow *d.* at Bury St. Edmunds, in or before 1777. Admon. 17 April 1777, to her da., Elizabeth WALKER, widow.(a)

IV. 1762. SIR MORDAUNT MARTIN, Baronet [1667], of Burnham Westgate Hall, co. Norfolk, and of Long Melford aforesaid, only s. and h. by 1st wife, *b.* 1740; *suc. to the Baronetcy*, 4 June 1762; was, sometime, Marshal of the Vice-Admiralty Court in Jamaica. He *m.* firstly, 5 Aug. 1765, Everilda Dorothea, 3d da. of the Rev. William SMITH, Rector of Burnham aforesaid, by Elizabeth, da. of Richard BEAUMONT, of Whitby Hall, co. York. She *d.* Sep. 1800. He *m.* secondly, 4 Aug. 1808, Catherine, widow of the Rev. Edward Roger NORTH, Vicar of Harlow, Essex, da. of the Rev. Armyne STYLEMAN, of Ringstead, Norfolk, by Ann, da. of James BLAKEWAY, R.N. He *d.* 24 Sep. 1815, aged 75. Will pr. 1816. His widow, by whom he had no issue, *d.* 29 April 1825, at Ringstead aforesaid, in her 66th year.

V. 1815, to 1854. SIR ROGER MARTIN, Baronet [1667], of Burnham Westgate Hall and Long Melford aforesaid, only s. and h. by 1st wife, *b.* 22 Feb. 1778, at Burnham; entered the East India Company's service (Bengal), 1795, and was, sometime, senior Judge of the Court of Appeal, at Moorshedabad, retiring in 1828, having *suc. to the Baronetcy*, 25 Sep. 1815. He *d.* unm., 16 Dec. 1854, at Burnham Westgate Hall, aged 76, when the *Baronetcy* became *extinct*. Will pr. Jan. 1855.

HASTINGS:

cr. 7 May 1667;

ex. Sep. 1668.

I. 1667, to 1668. "RICHARD HASTINGS, of Redlynch (near Bristol), co. Somerset, Esq.," 3d s. of Sir Henry HASTINGS, of Hamberston, co. Leicester, by Mabel, da. of Anthony FAUNT, of Foston, in that county (which Henry, who *d.* 1629, was 4th s. of Sir Edward HASTINGS, 4th s. of Francis, 2d EARL OF HUNTINGDON), was *cr. a Baronet*, as above, 7 May 1667. He *m.* Margaret, da. of Sir Robert POYNTZ, K.B., of Iron Acton, co. Gloucester. He *d.* s.p., and was *bur.* 3 Sep. 1668, in Bath Abbey, when the *Baronetcy* became *extinct*. Will pr. 1668. His widow *m.* 24 Sep. 1669, at Wells (registered at Wraxall, co. Somerset), Samuel GORGES, of the Inner Temple, London, 3d Justice of the Common Pleas [I.], 1684-86 (*bap.* 26 March 1635, at Wraxall, Somerset), who, surviving her, *d.* 23 Dec. 1686, desiring to be *bur.* with her at St. Mary's, Kilkenny.

HANHAM:

cr. 24 May 1667.

I. 1667. "WILLIAM HANHAM, of [Dean's Court, in] Wimborne, co. Dorset., Esq." 1st s. and h. of John HANHAM, of the same (*d.* 1662, aged 76), by Frances, sister of John DODINGTON, of Bremer, Hants, was *b.*, probably, about 1641, and was *cr. a Baronet* as above, 24 May 1667. He *m.* Elizabeth, da. of George COOPER, of Clarendon Park, Wilts (br. to the 1st EARL OF SHAFTESBURY), by Elizabeth, 1st da. of John OLDFIELD, Alderman of

(a) Probably a da. by a former husband.

London. He *d.* in May or June 1671. Will dat. 17 May and pr. 9 June 1671. The will of his widow, who was a prisoner in the Tower of London in 1689,(a) was pr. 1722.

II. 1671. SIR JOHN HANHAM, Baronet [1667], of Dean's Court, in Wimborne, aforesaid, only s. and h; *suc. to the Baronetcy* in May or June 1671. He *m.* Jane, da. and h. of William EYRE, of Neston Park, Wilts. He *d.* 1703. Will pr. July 1710. His widow(b) *d.* 1707.

III. 1703. SIR WILLIAM HANHAM, Baronet [1667], of Dean's Court, in Wimborne, and of Neston Park aforesaid, 1st s. and h., *b.*, probably, about 1690; *suc. to the Baronetcy* in 1703. He *m.*, in June 1717, Mary, 1st da. of William NORRIS, of Nonsuch, Wilts, by Eliza, da. of Jacob SELFE, of Beanacre in that county. He *d.* March 1762. Admon. 26 May 1762. His widow *d.* 22 Dec. 1774, aged 78.

IV. 1762. SIR WILLIAM HANHAM, Baronet [1667], of Dean's Court, in Wimborne, and of Neston Park aforesaid, 1st s. and h., *b.* 1718 at Nonsuch aforesaid; matric. at Oxford (New Coll.) 18 Nov. 1736, aged 18; *suc. to the Baronetcy* in March 1762; Lieut. Col. of the Dorset Militia. He *m.* firstly, in March 1744, Ann, da. of John JENNINGS, of Shiplake, Oxon, by Jane, da. of William CONSTANTINE, of Merly, Dorset. She *d.* s.p. He *m.* secondly, in June 1762, Mary, 3d da. of William LYNCH, D.D., Dean of Canterbury, by Mary, da. of William WAKE, D.D., Archbishop of Canterbury. She *d.* Oct. 1764. Admon. 18 Dec. 1764. Will pr. Feb. 1765. He *m.* thirdly, in Dec. 1765, Harriet, 3d da. of Henry DRAX, of Charborough, Dorset, by Elizabeth, da. and h. of Sir Edward ERNLE, 3d Baronet [1661]. He *d.*, after a long and painful illness, at Bath, 11 and was *bur.* 24 Feb. 1776, in Bath Abbey, aged 58. Will pr. 1776. His widow *d.* 2 April 1786. Will pr. June 1786.

V. 1776. SIR WILLIAM THOMAS HANHAM, Baronet [1667], of Dean's Court in Wimborne aforesaid, only s. and h., by 2d wife; *b.* June 1763; *suc. to the Baronetcy*, 11 Feb. 1776; matric. at Oxford (Corpus Christi Coll.), 30 Oct. 1781, aged 18. He *d.* unm. 19 Aug. 1791, aged 28. Will pr. Aug. 1791.

VI. 1791. SIR JAMES HANHAM, Baronet [1667], of Dean's Court, in Wimborne aforesaid, uncle and h., being yst. son of the 3d Baronet, *b.* at Calne about 1726; matric. at Oxford (Oriel Coll.), 17 Dec. 1744, aged 18; B.A., 1748; in Holy Orders; *suc. to the Baronetcy*, 19 Aug. 1791; was Rector of Winterborne, Selston and Pimperne, all in co. Dorset, 1800 till death. He *m.* in 1757, Jane, only child of Edward PHELIPS, of Wimborne (*bap.* 23 March 1706), niece and heir of William PHELIPS, of Corfe Mullen, Dorset, who *d.* s.p. 1747, aged 46. She, by whom he had twelve children, *d.*, apparently, before him. He *d.* at Dean's Court, 11 March 1806, aged 80. Will pr. 1806.

VII. 1806. SIR JAMES HANHAM, Baronet [1667], of Dean's Court, in Wimborne aforesaid, 1st s. and h., *b.* at Corfe Mullen aforesaid, 10 March 1760; matric. at Oxford (Trin. Coll.), 16 Dec. 1778, aged 18; in Holy Orders; was a Priest of the Colleg. Church of Wimborne and Rector

(a) She was the only woman among 25 prisoners, among whom were Judge Jefferies, the Earl of Peterborough, Lord Montgomery, Lord Preston, etc., and other adherents of James II. According to Playfair's *Baronetage* this lady alienated several estates, and kept her minor son out of all the profits till he was 25. It is certain that in 1674 an Act of Parl. was passed to pay the debts of her husband, the late Baronet, out of his real property.

(b) She is called an "incomparable lady." See Hutchins' *Dorset* (edit. 1868), vol. iii, p. 232, and Wotton's *Baronetage*, 1741.

of Winterborne Selston, 1806 till his death; *suc. to the Baronetcy*, 11 March 1806. He *m.* firstly, 16 April 1793, Anne, da. of Edward PYKE, R.N. She *d.* 15 July 1801. He *m.* secondly, 14 Dec. 1815, Eliza DEAN, da. of William PATEY, Lieut. R.N., of Wimborne aforesaid. He *d.* 2 April 1849, aged 89. Will pr. July 1849. His widow *d.* 5 June 1877, at Manston House, Dorset, in her 90th year.

VIII. 1849. SIR WILLIAM HANNAM, Baronet [1667], of Dean's Court, in Wimborne aforesaid, 1st s. and h., by 1st wife, *b.* 8 May 1798; Lieut. R.N., 1818; *suc. to the Baronetcy*, 2 April 1849. He *m.* 6 Nov. 1823, Harriet, da. of George MORGAN, of Mount Clare, in Roehampton, Surrey. She *d.* Feb. 1838. He *d.* s.p., 27 March 1877, at 30 St. James' square, Bath, aged 78.

IX. 1877. SIR JOHN ALEXANDER HANHAM, Baronet [1667], of Dean's Court, in Wimborne aforesaid, nephew and h., being 1st s. and h. of Capt. John HANHAM, by Amy Ursula, da. of Alexander COPLAND, of Wingfield, Berks, which John (who distinguished himself in the Sutlej campaign, and who *d.* 16 Sept. 1861, aged 38), was 3d s. of the 7th Baronet, being the 1st s. by the 2d wife. He was *b.* 5 July 1854, at Malvern; ed. at Wellington Coll.; matric. at Oxford (Mag. Coll.), 16 Jan. 1875, aged 20; B.A., 1878; M.A., 1885; Barrister (Inner Temple), 1881; Apparitor Gen. of the Province of Canterbury, 1885. He *m.*, 18 July 1896, at St. Paul's, Knightsbridge, Cordelia Lucy, 2d da. of Henry Charles (LOPES), 1st BARON LUDLOW OF HEYWOOD, by Cordelia Lucy, da. of Erving CLARK, of Efford, Devon.

TOPP:

cr. 25 July 1668;

dorm. or *ex.* 1733.

I. 1668. FRANCIS TOPP, of Tormarton, co. Gloucester, Esq.," presumably s. of John TOPP, of Salisbury and Stockton, Wilts (*d.* 13 Aug. 1632), by Mary, da. of John HOOPER, was *cr. a Baronet*, as above, 25 July 1668. He *m.*, in or before 1663, Elizabeth, said(a) to be a "kinswoman of the Duke of Newcastle." He *d.* in or before 1676. Will pr. 1676. The will of Dame Elizabeth Topp, of York, pr. 1703.

II. 1676? SIR JOHN TOPP, Baronet [1668], of Tormarton aforesaid, s. and h., *b.* about 1663; *suc. to the Baronetcy*, in or before 1676. He *m.* 31 March 1684, at St. Margaret's, Westm. (Lic. Fac. 29, he about 21 and she about 17), Barbara, sister of Henry, 1st VISCOUNT ST. JOHN, da. of Sir Walter ST. JOHN, 3d Baronet [1611], by Joanna, da. of Oliver ST. JOHN, Chief Justice of the Common Pleas. He, who was living "distract"(a), 1703, *d.* s.p.m.(b)

III. 1720? to 1733. SIR JEREMY TOPP, Baronet [1668], of Bremore, Hants, presumed to be br. and h. male, and, as such, to have *suc. to the Baronetcy* about 1720. He was *bur.* 1733, at Highgate, Midx., when the *Baronetcy* became *dormant* or *extinct*. M.I.

(a) Le Neve's MS. *Baronetage*.
(b) St. John, his da., *bap.* 10 March 1685/6, at Newark, Notts, inherited the Tormarton estate. She *m.*, firstly, John Hungerford, and, secondly, Thomas Peach.

LANGHORN:

cr. 28 Aug. 1668;

ex. 26 Feb. 1714/5.

I. 1668, to 1715. "WILLIAM LANGHORNE, of the Inner Temple, London, Esq.," 1st s. of William LANGHORNE, of London, was *b.* about 1634; was not improbably the "William, s. and h. of William LANGHORNE, of Hitchin, Herts, gent.," who was admitted, 7 July 1652, to Gray's Inn; was an East India merchant, and was *cr. a Baronet*, as above, 28 Aug. 1668. He, in 1680, purchased the manor and estate of Charlton, near Greenwich, Kent. He *m.* firstly, after 1694, Grace, DOWAGER VISCOUNTESS CHAWORTH OF ARMAGH [I.] 2d da. of John (MANNERS), 8th EARL OF RUTLAND, by Frances, da. of Edward (MONTAGU), BARON MONTAGU OF BOUGHTON. She, who was *b.* at Haddon, co. Derby, 1632, *d.* 15 and was *bur.* 24 Feb. 1699/700, at Charlton, in her 69th year. M.I. He *m.* secondly, 16 Oct. 1714, Mary, da. of (—) ASTON and Dorothy, afterwards wife of Rev. Robert WARREN, D.D. He *d.* s.p., 26 Feb. 1714/5, and was *bur.* at Charlton, aged 85, when the *Baronetcy* became *extinct*.(a) Will pr. 8 March 1714/5. His widow *m.*, 24 Sep 1717, at Lee, co. Kent, George JONES, of Twickenham, Midx., and *d.* his widow, 26 May 1730, aged 33, being *bur.* at Charlton. M.I. Admon. 17 May 1738.

Memorandum.—It is remarkable that after so many creations [E.], averaging upwards of forty a year, during eight years, 1660 to 1667, there are but two creations [E.] in 1668, and *none* in 1669.

MOSTYN:

cr. 28 April 1670.

I. 1670. "EDWARD MOSTYN, of Talacre, co. Flint, Esq.," 1st s. and h. of John MOSTYN, of the same, by Anne, da. of Henry FOX of Lehurst, Salop, was *cr. a Baronet*, as above, 28 April 1670. He *m.* firstly, Elizabeth, da. of Robert DOWNS, of Bodney, Norfolk, by whom he had eight children. He *m.* secondly, Eleanor, widow of Thomas POOL, of Pool, co. Chester, da. of Francis DRAYCOTT, of co. Stafford. She *d.* at St. Giles' in the Fields, Midx., 1685. Admon. 10 Dec. 1724 and May 1733. He *m.* thirdly, Mary, widow of Sir George SELBY, da. of Richard (MOLYNEUX), 1st VISCOUNT MOLYNEUX OF MARYBOROUGH [I.], by Mary, da. and coheir of Sir Thomas CARYLL. She was *bur.* 28 Jan. 1697/8, at St. Giles' aforesaid. Admon. 27 June 1698, to her husband. He *d.* before 1715.

II. 1700? SIR PYERS MOSTYN, Baronet [1670], of Talacre aforesaid, 2d but 1st surv. s. and h. by 1st wife; *suc. to the Baronetcy* between 1698 and 1715, on which last date he was "a Catholic Nonjuror" with an entailed estate of £512 a year. He *m.* Frances, da. of Sir George SELBY, of Wentington, co. Durham, by Mary his wife, both abovenamed. He *d.* 15 Nov. 1720. Will pr. 1721. The admon. of his wife or probably widow who *d.* at Llansasaph, co. Flint, was granted, 17 March, 1725/6, to his executor.

(a) The valuable estate of Charlton passed by entail to his nephew (s. of his sister Elizabeth), Sir John Conyers, 3d Baronet [1628], and on the death, s.p.m., in 1731, of the 4th Baronet (son of the above), to William Langhorn Games, on whose death it was inherited by the Rev. John Maryon, whence it passed to the family of Wilson, afterwards Maryon-Wilson, Baronet [1661]. See vol. iii, p. 171, note "b."

III. 1720. SIR PYERS MOSTYN, Baronet [1670], of Talacre aforesaid, 2d but 1st surv. s. and h.; *suc. to the Baronetcy* 15 Nov. 1720. He *d.* unm. 1735.

IV. 1735. SIR GEORGE MOSTYN, Baronet [1670], of Talacre aforesaid, br. and h., *suc. to the Baronetcy* in 1735. He *m.* firstly, Mary, 1st da. of Thomas CLIFTON, of Lytham, co. Lancaster, by Eleanora Alathea, da. of Richard WALMESLEY. She *d.* s.p. He *m.* secondly, in or before 1725, Teresa, da. of Charles TOWNLEY, of Townley, co. Lancaster, by Ursula, da. of Richard FERMOR, of Tusmore, Oxon. He *d.* at Talacre, 30 Sep. 1746. Admon. 21 Oct. 1746, to his widow. She *d.* 27 March 1766. Will pr. 1766.

V. 1746. SIR EDWARD MOSTYN, Baronet [1670], of Talacre aforesaid, 1st s. and h., *b.* 27 April 1725; *suc. to the Baronetcy*, 30 Sep. 1746. He *m.* June 1748, Barbara, da. and h. of Sir George BROWNE, 3d Baronet [1659], of Kiddington, Oxon, by his 1st wife, Barbara, da. of Edward (LEE), 1st EARL OF LICHFIELD. He was *bur.* 13 March 1755, at Kiddington. M.I. Will pr. 1755. His widow *m.* in or before 1760, Edward GORE, of Barrow Court, in Barrow Gurney, Somerset (who was *bur.* there 11 April 1801), and *d.* 1801, aged 72. Will pr. 1810.

VI. 1755. SIR PYERS MOSTYN, Baronet [1670], of Talacre aforesaid, 1st s. and h. 1st s. and h., *b.* 23 Dec. 1749; *suc. to the Baronetcy* in March 1755. He *m.* in or before 1784. Barbara, da. of (—) SLAUGHTER, of Ingatestone, Essex. She *d.* 2 Oct. 1815. He *d.* 29 Oct. 1823, aged 73. Admon. Nov. 1823.

VII. 1823. SIR EDWARD MOSTYN, Baronet [1670], of Talacre aforesaid, only s. and h., *b.* 10 April 1785; *suc. to the Baronetcy*, 29 Oct. 1823; was sometime Custos Brevium of the Court of Common Pleas. Sheriff of Flintshire, 1837-38. He *m.* firstly, 20 Oct. 1808, Frances, 1st da. of Nicholas BLUNDELL, *formerly* PEPPARD, of Crosby, co. Lancaster, by Clementina, da. of Stephen Walter TEMPEST, of Broughton, co. York. She *d.* 27 Jan. 1835, at Spring Bank, near Worcester, from the effects of a carriage accident.(a) He *m.* secondly, 2 Aug. 1836, his cousin, Constantina, 3d da. of Henry SLAUGHTER, of Furze Hall, Essex. He *d.* 18 July 1841, at Talacre, in his 56th year. Will pr. Aug. 1841. His widow *d.* 12 Dec. 1872.

VIII. 1841. SIR PYERS MOSTYN, Baronet [1670], of Talacre aforesaid, 1st s. and h. by 1st wife, *b.* 27 Sep. 1811, at Cooper Hill, Lancashire; *suc. to the Baronetcy*, 18 July 1841; Sheriff of Flintshire, 1843-44. He *m.* 9 May 1844, at the Roman Catholic church, Chelsea, Frances Georgiana, 2d da. of Thomas Alexander (FRASER), LORD LOVAT [S.], by Charlotte Georgiana, da. of George (JERNINGHAM), 8th LORD STAFFORD. He *d.* at Talacre, 14 May 1882, in his 71st year. Will pr. under £40,000. His widow, who was *b.* 20 Feb. 1826, *d.* 25 Dec. 1899, in her 74th year, at Haunton Hall, Tamworth.

IX. 1882. SIR PYERS WILLIAM MOSTYN, Baronet [1670], of Talacre aforesaid, 1st s. and h., *b.* there, 14 May 1846; *suc. to the Baronetcy*, 14 May 1882; Sheriff of Flintshire, 1893. He *m.* 4 Nov. 1880, at the Roman Catholic church of St. Joseph, Avon Dasset, Anna Maria, 5th da. of Thomas Aloysius PERRY, of Bitham House, co. Warwick.

Family Estates.—These, in 1883, consisted of 4,184 acres in Flintshire, valued then at £9,000 a year, but in 1878 at £10,568. In 1878 there was added thereto 2,025 acres in Carnarvonshire, and 292 in Denbighshire (worth together, £4,278 a year), belonging to the "trustees of Lady Mostyn." *Seat.*—Talacre, near Rhyl, co. Flint.

(a) See a full account thereof in the *Annual Register* for 1805.

STONHOUSE, *or* STONEHOUSE:

cr. 5 May 1670;

merged July 1740, in the Baronetcy *cr.* 7 May 1628.

I. 1670. "SIR GEORGE STONEHOUSE," 3d Baronet [1628], of Radley, Berks, wishing to debar his eldest son from succeeding to his title, was *cr. a Baronet*, as above, 5 May 1670, "for life (having surrendered his former patent by a fine(a)), with rem. to John STONEHOUSE, his 2d son, and to the heirs male of his body, and, for lack of such issue, to James, his 3d son, etc, with precedency to him and his sayd sons according to the first patent dated 7 May 1628." See fuller particulars of him in vol. ii, p. 37, under the creations of 1628. He *d.* 1675. Will pr. 1675.

II. 1675. SIR JOHN STONHOUSE, Baronet [1670], of Radley aforesaid, 2d s., *b* about 1639; matric. at Oxford (Queen's Coll.), 7 Nov. 1655; admitted to Gray's Inn, 28 Nov. 1656; *suc. to the Baronetcy*, according to the spec. rem. in its creation (as also to the family estates) on the death of his father, 1675; was M.P. for Abingdon (six Parls.), 1675-81, 1685-87, and Jan. to Feb. 1690. He *m.* (Lic. Vic. Gen. 10 Oct. 1668, he about 29 and she about 26), Martha, widow of Richard SPENCER, of London, merchant, da. and h. of Robert BRIGGES (a yr. s. of Sir Moreton BRIGGES, 1st Baronet [1641]), by Sarah, da. of Thomas MORETON, of Shiffnal, Salop. He *d.* about 1700. Will pr. Nov. 1700. The will of his widow, dat. 29 March 1705, pr. 5 Feb. 1711/2.

III. 1700? SIR JOHN STONHOUSE, Baronet [1670], of Radley aforesaid, s. and h., *b.* about 1673; matric. at Oxford (Queen's Coll.), 12 April 1690, aged 17; admitted to the Inner Temple, 1690; *suc. to the Baronetcy*, about 1700; was M.P. for Berks (nine Parls.) 1701 to his death in 1733; P.C., 7 April 1713, and Comptroller of the Household to Queen Anne, 1713-14. He *m.* firstly, Mary, da. and h. of Henry MELLISH, of Sanderstead, Surrey. She *d.* s.p.m., in or shortly before 1706. Her will pr. June 1715. He *m.* secondly, 29 Aug. 1706, at Kirtlington, Oxon, Penelope, da. of Sir Robert DASHWOOD, 1st Baronet [1684], of Northbrooke, Oxon, by Penelope, da. and coheir of Sir Thomas CHAMBERLAYNE, 2d Baronet [1642]. He *d.* 10 Aug. 1733. Will dat. 26 March 1732, pr. 3 Feb. 1734/5.

IV. 1733. SIR JOHN STONHOUSE, Baronet [1670], of Radley aforesaid, s. and h., *suc. to the abovenamed Baronetcy* [1670] on the death of his father, 10 Aug. 1733, and *suc. to the Baronetcy cr.* 7 May 1628, on the death of his cousin in July 1740. See "STONHOUSE" Baronetcy, *cr.* 7 May 1628, under the 7th Baronet.

CARTERET, *or* DE CARTERET:

cr. 4 June 1670;

ex. 6 June 1715.

I. 1670. "PHILIP CARTERET, of St. Ouen [in the Island of] Jersey, Esq.," only s. and h. of Sir Philip CARTERET,(b) Seignior of St. Ouen aforesaid, by Anne, da. of Sir Francis DOWSE, of Wallop, Hants, suc. his father in that Seignory, and was *cr. a Baronet*, as above, 4 June 1670. He, in 1675, was Bailiff of the Island of Jersey. He *m.* in 1649, Anne, da. of Abraham DUMARESQUE. He *d.* probably in 1672, but certainly before 1675.

(a) Such surrender, however, of an English dignity was, presumably, illegal.
(b) This Philip was uncle to Sir George Carteret, Joint Gov. of Jersey, who was *cr. a Baronet* 9 May 1645, and was ancestor of the Barons Carteret of Hawnes and Earls Granville.

II. 1675? SIR PHILIP CARTERET, *or* DE CARTERET, Baronet [1670], of St. Ouen aforesaid, only s. and h., *b.* about 1650; *suc. to the Baronetcy* before 25 April 1676. He *m.* (Lic. Vic. Gen., 25 April 1676, he a Baronet, aged 25, Bachelor, she about 13, with consent of her father) Elizabeth, only surv. child of Sir Edward CARTERET, Seigneur of Trinity, Gentleman Usher of the Black Rod, by Elizabeth, da. of Robert JOHNSON, Alderman of London. He *d.* in 1693. Will dat. 17 May 1688, pr. 16 Nov. 1693. His widow, who was *b.* 30 Dec. 1663, and *bap.* 12 Jan. 1663/4, at St. Martin's in the Fields, *d.* 26 and was *bur.* 20 March 1717, in Westm. Abbey, aged 52. M.I. Will dat. 23 July 1716 to 12 March 1716/7, pr. 1 April 1717.

III. 1693, to 1715. SIR CHARLES CARTERET, *or* DE CARTERET, Baronet [1670], of St. Ouen aforesaid, only s. and h., *bap.* 4 June 1679, at St. Margaret's, Westm., King Charles II and the Duke of Monmouth being his sponsors; *suc. to the Baronetcy* in 1693; was Gent. of the Privy Chamber to Queen Anne, and High Bailiff of Jersey. He *d.* s.p.s.(a) 3 or 6 and was *bur.* 8 June 1715, in Westm. Abbey, when the *Baronetcy* became *extinct.* M.I.(b).

SKIPWITH :
cr. 25 Oct. 1670 ;
ex. presumably 28 Jan. 1790.

I. 1670. "FULWAR SKIPWITH, of Newbold Hall [in Monk's Kirby], co. Warwick, Esq.," s. and h. of William SKIPWITH, by Elizabeth, da. and coheir of Richard REDDING, of Harrow on the Hill, Midx. (which William was only s. and h. of Henry SKIPWITH, by Margaret, da. of Richard FULWAR, of Copwood, Sussex), was elected Sheriff of Warwickshire, Nov. 1667, but did not act, and was *cr. a Baronet*, as above, 25 Oct. 1670. He *m.* firstly, Dorothy, da. of Thomas PARKER, of Anglesey Abbey, co. Cambridge. He *m.* secondly, Elizabeth, widow of Sir George CONY, da. of Edward SKIPWITH, of Grantham. He *d.* 1678. Will dat. 13 to 14 Dec. 1671, pr. 23 May 1678. The will of his widow dat. 12 Feb. 1689, pr. 11 July 1691, 20 June and 20 Dec. 1694.

II. 1678. SIR FULWAR SKIPWITH, Baronet [1670], of Newbold Hall aforesaid, grandson and h., being only s. and h. of Humberston SKIPWITH, by Elizabeth, da. and h. of Sir George CONY and Elizabeth his wife, both abovenamed, which Humberston was s. and h. ap. of the late Baronet, but *d.* v.p., 14 June 1677, aged 22. He was *bap.* 24 June 1676 and *suc. to the Baronetcy*, two years later. He was M.P. for Coventry, 1713-14. He *m.* (Lic. Fac. 18 Aug. 1703) Mary, da. of Sir Francis DASHWOOD, 1st Baronet [1707], of Wycombe, by his 1st wife, Mary, da. of John JENNINGS. He *d.* at Bath, 13 May 1728, aged 52. Will pr. 1728. His widow *d.* Aug. 1738. Admon., as at St. Geo. Han. sq., 9 Oct. 1738, to a creditor.

III. 1728. SIR FRANCIS SKIPWITH, Baronet [1670], of Newbold Hall aforesaid, 1st s. and h., *b.* probably about 1705; *suc. to the Baronetcy* 13 May 1728. He *m.* in 1734(c) Ursula, 2d and yst. da. of Thomas CARTWRIGHT, of Aynho, co. Northampton, by Airmine, 2d da. and coheir of Thomas (CREW), 2d BARON CREW OF STEYNE. She *d.* 1771. He *d.* 6 Dec. 1778. Admon. 16 Jan. 1779, and Sep. 1824.

(a) He had a son, James, *bap.* at Isleworth, 15 June 1694, who *d.* before him.
(b) His age on his monument is given as in his 34th year, and on his coffin plate as aged 34, but at the time of his burial he was, apparently, 36.
(c) Ped. of Cartwright in Baker's Northamptonshire, but query if this marriage was not in or before 1730.

IV. 1778, to 1790. SIR THOMAS GEORGE SKIPWITH, Baronet [1670], of Newbold Hall, aforesaid, 1st s. and h.; was M.P. for Warwickshire (two Parls.), March 1769 to 1780, and for Steyning, 1780-84, having *suc. to the Baronetcy*, 6 Dec. 1778. He *m.*, 13 Sep. 1785, at St. Marylebone, Midx., Selina, 1st da. of the Hon. George SHIRLEY, of Lower Eatington, co. Warwick (yr. s. of Robert, 1st EARL FERRERS), by Mary, da. of Humphrey STURT. He *d.* s.p. 28 Jan. 1790, aged, it is said, 60(a), and was *bur.* at Monks Kirby, co. Warwick, when the *Baronetcy*, presumably, became *extinct.* M.I. Will pr. Aug. 1790. His widow, who was *b.* 22 June and *bap.* 18 July 1752, at Lower Eatington, *d.* 28 March 1832, at Newbold Hall, aged 80, and was *bur.* at Monks Kirby. M.I.

SABINE, *or* SABIN :
cr. 22 March 1670/1 ;
ex. Nov. 1704.

I. 1671, to 1704. "SIR JOHN SABIN, of Eyne [or Ton House] in [Upper] Gravenhurst, co. Bedford, Knt.," s. and h. of John SABINE, of Patricksbourne, Kent (who *d.* 1658), by (—), da. of (—) SHERWOOD, of co. Cambridge, was *b.* about 1639; matric. at Oxford (Glouc. Hall), 21 March 1658/9, having been admitted to Lincoln's Inn, 6 Nov. 1652; Barrister, 1664, and was *cr. a Baronet*, as above, 22 March 1670/1, having been *Knighted* on the same day. He, in 1672, sold the Eyne estate. He *m.* (Lic. Vic. Gen., 24 July 1665, he 26 and she 18, with consent of her father), Elizabeth, da. and h. of William ALLEN, of Eyne aforesaid, by Eleanor, da. of the Rev. William GOLDSMITH, Rector of Campton-cum-Shefford, Beds. She was living 1673. He *d.* s.p.m.s.(b), and was *bur.* 26 Nov. 1704, at St. James', Clerkenwell, Midx.(c), when the *Baronetcy* became *extinct.* Will pr. June 1705.

CHAYTOR :
cr. 28 June 1671 ;
ex. Jan. 1720/1.

I. 1671, to 1721. "WILLIAM CHATER (*i.e.*, CHAYTOR), of Croft Hall [near Darlington], co. York, Esq.," 2d but 1st surv. s. and h. of Nicholas CHAYTOR, of Butterby, co. Durham, Col. in the Royal Service (*d.* 10 Feb. 1655), by Anne, da. and coheir of William LAMBTON, of Haughton-le-Field in that county, was *bap.* 5 Aug. 1639, and having, by the death in 1660 of the infant s. of (his 2d cousin, once removed) John CHAYTOR, of Croft aforesaid, *suc.* to that estate, entered his pedigree at the Visit. of Yorkshire in 1665, being then aged 25, and was *cr. a Baronet*, as above, 28 June 1671. He was Col. of the Richmondshire Militia in 1689. In 1695 he procured an Act of Parl. for making provision for younger children and payment of debts. He *m.* 21 Aug. 1675 (settlement 17), Peregrina, da. of Sir Joseph CRADOCK, of Richmond, co. York, by his 2d wife, Jane, da. and h. of the Rev. Anthony MAXTON, Preb. of Durham. She *d.* 16 and was *bur.* 19 June 1704 at Kensington. He *d.* s.p.m.s.,(d)

(a) But see p. 48, note "c," as to the marriage of his parents, said to have been in 1734.
(b) Margaret, his 1st da., *bap.* 12 Dec. 1668 at Upper Gravenhurst, *m.*, in or before 1692, Charles Milward, of Silsoe, Beds, and had issue.
(c) The burial entry is "John Sabin; it was said he was a Baronet."
(d) He had no less than eight sons and five daughters, none of whom survived him. Two of the sons, Henry and Thomas, served under the Duke of Marlborough, of whom Henry was a Major in the army, and *d.* at York 17 Oct. 1717, aged 31, being *bur.* at Croft.

a prisoner for debt, in the Fleet prison, where he had been seventeen years, and was *bur.* 7 Jan. 1720/1, at St. Bride's, London, aged 81, when the *Baronetcy* became *extinct.*(a)

CROFT :
cr. 18 Nov. 1671.

I. 1671. "HERBERT CROFT, of Croft Castle, co. Hereford [only] son and heir [ap.] to [Herbert CROFT] the Bishop of Hereford" (who *d.* 18 May 1691, aged 88), by Anne, da. of Jonathan BROWN, D.D., Dean of Hereford, was *b.* about 1652; matric. at Oxford (Magdalen Coll.), 27 June 1668, aged 16; entered the Middle Temple, 1668, and, "being a gentleman of good parts and judgment and a zealous Protestant,"(b) was v.p. *cr. a Baronet*, as above, 18 Nov. 1671; was M.P. for Herefordshire, March to July 1679 and 1690-98; elected Sheriff of that county 1682, but did not act. He *m.*, in or before 1678, Elizabeth, da. of Thomas ARCHER, of Umberslade, co. Warwick, by Anne, da. of Richard LEIGH, of London. She *d.* 1709. He *d.* 3 Nov. 1720. Will dat. 8 July 1716, pr. 4 Dec. 1720.

II. 1720. SIR ARCHER CROFT, Baronet [1661], of Croft Castle aforesaid, 1st s. and h., *bap.* 3 March 1683/4; matric. at Oxford (New Coll.), 15 April 1702, aged 17; *suc. to the Baronetcy*, 3 Nov. 1720; was M.P. for Leominster, 1722-27, for Winchilsea, Feb. to March 1728, and for Beeralston, March 1728 to 1734; was a Commissioner of Trade and Plantations, 1730. He *m.* 10 Jan. 1723, Frances, da. of Brig. Gen. Richard WARING. He *d.* 10 Dec. 1753, aged 69. Admon. 21 June 1770, limited as to the interest of the family of Dyer. His widow *d.* 6 May 1767, at her house at Kensington.(c) Will, in which she directs to be *bur.* at Thatcham, Berks, pr. 6 June 1767.

III. 1753. SIR ARCHER CROFT, Baronet [1671], of Croft Castle aforesaid, 1st s. and h., *b.* 1731; *suc. to the Baronetcy*, 10 Dec. 1753. He was an officer in the Court of Chancery, and a Vice-President of the [Lunatic?] Asylum. He sold the family estate of Croft Castle. He *m.* 24 April 1759, Elizabeth Charlotte (1st cousin of, the poet, William COWPER), 2d da. and coheir of Ashley COWPER, one of the Clerks to the House of Lords, by Dorothy, da. of John OAKES. He *d.* s.p.m.s., 30 Nov. 1792, at Salisbury. Will pr. Jan. 1793. His widow *d.* in or before 1808. Will pr. 1808.

IV. 1792. SIR JOHN CROFT, Baronet [1671], of Dunstan Honse in Thatcham, Berks, and of Russell Place, St. Pancras, Midx., br. and h. male, *b.*, probably, about 1735; *suc. to the Baronetcy*, 30 Nov. 1792. He *d.* unm. and s.p. legit., at Bath, 4 Dec. 1797. Will dat. 15 Oct. 1796, pr. 29 Dec. 1797.

V. 1797. SIR HERBERT CROFT, Baronet [1671], 2d cousin, once removed, and h. male, being 1st s. and h. of Herbert CROFT, of Waterhouse, Essex, Receiver of the Charter House estates (*d.* 7 July 1785, aged 67), by his 1st wife Elizabeth, da. of Richard YOUNG, of Midhurst, Sussex, which

(a) He was suc. in the estate of Croft by his nephew, Henry Chaytor, whose father, Henry, had *d.* 4 May 1719, aged 71. He *d.* Feb. 1774, aged 85, being father of William Chaytor, whose illegit. son, William Chaytor, was *cr. a Baronet* 30 Sep. 1831, as "of Croft, co. York, and of Witton Castle, co. Durham."
(b) Wotton's *Baronetage*, edit. 1741.
(c) The following strange notice of death on 25 Jan. 1805, occurs in the *Annual Register* for 1805, viz.:—"At Batheaston, Grace, Lady Croft, da. of [—] Bramston, Esq., and relict of Sir Archer Croft, Baronet, who died 1758 [*sic*], being the 2d who bore the title." This apparently refers to *Grace*, da. of Thomas *Bramston*, of Waterhouse, Essex, who *m.* in or before 1722, Francis Croft, 2d son of the 1st Baronet, and who was grandmother of the 5th and 6th Baronets. If so, however, she must have been aged about 100 years.

Herbert was s. and h. of Francis CROFT, of London, one of the six Clerks of the Court of Chancery, and Receiver for the Charter House estates. He was *b.* 1 Nov. 1751, at Dunster park, Berks; admitted to Lincoln's Inn, 26 June 1765; matric. at Oxford (Univ. Coll.), 16 March 1771, aged 19; B.C.L., 1785; was sometime a Barrister, but afterwards took Holy Orders, and was Vicar of Prittlewell, Essex, 1787; author of "*Love and Madness*" (1780),(a) and of several other publications. He *suc. to the Baronetcy*, 4 Dec. 1797. He *m.* firstly, Sophia, da. and h. of Richard CLEAVE. She *d.* 8 Feb. 1792. He *m.* secondly, 25 Feb. 1795 (by spec. lic.), at Ham House, Petersham, Surrey (the residence of her sister, the Countess of Dysart [S.]), Elizabeth, da. of David LEWIS, of Allesley and Solihull, co. Warwick. She *d.* Sep. 1815. He *d.* s.p.m., 25 April 1816, at Paris, having been a prisoner of war there for fifteen years, since 1801. Admon. Dec. 1816.

VI. 1816. SIR RICHARD CROFT, Baronet [1671], br. and h. male, *b.* 9 Jan. 1762, was sometime a surgeon at Tutbury, and afterwards for a short time at Oxford, where he was "privilegiatus" as "Chirurgus," 20 June 1788, and finally settled in London, where he was known as an eminent "accoucheur," attending as such the Princess Charlotte, whose death, 6 Nov. 1817, was the cause of his suicide, some three months later. He *suc. to the Baronetcy*, 25 April 1816. He *m.* 3 Nov. 1769, Margaret, sister of Thomas (DENMAN), 1st BARON DENMAN OF DOVEDALE, da. of Thomas DENMAN, M.D., by Elizabeth, da. of Alexander BRODIE. He shot himself through the head, at the house of a patient in Wimpole street, 13, and was *bur.* 18 Feb. 1818,(b) from his own house in Old Burlington street, at St. James', Westm., aged 57. Will pr. 1815. His widow *d.* 24 Sep. 1847, in Welbeck street, aged 77. Will pr. Oct. 1847.

VII. 1818. SIR THOMAS ELMSLEY CROFT, Baronet [1651], 3d but 1st surv. s. and h., *b.* 2 Sep. 1798; *suc. to the Baronetcy*, 13 Feb. 1818; F.S.A. He *m.* 9 Sep. 1824, at Caversham Park, Berks (by spec. lic.), Sophia Jane Lateward, only da. and h. of Richard Lateward LATEWARD, of Grove House, in Ealing, Midx. He *d.* s.p.m., 20 Oct. 1835, in Wellington sq., Hastings, aged 37. Will pr. Nov. 1835. His widow *m.* at Brussels (a few days later), 7 Nov. 1835, Col. William LYSTER, and *d.* 10 Dec. 1890.

VIII. 1835. SIR ARCHER DENMAN CROFT, Baronet [1671], br. and h. male, *b.* 7 Dec. 1801 in Welbeck street, Marylebone; admitted to Lincoln's Inn, 21 Aug. 1820, aged 19; *suc. to the Baronetcy*, 20 Oct. 1835; Barrister, 1839, and one of the Masters of the Court of Queen's Bench. He *m.* 31 Aug. 1837, Julia Barbara, widow of Athelstan CORBET, of Merionethshire, yst. da. of Major-Gen. John GARSTIN, E.I.C.S., of Calcutta. She *d.* 17 Nov. 1864, at 1 Sussex place, Hyde Park. He *d.* there very suddenly, from heart disease, 10 Jan. 1865 (being the evening of the day of his son's marriage), aged 63.

IX. 1865. SIR HERBERT GEORGE DENMAN CROFT, Baronet [1671], of Lugwardine Court, co. Hereford, only s. and h., *b.* 25 July 1838, and *bap.* 21 May 1839, at Acton, Midx.; ed. at Eton; matric. at Oxford (Merton Coll.), 12 March 1857, aged 18; B.A., 1860; M.A., 1864; Barrister (Inner Temple), 1861, being a member of the Oxford Circuit and a Revising Barrister; *suc. to the Baronetcy*, 10 Jan. 1865; was M.P. for Herefordshire, 1868-74.(c) He *m.* 10 Jan. 1865, at Weyhill, Hants, Georgiana Eliza Lucy, 1st da. and coheir of

(a) This romance was founded on the murder, in April 1779, of Martha Ray, an actress, by the Rev. James Hackman. It is called by Carlyle (in his *Reminiscences*), "a loose, foolish old book," but nevertheless went through seven editions.
(b) An interesting account of this tragedy (rendered more sad by the death of one of his patients, Mrs. Thackeray, on whom he was then in attendance) is in the *Gent. Mag.*, vol. 88, part 1, pp. 188 and 277.
(c) He excited some ridicule by presenting a petition (during the debate on the Burial Bill) which he stated was signed by some of his constituents who had "*lived* in their parish *for centuries.*"

Matthew Henry MARSH, of Ramridge House, Hants, by Eliza Mary Anne, da. of Henry Alworth MEREWETHER, Serjeant-at-Law. He *d.* 11 Feb. 1902, at Lugwardine Court, aged 63. Will pr. at £22.164. His widow living 1903.

X. 1902. SIR HERBERT ARCHER CROFT, Baronet [1671], of Lugwardine Court aforesaid, 1st s. and h., *b.* 5 Sep. 1868; sometime Lieut. in the Shropshire Light Infantry; *suc. to the Baronetcy*, 11 Feb. 1902. He *m.* firstly, 20 June 1892, Kathleen, 2d da. of John HARE, of Invercargill, New Zealand. She *d.* s.p.m., 25 Sep. 1898. He *m.* secondly, 3 Feb. 1903, at Grappenhall, co. Chester, Katharine Agnes, 1st da. of Joseph Charlton PARR, of Grappenhall Heyes, by Jessie Maria, da. of Col. George Lister LISTER-KAYE, 10th Royal Hussars.

SAINT AUBYN, *or* SAINT AUBIN:

cr. 11 Dec. 1671;

ex. 10 Aug. 1839.

I. 1671. "JOHN SAINT AUBIN, of Clowance, co. Cornwall, Esq.," 1st s. and h. ap. of John SAINT AUBYN, of the same (aged 10 at the Visit. of Devon, 1620, who purchased St. Michael's Mount, Cornwall, in 1657, and was Sheriff of that county, 1666-67), by Catharine, da. of Francis GODOLPHIN, of Treveneage, was *bap.* 6 April 1645, at St. Andrew's, Plymouth; matric. at Oxford (Exeter Coll.), 17 July 1663; and was v.p. *cr. a Baronet*, as above, 11 Dec. 1671; was M.P. for St. Michael (two Parls.), 1679-81. He suc. his father in Aug. 1684. He *m.* 14 Nov. 1665, at St. Columb Major, Anne, da. and coheir of James JENKYN, of Trekenning. He *d.* in 1687. Admon. 7 June 1687 to his widow, Anne. She *m.* 15 Oct. 1696, at St. Bride's, London (Lic. London 12, she aged 50, widow), William SPENCER, of Lancashire, then of St. Martin's in the Fields, aged 44, widower. She *m.* (for her 3d husband), 22 July 1708, at Paddington (Lic. London 20, she aged 55, widow), Richard PAGE, of Harrow on the Hill, aged 55, widower, who survived her, but who *d.* before July 1719. She *d.* in or before 1712.(a) Her admon. as "of Harrow on the Hill," 22 May 1712 and 13 July 1719.

II. 1687. SIR JOHN SAINT AUBYN, Baronet [1671], of Clowance aforesaid, 1st s. and h., *bap.* 13 Jan. 1670, at St. Columb Major; *suc. to the Baronetcy* in 1687. He was M.P. for Helston (two Parls.), 1689-95, and Sheriff of Cornwall, 1704-05. He *m.* 22 May 1695, at St. George's Chapel, Windsor, Mary, da. and coheir of Peter DELAHAY, of St. Margaret's, Westm. He *d.* 20 June 1714, and was *bur.* at Crowan, aged 44. M.I. The will of his widow is dat. 13 June 1717.

III. 1714. SIR JOHN SAINT AUBYN, Baronet [1671], of Clowance aforesaid, 1st s. and h., *b.* about 1703; *suc. to the Baronetcy* 20 June 1714; matric. at Oxford (Exeter Coll.), 12 June 1718, aged 15; *cr.* M.A. 19 July 1721; was M.P. for Cornwall (four Parls.), 1722, till his death in 1744. He *m.* 3 Oct. 1725(b) Catherine, sister and coheir [1750], of Sir William MORICE, 3d Baronet [1661], of Werrington, 1st daughter of Sir Nicholas MORICE, 2d Baronet [1661], by Catherine, da. of Thomas (HERBERT), EARL OF PEMBROKE AND MONTGOMERY. She *d.* 16 June 1740, and was *bur.* at Crowan. He was *bur.* there 23 Aug. 1744. Will dat. 25 July 1740, pr. 9 May 1745.

(a) It is stated [but query if not in error] in Vivian's *Visitations of Cornwall* that she was "buried at Woking, Surrey. M.I." In that work, also (but clearly in error), the burial of the 1st Baronet is said to have been "24 June 1699, at Crowan."

(b) Stated (as in note "a" above) to have been at St. James' Westm.

IV. 1744. SIR JOHN SAINT AUBYN, Baronet [1671], of Clowance aforesaid, only s. and h., *b.* there 12 Nov. 1726; *suc. to the Baronetcy* in Aug. 1744.; matric. at Oxford (Oriel Coll.), 19 Oct. 1744, aged 17; *cr.* M.A. 1 July 1747; M.P. for Launceston 1747-54, and 1758 till void in Feb. 1759; for Cornwall, 1761, till death in 1772. He *m.* 4 June 1756, at St. James' Westm. (by spec. lic. in her father's house in St. James' place), Elizabeth, da. of William WINGFIELD, of Washington, co. Durham, by Anne, da. of Sir William WILLIAMSON, 4th Baronet [1642]. He *d.* 12 Oct. 1772, and was *bur.* at Crowan, aged nearly 47. M.I. Will dat. 21 Feb. 1760, pr. 29 Oct. 1772. His widow *m.* 5 Oct. 1782, at St. James', Westm. (by spec. lic. at her house in New Bond street), John BAKER, of Orsett, Essex. She *d.* 28 Aug. 1796, and was *bur.* at Orsett. Admon. May 1800 and Nov. 1801.

V. 1772, to 1839. SIR JOHN SAINT AUBYN, Baronet [1671], of Clowance aforesaid, only s. and h., *b.* 17 May 1758, in Golden square, and *bap.* the same day at St. James', Westm.; *suc. to the Baronetcy*, 12 Oct. 1772; Sheriff of Cornwall, 1781-82; M.P. for Truro, Feb. to March 1784; for Penrhyn, 1784-90; and for Helston, 1807-12; F.R.S., F.S.A., etc. He *m.* 1 July 1822 (at the age of 64), at St. Andrew's, Holborn, Juliana, da. of (—) VINNICOMBE(a). He *d.* s.p. legit., 10 Aug. 1839, at Lime Grove, Putney Hill, Surrey, and was *bur.* at Crowan, aged 81, when the *Baronetcy* became *extinct*. Will pr. March 1840. His widow *d.* at Lime Grove aforesaid, 14 June 1856, aged 87. Will pr. Dec. 1856.

BALL:

I. 1672, to 1680. SIR PETER BALL, of Mamhead, co. Devon, who had been *Knighted* at Oxford, 7 Oct. 1642, was *cr. a Baronet*, 22 July 1672,(b) but appears never to have assumed the title, the warrant no doubt never having passed the Great Seal. He was *bur.* 4 Sep. 1680, at Mamhead, aged 81, but neither William BALL, his s. and h., nor Thomas BALL, the surv. s. and h. of the said William (which Thomas was *bur.* at Mamhead, 11 June 1749, aged 77, as "the last of his family"), were ever styled Baronets.

EDEN:

cr. 13 Nov. 1672;

sometime, 1811-1844 JOHNSON EDEN.

I. 1672. "ROBERT EDEN, of West Auckland, co. Durham, Esq.," 1st s. and h. ap. of John EDEN, of the same, by Catherine, da. of Sir Thomas LAYTON, of Layton, co. York, was *b.* about 1644; matric. at Oxford (Queen's Coll.), 2 Aug. 1661, aged 17, being aged 21, in the Her. Visit. of Durham, 1666; Barrister (Middle Temple), 1670; and was v.p. *cr. a Baronet*, as above, 13 Nov. 1672. He suc. his father in 1675, and was M.P. for co. Durham (seven Parls.), March to July 1679, 1690-95, 1698-1700 and 1702-13. He *m.* Margaret, da. and h. of John LAMBTON, of the City of Durham. He was *bur.* 17 May 1720, at St. Helen's, Auckland.

(a) By her, before marriage, he had (besides two daughters) no less than six sons, born from 1794 to 1811, of whom the 4th son Edward, *b.* 6 Nov. 1799, suc., under his will, to the family estates, and was *cr. a Baronet*, 31 July 1866, being father of John, 2d Baronet [1866], who was *cr.*, 4 July 1887, Baron St. Levan of St. Michael's Mount, Cornwall.

(b) *Ex inform.* H. Houston Ball. A good pedigree of the family and further particulars of Sir Peter Ball is in Col. Vivian's *Visitations of Devon.*

II. 1720. SIR JOHN EDEN, Baronet [1672], of Windleston, co. Durham and West Auckland aforesaid, 1st s. and h., *b.* probably about 1680; matric. at Oxford (Queen's Coll.), 25 Feb. 1694/5; M.P. for co. Durham (three Parls.), 1713-27; *suc. to the Baronetcy*, 17 May 1720. He *m.* 31 Jan. 1715, Catherine, da. of Mark SHAFTS, of Whitworth, co. Durham. He *d.* at Bath, 2 and was *bur.* 17 May 1728, at St. Helen's aforesaid. His widow *d.* 2 July 1730.

III. 1728. SIR ROBERT EDEN, Baronet [1672], of Windleston and West Auckland aforesaid, only s. and h. *b.* about 1718; *suc to the Baronetcy*, 2 May 1728; matric. at Oxford (Queen's Coll.), 4 June 1735, aged 18. He *m.* 8 May 1739, Mary, sister and coheir of Morton DAVISON, da. of William DAVISON, both of Beamish, co. Durham. He *d.* 25 June 1755. His widow *d.* 31 Jan. 1794. Will pr. 1795.

IV. 1755. SIR JOHN EDEN, Baronet [1672], of Windleston and West Auckland aforesaid, 1st s. and h.,(a) *b.* 16 Sep. 1740; *suc. to the Baronetcy*, 25 June 1755; ed. at Trin. Coll., Cambridge; M.A., 1761; was M.P. for co. Durham (three Parls.), 1774-90. He *m.* firstly, 26 June 1764, Catherine, da. of John THOMPSON, of Kirby Hall, co. York, by his 1st wife Elizabeth, da. of Stephen CROFT, of Stillington, in that county. She *d.* s.p. 12 March 1766. He *m.* secondly, 9 April 1767, Dorothea, da. and h. of Peter JOHNSON, Recorder of York. She *d.* 21 June 1792. He *d.* 23 Aug. 1812, aged 71.

V. 1812. SIR ROBERT JOHNSON-EDEN, Baronet [1672], of Windleston and West Auckland aforesaid, 1st s. and h.,(b) by 2d wife, *b.* 25 Oct. 1774; admitted to Lincoln's Inn, 16 Jan. 1795; ed. at Trin. Coll., Cambridge; B.A., 1796; M.A., 1800; took by Royal Lic., 15 Feb. 1811, the name of *Johnson* before that of *Eden*; *suc. to the Baronetcy*, 23 Aug. 1812. He *d.* unm. 4 Sep. 1844, at Windlestone, in his 70th year. Admon. Nov. 1844.

VI. and IV. 1844. SIR WILLIAM EDEN, Baronet [1672 and 1776], of Windleston aforesaid, and of Truir, co. Durham, cousin and h. male, being 2d s. of Sir Frederick Morton EDEN, 2d Baronet [1776], by Anne, da. and h. of James Paul SMITH, of London, which Frederick (who *d.* 14 Nov. 1809) was s. and h. of Sir Robert EDEN, 1st Baronet [1776], Gov. of the province of Maryland (*d.* 1786), who was yr. br. of Sir John EDEN, 4th Baronet [1672] and 2d s. of Sir Robert EDEN, 3d Baronet [1672]. He was *b.* 31 Jan. 1803; was ed. at Eton; matric. at Oxford (Ch. Ch.) 10 Nov. 1821, aged 18; *suc. to the Baronetcy* of 1776 (as 4th Baronet) on the death of his br., 24 Dec. 1814, and *suc. to the Baronetcy* of 1673 (as 6th Baronet) on the death of his cousin, as above, 4 Sep. 1844; was Custos Brevium of the Court of King's Bench; Major in the Durham Militia, 1846; Sheriff of co. Durham, 1848. He *m.* 23 April 1844, at Sherwell, Hants, Elfrida Susanna Harriet, yst. da. of Col. William IREMONGER, of Wherwell Priory, by Pennant, da. of Rice THOMAS, of Coed Helen, co. Carnarvon. He *d.* 21 Oct. 1873, at Ladington Hall, near Barnard Castle, in his 70th year. His widow *d.* 8 July 1882, at Bournemouth.

VII. and V. 1873. SIR WILLIAM EDEN, Baronet [1673 and 1776], of Windlestone aforesaid, 1st s. and h., *b.* 4 April 1849; sometime Lieut. 8th Hussars; *suc. to the Baronetcies*, 21 Oct. 1873; Lieut.-Col. 2d

(a) Of his yr. brothers (1) Robert Eden, was Governor of Maryland, and was *cr. a Baronet*, 19 Oct. 1796, being grandfather of the 4th Baronet [1796], who, on 4 Sep. 1844, inherited this Baronetcy [1672]. (2) William Eden, was *cr.*, on 18 Nov. 1789, Baron Auckland [I.], and on 22 May 1793, Baron Auckland [G.B.]; and (3) Morton Eden, was *cr.* 3 Nov. 1799, BARON HENLEY OF CHARDSTOCK [I.].

(b) His yr. brother, Morton John Eden, *b.* 30 June 1778, having suc. to the estate of Beamish, being that of his mother's family, took her name of Davison before that of Eden, by Royal Lic. 26 Oct. 1812, and *d.* unm. 28 June 1841.

Durham Light Infantry Volunteers. He *m.* 20 July 1886, at St. Paul's, Knightsbridge, Sybil Frances, 2d da. of Sir William GREY, K.C.S.I., by his 1st wife, Margaret HUNGERFORD, da. of Welby JACKSON, of the Bengal Civil Service. She was *b.* 9 April 1867.

WERDEN:

cr. 28 Nov. 1672;

ex. 13 Feb 1758.

I. 1672. "JOHN WERDEN, Esq. of [Cholmeaton] co. Chester, Secretary to His Royal Highness the Duke of York," s. and h. ap. of Lieut.-Gen. Robert WERDEN, of Cholmeaton, and of Leyland, co. Lancaster, a Col. of Horse in the service of Charles I (*d.* 23 Jan. 1689/90), by his 1st wife, Jane, da. of (—) BACKHAM, was *b.* 25 March 1640, at Cholmeaton; Barrister (Middle Temple), 1660; Baron of the Exchequer of Chester, 1664; Sec. to the Embassy to Spain and Portugal, and afterwards (1669) Envoy to Sweden and Holland, 1672; Sec. to James, Duke of York, and was *cr. a Baronet*, as above, 28 Nov. 1672. He was M.P. for Reigate, Jan. 1673, till void 28 of the same month; re-elected Feb. 1673 to 1679, and 1685-87; *cr.* D.C.L. of Oxford, 22 May 1683; was a Commissioner of Customs, 1685-94 and 1703-14. He *m.* firstly, Lucy, da. of [—] OSBORNE, D.D. She *d.* s.p. and was *bur.* 7 Feb. 1678/9, at St. Martin's in the Fields. He *m.* secondly, in or before 1682, Mary, da. of William OSBORNE, of Kenniford, Devon. She *d.* of the small-pox, and was *bur.* 22 Aug. 1683, at St. Martin's aforesaid. He *d.* 29 Oct., and was *bur.* there 7 Nov. 1716, in his 77th year. Will pr. Nov. 1716.

II. 1716, to 1758. SIR JOHN WERDEN, Baronet [1672], of Leyland and Cholmeaton aforesaid, and of Hollyport, Berks, only s. and h., by 2d wife, *b.* 28 April 1683; matric. at Oxford (Gloucester Hall), 23 Jan. 1697/8, aged 15; admitted to Inner Temple 1700; *suc. to the Baronetcy*, 7 Nov. 1716. He *m.* firstly, 9 July 1704, Elizabeth, sister of Nicholas and da. of Robert BRETON, of Norton, co. Northampton. He *m.* secondly, Judith, da. of John EYRE, of Maidford in that county. She *d.* s.p., 5 May 1726, in her 42d year, and was *bur.* at Bray, Berks. M.I. He *m.* thirdly, Elinor, da. of (—) VERNER, of London, merchant. She *d.* 24 March 1732/3, in her 28th year, and was *bur.* at Bray. M.I. He *m.* fourthly, in or before 1740, Susanna, da. and coheir of John STAVELEY, an officer in the Army, by Frances, his wife. He *d.* s.p.m.s.,(a) 13 Feb. 1758, in his 75th year, when the *Baronetcy* became *extinct*. Will pr. 1758. His widow *d.* at Chichester, in or before 1787. Admon. 17 Feb. 1787, to Susanna BAYNTON, widow, her only child.

ALLIN, *or* ALLEN:

cr. 7 Feb. 1672/3;

ex. Oct. 1696.

I. 1673. "THOMAS ALLEN [*or* ALLIN], of Blundeston, co. Suffolk, a Captain at Sea, sometime Admiral in the Streights, then Comptroller of the Navy and one of the Commissioners thereof," s. of Robert ALLEN, *or* ALLIN, was *b.* about 1613; was *Knighted* 24 Sep. 1665, being then Capt. of H.M. ship "The Old James," and was *cr. a Baronet*, as above, 7 Feb. 1672/3. He was sometime Comptroller of the Navy, Admiral in the

(a) He apparently left three daughters and coheirs, one by each of his 1st, 2d, and 4th wives respectively, viz.:—(1) Lucy, *m.* 13 Dec. 1722, Charles (Beauclerk), 2d Duke of St. Albans, and had issue; (2) Charlotte, *m.* 13 Dec. 1722, Lord William Beauclerk, br. to the above, by whom she was grandmother of the 4th Duke; (3), Susanna, *m.* Edward Bayntun, Consul Gen. at Algiers, and had issue.

IV

Straits, Capt. of Sandgate Castle, and Master of the Trinity House. He purchased the estate of Somerleyton, co. Suffolk. He *m.* firstly, Alice, da. of W. WHITING, of Lowestoft, Capt. R.N. He *m.* secondly (Lic. Vic. Gen., 3 July 1682, being then about 60 and a widower), Elizabeth (about 36, spinster), da. of Thomas ANGUISH, of Moulton, Norfolk, but by her had no issue. He was *bur.* at Somerleyton, 5 Oct. 1685, in his 73d year. Will pr. Oct. 1685.

II. 1685, to 1696. SIR THOMAS ALLIN, *or* ALLEN, Baronet [1673], of Somerleyton aforesaid, only s. and h.; was M.P. for Winwick Nov. 1678 to July 1679 and 1689 till void in Feb. of that year; *suc. to the Baronetcy* in 1685. He *m.* in 1672, Mary, da. of John CALDWALL, of London, Scrivener. He *d.* s.p., Oct. 1696, when the *Baronetcy* became *extinct.*(a) Admon. 10 Nov. 1696, and 14 Nov. 1698. The will of his widow, then of St. James', Westm., dat. 23 Aug. and pr. 20 Sep. 1699.

WARRE:

cr. 2 June 1673;

ex. 1 Dec. 1718.

I. 1673, to 1718. "FRANCIS WARRE, of Hestercombe, co. Somerset, Esq.," only s. and h. of Sir John WARRE, of the same (*d.* 1669), by Unton, da. of Francis (HAWLEY), 1st BARON HAWLEY OF DONAMORE [I.], was *b.* about 1659; matric. at Oxford (Oriel Coll.) 16 Oct. 1674, aged 15; was sometime Capt. in the Duke of Monmouth's regiment, and was *cr. a Baronet*, as above, 2 June 1673. He was M.P. for Bridgwater (four Parls.) 1685-87, 1689-95, and 1699-1700, and for Taunton (eight Parls.) 1701 till unseated 28 June 1715; was Col. of the Taunton regiment, and Vice-Admiral of Somerset and Bristol. He *m.* firstly, Anne, da. and h. of Robert CUFFE, of Michaelchurch, Somerset. She *d.* 24 Dec. 1690. He *m.* secondly, Margaret, da. of John HARBIN, of London, merchant. She *d.* 9 Jan. 1718/9. He *d.* s.p.m.s.(b) at Ghent, in Flanders, 1 and was *bur.* 11 Dec. 1718, at Kingston, Somerset, when the *Baronetcy* became *extinct*. Will dat. 28 Nov. 1718, pr. at Taunton, 19 Jan. 1718/9.

BRIDGEMAN:

cr. 12 Nov. 1673;

ex. Nov. *or* Dec. 1740.

I. 1673. "ORLANDO BRIDGEMAN, of Ridley, co. Chester, Esq., 2d son to Sir Orlando BRIDGEMAN, Knt. and Baronet [1660], Lord Keeper of the Great Seal of England" (*d.* 25 June 1674, aged 65), by his 2d wife, Dorothy, da. and coheir of John SAUNDERS, M.D., Provost of Oriel College, Oxford [1644-53], was *b.* about 1650, admitted to Inner Temple, 1658; Barrister, 1669; M.P. for Horsham, Oct. 1669 to 1679, and was v.p. *cr. a Baronet*, as above, 12 Nov. 1673. He *m.* (Lic. Fac. 28 Sep. 1670, he about 20 and she about 16), Mary, da. of Sir Thomas CAVE, 1st Baronet [1641], of Stanford, co. Northampton, by his

(a) The estates devolved on his nephew, Richard Anguish, s. and h. of his sister Alice, by Edmund Anguish, of Moulton, co. Norfolk. He assumed the additional name of Allin, or Allen, and was *cr. a Baronet*, 14 Dec. 1699, a dignity which became extinct in 1794.

(b) John Warre, his son and heir ap. (by his 1st wife) matric. at Oxford (Balliol Coll.) 15 June 1697, aged 19; was a Capt. of Dragoons; *d.* v.p. and s.p. about 1710, at Ghent, in his 33d year. Margaret, da. and h. (by his 2d wife), only surv. child, *m.* John Bamfylde (who *d.* 17 Sep. 1750, aged 60), by whom she had a son, Coplestone Warre Bampfylde, who suc. to the Hestercombe estate.

2d wife, Penelope, da. and coheir of Thomas (WENMAN), 2d VISCOUNT WENMAN OF TUAM [I.]. He *d.* 20 April 1701, aged 51, and his widow *d.* (a few weeks later) 8 June 1701, in her 50th year, both being *bur.* at St. Michael's, Coventry. M.I. His admon. (in which he is erroneously called "widower") 28 Nov. 1701, to his son.

II. 1701. SIR ORLANDO BRIDGEMAN, Baronet [1673], of Ridley aforesaid, and of Withy Brook, co. Warwick, only s. and h., *b.* about 1679; entered Rugby School, 24 Aug. 1689; matric. at Oxford (Trin. Coll.) 10 Nov. 1694, aged 15; *suc. to the Baronetcy*, 20 April 1701; was M.P. for Coventry, Feb. 1707 to 1710; for Calne, 1715-22; for Lostwithiel, Feb. 1724 to 1727; for Blechingley, 1727-34, and for Dunwich, Feb. 1734 to 1738; Auditor-Gen. to the Prince of Wales, afterwards (1727) George II; Commissioner of Trade, 8 Aug. 1727 till death in 1738; nominated Governor of Barbadoes, 1737, but never went there. He *m.* (Lic. Fac. 15 April 1702) Susanna (then about 17), da. of Sir Francis DASHWOOD, 1st Baronet [1707], of Wycombe, Bucks, by his 1st wife, Mary, da. of John JENNINGS. He (having been missing for some weeks) was found drowned in the Thames, near Limehouse, 10 June 1738.(a) Admon. 12 June 1751. His widow *d.* 4 Sep. 1747.

III. 1738, to 1740. SIR FRANCIS BRIDGEMAN, Baronet [1673], of Ridley aforesaid, only s. and h., *b.* Aug. 1713; *suc. to the Baronetcy* in June 1738. He *d.* unm., Nov. or Dec. 1740, on board ship in Sir Chaloner Ogle's fleet on the way to the West Indies, when the *Baronetcy* became *extinct*.

WINDHAM, *or* WYNDHAM:

cr. 18 Nov. 1673;

ex. April 1719.

I. 1673. "FRANCIS WINDHAM, of Trent, co. Somerset, Esq.," 4th surv. s. of Sir Thomas WINDHAM, *or* WYNDHAM,(b) of Kentsford, in St. Decumans in that County (*d.* in or before March 1634/5), by Elizabeth, da. of Richard CONINGSBY, of Hampton Court, co. Hereford, was *b.* about 1612 (being 6th of eight sons(c) all living at the Visit. of Somerset 1623, when he was aged 11), was M.P. for Minehead, April to May 1640; for Milborne Port, Aug. to Dec. 1660, and 1661 till death in 1676; a Col. in the army and a zealous Royalist; received and kept for some time concealed in his house at Trent, Charles II, when a fugitive after the battle of Worcester, in Sep. 1651, and was *cr. a Baronet*, as above, 18 Nov. 1673; was Governor of Dunster Castle. He *m.* in or before 1648, Anne, da. and coheir of Thomas GERARD, of Trent, co. Somerset, with whom he acquired that estate. He was *bur.* at Trent. 15 July 1676. Will dat. 8 Feb. 1675, pr. 18 Oct. 1676, by Anne his widow.

II. 1676. SIR THOMAS WYNDHAM, Baronet [1673], of Trent aforesaid, 1st s. and h., *b.* about 1648; matric. at Oxford (Merton Coll.), 1 April 1664, aged 16; admitted to Lincoln's Inn 1666; *suc. to the Baronetcy* in July 1676. He *m.* (Lic. Vic. Gen. 19 June 1676, he about 27 and she about 18),

(a) The burial 5 Dec. 1745, of "Sir Orlando Bridgeman, Knt. and Baronet" occurs in the par. reg. of St. Nicholas, Gloucester.

(b) This Thomas was elder br. of Hugh Wyndham, *cr. a Baronet*, 4 Aug. 1641, being 1st. s. and h. of Edmund Wyndham, of Kentsford aforesaid, 2d son of Sir John Wyndham of Orchard Wyndham, Somerset (*d.* 1573), the ancestor of the Wyndham, Baronets, so *cr.* 1661, afterwards Earls of Egremont.

(c) Sir Edmund Wyndham, the eldest of these, inherited Kentsford, and was Knight Marshal of England at the Restoration. He *d.* in 1682, being ancestor of the Wyndhams of Cathanger, Somerset, and of Tale, Devon.

I

Elizabeth, da. and coheir of Sir George CROKE, of Waterstock, Oxon., by Jane, da. of Sir Richard ONSLOW, of Clandon, Sussex. He *d.* s.p.m.(a) in 1693, apparently at Bruges in Flanders. Will dat. 29 Dec. 1692 (his wife being then living), pr. 23 May 1693.

III. 1693. SIR FRANCIS WYNDHAM, Baronet [1673], of Trent aforesaid, br. and h. male, *b.* about 1654; matric. at Oxford (Merton Coll.), 11 Nov. 1670, aged 16; admitted to Middle Temple, 1670; *suc. to the Baronetcy* in 1693; was M.P. for Ilchester (four Parls.), 1695-1700 and 1701-05. He *m.* firstly, Elizabeth, widow of John BERNEY, yst. da. of Sir Richard ONSLOW, abovementioned, by Elizabeth, da. and h. of Arthur STRANGEWAYS, of co. Durham. He *m.* secondly, 18 Feb. 1694/5, at the Chapel Royal, St. James', Hester, widow of Matthew INGRAM. She was *bur.* 24 April 1708, at Chelsea. He *m.* thirdly, 8 April 1712, at Whitehall Chapel (Lic. Fac. 3), Henrietta, widow of Sir Richard NEWDIGATE, 2d Baronet [1677], da. of Thomas WIGGINGTON, *or* WINTON, of Ham, co. Surrey. He *d.* at his house in Paradise Row, Chelsea, 22 March 1715/6. Will, directing his burial to be at Trent, dat. 24 Aug. 1714, to 14 March 1715, pr. 21 April 1716 and again 22 May 1740. His widow *m.* William LOWFIELD, of Chelsea, and *d.* there 26 June 1739.

IV. 1716, to 1719. SIR FRANCIS WYNDHAM, Baronet [1673], of Trent aforesaid, grandson and h., being only s. and h. of Thomas WYNDHAM (admitted to Lincoln's Inn, 28 March 1701), who was only s. and h. ap. of the late Baronet, but *d.* v.p., being (presumably) *bur.* 7 May 1713, at St. Margaret's, Westm.(b) He was *b.* about 1707; *suc. to the Baronetcy* 22 March 1715/6, and *d.* in boyhood, being *bur.* 16 April 1719, at St. Margaret's aforesaid, aged about 12, when the *Baronetcy* became *extinct*. Admon. 27 May 1719, in trust for his younger sister Frances Wyndham.

HARRIS:

cr. 1 Dec. 1673;

ex. Feb. 1685/6.

I. 1673, to 1686. "ARTHUR HARRIS, of [Hayne in Stowford], Devon, Esq.," only s. and h. of John HARRIS, of the same (aged 34 at the Her. Visit. of Devon in 1620), by his 2d wife Cordelia (*m.* Nov. 1631), da. of John (MOHUN), 1st BARON MOHUN OF OKEHAMPTON, was *b.* about 1650; suc. his father 6 March 1656/7; was M.P. for Okehampton (four Parls.), Jan. 1671 to 1681; and was *cr. a Baronet*, as above, 1 Dec. 1673. He *m.* (Lic. Fac., 5 June 1673, he about 22 and she about 21) Theophila, da. of John TURNER, of St. Bride's, London, and of York, Serjeant-at-Law. He *d.* s.p., and was *bur.* 20 Feb. 1685/6, at Lifton, Devon, when the *Baronetcy* became *extinct*. M.I. Admon. 25 Nov. 1686 to his widow, and again Jan. 1702/3. She *d.* at Greenwich and was *bur.* thence 27 July 1702, at Lifton. Will pr. Sep. 1702.

(a) Anne his da. and h., then aged about 20, *m.* June 1697 (Lic. Fac. 21), William James, of Ightham Court, Kent, and had issue.

(b) The following extracts from the Parish Registers of St. Margaret's, Westm., apparently belong to this family:—

Baptism. 1710, Aug. 22. "Frances, da. of Thomas Windham, Esq., and Lucy, *b.* 12."

Burials. 1713, May 7. "The Hon. Thomas Wyndham, Esq."

" 1716, March 31. "Madam Windham" [presumably his widow].

" 1719, April 16. "Sir Francis Windham, Bart.; mid chancel."

BLACKETT, *or* BLACKET:

cr. 12 Dec. 1673.

I. 1673. "WILLIAM BLAKET [*recte* BLACKET], of Newcastle, co. Northumberland, Esq.," 3d s.(a) of William BLACKETT, of Hoppyland, co. Durham (aged 40 in 1628), by Isabella, da. of William CROKE, of Wolsingham, in that county, was *b.* about 1620; was Alderman and sometime Mayor of Newcastle; M.P. for that town in three Parls., Dec. 1673 till death in 1680, and having "by the product of his mines and colleries acquired a very great fortune,"(b) was *cr. a Baronet*, as above, 12 Dec. 1673. He *m.* firstly, 10 July 1645, at Hamsterley, co. Durham, Elizabeth, da. of Michael KIRKLEY, of Newcastle aforesaid, merchant. She *d.* 7 April 1674, and was *bur.* at St. Nicholas', Newcastle. M.I. He *m.* secondly, Margaret, widow of Captain John ROGERS, da. of Ralph COCK, of Newcastle aforesaid. He *d.* 16 May 1680, aged about 61, and was *bur.* at St. Nicholas' aforesaid. M.I. Will dat. 9 March 1679/80, pr. at Durham, 1680. His widow, by whom he had no issue, survived him many years. Her will dat. 7 July 1703, pr. 13 Nov. 1710.

II. 1680. SIR EDWARD BLACKET, Baronet [1674], of Newby, co. York (an estate that he had purchased), 1st s. and h., by 1st wife, *b.* about 1649; was Sheriff of Northumberland, 1679-80; *suc. to the Baronetcy*, 16 May 1680; was M.P. for Ripon, 1689-90, and for Northumberland, 1690-1700. He *m.* firstly, Mary, only child of Thomas NORTON, of Langthorne, co. York. She *d.* s.p.s. He *m.* secondly, about 1680, Mary, da. of Sir John YORKE, of Richmond, co. York, by Mary, da. of Maulger NORTON and Ann, da. of Sir George WANDESFORD. She was *bap.* at Richmond, co. York, 27 Jan. 1657/8. He *m.* thirdly, 21 Oct. 1699, at St. Mary le Bow, Durham, Diana, widow of Sir Ralph DELAVAL, 2d Baronet [1660], da. of George (BOOTH), 1st BARON DELAMERE, by his 2d wife, Elizabeth, da. of Henry (GREY), EARL OF STAMFORD. She *d.* 7 Oct. 1713. He *d.* 23 April 1718, aged 66, and was *bur.* at Ripon. M.I. there to him and his three wives. Will pr. April 1718.

III. 1718. SIR EDWARD BLACKET, Baronet [1673], of Newby aforesaid, and of Hexham, co. Northumberland, 2d but 1st surv. s. and h. male,(c) by 2d wife, *b.* about 1683; was a captain in the Navy; *suc. to the Baronetcy*, 23 April 1718. He *m.* Mary, widow of Nicholas ROBERTS, of London, Merchant, da. of the Rev. Thomas JEKYLL, D.D., a br. of Sir Joseph JEKYLL, sometime [1717-38] Master of the Rolls. He *d.* s.p., 1 March 1756, aged 73. Will dat. 7 Feb. and pr. 14 April 1756. His widow *d.* a few months later, Dec. 1756, aged 82. Her will pr. Jan. 1775.

IV. 1756. SIR EDWARD BLACKET, *or* BLACKETT, Baronet [1673], of Hexham aforesaid, and of Matfen Hall, in Stamfordham, co. Northumberland, nephew and h., being 1st s. and h. of John BLACKET, of Newby aforesaid, by Patience, da. of Henry WISE, of Brompton park, Midx., and of Warwick Priory, which John was 3d son of the 2d Baronet, by his 2d wife. He was *b.* 9 April 1719, and *bap.* at St. Margaret's, Westm. He matric. at Oxford (Trin. Coll.), 16 Feb. 1736/7, aged 17; *suc. to the Baronetcy*, 1 March 1756; was, presumably (though described as "of Matfen, *Esquire*,"), Sheriff of Northumberland, 4 Feb. 1757 to 28 Jan. 1758; and was M.P. for Northumberland, 1768-74. He *m.*, Sep. 1751, Anne, da. and h. of Oley DOUGLAS, of Matfen Hall aforesaid (with whom he acquired that estate), and of Newcastle-upon-Tyne, by Mary, da. of Richard HARRIS, of London, merchant. He *d.* at Thorpe Lee, in Thorpe, co. Surrey (an estate of about 140 acres, which he had purchased), 3 Feb. 1804, aged 85. Will pr. 1804. His widow *d.* there 30 Dec. 1805, aged 80. Will pr. 1806.

(a) The eldest son, Christopher Blacket, was ancestor of the Blacketts, of Wylam, co. Northumberland.

(b) Wotton's *Baronetage* [1741].

(c) His elder br., William Blacket, *d.* v.p., leaving, by Diana, da. of Sir Ralph Delaval, 2d Baronet [1660], a da. and h., Diana, who *m.* Henry Mainwaring, and was mother of Sir Henry Mainwaring, 4th Baronet [1660].

V. 1804. SIR WILLIAM BLACKETT, Baronet [1673], of Matfen Hall aforesaid, 2d but 1st surv. s. and h., *b.* there 16 Feb. 1759; matric. at Oxford (Trin. Coll.), 30 March 1778, aged 20; *suc. to the Baronetcy*, 3 Feb. 1804; Sheriff of Northumberland, 1807-08. He *m.* 6 Aug. 1801, at St. Geo., Han. sq., Anne, da. of Benjamin KEENE, of Westoe Lodge, co. Cambridge, s. of Edmund KEENE, Bishop of Ely. He *d.* 27 Oct. 1816, at Westoe Lodge aforesaid, aged 57. Will pr. 1817. His widow, who resided at Thorpe Lee abovenamed, *d.* 7 Aug. 1859, at 34 Portman square, Marylebone.

VI. 1816. SIR EDWARD BLACKETT, Baronet [1673], of Matfen Hall aforesaid, 2d but 1st surv. s. and h., *b.* 23 Feb. 1805, in Edward street, Marylebone; *suc. to the Baronetcy*, 27 Oct. 1816; ed. at Eton; matric. at Oxford (Ch. Ch.), 30 April 1824, aged 19; was sometime an officer in the 1st Life Guards. He *m.* firstly, 1 May 1830, at St. Margaret's, Westm., Julia, 2d da. of Sir Charles Miles Lambert MONCK, *formerly* MIDDLETON, 6th Baronet [1662] by his 1st wife, Louisa Lucia, da. of Sir George COOKE, 7th Baronet [1661]. She, who was *b.* 23 April 1808, *d.* 15 June 1846. He *m.* secondly, 16 Oct. 1851, at Bywell St. Andrew, Northumberland, Frances Vere, widow of William Henry ORD, 5th da. of Sir William LORAINE, 4th Baronet [1664], being 1st da. by his 2d wife, Frances, da. and h. of Francis CAMPART. She, who was *b.* 12 Aug. 1800, and by whom he had no issue, *d.* 28 May 1874, at Matfen Hall. He *m.* thirdly, 15 June 1875, at Christ Church, Chertsey, Surrey, Isabella Helen, da. of John RICHARDSON, of Kirklands, co. Roxburgh. She *d.* s.p. at Matfen Hall, 28 Feb. 1879. He *m.* fourthly, 5 Aug. 1880 (at the age of 75), at Thorpe, co. Surrey, Alethea Riannette Anne, 2d da. of Major-Gen. William Henry SCOTT, of Thorpe House, by Harriett Alethea, da. of John Thomas (STANLEY), 1st BARON STANLEY OF ALDERLEY. He *d.* 23 Nov. 1885, at Matfen Hall, in his 81st year. Will dat. 8 Aug. 1880 to 25 May 1883, pr. 29 March 1885 above £33,000.(a) His widow, who *m.* 5 Aug. 1888, at Halton chapel, Henry Frederic Gisborne HOLT, of Ropley, Hants, was living 1903.

VII. 1885. SIR EDWARD WILLIAM BLACKETT, Baronet [1673], of Matfen Hall aforesaid, 1st s. and h. by 1st wife, *b.* 22 March 1831; ed. at Eton; entered the army 1851, serving in the Crimean war, 1854-55, and being severely wounded at the Redan; Major Rifle Brigade, 1862; Lieut.-Col. 1870; Colonel, 1878, and Hon. Major-General, 1881. Aide-de-Camp to Queen Victoria, 1878; Knight of the Legion of Honour, of France; *suc. to the Baronetcy* 23 Nov. 1885; Sheriff of Northumberland, 1889. He *m.* 23 Nov. 1871, at St. Mary's, Bryanston sq., Marylebone, Julia Frances, sister and coheir (17 Nov. 1868) of Hugh (SOMERVILLE), 18th LORD SOMERVILLE [S.], 5th and yst. da. of Kenelm, 17th LORD SOMERVILLE [S.], by Frances Louisa, da. of John HAYMAN. She was *b.* 24 May 1844.

Family Estates.—These, in 1883, consisted of 15,354 acres in Northumberland, 1,569 in the North Riding of Yorkshire, and 553 in Durham. *Total.*—17,476 acres, worth £16,183 a year. *Seat.*—Matfen Hall, near Newcastle-on-Tyne.

THOMPSON:

cr. 12 Dec. 1673;

afterwards, 1696-1745, BARONS HAVERSHAM;

ex. 11 April 1745.

I. 1673. "JOHN THOMPSON, of Haversham, co. Buckingham, Esq.," s. and h. of Maurice THOMPSON, of Lee, co. Kent (a prominent member of Cromwell's government, who *d.* 1671), was *b.* about 1647; admitted to Lincoln's Inn, 3 March 1663/4; Sheriff of Bucks, 1669-70, and was *cr. a Baronet*, as above, 12 Dec. 1673. He was M.P. for Gatton (four Parls.), 1685-96; was a vehement opposer of the measures of James II, and one of the earliest subscribers to the invitation to England sent to William of Orange; was a Commissioner of Public Accounts, 1695. He *m.* firstly, 14 July 1668, at St. James', Clerkenwell (Lic. Vic. Gen. 13, each aged about 20), Frances, widow of John WYNDHAM, da. of Arthur (ANNESLEY), 1st EARL OF ANGLESEY, by Elizabeth, da. of Sir James ALTHAM. She was living when he was *cr.*, 4 May 1696, BARON HAVERSHAM, co. Buckingham. In that Peerage this *Baronetcy* then *merged*, and so continued till the death of the 2d holder, 11 April 1745, when both became *extinct*.

(a) In it he leaves the Sockburn estates, co. York, to his 2d son, Charles Francis Blackett, and the Matfen and Fenwick estates (charged, however, with £40,000 for his younger children) and all the residue, to his eldest son.

TYNTE, *or* TINT:

cr. 26 Jan. 1673/4(a);

ex. 25 Aug. 1785.

I. 1674. "HALSEWELL TINT [*or* TYNTE], of Halsewell [in Goathurst], co. Somerset, Esq.," s. and h. of John TYNTE, of the same, and of Chelvey in that County, a zealous Royalist and one of the intended Knights of the Royal Oak (*bur.* 26 Aug. 1669, at Goathurst) by Jane, da. and h. of Hugh HALSEWELL, of Halsewell aforesaid (with whom he acquired that estate), was *bap.* 4 Feb. 1648/9 at Goathurst; matric. at Oxford (Hart Hall) 9 March 1665/6, aged 17; admitted to Middle Temple, 1667, and was *cr. a Baronet*, as above, 26 Jan. 1673/4(a); Sheriff of Somerset, 1674-75; M.P. for Bridgwater (four Parls.), 1679-97. He *m.*, in or before 1671, Grace, 1st da. and coheir of Robert FORTESCUE, of Filleigh, Devon, by his 1st wife Grace, da. of the well known Sir Bevill GRANVILLE, of Stow, co. Cornwall. She was *bur* 22 March 1694, at Goathurst, the same day as her son Fortescue Tynte. He was *bur.* there 9 April 1702, aged 53. Admon. 20 Sep. 1705 and 20 Nov. 1713.

II. 1702. SIR JOHN TYNTE, Baronet [1674], of Halsewell aforesaid, 3d but 1st surv. s. and h.(b); *bap.* 4 March 1683, at Goathurst, *suc. to the Baronetcy* in April 1702; matric. at Oxford (New Coll.), 19 April 1703, aged 15. He *m.* 25 Dec. 1704, at Clapton-in-Gordano, Somerset, Jane,(c) 1st da. of Sir Charles KEMEYS, 3d Baronet [1642] of Kevenmabley, co. Glamorgan, by Jane, da. of Philip (WHARTON) 4th BARON WHARTON. He was *bur.* 16 March 1709/10 at Goathurst, aged 27. Will dat. 4 March and pr. 27 Nov. 1710. His widow was *bur.* there 16 Oct. 1747. Will dat. at Bath 29 Sep. 1724, pr. 9 Nov. 1747.

III. 1710. SIR HALSEWELL TYNTE, Baronet [1674], of Halsewell aforesaid, and of Regilbury, co. Somerset, 1st s. and h., *b.* 15 and *bap.* 29 Nov. 1705, at Goathurst; *suc. to the Baronetcy* in March 1709/10; matric. at Oxford (New Coll.), 1 March 1722/3, aged 17; *cr.* M.A., 19 July 1726. M.P. for Bridgwater, 1727 till death in 1730. He *m.* 28 Sep. 1727, at Llanywerr, Brecon, Mary, da. of John WATERS,(a) of Brecon, by Jane, da. and coheir of Francis LLOYD, of Crickadarn, one of the Judges of North Wales. He *d.* s.p.s., and was *bur.*, 18 Nov. 1730, at Goathurst, aged 62. Admon. 2 Jan. 1730/1. His widow *m.* 1 Oct. 1736, Paulet ST. JOHN, of Farley, Hants, who (after her death) was *cr. a Baronet*, 9 Sep. 1772 (see that creation). She *d.* 17 Dec. 1758, at Farley. Admon. granted to her husband, 2 May 1759.

(a) This apparently is the correct date and is the one given in Le Neve's MS. *Baronetage* and in Beatson's List. The date given in Dugdale's *Catalogue* and elsewhere is "7 June xxvi Car. ii," *i.e.*, 1674, though the name is placed there *above* one creation in March, and three in May 1674.

(b) Of his two elder brothers (1) Halsewell Tynte *bap.* 5 Feb. 1672/3 at Goathurst; matric. at Oxford (Ball. Coll.), 19 Jan. 1690, aged (it is stated) 15; *d.* unm. and v.p. and was *bur.* 27 Feb. 1690, at Goathurst; (2) Fortescue Tynte, *bap.* 19 Feb. 1673/4, as above, *m.* and *d.* v.p. and s.p., being *bur.* 22 March 1694 at Goathurst, the same day as his mother.

(c) In consequence of this match their descendant, Col. Charles Kemeys Kemeys-Tynte, of Halsewell and Kevenmably abovenamed, claimed in 1843, as a coheir, the Barony of Wharton, alleging it to have been a creation (not by patent, but) by writ of 1544.

IV. 1730. SIR JOHN TYNTE, Baronet [1674], of Halsewell aforesaid, br. and h., *b.* 27 March, and *bap.* 21 April 1707, at Goathurst; matric. at Oxford (Queen's Coll.), 25 Nov. 1726, aged 19; took Holy Orders and was Rector of Goathurst aforesaid; *suc. to the Baronetcy* in Nov. 1730. He *d.* unm. 15, and was *bur.* 23 Aug. 1740, at Goathurst, aged 33. Will pr. 1740.

V. 1740, to 1785. SIR CHARLES KEMEYS TYNTE, Baronet [1674], of Halsewell, and, after his mother's death [1747], of Kevenmabley aforesaid, br. and h., *b.* 19 and *bap.* 22 May 1710, at Goathurst; *suc. to the Baronetcy*, 15 Aug. 1740; M.P. for Monmouth, March 1745 to 1747, and for Somerset 1747-74. Col. of the Somerset Militia; *cr.* D.C.L. of Oxford, 3 July 1759. He *m.* in March 1737/8, Anne, 1st da. and coheir of the Rev. Thomas BUSBY, LL.D., Rector of Addington, Bucks [1693—1725], by Anne, da. of John LIMBRY, of Hoddington, in Upton Gray, Hants. He *d.* s.p., 25 Aug., and was *bur.* 8 Sep. 1785, aged 75, when the *Baronetcy* became *extinct*.(b) Will pr. Sep. 1785 and June 1834. His widow was *bur.*, 24 March 1798, at Goathurst. Will pr. April 1798.

VAN TROMP:

cr. 25 March 1674;

ex. or *dormant* probably about 1710.

I. 1674. "CORNELIUS MARTIN TRUMP [*recte*, VAN TROMP], Vice-Admiral of Holland and West Friezland," s. of Sir Martin VAN TROMP, Knight of the Order of St. Michael (who was killed in 1658, in a sea fight between the English and the Dutch), took part with his country in the naval engagement off Harwich, 3 June 1665, conducting a skilful retreat from the victorious English, but, having visited London during the peace, was *cr. a Baronet*, as above, 5 March 1674. In 1677 he became Lieut.-Admiral-General of the United Provinces. He, who had just been made commander of a fleet destined to act against the French, *d.* 20 May 1691, and was *bur.* with his father at Delft.

II. 1691, to 1710? SIR MARTIN HARPERTSZOON VAN TROMP, Baronet [1674], s. and h., living 1705.(c) He apparently is the same as the "Maerten Harpertszoon TROMP, Lieut.-Admiral of Holland and West Friesland, whose da., Alida TROMP, was mother of the Baronetess Debora SPEELMAN."(d) He is presumed to have *d.* s.p.m.s., when apparently, the *Baronetcy* became *extinct* or *dormant*.

(a) See an account of this family in the *Her. and Gen.*, vol. ii, p. 386.

(b) The considerable estates both in Glamorganshire and Somersetshire devolved on his niece Jane, wife of Col. Johnson, da. and sole heir of his only sister Jane, who *m.*, 23 April 1737, at Gray's Inn chapel, Ruisshe Hassel, an officer of the Royal Horse Guards. Jane Hassel, their da. (niece of the testator, as above stated), *m.*, in 1765, Col. John Johnson (1st Foot Guards), who, with her (who *d.* 1825), took the name of *Kemeys-Tynte*, and *d.* 1807, leaving issue.

(c) Le Neve's MS. *Baronetage*.

(d) See "Speelman," Baronetcy, *cr.* 9 Sep. 1686.

ONSLOW:

cr. 8 May 1674 in reversion;

came into possession, 12 Oct. 1687;

afterwards, since 1716, BARONS ONSLOW OF ONSLOW AND CLANDON;

and, since 1801, EARLS ONSLOW.

I. 1687. "ARTHUR ONSLOW, of West Clandon, co Surrey, Esq.," 1st s. and h. of Sir Richard ONSLOW, of the same, and of Loseley in that county, Col. in the Parl. Army (*d.* 19 May 1664, in his 63d year), by Elizabeth, da. and h. of Arthur STRANGEWAYS, of co. Durham, was *bap.* 22 May 1624, at Cranley, co. Surrey; matric. at Oxford (Queen's Coll.), 24 May 1639, and then called 17; admitted to Lincoln's Inn, 10 June 1640; M.P. (when under age), for Bramber 1640, till void 16 Dec.: re-elected Jan. 1640/1, till secluded, 1648; for Surrey (jointly with his father), 1654-55; 1656-58 and 1659, and for Guildford, 1660, 1661-79, for Surrey (again, three Parls.) 1679-81, and was *cr. a Baronet*, as above, 8 May 1674, "*in reversion*, after the death of his father-in-law, Sir Thomas FOOTE, without issue male, who was [*i.e.*, who had been so] created, 21 Nov. 1660, and with the same precedency." He (shortly before his death) *suc. to the Baronetcy* [*cr.*, as before stated, 8 May 1674], on the death of the said Sir Thomas Foote, s.p.m. (aged 96), 12 Oct. 1687. He *m.* firstly, Rose, only surv. da. and h. of Nicholas STOUGHTON, of Stoughton, in Stoke, co. Surrey, by his 2d wife, Anne, da. of William EVANS. She, who was *b.* 29 April 1628, *d.* s.p.s. 11 March 1647/8, and was *bur.* at Stoke aforesaid. He *m.* secondly, in or before 1654, Mary, 2d da. and coheir of the abovenamed Sir Thomas FOOTE, Baronet [so *cr.* 21 Nov. 1660], sometime [1649-50], Lord Mayor of London, by Elizabeth, da. of William MOTT, of Plaistow, Essex. He *d.* 21 July 1688, aged 67, and was *bur.* at Cranley, Surrey. Will pr. Nov. 1688. His widow, who was *bap.* 24 Oct. 1630, at St. Benet's, Gracechurch, London, *d.* in or before 1706. Will pr. March 1706.

II. 1688. SIR RICHARD ONSLOW, Baronet [1674], of West Clandon aforesaid, 1st s. and h. by 2d wife, *b.* 22 or 23 June and *bap.* 9 July 1654, at Cranley; matric. at Oxford (St. Edmund Hall) 2 June 1671, aged 16; admitted to Inner Temple, 1674; M.P. for Guildford (four Parls.), 1679-81 and 1685-87; for Surrey (nine Parls.), 1689-1710; for St. Mawes, 1710-13, and for Surrey again, 1713, till raised to the Peerage in 1716, having *suc. to the Baronetcy* 21 July 1688; a Lord of the Admiralty, 1690-93; Speaker of the House of Commons,(a) 1708-10; P.C. 1710 and 1714; Chancellor of the Exchequer, 1714-15; one of the Tellers of the Exchequer (for life), 1715. He *m.* 31 Aug. 1676, at St. Dionis, Backchurch, London, Elizabeth, da. and h. of Sir Henry TULSE, sometime (1683-84), Lord Mayor of London, by Elizabeth, his wife. She was living when he was *cr.*, 19 June 1716, BARON ONSLOW OF ONSLOW, co. Salop, AND OF CLANDON, co. Surrey, with a spec. rem. in favour of the male issue of his father. In that Peerage this *Baronetcy* then *merged*, the 4th Baron and 5th Baronet being *cr.*, 17 June 1801, EARL ONSLOW. See *Peerage*.

PARKER:

cr. 22 May 1674;

ex. 19 April 1750.

I. 1674. "SIR ROBERT PARKER, of Ratton in the parish of Willingdon, co. Sussex," 1st surv. s. and h. of George PARKER, of the same (*d.* 12 July 1673, in his 53d year), by Mary, 2d da. of Sir Richard

(a) He must not be confounded with his more celebrated nephew, Arthur Onslow, who was thirty-three years Speaker, *i.e.*, 1727-60, being the whole of the reign of George II. The s. and h. of *that* Speaker was *cr.* (eight years after his death) 20 May 1776, Baron Cranley of Imbercourt, and suc. a few months later, 8 Oct. 1776, as the 4th Baron Onslow and 5th Baronet [1674], being *cr.*, 17 June 1801, Earl Onslow.

NEWDIGATE, 1st Baronet [1677], of Arbury, co. Warwick, was *b.* about 1655 and was *cr. a Baronet*, as above, 22 May 1674. He was M.P. for Hastings (three Parls.), 1679-81. He *m.* 5 Feb. 1673/4, at Camberwell, Surrey (Lic. Fac. 3, both aged about 19), Sarah, only da. of George CHUTE, of Brixton Causeway, in Lambeth. He *d.* 30 Nov. 1961, in his 37th year. Admon. 16 Dec. 1691. His widow *d.* 2 Aug. 1708, aged 55, both being *bur.* at Willingdon. M.I. Her will pr. Aug. 1708.

II. 1691. SIR GEORGE PARKER, Baronet [1674], of Ratton aforesaid, 1st s. and h., *b.* 1677, *suc. to the Baronetcy*, 30 Nov. 1691; was M.P. for Sussex (two Parls.), 1705-08 and 1710-13. He *m.* 25 Feb. 1692, Mary, 1st da. of Sir Walter BAGOT, 3d Baronet [1627], of Blithfield, co. Stafford, by Jane, da. and h. of Charles SALUSBURY. He *d.* 18 June 1726, in his 50th year. His widow, who was *b.* 2 Dec. 1672, *d.* 14 May 1727, in her 55th year. Both *bur.* at Willingdon. M.I.

III. 1726, to 1750. SIR WALTER PARKER, Baronet [1674], of Ratton aforesaid, 1st s. and h., *b.* probably about 1700; admitted to Lincoln's Inn, 21 Jan. 1716/7; *suc. to the Baronetcy*, 18 June 1726. He *d.* unm. 19 April 1750, when the *Baronetcy* became *extinct.*(a) Will pr. 1750.

SHERARD, *or* SHERRARD:
cr. 25 May 1674(b);
ex. 25 Nov. 1748.

I. 1674. "JOHN SHERRARD [*or* SHERARD], of Lopthorpe [in North Witham], co. Lincoln, Esq.," 1st s. and h. of Richard SHERARD, of the same (*d.* 12 Sep. 1668), by Margaret, da. of Lumley DEWE, of Bishop Upton, co. Hereford, was *b.* about 1662, and was, at about the age of 12, *cr. a Baronet*, as above, 25 May 1674, with a spec. rem., failing heirs male of his body to his brothers, RICHARD SHERARD and BROWNLOW SHERARD and the heirs male of their bodies respectively. He matric. at Oxford (Ch. Ch.), 31 July 1678, aged 16; was admitted to the Inner Temple, 1681; Sheriff of Lincolnshire, 1709-10. He *d.* unm. 1 Jan. 1724/5, in his 63d year, and was *bur.* at North Witham. M.I. Admon. 26 Jan. 1724/5 and 7 July 1730.

II. 1725. SIR RICHARD SHERARD, Baronet [1674], of Lopthorpe aforesaid, br. and h., *b.* about 1666; admitted to Gray's Inn, 2 May 1711; *suc. to the Baronetcy* (according to the spec. rem.) 1 Jan. 1724/5. He *d.* unm. 14 June 1730, in his 65th year, and was *bur.* at North Witham. M.I. Will pr. 1730.

III. 1730. SIR BROWNLOW SHERARD, Baronet [1674], of Lopthorpe aforesaid, only surv. br. and h., *b.* 7 Feb. 1667/8 (the year of his father's death) at North Witham; was Gent. Usher of the Privy Chamber to William III, Queen Anne, George I and George II; *suc. to the Baronetcy* 14 June 1730. He *m.* in or after 1699, Mary, widow of Sir Richard ANDERSON, 2d Baronet [1643], of Penley, Herts (who *d.* 16 Aug. 1699), formerly widow of Humphrey SIMPSON, da. of the Rt. Hon. John METHUEN, sometime Ambassador to Portugal, by Mary, da. of Seacole CHEVERS, of Cornerford, Wilts. He *d.* 30 Jan. 1735/6, in his 69th year, and was *bur.* at North Witham. M.I. Will pr. 1736.

(a) The chief estates passed to the family of Fuller, through that of Lidgiter and Trayton, Philadelphia, yst. sister of the last Baronet, having *m.* Nathaniel Trayton, of Lewes.

(b) The date in Dugdale's *Catalogue* is (apparently in error) given as "*20* May 1674," though placed after that of Parker, a creation of *22* May 1674.

IV. 1736, to 1748. SIR BROWNLOW SHERARD, Baronet [1674], of Lopthorpe aforesaid, and Newton Hall, in Great Dunmow, Essex, s. and h., *b.* probably about 1702; admitted to Gray's Inn, 12 Nov. 1719; *suc. to the Baronetcy*, 30 Jan. 1735/6. He *m.* 16 July 1738, Mary, 1st da. of Col. the Hon. Thomas SYDNEY, of Ranworth, Norfolk (yr. s. of Thomas, 4th EARL OF LEICESTER), by Mary, da. of Sir Robert REEVE, 2d Baronet [1663], of Thwaite. He *d.* s.p. 25 Nov. 1748, when the *Baronetcy* became *extinct*. Will pr. 1749. His widow *d.* at Hampton Court, 27 March 1758. Will pr. 1758.

CLARGES:
cr. 30 Oct. 1674;
ex. 17 Feb. 1834.

I. 1674. "WALTER CLEARGIS [*recte* CLARGES], of St. Martin's in the Fields, co. Middlesex, Esq.," only s. and h. ap. of Sir Thomas CLARGES,(a) (whose sister, Anne, *m.*, Jan. 1652/3, the celebrated General George MONK, *cr.* DUKE OF ALBEMARLE), by Mary, da. of George, sister and coheir of Edward PROCTER, of Norwell Woodhouse, Notts; was *b.* about 1654; matric. at Oxford (Merton Coll.) 3 Feb. 1670/1, aged 17, and was v.p. (when presumably aged but 20) *cr. a Baronet*, as above, 30 Oct. 1674; was M.P. for Colchester, 1679-81 and 1685-87; for Westminster, 1690-95 and 1702-05, having suc. his father 4 Oct. 1695. He *m.* firstly, Jane, only da. of Sir Dawes WYMONDSELL, of Putney, co. Surrey, by his 1st wife, Jane, da. of Sir Robert COOKE, of Highnam, co. Gloucester. She *d.* s.p.m. He *m.* secondly, in or before 1682, Jane, da. of the Hon. James HERBERT, of Kingsey, Bucks (yr. s. of Philip, 4th EARL OF PEMBROKE), by Jane, da. of Sir Robert SPILLER, of Laleham, Midx. She was living July 1688, but *d.* before July 1691. He *m.* thirdly, in or before 1691, Elizabeth, widow of Sir Robert WYMONDSELL, of Putney, da. and coheir of Sir Thomas GOLD(b), sometime (1675-76) Sheriff of London. He *d.* March 1705/6. Will pr. April 1706. His widow *d.* 20 April 1728. Her will pr. 1736.

II. 1706. SIR THOMAS CLARGES, Baronet [1674], of Aston, near Stevenage, Herts, 1st surv. s. and h. by 2d wife, *b.* 25 and bap. 31 July 1688, at St. James', Westm.; *suc. to the Baronetcy* in March 1705/6. M.P. for Lostwithiel, Cornwall, 1713-15. He *m.*, in or before 1721, Barbara, 2d and yst. da. and coheir of John (BERKELEY), 4th VISCOUNT FITZHARDINGE [I.], by Barbara, da. of Sir Edward VILLIERS. He *d.* 19 Feb. 1759. Will pr. 1759.

III. 1759. SIR THOMAS CLARGES, Baronet [1674], of Aston aforesaid, grandson and h., being only s. and h. of Thomas CLARGES, by Anne, da. of John (BARRINGTON, *formerly* SHUTE), 1st VISCOUNT BARRINGTON OF ARDGLASS [I.], which Thomas (who *d.* v.p. in France, 27 Nov. 1753, aged 32) was only s. and h. ap. of the late Baronet. He was *b.* 4 Oct. 1751 at Aix la Chapelle, and *suc. to the Baronetcy*, 19 Feb. 1759; matric. at Oxford (Ch. Ch.) 6 June 1770, aged 16; was M.P. for Lincoln, 1780 till his death in 1782. He *m.*,

(a) John Clarges, of St. Mary's Savoy, Midx., the father of this Thomas, appears to have been a Farrier. (*See* evidence in a trial at the King's Bench, 15 Nov. 1700, of "Wm. Sherwin *v.* Sir Walter Clarges," as also in "Pride *v.* Earl of Bath" [1 Salkeld, 120]). There is, however, an elaborate pedigree of him and his sister, the Duchess of Albemarle, deducing their descent from the family of De Glarges, in the province of Hainault, compiled 4 Feb. 1675, by the "chef de nom et famille de Montigny de Glarges."

(b) She is generally said to have been the widow of Sir Dawes Wymondsell, but Sir Thomas Gold's da., Elizabeth, *m.*, in Oct. 1684, Sir Robert (*not* Sir Dawes) Wymondsell, and was living as his wife in 1686, when she took out admon. to her father. The will of Sir Robert Wymondsell was pr. Sep. 1687.

20 Oct. 1777, Louisa, da. of (—) SKRINE, of Arlington street, St. James', Westm. He *d.* 23 Dec. 1782. Will pr. Jan. 1783. His widow, who was *b.* 6 July 1760, *d.* at Richmond 5 Aug. 1809, and was *bur.* at Petersham, Surrey. M.I. Will pr. 1809.

IV. 1782, to 1834. SIR THOMAS CLARGES, Baronet [1674], 1st s. and h., *b.* about 1780; *suc. to the Baronetcy*, 25 Dec. 1802; matric. at Oxford (Ch. Ch.) 23 Oct. 1799, aged 19; B.A., 1802. He *d.* unm. at Brighton, 17 Feb. 1834, in his 54th year, when the *Baronetcy* became *extinct*. Will pr. March and April 1834.(a)

WILLIAMS:(b)
cr. 12 [not 2] Nov. 1674(c);
ex. 12 July 1804.

I. 1674. "THOMAS WILLIAMS, of Eltham [a mistake for Elham, near Canterbury], co. Kent, Esq., His Majesty's Physician in Ordinary," yr. br. of William WILLIAMS, of Talyllyn, co. Brecon, both being sons of Thomas WILLIAMS, of Talyllyn aforesaid, by Mary, da. of John PARR, of Poston, co. Hereford, was *b.* about 1621; practised in Kent as a medical man, and was admitted, 11 Feb. 1659/60 ("medico-chirurgiam Eltham [Elham?] in comitatu Cantii exercens"), as an Extra Licentiate of the College of Physicians, London. He was created M.D. of the Univ. of Cambridge, *per lit. Regias*, 5 March 1669; Chymical Physician to Charles II, 19 June 1670, and was *cr. a Baronet*, as above, 12 Nov. 1674.(c) He was M.P. for Weobley 1675, till unseated 1678. He *m.* firstly, before 1653, Anne, da. of John HOGBEANE,(d) of Elham aforesaid, Barrister at Law. She, who was *bap.* at Elham, 10 June 1632, was *bur.* there, 18 Feb. 1664. He *m.* secondly (Lic. Vic. Gen., 21 Dec. 1666, he about 48 and she about 30), Grace CARWARDINE, of Madley, co. Hereford, widow, da. of Thomas LEWIS, of the Moor, co. Hereford. He was *bur.* 12 Sep. 1712, at Glasbury, co. Brecon.

II. 1712. SIR JOHN WILLIAMS, Baronet [1674], sometime of Elham aforesaid and of Fulham, Midx.; but subsequently of Pengethly in Sellack, co. Hereford, 1st s. and h.; *bap.* 24 Nov. 1653, at Elham; was *Knighted* v.p. before 8 Feb. 1674/5; was M.P. for Hereford (three Parls.) 1700-05; *suc. to the Baronetcy*, Sep. 1712. He *m.* (Lic. Vic. Gen. 8 and marriage settlement dat. 11 Feb. 1674/5) Mary (then aged 13), da. and h. of Sir William POWELL, *formerly* HINSON, Baronet [so *cr.* 23 Jan. 1660/1], of Fulham, co. Midx., and of Pengethly aforesaid, by his 1st wife, Mary, da. and h. of John PEARL, of

(a) In it he left land worth £10,000 a year and the bulk of his property to Major Hare, a distant kinsman.

(b) The particulars in this article have for the most part been kindly furnished by H. J. T. Wood, of 2 New square, Lincoln's Inn.

(c) The date *12* Nov. 1674 is from the original patent, enrolled Pat. Rolls, 26 Car. II, part 6, no. 2. "A search of the Patent Rolls and of the list of Baronets in Guillim's Heraldry shews that the only Thomas Williams who was created a Baronet before 1685 was Thomas Williams, of Elham, co. Kent. The Baronet, the doctor, and the M.P. of this name are identified in '*a seasonable argument to persuade all the Grand Juries of England to petition for a new Parliament.*' Amsterdam, 1677, p. 10." See "*a Breconshire Pedigree*" in the *Genealogist*, N.S., vol. xiv, p. 150, by H. J. T. Wood [see note "a" above], who therein fully sets out the ancestry of this Baronet, and who has also examined the original patent in the possession [1901] of the family of Wood, at Gwernyfed.

(d) "The proof of this is not quite complete, but compare will of Sir John Williams, Baronet [proved 24 July 1723], s. and h. of Sir Thomas, with the Elham Registers" [*Breconshire Pedigree*, as in note "c" next above].

Acornbury, co. Hereford. She, who was *bap.* 27 Jan. 1662/3, was *bur.* 12 Nov. 1704, at Sellack. M.I. Admon. 21 Nov. 1704. He *d.* s.p.m., 28 April 1723 aged 69, and was *bur.* at Sellack.(a) M.I. Will dat. 2 April and pr. 24 July 1723.

III. 1723. SIR DAVID WILLIAMS, Baronet [1674], of Gwernevet and Llangoed Castle, co. Brecon, nephew and presumably h. male, being 2d but apparently 1st surv. s. and h.(b) of Sir Edward WILLIAMS, of Gwernevet aforesaid, by Elizabeth, 1st da. and coheir(c) of Sir Henry WILLIAMS, 2d Baronet [1644] of Gwernevet, which Edward (who was *bap.* at Elham, 6 Nov. 1659, M.P. for Breconshire, 1697-98 and, 1705 till death in 1721, being *bur.* at Glasbury, co. Brecon, 28 July 1721) was yr. s. of the 1st Baronet. He, it is presumed, *suc. to the Baronetcy*, 28 April 1723. He *m.* in or before 1725, Susanna, da., and eventually coh., of Thomas WITHERSTONE, of the Lodge, in Burghill, co. Hereford. He was *bur.* 6 Feb. 1739/40, at Llyswen.(c) Will dat. 23 Jan., pr. 12 Feb. 1739/40, at Brecon. His widow *m.* Rev. Thomas JOHNSON, Rector of Merthyr Tydvil, co. Glamorgan, and was *bur.* 12 May 1775 at Llyswen.

IV. 1740. SIR HENRY WILLIAMS, Baronet [1674], of Gwernevet and Llangoed Castle aforesaid, 1st s. and h.; *suc. to the Baronetcy*, Feb. 1739/40. He *d.* unm. 15 and was *bur.* 17 Aug. 1741,(c) at Llyswen, aged 16. M.I.

V. 1741, to 1804. SIR EDWARD WILLIAMS, Baronet [1674], of Gwernevet and Llangoed Castle aforesaid, and of Clifton, co. Gloucester, br. and h.; *suc. to the Baronetcy*, 15 Aug. 1741; was M.P. for Breconshire, 1788-89. He *m.*, 2 Feb. 1748/9, at St. Geo. Han. sq. (settl. 31 Jan.), Mary, da. and coheir of Isaac LEHEUP, of Gunthorpe, co. Norfolk. She *d.* at Llangoed Castle, 1763, aged 34. He *m.* secondly, 2 May 1777, Mary, da. and coheir of John RILEY, of Epsom, Surrey, and of Bread street, London. He *d.*, s.p.m.s.,(d) 12 July 1804, at Clifton foresaid, aged 76, when the *Baronetcy* became *extinct* or *dormant.*(e) Admon. 1 Oct. 1804 and 8 June 1812. His widow *d.* 24 March 1812, aged 67. M.I. to both of them in Bristol cathedral.

FILMER:
cr. 26 Dec. 1674.

I. 1674. "ROBERT FILMER, of East Sutton, co. Kent, Esq.," 2d s. of Sir Robert FILMER of the same, a great sufferer for his loyalty to Charles I (*d.* 1653), by Anne (*m.* Aug. 1618), da. and coheir of Martin

(a) The date, 28 April 1723 (*not* 17 June, as in Wotton's *Baronetage*, 1741), is that on the monument of his daughters and coheirs (1) Mary, *m.* John Hurleston, of Rowton, co. Chester; (2) Elizabeth, *m.* Thomas Price, of Llanfoist, co. Monmouth; (3) Anne, *m.* William Martin; (4) Penelope, *m.* Thomas Symonds, of Sugwass, co. Hereford, who, in her right, obtained the Pengethly estate, and transmitted it to their descendants.

(b) Henry is described in a deed, dat. 28 March 1721 (recited in a deed of 19 Sep. 1722), as s. and h. of Sir Edward; David being therein described as yr. brother of the said Henry. Henry's will, dat. 6 April 1723, was pr. 9 Oct. following, but he is supposed to have died between 6 and 28 April, on which last day his uncle died. [*Ex inform.*, H. J. T. Wood; see p. 66, note "b."].

(c) See vol. ii, p. 224, notes "c" and "g," under "Williams," Baronet [1644].

(d) Of his children by his 1st wife, Edward Williams, only son, *bap.* 18 Nov. 1757 at Llyswen, sometime Major Commandant of the Brecon Militia, *d.* v.p. and s.p. 25 Nov. 1799, and was *bur.* at Brecon: Mary, only da. and h., *bap.* 23 March 1752 at Llyswen; *m.* 22 June 1776, at Littleton, Midx., Thomas Wood, of Littleton, and *d.* 18 July 1820, leaving issue, who inherited the Gwernevet (now [1901] called Gwernyfed) estate.

(e) It is by no means certain that the male issue of the 1st Baronet has failed. He is said to have had issue by his 2d wife. See Jones' *Brecon*.

Heton, D.D., Bishop of Ely [1599—1610], was *bap.* 28 Feb. 1621/2, at St. Margaret's, Westm.; matric. at Oxford (Ch. Ch.), 29 March 1639, aged 17; admitted to Gray's Inn, 18 Nov. 1639; Barrister, 1651; suc. his elder br., Sir Edward Filmer (who *d.* unm. in Paris), in the family estate, in Sep. 1669, and was *cr. a Baronet*, as above, 26 Dec. 1674. He *m.* (settlmt. 24 Feb. 1648), Dorothy, da. of Maurice Tuke, of Layer Marney, Essex, and h. to her mother Amy, da. of Reginald Kempe, of Ollantigh, Kent. She *d.* 10 June 1671. He *d.* 22 March 1675/6, aged 54. Will pr. 1676. Both *bur.* at East Sutton.

II. 1676. Sir Robert Filmer, Baronet [1674], of East Sutton aforesaid, 1st s. and h., *b.* 16 and *bap.* there 26 Oct. 1648; admitted to Gray's Inn, 29 Oct. 1670; *suc. to the Baronetcy*, 22 March 1675/6; Sheriff of Kent, 1688-89. He *m.* (Lic. Vic. Gen. 1 Aug. 1682, he about 32 and she about 24) Elizabeth, da. and coheir of Sir William Beversham, of Holbrook Hall, Suffolk, one of the Masters in Chancery, by his 1st wife, Frances, da. and coheir of Christopher Harries, of Margaretting, Essex. She *d.* 4 May 1717, aged 62. He *d.* 14 April 1720, aged 71. Will pr. 1720. Both *bur.* at East Sutton.

III. 1720. Sir Edward Filmer, Baronet [1674], of East Sutton aforesaid, 1st s. and h.; *bap.* there 30 May 1683; matric. at Oxford (New Coll.), 12 July 1700, aged 17; *suc. to the Baronetcy*, 14 April 1720. He *m.* 24 Feb. 1706/7, Mary, da. of John Wallis, of Soundness, Oxon, only s. and h. of John Wallis, D.D., Savilian Professor at Oxford. He *d.* 10 Feb. 1755, aged 72. His widow, by whom he had twenty children, *d.* 5 Jan. 1761, aged 62. Both *bur.* at East Sutton.

IV. 1755. Sir John Filmer, Baronet [1674], of East Sutton aforesaid, 4th but 1st surv. s. and h., *bap.* there 30 Sep. 1716; matric. at Oxford (University Coll.), 5 Dec. 1734, aged 18; Barrister (Middle Temple), 1741; *suc. to the Baronetcy*, 10 Feb. 1755; M.P. for Steyning, Feb. 1767 to 1774. He *m.* April 1757, Dorothy, da. of the Rev. Julius Deedes, of Great Mongham, Kent, Preb. of Canterbury, by Dorothy, da. of Nathaniel Denew, of St. Stephen's. He *d.* s.p. 22 Feb. 1797, aged 81. Will pr. March 1797. His widow *d.* 2 July 1818, aged 82 years and 6 months. Will pr. 1818. Both *bur.* at East Sutton.

V. 1797. Sir Beversham Filmer, Baronet [1674], of East Sutton, aforesaid, br. and h., *bap.* there 21 April 1719; was admitted (as "of Brandon in Cranbrook, Kent, Gent."), 29 April 1757, to Gray's Inn[a] and *suc. to the Baronetcy*, 22 Feb. 1797. He *m.* Feb. 1764, Dorothy, da. of William Hendley, of Gore Court in Sittingbourne, Kent. She *d.* 14 Oct. 1793, near Bedford Row, Holborn. He *d.* s.p. 31 Dec. 1805, aged 86. Will pr. Jan. 1806.

VI. 1805. Sir Edmund Filmer, Baronet [1674], of East Sutton aforesaid, br. and h., *bap.* there 7 May 1727; matric. at Oxford (Corpus Christi Coll.), 2 Dec. 1745, aged 18; B.A., 1749; M.A., 1752; in Holy Orders; Rector of Crundale, Kent; *suc. to the Baronetcy*, 31 Dec. 1805. He *m.* 13 May 1755, Annabella Christiana, 1st da. of Sir John Honywood, 3d Baronet [1660], by his 1st wife, Annabella, da. of William Goodenough. She *d.* 18 Oct. 1798, aged 70, and was *bur.* at Crundale. M.I. He *d.* 27 June 1810, at East Sutton, aged 83, and was *bur.* at Crundale. Will pr. 1810.

VII. 1810. Sir John Filmer, Baronet [1674], of East Sutton aforesaid, 2d but 1st surv. s. and h.[b]; *b.* 19 March and *bap.* 6 April 1760, at Crundale; matric. at Oxford (Univ. Coll.), 13 Nov. 1776 (the same time

(a) His uncle Beversham Filmer had been so admitted, 14 Nov. 1702, being afterwards admitted (as "of Gray's Inn, Esq.") 26 June 1723, to Lincoln's Inn. He, who was a Barrister of some note and master of the *Nisi Prius* Office, *d.* unm. 11 June 1763.

(b) Edward Filmer, the 1st son, *b.* 13 April 1759; matric. at Oxford (Univ. Coll.), 13 Nov. 1776, aged 17. He *d.* s.p. and v.p., 30 Sep. 1794, aged 36. Admon. 21 April 1795, to Mary, his widow.

as his elder brother), aged 16; B.A. (Mag. Coll.), 1780; M.A., 1783; Fellow, 1785-95; took Holy Orders; B.D., 1792; Vicar of Abbots Langley, Herts, 1785-1821; *suc. to the Baronetcy*, 27 June 1810. He *m.* firstly, 12 Feb. 1795, Charlotte, 1st da. of Joseph Portal, of Laverstoke, Hants, by Sarah, da. of Gen. John Peachy, of Gosport. She *d.* 31 Aug. 1813, aged 58, and was *bur.* at East Sutton. M.I. He *m.* secondly, May 1821, Esther, da. of John Stow, of Tenements St. Stephen, near Canterbury. He *d.* s.p. 15 July 1834, at East Sutton, aged 74. Will dat. 29 Dec. 1829, pr. 21 Aug. 1834. His widow *d.* 16 March 1842, at Kensington, aged 44. Admon. April 1842.

VIII. 1834. Sir Edmund Filmer, Baronet [1674], of East Sutton aforesaid, nephew and h., being only s. and h. of Edmund Filmer, Capt. in the Army, by Emily, da. of George Skene, M.D., of Aberdeen, which Edmund (who *d.* 30 March 1810, at Bath, aged 45), was yr. br. of the late and 4th s. of the 6th Baronet. He was *b.* 14 June 1809, at Walcot, near Bath; matric. at Oxford (Oriel Coll.), 29 May 1827, aged 17; *suc. to the Baronetcy*, 15 July 1834; was M.P. for West Kent (four Parls.), March 1838 till death in 1857. He *m.* 1 Sep. 1831, at Melcombe Regis, Dorset, Helen, 2d da. of David Monro, of Quebec, in Lower Canada. He *d.* at East Sutton Place, 8 Jan. 1857, aged 47. Will pr. May 1857. His widow *d.* 17 July 1888, aged 78, at "The Bourne," Maidenhead.

IX. 1857. Sir Edmund Filmer, Baronet [1674], of East Sutton aforesaid, 1st s. and h., *b.* 11 July and *bap.* there 31 Aug. 1835; ed. at Eton; sometime Capt. Gren. Guards; *suc. to the Baronetcy*, 8 Jan. 1857; M.P. for West Kent, 1859-65, and for Mid Kent, 1880, till resigned in 1884; Sheriff of Kent, 1870. He *m.* 21 Oct. 1858, at St. Geo. Han. sq., Mary Georgiana Carolina, 1st da. of Arthur Marcus Cecil (Sandys, *formerly* Hill), 3d Baron Sandys of Ombersley, by Louisa, da. of Joseph Blake. He *d.* at Brighton, 17 Dec. 1886 and was *bur.* at East Sutton, aged 51. His widow, who was *b.* 4 April 1838, *d.* at 22 Lowndes Street, Knightsbridge, 17 March 1903, aged 64, and was *bur.* at East Sutton.

X. 1886. Sir Robert Marcus Filmer, Baronet [1674], of East Sutton aforesaid, 2d but only surv. s. and h., *b.* 25 Feb. 1878; *suc. to the Baronetcy* (at the age of eight years), 17 Dec. 1886; ed. at Eton and at the Military College, Sandhurst; Lieut. Gren. Guards, serving in the Soudan, 1896, and in the Transvaal War, 1899-1902.

Family Estates.—These, in 1883, consisted of 6,596 acres in Kent (worth £9,221 a year), 5 in Berks (worth £150 a year) and 7 in Essex. *Total.*—6,608 acres, worth £9,395 a year. *Seat.*—East Sutton Park, near Staplehurst, Kent.

NEVILL:

cr. 24 Feb. 1674/5;

ex. 1686.

I. 1675, to 1686. "Sir Edward Nevill, of Grove, co. Nottingham, Knt.," s. and h. of Edward Nevill, of the same, by Mary, da. of [—] Scott, of Camberwell, Surrey, was *b.* about 1652; matric. at Oxford (Jesus Coll.), 26 March 1669, aged 17; *Knighted* 11 Dec. 1671, and was *cr. a Baronet*, as above, 24 Feb. 1674/5; was M.P. for East Retford, 1679-81, and 1685 till death in 1686. He *m.* firstly (Lic. Vic. Gen. 8 Nov. 1669, aged about 19, his parents dead, and with consent of guardians), Catharine Kederminster (then aged about 35), widow, said to be da. of [—] Holt, of Warwickshire. He *m.* secondly (Lic. Vic. Gen. 10 July 1684, he aged about 34, widower), Mary Bostock, of St. Mary Aldermary, London, then about 39, widow. He *d.* s.p. in 1686, when the *Baronetcy* became *extinct*. Will pr. May 1686.

TROMP, *or* VAN TROMP:

cr. 23 April 1675;

ex. or *dormant* since 29 May 1691.

I. 1675, to 1691. "Cornelius Martinus Tromp [*or* Van Tromp, of Amsterdam], Lord Admiral of Holland"[a] [*Qy.* Vice Admiral of Holland and West Friesland], s. of Martin Herbertson [*recte* Harpertszoon] Van Tromp, the famous Dutch Admiral who contended with Admiral Blake, was *b.* about 1630; distinguished himself in several sea fights against the English; was in command at Solebay, 28 May 1672, and is said to have effected a masterly retreat therefrom; was in London during the peace, 1674-5, and was *cr. a Baronet*, as above, 23 April 1675, with rem. of that dignity to the issue male of his body, failing which, with a spec. rem. to his brothers, "Harper Martin Tromp, Burgomaster of Delft," and "Adrian Martin Tromp, Capt. in the Prince of Orange's regiment,"[a] in like manner respectively. In 1677 he was made Lieut.-Admiral Gen. of the United Provinces. He was about to assume the command of a fleet destined to act against the French, when he *d.* 29 May 1691, in his 62d year and was *bur.* (with his father), at Delft. At his death the *Baronetcy* became presumably *extinct* or *dormant*.

MORE, *or* MOORE:

cr. 22 Nov. 1675[b];

ex. 21 May 1810.

I. 1675. "Edward Moore [*or* More], of Moore Hall [presumably of Bank Hall in Walton], co. Lancaster, Esq.," s. and h. of Col. John More, of the same (who was M.P. for Liverpool 1640-50, and who held that town against Charles I.), by Mary, da. of Alexander Rigby, of Burgh and Leyton, had the "*Recepi*" for a *Baronetcy*, 1 March 1661/2, which, however, did not pass the Great Seal till 22 Nov. 1675. He *m.* firstly, in or before 1664, Dorothy, da. and coheir of Sir William Fenwick, of Meldon, Northumberland. She was living 1667. He *m.* secondly, Mary, da. of (—) Ben, by Mary, afterwards (6 Jan. 1656/7), 2d wife of Sir Thomas Bludworth, Lord Mayor of London, 1666.[c] He *d.* at Bank Hall in or before 1679. Admon. 4 Aug. 1679, to his widow. She, by whom he had no male issue, *m.* Mun Browne, Merchant (whose will dat. 1 Oct. was pr. by Mary the relict, 27 Nov. 1674) and *d.* before 5 March 1715/6.[d]

II. 1679? Sir Cleave More, *or* Moore, Baronet [1675], of Bank Hall aforesaid, and afterwards of Swineshead Abbey, co. Lincoln, 3d but 1st surv. s. and h. by 1st wife, *b.* at Liverpool about 1664; matric. at Oxford (Ch. Ch.), 4 July 1682, aged 18; *suc. to the Baronetcy* in or before 1679;

(a) The description of this grantee and of those in remainder to the dignity is taken from a letter, 8 Feb. 1674/5 (when presumably the warrant had been already passed) among the "Fleming MSS. in the 7th app. to the 12th Report of the Hist. MSS. Commission. In Dugdale's *Catalogue* the grantee is called "Sir Richard Tulpe [*sic*], of Amsterdam in the province of Holland, Knt."

(b) This is inserted in Dugdale's *Catalogue* under the date of 1 March 1661/2, being that of the Receipt, instead of under 22 Nov. 1675, being that of the Patent.

(c) She was undoubtedly the da. of Mary, the 2d wife of Sir Thomas Bludworth, who married such wife at St. Dionis, Backchurch as "Mrs. Mary Ben, widow." Possibly, however, Lady Bludworth may have been her mother by a previous husband, *not* of the name of Ben.

(d) See will (pr. 2 Jan. 1716/7) of her uterine sister, Mary Cawthorne (*née* Bludworth) of that date, in which she speaks of "my poor nephew, Mun Browne, of London, Gent., son of my sister, Dame May Moore, deceased," and see also will of Mun Browne (his father) dat. 1 Oct. and pr. 27 Nov. 1674, in which he speaks of "my father-in-law, Sir Thomas Bludworth and my mother, his Lady."

sold the estate of Bankhall to the Earl of Derby; was M.P. for Bramber, Jan. 1709 to 1710. He *m.*, in or before 1689, Anne, da. and h. of Joseph Edmonds, of Cumberlow Green, in Clothal, Herts, son of Simon Edmonds, who fined for Alderman of London. She was *bur.* (with her family) 10 Nov. 1720, at St. Mary, Aldermanbury, London. Will pr. Oct. 1720. He *d.* a widower, 23 March 1729/30, in St. Anne's, Aldersgate, London, 23, and was *bur.* 27 March 1730 at St. Mary's aforesaid. Admon. 24 April 1730, and 22 March 1731/2.

III. 1730. Sir Joseph Edmonds More, Baronet [1675], only s. and h., *b.* about 1690; matric. at Oxford (Magdalen Coll.), 17 Oct. 1707, aged 17; *suc. to the Baronetcy*, 23 March 1729/30. He *m.* Osbaston Sophia, da. of (—) Newnam, or Newman, of Lincoln's Inn Fields. He *d.* 14 March 1731/2. Will pr. 1732. His widow *d.* in or before 1750. Her will pr. 1750.

IV. 1732. Sir Joseph Edmonds More, Baronet [1675], 1st s. and h., *b.* probably about 1715; *suc. to the Baronetcy*, 14 March 1731/2. He *m.*, in 1736, Henrietta Maria, da. of William Morris, of Fernam, near Faringdon, Berks. He *d.* 29 March 1741. Will pr. 1741. His widow *m.*, about 1750, Edward Smith.

V. 1741, to 1810. Sir William More, Baronet [1675], of Stamford, co. Lincoln, only s. and h., *bap.* 3 Oct. 1738, at Howell, co. Lincoln; *suc. to the Baronetcy*, 29 March 1741. He *m.*, probably before 1775, (—), da. of (—). He *d.* at Brompton, s.p.m.[a] 21, and was *bur.* 29 May 1810, at St. Anne's, Soho, aged 71, when the *Baronetcy* became *extinct*. Will pr. 1810.

SAMWELL:

cr. 22 Dec. 1675;

ex. 18 Oct. 1789.

I. 1675. "Thomas Samwell,[b] of Upton, co Northampton, Esq.," as also of Gayton in that county, only s. and h. of Richard Samwell, of the same, by Frances, 1st da. and coheir of Thomas (Wenman), 2d Viscount Wenman of Tuam [I.], was *b.* probably about 1645; suc. his father in 1662; and was *cr. a Baronet*, as above, 22 Dec. 1675. He was M.P. for Northamptonshire, 1689-90, and for Northampton, 1690 till his death in 1693/4. He *m.* firstly (Lic. Vic. Gen. 1 April 1673, aged 19), Elizabeth (also aged 19), da. and h. of George Gooday, of Bower Hall, in Pentlow, Essex. She was living 1678. He *m.* secondly, 7 July 1685, at St. Giles' in the Fields (Lic. Fac. 4), Anne, da. and h. of Sir John Godschalk, of Atherston upon Stour, co. Warwick. She was *bur.* from Westminster, at St. Paul's, Covent Garden, 15 April 1687. He was *bur.* 23 March 1693/4, at Upton. Will dat. 24 Feb. 1690/1 to 15 Dec. 1691, pr. 6 Feb. 1695/6.

II. 1694. Sir Thomas Samwell, Baronet [1675], of Upton aforesaid, only s. and h., by 2d wife, *bap.* there 14 April 1687; *suc. to the Baronetcy* in March 1693/4; was M.P. for Coventry, 1715-22. He *m.* firstly, 22 March 1709/10, Millicent (then aged 15), da. and h. of the Rev. Thomas Fuller, D.D., Rector of Hatfield, Herts. She was *bur.* 11 May 1716, at Upton. He *m.* secondly, 26 Jan. 1720/1, at St. Giles' in the Fields, Midx., Mary, widow of William Ives, of Bradden, co. Northampton, da. of Sir Gilbert Clarke, of Chilcot, co. Derby. He *d.* at Bradden 16 Nov. and was *bur.* 2 Dec. 1757, at Upton, aged 70. His widow *d.* 1 Aug. 1758, and was *bur.* there. Admon. 19 Aug. 1758.

(a) Elizabeth, his da. and h., *m.*, 1795, Charles Browning, of Horton Lodge, Surrey.

(b) See pedigree in Baker's *Northamptonshire*, vol. i, p. 224.

III. 1757. SIR THOMAS SAMWELL, Baronet [1675], of Upton aforesaid, 1st s. and h. by 1st wife, *b.* 28 Feb. 1710/1, at St. James', Westm., and *bap.* at Upton; *suc. to the Baronetcy*, 16 Nov. 1757. He *d.* unm. and s.p. legit. 3 and was *bur.* 12 Dec. 1779, at Upton, aged 68. Will pr. 1780.

IV. 1779, to 1789. SIR WENMAN SAMWELL, Baronet [1675], of Upton aforesaid, br. (of the half blood) and h. male, being 3d s. of the 2d Baronet, and 1st s. by the 2d wife; *b.* 24 Oct. 1728, at St. Geo. Han. sq., and *bap.* at Upton; *suc. to the Baronetcy*, 3 Dec. 1779. He *m.* Elizabeth, da. of Thomas SMITH, of East Haddon, co. Northampton. She *d.* 28 June and was *bur.* 4 July 1789, at Upton. He *d.* s.p., a few months later, 18 and was *bur.* there 26 Oct. 1789, aged nearly 61, when the *Baronetcy* became *extinct.*(a) Will pr. Jan. 1791.

RICH (b):

cr. 24 Jan. 1675/6;

ex. 8 Jan. 1799.

I. 1676. "CHARLES RICH of the City of London, Gent,"(c) nephew of Robert, 1st EARL OF WARWICK and grandson of Robert, 2d BARON RICH, being yst. s. of the Hon. Sir Edwin RICH, of Mulbarton and Newton Flotman, co. Norfolk (who *d.* before 26 Feb. 1647/8), by Honora, *or* Margaret, da. of Charles WOLRYCHE, of Wickham Brook and Cowling, co. Suffolk, was *b.* about 1619; was presumably a merchant of London; suc. his elder br. Sir Edwin RICH, 16 Nov. 1675, in the Norfolk estate and was *cr. a Baronet*, as above, 24 Jan. 1675/6, "for life, with a [special] remainder to Robert RICH, of Stondon, co. Essex, Esq.," who had married his younger daughter. He *m.* 28 Nov. 1641, at St. Martin's in the Fields (Lic. Lond. 26, he 23 and she 18, her parents dead), Elizabeth, da. of John CHOLMELEY, of Kirkby, Underwood, co. Lincoln, by Elizabeth, da. of Edmund PILKINGTON, of Staunton le Dale, co. Derby. He *d.* s.p.m.(d) and was *bur.* 30 May 1677, at Enfield, co. Midx. in his 59th year. M.I. Will dat. 27 April and pr. 7 July 1677. The will of his widow was pr. 1694.

II. 1677. SIR ROBERT RICH, Baronet [1676], of Roos Hall, in Beccles, co. Suffolk, son-in-law of the above, was 2d s. of Colonel Nathaniel RICH(e), of Stondon, co. Essex, by his 1st wife, Elizabeth, da. of Sir Edmund HAMPDEN, of Hampden, Bucks; was *b.* 1648; *Knighted* at Whitehall, 14 Feb. 1675/6, and *suc. to the Baronetcy* in May 1677, according to the spec. rem. in the patent thereof. He was M.P. for Dunwich (four Parls.), 1689 till death in 1699, and one of the Lords of the Admiralty, 1691-99. He *m.* 17 Feb. 1675/6, at St. Martin's in the Fields (both being then of St. Laurence, Pountney, London, and unm.), Mary 2d and yst. da. and coheir of Sir Charles RICH, 1st Baronet [1676], and Elizabeth, da. of John CHOLMELEY, all three abovenamed. He *d.* 1 Oct. 1699, aged 51, and was *bur.* at Beccles. M.I. Admon. 3 Feb. 1699/700. His widow was *bur.* there 23 Dec. 1714. Admon. 17 May 1715, to her da. [Dame] Elizabeth WHITE, widow.

(a) The estates devolved on his nephew, Thomas Samwell Watson, s. and h. of Thomas Atherton Watson, by Catherine, his only sister of the whole blood. He took the name of Samwell, by Act of Parl. 1790.

(b) Much of the information in this article has been kindly supplied by Sir Charles Henry Stuart Rich, 4th Baronet [1791], a descendant and representative of these Baronets.

(c) He is so styled in Dugdale's *Catalogue* where almost all the other grantees are described as "Esquires." This description, however (possibly adopted because he was in trade), seems anomalous for the grandson of a nobleman and the [then] eldest surv. son of a Knight. He is called in Le Neve's *Knights*, "of the New Exchange, London, Hosier," in the notice of the family, under 10 July 1666, the date of his elder brother Edwin's Knighthood.

(d) Elizabeth, the elder of his two daughters, *m.* Pierre de Ceville, a native of France, Capt. in a reg. of English Guards.

(e) This Nathaniel Rich was but a distant relative to the grantee, if (as is generally alleged), he was *seventh* in descent from Richard Rich, Alderman and sometime [1441-42] Sheriff of London, through his 1st son John, who *d.* v.p., inasmuch as the 1st Baronet was *sixth* in descent from the said Richard, through his yr. s. Thomas Rich.

III. 1699. SIR CHARLES RICH, Baronet [1676], of Roos Hall aforesaid, 1st s. and h., *b.* probably about 1680; *suc. to the Baronetcy* 1 Oct. 1699; was in the Navy, being Capt. of the "Feversham" man-of-war at his death in 1706. He *m.*, being then of St. Andrew's, Dublin (Lic. Prerog. [I.] 9 Jan. 1704/5), "Maria WHITE, of St. Bridget's, Dublin, spinster," da. of Col. Francis WHITE. He *d.* s.p., and was *bur.* 19 Oct. 1706, at St. Margaret's, Westm. Will dat. 14 Aug., and pr. Nov. 1706. His widow *m.* 27 March 1707, at the French church of St. Mary's, Dublin, as his 1st wife, Chamberlain WALKER, M.D., of Dublin, who was afterwards, 4 Nov. 1721, *Knighted*, and who *d.* 7 March 1731. She *d.* in or before 1712. Admon. 24 July 1712.

IV. 1706. SIR ROBERT RICH, Baronet [1676], of Roos Hall aforesaid, br. and h., *b.* 3 July 1685; was a Page of Honour to William III; *suc. to the Baronetcy* in Oct. 1706. He was an officer in the army, being wounded at Blenheim and Ramillies; Colonel, 24 Oct. 1709; General, 1745; Col. of the 4th Reg. of Dragoons till his death, and finally, 1757, FIELD MARSHAL. He was also a Groom of the Bedchamber to George, Prince of Wales, afterwards George II; was M.P. for Dunwich, 1715-20; for Beeralston, Feb. 1724 to 1727; and for St. Ives (two Parls.), 1727-41; was Governor of Chelsea Hospital, 1740 till his death in 1768. He *m.* 28 Sep. 1714, at Gawsworth, co. Chester, Elizabeth, 1st da. and coheir(a) of Col. Edward GRIFFITH, one of the Clerks of the Board of Green Cloth and Secretary to the Prince Consort, George, Prince of Denmark, by Elizabeth (*afterwards* BARONESS MOHUN), da. of Thomas LAWRENCE, 1st Physician to Queen Anne. He *d.* 1 Feb. 1768, and was *bur.* in South Audley street chapel, aged 82. Will dat. 31 Oct. 1767, pr. 6 Feb. 1768. His widow *d.* in Cleveland Row, St. James', 13 and was *bur.* 20 Oct. 1773, in Westm. Abbey, aged 81. Will dat. 15 Dec. 1770, pr. 3 Nov. 1773.

V. 1768. SIR ROBERT RICH, Baronet [1676], of Roos Hall aforesaid, 2d but 1st surv. s. and h., *b.* 1717; was an officer in the Army and held a command at the battle of Culloden, becoming eventually (1760) Lieut.-General; was Governor of Londonderry and of Culmore Fort, 1756; *suc. to the Baronetcy*, 1 Feb. 1768. He *m.* firstly, 31 May 1752, at St. Geo. Han. sq. (Lic. Lond.), Mary, sister of Peter, 1st EARL LUDLOW [I.], 2d da. of Peter LUDLOW, of Ardsallagh, co. Meath, by Mary, da. and h. of John PRESTON, of Ardsallagh aforesaid. She *d.* in childbirth, 6 Sep. 1755, at Montpelier, and was *bur.* in South Audley street chapel, aged 30. M.I. He *m.* secondly, 21 Sep. 1771, at Witham, co. Essex, Elizabeth WILLIAMS, widow, da. of Richard BELL, of Brampton, near Carlisle. He *d.* s.p.m.,(b) 19 May 1785, and was *bur.* in South Audley street chapel. Will dat. 29 May 1784, pr. June 1785. His widow *m.* James WALKER, Master of the Ceremonies at Margate, co. Kent, and *d.* 22 July 1788, aged 47, being *bur.* at Margate. M.I.

(a) Her sister Anne *m.*, about 1718, William (Stanhope), 1st Earl of Harrington, and *d.* in childbirth 18 Dec. 1719.

(b) Mary Frances, his only da. and h., by his 1st wife, *b.* 31 May 1755, *m.* 4 Jan. 1783, at New Windsor, Berks. the Rev. Charles Bostock, LL.D., who took the name of Rich, by Royal lic., 23 Dec. 1790, and was *cr. a Baronet*, 11 June 1791, a date, oddly enough, about eight years *before* the Baronetcy of Rich [1676] enjoyed by his wife's uncle, had become extinct. She *d.* his widow, 20 May 1833, and was *bur.* with her parents in South Audley street chapel. M.I. in Millbrook church, Hants.

VI. 1785, to 1799. SIR GEORGE RICH, Baronet [1676], of Letcombe Regis, co. Buckingham, br. and h. male, *b.* 13 June 1728; *suc. to the Baronetcy*, 19 May 1785. He *d.* unm. 8 Jan. 1799, and was *bur.* at Bucklebury in that county, aged 70, when the *Baronetcy* became *extinct.* M.I. Will dat. 14 Jan. 1783, pr. 17 Jan. 1799, by his niece, Dame Mary Frances RICH.

MADDOX, *or* MADDOKS:

cr. 11 March 1675/6;

ex. 14 Dec. 1716.

I. 1675, to 1716. "BENJAMIN MADDOX [*or* MADDOKS],(a) of Wormley, co. Hertford, Esq.," s. of Benjamin MADDOX, *or* MADDOKS, of Boughton Monchelsea, Kent, by Mary, da. of Sir Multon LAMBARDE, of Westcombe, in that county, was *b.* about 1638; matric. at Oxford (Wadham Coll.), 20 July 1654 (in which College he subsequently founded an Exhibition), and was *cr. a Baronet*, as above, 11 March 1675/6. He *m.* (Lic. Fac. 25 May 1664, he 26 and she 19), Dorothy, sister of Sir William GLASCOCK, Judge of the Admiralty in Ireland (*d.* 14 July 1688), da. of Sir William GLASCOCK, of Wormley aforesaid, by his 2d wife Mary, da. and h. of Arthur SHERE, of London, merchant. He *d.* s.p.m.,(b) 14 Dec. 1716, when the *Baronetcy* became *extinct*. Will pr. Feb. 1717. The will of his widow was pr. 1720.

BARKER :(c)

cr. 29 March 1676;

ex. 22 Oct. 1818.

I. 1676. "WILLIAM BARKER, of Bockinghall [in Bocking], co. Essex, Esq.," and afterwards of Curraghmore, co. Limerick, s. and h. of William BARKER,(d) of St. Andrew's, Holborn, Mercer, who fined for Alderman of London, by Martha, da. of William TURNER, of Highworth, Wilts, was *b.* about 1652; admitted to Gray's Inn, 12 July 1650, and was *cr. a Baronet*, as above, 29 March 1676. He *m.* firstly (indenture before marriage 23 June 1676), Elizabeth, one of the sixteen children of Sir Jerome ALEXANDER, Justice of the Common Pleas [I.], 1660 to 1670, by (—) da. of (—) HAVERS. She brought him an estate of £1,500 a year. Her will pr. [I.] 18 Dec. 1702. He *m.* secondly (Lic. Lond. 11 Nov. 1702, he aged 50 and widower), "Mrs. Letitia MOTHAM," then aged 20, spinster, both being of St. Margaret's, Westm. He, having mortgaged the Bocking estate, emigrated to Ireland. Will, as of Curraghmore, co. Limerick, dat. 11 Nov. 1710 to 6 Jan. 1710/1, pr. [I.] 13 Nov. 1719. A second will, as of the City of London, dat. 21 Aug. 1717, pr. [I.] 10 Dec. 1742.

II. 1719? SIR WILLIAM BARKER, Baronet [1676], of Ringsale Hall, co. Suffolk, s. and h., *b.* about 1677, *suc. to the Baronetcy*, in or before 1719; Sheriff of Suffolk, 1738-39. He *m.* Catharine Theresa, 1st da. and coheir of Samuel KECK, of the Middle Temple, London. He *d.* 5 May 1746. Will pr. 1746.

(a) He signs the allegation for his marriage licence, 25 May 1664, as "Maddoks."

(b) Of his two daughters and coheirs (1) Dorothy, *m.* Benjamin Rudyerd and had issue, and (2) Mary, *m.* Edward Pollen.

(c) Much of the information in this article has been kindly furnished by G. D. Burtchaell, of the Office of Arms, Dublin.

(d) This William was yr. s. of Sir Robert Barker, K.B., of Grimston Hall, Suffolk, who, by a former wife, was father of Sir John Barker, of the same, *cr. a Baronet*, 17 March 1621/2.

III. 1746. SIR WILLIAM BARKER, Baronet [1676], of Ringsale Hall aforesaid and of Kilcooley Abbey, near Kilkenny, co. Tipperary, 1st s. and h., by 1st wife, *b.* 1704; admitted to Trin. Coll., Dublin, as Fellow Commoner, 26 Feb. 1720; *suc. to the Baronetcy*, 5 May 1746. He *m.*, in 1736, Mary, da. of Valentine QUIN, of Adare, co. Limerick, by Mary, da. and coheir of Henry WIDENHAM, of Court, in that county. He *d.* 20 March 1770, at Kilcooley, aged 66. Will pr. [I.] 1770. His widow *d.* 16 Sep. 1776 at Kilkenny.

IV. 1770, to 1818. SIR WILLIAM BARKER, Baronet [1676], of Kilcooley Abbey aforesaid, only s. and h., *suc. to the Baronetcy*, 20 March 1770; Sheriff of co. Tipperary, 1764. He *m.* (Lic. Dublin, 23 Jan. 1760) Catharine, da. and h. of William LANE, of Dublin, by Dorothea, da. of William CONNER. He *d.* s.p. 22 Oct. 1818, when the *Baronetcy* became *extinct.*(a) Will pr. Nov. 1818. The will of his widow pr. 1830.

BROOKES, *or* BROOKE:

cr. 13 June 1676;

ex. 26 Jan. 1770.

I. 1676. "JOHN BROOKES, Esq., citizen of York," s. and h. of James BROOKES, *or* BROOKE, of Ellingthorpe, co. York (who fined for Sheriff of London), was admitted to Gray's Inn, 21 Oct. 1650, and was *cr. a Baronet*, as above, 13 June 1676; M.P. for Boroughbridge, 1679-81 and 1681. He *m.*, probably about 1670, Mary, da. of Sir Hardress WALLER, by Elizabeth, da. and coheir of Sir John DOWDALL. He *d.* 18 Nov. 1691, and was *bur.* at St. Martin's, Coney street, York. M.I.

II. 1691. SIR JAMES BROOKES, *or* BROOKE, Baronet [1676], of Shelton, Salop, 1st s. and h., *b.* about 1675(b); *suc. to the Baronetcy*, 18 Nov. 1691. He *m.* Bridget, da. of (—) WALKER. He *d.* 28 Aug. 1742.(c) His widow, who survived her son, the 3d Baronet, *d.* s.p.s. at Shelton, 20 Dec. 1778.

III. 1742, to 1770. SIR JOB BROOKES, *or* BROOKE, Baronet [1676], of Shelton aforesaid, and afterwards of Scawton-on-the-Moor, co. York, 1st and only surv. s. and h., *suc. to the Baronetcy*, 28 Aug. 1742. He, who was for many years a lunatic, *d.* unm. 26 Jan. 1770, at Scawton, when the *Baronetcy* became *extinct.*(d) Admon. 15 Nov. 1770, to "Anthony Procter, Esq., cousin german and one of the next of kin."

(a) Of his two sisters and coheirs, (1) Mary, *m.* firstly Chambre Brabazon Ponsonby, and had a son, who, on inheriting the estate of Kilcooley, took the name of Barker, after that of Ponsonby. She *m.* secondly, Sir Robert Staples, 7th Baronet [I. 1628]. (2) Hannah Maria, *m.* 1768, Eland Mossom.

(b) His yr. br. John Brooke, called also Brookes (the 2d s. of his parents), matric. at Oxford (Univ. Coll.) 1 July 1693, aged 16.

(c) This date from the *Gent. Mag.*, etc., is confirmed by the [MS.] diary of Gertrude Savile [*penes* Lord Hawkesbury], which states that "Sir James Brookes, a fool, Lady Savile's uncle, died Sep. 1742." This Lady Savile was Mary, wife of Sir George Savile, 7th Baronet [1611], by Mary, da. of John Pratt and Henrietta, sister of Sir James Brookes, 2d Baronet [1676], abovenamed. In Wotton's *Baronetage*, however, Sir James is said to have died at Hammersmith, Midx., in March 1735, his age being (elsewhere) given as 67.

(d) The following note by J. C. Brooke (sometime) York Herald, is in his edition of Wotton's *Baronetage*:—"Sir Job Brookes was many years a lunatic, and his brother Montagu dying before him, the estate of this family descended to his cousin, (—) Jenkins, wife of (—) Jenkins, of Sussex, only child of his uncle Henry Brookes."

HEAD:

cr. 19 June 1676;

ex. 28 Jan. 1868.

I. 1676. "RICHARD HEAD, of [Hermitage, near] Rochester, co. Kent, Esq.," 2d s. of Richard HEAD, of Rochester, by Anne, da. of William HARTRIDGE, of Cranbrook, in that county, was *b.* about 1609; was M.P. for Rochester, Nov. 1667 to 1669 and March to July 1679; was Alderman of that city, and was *cr. a Baronet*, as above, 19 June 1676. He entertained James II when a fugitive from London, in 1688, at his house in Rochester, and was presented by that King with an emerald ring.(a) He *m.* firstly, about 1640, Elizabeth, da. and coheir of Francis MERRICK, Alderman of Rochester. He *m.* secondly, before 1653, Elizabeth, da. and coheir of (—) WILLEY, of Wrotham, co. Kent. She was living 1661. He *m.* thirdly,(b) Anne, widow of John BOYS, of Hode, co. Kent, da. of William KINGSLEY, D.D., Archdeacon of Canterbury, by Damaris, da. of John ABBOTT, of Guildford, br. to George ABBOTT, Archbishop of Canterbury. He *d.* 18 Sep. 1689, in his 80th year, and was *bur.* in Rochester Cathedral. M.I. Will dat. 10 Sep. 1689, pr. same month. His widow, by whom he had no issue, *d.* 21 Feb. 1713, aged 81.

II. 1689. SIR FRANCIS HEAD, Baronet [1676], of Hermitage aforesaid, grandson and h., being only surv. s. and h. of Francis HEAD, by Sarah(c) (Lic. Fac. 1 July 1667), only da. of Sir George ENT, M.D., which Francis (who *d.* v.p. 16 Oct. 1678, aged 37, and was *bur.* at St. Margaret's, Rochester) was 1st s. and h, ap. of the late Baronet by his 1st wife. He was *b.* about 1670; admitted to Middle Temple, 1684; matric. at Oxford (Trin. Coll.), 19 Nov. 1686, aged 16; *suc. to the Baronetcy*, 18 Sep. 1689. He *m.* 5 May 1692, at St. Peter le Poor, London (Lic. Fac. 3, he 22, bachelor, she 17, spinster, with consent of her guardian, Sir Edward ABNEY), Margaret, 1st da. and coheir of James SMITHSBY (s. of Sir Thomas SMITHSBY, a great sufferer in the Royal cause), by (—), da. of John GREEN, Recorder of London. He *d.* Aug. 1716, aged about 46, and was *bur.* at St. Mildred's, Canterbury. M.I. Will pr. at Canterbury, 1716. The will of his widow was pr. 1733.

III. 1716. SIR RICHARD HEAD, Baronet [1676], of Hermitage aforesaid, 1st s. and h., *b.* about 1692; matric. at Oxford (Univ. Coll.), 13 Nov. 1711, aged 18; *suc. to the Baronetcy* in Aug. 1716. He *d.* unm., May 1721, and was *bur.* at Ickham, Kent.

IV. 1721. SIR FRANCIS HEAD, Baronet [1676], of Hermitage aforesaid, next br. and h., *b.* about 1693; matric. at Oxford (Ch. Ch.), 10 Oct. 1712, aged 18; B.A., 1716; M.A., 1719; *suc. to the Baronetcy*, in May 1721. He *m.*, in June 1726, Mary, da. and h. of Sir William BOYS, M.D., by Anne, da. of Sir Paul BARRETT, Serjeant at Law. He *d.* s.p.m.,(d) at Hermitage, 27 Nov. 1768, aged 75. Will pr. 1768. His widow *d.* in Cockspur street, Midx., 29 Oct. 1792, aged 92. Will pr. Nov. 1792.

V. 1768. SIR JOHN HEAD, Baronet [1676], only surv. br. and h. male, *b.* about 1702; matric. at Oxford (Ch. Ch.) 17 Oct. 1719, aged 17; B.A., 1723; M.A., 1726; in Holy Orders and apparently D.D., holding several preferments in co. Kent, being Rector of St. George's (Canterbury), 1730-60; Vicar of Selling, 1732; Rector of Burmarsh, 1737; Rector of Pluckley to 1760;

(a) This was stolen from the 7th Baronet [Playfair's *Baronetage*].

(b) His three wives are spoken of in his M.I. as "satis elegantes."

(c) This Sarah *m.*, as her 2d husband, Sir Paul Barrett, Serjeant at Law.

(d) Wilhelmina, 1st da. and coheir, Baroness Teynham, *d.* s.p., Nov. 1758, bnt Anne Gabriella, 2d da. and coheir, *m.* (for her 1st husband) Moses Mendez, and *d.* 1771, leaving by him two sons, both of whom took the name of Head, the younger, James Roper Head, being father of Sir Francis Bond Head, Baronet, so *cr.* 1 Jan. 1837.

and Rector of Ickham, 1760 till his death; besides being Preb. of Hereford, 1738-69; Archdeacon of Canterbury, 1748-69; Preb. of Canterbury, 1759-69; and Deputy Clerk of the Closet to George II, 1740. He *suc. to the Baronetcy* (a year before his death), 27 Nov. 1768. He *m.* firstly, about 1730, Jane, da. of the Rev. Peter LEIGH, Rector of Whitchurch, Salop, by Elizabeth, da. of the Hon. Thomas EGERTON. By her, who was *bur.* at Ickham, he had ten children, all of whom *d.* unm. and v.p. He *m.* secondly, 21 April 1751, Jane, sister of the Rev. William GECKIE, D.D., Archdeacon of Gloucester. He *d.* suddenly s.p.s., 4 Dec. 1769, and was *bur.* at Ickham. Will pr. 1769. His widow, by whom he had no children, *d.* 18 Jan. 1780, aged 85. Will pr. March 1780, and again 1803.

VI. 1769. SIR EDMUND HEAD, Baronet [1676], cousin and h. male, being 2d(a) s. of John HEAD, of Liverpool, merchant, by Hannah, da. of the Rev. Edmund WICKINS, Rector of Kirkby Thore, Westmoreland, which John (who *d.* 1739, aged 38) was only s. of Dawes HEAD,(b) of Ravenstonesdale, in that county (*d.* May 1705, aged 23), only s. of John HEAD, merchant of London (by Ann, da. and coheir of John DAWES, of Putney, Surrey), who *d.* 1687, being 5th s. (1st s. by 2d wife) of the 1st Baronet. He was *b.* 1733; emigrated to America and became a merchant at Charlestown, in South Carolina, about 1764; was President of the Court of Trade and Commerce; was, at the commencement of the war of independence, 1776-77, chosen a member of the American congress, but refused to act against his country, and was consequently banished and his property confiscated. He *suc. to the Baronetcy*, 4 Dec. 1769, but seems not to have assumed the title for some three or four years.(c) He was residing at Cook's Court, Carey street, London, in July 1794. He *m.* firstly, in or before 1771, at Charlestown aforesaid, Mary, only da. of Daniel RAINEAU, of Dublin, in Ireland. She *d.* 12 June 1775, aged 28, and was *bur.* at St. Michael's, in Charlestown. He *m.* secondly (a few months before his death), 12 May 1796, at St. Clement's Danes, Midx., Dorothy, da. of Maximilian WESTERN, of Cokethorpe, Oxon., a director of the East India Company, by (—) da. of (—) TAHOURDIN. He *d.* 21 and was *bur.* 27 Nov. 1796, aged 63, in Rochester Cathedral, near the 1st Baronet. M.I. Will pr. 1802. His widow, by whom he had no issue, *d.* 7 Jan. 1807, and is said to have been *bur.* with him.

VII. 1796. SIR JOHN HEAD, Baronet [1676], 2d but only surv. s. and h., *b.* 3 Jan. 1773; matric. at Oxford (Mag. Coll.), 3 Dec. 1793, aged 20; B.A. and M.A., 1800; admitted to Lincoln's Inn, 21 July 1794; *suc. to tho Baronetcy*, 21 Nov. 1796; took Holy Orders; was Incumbent of Egerton, co. Kent, 1807, and Rector of Rayleigh, co. Essex; purchased the estate of Wiarton place, in Boughton Monchelsea, Kent, before 1801. He *m.* 8 Oct. 1801, Jane, da. and h. of Thomas WALKER, of Russell place, Fitzroy square, Marylebone. He *d.* 4 Jan. 1838, aged 65, in John street, Adelphi, Midx. Will pr. July 1838. The admon. of "Dame Jane Head, Devon," granted Aug. 1842.

VIII. 1838, to 1868. SIR EDMUND WALKER HEAD, Baronet [1676], only s. and h., *b.* at Wiarton Place aforesaid, in 1805; ed. at Winchester; matric. at Oxford (Oriel Coll.), 11 June 1823, aged 18; B.A. and 1st Class Classics, 1827; M.A., 1830; Fellow of Merton Coll., 1830-37, and Principal Postmaster and Tutor; University Examiner, 1834-39; admitted to Lincoln's Inn, 29 April 1835; Assistant Poor-law Commissioner,

(a) John Head, the 1st son, *bap.* 26 Jan. 1729, at Appleby, was in the Naval service, and *d.* unm. at Barbadoes, 10 Feb. 1752.

(b) Dawes Head, *b.* at St. Swithen's, London, 16 April 1682, and called in his grandfather's will, 10 Sep. 1689, "my pretty grandchild of Ravenstone," run away from Westm. School at the age of 16 and married Jane Taylor, by whom, before his death, a few days over the age of 23 years, he had four children, his widow, who *d.* Sep. 1705, surviving him but four months.

(c) As early, however, as 1775, the death of his wife (12 June 1775) is spoken of as that of "The Lady of Sir Edmund Head, Bart." [*Annual Register*, etc.]

1836-41; Commissioner, 1841-47, having meanwhile *suc. to the Baronetcy*, 4 Jan. 1838; Gov. of New Brunswick, 1847-54; and Gov. Gen. of Canada, 1854-61; P.C., 1857; **K.C.B.**, 1860. Hon. D.C.L. of Oxford, 2 July 1862; Hon. LL.D. of Cambridge, 1862; F.R.S., etc.(a) He *m.* 27 Nov. 1838, at Ross, Anna Maria, da. of the Rev. Philip YORKE, Preb. of Ely (grandson of the 1st EARL OF HARDWICKE), by Anna Maria, da. of Charles (COCKS), 1st BARON SOMMERS OF EVESHAM. He *d.* s.p.m.s.(b) suddenly, of heart disease, 28 Jan. 1868, at 29 Eaton square, Midx., in his 63d year, when the *Baronetcy* became *extinct*. His widow *d.* 25 Aug. 1890, aged 82, at Shere, co. Surrey. Will pr. 5 Oct. 1890, over £39,000.

PENNINGTON:

cr. 21 June 1676;

afterwards, since 1793, BARONS MUNCASTER [I.].

I. 1676. "WILLIAM PENNINGTON, of Muncaster, co. Cumberland, Esq.," as also of Pennington, co. Lancaster, s. and h. of Joseph PENNINGTON, of the same places (*d.* 1659), by Margaret, da. of John FLEETWOOD, of Penwortham, co. Lancaster, was *bap.* at Muncaster, 16 March 1655, being 9 years old at the date of the Visit. of Lancashire in 1664, and was *cr. a Baronet*, as above, 21 June 1676(c), was Sheriff of Cumberland, 1685-86. He *m.*, in or before 1677, Isabel, 1st da. and coheir of John STAPLETON, of Wartre, *or* Warter, co. York, by Elizabeth, da. of Sir Wilfrid LAWSON, 1st Baronet [1688] of Isell. She, who inherited the estate of Wartre, was *bur.* 12 April 1687, at Waberthwaite. He *d.* 12 July 1730 at Wartre, aged 75.

II. 1730. SIR JOSEPH PENNINGTON, Baronet [1676], of Muncaster, Pennington and Wartre aforesaid, 1st s. and h., *b.* 4 and *bap.* 16 Oct. 1677, at Waberthwaite; matric. at Oxford (Queen's Coll.), 4 June 1695, aged 17; Comptroller of the Excise, 1723; *suc. to the Baronetcy*, 12 July 1730; M.P. for Cumberland (two Parls.), 1734-44; admitted to Middle Temple, 30 Dec. 1735. He *m.* 20 March 1706, at Lowther, Westmorland, Margaret, 4th da. of John (LOWTHER), 1st VISCOUNT LONSDALE, by Katherine, da. of Sir Henry Frederick THYNNE, 1st Baronet [1641]. She *d.* 15 Sep. 1738, at Bath, and was *bur.* in the Abbey there. He *d.* 3 Dec. 1744, aged 67. Will pr. 1745.

III. 1744. SIR JOHN PENNINGTON, Baronet [1676], of Muncaster, Pennington and Wartre aforesaid, 2d but 1st surv. s. and h.,(d) *b.* probably about 1710; was Comptroller of the Excise before 1741; *suc. to the Baronetcy*, 3 Dec. 1744; M.P. for Cumberland, (four Parls.), Jan. 1745 to 1768, and Col. of the Cumberland Militia, during the Rising of 1745; L.-Lieut. of Westmorland. He *d.* unm. 26 March 1768. Will pr. June 1768.

IV. 1768. SIR JOSEPH PENNINGTON, Baronet [1676], of Muncaster, Pennington and Wartre aforesaid, next surv. br. and h.,(e) being 4th and yst. s. of the 2d Baronet; *bap.* 20 Jan. 1718, at Wartre; was a Commissioner of the Customs, 1763-69; *suc. to the Baronetcy*, 26 March 1768. He *m.* Mary, da. and h. of John MOORE, of Somersetshire. She *d.* Aug. and was *bur.* 12 Sep. 1783, at Fulmer, Bucks. Admon. April 1785. He *d.* 3 Feb. 1793, at Wartre, aged 75.

(a) He was a first class scholar in Greek, Latin, German and Spanish; the author of several poems in all of those languages, as also of "*the Handbook of Spanish Painting*," etc.

(b) John Head, his only son, was drowned v.p., 25 Sep. 1859, in the River St. Maurice, Canada, aged 15.

(c) He was a patron of Lilly, the famons Astrologer.

(d) William Pennington, the eldest son, *d.* unm. and v.p. 8 April 1734.

(e) Lowther Pennington, his next elder brother, *d.* unm. and v.p. 4 May 1733, at Cambridge.

V. 1793. JOHN (PENNINGTON), BARON MUNCASTER [I.] (who had been so *cr.*, v.p., 21 Oct. 1783, with a spec. rem. of that dignity in favour of his brother), 1st s. and h., *suc. to the Baronetcy* [1676] as 5th Baronet, on the death of his father, 3 Feb. 1793, which dignity then *merged* in the above named peerage, and still so continues. See *Peerage*.

HOSKYNS:

cr. 18 Dec. 1676.

I. 1676. "BENET [*or* BENNET] HOSKYNS, of Harewood, co. Hereford, Esq.," as also of Morehampton in Abbey Dore, in that county, only s. and h. of John HOSKYNS, of the same, Serjeant at Law (who entertained James I at Morehampton, and who *d.* there 27 Aug. 1638, aged 62), by Benedicta (*m.* 1 Aug. 1601), da. of Robert MOYLE, of Buckwell, Kent, was *b.* 1609; admitted to Middle Temple, 16 May 1619; Barrister, 11 Feb. 1631, being Bencher in 1649 and Treasurer in 1664; was M.P. for Wendover, April to May 1640; for Hereford, 1640, till secluded in 1648, and for Herefordshire, 1656-58 and 1659; was one of the assessors of Herefordshire in 1657, and was *cr. a Baronet*, as above, 18 Dec. 1676. He *m.* firstly, in or before 1634, Anne, da. of Sir Henry (*or* Sir John) BINGLEY, of Templecombe, Somerset, Auditor of the Exchequer. He *m.* secondly,, in 1655, Dorothy, widow of John ABRAHALL, da. of Francis KYRLE, of Much Marle, co. Hereford. He *d.* 10 Feb., and was *bur.*, 2 March 1679/80, at Harewood. Will pr. Dec. 1683.

II. 1680. SIR JOHN HOSKYNS, Baronet [1676], of Harewood and Morehampton aforesaid, 1st s. and h. by 1st wife, *b.* 23 July 1634, in that county; ed. at Westm. school; matric. at Oxford (Ch. Ch.), 9 Dec. 1650; admitted to Middle Temple, 1647; Barrister, 1653; Bencher, 1671; Master in Chancery, 1676, till death in 1703; Fellow of the Royal Society, 1663; President, 1682-83, and Secretary thereof, 1685-87; was *Knighted* v.p. 24 Jan. 1675/6, and *suc. to the Baronetcy*, 10 Feb. 1679/80; M.P. for Herefordshire, 1685-87. He *m.* (Lic. Vic. Gen.(a), 29 Aug. 1671, he about 30 [37?], bachelor, and she about 20, spinster), Jane, da. of Sir Gabriel LOWE, of Newark, in Ozleworth, co. Glouc., by Lydia, da. of Sir Stephen SOAME, of Haydon, co. Essex. He *d.* 12 and was *bur.* 25 Sep. 1705, at Harewood, aged 71. Will pr. Dec. 1706. His widow was *bur.* 15 July 1724, at Harewood.

III. 1705. SIR BENNET HOSKYNS, Baronet [1676], of Harewood and Morehampton aforesaid, 1st s. and h., *b.* 28 Jan. and *bap.* 3 Feb. 1674/5, at Harewood; *suc. to the Baronetcy*, 12 Sep. 1705. He *m.* 2 Oct. 1707, at St. Barth. the Great, London (Lic. Fac. 1), Gertrude, widow of Sir Peter WHITCOMBE, da. of John (ARUNDELL), 2d BARON ARUNDELL OF TRERICE, by his 2d wife, Barbara, da. of Sir Henry SLINGSBY, 1st Baronet [S. 1638] of Scriven, co. York. She *d.* 23 Sep. and was *bur.* 9 Oct. 1709 at Harewood, in her 33d year. Her will pr. Oct. 1709, and again Jan. 1721. He *d.* 17 Dec. 1711, and was *bur.* 6 Jan. 1711/2, at Harewood, aged 36. Admon. 25 Feb. 1711/2 and 24 Nov. 1724.

IV. 1711. SIR HUNGERFORD(b) HOSKYNS, Baronet [1676], of Harewood and Morehampton aforesaid, br. and h., *b.* probably about 1677; served in the French wars under the Duke of Marlborough; *suc. to the*

(a) Another Lic. (Vic. Gen.), some two years before, *viz.*, 26 Nov. 1669, in which his age is described (more accurately) as "about 34" (he being in both licenses styled "John Hoskyns of the Middle Temple, Esq., bachelor"), was granted for marriage with Mrs. Dorothy Pakington, of Westwood, co. Worcester, about 22, spinster, with consent of her father, Sir John Pakington. This marriage, however, never took place.

(b) The name of Hungerford was that of his mother's grandmother, Anne, da. of (—) Hungerford, of Down Ampney, co. Gloucester, wife of Sir Gabriel Lowe (*d.* 1659, aged 80), the father of Sir Gabriel Lowe named in the text.

Baronetcy, 17 Dec. 1711; was M.P. for Hereford, March 1717 to 1722. He *m.*, in or before 1720, Mary, 3d da. of Theophilus LEIGH, of Addlestrop, co. Gloucester, by Mary, sister of James, 1st DUKE OF CHANDOS, da. of James (BRYDGES), 8th BARON CHANDOS OF SUDELEY. She *d.* at Hereford 9, and was *bur.* 15 July 1735, at Harewood. He *d.* at Harewood 21, and was *bur.* there 29 Dec. 1767, in his 91st year.

V. 1767. SIR CHANDOS HOSKYNS, Baronet [1676], of Harewood and Morehampton aforesaid, 1st s. and h., *bap.* 22 April 1720, at Harewood; matric. at Oxford (Balliol Coll.), 4 July 1737, aged 17; *suc. to the Baronetcy*, 21 Dec. 1767; Sheriff of Herefordshire, 1771-72. He *m.*, in or before 1753, Rebecca, da. of Joseph MAY, of London, Merchant. He *d.* 29 May, and was *bur.* 12 June 1773, at Harewood, aged 73. Will pr. Feb. 1775. His widow *d.* 14, and was *bur.* 28 Aug. 1782, at Harewood. Will pr. 1782.

VI. 1773. SIR HUNGERFORD HOSKYNS, Baronet [1676], of Harewood and Morehampton aforesaid, 1st s. and h., *b.* about 1753; matric. at Oxford (Balliol Coll.), 28 Dec. 1771, aged 18; *suc. to the Baronetcy*, 29 May 1773; Sheriff of Herefordshire, 1785-86. He *m.*, 14 Dec. 1774, at Stanwell, Midx., Catherine, da. of Edwin Francis STANHOPE, of Stanwell, Midx., Gentleman Usher to the Queen Consort, by Catherine, da. and coheir of John BRYDGES, *styled* MARQUESS OF CARNARVON, s. and h. ap. of James, 1st DUKE OF CHANDOS. She *d.* 15 and was *bur.* 19 Feb. 1790, at Harewood, aged 34. He *d.* in Stanhope street, May Fair, Midx., 10 July 1802, and was *bur.* at Harewood, in his 48th year. Will pr. 1802.

VII. 1802. SIR HUNGERFORD HOSKYNS, Baronet [1676], of Harewood aforesaid, 1st s. and h., *b.* 12 June, and *bap.* 12 July 1776 at Stanwell, Midx.; matric. at Oxford (Oriel Coll.), 22 Oct. 1794, aged 18; *suc. to the Baronetcy*, 10 July 1802; Sheriff of Herefordshire, 1813-14. He *m.* 4 Aug. 1803, at Bank (registered at Harewood), Sarah, yst. da. of John PHILIPS, of Bank Hall, near Stockport, by Sarah, da. of George LEIGH, of Oughrington, co. Chester. She *d.* 12 March 1860, aged 81, at Harewood. He *d.* 27 Feb. 1862, at Clevedon, Somerset, in his 86th year.

VIII. 1862. SIR HUNGERFORD HOSKYNS, Baronet [1676], of Harewood(a) aforesaid, 1st s. and h., *b.* 19 Sep. 1804, and *bap.* there; ed. at Eton; matric. at Oxford (Oriel Coll.) 23 June 1823, aged 18; B.A. and 3d Class Classics, 1827; M.A., 1830; Barrister (Middle Temple), 1830; *suc. to the Baronetcy*, 27 Feb. 1862. He *d.* unm. 21 Nov. 1877, aged 73, at Sandiwell Park, near Cheltenham.

IX. 1877. SIR JOHN LEIGH HOSKYNS, Baronet [1676], next surv. br. and h. male, being 3d s. of the 7th Baronet, *b.* 4 Feb. 1817, at Cheltenham; admitted to Rugby School, Aug. 1828; matric. at Oxford (Balliol Coll.), 10 May 1835, aged 18; was Demy of Mag. Coll., 1837-43; B.A. and 2d Class Classics, 1839; M.A., 1841; Fellow of Mag. Coll., 1843-45; took Holy Orders; Rector of Aston Tirrold, Berks, 1845; Select Preacher at Oxford, 1855-56; *suc. to the Baronetcy*, 21 Nov. 1877; Hon. Canon of Ch. Ch. Oxford, 1880. He *m.* 23 April 1846, at Lugwardine, co. Hereford, Phyllis Emma, da. of Commodore Sir John Strutt PEYTON, K.C.H. (*d.* 20 May 1838, aged 52), by Frances, his wife.

(a) This estate was for sale in 1876, and apparently was sold either by the 8th Baronet or his executors.

STANDISH:

cr. 8 Feb. 1676/7;

ex. 16 May 1812.

I. 1677. "RICHARD STANDISH, of [Duxbury], co. Lancaster, Esq.," 2d but 1st surv. s. and h. of Richard STANDISH, of Duxbury aforesaid, by Elizabeth, da. of Piers LEGH, of Lyme, co. Chester, was *cr. a Baronet*, as above, 8 Feb. 1676/7. He was M.P. for Wigan, 1690 till death. He *m.* Margaret, da. of Thomas HOLCROFT, of Holcroft, co. Lancaster. He *d.* about Dec. 1693. His widow, who was *b.* 27 Aug. and *bap.* 7 Sep. 1656 at Newchurch, co. Lanc., *m.*, after 1694, as his 2d wife, Sir Thomas STANLEY, 4th Baronet [1627], of Bickerstaffe, who *d.* 7 May 1714. She *d.* 14 Oct. 1735, "at a great age," *viz.*, 81.

II. 1693? SIR THOMAS STANDISH, Baronet [1677], of Duxbury aforesaid, 1st s. and h., *suc. to the Baronetcy* on the death of his father; was Sheriff of Lancashire, 1711-12. He *m.*, probably before 1710,(a) Jane, da. of Charles TURNOR, of Cleveland, co. York. He *d.* 13, or 21 Dec. 1756.

III. 1756, to 1812. SIR FRANK STANDISH, Baronet [1677], of Duxbury aforesaid, grandson and h., being 1st s. and h. of Thomas STANDISH, by Catherine, da. and coheir of Robert FRANK, of Pontefract, which Thomas, who *d.* v.p. 23 Dec. 1746, was 1st s. and h. ap. of the late Baronet. He was *b.* about 1746; *suc. to the Baronetcy* in Dec. 1756; matric. at Oxford (Brasenose Coll.), 31 Jan. 1763, aged 17; was M.P. for Preston, 1768, till unseated in Nov. of that year; Sheriff of Lancashire, 1782-83. He *d.* unm., 18 May 1812, when the *Baronetcy* became *extinct*.(b) Admon. June 1812.

ROBERTSON, *otherwise* COLYEAR(c):

cr. 20 Feb. 1676/7;

afterwards, 1699—1835, LORDS PORTSMORE AND BLACKNESS [S.];

and subsequently, 1703—1835, EARLS OF PORTMORE [S.];

ex. 18 Jan. 1835.

I. 1677. "ALEXANDER ROBERTSON, *alias* COLYEAR, of the Province of Holland," son of "Major David COLZEAR"(c) [*i.e.*, COLYEAR], assumed about 1670 (for what reason is not clear) the name of ROBERTSON, and was *cr. a Baronet*, as above, 20 Feb. 1676/7; was designated, when served heir gen. to his unm. sister Joanna, 24 March 1677, "Colonellus Alexander ROBERTSONE, *alias* COLZEAR, hæres Joannæ COLZEAR, filiæ Majoris Davidis COLZEAR, sororis germanæ," no notice being then taken of his Baronetcy. He settled in London and apparently *d.* there, being dead in or before 1691.

II. 1685? SIR DAVID COLYEAR, Baronet [1677], 1st s. and h., *b.* probably about 1655,(d) served (v.p.) in the army of the Prince of Orange; was in command of a Scotch regiment in the service of the States

---

(a) Turner [Turnor?] Standish, his 6th son, matric. at Oxford (Brasenose Coll.), 28 April 1737, aged 19.

(b) The estates devolved on the great grandson and h. of his aunt Margaret (*d.* 1776), by her 2d husband, Anthony Hall, of Flass, *viz.*, Frank Hall, who took the name of Standish, and *d.* s.p. in 1841, aged 42, being succeeded therein by his 2d cousin, William Standish Carr (who took the name of Standish, instead of Carr), whose grandfather, the Rev. Ralph Carr, had *m.* Anne, da. of Anthony Hall abovenamed, by Margaret, da. of Sir Thomas Standish, 2d Baronet [1677].

(c) See an article in the *Mis. Gen. et Her.*, new series, vol. iv, p. 85.

(d) His yr. br., Field Marshal Walter Philip Colyear, was *b.* about 1657, being said to have been aged 90 at his death in Nov. 1747.

of Holland; served under William III in Ireland, 1689-90, and afterwards in Flanders; *suc. to the Baronetcy* before April 1691,(a) and was naturalised by act of Parl. 1697. He *m.* in or shortly before Aug. 1696, Catharine, *suo jure* COUNTESS OF DORCHESTER (see *Peerage*), who was living when he was *cr.*, 1 June 1699, LORD PORTMORE AND BLACKNESS [S.], being afterwards *cr.*, 13 April 1703, EARL OF PORTMORE, etc. [S.]. In these peerages this *Baronetcy* then *merged*, and so continued till it and the other titles became *extinct* on the death, 18 Jan. 1835, of the 4th Earl and Baron and 5th Baronet. See *Peerage*.

DYKE, *or* DIKE:

cr. 3 March 1676/7.

I. 1677. "THOMAS DIKE, of Horeham [in Waldron], co. Sussex, Esq.," s. and h. of Sir Thomas DYKE, of the same (*d.* 13 Dec. 1669, aged 57), by Catherine (*m.* 7 Aug. 1639, at Roxwell, Essex), da. of Sir John BRAMSTON, of Skreens, in Roxwell aforesaid, Lord Chief Justice of the King's Bench (1635-43), was *b.* about 1650; matric. at Oxford (Ch. Ch.), 1 June 1666, aged 16; admitted to the Middle Temple, 1667, and was *cr. a Baronet*, as above, 3 March 1676/7; Sheriff of Sussex, 1684, but did not act; M.P. for Sussex, 1685-87, and for East Grinstead (three Parls.), 1689-98; Commissioner of Public Accounts, 1696. He *m.*, about 1695, Philadelphia, da. and coheir of Sir Thomas NUTT, of Mays, in Selmiston, co. Kent, by Catherine, da. of Sir Thomas PARKER, of Ratton, co. Sussex. He *d.* 31 Oct. 1706 in his 57th year, and was *bur.* at Waldron. M.I. Will pr. Nov. 1706. His wife survived him.

II. 1706. SIR THOMAS DYKE, Baronet [1677], of Horeham and Mays aforesaid, and, afterwards, of Lullingston Castle, co. Kent, 2d but only surv. s. and h., *b.* about 1700; *suc. to the Baronetcy*, 31 Oct. 1706; matric. at Oxford (Ch. Ch.), 2 Nov. 1715, aged 15; *cr.* M.A., 7 Nov. 1718, and D.C.L., 11 July 1733. He *m.*, 23 May 1728, at St. Helen's, Bishopsgate, London, Anne, widow of John BLUET, of Holcombe Regis, Devon, da. and h. of Percival HART,(b) of Lullingstone aforesaid, by Sarah (*m.* 28 Nov. 1689, at St. Andrew's, Holborn), da. of Edward DIXON, of Hilden, in Tunbridge. He *d.* 20, and was *bur.* 25 Aug. 1756, at Lullingstone. Will pr. 1756. His widow, who was *bap.* 1 Nov. 1692, at Lullingstone, *d.* 24 Nov. and was *bur.* there, 1 Dec. 1763. Will pr. 1763.

III. 1756. SIR JOHN DIXON DYKE, Baronet [1677], of Lullingstone Castle aforesaid, 3d but only surv. s. and h.; *b.* in Great Ormond Street, 23 Nov., and *bap.*, 4 Dec. 1732, at St. George's the Martyr, Midx.; matric. at Oxford (Ch. Ch.), 6 March 1749/50, and then called 16; *suc. to the Baronetcy*, 20 Aug. 1756. He *m.*, 3 May 1756, at Lullingstone, Philadelphia Payne, da. of George HORNE, of East Grinstead, co. Sussex. She *d.* 31 Jan. 1781. Will pr. 1804. He *d.* 6 and was *bur.* 13 Sep. 1810, at Lullingstone, aged nearly 78. Will pr. 1811.

IV. 1810. SIR THOMAS DYKE, Baronet [1677], of Lullingstone Castle aforesaid, 1st s. and h., *b.* 29 Dec. 1763 and *bap.*, 23 Jan. 1764, at St. James', Westm.; *suc. to the Baronetcy*, 6 Sep. 1810; Col. of the West Kent Militia. He *d.* unm., at Lullingstone Castle, 22, and was *bur.* 29 Nov. 1831, at Lullingstone, in his 68th year. Will pr. Dec. 1831.

(a) At that date he is spoken of in Luttrell's *Diary* as "Sir David Collier."

(b) This Percival was s. and h. of Sir Percival Hart, of Lullingstone aforesaid, whose ancestor, Sir John Peche, had acquired that estate in 1361.

V. 1831. SIR PERCIVAL HART DYKE, Baronet [1677], of Lullingstone Castle aforesaid, br. and h., *b.* 27 Dec. 1767; matric. at Oxford (Univ. Coll.), 15 July 1784, aged 17; B.A., 1789; *suc. to the Baronetcy*, 22 Nov. 1831; was an unsuccessful claimant in 1836 for the BARONY OF BRAYE, of which, through the families of HART and BRAYE, he was a coheir. He *m.* 26 July 1798, at St. Geo. Han. sq., Anne, 1st da. of Robert JENNER, of Chislehurst, co. Kent, by Anne, da. and h. of Peter BIRT, of Wenvoe Castle, co. Glamorgan. He *d.* 4 Aug. 1846, at Lullingstone Castle, in his 79th year. Will pr. Sep. 1846. His widow *d.* 27 Dec. 1847, in Devonshire place, Marylebone, aged 72. Will pr. Dec. 1847.

VI. 1846. SIR PERCYVALL HART DYKE, Baronet [1677], of Lullingstone Castle aforesaid, 1st s. and h., *b.* 9 June 1799, at Chislehurst aforesaid; ed. at Westm. School; matric. at Oxford (Ch. Ch.), 21 April 1819, aged 19, and was afterwards of St. Alban Hall, in that University; *suc. to the Baronetcy*, 4 Aug. 1846. He *m.* 25 June 1835, at Bromley, co. Kent, Eliza, yst. da. of John WELLS, of Bickley House, in that county. He *d.* 12 Nov. 1875, at Lullingstone Castle, in his 77th year. His widow *d.* 16 July 1888, at 34 Hill Street, St. Geo. Han. sq.

VII. 1875. SIR WILLIAM HART DYKE, Baronet [1677], of Lullingstone Castle aforesaid, 2d but 1st surv. s. and h., *b.* 7 Aug. 1837(a); ed. at Harrow; matric. at Oxford (Ch. Ch.), 15 Oct. 1856, aged 19; B.A., 1861; M.A., 1863; was M.P. for West Kent, 1865-68; for Mid Kent, 1868-85, and for North West Kent (Dartford division) since 1885, having *suc. to the Baronetcy* 12 Nov. 1875; was joint Patronage Sec. to the Treasury ("Conservative Whip"), 1874-80; P.C. [E.], 1880; P.C. [I.], 1885; Chief Sec. for Ireland, 1885-86; Vice-President of the Council on Education, 1887-92. He *m.* 30 May 1870, at St. Geo. Han. Sq., Emily Caroline, 1st da. of John William (MONTAGU), 7th EARL OF SANDWICH, by his 1st wife, Mary, da. of Henry William (PAGET), 1st MARQUESS OF ANGLESEY. She was *b.* 19 Dec. 1846.

Family Estates.—These, in 1883, consisted of 7,951 acres in Kent, 688 in Sussex, 223 in Herts, and 3 in Surrey. *Total*, 8,865 acres, worth £11,474 a year. *Chief Seat.*—Lullingstone Castle, near Dartford, co. Kent.

COTTON:

cr. 29 March 1677;

afterwards, since 1814, BARONS COMBERMERE;

and since 1827, VISCOUNTS COMBERMERE OF BHURTPORE.

I. 1677. "SIR ROBERT COTTON, of Combermere, co. Chester, Knt.," 2d s. of Thomas COTTON, being 1st s. by his 2d wife, Elizabeth (*b.* 1 Aug. 1609), sister and coheir of Sir Hugh CALVELEY, da. of Sir George CALVELEY, both of Lea, which Thomas (who *d.* v.p. before 1649) was only s. and h. ap. of George COTTON, of Combermere aforesaid, was *b.* about 1635; suc. his said grandfather in the family estate (his elder br., George COTTON, having *d.* in 1647 s.p.s.) in 1649; was *Knighted*, 25 June 1660; M.P. for Cheshire (eight Parls.), 1679-1702; and was *cr. a Baronet*, as above, 29 March 1677. He *m.* Hester, sister and h. (23 May 1684) of Sir John SALUSBURY, 3d Baronet, da. of Sir Thomas SALUSBURY, 2d Baronet [1629], of Llewenny, co. Denbigh, by Hester, da. of Sir Edward TYRRELL, 1st Baronet [1627], of Thornton, Bucks. She *d.* Dec. 1710. He *d.* 17 Dec. 1712, aged 77. Will pr. Dec. 1712.

(a) His elder br., Lieut. Percyvall Hart Dyke (Rifle Brigade), *b.* 29 Aug. 1836, *d.* unm. and v.p. in the Crimean War, 19 April 1855.

II. 1712. **Sir Thomas Cotton**, Baronet [1677], of Combermere and Llewenny aforesaid, 4th but only surv. s. and h.,(a) was *b.* probably about 1672; *suc. to the Baronetcy*, 17 Dec. 1712; Sheriff of Cheshire, 1712-13. He *m.* (Lic. Vic. Gen. 18 Nov. 1689, he about 17) Philadelphia (a minor 4 April 1694, but of full age 18 May 1698), da. and h. of Sir Thomas Lynch, of Esher, co. Surrey, thrice Governor of Jamaica,(b) by Vera, sister of Arthur (Herbert), Earl of Torrington, da. of Sir Edward Herbert. He *d.* 12 June 1715. Will pr. July 1715. His widow *m.* Thomas King, who, in his will, dat. 1722, describes himself as of Combermere. She *d.* 30 Dec. 1758 at a great age. Her will, as "of Finchley Lodge, co. Midx., widow," dat. 3 Nov. 1756 to 6 May 1758, pr. 8 Feb. 1759.(b)

III. 1715. **Sir Robert Cotton**, Baronet [1677], of Combermere and Llewenny aforesaid, 2d but 1st surv. s. and h.; *bap.* 2 Jan. 1694/5, at St. Margaret's, Westm.; matric. at Oxford (Brasenose Coll.), 8 July 1714, aged 15; *suc. to the Baronetcy*, 12 June 1715; was M.P. for Cheshire, 1727-34, and for Lostwithiel, 1741-47. He *m.* Elizabeth, da. of Lyonel (Tollemache), Earl of Dysart [S.], by Grace, da. and coheir of Sir Thomas Wilbraham, 3d Baronet [1621] of Woodhey. She *d.* 16 Aug 1745, aged 63. He *d.* s.p., 27 Aug. 1748, aged 53. Both *bur.* at Wrenbury, co. Chester. His will pr. 1749.

IV. 1748. **Sir Lynch Salusbury Cotton**, Baronet [1677], of Combermere and Llewenny aforesaid, next surv. br. and h., being 5th s. of the 2d Baronet, *b.* about 1705; *suc. to the Baronetcy*, 27 Aug. 1748; was M.P. for Denbighshire, 1749-74. He *m.* in or before 1738, Elizabeth Abigail, da. of Rowland Cotton, of Bellaport, Salop, and of Etwall, co. Derby, by Mary, da. of Sir Samuel Sleigh, of Etwall aforesaid. He *d.* 14 Aug. 1775, aged 70, and was *bur.* at Wrenbury. Will pr. Sep. 1775. His widow *d.* at St. Margaret's, Westm., 4 Jan. 1777, aged 64, and was *bur.* at Wrenbury. Admon. 23 Jan. 1777.

V. 1775. **Sir Robert Salusbury Cotton**, Baronet [1677], of Combermere and Llewenny aforesaid, 1st s. and h., *b.* about 1739; *suc. to the Baronetcy*, 14 Aug. 1775; was M.P. for Cheshire (four Parls.), 1780-96. He *m.* in 1767, Frances, yst. da. and coheir of James Russell Stapleton, of Bodrhyddan, co. Flint, Col. of the Guards, by Penelope, da. of Sir John Conway, 2d Baronet [1660], of Bodrhyddan aforesaid, and Penelope, his 2d wife. He, who had alienated estates to the amount of £20,000,(c) *d.* at Combermere Abbey, 24 Aug. 1809, in his 71st year. His widow *d.* 20 April 1825, at Penbedw, near Mold, the house of her sister Elizabeth, widow of Watkin Williams.

VI. 1809. **Sir Stapleton Cotton**, Baronet [1677], of Combermere and Llewenny aforesaid, 2d but 1st surv. s. and h.,(d) *b.* 14 Nov. 1773, at Llewenny Hall; ed. at Westm. School, 1785-89; joined the Army, 1790, and was in the Holland Campaign, 1793-94, becoming, in 1794 (at the age of 21), Lieut.-Col. of the 25th Dragoons, with whom he served at the Cape in 1796, and subsequently in India in 1799 against Tippoo Sahib at Malavelly, and at the siege of Seringapatam. He returned home (after his elder brother's death) in 1800; was M.P. for Newark (three Parls.), 1806-14; Col. in the Army and Lieut.-Col. of the 16th Light Dragoons, 1800; Major-General, 1805. In 1808-09 he served in Portugal with a brigade of the 14th and 16th Light Dragoons, and for his signal service at Talavera, 28 July 1809, received the thanks of Parl. He *suc. to the Baronetcy* and the Combermere estate, 24 Aug. 1809. Being in command of the 1st division of Cavalry, he covered the retreat (July to Sep. 1810) of Torres Vedras, and as Commander of the whole of the allied Cavalry (1811-14), led the famous charge at Salamanca (22 July 1812), which decided that victory, he being severely wounded in that battle, where he was 2d in command under Wellington. For this he received the thanks of Parl., and was nom. **K.B. (G.C.B.** after 1815), 18 Aug. 1812, and made Col. of the 20th Light Dragoons, 1813; Knight Grand Cross of the Tower and Sword of Portugal (11 March 1813); of St. Ferdinand of Spain and of Charles III of Spain. He was at the great and final victory of Toulouse, 10 April 1814, and was raised to the peerage five weeks after, as stated below. He *m.* firstly, 1 Jan. 1801, Anna Maria, 1st da. of Thomas (Pelham-Clinton), 3d Duke of Newcastle, by Anna Maria, da. of William (Stanhope), 2d Earl of Harrington. She, who was *b.* 29 July 1783, *d.* 31 May 1807, seven years before her husband was *cr.*, 17 May 1814, BARON COMBERMERE, co. Chester. In that peerage this *Baronetcy* then *merged*, and still [1903] so continues, the grantee (for his signal services in India, where he was Commander-in-Chief at the Capture of Bhurtpore) being subsequently *cr.*, 8 Feb. 1827, VISCOUNT COMBERMERE OF BHURTPORE in the East Indies and of Combermere, co. Chester. See *Peerage.*

(a) Of his brothers, two, John and Robert, *d.* in infancy. George *d.* unm. and v.p., 8 Jan. 1702, and was *bur.* at Wrenbury; while Hugh Calveley Cotton, who *m.* Mary, da. and h. of Sir William Russell, Baronet (so *cr.* 8 Nov. 1660), of Laugharne, co. Carmarthen, *d.* s.p.m. and v.p., leaving Catherine, his da. and h., who *m.* Thomas Lewis, of St. Pierre, and *d.* s.p.

(b) See abstract of wills of the Lynch family in *Mis. Gen. et Her.*, N.S., vol. iv, pp. 395-397.

(c) *Dict. Nat. Biog.*, under "Cotton, Sir Stapleton."

(d) His elder br., Robert Salusbury Cotton, *b.* 11 Sep. 1768, *d.* unm. and v.p., 1799.

WILLOUGHBY:

cr. 7 April 1677;

subsequently, since 1712, Barons Middleton.

I. 1677. "**Francis Willoughby**, of Wollaton,(a) co. Nottingham, Esq.," 1st s. and h. of Francis Willoughby, of Middleton, co. Warwick, F.R.S., the celebrated Naturalist (author of a book on *Ornithology*), by Emma (marr. lic. Vic. Gen., 19 Dec. 1667), 2d da. and coheir of Sir Henry Barnard, *or* Bernard, of Stoke and Bridgenorth, Salop, and Aconbury, co. Hereford, Turkey-Merchant, of London, was *b.* in 1668; suc. his father (who *d.* at the age of 37), 3 July 1672, and, in consequence, presumably, of his said father's literary attainments, was (when under nine years of age), *cr. a Baronet*, as above, 7 April 1677, "with [a special] remainder for lack of issue male to Thomas [Willoughby], his brother, and to the heirs male of his body." He *d.* unm. Sep. 1688, in his 20th year. Will pr. Dec. 1688.

II. 1688. **Sir Thomas Willoughby**, Baronet [1677], of Wollaton and Middleton aforesaid, only br. and h., was *b.* about 1670; *suc. to the Baronetcy* in Sep. 1688, under the spec. rem. in the creation thereof; was Sheriff of Notts, 1695-96; M.P. for that county (five Parls.), 1698-1710, and for Newark, 1710-12. He *m.*, about 1690, Elizabeth, da. and coheir of Sir Richard Rothwell, Baronet [so *cr.* 16 Aug. 1661], of Ewerby and Stapleford, co. Lincoln, by Elizabeth, formerly wife of [—] Rothwell. She was living when he was *cr.*, 1 Jan. 1711/2, BARON MIDDLETON of Middleton, co. Warwick. In that peerage this *Baronetcy* then *merged* and still [1903] so continues. See *Peerage.*

(a) Bridget, da. and coheir of Sir Francis Willoughby, of Wollaton and Cossal, Notts, *m.* Sir Percival Willoughby, of Bore place, Kent, whose only s. and h., Sir Francis Willoughby (*d.* 1665), was father of Francis Willoughby, the father of Francis Willoughby, the grantee.

WHITE, *otherwise* VITUS:

cr. 29 June 1677;

forfeited 1691.

I. 1677, to 1691. "**Ignatius Vitus**, *alias* **White**,(a) [Count D'Albi in the Holy Roman Empire]," 2d s.(b) of Sir Dominick White, of Limerick, in Ireland," sometime (1636), Mayor of that city, Baron(c) and Count D'Albi as aforesaid (having been *cr. a Count*, Aug. 1658, by the Emperor Leopold), by his 1st wife Christina, da. of Thomas Bourke, of Limerick, of the family of the Barons Castle Connell [I.], was *b.* about 1626; was many years Envoy of Charles II. to Brussels, and subsequently to Madrid; was Col. of a Reg. of Horse in Flanders, and was, in or before 1674, *cr.* BARON DE VICKE in Holland; was, as "Ignatius Vitus, Baron of Vicque," *cr.* D.C.L. of Oxford, 27 June 1674, and was *cr. a Baronet*, as above, 29 June 1677, with a spec. rem. "for want of issue male, to his nephew,(d) Ignatius Maximilian Vitus and to the heirs male of his body." He was P.C. and Sec. of State [I.], and was *cr.* 20 Aug. 1677, by the Emperor Leopold, MARQUIS D'ALBEVILLE in the Holy Roman Empire, a creation which, under the Earl Marshal's warrant, 30 Oct. 1686, was registered in the College of Arms, London; together with a recital that Charles II had, by royal signet, 7 April 1679, allowed "the Rt. Hon. Sir Ignatius White *alias* D'Alby, Knight Baronet of the Kingdom of England and Baron de Vigue [*i.e.*, Baron de Vicke in Holland], now Marquis D'Albyville, and Knight, Baron, Count and Marquis of the [Holy Roman] Empire, to receive honours from any King at amity with His Majesty." He was appointed,(a) 1686, Ambassador to the Hague, where he had a medal struck on the birth, 10 June 1688, of the heir apparent to the Crown. He accompanied James II into France, after the battle of the Boyne; was attainted in 1691; and proclaimed an outlaw at Dublin, 11 May in that year, whereby the *Baronetcy* became *forfeited*. He was, till his death in 1694, Secretary to the exiled King at St. Germain's. He *m.* firstly, in or before 1664, Mary, da. of Patrick (FitzMaurice), Baron Kerry and Lixnaw [I.], by Honora, da. of Edmond Fitzgerald. She *d.* s.p.m. about 1680, at St. Martin's in the Fields, and was *bur.* "near Covent Garden." Admon. 20 March 1683/4. He *m.* secondly, 19 May 1681, at S. James', Duke place, London, Mary Whorow, spinster. He *d.* 21 and was *bur.* 22 Aug. 1694, at St. Germain l'Auxerrois, Paris, aged "67-70." His widow was living June 1712, in the service of the Queen of Spain, at Madrid.

(a) See full account of this family in R. G. Maunsell's "*History of Maunsell or Mansel*," etc. [Cork, 1903], to whom, as also to the Marquis de Ravigny, the Editor is much indebted. The entries relating to this Baronetcy, from the registers of St. Germain's in Paris, have been most kindly supplied by Herbert Vivian.

(b) Of his brothers: (1) Sir Richard White, the eldest son, embarked, 1651-54, with 7,000 men from Ireland to Spain, where, apparently, he was Knighted. He *d.* s.p. and in the Fleet prison [Le Neve's MS. *Baronetage*]. His will, as "of London, Knt.," dat. 8 Sep. 1698 and pr. 3 June 1699, leaves his residue "to my nephew and nieces, children of my deceased brother Ignatius, Marquis of Albeville, and Mary, Marchioness of Albeville, his widow." (2) Andrew White, Count D'Albi, the 3d son, Governor of Barbadoes [Le Neve's MS. *Baronetage*], *m.* twice, but *d.* s.p.m., and was *bur.* at St. Margaret's, Westm., 15 Dec. 1687, as "Sir Andrew White, Count Alvey." (3) Francis White, 4th and yst. son, who *m.* a Flemish lady and had a son, Ignatius Maximilian Vitus, *or* White [presumably the nephew in remainder to the Baronetcy in June 1677], who [as stated in Le Neve's MS. *Baronetage*] "died young."

(c) His ancestor, Dominick White, of Limerick, having distinguished himself in the French wars, was *cr.* in 1513, by the Emperor Maximilian I, Baron D'Albi, of the Holy Roman Empire. See note "a" above.

(d) This nephew if (as is presumed) identical with Ignatius Maximilian, son of the grantee's brother, Francis White, *d.* young and in the lifetime of the grantee. See note "b" above.

II. 1694, to 1710. **Sir James(a) White**, Baronet(b) [1677], **Marquis D'Albeville**, etc., only surv. s. and h. by 2d wife; suc. to his father's dignities,(b) 21 Aug. 1694. He was in the French Service, being, apparently,(c) Lieut. in Galway's Irish Infantry, 1706-09, though sometimes called a Capt. in "the King of England's Reg. of Dragoons." He *d.* unm., being slain at the battle of Villa Viciosa, in Spain, 10 Dec. 1710 (in which he is said to have twice saved the life of Philip V. King of Spain).(d) when the *Baronetcy* became *extinct*, as did also all the male issue of the grantee and of his brothers.(e)

(a) His christian name is somewhat doubtful. He, in the will dated 1698, of his uncle, Sir Richard (see page 86, note "b"), is, unfortunately, only mentioned as "the son" of testator's deceased brother. One such son, Ignatius, [*b.* about 1684], had died v p. 3, and was *bur.* at St. Germain's in Paris 4 Sep. 1690, as "Ignace Dalbeville, agé de 6 ans, fils de Monsieur le Marquis Dalbeville, Anglois de nation." The only son ascribed to the grantee in Le Neve's MS. *Baronetage* is apparently (for the name has been altered, and, save for the final 'es," is not quite clear) named James. It is presumed, therefore, that he (whose death is not mentioned by Le Neve) was "*the son*" who survived his father, as is mentioned in his uncle's will of 1698. The grantee, however, may have had other sons, of whom one (possibly, even, one named Ignatius and born after the death, in Sep. 1690, of his brother of that name) may have been the son who survived him. It is clear, however, that the grantee was succeeded by a *son* and not by his nephew (Ignatius Maximilian, as to whom see page 86, note "b"), who was in spec. rem. to the Baronetcy, inasmuch as the Marquisate, which undoubtedly was held in 1710 by the grantee's successor, could only have been inherited by his *own* issue, and would not have passed to a nephew or any collateral. In O'Callaghan's *Irish Brigades* (p. 279) the father of the Marquis who was killed at Villa Viciosa, 10 Dec. 1710, is expressly stated to have been "King James II's Ambassador in Holland," *i.e.*, the first Baronet.

(b) Subject to the attainder of 1691.

(c) In reply to an enquiry sent to the French War Office by the Marquis de Ruvigny for information as to "White, Marquis of Albeville, killed at Villa Viciosa," the following answer was given:—"République Française, Ministre de la Guerre, Paris, le 14 Novembre 1903. White (sans autres indications) figure sur controle general de l'infanterie etabli in 1706, comme Lieutenant au regiment de Galway (infanterie Irlandaise).—Remplacé le 20 Juillet 1709." The Marquis adds that the same letter contained also an account of the services of sixteen other Jacobite officers, but that in this case *alone* no particulars were supplied, while in nearly every other case the full christian name and title, as also the dates and places of birth, were given. He concludes thus, "Indeed there is nothing [in this extract] to shew that it *is* the Marquis of Albeville, only that it appears to be the only White they can trace."

(d) Marshal Vendome writes, in his report of the battle, "The Lieut. Col. of the Regiment [Killmallock's Dragoons] received a musket shot through the body while charging the enemy, and the Marquis D'Albeville, one of his brave Captains, sabre in hand, all covered with wounds, lost his life, after having won admiration, by many brave and intrepid actions." See page 86, note "a."

(e) This appears to be conclusively proved by the following document [*ex inform.* the Marquis de Ruvigny] among the Stuart papers [Warrant Book IV of James III and VIII], dated at St. Germain, June 1712:—"Certificate that all the brothers of the late Sir Ignatius White, an Irishman, a Baronet of England and Marquis D'Albeville of the Holy Roman Empire (formerly Envoy Extraordinary to Holland of the late King, and his Secretary of State for Ireland) have died and that the sole heire of all these brothers are the daughters of the said Marquis D'Albeville, who are at present, with their mother, in the service of the Queen of

BARLOW :

cr. 13 July 1677 ;

ex. between 1756 and 1775.

I. 1677. "JOHN BARLOW, of Slebech, co. Pembroke, Esq.," 1st s. and h. of George BARLOW, of the same, by Joan, da. and coheir of David LLOYD, of Kily-Keithed in that county (which George was s. and h. of Col. John BARLOW, a zealous Royalist, and a great sufferer in that cause), was *b.* about 1652, and was *cr. a Baronet*, as above, 13 July 1677; was Sheriff of Pembrokeshire, 1680-81. He *m.*, 3 Feb. 1671/2 (Lic. Fac. 2, both aged about 20), Beatrice, sister and coheir [1674] of Sir John LLOYD, 2d Baronet, da. of Sir John LLOYD, 1st Baronet [1662], of Woking, Surrey, and the Forest, co. Carmarthen, by Beatrice, da. of Francis (ANNESLEY), VISCOUNT VALENTIA [I.]. She *d.* s.p.m. Admon. 7 July 1679. He *m.* secondly, Catharine. da. of Christopher MIDDLETON, of Middleton Hall, co. Carmarthen. He *d.* in 1695. Will dat. 17 Sep. 1694, pr. 27 June 1695 and [1.] 1701.

II. 1695. SIR GEORGE BARLOW, Baronet [1677], of Slebech aforesaid, 1st s. and h., by 2d wife; *b.* probably about 1680; *suc. to the Baronetcy* in 1695, and was under age in 1697. He made over the Slebech estate to his br., John BARLOW (who *d.* Nov. 1739), and resided chiefly in Lincolnshire. He *m.* 31 May 1695, at St. James', Duke Place, London, Winifred, da. of George HENEAGE, of Hainton, co. Lincoln, by his 1st wife, Mary, da. of Thomas KEMP, of Slindon, Sussex. He *d.* before 3 March 1725/6. His wife survived him. Her admon. of that date as "of Islington, Midx., widow."

Spain and the Prince of Asturias at Madrid." It is, however, alleged (see page 86, note "a") that the 2d Baronet and Marquis left a son and h., John White, who followed Prince Charles Edward to England and was slain at Culloden in 1746, leaving a son and h., Thomas White, who was (with his father) at the said battle, but who soon afterwards "made his way to Ireland," leaving a son and h., John White, Barrister [1784] and King's Counsel, who (by Isabella, da. of Capt. Ebenezer Warren, 62d Foot) left a son and h., Thomas White Warren, Barrister [1821], whose s. and h., John Warren White, 40th Regiment, claimed the Baronetcy in 1880, being then of St. Arnaud, Victoria, Australia. "After making a very exhaustive search, Sir J. Bernard Burke, Ulster, made a report, 2 Feb. 1881, coming to the conclusion that there was no evidence to show that the claimant's great grandfather, Thomas White, who was a stationer in the city of Cork, was descended from the family of Sir Ignatius White, the 1st Baronet." Of the daughters of the grantee, Mary the only child by his 1st wife, *d.* unm. and was *bur.* at St. Germain in Paris, 27 July 1691, aged 27. Of those by the 2d wife, Mary (born within a year of the death of her abovenamed sister of that name) was *bap.* 27 Feb. 1692, at St. Germain; Charlotte is described in the Stuart papers [vol. iv, James III and VIII] in a declaration, dat. 12 April 1726, as "Charlotte Whyte, Countess of Alby, Marchioness of Albeville of the Empire, Lady of Honour to the Queen of Spain, and legitimate da. of the late Sir Ignatius Whyte, of Ireland, Baronet of England, Count of Alby and Marquis of Albeville) late Ambassador to Holland of James II. and his Secretary for Ireland), wife of Sieur Antoine de Sartine"; [—], possibly the abovenamed Mary, *m.* Gen. Lacy, Commander of the Ulster regiment in Spain in 1732, and had issue, see page 86, note "a"; [—], possibly the abovenamed Mary, *m.* (apparently) Sir Timon Connock, s. and h. ap. of Sir William Connock, *cr.* a Baronet in 1732 by the titular King, James III, and *d.* v.p. It is, at all events, certain that this Timon *m.* before 21 March 1707 one of the Maids of Honour to Mary, Queen Dowger of James II, and that their son and heir, Sir Joseph Connor, called the 2d Baronet, is said (Gilbert's *Cornwall*) to have inherited the title of Count D'Alby, of the Empire, from bis mother, and to have been *cr.* Marquis D'Albeville. [*Ex inform.* Marquis de Ruvigny.]

III. 1720? to 1760? SIR GEORGE BARLOW, Baronet [1677], of Irnham, co. Lincoln, only s. and h.; *suc. to the Baronetcy* on his father's death, before 1726. He *m.*, before April 1741, Ursula. He *d.* s.p., in France, between 1756(a) and 1775, when the *Baronetcy* became *extinct.*(a) Will, as of Kirmond le Mire, co. Lincoln, dat. 24 April 1741 (leaving all to his wife) pr. 7 Dec. 1775. Her Admon., as of Irnham, co. Lincoln, widow granted 2 Dec. 1775 to Ann CHAPPLE, widow, niece and next of kin.

NEWDIGATE, *or* NEWDEGATE:

cr. 24 July 1677 ;

ex. 2 Dec. 1806.

I. 1677. "RICHARD NEWDIGATE [*or* NEWDEGATE(b)], of Arbury, co. Warwick, Serjeant-at-Law," 2d s. of Sir John NEWDEGATE of the same, and of Brakenbury in Harefield, Midx. (*bur.* there 12 April 1610, aged 40), by Anne, da. of Sir Edward FITTON, of Gawsworth, co. Chester, was *b.* 17 Sep. 1602; matric. at Oxford (Trin. Coll.), 6 Nov. 1618, aged 16; admitted to Gray's Inn (with his elder br. John), 3 July 1620; Barrister, 1628; Bencher, 1650; being, during the Protectorate, made Serjeant at Law, Jan. 1653/4; a judge of the Upper Bench, 1654-55, and again 1656; Chief Justice of the Upper Bench, Jan. to June 1660; M.P. for Tamworth, 1660, being in that year made Serjeant in Law, by the King, and (17 years later) being *cr. a Baronet*, as above, 24 July 1677. He, in 1642, had suc. his elder br. John(c) in the family estate of Arbury, etc., and (besides purchasing Astley Castle in Warwickshire) purchased in 1674 the Manor and principal estate at Harefield, Midx., which in 1586 had been alienated by his grandfather. He *m.* in 1630, Juliana, sister of Francis (LEIGH), EARL OF CHICHESTER, da. of Sir Francis LEIGH, K.B. of Newnham, co. Warwick, by Mary, da. of Thomas (EGERTON), 1st VISCOUNT BRACKLEY, better known as Lord Chancellor Ellesmere. He *d.* 14 Oct. 1678, aged 76, and was *bur.* at Harefield. M.I. Will dat. 6 June and pr. 18 Dec. 1678. His widow *d.* at Harefield, 1685, and was *bur.* there. M.I. Will dat. 1 Sep. 1683 to 24 June 1684, pr. 1 Jan. 1685/6.

II. 1678. SIR RICHARD NEWDIGATE, Baronet [1677], of Arbury and Harefield aforesaid, 3d but 1st surv. s. and h., *b.* 4 May 1644; admitted to Gray's Inn, 7 Feb. 1653/4; matric. at Oxford (Ch. Ch.), 21 March 1660/1; *suc. to the Baronetcy*, 14 Oct. 1678; M.P. for Warwickshire, 1681 and 1689-90. He *m.* firstly, in or before 1668, Mary, da. of Sir Edward BAGOT, 2d Baronet [1627], of Blithfield, co. Stafford, by Mary, da. of William LAMBARD, of Buckingham. She, who was *b.* 6 April 1646, *d.* 14 and was *bur.* 19 Sep. 1692, at Harefield. M.I. He *m.* secondly, 2 May 1704, Henrietta, da. of Thomas WIGGINGTON, *otherwise* WINTON, of Ham, co. Surrey. He *d.* in Brownlow Street, Holborn, 4 and was *bur.* 20 Jan. 1709/10, at Harefield aforesaid, in his 66th year. M.I. Will pr. June 1711. His widow *m.* (as his 3d wife) 8 April 1712, at Whitehall Chapel (Lic. Fac. 3), Sir Francis WYNDHAM, 3d Baronet [1673], of Trent, co. Somerset, who *d.* at Chelsea, 22 March 1715/6. She *m.* (for her 3d husband) William LOWFIELD, of Chelsea, and *d.* there 26 June 1739.

(a) On 10 Dec. 1756 occurs the death of "George Barlow, of Slebech, co. Pembroke, Esq." [*London Mag.*], being doubtless that of a son of John Barlow, of Slebech, the 2d s. of the 1st Baronet.

(b) Both he and his widow spell the name "Newdegate" in their respective wills.

(c) This John Newdigate, of Arbury, was Sheriff of Warwickshire, 1625. He *m.* Susanna, da. of Arnold Luls, but *d.* s.p. 1642, aged 42, and was *bur.* at Harefield. M.I.

III. 1710. SIR RICHARD NEWDIGATE, Baronet [1677], of Arbury and Harefield aforesaid, only surv. s. and h., *b.* 29 April and *bap.* 14 May 1668, at Chilvers Coton, co. Warwick; matric. at Oxford (Ch. Ch.) 20 Nov. 1685, aged 17; *suc. to the Baronetcy*, 4 Jan. 1709/10. He *m.* firstly, in 1694, Sarah, da. of Sir Cecil BISHOPP, 4th Baronet [1620], of Parham, Sussex, by Sarah, da. and h. of George BURY, of Culham, Oxon. She *d.* s.p., fifteen months afterwards, 5, and was *bur.* 12 Oct. 1695, at Harefield, in her 27th year. M.I. He *m.* secondly, in or before 1711, Elizabeth, da. of Sir Roger TWISDEN, 2d Baronet [1666], of Bradburne, Kent, by Margaret, da. of Sir John MARSHAM, 1st Baronet [1663]. He *d.* 22 July and was *bur.* 18 Aug. 1727, at Harefield, aged 59. Will dat. 28 Jan. 1722/3, pr. 12 Oct. 1727, by the widow. She, who was *b.* 31 May 1681, *d.* 14 Sep. 1765, at Astley Castle, co. Warwick, and was *bur.* at Harefield in her 85th year. M.I.

IV. 1727. SIR EDWARD NEWDIGATE, Baronet [1677], of Arbury and Harefield aforesaid, 1st surv. s. and h., by 2d wife, *b.* about 1715; ed. at Westm. School; *suc. to the Baronetcy*, 22 July 1727; matric. at Oxford (Univ. Coll.), 10 Oct. 1732, aged 17. He *d.* unm. 14 and was *bur.* 17 April 1734, at Harefield. Admon. 16 April 1741, to his brother.

V. 1734, to 1806. SIR ROGER NEWDIGATE, Baronet [1677], of Arbury and Harefield aforesaid, only surv. br. and h., being 7th and yst. s. of the 3d Baronet, was *b.* 20 May 1719(a); ed. at Westm. School (King's Scholar); *suc. to the Baronetcy*, 4 April 1734; matric. at Oxford (Univ. Coll.), 9 April 1736, aged 16; *cr.* M.A., 16 May 1738, and D.C.L., 13 April 1749; was M.P. for Middlesex, Aug. 1742 to 1747, and for Oxford University (five Parls), Jan. 1750 to 1784, in the "High Tory" interest. He was an active promoter of various canals, then first established, and was a collector of antiquities, many of which he presented to the University of Oxford, where he founded the annual prize for English poetry, called by his name, first awarded in 1806. He *m.* firstly, 31 May 1743, Sophia, da. of Edward CONYERS, of Copthall, Essex, by Matilda, da. of William (FERMOR), 1st BARON LEMPSTER. She, who was *b.* 20 Dec. 1718, *d.* 9 July 1774, after a long illness, and was *bur.* at Harefield. M.I. He *m.* secondly, 3 June 1776, Hester Margaretta, da. of Edward MUNDY, of Allstree and Shipley, co. Derby, by Hester, da. and h. of Nicholas MILLER, of Shipley aforesaid. She *d.* at Arbury, 30 Dec. 1800, and was *bur.* at Harefield. M.I. He *d.* s.p., at Arbury, 23 Nov. 1806, in his 88th year, and was *bur.* at Harefield, when the *Baronetcy* became *extinct.*(b) Will pr. 1806.

CUST :

cr. 29 Sep. 1677 ;

afterwards, since 1776, BARONS BROWNLOW OF BELTON ;

and, since 1815, EARLS BROWNLOW.

I. 1677. "RICHARD CUST, of Stamford, co. Lincoln, Esq.," only surv. s. and h. of Samuel CUST, of Boston in that County (who took part against Charles I in the Great Rebellion, and *d.* 5 March 1662/3), by Ann, da. of Richard BURRELL, of Dowsby, co. Lincoln, was *bap.* there 23 June 1622; admitted to the Inner Temple, 18 Feb. 1640/1; Barrister, 5 Feb. 1649/50; a Captain of the trained bands in the Parl. army, 31 Dec. 1642; M.P. for Lincolnshire, 1653, and subsequently (three Parls.), 1679-81, for Stamford, having been *cr. a Baronet*, as above, 29 Sep. 1677. He *m.* (settlement 16 March 1641/2, both being under age, the mar. lic. [preserved at Belton] 29 Dec. 1644), Beatrice, "an orphan heiress," da. and h. of William PURY, of Eversham place in Kirton, co. Lincoln, by Elizabeth, da. of Robert MILLETT, of Hayes, Midx. He *d.* 30 Aug., and was *bur.* 6 Sep. 1700, at St. George's, Stamford, aged 78. M.I. Will dat. 26 April 1699, pr. 2 Dec. 1700. His widow *d.* 1 and was *bur.* there 7 April 1715, aged 92. Will dat. 15 Dec. 1711.

(a) Richard Newdigate, his next elder br., was *b.* at Harefield 16 July 1716, and *d.* of the small-pox, at Westm. School, 16 April 1732, aged 15. M.I. at Harefield.

(b) The estates passed to the descendants of his cousin Millicent, wife of Christopher Parker, the only child that had issue of his uncle Francis Newdigate, of Nottingham. Of these, Francis Parker, of Kirkhallam, her 2d s., assumed the name of Newdigate.

II. 1700. SIR RICHARD CUST, Baronet [1677], of Stamford aforesaid, grandson and h., being s. and h. of Sir Pury CUST, by his 1st wife (of whom he was the only surv. s.), Ursula (*m.* 21 Aug. 1678), da. and h. of Edward WOODCOCK, of Newtimber, Sussex, which Pury, who was *Knighted* soon after 1660, was 5th but last surv. s. of the 1st Baronet and *d.* v.p. 21 Feb. 1698/9, aged 43. He was *bap.* 30 Oct. 1680, at St. George's, Stamford, and *suc. to the Baronetcy*, 30 Aug. 1700. He took little part in public life, though he was Sheriff of Lincolnshire, 1721. He *m.* in 1717, Anne, sister and h. [1754] of John (BROWNLOW), VISCOUNT TYRCONNEL [I.], da. of Sir William BROWNLOW, 4th Baronet [1641], of Great Humby and Belton, co. Lincoln, by Dorothy, da. and coheir of Sir Richard MASON. He *d.* 25 July 1734, aged 53, and was *bur.* at St. George's, Stamford. Will pr. Aug. 1734. His widow *d.* at a great age, at Grantham, co. Lincoln, 29 Dec. 1779, and was *bur.* 11 Jan. 1780, at St. George's, Stamford. Will pr. March 1780.

III. 1734. SIR JOHN CUST, Baronet [1677], of Stamford aforesaid, and afterwards [1754-70] of Belton, co. Lincoln, 1st s. and h., *b.* 29 Aug. and *bap.* 25 Sep. 1718, at St. Martin's in the Fields, Midx.; ed. at Eton; *suc. to the Baronetcy*, 25 July 1734; admitted to Benet's, *otherwise* Corpus Christi Coll., Cambridge; M.A., 1739; Barrister (Middle Temple), 26 Nov. 1742; M.P. for Grantham (Parls.), 1743, till death in 1770; Clerk of the Household to Frederick, Prince of Wales, 1747-51, and to George, Prince of Wales, 1751-60; Steward of the Household of the Dow. Princess of Wales, 1751; Col. of the south batt. of the Lincolnshire Militia, 1759; SPEAKER OF THE HOUSE OF COMMONS, 3 Nov. 1761 to the end of that Parl. in March 1768, and again (having been made P.C. 24 Jan. 1762), 10 May 1768, till he resigned, from ill-health, 19 Jan. 1770, five days before his death. He *m.* 8 Dec. 1743, Etheldred, da. and coheir of Thomas PAYNE, of Hough-on-the-hill, co. Lincoln, by Elizabeth, da. of Martin FOLKES, Barrister at Law. He *d.* at St. Margaret's, Westm., Midx., 24 Jan. and was *bur.* 8 Feb. 1770, at Belton, co. Lincoln, in his 52d year. M.I. Admon. 26 April 1770. His widow *d.* 22 Jan. 1775, aged 55, and was *bur.* with him. M.I. Will pr. Feb. 1775.

IV. 1770. SIR BROWNLOW CUST, Baronet [1677], of Belton aforesaid, 1st but only surv. s. and h., *b.* 3 Dec. 1744, in Norfolk street, St. Clement Dane's, Midx.; ed. at Eton, and at Corpus Christi College, Cambridge; M.A. 1766; was M.P. for Ilchester, 1768-74, and for Grantham, 1774 till raised to the Peerage in 1776, having *suc. to the Baronetcy*, 24 Jan. 1770; was *cr.* D.C.L. of Oxford, 7 July 1773. He *m.* firstly, 16 Oct. 1770, at St. Geo. Han. sq., Jocosa Katherina, 2d and yst. da. and coheir of Sir Thomas DRURY, Baronet [so *cr.* 1739], of Overstone, co. Northampton, by Martha, da. of Sir John TYRRELL, 3d Baronet [1666]. She, who was *b.* in Queen square 19 April, and *bap.* 12 May 1749, at St. George the Martyr, Midx., *d.* s.p.m., 11 Feb. 1772, in her 23d year, and was *bur.* at Belton. M.I. He *m.* secondly, 31 Aug. 1775, at St. James', Westm., Frances, only da. and h. of Sir Henry BANKES, of Wimbledon, Surrey, Alderman of London, by Frances, da. of Charles PEMBROOKE, of St. George's, Canterbury. She was living when he (in consideration, presumably, of his late father's services) was *cr.*, 20 May 1776, BARON BROWNLOW OF BELTON, co. Lincoln. In that peerage this *Baronetcy* then *merged*, and still [1903] so continues, the 2d Baron and 5th Baronet being *cr.*, 17 Nov. 1815, EARL BROWNLOW, etc. See *Peerage*.

ANDERTON:

cr. 8 Oct. 1677;

ex. 12 Feb. 1760.

I. 1677. "FRANCIS ANDERTON, of Lostock, co. Lancaster, Esq.," s. and h. of Christopher ANDERTON, of the same, by his 2d wife, ALETHEIA, da. of Sir Francis SMITH, *otherwise* CARRINGTON, of Wootton Wawen, co. Warwick, was *b.* about 1628; suc. his father 7 July 1650; was aged 36 when he entered his pedigree on the Her Visit. of Lancashire in 1664, and was *cr. a Baronet*, as above, 8 Oct. 1677. He *m.* in or before 1657, Elizabeth, da. and coheir of the Hon. Sir Charles SOMERSET, K.B. (yr. s. of Edward, 4th EARL OF WORCESTER), by Elizabeth, da. and h. of Sir William POWELL, of Llanpylt, co. Monmouth. He *d.* at Paris, 9 Feb. 1678, in his 51st year, and was *bur.* in the church of the English Benedictine monks there. M.I. The will of his widow was pr. Oct. 1706.

II. 1678. SIR CHARLES ANDERTON, Baronet [1677], of Lostock aforesaid, 1st s. and h., *b.* 1657, being 7 years old at the Heralds' Visit. of Lancashire, 1664; *suc. to the Baronetcy*, 9 Feb. 1678. He *m.* in or before 1676, Margaret, da. and h. of Laurence IRELAND, of Lydiate, co. Lancaster, by Anne, da. of Edward SCARISBRICK, of Scarisbrick. He *d.* 30 Dec. 1691. Will dat. 29 Dec. 1691, pr. 8 March 1693, at Chester. His widow *d.* in London, 26 Aug. 1720, in her 62d year, and was *bur.* at St. Pancras, Midx. M.I. Will dat. 12 Aug. 1720.

III. 1691. SIR CHARLES ANDERTON, Baronet [1677], of Lostock aforesaid, 1st s. and h., *suc. to the Baronetcy*, 30 Dec. 1691. He *d.* young and unm., at St. Omer's, in 1705.

IV. 1705. SIR JAMES ANDERTON, Baronet [1677], of Lostock aforesaid, br. and h., *suc. to the Baronetcy* in 1705. He *d.* a minor and unm., at St. Omer's, 5 Oct. 1710.

V. 1710. SIR LAURENCE ANDERTON, Baronet [1677], br. and h., *b.* about 1680, being aged 37 or 38 in May 1718; ed. at the Jesuits' Coll. of St. Omer's; joined the English Benedictines at Dieulwart, near Verdun; was for some time a monk at Lanspey, in Germany; *suc. to the Baronetcy*, 5 Oct. 1710, being in 1715 one of the English Catholic non-jurors, though, to save the estates, he renounced his religion, 21 May 1724, five months before his death. He *d.* unm. in London, 4 Oct. 1724. Will dat. 27 Oct. 1723 to 18 Jan. 1723/4.

VI. 1724, to 1760. SIR FRANCIS ANDERTON, Baronet [1677],(a) br. and h., wrongfully *assumed the Baronetcy* in 1710, in lieu of his elder br. abovenamed (who was a Priest), joined in the Stuart rising of 1715, and was (being then *styled* "Baronet") convicted of "high treason," forfeiting thereby his estate of Lostock, of which as early as 1705, in the lifetime of his brother James, he was in possession. He *suc. to the Baronetcy*, 4 Oct. 1724.(a) He *m.* in 1707 or 1708, Frances, da. of Sir Henry BEDINGFELD, 2d Baronet [1661], by his 2d wife, Elizabeth, da. of Sir John ARUNDELL, of Lanherne. She was dead "several years" before 1741.(b) He *d.* s.p. at Lydiate aforesaid 12 and was *bur.* 18 Feb. 1760, at Halsall, co. Lancaster, when the *Baronetcy* became *extinct*.

(a) On the presumption that he was not then under attainder for high treason, as, if so, the Baronetcy would have become forfeited on his accession thereto, 30 Sep. 1724.

(b) Wotton's *Baronetage*, 1741.

SIMEON:

cr. 18 Oct. 1677;

ex. 22 Dec 1768.

I. 1677. "JAMES SIMEON, of Chilworth, co. Oxford, Esq.," 5th and yst. s.(a) of Sir George SIMEON, of the same and of Baldwin Brightwell, in that county (who *d.* 4 May 1664), by his 2d wife, Margaret (*m.* Nov. 1624), da. of Sir Richard MOLYNEUX, 1st Baronet [1611], of Sefton, co. Lancaster, was *cr. a Baronet*, as above, 18 Oct. 1677. He *m.*, between 1663 and 1680, Bridget, yr. da. and finally sole h. of Walter HEVENINGHAM, of Aston, near Stone, co. Stafford, by Mary, da. of Richard MIDDLEMORE, of Edgbaston, co. Warwick. She *d.* 16 March 1691. He *d.* 15 Jan. 1708/9. Will pr. March 1709.

II. 1709, to 1768. SIR EDWARD SIMEON, Baronet [1677], of Aston and Baldwin Brightwell aforesaid, 1st s. and h., *b.* about 1682; *suc. to the Baronetcy*, 15 Jan. 1708/9; was one of the English Catholic non-jurors in 1715. He *d.* unm., 22 Dec. 1768, aged 86, when the *Baronetcy* became *extinct*.(b) Will dat. 15 June 1764, pr. 28 Jan. 1769.

POOLE:

cr. 25 Oct. 1677;

ex. 25 May 1821.

I. 1677. "JAMES POOLE, of Poole in Wirrall, co. Chester, Esq.," 2d s. of James POOLE, of the same, by Mary, sister of Sir Edward MOSTYN, 1st Baronet [1670], da. of John MOSTYN, of Talacre, co. Flint, was *b.*, presumably, about 1640.(c); was *cr. a Baronet*, as above, 25 Oct. 1677, with a spec. rem., "for lack of issue male. to William, his brother, and to the heirs male of his body." He *m.* firstly, Anne, da. of Thomas EYRE, of Hassop, co. Derby. She *d.* 24 Aug 1683, and was *bur.* at Wolverhampton. He *m.* secondly, in or after 1683, Ann, widow of Sir Thomas ESTCOURT, of Sherston Pinckney, Wilts (*d.* 1682-83), da. of (—) KIRKHAM, co. Derby. She was living 1 Feb. 1696,(d) but *d.* 8 March 1698, and was *bur.* at Easton, co. Chester. He *m.* thirdly, Frances, widow of Sir John CORBET, 3d Baronet [1627], of Stoke, Salop, da. and coheir of Major-Gen. Randolph EGERTON, of Betley, co. Stafford. He was living 8 Oct. 1706.

II. 1710? SIR FRANCIS POOLE, Baronet [1677], of Poole aforesaid, and of the Friary, in Lewes, co. Sussex, 3d but 1st surv. s. and h. by 1st wife, *b.* 1682(e) or 1683, the year of his mother's death, living 1704,

(a) Edward Simeon, one of the elder sons, *b.* 1632, was ed. at St. Omer, and became a Jesuit in 1656. He *d.* 17 Jan. 1701, aged 69.

(b) His estates devolved on his nephew, Thomas Weld (yr. s. of his sister Margaret, by Humphrey Weld, of Lulworth Castle, Dorset), who accordingly assumed the name of Simeon, and whose only child Mary, took the veil at Bruges.

(c) It is difficult to conjecture the dates in this pedigree, which are for the most part omitted in Ormerod's Cheshire. The grantee's eldest brother, Benjamin, *d.* Jan. 1646, leaving a da. and heir, so that the said Benjamin himself was probably born not later than 1626, and his yr. br. not later than 1640.

(d) On that date admon. of her son Charles Estcourt, late of Poole, co. Chester, but died beyond seas, was granted to her.

(e) James Poole, *b.* 4 June 1681, 2d s. of the 1st Baronet (the elder br., John, having *d.* an infant), *m.* Meliora Gumbleton, and *d.* s.p. and v.p. 8 Oct. 1706.

beyond the seas, *suc. to the Baronetcy*, after 8 Oct. 1706, on the death of his father. He was M.P. for Lewes, Dec. 1743 to 1754. He *m.* Frances, da. of Henry PELHAM, of Lewes, Sussex, Clerk of the Pells in the Exchequer (br. of Thomas, 1st BARON PELHAM OF LAUGHTON), by Frances, da. and coheir of John BINE, of Rowdell, in that county. She *d.* 30 April 1762. He *d.* 15 Feb. 1763, aged about 80. Will pr. 1763.

III. 1763. SIR HENRY POOLE, Baronet [1677], of Poole and Lewes aforesaid, 1st s. and h., *suc. to the Baronetcy*, 15 Feb. 1763; was a Commissioner of Excise, 1763, and again 1765. He *d.* unm. 8 July 1767. Admon. 6 Aug. 1767, and again Sep. 1843.

IV. 1767. SIR FERDINANDO POOLE, Baronet [1677], of Poole and Lewes aforesaid, only br. and h., *suc. to the Baronetcy*, 8 July 1767; Sheriff of Sussex, 1789-90. He *m.* in 1772 (—), da. of Thomas WHITE, of Horsham, Sussex. She *d.* 24 May 1786. He *d.* s.p., 8 June 1804, at Lewes.(a). Will pr. 1804.

V. 1804, to 1821. SIR HENRY POOLE, Baronet [1677], of Poole aforesaid and of the Hooke, near Lewes, Sussex, cousin and h. male, being only s. and h. of William POOLE, of the Hooke aforesaid, by his 2d wife, Dorothea, da. of the Rev. Daniel WALTER, Vicar of Cuckfield, Sussex, and Preb. of Chichester, which William, was only s. and h. of William POOLE (living 1677), next br. to the 1st Baronet, who was in spec. rem. to the Baronetcy. He was *b.* 29 Feb. 1744/5; was presumably the Henry POOLE, of Peterhouse, Cambridge, who took the degree of LL.B. in 1770; was in Holy Orders; Preb. of Chichester, 1783 till his death in 1821; Rector of Chailey and of Waldron, both co. Sussex, 1784; *suc. to the Baronetcy*, 8 June 1804. He *m.* Charlotte, da. and coheir of Jonathan BURWARD, of Woodbridge, Suffolk. She *d.* in or before 1808. Admon. Jan. 1808. He *d.* s.p.m. 25 May 1821, aged 76, when the *Baronetcy* became *extinct*.(b) Will pr. 1821.

WHARTON:

cr. 19 Dec. 1677;

ex. before 1741.

I. 1677. "GEORGE WHARTON, of Kirkby Kendall, co. Westmorland, Treasurer of the Ordnance," s. of George WHARTON, a Blacksmith at Kendal (*d.* in his son's infancy), was *b.* 4 April 1617, at Strickland, near Kendal; was a "sojourner," studying mathematics and astronomy, in Oxford, 1633, and subsequently (1643) was considered a member of Queen's College, Oxford, and is said to have been *cr.* M.A. of that University; raised a troop of horse for the King, which was defeated, 1643, at Stow, co. Gloucester; was Paymaster to the Artillery, 1645; was imprisoned by the Parl. 1649-50; Paymaster to the Ordnance Office, 1660, till his death, being *cr. a Baronet*, as above, 19 Dec. 1677. He was author of several pamphlets, some political, but chiefly astronomical. He *m.*, probably before 1650, Anne, da. of (—) BUTLER. She was living at Enfield, Midx., 7 July 1668.(c) He *d.* at Enfield, 12, and was *bur.* 25 Aug. 1681, in the church of St. Peter-ad-Vincula, in the Tower of London (where he had an official residence), aged 64. Will pr. 1681.

(a) Frances, his only sister, *m.* 6 Oct. 1767, as his 1st wife, Henry (Temple), 2d Viscount Palmerston [I.], and *d.* in childbed, 1 June 1769, s.p.s., in his house at the Admiralty, Whitehall, being *bur.* at Romsey, Hants. M.I.

(b) The estate of Poole was sold in 1820 by his daughters and coheirs, of whom Charlotte Elizabeth had *m.*, in 1815, Robert Willis Blencowe, afterwards of the Hooke abovenamed.

(c) Her da. Dorothy was *bap.* there at that date.

II. 1681, to 1730? SIR POLYCARPUS WHARTON, Baronet [1677], 2d but 1st surv. s. and h.,(a) *b.* probably about 1652; *suc. to the Baronetcy*, 12 Aug. 1681. He *m.* 15 April 1675, at St. Peter's-ad-Vincula aforesaid, Theophila, da. of Justinian SHERBURNE, br. of Sir Edward SHERBURNE. They were both living 1 Dec. 1687.(b) He *d.* s.p.m.s.(c) before 1741,(d) when the *Baronetcy* became *extinct*.

ACLAND, *or* ACKLAND:

cr. 21 Jan. 1677/8;

afterwards, since 1745, DYKE-ACLAND.

I. 1678. "HUGH ACKLAND [*rectius* ACLAND], of Columb-John [as also of Killerton, both in Broad Clyst], co. Devon, Esq.," 4th s. of Sir John ACLAND, 1st Baronet(e) [1644], by Elizabeth, da. of Sir Francis VINCENT, 1st Baronet [1620], was *b.* about 1639; matric. at Oxford (Exeter Coll.), 27 Nov. 1652; B.A., 22 June 1655; *suc.*, by the death, in 1672, of his nephew, Sir Arthur ACLAND, 5th Baronet(e) [1664], to *that Baronetcy*(e) and the family estates, and, though styled a Baronet in his marriage licence, 19 March 1673/4, was, nevertheless, *cr. a Baronet*, as above, *de novo*, 21 Jan. 1677/8, it being stated that "amidst the confusion of those Civil wars, the letters patents [of 1644] were destroyed, and new letters patents not being granted till 1677 (by reason of a long minority in this family), there was in them inserted *a special clause of precedency*(f) from the date of the first, *viz.*, 24 June 1644."(g) He was M.P. for Barnstaple, 1679, and for Tiverton, 1685-87; Sheriff of Devon, 1690-91. He *m.* (Lic. Vic. Gen., 19 March 1673/4, he, styled "Baronet," aged about 35, bachelor, and she about 20, spinster), Anne, da. of Sir Thomas DANIEL, of Beswick Hall, co. York. He was *bur.* 9 March 1713/4, at Broad Clyst. His widow was *bur.* there 15 March 1727/8, aged 77.

II. 1714. SIR HUGH ACLAND, Baronet [1678], of Killerton aforesaid, grandson and h., being 1st s. and h. of John ACLAND of Wooleigh, by Elizabeth (*m.* 24 March 1695/6), da. of Richard ACLAND, of Fremington and Barnstaple, Devon, which John was 1st s. and h. ap. of the late Baronet, but *d.* v.p., and was *bur.* 20 May 1703, at Broad Clyst, aged 28. He was *bap.* there, 26 Jan. 1696/7; was M.P. for Barnstaple (two Parls.), 1721-27; *suc. to the Baronetcy* in March 1713/4. He *m.* (Lic. at Wells, 9 May 1721), Cicely, 1st da. and coheir (eventually sole h.), of Sir Thomas WROTH, 3d Baronet [1660], of Petherton Park and Newton Manor, both co. Somerset, by Mary, da. and h. of Francis OSBALDESTON, of Aldersbrook, Essex. He *d.* 29 July, and was *bur.* 3 Aug. 1728, at Broad Clyst, aged 31. Will pr. 1728. His widow *m.* there, 13 Aug. 1729, Rev. Thomas TROYTE, of Silverton, Devon, who was *bur.* there 15 Dec. 1750.

(a) George Wharton, the 1st s. was a captain in the army, but *d.* unm. and v.p.; Richard, the 3d son, was an engineer; and William. the 4th and yst. son, was also a captain in the army.

(b) "James, s. of Sir Polycarpus Wharton and Theophila," was *b.* and *bap.* 1 Dec. 1687, at Allhallows', Barking.

(c) Besides James, mentioned in note "b" above, they had a son George, *bap.* 13 Sep. 1676 at St. Peter's-ad-Vincula.

(d) The Baronetcy is placed among those that were then extinct in Wotton's *Baronetage*, 1741.

(e) The creation of the Baronetcy of Acland, 24 June 1644, not having ever passed the seals, was considered invalid, so that the heir thereto was (as an "Esq."), *cr. a Baronet, de novo*, 21 Jan. 1677/8, though with the precedency of the former creation.

(f) The creation of the Baronetcy of Boothby, 13 July 1660, was practically a similar case, and that of Edwards, 22 April 1678 (the next creation following this one), was precisely similar.

(g) Wotton's *Baronetage*, 1741, vol. ii, p. 410.

III. 1728. SIR THOMAS ACLAND, afterwards [1745-85] DYKE-ACLAND, Baronet [1678], of Killerton and Petherton aforesaid, 1st s. and h., *b.* about 1723; matric. at Oxford (Balliol Coll.), 3 May 1740, aged 17; *suc. to the Baronetcy*, 29 July 1728; M.P. for Devon, 1746-47, and for Somerset, 1767-8; Sheriff of Somerset, Dec. 1750 to Jan. 1752. He *m.* 7 Jan. 1744/5, at Kingston, Somerset, Elizabeth, da. and h. of Thomas DYKE, of Tetton in Kingston, and of Pixton in that county. On that occasion he assumed the name of DYKE before that of ACLAND. She was *bur.* 13 July 1753, at Broadclyst. Admon. 2 Nov. 1753. He *d.* at Bath, 24 Feb., and was *bur.* 8 March 1785, at Broadclyst. Will dat. 6 July 1784, pr. 6 April 1785.

IV. 1785. Feb. SIR JOHN DYKE-ACLAND, Baronet [1678], of Killerton and Petherton aforesaid, grandson and h., being only s. and h. of Major John DYKE-ACLAND, 20th Foot, by Christiana Harriet Caroline (*m.* 3 June 1750), da. of Stephen (FOX-STRANGWAYS), 1st EARL OF ILCHESTER, which John was 1st. s. and h, ap. of the late Baronet, but (after having served in General Burgoyne's Expedition, and been severely wounded in Canada), *d.* v.p., 31 Oct. 1778.[a] He, who was *b.* 1778, *suc. to the Baronetcy*, 24 Feb. 1785, and *d.* two months later, being *bur.* 23 April 1785, at Broad Clyst, aged about 7 years.[b] Admon. March 1786.

V. 1785. April. SIR THOMAS DYKE-ACLAND, Baronet [1678], of Killerton aforesaid, and of Holnicote, Somerset, uncle and h. male, *bap.* 18 April 1752, at Selworthy, Somerset; ed. at Eton; matric. at Oxford (Univ. Coll.), 5 May 1770, aged 17; *suc. to the Baronetcy* in April 1785. He *m.* 4 July 1785, at Barnes, Surrey, Henrietta Anne, da. of Sir Richard HOARE, 1st Baronet [1786], of Stourhead, Wilts, by his 2d wife, Frances Anne, da. of Richard ACLAND, of London, merchant. He *d.* 17 and was *bur.* 29 May 1794, at Broad Clyst, aged 42. Will dat. 3 March, 1793, pr. 26 June, 1794. His widow *m.* 6 June 1795, Capt. the Hon. Matthew FORTESCUE, R.N., who *d.* 19 Nov. 1842, aged 78, and was *bur.* at Barnes. She *d.* 2 Sep. 1841, and was *bur.* there.

VI. 1794. SIR THOMAS DYKE-ACLAND, Baronet [1678], of Killerton and Holnicote aforesaid, 1st s. and h., *b.* in South Audley street, 29 March, and *bap.* 18 April 1787, at St. George's, Han. sq.; ed. at Harrow; *suc. to the Baronetcy*, 17 May 1794; matric. at Oxford (Ch. Ch.), 29 May 1805, aged 18; B.A., 1808; M.A., 1824, being *cr.* D.C.L., 15 June 1831; Sheriff of Devon, 1809-10; M.P. for that county, 1812-18, and 1820-31; for North Devon, 1837-57. He *m.* 7 April 1808, at Mitcham, Surrey, Lydia Elizabeth, da. of Henry HOARE, of Mitcham Grove, by Lydia Henrietta, da. of Isaac MALLORTIE, of London, Merchant. She, who was *b.* 16 Sep. 1786, *d.* 25 June 1856, aged 69. He *d.* 22 July 1871, at Killerton, aged 84.

VII. 1871. SIR THOMAS DYKE-ACLAND, Baronet [1678], of Killerton and Holnicote aforesaid, 1st s. and h.[c] *b.* at Killerton 25 May, and *bap.* 15 June 1809, at Broad Clyst; ed. at Harrow, where, in 1826, he won the Peel prize; matric. at Oxford (Ch. Ch.), 28 June 1827, aged 18; B.A. and double first class (classics and mathematics), 1831; Fellow of All Souls' Coll., 1831-39; M.A., 1835, being *cr.* D.C.L. 14 June 1858; was v.p. M.P. (as a Conservative) for West Somerset (two Parls.), 1837-47, being afterwards (as a Liberal), M.P. for North Devon, 1865-85, and for West Somerset, 1885-86, when he voted in favour of the "Home Rule" Bill. He was Lieut.-Col. of the 3d Devon Volunteer Rifles,

(a) His wife, Lady Harriet Acland, accompanied him to Canada in 1776, where she underwent many terrible hardships [Betham's *Baronetage*, vol. ii, p. 34]. She *d.* 21 July 1815, aged 65.

(b) His only sister and h., Elizabeth Kitty, *b.* 13 Dec. 1773, inherited some of the estates. She *m.* 26 April 1796, Henry George (Herbert), 2d Earl of Carnarvon, and *d.* 5 March 1813, leaving issue.

(c) The 4th son was the well-known Sir Henry Wentworth Dyke-Acland, for forty years Regius Professor of Medicine at Oxford, and the leading Physician of that University, where he *d.* 16 Oct. 1900, aged 85, having been made **K.C.B.** in 1884, and *cr. a Baronet* in 1890.

1860-81; was second Church-estates Commissioner, 1869-74, and *suc. to the Baronetcy*, 22 July 1871; P.C., 1883. He *m.* firstly, 14 March 1841, at Walton, co. Warwick, Mary, 1st da. of Sir Charles MORDAUNT, 8th Baronet [1611], by Marianne, da. of William HOLBECH, of Farnborough in that county. She *d.* at Tetton, Somerset 11, and was *bur.* 17 June 1851, at Broad Clyst, aged 58. He *m.* secondly, 18 June 1856, Mary, da. of John ERSKINE, Commissary Gen. of the British forces in Portugal (br. of James, 2d EARL OF ROSSLYN), by Mary, da. of Sir John MORDAUNT, 7th Baronet [1611]. She *d.* 14 May 1892. He *d.* at Killerton, 29 May 1898, in his 90th year. Will pr. at £74,141, gross.

VIII. 1898. SIR CHARLES THOMAS DYKE-ACLAND, Baronet [1678], of Killerton and Holnicote aforesaid, 1st s. and h., *b.* 16 July 1842, in Queen Anne Street; ed. at Eton; matric. at Oxford (Ch. Ch.), 23 May 1861, aged 18; B.A., 1866; M.A., 1868; Barrister (Inner Temple), 17 Nov. 1869; M.P. for East Cornwall, 1882-85, and for North Cornwall, 1885-92; Church-estates Commissioner, 1886; Parl. Sec. to Board of Trade, Feb. to Aug. 1886; Dep. Warden of the Stanneries; sometime Lieut.-Col. of 1st Devon Yeomanry Cavalry; *suc. to the Baronetcy*, 29 May 1898. He *m.*, 1 Nov. 1879. at All Saints' chapel, Bradfield, in Uffculme, Devon, Gertrude, 3d da. of Sir John Walrond WALROND *(formerly* DICKINSON), 1st Baronet [1876], by Frances Caroline, da. of Samuel (HOOD), 2d BARON BRIDPORT [I.]. She was *b.* 8 Aug. 1853.

Family Estates.—These, in 1883, consisted of 20,300 acres in Somerset, 15,018 in Devon, and 4,578 in Cornwall. *Total.*—39,896 acres, worth £34,785 a year. *Principal Seats.*—Killerton Park, near Exeter, Devon, and Holnicote, near Taunton, Somerset.

EDWARDS, *or* EDWARDES:

cr. 22 April 1678;

ex. 24 Aug. 1900.

I. 1678. "FRANCIS EDWARDS, of Shrewsbury, co. Salop, Esq.," 2d but 1st surv. s. and h. of Sir Thomas EDWARDS, 1st Baronet[a] [1645], of Grete, co. Salop, and of Shrewsbury aforesaid, by his 2d wife, Cicely, da. of Edward BROOKES, of Stretton, Salop, was *b.* probably about 1645; *suc. to the Baronetcy*[a] [1647], 27 April 1660, and matric. (as a Baronet) at Oxford (Balliol Coll.), 26 Oct. 1660, but was, nevertheless, *cr. a Baronet*, as above, *de novo*, it being stated that "in the Civil Wars, 'tis supposed the Baronet's patent [of 1644/5] was lost, for in April 1678, a new one was granted[b] to Francis (then Sir Francis) EDWARDS, of Shrewsbury, and to the heirs male of his body, with remainder to [his brothers] Thomas, Benjamin, Herbert, and Jonathan, and the heirs male of their bodies, etc. [and] with a special clause of precedency before all Baronets created after the year 1644, viz., according to the former patent"[c] [*i.e.*, the date of 21 March 1644/5]. He was M.P. for Shrewsbury, 1685-87, and 1689-90; was Col. of a Company of Foot, and fought on behalf of William III. at the battle of the Boyne. He *m.* Eleanor, da. of Sir George WARBURTON, 1st Baronet [1660] of Arley, by his 1st wife Elizabeth, da. of Sir Thomas MYDDLETON. She was *bur.*, 24 July 1675, at St. Chad's, Shrewsbury. He (according to some accounts) *d.* in 1690, in Ireland, and was *bur.* there. Admon., as of Shrewsbury, 23 Dec. 1690.

(a) The creation of the Baronetcy of Edwards not having ever passed the Seals was considered invalid, so that the heir thereto was (as an "Esq.") *cr. a Baronet, de novo*, 22 April 1678, though with the precedency of the former creation.

(b) See p. 95, note "f," under "Acland."

(c) Wotton's *Baronetage*, 1741, vol. ii, p. 416.

II. 1690? SIR FRANCIS EDWARDS, Baronet [1678], of Shrewsbury aforesaid, and afterwards of Grantham, co. Lincoln, and Edmonton, Midx., only surv. s. and h.; *suc. to the Baronetcy* in or before 1690, being then a minor. He *m.* in or before 1699, Susan, da. of Robert HARVEY, of Stockton, co. Warwick. He *d.* at Easton, co. Lincoln, and was *bur.* 23 Oct. 1701, at Grantham, in that county.[a]

III. 1701. SIR FRANCIS EDWARDS, Baronet [1678], of Shrewsbury aforesaid, only s. and h., *bap.* 17 April 1699 at Grantham aforesaid; *suc. to the Baronetcy*, in Oct. 1701; admitted to Rugby School, 26 Oct. 1713.[b] He *m.* firstly, Anne, da. and coheir of Thomas ROCKE, of Shrewsbury. She *d.* s.p. 15 March 1726. He *m.* secondly, 10 June 1726, at Middle, Salop, Hester, da. and coheir of John LACON, of West Coppies, Salop. He *d.* s.p.m.,[c] 5 Aug. 1734, and was *bur.* in Meol Church, Salop, aged 35. Will pr. 1739.

IV. 1734. SIR HENRY EDWARDS, Baronet [1678], of Shrewsbury aforesaid, cousin and h. male, being s. and h. of Thomas EDWARDS, Town Clerk of Shrewsbury, by Mary (mar. lic. fac. 23 July 1688), da. and coheir of John HAYNES, of Soresby, Salop, which Thomas, who *d.* 28 Jan. 1726/7, aged 82, was next br. to the grantee of 1678, and was in rem. to that Baronetcy under the spec. clause in its creation. He, accordingly, *suc. to the Baronetcy*, 5 Aug. 1734. He *m.* in 1727, his cousin Eleanor, only da. of Sir Francis EDWARDS, 2d Baronet [1678] abovenamed, by Susan, da. of Robert HARVEY, of Stockton, co. Warwick. He *d.* at Shrewsbury, 26 March 1767. Will pr. Dec. 1771.

V. 1767. SIR THOMAS EDWARDS, Baronet [1678], of Shrewsbury aforesaid, and of Ealing, Midx., 1st s. and h., *b.* probably about 1730; *suc. to the Baronetcy*, 26 March 1767. He *m.* in 1760, Anne, only da. and h. of John BARRETT, of Ealing aforesaid. She *d.* 16 April 1785. He *d.* s.p.m.,[d] at Deal, co. Kent, 13 Nov. 1790. Will pr. Jan. 1791.

VI. 1790. SIR THOMAS EDWARDES, Baronet [1678], cousin and h. male, being only s. and h. of the Rev. Thomas EDWARDES, Rector of Grete and Vicar of Chirbury, both co. Salop, by Martha, da. and coheir of Thomas MATTHEWS, of Guerendda, co. Montgomery, which Thomas Edwardes (who was *bap.* 12 May 1697, and *bur.* 27 Jan. 1756, both at Chirbury), was 2d and yst. s. of the Rev. Jonathan EDWARDES, *or* EDWARDS (*bap.* at Grete, 3 Oct. 1653, and *d.* 1705), Rector of the second portion of Westbury, Salop, yst. br. of the grantee of 1678, and in rem. to the Baronetcy, granted at that date, under the spec. clause in its creation. He was *b.* at Grete aforesaid, 7 Jan. 1727; matric. at Oxford (Pemb. Coll.), 2 March 1743/4, aged 17; B.A., 1748; was in Holy Orders; Rector of Frodesley, Salop, and of Tilston, Cheshire; *suc. to the Baronetcy*, 13 Nov. 1790. He *m.* Juliana, only surv. da. of John THOMAS, of Aston, co. Montgomery. She *d.* at Frodesley, July 1778, aged 56. He *d.* 22, and was *bur.* there 24 Sep. 1797.

VII. 1797. SIR JOHN THOMAS CHOLMONDELEY EDWARDES, Baronet [1678], 1st s. and h., *b.* about 1764, at Acton Scot, Salop; matric. at Oxford (Pemb. Coll.), 12 March 1781, aged 17; B.A., 1784; in Holy Orders; Rector of Frodesley, Salop; *suc. to the Baronetcy*, 22 Sep. 1797. He *m.* 8 Nov. 1785, Frances, da. of John GASK, of Tickhill, co. York, and Wellclose square, London. He *d.* 23 Feb. 1816, aged 52. Will pr. 26 Aug. 1816. His widow *d.* 15 June 1859, aged 96.

(a) In the burial entry there is inserted "Certified to Edmunton."

(b) As "Baronettus de Salopia."

(c) Hester, his only da. and h., by his 2d wife, *m.* 19 Jan. 1746/7, George Cholmondeley, *styled* Viscount Malpas, and was mother of the 4th Earl (1st Marquess) Cholmondeley.

(d) Ellen Esther Mary, his only da. and h., *m.* John Thomas Hope, of Netley Hall, in Dorrington, Salop, and *d.* 4 June 1837, leaving issue.

VIII. 1816. SIR HENRY EDWARDES, Baronet [1678], of Meole Brace, Salop, 1st s. and h., *bap.* 14 Aug. 1787, at Ford; *suc. to the Baronetcy*, 23 Feb. 1816. He *m.* 19 June 1828, Louisa Mary Anne, sister of Thomas Henry HOPE-EDWARDES, only da. of John Thomas HOPE, both of Netley Hall, in Dorrington, Salop, by Helen Hester Mary, only da. and h. of Sir Thomas EDWARDS, 5th Baronet [1678], abovenamed. He *d.* 26 Aug. 1841, at Ruyton, Salop, aged 54. Admon. Jan. 1842. His widow *m.*, 20 Feb. 1846, James Murray MARTIN, Major in the East India Company's service, who *d.* 19 April 1870.

IX. 1841, to 1900. SIR HENRY HOPE EDWARDES, Baronet [1678], of Wootton Hall, near Ashbourne, co. Derby, 1st s. and h., *b.* 10 April 1829, at Meole Brace aforesaid; *suc. to the Baronetcy*, 26 Aug. 1841; ed. at Rugby school; sometime, 1851-53 Lieut. 85th Foot. He *d.* unm. at Wootton Hall aforesaid, 24, and was *bur.* 29 Aug. 1900 (from Netley Hall, Salop), at Frodesley, aged 71, when the *Baronetcy* became *extinct*. Will pr. at £46,494, the net personalty being £17,726.

OXENDEN:

cr. 8 May 1678;

afterwards, since 1895, DIXWELL-OXENDEN.

I. 1678. "SIR HENRY OXENDEN, of Deane [in Wingham], co. Kent, Knt.," 1st s. and h.[a] of Sir James OXENDEN, of the same, by Margaret, da. of Thomas NEVINSON, of Eastry in that county, was *b.* 28 April 1614; admitted to Gray's Inn, 2 June 1632; suc. his father 24 Sep. 1657; was M.P. for Winchilsea, Oct. 1645 till secluded Dec. 1648; for Kent, 1654-55 and 1656-58, and for Sandwich, 1660; *Knighted*, 8 June, or 11 July, 1660, and was *cr. a Baronet*, as above, 8 May 1678. He *m.* firstly, Mary, da. and h. of Robert BAKER, of St. Martin's in the Fields. She *d.* s.p.m.[b] in childbirth, and was *bur.* there 5 Dec. 1638. He *m.* secondly, 14 Aug. 1640, at Leeds, co. Kent, Elizabeth, 6th da. of Sir William MEREDITH, 1st Baronet [1622], of Leeds Abbey, by Susanna, da. of Francis BARKER, of London. She, by whom he had thirteen children, *d.* 19 Aug. 1659. He *m.* thirdly, 18 Feb. 1661, Elizabeth, widow of Mark DIXWELL, of Broomhouse, da. and coheir of Matthew READ, of Folkestone, but by her had no issue. He *d.* Aug. 1686. Will pr. Sep. 1686.

II. 1686. SIR JAMES OXENDEN, Baronet [1678], of Deane aforesaid, 1st s. and h. by 2d wife, *b.* about 1643; admitted to Gray's Inn, 28 Nov. 1657; was *Knighted*, v.p. 22 March 1671/2; *suc. to the Baronetcy*, Aug. 1686; was M.P. for Sandwich (four Parls.), 1679-90; for Kent, 1698-1700, and for Sandwich (again), 1701-02. He *m.* firstly (Lic. Fac., 17 May 1673, he about 30 and she about 17), Elizabeth, da. of Edward CHUTE, of Bethersden, Kent, by Elizabeth, da. of (—) DIXWELL. He *m.* secondly, Arabella, sister of Lewis, 1st EARL OF ROCKINGHAM, da. of Edward (WATSON), 2d BARON ROCKINGHAM, by Anne, da. of Thomas (WENTWORTH), EARL OF STRAFFORD. He *d.* s.p., 29 Sep. 1708. Will pr. Oct. 1708. His widow *d.* 14 Jan. 1735. Will pr. 1735.

III. 1708. SIR HENRY OXENDEN, Baronet [1678], of Deane aforesaid, br. and h., *b.* probably about 1645; was sometime Deputy-Governor of Bombay in East India; *suc. to the Baronetcy*, 29 Sep. 1708, but *d.* unm. soon afterwards, in Feb. 1708/9. Will pr. March 1709, and May 1712.

IV. 1709. SIR HENRY OXENDEN, Baronet [1678], of Deane aforesaid, nephew and h., being 1st s. and h. of George OXENDEN, LL.D., Vicar Gen. to the province of Canterbury, and sometime Master of Trinity Hall,

(a) The 3d son, Sir George Oxenden, Governor of Bombay and President of the East India Company, *d.* in or before 1673. Will pr. 1673.

(b) The only child of the first marriage, Mary, was *bap.* 25 Nov. 1638 at St. Martin's in the Fields.

Cambridge, by Elizabeth, da. of Sir Basil DIXWELL, 1st Baronet [1660], of Broome, in Barham, co. Kent, which George (who *d.* 21 Feb. 1702/3) was yr. br. of the 2d and 3d Baronets and 3d s. of the 1st Baronet. He was *b.* about 1690, and *suc. to the Baronetcy* in Feb. 1708/9, was M.P. for Sandwich, 1713, till death in 1720. He *m.* 27 July 1712, at St. Paul's Cathedral, London, Anne, da. of John HOLLOWAY, of Oxford, Barrister. He *d.* s.p., 21 April 1720. Will pr. 1720. His widow *m.*, 4 May 1721, at St. Giles' in the Fields, Richard (COOTE), 2d EARL OF BELLOMONT [I.], who *d.* 10 Feb. 1766, aged 63. She *d.* 13 and was *bur.* 20 Feb. 1723/4, at St. Anne's, Soho, Midx.

V. 1720. SIR GEORGE OXENDEN, Baronet [1678], of Deane aforesaid, br. and h., *b.* 26 Oct. 1694, ed. at Trin. Hall, Cambridge; LL.B., 1715; *suc. to the Baronetcy*, 21 April 1720; was M.P. for Sandwich, 1720-54; a Lord of the Admiralty, 1725-27; a Lord of the Treasury, 1727-37; a Groom of the Bedchamber to the Prince of Wales, 1742. He *m.* in 1720, Elizabeth, 1st da. and coheir of Edmund DUNCH, of Little Wittenham, Berks, Master of the Household to Queen Anne and to George I, by Elizabeth, da. of Col. Charles GODFREY, Master of the Jewel Office. He *d.* 20 Jan. 1775, aged 81. Will pr. Jan. 1775. His widow *d.* 25 Feb. 1779. Will pr. March 1779.

VI. 1775. SIR HENRY OXENDEN, Baronet [1678], of Deane and Little Wittenham, as also of Broome aforesaid, 1st s. and h.,(a) *b.* 5 and *bap.* 17 Sep. 1721, at St. Martin's in the Fields; admitted to Lincoln's Inn, 16 July 1737; suc. to the estate of Broome, soon after 1753, and *suc. to the Baronetcy*, 30 Jan. 1775. He *m.* 31 July 1755, at Westm. Abbey (Lic. Fac. 28 both above 21), Margaret, yst. da. and coheir of Sir George CHUDLEIGH, 4th Baronet [1622], by Frances, da. and coheir of Sir William DAVIE, 4th Baronet [1641]. She *d.* at Broome House, 30 March 1803, aged about 70, and he *d.* there 15 June following, aged 81, both being *bur.* at Wingham. His will pr. 1803.

VII. 1803. SIR HENRY OXENDEN, Baronet [1678], of Broome House aforesaid, only s. and h., *b.* in Albemarle street, St. Geo. Han. sq., 14 and privately *bap.* there 20 May 1756, received into the Church 20 July following, at Little Wittenham; ed. at Eton and at St. John's Coll., Cambridge; B.A., 1778; was for fifty years a Commissioner of Dover Harbour; and *suc. to the Baronetcy*, 15 June 1803. He *m.*, 20 June 1793, Mary, da. of Col. GRAHAM, of St. Lawrence House, near Canterbury (sometime Governor of Georgia), by whom he had nine children. He *d.* 22 Sep. 1838, at Broome House aforesaid, aged 82. Will pr. Jan. 1839.

VIII. 1838. SIR HENRY CHUDLEIGH OXENDEN, Baronet [1678], of Broome House (*otherwise* Broome Park) aforesaid, 1st s. and h.,(b) *b.* 24 June 1795; ed. at Eton and at St. John's Coll., Cambridge; *suc. to the Baronetcy*, 22 Sep. 1838. He *m.* firstly, in 1830, Charlotte, da. of Capt. BROWNE, R.N. She *d.* March 1843. He *m.* secondly, 28 July 1848, at St. Geo. Han. sq., Elizabeth Phœbe, 3d da. of James KING, of Rupert street, Midx., and of Brighton. She *d.* 13 Sep. 1877, at Broome Park. He *d.* there s.p., 14 Aug. 1889, in his 95th year, and was *bur.* at Barham.

IX. 1889. SIR HENRY MONTAGU OXENDEN, Baronet [1678], of Broome Park aforesaid, nephew and h., being 1st s. and h. of the Rev. Montagu OXENDEN, Rector of Eastwell and Luddenham, co. Kent, by his 1st wife, Elizabeth, da. of Richard WILSON, of Bildeston, Norfolk, which

(a) George Oxenden, the 2d and yst. son, inherited the estate of Broome under the will of his kinsman, Sir Basil Dixwell, 2d Baronet [1660], who *d.* 25 March 1750, and in consequence took the name of Dixwell. He *d.* unm., 20 Oct. 1753, devising the same to his father, the 5th Baronet, who immediately made it over to his only surv. son, Henry, afterwards the 6th Baronet.

(b) Ashton Oxenden, the 5th son, *b.* 28 Oct. 1808, Rector of Pluckley, Kent, 1848-70, Bishop of Montreal and Metropolitan of Canada 1869-78, Vicar of St. Stephen's, Canterbury, 1879-85, was author of several well-known religious works. He *d.* 22 Feb. 1892.

Montagu, who *d.* 25 Jan. 1880, aged 80, was next br. to the late and 2d s. of the 7th Baronet. He was *b.* 20 June 1826; *suc. to the Baronetcy*, 14 Aug. 1889, and *d.* unm. Sep. 1895.

X. 1895. SIR PERCY DIXWELL NOWELL DIXWELL-OXENDEN, Baronet [1678], of Broome Park aforesaid, br. and h., *b.* 6 June 1838; sometime Capt. in the Kent Yeomanry Cavalry; took by royal lic. in 1890 the name of DIXWELL before that of OXENDEN; *suc. to the Baronetcy*, Sep. 1895. He *m.* 26 Nov. 1868, Isabella, 3d and yst. da. of Rev. the Hon. Daniel Heneage FINCH-HATTON (br. of George William, EARL OF WINCHELSEA), by Louisa, da. of the Hon. Robert FULKE GREVILLE, and Louisa, *suo jure* COUNTESS OF MANSFIELD.

Family Estates.—These, in 1883, consisted of 5,266 acres in Kent, worth £4,368 a year. *Seat.*—Broome Park, near Canterbury.

BOWYER:

cr. 18 May 1678;

afterwards, since 1680, GORING.

I. 1678. "SIR JAMES BOWYER, [3d] Baronet [1627], of Leighthorne [in North Mundham], co. Sussex," yr. s. of Sir Thomas BOWYER, Baronet, so *cr.* 23 July 1627 [see full particulars of these Baronets under that date in vol. ii, pp. 31-32], *suc. to the Baronetcy* in 1659, but, having no issue and there being no one in succession to that dignity, "on surrendering his patent had now a new creation to that dignity, for life only, the remainder to Henry GORING, of Highden in the same county, Esq., and to the heirs males of his body, with the same precedency [viz., that of 23 July 1627] as the said Sir Thomas BOWYER enjoyed."(a) He *d.* s.p. and was *bur.* 28 Feb. 1679/80.

II. 1680. SIR HENRY GORING, Baronet [1678], of Highden, in Washington, co. Sussex, only surv. s. and h. of Henry GORING, of the same (*d.* 26 Feb. 1655), by Mary, da. of Sir Thomas EVERSFIELD, of Denne, in Horsham, Sussex, was *bap.* 22 May 1622, at Washington; was, possibly,(b) admitted to the Inner Temple, 1637, becoming a Barrister, 1645; was M.P. for Sussex, 1660; for Steyning, 1661-79, and for Sussex again, 1685-87; and *suc. to the Baronetcy* in Feb. 1679/80, under the spec. rem. in the patent of its creation. He *m.*, 2 May 1642, in London, Frances, 1st da. of Sir Edward BISHOPP, 2d Baronet [1620], of Parham, Sussex, by Mary, da. of Nicholas (TUFTON), 1st EARL OF THANET. She *d.* 14 Dec. 1694, and was *bur.* at Washington. He *d.*, 3 April 1702, in his 80th year, and was *bur.* at Billinghurst.(c) Will dat. 6 June 1695 to 25 Aug. 1700, pr. 15 June 1702.

III. 1702. SIR CHARLES GORING, Baronet [1678], of Highden aforesaid, grandson and h., being 1st s. and h. of Henry GORING, of Wappingthorn, in Steyning, Sussex; a Capt. in a Regiment of Foot, and Sheriff of Sussex, 1681-82, by his 1st wife Elizabeth (mar. lic. Fac. 3 Oct. 1667, he 21 and she 16), da. and coheir of Anthony MOREWOOD, of Alfreton, co. Derby, which Henry was 1st s. and h. ap. of the late Baronet, but *d.* v.p., being slain by Sir Edward DERING, 3d Baronet [1626], in 1687, aged about 40. He was *b.* probably 1668, and *suc. to the Baronetcy*, 3 April 1702. He *m.*

(a) See vol. ii, p. 32, notes "a" and "b," as to this surrender and as to the possible reason of this transaction. Le Neve (in his MS. *Baronetage*) says of him that, at the time when he surrendered his patent, "he was a poor scholar of Winton and Fellow of New College, Oxon; having no estate he went into orders."

(b) The Henry Goring, of Highden, Sussex, so admitted, is called "s. and h. of *Edward*," and may be a son of the Baronet's uncle, Edward Goring, of Cobden, Sussex, who *d.* 1657, leaving issue.

(c) An oval portrait of him (half length and in armour), said to be by Sir Peter Lely, which was sometime in possession of his great nephew, Col. Pocklington, was sold by auction, 8 Jan. 1876, at Christie's.

16 Nov. 1699, at Knightsbridge Chapel, Midx., and again 12 May 1700, at St. Martin's in the Fields, Elizabeth, yst. da. of Richard BRIDGER, of Combe Place, in Hamsey, Sussex, by Frances, da. of Walter BURRELL, of Cuckfield, in that county. He *d.* s.p. and was *bur.* 13 Jan. 1712/3, at Billinghurst. Will dat. 16 April 1712, pr. 17 March 1713. His widow *d.* 27 March 1741, and was *bur.* at Worminghurst. Will dat. 27 Nov. 1733, pr. 8 April 1741.

IV. 1713. SIR HARRY GORING, Baronet [1678], of Highden aforesaid, br. of the half blood and h. male, being s. of Captain Henry GORING, abovenamed, by his 2d wife, Mary (*m.* 1676), yst. da. and coheir of Sir John COVERT, Baronet (so *cr.* 2 July 1660), of Slaugham, Sussex. He was *bap.* 16 Sep. 1679, at Slaugham; was in the army and eventually Col. of the 31st Foot; was M.P. for Horsham, April 1707 to 1708, for Steyning, Feb. 1709 to 1715, and for Horsham (again), 1715, till unseated June 1715. He *suc. to the Baronetcy*, Jan. 1712/3. He *m.* (settlement after marriage, 25 Feb. 1714) Elizabeth, 1st da. and coheir of Admiral Sir George MATHEW, of Southwark, Surrey, and Twickenham, Midx. He *d.* at Horsham, 12, and was *bur.* 16 Nov. 1731, at Billinghurst, aged 52. Will dat. 25 July 1731, pr. 26 Nov. 1732. His widow, by whom he had nine sons, *d.* 28 July 1768, aged 100. Will dat. 17 Oct. 1767, pr. 10 Aug. 1768.

V. 1731. SIR CHARLES MATHEW GORING, Baronet [1678], of Highden aforesaid, 1st s. and h., *b.* 15 and *bap.* 26 May 1706, at St. James', Westm.; matric. at Oxford (Mag. Coll.), 4 May 1725, aged 18; *suc. to the Baronetcy*, 12 Nov. 1731. He *m.* firstly, 15 July 1731, at St. Paul's Cathedral, London, Mary, yst. da. of William BLACKBURN, of Morton Ash and High Ongar, Essex, Sheriff of that county, 1714. She *d.* April and was *bur.* 5 May 1739, at Washington aforesaid. He *m.* secondly, 20 April 1743, at Wiston, Sussex, Elizabeth, elder of the two sisters and coheirs of Sir Robert FAGGE, 4th Baronet [1660], of Wiston aforesaid, da. of Sir Robert FAGGE, 3d Baronet [1660], by Christian, da. of Sir Cecil BISHOPP, 3d Baronet [1611]. He *d.* Aug. and was *bur.* 2 Sep. 1769, at Wiston, aged 63. Will dat. 5 May 1768, pr. 2 Sep. 1769, at Chichester. His widow, who was *bap.* 5 May 1703, *d.* 23 Feb. 1784, and was *bur.* at Wiston.(a) M.I.

VI. 1769. SIR HARRY GORING, Baronet [1678], of Highden aforesaid, 1st s. and h. by 1st wife, *b.* 26 April and *bap.* 29 June 1739, at Washington; matric. at Oxford (Mag. Coll.), 1 Nov. 1757, aged 18; B.A., 1760; M.A., 1763; *suc. to the Baronetcy* in Aug. 1769; M.P. for Shoreham, 1790-96. He *m.* firstly, 8 Sep. 1767, at St. Geo. the Martyr, Queen sq., Midx., John Anna, only child of John FORSTER, Governor of Fort William, Bengal. She, who was *b.* 27 April and *bap.* there 27 May 1748, *d.* 4 June 1774, and was *bur.* at Wanstead, Essex. M.I. Admon. June 1792. He *m.* secondly, 23 Oct. 1777, at St. Andrew's, Holborn, Elizabeth, da. of Thomas FISHER, of Barbadoes. She *d.* 10 July 1780 and was *bur.* at Washington, aged 85. He *d.* 1 Dec. 1824. Admon. Dec. 1824.

VII. 1824. SIR CHARLES FOSTER GORING, Baronet [1678], of Highden aforesaid, 1st s. and h. by 1st wife, *b.* 11, and *bap.* 26 July 1768, at St. Giles' in the Fields; matric. at Oxford (Mag. Coll.), 3 Nov. 1786, aged 18; *suc. to the Baronetcy*, 1 Dec. 1824. Sheriff of Sussex, 1827-28. He *m.*, 9 Nov. 1799, at All Saints', Canterbury, Bridget, da. of Henry DENT, of Canterbury. She, who was *b.* 21 April 1773, *d.* 12 Jan. 1816, and was *bur.* at Washington. He *d.* at Highden, 26 March 1844, aged 75, and was *bur.* at Twineham, Sussex. Will pr. April 1844.

VIII. 1844. SIR HARRY DENT GORING, Baronet [1678], of Highden aforesaid, 1st s. and h., *b.* 30 Dec. 1801, in Devonshire place, Marylebone, and *bap.* 10 Feb. 1802, at Washington; matric. at Oxford (Mag. Coll.), 10 Nov. 1820, aged 17; B.A., 1824; M.A., 1829; was M.P. for Shoreham, 1832-41; *suc. to the Baronetcy*, 26 March 1844; was Sheriff of Anglesey, 1848. He *m.* firstly, 2 Aug. 1827, at Thorpe, co. Norfolk, Augusta, sister of Gen. Sir

(a) Her only child, Charles Goring, inherited the Wiston estate from her, and *d.* Dec. 1829, aged 86, being ancestor of the Goring family of that place.

Robert John HARVEY, K.C.B., da. of John HARVEY, of Thorpe lodge, in Thorpe aforesaid, by Frances, da. of Sir Roger KERRISON. She was divorced by Act of Parl., 21 June 1841.(a) He *m.* secondly, 11 May 1842, at Hove, Sussex, Mary Elizabeth, widow of Jones PANTON, of Plâs Gwyn, co. Anglesey, da. and h. of John Griffith LEWIS, of Llanddyfian in that county. He *d.* 19 April 1859, at the Hotel Windsor, Rue Rivoli, Paris, aged 57. His widow *d.* 20 Oct. 1871.

IX. 1859. SIR CHARLES GORING, Baronet [1678], of Highden aforesaid, only s. and h., by 1st wife; *b.* 2 June 1828, in Portugal street, St. Geo. Han. sq., and *bap.* 2 Aug. following, at Yapton, Sussex; sometime an officer in the 12th Lancers; *suc. to the Baronetcy*, 19 April 1859; Capt. 8th Sussex Rifle Volunteers, 1860. He *m.* firstly, 11 Feb. 1850, at Trinity, Paddington, Margaret Anne, 2d da. of Jones PANTON abovenamed. She *d.* 1856. He *m.* secondly, 21 April 1857, at St. James', Paddington, Eliza, 2d da. of the Rev. Capel MOLYNEUX, Vicar of St. Paul's, Onslow square, Midx., by his 1st wife Maria, da. of Admiral CARPENTER. He *d.* s.p., at Highden, 3 Nov. 1884, aged 56. His widow *m.*, 22 Jan. 1885, Col. Robert Ashworth Godolphin COSBY, of Stradbally Hall, Queen's County, "whose name she assumed [in] 1893 [and] is now [1904] known as Mrs. Cosby."(b)

X 1884. SIR CRAVEN CHARLES GORING, Baronet [1678], of Strettington, near Chichester, Sussex, cousin and h. male, being s. and h. of the Rev. Charles GORING, Rector of Twineham, Sussex, by Maria Arabella, da. of the Hon. Frederick ST. JOHN (2d s. of Frederick, 2d VISCOUNT BOLINGBROKE), which Charles, who *d.* 4 Aug. 1859, aged 54, was yr. br. of the 8th, and 2d s. of the 7th Baronet. He was *b.* 24 Oct. 1841; was sometime Capt. 33d Foot and Hon. Col. of the 3d and 4th batts. of the Sussex Militia. He *suc. to the Baronetcy*, 3 Nov. 1884. He *m.*, 14 Dec. 1869, Agnes, 2d da. of Charles A. STEWART, of West Hall, High Legh, Cheshire. He *d.* s.p.m. 14 March 1897, in Ebury Street, Pimlico, and was *bur.* at Boxgrove, Sussex, aged 55. His widow living 1904.

XI. 1897. SIR HARRY YELVERTON GORING, Baronet [1678], cousin and h. male, being 1st s. and h. of Forster GORING, of Wellington, New Zealand, sometime of Portumna, co. Galway, and of Oriental place, Brighton, by Sydney Eloisa, da. of Barry John (YELVERTON), 3d VISCOUNT AVONMORE [I.], which Forster, who *d.* 8 Dec. 1893, aged 83, was uncle to the late and 3d s. of the 7th Baronet. He was *b.* 19 July 1840; was sometime Sergeant-Major and Warrant Officer, 38th Regimental District, retiring 1886; *suc. to the Baronetcy*, 14 March 1897; "is in business as a tobacco merchant at Tamworth"(b) [7 Silver street]. He *m.*, 19 July 1875, Sarah Anne, da. of John HICKIN, of Lichfield.

CURLE, *or* CURLL:

cr. 20 June 1678;

ex. in or before 1679.

I. 1678, to 1679? "WALTER CURLE [*or* CURLL], of Soberton, co. Southampton, Esq.," said to be son,(c) but who probably was a more distant relative of Walter CURLL, D.D., Bishop of Winchester (who *d.* 1647 in his 73d year), was *cr. a Baronet*, as above, 20 June 1678. He *m.* Barbara, da. of [—]. He *d.* s.p. in or before Jan. 1678/9, when the *Baronetcy* became *extinct*. Admon. 28 Jan. 1678/9 to his widow.

(a) She *m.*, subsequently, E. Trelawny.

(b) Dodd's *Baronetage* for 1904.

(c) One of the Bishop's sons, William, was *bap.* as late as 26 Dec. 1629, at Bromley, co. Kent. A grandson, Walter Curle, of Buttermere, Wilts (s. and h. of John Curle, of the same, who *d.* about 1661), was living in 1681, being then aged 46 and married.

IV

DUTTON:

cr. 22 June 1678;

ex. 1 Feb. 1742/3.

I. 1678. "RALPH DUTTON, of Sherborne, co. Gloucester, Esq.," 2d s. of Sir Ralph DUTTON, of Standish in that county, Gentleman of the Privy Chamber, by Mary (mar. lic., London, 25 May 1624), da. of William DUNCOMBE, of London, suc. his elder br., William DUTTON, of Sherborne, in that estate about 1670 (after 8 Nov. 1664), and was *cr. a Baronet*, as above, 22 June 1678. He was M.P. for co. Gloucester (six Parls.), 1679-81 and 1689-98, and was "one of the chief men for the sport" of greyhound-coursing. He *m.* firstly (settlmt. 13 Aug. 1674), Grizel, da. of Sir Edward POOLE, of Kemble, Wilts. She *d.* s.p.m. He *m.* secondly, 19 Jan. 1678/9, at Westm. Abbey (settlmt. 31 Dec. 1678), Mary, only surv. da. of Peter BARWICK, M.D., Physician in Ordinary to Charles II, by Anne, his wife. He *d.* in 1720 or 1721. Will, in which he styles himself "of Rathfarnham, co. Dublin," dat. 12 Oct. 1720, pr. 21 March 1720/1. The will of his widow, as "of St. Martin's in the Fields," dat. 22 July 1721, pr. 4 Oct. 1723.

II. 1721? to 1743. SIR JOHN DUTTON, Baronet [1678], of Sherborne aforesaid, 2d but 1st surv. s. and h. by 2d wife, *bap.* 2 Jan. 1683/4, at St. Margaret's, Westm.; *suc. to the Baronetcy* in 1720 or 1721. He *m.* firstly (settlement 17 June 1714), Mary, da. and h. of Sir Rushout CULLEN, 3d Baronet [1661], by his 1st wife, Mary, da. of Sir John MAYNARD. He *m.* secondly, 1 June 1728 at Hampstead, Midx. (registered at Ely chapel, Holborn, by the Bishop of Ely), Mary (settlement 7 May 1728, she a fortune of £20,000), da. of Francis KECK, of Great Tew, Oxon, by Jane, or Mary, da. of Maijor DUNCH, of Pusey, Berks. She *d.* in childbirth, June 1729. He *d.*, s.p.s., 1 and was *bur.* (at midnight) 4 Feb. 1742/3, at Sherborne, in his 60th year, when the *Baronetcy* became *extinct*.(a) Will pr. 1743.

DYER:

cr. 6 July 1678.

I. 1678. "WILLIAM DYER, of Tottenham, co. Middlesex, Esq.," and afterwards of Newnham, Herts, only surv. s. and h. of George DYER, of Heytesbury, Wilts, by Sarah, da. of [—] ROLPH, of Enford in that county, was a Barrister of the Inner Temple, London; entered and signed his pedigree at the Heralds' Visit. of Midx. in 1664, having then six children; was Sheriff of Essex, 1677-78, and was *cr. a Baronet*, as above, 6 July 1678. He *m.* in or before 1650, Thomazine (a fortune of above £30,000), da. and h. of Thomas SWINNERTON, of Stanway, Essex, by Joanna, da. of Thomas SYMONDS, of London, her father being s. of Sir John SWINNERTON, Lord Mayor of London, 1612-13. He *d.* 27 Jan. 1680/1, and was *bur.* at Newnham aforesaid. M.I. Will dat. 3 April 1680, pr. 21 Feb. 1680/1. His widow, who was *bap.* 5 Jan. 1623/4, at St. Barth. the Less, London, *m.* 8 Aug. 1683, John HOPWOOD, of Tottenham, and afterwards of Stanway aforesaid. She *d.* 13 April 1697, aged 73, and was *bur.* at Newnham. M.I. Will dat. 28 July 1687, pr. 30 April 1697.

(a) The estates passed to his nephew, James Lennox Naper, of Loughcrew, co. Meath, son of his sister Anne, by James Naper, of Loughcrew. He took the name of Dutton accordingly, and was father of James Dutton, who was *cr.* 20 May 1784, Baron Sherborne, co Gloucester.

II. 1681. SIR JOHN SWINNERTON DYER, Baronet [1678] of Newton Hall in Great Dunmow, Essex, 2d but 1st surv. s. and h.,(a) *b.* about 1656; *suc. to the Baronetcy*, 27 Jan. 1680/1. He *m.* in or before 1687, Elizabeth, da. of Rowland JOHNSON, of Gray's Inn, Midx. He *d.* 17 and was *bur.* 21 May 1701, aged 44, at Great Dunmow. Will dat. 2 Oct. 1690 to 23 Dec. 1696, pr. 7 July 1701. His widow *d.* 30 May, and was *bur.* 7 June 1727, aged 57, at Great Dunmow.

III. 1701. SIR SWINNERTON DYER, Baronet [1678], of Newton Hall aforesaid, and afterwards of Spains Hall in Finchingfield, Essex, 2d but 1st surv. s. and h.,(b) *bap.* 15 Feb. 1687/8, at St. Andrew's Holborn; admitted, as Fellow Commoner, to Benet's Coll., Cambridge; *suc. to the Baronetcy*, 17 May 1701. He *m.* firstly, 6 Sep. 1712, at St. Benet's, Paul's Wharf, London, Anne, 4th da. of Edward BELITHA, of Kingston-on-Thames. She *d.* s.p.m., and was *bur.* 28 Aug. 1714, at Great Dunmow. M.I. He *m.* secondly, 21 Dec. 1727, at St. Paul's, Covent Garden, Mary, sister and heir of John KEMPE, da. of another John KEMPE, both of Spains Hall aforesaid. She *d.* s.p. at Bath, and was *bur.* 30 Oct. 1730, at Finchingfield. Will dat. 10 March 1728, pr. 23 Oct. 1730. He *d.* s.p.m.,(c) at Kensington, 4 and was *bur.* 14 March 1735/6, at Finchingfield, aged 48. Will dat. 9 Oct. 1734, pr. 8 March 1735/6.

IV 1736. SIR JOHN SWINNERTON DYER, Baronet [1678], of Spains Hall aforesaid, br. and h. male; *b.* probably about 1692; *suc. to the Baronetcy*, 4 March 1735/6. He *d.* unm. 3 and was *bur.* 12 Feb. 1754, at Finchingfield. Will dat. April 1750, pr. 29 July 1758.

V. 1754. SIR THOMAS DYER, Baronet [1678], of Spains Hall aforesaid, br. and h. male, being 5th and yst. s. of the 2d Baronet; *bap.* 12 March 1694, at Great Dunmow; *suc. to the Baronetcy* 3 Feb. 1754, as also the estate of Spains Hall, which he sold in 1760, and resided at St. John's Square, Westm. He *m.*, 25 Sep. 1735, at St. Margaret's, Westm. (settlmt. 28), Elizabeth, da. of Col. [—] JONES. Her will dat. 13 Jan. 1777, pr. the same year. He *d.* 1780, aged about 86. His will dat. 13 Jan. 1777, pr. 9 Oct. 1780.

VI. 1780. SIR JOHN SWINNERTON DYER, Baronet [1678,] 1st s. and h.; *bap.* 20 Nov. 1738, at Finchingfield; was a Col. in the army and Capt. of a Company of Guards; sometime Groom of the Bedchamber to George, Prince of Wales, afterwards George III; *suc. to the Baronetcy* in 1780. He *m.* Susanna, da. of [—] VICARY, of Windsor, Berks. She is said to have been *bur.* at St. Margaret's, Westm., 17 April 1773. He *d.*, having "shot himself in a fit of insanity," 21 and was *bur.* 28 March 1801, at St. Mary's, Aldermanbury, aged 62. Will dat. 22 Sep. 1790, pr. 21 July 1801.

VII. 1801. SIR THOMAS RICHARD SWINNERTON DYER, Baronet [1678], only s. and h.; *b.* probably about 1770; served in the Expedition to Egypt in 1801; being sometime Lieut. Col. in the Foot Guards, and finally Lieut. Gen. both in the English and Spanish service; *suc. to the Baronetcy*, 21 March 1801. He *m.* 14 April 1814, at North Stoneham, Hants, Elizabeth, da. and h. of James STANDERWYKE, of Ovington House, in that county. He *d.* s.p. 12 April 1838, in Clarges street, Midx., and was *bur.* at Ovington. Will dat. 14 June 1833, pr. 10 May 1838. His widow *m.*, 30 May 1839, at Ovington, Frederic, BARON VON ZANDT, of the Kingdom of Bavaria, Chamberlain to the King thereof.

(a) The eldest son, Swinnerton Dyer, aged 13 at the Her. Visit. of Midx., 1664, was admitted to Lincoln's Inn, 13 April 1670, but *d.* v.p. and unm., being *bur.* 29 Jan. 1676/7 at St. Mary's Aldermanbury, London.

(b) The eldest son, another "Swinnerton Dyer," *b.* in High Holborn, and *bap.* 13 Jan. 1686/7, at St. Andrew's, Holborn, *d.* in infancy, and was *bur.* 26 April 1687, at St. Mary's, Aldermanbury.

(c) Anne, his only da. and h., by 1st wife, *m.* Paul Whitehead, of Twickenham, Midx., and *d.* s.p. 1768, being *bur.* at Teddington. M.I.

VIII. 1838. SIR THOMAS SWINNERTON DYER, Baronet [1678], of Swinnerton Lodge, in Tunstal, Devon, cousin and h. male, being 2d but 1st surv. s. of Thomas DYER, of the Treasury Office, by his 1st wife Mary, da. of Richard SMITH, of London, Merchant, which Thomas, who *d.* 9 Aug. 1800, aged 56, was 2d son of the 5th Baronet. He was *b.* 6 Oct. and *bap.* 5 Nov. 1770, at St. Margaret's, Westm.; was a Commander in the Royal Navy in 1810, and *suc. to the Baronetcy*, 12 April 1838. He *m.* 11 April 1814 (Lic. Fac.), Mary, da. of John DAVIS. He *d.* s.p. legit.,(a) 27 Nov. 1854, at Dartmouth, and was *bur.* there, aged 84. Will dat. 9 Sep. 1853, pr. 12 June 1854. His widow *d.* 1855.

IX. 1854. SIR THOMAS DYER, Baronet [1678], of Westcroft lodge, in Chobham, Surrey, nephew and h., being only s. and h. of Sir John DYER, K.C.B., Lieut. Col. R.A., by Jane, da. of Simon HALLIDAY, of Westcombe park, Kent, which John, who *d.* 2 July 1816, aged 44, was br. of the whole blood to the late Baronet. He was *b.* 10 Dec. 1799, and *bap.* 9 Jan, 1800, at Cottingham, co. York; ed. at Woolwich Academy; entered the Royal Artillery, 1825, but retired as Captain in 1832; *suc. to the Baronetcy*, 27 Nov. 1854. He *m.* 7 Feb. 1832, at Woolwich, Mary Anne, da. of John Albeck CLEMENT, of Steppe, Hants, Col. R.A. He *d.* 31 Oct. 1878, at 14 Redcliffe square, South Kensington, aged nearly 79. His widow *d.* there 9 Feb. 1880, aged 77.

X. 1878. SIR SWINNERTON HALLIDAY DYER, Baronet [1678], of Westcroft lodge aforesaid, 1st s. and h., *b.* there 4 June 1833; entered the army, 1851; Capt. 17th Foot, 1855, and subsequently in the 8th Foot; served at the capture of Sebastopol; had the Crimean medal and clasp, and the Turkish Order of the Medjidie; *suc. to the Baronetcy*, 31 Oct. 1878. He *m.* 29 July 1858, Helen Maria, 1st da. of the Rev. Robert CROKER, of Athlacca, by Margaret, da. of Standish O'GRADY, of the Grange, co. Limerick. He *d.* 16 March 1882, aged 48, at Westcroft lodge. His widow living 1904.

XI. 1882. SIR THOMAS SWINNERTON DYER, Baronet [1678], of Westcroft lodge aforesaid, only s. and h., *b.* 3 Oct. 1859; ed. at Rugby, and at Magdalen Coll., Cambridge; *suc. to the Baronetcy*, 16 March 1882. He *m.* 21 Jan. 1886, at St. Stephen's, South Kensington, Dona Edith, 3d da. of Sir Charles Roderic MCGRIGOR, 2d Baronet [1831], by Elizabeth Anne, da. of Major-Gen. Sir Robert NICKLE, K.B.

CHILD, *or* CHILDE:

cr. 16 July 1678;

afterwards, 1718-84, VISCOUNTS CASTLEMAINE [I.],

and subsequently, 1732-84, EARLS TYLNEY [I];

ex. 17 Sep. 1784.

I. 1678. "JOSIAS CHILDE, of Wanstead, co. Essex, Esq," 2d s. of Richard CHILD, of London, merchant, by Elizabeth, da. of (—) ROYCROFT, of Weston's Wick, Salop, was *b.* about 1630; acquired a considerable fortune as a London merchant; was sometime Gov. of the East India Company; was M.P. for Petersfield, 1659 till void, 22 March 1659, for Dartmouth, Feb. 1673 to 1679, and for Ludlow, 1685-87; purchased in 1673 the estate of Wanstead,(b) and was *cr. a Baronet*, as above, 16 July 1678; Sheriff of Essex,

(a) His illegitimate son, Richard Thomas Swinnerton Dyer, a Clerk in the Exchequer and Audit Department, appears for some years to have styled himself a Baronet.

(b) He is said to have incurred "a prodigious cost in planting walnut trees and making fish ponds many miles in circuit."

1688-89. He *m.* firstly, 26 Dec. 1654, at Portsmouth, Hannah, da. of Edward BOATE, master shipwright, of that town, by his 1st wife. She, by whom he had three children,(a) was *bur.* there, 29 July 1662. He *m.* secondly (Lic. Fac., 14 June 1663, he of St. Botolph's, Billingsgate, aged 32, widower, and she of St. Margaret's, Lothbury, aged 20, widow), Mary, widow of Thomas STONE, of London, merchant, da. of William ATWOOD, of Hackney, Midx. He *m.* thirdly (Lic. Fac. 8 Aug. 1676), Emma, widow of Francis WILLOUGHBY, of Middleton, co. Warwick, 2d da. and coheir of Henry BARNARD, or BERNARD, of Stoke, and Bridgnorth, Salop, and of Aconbury, co. Hereford, Turkey-merchant, of London. He *d.* 22 June 1699, aged 69, and was *bur.* at Wanstead. M.I. Will dat. 22 Feb. 1696, pr. 6 July 1699. His widow *d.* 16 Oct. 1725, at a great age.

II. 1699. SIR JOSIAH CHILD, Baronet [1678], of Wanstead aforesaid, 3d but 1st surv. s. and h., being 1st s. by the 2d wife, *b.* about 1668; *suc. to the Baronetcy*, 22 June 1699; was M.P. for Wareham, 1702 till death in 1704. He *m.*, at Hackney, Midx., 10 March 1690/1 (Lic. Fac. 27 Feb., he about 22 and she about 19), Elizabeth, da. of Sir Thomas COOKE, of Hackney. He *d.* s.p. 20 Jan. and was *bur.* 4 Feb. 1703/4, at Hackney. Will pr. Feb. 1704. His widow is supposed to have *m.* "Jo. CHADWICK, Esq.," who (so described) was *bur.* 8 Dec. 1713, at Hackney. She, as "Dame Elizabeth CHILD, widow," was *bur.* there 26 Jan. 1740/1.

III. 1704. SIR RICHARD CHILD, Baronet [1678], of Wanstead aforesaid, br. of the half blood and h. male, being s. of the 1st Baronet by his 3d wife, was *bap.* 5 Feb. 1679/80, at Wanstead, and *suc. to the Baronetcy*, 20 Jan. 1703/4; was M.P. for Malden, 1708-10; for Essex, 1710-22 and 1727-34. He, about 1715, built the magnificent structure (260 feet in length) of Wanstead House. He *m.* at Wanstead, 22 April 1703 (Lic. London, same date, both aged 21), Dorothy, only surv. da. and h. of John GLYNNE, of Henley Park, Surrey, and of Bicester, Oxon, by Dorothy, da. of Francis TYLNEY, of Rotherwick, Hants. She was living when he was *cr.*, 24 April 1718, VISCOUNT CASTLEMAINE, *cr.*, Kerry [I.], being afterwards *cr.*, 11 June 1731, EARL TYLNEY OF CASTLEMAINE, co. Kerry [I.]. In these peerages this *Baronetcy* then *merged* and so continued till all of them became *extinct*, on the death, 17 Sep. 1784, of the 2d Earl and Viscount, and 4th Baronet, who had, by Act of Parl. 1734, taken the name of TYLNEY instead of CHILD.

SKIPWITH:

cr. 27 July 1678;

ex. 4 June 1756.

I. 1678. "SIR THOMAS SKIPWITH, of Metheringham, co. Lincoln, Knt.," 2d s.(b) of Edward SKIPWITH, of Gosberton and Grantham, in that county, by Elizabeth (*m.* 18 May 1617), da. of Sir John HATCHER, of Careby, co. Lincoln, was *b.* probably about 1620; admitted to Gray's Inn, 30 April 1638; Barrister and (in 1670) Reader of that Society; M.P. for Grantham, 1659 and 1660; *Knighted*, 29 May 1673; Serjeant at Law, 21 April 1675, and was *cr. a Baronet*, as above, 27 July 1678. He *m.* firstly, probably about 1650, Elizabeth, da. and h. of Ralph LATHAM, of Upminster, Essex. He *m.* secondly, 30 April 1673, at Westm. Abbey (Lic. Fac. same date), Elizabeth, widow of Edward MADDISON, of Caistor, co. Lincoln (*bur.* there 30 March 1672), da. of Sir John REA, of Richmond, Surrey, and of London,

(a) Elizabeth, the only one of these three children that survived infancy, *m.* John Howland, and was mother of Elizabeth, Duchess of Bedford.

(b) His elder br., William Skipwith, *m.* Dorothy, da. of Anthony Hawkridge, which Dorothy was living, as his widow, Aug. 1688.

Scrivener, by his 1st wife (—), da. of Lancelot BURTON. He *d.* at his house in Lincoln's Inn Fields, 2 and was carried thence, 18 June 1694, for burial at Upminster. Will dat. Aug. 1688, pr. 7 June 1694. His widow, by whom he had no issue, was *bur.* 19 March 1697/8, at Caistor aforesaid. Will dat. 8, and pr. 10 March 1697/8.

II. 1694. SIR THOMAS SKIPWITH, Baronet [1678], of Metheringham aforesaid, only s. and h., by 1st wife; *b.* probably about 1652; admitted to Gray's Inn, 5 Aug. 1670; *suc. to the Baronetcy,* 2 June 1694; was M.P. for Malmesbury, Dec. 1696 to 1698. He *m.* Margaret, widow of William BROWNLOW, of Snarford, co. Lincoln (who *d.* in or before 1675), da. and coheir of George (BRYDGES), 6th BARON CHANDOS OF SUDELEY, by his 1st wife, Susan, da. of Henry (MONTAGU), 1st EARL OF MANCHESTER. He *d.* at Bath, 15 June 1710, and was *bur.* at Upminster. Will pr. 8 July 1710. His widow *d.* 1 and was *bur.* 8 Jan. 1731/2 in Westm. Abbey, aged 94.

III. 1710, to 1756. SIR GEORGE BRYDGES SKIPWITH, Baronet [1678], of Metheringham aforesaid, only s. and h., *b.* 7 and *bap.* 14 Nov. 1686, at St. Giles' in the Fields; *suc. to the Baronetcy,* 15 June 1710. He *m.* before 1741,(a) Martha, da. and h. of Robert PITT, M.D. She *d.* 5 Aug. 1741. He *d.* s.p. 4 June 1756, when the *Baronetcy* became *extinct.* Will dat. 29 June 1729 to 22 April 1738, pr. 18 Jan. 1759.

HAWKESWORTH:

cr. 6 Dec. 1678;

ex. 17 March 1735.

I. 1678. "WALTER HAWKESWORTH, of Hawkesworth, co. York, Esq.," s. and h. of Walter HAWKESWORTH, of the same, by Alice (*m.* 20 Oct. 1652), da. of Sir William BROWNLOW, 1st Baronet [1641], was *b.* 22 Nov. 1660; aged 5 years at the Heralds' Visit. of Yorkshire, in April 1666; suc. his father (who *d.* aged 52) in Dec. 1677, and was *cr. a Baronet,* as above, 6 Dec. 1678. He *m.*, probably about 1690, Anne, da. of Sir Robert MARKHAM, 1st Baronet [1642], of Sedgbrook, by Rebecca, da. of Sir Edward HUSSEY, 1st Baronet [1611], of Honington. He *d.* 21 Feb. 1683, and was *bur.* at Guiseley, co. York. M.I. Will dat. 2 Feb. 1683. His widow was *bur.* 27 May 1716, at St. Mary's, Nottingham.

II. 1683, to 1735. SIR WALTER HAWKESWORTH, Baronet [1678], of Hawkesworth aforesaid, only s. and h., *suc. to the Baronetcy* in Feb. 1683. He *m.* in or before 1697, Judith, 1st da. and coheir of John AYSCOUGH, of Osgodby, co. Lincoln, s. and h. of Sir William AYSCOUGH, of the same. He *d.* s.p.m.s.(b) at York, 17 and was *bur.* 20 March 1735, at St. Helen's, in that city, when the *Baronetcy* became *extinct.* His widow was *bur.* there, 2 Oct. 1724.

(a) Wotton's *Baronetage,* 1741.

(b) Of his two surv. daughters and coheirs, Frances, *bap.* 11 Oct. 1702, at Otley, co. York, *m.* there, 7 March 1721/2, Thomas Ramsden, of Crowstone, by whom she had a son, Walter Ramsden, who took the name of Hawkesworth on inheriting the estates of his maternal grandfather. His s. and h., however, took the name of Fawkes, on inheriting the estates of that family at Fernley, co. York.

IV

KENRICK:(a)

cr. 29 March 1679;

ex. 1699.

I. 1679. "WILLIAM KENRICK, of Whitley [near Reading], co. Berkshire, Esq.," 1st s. and h. of Thomas KENRICK,(b) of Reading, by Martha, da. of Sir Henry DAVY, was *bap.* 26 Dec. 1631, at St. Giles', Reading;(c) suc. his father in Oct. 1664; entered his pedigree in the Heralds' Visit. of Berks, 1664, and was *cr. a Baronet,* as above, 29 March 1679. He was Sheriff of Berks, 1680-81. He *m.* in or before 1662, Grace, da. and h. of Peter KIBLEWHITE, of Swindon, Wilts. She *d.* before Aug. 1684. He was *bur.* 8 Sep. 1684, at St. Mary's, Reading. Will dat. 28 Aug. 1684, pr. 21 May 1685.

II. 1684, to 1699. SIR WILLIAM KENRICK, Baronet [1679], of Whitley aforesaid, 1st s. and h., *b.* 1665, at Swindon; matric. at Oxford (Wadham Coll.), 22 July 1684, aged 19; *suc. to the Baronetcy* in Sep. 1684. He *m.* in or before 1685,(d) Mary, da. of (—) HOUSE, of Whitley. He *d.* s.p.m.s.(e) and was *bur.* at St. Mary's aforesaid in [the month not being stated] 1699, when the *Baronetcy* became *extinct.* Will dat. 29 Sep. 1696, pr. 21 Oct. 1699, by his widow. Her will pr. Jan. 1705/6.

SNOW:

cr. 25 June 1679;

ex. 16 Nov. 1702.

I. 1679, to 1702. "JEREMY SNOW, of Salisbury [*otherwise* the manor of Shenley Hall, in Shenley], co. Hertford, Esq.," s. of Robert SNOW, of Allhallows, Lombard Street, London, Goldsmith (*d.* Aug. 1638), by Frances, da. of (—) LAMBORN, *or* SAMBORN, of Wykin, co. Northampton, purchased the manor of Shenley Hall in 1669, and was *cr. a Baronet,* as above, 25 June 1679. He *m.* Rebecca, da. of Thomas WARD, of London, Merchant. He *d.* s.p. 16 Nov. 1702, in his 74th year, and was *bur.* at Shenley, when the *Baronetcy* became *extinct.*(f) M.I. Will pr. Nov. 1702. His widow *d.* 26 Oct. 1703, and was *bur.* there. M.I. Will pr. 1703.

(a) See *Her. & Gen.*, vol. vii, pp. 550-552.

(b) This Thomas was only s. of William Kenrick, *or* Kendrick, Mayor of Reading, 1632, br. of John Kendrick, citizen and draper of London, a great benefactor to the towns of Reading and Newbury, both being sons of Thomas Kendrick, Mayor of Reading, 1580.

(c) "William Kenrick, Esq.," was M.P. for Kent, 1653, and for Hythe, 1659, but probably was not the same person as the future Baronet.

(d) A son Charles, *bap.* 1685, at St. Mary's, was *bur.* 3 May 1686, at St. Giles', Reading.

(e) Of his three daughters (Frances, Mary and Grace, all living in Sep. 1696), Mary was *bur.* 4 Jan. 1712/3, at St. Mary's, Reading. See Chambers' *Book of Days*, i., 439, as to the curious legend about one of them.

(f) The Shenley estate devolved on his nephew, John Snell (son of his sister Susanna, by George Snell), who was *bur.* at Shenley, 20 Dec. 1724, leaving issue.

MAROW, *or* MARROW:

cr. 16 July 1679;

ex. between 1683 and 1699.

I. 1679, to 1690? "SIR SAMUEL MARROW [*or* MAROW], of Berkswell, co. Warwick, Knt," s. and h. of Thomas MAROW, of the same (*d.* in or before 1669), by Anne, da. of Sir Thomas GRANTHAM, of Goltho', co. Lincoln, was *b.* about 1652; admitted to Gray's Inn, 5 May 1669, and was *cr. a Baronet,* as above, 16 July 1679, being subsequently *Knighted* 29 Oct. 1669. He *m.* (Lic. Vic. Gen., 13 Oct. 1669, both aged about 17) Mary, da. of Sir Arthur CAYLEY, of Newland, co. Warwick. He was living 1683, aged about 30, but *d.* s.p.m. in or before 1699, when the *Baronetcy* became *extinct.* His widow *m.* in or before that year,(a) Francis FISHER, of Berkswell aforesaid, living Dec. 1699. She *d.* a widow 19 and was *bur.* 22 Oct. 1714, at St. James', Westm., in her 63d year.(b) M.I. Will pr. Oct. 1714.

BRADSHAIGH:

cr. 17 Nov. 1679;

ex. in or shortly before 1779.

I. 1679. "SIR ROGER BRADSHAIGH, of Haigh [in Wigan], co. Lancaster, Knt.," 3d but 1st surv. s. and h. of James BRADSHAIGH ("Scholar and Poet," who *d.* v.p. 1631), by Anne, da. of Sir William NORRIS, K.B., of Speke in that county, was *b.* 1627; suc. his grandfather, Roger BRADSHAIGH, in the estate of Haigh 16 May 1641; was the first of his family who conformed to the established religion; fought for the King in the Civil Wars, and was sometime a prisoner in Chester Castle; was *Knighted,* 18 June 1660; entered his pedigree at the Heralds' Visit. of Lancashire in 1664, being then aged 36; was admitted to Gray's Inn, 2 Feb. 1672/3, and was *cr. a Baronet,* as above, 17 Nov. 1679. He was M.P. for Lancashire, 1660, and for Wigan, 1661-79. He *m.*, in or before 1650, Elizabeth, da. of William PENNINGTON, of Muncaster, Cumberland, by Catherine, da. of Richard SHERBORNE, of Stonyhurst, co Lancaster. He *d.* at Chester, 31 March and was *bur.* 4 April 1684, at Wigan. M.I. Admon., 1684. His widow *d.* April 1695.

II. 1684. SIR ROGER BRADSHAIGH, Baronet [1679], of Haigh aforesaid, 1st s. and h., *b.* about 1649, being aged 15 in 1664; was *Knighted* v.p., 8 March 1678/9; was Sheriff of Lancashire, 1678-79; M.P. for Wigan, 1679, and for Lancashire, 1685-87, having *suc. to the Baronetcy,* 31 March 1684. He *m.* 7 April 1673 (Lic. Fac., same date, he 22 and she 18), Mary, da. and coheir of Henry MURRAY, Groom of the Bedchamber, by Anne, *suo jure* VISCOUNTESS BAYNING, both then deceased. He *d.* 17 June 1687. Will pr. at Chester, 1687. His widow *d.* 1 Dec. 1713.

III. 1687. SIR ROGER BRADSHAIGH, Baronet [1679], of Haigh aforesaid, 1st s. and h., *b.* probably about 1675; *suc. to the Baronetcy,* 17 June 1687; was (when under age) M.P. for Wigan, 1695, and continued to be so (fourteen Parls.) for forty-six years till death in 1747; was Col. of a Regt. of Foot, *temp.* Queen Anne. He *m.* Rachel, 2d da. of Sir John GUISE, 2d Baronet [1661], of Elmore, co. Gloucester, by Elizabeth, da. of John Grubham HOWE. She *d.* 12 Sep. 1743. He *d.* 25 Feb. 1746/7. Will pr. 1747.

(a) On 13 Dec. 1699, she, being then the wife of Francis Fisher, gave consent (Lic. Fac.) to the marriage of her da., Mary Marow (about 22, spinster), to John Knightley, *otherwise* Wightwick, of Offchurch, co. Warwick.

(b) Her character and good works are set forth in Wilford's *Memorials.*

IV. 1747, to 1779? SIR ROGER BRADSHAIGH, Baronet [1679], of Haigh aforesaid, 1st s. and h., *b.* probably about 1710; *suc. to the Baronetcy,* 25 Feb. 1746/7. He *m.*, April 1731, Dorothy, da. of William BELLINGHAM, of Lévens, Westmorland. He *d.* s.p., probably in or shortly before 1779, but certainly between 1764 (the date of his will) and 1779, when the *Baronetcy* became *extinct.*(a) Will pr. at Chester, 1779. His widow *d.* Aug. 1785. Will pr. March 1786.

STAPLETON:

cr. 20 Dec. 1679;

sometime, 1788—1831, LORD LE DESPENCER.

I. 1679. "WILLIAM STAPLETON, Esq, Governor of the Leeward Islands in America," yr. br. of Edmund STAPLETON, Governor of Nevis (who *d.* s.p.), and elder br. of Redmund STAPLETON, Governor of Montserrat, all being sons of Redmund STAPLETON, of Thurlesbegg, co. Tipperary, by Sarah, da. of (—) MCEGAN, accompanied Charles II when an exile in France, and was, after the Restoration, made Governor of the Leeward Islands and Capt. Gen. of the forces there. He *m.* in or before 1672, Anne, sister of Sir James and da. of Col. Randolph RUSSELL, both Governors of Nevis. He *d.* 3 Aug. 1686, at Paris. Will pr. 1686. His widow was living in London, 1702. She appears to have *m.* Col. Walter HAMILTON, Governor of Nevis (who *d.* 18 April 1722), and to have *d.* as his widow, 8 July 1722.(b) Will pr. 1722.

II. 1686. SIR JAMES STAPLETON, Baronet [1679], of London, 1st s. and h., *b.* 24 Sep. 1672, *suc. to the Baronetcy,* 3 Aug. 1686. He *d.* unm., aged 17, and was *bur.* 29 July 1690, at St. Nicholas', Liverpool.

III. 1690. SIR WILLIAM STAPLETON, Baronet [1679], br. and h., *b.* 14 Nov. 1674; ed. at Paris; *suc. to the Baronetcy* in July 1690. He *m.* 23 Jan. 1696/7, at Stepney, Midx., Frances, 3d da. of his maternal uncle, Sir James RUSSELL, Governor of Nevis, by Penelope, da. of Sir Timothy TYRRELL, of Oakley, in Shotover, Oxon. He *d.* abroad, presumably at Nevis, 6 or 7 Dec. 1699. Will as "of the island of Nevis," dat. 6 Dec. 1699, (the sanity of the testator being sworn to, 8 Dec. 1699 and 13 Jan. 1699-1700), pr. 14 March 1700/1. His widow *d.* 14 Jan. 1746. Will pr. 1746.

IV. 1699. SIR WILLIAM STAPLETON, Baronet [1679], 1st s. and h., *b.* 1698, presumably at Nevis; *suc. to the Baronetcy,* as an infant, in Dec. 1699; matric. at Oxford (Ch. Ch.), 17 April 1714, aged 15, and was *cr.* D.C.L., 11 July 1733. He, who was of Grey's Court, in Rotherfield Greys, Oxon, was M.P. for that county, 1727, till death in 1740. He *m.* 28 April 1724, at the Temple Church, London, Catherine, da. and h. of William PAUL, of Braywick, Berks, by Catherine, da. of Vere (FANE), 4th EARL OF WESTMORLAND

(a) The magnificent estate of Haigh, "reckoned one of the best situations in the north of England" [Wotton's *Baronetage,* 1741], passed to the family of Lindsay, Earls of Crawford [S.], through the marriage, in 1731, of Elizabeth, sister of the last and da. of the 3d Baronet, to John Edwin, whose da. and h., another Elizabeth, *m.* Charles Dalrymple, and was mother of a third Elizabeth, who *m.*, 1 June 1780, Alexander (Lindsay), 6th Earl of Balcarres [S.], to whose son, James, the 7th Earl, the ancient Earldom of Crawford [S.] was, in 1848, allowed.

(b) This Walter Hamilton is usually made to be the husband of her da. in law, Frances, widow of the 3d Baronet, but the following extracts of deaths given in Musgrave's *Obituary*, confirm the account in the text:—

"1722 April 18. HAMILTON, Brig. Gen. and Gov. of the Leeward Islands."

"1722 July 8. STAPYLTON, Lady, relict of (—) Hamilton, Gov. of the Leeward Islands, mother of Sir Thomas [*sic*] 5 Baronet."

"1746 Jan. 14. STAPLETON, Frances, Lady Dow., mother of Sir William S."

and LORD LE DESPENCER. He *d.* 12 Jan. 1739/40, at Bath, and was *bur.* at Rotherfield Grays, aged 41. Admon. 5 March 1739/40, 13 June 1754, and April 1817. His widow *m.* Rev. Matthew DUTTON (living 17 July 1753), and *d.* 28 June 1753, being *bur.* at Rotherfield Greys. Admon. 17 July 1753.

V. 1740. SIR THOMAS STAPLETON, Baronet [1679], of Grey's Court aforesaid, 2d but 1st surv. s. and h.,(a) *b.* 24 Feb. 1727; *suc. to the Baronetcy*, 12 Jan. 1739/40; matric. at Oxford (St. Mary Hall), 27 Feb. 1743/4, aged 17, and was *cr.* D.C.L. 3 July 1754. He was M.P. for Oxford, Nov. 1759 to 1768. He *m.* 27 Nov. 1765, at Lewknor, Oxon, Mary, da. of Henry FANE, of Wormsley, in that county (br. of Thomas, 8th EARL OF WESTMORLAND), by his 2d wife, Anne, da. of John WYNNE, D.D., Bishop of Bath and Wells. He *d.* 1 Jan. 1781. Will pr. Nov. 1781. His widow *d.* 26 Feb. 1835, in her 91st year. Will pr. May 1835.

VI. 1781. SIR THOMAS STAPLETON, Baronet [1679], of Grey's Court aforesaid, 1st s. and h., *b.* 10 Nov. 1766; *suc. to the Baronetcy*, 1 Jan. 1781. By the death s.p., 16 May 1788, of Rachel, widow of Sir Robert AUSTEN, 4th Baronet [1660], (which Lady, though only a coheir to the dignity, had styled herself BARONESS LE DESPENCER), he became, on the consequent termination of the abeyance (1781-88) of that ancient Barony, LORD LE DESPENCER in right of his grandmother, Catherine abovenamed, he being, after 1788, the sole representative of her grandfather, Vere (FANE), 4th EARL OF WESTMORLAND, LORD LE DESPENCER. He *m.* 29 July 1791, at St. Marylebone, Elizabeth, 2d da. of Samuel ELIOT, of Antigua, by Alice, da. of Col. William BYAM, of Byams in Antigua. He *d.* in London, 3 Oct. 1831, aged 64. Will pr. March 1832. His widow *d.* 3 Jan. 1848, at Bath, aged 90. Will pr. 1848. At his death the Barony devolved on his grand-daughter and *heir general* (the only da. and h. of the Hon. Thomas STAPLETON, his eldest son, who had *d.* v.p. and s.p.m., 1 June 1829, aged 37), but the Baronetcy descended to his *heir male*, as below.

VII. 1831. HON. SIR FRANCIS JARVIS STAPLETON, Baronet [1679], of Grey's Court aforesaid, 4th and yst. but only surv. s. and h. male, *b.* Aug. 1807, in Hanover square; ed. at Trin. Coll., Cambridge; M.A., 1831; in Holy Orders; Rector of Mereworth, 1827-74, and Vicar of Tudeley, 1832-74, both in co. Kent, having *suc. to the Baronetcy*, 3 Oct. 1831. He *m.*, 17 May 1830, at Florence, Margaret, 1st da. of Lieut. Gen. Sir George AIREY, K.C.H., by Catharine, da. of Richard TALBOT, of Malahide Castle, co. Dublin, and Margaret, *suo jure* BARONESS TALBOT DE MALAHIDE [I.]. He *d.* 11 Feb. 1874, at Mereworth Rectory, in his 67th year. His widow *d.* 7 Feb. 1880, at 51 Onslow Gardens, Midx.

VIII. 1874. SIR FRANCIS GEORGE STAPLETON, Baronet [1679], of Grey's Court aforesaid, 1st s. and h., *b.* 19 March 1831, at Clifton, near Bristol; entered the Army, 1849, serving with the 43d Light Infantry in the Kaffir War, 1851-53; Capt. Grenadier Guards, 1855; *suc. to the Baronetcy*, 4 Feb. 1874; Sheriff of Oxon, 1886. He *m.*, 5 Sep. 1878, at Shortlands, Kent, Mary Catherine, 2d da. of Adam Steuart GLADSTONE, of Hazlewood, Hants, by Caroline, da. of Joseph Need WALKER, of Calderstone Hall, co. Lancaster. He *d.* s.p.m. of paralysis, at Grey's Court aforesaid, 30 Oct. 1899, in his 69th year. His widow living 1904.

IX. 1899. SIR MILES TALBOT STAPLETON, Baronet [1679], of Grey's Court aforesaid, nephew and h. male, being only s. and h. of Richard Talbot Plantagenet STAPLETON, Lieut. Col. 19th Hussars, by Emma, da. of the Rev. John Duncombe SHAFTO, which Richard (who *d.* 28 April 1899, aged 65) was next br. of the late Baronet. He was *b.* 26 May 1893, and *suc. to the Baronetcy*, 30 Oct. 1899.

(a) Will Stapleton, Lieut. R.N., the eldest son, *d.* unm. and v.p., being killed by the bursting of a cannon at Port Royal, in Jamaica.

BLOUNT:

cr. 27 Jan. 1679/80;

ex. 8 Oct. 1757.

I. 1680. "THOMAS POPE BLOUNT, of Tittenhanger [in the parish of Ridge], co. Hertford, Esq.," 1st s. and h. ap. of Sir Henry BLOUNT, of the same (a celebrated traveller, who *d.* 9 Oct. 1682, in his 80th year), by Hester, relict of Sir William MAINWARING, 1st da. and h. of Christopher WASE, of Upper Holloway, in Islington, Midx., was *b.* 12 Sep. 1649, at Upper Holloway; admitted to Lincoln's Inn, 1 Dec. 1668; suc. his mother in the estate of Tittenhanger (which had been settled on her) in Nov. 1678, and was *cr. a Baronet*, as above, 27 Jan. 1679/80. He suc. his father in the rest of the family estates, 9 Oct. 1682; was M.P. for St. Albans (three Parls.), 1679-81; and for Herts (three Parls.), 1689, till his death in 1697; a Commissr. of Public Accounts, 1694-97. He *m.* 22 July 1669, at St. Olave's, Hart street, London (Lic. Vic. Gen. 19), Jane (then "about 17"), da. of Sir Henry CÆSAR, *otherwise* ADELMARE, of Bennington place, Herts, by Elizabeth, da. and h. of Robert ANGELL, of London, Merchant. He *d.* at Tittenhanger, 30 June, and was *bur.* 8 July 1697, at Ridge.(a) Will pr. 1697. His widow, who was *b.* 2 Oct. 1650, *d.* at Kensington gravel pits, Midx., 14 and was *bur.* 17 July 1726, at Ridge, aged 76.

II. 1697. SIR THOMAS POPE BLOUNT, Baronet [1680], of Tittenhanger aforesaid and of Twickenham, Midx., 1st s. and h., *b.* 19 May 1670 in the Strand, St. Mary le Savoy, Midx.; *suc. to the Baronetcy*, 30 June 1697. He *m.* in King street chapel [*Qy.* Westm.], 8 Dec. 1695(b) (Lic. Fac. same date, he 24 and she 18), Katherine, 2d but 1st surv. da. of James BUTLER, of Amberley Castle and Thakeham, Sussex, by Grace, da. of Richard CALDECOT. He *d.* at Twickenham 17 and was *bur.* 22 Oct. 1731, at Ridge, aged 61. Will dat. 19 Nov. 1729, pr. 20 Oct. 1731. His widow, who was *bap.* 8 April 1676, at Amberley, *d.* 20 Dec. 1752, and was *bur.* at Ridge in her 77th year. Will pr. 1753.

III. 1731, to 1757. SIR HARRY POPE BLOUNT, Baronet [1680], of Tittenhanger and Twickenham aforesaid, 2d but 1st surv. s. and h.,(c) *b.* 13 Sep. 1702, "in the Terrace, in St. James' street," Midx.; matric. at Oxford (Trin. Coll.), 18 July 1720, aged 18; *suc. to the Baronetcy*, 17 Oct. 1731; was a "diligent and faithful antiquary."(d) He *m.* 19 Sep. 1728, at St. Peter's Cornhill, London, Anne (£10,000 fortune) yst. da. and coheir of Charles CORNWALLIS, of Medlow, co. Huntingdon. He *d.* s.p., 8 October 1757, and was *bur.* at Ridge, aged 55, when the *Baronetcy* became *extinct.*(e) Will pr. 1758. His widow *d.* 29 Sep. 1761, at Wild Hill, in Bishop's Hatfield, Herts, and was *bur.* at Ridge, aged 57. Admon. 14 Oct. 1761 to a creditor; Margaret CORNWALLIS, spinster, sister and only next of kin, having renounced.

(a) He was author of a work called "*De re Poetica*" and of various treatises.

(b) 8 *Nov.* 1695, according to the pedigree in Clutterbuck's *Hertfordshire* (vol. i, p. 212). The marriage is, apparently, not recorded in the parish register of St. James' or St. Margaret's, Westm., St. Martin's in the Fields, or St. Anne's, Soho.

(c) The 1st son, Thomas Pope Blount, was *b.* in Park place, St. James', Westm., 19 June 1700, and *d.* 30 Jan., being *bur.*, 2 Feb. 1701/2, at Ridge. Neither of the baptisms of these two brothers is, apparently, recorded in the parish register of St. James', Westm.

(d) Warton's *Life of Sir Thomas Pope.*

(e) Katharine, his sister, *b.* 9 April 1704, at Twickenham (the only child of his parents that had issue), *m.* 21 Feb. 1730/1, at St. Anne's, Soho, William Freeman, of Aspeden, Herts, and had an only da. and h., Katharine, who *m.* 19 May 1755, the Hon. Charles Yorke, Lord Chancellor, and was mother of Philip, 3d Earl of Hardwicke. She, who *d.* 10 July 1759, inherited the Tittenhanger estate, and transmitted it to her posterity.

WALKER:

cr. 28 Jan. 1679/80;

ex. before 1703.

I. 1680. "SIR GEORGE WALKER, of Bushey, co. Hertford, Knt.," s. and h. of Sir Walter WALKER, of Barton, co. Stafford, Doctor of Laws, Judge Advocate to the Queen Consort Catherine (*d.* 1674), by Mary, da. of (—) LYNN, of Southwick, co. Northampton, was *b.* about 1643; *Knighted*, 22 Nov. 1676, at Whitehall, and was *cr. a Baronet*, as above, 28 Jan. 1679/80. He *m.* 13 June 1677 (Lic. Vicar Gen. 7, he 34 and she 19), Susanna, da. and coheir of John BYNE, of Rowdell in Washington, co. Sussex, by Mary, or Susan, da. of Goldsmith HUDSON. She *d.* before him. He, having wasted his fortune and alienated his estate,"(a) *d.* in the King's Bench Prison, St. George's, Southwark, in 1690. Admon. (as "late of Bushey Hall, Herts") to a creditor, 29 Oct. 1690, and 12 March 1690/1.

II. 1690, to 1700? SIR WALTER WALKER, Baronet [1680], of Rowdell aforesaid, only s. and h., *b.* about 1682, being about 8 years old when he *suc. to the Baronetcy* in 1690. He, who inherited some property from his mother, *d.* a minor and unm. before 1703, when the *Baronetcy* became *extinct.*

SAS-VAN-BOSCH:

cr. 22 Oct. 1680;

ex. or dormant, probably about 1720.

I. 1680, to 1720? "GELEBRAND SAS-VAN-BOSCH, a servant to the Prince of Orange," a native of Holland, and Secretary to the Admiralty at Rotterdam, was *cr. a Baronet*, as above, 22 Oct. 1680, which dignity probably became *extinct* or *dormant* at his death.

ROBERTS:

cr. 2 Feb. 1680/1;

ex. 14 Dec. 1692.

I. 1681, to 1692. "JOHN ROBERTS, of Bowe [*i.e.* Bromley St. Leonard's, *otherwise* Bromley by Bow], co. Essex [*i.e.* Middlesex], Esq." (whose parentage is unknown), *b.* about 1620, was *cr. a Baronet*, as above, 2 Feb. 1680/1. He *m.* firstly, Mary, da. of William AMY, of Exeter, merchant. He *m.* secondly (Lic. Vic. Gen., 6 April 1691, he of Bromley, Midx., above 70, widower), Deborah BOVETT, then of St. Augustine's, London, about 34, widow, relict of (—) BOVETT, of London, silkman, da. of (—) POWELL, of Bristol, merchant. He *d.* s.p. 14 and was *bur.* 29 Dec. 1692, at Bromley aforesaid, when the *Baronetcy* became *extinct.* M.I. Will dat. 4 April 1692, pr. 22 March 1692/3 by the widow. She *m.* (Lic. Fac. 18 May 1694, being then of Bromley, Midx., aged 35, widow) Joseph TITY, then "of Lincoln's Inn, Esq., aged 40, widower."

(a) The estate of Bushey Hall appears to have been purchased, before 1685, by Sir John Marsham, 1st Baronet [1663], who died there 26 May 1685.

BECKWITH:

cr. 15 April 1681;

ex. apparently soon after 1811.

I. 1681. "ROGER BECKWITH, of Aldborough, co. York, Esq.," 2d but 1st surv. s. and h. of Arthur BECKWITH, of the samo (a Capt. in the Parl. army, who was slain in 1642, aged 27), by Mary, da. of Sir Marmaduke WYVILL, 2d Baronet [1611], was *cr. a Baronet*, as above, 15 April 1681. He *m.* firstly, Elizabeth, da. of Sir Christopher CLAPHAM, of Beamsley, co. York, by his 2d wife, Margaret, da. of Anthony OLDFIELD, of Spalding, co. Lincoln. She was *bur.* 1 Dec. 1673, at Masham, co. York. M.I. He *m.* secondly, at Ripon, Elizabeth, da. of Sir Edmund JENINGS, of Ripon. He *d.* (having shot himself) 6 Dec. 1700, and was *bur.* at Ripon. M.I. Will dat. 7 May 1690, pr. 28 Feb. 1700/1. His widow was *bur.* there. Her will dat. 6 Jan. 1701, pr. 1711.

II. 1700. SIR ROGER BECKWITH, Baronet [1681], of Aldborough aforesaid, 1st surv. s. and h.,(a) being 1st s. by 2d wife, *b.* 13 June 1682; *suc. to the Baronetcy*, 6 Dec. 1700; Sheriff of Yorkshire, 1706-07. He *m.* 10 Oct. 1705, Jane, da. and h. of Benjamin WADDINGTON, of Allerton Gledhow, co. York, by Mary, da. of John PARKER, of Extwisle, co. Lancaster. She, who was *b.* Dec. 1686, at Leeds, *d.* Dec. 1713, and was *bur.* at Masham. He *d.* s.p.m.s. (having shot himself), May 1743, aged 60. Will dat. 26 March 1730, pr. Jan. 1749.(b)

III. 1743. SIR MARMADUKE BECKWITH, Baronet [1681], only surv. br. and h. male, *b.* Jan. 1687; was a merchant in Virginia and Clerk of the Peace there; *suc. to the Baronetcy* in May 1743; was living, with male issue, Dec. 1748,(c) and apparently 1771.(d)

IV. 1780? to 1815? SIR JONATHAN BECKWITH, Baronet [1681], s. and h., is called "the present Baronet" both in 1803 and 1811,(e) on whose death, presumably, the *Baronetcy* became *extinct*, or, at all events, *dormant.*

PARKYNS:

cr. 18 May 1681;

sometime, 1806-50, BARON RANCLIFFE [I.].

I. 1681. "THOMAS PARKYNS, of Bunney, co. Nottingham, Esq.," s. of Isham PARKYNS, of the same, a Col. in the royal army during the Civil War, by Catharine, da. of Henry CAVE, of Barrow, co. Leicester (which Isham was s. and h. of Sir George PARKYNS, Capt. of Walmer Castle), was *bap.* 7 July 1639, at Bunny; admitted to Gray's Inn, 26 May 1655; matric. at Oxford (Wadham Coll.), 7 Nov. 1655; suc. his father, 21 June 1671; Sheriff of Notts, 1671-72, and was *cr. a Baronet*, as above, 18 May 1681. He *m.* in or before 1662, Anne, da. and h. of Thomas CRESSY, major in the army, of Fulsby in Kirkby on Bain, co.

(a) Arthur, his elder br. (only child by 1st wife), is said to have *d.* s.p. in 1700 (shortly before his father), beyond the seas.

(b) According to some accounts the *Baronetcy* became then *extinct*, and it is so dealt with in Clay's *Dugdale's Visitation of Yorkshire.* Joane, his sister, only da. and h. of the 2d Baronet, *m.* Beilby Thompson, of Escrick.

(c) The death in England, 27 Dec. 1748, of "Tarply, son of Sir Marmaduke Beckwith, of Virginia," is recorded in the *Gent. Mag.*

(d) According to Kimber's *Baronetage* [1771], he was the then Baronet, and had (besides the son mentioned in note "c" above) a son, "Marmaduke, now [1771] living in Virginia," who, possibly, was his successor.

(e) Betham's *Baronetage*, 1803, and Playfair's *Baronetage*, 1811.

Lincoln, by Elizabeth, da. of Sir Henry GLEMHAM and Anne, da. of Thomas (SACKVILLE), EARL OF DORSET. He was *bur.* 25 July 1684, at Bunny, aged 45. His widow *d.* 11 Jan. 1725/6, aged 86 or (as is sometimes said) 92 or 96, and was *bur.* there.

II. 1684. SIR THOMAS PARKYNS, Baronet [1681], of Bunny aforesaid, 2d but 1st surv. s. and h., *bap.* 10 Nov. 1662, at Bunny; ed. at Westm. School, and (2½ years, 1680-83) at Trinity Coll., Cambridge; admitted to Gray's Inn, 18 May 1682; *suc. to the Baronetcy* in July 1684; was Sheriff of Notts, March to Nov. 1689. He had a good knowledge of mathematics, hydraulics, architecture, grammar and, above all, of wrestling, on which he wrote a treatise.(a) He *m.* firstly, in or before 1686, Elizabeth, da. and h. of John SAMPSON, of Beason, co. Derby, s. and h. of John SAMPSON, of Hewby, co. York, Alderman of London. She, who by deed dat. 1704, agreed to live apart from her husband, *d.* Sep. 1727. Admon. 5 Jan. 1730/1, to her husband. He *m.* secondly, 7 Feb. 1727/8, at Bunny, Jane, 1st da. of George BARNET, Alderman of York. She *d.* 27 Aug. 1740, aged 33, and was *bur.* at Bunny. He *d.* 29 March 1741, and was *bur.* there. Will pr. 1741.

III. 1741. SIR THOMAS PARKYNS, Baronet [1681], of Bunny aforesaid, 3d but 1st surv. s. and h. male,(b) being 1st s. by 2d wife, *bap.* 8 Dec. 1728, at Bunny; *suc. to the Baronetcy*, 29 March 1741; Sheriff of Notts, 1755-56. He *m.* firstly, 7 April 1747, at the Chapel of Chelsea Hospital, Midx., his great niece(c) (of the half blood), Jane, da. and h. of Thomas PARKYNS, of Wimeswold, co. Leicester, by Elizabeth, da. of DANIEL WOODROFFE, of London, Thomas (who *d.* 1 June 1735, aged 25) was only surv. s. and h. of Sampson merchant, which PARKYNS, of Great Leake, Notts, 1st s. and h. ap. of the 2d Baronet, by his 1st wife, but who *d.* v.p., 17 April 1713, aged 27. She *d.* 24 Dec. 1760, and was *bur.* 2 Jan. 1761, at Bunny. He *m.* secondly, in 1765, Sarah, da. of Daniel SMITH, of Bunny aforesaid. She *d.* 22 March 1796, and was *bur.* there. He *m.* thirdly, 1 Sep. 1796, Jane, da. of Joseph BOULTBEE, of Leicester. He *d.* at Bunny park, 17 March 1806, aged 77. Will pr. 1806. His widow *d.* in or before 1841. Her will pr. Oct. 1841 and Oct. 1845.

IV. 1806. GEORGE AUGUSTUS HENRY ANNE (PARKYNS), 2d BARON RANCLIFFE [I.], and 4th Baronet [1681], grandson and h., being only s. and h. of Thomas Boothby (PARKYNS), BARON RANCLIFFE [I.] (so *cr.* 3 Oct. 1795), by Elizabeth Anne, da. of Sir William JAMES, 1st Baronet [1778], which Thomas, was s. and h. ap. of the 3d Baronet, but *d.* v.p. 17 Nov. 1800, aged 45. He was *b.* 10 June 1785, in Arlington street, St. James', Westm. (George Augustus, Prince of Wales, afterwards George IV, being one of his sponsors); *suc. to the peerage* [I.] on the death of his father, 17 Nov. 1800, and *suc. to the Baronetcy*, and an unencumbered property of £21,000 a year,(d) on the death of his grandfather, 17 March 1806; sometime an officer 10th Hussars; Equerry to (his godfather) the Prince of Wales; M.P. for Minehead, 1806-07, and for Nottingham after ten days' contest), 1812-20, and 1826-30. He *m.* 15 Oct. 1807 (spec.lic.), at Castle Forbes, co. Longford, Elizabeth Mary Theresa, 1st da. of George (FORBES), 6th EARL OF GRANARD [I.], by Selina Frances, da. of John (RAWDON), 1st EARL OF

(a) He is spoken of as "*Luctator.*" On his monument is a statue of him "wrestling" with Time.

(b) Of his two elder brothers of the half blood, Thomas was admitted to Gray's Inn, 4 July 1704, and *d.* unm., Sep. 1706, aged 19. Sampson Parkyns, the eldest son, was admitted to the Middle Temple, 18 Sep. 1702, and to Gray's Inn, 17 Nov. 1704; *m.* Alice Middlemore, and *d.* v.p., 17 April 1713, aged 27, leaving issue Thomas Parkyns, sometime [1713-25] heir ap. to the Baronetcy, who *m.*, but *d.* s.p.m. 1 June 1735 aged 25, in the lifetime of his grandfather, the 2d Baronet, leaving Jane, his da. and h., who *m.*, in 1747, her great-uncle the 3d Baronet.

(c) The marriage with a *great* niece (unlike that with a niece) is not within the degrees that are canonically prohibited.

(d) *Gent. Mag.*, 1807.

MOIRA [I.] From her he was separated in or soon after 1815.(a) He *d.* s.p. legit.(b) at Bunny park, 6 Nov. 1850, aged 65, when the *peerage* became *extinct*. Will pr. June 1851.(c) His widow, who was *b.* 3 Dec. 1786, *d.* at Paris, Jan. 1852, aged 65. Admon. May 1852.

V. 1850. SIR THOMAS GEORGE AUGUSTUS PARKYNS, Baronet [1681], of Ruddington Manor, Notts, cousin and h. male, being 1st s. and h. of Thomas Boultbee PARKYNS, of Ruddington aforesaid, and of Newland co. Gloucester, by Charlotte Mary, da. of George SMITH, of Edwalton, Notts, and Foellart, co. Cardigan, which Thomas last named, who *d.* in Italy, 1833, aged 35, was yst. s. of the 3d Baronet, being only s. of the 3d wife. He was *b.* 26 June 1820, at Mondeville, near Caen in Normandy; matric. at Oxford (Univ. Coll.), 14 June 1838, aged 17; *suc. to the Baronetcy* (but not to the estates), 1 Nov. 1850. He *m.* in 1843. Annie, da. of W. JENNINGS. She *d.* 23 Dec. 1888. He *d.* 7 March 1895, aged 74.

VI. 1895. SIR THOMAS MANSFIELD FORBES PARKYNS, Baronet [1681], 1st s. and h.,(d) *b.* 30 April 1853, at Ruddington aforesaid; ed. at Eton; matric. at Oxford (Brasenose Coll.), 23 May 1872, aged 19; Barrister (Inner Temple), 1879; *suc. to the Baronetcy*, 7 March 1895. He *m.*, 14 July 1886, Beatrice, da. of Arthur Travers CRAWFORD, C.M.G., Bombay Civil Service.

BUNBURY:

cr. 29 June 1681.

I. 1681. "THOMAS BUNBURY, of Bunbury and [of] Stanney [in Stoke], co. Chester, Esq.," 1st s. and h. of Henry BUNBURY, of the same, by Ursula, da. of Sir John BAILEY, of Hoddesdon, Herts, suc. his father (who *d.* aged 66), 1 Feb. 1664, was Sheriff of Cheshire, 1673-74, and was *cr. a Baronet*, as above, 29 June 1681. He *m.* firstly, before 1657, Sarah, da. of John CHETWODE, of Okeley, co. Stafford, by Eleanor, da. and h. of William STEPHENTON, of Dothill, Salop. She *d.* 1671, aged 45, and was *bur.* at Thornton, co. Chester. He *m.* secondly, Mary, da. of Humphrey KELSALL, of Heathside, co. Chester. He *d.* 22 Aug. 1682, and was *bur.* at Stoke aforesaid. M.I.

II. 1682. SIR HENRY BUNBURY, Baronet [1681], of Bunbury and Stanney aforesaid, only surv. s. and h. by 1st wife; *b.* about 1657, being aged 6 years at the Heralds' Visit. of Cheshire, 1663; *suc. to the Baronetcy*, 22 Aug. 1682. He *m.* Mary, da. of Sir Kendrick EYTON, of Eyton, co. Denbigh, one of the Welsh Judges. She *d.* s.p.m., and was *bur.* at Thornton aforesaid. He *d.* 20 Dec. 1687, and was *bur.* there.

III 1687. SIR HENRY BUNBURY, Baronet [1681], of Bunbury and Stanney aforesaid, 1st surv. s. and h.; *suc. to the Baronetcy*, 20 Dec. 1687; was Sheriff of Cheshire, 1699-1700; M.P. for Chester (nine Parls.),

(a) He accused her of "improper intimacy with a French nobleman." [Obituary notice in *Gent. Mag.*, 1850].

(b) He devised the Bunny estate and all his property whatsoever to Mrs Burth, who had been his mistress for the last twenty years of his life. [*Gent. Mag.* 1850].

(c) Of his three sisters (1), Elizabeth Anne *m.*, 3 Dec. 1810, Sir Richard Levinge, 6th Baronet [I. 1704], and *d.* 28 Oct. 1853, leaving issue; (2), Henrietta Elizabeth, *m.* 13 July 1809, Sir William Rumbold, 3d Baronet [1779], and *d.* 8 Sep. 1830, leaving issue; (3), Maria Charlotte, *m.* firstly, in 1817, the Marquis de Choiseul, who *d.* in 1823; she *m.* secondly, 2 June 1824, Prince Augustus Jules Armand de Polignac, minister to Charles X, King of France.

(d) His yr. br., Mansfield Parkyns, the well known traveller in Abyssinia, *d.* s.p.m. 19 Jan. 1894, aged 70, and was *bur.* at Woodborough, Notts.

1700-27; a Commissioner of the Revenue [I.], 1711. He *m.*, in or before 1700, Susanna, sister of Sir Thomas HANMER, 4th Baronet [1620], da. of William HANMER, of Bettisfield, co. Flint, by Peregrine, da. of Sir Henry NORTH, 1st Baronet [1660], of Mildenhall, Suffolk. He *d.* 12, and was *bur.* 16 Feb. 1732/3, at Stoke aforesaid. M.I. His widow *d.* 23 Sep. 1744, and was *bur.* there. M.I.

IV. 1733. SIR CHARLES BUNBURY, Baronet [1681], of Bunbury and Stanney aforesaid, 3d but 1st surv. s. and h., *bap.* 9 Feb. 1707/8, at Chester Cathedral; M.P. for Chester, March 1733 till death in 1742; *suc. to the Baronetcy*, 12 Feb. 1732/3. He *d.* unm., after a long illness, 10, and was *bur.* 23 April 1742, at Stoke aforesaid, aged 34. M.I. Will pr. 1742.

V. 1742. SIR WILLIAM BUNBURY, Baronet [1681], of Bunbury and Stanney aforesaid, br. and h., *b.* about 1710; ed. at St. Catharine's Hall, Cambridge; B.A., 1730; M.A., 1734, and Fellow; took Holy Orders; was Vicar of Mildenhall, co. Suffolk; *suc. to the Baronetcy*, 10 April 1742. He inherited, under the will of his uncle, Sir William HANMER, 4th Baronet [1620] (who *d.* s.p. 7 May 1746), the estates of Barton Hall and of Mildenhall, both co. Suffolk, of which the former had belonged to the family of FOULKES, and had been acquired by the said Sir William, through marriage, and the latter (the inheritance of the family of NORTH) had been inherited by him through his mother, Peregrine NORTH, the maternal grandmother of the devisee. He was *cr.* D.D. of Oxford, 23 June 1755. He *m.*, in or before 1735, Eleanor, da. and coheir of VERE GRAHAM, of Wix Abbey, Essex, and of Holbrooke Hall, in Waldingfield, Suffolk, by (—), da. and coheir of Samuel WARNER, of Holbrooke Hall aforesaid. She *d.* 14 Feb. 1762. He, who resided latterly at Mildenhall, *d.* 11 June 1764. Will pr. 4 July 1764.

VI. 1764. SIR THOMAS CHARLES BUNBURY, Baronet [1681], of Bunbury and Stanney, as also of Barton Hall and Mildenhall aforesaid, 1st s. and h., *b.* May 1740; ed. at St. Catharine's Hall, Cambridge; M.A., 1765, having *suc. to the Baronetcy*, 11 June 1764; was for forty-three years M.P. for Suffolk (nine Parls.), 1761-84, and 1790-1812; Sheriff of Suffolk, 1788-89. He sold the estate of Bunbury, which had long ceased to be the residence of the family. He *m.* 2 June 1762, in the chapel of Holland House, Kensington, Sarah, 4th da. of Charles (LENNOX), 2d DUKE OF RICHMOND, by Sarah, da. and coheir of William (CADOGAN), 1st EARL CADOGAN. She, who was *b.* 15 Feb. 1744, and who was the Lady Sarah LENNOX of whom George III (when Prince of Wales) was supposed to have been enamoured, was divorced by act of Parl., 14 May 1776.(a) He *m.* secondly, Margaret. He *d.* s.p. at his house in Pall Mall, 31 March 1821, in his 81st year.(b) Will pr. June 1821. His widow *d.* there, 6 Feb. 1822, in her 78th year. Will pr. 7 March 1822.

VII. 1821. SIR HENRY EDWARD BUNBURY, Baronet [1681], of Stanney, as also of Barton Hall and Mildenhall aforesaid, nephew and h., being 2d but 1st surv. s. and h. of Henry William BUNBURY, the celebrated Caricaturist, by Catherine,(c) da. of Kane William HORNECK, Capt. Royal Engineers, and Lieut. Col. in the army of Sicily, which Henry William, who *d.* 7 May 1811, aged 60, was br. to the late, and 2d s. of the 5th Baronet. He was *b.* in London, 4 May 1778; ed. at Westm. School; entered the Coldstream Guards, 1795; served on the Staff of H.R.H. the Duke of York, in Holland, in 1799; as also at Naples and in Sicily, 1805-06, distinguishing himself at the battle of Maida, 4 July 1806, and becoming, finally, Lieut. General. He was Under Secretary for

(a) The cause was *crim. con.* with her cousin, Lord William Gordon, which, however, did not prevent her marriage, 27 Aug. 1781 (as his 2d wife) with Col. the Hon. George Napier, by whom she was mother of eight children, of whom the three elder sons were well known Generals, viz., Sir Charles James Napier, G.C.B., sometime Commander-in-Chief in India, who *d.* 29 Aug. 1853; Sir George Thomas Napier, K.C.B., who *d.* 3 Sep. 1855; and Sir William Francis Patrick Napier, K.C.B., author of the *History of the Peninsular War*, who *d.* 12 Feb. 1860.

(b) He was well known on the racecourse, and was owner of the winner of the first "Derby."

(c) She was the "*Little Comedy*" of Oliver Goldsmith.

War, 1809-16; K.C.B., 1815; *suc. to the Baronetcy*, 31 March 1821; was Sheriff of Suffolk, 1825-26, and M.P. for that county (on the Reform interest), 1830 and 1831; F.S.A. He, in 1859, sold the estate of Stanney, said to have been in the family since the reign of Edward III. He *m.* firstly, 4 April 1807, in Sicily, Louisa Amelia, 1st da. of Gen. the Hon. Henry Edward Fox (4th s. of Henry, 1st BARON HOLLAND), by Marianne, sister of Sir William CLAYTON, 4th Baronet [1732], and da. of William CLAYTON. She *d.* at Genoa, Sep. 1828. He *m.* secondly, 22 Sep. 1830, at Pau, in France, Emily Louisa Augusta, da. of Col. the Hon. George NAPIER, by his 2d wife, Sarah (divorced wife of Sir Thomas Charles BUNBURY, 7th Baronet [1681]), da. of Charles (LENNOX), 2d DUKE OF RICHMOND abovenamed. He *d.* 13 April 1860, aged 81, at Barton Hall aforesaid.(a) His widow, who was *b.* 11 July 1783, *d.* 18 March 1863, in her 80th year, at Abergwynant, in North Wales.

VIII. 1860. SIR CHARLES JAMES FOX BUNBURY, Baronet [1681], of Barton Hall and Mildenhall aforesaid, 2d but 1st surv. s. and h. by 1st wife, *b.* 4 Feb. 1809, at Messina, in Sicily; ed. at Trinity Coll., Cambridge; *suc. to the Baronetcy*, 13 April 1860; Sheriff of Suffolk, 1868. He *m.* 31 May 1844, at St. Geo. Bloomsbury, Francess Joanna, 2d. da. of Leonard HORNER, F.R.S., of Bedford place, Midx. He *d.* s.p. at Barton Hall, 18 June 1886, aged 77.(b) Will pr. 6 Sep. 1886, over £38,000. His widow *d.* 21 July 1894, at Mildenhall, aged 80. Will pr. at £14,088.

IX. 1886. SIR EDWARD HERBERT BUNBURY, Baronet [1681], of Barton Hall and Mildenhall aforesaid, br. of the whole blood, and h., *b.* 8 July 1811, at Brighton; ed. at Trinity Coll., Cambridge; B.A. (Senior Classic and Chancellor's Medallist), 1833; M.A., 1836; Barrister (Inner Temple), 1841; M.P. for Bury St. Edmund's, 1847-52; *suc. to the Baronetcy*, 18 June 1886. He *d.* unm., 5 March 1895, aged 83, at Brighton, and was *bur.* at Great Barton. Will pr. at £32,411.

X. 1895. SIR HENRY CHARLES JOHN BUNBURY, Baronet [1681], of Barton Hall and Mildenhall aforesaid, nephew and h., being 1st s. and h. of Col. Henry William St. Pierre BUNBURY, C.B., of Marchfield, Berks, by Cecilia Caroline, da. of Lieut. Gen. Sir George Thomas NAPIER, K.C.B.,(c) which Henry last named, who *d.* 18 Sep. 1875, aged 63, was br. of the whole blood to the late Baronet. He was *b.* 9 Jan. 1855, at Clapham; was sometime in the Royal Navy; *suc. to the Baronetcy*, 5 March 1895. He *m.* 11 March 1881, Laura Lavinia, 3d da. of Lieut. Gen. Thomas WOOD, of Littleton, Midx., and of Gwernyfed park, Brecon, by Frances, da. of John Henry SMYTH, of Heath Hall, co. York. She was *b.* 14 Aug. 1854.

Family Estates.—These, in 1883, consisted of 9,831 acres in Suffolk, worth £11,924 a year. *Seats.*—Barton Hall, near Bury, and Mildenhall Manor house, both in co. Suffolk.

PARKER:

cr. 1 July 1681.

I. 1681. "HUGH PARKER, of the City of London, Esq.," 3d s. of Hugh PARKER (living 1623), of Shoreditch, co. Somerset [*Qy.* Midx.], by Mary, only da. of Thomas HUTCHINS, *otherwise* LAWRENCE, of Holway

(a) He was author of some historic and military publications of considerable merit.

(b) Author of a *Journal of a Residence at the Cape of Good Hope*, and of some scientific treatises.

(c) See his parentage, p. 118, note "a."

in co. Somerset, was *b.* about 1607; was a Merchant of London; fined for the Aldermancy of Bridge ward Without, 1663, and was *cr. a Baronet*, 4 July 1681, as above, with a spec. rem., failing heirs male of his body, to "Henry PARKER, of Honington, co. Warwick, Esq.," his nephew. He *m.* Rachel, da. of (—) BROWN, of Louth, co. Lincoln. He *d.* s.p. 5, and was *bur.* 16 March 1696/7, at St. Bride's, London, aged 89. Will dat. 13 March 1694, pr. 1 April 1697. His widow was *bur.* there 3 March 1697/8. Her will pr. 1698.

II. 1697. SIR HENRY PARKER, Baronet [1681], of Honington, co. Warwick, nephew, being s. of Henry PARKER, by Margaret, da. of John WHITE, both of London, which Henry (who *d.* 1670), was br. of the late Baronet. He was *b.* about 1640; was admitted to the Middle Temple; M.P. for Evesham (six Parls.), 1679 to 1700, and for Aylesbury, Nov. 1704 to 1705; Recorder of Evesham, 1684-88; *suc. to the Baronetcy*, 5 March 1696/7, according to the spec. rem. in the patent, and rebuilt the mansion and church at Honington. He *m.* 29 March 1665 at St. Dionis Backchurch, London (Lic. Fac. 20, he about 25 and she about 17), Mary, da. (whose issue became heir) of Alexander HYDE, Bishop of Salisbury [1665-67], by Mary, da. of Robert TOUNSON, Bishop of Salisbury [1620-21], and Margaret, sister of John DAVENANT, Bishop of Salisbury [1621-41]. He *d.* 25 Oct. 1713 in his 74th year, and was *bur.* at Honington. M.I. Will pr. Nov. 1713. His widow *d.* 6 Jan. 1728/9. Her will pr. 1729.

III. 1713. SIR HENRY JOHN PARKER, Baronet [1681], of Honington aforesaid, as also of Talton, co. Somerset, and Hatch, co. Berks, grandson and h., being 1st s. and h. of Hugh PARKER, M.P. for Evesham, 1701/08, by Anne (afterward COUNTESS OF CLANRICARDE [I.]), da. of John SMITH, Commissioner of the Excise, which Hugh was 1st s. and h. ap. of the late Baronet, but *d.* v.p. 2 Feb. 1712, aged 39. He was *b.* about 1704; *suc. to the Baronetcy*, 25 Oct. 1713; matric. at Oxford, 7 July 1721, aged 17. He *m.* firstly, 23 Oct. 1728, Anne, da. and h. of Simon BARWELL, of Leicester. She *d.* s.p.m. 29 Oct. 1733, aged 19. He *m.* secondly, Catherine, da. of John PAGE, of Wandsworth, Surrey. She *d.* 1758. He *d.* s.p.m.s.(a) 7 Oct. 1771, at Talton aforesaid. Will pr. Nov. 1771.

IV. 1771. SIR HENRY PARKER, Baronet [1681], cousin and h. male, being 1st surv. s. and h. of the Rev. Hyde PARKER, Rector of Tredington, co. Worcester (1703-26), by Mary, da. of John REEVES, which Hyde (*bap.* 7 March 1707/8, at St. Andrew's, Holborn, and *d.* 24 May 1726) was yst. br. of the late Baronet. He was *b.* about 1713; matric. at Oxford (Trinity Coll.), 22 June 1731, aged 18; B.A. and Fellow, 1735; M.A., 1738; B.D., 1755; D.D., 1760; Rector of Rotherfield Greys, Oxon, 1767, and of Glympton, in that county, 1776-82, having *suc. to the Baronetcy*, 7 Oct. 1771. He *d.* unm. 10 July 1782, aged 70.

V. 1782. SIR HYDE PARKER, Baronet [1681], br. and h., *b.* 1 and *bap.* 25 Feb. 1713/4, at Tredington aforesaid; entered the Navy, serving first, 1728-38, in the Merchant Service; Lieut. R.N., 1745, becoming, finally, 26 Sep. 1780, Vice-Admiral of the Blue; served on the Indian coast, 1760-64; in the West Indies, 1770-80; serving as Commander of a squadron in the North Sea in March, 1781, where he had a severe, but not very decisive, engagement with the Dutch Squadron on the Doggerbank; was made Commander-in-Chief in the East Indies; and shortly afterwards *suc. to the Baronetcy*, 20 July, 1782. He *m.* in 1734, Sarah, da. of Hugh SMITHSON, of Northumberland. She *d.* about 1766. He set sail in Oct., and left Rio de Janeiro, 12 Dec. 1782, for the East Indies, after which date he was no more heard of, being lost at sea. Will pr. April 1784.

(a) John Parker, his only son (by 2d wife), *d.* unm. and v.p., at Stratford-on-Avon, Sep. 1769.

VI. 1783? SIR HARRY PARKER, Baronet [1681], of Melford Hall, Suffolk, 1st s. and h.,(a) *b.* about 1735; *suc. to the Baronetcy* on the death of his father, in 1782 or 1783; Sheriff of Suffolk, 1803-04. He *m.* in 1765 or 1766, Bridget, da. of William CRESWELL, of Creswell, co. Northumberland, by Grace, da. of Joseph FORSTER, of Low Buston. He *d.* 15 Jan. 1812, aged 77. Will proved 1812.

VII. 1812. SIR WILLIAM PARKER, Baronet [1681], of Melford Hall aforesaid, 1st s. and h., *b.* about 1770, in Westminster; matric. at Oxford (Ch. Ch.), 29 April 1789, aged 19; B.A., 1792; *suc. to the Baronetcy*, 15 Jan. 1812; Col. of the West Suffolk Militia. He *d.* unm. 21 April 1830. Will pr. July 1830.

VIII. 1830. SIR HYDE PARKER, Baronet [1681], of Melford Hall aforesaid, br. and h.; *b.* 1785; *suc. to the Baronetcy*, 21 April 1830; was M.P. for West Suffolk, 1832-35. He d. unm. 21 March 1856, at Government House, Devonport, aged 71.

IX. 1856. SIR WILLIAM PARKER, Baronet [1681], of Melford Hall aforesaid, cousin and h. male, being yst. but only surv. s. and h.(b) of Vice-Admiral Hyde PARKER, C.B., by Caroline, da. of Sir Frederick Morton EDEN, 2d Baronet [1776], of Maryland, which Hyde (who *d.* 26 May 1854) was s. of Admiral Sir Hyde PARKER (*d.* 16 March 1807, aged 68), br. of the 6th and yr. s. of the 5th Baronet. He was *b.* 2 Sep. 1826; was sometime Capt. 44th Foot, but retired 1859; *suc. to the Baronetcy*, 21 March 1856; Capt. 11th Suffolk Rifle Volunteers, 1860. He *m.* 22 Nov. 1855, at St. Geo. Han. sq., Sophia Mary, 2d da. of Nathaniel Clarke BARNARDISTON, of the Ryes, Sudbury, Suffolk. He *d.* 24 May 1891, aged 75, at Melford Hall aforesaid. His widow *d.* 16 May 1903, aged 66, at Westgate House, in Long Melford, Suffolk.

X. 1891. SIR WILLIAM HYDE PARKER, Baronet [1681], of Melford Hall aforesaid, 2d but 1st surv. s. and h.,(c) *b.* 8 April 1863; ed. at Clare Coll., Cambridge; B.A., 1885; took Holy Orders, 1886; Curate of All Saints', Wokingham, 1886-90; Chaplain to the Bishop of Barbadoes, 1890-91; *suc. to the Baronetcy*, 24 May 1891. He *m.* 18 Nov. 1890, at Christ Church, Lancaster Gate, Paddington, Ethel, da. of John LEECH, of Gorse Hall, Dukinfield, Cheshire.

Family Estates.—These, in 1883, consisted of 3,482 acres in Suffolk, of the value (said to be "considerably understated") of £4,720 a year; besides land in Middlesex, worth £160 a year. *Seat.*—Melford Hall, in Long Melford, co. Suffolk

SEYMOUR:

cr. 4 July 1681;

ex. April 1714.

I. 1681, to 1714. "HENRY SEYMOUR, Esq. [only] s. and h. [ap.] to Henry SEYMOUR, one of the Grooms of His Majesty's Bedchamber," of Langley, Bucks (an estate he had purchased in 1669), by his 2d wife, Ursula, relict of George STAWELL, da. of Sir Robert AUSTEN, 1st Baronet [1660], (which Henry, was yr. s. of Sir Edward SEYMOUR, 2d Baronet [1611], of Berry Pomeroy), was *b.* 20 Oct. 1674, and was, when in his 7th year, *cr. a Baronet*, as above, 4 July 1681, in consideration of his

(a) His yr. br., Admiral Sir Hyde Parker (*Knighted* 21 April 1779), served in the American War, and at Copenhagen in 1801, from which, however, he was recalled. He *d.* 16 March 1807, aged 68, being grandfather of William Parker, who in 1856 suc. as 9th Baronet.

(b) His elder br., Hugh Parker, Capt. R.N., *d.* unm., being killed in action at Sulina, on the Danube, 8 July 1854.

(c) His elder br., Hyde Parker, Lieut. King's Liverpool Regiment, *d.* unm. and v.p., 10 Dec. 1887, aged 26.

R

father's services, with a spec. rem., failing heirs male of his body, "to the said Henry, the father, and to the heirs male of his body." He suc. his father (who *d.* aged 74), 9 March 1686, and was M.P. for East Looe (seven Parls.), Jan. 1699 to 1713. He *d.* unm. in London, April 1714, and was *bur.* at Langley, when the *Baronetcy* became *extinct.*(a) Admon. 4 May 1714, to his uterine sister, Dame Elizabeth AUSTEN, widow,(b), and again, after her death, 8 April 1727.

JEFFREYS, *or* JEFFERYS:

cr. 17 Nov. 1681;

afterwards, 1685-1702, BARONS JEFFREYS OF WEM;

ex. 9 May 1702.

I. 1681. "SIR GEORGE JEFFERYS [*or* JEFFREYS], of Bulstrode(c) [in Hedgerley], co. Buckingham, Knt., one of His Majesty's Serjeants at Law, and Chief Justice of Chester," 6th son of John JEFFREYS, of Acton, near Wrexham, co. Denbigh, by Margaret, da. of Sir Thomas IRELAND, of Beansay, co. Lancaster, was *b.* 1648, at Acton; ed. at Shrewsbury, at St. Paul's School, London (1659), at Westm. School (1661), and at Trinity Coll., Cambridge (as a pensioner), 15 March 1662; admitted to Inner Temple. 19 May 1663; Barrister, 22 Nov. 1668, becoming a Bencher, Jan. 1678; Common Serjeant of London, 16 March 1671; Solicitor Gen. to H.R.H. the Duke of York, being *Knighted* at Whitehall, 14 Sep. 1677; Recorder of London, 22 Oct. 1678, an office he resigned, 2 Dec. 1680; Chief Justice of Chester, 30 April; and Serjeant at Law, 12 May 1680; being *cr. a Baronet*, as above, 17 Nov. 1681, with a spec. rem. "to the heirs male of his body by Ann, his now wife, and for default of such issue to the heirs male of his body." He was made Chief Justice of the King's Bench, 29 Sep. 1683; P.C., 4 Oct. 1683; presided at the trials, for high treason, of Algernon Sidney, in Nov. 1683, and of Titus Oates, in May 1685. He *m.* firstly, 23 May 1667, at Allhallows', Barking,(d) Sarah, da. of the Rev. Thomas NEESHAM, M.A. She, who, besides five other children, was mother of his only surv. s. and h., *d.* 14 and was *bur.* 18 Feb. 1677/8, at St. Mary's, Aldermanbury, London. He *m.* secondly (Lic. London, 6 June 1679, he about 32 and she about 23), Anne, widow of Sir John JONES, of Finmon, co. Glamorgan, da. of Sir Thomas BLUDWORTH, sometime (1665-66) Lord Mayor of London, by Mary, his 2d wife, formerly Mary BENN, widow. She was living when he was *cr.* 15 May 1685, BARON JEFFREYS OF WEM, co. Salop,(e) with spec. rem. like to that of his Baronetage, in which peerage this *Baronetcy* then *merged*, till both became *extinct*, by the death, 9 May 1702, of the 2d Baron and Baronet. See *Peerage.*

(a) The estate of Langley passed to his cousin, Sir Edward Seymour, 5th Baronet [1611], who sold it to Lord Masham, and *d.* Jan. 1740/1, aged 80, being ancestor of the Dukes of Somerset.

(b) She was da. of his mother by George Stawel, her 1st husband.

(c) According to Lipscomb's *Bucks*, he did not purchase the estate of Bulstrode from Sir Roger Hill till 1686, but as that date appears in the parts of the mansion there that was built by him, it is likely that the actual purchase was some years earlier. It was sold by his son-in-law, Charles Dyve, to the Duke of Portland.

(d) *Dict. Nat. Biogr.* There is, however, no entry thereof, a hiatus occurring in these registers between the marriages of 19 April 1666 and 10 Dec. 1667.

(e) He was raised to the peerage about three months after the accession of his patron, James II, to the throne, and "as no Chief Justice had ever been made a Lord of Parliament since the judicial system had been remodelled in the thirteenth century, this was an exceptional mark of Royal approbation" [*Dict. Nat. Biogr.*]. Some three months after this creation he started for his well known "Bloody circuit" in the West, on his return from which, 20 Sep. 1685, the King, "taking into his Royal consideration the many eminent and faithful services" which he had performed, made him Lord Chancellor, a post he retained till the end of that reign.

MIDDLETON, MIDDELTON, *or* MYDDELTON:

cr. 6 Dec. 1681(a);

ex., presumably, March 1702.

I. 1681, to 1702? "HUGH MIDDLETON, of Hackney, co. Middlesex, Esq.," 1st surv. s. and h. of Simon MIDDLETON,(b) of Hurst Hall, Edmonton, in that County, Draper, Citizen and Goldsmith of London, by the 2d of his four wives, Mary, da. of John SOAME, of Burnham Market, Norfolk, which Simon (whose will, dat. 25 July 1678, was pr. 29 Nov. 1680) was the yst. surv. s. of Sir Hugh MIDDLETON, 1st Baronet [1622], the projector of the New River Company. He was probably *b.* about 1658, and was, soon after his father's death, *cr. a Baronet*, as above, 6 Dec. 1681. He *m.* 17 July 1677, at Knightsbridge Chapel, Dorothy, da. of Sir William OGLANDER, 1st Baronet [1665], by Dorothy, da. of Sir Francis CLERK, of Hitcham, Bucks. She obtained a separation from him, and in May 1690, an Act passed to confirm a previous settlement on her, and to sell various estates for his debts. She *d.* 8 Jan. 1701/2, aged 45, and was *bur.* at Long Melford, Suffolk. M.I. Will dat. 20 March 1699/700, and pr. 9 Feb. 1701/2, in which she directs the inscription on her monument to state that she was "the unhappy wife of Sir Hugh MIDDLETON, Baronet." He, who had wasted all his property, *d.* s.p.m.,(c) in great obscurity, being presumably the "William RAYMOND, Gentleman, so called, otherwise called by the name of Hugh MIDDLETON, *d.* 10 March 1702" (who resided at Kemberton, Salop), whose burial is thus entered in the parish register of Shiffnal, in that county. At his death the *Baronetcy* became *extinct.*

ALSTON:

cr. 20 Jan. 1681/2;(d)

ex. 6 March 1819.

I. 1682. "JOSEPH ALSTON, the Elder, of Chelsea, co. Middlesex, Esq.," as also of Bradwell Abbey, Bucks (an estate he had purchased about 1660), 2d s. of Edward ALSTON, of Edwardston, co. Suffolk, by Margaret, da. of Arthur PENNING, of Kettleborough, in that county, was *b.* at Edwardston(e), and was *cr. a Baronet*, as above, 20 Jan. 1681/2. He *m.* firstly, about 1640, Mary (a fortune of about £12,000), da. and coheir of (—) CROOKENBERG, of Bergen-op-Zoom, in Brabant, Merchant. She was *bur.* 7 Feb. 1670/1, at Chelsea.(f) He *m.* secondly, Anne, widow of (—) STRATTON, of London, da. of (—) PHEASANT.

(a) This is the last creation given in Dugdale's *Catalogue*; see *Memorandum*, vol. iii, p. 1. The well known Sir William Dugdale, Garter, died about three years afterwards, 10 Feb. 1685/6, in his 81st year.

(b) This article is compiled from W. D. Pink's exhaustive account of the *Middleton Family*, contributed to the *Cheshire Courant*, July to Nov. 1891.

(c) Dorothy, his only surv. da. (unm. in March 1699/700) *m.* (Lic. Fac. 22 Dec. 1702, he 26 and she 23), Henry Berkeley, Barrister [1696], of the Middle Temple, London, who *d.* 1735.

(d) This is the first creation given in the *Continuation* (1682 to 1809) of Dugdale's *Catalogue*. See *Memorandum*, vol. iii, p. 1.

(e) There is a statement by P. Le Neve, dated Nov. 1714 (inserted in Le Neve's MS. *Baronetage*), that Mr. Mynheer, of Staple Inn, Holborn, Attorney, informed him that the grantee himself had stated that he came up to London with but 5s., was apprenticed to a Norwich factor, and *d.* worth £40,000.

(f) Her funeral sermon is given in Wilford's *Memorials*.

He was *bur.* 31 May 1688, at Chelsea. Will pr. June 1688. The will of his widow, describing herself as of Chelsea, and directing her burial to be at East Moulsey, Surrey, was dat. 19 April 1694, and pr. 29 July 1696, by her niece and residuary legatee, Dame Anne CLARKE, wife of Sir James CLARKE, of East Moulsey.

II. 1688. SIR JOSEPH ALSTON, Baronet [1682], of Bradwell Abbey aforesaid, 1st s. and h., *b.* about 1640; Sheriff of Bucks, 1670; *suc. to the Baronetcy* in May 1688. He *m.* 30 Sep. 1662, at Lee, co. Kent, Elizabeth, sister of John, 1st BARON HAVERSHAM, da. of Maurice THOMPSON, of Haversham, Bucks, Merchant of London, by Dorothy (or Ellen) da. of John VAUX, of Pembrokeshire. He *d.* 14 and was *bur.* 21 March 1688/9, at Bradwell, aged 49. Will pr. June 1689. The will of Dame Elizabeth Alston was pr. Dec. 1709.

III. 1689. SIR JOSEPH ALSTON, Baronet [1682], of Bradwell Abbey aforesaid, 1st s. and h., *b.* probably about 1665; *suc. to the Baronetcy*, 14 March 1688/9; Sheriff of Bucks, 1702-03; was sometime a prisoner for debt in Fleet street prison. He *m.* firstly, 23 June 1690, at Long Ditton, Surrey, Penelope, 3d da. and coheir of Sir Edward EVELYN, Baronet [so *cr.* 1683], of Long Ditton aforesaid, by Mary, da. and coheir of Charles BALAM. She, who was *b.* 3 Oct. 1672, at Long Ditton, and by whom he had seventeen children, *d.* 22 and was *bur.* there 28 June 1714, in her 42d year. He *m.* secondly, Charlotte, widow of Benjamin ALBIN, sister of Charles, 3d EARL OF PETERBOROUGH and 1st EARL OF MONMOUTH, 1st da. of John (MORDAUNT), 1st VISCOUNT MORDAUNT OF AVALON, by Elizabeth, da. and h. of the Hon. Thomas CAREY. He *d.* at Bath, and was *bur.* 29 Jan. 1715/6, at Long Ditton aforesaid. M.I. Admon. 6 June 1716 and 15 Sep. 1726. His widow *d.* between June 1716 and 1720. Will pr. 1720.

IV. 1716. SIR JOSEPH ALSTON, Baronet [1682], of Bradwell Abbey and Long Ditton aforesaid, 1st s. and h. by 1st wife, *bap.* 15 Sep. 1691, at Long Ditton; *suc. to the Baronetcy* in Jan. 1715/6, and soon afterwards sold the estate of Bradwell Abbey. He *m.* Lucy, only child of Richard THURSBY, of Hanslope, Bucks, and Abington, co. Northampton, by Elizabeth, da. of the Hon. Edward MONTAGU. He *d.* s.p. in 1718, aged about 27. Admon. 3 Dec. 1718, his widow being then a minor, and again, 3 Aug. 1737, after her death.

V. 1718. SIR EVELYN ALSTON, Baronet [1682], of Long Ditton aforesaid, br. and h. of the whole blood; *b.* 12 and *bap.* 14 Nov. 1692, at Long Ditton; *suc. to the Baronetcy* in 1718, and sold the estate of Long Ditton in 1721. He *m.* about 1720, Sarah,(a) da. of (—). He, having wasted all his estate, resided at Redstones, in Reigate, Surrey, where he was *bur.* 15 April 1750, aged 57. His widow *d.* 30 March 1753.

VI. 1750. SIR EVELYN ALSTON, Baronet [1682], 1st s. and h., *b.* in or before 1721; *suc. to the Baronetcy* in April 1750. He *m.* 13 March 1766, at St. Marylebone, Midx., Elizabeth MAY, widow. He *d.* s.p. 1783. Will pr. March 1783. His widow *d.* in or before 1808. Will pr. 1808.

VII. 1783. SIR WILLIAM ALSTON, Baronet [1682], br. and h., *b.* 10 and *bap.* 14 April 1722, at Reigate; *suc. to the Baronetcy* in 1783. He *m.* 10 Sep. 1745, at the Fleet Chapel, London, Elizabeth WEARE. She, who was *b.* 19 Sep. 1721, *d.* 21 June 1800. He *d.* at Oxtead, Surrey, Nov. 1801.

(a) His wife's name, and most of the subsequent account of this family, was kindly supplied by Lionel Cresswell, of Wood Hall, Calverley, Yorkshire.

VIII. 1801, to 1819. SIR WILLIAM ALSTON, Baronet [1682], s. and h., *bap.* 1746, at Lingfield, Surrey; *suc. to the Baronetcy* in Nov. 1801. He *m.* 18 Dec. 1770, at Lingfield, Mary ROSE. She *d.* 3 Feb. 1782, and was *bur.* there, aged 33. He *d.* s.p.m.s.,(a) 6 March 1819, when the *Baronetcy* became *extinct*.

ROBINSON:

cr. 26 Jan. 1681/2;

ex. 21 April 1743.

I. 1682. "THOMAS ROBINSON, of Kentwell [Hall, in Long Melford], co. Suffolk, Esq.," s. of (—) ROBINSON, of Westminster, *b.* about 1618; was admitted to the Inner Temple, Nov. 1656; Barrister, and subsequently [1677], Bencher and Treasurer; one of the Prothonotaries of the King's Bench; purchased the estate of Kentwell Hall, and was *cr. a Baronet*, as above, 26 Jan. 1681/2. He *m.* in 1648, Jane, 1st da. of Lumley DEW, of Upton Bishop, co. Hereford. She *d.* in the house of Sir John DAVIES, at Pangbourne, Berks, 22 Nov. 1665, in her 49th year, and was *bur.* at Pangbourne. M.I. He *d.* (being killed by leaping from his window in the Temple, to avoid being burnt) 2, and was *bur.* 7 Aug. 1683, in the Temple Church, aged 65.(b) Admon. 17 Aug. 1683, 23 June 1684, 2 Nov. 1692, and 4 March 1708/9.

II. 1683. SIR LUMLEY ROBINSON, Baronet [1682], of Kentwell Hall aforesaid, only surv. s. and h., *b.* about 1649; matric. at Oxford (Ch. Ch.), 13 May 1665, aged 16; Barrister (Inner Temple), 1673; *suc. to the Baronetcy*, 7 Aug. 1683. He *m.* (Lic. Vic. Gen., 26 July 1680), Anne (then aged about 22), only surv. da. and h. of John LAURENCE, of St. Margaret's, Westm., sometime Secretary to the Chancellor of the Exchequer, by Amy, da. of Richard WILLIAMS, of Chichester. He *d.* 6 and was *bur.* 10 June 1684,(b) in Westm. Abbey, in his 35th year. Admon. 23 June 1684 and 20 June 1707. His widow *m.*, 2 Aug. 1688, at St. Mary Aldermary, London (Lic. Vic. Gen., 1), William FOULIS, then about 30, Bachelor, who, after her death, became, 23 March 1694/5, 4th Baronet [1620], and was *bur.*, 7 Oct. 1741, aged 83, at Ingleby, co. York. She was *bur.*, 13 Dec. 1690, with her parents and her 1st husband, in Westm. Abbey. Will dat. 4 March 1689/90, pr. 7 Jan. 1690/1.

III. 1684, to 1743. SIR THOMAS ROBINSON, Baronet [1682], of Kentwell Hall aforesaid, only s. and h.; *bap.* 14 July 1681, at Westm. Abbey, and *suc. to the Baronetcy*, 6 June 1684; matric. at Oxford (Balliol Coll.), 23 Sep. 1695, aged 14. He *m.* 30 May 1710, at Knightsbridge Chapel, Midx. (Lic. Fac., 29), Elizabeth, da. of Sir Thomas HARE, 2d Baronet [1641] of Stow Bardolph, Norfolk, by Elizabeth, da. of George DASHWOOD, of Northbrooke, Oxon.(c) He *d.* s.p. 21 April 1743, aged 62, when the *Baronetcy* became *extinct*.(d)

(a) William Alston, his s. and h. ap., *m.* 2 Jan. 1793, at Lingfield, Surrey, Elizabeth, da. of John Brister, of Crowhurst, and *d.* v.p. and s.p.m., 23 March 1802, in his 32d year, leaving three daughters and coheirs.

(b) Burial also registered at Long Melford.

(c) Admon. of "Dame Elizabeth Robinson, commonly called Lady Lechmere," of St. Martin's in the Field's, Midx. was granted 1 April 1739, to her husband, "Sir Thomas Robinson, Baronet." It seems likely that this refers to this Elizabeth, but in that case the word "Lechmere" (unless a mistake for "Robinson") is unintelligible.

(d) His sister, Anne, *bap.* 5 Oct. 1682, at Westm. Abbey, *m.* (Lic. Fac. 5 Dec. 1705) Sir Comport Fytche, 2d Baronet [1688], and had issue.

MAYNARD;

cr. 1 Feb. 1681/2;

afterwards, 1775-1865, VISCOUNTS MAYNARD;

ex. 18 May 1865.

I. 1682. "WILLIAM MAYNARD, of Walthamstow, co. Essex," 3d but 1st surv. s. and h. of Charles MAYNARD,(a) Auditor of the Exchequer, by Mary (marr. lic. London, 16 July 1633), da. of Zeager CORSELLIS, of London, Merchant, was *b.* about 1640; suc. his father, Nov. 1665, and was *cr. a Baronet*, as above, 1 Feb. 1681/2; was M.P. for Essex, 1685 till death in same year. He *m.* (Lic. Vic. Gen., 10 May 1667, he about 26 and she about 20), Mary, da. of William BAYNBRIGG, Citizen and Merchant Tailor of London. He *d.* 7 Nov. 1685, and was *bur.* at Walthamstow. Admon. 4 Dec. 1685, to his widow.

II. 1685. SIR WILLIAM MAYNARD, Baronet [1682], of Walthamstow aforesaid, 3d but 1st surv. s. and h., *b.* about 1676; *suc. to the Baronetcy*, 7 Nov. 1685; matric. at Oxford (St. John's Coll.), 7 July 1694, aged 18. He *d.* unm. 15 Dec. 1715.

III. 1715. SIR HENRY MAYNARD, Baronet [1682], of Walthamstow aforesaid, and of Waltons, in the parish of Ashdon, co. Essex, br. and h.; was a Turkey Merchant, and sometime Resident at Aleppo; *suc. to the Baronetcy*, 15 Dec. 1715; was Verderer of Waltham Forest, 1725. He *m.* 22 March 1719/20, Catharine, sister of Sir Charles Gunter NICOLL, K.B., da. of George GUNTER, of Racton, Sussex. He *d.* 16 Nov. 1738, and was *bur.* at Walthamstow. Will pr. 1738. His widow *d.* 6 Nov. 1744, and was *bur.* there. Will pr. 1745.

IV. 1738. SIR WILLIAM MAYNARD, Baronet [1682], of Waltons aforesaid, only s. and h., *b.* 19 April 1721; entered Winchester School, 1731; *suc. to the Baronetcy*, 16 Nov. 1738; matric. at Oxford (Queen's College), 22 March 1738/9, aged 17; was Recorder of Saffron Walden, and M.P. for Essex (three Parls.), 1759 till death in 1772. He *m.* 13 Aug. 1781, at Westm. Abbey (Lic. Fac. 8, he above 30 and she 20), Charlotte, 2d da. of Sir Cecil BISHOPP, 6th Baronet [1620], by Anne, da. of Hugh (BOSCAWEN), 1st VISCOUNT FALMOUTH. She *d.* 16 and was *bur.* 21 May 1762, at Little Easton, Essex. He *d.* 18 and was *bur.* there 27 Jan. 1772, aged 50. Will dat. 22 June 1762 to 18 Jan. 1772, pr. 23 March 1772.

V. 1772. SIR CHARLES MAYNARD, Baronet [1682], of Waltons aforesaid, 1st s. and h., *b.* there 9. Aug. 1752; ed. at Eton, and at Sidney Sussex Coll., Cambridge; M.A., 1772; *suc. to the Baronetcy*, 18 Jan. 1772, and *suc. to the Peerage* as the 2d VISCOUNT MAYNARD OF EASTON LODGE, co. Essex, on the death, 30 June 1775, of his 3d cousin, Charles (MAYNARD), the 1st Viscount, in consequence of a spec. rem. in the creation of that Viscountcy,(b) 28 Oct. 1766. In that peerage this *Baronetcy* then *merged*, till both became *extinct*, on the death, s.p.m.s., 19 May 1865, of his s., the 3d Viscount and 6th Baronet. See *Peerage*.

(a) This Charles was 3d and yst. s. of Sir Henry Maynard, of Estaines, co. Essex, Secretary to the Lord Treasurer Burghley, *temp.* Eliz. His eldest br., William, was *cr. a Baronet* in 1611, and subsequently *cr.* [1620] Baron Maynard [I.] and [1628] Baron Maynard of Estaines [E.]. His great-grandson Charles, the 6th Baron, was *cr.* 18 Oct. 1766, Viscount Maynard of Easton Lodge, co. Essex, etc., with a spec. rem., failing male issue, to his father's 2d cousin, Sir William Maynard, 4th Baronet [1682], whose son, the 5th Baronet, on his Lordship's death s.p., 20 June 1775, aged 85, suc. to the abovenamed Viscountcy.

(b) See note "a" above as to this spec. rem.

NAPIER:

cr. 25 Feb. 1681/2;

existing, 1743 and possibly later.

I. 1682. "SIR ROBERT NAPIER, of Puncknoll, co. Dorset, Esq.," [*sic.*, but should be "Knight"], s. and h. ap. of Robert NAPIER,(a) of the same, Master of the Hanaper Office, by his 1st wife, Anne (mar. lic. London, 12 July 1637), Anne, da. of Alan CORRANCE, of Wykin, Suffolk, was *b.* about 1642; matric. at Oxford (Trinity Coll.), 1 April 1656; Barrister (Middle Temple), 1660; Sheriff of Dorset, 1680; *Knighted* at Windsor, 27 Jan., and was *cr. a Baronet*, v.p., as above, 25 Feb. 1681/2; suc. his father, 1686; was M.P. for Weymouth, 1689-90; for Dorchester, 1690 till unseated, 6 Oct. 1690, and again, 1698 till death in 1700. He *m.* 21 Nov. 1667, at the Savoy Chapel, Midx. (registered at Long Ditton, Surrey), Sophia, da. of Charles EVELYN, of Godstone, Surrey (an officer of the Guards to Sophia, Electress of Hanover), by Jane, da. of Sir Thomas EVELYN, of Long Ditton, in that county. He *d.* 31 Oct. 1700, and was *bur.* at Puncknoll. Will pr. Dec. 1700.

II. 1700, to 1743. SIR CHARLES NAPIER, Baronet [1682], of Puncknoll aforesaid, only surv. s. and h.; was 23 years old and in the Fleet prison for debt, about 1696;(b) *suc. to the Baronetcy*, 31 Oct. 1700, sold the estate of Puncknoll, and was, in 1741,(c) residing at "Sowdley House [*Qy.* Salden, in Mursley], Bucks," having *m.* "Melony, da. of Arthur ALIBONE, Citizen of London," by whom he had at that date, "issue living, two sons, George and Robert NAPIER." He *d.* 1743,(d) after which date *nothing authentic*(e) *is known of the Baronetcy.*

DAVERS:

cr. 12 May 1682;

ex., or *dormant*, 4 June 1806.

I. 1682. "ROBERT DAVERS, of Rougham, co. Suffolk, Esq.," whose parentage is unknown, was, in all probability, the Robert DAVERS, *b.* about 1620, who as a boy, aged 14, sailed with 78 others in April 1635 for Barbadoes. He, in 1673, was proprietor of 600 acres, being among the "most eminent planters" there,(f) and having "got an estate of the value of £30,000,"(g) returned to England about 1680, purchased soon afterwards the estate of Rougham from the family of BURWELL, and was *cr. a Baronet*, as above, 12 May 1682. He *m.* in or before 1653, Eleanor, probably sister of George LUKE.(h) She was living in July 1679, but probably *d.* in Barbadoes

(a) This Robert was yr. br. of Sir Gerard Napier, of Middlemarsh Hall, Dorset *cr. a Baronet*, 25 June 1641, a dignity which became extinct, 25 Jan. 1765.

(b) Le Neve's MS. *Baronetage.*

(c) Wotton's *Baronetage* [1741]. The account in Kimber's *Baronetage* [1771], is much the same, no notice being made of the death of the 2d Baronet, who indeed is there called "the *present* Baronet" (though his age would have been above 100), and the words "he had issue" being substituted for "he has issue living."

(d) Courthope's *Extinct Baronetage.*

(e) In the pedigree in Hutchins' *Dorset*, his eldest son is called "*Sir George.*"

(f) This article is mainly taken from the account of the family in the admirable annotations to the *Rushbrook Parish Registers*, 1567-1850, by "S.H.A.H.," pub. by Geo. Booth, Church Street, Woodbridge, Suffolk, 1903, 4to, pp. 486.

(g) Le Neve's MS. *Baronetage.*

(h) The 1st Baronet in his will, dat. 4 July 1679, leaves £500 "to my brother, George Luke."

before him. He was *bur.* 21 June 1684, at Rougham. Will, as of St. George's in Barbadoes, dat. 4 to 19 July 1679, pr. 29 June 1688.

II. 1684. SIR ROBERT DAVERS, Baronet [1682], of Rougham aforesaid, only s. and h., *b.* in Barbadoes, 1653; was in England, 1680-82, but, returning to Barbadoes, took his seat in the Council there, 13 June 1682, and was, 30 Nov. 1683, one of the Barons of the Court of Exchequer and of Pleas there; *suc. to the Baronetcy* in June 1684; was elected Sheriff of Suffolk, Dec. 1684, but did not act, and came over to England finally in 1687; M.P. (in the Tory interest) for Bury St. Edmunds (six Parls.), 1689-1701, and Nov. 1703 to 1705; for Suffolk (six Parls.), 1705, till his death in 1722. He *m.*, 2 Feb. 1681/2, at Rushbrook, Suffolk, Mary, 1st da. and coheir [1703] of Thomas (JERMYN), 2d BARON JERMYN OF ST. EDMUNDSBURY, by Mary, da. of Henry MERRY, 1st s. of Sir Henry MERRY, of Derbyshire. By this marriage he acquired in 1703 one-fifth of the Rushbrook estate, of which he purchased the other parts from his wife's sisters. He sold the estate of Rougham between 1705 and 1710 to his son in law, Clement CORRANCE. He *d.* 1 and was *bur.* 7 Oct. 1722, at Rushbrook, aged 69. Will, in which he directs his Barbadoes estate to be sold, dat. 14 March 1714, pr. 13 Dec. 1722. His widow, who was *b.* in 1663, probably in Jersey, *d.* four days after him, 11 and was *bur.* with him 14 Oct. 1722, aged 69. Admon. 13 Dec. 1722 and 18 July 1723.

III. 1722. SIR ROBERT DAVERS, Baronet [1682], of Rushbrook aforesaid, 1st s. and h., *b.* about 1684 possibly in Barbadoes; matric. at Oxford (Ch. Ch.), 25 Jan. 1702/3, aged 17 [*sic*]; Auditor of the Excise, 1713; *suc. to the Baronetcy*, 1 Oct. 1722. He *d.* unm. 20 and was *bur.* 23 May 1723, at Rushbrook, aged 39. [*sic*] M.I. Will dat. 28 Nov. 1722 to 26 Feb. 1722/3, pr. 18 July 1723.

IV. 1723. SIR JERMYN DAVERS, Baronet [1682], of Rushbrook aforesaid, br. and h., *b.* about 1686 possibly in Barbadoes; matric. at Oxford (Ch. Ch.), 14 March 1703/4, aged 17; was M.P. for Bury St. Edmunds, 1722-27, and for Suffolk (three Parls.), 1727, till death in 1743; *suc. to the Baronetcy*, 20 May 1723. By the death, 12 Oct. 1726, of Judith, widow of his great uncle, Henry (JERMYN), 3d BARON JERMYN OF ST. EDMUNDSBURY and 1st BARON DOVER, he inherited considerable estates, of which he sold that of Cheveley, in Cambridgeshire, in 1732. He *m.* 21 Oct. 1729 [*Qy.* 1728], at Rushbrook, Margaretta, 1st da. and coheir of the Rev. Edward GREEN, Rector of Drinkstone, Suffolk [1692-1740], and Margaret, his wife. He *d.* 20 and was *bur.* 27 Feb. 1742/3, at Rushbrook. Will dat. 20 Aug. 1740 to 4 Feb. 1742/3, pr. 31 Oct. 1743. His widow *d.* at Angel Hill, Bury St. Edmunds, 5 Feb. 1780, aged 85. Will dat. 16 and 17 Aug. 1771, directing her burial to be with her parents at Drinkstone, pr. 17 April 1780 at the Archdeacon's Court at Sudbury.

V. 1743. SIR ROBERT DAVERS, Baronet [1682], of Rushbrook aforesaid, 1st s. and h., *b.* presumably(a) about 1730 (*i.e.*, after his parents' marriage in Oct. 1729), admitted to Bury Grammar School, July 1742;

(a) It is not, however, very clear whether he was not *b.* (as indicated below) in Jan. 1729/30, some ten months before his parents' marriage, though of course that birth may apply to another child of the same name, who possibly *d.* in infancy. The following baptisms at St. Margaret's, Westm., illustrate the subject: (1) Jermyn, s. of Jermyn and Margaretta Davers, *b.* 4 and *bap.* 10 Dec. 1720; (2) Margaretta Maria, da. of Sir Jermyn Davers and Dame Margaretta, *b.* 29 Sep. and *bap.* 5 Oct. 1723; (3) Mary, da. of the same, *b.* 4 and *bap.* 5 Aug. 1725; (4) Mary, da. of the same, *b.* 28 Feb. and *bap.* 1 March 1726/7; (5) Robert, s. of same, *b.* 20 and *bap.* 21 Jan. 1728/9. The burial of the first-named Mary is recorded there, 26 Aug. 1725, as "Mrs Mary Davers, C." Sir Jermyn Davers, in his will dat. 20 Aug. 1740, leaves annuities to his "two natural sons, James and Jermyn Davers," but mentions Robert Davers as his eldest s., whom he places first in the entail of the estate.

suc. to the Baronetcy, 20 Feb. 1742/3. After travelling in 1756 in Italy, he left England for North America in 1761, being presumably in the army, as in May and June 1762, "while at Fort Detroit, an English garrison in North America," he made a will, which he placed in the custody of "Lieut. Leslye, of the 1st battalion of Royal Americans," from whom, "being in garrison at an English fort in North America, called Fort Michilunackinac," in July 1763, it was "taken by the Indians" and "either lost or destroyed. He *d.* unm., June 1763, being killed (when in a boat) by the Indians near Lake Huron in Canada. Admon. 20 March 1764, in which the fate of his will (as mentioned above) is recited.

VI. 1763, to 1806. SIR CHARLES DAVERS, Baronet [1682], of Rushbrook aforesaid, br. and h., *b.* 4 June 1737; entered in March 1758, the 48th Foot, then engaged against the French in Canada; Capt., 99th Foot, Jan., and 44th Foot, Oct. 1761, retiring on half pay in 1766, having *suc. to the Baronetcy* in June 1763. Was M.P. for Weymouth, 1768-74, and for Bury (four Parls.), 1774, till 1802. He *d.* 4 June 1806, on his birthday of 69, and was *bur.* at Rushbrook, presumably unm.,(a) and s.p. legit., when the *Baronetcy* became *extinct*, or possibly only *dormant*.(b) Will pr. 1806.

JAMES:

cr. 28 June 1682;

ex. 29 Sep. 1741.

I. 1682. "[JAMES] CANE JAMES, of Chrishall [*otherwise* CRESHALL], co. Essex," *formerly* James CANE, s. of Adam CANE, Citizen and Vintner of London, by Emlin, da. of Richard and sister of Sir John JAMES, of Creshall aforesaid, was *b.* about 1656; admitted to Gray's Inn, 1 June 1674; matric. at Oxford (St. John's Coll.), 18 May 1677, aged 19; suc. his said uncle (who *d.* unm. 17 Feb. 1676, aged 72) in the Creshall estate, and, having taken the surname of *James*, was *cr. a Baronet*, as above, 28 June 1682; Sheriff of Essex, 1685-86. He *m.* firstly (Lic. Fac. 6 July 1680), Susanna (then aged 16), 1st da. of Sir Peter SOAME, 2d Baronet [1685], of Heydon, Essex, by Susanna, da. of Ralph FREEMAN. She *d.* s.p., 5 months later, 28 Dec. 1680, aged 17, and was *bur.* at Heydon. M.I. He *m.* secondly, in or before 1692, Anne, da. and coheir of Francis PHILLIPS, of the Inner Temple, London, and of Kempton park, Midx., by Anne, da. of William JOLLIFFE, of Leak, co. Stafford. He *d.* 19 May 1736, aged 80, at Bury St. Edmunds, Suffolk. Will pr. 1736. The will of Dame Anne James was pr. 1739.

(a) As to his possible marriage and legit. issue, "S.H.A.H." (see p. 127, note "f") states that "Dr. G. B. Jermyn's MS. book says he married in America the da. of a miller, by whom he had one son, who afterwards served as a private soldier in the American army, who is also reported to have *m.* and to have had a family. I do not know how much truth there is in this, nor what the consequences would be if a descendant of the supposed family were to turn up. In another place Dr. Jermyn says that the wife of Sir Charles was the da. of an American planter, whose name was Coutts. At any rate no Lady Davers seems ever to have come to England." He had five illegit. sons, *bap.* at Rushbrook, April 1770 to July 1785, and three daughters, all by Frances Treice. At his death his estates went to his nephew and (apparently) heir at law, Frederick William (Hervey), 5th Earl (and afterwards 1st Marquess) of Bristol, who, three years later, sold them in 1808 to Robert Rushbrooke, who had *m.*, 23 May 1808, at St. James, Westm., Frances, illegit. da. of the 6th and last Baronet.

(b) Of the four brothers he was the only one who *d.* a natural death. The eldest (the 5th Baronet) was murdered; Henry Davers, the 2d s., admitted to Bury School in 1743, shot himself, on board ship, about 1760, and the Rev. Thomas Davers, M.A., Rector of Stow Langloft and Little Whelnetham, "shot himself in his mother's greenhouse at Bury," 30 June 1766. Of his two surviving sisters and coheirs (1) Mary *d.* unm., Aug. 1805, at Bury, aged 75, and (2) Elizabeth, *bap.* at Rushbrook, 1 Feb. 1732/3, *m.* there, 10 Aug. 1752, Frederick (Hervey), 4th Earl of Bristol, and *d.* at Ickworth Lodge, July 1803, leaving issue.

II. 1736, to 1741. SIR JOHN JAMES, Baronet [1682], of Creshall aforesaid, s. and h, *b.* about 1692; matric. at Oxford (St. John's Coll.), 13 March 1708/9, aged 16; *suc. to the Baronetcy*, 19 May 1736. He *d.* unm. 29 Sep. 1741, aged 47, and was *bur.* at Creshall, when the *Baronetcy* became *extinct*. Will dat. 15 May 1740, pr. 1741.(a)

GANS:

cr. 29 June 1682;

dormant or *extinct* on death of grantee.

I. 1682, to 1700? "CORNELIUS GANS, of Holland," a nephew of the celebrated Admiral TROMP,(b) was *cr. a Baronet*, as above, 29 June 1682, with a spec. rem., failing heirs male of his body, to "Stephen GROUBERT, *or* GROUBERT, Esq.," presumably (also) of Holland. At his death, however, the *Baronetcy* became *dormant* or *extinct*.

THORNHILL:

cr. 24 Dec. 1682;

ex. 1693.

I. 1682, to 1693. "TIMOTHY THORNHILL, of the island of Barbadoes and of Kent, Esq.," s. of Col. Timothy THORNHILL,(c) of Barbadoes, was *b.* about 1660 (being about 36 years old in 1696(d)), and was *cr. a Baronet*, as above, 24 Dec. 1682. He *m.* (—), da. of (—) BARRETT, of Barbadoes. He *d.* s.p. 1693, in or shortly before April,(e) when the *Baronetcy* became *extinct*. His widow *m.* Col. BLACKSTONE, of Barbadoes.

EVELYN:

cr. 17 Feb. 1682/3;

ex. 3 May 1692.

I. 1683, to 1692. "SIR EDWARD EVELYN, of Long Ditton, co. Surrey, Knt.," s. and h. of Sir Thomas EVELYN, of the same, by Anne, da. and h. of Hugh GOLD, of London, Merchant. was *b.* 25 and *bap.* 31 Jan. 1625/6, at Long Ditton; suc. his father (who *d.* aged 72), 4 Aug. 1659; was *Knighted*, at Worcester park, Surrey, 13 Sep. 1676, and was *cr. a Baronet*, as above, 17 Feb. 1682/3. He was M.P. for Surrey, 1685-87. He *m.* 15 Sep. 1659, at St. Dionis Backchurch, London, Mary, da. and coheir of Charles(f) BALAM, of Sawston, co. Cambridge, by Elizabeth, da. and h. of John

(a) He left his estates to the Hospitals of Christ Church, Bethlehem and St. George, but this devise being invalid under the Mortmain Act of Geo. II, they passed to the heir at law, Haestrect James, whose only child, Elizabeth, *m.* William James, of Ightham, co. Kent, leaving a son, Richard James, who *d.* s.p. 1807, having devised them to his cousin, Demetrius Gervis James.

(b) Not "Van Tromp."

(c) Possibly some relation of Sir Timothy Thornhill, of Ollantigh, co. Kent, Knt., who was admitted to Gray's Inn, 2 Feb. 1615/6 and whose will was pr. in 1648.

(d) Le Neve's MS. *Baronetage*.

(e) Luttrell's *Diary*, 11 April 1693, "Wrote from Barbadoes that Sir Timothy Thornhill and Mounsieur Dubois have died of the sicknesse."

(f) Often (erroneously) called *Anthony* Balam.

BYATT, of the same. He *d.* s.p.m.s.(a) 3 and was *bur.* 12 May 1692, at Long Ditton, aged 66, when the *Baronetcy* became *extinct*. Will dat. 12 Oct. 1691, pr. 1 July 1692. His widow, who was *bap.* at Sawston, 1632, was *bur.* 10 July 1696, at Long Ditton. Will pr. 18 Nov. 1696.

LEAR:

cr. 2 Aug. 1683;

ex. in or before 1736.

I. 1683. "THOMAS LEAR, of Lindridge [in Bishops Teignton], co. Devon, Esq.," s. of Sir (?) Thomas LEAR(b), of the same, and nephew and h. of Sir Peter LEAR, Baronet (so *cr.* 2 July 1660), a West India merchant, to whose estates he succeeded, was *b.* about 1672, and was, when apparently about 11 years of age, *cr. a Baronet*, as above, 2 Aug. 1683, with a spec. rem., failing heirs male of his body, "to John and Walter LEAR, his brothers, and their issue male respectively, and, in default, to Thomas LEAR, of Barbadoes, and his issue male." He matric. at Oxford (Wadham Coll.), 2 July 1687, aged 15; was M.P. for Ashburton, 1701-05. He *m.* (mar. lic. at Exeter, 17 March 1690) Isabella, da. of Sir William COURTENAY, 1st Baronet [1644], of Powderham, Devon, by Margaret, da. of Sir William WALLER, the Parly. General. She (or possibly an elder sister of the same name), was *bap.* at Powderham, 18 Dec. 1660. He *d.* s.p. Dec. 1705. Will pr. June 1706.(c)

II. 1705, to 1736. SIR JOHN LEAR, Baronet [1683], of Lindridge aforesaid br. and h., *suc. to the Baronetcy* in Dec. 1705 in accordance with the spec. rem. in the creation of that dignity; Sheriff of Devon, Dec. 1708 to Jan. 1708/9 and Jan. to Dec. 1710. He *m.* (—), da. of Christopher WOLSTON, of Devon. He *d.* s.p.m.(d) in or before 1736, when the *Baronetcy* became *extinct*.

WYTHAM, *or* WITHAM:

cr. 13 Dec. 1683;

ex. 15 Nov. 1689.

I. 1683, to 1689. "JOHN WYTHAM, of Goldesborough, co. York, Esq.," *b.* about 1644; was admitted to the Inner Temple; was sometime Chief Magistrate in Barbadoes, and was *cr. a Baronet*, as above, 13 Dec. 1683. He *m.* and had one child, who *d.* before him. He *d.* s.p.s. 15 and was *bur.* 28 Nov. 1689, in the Inner Temple, aged 45, when the *Baronetcy* became *extinct*. M.I. Will dat. 26 Oct. to 7 Nov. 1689, pr. 21 Feb. 1689/90.

(a) Of his surviving daughters and coheirs, (1) Anne, *b.* 26 March and *bap.* 5 April 1661 at Long Ditton, *m.* there 22 June 1682, William Hill, of Teddington, Midx. (2) Mary, *b.* 14 and *bap.* 23 July 1662 as aforesaid, *m.* 5 July 1688, at St. Giles' in the Fields (reg. at Long Ditton), Sir William Glynne, 3d Baronet [1661]. (3) Penelope, *b.* 3 and *bap.* 7 Oct. 1672 as aforesaid, *m.* 23 June 1690, at Long Ditton, Sir Joseph Alston, 3d Baronet [1681]. (4) Sophia, *b.* 1 and *bap.* 3 March 1675/6 as aforesaid, *m.* before 1696, Sir Stephen Glynne, 4th Baronet [1661], *d.* 5 and was *bur.* 8 Jan. 1738, at Long Ditton, leaving issue.

(b) Described as "Eques auratus" in his son's matriculation, but called in Le Neve's MS. *Baronetage* "Thomas Lear, a farmer of Devon, son of (—) Lear, near Totness, a very mean person," and brother of Sir Peter Lear, Baronet [1660], 'a scrivener,' who was first a servant, then a planter at Barbadoes."

(c) The will of Dame Susanna Lear, *alias* Susanna Rolle, was pr. Jan. 1713.

(d) Mary, his only da. and h., *m.* firstly Sir Thomas Tipping, 2d Baronet [1698], who *d.* s.p. 20 Feb. 1725, and secondly Thomas Comyns, who sold Lindridge house in 1736 to Dr. Finney.

RICHARDS:

cr. 22 Feb. 1683/4;

ex. or *dormant* after 1741.

I. 1684. "JAMES RICHARDS, of Brambletye House [in East Grinstead], co. Sussex, Esq.," yst. s. of John RICHARDS, of Toulouse, in France (who came to England with Henrietta Maria, Queen Consort of Charles I), having distinguished himself in the Navy, was *cr. a Baronet*, as above, 22 Feb. 1683/4. He was suspected of high treason (large supplies of arms, etc., being found at his house), and escaped to Spain. He *m.* firstly, Anne POPELEY, of Redhouse, Bristol. He *m.* secondly, in or before 1685, Beatrice HERRERA. He *d.* in Spain in or before 1705. Admon. 5 Dec. 1705 to a creditor.

II. 1705? SIR JOHN RICHARDS, Baronet [1684], 1st s. and h., by 1st wife; was Colonel of a reg. of foot in the Spanish service before he was 21, but afterwards became a merchant at Cadiz; *suc. to the Baronetcy* in or before 1705. He *d.* unm.(a)

III. 1729? SIR JOSEPH RICHARDS, Baronet [1684], br. of the half blood and h. male, being 3d s. of the 1st Baronet, but 1st by the 2d wife; *b.* about 1685; *suc. to the Baronetcy* on the death of his brother. He *d.* unm. 2 June 1738, aged 53, and was *bur.* at St. Pancras, Midx. M.I. Will pr. 1738.

IV. 1738, to 1750? SIR PHILIP RICHARDS, Baronet [1684], next br. and h. male; *suc. to the Baronetcy*, 2 June 1738. He *m.*, in or before 1741, [—], da. of the Duc DE MONTEMAR, General in the Spanish army. He was living, with issue, in 1741,(b) but on his death the *Baronetcy* became either *extinct* or *dormant*.(c)

DASHWOOD:

cr. 16 Sep. 1684.

I. 1684. "SIR ROBERT DASHWOOD, of Northwood, co. Oxon, Knt.," 1st s. and h. of George DASHWOOD, of Hackney, Midx., Alderman of London, Farmer of the revenue of Ireland and a Commissioner of Excise (who is said to have had a warrant for a Baronetcy), by Margaret,(d) dau. of William PERRY, of Thorpe, Surrey, was *bap.* 6 Nov. 1662, at St. Margaret's, Westm.; matric. at Oxford (Trin. Coll.), 19 July 1679, aged 17; admitted to Inner Temple, 1679; suc. his father in 1682; was Sheriff of Oxon, 1683-84; was *Knighted* at Windsor, 4 June 1682, being then a merchant of London, and was *cr. a Baronet*, as above, 16 Sep. 1684, with a spec. rem., failing male issue, to that of his deceased father. He was M.P. for Banbury 1689-98, and for Oxon, Nov. 1699 to 1700. He *m.* (Lic. Vic. Gen., 9 June 1682, he about 20 and she about 19) Penelope, da. and coheir of Sir Thomas CHAMBERLAYNE, 2d Baronet [1642], of Wickham, Oxon, by Margaret, da. of Edmund PRIDEAUX. He was *bur.* 20 July 1734, at Kirtlington, Oxon. Will pr. 1734. His widow was *bur.* there 22 Feb. 1734/5.

(a) "*Mr.* [possibly a mistake for '*Sir*'] John Richards, an eminent Spanish merchant," *d.* 11 April 1729 [*Hist. Reg.* 1729].

(b) Wotton's *Baronetage*, 1741.

(c) It is not known whether he left male issue, but he had two younger brothers, James and Lewis.

(d) She is said to have been granted the precedence of the *widow of a Baronet*, in the same patent wherein her son was *cr.* a Baronet. Her will, as "Dame Margaret Dashwood," was proved May 1714.

II. 1734. SIR JAMES DASHWOOD, Baronet [1684], of Kirtlington Park, Oxon, grandson and h., being 2d but 1st surv. s. and h. of Robert DASHWOOD, by Dorothea, sister and coheir of Sir John READE, 3d Baronet [1642], da. of Sir John READE, 2d Baronet, of Brocket Hall, Herts, which Robert, who *d.* v.p. at Paris, and was *bur.* 5 Nov. 1728, at Kirtlington, aged 41, was 3d but 1st surv. s. of the 1st Baronet. He was ed. at Abingdon Grammar School; *suc. to the Baronetcy* in July 1734; was Sheriff of Oxon, 1738-39; M.P. for that county (five Parls.), 1740 till unseated in April 1753, and again 1761-68; was *cr.* D.C.L. of Oxford, 25 Aug. 1743, and was High Steward of that University. He *m.* 17 Feb. 1738/9, at Keith's Chapel, Mayfair, Midx., Elizabeth (sister of Anne, DUCHESS OF HAMILTON), da. and coheir of Edward SPENCER, of Rendlesham, Suffolk, by Anne, his wife.(a) He *d.* 10 Nov. 1779. Will pr. Nov. 1779. His widow *d.* 19 April 1798. Will pr. April 1798.

III. 1779 SIR HENRY WATKIN DASHWOOD, Baronet [1684], of Kirtlington park aforesaid, 2d but 1st surv. s. and h., *b.* 30 Aug. 1745; matric. at Oxford (Brasenose Coll.), 16 April 1763, aged 17; *cr.* M.A. 29 April 1766, and D.C.L., 8 July 1773; *suc. to the Baronetcy*, 10 Nov. 1779; was for thirty-six years M.P. for Woodstock (eight Parls.), 1784-1820; Gent. of the Privy Chamber, 1784. He *m.* 17 July 1780, at Gatton park, Surrey, Helen Mary, da. of John GRAHAM, of Kinross, Scotland, sometime a member of the Supreme Court of Calcutta, by Helen, sister of William (MAYNE), BARON NEWHAVEN OF CARRICK MAYNE [I.], da. of William MAYNE, of Pile, co. Stirling. She, who was Lady of the Bedchamber and Governess to the Royal Princesses, *d.*, after a long illness, 12 Oct. 1796. Admon. Nov. 1796. He *d.* 10 June 1828, at Kirtlington park, aged 82.

IV. 1828. SIR GEORGE DASHWOOD, Baronet [1684], of Kirtlington park aforesaid, 1st surv. s. and h.,(b) *b.* there 17 Sep. 1786; was one of the Pages at Court, 1796; *suc. to the Baronetcy*, 10 June 1828; was M.P. for Truro, April 1814 to 1818. He *m.* 8 Sep. 1815, Marianne Sarah, 1st da. of Sir William ROWLEY, 2d Baronet [1786], of Tendring, Suffolk, by Susanna Edith, da. of Admiral Sir Robert HARLAND, 1st Baronet [1771]. He *d.* 12 Sep. 1861, at Kirtlington park, aged nearly 75. His widow *d.* there 24 March 1877, aged 88.

V. 1861. SIR HENRY WILLIAM DASHWOOD, Baronet [1684], of Kirtlington park aforesaid, 1st s. and h., *b.* 17 Oct. 1816, in Wimpole street, Marylebone; ed. at Harrow; matric. at Oxford (Corpus Christi Coll.), 23 Oct. 1834, aged 18; *suc. to the Baronetcy*, 12 Sep. 1861; Sheriff of Oxon, 1867, and sometime L. Lieut. of that county. He *m.* 18 Sep. 1845, at Sherborne, co. Warwick, Sophia, da. and h. of John DRINKWATER, of Sherborne aforesaid, by Ellen, da. of Nathan HYDE, of Ardwick, co. Lancaster. He *d.* 25 Jan. 1889, at Kirtlington park, aged 72. His widow *d.* 15 Oct. 1894, at 33 Eaton square, aged 76.

VI. 1889. SIR GEORGE JOHN EGERTON DASHWOOD, Baronet [1684], of Kirtlington park aforesaid, 1st s. and h., *b.* 12 Sep. 1851, in Wilton crescent; ed. at Eton; sometime Capt. Scots Fusileer Guards; *suc. to the Baronetcy*, 25 Jan. 1889; Hon. Major in the Oxon Light Infantry Militia. He *m.* 12 Aug. 1875, at Arrow, co. Warwick, Mary Margaret, 5th and yst. da. of Francis Hugh George (SEYMOUR), 5th MARQUESS OF HERTFORD, by Emily, da. of William (MURRAY), EARL OF MANSFIELD. She was *b.* 27 June 1855.

Family Estates.—These, in 1883, consisted of 7,515 acres in Oxfordshire and 115 in Lancashire. *Total.*—7,630 acres, worth £12,507 a year. *Seat.*—Kirtlington park, Oxon.

(a) This Anne was afterwards (1731) 2d wife to Sir William Barker, 5th Baronet [1622], of Grimston, Suffolk.

(b) His elder br., Henry George Mayne Dashwood, *d.* unm. and v.p. 24 Oct. 1803, aged 21.

CHUTE:

cr. 17 Sep. 1684;(a)

ex. 4 Feb. 1721.

I. 1684, to 1721. "SIR GEORGE CHUTE, of Hinxhill place [in Hinxhill], co. Kent, Knt.," as also of Surrenden in Bethersden, in that county, posthumous s. and h. of Sir George CHUTE, of the same (*bur.* 8 June 1664, at Bethersden), by Cicely (*m.* April 1661), da. and coheir of Ralph FREKE, of Hannington, Wilts, was *bap.* at Bethersden, 10 Feb. 1664/5, and, having been *Knighted*, was *cr. a Baronet*, as above, 17 Sep. 1684; was M.P. for Winchilsea, Nov. 1696 to 1698. He *d.* unm. 4 and was *bur.* 13 Feb. 1721 at Bethersden, aged 57, when the *Baronetcy* became *extinct*. Will dat. 26 Aug. 1718, pr. 1 Sep. 1722.

SHIERS, *or* SHEERS:

cr. 16 Oct. 1684;

ex. 18 July 1685.

I. 1684, to 1685. "SIR GEORGE SHEERS [*or* SHIERS], of Slyfield House [in Great Bookham], co. Surrey, Knt.," 1st s. and h. of Robert SHIERS, of the same (*bur.* 28 June 1668, at Great Bookham), by Elizabeth, his wife, was *b.* about 1660; matric. at Oxford (Exeter Coll.), 18 July 1679, aged 18, and, having been *Knighted*, was *cr. a Baronet*, as above, 16 Oct. 1684. He *m.* 3 July 1685, at the Temple Church, London, Elizabeth (*b.* Aug. 1670), only child of Edmund DICKENSON, M.D., Physician to Charles II, by Elizabeth, da. of the Rev. Stephen LODINGTON, Archdeacon of Stow, co. Lincoln. He *d.* s.p. 18 July 1685, a few days after his marriage, when the *Baronetcy* became *extinct*. He devised his estates to his mother.(b) His widow *m.* 18 Sep. 1687, at St. Sepulchre's, London (Lic. Fac. 17, he 29, Bachelor), Charles John, BARON BLOMBERG in Prussia, who survived her. She *d.* 1744, and was *bur.* at Hollingbourne, Kent. Will dat. 30 June 1738, pr. 1744.

SANDYS, *or* SANDS:

cr. 15 Dec. 1684;

ex. 5 May 1726.

I. 1684, to 1726. "RICHARD SANDS [*or* SANDYS], of Northborne, co. Kent, Esq.," s. and h. of Sir Richard SANDYS, of the same (*d.* 1669), by Mary (*b.* 28 April 1643, at Blackfriars), da. of Sir Henry HEYMAN, 1st Baronet [1641], was *b.* 6 and *bap.* 12 Jan. 1670, at Northbourne, and was *cr. a Baronet*, as above, 15 Dec. 1684. He *m.* firstly (Lic. Vic. Gen., 12 April 1694, he about 24 and she 16), Jane, da. of the Rev. Thomas WARD, Preb. of Salisbury. She was *bur.* at Northbourne, 16 Oct. 1696, being carried away for burial from St. Giles' in the Fields. He *m.* secondly, Mary, da. of Sir Francis ROLLE, of Shapwick, Somerset, by Priscilla, da. and coheir of Sir Thomas FOOTE, Baronet [*cr.* 1660]. She *d.* at Westham, Essex, and was *bur.* at Northbourne 5 Oct. 1709. Admon. 31 Oct. 1709 to her husband. He *d.* s.p.m.(c) 5 and was *bur.* 15 May 1726 at Northbourne, when the *Baronetcy* became *extinct*. Will dated 7 Jan. 1722.

(a) In the continuation of Dugdale's *List*, the date is given as 16 Sep., and it is placed before "Dashwood."

(b) She (as Elizabeth Shiers, widow) *d.* 14 Aug. 1700, devising considerable estates to Exeter College, Oxford, where, consequently, some additional buildings, erected out of such bequest, are known by her name.

(c) Of his married daughters and coheirs (1), Priscilla, 3d but 1st surv. da., *m.* her 3d cousin, Henry Sandys, of Down, Kent, and had a son, Richard Sandys, who inherited Northbourne Court, and *d.* 1763, leaving issue; (2) Mary, 4th but 2d surv. da., *m.* William Roberts, of Harbledown, Kent; (3) Anne, 7th but 3d surv. and yst. da., *m.* Charles Pyott, who *d.* s.p.m., 1789.

BLACKET, *or* BLACKETT:

cr. 23 Jan. 1684/5;

ex. 25 Sep 1728.

I. 1685. "SIR WILLIAM BLACKET, of Newcastle-upon-Tyne, co. Northumberland, Knt.," as also of Wallington in that county, 3d and yst. s. of Sir Edward BLACKET, 1st Baronet [1673], of Newcastle aforesaid (*d.* 16 May 1680), by his 1st wife Elizabeth, da. of Michael KIRKLEY, Merchant of that town, was *b.* about 1657, and was *cr. a Baronet*, as above, 23 Jan. 1684/5. He was M.P. for Newcastle, 1685-90, 1695-1700, and 1705 till death in that year; was Sheriff of Northumberland, 1688-89, and was considered "a good speaker in the House of Commons."(a) He *m.* 27 Jan. 1684/5, at St. Nicholas', Newcastle (Lic. Fac. 22, he 27 and she 16), Julia, da. of Sir Christopher CONYERS, 2d Baronet [1628], of Horden, by his 2d wife, Julia, da. of Richard (LUMLEY), 1st VISCOUNT LUMLEY OF WATERFORD [I.]. He *d.* Dec. 1705. Will pr. Feb. 1706. His widow *m.* Sir William THOMSON, Recorder of London [1714-39], and one of the Barons of the Court of Exchequer (1729-39) and *d.* before him 16 Aug. 1722 being *bur.* at Hampstead, Midx. M.I.

II. 1705, to 1728. SIR WILLIAM BLACKET, Baronet [1685], of Wallington aforesaid, only surv. s. and h., *b.* about 1690; matric. at Oxford (University Coll.), 14 May 1705, aged 15; *suc. to the Baronetcy*, Dec. 1705; was M.P. for Newcastle-on-Tyne, 1710 till death in 1728. He *m.* 20 Sep. 1725, at Hampstead aforesaid, Barbara, only da. of William (VILLIERS), 2d EARL OF JERSEY, by Judith, da. of Frederick HERNE, of London. He d. s.p. legit.,(b) 25 Sep. and was *bur.* (with great state) 7 Oct. 1728, at St. Nicholas', Newcastle, when the *Baronetcy* became *extinct*. His widow *m.* 13 March 1728/9, Bussy (MANSELL), 3d BARON MANSELL OF MARGAM (who *d.* s.p. 29 Nov. 1750), and *d.* 11 June 1761, being *bur.* at Newick, Sussex. Will pr. 1761.

CHILD:

cr. 4 Feb. 1684/5;(c)

ex. 24 Sep. 1753.

I. 1685. "SIR JOHN CHILD, of the City of London, Knt.," and of Surat, in the East Indies, s. of Theophilus CHILD,(d) of Newton, co. Northampton, sometime "Clerk of the Stockmarket," London (living at a great age Jan. 1689/90), by Frances, sister of John GOODYEAR, Dep. Gov. of Bombay, da. of Francis GOODYEAR, of co. Hereford, was an East India merchant and President of the Council at Surat, describing himself in his will, as "Generall for the East India Company's affairs in India, Persia," etc. He *m.*, in India, in or before 1678, Susanna, da. of John SHACKSTONE, Dep. Governor of Bombay. He *d.* on board ship in or near the Bombay roads early in 1690, leaving a fortune of £100,000. Will dat. 25 Jan. 1689/90, "then truly sick and very weak," pr. 25 Feb. 1700/1 and 2 April 1725. His widow *m.* George WELDON, an East India merchant (will dat. 14 June 1697, pr. 11 March 1697/8, directing £1,000 to be spent on a monument to her), and *d.* at sea, on voyage home in his lifetime, in or before 1697. Admon. 25 Feb. 1700/1 and 10 May 1725.

(a) Wotton's *Baronetage*, 1741.

(b) He left his vast estates to his illegitimate da., Elizabeth, who *m.* Walter Calverley, afterwards Sir Walter Calverley-Blackett, 2d Baronet [1711], on whose death s.p.s., in 1777, they passed to the family of Beaumont.

(c) In the continuation of Dugdale's *List* the date is given as 5 Feb. 1684/5.

(d) This Theophilus is said to have been the son of John Child, of Brentford and Colebrook, Midx. (*b.* at Reading), by Margaret, da. of [—] Reade, of Brentford. The relationship to Sir Josiah Child, 1st Baronet [1678], is not clear, but that Baronet is mentioned in the will (25 Jan. 1689/90) of Sir John Child, the 1st Baronet [1685] of this line.

II. 1690. SIR CÆSAR CHILD, Baronet [1685], of Cleybury, in Barking, co. Essex, 1st s. and h., *b.* about 1678; *suc. to the Baronetcy* in 1690; was Sheriff of Northants, 1701-02. He *m.* at Woodford, Essex, 1 Dec. 1698 (Lic. Fac. 26 Nov., he above 19 and she above 15), Hester, da. of John EVANCE, of London (then deceased), by Hester (then Hester GOODYER), niece of Sir Stephen EVANCE. He *d.* of the small pox 7 March 1724/5. Will pr. 1725. His widow was *bur.* 14 Mar. 1732/3, at Woodford aforesaid. Will pr. March 1733.

III. 1725, to 1753. SIR CÆSAR CHILD, Baronet [1685], of Wyvenhoe, co. Essex, 1st s. and h., *b.* 8 Feb. 1701/2, and *bap.* at Woodford aforesaid; admitted to Lincoln's Inn, 19 Oct. 1719; *suc. to the Baronetcy*, 7 March 1724/5. He *d.* unm. 24 Sep. 1753, aged 51, and was *bur.* at Wyvenhoe, when the *Baronetcy* became *extinct*. M.I. Will pr. 1753.

SOAME:

cr. 5 Feb. 1684/5;

ex. 7 Sep. 1798.

I. 1685. "SIR WILLIAM SOAME, of Thurlow, co. Suffolk, Knt.," only surv. s. and h. of Stephen SOAME of the same (will dat. 15 Nov. 1657, pr. 22 Feb. 1658/9), by his 1st wife, Mary, da. and coheir of Sir John DYNHAM, of Bourstall, Bucks (which Stephen was 1st s. and h. of Sir William SOAME, of Thurlow aforesaid, 1st s. and h. of Sir Stephen SOAME, also of Thurlow, L. Mayor of London, 1598-99), was *b.* about 1645; Sheriff of Suffolk, 1672-73, and, having been *Knighted*, 21 Feb. 1673/4, was *cr. a Baronet*, as above, 5 Feb. 1684/5, with a spec. rem., failing issue male of his body, to [his father's first cousin] Peter SOAME, of Heydon, co. Essex.(a) He *m.* firstly (Lic. Vic. Gen. 10 Feb. 1668/9, he about 24 and she about 23), Beata, da. of Thomas (POPE), 3d EARL OF DOWNE [I.], by Beata, da. of Sir Henry POOLE, of Saperton, co. Gloucester. She *d.* s.p. Admon. 23 Nov. 1680 and 23 Nov. 1700. He *m.* secondly, Mary, da. of Sir Gabriel HOWE, of Wotton under Edge, co. Gloucester. He *d.* s.p. at Malta in 1686. Will pr. Dec. 1686. The will of his widow was pr. March 1688.

II. 1686. SIR PETER SOAME, Baronet [1685], of Heydon, co. Essex, and Brickenden, Herts, cousin of the above,(a) being 1st s. and h. of Sir Stephen SOAME, of the same, Sheriff of Essex, 1620, by Elizabeth, da. of Sir Thomas PLAYTERS, 1st Baronet [1623], which Stephen (whose will was pr. 1640) was yr. s. of Sir Stephen SOAME, L. Mayor of London, 1598-99, and consequently great uncle of the grantee. He was *b.* 1634 (being six months old at the Her. Visit. of Essex, 1634), and *suc. to the Baronetcy*, according to the spec. rem. in its creation, in 1686. He, as Lord of the manor of Heydon, claimed to hold the basin, ewer and towel at the Coronation of James II. He *m.* 10 Dec. 1656, at Aspeden, Herts, Susanna, da. of Ralph FREEMAN, of Aspeden, by Mary, da. of Sir William HEWITT. He *d.* 1693 or 1694. Will dat. 13 April 1693, pr. 20 Feb. 1695/6. His widow *d.* shortly afterwards. Her will dat. 9 June 1694, pr. (with her husband's) 20 Feb. 1695/6.

III. 1693? SIR PETER SOAME, Baronet [1685], of Heydon aforesaid, 1st s. and h., *b.* about 1675; *suc. to the Baronetcy* in 1693 or 1694. He *m.* (Lic. Fac. 5 March 1694/5, he about 20 and she about 18) Joane, da. of George CHUTE, of Stockwell, Surrey, by Joane, da. of Sir Walter ST. JOHN, 3d Baronet [1611]. He *d.* of the small pox, at West Chester, early in 1709. Admon. 18 Feb. 1708/9, and 17 Jan. 1717/8. His widow *d.* in or before 1717. Admon. 14 June 1717 and 17 Jan. 1717/8.

(a) This Peter was by no means the nearest male relative to the grantee, whose father had no less than seven younger brothers, of whom six were married and two (at least) had male issue. To one of these uncles, Bartholomew Soame, he devised the family estate of Thurlow.

IV. 1709, to 1798. SIR PETER SOAME, Baronet [1685], of Heydon aforesaid, only s. and h., *b.* about 1707; *suc. to the Baronetcy* in 1709; matric. at Oxford (Ch. Ch.), 21 Jan. 1724/5, aged 17; was a Gent. of the Privy Chamber. He *m.* 23 April 1729, at Stanwell, Midx., Alethea, da. of "Governor PHILLIPS," of that place. She *d.* March 1745. He *d.* s.p.m.s.(a) 7 Sep. 1798, aged above 90, when the *Baronetcy* became *extinct*.(b)

CREATIONS BY JAMES II,

6 Feb. 1684/5 to 11 Dec. 1688.(c)

SUDBURY:

cr. 25 June 1685;

ex. 27 March 1691.

I. 1685, to 1691. "SIR JOHN SUDBURY, of Eldon, co. Durham, Knt.," s. of [—] SUDBURY, of Coggershall, ce. Essex, Clothier,(d) by Elizabeth (living March 1690/1), and nephew of John SUDBURY, D.D., Dean of Durham [1661-84]; was ed. at Trin. Hall, Cambridge; Fellow and LL.B., 1683, and was, after having been *Knighted*, *cr. a Baronet*, as above, 25 June 1685. He *m.* Bridget, da. of Sir Thomas EXTON, LL.D., Dean of the Arches Court and Vicar Gen. of the Province ef Canterbury, by Isabella (relict of Thomas PRUJEAN, M.D.), da. of Robert HORE, citizen and apothecary of London. He *d.* s.p.m.(e) 27 March, and was *bur.*, 3 April 1691, at Hornchurch, Essex, when the *Baronetcy* became *extinct*. Will, as "of Beadles," co. Essex, dat. 16 March 1690/1, pr. 4 April 1691. His widow, who was *bap.* 12 Sep. 1667, at St. Margaret's, Westm., *m.*, before 1696, Thomas CLUTTERBUCK, of Ingatestone, Essex. She *m.* (as her 3d husband), 21 Nov. 1699, at Westm. Abbey (Lic. Fac. 20, each aged about 30), Edward CARTERET, of Dagenham, Essex, Joint Postmaster General (who, surviving her, *d.* 15 April 1739), and *d.* 18, being *bur.* 26 Sep. 1735 at Hornchurch aforesaid, aged 68. Admon. 27 July 1758.

(a) Peter Soame, his only son, *d.* v.p. and unm. 20 April 1757.

(b) He devised his estates to Buckworth Herne, who by royal lic., 12 Dec. 1806, took the surname of Buckworth-Herne-Soame, and who by the death (15 July 1814) of his father, Sir Everard Buckworth-Herne, 5th Baronet [1697], became 6th Baronet [1697]. There was not, however, any relationship between him and the testator.

(c) During the interregnum, 12 Dec. 1688 to 12 Feb. 1688/9, no creations were made.

(d) "A person of a mean fortune" according to Le Neve's MS. *Baronetage*.

(e) Anne, his only da., *d.* shortly after him, aged 3 years, and was *bur.* 12 Sep. 1691, at Hornchurch. Her aunt Elizabeth, only sister of her father, wife of William Tempest, of Durham, was her heir.

T

JENKINSON:

cr. 17 Dec. 1685;

ex. 28 June 1739.

I. 1685. "PAUL JENKINSON, of Walton, co. Derby, Esq.," s. of Richard JENKINSON, Merchant, by Frances, da. of Thomas BENNET, of Derbyshire, was *cr. a Baronet*, as above, 17 Dec. 1685. He was Sheriff of Derbyshire, 1686-87. He *m.* Barbara, 3d da. of John COTES, of Woodcote, Salop. He *d.* 1714. His widow *m.* General WIGHTMAN, whom she survived, and *d.* 3 April 1723. Will pr. 1723.

II. 1714. SIR PAUL JENKINSON, Baronet [1685], of Walton aforesaid, 1st s. and h.; *suc. to the Baronetcy* in 1715. He *m.* Catherine (*b.* about 1695), sister and coheir of William REVEL (d. 1706, aged 12), 2d and yst. da. of John REVEL, of Ogston, co. DERBY, by Elizabeth, da. of Robert COPLEY, of Doncaster. He *d.* s.p.m.(a) at Walton 14 and was *bur.* 17 Jan. 1721/2, at Chesterfield. His widow *m.* William WOODYEARE, of Crookhill, near Doncaster.(b).

III. 1722, to 1739. SIR JONATHAN JENKINSON, Baronet [1685], br. and h. male, *suc. to the Baronetcy*, 14 Jan. 1721/2. He *m.* Mary, 3d da. of Sir Robert CLERKE, of Watford, co. Northampton.(b) He *d.* s.p.m. 28 June 1739, when the *Baronetcy* became *extinct*.

DAVIES, *or* DAVIS:

cr. 11 Jan. 1685/6;

ex. or *dormant* 4 Dec. 1705.

I. 1686, to 1705. "GEORGE DAVIES [*or* DAVIS], Esq. [of London], Consul and Agent at Naples," was *cr. a Baronet*, as above, 11 Jan. 1685/6. He *d.* at Leghorn 4 Dec. 1705, and was *bur.* in the Protestant cemetery there, when the *Baronetcy* became *extinct* or *dormant*. M.I.(c)

SHERBOURNE, *or* SHERBURNE:

cr. 4 Feb. 1685/6;

ex. 14 Dec. 1717.

I. 1686, to 1717. "NICHOLAS SHERBURNE [*or* SHERBOURNE], son of Richard SHERBURNE [*or* SHERBOURNE], of Stonyhurst, co. Lancaster, Esq.," 1st s. and h. ap. of Richard SHERBOURNE, of the same, by Isabel, da. of John INGLEBY, of Lewkland, was v.p. *cr. a Baronet*, as above, 4 Feb. 1685/6, and suc. his father, 16 Aug. 1689. He *m.*, in or before 1693, Catherine, da. and coheir of Sir Edward CHARLTON, Baronet

(a) Elizabeth, his da. and h., inherited the Walton estate, which she gave to her mother, whose second husband became possessed of it. His heir, John Woodyeare, sold it in 1813.

(b) "Lady Jenkinson died at Bath" 1748. Possibly this was the relict of the 2d or 3d Baronet.

(c) The inscription is printed in the *Mis. Gen. et Her.*, 3d s., II, 150.

[*cr.* 1645], of Hesleyside, co. Northumberland, by Mary, da. and coheir of Sir Edward WIDDRINGTON, Baronet [*cr.* 1642], of Cartington in that county. He *d.* s.p.m.s.(a) 14 Dec. 1717, when the *Baronetcy* became *extinct*. Will dat. 9 Aug. 1717, pr. June 1718. His widow *d.* 27 Jan. 1727/8, in Cork street, Burlington gardens, Midx. Will pr. 1728.

GULDEFORD:

cr. 4 Feb. 1685/6;

ex. in 1740, or Jan. 1740-1.(b)

I. 1686, to 1740? "ROBERT GULDEFORD, of Hempstead place [in Benenden], co. Kent, Esq., s. and h. of Edward GULDEFORD, of the same, by Anne, da. of Sir Robert THROCKMORTON, 1st Baronet [1642], of Coughton, suc. his father in 1678, and was *cr. a Baronet*, as above, 4 Feb. 1685/6. He *m.* (settlmt. 15 Nov. 1695) Clara (then aged 14), da. and coheir of Anthony MONSON, of Northorpe, co. Lincoln, by Dorothy, da. of (—) WITHERING. She, who was *bap.* 1 April 1681, at Northorpe, and who had sold that estate, 12 June 1705, *d.* in 1738. Will dat. 20 July and pr. 14 Nov. 1738. He, who had many years before [1716-17?] sold Hempstead and all other his estates, *d.* s.p. between 20 Sep. 1740 and 26 Jan. 1740/1, probably at Comber, co. Sussex [*Hasted* iii, 83], when the *Baronetcy* became *extinct*. Will dat. 30 Sep. 1740, pr. 26 Jan. 1740/1.

BLOIS:

cr. 15 April 1686.

I. 1686. "CHARLES BLOIS, of Grundesburgh, co. Suffolk, Esq.," only surv. s. and h. of Sir William BLOIS, of the same, by his 1st wife, Martha, da. and coheir of Sir Robert BROOKE, of Cockfield Hall, in Yoxford, co. Suffolk, was *bap.* 14 Sep. 1657, at Yoxford; suc. his father, 25 Nov. 1675, and was *cr. a Baronet*, as above, 15 April 1686; M.P. for Ipswich, May 1689 to 1695, and for Dunwich, Jan. 1700 to 1709. In 1696, by the death of his maternal aunt, he inherited the estate of Cockfield Hall. He *m.* firstly, 11 May 1680, at Ubbeston, co. Suffolk, Mary, da. of Sir Robert KEMP, 2d Baronet [1641], of Gissing, Norfolk, by Mary, da. and h. of John SOANE, of Ubbeston aforesaid. She *d.* 18 and was *bur.* 19 Jan. 1692/3, at Grundisburgh. He *m.* secondly (Lic. Fac. 18 April 1694), Anne (aged 25), da. of Ralph HAWTREY, of Riselip, Midx., by Barbara, da. of Sir Robert DE GREY, of Merton, Suffolk. She *d.* 29 Nov. 1727, and was *bur.* at Grundisburgh. He *d.* 9 April 1738,(c) aged 80, and was *bur.* there. Will pr. 1738.

II. 1738. SIR CHARLES BLOIS, Baronet [1686], of Cockfield and Grundisburgh aforesaid, grandson and h., being only s. and h. of William BLOIS, by Jane, da. of Sir Robert KEMP, 3d Baronet [1641], of Gissing,

(a) Richard Francis Sherburne, his only son, *d.* v.p. in 1702, aged 9 years. Maria Winifred Frances, only da. and h., *m.* firstly, 26 May 1709, Thomas (Howard), Duke of Norfolk, and *d.* s.p. 25 Sep. 1754, when the Stonyhurst estate devolved on the family of Weld (descended from William Weld by Elizabeth, her paternal aunt), who, in 1794, leased it as a College for English Roman Catholics.

(b) The information in this article has been kindly supplied by W. D. Pink, chiefly from the *Addit. MSS.* 5711, p. 69 (Brit. Museum) compared with J. J. Howard's *Catholic Families*, I, 80. It entirely disproves the date of death "1716-17" (which probably is that of the sale of some of the estates) as given in Courthope's *Extinct Baronetage*.

(c) His religious habits, hospitality and charity are greatly extolled in Wotton's *Baronetage* (1741).

which William (who *d.* v.p. 24 May 1734, aged 43) was 2d but 1st surv. s. of the late Baronet,(a) by his 1st wife. He was *bap.* at Yoxford, 25 June 1733; *suc. to the Baronetcy*, 9 April 1738, but *d.* unm. 26 Feb. 1760, and was *bur.* there, aged 26. Admon. 22 April 1760 and 29 April 1778.

III. 1760. Sir Charles Blois, Baronet [1686], of Cockfield and Grundisburgh aforesaid, uncle and h. of the whole blood; *bap.* 3 April 1692, at Grundisburgh; was a lunatic; *suc. to the Baronetcy*, 26 Feb. 1760, but *d.* unm., and was *bur.* 27 Dec. 1761, at Grundisburgh, aged 69.

IV. 1761. Sir Ralph Blois, Baronet [1686], of Cockfield and Grundisburgh aforesaid, br. of the half blood and h., being s. of the 1st Baronet, by his 2d wife. He was *bap.* 16 June 1706, at Yoxford; ed. at Woodbridge and Bury Schools; admitted as Pensioner to Caius Coll., Cambridge, 20 Nov. 1724, aged 18; Scholar, 1725-32; B.A., 1728/9; M.A., 1732; Fellow, 1732-38; in Holy Orders, and (as such) admitted to Gray's Inn, 1 Feb. 1752; *suc. to the Baronetcy* in Dec. 1761. He *m.* 24 Oct. 1738, at Bramfield, Suffolk, Elizabeth, 1st da. of Reginald Rabett, of Bramfield aforesaid. He *d.* at Hampstead, 8 May 1762, and was *bur.* at Yoxford, aged 56. Will pr. 1762. His widow *m.*, 14 Oct. 1765, Osborn Fuller, of Carlton, Suffolk, and *d.* 7 Jan. 1780.

V. 1762. Sir John Blois, Baronet [1686], of Cockfield and Grundisburgh aforesaid, only surv. s. and h., *bap.* 21 Nov. 1740 at Yoxford; ed. at Emman. Coll., Cambridge; M.A., 1762; admitted to Gray's Inn, 12 May 1762, having *suc. to the Baronetcy*, 8 May 1762; Sheriff of Suffolk, 1764. He *m.* firstly, 3 Feb. 1762, Sarah, sister of Thomas Thornhill, of Fixby, co. York, da. of George Thornhill, of Diddington, co. Huntingdon, by Sarah, da. of John Barne, of London. She *d.* 17 May 1766. He *m.* secondly, 21 April 1772, Lucretia, da. and eventually heir of Thomas Offley, of the Isle of St. Christopher. She *d.* 11 July 1808. He *d.* 17 Jan. 1810. Admon. Feb. 1810.

VI. 1810. Sir Charles Blois, Baronet [1686], of Cockfield and Grundisburgh aforesaid, 1st s. and h. by 1st wife; *bap.* 4 March 1766, at Yoxford; Lieut.-Col. of the Ouse and Derwent Vol. Corps of infantry; *suc. to the Baronetcy*, 17 Jan. 1810. He *m.* 19 Jan. 1789, at Drax, co. York, Clara, da. of Jocelyn Price, of Camblesforth Hall, co. York. She *d.* 22 Feb. 1847, at Coxfield hall, aged 78. He *d.* 20 Aug. 1850, aged 84. Will pr. Sep. 1850.

VII. 1850. Sir Charles Blois, Baronet [1686], of Cockfield and Grundisburgh aforesaid, 1st s. and h., *b.* April 1794, at Sway, Hants; was an officer in the army, and present at the battle of Waterloo; sometime Major in the 1st Dragoons; Lieut. Col. in the East Suffolk militia, 1844-53; *suc. to the Baronetcy*, 20 Aug. 1850. He *d.* unm. at Cockfield Hall, 12 June 1855, in his 62d year.

VIII. 1855. Sir John Ralph Blois, Baronet [1686], of Cockfield and Grundisburgh aforesaid, nephew and h., being 1st s. and h. of John Ralph Blois, Commander R.N., by Elizabeth, da. of the Rev. John Barrett, Rector of Inniskeel, co. Donegal, which John Ralph, who *d.* 19 June 1853, aged 58, was 2d s. of the 6th Baronet. He was *b.* 18 August 1830, at Wexford; ed. at the Royal Naval College; served in the Royal Navy; *suc. to the Baronetcy*, 12 June 1855; Sheriff of Suffolk, 1862. He *m.* 25 Jan. 1865, at St. Michael's, Chester sq., Eliza Ellen, yst. da. of Alfred Chapman, Captain R.N., of 90 Eaton place, Pimlico. He *d.* at Cockfield Hall, 31 Dec. 1888, aged 58. His widow was living 1904.

IX. 1888. Sir Ralph Barrett Macnaghten Blois, Baronet [1686], of Cockfield and Grundisburgh aforesaid, 1st s. and h., *b.* at Cockfield Hall, 21 Nov. 1866; ed at Wellington College; sometime Lieut. Scots Guards; *suc. to the Baronetcy*, 31 Dec. 1888; Capt. Royal Guards Reserve regiment, 1900. He *m.* 30 April 1898, at Christ Church, Mayfair, Midx., Winifred Grace Hegan, yr. da. of Col. Edmund Hegan Kennard, by Agnes, 2d da. and coheir of Joseph Hegan, of Dawpool, co. Chester.

(a) Robert Blois, his elder brother, *m.* Amy, da. of John Burrows, of Ipswich, but *d.* (before him) s.p. and v.p. 21 March 1728, aged 46.

Family Estates.—These, in 1883, consisted of 6,057 acres in Suffolk, and 250 in Norfolk. *Total.*—6,307, worth £8,212 a year. *Seat.*—Cockfield Hall, near Saxmundham, co. Suffolk.

COMPTON:

cr. 6 May 1686;

ex. 29 Aug 1773.

I. 1686. "Sir William Compton, of Hartbury, co. Gloucester, Knt.," as also of Hindlip, co. Worcester, s. and h. of William Compton, of the same, by Mary, da. of Thomas Habington, *or* Abington, of Hindlip aforesaid, was, after having been *Knighted, cr. a Baronet*, as above, 6 May 1686. He *m.* Catherine, sister of Sir Thomas Bond, 1st Baronet [1658], da. of Thomas Bond, M.D., of Hoxton, Midx., by Catherine, da. and h. of John Osbaldeston, of Harbens, co. Warwick. He *d.* in or before 1698. Admon. 15 July 1698. Admon. at the same date, of his widow.

II. 1698? Sir William Compton, Baronet [1686], of Hartbury and Hindlip aforesaid, s. and h.; *suc. to the Baronetcy* in or shortly before 1698. He *m.* Jane, da. and h. of (—) Hyde, of Hinton in Hurst, Berks. She *d.* 3 Feb. 1728/9. He *d.* at Hurst, 5 June 1731. Admon. 25 Nov. 1731.

III. 1731. Sir William Compton, Baronet [1686], of Hartbury, Hindlip, and Hurst aforesaid, 1st s. and h.; *suc. to the Baronetcy*, 5 June 1731. He *m.* (—), da. of (—) Holder. He *d.* 3 May 1758.

IV. 1758. Sir William Compton, Baronet [1686], of Hartbury and Hindlip aforesaid, 1st s. and h.; *suc. to the Baronetcy*, 3 May 1758. He *m.* (—) da. of (—) Bradnock. He *d.* s.p., Jan. 1760. Will pr. 1760.

V. 1760, to 1773. Sir Walter Abington Compton, Baronet [1686], of Hartbury and Hindlip aforesaid, br. and h.; *suc. to the Baronetcy* in Jan. 1760. He *m.* 20 Sep. 1765, at Haddington, in Scotland, Anne Sarah Bennet Mosley, of Chipping Campden, co. Gloucester. He *d.* s.p. 29 Aug. 1773, when the *Baronetcy* became *extinct.*(a) His widow *d.* at Hartbury, Nov. 1776. Will pr. Dec. 1776.

CHARLTON:

cr. 12 May 1686;

ex. 3 Dec. 1784.

I. 1686. "Sir Job Charlton, of Ludford, co. Hereford, Knt.," only surv. s. and h. of Robert Charlton, of Whitton, Salop, and of London, by his 1st wife, Emma, sister of Sir Job and da. of Thomas Harby, of Adston, co. Northampton, was *b.* in London about 1615; matric. at Oxford (Mag. Hall), 20 April 1632, aged 17; B.A., 1632; admitted to Lincoln's Inn, 19 Nov. 1633; Barrister, 18 Nov. 1644; Bencher, 1659; M.P. for Ludlow, 1659, 1660, and 1661-79; Serjeant at Law, 1660; Chief Justice of Chester, 1662-80 and again 1686 till death in 1697; *Knighted*, 1662; King's Serjeant at Law, 1668; Speaker of the House of Commons, 4 to 18 Feb. 1673; Justice of the Court of Common Pleas, 1680 till displaced, 20 April 1686, when he was restored to the Chief Justiceship of Chester, being *cr. a Baronet*, as above, 12 May 1686. He *m.* firstly, in or before 1650, Dorothy, da. and h. of William Blunden, of Bishop's Castle, Salop, by whom he had seven children. He *m.* secondly, Lettice, da. of Walter Waring, of Oldbury. He *d.* 27 May 1697. Will pr. 1697.

(a) The estates passed eventually to his two nieces, daughters and coheirs of his sister, Jane, by her husband, John Berkeley, viz. (1), Catherine, who inherited Hartbury, *m.* Robert Canning, of Foxcote, co. Warwick, and *d.* 1823; (2), Jane, who inherited Hindlip, *m.* 14 May 1799, Thomas Anthony (Southwell), 3d Viscount Southwell of Castle Mattress [I.], but *d.* s.p.m.s. 26 Oct. 1853.

II. 1697. Sir Francis Charlton, Baronet [1686], of Ludford and Whitton aforesaid, and of Envill, co. Stafford, 1st s. and h. by 1st wife, *b.* about 1651; admitted to Lincoln's Inn, 1 Jan. 1661/2; matric. at Oxford (St. Edm. Hall), 30 March 1666, aged 15; M.P. for Ludlow, 1679-81, and for Bishop's Castle, 1685-87; *suc. to the Baronetcy*, 27 May 1697; Sheriff of Salop, 1698-99; of Herefordshire, 1708-09. He *m.* firstly, in or before 1682, Dorothy, da. and coheir of the Rev. [—] Bromwych. He *m.* secondly, 13 March 1706/7, at St. Bride's, London (Lic. Vic. Gen. 11, he about 56, widr., and she about 26), Mary, da. of Joseph Came, of St. Mary's, Aldermanbury, London, merchant. He *d.* 21 April 1729. Will pr. 1729. The will of his widow pr. Feb. 1742.

III. 1729. Sir Blunden Charlton, Baronet [1686], of Ludford and Whitton aforesaid, s. and h., only child by 1st wife; *b.* about 1682; matric. at Oxford (St. Edm. Hall), 28 March 1698, aged 16; *suc. to the Baronetcy*, 21 April 1729. He *m.* Mary, sister of Thomas, 1st Baron Foley of Kidderminster, 4th da. of Thomas Foley, of Whitley Court, co. Worcester, by Elizabeth, da. of Edward Ashe, of Heytesbury. He *d.* Dec. 1742.

IV. 1742, to 1784. Sir Francis Charlton, Baronet [1686], of Ludford and Whitton aforesaid, 1st s. and h., *b.* at Burford, Salop, about 1707; matric. at Oxford (Ch. Ch.), 6 July 1721, aged 14; was a Gent. of the Privy Chamber and Treasurer of the General Post Office; *suc. to the Baronetcy* in Dec. 1742. He *d.* unm. 3 Dec. 1784, when the *Baronetcy* became *extinct.*(a) Will pr. Dec. 1784.

SPEELMAN:(b)

cr. 9 Sep. 1686.

I. 1686, to 1695. Debora Speelman, *otherwise* Kievit, widow, relict of John Cornelis Speelman, (who *d.* before the Royal warrant directing his creation as a Baronet had passed the Great Seal), was *raised to the rank of a Baronet's widow* for the term of her life, by letters patent, 9 Sep. 1686,(c) being those wherein her infant son, Cornelius Speelman, was *cr. a Baronet*, as mentioned below. She was da. of John Nicolaes Kievit, Member of the Municipality and Pensionary of Rotterdam, Attorney Fiscal to the Admiralty of the Maes, by Alida, da. of Maerten Tromp, Lieut. Admiral of Holland and West Friesland; was *b.* about 1655; *m.*, in or before 1683, the above named John Cornelis Speelman. He who was s. of Cornelis Speelman, Gov. Gen. of East India for the States Gen. of the United Netherlands (*d.* 11 Jan. 1684), by Petronella Maria Wonderaer, his wife, was *b.* 1 Feb. 1659, in Batavia, and *d.* 4 June, 1686, before (as above stated) his creation as a Baronet had passed the Great Seal. His widow, the *suo jure Baronetess*, *d.* at Rotterdam, 25 Sep. 1695, aged 40, and was *bur.* in the "Groote Kerk" there.

(a) The estates passed to his nephew, Nicholas Lechmere, of Hanley Castle, co. Worcester, son of his sister Elizabeth, by Edmund Lechmere. He assumed the name of Charlton after that of Lechmere.

(b) The information in this article has been kindly supplied by George W. Gray, who obtained the same from the present [1903] Baronet, together with a copy of the patent, the original of which has remained since its issue in the possession of each successive holder of the title.

(c) The words in the patent are as under. "Cumque ex gratia nostra speciali statuimus preficere constituere et creare Johannem Cornelium Speelman et heredes suos masculos ad et in statum, gradum et dignitatem Baronetti (Anglice *of a Baronett*) hujus regni nostri Anglie, et warrantum ad inde requisitum signaverimus, quod, per mortem predicti Johannis Cornelii Speelman intervenientem, ad magnum sigillum nostrum non prosecutum fuit, Igitur Volumus ac per presentes de gratia nostra speciali ac ex certa scientia et mero motu nostris pro nobis, heredibus et successoribus nostris Erigimus preficimus et creamus Deboram Speelman, *alias* Kievit, viduam et relictam dicti Johannis Cornelii Speelman, ad et in statum dignitatem et gradum Baronetti (Anglice *of a Baronett's widow*) habendum tenendum et gaudendum eidem Deborae Speelman, viduae, pro et durante vita sua naturali, unacum inscriptione, titulo, privilegio, loco et preheminencia uxoris, sive vidue, Baronetti hujus regni nostri Anglie ullo modo spectanti sive pertinenti."

I. 1686. "Cornelis Speelman, a subject of the States General of the United Netherlands, grandson (by the son) of Cornelis Speelman, late Governor General of East India for the abovenamed States General" (*d.* 11 Jan. 1684), was *b.* 19 Jan. 1684, being only s. and h. of John Cornelis Speelman (*d.* 4 June 1686, aged 26), by Debora his wife, both abovementioned, and was, at the age of 2 years, *cr. a Baronet*, as above,(a) 9 Sep. 1686, his said mother being raised to the rank of a Baronetess in the same patent. He, who was Lord of Nieland Scabinus at Bois-le-Duc, was in 1719, a Counsellor, and subsequently an Alderman there. He *m.* there 11 Jan. 1716, Agatha Vander Houven, Lady of Heeswyk and Diuther, da. of Jacob Jacobsr(b) Vander Houven. He *d.* 30 April 1746, aged 62, and was *bur.* at Heeswyk. His wife survived him.

II. 1746. Sir Cornelis Speelman, Baronet [1686], Lord of Heeswyk and Diuther aforesaid, 4th but 1st surv. s. and h., *b.* 5 Oct. 1722, at Bois-le-Duc; *suc. to the Baronetcy*, 30 April 1746. He *m.* 10 June 1745, at Leyden, Cornelia Clara, da. of Jacob Jacobsr(b) Van der Meer. She, who was *b.* 8 April 1720, *d.* 7 Aug. 1764, at Leyden, and was *bur.* in the "Hooglandsche Kerk" there. He *d.* at Leyden, 19 Sep. 1787, and was *bur.* as above.

III. 1787. Sir Cornelis Jacob Speelman, Baronet [1686], Lord of Heeswyk and Diuther aforesaid, 1st s. and h., *b.* 26 May 1747, at Leyden; *suc. to the Baronetcy*, 19 Sep. 1787; was a member of the Legislative College, 1802. He *m.* 18 May 1779, at Bois-le-Duc, Catherina, da. of Abraham Verster. She, who was *b.* 19 June 1749, *d.* 20 Feb. 1811, and was *bur.* at Heeswyk. He *d.* 14 June 1825, at Bois-le-Duc, and was *bur.* at Heeswyk aforesaid.

(a) The words in the patent are as under:—"Creamus dilectum nostrum Cornelium Speelman, Dominorum Ordin. Gen. Federati Belgii subditum, et Cornelii Speelman, nuper Gubernatoris Gen. Indiae Orientalis, ad supramemoratos Dominos Ord. Gen. spectantis nepotem ex filio, virum familiâ, patrimonio," etc.

This conferring of an English hereditary title on a foreign subject, an infant, whose grandfather's services (for which, apparently, they were granted) were neither in, nor on behalf of, England, seems very unusual. This remark also applies to the Baronetcy promised to the grantee's father, who died aged 26, never, apparently, having had any connection with England.

(b) Meaning "son of Jacob."

IV. 1825. SIR ABRAHAM FLORENTIUS SPEELMAN, Baronet [1686], Lord of Mulverhost, 2d but 1st surv. s. and h.; *b.* 3 Sep. 1784, at Heeswyk; *suc. to the Baronetcy*, 14 June 1825; was a member of the Nobles of North Brabant, and Burgomaster of Boxtel. He *m.* 1 April 1818, at Dordrecht, Sophia Balthina STOOP, da. of Anthony Balthasar STOOP, by Clara Cornelia VANDER POT, his wife. He *d.* 25 Aug. 1840, at Boxtel, and was *bur.* there. His widow *d.* 25 March 1863 at Berlicum, and was *bur.* there, aged 82.

V. 1840. SIR CORNELIS JACOB ABRAHAM SPEELMAN, Baronet [1686], s. and h., *b.* 5 Jan. 1823; *suc. to the Baronetcy*, 25 Aug. 1840; was an officer in the Artillery, obtaining finally the rank of General. He *m.* 25 April 1865, at Groningen, Anna Judith HORA-SICCANA, da. of Jonkheer(a) Jean Herman Martens HORA-SICCANA, by Isabelle Antoinette, BARONESS VAN IMHOFF, his wife. He *d.* s.p.m.(b) 18 Jan. 1898.

VI. 1898. SIR HELENUS MARINUS SPEELMAN, Baronet [1686], cousin and h. male, being s. and h. of Jonkheer(a) Cornelis Jacob SPEELMAN, Member of the Nobles of Friesland and President of the Court of Justice, by Elizabeth Woltera Sandrina, da. of Jacobus ENSCHEDÉ, which Cornelis (*b.* 17 Dec. 1817, and *d.* 7 March 1891) was s. and h. of Jonkheer(a) Helenus Marinus SPEELMAN-WOBMA,(c) also Member of the Nobles of Friesland and President of the Court of Justice (*b.* 29 Oct. 1787, and *d.* 20 March 1867), who was 4th and yst. s. of the 3d Baronet. He was *b.* 27 July 1852; was sometime, 1870-83, an officer in the Royal Dutch navy, and afterwards Burgomaster of Harlingen; *suc. to the Baronetcy*, 18 Jan. 1898. He *m.*, 27 March 1884, at Groningen, Jonkvrouwe(a) Wendelina Cornera VAN PANHUYS, da. of Jonkheer(a) Johan Æmilius Abraham VAN PANHUYS, Governor of Groningen and afterwards Vice-President of the Council of State, by Jonkvrouwe(a) Catharina Johanna VAN SMINIA, his wife.

HUMBLE:

cr. 17 March 1686/7;

ex. 12 Aug. 1709.

I. 1687, to 1705. "SIR WILLIAM HUMBLE, of Kensington, co. Middlesex, Knt., 2d s. of Sir William HUMBLE, 1st Baronet [1660], by Eliza, da. of John ALLANSON, was *b.* about 1650, and, having been *Knighted*, was *cr. a Baronet*, as above, 17 March 1686/7. He *m.* firstly (Lic. Fac. 15 Nov. 1681, aged 25 [*Qy.* 31], Frances HASLERIGGE, of St. Clement Danes, widow, who is generally said to have been da. of Sir Arthur HESILRIGE, 2d Baronet [1622], by his 2d wife, Dorothy, da. of Fulke GREVILLE. She was *bur.* 5 Sep. 1693, at Twickenham. He *m.* secondly, 14 Feb. 1694/5, at Isleworth, Mary, da. of (—) FISHER, of Isleworth. He *d.* s.p. 12 and was *bur.* 16 Aug. 1705, at Twickenham, in his 56th year, when the *Baronetcy* became *extinct*. Will pr. 22 April 1706. His widow *d.* at Isleworth 13 and was *bur.* 20 June 1752, at Twickenham, aged 76. Will pr. 1760.

(a) The meaning of the words *Jonkheer* and *Jonkvrouwe*, as also the position of the Speelman family in their native country, is thus elucidated:—"When, in 1817, a bill had passed for the regulation of the Nobility in the Netherlands, lists of names were published by the Government, including the names of all persons who were incorporated into the Dutch Nobility. Those persons [to] whom were given no special title (Count or Baron) had to bear the predicate *Jonkheer*, or, for the females, *Jonkvrouwe*. This predicate is always put before the christian names. It is generally abbreviated and put down thus, *Jhr.* and *Jkvre.* In 1817, Cornelis Jacob Speelman established his rights with regard to the Dutch Nobility, and his name was included in the first list of names of Nobles published by the Government; [accordingly] since that time *all* the descendants bear the predicate of the Dutch Nobility. Thus, since 1817, all the male descendants have before their christian names *Jonkheer*, or, by abbreviation, *Jhr.*; and the female descendants *Jonkvrouwe*, or *Jkvre.*" [G. W. Gray, see note "a" above, from information supplied by Sir Helenus M. Speelman, Baronet.]

(b) Cornelis Jacob Speelman, his only son, *b.* 30 March 1863, at Groningen, *d.* there an infant, 20 Nov. 1864.

(c) He was the only member of the family who had the addition of "Wobma" to his surname.

DUCK, *or* DUKE:

cr. 19 March 1686/7;

ex. 26 Aug. 1691.

I. 1687, to 1691. "JOHN DUKE [*i.e.*, DUCK], of Haswell on the Hill, co. Durham, Esq.," whose parentage is unknown, was *b.* about 1632, and having, by the trade of a Butcher, become "the wealthiest burgess on the civil annals of the city of Durham,"(a) was Mayor of that city 1681, building therein, (in Silver street), a splendid mansion and founding a hospital at Lumley in that county, and was *cr. a Baronet*, as above, 19 March 1686/7. He *m.* 30 July 1655, at St. Nicholas', Durham, Anne, da. of (his former master), John HESLOP, of that city, Butcher. He *d.* s.p. 26 and was *bur.* 31 Aug. 1691, at St. Margaret's, Durham, aged 59, when the *Baronetcy* became *extinct*.(b) His widow *d.* 14 and was *bur.* there 18 Dec. 1695, as "Madam Duck," aged 60.

FULLER:

cr. 1 Aug. 1687;

ex. 1709.

I. 1687, to 1709. "JOHN [*but should be* "JAMES"] CHAPMAN FULLER, of the Inner Temple, London, Esq.," was *cr. a Baronet*, as above, 1 Aug. 1687. He *m.* firstly, Frances, da. of John FINCHAM, of Upwell. He *m.* secondly, Emma, widow of Sir Edward WINTOUR, da. of Richard Hoo, of Norfolk. He *d.* s.p. in the Fleet prison, London, 1709, when the *Baronetcy* became *extinct*.

PYNSENT:

cr. 13 Sep. 1687;

ex. 30 Jan. 1765;

assumed till 2 Oct. 1781.

I. 1687. "WILLIAM PYNSENT, of Erchfont [near Devizes], co. Wilts, Esq.," only s. and h. of William PYNSENT, of London (*d.* in or before 1667), by Ann, sister and h. of John LANCELOTT, Gentleman of the Privy Chamber, da. of John LANCELOTT, Citizen of London, was *b.* probably about 1650; admitted to Lincoln's Inn, 11 Nov. 1667; became heir male, 29 Aug. 1668, to his uncle John PYNSENT, Prothonotary of the Court of Common Pleas, and was *cr. a Baronet*, as above, 13 Sep. 1687. Sheriff of Wilts, 1688-89 and 1693-94; M.P. for Devizes, 1689-90. He *m.*, in or before 1681, Patience, da. of John BOND, Alderman of London. He *d.* in or before 1719. Will pr. Oct. 1719.

(a) Burke's *Extinct Baronetage*, in which a full and interesting account of his career is given.

(b) His estates devolved on two nieces of his wife, viz., (1) Elizabeth Heslop, who *m.* George Tweddell, Alderman of London, and (2) Jane Heslop, who *m.* firstly, James Nicholson, of Durham, Cordwainer, and secondly, Richard Wharton, Attorney. By her first husband she was mother of James Nicholson, of West Rainton, M.P. for Durham, 1708, who *d.* 1727, leaving three daughters and coheirs, of whom (1) Jane, "worth £20,000," *m.* 28 July 1736 Thomas (Lyon), 6th Earl of Strathmore and Kinghorn [S.], and had issue; (2) Anne, *m.* Hon. Patrick Lyon; and (3) Mary, *d.* unm.

II. 1719? to 1765. SIR WILLIAM PYNSENT, Baronet [1687], of Erchfont aforesaid, 1st s. and h., *b.* about 1681; *suc. to the Baronetcy* in or before 1719; was M.P. for Taunton, Aug. 1715 to 1722; Sheriff of Somerset, 1741-42. He *m.* Mary, widow of Edmund STAR, of New Court, da. and coheir of Thomas JENNINGS, of Burton, in Curry Rivel, co. Somerset, with whom he acquired that estate, afterwards called Burton-Pynsent. He *d.* s.p.s.(a), and was *bur.* 30 Jan. 1765 at Erchfont, aged 84,(b) when the *Baronetcy* became *extinct*.(c) Will, in which he left all his estates (worth £3,000 a year) to William PITT,(d) afterwards the celebrated EARL OF CHATHAM, as an admirer of his patriotism, pr. Jan. 1765.

III. 1765, to 1781. SIR ROBERT PYNSENT, Baronet [1687],(e) *formerly* ROBERT PINSENT, was only s. and h. of Robert PINSENT, of Athy, co. Kildare, by Edith, da. of Oliver WALSH, of Dollardstown in that county, which Robert (will dat. 21 Feb. 1729/30, pr. [I.] 2 March 1732/3), was son and administrator (8 Jan. 1705 [I.] of William PINSENT, of Athy (*b.* there 1629, and admitted to Trin. Coll., Dublin, 28 Nov. 1664, aged 15), who was s. of the Rev. William PINSENT (admon. [I.] 1653), Rector of Athy aforesaid.(f) He was *b.* at Athy about 1707; entered Trin. Coll. Dublin, 12 July 1725, aged 18; B.A. 1730; in Holy Orders; Vicar of Kilmurry and Dunmoylin, 1741-72; *assumed the Baronetcy* in Jan. 1765, on the grounds of being heir male of the body of the grantee, which the above recited pedigree disproves. He was Preb. of Donoughmore, in dio. Limerick, 1765-68; Rector and Vicar of Macroom, co. Cork, 1767-72; Vicar Choral of Limerick Cathedral, 1773-78; Preb. of Moville, in dio. Derry, 1772 till death in 1781. He *m.* Mary, da. of (—) NUTHALL, of co. Kildare. He *d.* s.p.(g) 2 Oct. 1781, when the *assumption of the Baronetcy* ceased. Will dat. 4 Sep 1780, pr. 4 Dec. 1785 [I.].

(a) William Pynsent, his only son, *m.* (—), widow of Edward Wadman, but *d.* v.p. and s.p. 15 June 1754, being frequently (though in error) considered to have been the 3d Baronet. Eleanor Anne, his last surv. da., who had inherited estates from the family of Tothill, which passed at her death to her father, *d.* unm. in 1763, two years before him.

(b) See *N. & Q.*, 4th S., ii, 546.

(c) The title is given as "extinct" in Kimber's *Baronetage* (1771); as to this fact "E.W." states in *N. & Q.* (4th S., iii, 383) that "in 1765 the Baronetcy certainly became extinct, the second Baronet's only son (who married the widow of Edward Wadman, Esq.), dying 1754 s.p., and the other sons of the first Baronet having all died s.p. The *Extinct Baronetage* speaks of the Rev. Sir Robert as 4th Baronet, and descended from a younger son of the 1st Baronet. He may have assumed the title previous to his death in 1781, s.p., but it is certain that the 2d Baronet was the only son of the 1st Baronet who had issue male or ever married, [and] consequently thus, in 1765, the title became extinct."

(d) He accordingly when raised to the peerage, 4 Aug. 1766, was *cr.* Viscount Pitt *of Burton Pynsent*, co. Somerset, and Earl of Chatham.

(e) According to the assumption in Jan. 1765.

(f) The information as to this Irish family of Pinsent has been kindly supplied by G. D. Burtchaell, Office of Arms, Dublin Castle.

(g) He had a sister mentioned in her parent's will (that of her mother, was dat. 5 Sep. 1741, and pr. [I.] 28 Nov. 1749), but not in his own, viz., Henrietta, who *m.* Henry Bunbury.

STYCH:

cr. 8 Oct. 1687;

ex. 11 May 1725.

I. 1687. "WILLIAM STYCH, of Newbury [Grange, in Barking], co. Essex, Esq.," as also of Enfield, co. Midx., 1st s. and h. of William STYCH, of Newbury Grange aforesaid, by Magdalen, da. of Walleston BETHAM, of Rowington Hall, co. Warwick, suc. his father (who was *bur.* at Barking, 26 July 1678), and was *cr. a Baronet*, as above, 8 Oct. 1687, with a spec. rem., failing his issue male, to Richard STYCH, his brother, in like manner. He *m.* firstly, Margaret, da. of Sir Thomas LONGUEVILLE, 2d Baronet [S. 1638], by his 1st wife, Mary, da. of Sir William FENWICK. She was *bur.* 3 Dec. 1677, at Barking. He *m.* secondly, Elizabeth, da. of [—]. She was *bur.* 31 Aug. 1688, at Barking aforesaid. He *d.* s.p.m.s.(a) and was *bur.* there 12 March 1696/7. Will dat. 4 March 1696/7, pr. 10 April 1699.

II. 1697, to 1725. SIR RICHARD STYCH, Baronet [1687], of Newbury Grange aforesaid, br. and h. male, *suc. to the Baronetcy* in March 1696/7, according to the spec. rem. in the creation thereof. He *d.* s.p., presumably unm., 11 May 1725, in London, when the *Baronetcy* became *extinct*.

LAWSON:

cr. 31 March 1688;

ex. 14 June 1806.

I. 1688. "WILFRID LAWSON, of Isell, co. Cumberland, Esq.," s. and h. of William LAWSON, of the same, by (—), da. of (—) BEWLEY, of Hesketh, in that county (which William inherited the estate of Isell on the death, aged 87, of his uncle, Sir Wilfrid LAWSON, 16 April 1632), was presumably the "Wilfrid LAWSON," who (though described as the son of a Gentleman of *Cornwall* [probably a mistake for *Cumberland*]) matric. at Oxford (Queen's Coll.), 21 Nov. 1628, aged 17. He was Sheriff of Cumberland, 1635-36 and 1652-53; was *Knighted*, 26 Feb. 1640/1, at Whitehall; was Assessment Commsr. for Cumberland; M.P. for that county 1659 and 1660; and for Cockermouth, 1661-78; and was *cr. a Baronet*, as above, 31 March 1688. He *m.* Jane, da. of Sir Edward MUSGRAVE, 1st Baronet [S. 1638], of Hayton Castle, Cumberland, by Mary, da. of Sir Richard GRAHAM, 1st Baronet [1629], of Esk, having by her thirteen children. He *d.* 1689.

II. 1689. SIR WILFRID LAWSON, Baronet [1688], of Isell aforesaid, grandson and h., being 2d but only surv. s. of William LAWSON, by Mildred, da. of Sir William STRICKLAND, 1st Baronet [1641], which William was 1st s. and h. ap. of the late Baronet, but *d.* v.p. He was *b.* about 1665; admitted to Gray's Inn, 4 March 1680/1; matric. at Oxford (Queen's Coll.), 22 March 1680/1, aged 16; *suc. to the Baronetcy* in 1689; was Sheriff of Cumberland, 1689-90; M.P. for Cockermouth, 1690-95. He *m.*, in or before 1697, Elizabeth, da. and h. of George PRESTON, of Holker, co. Lancaster, by Mary, sister of John, 1st VISCOUNT LONSDALE, da. of Col. John LOWTHER, of Lowther. He *d.* 1705.(b) Will pr. March 1705. His widow *d.* 3 April 1734. Will pr. 1735.

(a) William, s. of Sir William Stitch, was *bur.* 31 Aug. 1687, at Barking.

(b) His conscientiousness in restoring impropriate tithes to the Church and in sending £600 to the Government on discovering that his estate had been undertaxed to that amount, is recorded in Wotton's *Baronetage* [1740].

III. 1705. Sir Wilfrid Lawson, Baronet [1688], of Isell aforesaid, 1st s. and h., *b.* 1697; *suc. to the Baronetcy* in 1705; matric. at Oxford (Queen's Coll.), 25 April 1713, aged 16; admitted to Inner Temple, 1715; Groom of the Bedchamber to George I; F.R.S., 1718; M.P. for Boroughbridge, Jan. 1718 to 1722, and for Cockermouth, 1722 till death in 1737. He *m.* 14 March 1723/4, at Fulham, Midx., Elizabeth Lucy, niece of the well known Charles, 3d Earl of Peterborough and 1st Earl of Monmouth, da. of Lieut. Gen. the Hon. Harry Mordaunt, by his 1st wife, Margaret, da. of Sir Thomas Spencer, 3d Baronet [1611] of Yarnton. He *d.* 13 July 1737, aged about 40. Will pr. 1738. His widow was *bur.* 29 Nov. 1765 at Fulham.

IV. 1737. Sir Wilfrid Lawson, Baronet [1688], of Isell aforesaid, 1st s. and h., *b.* about 1732; *suc. to the Baronetcy*, 13 July 1737. He *d.* at Kensington, "of a mortification of the bowels," 2 and was *bur.* 4 May 1739 at Fulham, aged about 7 years.

V. 1739. Sir Mordaunt Lawson, Baronet [1688], of Isell aforesaid, only br. and h., *b.* about 1733; *suc. to the Baronetcy*, 2 May 1739. He *d.* 8 and was *bur.* 13 Aug. 1743, at Fulham, aged about 10 years.

VI. 1743. Sir Gilfrid Lawson, Baronet [1688], of Isell aforesaid and of Brayton, co. Cumberland, cousin and h. male, being s. and h. of Wilfrid Lawson, of Brayton aforesaid, by Sarah, da. and coheir of (—) James, of Washington, co. Durham, which Wilfrid (who was admitted to Gray's Inn, 7 Feb. 1653/4) was 2d s. of the 1st Baronet He, who was M.P. for Cumberland (seven Parls.), 1702-05 and 1708-34; *suc. to the Baronetcy*, 8 Aug. 1743. He *d.* s.p. 23 Aug. 1749.

VII. 1749. Sir Alfred (sometimes called Alured) Lawson, Baronet [1688], of Isell aforesaid, br. and h.(a); *suc. to the Baronetcy*, 23 Aug. 1749. He *m.* (—). He *d.* 14 Feb. 1752. Will pr. 1752.

VIII. 1752. Sir Wilfrid Lawson, Baronet [1688], of Isell and Brayton aforesaid, 1st s. and h.; *suc. to the Baronetcy*, 14 Feb. 1752; Sheriff of Cumberland, 1756-57; M.P. for that county, 1761 till death next year. He *d.* s.p. 1 Dec. 1762.

IX. 1762. Sir Gilfrid Lawson, Baronet [1688], of Isell and Brayton aforesaid, br. and h., *b.* about 1710; *suc. to the Baronetcy*, 1 Dec. 1762; Sheriff of Cumberland (being, however, called "Wilfrid"), 1768-69. He *m.* in or before 1764, Emilia, da. of John Levitt. She *d.* 30 May 1769. He *d.* 26 June 1794, aged 84. Will pr. July 1794.

X. 1794, to 1806. Sir Wilfrid Lawson, Baronet [1688], of Isell and Brayton aforesaid, s. and h., *b.* about 1764; ed. at St. John's Coll., Cambridge; B.A. 1786; M.A. 1789; *suc. to the Baronetcy*, 26 June 1794; Sheriff of Cumberland, 1801-02. He *m.* Anne, da. of John Hartley, of Whitehaven. He *d.* s.p. at Cheltenham, 14 June 1806, in his 43d year, when the *Baronetcy* became *extinct*.(b) Will pr. 1806. His widow *d.* 30 Nov. 1811, aged 48. Will pr. 1812.

(a) Among the graduates of Cambridge University is "Alfred Lawson, B.A., 1738; M.A., 1742; St. John's College," which, possibly refers to a son of this Baronet.

(b) He devised his estates to his wife's nephew, Thomas Wybergh, s. of her sister Isabel, by Thomas Wybergh, of Clifton Hall, Westmorland. This Thomas took the name of Lawson, 21 July 1806, but *d.* at sea, v.p. and unm., 2 May 1812, aged 23, being suc. in the Lawson estates by his yr. br., Wilfrid Wybergh, who, accordingly, took the name of Lawson 26 Sep. 1812, and was *cr. a Baronet*, as "of Brayton house, co. Cumberland," 30 Sep. 1831.

WILLIAMS:

cr. 6 July 1688;

afterwards, since 1740, Williams-Wynn.

I. 1688. "Sir William Williams, of Gray's Inn, co. Midx., Knt., Solicitor-General," being also of Glascoed, in Llansilin, co. Denbigh, was 2d s. of Hugh Williams, D.D., Rector of Llantrisant, co. Anglesey, and Canon of Bangor (*d.* 1670, aged 74), by Emma, da. and h. of John Dolben, of Caeau Gwynion, co. Denbigh, was *b.* 1634, at Nantanog in Llantrisant aforesaid; matric. at Oxford (Jesus Coll.), 7 Nov. 1650, and admitted to Gray's Inn 5 days later; Barrister, 1658, becoming Treasurer in 1681; Recorder of Chester, 1667-84 and 1687—1700, and, being an active politician in the Whig interest, was M.P. for Chester, June 1675 to 1681, for Montgomery for a few months, till void in June 1685, and for Beaumaris 1689-90 and 1695-98; was Speaker of the House of Commons, Oct. 1680 to March 1680/1, and was fined, in 1686, £10,000 (though payment of £8,000 was accepted) for having, as Speaker, licenced the publication of Dangerfield's libellous *Narrative*. He was, however, on 13 Dec. 1687, made Solicitor-General (being *Knighted* 11 Dec. 1687), and, as such, had, on behalf of the Crown, the conduct of the (unsuccessful) prosecution of the seven Bishops(a) in June 1688, being the next week *cr. a Baronet*, as above, 6 July 1688. Though an active supporter of the Revolution he was not continued in office, but was made King's Counsel in 1689, and continued to practise at the Bar till his death. He was L. Lieut. of Merionethshire Oct. 1689 to March following. As early as 1665 he had purchased the estate of Llanforda, Salop, but apparently resided chiefly at that of Glascoed.(b) He *m.*, 14 April 1664, Margaret, 1st da. and coheir of Watkin Kyffin, of Glascoed aforesaid. He *d.* at Gray's Inn, 11 July 1700, aged 66, and was *bur.* at Llansilin. M.I. Admon. 16 Sep. 1700. His widow was *bur.* there 10 Jan. 1705.

II. 1700. Sir William Williams, Baronet [1688], of Llanforda and Glascoed aforesaid, 1st s. and h.,(c) *b.* about 1665; *suc. to the Baronetcy*, 11 July 1700; was M.P. for Denbigh, 1708-10. He *m.* firstly, in 1689, Jane (*b.* 25 Dec. 1665), 1st da. and coheir of Edward Thelwall, of Plas-y-Ward, co. Denbigh, by Sidney, only da. of William Wynn, of Branas in Edeirnion, co. Merioneth, which William was 6th s. of Sir John Wynn, 1st Baronet [1611], of Gwydir, co. Carnarvon. He *m.* secondly, Catharine, da. of Mytton Davies, of Gwysaney, co. Flint, but by her had no issue. He *d.* 20 Oct. 1740, aged about 75. Will pr. 1741.

III. 1740. Sir Watkin Williams-Wynn, Baronet [1688], of Wynnstay, co. Denbigh, *formerly* Watkin Williams, 1st s. and h. by 1st wife, was *b.* 1692; matric. at Oxford (Jesus Coll.), 18 Dec. 1710, aged 17, and was *cr.* D.C.L., 19 Aug. 1732; was M.P. for Denbighshire (six Parls.), June 1716 till death in 1749. By the death, 7 Jan. 1718/9, of his mother's cousin, Sir John Wynn, 5th and last Baronet [1611], he acquired the estate of Wynnstay,(d) and other considerable estates, and assumed the name of *Wynn* after that of *Williams*. He was Mayor of Oswestry, 1728, and of Chester, 1732; *suc. to the Baronetcy*, 20 Oct. 1740; was known in North Wales as "the Great Sir Watkin;"

(a) "It was said that the King had promised that if Williams had secured a conviction he should replace his old enemy [Jeffreys] as Chancellor. This seems to be referred to in Williams's epitaph, where he is described as *tantum non-purpuratis adscriptus*" [*Dict. Nat. Biogr.*].

(b) He is described "as being even then [1665, when only 31] *the Leviathan of our Laws and Lands*" [*Dict. Nat. Biogr.*].

(c) The 2d son, John Williams, inherited the estate of Bodelwyddan, co. Flint, and was ancestor of Sir John Williams, of the same, *cr. a Baronet*, 24 July 1798.

(d) The name was formerly Watstay, but was thus changed by Sir John Wynn, who himself had acquired it by marriage. See vol. i, p. 65.

was a strong opposer of Walpole's ministry, and one of the most influential Jacobites in Parl., being somewhat implicated in the Rising of 1745. He *m.* firstly, Anne, da. and h. of Edward Vaughan, of Glanllyn and of Llwydiarth, co. Montgomery, and Llangedwin, co. Denbigh, by Catherine, da. and h. of Maurice Roberts, of Llangedwin aforesaid. She *d.* s.p.s. 14 March 1748, devising all her estates to her husband. He *m.* secondly, 19 July 1748,(a) at Wraysbury, Bucks, Frances, da. of George Shakerley, of Hulme, co. Chester, and of Gwersyllt, by Anne, da. of Sir Walter Bagot, of Blithfield, co. Stafford. He *d.*, in consequence of a fall from his horse, 23 Sep. 1749, and was *bur.* at Rhuabon. Will pr. 1750. His widow *d.* 19 April 1803. Will pr. 1803.

IV. 1749. Sir Watkin Williams-Wynn, Baronet [1688], of Wynnstay aforesaid, 1st s. and h. by 2d wife, *b.* 1749 and *suc. to the Baronetcy*, 23 Sep. 1749; matric. at Oxford (Oriel Coll.), 9 May 1766, aged 17, and was *cr.* D.C.L., 4 July 1771; was M.P. for Salop, 1772-74, and for Denbighshire, 1774 (four Parls.) till death in 1789. He *m.* firstly, 11 April 1767, Henrietta, 4th da. of Charles Noel (Somerset), 4th Duke of Beaufort, by Elizabeth, da. of John Berkeley. She *d.* s.p. 24 July following, at Kensington. He *m.* secondly, 21 Dec. 1771, Charlotte, sister of George, 1st Marquess of Buckingham, da. of the Rt. Hon. George Grenville, by Elizabeth, da. of Sir William Wyndham, 3d Baronet [1661]. He *d.* 24 July 1789, and was *bur.* at Rhuabon, aged about 40. Will pr. 1789. His widow, who was *b.* 14 Sep. 1754, *d.* 29 Sep. 1832. Will pr. Oct. 1832 and July 1851.

V. 1789. Sir Watkin Williams-Wynn, Baronet [1688], of Wynnstay aforesaid, 1st s. and h., by 2d wife, *b.* 25 Oct. 1772; *suc. to the Baronetcy*, 29 July 1789; matric. at Oxford (Ch. Ch.), 15 Oct. 1789, aged 16, being *cr.* D.C.L. 4 July 1793; M.P. for Beaumaris, 1794-96, and for Denbighshire, (fourteen Parls.) 1796 till death in 1840, being a supporter of Pitt's administration; L. Lieut. of Denbighshire and Merionethshire; sometime aide-de-camp to William IV; was, from his great influence in his district, called "the Prince of Wales"(b). He *m.*, 4 Feb. 1817, at St. Geo. Han. sq., Henrietta Antonia, 1st da. of Edward (Clive), 1st Earl of Powis [1804], by Henrietta Antonia, da. of Henry Arthur (Herbert), 1st Earl of Powis [1748], sister and heir of the 2d Earl. She, who was *b.* 5 Sep. 1786, *d.* 22 Dec. 1835. He *d.* at Wynnstay, 6, and was *bur.* 15 Jan. 1840, at Rhuabon, in his 68th year. Will pr. April 1840 and Sep. 1851.

VI. 1840. Sir Watkin Williams-Wynn, Baronet [1688], of Wynnstay aforesaid,(c) 1st s. and h., *b.* 22 May 1820, at 18 St. James' Square, Midx.; ed. at Westm. School; matric. at Oxford (Ch. Ch.), 11 May 1837, aged 16; Cornet 1st Life Guards, July 1839, retiring as Lieut. in 1843; *suc. to the Baronetcy*, 6 Jan. 1840; M.P. for Denbighshire (nine Parls.), 1841 till death in 1885, during the whole of which time he hunted a large country four days a week at his own expense; Lieut.-Col. com. Montgomery Yeomanry, 1844-77, and Hon. Col., 1877 till death; Lieut.-Col. Denbighshire Rifle Vols., 1862 till death; Vol. aide-de-camp to Queen Victoria, 1881. He *m.*, 28 April 1852, at St. James', Westm., Marie Emily, 3d da. of his uncle, the Rt. Hon. Sir Henry Watkin Williams-Wynn, G.C.H. and K.C.B., by Hester Frances, da. of Robert (Smith), 1st Baron Carrington of Upton. He *d.* at Wynnstay, 9 May 1885, in his 65th year. Will dat. 7 Oct. 1884, pr. 12 Sep. 1885, above £105,000. His widow living 1904.

(a) This marriage was "at the request of the late Lady, under her hand" [*Gent. Mag.*, as quoted in the *Dict. Nat. Biogr.*].

(b) *Annual Register*, 1840. It was a current speech among the poor in his vast district, that "if God was to die we should still have Sir Watkin."

(c) This house was entirely destroyed by fire 6 March 1858, at the loss of £70,000, as also of many valuable MSS., the whole of the library, pictures, and works of art. It was rebuilt shortly afterwards.

VII. 1885. Sir Herbert Lloyd Watkin Williams-Wynn, Baronet [1688], of Wynnstay aforesaid, nephew and h. male, being 2d but 1st surv. s.(a) of Lieut.-Col. Herbert Watkin Williams-Wynn, by Anna, da. and h. of Edward Lloyd, of Cefn, co. Denbigh, which Herbert (who *d.* 22 June 1862, aged 40) was next br. to the late Baronet. He was *b.* 6 June 1860; ed. at Wellington Coll. and at Trin. Coll., Cambridge; B.A., 1883; *suc. to the Baronetcy*, 9 May 1885; was M.P. for Denbighshire, May to Nov. 1885; Sheriff thereof, 1890; Lord Lieutenant of Montgomeryshire, 1891; Lieut.-Col. com. Montgomeryshire Yeomanry; a director of the Great Western Railway. He *m.* 26 Aug. 1884, Louise Alexandra, only surv. da. and h. of his uncle, Sir Watkin Williams-Wynn, 6th Baronet [1688], by Mary Emily, his wife, both abovenamed.

Family Estates.—These, in 1883, consisted of 70,559 acres in Montgomeryshire (worth but £18,139 a year), 42,044 in Merionethshire (worth but £7,438 a year), 28,721 in Denbighshire, 3,856 in Shropshire, 361 in Cardiganshire, 224 in Flintshire, and 5 in Cheshire. *Total*, 145,770 acres, worth £54,575 a year. *Principal Seat.*—Wynnstay, near Ruabon, co. Denbigh.

ASHURST:

cr. 21 July 1688;

ex. 17 May 1732.

I. 1688. "Sir Henry Ashurst, of Waterstock,(b) Oxon, Knt.," 1st s. and h.(c) of Henry Ashurst, of London, Merchant, eminent for his piety and good works (who was *bur.* 1 Dec. 1680, at St. Augustine's, Watling street), by Judith, da. of (—) Reresby, of co. York, was *b.* 8 and *bap.* 14 Sep. 1645, at St. Augustine's aforesaid, was, apparently, a Merchant of London, and having been *Knighted*, was *cr. a Baronet*, as above, 21 July 1688. He was M.P. for Truro, 1681-95, and for Wilton, Wilts, 1698—1702; Commissr. of Hackney Coaches, 1694. He *m.* (Lic. Vic. Gen., 26 March 1670, he of Hackney, Midx., about 24 and she about 22) "the Hon. Mrs. Dyana Pagett, of West Drayton, Spinster," da. of William (Paget), Lord Paget, by Frances, da. of Henry (Rich), 1st Earl of Holland. She was *bur.* 3 Sep. 1707, at Waterstock. He *d.* 13 and was *bur.* there 28 April 1711, aged 65. Will dat. 9 Dec. 1710, pr. 11 May 1711.

II. 1711, to 1732. Sir Henry Ashurst, Baronet [1688], of Waterstock aforesaid, only s. and h.; *suc. to the Baronetcy*, 13 April 1711; M.P. for Windsor, 1715-22. He *m.* in or before Jan. 1711, Elizabeth, 2d and yst. da. and coheir of Sir Thomas Draper, Baronet (so *cr.* 9 June 1660), of Sunninghill, Berks, by Mary, da. and h. of (—) Carey, of Sunninghill aforesaid. He *d.* s.p. 17 May 1732, when the *Baronetcy* became *extinct*.(d) Will pr. 1732. His widow *d.* at Sunninghill, in or before 1738. Admon. 23 March 1737/8, to "John Baber, Esq.," nephew and next of kin.

(a) His elder br., Edward Watkin Williams-Wynn, Lieut. Scots Guards, *d.* unm. 8 Sep. 1880, being drowned in the Thames, aged 23.

(b) Of "Emington, Oxon," according to Heylin's *list*.

(c) The 2d s., Sir William Ashurst, Lord Mayor of London, 1693-94, was *b.* 26 April and *bap.* 2 May 1647, at St. Augustine's aforesaid. He *m.* (Lic. Vic. Gen. 31 Aug. 1688) Elizabeth, da. of Robert Thompson, of Newington Green, Midx. He *d.* 12 Jan. 1719/20.

(d) Frances, his sister and h., *m.* Sir Richard Anguish, *otherwise* Allin, 1st Baronet [1699], by whom, besides male issue, she had Diana, only da., who *m.* William Henry Ashurst, of Ashurst, co. Lancaster, and was father of Sir William Henry Ashurst, of Waterstock aforesaid, Justice of the Court of King's Bench, 1770-1800.

FYTCHE:

cr. 7 Sep. 1688;

ex. 13 June 1736.

I. 1688. "SIR THOMAS FYTCHE, of Eltham, co. Kent, Knt.," and of Mount Mascall, North Cray, in that County, 1st surv. s. and h. of William FYTCHE, of Barkway, Herts, and of Steeple Bumstead, Essex, by Alice, da. of (—), LARKIN, was *bap.* 17 Dec. 1637, at Barkway, was *Knighted*, 7 Dec. 1679, and was *cr. a Baronet*, as above, 7 Sep. 1688. He *m.* in or before 1676, Anne, da. and h. of Richard COMPORT, of Southend, near Eltham aforesaid (*bur.* 8 Jan. 1683, at Eltham), by Jane, da. of (—) BURSTON, of Kent. He *d.*, a few days after his creation, 16 and was *bur.* 19 Sep. 1688, at Eltham, aged 50. Burial registered also at St. Anne's, Blackfriars, London. Admon. 25 Sep. 1688, to his widow. She *d.* in or before 1716. Admon. as of Southend, near Eltham, 21 Aug. 1716, 3 Nov. 1722, and 10 May 1737.

II. 1688. SIR COMPORT FYTCHE, Baronet [1688], of Eltham and Mount Mascall aforesaid, 1st s. and h., *b.* 18 Oct. 1676; *suc. to the Baronetcy*, 16 Sep. 1688; matric. at Oxford (New Coll.), 19 Dec. 1693, aged 17. He *m.* 6 Dec. 1705, at St. Vedast's, London (Lic. Fac. 5), Anne, only da. of Sir Lumley ROBINSON, 2d Baronet [1682], by Anne, da. and h. of John LAURENCE, of Westminster. He *d.* at Bath 29 and was carried thence for burial [presumably at Eltham], 30 Dec. 1720, aged 44. Will pr. 1721. His widow, who was *bap.* 5 Oct. 1682, at Westminster Abbey, was *bur.* 29 April 1737, at Eltham. Admon. 10 May 1737 to her only da. Alice FYTCH.(a)

III. 1720, to 1736. SIR WILLIAM FYTCHE, Baronet [1688], of Eltham and Mount Mascall aforesaid, only s. and h., *b.* about 1714; *suc. to the Baronetcy*, 29 Dec. 1720; matric. at Oxford (New Coll.), 2 June 1731, aged 17, and was *cr.* M.A. 5 March 1733. He *d.* unm. 13 and was *bur.* 19 June 1736, at Eltham, when the *Baronetcy* became *extinct*.(b)

MORDEN:

cr. 20 Sep. 1688;

ex. 6 Sep. 1708.

I 1688, to 1708. "JOHN MORDEN, of [Wricklemarsh, in] Blackheath, co. Kent, Esq.," only s. of George MORDEN, of St. Bride's, London, Citizen and Goldsmith (*d.* Sep. 1624), by Martha (*m.* Oct. 1619), da. of Thomas HARRIS, of London, was *b.* 13 Aug. 1623 at (it is said) St. Bride's, London; traded at Aleppo as a Turkey merchant; was a member of the East India Company, and, having purchased considerable estates at Charlton, Lewisham, etc., co. Kent, was *cr. a Baronet*, as above, 20 Sep. 1688. He was a Commissr. of Excise, 1691, and was M.P. for Colchester, 1695-98. He founded the well-known Morden College, Blackheath (opened in June 1700) for decayed Merchants. He *m.* (Lic. Fac. 31 May 1662, he about 36 of St. Martin's Outwich, Merchant, and she about 22),

(a) See *N. & Q.*, 8th S., iv, 151, as to this admon. and as to the administratrix being Alice and not Anne. On the same date, 10 May 1737, was granted the additional admon. of Dame Anne Fytch [widow of the 1st Baronet] to her da., Anne Fytch, Spinster, *de bonis non* administered by her da. Christian Fytch, 3 Nov. 1722. This last named Anne was presumably the "Mrs. Anne Fytch," *bur.* at Eltham, 22 April 1740. [See Drake's *Hundred of Blackheath*, p. 212].

(b) The estates devolved on his only surv. sister Alice, who *m.* 28 Oct. 1740, for her first husband, Sir John Barker, 6th Baronet [1622], whose only s. and h., Sir John Fytch Barker, 7th Baronet, *d.* s.p. 3 Jan. 1766, aged 24, and devised them to a stranger in blood.

Susan, da. of Joseph BRAND, of Edwardstone, Suffolk, by Thomazine, da. of Thomas TROTTER, of London, Merchant. He *d.* s.p. 6 and was *bur.* 20 Sep. 1708, in his 86th year, in the Chapel at Morden College, when the *Baronetcy* became *extinct*. Will dat. 15 Oct. 1702 to 9 March 1702/3, pr. Oct. 1708.(a) His widow was *bur.* with him 10 June 1721. Will pr. 1721.

NARBOROUGH, *or* NARBROUGH:

cr. 15 Nov. 1688;

ex. 22 Oct. 1707.

I. 1688, to 1707. "JOHN NARBOROUGH [*or* NARBROUGH], of Knowlton, co. Kent, Esq., eldest s. of Sir John NARBOROUGH [*or* NARBROUGH], Knt.,"(b) a well known Admiral (*d.* 27 May 1688, in his 49th year), by his 2d wife, Elizabeth (*m.* 20 June 1681, at Wanstead, Essex), da. of Capt. John HILL, of Shadwell (afterwards wife [*m.* 10 March 1690/1, at Allhallows', Staining] of the celebrated Admiral, Sir Cloudesly SHOVELL), was *b.* 14 and *bap.* 21 Oct. 1684, at St. Olave's, Hart street, London, and was, when but four years old, in respect of his father's services, *cr. a Baronet*, as above, 15 Nov. 1688, with a spec. rem., failing heirs male of his body to his br. James NARBOROUGH [*or* NARBROUGH] (*b.* and *bap.* 2 Nov. 1685 at St. Olave's aforesaid) in like manner. He (with his said br. James,(c) then aged 17) matric. at Oxford (Ch. Ch.), 7 July 1703, aged 18. Both were Lieuts. in the Navy, and *d.* unm. three years later, on the same day, 22 Oct. 1707, being lost at sea, off the Scilly islands (with their stepfather, Sir Cloudesly SHOVELL), when the *Baronetcy* became *extinct*.(d) M.I. at Knowlton. Will dat. 14 June 1706, pr. 13 Jan. 1707/8.

CREATIONS BY WILLIAM III AND MARY II.

13 Feb 1688/9(e) to 27 Dec. 1694.

(a) He left his estates, after his wife's death, in trust for Morden College, having no very near relatives. The only Morden mentioned in his will is his cousin, "John Morden, Calendar," to whom he leaves £100. Possibly this is the John Morden, of Great Bradley, Suffolk, and of Suffield, Norfolk, who was 4th in descent from testator's great grandfather, John Morden, of Exning. This John *d.* 1726, leaving a s. and h., William Morden, who, on inheriting the estates of his maternal great uncle, Sir Charles Harbord, took that name and was *cr. a Baronet* in 1745. See pedigree of Morden in J. J. Muskett's *Suffolk Manorial Families*, vol. ii, p. 120.

(b) See full account of the family by the Hon. Robert Marsham Townshend, in *N. & Q.*, 7th S., vi, p. 420.

(c) There is a monument in Christ Church Cathedral, Oxford, to this James, who possibly was a benefactor to that University. His will, dat. "1707," was pr. 13 Jan. 1707/8, as was that of his brother.

(d) Elizabeth, his only surv. sister and h., *b.* 9 and *bap.* 27 April 1682, at St. Olave's, Hart street, *m.* 23 Jan. 1700/1, at St. Dionis Backchurch, Thomas D'Aeth, *cr. a Baronet*, 16 July 1716, and *d.* 24 June 1721, being *bur.* at Knowlton.

(e) During the interregnum 12 Dec. 1688 to 12 Feb. 1688/9, no creations were made.

V

MOLESWORTH:

cr. 19 July 1689.

I. 1689, July. "HENDER MOLESWORTH, of Spring Gardens, Westminster, co. Middlesex, Governor of Jamaica," 2d s. of Hender MOLESWORTH,(a) of Pencarrow, co. Cornwall (*d.* 1647, aged about 50), by Mary, da. of John SPARKE, of the Friary, Plymouth, was *b.* about 1638; was a merchant at St. Katharine's, Jamaica, being sometime President of the Council there and Deputy Governor of that Island; was Governor thereof, Nov. 1688 till death, and, being a supporter of the Revolution, was *cr. a Baronet*, as above, 19 July 1689, with a spec. rem., failing heirs male of his body, to his eldest br., "Sir John MOLESWORTH, of Pencarrow, co. Cornwall, Knt." He *m.* firstly, Grace, widow of Thomas TOTTLE, of Jamaica, merchant, da. of Capt. George MANGYE, of Jamaica, formerly a Goldsmith of London. She *d.* s p. 31 Aug. and was *bur.* 6 Sep. 1687, at St. Anne's, Soho, Midx. He *m.* secondly, 12 Feb. 1688/9, at St. Martin's in the Fields (Lic. Fac. 11, he about 50, widower, and she about 22), Mary, widow of Sir Thomas LYNCH, Gov. of Jamaica, da. and coheir of Thomas TEMPLE, of Franckton, co. Warwick. He *d.* s.p. a month after his creation, and was *bur.* 12 Aug. 1689, at St. Anne's, Soho. Will dat. 2 April, pr. 5 Sep. 1689. His widow *d.* 11 and was *bur.* 14 July 1721, at St. Anne's aforesaid. Will pr. 11 July 1721.

II. 1689, Aug. SIR JOHN MOLESWORTH, Baronet [1689], of Pencarrow aforesaid, 1st br. and h., *bap.* 27 May 1635, at St. Andrew's, Plymouth; suc. his father, 1647; matric. at Oxford (Balliol Coll.), 20 July 1654; admitted to the Inner Temple, Nov. 1656; *Knighted*, 18 June 1675; *suc. to the Baronetcy*, under the spec. rem. in the creation thereof, Aug. 1689; Vice-Admiral of Cornwall, temp. Car. II, till death; Sheriff thereof, 1690-91; M.P. for Lostwithiel, 1700-01; for Bossiney, 1701-02; and for Lostwithiel again, 1702-05. He *m.* firstly, 7 Oct. 1663, at Maristow, Devon (Lic. 29 July), Margery, sister of Sir Edward WISE, K.B., 1st da. of Thomas WISE, of Sidenham, Devon, by Mary, sister of Arthur (CHICHESTER), 1st EARL OF DONEGAL [I.], da. of Edward, 1st VISCOUNT CHICHESTER OF CARRICKFERGUS [I.]. She was *bur.* 19 June 1671, at Egloshayle, Cornwall. He *m.* secondly, Margaret (*bap.* 20 Feb. 1630/1, at Plympton St. Mary), da. of Sir Nicholas SLANNING, of Maristow, Devon, by Gertrude, da. of Sir James BAGGE. She *d.* s.p. and was *bur.* 12 Feb. 1682, at Egloshayle. He was *bur.* there 18 Oct. 1716, aged 31.

III. 1716. SIR JOHN MOLESWORTH, Baronet [1689] of Pencarrow aforesaid, 1st s. and h. by 1st wife, *bap.* 23 June 1668, at Egloshayle; matric. at Oxford (Exeter Coll.), 12 May 1687, aged 18; admitted to the Middle Temple, 1688; *suc. to the Baronetcy* in Oct. 1716. He *m.* 19 Sep. 1699, at Tetcott, Devon (settlement 7 Sep. 1704), Jane, da. of John ARSCOTT, of Tetcott, Devon, by his 2d wife, Prudence, da. of (—). She, who was *bap.* 19 June 1678, at Tetcott, was *bur.* 6 May 1719 at Egloshayle. He was *bur.* there 20 June 1723, aged 55. Will dat. 3 Sep. 1720, pr. 14 Oct. 1724, and 2 June 1728.

IV. 1723. SIR JOHN MOLESWORTH, Baronet [1689], of Pencarrow aforesaid, 1st s. and h., *bap.* 28 Feb. 1705 at Egloshayle; *suc. to the Baronetcy* in June 1723; was M.P. for Newport, co. Cornwall, 1734-41, and for Cornwall (three Parls.), Dec. 1744 to 1761. He *m.* in 1728, Barbara, 2d da. of Sir Nicholas MORICE, 2d Baronet [1661], of Werrington, Devon, by Catherine, da.

(a) This Hender Molesworth was s. and h. of John Molesworth, of Pencarrow, who entered his pedigree at the Visit. of Devon 1620 (*bur.* 26 Jan. 1634, at St. Kew), by his 1st wife, Catherine, da. and coheir of John Hender, of Botreaux Castle, Cornwall.

of Thomas (HERBERT), 8th EARL of PEMBROKE. She *d.* of the small-pox, at Staines, Midx., 17 and was *bur.* 31 May 1735, at Egloshayle, aged 24. M.I. He *d.* 4 and was *bur.* there 14 April 1766. Will dat. 27 Feb., pr. 22 April 1766.

V. 1766. SIR JOHN MOLESWORTH, Baronet [1689], of Pencarrow aforesaid, 1st s. and h., *b.* 12 March and *bap.* 9 April 1729, at Egloshayle; matric. at Oxford (Balliol Coll.), 14 March 1748/9, aged 19, and was *cr.* M.A., 17 May 1751; *suc. to the Baronetcy*, 4 April 1766; M.P. for Cornwall, May 1765 till death in 1775. He *m.* firstly, 28 Sep. 1755, Frances, da. and coheir of James SMYTH, of St. Audrie's, Somerset. She *d.* 1 and was *bur.* 9 July 1758, at Egloshayle. He *m.* secondly, 22 July 1762, at Egloshayle, his cousin, Barbara, da. of Sir John ST. AUBYN, 3d Baronet [1671], of Clowance, by Catherine, 1st da. of the abovenamed Sir NICHOLAS MORICE, 2d Baronet [1661]. He *d.* 20 and was *bur.* 26 Oct. 1775, at Egloshayle, aged 46. Will pr. 1777. His widow *d.* 14 Aug. 1814. Will pr. 1814.

VI. 1775. SIR WILLIAM MOLESWORTH, Baronet [1689], of Pencarrow aforesaid, 1st s. and h., only child by 1st wife, *b.* 30 June 1758, at Langdon, near Plymouth; *suc. to the Baronetcy*, 20 Oct. 1775; admitted to St. John's Coll., Cambridge, 1779; M.P. for Cornwall, Feb. 1784 to 1790; Sheriff thereof, 1791-92. He *m.* 27 May 1786, Catherine Treby, yst. da. of Paul Henry Treby OURRY,(a) Commissr. of Plymouth Dockyard, by Charity, 1st da. and coheir of the Rt. Hon. George TREBY, Sec. at War. He *d.* in London, 22 Feb. and was *bur.* 8 March 1798, at Egloshayle, in his 40th year. Will pr. April 1798. His widow, who was *b.* 26 June 1761, *d.* at Cobham, co. Surrey, 10 Dec. 1842, aged 81. Will pr. Feb. 1843.

VII. 1798. SIR ARSCOTT OURRY MOLESWORTH, Baronet [1689], of Pencarrow aforesaid, 1st s. and h., *b.* 1789; *suc. to the Baronetcy*, 22 Feb. 1798; ed. at St. John's Coll., Cambridge; B.A., 1809; Sheriff of Cornwall, 1816-17. He *m.* 7 July 1809, Mary, 1st da. of Patrick BROWN, of Edinburgh. He *d.* at Pencarrow, 26 Dec. 1823, and was *bur.* 3 Jan. 1824, at Egloshayle, aged 34. M.I. Will pr. 1824. His widow *d.* in Lowndes street, Midx., 16 April 1877, in her 97th year.

VIII. 1823. SIR WILLIAM MOLESWORTH, Baronet [1689], of Pencarrow aforesaid, 1st s. and h., *b.* 23 May 1810, in Upper Brook street and *bap.* at St. Geo. Han. sq.; *suc. to the Baronetcy*, 26 Dec. 1823; ed. at a school at Offenbach, in Germany; was for two years at Trin. Coll., Cambridge,(b) and subsequently (about 1828) at the Univ. of Edinburgh; was an advanced "Liberal,"(c) and, as such, M.P. for East Cornwall, 1832-37; for Leeds, 1837-41; for Southwark, Sep. 1845 till death in 1855; Sheriff of Cornwall, 1842. Privy Councillor, 1852; a Commissr. of Works, 1852-55, and for a few months before his death (July to Oct. 1855), Colonial Secretary. He *m.* 4 July 1844, at St. Geo. Han. sq., Andalusia Grant, widow of Temple WEST, of Mathou Lodge, co. Worcester, only da. of James Bruce CARSTAIRS.(d) He *d.* s.p. 22 Oct. 1855, at

(a) See *Mis. Gen. et Her.*, 3d S., vol. v, p. 12, for a pedigree of the Huguenot family of Ourry.

(b) He was expelled thence, having challenged his tutor to fight a duel.

(c) "In Germany he had become democratic; in Scotland sceptical," while, during his Cambridge career, "the utilitarian propaganda had been actively carried on." Several incidents connected with him appear in *The Philosophical Radicals* of 1832, written by Mrs. Grote and privately printed in 1866. He edited, (in no less than sixteen vols. [!]), *Hobbes's Works*, and had meant to have added thereto a life of Hobbes. He also wrote some articles in the *London and Westminster Review* [see *Dict. Nat. Biogr.*].

(d) To him, who died at his said daughter's house, there is the following monumental inscription at [presumably] Egloshayle:—"JAMES BRUCE CARSTAIRS, Esq., the last surviving member of the family of SIR JAMES BRUCE, Baronet, of Kinross, N.B., died 10 Sep. 1845, aged 75 years."

87 Eaton Place, Pimlico, in his 46th year, and was *bur.* in Kensal Green cemetery. Will pr. March 1856. His widow, to whom he left his estates (though possibly only for her life), and who, for above forty years, was a leading member in fashionable society, *d.* in Eaton Place aforesaid 16 May 1888, and was *bur.* with him.

IX. 1855. SIR HUGH HENRY MOLESWORTH, Baronet [1689], cousin and h. male, being 1st s. and h. of the Rev. William MOLESWORTH, Rector of Beaworthy, Devon, and of St. Breock and St. Ervan, co. Cornwall, by his 1st wife, Katharine, da. of Paul Treby TREBY, *formerly* OURRY, of Goodamoor, Devon, br. of Dame Catherine Treby MOLESWORTH, wife of the 6th Baronet, which William (who *d.* 28 March 1851, aged 58), was br. of the 7th and son of the 6th Baronet. He was *bap.* 13 Oct. 1818, at St. Breock; ed. at Eton and St. John's Coll., Cambridge; B.A., 1840; took Holy Orders, 1842; Rector of Little Petherick *or* St. Petrock Minor, Cornwall, 1848 till death; *suc. to Baronetcy*, 22 Oct. 1855. He *m.* 15 July 1856, at St. Geo. Han. sq., Beatrice Anne, 3d da. of Charles PRIDEAUX-BRUNE, of Prideaux place in Padstow, Cornwall, by Mary, da. and coheir of Edmund John GLYNN, of Glynn, co. Cornwall. He *d.* s.p.s. 6 and was *bur.* 11 Jan. 1862, at Little Petherick, aged 43. His widow *d.* 3 March 1903, at 70 Elm Park gardens, London, S.W., and was *bur.* at Kensal Green cemetery.

X 1862. SIR PAUL WILLIAM MOLESWORTH, Baronet [1689], br. of the whole blood and h., *bap.* 13 Jan. 1821, at St. Breock aforesaid; ed. at Eton and at St. John's Coll., Cambridge; B.A., 1843; M.A., 1846; took Holy Orders, and was Rector of Tetcott, Devon, 1846 till he resigned, on becoming a Roman Catholic, in 1860; *suc. to the Baronetcy*, 6 Jan. 1862. He *m.* 25 Sep. 1849, at Trewarthenick, Cornwall, Jane Frances, 1st da. of Gordon William Francis Booker GREGOR, of the same. He *d.* at "The Tower," Newquay, Cornwall, 23 Dec. 1889, aged 68. Will pr. 1 Feb. 1890, above £9,000, his widow being then living.

XI. 1889. SIR LEWIS WILLIAM MOLESWORTH, Baronet [1689], 1st s. and h., *b.* 31 Oct. and *bap.* 4 Dec. 1853, at Cornelly, Cornwall; ed. at Beaumont and Stonyhurst Colleges; *suc. to the Baronetcy*, 23 Dec. 1889; Sheriff of Cornwall, 1899; M.P. for Bodmin Division of Cornwall, since 1900. He *m.* 3 June 1874, at the Roman Catholic Church of St. Lawrence, St. Louis, State of Missouri, in North America, Jane Graham, 2d surv. da. of Brig.-Gen. Daniel Marsh FROST, of the city of St. Louis aforesaid, by Eliza, 1st da. of Richard GRAHAM and Catharine, da. of John MULLANPHY.

Family Estates.—These, in 1883, being then owned by the Dowager Lady Molesworth, of Pencarrow, consisted of 8,967 acres in Devon, 8,064 in Cornwall, and 3 in Huntingdonshire. *Total.*—17,034 acres, worth £10,997 a year.

RAMSDEN:

cr. 30 Nov. 1689.

I. 1689. "JOHN RAMSDEN, of Byrom [in Brotherton], co. York, Esq.," as also of Longley Hall in Almondbury in the same county, 1st s. and h of William RAMSDEN,(a) of the same, by Elizabeth, da. and h. of George PALMES, of Naburn in that county, was *b.* April and *bap.* May 1648, at Almondbury; was v.p. Sheriff of Yorkshire, 1672-73; suc. his father, 26 Sep. 1679,

(a) This William was s. and h. (by his 1st wife, Margaret, da of Sir Peter Frescheville, of Staveley, co. Derby) of Sir John Ramsden, aged 17 at the Visit. of Yorkshire, 1612, who, being a Col. in the service of Charles I, was taken prisoner at Selby, and died in Newark Castle, 22 Aug. 1644.

and was *cr. a Baronet*, as above, 30 Nov. 1689. He *m.* 7 March 1670/1 (settlement 22 Jan. previous), at Armthorpe, co. York (registered at Doncaster), Sarah (then aged 21), da. and h. of Charles BUTLER, of Coates by Stow, co. Lincoln, by Susan, da. of Brian COOKE, of Doncaster. She *d.* 14 and was *bur.* 15 Jan. 1683/4, at Brotherton. He *d.* 11 June 1690, and was *bur.* there aged 42. Will dat. 26 Dec. 1687, pr. 19 Aug. 1690, at York.

II. 1690. SIR WILLIAM RAMSDEN, Baronet [1689], of Byrom and Longley Hall aforesaid, 1st s. and h., *bap.* 22 Oct. 1672, at Brotherton; *suc. to the Baronetcy*, 11 June 1690. He *m.* 6 Aug. 1695, at Lowther, co. Westmorland, Elizabeth, sister and coheir (12 March 1750/1) of Henry (LOWTHER), 3d VISCOUNT LONSDALE, da. of John, 1st VISCOUNT LONSDALE, by Katharine, da. of Sir Henry Frederick THYNNE, 1st Baronet [1641]. He *d.* 27 June and was *bur.* 1 July 1736, at Brotherton, aged 63. Will dat. 10 April 1731, pr. 10 May 1737. His widow was *bur.* there 9 Oct. 1764. Will dat. 28 June 1763, pr. 19 Oct. 1764, at York.

III. 1736. SIR JOHN RAMSDEN, Baronet [1689], of Byrom and Longley Hall aforesaid, 1st s. and h., *bap.* 21 March 1698/9, at Brotherton; was M.P. for Appleby (four Parls.), 1727-54; *suc. to the Baronetcy*, 27 June 1736. He *m.* (Lic. 8 Aug. 1748 to be *m.* at Ackworth, co. York), Margaret, widow of Thomas BRIGHT, *formerly* LIDDELL, of Badsworth, co. York, only surv. da. and h. of William NORTON, of Sawley, near Ripon, by Margaret, da. of Ralph LOWTHER. He *d.* at Byrom, 10 and was *bur.* 17 April 1769, at Brotherton, aged 70. Will dat. 2 April 1767, pr. 13 May 1769. His widow was *bur.* there 7 June 1775. Will dat. 14 April 1774, pr. 2 June 1775.

IV. 1769. SIR JOHN RAMSDEN, Baronet [1698], of Byrom and Longley Hall aforesaid, 2d but only surv. s. and h., *bap.* 1 Dec. 1755, at Brotherton; *suc. to the Baronetcy*, 10 April 1769; matric. at Oxford (Univ. Coll.), 5 April 1774, aged 18, and was M.P. for Grampound, 1780-84; Sheriff of Yorkshire, 1797-98. He *m.* 7 July 1787, at her mother's house in Stanhope street, Mayfair, Louisa Susanna, 5th and yst. da. and coheir of Charles (INGRAM, *or* INGRAM-SHEPHERD), 9th and last VISCOUNT IRVINE, by Frances his wife, formerly Frances GIBSON, *or* SHEPHERD, Spinster. He *d.* in Hamilton place, Piccadilly, 15 July 1839, and was *bur.* at Brotherton, aged 83. Will pr. Dec. 1839. His widow *d.* at Byrom Hall 22 Nov. 1857, aged 91, and was *bur.* with him.

V. 1857. SIR JOHN WILLIAM RAMSDEN, Baronet [1689], of Byrom and Longley Hall aforesaid, and of Ardverikie, co. Inverness, grandson and h., being 2d but only surv. s. and h. of John Charles RAMSDEN, of Newby Park, in Topcliffe, co. York, by Isabella, da. of Thomas (DUNDAS), 1st BARON DUNDAS OF ASKE, which John (who was M.P. for Malton, 1812-31, for Yorkshire 1831-33, and for Malton again 1833 till his death) was 1st s. and h. ap. of the late Baronet, but *d.* v.p. 20 Dec. 1836, aged 48. He was *b.* at Newby park 14 and was *bap.* 16 Sep. 1831, at Topcliffe aforesaid; *suc. to the Baronetcy*, 15 July 1839; was ed. at Eton and at Trinity Coll., Cambridge; M.A., 1852; was M.P. for Taunton, May 1853 to 1857; for Hythe, 1857-59; for the West Riding of Yorkshire, 1859-65; for the Monmouthshire boroughs, 1868-74, and for the West Riding (again), 1880-85 and 1885-86; Under Secretary of State for War, May 1857 to March 1858; Hon. Col. 1st West Riding Artillery Vols., 1862; Sheriff of Yorkshire, 1868. He *m.* 2 Aug. 1865, at St. Martin's in the Fields, Midx., Helen Gwendolen, 3d and yst. da. and coheir of Edward Adolphus (SEYMOUR), 12th DUKE OF SOMERSET, by Jane Georgiana, da. of Thomas SHERIDAN. She was *b.* 14 Nov. 1846.

Family Estates.—These, in 1883, consisted of 11,248 acres in the West Riding of Yorkshire (worth £168,420 a year), and 800 in Lincolnshire; besides 138,000 (worth £11,474 a year) in Inverness-shire. *Total.*—150,048 acres, worth £181,294 a year, inclusive of a rental of £1,819 belonging to the Hon. Mrs. Ramsden,

mother to the owner. The following remark, however, is appended thereto [Bateman's *Great Landowners*, 1883]: "This is one of the cases specially noted in the return where (in Yorkshire) the gross estimated rental forms no criterion of the income received by the landlord." *Principal Seats.*—Byrom, near Ferrybridge, co. York; Longley Hall, near Huddersfield, in that county; also Ardverikie, near Kingussie, co. Inverness.

ROBINSON:

cr. 13 Feb. 1689/90:

afterwards, since 1792, BARONS GRANTHAM;

since 1833, EARLS DE GREY;

and, since 1871, MARQUESS OF RIPON.

I. 1690. "SIR WILLIAM ROBINSON, of Newby, co York, Knt.," 1st s. of Thomas ROBINSON, of York, Turkey merchant (*bur.* at St. Crux, York, 16 July 1678), by Elizabeth da. of Charles TANKARD, of Arden, in that county, was *b.* about 1656; suc. to the estate of Newby, 6 Feb. 1688/9, on the death s.p., of his uncle Sir Metcalfe ROBINSON, Baronet (so *cr.* 30 July 1660), and was himself *cr. a Baronet*, as above, 13 Feb. 1689/90, having, apparently, been *Knighted* a short time before.(a) He was Sheriff of Yorkshire, 1689-90; was M.P. for Northallerton, 1689-90 and 1790-95; for York (nine Parls.) 1698-1722, and Lord Mayor of York, 1700. He *m.* 8 Sep. 1699, at Wheldrake, Mary (*b.* 25 Aug. 1664), da. of George AISLABIE, of Studley Royal, co. York, by his 2d wife, Mary, da. and coheir of Sir John MALLORY, of Studley Royal aforesaid. He *d.* 22 Dec. 1736, and was *bur.* at Topcliffe, aged 80.

II. 1736, Dec. 22. SIR METCALFE ROBINSON, Baronet [1690], of Newby aforesaid, 1st surv. s. and h.,(b) *b.* probably about 1683; *suc. to the Baronetcy*, 22 Dec. 1736, but *d.* unm. four days later 26 Dec. 1736, and was *bur.* at Topcliffe. Will pr. 1737.

III. 1736. Dec. 26. SIR TANCRED ROBINSON, Baronet [1690], of Newby aforesaid, br. and h., *b.* probably about 1685; was in the Navy, becoming, finally, Rear Admiral, 1734, but resigning 1741; was L. Mayor of York, 1718 and again 1738, having *suc. to the Baronetcy*, 26 Dec. 1736. He *m.* in or before 1713 his cousin, Mary, only da. and h. of Rowland NORTON, of Dishforth, co. York, by Margaret, sister of the 1st Baronet and da. of Thomas ROBINSON abovenamed. She was *bur.* 26 July 1748, at St. Crux. He *d.* 3, and was *bur.* there 7 Sep. 1754.

IV. 1754. SIR WILLIAM ROBINSON, Baronet [1690], of Newby aforesaid, 1st surv. s. and h., *b.* 1713; *suc. to the Baronetcy*, 3 Sep. 1754. He *m.* Dorothea, da. of John THORNHILL, of Stanton, co. Derby. He *d.* s.p. 4 March 1770. Will pr. March 1770. His widow *d.* 25 March 1789. Will pr. 1789.

V. 1770. SIR NORTON ROBINSON, Baronet [1690], of Newby aforesaid, br. and h., *b.* probably about 1715; *suc. to the Baronetcy*, 4 March 1770. He *d.* unm. Feb. 1792. Admon. Feb. and April 1793.

VI. 1792. THOMAS PHILIP (ROBINSON), 3d BARON GRANTHAM and 6th Baronet [1690], cousin and h. male, being s. and h. of Thomas, 2d BARON GRANTHAM (*d.* 20 July 1786, aged 47), who was s. and h. of Thomas, 1st BARON GRANTHAM, so *cr.* 7 April 1761 (*d.* 30 Sep. 1770, aged about

(a) He was returned for Northallerton as "Esq." in Jan. 1688/9, but as "Baronet" on 4 March 1689/90.

(b) Metcalfe Robinson, an elder son, *d.* young, and was *bur.* 29 April 1681, at St. Crux, York.

77), who was br. of the 2d and 3d Baronets and yr. s. of the 1st Baronet. He was *b.* 8 Dec. 1781, suc. to the Peerage, as above, 20 July 1786, and *suc. to the Baronetcy* in Feb. 1792, which thenceforth became *merged in the said Peerage.* He subsequently, 4 May 1833, suc. as EARL DE GREY (a creation dat. 25 Oct. 1816) his nephew and successor in all these dignities, being *cr.*, 23 June 1871, MARQUESS OF RIPON. See *Peerage*.

EDWARDS:

cr. 7 Dec. 1691;

ex. 10 March 1764.

I. 1691. "JAMES EDWARDS, of the city of York, Esq.," whose parentage is unknown, but who was nephew of Sir James EDWARDS,(a) L. Mayor of London, 1678-79 (who is said to have lent £30,000 to Charles II when in exile, and who *d.* 13 Feb. 1689/90), as also of Michael EDWARDS, of Kingston on Thames, and of Garston in Blechingley, co. Surrey (who by will dat. 18 Dec. 1696, devised his estates to him), was *cr. a Baronet*, as above, 7 Dec. 1691. He was of Reedham Hall, co. Norfolk; was Sheriff of Norfolk, 1695-96, and was a Gentleman of the Privy Chamber. He *m.* firstly, in or before 1689, (—), da. of (—) WRIGHT, Alderman of York. He *m.* secondly, in or before 1689, Rebecca, da. of (—) HOLWELL, *or* HOLLOWAY, of Hackney, Midx., Tobacconist. He *d.* March 1701/2. Will pr. April 1702. His widow *d.* 12 March 1753(b) and was *bur.* at Weybridge, Surrey. M.I.

II. 1702 SIR JAMES EDWARDS, Baronet [1691], of Reedham Hall aforesaid, 1st s. and h. by 1st wife, *b.* about 1689, being aged about 20 in 1709; *suc. to the Baronetcy* in March 1701/2; F.R.S, 1731. He *m.* in April 1718, Mary, only surv. da. and h. of the Rev. Matthew KIRBY, D.D., of Walton upon Thames, Surrey, and Elizabeth his wife. She *d.* 31 Oct. 1739, aged 42, and was *bur.* there. M.I. He *d.* s.p. 1744, and was *bur.* there also. M.I. Admon. 22 Jan. 1744/5 to his sister (of the whole blood) Jane,(c) wife of Jenkin Thomas PHILIPPS, Esq., and again (after her death), 23 June 1746, to his brother, the 3d Baronet.

III. 1744, to 1764. SIR NATHANIEL EDWARDS, Baronet [1691], br. of the half blood and h. male, being s. of the 1st Baronet by his 2d wife; *b.* about 1699, being aged 10 in 1709; was in Holy Orders; Rector of Weybridge, Surrey, Oct. 1736 till death; *suc. to the Baronetcy*, in 1744. He *d.* unm. 4 March 1764, and was *bur.* there, when the *Baronetcy* became *extinct:* M.I. Admon. 16 Oct. 1765 to James TAYLOR, "Esq.," nephew and next of kin, and again, July 1796.

DUDDLESTONE:

cr. 11 Jan. 1691/2;

ex., probably about 1750.

I. 1692. "SIR JOHN DUDDLESTONE, of the city of Bristol, co. Somerset, Knt," whose parentage is unknown, was a tobacconist (though sometimes called a "bodice maker") of that city, and, having risen to some

(a) This Sir James was son of John Edwards, of Garton, co. York, yeoman.

(b) "1763" is the date (erroneously) given on the monument.

(c) She was unm. in the pedigree [1709] in Le Neve's MS. *Baronetage*, having two sisters (both of the whole blood), *viz.* (1), Sarah, wife [1709] of (—) Marsh, of Chancery Lane, Lawyer; and (2), Alathea, widow [1709] of (—) Haire, Merchant.

position, was *Knighted* by King Charles II, 7 Sep. 1690,(a) and was subsequently *cr. a Baronet*, as above, 11 Jan. 1691/2. He, however, having lost above £20,000 by reason of a great storm at sea in Nov. 1704, became greatly impoverished. He *m.* (—). He *d.* in or before 1716, and was *bur.* (as was his wife) at All Saints, Bristol. Will pr. Aug. 1716.

II. 1716? to 1750? SIR JOHN DUDDLESTON, Baronet [1692], of Bristol aforesaid, grandson and h., *suc. to the Baronetcy* in or before 1716; was in an under post in the Customs at Bristol, 1727. He *d.* s.p.m. probably about 1750, when the *Baronetcy* became *extinct.*

WENTWORTH:

cr. 28 July 1692;

ex. 3 Dec. 1741.

I. 1692 "JOHN WENTWORTH, of North Emsall [*i.e.*, Elmshall], co. Gloucester [*sic*, but should be "York"], Esq.," as also of Brodsworth in co. York, 1st s. and h. of Henry WENTWORTH, of Brodsworth aforesaid, by Susan, da. of [—] BRADSHAW, of Lancashire, which Henry (who was aged 19 in the Visit. of Yorkshire, 1666, and who was *bur.* at South Kirkby, 28 Oct. 1684) was yr. br. of Sir John WENTWORTH, of North Elmshall (whose issue became *extinct*, 8 Aug. 1689), and 2d s. of Thomas WENTWORTH, of the same, who *d.* 10 May 1653, aged 33. He was *bap.* 18 Nov. 1673, at Brodsworth; suc. to the estate of North Elmshall on the death of his cousin, Thomas WENTWORTH, 8 Aug. 1689, and was *cr. a Baronet*, as above, 28 July 1692. He *m.* firstly (settlement Feb. 1692), Mary, da. of John (LOWTHER), 1st VISCOUNT LONSDALE, by Catherine, da. of Sir Henry Frederick THYNNE, 1st Baronet [1641]. She *d.* s.p.m. 16, and was *bur.* 19 April 1706, in Bath Abbey, aged 30. He *m.* secondly, in or before 1710, Elizabeth, da. of William (CAVENDISH), 1st DUKE OF DEVONSHIRE, by Mary (*m.* 27 Oct. 1662), da. of James (BUTLER), 1st DUKE OF ORMONDE. He *d.* 25 April and was *bur.* 4 May 1720, at South Kirby, aged 46. M.I. Will dat. 18 Jan. 1719/20, pr. 24 Dec. 1720. His widow was *bur.* with him, 29 Aug. 1741, aged 70. Will pr. 1741.

II. 1720, to 1741. SIR BUTLER CAVENDISH WENTWORTH, Baronet [1692], of North Elmshall and Brodsworth aforesaid, as also of Howsham, co. York, only s. and h., by 2d wife, *b.* about 1710; *suc. to the Baronetcy*, 25 April 1720. He *m.* Bridget, 1st da. of Sir Ralph MILBANKE, 3d Baronet [1661], of Halnaby, co. York, by his 1st wife, Elizabeth, da. of John (DARCY), LORD CONYERS. He *d.* s.p., 3 Dec. 1741, aged 31, when the *Baronetcy* became *extinct*. Will pr. 1746. His widow *m.*, 3 Oct. 1748, at York Minster, John MURRAY, sometime Ambassador to Turkey (who *d.* 9 Aug. 1775), and *d.* 3 Sep. 1774.

LEIGHTON:

cr. 2 March 1692/3.

I. 1693. "EDWARD LEIGHTON, of Wattlesborough, co. Salop, Esq.," s. and h. of Robert LEIGHTON, of the same, M.P. for Shrewsbury, 1661-78, by Gertrude, da. of Edward BALDWIN, of Diddlebury, co. Salop, was *b.* about 1650; matric. at Oxford (Ch. Ch.), 5 Aug. 1668, aged 18; suc. his father 1689, and, being a zealous supporter of the Revolution, was *cr. a*

(a) The King was accompanied on this visit by Prince George of Denmark, to whom, according to popular tradition, the grantee owed his promotion. The amusing story in the *Percy Anecdotes*, attributing these honours to the reign of Queen Anne, is manifestly an anachronism, though possibly there may be ground for some of the statements therein.

Baronet, as above, 2 March 1692-3; was M.P. for Salop, 1698-1700, and for Shrewsbury, Dec. 1709 to 1710. He *m.* firstly, 24 May 1677, at Alberbury, Salop, Dorothy, da. of Sir Job CHARLTON, 1st Baronet [1686], of Ludford, co. Hereford, sometime one of the Justices of the Common Pleas, by his 1st wife, Dorothy, da. and h. of William BLUNDEN. She was *bur.* 23 April 1688, at Alberbury. He *m.* secondly, 29 July 1693, at St. Chads, Shrewsbury, Jane, da. of Daniel NICHOLL, of London. He was *bur.* 6 April 1711, at Alberbury. Will pr. May 1711. His widow *d.* in or before 1746. Will pr. 1746.

II. 1711. SIR EDWARD LEIGHTON, Baronet [1693], of Wattlesborough aforesaid, 2d but 1st surv. s. and h., by 1st wife, *bap.* 11 Aug. 1681, at Alberbury; *suc. to the Baronetcy* in 1711. He changed the family residence from Wattlesborough to Loton Park, Salop, where he rebuilt the mansion; was Sheriff of Salop, Nov. to Dec. 1726. He *m.* firstly, 11 May 1709, at Norton in Hale, Rachel, da. of Sir William FORESTER, of Dothill, Salop, by Mary, da. of James (CECIL), 3d EARL OF SALISBURY. She, by whom he had nine children, was *bur.* 22 Feb. 1720/1, at Alberbury. He *m.* secondly, Judith, widow of Capt. THWAITES, East India Company's service, da. of John ELWICK, *or* ELLIOTT, of Mile End, Midx., a Director of that Company. He *d.* 6, and was *bur.* 9 May 1756, at Alberbury, aged 74. Will pr. 1756. His widow, by whom he had no issue, *d.* at Bath, 1764. Admon. 29 Nov. 1764, to Dame Judith CLIFTON, widow, her only child.

III. 1756. SIR CHARLTON LEIGHTON, Baronet [1693], of Loton park aforesaid, 2d but 1st surv. s. and h.(a) by 1st wife, *b.* about 1715; was an ensign in the army and subsequently, 1739, Capt., and 1745, Major of Marines, serving at Carthagena and elsewhere, retiring 1765, having been Sheriff of Shropshire, 1749-50, and having *suc. to the Baronetcy*, 6 May 1756. He was Col. of the Shropshire Militia; M.P. for Shrewsbury, 1774, till void 8 March 1775. He *m.* firstly, Anna Maria, da. of Richard MYTTON, of Halston, Salop, by Lætitia, sister and h. of Thomas OWEN, of Condover, in that county. She *d.* Aug. 1750. He *m.* secondly, 22 Oct. 1751, Emma, 2d da. of Sir Robert MAUDE, 1st Baronet [I. 1705], by Elizabeth, da. and h. of Francis CORNWALLIS, of Albermarles, co. Carmarthen. He *d.* at Shrewsbury, 5 May 1780. Admon. July and Oct. 1784.

IV. 1780. SIR CHARLTON LEIGHTON, Baronet [1693], of Loton park aforesaid, 1st s. and h., by 1st wife, *b.* about 1747; *suc. to the Baronetcy*, 3 May 1780; M.P. for Shrewsbury, 1780 till death in 1784. He *d.* unm., 9 Sep 1784. Will pr. March 1786.

V. 1784. SIR ROBERT LEIGHTON, Baronet [1693], of Loton park aforesaid, br. of the half blood and h., being s. of the 3d Baronet by his 2d wife; *b.* 1752; *suc. to the Baronetcy*, 9 Sep. 1784; was Sheriff of Shropshire, 1786-87. He *d.* unm., Feb. 1819, aged about 67. Will pr. 1819.

VI. 1819. SIR BALDWIN LEIGHTON, Baronet [1693], of Loton park aforesaid, cousin and h. male, being 2d s.(b) of Baldwin LEIGHTON, of Shrewsbury, Capt. 9th Foot, by Anne, da. of Capt. [—] SMITH, which Baldwin (*b.* 1717) was next br. to the 3d and s. of the 2d Baronet. He was *b.* 15 Jan. 1747; served in the army and was wounded in the American war; was Brig.-General in Portugal, 1798, and in the West Indies, 1801; Major-Gen. in the army, 1803; Lieut.-Gen., 1809, and full General, 1819; was on the Home Staff at Sunderland and Newcastle, 1803, and on that in Jersey, 1807; Gov. of Carrickfergus, 1817; *suc. to the Baronetcy*, Feb. 1819. He *m.* firstly, in May 1780, Anne, da. of the Rev. William PIGOTT, Rector of Edgmond, Salop. She *d.* s.p. He *m.* secondly, 25 Nov. 1802, Louisa Margaretta Anne, sister of John Thomas, 1st BARON

(a) The eldest son, Forester Leighton, who was a Capt. in a regiment raised in 1745, *d.* unm. and v.p. at Bath.

(b) The eldest son, Edward Leighton, matric. at Oxford (Pemb. Coll.), 14 April 1764, aged 18; B.A., 1767; was in Holy Orders; Rector of Cardiston, Salop, and of Pontesbury (2d portion), 1769. He *d.* s.p., 21 May 1804.

STANLEY OF ALDERLEY, 2d da. of Sir John Thomas STANLEY, 6th Baronet [1660], by Margaret, da. and h. of Hugh OWEN. He *d.* 13 Nov. 1828, at Loton park, aged 81. Will pr. Dec. 1828. His widow *d.* 3 Jan. 1842, at Bath. Will pr. March 1842.

VII. 1828. SIR BALDWIN LEIGHTON, Baronet [1693], of Loton park aforesaid, only s. and h., by 2d wife, *b.* 14, *bap.* 31 May 1805, and received into the church, 12 July following at Sunderland; admitted to Rugby School, 1817; matric. at Oxford (Mag. Coll.), 15 March 1823, aged 17; *suc. to the Baronetcy*, 13 Nov. 1828; was M.P. for South Shropshire, Sep. 1859 to 1865. He *m.* 9 Feb. 1832, at Oswestry, Mary, sister and h. of the Rev. John PARKER, of Sweeny Hall, Salop, da. of Thomas Netherton PARKER, of the same. She *d.* 5 March 1864, at Loton park. He *d.*, of bronchitis, 26 May 1871, at Norton Hall, near Daventry, co. Northampton, aged 66.

VIII. 1871. SIR BALDWIN LEIGHTON, Baronet [1693], of Loton Park aforesaid, 1st s. and h., *b.* 27 Oct. 1836; ed. at Eton; matric. at Oxford (Ch. Ch.), 8 June 1854, aged 17; B.A., 1859; M.A., 1864; admitted to Lincoln's Inn, 5 June 1858; *suc. to the Baronetcy*, 26 May 1871; M.P. for South Shropshire, Aug. 1877 to 1885. He *m.* 30 Jan. 1864, Eleanor Leicester, sister and coheir of John Byrne Leicester (WARREN), 3d BARON DE TABLEY (who *d.* unm. 22 Nov. 1895, aged 60), 3d da. of George, 2d BARON DE TABLEY, by Catharina Barbara, da. of Jerome, COURT DE SALIS. He *d.* 22 Jan. 1897, of pneumonia, at Loton park, aged 60. Will pr. at £22,504 gross personalty. His widow who was *b.* 1841, having suc. to the estates of her brother, took by deed poll, 24 May 1900, the name of *Leighton-Warren*, in lieu of that of *Leighton*. She was living 1904.

IX. 1897. SIR BRYAN BALDWIN MAWDDWY LEIGHTON, Baronet [1693], of Loton Park aforesaid, 1st s. and h., *b.* 26 Nov. 1868; *suc. to the Baronetcy*, 22 Jan. 1897; served in the Cuban campaign with the U.S. cavalry in 1898, and in the Transvaal war, 1899; A.D.C. to the Viceroy of Ireland, 1902. He *m.* 3 Dec. 1890, at St. Mary's, Margam, co. Glamorgan, Margaret Frances, 3d da. of John Fletcher FLETCHER, of Saltoun Hall, co. Haddington, by Bertha Isabella, da. of Christopher Rice MANSELL, of Margam aforesaid.

Family Estates.—These, in 1883, consisted of 4,085 acres in Shropshire, and 11 in Montgomeryshire. *Total.*—4,096 acres, worth £5,421 a year. *Principal Seat.*—Loton Park, near Shrewsbury, Salop.

COLT:

cr. 2 March 1693/4.

I. 1694. "HENRY DUTTON COLT, of [St. James', in] the city of Westminster, Esq.," senior,(a) 4th s. of George COLT, of Grays, *otherwise* Cotts Hall, in Cavendish, co. Suffolk, and of Clay Hall, in Barking, and Parndon Hall, both in co. Essex, by Elizabeth, da. and coheir of John DUTTON,(b) of Sherborne, co. Gloucester, which George (*bap.* 17 Aug. 1614, at Cavendish) was a zealous Royalist, and fled to Holland after the battle of Worcester, being

(a) So styled in the patent, probably to distinguish him from Henry Colt, s. of his brother Sir William Colt.

(b) This John Dutton, who was a Cromwellian, is said (in the interesting account of the family contributed by Mary Dutton Colt, a niece of the 1st Baronet to Wotton's *Baronetage*) to have offered to settle his estates on his son-in-law, George Colt, if he would leave the Royal cause, but, on his refusal, to have entailed them on his own heirs male collateral.

drowned on his passage to Ireland, 20 Jan. 1658,(a) in his 45th year, and *bur.* at Girtringdunbark). He was *b.* about 1646,(b) was, sometime, Adjutant to Prince Rupert, and, having been a promoter of the Revolution, was *cr. a Baronet*, as above, 2 March 1693/4, with a spec. rem., failing heirs male of his body, to his eldest brother John Dutton COLT, of Letton, co. Hereford, in like manner, whom failing to the heirs male of the body of his late br., Sir William Dutton COLT, deceased.(c) He was M.P. for Newport (Isle of Wight), 1695-98, and for Westminster, 1701-02, and 1705-08. He *m.* Cecilia, widow of William NUTHILL, of Thames Ditton, Surrey, formerly wife of Sir Robert HATTON, of the same (*d.* 1684), da. of Francis BREWSTER, of Wrentham, co. Suffolk. She *d.* Oct. 1712. Will pr. Oct. 1712. He *d.* s.p., 25 April 1731.

II. 1731. SIR JOHN DUTTON COLT, Baronet [1694], of Leominster, co. Hereford, great nephew and h., being only s. and h. of John Dutton COLT, of the same, by Mary, da. of John ARNOLD, of Llanvihangel Crucorney, co. Monmouth, which John (*bap.* 20 Sep. 1686, at Camberwell, Surrey, and *d.* 2 Feb. 1729) was 1st s. and h. of John Dutton COLT,(d) abovementioned (*d.* 29 April 1722), the eldest br. of the 1st Baronet. He was *b.* 1725, and *suc. to the Baronetcy*, 25 April 1731, under the spec. rem. in the creation thereof. He was in Holy Orders, being Rector of Letton, Willersley, and Cold Weston, co. Hereford. He *m.* 24 June 1747, Margaret, or Mary, da. of John POWELL, of London. He was *bur.* 4 May 1809, at Leominster, aged 84.(e)

III. 1809. SIR JOHN DUTTON COLT, Baronet [1694], s. and h., *b.* probably about 1750; *suc. to the Baronetcy*, May 1809. He *m.* in 1774, Malet, 1st da. of George LANGLEY, of Goulding Hall, Salop, Capt. in the Royal Marines, by Malet, da. of John (VAUGHAN), 1st VISCOUNT LISBURNE [I.]. He was *bur.* 29 June 1810, at Cound, Salop. His widow *d.* 24 Jan. 1824.

IV. 1810. SIR JOHN DUTTON COLT, Baronet [1694], 1st s. and h., *b.* 8 Oct. 1774; *suc. to the Baronetcy* in June 1810. He *d.* unm., 10 Jan. 1845, at Hill Court, near Berkeley, in his 73d year. Will pr. March 1845.

V. 1845. SIR EDWARD VAUGHAN COLT, Baronet [1694], of Trawscoed, co. Radnor, only surv. br. and h., *b.* about 1781; *suc. to the Baronetcy*, 10 Jan. 1845. He *m.* in 1805, Frances Martha, da. of Harry GOUGH, of Weobley, Capt. R.N. He *d.* 9 June 1849, at Trawscoed, aged 68. His widow *d.* there 10 July 1865, aged 83.

(a) See the account of him by his grand-daughter (p. 162, note "b,") where it is also said that at his death "there was found in his pocket a warrant for being an Earl." It is not likely that the date of death (20 Jan. 1658) assigned to him by his grand-daughter is wrong, especially as she mentions that he was then in his 45th year (which accords with his date of baptism, a date which she does not mention), but the date of death assigned to him in J. J. Howard's, *Visit. of Suffolk*, is 1674, and the birth of Edward, the 6th of his nine sons, was as late as 1663, if the statement of his age as being 35 on 13 Sep. 1698, as given in his allegation for a marriage license (Fac. Office) of that date, is correct.

(b) His eldest br. was 16 years old at his father's death in 1658, and he himself was the fourth of nine sons.

(c) This William was *Knighted*, 26 Nov. 1684, six days after his marriage, 20 Nov. 1684 (at Westm. Abbey), to Mary Shipman, widow, his 3d wife. He was afterwards Resident at the Court of Hanover, where he died. Will dat. 4 May 1689 to 29 Aug. 1673, pr. 18 Jan. 1693/4.

(d) This John acquired lands in Herefordshire by his 1st wife (the mother of his nine children), Mary, da. and h. of John Booth, of Letton, in that county. His unyielding conduct in refusing the surrender (required by the Crown) of the Charter of Leominster and the suffering that it brought upon him are fully dwelt upon by his daughter (see note "a" above). He sold Colt Hall and other family estates.

(e) Playfair's *Baronetage* [1811].

VI. 1849. SIR EDWARD HARRY VAUGHAN COLT, Baronet [1694], 1st s. and h., *b.* April 1808, at Lescroft, co. Stafford; matric. at Oxford (Queen's Coll.), 19 Sep. 1827, aged 20; B.A., 1836; took Holy Orders; Vicar of Hill, near Thornbury, co. Gloucester, 1839 till death in 1882; *suc. to the Baronetcy*, 9 June 1849. He *m.* 6 March 1844, at Adbaston, co. Stafford, Ellen Cotton, yst. da. of Francis Flicken NORTHEN, M.D., of Lea House, co. Stafford. She *d.* 30 April 1870, at Hill Vicarage, co. Gloucester, aged 60. He *d.* there s.p.m. 15 Oct. 1882, aged 74.

VII. 1882. SIR THOMAS ARCHER COLT, Baronet [1694], br and h. male, *b.* 6 Nov. 1815; ed. at Glasgow Univ.; M.A. and M.D., 1840; practised as a Physician at Torquay, Devon; *suc. to the Baronetcy*, 15 Oct. 1882. He *m.* 13 Sep. 1849, at Puddlestone, co. Hereford, Frances, yst. da. of Elias CHADWICK, of Swinton Hall, co. Lancaster, by Alice, da. of Henry ARROWSMITH, of Astley, in that county. She *d.* 31 March 1892, aged 77, at Rock House, Maidencombe, St. Marychurch, Devon. Will pr. 6 Oct. 1892, over £14,000. He *d.* 26 Feb. 1893, aged 77, at Maidencombe aforesaid.

VIII. 1893. SIR EDWARD HARRY DUTTON COLT, Baronet [1694], 1st s. and h., *b.* 3 Oct. 1850, at Gloucester; ed. at Shrewsbury School; matric. at Oxford (non collegiate) 28 Nov. 1870; B.A. (Merton Coll.), 1875; M.A., 1881; in Holy Orders; sometime Curate of Atworth, Wilts; Rector of Monk Okehampton, Devon, 1889-97; *suc. to the Baronetcy*, 26 Feb. 1893. He *m.* 4 Sep. 1889, Alice, da. of William Jefferys STRANGE, of Mile House, Sulhamstead, Berks.

SMITH:

cr. 20 April 1694;

ex. 11 Oct. 1760.

I. 1694. "JOHN SMITH, of Isleworth, co. Middlesex, Esq.," 2d[a] s. of Sir John SMITH, Alderman, and sometime [1669-70] Sheriff of London (*d.* 18 June 1673), being 1st s. by his 2d wife, Jane, da. and h. of Robert DEANE, of Yorkshire, was, apparently, a merchant of London, and having "advanced several sums of money towards carrying on the war against France,"[b] was *cr. a Baronet*, as above, 20 April 1694. He was subsequently a Gentleman of the Privy Chamber. He *m.* 22 Sep. 1691, Mary, da. of Sir John EYLES, of South Broom, Wilts, Lord Mayor of London [October to Nov. 1688], by (—), da. of (—) COWPER, citizen of London. She was *bur.* 8 Jan. 1724/5, at St. Mary's, Aldermary, London. He *d.* at his house in Queen street 16, and was *bur.* with his wife, 26 Aug. 1726. Will pr. 1726.

II. 1726, to 1760. SIR JOHN SMITH, Baronet [1694], of Isleworth aforesaid, 1st s. and h., *suc. to the Baronetcy*, 16 Aug. 1726. He *d.* unm., 11 Oct. and was *bur.* 20 Nov. 1760, at St. Mary's, Aldermary, aforesaid, when the *Baronetcy* became *extinct*. Will pr. 1761.

---

[a] The eldest son (only child of the 1st wife), James Smith, *m.* Sarah Burrell (who *d.* 8 Dec. 1691), and *d.* s.p. 1703.
[b] Wotton's *Baronetage*, 1741.

THOMAS:

cr. 24 Dec. 1694.

I. 1694. "JOHN THOMAS, of Wenvoe, co. Glamorgan, Esq.," 1st s. and h. of William THOMAS, by Sarah, da. and h. of John POWELL, of Flemingston in that county, having acquired, by marriage with his cousin, the estate of Wenvoe (which formerly was that of his great grandfather, Edmund THOMAS), was *cr. a Baronet*, as above, 24 Dec. 1694, with a spec. rem., failing heirs male of his body, to his brothers, Edmund THOMAS and William THOMAS respectively, in like manner. He was Sheriff of Gloucestershire, 1699—1700. He *m.* in 1692, Elizabeth, widow of the well known Gen. Edmund LUDLOW (*d.* 26 Nov. 1692, in his 73d year), sister and h. (May 1677) of Edmund, and da. of William THOMAS (*d.* 9 June 1636, aged 25), of Wenvoe aforesaid, by Jane, da. of Sir John STRADLING, 1st Baronet [1611]. He *d.* s.p. and intestate, 17 Jan. 1702/3. His widow *d.* 8 Feb. following, aged 72. Both *bur.* at Wenvoe.

II. 1703. SIR EDMOND THOMAS, Baronet [1694], of Wenvoe aforesaid, next br. and h.; *b.* 1667; *suc. to the Baronetcy*, 17 Jan. 1702/3, under the spec. rem. in the creation of that dignity. He *m.* (settlement 25 Dec. 1711) Mary, da. of the Rt. Hon. John GRUBHAM-HOWE, of Stowell, co. Gloucester, by Annabella, illegit. (but legitimated) da. of Emmanuel (SCROPE), EARL OF SUNDERLAND. He *d.* 1723. His widow *m.* Anthony POWELL, of Coytrehen, co. Glamorgan, and *d.* 26 April 1745.

III. 1723. SIR EDMOND THOMAS, Baronet [1694], of Wenvoe aforesaid, 1st s. and h., *bap.* 9 April 1712; *suc. to the Baronetcy*, 1723; matric. at Oxford (Queen's Coll.), 23 Jan. 1729/30, aged 17; M.P. for Chippenham, 1741-54, and for Glamorganshire, 1762, till death in 1767. He sold the estate of Wenvoe in 1765. He *m.*, May 1740, Abigail, widow of William NORTHEY, of Compton Basset, Wilts, da. of Sir Thomas WEBSTER, 1st Baronet [1703], by Jane, da. and h. of Edward CHEEKE. He *d.* 10 Oct. 1767, aged 55. Will pr. 1768. His widow *d.* 9 May 1777.

IV. 1767. SIR EDMOND THOMAS, Baronet [1694], 1st s. and h., *b.* about 1742, matric. at Oxford (Queen's Coll.), 28 Nov. 1758, aged 16; *suc. to the Baronetcy*, 10 Oct. 1767. He *d.* unm. in the Isle of Jersey, 1789. Admon. March 1789.

V. 1789. SIR JOHN THOMAS, Baronet [1694], only surv. br. and h., *b.* 6 July 1749; *suc. to the Baronetcy* in 1789. He *m.*, in 1782, Mary, da. of John PARKER, of Hasfield Court, co. Gloucester. He *d.* 14 Dec. 1828, aged 79. Will pr. Jan. 1829. His widow *d.* at Southampton, May 1845. Will pr. July 1845.

VI. 1828. SIR JOHN GODFREY THOMAS, Baronet [1694], 1st s. and h., b. 1 Sep. 1784; matric. at Oxford (St. Mary Hall), 8 Nov. 1800, aged 16; B.A. (Wadham Coll.), 1803; M.A., 1806; took Holy Orders; was Vicar of Bodiam, 1809, and of Wartling, both in co. Sussex, 1811, till death in 1841; *suc. to the Baronetcy*, 14 Dec. 1828. He *m.* firstly, 1 April 1808, Frances, da. of Stephen RAM, of Ramsfort, co. Wexford, by Charlotte, da. of James (STOPFORD), 1st EARL OF COURTOWN [I.] She *d.* Jan. 1816. He *m.* secondly, 10 March 1817, Elizabeth Anne, widow of Lieut.-Col. GREY, 30th Foot (killed at Badajoz, April 1812), 1st da. of the Rev. John VIGNOLES, of Cornahir, co. Westmeath. He *d.* 7 May 1841, at Bodiam Vicarage, aged 56. Will pr. July 1841. His widow *d.* 5 May 1854, at Clifton, co. Gloucester, aged 67. Will pr. Dec. 1854.

VII. 1841. SIR EDMOND STEPHEN THOMAS, Baronet [1694], 1st s. and h., being only s. by 1st wife, *b.* 6 Feb. 1810; was an officer in the army, becoming Major in the 69th Foot in 1846 (retiring 1850), having *suc. to the Baronetcy*, 7 May 1841. He d. unm. at Cork, 6 Feb. 1852, aged exactly 42.

VIII. 1852. SIR GODFREY JOHN THOMAS, Baronet [1694], of Cornahir, co. Westmeath, br. of the half blood and h., being s. of the 6th Baronet by his 2d wife; *b.* 16 June 1824; *suc. to the Baronetcy*, 6 Feb. 1852. He *m.* 25 Oct. 1853, at Llanelly, co. Carmarthen, Emily, 1st da. of William CHAMBERS, of Llanelly House, and of Hafod in that county. He *d.* 13 July 1861, aged 37, "at his residence, Whitehall, Essex."[a] His widow living 1904.

IX. 1861. SIR GODFREY VIGNOLES THOMAS, Baronet [1694], of Cornahir aforesaid, 1st s. and h., *b.* 27 March 1856, at Hafod aforesaid; *suc. to the Baronetcy*, 13 July 1861; ed. at Brighton Coll., and at the Royal Academy, Woolwich; entered the Royal Artillery, in which he subsequently became Lieut Col.; served in the Afghan campaign, 1878-79; in Egypt, 1882; in the Soudan, 1884 (4th Class Medjidie); in the Transvaal war, 1899-1901; **D.S.O.**, 1901. He *m.* 30 April 1887, Mary Frances Isabella, 1st da. of Charles OPPENHEIM, of Great Cumberland Place, Hyde Park.

CREATIONS BY WILLIAM III (Alone),
28 Dec. 1694 to 8 March 1701/2.

BLACKHAM:

cr. 13 April 1696;

ex. 2 July 1728.

I. 1696. "RICHARD BLACKHAM, of the city of London, Esq.," being a Turkey merchant and one of the largest woollen manufacturers, was *cr. a Baronet*, as above, 13 April 1696. He *m.* probably about 1670, Elizabeth, da. of Thomas APPLEYARD, of Ulceby, co. Lincoln, by Mary, sister of Sir John, and da. of Thomas BOYNTON, of Rockliffe, co. York. He *d.* 29 June and was *bur.* 9 July 1728, at St. Benet's, Gracechurch, London. Will pr. 1730. His widow living, but incapable, 8 July 1730, *d.* at St. Cath. Coleman, London, and was *bur.* 11 Dec. 1731, at St. Benet's aforesaid. Admon. 5 May 1733, to "Elizabeth, wife of Richard LANGLEY, Esq., and Judith, wife of John TWISLETON, Esq.," nieces by sister, and next of kin.

II. 1728. June to July. SIR JOHN BLACKHAM, Baronet [1696], of Lyons Inn, St. Clement Danes, Midx., only s. and h., *suc. to the Baronetcy*, 29 June 1728, but *d.* unm., a few days afterwards, 2 July 1728, when the *Baronetcy* became *extinct*. He was *bur.* on the same day and in the same place as his father. Admon. 10 July 1728, to sister Frances BLACKHAM, spinster, and again, 8 July 1730, after her death (Feb. 1729/30), to Judith TWISLETON and Elizabeth LANGLEY, both abovementioned.

WHEATE:

cr. 2 May 1696;

ex. 14 July 1816.

I. 1696. "THOMAS WHEATE, of Glympton, co. Oxford, Esq.," only s. and h. of Thomas WHEATE, of the same, by Frances, da. of Sir Robert JENKINSON, of Walcot, Oxon, was *cr. a Baronet*, as above, 2 May 1696. He was M.P. for Woodstock, 1690-95, 1708-10, 1710-13, 1713 till void, and 1715 till death in 1721; Sheriff of Oxon, 1696-97; and Keeper of the Stores of the Ordnance. He *m.* in or before 1695, Anne, da. and coheir of George SAWBRIDGE, of London, Bookseller, who fined for Alderman. She *d.* 14 Jan. or June 1719, and was *bur.* at Glympton. He *d.* 25 Aug. 1721. Will pr. 1721.

---

[a] *Annual Register* for 1861.

II. 1721. SIR THOMAS WHEATE, Baronet [1696], of Glympton aforesaid, 1st s. and h., *b.* about 1695; admitted to the Inner Temple, 1706; matric. at Oxford (Wadham Coll.), 31 March 1712, aged 17; *suc. to the Baronetcy*, 25 Aug. 1721; was M.P. for Woodstock, 1722-27. He *m.* in or before 1724, Mary, da. and coheir of Thomas GOULD, of Oak End, in Iver, Bucks. He *d.* s.p.m., May 1746. Will pr. 1746. His widow *d.* 1765. Will pr. 1766.

III. 1746. SIR GEORGE WHEATE, Baronet [1696], br. and h. male, *b.* probably about 1700; admitted to the Inner Temple; Barrister at Law and Recorder of Banbury; *suc. to the Baronetcy* in May 1746, and was admitted (from the Inner Temple) to Lincoln's Inn 23 Feb. 1746/7. He *m.*, in May 1742, Avice, da. of Sir Jacob ACWORTH, Surveyor of the Royal Navy. He *d.* 5 June 1751. Will pr. 1751. His widow *d.* in or before 1803. Her admon. Jan. 1803.

IV. 1751. SIR GEORGE WHEATE, Baronet [1696], 1st s. and h.; Lieut. Royal Artillery; *suc. to the Baronetcy*, 5 June 1751. He *d.* unm. 26 Jan. 1760.

V. 1760. SIR JACOB WHEATE, Baronet [1696], of Lechlade, co. Gloucester, br. and h.; sometime Commander in the Royal Navy; *suc. to the Baronetcy*, 26 Jan. 1760. He *m.*, in Dec. 1782, Maria, da. of David SHAW, of New York, in North America. He *d.* s.p. Feb. 1783. Will pr. Aug. 1783. His widow *m.*, April 1788, Admiral the Hon. Sir Alexander Forrester Inglis COCHRANE, **G.C.B.** (a yr. s. of Thomas, 8th EARL OF DUNDONALD [S.]), who *d.* 29 June 1832, aged 73, and *d.* 18 March 1856 in Eaton place, at a great age.

VI. 1783, to 1816. SIR JOHN THOMAS WHEATE, Baronet [1696], of Lechlade aforesaid, yst. br. and h. male, *b.* in Bedford Row, and *bap.*, 17 Oct. 1749, at St. Andrew's, Holborn; matric. at Oxford (Trin. Coll.), 13 Oct. 1767, and then aged 18; B.A. 1771; M.A. 1775; took Holy Orders; Vicar of Lechlade, 1774, and Rector of Great Penton, co. Lincoln; *suc. to the Baronetcy* in Feb. 1783. He *d.* unm. 14 July 1816, aged 66, when the *Baronetcy* became *extinct*. Will pr. 1816.

AYSHCOMBE:

cr. 28 May 1696;

ex. in or before 1727.

I. 1696, to 1727? "OLIVER AYSHCOMBE, of Lyford, co. Berks, Esq.," was presumably the Oliver next br. to John AYSHCOMBE, of Lyford (aged 20 at the Visit. of Berks, 1664), both being sons of John AYSCOMBE, of the same (who *d.* 17 March 1662, aged 64), by Joan, da. of (—) BANNINGES. He was *cr. a Baronet*, as above, 28 May 1696. He *m.* Elizabeth (unm. 1686), sister of Sir William CHAPMAN, 1st Baronet [1720], da. of Sir Jasper CHAPMAN, sometime (1688-89) Lord Mayor of London, by his 2d wife, Elizabeth, da. of Anthony WEBB, of Hackney, Midx. Her will pr. 1719. He *d.* s.p. in or before 1727, when the *Baronetcy* became *extinct*. Will pr. Feb. 1726/7.

MANSEL, *or* MANSELL:

cr. 22 Feb. 1696/7;

ex. 6 April 1798.

I. 1697. "EDWARD MANSELL, of Trimsaran, co. Carmarthen, Esq.," only s. and h. of Henry MANSEL, *or* MANSELL,(a) of Stradey in that county (*d.* before 1683), by Frances, da. and h. of Sir John STEPNEY, 2d Baronet [1621], of Prendergast, co. Pembroke, was admitted to Lincoln's Inn, 25 June 1683, and having acquired the estate of Trimsaran by marriage, was Sheriff of Carmarthenshire, 1689, and was *cr. a Baronet*, as above, 22 Feb. 1696/7. He *m.* Dorothy, widow of (—) LLOYD, sister and h. [1683] of Edward VAUGHAN, of Trimsaran aforesaid, da. of Philip VAUGHAN, of the same. He *d.* 19 Feb. 1719/20. His widow, by whom he had 11 children, *d.* Sep. 1721.

II. 1720. SIR EDWARD MANSEL, Baronet [1697], of Trimsaran and Stradey aforesaid, 1st s. and h.; *suc. to the Baronetcy*, 19 Feb. 1719/20; Sheriff of Carmarthenshire, 1728-29. He *m.* firstly Anne, da. of Thomas PRICE, of Garth Llwyn, co. Carnarvon. She *d.* s.p. 1 Nov. 1731, at Hampstead, Midx. He *m.* secondly, Nov. 1740, Mary, widow of [—] BAYLEY, of the Vineyard, near Hereford. He *d.* 10 May or 4 Nov. 1754. His widow *d.* in or before 1788. Will pr. 1788.

III. 1754. SIR EDWARD VAUGHAN MANSEL, Baronet [1697], of Trimsaran and Stradey aforesaid, presumably s. and h., by 2d wife, but possibly nephew and h. as s. and h. of Rawleigh MANSEL (*d.* 1748), a yr. br. of the late Baronet;(b) *suc. to the Baronetcy* in 1754; Sheriff of Carmarthenshire, 1778. He *m.* Mary, da. of Joseph SHEWEN, of Swansea. He *d.* Jan. 1788. Will dat. 21 Oct. 1786, pr. 1789. His widow *d.* in or before 1806. Admon. Sep. 1806.

IV. 1788, to 1798. SIR EDWARD JOSEPH SHEWEN MANSEL, Baronet [1697], of Trimsaran and Stradey aforesaid, s. and h.; *suc. to the Baronetcy* in Jan. 1788. He *d.* unm., 6 April 1798, at Llanelly, co. Carmarthen, when the *Baronetcy* became *extinct*.

HODGES:

cr. 31 March 1697;

ex. 1 April 1722.

I. 1697. "WILLIAM HODGES, of [ ], co. Middlesex, Esq.," s. of John HODGES, of Cotterstock, co. Northampton [*d.* about 1665], was a merchant trading in Cadiz in Spain, and was *cr. a Baronet*, as above, 31 March 1697, for services rendered to the fleet when off Cadiz in 1695. He was M.P. for St. Michael (two Parls.), 1705-10. He *m.*, in or before 1698, Sarah, da. and coheir of Joseph HALL, of London, merchant. He *d.* 31 July 1714, and was *bur.* at St. Stephen's, Coleman street. Will pr. 1714. His widow *d.* 25 April 1717, and was *bur.* with him. Admon. 22 May 1717, as of Allhallows in the Wall, London.

II. 1714, to 1722. SIR JOSEPH HODGES, Baronet [1697], s. and h., *suc. to the Baronetcy*, 31 July 1714, being then aged about 10 years; F.R.S., 1716. He dissipated the whole of his fortune, about £7,000 or £8,000 a year, and resided abroad, chiefly in France, and subsequently in Spain, "where he lives, 1718, and goes for a Lord."(c) He *d.* of dropsy, unm., in London, 1 April 1722, when the *Baronetcy* became *extinct*. Will pr. 1722.

(a) This Henry was s. and h. of John Mansel, who was 6th s. (1st s. by 2d wife) of Sir Francis Mansel, 1st Baronet [1622], of Muddlescombe.

(b) That is the affiliation assigned to him in R. G. Maunsell's *History of Maunsell or Mansel* [1903].

(c) Le Neve's MS. *Baronetage*.

BUCKWORTH:

cr. 1 April 1697;

sometime, 1801-14, BUCKWORTH-HERNE;

afterwards, since 1814, BUCKWORTH-HERNE-SOAME.

I. 1697. "SIR JOHN BUCKWORTH, of [West] Sheen [in Richmond], co. Surrey, Knt.," only s. and h. of Sir John BUCKWORTH, Alderman of London [1683-86], Dep. Gov. of the Turkey Merchants (*d.* Dec. 1687, aged 65), by his 2d wife, Hester (Lic. Vic. Gen., 4 Jan. 1661/2), relict(a) of Moses GOODYEAR, of London, merchant, was *b.* 18 and *bap.* 28 Oct. 1662, at St. Olave's, Hart street, London; was a citizen and fishmonger of London; *Knighted* 2 Dec. 1693, at Petersham, Surrey, and was *cr. a Baronet*, as above, 1 April 1697. He, though never an Alderman, was Sheriff of London, 1704-05. He *m.* 27 Oct. 1687, at Westm. Abbey (Lic. Vic. Gen. 24, he aged 25 and she 16), Elizabeth, da. of John HALL, of Yarmouth, co. Norfolk, merchant of London, by (—), who was living Oct. 1687. He *d.* at Sheen 12, and was *bur.* 24 June 1709, at St. Peter le Poor, London, aged 46.(b) Will dat. 23 July 1708, pr. 18 June 1709. His widow *m.* 13 Aug. 1712, also in Westm. Abbey, John HICCOCKS, one of the Masters in Chancery (1702-23), who *d.* 5 and was *bur.* 19 April 1726, in the Temple Church, London, aged 57. She *d.* at Sheen, 20 and was *bur.* 27 May 1737, at St. Peter le Poor aforesaid. Will dat. 25 July 1736, pr. 6 June 1737.

II. 1709. SIR JOHN BUCKWORTH, Baronet [1697], of West Sheen aforesaid, 1st s. and h., *bap.* 5 April 1704, at Richmond; *suc. to the Baronetcy*, 12 June 1709; was, presumably, ed. at Eton; M.P. for Weobley, 1734-41. He was unm. 1741,(c) but *m.* subsequently Mary Jane, da. of [—], and sister of Angelique Faicho CLERMONT, who was living Dec. 1758, and was *bur.* at Twickenham 1783. He *d.* s.p.m. legit.(d) 3 Jan. 1759, in Rathborne Place, Marylebone, aged nearly 55, and was *bur.* in the dormitory of Eton College Chapel. Will dat. 25 Dec. 1758, pr. 23 Jan. 1759. His widow *d.* 26 Jan. and was *bur.* 2 Feb. 1775, at Twickenham, aged 64. M.I. Will dat. 11 Jan. 1772, pr. 7 March 1775.

III. 1759. SIR EVERARD BUCKWORTH, Baronet [1697], br. and h. male, *bap.* 23 April 1704, at Richmond; admitted to Linc. Inn 5 May 1720; Master of the Horse to the Princesses, and sometime Assistant Gentleman Usher to George II; *suc. to the Baronetcy*, 3 Jan. 1759. He *m.* in or before 1726, Mary, da. of William DIPPLE, *or* DOBELL, of co. Worcester. She *d.* 29 Nov. 1767, and was *bur.* at Sunninghill Church, Berks. He *d.* 2 Feb. 1779, aged 74, and was *bur.* with his wife. Will pr. Feb. 1779.

(a) She, in the licence of Jan. 1661/2, is incorrectly described as "spinster," about 34, and at own disposal. See, however, the marr. lic. (Vic. Gen.), 16 Oct. 1671, for marriage of Jerome Rawstorn with her da., "Mrs Hester Goodyeare, about 18, spr," granted with consent of the mother, "Mrs Hester Buckworth, *alias* Goodyeare." See also Col. Chester's *Westm. Abbey Registers* (p. 332, note 6), in the note to the burial, 16 June 1731, of Dame Mary Hussey, another such daughter.

(b) "A person of extraordinary parts, and spoke Latin as fluent as he did English (though few spoke English better), and having been well grounded in classical learning, travelled into Turkey and other places, where he improved his natural and acquired abilities, and returning from abroad a complete gentleman, was universally esteemed by all that knew him." [Wotton's *Baronetage*, 1741.]

(c) Wotton's *Baronetage*, 1741.

(d) In his will he leaves all his estates to his two sons (1) Charles Buckworth, Lieut. in the Fusileers, and (2) Francis Buckworth, an officer of the Royal Navy, and, failing their issue, to his da. Frances Mary, wife (*m.* 11 Feb. 1752, at St. Marylebone) of Nathaniel Gould, with rem., failing her issue, to his br. Everard Buckworth.

IV. 1779. SIR JOHN BUCKWORTH, Baronet [1697], 1st s. and h., *bap.* 8 July 1726, at Richmond; *suc. to the Baronetcy*, 2 Feb. 1779. He *d.* unm. at Brussels, 10 June 1801, aged 74, and was *bur.* there. Will pr. Dec. 1801.

V. 1801. SIR EVERARD HERNE, *or* BUCKWORTH-HERNE, Baronet [1697], *formerly* Everard BUCKWORTH, br. and h., *bap.* 12 Nov. 1732, at Richmond; admitted to Lincoln's Inn, 20 July 1747; was, as "Everard BUCKWORTH, Esq.," *cr.* M.A. of Oxford, 8 July 1763, and presumably was *cr.* LL.D. of Cambridge (Trin. Hall) *per litteras regias*, 1768; was a Gentleman Pensioner and Exon of the Yeomen of the Guard to Geo. II and Geo. III. He assumed the name of *Herne*, after or in lieu of that of *Buckworth*, in consequence of his marriage. He *suc. to the Baronetcy*, 10 June 1801. He *m.*, in or before 1762, Anne, illegit. da. of Paston HERNE,(a) of Heverland Hall, Norfolk. She *d.* Oct. 1806, and was *bur.* at Heydon, Essex. Will pr. 1807. He *m.* secondly, [—]. He *d.* 15 July 1814, aged 81. Will pr. 1815.

VI. 1814. SIR BUCKWORTH BUCKWORTH-HERNE-SOAME, Baronet [1697], of Heydon House, co. Essex, *formerly* Buckworth HERNE, 1st s. and h., by 1st wife, *b.* 17 April 1762. By royal lic., 12 Dec. 1806, he took the name of *Buckworth-Herne-Soame* in compliance with the will of Sir Peter SOAME, 4th and last Baronet [1685] of Heydon House aforesaid, whose estates he inherited, though he was not any relation to the testator. He *suc. to the Baronetcy*, 15 July 1814. He *m.*, in or before 1793, Susan, da. of Stephen SIMPERINGHAM, of Cambridge. She *d.* 6 Dec. 1819 He *d.* 21 Jan. 1822, aged 59.

VII. 1822. SIR PETER BUCKWORTH-HERNE-SOAME, Baronet [1697], of Heydon House aforesaid, 1st s. and h., *b.* 24 April 1793, at Pampisford, co. Cambridge; was sometime an officer in the army; *suc. to the Baronetcy*, 21 Jan. 1822. He *m.* 13 Oct. 1830, Mary, da. of William BRADSHAW. He *d.* s.p. at Little Chishill, Essex, 25 Feb. 1860, aged 66. His widow *d.* 17 Oct. 1888, at 7 Tregunter Road, South Kensington, aged 88.

VIII. 1860. SIR JOHN BUCKWORTH-HERNE-SOAME, Baronet [1697], br. and h., *b.* 21 June 1794; was sometime a tenant farmer at Little Chishill and Great Parndon, both in co. Essex; *suc. to the Baronetcy*, 25 Feb. 1860. He *m.* 17 Jan. 1833, Lydia, da. of H. HAGGER. She *d.* 6, and was *bur.* 13 April 1863, at Great Parndon aforesaid, aged 63. M.I. He *d.* s.p.m.s.(b) 4 Feb. 1888, at Ware, Herts, aged 93.

IX. 1888. SIR CHARLES BUCKWORTH-HERNE SOAME, Baronet [1697], nephew and h., being 1st s. of Charles BUCKWORTH-HERNE-SOAME, by Hannah, da. of Richard PROCTOR, of Hay, co. Brecon, which Charles (*b.* 23 April 1798 and *d.* 6 Dec. 1863) was yr. br. of the late Baronet. He was *b.* 29 May 1830; ed. at Bedford Grammar School, and at St. Bartholomew's Hospital, London; member of the Royal Coll. of Surgeons; *suc. to the Baronetcy*, 4 Feb. 1888. He *m.* 29 March 1855, Mary, da. of his maternal uncle, Richard Fellows PROCTOR, of Ironbridge, Salop. She *d.* 24 Dec. 1893.

(a) This Paston Herne was only s. and h. of Thomas Herne, of Heverland Hall aforesaid (*d.* 30 Oct. 1736), by Charlotte, 1st da. and coheir of William (Paston), 2d and last Earl of Yarmouth.

(b) Charles Buckworth-Herne-Soame, his only son, *d.* unm. and v.p. 9 Dec. 1878, at Boston, in North America.

LOWTHER:

cr. 15 June 1697;

ex. 3 Feb. 1753.

I. 1697. "WILLIAM LOWTHER, of Marske, co. York, Esq.," as also of Holker, co. Lancaster, 1st surv. s. and h. of Anthony LOWTHER,(a) of the same, sometime (1678-79) M.P. for Appleby, (*d.* 27 Jan. 1692), by Margaret, (*m.* Feb. 1666/7), da. of Admiral Sir William PENN, was *b.* probably about 1670, and was *cr. a Baronet* as above, 15 June 1697; was M.P. for Lancaster, 1702-05 He *m.* Catherine, da. and h. of Thomas PRESTON, of Holker aforesaid, by Elizabeth, da. of Sir Roger BRADSHAIGH, 1st Baronet [1679], of Haigh, co. Lancaster. He *d.* April 1705. Will pr. July 1705.

II. 1705. SIR THOMAS LOWTHER, Baronet [1697], of Marske and Holker aforesaid, only s. and h.; *suc. to the Baronetcy* in April 1705; was M.P. for Lancaster (four Parls.), 1722 till death in 1745. He *m.* July 1723, Elizabeth, 3d da. of William (CAVENDISH), 2d DUKE OF DEVONSHIRE, by Rachel, sister of Wriothesley, 2d DUKE OF BEDFORD, da. of William RUSSELL, *styled* LORD RUSSELL. He *d.* at Bath, 23 March 1745. Admon. 17 Aug. 1745, 23 May 1748, and Nov. 1821. His widow, who was a lunatic, *d.* 7 and was *bur.* 14 Nov. 1747, at Chelsea.

III. 1745, to 1753. SIR WILLIAM LOWTHER, Baronet [1697], of Marske and Holker aforesaid, only s. and h., *b.* in 1727; *suc. to the Baronetcy*, 23 March 1745. He *d.* unm. 3 Feb. 1753, when the *Baronetcy* became *extinct*.(b)

TICHBORNE:(c)

cr. 12 July 1697;

afterwards, 1715-31, BARON FERRARD OF BEAULIEU [I.];

ex. Oct. 1731.

I. 1697, to 1731. "SIR HENRY TICHBORNE, of Beaulieu, co. Louth, Ireland, Knt.," 1st s. and h. of Sir William TICHBORNE,(d) of the same and of Blessingbourne, co. Tyrone, sometime (1661-66) M.P. [I.] for Swords and (1692-93) for co. Louth, (*d.* 12 March 1693/4), by Judith, relict of Robert MOLESWORTH, of Dublin, da. of John BYSSHE, sometime [1660-79] L. Ch. Baron of the Exchequer [I.], was *b.* in Dublin 1662; admitted to Trin. Coll., Dublin (as Fellow Commoner) 4 Dec. 1677, aged 15; Sheriff of co. Louth, 1692; M.P. [I.] for Ardee, 1692-93; for co. Louth, 1695-99, and 1710-13, having suc. his father 12 March 1693/4; Mayor of Drogheda, 1694; *Knighted* by the L. Justices [I.] 28 March 1694, and, having forwarded the cause

(a) This Anthony was s. of Robert Lowther, a Merchant at Leeds and London (*bur.* 9 Jan. 1655 at Lothbury), who was a yr. br. of Sir John Lowther, ancestor of the Earls of Lonsdale, both being sons of Sir Christopher Lowther, of Cumberland.

(b) He devised Holker and the other estates inherited from the family of Preston to his maternal cousin, Lord George Augustus Cavendish, who *d.* unm. 2 May 1794, when they passed to the Dukes of Devonshire.

(c) The information in this article has been kindly supplied by G. D. Burtchaell, of the Heralds' Office, Dublin.

(d) This William was s. and h. of Field Marshal Sir Henry Tichborne, L. Ch. Justice of Ireland, 1642 (*d.* 1667, aged 82), who was 4th s. of Sir Benjamin Tichborne, 1st Baronet [1621].

of William III, in Ireland, was *cr. a Baronet*, as above, 12 July 1697; was Sheriff of co. Armagh, 1708, and was subsequently by George I, *cr.* 9 Oct. 1715, BARON FERRARD OF BEAULIEU, co. Louth [I.] He *m.* 28 July 1683, at Combermere, co. Chester, Arabella, 6th da. of Sir Robert COTTON, 1st Baronet [1677], by Hester, da. of Sir Thomas SALUSBURY, 2d Baronet [1619]. He *d.* s.p.m.s.(a) in Oct. 1731, aged 70, when *all his honours* became *extinct*. Will dat. 16 March 1730/1, pr. [I.] 30 Oct. 1731.

FARINGTON, *or* FARRINGTON:

cr. 17 Dec. 1697;

ex. 7 Aug. 1719.

I. 1697, to 1719. "RICHARD FARRINGTON [*or* FARINGTON], of Chichester, co. Sussex, Esq.," 1st s. and h. of Sir John FARINGTON, of the same, and of Gray's Inn, Midx. (*d.* 1685, aged 76), by Anne, da. of John MAY, of Rawmere, Sussex, was *b.* probably about 1650, and was *cr. a Baronet*, as above, 17 Dec. 1697. He was Sheriff of Sussex, 1656-57; M.P. for Chichester, 1681, 1698-1700, 1708-10, 1710-13, and 1715 till death in 1719. He *m.* in or before 1675,(b) Elizabeth, da. and h. of John PEACHEY, of Eartham. He *d.* s.p.s.(c) 7 Aug. 1719, when the *Baronetcy* became *extinct*. Will pr. 1 Oct. 1719, by his widow. She *d.* in or before 1739. Will pr. 1739.

TIPPING:

cr. 24 March 1697/8;

ex. 20 Feb. 1724/5.

I. 1698. "WILLIAM [should be "THOMAS"] TIPPING, of Wheatfield, co. Oxford, Esq.," 1st surv. s. and h. of Sir Thomas TIPPING, of the same (*d.* 1 March 1693, in his 79th year), by Elizabeth, da. of Sir White BECONSHAW, of Moyles Court, co. Southampton, was *bap.* at Wheatfield, 29 April 1653; matric. at Oxford (Trin. Coll.), 16 Nov. 1669, aged 17; admitted to Lincoln's Inn, 23 Nov. 1672; was M.P. for Oxon, 1685-87; for Wallingford, 1689-90, and 1695-1700, having been *cr. a Baronet*, as above, 24 March 1697/8. He *m.* in or before 1699, Anne, da. and eventually h. of Thomas CHEEKE, of Pirgo, in Havering, co. Essex, sometime Lieut. of the Tower of London, by Lætitia, sister of Edward, EARL OF ORFORD, da. and eventually heir of the Hon. Edward RUSSELL. He *d.* 1 July 1718 in St. George's, Southwark [*Qy.* the King's Bench prison], Surrey. Admon. 21 April 1719, to a creditor. His widow *d.* at Pirgo, 21, and was *bur.* 29 Jan. 1727/8, at Havering aforesaid. Will pr. 1728.

(a) Besides a son, Cotton Tichborne, who *d.* an infant, and a da., Salusbury, who *m.* William Aston, of co. Louth, he had two sons, viz. (1) Henry Tichborne, *b.* 20 April 1684; Sheriff of co. Louth, 1706; *m.* Mary, da. of John Fowke, of Ardee, and *d.* s.p.s., being drowned off Liverpool 1709; (2) Capt. William Tichborne, M.P. [I.] for Philipstown, 1715-17; *m.* in 1712, Charlotte Amelia, da. of Robert (Molesworth), 1st Viscount Molesworth of Swords [I.], and had issue (1) Arabella, who *m.* May 1744, Francis Wyatt, of Shackelford, Midx, and (2) Wilhelmina, who *d.* unm.

(b) There is a marriage lic., 28 Feb. 1670/1 (Vic. Gen.), of Richard Farrington, Gent., of Chichester, about 27, Bachelor, and Elizabeth Merlett of the same, about 23, Spinster. This probably refers to him, but whether or no the marriage ever took place is not known.

(c) His three sons, John, Thomas and Richard, all *d.* v.p. and s.p., the eldest as "John Farrington, of Chichester, Esq., aged above 21, Bach.," had lic. (Fac.) 9 April 1697, to marry Elizabeth Muller of the same, aged above 21.

II. 1718, to 1725. SIR THOMAS TIPPING, Baronet [1698], of Wheatfield aforesaid, only s. and h., *bap.* 6 March 1699/700, at St. Paul's, Covent Garden, Midx.; *suc. to the Baronetcy*, 1 July 1718. He *m.* (settlmt. dat. 26 Dec. 1724), Mary, da. and h. of Sir John LEAR, 2d Baronet [1683], of Lindridge, Devon, by (—), da. of Christopher WOLSTON, of Devon. He *d.* s.p. 20 Feb. 1724/5,(a) aged 24, when the *Baronetcy* became *extinct*.(b) Will pr. 1727.

GERMAIN, *or* GERMAINE:

cr. 25 March 1698;

ex. 11 Dec. 1718.

I. 1698, to 1718. "SIR JOHN GERMAINE, of the city of Westminster, Knt.," said to have been "the son of a private soldier in the Life Guards of William II, Prince of Orange," by a "mother who was very handsome," and who was "stated to have been that Prince's mistress,"(c) was *b.* about 1650, accompanied William III to England in 1688, serving with him afterwards in Ireland and Flanders; was, though he had "a total want of education," of distinguished "personal appearance"; was *Knighted* at Kensington, 26 Feb. 1697/8, and *cr. a Baronet*, as above, 25 March 1698.(d) He was M.P. for Morpeth, 1713-15, and for Totness, April 1717 till death in 1718. He *m.* firstly (Lic. Fac. 15 Sep. 1701, he stated to be about 47, Bachelor, she, described as "Lady Mary MORDANT, about 40, Spinster" [*sic*]), Mary, *suo jure* BARONESS MORDAUNT, divorced wife(e) of Thomas (HOWARD), DUKE OF NORFOLK, da. and h. of Henry (MORDAUNT), 2d EARL OF PETERBOROUGH, by Penelope, da. of Barnabas (O'BRIEN), 6th EARL OF THOMOND [I.]. She *d.* s.p. 17 Nov. 1705, aged 46, and was *bur.* at Lowick, co. Northampton, having devised Drayton and other considerable estates in that county and elsewhere (which she had inherited on the death of her father, 19 June 1697), to her husband. Her admon., as "*Mary, Dow. Duchess of Norfolk,*" a description strangely contradicting that of 1701 as "spinster") granted 14 March 1705/6 to him. He *m.* secondly, in Oct. 1706, Elizabeth, 2d da. of Charles (BERKELEY), 2d EARL OF BERKELEY, by Elizabeth, da. of Baptist (NOEL), 3d VISCOUNT CAMPDEN. He *d.* s.p.s. 11 and was *bur.* 17 Dec. 1718, at Lowick aforesaid, aged 68, leaving all his vast property to his wife. Will pr. 12 Dec. 1718. His widow, who survived him more than half a century, and was well known in fashionable, literary, and even political society, *d.* in St. James' square, 10 Dec. 1789, leaving, besides vast estates, £120,000 in the funds. Will pr. 22 Dec. 1769.(f)

(a) In the *Hist. Reg.* for 1723 (p. 38) the death is recorded on 1 Sep. 1723, of "Sir *Francis* Tipping, of Thame, co. Oxford, Baronet, succeeded in honour and estate by his son of the same name."

(b) Of his two sisters and coheirs, who, in 1728, became coheirs to their mother (1) Lætitia, *m.* 9 June 1725, Samuel (Sandys) 1st Baron Sandys of Ombersley, and *d.* May 1779, leaving issue; (2) Katherine (who inherited the estate of Pirgo) *m.* Aug. 1726, Thomas (Archer) 1st Baron Archer of Umberslade, and *d.* 20 July 1754, at Pirgo, leaving issue.

(c) *Dict. Nat. Biogr.*

(d) He is described by Evelyn [April 1700] as "a Dutch gamester, of mean extraction, who had got much by gaming."

(e) She and Sir John Germain were in 1690 charged with *crim. con.*, and several bills for divorce were introduced, but none passed till 1701.

(f) She, according to her husband's wish, in the event of her having no issue, devised the Drayton estate (with £20,000) to Lord George Sackville, 2d s. of Lionel, Duke of Dorset, by Elizabeth da. of Lieut. Gen. Walter Philip Colyear, who had been a colleague with Sir John Germain in the Dutch service. He accordingly took the name of Germain (being well known as such, 1770-82), and was *cr.* 11 Feb. 1782, Viscount Sackville of Drayton, co. Northampton.

POWELL:

cr. 19 July 1698;

ex. 21 March 1720/1.

I. 1698. "THOMAS POWEL [*or* POWELL], of Broadway [near Langharne], co. Carmarthen, Esq.," s. and h. of Sir John POWELL, of the same, sometime (1686-96) one of the Justices of the Court of Common Pleas and of the King's Bench, was *b.* about 1666; suc. his father, 7 Sep. 1696, and was *cr. a Baronet*, as above, 19 July 1698. He was M.P. for Carmarthenshire (two Parls.), 1710-15. He *m.* firstly [—]. He *m.* secondly, 27 July 1698, at Stoke Newington, co. Midx. (Lic. London, same date, he 32, widower, and she 18, spinster), Judith, da. of Sir James HERBERT, of Colebrook, co. Monmouth. He *d.* 24 Aug. 1720, at Broadway. Will pr. 1729.

II. 1720, to 1721. SIR HERBERT POWELL, Baronet [1698], of Broadway and Colebrooke aforesaid, only s. and h., *b.* probably about 1700; *suc. to the Baronetcy*, 24 Aug. 1720, but *d.* unm. a few months later, 21 March 1720/1, when the *Baronetcy* became *extinct*. Admon. 17 June 1729 to use of Dame Elizabeth, wife of Sir John PRYCE [5th] Baronet [1628], and Mary, wife of Charles POWELL, sisters and next of kin.(a)

CLARKE, *or* CLARK:

cr. 25 July 1698;

ex. 23 May 1806.

I. 1698. "SAMUEL CLARK [*or* CLARKE], of Snailwell, co. Cambridge, Esq.," only s. and h. of John CLARKE, of Bury St. Edmunds, Suffolk, by Margaret, da. of (—) BOURNE, of Bury aforesaid, was admitted to Gray's Inn, 11 Nov. 1662; suc. his father about 1681, and was *cr. a Baronet*, as above, 25 July 1698. He *m.* about 1680, Mary, da. of Robert THOMPSON, of Newington Green. He *d.* 8 March 1719. The will of his widow dat. 3 Aug., pr. 12 Dec. 1720.

II. 1719. SIR ROBERT CLARKE, Baronet [1698], of Snailwell aforesaid, 1st s. and h.; admitted to Gray's Inn, 23 June 1701; was M.P. for Cambridgeshire, April 1717 to 1722; *suc. to the Baronetcy*, 8 March 1719. He *m.*, in or before 1712, Mary, da. of Arthur BARNARDISTON, of Hoxton, Midx., by Mary, da. of Sir Richard LLOYD, of Hallom, Notts. She *d.* Jan. 1732/3. He *d.* Nov. 1746. Will pr. 1747.

III. 1746. SIR SAMUEL CLARKE, Baronet [1698], of Snailwell aforesaid, 1st s. and h., *b.* 12 May 1712; admitted to Gray's Inn, 8 March 1726/7; *suc. to the Baronetcy* in Nov. 1746; Sheriff of the Counties of Cambridge and Huntingdon, 1753-54. He *d.* unm., 10 Nov. 1758, aged 43. Will pr. 1758.

IV. 1758. SIR ROBERT CLARKE, Baronet [1698], of Snailwell aforesaid, br. and h., *b.* 22 Jan. 1714; admitted to Gray's Inn, 17 April 1731; *suc. to the Baronetcy*, 10 Nov. 1758. He *m.*, before 1763, Elizabeth, da. of (—) LITTEL, of Bow lane, London. He *d.* 18 Aug. 1770, aged 56. Will pr. Nov. 1770. His widow living 17 Nov. 1787.

V. 1770. SIR JOHN CLARKE, Baronet [1698], of Snailwell aforesaid and of Feckenham, Suffolk, only s. and h., *b.* about 1763; *suc. to the Baronetcy*, 18 Aug. 1770. He *d.* unm. 8 Nov. 1782, aged 19. Admon. July and Nov. 1787.

(a) "He left two sisters, to whom an estate of £3,000 a year." [Mawson's *Obits.*]

VI. 1782, to 1806. SIR ARTHUR CLARKE, Baronet [1698], of Snailwell aforesaid, uncle and h., being 3d s. of the 3d Baronet, *b.* 6 Feb. 1715; *suc. to the Baronetcy*, 8 Nov. 1782, and sold the estate of Snailwell. He *m.*, but *d.* s.p. 23 May 1806, when the *Baronetcy* became *extinct*. Will pr. 1806.

FIREBRACE:

cr. 28 July 1698;

ex. 28 March 1759.

I. 1698. "SIR BASIL FIREBRACE, of London, Knt," 2d(a) s. of Sir Henry FIREBRACE, Chief Clerk of the Kitchen to Charles I and Charles II, whose services to the former, when a prisoner at Carisbrooke, are well known(b) (*d.* 27 Jan. 1690/1, aged 71, and was *bur.* at Stoke Golding, co. Leicester), by his 1st wife, Elizabeth, da. of Thomas DARILL, of Stoke Golding aforesaid, was *b.* about 1653, being aged 29 in the Heralds' Visit. of Leicestershire, 1682; was a Citizen and Wine Merchant (apparently "Vintner") of London; Sheriff of that city, 1687-88, being *Knighted*, at Windsor, 2 Aug. 1687, (when "Sheriff elect,"); was M.P. for Chippenham, Dec. 1690 till unseated 22 Jan. 1691/2, and was *cr. a Baronet*, as above, 28 July 1698. He *m.* 7 Sep. 1671, at St. Margaret's, Westm. (Lic. Fac. 5, he of Allhallows', Barking, about 21, bachelor, and she 19, spinster), Mary, da. of Thomas HOUGH, of St. Botolph's, Bishopsgate, Milliner. He *d.* 7, and was *bur.* 11 May 1724, at St. Margaret's, Westm., aged 71.(c)

II. 1724. SIR CHARLES FIREBRACE, Baronet [1698], of Stoke Golding aforesaid, and afterwards of Long Melford, co. Suffolk, 5th but 1st surv. s. and h., was *b.* 5 and *bap.* 18 June 1680,(c) being aged 3 in 1682; *suc. to the Baronetcy*, 7 May 1724. He *m.* (Lic. Lond., 3 July 1710, he of Stoke Golding, aged 30, and she of St. Andrew's Holborn, aged 28) Margaret, 2d and yst. sister and coheir (May 1704) of Sir John CORDELL, 3d Baronet, da. of Sir John CORDELL, 2d Baronet [1660], of Long Melford aforesaid, by Elizabeth, da. of Thomas WALDEGRAVE, of Smallbridge, Suffolk. She, who was *bap.* 8 Feb. 1676, was *bur.* 21 May 1712, both at Long Melford. He *d.* 2 and was *bur.* there 10 Aug. 1727, aged 47. Will pr. Nov. 1727.

III. 1727, to 1759. SIR CORDELL FIREBRACE, Baronet [1698], of Long Melford aforesaid, only s. and h., *b.* in King's street, Bloomsbury, 20 Feb.(c) and *bap.* 15 March 1711/2, at St. Giles' in the Fields; *suc. to the Baronetcy*, 2 Aug. 1727; matric. at Oxford (St. John's Coll.), 9 May 1729, aged 17; M.P. for Suffolk, March 1735 till death in 1759. He *m.* 26 Oct. 1737, at Somerset House Chapel, Bridget ("£25,000 fortune"),(d) widow of Edward EVERS, of Ipswich and of Washingley, co. Lincoln (who devised the Washingley estate to her), 3d da. of Philip BACON, of Ipswich, the 2d s. of Sir

---

(a) The 1st son, Henry Firebrace, D.D., Fellow of Trin. Coll., Cambridge, aged 32 in 1682, was apparently the "Dr. Henry Firebrace, *bur.* 27 Nov. 1708," in the south aisle of St. Helen's, Bishopsgate, London.

(b) An elaborate account of them from the "Life of Dr. Barwick" is in Wotton's *Baronetage* [1742].

(c) *Mem.* on fly leaves of an old Bible, printed in J. J. Howard's edition of the *Visitation of Suffolk, 1561* (vol i, p. 247), under "CORDELL."

(d) *Notes & Queries*, 8th S., i, 155. Another marriage, in Aug. 1736 (a year previous) is, however assigned to him (7th S., ix, 267 and 433, and 8th S. i, 520), *viz.*, to "Miss Dashwood, da. of George Dashwood, of Heveningham," Suffolk, "an heiress." This marriage presumably never took place; at all events the marriage in Oct. 1737, with Bridget Evers, is the one (and the only one) given, "*ex inform.* Dom. Cor. Firebrace, Bar.," in Wotton's *Baronetage* [1741].

Nicholas BACON, K.B., of Shrubland Hall, Suffolk.[a] He *d.* s.p. 28 March 1759, aged 47, when the *Baronetcy* became *extinct.*[b] Will pr. Nov. 1759. His widow (to whom he devised the Long Melford estate) *m.* 7 April 1762, as his 2d wife, William CAMPBELL (br. to John, 4th DUKE OF ARGYLL [S.]), who *d.* 8 Sep. 1787 at Liston hall, co. Suffolk, and *d.* before him s.p. at Long Melford, 3 July 1782, aged above 80. Will pr. July 1782.

NORRIS:

cr. 3 Dec. 1698;

ex. 10 Oct. 1702.

I. 1698, to 1702. "WILLIAM NORRIS, of Speke, co. Lancaster, Esq., Ambassador to the Great Mogul," 2d s.[c] of Thomas NORRIS, NORRES, *or* NORREYS, of Speke, co. Lancaster (aged 46 in the Heralds' Visit. of Lancashire, 1664), by Catherine, da. of Sir Henry GARROWAY, L. Mayor of London (1639-40), was aged 6 years in 1664; ed. at Trin. Coll., Cambridge, of which he became a Fellow; B.A., 1678; M.A., 1682; was M.P. for Liverpool, 1695-1701; a Commissr. of Public Accounts, 1697; was appointed Ambassador to the Great Mogul, and was *cr. a Baronet*, as above, 3 Dec. 1698. He *m.* (Lic. Fac., 13 Dec. 1689, being then of Trin. Coll. aforesaid, aged 31) Elizabeth POLLEXFEN, of St. Clement Danes, widow of Nicholas POLLEXFEN, and formerly of Isaac MEYNELL, both of London. He *d.* s.p. 10 Oct. 1702, on his journey back from India, when the *Baronetcy* became *extinct.* Will pr. April 1703. The will of Dame Elizabeth NORRIS was pr. 1713.

ROGERS:

cr. 21 Feb. 1698/9;

sometime, 1871 to 1889, BARON BLACHFORD;

ex. 9 March 1895.

I. 1699. "JOHN ROGERS, of Wisdome, co. Devon, Esq.," as also of Blachford, both in Cornwood, in that county, 1st s. of John ROGERS, sometime Puritan minister of Purleigh, co. Essex, and afterwards a Physician at St. Mary Mag., Bermondsey, a well known "Fifth Monarchy man,"[d] by Elizabeth, da. of Sir Robert PAYNE, of Midlow, co. Huntingdon, was *b.* about 1649 (being aged 13 at the Heralds' Visit. of Surrey in 1662), was a merchant at Plymouth, near which place he purchased the abovementioned estates, was M.P. of that town, 1698-1700, and was *cr. a Baronet*, as above, 21 Feb. 1698/9. He was Sheriff of Devon, 1701-02. He *m.* in or before 1676, Mary, da. of Spencer VINCENT, of Lombard Street, London, merchant, Alderman of that city. He *d.* at Plymouth, and was *bur.* 23 April 1710, at Charles

[a] She is commemorated by the great Dr. Johnson in some silly verses to *Lady Firebrace at Bury Assizes*, printed in the *Gent. Mag.* for Sep. 1738, in which he calls her (who was then about 40 and the wife of the second of her three husbands) not only "a muse and grace," but even a "bright nymph."

[b] The representation of the family devolved on the Earls of Denbigh, his aunt Hester (aged 6 in 1682) having *m.*, 22 June 1695, Basil (Feilding), 4th Earl of Denbigh, and having left issue.

[c] Thomas Norreys, the eldest son, aged 11 in 1664, suc. his father in 1700, but *d.* s.p.m., leaving a da. and h., Mary, who *m.* Lord Sydney Beauclerk, and inherited the estate of Speke, which passed to her issue, and was sold by her grandson in 1797.

[d] The date of his death has not been ascertained, he was living in 1665, and there is the burial at Bermondsey of "John Rogers" on 22 June 1670, which not improbably refers to him. He was *b.* 1627, at Messing, Essex.

church, in that town. Will dat. 25 Sep. 1708, pr. 11 May 1710. His widow *m.* 5 Sep. 1710, at St. Andrew's, Plymouth, as his 3d wife, Sir Edmund PRIDEAUX, 4th Baronet [1622], who *d.* 6 Feb. 1719/20, aged about 72. She *m.* thirdly, 31 Jan. 1722/3, Col. John ARUNDELL (*bur.* 5 July 1725, at St. Margaret's, Westm.), and *d.* a few weeks after that marriage 12 March 1722/3, aged about 80. Will dat. 10 and pr. 21 March 1722/3.

II. 1710. SIR JOHN ROGERS, Baronet [1699], of Wisdome and Blachford aforesaid, only surv. s. and h., *bap.* 14 June 1676, at St. Andrew's, Plymouth; *suc. to the Baronetcy* in April 1710; was M.P. for that town, 1713-22, and Recorder thereof. He *m.* 9 May 1698, at St. Giles' in the Fields, Mary, da. of Sir Robert HENLEY, of the Grange, co. Southampton, Prothonotary of the King's Bench, by his 2d wife, Barbara, da. of John EVERY, of Wootton Glanville, Dorset. He *d.* 21 and was *bur.* 27 Jan. 1743/4, at Cornwood aforesaid, in his 68th year. M.I. Will dat. 23 June 1742, pr. 9 Feb. 1743/4. His widow *d.* at Exeter, and was *bur.* 8 Dec. 1760, at Cornwood, aged 77. Will dat. 13 Nov. 1753, pr. 23 June 1761.

III. 1744. SIR JOHN ROGERS, Baronet [1699], of Wisdome and Blachford aforesaid, 1st s. and h., *bap.* 31 Aug. 1708, at Cornwood; matric. at Oxford (New Coll.), 13 Aug. 1724, aged 18; B.A., 1 March 1726/7; was unduly elected M.P. for Plymouth, June 1739 till void Jan. 1739/40; Recorder of that town; *suc. to the Baronetcy*, 21 Jan. 1743/4; Sheriff of Devon, 1749, (but did not serve,) and 1755-56; Col. of the South Devon Militia. He *m.* 28 Oct. 1742, at St. Benet's, Paul's wharf, London, Hannah, da. of Thomas TREFUSIS. She, who was the Foundress of "Lady Rogers' Church Schools at Plymouth" (afterwards removed to Ivybridge), *d.* 18 and was *bur.* 23 April 1766, at Cornwood, aged 48. M.I. Will dat. 8 Sep. 1764, pr. 16 May 1766. He *d.* s.p. at Blachford 20 and was *bur.* 24 Dec. 1773, at Cornwood, aged 65. Will dat. 22 Aug. 1763, pr. 15 Feb. 1774.

IV. 1773. SIR FREDERICK ROGERS, Baronet [1699], of Wisdome and Blachford aforesaid, br. and h., *bap.* 24 Oct. 1716, at Cornwood; was Recorder of Plymouth; Capt. in the Navy and Commissioner of Plymouth Dockyard; *suc. to the Baronetcy*, 20 Dec 1773. He *m.* firstly, 19 April 1742, at East Stonehouse, Devon, Grace, da. and eventually h. of Nathaniel COOPER, *afterwards* COOPER-LEMAN, of Norwich and Plymouth, Clerk to the Victualling Board in London,[a] by Mary, da. of Kenrick EDISBURY, of Harwich, Essex. She, who assumed the name of *Leman* after that of *Rogers*, *d.* 6 and was *bur.* 13 Jan. 1766, at Cornwood, aged 48. He *m.* secondly, 17 May 1768, at Stoke Damerel, Devon, Catherine, widow of Vice-Admiral Philip DURELL, da. of Thomas VINCENT, of Plymouth. He *d.* at Bath 7 and was *bur.* 13 June 1777, at Cornwood, aged 60. Will dat. 8 Aug. 1775, pr. 2 July 1777. His widow *d.* 1803. Will dat. 22 Feb., pr. 7 July 1803 and 14 Dec. 1819.

V. 1777. SIR FREDERICK ROGERS, Baronet [1699], of Wisdome and Blachford aforesaid, 1st s. and h. by 1st wife, *b.* 23 July 1746, at Plymouth; *suc. to the Baronetcy*, 7 June 1777; was Recorder of Plymouth and M.P. thereof, May 1780 to 1784, and 1790-97. He *m.* 21 Dec. 1769, at Gretna Green, and subsequently 27 June 1770, at Plympton St. Maurice, Devon, Jane, da. of John LILLICRAP, of Stoke Damerel, Devon, Warrant Officer at Gibraltar. He *d.* at Speenhamland, Berks, 21 June 1797, and was *bur.* at Cornwood, aged 50. M.I. Will dat. 22 Nov. 1783, pr. 5 Dec. 1798. His widow *d.* at Bath 10 and was *bur.* 16 Oct. 1800, at Cornwood. M.I. Will dat. 26 Oct. 1797, pr. 11 Nov. 1801.

VI. 1797. SIR JOHN LEMAN ROGERS, Baronet [1699], of Wisdome and Blachford aforesaid, 1st s. and h., *b.* at Plymouth 18 April and *bap.* 5 Oct. 1780 at Cornwood; admitted to Winchester School, 1795; *suc. to the*

[a] His father, another Nathaniel Cooper, *m* Ann (living 1664), only surv. da. of Thomas Leman, of Wenhaston, Suffolk.

Baronetcy, 21 June 1797; sometime Capt. 2d Dragoon Guards; M.P. for Callington, 1812-13; Sheriff of Devon, 1838. He *d.* unm., 10 Dec. 1847, aged 67, and was *bur.* at Cornwood. Will dat. 11 June 1821 [*sic*], pr. 3 May 1848.

VII. 1847. SIR FREDERICK LEMAN ROGERS, Baronet [1699], of Wisdome and Blachford aforesaid, br. and h., *b.* at Hoe House, Plymouth, 11 and *bap.* 27 Feb. 1782, at Cornwood; *suc. to the Baronetcy*, 10 Dec. 1847. He *m.* 12 April 1810, at St. Marylebone, Midx., Sophia, 2d da. and coheir of Lieut.-Col. Charles Russell DEARE, Bengal Artillery (killed in action, 13 Sep. 1790), by Catherine, da. of the Rev. Thomas STARK, M.A., Minister of Ballindean, in Balmerino, co. Fife. He *d.* at Blachford 13 and was *bur.* 20 Dec. 1851, at Cornwood, in his 70th year. M.I. Will dat. 26 Dec. 1848, pr. 4 Feb. 1852. His widow who was *b.* 26 May 1786, at Fort William, Calcutta, *d.* at Blachford 16 and was *bur.* 22 Feb. 1871 at Cornwood, aged 84.

VIII. 1851. SIR FREDERIC ROGERS, Baronet [1699], of Wisdome and Blachford aforesaid, 1st s. and h., *b.* 31 Jan. and *bap.* 18 May 1811, at St. Marylebone; ed. at Eton, 1822-28; matric. at Oxford (Oriel Coll.), 2 July 1828, aged 17; Craven Scholar, 1829; admitted to Lincoln's Inn, 28 October, 1831; B.A. (Oxford), and double first class, 1832; Fellow of Oriel Coll., 1833-45; Vinerian Scholar, 1834; M.A., 1835; Vinerian Fellow and B.C.L., 1838; Barrister (Lincoln's Inn), 26 Jan. 1837; Registrar of Joint Stock Companies, 1844-45; Emigration Commissioner, 1845-60; *suc. to the Baronetcy*, 13 Dec. 1851; West India Estates Commissioner, 1857; Permanent Under Sec. of State for the Colonies, 1860-71, and, while such, was made K.C.M.G., 1869; P.C., 1871, and finally raised to the peerage,[a] being *cr.* 1 Nov. 1871, BARON BLACHFORD of Wisdome and Blachford, co. Devon. He was Cathedral Commissioner, 1880-84; G.C.M.G., 1883. He *m.* 29 Sep. 1847, at Dunfermline, co. Fife, Georgiana Mary, da. of Andrew COLVILLE, *formerly* WEDDERBURN, of Ochiltree and Craigflower, by his 2d wife, Maria Louisa, da. of William (EDEN), 1st BARON AUCKLAND. He *d.* s.p. at Blachford, 21 Nov. 1889, and was *bur.* at Cornwood, aged 78,[b] when the *Peerage* became *extinct*, but the Baronetcy devolved as below. His widow *d.* at Blachford aforesaid, 13 July 1900, and was *bur.* with him, aged (also) 78. Her will pr. at £25,322 gross, and £24,153 net personalty.

IX. 1889. SIR JOHN CHARLES ROGERS, Baronet [1699], of Wisdome and Blachford aforesaid, br. and h., *b.* 10 April and *bap.* 18 June 1818, at St. Marylebone; *suc. to the Baronetcy*, 21 Nov. 1889. He *d.* unm. at Blachford, being accidentally drowned in the lake there, 25 March 1894, in his 76th year, and was *bur.* at Cornwood. Will pr. at £38,084 gross, and £23,962 net personalty.

X. 1894, to 1895. SIR EDWARD ROGERS, Baronet [1699], of Wisdome and Blachford aforesaid, only surv. br. and h., *b.* 5 Sep. 1819, and *bap.* 17 Feb. 1820, at St. Marylebone; matric. at Oxford (Ch. Ch.), 11 May 1837, aged 17; Student of Ch. Ch., 1839-76; B.A., 1841; M.A., 1843; in Holy Orders; Rector of Odcombe, Somerset, 1875-90; *suc. to the*

[a] This appears to have been the first peerage conferred on a member of the Civil Service, the grantee being in this case a personal friend of the Prime Minister, Gladstone. The precedent was, however, shortly followed by many similar creations, *viz.*, that of Cottesloe (Fremantle) and Hammond, both in 1874; of Hobhouse and Lingen, both in 1885; of Thring in 1886, of Sandford in 1891, of Playfair in 1892, of Farrer in 1893, and of Welby in 1894. Of these ten creations all but one (Sandford) were owing to the recommendation of the *same* Premier, *viz.*, Gladstone. [*Ex inform.* Hon. Vicary Gibbs.].

[b] "He was the most gifted, the most talented, and of the most wonderful grasp of mind of any of his contemporaries." [John H. Newman]. He was also a thoroughly earnest churchman, of the type of his two friends, Gladstone, the Prime Minister, and Dr. Church, Dean of St. Paul's. He was one of the promoters of *The Guardian* newspaper in 1846, and a copious contributor of various highly cultured articles to the *Reviews* and *Magazines* of his period.

Baronetcy, 25 March 1894. He *d.* unm. at Blachford, of paralysis, 9 March 1895, aged 75, and was *bur.* at Cornwood, when the *Baronetcy* became *extinct.* Will pr. at £45,437 gross personalty.

Family Estates.—These, in 1883, consisted of 2,919 acres in Devon, worth £2,575 a year.[a] *Principal Residence.*—Blachford, near Ivybridge, Devon.

STANLEY:[b]

cr. 13 April 1699;

ex. 30 Nov. 1744.

I. 1699, to 1743. "JOHN STANLEY, of Grange Gorman, co. Dublin, Esq.," 3d s.[c] of Sir Thomas STANLEY,[d] of Dublin, by Jane, da. of (—) BORROWES, was *b.* 1663, at Tickencor, co. Waterford; admitted to Trin. Coll., Dublin, 21 Oct. 1676, aged 13; M.A., 1684; Sec. to various Lords Chamberlain of the Household, 1689-99 and 1700-14; Commissioner of Stamp Duties, Sep. 1698 to Dec. 1700, and was *cr. a Baronet*, as above, 13 April 1699; Commissioner of Customs, May 1708 till death in 1744; M.P. [I.] for Gorey, *otherwise*, Newborough, 1713-14. He *m.* Anne, sister of George, BARON LANSDOWN OF BIDEFORD, da. of Bernard GRANVILLE, of Stow, co. Cornwall, Master of the Horse, by Anne, da. and h. of Christopher MORLEY, of Hornby, co. York. She *d.* 29 March 1729/30. He *d.* s.p. 30 Nov. 1744, aged about 81, when the *Baronetcy* became *extinct.*[e] Will, as of North End in Fulham, Midx., dat. 23 Sep. 1737, pr. 1744, and pr. [I.] 18 July 1745.

[a] The estate of Blachford was devised by the 9th Baronet, Sir John Charles Rogers, after the death of his brother Edward, and his sister in law, Lady Blachford (who *d.* 13 July 1900, being the survivor of the two), to his maternal cousin, Col. Robert Elphinstone Deare, with rem. to the Colonel's two sisters. These, inasmuch as Col. Deare *d.* before Lady Blachford, succeeded thereto on her death in July 1900.

[b] The information in this article has been kindly supplied by G. D. Burtchaell, of the Office of Arms, Dublin.

[c] Of his elder brothers, Thomas *d.* unm, while Stephen, *b.* 1659 in co. Tipperary, was admitted to Trin. Coll., Dublin, 5 June 1675, as Fellow Commoner, aged 16; was M.P. [I.] for co. Waterford, 1717-25; *m.* (Lic. Prerog. [I.], 23 Sep. 1676) Margaret, only da. of Sir William Tichborne of Beaulieu, and *d.* s.p. 1725. This Stephen and his said wife are (erroneously) given as the parents of the Baronet in Wotton's *Baronetage* [1741].

[d] This Thomas had a grant of arms, 7 April 1649, from Roberts, Ulster, being then Sergeant-Major under Sir John Borlase; was *Knighted* by the Lord Deputy [I.] Henry Cromwell, 4 Jan. 1658, in which year he was Sheriff of the counties of Waterford and Tipperary; was M.P. [I.] for co. Louth, 1661-66, and *d.* 27 Aug., being *bur.* 2 Sep. 1674, at St. Michan's, Dublin. Will dat. 18 July 1673, pr. [I.] 1674. He had an elder br., Stephen Stanley, *b.* at Maryborough, Queen's county, in 1621, who was admitted to Trin Coll., Dublin, as Scholar, 14 May 1639, aged 18. Their sister, Abigail, *m.* 25 July 1652, William Handcock, and had issue. The father of Thomas Stanley, the grantee of 1649, was the Rev. Thomas Stanley.

[e] He entailed his estate on his nephew, Charles Monck, Barrister at Law, 2d s. of his only sister, Sarah (*m.* 1 May 1673, and *bur.* 8 April 1710, at St. Michan's, Dublin), by Henry Monck, who was *bur.* there 23 Aug. 1715. This Charles *d.* 1752, being ancestor of the Viscounts Monck [I.], sometime, 1822-48, Earl of Rathdowne [I.].

DENTON:

cr. 12 May 1699;

ex. 4 April 1714.

I. 1699, to 1714. EDMUND DENTON, of Hillesden, co Buckingham, Esq.," 1st s. and h. of Alexander DENTON, of the same (*d.* 17 Oct. 1698, aged 44), by Hester, da. and h. of Nicholas HERMAN, of Middleton Stoney, Oxon, was *bap.* 25 Oct. 1676, at Hillesden; matric. at Oxford (Wadham Coll.), 21 Feb. 1694/5, aged 16; admitted to Middle Temple, 1697; suc. his father, 17 Oct. 1698; M.P. for Buckingham (five Parls.) Dec. 1698 to 1708, and for Bucks 1708-13, and was *cr. a Baronet*, as above, 12 May 1699. He *m.* 18 May 1700, at St. Dionis Backchurch, London, Mary, 1st da. and coheir of Anthony ROWE, of Muswell Hill, in Hackney, Midx., and of North Aston, Oxon, Clerk of the Green Cloth, by Mary, da. of Robert MANLEY. He *d.* s.p. 4, and was *bur.* 11 May 1714, at Hillesden, aged 37, when the *Baronetcy* became *extinct.* M.I. Will pr. June 1714. His widow, who was *b.* 15 and *bap.* 19 Feb. 1683/4, at St. Martin's in the Fields, *m.* in or before 1718, Trevor (HILL), 1st VISCOUNT HILLSBOROUGH [I.], who *d.* 5 May 1742, and was *bur.* at Hillsborough. She *d.* (on her journey to Bath) a few months later, 23 Aug. 1742, aged 58, and was *bur.* at Hillesden. M.I.

VANDERBRANDE:

cr. 9 June 1699;

ex., presumably, soon after 1713.

I. 1699. JOHN "PETER VANDERBRANDE, of Kleverskirke, in Holland, Esq.," Burgomaster of Middleburgh, Representative for Zealand at the States General, and Ambassador from the United Provinces to William III of England, was *cr. a Baronet*, as above, 9 June 1699. He *d.* in or before 1713. Will pr. June 1713.

II. 1713, to 1720? SIR CORNELIUS VANDERBRANDE, Baronet [1699], s. and h., *suc. to the Baronetcy* on his father's death, and proved his will in June 1713; after which date no more is known of him, and the *Baronetcy* is *presumed* to have become *extinct* on his death.[a]

BROWN:

cr. 14 Dec. 1699;

ex., presumably, about 1760.

I. 1699. "WILLIAM BROWN, of London, Esq.," was made Burgess and Guild Brother of Edinburgh, in 1684; registered Arms, 20 March 1693, at the Lyon Office, as "a Scotsman in origin, descended from that family of Browns in the Shiredom of Angus, now [1693] represented by George Brown, of Horn, late Provost of Dundie,"[b] acquired a considerable fortune as a merchant at Dantzic and in London, and was *cr. a Baronet*, as above, 14 Dec. 1699. He returned to Dantzic, where he was living 1717 in the Langmarkt,[b] and *d.* there before 1735.

(a) It is placed in Wotton's *Baronetage* (1741), vol. iv, p. 268, among those Baronets "whereof no certain information can be had."

(b) *Ex inform.* Sir James Balfour Paul, Lyon, who adds that the grantee's sister *m.* a Dantzic merchant named Nisson, and had a da., Janet, who in 1713 *m.* John Nicholson, shoemaker in Dundee, son of another Dantzic merchant. From "*The Scots in Eastern and Western Prussia,*" by Th. Fischer [1903] it appears that Brown of Dantzic "was made Burgess and Guild brother of Edinburgh in 1684. He also received a Baronetcy. The patent [*sic*] is still preserved at Dantzic, and is signed by Sir George Drummond. In 1717 he possessed a fine house on the Langmarkt." The word "patent," as above, must, however, mean "Burgess ticket," as Sir George Drummond was Provost of Edinburgh at that time.

II. 1720? SIR JOHN BROWN, Baronet [1699], of Kew Green, Surrey,[a] s. and h., *suc. to the Baronetcy* on the death of his father; resided in Pall Mall. He *m.* firstly (—). He *m.* secondly, Oct. 1723 (—), da. of (—) CHRISTMAS.[b] Admon. of "Dame Elizabeth BROWN, of Chelsea, Midx.," 13 Oct. 1735, to her husband "Sir John BROWN, Baronet." Death of "Sir John BROWN, Baronet," June 1738, in Fetter Lane, Holborn.

III. 1738? to 1760? SIR [—] BROWN, Baronet, s. and h., *suc. to the Baronetcy* on the death of his father; was living 1741 in Poland,[b] and *d.* there,[c] but nothing further is known of him, and the *Baronetcy* is *presumed* to have become *extinct* at his death.

ANGUISH, *otherwise* ALLEN, *or* ALLIN:

cr. 14 Dec. 1699;

ex. 30 April 1794.

I. 1699. "WILLIAM [*recte* RICHARD] ANGUISH, *otherwise* ALLEN [*or* ALLIN], of Somerleyton, co. Suffolk, Esq.," s. and h. of Edmund ANGUISH, of Moulton, Norfolk, by Alice, the only child that left issue of Admiral Sir Thomas ALLEN, *or* ALLIN, 1st Baronet [1673], of Blundeston, co. Suffolk, having in Oct. 1696, inherited the estate of Somerleyton etc., by the death of his maternal uncle, Sir Thomas ALLEN, *or* ALLIN, the 2d and last Baronet [1673], assumed the name of ALLEN, *or* ALLIN, and was *cr. a Baronet*, as above, 14 Dec. 1699. He was M.P. for Dunwich, 1703-10. He *m.* probably about 1710, Frances, the only child that left issue of Sir Henry ASHHURST, 1st Baronet [1688] of Waterstock, Oxon, by Diana, da. of William (PAGET), LORD PAGET DE BEAUDESERT. He *d.* 19 Oct. 1725. Will pr. 1730. His widow *d.* 23 June 1743. Will pr. 1743.

II. 1725. SIR THOMAS ALLEN, ALLIN, *or* ANGUISH, Baronet, of Somerleyton aforesaid, 1st s. and h.; *suc. to the Baronetcy,* 19 Oct. 1725; sometime (till 1729) Land waiter for the port of London; Sheriff of Suffolk, Jan. to Dec. 1730; Serjeant at Arms to the Treasury, 1743. He *d.* unm. 12 Aug. 1765. Will pr. 1765.

III 1765. SIR ASHURST ALLEN, *or* ALLIN, Baronet [1699], of Somerleyton aforesaid, br. and h., *b.* about 1720; ed. at Emman. Coll., Cambridge; B.A., 1739; in Holy Orders; Rector of Blunston cum Flixton; *suc. to the Baronetcy,* 12 Aug. 1765. He *m.*, before 1741; Thomazine, widow of [—] NORRIS, of Norfolk, da. of Col. PLAYTERS, by Caroline, his wife. He *d.* 6 Nov. 1770. Will pr. March 1773.

IV. 1770, to 1794. SIR THOMAS ALLEN, *or* ALLIN, Baronet [1699], of Somerleyton aforesaid, only s. and h.; *suc. to the Baronetcy,* 6 Nov. 1770. He *d.* unm. 30 April 1794, when the *Baronetcy* became *extinct.*[d]

(a) His "seat at Kew Green was purchased by Queen Caroline," wife of George II. See note "d" below.

(b) Wotton's *Baronetage,* 1741.

(c) See p. 180, note "b."

(d) The estate of Somerleyton and others passed to his cousin and heir male Thomas Anguish, great grandson of Edmund Anguish (*d.* 1708), next br. to the 1st Baronet, both being sons of Edmund Anguish, by Alice, da. of Admiral Sir Thomas Allen, or Allin, 1st Baronet [1678], of Blundeston [Burke's *Commoners,* vol. ii, p. 419, edit. 1837].

NEWMAN:

cr. 20 Dec. 1699;

ex. 4 June 1747.

I. 1699. "RICHARD NEWMAN, of Fifehead Magdalen, co. Dorset, Esq.," as also of Evercreech park, co. Somerset, only s. and h. of Richard NEWMAN, of the same (*d.* June 1682, aged 32), by Grace, da. and coheir of Henry EDMONDES, of Preston Hall, in Preston Deane, co. Northampton, was *b.* about 1675; matric. at Oxford (Pemb. Coll.), 8 April 1693, aged 18, and was *cr. a Baronet*, as above, 20 Dec. 1699. He was M.P. for Milborne Port, 1700-01, and Sheriff of Northamptonshire, 1706-07. He *m.* (Lic. Lond. 1 June 1696, each being about 20) Frances, da. of Sir Thomas SAMWELL, 1st Baronet [1675], of Upton, co. Northampton, by his 1st wife, Elizabeth, da. and h. of George GOODAY. He *d.* 30 Dec. 1721, at Preston aforesaid, and was *bur.* 3 Jan. 1721/2, at Fifehead. M.I. Will dat. 10 Sep. 1712, to 29 Dec. 1721, pr. 28 Dec. 1722. His widow *d.* at Bath, 4 Dec. 1730, and was *bur.* there. M.I. Admon. 26 Jan. 1730/1.

II. 1721, to 1747. SIR SAMUEL NEWMAN, Baronet [1699], of Fifehead Magdalen, Evercreech park and Preston Hall aforesaid, only s. and h., *b.* about 1700; *suc. to the Baronetcy,* 30 Dec. 1721, and pr. his father's will 28 Dec. 1722; was Sheriff of Northamptonshire, 1746-47. He *d.* unm., at St. Margaret's Westm., 4 June 1747, and was *bur.* at Fifehead, when the *Baronetcy* became *extinct.*[a] M.I. Admon. 16 July 1747, and again April 1805.

WESCOMBE, *or* WESTCOMBE:

cr. 23 March 1699/700;

ex., presumably, 6 Dec. 1752.

I. 1700. "MARTIN WESTCOMBE [*or* WESCOMBE], of [—], co. Dorset, Esq., Agent and Consul at Cadiz," 1689, who was for a long time resident in Spain, was *cr. a Baronet*, as above, 23 March 1699/700. He *m.*, in or before 1708 [—]. He *d.* between 1708 and 1736.

II. 1720? to 1752. SIR ANTHONY WESCOMBE, Baronet [1700], s. and h., *b.* about 1708; *suc. to the Baronetcy* on the death of his father; was Deputy Commissary Gen., Deputy Judge Advocate and Commissary of the Musters at Minorca, in or before 1741. He *m.* 1 April 1736, in Duke street Chapel, St. Margaret's, Westm. (being then of St. Geo. Han. sq., about 28 bachelor), Anna Maria (then aged 25 [35?] da. of Josias CALMADY, of Langdon and Leawood, Devon, by his 2d wife, Jane, da. of Sir John ROLT, of Milton, Beds. She, who was *bap.* 10 Feb. 1701/2, at Wembury, Devon, *d.* s.p. at St. Marylebone, before her husband. Admon. 10 May 1769. He *d.* presumably s.p. 6 Dec. 1752, when the *Baronetcy* is supposed to have become *extinct.*[b] Will pr. 1752.

(a) The estates devolved on his three sisters, who all *d.* s.p., and on the death of the survivor, 25 Aug. 1775, passed to the grandchildren of Ashburnham Toll, of Graywell, Hants, by Anne (*m.* May 1696), sister of the 1st Baronet.

(b) In Kimber's *Baronetage* [1771] "SIR ANTHONY WESCOMBE, son and heir" of the 2d Baronet, is given as "the present Baronet." If he was such son, he must have been by a marriage after that in 1736, for the admon. of Dame Anna Maria Wescombe, proves that *she* died without issue, though before her husband. In Kensington churchyard is a M.I. to "DAME REBECCA WESCOMBE, widow of SIR WILLIAM WESCOMBE, Baronet, died 3 Jan. 1789, aged 77," which William may possibly have been a yr. br. of the 2d Baronet, who, however, is often called *only* s. and h. of the 1st Baronet. She was mother [possibly, however, not by her said husband] of Elizabeth (*d.* 16 Dec. 1808, aged 67) wife of "Malcolm McDuffe, Esq., late of the island of Jamaica," who died 29 July, 1812, aged 75.

CHETWODE:[a]

cr. 6 April 1700;

sometime, 1845-73, NEWDIGATE-LUDFORD-CHETWODE.

I. 1700. "JOHN CHETWODE, of Oakley, co. Stafford, Esq.," as also of Chetwode, Bucks, 1st s. and h. of Philip CHETWODE, of the same (aged 21 in the Visit. of Staffordshire 1663), by Hester, 1st da. and coheir of William TOUCHET, of Nether Witley, co. Chester, was *bap.* 4 Sep. 1666, at Mucklestone, co. Stafford; suc. his father (who *d.* aged 37) in Oct. 1678; was Sheriff of Staffordshire, Jan. to Dec. 1698, and was *cr. a Baronet*, as above, 6 April 1700. He *m.* firstly, 13 Sep. 1695, at Allhallows', London, Mary, 3d da. of Sir Jonathan RAYMOND, of Barton Court, Berks, Alderman, and sometime (1679-80) Sheriff of London, by Anne, da. and h. of Philip JEMMETT, of Kintbury, Berks. She *d.* 12, and was *bur.* 15 Jan. 1702 at Mucklestone. M.I. He *m.* secondly, Catherine, 3d da. of John TAYLEUR, of Rodington, Salop. She *d.* s.p., at Chester, 14 and was *bur.* 19 Oct. 1717, at Mucklestone, her death being "occasioned by a fall from her coach, 6 Dec. 1716."[a] M.I. He *d.* at Oakley 22, and was *bur.* 27 April 1733 at Mucklestone, aged 66. M.I. Will dat. 9 March 1732, pr. 20 Dec. 1733.

II. 1733. SIR PHILIP TOUCHET CHETWODE, Baronet [1700], of Oakley, Chetwode, and Witley aforesaid, only son and h., by 1st wife; *b.* 22 July, and *bap.* (as "Touchet" only) 6 Aug. 1700, at Winwick, the baptism being reg. at Chetwode aforesaid; was confirmed, 8 July 1711, at Eccleshall, co. Stafford, "and did then and there receive the name of Philip, to be used from thenceforth as his Christian name"; *suc. to the Baronetcy,* 22 April 1733. He *m.* (settmt. 10 Jan. 1727) Elizabeth, da. and h. of George VENABLES, of Agden, co. Chester, by Theophania, da. of Charles HUTCHINSON, of Lichfield. She *d.* at Oakley, 14, and was *bur.* 17 Sep. 1745, at Mucklestone, aged 39. M.I. He *d.* at Oakley 15, and was *bur.* 21 Nov. 1764, at Mucklestone, aged 64. M.I. Will pr. 1764.

III. 1764. SIR JOHN [*or* JOHN TOUCHET] CHETWODE, Baronet [1700], of Oakley, Chetwode, and Witley aforesaid, 1st s. and h., *b.* 29 April 1732 and *bap.* at Rostherne, co. Chester; was Sheriff of Staffordshire (as "John Touchet Chetwode, Esq."), 1756-57, and *suc. to the Baronetcy,* 15 Nov. 1764. He *m.*, in 1756, Dorothy, 3d da. and coheir of Tobias BRETLAND, of Thorncliffe, co. Chester. She, who was *b.* 1737, *d.* 30 Dec. 1769, and was *bur.*, 9 Jan. 1770, at Mucklestone. M.I. He *d.* 25 May, and was *bur.* there 10 June 1779, aged 47. M.I. Will pr. July 1779 and Jan. 1834.

IV. 1779. SIR JOHN CHETWODE, Baronet [1700], of Oakley, Chetwode, and Witley aforesaid, 1st surv. s. and h., *b.* 11 May 1764, and *bap.* at Stockport, Cheshire; *suc. to the Baronetcy,* 25 May 1779; was Sheriff of Cheshire, 1789; M.P. for Newcastle-under-Lyme, July 1815 to 1818, and for Buckingham, 1841 till death in 1843. He *m.* firstly, 26 Oct. 1785 (spec. lic.), at Dunham Massey, co. Chester, Elizabeth, 1st da. of George Harry (GREY), 5th EARL OF STAMFORD and 1st EARL OF WARRINGTON, by Henrietta, da. of William (CAVENDISH-BENTINCK), 2d DUKE OF PORTLAND. She who was *b.* 20 April 1764, at St. James', Westm., *d.* 12 July 1826, and was *bur.* at Mucklestone. M.I. He *m.* secondly, 16 May 1827, at Hammersmith, Elizabeth, da. of John BRISTOW, of Lincolnshire, an officer in the army. He *d.*, at Bognor, Sussex, 17 Dec. 1845, aged 81, and was *bur.* at Mucklestone. M.I. Will pr. Feb. 1846. His widow, by whom he had no issue, *m.*, 22 May 1848, at St. John's, Hampstead, Andrew Kennedy HUTCHINSON, of Chester square, Pimlico.

V. 1845. SIR JOHN NEWDIGATE-LUDFORD-CHETWODE, Baronet [1700], of Oakley, Chetwode and Witley aforesaid, and of Ansley Hall, co. Warwick, 1st s. and h., *b.* 12 and *bap.* 13 Nov. 1788, at Mucklestone; took by royal lic. 1 Aug. 1826, the name of *Newdigate-Ludford* before that of *Chetwode,* in consequence of his marriage; *suc. to the Baronetcy,* 17 Dec. 1845.

(a) See pedigree in *Mis. Gen. et Her.,* 2d S., vol. i, pp. 85-91.

Sheriff of Warwickshire, 1852. He *m.* firstly, 16 Oct. 1821, at Ansley (settlemt. 27 Oct. 1821) Elizabeth Juliana, 1st da. and coheir of John NEWDIGATE-LUDFORD, of Ansley Hall aforesaid. She *d.* there 17 June 1859, aged 79, and was *bur.* at Ansley. M.I. He *m.* secondly, 17 Jan. 1861, at St. Thomas', Portman square, Marylebone, Arabella Phyllis, widow of James READE, of Lower Berkeley street, only child of Samuel DENTON. She *d.* 26 June 1873, and was *bur.* at Mucklestone. M.I. He *d.* s.p., about ten weeks afterwards, 8 Sep. 1873, at Oakley, in his 85th year, and was *bur.* with her. M.I.

VI. 1873. SIR GEORGE CHETWODE, Baronet [1700], of Oakley, Chetwode and Witley aforesaid, nephew and h., being 2d but 1st surv. s. of the Rev. George CHETWODE, of Chilton House, Bucks, Rector of Ashton under Lyne, co. Lancaster, by his 1st wife Charlotte Anne, sister of the 1st BARON HATHERTON, da. of Morton WALHOUSE, of Hatherton, co. Stafford, which George (who was *b.* 1 Nov. 1791, and *d.* Aug. 1870), was yr. br. of the whole blood, to the late Baronet. He was *b.* 20 July 1823, at Chesterton, Oxon; joined the army (4th Foot) 1840, being eventually Lieut.-Col. 8th Hussars; serving in the Crimean War (5th Class Medjidie, 1851), and in the Indian campaigns; *suc. to the Baronetcy*, 8 Sep. 1873. He *m.* 21 Oct. 1868, Alice Jane, sister of the 1st BARON BURTON, 2d da. of Michael Thomas BASS, of Rangemore, co. Stafford, by Eliza Jane, da. of Major Samuel ARDEN, of Longcroft, in that county. She was *b.* 1 Aug. 1843.

Family Estates.—These, in 1883, consisted of 1,617 acres in Cheshire (worth £3,361 a year); 1,158 in Staffordshire; 917 in Salop, and 413 in Bucks. *Total.*—4,105 acres, worth £7,071 a year. *Principal Seats.*—Oakley Hall, near Market Drayton, co. Stafford; Agden, co. Chester and Chetwode, co. Buckingham.

VANACKER:(a)

cr. 31 Jan. 1700/1;

afterwards, 1711-54, SAMBROOKE, *or* VANACKER-SAMBROOKE;

ex. 4 Oct. 1754.

I. 1701. [SIR] "NICHOLAS VANACKER, of London, merchant," 3d s. of Nicholas VANACKER, merchant, of the same, Lord of the Manor of Erith, co. Kent (*b.* at Belle, near Ypres in Flanders; will pr. 10 May 1669), by Susanna, da. of James BUTLER, of Amberley Castle, Sussex, was *b* in or soon after 1651;(b) ed. at Leyden Univ.; was a Turkey merchant, and fined, in 1699, for the Shrievalty of London; was *Knighted* at Kensington, 21 and was *cr. a Baronet*, as above, 31 Jan. 1700/1, with a spec. rem. "in default of male issue to his brother John VANACKER, with further remainder, in default of male issue to Jeremy SAMBROOKE, Esq., eldest son of Sir Jeremy SAMBROOKE, Knt." He *d.* s.p. and was *bur.* 19 Feb. 1701/2, at St. Andrew's Undershaft. Will pr. Feb. 1701/2.

II. 1702. SIR JOHN VANACKER, Baronet [1701], br. and h., *suc. to the Baronetcy* in Feb. 1701/2, according to the spec. rem. on its creation. He probably was a merchant in London. He *d.* s.p.(c) in Chancery lane, and was *bur.*, 24 March 1710/1, at St. Andrew's, Undershaft, London.(d) Will pr. March 1711.

(a) See A. W. Crawley-Boevey's "*Perverse Widow*" [*Boevey Family, &c.*], as also *N. & Q.*, 8th Series, i, 218.

(b) His next elder br. was *bap.* 3 Nov. 1650, at the Dutch Church, London.

(c) The following mar. lic. at the Faculty Office not improbably refers to him:—1680, Aug. 11, "John Vanacker and Sarah Bax."

(d) The following entries of burials are, however, somewhat contradictory, viz., that at St. Andrew's, Holborn, 11 April 1711 [*Qy.* if not an insertion made some time after date], of "Sir John Van Anker, from Chancery lane"; and that at St. Andrew's, Undershaft, 24 March 1710/1, of "Sir John Vanuaker, Knt."

III. 1711. SIR SAMUEL SAMBROOKE, *or* VANACKER-SAMBROOKE, Baronet [1701], nephew and h., being 1st s. and h. of Sir Jeremy SAMBROOKE, Merchant of London, a Director of the East India Company, and F.R.S. (*d.* 27 April 1705), by Judith (will pr. 1744), sister of the last two Baronets, da. of Nicholas VANACKER, all abovenamed.(a) He was *b.* about 1678, and *suc. to the Baronetcy* in March 1710/1, according to the spec. rem. in its creation; was M.P. for Great Hedworth, 1708-10. He *m.* at St. Giles' in the Fields, 21 Jan. 1700/1 (Lic. 20, he of St. Michael's, Bassishaw, "Esq.," aged 22 and she aged 18), Elizabeth, da. of the Right Hon. Sir Nathan WRIGHT, then L. Keeper of the Great Seal, by Elizabeth, da. of George ASHBY, of Quenby, co. Leicester. He *d.* 27 Dec. 1714, in Chancery lane, and was *bur.* 4 Jan. 1714/5, at Edmonton, Midx. Will pr. Jan. 1714/5. His widow *d.* 7 Dec. 1775, aged 94. Will pr. Dec. 1775.

IV. 1714. SIR JEREMY SAMBROOKE, *or* VANACKER-SAMBROOKE, Baronet [1701], only s. and h.; *suc. to the Baronetcy*, when a minor, 27 Dec. 1714; was M.P. for Beds, Jan. 1730/1, till his death in 1740. He *d.* unm. at Bush Hill, near Enfield, 5, and was *bur.* 13 July 1740, at Edmonton. Admon. 31 July 1740 to his sister Susanna, wife of John CRAWLEY, Esq., the mother, Dame Elizabeth VANACKER-SAMBROOKE, widow, renouncing.

V. 1740, to 1754. SIR JEREMY SAMBROOKE, Baronet [1701], of Gobions, in North Mims, Herts, uncle and h. male; *suc. to the Baronetcy*. 5 July 1740. He *d.* unm. 4, and was *bur.* 12 Oct. 1754, at North Mims, when the *Baronetcy* became *extinct*. Will pr. 1754.

MOYER, *or* MAYER:

cr. 25 March 1701;

ex. 17 April 1716.

I. 1701, to 1716. "SAMUEL MAYER [*recté* MOYER], of Pitsey Hall, co. Essex, Esq.," as also of St. Stephen's, Walbrook, London, Turkey merchant, s. and h. of Samuel MOYER, of Pitsey Hall aforesaid (Alderman of London and sometime M.P. thereof, and one of the Judges of the Court of Probate during the Commonwealth), by Rebecca, da. of [—] THOROLD, was *b.* about 1643; admitted by patrimony to the Mercers' Company, London, in 1669; suc. his father in July 1683; was Sheriff of Essex, 1698, and was *cr. a Baronet*, as above, 25 March 1701. He *m.* 2 March 1670/1, at St. Martin's Outwich, London (Lic. London, 25 Feb., he of St. Giles', Cripplegate, aged 28, bachelor) Rebecca (then aged 19), sister of Sir William JOLLIFFE, da. of John JOLLIFFE, Alderman of London. He *d.* s.p.m.(b) 17 April, and was *bur.* 7 May 1716, at St. Stephen's, Walbrook, when the *Baronetcy* became *extinct*.(c) Will dat. 17 May 1711, pr. May 1716. His widow, who was *b.* 9 Jan. 1650, *d.* 28 Jan., and was *bur.* 12 Feb. 1723/4, at St. Stephen's aforesaid. Her will dat. 10 Dec. 1722, pr. 21 Feb. 1723/4.

(a) Susanna, the only other sister, *d.* in childbirth, 6 July 1683, at Hugli, in India, being then the 1st wife of William Hedges, chief of the Company's affairs in Bengal, 1681-87. He, who was afterwards Sheriff [1693-94] and Alderman of London and a Director of the Bank of England, and who was knighted 6 March 1688, was *bur.* with her, 15 Aug. 1701, at Stratton St. Margaret's, Wilts.

(b) Of his three daughters and coheirs (1) Rebecca *m.* 24 April 1710, at St. Stephen's, Walbrook, Edward Pauncefort, and *d.*, probably s.p., before 1722; (2) Mary, *b.* and *bap.* 8 Nov. 1675, at St. Stephen's aforesaid, *m.* there, 24 July 1711, Charles Samborn Le Bas, of Pipwell Abbey, co. Northampton, and *d.* July 1722, leaving an only child, Rebecca, who *m.*, Oct. 1735, Simon (Harcourt), 1st Earl Harcourt; (3) Elizabeth, *b.* 16 and *bap.* 17 March 1678/9 at St. Stephen's aforesaid, *m.* (—) Jenyns (who *d.* before 1722), and *d.* s.p. 30 March 1758, when admon. of her estate was granted to her niece and only next of kin, Rebecca, Countess Harcourt.

(c) The estate of Pitsey passed to Benjamin Moyer, his nephew and heir male, who *d.* 29 May 1759, leaving a son John, who *d.* 11 Jan. 1773, at Walthamstow, aged 70.

THORNYCROFT:

cr. 12 Aug. 1701;

ex. 23 June 1743.

I. 1701. "JOHN THORNYCROFT, of Milcomb, co. Oxford, Esq.," 2d s. of John THORNYCROFT, of Bloxham in that county, Bencher of Gray's Inn, Midx., by Dorothy, da. of Sir John HOWEL, Recorder of London, *b.* 16 Nov. 1659; admitted to Gray's Inn, 16 Nov. 1675; Barrister, 1686; suc. his father (who *d.* aged 71), 25 Sep. 1687, and was *cr. a Baronet*, as above, 12 Aug. 1701;(a) Sheriff of Oxon, 1701-02. He *m.* 17 Feb. 1686/7 (Lic. Lond. 16, he aged 27, and she, of Milcomb aforesaid, but then of St. Andrew's, Holborn, aged 21), Elizabeth, da. and h. of Josiah KEY, of Milcomb. She *d.* there 6 March 1703, aged 38. He *d.* 8 and was *bur.* 21 Dec. 1725, at St. Andrew's, Holborn, aged 66. Will pr. 1725.

II. 1725, to 1743. SIR JOHN THORNYCROFT, Baronet [1701], of Milcomb aforesaid, 1st s. and h., *b.* 1691; *suc. to the Baronetcy*, 8 Dec. 1725. He *m.* Terceira, da. of Andrew BONNELL, of St. Dunstan's in the East, merchant, by Anne, da. of Sir Thomas ALLEN, 1st Baronet [1660], of London. He *d.* s.p. in the King's Bench prison, 23 June 1743, aged 52, when the *Baronetcy* became *extinct*. Will pr. 1743.

CREATIONS BY QUEEN ANNE,

8 March 1701/2 to 1 May 1707,

being the date of the Union with Scotland, when the creation of English (as well as of Scotch) Baronetcies ceased and those of Great Britain began.

WINFORD:

cr. 3 July 1702;

ex. 19 Jan. 1743/4.

I. 1702. July, to Sep.? "THOMAS WINFORD, of Grashampton, co. Worcester, Esq.," s.(b) of Sir John WINFORD, of Crowle and Ashley, in that county, who fought for Charles II, at the battle of Worcester (*d.* 2 July 1682), by Elizabeth, da. of Sir Henry WILLIAMS, Baronet [1644], of Gwernevet, was admitted to Lincoln's Inn, 18 June 1678; was second Prothonotary in the Court of Common Pleas (till his death in 1702, and was *cr. a Baronet*, as above, 3 July 1702, with a spec. rem., failing heirs male of his body to those of his br. "Henry WINFORD, of Glashampton, Esq."(c) He *m.* Sarah, da. and coheir of Michael PEARCE, of Drury Lane, Midx, Apothecary. He *d.* s.p. between July and Sep. 1702. Will pr. Sep. 1702. His widow *d.* 17 Sep. 1735, and was *bur.* at Hillingdon, Midx. Will pr. 1735.

(a) In Dec. 1696, Sir Anthony Mayney, *or* Mayne, 2d Baronet [1641] petitions to surrender his Baronetcy for one to be granted to him for life with rem. to his "kinsman, John Thornicroft, of Gray's Inn." This, however, was never done, and the petitioner *d.* unm. in 1706. See vol. ii, p. 460, being corrigenda to page 93, *sub* "Mayney, *or* Mayne."

(b) In his admission to Lincoln's Inn he is called "son and heir ap.," though he is generally spoken of as the 2d son.

(c) Wotton's *Baronetage*, 1741.

II. 1702, to 1744. SIR THOMAS COOKES WINFORD, Baronet [1702], of Glashampton aforesaid, and of Norgrove, co. Worcester, nephew and h., being s. and h. of Henry WINFORD, of Ashley, co. Worcester, and of Glasford aforesaid, by Mercy, sister and heir of Sir Thomas COOKES, 2d Baronet [1664], only da. of Sir William COOKES, 1st Baronet [1664], both of Norgrove aforesaid, which Henry (who *d.* before Nov. 1687), was br. of the late Baronet. He, who was *b.* about 1674, was admitted to Lincoln's Inn, 10 Nov. 1687; *suc. to the Baronetcy*, in or shortly before Sep. 1702, according to the *spec. rem.* in the creation of that dignity; was M.P. for Worcestershire, Dec. 1707 to 1710; Sheriff of that county, 1721-22. He *m.* firstly, Beata, yst. da. of Sir Henry PARKER, 1st Baronet [1681], of Honington, co. Warwick. He *m.* secondly (Lic. Worcester, 12 Nov. 1718, he about 44, widower, she about 17, spinster), Elizabeth, da. of [—] WILMOT, of Bromsgrove, co. Worcester. He *d.* s.p. 19 Jan. 1743/4, aged about 70, when the *Baronetcy* became *extinct*. Will pr. 1743. His widow *d.* 29 Nov. 1753.

SEDLEY, *or* SIDLEY:

cr. 10 July 1702;

ex. 23 Aug. 1778.

I. 1702. CHARLES SEDLEY, *or* SIDLEY, of Southfleet, co. Kent, Esq.,(a) s. and h. of Sir Charles SEDLEY (*Knighted*, when under age, 12 March 1688/9), by Frances, da. of Sir Richard NEWDIGATE (which Charles last named was an illegit. son, by Catherine AYSCOUGH, spinster,(b) of the celebrated wit, Sir Charles SEDLEY, 5th Baronet [1611], but *d.* v.p., being *bur.* from St. Giles' in the Fields, at Southfleet, 29 May 1701), was *b.* probably about 1695(c); suc. in his infancy to the family estates in Kent (which he subsequently sold) on the death of his grandfather, the 5th Baronet [1611] abovenamed, 20 Aug. 1701, and was *cr. a Baronet*, as above, 10 July 1702. He *m.* in 1718, Elizabeth, da. of William FRITH and Mary his wife (possibly a da. and coheir of [—] COLLINGE, of Nuthall), and by her acquired the estate of Nuthall, Notts, and the manors of Hayford and Harleigh. He *d.* 18 Feb. 1729/30. Will pr. 1730. His widow *d.* 20 April 1738.

II. 1730, to 1778. SIR CHARLES SEDLEY, Baronet [1702], of Nuthall aforesaid, only s. and h., *b.* about 1721; *suc. to the Baronetcy*, 18 Feb. 1729/30; matric. at Oxford (Univ. Coll.), 22 Feb. 1738/9, aged 17; M.P. for Nottingham, May 1747 to 1754, and 1774 till death in 1778; purchased the estate of Kirby Belers, co. Leicester. He *d.* unm.(d) at Nuthall, 23 Aug. 1778, when the *Baronetcy* became *extinct*. Will pr. May 1781.

(a) The [erroneous] description of the grantee in the continuation of Dugdale's *List* has not, in this case, been followed. It is "Sir Charles Sedley, of Southfleet, co. Kent, Knt., natural son of Sir Charles Sidley or Sedley, Baronet."

(b) She is said to have gone through the ceremony of marriage with him in the lifetime of his existing wife.

(c) "Ann, da. of Sir Charles Sidley, Knt., and Frances," was *bap.* 26 March 1700 at St. Giles' in the Fields.

(d) The estates passed to his illegit. da., Elizabeth Rebecca Anne, who *m.* 14 Feb. 1779, Henry Venables Vernon, afterwards Sedley. She *d.* 18 July 1793, being by her said husband, who became, in June 1813, 3d Baron Vernon of Kinderton, ancestress of the succeeding Lords.

WEBSTER:

cr. 21 May 1703;

sometime, 1795-97, VASSAL.

I. 1703. "THOMAS WEBSTER, of Copthall, co. Essex, Esq.," s. and h. ap. of Godfrey WEBSTER (afterwards, 2 Aug. 1708, *Knighted*), of Nelmes in Havering, co. Essex, Citizen of London[a] (will pr. 1720), by Abigail, da. and coheir of Thomas GORDON, of the Mere, co. Stafford, having purchased in 1700 the estate of Copthall;[b] aforesaid; was *cr. a Baronet,* as above, 21 May 1703. Before 1708 he purchased the historic estate of Battle Abbey, co. Sussex,[c] and in 1726 that of Albury Hatch, in Barking, co. Essex. He was Sheriff of Essex, 1703-04; M.P. for Colchester, 1705-08; 1708-10; 1710 till unseated in Jan. 1711; 1713 till unseated May 1714, and 1722-27; Verderer of the forest of Waltham. He *m.* Jane, da. and h. of Edward CHEEK, of Sandford Orcas, Somerset, by Mary, da. and coheir of Henry WHISTLER, of Epsom, Surrey. He *d.* 30 May, and was *bur.* 12 June 1751 at Battle. Will pr. 1751. His widow was *bur.* there 8 Feb. 1760. Will pr. 1760.

II. 1751. SIR WHISTLER WEBSTER, Baronet [1703], of Battle Abbey aforesaid, 1st s. and h., *b.* probably about 1690; M.P. for East Grinstead (three Parls.), 1741-61; *suc. to the Baronetcy,* 30 May 1751. He *m.* Martha, da. of the Rev. [—] NAIRNE, Dean of Battle. He *d.* s.p. 21 Sep. 1779. Will pr. Nov. 1779. His widow *d.* 25 Dec. 1810. Will pr. 1811.

III. 1779. SIR GODFREY WEBSTER, Baronet [1703], of Battle Abbey and Nelmes aforesaid, br. and h., *b.* probably about 1695; *suc. to the Baronetcy,* 21 Sep. 1779. He *m.* in or before 1719, Elizabeth, da. of Gilbert COOPER, of Lockington, co. Derby, and Thurgarton, Notts. He *d.* 6 May 1780. Will pr. May 1780. His widow *d.* 17 June 1807. Will pr. 1807.

IV. 1780. SIR GODFREY WEBSTER, *sometime* (1795-97) VASSAL, Baronet [1703], of Battle Abbey aforesaid, s. and h., *b.* 1719 at Epsom; matric. at Oxford (Oriel Coll.), 8 July 1737, aged 18; *suc. to the Baronetcy,* 6 May 1780; M.P. for Seaford, March 1786 to 1790, and for Wareham, 1796, till death in 1800; took by royal lic., 21 Aug. 1795, the surname of VASSAL only, which, however, he discontinued to use after his wife's divorce in 1797. He *m.* 27 June 1786, Elizabeth, da. and h. of Richard VASSAL, of Jamaica, by Mary, da. of Thomas CLARKE, of New York. She, however, was divorced by Act of Parl. in 1797.[d] He, who had had "ill luck at play, shot himself at his house in Tenterden street, Hanover square, 3 June 1800," aged about 80, the verdict being one "of lunacy."[e] Will pr. Aug. 1800 and Sep. 1853.

(a) He was, according to Le Neve's *Knights,* "a Packer by trade."

(b) The vendor was Charles (Sackville), Earl of Dorset. This estate, however, he sold long before his death to Edward Conyers, whose son John, in 1753, built a new house in Epping parish. The old "Copthall," which was "a noble large house" [Morant's *Essex*], was in the parish of Waltham.

(c) The vendor was Francis (Browne), 4th Viscount Montagu [who inherited that title in 1682, and died in 1708], to whose ancestor, Sir Anthony Browne, K.G., it was granted by Henry VIII in 1539. Sir Anthony converted it into a dwelling-house, and built the banqueting hall, etc. In 1857, however, the estate was sold, by the Webster family, to Lord Harry George Vane, afterwards (1864-91) 4th Duke of Cleveland, on the death of whose widow (18 May 1901) it was sold by auction, 27 Nov. 1901 (6,000 acres, with a rent roll of £5,000), for £200,000, to the 8th Baronet, s. and h. of the 7th Baronet, who had alienated it in 1857, as above.

(d) She *m.* 9 July 1797, at Rickmansworth, Herts. Henry Richard (Fox) 3d Baron Holland, from whom her husband had obtained £6,000 damages in an action for *crim. con.*

(e) Betham's *Baronetage,* 1803.

V. 1800. SIR GODFREY VASSAL WEBSTER, Baronet [1703], of Battle Abbey aforesaid, 1st s. and h., *b.* 6 Oct. 1789; *suc. to the Baronetcy,* 3 June 1800; was M.P. for Sussex, 1812-20. He *m.* 22 Aug. 1814, at St. Geo. Han. sq., Charlotte, 1st da. of Robert ADAMSON, of Westmeath, and of Hill street, St. Geo. Han. sq. He *d.* 17 July 1836, aged 46. Admon. Nov. 1841. His widow *d.* at 29 Warrior square, St. Leonard's on Sea, 30 Jan., and was *bur.* 7 Feb. 1867, aged 76, at Hollington, Sussex.

VI. 1836. SIR GODFREY VASSAL WEBSTER, Baronet [1703], of Battle Abbey aforesaid, 1st s. and h., *b.* 3 July 1815; entered the navy, becoming Commander R.N. in 1850, having *suc. to the Baronetcy* 17 July 1836. He *m.* 10 July 1851, at St. Paul's, Knightsbridge, Sarah Joanna, widow of the Hon. Charles ASHBURNHAM, yst. da. of William MURRAY, of St. James', Jamaica. He *d.* s.p. 4 May 1853, in his 38th year, at Battle Abbey aforesaid. Will pr. June 1853. His widow, who was *b.* in Jamaica, in 1807, *d.* 19 Dec. 1889, at 2 Argyll road, Kensington.

VII. 1853 SIR AUGUSTUS FREDERICK GEORGE DOUGLAS WEBSTER, Baronet [1703], of Battle Abbey aforesaid, br. and h., *b.* 19 April 1819; entered the Navy, becoming eventually Commander R.N.; *suc. to the Baronetcy,* 4 May 1853. He sold the estate of Battle Abbey[a] in 1857, and resided at Hildon House, near East Tytherley, Hants. He *m.* 31 May 1862, at St. Peter's, Pimlico, Amelia Sophia, da. of Charles Frederick Augustus PROSSER-HASTINGS, of Taunton. He *d.* at Hildon House aforesaid, 27 March 1886, aged 66. Will pr. May 1886, over £4,000. His widow *d.* 30 April 1891.

VIII. 1886. SIR AUGUSTUS FREDERICK WALPOLE EDWARD WEBSTER, Baronet [1703], of Hildon House, and afterwards [1901] of Battle Abbey aforesaid, 1st s. and h., *b.* 10 Feb. 1864; ed. at Eton; sometime Capt. (2d Batt.) Gren. Guards; *suc. to the Baronetcy,* 27 March 1886; repurchased in 1901 the estate of Battle Abbey.[a] He *m.* 12 Nov. 1895, Mabel, only da. of Henry CROSSLEY, of Aldborough Hall, co. York.

Family Estates.—That of Battle Abbey, in 1883, consisted of 6,025 acres, worth £6,491 a year, and when repurchased by the family[a] in 1901, was described as 6,000 acres, with a rent roll of £5,000 a year. *Principal Seat.*—Battle Abbey, Sussex.

DOLBEN:

cr. 1 April 1704;

ex. 27 Sep. 1837.

I. 1704. GILBERT[b] DOLBEN, of Finedon, co. Northampton, Esq., 1st s. and h. of John DOLBEN, D.D., Archbishop of York (1683-86), by Catharine, da. of Ralph SHELDON, of Stanton, co. Derby (br. to Gilbert, Archbishop of Canterbury), was *b.* about 1658; ed. at Westm. School; matric. at Oxford (Ch. Ch.) 18 Sep. 1674, aged 15; Barrister (Inner Temple) 1680, being Bencher 1706, and Treasurer, 1721; suc. his father (who *d.* aged 62) 11 April 1686; was M.P. for Ripon 1685-87; for Peterborough (eight Parls.) 1689-98 and 1701-10, and for Yarmouth (Isle of Wight), 1710-14; was for nearly twenty years (1701-20) a Justice of the Common Pleas in Ireland, and was *cr. a Baronet,* as above, 1 April 1704. He *m.* in or before 1683, Anne, 1st da. and coheir of Tanfield MULSO, of Finedon (*otherwise* Thingdon) aforesaid, by Mary, da. of (—) LUTHER. He *d.* 22 Oct. 1722, in his 64th year. Will pr. 21 March 1722/3. His widow *d.* Dec. 1744, aged 83.

(a) See p. 188, note "c."

(b) Wrongly called "George" in the continuation of Dugdale's *List.*

II. 1722. SIR JOHN DOLBEN, Baronet [1704], of Finedon aforesaid, only s. and h., *b.* 12 Feb. 1683/4 at his grandfather's house, Bishopsthorpe, co. York; ed. at Westm. School; matric. at Oxford (Ch. Ch.), 11 May 1702, aged 17; Student, 1702; B.A., 22 Jan. 1704/5; M.A. 1707, being B.D. and D.D. 1717; in Holy Orders; Vicar of Finedon aforesaid, 1714; Preb. of Durham, 1718, obtaining the "golden stall" 1719; Rector of Burton Latimer, co. Northampton, 1719; *suc. to the Baronetcy,* 22 Oct. 1722; was Visitor of Balliol College, Oxford, 1728. He *m.,* 28 July 1720, at Sherborne Castle, Dorset, Elizabeth, da. of William (DIGBY), 5th BARON DIGBY OF GEASHILL [I.], by Jane, da. of Edward (NOEL), 1st EARL OF GAINSBOROUGH. She *d.* 4 Nov. 1730, at Aix, in Provence. He *d.* 20 Nov. 1756, aged 72, at Finedon, and was *bur.* there. Will pr. 1805.

III. 1756. SIR WILLIAM DOLBEN, Baronet [1704], of Finedon aforesaid, only surv. s. and h., *b.* about 1727; ed. at Westm. School; matric. at Oxford (Ch. Ch.), 28 May 1744, aged 17; Student, 1744; being *cr.* D.C.L. 7 July 1763; *suc. to the Baronetcy,* 20 Nov. 1756; was Sheriff of Northamptonshire, 1760-61; M.P. for Oxford Univ., 3 Feb. to 11 March 1768; for Northamptonshire, 1768-74, and for Oxford Univ. (again, five Parls.), 1780—1806; Verderer of Rockingham forest, 1765. He *m.* firstly, 17 May 1748, at Westm. Abbey, Judith, da. and h. of Somerset ENGLISH, Housekeeper of Hampton Court palace, Midx., by Judith, da. and eventually heir of Hugh PEARSON, of Hampnett, Sussex. She *d.* 6 Jan. 1771, aged 40. Her admon. 27 Aug. 1773. He *m.* secondly, 14 Oct. 1789, Charlotte, widow of John SCOTCHMER, da. of Gilbert AFFLECK, of Dalham Hall, Suffolk, by Anne, da. of John DOLBEN, brother to the 1st Baronet. He *d.* at Bury St. Edmunds, 20 March 1814, aged about 88. Admon. June 1814 and Dec. 1818. His widow, by whom he had no issue, *d.* 12 March 1820. Will pr. 1820.

IV. 1814, to 1837. SIR JOHN ENGLISH DOLBEN, Baronet [1704], of Finedon aforesaid, only s. and h., by 1st wife; *b.* about 1750; ed. at Westm. School; matric. at Oxford (Ch. Ch.), 1 June 1768, aged 18; B.C.L. 1775, being *cr.* D.C.L. 27 June 1788; F.S.A., 1780[a]; *suc. to the Baronetcy,* 20 March 1814. He *m.* in Oct. 1779, Hannah, da. of William HALLET, of Canons in Edgware, co. Midx., and heir to her mother, (—), da. and coheir of John HOPKINS, of Brittons, co. Essex. He *d.* s.p.m.s.,[b] after a short illness, 27 Sep. 1837, at Finedon hall, in his 88th year, when the *Baronetcy* became *extinct.* Admon. Oct. 1843.

IRBY:

cr. 13 April 1704;

afterwards, since 1761, BARONS BOSTON.

I. 1704. "EDWARD IRBY, of Boston, co. Lincoln, Esq.," 1st s. and h. of Anthony IRBY, of the same,[c] by Mary, da. and h. of John STRINGER, of Ashford, co. Kent, was M.P. for Boston, 1702-08, and was *cr. a Baronet,* as above, 13 April 1704. He *m.* in or before 1706, Dorothy, da. of the

(a) He was a good antiquary and classic, and a zealous Churchman, though somewhat eccentric. "He had his cards printed in black letter type, saying that he was himself *Old English.*" See an account of him in the *Gent. Mag.* for 1837.

(b) William Somerset Dolben, his only son, *b.* 1780; *m.* Frances, da. of Capt. Walter Saunders, and *d.* s.p.m. and v.p. in 1817, leaving two daughters and coheirs, of whom Frances *m.,* 1 July 1835, William Harcourt Isham Mackworth, who by royal lic. took the name of Dolben.

(c) This Anthony was s. and h. of Sir Anthony Irby of the same, whose estate "at Boston" was estimated at "about £1,000 [a year] in Sir Joseph Williamson's Lincolnshire Families, *temp.* Car. II" [*Her and Gen.* ii, 122].

Hon. Henry PAGET, of St. Michan's, Dublin,[a] yr. s. of William, LORD PAGET DE BEAUDESERT. He *d.* at Kingscliffe, co. Northampton, and was *bur.* 11 Nov. 1718, at Whaplode, co. Lincoln. Admon. 4 June 1719, to a creditor. His widow was *bur.* Oct. 1734, at Drayton, co. Midx., with her ancestors.

II. 1718. SIR WILLIAM IRBY, Baronet [1704], of Boston aforesaid, only s. and h., *b.* 8 March 1706/7; *suc. to the Baronetcy,* Nov. 1718; Page of Honour to George I, 27 Feb. 1723/4, and to George II, 22 Jan. 1728; Equerry to the Prince of Wales, 10 Dec. 1728; M.P. for Launceston, March 1735 to 1747, and for Bodmin 1747, till raised to the peerage in 1761; Vice-Chamberlain to the Princess of Wales, 1 Aug. 1736, and Lord Chamberlain to her in 1760. He *m.* 26 Aug. 1746, Albinia (sometime Maid of Honour to the said Princess), da. of Henry SELWYN, of Matson, co. Glouc., by Ruth, da. of Anthony COMPTON, of Gainslaw, Northumberland. She was living when he was *cr.* 10 April 1761, BARON BOSTON of Boston, co. Lincoln. In that peerage this *Baronetcy* then *merged,* and still [1904] so continues. See *Peerage.*

FOWLER:

cr. 1 Nov. 1704;

ex. 1 March 1771.

I. 1704. "WILLIAM FOWLER, of Harnage Grange, co. Salop, Esq.," yr. s. of Richard FOWLER, of the same, by Margaret, da. of Richard (NEWPORT), 1st BARON NEWPORT OF HIGH ERCALL, suc. his elder br. Francis Leveson FOWLER (who *d.* s.p.m.) in the family estates, and was *cr. a Baronet,* as above, 1 Nov. 1704; Sheriff of Salop, 1711-12. He *m.,* probably about 1630, Mary, 2d da. of Sir Robert COTTON, 1st Baronet [1677], of Combermere, co. Chester, by Mary, da. of Sir Thomas SALUSBURY, 2d Baronet [1619], of Llewenny. He *d.* 1717, and was *bur.* at Cound, Salop. Will pr. Aug. 1717. His widow *d.* in or before 1742. Will, as of St. James', Westm., in which she directs to be *bur.* at Esher, Surrey, dat. 21 March 1728, pr. 1 Feb. 1741/2.

II. 1717. SIR RICHARD FOWLER, Baronet [1704], of Harnage Grange aforesaid, 1st s. and h.; *suc. to the Baronetcy* in 1717. He *m.* 19 Sep. 1706, at St. Paul's Cathedral, London, Sarah, da. of William SLOANE, of Portsmouth (br. of Sir Hans SLOANE, Baronet [1716]), by Jane, da. of Alexander HAMILTON, of Killileagh, co. Down. He *d.* in or before 1731. Will pr. 1731. His widow *m.* Aug. 1737 (as his 3d wife), Francis ANNESLEY, of Thurgunby, co. York, who *d.* 7 April 1750, aged 80. She *d.* 14 Sep. 1763, at Kentish-town, St. Pancras, Midx. Will pr. 1763.

III. 1731? SIR WILLIAM FOWLER, Baronet [1704], of Harnage Grange aforesaid, 1st s. and h., *b.* about 1718 at St. Giles', Shrewsbury; matric. at Oxford (Wadham Coll.), 15 Feb. 1725/6, aged 18; *suc. to the Baronetcy* about 1731. He *m.* in 1728/9, (—), da. of Brig. Gen. NEWTON. She *d.* at Shrewsbury, in childbirth, 18 March 1738/9. He *d.* in or shortly before 1746, having embarked for Calcutta on board an East India ship which was lost at sea. Will pr. 1746.

(a) This Henry Paget *m.* firstly Anne Sandford, who was *bur.* 15 Dec. 1683, at St. Michan's, Dublin), and, secondly, 24 March 1684, at St. Kevin's, Dublin, Mary Bourke, or Rourke. It is not, however, certain which was the mother of Dorothy Irby.

IV. 1746? SIR WILLIAM FOWLER, Baronet [1704], of Harnage Grange aforesaid, only s. and h.; *suc. to the Baronetcy* about 1746; was a Cornet of Dragoons and an officer in the Prussian army. He *d.* unm., at the Hague in Germany, 25 Nov. 1760.(a) Will pr. 1760.

V. 1760, to 1771. SIR HANS FOWLER, Baronet [1704], of Abbeycwmhir, co. Radnor, uncle and h. male; sometime an officer in the Prussian Army; *suc. to the Baronetcy*, 25 Nov. 1760. He *m.* Sarah, da. of [—] DIBBS, of Dodington, Oxon. He *d.* s.p. 1 March 1771, when the *Baronetcy* became extinct.(b) Will pr. 1771. His widow *d.* 14 April 1775. Will pr. 1775.

FLEMING:

cr. 4 Oct. 1705;

afterwards, since, apparently, 1857, LE FLEMING.(c)

I. 1705. "WILLIAM FLEMING, of Rydal, co. Cumberland [*recte* Westmorland], Esq.," 1st s. and h. (out of eleven sons) of Sir Daniel FLEMING, of the same, sometime Sheriff of Cumberland (*d.* 25 March 1701, aged 67), by Barbara, da. of Sir Henry FLETCHER, 1st Baronet [1641] of Hutton, was *b.* 15 March 1656, at Rydal Hall; was lame all his life through a fall when only two years old; was M.P. for Westmorland, Nov. 1696 to 1698; 1698—1700, and Nov. 1704 to 1705, being in 1698 made a Commissioner of Excise, and was *cr. a Baronet*, as above, 4 Oct. 1705, with a spec. rem., failing heirs male of his body to those of his said father. He *m.* 1 Aug. 1723, Dorothy, da. of Thomas ROWLANDSON, of Kendal. He *d.* s.p.m.,(d) 29 Aug. 1736, at Rydal Hall, and was *bur.* at Gresmere, aged 80. "Lady FLEMING, relict of (—)" (presumably his widow), *d.* 31 March 1757.

II. 1736. SIR GEORGE FLEMING, Baronet [1705], BISHOP OF CARLISLE [1735-47], next surv. br. and h. male, being 5th s. of Sir Daniel FLEMING and Barbara, both abovenamed, was *b.* about 1670; matric. at Oxford (St. Edmund's Hall), 14 July 1688, aged 18; B.A., 1692; M.A., 7 March 1694/5; in Holy Orders: Vicar of Aspatria, Cumberland, 1695; Canon of Carlisle, 1701; Rector of Stanwix, 1703; Vicar of Kirkland, 1703; Rector of Salkeld, 1705; Archdeacon of Carlisle, 1705; Rector of Ullesby, Cumberland, 1719; *cr.* LL.D. (Lambeth degree), 22 Feb. 1726/7; Dean of Carlisle, 1727; Rector of Grasmere, 1729, and, finally, Bishop of Carlisle, 1735 till death; *suc. to the Baronetcy* (according to the spec. rem. in the creation thereof), 29 Aug. 1736. He *m.* 28 Oct. 1708, Catherine, da. of Robert JEFFERSON, of Carlisle, coheir of Thomas JEFFERSON. She *d.* at the Deanery, 1, and was *bur.* 4 May 1736 in the Cathedral of Carlisle, in her 57th year. M.I. He *d.* s.p.m.s.(e) 2 July 1747, said to be aged nearly 81.

(a) Of his three sisters and coheirs, (1) Lucy *m.* John Jones, of London, and had issue; (2) Lætitia *m.* Launcelot Baugh, of Lentwardine; and (3) Harriot *m.* Joseph Hughes, of the Auditor's Office.

(b) Sarah, his only sister, *m.* Col. Thomas Hodges, of the Guards, and had a son Thomas, who took the name of Fowler, and inherited the estate of Abbey-cwmhir, and a da. Sarah, wife of Col. George Hastings (*d.* 1802), and mother of the 11th Earl of Huntingdon.

(c) See p. 193, note "c."

(d) Of his three daughters and coheirs (1) Dorothy *m.* Edward Wilson, of Dallam Tower; (2) Barbara *m.* Edward Parker, of Browsholme, and (3) Catherine *m.* Sir Peter Leicester, *formerly* Byrne, 4th Baronet [I. 1671].

(e) His only son, William Fleming, *b.* about 1710; matric. at Oxford (Queen's Coll.), 20 April 1727, aged 17; B.A., 1731; M.A., 1733; B.C.L. and D.C.L., 1742; was in Holy Orders; Archdeacon of Carlisle, 1735-43. He *m.* 27 Dec. 1739, Dorothy, da. of Daniel Wilson, of Dallam Tower, but *d.* v.p. and s.p.m. in or before April 1743, leaving a da. and h., Catherine, who *m.* Thomas Ayscough.

III. 1747. SIR WILLIAM FLEMING, Baronet [1705], of Rydal aforesaid, nephew and h. male, being s. and h. of Michael FLEMING, Major in the army and sometime [1707-08] M.P. for Westmorland, by Dorothy, da. of [—] BENSON, which Michael was yr. br. of the late as also of the 1st Baronet, being 6th s. of Sir Daniel FLEMING and Barbara, his wife, both abovenamed. He was sometimes Ensign in Howard's Foot. He *suc. to the Baronetcy* (according to the spec. rem. in the creation thereof), 2 July 1747; Sheriff of Cumberland, 1754-55; M.P. for that county, May 1756 till death. He *m.* Elizabeth, da. of Christopher PETYT, *or* PETTY, of Skipton-in-Craven, co. York. He *d.* 31 March 1757. His widow *d.* 22 April 1788, aged 88.

IV. 1757. SIR MICHAEL-LE(a) FLEMING, Baronet [1705], of Rydal aforesaid, only s. and h., *suc. to the Baronetcy*, 31 March 1757, being then a minor; was M.P. for Westmorland (— Parls.) from 1774, and Lt.-Col. of the Cumberland Militia, from 1779 till death in 1806. He *m.* 23 Nov. 1782, Diana, da. and h. of Thomas (HOWARD), 14th EARL OF SUFFOLK and 7th EARL OF BERKSHIRE, by Elizabeth, da. of William KINGSCOTE, of Kingscote, co. Gloucester. He *d.* s.p.m. 19 May 1806. Admon. Sep. 1806. His widow, who was *b.* 23 July 1748, *d.* June 1816. Will pr. 1817.

V. 1806. SIR DANIEL FLEMING, Baronet [1705], of Rydal aforesaid, cousin and h. male, being 1st s. and h. of Roger FLEMING, of Whitehaven, by Isabella, da. of William HICKS, of the same, which Roger was 1st s. and h. of Daniel FLEMING, Land Surveyor of the port of Whitehaven aforesaid, only s. of the Rev. Roger FLEMING, M.A., for 32 years Vicar of Brigham, co. York (*d.* 1736, aged 65), who was yr. br. of the 1st and 2d Baronets, being 8th of the 11 sons of Sir Daniel FLEMING and Barbara his wife, both abovenamed. He was *b.* probably about 1785; *suc. to the Baronetcy*, 19 May 1806, soon after which he *m.*, 4 Feb. 1807, at St. Geo. Han. sq., his cousin Anne Frederica Elizabeth le,(b) da. and h. of his predecessor, Sir Michael le FLEMING, 4th Baronet [1705], by Diana his wife, both abovenamed. He *d.* s.p. 1821. His widow *d.* 5 April 1861, aged 76, at Rydal Hall aforesaid.

VI. 1821. SIR RICHARD FLEMING, Baronet [1705], br. and h., *b.* 4 Nov. 1791 at Whitehaven; ed. at Trinity Hall, Cambridge; M.A., 1823; took Holy Orders, and was Rector of Grasmere and Windermere, co. Westmorland, and of Bowness, co. Cumberland; *suc. to the Baronetcy*, in 1821. He *m.* 6 Sep. 1825, at Over Kellet, Sarah, 3d da. of W. B. BRADSHAW, of Halton Hall, co. Lancaster. She left her husband. He *d.* 3 April 1857, aged 65. Admon. July 1857.

VII. 1857. SIR MICHAEL FLEMING, *or* LE FLEMING,(c) Baronet [1705], 1st s. and h., *b.* 6 April 1828, at Grasmere Rectory; *suc. to the Baronetcy*, 3 April 1857, being then a resident at Dalemaine, Rangiora, near Canterbury, in New Zealand. He *m.* in 1853, Mary, yst. da. of Capt. BODDIE, of the Russian Navy. He *d.* in 1883, aged 55. His widow *d.* apparently in 1903.(d)

(a) The 3d Baronet, "Sir William, from his veneration for antiquity, was desirous to restore the primitive orthography of the family name by inserting the particle *le*, and in this instance effectually performed it by incorporating the particle with his son's christian name at his baptism, who thereby bears the name with the first founders of the family" [Betham's *Baronetage*, 1801-05].

(b) See note "a," above, as to the probable cause of the "le" in her name.

(c) He apparently assumed the name of "Le Fleming" in lieu of that of "Fleming." See note "a," above.

(d) She is mentioned as living in Dod's *Baronetage* for 1903, but omitted in that for 1904.

VIII. 1883. SIR ANDREW-FLEMING-HUDLESTON LE FLEMING, Baronet [1705], only s. and h., *b.* 1855, at Essedale, Nook Station, near Canterbury, in New Zealand; *suc. to the Baronetcy* in 1883.

Family Estates.—These, in 1876, being then the property of Gen. George Cumberland Hughes of Rydal Hall (who *d.* June 1877) consisted of 3,611 acres in Westmorland; 1,169 in Cumberland, and 640 in Lancashire. *Total.*—5,420 acres, worth £3,228 a year.

MILLER:

cr. 29 Oct. 1705.

I. 1705. Oct. "WILLIAM [should be "THOMAS"] MILLER, of Chichester, co. Sussex, Esq." [but should be "Knight"], s. of Mark MILLER, Alderman of that city, by Mary, sister and coheir of John COMBER, sometime Sheriff for the counties of Sussex and Hants, was *b.* 1635, and having inherited a large fortune from his uncle, was Alderman and several times Mayor of Chichester; M.P. for that city, 1688 and 1690; *Knighted* at Whitehall, 23 Dec. 1689, and was *cr. a Baronet*, as above, 29 Oct. 1705. He *m.* in or before 1665, Hannah, da. of [—]. He *d.* 2 Dec. 1705, aged 70, a few weeks after his creation. His widow *d.* 11 Jan. 1706, aged also 70. Both were *bur.* in Chichester Cathedral. M.I.

II. 1705. Dec. SIR JOHN MILLER, Baronet [1705], of Chichester aforesaid, *b.* about 1665; admitted to Lincoln's Inn, 6 Dec. 1684; M.P. for Chichester, 1698—1710; for Sussex, 1700-01; for Chichester (again) 1701-02, 1702-05 and 1710-13; Sheriff of Sussex, 1706-07, having *suc. to the Baronetcy*, 2 Dec. 1705. He *m.* firstly, in or before 1689, Margaret, da. of John PEACHEY, of Chichester. She *d.* 23 Sep. 1701, aged 38. He *m.* secondly, Anne, da. of William ELSON, of Groves, Sussex, by Jane (living July 1725) his wife. She *d.* s.p.s., 6 May 1709, aged 29. M.I. as above. Admon. 23 June 1725, to William ELSON, her nephew. He *m.* thirdly, 2 May 1710, at St. Dunstan's in the West, London, Elizabeth, 1st da. of Sir William MEUX, 2d Baronet [1641], by his 2d wife Elizabeth, da. of George BROWNE. He *d.* 29 Nov. 1721, aged 56. M.I. as above. Will pr. 1732. His widow, who was *bap.* 19 July 1677, at Kingston, in the Isle of Wight, *d.* s.p.m., 22 April 1756.

III. 1721. SIR THOMAS MILLER, Baronet [1705], of Lavant, near Chichester, s. and h., by 1st wife, *b.* about 1689; matric. at Oxford (New Coll.), 29 Jan. 1706/7, aged 18; M.P. for Chichester, 1715-27, having *suc. to the Baronetcy*, 29 Nov. 1721. He *m.* Jane, da. of Francis GOTHER, *or* GOATER, Alderman of Chichester. He *d.* at Lavant Nov. 1733. Will pr. 1734. His widow *d.* Dec. 1734.

IV. 1733. SIR JOHN MILLER, Baronet [1705], of Lavant aforesaid, 1st s. and h.; *suc. to the Baronetcy* in Nov. 1733. He *m.* about 1735, Susan, da. of Matthew COMBE, M.D., of Winchester. He *d.* 19 April 1772. Will pr. July 1772. His widow *d.* 26 June 1788.

V. 1772. SIR THOMAS MILLER, Baronet [1705], of Lavant aforesaid, and afterwards of Froyle, Hants, 1st s. and h., *b.* about 1735; *suc. to the Baronetcy*, 19 April 1772; was M.P. for Lewes, 1774-78, and for Portsmouth, 1806 till death in 1816. He *m.* firstly, Hannah, da. of [—] BLACK, Alderman of Norwich. She *d.* s.p.m. He *m.* secondly, in or before 1780, Elizabeth, da. and h. of [—] EDWARDS. The will of "Dame Elizabeth MILLER; Southon," is pr. Aug. 1800. He *d.* 4 Sep. 1816 in his 81st year. Will pr. 1817.

VI. 1816. SIR THOMAS COMBE MILLER, Baronet [1705], 2d and yst., but only surv. s. and h.,(a) by 2d wife; *b.* 1780; ed. at St. John's Coll., Cambridge; LL.B., 1802; took Holy Orders, and was Vicar of Froyle, Hants, 1803-64; *suc. to the Baronetcy*, 4 Sep. 1816. He *m.* 5 May 1824, Martha, 1st da. of the Rev. Thomas HOLMES, of Brooke Hall, Norfolk, and of Bungay, Suffolk. He *d.* 29 June 1864, at Froyle, aged 84. His widow *d.* 28 June 1877, in her 77th year, at 16 Lower Berkeley street, Midx.

(a) His elder br., John Miller, *d.* unm. and v.p. 22 April 1804.

VII. 1864. SIR CHARLES HAYES MILLER, Baronet [1705], of Froyle, Hants, 1st s. and h., *b.* 6 Feb. 1829, at Froyle; ed. at Eton; was sometime (1847) Cornet 2d Life Guards; *suc. to the Baronetcy*, 29 June 1864. He *m.* 9 April 1856, Catherine Maria, 2d da. of James Winter SCOTT, of Rotherfield Park, Hants, by Lucy, da. of Sir Samuel CLARKE-JERVOICE, 1st Baronet [1813], of Idsworth, in that county. He *d.* 12 Jan. 1868, at Froyle, after a few hours' illness, aged 38. His widow living 1904.

VIII. 1868. SIR CHARLES JOHN HUBERT MILLER, Baronet [1705], of Froyle aforesaid, 1st s. and h., *b.* 12 Sep. 1858, at Anstey Manor, near Alton, Hants; *suc. to the Baronetcy*, 12 Jan. 1868; ed. at Eton; sometime (1880-92) an officer in the Coldstream Guards, retiring as Captain.

Family Estates.—These, in 1883, consisted of 4,008 acres in Hants, valued at £4,667 a year. *Seat.*—Froyle Place, near Alton, Hants.

HALFORD, *or* HOLFORD:

cr. 27 June 1706;

ex., apparently, 25 March 1720.

I. 1706. "SIR WILLIAM HALFORD [*or* HOLFORD], of Welham, co. Leicester, Knt.," s. and h. of Sir William HALFORD of the same (will dat. 31 July 1678, pr. 3 Jan. 1682/3), by Elizabeth, da. of Sir John PRETYMAN, 1st Baronet [S. 1660?] was *b.* at Stokeston, co. Leicester, 1663, being aged 18 at the Visit. of Leicestershire in 1681; admitted to Gray's Inn, 29 Nov. 1680; was *Knighted* 14 Aug. 1683, and was *cr. a Baronet*, as above, 27 June 1706. He *m.* firstly, in or before 1692, Frances, 2d da. of James (CECIL) 3d EARL OF SALISBURY, by Margaret, da. of John (MANNERS), 8th EARL OF RUTLAND. He *m.* secondly, Elizabeth, da. of Henry HARBIN, merchant (*bur.* at Allhallows', Stepney, London, 25 Feb. 1700/1), da. of (—) LEWIS, of Stanton St. John, Oxon, Coachman.(a) He *d.* 1 March 1708/9, and was *bur.* at Allhallows' aforesaid. His widow, by whom he had no issue, was *bur.* there "in great state," 17 Nov. 1720, aged about 70. Will dat. 19 Nov. 1717, in which she founded eleven exhibitions at Oxford, pr. Jan. 1720/1.(a)

II. 1709. SIR JAMES HALFORD, *or* HOLFORD, Baronet [1706], of Welham aforesaid, 1st s. and h. by 1st wife; *suc. to the Baronetcy*, 1 March 1708/9, living unm. 1710;(b) was an officer in the Queen's Life Guards 1712, but appears to have *d.* soon afterwards s.p.m., and probably unm.

III. 1715? to 1720. SIR WILLIAM HALFORD, *or* HOLFORD, Baronet [1706], of Welham aforesaid, br. and h. of the whole blood, *b.* about 1693; matric. at Oxford as "*William Holford*" (Trin. Coll.), 21 Oct. 1713, aged 20; B.A. (New Coll.), 1718, being a Fellow thereof; *suc. to the Baronetcy* on the death of his brother; was "a rakish, drunken sot."(b) He died "poor," and probably unm. 25 March 1720, when the *Baronetcy* is presumed to have become *extinct*.(c)

[On 1 May 1707, the Union with Scotland took place, after which date the creation of *Baronetcies of England* (as well as *of Scotland*) ceased, and that of *Baronetcies of Great Britain* began].

(a) *N. & Q.*, 9th S., i, 371.

(b) Le Neve's MS. *Baronetage*.

(c) He had a yr. br. named John.

Baronetcies of Ireland.(a)

1619—1800.

FOURTH PART.

VIZ.,

CREATIONS,

1 Jan. 1664/5 to 1 May 1707.(b)

KENNEDY :(c)

cr. 25 Jan. 1664/5 ;(d)

forfeited 1710 ;

ex. shortly after 1727.

I. 1665. ROBERT KENNEDY, of Ballygarvey, *otherwise* Mount Kennedy, co. Wicklow,(e), 1st s. of Robert KENNEDY, was Joint Chief Remembrancer of the Exchequer [I.], 1625-34; Sheriff of co. Wicklow, 1643; M.P. [I.] for the borough of Kildare, 1643-49, and was *cr.* a Baronet [I.], by patent, dated 25 Jan. 1664/5,(d), which, however, was never enrolled, as neither were the King's Letters, but the Privy Seal was dat. 28 Oct. 1663 [*Carte Papers*]. He *m.* firstly, probably before 1620, Constance, 1st da. of Jonas SILYARD, of Dublin, by Margaret, da. of Ralph SANKEY, of Fassaroe, co. Dublin. He *m.* secondly (as her 4th husband), Elizabeth, widow (as 2d wife) of Randolph BARLOW, Archbishop of Tuam (*d.* 22 Feb. 1637), formerly wife of John TANNER, Bishop of Derry (*d.* 14 Oct. 1615), and, before that, of the Rev. Luke CHALONER, D.D., Vice Chancellor of the Univ. of Dublin (*d.* 27 April 1613), da. of Christopher PERCEVAL. She *d.* s.p. 30 Jan. and was *bur.* 3 Feb. 1658/9, at St. Nicholas', Dublin. Funeral entry. He *d.* March 1667/8, and "was *bur.* in the country." Funeral entry. Admon. [I.] 11 June 1677, to a creditor.

(a) See vol. i, p. 223, note "a," for acknowledgment of the kind assistance of Sir Arthur Vicars, Ulster King of Arms, and others, and more especially of the copious and invaluable information given by G. D. Burtchaell (of the College of Arms, Dublin), as to the Irish Baronetcies.

(b) See page 1, note "a," as to these dates.

(c) The information in this article has been entirely furnished by G. D. Burtchaell. See note "a" above. There is a very incorrect pedigree of the family in Burke's *Patrician*, vol. v.

(d) List of Baronets in Ulster's office.

(e) The description (as well as the dates) of the grantees of these Irish Baronetcies is, in most cases, placed within inverted commas as being taken from the *Liber Munerum Publicorum Hiberniæ* (see vol. i, p. 223, note "b"). This, however, is not the case in this instance, inasmuch as the creation of "Kennedy" has been omitted in that work.

II. 1668. SIR RICHARD KENNEDY, Baronet [I. 1665], of Mount Kennedy aforesaid, 2d but 1st surv. s. and h.,(a) by 1st wife; admitted to Lincoln's Inn, London, 25 Aug. 1638, and to the King's Inns, Dublin, 28 Jan. 1656; was M.P. [I.] for Mullingar, 1647-49; *Knighted* 29 Aug. 1660, being made, 27 Sep. following, Joint Chief Remembrancer of the Exchequer [I.], and 8 Nov. in the same year, Second Baron of the Exchequer [I.], an office he resigned in 1681. He *suc. to the Baronetcy*(b) in March 1667/8. He *m.*, about 1650, Anne, da. of Christopher BARKER, by Sarah, da. of Bonham NORTON. He, in 1682, settled Mount Kennedy and his other land in tail male. He *d.* Jan. 1684/5.(c) Funeral entry. Will dat. 19 Feb. 1679/80, pr. 8 Sep. 1701, in Prerog. Court [I.]. The will of his widow dat. 10 Jan. 1698/9, pr. there 15 Oct. 1703.

III. 1685. SIR ROBERT KENNEDY, Baronet [I. 1665], of Mount Kennedy aforesaid, 1st s. and h., *b.* about 1650; entered Trin. Coll., Dublin, as Fellow Commoner, 23 Feb. 1665/6, aged 15; admitted to Lincoln's Inn, London, 9 Feb. 1670/1; *suc. to the Baronetcy*, Jan. 1684/5; was Sheriff of co. Wicklow, 1686.(d) He *m.* (Lic. 20 Oct. 1682) Frances, sister of Robert HOWARD, Bishop of Elphin [1729-40], da. of Ralph HOWARD, of Shelton Abbey, co. Wicklow, by Catherine, da. of Roger SOTHEBY. He *d.* 1688.(c) Funeral entry.

IV. 1688, to 1710. SIR RICHARD KENNEDY, Baronet [I. 1665], of Mount Kennedy aforesaid, 1st s. and h.; *b.* there about 1686; *suc. to the Baronetcy* in 1688; entered Trin. Coll., Dublin, 22 Jan. 1703/4, aged 16. He, when of full age, suffered a recovery of the entailed estates, thereby vesting them in himself absolutely. He was Sheriff of co. Dublin, 1709. He *m.* Katharine, da. of Sir Francis BLAKE, of Oxfordshire. He *d.* s.p.m.,(e) aged 23, being killed in a duel, by Mr. Dormer in April 1710. Will dat. 22 July 1707, pr. at Dublin 25 Sep. 1710. His widow *m.* Lord Frederick Henry HOWARD (yr. s. of Henry, DUKE OF NORFOLK), who *d.* 16 March 1726/7, aged 42. She *d.* 22 Jan. 1731/2.

V. 1710, to 1730? SIR WILLIAM KENNEDY, Baronet [1665], uncle and h. male, being 2d s. of the 2d Baronet; *b.* 1664; entered Trin. Coll., Dublin, 19 Jan. 1678/9, aged 14; M.A., 1686. Being an adherent of James II, he was *attainted* 3 April (1694), 6 and 7 William and Mary, and, consequently, when *he became heir to the Baronetcy* in April 1710, was not legally entitled thereto. He became a monk in the English Monastery at Paris, and was living in France in 1727. On his death the *Baronetcy* presumably became *extinct*.

(a) His elder br. Silvester Kennedy was admitted to Lincoln's Inn, 8 March 1630/1, by spec. favour. He *m.* Mary, da. of William Crofton, but *d.* s.p. and v.p. His widow *m.* (as his 3d wife) Sir Paul Davys, Sec. of State [I.].

(b) He is called "Sir R. Kennedy, *Bart.* [apparently a mistake for 'Knight'], Second Baron," etc., in Royal letters, dated 3 Oct. 1662. [Smyth's *Law Officers of Ireland*, 1839, p. 154].

(c) The statement in *Notes and Queries* [8th S., vi. 15] that the 2d Baronet *d.* in London, 10 May 1703, and was *bur.* at St. Margaret's, Westminster, is clearly an error. He is stated in the printed claim of Sir Wm. Dudley to the Kennedy estate to have *d.* in 1684, and his son, the 3d Baronet, in 1688.

(d) "If to be judged by his intimates, extremely Whiggish" [D'Alton's "King James' Irish Army List, 1689," where also, among the outlawries of 1691, occurs the name of "William Kennedy, of Mount Kennedy, co. Wicklow, popularly called Lord William Kennedy"].

(e) Elizabeth, his only da. and h., *m.* 12 Dec. 1719, Sir William Dudley, 3d Baronet [1660], who *d.* s.p. 15 June 1764, aged 67, having previously advanced a claim to the Kennedy estates.

DIXON :(a)

1665? to 1726.

SIR WILLIAM DIXON, of Dublin and of Colverstown, co. Kildare, 1st s. and h. of Sir Robert DIXON, Mayor of Dublin, 1633-34 (*bur.* 1 Sep. 1654, at St. John's, Dublin), by Maud, da. of [—] BEE, of Dublin, was M.P. [I.] for Donegal Borough, 1639-49, and for Jamestown, 1661, till death in 1666; was *Knighted* by the Lords Justices [I.], 23 April 1661; Sheriff of co. Dublin, 1665; and was in 1687 (21 years after his death) *styled*, in error, "*Baronet*" [Qy. I.].(a) He *m.* probably about 1640, Margaret, 2d da. of Capt. Erasmus SAUNDERS. She *d.* 30 April and was *bur.* 5 May 1662, at St. Werburgh's, Dublin. Funeral entry. He *d.* 25 Jan. and was *bur.* there 2 Feb. 1665/6. Funeral entry. Will dat. 28 Oct. 1665, pr. [I.] 1666.

RICHARD DIXON, *subsequently*, after 1683/4, SIR RICHARD DIXON, of Colverstown aforesaid, 1st s. and h.; admitted to Lincoln's Inn, 26 Oct. 1659; suc. his father, 25 Feb. 1665/6; was Sheriff of co. Kildare, 1667; *Knighted* by the Lord Deputy [I.], 24 Feb. 1683/4, and was in 1687 (about three years after his death) *styled*, in error, "*Baronet*."(a) He *m.* at St. Werburgh's aforesaid, 18 Jan. 1662/3 (Lic. 29 Dec. 1662) Mary, niece of Sir Maurice EUSTACE, Lord Chancellor [I.], da. of William EUSTACE, of Blackrath, co. Kildare, by Anne, da. of James NETTERVILLE, of Castletown Kilpatrick, co. Meath. She *d.* 3 Jan. 1678/9, and was *bur.* at Kilcullen, co. Kildare. Funeral entry. He *d.* 19 and was *bur.* there 22 July 1684. Funeral entry. Will dat. 13 March 1683/4, pr. [I.] 16 Aug. 1684.

ROBERT DIXON, of Colverstown aforesaid, only s. and h., *b.* 1674, being 10 years old when he suc. his father 19 July 1684, and being in an inquisition at Kilmainham, 13 Oct. 1687, *styled*, in error, "*Baronet*."(a) This title, however, he never assumed. He was M.P. [I.] for Randalstown, 1692-93, and for Harristown, 1703-13, being Sheriff of co. Kildare 1709. He *d.* unm. in Jervis street, Dublin,(b) and was *bur.* (as "Colonel Dixon") at Kilcullen, 9 March 1725/6. Funeral entry.

(a) No such Baronetcy as this ever existed or even was ever claimed or assumed. Its suggested existence is founded solely on error as below. "A Jury of good and lawful men of the county of Dublin on an inquisition at Kilmainham, 13 Oct. 1687, found upon their oaths that William Dixon, *Baronet*, was seized of the town and lands of Barrettstown, and died 25 Jan. 1665; that Richard Dixon, *Baronet*, was his son and heir, and died 19 July 1684, and that Robert Dixon, *Baronet*, was his son and heir. Now none of these persons were Baronets. Possibly from three Dixons, in succession, being *Knights*, the Jurors may have imagined they possessed an hereditary title. Yet this seems strange, as an interval of 17 years elapsed between the death of Sir William Dixon and the Knighting of his son, Sir Richard, who enjoyed his title only five months. Sir Richard's son, Robert, was never known as *Sir*. The inquisition is in print (*Inquisitionum Cancellariæ Hiberniæ Repertorium*, vol. i). I have examined the original, and there is no doubt about the description of *Baronet*." [G. D. Burtchaell (see p. 196, note "a") by whom also the pedigree of the Dixon family is kindly supplied.

(b) He had six sisters and coheirs, viz —(1) Mary; (2) Margaret, who *m.* (Lic. 17 Dec. 1681) Robert Johnson, a Baron of the Exchequer [I.] 1703-13, and had issue; (3) Charity, *m.* John O'Neill, of Shane's Castle, co. Antrim, and had issue; (4) Anne; (5) Elizabeth, *m.* Sir Kildare Borrowes, 3d Baronet [I. 1646]; (6) Catherine.

BERESFORD :

cr. 5 May 1665 ;

afterwards, since 1720, VISCOUNTS TYRONE [I.];

since 1746, EARLS OF TYRONE [I.];

and, since 1789, MARQUESSES OF WATERFORD [I.]

I. 1665. "TRISTRAM BERESFORD, Esq. [*sic*, but should be "Knight") of Coleraine, co. Londonderry,"(a) 1st s. and h. of Tristram BERESFORD, of the same (*b.* 1574), Manager for the Corporation of London of the Plantation in Ulster, called Londonderry, by (—), da. of (—) BROOKE, of London, was M.P. [I.] for co. Derry, 1634, being M.P. [E.] for the counties of Derry, Donegal, and Tyrone, 1656-58, and M.P. [I.] for co. Londonderry, 1661-66; was *Knighted* in 1664 by the Lord Deputy Ossory [I.], and was, in "consideration of his faithful services and sufferings,"(b) *cr. a Baronet* [I.], as above, by patent dated at Dublin, 5 May 1665, the privy seal being dated at Whitehall, 24 March 1664/5. He *m.* firstly Anne, 1st da. of John ROWLEY, of Castle Roe, co. Londonderry, by Mary, da. of Robert GAGE, of Raundes, co. Northampton. He *m.* secondly, Sarah, da. of [—] SACKVILLE. He *d.* 15 and was *bur.* 18 Jan. 1673, at Coleraine. Will pr. [I.] 1674.

II. 1673. SIR RANDAL BERESFORD, Baronet [I. 1665], of Coleraine aforesaid, s. and h., being only s. by 1st wife; was M.P. [I.] for Coleraine, 1661-66 (being, erroneously, styled "Baronet"); *suc. to the Baronetcy*, 15 Jan. 1673. He *m.* (Lic. Vic. Gen., 20 Feb. 1662/3, being then "of Fulraigne, co. Londonderry, Esq., about 27, bachelor"), Catherine (then about 20) yst. da. of Francis (ANNESLEY), VISCOUNT VALENTIA [I.] by his 2d wife, Jane, da. of Sir John STANHOPE. He was *bur.* 19 Oct. 1681, at St. Martin's in the Fields. Midx. Will dat. 4 Oct. 1681, pr. 26 July 1682. His widow *d.* 3 April 1701, and was *bur.* at St. Michan's, Dublin. Her will pr. [I.] 1701.

III. 1681. SIR TRISTRAM BERESFORD, Baronet [I. 1665], 2d but only surv. s. and h., *b.* 1669; *suc. to the Baronetcy* in Oct. 1681; was a zealous Protestant, and commanded a Reg. of Foot against James II, by whose Parl. [I.] of 1689 he was consequently attainted; was M.P. [I.] for co. Londonderry, 1695. He *m.* in Feb. 1687, Nicola Sophia, yst. da. and eventually coheir of Hugh (HAMILTON), 1st BARON HAMILTON OF GLENAWLY [I.], by his 2d wife Susanna, da. of Sir William BALFOUR. He *d.* 16 June 1701. Will dat. 4 March 1698, directing his burial to be at Coleraine. His widow, who was *b.* 23 Feb. 1666, *m.* in 1704 (as his 1st wife, Lieut.-Gen. Richard GORGES, of Kilbrew, co. Meath (who *d.* 12 April 1728), and *d.* 23 Feb. 1713, on her birthday of 47.(c)

IV. 1701. SIR MARCUS BERESFORD, Baronet [I. 1665], of Coleraine aforesaid, only s. and h., *b.* 16 and *bap.* 27 July 1694; *suc. to the Baronetcy*, 16 June 1701; was M.P. [I.] for Coleraine, 1715 till raised to the Peerage [I.] in 1720. He *m.* 16 July 1717, Catharine, only da. and h. of James (POWER), 3d and last EARL OF TYRONE [I.], by Anne, da. and coheir of Andrew RICKARDS. She, who was *b.* 29 Nov. 1701, was living when he was *cr.* 4 Nov. 1720, VISCOUNT TYRONE, &c. [I.], and, subsequently, 18 July 1746, EARL OF TYRONE [I.] In that Peerage this *Baronetcy* then merged, and still [1904], so continues, the 2d Earl and 5th Baronet being *cr.*, 19 Aug. 1789, MARQUESS OF WATERFORD [I.]. See *Peerage*.

(a) See p. 196, note "e," *sub* Kennedy.

(b) Lodge's *Irish Peerage*, 1789, vol. ii, p. 297.

(c) The date of her death had been predicted to her (according to the well-known ghost story) by the apparition after death, 14 Oct. 1693, of her early friend John (Power), 2d Earl of Tyrone [I.]. See full account in *Complete Peerage*, by G.E.C., vol. vii, p. 452, note "d."

RAWDON:

cr. 20 May 1665;

afterwards, 1750-1868, BARONS RAWDON OF MOIRA [I.];

and, 1761-1868, EARLS OF MOIRA [I.];

subsequently, 1816-68, MARQUESSES OF HASTINGS;

ex. 10 Nov. 1868.

I. 1665. "SIR GEORGE RAWDON, Knt., of Moyra, co. Down," was *cr. a Baronet* [E.], as above (though described as "Esq.") 10 Nov. 1665, and possibly also a Baronet of Ireland, as his name appears in the list of such creations under the same date in the *Liber Munerum Hiberniæ*, though the patent is there stated to be (not at Dublin, but) at Westminster.([a]) See an account of this Baronetcy on p. 14.

TRESWELL:

cr. 6 June 1665.

ex. 28 May 1670.

I. 1665, to 1670. "COLONEL DANIEL TRESWELL," sometime [1644] Captain in the Earl of Leicester's Regiment [I.], was in 1662 Colonel of the Battle Axe Guards [I.], and was *cr. a Baronet* [I.], as above, by patent dat. at Dublin, 6 June 1665, the privy seal being dat. at Whitehall, 20 Nov. 1661. He was M.P. [I.] for Downpatrick, 1665-66. He *m.* Katharine, yr. da. of Francis PLOWDEN, of Plowden, by his 2d wife Katharine (relict of Richard BUTLER, of Callan, co. Kilkenny), da. and coheir of Thomas AUDLEY, of Morton, co. Norfolk. He *d.* s.p., 28 and was *bur.* 30 May 1670, in the old church at St. Canice, Finglass, co. Dublin, when the *Baronetcy* became *extinct*. M.I. Funeral entry in Ulster's Office. Will dat. 27 May 1670, pr. [I.] 1670. The will of his widow was pr. [I.] 1671.([b])

BARRET, *or* BARRETT:

cr. 4 July 1665;

ex. 16 Feb. 1672/3.

I. 1665, to 1673. "WILLIAM BARRETT, Esq., of Castlemore, co. Cork," only s. and h. of Sir Andrew BARRETT, *or* BARRET, of Inniscarry, co. Cork (*bur.* 6 Nov. 1646, in Christ Church, Cork), by Barbara (who was afterwards wife of Heyward ST. LEGER, and who *d.* his widow in 1685), was *b.* probably about 1640, and was *cr. a Baronet* [I.], as above (no patent however being on record), the privy seal being dat. at Hampton Court, 4 July 1665. He *d.* unm. at Bristol, on his return from foreign travel, 16 Feb. 1672/3, when the *Baronetcy* became *extinct*. Will dat. the said 16 Feb. 1672/3, pr. [I.] 1674.([c])

([a]) See creations of "Saint George," 5 Sep. 1660, of Lane, 9 Feb. 1660/1, and of "Gifford," 4 March 1660/1, for somewhat similar cases.

([b]) Her nephew Richard Plowden (son of her br. Edmund) assumed the name of Treswell after that of Plowden, but *d.* unm. Will dat. 22 Aug. 1672, pr. [I.] 1672.

([c]) See Lodge's *Irish Peerage* [1789], vol. vi, p. 117, for an abstract of his will in which he left all, save what was entailed on his right heir, to his uncle [*sic*] John St. Leger.

GETHIN, *or* GETHING:([a])

cr. 1 Aug. 1665.

I. 1665. "RICHARD GETHING [*or* GETHIN], Esq., of Moyallow, co. Cork," whose parentage is unknown, was *b.* probably about 1615; was M.P. [I.] for Clonmell, 1639-49, and for Newtown Limavady, 1661-66, and, having obtained a considerable grant of lands in co. Cork, subsequently called Gethins Grot, was *cr. a Baronet* [I.] as above, by patent, dat. 1 Aug. 1665, the privy seal being dat. 7 July previous at Hampton Court. He *m.* in or before 1641, (—), supposed to have been a da. of Arthur FREKE, of Castle Freke, co. Cork, by Dorothy, da. of Sir Richard SMYTH, of Ballynatray, co. Waterford. He, who was one of the Council of the Government of Munster, was living 1679.

II. 1685? SIR RICHARD GETHIN, Baronet [I. 1665], of Gethins Grot aforesaid, grandson and h., being s. and h. of Richard GETHIN, of Ballyfenatur, co. Cork, by Jane, da. of Anthony STAWELL, which Richard (*b.* in co. Cork 1641, and whose will dat. 6 Feb. 1678/9, was pr. 20 June 1679), *d.* v.p. in 1679. He was *b.* 1674, and *suc. to the Baronetcy*, on the death of his grandfather; was B.A. of Dublin Univ. 1696. He *m.* firstly (Lic. Lond. 15 Feb. 1696/7, being then about 22, bachelor), Grace, only surv. child of Sir George NORTON, of Abbotsleigh, Somerset (*d.* s.p.s. 26 April 1715, aged 67), by Frances, da. of Ralph FREKE, of Hannington, Wilts. She *d.* s.p. 11 Oct. 1697, in her 21st year. M.I. in Westm. Abbey and in Bath Abbey. He *m.* secondly, in 1698, Sarah, 3d da. of Henry FARNHAM, of Nether Hall, co. Leicester, by Martha, da. of Thomas MOULSEY, of Staffordshire. He *d.* 1709, aged about 35. Will dat. 3 Aug. 1709, pr. [I.] 1709. His widow, who was *b.* 1673, *m.* [—] BOYLE.

III. 1709. SIR RICHARD GETHIN, Baronet [I. 1665], of Gethins Grot aforesaid, 1st s. and h., *b.* 1698, in Leicestershire; *suc. to the Baronetcy* in 1709; entered Trin. Coll., Dublin, 1 June 1713; was Sheriff of co. Sligo, 1724. He *m.*, probably about 1725, Margaret, da. of Col. [—] EAMES. He *d.* before 1774. Admon. [I.] to his widow, 4 Jan. 1774. The will of his widow, dat. 15 Oct. 1774, pr. [I.] 1778.

IV. 1765? SIR RICHARD GETHIN, Baronet [I. 1665], of Gethins Grot aforesaid, 1st s. and h.; *b.* probably about 1725; *suc. to the Baronetcy* on the death of his father. He *m.* 15 Aug. 1750 (Lic. 7, being then "Esq.," Prerog. [I.]) Mary, sister of Thomas, 1st EARL OF HOWTH [I.], 1st da. of William (ST. LAWRENCE), BARON HOWTH [I.], by Lucy, da. of Lieut.-Gen. Richard GORGES. He, who was living 1776, *d.* before 1780, probably about 1778. His widow, who was *b.* 17 May 1729, *d.* in France 4th Oct. 1787.

V. 1778? SIR PERCY GETHIN, Baronet [I. 1665], of Percy Mount, co. Sligo, only s. and h.; *suc. to the Baronetcy* on the death of his father; was Sheriff of co. Sligo, 1780. He *m.* May 1786, Anne, sister of Sir Richard NAGLE, 1st Baronet (1813), da. of Thomas NAGLE, of Mount Nagle, co. Cork, and of Jamestown, co. Westmeath, by Mary, da. of Kedagh GEOGHEGAN. He *d.* 10 Oct. 1837.

VI. 1837. SIR RICHARD GETHIN, Baronet [I. 1665], grandson and h., being 1st s. and h. of Richard GETHIN, Capt. in the army (who served through the Peninsular War), by Jane, da. of Lieut.-Col. SOUTH, of Heavitree, Devon, which Richard (who *d.* v.p., 5 Jan. 1835, was 1st s. and h. ap. of the late Baronet. He was *b.* 28 Dec. 1823, in Baring Crescent, Heavitree, and *suc. to the Baronetcy*, 10 Oct. 1837; was Lieut. 1st Dragoon Guards; exchanged, 1846, to 83d Foot, and then retired; served with the Turkish contingent,

([a]) The pedigree in Playfair's *Baronetage* "has been hopelessly mixed up." [G. D. Burtchaell, see p. 196, note "a."]

receiving the local rank of Capt. in the Crimean War in 1856. He *m.* 25 June 1846, at Boxted, Suffolk, Frances, yst. da. of George WELLER-POLEY, of Boxted Hall, by Helen Sophia, da. of James FISHER, of Browston Hall, in that county. This marriage was, however, dissolved Jan. 1862. He *d.* 11 June 1885, in his 62d year. She was living 1904.

VII. 1885. SIR RICHARD CHARLES PERCY GETHIN, Baronet [I. 1665], 1st s. and h., *b.* 20 Nov. 1847, at Boxted Hall aforesaid. Barrister at Law (Inner Temple), 1879; *suc. to the Baronetcy*, 11 June 1885; was sometime Capt. and Hon. Major 4th Suffolk Reg. of Militia, serving in the Transvaal War. He *m.* 5 June 1876, Catharine, 1st da. of Frederick Edward Burton SCOTT, of Ingham Lodge, Claughton, Cheshire.

O'NEILE, *or* O'NEILL:

cr. 23 Feb. 1665/6;

forfeited 1691.

I. 1666. "SIR HENRY O'NEILE [*or* O'NEILL], Knt.," of Killelagh, co. Antrim, s. of Neill Oge O'NEILL, of the same (*d.* 1628), by Alice, da. of [—] O'DONELL, was *b.* 1625, and was *cr. a Baronet* [I.], as above, by privy seal, dat. at Whitehall, 23 Feb. 1665/6, no patent, however, being recorded. He *m.*, probably about 1655, Eleanor, 8th and yst. da. of Sir William TALBOT, 1st Baronet [I. 1623], of Carton, by Alison, da. of John NETTERVILLE, of Castletown, Kilpatrick, co. Meath. He *d.* [—]. His widow *m.* Hon. James NETTERVILLE, 4th s. of John, 2d VISCOUNT NETTERVILLE OF DOWTH [I.].

II. 1680? SIR NEILL O'NEILL, Baronet [I. 1666], of Killelagh aforesaid, s. and h., *b.* about 1658; *suc. to the Baronetcy* on the death of his father; was a Capt. of Dragoons in the Army of James II, in 1687; Lord-Lieut. of co. Antrim, 1689. He *m.* Jan. 1677, Frances, 1st da. of Caryl (MOLYNEUX), 3d VISCOUNT MOLYNEUX OF MARYBOROUGH [I.], by Mary, da. of Alexander BARLOW. He *d.* s.p.m., 8 July 1690, aged 32 years and 6 months, from wounds received at the battle of Boyne, fighting on the side of James II, and was consequently (after death) attainted in 1691. He was *bur.* in the Franciscan Priory, Waterford. M.I. The will of his widow was pr. [I.] 1732.

III. 1690, to 1691. SIR DANIEL O'NEILL, Baronet [I. 1666], of Killelagh aforesaid, br. and h. male; *suc. to the Baronetcy*, 8 July 1690, which, however, by the posthumous attainder in 1691 of the late owner became *forfeited*. He was M.P. [I.] for Lisburne, in the parl. of James II, 1689. He *m.*, probably about 1690, Mary, 1st da. of Sir Gregory BYRNE, 1st Baronet [I. 1671], of Timogue, Queen's County, by Margaret, da. and coheir of Colonel Christopher COPLEY, of Wadworth, co. York. He *d.* s.p.m.([a]) His widow, who was *b.* 1671, *m.* before 1705/6 (as his 2d wife) Mark BAGOTT, of Mount Arran, co. Carlow, and of Dublin (who was *bur.* at St. Audoen's, Dublin, 30 Jan. 1717/8, and whose will dat. 1705/6, was pr. [I.] 1718), and *d.* at a "very advanced age," in Russel's Court, Church street, Dublin, being *bur.* 29 Aug. 1759, at St. Audoen's aforesaid.

([a]) Elinor, his only da. and h., *m.* Hugh O'Reilly, of Ballinlough, co. Westmeath, and was grandmother of James O'Reilly, of the same, *cr. a Baronet* [I.], 23 July 1795.

BATH:

cr. 7 May 1666;

ex. 10 May 1686.

I. 1666. "LUKE BATH, Esq., of Athcarne, co. Meath," 1st s. and h. of James BATH, of the same (*d.* before 1660), and nephew of Sir John BATH (will pr. [I.] 1630), was *cr. a Baronet* [I.], as above, by patent dat. at Dublin, 7 May 1666, the privy seal being dat. at Whitehall, 15 March 1661/2. He *m.* Cicely, da. of Nicholas DOWDALL, of Brownstown, co. Meath, by his 2d wife Jane, da. of Thomas AYLMER, of Lyons, co. Kildare. He *d.* 1674. Admon. [I.], 22 June 1698.

II. 1674. SIR PETER BATH, Baronet [I. 1666], of Athcarne aforesaid, only s. and h.; *suc. to the Baronetcy* in 1674. He *m.* (articles 2 March 1684/5), Margaret, 1st da. of John TALBOT, of Belgard, co. Dublin. He *d.* s.p.m.,([a]) 10 May 1686, when the *Baronetcy* became *extinct*. Will dat. 30 Jan. 1685/6, pr. [I.], 12 Feb. 1686/7. The will of his widow, then "of Belgert, co. Dublin," dat. 2 June 1732, was pr. [I.] 8 June 1733.

BELLINGHAM:([b])

cr. 18 March 1666/7;

ex. June 1699.

I. 1667. "SIR DANIEL BELLINGHAM, Knt., Alderman of Dublin," one of the sons([c]) of Robert BELLINGHAM, Sheriff of co. Longford, 1611-12, and sometime (between 1616 and 1620) Attorney to the 2d Remembrancer of the Exchequer [I.] (*bur.* at Kendal, 1639), by Margaret (*d.* 11 Nov. 1668, being *bur.* at St. Werburgh's, Dublin), da. of [—] WHITE, of the house of Clongell, co. Meath, was *b.* about 1620; sworn of the Goldsmiths' Guild, Dublin, 1644; Freeman, Easter 1648; Sheriff, 1655; Alderman, 1656; Major of the city Militia, 1659; *Knighted* by the Viceroy [I.], 30 Sep. 1662; Lord Mayor([d]) of Dublin, 1665-66; being *cr. a Baronet* [I.], as above, by patent dat. at Dublin, 18 March 1666/7, the Privy Seal being dated at Whitehall 14 Feb. previous. He *m.* about 1645, Jane, da. of Richard BARLOW, of Cheshire. He *d.* in 1672, and was *bur.* (with his mother) at St. Werburgh's, Dublin. Will dat. 27 April, and pr. 12 July 1672 [I.]([e]). His wife survived him.

II. 1672, to 1699. SIR RICHARD BELLINGHAM, Baronet [I. 1667], of Dubber, co. Dublin, only s. and h.; *bap.* 21 Oct. 1648 at St. Werburgh's aforesaid; admitted to Trin. Coll., Dublin (as Fellow Commoner), 4 Jan. 1666/7; B.A., 1669; admitted to Lincoln's

([a]) Cecilia, his only child (posthumous), *d.*, aged two months. Her admon. [I.] 1 Nov. 1687.

([b]) The information in this article is chiefly supplied by the Rev. A. R. Maddison (Canon of Lincoln), who disproves, on reliable evidence, many statements in the generally received pedigree of the Irish branch of this family. Richard Langrishe, V.-P. of the Soc. of Antiquaries [I.], has also gone into the evidence showing the descent of the grantee from the family of Bellingham, of Levens, co. Westmorland.

([c]) Another son, Henry Bellingham, of Germondstown (now Castle Bellingham), Citizen and Goldsmith of Dublin (*d.* 1676), was father of Col. Thomas Bellingham (*d.* 15 Sep. 1721) of the same, who was great-grandfather of Sir William Bellingham, Baronet, so. *cr.* 19 April 1796.

([d]) He was the first Mayor of that city that used the prefix "Lord." The style of *Lord Mayor* was granted by Charles I, 29 July 1641, but was not used till the attention of the municipal council was directed to it by the Duke of Ormonde, when Viceroy, 20 Sep. 1665. [*Ex inform.*, G. D. Burtchaell.]

([e]) He granted lands at Finglass, co. Dublin, for the relief of debtors, but the trust was never carried out.

Inn, 15 Sep. 1670; *suc. to the Baronetcy* in 1672; was Sheriff of co. Dublin, 1684. He *d.* s.p. and was *bur.* June 1699 at St. Werburgh's, aged 50, when the *Baronetcy* became *extinct*. Will dat. 13 June and pr. 25 July 1699 [I.].(a)

LANGFORD:

cr. 19 Aug. 1667;

ex. in or shortly before 1725.

I. 1667. "HERCULES LANGFORD, Esq., of Kilmackevett, co. Antrim," as also of Summer Hill, co. Meath, 1st s. of Arthur LANGFORD, of Kilmackevett aforesaid, was *b.* 1626 at Ballygarry, co. Antrim, being erroneously described as 1st s. of a *Knight*,(b) when he entered Trin. Coll., Dublin, as Fellow Commoner, 12 Aug. 1641; was Sheriff of co. Antrim, 1661, and was *cr. a Baronet* [I.], as above, by patent dat. at Dublin 19 Aug. 1667, the Privy Seal being dat. at Hampton Court, 1 July 1665; was Sheriff of co. Meath, 1677. He *m.*, probably about 1650, Mary, da. of Henry UPTON, of Castle Norton, co. Antrim, by Mary, sister of John, 1st VISCOUNT MASSEREENE [I.], da. of Sir Hugh CLOTWORTHY. He *d.* 18 and was *bur.* 21 June 1683, at St. Michan's, Dublin, aged 57. Funeral entry. Will dat. 28 May 1680, pr. [I.] 7 Dec. 1683. His widow, who was *b.* 26 Feb. 1629, *d.* in or shortly before 1692. Will dat. 15 July 1690, pr. [I.] 1692.

II. 1683. SIR ARTHUR LANGFORD, Baronet [I. 1667], of Summer Hill aforesaid, 1st s. and h., *b.* probably about 1652; entered Trin. Coll., Dublin, as Fellow Commoner, 9 July 1670; *suc. to the Baronetcy*, 18 June 1683; was attainted by the Irish Parl. of James II, in 1689; was M.P. [I.] for Duleek, 1692-93; for Coleraine, 1695-99 and 1702-13, and for co. Antrim, 1715 till death next year. He *d.* unm. 29 March 1716. Will dat. 1 Dec. 1715, pr. [I.] 6 April 1716.

III. 1716, to 1725. SIR HENRY LANGFORD, Baronet [I. 1667], of Kings Kerswell, Devon (an estate purchased in 1710), only surv. br. and h.; was M.P. [I.] for St. Johnstown, co. Donegal, 1695-99; *suc. to the Baronetcy*, 29 March 1716; was Sheriff of Devon, 1716-17. He *d.* s.p., in or shortly before 1725, and was *bur.* at Kings Kerswell, when *the Baronetcy* became *extinct*.(c) Will, in which he leaves that estate to his godson, Thomas BROWN, of Gray's Inn, pr. 1725.

(a) He left four stone statues (still [1904] at Castle Bellingham) to Col. Thomas Bellingham, the son of his paternal uncle, Henry Bellingham (see p. 203, note "c" above). The abovenamed Henry was accordingly son of Robert Bellingham of Ireland, abovenamed (father of the grantee), and was not (as often conjectured) identical with Henry, son of Alan Bellingham, of Levens, co. Westmorland, by Susan, da. of Marmaduke Constable. This last named Henry, indeed (who was of Whitstable), *d.* s.p.m., leaving an only da. and h., who *m.* Sir Reginald Graham. [*Ex-inform.* A. R. Maddison, see p. 203, note "b"].

(b) Sir Roger Langford (Knighted 14 Dec. 1630) was but 16 at the time of this Baronet's birth (1626), being a posthumous son of Roger Langford, of Muckmayer, who *d.* in 1609. The lastnamed Roger was nephew of Sir Hercules Langford (Knighted 19 Aug. 1621) who *d.* s.p. 16 April 1639.

(c) His yr. brother Theophilus Langford, of Kinsale, *d.* unm. before him. Will pr. 31 Aug. 1713. Mary, 1st sister and coheir, *m.* in 1671, Sir John Rowley, of Castle Roe, M.P. [I.] for Londonderry, and was ancestress of the Viscounts Langford [I.], *cr.* 1776, *ex.* 1796, and of the Barons Langford of Summerhill [I.], *cr.* 1800. Susanna, 2d and yst. sister and coheir, *d.* unm. Will dat. 22 March 1725, pr. 8 Nov. 1726. See *N. & Q.*, 8th S., iii, 308 and iv, 34.

BYRNE:

cr. 17 May 1671;

afterwards, since 1744, LEICESTER;

sometime, 1826—1895, BARONS DE TABLEY OF TABLEY HOUSE.(a)

I. 1671. "GREGORY BYRNE, of Timogue, Queen's County," 1st s. and h. ap. of Daniel BYRNE,(b) of Timogue aforesaid, a clothier in Dublin (who, having made a fortune by a contract to clothe the Army in Ireland, was *bur.* 24 Jan. 1683/4, at St. Audoen's, Dublin), by Anne, da. of Richard TAYLOR, of Swords, co. Dublin, was admitted to Gray's Inn, London, 23 June 1662; was M.P. [I.] for Ballynakill, 1689, in the parl. of James II, and was v.p., *cr. a Baronet*, as above, by patent dat. at Dublin, 17 May 1671, the Privy Seal being dat. at Whitehall, 16 Jan. 1666/7. He suc. to the family estates on the death of his father, 24 Jan. 1683/4; was Tax Assessor for Queen's County, under James II, and was Sheriff thereof, 28 Nov. 1689 to 10 June 1690. He *m.* firstly (Lic. 15 and settlement 17 March 1669/70) Margaret, or Penelope, da. and coheir of Christopher COPLEY, of Wadworth, co. York, Col. in the Army, by his 2d wife, Mary, relict of the Hon. John CHICHESTER, da. of Roger (JONES), 1st VISCOUNT RANELAGH [I.], Lord President of Connaught. She *d.* 20 and was *bur.* 23 July 1685, at St. Audoen's, Dublin. Funeral entry. He *m.* secondly, in 1690, Alice, sister of Christopher (FLEMING), VISCOUNT LONGFORD [I.], da. of Randal (FLEMING), LORD SLANE [I.], by his 2d wife Penelope, da. of Henry (MOORE), 1st EARL OF DROGHEDA [I.]. He *d.* March 1712.(c) His widow *m.* Col. Thomas WARREN, an officer in the German Service, and *d.* 13 Dec. 1753.

II. 1712. SIR DANIEL BYRNE, Baronet [I. 1671], of Timogue aforesaid, 1st surv. s.(d) and h., by 1st wife, *b.* 1676; *suc. to the Baronetcy* in 1712. He *m.* in or before 1704, Anna Dorothea (*b.* 26 April 1682), only da. (whose issue, in Feb. 1826, became sole heir) of Edward WARREN, of Poynton, co. Chester, by his 1st wife Dorothy, da. and h. of John TALBOT, of Salebury and Dinkley, co. Lancaster. He *d.* 25 Sep. 1715, in his 39th year, and was *bur.* at Timogue. M.I. Will dat. 4 Jan. 1714/5, pr. [I.] 8 May 1717. His widow *d.* in or before 1755. Her admon. [I.] 30 June 1755.

III. 1715. SIR JOHN BYRNE, Baronet [I. 1671], of Timogue aforesaid, 1st surv. s.(e) and h., *b.* probably about 1705; *suc. to the Baronetcy*, 25 Sep. 1715; was Sheriff of Cheshire, Feb. to Dec. 1740. He *m.* in 1728, Meriel, widow of Fleetwood LEGH, of Bank (*d.* s.p.m.s., 21 Jan. 1725), da. and h. of Sir FRANCIS LEICESTER, 3d and last Baronet [1660], of Tabley, co. Chester, by Frances, da. and h. of Joshua WILSON, of Colton, co. York. She, who was *b.* 25 Nov. and *bap.* 2 Dec. 1705, at Tabley, was *bur.* at Great Budworth, co.

(a) "A tautologous designation that was sufficiently unmeaning," the title being, according to the nineteenth century fashion "*entirely new*, but *formed on the antique pattern* like a modern Gothic Castle." [*Her. and Gen.*, vol. i, p. 151].

(b) See O'Donovan's *Annals of Four Masters*, p. 1703, note, for "some racy details" respecting this Daniel Byrne. [*Ex inform.*, C. M. Tenison].

(c) He is often stated to have been *bur.* at St. Audoen's, Dublin, in 1714, where under 18 July 1714, the following burial is registered "Mrs. Margaret Byrn, da. to Sir Gregory Byrn," which, presumably, some careless person took to refer to Sir Gregory himself. The Parish Register of St. Audoen is complete from 1672, and his burial does not appear therein. [*Ex inform.*, G. D. Burtchaell, who adds that the date of March 1712, was arrived at, after looking up all the references he could find].

(d) An elder son was *bur.* 7 Dec. 1672, at St. Audoen's.

(e) Charles, an elder son, *b.* 1704, *d.* 1 Nov. 1713, in his 9th year, and was *bur.* at Timogue. M.I.

Chester. He *d.* at York, Jan. and was *bur.* 2 Feb. 1741/2, at Great Budworth. Will, dat. 6 March 1738, directing all who suc. to his estates to bear the name of BYRNE, pr. [I.] 1742. His widow *d.* Aug. 1742.

IV. 1742. SIR PETER BYRNE, *afterwards* (1744-70) LEICESTER, Baronet [I. 1671], of Timogue and Tabley aforesaid, 1st s. and h., *b.* Dec. 1732; *suc. to the Baronetcy*, Jan. 1741/2. He, by act of Parl. 1744 (17 Geo. II), was enabled to sell his Irish estates and to take the name of *Leicester* instead of *Byrne*, in compliance with the will of his maternal grandfather, the abovenamed Sir Francis LEICESTER, 3d and last Baronet [1660] (who *d.* s.p.m. 5 Aug. 1742), to whose estate of Tabley he succeeded. He matric. at Oxford (Brasenose Coll.), 30 May 1750, aged 17; was *cr.* M.A., 23 June 1753; was M.P. for Preston, March 1767 to Nov. 1768. He *m.* 6 July 1755, Catherine, 3d da. and coheir of Sir William FLEMING, 1st Baronet [1705], of Rydal, by Dorothy, da. of Thomas ROWLANDSON, of Kendal. He *d.* at Tabley 12, and was *bur.* 20 Feb. 1770, at Great Budworth, aged 37. Will pr. 1788. His widow *d.* 8, and was *bur.* 13 Dec. 1786, at Great Budworth. Will pr. May 1787.

V. 1770. SIR JOHN FLEMING LEICESTER, Baronet [I. 1671], of Tabley aforesaid, 4th but 1st surv. s. and h., *b.* 4 April 1762 at Tabley; *suc. to the Baronetcy*, 12 Feb. 1770; ed. at Trin. Coll., Cambridge; M.A., 1784; was M.P. for Yarmouth (Isle of Wight), 1790-96; for Heytesbury, 1796-1802; and for Stockbridge, Jan. to April 1807; was a liberal patron of the fine arts, etc. He *m.* 10 Nov. 1810 (by spec. lic.,) at Hampton Court Palace, Georgina Maria, yst. da. of Josiah COTTIN, Lieut.-Col. in the Army. She was living when (a year before his death) he was *cr.*, 10 July 1826, BARON DE TABLEY OF TABLEY HOUSE,(a) co. Chester. In that peerage this *Baronetcy* then merged, till the former became *extinct*, 22 Nov. 1895. He *d.* 18 June 1827, aged 65.

VI. 1827. GEORGE (LEICESTER, *afterwards* WARREN), 2d BARON DE TABLEY OF TABLEY HOUSE,(a) and 6th Baronet [I. 1671], 1st s. and h., *b.* 28 Oct. 1811; *suc. to the Peerage and Baronetcy*, 18 June 1827; took the name of *Warren*(b) in lieu of *Leicester* by royal lic., 18 Feb. 1832. He *d.* 19 Oct. 1887, aged nearly 76.

VII. 1887. JOHN BYRNE LEICESTER (WARREN), 3d BARON DE TABLEY OF TABLEY HOUSE(a) and 7th Baronet [I. 1671], 1st and only surv. s. and h., *b.* 26 April 1835; *suc. to the Peerage and the Baronetcy*, 19 Oct. 1887. He *d.* unm. 22 Nov. 1895, aged 60, when the *peerage* became *extinct*.

[Bracketed beside V.–VII.: *See fuller particulars in Peerage.*]

VIII. 1895. SIR PETER FLEMING FREDERIC LEICESTER, Baronet [I. 1671], cousin and h. male, being 1st s. and h. of the Rev. Frederic LEICESTER, M.A. (Oxford), by his 2d wife, Amelia Susanna, da. of Lt.-Col. John CAMPBELL, which Frederic (who *d.* 16 April 1873, aged 70), was 1st s. and h. of Charles LEICESTER (*d.* 1815, aged 48), who was yr. br. of the 5th and 3d s. of the 4th Baronet. He was *b.* 25 Jan. 1863; sometime Lieut. 51st King's Own Light Infantry, and *suc. to the Baronetcy*, but to none of the family estates, 22 Nov. 1895.

(a) See p. 205, note "a."

(b) Under the will of his distant cousin, Elizabeth Harriet, Dow. Viscountess Bulkeley [I.], da. and h. of Sir George Warren, K.B., and in right of his descent from Dorothea, da. of Edward Warren, the wife of his great-great-grandfather abovementioned. The old lady, however, though she left him some property, chiefly in Lancashire, did not leave him the estate of Poynton, co. Chester, which had been for centuries the inheritance of his ancestors, of the name of Warren. See fuller particulars in the *Complete Peerage*, by G.E.C., vol. iii. p. 97, note "d."

HUME:

1671-1750.

In Burke's *Extinct Baronetcies* (edit. 1841, p. 603), a Baronetcy [I.] of "Hume, of Castle Hume, co. Fermanagh," is treated of, and is alleged to have been created in 1671, and to have become *extinct* about 1750. This, however, is a mistake for the Nova Scotia Baronetcy of HOME, or HUME, of North Berwick, *cr.* about 1638 (afterwards of Tully *or* Castle Hume, co. Fermanagh), which became *extinct* in 1747. See vol. ii, p. 443.

BULKELEY:

cr. 9 Dec. 1672;

ex. 7 April 1710.

I. 1672. "RICHARD BULKELEY, Esq., of Dunlavan, co. Wicklow," as also of Old Bawn, co. Dublin, 1st s. and h. of the Rev. William BULKELEY, D.D., Archdeacon of Dublin, by Elizabeth, da. of Henry MAINWARING, of Kilkenny, one of the Masters in Chancery [I.], and (though a layman) Archdeacon of Ossory (which William was 1st s. of Lancelot BULKELEY, Archbishop of Dublin), was *b.* 7 Sep. 1634, at Tallaght, co. Dublin; was M.P. [I.] for Baltinglass, 1665-66; Sheriff of co. Wicklow, 1666; suc. his father in Feb. 1670/1, and was *cr. a Baronet* [I.], as above, by patent, dat. at Dublin, 9 Dec. 1672, the Privy Seal being dat. at Whitehall, 24 Sep. previous. He *m.* firstly, in 1659, Catherine, da. and coheir of John BYSSE, sometime [1660-79] Ch. Baron of the Exchequer [I.], by Margaret, relict of John KING, da. of Francis EDGWORTH, sometime [1606-26] Clerk of the Crown and Hanaper [I.]. She *d.* 8 and was *bur.* 14 Feb. 1661/2, at St. Patrick's Cathedral, Dublin. Funeral entry. He *m.* secondly, 8 Feb. 1684/5, at St. Nicholas within, Dublin, Dorothy, da. of Henry WHITFIELD. He *d.* 17 March 1684/5, aged 50. Funeral entry. Will dat. 17 Jan. 1684/5, pr. [I.] 1685. His widow, by whom he had no issue, *m.* in 1687, William WORTH, sometime [1681-86] Baron of the Exchequer [I.] (who *d.* 23 Dec. 1721), and *d.* 12, being *bur.* 13 Jan. 1704/5, at St. Patrick's aforesaid.

II. 1685, to 1710. SIR RICHARD BULKELEY, Baronet [I. 1672], of Old Bawn aforesaid, 1st s. and h., by 1st wife, *b.* 17 Aug. 1660, entered Trin. Coll., Dublin, as Fellow Commoner, 4 Sep. 1676; B.A., 1680; Fellow, 1681-82; M.A., 1682; was *cr.* B.A. (Ch. Ch.), Oxford, 21 May 1680; *suc. to the Baronetcy*, 17 March 1684/5; was attainted (as "Sir Richard Buckley") by the Irish Parl. of James II, in 1689; was M.P. [I.] for Fethard, co. Wexford, 1692-93, 1695-99, and 1703 till death in 1710; was F.R.S., etc.(a) He *m.* 16 Feb. 1685/6, at Westm. Abbey (Lic. Vic. Gen. 15, he about 26 and she about 20), Lucy, 3d da. of Sir George DOWNING, 1st Baronet [1663], by Frances, sister of Charles, 1st EARL OF CARLISLE, da. of Sir William HOWARD, of Naworth. He *d.* s.p. 7 April 1710, in his 50th year, and was *bur.* at Ewell, Surrey, when the *Baronetcy* became *extinct*. M.I. His widow, who *m.* a few months later, in Aug. 1710, the abovenamed William WORTH (the widower of her husband's step mother), *d.* 9 Oct. following in her 47th year, and was *bur.* at Ewell aforesaid. M.I. Admon. [I.], 16 Feb. 1719/20, to her said husband, who himself *d.* 23 Dec. 1721, aged 75.

(a) He was author of several treatises. "Later in life he became a convert to certain French Enthusiasts, pretending to the gift of prophecy and the power of working miracles." [*Dict. Nat. Biogr.*].

READING:

cr. 27 Aug. 1675;

ex. March 1689.

I. 1675, to 1689. "ROBERT READING, of Dublin, Esq.," whose parentage is unknown, was probably the "Robert Reading, Esq.," who matric. at Oxford (Ch. Ch.), 28 March 1655, being B.A., 14 Dec. 1658; and presumably he, who, as "of London, gent.," was admitted to the Inner Temple, 1659. He was M.P. [I.] for Ratoath, 1662-66; and was *cr. a Baronet* [I.], as above, by patent, dat. at Dublin, 27 Aug. 1675, the Privy Seal being dat. at Windsor, 11 of same month. He was living in 1683 at St. Martin's in the Fields, Midx., and was attainted by the Irish Parl. of James II, in 1689, and then described as "of Brazeil, co. Dublin." He *m.* about 1662, Jane, widow of Charles (COOTE), 1st EARL OF MOUNTRATH [I.] (who *d.* 18 Dec. 1661), da. of Sir Robert HANNAY, 1st Baronet [S. 1630], by Jane, da. of (—) STEWART. Her burial, 18 Nov. 1684, at Westm. Abbey, is recorded also on 22 Nov. 1684, at St. Michan's Dublin.(a) He *d.* s.p.m.(b) and was *bur.* 25 March 1689, at Newark, Notts, when the *Baronetcy* became *extinct.*

SANDS, *or* SANDYS:

cr. 21 Dec. 1676;

ex. in or before 1704.

I. 1676. "WILLIAM SANDYS [*rightly* SANDS], Esq., of Dublin," and of Blackhall, co. Kildare, s. of Isaac SANDS, of Dublin, Clothier (admitted as a Freeman, 1648), was Sheriff of co. Kildare, 1671, and of the city of Dublin, 1674-75, and was *cr. a Baronet* [I.], as above, by patent dat. at Dublin, 21 Dec. 1676, the Privy Seal being dat. at Whitehall, 13 Nov. previous. He *m.* firstly, Catherine, da. of Richard BROOKE.(c) He *m.* secondly (Lic. Prerog. [I.] 25 July 1681), Grace,(d) widow of William HAWKINS, of Dublin (*d.* 22 Dec. 1680), da. of William THWAITES. He *d.* in London 14, and was *bur.* (as "Sir William SANDS"), 16 Aug. 1687, at St. Michael's, Cornhill. Funeral entry. Will dat. 13 June 1687, pr. [I.] that year. His widow *d.* in Jervis street, and was *bur.* at St. Werburgh's, Dublin. Her will, dat. 24 Aug. 1711, pr. [I.] 16 Dec. 1714.

II. 1687, to 1704? SIR JOHN SANDS, only s. and h., by 1st wife, *suc. to the Baronetcy* in 1687; was an officer in the regiment of Lord North and Grey. He *m.* firstly, in 1692, Jane 2d da. of James WARE (1st s. of Sir James WARE the Historian), by his 2d wife Barbara, da. of [—] STONE. She *d.* about a year afterwards. Admon. [I.], 13 Jan. 1693/4, to her husband. He *m.* secondly (Lic. Prerog. [I.], 10 Dec. 1693), Charity, da. of Robert COPINGER, by Margaret, da. of Sir William DIXON, of Colverstown, co. Kildare. He *d.* s.p., at Hochstadt, in Germany, in or before 1704 (being in all probability killed at the battle of Blenheim, 2 Aug. 1704), when the *Baronetcy* became *extinct.* Admon. 6 Oct. 1704, to a creditor. Admon. [I.], 20 Feb. 1713/4, 12 Nov. 1714, and 31 May 1725, to creditors. His widow was *bur.* at St. Werburgh's 1722. Will dat. 3 Feb. 1721/2, pr. [I.] 29 March 1722.

(a) See note in Chester's *Westm. Abbey Registers.*

(b) Elizabeth, his da. and h., *m.* when about 15, in 1684 (Lic. Fac. 24 Jan. 1683/4) James Hamilton, of Donalong, afterwards 6th Earl of Abercorn [S.] and was ancestress of the succeeding Peers.

(c) This Richard is said to have been 2d son of Sir Robert Brooke of Norton, Cheshire, in the Funeral entry of Sir William Sands; but *query.*

(d) She by her 1st husband was mother of William Hawkins, Ulster King of Arms, 1698—1736.

IRVINE:

cr. 31 July 1677;

ex. Oct. 1689;

assumed, 1810, or 1814, to 1847.

I. 1677, to 1689. "GERARD IRVINE, Esq., of Lowtherstown, co. Fermanagh," and of Ardscragh, co. Tyrone, 2d s. of Christopher IRVINE, Barrister at Law (who emigrated to Ireland and received large grants of land there, and was *bur.* at Lowtherstown, 1666), by his cousin Blanche, da. of Edward IRVINE, Laird of Stapleton, was Lieut. Col. in the Army of Charles II at Worcester, being subsequently taken prisoner; was Sheriff of co. Fermanagh, 1672,(a) and was *cr. a Baronet* [I.], as above, by patent dat. at Dublin, 31 July 1677, the Privy Seal being dat. at Whitehall 30 June previous. He *m.* firstly, Catharine, da. of Capt. Adam CATHCART, of Bandoragh, Scotland, and of Drumslager, co. Tyrone. She *d.* s.p. He *m.* secondly, in or before 1654, Mary, da. of Major William HAMILTON, Laird of Blair. She *d.* at Castle Irvine, co. Fermanagh, in 1685. He *d.* s.p.m.s.,(b) at the Camp at Dundalk, being then Lieut. Col. in Granard's Regiment, in the service of William III, in Oct. 1689, when the *Baronetcy* became *extinct.* He was *bur.* at Dundalk.

The Baronetcy was, however, claimed and assumed as under.

II. 1810. WILLIAM IRVINE, of Castle Irvine, co. Fermanagh, s. and h. of Christopher IRVINE, of the same, by his 2d wife Elinor, da. of Mervyn AUDLEY, of Trillick, co. Tyrone, which Christopher, (who *d.* 1755, aged 58), was s. and h. of Col. Christopher IRVINE (who inherited in 1714 the estate of Castle Irvine aforesaid, and *d.* 1723), who was s. and h. of William IRVINE, of Ballindulla, Sheriff of co. Fermanagh, 1681, yst. br. of the grantee. He was *b.* 15 July 1734; Sheriff of co. Fermanagh, 1758; of co. Tyrone, 1768; M.P. [I.] for Ratoath, 1790-97; *claimed and, probably, assumed this Baronetcy* in 1810, on the ground that his grandfather, the said Col. Christopher IRVINE, was grandson [instead of nephew] to the grantee.(c) He *m.* firstly, 10 Dec. 1755, Flora Caroline, da. of John (COLE), 1st BARON MOUNTFLORENCE [I.], by Elizabeth, da. of Hugh Willoughby MONTGOMERY. She *d.* s.p.m.s., 20 Oct. 1757. He *m.* secondly, 23 Feb. 1760, Sophia, da. of Gorges LOWTHER, of Kilrue, co. Meath, by Judith, da. of John USHER. He *d.* 12 May 1814, aged 79. Will as "Esq.," dat. 9 March, 1813, pr. 1814.

(a) "His Arms as Lieut. Col. Gerard Irvine of Castillfartagh, were confirmed and matriculated 1 Sep. 1673, by Ch. Araskine [Erskine], Lyon. Certificate in Ulster's Office." [G. D. Burtchaell].

(b) Of his three sons (1) Christopher, *b.* 1654, *m.* Deborah, da. and coheir of Henry Blemerhasset, but *d.* s.p. and v.p. 1680; (2) Charles, Lieut. of Horse, *d.* unm. and v.p. 1684; (3) Gerard, drowned while at Enniskillen School. Margaret, his only da. and h., *m.* John Creighton, of Crom, co. Fermanagh.

(c) This claim was supported by the affidavit, sworn 15 May 1810, and lodged in Ulster's office, of Gerard Johnston the elder, of Moneykee, co Fermanagh, aged upwards of 79 years, in which he states "that he knows William Irvine, late of Castle Irvine, but now of the city of Dublin, to be the legitimate son of Christopher Irvine, formerly of Castle Irvine, deceased, and Elinor Irvine, otherwise Mervyn, his wife, and had heard and believed the said Christopher Irvine, the father, was legitimate son of Col. Christopher Irvine and Dorothy Anne Brett, his wife, and the said Col. Christopher Irvine, the grandfather, was the legitimate grandson of Sir Gerard Irvine, Baronet," etc., etc. [*Ex inform.*, G. D. Burtchaell].

III. 1814, to *1847.* SIR GORGES MARCUS D'ARCY-IRVINE, Baronet(a) [I. 1677], of Castle Irvine aforesaid, 1st s. and h., by 2d wife, *b.* 26 Nov. 1760; *assumed the Baronetcy,* on the death of his father, in May 1814. He *m.* firstly, 31 March 1788, Elizabeth, da. and h. of Judge D'ARCY, of Dunmow Castle, co. Meath, by Elizabeth, da. and h. of Richard NUGENT, of Robinstown, and, apparently in consequence of this marriage, assumed the name of D'ARCY before that of *Irvine.* She *d.* 1829. He *m.* secondly, Sarah, da. of [—]. He *d.* abroad, 28 Nov. 1847, aged 87, leaving male issue, but, after his death the *assumption of the Baronetcy* ceased.(b) His will (as that of a Baronet) pr. June 1848. His widow *m.* 5 Feb. 1849 (as the widow of a Baronet), Louis Maximilian TIMMERMAN, Chevalier of the Legion of Honour.

PARSONS:

cr. 15 Dec. 1677;

afterwards, since 1807, EARLS OF ROSSE [I.].

I. 1677. "LAURENCE PARSONS, Esq., of Parsonstown [*otherwise* BIRR], King's County," 1st s. and h. of William PARSONS,(c) of the same (who held Birr Castle, of which he was Governor, for Charles I during a siege of fifteen months, terminating 20 Jan. 1642, and who *d.* in 1652), by Dorothy (*m.* 19 July 1636), da. of Sir Thomas PHILIPS, of Newtown Limavady, co. Derry, was *b.* in or soon after 1637, was Sheriff of King's County, 1662 and 1690, and was *cr. a Baronet* [I.], as above, by patent dat. at Dublin 15 Dec. 1677, the Privy Seal being dated at Whitehall, 23 Nov. previous. He was attainted by the Irish Parl. of James II in 1689, and condemned to death. He *m.* Frances, yst. da. and coheir of William SAVAGE, of Castle Rheban, co. Kildare (son of Sir Arthur SAVAGE), by Frances da. of Walter WELDON, of St. John's Bower, Athy, co. Kildare. He *d.* 1698. His widow *d.* at Carrick on Suir, 2 and was *bur.* 6 Nov. 1701, at Birr.

II. 1698. SIR WILLIAM PARSONS, Baronet [I. 1677], of Birr Castle aforesaid, 1st s. and h.; was M.P. [I.] for King's County, 1692-93, 1695-99, 1703-13 and 1715 till death in 1741, having *suc. to the Baronetcy* in 1698; Sheriff of co. Tipperary, 1709. He *m.* firstly, Elizabeth, da. of Sir George PRESTON, of Craigmillar. She *d.* 15 and was *bur.* 19 Nov. 1701 at Birr. He *m.* secondly (Lic. 10 Feb. 1718/9), Elizabeth, widow of the Rev. Dillon ASHE, D.D., of Finglas, co. Dublin, 1st da. and coheir of Sir George ST. GEORGE, of Dunmore, co. Galway, by Elizabeth, da. of Sir Robert HANNAY, apparently the 2d (not the 1st) Baronet(d) [S. 1630]. She *d.* s.p. 6 Feb. 1739/40. He *d.* 17 March 1740/1, at a great age, and was *bur.* at Birr. Will dat. 9 March 1740/1, pr. [I.] 9 Nov. 1741.

(a) According to the claim made in 1810 to that dignity.

(b) The true pedigree of the family having, presumably, been ascertained.

(c) This William was br. and h. of Richard Parsons, of Birr (*d.* s.p. 22 May 1634), both being sons of Sir Lawrence Parsons, Attorney Gen. for the province of Munster, who was yr. br. of Sir William Parsons, sometime Lord Deputy [I.], who was *cr.* a Baronet [I.], 10 Nov. 1620. That dignity together with the Viscountcy of Rosse [I.] (which had been conferred, 2 July 1681, on the 3d Baronet), and the Earldom of Rosse [I.] (which had been conferred, 16 June 1718, on the 2d Viscount and 4th Baronet, became extinct (together with the said Peerages) on the failure of the grantee's male issue, 27 Aug. 1764.

(d) It would appear from the Admon. of the *first* Baronet that he had only two daughters, Lady Coote and Lady Acheson.

III. 1741. SIR LAURENCE PARSONS, Baronet [I. 1677], of Birr Castle aforesaid, grandson and h., being 1st s. and h. of William PARSONS, by Martha (*m.* Feb. 1705/6), da. of Thomas PIGOTT, of Chetwynd, co. Cork, by Jane, da. of Sir Emanuel MOORE, 1st Baronet [I. 1681], which William, who was 1st s. and h. ap. of the 1st Baronet, was living 1707, but *d.* v.p. before 1741. He was *b.* 1707; admitted to Trin. Coll., Dublin, as Fellow Commoner, 7 Feb. 1723/4, aged 16; *suc. to the Baronetcy,* 17 March 1740/1; was M.P. [I.] for King's County, 1741 till death in 1756. He *m.* (Lic. [I. Prerog.] 5 Sep. 1730) Mary, da. and coheir of William SPRIGGE, of Cloonivoe, in King's County, by Catherine, da. of Edward DENNY, of Tralee, co. Kerry. He *m.* secondly (Lic. [I. Prerog.] 16 Feb. 1742/3, Anne, only da. of Wentworth HARMAN, of Moyne, co. Carl[illegible], by Lucy, da. of Audley MERVYN, of Trillick, co. Tyrone. He *d.* at Birr, 24 [illegible] 1756, aged 49. Admon. [I.] 22 Dec. 1756. The will of his widow, dat. [illegible] Oct. 1773, pr. [I.] 23 Dec. 1777 or 1779.

IV. 1756. SIR WILLIAM PARSONS, Baronet [I. 1677], of Birr Castle aforesaid, 1st s. and h., by 1st wife; *bap.* 6 May or Aug. 1731; Sheriff (v.p.) for King's County, 1753, and again 1779; *suc. to the Baronetcy,* 24 Oct. 1756; was M.P. [I.] for King's County 1757, till death in 1791. He *m.* (Lic. [I. Prerog.] 28 June 1754) Mary, da. and h. of John CLEARE, of Kilburry, co. Tipperary, by Margaret, da. of the Rev. Lawrence CLOTTERBOOK [CLUTTERBUCK], of Derryloskan, co. Tipperary. He *d.* 1 May 1791, aged about 60.

V. 1791. SIR LAURENCE PARSONS, Baronet [I. 1677], of Birr Castle aforesaid, 1st s. and h., *b.* 21 May 1758; ed. at Trin. Coll., Dublin; B.A., 1780; LL.B., 1783; LL.D., 1790; was M.P. [I.] for the Univ. of Dublin, 1789-90, and for King's County, 1791—1800 (distinguishing himself by his efforts against the Irish Union) being again M.P. [U.K.] for that county 1801-07. He *suc. to the Baronetcy,* 1 May 1791; P.C. and one of the Lords of the Treasury [I.], 9 May 1805; Joint Postmaster Gen. [I.]. He *m.* (mar. lic. 1 May 1797) Alice, da. of John LLOYD, of Gloster, in King's County, by Jane, da. and coheir of Thomas LE HUNTE, of Artramont, co. Wexford. She was living when, on 20 April 1807, he became EARL OF ROSSE and BARON OXMANTOWN [I.] by the death of his paternal uncle, who had been elevated to the Barony, 26 Sep. 1792, and to the Earldom 3 Feb. 1806, with, in each case, a special remainder of the dignity. In these Peerages this *Baronetcy* then *merged,* and still [1904] so continues. See *Peerage.*

REYNELL:

cr. 27 July 1678;

ex. 10 Feb. 1848.

I. 1678. "SIR RICHARD REYNELL, Knt., of Dublin, Justice of the King's Bench" [I.], 2d s. of Sir Richard REYNELL, of East Ogwell, Devon (*d.* 10 Feb. 1648, aged 60), by Mary (*m.* 12 Jan. 1616), da. and coheir of Richard REYNELL, of Credy Widger, Devon, Bencher of the Middle Temple, London, was *b.* probably about 1630; admitted to the Middle Temple, and, subsequently to King's Inns, Dublin, 1658; was M.P. [I.] for Athboy, 1661-66; 2d Serjeant at Law [I.], 11 May 1673; was *Knighted* by the Viceroy [I.], 1673; 3d Justice of the King's Bench [I.], 26 May 1674, till removed 1686, being *cr. a Baronet* [I.], as above, by patent dat. at Dublin, 27 July 1678, the Privy Seal being dat. at Whitehall, 20 June previous; P.C. [I.], 26 July 1682; M.P. for Ashburton, 1689-90; Ch. Justice of the King's Bench [I.], 9 Dec. 1690, till his resignation in May 1695. He *m.*, 20 Nov. 1660, at the King's Inns, Hester, yr. da. of Randal BECKET, of the King's Inns aforesaid, and Anne, his wife. She *d.* of consumption, 17 July 1682, at Abbeville, in France, and was *bur.* at East Ogwell. He *d.* in London 18 and was *bur.* 30 Oct. 1699, at East Ogwell. Will dat. 19 May 1699, registered 18 Oct. 1699, pr. May 1700.

II. 1699. SIR RICHARD REYNELL, Baronet [I. 1678], of Laleham, Midx., 1st s. and h., *bap.* 8 Dec. 1673, at St. Nicholas within, Dublin; matric. at Oxford (Mag. Coll.), 28 Aug. 1689, aged 15; admitted to Inner Temple, 1689; M.P. [I.] for Wicklow Borough, 1692-93; *suc. to the Baronetcy,* 18 Oct. 1699. He *m.*, in or before 1699, Elizabeth, da. and h. of Thomas REYNELL, of Laleham aforesaid, by Anne, da. and coheir of Charles BALAM, of Cambridge, which Thomas (who *d.* Jan. 1670, aged 72), was s. and h. of Sir Thomas REYNELL, by Katharine, da. and h. of Sir Henry SPILLER, of Laleham aforesaid. She *d.* 2 April 1706, and was *bur.* at Laleham, aged 39. He *d.* June 1723, aged 49, and was *bur.* there. Admon. 21 Aug. 1723.

III. 1723. SIR THOMAS REYNELL, Baronet [I. 1678], of Laleham aforesaid, only s. and h., *b.* 1699; matric. at Oxford (Balliol Coll.), 21 Aug. 1716, aged 17; *suc. to the Baronetcy* in June 1723. He *m.* 26 Aug. 1730, at the Fleet Chapel, London, Sarah, da. and coheir of Richard RIGHTON, of Chipping Norton, Oxon. He *d.* at Chelsea 15 and was *bur.* 19 Sep. 1775, at Kensington, aged 76. Will pr. April 1784. His widow *d.* in 1782.

IV. 1775. SIR RICHARD REYNELL, Baronet [I. 1678], of Laleham aforesaid, 1st s. and h., *b.* probably about 1735; *suc. to the Baronetcy,* 15 Sep. 1775; was made Commissr. for the Salt Duties, 3 April 1784, and Sec. to the L. Steward of the Household. He *d.* unm. at his house in Margaret street, Cavendish square, Marylebone, 17 Nov. 1798. Will pr. Nov. 1798.

V. 1798. SIR RICHARD LITTLETON REYNELL, Baronet [I. 1678], nephew and h., being 1st s. and h. of Lieut. Thomas REYNELL, by Anne, da. of Samuel CARTY, of Kinsale, which Thomas (who was killed at the battle of Saratoga, 7 Oct. 1777) was 2d s. of the 3d Baronet. He was *b.* 30 April 1772; *suc. to the Baronetcy,* 17 Nov. 1798; settled in the United States of America; was a military officer; and *d.* s.p.m. (probably unm.) 4 Sep. 1829, at Baltimore, aged 57.

VI. 1829, to 1848. SIR THOMAS REYNELL, Baronet [I. 1678], K.C.B., yst. but only surv. br. and h.,(a) *b.* 9 April 1777; entered the army, becoming eventually (1837) Lieut. Gen.; served in Flanders; was, in 1796, at the capture of Friesland; in 1798 was Adjutant Gen. to the forces at San Domingo; served with the 40th regiment in Egypt, obtaining the Turkish medal in 1801; was aide-de-camp to Marquess Cornwallis in India, and Dep. Quartermaster Gen. to the troops there; served in Portugal with the 71st Foot, and was at the action of Sobrale; commanded that regiment at Waterloo, where he was wounded, being made a Knight of the Austrian Order of Maria Theresa, and of the Russian Order (4th class) of St. George; was made K.C.B., 26 Dec. 1826, receiving the thanks of Parl. for services at the siege of Bhurtpore; *suc. to the Baronetcy,* 4 Sep. 1829; was Col. of the 99th Foot, 1832-34; of the 87th, 1834-51; and of (his old regiment) the 71st Foot, 1841 till his death. He *m.* 12 Feb. 1831, Elizabeth Louisa, widow of Major Gen. Sir Denis PACK, K.C.B., 4th da. of George de-la-Poer (BERESFORD), 1st MARQUESS OF WATERFORD [I.], by Elizabeth, da. and h. of Henry MONCK. He *d.* s.p. 10 Feb. 1848, at Avisford, near Arundel, Sussex, aged 70, when the *Baronetcy* became *extinct.* Will pr. March 1848. His widow, who was *b.* 2 Feb. 1783, *d.* 6 Jan. 1856, at Avisford aforesaid, aged nearly 73. Will pr. Feb. 1856.

(a) His next elder br. Major Samuel Reynell, *b.* 31 Oct. 1775, *d.* at Kinsale in 1821.

MAGILL: (a)

cr. 10 Nov. 1680;

ex. 18 Jan. 1699/700.

I. 1680, to 1700. "JOHN MAGILL, Esq., of Gill Hall, co. Down," *formerly* John JOHNSTON, 1st s. of William JOHNSTON, Lieut. of Dragoons,(b) by Susanna, only child of John MAGILL, of Gill Hall aforesaid, sometime (1660) Sheriff of co. Down, suc. to the estates of his said maternal grandfather, in 1677; assumed the name of MAGILL in lieu of that of JOHNSTON; was *Knighted*, 5 Nov. 1680, by the Viceroy [I.], and was *cr. a Baronet* [I.], as above, by patent dat. at Dublin, 10 Nov. 1680, the Privy Seal being dat. at Whitehall, 30 Sep. previous. He was M.P. [I.] for Hillsborough, 1692-93, and for Downpatrick, 1695-99. He *m.* firstly (Lic. [I. Prerog.], 13 Oct. 1677), Elizabeth, 2d da. of WILLIAM HAWKINS, of Dublin,(c) by his 2d wife Anna, da. of (—) THOMPSON, of London. She *d.* s.p. He *m.* secondly (Lic. Dublin, 2 July 1683), Arabella Susanna, 2d da. and eventually coheir of Hugh (HAMILTON), 1st BARON HAMILTON OF GLENAWLY [I.], by Susanna, yst. da. of Sir William BALFOUR, of Pitcullo, co. Fife. He *d.* s.p. in Dublin, 18, and was *bur.* 27 Jan. 1699/700, in the church of Dromore, when the *Baronetcy* became *extinct.* Funeral entry. Will dat. 13 June 1698, pr. [I.] 13 Feb. 1699/700.(d) His widow, who was *bap.* 7 Feb. 1666/7, at St. Margaret's, Westm., *m.* (Lic. 2 May 1700) Marcus (TREVOR), 3d VISCOUNT DUNGANNON [I.], who *d.* s.p.m. in Spain, 8 Nov. 1706. She *m.* thirdly, 17 July 1708, at St. Mary's, Wolnoth, London, the Hon. Henry BERTIE (who *d.* Dec. 1735, aged 60), and *d.* shortly after such marriage, 10, being *bur.* 16 Dec. 1708, in Westm. Abbey. Admon. 24 Dec. 1708.

HARTSTONGE:

cr. 20 April 1681;

ex. 1797.

I. 1681. "STANDISH HARTSTONGUE [*or* HARTSTONGE], Esq., of Bruffe, co. Limerick, Baron of the Exchequer" [I.], s. of Francis HARTSTONGE, of South Repps, Norfolk (*d.* before 1635), by Elizabeth,(e) da. and coheir of Sir Thomas STANDISH, of Bruff aforesaid, was *b.* probably about 1630; admitted to Middle Temple, London, 4 Nov. 1647; to King's Inns, Dublin, 11 Feb. 1658; was Recorder of Limerick; M.P. [I.] for that city, 1661-66; 2d Justice of Munster, 12 Feb. 1666/7, till that Court was abolished in 1672; 3d Baron of

---

(a) Some of the information in this article (which for the most part has, as usual, being supplied by G. D. Burtchaell) is from Col. Johnston, of Market Hill, co. Armagh.

(b) This William was 2d s. of Richard Johnston, and yr. br. of David Johnston, who emigrated to Ireland from Scotland.

(c) This William Hawkins was father, by his 3d wife, of William Hawkins, Ulster King of Arms, 1698—1736. See p. 208, note "d."

(d) The Gill Hall estate devolved on his nephew John Hawkins (s. of his eldest sister, Mary, by John Hawkins, of Rathfriland), who took the name of Magill, and *d.* 5 Sep. 1713, being suc. by his only s., Robert, who *d.* s.p.m., 10 April 1745, leaving a da. and h., Theodosia, who *m.* 29 Aug. 1765, John (Meade), 1st Earl of Clanwilliam [I.], and had issue. The Gilford estate, co. Down, devolved upon his nephew, William Johnston (son of his 2d sister, Susanna, by her cousin, Richard Johnston, of co. Monaghan), who was *Knighted* in 1714; Sheriff of co. Down, 1717, and of co. Armagh, 1721, being father of Richard Johnston, of Gilford aforesaid (*d.* 11 Feb. 1758, aged 48) and grandfather of Richard Johnston, who was *cr. a Baronet* [I.], as of Gilford, 27 July 1772, a dignity which became *extinct* in Feb. 1841.

(e) This Elizabeth *m.* for her 2d husband, before Nov. 1635, (—) Raynes.

the Exchequer [I.], 10 March 1678/9, but removed May 1686, though re-appointed, 10 Dec. 1690, but retired, or was again removed, in 1692 or 1695.(a). He was *cr. a Baronet* [I.], as above, by patent, dat. at Dublin, 20 April 1681, the Privy Seal being dat. at Whitehall, 28 Feb. previous. He was attainted by the Irish Parl. of James II in 1689, together with his son "Standish HARTSTONGUE, Esq." He *m.* firstly, about 1650, Elizabeth, da. of Francis JERMY, of Gunston, by Alice, da. of Sir Anthony IRBY, of Boston. She, by whom he had eleven children, *d.* 5 April 1663, and was *bur.* in Limerick Cathedral. M.I. He *m.* secondly (Lic. Dublin, 14 July 1664), Anne, sister and coheir of Sir Thomas BRAMHALL, da. of John BRAMHALL, Archbishop of Armagh [1661-62], by Eleanor, da. of William HAWLEY, of York. She *d.* s.p. Will p. [I.] 1682. He *m.* thirdly, in 1684, Joanna, da. of Rowland GWYNNE, of Radnorshire. He *d.* in England, possibly at Hereford, after Aug. 1695,(b) and probably before Aug. 1697. The will of his widow was pr. Nov. 1718.

II. 1697? SIR STANDISH HARTSTONGE, Baronet [I. 1681], of Bruff aforesaid, grandson and h., being s. and h. of Francis HARTSTONGE, by his 1st wife, Mary, da. and coheir of Richard BRETTRIDGE, of Castle Brettridge, co. Cork, which Francis (who was *b.* 1651, and entered Trin. Coll., Dublin, 1668), was s. and h. ap. of the late Baronet, but *d.* v.p. between 29 May 1683 and 9 Nov. 1688.(c) He was *b.* about 1673, and "did in his grandfather's time behave himself disobediently,"(d) but *suc. to the Baronetcy* on his death. He was M.P. [I.] for Kilmallock, 1695-99; for Ratoath, 1703-13; and for St. Canice, 1713-14, and 1715-27. He *m.* in or before 1689 (—), da. of (—) PRICE? He *d.* "at a very advanced age," 20 July 1751, and was *bur.* at St. Anne's, Dublin. Will dat. 24 April 1748, pr. [I.] 8 Aug. 1751.

III. 1751, to 1797. SIR HENRY HARTSTONGE, Baronet [I. 1681], of Bruff aforesaid, grandson and h., being s. and h. of Price HARTSTONGE, M.P. [I.] for Charleville, 1727, till his death, by Alice, da. and h. of Henry WIDENHAM, of Court, co. Limerick, which Price, who was s. and h. ap. of the late Baronet, *d.* v.p. 3 Feb. 1743/4, aged 54, and was *bur.* at St. Anne's, Dublin. He was *b.* probably about 1725; *suc. to the Baronetcy,* 20 July 1751; was M.P. [I.] for co. Limerick, 1783-89. He *m.* 23 Dec. 1751, Lucy, sister of Edmond Sexten (PERY), VISCOUNT PERY OF NEWTOWN PERY (many years Speaker of the Irish House of Commons), 5th da. of the Rev. Stackpole PERY, of Stackpole Court, co. Clare, by Jane, da. of the Rev. William TWIGGE, Archdeacon of Limerick. She *d.* 20 March 1793. He *d.* s.p. in 1797, when the *Baronetcy* became *extinct.*(e) Will dat. 2 June 1796, pr. [I.] 28 March 1797.

(a) By patent at Dublin 16 Feb., 5 William and Mary [1692/3], "Sir Henry Echlin, Baronet," was made Baron of the Exchequer [I.], *vice* "Hartstongue *deceased.*" [C. J. Smyth's *Law Officers of Ireland*]. The word "deceased" is, however, undoubtedly a mistake. Luttrell, in his *Diary,* under 1 June 1695, writes that "the Lord Cheif Justice Reynolds and Baron Hartstongue are displaced, Sir Richard Pine succeeds the former, and Mr. Donneland the latter."

(b) At that date his grandson and future successor was returned to Parl. as "Esq." Another Standish Hartstonge, viz., the 2d s. of the 1st Baronet, was also M.P. in the same Parl., and as, on 25 Aug. 1697, "Mr. Hartstonge" appears as a Teller in the Commons Journal without any distinction (as "Senr" or "Junior") the inference is that there was then but *one* Mr. Hartstonge in the house, and that the other had become "Sir." It seems not improbable that the first Baronet *d.* at Hereford, as he is described thereof in the entry of his son Gwynne Hartstonge to the Middle Temple in 1699.

(c) The respective dates of the making and proving of his will.

(d) Will of his uncle Standish Hartstonge, Recorder of Kilkenny, dat. 9 June 1704, who accordingly leaves him nothing.

(e) C. M. Tenison writes (from Hobart, Tasmania): "I have heard that a man named Hartstongue, who was a small jeweller and silversmith in Dublin, in the early part of the nineteenth century, was supposed to have a claim to this Baronetcy."

MOORE:

cr. 29 June 1681.

I. 1681. "CAPTAIN EMANUEL MOORE, of Ross Carbery, co. Cork," whose parentage is unknown,(a) is said to have been in command of the second troop of horse in Munster; was Sheriff of co. Cork, 1677; was attainted by the Irish Parl. of James II in 1689, and was *cr. a Baronet* [I.] by patent dat. at Dublin, 29 June 1681, the Privy Seal being dat. at Windsor, 14 May previous. He *m.* about 1660, Martha, sister of Sir Richard HULL, da. of William HULL, of Leamcon, co. Cork, by his 1st wife, Jane, da. of Richard BOYLE, Archbishop of Tuam (1638-45). He *d.* about 1692. Will dat. 8 June 1691, pr. [I.] 3 Feb. 1692/3.

II. 1692? SIR WILLIAM MOORE, Baronet [I. 1681], of Ross Carbery aforesaid, 1st s. and h., *b.* 1663; admitted to Trin. Coll., Dublin (as Fellow Commoner), 30 June 1679, aged 16; *suc. to the Baronetcy* on his father's death; was M.P. [I.] for Bandon, 1692-93. He *m.* 19 Oct. 1683, Catherine, da. of Sir John PERCEVAL, 1st Baronet [I. 1661], by Catherine, da. of Robert SOUTHWELL of Kinsale. He *d.* 28 Aug. 1693, and was *bur.* in the Cathedral of Ross, co. Cork, aged 31. M.I. Will dat. 24 Aug. 1692, pr. 21 Nov. 1693. His widow, who was *b.* 19 April 1662, *m.* in 1696, Major John MONTGOMERY, of Ballyleck, co. Monaghan. She *m.* thirdly in 1699, Brig. Gen. George FREKE, sometime M.P. [I.] for Cloughnakilty.

III. 1693. SIR EMANUEL MOORE, Baronet [I. 1681], of Ross Carbery aforesaid, and Dunmore, co. Cork, 1st. s. and h., *b.* 1685; *suc. to the Baronetcy,* 28 Aug. 1693; admitted to Trin. Coll., Dublin, as "*Nobilis,*" 2 Aug. 1703, aged 18; was M.P. [I.] for Downpatrick, 1715-27. He *m.* (Lic. 17 Feb. 1707/8), Catherine, da. and h. of Charles ALCOCK, of Powerstown, co. Tipperary, by Mary, his wife.(b) He *d.* in or shortly before 1733. Will dat. 29 March 1731, pr. [I.] 23 Nov. 1733.

IV. 1733? SIR CHARLES MOORE, Baronet [I. 1681], only s. and h.; *suc. to the Baronetcy* about 1733; was appointed 8 Feb. 1749/50, Keeper of the Records in the Birmingham Tower, Dublin Castle. He *d.* unm., suddenly, 6 Oct. 1754. Will dat. 17 Sep., pr. 17 Oct. 1754.

V. 1754. SIR ROBERT MOORE, Baronet [I. 1681], of Holystone, co. Northumberland, uncle and h., being yr. s. of the 2d Baronet; was a Major in the army; *suc. to the Baronetcy,* 6 Oct. 1754. He *m.* Anne, da. of the Rev. (—) DRAPER. He *d.* in or shortly before 1758. Will dat. 17 July 1756, pr. 20 April 1758.

VI. 1758? SIR WILLIAM MOORE, Baronet [I. 1681], of Cork, only s. and h.; was Capt. in 61st Regt. of Foot; *suc. to the Baronetcy* in or shortly before 1758. He *d.* unm. in 1783 or 1784. Will dat. 15 Aug. 1783, pr. [I.] 28 Jan. 1784.

VII. 1783? SIR EMANUEL MOORE, Baronet [I. 1683], of Maryborough, co. Cork, 2d cousin and h. male, being s. and h. of Richard MOORE, of Maryborough, by Alice, da. of (—) LAMB, which Richard (who was *b.* 1694), was s. and h. of Emanuel MOORE, of Maryborough (*d.* 1727, aged 61), who was br. of the 2d and yr. s. of the 1st Baronet. He was *b.*

(a) In Playfair's *Baronetage* [1811], he is stated to have been grandson of "Thomas Moore, Esq., of the Priory of Taunton, Somerset" (who *d.* 1575), though how such a conclusion is arrived at is not explained.

(b) This Catherine was third cousin to her husband, her paternal grandfather, Charles Alcock, having *m.* Catherine, da. of John Mulys, of Halyngton, Devon, by Norrys, da. of Richard Perceval, and sister of Sir Philip Perceval, paternal grandfather to Catherine, her said husband's mother.

17 March 1721/2; was Sheriff of co. Cork 1764, and *suc. to the Baronetcy* in 1783 or 1784. He *m.* in July 1742, Anne, da. and h. of Allen BROWNE, of Surmount, co. Cork, by Catherine, da. of Col. Edward HASTINGS, Gov. of Upnor Castle. He *d.* Aug. 1793, aged 71. Will dat. 18 July 1793, pr. [I.] 27 Jan. 1795.

VIII. 1793. SIR RICHARD MOORE, Baronet [I. 1683], of Cork, 1st s. and h., *b.* 7 April 1744; *suc. to the Baronetcy* in Aug. 1793. He *m.* 6 July 1770, Jane, 1st da. of Boyle TRAVERS, Banker and Alderman of Cork, by Catherine, da. of (—) CROSS. She, by whom he had ten children, *d.* 10 March 1801. He was living 1811.(a)

IX. 1815? SIR EMANUEL MOORE, Baronet [I. 1683], of Cork aforesaid, 1st surv. s. and h., *b.* 1786; *suc. to the Baronetcy* on the death of his father. He *m.* firstly, 28 Sep. 1809, Ellen, da. of Herbert GILLMAN, of Old Park, co. Cork. He *m.* secondly in 1844, (—), widow of Richard ASHE.(b) He *d.* 1849.

X. 1849. SIR RICHARD EMANUEL MOORE, Baronet [I. 1683], of Cork aforesaid, 1st s. and h. by 1st wife, *b.* 1810, at Maryborough; *suc. to the Baronetcy* in 1849. He *m.* firstly, 18 Oct. 1829, Mary Anne, 1st da. of A. Ryan O'CONNOR, of Kilgobbin House, co Cork. She *d.* 1848. He *m.* secondly in 1851, Margaret Matilda, da. of Roger O'CONNOR, of Dublin. He *d.* 24 June 1882, "in very poor circumstances," aged 71. His widow living 1904.

XI. 1882. SIR THOMAS O'CONNOR MOORE, Baronet [I. 1683], of Blackpool in Cork, coal dealer, 1st s. and h., by 1st wife; *b.* 5 Nov. 1845; *suc. to the Baronetcy*, 24 June 1882; living unm. 1904.

EATON:

cr. 21 Feb. 1681/2;

ex. Dec. 1697.

I. 1682, to 1697. "SIMON EATON, Esq., of Dunmoylin, co. Limerick," who was apparently a Cromwellian grantee of lands in that county, and in co. Clare; was Sheriff of co. Limerick, 1661, and of co. Kerry, 1676; and was *cr. a Baronet* [I.], as above, by patent dat. at Dublin, 21 Feb. 1681/2, the Privy Seal being dat. at Whitehall, 21 Dec. 1681. He, who was attainted by the Irish Parl. of James II in 1689, was Sheriff of co. Kerry, 1697. He *m.* about 1659, Susanna, widow of Chichester PHILIPPS, da. of the Rev. Thomas WARNER, by (—), da. of (—) EATON.(c) He *d.* s.p.m.s.,(d) and was *bur.*, 16 Dec. 1697, at St. James', Westm., when the *Baronetcy* became *extinct.* M.I. Will dat. 1 March 1696/7, pr. [E.] 1697 and [I.] 1698. The will of his widow was pr. [I.] 1701.

(a) Playfair's *Baronetage* [1811].

(b) Dod's *Baronetage*, etc., 1849.

(c) According to C. M. Tenison (see vol. i, p. 223, note "a"), her parents were Edward Warner, and Eleanor, 10th da. of Robert Magner, of Castle Magner, co. Cork. He adds that this Edward Warner gave him, in exchange for an estate in England, the estate of Curragh, near Newtown, co. Cork, and put him in possession of it, but Sir Simon never gave Warner the estate in England which he was to have had in lieu thereof.

(d) His son, Simon Eaton, *b.* 1660, admitted 8 Oct. 1676, as Fellow Commoner, to Trin. Coll., Dublin, aged 16, *m.* 1678 (Lic. Cork), Mary, da. of Sir Richard Aldworth, of Newmarket, co. Cork. He *d.* v.p. 19, and was *bur.* 20 Nov. 1684, in St. Patrick's Cathedral, Dublin. Funeral entry. Aldworth Eaton, only son of the above, *d.* young and before his grandfather. Martha, the only surv. da., *m.* George Mathew, of Thurles, co. Tipperary.

KING:

cr. 27 Sep. 1682;

sometime, 1748-55, BARON KINGSBOROUGH [I.];

afterwards, since 1764,

BARON KINGSTON OF ROCKINGHAM [I.];

since 1766, VISCOUNTS KINGSBOROUGH [I.];

and, since 1768, EARLS OF KINGSTON [I.].

I. 1682. "ROBERT KING, Esq., of Boyle Abbey, co. Roscommon," yr. br. of John (KING), 1st BARON KINGSTON [I.] (so *cr.*, 4 Sep. 1660, whose issue male became extinct 28 Dec. 1761), both being sons of Sir Robert KING, of Boyle Abbey aforesaid, Muster Master Gen. [I.] (*d.* 1657), by his 1st wife Frances, da. of Henry (FOLLIOTT), 1st BARON FOLLIOTT OF BALLYSHANNON [I.], was *b.* probably about 1625; was ed. at All Souls' College, Oxford, of which he was constituted Fellow in 1649 by the "Visitors"; B.C.L., 18 Dec. 1649; was M.P. [I.] for Ballyshannon, May 1661 to 1666; for co. Roscommon, 1692-93 and 1695-99; for Boyle 1703 till death in 1708; was P.C. [I.], and was *cr. a Baronet* [I.], as above, by patent, dat. at Dublin, 27 Sep. 1682, the Privy Seal, being dat. at Windsor 21 Aug. previous. He was *Knighted* 12 Oct. 1682. He was attainted by the Irish Parl. of James II in 1689. He *m.* about 1670, Frances, da. and h. of Lieut. Col. Henry GORE (yr. s. of Sir Paul GORE, 1st Baronet [I. 1622]), by Mary, da. and coheir of Robert BLAYNEY, of Tregonan, co. Montgomery. He *d.* in 1708. Will pr. [I.] 17 July 1708. His widow *m.* Robert CHOPPYNE, of Newcastle, co. Longford.

II. 1708. SIR JOHN KING, Baronet [I. 1682], of Boyle Abbey aforesaid, 2d but 1st surv. s. and h.,(a) *b.* before 1675; was M.P. [I.] for Boyle, 1695-99, 1703-13, 1713-15, and for co. Roscommon, 1715 till death, 1720; *suc. to the Baronetcy* in 1708. He *m.* Elizabeth, sister and coheir of Henry SANKEY, 1st da. of John SANKEY, of Tenelick, co. Longford, by Eleanor, da. of Robert MORGAN, of Cottelstown, co. Sligo. He *d.* s.p. 19 March 1720. Will pr. [I.] 1722. His widow *m.* (as his 2d wife) John (MOORE), 1st BARON MOORE OF TULLAMORE [I.], who *d.* 8 Sep. 1725. She *m.* thirdly (also as 2d wife) Brabazon (PONSONBY), 1st EARL OF BESSBOROUGH [I.] (who *d.* 4 July 1758, aged 80), and *d.* 17 July 1738, aged 58, being *bur.* at Fidowne.

III. 1720. SIR HENRY KING, Baronet [I. 1682], of Boyle Abbey aforesaid, br. and h., *b.* 1680 at Rockingham, co. Roscommon; admitted to Trin. Coll., Dublin, 26 Aug. 1695, aged 15; M.P. [I.] for Boyle (three Parls.), 1707-27, and for co. Roscommon, 1727 till death in 1740: *suc. to the Baronetcy*, 19 March 1720; P.C. [I.], 26 Oct. 1733. He *m.* April 1722, Isabella, sister of Richard, 1st VISCOUNT POWERSCOURT [I.], da. of Edward WINGFIELD, of Powerscourt, co. Wicklow, by his 1st wife Eleanor, da. of Sir Arthur GORE, of Newton Gore, co. Mayo. He *d.* at Spa, in Belgium, 1 Jan. 1740, in his 60th year. Will pr. [I.] 1741. His widow *d.* at Bath, 23 Oct. 1764.

IV. 1740. SIR ROBERT KING, Baronet [I. 1682], of Boyle Abbey aforesaid, 1st s. and h., *bap.* 18 Feb. 1724; *suc. to the Baronetcy*, 1 Jan. 1740; was M.P. [I.] for Boyle, 1745-48, and was *cr.* 13 June 1748, BARON KINGSBOROUGH [I.], taking his seat 8 Nov. 1749.(b) He was *Custos Rot.* for co. Roscommon. He *d.* unm. 22 May 1755, aged 31, when the *peerage* became *extinct.*

(a) His elder br., Robert King, *d.* v.p., and was *bur.* 28 March 1684, at St. Michan's, Dublin.

(b) The preamble is given in Lodge's *Irish Peerage* [1789], vol. iii, p. 236.

V. 1755. SIR EDWARD KING, Baronet [I. 1682], of Boyle Abbey aforesaid, br. and h., *b.* 29 March 1726; was M.P. [I.] for co. Roscommon, 1749-60, and for co. Sligo, 1761-64, having *suc. to the Baronetcy*, 22 May 1755; was Sheriff of co. Roscommon, 1761. He *m.* 5 May 1752, Jane, da. [*Qy.* illegit.?] of Thomas CAULFIELD, of Donamon, co. Roscommon. She was living when he was *cr.* 13 July 1764, BARON KINGSTON OF ROCKINGHAM, co. Roscommon [I.], being subsequently *cr.*, 15 Nov. 1766, VISCOUNT KINGSTON OF KINGSBOROUGH, co. Sligo, and, finally, on 25 Aug. 1768, EARL OF KINGSTON [I.]. In these peerages this *Baronetcy* then *merged*, and still [1904] so continues.

WARD:

cr. 9 Dec. 1682;

ex. 1691.

I. 1682, to 1691. "SIR ROBERT WARD, Knt., of Killogh, co. Down," 2d s. of Nicholas WARD, Surveyor Gen. of the Ordnance in Ireland [1599], by Mary, da. of Ralph LEYCESTER, of Toft, co. Chester, was *b.* 1610; was Sheriff of co. Down, 1661 and 1667; was *Knighted* about 1670, and was *cr. a Baronet* [I.], as above, by patent dat. 9 Dec. 1682, at Dublin, the Privy Seal bearing date 31 Oct. previous, at Whitehall. He *m.* before April 1661, Mary, widow of Robert ECHLIN, of Ardquin, co. Down,(a) da. of Henry LESLIE, Bishop of Meath (1660-61), by Jane, da. of Robert SWINTON, of Swinton. He *d.* s.p.m.s.,(b) 1691, aged about 81, when the *Baronetcy* became *extinct.*

EVANS:

cr. 19 Feb. 1682/3

ex. May 1690.

I. 1683, to 1690. "WILLIAM EVANS, Esq., of Kilkreene, in city of Kilkenny," 1st s. and h. of Capt. Thomas EVANS, of Kilcreen aforesaid, sometime (1661-66) M.P. [I.] for the city of Kilkenny (*d.* 1677) by Katherine, da. of Walter WELDON, of St. John's Bower, Athy, co. Kildare, was *b.* 1662; admitted to Trin. Coll., Dublin, as Fellow Commoner, 3 Aug. 1676, aged 14, and was *cr. a Baronet* [I.], as above, by patent dat. 19 Feb. 1682/3, at Dublin, the Privy Seal bearing date 28 Sep. 1682, at Whitehall; Sheriff of co. Kilkenny, 1686. He was attainted by the Irish Parl. of James II in 1689. He *m.* Jane, da. and coheir of Col. the Hon. Richard COOTE, of Tullaghmaine, co. Kilkenny (yr. s. of Charles, 1st EARL OF MOUNTRATH [I.]), by Penelope, da. of Arthur HILL, of Hillsborough, co. Down. He *d.*, s.p.m.s.,(c)

(a) By whom, with other issue, she had Sir Henry Echlin, *cr. a Baronet* [I.] in 1721.

(b) His only son, Charles Ward, *b.* 1662; entered Trin. Coll., Dublin (as Fellow Commoner), 1 Feb. 1677/8; was Sheriff of co. Down, 1685; *m.* 15 Dec. 1681, Catharine, 1st da. of Sir John Temple, Attorney Gen. and sometime (1661-66) Speaker of the House of Commons [I.], and *d.* s.p. and v.p. His will pr. [I.] 1692. His widow, who was *bap.* 4 Sep. 1664, *m.* Charles King, of Dublin, and *d.* 1694. Her will, as "wife of Charles King, and late wife and executrix to Charles Ward of Killough, co. Down, Esq.," dat. 4 and pr. 20 [I.] Aug. 1694.

(c) Thomas Evans, his only son, *d.* in infancy. Of his four daughters, Jane and Dorothy, *d.* unm.; Penelope *m.* in 1698, Richard Cole, of Archersgrove, co. Kilkenny, and *d.* s.p.; while Catharine, who became eventually the sole heir, *m.* in Aug. 1707, Francis Morres, of Castle Morres, co. Kilkenny, her eldest son being *cr.* in 1756 Baron, and in 1763, Viscount Mountmorres [I.]; her second son, Sir William Evans Morres, being *Knighted* 28 Aug. 1755, and *cr. a Baronet* [I.], 24 April 1758, and her third son being father of Lodge Evans Morres, *cr.* in 1800 Baron, and, in 1816, Viscount Frankfort de Montmorency [I.].

May 1690, aged 28, when the *Baronetcy* became *extinct.* Admon. [I.] 16 Sep. 1691, to the widow. She *m.* (as his 2d wife) Henry GORGES, of Somerset, co. Derry, who *d.* 1695. She *m.* thirdly, Jervais (or Jeremiah) PRICE, of the Inner Temple, London. She *m.* fourthly, in 1703, Major William BILLINGSLEY, of the Three Castles, co. Kilkenny. She *d.* 25 June 1729, and was *bur.* at St. Michan's, Dublin.

HAMILTON:

cr. 19 Feb. 1682/3;

ex. in 1729 or 1730.

I. 1683. "SIR ROBERT HAMILTON, Knt., of Mount Hamilton, co. Armagh," whose parentage is unknown, was *Knighted* about 1670; Commissr. of the Revenue [I.], 25 Sep. 1678; King's Counsel 30 Sep. 1678, and, presumably, in consequence of his marriage, was *cr. a Baronet* [I.], as above, by patent, dat. at Dublin 19 Feb. 1682/3, the Privy Seal bearing date 24 Jan. previous, at Whitehall. He *m.* before 1676, Sarah, only child of Sir Hans HAMILTON,(a) Baronet [I. so *cr.* 6 April 1662], of Monella and of Hamilton's Bawn, co. Armagh, by Magdalen, da. of Sir Edward TREVOR, and, apparently, inherited those estates on the death, 14 Feb. 1681/2, of his said father in law, whom he had also suc. as *Custos Rot.* for co. Armagh. His wife *d.* before her said father, probably about 1680. He himself *d.* 1703.

II. 1703, to 1730? SIR HANS HAMILTON, Baronet [I. 1683], of Hamilton's Bawn aforesaid, only s. and h., *b.* 1673; *suc. to the Baronetcy* in 1703; was M.P. [I.] for co. Armagh, 1703-13. He *m.*, probably about 1705, Jane, 1st da. of Clotworthy (SKEFFINGTON), 2d VISCOUNT MASSEREENE [I.], by Rachel (*m.* 1680), da. of Sir Edward HUNGERFORD, K.B. He *d.* s.p.m.,(b) at Utrecht in 1729 or 1730, aged about 56, when the *Baronetcy* became *extinct.* Admon. [I.] 7 Sep. 1741.

CALDWELL:(c)

cr. 23 June 1683;

ex. 13 Oct. 1858.

I. 1683. "JAMES CALDWELL, Esq., of Wellsburrow [*i.e.*, Wellsborough], co. Fermanagh," 2d s. of John CALDWELL, of Enniskillen, merchant (*b.* at Prestwick, co. Ayr, and *d.* in Dublin 19 Feb. 1639/40), being 1st s. by 2d wife Mary, da. of Anthony SWETTENHAM, of Shotwick, co. Chester, was *b.* before 1634, probably about 1630; settled at Rossbeg, *afterwards* called Castle Caldwell, in Templecarne, co. Fermanagh; was Sheriff of that county 1677,(d) having purchased the estate of Wellsborough therein in 1671, and was *cr. a Baronet* [I.], as above, by patent, dat. at Dublin 23 June 1683, the

(a) See an account of this family in Lodge's *Irish Peerage* [1789], vol. i, p. 270, note.

(b) Anne, his only da. and h., *m.* James Campbell, who assumed the name of Hamilton, and *d.* in London, 7 July 1749, aged 80.

(c) Much of the information contained in this article has been kindly supplied by W. H. Greaves-Bagshawe, of Ford Hall, near Chapel en le Frith, a descendant of the 3d Baronet, through the marriage (25 March 1751, at Castle Caldwell) of that Baronet's da., Catherine, with Col. Samuel Bagshawe, of Ford Hall aforesaid.

(d) The Sheriff of that county in 1664 was William Caldwell, of Drumboory.

Privy Seal being dat. 30 April previous at Windsor. He and his "son and heir Charles" were attainted in 1689 by the Irish Parl. of James II, in which year he was Col. of a Reg. of Foot and Capt. of a troop of Horse, being a vigorous supporter of the cause of William III, and receiving several extensive grants accordingly.(a) He *m.* firstly, apparently about May 1657, Catharine, sister of Charles CAMPBELL, sometime M.P. [I.] for Newtown Ards, da. of Charles CAMPBELL, of Ikeldon, co. Ayr, and of Newtown Montgomery. She was living May 1657, and *d.*, apparently, shortly before 15 March 1689. He *m.* secondly (Lic. Vic. Gen., 23 July 1690, being then of St. Margaret's, Westm., about 45 [*Qy.* 60?], widower), "Mrs. Susanna BECKE, of St. James', Clerkenwell, about 40, widow." He *d.* shortly before 13 Feb. 1716/7, aged about 87. Will dat. 30 May 1711 to 20 March 1712/3, pr. [I.] 28 March 1717.

II. 1717? SIR HENRY CALDWELL, Baronet [I. 1683], of Castle Caldwell aforesaid, 2d but only surv. s. and h.,(b) was, with his father and brothers, very active in the cause of King William III; was Sheriff of co. Fermanagh, 1693; is said to have lived (v.p.) as a merchant at Killibegs, co. Donegal, and (1714) at Ballyshannon; *suc. to the Baronetcy* in or shortly before Feb. 1716/7. He *m.* firstly, Catharine, da. of Sir John HUME, 2d Baronet [S. 1638?] of Castle Hume, co. Fermanagh, by Sidney, da. and coheir of James HAMILTON, of Castle Hamilton, co. Leitrim. He *m.* secondly, shortly after 14 July 1722, "a person of considerably lower position than himself." He *d.* shortly before 5 Nov. 1726. Will dat. 21 June 1721, not mentioning his own family, but leaving all to Mrs. Ann Hewetson, pr. [I.] 19 Jan. 1726.

III. 1726? SIR JOHN CALDWELL, Baronet [I. 1683], of Castle Caldwell aforesaid, only s. and h.; *suc. to the Baronetcy* in or shortly before Nov. 1726; was Sheriff of co. Fermanagh, 1730. He *m.* 11 July 1719, at St. Bridget's, Dublin (settlement same date), Mary, 1st da. of John TRENCH, D.D., Dean of Raphoe, by Anne, da. of Richard WARBURTON, of Garryhinch, in Queen's County. He *d.* between 14 and 18 Feb. 1743/4. Will dat. 5 Jan. 1742/3 to 14 Feb. 1743/4, pr. [I.] 14 or 19 May 1744. His widow *d.* soon after 7 Nov. 1769.(c)

IV. 1744. SIR JAMES CALDWELL, Baronet [I. 1683], of Castle Caldwell aforesaid, 1st s. and h., *b.* about 1722; ed. at Dundalk School, 1734; Fellow Commoner of Trin. Coll., Dublin; B.A., 1740; a Freeman of Londonderry, 1741; *suc. to the Baronetcy* in Feb. 1743/4, being then in France. Having distinguished himself in the Austrian Service, he was *cr.* by the Empress Maria Theresa, 15 March 1749, a COUNT OF MILAN IN THE HOLY ROMAN EMPIRE, with rem. to the heirs male of his body. Dep. Gov. of co. Fermanagh, and Col. of a Reg. of Militia, 1752; F.R.S., Feb. 1753; Sheriff of co. Fermanagh, 1756. He raised, 12 Jan. 1760, a Reg. of Light Horse (20th Dragoons) for the defence of Ireland, which was disbanded, 1763; P.C. [I.], 30 Jan. 1762; is said to have declined an Irish Peerage, as also the office of Chamberlain to the Empress of Germany. He *m.* 18 Dec. 1753, at St. Anne's, Dublin, Elizabeth (£5,000 portion), sister of Sir John HORT, 1st Baronet [I. 1767],

(a) A very full account of his actions is given in Playfair's *Baronetage* [1811].

(b) Charles Caldwell, the eldest son, eventually (before July 1694) Lieut. Col. was, with his brothers Henry, Hugh and John, most active in the cause of William III. He *d.* unm. and v.p. presumably after 1702.

(c) In 1766 she received from Maria Theresa, Empress of Germany, a snuff box, in memory of her son Col. Hume Caldwell, who was killed in the Austrian Service, 15 Aug. 1762, in his 27th year, and who, had he survived, was to have been made a General, and Chamberlain to the said Empress. See an interesting (but extremely lengthy) account of him in Playfair's *Baronetage* [1811].

1st da. of Josiah HORT, D.D., Archbishop of Tuam, by Elizabeth, da. of Lieut. Col. the Hon. William FITZMAURICE, of Gallane, co. Kerry, br. of Thomas, 1st EARL OF KERRY [I.]. She, who was *bap.* 26 Dec. 1729, *d.* 11 Sep. 1778, in Dublin, and was *bur.* there. He *d.* Feb. 1784, at Castle Caldwell, and was *bur.* in the chapel there. Will pr. [I.] 1784.

V. 1784. SIR JOHN CALDWELL, Baronet [I. 1683], of Castle Caldwell aforesaid, a COUNT OF THE HOLY ROMAN EMPIRE, 1st s. and h., *b.* 16 Aug. 1756; entered the Army, 1774; Lieut. 1777; Aide de Camp to the Viceroy of Ireland, 1782; *suc. to the Baronetcy* in Feb. 1784; Gov. of co. Fermanagh, 1793; Lieut. Col. of the Fermanagh Militia, 1794; Sheriff of that county, 1798; Capt. of the Belleek infantry, 1802. He *m.* 16 May 1789, at Queen's Square chapel, Bath, Harriett, da. and coheir of Godfrey MEYNELL, of Yeldersley and Bradley, co. Derby, by Frances, da. of [—] DEALTRY. She *d.* at Bath, 1795. Admon. Feb. 1818. He *d.* s.p.m.,(a) 17 June 1830, aged 73, at Ramsgate, co. Kent, when the Countship of the Holy Roman Empire became extinct.

VI. 1830. SIR JOHN CALDWELL, Baronet [I. 1683], of Belmont, in Canada, Treasurer Gen. of that dominion, cousin and h. male, being only s. and h. of Lieut. Col. Henry CALDWELL, of Caldwell manor, near Quebec, in Canada aforesaid,(b) Receiver Gen. of Lower Canada [1793], by Anne, da. of Alexander HAMILTON, of Knock and Hampton, co. Dublin, which Henry, who *d.* at Quebec 28 May 1810, aged 72, was yr. br. of the 4th, and 4th son of the 3d Baronet. He was *bap.* 25 Feb. 1775, at Quebec; was made Treasurer Gen. of Canada, about April 1810; *suc. to the Baronetcy*, 17 June 1830. He *m.* 21 Aug. 1800, at Quebec, Jane (then aged 18) da. of James DAVIDSON, Surgeon to the 2d Batt. of the Royal Canadian Volunteers. She *d.* at Quebec 1805, and was *bur.* there. He *d.* at Fremont House, Boston, United States of America, 26 Oct. 1842, aged 67, and was *bur.* at Boston. Will pr. Feb. 1844.

VII. 1842, to 1858. SIR HENRY JOHN CALDWELL, Baronet [I. 1683], of Belmont, in Canada aforesaid, only s. and h., *b.* 22 Oct. and *bap.* 28 Nov. 1801, at the Protestant Church at Quebec; was a Member of the Canadian Parl. in 1831; *suc. to the Baronetcy*, 26 Oct. 1842. He *m.* 18 Dec. 1839, at Walcot, near Bath, Sophia Louisa, 1st da. of David Runwas PAYNTER, of Dale Castle, co. Pembroke, by Sophia Catherine, da. and h. of Howel PRICE, of Berthlewydd, co. Carmarthen. He *d.* s.p. 13 Oct. 1858, at Marlborough Buildings, Bath, in his 57th year, and was *bur.* at Lansdown Cemetery there, when the *Baronetcy* became *extinct.*(c) M.I. Will dat. at Quebec 18 Jan. 1845, pr. (with two codicils) 15 Nov. 1858. His widow, who was *b.* 25 Nov. 1818, *d.* at Marlborough Buildings aforesaid, 22 Sep. 1864.

(a) Of his two surv. daughters and coheirs (1) Frances Arabella, *b.* at Bath in or shortly before March 1790, *m.* 11 June 1817, at Brighton, John Colpoys Bloomfield, of Redwood, co. Tipperary, inherited her father's estate of Castle Caldwell, and *d.* 1872, leaving issue John Caldwell Bloomfield, of Castle Caldwell, Sheriff for co. Fermanagh, 1874. (2) Louisa Georgiana, *b.* 1794 or 1795, *m.* 31 March 1823, at Bathwick, Sir Josiah William Hort, 2d Baronet [1767].

(b) This Henry possessed in that dominion 600,000 acres, of which an estate of about 40,000 was opposite Quebec. He distinguished himself at the taking of Louisbourg and Quebec, and is said to have declined a Baronetcy offered to him for his services.

(c) Anne, his only sister, *b.* Aug. 1805, *m.* at Quebec in Aug. 1829 (as his 1st wife) Lieut. Gen. John Eden, C.B. (who *d.* 6 Oct. 1864, aged 75), and *d.* Nov. 1841, being *bur.* at Montreal, leaving issue,

FRANCKLIN:

1684? existing 1689.

"SIR WILLIAM FRANCKLIN, Baronet [I.?] of Belfast," is said to have been attainted by James II(a) [probably by the Irish Parl. in 1689], and, if rightly described, must presumably have possessed a Baronetcy created before the reign of that King. Nothing further is known of him.

CREATIONS BY JAMES II,

6 Feb. 1684/5 to 11 Dec. 1688.

EUSTACE:

cr. 23 Dec. 1685;

forfeited 1691.

I. 1685, to 1691. "MAURICE EUSTACE, Esq., of Castle Martin, co. Kildare," s. and h. of John EUSTACE, of the same (*d.* 1684), by Margaret, da. of Edmund KEATING, of Narraghmore, in that county, and Elinor, sister of Sir Maurice EUSTACE, sometime [1660-65], Lord Chancellor of Ireland (*d.* s.p. legit. 22 June 1665), da. of John EUSTACE, of Harristown, co. Kildare. He was *cr. a Baronet* [I.], as above, by patent dat. at Dublin, 23 Dec. 1685, the Privy Seal bearing date at Windsor, 12 Sep. previous. He was P.C. [I.] 1686; was Colonel of the 19th Foot in the army of James II at the siege of Derry in 1689. He *m.* (Lic. 22 Oct. 1684) Margaret, 4th da. of Sir Thomas NEWCOMEN, of Sutton, co. Dublin, by Frances, sometime wife of James CUSACK, sister of Richard, DUKE OF TYRCONNEL [I.], da. of Sir William TALBOT, 1st Baronet [I. 1623], of Carton, co. Kildare. He was *attainted* in 1691, whereby *the Baronetcy* became *forfeited*. He retired to France, where he *d.* s.p.m.(b) 15 Oct. 1693, when the *Baronetcy* became *extinct.*(c) His widow *d.* 30 June 1738. Her will dat. Jan. pr. [I.] 1 Feb. 1738/9.

(a) *Ex inform.* C. M. Tenison.

(b) Of his daughters and coheirs (1) Frances *d.* young, (2) Maria Henrietta *d.* unm. before 8 June 1717, when her mother took out admon. to her.

(c) He is not to be confused with his mother's 1st cousin, Sir Maurice Eustace, of Harristown, s. of William Eustace (who *d.* 1 Feb. 1674) and nephew of the Lord Chancellor [I.]. That Maurice *d.* s.p.m.s., 13 April 1703, leaving a br., Sir John Eustace (who *d.* s.p. in Oct. 1704), and three daughters and coheirs, viz., by his 1st wife, Anne Colvill: (1) Anne, who *m.* Benjamin Chetwode, and was mother of John Chetwode-Eustace; (2) Penelope, *m.* firstly Robert Echlin, and secondly Edward Stratford; and, by his 2d wife, Clotilda Parsons, (3) Clotilda, *m.* 23 April 1726, at St. James', Dublin, Thomas Tickell, the "Poet" (who *d.* 23 April 1740, aged 54), and was *bur.* with him at Glasnevin, co. Dublin, in 1792. [*Mis. Gen. et Her.*, new series, vol. ii, p. 472].

TYRRELL:

cr. 20 May 1686;

forfeited 1691;

but assumed later.

I. 1686, to 1691. "EDWARD TYRRELL, Esq., of Lynn, co. Westmeath," as also of Longwood, co. Meath, s. of Thomas TYRRELL,(a) of Simonstown, co. Westmeath, "a lawyer of very small estate," was Sheriff of co. Westmeath, 1669, 1678, and 1679; of co. Meath, 1685; was a Capt. in Luttrell's Dragoons, and was *cr. a Baronet* [I.], as above, by patent dat. at Dublin 20 May 1686, the Privy Seal being dat. at Whitehall, 18 March previous, with a special remainder, failing heirs male of his body, to his nephew, Edward TYRRELL, and his "heirs male." He was M.P. [I.] for Belturbet, 1689, in the Parl. of James II, and was by that King (whose cause he adopted), made 7 April 1690, Supervisor of the counties of Cork, Waterford and Kerry. He *m.* Eleanor, widow of George COLLEY, of Edenderry, and formerly of Col. William DUCKINFIELD, yr. da. of Sir Dudley LOFTUS, of Killyan, by Cecilia, da. of Sir James WARE, the elder. He was made prisoner at the surrender of Cork in 1690, and so continued till his death, 7 Feb. 1690/1, "and was never brought to trial or outlawed until 16 April 1691, when he was dead and in his grave."(b) He *d.* s.p.m.,(c) but the *Baronetcy*, by this attainder (though two months after death) was presumably, *forfeited.*

The Baronetcy was assumed as under:—

II. 1691, to *1720?* SIR EDWARD TYRRELL, Baronet(d) [I. 1686], nephew of the grantee, being s. and h. of Thomas TYRELL, of Simonstown aforesaid, br. of the late Baronet, *assumed the Baronetcy* in Feb. 1690/1 (notwithstanding the attainder), as being entitled thereto under the spec. rem. in the creation thereof. He, apparently, *m.* Rebecca, da. of [—]. Nothing more is known of him or of any subsequent assumption of the dignity. "Rebecca, relict of Sir Edward TYRRELL, Baronet, Northants" [*sic*], presumably his widow, *d.* 29 May 1750, aged 95.(e)

TRANT:

cr. 29 July 1686;

forfeited 10 April 1691;

but assumed till or after 1728.

I. 1686, to 1691. "PATRICK TRANT, Esq., of Portarlington, Queen's County," s. of (—) TRANT, of Dingle, said to have been a London Merchant, was Commissioner of Excise and Hearth Money [I.], 10 April 1684 to 11 March 1685, and was *cr. a Baronet* [I.], as above, by patent, dat. at Dublin, 29 July 1686, the Privy Seal bearing date at

(a) This Thomas was admitted to Gray's Inn, 10 Aug. 1627 (as son of Richard Tyrrell, of Kilbride), and, subsequently, 8 Feb. 1633, to King's Inns, Dublin.

(b) See claim of Robert Edgworth and Catharine, his wife, da. and h. of the deceased. [*Forfeited Estates*, at Chichester House, Dublin].

(c) Catherine, his da. and h., *m.* before his death Robert Edgworth, of Clonbrony, co. Longford, and had issue to whom (being Protestants) the Longwood and other estates were restored.

(d) According to the assumption of that dignity.

(e) *London Magazine*, 1750, p. 285.

Whitehall, 22 May previous. He was M.P. [I.] for Queen's County, 1689, in the Parl. of James II, who is said to have promised him a peerage as BARON MARYBOROUGH [I.]. He *m.* Helen, who, with him, was attainted 10 April 1691, when the *Baronetcy* was *forfeited*. He followed James II into France, and *d.* there before 1702. The will of his widow, as "of St. Anne's, Soho, Midx., dat. 26 Oct. 1721, pr. 6 Feb. 1728/9.

The Baronetcy was assumed as under :—

II. 1700? SIR JOHN TRANT, Baronet(a) [I. 1686], s. and h.(b); *assumed the Baronetcy* notwithstanding the attainder. He *d.* unm. 5 May 1702, being "found dead in Covent Garden, in a duel."(c)

III. 1702. SIR CHARLES TRANT, Baronet(a) [I. 1686], br. and h., *assumed the Baronetcy*, as above, in May 1702. He *d.* unm. in or before 1711. Admon. [I.] 21 Nov. 1711, to his mother.

IV. 1711? to *1730?* SIR LAURENCE TRANT, Baronet(a) [I. 1686], br. and h., *assumed the Baronetcy*, as above, in or before 1711. He was living 1728, after which date nothing further is known of him.

O'SHAUGNESSY, *or* SHAGNESSY:

1686? to 1690.

"SIR ROGER O'SHAGNESSY, of Gortinhegouragh, co. Galway," is described as "*Baronet*" in Archdall's edit. of Lodge's *Irish Peerage* [1789, vol. ii, p. 35] in the account of Connor (O'BRIEN), 2d VISCOUNT CLARE [I.], whose da., Ellen, he married. This description of him is, however, a mistake, for (though his father, grandfather and great great grandfather were Knights) he (himself) was neither Knight nor Baronet. He fought as Capt. in "Clare's Dragoons" (the regiment of his said father-in-law), for the cause of James II, at the battle of the Boyne, 1 July 1690, and *d.* ten days afterwards at his castle of Gort, and was attainted as an "Esquire" (only) in 1697, his estates being granted to Thomas Prendergast, who was *cr. a Baronet* [I.] by William III.

(a) According to the assumption of that dignity.

(b) In a pedigree furnished by C. M. Tenison he is made *grandson* and heir, viz., s. and h. of Richard Trant, stated to have been 1st s. and h. ap. of the grantee. The 1st Baronet had a br. Richard, who was Governor of Barbadoes, and who left a son, James, and a da., Margaret, wife of Richard (Lambart), 4th Earl of Cavan [I.].

(c) *Top. and Gen.*, vol. iii, p. 41, and Luttrell's *Diary*. His antagonist was "one Mr. Weedon" (with whom he had "quarrelled at play"), who escaped.

CHAMBERS.

1686? or, not improbably 1663, to 1694.

"SIR RICHARD CHAMBERS, Baronet" [*Qy.* I.] is referred to as "deceased" in an inquisition(a) taken at Dublin, 31 Oct. 1694, on his widow, "Donna Mariana CHAMBERS," a foreigner born at Xeres in Spain and never naturalised. The mention of his interest in the estate of "the late Earl of Limerick" makes it probable that (like that Earl) he was an adherent of and obtained his title from James II,(b) but it is not improbable that it was given in 1663, and that he is the person indicated, 24 Oct. 1663, in the warrant for creating [—] CHAMBERS, a Baronet. [*Calendar of State Papers.* Entry Book, 15.]

O'BRIEN:

cr. 9 Nov. 1686;

afterwards, since 1855, BARONS INCHIQUIN [I.]

I. 1686. "DONOUGH O'BRIEN, Esq., of Leminnegh, co. Clare," as also of Dromoland, in that county, 1st s. and h. of Connor O'BRIEN, of the same, by Mary, da. of Sir Turlogh MAC MAHON, 1st [*Qy.*] Baronet [I. 1628], which Connor (who was a Colonel in the army and was slain in battle 1651, aged 34) was s. and h. of Donough O'BRIEN, of the same (*d.* 10 Jan. 1634), who was s. and h. of Connor O'BRIEN, of the same (*d.* 2 Jan. 1602), who was s. and h. of Donough O'BRIEN, of the same, which Donough (*d.* Sep. 1582) was yr. br. of Dermod (O'BRIEN), 2d BARON INCHIQUIN [I.] (ancestor of the EARLS OF INCHIQUIN [I.], 1654-1855, MARQUESSES OF THOMOND [I.], 1800-1855), both being sons of Murrough O'BRIEN, sometime KING OF THOMOND, who was *cr.*, 1 July 1543, EARL OF THOMOND [I.] for life and BARON INCHIQUIN [I.], with rem. to heirs male of his body. He was *b.* 1642; ed. in London; was Sheriff of co. Clare, 1690; M.P. for that county, 1692-93, 1695-99 and 1703-14, being *cr. a Baronet* [I.], as above, by patent dat. at Dublin, 9 Nov. 1686, the Privy Seal bearing date, 16 Oct. previous, at Whitehall. He was P.C. to Queen Anne. He *m.* firstly (contract 24 July 1674), Lucia, da. of Sir George HAMILTON, 1st Baronet [S. or I. 1634], by Mary, sister of James, 1st DUKE OF ORMONDE, da. of Thomas BUTLER, *styled* VISCOUNT THURLES. She *d.* 1676. He *m.* secondly (Lic. 23 July 1677), Elizabeth, widow of Henry GREY, da. of Major Joseph DEANE, of Crumlin, co. Dublin, by his 1st wife, Anne. She *d.* 16 Jan. and was *bur.* 18 Feb. 1683/4, at St. Bride's, Dublin. Funeral entry. He *d.* 17 Nov. 1717, aged 75, and was *bur.* at Killenasulagh, co. Clare. M.I. Will dat. 18 Nov. 1717, pr. 1 April 1718.

(a) The purport of this Inquisition, which is in Latin, is as under:—

The Tholsel, Dublin, 31 Oct. 6 Wm. & M.

Donna Mariana Chambers, widow of Richard Chambers, Baronet, deceased, is a foreigner born in Xeres in the Kingdom of Spain, under the allegiance of the King of Spain, and was not naturalized at any time in any of the dominions of our Lord the King, but what estate or interest the said donna Marianna, or any other in trust for her, has or had in the Kingdom of Ireland, and what are the incumbrances forfeited to the King upon any lands heretofore appertaining to the late Earl of Limerick in the county of the City of Dublin, the jurors are ignorant. [*Inquisitionum Cancellariæ Hiberniæ repertorium*, vol. i].

(b) Euphemia Maria, da. of Richard Chambres [Chambers?], a lady of Spanish domicile, *m.* before May 1664 (probably about 1660) at Xeres in Spain, William (Dungan), 1st Earl of Limerick [I.], to whom she brought a portion of £30,000. She was living as his widow in 1703, and her will is pr. [I.] in 1703.

II. 1717. SIR EDWARD O'BRIEN, Baronet [I. 1686], of Dromoland aforesaid, grandson and h., being s. and h. of Lucius O'BRIEN, M.P. [I.] for co. Clare, 1703-14, by Catherine, da. of Thomas KEIGHTLEY, of Hertingfordbury, and Frances, da. of Edward (HYDE), 1st EARL OF CLARENDON, which Lucius, was s. and h. ap. of the late Baronet by his 1st wife, but *d.* v.p. 6 Jan. 1716/7. He was *b.* 7 April 1705; matric. at Oxford (Balliol Coll.), 12 Oct. 1721, aged 16; *suc. to the Baronetcy*, 17 Nov. 1717; was M.P. for Peterborough, 1727-28, and M.P. [I.] for co. Clare 1727, till death in 1765; was Colonel of the Militia Dragoons of that county. He *m.* about 1730, Mary, da. of Hugh HICKMAN, of Fenloe, co. Clare, by Anne, da. of George HASTINGS, of Daylesford, co. Worcester. She *d.* 20 Feb. 1760. He *d.* 26 Nov. 1765, aged 60. Will dat. 2 Aug. 1765, pr. 30 May 1767.

III. 1765. SIR LUCIUS HENRY O'BRIEN, Baronet [I. 1686], of Dromoland aforesaid, 1st s. and h., *b.* 2 Sep. 1731; ed. at Trin. Coll., Dublin; B.A., 1752; admitted to Middle Temple, 18 Sep. 1753; Barrister (King's Inns, Dublin), 17 Nov. 1758; M.P. [I.] for Ennis, 1761-68; *suc. to the Baronetcy*, 26 Nov. 1765; was M.P. [I.] for co. Clare, 1768-83; for Tuam, 1783-90, and for Ennis (again) 1790, till death in 1795; was Clerk of the Crown and Hanaper [I.], 16 Jan. 1788, till the grant was revoked in 1795; P.C. [I.], 10 Feb. 1786; F.R.S. [I.]. He *m.* 26 May 1768 (Lic. 18), Anne, da. of Robert FRENCH, of Monivae, co. Galway, by Nichola, sister of Archibald, 1st VISCOUNT GOSFORD [I.], da. of Sir Archibald ACHESON, 5th Baronet [S. 1628]. He *d.* 15 Jan. 1795, aged 63. Will dat. 20 June 1792, pr. 17 Feb. 1798.

IV. 1795. SIR EDWARD O'BRIEN, Baronet [I. 1686], of Dromoland aforesaid, 1st s. and h., *b.* 17 April 1773; *suc. to the Baronetcy*, 15 Jan. 1795; was M.P. [I.] for Ennis (two Parls.), 1795—1800, and [U.K.] for co. Clare, 1802-26; Lieut. Col. of the Clare Militia. He *m.* 12 Nov. 1799, Charlotte, 1st da. and coheir of William SMITH, of Cahirmoyle, co. Limerick. He *d.* 13 March 1837, aged 63, at Dromoland. His widow *d.* 28 Sep. 1856, at Dromoland aforesaid.

V. 1837. SIR LUCIUS O'BRIEN, Baronet [I. 1686], of Dromoland aforesaid, 1st s. and h.,(a) was *b.* 5 Dec. 1800, at Dromoland; ed. at Trin. Coll. Cambridge; B.A., 1825; M.A., 1828. He was M.P. for co. Clare, 1826-30, and 1847-52, being Sheriff of that county 1835; *suc. to the Baronetcy*, 13 March 1837 and was Lord Lieut. of co. Clare, 1843. He *m.* firstly, 21 Feb. 1837, Mary, 1st da. of William FITZGERALD, of Adelphi, co. Clare, by Julia Cecilia, da. of Maurice FITZGERALD, of Lifford. She *d.* 26 May 1852, aged 33. He *m.* secondly, 25 Oct. 1854, at Limerick Cathedral, Louisa, da. of James FINUCANE, Major in the Army, by Jane, da. of Matthias FINUCANE, sometime (1794—1806) a Justice of the Common Pleas [I.]. She was living when by the death, 3 July 1855, of his distant cousin James (O'Bryen), 3d MARQUESS OF THOMOND, 7th EARL OF INCHIQUIN and 12th BARON INCHIQUIN [I.], he became BARON INCHIQUIN [I.] as heir male of the body of the grantee, who was so *cr.* (as above mentioned) 1 July 1543. His right thereto was confirmed by the Committee for privileges 11 April 1862. In that Barony this *Baronetcy* then *merged*, and still [1904] so continues.

(a) His next yr. br. William Smith-O'Brien, on inheriting the estate of Cahirmoyle at the death of his maternal grandfather, took the additional name of Smith, and after a turbulent career as an Irish agitator, was found guilty of high treason and sentenced to be hanged in Oct. 1848, which sentence was, however, commuted to transportation. His arrest in a cabbage garden, where he was hiding, brought great ridicule on the "Patriot" cause. He *d.* 18 June 1864, aged 60, having been pardoned in 1854.

DOMVILE:

cr. 21 Dec. 1686;

ex. 13 March 1768.

I. 1685. "THOMAS DOMVILE, Esq., Clerk of the Crown and Hanaper in Chancery, of Temple Oge, co. Dublin," 2d s. of Sir William DOMVILE, sometime, 1660-86, Attorney General [I.] (*bur.* 14 July 1689, at St. Bride's, Dublin), by Bridget, da. of Sir Thomas LAKE, of Canons in Edgware, Midx., Prin. Sec. of State [E.], was *b.* probably about 1650; was made Joint Clerk of the Crown and Hanaper [I.], 16 April 1674, and was, v.p., *cr. a Baronet* [I.], as above, by patent dat. at Dublin, 21 Dec. 1686, the Privy Seal bearing date at Whitehall the 6th day of the same month. He was M.P. [I.] for Mullingar, 1692-93. He *m.* firstly, his cousin Elizabeth, da. of Sir Lancelot LAKE, of Canons aforesaid. She *d.* s.p.m. He *m.* secondly, Frances, da. of Sir John COLE, 1st Baronet [I. 1661], by Elizabeth, da. of the Hon. John CHICHESTER. She *d.* s.p. He *m.* thirdly, in or before 1686, Anne, 2d da. of the Hon. Sir Charles COMPTON (2d s. of Spencer, 2d EARL OF NORTHAMPTON), by Mary, da. of Sir Hatton FERMOR, of Easton Neston, co. Northampton. He *d.* 15, and was *bur.* 17 April 1721, in St. Patrick's Cathedral, Dublin. Will dat. 29 March, pr. [I.] 27 Nov. 1721. His widow was *bur.* at St. Patrick's aforesaid, 8 Jan. 1730. Will dat. 22 July 1726, pr. [I.] 2 June 1730.

II. 1721, to 1768. SIR COMPTON DOMVILE, Baronet [I. 1686], of Templeogue aforesaid, only s. and h., *b.* about 1686; entered Trin. Coll. Dublin, as Fellow Commoner, 19 Jan. 1699/700, aged 14; Clerk of the Crown and Hanaper [I.], 10 Nov. 1708; *suc. to the Baronetcy*, 15 April 1721; was Sheriff of co. Dublin, 1724; M.P. [I.] for that county for forty years, viz., 1727 till death in 1768; P.C. [I.], 27 May 1743. He *d.* unm. at his house in Merrion street, Dublin, 13, and was *bur.* 16 March 1768, in St. Patrick's aforesaid, when the *Baronetcy* became *extinct*.(a) Will dat. 27 July 1761, pr. 1768.

DOWDALL:

1688?(b) to 1691;

assumed till 1742.

I. 1688? SIR LUKE DOWDALL, of Athlumney, co. Meath, Knight, s. and h. of Lawrence DOWDALL, of the same, Sheriff of that county 1641 (admon. [I.] 18 April 1660), by Joan, da. of Luke (PLUNKETT), 1st EARL OF FINGALL, was *Knighted* about 1665, and is said(c) to have been *cr. a Baronet* [I.] by James II, probably about 1688 or 1689,(b) and, though no patent or Privy Seal exists, was described *as a Baronet* in the act of attainder,(c) 6 April 1691.

(a) The estates devolved on his nephew, Charles Pocklington, only s. of his sister Elizabeth (*m.* 29 Sep. 1722), by Admiral Christopher Pocklington. He accordingly took the name of Domvile only, and *d.* April 1810, leaving a son and h., who was *cr. a Baronet*, 22 May 1815.

(b) The grantee "is described as *Baronet* in a grant (as printed) under the Act of Settlement, 27 June 1677, but in a subsequent grant, 22 July 1678, as a *Knight*. He also appears as a *Knight* (only) in Chancery Bill, 14 May 1687. The first description as Baronet is clearly an error. Betham says he was made a Baronet by James II, so I think he should appear as a creation of his under 1688 or 1689. The title was fully acknowledged, as he was attainted *as a Baronet*, 6 April 1691, and he is so described in the petition of his widow to the trustees of Forefeited estates." [G. D. Burtchaell].

(c) Sir William Betham, Ulster.

He *m.* in or before 1678(a) Catherine, widow of John WALSH, of Old Connaught, co. Dublin, sister of Sir Gregory BYRNE, 1st Baronet [I. 1671], da. of Daniel BYRNE, of Dublin, by Anne, da. of Richard TAYLOR, of Swords. He *d.* 31 Aug. 1689. Nunc. will of same date, pr [I.] 17 Feb. 1689/90. He was attainted for high treason (about a year after his death), 6 April 1691, whereby *the Baronetcy* was *forfeited*. His widow petitioned the trustees of forfeited estates.

II. 1689, to 1691. SIR LAURENCE DOWDALL, Baronet [I. 1688?] 1st s. and h., *suc. to the Baronetcy*, 31 Aug. 1689, *which*, however, by the above recited attainder, *became forfeited* 6 April 1691. He *d.* under age and unm. before 22 July 1700.

The title was, however, assumed, notwithstanding the attainder, as under:—

III. 1700? SIR DANIEL DOWDALL, Baronet [I. 1688?],(b) br. and h., *assumed the Baronetcy* on the death of his brother. He took Holy Orders in the Church of Rome, and was Priest of Arran Quay Chapel, Dublin. He *d.* unm. in or before 1729. Admon. [I.] 9 May 1729, to his brother "Sir James DOWDALL."(b)

IV. 1729? to 1742. SIR JAMES DOWDALL, Baronet [I. 1688?](b) br. and h., *assumed the Baronetcy* in or before 1729. He *d.* unm., suddenly at Loughboy, co. Dublin, 9 Dec. 1742, and was *bur.* in St. James' Churchyard, aged 52, when the *Baronetcy* (which had been forfeited in 1691) became *extinct*. Admon [I.] 21 May 1744, to a creditor, the sisters Thomazine CLERK, widow, and Mary WALE, of Staplestown, co. Carlow, widow, consenting.

BELLEW:

cr. 11 Dec. 1688;(c)

afterwards, since 1848, BARONS BELLEW OF BARMEATH [I.].

I. 1688. "PATRICK BELLEW, Esq., of Barmeath, co. Louth," s. and h. of John BELLEW, of the same (will dat. 17 Feb. 1672, pr. [I.] 27 May 1679), by Mary, da. of Robert DILLON, of Clonbrock, obtained (under the act of settlement, 1678, and the act of grace, 6 Jan. 1684) lands, co. Galway and Louth, to be called Castle Bellew; was Sheriff of co. Louth, 1687, and was *cr. a Baronet* [I.], as above, by patent, dat. at Dublin, 11 Dec. 1688,(c) the Privy Seal bearing date at Whitehall, 25 April 1687. He *m.*, probably about 1660, Elizabeth, da. of Sir Richard BARNEWALL, 2d Baronet [I. 1623], by his 2d wife Julia, da. of Sir Gerald AYLMER, 1st Baronet [I. 1622]. He *d.* Jan. 1715/6.

(a) One of his sons, Patrick Dowdall, was *bur.* at St. Audoen's, Dublin, 26 March 1678.

(b) According to the assumption of the Baronetcy, notwithstanding its forfeiture on 6 April 1691.

(c) The last day of the reign of James II as terminated by the Act of Parl. in 1689.

II. 1716. SIR JOHN BELLEW, Baronet [I. 1688], of Barmeath and Castle Bellew aforesaid, 1st s. and h., *b.* probably about 1660; *suc. to the Baronetcy* in Jan. 1715/6. He *m.* firstly, 1 Dec. 1685, Clare, sister and h. of Nicholas TAYLOR, of Dublin, da. of Edward TAYLOR, of the same, by Clare, relict of Patrick MALPAS, da. of (—) HUMPHRIES. She, by whom he had six children, *d.* 1708. He *m.* secondly, Elizabeth, da. of Edward CURLING, Storekeeper of Derry during the siege of 1689. He *d.* 23 July 1734. Will dat. 26 May 1733, pr. [I.] 3 Aug. 1734. His widow, by whom he had ten children, *m.* St. Laurence BERFORD, and *d.* shortly afterwards, 3 Jan. 1735.

III. 1734. SIR EDWARD BELLEW, Baronet [I. 1688], of Barmeath aforesaid, 2d but 1st surv. s. and h.(a) by 1st wife, *b.* probably about 1695; *suc. to the Baronetcy*, 23 July 1734 He *m.* in or before 1728, Eleanor, 1st da. and coheir of Michael MOORE, of Drogheda, by Alice, da. of William ALCOCK, of Clogh (afterwards Witton), co. Wexford. He *d.* in Flanders, Oct. 1741. Will dat. 13 Aug. 1741, pr. [I.] 4 June 1742.

IV. 1741. SIR JOHN BELLEW, Baronet [I. 1688], of Barmeath aforesaid, 1st s. and h., *b.* 1728; *suc. to the Baronetcy*, Oct. 1741. He *d.* unm. 2 Nov. 1750, aged 22. Will dat. 14 Jan. 1748/9, pr. [I.] 9 Jan. 1750/1.

III. 1750. SIR PATRICK BELLEW, Baronet [I. 1688], of Barmeath aforesaid; br. and h.,(b) *b.* probably about 1735; *suc. to the Baronetcy*, 2 Nov. 1750. He *m.* (Lic. Dublin, 18 Aug. 1756) Mary, da. and coheir of Matthew HORE, of Shandon, co. Waterford, by Mabella, da. of (—) He *d.* 5 March 1795.

IV. 1795. SIR EDWARD BELLEW, Baronet [I. 1688], of Barmeath aforesaid, 1st s. and h., *b.* probably about 1760; *suc. to the Baronetcy*, 5 March 1795. He *m.* 13 Aug. 1786, in Great George street, Dublin (Lic. Prerog. [I.], 12), Mary Anne, da. and h. of Richard STRANGE, of Rockwell Castle, co. Kilkenny. He *d.* 15 March 1827. His widow *d.* 14 May 1837, in Conduit street, Midx., aged 76.

V. 1827. SIR PATRICK BELLEW, Baronet [I. 1688], of Barmeath aforesaid, 1st s. and h.; *b.* 29 Jan. 1798 in London; *suc. to the Baronetcy*, 15 March 1827; was Sheriff of co. Louth, 1831; M.P. for that county (two Parls.), 1834-37, and sometime Lord Lieutenant thereof; P.C. [I.], 17 Jan. 1838. He *m.*, 19 Jan. 1829, by spec. lic., at the Manor House, Bathampton, Somerset, Anna Fermina, da. of Don José Maria DE MENDOZA-Y-RIOS, of Seville. She was living when he was *cr.*, 10 July 1848, BARON BELLEW OF BARMEATH, co. Louth [I.] In that peerage this *Baronetcy* then *merged* and still (1904) so continues. See *Peerage*.

(a) His elder br., Patrick Bellew, *m.* firstly, July 1713, Mary, da. of Richard (Bourke), Earl of Clanricarde [I.]. She *d.* 12 Jan. following. He *m.* secondly, in or after 1714, Frances, Dow. Viscountess Dillon [I.], da. of Sir George Hamilton, Count Hamilton in France. He *d.* s.p. and v.p. 12 June 1720. Admon. 30 June 1720 to his widow.

(b) Michael Bellew, the 3d brother, is sometimes (erroneously) stated to have been great great grandfather of Michael Dillon Bellew, *cr. a Baronet*, 15 Aug. 1838, as of Mount Bellew, co. Galway. That family however was descended from Christopher Bellew, a *brother* of the 1st Baronet.

CREATIONS BY WILLIAM III AND MARY II.
AS ALSO BY WILLIAM III ALONE.

13 Feb. 1688/9(a) to 8 March 1701/2.

EDGWORTH:

alleged to have been *cr.* by William III;

assumed from about 1800 to 1818.

ESSEX WHYTE EDGWORTH, of Pallasnore, co. Longford, living at Bath, 18 Feb. 1809, *styled himself a Baronet*,(b) on the ground that his great [should, however, be "great-great"] grandfather, Sir John EDGWORTH, Capt. of the Guards in Ireland to Charles II, (who was *Knighted* at Whitehall 21 July 1672) had been *cr. a Baronet* [I.] by William III. This Sir John (whose will dat. 15 Feb. 1692/3, was pr. [I.] in 1727), he states to have *d.* soon after the battle (1 July 1690) of the Boyne. There is, however, no trace of his having ever been *cr. a Baronet*, and, even if he had been, his eldest son Francis EDGWORTH, of Edgworth's Town, co. Longford (who *d.* 1722), and his 2d son, Robert EDGWORTH, of Longwood, co. Meath (who *d.* 1730), both left male issue, who would be entitled to that dignity in preference to the issue of the 3d son, Henry EDGWORTH, of Lisard, co. Longford (who *d.* 1725), of whom the claimant, through a 2d son (the elder son Henry EDGWORTH, of Lisard, having also left male issue), was great grandson. Essex EDGWORTH, of Pallasmore, co. Longford, 2d son of the said Henry, *d.* Oct.

(a) During the interregnum, 12 Dec. 1688 to 12 Feb. 1688/9, no creations were made.

(b) Sir Arthur Vicars, Ulster, kindly supplies from "the Betham correspondence," now in his possession, the following letter, endorsed "Essex Edgeworth, Esq., soi disant Baronet":—

"Bath, 18th Febry., 1809.

"Sir,—I received your letter informing me you are about publishing a History of the Irish Baronets, and that you cannot find any traces of my family, which I suppose must be owing to some neglect in the Irish Registry or perhaps on account of the title lying so long dormant, since the death of Sir John Edgworth, my great grandfather, which happened soon after the Battle of the Boyne. He received that honor from King William, for his distinguished services, and at the same time was honored with the Command of the 18th Regiment or Royal Irish, as you may see by referring to the succession of Colonels in the Army List. The deeds and grants (*sic*) made to him by King William of the different lands in the Counties of Longford, Leitrim and Cavan give me a right to the title as well as the estates I now hold under said deeds, as already appeared on the documents being laid before Council previous to my being presented in December 1796, as may be seen in the *Gazette* and newspapers. When I go to Ireland shall be happy to give you any further information in my power, and have

"The honor to be, Sir, your hble. servant,

"E. W. Edgworth."

Among the same correspondence is a letter, dated 16 March 1809, from "C. L. T." (the Hon. Charles Ludlow Tonson, an accomplished Genealogist) in which the writer states "The assumption of the Baronetage in [the cases of] Crofton and Giffard is not so extraordinary as in [those of] Sheridan and Edgeworth, and it is possible that it might have been assumed under a mistaken impression of right, but in the latter instances there must have been wilful imposture in the assumer."

1764, being suc. by his son Francis Whyte EDGWORTH, who *m.* in May 1768, Susanna, da. of the Rev. Richard HANDCOCK, Dean of Achonry, and *d.* in or shortly before 1799 (never having styled himself a Baronet), leaving seven sons, of whom the said Essex Whyte EDGWORTH, who styled himself "Baronet" (as abovementioned) was the eldest. His will dat. 30 June 1807, was proved as that of a Baronet, 27 July 1810, but after his death nothing more is known of this assumption.

VESEY:

cr. 28 Sep. 1698;

afterwards, since 1750, BARONS KNAPTON [I.];

and, since 1776, VISCOUNTS DE VESCI OF ABBEY LEIX [I].

I. 1698. "THOMAS VESEY, Esq., of Abbey Leix, Queen's County, afterwards [1714-30] Bishop of Ossory," 1st s. and h. ap. of John VESEY, Archbishop of Tuam [1678 till his death 28 March 1716] by his 1st wife, Rebecca, da. of (—) WILSON, of Cork House, co. Dublin, was *b.* 1673 at Cork (of which city his father was then Dean); ed. at Eton; matric. at Oxford (Ch. Ch.), 13 July 1689, aged 16; B.A., 1693; Fellow of Oriel Coll., Oxford, 1695; M.A., 1697, and was v.p. *cr. a Baronet*, as above, at the age of 25, by patent dat. at Dublin 28 Sep. 1698, the Privy Seal being dat. at Kensington 13 July previous. He soon afterwards took orders, being ordained Deacon, 28 Oct. 1699, and Priest 24 June 1700; was Archdeacon of Tuam, 25 June 1700, and Rector of Moore and Drum in that diocese till 1703; Chaplain to the Duke of Ormonde, when Viceroy [I.]; was *cr.* LL.D. of Dublin, *honoris causâ*, 1712; Bishop of Killaloe, 12 June 1713, and Bishop of Ossory, 28 April 1714, till death in 1730. He *m.* Mary, only surv. da. and h. of Denny MUSCHAMP, of Horsley, Surrey, Muster Master Gen. [I.], by Elizabeth, da. of Michael BOYLE, Archbishop of Armagh. He *d.* 6 Aug. 1730, aged 57, and was *bur.* at St. Anne's, Dublin. His widow *d.* 26 Feb. 1746.

II. 1730. SIR JOHN DENNY VESEY, Baronet [I. 1698], of Abbey Leix aforesaid, only s. and h., *b.* there 1709; matric. at Oxford (Ch. Ch.), 3 July 1727, aged 18, being in that year M.P. [I.] for Newtown Ards till raised to the peerage [I.] in 1751; *suc. to the Baronetcy*, 6 Aug. 1730. He *m.* 15 May 1732 (Lic. Prerog. [I.]), Elizabeth, 1st da. of William BROWNLOW, of Lurgan, co. Armagh, by Elizabeth, da. of James (HAMILTON), 6th EARL OF ABERCORN [S.]. She was living when he was *cr.*, 10 April 1750, BARON KNAPTON, Queen's County [I.], his son and heir, the 2d Baron being *cr.*, 19 July 1776, VISCOUNT DE VESCI. OF ABBEY LEIX, Queen's County [I.]. In these peerages this *Baronetcy* then *merged*, and still (1904) so continues. See *Peerage*.

PRENDERGAST:

cr. 15 July 1699;(a)

ex. 23 Sep: 1760.

I. 1699. "THOMAS PRENDERGAST, Esq.," said to have been son of Thomas PRENDERGAST, of Croane, co. Limerick, by Eleanor, da. and coheir of David CONDON,(b) served in the Irish Army on behalf of William III,

(a) This creation is given in the *Liber Mun. Hib.*, and placed between the creation of Vesey and Meade, but no date is therein assigned to it.

(b) *N. & Q.*, 8th S., ix, 341. In this the Baronet's pedigree is set forth as given in the foot notes to the Aldine edition of Swift's *Works*, where the grantee's father

and, having disclosed (by turning informer against his associates) a plot against that King, was rewarded with the estate of Gort, co. Galway (forfeited by the O'Shagnessy family), and was *cr. a Baronet* [I.], as above, 15 July 1699, but "no King's letter [is] inrolled nor did ever any patent pass."(a) He was M.P. [I.] for the borough of Monaghan, 1703, till his death in 1709, and a Brigadier Gen. in the Army of Queen Anne. He *m.* (Lic. Prerog. [I.], 10 Aug. 1697) Penelope, sister of William, 1st EARL CADOGAN, only da. of Henry CADOGAN, of Liscartan, co. Meath, by Bridget, da. of Sir Hardress WALLER, of Castletown, co. Limerick, the Regicide. He *d.* 9 Feb. 1709; being slain at the battle of Malplaquet. Admon. 22 Nov. 1709. Will dat. 15 Sep. 1705, pr. [I.] 2 Dec. 1710. The will of his widow dat. 1 Feb. 1745/6, pr. Nov. 1710, 11 May 1711, and 13 July 1737, and pr. [I.] 18 Oct. 1746.

II. 1709, to 1760. SIR THOMAS PRENDERGAST, Baronet [I. 1699], *suc. to the Baronetcy* 9 Feb. 1709; was M.P. [I.] for Clonmel, 1727 till death in 1760, and M.P. [E.] for Chichester, 1733-34; Postmaster-Gen. [I.] and P.C., 17 Aug. 1733. He is said to have had a promise of being raised to the peerage [I.] as VISCOUNT CLONMEL. He *m.* in 1739, Anne, da. and h. of Sir Roger WILLIAMS, of Marle, co. Carnarvon. He *d.* s.p. 23 Sep. 1760, when the *Baronetcy* became *extinct.*(b) Will pr. [I.] 1760. His widow *m.* Terence PRENDERGAST, who accordingly took the additional name of WILLIAMS in accordance with an indenture dat. 27 Jan. 1761, and was *bur.* 3 Oct. 1776, at Llan-Rhos, co. Carnarvon. She *d.* at Nantgwilym, in Bodfari, co. Flint, and was *bur.* 21 Dec. 1770 at Rhos aforesaid.(c) Her will as "Dame Anne PRENDERGAST, otherwise WILLIAMS, of Pantglas, co. Carnarvon," pr. 8 Feb. 1771 at St. Asaph (and also [I.] 1771) by William ROBERTS, Lieut. R.N. (*d.* July 1794), the residuary legatee.

CREATIONS BY QUEEN ANNE

8 March 1701/2 to 1 May 1707,

being the date of the Union with Scotland.

MEADE:

cr. 29 May 1703;

afterwards, since 1766, VISCOUNTS CLANWILLIAM [I.];

and, since 1776, EARLS OF CLANWILLIAM [I.].

I. 1703. "SIR JOHN MEADE, Knt., of Ballintobera, co. Cork," 1st s. and h. of Lt.-Col. William MEADE, of Ballintubber, co. Cork, a freeman (29 May 1660) of that city, by Elizabeth, da. of Sir Robert TRAVERS,

---

is called "a poor thieving cottager under Mr. Moore, condemned to be hanged for stealing cows." It is there observed that the name is "plentiful amongst the lower orders" in co. Tipperary. The 1st Baronet in his will, dat. 15 Sep. 1705, leaves an annuity of £14 to his father, which seems to indicate that the family was in a somewhat humble position.

(a) See p. 231, note "a."

(b) The Gort estate devolved on his nephew John Smyth, s. of his sister Elizabeth, by her 2d husband, Charles Smyth. He in 1760 took the name of Prendergast, and was *cr.*, on 13 May 1810, BARON KILTARTON OF GORT, co. Galway [I.], and on 22 Jan. 1816 VISCOUNT GORT, co. Galway [I.].

(c) *N. & Q.*, 8th S., xi, 285.

was *b.* in Cork, 1642; ed. at Kinsale; admitted to Trin. Coll., Dublin, 28 May 1658, as a Sizar,(a) aged 16; admitted to the King's Inns, Dublin, 28 May 1668, as from Gray's Inn(b); was *Knighted* at Cork, Aug. 1678, by the Viceroy [I.]; King's Counsel, 11 April 1685; Attorney Gen. [I.] and subsequently Judge of the Palatinate of Tipperary; M.P. [I.] for Dublin Univ., 1689, in the Parl. of James II, and for co. Tipperary 1692-93, 1695-99 and 1703 till death in 1707; a Commissr. of Applotment for co. Cork, 10 April 1690, and was *cr. a Baronet* [I.], as above, by patent dat. at Dublin, 29 May 1703, the Privy Seal bearing date at St. James' 26 April previous. He *m.* firstly (Lic. Cork, 1671), Mary, da. and h. of James COPPINGER. She *d.* s.p. He *m.* secondly, 14 June 1680, Elizabeth, da. and coheir of Major Daniel REDMAN, of Ballylinch, co. Kilkenny, by Abigail, da. of Roger OTWAY, of Bickside Hall, Westmorland. She *d.* s.p.m. He *m.* thirdly, 14 June 1688, Elizabeth, da. of Pierce (BUTLER), 2d VISCOUNT IKERRIN [I.], by Eleanor, da. of John BRYAN, of Bawnmore, co. Kilkenny. He *d.* 12 Jan. 1706/7, aged 64. Will dat. 12 Feb. 1704/5, pr. [I.] 9 Sep. 1707. His widow *d.* in Abbey Street, Dublin, Dec. 1757, aged 88.

II. 1707. SIR PIERCE MEADE, Baronet [I. 1703], of Ballintubber aforesaid, 3d but 1st surv. s. and h.(c) by 3d wife, *b.* there 1693; *suc. to the Baronetcy*, 12 Jan. 1706/7, and was as "*Eques Auratus*" admitted to Trin. Coll., Dublin, 13 April 1707, aged 14; B.A., 1711. He *d.* unm. and under age and was *bur.* 18 July 1711, in Christ Church, Dublin. Funeral entry. Admon. [I.] 4 May 1716 to his mother.

III. 1711. SIR RICHARD MEADE, Baronet [I. 1703], of Ballintubber aforesaid, br. and h., *b.* 1697; *suc. to the Baronetcy* in July 1711, and was as "*Eques Auratus*" admitted to Trin. Coll., Dublin, 5 Oct. 1712, aged 15; B.A., 1715; was M.P. [I.] for Kinsale, 1725 till death in 1744. He *m.* in 1736, Catherine, da. of Henry PRITTIE, of Dunalley, co Tipperary, by Elizabeth, da. and h. of Col. James HARRISON, of Cloghjordan, in that county. He *d.* 26 May 1744. Will dat. 26 May, pr. [I.] 3 July 1744. His widow *m.*, as his 2d wife, 6 Oct. 1748, Sir Henry CAVENDISH, 1st Baronet [1758], of Doveridge, co. Derby, who *d.* 31 May 1776, and *d.* 21 March 1779.

IV. 1744. SIR JOHN MEADE, Baronet [I. 1703], of Ballintubber aforesaid, only s. and h., *b.* 21 April 1744, and *suc. to the Baronetcy*, when but a month old, 26 May following; ed. at Trin. Coll., Dublin; B.A., 1764; was M.P. [I.] for Banagher 1764 till raised to the peerage in 1766. He *m.* 29 Aug. 1765 (Lic. Prerog. [I.] 10 July), Theodosia, da. and h. of Robert Hawkins MAGILL, of Gill Hall, co. Down, by his 2d wife, Anne, da. of John (BLIGH), 1st EARL OF DARNLEY [I.]. She was living when he was *cr.* 17 Nov. 1766, BARON GILFORD, of the Manor of Gilford, co. Down, and VISCOUNT CLANWILLIAM, of co. Tipperary [I.], being subsequently *cr.* 20 July 1776, EARL OF CLANWILLIAM [I.]. In these peerages this *Baronetcy* then *merged*, and still [1904] so continues. See *Peerage*.

(a) The Civil War had probably reduced the means of the family, but the entry almost certainly relates to him.

(b) There does not however appear to be any such admission at that Inn.

(c) Of his elder brothers, (1) William *d.* aged 13, and (2) James *d.* young.

TAYLOR:

cr. 12 June 1704;

afterwards, since 1760, BARONS HEADFORT [I.];

since 1762, VISCOUNTS HEADFORT [I.];

since 1766, EARLS OF BECTIVE [I.],

and, since 1800, MARQUESSES OF HEADFORT [I.].

I. 1704. "THOMAS TAYLOR, Esq., of Kells, co. Meath," only s. and h. of Thomas TAYLOR, of Kells aforesaid, Treasurer of War [I.] (who emigrated to Ireland in 1652, and *d.* 1 Aug. 1682, aged 51), by Anne, da. of William AXTELL, of Berkhamstead, Berks, was *b.* in Dublin 20 July 1662; ed. at Kilkenny; entered Trin. Coll., Dublin, as Fellow Comm., 15 Nov. 1677, aged 15; was M.P. [I.] for Kells, 1692-93, 1695-99, 1713-14, and 1727 till death 1736; Sheriff of co. Meath, 1701, and was *cr. a Baronet* [I.], as above, by patent dat. at Dublin 12 June 1704, the Privy Seal being dated at St. James' 15 May previous. He was P.C. [I.], 1 June 1726. He *m.* 20 June 1682, Anne, da. of Sir Robert COTTON, 1st Baronet [1677] of Combermere, co. Chester, by Hester, da. of Sir Thomas SALUSBURY, 2d Baronet [1619]. She *d.* 22 Aug. 1710. He *d.* 8 Aug. 1736, aged 74. Will dat. 10 July, pr. [I.] 19 Aug. 1736.

II. 1736. SIR THOMAS TAYLOR, Baronet [I. 1734], of Kells aforesaid, 1st s. and h., *b.* probably about 1690; was M.P. [I.] for Kells, 1713 till death 1757; Sheriff of co. Meath, 1714; *suc. to the Baronetcy*, 8 Aug. 1736; was P.C. [I.], 15 Nov. 1753. He *m.* (settl. 14, and Lic. Prerog. [I.] 15 Nov. 1714) Sarah, da. of John GRAHAM, of Platten, co. Meath, by Charity, da. of (—) NEWTON, of Drogheda. He *d.* Oct. 1757. Will dat 11 June, pr. [I.] 5 Nov. 1757.

III. 1757. SIR THOMAS TAYLOR, Baronet [I. 1704], of Kells aforesaid, 2d but only surv. s. and h., *b.* 20 Oct. 1724; was M.P. [I.] for Kells, 1747 till raised to the Peerage [I.] in 1760; Sheriff of co. Meath, 1756; *suc. to the Baronetcy* in Oct. 1757. He *m.* 4 July 1754 (Lic. Prerog. [I.] 11 June) Jane, 1st da. of the Rt. Hon. Hercules Langford ROWLEY, by Elizabeth, *suo jure* VISCOUNTESS LANGFORD [I.]. She was living when he was *cr.*, 6 Sep. 1760, BARON HEADFORT, co. Meath [I.], and subsequently, 12 April 1762, VISCOUNT HEADFORT [I.], being finally *cr.*, 24 Oct. 1766, EARL OF BECTIVE, of Bective Castle, co. Meath [I.]; the 2d Earl and 4th Baronet being *cr.* 29 Dec. 1800, MARQUESS OF HEADFORT [I.]. In these peerages this *Baronetcy* then *merged* and still [1904] so continues. See *Peerage*.

LEVINGE:

cr. 26 Oct. 1704.

I. 1704. "SIR RICHARD LEVINGE, Knight, of Dublin, afterwards [1720-24] Ch. Justice of the Common Pleas" [I.] being also of Mullalea (*afterwards* High Park), co. Westmeath, yr. s. of Richard LEVINGE, of Parwich, co. Derby, Barrister at Law and Recorder of Chester (1662-67), by Anne, da. of George PARKER, of Park Hill, co. Stafford, was *b.* 2 May 1656 at Leek, co. Stafford; admitted to Inner Temple, 9 Sep. 1671; Barrister, Nov. 1678; Recorder of Chester, 1686-87, and afterwards of Derby; M.P. [E.] for Chester, 1690-95, and for Derby, 1710-11; M.P. [I.] for Blessington, 1692-93; for Longford, 1698-99 and 1703-13; for Kilkenny city, 1713-14. He was Solicitor-Gen. [I.] for the 1st time, 29 Dec. 1690, resigning May 1695; was admitted to King's Inns, Dublin, 6 May 1691; *Knighted*, 23 Sep. 1692; Speaker of the House of Commons [I.], 26 Oct. 1692;

Solicitor-Gen. [I.] for the 2d time, 15 April 1704 till removed in Sep. 1709, and was *cr. a Baronet* [I.], as above, by patent dated at Dublin 26 Oct. 1704, the Privy Seal being dated at Windsor 14 Aug. previous; Attorney-Gen. [I.], 5 July 1711, till removed Nov. 1714; Ch. Justice of the Common Pleas [I.], 13 Oct. 1720 till death in 1724; P.C. [I.] 6 May 1721. He *m.* firstly, about 1690, Mary, da. and coheir of Gawen CORBYN, of London, Linendraper, and by her had seven children. The will of Dame Mary Levinge was pr. 1720. He *m.* secondly, Mary, da. of Robert JOHNSON, 3d Baron of the Exchequer [I. 1703-13], by Margaret (mar. lic. 17 Dec. 1681), da. of Sir Richard DIXON, of Calverstown, co. Kildare. He *d.* 13 July 1724, aged 68. Will dat. 9 July 1723, pr. [I.] 22 July 1724. His widow *m.* (Lic. Dublin 9 Nov. 1732), CHARLES ANNESLEY, Capt. Battleaxe Guards, who *d.* s.p. 23 Feb. 1746. She *d.* 2 Dec. 1756. Admon. [I.] 18 Jan. 1757.

II. 1724. SIR RICHARD LEVINGE, Baronet [I. 1704], of Mullalea, othewise High Park aforesaid, 1st s. and h. by 1st wife, *b.* about 1690; was v.p. M.P. [I.] for co. Westmeath, 1723-27, and for Blessington, 1727 till death in 1748; *suc. to the Baronetcy*, 13 July 1724. He *m.* (Lic. Prerog. [I.] 9 April 1719) Isabella, da. of Sir Arthur RAWDON, 2d Baronet [1665], of Moira, by Helen, da. and h. of Sir James GRAHAM. She *d.* 2 Nov. 1731. He *d.* s.p., 27 Feb. 1747/8. Will dat. 15 Jan. 1744/5, pr. [I.] 9 March 1747/8.

III. 1748. SIR CHARLES LEVINGE, Baronet [I. 1704], of High Park aforesaid, br. and h., *b.* 1693; *suc. to the Baronetcy*, 27 Feb. 1747/8. He *m.* in 1722, Anne, da. and coheir of Major Samuel GREENE, of Killaghy Castle, co. Tipperary, sometime M.P. [I.] for Cashel. He *d.* 29 May 1762, aged about 70. Will dat. 24 Feb. 1762, pr. [I.] 6 Aug. 1766.

IV. 1762. SIR RICHARD LEVINGE, Baronet [I. 1704], of High Park aforesaid, only s. and h., *b.* 1723 or 1724; *suc. to the Baronetcy*, 29 May 1762; Sheriff of co. Westmeath, 1764. He *m.* firstly, 17 April 1744, his cousin, Dorothea, da. of William KENNEDY, of Mullow, co. Longford, by Grace, da. of Sir Richard LEVINGE, 1st Baronet [I. 1704] abovenamed. He *m.* secondly, probably about 1760, Mary, illegit. da. of Sir Henry TUITE, 6th Baronet [I. 1622]. He *d.* 30 Oct. 1786, aged about 63. Will dat. 23 April 1782, pr. [I.] 1786.

V. 1786. SIR CHARLES LEVINGE, Baronet [I. 1704], of High Park aforesaid, 1st s. and h. by 1st wife, *b.* 17 April 1751; *suc. to the Baronetcy*, 30 Oct. 1786; was Sheriff of co. Westmeath, 1791. He *m.* 26 June 1779 (Lic. Prerog. [I.] 19), Elizabeth Frances, da. of Nicholas REYNELL, of Reynella, co. Westmeath, by Frances, da. of (—) BRUSH. He *d.* 19 Jan. 1796, aged 44. Admon. [I.] 14 March 1796. His widow *d.* 19 May 1828.

VI. 1796. SIR RICHARD LEVINGE, Baronet [I. 1704], of High Park aforesaid, 1st s. and h., *b.* 29 Oct. 1785; *suc. to the Baronetcy*, 19 Jan. 1796; admitted to Rugby School, 31 July 1797, aged 12; Sheriff of co. Westmeath, 1808. He *m.* 3 Dec. 1810 (Lic. Prerog. [I.] 19 Oct.), Elizabeth Anne, 1st sister and coheir of George Augustus Henry Anne (PARKYNS), 2d BARON RANCLIFFE [I.], da. of Thomas Boothby (PARKYNS), 1st BARON RANCLIFFE [I.], by Elizabeth Anne, da. of Sir William JAMES, 1st Baronet [1778], of Eltham. He *d.* 12 Sep. 1848, aged 62. Will pr. March 1849. His widow *d.* 28 Oct. 1853.

VII. 1848. SIR RICHARD GEORGE AUGUSTUS LEVINGE, Baronet [I. 1704], of High Park aforesaid, and of Knockdrin Castle, co. Westmeath, 1st s. and h., *b.* 1 Nov. 1811 in Hertford street, Mayfair; served in the army fourteen years; sometime Capt. 5th Dragoons; *suc. to the Baronetcy*, 12 Sep. 1848; Sheriff of co. Westmeath, 1851; M.P. for that county, 1857-65; Lieut.-Col. of the Westmeath Militia. He *m.* firstly, 20 March 1849, Caroline Jane, widow of Lieut.-Col. J. HANCOX (7th Dragoon Guards), 1st da. of Col.

Lancelot ROLLESTON, of Watnall Hall, Notts. She *d.* 5 May 1848. He *m.* secondly, 10 Feb. 1870, Margaret Charlotte, widow of David JONES, of Pantglas, co. Carmarthen, da. of Sir George CAMPBELL, of Edenwood, co Fife, by Margaret, da. of Andrew CHRISTIE, of Ferrybank. She *d.* 5 Nov. 1871, in Lowndes square, in her 47th year. He *d.* s.p. 28 Sep. 1884, aged 72, at Brussels.(a) Will pr. over £10,000.

VIII. 1884. SIR VERE HENRY LEVINGE, Baronet [I. 1704], of Knockdrin Castle aforesaid, next surv. br. and h., *b.* 28 Nov. 1819; ed. at Haileybury College; was in the Madras Civil Service, 1857-67; *suc. to the Baronetcy,* 28 Sep. 1884. He *d.* unm. 22 March 1885, aged 65, at Madras. Will dat. 1 Feb. and pr. 11 Nov. 1885, by Harry Corbyn LEVINGE, br. and universal legatee.

IX. 1885. SIR WILLIAM HENRY LEVINGE, Baronet [I. 1704], of Knockdrin Castle aforesaid, and formerly of Lurgo, co. Tipperary, nephew and h., being 1st s. and h. of William James LEVINGE, of Dublin, by Anne Maria, da. of John Michael Henry, BARON DE ROBECK in the Kingdom of Sweden, which William James (who *d.* 22 Oct. 1867, aged 46), was br. to the late and 7th s. of the 6th Baronet. He was *b.* 21 May 1849, at Merrion square, Dublin; matric. at Oxford (Oriel Coll.), 19 Oct. 1867, aged 18; B.A. and 3d Class Law and Modern History, 1871; M.A., 1874; *suc. to the Baronetcy,* 22 March 1885. He *m.* 2 Nov. 1876, Emily Judith, 2d da. of Sir Richard SUTTON, 4th Baronet [1772] of Benham Park, Berks, by his 2d wife Harriet Anne, da. of William Fitzwilliam BURTON, of Burton Hall, co. Carlow. He *d.* 17 April 1900, at Knockdrin Castle aforesaid, in his 51st year. Will pr. at £1,023. His widow living 1904.

X. 1900. SIR RICHARD WILLIAM LEVINGE, Baronet [I. 1704], of Knockdrin Castle aforesaid, 1st s. and h., *b.* 12 July 1878; *suc. to the Baronetcy,* 17 April 1900; sometime Lieut. 8th Hussars, serving in the Transvaal War.

MAUDE:

cr. 9 May 1705;

sometime, 1776-77, BARON DE MONTALT [I.];

afterwards, since 1785, BARONS DE MONTALT [I.];

and, since 1791, VISCOUNTS HAWARDEN [I.];

sometime, 1886-19[—], EARL DE MONTALT.

I. 1705. "ROBERT MAUDE, of Dundrum, co. Tipperary," s. of Anthony MAUDE, of Dundrum aforesaid, by his 2d wife, Alice, 1st da. of Sir Standish HARTSTONGE, 1st Baronet [1681], of Bruff, co. Limerick, was *b.* at Limerick about 1676; admitted to Trin. Coll., Dublin, as Fellow Commoner, 10 July 1693; was M.P. for Gowran, 1703-13; for St. Canice (two Parls.), 1713-27, and for Bangor, 1727-30, being *cr. a Baronet* [I.], as above, by patent dated at Dublin, 9 May 1705, the Privy Seal being dat. at St. James', 8 Feb. previous. He *m.*, Jan. 1718, Elizabeth or Eleanor, sister and coheir of Francis CORNWALLIS, da. of Thomas CORNWALLIS, of Acton, Midx., and of Albemarlais, co. Carmarthen, by Emma, da. of Sir Job CHARLTON, 1st Baronet [1686]. He *d.* of the gout, 4 Aug. 1750, aged about 74. M.I. at St. Anne's, Dublin. Will dat. 23 June 1706 (?), pr. [I.] 29 Aug. 1750.

(a) He was the author of *Historical Records of the 43rd Regiment,* etc.

II. 1750. SIR THOMAS MAUDE, Baronet [I. 1705], of Dundrum aforesaid, 1st s. and h., *b.* probably about 1725; *suc. to the Baronetcy,* 4 Aug. 1750; was M.P. [I.] for co. Tipperary (two Parls.), 1761-76; Sheriff of that county, 1765; P.C. [I.], 9 June 1768; Governor of co. Tipperary, 1770. He was *cr.*, 18 July 1776, BARON DE MONTALT OF HAWARDEN, co. Tipperary [I.], but, within a year, *d.* unm., 17 May, 1777, when that *peerage* became *extinct.* Will dat. 3 June 1773, pr. [I.] 14 April 1778.

III. 1777. SIR CORNWALLIS MAUDE, Baronet [I. 1705], yst. br. and h., *bap.* 19 Sep. 1729; *suc. to the Baronetcy,* 17 May 1777; was M.P. [I.] for the borough of Roscommon, 1783 till raised to the peerage [I.] in 1785. He *m.* firstly, 8 Aug. 1756, at St. Geo. Han. sq., his cousin, Lætitia, da. of Thomas VERNON, of Hanbury Hall, co. Worcester, by Jane, da. of Thomas CORNWALLIS. She *d.* s.p.m., 1757. He *m.* secondly, 10 June 1766, Mary, da. of Philip ALLEN, niece of Ralph ALLEN, of Prior Park, Bath. She *d.* 1775. He *m.* thirdly (Lic. Prerog. [I.], 18 June 1778(a)), Anne Isabella, sister of Charles Stanley, 1st VISCOUNT MONCK [I.], da. of Thomas MONCK, of Dublin, Barrister, by Judith, da. of Robert MASON. She was living when he was *cr.* 29 June 1785, BARON DE MONTALT OF HAWARDEN, co. Tipperary [I.], being subsequently *cr.*, 10 June 1791, VISCOUNT HAWARDEN, of co. Tipperary [I.]. In these peerages this *Baronetcy* then merged, and still (1904) so continues, the 5th Viscount being *cr.*, 9 Sep. 1886, EARL DE MONTALT, a dignity which expires at his death. See *Peerage.*

COX:

cr. 21 Nov. 1706;

ex., apparently, 17 Oct. 1873;

but assumed (by two parties), since 1873.

I. 1706. "SIR RICHARD COX, of Dunmanway, co. Cork, Lord Chancellor" [I. 1703-07], only s. and h. of Richard Cox,(b) Capt. in Major General Jephson's Dragoons (who fought firstly for and secondly against Charles I, and who was murdered by a brother officer in July 1652), by Catherine, relict of Capt. Thomas BATTEN, da. of Walter BIRD, *or* BOORDE, sometime Recorder of Clonakilty, was *b.* at Bandon Bridge, co. Cork, 25 March 1650; ed. at Clonakilty; admitted to Gray's Inn, 17 Aug. 1671; Barrister, 9 Aug. 1673, having practised previously as an Attorney; admitted to King's Inns, Dublin, 9 Nov. 1674; Recorder of Kinsale, and afterwards of Waterford; second Justice of the Common Pleas [I.], 2 Sep. 1690; Chief Justice thereof, and P.C. [I.] 16 May 1701, being *Knighted* at Dublin Castle, 5 Nov. 1692; Lord High Chancellor [I.] 6 Aug. 1703, till removed, June 1707, being *cr. a Baronet* [I.] by patent dat. at Dublin, 21 Nov. 1706, the Privy Seal bearing date at Kensington, 17 Oct. previous; was Chief Justice of the Queen's Bench [I.] 5 July 1711, till removed Sep. 1714. He was three times one of the Lord's Justices [Regents] of Ireland during the absence of the Viceroy. He *m.* 26 Feb. 1673, Mary, da. of John BOURNE, of Carbery, co. Cork. She *d.* 1 June 1715, and was *bur.* at Dunmanway, aged 56. M.I. He *d.* there 3 May 1733, aged 83.(c) Will dat. 21 April, pr. [I.] 26 May 1733, by his son Michael Cox.

(a) The date of this marriage is generally given as 3 June 1777.

(b) This Richard was son of Michael Cox, who emigrated from Bishop's Canning, Wilts, to co. Cork, and *d.* between 1610 and 1625.

(c) He was author of a History of Ireland from its Conquest by the English to 1653. His own *Autobiography,* ed. by Richard Caulfeild, B.A., was published by J. R. Smith, London, 1860, 8vo, pp. 22. See also an account of him in O'Flanagan's "Lives of the Lord Chancellors of Ireland."

II. 1733. SIR RICHARD COX, Baronet [I. 1706], of Dunmanway aforesaid, grandson and h., being s. and h. of Richard Cox, M.P. [I.] for Tallaght 1705 and for Clonakilty 1717-25, by his 1st wife, Susanna FRENCH (who *d.* 1716), which Richard was 1st s. and h. ap. of the late Baronet, but *d.* v.p. 15 April 1725, aged 47. He was *b.* 23 Nov. 1702; matric. at Oxford (St. John's Coll.), 4 May 1720, aged 17; was Sheriff of co. Cork, 1727, and M.P. [I.] for Clonakilty, 1727 till death in 1766; *suc. to the Baronetcy,* 3 May 1733; was Collector of Customs of the port of Cork, and was Sheriff of that city 1744. He *m.* 13 Sep. 1725, Catharine, sister of George, 1st BARON CARBERY [I.], da. of the Rt. Hon. George EVANS, of Bulgaden hall, co. Limerick, by Mary, da. of John EYRE, of Eyre court, co. Galway. He *d.* Feb. 1766. Will dat. 1763, pr. [I.] 1766. His widow *d.* Jan. 1768.

III. 1766. SIR MICHAEL COX, Baronet [I. 1706], of Dunmanway aforesaid, 2d but 1st surv. s. and h.,(a) *b.* probably about 1730; ed. at Trin. Coll., Dublin; B.A., 1757; M.A., 1760; took Holy Orders, 21 Sep. 1760; *suc. to the Baronetcy,* Feb. 1766; Archdeacon of Cashel, 3 Aug. 1767; Preb. of Doon (dio. of Emly), 18 Sep. 1767; Vicar of Drinagh and Fanlobbus, co. Cork, 21 Dec. 1768, holding all three preferments till his death in 1772. He *m.* 7 Jan. 1762 (Lic. 6), Elizabeth, widow of John ARTHUR, of Seafield, co. Dublin, only da. of Hugh (MASSY), 1st BARON MASSY [I.], by his 1st wife, Mary, da. and h. of James DAWSON. He *d.* s.p. 18 July 1772. Will dat. 7 Oct. 1769, pr. [I.] 2 Feb. 1773. His widow *d.* 12 March 1825, aged 98. M.I. at St. Anne's, Dublin.

IV. 1772. SIR RICHARD EYRE COX, Baronet [I. 1706], of Dunmanway aforesaid, 2d but only surv. s. and h., *b.* probably about 1765; *suc. to the Baronetcy,* 18 July 1772; was Lieut. 68th Foot. He *m.* 2 Feb. 1780, Maria, sister of William, the 2d, and of James, the 3d MARQUESS OF THOMOND [I.], 1st da. of Edward O'BRIEN, by Mary, da. of (—) CARRICK. He *d.* s.p. 6 Sep. 1783, being accidentally drowned near Dunmanway.(b) Admon. [I.] 17 Sep. 1783. His widow *m.* in Jan. 1786, Rt. Hon. William SAURIN, sometime Attorney-Gen. [I.]. She *d.* 28 Jan. 1840.

V. 1783. SIR RICHARD COX, Baronet [I. 1706], cousin and h. male, being 1st s. and h. of Michael COX, Lieut. Col. in the Guards, by Anna Maria (*m.* Jan. 1765), da. of Daniel SHEA, of the West Indies, planter, which Michael, who *d.* 4 Feb. 1782, was 2d s.(c) of John COX, of Bandon, co. Cork (*b.* 14 April 1705), only br. of the 2d Baronet. He was *b.* 6 June 1769; *suc. to the Baronetcy* (but not to the estate) 6 Sep. 1783. He *d.* unm. in Sep. 1786, aged 17, being lost at sea in the Severn packet on his passage home from Bengal.

VI. 1786. SIR JOHN COX, Baronet [I. 1706], br. and h.; *b.* 4 April 1771; *suc. to the Baronetcy;* an officer in the Life Guards. He *d.* s.p. 23 Dec. 1832, aged 61. Admon. June 1833.

VII. 1832. SIR GEORGE MATTHIAS COX, Baronet [I. 1706], only surv. br. and h., *b.* 24 Feb. 1777; an officer in the Bombay Army, being sometime in command of the 14th Light Infantry, and becoming, eventually, Major General; *suc. to the Baronetcy,* 23 Dec. 1832. He *d.* unm. 28 Jan. or June 1838, aged 61. Will pr. July 1838.

(a) His elder br., Richard Cox, *m.* 28 Oct. 1758, Eliza Turner, da. of John Becher, of Aghadown, co. Cork, but *d.* v.p. and s.p.

(b) On his death the Dunmanway estate devolved on his 1st cousin, Henry Hamilton, s. of Joshua Hamilton (grandson of the 1st Viscount Boyne [I.]), by Mary, da. of Sir Richard Cox, the 2d Baronet, according to the will of that Baronet in case of the failure of his issue male. He took the name of Cox after that of Hamilton, in 1784, and *d.* 1821, leaving issue.

(c) Richard Cox, the 1st son, Capt. 46th Foot, *d.* unm. at Havannah. John Cox, 3d and yst. son, Major in the East India Service, *d.* s.p.

VIII. 1838. SIR RICHARD COX, Baronet [I. 1706], of Castletown, co. Kilkenny, cousin and h. male, being s. and h. of Michael Cox, of Castletown aforesaid, by Mary, da. of Henry Sadleir (PRITTIE), 1st BARON DUNALLEY [I.], which Michael (who was *b.* 14 April 1768, and *d.* 1836), was 1st s. and h. of Richard Cox, of Castletown aforesaid (*b.* 15 Jan. 1745, and *d.* July 1790), only s. (by 2d wife) of Michael Cox, D.D., Archbishop of Cashel, 1754-79 (*b.* 2 Nov. 1691, and *d.* 28 May 1779), 6th s. of the 1st Baronet. He was Sheriff of co. Kilkenny, 1829; and *suc. to the Baronetcy,* 28 Jan., or June 1838. He *d.* s.p. 7 May 1846.(a)

IX. 1846. SIR FRANCIS COX, Baronet [I. 1706], uncle and h. male, *b.* 23 July 1769; *suc. to the Baronetcy,* 7 May 1846. He *m.* Aug. 1803, Anna Maria, 2d da. of Sir John FERNS. He *d.* s.p., 6 March 1856, aged 86.

X. 1856. SIR RALPH HAWTREY COX, Baronet [I. 1706], of Borrisokane, co. Tipperary, nephew and h. male, being 1st s. and h. of the Rev. Richard Cox, Rector of Cahirconlish, co. Limerick, by Sarah, da. of the Rev. Ralph HAWTREY, which Richard (*b.* 20 Sep. 1771, and *d.* 1834), was next yr. br. of the late Baronet. He was *b.* at Cahirconlish, 1808, and ed. at Sion College, Bath; *suc. to the Baronetcy,* 6 March 1856. He *m.* 1857, Elizabeth, widow of Henry HONE. He *d.* s.p. 12 April 1872, at Kingstown, near Dublin. His widow living 1875.

XI. 1872, April. SIR MICHAEL (sometimes called 'MICHAEL FRANCIS HAWTREY") COX, Baronet, [I. 1706], next br. and h., *b.* 1810, who, owing to a fall from his horse in his youth, was out of his mind; *suc. to the Baronetcy,* 12 April 1872, and *d.* a few weeks later, 15 June 1872, at Kilkenny.

XII. 1872, June, to 1873. SIR FRANCIS HAWTREY COX, Baronet [I. 1706], br. and h., *b.* about 1816; *suc. to the Baronetcy,* 15 June 1872,(b) He *m.* 6 March 1853, Emma Catherine, yst da. of Duncan MCKELLAR. He *d.* s.p., 17 Oct. 1873, at Brecart Lodge, co. Antrim, aged 57, when the *Baronetcy* became *extinct.*(c) His widow *m.*, 26 Feb. 1876, at Trinity Church, Clapham, Surrey, Rev. Hugh Martin SHORT, of West Heslerton, co. York, sometime (1858-81) Vicar of Thornthwaite, Cumberland, who *d.* at Whitby, 9 June 1898. She was living 1904.

The *Baronetcy* was *assumed* by two parties, as below.

XIII. 1873. SIR EDMUND COX, Baronet [I. 1706],(d) of Endiang Kingsey, in the Dominion of Canada, retired Col. in the Canadian service, and formerly Capt. in the 87th (Royal Irish Fusiliers) Regt. (having served in the first Burmese War), *assumed the Baronetcy* 17 Aug. 1876, stating that it had devolved on him, on the death, without issue, in 1873, of "Sir William Saurin Cox,"(c) as "being in direct descent

(a) The estate of Castletown devolved on his nephew, H. J. R. Villiers-Stuart, s. and h. of his sister Catherine (*m.* 1833), by Lieut. Col. William Villiers-Stuart (*d.* 1873), 2d s. of Lord Henry Stuart, 5th s. of the 1st Marquess of Bute.

(b) Of these twelve Baronets, only two (viz., the 2d Baronet in 1766, and the 3d Baronet in 1772) were succeeded by a son, and in no case was any one of them succeeded by the eldest son.

(c) The 12th Baronet had a br. [but *query* if not older than himself] William Saurin Cox, who *m.* Mary, da. of Major Miller, of co. Derry, and *d.* s.p.s., apparently in the lifetime of the eldest br., the 10th Baronet. He, however, is sometimes said to have *suc. to the Baronetcy* on the death of the said 12th Baronet, 17 Oct. 1873, and to have *d.* s.p within three months of such succession.

(d) According to the assumption in 1873 of that dignity.

from William, the youngest son of Sir Richard Cox, who was *cr. a Baronet* [I.] in 1706.(a) He was 2d s.(b) of William Nicholas Cox, Col. R.A., by Jane, da. of James WALKER, of Quebec, which William (who *d.* 1811, aged 46, at the Cape of Good Hope) was 1st s. of Nicholas Cox, Major in the army (*bur.* 11 Jan 1794 at Quebec), who was only s. of William Cox (by Frances, da. of Richard WINSLOW), which William is alleged to have been yst. s. of the grantee.(c) He, who was *b.* 1797, was (besides his military appointments abovenamed) sometime Registrar of co. Drummond, in Canada. He *m.* in 1832, his cousin, Anne Eleanor Mary, da. of Col. Edmund FAUNCE, by Brydges, da. of Major Nicholas Cox, abovenamed. He *d.* s.p.m.s., 26 Aug. 1877, at Endiang Kingsey aforesaid, aged 80.

XIV. 1877. SIR GEORGE WILLIAM COX, Baronet [I. 1706].(d) nephew and h. male, being 1st s. and h. of George Hamilton Cox, Capt. in the Bengal Native Infantry, by Eliza Kearton, da. of John HORNE, of St. Vincent, a West Indian planter, which George (*b.* in Newfoundland 1800, and *d.* in India 1841), was next br. to the late Baronet.(d) He was *b.* at Benares, East India, in 1827; ed. at Rugby; matric at Oxford (Trin. Coll.), 19 May 1845, aged 18; S.C.L. and 2d Class Classics, 1849; B.A. and M.A., 1859; in Holy Orders; sometime (1860-61) one of the Masters at Cheltenham College; *suc. to the Baronetcy*,(d) 26 Aug. 1877; Rector of Scrayingham, co. York, 1881-97, being presented thereto, "under the title of Baronet," by Queen Victoria "under the great seal in the Court of Chancery."(e) He *m.* 1850, Emily Maria, da. of Lt.-Col. William STIRLING, of the 17th Bombay infantry. She *d.* 1898. He *d.* 9 Feb. 1902, aged 75, at Ivy House, Walmer, the residence of Dr. Sidney Hulke.(f)

(a) The following is a copy of an advertisement inserted in *The Times* for 27 Sep. 1876 (page 1, column 2) :—"I, Edmund Cox, of Endiang, Kingsey, in the Dominion of Canada, retired Colonel in the Canadian Militia and formerly Captain in the 87th Regiment (Royal Irish Fusileers), hereby give notice that being in direct descent from William, the youngest son of Sir Richard Cox, Lord Chancellor of Ireland, who was created a Baronet in 1706, I have ASSUMED the TITLE which devolved upon me by the death, without issue, of Sir William Saurin Cox in the year 1873 and that I shall henceforth be known as SIR EDMUND COX, BART. [Signed] Ed. Cox. August 17th, 1876."

(b) His elder br., William Cox, *d.* unm., being drowned in the St. Laurence river 1816, aged 21.

(c) Sir Richard Cox in his autobiography (see p. 237, note "c") writes, under Aug. 1706, "I paid £40 to bind William Cox apprentice to Mr. Minchen, Chyrurgeon." There is, however, nothing to shew that this William was his child, indeed the natural inference would be that he was not. He had a son William, *b.* 1686, who *d.* Aug. 1693, and it is conjectured that another William (*i.e.* the apprentice) was *b.* subsequently in that same year, but as a son Robert was *b.* 30 Dec. 1692, the birth could hardly have been till after Oct. 1693, making the child but twelve at the date of the apprenticeship. Moreover, the William Cox, who was ancestor to "Sir Edmund," *m.* Frances Winslow (whose grandmother was a Downing), and is described in a pedigree of the Downing family, as "William Cox, Rector," at the time of his marriage, whereas William, the apprentice, would presumably have become a surgeon, and anyhow there is no identity between them.

(d) See p. 239, note "d."

(e) "Copy of Declaration of Sir George W. Cox, Baronet," made at York, 9 Oct. 1888 (pp. 14, 4to.), printed circa 1889.

(f) He was author of various educational works, as also of the "Life of Bishop Colenso of Natal," and is said to have been himself *nominated*, in 1886, Bishop of Natal, such election, however, not being confirmed by the Crown.

XV. 1902. SIR EDMUND CHARLES COX, Baronet [I. 1706],(a) 2d but 1st surv. s. and h., *b.* 1856; ed. at Marlborough School and at Trin. Coll., Cambridge; Assistant Inspector General of Police at Bombay; *suc. to the Baronetcy*,(a) 9 Feb. 1902. He *m.* in 1891, Ella Marion, da. of George William BORRADAILE, C.B., Col. in the Royal Artillery, by (—), da. of Surgeon Gen. Charles Doyle STRAKER.

The second of the two parties who *assumed the Baronetcy* in 1873, was as under.

XIII. bis, 1873. SIR JOHN HAMILTON COX, Baronet [I. 1706].(a) Major-Gen. in the Gordon Highlanders and C.B. (having served with distinction in the Indian Mutiny), *assumed the Baronetcy* on the death, 17 Oct. 1873, of his maternal cousin, the 12th Baronet, as the heir male of the body of the grantee. He was s. and h. of William Cox, General in the Rifle Brigade and 1st Royal Dragoons, K.H., by his 1st wife, Catherine (sister of Sarah, mother of the 10th, 11th and 12th Baronets), da. of the Rev. Ralph HAWTREY, which William (*b.* 16 March 1790, and *d.* 1857), was s. of John Cox of Carrick on Suir (by Mary, da. of [—] RIX, of Kilkenny), which John (*b.* 1724, *d.* 25 June 1795), was stated (no parentage being named) to have been a nephew of Archbishop Cox, and, consequently, a grandson of the 1st Baronet.(b) He was *b.* 30 Aug. 1817. He *m.* 1860, Mary Hall, 2d da. of John ANDREWS, of Rathenny park, King's County, by Elizabeth, da. of Robert HALL, of Merton Hall, co. Tipperary. He *d.* 10 March 1887, at 37 Sterndale road, West Kensington, and was *bur.* at Cheltenham, in his 70th year.

XIV. bis, 1887. SIR JOHN HAWTREY REGINALD COX, Baronet [I. 1706],(a) 1st s. and h., *b.* 23 April 1861; ed. at Dulwich; Capt. 6th Inniskilling Dragoons, and Major in the Antrim Artillery; served in Zululand, 1884 and 1888, and in the Bechuanaland Expedition, 1884-85; *suc. to the Baronetcy*,(a) 10 March 1887. He *m.* 14 July 1902, at St. Paul's, Knightsbridge, Margaret Rodger, yst. da. of George THOMSON, of Dalling Mohr, co. Argyll, and of Glasgow.

(a) See p. 239, note "d."

(b) The affiliation of this John was, subsequently, attributed to the Archbishop himself, of whom he was conjectured to be a son by his 1st wife, Anne, da. of Toby Purcell, though *b.* (1725) twelve years after their marriage, 22 May 1712. In that case, however, William, s. and h. of the said John, ought to have *suc. to the Baronetcy* 28 Jan. 1838, in lieu of the 8th, 9th, 10th, 11th and 12th Baronets, whose right thereto was never disputed by the said Gen. William Cox, or by his son, who only assumed it *after* the death of the 12th Baronet in 1873. The will of this John Cox, dat. 7 March 1795, was pr. 14 Aug. following by Michael Cox, of Castletown (*b.* 1768), called by testator his "trusty friend," to whom he (if a son of the Archbishop by his 1st wife) would have been uncle of the half blood and between forty and fifty years his senior. The date of the birth of this John (1724) makes it impossible for him to be a *grandson* of the Archbishop, who was *b.* in 1691, and did not marry till 1712.

Baronetcies of Scotland.(a)

1625—1707.

THIRD AND LAST PART,

VIZ.,

CREATIONS,

1 Jan. 1664/5(b) to 1 May 1707, the date of the Union [S.].

RAMSAY :(c)

cr. 2 June 1665;

ex. 22 Oct. 1744.

I. 1665. "JOHN RAMSAY, of Whitehill," co. Edinburgh, 2d s. of Simon or Simeon RAMSAY,(d) of the same and of Fawside, co. Haddington, and Priorletham, co. Fife, by his 1st wife, Elizabeth, da. of James STEVENSON, of Hermieshiels, co. Edinburgh, was *b.* 1624; was an Advocate; lent £600 to the Parl. in 1644; was served heir, 11 March 1654 to his elder br., John RAMSAY, of Whitehill aforesaid, and was *cr. a Baronet* [S.] as above, 2 June 1665, with rem. to heirs male of the body, an honour "most deservedly conferred upon him by his Majesty." He *m.* (contract 18 Feb. 1643, tocher 8,000 merks) Anne, 1st da. of James BAIRD, of Newbyth, Advocate by Bethia DEMPSTER. He *d.* 5 June 1674, aged 56. His widow *d.* 14 April 1680, aged (also) 56.

II. 1674. SIR JOHN RAMSAY, Baronet [S. 1665], of Whitehill aforesaid, s. and h, *b.* 26 Feb. 1645; *suc. to the Baronetcy*, 5 June 1674, between which date and 1678 he registered armorial ensigns at the Lyon Office. On 24 April 1667 he was served h. to his father in the Barony of Ednam, co. Roxburgh, as also to his uncle, John RAMSAY, and his aunt Margaret in other

(a) See Vol. ii, p. 275, note "a," as to the very great assistance, in the account of these dignities given by Sir James Balfour Paul, Lyon King of Arms. Thanks are also due to Francis James Grant, Rothesay Herald and Lyon Clerk, as also to James R. Anderson, of Glasgow, who has compiled a valuable list of all the Scotch Baronetcies created by Charles II and his successors, which has for the most part been followed in this work.

(b) See Vol. iii, p. 1, note "a" as to this date, which represents about half of the creations made between the death of Charles I and the Union with Scotland.

(c) The information in this article was chiefly furnished by the late R. R. Stodart, Lyon Clerk Depute [1863-86].

(d) This Simon graduated at the Univ. of Edinburgh, 25 July 1607, and up to the time of his purchase of Whitehill (26 June 1623, from William Ramsay) is always styled "Indweller in Edinburgh." On 27 Aug. 1618 he was served h. gen. of his br. Henry Ramsay, Merchant Burgess of Coline, in the Duchy of Spruce and Kingdom of Poland.

properties. He was, however, in embarrassed circumstances, and the management of his estates was given to his 2d s., Andrew RAMSAY, then a successful lawyer. These, accordingly, were settled by two deeds, 1708 and 1712, (1) on the said Andrew and the heirs male of his body; (2) on the Baronet's first son, John RAMSAY; (3) on his 3d son, Charles RAMSAY; (4) on his nephew, Ensign John RAMSAY,(a) in like manner; and (5), on the eldest heir female without division. He *m.* firstly, 29 Aug. 1671, Anna, only da. of Sir John CARSTAIRS, of Kilconquhar, co. Fife, by Isabella, da. of Andrew AINSLIE, of Edinburgh, Merchant. She *d.* 19 April 1689, aged 37. He *m.* secondly, Rosina, widow of James DEANS, of Woodhouselee, co. Edinburgh, Advocate, and da. of Sir William PURVES, of Woodhouselee. She *d.* s.p.m. He *d.* 14 April 1715, aged 70, and was *bur.* at Primrose, *otherwise* Carringtoun.

III. 1715. SIR JOHN RAMSAY, Baronet [S. 1665], s. and h., by 1st wife, was, on 23 Nov. 1693, served h. to his mother; *suc. to the Baronetcy*, 14 April 1715, was, on 31 Jan. 1717, served h. gen. to his maternal grandmother, and on 30 March 1717, h. gen. of his father. He *m.* Marjory DEANS. He *d.* Saturday, 5 Oct. 1717, s.p., and was *bur.* 7, in the churchyard of Carringtoun. His widow *m.* Major William DRUMMOND (of the family of Hawthornden), and was living, as his wife, 1720.

IV. 1717. SIR ANDREW RAMSAY, Baronet [S. 1665], of Whitehill aforesaid, next br. and h., *b.* 26 June 1678; Advocate, 29 Jan. 1704; sometime Sheriff Depute of Edinburgh; universal legatee of the will of his br., George RAMSAY, pr. 10 Dec. 1701; *suc. to the Baronetcy*, 5 Oct. 1717, and had service to his elder br., 13 March and 3 July 1718. He *m.* (contract 30 April 1716) Elizabeth, da. of Thomas LEIRMONTH, Advocate, with a fortune of 16,000 merks. He *d.* 24 and was *bur.* 27 Dec. 1721, in the old churchyard of Carringtoun, aged 43. His widow *d.* 12 and was *bur.* there on the 16 Nov. 1763.

V. 1721, to 1744. SIR JOHN RAMSAY, Baronet [S. 1665], of Whitehill aforesaid, s. and h., *b.* 1720, and *suc. to the Baronetcy*, 24 Dec. 1721. Had service to his father, 22 Jan. 1726 and 10 July 1744. He *d.* unm. 22 and was *bur.* 26 Oct. 1744, with his parents, aged 24, when the *Baronetcy* became *extinct*.(b)

GRAHAM :

cr. 28 June 1665;

ex. 12 July 1708.

I. 1665. "WILLIAM GRAHAM, of Gartmore," co. Stirling, probably s. of John GRAHAM, of Poldare in that county (1644), bought the estate of Gartmore, and had Crown Charter thereof, 17 March 1645, and was *cr. a Baronet* [S.], as above, 28 June 1665, with rem. to heirs male of the body. He registered arms in the Lyon Office, 21 July 1673, and had an act for a weekly market at Middlethird in 1681. He *m.* (contract, 19 Dec. 1663) Elizabeth, sister of William (GRAHAM), EARL OF AIRTH AND MENTEITH [S.] (who *d.* s.p. 12 Sep. 1694), 2d da. of John GRAHAM, *styled* LORD KINPONT, by Mary, da. of William (KEITH), 6th EARL MARISCHAL [S.]. She *d.* 1672. He *d.* Dec. 1684.

(a) This John was s. of James Ramsay, 3d s. of the 1st Bart., and appears to have *d.* between 1708 and 1712, as he is not mentioned in the settlement of the latter date.

(b) Ann, his only surv. sister, *m.*, 3 June 1736, Robert Balfour, of Balbirnie, co. Fife, who assumed the name of Ramsay after that of Balfour. She was served, 24 April 1745, as h. of line entail and provision separate to her br. in all the estate. She *d.* Feb. 1766, leaving issue.

II. 1684, to 1708. Sir John Graham, Baronet [S. 1665], of Gartmore aforesaid, only s. and h., who, with his father, had a Crown Charter of that estate, 23 April 1672; *suc. to the Baronetcy* in Dec. 1684, was served heir general of his father, 16 Feb. 1687, and heir spec. in the estate of Gartmore, 12 Feb. 1695. He became insane 1696. He *d.* unm. 12 July 1708, when *the Baronetcy* became *extinct*.(a)

PURVES:

cr. 5, 6, or 25 July 1665;

afterwards, since 1812, Purves-Hume-Campbell.

I. 1665. "Sir William Purves, of Purves Hall," co. Berwick, only s. of Robert Purves, of Abbeyhill, co. Edinburgh, Burgess of that city (*d.* 1655), by Anne Douglas, his wife, was an officer in the Court of Session, holding afterwards, 1656, an office in the Court of Exchequer; an Advocate, and, 13 Nov. 1662, Solicitor-Gen. [S.]; was *Knighted* and subsequently *cr. a Baronet* [S.], as above, 5, 6, or 25 July 1665, there being, however, no record of such creation in the Great Seal Register. He *m.* Margery, da. of Robert Fleeming, of Restalrig. He *d.* in 1684 or 1685(b).

II. 1685? Sir Alexander Purves, Baronet [S. 1665], of Purves Hall aforesaid, 1st s. and h. He obtained by patent, 2 May 1666, the reversion, after his father's death, of the office of Solicitor-Gen. [S.]. He *suc. to the Baronetcy* in 1684 or 1685. He *m.* (—) da. of (—) Hume, of Ninewells. He *d.* 1701.

III. 1701. Sir William Purves, Baronet [S. 1665], of Purves Hall aforesaid, 1st s. and h.; *suc. to the Baronetcy* in 1701. He *m.* in or before 1700, his cousin Elizabeth, da. of (—) Deans, of Woodhouselee, co. Edinburgh, by Rosina, da. of Sir William Purves, 1st Baronet [S. 1665]. He *d.* 1730. His widow *d.* 8 Sep. 1764.

IV. 1730. Sir William Purves, Baronet [S. 1665], of Purves Hall aforesaid, 1st s. and h., *bap.* 14 Jan. 1701; *suc. to the Baronetcy* in 1730. He *m.* in or before 1736, Anne, 1st da. of Alexander (Hume-Campbell), 2d Earl of Marchmont [S.] by Margaret, da. and h. of Sir George Campbell, of Cessnock, co. Ayr. He *d.* 18 June 1762, aged 62. His widow, who was *b.* 3 Aug. 1698, *d.* at Berwick, 2 April 1784, aged 86.

V. 1762. Sir Alexander Purves, Baronet [S. 1665], of Purves Hall aforesaid and of Eccles, co. Berwick, 2d but 1st surv. s. and h.; *bap.* 15 Jan. 1739; *suc. to the Baronetcy*, 18 June 1762; was an officer in the Army, retiring in 1781, as Major in the 18th Foot. He *m.* firstly, 23 Aug. 1766, Catherine, da. of [—] Le Blanc, of London. She *d.* 12 Feb. 1772, at Purves Hall. He *m.* secondly, 21 June 1775, at Haddington, Mary Home ["of Coldingham"], da. of Sir James Home, of Manderston (*Qy.* Baronet [S.]). She *d.*

(a) Gartmore was sold by Mary Hodge, his niece and heir, she being only child of his sister Mary, by James Hodge, of Gladsmuir, Advocate. She *m.* 28 Feb. 1701, her cousin, William Graham, and her son and heir, William Graham, assumed the Earldom of Menteith [S.] and voted, as such Earl, in various elections of Scottish Representative Peers, 1744 to 1761, till forbidden, 2 March 1762, to do so. He *d.* unm. 30 June 1783.

(b) He is presumed to have been the "Sir William Worthy" delineated in Allan Ramsay's "*Gentle Shepherd.*"

4 July 1785. He *m.* thirdly, 9 Nov. 1785, Magdalen, da. of James Edmonston, of Longfaugh. She *d.* 22 Aug. 1788. He *m.* fourthly, 19 Jan. 1789, Isabella, da. of James Hunter, of Frankfield. He *d.* 13 Nov. 1812, aged 74. The will of his widow was pr. Jan. 1848.

VI. 1812. Sir William Purves-Hume-Campbell, Baronet [S. 1665], of Marchmont House, co. Berwick, 1st s. and h., by 1st wife, *b.* 4 Oct. 1767; assumed the additional names of Hume-Campbell in 1794, in compliance with the will of his grand uncle (br. to his paternal grandmother) Hugh (Hume-Campbell), 3d Earl of Marchmont [S.], whose estate at Marchmont he inherited; *suc. to the Baronetcy*, 13 and was served heir of entail 30 Nov. 1812. He *m.* 2 May 1812, Charlotte, widow of Anthony Hall, of Plass, co. Durham, da. of [—] Rey. He *d.* 9 April 1833, at Marchmont, aged 65.

VII. 1833. Sir Hugh Purves-Hume-Campbell, Baronet [S. 1665], of Marchmont House aforesaid, only s. and h., *b.* 15 Dec. 1812, at Edinburgh; ed. at Eton and at Trin. Coll., Cambridge; *suc. to the Baronetcy*, 9 April 1833; M.P. for Berwickshire (four Parls.), 1834-47; Brig. Gen. of the Royal Company of Archers, the Queen's body guard [S.]. He *m.* firstly, 30 Jan. 1834, at Spottiswoode, co. Berwick, Margaret Penelope, yr. da. of John Spottiswoode, of Spottiswoode aforesaid, by Helen, da. of Andrew Wauchope, of Niddrie. She *d.* 16 Oct. 1839, suddenly, at Paris. He *m.* secondly, 9 Oct. 1841, at St. Geo. Han. sq., Juliana Rebecca, only da. of Lieut. Gen. Sir Joseph Fuller, G.C.H. She *d.* at Marchmont House, 11 and was *bur.* 19 Oct. 1886, in Kensal Green Cemetery. Will pr. 14 Dec. 1886, above £65,000. He *d.* s.p.s.,(a) 30 Jan. 1894, at 18 Hill street, Berkeley square, in his 82d year.

VIII. 1894. Sir John Home Purves-Hume-Campbell, Baronet [S. 1665], of Marchmont House aforesaid, cousin and h. male, being only s. and h. of Charles Hyde Home Purves, of Purves Hall aforesaid, sometime Lieut. Rifle Brigade, by Frances Mabel, da. of Clement Archer, of Hill House, Hampton, Midx., which Charles (who *d.* 19 Jan. 1881, aged 31), was s. and h. of John Home Purves, of Purves Hall aforesaid, Col. in the Grenadier Guards (*d.* 2 July 1867) who was s. and h. of John Home Purves, Capt. Scots Greys, the 2d s. of the 5th Baronet, being eldest s. of his 2d wife. He was *b.* 9 Aug. 1879; ed. at Eton; *suc. to the Baronetcy* and the Marchmont estate, 30 June 1894, when he assumed the additional names of Hume-Campbell; sometime Lieut. 2d Life Guards, and served in the Transvaal War. He *m.*, 1 Oct. 1901, at Hampton, Midx., Emily Jane, only da. of the Rev. Robert Digby Ram, M.A. (Cambridge), Vicar of Hampton aforesaid, and Preb. of St. Paul's, London.

Family Estates.—These, in 1883, consisted of 20,180 acres in Berwickshire, worth £17,976 a year. *Principal Residence.*—Marchmont House, near Dunse, co. Berwick.

MALCOLM:

cr. 25 July 1665.

I. 1665. "John Malcolm, of Balbedie," co. Fife, 1st s. and h. ap. of John Malcolm, of Balbedie, Lochore and Innerteil, sometime (1641) Chamberlain of Fife (*d.* 6 Feb. 1692, aged 81), by Margaret, da. of Sir Michael Arnot, of Arnot, co. Kinross; was *b.* 1646, and was v.p. when

(a) Helen, his only child (by his 1st wife) *m.* 13 July 1854, Sir George Warrender, 6th Baronet [1715], and *d.* s.p. and v.p. 11 March 1875.

under age; *cr. a Baronet* [S.], as above,(a) 25 July 1665, the creation, however, not being recorded in the Great Seal Register [S.]. He was M.P. for Kinross-shire, 1711-13. He *m.*, before 4 Aug. 1680, Emilia, 3d da. of John (Balfour), 3d Lord Balfour of Burleigh [S.], by Isabel, da. of Sir William Balfour, of Pitcullo. He *d.* 30 March 1729.(b) His widow *d.* 12 Jan. 1732, at Lochore, aged about 74, and was *bur.* at Ballingry, co. Fife.

II. 1729. Sir John Malcolm, Baronet [S. 1665], of Lochore and Innerteil aforesaid, 1st s. and h., *bap.* 4 May 1681; *suc. to the Baronetcy*, 30 March 1729. He *m.* (contract 27 Jan. and 11 July 1709), Isabel, 1st da. of his maternal uncle, Lieut.-Col. The Hon. John Balfour, of Ferny, by Barbara, da. of Arthur Ross, Archbishop of Glasgow. He *d.* at Lochore, 12 Aug. 1753, aged 72. His widow *d.* at Kirkcaldy, 14 Dec. 1763.

III. 1753. Sir Michael Malcolm, Baronet [S. 1665], of Lochore and Innerteil aforesaid, 3d but 1st surv. s. and h. male;(c) *suc. to the Baronetcy*, 12 Aug. 1753; was served heir to his father 20 Dec. 1784, and sold the estate of Lochore about 1790. He *m.*, 1 Feb. 1752, Katharine, da. of Peter Bathurst, of Clarendon Park, Wilts, by Selina, da. of Robert (Shirley), 1st Earl Ferrers. He *d.* s.p.s., 5 May 1793, in Edinburgh. His widow *d.* there 30 Oct. 1794.

IV. 1793. Sir James Malcolm, Baronet [S. 1665], of Grange, co. Fife, and Balbedie aforesaid, cousin and h. male, being only surv. s. of Robert Malcolm, of Grange, by Isabella, da. of Robert Herries, of Halldykes, co. Dumfries, which Robert Malcolm (who *d.* abroad, 3 June 1769, aged 87) was 2d s. of the 1st Baronet. He, who was in the army, *suc. to the Baronetcy*, 5 May 1793, and was Lieut.-Gov. of Sheerness in 1794. He *d.* s.p., 25 Oct. 1805. Will pr. 1805.

(a) It has been suggested that the Baronetcy was conferred on his father (whose name was also John) and not on himself, but such was not the case. There is a charter as early as 5 March 1667 of the lands of Bynn, etc., co. Fife, to John Malcolm, of Balbedie, and to his son, Sir John Malcolm, Knt. and Baronet, as also another, 14 March 1680, of the lands of Innerteil to the same parties and the heirs male of the latter, by Emily Balfour his wife, while the entry of the burial of the former in the parish register of Ballingry, co. Fife, is as follows:—"John Malcolm, of Balbedie, Lochoir and Innerteil, patron of this church, died Feb. 8, 1692 at 11 before noon, buried in his isle, aged 81."

(b) Of the younger brothers of the 1st Baronet (1) Michael Malcolm, of Balbedie (who appears to have inherited that estate, while those of Lochore and Innerteil passed to his eldest brother) *d.* s.p., 19 June 1733, aged 86, having entailed the lands of Balbedie, 9 Oct. 1725 on his nephew, Michael Malcolm, of Balbedie, the father of the 5th Baronet; (2) Alexander Malcolm, a person of some note, whose death is thus recorded in the parish register of Ballingry, co. Fife, where most of the family (including the father, who died the same year) are buried, "1692, Sep. 17, Died at Cupar in the Barony, Alexander Malcolm, Lord Lochoir, of an fluxe about six in the morning, Saturday, and buried in the said isle, 22 September, on the north wall, with his head to the west wall. Is third son to the said John Malcolm and Margaret Arnot, da. to Sir Michael Arnot. Born 13 Dec. 1650 between 4 and 5 in the morning: was a Lord of Session, 1687, and a Lord of the Privie Counsell to King James the 7th and by patent, 1688, Lord Justice Clark." [*Ex inform.* of the present (1904) Baronet, who has kindly supplied many other particulars in this article].

(c) Of his elder brothers (1) James, *d.* s.p. and v.p. 20 June 1737, aged 28; (2) Robert, *d.* v.p. and s.p.m., leaving a da., Anne, who *m.* Alexander Graham, an Attorney, at Jamaica, and left an only surv. child, Ann Katherine, who was served heir, 9 Feb. 1796, to her grand uncle, Sir Michael Malcolm, the 3d Baronet, and who *m.* David Littlejohn, of Kingston, in Jamaica.

V. 1805. Sir John Malcolm, Baronet [S. 1665], of Balbedie and Grange aforesaid, cousin and h. male, being yst. but last surv. s. of Michael Malcolm, of the same, by his 2d wife, Anne, da. of (—) Blackwood, which Michael (who *d.* 10 April 1754, aged 71) was 3d s. of the 1st Baronet. He was *b.* 1 April 1749; was served heir to his br. (of the half blood), James Malcolm, of Balbedie (who *d.* s.p., 11 Aug. 1798, aged 71), 8 Oct. 1799, and *suc. to the Baronetcy*, 25 Oct. 1805. He *m.* Jean, da. of (—) Hutton. He *d.* 23 May 1816, aged 67. His widow *d.* 5 Dec. 1826, at Leslie, co. Fife.

VI. 1816. Sir Michael Malcolm, Baronet [S. 1665], of Balbedie and Grange aforesaid, served heir to his father and to his cousin, Sir James Malcolm, of Grange, 10 Dec. 1818; *suc. to the Baronetcy*, 23 May 1816. He *m.* firstly, 18 Dec. 1809, at Kirkcaldy, Isabella, da. of Thomas Davie, of Kirkcaldy, merchant. She *d.* s.p. in 1824, and was *bur.* at Ballingry. He *m.* secondly, June 1824, Mary, yst. da. of John Forbes, of Bridgend, co. Perth. He *d.* 8 Oct. 1828. His widow *d.* 13 Feb. 1897, at Eldon road, Kensington, at a great age, and was *bur.* at Ballingry aforesaid.

VII. 1828. Sir John Malcolm, Baronet [S. 1665], of Balbedie and Grange aforesaid, only s. and h. by 2d wife, *b.* 1 April 1828, at Balbedie, and *suc. to the Baronetcy*, 8 Oct. following, being served heir to his father, 22 Nov. 1828. He *m.* 1 Oct. 1861, Jane, da. of John MacDougal. He *d.* s.p. 24 Dec. 1865, at Burntisland, co. Fife, aged 37. His widow *d.* 7 Nov. 1875, at 16 Montgomery street, Edinburgh, aged 47.

VIII. 1865. Sir James Malcolm, Baronet [S. 1665], cousin and h. male, being 2d and yst. but last surv. s. of James Malcolm, by Helen, da. of James Duncan, of Abernethy, co. Perth, which James (who *d.* 25 June 1826) was yr. br. of the 6th, and s. of the 5th Baronet. He was *b.* 11 April 1823; was sometime a merchant at Liverpool, but was in the Commission of Peace for the county of Fife; *suc. to the Baronetcy*, 24 Dec. 1865, and was served heir to his cousin, 23 Feb. 1866. He *d.* unm. 8 June 1901, aged 78.

IX. 1901. Sir James William Malcolm, Baronet [S. 1665], of Hoveton Hall, Norfolk, cousin and h. male, being 1st surv. s. of James Malcolm, by his 2d wife, Adeline, da. of Capt. James Attye, of Pinchbeck, co. Lincoln, sometime Capt. 52d Foot, which James Malcolm (who *d.* 16 July 1878, aged 73) was s. of William Malcolm (*d.* 3 Aug. 1838, aged 70), s. of Alexander Malcolm (*d.* at Olrig, 11 Sep. 1809, aged 89), s. of Charles Malcolm (*bap.* 19 Aug. 1687), 4th s. of the 1st Baronet. He was *b.* 29 March 1862; ed. at Mag. Coll., Cambridge; was sometime Capt. in the Pembroke Artillery Militia; in the Commission of Peace for co. Norfolk; *suc. to the Baronetcy*, 8 June 1901, having previously, 17 March 1897, recorded his pedigree in the Lyon office. He *m.*, 14 Nov. 1885, Evelyn Alberta, 3d da. of Albert George Sandeman, of Presdales, Herts, one of the Directors of the Bank of England, by Maria Carlotta Perpetua da Sarmento, da. of the Viscount da Torre de Moncorvo, of the Kingdom of Portugal, sometime Portuguese Ambassador to England.

MENZIES:

cr. 2 Sep. 1665.

I. 1665. "Sir Alexander Menzies, of that ilk," as also of Weem, co. Perth, 1st s. and h. of Duncan Menzies, of the same, by Jean, da. of the Hon. James Leslie, Master of Rothes, having, apparently, been *Knighted*, was *cr. a Baronet* [S.], as above, 2 Sep. 1665, with rem. to heirs male of the body. He was M.P. [S.] for Perthshire 1693, till his death in 1695. He *m.* Agnes, 1st da. of Sir John Campbell, 4th Baronet [S. 1625], of Glenorchy, by his 1st wife, Mary, da. of William (Graham), Earl of Strathern, Menteith and Airth [S.]. He *d.* in 1695, shortly before 16 April.

II. 1695. SIR ALEXANDER MENZIES, Baronet [S. 1665], of Castle Menzies and Weem aforesaid, grandson and h., being 1st s. and h. of Capt. Robert MENZIES, by Anne, da. of Walter (SANDILANDS), 6th LORD TORPICHEN [S.], which Robert was 1st s. and h. ap. of the late Baronet, but *d.* v.p. 1691. He *suc. to the Baronetcy* in 1695. He *m.* his cousin, Christian, da. of Lord Neil CAMPBELL (yr. s. of the MARQUESS OF ARGYLL [S.]), by his 2d wife Susan, da. of Sir Alexander MENZIES, 1st Baronet [S. 1665]. He *d.* before 1736. His widow *d.* April 1736.

III. 1730? SIR ROBERT MENZIES, Baronet [S. 1665], of Castle Menzies and Weem aforesaid, only s. and h., *suc. to the Baronetcy* on the death of his father. He *m.* Mary, 1st da. of James (STEWART), 2d EARL OF BUTE [S.], by Anne, da. of Archibald (CAMPBELL), 1st DUKE OF ARGYLL [S.]. She *d.* 30 Dec. 1773, at Castle Menzies. He, who executed an entail of the Baronies of Menzies and Rannoch, *d.* s.p. 4 Sep. 1786.

IV. 1786. SIR JOHN MENZIES, Baronet [S. 1665], of Castle Menzies aforesaid, cousin and heir male, being only s. and h. of James MENZIES, of Edinburgh, Merchant, by Janet, da. of (—) STEVENSON, which James was s of Capt. James MENZIES, of Comrie, who was 2d s. of the 1st Baronet. He *suc. to the Baronetcy*, 4 Sep. 1786. He *m.* 4 March 1797, at St. Geo. Han. sq., Charlotte, 1st da. of John (MURRAY), 4th DUKE OF ATHOLL [S.], by his 1st wife, Jean, da. of Charles Schaw (CATHCART), 9th LORD CATHCART [S.]. He *d.* s.p. at Castle Menzies, 26 March 1800. Will pr. July 1800. His widow, who was *b.* in Grosvenor place, Midx., 23 Oct. and *bap.* 19 Nov. 1775, *m.* 28 May 1801, Admiral Sir Adam DRUMMOND, K.C.H., who *d.* 3 May 1849, aged 78. She *d.* in London, 31 May 1832.

V. 1800. SIR ROBERT MENZIES, Baronet [S. 1665], of Castle Menzies aforesaid, cousin and h. male, being only s. and h. of Neil MENZIES, of Perth, Surgeon, by Mary (*d.* 24 Nov. 1783), da. of Henry (BOTHWELL), LORD HOLYROODHOUSE [S.], which Neil was 3d s. of Capt. James MENZIES, of Comrie abovementioned, the 2d s. of the 1st Baronet. He, who was *b.* before 1760, *suc. to the Baronetcy*, 26 March 1800. He *m.* in or before 1780, Catherine, da. of Duncan OCHILTREE, of Linsaig, co. Argyll, by Vere, da. of Robert FLEMING, of Moness. He *d.* 8 March 1813 [*not*, as often stated, 1814]. Will pr. 1820.

VI. 1813. SIR NEIL MENZIES, Baronet [S. 1665], of Castle Menzies aforesaid, only s. and h., *b.* 16 Aug. 1780; Advocate [S.], 6 March 1802; *suc. to the Baronetcy*, 8 March 1813; Lieut.-Col. of the Royal Highland Perthshire Militia. He *m.* firstly, 6 June 1808, Emilia, da. of Francis BALFOUR, of Fernie, co. Fife, by (—), da. of (—) BALFOUR, of Dunbog. She *d.* s.p.m. 1 Nov. 1810. He *m.* secondly, 3 Dec. 1816, Grace Charlotte Conyers, sister of Fletcher (NORTON), 3d BARON GRANTLEY, 1st da. of the Hon. Fletcher NORTON, by Caroline Elizabeth, da. of James BALMAIN. He *d.* 20 Aug. 1844, at Edinburgh, aged 64. His widow, who was *b.* at Edinburgh, May 1794, and who by Royal Warrant was raised in 1831 to the rank of the da. of a Baron, *d.* 3 Jan. 1877, aged 83, at 13 Grosvenor street, Edinburgh.

VII. 1844. SIR ROBERT MENZIES, Baronet [S. 1665], of Castle Menzies aforesaid, 1st s. and h. by 2nd wife, *b.* 26 Sep. 1817, at Abbey Hill, Edinburgh; mat. at Oxford (Univ. Coll.), 23 June 1837, rowing in the University Eight; S.C.L., 1842; *suc. to the Baronetcy*, 20 Aug. 1844; Capt. in the Perthshire Militia, 1855-56; Hon. Col., 5th Vol. Batt. Black Watch. He *m.* 10 June 1846, Annie Balcarres, 6th da. of Major James Alston STEWART, of Urrard, co. Perth. She *d.* 29 April 1878, at Farlayer, in that county. He *d.* 22 April 1903, at Camserney Cottage, Aberfeldy, and was *bur.* at St. David's, Weem, aged 85.

VIII. 1903. SIR NEIL JAMES MENZIES, Baronet [S. 1665], of Castle Menzies aforesaid, 1st and only surv. s. and h., *b.* 5 March 1855; sometime Capt. in the Scots Guards, serving in the Suakim expedition, 1885, but retired 1892; *suc. to the Baronetcy*, 22 April 1903.

Family Estates.—These, in 1883, consisted of 98,284 acres in Perthshire, worth £11,467 a year. *Principal Seats.*—Castle Menzies, Foss House and Rannoch Lodge, all in co. Perth.

DALZELL:

cr. 11 April 1666;

afterwards, since June 1702, EARLS OF CARNWATH [S.];

but forfeited, 1716 to 1826.

I. 1666. "ROBERT DALZELL, of Glenae," co. Dumfries, only s. and h. ap. of the Hon. John DALZELL, of the same, by Agnes, da. of [—] NISBET, of Dean (the said John, who *d.* 24 Feb. 1689, being 2d s. of Robert, 1st EARL OF CARNWATH [S.]), was v.p. *cr. a Baronet* [S.], as above, 11 April 1666, with rem. to heirs male of his body. He was M.P. [S.] for Dumfries sheriffdom, 1665, 1667, 1669-74, 1681-82, and 1685 till death in Sep. 1685. He is sometimes said to have *m.* firstly (—), da. of (—) SANDILANDS, who (in that case) *d.* s.p.m.[a] He undoubtedly *m.* (contract 11 Oct. 1654) Margaret, 3d da. of James (JOHNSTONE), 1st EARL OF HARTFELL [S.], by his 1st wife Margaret, da. of William (DOUGLAS), 1st EARL OF QUEENSBERRY [S.]. She *d.* s.p. Oct. 1655. He *m.* finally, Violet, da. of [—] RIDDELL, of Haining. He *d.* v.p. in Sep. 1685.

II. 1685. SIR JOHN DALZELL, Baronet [S. 1666], of Glenae aforesaid, 1st s. and h., by 3d wife; *suc. to the Baronetcy*, Sep. 1685, and was served heir to his father, 2 Sep. 1686; M.P. [S.] for Dumfries sheriffdom, April to June 1686 and 1689 till death in that year; suc. his grandfather 24 Feb. 1689. He *m.*, 16 June 1686, his cousin, Henrietta (*b.* 10 May 1661), 2d da. of Sir William MURRAY, 1st Baronet [S. 1664], of Stanhope, by Janet, da. of James (JOHNSTONE), 1st EARL OF HARTFELL [S.] abovenamed. He *d.* March 1689.

III. 1689. SIR ROBERT DALZELL, Baronet [S. 1666], of Glenae aforesaid, 1st s. and h., *b.* probably about 1687; *suc. to the Baronetcy* in March 1689; was ed. at Cambridge. He became EARL OF CARNWATH, etc. [S.] by the death, in June 1702, of his cousin the 5th Earl. In that peerage this *Baronetcy* then *merged*, and still (1904) so continues, though both were *forfeited* in 1716, but restored in 1826. See *Peerage*.

LINDSAY[b]:

cr. 15 April 1666;

ex. 6 March 1799.

I. 1666. "ALEXANDER LINDSAY, of Evelick," in the Sheriffdom of Perth, s. and h. of Alexander LINDSAY, of the same (s. of Alexander LINDSAY, Bishop of Dunkeld), was retoured heir to his father, 8 Nov. 1665,

[a] This lady is sometimes stated to have been his *mother*, not his wife.

[b] W. A. Lindsay, K.C., Windsor Herald, has kindly furnished much of the information in this article, but little seems known about the earlier Baronets. In right of descent from William, *third* son of David, 3d Earl of Crawford [S.], the Lindsays of Evelick stood next, in the entail of the *Comitatus*, to the Lindsays of Edzell (lineal ancestors of the present Earls), who were the descendants of Walter, *second* son of the said Earl; but the Baronets were not the heirs male of the said William, the Bishop of Dunkeld, having had an elder (though ousted) brother.

and was *cr. a Baronet* [S.], as above, 15 April 1666, but the creation is not recorded in the Great Seal Register [S.]. He *m.* firstly (contract 26 April, proclamation, 11, 18 and 25 April 1658, in the Kilspindie parish register), Jeane (20,000 merks), sister and coheir of Alexander, da. of Thomas FOTHERINGHAM, both of Powrie. He *m.* secondly, 10 July 1679, Rachel KIRKWOOD. He *d.* about 1690.

II. 1690? SIR ALEXANDER LINDSAY, Baronet [S. 1666], of Evelick aforesaid, s. and h., *bap.* 26 Feb. 1660, at Kilspindie; *suc. to the Baronetcy* on the death of his father, and was excommunicated by the Presbytery of Perth, 1709. He *m.* (contract 3 March 1681) Elizabeth, sister of Sir Henry WARDLAW, 1st Baronet [S. 1631], da. of Cuthbert WARDLAW, tenant in Balmule.[a] He was living 1709.

III. 1720? SIR ALEXANDER LINDSAY, Baronet [S. 1666], of Evelick aforesaid, s. and h., *suc. to the Baronetcy* on the death of his father. He *m.* (contract, 22 and 28 April 1720; registered 15 April 1766) Amelia, sister of William, 1st EARL OF MANSFIELD, 4th da. of David (MURRAY), 5th VISCOUNT STORMONT [S.], by Marjory, da. of David SCOTT, of Scotstarvet. He *d.* at Evelick, 6 May 1762. His widow *d.* at Edinburgh, 18 Feb. 1774.

IV. 1762. SIR DAVID LINDSAY, Baronet [S. 1666], of Evelick aforesaid, 1st s. and h.,[b] *b.* probably about 1732, *suc. to the Baronetcy*, 6 May 1762; was retoured heir general of his father, 4 Feb. 1772; was Capt. 3d Reg. of Foot Guards, 1758-76; Lieut.-Col. of the 59th Foot, 1776; Major-Gen., 1777; Lieut.-Gen., 1779, and General, 1796; was also *Custos Brevium* of the Court of King's Bench. He *m.* Susanna Charlotte, widow of George ELLIS, of Jamaica, da. of Samuel LONG, of the same. He *d.* 6 March 1797, in Cavendish square, Marylebone. Will pr. March 1797. His widow *d.* 7 July 1818, in Berkshire. Admon. July 1818.

V. 1797, to 1799. SIR CHARLES SCOTT LINDSAY, Baronet [S. 1666], of Evelick aforesaid, yst. but only surv. s. and h.,[c] *suc. to the Baronetcy*, 6 March 1797. He was an officer in the Royal Navy, and had (but a few days before his succession) distinguished himself as Commander of *La Bonne Citoyenne* at the defeat of the Spanish fleet, 14 Feb. 1797, off Cape St. Vincent, being made Capt. R.N. 7 March following. He *d.* unm., being drowned while in command of the *Daphne*, 6 March 1799, off Demarara, in the West Indies, when the *Baronetcy* became *extinct*.[d] Admon. July 1799.

ERSKINE, *or* ARSKIN:

cr. 30 April 1666;

afterwards, since 1789, ST. CLAIR-ERSKINE;

and, since 1805, EARLS OF ROSSLYN.

I. 1666. "CHARLES ERSKINE [*or* ARSKIN], of Alva," 3d but 1st surv. s. of the Hon. Sir Charles ERSKINE, of Alva and Cambus Kenneth, by Mary, da. of Sir Thomas HOPE, 1st Baronet [S. 1628],

[a] In Oct. 1693 and afterwards the baptism of some of his children occurs at Kilspindie, but no son named Alexander is among them.

[b] His yr. br., Rear Admiral Sir John Lindsay, K.B., who distinguished himself at the siege of Havannah in 1760, *d.* s.p. legit., 7 June 1788, aged 51, and was *bur.* in Westm. Abbey.

[c] His elder br., William Lindsay, Governor of Tobago, who in 1791 was Ambassador to Venice, *d.* unm. and v.p.

[d] His sisters Amelia and Elizabeth were retoured 8 Nov. 1799 as heirs portioners. The former had *m.*; 3 Sep. 1785, the Rt. Hon. Thomas Steele, and had issue. The latter *m.* Augustus Schultze, of Sunning Hill, Berks.

of Craighall, which Charles was a yr. s. of John, EARL OF MAR [S.], by his 2d wife, Mary, da. of Esme (STEWART), DUKE OF LENNOX [S.], was *b.* 4 July 1643; suc. his father, 8 July 1663, being served his heir 15 July 1665, and was *cr. a Baronet* [S.], as above, 30 April 1666, with rem. to the heirs male of his body. He was M.P. [S.] for Clackmannanshire, 1665 and 1667, and for Stirlingshire, 1689 till death in 1690. He *m.*, about 1670, Christian, da. of Sir James DUNDAS, of Arnistoun. He *d.* 4 June 1690, aged 46.

II. 1690. SIR JAMES ERSKINE, Baronet [S. 1666], of Alva aforesaid, 1st s. and h., *b.* probably about 1670; *suc. to the Baronetcy*, 4 June 1690. He *d.* unm., being killed at the battle of Landen, 23 July 1693.

III. 1693. SIR JOHN ERSKINE, Baronet [S. 1666] of Alva aforesaid, br. and h.,[a] *b.* about 1673; *suc. to the Baronetcy*, 23 July 1693; was served heir to his br. 1 May 1694, and to his father, 24 May 1696; admitted an Advocate 1700; was M.P. [S.] for Clackmannanshire, 1700-02; for Burntisland, 1702-07 (being a supporter of the treaty of the Union [S.]) and was M.P. [G.B.] for the same, 1707-08, and for Clackmannanshire, again, 1713-15. He *m.* Catharine (*b.* 14 Jan. 1685), 2d da. of Henry (ST. CLAIR), LORD SINCLAIR [S.], by Grizel, da. of Sir James COCKBURN. He *d.* in the Isle of Man, owing to a fall from his horse, 12 March 1739, in his 67th year.

IV. 1739. SIR CHARLES ERSKINE, Baronet [S. 1666], of Alva aforesaid, 1st s. and h.; *suc. to the Baronetcy*, 12 March 1739; was Major in the Royal Scots Reg. of Foot. He *m.*, in or before 1743, Henrietta, da. of Col. FRASER, of Dunballock. He *d.* s.p.m., being killed at the battle of Laffeldt, 2 July 1747.

V. 1747. SIR HENRY ERSKINE, Baronet [S. 1666], br. and h., was Deputy Quarter Master General (with rank of Lieut.-Col.) in the Expedition to Port L'Orient, where he was wounded, 21 Sep. 1746; was in command of the 67th Foot, 1758; of the 25th Foot, 1761, and of the Royal Scots, 1762, becoming finally Lieut.-Gen. in the Army; *suc. to the Baronetcy*, 2 July 1747; was M.P. for Ayr burghs, 1749-54, and for Anstruther Easter burghs, 1754-61; Sec. of the Order of the Thistle, 1765. He *m.* in 1761, Janet, sister of Alexander (WEDDERBURN), 1st EARL OF ROSSLYN, Lord Chancellor [1793—1801], only da. of Peter WEDDERBURN, of Chesterhall, co. Haddington (a Lord of Session under the style of Lord Chesterhall), by Janet, da. of David OGILVIE. He *d.* 7 Aug. 1765, at Marylebone, Midx. Admon. 17 March 1766. Will pr. July following. His widow *d.* June 1767.

VI. 1765. SIR JAMES ERSKINE, *afterwards* ST. CLAIR-ERSKINE, Baronet [S. 1666], 1st s. and h., *b.* 6 Feb. and *bap.* 3 March 1762, at St. Marylebone; *suc. to the Baronetcy*, 7 Aug. 1765; was for 23 years in the House of Commons, being M.P. for Castle Rising, 1782-84; for Morpeth, 1784-96, and for the Kirkcaldy burghs, 1796—1805, being one of the Managers of the House of Commons at the trial of Warren Hastings, 1787, and generally voting in opposition to Pitt. He was made Director of the Chancery of Scotland, 1785, for life. He took the name of ST. CLAIR before that of ERSKINE, by royal lic. 9 June 1789, on succeeding to the estates at Rosslyn, Dysart, etc., through his descent from LORD SINCLAIR [S.], the father of his paternal grandmother above-

[a] The 3d br., Charles Erskine, of Tinwald, co. Dumfries, was a Lord of Session, 1742, under the style of Lord Tinwald and Lord Justice Clerk for life in 1748. He purchased the family estate of Alva, and *d.* 5 April 1763, aged 83, and was suc. by his only surv. s., James Erskine, of Barjarg, co. Dumfries (in right of his wife), who was also a Lord of Session, 1761, under the style of Lord Barjarg, and afterwards of Lord Alva. He *d.* 13 May 1796, aged 74, leaving issue.

named. Having joined the Army in 1778, he became Lieut.-Col. 12th Light Dragoons, 1792, serving as Adjutant General at Toulon, 1793, and in Portugal, 1796, being at the siege of Copenhagen, and, in 1809, in the Walcheren expedition, becoming in 1801 Col. of the 9th Lancers and finally, in 1813, General in the Army. He *m.* 4 Nov. 1789, at St. James', Westm. (by spec. lic. in her father's house in Old Bond street), Harriet Elizabeth, 1st da. of the Hon. Edward BOUVERIE (2d s. of Jacob, 1st VISCOUNT FOLKESTONE), by Henrietta, da. of Sir Everard FAWKENER, K.B. She (who was *b.* 1771) was living when by the death of his maternal uncle, 3 Jan. 1805, he suc. as 2d EARL OF ROSSLYN and BARON LOUGHBOROUGH, under the spec. rem. in the creation of those dignities. In those peerages this *Baronetcy* then *merged*, and still (1904) so continues. See *Peerage*.

STIRLING :(a)
cr. 30 April 1666.

I. 1666. "GEORGE STIRLING, of Glorat," co. Stirling, s. and h. of Sir Mungo STIRLING, of the same (said to have been "a staunch cavalier"), was *cr. a Baronet* [S.], as above, 30 April 1666, no record of such creation being in the Great Seal register [S.], though there is a copy thereof, at Glorat, stating the limitation to be to the heirs male of the body. He recorded his Arms in the Lyon office about 1673. He *m.* firstly (contract 11 July 1657) Mary, da. of Sir George SETON, of Hales. She *d.* s.p.m. Aug. 1659. He *m.* secondly (contract 16 Feb. 1661) Marjory, da. of Sir William PURVES, 1st Baronet [S. 1665], of Purves Hall, by Margery, da. of Robert FLEEMING, of Restalrig. He was living about 1673.

II. 1680? SIR MUNGO STIRLING, Baronet [S. 1666], of Glorat aforesaid, 1st s. and h., *suc. to the Baronetcy* on the death of his father. He *m.*, about 1705, Barbara, widow of John DOUGLAS, of Maine, da. of Hugh CORBET, of Hardgray. He *d.* 21 April 1712.

III. 1712. SIR JAMES STIRLING, Baronet [S. 1666], of Glorat aforesaid, s. and h., *suc. to the Baronetcy*, 21 April 1712. He *m.* firstly, May 1728, Martha LUKE. She was *bur.* 7 July 1733, in the Cathedral churchyard, Glasgow.(b) He *m.* secondly, 28 Jan. 1751, Jean, only da. of Capt. John STIRLING, of Herbertshire [*Qy.* Hertfordshire]. He *d.* s.p. 30 April 1771, at Glorat. His widow *m.* (as 2d wife) James ERSKINE, a Lord of Session, styled LORD ALVA, who *d.* 13 May 1796, aged 74,(c) and *d.* 1797.

IV. 1771. SIR ALEXANDER STIRLING, Baronet [S. 1666], of Glorat aforesaid, and sometime of St. Albans, cousin and h. male, being s. and h. of John STIRLING, Writer, in Edinburgh, by Elizabeth, 1st da. and coheir of Sir Alexander HOME, of Renton, which John was 2d s. of the 1st Baronet. He was *b.* 1715, and *suc. to the Baronetcy*, 30 April 1771. He *m.* Mary, 1st da. of Robert WILLIS, of Stroud, near Rochester. He *d.* 22 Feb. 1791. "The Dow. Lady STIRLING" *d.* 7 Jan. 1814, in her 90th year.

V. 1791. SIR JOHN STIRLING, Baronet [S. 1666], of Glorat aforesaid, s. and h., *suc. to the Baronetcy*, 22 Feb. 1791; Chairman of the Chamber of Commerce, 1801. His marriage (evidently a second ceremony, the first being apparently before 1771) is recorded, 28 Jan. 1774, at St. Andrew's

(a) A book called "The Stirlings of Craigbarnet and Glorat," by Joseph Bain, was published at Edinburgh, 1883.
(b) This marriage is not mentioned in Playfair's *Baronetage*.
(c) See p. 251, note "a."

Episcopal Church, Glasgow, with "Gloryanah STIRLING, late FOLSOME,"(a) *viz.*, Gloriana, da. of Samuel FOLSOME, of Stratford, in North America, said to have been a Blacksmith.(b) He *d.* 16 March 1818. His widow *d.* 4 Jan. 1826.

VI. 1818. SIR SAMUEL STIRLING, Baronet [S. 1666], of Glorat aforesaid, 1st surv. s. and h., *b.* 28 July 1783, at Glorat; Advocate, 25 June 1808; *suc. to the Baronetcy*, 16 March 1818. He *m.* (contract 13 Sep. 1842) Mary Anne, only da. of Robert BERRIE, Major in the East India Company's Service. She *d.* 8 Oct. 1856. He *d.* s.p. 3 May 1858, at the Hotel Windsor, Paris, aged 74.

VII. 1858. SIR SAMUEL HOME STIRLING, Baronet [S. 1666], of Glorat aforesaid, nephew and h., being 1st s. and h. of George STIRLING, Capt. 9th Foot, by his 1st wife, Anne Henrietta, da. of William GRAY, of Oxgang, which George (who *d.* 21 Feb. 1852, aged 66), was yr. br. of the late Baronet. He was *b.* 28 Jan. 1830; *suc. to the Baronetcy*, 3 May 1858; was Capt. Linlithgow Militia Artillery, 1860. He *m.* 11 Oct. 1854, Mary Harriet Thornton, yst. da. of Col. Thomas Stirling BEGBIE, 44th Foot. He *d.* s.p.m. at Glorat, 19 Sep. 1861, aged 31. His widow *d.* 12 Jan. 1895, at Cairnbank, near Duns, in Scotland, aged 65.

VIII. 1861. SIR CHARLES ELPHINSTONE FLEMING STIRLING, Baronet [S. 1666], of Glorat aforesaid, br. and h. male, *b.* 31 July 1831; *suc. to the Baronetcy*, 19 Sep. 1861. He *m.* 24 April 1867, at St. Mary's, Bryanston square, Marylebone, Anne Georgina, 1st da. of James MURRAY, of Ancoats Hall, near Manchester, and Bryanston square aforesaid.

STIRLING :
cr. 2 May 1666;
ex. 9 May 1808.

I. 1666. HENRY STIRLING,(c) of Ardoch," 1st s. and h. of William STIRLING, of the same, by Margaret (marr. contract 15 May 1602), da. of James MURRAY, Junior, of Strowan, suc. his father in 1652, and was *cr. a Baronet* [S.], as above, 2 May 1666, with rem. to heirs male of his body. He *m.* Isobel, da. of John HALDANE, of Gleneagles. He *d.* Feb. 1669.

II. 1669. SIR WILLIAM STIRLING, Baronet [S. 1666], of Ardoch aforesaid, s. and h.; *suc. to the Baronetcy*, in Feb. 1669. He *m.* firstly (contract 22 Jan. 1685), Mary, 1st da. of Sir Charles ERSKINE, 1st Baronet [S. 1666], of Alva, by Christian, da. of Sir James DUNDAS. He *m.* secondly (contract 24 May 1699), Janet, da. of John MURRAY, of Touchadam. He *d.* Feb. 1702. His widow *m.* 3 Dec. 1702, Robert MURRAY, s. of Sir Robert MURRAY, of Abercairney.

III. 1702. SIR HENRY STIRLING, Baronet [S. 1666], of Ardoch aforesaid, s. and h. by 1st wife, *b.* 18 Nov. 1688; *suc. to the Baronetcy*, in Feb. 1702; admitted as Advocate, 29 Nov. 1710. He *m.* 31 Dec. 1726, Anna, da. of Thomas GORDON, Governor of Cronstadt and Admiral of the Russian Fleet. He *d.* 24 Nov. 1753. His widow *d.* 23 Sep. 1776 in Grosvenor square, Midx.

(a) *Scottish Antiquary*, vol. x, p. 21. In Playfair's *Baronetage* [1811] it is stated that by her he had "19 children in the first 18 years of their marriage."
(b) See "*Recollections of Curious Character*" as to this romantic marriage. The first child seems to have been born in America.
(c) He is sometimes, but incorrectly, called Alexander Stirling.

IV. 1753. SIR WILLIAM STIRLING, Baronet [S. 1666], of Ardoch aforesaid, 1st s. and h., *b.* in Russia about 1730; was a Lieut. in Gen. HALKET'S regiment in the Dutch service; *suc. to the Baronetcy*, 24 Nov. 1753. He *m.* 17 April 1763, Christian, da. of John ERSKINE, of Carnock, Advocate. She *d.* 7 Sep. 1788. He *d.* s.p.m.(a) 26 July 1799. Admon. Dec. 1801.

V. 1799, to 1808. SIR THOMAS STIRLING, Baronet [S. 1666], of Strowan, co. Perth, br. and h. male, *b.* Oct. 1733; served in the Dutch, 1747, and afterwards in the English service, being at the capture of Martinique in 1759 and of the Havannah in 1762, and at the conquest of Canada, 1763. He served in the American war till 1780, when he was severely wounded; was sometime (1782) Col. of the 71st Foot, and subsequently, 1790, of the 41st Foot, becoming full General in 1801. He purchased the estate of Strowan in 1794, and *suc. to the Baronetcy*, 26 July 1799. He *d.* at Strowan, unm., 8 May 1808, when the *Baronetcy* became *extinct*.(b) Will pr. 1808.

WOOD :
cr. 11 May 1666;
ex., apparently, 3 May 1738;
but assumed subsequently.

I. 1666. "JOHN WOOD, of Bonyngtoun,"(c) co. Forfar, 2d s. of Patrick WOOD, of the same (*d.* before 1653), by Anne, da. of John (CARNEGIE), 1st EARL OF NORTHESK [S.], was *b.* about 1638; suc. to the family estates on the death of his elder br., Henry WOOD; had spec. service, 17 Oct. 1661, to his father in the estates of Bonyngtoun, Letham, Kimblethmont, etc., and was *cr. a Baronet* [S.], as above, 11 May 1666, such creation, however, not being recorded in the Great Seal Register. He, however, registered his arms and supporters as a Baronet, in the Lyon office, in 1672. He, who "ruined his estate," sold Kimblethmont in 1678. He *m.* (contract, 10-13 Feb. 1660; tocher, 6,000 merks) Anne, 1st da. of James (OGILVY), 2d EARL OF AIRLIE [S.], by his 1st wife, Helen, da. of George (OGILVY), 1st LORD BANFF [S.]. He *d.* Jan. 1693.

II. 1693, to 1738. SIR JAMES WOOD, Baronet [S. 1666], of Bonytoun aforesaid, s. and h.; *suc. to the Baronetcy*, Jan. 1693, and was served heir gen. and heir special in Bonytoun, 10 Aug. 1704. He served sometime in the Dutch army; was Gov. of Dendermonde; was subsequently Major in Strathnaver's regiment; Col. 21st Foot; Col. of the Royal Scots Fusileers; Major-Gen. in the army, 27 Oct. 1735, and Brig.-Gen. in Dublin. He *m.*, 22 Feb. 1731, Anne, only da. of Edward JONES, Master of the Royal Vineyard in St. James' Park, Westm. He *d.* s.p.m., 3 May 1738,(d) when the *Baronetcy*, apparently, *became extinct*. His widow *d.* at Delft, in Holland, in or before 1748. Admon. 25 Aug. 1748, for benefit of her grandson and next of kin, James ALLARDICE-WOOD, of Aberbrothock, in Scotland.

(a) His da. and h. *m.* Col. Charles Moray, of Abercairney, co. Perth, and her second son, William, took the name of Moray-Stirling on inheriting the estate of Ardoch.
(b) He left the Strowan estate to his nephew (son of his sister), Thomas Graham, of Airth, with rem. to the 2d son, who accordingly took the additional name of Stirling.
(c) The estate was acquired by this family about 1490 by the marriage of Walter Wood with Dorothea Tulloch, the heiress of Bonyngtoun.
(d) This is the date given in his grandson's service. It is elsewhere given as 23 Feb. 1738.

The title was assumed as under.

III. 1750? JAMES ALLARDYCE-WOOD, grandson and heir of line, being s. and h. of (—) ALLARDYCE, by (—) elder of the two daughters and coheirs of the late Baronet, was, on 23 April 1739, served heir spec. to his maternal grandfather in the estates of Bonyngtoun, Letham, etc., and on 3 May 1748, heir of line and provision general. He appears shortly after that date to have *assumed the Baronetcy*. He *m.* Jane MACKENZIE, who survived him, and *d.* in 1802, being described as "widow of Sir James ALLARDYCE-WOOD, of Letham, *Baronet*."

RUTHVEN :
cr. 11 July 1666;
ex. about 1700.

I. 1666, to 1700? "FRANCIS RUTHVEN, of Redcastle," co. Forfar, was *cr. a Baronet* [S.], as above, 11 July 1666, with rem. to heirs male of the body. He *m.* Elizabeth, 2d da. of Thomas (RUTHVEN), 1st LORD RUTHVEN OF FREELAND [S.], by Isabel, da. of Robert (BALFOUR, *formerly* ARNOT), LORD BALFOUR OF BURLEIGH [S.]. This Elizabeth, who *d.* before Oct. 1674, was 2d of the three sisters of the 2d Lord, who *d.* unm. April 1701. Sir Francis *d.* s.p.m.,(a) when the *Baronetcy* became *extinct*.

ERSKINE :
cr. 20 Aug. 1666;
afterwards, 1797-1829, EARLS OF KELLIE [S.];
ex. 3 Dec. 1829.

I. 1666. "CHARLES ERSKINE, of Cambo," co. Fife, 3d s. of Alexander ERSKINE, *styled* VISCOUNT FENTOUN (s. and h. ap. of Thomas, 1st EARL OF KELLIE [S.], but *d.* v.p. Feb. 1633), by Anne, da. of Alexander (SETON), 1st EARL OF DUNFERMLINE [S.], was *b.* probably about 1620; joined the Royalist troops and was taken prisoner, Nov. 1654, in the Braes of Angus; was installed Lyon King of Arms, 25 Nov. 1663, and was *cr. a Baronet* [S.], as above, 20 Aug. 1666, with rem. to heirs male of the body. He had a charter of the Barony of Cambo (which he had purchased), 27 Oct. 1669. He *m.* in or before 1665, Penelope, da. of Arthur BARCLAY, of Colhill, Gentleman of the King's Chamber. He *d.* Feb. 1677.

II. 1677. SIR ALEXANDER ERSKINE, Baronet [S. 1666], of Cambo aforesaid, only s. and h., *b.* 1665; *suc. to the Baronetcy* in Feb. 1677, though not served heir to his father till 12 Oct. 1686; was, when under age, installed Lyon King of Arms, 27 July 1681, an office which, under the Great Seal, 29 Jan. 1702, he held with rem. to his son, Alexander Erskine (who predeceased him); was Joint Keeper of the Signet, 1711; M.P. [S.] for Fifeshire (two

(a) Isobel, his 1st da. and coheir, became in Oct. 1622, heir of line to her maternal grandfather, Thomas (Ruthven), 1st Lord Ruthven of Freeland [S.], and inherited the estates of that family. She assumed that peerage (on the ground that it had been granted to the heir general) which was borne by her son and has continued to be so by the heirs of his body.

Parls.) 1710-15; joined the Jacobite rising in Aug., but surrendered, 17 Sep. 1715, and was imprisoned at Edinburgh till it was put down. He *m.* in 1680, Mary, 1st da. of his paternal uncle, Alexander (ERSKINE), 3d EARL OF KELLIE, by his 1st wife, Mary, da. of Col. KIRKPATRICK. He *d.* (not in 1735 but) in 1727.

III. 1727. SIR CHARLES ERSKINE, Baronet [S. 1666], of Cambo aforesaid, 1st s. and h.; Bute Pursuivant, 1707-15; Lyon Clerk, 1715-24; *suc. to the Baronetcy* in 1727. He *d.* unm., 8 Feb. 1753.

IV. 1753. SIR JOHN ERSKINE, Baronet [S. 1666], of Cambo aforesaid, br. and h.; Kyntyre Pursuivant, 1707-26; Albany Herald, 1726-53; *suc. to the Baronetcy*, 8 Feb. 1753. He *d.* unm., 20 July 1754.

V. 1754. SIR WILLIAM ERSKINE, Baronet [S. 1666], of Cambo aforesaid, br. and h.; Unicorn Pursuivant, 1707-15; *suc. to the Baronetcy*, 20 July 1754. He *d.* unm., 30 Oct. 1780.

VI. 1780. SIR CHARLES ERSKINE, Baronet [S. 1666], of Cambo aforesaid, nephew and h., being 1st s. and h. of David ERSKINE, by his 2d wife, (—), da. of (—) YOUNG, of Edinburgh, which David was next br. of the late and 4th s. of the 2d Baronet. He *suc. to the Baronetcy*, 30 Oct. 1780. He *m.* about 1760, Peggy, da. of (—) CHIENE.(a) He *d.* 6 March 1790, at Cambo.

VII. 1790. SIR WILLIAM ERSKINE, Baronet [S. 1666], of Cambo aforesaid, 1st s. and h., *b.* about 1760; *suc. to the Baronetcy*, 6 March, 1790; was a Lieut. in the 26th Foot. He *d.* unm., at Niagara in America, 2 Oct. 1791.

VIII. 1791. SIR CHARLES ERSKINE, Baronet [S. 1666], of Cambo aforesaid, only surv. br. and h., *b.* about 1764; *suc. to the Baronetcy*, 2 Oct. 1791. By the death, 8 May 1797, of his cousin, Archibald (ERSKINE), 7th EARL OF KELLIE [S.], he became EARL OF KELLIE. etc. [S.] In that peerage this *Baronetcy* then merged, till it became *extinct* by the death, 3 Dec. 1829, of the 10th Earl and 10th Baronet, though the peerage still continued. See *Peerage*.

SCOTT:

cr. 22 Aug. 1666(b);

afterwards, since 1725, LORDS NAPIER OF MERCHISTOUN [S.].

I. 1666. "FRANCIS SCOTT, of Thirlestane," co. Selkirk, 1st s. and h. of Patrick SCOTT, of the same, by Isabel, da. of Sir John MURRAY, of Blackbarony, co. Peebles, was *b.* 11 May 1645; suc. his father, 22 June 1666, and was *cr. a Baronet* [S.], as above, 22 Aug. 1666,(b) with rem. to the heirs male of the body, being served heir to his father, 29 Nov. 1667. He

(a) The following distich on her was written on a window pane at Craie:—

"*To Miss Peggy Chiene.*
Oh blest by Nature, blest by art,
To please the eye, to win the heart.
Where beauty forms the second praise,
Lost in thy worth's superior blaze."

(b) According to Wood's *Douglas' Peerage* [S.], Milne's *List* and the *Lists* in Chamberlayne and Miege, the date was 22 *August* 1666, but it is sometimes given as 22 *April* 1666. Considering that the death of the grantee's father took place 22 June 1666, the former date seems more probable.

was M.P. [S.] for co. Selkirk, 1669-74, 1685-86, and 1693-1701; was Master of the Works, 17 Oct. 1704. He *m.* (contract 27 Nov. 1673), Henrietta, 6th da. of William (KERR), EARL OF LOTHIAN [S.], by Anne, *suo jure* COUNTESS OF LOTHIAN [S.]. He *d.* at Edinburgh, 7 March 1712, in his 67th year. His widow *d.* there 30 June 1741, aged 90.

II. 1712. SIR WILLIAM SCOTT, Baronet [S. 1666], of Thirlestane aforesaid, 1st but only surv. s. and h., *b.* probably about 1680; admitted an Advocate, 25 Feb. 1702; *suc. to the Baronetcy*, 7 March 1712. He *m.* firstly (contract 15 Dec. 1699) Elizabeth, "Mistress of Napier," only surv. child and h. presumptive of Margaret, *suo jure* BARONESS NAPIER [S.], by John BRISBANE, Envoy to Portugal. She *d.* 21 Aug. 1705. He m. secondly (contract, 30 June 1710), Jean, widow of Sir William SCOT, of Harden, da. of Sir John NISBET, of Dirletoun. He *d.* 8 Oct. 1725.(a)

III. 1725. Francis (NAPIER, *formerly* SCOTT) LORD NAPIER [S.], only s. and h. by 1st wife, *b.* 16 Nov. 1705; suc. to the Peerage [S.], as above, in Sep. 1706, on the death of his maternal grandmother, Margaret, *suo jure* BARONESS NAPIER [S.] abovenamed, when, apparently, he took the name of *Napier* in lieu of *Scott*. He *suc. to the Baronetcy* and to the estate of Thirlestane, 8 Oct. 1725 (on the death of his father), when that *Baronetcy became merged in the Peerage*, and still (1904) so continues. See *Peerage*.

BLAIR:

cr. 18 Sep. 1666;

but, apparently, never confirmed.

WILLIAM BLAIR, of Kinfauns, co. Perth (which he acquired in 1654, having formerly been of Williamstoun), was *cr. a Baronet* [S.], as above, 18 Sep. 1666, with rem. to his heirs male,(b) but the creation is not recorded in the Great Seal Register. He *m.* Agnes MURRAY, and *d.* s.p.m.(c)

(a) He was the author of several Latin poems.

(b) *Ex inform.* Francis J. Grant, Rothesay Herald and Lyon Clerk, who adds that, according to the Inventory of Deeds, "the patent of Knight Baronetcy," so granted, is (1904) at Kinfauns.

(c) He had two daughters and coheirs, viz. (1) Elizabeth, who apparently *d.* unm., and (2) Anna, who *m.*, in or before 1682 (as his 1st wife), the Hon. Alexander Carnegie, 4th s. of David, 2d Earl of Northesk [S.]. Their son, Alexander Carnegie, *otherwise* Blair, was served heir to his mother in the Barony of Kinfauns, 17 April 1695. He *m.* in 1697, at the age of 15, Jean, da. of James Carnegie, of Finhaven. They did not live together for some years, but afterwards cohabited for a few months, after which he went abroad for several years. During his absence she had a child. He returned home in Feb. 1720, and his wife gave birth on 6 Aug. following, at Berwick, to a da., named Margaret, having subsequently another daughter. The paternity of these children was disputed by the next heirs (on the ground of want of access and of the impotency of the father), but apparently unsuccessfully, as the said Margaret Blair became heiress of Kinfauns. She *m.* 17 Oct. 1741 John (Gray), 11th Lord Gray [S.] (who *d.* 28 Aug. 1782, aged 66, at Kinfauns), and *d.* 22 Jan. 1790, being ancestress of the succeeding Peers. See note "b" above.

ELIOTT:

cr. 3 Dec. (or 3 Sep.) 1666.(a)

I. 1666. "SIR GILBERT ELIOTT, of Stobbs," co. Roxburgh, 1st s. and h. of William ELIOTT, of the same, sometime (1640-51) M.P. for Roxburghshire, by Elizabeth, da. of Sir James DOUGLAS, of Cavers, was *Knighted* at Largo, 14 Feb. 1651, by Charles II; was M.P. [S.] for Roxburghshire, 1661-63, 1667 and 1669-74, and was *cr. a Baronet* [S.], as above, 3 Dec. (or 3 Sep.) 1666,(b) with rem. to heirs male of the body. He *m.* firstly, Isabella, da. of the Hon. James CRANSTOUN, Master of Cranstoun (s. and h. ap. of John, 2d LORD CRANSTOUN [S.]), by his 2d wife, Elizabeth, da. of Francis (STEWART), EARL OF BOTHWELL [S.]. He *m.* secondly, Magdalen, da. of Sir John NICOLSON, 2d Baronet [S. 1629], of Lasswade, by Elizabeth, da. of Sir William DICK, of Braid. She *d.* as his widow, and was *bur.* 24 Feb. 1699.

II. 1680? SIR WILLIAM ELIOTT, Baronet [S. 1666], of Stobs aforesaid, 1st s. and h., by 1st wife; *suc. to the Baronetcy* on the death of his father; was M.P. [S.] for Roxburghshire, 1689, and again 1689 till 29 April 1693, when (not having taken the oath of allegiance) his seat was declared vacant. He *m.* firstly, Elizabeth, 1st da. of Sir John SCOTT, 1st Baronet [S. 1671], of Ancrum, by his 1st wife, Elizabeth, da. of Francis SCOTT, of Mangerston. He *m.* secondly, Margaret, da. of Charles MURRAY, of Haldon. He *d.* 1694. His widow living 15 April 1702.

III. 1694. SIR GILBERT ELIOTT, Baronet [S. 1666], of Stobs aforesaid, 1st s. and h., *b.* about 1681; *suc. to the Baronetcy* in 1694; was M.P. for Roxburghshire (three Parls.) 1708-15, and 1726-27. He *m.* 23 April 1702, at St. Bride's, London (Lic. Vic. Gen. 15, he above 21, with consent of mother), Eleanor (then above 17), da. of William ELIOTT, of Wells, co. Roxburgh, and of St. Martin's in the Fields, Westminster, laceman. She *d.* 1728. He *d.* 27 May 1764, at a great age.

IV. 1764. SIR JOHN ELIOTT, Baronet [S. 1666], of Stobs aforesaid, 1st s. and h.,(c) *b.* probably about 1705; *suc. to the Baronetcy*, 27 May 1764. He *m.* Mary, da. of (—) ANDREWS, of London. He *d.* 31 Dec. 1767. Will pr. Jan. 1768. His widow *d.* in London, 12 Jan. 1771. Will pr. Jan. 1771.

V. 1767. SIR FRANCIS ELIOTT, Baronet [S. 1666], of Stobs aforesaid, only s. and h., *suc. to the Baronetcy*, 31 Dec. 1767. He *m.* Euphan., da. of (—) DIXON. He *d.* 20 June 1791.

VI. 1791. SIR WILLIAM ELIOTT, Baronet [S. 1666], of Stobs aforesaid, 1st s. and h., *suc. to the Baronetcy*, 20 June 1791. He *m.* 14 April 1790, in Edinburgh, Mary, da. of John RUSSELL, of Roseburn, Writer to the Signet. He *d.* 14 May 1812. His widow *d.* at Edinburgh, 6 June 1850. Will pr. July 1850.

VII. 1812. SIR WILLIAM FRANCIS ELIOTT, Baronet [S. 1666], of Stobs aforesaid, 1st s. and h., *b.* 1792; *suc. to the Baronetcy*, 14 May 1812. In 1818, on the death of his cousin, the Rt. Hon. William ELIOTT (great

(a) The date "3 *Dec.* 1666" is that given in Milne's *List* (as also in the *Lists* of Chamberlayne and Miege), where it is added "the same day with Bamffe Ramsay," which creation (undoubtedly one of 3 Dec. 1666) is, also, stated therein to have been "the same day as Elliot of Stobs."

(b) He is sometimes said to have been made "Knight Banneret at the battle of Scone, 1643," but there never was such a battle, neither was the King in Scotland in that or even in the previous year.

(c) The eighth and yst. s., Gen. George Augustus Eliott (*b.* at Wells, co. Roxburgh, 25 Dec. 1717), is famous for his defence of Gibraltar (1779-83), and was *cr.*, 6 July 1787, Baron Heathfield of Gibraltar, a peerage which became *extinct* on the death of his son, the 2d Baron, 26 Jan. 1813.

nephew to Eleanor, wife of the 3d Baronet), he suc. to the estate of Wells, co. Roxburgh. He *m.*, 22 March 1826, at Clifton, Theresa, 1st da. of Sir Alexander BOSWELL, 1st Baronet [1821], of Auchinleck. She *d.* 1836. He *d.* in London, 3 Sep. 1864, aged 72.

VIII. 1864. SIR WILLIAM FRANCIS AUGUSTUS ELIOTT, Baronet [S. 1666], of Stobs aforesaid, 1st s. and h., *b.* at Stobs Castle, 2 Feb. 1827; ed. at Eton; was sometime an officer in the 93d Highlanders; *suc. to the Baronetcy*, 3 Sep. 1864. F.R.S. He *m.* firstly, 1 Dec. 1846, Charlotte Maria, da. of Robert WOOD, of Quebec. She *d.* s.p.m., 29 Nov. 1878, at Ruberslaw, near Crieff, co. Perth. He *m.* secondly, 22 April 1879, at St. Michael's, Mickleham, Surrey, Hannah Grissell, widow of Henry KELSALL, da. of H. T. BIRKETT, of Foxbury, Surrey.

Family Estates.—These, in 1883, consisted of 19,345 acres in Roxburghshire, valued at £11,509 a year, of which £2,575 belonged to the trustees of the late Baronet. *Principal Seat.*—Stobs Castle, near Hawick, co. Roxburgh.

RAMSAY:

cr. 3 Dec. 1666.

I. 1666. "SIR GILBERT RAMSAY, of Bamff," co. Perth, s. and h. of Gilbert RAMSAY, of the same, by Isobel, da. of (—) OGILVY, of Clova, having distinguished himself at the defeat of the Covenanters, at Pentland Hills, 28 Nov. 1666, and, having been *Knighted*, was *cr. a Baronet* [S.], as above, 3 Dec. 1666, with rem. to heirs male of the body. He *m.* Elizabeth da. of Thomas BLAIR, of Balthyock.

II. 1686? SIR JAMES RAMSAY, Baronet [S. 1666], of Bamff aforesaid, 2d s. and h. male;(a) *suc. to the Baronetcy* on the death of his father; was M.P. [S.] for Perthshire, 1689, and again in 1689 till 28 April 1693, when (not having taken the oath of allegiance) his seat was declared vacant. He *m.* firstly, probably about 1665, Christian, da. and coheir of Sir Thomas OGILVY (2d s. of James, 1st EARL OF AIRLIE [S.]), by Christian, relict of Col. Thomas KER, da. of Patrick (RUTHVEN), EARL OF BRENTFORD. He *m.* secondly (—), and left issue by both wives. He *d.* 1730, at a great age.

III. 1730. SIR JOHN RAMSAY, Baronet [S. 1666], of Bamff aforesaid, 1st s. and h., by 1st wife, *b.* probably about 1670; *suc. to the Baronetcy* in 1730. He *m.*, in or before 1706, Lilias, 1st da. of Thomas GRÆME, of Balgowan. He *d.* 1738. His widow *d.* 4 March 1757, aged 85.

IV. 1738. SIR JAMES RAMSAY, Baronet [S. 1666], of Bamff aforesaid, 1st s. and h., *b.* about 1706; *suc. to the Baronetcy* in 1738; was "a man remarkable for his piety, honesty and integrity."(b) He *m.* Elizabeth, da. of Dr. George RAIT, of Annistoun. He *d.* 23 March 1782, aged 76.

V. 1782. SIR JOHN RAMSAY, Baronet [S. 1666], of Bamff aforesaid, 1st s. and h.; admitted as Advocate, 12 Dec. 1772; *suc. to the Baronetcy*, 23 March 1782; was Sheriff of Kincardineshire. He *d.* unm., 20 April 1783.

(a) Thomas Ramsay, the 1st s., *m.* Jean, da. of Sir Thomas Lumsden, of Innergelly, co. Fife, and *d.* v.p. and s.p.m., leaving a da., who *d.* unm.

(b) Playfair's *Baronetage* [1811].

VI. 1683. SIR GEORGE RAMSAY, Baronet [S. 1666], of Bamff aforesaid, br. and h.; *suc. to the Baronetcy*, 20 April 1783. He *m.* 29 Aug. 1786, Eleanora (*b.* 1766), 3d and yst da. of George (FRASER), LORD SALTOUN [S.], by Helen, da. of John GORDON, of Kinnellar. He *d.* s.p., 16 April 1790, of wounds received (two days before) in a duel with Capt. MACRAE, near Musselburgh. His widow *m.* 6 July 1792, at Hatton, co. Stirling, Lieut.-Gen. Sir Duncan CAMPBELL, of Lochnell, co Argyll, and *d.* about 1821.

VII. 1790. SIR WILLIAM RAMSAY, Baronet [S. 1666], of Bamff aforesaid, br. and h.; *suc. to the Baronetcy*, 16 April 1790. He *m.* 5 Aug. 1796, Agnata Frances, da. of Vincent Hilton BISCOE, of Hookwood, Surrey. He *d.* 17 Feb. 1807. Will pr. 1807.

VIII. 1807. SIR JAMES RAMSAY, Baronet [S. 1666], of Bamff aforesaid, 1st s. and h., *b.* 26 Sep. 1797, at Edinburgh; *suc. to the Baronetcy*, 17 Feb. 1807; matric. at Oxford (Ch. Ch.), 30 May 1816, aged 18; 2d class Classics, 1819. He *m.* 9 Feb. 1828, Jane, da. and h. of John Hope OLIPHANT, sometime first member of the Council in Prince of Wales' Island, by Jean, 2d da. of Sir John WEDDERBURN, 6th Baronet [S. 1704]. She *d.* 2 June 1842. He *d.* s.p., 1 Jan. 1859, aged 61.

IX. 1859. SIR GEORGE RAMSAY, Baronet [S. 1666], of Bamff aforesaid, br. and h., *b.* 10 March 1800, at Edinburgh; ed. at Harrow and at Trin. Coll., Cambridge; B.A., 1823; B.M., 1826; *suc. to the Baronetcy*, 1 Jan. 1859. He *m.* 9 Oct. 1830, at Paris, Emily Eugenia, da. of Henry LENNON, of Westmeath, Capt. 49th Foot. He *d.* at Bamff, 22 Feb. 1871, aged 71. His widow *d.* 28 Jan. 1885, aged 78, at Carlton Crescent, Southampton.

X. 1871. SIR JAMES HENRY RAMSAY, Baronet [S. 1666], of Bamff aforesaid, 1st s. and h., *b.* 21 May 1832, at Versailles, in France; ed. at Rugby School; matric. at Oxford (Ch. Ch.), 26 June 1851, aged 19; 1st class Classics, 1854; 1st class Law and Modern History, 1855; B.A., 1855; M.A., 1858; Barrister (Lincoln's Inn), 1863; *suc. to the Baronetcy*, 22 Feb. 1871; is author of *Lancaster and York* and other historical works. He *m.* firstly, 24 July 1861, at St. Andrew's, Kelso, Elizabeth Mary Charlotte, 1st da. of William SCOTT-KERR, of Chatto and Sunlaws, co. Roxburgh, by his 1st wife, Hannah Charlotte, relict of Sir John James SCOTT-DOUGLAS, 3d Baronet [1786], da. and h. of Henry SCOTT, of Belford, co. Roxburgh. She *d.* s.p.m., 28 Aug. 1868, at Bamff, aged 29. He *m.* secondly, 20 Aug. 1873, at St. John's, Edinburgh, Charlotte Fanning, only surv. child of William STEWART, of Ardvorlich, by Jane Emily, da. of John WILLSON, of Purdiesburn, co. Down.

Family Estates.—These, in 1883, consisted of 12,845 acres in co. Perth, and 1,027 in co. Forfar. *Total*, 13,872 acres, worth £4,570 a year. *Principal Seat.*—Bamff, near Alyth.(a)

HAY:

cr. 26 March 1667;

ex. 20 Dec. 1751.

I. 1667. "JAMES HAY, of Linplum," 1st s. and h. of the Hon. Sir William HAY, of Linplum aforesaid, by Anne, da. of (—) MURRAY (which William was yr. br. to John, 1st EARL OF TWEEDDALE [S.], both being sons of John, 8th LORD HAY OF YESTER [S.]), was M.P. [S.] for Haddington Constabulary 1669-74, and was *cr. a Baronet* [S.], as above, 26 March

(a) The following note is added in Bateman's *Great Landowners* [1883], "This estate has been held in male line by charter since 1232."

1667, with rem. to heirs male of the body. He *m.* firstly (contract 4 Feb. 1661) Jean, sister of Sir Francis SCOTT, 1st Baronet [S. 1666], 1st da. of Sir Patrick SCOTT, of Thirlestane, by Isabel, da. of Sir John MURRAY, of Blackbarony. He *m.* secondly, 27 April 1682, Anna LEVINGTOUN. He *d.* 1704.

II. 1704, to 1751. SIR ROBERT HAY, Baronet [S. 1667], of Linplum aforesaid, 2d but only surv. s. and h. male,(a) by 1st wife, *b.* about 1673; was an officer in the army, becoming eventually Lieut.-Col. of the (Scots Greys) 2d Reg. of Dragoons; *suc. to the Baronetcy* in 1704. He *d.* s.p., presumably unm., at Linplum, 20 Dec. 1751, in his 79th year, when the *Baronetcy* became *extinct*.(b)

STEWART:

cr. 27 March 1667;

afterwards, since 1796, SHAW-STEWART.

I. 1667. "ARCHIBALD STEWART, of Blackhall," co. Renfrew, 2d s. of John STEWART, by Mary (*m.* 1633), da. of Sir James STIRLING, of Keir, which John, who *d.* v.p. before 1658, was s. and h. ap. of Sir Archibald STEWART, of Blackhall aforesaid, was *b.* probably about 1635; suc. his elder br. John STEWART, who *m.* but *d.* s.p. in 1658, and suc. his said grandfather (in the family estate) in 1665; was M.P. [S.] for Renfrewshire 1667, and was *cr. a Baronet* [S.], as above, 27 March 1667, and, though there is no record of such creation in the Great Seal Register, "he takes out his arms as Barronet."(c) He *m.* firstly (contract 12 March 1659), Anne, da. and coheir of Sir John CRAUFURD, 1st Baronet [S. 1638], of Kilbirnie, by his 2d wife, Magdalen, da. and coheir of David CARNEGY, *styled* LORD CARNEGY, s. and h. of David, 1st EARL OF SOUTHESK [S.]. He *m.* secondly, Agnes DALMAHOY, probably Agnes (*bap.* 1 Sep. 1648), da. of Sir Alexander DALMAHOY, of that ilk, by Marion, da. of James NISBET, of Dean. She *d.* s.p. He *m.* thirdly, Mary, da. of (—) DOUGLAS. He, who was living April 1713, *d.* probably in or about 1722.

II. 1722? SIR ARCHIBALD STEWART, Baronet [S. 1667], of Blackhall aforesaid, grandson and h., being 1st s. and h. of John STEWART, Advocate [2 July 1692], M.P. [S.] for Renfrewshire (two Parls.) 1700-04, by Rebecca (*m.* 13 March 1700, at Glasgow), da. of Michael WALLACE, of Glasgow, Physician,(d) which John, who *d.* v.p. April 1713, was 2d s. (his elder br. dying v.p. and s.p.) of the late Baronet. He, who was served heir to his father, 17 Sep. 1717, was admitted as Advocate, 12 Dec. 1718; and *suc. to the Baronetcy* on the death of his grandfather, probably about 1722. He *d.* unm. April 1724.

III. 1724. SIR MICHAEL STEWART, Baronet [S. 1667], of Blackhall aforesaid, br. and h., *b.* about 1712; *suc. to the Baronetcy* in April 1724; admitted as Advocate, 19 July 1735. He *m.*, June 1738, Helen, sister and coheir of Sir John HOUSTON, 4th Baronet (who *d.* s.p. 27 July 1751), da. of Sir John HOUSTON, 3d Baronet [S. 1668], of Houston, by Margaret, da. of Sir John SHAW, 2d Baronet [S. 1687], of Greenock, co. Renfrew, and Eleanor, his wife, 1st da. of Sir Thomas NICOLSON, 2d Baronet [S. 1637], of Carnock, co. Stirling. She *d.* at Glasgow, 19 July 1746. He *d.* 20 Oct. 1796, aged 84.

(a) The eldest son, John Hay, *m.* 4 July 1685, Jean Foulis, and *d.* v.p. and s.p.m., before 16 May 1687, leaving an only da. and h. Margaret, *b.* 31 June 1686, who *m.* her cousin, Lord William Hay, of Newhall, and had numerous issue.

(b) He devised his estate to his cousin, Major-Gen. Lord Charles Hay (yr. s. of Charles, 3d Marquess of Tweeddale [S.]), who *d.* unm. May 1750.

(c) Milne's *List*.

(d) Her burial at the High [*i.e.*, Cathedral] Churchyard, Glasgow, is thus recorded, under 21 May 1740, "Rebekca Wallace, relik to the desised Sir John Stewart, of Blakhall." She *d.* in her 58th year.

IV. 1796. SIR JOHN SHAW-STEWART, Baronet [S. 1667], of Greenock and Blackhall aforesaid, 1st s. and h., *b.* probably about 1740; suc. as heir to his mother, on the death s.p.m. in 1752, of her maternal uncle, Sir John SHAW, 3d and last Baronet [S. 1687], to the estate of Greenock (under a settlement dated 1700), and took the name of SHAW before that of STEWART accordingly; was M.P. for Renfrewshire, 1780 to 21 Aug. 1783, and (two Parls.) 1786-96; *suc. to the Baronetcy* and the estate of Blackhall, 20 Oct. 1796. He *m.* in April 1786, Frances, widow of Sir James MAXWELL, 7th Baronet [S. 1682], of Pollok, 2d da. of Robert COLHOUN, of the island of St. Christopher. He *d.* s.p. 7 Aug. 1812. His widow *d.* at Glasgow 21 March 1818.

V. 1812. SIR MICHAEL SHAW-STEWART, Baronet [S. 1667], of Greenock, Blackhall and Carnock aforesaid, *formerly* Michael STEWART-NICOLSON, nephew and h., being only s. and h. of Houston STEWART-NICOLSON, of Carnock, by Margaret (*m.* 19 March 1765, at Edinburgh), da. of Boyd PORTERFIELD, of that ilk, which Houston, who took the name of NICOLSON after that of STEWART, on succeeding, in 1752, to the estate of Carnock (on the death s.p. of his mother's brother, Sir John HOUSTON, 4th Baronet [S. 1668]), was next br. to the late Baronet, and *d.* 1785. He was *b.* 10 Feb. 1766(a); *suc. to the Baronetcy* and the Greenock estate, 7 Sep. 1812, when he took the name of SHAW-STEWART in lieu of STEWART-NICOLSON; was sometime Lord Lieut. of Renfrewshire. He *m.* 24 Sep. 1787, his cousin Catherine, 2d and yst. da. of Sir William MAXWELL, 3d Baronet [S. 1683], of Springkell, by Margaret, da. of Sir Michael STEWART, 3d Baronet [S. 1667] abovenamed. He *d.* 25 Aug. 1825, at Ardgowan House, Greenock, in his 60th year. His widow *d.* 10 May 1849, in Park lane, at the residence of her da., the Duchess of Somerset.

VI. 1825. SIR MICHAEL SHAW-STEWART, Baronet [S. 1667], of Greenock and Carnock aforesaid, *formerly* Michael STEWART-NICOLSON, 1st s. and h., *b.* 1788 at Kirkpatrick, co. Dumfries; matric. at Oxford (Ch. Ch.), 29 Jan. 1807, aged 18; admitted to Lincoln's Inn, 1810; *suc. to the Baronetcy*, 25 May 1825; was M.P. for Lanarkshire, 1827-30; for Renfrewshire (four Parls.), 1830 till death in 1837. He *m.* 16 Sep. 1819,(b) at St. Marylebone,

(a) "Mrs. Nicolson, wife of Mr. Nicolson, of Carnock, of a son" [*Scot's Mag.*, under 10 Feb. 1766].

(b) Another wife is sometimes attributed to him, viz., "Eliza Mary, 2d da. of J. Murdoch," called *first* wife in Foster's *Members of Parl.* [S.]. A claim was made by James Gilmour (see two tracts, without date, but subsequent to 19 Feb. 1897, published by himself at "24 Iona place, Mount Florida, Glasgow," viz., "The Greenock paternity case" and "Glasgow Corporation baby farming plainly exposed") that he himself was son of "Sir Michael Shaw Stewart [*i.e.*, the 6th Baronet] and his wife, Eliza Mary Murdoch, of 13 Portland place, London." It is stated that she, who is called a West Indian heiress, married in London about 1826 (before 1829), and was living 1839. Of this marriage the said James Gilmour, born 29 Jan. 1840, who was placed under that name in the Glasgow hospital, alleges himself to be the surviving son and heir, and consequently entitled, on his father's death, to the Baronetcy. The date of the death of his father (said to have been aged about 18 on the death of *his* father in 1825), is, however, never given. It will be noticed that the 6th Baronet, whom he claims as his father, married [as stated in the text] some ten years previously (16 Sep. 1819) Eliza Mary Farquhar, by whom he had a son (born in 1826) who did (*de facto*) succeed to the Baronetcy in 1836. This difficulty is, however, disposed of by saying that Miss Farquhar's husband, though (by means of foreclosing the mortgage of £25,000 made by the 5th Baronet to her father, Robert Farquhar) he obtained possession of the Greenock estates, was *not*, in reality, the son of the 5th Baronet but assumed the Baronetcy, which rightfully belonged to James Gilmour's father, like whom (who, it is stated, *was* such son), he styled himself "SIR MICHAEL SHAW STEWART, [6th] Baronet," so that from and after 1825 till the death of one of the said parties, there were *two contemporary* persons thus designated. The marriage with Miss Murdoch is there stated to be mentioned in *Lodge's Peerage* for 1834, as also in *Oliver and Boyd's Almanack* for 1837.

Eliza Mary, only child of Robert FARQUHAR, of Newark, co. Renfrew. He *d.* 19 Dec. 1836, at the Douglas Hotel, Edinburgh, aged 48. His widow, who was *b.* 14 Jan. 1799, *d.* suddenly 25 Jan. 1852, in Belgrave square.

VII. 1836. SIR MICHAEL ROBERT SHAW-STEWART, Baronet [S. 1667], of Greenock, 1st s. and h., *b.* 26 Nov. and *bap.* 25 Dec. 1826, at Ardgowan; ed. at Eton; *suc. to the Baronetcy*, 19 Dec. 1836; matric. at Oxford (Ch. Ch.), 31 May 1844; sometime, 1845-46, an officer in the 2d Life Guards; M.P. for Renfrewshire, 1855-65; Lieut.-Col. 1st Renfrew Vols., 1860 till death; Grand Master Mason of Scotland, 1863; Sheriff of Wilts, 1883. He *m.* 28 Dec. 1852, at St. Geo. Han. sq., Octavia, 6th da. and 8th child of Richard (GROSVENOR), 2d MARQUESS OF WESTMINSTER, by Elizabeth Mary, da. of George Granville (LEVESON-GOWER), 1st DUKE OF SUTHERLAND. He *d.* at Ardgowan 10, and was *bur.* there 15 Dec. 1903 (after an operation, six days before death), aged 77. Will pr. at £120,902. His widow, who was *b.* 22 Sep. 1829, living 1904.

VIII. 1903. SIR MICHAEL HUGH SHAW-STEWART, Baronet [S. 1667], of Greenock, 1st s. and h., *b.* 11 July 1854, in Belgrave square; ed. at Eton; matric. at Oxford (Ch. Ch.), 23 May 1872, aged 17; sometime Capt. 4th Batt. Sutherland and Argyll Highlanders; M.P. for East Renfrewshire since 1886. He *m.* 14 Nov. 1883, at St. Geo. Han. sq., Alice Emma, 1st da. of John Alexander (THYNNE), 4th MARQUESS OF BATH, by Frances Isabella Catherine, da. of Thomas (VESEY), 2d VISCOUNT DE VESCI [I.]. She was *b.* 27 Jan. 1864.

Family Estates.—These, in 1883, consisted of 26,376 acres in Renfrewshire and 92 in Ayrshire. *Total*—26,468 acres, worth £7,378 a year. *Principal Seat.*—Ardgowan, near Greenock, co. Renfrew, and Fonthill Abbey, Wilts, though no land in Wiltshire is, in 1883, attributed to the family.

DON:

cr. 7 June 1667;

afterwards, since 1862, DON-WAUCHOPE.

I. 1667. "ALEXANDER DON, of Newton," *otherwise* Newton Don, co. Berwick, s. of (—) DON, of the same, by (—) MUSHET, of Burnbank, was *cr. a Baronet* [S.], as above, 7 June 1667, with rem. to heirs male of his body. He executed an entail of his estate in 1681. He *m.* Isabella, da. of [—] SMITH, of Duns. He *d.* 1687, before 22 July.(a)

II. 1687. SIR JAMES DON, Baronet [S. 1667], of Newton Don aforesaid, 1st s. and h.; *suc. to the Baronetcy* in 1687. He *m.*, 3 July 1680, Marion, da. of [—] SCOT, of Goranbery.

III. 1710? SIR ALEXANDER DON, Baronet [S. 1667], of Newton Don aforesaid, only s. and h.; *suc. to the Baronetcy* on his father's death. He *m.*, before 1717, Margaret, da. of John CARRE, of Cavers. He *d.* 13 April 1749. His widow *d.* at Coldstream, 24 Aug. 1767, at a very advanced age.

IV. 1749. SIR ALEXANDER DON, Baronet [S. 1667], of Newton Don aforesaid, 1st s. and h.,(b); *suc. to the Baronetcy*, 13 April 1749. He *m.* in 1750, Mary, da. of John MURRAY, of Philiphaugh, Heritable Sheriff of Selkirk. He *d.* 2 Oct. 1776, at Newton house.

V. 1776. SIR ALEXANDER DON, Baronet [S. 1667], of Newton Don aforesaid, 2d but only surv. s. and h.(c); *suc. to the Baronetcy*, 2 Oct. 1776; was sometime an officer in the army, and was, in

(a) In the Laing Charters, but by an evident mistake, his death is given as 1674.

(b) Patrick Don, a Capt. in the army, his only brother, *d.* 22 Feb. 1811, in his 94th year.

(c) James Don, his eldest brother, *d.* unm. and v.p. Sep. 1743.

IV

1778, Capt. of a reg. of Southern Fencibles. He *m.* in 1778, Henrietta, sister and coheir [1796] of John (CUNNINGHAM), 15th EARL OF GLENCAIRN [S.], da. of William, the 13th Earl, by Elizabeth, da. and coheir of Hugh MACGUIRE. She *d.* 12 March 1801. He *d.* 5 June 1815.(a)

VI. 1815. SIR ALEXANDER DON, Baronet [S. 1667], of Newton Don aforesaid, only s. and h., *b.* 1779; ed. at Eton, 1791-96; sometime an officer in the Dumfries Militia. On the death, 24 June 1801, of his grandmother, the COUNTESS OF GLENCAIRN [S.], he suc. to the estate of Ochiltree in Ayrshire. Being in France in 1801 he was detained there as prisoner; *suc. to the Baronetcy*, 5 June 1815; was M.P. for Roxburghshire (three Parls.), 1814 till death in 1826. He *m.* firstly, in 1809, Lucretia, 2d da. of George MONTGOMERIE, *formerly* MOLYNEUX, of Garboldisham hall, Norfolk, by Elizabeth, da. of Michael WHITE, Governor of the Leeward islands. She *d.* s.p. 1815. He *m.* secondly, in Aug. 1824, Grace, da. of John STEIN, of Edinburgh (sometime M.P. for Bletchingley), by (—), da. of John BUSHBY, of Tinwald Downs. He *d.* 11 April 1826, aged 47. His widow *m.*, in 1836, Gen. Sir James Maxwell WALLACE, K.H., who *d.* 3 Feb. 1867 at Dinderly hall, Northallerton, aged 82. She *d.* 13 March 1878, at Duncombe place, York.

VII. 1826. SIR WILLIAM HENRY DON, Baronet [S. 1667], of Newton aforesaid, only s. and h., by 2d wife, *b.* 4 May 1825; *suc. to the Baronetcy* in his infancy, 11 April 1826; ed. at Eton, 1838-41; was a Page in the "Eglinton tournament," Aug. 1839; an officer in the 5th Dragoon Guards, 1842-45; was owner of steeplechase horses and was well known on the turf; sold the estate of Newton Don for £85,000, and went on the stage in America, 1850-55; in Great Britain, 1855-61, and in Australia, 1861, till death in 1862. He *m.* firstly, June 1847, Antonia, da. of [—] LEBRUN, of Hamburg. He *m.* secondly, 17 Oct. 1857, at St. Marylebone, "a charming actress,"(b) sometime of the Queen's theatre, Dublin, *viz.*, Emily Eliza Grace, 1st da. of John SAUNDERS, of the Adelphi theatre, London, himself a popular actor. He *d.* s.p.m. 19 March 1862, after less than four days' illness, at Webb's hotel, Hobart town, Tasmania, aged 36. His widow, who continued her career as an actress till 1867, and subsequently sang at the music halls, *d.* of a rapid consumption 20 Sept. 1875, at Edinburgh.

VIII. 1862. SIR JOHN DON-WAUCHOPE, Baronet [S. 1667], of Edmonstone, co. Midlothian, *formerly* John WAUCHOPE, cousin and h. male, being only s. and h. of John WAUCHOPE, of Edmondstone aforesaid, Lieut.-Col. of the Edinburgh Militia, by Henrietta Warrender Cecilia, da. of Sir James Gardiner BAIRD, 4th Baronet [S. 1696], which John, who *d.* June 1837, aged about 70, was 2d but 1st surv. s. and h. of John WAUCHOPE, of Edmondstone (who *d.* 1810, aged 68), the s. and h. of James WAUCHOPE, *formerly* James DON, of the same, Advocate 1716, the only son that had issue of Patrick DON, of Altouneburn, by Anne, da. of (whose issue became heir of line to) John WAUCHOPE, of Edmondstone aforesaid, a Lord of Session [S.] under the style of Lord Edmondstone), the said Patrick being 3d s. of Sir Alexander DON, the 1st Baronet [S. 1667]. He was *b.* 10 July 1816, at Edmondstone; suc. his father in that estate, June 1837; ed. at Trin. Coll., Cambridge; B.A., 1837; M.A. 1842; Capt. Midlothian Yeomanry Cavalry, 1837-52; *suc. to the Baronetcy*, 19 March 1862, when he took the name of DON before that of WAUCHOPE; Chairman of Board of Lunacy [S.], 1863, and of Board of Education [S.], 1872. He *m.* 26 April 1853, Bethia Hamilton, 1st da. of Andrew Buchanan, of Greenfield, co. Lanark, by Bethia Hamilton, da. of William RAMSAY, of Gogar. He *d.* 12 Dec. 1893, in his 78th year, at 12 Ainslie place, Edinburgh. Personalty, £73,811. His widow living 1904.

(a) His two daughters, Elizabeth and Mary, were both drowned, 12 June 1795, in the Eden river, near Kelso.
(b) *N. & Q.*, 9th S., x, 108.

IX. 1903. SIR JOHN DOUGLAS DON-WAUCHOPE, Baronet [S. 1667], of Edmonstone aforesaid, 1st s. and h., *b.* 15 Sep. 1859; ed. at Trin. Coll., Cambridge; B.A., 1881; sometime Lieut. 3d Batt. Royal Scots; *suc. to the Baronetcy*, 12 Dec. 1903.

CAMPBELL :(a)
cr. probably between 23 Jan. 1667 and 16 May 1668,
but certainly before 1672.

I. 1668? "COLIN CAMPBELL, of Aberuchill," co. Perth, s. and h. of James CAMPBELL(b) of the same, a staunch adherent of the Royal Cause, by Ann, da. of Patrick HEPBURN, of Woolling, and Janet NAPIER, his wife; suc. his father in Nov. 1640, being then a minor, and was *cr. a Baronet* [S.], as above, probably between 23 Jan. 1667 and 16 May 1668, but certainly before 1672, though no record of such creation is on the Great Seal Register [S.].(c) He was admitted an Advocate, 4 Nov. 1664; was Sheriff Depute of Argyllshire, 1668; M.P. [S.] for Inverary, 1669-74 (being then "Provost"), and for Perthshire, 1690-1702. In 1669 he acquired the Barony and Castle of Kilbryde, co. Perth; was Senator of the College of Justice [S.] under the style of *Lord Aberuchill*, 1689; Lord of Justiciary and P.C. [S.], 1690. He estimated the losses he had received from the Highland army, under Dundee, at £17,201 Scots, but, though promised compensation by Act of Parl., appears never to have received it. He *m.* firstly, Margaret, or Janet, da. of Alexander FOULIS, of Ratho. She was *bur.* 5 June 1666. He *m.* secondly (contract 9 Aug. 1667), Catherine, sister of George, 1st EARL OF CROMARTY [S.]. 5th and yst. da. of Sir John MACKENZIE, 1st Baronet [S. 1628], of Tarbat, by Margaret, da. and coheir of Sir George ERSKINE, of Innerteil. He *d.* at Edinburgh, 16 Feb. 1704.

II. 1704. SIR JAMES CAMPBELL, Baronet [S. 1668?] of Aberuchill and Kilbryde aforesaid, 2d but 1st surv. s. and h. by 2d wife(d), *b.* about 1672; *suc. to the Baronetcy*, 16 Feb. 1704. He *m.* firstly Jean, da. and h. of Sir John DEMPSTER, of Pitliver, co. Fife. He *m.* secondly his cousin Jean, 2d da. of James (CAMPBELL), 2d EARL OF LOUDOUN [S.], by Margaret, da. of Hugh (MONTGOMERY), EARL OF EGLINTON [S.], but by her he had no issue. He *d.* 10 May 1754, aged 82.

III. 1754. SIR JAMES CAMPBELL, Baronet [S. 1668?] of Aberuchill and Kilbryde aforesaid, grandson and h., being s. and h. of Colin CAMPBELL, of Pitliver aforesaid, Advocate, by Catherine, da. of William NISBET, of Dirleton in East Lothian, which Colin, who was only s. and h. ap. of the late Baronet by his 1st wife (whose estate of Pitliver he inherited and sold) *d.* v.p. about 1738. He was *b.* 1723; was an officer in the Scots Greys and present at the battle of Fontenoy, 30 April 1745; *suc. to the Baronetcy*, 10 May 1754. He sold the estate of Aberuchill in 1772, and entailed that of Kilbryde in 1800. He *m.* firstly, 4 March 1754, Margaret, da. and h. of Capt. William Conductor BALL (*or* BALD), of Hatton Garden, London, niece of Alexander LE GRAND, a Commissr. of Customs. She *d.* 19 Sep. 1766, at Kilbryde. He *m.* secondly, Mary Ann, da. of Joseph BURN. He *d.* March 1812.

(a) See *Her. and Gen.*, vol. v, pp. 266-270, where the pedigree, as registered in the Lyon office, is set out.
(b) This James is often said to have been at the battle of Worcester, 3 Sep. 1651, an event, which took place eleven years after his death. He was s. and h. of Colin Campbell, of Aberuchill (living 1612), and was yr. br. of Sir James Campbell, of Lawess, father of John, 1st Earl of Loudoun [S.].
(c) He registered his Arms as Baronet in the Lyon office no less than four times between 1672 and 1703.
(d) Archibald Campbell, his elder br. of the half-blood, *d.* unm. and v.p.

IV. 1812. SIR ALEXANDER CAMPBELL, Baronet [S. 1668?], of Kilbryde aforesaid, 2d but 1st surv. s. and h., by 1st wife,(a) *b.* 16 Aug. 1757; *suc. to the Baronetcy* in March 1812. He *m.* (when in his 59th year) 31 July 1816, Margaret, da. of Alexander COLDSTREAM, of Crieff. He *d.* 13 Dec. 1824, at Kilbryde Castle, aged 67. His widow *d.* (37 years later) in 1871.

V. 1824. SIR JAMES CAMPBELL, Baronet [S. 1668?], of Kilbryde aforesaid, and of Redhill near Lydney, co. Gloucester, 1st s. and h., *b.* in Edinburgh, 5 May 1818; ed. at the High School and College there; *suc. to the Baronetcy*, 13 Dec. 1824; Dep. Surveyor of Dean Forest, 1855-93; Lieut.-Col. of the Gloucestershire Volunteers, 1872-86. He *m.* 28 July 1840, at St. Geo. Han. sq., Caroline, 2d da. of Admiral Sir Robert Howe BROMLEY, 3d Baronet [1757], by Anne, da. of Daniel WILSON, of Dallam Tower, Westmorland. She *d.* 9 Dec. 1900, at Redhill aforesaid. He *d.* 27 March 1903, in his 85th year, at Plas Heaton, near Trefnant, North Wales.

VI. 1903. SIR ALEXANDER CAMPBELL, Baronet [S. 1668?], of Kilbryde aforesaid, only s. and h., *b.* 10 Aug. 1841, at Stoke Hall near Newark; ed. at Harrow; entered Royal Artillery, 1861, becoming Lieut.-Col. 1889 and Col. (retired) 1894; *suc. to the Baronetcy*, 27 March 1903. He *m.* firstly, 6 Feb. 1871, Edith Frances Arabella, only da. of Alexander S. JAUNCEY. She *d.* 1884. He *m.* secondly, 4 Oct. 1893, Annie Augusta, widow of Walter JAMES, of Elvaston Hall, Ryton-on-Tyne, da. of Robert Henry MITFORD, of Weston Lodge, Hampstead, Midx.

DOUGLAS :
cr. 26 Feb. 1668.(a);
afterwards, since 1810, MARQUESSES OF QUEENSBERRY [S.].

I. 1668. JAMES DOUGLAS, of Kelhead, 2d but 1st surv. s. and h. ap. of the Hon. Sir William DOUGLAS, of Kelhead aforesaid, sometime (1647), Governor of Carlisle, by his 1st wife, Agnes, da. and h. of George FAWSIDE, of Fawside, which William was 2d s. of William, 1st EARL OF QUEENSBERRY [S.], was *b.* 19 Feb. 1639, and was v.p. *cr. a Baronet* [S.], as above, 26 Feb. 1668,(b) with rem. to the heirs male of his body. He suc. his father in the family estate, 1673. He *m.* (contract 28 Oct. 1667) Catherine, 2d da. of his paternal uncle, James (DOUGLAS), 2d EARL OF QUEENSBERRY [S.], by his 2d wife, Margaret, da. of John (STEWART), 1st EARL OF TRAQUAIR [S.]. He was living 8 Sep. 1705, but *d.* before April 1708.

II. 1707? SIR WILLIAM DOUGLAS, Baronet [S. 1668], of Kelhead aforesaid, only s. and h., *b.* probably about 1675; *suc. to the Baronetcy* on his father's death. He *m.* (contract 8 Sep. 1705), Helen, da. of Col. John ERSKINE, Dep. Gov. of Stirling Castle. He *d.* 10 Oct. 1733. His widow, by whom he had fourteen children, *d.* 26 July 1754.

III. 1733. SIR JOHN DOUGLAS, Baronet [S. 1668], of Kelhead aforesaid, 1st s. and h.; *b.* probably about 1708; *suc. to the Baronetcy*, 10 Oct. 1733; was M.P. for Dumfries burghs, 1734, till unseated 13 Feb. 1736; for Dumfrieshire, 1741-47; was committed to the Tower of London, 14 Aug. 1746, on suspicion of being concerned in the Jacobite rising, but released in March

(a) Colin Campbell, his elder br., Capt. 19th Foot and Lieut.-Col. of the Perth Militia, *d.* unm. 1811, a year before his father.
(b) The date given in Milne's (very accurate) *List*, as also in those of Miege and Chamberlayne and in Wood's *Douglas's Peerage*, vol. ii, p. 389, is 26 Feb. 1668, but in the last named work on p. 386 it is given as 20 Feb. 1668, and the grantee is made to be Sir *William* Douglas, *father* of the Sir James, the grantee given in the text.

1748. He *m.* about 1730, Christian, 6th da. of Sir William CUNNINGHAM, 2d Baronet [S. 1669], of Lambrughton and Caprington, by Janet, da. and h. of Sir James DICK, 1st Baronet [S. 1707], of Prestonfield. She, who was *b.* 23 April 1710, and by whom he had eight children, *d.* Nov. 1741. He *d.* at Drumlanrig, 13 Nov. 1778.

IV. 1778. SIR WILLIAM DOUGLAS, Baronet [S. 1668], of Kelhead aforesaid, 1st s. and h., *b.* probably about 1730; was M.P. for Dumfries burghs (two Parls.), 1768-80; *suc. to the Baronetcy*, 30 Nov. 1778. He *m.* 21 May 1772, at Edinburgh, Grace, 1st da. and coheir of William JOHNSTON of Lockerby, co. Dumfries. He *d.* 16 May 1783. His widow *d.* 25 March 1836, at Glen Stuart, in her 93d year.

V. 1783. SIR CHARLES DOUGLAS, Baronet [S. 1668], of Kelhead aforesaid, 1st s. and h., *b.* March 1777; *suc. to the Baronetcy*, 16 May 1783. He *m.* 13 Aug. 1803, at Richmond, co. Surrey, Caroline, 3d da. of Henry (SCOTT), DUKE OF BUCCLEUCH AND QUEENSBERRY [S.], by Elizabeth, da. and h. of George (MONTAGU, *formerly* BRUDENELL), 1st DUKE OF MONTAGU and 4th EARL OF CARDIGAN. She was living when, by the death of his cousin, William (DOUGLAS), 4th DUKE, 5th MARQUESS and 7th EARL OF QUEENSBERRY [S.], he, as heir male, succeeded him as MARQUESS AND EARL OF QUEENSBERRY [S.] the 3d Earl having been *cr.*, 11 Feb. 1681/2, MARQUESS OF QUEENSBERRY [S.], with rem. to his heirs male whatsoever. In that Peerage this *Baronetcy* then *merged*, and still (1904) so continues. See *Peerage*.

STEWART :
cr. 29 Feb. 1668;(a)
ex. 15 Jan. 1797.

I. 1668. "ARCHIBALD STEWART, of Castlemilk," *or* Castletoun (near Glasgow), co. Lanark, and of Gourock, co. Renfrew, only s. of Sir Archibald STEWART, of the same (a zealous Royalist), by Mary, da. of John (FLEMING), EARL OF WIGTOUN [S.], suc. his father soon after 1660, and was *cr. a Baronet* [S.], as above, 29 Feb. 1668,(a) and, though there is no record of such creation in the Great Seal Register [S.], took out his Arms as a Baronet in the Lyon office. He was M.P. [S.] for Renfrewshire, 1669-70. He *m.* (contract 2 Sep. 1665) Mary, sister of John, 1st EARL OF HYNDFORD [S.], 1st da. of the Hon. William CARMICHAEL, Master of Carmichael, by Grizel, da. of William (DOUGLAS), 1st MARQUESS OF DOUGLAS [S.]. He *d.* about 1670.

II. 1670? SIR WILLIAM STEWART, Baronet [S. 1668], of Castlemilk aforesaid, 1st s. and h., *suc. to the Baronetcy* on the death of his father; was M.P. [S.] for Lanarkshire, 1696-1702. He *m.* Margaret, da. and h. of John CRAWFURD, of Milton. He *d.* Nov. 1715. His widow *d.* 28 March 1737, in her 49th year.(b)

III. 1715. SIR ARCHIBALD STEWART, Baronet [S. 1668], of Castlemilk aforesaid, 1st s. and h.; *suc. to the Baronetcy* in Nov. 1715. He *m.*, April 1742, Frances, da. of James STIRLING, of Keir. She *d.* at Gourock, 12 Sep. 1757. He *d.* s.p.m., 5 Jan. 1763.

IV. 1763. SIR JOHN STEWART, Baronet [S. 1668], of Castlemilk aforesaid, *formerly* John CRAWFURD, of Milton aforesaid, br. and h. male, who had inherited the estate of John CRAWFURD, his maternal grandfather and taken his name; *suc. to the Baronetcy* on the death of his brother, 5 Jan. 1763, and resumed his patronymic of STEWART. He *m.* Helen, da. of John ORR, of Borrowfield. He *d.* 1 April 1781. His widow *d.* 17 May 1782.

(a) Douglas' *Baronage* [S.], p. 516, where the patent is stated to be "*in pub. archiv.*"
(b) *View of the Merchants House of Glasgow* (1866), p. 583.

V. 1781, to 1797. **Sir John Stewart**, Baronet [S. 1668], of Castlemilk aforesaid, 1st s. and h.,(a) *b.* probably about 1740; *suc. to the Baronetcy*, 1 April 1781. He *m.*, probably about 1770, Anne, da. and h. of his uncle, Sir Archibald Stewart, 3d Baronet [S. 1668], by Frances, da. of James Stirling. He *d.* s.p. 15 Jan. 1797, when *the Baronetcy* became *extinct*. His widow *d.* 26 Dec. 1821.

HOUSTON:

cr. 29 Feb. 1668;

not assumed after 1795, but existing 1881.

I. 1668. "Patrick Houston, of that ilk," co. Renfrew, as also of Leny, co. Midlothian, 1st s. and h. of Sir Ludovick Houston, of the same, many years M.P. [S.] for Dumbartonshire and Renfrewshire, by Margaret, da. of Patrick Maxwell, of Newark, co. Renfrew, suc. his father in 1662; was M.P. [S.] for Renfrewshire, 1661, and for Dumbartonshire, 1678 and 1681-82, and was *cr. a Baronet* [S.], as above, 29 Feb. 1668,(b) with rem. to the heirs male of his body. He had Crown Charter, 23 Feb. 1671, of the old Barony of Houston. He *m.* Anne, da. of John (Hamilton), 1st Lord Bargeny [S.], by Jane, da. of William (Douglas), 1st Marquess of Douglas [S.]. She *d.* 12 March 1678. He *d.* 1696.

II. 1696. **Sir John Houston**, Baronet [S. 1668], of Houston aforesaid, 1st s. and h.; was M.P. [S.] for Renfrewshire, 1685-86, for Stirlingshire, 1689 and 1689-1702, and for Renfrewshire (again), 1702-07, having *suc. to the Baronetcy* in 1696. He *m.* Anne, 1st da. of John (Drummond), 1st Earl of Melfort [S.], by his 1st wife, Sophia (heiress of Lundin), da. of Robert Maitland. He *d.* Dec. 1717. His widow, who was *b.* 3 March 1671, *d.* April 1738, aged 67.

III. 1717. **Sir John Houston**, Baronet [S. 1668], of Houston aforesaid, s. and h.; was M.P. for Linlithgowshire (three Parls.), 1708-15; Commissary of Glasgow; *suc. to the Baronetcy* in Dec. 1717. He *m.* Margaret, da. of Sir John Shaw, 2d Baronet [S. 1687], of Greenock, by Margaret, da. of Sir Thomas Nicolson, 2d Baronet [S. 1637] of Carnock. He *d.* 11 Feb. 1722, "in the flower of his age," leaving his estate burdened with some £200,000 debt.(a) His widow *d.* (a year before her son) 29 Jan. 1750.

IV. 1722. **Sir John Houston**, Baronet [S. 1668], of Houston aforesaid, only s. and h.; *suc. to the Baronetcy*, 11 Feb. 1722, and sold the much encumbered estate of Houston in 1740. He (though impotent) *m.* 12 Feb. 1744, at Edinburgh, his cousin Eleanora, 1st da. of Charles (Cathcart), 8th Lord Cathcart [S.], by his 1st wife, Marion, only child of Sir John Shaw, 3d and last Baronet [S. 1687], of Greenock. She, who was *b.* in Edinburgh, 3 March 1720, brought him £3,500, but (though aware before her marriage of her husband's state) sued for a divorce.(c) He *d.* s.p. in London

(a) The 2d son, William Stewart, took the name of Crawfurd in 1781, on inheriting in that year the estate of Milton, formerly that of his maternal grandfather, John Crawfurd. He *d.* s.p.m. before his elder brother.

(b) See *N. & Q.*, 3d S., x, p. 64, where (*inter alia*) it is stated that the warrant was dated at Whitehall on the last of Feb. 1668, inferring that the creation was not recorded on the Great Seal Register [S.], but in Milne's *List* there is no mark to denote that it had not been so registered.

(c) See *N. & Q.*, 3d S., x., pp. 81-83, for very full particulars as to this unhappy marriage, and of the two comedies (*The Coquette* and *In Foro*) of which she was the author. In Jones's *Biographia Dramatica* she is [erroneously] said to have died 30 July 1780. At that date there certainly does occur the death, at Bath, of "Hon. Lady Susan Houston, relict of Sir Thomas," an entry not easy of explanation.

27 and was *bur.* 31 July 1751, at St. Martin's in the Fields.(a) His widow *d.* 3 Nov. 1769, in her 50th year.

V. 1751. **Sir Patrick Houston**, Baronet [S. 1668], of Savanna, in Georgia, cousin and h. male,(b) being 2d s. but eventually (before Dec. 1747) h. male of Patrick Houston, Merchant, of Glasgow, by Isabel, da. and h. of George Johnstone, also of Glasgow, Merchant, which Patrick, who *d.* before 1717, was 2d s. of the 1st Baronet. He, who was *b.* about 1698 and was Comptroller of the Customs at the Port of Glasgow in 1723 and Chamberlain of of Kinneil, 1730; emigrated to America(c) about 1740, and became President of the Council at Georgia. He *suc. to the Baronetcy*, but not to any of the family estates, 27 July 1751. He *m.* Priscilla Dunbar. He *d.* 5 Feb. 1762, at Savanna, aged 64. His widow *d.* 26 Feb. 1775, aged 70. M.I. to both of them in the cemetery at Savanna.

VI. 1762. **Sir Patrick Houston**, Baronet [S. 1668], of Savanna aforesaid, 1st s. and h.; *b.* about 1743; *suc. to the Baronetcy*, 5 Feb. 1762; was a Lawyer. He, in the American War of Independence, took the part of the Crown and subsequently returned to England. He *d.* unm. at Bath, 24 and was *bur.* 28 March 1785, in Bath Abbey, in his 43d year. M.I. there.

VII. 1785. **Sir George Houston**, Baronet [S. 1668], of Georgia aforesaid, br. and h., *b.* probably about 1745; *suc. to the Baronetcy*, 24 March 1785. He *m.* Anne, da. of Thomas Moodie, of Georgia aforesaid, formerly of Dumbarton, co. Fife. He *d.* in Georgia 1795. His widow *d.* 1820.

VIII. 1795. **Patrick Houston**, of Georgia aforesaid, s. and h., *suc. to the Baronetcy* in 1795, but did not assume the title. He *m.* Eliza Macqueen.

IX. 1835? **George Houston**, of Georgia aforesaid, Planter, s. and h., *suc. to the Baronetcy* on the death of his father, but did not assume the title. He *m.* (—) Hazelhurst. He *d.* s.p. March 1881.

X. 1881. **Patrick Houston**, of Tallahassee in Florida, nephew and h. male, being s. and h. of Edward Houston, of Florida, Planter, by Claudia Bond. He *suc. to the Baronetcy* in March 1881, but did not assume the title. He *m.* Martha Brash.

[The devolution of the Baronetcy is unknown after this period.]

BRUCE:

cr. 21 Oct. 1668;

ex. 19 March 1710.

I. 1668. "William Bruce, of Balcaskie," co. Fife, 2d s. of Robert Bruce, of Blairhall (living 1633), by Catherine, da. of Sir

(a) He left a general disposition of his estate to his distant cousin, George Houston, of Johnstone, co. Renfrew, a great grandson of George Houston, of the same, who was a younger *brother* of the 1st Baronet. He thereby excluded his heir male (the grandson of Patrick Houston, 2d *son* of the said 1st Baronet), as also his own two sisters (or their issue), *viz.*, (1) Helena, who *m.* Sir Michael Stewart, 3d Baronet [S. 1667] of Blackhall, and (2) Anne, who *m.* Col. William Cunningham, of Enterkine.

(b) The information as to this Baronetcy after 1751 was kindly supplied by the late R. R. Stodart, sometime [1863-86], Lyon Clerk Depute.

(c) Taking with him portraits of his father and mother, as also of his grandfather, the 1st Baronet, which, together with some old plate, were in possession of the family in 1880, and probably later.

John Preston, of Valleyfield, took a leading part in the Restoration; was made Clerk of the Bills, 1660; acquired the estate of Balcaskie, and was *cr. a Baronet* [S.], as above, 21 Oct. 1668, with rem. to the heirs male of his body. He subsequently purchased the lands and Barony of Kinross. He was M.P. [S.] for Fifeshire, 1669-74, and for Kinross-shire, 1681-82 and 1685-86; was made Master of the King's Works, and, as such, completed the palace of Holyrood. He *m.* firstly, Mary, da. of Sir James Halkett, of Pitfirrane, by Margaret, da. of Sir Robert Montgomery, of Skelmorlie. He *m.* secondly, Magdalen Scot, by whom he had no issue. "Sir William Bruce, Kinross, his Lady, *d.* 30 May 1699."(b) He *d.* at Edinburgh, 1 Jan. 1710,(b) at a great age.

II. 1710, Jan. to Mar. **Sir John Bruce**, Baronet [S. 1668], of Kinross and Balcaskie aforesaid, only s. and h. by 1st wife; was M.P. [S.] for Kinross-shire, 1702-07 and [G.B.] 1707-08; *suc. to the Baronetcy*, 1 Jan. 1710. He *m.* May 1687, Christian, Dow. Marchioness of Montrose [S.], 2d da. and coheir of John (Leslie), Duke of Rothes [S.], by Anne, da. of John (Lindsay), Earl of Crawford and Lindsay [S.]. He *d.* shortly after his father, s.p.m., at Glasgow, 19 March 1710,(b) when the *Baronetcy* became *extinct*,(a) but the estate of Kinross devolved on his only sister(c) and the heirs *male* of her body, subject to taking the name of Bruce of Kinross. His widow *d.* at Edinburgh, 21 April and was *bur.* 1 May 1710, in the Abbey church there. Funeral entry in Lyon office.

BARCLAY:

cr. 22 Oct. 1668.(d)

I. 1668. "Sir Robert Barclay, of Pierston," co. Ayr, s. and h. of William Barclay, of the same, suc. his father in 1628, and having been *Knighted* was *cr. a Baronet* [S.], as above, 22 Oct. 1668(d) (the warrant being dat. at Whitehall), with rem. to the heirs male of his body. He *m.* firstly, 4 Aug. 1653, Catharine, da. of Alexander Lockhart, of Edinburgh, Merchant. He *m.* secondly, 28 Sep. 1659, Barbara, da. of (—) Deans, said to have been Clerk of the Signet. He *d.* 1694, or possibly 1695. Will confirmed 20 Dec. 1695.

II. 1694? **Sir Robert Barclay**, Baronet [S. 1666], of Pierston aforesaid, 2d but 1st surv. s. and h.(e) by 1st wife; *b.* 21 Feb. 1658; *suc. to the Baronetcy* in 1694 or 1695. He *m.* Bethia, da. of Sir Robert Baird, 1st Baronet [S. 1696], of Saughton Hall, by Elizabeth, da. of Michael Fleming. He *d.* at Pierston, before 1717. His widow, under the style of "Dame Martha [*sic*] Baird, relict of Sir Robert Barclay, of Pierston," was *bur.* 21 Jan. 1731, in the High churchyard, Glasgow.

(a) In Douglas' *Baronage* [S.] it is stated that "the Baronetship went to his cousin and heir male, Sir Alexander Bruce (second son of [his paternal uncle, Thomas Bruce] the 4th Baron of Blairhall), who, dying unmarried, these honours became extinct." There is, however, nothing to support this statement, and the entail of all his lands by the 1st Baronet on his daughter's children (failing those of his son) seems against it. If, however, it be correct, one must suppose that the patent was to heirs male whatsoever, in which case the title would not be extinct, the male descendants of the grantee's great grandfather (Sir Edward Bruce, of Blairhall) represented by the Earl of Elgin [S.] being numerous.

(b) Masterton papers [*Scottish History Society Miscellany*, pp. 473, 483, 484].

(c) This was Anne, who *m.* firstly Sir Thomas Hope, 4th Baronet [S. 1628], of Craighall, and secondly Sir John Carstairs, of Kilconquhar, and had by both husbands male issue, who successively took the name of Bruce and inherited the estate of Kinross.

(d) In Playfair's *Baronetage* the date is given as 2 Oct. 1668.

(e) His elder br. Alexander, *bap.* 17 Dec. 1654, was living 1662, but *d.* v.p. and unm.

III. 1710? **Sir Robert Barclay**, Baronet [S. 1668], of Pierston aforesaid, 1st s. and h.; *suc. to the Baronetcy* on the death of his father, to whom he was served heir in 1717. He sold the estate of Pierston. He joined the Jacobite rising in 1715 and escaped abroad. He, who was living 1717, *d.* unm., probably not long afterwards, at Aix la Chapelle.

IV. 1720? **Sir James Barclay**, Baronet [S. 1668], br. and h., *suc. to the Baronetcy* on the death of his brother; was M.D. of the Univ. of Glasgow, 1734, and was a Surgeon in the Royal Navy. He *m.* about 1710, (—), 1st da. and coheir of William Bloyes, of Taunton Dean, Somerset, Capt. R.N. (who *d.* 9 April 1720), by (—), his 1st wife. He *d.* in London 12 Jan. 1755.

V. 1755. **Sir William Bloyes Barclay**, Baronet [S. 1668], only s. and h., *b.* about 1710, in Craven street, Westminster; was a Purser in the Royal Navy; *suc. to the Baronetcy*, 12 Jan. 1755. He *m.*, 18 March 1746/7, at the Fleet chapel (by the Rev. Mr. Wyatt), Susanna, da. of William Church, of Gloucester, Surgeon. He *d.* 7 June 1756, on board H.M.S. "Bedford." Will dat. 23 Aug. 1743, pr. 26 June 1756. His widow *d.* at Barnes terrace, 28 March, and was *bur.* 3 April 1791, at Mortlake, Surrey, aged 75.

VI. 1756. **Sir William Barclay**, Baronet [S. 1668], 1st s. and h., *b.* and *bap.* 22 May 1748, at St. John's, Westm.; *suc. to the Baronetcy*, 7 June 1756, but possibly never assumed the same; was sometime a Capt. in the Guards, but afterwards was Lieut.-Col. in the East India Service and accompanied Clive to India in 1765. He *d.* unm. at Calcutta, "aged 21," *i.e.*, in 1769.(a)

VII. 1769. **Sir James Mantle Barclay**, Baronet [S. 1668], br. and h., *b.* at Kingston, Hants, 2 Oct. and *bap.* 2 Nov. 1750, at Portsea; entered the Royal Navy and was at the taking of Havannah in 1762, becoming finally Capt. R.N.; *suc. to the Baronetcy* in 1769. He *d.* unm. 12 June 1793, aged 42, at Aix la Chapelle, and was *bur.* in the French Walloon Protestant church at Maestricht, with military honours.

VIII. 1793. **Sir Robert Barclay**, Baronet [S. 1668], br and h., *b.* 13 Sep. 1755, at Gosport, Hants; *suc. to the Baronetcy*, 12 June 1793; was taken prisoner by the French in 1798, and tried for complicity with a mission held at Hamburg, 1796-98, but acquitted and released, 19 Nov. 1799; was M.P. for Newtown (Isle of Wight), 1802-06, and 1806-07. He *m.* firstly, 30 Nov. 1780, at Ghent, Elizabeth, da. of John Tickell, of Glasnevin, co. Dublin. She *d.* 13 March 1788, at Maestricht, and was *bur.* in the French Walloon Protestant church there, aged 32. He *m.* secondly, 20 June 1802, at the church of the British Factory at Hamburg, Harriette Alicia, widow of Baron de Cronstedt (of Sweden), da. of Col. [Solomon ?] Durell, Equerry to George III, by Martha, da. of Urban Hall, of Park hall, Notts. He *d.* 14 Aug. 1839, at Mauritius, aged nearly 84. Will pr. April 1840. His widow was *b.* 15 July 1777, *d.* 16 Feb. 1859, in Brook street, Bath, in her 82d year.

IX. 1839. **Sir Robert Barclay**, Baronet [S. 1668], grandson and h., being s. and h. of Robert Brydges Barclay, Major 71st Foot, by Jane, da. of Arthur Williams, of Dungannon, co. Tyrone, which Robert, who *d.* v.p. 8 Aug. 1825, aged 43, was 1st s. and h. ap. of the late Baronet by his 1st wife. He was *b.* at Dungannon, 24 July and *bap.* 18 Aug. 1819, at Drumglass, co. Armagh; *suc. to the Baronetcy*, 14 Aug. 1839, and was served heir to his grandfather, 6 March 1841, at Edinburgh; Lieut. 25th Foot, 1846; Lieut. Lancashire Artillery Militia, 1855. He *d.* unm. 19 May 1859, at Dungannon, aged nearly 40.

(a) In the pedigree recorded in the College of Arms and signed by both his brothers, James and Robert, 13 April 1792, he is not styled "Baronet." The entry runs thus: "William, 1st son, *b.* 22 May 1748, and *bap.* the same day at St. John's, Westm., *d.* unm. in the East Indies, aged 21." If, however, he was born 1748 and was aged twenty-one when he died, he must have been entitled to the Baronetcy for thirteen years.

X. 1859. SIR DAVID WILLIAM BARCLAY, Baronet [S. 1668], uncle of the half blood and h. male, being s. of the 8th Baronet by his 2d wife. He was b. 5 Sep. 1804; sometime Capt. 99th Foot; aide-de-camp to the Gov. of the Mauritius; *suc. to the Baronetcy*, 19 May 1859; member of the Legislative Council at the Mauritius, 1846-64. He m. firstly, 16 Feb. 1829, Elise Josephe DE RUNE, yst. da. of Charles Malo, MARQUIS DE RUNE, of Warsy, in Picardy. She d. 22 March 1867, very suddenly, at 137 Westbourne terrace, Paddington, aged 57. He m. secondly, 19 Sep, 1872, Emily, 2d da. of James Edmeed STACEY, of Kingston, Surrey. He d. 23 Nov. 1888, at 42 Holland Road, Kensington, aged 84, and was *bur.* in the Paddington cemetery, in Willesden lane, Midx. His widow living 1904.

XI. 1888. SIR COLVILLE ARTHUR DURELL BARCLAY, Baronet [S. 1668], 1st s. and h. by 1st wife, b. 20 Dec. 1829; ed. at Grosvenor College, Bath; entered the Colonial Civil Service, 1846; sometime Auditor Gen. of Ceylon; Collector of Customs and Receiver Gen. of the Mauritius, and was, in both those Colonies, a member of the Executive and Legislative Council; C.M.G., 1870; *suc. to the Baronetcy*, 23 Nov. 1888; Commander of the Legion of Honour, 1889, having first received that order in 1878 for services at the International Exhibition of Paris. He m. 10 July 1855, Louise Melanie, yst. da. and coheir of Edoard Julien DE BELZIM, of the Mauritius. He d. 18 Feb. 1896, at 1 Rue Francois, Champs Elysées, Paris, aged 66. Personalty sworn at £2,676. His widow living 1904.

XII. 1896. SIR DAVID EDWARD DURELL BARCLAY, Baronet [S. 1668], 1st s. and h., b. 30 March 1858; sometime Capt. 19th Hussars, serving in Egypt, 1882 (wounded at Tel-el-Kebir), and in the Soudan, 1884 (medal, 3 clasps, and Khedive's star); *suc. to the Baronetcy*, 18 Feb. 1896. He m. 9 Oct. 1889, Lætitia, 4th da. of the Hon. Amias Charles ORDE-POWLETT, of Thorney Hall, co. York (br. of William Henry, 3d BARON BOLTON), by Anne Martha, da. of Christopher TOPHAM, of Middleham Hall, co. York. She was b. 25 April 1859.

BARCLAY.[a]

cr. date unknown;

afterwards, WASTELL.

A Baronetcy [S.] was assumed, as under, by a family of WASTELL, in right of an alleged devolution thereof, from a family of BARCLAY, on whom it is said to have been conferred.

[——]. SIR WILLIAM WASTELL, Baronet[b] [S.]; m. firstly [—], da. of Sir Jonathan MILES. She d. s.p.m. He m. secondly, Agatha, da. of Col. WHALLEY.

[——]. SIR WILLIAM HENRY WASTELL, Baronet[b] [S.], s. and h. by 2d wife; *suc. to the Baronetcy*[b] on the death of his father. He m. firstly, Philadelphia, da. of [—] TANNER. He m. secondly, in 1884, Elizabeth Adelaide, da. of Major Robert Onslow Bellerophon HICKSON. He d. 1900.

[—]. 1900. CHARLES WASTELL, s. and h. by 1st wife; *suc. to the Baronetcy*,[b] in 1900, but did not assume the title. He m. [—].

[a] *Ex inform.* Sir E. M. Mackenzie, Baronet [S. 1703].
[b] According to the assumption of that dignity.

RAMSAY:[a]

cr. 23 June 1669;

ex. 1709.

I. 1669, to 1709. "ANDREW RAMSAY, of Abbotshall," co. Fife, as also of Waughton, co. Haddington, s. and h. ap. of Sir Andrew RAMSAY, of Abbotshall aforesaid, sometime (1654-57 and 1662-73) Lord Provost of Edinburgh, and (1671-73) a Lord of Session under the style of *Lord Abbotshall*,[b] by Janet CRAW, his wife, was *bap.* 24 Dec. 1648, at the Grey Friars church, Edinburgh;[c] was M.P. [S.] for North Berwick, 1669-74, and was *cr. a Baronet* [S.], as above, 23 June 1669, with rem. to heirs male of the body. He suc. his father (who d. aged 69), 17 Jan. 1688. He m. Anne, da. of Hugh (MONTGOMERIE), EARL OF EGLINTOUN [S.], by his 2d wife, Mary, da. of John (LESLIE), EARL OF ROTHES [S.]. He d. s.p.s. 1709, and was *bur.* at Abbotshall, when the *Baronetcy* became *extinct*.[d]

CUNNINGHAM:

cr. 19, or 21, Sep. 1669;

sometime, 1829-45, DICK;

and afterwards, since 1845, DICK-CUNYNGHAM.

I. 1669. "JOHN CUNNINGHAM, of Lambrughton," co. Ayr, s. and h. of John CUNNINGHAM, of Brownhill in Tarbolton and of Geiss, co. Caithness, member of the Committee of War, by his 2d wife, Elizabeth, da. of Sir John SINCLAIR, of Ratter, was admitted an Advocate and became a lawyer of some distinction; purchased the estate of Lambrughton soon after 1663; was M.P. [S.] for Ayrshire, 1665, and again, 1681-82; sold the estate of Brownhill in 1667, and was *cr. a Baronet* [S.], as above, 19 or 21 Sep. 1669. He purchased, in 1683, the old family estate of Caprington, in the parish of Riccarton, co. Ayr. He m. Margaret, da. of John MURRAY, of Touch Adam and of Polmaise, co. Stirling. He was *bur.* 20 Nov. 1684.

II. 1684. SIR WILLIAM CUNNINGHAM, Baronet [S. 1669], of Caprington and Lambrughton aforesaid, 1st s. and h.; *bap.* 7 Feb. 1664; *suc. to the Baronetcy* in Nov. 1684. He executed an entail of the Barony of Caprington, 27 Feb. 1719. He m., in or before 1696, Janet, only surv. da. and h. of Sir James DICK, 1st Baronet [S. 1677 and 1707], of Prestonfield, co. Edinburgh, by Anne, da. of William PATERSON, of Dunmore, co. Fife. He d. 1740, aged 76. His widow d. 20 June 1753, in her 81st year, at Prestonfield.

III. 1740. SIR JOHN CUNNINGHAM, Baronet [S. 1669], of Caprington aforesaid, 1st s. and h., b. about 1696; one of the best scholars of his time; *suc. to the Baronetcy* in 1740, and was served heir gen. of his

[a] Most of the information in this Article has been kindly furnished by Thomas Colyer Fergusson.
[b] This Andrew was 3d son of the Rev. Andrew Ramsay, Minister of the Grey Friars church, Edinburgh (d. 30 Dec. 1659, aged 85), who was yr. br. of Sir Gilbert Ramsay, 1st Baronet [S. 1625], of Balmain.
[c] He is said (Milne's *List*) to have been "first Knighted by the Usurper Cromwell," but as he was but 12 at the time of the Restoration (1660) such Knighthood is hardly probable.
[d] The Baronetcy assumed by James Ramsay in 1806 was probably not meant to be this one, the said James (son of David Ramsay of Prestonpans) being descended from a brother of this Baronet. See vol. ii, p. 302, and note "b" to the same.

father, 7 April 1750, and h. male and of provision gen. 7 Nov. 1753. He m. in 1749, Elizabeth, da. of Alexander (MONTGOMERIE), EARL OF EGLINTOUN [S.], by his 3d wife, Susanna, da. of Sir Archibald KENNEDY, 1st Baronet [S. 1682], of Culzean. He d. of apoplexy 30 Nov. 1777, in his 82d year. His widow d. at Edinburgh, 9 Feb. 1800, aged 93.

IV. 1777. SIR WILLIAM CUNNINGHAM, Baronet [S. 1669], of Caprington aforesaid, 1st s. and h., b. 19 Dec. 1752; *suc. to the Baronetcy*, 30 Nov. 1777; was served heir gen. of his father, 25 March 1778, and h. male and of provision gen., 29 Sep. 1779. He m. 19 Nov. 1799, at Edinburgh, Mary (then of St. Andrew's square in that city), widow of Capt. John GRAEME, da. of [—] SWINDELL. She d. 1810. He d. s.p. 16 Jan. 1829,[a] aged 76.

V. and VII. 1829. SIR ROBERT KEITH DICK, *afterwards*, since 1845, DICK-CUNYNGHAM, Baronet [S. 1669 and 1707], of Prestonfield, co. Edinburgh, cousin and h. male, being 3d and yst. s. but eventually h. male of Sir Alexander DICK, 3d Baronet [S. 1707], formerly Alexander CUNNINGHAM, by his 2d wife, Mary, da. of Edward BUTLER, of Pembroke, which Alexander (who d. 10 Nov. 1785, aged 82) was a yr. son of Sir William CUNNINGHAM, 2d Baronet [S. 1669] abovementioned, by Janet, da. and h. of Sir James DICK, 1st Baronet [S. 1677 and 1707], also abovementioned, to whose Baronetcy [S. 1707] he succeeded on the death, 14 Jan. 1746, of his next elder brother, Sir William DICK, 2d Baronet [S.], who had inherited the same (under the spec. rem. in the creation of that dignity on the death, in 1728, of their maternal grandfather, the said Sir James DICK, 1st Baronet [S. 1677 and 1707]. He was b. 14 April 1773, and by the death, of his next elder brother, Sir John DICK, 6th Baronet [S. 1707], *suc. to that Baronetcy*, 14 Dec. 1812. By the death of his cousin, Sir William CUNNINGHAM, 4th Baronet [S. 1669], he *suc. to that Baronetcy*, 16 Jan. 1829. In 1845, by private Act of Parl. he took the name of DICK-CUNYNGHAM, in lieu of that of DICK, and was enabled to dispose of certain estates. He m. 15 May 1807, Harriet, 3d da. of Thomas HANMER, of Stapleton, co. Gloucester. He d. 14 Dec. 1849, aged 76. His widow d. 27 Jan. 1857.

VI. and VIII. 1849. SIR WILLIAM HANMER DICK-CUNYNGHAM, Baronet [S. 1669 and 1707], of Prestonfield aforesaid, 1st s. and h., b. 22 Oct. 1808, at Sylhet, in Bengal, East India; sometime Lieut. 1st Dragoon Guards; *suc. to the Baronetcies*, 14 Dec. 1849. He m. 17 Feb. 1836, Susan, 3d da. of Major James Alston STEWART, of Urrard, co. Perth. He d. suddenly, 20 Feb. 1871, at Prestonfield, aged 62. His widow d. 26 April 1892, at 17 Eccleston square, Pimlico.

VII. and IX. 1871. SIR ROBERT KEITH ALEXANDER DICK-CUNYNGHAM, Baronet [S. 1669 and 1707], of Prestonfield aforesaid, 1st s. and h., b. 21 Dec. 1836, at Urrard, co. Perth; was an officer in the 93d Foot, 1855-63, serving throughout the Indian Mutiny, 1857-59, and being severely wounded at the siege of Lucknow (Lucknow clasp); *suc. to the Baronetcies*, 20 Feb. 1871. He m. 30 March 1864, Sarah Mary, da. of William HETHERINGTON, of Birkenhead, co. Chester. He d. 2 May 1897, at "Polefield," Lansdown road, Cheltenham, aged 60. His widow living 1904.

[a] The family estate of Caprington devolved at his death, in 1829, on his cousin, Anne, wife of John Smith, Writer to the Signet, the second of the four sisters and coheirs of Sir Alexander Dick, 5th Baronet [S. 1707], who was son of the 4th Baronet and grandson of Sir Alexander Dick, 3d Baronet [S. 1707], formerly Alexander Cunningham, a yr. br. of Sir John Cunningham, 3d Baronet [S. 1669], abovenamed, both which last were maternal grandsons of Sir James Dick, 1st Baronet [S. 1707]. She d. soon afterwards, 1 March 1830, leaving a son, who took the name of Cunningham.

VIII. and X. 1897. SIR WILLIAM STEWART DICK CUNYNGHAM, Baronet [S. 1669 and 1707], of Prestonfield, 1st s. and h., b. 20 Feb. 1871; ed. at Harrow and at Sandhurst Coll.; was an officer in the Black Watch; *suc. to the Baronetcies*, 2 May 1897; served in the Transvaal War, 1900-01, retiring as Capt. in 1903. He m. 7 Nov. 1903, at Christ Church, Lancaster Gate, Paddington, Evelyn Eleanora, 1st da. of Arthur FRASER, of 10 Craven Hill, Hyde Park.

NISBET:

cr. 2 Dec. 1669;

ex., 18 Sep. 1827.

I. 1669. "PATRICK NISBET, of Craigintinny," 1st s. and h. of Sir Henry NISBET, of the same, by Isabella, da. of Thomas NICHOLSON, of Cockburnspath, was *cr. a Baronet* [S.], as above, 2 Dec. 1669, with rem. to heirs male of the body. He, in 1672, exchanged his paternal estate with his 2d cousin, Alexander NISBET, of Dean, for the Barony of Dean, co. Midlothian. He m. Agnes, da. of James BROWN, of Stevenston. He d. 1682, when he is said to have been in his 100th year.

II. 1682. SIR HENRY NISBET, Baronet [S. 1669], of Dean aforesaid, 2d but 1st surv. s. and h.; *suc. to the Baronetcy*, in 1682. He m. firstly, 9 Nov. 1657, Christian, da. of Sir John RIDDELL, 3d Baronet [S. 1628], by his 2d wife, Helen, da. of Sir Alexander MORRISON. He m. secondly, Margaret SINCLAIR. He d. Aug. 1713.

III. 1713. SIR JOHN NISBET, Baronet [S. 1669], of Dean aforesaid, 1st s. and h. by 1st wife; *suc. to the Baronetcy*, Aug. 1713. He m. (contract 23 Aug. 1717) Anne, da. of Sir Andrew MYRTON, 1st Baronet [S. 1701], of Gogar. He d. 30 March 1728. His widow living 13 March 1748/9. She possibly d. 13 June 1768, at Edinburgh.[a]

IV. 1728. SIR HENRY NISBET, Baronet [S. 1669], only s. and h., *suc. to the Baronetcy* in 1728; was a Capt. in Col. Graham's Reg. of Foot. He d. unm., being slain at the battle of Raucoux, 11 Oct. 1746. Admon. 13 March 1748/9, to his mother.

V. 1746. SIR ALEXANDER NISBET, Baronet [S. 1669], of Dean aforesaid, uncle and h. male, being yr. son of the 2d Baronet; *suc. to the Baronetcy* and estate, 11 Oct. 1746. He m. in Oct. 1742, Molly, da. of John RUTHERFORD. He d. 7 Oct. 1753, at Charlestown, South Carolina, in America. His widow d. 19 June 1797.

VI. 1753. SIR HENRY NISBET, Baronet [S. 1669], of Dean aforesaid, 1st s. and h.; *suc. to the Baronetcy*, 7 Oct. 1753. He d. unm. in 1762. The will of "Henry NISBIT, Baronet, of Agmore, co. Longford," pr. [I.] 1789 [*sic*].

[a] 1768, June 13, died "Lady Nesbit, relict of Sir John, Bart., of Edinburgh."

VII. 1770? Sir John Nisbet, Baronet [S. 1669], br. and h.; was a Cornet of the 2d or North British Dragoons in 1764; *suc. to the Baronetcy* on the death of his brother. He *m.* Claudine Favre, a French woman. He *d.* 1776.

VIII. 1776, to 1827. Sir John Nisbet, Baronet [S. 1669], s. and h.; *suc. to the Baronetcy* in 1776; was residing in North America in 1811.(a) He *m.* Nov. 1797, "Miss Alston," an American actress, *i.e.*, Mary, da. of William Alston, of South Carolina. He *d.* s.p.m. at Naples, 18 Sep. 1827, when the *Baronetcy* became *extinct*. Will pr. June 1828. His widow (possibly a *second* wife) *d.* 18 Jan. 1839, in Montagu place, Midx.(b) Her will, as "Rosina Byron, commonly called Lady Nisbet" (Midx.) was pr. June 1839.

HAMILTON:

cr. 11 Feb. 1669/70;

extinct, presumably, about 1710.

I. 1670. "Alexander Hamilton, of Haggs," s. of Alexander Hamilton, of the same (said to have been a scion of the Hamiltons of Orbistoun derived from Provost Gavin Hamilton, 4th s. of Sir James Hamilton, of Cadyow), by Jean, da. of Patrick Maxwell, of Newark, suc. his father in Oct. 1649, and was *cr. a Baronet* [S.], as above, 11 Feb. 1669/70, though no record of such creation is in the Great Seal Register. The remainder is said (in Milne's *List*) to have been to heirs male of the body. He *d.* before 1700.

II. 1700? to 1710? Sir Alexander Hamilton, Baronet [S. 1670], of Haggs aforesaid, s. and h., *suc. to the Baronetcy* about 1700, and was admitted as Writer to the Signet, 15 July 1700. He *d.* unm. about 1710, when the *Baronetcy* became *extinct*.

WALLACE:

cr. 8 March 1669/70;

ex. 18 Aug. 1770;

but assumed 1771-1892,

as Dunlop-Wallace,

or Dunlop-Agnew-Wallace.

I. 1670. "Sir Thomas Wallace, of Craigie," *otherwise* Craigie-Wallace, as also of Newton, both in co. Ayr, 1st s. of William Wallace, of Failford, in that county, by Agnes, da. of Sir Thomas Boyd, of

(a) Playfair's *Baronetage*, 1811.

(b) 1839, Jan. 18. Died "in Montagu place, at the residence of her daughter, the Countess of Montara, Lady Nisbett, relict of Sir J. Nisbett, Bart." [*Annual Reg.* 1839].

Bollinshaw, which William was s. and h. of the Rev. William Wallace, Minister of Failford (a yr. br. of Sir John Wallace, of Craigie Wallace aforesaid), was admitted an Advocate, 4 July 1661, and having suc. to the estate of Craigie-Wallace, by the death of his 2d cousin, Sir Hugh Wallace,(a) of the same (grandson of Sir John Wallace abovenamed), was *Knighted* before 1665; was M.P. [S.] for Ayrshire, 1665 and 1667, and was *cr. a Baronet*, as above, 8 March 1669/70, with rem. to heirs male of the body, the patent stating that the said Sir Hugh had "disponed his estates and the title of Knight Baronet to him.(b) He was appointed a Senator of the Court of Justice, 28 June 1671, and Lord Justice Clerk, 9 July 1675. In 1678 he bought the estate of Ellerslie, co. Renfrew, and settled it on his 2d son, Thomas. He *m.*, probably about 1660, Eupheme, da. and h. of William Gemmell, of Templeland and Garrive, co. Ayr, by (—), da. of (—) Craufórd, of Camlarg. He *d.* 26 March 1680, at Newton aforesaid.

II. 1680. Sir William Wallace, Baronet [S. 1670], of Craigie Wallace aforesaid, 1st s. and h., *suc. to the Baronetcy*, 26 March, and was served, 27 Aug. 1680, heir to very extensive estates united with the Barony of Craigie. He was Col. of Horse (under "Claverhouse") at Killiecrankie; served in Ireland in 1690, and was in France 1695. He *m.* firstly, in 1682, Eupheme (tocher 20,000 merks), da. of William Fullarton, of Fullarton, co. Ayr. She *d.* s.p. He *m.* secondly, Jean, da. of William Menzies, of Pitfoddels, co. Kincardine. He *m.* thirdly, before 1698, Elizabeth, da of Andrew Wauchope, of Niddrie Marischal, co. Edinburgh. He *d.* s.p m.,(c) and was *bur.* 25 Jan. 1700, at Craigie.

III. 1700. Sir Thomas Wallace, Baronet [S. 1670], of Craigie Wallace and Ellerslie aforesaid, br. and h. male, *b.* 27 and *bap.* 29 Jan. 1665; Advocate, 10 Dec. 1687; *suc. to the Baronetcy* in Jan. 1700, in which year he sold the estate of Ellerslie. In 1704 he took the oath of allegiance to qualify for practising at the Bar. He *m.*, in or before 1702, Rachel, da. of Sir Hew Wallace, of Woolmet. He *d.* 21 Jan. 1728, in Edinburgh.

IV. 1728, to 1770. Sir Thomas Wallace, Baronet [S. 1670], of Craigie-Wallace aforesaid, s. and h., *b.* Feb. 1702; Advocate 17 Dec. 1723; *suc. to the Baronetcy*, 21 Jan. 1728; was served heir gen. of his father, 27 April 1736; heir of conquest gen. to his br., William Wallace, 31 Jan. 1737, and heir gen. to his grandfather, 8 Nov. 1743. He *m.* in 1725, Eleanor, sister and h. (Feb. 1736) of Thomas Agnew, of Lochryan, co. Wigtoun, da. of Col. Agnew, of the same. She *d.* 19 and was *bur.* 21 Aug. 1761, in Glasgow Cathedral, aged 55. He *d.* s.p.m.s.(d) 18 Aug. 1770, in his 69th year, when the *Baronetcy* became *extinct*.

(a) This Sir Hugh Wallace is often considered to have been himself a Baronet [S.], and is said [Playfair's *Baronetage*] to have been so *cr.* in 1669, though there is no record of such creation and, apparently, no recognition of it, save as in the allusion in note "b" below. He *m.* Esther, da. of [—] Ker, of Littleden, and had one son, Hugh, who was "fatuus," and who *d.* unm. and probably v.p.

(b) Milne (in his *List*) observes, "He seems to have a former patent disponed to him by the last Sir Hewgh Wallace, which is ratyfied 8 March 1670, bot maketh him not to take place conforme to date of the said patent."

(c) Of his two daughters and coheirs, (1) Margaret, *d.* unm. at Niddrie, 19 March 1712, and (2) Jane, *m.* 20 April 1710, James Wauchope, Merchant of Edinburgh, and *d.* 5 Dec. 1715, leaving issue (the Wauchope family of Niddrie), among whom (and not among the issue of his younger brother, the 3rd Baronet), the heir general of the Baronetcy is to be found.

(d) His only son, a Capt. in the Guards, *d.* unm. and v.p. 9 Oct. 1755, aged 26.

The Baronetcy was, however, assumed as below.

V. 1771. Sir Thomas Dunlop-Wallace, Baronet [S. 1670],(a) of Craigie and Lochryan aforesaid, grandson and heir of line to the 3d (but not to the 1st or 2d) Baronet, being s. and h. of John Dunlop, of Dunlop, by Frances Anne, (*b.* 16 April 1730), da. and h. of the late Baronet. He was served, 22 Feb. 1771, heir of provision general to his said maternal grandfather, the 3d Baronet, when he (unwarrantably) *assumed the Baronetcy*, and obtained a royal warrant, 23 July 1773, for supporters under the name of "Sir Thomas Wallace, of Craigie, Baronet." This, however, was cancelled on the explanation of Lyon King of Arms that "Mr. Dunlop" had no right to the title of Baronet, which title, however, he continued to use. His affairs having fallen into disorder, he sold, in 1776, the estate of Failford, and, in 1784, the ancestral estate of Craigie. From 1800 to 1814 he was one of the Englishmen detained as prisoners in France. He *m.* firstly, in Sep. 1772, Eglantine, da. of William Maxwell, 3d Baronet [S. 1661], of Monreith, by Magdalen, d. of William Blair, of Blair. She, however, was divorced.(b) He *m.* secondly, 1783, in London, Elizabeth Brunsdon, a native of Scotland. Her he deserted, and she brought an action of divorce against him in 1789, in Scotland, which was dismissed on final appeal for want of jurisdiction. He *d.* 1835.(c)

VI. 1835. Sir John Alexander Dunlop-Agnew-Wallace, Baronet [S. 1670],(a) of Lochryan aforesaid, K.C.B. [1833], only s. and h. by 1st wife, *b.* 1774; entered the Army, 1787, becoming eventually Lieut. Gen. in 1837, and General, 11 Nov. 1851; served against Tippoo-Sahib, 1791-92, and at the siege of Seringapatam, was at the capture of Minorca, 15 Nov. 1798; in the Egyptian Campaign, 1801, and in the Peninsular War (at Busaco, 1810, where he distinguished himself, Fuentes de Onoro and Salamanca), 1809-12, and was in command of a Brigade in the Army of Occupation of France, 1815; C.B., 4 June 1815; was Col. of the 88th Foot, 1831 till death in 1857; K.C.B., 16 Sep. 1833, and *suc. to the Baronetcy*(a) soon afterwards, 1835. He *m.*, in or before 1830, Janet, da. of William Rodger, of Glasgow, Timber Merchant. He *d.* 10 Feb. 1857, aged 83, at Lochryan House. His widow *d.* there 16 Aug. 1862, aged 99.

VII. 1857, to 1892. Sir William Thomas Francis Agnew Dunlop-Agnew-Wallace, Baronet [S. 1670],(a) of Lochryan aforesaid, 1st s. and h., *b.* 27 May 1830; entered the Army, becoming finally Lieut. Col. Grenadier Guards in 1859, but retiring in 1860. He *suc. to the Baronetcy*,(a) 10 Feb. 1857. He *d.* unm. in London, 28 Jan, 1892, aged 61, when the *assumption of this Baronetcy ceased*.(d)

(a) According to the assumption of the Baronetcy in and after 1771.

(b) She, who, notwithstanding, continued to style herself "Lady Wallace," was a person of talent though of great eccentricity, as was her sister Jane, Duchess of Gordon [S.]. She was arrested in Paris in 1789; was knocked down and bruised at Margate in 1794, being taken for a person of bad character. She (or, perhaps, her successor) is possibly "The Dowager Lady Wallace, relict [*sic*] of Sir Thomas, Bart.," who died 17 Oct. 1791. At all events her will was pr. in 1803.

(c) This date of death is given in various accounts of his son.

(d) His nephew and h., John Alexander Dunlop-Agnew-Wallace decided not to continue the assumption of the title.

FALCONER:

cr. 20 or 30 March 1670;

afterwards Lord Falconer of Halkertoun [S.];

ex. 17 March 1727.

I. 1670. "Alexander Falconer, of Glenfarquhar," 1st s. and h. of Sir David Falconer, of the same, by Margaret, da. of [—] Hepburn, of Bearford, was *cr. a Baronet* [S.], as above, 20 or 30 March 1670, being then, apparently, styled the "younger,"(a) with rem. to the heirs male of his body. He (being then styled "Knight and Baronet") was M.P. [S.] for Kincardineshire, 1678

II. 1700? to 1727. Sir Alexander Falconer, Baronet [S. 1670], of Glenfarquhar aforesaid, only s. and h., *suc. to the Baronetcy* on the death of his father. Many years afterwards, *viz.* in Feb. 1724, he suc. his cousin, to whom he was heir male, as Lord Falconer of Halkertoun [S.], a peerage *cr.* 20 Dec. 1647, with rem. to heirs male whatsoever. He *d.* s.p. 17 March 1727, when the *Baronetcy* became *extinct*, but the peerage devolved on his cousin and heir male. See *Peerage*.

BENNET:(b)

cr. 18 Nov. 1670;

ex. about 1765.

I. 1670. "William Bennet, of [Marlefield, in] Grubet," co. Roxburgh, s. and h. of the Rev. William Bennet, Minister of Ancrum, in that county, by Margaret, da. of William Eliott, of Stobbs, suc. his father in 1647, and was *cr. a Baronet* [S.], as above, 18 Nov. 1670, with rem. to heirs male of the body. He *m.* Christian, da. of Alexander Morison, of Prestongrange. He was living 1693 and 1708.(d)

II. 1710? Sir William Bennet, Baronet [S. 1670], of Grubet aforesaid, s. and h.;(c) was a Capt. in the Army; attended William III from Holland in 1688, raising fifty men at his own cost, and having, in 1691, an Act of Parl. in his favour. He was (v.p.) M.P. [S.] for Roxburghshire, 1693-1702, and again 1702-07, being (still as an "Esq.") M.P. thereof [G.B.], 1707-08.(d) He *suc. to the Baronetcy*, probably soon after 1708. He *m.* firstly,

(a) Milne's *List*. The designation of "younger," however, if it exists in the original, seems somewhat to imply that the Baronetcy was granted to the Alexander here made the 2d Baronet in his father's lifetime, and not to Alexander Falconer, the father. The grantee's cousin, however, Alexander Falconer, afterwards (1 Oct. 1671), 2d Lord Falconer, of Halkertoun [S.], may have been the "Senior," to whom the grantee was "Junior."

(b) The information in this article was chiefly furnished by the late R. R. Stodart, Lyon Clerk Depute [1863-86].

(c) His sister *m.* Charles Stuart, of Dunearn (grandson of James, Earl of Moray [S.], and was mother of Alexander Stuart, well-known for his valuable collection of books, pictures, etc.

(d) In the collection of J. J. Howard, LL.D., was (1895) the bookplate of "Sir William Bennet, of Grubett, Baronet, 1707." Arms:—*Or*, a cross pattée between 3 mullets, *gules*; a chief *of the last*; on a canton the badge of a Nova Scotia Baronet. Crest:—A dexter arm, grasping a [—]. Motto:—"Benedictus qui tollit crucem."

Jean, da. of Sir John KERR, of Lochtour. He *m.* secondly, Margaret SCOUGALL, heiress of Whitekirk, co. Haddington. She *d.* s.p. He *m.* thirdly, Elizabeth, da. and h. of Sir David HAY, M.D. He *d.* Dec. 1729.(a)

III. 1729. SIR WILLIAM BENNET, Baronet [S. 1670], of Grubet aforesaid, s. and h. by 1st or 3d wife; *suc. to the Baronetcy* in Dec. 1729. He *d.* s.p. 3 Jan. 1733.

IV. 1733. SIR DAVID BENNET, Baronet [S. 1670], of Grubet aforesaid, br. and h., being s. of the 2d Baronet, probably by the 3d wife; *suc. to the Baronetcy*, 3 Jan. 1733. He *d.* s.p. April 1741.

V. 1741, to 1765? SIR JOHN BENNET, Baronet [S. 1670], of Grubet aforesaid, uncle and h., *suc. to the Baronetcy* in April 1741. He *d.* s.p. about 1765, when the *Baronetcy* became *extinct*.(b)

SETON:

cr. 24 Jan. 1670/1;

ex. Nov. 1671.

I. 1671, Jan. to Nov. The Hon. "ROBERT SETON, of Windygoul," 11th and yst. s. of George (SETON), 3d EARL OF WINTOUN [S.] (*d.* 17 Dec. 1650, aged 65), being 6th s. of his 2d wife, Elizabeth, da. of John (MAXWELL), LORD HERRIES [S.], was *b.* 10 Nov. 1641, at Tranent, and was *cr. a Baronet* [S.], as above, 24 Jan. 1670/1, with rem. to heirs male of the body. He *d.* s.p. Nov. 1671, aged 30 (his next elder br., the Hon. Sir John SETON, 1st Baronet [S. 1664], of Garletoun, being, 20 Feb. 1671/2, served his heir), when the *Baronetcy* became *extinct*.

HALKETT:

cr. 25 Jan. 1670/1.(c)

See Vol. iii, p. 334, under 25 Jan. 1661/2.

HOME, *or* HUME:

cr. 25 Jan. 1670/1;

sometime, 1878-87, HOME-SPEIRS.

I. 1671. "JOHN HOME [*or* HUME], of Blackadder," co. Berwick, 1st s. and h.(d) of Sir John HOME, *or* HUME, of the same, sometime M.P. [S.] for Berwickshire, by Mary, da. of Sir James DUNDAS, of Arniston, co.

(a) This Baronet was well known in the literary circles of his day; was a friend of Allan Ramsay, etc.

(b) The niece of the last Baronet, sister of the 3d and 4th Baronets, *m.* her cousin german, William Nisbet, of Dirletoun, and conveyed the estates to that family, who sold them to the family of Hay, Marquesses of Tweeddale [S.].

(c) In Milne's *List* the Creation of "Charles Hacket, of Pitfirrin," is given as on 25 Jan. 1671, "the same day with Hume of Blaccator," but the more probable date is 25 Jan. 1661/2.

(d) His yr. br., Sir David Home, of Crossrigs, *b.* 1643, who, in 1673, was a Brewer, was admitted an Advocate 1687, and, "to his great surprise," became a Lord of Session, 1689, under the style of Lord Crossrigs, and a Lord of Justiciary in 1690. He *d.* 12 April 1707, leaving issue.

Midlothian, was *b.* about 1640; suc. his father in 1655, being served heir to him in 1663, and was *cr. a Baronet* [S.], 25 Jan. 1670/1, with rem. to heirs male of the body. He *m.* in 1660, Mary, da. of his maternal uncle, Sir James DUNDAS, of Arniston, by his 1st wife, Marian, da. of Robert (BOYD), LORD BOYD [S.]. She *d.* 1672. He *d.* in France, 23 Jan. 1675.

II. 1675. SIR JOHN HOME, Baronet [S. 1671], of Blackadder aforesaid, 1st s. and h.; *suc. to the Baronetcy*, 23 Jan. 1675; was M.P. [S.] for Berwickshire, 1690 till death in 1706. He *m.* Catherine, da. of Sir John PRINGLE, 1st Baronet [S. 1683], of Stichel, by Margaret, da. of Sir John HOPE, a Lord of Session under the style of LORD CRAIGHALL. He *d.* 4 April 1706. His widow *d.* 6 June 1755.

III. 1706. SIR JOHN HOME, Baronet [S. 1671], of Blackadder aforesaid, 1st s. and h.; *suc. to the Baronetcy*, 4 April 1706. He *m.* Anne, da. of William NISBET, of Dirletoun. His widow *d.* (at apparently a great age) 1 Jan. 1779.

IV. 1730? SIR WILLIAM HOME, Baronet [S. 1671], of Blackadder aforesaid, 1st s. and h.; *suc. to the Baronetcy* on the death of his father. He *d.* young and unm.

V. 1735? SIR JOHN HOME, Baronet [S. 1671], of Blackadder aforesaid, br. and h.; *suc. to the Baronetcy* on the death of his brother. He *d.* unm. and was *bur.* 9 April 1737, in the Greyfriars, Edinburgh. M.I.

VI. 1737. SIR JAMES HOME, Baronet [S. 1671], of Blackadder aforesaid, uncle and h. male; was a Writer to the Signet, 1726; *suc. to the Baronetcy*, April 1737. He *m.* Catherine, da. of George LIVINGSTONE, one of the Depute Clerks of Session. He *d.* 28 March 1755. His widow *d.* at Edinburgh, 30 Aug. 1788.

VII. 1755. SIR GEORGE HOME, Baronet [S. 1671], of Blackadder aforesaid, only s. and h.; entered the Royal Navy when young, becoming finally, 1797, Admiral; *suc. to the Baronetcy*, 20 March 1755. He *m.* 13 Sep. 1785, his cousin Helen, da. and coheir of James BUCHANAN, of Drumpellier, Commissr. of Customs at Edinburgh, by Margaret, da. of the Hon. John HAMILTON (2d s. of the 6th EARL OF HADDINGTON [S.]), and Margaret, his wife, da. of Sir John HOME, 3d Baronet [S. 1671]. He *d.* at Darnhall, 2 May 1803. Will pr. 1804.

VIII. 1803. SIR JAMES HOME, Baronet [S. 1671], of Blackadder, aforesaid, 1st s. and h., *b.* 17 March 1790; sometime in the service of the East India Company; *suc. to the Baronetcy*, 2 May 1803. He *m.* 12 July 1828, Anna, 1st da. of Andrew STIRLING, of Drumpellier, co. Lanark, and of London, Factor, by Ann, da. of Sir Walter STIRLING. He *d.* 12 March 1836. Admon. May 1839. His widow *d.* 8 June 1866, at 19 Rutland street, Edinburgh.

IX. 1836. SIR JOHN HOME, Baronet [S. 1671], 1st s. and h., *b.* 4 Aug. 1829; *suc. to the Baronetcy*, 12 March 1836; was an officer in the Royal Navy. He *d.* unm. 26 March 1849, in his 20th year.

X. 1849. SIR GEORGE HOME, *afterwards*, 1878-87, HOME-SPEIRS, Baronet [S. 1671], of Culcreugh, co. Stirling, br. and h.; *b.* 3 Sep. 1832; *suc. to the Baronetcy*, 26 March 1849; admitted an Advocate, 1854; Capt. of the City of Edinburgh Vol. Rifles, 1859. In 1878 he assumed the name of SPEIRS (being that of his wife) after that of HOME. He *m.* 9 March 1858, at Whitehouse, near Edinburgh, Anne Oliphant, only da. and h. of Robert Graham SPEIRS, Advocate (then deceased), sometime Sheriff of Midlothian. He *d.* 20 July 1887, at 1 Ralston street, Tedworth square, Midx., in his 55th year. His widow living 1904.

XI. 1887. SIR JAMES HOME, Baronet [S. 1671], 1st s. and h., *b.* 28 Sep. 1861; served as Lieut. in the Black Watch Highlanders in Egypt, 1882 and 1884-85 (medal with clasps and bronze star); *suc. to the Baronetcy*, 20 July 1887. He *m.* 30 Aug. 1892, at St. Geo. Han. sq., Amy Eliza, yr. da. of William Arthur GREEN, of San Francisco, in California.

COCKBURN:(a)

cr. 24 May 1671;(b)

ex. or *dormant*, 9 Jan. 1800;

but assumed till 1841.

I. 1671. "JAMES COCKBURN, of that ilk," br. and h. of William COCKBURN, of the same, both being sons of JOHN COCKBURN, of that ilk (*d.* 1652), by Elspeth, da. of Sir William OLIPHANT, of Newtown, King's Advocate [S.], was *b.* 7 Nov. 1628; was a Merchant in Edinburgh, being made a Burgess, 3 March 1658; was joint farmer of the Revenue [S.]; suc. his br., William COCKBURN, in 1663, and was *cr. a Baronet* [S.], by warrant, dat. 24 May 1671,(b) at Whitehall, the patent, however, not being signed, "though officially docqueted as duly put on record."(c) He *m.* in or before 1658, Grissel, da. of Alexander HAY, of Barra. He *d.* 1 and was *bur.* 3 Jan. 1704, at Greyfriars, Edinburgh.(d)

II. 1704. SIR WILLIAM COCKBURN, Baronet [S. 1671], of that ilk, 2d but only surv. s. and h.; *b.* 11 Sep. 1662; admitted an Advocate 9 Nov. 1686; *suc. to the Baronetcy*, 1 Jan. 1704. He *m.* Helen LERMOWTH. He *d.* at Dalkeith 4 and was *bur.* 11 Jan. 1751, at Greyfriars aforesaid, in his 89th year.(d). His widow *d.* 28 Nov. 1764.

III. 1751. SIR JAMES COCKBURN, Baronet [S. 1671], of that ilk, only s. and h.; entered the Army, 1747; *suc. to the Baronetcy*, 4 Jan. 1751, being retoured heir to his father and his heir special in Langton and the office of Usher [S.], 25 Nov. 1754.(e) He is styled "Baronet" when he became Lieut. (42d Foot) in March 1755; Capt. (48th Foot), March 1758, being wounded at Quebec, 28 April 1760; Major, March 1769; Lieut. Col., Aug. 1777. He *m.* 8 April 1764, at Edinburgh, Mary, da. of Robert ROCHEAD, of Mastertoun. She *d.* 6 Sep. 1766. He appears to have *m.* secondly (though such marriage is denied) Phœbe SHARMAN, of Bandon, co. Cork, spinster. He *d.* there 13 March 1780. Admon. 5 May 1780, as "of Blandon [*sic*], co. Cork," to his widow, the relict, "Dame Phœbe Cockburn." Her will (in which she is also thus described) dat. 28 Jan. and pr. 12 June 1798.(f)

(a) As to the pedigrees of this family, see vol. ii, p. 327, note "c," *sub* "Cockburn of Langton."

(b) Domestic Calendars of State Papers temp. Car. II.

(c) *Ex inform.* Sir J. Balfour Paul, Lyon King of Arms. The creation is not, however, mentioned in Milne's *List*.

(d) Cockburn MS. pedigree; see note "a" above.

(e) The estate of Langton and the office of Usher [S.] had been disponed 6 May 1690 by Sir Archibald Cockburn, 4th Baronet [S. 1627], and his son Archibald in favour of Sir James Cockburn, 1st Baronet [S. 1671], and his son, William, afterwards the 2d Baronet. See vol. ii, p. 329, note "b," *sub* "Cockburn of Langton."

(f) In it she mentions her three sons, viz., (1) James, who assumed the Baronetcy in 1800; (2) George, then a Surgeon in the Cape of Good Hope; afterwards an Ensign in the Guards, who committed suicide, 25 Oct. 1800; and (3) Robert, then under 25 years of age; afterwards an officer in 26th Dragoons,

IV. 1780, to 1800. SIR WILLIAM JAMES COCKBURN, Baronet [S. 1671], of that ilk, said to be only legit. s. and h.(a) and only child by 1st wife; *suc. to the Baronetcy*, 13 March 1780, and three months later, being then styled "Baronet," became Ensign (26th Foot) in May 1780; Lieut. (1st Foot) in Oct. 1783, and subsequently Major; Lieut. Col. in the Army. He *d.* unm. at Athlone, 9 Jan. 1800. Will, of same date, pr. April 1800. On his death the *Baronetcy* became apparently *extinct* or *dormant*.(b)

The *Baronetcy*, however, was *assumed*, as below.

V. 1800, to 1841. SIR JAMES COCKBURN, Baronet [S. 1671],(c) who, if legitimate, was br. of the half blood to the late Baronet, and s. (by Phœbe SHARMAN, abovenamed) of the 3d Baronet, was *b.* probably about 1770; Capt. 60th Foot in or earlier than 1798, leaving the Service in 1801; *assumed the Baronetcy* in Jan. 1800; was a Clerk in the Navy office. He *m.* Barbara SPETTIGUE. He *d.* s.p. early in 1841, at 6 Pratt street, Lambeth, Surrey, and was *bur.* at Lambeth. Will (as "Sir James COCKBURN, Baronet," dat. 19 Jan. pr. 20 March 1841, under £160. The will of his widow and universal legatee (as "Dame Barbara COCKBURN"), of 6 Pratt street aforesaid (who was also *bur.* at Lambeth), dat. 14 Jan. and pr. 29 March 1846, under £600.

BENNET, *or* BENNETT:

cr. 28 July 1671;

ex. apparently about 1700.

I. 1671, to 1700? "GEORGE BENNETT [*or* BENNET], in the shire of Fife," s. of Rev. William BENNET, minister of the College Kirk of Edinburgh," was in service of Cassimor, King of Poland, and was one of his noblemen, and came to great riches,"(d) and was *cr. a Baronet* [S.] as above, 28 July 1671, with rem. to heirs male of the body. His arms with the badge of Baronetcy are reg. in the Lyon Office, but no account of him is there given. He was living in Poland when [1690?] Nisbet wrote his treatise on Heraldry, but is supposed to have *d.* s.p.m. about 1700, when (if so) the *Baronetcy* became *extinct*.

who *d.* at Newry, July 1800. She appears to have been on good terms with [her stepson?] the 4th Baronet, whom she makes a trustee of her will, and who, in his own will, leaves the bulk of his property to his three brothers, giving his badge as a Baronet of Nova Scotia to his "brother" James.

(a) See p. 282, note "c."

(b) The limitations of this Baronetcy being unknown, it is claimed as heir male collateral by Sir E. C. Cockburn, of Pennockstone, co. Hereford (see vol. ii, p. 333, note "c"), who in a letter, dated 30 July 1901, writes:—"My grandfather, William Cockburn, Major 73d, was in India when Sir W. J. Cockburn died at Athlone, but, returning in 1801, he took up the Baronetcy of that ilk."

(c) According to the assumption of that dignity in 1800.

(d) Milne's *List*.

SCOTT:
cr. 27 Oct. 1671;
ex. 21 May 1902.

I. 1671. "JOHN SCOTT, of Ancrum," co. Roxburgh, 1st s. and h. of Patrick SCOTT, of the same, formerly of Kirkstyle, co. Perth, by his 1st wife, Elizabeth, da. of David SIMSON, of Monturpie, co. Fife, got a charter, under the Great Seal, of the Barony of Ancrum, etc., in 1670, and was *cr. a Baronet* [S.], as above, 27 Oct. 1671, with rem. to heirs male of the body. He *m.* firstly, Elizabeth, da. of Francis SCOTT, of Mangerton, by whom he had ten children. He *m.* secondly, Elizabeth, da. of Sir William BENNETT, Baronet [S. 1670], of Grubet. She *d.* s.p.m. He *m.* thirdly, April 1708, at Cornhill, Barbara, da. of Walter KER, of Littledean. He *d.* 1712.

II. 1712. SIR PATRICK SCOTT, Baronet [S. 1671], of Ancrum aforesaid, 1st s. and h.; admitted as Advocate, 25 Nov. 1676, becoming of some eminence at the Bar; was M.P. [S.], 1685-86, 1689, and 1689 to 23 April 1698, when his seat was declared vacant because he had not signed the assurance; *suc. to the Baronetcy* in 1712. He *m.* firstly, Anne (a considerable fortune), da. of William WALLACE, of Helington. She *d.* s.p.s. He *m.* secondly, Margaret, da. of Sir William SCOTT, of Harden, by Christian, da. of Robert (BOYD), 6th LORD BOYD [S.]. He *d.* 1734.

III. 1734. SIR JOHN SCOTT, Baronet [S. 1671], of Ancrum aforesaid, 1st s. and h. by 2d wife; *suc. to the Baronetcy* in 1734. He *m.* Christian, da. of William NISBET, of Dirletoun. He *d.* at Edinburgh, 21 Feb. 1746.

IV. 1746. SIR WILLIAM SCOTT, Baronet [S. 1671], of Ancrum aforesaid, 2d but 1st surv. s. and h.(a); *suc. to the Baronetcy*, 21 Feb. 1746, being at that time Lieut. in Barrel's reg. of Foot. He *d.* unm. 16 June 1769.

V. 1769. SIR JOHN SCOTT, Baronet [S. 1671], of Ancrum aforesaid, nephew and h., being s. and h. of John SCOTT, of Craigintinnie, by Margaret, da. of Chambres LEWIS, Collector of Customs at Leith, which John (who inherited the estate of Craigintinnie from his mother) was next br. of the late Baronet. He was an officer in the army, and *suc. to the Baronetcy* 16 June 1769. He *m.*, 10 July 1794, Harriet, da. of William GRAHAM, of Gartmore. He *d.* 24 Dec. 1812.

VI. 1812. SIR WILLIAM SCOTT, Baronet [S. 1671], of Ancrum aforesaid, 2d and yst. but only surv. s. and h.(b); *b.* 26 July 1803; *suc. to the Baronetcy*, 24 Dec. 1812; sometime Lieut. 2d Life Guards; M.P. for Carlisle, 1829-30, and for Roxburghshire, 1859-70. He *m.* 1828, Elizabeth, da. and h. of David ANDERSON, of Balgay, co. Forfar. He *d.* 12 Oct. 1871, at Ancrum, aged 68. His widow *d.* 11 April 1878, at 16 Lowndes square.

VII. 1871, to 1902. SIR WILLIAM MONTEITH SCOTT, Baronet [S. 1671], of Ancrum aforesaid, 1st s. and h., *b.* in Clarges Street, 1829; sometime Lieut. 79th Foot; Capt. Roxburgh Vol. Rifles, 1859; *suc. to the Baronetcy*, 12 Oct. 1871. He *m.* 17 Jan. 1861, at St. Geo. Han. sq., Amelia Murray, 1st da. of Gen. Sir Thomas Monteath DOUGLAS, K.C.B., of Douglas-support and Stonebyres, co. Lanark. She *d.* 3 Nov. 1890. He *d.* s.p.m.s.,(c) 21 May 1902, in Paris, when the *Baronetcy* became *extinct*.

(a) Patrick Scott, the 1st son, was a Cornet in Cope's Dragoons, but *d.* unm. and v.p. at Ghent, 28 Sep. 1742.
(b) John Scott, the 1st s., *b.* 14 July 1798, at Athlone, was apparently living in 1811, but *d.* unm. and v.p.
(c) William Michael Augustus Scott, his only son, was *b.* 19 June 1865, and *d.* 21 Jan. 1870.

CUNINGHAME, *or* CUNNINGHAM(a):
cr. 26 Feb. 1671/2;
afterwards, since 1770, MONTGOMERY-CUNINGHAME.

I. 1672. "ALEXANDER CUNNINGHAM [*or* CUNINGHAME], of Corshill," in the parish of Stewarton, co. Ayr, only s. and h. of Alexander CUNINGHAME, by Anne, da. of John CRAWFORD, of Kilbirnie, which Alexander (who *d.* v.p. in or before 1646) was 1st s. and h. ap. of Alexander CUNINGHAME,(b) of Corshill aforesaid, was *b.* about 1643; suc. his said grandfather (who was living 1663) in or about 1667, and was *cr. a Baronet* [S.], as above, 26 Feb. 1671/2, with rem. to heirs male of the body, and registered arms as a descendant of a second son of the house of Glencairn. He *m.* about 1665, Mary, sister of Sir Archibald STEWART, 1st Baronet [S. 1667], da. of John STEWART, of Blackhall, co. Renfrew, by Mary, da. of Sir James STIRLING, of Keir. He became a ruined man, from having been surety to the spendthrift, Sir David CUNINGHAM, 4th Baronet [S. 1630], and *d.* March 1685.

II. 1685. SIR ALEXANDER CUNINGHAME, Baronet [S. 1672], of Corshill aforesaid, only s. and h., *suc. to the Baronetcy* in March 1685, being then a minor, and was, ill-advisedly, served heir general to his father, 25 March 1685, and heir special in the Barony of Robertland. By this service not only his estate but that of his wife was given up to his father's creditors, and he had to subsist "by the effects of his industry." He *m.* in 1686, Margaret, sister of David (BOYLE), 1st EARL OF GLASGOW [S.], da. of John BOYLE, of Kelburn, by his 1st wife, Maria, da. of Sir Walter STEWART, of Allantoun. He *d.* 1730.

III. 1730. SIR DAVID CUNINGHAME, Baronet [S. 1672], of Corshill aforesaid, only s. and h., *suc. to the Baronetcy* in 1730. He *m.* Penelope, da. of Alexander MONTGOMERY, of Assloss, co. Ayr, by Margaret, da. of Alexander MONTGOMERY, of Kirktonholm, co. Lanark. She *d.* before 4 Feb. 1742, when her son Alexander was served her heir. He *d.* 4 July 1770, at Corshill, at a great age.(c)

IV. 1770. SIR WALTER MONTGOMERY-CUNINGHAME, Baronet [S. 1672], of Kirktonholm aforesaid, grandson and h., being 1st s. and h. of Capt. Alexander MONTGOMERY-CUNINGHAME, by Elizabeth, 1st da. of David, and heir (1767) to her br. James MONTGOMERY, both of Lainshaw, co. Ayr, which Alexander, who took the name of MONTGOMERY before that of CUNINGHAME (as heir, 11 May 1761, to his maternal aunt, Anne MONTGOMERY) on succeeding to the estate of Kirktonholm (formerly that of his maternal great uncle, Sir Walter MONTGOMERY), was 1st s. and heir ap. of the late Baronet, was served heir to his mother, but *d.* v.p., a few months before his father, in Jan. 1770. He *suc. to the Baronetcy*, 4 July 1770. He was served, 2 May 1776, heir male of provision special to his mother, whose estate of Lainshaw he sold in 1779. He was an unsuccessful claimant to the EARLDOM OF GLENCAIRN [S.], in July 1797.(d) He *d.* unm. March 1814.

(a) Much of the information in this article was supplied by the late R. R. Stodart, Lyon Clerk Depute [1863-86].
(b) This Alexander was s. and h. of another Alexander (*d.* 1646), s. and h. of Cuthbert (*d.* 1575), s. and h. of Andrew, all of Corshill aforesaid, the said Andrew being 2d s. of William (Cuninghame), 4th Earl of Glencairn [S.], from whom, in 1532, he received the Corshill estate. From this descent it would seem that, if no nearer male heir exists, this family has a good claim as heir male to the Earldom of Glencairn.
(c) The estate was then sold and fenced out, all that devolved on his grandson was one farm and the ruined fragment of the Castle.
(d) See note "b" above.

V. 1814, March. SIR DAVID MONTGOMERY-CUNINGHAME, Baronet [S. 1672], of Kirktonholm aforesaid. br. and h., sometime Lieut. in the North British Dragoons; *suc. to the Baronetcy* in March 1814, but *d.* unm. a few months later, in Nov. 1814.

VI. 1814, Nov. SIR JAMES MONTGOMERY-CUNINGHAME, Baronet [S. 1672], of Kirktonholm aforesaid, only surv. br. and h., being 5th s. of the 3d Baronet; *suc. to the Baronetcy*, Nov. 1814. He *m.* in 1802, Janet, da. of Thomas CUMING, of Edinburgh, Banker. He *d.* March 1837.

VII. 1837. SIR ALEXANDER DAVID MONTGOMERY-CUNINGHAME, Baronet [S. 1672], of Kirktonholm aforesaid, 1st s. and h., *suc. to the Baronetcy* in March 1837. He *d.* 8 June 1846.

VIII. 1846. SIR THOMAS MONTGOMERY-CUNINGHAME, Baronet [S. 1672], br. and h.; *suc. to the Baronetcy*, 8 June 1846; Lieut. Col. Royal Ayrshire Rifles, 1850-58. He *m.* in 1832, Charlotte, only da. and h. of Hugh HUTCHESON, of Southfield, co. Renfrew. He *d.* 30 Aug. 1870, at 16 Princes Terrace, Hyde Park. His widow *d.* probably in 1902.(a)

IX. 1870. SIR WILLIAM JAMES MONTGOMERY-CUNINGHAME, Baronet [S. 1672], of Glenmoor, co. Ayr, 1st but only surv. s. and h., *b.* 20 May 1834; ed. at Harrow; entered the Army, 1853; Capt. Rifle Brigade, 1855, serving through the Russian War, receiving medal and 4 clasps; 5th Class of the Medjidie, and (for personal valour) the Victoria Cross; became Major in 1867, but placed on half-pay 1871; *suc. to the Baronetcy*, 30 Aug. 1870; M.P. for Ayr district, 1874-80; sometime Major 4th Batt. Royal Scots Fusileers (Militia); Col. of the Clyde Vol. Brigade, 1888. He *m.* 22 April 1869, Elizabeth, yst. da. of Edward Bourchier HARTOPP, of Dalby Hall, co. Leicester, by Honora, da. of Gen. William GENT. He *d.* 11 Nov. 1897, aged 63, at Gunton Old Hall, Suffolk. His widow living 1904. Will pr. at £13,281.

X. 1897. SIR THOMAS ANDREW ALEXANDER MONTGOMERY-CUNINGHAME, Baronet [S. 1672], of Glenmoor aforesaid, 1st s. and h., *b.* 30 March 1877; ed. at Eton and at Sandhurst Mil. College; Lieut. Rifle Brigade; *suc. to the Baronetcy*, 11 Nov. 1897. He served and was wounded in the Transvaal war, 1899-1901.

Family Estates.—These, in 1883, consisted of 3,209 acres in Ayrshire and 161 in Lancashire. *Total*, 3,370 acres, worth £3,329 a year. *Principal Residence.*—Glenmoor, near Maybole, co. Ayr.

LOCKHART:
cr. 28 Feb. 1671/2(b);
sometime, 1758-60, ROSS-LOCKHART;
afterwards, since 1778, LOCKHART-ROSS.

I. 1672. "WILLIAM LOCKHART, of Carstairs," co. Lanark, s. of Sir William LOCKHART, of the same, by Mary, da. of (—) CARMICHAEL, was *cr. a Baronet* [S.], as above, 28 Feb. 1671/2,(b) with rem. to heirs male of the body. He *m.* Isabel, 5th da. of James (DOUGLAS), 2d EARL OF QUEENSBERRY [S.], by his 2d wife, Margaret, da. of John (STEWART), 1st EARL OF TRAQUAIR [S.]. He *d.* 1710.

(a) She is inserted in Dod's *Baronetage* for 1902, but not in that for 1903.
(b) According to Playfair's *Baronetage* [1811], the creation was on the last day of Feb. *1668*.

II. 1710. SIR JAMES LOCKHART, Baronet [S. 1672], of Carstairs aforesaid, s. and h., *suc. to the Baronetcy* and was retoured heir to his father, in 1710. He *m.*, in or before 1715, Grizel, 3d da. of William (Ross), 12th LORD ROSS OF HALKHEAD [S.], by his 1st wife, Agnes, da. and h. of Sir John WILKIE. He *d.* 31 July 1755.

III. 1755. SIR WILLIAM LOCKHART, Baronet [S. 1672], of Carstairs aforesaid, 1st s. and h., *b.* about 1715; *suc. to the Baronetcy*, 31 July 1755. He *m.* firstly, 25 July 1751, Philadelphia, da. of Major James AGNEW, 4th s. of Sir James AGNEW, of Lochnaw. She *d.* s.p. He *m.* secondly, 13 Jan. 1755, Catherine, 2d da. of John PORTERFIELD, of Fullwood, Advocate. He *d.* s.p.m. (two days after a carriage accident), 26 June 1758. His widow *d.* 15 March 1807.

IV. 1758. SIR JAMES ROSS-LOCKHART, Baronet [S. 1672], of Carstairs aforesaid, and of Balnagowan, co. Ross, br. and h., *b.* about 1717; was an officer in the army, being wounded at the battle of Culloden in 1745, becoming eventually Major-General, and being Col. of the 38th Foot. He took the name of Ross before that of LOCKHART, on succeeding to the estate of Balnagowan, on the death, 19 Aug. 1754, of his cousin, William (Ross), 14th LORD ROSS OF HALKHEAD [S.]. He *suc. to the Baronetcy*, 26 June 1758. He *m.* Elizabeth, da. of Major John CROSBIE. He *d.* s.p.m.,(a) and was *bur.* 30 Sep. 1760, at Paddington, in his 44th year. Admon., as "of St. Geo. Han. sq.," to "Charles Ross, Esq., a creditor, the widow renouncing. She *d.* April 1814, aged 85. Will pr. 1814.

V. 1760. SIR GEORGE LOCKHART, Baronet [S. 1672], of Carstairs aforesaid, br. and h. male, *b.* about 1718; *suc. to the Baronetcy* in Sep. 1760, and sold the estate of Carstairs in 1762. He *d.* unm., 13 Aug. 1778, at Bonnington, co. Lanark.

VI. 1778. SIR JOHN LOCKHART-ROSS, Baronet [S. 1672], of Balnagowan aforesaid, br. and h., *b.* 11 Nov. 1721; entered the Navy in 1735, distinguishing himself as Capt. of the "Tartar" frigate (28 guns) in 1759, wherewith he captured nine ships of war from the French within the space of fifteen months, becoming Admiral in 1779. He suc. to the Balnagowan estate on the death of his elder br. (the 4th Baronet) in Sep. 1760, and thereupon took the name of Ross after that of LOCKHART. He was M.P. for the Borough of Lanark, 1761-68, and for Lanarkshire, 1768-74. He *suc. to the Baronetcy*, 13 Aug. 1778. He *m.* 6 Sep. 1762, Elizabeth, da. of Robert DUNDAS, of Arnistoun, President of the Court of Session, by his 1st wife (to whom she was heir), Henrietta, da. and h. of Sir James CARMICHAEL, of Bonnington, co. Lanark, by Margaret, da. and h. of William BAILLIE, of Lamington. He *d.* 9 June 1790, aged 70.

VII. 1790. SIR CHARLES LOCKHART-ROSS, Baronet [S. 1672], of Balnagowan and Bonnington aforesaid, 1st s. and h., *b.* about 1763; was an officer in the Army, becoming finally, in 1805, Lieut. Gen., and being Col. of the 86th Foot; was M.P. for the Wick burghs, 1786-96, for Ross-shire, 1796-1806, and for Linlithgow burghs, 1806-07; *suc. to the Baronetcy*, 9 June 1790. He *m.* firstly, about 1788, Matilda Theresa, a Countess in the Holy Roman Empire, da. of James LOCKHART-WISHART, Count of the Holy Roman Empire, Lieut. Gen. in the Austrian Service, by his 1st wife, Matilda, da. of Sir John LOCKHART, of Castle Hill. She *d.* 1 Feb. 1791, aged 24, and was *bur.* at Kensington.(b) M.I. He *m.* secondly, 15 April 1799, Mary Rebecca, 1st

(a) His only child "John [Joan?] Elizabeth Ross," an infant in Nov. 1760, was presumably a daughter.
(b) Of her issue, John, the only son, *d.* in boyhood, 5 July 1797, while Martha, the only da., inherited the Lamington property, took the name of Ross-Wishart, and *m.*, 6 Jan. 1812, as his first wife, Admiral Sir Thomas John Cochrane, G.C.B., being mother of Alexander Napier Ross Cochrane-Wishart-Baillie, who was *cr.* in 1880 Baron Lamington, co. Lanark.

da. of William Robert (FITZGERALD), 2d DUKE OF LEINSTER [I.], by Emilia Olivia, da. and h. of St. George (USHER-ST. GEORGE), BARON ST. GEORGE OF HATLEY ST. GEORGE [I.]. He *d.* 8 Feb. 1814, in his 52d year. His widow, who was *b.* 6 May 1777, *d.* 28 Feb. 1842.

VIII. 1814. SIR CHARLES WILLIAM FREDERICK AUGUSTUS LOCKHART-ROSS, Baronet [S. 1672], of Balnagowan and Bonnington aforesaid, 3d and yst. but only surv. s. and h., being 2d s. by the 2d wife, *b.* 19 Jan. 1812, at Cheltenham; *suc. to the Baronetcy,* 8 Feb. 1814; ed. at Eton; matric. at Oxford (Ch. Ch.), 18 April 1831, aged 19; took no interest in public affairs, and never filled any office. He *m.* firstly, 9 Feb. 1841, Elizabeth Baillie, da. of his uncle, Col. Robert LOCKHART-ROSS, 4th Dragoon Guards (5th s. of the 6th Baronet), by Caroline, da. of John MACBEAN. She *d.* s.p. 4 Nov. 1853, at Bonnington, aged 32. He *m.* secondly, 2 March 1865 (ceremony performed by the Minister of Lanark), Rebecca Sophia, 3d surv. da. of Henry BARNES, of Tufnell Park. He *d.* 26 July 1883, at Balnagowan, aged 71. His widow living 1904.

IX. 1883. SIR CHARLES HENRY AUGUSTUS FREDERICK LOCKHART-ROSS, Baronet [S. 1672], of Balnagowan and Bonnington aforesaid, only s. and h. by 2d wife, *b.* at Balnagowan, 4 April 1872; *suc. to the Baronetcy,* 26 July 1883; ed. at Eton and at Trin. Coll., Cambridge, where he rowed in the Eight; sometime Lieut. Seaforth Highlanders Militia, serving in the Transvaal War (1899-1901), in the Corps of Gillies, to whom he presented "Ross's Battery"; was inventor of the Ross magazine rifle. He *m.* firstly, 26 April 1893, Winifred, yst da. and coheir of Alexander Augustus BERENS, by Louisa Winifred, da. of the Rev. Edward STEWART, Rector of Lainston, Hants. This marriage was dissolved in 1897.(a) He *m.* secondly, in 1901, Patricia Burnley, da. of Andrew ELLISON, of Louisville, Kentucky, U.S.A.

Family Estates.—These, in 1883, consisted of 300,000(b) acres in Ross-shire, 55,000 in Sutherlandshire, and 1,500 in Lanarkshire. *Total.*—356,500 acres, worth £17,264 a year. *Principal Seats.*—Balnagowan, near Parkhill, co. Ross, and Bonnington, co. Lanark.

MAITLAND:

cr. 12 March 1671/2(c);

dormant in or shortly before 1704.

I. 1672. "RICHARD MAITLAND, of Pitrichie," in the parish of Udny, co. Aberdeen,(d) s. and h. of Patrick MAITLAND, of the same, by Katharine, da. of Alexander BURNETT, of Leys, had spec. service to his

(a) She *m.* in 1901, Capt. Noel Llewellyn, D.S.O., District Commandant of the South African Constabulary.

(b) "The return only gives Sir Charles 110,000 acres in Ross" [Bateman's *Great Landowners*, 1883].

(c) On this same date, according to Wood's *Douglas Peerage* of Scotland [vol. ii, p. 72], the Hon. Charles Maitland, of Hatton [*i.e.*, Haltoun], co. Edinburgh, yst s. of the 1st Earl of Lauderdale [S.], is said to have been *cr. a Baronet* [S.]. This, however, seems to be a confusion with the creation as in the text, the grantee of which was, however, no near relative of this Charles. This Charles succeeded, 24 Aug. 1682, as (3d) Earl of Lauderdale [S.], and had four sons, of whom John Maitland, the 2d son, was *cr. a Baronet* [S.] 18 Nov. 1680 (a fact omitted in the said peerage), and succeeded, 18 Sep. 1734, as (5th) Earl of Lauderdale [S.], in which peerage that Baronetcy then became merged and still so continues. The Baronetcy [S.] therefore enjoyed by these Earls is apparently one of the date of 18 Nov. 1680, and not (as stated in the said peerage) one of 12 March 1671/2.

(d) In Milne's *List* he is called "the elder."

father, 12 July 1643; was a Senator of the College of Justice, Dec. 1671, and was *cr. a Baronet* [S.], as above, with rem. to heirs male whatsoever, 12 March 1672. In that year he reg. arms in the Lyon Office. He had Crown Charter of the Barony of Gight, co. Aberdeen, as a Free Barony, 6 July 1672. He *m.* Margaret, da. of Robert GORDON, of Straloch and Pitlurg, the well-known Geographer. He *d.* 22 Feb. 1677.

II. 1677 SIR RICHARD MAITLAND, Baronet [S. 1672], of Pitrichie aforesaid, s. and h., *suc. to the Baronetcy,* 22 Feb. 1677, and had spec. service to his father, 31 May 1678. He *d.* s.p. between June and Oct. 1679.

III 1679. SIR CHARLES MAITLAND, Baronet [S. 1672], of Pitrichie aforesaid, br. and h., *suc. to the Baronetcy,* in 1679, and had service to his br. in the Barony of Gight, and other lands; was M.P. [S.] for Aberdeenshire, 1685-86. He *m.* firstly, Jean, da. of Sir John FORBES, 3d Baronet [S. 1626], of Monymusk, by his 1st wife, Margaret, da. of Robert (ARBUTHNOTT), 1st VISCOUNT ARBUTHNOTT [S.]. He *m.* secondly, in 1696, Nichola, widow of Sir Alexander BURNETT, of Craigmyle, da. of Peter YOUNG, of Auldbar. He *d.* 1700.

IV. 1700, to 1704? SIR CHARLES MAITLAND, Baronet [S. 1672], of Pitrichie aforesaid, only s. and h.; *suc. to the Baronetcy* in 1700, and was served heir gen. of his father, 23 March 1702/3. He *m.* before 23 June 1703,(a) Margaret BURNETT, the step da. of his father. He *d.* s.p., in or shortly before 1704 (before 6 May 1704(a)), when the heirs male of the body of the grantee became, presumably, extinct,(b) and the *Baronetcy* became *dormant* or *extinct.*

JARDINE:

cr. 25 May 1672.

I. 1672. "ALEXANDER JARDINE, of Applegirth," co. Dumfries, s. of Alexander JARDINE, of the same, was *cr. a Baronet* [S.], as above, 25 May 1672, with rem. to heirs male of the body. He was retoured heir to his said father, 20 April 1691. He *m.* in or before 1675, Margaret, da. of James (DOUGLAS), 2d EARL OF QUEENSBERRY [S.], by his 2d wife, Margaret, da. of John (STEWART), 1st EARL OF TRAQUAIR [S.]. He *d.* between 1691 and 1699. His widow *m.* Sir David THOIRS.

II. 1695? SIR ALEXANDER JARDINE, Baronet [S. 1672], of Applegirth aforesaid, 1st s. and h., *suc. to the Baronetcy* on the death of his father. He *d.* unm. and was *bur.* 6 Feb. 1699.(c)

III. 1699. SIR JOHN JARDINE, Baronet [S. 1672], of Applegirth aforesaid, br. and h., *b.* 1683; *suc. to the Baronetcy* in Feb. 1699. He *m.* firstly, in or before 1712, Catherine, da. of Sir James LOCKHART, of Carstairs. He *m.* secondly, Jane, da. of (—) CHARTERIS, of Amisfield. He *d.* 1737. His widow *d.* 7 Feb. 1762.

(a) Town House Papers, Aberdeen.

(b) Of his six sisters and coheirs, Jean, the eldest, who was served his heir gen. and of entail, 6 May 1704, *m.* Hon. Alexander Arbuthnott (who took the name of Maitland and *d.* 1721), and *d.* 22 Oct. 1746, leaving, besides two daughters (who, under the Pitrichie entail, did not inherit that estate), an only s. and h., Charles Maitland, of Pitrichie, M.P. for Aberdeen Burghs, 1748 till he *d.* 10 Feb. 1751. On his death, unm., the estate devolved on his 1st cousin, Arthur Forbes, afterwards Forbes-Maitland of Pitrichie, s. and h. of Thomas Forbes, of Echt, by Mary, 2d sister and coheir of the last Baronet.

(c) "Account book of Foulis of Ravelston" [*Scottish History Society*].

IV. 1737. SIR ALEXANDER JARDINE, Baronet [S. 1672], of Applegirth aforesaid, 1st s. and h., by 1st wife, *b.* 1712; *suc. to the Baronetcy* in 1737. He resided principally abroad; became a Roman Catholic; entered the military service and was elected one of the Knights of Malta. He *d.* unm. at Brussels, Dec. 1790. Admon. March 1791.

V. 1790. SIR WILLIAM JARDINE, Baronet [S. 1672], of Applegirth aforesaid, br. of the half blood and h., being s. of the 3d Baronet by his 2d wife; *suc. to the Baronetcy* in Dec. 1790. He *m.* Barbara DE LA MOTTE, a French lady. He *d.* 17 March 1807.

VI. 1807. SIR ALEXANDER JARDINE, Baronet [S. 1672], of Applegirth aforesaid, only s. and h.; *suc. to the Baronetcy,* 17 March 1807. He *m.*, in or before 1799, Janet, da. of Thomas MAULE, Lieut. of Invalids, grandson of Henry MAULE, Bishop of Meath, 1744-58. He *d.* 1821. His widow *d.* at Madeira, 9 Aug. 1825.

VII. 1821. SIR WILLIAM JARDINE, Baronet [S. 1672], of Jardine Hall, co. Dumfries, 1st s. and h., *b.* 13 Feb. 1800 in North Hanover street, Edinburgh; *suc. to the Baronetcy* in 1821; was a Commissr. of the Salmon Fisheries, 1860. He *m.* firstly, 28 June 1820, Jane Home, da. of Daniel LIZARS, of Edinburgh. She *d.* 2 March 1871, at Jardine Hall. He *m.* (eight months subsequently) 18 Nov. 1871, at Pendock, co. Worcester, Hyacinthe, only da. of the Rev. William Samuel SYMONDS, Rector of Pendock. He *d.* 9 Nov. 1874, at "Riston," Sandown, Isle of Wight, aged 74. His widow *m.* (as his 2d wife), 22 Aug. 1876, at St. Nicholas, Hereford, Sir Joseph Dalton HOOKER, G.C.S.I., Director of the Royal Gardens at Kew, 1865-85, and was (as was he) living 1904.

VIII. 1874. SIR ALEXANDER JARDINE, Baronet [S. 1672], of Jardine Hall aforesaid, 1st s. and h., by 1st wife, *b.* there 10 Feb. 1829; ed. at Edinburgh and at Woolwich; *suc. to the Baronetcy,* 9 Nov. 1874. He *m.*, 28 Dec. 1861, Henrietta, 3d da. of William YOUNGER, of Craigielands, co. Dumfries, by Isabella, da. of Henry JOHNSTON, M.D., of Corstorphine House, co. Edinburgh. He *d.* 14 Jan. 1893, aged 63, at Gunton House, Edinburgh. His widow living 1904.

IX. 1893. SIR WILLIAM JARDINE, Baronet [S. 1672], of Jardine Hall aforesaid, 1st s. and h., *b.* 11 June 1865; ed. at Fettes College, Edinburgh; *suc. to the Baronetcy,* 14 Jan. 1893; sometime Lieut. 1st Vol. Batt. Cheshire reg. and Calcutta Light Horse, serving in the Transvaal war in 1900; member of the Royal Company of Archers (Queen's body guard for Scotland), and Capt. 3d Batt. King's Own Scottish Borderers militia.

Family Estates.—These, in 1883, consisted of 5,538 acres in co. Dumfries, worth £5,818 a year. *Principal Seat.*—Jardine Hall, near Lockerby, co. Dumfries.

HOPE:

cr. 30 May 1672;

ex., presumably, in or before 1794.

I. 1672. "ALEXANDER HOPE, of Kerse," co. Stirling, s. and h. of Sir Thomas HOPE, of the same, Lord Justice General [S.], 1641-43 (who was *b.* 2 Aug. 1606, being 2d s. of Sir Thomas HOPE, 1st Baronet [S. 1628] of Craighall), was *b.* 12 Dec. 1637; suc. his father, 23 Aug. 1643; was *Knighted* before (probably long before) 1659, and was *cr. a Baronet* [S.] as above, 30 May 1672, "provydit to the heirs male of his own body and their descendants in a right lyne for ever."(a) He *m.*, 12 Nov. 1659, at Delft in the Netherlands,

(a) Milne's *List.*

"Mistress Louisa HUNTER."(a) He *d.* Dec. 1673, and was *bur.* 1 Jan. 1693/4, at Greyfriars, Edinburgh, aged 36.

II. 1673. SIR ALEXANDER HOPE, Baronet [S. 1672], of Kerse aforesaid, s. and h., *b.* 13 Aug. 1663; *suc. to the Baronetcy* in Dec. 1673. He *m.*, 14 April 1690, Nicolas, only da. of William (HAMILTON), 2d LORD BARGENY [S.], by his 1st wife, Margaret, da. of William (CUNINGHAME), 9th EARL OF GLENCAIRN [S.]. He *d.* 10 and was *bur.* 13 Feb. 1719,(b) at Greyfriars, Edinburgh, aged 55. M.I.

III. 1719. SIR ALEXANDER HOPE, Baronet [S. 1672], of Kerse aforesaid, s. and h., *b.* 3 Jan. 1697; *suc. to the Baronetcy,* in Feb. 1719. He *m.* Anne, 3d da. of David (CARNEGIE), 4th EARL OF NORTHESK [S.], by Margaret, sister of David, EARL OF WEMYSS [S.], da. of James (WEMYSS), LORD BURNTISLAND [S.]. She *d.* 1 Feb. 1733. He *d.* 24 Feb. 1749.

IV. 1749, to 1794? SIR ALEXANDER HOPE, Baronet [S. 1672], of Kerse aforesaid, only s. and h.; *suc. to the Baronetcy,* 24 Feb. 1749. He sold the estate of Kerse to the family of Dundas. On his death, in or before 1794, the male issue of the grantee as also, presumably, the *Baronetcy* became *extinct.* Admon. March 1794.

MURRAY:

cr. 7 June 1673;(c)

afterwards, since 1837, KEITH-MURRAY.

I. 1673. "WILLIAM MURRAY, of Ochtertyre," co. Perth, s. and h. ap. of Patrick MURRAY, of the same (who *d.* 2 Feb. 1677, aged 86, and was *bur.* at Monivaird), by Mary, da. of Sir William MORAY, of Abercairn, was *b.* 30 Oct. 1615, at Ochtertyre; was a Royalist, and was fined by Parl.; got a charter of lands, on his father's resignation, 30 Jan. 1662, and was (v.p.) *cr. a Baronet* [S.], as above, 7 June 1673,(c) such creation, however, not being recorded in the Great Seal Register, but he "gets his Arms as Baronet out of the Lyon office."(d) He was M.P. [S.] for Perthshire, 1673-74. He *m.* 7 June 1649, Isabel, da. of John OLIPHANT, of Bachilton. He *d.* 18 Feb. 1681, in his 66th year. His widow *d.* 6 April 1683.

II. 1681. SIR PATRICK MURRAY, Baronet [S. 1673], of Ochtertyre aforesaid, 2d but 1st surv. s. and h., *b.* at Dollery, 21 Jan. 1656; *suc. to the Baronetcy,* 18 Feb. 1681; was employed by the Government in distributing the money to quiet the Highland clans after the Revolution, of 1688, and acquired a considerable fortune and extensive estates, whereof he executed a strict entail;(e) was M.P. [S.] for Perthshire, 1702-07. He, however, was committed to Edinburgh Castle on suspicion of being implicated in the

(a) In the register of marriages at the church at Delft noticed in Wm. Stevens's *History of the Scottish Church, Rotterdam* [Edinburgh, 1833, p. 296, note], occurs, under 12 Nov. 1659, that of "Sir Alexander Hope, of Kerse, Knt. Bart., and Mris. Louisa Hunter" [*ex inform.* J. R. Anderson]. It is possible that this designation was owing to his having obtained a Baronetcy from the Protector Cromwell, as was the case with many of the grantees of Charles II.

(b) Index to services of heirs.

(c) 3 June 1673 according to Chamberlayne's *List,* and 3 Jan. 1673 according to that of Miege.

(d) Milne's *List.*

(e) In it is this remarkable clause, which probably would be inoperative at law, as to the forfeiture threatened, that "hail heirs of entail succeeding to the aforesaid lands and estates, shall neither take nor receive from the fountain of honour, nor from any other person by succession, any higher title at any time than that which I presently enjoy, *viz.*, a Knight Baronet," under penalty of forfeiture of the estate.

Jacobite Rising, but was admitted to bail, 29 Sep. 1715. He *m.* 15 Feb. 1681, at Gleneagles, Margaret, 1st da. of Mungo HALDANE, of Gleneagles, by (a presumed marriage with) Anne GRANT. She, who was *b.* 22 July 1657, *d.* 17 Feb. 1722, aged 65, and was *bur.* at Monivaird. He *d.* 25 Dec. 1735, and was *bur.* there in his 80th year.

III. 1735. SIR WILLIAM MURRAY, Baronet [S. 1673], of Ochtertyre aforesaid, 1st s. and h., *b.* at Foulis, 22 Feb. 1682; is said(a) to have been bred at the Univ. of Oxford, and to have been an accomplished scholar; was (with his father) cited on suspicion of being concerned in the Jacobite rising of 1715; *suc. to the Baronetcy*, 25 Dec. 1735. He *m.* 25 July 1706, at Perth, Catherine, 3d da. of Hugh (FRASER), LORD LOVAT [S.], by Amelia, da. of John (MURRAY), 1st MARQUESS OF ATHOLL [S.]. He *d.* 20 Oct. 1739, in his 57th year at Edinburgh, and was *bur.* in St. Giles' church there. His widow *d.* 4 March 1771, aged 81, at Foulis, and was *bur.* there.

IV. 1739. SIR PATRICK MURRAY, Baronet [S. 1673], of Ochtertyre aforesaid, 1st s. and h., *b.* at Monivaird, 21 Aug. 1707; *suc. to the Baronetcy*, 20 Oct. 1739; was an officer in the army, and was taken prisoner in 1745 by the Insurgents at the battle of Prestonpans. He *m.* 18 Feb. 1741, Helen, 1st da. of John HAMILTON, Writer to the Signet, by Jean, da. of (—) GARTSHORE, of Gartshore. He *d.* at Ochtertyre, 9 Sep. 1764, aged 57, and was *bur.* at Monivaird. His widow *d.* at Gorthie, 18 July 1773, and was *bur.* at Monivaird.

V 1764. SIR WILLIAM MURRAY, Baronet [S. 1673], of Ochtertyre aforesaid, only s. and h., *b.* there 23 Oct. 1746; was sometime an officer in the army; *suc. to the Baronetcy*, 9 Sep. 1764, and rebuilt the house at Ochtertyre. He *m.* 6 March 1770, Augusta, yst. da. of George (MACKENZIE), 3d EARL OF CROMARTIE, by Isabel, da. of Sir William GORDON, Baronet [S. 1704], of Dalpholly. He *d.* 6 Dec. 1800 at Ochtertyre, and was *bur.* at Monivaird, aged 54. His widow *d.* 20 Jan. 1809 at Liverpool, aged 62, and was *bur.* at St. James' there. M.I.

VI. 1800. SIR PATRICK MURRAY, Baronet [S. 1673], of Ochtertyre aforesaid, 1st s. and h.,(b) *b.* there 3 Feb. 1771; admitted as Advocate, 1793; King's Remembrancer of the Court of Exchequer [S.], for life, 1799; *suc. to the Baronetcy*, 6 Dec. 1800; Lieut.-Col. Commandant of the Strathearn Infantry, 1803, and, shortly afterwards, Provincial Grand Master of the Perthshire Freemasons; M.P. for Edinburgh city (two Parls.), 1806-12; Lieut.-Col. of the Western Reg. of the Perthshire Militia, and one of trustees of the Scotch fishery in 1808; Sec. for the affairs of India, 1810. He *m.* 13 Dec. 1794, at Edinburgh, Mary Ann, yst. da. of John (HOPE), 2d EARL OF HOPETOUN [S.], by his 3d wife, Elizabeth, da. of Alexander (LESLIE), 5th EARL OF LEVEN [S.]. He *d.* 1 June 1837, aged 66. His widow, who was *b.* 12 July 1773, *d.* 21 Feb. 1838.

VII. 1837. SIR WILLIAM KEITH MURRAY, Baronet [S. 1673], of Ochtertyre aforesaid, 1st surv. s. and h., *b.* there 19 July 1801; assumed, apparently, the name of KEITH before that of MURRAY in consequence of his marriage in 1833, and *suc. to the Baronetcy*, 1 June 1837; sometime Lieut. Col. of the Perthshire Militia, and subsequently (1860) of the 1st Batt. of the Perthshire Rifle Vols. He *m.* firstly, 28 Nov. 1833, Helen Margaret Oliphant,

(a) Playfair's *Baronetage* [1811].

(b) His yr. br., Gen. Sir George Murray, G.C.B., *b.* 6 Feb. 1772 at Ochtertyre, distinguished himself in Flanders, Egypt, and the Peninsula; was M.P. for Perthshire (four Parls.), 1824-32; Gov. of Fort George and Master Gen. of the Ordnance. He *d.* s.p.m., 28 July 1846, aged 74.

only da. and h. of Sir Alexander KEITH, of Dunnottar, Knight Marischal of Scotland. She *d.* 28 Oct. 1852. He *m.* secondly, 8 July 1854, at Heckfield, Hants, Adelaide Augusta Lavinia, 4th da. of Francis (RAWDON-HASTINGS), 1st MARQUESS OF HASTINGS, by Flora, *suo jure* COUNTESS OF LOUDOUN [S.]. She, who was *b.* 25 Feb. 1812, *d.* s.p. 6 Dec. 1860. He *d.* 16 Oct. 1861, at Ochtertyre, aged 60.

VIII. 1861. SIR PATRICK KEITH MURRAY, Baronet [S. 1673], of Ochtertyre aforesaid, 1st s. and h. by 1st wife, *b.* 27 Jan. 1835; ed. at Trin. Coll., Cambridge; entered the Army, 1854, becoming Capt. Gren. Guards, 1857, but retired in 1861; *suc. to the Baronetcy*, 16 Oct. 1861. He *m.* firstly, 23 Aug. 1870, at St. Columba's Chapel, Crieff, Frances Amelia Jemima, 6th da. of Anthony MURRAY, of Dollerie, co. Perth,(a) by Georgina, 3d da. of Sir Patrick MURRAY, 6th Baronet [1673], of Ochtertyre abovenamed. She *d.* 7 Oct. 1874, at Aberturret, Crieff, aged 31. He *m.* secondly, 30 March 1876, Ioné Campbell, da. of William PENNEY, of Kinloch, a Lord of Session [S.] under the style of *Lord Kinloch*. She *d.* 5 March 1881, at Ochertyre, aged 35.

Family Estates.—These, in 1833, consisted of 17,876 acres in Perthshire, worth £11,051 a year. *Principal Seat.*—Ochtertyre, near Crieff, co. Perth.

FRASER :(b)

cr. 2 Aug. 1673;

ex. 10 May 1729.

I. 1673. ALEXANDER FRASER, of Dores," co. Kincardine,(c) only s. of Adam FRASER, by (—), da. of (—) DUFF, of Drummure, which Adam was 2d s. of Thomas FRASER, of Dores aforesaid (by Helen, da. of James GORDON, of Abergeldie), was *b.* about 1607; ed. at the Univ. of Aberdeen and of Leyden; M.D. of Montpelier, 1 Oct. 1635, being incorporated at Cambridge, 9 March 1637; Candidate of the Coll. of Physicians, 30 March 1640; Fellow, 23 Nov. 1641; "Elect," 26 July 1666. He was made Court Physician in Ordinary (to Charles I) in 1645,(d) continuing as such (till death) to Charles II, both during his exile, his visit to Scotland in 1650, and afterwards at his Restoration. He was one of the Founders of the Royal Society, of which, in 1663, he was a Fellow. He re-purchased his grandfather's estate of Dores, which had been alienated by his cousin, had a Crown charter thereof in 1665, and was *cr. a Baronet* [S.], as above, 2 Aug. 1673, "provydit to whatsoever of his sons succeeds him in the Barony of Doores and the aires male [of his (said son's) body]."(e)

(a) See a good account of the family of Murray of Dollerie in *The Genealogist*, Orig. Series, vol. vii, pp. 15-19.

(b) Much of the information contained in this article has been kindly supplied by James R. Anderson, of Glasgow, who possesses a copy of the sermon preached by John MENZIES (of Aberdeen), at the funeral of "Sir Alexander Fraiser, of Doores," printed at Edinburgh, 1681, in which various particulars of his career are given. Selections therefrom and other particulars relating to the Baronet are in a work called "*Scotish Elegiac Verses*," 1629-1729, Edinburgh 1842, 8vo.

(c) See an account of the family of Fraser, "of the House of Dores," co. Kincardine, in Macfarlane's *Genealogical Collections* (vol. ii, pp. 316-331), pub. by the Scottish History Society (vol. xxxiv.) in 1900, as also in Stodart's *Scottish Arms*, vol. ii, p. 257.

(d) Macfarlane (as in note "c" above), states that "this information" was from "his own son," Sir Peter Fraser.

(e) Milne's *List*. The words are "cuicunque ejus filiorum Baroniam de Dores providebit et heredibus masculis de corpore dicti filii."

He *m.* firstly, "when he was a more private character than it that [*sic*; probably meaning 'than that in which'] he afterwards shone, a Lady sirnamed [Elizabeth] DOWCHLY, a gentleman's da., near Bristoll, who bore to him two sons and a daughter."(a) He *m.* secondly, after 1659, Mary, widow of Dudley WYLDE, of Canterbury (will dat. 15 July, pr. 8 Sep. 1653), 4th da. of Sir Ferdinando CAREY (*d.* 1638), by Philippa, da. of Sir William THOCKMORTON. He *d.* at Whitehall, in his 75th year, 28 April, and was *bur.* 20 July 1681, at Dores aforesaid.(b) Will dat. 9 Oct. 1679, pr. 7 July 1681 and 12 Dec. 1720. His widow was *bur.* 22 Dec. 1695, at Fulham, co. Midx. Will dat. 15 Dec. 1695, pr. 21 Jan. 1695/6 by her da. Carey, Countess of Monmouth, the universal legatee.

II. 1681, to 1729. SIR PETER FRASER, Baronet [S. 1673], of Dores aforesaid, 3rd and yst. s., being only s. by 2d wife, was *b.* after 1659, being under age in 1679; *suc. to the Baronetcy* on the death of his father, 26 April 1681, under the spec. rem. in the limitation of that dignity in consequence of the Dores estate having been entailed on him.(c) He was Lord Lieut. of Kincardineshire. He *m.*, probably about 1700, Anne, sister and coheir of Henry HERON, of Cressy Hall, in Surfleet, co. Lincoln (who *d.* s.p.s. 10 Sep. 1730, aged 56), da. of Sir Edward HERON, K.B., by Dorothy, da. of Sir James LONG, 2d Baronet [1662], of Draycot. He *d.* s.p. 10 May 1729, when the

(a) Viz., (1) "Alexander Fraser, *Esq.* [*not* called "Baronet"], his eldest son, who was Capt. of a troop of horse in H.M.'s forces in Ireland. He *m.* the only da. of Sir Robert Weirs, and had with her a fair estate near the City of Dublin, but *d.* s.p.m.s." He in his father's will dat. 9 Oct. 1679, is called "eldest son," and receives £50 only, testator "having been very bountiful to him heretofore." (2) "Charles Fraser, Esq., a learned and ingenious gentleman as any in his time. He translated some of Plutarch's *Lives*, and was generally supposed the author of *The Turkish Spy*. He died unm." He is not mentioned in his father's will, but was apparently the "Charles Fraiser, M.D., ed. at Westm. School and at Trin. Coll., Cambridge, of which he was afterwards Fellow; B.A., 1670; M.A., 1674; M.D. by Royal mandate, 1678; Physician in Ord. to Charles II, and, as such, admitted Fellow of the College of Physicians, 1684. Of him Peter Le Neve, in his *Memoranda*, after mentioning "Lady Frazier's" burial at Fulham, 22 Dec. 1695, speaks in a subsequent addition to that note "Dr. Frazier, her son [but should be "*step* son"], mad 1698." The da. Elizabeth, *m.* firstly, "Mr. Broomley [*Qy.* Gerard] (br. to the Lord Broomley [*Qy.* Gerard of Bromley]), slain in the second Dutch War, leaving no issue." She *m.* secondly James Graham, "Privy Purse to the late King James VII" [S.], br. to Richard, 1st Viscount Preston [S.].

(b) He was a great favourite with the King, and was much employed in Court affairs. "Dr. Pierce" told Pepys (*Diary* 19 Sep. 1664) that Fraser's influence was owing to his being "so great with all the Ladies of the Court in helping them to slip their calves when there is occasion, and with the great men in curing them." In the *Dict. Nat. Biogr.* this Pierce is spoken of as "a groom of the Privy Chamber, who repeated "backstairs' gossip," it being there, also, stated that Sir John Denham's "attacks" on Fraser are "founded on personal enmity."

(c) In the funeral sermon (see p. 293, note "b") it is said that the 1st Baronet, "having provided his other worthy and well deserving children of riper years, hath transmitted this old heretage of his Progenitors [*i.e.*, the estate of Dores] *with all its dignities* to his hopeful son here present, who by the mother is descended of the honourable name of Caries in England. . . . This, *his youngest son*, he sent hither to be educated." In a pedigree of Carey, entered at the Heralds' College, in which the 1st Baronet's second marriage with Mary Carey is set out, and which is signed by himself on 1 Aug. 1677, he mentions three children by that wife, *viz.*, "Peter Fraser, Esq., only son, 1677; Caria, 1677, (and) Catherina, 1677." As to the "exceeding fine parts" of this Sir Peter, see Macfarlane, as on p. 293, note "c."

Baronetcy became *extinct*.(a) His widow, who was *bap.* 11 Nov. 1677, at Surfleet, and who enjoyed the estate of Dores for her life,(b) *d.* at Cressy Hall, 25 Aug. 1769, in her 92d year, and was *bur.* at Surfleet. M.I.

CUNINGHAM :

cr. 3 Aug. 1673;

ex. in or before Aug. 1674.

I. 1673. "ROBERT CUNINGHAM, of Auchenharvie," in the parish of Stewarton, co. Ayr, 2d s. of the Rev. John CUNINGHAM,(c) of Raidland, in Dalry, co. Ayr, Minister of Dalry (1604), by his 2d wife, Jean, da. of Robert KER, of Trearne, co. Ayr, fought on the King's side at the battle of Worcester; was Physician for Scotland to Charles II; had a Crown charter of Auchenharvie, 20 March 1667, ratified 1669, and, having probably been *Knighted*, was *cr. a Baronet* [S.], as above, 3 Aug. 1673, the limitation of the dignity being unknown, as no record of such creation exists in the Great Seal Register, nor is it in Milne's *List*. He, however, registered his arms *as a Baronet*, 10 Sep. 1673, in the Lyon office. He *m.* firstly, before 1653, Elizabeth, da. of [—] DUNDAS, by (—) BUSBY, of Addington. He *m.* secondly, before 1661, Elizabeth, da. of Sir John HENDERSON, of Fordell, co. Fife, by Margaret MONTEITH, heiress of Randifoord. He *d.* late in Feb. and was *bur.* 4 March 1673/4 in Greyfriars, Edinburgh.(d)

II. 1674, Feb. to Aug? SIR ROBERT CUNINGHAM, Baronet [S. 1673], of Auchenharvie aforesaid, only s. and h. by 2d marriage; *bap.* 7 Aug. 1662; *suc. to the Baronetcy* in Feb. 1673/4. He *d.* s.p. a few months later, before 29 Aug. 1674, when the *Baronetcy* is presumed to have become *extinct*.(e)

(a) Index to service of heirs. The date is usually given as 23 May. Of his two sisters of the whole blood and coheirs, (1) Carey, maid of honour to the Queen Consort Catharine, *m.* as his 1st wife, shortly after 1677, the well-known Charles (Mordaunt), Earl of Peterborough and Monmouth, who *d.* 25 Oct. 1735, aged about 77. She *d.* 13 and was *bur.* 16 May 1709, at Turvey, Beds. (2) Catharine *m.*, after 1677, Charles Scarburgh, Clerk of the Green Cloth, and *d.* s.p.m.

(b) The estate of Dores, or Durris, then devolved on Charles (Mordaunt), 4th Earl of Peterborough, grandson of the 3d Earl by his 1st wife, Carey, sister of Sir Peter Fraser abovenamed. It was sold in 1826 by Alexander (Gordon), 4th Duke of Gordon [S.], who in 1819 had become heir to the Mordaunt family in right of his grandmother, Henrietta, Duchess of Gordon [S.], da. of Charles (Mordaunt), Earl of Peterborough and Monmouth, by Carey, (see note "a" above), da. of Sir Alexander Fraser, 1st Baronet [S. 1673], of Dores aforesaid.

(c) This John was s. of Robert Cuningham, of Raidland aforesaid (living 1567), who was 3rd son of William Cuningham, of Craigends, co. Renfrew, whose relationship to Sir David Cuningham, 1st Baronet [S.], of Auchenharvie (so *cr.* 23 Dec. 1633) is unknown. See (*inter alia*) "General Account of Ayrshire Families," by Geo. Robertson, 1833, vol. i, p. 274.

(d) In Robert Law's *Memorials* [Edin. 1818, p. 62] is this note:—"Feb. 1674, the end of it, dyed Sir Robert Cuningham, Doctor of Medicine, in a day's sickness, of an iliack passion; a worthy man and very usefull in his tyme."

(e) Anne, his only sister and h. of the whole blood, *d.* unm. 1677, when her uncle Robert Cuningham, of Edinburgh, apothecary, (who was served her heir of entail), succeeded to Auchenharvie. He, however, nearly ruined himself by speculative improvements, and having *m.* Anne Purves, *d.* 10 July 1715, being suc. by his son and heir, James Cuningham, who *m.* Marion, da. of (—) Fullarton, of Fullarton, and *d.* Dec. 1728, leaving an only s. and h., Robert Cuningham, who *d.* under age and unm., in Dec. 1733. None of these, however, assumed the

KENNEDY:

cr. 4 Aug. 1673;

ex., apparently, June 1740.

I. 1673. "John Kennedy, of Girvanmains," in Girvan, co. Ayr (who appears to have been a grandson of Gilbert KENNEDY, of the same, living 1662), reg. arms in the Lyon office, 1672,(a) and was *cr. a Baronet* [S.], as above, 4 Aug. 1673, with rem. to heirs male of the body; was admitted a Burgess of Ayr, 1674. On 22 Aug. 1678 he was served heir of conquest to his uncle, John KENNEDY, in the Barony of Dalwarton, co. Ayr. He, who appears to have been ruined, sold his estates to Sir Thomas KENNEDY, of Kirkhill, Provost of Edinburgh, etc., who was thence, sometimes, styled "of Girvanmains."(b)

II. 1700? to 1740. SIR GILBERT KENNEDY, Baronet [S. 1673], of Girvanmains aforesaid [*Qy.* his relationship to the above?]; presumably *suc. to the Baronetcy*. He was Falconer to the King in Scotland at a salary of £50. He *m.* Jean, da. of Sir Archibald KENNEDY, 1st Baronet [S. 1682], of Culzean, by Elizabeth, da. of David (LESLIE), 1st LORD NEWARK [S.]. He *d.* June 1740, when the *Baronetcy* became apparently *extinct*.

MACKENZIE:

cr. 16 Oct. 1673;(c)

forfeited 13 Nov. 1715;

but assumed since about 1720.

I. 1673. KENNETH(d) MACKENZIE, of Coul, in the parish of Contin, co. Ross, 2d s. of Alexander MACKENZIE, of Coul aforesaid, being 1st s. by 2d wife(e) Christian (*m.* in or before 1617), da. of Hector MONRO, of Assynt, which Alexander (who *d.* 1650, at a great age) was illegit. s. of Colin MACKENZIE, of Kintail,(f) by Mary (sometimes called his 2d wife), da. of Roderick MACKENZIE, of Davochmaluach, was *b.* probably about 1620; suc. to the estate of Coul on the death of his father, and was *cr. a Baronet* [S.], as above, 16 Oct. 1673, with rem. to the heirs male of his body, such creation however, not being recorded in the Great Seal Register. He was Sheriff of the united counties of Ross and Inverness. He *m.* firstly, Jean, 1st da. of Alexander CHISHOLM, of Comar. He *m.* secondly (—), da. of Thomas MACKENZIE, of Inverlast. He *d.* in or before 1681.

Baronetcy to which, if the limitation was to heirs male whatsoever, they would have been entitled, though the first one (the harbour builder) is in some notices (though never in any service) styled "Sir Robert." Auchenharvie passed to Anne, sister of the last named Robert, who *m.* in 1737, John Reid, and had issue Robert Reid-Cuningham, of Auchinharvie.

(a) These were: "*Arg.* on a chevron, *gu.*, between 3 cross-crosslets, *sa*, a boar's head, *of the 1st*; in middle chief a man's heart, *of the 2nd*." Now, as the boar's head, apparently, indicates the mother (GORDON) of the first Kennedy of Girvanmains, it has been suggested that the man's heart might indicate that a DOUGLAS was the mother of the grantee.

(b) The following almost inexplicable entry may *possibly* refer to some member of this family:—"Sir John Ven Kennedy, Baronet, and Elizabeth Charlton, widow, both of St. Martin's in the Fields," were *m.* 19 Feb. 1726/7, at St. Bennet's, Paul's wharf, London.

(c) In Beatson's *List* given as 1679.

(d) The grantee is (erroneously) called "Alexander," both in Milne's and in Beatson's *List*.

(e) His elder br. of the half-blood, Roderick (who *d.* v.p.), was ancestor of the family of Mackenzie, of Applecross.

(f) See tabular pedigree *under* "Mackenzie, of Scatwell," *cr.* 1703.

II. 1680? SIR ALEXANDER MACKENZIE, Baronet [S. 1673], of Coul aforesaid, 1st s. and h. by 1st wife; *suc. to the Baronetcy* in or before 1681, when his lands were erected into a free Barony, which, in 1702, he entailed on the heirs male of his body. He was M.P. [S.] for Ross-shire, 1692 till death in 1702. He *m.* firstly, before 1673, Jean (*b.* 3 Jan. 1636, in Salisbury), 4th da. of Sir Robert GORDON, 1st Baronet [S. 1625], of Gordonstoun, by Louisa, da. and h. of John GORDON, of Glenluce, Dean of Salisbury. He *m.* secondly, Janet JOHNSTONE, of Warriston. He *d.* 1702.

III. 1702, to 1715. SIR JOHN MACKENZIE, Baronet [S. 1673], of Coul aforesaid, 1st s. and h. by 1st wife, *b.* in or before 1673; *suc. to the Baronetcy* in 1702; joined in the rising of 1715, and, not having rendered himself up to justice before 30 June 1716, was attainted, under the Act, 13 Nov. 1715. He *m.* firstly, Margaret, da. of Hugh ROSE, of Kilravock. He *m.* secondly, in 1703, Helen (*b.* 27 Feb. 1683), 4th da. of Patrick (MURRAY), 3d Lord ELIBANK [S.], by Anne, da. of Alexander BURNET, Archbishop of St. Andrew's. He *d.* s.p.m. soon after 1715, the *Baronetcy*, by his abovementioned attainder in that year, having previously become *forfeited*.(a)

The Baronetcy, notwithstanding the forfeiture,(a) was assumed as below.

IV. 1720? SIR COLIN MACKENZIE, Baronet [S. 1673],(b) of Coul aforesaid, br. of the whole blood and h. male; *b.* 1674; admitted as Advocate [S.], 8 Feb. 1701; Clerk to the Pipe in the Exchequer [S.] till death; suc. under the entail of 1702 to the family estate on the death of his brother, when he *assumed the Baronetcy*(b) also. He *m.*, June 1705, Henrietta, widow of Andrew BROWN, of Braid, da. of Sir Patrick HOUSTON, 1st Baronet [S. 1668], by Anne, da. of John (HAMILTON), 1st LORD BARGENY [S.]. He *d.* Oct. 1740, in his 67th year.

V. 1740. SIR ALEXANDER MACKENZIE, Baronet [S. 1673],(b) of Coul aforesaid, 1st s. and h.; *suc. to the Baronetcy*(b) in Oct. 1740, and had a charter under the Great Seal of the whole estate of Coul in 1743, as heir to his grandfather. He *m.* Janet, da. of Sir James MACDONALD, 6th Baronet [S. 1625], by his 1st wife, Janet, da. of Alexander MACLEOD, of Grishernish. He *d.* 1792.

(a) In Douglas's *Baronage* [S.], after mentioning that the 3d Baronet "was attainted for high treason," it is added (without comment) that "he was succeeded in his estate and titles by his brother, Sir Colin Mackenzie, 4th Baronet, of Coul." In Playfair's *Baronetage* [S.] it is stated (apparently without any foundation) that "the Act of attainder for high treason [whereby he, together with George, Earl Marischall [S.], William, Earl of Seaforth [S.], and others, was attainted], not extending in its purview to the other branches of his family, both the estate and the title devolved to his brother, Sir Colin Mackenzie, who was 4th Baronet, of Coul." It is remarked thereon (by J. Anderson, Writer to the Signet) that "This reasoning is inconclusive. There is no resignation of the title of Baronet, so that the limitation of the Patent (Paper Register, lib. 21), 16 Oct. 1673, to Kenneth Mackenzie and *the heirs male of his body* fell, with the attainder of *Sir John Mackenzie of Cowl*, in 1715, and though his brother (as heir male to Sir Alexander), under the entail of 1701, might be entitled to the *estate*, he could have *no right to the title of Baronet*, as established by the Act of Queen Anne regulating the treason laws of Scotland and England."

(b) Presuming (though there appears to be no good reason for such presumption) that the forfeiture of 1715 became void after the death s.p.m. of the attainted Baronet.

VI. 1792. SIR ALEXANDER MACKENZIE, Baronet [S. 1673],(a) of Coul aforesaid, 1st s. and h., was in the East India Company's service, becoming finally Major General, and being Provincial Commander in Chief at Bengal, 1790-92; *suc. to the Baronetcy*(a) in 1792. He *m.* at Leith, 30 April 1778, Katharine, da. of Robert RAMSAY, of Camno. He *d.* 14 Sep. 1796.

VII. 1796. SIR GEORGE STEUART MACKENZIE, Baronet [S. 1673],(a) of Coul aforesaid, only s. and h., *b.* 22 June 1780; *suc. to the Baronetcy*(a) in 1796; was Ensign General in the Royal Scottish Archers; F.R.S. and Vice-President of the Royal Society of Edinburgh.(b) He *m.* firstly, 8 June 1802, Mary, 5th da. of Donald MACLEOD, of Geanies, co. Ross. She *d.* 18 Jan. 1835. He *m.* secondly, 27 Oct. 1836, Catharine, widow of John STREET, Capt. R.A., 2d da. of Sir Henry JARDINE, of Harwood, aged 68. He *d.* Oct. 1848. His widow *d.* 2 Aug. 1857.

VIII. 1848. SIR ALEXANDER MACKENZIE, Baronet [S. 1673],(a) of Coul aforesaid, 1st s. and h. by 1st wife, *b.* 10 Jan. 1805; entered the East India Company's military service, 1824; Capt. Bengal Native Infantry, 1825; was at the siege and capture of Bhurtpore, 1825-26, and at the battle of Maharajpore (where his horse was killed under him), 29 Dec. 1843; served, as Dep. Judge Gen., with the Army at Gwalior; was in the first campaign (1845-46) on the Sutlej, retiring in 1851. He, who *suc. to the Baronetcy*(a) in Oct. 1848, obtained in 1855 the local rank of Major in the East Indies. He *d.* unm. 3 Jan. 1856, aged nearly 57, at Coul.

IX. 1856. SIR WILLIAM MACKENZIE, Baronet [S. 1673],(a) of Coul aforesaid, br. of the full blood and h., *b.* 20 May 1806, at Coul; ed. at the High School and Univ. of Edinburgh; entered the Maritime Service of the East India Company in 1826, serving subsequently in the Bombay and China country Service; resided some time in New South Wales; *suc. to the Baronetcy*(a) 3 Jan. 1856. He *m.* 16 Aug. 1858, at Dublin, Agnes, 2d da. of Ross Thompson SMYTH, of Ardmore, co. Londonderry. He *d.* s.p. 21 Dec. 1868, at Coul house, aged 62. His widow *m.* Sep. 1881, BARON DI SAN FELICE, of Naples, and was living at Rome, 1904.

X. 1868. SIR ROBERT RAMSAY MACKENZIE, Baronet [S. 1673],(a) of Coul aforesaid, br. of the full blood and h.; *b.* 21 July 1811; was sometime Treasurer and Premier of the Executive Council of the Colony of Queensland; *suc. to the Baronetcy*,(a) 21 Dec. 1868. He *m.* 29 Sep. 1846, Louisa Alexandrina, da. of Richard JONES, of New Farm, Brisbane, Queensland, Member of the Legislative Assembly of New South Wales and Treasurer of the Colony of Queensland. He *d.* 19 Sep. 1873, at 6 Atherstone Terrace, South Kensington, aged 62. His widow living 1904.

XI. 1873. SIR ARTHUR GEORGE RAMSAY MACKENZIE, Baronet [S. 1673],(a) of Coul aforesaid, only s. and h., *b.* 2 May 1865; *suc. to the Baronetcy*,(a) 19 Sep. 1873. He *m.* 11 May 1901, at St. Paul's, Knightsbridge, Evelyn Mary Montgomery, 4th and yst. da. of Major Gen. Sir Edward Wolstenholm WARD, K.C.M.G., Member of the Leg. Council of New South Wales, by Anne Sophia, da. of Robert CAMPBELL.

Family Estates.—These, in 1883, consisted of 43,189 acres in Ross-shire, valued at £5,214 a year. *Principal Seat.*—Coul House, near Dingwall, co. Ross.

(a) See p. 297, note "b."

(b) He was author of "*An Agricultural and Political Survey of Ross and Cromartyshire*," as well as of some scientific treatises.

COCHRANE:

cr. 1673;

afterwards, since 9 July 1758,

EARLS OF DUNDONALD [S.].

I. 1673. THE HON. SIR JOHN COCHRANE, of Ochiltree, 2d s. of William (COCHRANE), 1st EARL OF DUNDONALD [S.], by Eupheme, da. of Sir William SCOT, of Ardross, M.P. [S.] for Ayrshire, 1667, 1669-74, 1678 till void, and 1681-82, is said, but apparently in error, to have been *cr. a Baronet* [S.] in 1673.(a) He was implicated in the rebellion of 1683, was "forfeited" 22 May 1685 (the forfeiture being subsequently remitted), and was living 1693, being suc. by the 1st s. (II), WILLIAM COCHRANE, of Ochiltree, who *d.* 1728, being suc. by his s. (III), CHARLES COCHRANE, of Ochiltree, who *d.* unm. 19 Sep. 1752, and was suc. by his next surv. br. (IV), LIEUT.-GEN. JAMES COCHRANE, of Ochiltree, who *d.* s.p. 29 June 1758, being suc. by his next br. (V), THOMAS COCHRANE, of Ochiltree, who next month, 9 July 1758, suc. his distant cousin as 8th EARL OF DUNDONALD [S.]. None of these persons, however, appear to have assumed the title of Baronet, and the title, if ever promised, was apparently never confirmed. See full accounts of them in the Scot's Peerage, *sub* "Dundonald."

HAMILTON:

cr. 5 Nov. 1673;

dormant after 1701;

but reassumed, in 1816 or 1834;

afterwards, since 1889, STIRLING-HAMILTON.

I. 1673. "WILLIAM HAMILTON, of Preston," co. Haddington, 1st s. and h. of Sir Thomas HAMILTON, of Preston and Fingalton, by his 2d wife, Anne, da. of Sir James HAMILTON, of Preston, was *b.* about 1645, suc. his father in 1672, and was *cr. a Baronet* [S.], as above, 5 Nov. 1673, with remainder, presumably, to heirs male whatsoever,(b) but no record of such creation exists in the Great Seal Register.(c) He *m.*, in 1670, Rachel, da. of Sir Thomas NICOLSON, of Cockburnspath. He, having alienated his estates to his brother-in-law, Sir James OSWALD, retired to Holland, and *d.* s.p.m.

II. 1690? to 1701. SIR ROBERT HAMILTON, Baronet [S. 1673], br. and h. male; *b.* 1650; *suc. to the Baronetcy*, on the death of his brother. He *d.* unm. in 1701, when the *Baronetcy* became *dormant*, and so continued for above a century.(d)

(a) No mention of such creation is made in Milne's *List*, but in Beatson's *List* that of "COCHRANE OF OCHILTREE, now Earl of Dundonald," occurs under "1673."

(b) The devolution of this dignity on the brother of the grantee implies the remainder to have been to heirs male whatsoever.

(c) The creation is also omitted in Milne's *List*.

(d) No mention of it is made in Playfair's *Baronetage* of 1811, when probably it was considered as extinct.

The right to the title, according to the service of a Scotch Jury in 1816, was as under—

III. 1701. SIR ROBERT HAMILTON, Baronet [S. 1673],[a] of Airdrie, cousin and h. male, being s. and h. of Gavin HAMILTON, of the same, by Jane, da. of Robert MONTGOMERY, of Hazlehead, which Gavin (who *d.* 29 Dec. 1681), was s. of John HAMILTON, of Airdrie (*b.* 1569), s. of Gavin HAMILTON, of the same (*d.* 1591), s. of John HAMILTON, also of Airdrie (slain at Flodden, 9 Sep. 1513), who was yr. br. of Robert HAMILTON, of Preston (both being sons of Sir Robert HAMILTON, of Preston, living 1516), which Robert was father of Robert, the father of Sir David, father of George (*d.* 1608), all of Preston aforesaid, the said George having for his 3d s. Robert HAMILTON, of Newhaven, whose son, Sir Thomas HAMILTON, succeeded to the estates of Preston and Fingalton, and was father of the 1st Baronet. He *suc. to the Baronetcy*[a] (but not to the Preston estate), on the death of his cousin, the 2d Baronet in 1701, but did not assume the title. He *m.*, in or before 1681, Elizabeth, da. of William COCHRANE, of Rochsoles.

IV. 1720? WILLIAM HAMILTON, of Airdrie aforesaid, s. and h., *b.* 6 March 1681; was ordained Minister of Bothwell, 28 Sep. 1709; *suc. to the Baronetcy*[a] on the death of his father, but did not assume the title. He *m.* in or before 1714, Margaret, da. and h. of John BOGLE, of Sandyhills. He *d.* 25 May 1749, aged 68. His widow *d.* 2 April 1773.

V. 1749. ROBERT HAMILTON, of Airdrie aforesaid, s. and h., *b.* 1714; *suc. to the Baronetcy*[a] in 1749, but did not assume the title. He became involved in unfortunate speculations, which forced him to sell Airdrie and all that remained of the family estates. He *m.* in or before 1748, Mary, da. of John BAIRD, of Craigton. He *d.* 1756.

VI. 1756. WILLIAM HAMILTON, s. and h., *b.* 1748; *suc. to the Baronetcy*[a] in 1756, but did not assume the title. He *d.* unm. in the same year.

VII. 1756. JOHN HAMILTON, br. and h., *b.* about 1750; *suc. to the Baronetcy*[a] in 1756, but did not assume the title. He *d.* unm. in the West Indies, 1778.

VIII. 1778. ROBERT HAMILTON, br. and h., *b.* 1754; *suc. to the Baronetcy*[a] in 1778, but did not assume the title. He *d.* unm. at St. Helena, 8 June 1799, aged 45

IX. 1799, and 1816. SIR WILLIAM STIRLING HAMILTON, Baronet [S. 1673],[a] cousin and h. male, being 1st s. and h. of William HAMILTON, Professor of Anatomy at the Univ. of Glasgow, by Elizabeth, da. of William STIRLING, of Drumpelier, which William HAMILTON (who *d.* 1793, aged 33) was s. and h. of Thomas HAMILTON, (also) Professor of Anatomy, as above (*d.* 1781, aged 53), yr. br. of the 5th and 4th s. of the 4th Baronet.[a] He was *b.* in Glasgow, 1788; matric. at Oxford (Balliol Coll.), 7 May 1807, aged 19; 1st Class (Classics), 1810; B.A., 1811; M.A., 1814; Advocate [S.], 1813; Professor of logic and metaphysics at the Univ. of Edinburgh 1836, till death in 1856. He, who had *suc. to the Baronetcy*,[a] 8 June 1799, but who did not assume the title till many years later, was in 1816 served by a Jury before the Sheriff of Edinburgh, heir male to the 2d Baronet (who *d.* 1701), and, consequently, though apparently not till 1834,[b] *assumed the Baronetcy*. He *m.* in 1829, his cousin, Janet, da. of Hubert MARSHALL. He *d.* at Edinburgh, 6 May 1856, aged 68. His widow *d.* there, at 16 Great King street, 24 Dec. 1877.

[a] According to the service in Edinburgh, 1816.
[b] Debrett's *Baronetage* [1900].

X. 1856. SIR WILLIAM HAMILTON, *afterwards*, since 1889, STIRLING-HAMILTON, Baronet [S. 1673],[a] 1st s. and h.,[b] *b.* 17 Sep. 1830, at Edinburg; ed. there and at Addiscombe; *suc. to the Baronetcy*, 6 May 1856;[a] was an officer in the Bengal Artillery; Engineer in Peshawar Valley, 1855-57, being severely wounded in one of the frontier expeditions in those years; was also wounded in the Indian Mutiny campaign, 1857 (medal with clasp); Capt. R.A., 1866; Major, R.H.A., 1872, and Lieut.-Col. 1875; was in command of the R.A., western district, 1881-85, becoming, finally, 1889, Lieut.-Gen. and Gen. and Col. Commandant 1895. By deed poll in 1889 he assumed the name of STIRLING, before that of HAMILTON. He *m.* 15 Oct. 1856, at Peshawar, Eliza Marcia, 1st da. of Major Gen. BARR, Royal Horse Artillery.

ERSKINE:

cr. 3 July 1674;

but the patent never passed,

nor was the title ever assumed.

I. 1674. JOHN ERSKINE, of Balgonie, had the royal warrant dat. 3 July 1674, at Hampton Court, to be *cr. a Baronet* [S.] with rem. to heirs male of the body, but the patent never passed the Great Seal, nor was the title ever assumed.[c]

SINCLAIR, *or* ST. CLAIR:[d]

an alleged creation, probably about 1675;[e]

existing about 1780.

I. 1675? JAMES SINCLAIR, *or* ST. CLAIR,[f] of Kinnaird, co. Fife (an estate which he purchased of the Balfour family, 5 Sep. 1675), and of Auldbar, co. Forfar (which he purchased about 1650, and sold, in portions, between 1670 and 1678), is said to have been *cr. a Baronet* [S.] probably about 1675.[e] He *m.* Isabel BALFOUR, possibly a da. of Sir James BALFOUR, 1st Baronet [S. 1633], Lyon King of Arms, by his 3d wife, Margaret, da. of Sir James ARNOT. He *d.* in or shortly before 1702.

[a] According to the service in Edinburgh, 1816.
[b] His yr. br. Thomas Hamilton, an officer in the Army, was author of *Annals of the Peninsular Campaign*, and other works. He *d.* s.p. 27 Aug. 1875.
[c] "I have seen the authentic registration of a signature under the hand of Charles II, '*given at His Majesties honour at Hampton Court*,' the 3d of July 1674, and countersigned by the Duke of Lauderdale, the Sec. of State, for a patent of the dignity of a Knight Baronet to John Erskine, of Balgonie, and the heirs male of his body. It did not pass the Great Seal, and the disponee therefore did not take the dignity. In 1689 and 1690 (Acts of Parl., vol. ix, pp. 29-140) he still figures as '*John Erskine, of Balgonie*,' nor can the Baronetcy be proved to have vested in his family, who continued at least till 1764." [Riddell's *Law in Scottish Peerages*, 1842, vol. i, pp. 66-67].
[d] The information in this article is chiefly from the late R. R. Stodart, Lyon Clerk Depute, 1863-86.
[e] Not only is the date of creation unknown, but the actual existence of this Baronetcy is very doubtful.
[f] There is no certainty as to his parentage, but in all probability he was one of the three children (under age at their mother's death, 19 July 1645) of James Sinclair (2d s. of Sir John Sinclair, 1st Baronet [S. 1636] of Stevenson), by Jean, da. of Sir James Durham, of Pitkerro, co. Forfar, afterwards 2d wife to Sir James Balfour, Lyon King of Arms.

II. 1702? SIR GEORGE SINCLAIR, *or* ST. CLAIR, Baronet [S. 1675?], of Kinnaird aforesaid, s. and h., *suc. to the Baronetcy*, on the death of his father, to whom he was served heir, 22 Sep. 1702, in the Barony of Kinnaird. This he sold, 24 Jan. 1726. He *m.* Margaret CRAWFORD. He *d.* 1726.

III. 1726. SIR JOHN SINCLAIR, *or* ST. CLAIR, Baronet [S. 1675?], s. and h., *suc. to the Baronetcy*, on the death of his father, to whom he was served heir general, 10 Nov. 1726; entered the army, serving on the continent and in Minorca; Major, 7 Oct. 1754; Quarter-Master Gen. in America, with local rank of Lieut.-Col. He *m.*, 17 March 1762, at Burlington, Elizabeth, da. of John MOLAND, *or* MORDAN, an eminent lawyer, at Philadelphia. He *d.* at Bolville, 26 Nov. or 25 Dec. 1767, and was *bur.* in St. John's Church, Elizabethtown. Will pr. 1769. His widow *m.* 14 March 1769, Lieut.-Col. Dudley TEMPLER, 25th Foot, and *d.* in London, 29 Oct. 1783.

IV. 1767. SIR JOHN SINCLAIR, *or* ST. CLAIR, Baronet [S. 1675?], s. and h., *b.* 1763; and *suc. to the Baronetcy*, when an infant, in Nov. or Dec. 1767. He *m.* [—],[a] da. of Sir William ERSKINE, 1st Baronet [1791], of Torry, by Frances, da. of James MORAY, of Abercairny. Nothing further is known of him or of his successors, if any.

HOME, *or* HUME:[b]

cr. between 1672 and 1678;

ex. (apparently) 1 Jan. 1788.

I. 1672-78. SIR ALEXANDER HOME, *or* HUME, Knt., of Renton, in the parish of Coldingham, co. Berwick, 1st s. and h.[c] of Sir John HOME, *or* HUME, of the same, sometime (1663-71) a Lord of Session and Lord Justice Clerk, by Margaret, da. of (whose issue became heir to) the Hon. John STEWART, Commendator of Coldingham (2d s. of Francis, 1st Earl of BOTHWELL [S.]), suc. his father in 1671, to whom, being then a Knight, he was served heir special in Northfields and Fewlls, and was *cr. a Baronet* [S.], as above, between 1672 and 1678, there being, however, no record of such creation in the Great Seal Register, and no date being assigned to it in Milne's *List*, where, however, it is noted that he "gets his arms as Barronet out of the Lyon office." He was served, 2 June 1690, heir. gen. of his father, and heir spec. in the Barony of Renton, the office of Forester, etc. He was, however, nearly ruined by his yr. br., Sir Patrick HOME, 1st Baronet [S. 1697], of Lumsden, who (wrongfully) held from him the estate of Renton, and whom, in 1685, he accused of forgery. He *m.* Agnes, or Margaret, da. of Sir William SCOT, of Clerkington, from whom he was afterwards separated. He *d.* 28 May 1698.

II. 1698. SIR ROBERT HOME, *or* HUME, Baronet [S. 1672-78], s. and h., *suc. to the Baronetcy*, 28 May 1698, and was, on 14 July following, served heir male and of provision general. He *m.* Jean, da. of William DALMAHOY, of Ravelrig. He was living 1716, but *d.* before March 1733.

[a] Probably Magdalen, yst da., *b.* 24 Feb. 1787. See Wood's *Douglas' Peerage* [S.], vol. i, p. 274, where she is the only da. whose marriage or death is not given.
[b] Much of the information in this article was supplied by the late R. R. Stodart, Lyon Clerk Depute, 1863-86.
[c] The 2d son, Sir Patrick Home, *or* Hume, was *cr. a Baronet* [S.], 31 Dec. 1697, as of Lumsden.

III. 1730? SIR ALEXANDER HOME, *or* HUME, Baronet [S. 1672-78], s. and h., *suc. to the Baronetcy*, on the death of his father, to whom he had service as heir gen., 9 March 1733. He *d.* s.p. in Edinburgh, 17 Feb. 1737, and was *bur.* at Coldingham.

IV. 1737, to 1788. SIR JOHN HOME, *or* HUME, Baronet [S. 1672-78], of Renton aforesaid, br. and h., *suc. to the Baronetcy*, 17 Feb. 1737, and was served heir gen. of his br., 28 Nov. 1738, and heir male of provision gen. to his father, 3 Nov. 1739. He was an unsuccessful claimant for the *Earldom of Dunbar* [S.], *cr.* 1605. He *d.* s.p. 1 Jan. 1788, when the *Baronetcy* became (apparently) *extinct*.[a]

CARMICHAEL:[b]

cr., apparently, about 1676;[c]

afterwards, 1727-38, CARMICHAEL-BAILLIE;

ex. or *dormant*, July 1738.

I. 1676? THE HON. SIR JAMES CARMICHAEL, of Bonington, co. Lanark, 5th and yst. s. of James (CARMICHAEL), 1st LORD CARMICHAEL [S.], by Agnes, da. of William WILKIE, of Foulden, was *Knighted* at Oatlands, Surrey, 2 July 1632; was executor to his yr. br., Capt. the Hon. John CARMICHAEL, in 1644; was a Col. in the Army of Charles II at Dunbar, in 1650, and having purchased probably about 1676,[d] a blank warrant for a Baronetcy, for £100,[e] was apparently "at once recognised as a Baronet,"[f] as, undoubtedly, his son was, though there is no record of such creation in the Great Seal Register or apparently elsewhere, and neither pedigree nor arms are recorded. He *m.* Margaret, da. of Sir John GRIERSON, of Lag. She *d.* before 27 July 1665.[g] He *d.* in or shortly before 1681.

[a] The Coldingham estate devolved on his cousin, Sir Alexander Stirling, 4th Baronet [S. 1666], of Glorat, s. and h. of John Stirling, by Elizabeth, only da. of Sir Alexander Home, *or* Hume, the 1st Baronet.
[b] The information in this article is chiefly from the late R. R. Stodart, Lyon Clerk Depute, 1863-86.
[c] The date of 4 Dec. 1632 is sometimes (though on what ground is unknown) given as that of this creation, but is probably erroneous. See note "d" below.
[d] See note "c" above. The seven sons of the Duchess of Hamilton (who obtained this warrant for their tutor, [see note "e" below]), were born between 1658 and 1673.
[e] "Mr. John Bannatine, Minister of Lanark, having taken charge of the sons of the Duchess of Hamilton, her Grace procured for him a warrant of this nature [*i.e.*, a blank warrant, to be sold by the recipient, for nominating the purchaser a Baronet], which he sold for £100 to his parishioner, CARMICHAEL OF BONINGTON, who was at once recognised as a Baronet. The title was held without dispute by his descendants till they became extinct in the male line on the death of Sir William Carmichael-Baillie, of Lamington and Bonington, in July 1738." [*Notes on the traffic in Baronetcies*, by "S***" (*i.e.*, R. R. Stodart), see note "b" above]. *Genealogist*, Orig. Series, vol. iii, p. 66.
[f] See note "e" above, but the writer thereof subsequently conjectured that the warrant "acquired validity by Crown ratification or recognition *in the person of the son* of the purchaser, who *himself* is always styled a Knight." Such designation, however, is frequently at this period applied to a Baronet. The date of the evolution of the warrant into a recognised Baronetcy is not clear, but the fact is certain. See vol. ii, p. 452, notes "a" and "b" (under "Turing") for some similar cases.
[g] At that date her eldest son, James Carmichael (who *d.* v.p. and s.p.) was (in her right) served heir to her aunt Jane, da. of Sir John Grierson.

II. 1681? SIR JOHN CARMICHAEL, Baronet [S. 1676?], of Bonington aforesaid, 2d but 1st surv. s. and h.; *suc. to the Baronetcy* (which, however, he may possibly not have assumed till a somewhat later date) on the death of his father, to whom he was served heir general, 5 Nov. 1681. He *m.* 15 May 1684, at Edinburgh, Henrietta, 3d da. of James (JOHNSTONE), 1st EARL OF ANNANDALE [S.], by Henrietta, da. of William (DOUGLAS), 1st MARQUESS OF DOUGLAS [S.]. She was *bur.* 29 Nov. 1689, at Carmichael. He was *bur.* there 28 Jan. 1691, being styled "Baronet" in his funeral entry at the Lyon office and having the badge thereof in his arms.

III. 1691. Jan. SIR WILLIAM CARMICHAEL, Baronet [S. 1676?], of Bonington aforesaid, 1st s. and h., *b.* about 1686; *suc. to the Baronetcy* in Jan. 1691; *d.* unm. 5 June following, five months after his father.

IV. 1691. June. SIR JAMES CARMICHAEL, Baronet [S. 1676?], of Bonington, br. and h., *b.* about 1690; *suc. to the Baronetcy*, on the death of his brother, and was, 20 June 1691, served heir gen. of his father, Sir John CARMICHAEL, "Baronet," and of his grandfather, Sir James CARMICHAEL, "Knight,"(a) being served heir special of his father, 12 April 1692, in the Barony of Thankerton, co. Lanark. He was M.P. for Linlithgow burghs, 1713-15, and for Linlithgowshire, till unseated on petition, 8 April 1714. He *m.* (contract 7 Jan. 1715) Margaret, 1st of the two daughters and coheirs of William MAXWELL, *otherwise* BAILLIE, of Lamington, co. Lanark, by his 2d wife, Henrietta, da. of William (LINDSAY), EARL OF CRAWFORD AND LINDSAY [S.]. She, who was *b.* 1696, suc. her father in all his lands, 27 Dec. 1725, and took the name of BAILLIE. He *d.* in Edinburgh, 16 July 1727, aged 37, and was *bur.* at Lamington. His widow (*Lady Carmichael-Baillie*, the heiress of Lamington) *d.* 14 Sep. 1759, aged 63, at Edinburgh.

V. 1727, to 1738. SIR WILLIAM CARMICHAEL-BAILLIE, Baronet [S. 1676?], of Bonington aforesaid, only s. and h.; *suc. to the Baronetcy*, 16 July 1727; was served heir special of his father, 7 Feb. 1732, and again 15 Feb. 1733, in the Baronies of Thankerton abovenamed, Blackburn, co. Linlithgow, Craigend, co. Fife, etc. He appears to have assumed his mother's surname in expectation of inheriting the Baillie estates. He *d.*, however, in her lifetime, unm., July 1738, when the *Baronetcy* became *extinct* or *dormant*.(b)

(a) See p. 303, note "f."

(b) Henrietta, his sister and heir, *m.* 17 Oct. 1741, as his 1st wife, Robert Dundas, of Arniston, Lord President of the Court of Session, and *d.* in her mother's lifetime, 13 May 1755, leaving issue one son William, who took the name of Baillie in lieu of Dundas on succeeding to the estate of Lamington, on his grandmother's death in Sep. 1759. He *d.* unm. and a minor soon afterwards 17 June 1760, and was suc. in his estates by Elizabeth, his elder sister, who *m.* 6 Sep. 1762, Admiral Sir John Lockhart-Ross, 6th Baronet [S. 1672], whose granddaughter, Matilda (1st da. but not coheir of the 7th Baronet), *m.* 6 Jan. 1812, Admiral Sir Thomas John Cochrane, G.C.B., and took the name of Wishart. She *d.* 4 Sep. 1819, leaving a son and heir Alexander Dundas Ross Cochrane-Wishart-Baillie (*b.* 24 Nov. 1816), who, having inherited the Lamington estate, was *cr.* 3 May 1880, Baron Lamington.

MURRAY :(a)

cr. 2 July 1676;

afterwards, from about 1703, HEPBURN-MURRAY;

ex. about 1774.

I. 1676. "THOMAS MURRAY, of Glendoick," co. Perth, 2d s. of Sir Thomas MURRAY,(b) of Woodend in that county, sometime Sheriff thereof (*d.* 1606), was admitted an Advocate, 1661; had charter of the Barony of Glendoick, 2 Feb. 1672; was a Lord of Session, 18 May 1674, and was *cr. a Baronet* [S.], as above, 2 July 1676, with rem. to heirs male of the body; was Lord Clerk Register, 1 Nov. 1677, but was deprived of all office in 1680.(c) He *m.* Barbara, 1st da. and coheir of the Rev. Thomas HEPBURN, of Blackcastle, Minister of Oldhamstocks. He *d.* 1684.

II. 1684. SIR THOMAS MURRAY, Baronet [S. 1676], of Glendoick 1st s. and h., *suc. to the Baronetcy* in 1684. He *d.* Dec. 1701.

III. 1701. SIR JOHN MURRAY, *afterwards* HEPBURN-MURRAY, Baronet [S. 1676], of Glendoick, and afterwards of Blackcastle aforesaid, br. and h.; *suc. to the Baronetcy* in Dec. 1701; admitted an Advocate, 1702; suc. to the estate of Blackcastle on the death s.p. in or before 1703, of his maternal aunt, Margaret, widow of (her cousin) Sir Patrick HEPBURN, when he assumed the name of HEPBURN before that of MURRAY. He *m.* 23 July 1703, Mary, 2d da. of Sir Patrick MURRAY, 2d Baronet [S. 1673], of Ochtertyre, by Margaret, da. of Mungo HALDANE, of Gleneagles. He *d.* 8 Jan. 1714. His widow *d.* 25 Aug. 1766.

IV. 1714. SIR PATRICK HEPBURN-MURRAY, Baronet [S. 1676], of Glendoick and Blackcastle aforesaid, and afterwards of Balmanno, co. Perth, only s. and h., *bap.* 2 Nov. 1706; *suc. to the Baronetcy*, 8 Jan. 1714; was a Captain in Cochrane's Marines. He, presumably (or possibly his father), suc. to the estate of Balmanno on the death s.p. of his uncle, Anthony MURRAY, Merchant, of Edinburgh, by whom it had been purchased. He sold the estate of Glendoick. He *m.*, 14 Nov. 1751, Anne, 1st da. of Alexander HAY, of Drummelzier, co. Peebles. He *d.* 5 April 1756, at Balmanno. Admon. 5 May 1770. His widow *m.* 7 Oct. 1762, Archibald STIRLING, of Keir, and *d.* 14 Oct. 1807.

V. 1756, to 1774? SIR ALEXANDER HEPBURN-MURRAY, Baronet [S. 1676], of Balmanno and Blackcastle aforesaid, only s. and h., *b.* 4 Dec. 1754; *suc. to the Baronetcy* in April 1756. Was an officer in the army. He *d.* unm., being slain in America, about 1774, when the *Baronetcy* became *extinct*.(d)

(a) The information in this article was chiefly supplied by the late R. R. Stodart, Lyon Clerk Depute, 1863-86.

(b) This Thomas was s. and h. of Alexander Murray, of Woodend, s. and. h. of Patrick Murray, Chamberlain of Inchaffray, who acquired the estate of Woodend, and *d.* in 1590. He was 2d s. of Anthony Murray, of Dollerie (living 1554), who was 2d s. of David Murray, of Ochtertyre, co. Perth.

(c) The occasion was the fall from power of the well known Duke of Lauderdale [S.], whose wife, *suo jure* Countess of Dysart [S.], was the Baronet's distant cousin and patroness.

(d) Of his two sisters and coheirs (1) Anne *m.* John Stirling, of Craigbarnet, co. Stirling, and *d.* s.p., (2) Mary, who inherited Balmanno and Blackcastle, *m.* 30 May 1777, her cousin, Col. John Belshes, of Invermay, who took the additional name of Hepburn. They registered arms in 1804, and left a son and h., Alexander Hepburn-Murray-Belshes, who sold the estate of Blackcastle about 1825. He *d.* unm. about 1864, when the estates of Balmanno and Invermay devolved on his cousin, Sir John Stuart Forbes, *afterwards* Hepburn-Forbes, 8th Baronet [S. 1626], of Pitsligo, descended from his paternal great aunt, Emilia (da. of the 1st Baronet), wife of Alexander Belshes, of Invermay.

DICK :

cr. 2 March 1677;

ex. 1728.

I. 1677, to 1728. "JAMES DICK, of Prestonfield," *or* Priestfield, co. Midlothian, yr. s. of Alexander DICK,(a) of Heugh, in East Lothian (*d.* 1663, being 4th s. of the well known and opulent Sir William DICK, of Braid, sometime, 1638-39, Provost of Edinburgh, by Helen (*m.* 1641), da. of Sir James ROCHEAD, 1st Baronet [S. 1704], of Innerleith, was *b.* about 1644, acquired considerable wealth as a merchant in Edinburgh, purchased the estate of Prestonfield (where, in 1687, he built the mansion) and Corstorphine, and was *cr. a Baronet* [S.], as above, 2 March 1677, with, presumably, rem. to heirs male of the body.(b) He was M.P. [S.] for Edinburgh, 1681-82, and Lord Provost of that city, 1682-83. In 1682, he was one of the few who were saved (with the Duke of York, whom he was accompanying from London) in the wreck of the "Gloucester" frigate.(c) Having no surviving male issue, he was again *cr. a Baronet* [S.], 22 March 1707, with a spec. rem. in favour of the male issue of his only surviving da. He *m.* Anne, da. of William PATERSON, a yr. s. of the house of Dunmure. She *d.* 1710. He *d.* s.p.m. at Prestonfield, 15 Nov. 1728 in his 85th year, when the *Baronetcy* of 1707 *devolved according to the spec. rem.*, but the *Baronetcy* of 1677 became *extinct*.

GILMOUR :

cr. 1 Feb. 1678;

ex. 27 Dec. 1792.

I. 1678. "ALEXANDER GILMOUR, of Craigmiller," co. Edinburgh, s. and h. of Sir John GILMOUR, of the same, sometime (1661-70) Lord President of the Court of Session, and P.C. [S.] by his 3d wife Margaret, da. of Sir Alexander MURRAY, 2d Baronet [S. 1628], of Blackbarony, was *bap.* 6 Dec. 1657, at Edinburgh, served heir gen. of his father, 26 Sep. 1671, and was *cr. a Baronet* [S.], as above, 1 Feb. 1678, with rem. to heirs male of the body. Though the patent was recorded in the Great Seal Register he did not apparently assume the title till about twelve years later. He was M.P. [S.] for co. Edinburgh, 1690—1702. He *m.* Grizel, da. of George (Ross), 11th LORD ROSS OF HALKHEAD [S.], by his 1st wife, Grizel, da. of William (COCHRANE), 1st EARL OF DUNDONALD [S.] He *d.* 29 Oct. 1731, aged 74. His widow *d.* at Inch, 10 June 1732.

II. 1731. SIR CHARLES GILMOUR, Baronet [S. 1678], of Craigmiller aforesaid, only surv. s. and h., *suc. to the Baronetcy*, 29 Oct. 1731; M.P. for co. Edinburgh (two Parls.) 1737-47; Paymaster of the Board of Works, 1742; Commissioner for trade and plantation, 1747 till death in 1751. He *m.* March 1733, Jean, da. of Sir Robert SINCLAIR, 3d Baronet [S. 1664], of Longformacus, by Christian, da. of Adam COCKBURN, of Ormiston, Lord Justice Clerk. He *d.* at Montpelier, in France, 9 Aug. 1750. His widow *d.* in London, 1 Feb. 1782.

III. 1750, to 1792. SIR ALEXANDER GILMOUR, Baronet [S. 1678], of Craigmiller aforesaid, only s. and h.; *b.* probably about 1735; *suc. to the Baronetcy*, 9 Aug. 1750, and had service to his father, 4 April 1752. In 1754 he claimed, unsuccessfully, the estate of Balnagowan on the death of his cousin William (Ross), 14th and last LORD ROSS OF HALKHEAD [S.]. He was an officer in the Foot Guards; was one of the Clerk Comptrollers of the Board of Green Cloth, 1765; M.P. for co Edinburgh (three Parls.), 1761-74. He *m.* [—]. She *d.* Jan. 1780. He *d.* s.p. in France, 27 Dec. 1792, when the *Baronetcy* became *extinct*.(c)

(a) See *Her. and Gen.*, vol. viii, pp. 257-269, for a good account of this family.

(b) The creation is not given in Milne's *List*, and is apparently not entered on the Great Seal Register.

(c) His long and interesting letter, dat. 9 May 1682, as to this escape is given n Playfair's *Baronetage* [1811].

CAMPBELL :(b)

cr. 23 March 1679;

ex. 5 July 1752.

I. 1679. "COLIN(c) CAMPBELL, of Ardkinglass," co. Argyll, s. and h. of James CAMPBELL, of the same, M.P. [S.] for Argyllshire, 1646-49, by Mary, da. of Sir Robert CAMPBELL, of Glenorchy, co. Perth. was *b.* probably about 1640, and was *cr. a Baronet* [S.], as above, 23 March 1679, with rem. to heirs male of the body. He was imprisoned in 1684 on (apparently unfounded) suspicion of high treason, and was afterwards M.P. [S.] for Argyllshire 1693-1702. He *m.* Helen, da. of Sir Patrick MAXWELL, of Newark. He *d.* April 1709.

II. 1709, to 1752. SIR JAMES CAMPBELL, Baronet [S. 1679], of Ardkinglass aforesaid, s. and h., *b.* about 1666; was v.p., M.P. [S.] for Argyllshire, 1702-07, and M.P. thereof [G.B.] (seven Parls.), 1707-34, and for Stirlingshire, 1734-41; *suc. to the Baronetcy* in April 1709, and was served heir to his father, 2 Feb. 1711. He *m.* firstly, Margaret, heiress of Gargunnock, co. Stirling, da. and coheir of Adam CAMPBELL, of Gargunnock aforesaid. By her he had nine children. He *m.* secondly (contract 23 Aug. 1731), Anne, widow of Col. John BLACKADER, da. of John CALLANDER, of Craigforth. By her he had no issue. He *d.* s.p.m.s.,(d) 5 July 1752, at Gargunnock, aged 86, when the *Baronetcy* became *extinct*.

CLERK :

cr. 24 March 1679.

I. 1679. "JOHN CLERK, of Penicuick,"(e) co. Edinburgh, 1st s. and h. of John CLERK, of the same (who was *b.* at Fettercairn, 22 Dec. 1611, settled in Paris, 1634, and having acquired a large fortune, purchased the Barony of Penicuick in 1646), by Mary, da. of Sir William GRAY, of

(a) His aunt, Helen, da. of the 1st Baronet, *m.* William Little, *formerly* Ranken, of Over Liberton, co. Edinburgh, and *d.* 17 Feb. 1758, leaving Grizel, her only da. and h., who was ancestress of the family of Little, *afterwards* Little-Gilmour, of Craigmiller.

(b) There is a good account of this family by "A.W.G.B.," in *N. and Q.*, 9th S., viii, 106.

(c) Called (erroneously) "James" in Miege's *List*.

(d) His only son was drowned when a boy. Of his eight daughters, by his 1st wife, (1) Jane, the eldest, *m.* John Macnaughton, of Dunderawe, and had one son, who also was drowned in boyhood; (2) Helen *m.* Sir James Livingstone, 2d Baronet [S. 1685], who *d.* 2 May 1771, being mother of Sir James Livingston, afterwards Sir James Campbell, 3d Baronet [S. 1685], who took the name of Campbell on succeeding to the estate of Ardkinglass and *d.* 21 Nov. 1688, leaving a son and h., Sir Alexander Campbell, 4th Baronet [S. 1685], who *d.* s.p. in 1810, when the *Baronetcy* of 1685, became *extinct*. Mary, aunt of this last, and da. of the 2d Baronet, *m.* John Callander, of Craigforth, and was great grandmother of John Henry Callander, M.P. for Argyllshire, 1833-34, who inherited the estate of Ardinglass.

(e) See "Memoirs of Clerk of Penicuick," one of the publications of the *Scottish History Society*, for many particulars as to the earlier Baronets of this family.

Pittendrum, suc. his father in 1674, and was *cr. a Baronet* [S.], as above, 24 March 1679, with rem to heirs male of the body. He was M.P. [S.] for Edinburghshire, 1690-1702, and purchased in 1700 the lands and Barony of Lasswade. He *m.* firstly, 1674, Elizabeth, da. of Henry HENDERSON, of Elrington, and had by her six children. He *m.* secondly, Christian, da. of the Rev. James KIRKPATRICK, and had eight more children by her. He *d.* 1722.

II. 1722. SIR JOHN CLERK, Baronet [S. 1679], of Penicuick aforesaid, 1st s. and h. by 1st wife; was *b.* 8 Nov. 1676; admitted an Advocate, 20 July 1700; was v.p. M.P. [S]. for Withorn, 1702-07, being also M.P. [G.B.] thereof, 1707-08, having been one of the Commissioners for the Union; was a Baron of the Exchequer [S.], 1707 till death in 1755; *suc. to the Baronetcy*, 1722; F.S.A., 1725; F.R.S., 1728, being an antiquary of some note. He *m.* firstly, 23 Feb. 1701, Margaret, 1st da. of Alexander (STEWART), 3d EARL OF GALLOWAY [S.], by Mary, da. of James (DOUGLAS), 2d EARL OF QUEENSBERRY [S.]. She *d.* in childbirth,(a) 26 Dec. 1701. He *m.* secondly, 15 Nov. 1709, Janet, 5th da. of Sir John INGLIS, 2d Baronet [S. 1687], of Cramond, by Anne, da. of Adam COCKBURN, of Ormiston, Lord Justice Clerk. By her he had thirteen children. He *d.* 4 Oct. 1755. His widow *d.* 29 Jan. 1760.

III. 1755. SIR JAMES CLERK, Baronet [S. 1679], of Penicuick aforesaid, 2d but 1st surv. s. and h., being 1st s. by 2d wife; *b.* probably about 1710; *suc. to the Baronetcy*, 4 Oct. 1755, and enlarged the mansion of Penicuick. He *m.* Elizabeth, da. of the Rev. John Cleghorn, minister of Wemyss. He *d.* s.p. 6 Feb. 1783.

IV. 1783. SIR GEORGE CLERK, Baronet [S. 1679], of Penicuick aforesaid, next surv. br. and h.; was a Commissioner of the Customs, and a Remembrancer in the Exchequer; *suc. to the Baronetcy*, 6 Feb. 1783. He *m.* Dorothea, da. and h. of his paternal uncle, William CLERK-MAXWELL, *formerly* CLERK, by Agnes MAXWELL, heiress of Middleby, co. Dumfries. He *d.* 29 Jan. 1784. Admon. April 1796. His widow *d.* 28 Dec. 1793.

V. 1784. SIR JOHN CLERK, Baronet [S. 1679], of Penicuick aforesaid, 1st s. and h.; *suc. to the Baronetcy*, 24 Jan. 1784. He *m.* Rose Mary, da. of Joseph DACRE-APPLEBY, of Kirklington, co. Cumberland, by Catharine, da. of Sir George FLEMING, 2d Baronet [1705], Bishop of Carlisle. He *d.* s.p. 1798.(b)

VI. 1798. SIR GEORGE CLERK, Baronet [S. 1679], of Penicuick *or* Penicuik aforesaid, nephew and h., being s. and h. of James CLERK, an officer of the East India Company, by Janet (*m.* 18 Oct. 1786), da. of George IRVING, of Newton, which James, who *d.* 1793, was 3d s. of the 4th Baronet. He was *b.* 1787, and *suc. to the Baronetcy* in 1798; matric. at Oxford (Trin. Coll.), 21 Jan. 1806, aged 18, being *cr.* D.C.L., 5 July 1810; M.P. for Edinburghshire (three Parls.) 1811-20; for Stamford, 1838-47, and for Dover, 1847-52; F.R.S., 1819; a Lord of the Admiralty, 1819-27 and 1828-30, being one of the Council to the Lord High Admiral, 1827-28; Under-Secretary of Home Department, 1830-35; Secretary to the Treasury, 1841; P.C., 1845; Master of the Mint and V.P. of Board of Trade, 1845-46. He *m.* 13 Aug. 1810, Maria Anne, 2d da. of Ewan LAW, of Horsted place, Sussex, by Henrietta Sarah, da. of William MARKHAM, Archbishop of York. She *d.* 7 Sep. 1866, at 118 Eaton square, Pimlico. He *d.* 23 Dec. 1867, at Penicuik house, in his 81st year.

(a) Her child, John Clerk, "a young gentleman of extraordinary qualifications" [Playfair's *Baronetage*, 1811], *d.* unm. and v.p. 1722.

(b) "Lady Clerke [possibly his relict], wife of Rev. Jos. Townsend, Rector of Pewsey," died June 1814.

VII. 1867. SIR JAMES CLERK, Baronet [S. 1679], of Penicuik aforesaid, s. and h., *b.* 17 July 1812; Capt. Commandant of the 3d Midlothian Volunteers; *suc. to the Baronetcy*, 23 Dec. 1867. He *m.* 26 June 1851, Jane Calvert, 1st da. of Major-Gen. Mercer HENDERSON, C.B. He *d.* 17 Nov. 1870, at Clifton, co. Gloucester, aged 58. His widow *d.* 29 Sep. 1895, at Penicuik house.

VIII. 1870. SIR GEORGE DOUGLAS CLERK, Baronet [S. 1679], of Penicuik aforesaid, *b.* in London 1852, ed. at Eton; matric. at Oxford (Exeter Coll.), 15 Oct. 1870, aged 18, and *suc. to the Baronetcy*, a month later, 17 Nov. following; sometime, 1872-74, Lieut. 2d Life Guards; Lieut. Col. commanding 6th Vol. Batt. Royal Scots; served in the Transvaal War. He *m.* 4 Jan. 1876, at St. John's Church, Johnstone, Aymée Elizabeth Georgiana, 2d da. of Sir Robert John MILLIKIN-NAPIER, 9th Baronet [S. 1627], by Anne Salisbury Meliora, da. of John Ladeveze ADLERCRON.

Family Estates.—These, in 1883, consisted of 12,696 acres in Midlothian, and 500 in Peebleshire. *Total.*—13,196 acres, worth £8,993 a year, exclusive of £2,421 for mines. *Residence.*—Penicuik House, near Edinburgh.

DALMAHOY:(a)

cr. 17 Dec. 1679;

extinct 10 Oct. 1800.

I. 1679. "JOHN DALMAHOY, of that ilk," in Ratho', co. Edinburgh, s. and h. of Sir Alexander DALMAHOY,(b) of the same, by Marian, da. of James NISBET, of Dean, was *bap.* 20 Jan. 1637; was served heir to his grandfather Sir John DALMAHOY, in lands called Whelpside, in Currie, co. Edinburgh, and was *cr. a Baronet*, as above, 17 Dec. 1679, with rem. to heirs male of the body. He *m.* firstly, Lilias, da. of (—) ELPHINSTONE, of Quarrel, said to be a br. to LORD ELPHINSTONE [S.]. He *m.* secondly (—), but by her had no male issue.

II. 1700? SIR ALEXANDER DALMAHOY, Baronet [S. 1679], of Dalmahoy, 1st s. and h. by 1st wife; *suc. to the Baronetcy* on the death of his father. He *m.* Alicia, da. of John PATERSON, Archbishop of Glasgow, by Margaret, da. of Henry WEMYSS, of Conland. She survived him, but was dead before 1741.

III. 1730? SIR ALEXANDER DALMAHOY, Baronet [S. 1679], of Dalmahoy aforesaid and of Blackness, co. Edinburgh, 1st s. and h.; *suc. to the Baronetcy* on the death of his father, before 14 Feb. 1741, when he was served heir to his mother. He *m.*, before 5 March 1751, Elizabeth, da. of Walter CORNWALL, of Bonhard. She *d.* at Edinburgh, 26 March 1763. He *d.* 29 Oct. or 9 Nov. 1773.

IV. 1773. SIR ALEXANDER DALMAHOY, Baronet [S. 1679], of Dalmahoy aforesaid and of Carriden, near Linlithgow, only s. and h.; *suc. to the Baronetcy* in Oct. or Nov. 1773; was an officer in the French Service;

(a) See *Her. and Gen.*, vol. v, p. 379-381, for a review of "*The family of Dalmahoy, of Dalmahoy, Ratho'*, co. Edinburgh, privately printed. London, royal 8vo, pp. 55. No date," Of that family the author, Mr. Falconer, was a descendant.

(b) Col. Thomas Dalmahoy, a yr. br. of this Sir Alexander, was of the Friary, near Guildford, was M.P. for that town, 1664-79, and was Master of the Buckhounds to Charles II. He *m.* 19 June 1655, at St. Martin's in the Fields, Elizabeth, Dow. Duchess of Hamilton [S.], who was *bur.* there 2 Sep. 1659. He *d.* s.p. 24 and was *bur.* 27 May 1682, at St. Martin's aforesaid. Will dat. 1681.

Knight of St. Louis, in France. He *d.* s.p. (presumably unm.), 4 Jan. 1800, at Appin House, co. Argyll.

V. 1800, Jan. to Oct. SIR JOHN HYDE DALMAHOY, Baronet [S. 1679], cousin and h. male, being s. and h. of Alexander DALMAHOY, of Walthamstow, Essex, and (after 1746) of Ludgate Hill, London, Chemist, by Elizabeth, da. of John BOARD, of Paxhill park, in Lindfield, Sussex, which Alexander (who *d.* 10 Oct. 1781) was s. of William DALMAHOY, yr. br. of the 3d and s. of the 2d Baronet. He was *b.* about 1768; matric. at Oxford (Hertford Coll.), 28 May 1789, aged 21; B.A., 4 March 1794, and took Holy Orders; *suc. to the Baronetcy*, 4 Jan. 1800. He *d.* a few months later, s.p., probably unm., 10 and was *bur.* 17 Oct. 1800, at Westerham, Kent, aged 32, when the *Baronetcy* became *extinct*. Will pr. Dec. 1800.

BAIRD:

cr. 4 Feb. 1679/80;

ex. Sep. 1745.

I. 1680. "WILLIAM BAIRD, of Newbyth," co. Haddington, 1st s. and h. ap. of Sir John BAIRD, of the same, a Lord of Session under the style of *Lord Newbyth*, by Margaret, da. of Sir William HAY, of Linplum, was *b.* 12 Nov. 1654, and was, v.p., *cr. a Baronet* [S.], as above, 4 Feb. 1679/80, with rem. to heirs male of the body. He was admitted an Advocate 31 July 1680, and suc. his father, in the family estate, 27 April 1698. He *m.* firstly, Helen, da. of Sir John GILMOUR, of Craigmiller, Lord President of the Court of Session. She *d.* 22 and was *bur.* 25 April 1701, at Liberton. He *m.* secondly, Mary, 3d da. of Henry (ST. CLAIR), LORD SINCLAIR [S.], by Grizell, da. of Sir James COCKBURN of Cockburn. He *d.* at Edinburgh 17, and was *bur.* 22 Feb. 1737, at Liberton. His widow, by whom he had no issue, *d.* 22 Oct. 1756, aged about 70.

II. 1737, to 1745. SIR JOHN BAIRD, Baronet [S. 1680], of Newbyth aforesaid, 1st s. and h. by 1st wife, *b.* 13 Oct. 1685; was M.P. for Edinburghshire, 1715-22, and *suc. to the Baronetcy*, 17 Feb. 1737. He *m.* Janet, da. of the Hon. Sir David DALRYMPLE, 1st Baronet [S. 1700] of Hailes, by Janet, da. of Sir James ROCHEAD. He *d.* s.p. Sep. 1745, aged nearly 70, when the *Baronetcy* became *extinct*.(a) His widow, who was *b.* 31 March 1698, *m.* General the Hon. Sir James ST. CLAIR, of Dysart (who *d.* there s.p. 30 Nov. 1762), and *d.* in London, 8 Jan. 1766, aged 68.

MAITLAND:

cr. 18 Nov. 1680;(b)

sometime, 1693-95, LAUDER;

afterwards, since 1695, EARLS OF LAUDERDALE [S.].

I. 1680. "JOHN MAITLAND, of Ravelrig," 2d s. of the Hon. Charles MAITLAND (afterwards [1682], 3d EARL OF LAUDERDALE [S.]), by Elizabeth (*m.* 18 Nov. 1652), 2d da. and coheir (but heir to the estate)

(a) He entailed the Newbyth estate, 4 Aug. 1737, failing his own issue, on his father's first cousin, William Baird, of Edinburgh, Merchant (*d.* Sep. 1737), whose son, William Baird, succeeded thereto in 1745, and was father of Lieut.-General Sir David Baird, *cr. a Baronet*, 13 April 1809, whose successors are still (1904) owners thereof.

(b) See p. 288, note "c," under "Maitland," as to a Baronetcy [S.], supposed to have been conferred 12 March 1671/2, on the Hon. Charles Maitland (afterwards [1682] 3d Earl of Lauderdale [S.]), the father of the grantee of 18 Nov. 1680.

of Richard LAUDER, of Haltoun, co. Edinburgh, was *b.* probably about 1655, admitted an Advocate 30 July 1680, and was v.p. *cr. a Baronet* [S.], as above, 18 Nov. 1680, with rem. to heirs male of the body; was M.P. [S.] for Edinburghshire, 1685-86, 1689 (conv.) and 1689, till he *suc. to the peerage* [S.] in 1695; was a Lord of Session, 28 Nov. 1689, under the style of *Lord Ravelrig*, till his death in 1710; P.C. and Col. of the Edinburghshire Militia, 1689; assumed the designation of *Lauder*, of Haltoun, 1693, in lieu of that of *Maitland*, of Ravelrig. He *m.*, about 1680, Margaret, da. and h. of ALEXANDER (Cunningham), 10th EARL OF GLENCAIRN [S.], by Nicola, da. of Sir James STEWART. She was living when, by the death of his brother in 1695, he became 5th EARL OF LAUDERDALE [S.], etc. In that peerage this *Baronetcy* then *merged*, and still [1904] so continues. See *Peerage*.

MAXWELL:

cr. 8 Jan. 1680/1.

I. 1681. "WILLIAM MAXWELL, of Monreith," co. Wigton, 2d s. of William MAXWELL, of the same (*d.* 1670), by Margaret (*m.* 1632), da. of John MACCULLOCH, of Myretoun, was *b.* probably about 1635; suc. his nephew, William MAXWELL (sometime 1667 and 1669-72; M.P. [S.] for Wigtonshire), in the estate of Monreith in 1679 (being retoured as his heir male of entail and provision, 2 June 1681), and was *cr. a Baronet* [S.], as above, 8 Jan. 1680/1, with rem. to heirs male whatsoever. He *m.* firstly, Oct. 1685, Joanna, da. of Patrick MACDOUALL, of Logan. He *m.* secondly, Elizabeth, da. of Sir Thomas HAY, 1st Baronet [S. 1663], of Park, by Marion HAMILTON. He *d.* April 1709.

II. 1709. SIR ALEXANDER MAXWELL, Baronet [S. 1681], of Monreith aforesaid, 2d but 1st surv. s. and h.(a) by 2d wife; *suc. to the Baronetcy* in April 1709; was M.P. for the Wigton burghs, 1713-15. He *m.*, 29 Dec. 1711, Jean, 4th da. of Alexander (MONTGOMERIE), EARL OF EGLINTON [S.], by his 1st wife, Margaret (*m.* 1676), sister of John, 2d EARL OF DUNDONALD [S.], da. of William COCHRANE, *styled* LORD COCHRANE. He *d.* 23 May 1730. His widow *d.* 20 Feb. 1745, in Edinburgh.

III. 1730. SIR WILLIAM MAXWELL, Baronet [S. 1601], of Monreith aforesaid, 1st s. and h., *b.* about 1715; *suc. to the Baronetcy*, 23 May 1730.(b) He *m.*, probably before 1750, Magdalen, da. of William BLAIR, *formerly* SCOTT, of Blair, by his 2d wife, Catharine, da. of Alexander TAIT, of Edinburgh. She *d.* 28 Jan. 1765. He *d.* at Edinburgh, 22 Aug. 1771.

IV. 1771. SIR WILLIAM MAXWELL, Baronet [S. 1681], of Monreith aforesaid, 1st s. and h.; *suc. to the Baronetcy*, 22 Aug. 1771. He *m.* in 1776, Catherine, da. and h. of Adam BLAIR, of Adamton, by Anne (maternal aunt of her husband), da. of the abovenamed William BLAIR, *formerly* SCOTT, of BLAIR. She *d.* 2 April 1798. He *d.* Feb. 1812, at Edinburgh.

V. 1812. SIR WILLIAM MAXWELL, Baronet [S. 1681], of Monreith aforesaid, 1st s. and h., *b.* 5 March 1779; entered the army, and served as Lieut.-Col. of the 26th Foot (of which he raised a battalion) in Spain, losing his left arm at the battle of Corunna, 16 Jan. 1809, and being wounded at the siege of Walcheren later in that year. He was M.P. for Wigtonshire (five Parls.), 1806-12 and 1822-30, having *suc. to the Baronetcy* in Feb. 1812. He *m.* 23 April 1803, Catherine, yst da. of John FORDYCE, of Ayton, co. Berwick. He *d.* 22 Aug. 1838, at Monreith, in his 60th year. Will pr. Dec. 1838. His widow *d.* 19 July 1857, at Kilduff, in East Lothian, aged 76.

(a) William Maxwell, the 1st son, *d.* unm. and v.p. 1707, being drowned in the Firth.

(b) In Playfair's *Baronetage* (1811) is an account of how he assisted in 1750 in the saving of the money and storage of a Spanish ship, wrecked near Kirkmedden.

VI. 1838. SIR WILLIAM MAXWELL, Baronet [S. 1681], of Monreith aforesaid, 1st s. and h., *b.* there 2 Oct. 1804; was sometime Capt. 14th Light Dragoons, but retired in 1844; *suc. to the Baronetcy*, 22 Aug. 1838; Lieut.-Col. Galloway Rifles Militia, 1854-59. He *m.* 10 June 1833, Helenora, 3d and yst da. of Sir Michael SHAW-STEWART, 5th Baronet [S. 1667], by Catherine, da. of Sir William MAXWELL, 3d Baronet [S. 1683], of Springkell. She *d.* 27 Oct. 1876, at Bournemouth. He *d.* there 29 March 1877, aged 71.

VII. 1877. SIR HERBERT EUSTACE MAXWELL, Baronet [S. 1681], of Monreith aforesaid, 4th but only surv. s. and h., *b.* 8 Jan. 1845, at 14 Abercromby place, Edinburgh; ed. at Eton; matric. at Oxford (Ch. Ch.), 12 Dec. 1863, aged 18; *suc. to the Baronetcy*, 29 March 1877; M.P. for Wigtonshire (six Parls.) since 1880; a Junior Lord of the Treasury, 1886-92, and "Conservative Whip," 1886-95; P.C., 1897; sometime Lieut.-Col. 3d Batt. Royal Scots Fusileers Militia; President of the Society of Scottish Antiquaries; LL.D.; F.R.S. He *m.* 20 Jan. 1869, Mary, 1st da. of Henry FLETCHER-CAMPBELL, of Boquhan, co. Stirling.

Family Estates.—These, in 1883, consisted of 16,877 acres in co. Wigton, worth £15,569 a year.(a) *Seat.*—Monreith, near Whauphill, Wigtonshire.

STEWART, STEUART, *or* STUART:
cr. 23 Sep. 1681;
afterwards, 1701-35, EARL OF MORAY [S.];
ex. 7 Oct. 1735.

I. 1681, to 1735. THE HON. CHARLES STEWART, STEUART, *or* STUART, 2d s. of Alexander, 5th EARL OF MORAY [S.], by Emilia, da. of Sir William BALFOUR, of Pitcullo, was *b.* about 1665, and was v.p., *cr. a Baronet* [S.], 23 Sep. 1681, with rem. to heirs male of the body. On the death, s.p.m., of his elder br. James STEWART, *styled* LORD DOUNE, in 1685, he became 1st s. and h. ap. of his father, and as such was *styled* LORD DOUNE, and on the death of his father, 1 Nov. 1701, *suc. to the Peerage* as EARL OF MORAY [S.]. He *m.*, in or after 1695, his cousin, Anne, Dowager COUNTESS OF LAUDERDALE [S.], 2d da. of Archibald (CAMPBELL), 9th EARL OF ARGYLL [S.], by his 1st wife, Mary, da. of James (STEWART), 4th EARL OF MORAY [S.]. She *d.* at Dunnibirsil, 18 Sep. or Dec. 1734, in her 76th year. Funeral entry in Lyon office. He *d.* there s.p., 7 Oct. 1735, also in his 76th year, when *the Baronetcy* became *extinct*, though the Earldom devolved on his br. and h. male.

MAXWELL:(b)
cr. 12 April, sealed 25 May 1682;(c)
afterwards, since 1865, STIRLING-MAXWELL.

I. 1682. "JOHN MAXWELL, of Pollok," *or* Nether Pollok, co. Renfrew, 1st s. and h. of Sir George MAXWELL, of the same,(c) formerly of Auldhouse, in that county, by Annabella (*m.* Dec. 1646), da. of Sir Archibald STEWART, of Blackhall and Ardgowan, was *b.* Jan. 1648, suc. his

(a) The following note is added in Bateman's *Great Landowners* [1883]:—"This property has been in this family since 1481."
(b) See an article on this Baronetcy in *Her. and Gen.*, vol. iii, p. 545.
(c) According to Milne's *List* and Douglas's *Baronage* (p. 452), the date was 12 April 1682, and according to Chamberlayne's and Miege's *Lists* 12 Aug. 1682.

father in April 1677, and was *cr. a Baronet* [S.], as above, 12 April, sealed 25 May 1682,(a) with rem. to "aires male of his body,(b) bot ratified provydit to heirs of tailzee by ane new patent, dated 27 March 1707."(c) He was fined £93,600 Scots for refusing to take "the test," and imprisoned July 1683, but the fine was remitted at the Revolution, and he was M.P. [S.] for Renfrewshire, 1689 [conv.] 1689-93, 1695-96, and 1698, till appointed Lord Justice Clerk, 6 Feb. 1699, an office he held till 1703. He had previously, 1695, been P.C., a Lord of the Treasury and Exchequer [S.], and, somewhat later, an ordinary Lord of Session under the designation of *Lord Pollok*. He was Lord Rector of Glasgow, 1691—1717. Having no issue and no brother, he executed a deed of entail, 1 Aug. 1718, of the estate and Baronetcy (in accordance with the patent of 27 March 1707) in favour of John MAXWELL (his successor) and the heirs male of his body, whom failing to the eldest heir female. He *m.* (contract 23 Feb. 1671), Marion, sister of Sir James STEWART, Lord Advocate, da. of Sir James STEWART, of Kirkfield. She *d.* 1706. He *d.* s.p.s. 4 July 1732, aged 84.

II. 1732. SIR JOHN MAXWELL, Baronet [S. 1682], of Pollok aforesaid, formerly of Blawerthill, cousin and heir male and heir of entail, being s. and h. of Zacharias MAXWELL, of Blawerthill aforesaid, and of Glasgow, Merchant, by Jean (*m.* 1671), da. of John MAXWELL, of Southbar, which Zacharias (who *d.* April 1698) was yr. br. of Sir George MAXWELL, father of the late Baronet, both being sons of the Rev. John MAXWELL, of Auldhouse, Rector of the University of Glasgow. He, who was *b.* 1686, suc. his father in April 1698, was admitted an Advocate, Nov. 1707, and *suc. to the Baronetcy*, 4 July 1732, as heir of entail of the late owner, under the spec. provision in the patent of 27 March 1707. He *m.* firstly, 8 April 1709, Anne, 3d and yst. da. of John (CARMICHAEL), 1st EARL OF HYNDFORD [S.], by Beatrix, da. of David (DRUMMOND) 3d LORD MADERTY [S.] She *d.* about 1720. He *m.* secondly, Aug. 1727, Barbara, da. of Walter STEWART, of Blairhall, Advocate, by Elizabeth, da. and h. of Robert STEWART, of Pardovan. She was living March 1735. He *m.* thirdly, 27 Dec. 1739, Margaret, da. of John CALDWELL, of Caldwell, by Margaret, da. of Sir Walter STEWART, of Allanton. He *d.* 24 Dec. 1752, aged 66. His widow *d.* s.p. at Hamilton, 25 March 1758.

III. 1752. SIR JOHN MAXWELL, Baronet [S. 1682], of Pollok aforesaid, 1st s. and h., by 1st wife, *b.* 27 March 1720; *suc. to the Baronetcy*, 24 Dec. 1752. He *d.* unm., 14 Sep. 1758, aged 38.

IV. 1758. SIR WALTER MAXWELL, Baronet [S. 1682], of Pollok aforesaid, br. of the half blood and h., being s. of the 2d Baronet by his 2d wife; *b.* 15 Feb. 1732; *suc. to the Baronetcy*, 14 Sep. 1758. He *m.* 10 Feb. 1760, Darcy, da. of Thomas BRISBANE, of Brisbane, by Isabel, da. of Thomas NICOLSON. He *d.* 29 April 1762, aged 30. His widow *d.* 2 July 1810.

V. 1762, April. SIR JOHN MAXWELL, Baronet [S. 1682], of Pollok aforesaid, only s. and h., *b.* 27 Nov. 1761; *suc. to the Baronetcy*, 29 April 1762, and *d.* in infancy, 25 July following, aged 7 months.

(a) He suc. to that estate on the death (s.p. 1 Nov. 1647) of his distant cousin, Sir John Maxwell, of Pollok, who had been *cr. a Baronet* [S.], 25 Nov. 1630, and had entailed that estate on him in the event of his death without issue. See vol. ii, p. 384, note "d."
(b) In the petition for the grant of this Baronetcy, it was asked (though not granted) that "the title might be revived and a patent granted bearing precedence from the date of the former," *i.e.*, the Baronetcy [S.] *cr.* 25 Nov. 1630. See vol. ii, p. 384, note "a," and see also p. 312, note "b."
(c) Milne's *List*. The words of the patent are, "dicto domino Johanni et hæredibus masculis ex suo corpore, quibus deficientibus, aliis suis hæredibus talziæ quibuscumque, in ejus infeofamentis terrarum suarum et status contentis." See p. 312, note "b."

VI. 1762, July. SIR JAMES MAXWELL, Baronet [S. 1682], of Pollok aforesaid, uncle and h., being next br. of the whole blood to the 4th Baronet; *b.* 26 March 1735; *suc. to the Baronetcy*, 25 July 1762. He *m.* 3 Dec. 1764 (contract 19 and 23 Nov.), Frances, 2d da. of Robert COLHOUN, of the island of St. Christophers. He *d.* 3 May 1785, aged 50. His widow *m.* in April 1786, Sir John SHAW-STEWART, 4th Baronet [S. 1667], who *d.* s.p. 7 Aug. 1813, and *d.* as his widow, at Glasgow, 21 March 1818.

VII. 1785. SIR JOHN MAXWELL, Baronet [S. 1682], of Pollok aforesaid, 1st s. and h., *b.* 31 Oct. 1768; *suc. to the Baronetcy*, 3 May 1785; was Master of the Renfrewshire and Lanarkshire Foxhounds; M.P. for Paisley, 1833-34. He *m.* in 1788, Hannah Anne, da. of Richard GARDINER, of Aldborough, Suffolk, and Ingoldsthorpe, Norfolk, by Anne,(a) da. of Benjamin BROMHEAD, of Thurlsby, co. Lincoln. She *d.* 21 July 1841. He *d.* 30 July 1844, aged 75.

VIII. 1844. SIR JOHN MAXWELL, Baronet [S. 1682], of Pollok aforesaid, only s. and h., *b.* there 12 May 1791; matric. at Oxford (Ch. Ch.), 26 Oct. 1809, aged 18; was v.p., M.P. for Renfrewshire (three Parls.), 1818-30, and for Lanarkshire (two Parls.), 1833-37; Lt. Col. Renfrewshire Militia; *suc. to the Baronetcy*, 30 July 1844. He *m.* 14 Oct. 1839, at Milverton, Matilda Harriet, 2d da. of Thomas (BRUCE), 7th EARL OF ELGIN [S.], by his 1st wife, Mary, da. of William Hamilton NISBET. She, who was *b.* 23 Sep. 1802, *d.* 31 Aug. 1857, at Pollok. He *d.* s.p. 7 June 1865, at Pollok, aged 74, when the issue male of all the preceding Baronets appears to have become *extinct*.

IX. 1865. SIR WILLIAM STIRLING, *afterwards* (since 1866) STIRLING-MAXWELL, Baronet [S. 1682], of Pollok aforesaid, and of Keir, co. Perth, nephew and h., being only s. and h. of Archibald STIRLING, of Keir aforesaid, for twenty-five years a Planter in Jamaica (*d.* 9 April 1847, aged 77), by Elizabeth (*d.* 5 Sep. 1822), 2d and yst. sister(b) of the late and the only child that had issue of the 7th Baronet. He was *b.* at Kenmure, near Glasgow, 8 March 1818; admitted to Trin. Coll., Cambridge, 1835; B.A., 1839; M.A., 1843; suc. to the estate of Keir on his father's death, 9 April 1847; was M.P. for Perthshire (four Parls.), 1852-68 and 1874 till death in 1878; Dean of Faculties at Glasgow Univ., 1857-60; LL.D. (Edinburgh), 1861; Rector of St. Andrew's Univ., Nov. 1862; *suc. to the Baronetcy*, 7 June 1865, as heir of entail under the deed of 1 Aug. 1718, executed by the 1st Baronet, but did not assume the title till March 1866, when he had obtained an opinion from as many as four Counsel in his favour as to his right thereto.(c) On this date also

(a) This Anne *d.* 17 Feb. 1802, in her 67th year. M.I. at St. Peter's Gowts, Lincoln.
(b) Her eldest sister, Harriet Anne, *d.* unm. and v.p. 18 Oct. 1841, aged 52.
(c) Sir William Fraser printed 50 copies of a statement of this right with the opinions of Counsel annexed. The following remarks on this succession were made by the late R. R. Stodart, Lyon Clerk Depute, 1863-86:—
"He was never served and never matriculated here [*i.e.*, at the Lyon office] as a Baronet, though he spoke and wrote about the step.
John [Maxwell] of Pollock was cr. a Baronet by patent dat. at Whitehall, 12 April 1682, with rem. to the heirs male of his body (Great Seal Reg.). Sir John, having no child and no brother, obtained upon his own resignation a renewed patent extending the limitation, failing heirs male of his body, to other heirs of entail whomsoever. (Kensington, 27 March 1707, Great Seal Reg.). The late Sir John [*i.e.*, the 8th Baronet], who died in 1865, was his heir male and heir under the deed of entail, 1 August 1718, which calls the eldest heir female to the succession, with a stringent clause as to the surname and arms of Maxwell, to be the principal name and [the] arms [to be] in the first quarter. So far, so good, [and] under this Mr. Stirling's right to the Baronetcy would be indisput-

he assumed the name of *Maxwell* in lieu of that of *Stirling*. He was Rector of the University of Edinburgh, 1872-74; LL.D. (Glasgow), 1873; Hon. LL.D. (Cambridge), 1874; Chancellor of the University of Glasgow, 1875-78; Hon. D.C.L. (Oxford), 1876; **K.T.**, 9 Dec. 1876(a); well known as an author of historical and other works,(b) and as a collector of sixteenth century engravings. He *m.* firstly, 26 April 1865, at Paris, Anna Maria, 2d da. of David (LESLIE-MELVILLE), EARL OF LEVEN AND MELVILLE, [S.], by Elizabeth Anne, da. of Sir Archibald CAMPBELL, 2d Baronet [1808], of Succoth. She, who was *b.* Dec. 1826, *d.* 8 Dec. 1874 (from the effects of a burn on 21 Nov. previous), at Keir. He *m.* secondly, 1 March 1877 (by spec. lic., the bride being too ill to leave her bed), Caroline Elizabeth Sarah, widow of the Hon. George Chapple NORTON, Recorder of Guildford, 2d da. of Thomas SHERIDAN(c), by Caroline Henrietta, da. of James CALLANDER, of Craigforth, *afterwards* James CAMPBELL, of Ardinglass. She, who was *b.* at 11, South Audley street, in 1808, *d.* 15 June 1877, at 10 Upper Grosvenor street (about three months after her marriage), and was *bur.* at Keir, aged about 69.(d) He *d.* (seven months later) at Venice, of typhoid fever, 15 Jan. 1878, in his 60th year, and was *bur.* in Lecropt church.

X. 1878. SIR JOHN MAXWELL STIRLING-MAXWELL, Baronet [S. 1682], of Pollok aforesaid, 1st s. and h., by 1st wife, *b.* 6 June 1866; *suc. to the Baronetcy*, 15 Jan. 1878; ed. at Eton and at Trin. Coll., Cambridge; B.A., 1894; sometime Assistant Private Secretary to the Secretary of State for the Colonies; a Scottish University Commissioner, 1892; M.P. for Glasgow, 1895-1900; Hon. Col. 3d Lanarkshire Rifle Volunteers. He *m.* 12 Nov. 1901, Ann Christian, 1st da. of the Rt. Hon. Sir Herbert Eustace MAXWELL, 7th Baronet [S. 1681], of Monreith, by Mary, da. of Henry FLETCHER-CAMPBELL, of BOQUHAN, co. Stirling. She was *b.* 5 Sep. 1871.

Family Estates.—These, in 1883, as held by the [then] late Baronet, consisted of 8,863 acres in co. Perth (worth £5,731 a year), 5,691 in co. Lanark (worth £8,741 a year), 4,773 in co. Renfrew (worth £13,012 a year), and 1,487 in co.

able, but Sir John Maxwell [the 8th Baronet] either did break this entail or tried to do so, or thought he had done so, for on 23 July 1863 he executed a new entail, as if he had been owner in fee of the entire estate, in favour of '*William Stirling, Esq., of Keir, my nephew, who as my heir at law (!) shall also have right to the Baronetcy held by me.*' [The said] heir '*to bear use and retain surname of Maxwell, as last or only surname, and the arms and designation of Maxwell of Pollock.*' Keir and Pollock never to be held by the same person. The deed is one of the longest and most involved I ever toiled through, and contains many provisions and burdens the estate to an extent quite incompatible with the maintenance of the 1718 entail. I leave you to draw your own conclusion. An absurd state of things might arise under the 1863 entail if the eldest son chooses Keir and Cadder of course retaining the Baronetcy [and] the second is [*i.e.*, should remain] Mr. Maxwell of Pollock."
(a) He was the only Commoner who was a Knight of the Thistle since the revival of that Order by James II. in 1687.
(b) *e.g.*, "Annals of the Artists of Spain" [1848], "The Cloister Life of the Emperor Charles V" [1852], "Don John of Austria" [1883]; etc.
(c) A notice of the accomplished family of Sheridan is in *The Ancestor*, No. IX [April 1904].
(d) She was one of three sisters noted for their beauty and cleverness, of whom the yst. was Jane Georgiana, Duchess of Somerset, who, as Lady Seymour, was the *Queen of Beauty* at the Eglinton tournament in 1839. The eldest, Helen Selina, Baroness Dufferin and Claneboye [I.] was perhaps the most clever and witty of the three, but the "Hon. Caroline Norton" (by which designation she was generally known), was a poetess of no mean power, and the authoress of *Stuart of Dunleath* and other works. She was separated from her first husband in 1840, who had failed in an action for *crim. con.*, tried 23 June 1836, against her and Viscount Melbourne.

Stirling (worth £2,370 a year). *Total.*—20,814 acres, worth £29,854 a year; exclusive of £4,389 for quarries and minerals. "These estates are to be divided between the present [*i.e.*, the 10th] Baronet and his younger brothers, both minors" [Bateman's *Great Landowners*, edit. 1883]. The yr. br. Archibald, *b.* 14 Sep. 1867, relinquished the name of Maxwell, on coming of age, and took that of Stirling only, on inheriting Keir and other estates of the Stirling family.

KENNEDY:

cr. 8 Dec. 1682;(a)

afterwards, 1759-92, EARLS OF CASSILLIS [S.];

ex. 18 Dec. 1792.

I. 1682. "ARCHIBALD KENNEDY, of Culzean," co. Ayr, s. and h. of John KENNEDY, of the same (*d.* 1665), by Margaret, da. of John (HAMILTON), 1st LORD BARGENY [S.], which John was 1st s. and heir of Sir Alexander KENNEDY, of Culzean (*d.* Sep. 1652), 3d and yst. s. but eventually heir to the estate of the Hon. Sir Thomas KENNEDY, of Culzean aforesaid (*d.* 1611), 2d s. of Gilbert (KENNEDY), 3d EARL OF CASSILLIS [S.], suc. his father in 1665, being served heir to him, 17 April 1672, and was *cr. a Baronet* [S.], as above, 8 Dec. 1682, with rem. to heirs male of the body. He *m.*, when a minor (probably before 1680), Elizabeth, 1st da. of David (LESLIE), 1st LORD NEWARK [S.], by Jean, da. of Sir John YORKE. She was living 4 March 1693. He *d.* 1710.

II. 1710. SIR JOHN KENNEDY, Baronet [S. 1682], of Culzean aforesaid, 1st s. and h., *suc. to the Baronetcy* in 1710, and was served heir to his father, 12 March 1711. He *m.* in London (contract, 15 March 1706), Jean DOUGLAS, of the family of DOUGLAS, of Mains, co. Dumbarton. He *d.* July 1742. His widow, by whom he had twelve sons and eight daughters, *d.* 1 Feb. 1767, at Craigbowie.

III. 1742. SIR JOHN KENNEDY, Baronet [S. 1682], of Culzean aforesaid, 1st surv. s. and h., *suc. to the Baronetcy* in July 1742, and was served heir of his father 28 Feb. 1743. He *d.* unm., at Ayr, 10 April 1744.

IV. 1744. SIR THOMAS KENNEDY, Baronet [S. 1682], of Culzean aforesaid, next surv. br. and h.; was an officer in the Army, and served in Flanders; *suc. to the Baronetcy*, 10 April 1744. By the death, 7 Aug. 1759, of his distant cousin John (KENNEDY), 8th EARL OF CASSILLIS [S.], he became entitled to that dignity as heir male, and, though his claim was disputed by the heir general, it was confirmed to him by the House of Lords, 27 Jan. 1762, and he became accordingly EARL OF CASSILLIS AND LORD KENNEDY [S.]; was a REP. PEER [S.] 1774, and *d.* unm. at Culzean, 30 Nov. 1775. Will pr. March 1776.

V. 1775, to 1792. DAVID (KENNEDY), EARL OF CASSILLIS and LORD KENNEDY [S.], also a Baronet [S. 1682], only surv. br. and h., was in 1752 an Advocate, and was M.P. for Ayrshire, 1768-74. He *suc. to the Peerage and Baronetage*, 30 Nov. 1775; was a REP. PEER [S.] in three Parls., 1776-90. He *d.* of the gout at Culzean, unm., 18 Dec. 1792, when the issue male of the 1st Baronet, and the *Baronetcy* became *extinct*, but the Peerage devolved on his 3d cousin and heir male, Archibald KENNEDY, great grandson of Alexander KENNEDY, of Craigoch, uncle of the 1st Baronet.

(a) According to Wood's *Douglas's Peerage* [S.], vol. i, p. 336, it was "16 Dec. 1682" (probably the date of the sealing) though in the same work [vol. i, p. 338] it is given (as in the text), "8 Dec. 1682."

BANNERMAN:(a)

cr. 28 Dec. 1682.

I. 1682. "ALEXANDER BANNERMAN OF ELSICK," co. Kincardine, s. and h. of Alexander BANNERMAN, of the same, by his 1st wife, Marion, da. of Alexander HAMILTON, of Easter Binning, co. Linlithgow, *suc.* his father between 1661 and 1670; registered arms about 1672,(b) and was *cr. a Baronet* [S.], as above, 28 Dec. 1682, with rem. to heirs male of his body. This creation is said to have been "on account of his constant loyalty during the rebellion and of the heavy calamities he [but query if not *his father*] had suffered on that account." He again registered arms, but with the additions of supporters, March 1692. He *m.* (contract dat. 15 Feb. 1670) Margaret, 2d da. of Patrick SCOTT, of Thirlestane, co. Selkirk, by Isabel, da. of Sir John MURRAY, of Blackbarony. He *d.* 11 April 1711.

II. 1711. SIR ALEXANDER BANNERMAN, Baronet [S. 1682], of Elsick aforesaid, s. and h., *suc. to the Baronetcy*, 11 April 1711, and was, 26 March 1713, served heir gen. of his father, and heir spec. in Strachan, Findoun, etc. He *m.* Isabella, da. of Sir Donald MACDONALD, 3d Baronet [S. 1625], of Slate, by Mary, da. of Robert (DOUGLAS), 8th EARL OF MORTON [S.]. He *d.* Feb. 1742. His widow *d.* 13 June 1743.

III. 1742. SIR ALEXANDER BANNERMAN, Baronet [S. 1682], of Elsick aforesaid, s. and h., *suc. to the Baronetcy*, Feb. 1742. He joined the Jacobite rising in 1745 and was present at the battle of Culloden, after which he fled to France. He *m.* Isabella, da. and h. of [—] TROTTER, with whom he acquired the estate of Horsley, or Harlesy, in Yorkshire. He *d.* at Paris, 1747.

IV. 1747. SIR ALEXANDER BANNERMAN, Baronet [S. 1682], of Elsick aforesaid, s. and h.; *suc. to the Baronetcy*, 1747, and was served heir gen. of his father, 9 March 1749. Being envolved in lawsuits and threatened with forfeiture under suspicion of complicity in the Jacobite rising of 1745, he, in 1756, sold the estate of Elsick to the Corporation of Aberdeen. He *m.* 1764, Elizabeth, da. of Marmaduke SEDGWICK, of co. York. He *d.* s.p.m., at Horsley aforesaid, 13 June 1770.

V. 1770. SIR EDWARD TROTTER BANNERMAN, Baronet [S. 1682], br. and h., *suc. to the Baronetcy*, 13 June 1770; Major of the 36th Reg. of Foot in 1778. He *d.* unm. at Aberdeen, 1 Oct. 1796.

VI. 1796. SIR ALEXANDER BANNERMAN, Baronet [S. 1682], of Kirkhill, co. Aberdeen, formerly ALEXANDER BURNETT, cousin and h., being s. and h. of Alexander BANNERMAN, of Aberdeen, merchant (*d.* 1782, aged 67), by Margaret, 1st da. and coheir of Thomas BURNETT, of Kirkhill aforesaid, which Alexander was s. and h. of Sir Patrick BANNERMAN, sometime (1715) Provost of Aberdeen (*d.* 1733), who was 2d s. of the 1st Baronet. He was *b.* 22 Dec. 1741; was M.D. and Professor of Medicine of the Univ. of Aberdeen, and Physician in that city. On 16 April 1777 he was served heir of provision gen. to his grand uncle, Alexander BURNETT, of Kirkhill aforesaid, when he took the name of BURNETT in lieu of that of BANNERMAN. He *suc. to the Baronetcy*, 1 Oct. 1796, when he resumed his patronymic of BANNERMAN. He *m.* 1768, Mary, da. of James GORDON, of Banchory, by Mary, da. of [—] BUCHAN, of Auchmacoy. He *d.* 29 Dec. 1813, aged 72.

(a) Much of the information in this article was kindly supplied by the late R. R. Stodart, sometime (1863-86) Lyon Clerk Depute.

(b) This is the first appearance of what is often called "the ancient coat of the family." It is to be noted that this is not the same family as that of Bannerman of Watertown. See note "a" above.

VII. 1813. SIR ALEXANDER BANNERMAN, Baronet [S. 1682], of Kirkhill aforesaid, 2d but 1st surv. s. and h.(a), *b.* 19 Dec. 1769; *suc. to the Baronetcy*, 29 Dec. 1813. He *m.* 1800, Rachel, da. of John IRVING, of Auchmunziel. He *d.* s.p., 31 May 1840, at Aberdeen, aged 70. Will pr. Dec. 1840. His widow, who was *b.* 29 Jan. 1779, *d.* 13 Nov. 1847.

VIII. 1840. SIR CHARLES BANNERMAN, Baronet [S. 1682], of Kirkhill abovenamed, and of Crimmonmogate, co. Aberdeen,(b) br. and h., *b.* 18 Aug. 1782, was sometime a manufacturer in Aberdeen; *suc. to the Baronetcy*, 31 May 1840. He *m.* 14 Aug. 1821, Anne, 3d da. of his uncle, Charles BANNERMAN, an advocate in Aberdeen, by Margaret, da. of Patrick WILSON, of Finzeauch. She *d.* 1838. He *d.* 18 June 1851, aged 68. Will pr. Aug. 1851.

IX. 1851. SIR ALEXANDER BANNERMAN, Baronet [S. 1682], of Crimmonmogate and Kirkhill aforesaid, only s. and h., *b.* 6 April 1823, in Aberdeen; ed. at Trin. Coll., Cambridge; attached to the Legation at Florence, 1844 to 1847; *suc. to the Baronetcy*, 18 June 1851. He *m.* firstly, 25 Sep. 1860, Arabella Diana, yst. da. of John (SACKVILLE-WEST), 5th EARL DELAWARR, by Elizabeth, *suo jure* BARONESS BUCKHURST. She, who was *b.* 10 Jan. 1835, *d.* s.p.m., 9 Feb. 1869, at 46 Grosvenor place. He *m.* secondly, 20 Jan. 1874, Katharine, 1st da. of Bertram (ASHBURNHAM), 4th EARL ASHBURNHAM, by Catharine Charlotte, da. of George BAILLIE, of Jerviswood. He *d.* s.p.m., 21 April 1877, after three days' illness, at 46 Grosvenor place aforesaid, aged 54. His widow, who was *b.* 23 Nov. 1841, *d.* 30 Sep. 1885 at Eastbourne, Sussex, and was *bur.* at Crimmonmogate. Will pr. 18 Dec. 1885.

X. 1877. SIR GEORGE BANNERMAN, Baronet [S. 1682], cousin and h., being s. and h. of Thomas BANNERMAN, of Aberdeen, manufacturer, by Jane, da. of George HOGARTH, which Thomas (who *d.* 14 April 1863, aged 67) was 2d s.(c) of Thomas BANNERMAN, wine merchant, of Aberdeen (*d.* Jan. 1820, aged 57), who was next br. to the 6th Baronet. He was *b.* 4 June 1827, at Aberdeen; was Capt. Royal Engineers, and *suc. to the Baronetcy*, 21 April 1877. He *m.*, 5 Oct. 1869, Anne Mary, 1st da. of Richard BROOKE, of Handford, Cheshire, F.S.A.

Family Estates.—That of "Miss Bannerman, of Elsick, co. Aberdeen" (da. and h. of the 9th Baronet) consisted, in 1883, of 7,660 acres in Aberdeenshire and 500 in Kincardineshire. Total, 8,160 acres, worth £8,446 a year.

PRINGLE:

cr. 5 Jan. 1682/3.(d)

I. 1683. "ROBERT PRINGLE, of Stichell," co. Roxburgh, 1st s. and h. of John PRINGLE, by Margaret SCOTT, illegit. da. of Walter (SCOTT), 1st EARL OF BUCCLEUCH [S.], which John, who *d.* v.p., was 1st s. and h. ap. of Robert PRINGLE (who purchased the estate of Stichell in 1628, and who was M.P. [S.] for Roxburghshire, 1639-41), suc. his said grandfather in 1649; suc. to the estate of Newhall, co. Selkirk, on the death of his cousin,

(a) Thomas Bannerman, the eldest son, *d.* unm. and v.p. in India.

(b) This estate and a large fortune were inherited from his cousin Patrick Milne, s. and h. of Alexander Milne, of Crimmonmogate aforesaid, by Margaret, da. of Sir Patrick Bannerman, grandfather of the 6th Baronet.

(c) The first son was Sir Alexander Bannerman, M.P. for Aberdeen, 1833-47; Lieut.-Governor of Prince Edward Island, 1851-54; Governor of Bahamas, 1854-57, and of Newfoundland, 1857-64. He *d.* s.p. 30 Dec. 1864, aged 76.

(d) The date of 5 July 1683 is given in Playfair's *Baronetage* (1811), and is adopted in Burke's *Baronetage*.

Robert PRINGLE, of Newhall, in 1672; was M.P. [S.] for Roxburghshire, 1678 and 1681-82, and was *cr. a Baronet* [S.], as above, 6 Jan. 1682/3,(a) with rem. to heirs male of the body. He *m.* in 1660, Margaret, da. of Sir John HOPE, 2d Baronet [S. 1628], of Craighall, a Lord of Session under the style of *Lord Craighall*, by Margaret, da. of Sir Archibald MURRAY, 1st Baronet [S. 1628], of Blackbarony. By her he had nineteen children, of whom six sons and seven daughters attained full age.

II. 1700? SIR JOHN PRINGLE, Baronet [S. 1683], of Stichell aforesaid, 1st s. and h., *bap.* 2 July 1662; *suc. to the Baronetcy*, on the death of his father. He *m.* in 1685, Magdalen, da. of Sir Gilbert ELIOTT, 1st Baronet [S. 1666], of Stobbs, by his 2d wife, Magdalen, da. of Sir John NICOLSON, 2d Baronet [S. 1629], of Lasswade. He *d.* April 1721, aged about 59. His widow *d.* Dec. 1739.

III. 1721. SIR ROBERT PRINGLE, Baronet [S. 1683], of Stichell aforesaid, 1st s. and h., *bap.* 6 Oct. 1690; *suc. to the Baronetcy* in April 1721. He *m.*, in 1723, Catherine, da. of James PRINGLE, of Torwoodlee, co. Selkirk. She *d.* 28 May 1745. He *d.* 14 Dec. 1779, aged 89.

IV. 1779. SIR JAMES PRINGLE, Baronet [S. 1683], of Stichell aforesaid, 2d but 1st surv. s. and h.,(b) *bap.* 6 Nov. 1726; was an officer in the British Fusiliers, Lieut.-Col. 59th Foot, and, subsequently, of the Buccleuch Fencibles; was M.P. for Berwickshire (four Parls.) 1761, till his resignation in April 1779; *suc. to the Baronetcy*, 14 Dec. 1779. Master of the Works [S.]. He *m.* 11 Sep. 1767, Elizabeth, da. of Norman MACLEOD, of Macleod, by his 2d wife, Anne, da. of William MARTIN, of Inchfure. He *d.* 7 April 1809, aged 82. Will pr. 1811. His widow *d.* 9 Oct. 1826, at Mellerstein.

V. 1809. SIR JOHN PRINGLE, Baronet [S. 1683], of Stichell aforesaid, 2d but 1st surv. s. and h.,(c) *b.* there 20 Jan. 1784; Captain 12th Light Dragoons, having been ten years in that regiment; *suc. to the Baronetcy*, 7 April 1809. He *m.* firstly, 2 June 1809, Emilia Anne, 2d da. of his maternal uncle, Lieut.-Gen. Norman MACLEOD, of Macleod, by his 2d wife, Sarah, da. of N. STACKHOUSE, "Second in Council" at Bombay. She *d.* 22 Feb. 1830, at Stichell. He *m.* secondly, 10 Oct. 1831, at Langton, co. Berwick, Elizabeth Maitland, 1st da. of John (CAMPBELL), 1st MARQUESS OF BREADALBANE, by Mary Turner, da. and coheir of David GAVIN, of Langton aforesaid. He *d.* s.p.m.s.,(d) at Langton, 15 June 1869, aged about 85. His widow, who was *b.* 25 July 1794, *d.* 17 Feb. 1878, at Langton, aged 83.

VI. 1869. SIR NORMAN PRINGLE, Baronet [S. 1683], br. and h. male, *b.* 22 July 1787, at Edinburgh; second-Lieut. 21st Fusiliers, 1804; served in Sicily, 1806; in Egypt, 1807; at the defence of Scylla Castle, 1808; in Spain, with the Catalonian army, 1812; in Italy, 1814, being at the capture of Genoa; also in North America, being in the actions of Baltimore, New

(a) See p. 318, note "d."

(b) His elder br., John, *d.* v.p. unm. and under age in 1740.

(c) His elder br., Robert Pringle, who *d.* v.p. and s.p., *m.* 22 April 1806, Sarah, 1st da. of his maternal uncle, Lieut.-Gen. Norman MACLEOD. She *d.* in the June following in her 20th year, and he a few months later.

(d) Besides seven daughters (four of whom married) he had (by his 1st wife) three sons, who all *d.* v.p., *viz.* (1) James Pringle, who *d.* unm. 21 Aug. 1865; (2) Norman Pringle, of the Royal Engineers, who also *d.* unm., being drowned when a cadet at Woolwich; (3) John Robert Pringle, in the Madras Civil Service, who *m.* 21 Aug. 1844, and *d.* 5 Sep. 1847, leaving a da. and h., Emily Eliza Steele, who *m.* firstly, 19 Dec. 1865, John Gordon, of Cluny (who *d.* s.p. 3 March 1878), and secondly, 5 Dec. 1880, Sir Reginald Archibald Edward Cathcart, 6th Baronet [S. 1703].

Orleans, etc.; became Major 21st Fusiliers in 1814, retiring in 1815; was Consul at Stockholm, 1846-57, and at Dunkirk, 1857, till death in 1870; *suc. to the Baronetcy* (in his 83d year) 15 June 1869, but not, apparently, to the estates. He *m.*, 17 Jan. 1826, at Alderston, in Scotland, Anne, 1st da. of Robert STEUART, of Alderston. He *d.* 17 April 1870, aged 82, at the British Consulate, Dunkirk. His widow *d.* 4 Aug. 1883, at 85 St. George's Road, Pimlico.

VII. 1870. SIR NORMAN WILLIAM DRUMMOND PRINGLE, Baronet [S. 1683], 1st s. and h., *b.* at Edinburgh, 16 April 1836; entered the army, 1858; Captain 38th Foot, 1868; *suc. to the Baronetcy*, 17 April 1870; Major, 1878; Lieut.-Col., 1882; served in Egypt, 1882 (medal and star); on the Upper Nile, 1885-86, being in command of the South Staffordshire Reg., 1885-86; Colonel, 1886, retiring from the service 1892; member of the Royal Archers, the Queen's bodyguard of Scotland. He *m.* 10 Jan. 1871, at St. Barnabas, Pimlico, his cousin, Louisa Clementina, yst da. of Robert STEUART, of Alderston. He *d.* 21 July 1897, aged 61, in Welbeck street, Marylebone. Will pr. at £26,389. His widow living 1904.

VIII. 1897. SIR NORMAN ROBERT PRINGLE, Baronet [S. 1683], 1st s. and h., *b.* 18 Oct. 1871, in Belgrave road, Pimlico, *suc. to the Baronetcy*, 21 July 1897.

Family Estates.—These, in 1884, then belonging to "the late Lady E. Pringle" [*i.e.* the widow of the 5th Baronet], consisted of 8,121 acres in Berwickshire and 12 in Hants. *Total*, 8,133 acres, worth £8,785 a year. *Residence*, Langton house, near Dunse, Scotland.

MAXWELL:

cr. 7 Feb. 1682/3;

afterwards, since 1804, HERON-MAXWELL.

I. 1683. "SIR PATRICK MAXWELL, of Springkell," in Annandale, co. Dumfries, 1st s. and h. ap. of William MAXWELL, of the same, by Jane (marr. contract 20 May 1637), da. of Patrick STEWART, of Rosland, co. Bute, Minister of Rothesay, was *b.* probably about 1640, and was, v.p., *cr. a Baronet* [S.], as above, 7 Feb. 1682/3, with rem. to heirs male of the body, the creation, however, not being recorded in the Great Seal Register.(a) He suc. his father about 1695, and joined the insurgents (under Lord Kenmure) in 1715, with sixteen mounted men. He *m.* firstly (—), da. of Joseph DACRE-APPLEBY, of Kirklington. She *d.* s.p. He *m.* secondly, in or before 1703, Mary, da. of Alexander (GORDON), 5th VISCOUNT KENMURE [S.], by his 3d wife, Grizel, da. of James (STEWART), 2d EARL OF GALLOWAY [S.]. He *d.* April 1723, aged 83.

II 1723. SIR WILLIAM MAXWELL, Baronet [S. 1683], of Springkell aforesaid, only s. and h. by 2d wife, *b.* 10 Aug. 1703; *suc. to the Baronetcy* in April 1723. He *m.* 11 Oct. 1725, Catherine, 1st da. of Sir William DOUGLAS, 2d Baronet [S. 1668], of Kelhead, by Helen, da. of Col. John ERSKINE. He *d.* 14 July 1760, aged nearly 57. His widow *d.* at Springkell, 29 Sep. 1761, in her 54th year.

III. 1760. SIR WILLIAM MAXWELL, Baronet [S. 1683], of Springkell aforesaid, only surv. s. and h., *b.* about 1740; *suc. to the Baronetcy*, 14 July 1760. He *m.* 24 March 1764, Margaret, da. of Sir Michael STEWART, 3d Baronet [S. 1677], of Blackhall, by Helen, da. of Sir John HOUSTON, 4th Baronet [S. 1668], of Houston. He *d.* 4 March 1804, in his 65th year. His widow *d.* March 1816, aged 74.

(a) In Milne's *List* he is called "Patrick younger of Springkell." He was indeed the "younger of Springkell," his father being alive, but not apparently the younger of the name of "Patrick."

IV. 1804. SIR JOHN SHAW STEWART HERON-MAXWELL, Baronet [S. 1683], of Springkell aforesaid and of Kirouchtree, co. Galloway, 4th and yst., but only surv. s. and h.(a); *b.* 29 June 1772; was an officer in the Army; Lieut.-Col. 23d Light Dragoons and eventually Lieut.-Gen.; took the name of HERON before that of MAXWELL, on the death, 9 June 1803, of his wife's father; *suc. to the Baronetcy*, 4 March 1804; was M.P. for Dumfries burghs, 1807-12. He *m.* 4 Jan. 1802, at Kirouchtree aforesaid, Mary, only surv. da. and h. of Patrick HERON, of Heron in Kirouchtree, sometime (1795-1803) M.P. for Kirkcudbright Stewartry, by Elizabeth, da. of Thomas (COCHRANE), 8th EARL OF DUNDONALD [S.]. He *d.* 29 Jan. 1830, aged 57. Will pr. Nov. 1830. His widow *d.* 18 June 1856, at Kirouchtree, aged 79.

V. 1830. SIR PATRICK HERON-MAXWELL, Baronet [S. 1683], of Springkell aforesaid, 2d but 1st surv. s. and h., *b.* 1 Jan. 1805, *suc. to the Baronetcy*, 29 Jan. 1830. He *d.* unm., from injuries by a fall from his horse 27 Aug. 1844, aged 39.

VI. 1844. SIR JOHN HERON-MAXWELL, Baronet [S. 1683], of Springkell aforesaid, br. and h., *b.* 7 March 1808, in Edinburgh; Lieut. Royal Navy, 1828; appointed to the Coast Guard [S.], 1838; *suc. to the Baronetcy*, 27 Aug. 1844; Commander Royal Navy, 1864. He *m.* 6 Nov. 1833, at Hampstead, Caroline, 6th da. of the Hon. Montgomery Granville John STEWART (4th s. of John, 7th EARL OF GALLOWAY [S.]), by Catherine, da. of Patrick HONYMAN. He *d.* 22 Aug. 1885, in Charing Cross hospital, aged 77. His widow, who was *b.* 28 Nov. 1813, *d.* 22 Oct. 1896, in her 83d year, at 50 St. George's square, London, and was *bur.* in Putney Vale cemetery.

VII. 1885. SIR JOHN ROBERT HERON-MAXWELL, Baronet [S. 1683], of Springkell aforesaid, 1st s. and h., *b.* 4 June 1836, at Bargaly, co. Kirkcudbright; ed. at Harrow; matric. at Oxford (Exeter Coll.), 13 May 1856, aged 19; Lieut. 15th Light Dragoons, 1860; Capt., 1863; *suc. to the Baronetcy*, 22 Aug. 1885; member of the Royal Archers, King's Bodyguard for Scotland. He *m.* 7 Aug. 1866, at Avoca, co. Wicklow, Caroline Harriet, 3d da. of Richard HOWARD-BROOKE, of Castle Howard in that county, by Frances Caroline, da. of Hans HAMILTON, of Abbotstown, co. Dublin. She *d.* 20 Feb. 1900.

Family Estates.—These, in 1883, consisted of 13,391 acres in Dumfriesshire, worth £8,758 a year. *Seat*, Springkell, near Ecclefechan.

SHARP(b):

cr. 21 April 1683;

dormant or *extinct*, since 13 Feb. 1780.

I. 1683. "WILLIAM SHARP, of Scotscraig,"(c) co. Fife, only s. and h. of James SHARP, Archbishop of St. Andrews (1662-79), by Helen (*m.* 6 April 1653), da. of William MONCREIFF, of Banderston,

(a) Of the three elder sons, who all *d.* unm. and v.p. (1) William Maxwell, *b.* 22 Jan. 1765; *d.* on his passage from Bombay to China, 19 Aug. 1784. (2) Michael Stewart Maxwell, Col. of the Dumfriesshire Light Dragoons, *b.* 21 July 1768, *d.* at Springkell, 15 Oct. 1803, aged 35. (3) Patrick Maxwell, Ensign, 6th Foot, *b.* 9 June 1770, *d.* 10 July 1790, being drowned in Nova Scotia.

(b) Most of the information in this article has been kindly furnished by Alexander Bethune, s. and h. of Alexander Bethune, of Blebo, co. Fife (on whose death, about 1895, that estate was sold), which Alexander last named, was s. and h. of Major-Gen. Alexander Bethune, *formerly* Sharp, who, after considerable litigation, and an arrangement with the creditors, came, in 1815, into possession of the estate of Blebo, which had been held by William Bethune, *formerly* Chalmers (2d and surviving husband of Margaret, relict of the 6th Baronet and heiress of the family of Bethune of Blebo) till his death 25 Feb. 1807.

(c) This comprised the whole parish of Ferryport on Craig, and was bought in 1664 by the Archbishop for 9,500 merks.

was *b.* probably about 1655; suc. his father (who was murdered at the age of 66), 3 May 1679, in the estates of Scotscraig(a) aforesaid and of Strathtyrum in the parish of St. Andrews, being served his heir general, 6 May 1680, and was *cr. a Baronet* [S.], as above, 21 April 1683, with rem. to heirs male of the body. He suc. to the considerable estate of Stoniehill, co. Edinburgh, on the death of his uncle, Sir William SHARP, Deputy Keeper of the Signet, to whom he was served heir and of which he had a Crown charter 31 July 1706. He was M.P. [S.] for Clackmannanshire, 1681-82. He *m.* Margaret, da. of Sir Charles ERSKINE, 1st Baronet [S. 1666], of Cambo, Lyon King of Arms, by Penelope, da. of Arthur BARCLAY, of Colhill. He *d.* at Stoniehill, and was *bur.* 27 Jan. 1711/2, at Inveresk. Will dat. 5 May 1690, registered at Edinburgh 22 Aug. 1712. His widow *d.* March 1726, and was *bur.* at St. Andrews.

II. 1712. SIR JAMES SHARP, Baronet [S. 1683], of Scotscraig, Stoniehill and Strathtyrum aforesaid, 1st s. and h., *suc. to the Baronetcy* in Jan. 1711/2; served heir to his father, 22 Oct. 1712, in the estates of Scotscraig and Stoniehill, and heir spec. to his grandfather, 24 Sep. 1719, in that of Strathtyrum. In 1728 he sold the estate of Stoniehill, and, about 1735, sold that of Scotscraig. He *m.* between 1707 and 11 Nov. 1718, Mary, widow of Gideon SCOTT, of Highchester (who *d.* 1707), da. of John (DRUMMOND), 1st EARL OF MELFORT [S.], by his 1st wife, Sophia, da. and h. of Robert MAITLAND, of Lundin. He *d.* 25 April 1738. His widow *d.* 4 Oct. 1754.

III. 1738. SIR JAMES SHARP, Baronet [S. 1683], of Strathtyrum aforesaid, only s. and h., matric. at the Univ. of St. Andrews, 23 March 1737; *suc. to the Baronetcy*, 25 April 1738. He, who on 26 July 1744, was seized of the estate of Strathtyrum, which he apparently then sold, *d.* s.p. legit., presumably unm., shortly afterwards at St. Andrews. Will confirmed 20 April 1753, reg. at St. Andrews 1 Jan. following.(b)

IV. 1748? SIR WILLIAM SHARP, Baronet [S. 1683], uncle and heir male, merchant at St. Andrews; *suc. to the Baronetcy* on the death of his nephew. He *m.* firstly, in or before 1723, Ann MORE, by whom he had eight children.(c) She was living Jan. 1731/2. He *m.* secondly, in 1734, Sophia, 1st da. of his maternal uncle, Sir Alexander ERSKINE, 2d Baronet [S. 1666], of Cambo, by Anne, da. of Alexander (ERSKINE), 3d EARL OF KELLIE [S.]. She was *bur.* 6 June 1735, at St. Andrews. He, who *d.* s.p.s.,(d) survived her, probably as late as until 1754.

V. 1754? SIR ALEXANDER SHARP, Baronet [S. 1683], br. and h. male, matric. at St. Leonard's Coll., 12 Feb. 1712; was a merchant at St. Andrews; joined in the Jacobite rising of 1745; *suc. to the Baronetcy* on the death of his brother. He *m.* in or before 1728, Margaret HAMILTON. He was living April 1769, but *d.* shortly afterwards, before 1771. His widow *d.* 11 Dec. 1783.

(a) See p. 321, note "c."

(b) Mary Lilian, his only sister and h., *m.* Dec. 1739, James Lumsdaine, of Rennyhill, co. Fife, and had issue, who inherited Lely's portrait of the Archbishop. She was served, 25 July 1766, heir gen. and of provision gen. to her father.

(c) They were *bap.* at St. Andrews aforesaid from June 1723 to Jan. 1731/2.

(d) The admon. (in C.P.C.) 26 Sep. 1750, of "Sir William Sharpe, *Baronet*, of St. Mary Rotherhithe, Surrey," granted "to the relict Dame Anne" ("penalty £100") is generally presumed *not* to refer to him, though it is otherwise, inexplicable, and the date seems compatible. It would of course entail on him a third wife (of whom there is no other trace), viz., Anne, who survived him. This Anne is doubtless the "Lady Sharp, relict of Sir William Sharp, Baronet, wife of (—) Perrot, Surgeon at Earl Shilton, Leicestershire," who *d.* 10 Oct. 1791, aged 62. [*Gent. Mag.*]

VI. 1770? to 1780. SIR WILLIAM SHARP, Baronet [S. 1683], 1st s. and h., *b.* 28 and *bap.* 29 Jan. 1729 at St. Andrews; joined the Jacobite rising of 1745, and (though very young) was sentenced to death and attainted in 1746; fled to France and served in the French army till 1761, when he entered that of Portugal, becoming finally Major-General in the Portuguese service and Governor of Minho; returned to England and obtained pardon, v.p., by Royal warrant, 3 April 1769, shortly after which date he *suc. to the Baronetcy*. He *m.* in or before 1771,(a) Margaret, 1st sister and eventually heir of line to Henry BETHUNE, of Blebo, co. Fife (who *d.* s.p. in 1782), da. of John BETHUNE, of Blebo. He *d.* in Great Tichfield street, 13 and was *bur.* 14 Feb. 1780, at St. Marylebone, when the *Baronetcy* became *dormant* or *extinct*.(b) His widow *m.* (contract 1782) William CHALMERS, a Writer, in Edinburgh, on whom, 5 June 1783, she settled the estate of Blebo for his life, with rem. to their issue, failing which to her "son, Alexander SHARP." She *d.* in 1791, and her husband (who took the name of Bethune and retained for life the estate of Blebo) *d.* 25 Feb. 1807.(c)

STEWART:

cr. 2 June 1683(d);

sometime, 1827-90, DRUMMOND-STEWART;

ex. 20 Sep. 1890.

I. 1683. "THOMAS STEWART, of Blair" as also of Balcaskie, co. Fife, 1st s. of Henry STEWART, Advocate, by Mary, da. of Colin CAMPBELL, of Aberuchill (which Henry was 4th and yst. s. of Sir William STEWART, of Grandtully and Murtly, co. Perth), acquired the lands of Balcaskie

(a) There appears to be no record of this marriage. It may, however, be inferred by the following extracts from the Episcopal Register of St. Andrews:—1771 Aug. 20. "Alexander Sharp, son to Sir William Sharp, was baptized. Mr. Bethune of Blebo, the mother's father, and my Lady Sharp, the father's mother, were sponsors." Again, 1772 Nov. 17, "At Rungally, Charles, lawful son to the Rev. Mr. James Autchinson, was baptized. Mr. John Drummond, of Drumachie, Mr. Robert Bell, merchant in Cupar, and my *Lady Sharp, Blebo's daughter*, were sponsors." Notwithstanding the above evidence, there seems some doubt as to the legitimacy of the Alexander Sharp born in 1771, and possibly the marriage of his parents (though thus recognised) was invalid. The Baronet may, possibly, have had a previous wife still alive. There is a blank in the register of Alexander's baptism before the word "son," as though the Clerk was doubtful whether the word "lawful" (as in the entry of 1772) should or should not be inserted. Again, the non assumption of the Baronetcy at his father's death, in Feb. 1780, and above all the contesting of his right (see note "c" below) to the Blebo estate by his mother's *younger* sister, Janet Bethune (when the succession thereto opened 25 Feb. 1807), tend to create a doubt as to his being the *legitimate* son (and consequently heir) of his parents.

(b) The death, 8 Oct. 1780, "at Bletchingley, Surrey," of "Sir William Sharp, aged 97," is recorded in the *Scot's Mag.* He appears to have left £2,000 to build almshouses there, and his will is proved in 1781. Whoever he was, he was certainly not *identical* with the Baronet of the same name, who died eight months before him, on whose death, however, it is not impossible that he may have assumed the Baronetcy. There appears to be no record of his having been made a Knight, nor, on the other hand, is there any known place for him in the Baronet's pedigree.

(c) The right to the Blebo estate was contested in 1807 by Janet Bethune, younger sister of Margaret, Lady Sharp, as against Alexander Sharp, afterwards Bethune, the son of the said Margaret, who in 1782 was the heiress thereof. It was, however, then in the hands of creditors, from whom in 1815 it was redeemed by the said Alexander. See p. 321, note "b" and note "a" above.

(d) The date given in the *Lists* of Chamberlayne and Miege is 2 Jan. 1683.

and was *cr. a Baronet* [S.], as above, 2 June 1683 with rem. to heirs male of the body. He was a Lord of Session, 7 Nov. 1683, under the style of *Lord Balcaskie*; was M.P. [S.] for Fifeshire, 1685-86, and was a Lord of Justiciary, 28 July 1688, but deprived of office at the Revolution. He *m.*, in July 1682, Jean (*b.* at Edinburgh, 11 July 1661), 3d da. of George (MACKENZIE), 1st EARL OF CROMARTY [S.], by his 1st wife Anne, da. of Sir James SINCLAIR, 1st Baronet [S. 1631] of Cannisbay and Mey. He *d.* before 1717.

II. 1710? SIR GEORGE STEWART, Baronet [S. 1683], of Blair and Balcaskie aforesaid, 1st s. and h., *b.* 12 Oct. 1686; *suc. to the Baronetcy* on the death of his father, and suc. to the family estates of Grandtully, Murtly, etc., on the death of his cousin John STEWART, of the same, in 1720, under a deed which entailed the same on heirs male. He *m.* Anne, da. of Sir Archibald COCKBURN, 4th Baronet [S. 1627] of Langton, by Mary, da. of John (CAMPBELL), 1st EARL OF BREADALBANE [S.]. She *d.* at Dundee 20 Aug. 1757. He *d.* 1 Nov. 1759, aged 73.

III. 1759. SIR JOHN STEWART, Baronet [S. 1683], of Grandtully and Murtly aforesaid, br. and h., *b.* 29 Sep. 1687; an officer, eventually Col., in the Army; *suc. to the Baronetcy*, 1 Nov. 1759. He *m.* firstly, 13 Jan. 1725, Elizabeth, 2d and yst. da. and coheir of his maternal uncle, the Hon. Sir James MACKENZIE, 1st Baronet [S. 1704], of Roystoun, a Lord of Session under the style of *Lord Roystoun* (3d s. of George, 1st EARL OF CROMARTY [S.]), by Elizabeth, da. of Sir George MACKENZIE, of Rosehaugh. He *m.* secondly, 4 Aug. 1746, Jane, only sister of Archibald (DOUGLAS), DUKE OF DOUGLAS [S.], da. of James, 2d MARQUESS OF DOUGLAS [S.], by his 2d wife, Mary, da. of Robert (KERR), 1st MARQUESS OF LOTHIAN [S.]. She, who was *b.* at Douglas Castle, 17 March 1698, *d.* 22 Nov. 1753, at Edinburgh, and was *bur.* at Holyrood House, in her 56th year.(a) He *m.* thirdly, 12 Sep. 1761, at Edinburgh, Helen, 6th and yst. da. of Alexander (MURRAY), 4th LORD ELIBANK [S.], by Elizabeth, da. of George STIRLING, of Edinburgh, surgeon. He *d.* 14 June 1764, aged 76. His widow *d.* s.p., 28 Dec. 1809, at Ormistoun, aged 93.

IV. 1764. SIR JOHN STEWART, Baronet [S. 1683], of Grandtully and Murtly aforesaid, 2d but 1st surv. s. and h., by 1st wife, *b.* about 1726; *suc. to the Baronetcy*, 14 June 1764. He *m.*, 10 Aug. 1749, Clementina, da. of Charles STEWART, of Ballechin. She *d.* 10 Feb. 1789. He *d.* 6 Oct. 1797, aged 71.

V. 1797. SIR GEORGE STEWART, Baronet [S. 1683], of Grandtully and Murtly aforesaid, 1st s. and h., *b.* 17 Oct. 1750; admitted as Advocate, 3 Aug. 1776, and admitted to Lincoln's Inn, 5 Nov. following; *suc. to the Baronetcy*, 6 Oct. 1797. He *m.* 16 April 1792, Catherine, 1st da. of John DRUMMOND, of Logie Almond. She *d.* 1823. He *d.* at Murtly, 9 Dec. 1827, aged 77.

VI. 1827. SIR JOHN ARCHIBALD DRUMMOND-STEWART, Baronet [S. 1683], of Grandtully, Murtly, and Logie Almond aforesaid, 1st s. and h., *b.* 26 Oct. 1794; suc. to the estate of Logie Almond on his mother's death in 1823, and took the name of DRUMMOND before that of STEWART; *suc. to*

(a) She, at the age of 50, gave birth, 10 July 1748, at Paris, to twin sons, of whom the youngest *d.* in infancy. The elder, Archibald James Edward Stewart, was served, 9 Sep. 1761, heir of entail and provision to his maternal uncle, the Duke of Douglas [S.], and took the name of Douglas in lieu of that of Stewart. His right was opposed on the ground of his being a supposititious child, but, after very great litigation, was confirmed, 27 Feb. 1769. He was *cr.*, 8 July 1790, BARON DOUGLAS OF DOUGLAS, co. Lanark, a title which became extinct on the failure of his issue male, 6 April 1857.

the Baronetcy and his paternal estates, 9 Dec. 1827. He *m.* 25 Jan. 1832, Jane, 1st da. of Francis (STUART), EARL OF MORAY [S.], by his 2d wife, Margaret Jane, da. of Sir Philip AINSLIE. He *d.* s.p. at Paris, 20 May 1838, aged 43. Will pr. Dec. 1838. His widow *m.* 25 Aug. 1838 (four months after his death), Jeremiah Lonsdale POUNDEN, of Brownswood, co. Wexford (who *d.* 3 March 1887) and *d.* 14 March 1880,(a) at St. Leonard's-on-Sea.

VII. 1838. SIR WILLIAM GEORGE DRUMMOND STEWART, Baronet [S. 1683], of Grandtully, Murtly, and Logie Almond aforesaid, br. and h., *b.* 26 Dec. 1795; *suc. to the Baronetcy*, 20 May 1838, and assumed the name of DRUMMOND before that of STEWART. He *m.* in May 1830, Christian Mary, da. of (—) STEWART. She *d.* 1 Oct. 1856 at Grandtully. He *d.* s.p.s.(b) 28 April 1871, at Murthly Castle, aged 75.

VIII. 1871, to 1890. SIR ARCHIBALD DOUGLAS DRUMMOND-STEWART, Baronet [S. 1683], of Grandtully, Murtly and Logie Almond aforesaid, yst. and only surv. br. and h., *b.* 29 Aug. 1807; *suc. to the Baronetcy*, 28 April 1871. He *m.* 4 May 1875, at St. Mary's, Bryanston square, Hester Mary, 1st da. of John FRASER, of Bunchrew, co. Inverness, and Netley Park, co. Surrey. He *d.* s.p. at Murtly Castle, 20 Sep. 1890, aged 83, when *the Baronetcy* became *extinct*. Personalty sworn above £240,000 His widow living 1904.

Family Estates.—These, in 1883, consisted of 33,274 acres in Perthshire, worth £18,040 a year. A note [in Bateman's *Great Landowners*, 1883], states that "Grantully has been held since 1417." By an old entail the estates of Grandtully and Murtly passed in 1890 to Mr. Fotheringham, of Fotheringham, co. Forfar.

SETON :

cr. 15 Jan. 1683/4.(c)

I. 1684. "SIR ALEXANDER SETON, of Pitmedden," in the parish of Nony, co. Aberdeen, 2d s. of John SETON, 3d Laird of Pitmedden (slain, while in charge of the Royal Standard, at the battle of the Bridge of Dee, June 1639, in his 29th year), by Elizabeth, da. of Sir Samuel JOHNSTONE, 1st Baronet [S. 1628], of Elphinstone, was admitted an Advocate, 10 Dec. 1661; *Knighted*, 1664; suc. to the estate of Pitmedden, on the death of his br., James SETON, in 1667; had a Crown charter, 1 June 1677, of Pitmedden, and various other lands erected into the Barony of Orchardtown; was a Senator of the College of Justice, 31 Oct. 1677, under the style of *Lord Pitmedden*; M.P. [S.] for Aberdeenshire, 1681-82, and 1685-86; and was *cr. a Baronet* [S.], as above, 15 Jan. 1683/4, with rem. to heirs male of the body. He was removed from office, 12 May 1686, for opposing the Test Act. He *m.* in or before 1673, Margaret, da. and h. of William LAUDER, Clerk of Council and Session, by Katharine, da. of Thomas HUNTER, of Hagburn. He *d.* 1719, at a great age. His widow *d.* at Gateside, near Edinburgh, 19 Oct. 1723, and was *bur.* in the Greyfriars there.

(a) By her second husband she had an only surv. child, Eveleen, *b.* 3 May 1841, who on the death, 16 March 1895, of her maternal uncle, George Philip (Stuart), Earl of Moray and Lord Gray [S.], became *suo jure* Baroness Gray [S.].

(b) His only son, William George Stewart, *b.* 1831, entered the Army 1848; Captain, 1854; Major, 1858; served in the Indian Mutiny, 1857-59, receiving the **V.C.** for personal bravery; *d.* unmar. and v.p. 26 Oct. 1863, aged 37.

(c) The date is given as 11 Dec. 1683 in Milne's *List*, as also in those of Chamberlayne and Miege.

II. 1719. SIR WILLIAM SETON, Baronet [S. 1684], of Pitmedden aforesaid, 1st s. and h., *bap.* 6 March 1673, was author of "a memorial to members of Parliament of the Court Party," which was publicly burnt 16 Nov. 1700 and for which he was imprisoned in 1702. M.P. [S.] for Aberdeenshire, 1702-07 and again [G.B.] 1707-08, and was a Commissioner to treat for the Union; *suc. to the Baronetcy* in 1719. He *m.*, 1702, Catherine, 1st da. of Sir Thomas BURNETT, 3d Baronet [S. 1626], of Leys, by Margaret, da. of Robert (ARBUTHNOTT) 2d VISCOUNT ARBUTHNOTT [S.]. He *d.* 1744, aged 71. His widow *d.* 1749.

III. 1744. SIR ALEXANDER SETON, Baronet [S. 1684], of Pitmedden aforesaid, 1st s. and h., *bap.* 19 Jan. 1703, an officer in the Guards; *suc. to the Baronetcy* in 1744, and was served h. of provision gen. to his father, 21 Feb. 1750. He *d.* unm. 21 July 1750, aged 47.

IV. 1750. SIR WILLIAM SETON, Baronet [S. 1684], of Pitmedden aforesaid, br. and h., *suc. to the Baronetcy*, 21 July 1750, and was served h. male and of provision gen. to his br. 7 Feb. 1751. He *d.* unm. 11 Oct. 1774, at Pitmedden.

V. 1774. SIR ARCHIBALD SETON, Baronet [S. 1684], of Pitmedden aforesaid, br. and h., Lieut. R.N., *suc. to the Baronetcy*, 11 Oct. 1774. He *d.* s.p. 26 May 1775.

VI. 1775. SIR WILLIAM SETON, Baronet [S. 1684], of Pitmedden aforesaid, nephew and h., being s. and h. of Charles SETON, who was 6th and yst. s. of the 2d Baronet. He *suc. to the Baronetcy*, 26 May 1775. He *m.* 23 Nov. 1775, Margaret, da. of James LIGERTWOOD, of Tillery, co. Aberdeen. He *d.* 16 Feb. 1818, at his house in Union place, Aberdeen.

VII. 1818. SIR WILLIAM COOTE SETON, Baronet [S. 1684], of Pitmedden aforesaid, grandson and h., being only s. and h. of James SETON, Major in the 92d Highlanders, by Frances, da. of Capt. George COOTE, which James (who *d.* v.p. in 1814 from wounds received in the Peninsular wars), was 1st s. and h. ap. of the late Baronet. He was *b.* 19 Dec. 1808; *suc. to the Baronetcy*, 16 Feb. 1818; was admitted an Advocate, 1831; Lieut.-Col. 2d Aberdeen Rife Volunteers, 1863. He *m.* 26 Nov. 1834, Eliza Henrietta, widow of John Peter WILSON, Capt. E.I C.S., 2d da. of Henry LUMSDEN, of Cushney, co. Aberdeen, a director of the E.I.C. She *d.* 24 April 1873, at Pitmedden house. He *d.* 30 Dec. 1880, in his 73d year, at Portobello, near Edinburgh.

VIII. 1880. SIR JAMES LUMSDEN SETON, Baronet [S. 1684], of Pitmedden and Cushnie aforesaid, 1st s. and h., *b.* 1 Sep. 1835; entered the Madras army, 1852; served in Pegu and in the Indian and Abyssinian campaigns (medals, etc.), being Captain 102d Foot in 1862, but retiring in 1870; *suc. to the Baronetcy*, 30 Dec. 1880. He *m.* 20 Oct. 1870, Elizabeth, da. of George CASTLE, of Oxford. He *d.* s.p. 26 Sep. 1884, aged 49, at 3 Roland mansions, Gloucester road, Kensington, having "committed suicide while of unsound mind" by cutting his throat. His widow living 1904.

IX. 1884. SIR WILLIAM SAMUEL SETON, Baronet [S. 1684], of Pitmedden and Cushnie aforesaid, br. and h., *b.* 22 May 1837; served as Midshipman in the Persian expedition, 1856-57; sometime an officer in the 4th Rifles; served in Afghanistan, 1880; Col. Bengal Staff Corps; Assistant Adju. Gen., Poona division, 1885-90; *suc. to the Baronetcy*, 26 Sep. 1884. He *m.* 15 March 1876, Eva Kate St. Leger, only da. of Major Gen. Sir Henry Hastings Affleck WOOD, K.C.B., by Catherine, da. of Henry SANKEY, of Preston house, Kent, Commander R.N.

GORDON :(a)

1685? to 1700?

SIR GEORGE GORDON, of Gight, in Fyvie, co. Aberdeen, the 9th Laird of Gight, s. and h. of George GORDON, the 8th Laird (living 1644), and great-great-grandson of Sir William GORDON, 1st Laird of Gight (slain at Flodden, 1513) who was a yr. s. of George, 2d EARL OF HUNTLY [S.] is described (presumably in error) 30 Jan. 1685, as *Knight Baronet* [S.?] in an Aberdeenshire sasine of 12 Feb. 1708.(b) He *m.* his kinswoman Elizabeth, da. of Patrick URQUHART, of Meldrum. He *d.* s.p.m.,(c) when the male line of these Lairds and the *Baronetcy*, if indeed, it ever existed, *ceased*.

CREATIONS BY JAMES II [E.] AND VII [S.].

6 Feb. 1684/5 to 11 Dec. 1688.

GRIERSON, *or* GRIER :(d)

cr. 25 March 1685.(e)

I. 1685. "ROBERT GRIERSON, of [Rock Hall, in] Lag," co. Dumfries, s. and h. of William GRIERSON, *or* GRIER, of Farquhar, by Margaret (mar. contract June 1654), da. of Sir James DOUGLAS, of Mouswald (which William was 2d s. of Sir Robert GRIERSON, *or* GRIER, of Lag, sometime, 1628-33, 1639-41, 1643, 1644-47 and 1648, M.P. [S.] for Dumfries Sheriffdom, who *d.* about 1654), was served h., 9 April 1669, to his cousin Robert (s. and h. of Sir John GRIERSON, of Lag), who had *d.* 17 March

(a) The Editor is indebted to J. M. Bulloch (author of "The House of Gordon," New Spalding Club, Aberdeen, vol. i, pp. 165-310) for the notice of this Baronetcy.

(b) The exact copy of the entry in the ABERDEEN SASINES (vol. xii, fo. 171) is as below:—1685, Jan. 30; "Cum avisamento et consensu DOMINI GEORGII GORDON DE GICHT, Militis Baroneti pro sasina et possessione danda præfato Capitano Joanni Gordon, nuper tutori de Glanbucket," etc. The Rev. Walter MacLeod, of Edinburgh (well known for his antiquarian research), writes (28 Oct. 1902) that he has "a complete list of Baronets and none are of Gicht, but George [Gordon] might *inherit* the title in some way; many Gordons had it."

(c) Mary, his da. and h., *m.* Alexander Davidson, and was mother of Alexander Davidson *afterwards* Gordon, of Gight, and great grandmother of Catherine Gordon (the 13th and last of Gight), an Aberdeenshire heiress, who as "a stout, dumpty coarse looking woman, figured at Bath," who sold Gight in 1787, who, in 1788, was (by Captain the Hon. John Byron) mother of the famous poet, George Gordon (Byron), 6th Baron Byron of Rochdale, and who "died alone in 1811, in a fit of rage, over an upholsterer's bill." See "The marvellous record of the Gordons of Gight," in "*The Cocks of the North*," by "O.B." [*Ancestor*, no. 9 (April 1904), pp. 92-102, and no. 10 (July 1904), pp. 229—230].

(d) Much of the information in this article was given by the late R. R. Stodart, Lyon Clerk Depute, 1863-86.

(e) The date is given as 28 March 1685 in Playfair's *Baronetage* (1811) and in the *Lists* of Chamberlayne and Miege.

1666, at the age of 18;(a) was M.P. [S.] for Dumfries Sheriffdom, 1678, 1681-82 and 1685-86; was Steward of Kirkcudbright, making himself notorious by his vehement persecution of the Covenanters,(b) and was *cr. a Baronet* [S.], as above, 25 March 1685,(c) with rem. to heirs male whatsoever and with a pension of £200 a year. In April 1685, he presided at the trial and execution for refusing to take the abjuration oath of the two women known as "the Wigtown martyrs." After the Revolution he suffered many fines and imprisonments. He executed various entails 26 Oct. 1713, 28 Aug. 1719, 22 Oct. 1725, and 20 Dec. 1733, chiefly in favour of his 4th and yst. s., Gilbert, and to the exclusion of his eldest son. He *m.* Henrietta, 3d da. of James (DOUGLAS), 2d EARL OF QUEENSBERRY [S.], by his 2d wife Margaret, da. of John (STEWART), 1st Earl of TRAQUAIR [S.]. He *d.* 15 April 1736.(d)

II. 1736. SIR WILLIAM GRIERSON, *or* GRIER, Baronet [S. 1685], of Rock Hall, in Lag, aforesaid, 1st s. and h., was (together with his father) a Commissioner of Supply in 1704, and was v.p. M.P. [S.] for Dumfriesshire (two Parls.) 1709-10 and 1710, till unseated in Feb. 1711. He joined the Jacobite rising of 1715, and was fined and pardoned in 1724. He quarrelled with his father concerning the sale of some lands, and having been disinherited by him, *suc. to the Baronetcy*, but not to the estate, 15 April 1736, though he had gen. service to his father, 5 Jan. 1740. He *m.* in 1720, Ann, 3d da. of Sir Richard MUSGRAVE, 2d Baronet [S. 1638], of Hylton Castle, by Dorothy, da. and coheir of William JAMES, of Washington, co. Durham. She *d.* 16 Dec. 1749. He *d.* s.p. 1760.

III. 1760. SIR JAMES GRIERSON, Baronet [S. 1685], of Rock Hall, in Lag, aforesaid, nephew and h., being s.(e) of James GRIERSON, by Elizabeth, da. of (—) FERGUSON, which James (who *d.* in or before 26 March 1722) was 2d s. of the 1st Baronet. He had spec. service to his father, 26 March 1722, and *suc. to the Baronetcy* in 1760, when he tried unsuccessfully to recover the family estates from his uncle Gilbert. He *d.* s.p. 1765.

IV. 1765. SIR GILBERT GRIERSON, Baronet [S. 1685], of Rock Hall in Lag, aforesaid, uncle and h. male, being 4th and yst. s. of the 1st Baronet. He joined the Jacobite rising in 1715; was Writer and Chamberlain to the Duke of Buccleuch [S.], in 1733; suc., on the death of his father in April 1736, to the principal family estates, and was served heir of entail and provision to his br. William [the 2d Baronet] 24 Nov. 1760. He *suc. to the Baronetcy* in 1765. He *m* Elizabeth, da. of Robert MAITLAND, Col. of the Foot Guards. He *d.* 7 Feb. 1766. His widow *d.* 8 April 1788.

V. 1766. SIR ROBERT GRIERSON, Baronet [S. 1685], of Rock Hall, in Lag, aforesaid, s. and h., *b.* about 1737; entered the army as Ensign in 6th Foot, becoming Lieut. in 11th Foot, 10 Oct. 1761, retiring, apparently, 1763, as he "drew half pay for the extraordinary period of seventy-six years"(f); he *suc. to the Baronetcy*, 7 Feb. 1766. He *m.* in 1778, Margaret, 1st da. of Alexander DALZELL, of Glenae, co. Dumfries, *titular* EARL OF CARNWATH [S.], by Elizabeth, da. of (—) JACKSON. He *d.* at Rock Hall, 8 and was *bur.* 15 Aug. 1839, in Mouswald church, aged, it is said, 102 years. Will pr. July 1842.

(a) This Robert had suc. to the Lag estate on the death of his father in April 1658.

(b) He is the "Sir Robert Redgauntlet" of Wandering Willie's tale in Sir Walter Scott's *Redgauntlet*. A gruesome account of the cruelty of the "Laird of Lag" is given in Wodrow's *Sufferings* and many other works.

(c) See p. 327, note "e."

(d) The account of his funeral expenses shews that there was heavy drinking (a habit in which he himself much indulged) thereat for ten days!

(e) He was apparently a 2d or yr. s., as Robert Grierson is mentioned by the 1st Baronet, 28 Aug. 1719, as the [then] eldest son of this James.

(f) *Annual Register*, 1839.

VI. 1839. SIR ALEXANDER GILBERT GRIERSON, Baronet [S. 1685], of Rock Hall, in Lag, aforesaid, 1st s. and h., *b.* probably about 1780; *suc. to the Baronetcy*, 8 Aug. 1839. He *m.* Elizabeth (*b.* 1736), only da. and h. of his maternal uncle, Richard DALZELL, styling himself LORD DALZELL, by Elizabeth, da. of (—) JOHNSTON. He *d.* 1840.

VII. 1840. SIR RICHARD GRIERSON, Baronet [S. 1685], of Rock Hall, in Lag, aforesaid, 2d but 1st surv. s. and h.,(a) *suc. to the Baronetcy* in 1840. He *m.* Helen. He *d.* s.p. 1846. His widow *m.* 8 Oct. 1850, Lieut. Alexander BUCHANAN (who *d.* s.p. 18 Dec. 1855), and *d.* 2 Oct. 1854.

VIII. 1854. SIR ALEXANDER WILLIAM GRIERSON, Baronet [S. 1685], of Rock Hall, in Lag, aforesaid, br. and h.; sometime an officer in the 78th Foot (Rosshire Highlanders); *suc. to the Baronetcy*, 2 Oct. 1854. He *m.* Anne, yst. da. of Robert DAY, of Hants. He *d.* s.p., 27 Dec. 1879, at Southsea, Hants. His widow *d.* 3 Jan. 1891.

IX. 1879. SIR ALEXANDER DAVIDSON GRIERSON, Baronet [S. 1685], of Rock Hall, in Lag, aforesaid, nephew and h., being 1st s. and h. of William Charles GRIERSON, Commander R.N., by Emma Sophia, relict of Thomas WEST, R.N., da. of Michael COMERFORD, of Portsmouth, stationer, which William (who *d.* 8 Feb. 1871, aged 55) was yr. br. of the late and 3d s. of the 6th Baronet. He was *b.* 30 Nov. 1858; *suc. to the Baronetcy*, 27 Dec. 1879; Major 3d Batt. King's Own Scottish Borderers militia. He *m.* 7 Dec. 1882, Fannie, da. of Major George WHITE, of Westcombe Park, Blackheath.

Family Estates.—These, in 1883, consisted of 3,700 acres in co. Dumfries and 13 acres in Hants. *Total.*—3,713 acres, worth £3,546 a year. *Seat.*—Rock Hall, in Lag, co. Dumfries, which estate is said to have been in the family since 1438.

KIRKPATRICK:

cr. 26 March 1685.(b)

I. 1685. "THOMAS KIRKPATRICK, of Closeburn," co. Dumfries, 1st s. and h. of Robert KIRKPATRICK,(c) of the same, by Grizel, da. of Sir William BAILLIE, of Lamington, suc. his father about 1664; is said to

(a) The eldest son, Robert Grierson, an officer in the navy, is mentioned in very flattering terms in 1815 by Capt. Houston Stewart, R.N. He *d.* unm. and v.p.

(b) The date of 25 March is given in Milne's *List*, where the grantee is called "Thomas Kilpatrick"—that of 29 March is given in the 15th Rep. Hist. MSS., app. 8, p. 81, but that of 26 March (as in the text) is in the *Lists* of Chamberlayne and Miege, as also in Playfair's *Baronetage* (1811), where the patent [*Qy.* royal warrant] is stated to be dated at Whitehall.

(c) Eugenie-Marie de Guzman, Empress of the French (*b.* at Grenada, 5 May 1826; *m.* 29 Jan. 1853, Napoleon III), 2d and yst. da. and coheir of Cyprian, 8th Count of Montijo, a grandee of Spain (*d.* 1839), was, through her mother, descended from this family. That Lady, Mary Manuela, was da. of William Kirkpatrick, American Consul at Malaga, by Fanny, da. of Baron Grivegnee, of Malaga, which William was a descendant in the male line from Alexander Kirkpatrick, of Kirkmichael, yr. br. of Sir Thomas Kirkpatrick, of Closeburn (*d.* 1502), the lineal male ancestor of the Baronets of that name. See *N. & Q.*, 4th s., vol. xi, pp. 90, 200, 426, and 453. The Countess de Montijo, after a widowhood of forty years, *d.* 22 Nov. 1879, aged 86. Her eldest da., Maria-Francisca de Guzman, *b.* 29 Jan. 1825, *m.* 14 Feb. 1844, in Madrid, James Louis Francis Paul Raphael Stuart-FitzJames, 15th Duke of Alba, 8th Duke of Liria and Xerica, etc., in Spain, who, but for the attainder, would have been 8th Duke of Berwick [E.]. She *d.* in her mother's lifetime, 16 Sep. 1860, in Paris, aged 35, leaving issue. Her husband *d.* 10 July 1881, aged 60.

have refused a peerage,(a) and was *cr. a Baronet* [S.], as above, 26 March 1685, the rem. being stated to be to heirs male whatsoever, though there is no record of such creation in the Great Seal Register. He was M.P. [S.] for the Dumfries Sheriffdom, 1690—1702, and Lieut.-Col. of the militia of that county, 1691. He built a stately house at Closeburn, using for the purpose the materials (save only those of the keep) of the old castle. He *m.* firstly (contract 25 April 1666), Isabel, 1st da. of John (SANDILANDS), 4th LORD TORPICHEN [S.], by Isabel, da. of Sir Walter DUNDAS. He *m.* secondly (contract 7 Dec. 1672), Sarah, da. of Robert FERGUSSON, of Craigdarroch. He *m.* thirdly, in 1686, Grizel, widow of (—) INGLIS, of Murdiestoun, da. of Gavin HAMILTON, of Raploch. By her he had no issue. He was living 1691.

II. 1695? SIR THOMAS KIRKPATRICK, Baronet [S. 1685], of Closeburn aforesaid, 1st s. and h., by 1st wife; *suc. to the Baronetcy* on the death of his father. He *m.* firstly, 18 Feb. 1691, Hellenor, 1st da. and coheir of the Hon. Robert STEWART, of Ravenstone (2d s. of James, 2d EARL OF GALLOWAY [S.]), by Elizabeth, da. of Sir David DUNBAR, Baronet [S. 1664], of Baldoon. She *d.* s.p. He *m.* secondly, in 1702, Isabel, da. of Sir William LOCKHART, 1st Baronet [S. 1672], by Isabel, da. of James (STEWART), 2d EARL OF QUEENSBERRY [S.]. He was living 1711, and probably long afterwards.

III. 1730? SIR THOMAS KIRKPATRICK, Baronet [S. 1685], of Closeburn aforesaid, 1st s. and h., by the 2d wife; *b.* 1704; *suc. to the Baronetcy* on the death of his father. The mansion at Closeburn, with all therein, was destroyed by fire 29 Aug. 1748, and the Baronet removed to the keep of the old castle. He *m.* Susanna, da. and h. of James GRIERSON, of Capenoch. He *d.* Oct. 1771, aged 67.

IV. 1771. SIR JAMES KIRKPATRICK, Baronet [S. 1685], of Closeburn aforesaid, 2d but 1st surv. s. and h.; admitted Advocate, 4 Jan. 1758; *suc. to the Baronetcy*, Oct. 1771, and sold the estate of Closeburn in 1783 to Mr. Menteith. He *m.* in or before 1771, Mary, da. of (—) JARDINE. He *d.* 7 June 1804.

V. 1804. SIR THOMAS KIRKPATRICK, Baronet [S. 1685], 1st s. and h., *b.* 1777; admitted an Advocate 23 June 1798; *suc. to the Baronetcy*, 7 June 1804. He *m.* 7 June 1804, his cousin Jane, sister of Charles KIRKPATRICK-SHARPE, the well-known Scottish Antiquary (who *d.* 1851, aged 70), 2d da. of Charles KIRKPATRICK-SHARPE, formerly KIRKPATRICK,(b) of Hoddam, co. Dumfries, by Eleanor, da. of John RENTON, of Lamerton. He *d.* 1844.

VI. 1844. SIR CHARLES SHARPE KIRKPATRICK, Baronet [S. 1685], 2d and yst. but only surv. s. and h.,(c) *b.* May 1811; *suc. to the Baronetcy* in 1844. He *m.* 24 March 1837, Helen Stuart, da. of Thomas KIRK, of Keir Mill, co. Dumfries. He *d.* 9 Oct. 1867, at Libertad, Central America, on his journey to England, aged 56. His widow *d.* 29 Sep. 1877, in her 63d year.

VIII. 1867. SIR THOMAS KIRKPATRICK, Baronet [S. 1685], 1st s. and h., *b.* 26 April 1839; *suc. to the Baronetcy*, 29 Sep. 1877. He *m.* 23 Oct. 1886, Sophia Anne, da. of William BLANTON, of Frampton-on-Severn. She *d.* 31 July 1879, at Grove Villa, New Southgate, Midx. He *d.* s.p., on his yacht, "The Eva," in Dover Harbour, 23 June 1880, aged 42.

(a) "It is reported that at the Revolution he had the offer of a coronet with the style and dignity of Earl of Closeburne but he rejected the honour, doubtless for some good reason, which is not over apparent to his posterity" [Playfair's *Baronetage*, 1811].

(b) This Charles (who *d.* 1813, aged 63), was 2d s. of William Kirkpatrick, of Alisland, M.P. for Dumfries Burghs 1736-38, Clerk of the Court of Session 1738, who *d.* 22 May 1778, being 3d s. of the 2d Baronet.

(c) James Kirkpatrick, the 1st s., *b.* 1808, was an officer R.N., but *d.* unm. and v.p.

IX. 1880. SIR JAMES KIRKPATRICK, Baronet [S. 1685], br. and h., *b.* 22 March 1841; a Clerk in the Admiralty and sometime Private Sec. to the first Lord; *suc. to the Baronetcy*, 23 June 1880. He *m.* 24 April 1872, Mary Stewart, yst. da. of Charles John FEARNLEY, of Peckham, Surrey. He *d.* intestate, 20 Nov. 1899, at 296 Stanstead Road, Forest Hill, Essex, aged 58. Admon. £11,736, of which £384 was net personalty. His widow living 1904.

X. 1899. SIR CHARLES SHARPE KIRKPATRICK, Baronet [1685], 1st s. and h., *b.* 2 Feb. 1874; *suc. to the Baronetcy*, 20 Nov. 1899. He *m.* 4 Dec. 1900, Alice Wilhelmina, 3d da. of J. Parnell MAYNE.

LAURIE:

cr. 27 March 1685;

ex. 7 Jan. 1848.

I. 1685. "ROBERT LAURIE, of Maxwelton," co. Dumfries, s. and h. of John LAURIE(a), of the same, M.P. [S.] for Dumfries Sheriffdom, 1643 (*d.* 1672), and grandson of Stephen LAURIE (*d.* 14 Dec. 1637), the purchaser of that estate from the Earls of Glencairn [S.], "having distinguished himself by his loyalty in those troubled times"(b) was *cr. a Baronet* [S.], 27 March 1685, as above, with rem. to heirs male of the body. He *m.* firstly, Maria, da. of the Hon. Sir John DALZELL, 1st Baronet [S. 1666], of Glenae, by his 1st wife (—) da. of (—) SANDILANDS. She *d.* s.p.m. He *m.* secondly, 27 July 1674, at the Tron Kirk, Edinburgh, Jean, da. of Walter RIDDELL, of Minto, by Catherine, da. of Sir Patrick NISBET, of Eastbank. He *d.* April 1698.(c) Funeral escutcheon, 26 April 1698.(a)

II. 1698. SIR ROBERT LAURIE, Baronet [S. 1685], of Maxwelton aforesaid, 1st s. and h., by 2d wife, *b.* in or after 1674; *suc. to the Baronetcy* in April 1698. He *d.* unm., from a fall from his horse,(b) in 1702.

III. 1702. SIR WALTER LAURIE, Baronet [S. 1685], of Maxwelton aforesaid, br. of the whole blood and h.; *suc. to the Baronetcy* in 1702. He is said to have *m.* firstly, in 1708, Jean, da. of (—) NISBET, of Dean, and to have *m.* secondly, Henrietta, da. of Sir Robert GRIERSON, 1st Baronet [S. 1685], by Henrietta, da. of James (DOUGLAS), 2d EARL OF QUEENSBERRY [S.]. He *d.* 23 Nov. 1731.(d)

IV. 1731. SIR ROBERT LAURIE, Baronet [S. 1685], of Maxwelton aforesaid, s. and h.; *suc. to the Baronetcy*, 23 Nov. 1731; was M.P. for Dumfries burghs, 1738-41. He *m.* 4 Feb. 1733, Christian, 1st da. of Charles ERSKINE, of Alva (sometime a Lord of Session under the style of *Lord Tinwald*), Lord Justice Clerk, by his 1st wife, Grizel GRIERSON, heiress of Barjarg, co. Dumfries. She was *b.* 20 Dec. 1715, and *d.* at Edinburgh 21 Aug. 1755. He *d.* at Maxwelton, 28 April 1779.

(a) The funeral escutcheon, 26 April 1698, of this Baronet, shews that Stephen's mother's name was Ferguson [Stodart's *Scottish Arms*, ii, 199]. The 1st Baronet is sometimes said to be the son of William, who was son of John, the son of Stephen.

(b) Playfair's *Baronetage* [1811], in which is a note concerning the death of the 2d Baronet, and a very lengthy account of the naval services of the 6th.

(c) The "Bonnie Annie Laurie" celebrated in the pathetic lyric, by William Douglas, of Fingland, co. Kirkcudbright (her rejected suitor), was a da. of this Baronet, by his second marriage, and was *b.* 16 Dec. 1682. She *m.* in 1709, Alexander Fergusson, of Craigdarroch. M.P. for Dumfries burghs, 1715-22. See *N. & Q.*, 4th S. vii, 491.

(d) Index to services of Heirs.

V. 1779. SIR ROBERT LAURIE, Baronet [1685], of Maxwelton aforesaid, only s. and h.; was M.P. for Dumfries-shire for 30 years (six Parls.) 1774 till his death in 1804; *suc. to the Baronetcy*, 28 April 1779; entered early into the Army; was in 1779 Lieut.-Col., 16th Light Dragoons; Major-General in 1798, and finally, 1883, General; Knight Marshal of Scotland, 1785 till death. He *m.* firstly, 18 July 1763, at Edinburgh, Mary Elizabeth, da. of James (RUTHVEN), LORD RUTHVEN OF FREELAND [S.], by his 2d wife Anne, da. of James (STEWART), 2d EARL OF BUTE [S.]. She was living 1769. He *m.* secondly, at Ipswich, 25 April 1778, Judith, widow of Robert WOLLASTON, da. of (—) HATLEY. He *d.* 10 Sep. 1804, at Dumfries. Admon. Jan. 1805. His widow, by whom he had no issue, *d.* 25 Jan. 1824, in Upper Seymour street, aged 76. Will pr. 1824.

VI. 1804, to 1848. SIR ROBERT LAURIE, Baronet [S. 1685], of Maxwelton aforesaid, only s. and h., *b.* 25 May 1764; entered the Royal Navy, distinguishing himself as Lieut. of "The Queen," in Admiral Howe's action, 1794; as also, off Cuba, in 1801, and in the action with the Ville de Milan in 1805,(a) becoming eventually, 1821, Admiral; *suc. to the Baronetcy*, 10 Sep. 1804; K.C.B., 13 Sep. 1831. He *d.* unm. at Maxwelton House, 7 and was *bur.* 14 Jan. 1848, at Glencairn, in his 84th year, when the *Baronetcy* became *extinct*.(b)

STRACHAN:

cr. 8 May 1685;

extinct, presumably, on death of grantee.

I. 1685, to 1700? "THOMAS STRACHAN," believed "to be son of Thomas STRACHAN, brother of John STRACHAN, of Mureton, near Laurence Kirk, Farmer"(c) (both brothers being living 8 May 1638), served in the army of Leopold I, Emperor of Germany, and was *cr. a Baronet* [S.], 8 May 1685, with rem. to heirs male of the body,(d) without any territorial description, being described as "our beloved subject at present serving in the wars under his Imperial Majesty," and as being "sprung from the house of Thornton."(c) It is stated(c) that "to distinguish his Baronetcy from that of the elder branch he assumed the territorial designation of Inchtuthill."(e) He appears to have *d.* s.p.m., probably unm., in which case the *Baronetcy*, which was limited to the heirs male of his body, then became *extinct*.(f)

(a) See p. 331, note "b."

(b) His nephew, John Minet Fector, to whom on 22 April 1844, he had disponed the Maxwelton estate, suc. him therein, and took the name of LAURIE, 12 Feb. 1848. He was only s. of the Baronet's only sister Anne, *b.* 13 June 1769, who *m.* 22 Feb. 1794, John Minet Fector, of Updown, co. Kent, a Banker at Dover, and was living a widow in 1848. Her son, the said John Minet Laurie, of Maxwelton, *d.* s.p., 24 Feb. 1868, aged 55.

(c) *Strachan and Wise Families*, by Rev. Charles Rogers, LL.D., 2d edit., 1877, where the patent (rendered into English) is printed.

(d) Milne's *List*. The words there are "sub Cæsaris Majestatis auspiciis in bellis suis militans."

(e) This, however, appears to be a mistake. See vol. ii, p. 286, note "c" (under Strachan Baronetcy [S.], *cr.* 1625), as to the Inchtuthill estate.

(f) See vol. ii, p. 288, note "a," as to the conjecture that *this* Baronetcy [not the Baronetcy [S.] *cr.* 28 May 1625] was the one assumed, about 1765, by Sir John Strachan, and subsequently, 1777 to 1828, by his nephew and successor, the well known Admiral Sir Richard John Strachan.

LIVINGSTON:

cr. 20 July 1685;

afterwards, 1771—1810, CAMPBELL;

ex. or *dormant*, 1810.

I. 1685. "ALEXANDER LIVINGSTON, of Glentirran," illegit. s. of Alexander (LIVINGSTON), 2d EARL OF CALLENDER [S.], by (—), da. of (—) ELPHINSTONE, of Quarrel, co. Stirling, was *cr. a Baronet* [S.], as above, 20 July 1685, with rem. to heirs male whatsoever. He *m.* (—), da. of William BARTLEWICK, of Edinburgh, Surgeon Apothecary. He *d.* July 1698.(a)

II. 1698. SIR JAMES LIVINGSTON, Baronet [S. 1685], of Glentirran aforesaid and Dalderse, 5th but 1st surv. s. and h., *suc. to the Baronetcy* in July 1698. He *m.* Helen, da. and coheir (5 July 1752) of Sir James CAMPBELL, 2d Baronet [S. 1679], of Ardkinglass, co. Argyll, by his 1st wife Margaret, da. and coheir of Adam CAMPBELL, of Gargunnock, co. Stirling. She *d.* 29 March 1767. He *d.* 30 April 1771, at Bantaskine, at, presumably, a great age.

III. 1771. SIR JAMES CAMPBELL, Baronet [S. 1685], of Ardkinglass aforesaid, *formerly* James LIVINGSTON, s. and h.; was M.P. for Stirlingshire (three Parls.), 1747-68; Governor of Stirling Castle, 1763. Having inherited the estate of Ardkinglass, being that of his maternal ancestors, he took the name of CAMPBELL in lieu of that of LIVINGSTON. He *suc. to the Baronetcy*, 30 April 1771. He *m.* in 1752, Katherine, da. and coheir of Walter CAMPBELL, Receiver Gen. of the Customs. He *d.* 21 Nov. 1788.

IV. 1788, to 1810. SIR ALEXANDER CAMPBELL, Baronet [S. 1685], of Ardkinglass aforesaid, s. and h., *suc. to the Baronetcy*, 21 Nov. 1788. He *m.* in 1792 Marianne, only da. of John CHEAPE, a scion of the family of CHEAPE, of Sauchie. He *d.* s.p. in 1810 when the *Baronetcy* became *extinct* or *dormant*. His widow *m.* (as his 3d wife) 8 Dec. 1817, at Charlotte street Chapel, Edinburgh, Thomas (LYON-BOWES) EARL OF STRATHMORE AND KINGHORN [S.] and *d.* his widow at Holyrood house 23 being *bur.* in the chapel there 27 Oct. 1849, aged 77.(b)

KINLOCH:

cr. 5 Sep. 1685;

forfeited 1746.

I. 1685. "DAVID KINLOCH, of Kinloch," co. Fife, s. and h. of James KINLOCH, of the same, by (—), da. of David [?] GRAHAM, of Fintry, co. Forfar (which James was s. and h. of David KINLOCH, of Kinloch, a Physician and Traveller of considerable note, who *d.* 1617) was *cr. a Baronet* [S.], 5 Sep. 1685, with rem. it is said(c) to heirs male whatsoever, though no record of such creation exists in the Great Seal Register. He *m.* firstly, Elizabeth, only child of David BETHUNE, 2d s. of John BETHUNE, of Balfour. She *d.* s.p. He *m.* secondly, his cousin, Margaret, da. of James GRAHAM, of Fintry.

(a) Index to the services of heirs, 1718.

(b) See p. 307, note "d," *sub* "Campbell" for the subsequent devolution of the Ardkinglass estate.

(c) Milne's *List*.

II. 1700? SIR JAMES KINLOCH, Baronet [S. 1685], of Kinloch aforesaid, 1st s. and h. by 2d wife; *b.* probably about 1680; *suc. to the Baronetcy* on the death of his father. He *m.* Elizabeth, heiress of John NEVAY, of Nevay, co. Forfar. He *d.* 1744. His widow, by whom he had seven sons and five daughters, *d.* 6 May 1760, aged 77.

III. 1744, to 1746. SIR JAMES KINLOCH, Baronet [S. 1685], of Kinloch aforesaid, s. and h., *suc. to the Baronetcy* in 1744. He joined the Jacobite rising of 1745, was tried and condemned to death, and being attainted in 1746, the *Baronetcy* became *forfeited*. He, who escaped to France, and was subsequently pardoned, having inherited his mother's estate, took the name of NEVAY after that of KINLOCH. He *m.* Janet DUFF, said to be sister of the [1st] EARL FIFE [I.].(a) He, as "*Sir James Kinloch-Nevay, Baronet*," *d.* 5 Feb. 1766.(b)

DALZIELL, *or* DALYELL:

cr. 7 Nov. 1685;

ex., apparently, 11 May 1719;

but assumed from about 1726 to 1886.

I. 1685. CAPTAIN "THOMAS DALZIELL [*or* DALYELL], of Binns,"(c) co. Linlithgow, s. and h. of Gen. Thomas DALYELL, of the same, a distinguished cavalier, held a command at the battle of Worcester, and who, after the Restoration, was Commander in Chief of the forces in Scotland,(d) by Agnes, da. of John KER, of Cavers, was a Capt. in the army; suc. his father 1 Oct. 1685, on account of whose services, apparently, he was, a month later, *cr. a Baronet* [S.], 7 Nov. 1685, as above "provydit to his eldest son and heirs male and tailzie succeiding him in estate of Binns"(e). He *m.* Katharine, da. of Sir William DRUMMOND, of Riccaton, by Magdalen, da. of Thomas DALYELL, of Binns.

II. 1700? to 1719. SIR THOMAS DALZIELL, *or* DALYELL, Baronet [S. 1685], of Binns aforesaid, only s. and h.; *suc. to the Baronetcy* on his father's death. He *d.* unm. 4 May 1719 when the *Baronetcy*, apparently, became *extinct*.

(a) Burke's *Peerage*, 1902, under "Kinloch" Baronetcy, *cr.* 1873.

(b) The estate of Kinloch was purchased by his friends and restored to him, with reversion to his son William Kinloch, who lived in England but *d.* s.p., having sold Kinloch to his cousin, Capt. George Oliphant Kinloch, great grandson of James Kinloch, a yr. br. of the 1st Baronet [S. 1685] and grandfather of George Kinloch, *cr. a Baronet* 16 April 1873. It is stated (see note "a" above) that the "male heir and representative" of the attainted Baronet was [in 1902] "General Kinloch, of Kilrie and Logie."

(c) The estate of Binns was bought in 1629 by Thomas Dalyell, Steward to the Lord Bruce of Kinloss [S.].

(d) He raised the celebrated regiment called "the Scots Greys," the letters of service for raising which are dated 25 Nov. 1681 [Playfair's *Baronetage*, 1811].

(e) The words of the creation are "ac post ejus decessum in Thomam Dalziell, ejus filium legitimum natu maximum, et hæredes ejus masculos et talliæ sibi in jure hereditario statu, ac familiæ de Binns succedentes." The "innumerable faithful and eminent services" of the grantee's father are mentioned in the patent.

The Baronetcy was, however, assumed at some date between 1723 and 1728, as under.

III. 1726? SIR JAMES DALYELL, *or* DALZIELL, Baronet [S. 1685],(a) of Binns aforesaid, *formerly* James MENTEITH, nephew (by the *sister*) and h. or coheir (but certainly not heir *male*), being s. and h. of James MENTEITH, of Auldcathy, by Magdalen (*m.* 1688), sister of the late and 1st da. of the 1st Baronet. He was *b.* probably about 1690; was an officer in the Army, took the name of DALYELL, *or* DALZIELL, in lieu of that of MENTEITH about 1719 and *assumed the Baronetcy* between 1723 and 1728(b) He *m.* Helen, da. of (—) CAMPBELL, of Netherplace, co. Ayr. He *d.* 28 Feb. 1747. His widow *d.* 29 Jan. 1774 at Binns.

IV. 1747. SIR ROBERT DALYELL, *or* DALZIELL, Baronet [S. 1685],(a) of Binns aforesaid, 1st s. and h.; was an officer in the army, and served on the Continent; *suc. to the Baronetcy*,(a) 28 Feb. 1747. He *m.* 22 Sep. 1773, Elizabeth, da. of Nicol GRAHAM, of Gartmore, by Margaret, da. of William (CUNNINGHAM), 12th EARL OF GLENCAIRN [S.]. He *d.* 10 Oct. 1791. His widow, by whom he had eleven children, *d.* at Edinburgh, 31 July 1825.

V. 1791. SIR JAMES DALYELL, *or* DALZIELL, Baronet [S. 1685],(a) of Binns aforesaid, 1st s. and h., *b.* 7 July 1774; *suc. to the Baronetcy*,(a) 10 Oct. 1791; was an officer in the army, and served in Flanders, 1793. He *d.* unm. 1 Feb. 1841.

VI. 1841. SIR JOHN GRAHAM DALYELL, *or* DALZIELL, Baronet [S. 1685],(a) of Binns aforesaid,(c) br. and h., *b.* about 1778; was admitted as Advocate 1797; author of several scientific and historical works; V.P. of the Soc. of Antiquaries [S.], etc.; was *Knighted* 1836; *suc. to the Baronetcy*,(d) 1 Feb. 1841. He *d.* unm. 7 June 1851, at Edinburgh, in his 74th year. Will pr. Nov. 1851.

VII. 1851. SIR WILLIAM CUNNINGHAM DALYELL, *or* DALZIELL, Baronet [S. 1685],(a) of Binns aforesaid,(c) br. and h., being 5th and yst. s. of the 4th Baronet, *b.* 27 April 1784; was an officer in the Navy, 1792, receiving no less than sixteen wounds in various actions, and being many years a prisoner in France; becoming finally Capt. R.N. and commander of Greenwich Hospital. He *suc. to the Baronetcy*,(a) 7 June 1851. He *m.* in 1820, Maria, sister of Anthony SAMPAYO, French Minister at Hesse, da. of Anthony Teixiera SAMPAYO, of Peterborough House, Fulham, Midx. He *d.* 16 Feb. 1865, at his residence in Greenwich Hospital, in his 81st year. His widow *d.* 20 Oct. 1871 aged 72, at 120 Belgrave road, Pimlico.

(a) According to the assumption of that dignity, 1723-28.

(b) He executed an entail of the Auldcathy estate in 1723 as "James Dalyell of Binns," but on 29 Dec. 1728 he is styled "*Sir* James Dalyell" in a service to his cousin, James Menteth, of Miln Hall, as heir male. [*Ex inform.* R. R. Stodart, late (1863-86) Lyon Clerk Depute.] There can be no question that he was not the heir *male* of entail to the Baronetcy—and, indeed, no deed of entail thereof was apparently ever made.

(c) "It is understood that the estate of Binns, referred to in the remainder [of the Baronetcy] passed from the family in 1841" [Foster's *Baronetage*, 1883]. This, however, seems apparently not to have been the case.

VIII. *1865, to 1886.* Sir Robert Alexander Osborne Dalyell, *or* Dalziell, Baronet [S. 1685],(a) of Binns aforesaid,(b) 1st but only surv. s. and h., *b.* 1821; ed. at Trin. Coll., Cambridge; M.A., 1847; Barrister (Inner Temple), 1849; served in the Consulate at Bucharest, 1855-58; Acting Consul Gen. at Belgrade, 1858-59; Consul at Erzeroom, 1859; at Jassy in Moldavia, 1862, and at Roustchouk, 1865-74; *suc. to the Baronetcy*,(a) 16 Feb. 1865. He *d.* unm., 21 Jan. 1886, at "The Binns," aged 65, when the male issue of the 3d Baronet(a) became *extinct*, and the *assumption of this Baronetcy ceased*.(c)

MONCREIFFE:

cr. 30 Nov. 1685.

I. 1685. Thomas Moncreiffe, of Moncreiffe, co. Perth,(d) 2d s.(e) of David Moncreiffe, of Rapness, in Orkney (*d.* before 1649),(e) by his 1st wife, Barbara, da. of (—) Baikie, of Tankerness, was *b.* about 1627; was Clerk of the Exchequer and Treasury [S.], and, having acquired great wealth, bought in 1663, the Lordship of Moncreiffe from Sir John Moncreiffe, 2d Baronet [S. 1626], and was *cr. a Baronet* [S.] 30 Nov. 1685, with rem. to heirs male whatsoever. He *m.* firstly, Bertha Hamilton, "da. to the Laird of Bothwell." He *m.* secondly in 1703, Margaret (*b.* 1639), widow of Sir John Young, of Leny (who *d.* before 15 Aug. 1690), da. of Sir Thomas Hope, of Kerse. He *d.* s.p. 15 Jan. 1715, in the 89th year of his age. His widow was *bur.* 24 Nov. 1723, at Cramond, aged 84.(g)

II. 1715. Sir Thomas Moncreiffe, Baronet [S. 1685], of Moncreiffe aforesaid, nephew and h., being 1st s. and h. of Harry Moncreiffe, by Barbara, da. of Harry Herbert, of Cardiff, which Harry Moncreiffe was next br. of the full blood to the late Baronet. He *suc. to the Baronetcy*, as heir male, on the death of his uncle, 15 Jan. 1715. He *m.* Margaret, da. of David Smythe, of Methuen. He *d.* May 1738, at Glasgow.

(a) See p. 335, note "a."
(b) See p. 335, note "c."
(c) Of his sisters (1) Maria Christiana, *m.* 1855, Major Gen. Sir Charles Taylor Du Plat, K.C.B. (who *d.* 2 Nov. 1900), and *d.*, before her brother, 7 April 1867; (2) Elizabeth Grace, *m.* 11 April 1861, Gustavus Charles Cornwall and having inherited in 1886 the estate of Binns, assumed the name of Dalyell.
(d) Called in J. R. Anderson's *List* (see p. 242, note "a") "of Tullibole."
(e) David Moncreiffe, the 1st son, *m.* Margaret Anderson, of Holmsound, but *d.* s.p.m.
(f) *N. & Q.*, 3d s., iv, 229, under "Herbert of Cardiff."
(g) It is presumed from her age that this lady was the widow of the *first* Baronet, but it is possible she was a 1st wife of the 2d Baronet. The extract, as below, calls her *wife* (not *widow*) of Sir Thomas, but that is a very frequent confusion. "Dame Mary Hope, da. of Sir Thomas Hope, of Kerse, widow of Sir John Young, of Leny, and wife of Sir Thomas Moncrieff, of Moncrieff, buried at Cramond 24 Nov. 1723, aged 84 years" [Wood's *Cramond*, p. 20].

III. 1738. Sir Thomas Moncreiffe, Baronet [S. 1685], of Moncreiffe aforesaid, 1st s. and h., *b.* 31 Dec. 1704, *suc. to the Baronetcy* in 1739. He *m.* 2 June 1730, Catherine (*b.* 7 June 1711), 2d da. of Sir William Murray, 3d Baronet [S. 1673], of Ochtertyre, by Catherine, da. of Hugh [Fraser], Lord Lovat [S.]. He was *bur.* 8 May 1739 in the High churchyard, Glasgow, aged 34. His widow *d.* 30 Jan. 1763.

IV. 1739. Sir Thomas Moncreiffe, Baronet [S. 1685], of Moncreiffe aforesaid, 1st s. and h., *b.* 11 Feb. 1732; *suc. to the Baronetcy*, May 1739. He *m.* Clara, da. of Robert Guthrie, of Craigie in Angus. He *d.* 28 Sep. 1784, aged 52. His widow *d.* 31 March 1785.

V. 1784. Sir Thomas Moncreiffe, Baronet [S. 1685], of Moncreiffe aforesaid, only s. and h., *b.* 7 June 1758; *suc. to the Baronetcy*, 28 Sep. 1784. He *m.* 13 Aug. 1786, at Dalhousie castle, Elizabeth, 2d da. of George (Ramsay), 8th Earl of Dalhousie [S.], by Elizabeth, da of Andrew Glen. He *d.* 26 March 1818, aged 59. His widow, who was *b.* 6 Sep. 1769, *d.* 3 June 1848 in Chapel street, Belgrave square, from injuries caused by her dress taking fire, aged 78. Will pr. Dec. 1848.

VI. 1818. Sir David Moncreiffe, Baronet [S. 1685], of Moncreiffe aforesaid, only s. and h., *b.* 31 Dec. 1788; *suc. to the Baronetcy*, 26 March 1818. He *m.* 12 Jan. 1819, Helen, 2d da. of Æneas Mackay, of Scotstown, co. Peebles. He *d.* 20 Nov. 1830, at Moncreiffe House, aged 41. His widow *m.* (as his 2d wife) 30 Oct. 1849, at St. Peter's, Pimlico, George Augustus Frederick Henry (Bridgeman), 6th Earl of Bradford (who *d.* 22 March 1865, in his 76th year) and *d.* at Cannes, 22 April 1869.

VII. 1830. Sir Thomas Moncreiffe, Baronet [S. 1685], of Moncreiffe aforesaid, 1st s. and h., *b.* there 9 Jan. 1822; *suc. to the Baronetcy*, 20 Nov. 1830; sometime Lieut. 1st Foot Guards, retiring 1848; Lieut.-Col. Perthshire Militia, 1846; Lieut.-Col. Commandant (with rank of Honorary Colonel), 1855. He *m.* 2 May 1843, at St. Geo. Han. sq., Louisa, 1st da. of Thomas Robert (Hay), 10th Earl of Kinnoull, [S.], by Louisa Burton, da. of Admiral Sir Charles Rowley, G.C.B., 1st Baronet [1836]. He *d.* 15 Aug. 1879, at Moncreiffe house in his 58th year. His widow, who was *b.* 5 June 1825, *d.* 4 Sep. 1898, at Shilston house, near Leamington, co. Warwick, and was *bur.* at Moncreiffe, aged 73.(a)

VIII. 1879. Sir Robert Drummond Moncreiffe, Baronet [S. 1685], of Moncreiffe aforesaid, 1st s. and h., *b.* there 3 Nov. 1856; ed. at Harrow; sometime Lieut. Scots Guards, retiring 1881; *suc. to the Baronetcy*, 15 Aug. 1879; Lieut.-Col. 4th Vol. Batt. Black Watch (Royal Highlanders). He *m.* 6 April 1880, at St. Paul's, Knightsbridge, Evelyn Elizabeth Vane, 1st da. of his maternal uncle Col. the Hon. Charles Rowley Hay-Drummond, of Cromlix co. Perth, by Arabella Augusta, da. of Col. William Henry Meyrick. She was *b.* 27 Oct. 1858.

Family Estates.—These, in 1883, consisted of 4,743 acres in Perthshire, worth £7,247 a year. *Seat.*—Moncreiffe house, near Bridge of Earn, co. Perth.

(a) Of her eight daughters all famous for their beauty and all well married—(1) Louisa was Duchess of Atholl [S.]; (2) Helen *m.* Sir Charles John Forbes, 4th Baronet [1823]; (3) Georgina Elizabeth, was Countess of Dudley; (4) Harriet Sarah, *m.* (as first wife) Sir Charles Mordaunt, 10th Baronet [1611]; (6) Frances Rose, *m.* Sir Alexander Muir-Mackenzie, 3d Baronet [1805] etc.

NICOLSON:

cr., as (erroneously?) alleged, 1686.(a)

"John Nicolson, of Tulliecultrie" [*i.e.* Tillicoultrie] is stated to have been *cr. a Baronet* [S.], though no *date* of such creation is given in Milne's *List*, where it is added "no document, bot is so designed in papers." The date of 1686 is however, frequently assigned,(a) though in all probability, if such creation was ever made, it was in or before 1683, as the person indicated must be Sir John Nicolson, of Tillicoultrie, who *d.* 1683, and whose s. and h., Thomas, *suc.*, 9 June 1686, *to the Baronetcy* [S.] conferred 16 Jan. 1636/7 on Thomas Nicolson, of Carnock, co. Stirling. See vol. ii, pp. 424-426, for that Baronetcy, in which this creation, if it ever existed, must be merged.

BROUN:(b)

cr. 16 Feb. 1685/6.

I. 1686. "Patrick Broun, of Coulstoun," co. Haddington, 2d s. of James Broun, of the same (*d.* 1669), by Anna (*m.* 1625), da. and h. of Robert Heriot, of Trabroun, was *b.* probably about 1630; was served heir male, 6 May 1658, to his elder br. George Broun, of Coulston aforesaid (who *d.* s.p.m.(c) 1657), and was *cr. a Baronet* [S.], as above, 16 Feb. 1685/6, with rem. to heirs male for ever.(d) He *m.* firstly, Alison, da. of James Sinclair. He *m.* secondly, Jean, widow of the Rev. Robert Ker, Minister of Haddington, da. of John Ramsay, of Edington. He *d.* 1688.

(a) Beatson's *List* ("Nicholson, of Tillicoultry: extinct") as also other various authorities. The following remarks are made by James R. Anderson (see p. 242, note "a"), "This creation is given without date by Milne, Chamberlayne, and Miege. The year 1686 is assigned to a Nicolson creation by various authorities, [*e.g.*] Dod (1864, 1891), Lodge (1858), Debrett (1808, p. 1063), and a number of other lists such as in the early edition of Oliver and Boyd, etc. In all the above lists, however, the Baronet mentioned belongs to the 1636/7 creation, but there never was a Sir *John* in that line. Possibly 1686 is a mistake for 1636, and does not refer to the Tillicoultrie creation. In the *Scottish Antiquary* (vol. iii, pp. 56 and 145) the Nicolson Baronets are treated, but no mention is made of this creation."
(b) An elaborate account of this family is given in "*The Baronetage for 1844*, by Sir Richard Broun, Eq. Aur., K.J.J., Hon. Secretary of the Committee of the Baronetage for privileges," the author being s. and h. ap. of "the Hon. Sir James, 7th Bt. and present chief of the name in Scotland." In it it is stated that "This very ancient and noble family claims descent from and bears the arms of the Royal House of France." The *red* ground and the *chevron* between the three fleur-de-lis, as borne by the Broun family [Burke's *Baronetage*, 1902], however, militate against this statement.
(c) Lilias, the da. and h. of this George, did not however inherit the Coulston estate. She *m.* James Bannatyne, of Newhall.
(d) Equivalent, doubtless, to heirs male whatsoever.

II. 1688. Sir George Broun, Baronet [S. 1686], of Coulston aforesaid, s. and h. by (—) wife, *suc. to the Baronetcy* in 1688. He *m.* Elizabeth, 2d da. of George (Mackenzie), 1st Earl of Cromarty [S.], by his 1st wife, Anne, da. of Sir James Sinclair, 1st Baronet [S. 1631], of Mey. He *d.* s.p. 1718,(a) when the issue male of the grantee became extinct. His wife survived him.(b)

III. 1718 Sir George Broun, Baronet [S. 1686], of Thornydikes, co. Berwick, cousin and, presumably, heir male,(c) being s. of Alexander Broun, of Bassendean, in that county, by his 1st wife Catharine, da. of Sir Alexander Swinton, of Swinton, which Alexander Broun was s. and h. of George Broun, of Thornydikes, yr. br. of James Broun, of Colstoun, father of the 1st Baronet, both being sons of George Broun, of Colstoun. He, on the ground of being heir male, *suc. to the Baronetcy*(c) in 1718. He *m.* Janet, da. of Alexander Spottiswoode, of Warristoun, by his 2d wife Helen, da. of John Trotter, of Mortonhall. He *d.* s.p., 16 Feb. or 15 Aug. 1734.

IV. 1734. Sir Alexander Broun, Baronet [S. 1686], of Bassendean, co. Berwick, br. and h., *suc. to the Baronetcy* in 1734. He *m.* Beatrix, da. of Alexander Swinton, of Mersington, a Lord of Session [S.]. He *d.* 1750.

(a) The estate of Colstoun devolved on his niece, Jean, 1st da. and heir of line of his brother, Robert Broun, who (with his two sons) was drowned 31 May 1703. She *m.* Charles Broun, of Cleghornie, and their son George Broun, of Colstoun, was a Lord of Session [S.] under the style of "Lord Colstoun," being father of Charles Broun, of Colstoun, whose da. and h., Christian, *m.* 14 May 1805, George (Ramsay), 9th Earl of Dalhousie [S.], and is ancestress of the present [1904] Earl, the now owner thereof.
(b) She is the heroine of a romantic story, which has been versified under the name of "*The charmed Cornac of Colstoun*, by Edward Mackenzie Mackenzie, Baronet." The story states that, by recklessly biting (or dreaming that she had eaten) this magic pear (or cornac) which had been some three centuries in the family of her husband, she brought misfortune thereon, he, himself, dying without issue, his only brother (with two sons) having previously died leaving no male issue. [See note "a" above.] This pear is said to have been presented by Hugh Gifford, of Yester (who *d.* s.p.m. about 1409, being great grandson of another Hugh Gifford, of Yester, *the wizard*, who *d.* 1267, by whom perhaps it had been bewitched), to his da. Joan, on her marriage about 1400 to Sir William Hay, with the prophecy that so long as it was preserved unharmed, her race would flourish. It continued in the family of Hay, of Yester, till about 1550, when it formed part of the marriage dower of Jean, da. of John (Hay), 3d Lord Hay of Yester [S.], with George Broun, of Colstoun, whence it acquired the name of *the charmed Cornac of Colstoun*. Their descendant the 2d Baronet inherited it in 1688 "unharmed" but at his death in 1718 it passed, with the estate of Colstoun (see p. 338, note "c") to the heir female. In Broun's *Baronetage, 1844*, it is thus spoken of—"This pear, now nearly six [*sic*] centuries old is still [1844] preserved at Colstoun House . . . and . . . is perhaps the most singular vegetable curiosity in the Kingdom." See *N. & Q.*, 3d S., 111, 466.
(c) In a pedigree drawn up from the MS. notes of Sir Richard Broun, who *d.* 1781, by Edward M. Mackenzie (see note "b" above), it is stated that this Sir George had an *elder* br. Archibald Broun, who, in 1715, raised a troop of Horse for the Chevalier in the Jacobite rising. He, who probably was attainted, is said to have *m.* a da. of (—) Trotter, and to have left a son [*Qy.* if legitimate?] who was a Physician in Charlestown, in America, who left a son, Archibald, who *d.* unm. The first named Archibald may, however, possibly have died before the 2d Baronet, but if he left legitimate male issue, such issue would precede this Sir George in the right to the Baronetcy. Moreover this George is not called a Baronet in the pedigree of Spottiswoode (his wife's family), given in Douglas's *Baronage* [S.].

V. 1750, to 1776. SIR ALEXANDER BROUN, Baronet [S. 1686], of Bridgeness, only s. and h.; *suc. to the Baronetcy* in 1750. He *m.* in 1755, Mally, da. of Adam COLQUHOUN, of Glins, an officer of the Salt Duty at Borrowstonness. She was living 1766. He *d.* s.p.m.(a) 1776, when the *Baronetcy* became *dormant* and so remained for fifty years(b).

* * * * * * *

VI. 1776. THE REV. RICHARD BROUN, Minister of the Gospel, at Lochmaben, co. Dumfries, was, according to a service, 12 Jan. 1826 (see below), *entitled to the Baronetcy* in 1776 as heir male, he being 1st s. of James BROUN, tenant of Hume Castle, in the parish of Stichill, co. Berwick, by Alison, da. of William BRODIE, which James was 1st s. of George BROUN,(c) 1st s. of Alexander BROUN, both in Hume aforesaid, which Alexander was 1st s. of George BROUN, yr. br. of Alexander BROUN (father of the 3d and 4th and grandfather of the 5th Baronet) both being sons of George BROUN, of Thornydike.(d) He, who was sometime Minister of Bute, Kingarth, and (finally) of Lochmaben, entered his pedigree at the Lyon office, but *never assumed the Baronetcy.* He *m.* in 1765, Robina, da. of Col. Hugh MACBRIDE, of Beadland, co. Ayr. He *d.* 13 Dec. 1781. His widow *d.* 5 Feb. 1819.

VII. *1781,* or 1826. SIR JAMES BROUN, Baronet [S. 1686],(e) of Mayfield in Lochmaben, co. Dumfries (the name of which he changed to "Coulston Park") 1st s. and h., *b.* 12 March 1768; was an officer in the 30th Foot, serving ten years in the West Indies, during the Carib insurrection; *suc. to the Baronetcy,*(e) 13 Dec. 1781, but did not assume the title till 19 March 1826, after having been (in compliance with his claim(f) "served lawful heir male in general to Sir Alexander Broun, Baronet," by a Jury at Lochmaben, 12 Jan. previous. He in 1799 had raised a troop called the Lockerbie Volunteers. He *m.* firstly, 31 July 1798, Marion, sister of John Irvine HENDERSON, 1st da. of Robert HENDERSON, of Cleugheads and Whitecroft, by Janet, da. and h. of F. CARRUTHERS, of Whitecroft. She *d.* suddenly, 20 Aug. 1825. He *m.* secondly, 29 April 1835, Janet, 1st da. of Robert WATSON, of Edinburgh. He *d.* 30 Nov. 1844, at Moffat, co. Dumfries, aged 76. His widow *d.* 17 June 1868, at Seafield, near Leith, aged 84.

(a) He had two daughters and coheirs, Agnes and Beatrix, of whom the former was living unm. at Edinburgh in Jan. 1826, aged 60 and upwards, when she gave important evidence in favour of the claim to the Baronetcy then before the Jury.

(b) No notice of this Baronetcy is given in Playfair's *Baronetage* [S.], 1811, it being then, doubtless, considered to be extinct.

(c) This George is generally omitted, but is included in the statement of the claimant in 1826, to whom, if this George were omitted, "George Broun, first of Thornydike" would not be (as affirmed) "great great great great grandfather."

(d) See note "f" below as to his son's claim to the Baronetcy.

(e) According to the service of the Scotch Jury, 12 Jan. 1826.

(f) The statement in the "Claim for Capt. James Broun to be served nearest and lawful heir male in general to Sir Alexander BROUN, Baronet," was as follows:—"Honourable persons and good men of inquest, I, Captain James BROUN, of Mayfield, in the parish of Lochmaben and county of Dumfries say unto your Wisdoms that I am eldest lawful son of the late Rev. Richard BROUN, Minister of the Gospel in the parish of Lochmaben, who was eldest lawful son of James BROUN in Hume Castle, near Kelso, who was eldest lawful son of George BROUN in Hume, who was eldest lawful son of Alexander BROUN in Hume, who was eldest lawful son of George BROUN, who was third son of George BROUN, first of Thornydyke, my great, great, great, great grandfather [who was] great grandfather to the late Sir Alexander Broun, of Bassendean, Baronet, my cousin. And that the said deceased Sir Alexander Broun, Baronet, died at [*Qy.* in] the faith and peace of our Sovereign Lord the King and that I am the nearest and lawful heir male in general to the said Sir Alexander Broun, Baronet, my cousin." This

VIII. 1844. SIR RICHARD BROUN, Baronet [S. 1686],(a) of Coulston Park aforesaid, 1st s. and h., by 1st wife, was *b.* 22 April 1801, at Lochmaben. "Previous to succeeding his father, he demanded inauguration as a Knight, in the capacity of a Baronet's eldest son, but the Lord Chancellor having refused to present him to the Queen for this purpose, he *assumed the title of Sir* and the addition of *Eques auratus* in June 1842,"(b) and styled himself (when heir ap. to the Baronetcy of Broun) in the *Baronetage* (1844), edited by himself, "Sir Richard BROUN, Eques auratus, Hon. Sec. to the Committee of the Baronetage for privileges, a Knight Commander of the Sovereign Order of St. John of Jerusalem, and Grand Sec. of the Langue of England." He *suc. to the Baronetcy,*(a) 30 Nov. 1844, and describes himself in 1856 as "feudal Baron of Colstoun, Haddingtonshire, and chief of his race in North Britain."(c) He was for many years Sec. to the Central Agricultural Society, was a great promoter of extra-mural burial and was, in 1849, the projector of "the London Necropolis" at Woking. He *d.* unm. 10 Dec. 1858, at Sphinx Lodge, Chelsea, Midx., in his 58th year.

IX. 1858. SIR WILLIAM BROUN, Baronet [S. 1686],(a) of Dumfries, br. of the whole blood, and h., *b.* July 1804, at Lochmaben; was a Solicitor at Dumfries; *suc. to the Baronetcy,*(a) 10 Dec. 1858. He *m.*, at Dumfries, 18 July 1843, Elizabeth, 2d da. of John SMITH, of Drongan, co. Ayr. He *d.* 10 June 1882, at 7 Irving street, Dumfries, in his 78th year, and was *bur.* at Lochmaben. His widow *d.* 19 Aug. 1899, at "Glenshee," Cambridge Park, Twickenham, Midx., aged 80, and was *bur.* at Lochmaben.

X. 1882. SIR WILLIAM BROUN, Baronet [S. 1686],(a) of Somerton, in New South Wales, 2d but 1st surv. s. and h.,(d) *b.* 18 Dec. 1848, at Dumfries; *suc. to the Baronetcy,*(a) 10 June 1882. He *m.* 12 April 1871, at Sydney, in New South Wales, Alice Jane, 2d da. of James Cornelius PETERS, of Manley Beach, Sydney, New South Wales, Under Treasurer of that Colony, by Elizabeth, da. of James CHAMBERS, of Edinburgh.

---

was accompanied by a tabular pedigree beginning with "George, 1st of Thorndike, brother [*sic*] of Sir Patrick Broun, of Colstoun, Baronet." This George is also stated to have been "*brother* german of Sir Patrick Broun, of Colstoun, Baronet," in the "genealogical account" of the family by his great grandson Sir Alexander Broun, Baronet, compiled June 1763 at Bridgeness. George, however, appears to have been *uncle* (not brother) of the 1st Baronet, but the service of 1826 was as heir male to Sir Alexander, the 5th Baronet (who *d.* in 1776) whose right to the title was not questioned, so that the claimant's relationship to the *first* Baronet (a collateral relative) was not set forth. See, however, p. 339, note "c." "The claim of Sir Richard and his father Sir James to be Baronets of Nova Scotia will be found discussed in a work of W. B. D. D. Turnbull, entitled '*British American Association and Nova Scotia Baronets*; report of the action of damages for alleged libel, Broun (*soi-disant*) Sir Richard, against the *Globe* newspaper; with introductory remarks relative to the above scheme and the *illustrious* order connected with it.' 1846, 8vo." [*N. & Q.*, 7th S., iv, p. 191.] See also *Her. and Gen.*, vol. ii, p. 176, where it is mentioned that shortly after Turnbull's publication "the service of heirs was placed on its present greatly improved footing by the Act 10 and 11 Vict., c. 47." See also Seton's *Scottish Heraldry*, p. 304.

(a) See p. 340, note "e."

(b) Dod's *Peerage and Baronetage*, 1858. It has been stated that the Law Officers of the Crown reported against the claim on the ground of there being no clause of Knighthood in the patent of the Baronetcy.

(c) *Dict. Nat. Biogr.*

(d) James Broun, Royal Engineers, the 1st s., *d.* unm. and v.p. 31 Jan. 1872, on board H.M.S. "Jumna," aged 28.

PATERSON:

cr. 16 March 1685/6;(a)

forfeited 1716.

I. 1686. "HUGH PATERSON, of Bannockburn," presumably s. of Hugh PATERSON, of Bannockburn, sometime Writer to the Signet, by Elizabeth (*m.* 18 Aug. 1654, at Edinburgh), da. of Sir Thomas KER, of Fernyhurst, was *cr. a Baronet* [S.], as above, 16 March 1685/6,(a) with rem. to heirs male whatsoever. He *m.* Barbara, da. of Sir William RUTHVEN, of Dunglass. He *d.* Oct. 1696, *or* 21 Dec. 1701.(b)

II. 1696? to 1716. SIR HUGH PATERSON, Baronet [S. 1686], of Bannockburn, *b.* Jan. 1686, presumably s. and h.; *suc. to the Baronetcy* in 1696, or 1701, and, as a Baronet, was, in 1708, unduly elected M.P. for Stirlingshire but unseated in 1709, being, however, M.P. thereof (three Parls.) 1710-15; Commissioner of Trade [S.], 1711; joined in the Jacobite rising of 1715 and was attainted, whereby the *Baronetcy* became *forfeited* in 1716. He entertained Prince Charles Edward at Bannockburn house, 14 Sep. 1745, who made it his headquarters in Jan. 1745/6.(c) He *m.* 2 March 1711/2, at Twickenham, Midx., Jean, only da. of Charles (ERSKINE), EARL OF MAR [S.], by Mary, da. of George (MAULE), 2d EARL OF PANMURE [S.]. She *d.* 16 Nov. 1763, at Bannockburn. He *d.*, at Touch, 23 March 1777, aged 91 years and 2 months.(d)

MYLNE, *or* MILNE:

cr. 19 March 1685/6;

extinct or *dormant* 11 May 1791.

I. 1686. "ROBERT MYLNE [*or* MILNE], of Barnton," co. Dumfries, was *cr. a Baronet* [S.], as above, "by patent or diploma dated at Whitehall,"(e) 19 March 1685/6, with rem. to heirs male whatsoever.

* * * * * * *

II? 1730? SIR JOHN MYLNE, Baronet [S. 1686], of Barnton aforesaid, possibly grandson and h., *b.* about 1701; was Captain of Invalids, and *d.* 11 May 1791, aged 90. Will pr. June 1791. At his death the *Baronetcy* is presumed to have become *dormant* or *extinct.*(f)

(a) Milne's *List*; the date in the *Lists* of Chamberlayne and Miege is 6 March 1686, and that in the *Scottish Antiquary* (iv, 141) is 29 March 1686.

(b) In "the Masterton papers" [*Scot. Hist. Soc. Miscellany*] mention is made [p. 472] of the death of "Sir Hugh Paterson" in Oct. 1696, as also [p. 476] of the death of the "Laird of Bannockburn" on 21 Dec. 1701. Presumably the same person is indicated, but possibly the latter may have been the successor of the former.

(c) Anderson's *Scottish Nation*, in which, however, Lady Jean Erskine, is called, "mother" (not "wife") of Sir Hugh. It is there added that "Sir Hugh's granddaughter is said to have been privately *m.* to the Prince, but she released him to promote the Stuart cause."

(d) He left an only son, Hugh Paterson, who *m.* Elizabeth Seton, heiress of Touch, and *d.* s.p. [Wood's *Douglas' Peerage of Scotland*, under "Mar."]

(e) Nisbet's *Heraldry*, vol. ii, p. 127 (1816).

(f) In Playfair's *Baronetage* [S.], 1811, no account of the Baronetcy of Mylne is given, though in vol. iii, on p. 291, there is a reference to the appendix "for the account of this ancient family," in which, however, *no* account is given. In Burke's *Baronetage* for 1841 mention is made of "Sir John Milne, of Barnton, co. Dumfries," and it is stated that he "*is* [but *Qy.* if it should not read *was*, some fifty years before that date] the representative" of the 1st Baronet.

INNES:

cr. 20 March 1685/6;(a)

extinct or *dormant* 1882.

I. 1686. "ALEXANDER INNES, of Coxtoun," s. and h. of James INNES, who was s. of John INNES, of Coxtoun, by (—), da. and h. of (—) GORDON, of Rothiemay, by his wife the heiress of the family of BARCLAY, of Towie,(b) was M.P. [S.] for Elgin and Forresshire, 1685-86, and was *cr. a Baronet* [S.], as above, 20 March 1685/6, with rem. to heirs male whatsoever. He having inherited the Towie estate, formerly that of his maternal ancestors, took the name of BARCLAY in lieu of INNES.(c) He apparently *d.* s.p.m. before 20 Jan. 1736, when Jean BARCLAY was served heir to her father, "SIR ALEXANDER BARCLAY, of Towie, Baronet."(d)

The devolution of the Baronetcy on the heir male seems somewhat uncertain, but apparently was as under:—

II? 1730? SIR JOHN INNES, Baronet [S. 1686], of Aberdeen, apparently heir male, *suc. to the Baronetcy* possibly as early as 1730. He *m.* (—). He *d.* 30 Oct. 1768, at Aberdeen.(d)

III? 1768. SIR JAMES INNES, Baronet [S. 1686], of Coxtoun aforesaid, s. and h., *b.* about 1715; *suc. to the Baronetcy,* 30 Oct. 1768. He *m.* (—). She *d.* 16 Oct. 1786. He *d.* June 1790, aged 75.(e)

IV? 1790? SIR DAVID INNES, Baronet [S. 1686], apparently heir male, possibly s. and h. of above, *suc. to the Baronetcy,* probably in June 1790. He was *bur.* 8 Oct. 1803, at St. James', Westm. Will pr. (as a Baronet) 1803.

V? 1803? SIR DAVID INNES, Baronet [S. 1686], of Edinburgh, apparently heir male, was s. of George INNES, Inspector Gen. of Stamp Duties (*d.* March 1790), by (—), da. of Sir James INNES, of Colstoun; was *b.* 1781, at Parkside, Edinburgh; was sometime an officer in the 98th Foot; *suc. to the Baronetcy* possibly in 1803, but certainly before 1842.(f) He *m.* in 1833, Mary Anne, da. of (—) WILLIAMSON, of Stewarton, co. Ayr. He *d.* 1866, at Edinburgh. His widow living 1882.(g)

(a) Milne's *List*, but the date in that of Chamberlayne is 22 March 1686.

(b) Playfair's *Baronetage*, 1811, vol. iii, p. 236 *bis* [*rectius* p. 292], under "Berkeley, now Barclay."

(c) "Sir Alexander Innes, in right of his mother, who was an heiress, succeeded to the estate and name of Towie Barclay, and calls himself Innes, *alias* Barclay, of Towie" [*Innes family* (Spalding Club), p. 257].

(d) See vol. ii, p. 338, note "f," as to the admon., 2 Nov. 1769, of "Dame Isabel Innes, of Killswell, co. Aberdeen, widow," who possibly may be a widow of this Baronet.

(e) "James Innes, Capt. in the Army, 1st son of Sir James Innes, Baronet, near Aberdeen," *d.* v.p. 5 Aug. 1781.

(f) He appears in Dod's *Baronetage* of 1842; but in that of the previous year no account is given of this Baronetcy.

(g) Dod's *Baronetage*, 1882. She is not in that of 1883.

VI? 1866, to 1882. SIR GEORGE INNES, Baronet [S. 1686], of Park Villas, Richmond, co. Surrey, only s. and h., *b.* 1834, in Brandon street, Edinburgh; sometime Lieut. 22d Bombay Native Infantry, retiring 1859; Adjutant 5th Lanarkshire Rifle Volunteers, 1860-65; *suc. to the Baronetcy* in 1866; Capt. Hants Militia, 1870; Musketry Instructor, 1871. He *m.* firstly in 1855 (—), only surv. da. of William Colquhoun STIRLING, of Law and Edinbarnet. She *d.* 1864. He *m.* secondly, in 1865, Elsie, widow of J. W. HENDERSON, K.H., Major 50th Foot, da. of H. WATTS, of the Grove, near Bath. He *d.* s.p. in 1882, when the *Baronetcy* became *dormant* or *extinct*. His widow living 1904.(a)

GORDON :(b)

cr. 21 Aug. 1686;

assumed, wrongfully, 1782—1804;

dormant or *extinct*, 23 July 1835.

I. 1686. "JOHN GORDON, of Park," co. Banff, s. and h. of SIR JOHN GORDON,(c) of Park aforesaid, by Helen, da. of Sir James SIBBALD, 1st Baronet [S. 1630], of Rankeillour, was fined £1,200 in 1662 (when his father was fined £3,000), *suc.* his said father about 1672, registered arms soon afterwards, and was *cr. a Baronet* [S.], as above, 21 Aug. 1686, with rem. to heirs male whatsoever. He *m.* firstly, (—), da. of (—) GRAHAM, younger s. of (—) GRAHAM, of Claverhouse. He *m.* secondly, [Jean ?], da. of [Walter ?] FORBES, of Tolquhoun, co. Aberdeen. He *m.* thirdly, Katherine, da. of (—) OGILVIE, of Kempcairn. By these three wives he had no male issue. He *m.* fourthly, 3 March 1686, Helen, da. of James (OGILVY), 2d EARL OF AIRLIE [S.], by his 1st wife Helen, da. of George (OGILVY), 1st LORD BANFF [S.]. He *d.* Feb. 1713.

II. 1713. SIR JAMES GORDON, Baronet [S. 1686], of Park aforesaid, s. and h., by 4th wife, *suc. to the Baronetcy* in Feb., and had spec. service to his father 28 April 1713. He executed an entail of the Barony of Park on 19 Oct. following. He *m.* firstly, Helen, 1st da. of William (FRASER), LORD SALTOUN [S.], by Margaret, da. of James SHARPE, Archbishop of St. Andrews. He *m.* secondly, about 1720, Margaret, widow of George, Count LESLIE, of Balquhain, da. of John (ELPHINSTONE), 8th LORD ELPHINSTONE [S.], by Isabel, da. of Charles (MAITLAND), 3d EARL OF LAUDERDALE [S.]. He *d.* of apoplexy at Pool Wells, on the way to Aberdeen, 15 Dec. 1727. His widow *m.* John FULLERTON, of Dudwick.

(a) Dod's *Baronetage*, 1904.

(b) Much of the information in this article was supplied by the late R. R. Stodart, Lyon Clerk Depute, 1863-86, and by J. M. Bulloch, author of "*The House of Gordon*." See p. 327, note "a."

(c) This John, in 1631, suc. his father, Sir Adam Gordon (*Knighted* 1618), who bought the estate of Park from Lord Saltoun [S.] in 1600, which Adam was 2d s. of John Gordon, of Cairnbarrow, co. Banff, who was descended from "Jock" Gordon, of Sundargue, illegitimate cousin of Elizabeth Gordon, who married Alexander Seton, and was ancestress of the Earls and Marquesses of Huntly and of the Dukes of Gordon [S.].

III. 1727. SIR WILLIAM GORDON, Baronet [S. 1686], of Park aforesaid, s. and h., only s. by 1st wife, *suc. to the Baronetcy* on the death of his father, 15 Dec. 1727, to whom he was served heir general, 23 April 1728. He joined the Jacobite rising of 1745, and was attainted," but the attainder was afterwards reversed,"(a) apparently in his lifetime. To save the estate, however, he had made it over to his half br., Capt. John GORDON, who contrived to keep possession of it, though the Court had decided that though Sir William's life interest was forfeited, on his death the next heir male of entail would be entitled. He escaped to France, and became Lieut.-Col. of Ogilvie's regiment in the service of that kingdom. He also served the Emperor of Germany, and had recognition of nobility in Hungary. He *m.* 1745, Janet, da. of William (DUFF), 1st EARL FIFE [I.], by his 2d wife, Jean, da. of Sir James GRANT, *or* COLQUHOUN, 6th Baronet [S. 1625]. He *d.* at Douay, 5 June 1751. His widow *m.* George HAY, of Mountblairy, co. Banff, and *d.* 3 March 1758.

IV. 1751. SIR JOHN JAMES GORDON, Baronet [S. 1686], 1st s. and h., *b.* at Boulogne in France, 26 March 1749; *suc. to the Baronetcy* (but to no estate), 5 June 1751; entered the Royal Legion of France, 1774, but afterwards joined the East India Company's service. He *m.* in India, Hannah, da. of T. CORNER, of Middlesex. He *d.* 11 Dec. 1780, aged 31, being slain at the siege of Bassein, on the coast of Malabar, in India, leaving a son as mentioned below. His widow *d.* in Sloane street, Chelsea, 28 Jan. 1792. Admon. March 1798.

[Shortly (*i.e.* two years) after the death of the 4th Baronet in India, the fact of his having left an infant s. and h., was ignored, and the title was assumed as under].

V. bis 1782. SIR ERNEST GORDON, Baronet [S. 1686],(b) of Park aforesaid, and of Cobairdy, co. Aberdeen, s. and h. of James GORDON, of Cobairdy, by Mary, da. of James (FORBES), 15th LORD FORBES [S.], which James GORDON, was yr. br. to Capt. John GORDON abovenamed, of Park aforesaid, both being sons of the 2d Baronet by his 2d wife. He was *b.* about 1745; *suc.* his father, May 1773, in the estate of Cobairdy, and *suc.* his said uncle Sep. 1781, in the estate of Park,(c) being served, 12 Feb. 1782, his heir of entail and provision general, and also (though erroneously) heir male general of his great grandfather, Sir John GORDON, 1st Baronet [S. 1686], of Park aforesaid, after which service he *assumed the Baronetcy*, and on 25 Sep. 1782, was served (as Sir Ernest GORDON, Baronet), h. of entail special of the Barony of Park. He *m.* Mary, da. of General Robert DALRYMPLE-HORN-ELPHINSTONE, of Logie Elphinstone and Westall. He *d.* at Park, 5 Nov. 1800, aged 55. His widow *d.* at Edinburgh, 3 July 1812.

VI. 1800, to 1804. SIR JOHN GORDON, Baronet [S. 1686],(b) of Park aforesaid, only s. and h.; *suc. to the Baronetcy*,(b) 5 Nov. 1800, and had services to his father, 11 and 31 March 1801. He *d.* s.p., 10 June 1804, at Rothbury, co. Northumberland, when the (wrongful) assumption of the Baronetcy ceased.(d)

(a) Playfair's *Baronetage* [S.], 1811.

(b) According to the (erroneous) service, 12 Feb. 1782.

(c) The estate of Park had been made over to this John Gordon by the 3d Baronet. See in text.

(d) His only sister Mary Elizabeth, was, 27 Feb. 1807, served his heir special of lands in the parish of Insch, which had devolved on their grandfather, James GORDON, from the family of LESLIE, of Balquhain. She *d.* unm. The estate of Park appears to have followed the entail of 1813. It is now (1878) held by Lachlan Duff GORDON-DUFF, s. of Lachlan DUFF (afterwards Lachlan GORDON, of Park aforesaid), who was s. and h. of John DUFF, of Culbin, co. Moray (who *d.* 1767), by Helen, sister, of the whole blood, of the 3d Baronet. The heir general would appear to be among the issue of Richard CREED, of London (*d.* 1867), by Jessy Hannah, only sister of Sir John Bury Gordon, the 5th and last Baronet.

V. 1780, to 1835. SIR JOHN BURY GORDON, Baronet [S. 1685], only s and h. of Sir John James GORDON, 4th Baronet, by Hannah, his wife, both abovenamed, *b.* 5 April 1779, in India, his birth being ignored by his cousin Ernest GORDON, of Park, who assumed the Baronetcy in 1782, as above stated. He *suc. to the Baronetcy*, 11 Dec. 1780, in his 2d year; was sometime Capt. in the 13th Light Dragoons, and subsequently (1828), Major in the 15th Hussars. He, in 1826, raised a regiment for the Nizam of Hyderabad, now known as (Gordon's Horse) the 30th Lancers. He *m.* 9 Jan. 1798, Pyne, da. of Hon. Maurice CROSBIE, Dean of Limerick, by Pyne, da. of Sir Henry CAVENDISH, 1st Baronet [1755]. In 1806 she was divorced.(a) He *m.* secondly, Sep. 1815, Margaret Erskine, 4th da. of Richard CAMPBELL, of Craigie, co. Ayr. He *d.* s.p., at Madras, 23 July 1835, aged 56, when the issue male of the 1st Baronet is presumed to have failed, and the *Baronetcy* became *dormant* or *extinct*. His widow *m.* 1836, Gerhardt Anthonie VAN BARNEVELD, in whose lifetime she *d.* in London 13 Jan. 1867.

KINLOCH :

cr. 16 Sep. 1686.

I. 1686. "FRANCIS KINLOCH, of Gilmerton," s. of Andrew KINLOCH, a merchant of Rochelle, purchased the estates of Gilmerton, Athelstaneford and Markle, all in co. Haddington, having a charter of Markle, 24 July 1664; was a Commissioner of Supply; was, before 1674, Lord Provost of Edinburgh; M.P. [S.] for Edinburghshire, 1678, and was *cr. a Baronet* [S.], as above, 16 Sep. 1686, with rem. to heirs male of the body. He *m.* Magdalen, da. of (—) MACMATH, of Newbyres. She *d.* 16 Nov. 1674, aged 59, and was *bur.* in the Greyfriars, Edinburgh. M.I. He was *bur.* there, 17 Dec. 1691.

II. 1691. SIR FRANCIS KINLOCH, Baronet [S. 1686], of Gilmerton aforesaid, only s. and h., had a charter of Gilmerton from his father, 3 March 1680; *suc. to the Baronetcy* in Dec. 1691, and was served heir to his father 5 Feb. 1692. He *m.* in or before 1676, Mary (*b.* 1656), da. of David (LESLIE), 1st LORD NEWARK [S.] (the famous General) by Jean, da. of Sir John YORKE. He was *bur.* 11 Sep. 1699, at Greyfriars aforesaid. His widow *m.* 18 Jan. 1702, as his 2d wife, Sir Alexander OGILVY, 1st Baronet [S. 1701], of Forglen, a Lord of Session (who *d.* 1727), and *d.* at Edinburgh, 24 March 1748, in her 93d year.

III. 1699. SIR THOMAS KINLOCH, Baronet [S. 1686], of Gilmerton aforesaid, 1st s. and h., *bap.* at Edinburgh, 23 June 1676; *suc. to the Baronetcy* in Sep. 1699, and was served heir of his father 16 Nov. following. He *m.* in or before 1705, his cousin, Mary, sister and (in 1737) coheir of Sir James ROCHEAD, 1st Baronet [S. 1704], da. of Sir James ROCHEAD, of Innerleith, co. Edinburgh, Town Clerk of Edinburgh, by Magdalen, da. of Sir Francis KINLOCH, 1st Baronet [S. 1686]. He *d.* 2 March 1747, aged 70. She *d.* at Gilmerton, 2 April 1749, and was *bur.* at Athelstaneford.

IV. 1747. SIR JAMES KINLOCH, Baronet [S. 1686], of Gilmerton aforesaid, 1st s. and h.,(b) *bap.* 8 Aug. 1705 at Athelstaneford aforesaid, *suc. to the Baronetcy*, 2 March 1747. He *m.* April 1730, Margaret,

(a) For *crim. con.* with Hon. Henry Otway Brand, afterwards (1851) Lord Dacre, who was mulcted in £3,000 damages. They were subsequently *m.* 24 July 1806. See *Peerage*.

(b) Alexander Kinloch, the 4th and yst. s., took his mother's name of Rochead, inherited Inverleith (the estate of that family), and *d.* 11 May 1755, leaving issue.

2d da. of William FOULIS, of Woodhall. She, it is presumed, *d.* within eighteen months, as he *m.* (subsequently) 9 Oct. 1731, at Pormy, near Berne,(a) in Switzerland, Anne Marguerite, da. of Jean Rodolphe WILD, of Berne, by Anne Barbille IMHOFF. She, by whom he had eleven children, was living May 1751. He *d.* 25 March 1778, at Giez, in Switzerland, aged 72.(b)

V. 1778. SIR DAVID KINLOCH, Baronet(c) [S. 1686], of Gilmerton aforesaid, br. and h. male,(c) *b.* about 1710; *suc. to the Baronetcy*(c) 25 March 1778; was Writer to the Privy Seal, and was, in 1749, Commissioner of Fisheries, as also Governor of the British Linen Company. He *m.* 16 Jan. 1746, Harriett, da. of Sir Archibald COCKBURN, 7th Baronet [S. 1627], of Langton, by Mary (*m.* 1719), da. of John (CAMPBELL), 1st EARL OF BREADALBANE [S.]. She *d.* 29 July 1757.(d) He *d.* 18 Feb. 1795, aged 85.

VI. 1795, Feb. SIR FRANCIS KINLOCH, Baronet(c) [S. 1686], of Gilmerton aforesaid, 1st s. and h., *b.* about 1747; was endowed with great mechanical talent; *suc. to the Baronetcy*,(c) 18 Feb. 1795, but *d.* unm.(e) a few months later, 16 April 1795, in his 48th year.

VII. 1795, April. SIR ARCHIBALD GORDON KINLOCH, Baronet(c) [S. 1686], of Gilmerton, br. and h.; was a Major in the Army; *suc. to the Baronetcy*,(c) 16 April 1795. He *d.* unm. 1800.

VIII. 1800. SIR ALEXANDER KINLOCH, Baronet(f) [S. 1686], of Gilmerton aforesaid, br. and h., Collector of Customs at Preston Pans; *suc. to the Baronetcy*(f) in 1800. He *m.* 20 June 1801, Isabella, da. and coheir of John STOWE, of Newton, co. Lincoln. He *d.* 12 Feb. 1813. His widow *d.* 10 March 1861, at Nice, aged 88.

IX. 1813. SIR DAVID KINLOCH, Baronet [S. 1686], of Gilmerton aforesaid, only s. and h., *b.* there 1 Sep. 1805; *suc. to the Baronetcy*, 12 Feb. 1813. He *m.* 5 June 1829, Eleanor Hyndford, 1st da. of Sir Thomas

(a) The marriage, April 1730, of James Kinloch, eldest s. of Sir Francis Kinloch, of Gilmerton, with Margaret, 2d da. of William Foulis, of Woodhall, is recorded in the "Foulis of Ravelston account book," [*Scott. Hist. Soc.*, p. lxix.]

(b) See "Descendants of Sir James Kinloch, [the 4th] Baronet, by Henry Wagner, F.S.A. [*Genealogist*, N.S., vol. xiv, pp. 200-203].

(c) Presuming that James Kinloch, yst. and only surv. s. of James, the 4th Baronet (by Anne Marguerite Wild), was not entitled to succeed to his father's dignity. He was *bap.* 29 Jan. 1748/9, at Yverdon, was a Burgess of Cronay and Giez; *m.*, 28 Dec. 1791, Marianne Esther, da. of (—) Berdez (who *d.* his widow 13 June 1812), and *d.* s.p., being *bur.* 22 Oct. 1802 at Yverdon. His non-assumption of the Baronetcy certainly throws some doubt on the validity of his mother's marriage, but the issue thereof was recognised by the parents of the father, whose mother, "Noble Marie Kinloch, neé de Rochead," was, in 1732, sponsor to the 1st child, and whose father (the 4th Baronet) was sponsor, in 1733, to the 2d child," etc. (See note "b" above.) The explanation for this non-succession given in Playfair's *Baronetage* [S.] is hardly satisfactory, viz., "The children not being naturalised in Great Britain were incapable of succession," for, even allowing this statement to be true, such incapacity would not entitle the next heir to inherit the Baronetcy.

(d) She "was considered for mind, manners, and personal beauty as unequalled in her time. On this lady's death an elegant tribute was paid to her memory which we cannot omit inserting." Here follows 132 lines of verse (Playfair's *Baronetage*, 1811.)

(e) He is said to have been shot by his brother and successor, Archibald, who was tried for the murder in 1795, but acquitted as insane. See p. 242, note "c."

(f) See note "c" above, but on the death s.p. in Oct. 1802, of James Kinloch, there would be no doubt of the right of this Alexander to the Baronetcy, as heir male of the body of the grantee.

GIBSON-CARMICHAEL, 7th Baronet [S. 1702], by Janet, da. of Major Gen. Thomas DUNDAS, of Fingask. She *d.* at Edinburgh 15 Oct. 1849. He *d.* at Gilmerton, 23 Feb. 1879, aged 73.

X. 1879. SIR ALEXANDER KINLOCH, Baronet [S. 1686], of Gilmerton aforesaid, only s. and h., *b.* 1 Feb. 1830, at Castle Craig, co. Peebles; ed. at Eton; sometime Captain in the Grenadier Guards, serving with them in the Crimean War (medal, four clasps and Turkish medal) 1854-56; *suc. to the Baronetcy*, 25 Feb. 1879. He *m.* 12 Aug. 1852, Lucy Charlotte, 1st da. of Sir Ralph Abercromby ANSTRUTHER, 4th Baronet (S. 1694), of Balcaskie, by Mary Jane, da. of Major-Gen. Sir Henry TORRENS, K.C.B. She *d.* 14 Nov. 1903, at Kilduff, aged 70.

Family Estates.—These, in 1883, consisted of 2,846 acres in Haddingtonshire, worth £7,673 a year. *Seat.*—Gilmerton, co. Haddington.

CALDER(a):

cr. 5 Nov. 1686;

ex. or *dorm.* 14 May 1887.

I. 1686. "JAMES CALDER, of Muirton," in the parish of Kinloss, co. Moray, only surv. s. of Thomas CALDER, of Sheriffmill, near Elgin (which he purchased 29 Jan. 1639), Provost of Elgin, 1665-67, was Merchant Burgess and Councillor of Elgin, M.P. [S.] thereof, 1669-72, and for Elgin in Forres-shire, 1685-86; was in 1678 infeft of all his father's lands, and having purchased, before 1682, the estate of Muirton, was *cr. a Baronet* [S.], as above, the privy seal being dated at Whitehall, 5 Nov. 1686, with rem. to heirs male whatsoever. From his fidelity to James II (to whom, shortly before his deposition, he, as joint receiver of the customs of Scotland, paid a large sum which was re-demanded of him by the ensuing Government), he suffered much loss and was compelled to part with all the estates, though that of Muirton when sold in 1710 was subject to the life residence therein of his widow. He *m.*, in or before 1682, Grizel, da. of Sir Robert INNES, 2d Baronet [S. 1625], of Innes, by Jean [*not* Mary], da. of James (Ross), 5th LORD ROSS OF HALKHEAD [S.]. He *d.* in 1711. His widow continued to reside at Muirton till her death in 1742. Both were *bur.* in Elgin Cathedral.

II. 1711. SIR THOMAS CALDER, Baronet [S. 1686], 1st s. and h., *b.* 6 June 1682, at Muirton; *suc. to the Baronetcy*, but to none of the estates, in 1711; was implicated in the Jacobite rising of 1715, but, though imprisoned, was never attainted. He *m.* 7 Dec. 1711, at Edinburgh (contract 28 and 31 March 1712), Christian, da. of Sir John SCOTT, 1st Baronet [S. 1671], of Ancrum, by his 2d wife, Elizabeth, da. of Sir William BENNETT, Baronet [S. 1670], of Grubet. She, who was *b.* at Ancrum, 16 March 1688, and by whom he had twelve children, *d.* at Elgin 1743, and was *bur.* there. He *d.* at Edinburgh, and was *bur.* in Canongate there 31 Jan. 1760, in his 78th year.

III. 1760. SIR JAMES CALDER, Baronet [S. 1686], of Park House, near Maidstone, co. Kent, 1st s. and h., *b.* 10 Oct. 1712, at Muirton; ed. abroad, and resided many years at Leyden; purchased the estate of Park House abovenamed, and *suc. to the Baronetcy* Jan. 1760. He *m.* firstly, Feb. 1735, Alice, da. and coheir of Admiral Robert HUGHES. She *d.* 18 April

(a) Much information about this family (especially as to their earlier ancestry) will be found in some letters inserted in the copy of Douglas' *Baronage* [S.] which is in the Mitchell Library of Glasgow. They were written in 1800 by Amelia, wife of Sir Robert Calder, Baronet [1797], a yr. s. of Sir James Calder, 3d Baronet [S. 1686].

1768, and was *bur.* at Deptford. He *m.* secondly, 6 Oct. 1768, at St. Geo. Han. sq., Catharine, widow of Wentworth ODIARNE, Serjeant at Arms to the House of Commons, da. and coheir of (—) CAMEN, of Thetford, Norfolk. He *d.* at Bayswater house, Midx., 19 Sep. 1774, aged 62, and was *bur.* at Deptford. Will dat. 9 May 1771, pr. 6 Oct. 1774. His widow, by whom he had no issue, *d.* 26 Oct., and was *bur.* 6 Nov. 1776 at Deptford, aged 76. Will dat. 25 March, pr. 13 Nov. 1776.

IV. 1774. SIR HENRY CALDER, Baronet [S. 1686], of Park House aforesaid, 2d but 1st surv. s. and h.,(a) *b.* probably about 1740, entered the Army, becoming finally Major-General, Col. of the 30th Foot, and Lieut. Gov. of Gibraltar; *suc. to the Baronetcy*, 19 Sep. 1774. He *m.* firstly (settlement 1 March 1767), Elizabeth, yst. da. and coheir of Augustine EARLE, of Heydon, Norfolk. She *d.* s.p. Will dat. 2 May, pr. 9 June 1786. He *m.* secondly, 18 Jan. 1789, at St. Marylebone, Louisa, da. of Admiral Henry OSBORNE. He *d.* 3 Feb. 1792, at Bath. Admon. Feb. 1793. His widow living 1800.

V. 1792. SIR HENRY RODDAM CALDER, Baronet [S. 1686], of Park House aforesaid, only s. and h., *b.* there 15 March 1790, and *bap.* at Maidstone; *suc. to the Baronetcy*, in his 2d year, 3 Feb. 1792. He *m.* 3 Aug. 1819, Frances Selina, 4th da. of Edmond Henry (PERY), 1st EARL OF LIMERICK [I.], by Mary Alice, da. and h. of Henry ORMSBY, of Cloghan, co. Mayo. She, who was *b.* 30 July 1795, *d.* 11 June 1855, at Rutland square, Edinburgh, aged 65. Admon. Dec. 1855. He *d.* 13 Aug. 1868, at 43 Prince's Gardens, aged 78.

VI. 1868, to 1887. SIR WILLIAM HENRY WALSINGHAM CALDER, Baronet [S. 1686], only surv. s. and h., *b.* 14 Sep. 1821; *suc. to the Baronetcy*, 13 Aug. 1868. He *m.* in 1842, Julia, 1st da. of Julius HUTCHINSON, of Manor Vill, Tunbridge Wells, Kent. She *d.* 10 Dec. 1875. He *d.* s.p. 14 May 1887, aged 65, when the *Baronetcy* became *extinct* or *dormant*.

INGLIS(b):

cr. 22 March 1686/7;

ex. or *dorm.* 24 Nov. 1817.

I. 1687. "JAMES INGLIS, of Cramond," co. Edinburgh, 2d but only surv. s. and h.(c) of John INGLIS, of Cramond (*bur.* 1 April 1686, at Greyfriars, Edinburgh, aged 74), by Janet (*m.* 12 June 1632), da. of John ELLIS, of Southside, was *b.* 17 May 1660 ("28 years after his parents' marriage")(b) and was, within a year after his father's death, *cr. a Baronet* [S.], as above, 22 March 1686/7, with rem. to heirs male whatsoever. He *m.*, 31 Oct. 1682, Anne, 2d da. of Sir Patrick HOUSTON, 1st Baronet [S. 1668], of Houston, by Anne, da. of John (HAMILTON), 1st LORD BARGENY [S.]. He was *bur.* 6 Dec. 1688 at Greyfriars aforesaid, aged 28. His widow *m.*, 30 Sep. 1700, Sir William HAMILTON, of Whitelaw, a Lord of Session, under the style of *Lord Whitelaw*

(a) Thomas Calder, the 1st son, *d.* unm. and v.p., being lost on board the *Namur* (man-of-war) in the East Indies. The 4th and yst. son, Sir Robert Calder, K.C.B., *cr. a Baronet*, 22 Aug. 1798 (a dignity which became *extinct* 31 Aug. 1818, at his death), was a distinguished Admiral. His services are set forth at great length in above three closely printed pages in Playfair's *Baronetage* [S.] 1811, under his father's [S.] Baronetcy.

(b) Many particulars of this family are from J. P. Wood's *Parish of Cramond*.

(c) The elder son John Inglis (who would have been a good deal senior to the Baronet) was "a youth of promising parts, who *d.* of a fever at Paris, 20 June 1664," unm. and v.p. [Playfair's *Baronetage*, 1811].

and (1704) Lord Justice Clerk, who *d.* 14 Dec. 1704. She *m.* (as her 3d husband and his 2d wife) Adam COCKBURN, of Ormistoun, a Lord of Session under the style of *Lord Ormistoun* and Lord Justice Clerk, who *d.* 16 April 1735. She *d.* at Cramond, 18 Jan. 1721 and was *bur.* there.

II. 1688. SIR JOHN INGLIS, Baronet [S. 1687], of Cramond aforesaid, only s. and h., *b.* 23 Sep. 1683; *suc. to the Baronetcy* in Dec 1688. He *m.* Anne, da. of his step father, the abovenamed Adam COCKBURN, by his 1st wife, Susan, da. of John (HAMILTON), 4th EARL OF HADDINGTON [S.]. He *d.*, "without suffering as much as one day's confinement by sickness,"(a) 3 March 1771, aged 87. His widow *d.* 23 Nov. 1772, and was *bur.* at Cramond.

III. 1771. SIR ADAM INGLIS, Baronet [S. 1687], of Cramond aforesaid, 2nd but 1st surv. s. and h., *b.* 21 Oct. 1714; admitted Advocate, 1736; studied the Law at Leyden Univ.; *suc. to the Baronetcy*, 3 March 1771. He *m.* 22 Nov. 1766, at Barnbougle castle, Dorothea, 2d and yst. da. of James (PRIMROSE), 2d EARL OF ROSEBERY [S.], by Mary, da. of the Hon. John CAMPBELL, of Mamore. He *d.* s.p. at Cramond, 9 Nov. 1772, aged 58. She *d.* at Bath, 3 Dec. 1783. Will pr. Feb. 1784.

IV. 1772. SIR JOHN INGLIS, Baronet [S. 1687], of Cramond, br. and h., *b.* probably about 1716; was sometime a merchant and Dep. Barrack Master for Scotland; *suc. to the Baronetcy*, 9 Nov. 1772, and devoted himself much to the improvement of his estate. He *m.* in or before 1760, Christian, da. of Sir Robert SINCLAIR, 3d Baronet [S. 1664], of Longformacus, by Christian, da. of Adam COCKBURN abovenamed, L. Justice Clerk. She *d.* 15 July 1790, at Cramond. He *d.* s.p.m.s.(a) 5 April 1799. Will pr. June 1799.

V. 1799, to 1817. SIR PATRICK INGLIS, Baronet [S. 1687], of Cramond aforesaid, br. and h. male, *suc. to the Baronetcy*, 5 April 1799. He *d.* unm. 24 Nov. 1817 at Edinburgh, when the *Baronetcy* became *extinct* or *dormant*.

SHAW, *or* SCHAW:

cr. 28 June 1687;(b)

ex. 5 April 1732.

I. 1687. SIR "JOHN SHAW [*or* SCHAW], of Greenock," co. Renfrew, s. and h. of John SHAW, *or* SCHAW, of the same, sometime M.P. [S.] for Renfrewshire, by Helen, da. of John HOUSTON, of Houston, was in 1651 Lieut.-Col. of Dunfermline's Horse, and distinguished himself in the Royal cause at the battle of Worcester, 3 Sep. 1651, where he was *Knighted*; was M.P. [S.] for Renfrewshire, 1669-74, 1678, and 1681-82, and, having suc. his father in 1679, was *cr. a Baronet* [S.], as above, the Privy Seal being dat. at Windsor, 28 June 1687,(b) with rem. to heirs male of the body. He *m.* firstly, Jean (by whom he had six children), da. of Sir William MUIR, of Rowallan. He *m.* secondly, Janet, da. of (—) SCOTT. He *d.* at Edinburgh 16 and was *bur*

(a) His only son, Adam Inglis, of Southfield, was called to the Bar in 1782, but *d.* unm. and v.p. 1 Sep. 1794, aged 34. His only da., Anne, *m.* 6 April 1795, James (Sandilands), 9th Lord Torpichen [S.], who *d.* s.p. 7 June 1815, aged 55, and was apparently living as his widow in 1828.

(b) "Diploma of the title and dignity of Knight Baronet conferred by King James VII [S.] on Sir John Shaw of Grinock and the heirs male of his body. Windsor, 28 June 1687." Among the Laing Charters in the Univ. of Edinburgh. See Calendar No. 2857.

28 April 1693, in the Abbey Church of Holyrood. Funeral entry at Lyon Office.(a) His widow, as "Dame Janet SCOTT, relict of Sir John SHAW, of Groomnoch, aged about 70," was *bur.* 8 Feb. 1719, at Grey Friars, Edinburgh.

II. 1693. SIR JOHN SHAW, *or* SCHAW, Baronet [S. 1687], of Greenock aforesaid, only s. and h., *suc. to the Baronetcy*, 16 April 1693, and was by precept, 18 April 1694, infeoffed as heir of his father. He was "one of His Majesty's Principal Tacksmen for the Customs and Excise" [S.](b) He *m.* Eleanor, 1st da. (whose issue became coheir) of Sir Thomas NICOLSON, 2d Baronet [S. 1637], of Carnock, co. Stirling, by Margaret, da. of Alexander (LIVINGSTONE), 2d EARL OF LINLITHGOW [S.]. He *d.* suddenly at Edinburgh, April 1702.(c)

III. 1702, to 1752. SIR JOHN SHAW, *or* SCHAW, Baronet [S. 1687], of Greenock aforesaid, s. and h., *suc. to the Baronetcy* in April 1702; was M.P. for Renfrewshire, 1708-10; for Clackmannanshire, 1722-27, and for Renfrewshire, again, 1727-34. He *m.* 15 March 1700 (contract 1 March), Margaret, 1st da. of the Hon. Sir Hugh DALRYMPLE, 1st Baronet [S. 1698], of North Berwick, sometime President of the Court of Session, by his 1st wife, Marion, da. of Sir Robert HAMILTON, of Pressmennan. He *d.* s.p.m.(d) 5 April 1752, when the *Baronetcy* became *extinct*.(e) His widow, who was *b.* 6 March 1683, *d.* 8 Oct. 1757, aged 74.

PATERSON:(f)

cr. 2 July 1687;(g)

dormant, 14 Jan. 1782.

possibly ex., 14 May 1789,

I. 1687. "SIR WILLIAM PATERSON, Clerk of Council,"(g) 3d s. of John PATERSON, Bishop of Ross [1662-79], by Elizabeth, da. of (—) RAMSAY, was *b.* about 1630; was Advocate Regent of Philosophy in the Univ. of Edinburgh, 1667; Clerk of the Privy Council, 1679; was *Knighted* about 1680, and was *cr. a Baronet* [S.], as above, 2 July 1687,(g) with rem. to heirs male

(a) This was in error applied to "Sir John *Skeane*" in vol. ii, p. 345. See "Skeane."

(b) He is so described in an elegy "on the much to be lamented death (17 April 1702) of the Rt. Hon. Sir John Shaw, of Greenock, Knt.," in *Scotish Elegiac Verses* (ed. 1842), p. 144.

(c) Masterton Papers, p. 477.

(d) Marion, his only surv. child and heir, *b.* 7 Dec. 1700 at Edinburgh, *m.* as his 1st wife, 29 March 1718, at St. Mary Mag., Old Fish street, London, Charles (Cathcart), 8th Lord Cathcart [S.], and *d.* 21 March 1733, being ancestress of the later peers, who, afterwards, in commemoration of this descent, became *Barons Greenock* and Viscounts Cathcart, in 1807, being Earls Cathcart in 1811. These, however, who represented the house of Shaw of Sauchie, though they inherited Sauchie and other estates, did not inherit the estate of Greenock, which (by settlement) passed on the death of the 3d Baronet, in 1752, to the heirs of his sister, Lady Houston. See note "e" below.

(e) His five yr. brothers all *d.* unm., no less than four of them (Alexander, George, Hugh, and Thomas) being killed in the wars in the Low Countries. Margaret, the only married sister, was mother, by Sir John Houston, 3d Baronet [S. 1668], of Helena, who *m.* Sir Michael Stewart, 3d Baronet [S. 1667], and had issue who inherited the estates of Greenock and Carnock, formerly those of the Shaw and Nicolson families, and who, in 1752, took the name of Shaw before that of Stewart. See p. 262.

(f) See p. 242, note "c."

(g) The date and description are those given in Milne's *List* and in Stodart's MS. (see note "a" above). The date of 28 July 1687 is given in Chamberlayne's and Miege's *List*, as also in the list of James R. Anderson (see p. 242, note "a"), where the grantee is described as "William Paterson, of Eccles."

whatsoever. In 1688 he bought the estate of Grantoun, co. Edinburgh. He *m.*, about 1670, Alison, da. of (—) HAMILTON. She was *bur.* 10 Aug. 1698, at the Grey Friars, Edinburgh.(a) He *d.* at Leith, 29 Sep. 1709.(b)

II. 1709. SIR JOHN PATERSON, Baronet [S. 1687], of Eccles, co. Berwick, s. and h., *b.* 11 April 1673: *suc. to the Baronetcy*, 29 Sep. 1709; sold the estate of Grantoun shortly afterwards, and altered, 22 Oct. 1755, the entail of the estate of Eccles. He *m.* 11 Sep. 1703, Margaret, 1st da. of Sir William ELIOTT, 2d Baronet [S. 1666], of Stobs, by Margaret, da. of Charles MURRAY, of Haldon. He *d.* 14 Dec. 1759.

III. 1759, to 1782. SIR JOHN PATERSON, Baronet [S. 1687], of Eccles aforesaid, grandson and h., being s. and h. of John PATERSON, by Margaret, da. of Sir William SETON, 2d Baronet [S. 1684], of Pitmedden, which John (who *d.* v.p. in or before 1743) was s. and h. ap. of the late Baronet. He *suc. to the Baronetcy*, 14 Dec. 1759, and was served, 6 May 1760, heir gen. of his grandfather. He was M.P. for Berwickshire, 1779-80. He *m.* 2 Oct. 1755, at Redbraes, co. Edinburgh, Anne, *de jure* (10 Jan. 1794) *suo jure* BARONESS POLWARTH(c) [S.], da. of Hugh (HUME-CAMPBELL), 3d EARL OF MARCHMONT and LORD POLWARTH [S.], by his 1st wife, Anne, da. and coheir of Robert WESTERN, of London. He *d.* s.p.m.(d) at Bath, 14 Jan. 1782, when the *Baronetcy* became *dormant*. His widow *d.* at Newcastle, 27 July 1790, aged 56.

[The heirs male *of the body* of the grantee were probably extinct in 1782, but those of the grantee's *father* undoubtedly existed till 1789. Among these was:—

JAMES PATERSON-SINCLAIR, of Dysart, co. Fife, only s. and h. of John PATERSON, of Preston Hall, co. Fife (one of the Jacobite insurgents in 1715), by Grizel, da. and coheir of Henry (SINCLAIR), 7th LORD SINCLAIR [S.], which John, was s. and h. of John PATERSON (the well known) Archbishop of Glasgow (1687-1708), who was eldest br. of the 1st Baronet. He, in Nov. 1762, on the death of his maternal uncle, suc. to the Sinclair estates, and took the name of SINCLAIR, after that of PATERSON. Failing any nearer heir male,(e) he would have *suc. to the Baronetcy*, on the death of the 3d Baronet, 14 Jan. 1782. He *d.* unm., at Dysart, 14 May 1789, when the issue male of the grantee's father became probably *extinct*.(f)]

(a) Not long after her death he, in 1700, at the age of nearly 70, was publicly rebuked by the Kirk Session of Cramond for having begotten in fornication a bastard child of one Mary Miller.

(b) Masterton papers (*Scottish Hist. Soc. Miscellany*, vol. i, p. 483).

(c) The Barony of Polwarth [S.] was allowed in 1835 to Hugh Scott, s. and h. of her younger sister, Diana.

(d) Anne, his da. and h., inherited the estate of Eccles and *m.* there, 17 Feb. 1778, Philip Anstruther, M.P. for Anstruther Easter Burghs 1774-78, who, about 1782, took the name of Paterson, and who on the death of his father, 4 July 1799, suc. him as 4th Baronet [S. 1700] of Anstruther. He *d.* s.p. 5 Jan. 1808, the estate of Eccles having been already sold. His widow, who, in 1818, claimed the Barony of Polwarth [S.], *d.* s.p. 11 March 1822.

(e) As to these heirs male, the 3d Baronet had three brothers, *viz.*, William and Robert, both living 1743, and Capt. Alexander Paterson, who *d.* 20 Feb. 1763. The 2d Baronet had two younger sons, viz., James and Alexander, both living in 1743. There were three surviving brothers of the 1st Baronet, viz. (1) Robert Paterson, next youngest, Regent of Marischal College, Aberdeen, living about 1673; (2) George Paterson, of Innerwhinnery, co. Ross, the next eldest, living 1685, who had two sons, viz., John Paterson, his heir male and of provision, 30 Aug. 1698, and Robert Paterson, of Innerwhinnery, 1704; (3) John Paterson, Archbishop of Glasgow, abovenamed, eldest brother of the grantee.

(f) His uncle, Col. Alexander Paterson, 2d and yst. s. of the Archbishop, left a son John Paterson, who was M.P. and Chairman of Committees of Ways and Means. He *d.* in 1789 in his 85th year.

STEUART, *or* STEWART:

cr. 15 Aug. 1687;

dormant 29 Jan. 1849.

I. 1687. "ROBERT STEWART [*or* STEUART], of Allanbank," co. Berwick, 7th and yst. s.(a) of Sir James STEWART, *or* STEUART, of Kirkfield and Coltness, co. Lanark, Lord Provost of Edinburgh (*d.* 31 March 1681), by his 1st wife, Anne, sister of Sir Thomas HOPE, 1st Baronet [S. 1628], of Craighall, was *b.* 1643; was a merchant at Leith, and, having purchased the estate of Allanbank, was *cr. a Baronet* [S.], as above, 15 Aug. 1687, with rem. to heirs male whatsoever. He was M.P. [S.] for North Berwick, 1698-1702. He *m.* firstly, in 1682, Jean, sister of Sir Alexander GILMOUR, 1st Baronet [S. 1678], da. of Sir John GILMOUR, of Craigmillar, President of the Court of Session. He *m.* secondly, in 1692, Helen, da. of Sir Alexander COCKBURN, of Langton, co. Berwick. He *d.* 1707.

II. 1707. SIR JOHN STEUART, Baronet [S. 1687], of Allanbank aforesaid, 1st s. and h. by 1st wife, *b.* about 1685; *suc. to the Baronetcy* and was served heir to his father in 1707. He *m.* Margaret, da. of John KERR, of Morriston. He *d.* 19 May 1753, aged 68.

III. 1753. SIR JOHN STEUART, Baronet [S. 1687], of Allanbank aforesaid, 1st s. and h., *b.* 1714; admitted an Advocate, 1737; *suc. to the Baronetcy*, 19 May 1753; Sheriff of Berwickshire, 1755; Solicitor for the Stamp Duties [S.]. He *m.* 9 Oct. 1750 (settlement 13 March 1752), Margaret Agnes, sister of Hugh SMITH, *otherwise* SETON, da. of Charles SMITH, of Boulogne, wine merchant. She *d.* 23 Sep. 1807, in her 79th year. He *d.* 7 Oct. 1796, in his 82d year.

IV. 1796. SIR JOHN STEUART, Baronet [S. 1687], of Allanbank aforesaid, 1st s. and h., *b.* 1754; *suc. to the Baronetcy*, 7 Oct. 1796. He *m.* 16 Sep. 1778, his cousin, Frances, da. of James COUTTS, of Hampton and Whitsom Hill, Banker of London (M.P. for Edinburgh, 1762-68), by Polly PEAGRIM, his wife, which James was s. of John COUTTS, Provost of Edinburgh, by Jean, da. of Sir John STEUART, 2d Baronet [S. 1686]. She *d.* at Flushing, co. Cornwall, 26 Oct. 1809.(b) He *d.* 1817, aged 63.

V. 1817, to 1849. SIR JOHN JAMES STEUART, Baronet [S. 1687], of Allanbank aforesaid, 1st s. and h., *b.* at Rome 1779; *suc. to the Baronetcy* in 1817. He *m.* firstly, Elizabeth, only da. of Elborough WOODCOCK. She *d.* 5 Oct. 1828. He *m.* secondly, 1 June 1835, at Edinburgh, Katharine, 2d da. of Alexander MUNRO, M.D., of Craiglockart, Professor of Anatomy in the Univ. of Edinburgh. He *d.* s.p., 29 Jan. 1849, at his house in Edinburgh, aged 70, when the *Baronetcy* became *dormant*.

HALL:

cr. 8 Oct. 1687.

I. 1687. "JOHN HALL, of Dunglass,"(c) co. Haddington, generally said to be only s. and h. of Robert HALL, of Dunglass

(a) Of his elder brothers, (1) Thomas Steuart, of Coltness, was *cr. a Baronet* [S.], 29 Jan. 1698, while (2) Sir James Steuart, of Goodtrees, Lord Advocate 1692 and 1711, was father of James Steuart, of Goodtrees, *cr. a Baronet* [S.] v.p. 22 Dec. 1705.

(b) See Playfair's *Baronetage* (1811) as to her "many virtues," and her "pious and exemplary life."

(c) "Dunglass is the spot made famous by Sir Walter Scott, in *The Bride of Lammermoor*, under the name of *Ravenswood*. The real story occurred in Wigtonshire" [*Ex inform.*, Lieut. E. M. Mackenzie].

aforesaid, by Helen, da. of David CRICHTON, of Longtoun,(a) but who apparently was s. of John HALL, by Janet, da. of (—) HIGGINS, was *cr. a Baronet* [S.], as above, 8 Oct. 1687, with rem. to heirs male whatsoever. He was Lord Provost of Edinburgh, and was M.P. [S.] thereof 1689 till his death in 1696, being Præses of the Edinburgh Committee for taking the oaths of the members of the Universities to the confession of faith, etc. He *m.* firstly, Catherine, widow of John MEIN, of Craigcrook (whom she *m.* 16 Feb. 1662), da. of James LOCH, of Drylaw.(b). She was *bur.* 13 Nov. 1690, in the Greyfriars, Edinburgh. He *m.* secondly, Margaret, da. of George FLEMING, of Kilconquhar, by Margaret, da. of Stephen PHILIP, of Philipton. He was *bur.* 18 Oct. 1695, in the Greyfriars aforesaid.

II. 1695. SIR JAMES HALL, Baronet [S. 1687], of Dunglass aforesaid, s. and h. by 1st wife; *suc. to the Baronetcy* in Oct. 1695. He *m.* firstly, in 1698, Anne, 3d da. of Patrick (HUME), 1st EARL OF MARCHMONT [S.], by Grizel, da. of Sir Thomas KER, of Cavers. She, who was *b.* 4 Nov. 1677, *d.* s.p. at the Dean, near Edinburgh, 24, and was *bur.* 30 Jan. 1699.(c) He *m.* secondly, Margaret, da. of Sir John PRINGLE, 2d Baronet [S. 1683], of Stichell, by Magdalen, da. of Sir Gilbert ELIOTT, 1st Baronet [S. 1666], of Stobs. He *d.* 27 March 1742. His widow *d.* 9 April 1756, at a great age.

III. 1742. SIR JOHN HALL, Baronet [S. 1687], of Dunglass, s. and h., by 2d wife; *suc. to the Baronetcy*, 27 March 1742, and was one of the grand jury at Edinburgh for the trial of the Jacobite insurgents of 1745. He *m.* 16 Oct. 1759, Magdalen, 2d da. of his maternal uncle, Sir Robert PRINGLE, 3d Baronet [S. 1683], by Catharine, da. of James PRINGLE, of Torwoodlee, co. Selkirk. She *d.* 8 June 1763. He *d.* 3 July 1776.

IV. 1776. SIR JAMES HALL, Baronet [S. 1687], of Dunglass aforesaid s. and h., *b.* 17 Jan. 1761; ed. at Christ's College, Cambridge; *suc. to the Baronetcy*, 3 July 1776; Vice-President of the Soc. of Antiquaries [S.] 1798, and F.R.S.; M.P. for St. Michael's, in Cornwall, 1807-12. He *m.* 9 Nov. 1786, at St. Mary's Isle, near Kirckudbright, Helen, 2d da. of Dunbar (DOUGLAS, *formerly* HAMILTON), 4th EARL OF SELKIRK [S.], by Helen, da. of the Hon. John HAMILTON. He *d.* 23 June 1832, at Edinburgh, aged 72.(d) His widow *d.* there 12 July 1837, aged 76.

V. 1832. SIR JOHN HALL, Baronet [S. 1687], of Dunglass aforesaid, 1st s. and h.,(e) *b.* 16 Sep. 1787, in Edinburgh; *suc. to the Baronetcy*, 23 June 1832. He *m.* 23 Jan. 1823, Julia, da. of James WALKER, of Dalry, in Midlothian, by his 2d wife, Marion Anne, da. of John HOPE, M.D. He *d.* 2 April 1860, at 63 Lowndes square, aged 72. His widow *d.* there 3 Oct. 1874, aged 74.

VI. 1860. SIR JAMES HALL, Baronet [S. 1687], of Dunglass aforesaid, 1st s. and h., *b.* 1824; *suc. to the Baronetcy*, 2 April 1860. He *d.* unm. 1 May 1876, aged 52.

(a) Playfair's *Baronetage* (1811), etc., but, *per contra*, in Stodart's *Scottish Arms* (ii, p. 385) it is stated that "From the funeral escotcheon of Sir James Hall, 2d Baronet, of Dunglas, the 1st Baronet was son of John Hall and Janet Higgins, his wife, and her mother was a Goodlet."

(b) Wood's *Cramond*, p. 161.

(c) "The pleasantest, sprightliest young lady I ever knew" [Diary of George Home].

(d) Author of an "Essay on Gothic Architecture," 1813, and other treatises.

(e) His next br. Capt. Basil Hall, R.N. (*b.* 31 Dec. 1788) was the author of *Voyages and Travels*, *Schloss Hainfeld*, etc. He *d.* 11 Sep. 1844.

VII. 1876. SIR BASIL FRANCIS HALL, Baronet [S. 1687], of Dunglass aforesaid, br. and h., *b.* 1 June 1832, at Edinburgh; *suc. to the Baronetcy*, 1 May 1876. He *m.* 10 March 1877, Adelaide Catherine, da. of Robert Kerr ELLIOT, of Harwood and Clifton, co. Roxburgh.

Family Estates.—These, in 1883, consisted of 7,948 acres in Berwickshire and 887 in Haddingtonshire. *Total.*—8,835 acres, worth £10,187 a year. *Seat.*—Dunglass, near Dunbar.

STEWART:(a)

cr. 4 Nov. 1687;

dormant 24 Aug. 1746.

I 1687. "ARCHIBALD STEWART, of Burray," in Orkney, 4th but last surv. s. of William STEWART, of Mains, in Galloway, by Barbara, da. and h. of James STEWART, of Burray aforesaid, which William was only br. to Alexander, 1st EARL OF GALLOWAY [S.], was in Hamilton's army, 1648, for the rescue of the King, being afterwards in that of Montrose; held a command at the battle of Worcester, and was taken prisoner; was in 1683 Lieut.-Col. of the Orkney militia, and, having suc. his elder br., William STEWART, in the estates of Mains and Burray, was *cr. a Baronet* [S.], as above, with rem. to heirs male whatsoever, the Privy Seal being dated 4 Nov. 1687, at Whitehall.(a) He *m.* firstly, Isabel, da. of Sir William MURRAY, of Abercairny. She *d.* 3 Aug. 1683.(b) He *m.* secondly, a few weeks later, 16 Sep. 1683, his maidservant, Katharine, da. of Patrick ROWSAY, indweller in Stronsay.(b) She *d.* in childbed s.p.m., 26 June 1684.(b) He *d.* at Burray 13, and was *bur.* there 17 May 1689.(b)

II. 1689. SIR ARCHIBALD STEWART, Baronet [S. 1687], of Burray aforesaid, 1st s. and h., *suc. to the Baronetcy*, 13 May 1689; was M.P. [S.] for Orkney and Zetland, 1702-07. He *m.* Margaret, 1st da. of the Hon. Archibald STUART, of Dunearn, co. Fife (yr. s. of James, EARL OF MORAY [S.]), by [—], da. of Sir John HENDERSON, of Fordel. He *d.* 1704. His widow *m.* David (LESLIE), 5th LORD LINDORES [S.] (who *d.* s.p. July 1719), and *d.* a few months after him, Oct. 1719.

III. 1704, to 1746. SIR JAMES STEWART, Baronet [S. 1687], of Burray aforesaid, 1st s. and h.; *suc. to the Baronetcy* on the death of his father, in 1704. He *m.* Anne, 1st da. of David CARMICHAEL, of Balmeady. He *d.* s.p. a prisoner, under suspicion of high treason,

(a) See Nisbet's *Heraldry* (1816), vol. ii, p. 162, app., for an account of this family.

(b) The following interesting extracts (kindly furnished by James R. Anderson, of Glasgow, see p. 242, note "a") illustrate this race, of whom very little seems known. They are from *The Diary of Thomas Brown, Writer in Kirkwall, 1675-1693*, published at Kirkwall, 1898, 8vo:—

1683 Aug. 3. "Fryday's morning: Issobell Murray, spous to Archibald Stewart, of Burray, depairted this lyff" (p. 26).

1683 Sep. 16. "Sabbath night, about ten houres or yrby., Archibald Stewart, of Burray was meried to Katherine Rowsay his servatrix and da. to Patrick Rowsay, indweller in Stronsay" (p. 27).

1684 June 6. "Fryday's night, Katherine Rowsay, the Lady Burray, was browght to bed of a woman chyld" (p. 31).

1684 June 26. "Wedinsday's night, about twelff or yrby, the above namit Katherine Rowsay depairted this lyfe" (p. 31).

1689 May 13. "Munday's morning, betwixt twa and thrie or thairby, Archibald Stewart, of Burray, depairted this life, in his manner house of Burray and was intered in the Kirk yrof upon Friday the 17th instant" (p. 54).

in the new gaol, Southwark, 24 Aug. 1746, when the issue male of the grantee expired, and the *Baronetcy* became *dormant*.(a) His widow *d.* 19 Jan. 1779. Will recorded 25 Sep. 1779, in the Commissariot Court at Edinburgh.

THRIEPLAND, *or* THREIPLAND:

cr. 10 Nov. 1687;
forfeited in 1715;
restored 26 May 1826;
dormant, or *extinct*, 30 April 1882.

I. 1687. SIR "PATRICK THRIEPLAND, of Fingask," co. Perth, s. of Andrew THRIEPLAND, Burgess of Perth (1628), was a Merchant Trafficker of Perth; Treasurer, 1657; Baillie, 1659-62; Dean of Guild, 1661; Provost, 1664-69, 1671-75, 1676-77, and 1687; was M.P. [S.] for Perth, 1661-63, 1665, 1667 and, 1669-74; purchased the estate of Fingask in 1672; was *Knighted* in 1674, and was *cr. a Baronet* [S.], as above, the Privy Seal being dat. at Whitehall, 10 Nov. 1687, with rem. to heirs male whatsoever. He *m.* 13 March 1665, Euphemia, da. of John CONQUEROR, of Frierton. He *d.* 1689, after 18 Feb., being then a prisoner in Stirling Castle.

II. 1689, to 1715. SIR DAVID THRIEPLAND, Baronet [S. 1687], of Fingask aforesaid, only s. and h.; *suc. to the Baronetcy* in 1689. He took an active part in the Jacobite rising of 1715, and was consequently attainted, whereby the *Baronetcy* was *forfeited* and his estates annexed to the Crown. He *m.* firstly, in 1688, Elizabeth, 1st da. of Sir John RAMSAY, 2d Baronet [S. 1666], of Bamff, by his 1st wife Christian, da. of Sir Thomas OGILVIE, and by her had seven sons and three daughters. He *m.* secondly, in 1707, Catharine, widow of [—] WILLIAMSON, a merchant of Perth, 1st da. of David SMITH, of Barnhill, by his 2d wife, Barbara, da. of Alexander BRUCE, of Cultmalindy. He *d.* 1746. His widow *d.* 18 March 1762, at Fingask, aged 83.

> The Baronetcy was assumed, notwithstanding the attainder of 1715, as under(b):—
>
> *III. 1746.* SIR STUART THRIEPLAND, Baronet [S. 1687],(c) 9th and yst., but only surv. s. and h. by 2d wife, *b.* 26 May 1716; joined the Jacobite rising of 1745 and escaped to France, returning however after the act of indemnity, having *suc. to the Baronetcy*(c) in 1746. He was a member of the College of Physicians at Edinburgh, of which he was President, 4 Dec. 1766. He repurchased the estate of Fingask in 1782. He *m.* firstly, 5 March 1753, at St. Paul's, Edinburgh, Janet, 1st da. of David SINCLAIR, of Southdun, co. Caithness. He *m.* secondly, 19 Aug. 1761, at St. Paul's aforesaid, Janet BUDGE-MURRAY, spinster, of Pennyland and Toftingall, co. Caithness, da. of William BUDGE. He *d.* 2 Feb. 1805, at Fingask, aged 88.

(a) The heirs male, who apparently are entitled to the Baronetcy, are the Earls of Galloway [S.], and, accordingly, 24 June 1747, the then Earl was served heir to Sir Archibald Stewart, of Burray.

(b) No mention whatever is made of such attainder in Playfair's *Baronetage* (1811), the successor to the 2d Baronet being therein called "Sir Stuart Thriepland, the 3d Baronet," though it is stated that his eldest son (who suc. him 2 Feb. 1805) "Patrick Murray Thriepland, of Fingask, Esq., has not taken up the title."

(c) According to the assumption of the Baronetcy notwithstanding its forfeiture in 1715.

IV. 1805. III. 1826. SIR PATRICK MURRAY THRIEPLAND, *or* THREIPLAND, Baronet [S. 1687], of Fingask aforesaid, 2d but 1st surv. s. and h., being 1st s. by 2d wife, *b.* Nov. 1762; admitted Advocate, 31 July 1784; *suc. to the Baronetcy*,(a) 2 Feb. 1805, but did not assume the [forfeited] title till (the Royal assent having been given 25 April 1826), the attainder of his grandfather in 1715 was repealed by act of Parl., 26 May 1826,(b) and he was consequently *restored "to the dignity of a Baronet."* He *m.* 27 March 1792, Jessy Murray, da. of William Scott KERR, of Chatto, co. Roxburgh. He *d.* 11 Jan. 1837, aged 74. His widow *d.* 19 Jan. 1855, aged 87.

IV. 1837, to 1882. SIR PATRICK MURRAY THREIPLAND, Baronet [S. 1687], of Fingask aforesaid, only surv. s. and h., *b.* 26 May 1800, at Edinburgh; *suc. to the Baronetcy*, 11 Jan. 1837; sometime Major of the Perthshire militia, retiring in 1843. He *d.* unm. at Fingask Castle, 30 April 1882, in his 82d year, when the *Baronetcy* became *dormant*, or *extinct*.

LAUDER:

cr. 17 July and sealed 10 Aug. 1688;
cancelled 19 Feb. 1692.(c)

I. 1688, to 1692. "JOHN LAUDER [called 'late Baillie in Edinburgh'],(d) of Idington," co. Berwick, but better known as of Fountainhall, co. Haddington, having purchased the estate of Idington from the impoverished father of his 3d wife, Margaret (*m.* 15 Feb. 1670), da. of George RAMSAY, of Idington aforesaid, settled the same on his issue by that wife, and was *cr. a Baronet* [S.], 17 July 1688, with a spec. rem. (to the exclusion of his issue male by his former wives) to his son George RAMSAY and other the heirs male of his body by this marriage.(e) His eldest son, however, Sir John LAUDER (a Lord of Session [1689] under the style of *Lord Fountainhall*), considering such limitation to be unjust, obtained a new creation, dated 25 Jan. 1690, whereby (his father) the said grantee (then designated as "of Fountainhall") was *cr. a Baronet* [S.] with rem. to the heirs male of his body. The creation of 17 July 1688 was annulled by decree of Privy Council, 19 Feb. 1692, and the sons therein indicated were forbidden to assume the title

(a) See p. 356, note "c."

(b) By the same act the Earldoms of Wemyss, Airlie and Carnwath and the Barony of Duffus [S.], which were under similar attainder, were restored.

(c) *Ex inform.* R. R. Stodart, late (1863-86) Lyon Clerk Depute, who also supplied many other particulars of this family.

(d) Milne's *List.*

(e) He "with a view of gratifying his [3d] wife's vanity and ambition obtained in 1688 the honour of a Baronetcy, but, not satisfied with this distinction she succeeded in having the destination of the grant appropriated to his son [by the 3d marriage] George or [other] the heirs male of [the grantee's body by] Margaret Ramsay, his present spouse. [Sir John Lauder, *styled*] Lord Fountainhall [his eldest son], conceiving that such a destination, passing over himself and his brothers of the 2d marriage, was unjust, obtained on 16 May an order of Privy Council that the patent should remain in the Clerk's hands until it was rectified. Although this was done with her husband's sanction, she nevertheless contrived, by misrepresenting his eldest son, Sir John, as disaffected to the late Government, to have the patent [in favour] of her son George passed under the Great Seal on the 17th of July 1688. Having brought an action of reduction of this patent, a new charter conferring on John Lauder, Senior, of Fountainhall, whom failing to his eldest son, the title and dignity of a Knight Baronet was obtained 25 Jan. 1690." [Lord Fountainhall's *Historical Notices of Scottish Affairs*, Bannatyne Club, 1848 (Preface), edited by David Laing].

created by it.(a) The grantee *d.* (soon afterwards) in April 1692, in his 97th year. See fuller particulars below, under "LAUDER" Baronetcy [S.], *cr.* 25 Jan. 1690.

> The Baronetcy was, however, assumed, as below, under the limitation of the patent of 17 July 1688, notwithstanding its having been annulled on 19 Feb. 1692.
>
> *II. 1692, to 1700?* SIR GEORGE LAUDER, Baronet [S. 1688], of Idington aforesaid, younger s. of the grantee,(b) being 1st s. by his 3d wife, *b.* 31 May 1673; *assumed the Baronetcy* (notwithstanding the creation thereof had been annulled) in April 1692, on the death of his father, under the annulled patent of 17 July 1688, and was styled "Baronet" in certain acts of Parl. 1696.(c) He inherited the estate of Idington under his father's settlement. He *d.* s.p. in or before 1700, when the *assumption of the Baronetcy ceased.*(d)

GRANT:(e)

cr. 10 Aug. 1688.

I. 1688. "JAMES GRANT, of Dalvey," in the parish of Cromdale, co. Elgin, as also of Gartenbeg, in the parish of Dathel, s. and h. of Sweton GRANT, of Gartenbeg aforesaid, by (—), da. of (—) FARQUHARSON, of Inverey, was Advocate and Solicitor Gen. [S.] to James II, and having purchased the estate of Dalvey, was *cr. a Baronet* [S.], as above, 10 Aug. 1688, with rem. to heirs male whatsoever. For his fidelity to that King he was imprisoned, 15 May 1689, in the Tolbooth, Edinburgh. He *m.* (contract 8 April 1687), Agnes, sister of Walter, EARL OF TARRAS [S.], 3d da. of Sir Gideon SCOTT, of Highchester, co. Roxburgh, by Margaret, da. of Sir Thomas HAMILTON, of Preston. He *d.* s.p. legit. 1695. His widow *m.* Dr. William RUTHERFORD, of Barnhills.

II. 1695. LUDOVIC GRANT, of Dalvey aforesaid, br. and h., *suc. to the Baronetcy* (as heir male) in 1695, and was retoured heir gen. and heir special in Dalvey to his br., 14 May 1695. He, however, probably from political motives, *did not assume the Baronetcy.* He *d.* s.p. legit. 4 Jan. 1701.

III. 1701. SWETON GRANT, of Dalvey aforesaid, 2d cousin and h. male, being s. and h. of Duncan GRANT, s. and h. of Donald GRANT, yr. br. of John GRANT, of Gartenbeg, grandfather of the 1st Baronet, the said John and Donald being sons of Duncan GRANT, who first settled at Gartenbeg. He *suc. to the Baronetcy* (as heir male) 4 Jan. 1701, and was retoured heir spec. to his cousin, Ludovic GRANT, in the estate of Dalvey, 24 Feb. 1701 (which, however, he sold in that year to his wife's brother), but *did not assume the Baronetcy.* He *m.* Margaret, da. of Donald GRANT, of Inverlaidnan.

(a) "The original, partly burnt, with the seal torn off is in the possession of the family." See p. 357, note "c."

(b) The legitimacy of the three children by the 3d wife of the grantee, who was 75 when he married her, is questionable. His s. and h., Lord Fountainhall, states that his termagant stepmother was over intimate with her cousin, Ramsay, of Witstoun. See p. 357, note "c."

(c) See p. 357, note "c."

(d) He was suc. in the estate of Idington by his only surv. brother of the full blood, Archibald Lauder, *b.* 16 May 1679, who however does not appear to have assumed the Baronetcy. He *d.* s.p. Feb. 1704, when the heirs to the Baronetcy of 1688 became extinct, and the estate was inherited by his only sister, Elizabeth (*b.* 25 Oct. 1676), who *m.* John Cunningham, of Woodhall, co. Edinburgh, and had issue.

(e) Many of the particulars in this article have been kindly supplied by F. J. Grant, Rothesay Herald and Lyon Clerk. See also p. 242, note "c."

IV. 1752. SIR PATRICK GRANT, Baronet [S. 1688],(a) of Inverlaidnan, co. Inverness, cousin and h. male, being s. and h. of Donald GRANT, of the same, by Mary, da. of Lieut.-Col. Patrick GRANT (yr. s. of Sir John GRANT, of Grant), which Donald was s. and h. of John GRANT, s. and h. of John GRANT, s. and h. of Sweton GRANT, all of Inverlaidnan aforesaid, the said Sweton being 3d s. of Duncan GRANT, who first settled at Gartenbeg and who was ancestor of all the previous Baronets. He, who was *b.* about 1655, and who is said to have been at one time a barber,(b) was served heir male general to Sir James GRANT, the 1st Baronet, 22 Aug. 1752, and consequently *assumed the Baronetcy*, the estates, however, having been alienated. He *m.* Lydia, sister of Brig. Gen. MACKINTOSH, da. of William MACKINTOSH, of Borlum, co. Inverness. He *d.* 10 April 1755, in his 101st year, at his son's house, called Dalvey, formerly Grangehill, co. Elgin.

V. 1755. SIR ALEXANDER GRANT, Baronet [S. 1688],(a) of Dalvey, formerly Grangehill, co. Elgin, 1st s. and h.; acquired a large fortune in the West Indies; purchased the estate of Grangehill in 1749, and other lands in the parish of Dyke, co. Elgin (to which he gave the name of Dalvey), and *suc. to the Baronetcy*,(a) 10 April 1755. In 1758 he purchased the estate of Kincarth, also in the said parish of Dyke. He was also of Bookham Grove, in Leatherhead, co. Surrey. Had a grant of supporters from the Lyon Office, 8 July 1761; was M.P. for the Inverness burghs, 1761-68. He *m.* Elizabeth, da. of Robert COOKE, of Jamaica. He *d.* s.p. in Great George street, Westm., 1 Aug. 1772. Will pr. Nov. 1772. His widow *d.* 30 July 1792, aged 75.

VI. 1772. SIR LUDOVIC GRANT, Baronet [S. 1688],(a) of Dalvey and Grangehill aforesaid, only br. and h., *suc. to the Baronetcy*,(a) 1 Aug. 1772, and was served heir gen. to his br. 5 May 1773, and heir special in Dalvey, etc., 16 March 1774, "cum beneficio inventarii." He *m.* Margaret, da. of Sir James INNES, 5th Baronet [S. 1628], of Balveny, by Margaret, da. of Thomas FRASER, of Cairnbiddie. She *d.* 12 March 1782. He *d.* 17 Sep. 1790, at Moy Hall, co. Inverness.

VII. 1790. SIR ALEXANDER GRANT, Baronet [S. 1688],(a) of Dalvey aforesaid, 1st s. and h., *b.* probably about 1750; *suc. to the Baronetcy*,(a) 17 Sep. 1790, and sold the estate of Dalvey. He *m.* 13 July 1775, Sarah, da. and h. of Jeremiah CRAY, of Ibsley, Hants, by Sarah, sister of Sir James COLEBROOKE, of Chilham Castle, Kent. She *d.* at Paris, 4 Feb. 1803. He *d.* in London, 26 July 1825. Will pr. Sep. 1825.

VIII. 1825. SIR ALEXANDER CRAY GRANT, Baronet [S. 1688],(a) 1st s. and h., *b.* 30 Nov. 1782, at Bowrings Leigh, Devon; ed. at St. John's Coll., Cambridge; B.A., 1803; M.A., 1806; was M.P. for Tregony, 1812-18; for Lostwithiel (two Parls.), 1818-26; for Aldborough, co. York, 1826-30; for Westbury, 1830-31; for Cambridge town, 1840 and 1841-43, having *suc. to the Baronetcy*,(a) 26 July 1825; was Chairman of Committees of the House of Commons, 1826-32; Member of the Board of Control for India, 1834-35, and a Commissioner for auditing the public accounts (salary £1,200 a year), 1843 till death. He *d.* unm. 29 Nov. 1854, on the eve of his 72d birthday. Will pr. Jan. 1855.

IX. 1854. SIR ROBERT INNES GRANT, Baronet [S. 1688],(a) yst. but only surv. br. and h., being 3d s. of the penultimate Baronet, *b.* 8 April 1794, at Malsanger, Hants; *suc. to the Baronetcy*,(a) 29 Nov. 1854. He *m.* 17 Dec. 1825, Judith Towers, 1st da. of Cornelius Durant BATTELE, of the island of St. Croix, in the West Indies. He *d.* 1 Aug. 1856, aged 62. His widow *d.* 6 March 1884, aged 79, at her son's house, 21 Lansdowne crescent, Edinburgh.

(a) According to the service of 22 Aug. 1752.

(b) Among the Jury on this service were "Alexander Grant, Barber," and "Daniel Grant," Tailor," both probably relatives. See p. 242, note "c."

X. 1856. SIR ALEXANDER GRANT, Baronet [S. 1688],(a) 1st s. and h.,(b) b. at New York 23 Sep. 1826; ed. at Harrow School; matric. at Oxford (Balliol Coll.), 30 Nov. 1844, aged 18; Scholar, 1844-49; B.A. and 2nd class classics, 1848; Fellow of Oriel Coll., 1849-60, being Hon. Fellow in 1882; M.A., 1852; Examiner for India Civil Service, 1855; *suc. to the Baronetcy*,(a) 1 Aug. 1856; Examiner in Classical School, Oxford, 1857; Inspector of Schools in Madras Presidency, 1858; Professor of History, etc., in Elphinstone College, 1860; Principal thereof, 1862; Vice-Chancellor of the Univ. of Bombay, 1863; Director of Public Instruction, 1865, and member of the legislative Council in that Presidency, 1868; Principal and Vice-Chancellor of Edinburgh Univ., 1868 till death in 1884; and member of the Board of Education [S.], 1872-78. He was also Hon. LL.D. of Edinburgh Univ., 1865; of Glasgow Univ., 1879, and D.C.L. of Oxford Univ., 9 June 1880. He *m.* 2 June 1859, at St. Andrew's, Scotland, Susan, 2d da. of James Frederick FERRIER, Professor of Moral Philosophy, etc., of that Univ. He *d.* 30 Nov. 1884, at 21 Lansdowne crescent, Edinburgh, aged 58. His widow *d.* 20 March 1895, at St. Andrews, aged 54.

XI. 1884. SIR LUDOVIC JAMES GRANT, Baronet [S. 1688],(a) 2d but 1st surv. s. and h., *b.* at Bombay 4 Sep. 1862; matric. at Oxford (Balliol Coll.), 18 Oct. 1881, aged 19; Exhibitioner, 1881-86; B.A., 1886; having *suc. to the Baronetcy*(a) 30 Nov. 1884; admitted Advocate, 1887; Regius Professor of Public Law, etc., at Edinburgh Univ., 1890. He *m.* 17 July 1890, Elizabeth Ethel Graham, 1st da. of Henry Hill LANCASTER, of Edinburgh, Advocate.

CREATIONS BY WILLIAM III AND MARY II, AS ALSO BY WILLIAM III ALONE.

13 Feb. 1688/9(c) to 8 March 1701/2.

LAUDER:(d)

cr. 25 Jan. 1690;

afterwards, in 1769, LAUDER-DICK;

and subsequently, DICK-LAUDER.

I. 1690. "JOHN LAUDER, of Fountainhall," in the parish of Pencaithland, co. Haddington, s. of Andrew LAUDER,(e) of Edinburgh, merchant, by Janet,(f) da. of David RAMSAY, of Hillhead, near Lasswade, was *bap.* 17 Aug. 1595; acquired a large fortune as a merchant and Burgess of Edinburgh; was Treasurer of that city, 1652; Baillie, 1657-61. He purchased before 1672 (about which time he registered arms at the Lyon office) the estate of Newington, near Edinburgh, and subsequently, 10 June 1681, other estates (Woodhead, Templehall, etc.) in the counties of Haddington and Edinburgh, which by Crown charter, 13 Aug. 1681, were created into the Barony of Fountainhall. He was *cr. a Baronet* [S.], 17 July 1688, with a spec. rem. of that dignity (at the instigation of his 3d wife) to his issue male by his then wife. This patent, however, was cancelled 19 Feb. 1692. See fuller account thereof under 17 July 1688, on pp. 357-358. He was again *cr. a Baronet* [S.], as above, 25 Jan. 1690, with rem. to his eldest son in tail male and his heirs male successively. He *m.* firstly, 20 Nov. 1639, Marion, *or* Margaret, SPEIRS, by whom he had two sons, who *d.* young. She *d.* 1643. He *m.* secondly, 17 July 1645, Isabel, da. of Alexander ELLIS, of Mortonhall, near Edinburgh, by Margaret, da. of Nichol UDWART, Dean of Guild. By her he had fourteen sons. He *m.* thirdly (at the age of 75), 15 Feb. 1670, Margaret, da. of George RAMSAY, of Idington, co. Berwick, by whom he had three sons who were next in remainder to the Baronetcy [S.] conferred on him 17 July 1688, as abovementioned. He, having had in all twenty-four children, *d.* in his 97th year, and was *bur.* 7 April 1692. His widow *m.* in 1695 (as his 2d wife), William CUNNINGHAM, of Brownhill, Provost of Ayr.

(a) See p. 359, note "a."

(b) The 2d and yst. son, Robert Innes Grant, Lieut. and Adjutant of the 1st Sikh infantry, *b.* 1833, was slain in action against greatly superior numbers of the Sepoy rebels, near the Jerwah pass on the Oude frontier.

(c) During the Interregnum, 12 Dec. 1688 to 12 Feb. 1688/9, no creations were made.

(d) See p. 242, note "c."

(e) This Andrew was s. of Robert Lauder, by (—), da. of (—) Inglis. See the funeral escutcheon of the 1st Baronet. There is no authority for considering her to be of the family of Bellenden, *or* Bannatyne, of Lasswade. The modern pedigrees confuse this Andrew with an Andrew Lauder, of Lasswade (living with two sons in 1635), who was great grandson of William Lauder, Burgess of Lauder (1542), and Alison Bannatyne, his wife.

(f) The mother of this Janet was da. of (—) Nesbit, as is shewn by the funeral escutcheon (see note "c" above), though the modern pedigrees make her to be of the old family of Sinclair, of Rosslyn.

II. 1692. SIR JOHN LAUDER, Baronet [S. 1690], of Fountainhall aforesaid, 3d but 1st surv. s. and h., being 1st s. of the 2d wife, *b.* 2 Aug. 1646 in Edinburgh; admitted Advocate, 5 June 1668; *Knighted* about 1680; M.P. [S.] for Haddington Constabulary, 1685-86, 1690-1702, and 1702-07; Counsel for the Earl of Argyll at his trial in 1681; a Lord of Session in Ordinary, under the style of *Lord Fountainhall*, 1 Nov. 1689, and a Lord of Justiciary, 1690-1707, declining the post of Lord Advocate in 1692. He *suc. to the Baronetcy* in April 1692, and registered arms in the Lyon office, 15 June 1699.(a) He *m.* firstly, 21 Jan. 1669, at the Tron Church, Edinburgh, Janet, da. of Sir Andrew RAMSAY, of Abbotshall, co. Fife, Lord Provost of Edinburgh and Senator of the Court of Justice.(b) She, who was *bap.* 26 Sep. 1652, at the Grey Friars, Edinburgh, and with whom he had 10,000 merks, *d.* v.p. 27 Feb. 1686. He *m.* secondly, 26 March 1687, Marion, da. of the Rev. John ANDERSON, of Balram, Minister of Dysart. He *d.* at Edinburgh 20 and was *bur.* 23 Sep. 1722, in the Grey Friars there, aged 76. Will dat. 2 Dec. 1706, pr. (with two codicils) more than sixteen years later.

III. 1722. SIR JOHN LAUDER, Baronet [S. 1690], of Fountainhall aforesaid, 1st s. and h., by 1st wife, *bap.* 5 Dec. 1669; *suc. to the Baronetcy*, 20 Sep. 1722. He *m.* 10 Aug. 1696 (the estate of Fountainhall being settled on their issue) Margaret, 2d da. of Sir Alexander SETON, 1st Baronet [S. 1683], of Pitmedden, a Lord Justiciary under the style of *Lord Pitmedden*, by Margaret, da. and h. of William LAUDER. He *d.* Feb. 1728, aged 58.

IV. 1728. SIR ALEXANDER LAUDER, Baronet [S. 1690], of Fountainhall aforesaid, 1st s. and h., *b.* 6 Nov. 1698; *suc. to the Baronetcy* on the death of his father, in Feb. 1728. He *d.* unm. 17 May 1730, aged 31.

V. 1730. SIR ANDREW LAUDER, Baronet [S. 1690], of Fountainhall aforesaid, br. and h., *bap.* 8 May 1702; *suc. to the Baronetcy*, 17 May 1730. He *m.* his cousin, Isabel, da. and h. of William DICK, of Grange, co. Edinburgh, by Anne, da. of Sir Alexander SETON, 1st Baronet [S. 1683], abovenamed. She *d.* at Grange House, 7 Nov. 1758. He *d.* 6 March 1769, aged 66.

VI. 1769. SIR ANDREW LAUDER-DICK, and, possibly afterwards, DICK-LAUDER, Baronet [S. 1690], of Fountainhall and Grange aforesaid, 3d and yst. but only surv. s. and h.,(c) suc. to the Grange estate on

(a) He appears to have been the author of the story of the family descent from Bellenden. See p. 360, note "e."

(b) This Sir Andrew Ramsay *d.* 17 Jan. 1688.

(c) William Lauder, the 1st son, *d.* s.p. and v.p. at Calcutta, 4 Jan. 1763.

the death of his mother, 7 Nov. 1758, and took the name of DICK in addition to that of LAUDER, and *suc. to the Baronetcy*, 6 March 1769, expending large sums of money in the improvement of his estates. He *m.* 25 Oct. 1783, Elizabeth, 1st da. of Thomas BROUN, of Johnstonburn, co. Haddington. She *d.* 21 Jan. 1787. He *d.* 16 Dec. 1820.

VII. 1820. SIR THOMAS DICK-LAUDER, Baronet [S. 1690], of Fountainhall and Grange aforesaid, only s. and h., *b.* 13 Aug. 1784; *suc. to the Baronetcy*, 16 Dec. 1820. He *m.* 8 Feb. 1808, at Relugas, Charles Anne, only da. and h. of George CUMIN, of Relugas aforesaid, by Susanna Judith, da. of Col. CRAIGIE-HALKETT, of Hall Hill, co. Fife. He, having sold the said estate of Relugas, *d.* 29 May 1848, at Grange House, aged 63.(a) His widow *d.* 22 Nov. 1864, at Greenhill House, Edinburgh, aged 79.

VIII. 1848. SIR JOHN DICK-LAUDER, Baronet [S. 1690], of Fountainhall and Grange aforesaid, 1st s. and h., *b.* 21 April 1813, at Relugas; served for fourteen years on the Bengal military establishment of the E.I.C.; *suc. to the Baronetcy*, 29 May 1848. He *m.* 22 May 1845, Anne, 2d da. of North (DALRYMPLE), 9th EARL OF STAIR [S.], by his 1st wife Margaret, da. of James PENNY. He *d.* 23 March 1867, at Bournemouth, Hants, aged 53(b). His widow, who was *b.* 2 July 1820, living 1904 at Edinburgh.

IX. 1867. SIR THOMAS NORTH DICK-LAUDER, Baronet [S. 1690], of Fountainhall and Grange aforesaid, 1st s. and h., *b.* 28 April 1846, at Grange House aforesaid; entered the 60th Foot, 1864, Lieut. 1867, retiring 1869; *suc. to the Baronetcy*, 23 May 1867; Knight of Justice of the Order of St. John of Jerusalem.

HAMILTON:

cr. 1 March 1692;

ex. presumably 1726.

I. 1692, to 1726. "GEORGE HAMILTON, of Barnton," of whom little seems to be known, but whose father was "a lawful son of the house of Binning" [Lyon Register], was *cr. a Baronet* [S.], as above, 1 March 1692 (being the 2d person so created(b) in the new reign), with rem. to heirs male of the body. He *m.* Helen BALFOUR, probably da. of Sir Andrew BALFOUR, M.D. He, "before his death, which happened 26 Oct. 1726, was a common beggar in the streets of Edinburgh."(c) It is presumed that he *d.* s.p.m., and that the *Baronetcy* on his death became *extinct*. "After his death, his Lady, who was as proud as Lucifer himself, and a great phanatick, turned Papist for bread."(d)

(a) He was author of the *Wolf of Badenoch*, and other historical romances. He claimed to be descended from the family of Lauder of Bass, but utterly failed to prove such descent. Thereupon he put up a monument to the Lauder family in the Greyfriars Churchyard, Edinburgh, stating thereon the pedigree as he wished it to be. See p. 242, note "c."

(b) A most favourable character of him is given in Anderson's *Scottish Nation*.

(c) Milne's *List*.

(d) Interpolations of Robert Mylne, the antiquary, in the extracts from the Fountainhall MSS., published by Sir Walter Scott in 1822, and printed in appendix to the preface of the Bannatyne Club edition of the *Historical Notices of Scottish Affairs*, p. xxix. [This and similar extracts from these interpolations have been kindly furnished by James R. Anderson, of Glasgow.]

DENHAM:(a)

cr. 31 Jan. 1693;(b)

sometime, 1756-73, STEUART-DENHAM;

afterwards, 1773-76, LOCKHART-DENHAM;

extinct, presumably, 24 June 1776.

I. 1693. "WILLIAM DENHAM, of Westshield," in the Barony of Carnwath, co. Lanark, s. and h. of Robert DENHAM, *or* DENHOLM, of Westshield aforesaid, by Marion, da. of (—) LOCKHART, of Waygateshaw, co. Lanark, was *b.* 1630; acquired the superiority of the estate of Westshield from the EARLS OF CARNWATH [S.]; registered arms in the Lyon office about 1673; incurred forfeiture in 1685 for alleged complicity in the Rye house plot, but escaped to Holland; was pardoned 1690; M.P. [S.] for Lanarkshire, 1690-1702; Master of the Mint [S.], and was *cr. a Baronet* [S.], as above, 31 Jan. 1693,(b) with a spec. rem., failing heirs male of his body, to his assignees. He accordingly, a year before his death, executed 14 July 1711 an entail of his estates and the Baronetcy.(c) He *m.* firstly, 13 Oct. 1670, Anne, da. and coheir of Sir William MAXWELL, of Sauchton hall, co. Edinburgh. He *m.* secondly, Elizabeth, da. of Sir John HENDERSON, of Fordell, co. Fife. He *m.* thirdly, Catherine, 1st da. of Henry (ERSKINE), 3d LORD CARDROSS [S.], by Catherine, da. of Sir James STEWART, of Kirkhill. He *d.* s.p. 1 Jan. 1712, aged about 82. His widow *m.* 4 April 1714, Daniel CAMPBELL, of Shawfield.

II. 1712. SIR ROBERT DENHAM, Baronet [S. 1693], of Westshield aforesaid, formerly Robert BAILLIE, nephew and h., being s. and h. of the Rev. William BAILLIE, of Hardington, co. Lanark, Minister of Lamington, by Grizel (relict of John WEIR), elder sister to the 1st Baronet, and da. of Robert DENHAM abovenamed. He *suc. to the Baronetcy*, 1 Jan. 1712, under the entail of that dignity, and was, 3 March 1713, served heir of provision general to his said uncle. He *m.* Margaret, da. of (—). He *d.* before 25 Oct. 1737. Admon. at that date of his widow as "DAME MARGARET DENHAM, of Old Place, co. Lanark, widow," granted to her son Alexander DENHAM, and again 4 Jan. 1748/9 as "DAME MARGARET DENHAM, of Westshields, co. Lanark, widow," to her son "Sir Robert DENHAM, Baronet."

III. 1730? ALEXANDER DENHAM, of Westshield aforesaid, 1st s. and h., *suc. to the Baronetcy* on the death of his father, to whom he was served heir of entail and provision general, 22 Oct. 1744, but never assumed the title. He *d.* s.p. before Jan. 1748/9.

IV. 1748? SIR ROBERT DENHAM, Baronet [S. 1693], of Westshield aforesaid, br. and h., *suc. to the Baronetcy* on the death of his brother, to whom he was served heir of entail and provision general, 10 Jan. 1751. He *d.* s.p. 29 Sep. 1756.

(a) See p. 242, note "c."

(b) This creation, though omitted in Milne's *List* and various others, is recorded in the Great Seal Register (*N. & Q.*, 7th s., xii, p. 386), where a notice of the family of Denham, or Denholme, in the *Northern N. & Q.* or *Scottish Antiquary* (vol. v., p. 83) is mentioned, in which it is [erroneously] stated that there is no authority for this creation.

(c) This entail was in favour (1) of the heirs male and female of his own body; (2) of his nephew Robert Baillie, and the heirs male of his body; (3) of his nephew Archibald Stewart, in like manner; (4) of his grandnephew William Lockhart, in like manner; (5) of his grandnephew William Kennedy, in like manner; and (6) to the eldest heir female of the said remainder men in the same order. Of these four persons no less than three succeeded to the Baronetcy, but (the fourth) William Kennedy (who was s. of Sir Andrew Kennedy, 1st Baronet [S. 1698], of Clowburn, co. Ayr, by Margaret, da. of John Weir, of Clowburn aforesaid, by Grizel, his wife, elder sister to the 1st Baronet and da. of Robert Denham abovenamed) *d.* s.p. before (probably long before) 1776.

V. 1756. SIR ARCHIBALD STEUART-DENHAM, Baronet [S. 1693], of Westshield aforesaid, formerly Archibald STEUART, nephew of the grantee, being yst. s. of Sir Thomas STEUART, 1st Baronet [S. 1698], of Coltness, and his only surv. s. by his 2d wife Susan, relict of William LOCKHART, yr. of the two sisters of Sir William DENHAM, 1st Baronet [S. 1693], and da. of Robert DENHAM abovenamed. He was *b.* at Utrecht, 20 July 1683; was admitted an Advocate; *suc. to the Baronetcy*, as also to the Westshield estate, 29 Sep. 1756, under the entail, made by his maternal uncle, the 1st Baronet,(a) and took the name of DENHAM, after that of STEUART. To him he was served heir of entail, and provision general. In 1758, by the death of his nephew, John STEUART, *de jure*, 5th Baronet [S. 1698], he *suc. to that Baronetcy*. He *m.* in 1724, Jane, 1st da. of Sir George WARRENDER, 1st Baronet [1715], of Lochend, by his 2d wife Grizel, da. of Hugh BLAIR, of Edinburgh. She *d.* 2 Feb. 1770. He *d.* s.p.s.,(b) 12 June 1773, in his 90th year, when the Baronetcy of Steuart [S. 1698], devolved on his cousin and heir male. (See "STEUART" Baronetcy [S.], *cr.* 29 Jan. 1698), but the Baronetcy of Denham devolved as under.

VI. 1773, to 1776. SIR WILLIAM LOCKHART-DENHAM, Baronet [S. 1693], of Westshield aforesaid, formerly William LOCKHART, great nephew of the grantee, being s. and h. of William LOCKHART, by Elizabeth LAURIE, his wife, which William, was s. and h. of William LOCKHART, of Waygateshaw, by Susanna (afterwards wife of Sir Thomas STEUART, 1st Baronet [S. 1698], abovenamed), yr. of the two sisters of Sir William DENHAM, 1st Baronet [S. 1693], and da. of Robert DENHAM abovenamed. He *suc. to the Baronetcy*, as also to the Westshield estate, 12 June 1770, under the entail made by his father's maternal uncle, the 1st Baronet,(a) when he took the name of DENHAM, after that of LOCKHART. On 29 Sep. 1773, he was served heir of entail and provision special to Sir Robert DENHAM, Baronet [S.], as also to Sir Archibald STEUART-DENHAM, Baronet [S.], in the lands of Murehall, etc., co. Lanark. He *d.* s.p. 24 June 1776, when, there being no one who could take under the grantee's entail of 14 July 1711, the *Baronetcy* became, presumably, *extinct*.(c)

DUNBAR:

cr. 29 March 1694.

I 1694. "JAMES DUNBAR, of Mochrum," co. Wigtown, s. and h. of Thomas DUNBAR, of Mochrum, by Christian, da. of Major James Ross, of Balneil, was served heir to his father, 29 June 1675; had a Great Seal charter of the Barony of Mochrum, 1 June 1677, and was *cr. a Baronet* [S.], as above, 29 March 1694, with rem. to heirs male of the body. He *m.* firstly, 11 Feb. 1679, Isabel, da. and eventually coheir of Sir Thomas NICOLSON, 2d Baronet [S. 1637], of Carnock, by Margaret, da. of Alexander [LIVINGSTONE], 2d EARL OF LINLITHGOW [S.]. With her he acquired the estate of Plean, co. Stirling. He *m.* secondly, Jane da. of (—) KENNEDY, of Miunnchen, but by her had no male issue. He *d.* 1718.

II. 1718. SIR GEORGE DUNBAR, Baronet [S. 1694], of Mochrum aforesaid, 1st s. and h.(d) by 1st wife; sometime Capt. in the Scots Dragoons, serving in the continental wars under Marlborough; *suc. to the*

(a) See p. 263, note "c."

(b) His only son, Thomas Steuart-Denham, Capt. 8th Foot, *d.* v.p. and s.p., 22 March 1761.

(c) He left the estate of Westshield to his distant kinsman, Sir James Steuart, 7th Baronet [S. 1698], who thereupon took the name of Denham after that of Steuart, though he had no descent from that family.

(d) John Dunbar, the 2d and yst. son, a Cornet in the Scots' Dragoons, *d.* of wounds received at the battle of Teniers.

Baronetcy in 1718, and sold the estates of Mochrum and Pankill in the south of Scotland, purchasing that of Woodside, co. Stirling, where he built the mansion called Dunbar house. He *m.* Janet, da. of Sir John YOUNG, of Lenie. He *d.* Oct. 1747. His widow *d.* 18 May 1764.

III. 1747. SIR JAMES DUNBAR, Baronet [S. 1694], of Dunbar house, in Woodside aforesaid, 1st s. and h.; admitted an Advocate, becoming afterwards, 9 Feb. 1768, Judge Advocate Gen. [S.]; *suc. to the Baronetcy* in Oct. 1747. He *m.* 31 Oct. 1760, Jacobina, 2d and yst. da. and coheir of John HAMILTON, of Newton, Clerk to the Signet, by Jean, da. of (—) GARTHSHORE, of Garthshore, which John was yr. s. of William HAMILTON, of Wishaw. He *d.* 16 April 1782. Admon. July 1783. His widow *d.* at Edinburgh, 29 Jan. 1792.

IV. 1782. SIR GEORGE DUNBAR, Baronet [S. 1694], of Dunbar house, in Woodside aforesaid, only s. and h.; sometime Lieut.-Col. of the 14th Light Dragoons; *suc. to the Baronetcy*, 16 April 1782. He *m.* Maria, 1st da. of the Rev. Gustavus HAMILTON (grandson of Gustavus, 1st VISCOUNT BOYNE [I.]), by his 2d wife, Alicia, da. of Col. Lodowick PETERSON. He *d.* s.p. 15 Oct. 1799, having shot himself at Norwich. Will pr. Nov. 1800. His widow *d.* 24 June or 31 Aug 1808. Will pr. 1808.

V. 1799. SIR GEORGE DUNBAR, Baronet [S. 1694], cousin and h. male, being 1st s. and h. of Thomas DUNBAR, of Liverpool, merchant, by Tryphena (*m.* 1748), da. of J. PINCOCK, of London, merchant, which Thomas was 3d s. of the 2d Baronet. He was *b.* about 1750, and *suc. to the Baronetcy*, 15 Oct. 1799. He *m.* in 1775, Jane, da. and coheir of William ROWE, of Liverpool. He *d.* 10 Oct. 1811, near Liverpool, aged 61. His widow *d.* 28 Dec. 1830.

VI. 1811. SIR WILLIAM ROWE DUNBAR, Baronet [S. 1694], 1st s. and h., *b.* 19 Oct. 1776; sometime Capt. 21st Light Dragoons; *suc. to the Baronetcy*, 10 Oct. 1811. He *m.* 24 Aug. 1798, his cousin, Jacobina Anne, only da. and h. of William COPLAND, of Colliston, co. Dumfries, by Helen, da. of Sir James DUNBAR, 3d Baronet [S. 1694]. She *d.* 1807. He *d.* s.p.s., 22 June 1841, aged 64. Will pr. Dec. 1842.

VII. 1841. SIR WILLIAM DUNBAR, Baronet [S. 1694], of the Grange, in Bladenoch, co. Wigtown, afterwards (though not in the parish of Mochrum) called Mochrum park, nephew and h., being 1st s. of James DUNBAR, an officer in the 21st Light Dragoons, by Anna Catharina, da. of William Ferdinand, BARON DE REEDE D'OUDTSHOORN, in Holland, which James (who *d.* 31 Jan. 1840, aged 62) was next br. of the late Baronet. He was *b.* 2 March 1812; ed. at the Univ. of Edinburgh; admitted Advocate, 1835; *suc. to the Baronetcy*, 22 June 1841; M.P. for Wigtown burghs (two Parls.), 1857-65; a Lord of the Treasury and Keeper of the Privy Seal to the Prince of Wales, 1859-65; Keeper of the Great Seal in Scotland and one of the Council of the Duchy of Cornwall to that Prince, 1863-65; sometime Comptroller and afterwards, 1867-88, Auditor Gen. of the Exchequer. He *m.* 7 Jan. 1842, Catherine Hay, 1st da. of(James PATERSON, of Carpow, co. Perth, by Jane, da. of John Balfour HAY, of Leys and Randerston. He *d.* 18 Dec. 1889, at Mochrum park, aged 76, and was *bur.* at All Saints, Challock, co. Wigtown. His widow *d.* there 2 April 1890, aged 82.

VIII. 1889. SIR UTHRED JAMES HAY DUNBAR, Baronet [S. 1694], of Mochrum park aforesaid, 1st s. and h., *b.* 26 Feb. 1843; ed. at Glenalmond College, Perth; matric. at Oxford (Exeter Coll.), 11 June 1862, aged 19; B.A., 1866; Barrister (Inner Temple), 30 April 1869; Private Sec. to his father when Comptroller of the Exchequer, 1870-88; *suc. to the Baronetcy*, 18 Dec. 1889. He *m.* 20 April 1882, at Christ Church, Marylebone, Lucy Blanche Cordelia, 1st da. of Charles Thomas Constantine GRANT, of Kilgraston and Pitkeathly, by Janet Matilda, da. of William HAY, of Dans Castle, co. Berwick. She was *b.* 5 Aug. 1857. He *d.* s.p. 4 Sep. 1904, at Mochrum park, aged 61. His widow living 1904.

IX. 1904. SIR WILLIAM COSPATRICK DUNBAR, Baronet [S. 1694], of Mochrum park aforesaid, only br. and h., *b.* 20 July 1844; was Private Sec. to Under Sec. of State at Home Office, 1876-85; Assistant Under Sec. for Scotland, 1885-91; C.B., 1887; Registrar Gen. since 1892; *suc. to the Baronetcy*, 4 Sep. 1904. He *m.* 30 July 1878, Nina Susanna, 4th da. of Alfred DOUGLAS-HAMILTON, of The Firs, near Romford, Essex, by his 1st wife, Adelaide, da. and coheir of Alexander BLACK, of Gidea Hall, in that county.

Family Estates.—These, in 1883, consisted of 3,680 acres in co. Wigtown, and 8 in co. Perth. *Total.*—3,688 acres, worth £3,603 a year. *Seat.*—Mochrum Park, co. Wigtown.

ANSTRUTHER:

cr. 28 Nov. 1694.

I. 1694. "ROBERT ANSTRUTHER, of Wrae," co. Linlithgow (an estate he had acquired by marriage), 3d s.(a) of Sir Philip ANSTRUTHER, of Anstruther, co. Fife (*d.* 1702), by Christian, da. of Sir James LUMSDEN, of Innergelly (a General in the service of the King of Sweden), was *bap.* 24 Sep. 1658, at Anstruther-Easter; was a Merchant Burgess, and one of the Receivers of the Customs; M.P. [S.], for Anstruther-Easter, 1681-82, for Anstruther-Wester, 1702-07, and [G.B.] for Fifeshire, 1709-10, being *cr. a Baronet* [S.], as above, 28 Nov. 1694, with rem. to heirs male of the body. He purchased the estate of Balcaskie, in the parish of Carnbee, co. Fife, in 1698. He *m.* firstly, Sophia, da. and coheir of David KINNEAR, of Kinnear, in Kilmany, co. Fife, and for a time assumed the name of KINNEAR. She, however, *d.* s.p. He *m.* secondly, 12 March 1687, at Edinburgh, Jean, da. and h. of William MONTEITH, of Wrae aforesaid, by Margaret, da. of (—) DUNDAS. By her he had six sons. He *m.* thirdly, 13 Sep. 1703, at Edinburgh, Marion, da. of Sir William PRESTON, 2d Baronet [S. 1637], of Valleyfield, by Anne, da. of Sir James LUMSDEN. He *d.* March 1737 aged 78. His widow *d.* April 1743.

II. 1737. SIR PHILIP ANSTRUTHER, Baronet [S. 1694], of Balcaskie aforesaid, 1st s. and h., by 2d wife, was an Advocate, 1711, and one of the principal Clerks to the Bills; *suc. to the Baronetcy* in March 1737, and was served heir gen. 2 Feb. 1742. He *m.*, in or before 1733 (post nuptial settlement 21 Aug. and 4 Sep. 1738), Catherine, 1st da. of Lord Alexander HAY, of Spott, co. Haddington (yr. s. of John, 1st MARQUESS OF TWEEDDALE [S.]), by Catherine, da. of (—) CHARTERIS. She, by whom he had seven sons, *d.* at Balcaskie, 11 Feb. 1759. He *d.* 27 May 1763.

III. 1763. SIR ROBERT ANSTRUTHER, Baronet [S. 1694], of Balcaskie aforesaid, 1st s. and h., *b.* 19 and *bap.* 21 April 1733, at Carnbee; was (like his father) an Advocate, and one of the principal Clerks to the Bills; *suc. to the Baronetcy*, 27 May 1763. He *m.* 17 Aug. 1763, Janet, sister and coheir [1795] of Archibald (ERSKINE), 7th EARL OF KELLIE [S.], 3d and yst. da. of Alexander, the 5th Earl, by his 2d wife, Janet, da. of Archibald PITCAIRN, M.D. She, who was *b.* 9 and *bap.* 10 March 1742, at Carnbee, *d.* 17 Oct. 1770, at Balcaskie. He *d.* there 2 Aug. 1818, and was *bur.* at Carnbee, in his 86th year.

(a) He was one of five brothers, all of whom were *Knighted—viz.* (1) Sir William Anstruther, of Anstruther, who *d.* 24 Jan. 1711, being father of John Anstruther, of Anstruther, *cr. a Baronet* [S.], v.p., 6 Jan. 1700; (2) Sir James Anstruther, of Airdrie, whose only son Lieut.-Gen. Philip Anstruther, Gov. of Minorca, *d.* unm. 11 Nov. 1760; (3) Sir Robert Anstruther, Baronet [S.], so. *cr.* 28 Nov. 1694; (4) Sir Philip Anstruther, of Anstrutherfield, who *d.* 1722, leaving issue; and (5) Sir Alexander Anstruther, who *d.* 1743, leaving issue.

IV. 1818. SIR RALPH ABERCROMBY ANSTRUTHER, Baronet [S. 1694], of Balcaskie aforesaid, grandson and h., being 1st s. and h. of Brig.-General Robert ANSTRUTHER, by Charlotte Lucy (*m.* 16 March 1799, at Margate), only da. and h. of Lieut.-Col. James HAMILTON, Coldstream Guards,(a) which Robert (*b.* 3 March 1768), *d.* v.p. 14 Jan. 1809, and was *bur.* at Corunna, having greatly distinguished himself in the Peninsular wars. He was *b.* in Grosvenor street 1 March, and *bap.* 13 May 1804 at Carnbee; *suc. to the Baronetcy*, 2 Aug. 1818; ed. at Trin. Coll., Cambridge; M.A., 1822; Capt. in the Grenadier Guards; Rector of the Univ. of St. Andrew's, 1859. He *m.* 2 Sep. 1831, at Lambeth, Mary Jane, 1st da. of Major Gen. Sir Henry TORRENS, K.C.B., by (—), da. of (—) PATON, Governor of St. Helena. He *d.* 18 Oct. 1863, at Balcaskie, aged 59. His widow, who was *b.* 1 Feb. 1811, *m.* 14 Nov. 1868, at Edinburgh (as his 3d wife), William Talbot CROSBIE, of Ardfert Abbey, co. Kerry, and *d.* 26 Aug. 1886, being *bur.* at Ardfert.

V. 1863. SIR ROBERT ANSTRUTHER, Baronet [S. 1694], of Balcaskie aforesaid, and of Braemore, co. Caithness, 1st. s. and h.,(b) *b.* 28 Aug. 1834 at Edinburgh; ed. at Harrow; entered the Grenadier Guards, 1853; Lieut.-Col., 1861; *suc. to the Baronetcy*, 18 Oct. 1863; M.P. for Fifeshire (four Parls.), 1864-80, and for St. Andrew's burghs, 1885-86; Lieut. of that county, 1864 till death, 1886. He *m.* 29 July 1859, at Beckenham, co. Kent, Louisa Anne Chowne, 1st da. of the Rev. William Knox MARSHALL, B.D., Vicar of Wragby, co. Lincoln, and Preb. of Hereford, by Louisa, da. of the Rev. William MARSH, D.D., of Beckenham aforesaid, Rector of Beddington, co. Surrey.(c) He *d.* 21 July 1886, at Balcaskie, in his 52d year. His widow living 1904.

VI. 1886. SIR RALPH WILLIAM ANSTRUTHER, Baronet [S. 1694], of Balcaskie and Braemore aforesaid, 1st s. and h., *b.* 5 July 1858, and *bap.* at Beckenham aforesaid; ed. at Eton; sometime (1877-90) in the Royal Engineers, serving in the Egyptian campaign, 1883, and in the Bechuanaland expedition, 1885; *suc. to the Baronetcy*, 21 July 1886; Lieut.-Col. Com. 6th Fifeshire Vol. Batt. Royal Highlanders. He *m.* 5 Aug. 1885, at St. Mark's, North Audley street, Mildred Harriet, da. of Edward HUSSEY, of Scotney Castle, Sussex, and of Lamberhurst, Kent, by Henrietta Sarah, da. of the Hon. Robert Henry CLIVE, and Harriett, *suo jure* BARONESS WINDSOR. She was *b.* 6 June 1863, and *bap.* at Lamberhurst aforesaid.

Family Estates.—These, in 1883, consisted of 22,597 acres in co. Caithness (worth £4,000 a year), and 2,121 in co. Fife. *Total.*—24,718 acres, worth £9,062 a year. *Principal Seats.*—Balcaskie, near Pittenweem, co. Fife, and Watten, co. Caithness.

WEIR:

cr. 28 Nov. 1694;

ex. 1735.

I. 1694. "GEORGE WEIR, of Blackwood," co. Lanark, 1st s. and h. of George WEIR, *formerly* LAURIE, of the same, and only child by his 1st wife, Anne,(d) da. of George CLELAND, was bap. 12 June 1674,(e) suc.

(a) This James, who *d.* 22 Jan. 1804, in his 58th year, was s. of Lord Anne Hamilton, 3d s. of James, Duke of Hamilton [S.].

(b) Henry Anstruther, the 2d son, Lieut. Royal Welsh Fusileers, *d.* unm. and v.p., being killed at the Alma in the Crimea, 20 Sep. 1854, aged 18.

(c) The life of this most exemplary clergyman, one of the most impressive preachers of the Evangelical school (who *d.* at Beckenham rectory, 24 Jan. 1864, in his 90th year), has been written by his da., Catherine Marsh, authoress of the *Memorials of Capt. Hedley Vicars*, etc.

(d) "Ann Clelland, wife of George Weir, of Blackwood," was buried 14 Aug. 1675 at the Greyfriars, Edinburgh.

(e) Nisbet's *Heraldic Plates*, p. 28.

his father April 1680, and was *cr. a Baronet* [S.], as above, 28 Nov. 1694, with rem. to heirs male of the body. He *m.* Catherine, da. of Sir John JARDINE, 1st Baronet [S. 1672], of Applegirth, by Margaret, da. of James (DOUGLAS) 2d EARL OF QUEENSBERRY [S.]. She was *bur.* 16 July 1711 in the Abbey Church of Holyrood. He *d.* 7 Jan. 1716, in his 42d year.

II. 1716. SIR WILLIAM WEIR, Baronet [S. 1694], of Blackwood aforesaid, 1st s. and h., *suc. to the Baronetcy*, 7 Jan. 1716. He *m.* firstly, Rachel, da. of James HAMILTON, of Pencaitland, Senator of the College of Justice, by Catherine, da. of John DENHAM, of Westshield. He *m.* secondly, Christian, da. of Sir Philip ANSTRUTHER, of Anstrutherfield, by Elizabeth, da. and h. of James HAMILTON. He *d.* s.p.m.,(a) 1722. His widow *m.* 1740, John (STEWART), 6th EARL OF TRAQUAIR [S.] (who *d.* 28 March 1779 in his 81st year) and *d.* at Traquair house, 12 Nov. 1771, in her 69th year.

III. 1722, to 1737. SIR GEORGE WEIR, Baronet [S. 1694], br. and h. male, sometime Captain in Scots Royal Regiment of Foot; *suc. to the Baronetcy* in 1722. He *d.* unm. 1735, when the *Baronetcy* became *extinct*.

DICKSON(b):

cr. 28 Feb. 1695(c);

ex. or *dormant* 1 Feb. 1760;

but, apparently, assumed in 1760.

I. 1695. Captain ROBERT DICKSON, of Sornbeg in the parish of Galston, co. Ayr, s. and h. of Archibald DICKSON, of Tourlands Kilmaurs in the same county, by (—) da. and coheir of Robert BARCLAY, of Montgomeryston, Provost of Irvine, suc. his father shortly after 1690; registered Arms at the Lyon Office, 14 Sep. 1692, and, having acquired considerable property in Ayrshire and in West and Mid Lothian, was *cr. a Baronet* [S.], as above, 28 Feb. 1695, with rem. to heirs male of the body and it is said(d) to "other heirs successively." He subsequently acquired the estate of Inveresk, by which he was generally known. He was M.P. [S.] for Edinburghshire, 1702-07, and voted for the Union [S.]. He *m.* (contract 31 Jan. 1693) Helen, yst. da. of Sir John COLQUHOUN, 2d Baronet [S. 1625] of Luss, by Margaret, da. of Gideon BAILLIE. He *d.* Oct. 1711.

II. 1711, to 1760. SIR ROBERT DICKSON, Baronet [S. 1695], of Inveresk aforesaid, only s. and h., *bap.* 12 Nov. 1694, *suc. to the Baronetcy* in Oct. 1711 and had spec. service to his father in Inveresk, Corstorphine, Smeaton, etc., 20 April 1712. In 1713, however, he sold Inveresk and most of his other estates, being styled latterly "of Carberry"; was Inspector General of Salt duties at an annual salary of £130; was a Councillor of Musselburgh till his death in 1760. He *m.* (—) da. of (—) DOUGLAS, of Dornock, co. Dumfries. He *d.* s.p.m.s.,(e) 1 Feb. 1760, at Musselburgh, aged 65, when the *Baronetcy* became *extinct* or *dormant*.

(a) Catherine, his da. and h. by 1st wife, suc. to the family estate and *m.* 1733 the Hon. Charles Hope, of Craigie, and *d.* 1743, leaving issue, William Hope-Weir, *or* Hope-Vere, of Craigie Blackwood aforesaid.

(b) See p. 242, note "c." The family is said to have been descended in the male line from that of Keith. See Nisbet's *Heraldry*.

(c) Milne's *List*, but the *Lists* of Chamberlayne and Miege give the date as 1 March 1695.

(d) J. Foster's additions to Milne's *List* as printed in Foster's *Baronetage*, 1883.

(e) His only son Robert *d.* unm. and v.p. in India. On 21 July 1778, the three daughters, Anne (who *d.* 15 July 1795), Margaret and Helen were served heirs portioners general of their father and of their said brother Robert Dickson.

III. 1760. "DAVID DICKSON, Esq., of Derrymore, King's County," *suc. to the Baronetcy*, 1 Feb. 1760, according to the *London Mag.* for 1760, and *Exshaw's Mag.* He, presumably, is the same person as "David DICKSON, of Dublin, Esq.," who, on 6 March 1756, had a lic. (Dublin) to marry "Elizabeth HAY, of St. Paul's, spinster," but no further trace of him can be found.(a)

BAIRD:

cr. 28 Feb. 1695.

I. 1695. "ROBERT(b) BAIRD, of Saughton Hall," co. Edinburgh, 2d s.(c) of James BAIRD, of Byth, co. Aberdeen, by Bethia, da. of Sir John DEMPSTER, of Pitliver, being a merchant of great reputation in Edinburgh, and having purchased in 1660, the estate of Saughton Hall abovenamed, was *cr. a Baronet* [S.], as above, 28 Feb. 1695, with rem. to heirs male of the body. He *m.* Elizabeth, da. of Malcolm, or Michael, FLEMING, of Rathobyres. She was *bur.* 18 Oct. 1676, at the Greyfriars, Edinburgh. He *d.* Feb. and was *bur.* there 2 March 1697.

II. 1697. SIR JAMES BAIRD, Baronet [S. 1695], of Saughton Hall aforesaid, 1st s. and h., *suc. to the Baronetcy* in Feb. 1697. He *m.* firstly, in or before 1689, Margaret, da. and coheir of (—) HAMILTON, of Mountainhall, co. Edinburgh. She was *bur.* 8 March 1694, at Greyfriars aforesaid. He *m.* secondly, his cousin, Elizabeth, da. of Sir John GIBSON, of Addiston, co. Edinburgh, by (—), da. of his maternal uncle, Malcolm, or Michael FLEMING aforesaid. He *d.* May 1715.

III. 1715. SIR ROBERT BAIRD, Baronet [S. 1695], of Saughton Hall aforesaid, 1st s. and h., by 1st wife, *b.* probably about 1690; *suc. to the Baronetcy*, May 1715. He *m.* firstly, in or before 1729, Janet, da. of Robert BAIKIE, of Tankerness in Orkney. She *d.* 11 June 1733. He *m.* secondly, Helen, da. of (—) HOPE. He *d.* 8 Sep. 1740. His widow *d.* March 1741.

IV. 1740. SIR DAVID BAIRD, Baronet [S. 1695], of Saughton Hall aforesaid, 1st s. and h., by 1st wife, *b.* about 1729; *suc. to the Baronetcy*, 8 Sep. 1740; was Lieut. in the Royals, serving in Flanders as a volunteer. He *d.* unm. at Lisle, 1 July 1745, in his 17th year, from wounds received at the battle of Fontenoy, 30 April previous.

V. 1745. SIR WILLIAM BAIRD, Baronet [S. 1695], of Saughton Hall, aforesaid, br. of the whole blood and h.; *suc. to the Baronetcy* 1 July 1745; was a Captain in the Royal Navy. He *m.*, in 1750, Frances, 1st da. of the celebrated Colonel James GARDINER, of Bankton (who was slain at the battle of Prestonpans, 21 Sep. 1745) by Frances, da. of David (ERSKINE), EARL OF BUCHAN [S.]. He *d.* at Saughton Hall, 17 Aug. 1771.

VI. 1771. SIR JAMES GARDINER BAIRD, Baronet [S. 1697]. of Saughton Hall aforesaid, 2d but only surv. s. and h.; *suc. to the Baronetcy* 17 Aug. 1771; entered the 17th Foot, 1772; Lieut., 1776; Capt. (71st Foot), 1777; serving through the whole of the American war and through two

(a) *Ex inform.*, G. D. Burtchaell, Office of Arms, Dublin.

(b) Called "James," erroneously, in Milne's *List*.

(c) John Baird of Newbyth, the eldest son, a Lord of Session under the style of *Lord Newbyth*, was the father of Sir William Baird, *cr. a Baronet* [S.] of Newbyth, 4 Feb. 1680, a dignity which became *extinct* in Sep. 1745.

Campaigns in Flanders; Captain 1st Batt. Scots Brigade, 1794; Lieut.-Colonel 28th Light Dragoons, but retired in 1796. He *m.* firstly, in 1781, Henrietta, 3d da. of Wynne JOHNSTONE, of Hilltown. He *m.* secondly, 15 July 1818, Mary, widow of James SYMINGTON, da. of Robert WATT. She *d.* 14 Jan. 1826. He *m.* thirdly, in 1827, Wortley Cornelia Anne, da. of William MOIR, of New Grove. He *d.* 23 June 1830.

VII. 1830. SIR JAMES GARDINER BAIRD, Baronet [S. 1695], of Saughton Hall aforesaid, grandson and h., being 1st s. and h. of William BAIRD, Captain in the Army, by Lucy, da. of Thomas DICKSON, of Prospect House, Southampton, which William (who *d.* v.p. in 1823) was 1st s. and h. ap. of the late Baronet, by his first wife. He was *b.* 20 Aug. 1813; *suc. to the Baronetcy*, 23 June 1830; sometime Captain 10th Light Dragoons, retiring 1842; Lieut.-Colonel Midlothian Coast Artillery; Ensign Gen. of the Royal Company of Archers [S.], and a Volunteer Aide-de-Camp to Queen Victoria. He *m.* 13 March 1845, at Edmondstone, co. Edinburgh, his cousin, Henrietta Mary, sister of Sir John DON-WAUCHOPE, 8th Baronet [S. 1667], 1st da. of John WAUCHOPE, of Edmondstone aforesaid, by his maternal aunt Henrietta Warrender Cecilia, da. of Sir James Gardiner BAIRD, 6th Baronet [S. 1695]. He *d.* 6 Jan. 1896, aged 82, at Wester Lea, Murrayfield, Midlothian. His widow *d.* there, ten months later, 3 Nov. 1896.

VIII. 1896. SIR WILLIAM JAMES GARDINER BAIRD, Baronet [S. 1695], of Saughton Hall aforesaid, 1st and only surv. s. and h., *b.* 23 Feb. 1854; sometime Lieut. 7th Hussars; *suc. to the Baronetcy* 6 Jan. 1896; Lieut.-Colonel Commanding and Hon. Colonel of the Lothian and Berwick Yeomanry Cavalry. He *m.* 3 April 1879, at Maudslie Castle, co. Lanark, Arabella Rose Evelyn, 1st da. of William Wallace (HOZIER) 1st BARON NEWLANDS OF NEWLANDS AND BARROWFIELD AND OF MAUDSLIE CASTLE, by Frances Anne, da. of John O'HARA, of Raheen.

CUMMING: (a)

cr. 28 Feb. 1695;(b)

dormant or *extinct* about 1793;

but assumed subsequently.

I. 1695. "ALEXANDER CUMMING, of Culter," co. Aberdeen, the younger,(c) 1st s. and h. ap. of Alexander CUMMING, of Culter aforesaid (*d.* about 1715), by Helen, da. of James ALLARDYCE, of that ilk, was *b.* about 1674; admitted as Advocate, 1691, and was v.p. *cr. a Baronet* [S.], as above, 28 Feb. 1695, with rem. to heirs male whatsoever. He was M.P. for Aberdeenshire (four Parls.) 1709-22; was "Conservator of the Scots' privileges in the Low Countries," 1705-06; is said to have "been the means of saving the life of King George II";(d) F.R.S., 1720, and was in that year a heavy loser in the South Sea stock panic.(e) He *m.* firstly, in or before 1690, Elizabeth, da. of

(a) Much information about this Baronetcy is given in an able article in the *Genealogist* (vol. iii, pp. 1-11), entitled "*Sir Kenneth William Cumming of Culter, Baronet, by H. Barr Tomkins, Barrister at Law.*" This has been followed in this article.

(b) The date of 28 Feb. *1672* is given (presumably in error) as that of this creation in Burke's *Baronetage*, 1834-41.

(c) According to Mrs. Cumming Bruce's "*History of the Bruces and the Cumyns,*" the 1st Baronet (who was probably born about 1650) was 8th [?] in descent from Sir Alexander Cuming who (some 85 years before) was present at the wedding of Mary, Queen of Scots, in 1565.

(d) Statement of the 2d Baronet. See *N. & Q.*, 1st S., v, p. 279.

(e) "Probably the £80,000 he is said traditionally to have lost thereby were *punds Scots*, and worth only one-twelfth of pounds sterling." See note "a" above.

Sir Alexander SWINTON, of Mersington, Senator of the College of Justice under the style of *Lord Mersington*, by his 2d wife, Alison, da. of John SKENE, of Hallyards. She *d.* April 1709. He *m.* secondly, Elizabeth, da. and coheir of William DENNIS, of Pucklechurch, co. Gloucester. He *d.* 7 Feb. 1724/5, aged 55, and was *bur.* in the church of Culter. Will pr. 1725. His widow *d.* soon after him, and was *bur.* with him.

II. 1725. SIR ALEXANDER CUMMING, Baronet [S. 1695], possibly of Culter aforesaid, 1st s. and h.;(a) by the 1st wife, *b.* 1690; entered the Army, 29 May 1703, at the age of 13, becoming, subsequently, a Captain, and serving in the wars in Flanders, and at the battle of Malplaquet (1709), in which his uncle, Col. SWINTON, was slain. He was admitted as Advocate 1714, but quitting the legal profession was "taken unto the secret service of the Crown at a salary of £300 a year," from Christmas 1718 to Christmas 1721.(b) He *suc. to the Baronetcy*, 7 Feb. 1724/5, and possibly (if, as is not improbable, it had not been previously sold) to the estate of Cutler. In 1729 he sailed for America, and on 3 April 1730, was made Chief of the Cherokee nation, being crowned at Nequisee, he and six Cherokee chiefs doing homage to the King, at Windsor, 22 June following. In 1737 and 1750 (and probably through all that period) he was a Prisoner in the Fleet for debt, but on 30 Dec. 1765, was nominated a Pensioner of the Charter House, London. He *m.* about 1737, Amy, (not Anne) da. of Lancelot WHITEHALL, Commissioner of the Customs [S.]. She *d.* at Chelsea, and was *bur.* 22 Oct. 1743, at East Barnet, Midx. He *d.* at the Charter House, 23 and was *bur.* 28 Aug. 1775, at East Barnet, aged 85. Will pr. Aug. 1775.

III. 1775, to 1793? SIR ALEXANDER CUMMING, Baronet [S. 1695], only s. and h., *b.* about 1737; was a Capt. in the Army, being in 1779 on half pay at the rate of more than £20 a year; *suc. to the Baronetcy*, 23 Aug. 1775. Was nominated a Pensioner of the Charter House 1779 and 1789, but refused each time on ground of his half pay. He, subsequently, became deranged, and *d.* unm. in a state of great indigence, near Red Lion street, Whitechapel, when the *Baronetcy* became *dormant* or *extinct*.

The Baronetcy, however, was assumed possibly soon after 1793, but more probably some eighty years afterwards, as under.

IV. 1793. ROBERT CUMMING of Airdrie, stated(c) to have been s. of Robert CUMMING of Allathen, by Anna (*m.* 1730), da. of Alexander LESLIE, of Pitcaple, which Robert last named is stated(c) to have been br. of the 2d and yr. s. of the 1st Baronet(d); *suc. to the*

(a) His yr. br. (of the half blood) presumably his *only* yr. br., James Cumming, inherited the estate of Breda House, near Alford, co. Aberdeen, which, however, he sold. He *m.* twice, and left but one son, who *d.* s.p. before 15 June 1790.

(b) See p. 370, note "d."

(c) The affiliation and other particulars of this Robert are taken from a letter, dated 4 March 1867, written by "K. W. Cumming" (who by deed poll, 28 Nov. 1877, assumed the Baronetcy) which is printed in Tomkins's article. See p. 370, note "a." It is, however, shewn in that article that it "is impossible" for the claimant "to establish the most important points" in the pedigree, *viz.*, "that his great grandfather married a Miss Leslie and was the younger son of the Sir Alexander Cumming mentioned in the advertisement."

(d) See, however, note "a" above, as to James Cumming being, presumably, the *only* yr. son of the 1st Baronet.

Baronetcy(a) on the death of his cousin about 1793 and "because his Uncle's [*Qy.* Grandfather's] executors had sold Culter and his father [had] disposed of the lands of Allathen would not assume the title."(b) He *m.*, in or before 1775, Grace, da. of John STALKER, of Foxmore.

V. 1799? SIR KENNETH CUMMING, Baronet [S. 1695],(a) 1st s. and h., *suc. to the Baronetcy*(a) on the death of his father and is stated(c) to have "been in possession thereof for forty years."(a) He was M.D. in the Royal Artillery. He *m.* Marion, da. of David JONES, of Giveldon, co. Pembroke. He *d.* abroad s.p.m. 1838 or 1839, leaving two daughters.

VI. 1839? ROBERT STEWART CUMMING, of Cummingswood, in Prince Edward's Island, North America (which he was granted for his services at the siege of Copenhagen, 1807) only br. and h. male; *b.* 1777; was M.D. in the Royal Artillery and 7th Hussars; *suc. to the Baronetcy*(a) in 1838 or 1839, but never assumed the title. He *m.* firstly, Jane KAY, who *d.* 1826. He *m.* secondly, in or before 1837, Jean, da. of William AITCHISON, of Sprouston. He *d.* in Edinburgh, 1847, aged about 70. His widow *d.* 1865.

VII. 1847. SIR KENNETH WILLIAM CUMMING, Baronet [S. 1695],(a) only s. and h., *b.* 1837; *suc. to the Baronetcy*(a) in 1847, and signified his assumption thereof by deed poll, 28 Nov. 1877(a); ed. at Edinburgh University; M.D. 1861; entered Army Medical Service, 1862; sometime, 1864-73 in the Royal Artillery; Surgeon-Major, 1876; was in medical charge of the garrison at Exeter, 1876-78; Hon. Brig.-Surgeon (retired) 1882.

(a) According to the deed poll of 28 Nov. 1877 (advertised in the *Times* of 2 March 1878) as under.

"Notice is hereby given that I, KENNETH WILLIAM CUMMING hitherto known as Kenneth William Cumming, M.D., Surgeon-Major in Her Majesty's Army (Medical Service) have by deed poll under my hand and seal, dated the 23rd day of November 1877, ASSUMED as my lawful right, to myself and the heirs male lawfully begotten of my body THE NAME, rank, style and title of SIR KENNETH WILLIAM CUMMING, of Culter in the County of Aberdeen, BARONET, which rank and style were conferred upon my great great grandfather Sir Alexander Cumming, of Culter aforesaid, M.P., and the heirs male lawfully begotten of his body, by their late Majesties King William and Queen Mary, by letters patent dated the 28th day of February 1695, and the said Baronetcy having regularly descended to my late uncle SIR KENNETH CUMMING, of Culter aforesaid, who, after having been in possession thereof for 40 years, died in or about the year 1839 without any heir male lawfully begotten of his body, leaving my father ROBERT STEWART CUMMING, of Cummingswood in Prince Edward's Island in North America, M.D., his only brother and heir at law, who died in the year 1847, without having assumed the title and leaving me his only son and heir at law. The aforesaid deed poll was executed by me in lieu of recording my pedigree in one of the Colleges of Arms and obtaining a certificate therefrom, as required by the order of his late Majesty, King George III, dated the 6th day of December 1782, such order having been subsequently revoked by his said Majesty, so far as it related to Baronetcies created by letters patent prior to 1783. Dated 28th February 1878. Kenneth William Cumming.

"Witness—Wm. F. Geare, 57 Lincolns-inn-fields, Solicitor."

(b) See p. 371, note "c."

(c) This statement, if it implies that during that period he styled himself "Baronet," seems doubtful. His nephew (see p. 371, note "c") calls him "19th of the line and last actual Baronet," and adds, "See Peerages, etc., about 1800 up till 1838."

NEWTON:(a)

cr. 23 April 1697;

ex., 1724-27.

I. 1697, to 1727? RICHARD NEWTON, of that ilk, co. Haddington, s. and h. of Richard NEWTON, of the same, by Julian, sister of Patrick (HUME), 1st EARL OF MARCHMONT [S.], da. of Sir Patrick HUME, 1st Baronet [S. 1637], of Polwarth, was *cr. a Baronet* [S.] 23 April 1697 (the same date that his said maternal uncle was *cr. an Earl* [S.]) and is styled "Baronet" in several retours and other writs, there being among the family papers a receipt for the fees on such creation, though it is not recorded in the Great Seal Register and is not in Milne's *List*. He *m.* before 1702, Helen, da. of John LIVINGSTONE, niece and heir of Sir James LIVINGSTONE, 1st Baronet [S. 1699], of Westquarter. He, having no near relatives, executed an entail, 18 June 1724, in favour of a distant cousin, Richard HAY (4th s. of Lord William HAY), who, however, had no descent from the family of Newton. He *d.* s.p. before 24 June 1727, when the *Baronetcy* became *extinct*.

WEDDERBURN:

cr. 31 Dec. 1697;(b)

afterwards, 1705-1904, HALKETT;

ex. or *dormant*, 8 March 1904.

I. 1697. "PETER WEDDERBURN, of Gosford," co. Haddington, 3d s. of Sir Peter WEDDERBURN, of Gosford aforesaid, a Lord of Session (1668) under the style of *Lord Gosford* (*d.* 11 Nov. 1679), being 2d s. by his 2d wife, Agnes, da. of John DICKSON, of Hartree, a Judge of the Court of Session, was *b.* 1660; suc. his elder br., John WEDDERBURN, 26 May 1688, being in that year served heir to him and to his father, and was *cr. a Baronet* [S.], as above, by royal warrant dat. 31 Dec. 1697,(b) at Kensington, with rem. to heirs male of the body, no patent, however, being recorded in the Great Seal Register. He was sometime Capt. of Grenadiers. He, by the death s.p., 19 May 1705, of his wife's brother, Sir James HALKETT, 2d Baronet [S. 1662], inherited the estate of Pitfirrane, co. Fife, and took for himself and his successors therein the name of HALKETT in lieu of that of WEDDERBURN, and was (under the name of HALKETT) M.P. [S.] for Dunfermline, 1705-07, and M.P. thereof [G.B.] 1707-08. He *m.* in or before 1695, Janet, sister and heir of line of Sir James HALKETT, 2d Baronet [S. 1662], abovenamed, 1st da. of Sir Charles HALKETT, 1st Baronet [S. 1662], of Pitfirrane, co. Fife, by Jane, da. of Sir Patrick MURRAY, of Pitdennis. He *d.* 20 March 1746, aged 86.

II. 1746. SIR PETER HALKETT, Baronet [S. 1697], of Pitfirrane aforesaid, 1st s. and h., *b.* in or before 1695, was v.p. M.P. for Stirling burghs, 1734-41; was Lieut.-Col. at the battle of Gladsmuir in 1745, and was taken prisoner by the Jacobite insurgents, dismissed on parole and refused to rejoin his regiment in Feb. 1746; *suc. to the Baronetcy*, 20 March 1746; was in command of the 44th Foot in America in 1754. He *m.* Amelia, da. of Francis (STUART), EARL OF MORAY [S.], by his 2d wife, Jean, da. of John (ELPHINSTONE), 4th LORD BALMERINO [S.]. He *d.* 9 July 1755, being slain near the river Monnogahela, in America, at the defeat of Gen. Braddock. Will pr. 1757. His widow *d.* at Inveresk, 18 May 1781.

(a) See p. 242, note "c."

(b) The date in the *Lists* of Milne, Chamberlayne and Miege is 30 Dec. 1697, but in *The Wedderburn Book* (vol. i, p. 374) it is stated that "in 1697 by patent dat. at Kensington, 31 December, he was cr. a Baronet of Nova Scotia by William of Orange, with rem. to the heirs male of his body."

III. 1755. SIR PETER HALKETT, Baronet [S. 1697], of Pitfirrane aforesaid, 1st s. and h.,(a) *suc. to the Baronetcy*, 9 July 1755. He *d.* unm. 1792.

IV. 1792. SIR JOHN HALKETT, Baronet [S. 1697], of Pitfirrane, formerly John WEDDERBURN, of Gosford aforesaid, cousin and h. male, being 1st s. and h. of Charles WEDDERBURN, of Gosford, by Mary, da. of Sir Henry WARDLAW, 3d Baronet [S. 1631], *b.* 6 Aug. 1720; was a Capt. in the army at the taking of Guadaloupe in 1758; *suc. to the Baronetcy* and the Pitfirrane estate in 1792, when he took the name of HALKETT in lieu of WEDDERBURN, and settled the estate of Gosford on his next yr. br., Capt. Henry WEDDERBURN. He *m.* firstly, 6 Feb. 1758, at Brunstain House, Elizabeth, da. of Andrew FLETCHER, of Saltoun, Lord Justice Clerk. She *d.* s.p.m., 18 Dec. 1758. He *m.* secondly, in or before 1764, Mary (*b.* 1740), 6th and yst. da. and coheir of the Hon. John HAMILTON (2d s. of Thomas, 6th EARL OF HADDINGTON [S.]), by Margaret, da. of Sir John HOME, 3d Baronet [S. 1671], of Blackadder. He *d.* at Pitfirrane, 7 Aug. 1793. His widow *d.* at Dalmahoy, 3 Dec. 1803.

V. 1793. SIR CHARLES HALKETT, Baronet [S. 1697], of Pitfirrane aforesaid, 1st s. and h., by 2d wife; *b.* 1764; *suc. to the Baronetcy*, 7 Aug. 1793; was Capt. of the Dunfermline troop of the Fifeshire Yeomanry Cavalry. He *d.* unm. 26 Jan. 1837, at Pitfirrane, aged 71.

VI. 1837. SIR PETER HALKETT, Baronet [S. 1697], of Pitfirrane aforesaid, next br. and h., *b.* 1765; entered the Royal Navy; was at the victory over the Dutch Fleet at Camperdown in Oct. 1797, becoming, eventually, Admiral of the Blue and **G.C.H.**; *suc. to the Baronetcy*, 26 Jan. 1837. He *m.* 14 Oct. 1802, at Edinburgh, Elizabeth, da. of William TODD, of London She *d.* 1814. He *d.* 7 Oct. 1839, at Pitfirrane, aged 74. Will pr. Nov. 1839.

VII. 1839. SIR JOHN HALKETT, Baronet [S. 1697], of Pitfirrane aforesaid, only s. and h., *b.* 15 Jan. 1805; served in the Royal Navy, becoming Commander in 1837; *suc. to the Baronetcy*, 7 Oct. 1839. He *m.* 8 April 1831, Amelia Hood, da. of Col. CONWAY. He *d.* at Southampton, 5 Aug. 1847, aged 42. Will pr. April 1848. His widow *d.* 13 Feb. 1880, at Ryde.

VIII. 1847, to 1904. SIR PETER ARTHUR HALKETT, Baronet [S. 1697], of Pitfirrane aforesaid, 1st s. and h., *b.* 1 May 1834; *suc. to the Baronetcy* 5 Aug. 1847; ed. at Cheltenham College; Ensign, 81st Foot, 1851; 42d Foot, 1853, carrying the Queen's colours at the Alma, and serving all through the Crimean war; Captain, 1855, exchanging to the 3d Light Dragoons in 1856; had Crimean medal with three clasps; Commander of the order of "Isabella la Catolica" in Spain. He *m.* 6 May 1856, at Elstree, Herts, his cousin, Eliza Anna, 1st da. of Capt. Richard Kirwan HILL, 52d Foot, by Jane Margaret, da. of Sir Peter HALKETT, 6th Baronet [S. 1697]. He *d.* s.p.m.s.,(b) 8 March 1904, at Dunfermline, in his 70th year, when the *Baronetcy* became *extinct* or *dormant*. Will pr. at £58,382. His widow living 1904.

(a) His two brothers both *d.* unm., viz., Francis, Major in the Black Watch, who *d.* 11 Nov. 1760, and James, Lieut. 44th Foot, who was slain with his father, 9 July 1755.

(b) His only son, Wedderburn Conway Halkett, Capt. 78th Highlanders, *d.* v.p., 23 Aug. 1885, aged 28, leaving an only son, Arthur Wedderburn Halkett, who *d.* 15 Oct. 1886, in his 5th year.

HOME, *or* HUME(a):

cr. 31 Dec. 1697;

ex. 26 Dec. 1783.

I. 1697. SIR "PATRICK HOME [*or* HUME], of Lumsden" in the parish of Coldingham, co. Berwick, 2d s. of Sir John HOME, *or* HUME, of Renton in Coldingham, Lord Justice Clerk (*d.* 1671), by Margaret, da. of the Hon. John STEWART, Commendator of Coldingham (2d s. of Francis, 1st EARL OF BOTHWELL [S.]), was *b.* about 1650; admitted Advocate, 12 Jan. 1667, in which profession he made a large fortune; was *Knighted* before 1685, in which year he was accused of forgery by his elder br., Sir Alexander HOME, *or* HUME, 1st Baronet [S. 1672-78], from whom he fraudently and successfully withheld the paternal estate of Lumsden; was *cr. a Baronet* [S.], as above, by royal warrant, dat. 31 Dec. 1697, at Kensington, with rem. to heirs male of the body.(b) He was M.P. for Berwickshire, 1702-07. He *m.* Jean, da. of William DALMAHOY, of Ravelrig, co. Edinburgh, Quartermaster of the King's troop of Guards (s. of Sir Alexander DALMAHOY, of that ilk), by Helen, da. of (—) MARTIN. He, having entailed the estate of Lumsden, etc., a few days previously, *d.* Feb. 1723. Funeral escutcheon at Lyon office. His widow, who was *bap.* 19 April 1688, *d.* 23 Jan. 1756.

II. 1723. SIR JOHN HOME, Baronet [S. 1697], of Lumsden aforesaid and afterwards of Manderston in the parish of Dunse, co. Berwick, s. and h.; was fined in 1708 for being concerned in a riot; was admitted Advocate, 10 Feb. 1709; *suc. to the Baronetcy*, Feb. 1723, and was served heir gen. to his father, 12 Nov. 1726. He *m.* Margaret, da. of Sir Robert BAIRD, 1st Baronet [S. 1696], of Saughton Hall, by Elizabeth, da. of Michael, *or* Malcolm, FLEMING, of Ratho Byres. She *d.* 12 Feb. 1746. He *d.* 21 Dec. 1756.

III. 1756, to 1783. SIR JAMES HOME, Baronet [S. 1697], of Lumsden and Manderston aforesaid, s. and h., *suc. to the Baronetcy*, 21 Dec. 1756. He *m.* (—). She *d.* 11 Nov. 1777. He *d.* s.p.m.s.(c) 26 Dec. 1783, when the *Baronetcy* became *extinct*.

STEUART, *or* STEWART:

cr. 29 Jan. 1698;

sometime, 1758-73 and 1776-1839, STEUART-DENHAM;

afterwards, 1839-51, STEUART-BARCLAY;

dormant or *extinct*, 1851.

I. 1698, Jan. SIR "THOMAS STEWART [*or* STEUART], of Coltness," co. Lanark, 1st s. and h.(d) of Sir James STEWART, of the same, Lord Provost of Edinburgh, 1649 and 1659, by his 1st wife, Anne (*m*

(a) See p. 242, note "c."

(b) "Diploma by King William III, granting to Sir Patrick Home, of Lumsden the title and dignity of a Knight Baronet, at Kensington, 31 Dec. 1697." [*Calendar of the Laing Charters*, iv, 2966.]

(c) John, his only son, *d.* s.p. and v.p. 1765. Of the two daughters and coheirs (1) Margaret inherited the Manderston estate and was served heir of provision gen. to her father, 10 June 1784. She *m.* (—) Baird, but *d.* s.p. before May 1797. (2) Mary *m.* 21 June 1775, at Haddington (as second of his three wives), Sir Alexander Purves, 5th Baronet [S. 1665], and *d.* 4 July 1785, leaving (besides other issue) Alexander and John, who successively inherited the Manderston estate and took the name of Home.

(d) Of his yr. brothers (1) Sir James Steuart, of Goodtrees, Lord Advocate, 1692 and 1711, was father of James Steuart, of Goodtrees, *cr. a Baronet* [S.] v.p. 22 Dec. 1705, (2) Robert Steuart, of Allanbank, co. Berwick, *cr. a Baronet* [S.], 15 Aug. 1687.

1630), da. and coheir of Henry HOPE,(a) br. of Sir Thomas HOPE, 1st Baronet [S. 1628], of Craighall, was *b.* 1631; admitted Advocate, 1660; suc. his father (who *d.* aged 73), 31 March 1681; opposed the Test Act of 1681, being a zealous Presbyterian, and was forced to withdraw to Holland, but returned in 1687; was M.P. [S.] for North Berwick, 1689, till death in 1698; was *Knighted* in 1690 and was *cr. a Baronet* [S.], as above, 29 Jan. 1698, "provydit to heires male of his body and their aires male for ever."(b) He *m.* firstly, in 1654, Margaret, da. of his step-mother, Marion, da. of David MACULLOCH, of Goodtrees, co. Edinburgh, Writer, by her 1st husband, John ELIOTT, Advocate. She, by whom he had nine sons, *d.* 8 June 1675. He *m.* secondly, 14 March 1677, Susan, widow of William LOCKHART, of Wicketshaw, 2d and yst. sister of Sir William DENHAM, 1st Baronet [S. 1693], da. of Robert DENHAM, of Westshield, co. Lanark. By her he had five sons. He *d.* (shortly after his elevation to the Baronetcy) 6 April 1698, aged about 67.

II. 1698, April. SIR DAVID STEUART, Baronet [S. 1698], of Coltness aforesaid, 1st s. h., by 1st wife, *b.* 1656; *suc. to the Baronetcy*, 6 April 1698, and was served heir to his father, 2 March 1700. He, in 1712, sold the family estate of Coltness to his uncle, Sir James STEUART, Lord Advocate, father of Sir James STEUART, 1st Baronet [S. 1705], of Goodtrees, co. Edinburgh, who thus became "of Coltness." He *m.* in 1696, Marion, da. of William LOCKART, of Wicketshaw. He *d. s.p.* 1723, aged about 67.

III. 1723. THOMAS STEUART, nephew and h. male, being s. and h. of Walter STEUART, by his 2d wife Hannah QUASH, which Walter, who was *b.* 1663, was yr. br. of the whole blood to the late and s. of the 1st Baronet. He was *b.* 1708; *suc. to the Baronetcy* in 1723, but having no estate never assumed the title. He was a surgeon, and *d.* unm. at St. Christophers in 1737, aged about 29.

IV. 1737. ROBERT STEUART, uncle and h. male, being yr. br. of the whole blood to the 2d and s. of the 1st Baronet, *b.* 1675; *suc. to the Baronetcy* in 1737, but having no estate, never assumed the title. He *m.* in 1706, Margaret, da. of Zachary MAXWELL, of Blawarthill. He *d.* before 1758. His widow *d.* Dec. 1763.

V. 1750? JOHN STEUART, only surv. s. and h., Professor of Natural Philosophy at Edinburgh Univ.; *suc. to the Baronetcy* on the death of his father, but having no estate, never assumed the title. He *d.* unm. 12 May 1759.

VI. 1759. SIR ARCHIBALD STEUART-DENHAM, Baronet [S. 1693 and 1698], of Westshield, co. Lanark, formerly Archibald STEUART, uncle of the half blood and h. male, being only surv. child of the 1st Baronet by his 2d wife. He, who was *b.* at Utrecht, 20 July 1683, was Advocate 26 June 1711. By the death, 29 Sep. 1756, of his maternal cousin, Sir Robert DENHAM, 4th Baronet [S. 1693], he *suc. both to the Baronetcy* of Denham [S.], *cr.* 31 Jan. 1693, and to the estate of Westshield, under the entail of his maternal uncle, Sir William DENHAM, the 1st Baronet [S. 1693], when he took the name of DENHAM after that of STEUART, and was served heir of entail and provision general to him. On 12 May 1759, by the death of his nephew, John STEUART, *de jure* 5th Baronet [S. 1698], as above, he *suc. to that Baronetcy* [S. 1698], also. He *m.* in 1724, Jane, 1st da. of Sir George WARRENDER, 1st Baronet [1715], of Lochend, by his 2d wife, Grizel, da. of Hugh BLAIR, of Edinburgh. She *d.* 2 Feb. 1770. He *d. s.p.*, 12 June 1773, in his 90th year, when the Baronetcy of Denham devolved on his maternal cousin, William LOCKHART, afterwards LOCKHART-DENHAM (see DENHAM, Baronetcy [S.], *cr.* 31 Jan. 1693), but the Baronetcy of Steuart devolved as under.

(a) See Playfair's *Baronetage*, 1811 (vol. iii, appendix, p. xxi, note), as to her parentage, which differs from most of the other accounts thereof.
(b) Milne's *List*.

VII. and II. 1773. SIR JAMES STEUART, *afterwards* (from 1776) STEUART-DENHAM, Baronet [S. 1698 and 1705], of Westshield aforesaid, and Coltness, co. Lanark, cousin and h. male, being s. and h. of Sir James STEUART, 1st Baronet [S. 1705], of Goodtrees, sometime (1709) Solicitor Gen. [S.], by his 1st wife Anne, da. of Sir Hew DALRYMPLE, 1st Baronet [S. 1647], was *b.* 10 Oct. 1713; ed. at North Berwick School,(a) and subsequently at the Univ. of Edinburgh; *suc. to the Baronetcy* [S. 1705], and the estates of Goodtrees and Coltness (at the age of 14) on the death of his father, in 1727; admitted as Advocate, 1734, and after a prolonged travel abroad, applied himself diligently to his profession. He joined the Jacobite rising in 1745, but was pardoned in 1771, and was presented to the King 21 March 1772. He had meanwhile sold the estate of Goodtrees in 1756. By the death, 12 June 1773, of his cousin Sir Archibald STEUART-DENHAM, Baronet [S. 1693 and 1698], next abovenamed, he *suc. to the Baronetcy of Steuart* [S. 1698], in which his paternal Baronetcy [S. 1705], then merged. Finally by the death in 1776 of his somewhat distant kinsman, Sir William LOCKHART-DENHAM, 6th and last Baronet [S. 1693], of Westshield, co. Lanark, he, under his will, suc. to that valuable estate, and took the name of DENHAM after that of STEUART, though he (unlike his predecessor) had no descent whatever from the family of DENHAM. He *m.* 14 Oct. 1743, at Dunrobin, co. Sutherland, Frances, 1st da. of James (WEMYSS), EARL WEMYSS [S.], by Janet, da. and h. of Col. Francis CHARTERIS. He *d.* at Edinburgh, Nov. 1780, aged 67.(b) His widow *d.* at Coltness, 29 June 1789, in her 67th year.

VIII. and III. 1780. SIR JAMES STEUART-DENHAM, Baronet [S. 1698 and 1705], of Westshield and Coltness aforesaid, only s. and h., *b.* Aug. 1744; was an officer in the army, becoming eventually General in the army and Col. of the 2d Reg. of Dragoons (Scots Greys); *suc. to the Baronetcies*, Nov. 1780; was M.P. for Lanarkshire (three Parls.), 1784-1802; G.C.H. He *m.* 30 Sep. 1772, Alicia, da. of John BLACKER, of Carrick-Blacker, co. Armagh. He *d. s.p.s.*, 12 Aug. 1839, at Cheltenham, in his 95th year, being then the senior officer in the army.

IX. and IV. 1839, to 1851. SIR HENRY STEUART-BARCLAY, Baronet [S. 1698 and 1705], 2d cousin of the half-blood), and h. male, being only s. and h. of William STEUART-BARCLAY, of Collernie, co. Fife, by his 2d wife, Elizabeth, da. of Peter HAY, of Leys, which William (who *d.* 1783, aged 47) was s. of Henry STEUART-BARCLAY, *formerly* STEUART (*b.* 1697), who, by his wife, Antonia, da. and h. of John BARCLAY (whose name he took in addition to his own), acquired the estate of Collernie and who was yr. br. (of the half blood) to Sir James STEUART, 1st Baronet [S. 1705], of Goodtrees, being s. of Sir James STEUART, of Goodtrees, the Lord Advocate, by his 2d wife, Margaret, da. of Alexander AIR, merchant, of Leith. He was *b.* 1765 and inherited the estate of Collernie on the death of his father in 1783, which he sold in 1785. He *suc. to the Baronetcies*(as heir male collateral), 12 Aug. 1839. He *m.* 2 June 1789, Elizabeth WILSON. He *d. s.p.*, 1851, aged about 86, when both *Baronetcies* became *dormant* or *extinct*.

DUNBAR(c):

cr. 29 Jan. 1698.

I. 1698. "WILLIAM DUNBAR, of Durne," in the parish of Fordyce, co. Banff, 3d s. of Ninian DUNBAR, of Grangehill, in parishes of Dyke and Moy, co. Moray, by his 1st wife Mary, da. of Walter

(a) His career at school and all through life is given at very great length, and with an unusual amount of detail, in Playfair's *Baronetage* [1811], vol. iii, appendix xxxi-xxxvii.
(b) He was author of the "Principles of Political Æconomy," a work which had a considerable reputation.
(c) See p. 242, note "c."

OGILVY, of Dunlugus and Banff, was *cr. a Baronet* [S.], as above, by royal warrant, dat. at Kensington, 29 Jan. 1698, with rem. to "heirs male of his body and their aires male for ever."(a) He *m.* in or before 1667, Janet, da. of John BRODIE, Dean of Auldearn.

II. 1710? SIR JAMES DUNBAR, Baronet [S. 1698], of Durne aforesaid, 1st s. and h., *bap.* 9 Jan. 1668 at Kintessack; *suc. to the Baronetcy* on the death of his father. He *m.* Margaret, da. of Sir James BAIRD, of Auchmedden. She *d.* 11 Nov. 1734. He *d.* Nov. 1737.

III. 1737. SIR WILLIAM DUNBAR, Baronet [S. 1696], of Durne aforesaid, 1st s. and h.; *suc. to the Baronetcy*, Nov. 1737. He *m.* firstly, in 1737, Clementina, 4th da. of Sir James GRANT, *otherwise* COLQUHOUN, 6th Baronet [S. 1625], by Anne, da. and h. of Sir Humphrey COLQUHOUN, 5th Baronet [S. 1625]. She *d.* 1 June 1765. He *m.* secondly, Jane, da. of (—) BARTLET, of Banff. He *d.* 28 Jan. 1786.

IV. 1786. SIR JAMES DUNBAR, Baronet [S. 1698], of Durne aforesaid, 1st s. and h., by 1st wife; *suc. to the Baronetcy*, 28 Jan. 1786, and sold the estate of Durne; was Major in the Inverness Militia. He *d.* unm., and was *bur.* 20 Jan. 1812, at the Greyfriars, Edinburgh, when the issue male of the 1st Baronet became extinct.

V. 1812. SIR ROBERT DUNBAR, Baronet [S. 1698], cousin and h. male, being 1st s. and h. of the Rev. John DUNBAR, Minister of Knockando (1764) and of Dyke (1788), by Janet, da. of George GRANT, of Aberdeen, which John was 1st s. and h. of the Rev. Robert DUNBAR, of Ballinspink, in the parish of Fordyce, co. Banff, Minister of Dyke aforesaid (1727) who was 2d but 1st surv. s. of John DUNBAR, of Kinkorth, Tutor of Grangehill, who was s. and h. of David DUNBAR, of Kirkhill (*d.* 14 Feb. 1691), the next elder br. of the 1st Baronet, he being a yr. br. of Sir Robert DUNBAR, of Grangehill (*d.* 1659), and 2d s. of Ninian DUNBAR, abovenamed. He was *b.* 6 Jan. 1780; was, in 1811, a Ship and Insurance Broker, at 16 Old London Street, London,(b) and *suc. to the Baronetcy*, as heir male collateral, in Jan. 1812. He *m.*, 22 Oct. 1801, Margaret, da. of William FYFE, M.D., of Jamaica. He *d.* 11 Nov. 1813, aged 33. His widow *d.* 14 Jan. 1831.

VI. 1813. SIR WILLIAM DUNBAR, Baronet [S. 1698], 1st s. and h., *b.* 16 May 1804, at Allhallows Stayning, London; *suc. to the Baronetcy*, 11 Nov. 1813; matric. at Oxford (Mag. Hall), 4 March 1828, aged 23; S.C.L., 1830; in Holy Orders. Minister of St. Paul's, Aberdeen, 1842; Incumbent of St. Paul's, Camden Town, Midx., 1855; Rector of Walwyns Castle, co. Pembroke, 1862-75, and Rector of Dummer, Hants, 1875-81. He *m.* 9 Feb. 1836, at St. Pancras, Midx., Anne, 1st da. of George STEPHEN, of Camden Town. He *d.* at Dummer Rectory, 27 Nov. 1881, in his 68th year. His widow *d.* 21 July 1889, at 5 Downshire Hill, Hampstead.

VII. 1881. SIR DRUMMOND MILES DUNBAR, Baronet [S. 1698], 2d and yst. but only surv. s. and h.,(c) *b.* 21 Nov. 1845, at Aberdeen; *suc. to the Baronetcy*, 27 Nov. 1881; sometime Chief Sanitary Inspector at Johannesburg, in South Africa, and was put on trial by the Boers for complicity in the rising of 1896. He *m.* 21 July 1873, Maria Louisa, 4th da. of John Hancorn SMITH, of Melville Park, Lower Albany, South Africa. He *d.* at Johannesburg, 4 Jan. 1903, aged 57. Will pr. May, 1904, at £305 gross, *nil* net. His widow living 1904.

(a) Milne's *List*. The diploma confers the dignity "in Gulielmum Dunbar de Durne, ob notam suam fidelitatem et integritatem, et post ejus decessum in heredes masculos de corpore suo, eorumque heredes masculos in perpetuum."
(b) Playfair's *Baronetage*, 1811.
(c) The eldest son, Alexander Stephen Dunbar, *m.* but *d. s.p.* and *v.p.*, 29 Jan. 1868, aged 30.

VIII. 1903. SIR GEORGE ALEXANDER DRUMMOND DUNBAR, Baronet, [S. 1698], 2d and yst. but only surv. s. and h.,(a) *b.* 10 May 1879, *suc. to the Baronetcy*, 4 Jan. 1903.

HOPE:

cr. 1 March 1698;

dormant 1763.

I 1698. SIR "WILLIAM HOPE, of Kirkliston," 9th and yst. but 2d surv. s.(b) of Sir James HOPE, of Hopetoun, co. Linlithgow (*d.* Nov. 1661, aged 47), by Anne, da. and h. of Robert FOULIS, of Leadhills, co. Lanark, was *b.* at Edinburgh, 15 April 1660; "served in the army; travelled much abroad; was an accomplished Cavalier, renowed for skill in fencing and horsemanship, and gracefulness and agility in dancing"(c); was formerly of Grantoun, in Midlothian, but subsequently of Kirkliston aforesaid, and, having been *Knighted*, was *cr. a Baronet* [S.], as above, 1 March 1698, with rem. to heirs male whatsoever. He was many years, and till his death, Deputy Governor, of Edinburgh Castle. In 1705 he purchased, for £7,500, the estate of Balcomie, co. Fife. He *m.*, in or before 1682, Elizabeth, da. of (—) CLERK. He *d.* at Edinburgh (of a fever caused by over-dancing), 1 Feb. 1724, and was *bur.* in the Canongate Church there, aged 63.

II. 1724. SIR GEORGE HOPE, Baronet [S. 1698], of Balcomie aforesaid, only s. and h., *b.* probably about 1685; was Capt. in a regiment of Foot; *suc. to the Baronetcy* 1 Feb. 1724. He *m.*, 29 Nov. 1724, Anne, da. of Sir John MACKENZIE, 3d Baronet [S. 1673], of Coul, by his 2d wife, Helen, da. of Patrick (MURRAY), 3d LORD ELIBANK [S.] He *d.* in Ireland, 20 Nov. 1729.

III. 1729 to 1763. SIR WILLIAM HOPE, Baronet [S. 1698], of Balcomie aforesaid, only s. and h., *suc. to the Baronetcy* when under 4 years of age, 20 Nov. 1729. He was a Lieutenant R.N., 1749, being afterwards Lieutenant 31st Foot, and subsequently Captain in the East India Company's service. He *m.* a Dutch lady.(d) He *d. s.p.*, being killed at Bengal in 1763(e), aged about 37, when the *Baronetcy* became *dormant*, the collateral heir male being the EARL OF HOPETOUN [S.], who, however, and whose successors, never assumed the same. His widow *m.* (—) LAMBERT, and *d.* 1766.(d)

DALRYMPLE:

cr. 28 April 1698;(f)

sometime, 1800? to 1810,

DALRYMPLE-HAMILTON-MACGILL;

afterwards, since 1810, HAMILTON-DALRYMPLE;

and finally, since 1840, EARLS OF STAIR [S.].

I. 1698. The Hon. "JAMES DALRYMPLE, of Killoch," formerly of Borthwick, subsequently of Killoch aforesaid, and finally of Cousland, 2d s. of James, 1st VISCOUNT STAIR [S.] (*d.* 25 Nov. 1695), by Margaret, da.

(a) The eldest son, William Dunbar, *d.* unm. and *v.p.*, 19 May 1900, aged 24.
(b) The 5th but 1st surv. s. and h., John Hope, of Hopetoun, was father of Charles, *cr.* 5 April 1703, Earl of Hopetoun [S.].
(c) Wood's *Douglas's Peerage* [S.], under "Hopetoun."
(d) Wood's *East Neuk of Fife*.
(e) This is the date in Wood's *Douglas' Peerage* (see note "c" above), but in Burke's *Extinct Baronetcies* it is given (probably by mistake) as "1773." No notice of his death is in Musgrave's *Obituary*, nor, apparently anywhere else.
(f) The dates of the two Dalrymple creations, 28 April 1698 and 29 April 1698 are (presumably in error) given in Playfair's *Baronetage* (1811) as 28 April 1697 and 29 April 1697.

and heir of line of James Ross, of Balniel, co. Wigtoun, was *b.* about 1650; Advocate, 25 June 1675; Commissary of Edinburgh and one of the principal Clerks of the Court of Session, and was *cr. a Baronet* [S.], as above, 28 April 1698,(a) with rem. "to heirs male of his body and their aires male for ever."(b) He was "a man of great learning and one of the best antiquarians of his time."(c) He *m.* firstly, 2 Jan. 1679, Catherine, 3d da. of Sir James DUNDAS, of Arnistoun, a Lord of Session, by his 1st wife, Marion, da. of Robert (BOYD), 6th LORD BOYD [S.]. She was *bur.* 17 Jan. 1689. He *m.* secondly, 4 Sep. 1691, Esther, widow of James FLETCHER, of Cranstoun, co. Midlothian, da. of John CUNNINGHAM, of Enterkine. Writer to the Signet. She *d.* in childbirth, and was *bur.* 7 April 1700, at Greyfriars, Edinburgh. He *m.* thirdly, 7 Sep. 1701, "Jean HALKETT, Lady DALPHOLLY." He *d.* May 1719.

II. 1719. SIR JOHN DALRYMPLE, Baronet [S. 1698], of Cousland and Cranstoun aforesaid,(d) 1st s. and h. by 1st wife, *b.* about 1682; admitted an Advocate, 1704; one of the principal Clerks of the Court of Session, upon his father's resignation in 1709; *suc. to the Baronetcy*, May 1719. He *m.* firstly (contract 7 Aug. 1702), Elizabeth, only surv. da. and h. of James FLETCHER, of Cranstoun aforesaid, by his step mother, Esther, da. of John CUNNINGHAM abovenamed. She was living 1714. He *m.* secondly, Sidney, da. of John SINCLAIR, of Ulbster, co. Caithness, by Jean, da. of Sir George MONRO, of Culraine. He *d.* 24 May 1743, aged about 60. His widow *d.* 20 Oct. 1759.

III. 1743. SIR WILLIAM DALRYMPLE, Baronet [S. 1698], of Cousland and Cranstoun aforesaid, 2d but 1st surv. s. and h. by 1st wife, *b.* 23 Sep. 1704; admitted Advocate, 27 Jan. 1730; *suc. to the Baronetcy*, 24 May 1743. He *m.* firstly, in or before 1726, Agnes, da. of William CRAWFORD, of Glasgow. She *d.* 13 Oct. 1755, at Edinburgh. He *m.* secondly, Ann, da. of (—) Philp. He *d.* at Cranstoun, and was *bur.* 20 March 1771, at Greyfriars, Edinburgh, aged 66.

IV. 1771. SIR JOHN DALRYMPLE, *afterwards* DALRYMPLE-HAMILTON-MACGILL, Baronet [S. 1698], of Cousland and Cranstoun aforesaid, as also of Fala and Oxenfoord, co. Edinburgh, 1st s. and h. by 1st wife, *b.* 1726; admitted as Advocate, 17 Dec. 1748; Solicitor to the Board of Excise; *suc. to the Baronetcy*, March 1771; was a Baron of the Court of Exchequer, 1776-1807.(e) "In consequence of his accession to several estates by marriage, towards the latter part of his life,"(f) he took the names of HAMILTON-MACGILL after that of DALRYMPLE. He *m.* 7 Oct. 1760, his cousin, Elizabeth, da. and h. of Thomas HAMILTON, afterwards HAMILTON-MACGILL, of Fala and Oxenford, by Elizabeth, da. of Sir John DALRYMPLE, 2d Baronet [S. 1698], abovenamed. He *d.* 26 Feb. 1810, aged 84, at Oxenfoord Castle. His wife survived him.

V. 1810. SIR JOHN HAMILTON-DALRYMPLE, Baronet [S. 1698], of Cousland, Cranstoun, Fala and Oxenfoord aforesaid, 4th but 1st surv. s. and h.,(g) *b.* 15 June 1771, in Edinburgh; Ensign, 100th Foot, 1790;

(a) See p. 379, note "f."

(b) Milne's *List*.

(c) See *Dict. Nat. Biog.*, where, however, no date of death is given, but merely the remark "floruit 1714."

(d) The estate of Killoch had been left to his yr. br. Robert Dalrymple, a Writer to the Signet, who *d.* 2 Dec. 1765, aged 81, leaving issue.

(e) He was author of "Memoirs of Great Britain and Ireland" [Edinburgh, 1771, 4to], in which, for (it is believed) the first time, the discreditable transactions (then recently discovered) of those much belauded "*patriots*" [!] Algernon Sidney and William, Lord Russell, were divulged.

(f) Playfair's *Baronetage*, 1811.

(g) Of the elder sons, besides one who *d.* an infant; (1) Thomas, *d.* at Edinburgh, 2 Feb. 1770, under 9 years of age; (2) William, an officer in the Royal Navy, was killed in action, 29 July 1782, in his 18th year, and is commemorated by a monument in Westminster Abbey.

Captain, 3d Foot Guards, 1798-1814; Colonel, 92d Foot, 1831-43; Colonel, 46th Foot, 1848 till death, becoming General, 1838; *suc. to the Baronetcy*, 26 Feb. 1810; was M.P. (in the Whig interest) for co. Edinburgh, 1833-34. He *m.* firstly, 23 June 1795, at Kenilworth, co. Warwick, Harriet, 1st da. of the Rev. Robert Augustus JOHNSON, of Kenilworth, by Anne Rebecca, sister to William (CRAVEN), 6th BARON CRAVEN OF HAMPSTED MARSHALL. She *d.* 16 Oct. 1823, and was *bur.* at Cranstoun. He *m.* secondly, 8 June 1825 (at the house of her widowed mother), Adamina, 4th da. of Adam (DUNCAN), 1st VISCOUNT DUNCAN OF CAMPERDOWN, by Henrietta, da. of the Right Hon. Robert DUNDAS. She was living when, by the death, 20 March 1840, of his cousin, the 7th EARL OF STAIR [S.], he *succeeded to that Peerage* as 8th EARL OF STAIR, etc. [S.]. In that peerage this *Baronetcy* then *merged* and still (1904) so continues. See *Peerage*.

DALRYMPLE:

cr. 29 April 1698(a);

afterwards, since 1796, HAMILTON-DALRYMPLE;

though, in 1800 to 1834, DALRYMPLE-HAMILTON.

I. 1698. The Hon "HEW DALRYMPLE, of North Berwick," co. Haddington, yr. br. of Sir James DALRYMPLE, 1st Baronet [S. 1698], of Killoch abovenamed, being 3d s. of James, 1st VISCOUNT STAIR [S.] (*d.* 25 Nov. 1695), by Margaret, da. and heir of line of James Ross, of Balniel, co. Wigtoun, was *b.* about 1653; Advocate, 23 Feb. 1677; was one of the Commissaries of Edinburgh; was Dean of the Faculty of Advocates, 1695-98; M.P. [S.] for New Galloway, 1696-1702, and for North Berwick, 1702-07, being one of the Commissioners to settle the Articles of the Union, and was *cr. a Baronet* [S.], as above, 29 April 1698,(a) with rem. "to heirs male of his body and their aires male for ever."(b) He was made, 7 June 1698, Lord President of the Court of Session (an office which had been vacant nearly three years, since his father's death), and continued so till his death in 1737. He *m.* firstly, 12 March 1682, Marion, da. of Sir Robert HAMILTON, of Presmennan, one of the Lords of Session. She was living June 1700. He *m.* secondly, in or before 1712, Elizabeth, widow of James HAMILTON, of Bangour, co. Linlithgow, da. of John HAMILTON, of Olivestob. He *d.* 1 Feb. 1737, in his 85th year. His widow *d.* at Edinburgh, 21 March 1742, aged 67.

II. 1737. SIR HEW DALRYMPLE, Baronet [S. 1698], of North Berwick aforesaid, grandson and h., being 1st s. and h.(c) of Sir Robert DALRYMPLE, of Castleton, by his 1st wife, Johanna (*m.* 23 Feb. 1707), da. and h. of the Hon. John HAMILTON, Master of Bargeny (1st s. and h. ap. of John, 2d LORD BARGENY [S.]), which Robert (who, after having been *Knighted*, *d.* v.p., 21 Aug. 1734) was s. and h. ap. of the late Baronet. He was *b.* probably about 1710; was admitted Advocate, 1730; *suc. to the Baronetcy*, 1 Feb. 1737; was M.P. for Haddington Burghs, 1742-47; for Haddingtonshire (two Parls.), 1747-61, and for Haddington Burghs (again), 1761-68. He was made King's Remembrancer [S.] in 1768. He *m.* firstly 12 July, 1743, Margaret, da. of (—) SAINTHILL, of London, surgeon. She *d.* at North Berwick, 31 Dec. 1748. Admon., as of St. James', Westm., 22 Feb. 1749/50. He *m.* secondly, 17 Aug. 1756, at St. James', Westm., in the house of Mrs. ASHBY, Saville Row, Martha, da. of Charles EDWIN, of Lincoln's Inn, Barrister, by his 1st wife, Martha, da. of (—) BARNARDISTON. She *d.* 12 Sep. 1782. He *d.* in London, 23 Nov. 1790. Will pr. April 1791.

(a) See p. 379, note "f."

(b) Milne's *List*.

(c) The 2d son, John Dalrymple (*b.* 4 Feb. 1715), who, on the death, 28 March 1736, of James, 4th and last Lord Bargeny [S.], inherited the estate of that family, and took the name of Hamilton, *d.* s.p. 12 Feb. 1796, aged 81.

III. 1790. SIR HEW DALRYMPLE, *afterwards*, since 1796, HAMILTON-DALRYMPLE, Baronet [S. 1698], of North Berwick aforesaid, 2d but 1st surv. s.(a) by the 1st wife, *b.* about 1746; sometime an Officer in the army; was v.p. M.P. for Haddingtonshire, 1780-84 and 1784 till made Auditor of the Excise [S.] in 1786; *suc. to the Baronetcy*, 23 Nov. 1790. By the death, 12 Feb. 1796, of his uncle, John HAMILTON, *formerly* DALRYMPLE, of Bargeny, co. Ayr, he inherited that estate and took the name of HAMILTON in addition to that of DALRYMPLE. He *m.*, in or before 1773, his cousin, Janet, 2d da. of William DUFF, of Crombie, co. Ayr, by Elizabeth, sister of the 2d Baronet and da. of Sir Robert DALRYMPLE abovenamed. He *d.* 13 Feb. 1800, at Bargeny. Will pr. April 1800.

IV. 1800. SIR HEW DALRYMPLE-HAMILTON, Baronet [S. 1698], of North Berwick and Bargeny aforesaid, *formerly* HAMILTON-DALRYMPLE, and before that DALRYMPLE, 1st s. and h., *b.* 3 Jan. 1774; was seven years in the Guards and one year in the Dragoons; was M.P. for Haddingtonshire (two Parls.), 1795-1800; for Ayrshire, 1803-06, 1806-07, 1811-12 and 1812-18, and for Haddington Burghs, 1820-26; *suc. to the Baronetcy*, 14 Feb. 1800, when he took the name of DALRYMPLE-HAMILTON; Lieut.-Col. Ayrshire Militia. He *m.* 19 May 1800, in London, Jane, sister of Robert, 1st EARL OF CAMPERDOWN, 1st da. of Adam (DUNCAN), 1st VISCOUNT DUNCAN OF CAMPERDOWN, by Henrietta, da. of the Right Hon. Robert DUNDAS. He *d.* s.p.m.,(b) 23 Feb. 1834, at Bargeny House, aged 60. His widow, who was *b.* 30 March 1778, and who was a celebrated beauty, was granted, by Royal warrant, 29 Oct. 1833, the precedence of the da. of an Earl, and *d.* at Paris, 7 March 1852, aged nearly 74.

V. 1834. SIR JOHN HAMILTON-DALRYMPLE, Baronet [S. 1698], of North Berwick aforesaid, br. and h. male, *b.* about 1776; entered the army, becoming eventually Major-Gen.; was M.P. for Haddington Burghs, 1805-06; *suc. to the Baronetcy* (but not to the Bargeny estate), 23 Feb. 1834. He *m.* 30 July 1806, at Lochend, co Haddington, Charlotte, only da. of Sir Patrick WARRENDER, 3d Baronet [1715], by H., da. of (—) BLAIR. He *d.* 26 May 1835, at Bruntsfield House, Edinburgh. Will pr. Jan. 1836. His widow *d.* 14 April 1871, at 20 Chesham Place, aged 87.

VI. 1835. SIR HEW HAMILTON-DALRYMPLE, Baronet [S. 1698], of North Berwick aforesaid, 1st s. and h., *b.* 21 Nov. 1814; entered the army and served in 1834, at the capture of Coorg, in the East Indies, becoming in 1847 Lieut.-Col. of the 71st Foot, but retiring in 1852; *suc. to the Baronetcy*, 26 May 1835; was Convener of Haddingtonshire, 1861. He *m.* 27 July 1852, at Sutton Scarsdale, co. Derby, Frances Elizabeth, only da. of Robert ARKWRIGHT, of Sutton aforesaid, by Frances Crawford, da. of Stephen George KEMBLE. He *d.* s.p., 27 April 1887, at Leuchie House, co. Haddington, aged 72, and was *bur.* at North Berwick. His widow *d.* at Leuchie House aforesaid, 28 Feb. 1894. Personalty sworn over £40,000.

VII. 1887. SIR JOHN WARRENDER DALRYMPLE, Baronet [S. 1698], of North Berwick aforesaid, br. and h., *b.* May 1824; entered, in 1842, the Bengal Civil Service, becoming, 1856-60, Civil and Sessions Judge at Hooghly, but retiring in 1872; *suc. to the Baronetcy*, 27 April 1887. He *m.*, 7 June 1847, at St. Geo. Han. sq., Sophia, yr. da. of James POTTLE, senior member of the service abovenamed. He *d.*, 28 Dec. 1888, at the Lodge, North Berwick, and was *bur.* at North Berwick, aged 64. His widow living 1904.

(a) The 1st son, Robert Stair Dalrymple, Capt. 11th Dragoons, *d.* unm. and v.p. at Manchester, 11 Sep. 1768, aged 24.

(b) His only da. and h., Henrietta-Dundas, who inherited the Bargeny estate, *m.* 16 June 1822, the Duc de Coigny, and *d.* 19 Dec. 1869, leaving issue, two daughters and coheirs, viz., the Countess of Stair and the Countess Manvers.

VIII. 1888. SIR WALTER DALRYMPLE, afterwards, since 1889, HAMILTON-DALRYMPLE, Baronet [S. 1698]., of North Berwick aforesaid, 2d but only surv. s. and h.,(a) *b.* 6 Jan. 1854; *suc. to the Baronetcy*, 28 Dec. 1888, and by royal lic., 1889, took the name of HAMILTON before that of DALRYMPLE. He *m.*, 7 Nov. 1882, Alice Mary, da. of Major-General the Hon. Sir Henry Hugh CLIFFORD, K.C.M.G. (yr. s. of Hugh Charles, 7th BARON CLIFFORD OF CHUDLEIGH), by Josephine Elizabeth, only child of Joseph ANSTICE, of Madeley Wood, Salop.

Family Estates.—These, in 1883, consisted of 3,039 acres in Haddingtonshire, worth £8,856 a year. *Residence.*—Leuchie house, North Berwick, co. Haddington.

KENNEDY: (b)

cr. 8 June 1698;

dormant or *extinct*, May 1729.

I. 1698. "ANDREW KENNEDY, of Clowburn," in the parish of Pettinain, co. Lanark, s. and h. of John KENNEDY, Provost of Ayr (1647-48), who was a scion of the family of KENNEDY, of Bargeny, registered arms at the Lyon office about 1680; was imprisoned in 1683 for having aided the fugitives at the battle of Bothwell bridge (1679); was a Commissioner of Supply, 1689-90; was appointed, in 1690, for life, and again, 1697, jointly with his eldest son, "Conservator of the Scots' privileges in the Low Countries," and, having acquired, by marriage, the abovenamed estate of Clowburn, was *cr. a Baronet* [S.], as above, 8 June 1690, with rem. to heirs male of his body and their heirs male successive.(c) Owing to malversation, his office of Conservator was given over 1705-06, to Sir Alexander CUMMING, 1st Baronet [S. 1695], and he was altogether deprived of it in Jan. 1708, shortly after which date the estate of Clowburn was sold. He *m.* Mary, da. and coheir, but eventually sole h., of John WEIR, of Clowburn aforesaid. He *d.* in or about Feb. 1716/7.

II. 1717, to 1729. SIR JOHN VERE(d) KENNEDY, Baronet [S. 1698], s. and h., was appointed in 1697 joint "Conservator of the Scots' privileges in the Low Countries" together with his father, and after his death to hold the same "during pleasure." He *suc. to the Baronetcy* about Feb. 1716/7. He *m.* firstly, in or before 1717, Elizabeth,(e) da. of (—). She was living June 1725.(f) He *m.* secondly, 19 Feb. 1726/7, at Bennet's, Paul's Wharf, London, Elizabeth CHARLTON, of St. Martin's in the fields, widow. He *d.* apparently, s.p.m.s., and was *bur.* at Chelsea, Midx., 26 May 1729, when the *Baronetcy* became *dormant* or *extinct*.(g) Will pr. 1729. "The Lady Kennedy" [possibly his widow] *d.* Aug. 1732, "at her house near Westminster Abbey."(h)

(a) Hew Dalrymple, the 1st. s., *b.* 21 April 1848, *d.* unm. and v.p. March 1868.

(b) See p. 242, note "c."

(c) Milne's *List*. The words therein are "provydit to his eldest son and heirs male of his body ejus que nostros [*Qy.* rectos] heredes masculos successive."

(d) His mother was of a Lanarkshire family of the name of Weir, who were descended (according to Sir James Dalrymple) from "Thomas *de Vere*," living 1266 [Burke's *Commoners*, vol. iii, p. 320].

(e) "John, s. of Sir John Kenedy and his Lady Elizabeth," *b.* 13 May, *bap.* 5 June 1717, at St. Martin's in the fields.

(f) "Alexander, of Sir John Kennedy, Bart., and Elizabeth," *bap.* 17 June 1725, at St. James', Westm.

(g) Marion, living 1750, the last surv. child of the 1st Baronet, left a house in Edinburgh to her remote kinsman, Robert Kennedy, of Auchtyfardle, co. Lanark.

(h) *London Mag.*, 1732, p. 262.

LIVINGSTON: (a)

cr. 30 May 1699;

not assumed from 1701 to about 1775;

dormant or *extinct*, 1 April 1853;

but assumed after 1859.

I. 1699 to 1701. "JAMES LIVINGSTON, of Westquarter," co. Stirling, yr. s. of the Hon. Sir William LIVINGSTON, of Culter (5th and yst. s. of William, 6th LORD LIVINGSTON [S.]), by Helen, da. of Alexander LIVINGSTON, and grand daughter and heir (8 July 1630) of Robert LIVINGSTON, of Westquarter aforesaid, *suc.* his elder br., Sir William LIVINGSTON, in the estate of Westquarter as heir male and was *cr. a Baronet* [S.], as above, by royal warrant, dat. at Kensington 30 May 1699, with rem. "to his eldest son and his aires male successive."(b) He *m.* (contract 28 June 1690) Mary, widow of Alexander (LIVINGSTON), 2d EARL OF CALENDAR [S.], 3d da. of William (HAMILTON), 2d DUKE OF HAMILTON, by Elizabeth, da. and coheir of James (MAXWELL), 1st EARL OF DIRLETOUN [S.]. He *d.* s.p., at Edinburgh, 27 Nov. 1701,(c) when the *Baronetcy* became *dormant* for about 70 years.(d) He left the estate of Westquarter to his widow, who *m.* (as her 3d husband and his 2d wife) James (OGILVY), 3d EARL OF FINDLATER [S.], who *d.* 1711, and *d.* s.p.m. 1705, before Aug., having entailed it on her said 2d husband for life, and, after his death, on the relatives of her 1st husband, as below.

* * * * * * *

II. 1701. ALEXANDER LIVINGSTON, of Bedlormie, co. Linlithgow, and afterwards (1711) of Westquarter aforesaid, 1st cousin twice removed and h. male, being s. and h. of Sir Alexander LIVINGSTON, of Craigengall, by Susanna, 1st da. and coheir of Patrick WALKER, of Bedlormie aforesaid, which Alexander (who *d.* May 1690), was s. and h. of William LIVINGSTON, of Craigengall and Ogilface, co. Linlithgow (*d.* 1649), s. and h. of the Hon. Sir George LIVINGSTON,(e) of Ogilface aforesaid (one of the adventurers of the forfeited estates in Ireland, where he died), next elder br. to the father of the 1st Baronet, both being yr. brs. of Alexander, 1st EARL OF LINLITHGOW [S.], and sons of William, 6th LORD LIVINGSTON [S.] abovenamed. He suc. to the Bedlormie estate on the death of his father in 1690, and *to the Baronetcy* (as heir male) on the death of his cousin abovenamed, 27 Nov. 1701, but did not assume the title. In 1711 he suc. to the estate of Westquarter, as abovementioned. He *m.* (contract Feb. and June 1683) Henrietta, da. of Alexander SCOTT, Goldsmith, Burgess of Edinburgh, and by her had seven sons. He *d.* 13 Nov. 1720.(f)

III. 1720. GEORGE LIVINGSTON, of Bedlormie aforesaid, 1st s. and h., *suc. to the Baronetcy* (though not, apparently, to the Westquarter estate) on the death of his father in 1720, but did not assume the title. He had general service to his father, 21 Feb. 1722. He *m.* in 1722, Frances,

(a) See p. 242, note "c."

(b) Milne's *List*. There are extracts bearing on the limitation printed in the *Scottish Antiquary*, vol. iii, p. 84.

(c) "The Laird of Westquarter dyd at Edinburgh 27 Nov" [1701]. See "Masterton Papers" in the *Scot. His. Soc. Miscellany*, p. 476.

(d) Helen, his niece and heir (who, however, did not inherit the Westquarter estate), *m.* before 1702, Sir Richard Newton, Baronet [S. 1697], who *d.* s.p. before 27 June 1727.

(e) It is stated (Playfair's *Baronetage*, 1811, and elsewhere) that "Ogleface" [*i.e.*, this George] was *cr. a Baronet* [S.] in 1625. This, however, is a mistake. The creation of 30 May 1625 (sealed 20 Aug. following) was that of Sir David Livingston, of Dunipace, and became dormant at his death, 1631-34.

(f) The will, proved Dec. 1718, of Sir Alexander Livingston, Baronet, who died in Holland, refers to the 3d and last Baronet [S. 1627], of Newbigging.

da. (but possibly illegit., though called "*lawful*" da. in her marr. contract, 21 April 1722. See *Reg. Mag. Sig.* 26 July 1722) of Lord John KERR, yr. s. of Robert, 1st MARQUESS OF LOTHIAN [S.]. He *d.* s.p., 1729.

IV. *1729.* ALEXANDER LIVINGSTON, of Bedlormie aforesaid, next br. and h., *suc. to the Baronetcy* in 1729 but did not assume the title. He had general service to his brother, 13 Nov. 1729. He was a surgeon at Dalkeith. He *m.* firstly, Christian, da. of John HAY, Collector of Customs. He *m.* secondly, Margaret, da. of John MURRAY, of Muirlawpen, co. Fife. He *d.* s.p., 1766.

V. 1766. WILLIAM LIVINGSTON, of Westquarter and Bedlormie aforesaid, next surv. br. and h., being 4th s. of his father; was a Capt. in the army. He was, 4 Feb. 1756, served heir of tailzie and provision general of Mary, COUNTESS OF FINDLATER [S.], relict of the 1st Baronet, and on 4 March 1765 recovered the estate of Westquarter, which had been possessed and illegally sold by his next eldest br., James LIVINGSTON, who *d.* s.p. in 1740.(a) He *suc. to the Baronetcy* in 1766, but did not assume the title. He *m.* Helen, da. of John PARKER, of London. He *d.* s.p., 22 Feb. 1769.

VI. 1769. SIR ALEXANDER LIVINGSTON, Baronet [S. 1699], of Westquarter and Bedlormie aforesaid, nephew and h., being s. and h. of Robert LIVINGSTON, by Isabella, da. of Thomas BAILLIE, of Polkemmet, co. Linlithgow, which Robert, who was an officer in the army, and who lost his right arm in battle against the Jacobite insurgents in 1745, *d.* in 1759. He *suc. to the Baronetcy* in 1769, but did not, apparently, assume the (long since dormant) title till some few years later, but, apparently, before 1778.(b) He, on 18 Aug. 1769, had spec. service to his uncle, George LIVINGSTON, in Bedlormie, part of Ogilface, etc., and, on 1 Jan. 1770, as heir male of entail and provision general to his uncle, William LIVINGSTON, in Westquarter.(c) In 1784 he claimed the EARLDOM OF CALLENDAR [S.]. He *m.* firstly, Ann, da. of John ATKINSON, of London, and by her had seven sons. She *d.* 27 Dec. 1778. He *m.* secondly, in 1782, Jane, only child of Capt. the Hon. William Henry CRANSTOUN (yr. s. of William, 5th LORD CRANSTOUN [S.], by Anne, sister of Sir David MURRAY, 4th Baronet [S. 1664], of Stanhope.(d) He *d.* 8 April 1795. His widow, who was *b.* 19 Feb. 1745, and by whom he had two more sons, had a pension of £100 a year, and *d.* at the Spittal, near Hexham, 7 July 1830, aged 84.

VII. 1795, to 1853. SIR THOMAS LIVINGSTONE, Baronet [S. 1699], of Westquarter and Bedlormie aforesaid, 3d but 1st surv. s. and h.(e) by 1st wife; was *b.* 20 Nov. 1769; entered the navy in Sep. 1782; was at the attack on Martinique, 1793; assisted to convey the Russian contingent to England, 1799; in command of the "Diadem;" was in the

(a) The Westquarter estate must apparently have been entailed on the 2d s. of this line, probably to keep it distinct from that of Bedlormie.

(b) The death of his wife, as "*Lady* Livingston, of Westquarter," is announced as on 27 Dec. 1778 [*Scot's Mag.*].

(c) An absurd story was current about his recovering the estate of Westquarter by accidently finding the title deeds at an inn. That estate, however, had been long before recovered by his uncle, the legal proceedings forming one of the leading cases in the law of Scotland. Moreover, the original deed of entail would not have been necessary, as it had been registered 10 Dec. 1719.

(d) See Wood's *Douglas' Peerage* [S.], under "Cranstoun."

(e) Alexander Small Livingston, the 1st s., *d.* v.p. and unm., 1790. Six other sons *d.* also unm., of whom George Augustus Livingston and David Livingston were killed in battle, and Francis Livingston was an officer in the 90th Foot. The other son, Thurstan Livingston, though married, *d.* s.p. legit.

expedition against Quiberon and Belleisle, in 1800; captured the "Vigilante" sloop of war (18 guns) on the coast of Egypt in 1806; becoming Vice-Admiral, 1838, and Admiral of the White in 1851. He *suc. to the Baronetcy*(a) in April 1795, and, subsequently, had spec. service to his father in the Barony of Bedlormie. In 1803 he had a grant for life of the custody of the palace of Linlithgow and the castle of Blackness, offices formerly held by his cousins, the Earls of Linlithgow [S.]. In 1821, he was served heir male general to James (LIVINGSTON), EARL OF CALLENDAR [S.], and accordingly laid claim to that Earldom. He, who considered himself the last heir male of the Livingston family, entailed his estates, shortly before his death, on the issue of his sister. He *m.* 24 Aug. 1809, Janet, da. of Sir James STIRLING, 1st Baronet [1792], sometime Lord Provost of Edinburgh, by Alison, da. of James MANSFIELD, of Edinburgh, Banker. She *d.* at Ardrossan, 1831. He *d.* s.p., at Westquarter, 1 April 1853, aged about 83, when the *Baronetcy* became *dormant* or *extinct*. Will pr. Aug. 1853.(b)

The Baronetcy was, however, assumed as under.

VIII. 1853, to *1859.* SIR ALEXANDER LIVINGSTON, Baronet [S. 1699](c), alleging himself to be nephew and h. male, as s. (alleging himself to be legit. s.) of Thurstan LIVINGSTON, of Rotherhithe, Surrey, Turner (formerly a seaman), by Catherine Anne (the validity of whose marriage, 7 Aug. 1808, was disputed), relict of John TICEHURST, da. of John DUPUIS, of Spitalfields, weaver, and sister of Susanna, 1st wife of the said Thurstan LIVINGSTON,(d) which Thurstan (who *d.* Dec. 1839), was yr. br. of the whole blood to the late Baronet. He, who was *b.* 13 June 1809, *assumed the Baronetcy* in April 1853, and claimed the estate of Bedlormie as heir of entail, which claim the Court of Session, in 1856, decided in his favour, but, however, in 1859, the House of Lords, though they held him to be legitimate in England, remitted to the Scotch Court the point of his *status* in Scotland, and finally the judgment was against him. He *d.* in poverty at Edinburgh, 20 Jan. 1859, in his 50th year.

(a) In Dod's *Baronetage* (1853) and elsewhere he is spoken of as the "10th Baronet," and his creation is given as "1625." This is on the [erroneous] supposition that his ancestor, Sir George Livingston, of Ogleface (see p. 384, note "e"), was made a Baronet, in which case the 1st Baronet of the creation of 1699 would have been the 4th of the [imaginary] creation of 1625, and this (the 7th), consequently, the 10th.

(b) The estates were inherited by his great nephew, Thomas Livingston Fenton, afterwards Fenton-Livingston, of Westquarter and Bedlormie, which latter estate he sold in 1873. He was only s. and h. of the Rev. John Fenton, Rector of Ousby and Vicar of Tarpenhoe, co. Cumberland, by Anne, 1st sister (only sister of the whole blood) of the late Baronet. The other sister, Elizabeth (only sister of the half blood), *m.* 26 July 1809, James Kirsopp, of the Spittal, co. Northumberland, and had issue.

(c) According to the assumption of the Baronetcy in 1853.

(d) It was on the ground of her being such sister that the validity of the marriage was disputed. In England the marriage with a deceased wife's sister, would (under the Act of Parl., 1835) have been valid, unless (before that date) it had been set aside during the lifetime of both parties. In Scotland, however, it was held that the law forbidding such marriages was (notwithstanding the Act of 1835), still in force.

ANSTRUTHER:

cr. 6 Jan. 1700;(a)

sometime, 1799-1808, ANSTRUTHER-PATERSON;

afterwards, since 1817, CARMICHAEL-ANSTRUTHER.

I. 1700. JOHN ANSTRUTHER, the younger, of Anstruther and of Elie House, co. Fife, s. and h. ap. of Sir William ANSTRUTHER, of the same, sometime (1707) a Lord of Justiciary (*d.* 24 Jan. 1711), by Helen, da. of John (HAMILTON), 4th EARL OF HADDINGTON [S.], was *b.* 1678, and was v.p. *cr. a Baronet* [S.], as above, by royal warrant dat. at Kensington, 6 Jan. 1700, but no patent is recorded in the Great Seal Register. He was M.P. [S.] for Anstruther Easter Burghs, 1702-07, and M.P. [G.B.] for same, 1708-10, 1710 till unseated in 1711, and 1713-15, as also for Fifeshire, 1715-41. He suc. his father in the family estates, 24 Jan. 1711; was Master of the Works [S.], 16 July 1717. He *m.* 24 Jan. 1716/7, at Edinburgh, Margaret, 1st da. (whose issue became heir) of James (CARMICHAEL), 2d EARL OF HYNDFORD [S.], by Elizabeth, da. of John (MAITLAND), 5th EARL OF LAUDERDALE [S.]. She *d.* 6 Nov. 1721, and was *bur.* at Elie Church. He *d.* at Elie House, 21 Sep. 1753, aged 75, and was *bur.* with her. Will dat. 18 Aug. 1746, pr. 28 Aug. 1754.

II. 1753. SIR JOHN ANSTRUTHER, Baronet [S. 1700], of Anstruther and Elie House aforesaid, 1st but only surv. s. and h., *b.* 27 Dec. 1718, at Edinburgh; *suc. to the Baronetcy*, 21 Sep. 1753; was M.P. for Anstruther Easter Burghs (three Parls.), 1766, till he resigned in 1782; and again 1790, till he resigned in 1793. He entailed all his estates, 18 Feb. 1778. He *m.* 4 Oct. 1750, at Edinburgh, Janet, da. of James FALL, of Dunbar, Merchant, sometime Provost and M.P. for that town, by Jean, da. of Patrick MURRAY, of Pennyland, in Caithness. He *d.* 4 July 1799, aged 80. Will pr. July 1799. His widow(b) *d.* 17 Feb. 1802, aged 85. Will pr. 1802.

III. 1799. SIR PHILIP ANSTRUTHER-PATERSON, Baronet [S. 1700], of Anstruther and Elie House aforesaid, formerly Philip ANSTRUTHER, 1st s. and h., *b.* 13 Jan. 1752, at Edinburgh; sometime Lieutenant

(a) Sir J. Balfour Paul, Lyon, writes, 8 April 1901, "Mr. Maitland Thomson, the Curator of the Historical Department, has just shewn me the original warrant by William III for a patent of Baronetcy to be made out in favour of *John Anstruther, the younger, of Anstruther, and his heirs male for ever.* The warrant is dated at Kensington, 6 Jan. 1700. The patent has never been put on record in the Register of the Great Seal. It is curious how neither Milne, in his *List of Baronets*, nor Nisbet, in his *Heraldry*, have got hold of this title, though they both wrote shortly after the date mentioned." From the number of Knights in this family, the father of the 1st Baronet being one of five brothers who were Knighted (see p. , note " "), and from the consecutive succession of Knights in four successive generations (the father, grandfather, great grandfather, and great great grandfather of the 1st Baronet having all been Knighted), it has often been supposed that the Baronetcy [S.] was one of the earliest date, indeed, Sibbald, in his *History of Fife*, states that Sir Robert Anstruther, great grandfather of the 1st Baronet, was himself, in his commission, dated 12 April 1627, as Ambassador to the Emperor of Germany, styled "Knight *and Baronet*." His son, Sir Philip (who *d.* 1702), who about 1672 registered arms as a *Knight*, is, in a pedigree, registered 17 June 1730 [erroneously] styled "*Baronet*," though no clue as to the creation of such Baronetcy is there given.

(b) "She is described by the Rev. Dr. Carlyle as a coquette and a beauty and elsewhere as a lady of great ability." Walter Simson, in the *History of the Gypsies*, mentions that she "was saluted by a rabble crowd at a contested election with the song of *The Gypsy Laddie*, a taunt which could only be apposite from her supposed [gypsy] descent." See account of the family of FALL, in the *Scottish Antiquary*, vol. xvi, pp. 127-132.

1st Dragoon Guards; M.P. for Anstruther Easter burghs, 1774, till he resigned in 1777; took the name of PATERSON after that of ANSTRUTHER about 1782, in consequence of his marriage; *suc. to the Baronetcy*, 4 July 1799. He *m.* 19 Feb. 1778, at Eccles, co. Berwick, Anne, da. and h. of Sir John PATERSON, 3d Baronet [S. 1687], of Eccles aforesaid, by Anne, *de jure* (10 Jan. 1794), *suo jure* BARONESS POLWARTH [S.], 1st da. and heir of line of Hugh (HUME-CAMPBELL), 3d EARL OF MARCHMONT and LORD POLWARTH [S.]. He *d.* s.p., 5 Jan. 1808, aged about 56, the estate of Eccles having already been sold. His widow, who in 1818, claimed the Barony of Polwarth [S.], *d.* s.p. 11 March 1822. Will pr. 1822.

IV. and I. 1808. SIR JOHN ANSTRUTHER, Baronet [S. 1700 and G.B. 1798], of Anstruther and Elie House aforesaid, br. and h., *b.* at Elie House, 27 March 1753; admitted to Lincoln's Inn, 12 Feb. 1774; Advocate, 30 July 1774; Barrister (Lincoln's Inn), 1779; M.P. for Anstruther Easter Burghs (two Parls.), 1783-90; for Cockermouth, 1790-96, and for Anstruther Easter Burghs (again), 1796-97, and 1806 till death, taking a leading part in the impeachment of Warren Hastings; was Chief Justice of the Supreme Court at Bengal, 1796-1806; *Knighted*, 4 Oct. 1797, and was *cr. a Baronet* [G.B.], 18 May 1798, as "of Fort William, Bengal"; P.C., 19 Nov. 1806; *suc. to the Baronetcy* [S. 1700], 5 Jan. 1808, and was, 14 March 1808, served heir of entail to his br., the late Baronet. He was *cr.* D.C.L. of the Univ. of Oxford, 3 July 1810. He *m.* in or before 1784, Maria Isabella, 1st da. of Edward BRICE, of Berners street, Marylebone. He *d.* 26 Jan. 1811, in Albemarle Street, aged 57. Will pr. 1811. His widow *d.* 14 June 1833, in Conduit street. Will pr. July 1833.

V. and II. 1811. SIR JOHN ANSTRUTHER, *afterwards* since 1817, CARMICHAEL-ANSTRUTHER, Baronet [S. 1700 and G.B. 1798], of Anstruther and Elie House aforesaid, 1st s. and h., *b.* in Lincoln's Inn Fields 1 June and *bap.* 1 July 1785, at St. Geo., Bloomsbury; ed. at Eton, 1799-1802; matric. at Oxford (Ch. Ch.), 21 Oct. 1803, aged 18; B.A., 1806; admitted to Lincoln's Inn, 1806; *suc. to the Baronetcies*, 26 Jan. 1811; was M.P. for Anstruther Easter Burghs (two Parls.), 1811 till death in 1818. By the death, 18 April 1817, of his cousin, Andrew (CARMICHAEL), 6th and last EARL OF HYNDFORD [S.], he inherited the estates of Carmichael and Westraw, co. Lanark, and took the name of CARMICHAEL before that of ANSTRUTHER. He *m.* 11 Jan. 1817, Jessie, da. of Major-Gen. David DEWAR, of Gilston House, co. Fife. He *d.* 28 Jan. 1818, aged 52. Admon. June 1821. His widow *m.* 27 March 1828, at Edinburgh, the Rev. Robert Bullock MARSHAM, D.C.L., of Caversfield, Oxon, Warden of Merton College, Oxford, 1826-80, who *d.* 27 Dec. 1880, aged 94. She *d.* 10 Nov. 1881, at Caversfield, aged 86.

VI. and III. 1818. SIR JOHN CARMICHAEL-ANSTRUTHER, Baronet [S. 1700 and G.B. 1798], of Anstruther and Elie House, as also of Carmichael and Westraw aforesaid, posthumous s. and h., *b.* 6 Feb. 1818, and *suc. to the Baronetcies* on his birth; ed. at Eton, where he *d.*, being accidentally shot by a playfellow, 31 Oct. and *bur.* 12 Nov. 1831, in the Chapel of Merton College, Oxford, aged 13.

VII. and IV. 1831. SIR WINDHAM CARMICHAEL-ANSTRUTHER, Baronet [S. 1700 and G.B. 1798], of Anstruther and Elie House, as also of Carmichael and Westraw aforesaid, uncle and h., *b.* 9 March 1793, at Lincoln's Inn Fields in the parish of St. Clement Danes; ed. at Eton, 1808; sometime an officer in the Coldstream Guards; *suc. to the Baronetcies* and to the very considerable estates of the family, 31 Oct. 1831; Major in the 1st Lanark Militia, 1831. "He was not long in possession before he became inextricably involved, and at length, after many years, succeeded in breaking the entail of his Anstruther estates, and sold them in 1856, together with the mansion of Elie House, to the brothers Baird [for £145,000, but he] still possessed the great Carmichael estates in Lanarkshire, which are in value equal to those he alienated."(a) He *m.* firstly in 1824, Meredith Maria, 2d da. of Charles WETHERELL. She *d.* 10 April 1841, at Brighton, aged 37. He *m.* secondly (a month later), 10 May 1841, Anne Constance, da. of Allen Williamson GREY. She *d.* 21 June 1856, at Boulogne, aged 44. He *m.* thirdly, 30 Sep. 1859, Mary Anne, 2d da. of John PARSONS. He *d.* 15 Sep. 1869, at Boulogne, in his 77th year. His widow living 1904.

VIII. and V. 1869. SIR WINDHAM CHARLES JAMES CARMICHAEL-ANSTRUTHER, Baronet [S. 1700 and G.B. 1798], of Carmichael and Westraw aforesaid, 1st s. and h., by 1st wife, *b.* about 1825 at Brussels; matric. at Oxford (Merton Coll.), 12 June 1843, aged 18; *suc. to the Baronetcies*, 15 Sep. 1869; was M.P. (Liberal interest) for South Lanarkshire, 1874-80. He *m.* 4 Sep. 1872, Janetta, only da. of Robert BARBOUR, of Bolesworth Castle, Cheshire. She *d.* 11 Sep. 1891, at Carmichael House. He *d.* there 26 Jan. 1898, aged 73. Will pr. at £151,906.

IX. and VI. 1898. SIR WINDHAM ROBERT CARMICHAEL-ANSTRUTHER, Baronet [S. 1700 and G.B. 1798], of Carmichael and Westraw aforesaid, only s. and h., *b.* 26 March 1877; ed. at Trin. Coll., Oxford; B.A. (honours in History), 1898; *suc. to the Baronetcies*, 26 Jan. 1898; was a great patron of "coursing." He *m.* 16 April 1901, at St. Michael's, Chester sq., Frederica Sylvia, yst. da. of Sir Frederick Matthew DARLEY, G.C.M.G., Lieut.-Gov. of New South Wales, by Lucy Forest, da. of Silvester BROWNE, of Melbourne, in Victoria. He *d.* 28 Oct. 1903, at Carmichael House, aged 26. Will pr. at £85,584 personalty. His widow living 1904.

X. and VII. 1903. SIR WINDHAM FREDERICK CARMICHAEL-ANSTRUTHER, Baronet [S. 1700 and G.B. 1798], of Carmichael and Westraw aforesaid, only s. and h., *b.* 1902; *suc. to the Baronetcies*, 28 Oct. 1903.

Family Estates.—These, in 1883, consisted of 11,814 acres in Lanarkshire, and 584 in Ayrshire. *Total.*—12,398 acres, worth £9,534 a year. *Seat.*—Carmichael House, near Thankerton, co. Lanark.

FORBES:

cr. 10 April 1700.

dormant, about, apparently, 1760.

I. 1700. "SAMUEL FORBES, of Foveran," co. Aberdeen, s. and h. of Alexander FORBES, of the same (who *d.* 1697) by his 1st wife, Margaret, da. of Samuel HAWKER, of Edinburgh, Apothecary, was *b.* there 1653; was M.P. [S.] for Aberdeenshire, 1693-98 and 1700-01, and was *cr. a Baronet* [S.], as above, 10 April 1700, with rem. to heirs male whatsoever. He *m.* (—) da. of (—) UDNY, of that ilk. He *d.* 16 July 1717, aged 54.(b)

II. 1717. SIR ALEXANDER FORBES, Baronet [S. 1700], of Foveran aforesaid, s. and h., *suc. to the Baronetcy*, 16 July 1717 and was served heir to his father, 13 March 1718. He *m.* Jane, da. of Major George SKENE, of Levaldstone. He *d.*, s.p.m.s., before 1755.

(a) Burke's *Vicissitudes of Families* (1859, 1st series, pp. 53-54). In a MS. note book of the late R. R. Stodart, some time (1863-86) Lyon Clerk Depute, it is stated that he was "a strolling player" when he suc. to the estates. An anecdote is added of how he cleverly forced his creditors to raise the allowance assigned to him, threatening to incur the forfeiture of the Lanarkshire estates by refusing (as desired in the deed of entail) to reside there some months each year.

(b) He was author of a *Description of Aberdeenshire*, printed by the Spalding Club in 1843.

III. 1750? to 1760? SIR JOHN FORBES, Baronet [S. 1700], of Knaperna, second cousin and h. male, being s. and h. of Samuel FORBES, of the same, by Margaret, da. of Hew CRAWFORD, of Jordan Hill, which Samuel was s. of John FORBES, of Knaperna,(a) yr. br. to the 1st Baronet. He suc. to the title before 1755, but, on his death, the *Baronetcy* became *dormant*.

DUNBAR:

cr. 10 April 1700.

I. 1700. "WILLIAM DUNBAR, of Hempriggs," co. Caithness, s. and h. of John DUNBAR, of the same, by Anne, da. of Andrew FRASER, Commissary of Inverness, was M.P. [S.] for Caithness-shire, 1678, and was *cr. a Baronet* [S.], as above, 10 April 1700, with rem. to heirs male whatsoever. He *m.* Margaret, 3d da. of Alexander SINCLAIR, of Lathron, by Jean, da. of John CUNNINGHAM, of Brownhill. He *d.* 1711, s.p.m.s.,(b) having devised the estate of Hempriggs to his daughter.(c)

II. 1711. SIR ROBERT DUNBAR, Baronet [S. 1700], only br. and h. male, *suc. to the Baronetcy* in 1711, but, not having inherited the estate of Hempriggs, was described as of Northfield. He *m.* in 1675, Mary, da. of Patrick SINCLAIR, of Ulbster. He *d.* 1742.

III. 1742, to 1763. SIR PATRICK DUNBAR, Baronet [S. 1700], of Northfield aforesaid, s. and h., *b.* about 1676; was M.P. for Caithness-shire, 1727-34, being then of Bowermadden, *suc. to the Baronetcy* in 1742. He *m.* firstly, in 1697 (—), da. of William SINCLAIR, of Dunbeath. He *m.* secondly, in 1722, Katherine, da. of Joseph BRODIE, of Mentown. He *d.* s.p.m.s.(d), 5 April 1763, aged 86, when the *Baronetcy* became *dormant*(e) for thirteen years till 1776.

* * * * * * * *

IV. 1763. ARCHIBALD DUNBAR, of Newton, Thunderton, and Duffus, co. Elgin, *b.* about 1693, matric. arms, v.p., in the Lyon office, 16 July 1734, as "descended from Kilbuiack, a third son of the family of Westfield."(f) He is said to have been cousin and h. male to the late Baronet, and, if so, would have been *entitled to succeed to the Baronetcy*,(g) 5 April 1763. He, however, never assumed, nor apparently ever claimed that title. He *m.* in 1735, Helen, yr. da. and coheir of his maternal uncle, Archibald DUNBAR, of Thunderstoun. He *d.* 13 Jan. 1769, aged 76.

(a) The estate of Knaperna was sold to George (Gordon), 3d Earl of Aberdeen [S.], 1746-1801.

(b) Benjamin Dunbar, his only son, *m.* Janet, da. of Patrick Dunbar, of Brins, but *d.* v.p. and s.p.

(c) Elizabeth, his da. and h., *m.* for her second husband, the Hon. James Sutherland, who took the name of Dunbar, and was *cr. a Baronet* [S.] 10 Dec. 1706, as "Dunbar of Hempriggs."

(d) John Dunbar, his only s., *d.* unm. and v.p., April 1749, aged 23.

(e) It is stated in Douglas' *Baronetage* [S.] to have become *extinct* in 1763; as also in Playfair's *Baronetage* (1811).

(f) The Dunbars of Kilbuick flourished about 1480. There is much about them in Stodart's *Scottish Arms* (vol. i, pp. 10-18). Among them was a James Dunbar of Newton, living 1604, an Archibald in 1670, whose eldest son Robert was living in 1689.

(g) According to the Service of 8 Oct. 1776, shewing that "Alexander Dunbar, of Thunderton, Esq.," was heir male to "Sir Patrick Dunbar, late of Northfield, Baronet," who was grandson to John Dunbar, of Hempriggs, "his [the said Alexander's] great great granduncle," the said John being brother of George Dunbar, of Arlish, the father of Archibald Dunbar, of Newton, the father of Robert Dunbar, of Newton, the father of Archibald Dunbar, who was father of the said Alexander Dunbar, of Thunderton, late of Newton aforesaid.

V. *1769, or 1776.* SIR ALEXANDER DUNBAR, Baronet [S. 1700],(a) of Northfield and Duffus House, co. Elgin, formerly of Thunderton and Newton aforesaid, s. and h., *b.* 12 Jan. 1742, was *entitled to succeed to the Baronetcy*(a) on his father's death, 13 Jan. 1769, though it was not till seven years later that he was, 8 Oct. 1776, served heir male to Sir Patrick DUNBAR, 3d Baronet, by a jury, before the Sheriff Depute of Elgin, when *he assumed the title*. He *m.* 21 April 1769, Margaret, yst. da. of John (ARBUTHNOTT), 6th VISCOUNT ARBUTHNOTT [S.], by his 2d wife Jean, da. of Alexander ARBUTHNOTT, of Findowrie. He *d.* 20 Dec. 1791, in his 50th year. His widow *d.* 8 June 1801.

VI. 1791. SIR ARCHIBALD DUNBAR, Baronet [S. 1700],(a) of Northfield and Duffus House aforesaid, 1st s. and h., *b.* 30 June 1772; *suc. to the Baronetcy*,(a) 20 Dec. 1791; Convener of the county of Elgin 1813, till his death in 1847; Lieut.-Col. of the Elginshire Militia. He *m.* firstly, 6 Nov. 1794, Helen, da. of Col. Sir Alexander Penrose CUMMING-GORDON, 1st Baronet [1804] of Altyre, by Helen, da. of Sir Ludovic GRANT, *formerly* COLQUHOUN, 7th Baronet [S. 1625]. She *d.* 16 March 1819. He *m.* secondly, 26 Sep. 1822, Mary, da. of John BRANDER, of Pitgaveny, co. Elgin. He *d.* at Northfield House, co. Elgin, 29 March 1847, aged 74. His widow, who became heir to her br. Lieut.-Col. James BRANDER, of Pitgaveny, took the name of BRANDER after that of DUNBAR in Nov. 1854, and *d.* 5 May 1869, at Northfield House aforesaid, in her 80th year.

VII. 1847. SIR ARCHIBALD DUNBAR, Baronet [S. 1700],(a) of Northfield and Duffus House aforesaid, 2d but 1st surv. s. and h.,(b) *b.* 5 July 1803, at Duffus House; sometime an officer in the 22d Foot; *suc. to the Baronetcy*,(a) 29 March 1847; Convener of Morayshire, 1847-88. He *m.* firstly, 12 June 1827, Keith Alicia, da. of George RAMSAY, of Barnton, Midlothian, by Jean, sister of William (HAMILTON), 7th LORD BELHAVEN AND STENTON [S.], da. of Robert HAMILTON, of Wishaw, the *de jure*, 6th Lord. She *d.* 15 March 1836. He *m.* secondly, 5 Nov. 1840, Sophia, yst. da. of George ORRED, of Tranmere Hall, Cheshire. He *d.* 7 Jan. 1898, aged 94. His widow living 1904.

VIII. 1898. SIR ARCHIBALD HAMILTON DUNBAR, Baronet(a) [S. 1700], of Northfield and Duffus House aforesaid, 1st s. and h. by 1st wife; *b.* 5 April 1828; ed. at Rugby; sometime Capt. 66th Foot; *suc. to the Baronetcy*,(a) 7 Jan. 1898.(c) He *m.* 15 July 1865, at Welford, Berks, Isabella Mary, 1st da. of Charles EYRE, of Welford Park.

NICOLSON (d):

cr. 15 April 1700;

existing, 1800;

dormant since about 1839.

I. 1700. "THOMAS NICOLSON, of Balcaskie," who, apparently, is more correctly described as "THOMAS NICOLSON, the younger, of Kemney,"(e) s. and h. ap. of Sir George NICOLSON, of Kemney, and sometime (1689-98) of Balcaskie, both co. Fife, a Lord of Session, under the style of *Lord Kemney* (*d.* 8 Feb. 1711), by Margaret, da. of (—) HALYBURTON, of Edinburgh,

(a) See page 390, note "g."

(b) Alexander Dunbar, the 1st son, *d.* v.p. and unm. in 1816.

(c) An acute and accurate genealogist, and the author of a work called "*Scottish Kings*," an excellent compendium of dates.

(d) See p. 242, note "c."

(e) Milne's *List*.

IV

merchant, was b. about 1664; admitted Advocate 29 Nov. 1687, and was v.p. cr. a Baronet [S.], as above, 15 April 1700, with rem. to heirs male whatsoever. He suc. to the estate of Upsetlingtoun, co. Berwick (purchased in 1708), on the death of his father, 8 Feb. 1711. He m., about 1688, Margaret, widow of James HAMILTON, of Ballencreiff, da. and eventually coheir of Sir Thomas NICOLSON, 2d Baronet [S. 1637], of Carnock. He d. s.p.m.,(a) 31 Aug. 1728.

II. 1728. SIR WILLIAM NICOLSON, Baronet [S. 1700], of Glenbervie, co. Kincardine, and Upsetlingtoun aforesaid, br. and h. male, b. probably about 1673, was sometime a merchant at Edinburgh, and Comptroller of the Customs at Aberdeen; purchased the estate of Glenbervie, 6 March 1721; suc. to the Baronetcy and to the Upsetlingtoun estate, 31 Aug. 1728; and was served heir 29 Jan. 1730. He m. firstly, 28 March 1697, Lilias, da. of (—) PRINGLE. She d. s.p.m., 20 April 1707, at Edinburgh. He m. secondly, 5 July 1713, Agnes, widow of Thomas BURNETT, of Glenbervie aforesaid, da. and coheir of Robert BURNETT, of Muchalls, co. Kincardine. She d. April 1736. He m. thirdly, in 1738, Mary, widow of James ALLARDICE, da. of Robert MILNE, of Balwyllie, Provost of Montrose. She d. 24 Dec. 1749. He m. fourthly (65 years after his first marriage, and when nearly 90), 1 June 1763, Helen (then aged 17), da. of John MILL, of Normanside, Old Montrose, and by her had children, one being but six weeks old at his death. He (who, altogether, had 22 children, most of whom d. young), d. 7 June 1766, at Edinburgh, aged about 93. His widow d. 4 Sep. 1783.

III. 1766. SIR JAMES NICOLSON, Baronet [S. 1700], of Glenbervie aforesaid, s. and h. by 2d wife, b. Jan. 1722; suc. to the Baronetcy, 7 June 1766, and had gen. service to his father 21 Nov. following. He m. 4 Aug. 1751, at Lauriston, Margaret, da. of John STRATON, of Lauriston aforesaid. He d. s.p.,(b) at Montrose, 11 March 1782, aged 60.

IV. 1782. SIR JAMES NICOLSON, Baronet [S. 1700], cousin and h. male, being s. and h. of James NICOLSON, of Trabroun, co. Berwick, a wine merchant in Leith, by Jean KERNOCHAN, a native of Ireland, which James (who, having been attainted in 1745, had sold the estate of Trabroun), was s. and h. of Thomas NICOLSON (d. v.p.), who was s. and h. ap. of James NICOLSON, of Trabroun aforesaid, yr. br. of Sir George NICOLSON, the father of the 1st Baronet. He, who suc. to the Baronetcy, 11 March 1782, was Capt. of Infantry in the Portuguese Service, 13 July following. He m. 25 July 1799, at Worksop, Notts, Margaret, da. of John WHARTON, of Frickley, near Doncaster, Major in the Army. He was living 1800, but d. presumably before 1818.(c) His widow was apparently living (between 1800 and 1818) at 31 Charlotte street, Somers Town, St. Pancras, Midx.

(a) Margaret, one of his daughters and coheirs, m. about 1710, as his 1st wife, William (Kerr), 3d Marquess of Lothian [S.], and d. 30 Sep. 1759, leaving issue.
(b) The Glenbervie estate passed to his sisters and, on their death, to Mrs. Badenoch, the descendant of one of them. She took the name of Nicolson, and d. 3 Oct. 1878, in her 78th year, leaving a son James Badenoch-Nicolson, of Glenbervie.
(c) The information supplied by R. R. Stodart (see p. 242, note "c") ends at the date of 1799. There is, however, a pedigree (compiled for his own use) by Francis Townsend, Windsor Herald, 1784-1818 (now remaining in the College of Arms, London, and marked "F.T.," vol. xxiii, p. 429), in which the birth of the 5th Baronet's son is mentioned, he being therein called "Sir Joseph," a designation which implies that his father was dead. There is also a mem. therein that "Lady Nicolson" was living at 31 Charlotte street, Somers Town. There is no account of this Baronetcy (or indeed of any Baronetcy of the name of Nicolson) in Playfair's Baronetage, 1811, but Burke's Baronetage, for 1841, gives "Sir James Nicolson, of Glenbervie, co. Kincardine" (no date of creation and no affiliation being stated) as "the present Baronet."

V. 1810? to 1839? SIR JOSEPH NICOLSON, Baronet [S. 1700], only child and h., b. 28 March 1800, at Worksop aforesaid; suc. to the Baronetcy, before 1818,(a) on the death of his father. He apparently d. in or about 1839,(b) when the Baronetcy became dormant.

ELLIOT:

cr. 19 April 1700;
afterwards, since 1778, ELLIOT-MURRAY-KYNYNMOUND;
since 1797, BARONS MINTO;
and since 1813, EARLS OF MINTO.

I. 1700. "SIR GILBERT ELLIOT, of Headshaw," 2d s. of Gavin ELLIOT, of Grange and Middlemilne, co. Roxburgh, who was 4th s. of Gilbert ELLIOT, of Stobs, co. Roxburgh, was implicated in the rebellion of 1679, being declared guilty of treason, 16 July 1685, which finding was, however, rescinded by Act of Parliament 22 July 1690; was Clerk to the Privy Council [S.], and having been Knighted, was cr. a Baronet [S.], as above, 19 April 1700, "provydit to his heirs male successivie for ever."(c) He, being then of Minto, co. Roxburgh, was a Lord of Session, 25 June 1705, under the style of Lord Minto, and a Lord Justiciary. He was M.P. [S.] for Roxburghshire, 1702-07. He m. firstly his cousin, Marion, or Helen, da. of Andrew STEVENSON, Burgess of Edinburgh, by Mary, da. of Andrew HAY, of Haystoun. She d. s.p.m. He m. secondly (contract 17 March 1692), Jean, da. of Sir Andrew CARRE, of Cavers, co. Roxburgh. He d. 1 May 1718, aged 67.

II. 1718. SIR GILBERT ELLIOT, Baronet [S. 1700], of Minto aforesaid, s. and h., by 2d wife, was b. about 1693; admitted Advocate, 26 July 1715; suc. to the Baronetcy, 1 May 1718; was M.P. for Roxburghshire, 1722, till appointed, 4 June 1726, a Lord of Session, under the style of Lord Minto; was a Lord of Justiciary, 13 Sep. 1733, and Lord Justice Clerk, 3 May 1763, till his death three years later. He m. about 1720, Helen, da. of Sir Robert STEUART, 1st Baronet [S. 1687], by his 2d wife, Helen, da. of Sir Alexander COCKBURN, of Langton. He d. 16 April 1766, aged about 73. His widow d. 22 June 1774.

III. 1766. SIR GILBERT ELLIOT, Baronet [S. 1700], of Minto aforesaid, s. and h.; admitted Advocate, 10 Dec. 1743; was M.P. for Selkirkshire (three Parls.) 1753, till he resigned in June 1765, and for Roxburghshire (three Parls.) 1765, till death in 1777; a Lord of the Admiralty, 1756-61; a Lord of the Treasury, 1761-62; P.C., 1762; Treasurer of the Chamber, 1762-70; suc. to the Baronetcy, 16 April 1766; Keeper of the Signet [S.], 1767; Treasurer of the Navy, 1770-77. He m. 14 Dec. 1746, Agnes, da. of Hugh DALRYMPLE-MURRAY-KYNYNMOUND, formerly DALRYMPLE, of Melgund, co. Forfar, and of Lochgelly and Kynynmound, co. Fife, all of which estates she inherited. He d. 11 Feb. 1777, at Marseilles. Will pr. 1777. His widow, who assumed the name of MURRAY-KYNYNMOUND, d. 30 Dec. 1778. Will pr. Jan. 1779.

IV. 1777. SIR GILBERT ELLIOT, afterwards, since 1778, ELLIOT-MURRAY-KYNYNMOUND, Baronet [S. 1700], of Minto aforesaid, 1st s. and h., b. 23 April 1751, at Greyfriars, Edinburgh: ed. at Paris; matric. at Oxford (Ch. Ch.), 9 Nov. 1768, aged 17; cr. M.A. 16 July 1772, and, subsequently, 4 July 1793; cr. D.C.L.; was v.p. M.P. for Morpeth, 1776-77, and, subsequently, for Roxburghshire (two Parls.), 1777-84; for Berwick, 1786-90, and for Helston, 1790-95, having suc. to the Baronetcy, 11 Feb. 1777. He assumed the name of MURRAY-KYNYNMOUND after that of ELLIOT, on his mother's death in Dec. 1778,

(a) See p. 392, note "c."
(b) In Solly's Titles of Honour (Index Society, 1880) the Baronetcy of "Nicolson, of Glenbervie," is given as "s.p. (?) 1839, presumed extinct."
(c) Milne's List.

which name was confirmed to him by royal lic. 2 Oct. 1797. He became P.C., 1793; Minister to the Italian States, March to May 1794; Viceroy of Corsica, June 1795 to Oct. 1796. He m. 3 Jan. 1777, at St. Geo. Han. sq., Anna Maria, 1st da. of Sir George AMYAND, 1st Baronet [1764], by Anna Maria, da. of John Abraham KORTEEN, of Hamburgh, merchant. She was living when he was cr. 20 Oct. 1797, BARON MINTO of co. Roxburgh, being, subsequently, 24 Feb. 1813, cr. VISCOUNT MELGUND, co. Forfar, and EARL OF MINTO. In that peerage this Baronetcy then merged, and still [1904] so continues. See Peerage.

JOHNSTONE:

cr. 25 April 1700;
sometime, 1792-1805, PULTENEY.

I. 1700. "JOHN JOHNSTON [or JOHNSTONE], of Westerhall" (otherwise Westraw, formerly Glendoning), in the Stewartry of Annandale, co. Dumfries, s. and h. of Sir James JOHNSTONE, Councillor, sometime, 1689-99, M.P. [S.] for Dumfries Sheriffdom, by Margaret, da. of John BANNATYNE, of Corehouse, co. Lanark, suc. his father, 18 Nov. 1699, to whom he had spec. service, 25 April 1700, and was cr. a Baronet [S.], as above, 25 April 1700, "provydit to his aires male successive for ever."(a) He was M.P. [S.] for Dumfries Sheriffdom (two Parls.), 1700-07, and M.P. [G.B.] thereof, 1707-08; was sometime Lieut.-Col. in Kerr's Dragoons. He m. (postnuptial settlement 21 March 1700), Rachel, 1st da. and coheir of James JOHNSTONE, of Sheens, co. Edinburgh, by Anne, da. of Sir John HAMILTON, Lord Clerk Registrar of Scotland. He possibly m. another wife, viz. Agnes, da. of the Hon. Sir John DALZELL, 1st Baronet [S. 1666], of Glenore. He d. s.p.m.,(b) at Tournay, 30 Sep. 1711.

II. 1711. SIR WILLIAM JOHNSTONE, Baronet [S. 1700], of Westerhall aforesaid, br. and h. male; was M.P. [S.], for Annan (two Parls.), 1698-1707, and M.P. [G.B.] for Dumfries burghs (three Parls.), 1708-15, and for Dumfriesshire (two Parls.), 1713-22.(c) He was a Councillor in or before 1702; suc. to the Baronetcy, 30 Sep. 1711, and was served heir spec. to his brother, 23 April 1712, and heir male gen. 17 June following. He m. before March 1701, Henrietta, da. and coheir of the abovementioned James JOHNSTONE, of Sheens, by Anne, da. of Sir John HAMILTON, all abovenamed. He d. 8 Oct. 1727.

III. 1727. SIR JAMES JOHNSTONE, Baronet [S. 1700], of Westerhall aforesaid, 1st s. and h.;(d) admitted Advocate, 18 June 1720; suc. to the Baronetcy, 8 Oct. 1727, and was served heir of line, etc., to his father, 27 Jan. 1728; Steward Depute of Annandale, 1743; M.P. for Dumfries burghs (two Parls.), 1743-54. He m. in 1719, Barbara, 1st da. of Alexander (MURRAY), 4th LORD ELIBANK [S.], by Elizabeth, da. of George STIRLING, of Edinburgh. He d. at Westerhall, 10 Dec. 1772. His widow, by whom he had fourteen children, d. there 15 March 1773.

IV. 1772. SIR JAMES JOHNSTONE, Baronet [S. 1700], of Westerhall aforesaid, 1st s. and h., b. 23 Jan. 1726; was a Lieut.-Col. in the Army; suc. to the Baronetcy, 10 Dec. 1772, and was served heir of line and provision gen. to his father, 28 July 1773; was M.P. for Dumfries burghs, 1784-90, and for Weymouth, 1791-94. He claimed, 12 June 1792, the MARQUESSATE OF

(a) Milne's List.
(b) Philadelphia, his da. and h., m. James Douglas, of Dornoch, and had issue.
(c) He (owing to the petition against his return for the county of Dumfries being left undecided) sat for the county as well as for the burghs of Dumfries throughout the Parl. of 1713-15.
(d) The 2d son Lieut.-Col. John Johnstone, was ancestor of the Johnstone, Baronets, so cr. 6 July 1795, afterwards, since 1881, Barons Derwent of Hackness.

ANNANDALE [S. 1700], as heir male collateral of the grantee.(a) He m. on or before 4 July 1759, Elizabeth Mary Louisa, widow of the Rev. (—) MERRICK, da. of (—) COLCLOUGH, by Elizabeth Mary Louisa, illegit. da. of Sir Thomas MONTGOMERY, of Ireland. He d. s.p. legit.(b) 3 and was bur. 17 Sep. 1794, in Westminster Abbey, aged 68. Will dat. 12 March 1790 to 28 Jan. 1794, pr. 21 March 1796. His widow d. 9 and was bur. there 17 April 1797. Will, in which she calls herself "Louisa Maria Elizabeth," dat. 2 Dec. 1794 to 15 March 1797, pr. 15 April 1797.

V. 1794. SIR WILLIAM PULTENEY, Baronet [S. 1700], of Westerhall aforesaid, formerly William JOHNSTONE, next surv. br.(c) and h., b. 19 Oct. 1729; admitted Advocate, 13 July 1751. He, in 1767, assumed the name of PULTENEY in lieu of JOHNSTONE on his wife succeeding to the vast estates of her father's first cousin, William (PULTENEY), EARL OF BATH, after the death, 26 Oct. 1767, of that Earl's brother. He was M.P. for Cromartyshire, 1768-74, and for Shrewsbury (six Parls.), 1775 till death in 1805; suc. to the Baronetcy, 3 Sep. 1794. He m. firstly, 10 Nov. 1760, at St. James', Westm., Frances, da. and eventually sole heir of Daniel PULTENEY, sometime Envoy to Denmark, by Margaret Deering, da. and coheir of Benjamin TICHBORNE, br. to Henry, BARON FERRARD OF BEAULIEU [I.]. She, who was b. 21 Oct. and bap. 14 Nov. 1725 at St. James' aforesaid, d. s.p.m.,(d) at Bath House, Piccadilly, and was bur. 8 June 1782, at Westm. Abbey, aged 56. Will dat. 3 Sep. 1773, pr. 18 June 1782. He m. secondly, 3 Jan. 1804 (being then 74 years old), at Dundas Castle, Margaret, widow of Andrew STEWART, of Castlemilk, da. and coheir of Sir William STIRLING, of Ardoch, 4th Baronet [S. 1666]. He d. s.p.m.,(d) 30 May and was bur. 11 June 1805, in Westm. Abbey, aged 75, being considered the richest commoner in the Kingdom (his funded estate reaching nearly two millions stirling), and the greatest American stockholder ever known.(e) Admon. 20 June 1805. His widow d. s.p. 1 Nov. 1849, in Piccadilly. Will pr. Dec. 1849, and May 1850.

VI. 1805. SIR JOHN LOWTHER JOHNSTONE, Baronet [S. 1700], of Westerhall aforesaid, nephew and h. male, being only s. and h. of George JOHNSTONE, sometime Gov. of Pensacola, West Florida, by Charlotte, da. of (—) DEE, which George (who d. 24 May 1787, aged 57), was next br. to the late Baronet. He was b. about 1783; suc. to the Baronetcy, 20 May 1805, succeeding also, at the same time, to the Westerhall estate, the Weymouth estate, and those in America, being served heir male and of provision gen. to his uncle, 10 Oct. 1806, and heir male and of provision gen. in Westerhall, 9 March 1808. He (as did his grandfather) claimed, 17 June 1805, the MARQUESSATE OF ANNANDALE [S. 1700].(a) He was M.P. for Weymouth from May till his death in Dec. 1811. He m. 14 Jan. 1804, Charlotte, da. of Charles GORDON, of Cluny, co. Aberdeen. He d. 24 Dec. 1811. Will pr. 1812. His widow m. 12 Sep. 1820, Richard WEYLAND, of Woodeaton, Oxon, Major in the Army (who survived her), and d. 1 Dec. 1845, at Torquay.

(a) His lineal ancestor Sir John Johnstone, father of the 1st Baronet, was cited in 1679 as nearest of kin to William (Johnstone), Earl of Annandale and Hartfell [S.], which Earl was cr. 4 June 1701, Marquess of Annandale [S.], with rem. to heirs male whatever.
(b) James Murray Johnstone, an illegit. s. (by Jean Swanston, of Romford, spinster), was living 12 March 1790, and then under 21 years of age.
(c) Alexander Johnstone, Lieut.-Col. 70th Foot, b. 18 July 1727, his next elder br. was of Grenada, but d. unm. 15 and was bur. 21 Jan. 1783, in Westminster Abbey.
(d) Henrietta Laura, b. 6 Dec. 1766, at Edinburgh, only da. and h., inherited the Pulteney estates in right of her mother, and was cr. 23 July 1792, BARONESS BATH, and, 26 Oct. 1803, COUNTESS OF BATH, which titles became extinct at her death, s.p., 14 July 1808.
(e) Gent. Mag.

VII. 1811. Sir Frederick George Johnstone, Baronet [S. 1700], of Westerhall aforesaid, only s. and h., b. Dec. 1810, at St. Marylebone, and *suc. to the Baronetcy*, in his infancy, 24 Dec. 1811; matric. at Oxford (Ch. Ch.), 21 Jan. 1829, aged 18; was M.P. for Weymouth, 1832-35. He (as did his father and great grandfather), claimed, 2 June 1834, the Marquessate of Annandale [S. 1700].(a) He m. 24 Oct. 1840, Maria Louisa Elizabeth Frederica, da. of William (Craven), 1st Earl of Craven, by Louisa, da. of John Brunton, of Norwich. He d. 7 May 1841, aged 31, being killed by a fall from his horse near Westerhall. Admon. Oct. 1842. His widow, who was b. 26 June 1815, m. 15 Aug. 1844, at St. Helens, Isle of Wight, Alexander Oswald, of Auchencruive, co. Ayr. (who d. 6 Sep. 1868), and d. 20 Oct. 1858, at Auchencruive.

VIII. 1841. Sir Frederick John William Johnstone, Baronet [S. 1700], of Westerhall aforesaid, 1st s. and h., being eldest of two posthumous sons, b. 5 Aug. 1841, at Gore House, Kensington; *suc. to the Baronetcy* on his birth, and was in July 1842 (by his guardians) a petitioner for the Marquessate of Annandale [S. 1700];(a) ed. at Eton; matric. at Oxford (Ch. Ch.), 7 Dec. 1858, aged 17; M.P. for Weymouth, 1874-85; Sheriff of Dorset, 1889. He m. 7 June 1899, at St. Geo. Han. sq., Laura Caroline, Dowager Countess of Wilton, 2d da. of William Russell, Accountant Gen. of the Court of Chancery (nephew of the 5th and 6th Dukes of Bedford), by Emma, da. of Col. John Campbell, of Schawfield.

Family Estates.—These, in 1883, consisted of 17,064 acres in co. Dumfries, and 200 (worth £2,716 a year), in co. Dorset. *Total.*—17,264 acres, worth £9,550 a year. *Seat.*—Westerhall, near Langholm, co. Dumfries.

CROUCH:
alleged creation, 1701;
assumed, 1904.

In Debrett's *Baronetage* for 1904 is a statement that a Baronetcy is "claimed and assumed by George Crouch, of Wynnstay and Annandale, Melbourne, Australia, claiming to be *5th Baronet* under a Nova Scotia patent of creation said to have issued in 1701, but of which there is no record whatever at the Lyon office," nor indeed, apparently, anywhere else. No further light can be thrown on this extraordinary statement, save that the address should, presumably, be "Wynstay *Road*, *Armadale*, Melbourne."

DALRYMPLE:
cr. 8 May 1701(b);
dormant, or *ex.*, 17 Oct. 1829.

I. 1701 The Hon. "David Dalrymple, of Hailes," co. Haddington, 5th s. of James (Dalrymple), 1st Viscount Stair [S.], by Margaret, da. of James Ross, of Balniel, co. Wigtown, was b. probably about 1665; admitted Advocate 3 Nov. 1688; M.P. [S.] for Culross (two Parls.),

(a) See p. 395, note "a."

(b) Milne's *List*, as also in the *lists* of Chamberlayne and Miege, but in Wood's *Douglas's Peerage* [S.], vol. ii, p. 525, as also in Playfair's *Baronetage* [1811], the date is given as 8 May 1700.

1697—1707, and M.P. [G.B.] thereof 1707-08, and for Haddington (four Parls.) 1708 till his death in 1721, having been a Commissioner for the treaty of the Union [S.]. He was *cr. a Baronet* [S.], 8 May 1701,(a) with rem. "to his heirs male successive for ever." He was sometime Solicitor-Gen. [S.] to Queen Anne, was Lord Advocate, 1709—1720, and Auditor of the Exchequer [S.] 1720 till his death next year. He m. 4 April 1691, at Edinburgh, Janet, widow of Alexander Murray, of Melgund, co. Forfar, da. of Sir James Rochead, of Inverleith. He d. 3 Dec. 1721. Will pr. Feb. 1724. His widow, who was b. 25 April 1662, d. 26 Dec. 1726.

II. 1721. Sir James Dalrymple, Baronet [S. 1701], of Hailes aforesaid, 1st s. and h., b. 24 July 1692 at Edinburgh; *suc. to the Baronetcy*, 3 Dec. 1721; was M.P. for Haddington burghs (three Parls.), 1722-34; Auditor-Gen. of the Exchequer [S.]; was, in 1737, one of the coheirs of his maternal uncle, Sir James Rochead, Baronet [S. 1704], of Inverleith. He m. in or before 1726, Christian, 2d and yst. da. of Thomas (Hamilton), 8th Earl of Haddington [S.], by Helen, da. of John Hope, of Hopetoun. He d. at New Hailes, 24 Feb. 1751, aged 58. His widow, by whom he had sixteen children, d. there 30 June 1770.

III. 1751. Sir David Dalrymple, Baronet [S. 1701], of Hailes aforesaid, 1st s. and h., b. at Edinburgh, 28 Oct. 1726; ed. at Eton, and subsequently (in Civil Law) at Utrecht; admitted an Advocate, 24 Feb. 1748; *suc. to the Baronetcy*, 24 Feb. 1751; cr. LL.D. of Edinburgh Univ., 1760; one of the Senators of the College of Justice, 6 March 1766, and a Lord of Justiciary, under the style of *Lord Hailes*, 3 May 1776, till his death in Nov. 1792, being much distinguished for his historical, literary, and legal knowledge.(b) He m. firstly, 12 Nov. 1763, Anne, da. of George Broun, of Colstoun, co. Haddington, a Lord of Session under the style of *Lord Colstoun*, by Elizabeth, da. of Hew Dalrymple, of Drummore. She d. 18 May 1768. He m. secondly, 20 March 1770, Helen, da. of Sir James Fergusson, 2d Baronet [S. 1703], of Kilkerran, a Lord of Session under the style of *Lord Kilkerran*, by Jean, da. and h. of James Maitland, *styled* Viscount Maitland, s. and h. ap. of John, 5th Earl of Lauderdale [S.]. He d. of apoplexy, s.p.m.,(c) 29 Nov. 1792, in his 67th year. His widow d. 10 Nov. 1810.

IV. 1792. Sir James Dalrymple, Baronet [S. 1701], nephew and h. male, being 1st s. and h. of John Dalrymple, merchant, and sometime Lord Provost of Edinburgh, by Anne Young (m. at Hermistoun), da. of Walter Pringle, of St. Kitts, which John (who d. 8 Aug. 1779), was yr. br. of the late and 6th s. of the 2d Baronet. He *suc. to the Baronetcy*, but not to the family estate, 29 Nov. 1792. He d. unm. Dec. 1800, being drowned in the shipwreck of Capt. Dempster's ship, in the Indian Seas.

(a) See p. 396, note "b."

(b) He is spoken of [Wood's *Douglas' Peerage* (S.), vol. i, p. 183], as "that honour to his country and to human nature." Among his historical works is one on the *Annals of Scotland*, from 1057 to 1370. His profound knowledge of the rules affecting the descent of Scotch peerages is shewn in *The additional case of Elizabeth, claiming the title of Countess of Sutherland* [S.], 1770, to which, in all probability, that Lady owed the decision in her favour, as against the heir male of that Earldom.

(c) Of his two daughters and coheirs (1) Christian, da. by the 1st wife, inherited the estate of Hailes, and d. unm. 9 Jan. 1838, leaving it to her nephew as below; (2) Jean, da. by the 2d wife, m. 8 Oct. 1799, her 1st cousin, Sir James Fergusson, 4th Baronet [S. 1703], and d. 6 May 1803, leaving a s. and h., Sir Charles Dalrymple Fergusson, 5th Baronet [S. 1703], who, in 1838, inherited the estate of Hailes from his aunt, Christian Dalrymple, as above stated.

V. 1800, to 1829. Sir John Pringle Dalrymple, Baronet [S. 1701], only br. and h.; sometime Lieut.-Col. of the Royal Regiment, and, subsequently, Col. in the Army; *suc. to the Baronetcy* in Dec. 1800. He m. 28 Dec. 1807, in the Isle of Wight, Mary, 2d da. of Edward Rushworth, of Farringford Hill, Isle of Wight. He d. s.p. 17 Oct. 1829, at Bath, when the issue male of the grantee became extinct,(a) and the *Baronetcy became dormant or extinct*. Will pr. Nov. 1829.

OGILVIE, or OGILVY:
cr. 24 June 1701(b);
subsequently, 1746-1803, Lords Banff [S.];
extinct, 4 June 1803.

I. 1701. The Hon. "Alexander Ogilvie [*or* Ogilvy], of Forglen," co. Banff, 2d s. of George (Ogilvy), 2d Lord Banff [S.], by Agnes, da. of Alexander (Falconer), 1st Lord Halkerton [S.], was admitted Advocate, and was *cr. a Baronet* [S.] 24 June 1701,(b) with rem. to heirs male of the body. He was M.P. [S.] for Banff (two Parls.), 1701-07, and a steady supporter of the Union [S.], but was in custody, in June 1703, for "undutiful behaviour in Parl." He was made a Senator of the College of Justice, 23 June 1705, and a Lord of Session, under the style of *Lord Forglen*, 23 July 1706. He m. firstly (contract 17 Nov. 1681), Mary (b. 8 Aug. 1663), 1st da. of Sir John Allardice, of Allardice, co. Kincardine, by whom he had eight children. He m. secondly, 18 Jan. 1702, Mary (b. about 1657), widow of Sir Francis Kinloch, 2d Baronet [S. 1686], of Gilmerton, da. of David (Leslie), 1st Lord Newark [S.], the famous General, by Jean, da. of Sir John Yorke. He d. 30 March 1727. His widow, by whom he had no issue, d. at Edinburgh, in her 92d year, 24 and was *bur.* 26 March 1748, with her 1st husband.

II. 1727. Sir Alexander Ogilvie, *or* Ogilvy, Baronet [S. 1701], of Forglen aforesaid, grandson and h., being only s. and h. of Alexander Ogilvie, *or* Ogilvy, by Jean, da. of Benjamin Frand, of Ballynachy, in Kings County, Ireland, which Alexander (who d. v.p.), was 2d s.(c) of the late Baronet. He *suc. to the Baronetcy*, 30 March 1727, and subsequently, by the death, Nov. 1746 of his cousin Alexander, 6th Lord Banff [S.] to the peerage as LORD BANFF [S.]. In that peerage this *Baronetcy then merged* till it became *extinct*, 4 June 1803, by the death of his son the 8th Lord and 3d Baronet, and the consequent failure of the issue male of the grantee. See *Peerage*.

MYRTON, or MYRETON:(d)
cr. 28 June 1701;(e)
ex. 5 Dec. 1774.

I. 1701. "Andrew Myreton [*or* Myrton], of Gogar," co. Edinburgh, sometime a merchant of Edinburgh, said to be descended

(a) His uncle, Alexander Dalrymple, Hydrographer to the Board of Admiralty, the last survivor of the sixteen children of the 2d Baronet, d. unm. 19 June 1808, in London, aged 70, "of vexation at being removed from that office." [Wood's *Douglas' Peerage* (S.), vol. ii, p. 526].

(b) Milne's *List*, but according to Wood's *Douglas's Peerage* [S.], vol. i, p. 193, the date was 29 June 1701, and according to the *Lists* of Chamberlayne and Miege, 25 July 1701.

(c) The eldest son, George Ogilvy, m. 10 Feb. 1710, Jean, widow of Sir Alexander Innes, of Coxtoun, da. of Patrick Meldrum, of Leathers, but d. s.p. and v.p.

(d) See p. 242, note "c."

(e) From the destinations in patents of Nova Scotia Baronetcies extracted from the original [in which the dates frequently differ from those in the general lists] as printed in *The Scottish Journal of Topography, Antiquities, Traditions, &c.*, vol. ii, p. 318 (July 1848).

from the family of Myrton, of Cambo, co. Fife, matric. Arms at the Lyon Office, 15 Feb. 1686, purchased the estate of Gogar in 1699, and was *cr. a Baronet* [S.], as above, 28 June 1701, with "rem. to heirs male of his own body only."(a) On 10 Nov. 1701, his arms were altered.(b) He was cited before Parl. for having received £12,000 interest on a loan of £36,000, but was exonerated. He entailed the Gogar estate 6 Aug. 1720. He m. before 1699, Jean, da. of Sir Richard Murray, of Priestfield and Melgund. He d. in or shortly after Aug. 1720.

II. 1720, to 1774. Sir Robert Myrton, Baronet [S. 1701], of Gogar aforesaid, only s. and h.; *suc. to the Baronetcy* in or shortly after Aug. 1720, and was served heir to his father in 1721. He m. Mary, da. of (—) Campbell, of Skipness, co. Argyll. She d. in childbirth, 21 Jan. 1750. He d. s.p.m.(c) at Gogar, 5 Dec. 1774, when the *Baronetcy* became *extinct*.

ELPHINSTONE:
cr. 2 Dec. 1701;(d)
dormant Jan. 1743.

I. 1701. "James Elphinstone, of Logie," *otherwise* Logie Elphinstone, co. Aberdeen, s. and h. of William Elphinstone,(e) of Ressiviot, in Durnoch, by Margaret, da. of (—) Forbes,(f) was b. about 1645; was writer to the Signet, 1671; M.P. [S.] for Aberdeenshire, 1693-1702; a Judge of the Commissary Court of Edinburgh, 1696 (with rem. of that office to his son), and, having purchased the estate of Craig House, in Midlothian, and that of Logie, &c., in co. Aberdeen, and being then "Generall Receaver,"(g) was "for his pure zeall to King William's government,"(g) *cr. a Baronet* [S.], as above, 2 Dec. 1701, with rem. to heirs male whatsoever. He was a Commissioner of the Signet, 1720. He m. 2 Sep. 1673, Cecilia, da. of John Denholme, of Muirhouse, Bailie of Edinburgh, by Catherine, da. of James Nairne, Merchant Burgess of that city, and Elizabeth his wife, da. of Robert Tod, also Merchant Burgess thereof. She d. 10 Nov. 1706. He d. 10 March 1722.

II. 1722. Sir John Elphinstone, Baronet [S. 1701], of Logie Elphinstone aforesaid, only s. and h., *bap.* 8 Aug. 1675; admitted Advocate, 15 Feb. 1699; was sometime, v.p., Sheriff of Aberdeenshire; *suc. to the Baronetcy*, 10 March 1722. He m. 23 Aug. 1703, Mary, da. of Sir Gilbert Elliot, 1st Baronet [S. 1700], of Headshaw and Minto, by his 1st wife, Marion, *or* Helen, da. of Andrew Stevenson, Burgess of Edinburgh. He d. 11 March 1732, aged 56. His widow d. 18 May 1767, at Pilrig, near Edinburgh.

III. 1732. Sir James Elphinstone, Baronet [S. 1701], of Logie Elphinstone aforesaid, 1st s. and h., b. probably about 1710; admitted Advocate, 23 Jan. 1728; *suc. to the Baronetcy*, 11 March 1732. He m. 4 Oct. 1733, Jean, 2d da. of Thomas Rattray, of Rattray and Craighall, co. Perth, D.D., Bishop of Dunkeld and Primus of the Scotch Episc. Church, by Marjory, da. of Thomas (Galloway), 2d Lord Dunkeld [S.]. He d. s.p.m., April 1739. His widow, who was b. 21 Jan. 1711, m. 2 April 1747, Lieut.-Col. George Mure, and d. 25 Sep. 1765.

(a) See p. 398, note "e."

(b) It seems that with the consent of Sir Robert Myrton, the ruined head of the family of Myrton, of Cambo, who "for grave and weighty considerations and motives," renounced all right to the arms thereof, that he obtained the same.

(c) Of his three daughters only one had issue, viz., Frances, who m. in 1768, as his 1st wife, Sir William Augustus Cunynghame, 4th Baronet [S. 1702], of Milncraig, and had issue.

(d) See p. 242, note "c."

(e) This William was s. of James Elphinstone, of Glack, co. Aberdeen, by Elizabeth, da. of (—) Wood, of Bonitoun, in that County.

(f) She is said (by Alexander Sinclair) to be a da. of (—) Forbes, o Tolquhoun, but there seems to be no proof of this.

(g) Milne's *List*.

Linlithgow; was Lieut.-Col. in Carmichael's reg. of Dragoon Guards; purchased the estate of Cliftonhall aforesaid, and had a royal warrant from William III, dated 19 April 1700, for a Baronetcy [S.], but, no patent having passed, was, by Queen Anne, *cr. a Baronet* [S.](a), as above, 17 June 1706, with rem., failing heirs male of the body, to "heirs whatsoever and their heirs male for ever."(b) On 4 Jan. 1718 he entailed the estates of Cliftonhall, Auedliston and other lands in co. Edinburgh and co. Linlithgow, on Fergusia,(c) his 2d da. and coheir expectant. He *m.* firstly, Anne, da. of Major Michael BARCLAY, a scion of the family of BARCLAY, seated at Colairny, co. Fife. She *d.* 29 May 1708. He *m.* secondly, Fergusia, da. of (—) MACCABIN. He, who was living Jan. 1718, *d.s.p.m.*(d) before Aug. 1722.

II. 1722? SIR WILLIAM STUART Baronet [S. 1706], of Colinton, co. Edinburgh, grandson and heir male of the heir general of the grantee, being only surv. s. of Daniel STUART,(e) a Commissioner for the Union [S.], by Margaret, 1st da. and heir of line.(f) of the late Baronet by 1st wife. He was,

(a) Riddell's *Scottish Peerage Law*, vol. i, p. 67.

(b) R. R. Stodart, Lyon Clerk Depute [1863-86], writes, 21 Jan. 1878, as follows—"My view as to the Wishart title is this: Sir George, when the patent in his favour passed, was an old man with three daughters and no prospect of having a son. To gratify his wish to perpetuate his honour the patent has the remainder, failing heirs male of his body [*ad*] *hæredes quoscumque eorumque hæredes masculos*. Perhaps it may not be well expressed, but I take it to mean that when the *male* line of Mrs. Stuart [the 1st da.] failed, the *male* line of Mrs. Lockhart [the 2d da.] is to succeed, otherwise why '*masculos*' at all. If the Baronetcy had been [meant] to go to the heirs general in the direct line of Margaret [the 1st da.] till every descendant of her body had died out, then the limitation should simply have been to *the heirs whatsoever* of Sir George's body. I do think the title became extinct on the failure [4 Aug. 1802] of the male line of the Lockharts. Of course, I see that there is, looking only at the words of the remainder, a great deal to be said for the view that the title vests in Lord Clinton's son, but then I rest my view on the *masculos*. Taken in conjunction with the fact that Baronetcies only descend to males, this rule is much strengthened by exceptions, because, when such are made, it is in cases of a man who is either childless or has no male issue, and then *for once* the title is made descendable through a female. I argue, therefore, that what is meant is the heirs male of the bodies of the daughters; ill expressed, as so many clauses of limitation in Scottish patents are, but still capable of that interpretation, which is, I think, almost forced upon us by the nature of the title. The object certainly was to perpetuate the Baronetcy. Suppose the second daughter to have had a line of direct male descendants, the eldest to have had daughters, the eldest of whom had only a daughter, and that this occurred again; surely this is a *reductio ad absurdum*, as the title would fall, on the death of the patentee, into abeyance, an abeyance from which it would not emerge for perhaps 150 years."

(c) Fergusia, da. most probably by the 2d wife, Fergiusa, and, if so, *b.* after 1708, *m.* 15 March 1727, George Lockhart, of Carnwath, co. Lanark. Their son, James Lockhart, was served heir of entail and provision general to his maternal grandfather, Sir George Wishart, the 1st Baronet [S. 1706], and assumed the name of Wishart. He, a Lieut.-Gen. in the Imperial service and a Baron of the Holy Roman Empire, *d.* 6 Feb. 1790, leaving (besides two daughters) one son Charles, Count Lockhart-Wishart, who *d.* s.p., 4 Aug. 1802, when the male issue of his grandmother, Fergusia, became extinct.

(d) Of his three daughters (1) Margaret, da. by the 1st wife, *m.* Daniel Stuart, and was mother of the 2d Baronet; (2) Fergusia, *m.* 1727, George Lockhart, see note "c" above; (3) Cordelia, *m.* William Sinclair, of Rosslyn, co. Edinburgh, but *d.* s.p.s.

(e) This Daniel, who *d.* 8 April 1708, was the 2d s. that left issue of Sir Archibald Stuart, 1st Baronet [S. 1668], of Castlemilk.

(f) If this Margaret survived her father, *she herself* (see note "b" above) as heir general of the grantee (and not her son) would, apparently, have had the right to the Baronetcy, on his death.

17 April 1719, served heir of entail and provision spec. of his br., George STUART, of Colinton, who *d.* a minor, June 1713. He *suc. to the Baronetcy*, on the death of his maternal grandfather, under the spec. rem. in the creation thereof and resided chiefly at Venice. He *m.* a Venetian lady, but *d.* s.p. at Paris, 6 Dec. 1777.

[On his death the issue male of the 1st da. of the 1st Baronet became *extinct*, and it has been held (see p. 436, note "b") that the dignity should, in Dec. 1777, have passed to James LOCKHART, s. and h. of the 2d da. It was, however, allowed as under.]

III.? 1777. EMILIA STUART BELSHES, widow, niece and h., being widow of William BELSHES, of Tofts, co. Berwick, da. of John BELSHES, of Invermay, co. Perth, and only child of her mother Mary (*d.* Dec. 1739), da. of Daniel STUART abovenamed and 1st surv. sister of the late Baronet. She *m.* in 1752, her cousin, William BELSHES abovenamed, who *d.* Oct. 1753, aged 36. She apparently was entitled to *succeed to the Baronetcy*(a) as heir general of the grantee, 6 Dec. 1777. She was served, 17 July 1797, heir general of her uncles, George STUART, and Sir William STUART, the 2d Baronet [S. 1706]. She *d.* 1807.

IV.? 1807, or 1777, to 1810. SIR JOHN BELSHES-WISHART, afterwards (1797-1810) SIR JOHN STUART, Baronet [S. 1706],(a) of Fettercairn, co. Kincardine, and previously John BELSHES, only s. and (in 1807) h. of the abovenamed Emilia Stuart BELSHES; was admitted Advocate; took the name of BELSHES-WISHART in lieu of BELSHES, and *suc. to the Baronetcy* in 1807, on his mother's death, or possibly 6 Dec. 1777, on the death of his mother's uncle, the 2d Baronet.(b), He was M.P. for Kincardineshire (two Parls.), 1797-1806. He took the name of STUART only in 1797, on succeeding to the estate of Fettercairn; was Baron of the Exchequer [S.], 1807. By the death of his mother in 1807, he became *heir of line to the Baronetcy*, which had been allowed to him in 1797. He *m.* 9 or 19 Nov. 1775, at Melville House, co. Fife, Jane, 1st da. of David (LESLIE-MELVILLE), 6th EARL OF LEVEN [S.], by Wilhelmina, 19th child of William NISBET, of Dirletoun, co. Haddington. He *d.* s.p.m., 5 Dec. 1810, since which date the *Baronetcy* has remained *dormant*.(c) His widow *d.* 28 Oct. 1829.

(a) On the theory that the limitation of the Baronetcy was equivalent to a remainder to heirs whatsoever. See, however, p. 436, note "b" as to a contrary view.

(b) According to the allowance in 1797 by the Lyon office of the Baronetcy to John Belshes-Wishart, although, at that date, he was not (though his mother was) heir of line to the Baronetcy, and who, certainly (as *nemo est hæres viventis*) was not, till his mother's death in 1807 (though her heir apparent, her actual heir. This allowance disallows the right in 1777, as to the Baronetcy of James Lockhart, s. and h. *male* of the *second* da. of the grantee, at which date the heir of the *first* da. was a *female*. See p. 436, notes "b" and "c."

(c) The heir of line would be his grandson, John Stuart Forbes, s. and h. ap. of his only da., Williamina (who *d.* v.p.). by Sir William Forbes, 7th Baronet [S. 1626], of Pitsligo. He, who, however, never appears to have assumed this Baronetcy, suc. his father, 24 Oct. 1828, as 8th Baronet [S. 1626], and *d.* s.p.m., 27 May 1866, leaving an only da. and h. (the heir of line to this Baronetcy), Harriet Williamina, Baroness Clinton, whose husband took the names of Hepburn-Stuart-Forbes, before that of Trefusis. She *d.* 4 July 1867, leaving a son and h., Charles John Robert Hepburn-Stuart-Forbes-Trefusis, who suc. his father, 29 March 1904, as Lord Clinton, and who is the heir of line to this Baronetcy.

The *Baronetcy* was, however, *assumed*, as under:—

V.? 1843, to *1855?* GEORGE WISHART, next br. to William WISHART, of Foxall, co. Linlithgow, Major in the 15th Foot, both being sons of William Thomas WISHART, of Foxall aforesaid, by Anne, da. of George BALFOUR, Writer to the Signet, which William Thomas was s. and h. of the Rev. William WISHART, Principal of the Univ. of Edinburgh, who was s. and h. of another Rev. William WISHART, also Principal of Edinburgh, who was 3d and yst. br. of Sir George WISHART, 1st Baronet [S. 1706]. He suc. his said br. William, 14 Aug. 1815, in the representation (though not to the estate) of his father, and was, on 18 July 1843, served heir male of the 1st Baronet, when he *assumed* the *Baronetcy*, on the (erroneous) belief that the remainder was to heirs male general. He *d.* unm., between 1850 and 1859, when the said assumption ceased.(a)

HOLBURN:

cr. 21 June 1706(b);

ex. or *dormant* 17 Dec. 1874.

I. 1706. "JAMES HOLBURN, of Menstrie," co Clackmannan, s. and h., of James HOLBURN, of Menstrie aforesaid, by Janet, da. of John INGLIS, of Cramond, was *cr. a Baronet* [S.], 21 June 1706(b), as above, with rem. to heirs male whatsoever. He *m.* (—). He *d.* Jan. 1736/7, in Edinburgh.

II. 1737. SIR JAMES HOLBURN, Baronet [S. 1706], of Menstrie, aforesaid, 1st s. and h.; *suc. to the Baronetcy*, Jan. 1736/7; was admitted Advocate, 23 Nov. 1714, being afterwards an Examiner in the Exchequer. He *m.* (—). He *d.* 26 July 1758, at Pennicuick.

III. 1758. SIR ALEXANDER HOLBURN, Baronet [S. 1706,] of Menstrie aforesaid, 2d but 1st surv. s. and h.(c) Capt. in the Royal Navy; *suc. to the Baronetcy*, 26 July 1758. He *m.* (—). He, who had for many years been a prisoner in the King's Bench, Southwark, and whose existence was, apparently, unknown in Edinburgh some ten years before his actual death,(d) *d.* s.p. 22 Jan. 1772, "in mean lodgings called Harrow Dunghill, Southwark."(e) His widow *m.* in 1774, John GRAHAM, of Newcastle, Surgeon.

IV. 1772. SIR FRANCIS HOLBURN, Baronet [S. 1706], cousin and heir male, being only s. and h. of Rear-Admiral Francis HOLBURN, sometime (1761) M.P. for Stirling and (1768-71) for Plymouth, Governor of Greenwich Hospital (for a few months before his death) by Frances, relict

(a) His next yr. br., Patrick Wishart, who, on the death, 14 Aug. 1815, of their eldest br., inherited the estates of Foxhall and Lidecote and sold them, left sons who *d.* unm. The yst. br., John Henry Wishart, a Surgeon in Edinburgh, left one son, also named John Henry Wishart, the last known male heir of this family, who *d.* at Swan Hill, Australia, 2 Feb. 1876.

(b) In the *lists* of Chamberlayne and Miege, and in Playfair's *Baronetage* (1811) the date of creation is 21 June 1706, but in that of Milne it is 22 July 1706.

(c) James Holburn, the 1st son, *d.* unm. and v.p., being slain in battle.

(d) On 5 Aug. 1762, the testament of Mrs. Jean Holburn, da. of the *deceased* Sir Alexander Holburn, was confirmed by the Commissary of Edinburgh.

(e) *Scot's Mag.*

of Edward LASCELLES, da. of Guy BALL, of Barbadoes, which Francis (who *d.* 15 and was *bur.* 23 July 1771, at Richmond, Surrey, aged 67) was 3d s. of the 1st Baronet. He *suc. to the Baronetcy*, 22 Jan. 1772. He *m.* 12 June 1786, Alicia, da. of Thomas BRAYNE, of co. Warwick. He *d.* 13 Sep. 1820, at Southampton. Will pr. 1821. His widow, who was *b.* 16 May 1766, *d.* 18 May 1829, and was *bur.* at Bath Abbey. M.I. Admon. June 1829.

V. 1820. to 1874. SIR THOMAS WILLIAM HOLBURN, Baronet [S. 1706], 2d but only surv. s. and h.(a) *b.* about 1793; was in the Royal Navy before 1811, being Commander in 1855; *suc. to the Baronetcy*, 13 Sep. 1820. He *d.* unm. at 10 Cavendish Crescent, Bath, 17 Dec. 1874, aged 81, when the *Baronetcy* became *extinct* or *dormant*.

GORDON:

cr. 9 July 1706.(b)

I. 1706. "Leivetenant Col. WILLIAM GORDON,(c) of Afton, 2d son of Umqll. Mr. William GORDON, of Earlstoun,"(d) co. Kirkcudbright (slain at Bothwell Bridge, 22 June 1679), by Mary, da. of Sir John HOPE, 2d Baronet [S. 1628], of Craighall, was *b.* 1654; served, in 1670, in the army of Frederick, Duke of Brandenburg; took part in the landing on the west of Scotland, 27 May 1685, in favour of the Duke of Monmouth's rebellion, as also in the landing at Torbay, 5 Nov. 1688, of the Prince of Orange, afterwards William III; fought at Steinkirk in July 1692, and in all King William's continental battles down to 1697, and, being then Lieut.-Col., was *cr. a Baronet* [S.], as above,(b) "provydit to the heires male of his body, then to ALEXANDER GORDON, of Earlstoun, his eldest br., and heires male of his body, for his eminent services to King William at the Revolution, 1688."(d) He was Gov. of Fort William. He, on 29 Sep. 1710, entailed his lands, but, having omitted the clause as to non-liability for debt, they were sold in 1743. He *m.* 28 Feb. 1692, Mary, da. and coheir of Sir George CAMPBELL, of Cessnock, co. Ayr. He *d.* s.p., in Parliament Close, Edinburgh, Dec. 1718. His widow, who accompanied him all through Flanders, *d.* 1733.

II. 1718. SIR ALEXANDER GORDON, Baronet [S. 1706], of Earlston and Afton aforesaid, 1st br. and h., *b.* 1650; joined (with his father) the insurrection of the Scots Covenanters, and was present (with him) at the battle of Bothwell Bridge, 22 June 1679, being accordingly declared guilty of high treason, 19 Feb. 1681; was captured, 21 Aug. 1683, but pardoned and released (after the Revolution), 5 Jan. 1688/9. He *suc. to the Baronetcy*, under the spec. rem., and to the estate of Afton, Dec. 1718. He *m.* firstly, 10 Nov. 1676, Janet, 1st da. of Sir Thomas HAMILTON, by Anne, da. and eventually h. of Sir James HAMILTON, of Preston. She, by whom he had thirteen children, *d.* 26 Feb. 1696, aged 43.(e) He *m.* secondly, 8 March 1698, Marion, da. of Alexander (GORDON) 5th VISCOUNT KENMURE [S.], by his 2d wife, Marion, da. of David MACULLOCH, of Ardwell. He *d.* 10 Nov. 1726, at Airds, aged 76, and was *bur.* in Dalry churchyard. Will pr. 28 Sep. 1729. His widow *d.* 20 Oct. 1748.

(a) Francis Holburn, the 1st son, an officer in the 3d Foot Guards serving in the Peninsular war; *d.* unm. and v.p. of wounds received at Bayonne, 14 April 1813.

(b) See p. 398, note "e," under "MYRTON," but in Playfair's *Baronetage* [1811] the date is given as 19 July 1706, and in the *Lists* of Milne, Chamberlayne and Miege, as 29 July 1706.

(c) Much of the information in this article was kindly supplied by J. M. Bulloch; see p. 327, note "a."

(d) Milne's *List*.

(e) She shared her husband's imprisonments, and her religious meditations, in the solitary dungeons of the Bass, are published under the title of *Lady Earlston's Soliloquies*.

III. 1726. SIR THOMAS GORDON, Baronet [S. 1706], of Earlston and Afton aforesaid, 1st surv. s. and h., by 1st wife, *b.* 26 Oct. 1685; *suc. to the Baronetcy*, 10 Nov. 1726. He became a bankrupt and alienated, 19 Nov. 1743, "the whole lands and Baronies of Earlston and Afton."(a) He *m.* firstly, 20 Jan. 1710, Anne (fortune 30,000 marks), 1st da. and coheir of William BOICK, BOIG, *or* BOYE, Merchant of Glasgow, by Anne, da. of William COCHRANE, of Rochsoles, co. Lanark. She *d.* 18 April 1751. He *m.* secondly, (—) GIBSON, Whitehaven, Spinster, by whom he had no issue. He *d.* of "iliack passion," 23 March 1769, aged 83, at Whitehaven.(b) His wife survived him.

IV. 1769. SIR JOHN GORDON, Baronet [S. 1706], 8th but 1st surv. s. and h. male,(c) *b.* 20 Dec. 1720; Capt. in the 70th Foot, serving for thirty-two years; *suc. to the Baronetcy*, 23 March 1769. He *m.*, 17 April 1775, Anne, yst. da. of Thomas MYLNE, of Powderhall. He *d.* s.p., 17 Oct. 1795, at Silver Knowes, near Cramond, in his 75th year. His widow *d.* 27 Aug. 1822, at her house in Edinburgh.

V. 1795. SIR JOHN GORDON, Baronet [S. 1706], of "Earlston" in St. Anne's parish, Montego Bay, Jamaica [1811], and afterwards of Earlston, co. Kirkcudbright,(d) nephew and h. male, being 1st s. and h. of James GORDON, of Jamaica, by Christiana, da. of James SCARLETT, of that island, which James GORDON (who *d.* 1794) was 9th and yst. s. of the 3d Baronet.(e) He was *b.* 4 Oct. 1780; *suc. to the Baronetcy*, 17 Oct. 1795; was in the 1st Reg. of Foot, and was living in Jamaica in 1811, but having, by the death, in 1816, of his very distant cousin, John GORDON, of Carleton in Scotland, suc. to that estate, he returned to that Kingdom. He *m.* firstly, 17 April 1811, at Water Valley, Jamaica, Juliana, da. of Jervis GALLIMORE, of Greenvale. She *d.* s.p., 13 Feb. 1824, at Senwick, co. Kirkcudbright. He *m.* secondly, 22 April 1825, in Edinburgh, Mary, only da. of William IRVING, of Gribton, co. Dumfries. He *d.* 8 Jan. 1843, at Earlston,(d) aged 62. His widow *d.* 8 March 1869, at Carlisle.

VI. 1843. SIR WILLIAM GORDON, Baronet [S. 1706], of Earlston aforesaid,(d) 2d but 1st surv. s. and h.,(f) *b.* 20 Oct. 1830, at Deebank, co. Kirkcudbright; *suc. to the Baronetcy*, 8 Jan. 1843; ed. at Cheltenham College; entered the Army, and was severely wounded before Sebastopol, 1854, and was in the famous charge of the Light Brigade at Balaclava(g); served subsequently in the Indian Mutiny, becoming Major in the Army, 1858; Lieut.-Col.

(a) The estate of Afton, however, appears to have been inherited by his granddaughter and heir general. See note "c" below.

(b) He "clandestinely" made a will in favour of his 2d wife and her family, "depriving his children of the smallest token of his. His wife and her niece received their daily subsistence after his death. We must brand the aunt the first of hypocrites." [MS. history of the family written by Sir John Gordon, the 4th Baronet, and belonging to the present [1904] one. See p. 439, note "c."

(c) Of his elder brothers (1), Thomas Gordon *d.* v.p. and s.p.m.s. in 1767, aged 54, leaving a da. and h., Catherine, who inherited the estate of Afton on the death of her grandfather in 1769, and who *m.*, 1 Feb. 1770, Major-Gen. Alexander Stewart, of Stair (*d.* 17 Dec. 1794), and died at Enterkin, Jan. 1818, being the person in whose honour Burns is said to have composed the poem of "Flow gently sweet Afton"; (2), Archibald Gordon, a Surgeon in the Royal Navy, who *d.* unm. and v.p., 11 June 1745, a prisoner at Brest, aged 30.

(d) The appellation of the estate of Carleton was changed to that of Earlston, in commemoration of the ancient ancestral estate of Earlston.

(e) His next elder br., Francis Gordon, an officer in the 60th Foot, *d.* unm. and v.p., having been massacred in cold blood by the Indians at Venango, when a prisoner (for the second time) in 1763, aged 35.

(f) The eldest son, John Gordon, *d.* unm. and v.p., 16 July 1842, aged 16.

(g) He was, on the occasion of the Jubilee of Balaclava, 25 Oct. 1904, presented with a solid silver piece, representing a 17th Lancer attacking the Russian guns.

17th Lancers, 1862; Knight of the French Legion of Honour (1856), having also the Turkish medal Medjidie. He *m.* firstly, 21 Sep. 1857, Catherine, widow of P. J. JOYCE, of Cultra Park, co. Galway, 2d da. of John PAGE, of Ireland. She *d.* at Bombay, 17 Jan. 1864. He *m.* secondly, 2 Aug. 1866, at Colly chapel, co. Kirkcudbright, Mary Grace, 1st da. of Sir William MAXWELL, 3d Baronet [1804], of Cardoness, by his 1st wife, Mary, da. of John SPROT, of London.

NAESMYTH, *or* NASMYTH:

cr. 31 July 1706.

I. 1706. "JAMES NAESMYTH [*or* NASMYTH], of Dawick," co. Peebles, said to be s. of John NASMYTH, by Isabella, da. of Sir James MURRAY, of Philiphaugh, was Advocate 17 March 1684, becoming a very successful lawyer (though at one time disbarred, but in 1696 re-instated), and having acquired in 1691 or 1692 the estate of Dawick from the family of VEITCH (of which he had crown charter, 17 Sep. 1703, ratified by Act. of Parl. 1705) was known as the *De'il of Daick*, and was *cr. a Baronet* [S.], as above, 31 July 1706, with rem. to heirs male whatsoever. He purchased, in or before 1709, the Barony of Posso, co. Peebles, from his cousin, Dr. Robert NASMYTH. He *m.* firstly in 1688, Jean, widow of Sir Ludovick GORDON, 2d Baronet [S. 1625], da. of John STEWART, of Ladywell. He *m.* secondly, Janet, 5th and yst. da. of Sir William MURRAY, 1st Baronet [S. 1664], of Stanhope, by Janet. da. of James (JOHNSTONE) 1st EARL OF HARTFIELD [S.]. He *m.* thirdly (contract 15 June 1702) BARBARA, 1st da. of Andrew PRINGLE, of Clifton, co. Roxburgh. He *d.* 20 July, 1720, having, 19 Nov. 1709, executed an entail of his dignities and lands, including the recently purchased estate of Posso. His widow *d.* 2 July 1768.

II. 1720. SIR JAMES NAESMYTH, *or* NASMYTH, Baronet [S. 1706], of Dawick and Posso aforesaid, 1st s. and h., by 3d wife, *b.* about 1704; *suc. to the Baronetcy*, 20 July 1720, being served heir gen. of his father, 8 July 1721, and to his mother, Barbara, 17 July 1776. He was an eminent Botanist, having studied under Linnæus, in Sweden. He was M.P. for Peeblesshire (two Parls.) 1732-41; and was F.R.S. 1767. He abandoned the house at Posso and called that at Dawick by the name of New Posso. He *m.* Jean, da. of Thomas KEITH(a). He *d.* at New Posso 4, and was *bur.* 9 Feb. 1779 at Greyfriars, Edinburgh, aged 75.

III. 1779. SIR JAMES NAESMYTH, *or* NASMYTH, Baronet [S. 1706], of Dawick or New Posso aforesaid, 1st s. and h.; *suc. to the Baronetcy*, 4 Feb. 1779, and was, 22 April following, served heir male, heir of line, entail and provision to his father in divers lands, many of which, apparently, he subsequently sold. He *m.* firstly, April 1785, Eleanor, da. of John MURRAY, of Philiphaugh, co. Selkirk, by (—) da. of (—) THOMSON. She by whom he had twelve children, *d.* after childbirth, 22 Feb. 1807, in York place, Edinburgh. He *m.* secondly (post nuptial settlement, July 1828), Harriet, da. of John JONES, of Westham, Sussex. He *d.* 4 Dec. 1829. His widow *d.* 21 April 1879, at Fern Lodge, Lower Norwood, Surrey, in her 88th year.

IV. 1829. SIR JOHN MURRAY NAESMYTH, Baronet [S. 1706], of Dawick aforesaid, 1st and only surv. s. and h., by 1st wife, *b.* there 30 Dec. 1803; entered at Rugby, Jan. 1818; *suc. to the Baronetcy*, 4 Dec. 1829; rebuilt the house at Dawick in a castellated style; was well known for his taste as a landscape gardener,(b) and was often professionally consulted in laying out

(a) This Thomas Keith is stated in Playfair's *Baronetage* (1811) to have been "a grandson of the Earl Marischall" [S.], but by no *legitimate* descent could that, apparently, be the case.

(b) "In addition to his ordinary gardens he created others for extensive botanical collections, with greenhouses for rare plants, and on these he put the strikingly appropriate motto, *Solomon, in all his glory, was not arrayed like one of these.*" [Anderson's *Scottish Nation.*]

pleasure grounds. He *m.* firstly, 19 May 1826, Mary, 4th da. of Sir John MARJORIBANKS, 1st Baronet [1815], by Alison, da. of William RAMSAY. She *d.* 20 Dec. 1836. He *m.* secondly, 8 July 1839, at Putney, Eleanor, 2d da. of Thomas (POWYS), 2d BARON LILFORD, by Henrietta Maria, da. and coheir of Robert Vernon ATHERTON. He *d.* 19 July 1876, in his 73d year, at Dawick aforesaid. His widow, who was *b.* 27 July 1800, *d.* 13 March 1880, at Tunbridge Wells, aged 79.

V. 1876. SIR JAMES NAESMYTH, Baronet [S. 1706], of Dawick aforesaid, only surv. s. and h., by 1st wife, *b.* 9 Feb. 1827; ed. at Haileybury Coll.; served in the Bengal Civil Service, 1847-73, being sometime Deputy Commissioner in the Punjaub; *suc. to the Baronetcy*, 19 July 1876; was a member of the Royal Scottish Archers. He *m.* firstly, 19 Nov. 1850, Eliza Gordon Brodie, 1st da. of Francis Whitworth RUSSELL, Bengal Civil Service, by Jane Anne Catherine, da. of James BRODIE, of Brodie. She *d.* 13 June 1887, at Barnes, Surrey. He *m.* secondly, in 1888, Agnes Carus Wilson, da. of the Rev. David Barclay BEVAN, of Courtlands, Tunbridge Wells. He *d.* s.p.,(a) 10 Oct. 1896, at Dawick aforesaid, aged 69. Personalty, £8,497. His widow *m.* in 1898, the Rev. Ernest Charles BEVAN, and was living 1904.

VI. 1896. SIR MICHAEL GEORGE NAESMYTH, Baronet [S. 1706], uncle of the half blood and h. male, being s. of the 3d Baronet, by his 2d wife, *b.* 19 Oct. 1828; was a Civil Engineer; *suc. to the Baronetcy*, 10 Oct. 1896. He *m.* 1 Aug. 1860, Mary Anne, da. of John NICHOLLS, Clerk to the Lord Chancellor's Court, Westm.

Family Estates.—These, in 1883, consisted of 15,485 acres, in co. Peebles, valued at £3,557 a year. *Seat.*—Dawick [since sold], near Stobo.

DUNBAR:

cr. 10 Dec. 1706;(b)

claiming to be LORDS DUFFUS [S.], 1827-75;

dormant, under the name of DUFF, 1875-97;

but resumed, under the name of DUNBAR, since 1897.

I. 1706. THE HON. JAMES DUNBAR, *formerly* SUTHERLAND, of Hempriggs, co. Caithness, next br. to Kenneth (SUTHERLAND), 3d LORD DUFFUS [S.], who was attainted in 1715, both being sons of James, 2d LORD DUFFUS [S.], by Margaret, da. of Kenneth (MACKENZIE), 3d EARL OF SEAFORTH [S.], having *m.* about 1705, Elizabeth, widow of Sir Robert GORDON, 3d Baronet [S. 1625], of Gordonstoun (who *d.* Oct. 1704), only child of Sir William DUNBAR, 1st Baronet [S. 1700] of Hempriggs aforesaid, by Margaret, da. of Alexander SINCLAIR, of Latheron, was, in the lifetime of his wife's father, *cr. a Baronet* [S.], as above, 10 Dec. 1706,(b) with rem. to heirs whatsoever.(c) He was M.P. [S.] for Caithness-shire, 1706-07, and M.P. [G.B.] thereof, 1710-13. He, on the death, s.p.m.s., in 1711, of his wife's father, the abovenamed Sir William DUNBAR, 1st Baronet [S. 1700]. succeeded to the estate of Hempriggs. He *d.* "in the country [Oct.?] 1724." Funeral entry at the Lyon office.

(a) Alice Mary, his only sister, *m.* 22 Sep. 1851, Francis Whitworth Russell, Major 5th Bengal Cavalry (*d.* 1872, aged 42), and *d.* 1892, leaving issue.

(b) This is the date given in Sir William Fraser's "*Sutherland book*" (vol. i, p. 515), and in Wood's *Douglas's Peerage* [S.], under "DUFFUS," but in the *Lists* of Milne, Chamberlayne and Miege it is given as 21 Dec. 1706.

(c) This remainder (though possibly it was not correctly copied by the scribe) is the one in the orig. patent. It is erroneously stated in Milne's *List* to have been to the grantees "aires *male* whatsoever."

II. 1724. SIR WILLIAM DUNBAR, Baronet [S. 1706], of Hempriggs aforesaid, 1st s. and h.,(a) *suc. to the Baronetcy* in 1724 when under age. He *m.* firstly, 6 Jan. 1729, Elizabeth, only child that had issue of Alexanger DUNBAR, of Westfield, Sheriff Principal of Moray, by Margaret, da. of Sir James CALDER, of Muirtoun. She *d.* s.p.m., 3 June 1746. He *m.* secondly, 21 March 1747, Jean, da. of David SINCLAIR, of Southdun. He *m.* thirdly, 21 Oct. 1749, Henrietta, da. of Hugh ROSE, of Kilravock, by his 2d wife Jane, da. of Hugh ROSE, of Broadby. He *d.* 12 June 1793. His widow, who was *b.* Sep. 1725, *d.* Sep. 1795 and was bur. in the Greyfriars, Edinburgh. M.I.

III. 1793. SIR BENJAMIN DUNBAR, Baronet [S. 1706], of Hempriggs aforesaid, only surv. s. and h., being 1st s. by 3d wife, *b.* 28 April 1761; *suc. to the Baronetcy*, 12 June 1793. He, on the death, 30 Jan. 1827, of his cousin James (SUTHERLAND) LORD DUFFUS [S.], who (by act of Parl., 25 May 1826) had been restored to that forfeited peerage, assumed the title of LORD DUFFUS [S.], as heir *male* of the body of the grantee (to whom, and not to the heir *general*, he alleged that the title belonged), and claimed to vote at the election of Scotch peers in 1830. In June 1838 he petitioned the House of Lords as to his right, but no decision thereon was made. He *m.*, 10 Dec. 1784, at Bighouse, Janet, 1st da. of George MACKAY, of Bighouse aforesaid. He *d.* at Hempriggs Castle, Feb. 1843, aged 81. His widow *d.* there 15 March 1857, aged 89.

IV. 1843, to 1875. SIR GEORGE SUTHERLAND DUNBAR, Baronet [S. 1706], of Hempriggs aforesaid, sometimes called LORD DUFFUS [S.], but who did not assume that title, 2d but only surv. s. and h., *b.* 6 Jan. 1799; *suc. to his father's title*, Feb. 1843. He *d.* unm., 28 Aug. 1875, at Ackergill Tower, near Wick, co. Caithness, when the male issue of the grantee of the peerage, as well as that of the grantee of the Baronetage, became *extinct*, and the *Baronetcy* remained *dormant* for above twenty years.

* * * * * * * *

V. 1875. BENJAMIN DUFF, nephew and heir of line, being 1st surv. s. and h. of Garden DUFF, of Hatton, by Louisa, eldest sister of the late Baronet. He, who was *b.* 1808, was sometime Capt. 92d (Gordon Highlanders), *suc. to the right to this Baronetcy*, 28 Aug. 1875, but did not assume the title. He *m.* in 1802, Emma, da. of Commissary Gen. HAINES, C.B., He *d.* 7 Dec. 1897.

* * * * * * * *

VI *1897*, *or* 1899. SIR GEORGE DUFF-SUTHERLAND-DUNBAR, Baronet [S. 1706], of Hempriggs and Ackergill aforesaid, grandson and h., being s. and h. of Garden Duff-DUNBAR, formerly DUFF, of the same, by Jane Louisa, da. of Lieut.-Col. James DUFF, of Knockleith, which Garden DUFF, who was an officer in the 79th (Cameron Highlanders), serving in the Indian Mutiny, having v.p., suc. to the above estates, took the name of DUNBAR after that of DUFF, and *d.* v.p. 1 June 1889. He was *b.* 29 May 1878; ed. at Harrow; Lieut.-Col. 2d Battalion Queen's Own Cameron Highlanders; *suc. to the Baronetcy*, 7 Dec. 1897 to which his right, as heir general, was acknowledged in 1899, at the Lyon Office. He *m.* 3 July 1903, at Trinity Church, Sloane street, Pimlico, Sibyl Hawtrey, da. of Col. C. W. H. TATE, Army Ordnance Department.

Family Estates.—These, in 1883, consisted of 26,880 acres in Caithness-shire, worth £11,045 a year. *Seats.*—Hempriggs Castle and Ackergill Tower, both near Wick, co. Caithness.

(a) James Dunbar, the 2d and yst. son, *d.* unm., being killed at the siege of Carthagena in 1741.

CRAIGIE :(a)

1707 to 1760 ?(b)

I. 1707. SIR WILLIAM CRAIGIE, Kt., of Gairsay, in the parish of Rendall in the island of Orkney, s. and h. of Hugh CRAIGIE, of Gairsay aforesaid, (M.P. [S.] for Orkney, etc., 1661, till death, 15 April 1663), by Margaret, da. of Major George CRICHTON, of Arveckie, and Jean, da. of Sir James STEWART, was under age in 1668; registered Arms in the Lyon Office about 1673; was M.P. [S.] for Orkney, etc., 1681-82, 1689 and 1689-1702; was tacksman of the Customs, etc., at Orkney, 1686, but was superseded at the Revolution, 1689, obtaining, however, damages of £25,000 Scots, in 1701, from the Exchequer; was fined for not having signed the assurance in 1693, between which date and 1696 he was *Knighted*, and is said to have been *cr. a Baronet* [S.], as above, in 1707.(b) He *m.* firstly (contract 20 Nov. 1678), Margaret, da. of Andrew HONYMAN, Bishop of Orkney. She *d.* 3 and was *bur.* 7 May 1689 at St. Magnus, Kirkwall. He *m.* secondly, 5 Feb. 1690, at St. Andrew's, Orkney, Anne, widow of John BUCHANAN, of Sandsyd (*d.* 12 Sep. 1689), da. of John GRAHAM, of Drechness. She *d.* 21 and was bur. 26 April 1692 at St. Magnus aforesaid. He *m.* thirdly, before 8 Sep. following, Anne, 2d da. of Sir Robert HAMILTON, 1st Baronet [S. 1646 ?], of Silvertonhill, by Anne, da. of John (HAMILTON), 1st LORD BELHAVEN [S.], but by her had no issue. He *d.* 9 April 1712, at Edinburgh.

II. 1712, to 1760 ? DAVID CRAIGIE, of Gairsay aforesaid, 2d but only surv. s. and h.,(c) was *served heir to his father* (as also to his grandfather and great grandfather), 1712, 1718 and 1736, but in none of these documents is he styled "Sir," nor is there any mention of any Baronetcy, as would almost certainly have been the case, if it had had any existence. He *m.* Marjorie DOUGLAS. In 1760 the estate of Gairsay was, presumably on the failure of his male issue, in the possession of William HONYMAN, s. of James, s. of William HONYMAN, of Gairsay, and the name of CRAIGIE was assumed by that family.

HILL :

cr. 4 Feb. 1707;

ex. or *dormant* 21 Nov. 1729.

I. 1707, to 1729. "COL. SCIPIO HILL,"(d) of Waughton, co. Haddington, an Englishman and a Protestant, whose parentage is unknown, served in the Army in Scotland from 1685 as a Captain of Horse, becoming subsequently a Colonel; was naturalised in Scotland, 25 March 1707, having been *cr. a Baronet* [S.], as above, 4 Feb. 1707, with,

(a) See pedigree in Stodart's *Scottish Arms* (vol. ii, p. 203), and see also many particulars of the then family in the *Diary of Thomas Brown, Writer, in Kirkwall, 1675—1693*, also *N. & Q.*, 5th S., v. 28.

(b) The creation in Beatson's *List* is given as "1707," it being the last creation of that year and of the Scottish Baronetcies, but as it does not appear at all in the more accurate *List* of Milne, nor in those of Chamberlayne and Miege, it is, presumably, a confusion with the undoubted Knighthood of the alleged grantee. See *N. & Q.*, 5th S., v. 28.

(c) William Craigie, the 1st son, *d.* v.p. and s.p., 1698.

(d) "Col. John Hill and Col. Scipio Hill, of Waughton (who was *cr. a Baronet*, N.S., 1707), were both Englishmen." [Stodart's *Scottish Arms*, ii, p. 155].

presumably, rem. to heirs male of the body. He is, as a Commissioner of Supply, described in that year as of Waughton aforesaid. He *d.* s.p. at his house in St. James', 21 and was *bur.* 26 Nov. 1729, at St. Margaret's, Westm., when the *Baronetcy* became *extinct* or *dormant*. Will pr. Nov. 1729, at the Court of the Dean and Chapter of Westminster.

GRAY :

cr. 5 March 1707;

ex. 14 Feb. 1773.

I. 1707. "JAMES GRAY," [*Qy.* of Denmiln], whose parentage is not known, was *cr. a Baronet* [S.], 5 March 1707, with rem. to heirs male of his body. He *m.* 12 June 1707, at Chiswick, Midx., Hester DODD, of Kensington. He *d.* 30 Oct. 1722 [1720 ?]. Will pr. 1720 [1722 ?]. His widow *d.* 24 and was *bur.* 31 Oct. 1781, at Kensington, aged "about 97." Will pr. Nov. 1781.

II. 1722. SIR JAMES GRAY, Baronet [S. 1707], 1st s and h., *b.* probably about 1708;(a) *suc. to the Baronetcy* on the death of his father; ed. at Clare Hall, Cambridge; M.A., 1729; sometime resident at Venice; Envoy to Naples, 1754, and one of the first who inaugurated the excavations at Herculaneum; Ambassador to Spain, 1769; **K.B.**, 1761, and P.C., 1 Nov. 1769. He *d.* s.p. legit.(b) 9 and was *bur.* 19 Jan. 1773, at Kensington. Will dat. 5 Aug. 1767, pr. by his mother 20 Feb. 1773.

III. 1773, Jan. to Feb. SIR GEORGE GRAY, Baronet, [S. 1707], br. and h., *b.* probably about 1710;(a) entered the Army, becoming in 1770, Lieut.-Gen., and being Col. of the 61st Foot 1759, and of the 37th Foot 1768; was also an amateur Architect; *suc. to the Baronetcy*, 9 Jan. 1773. He *m.* Charlotte, da. of (—). He *d.* s.p. 14 and was *bur.* 17 Feb. 1773, at Kensington, when the *Baronetcy* became *extinct*. Will dat. 29 Feb. 1760, pr. Feb. 1773. His widow was *bur.* there 10 June 1788. Will pr. 1788.

DICK :

cr. 22 March 1707;

merged, 1829, in the Baronetcy of CUNNINGHAM [S. 1669];

becoming *afterwards*, since 1845, DICK-CUNYNGHAM.

I. 1707. SIR JAMES DICK, Baronet [S. 1677], of Prestonfield or Priestfield, co. Midlothian (who had been *cr. a Baronet* [S.], 2 March 1677, with, presumably, rem. to heirs male of the body), having, in 1707, no surv. male issue, was again *cr. a Baronet* [S.], by royal warrant, dat. at Kensington 22 March 1707, with a spec. rem. "tailzied to aires male of his body, then to the aires male of Janet DICK, his da., by Sir William CUNINGHAM, of Capringtoun, sub iisdem conditionibus sicuti dicto Sir James DICK terris suis de Presitumfield per talliam dictis terris hactenus factam per illum succedere providentur."(c) He *d.* s.p.m., 15 Nov. 1728, in his 85th year, when the earlier *Baronetcy* [S. 1677] became *extinct*, but the later *Baronetcy* [S. 1707] devolved as under.

See fuller particulars of him, under *Baronetcy* [S.] *cr.* 2 March 1677, on p. 306.

(a) Five children of his parents were *bap.* at Kensington between 12 June 1712 and 6 July 1718, but neither James nor George are among them. These two indeed, were, presumably, born *previous* to 1712.

(b) He had two illegit. children, *viz.*, James Gray and Catherine Gray, both born at Naples.

(c) Milne's *List*.

II. 1728. SIR WILLIAM DICK, Baronet [S. 1707], of Prestonfield aforesaid, *formerly* William CUNNINGHAM, grandson, by Janet, da. and sole heir of the above, being her 3d son,(a) by Sir William CUNNINGHAM, 2d Baronet [S. 1669], of Caprington, co. Ayr. He was *b.* 12 June 1701, and *suc. to the Baronetcy*, 15 Nov. 1728, under the deed of his maternal grandfather, entailing the Prestonfield estates on the 3d and other the younger sons of his daughter in tail male successively. He, accordingly, on that date assumed the name of DICK in lieu of that of CUNNINGHAM. He *m.* Anne, da. and coheir of the Hon. Sir James MACKENZIE, 1st Baronet [S. 1704], of Roystoun, by Elizabeth, da. of Sir George MACKENZIE, of Rosehaugh. She *d.* 1741. He *d.* s.p., 14, and was *bur.* 20 Jan. 1746, in Duddingston Church, aged 49.

III 1746. SIR ALEXANDER DICK, Baronet [S. 1707], of Prestonfield aforesaid, formerly Alexander CUNNINGHAM, *or* CUNYNGHAM, next yr. br. and h., *b.* 22 Oct. 1703; studied medicine at Edinburgh; was M.D., 31 Aug. 1725, at the Univ. of Leyden, and, 23 Jan. 1727, at that of St. Andrew's in Scotland, being 7 Nov. 1727, Fellow of the Royal Coll. of Physicians, Edinburgh, and, after a long residence abroad, practised as a physician in Pembrokeshire. He *suc. to the Baronetcy*, 14 Jan. 1746, when he assumed the name of DICK in lieu of that of CUNNINGHAM, and was served, 22 April 1746, heir of entail and provision gen. to his brother, in Prestonfield, Corstorphine, etc. From 1756 to 1763 he was President of the Royal Coll. of Physicians at Edinburgh; was also a member of the Philosophical Soc. of Edinburgh, and one of the founders of the Royal Society. Registered arms (DICK only) at the Lyon office, 21 Dec. 1771. He *m.* firstly, 1 April 1736, Janet, 1st da. and coheir of his cousin Alexander DICK, of Edinburgh, by Margaret, da. of Patrick SCOT, of Rossie, which Alexander was s. of Lewis and grandson of Sir Andrew DICK, of Craighouse. She *d.* s.p.m. 26 Dec. 1760, at Prestonfield. He *m.* secondly, 23 March 1762, Mary, 1st da. of David BULTER, *or* BUTLER, of co. Pembroke. He *d.* 10 Nov. 1785, aged 82.

IV. 1785. SIR WILLIAM DICK, Baronet [S. 1707], of Prestonfield aforesaid, 1st s. and h., by 2d wife, *b.* 7 Jan. 1762; Adjutant in the 1st Foot Guards, 1778, and subsequently Capt. 10 Foot; *suc. to the Baronetcy*, 10 Nov. 1785; was Major in the Midlothian Fencible Cavalry. He *m.* 3 March 1786, at Paris, Joanna, da. and h. of William DOUGLAS, of Garvaldfoot, co. Peebles. She *d.* 4 Nov. 1794, at Prestonfield. He *d.* at Durham, 19 Nov. 1796, aged 34.

V. 1796. SIR ALEXANDER DICK, Baronet [S. 1707], of Prestonfield aforesaid, only s. and h., *b.* 8 Dec. 1786; *suc. to the Baronetcy*, 19 Nov. 1796. He *d.* unm. 2 June 1808, in his 22d year.(b)

VI. 1708. SIR JOHN DICK, Baronet [1707], of Prestonfield aforesaid, uncle and h. male, *b.* 10 June 1767; *suc. to the Baronetcy*, 2 June 1808. He *d.* unm., 14 Dec. 1812, aged 45.

VII. 1812. SIR ROBERT KEITH DICK, *afterwards*, since 1845, DICK CUNYNGHAM, Baronet [S. 1707], of Prestonfield aforesaid, br. and h., being yst. s. of the 3d Baronet, *b.* 14 April 1773; sometime in the East India Company (Bengal) Service; *suc. to the Baronetcy* 14 Dec. 1812. He *m.* 15 May 1807, Harriet, 3d da. of Thomas HANMER, of Stapleton, co. Gloucester. She was

(a) The eldest son, Sir John Cunningham, Baronet [S. 1669], *b.* about 1696, suc. his father as 3d Baronet in 1740, and was father of the 4th Baronet, on whose death, 16 Jan. 1829, that Baronetcy devolved on Sir Robert Keith Dick, 7th Baronet [S.], of the creation of 1707.

(b) Of his four sisters and coheirs, the 2d, Anne, *m.* John Smith, Writer to the Signet, and in 1820, on the death of Sir William Cunningham, *or* Cunyngham, 4th Baronet [S. 1669], of Caprington, inherited that estate, which had belonged to her paternal ancestors. She *d.* next year, and her s. and h. took the name of Cunningham. See p. 274, note "a."

living, when by the death, 16 Dec. 1829, of his cousin, Sir William CUNNINGHAM, *or* CUNYNGHAM, 4th Baronet [S. 1669], of Caprington, he *suc. to that Baronetcy*, in which this *Baronetcy* then *merged*, and he, by act of Parl., 1845, took the name of DICK-CUNYNGHAM. See pp. 273-275, under "CUNNINGHAM," Baronetcy [S.], *cr.* 19, *or* 21, Sep. 1669.

MAXWELL :

cr. 27 March 1707;

being a "*novodamus*" of the Baronetcy [S.] *cr.* 12 April 1682.

SIR JOHN MAXWELL, Baronet [S. 1682], of Pollok, co. Renfrew, who had been *cr. a Baronet* [S.], 12 April 1682, with rem. to heirs male of the body, received a "diploma regranting the title and extending the limitation, dat. at Kensington," 27 March 1707.(a) See MAXWELL Baronetcy [S.], of Pollok, *cr.* 12 April 1682, pp. 312-316.

STEWART, *or* STUART :

cr. 24 April 1707;

dormant 4 March 1767.

I. 1707. "ROBERT STEWART, of Tillicoultry," co. Clackmannan, 2d s. of Sir James STEWART, 1st Baronet [S. 1627] of Bute (*d.* 1662), by Isabella, da. of Sir Dugald CAMPBELL, 2d Baronet [S. 1628] of Auchinbreck, was *b.* probably about 1655; Advocate, 15 Nov. 1681; M.P. [S.] for Rothesay, 1689, and, again, in 1689 till vacated, 25 April 1693 (by refusing the oath of allegiance); for Dingwall, 1698-1702, and for Buteshire, 1702-07; Sheriff Principal of Clackmannan; Commissary of Edinburgh, 1696; a Lord of Session, 25 July 1701 till 1709,(b) under the style of *Lord Tillicoultry*; a Commissioner of Justiciary, 18 March 1707, and, having been a Commissioner and a zealous supporter of the treaty for the Union [S.], was *cr. a Baronet* [S.], as above, 24 April 1707,(c) with rem. to heirs male whatsoever. He *m.* firstly, 20 Oct. 1685, Violet, da. of Archibald HAMILTON, of Rosehall, by Elizabeth, da. of John JARDINE, of Edinburgh, Merchant. She was *bur.* 1 Feb. 1690 in the Greyfriars, Edinburgh. He *m.* secondly, 25 Aug. 1693, Cecil (*b.* 6 July 1676), sister of John, 2d LORD BELHAVEN [S.], da. of Robert HAMILTON, of Presmennan, a Lord of Session, under the style of *Lord Presmennan*, by Marion, da. of John DENHOLME, of Muirhouse. He *d.* 1 Oct. 1710.(d) His widow *d.* at Edinburgh, 21 Nov. 1762, aged 86.

II. 1710, to 1767. SIR ROBERT STEWART, Baronet [S. 1707], of Tillicoultry aforesaid, 1st s. and h., *b.* probably about 1700; *suc. to the Baronetcy*, 1 Oct. 1710. He *m.* Jean, da. of Sir William CALDERWOOD, of Polton, a Lord of Session. She *d.* 6 Nov. 1752. He *d.*, presumably s.p., 4 March 1767, when the *Baronetcy* became *dormant*.(e)

(a) Fraser's *Maxwell of Pollock*, vol. i, pp. 348-349.

(b) In 1709 he resigned his gown in favour of his nephew, Dugald Stewart of Blairhall.

(c) This creation was no less than seventy-nine years after his father had, similarly, been *cr. a Baronet* [S.].

(d) "My Lord Tillicultrie dyd 1st Oct." [1710]. See *Masterton Papers* [Scot. Hist. Soc. Miscellany, p. 484].

(e) Presuming there was no issue male of the 2d Baronet, and that his two brothers, Hugh Stewart and Col. James Stewart, *d.* unm. or s.p.m. (no wife is assigned to either of them in Wood's *Douglas's Peerage* [S.] under "Bute"), the Baronetcy would become merged (as was also the Baronetcy [S.] conferred 18 March 1627 on the grantee's father) with the Earldom of Bute [S.], and since 1796 with the Marquessate of Bute.

[On 1 May 1707 the Union with Scotland took place, after which date the creation of *Baronetcies of Scotland* (as well as of England) ceased, and that of *Baronetcies of Great Britain* began.]

Notwithstanding that Scotland had after 1707 ceased to exist as a separate kingdom, the following anomalous creation was alleged:—

BANKS:

1831 *to* 1854.

THOMAS CHRISTOPHER BANKS, a member of the Inner Temple, London, and a Genealogist of considerable note, having in 1830 assisted Mr. Humphreys, *alias* Alexander, in his claim to the Earldom of Stirling [S.], received from him (who alleged himself to be such Earl) a *grant of a Baronetcy of Nova Scotia*, dated 14 July 1831, together with a grant (in anticipation) of 16,000 acres in Canada. As to this creation the grantee remarks, "I consider the same to be perfectly as legal and as efficacious as if it had been conferred on me by the Crown itself." However, notwithstanding this assertion, he appears, in 1837, to have considered that a Baronetcy some 200 years more ancient, whose creation was of the more usual stamp (viz., the *Baronetcy of Norton* [S.], *cr.* 18 June 1633) would be preferable. Accordingly, in 1837, he petitioned Queen Victoria (a few months after her accession) for the lands, or for lands of like value, assigned to his "ancestor," viz., "Sir Walter BANKS, then bearing the name of NORTON," whose heir, he states, he is "by family settlements" [*sic*], alleging that the Baronetcy conferred on Sir Walter in 1633 was to heirs male and assigns whatsoever. It is not quite clear whether he considered the Norton *Baronetcy* (though the *estates* had been lost) to be already vested in him as such heir, but it is presumed that he did. Anyhow, the petition met with no success.

He was 1st s. of Thomas BANKS, one of the Gentlemen Pensioners, by (—) da. of (—) SHUTER, of Gough square, London; was *b.* in 1765; served on board H.M.S. the "Renown" (of which his relative Francis BANKS, who *d.* 12 Sep. 1777, was Captain), but soon afterwards studied the law and pursued genealogical studies, practising at Lyon's Inn, 1813-20, and subsequently at *the Dormant Peerage Office*, in John street, Pall Mall. The last and most valuable of his many works (one which displays considerable research and acumen (and which was published when he was nearly 80 years old), is the *Baronia Anglica, or Account of the Baronies in fee*, 2 vols., 4to, Ripon (1844). He was also author of a *Dormant and Extinct Baronage of England*, 4 vols, 4to (1807-09 and 1837), and of many other genealogical works. He *m.* (—), da. of (—) WESTON, of Kensington.

After a long and active life of literary labour, interspersed with vehement vituperation against his fellow genealogists and complaints against Government, he died in poor circumstances at Greenwich, 30 Sep. 1854, in his 90th year, having previously been an inmate of Tancred's Almshouses in Yorkshire. It is stated that "when the documents on which Humphrys founded his claims [to be Earl of Stirling] were discovered to be forgeries, Banks ceased to make use of his own title, but in his obituary notice he is styled *a Baronet of Nova Scotia* and *Knight of the Holy Order of St. John of Jerusalem.*"(a) Anyhow, on his death, 30 Sep. 1854, the *assumption of this Baronetcy ceased.*

(a) *Dict. Nat. Biog.* See also a memoir of him in the *Gent. Mag.* for Feb. 1855; also, *Notes & Queries*, 5th S., iv, 87, 150 and 377, where many interesting particulars (by "H.S.G.") are given of him.

CORRIGENDA ET ADDENDA.

p. 1; line 8, *for* "1809," *read* "1707"; note (a) line 5, *for* "Scotch Baronetcies ceased," *read* "English and Scottish Baronetcies ceased, and that of Baronetcies of Great Britain commenced."

p. 3; line 27, *for* "1664/3," *read* "1664/5(a)"; *and add as note* (a) "In Betham's Baronetage [but not in the older ones of Wotton and Kimber] it is stated that the final remainder was to the grantee's brother, Robert. This assertion, however, seems to have been made, merely, to account for the assumption of the dignity in 1790."

p. 6; line 6, *for* "1662," *read* "between Jan. and May 1662"; note (a), *conclude*, "He, who was of Farringdon, Berks, was elder br. of the grantee."

p. 7; lines 44 and 45, *for* "Northall," *read* "Northaw"; line 50, *after* "Bloomsbury," *add* "and was *bur.* 28 at Northaw."

p. 8; line 2, *for* "Northall," *read* "Northaw"; line 3, *for* "Mansell," *read* "Mansel."

p. 9; line 23, *conclude* "One of these two was doubtless the 'Edmund Godfrey Leman, who was served heir in June 1842 by an Edinburgh Court, and was bankrupt in 1846' [*ex inform.* C. E. Leman]"; line 24, *for* "Baronet," *read* "Baronet (a)"; line 26, *for* "ASHALL LEMAN," *read* "ASHALL LEMAN (b)," *and add as note* (b), "From the copy of a letter, dated 14 Jan. 1834, it appears that his claim was through Robert Leman, of Croft, co. Lincoln (1679 to 1709), said to have been 2d son of John Leman, s. and h. of John Leman, of Beccles, who (undoubtedly) was eldest br. of the 1st Baronet. The issue male of the elder brother (another John) of the abovenamed Robert is said to have become extinct in 1808 on the death of 'Sir Thomas Leman,' a physician in Bath, who had assumed the Baronetcy [*ex. inform.* W. J. Leeman]"; last line, *for* "(b)," *read* "(c)," and alter note "(b)" to note "(c)."

p. 13; line 2, *for* "in or before 1695," *read* "7 Feb. 1693/4, at Allhallows', Staining, London" line 3, *after* "of," *add* "St. Mary at Hill."

p. 18; line 5 from bottom, *after* "1726," *add* "aged 73. Will dat. 26 March and pr. 22 Oct. 1726, at York"; note (b), *conclude* "his heart being *bur.* at Catterick."

p. 19; line 29, *after* "Hall," *add* "and was *bur.* at Catterick, 16"; line 30, *after* "1834," *add* "His widow *d.* 13 Sep. 1834 and was *bur.* at Catterick. M.I."

p. 20; line 14, *for* "living 1904," *read* "*d.* 13 Nov. 1904, aged 79, at 2 Neville Street, Onslow square, S.W."; note (a), line 3, *after* "derived," *add* "was living 26 March 1726, but."

p. 21; line 29, *after* "extinct," *add* "Admon. as of Dublin, granted [I.], 8 May 1714, to a creditor."

p. 24; line 31, *after* "1704," *add* "ed. at Winchester, 1716-20"; line 38, *after* "1733," *add* "ed. at Winchester, 1749-50"; line 47, *after* "Parnham," *add* "ed. at Winchester, 1783-86."

p. 26; lines 13 to 15, *dele* "Utricia" to "Holland," and *insert* "Hester(cc)"; *add* (as note "cc") "Utricia Ogle, stated in Le Neve's MS. Baronetage to have been his wife, *m.* 18 Dec. 1645 at Utrecht [another] Sir William SWAN, who was Knighted, at Breda, in 1649. She was *bur.* at Hamburgh, 2 May 1674. He *d.* there 23 Aug. 1678, aged 59. Will pr. 6 March 1678/9 [See Sir Henry Ogle's *Ogle family*]."

p. 34; line 14, *after* "1701," *add* "ed. at Abingdon School."

p. 45; line 1, *for* "LANGHORN," *read* "LANGHORNE."

p. 48; line 16, *after* "s.p.s.," *add* "probably unm."; note (a), *dele* and *insert* "The wife and son attributed to him by Col. J. L. Chester (in his *Westminster Abbey Registers*, p. 283, note 3) are (which is very unusual in that most valuable work) incorrect. As to the alleged wife, *Mary, da. of Amias Carteret*, she *m.* (more than ten years before the Baronet was born) another Charles Carteret (son of Helier de Carteret) and had a son, Charles Carteret, Seigneur of Trinity, who was *b.* 1669 and *d.* 1712. As to the alleged son '*James, bap. at Isleworth, Midx., 16 June 1694*' (begotten when the Baronet, his alleged father was but 14), that child was, indeed, *bap.* as son of '*Sir Charles Carteret and the Lady Mary*,' but the Sir Charles there mentioned was not the Baronet, but was son of the Baronet's maternal uncle, Sir Edward Carteret, and was *Knighted*, Oct. 1687 [Luttrell's *Diary*]. That Sir Charles, who was M.P. for Milborne Port, 1690—1700, was afterwards attached to the Court of the exiled James II, at St. Germains, and, by his wife Mary Fairfax, sometime Maid of Honour to the Queen Consort, Mary of Modena, had a large family, of whom James, born in 1694, was one."

p. 50; line 15, *dele* "1709" to "1720," *and insert* "9 and was *bur.* 23 Jan. 1709 in the Chapel at Croft Castle. M.I. He *d.* 3 and was *bur.* with his wife 8 Nov. 1720. M.I."; line 17, *for* "1661," *read* "1671"; line 18, *for* "1st," *read* "2d but 1st surv."; *for* "3 March 1663/4," *read* "there, 3 April 1683"; line 21, *after* "1736," *add* "Governor of New York, 1739"; line 22, *after* "WARING," *add* "of Dunstan House, in Thatcham, Berks; line 28, *for* "69," *read* "70, and was *bur.* at Kensington"; line 29, *after* "Castle," *add* "and inherited that of his maternal grandfather at Thatcham, Berks"; line 30, *after* "1759," *add* "at St. Geo., Han. sq."; line 37, *after* "1797," *add* "and was *bur.* at Highworth, Wilts."

p. 51; line 2, *for* "1 Nov.," *read* "12 Nov."; line 11, *for* "Sep. 1815," *read* "21 Aug. 1815, and was *bur.* at Yardley, co. Warwick," *for* "25," *read* "26," *after* "Paris." *add* "and was *bur.* in the cemetery of Vaurigrand"; line 12, *after* "1801," *add* "M.I. at Prittlewell"; line 19, *for* "1769," *read* "1789 at St. James', Westm."; line 24, *for* "1815," *read* "15 April 1818"; lines 29 and 34, *for* "20," *read* "29"; line 22, *after* "1890," *add* "being *bur.* at Bethune, Pas de Calais, France"; line 26, *after* "1837," *add* "Tunbridge Wells."

p. 52; line 7, *after* "1892," *add* "at Sydney Cathedral, New South Wales"; line 8, *for* "25," *read* "26."

p. 62; *dele* lines 23 to end, as also notes "c" and "d."

p. 70; in margin, *dele* "to 1691"; line 3, *for* "since 29 May 1691," *read* "probably about 1710"; line 5, *for* "*Qy*," *read* "*i.e.*"; line 7, *for* "the," *read* "Knight of the Order of St. Michael (the"; line 8, *after* "Blake," *add* "and was slain in action, 1653)"; line 9, *after* "fights," *add* "(notably at Harwich, 3 June 1665)"; line 11, *after* "1765," *add* "(warrant dat. 25 March 1674)"; lines 17 and 18, *dele* "At" to "*dormant*," and *insert* as under:—

II. 1691, to 1710? SIR MARTIN HARPERTSZOON VAN TROMP, Baronet [1674], s. and h., living 1705.(b) He apparently is the same as the "Maerten Harpertszoon TROMP, Lieut.-Admiral of Holland and West Friesland, whose da., Alida TROMP, was mother of the Baronetess Debora SPEELMAN."(c) He is presumed to have *d.* s.p.m.s., when apparently, the *Baronetcy* became *extinct* or *dormant*.

lines 20, 30 and 33, and notes (b), (c) and (d), *for* (b), (c) and (d), *read* (d), (e) and (f).

(b) Le Neve's MS. *Baronetage.*

(c) See "Speelman," Baronetcy, *cr.* 9 Sep. 1686.

p. 72; note (d) *conclude*, "whose male issue became extinct in 1848."

p. 73; line 38, *after* "Culloden," *add* "(where he lost an arm and was reported dead)."

p. 75; between lines 17 and 18, *insert* "*but assumed*, 1770-1859"; after last line of text insert (within lines) as under:—

The Baronetcy was, however, *assumed* as under.(e)

IV. 1770. SIR SAMUEL BROOKE, Baronet [1676](f) *formerly* Samuel BROOKES, whose parentage is unknown (but who had a brother, Joseph BROOKES, of Dublin, Banker), was a Merchant of Dublin, 1760, residing in Lower Abbey Street, 1764, and was, in or before 1761, a Banker (presumably partner of Thomas Finlay and Co.) of that city; he *assumed the Baronetcy* in 1770 and, apparently, the name of BROOKE instead of BROOKES. He was residing at Leixlip, co. Dublin, in 1804, and in co. Anglesey, 1806-11. He (as "Samuel Brooks") *m.* (Lic. Dublin, 14 June 1760) Margaret, da. of Thomas FINLAY, of Dublin. She *d.* in childbirth (of twin sons), Aug. 1761, in Bachelor's Walk, Dublin. He *d.* in or about 1811 in co. Anglesey.

V. 1811? SIR JOSEPH BROOKE, Baronet [1676],(f) sometime of Chester, but afterwards of co. Tipperary and of Artane, co. Dublin, 1st s. and h.,(g) *b.* 6 Aug. 1761 in Bachelor's Walk, Dublin; entered the army, being a Major (20th Foot) in or before 1797, and Lieut.-Colonel (20th Foot) in or before 1800; *suc. to the Baronetcy*(f) in or about 1811. He *m.* firstly, Aug. 1797, Maria Isabella, da. of George DUNBAR. She *d.* s.p.m. He *m.* secondly, March 1800, Penelope, da. of John GRIMSHAW, of Preston, co. Lancaster. He *d.* 6 Feb. 1841, at Rockfield Cottage, in Artane aforesaid. Will dat. 26 Jan. 1823(h) at "Loches sur l'Indre et Loire," and codicil dat. 30 May 1830, pr. [I.] 20 Feb. 1841.

VI. 1841, to 1859. SIR HENRY WARREN BROKE, Baronet [1676],(f) of Curraghbane, co. Tipperary, 1st s. and h.(i) by second wife; was, apparently, a minor in Jan. 1823; *suc. to the Baronetcy*(f) 20 Feb. 1841. He *m.*, about June 1830, Elizabeth, da. of Capt. JUMP, of the Royal Navy. He, who sold his estate to his wife's nephew, John Heber Pemberton KOE, *d.* s.p. 16 Dec. 1859, at Curraghbane, when *the assumption of the Baronetcy ceased.* Will (in which he makes no mention of any of his own relations) dat. 21 May 1855, pr. [I.] 16 Jan. 1860, by the widow. She *d.* 3 March 1877, at Youghall Lodge, co. Tipperary. Will dat. 17 June 1870, pr. [I.] 17 April 1877.

p. 81; line 28, *for* "PORTSMORE," *read* "PORTMORE."

p. 92; line 41, *after* "possession," *for* "He," *read* "He (rightfully)."

(e) The information herein given was kindly supplied by G. D. Burtchaell, of the Office of Arms, Dublin.

(f) According to the assumption of the Baronetcy in 1770.

(g) The second and yst. son, Samuel Brooke, was *b.* also 6 Aug. 1761, being a twin.

(h) In this will he says "I think it right as there is a title of Baronet in the family [that] the eldest son ought to possess something more than the others."

(i) Charles Augustus Brooke, the 2d and yst. son, *m.*, apparently [Lic. Dublin, 1838], Caroline Adams, and probably *d.* s.p.m. before his brother. Of the two sisters, (1) Georgiana, *d.* unm. before 1823; (2) Harriet Louisa, *m.*, as first wife (Lic. Dublin, 1840), the Rev. Donelan Bolingbroke Seymour, M.A,

p. 103; line 39, *conclude*, "She *d.* at Tamworth, Aug. 1904."

p. 139; line 10, *after* "Esq.," *add* inverted commas.

p. 179; in margin, *for* "1743," *read* "1744."

p. 201; line 40, *for* "May 1786," *read* "it is said in May, 1786, but 1788 is the date of the marr. lic. at Dublin."

p. 202; line 28, *after* "s.p.m.," *add* "legit.,(a)" and *insert* as a note. "(a) The following death is in the *Annual Register* for 1791. On 7 September; *At Madrid, aged 100, Don Carlos Felix O'Neale. He was an old Lieut.-General of the Spanish Army, a great favourite of his Monarch, and had been Governor of the Havannah. He was the son of Sir Neale O'Neale, of the province of Ulster, who was killed at the battle of the Boyne.*"; line 39, for "s.p.m.(a)," *read* "s.p.m.(b)"; note (a), alter "(a)" to "(b)."

p. 203; in margin, *for* "1674," *read* "1674, to 1686."

p. 205; line 22, *for* "March," *read* "April"; line 26, *before* "1712," *insert* "April"; note (c), line 6, *dele* "the date," to end, and *insert* "in a Chancery bill, 12 July 1712, of *Dame Alice Byrne* v. *Sir Daniel Byrne, Baronet*, the said Alice, his widow, states that he died *in the month of April last past*]."

p. 209; in margin, and on line 4, *for* "1810," *read* "1810?"

p. 220; line 18, *for* "Catharine," *read* "before 1695, Catharine, 2d"; line 19, *after* "Sidney," *add* "elder"; line 25, *after* "h." *add* "by 1st wife."

p. 222; line 2, *for* "1684?" *read* "said, in error, to be"; line 3, *after* "Belfast," *add* "(s. of George FRANCKLIN, of Mavern, Beds.)"; lines 5 and 7, *dele* "and if," to end, and *insert*, "but this is a mis-description. In his will, dat. 10 March 1690/1 (pr. [E.] 24 April 1691, and [I.] 13 July 1691), he calls himself *Sir William Francklin, of Mavern, Beds., Knight*. He was *bur.*, as a *Knight*, 7 April 1691, at Bolnhurst Beds. His description as *of Belfast* was doubtless due to his wife Lætitia, the Dow. COUNTESS OF DONEGALL [I.], whom he *m.* in or after 1675, and who *d.* May 1691."

p. 224; in margin, *for* "*1700?*" *read* "*1696?*"; lines 4 and 5, *dele* "and *d.* there before 1702," and *insert* "presented a petition to the Privy Council [E.], 19 Jan. 1695/6; and *d.* in France before 28 April 1697.(c)"; line 8, *for* "s. and h.(b)" *read* "grandson and h., being s. and h. of Richard TRANT, who was 1st s. of the grantee, but *d.* v.p. He"; line 10, *for* "(c)," *read* "(d),"; line 11, *for* "br.," *read* "uncle"; line 17, *for* "O'SHAUGNESSY," *read* "O'SHAGNESSY"; line 21, *for* "35," *read* "33"; note (b), lines 2 and 3, *dele* from "viz.," to "grantee," *insert* "(as in the text) instead of (as usually stated) *son* and heir. The evidence for this is (1) that in the 1691 attainder, Lady Helen Trant and her sons, Richard, Laurence and Charles [but no son John] are mentioned; (2) that in 1700 the claimant to Sir Patrick Trant's confiscated estate was John Trant, son of Richard Trant, *i.e.*, doubtless s. and h. of the grantee's eldest son the abovenamed Richard"; note (c), *dele* "(c)," and *insert* "(d)," and place next above this note, "(c) On 28 April 1697, Sir *John* Trant is mentioned in an information by Ulysses Brown as to an assault upon the Earl of Monmouth [*Hist. MSS.*, Duke of Buccleuch, vol. ii, p. 463]."

p. 226; line 28, *after* "Limerick," *add* "by Grace, (relict of Nathaniel GARNER, of Dublin), da. of Robert STAVELY, of Cork."

p. 229; line 14, *for* "Witton," *read* "Wilton."

p. 233; line 31, *conclude* "Her will pr. [I.] 1779."

p. 236; line 35, *for* "19[—]," *read* "1905."

p. 238; line 25, *for* "1765," *read* "1763."

p. 239; line 31, *after* "SHORT," *add* "M.A."; line 32, *after* "sometime," *add* "Vicar of Kirkdale, near Leeds, and"; line 33, *for* "was living 1904," *read* "*d.* at the Rectory, Manor House, Fakenham, Norfolk, 2 Nov. 1904, aged 83. Will pr. at £29,504."

p. 240; note (c), line 7, *dele* "after."

p. 244; lines 2 and 1 from bottom, *dele* "HOME [of Coldingham], da.," and *insert* "2d da. and coheir"; last line, *after* "HOME," *add* "3d Baronet [S. 1697]; *dele* "(*Qy.* Baronet [S.]"; *for* "*d.*," *read* "(who had issue who took the name of HOME and inherited the estate of Manderston), *d.*"

p. 250; line 18, *for* "Feb. 1774," *read* "and was *bur.* 23 Feb. 1774, at the Chapel Royal, of Holyrood House."

p. 253; line 31, *conclude* "His widow *d.* June 1697(d)"; lines 36 and 37, *for* "Feb. 1702," *read* "19 Feb. 1702(d),.' and *add* note "(d) *Masterton Papers* [Scot. Hist. Soc. Miscellany, pp. 472 and 476]."

p. 260; line 37, *conclude* "She *d.* 10 Nov. 1904, at Killiecrankie House, aged 52.

p. 267; line 26, in margin, *for* "1670?" *read* "1680"; *after* "Castletoun," *add* "in the parish of Carumnoch"; line 35, *for* "about 1670," *read* "Oct. 1680. Will recorded in Glasgow commissariat, 2 July 1681. His wife survived him."; line 38, *after* "*m.*," *add* "23 June 1704, after being thrice proclaimed [Barony (Glasford) marr. regs.]."

p. 270; lines 24 and 25, *for* "s. and h. of," *read* "2d s. of Robert BARCLAY, of Pierston (*d.* 1638), by Agnes, da. of (—) WALLIS, suc. his elder br."; line 25, *for* "suc. his father in 1638," *read* "5 Sep. 1644"; line 29, *for* "28 Sep. 1689," *read* "before 19 Dec. 1679,(dd)" and as note "(dd) Annual rent charge of that date. The date of 28 Sep. 1689, as given in Playfair's Baronetage (1811), is clearly wrong and is inconsistant with the statement of her having been mother of eight sons"; line 34, *after* "*m.*," *add* "probably in 1677"; line 30, *after* "Michael," *add* "or Malcolm"; line 31, *for* "before," *read* "15 Aug."; *after* "widow," *add* "living as *Dame Bethia Baird*, 22 Aug. 1720, was *bur.*"; line 32, *dele* "was *bur.*"; note (b), *conclude*, "See also Paterson's *Ayr.*"; note (e), *for* "1662," *read* "16 Feb. 1676.'.

p. 271; in margin, *for* "1710?" *read* "1717"; *for* "1720?" *read* "1728"; line 3, *after* "father," *add* "15 Aug. 1717"; *for* "in," *read* "22 Oct."; line 4, *dele* "who was living 1717"; line 5, *for* "probably, not long afterwards," *read* "in 1728"; lines 7 and 8, *dele* "was M.D.," down to "and," and *insert* "in 1728, to whom he was served heir, 28 Nov. 1730"; line 8, *after* "Navy," *add* "and was made M.D. of the Univ. of Glasgow, *as a testimony of regard*, 22 Nov. 1734"; line 48, *for* "wife," *read* "wife(b)" and *add* as note "(b) The legitimacy of this Robert Brydges Barclay was disputed by his uncle, David William Barclay (who, in 1859, became the 10th Baronet) on the grounds (1) of his mother's marriage not being a legal one, and (2) of his having been born and bap. previous thereto. [See Dod's *Baronetage*, 1842 to 1854.] This last objection, however, would not have prevented him inheriting a *Scotch* dignity."

p. 274; line 24, *for* "by," *read* "was sometime in the East India Service at Bengal. By"; line 25, *before* "*suc.*," *insert* "he."

p. 279; line 3, *after* "*afterwards*," *add* "1724-27."

p. 286; line 32, *add* at end "**D.S.O.** He *m.*, 1 Nov. 1904, at St. Peter's, Eaton square, Alice, 1st da. of Sir William DES VOEUX, **G.C.M.G.**, sometime (1887-91) Gov. of Hong Kong, by Marion Denison, da. of Sir John PENDER, of Middleton Hall, co. Linlithgow."

p. 296; line 11, *dele* "(b)"; *dele* also note (b).

p. 302; in margin, *for* "1767," *read* "1767 to 1780?"; lines 2 and 3 from bottom, *dele* "He *m.*," down to "Ravelrig."

p. 307; note (d), last line, *for* "Ardinglass," *read* "Ardkinglass."

p. 346; line 19, *after* "KINLOCH," *add* "of Edinburgh, Merchant, acquired a large fortune as"; line 35, *for* "THOMAS," *read* "FRANCIS"; line 38, *for* "1705," *read* "1702"; line 39, *after* "ROCHEAD," *add* "or ROCHEID"; line 40, *before* "Innerleith," *read* "Inverleith, or"; line 42, *after* "she," *add* "who was *bap.* 22 Oct. 1669 at Edinburgh"; lines 43 and 44, *for* "of Gilmerton aforesaid, 1st," *read* "2d but 1st surv."; last line, *after* "1747," *insert* "but is said to have *relinquished the succession*(c)"; *insert* as note "(c) MSS. account of the Kentish family, by *J. P. Wood, of the Excise, Edinburgh, 8 June 1819* (the well known editor of Douglas' Peerage [S.]), now [1904] in the possession of (a descendant) Mrs. Briggs, Strathairly, Largo, Fife"; note (b), *commence* "Francis Kinloch, the 1st s., *b.* 12 May 1702; Advocate, 1730; had charter of Markle, 1740, but *d.* unm. and v.p."; line 2, *for* "Rochead," *read* "Rocheid."

p. 347; line 1, *for* "Woodhall," *read* "Woodhall(a)"; line 2, *for* "Berne(a)," *read* "Berne"; line 8, *after* "1778," *add* "having suc. to the *estate*, on his father's death in 1747 (see p. 346, note 'c,' as in the *Corrigenda*); note (c), line 9, *for* "the 4th," *read* "Sir Francis, the 3d"; line 10, *dele* the inverted commas *after* the word "child."

p. 397; line 7, *after* "Forfar," *add* "sister and coheir of Sir James ROCHEAD, 1st Baronet [S. 1704]"; line 8, *after* "Inverleith," *add* "by Magdalen, da. of Sir Francis KINLOCH, 1st Baronet [S. 1686]."

p. 400; in margin, *for* "1763," *read* "1763, to 1803."

p. 413; line 14, *for* "Grisell," *read* "Grizell"; line 18, *for* "only," *read* "first"; lines 18 and 26, *for* "Killetts," *read* "Kellits."

p. 414; lines 1 and 2, *for* "of Farenough aforesaid, 4th but," *read* "presumably"; line 9, *for* "13," *read* "19"; line 12, *after* "Jamaica," *add* "1st"; line 20, *for* "Taranore," *read* "Tavanore"; line 22, *for* "fifty," *read* "sixty"; line 37, *after* "*Baronetcy*," *add* "during the lifetime of his mother"; note (b), line 1, *for* "three," *read* "according to some accounts, four"; line 2, *for* "emigrated to," *read* "went from Jamaica to Maryland, in"; *after* "s.p.m.," *add* "and (4) Paul, *d.* unm. 1812."

p. 415; line 6, *for* "Victoria," *read* "Violetta."

INDEX

TO THE SURNAMES OF THE SEVERAL HOLDERS OF THE

BARONETCIES CREATED 1 JAN. 1664/5 TO 1 MAY 1707;

including not only those of the grantees themselves, but also those of their successors, to which is added the local (or, failing that, the personal) description of each grantee. The name of any Peerage dignity held with any such Baronetcy is not included, neither is the surname of the holder of any such peerage when different(a) from that of any Baronet who, as a Commoner, possessed the Baronetcy.

(a) See vol. i, p. 263, note "a."

IV

PROSPECTUS

OF THE

Complete Baronetage,

Whether Extant, Extinct, or Dormant,

EDITED BY

G. E. C.

EDITOR OF THE

"Complete Peerage."

Vol. i, BARONETCIES (English and Irish), created by JAMES I, 1611 to 1625; (issued April 1900); price, £1 1s. net.

Vol. ii, BARONETCIES (English, Irish and Scottish), created by CHARLES I, 1625 to 1649; (issued May 1902): price £1 11s. 6d. net.

Vol. iii, BARONETCIES (English, Irish and Scottish), created 1649 to 1664 by CHARLES II, including those created by the Lord Protector Oliver Cromwell, in 1657 and 1658; (issued Aug. 1903): price, £1 11s. 6d. net.

Vol. iv, BARONETCIES (English, Irish and Scottish), created 1665 to 1707 (the date of the Union with Scotland), when the creations of Scottish or Nova Scotia Baronetcies ceased; (issued Dec. 1904): price, £1 11s. 6d. net.

The succeeding Volumes will contain (1) the BARONETCIES of Great Britain and those of Ireland, 1707 to 1800 (the date of the Union with Ireland, when the creation of Irish Baronetcies ceased), and (2) those of the United Kingdom, viz., 1801 to 1901 (the accession of Edward VII), or, possibly, to the date of publication. Each Volume to be issued on the same terms as were Vols. ii, iii and iv., *viz.*, £1 1s. to Subscribers, the price, *after* publication, being raised to £1 11s. 6d. net.

[DECEMBER, 1904.]

Complete Baronetage

VOLUME FIVE
1707–1800

Complete Baronetage.

EDITED BY

G. E. C.

EDITOR OF THE

"Complete Peerage."

VOLUME V.

1707—1800.

EXETER:
WILLIAM POLLARD & Co. Ltd., 39 & 40, NORTH STREET.
1906.

IN MEMORY

OF

MY MUCH LOVED AND MUCH LOVING WIFE,

WHO,

AFTER ABOVE FORTY-NINE YEARS

OF MARRIED LIFE,

WAS,

THOUGH EIGHT YEARS MY JUNIOR

TAKEN FROM ME

AT MY AGE OF EIGHTY,

11 MARCH 1906.

"THY WILL BE DONE."

CONTENTS.

LIST OF SUBSCRIBERS.

Adams, Rev. H. W., 40, Eton Avenue, Hampstead, N.W.
Aldenham, Lord, St. Dunstan's, Regent's Park, N.W.
Amherst of Hackney, Lord, F.S.A., per Sotheran & Co., 140, Strand, W.C.
Anderson, J. R., 84, Albert Drive, Crosshill, Glasgow.
Annesley, Lieut.-Gen. A. Lyttelton, Templemere, Weybridge, Surrey.
Anstruther, Sir R., Bt., Balcaskie, Pillenweem, Scotland.
Armytage, Sir George, Bt., F.S.A., Kirklees Park, Brighouse.
Arnold, Charles T., Stamford House, West Side, Wimbledon.
Assheton, Ralph, Downham Hall, Clitheroe.
Athill, Charles H., F.S.A., Richmond Herald, College of Arms, E.C.
Attwood, T. A. C., 7, Hyde Park Mansions, W.

Bacon, Sir Hickman, Bt., per Sotheran & Co., 140, Strand, W.C.
Bain, J., Bookseller, 1, Haymarket, S.W. (5).
Batten, H. B., Aldon, Yeovil.
Beaven, Rev. A. B., Greyfriars, Leamington.
Bedford, Duke of, per Sotheran & Co., 140, Strand, W.C.
Bell & Sons, York Street, Portugal Street, W.C.
Bickers & Son, 1, Leicester Square, W.C.
Boase, F., 21, Boscobel Road, St. Leonards-on-Sea.
Boyle, Colonel the Hon. R. E., 95, Onslow Square, S.W.
Brigg, W., 14, Clifford's Inn, London, E.C.
Brooking-Rowe, J., Castle Barbican, Plympton.
Bruce Bannerman, W., F.S.A., The Lindens, Sydenham Road, Croydon, Surrey.
Bulloch, J. M., 118, Pall Mall, S.W.
Burke, Ashworth P., per Harrison & Sons, 45, Pall Mall, S.W.
Burke, Henry Farnham, C.V.O., F.S.A., Somerset Herald, College of Arms, E.C.
Burnard, Robert, Hunaby House, Princetown.
Byrom, E., Culver, near Exeter.

Carington, H. H. Smith, F.S.A., Ashby Folville Manor, Melton Mowbray.
Carmichael, Sir Thomas D. Gibson, Bt., Malleny, Balerno, Midlothian.
Carr, William, per Sotheran & Co., 140, Strand, W.C.

Chadwyck-Healey, C. E. H., F.S.A., per Sotheran & Co., 140, Strand, W.C.
Clements, H. J. B., Killadoon, Cellridge, co. Kildare, Ireland.
Clubs, *see under* Libraries.
Colyer-Fergusson, T. C., Ightham Mote, Ivy Hatch, near Sevenoaks.
Comber, John, High Steep, Jarvis Brook, Sussex.
Commin, J. G., 230, High Street, Exeter.
Conder, Edward, F.S.A., Conigree Court, Newent, Gloucester.
Cooper, Samuel J., Mount Vernon, near Barnsley.
Craig, Major A. Tudor, 96, York Mansions, Battersea Park, S.W.
Craigie, Edmund, The Grange, Lytton Grove, Putney Hill, S.W.
Crawford and Balcarres, Earl of, per Sotheran & Co., 140, Strand, W.C.
Crawley-Boevey, A. W., 24, Sloane Court, S.W.
Cresswell, L., Wood Hall, Calverley, Leeds.
Crisp, F. A., F.S.A., Grove Park, Denmark Hill, S.E.
Croft-Lyons, Lieut.-Colonel G. B., 3, Hertford Street, Mayfair, W.
Culleton, Leo, 92, Piccadilly, W.
Cullum, G. M. G., 4, Sterling Street, Montpelier Square, S.W.
Cust, Lady Elizabeth, 13, Eccleston Square, S.W.

Dalrymple, Hon. Hew, Oxenfoord Castle, Dalkeith.
Davies, Seymour G. P., English, Scottish, and Australian Bank, Ltd., Melbourne, Australia.
Davison, R. M., Grammar School, Ilminster.
Denny, A. & F., 147, Strand, W.C. (2).
Douglas-Crompton, S., per Sotheran & Co., 140, Strand, W.C.
Douglas, David, 10, Castle Street, Edinburgh.
Douglas & Foulis, 9, Castle Street, Edinburgh (6).
Duke, Rev. R. E. H., Maltby Rectory, Alford, Lincolnshire.
Duleep Singh, His Highness Prince, per Sotheran & Co., 140, Strand, W.C.
Dunkin, E. H. W., Rosewyn, 70, Herne Hill, S.E.

Edwardes, Sir Henry H., Bt., per Harrison & Sons, 45, Pall Mall, S.W.
Eland, H. S., High Street, Exeter.
Ellis & Elvey, 29, New Bond Street, W.

FitzGerald, Hon. J. D., K.C., per Sotheran & Co., 140, Strand, W.C.
Foley, P., F.S.A., Prestwood, Stourbridge, per A. & F. Denny, 147, Strand, W.C.
Fox, Charles Henry, M.D., 35, Heriot Row, Edinburgh.
Fox, Francis F., Yate House, Chipping Sodbury, Gloucester, per W. George's Sons, Bristol.
Fry, E. A., 124, Chancery Lane, W.C.

George, William Edwards, Downside, Stoke Bishop, near Bristol, per W. George's Sons, Bristol.
George's Sons, William, Top Corner Park Street, Bristol (6).
Gibbs, Antony, Tyntesfield, near Bristol.
Gibbs, H. Martin, Barrow Court, Somerset, per W. George's Sons, Bristol.
Gibbs, Rev. John Lomax, Speen House, near Newbury, Berks.
Gibbs, Hon. Vicary, St. Dunstan's, Regent's Park, N.W.
Glencross, R. M., Colquites, Washaway, R.S.O., Cornwall.
Gough, Henry, Sandcroft, Redhill, Surrey.
Graves, Robert Edmund, Lyndhurst, Grange Park, Ealing, W. (2).
Greaves-Bagshawe, W. H., Ford Hall, Chapel en le Frith.
Green & Sons, W., Law Booksellers, Edinburgh (2).
Gurney, Mrs. R., Gurney's Bank, Norwich.
Gutch, W., 4, Stone Buildings, Lincoln's Inn, W.C.

Harding, G., 64, Great Russell Street, W.C.
Hanson, Sir Reginald, Bt., 4, Bryanston Square, W.
Harben, H. A., 107, Westbourne Terrace, Hyde Park, W.
Hardy & Page, 21, Old Buildings, Lincoln's Inn, W.C.
Harrison & Sons, 45, Pall Mall, S.W. (7).
Haslewood, Rev. F. G., Chislet Vicarage, Canterbury.
Hatchards, 187, Piccadilly, W. (6).
Head, Christopher, 6, Clarence Terrace, Regent's Park, N.W.
Hesilrige, Arthur G. M., 160A, Fleet Street, E.C.
Hodges, Figgis & Co., Ltd., 104, Grafton Street, Dublin (3).
Hofman, Charles, 16, Grosvenor Street, W.
Hoskyns, H. W. P., North Perrott Manor, Crewkerne.
Hovenden, R., F.S.A., Heathcote, Park Hill Road, Croydon.
Hughes of Kinmel, H. R., Kinmel Park, Abergele, North Wales, per Sotheran & Co., 140, Strand, London, W.C.

Inns of Court, *see under* Libraries.
Iveagh, Viscount, F.S.A., per Sotheran & Co., 140, Strand, W.C.

Jarrold & Sons, Ltd., London Street, Norwich.
Johnston, G. Harvey, 22, Garscube Terrace, Murrayfield, Edinburgh, per W. & A. K. Johnston, Ltd., 7, Paternoster Square, E.C.
Johnston, Henry Augustus, Kilmore, Richhill, co. Armagh.
Johnston, Col. W., C.B., Newton Dee, Murtle, Aberdeen.
Larpent, Frederic de H., 36, Crystal Palace Park Road, Sydenham, S.E.
Lawton, William F., Librarian, Public Libraries, Hull.
Lea, J. Henry, South Freeport, Me., U.S.A.

Lee, W. B., Seend, Melksham.
Lefroy, Edward Heathcote, 65, Belgrave Road, S.W.
Lennard, Thos. Barrett, Horsford Manor, Norwich.
LIBRARIES, CLUBS, PUBLIC OFFICES, INNS OF COURT, ETC. :—
- Athenæum Club, per Jones, Yarrell & Poulter, 8, Bury Street, S.W.
- Baronetage, The Standing Council of the, per Sotheran & Co., 140, Strand, W.C.
- British Museum, Department of MSS., per Sotheran & Co., 140, Strand, W.C.
- Carlton Club, per Harrison & Sons, 45, Pall Mall, S.W.
- Central Free Public Library, Leeds, per F. Edwards, 83, High Street, Marylebone, W.
- Chicago; The Newberry Library, per H. Grevel & Co., 33, King Street, Covent Garden, W.C.
- Constitutional Club, per Sotheran & Co., 140, Strand, W.C.
- Exeter; The Exeter Royal Albert Memorial Museum.
- Guildhall Library, E.C., per C. Welch.
- Hull: The Hull Subscription Library, Royal Institution, Hull; William Andrews, Librarian.
- Incorporated Law Society, 103, Chancery Lane, W.C.; F. Boase, Librarian.
- Inner Temple Library, per Sotheran & Co., 140, Strand, W.C.
- Ireland; Office of Arms, Dublin Castle, per Hodges, Figgis & Co., Ltd., Dublin.
- „ King's Inn Library, per Hodges, Figgis & Co., Ltd., Dublin.
- „ National Library of Ireland, per Hodges, Figgis & Co., Ltd., Dublin.
- „ Kildare Street Club, Dublin.
- Junior Carlton Club, Pall Mall, per J. Rimell & Son, 53, Shaftesbury Avenue, W.
- Leeds; The Leeds Library, Commercial Street, Leeds: D. A. Cruse, Librarian.
- Lincoln's Inn Library, W.C.; A. F. Etheridge, Librarian.
- Manchester; The Manchester Free Library, per J. E. Cornish, 16, St. Ann's Square, Manchester.
- „ Rylands Library, Manchester, per Sotheran & Co., 140, Strand, W.C.
- National Portrait Gallery, per Wyman & Sons, Ltd., Fetter Lane, E.C.
- New University Club, St. James, S.W.— per J. Rimell & Son, 53, Shaftesbury Avenue, W.
- Oxford; Codrington Library, All Souls College.
- Oxford and Cambridge Club, per Harrison & Sons, 45, Pall Mall, S.W.
- Public Record Office, per Wyman & Sons, Ltd., Fetter Lane, E.C.
- Reform Club, Pall Mall, per Jones, Yarrell & Poulter, 8, Bury Street, S.W.
- Scotland; Mitchell Library, 21, Miller Street, Glasgow; F. T. Barrett, Librarian.

Libraries, Clubs, Public Offices, Inns of Court, etc., *continued*—
- Temple, see Inner Temple.
- United University Club, per Major H. C. Gibbings, 1, Suffolk Street, Pall Mall East, S.W.
- Wigan; The Wigan Public Library, per Sotheran & Co., 140, Strand, W.C.

Lindsay, Leonard C. C., F.S.A., 23, Belgrave Road, S.W.
Lindsay, W. A., K.C., F.S.A., Windsor Herald, College of Arms, E.C.
Littledale, Willoughby A., F.S.A., 26, Cranley Gardens, S.W.
Liverpool, Earl of, per Sotheran & Co., 140, Strand, W.C. (2).
Loraine, Sir Lambton, Bt., 7, Montagu Square, W.

Macdonald, W. R., Carrick Pursuivant, Neidpath, Wester Coates Avenue, Edinburgh.
MacGregor, J., 57, Grange Loan, Edinburgh.
Mackenzie, Lieut. E. Mackenzie, Reserve of Officers, Australia, c/o Head Quarters, Victoria Barracks, Melbourne, Australia.
MacLehose & Sons, J., 61, St. Vincent Street, Glasgow (2).
Macmillan & Bowes, Cambridge.
Maddison, Rev. Canon, F.S.A., Vicars' Court, Lincoln.
Magrath, Rev. John Richard, D.D., Queen's College, Oxford.
Malcolm, Sir J. W., Bt., Tostock Place, Suffolk.
Marshall, George W., LL.D., F.S.A., York Herald, Sarnesfield Court, Weobley, R.S.O.
Marsham-Townshend, Hon. Robert, F.S.A., Frognal, Foot's Cray, Kent.
Maskelyne, Anthony Story, Public Record Office, Chancery Lane, W.C.
Mayne, Campbell J. H., Oriental Club, Hanover Square, W.
Minson, Carnegy, The Quillet, Salisbury.
Menken, E., 50, Great Russell Street, British Museum, W.C.
Mocatta, A. C., per H. Sotheran & Co., 140, Strand, W.C.
Montagu, Col. H., 123, Pall Mall, S.W.
Mosley, Sir O., Bt., Rolleston Hall, Burton-on-Trent.
Murray, Keith W., F.S.A., 37, Cheniston Gardens, Kensington, W.
Myddelton, W. M., Spencer House, St. Albans.

Nudd, W. A., Bookseller, 2, The Haymarket, Norwich.

Offices, Public, *see under* Libraries.

Parker & Co., J., 27, Broad Street, Oxford.
Paul, Sir James Balfour, Lyon King of Arms, per W. Green & Sons, Edinburgh.
Penfold, Hugh, Rustington, Worthing.
Phillimore, W. P. W., 124, Chancery Lane, W.C.
Pixley, F. W., F.S.A., per Sotheran & Co., 140, Strand, W.C.

Pollard, W. & Co., Ltd., Exeter.
Price, Major E., 17, Penywern Road, Earl's Court, S.W.
Public Offices, *see under* Libraries.

Quaritch, B., 15, Piccadilly, W.

Ramsden, J. C., Willinghurst, Guildford, Surrey.
Ramsay, Sir James H., Bt., Bamff, Alyth, N.B.
Rees, Ltd., Hugh, 124, Pall Mall, S.W.
Rich, Sir Charles H. Stuart, Bt., F.S.A., Devizes Castle.
Richardson, W. H., F.S.A., 2, Lansdown Place, Russell Square, W.C.
Rye, Walter, St. Leonard's Priory, Norwich.
Rylands, J. Paul, F.S.A., 2, Charlesville, Birkenhead.
Rylands, W. H., F.S.A., South Bank Lodge, 1, Campden Hill Place, W.

Schomberg, Arthur, Seend, Melksham.
Scott-Gatty, Sir Alfred S., F.S.A., Garter King of Arms, College of Arms, E.C.
Seton, Sir Bruce Maxwell, Bt, Durham House, Chelsea, S.W.
Shadwell, Walter H. L., F.S.A., Trewollack, Bodmin.
Shaw, W. A., Hillcrest, Mountfield Road, Finchley, N.
Sherborne, Lord, 9, St. James's Square, S.W.
Simpkin, Marshall, Hamilton, Kent, & Co., Ltd., 4, Stationers' Hall Court, E.C.
Smith, J. Challoner, F.S.A., c/o Mr. R. Reedman, 80, Oxford Terrace, London, W. (2).
Sinclair Wemyss, Miss, of Southdon, per Harrison & Sons, 45, Pall Mall, S.W.
Sotheran & Co., 140, Strand, W.C. (26).
Stevens, Son, & Stiles, 39, Great Russell Street, W.C.
Stewart, C. P., Chesfield Park, Stevenage.
Strange, Hamon le, Hunstanton Hall, Norfolk.
Stoddart, A. R., Fishergate Villa, York.
St. Leger, James, White's Club, St. James's Street, S.W.

Tempest, Mrs., Broughton Hall, Skipton, Yorks.
Tempest, Sir Tristram, Bt., Tong Hall, Drighlington, Bradford, Yorks.
Tenison, C. M., Hobart, Tasmania.
Thompson, W. N., St. Bees, Cumberland.
Toynbee, Paget, Fiveways, Burnham, Bucks.
Turnbull, Alex. H., per Sotheran & Co., 140, Strand, W.C.

Vaughan, Capt. Wilmot, per Sotheran & Co., 140, Strand, W.C.

ABBREVIATIONS

USED IN THIS WORK.

Besides those in ordinary use the following may require explanation.

admon., administration of the goods of an intestate.

ap., apparent.

b., born.

bap., baptised.

bur., buried.

cr., created.

d., died.

da., daughter.

h., heir.

m., married.

M.I., Monumental Inscription.

pr., proved.

s., son.

s.p., sine prole.

s.p.m., sine prole masculo.

s.p.m.s., sine prole masculo superstite.

s.p.s., sine prole superstite.

suc., succeeded.

Wedderburn, Alexander, K.C., 47, Cadogan Place, S.W.
Weldon, William H., C.V.O., F.S.A., Norroy King of Arms, College of Arms, E.C.
Were, Francis, Gratwicke Hall, Flax Bourton, Somerset, per George's Sons, Bristol.
Wheler, E. G., Claverdon Leys, Warwick.
Wilson, Sir S. Maryon-, Bt., Fitzjohn, near Rugby.
Wood, F. A., Highfields, Chew Magna, Somerset, per George's Sons, Bristol.
Wood, H. J. T., Fingest Cottage, near High Wycombe, Bucks.
Wyman & Sons, Ltd., Fetter Lane, E.C. (3).

Yarborough, Countess of, per H. Sotheran & Co., 140, Strand, W.C.

Baronetcies of Great Britain,

1707—1800,

being the Creations made between 1 May 1707, the date of the Union with Scotland, and 1 Jan. 1801, the date of the Union with Ireland, when these (as well as the Irish) Creations ceased and the Creation of Baronetcies of the United Kingdom commenced.

CREATIONS BY QUEEN ANNE,

1 May 1707 to 1 Aug. 1714.

FURNESE:

cr. 27 June 1707;
ex. 28 March 1735.

I. 1707. SIR HENRY FURNESE, of Waldershare, Kent, Knt., said to have been s. of Henry FURNESE, of Sandwich, was *b.* about 1658; was a merchant of London and Member of the Drapers' Company; was *Knighted* 21 Oct. 1691 at the Hague; was M.P. for Bramber, 1698 till expelled 14 Feb. 1699; and for Sandwich 1700/1 till expelled 15 Feb. 1700/1, being re-elected 1701 till his death in 1712; was Sheriff of London, 1700-01, and was *cr. a Baronet*, as above, 27 June 1707. He was, in May 1711, shortly before his death, Alderman of Bridge Ward Within. He *m.* firstly (Lic. Vic. Gen., 4 Nov. 1684, he of St. Austin Friars, merchant, about 26), Anne (then aged 19), da. of Robert BROUGH, of St. Lawrence Jewry, Linendraper. She was *bur.* there, 30 June 1695. He *m.* secondly Matilda, widow of Anthony BALAM, da. of Sir Thomas VERNON, of London, merchant. He *d.* 30 Nov. 1712, aged 54. Will pr. Dec. 1712. His widow *d.* s.p.m.(a) 8 May 1732.(b)

II. 1712. SIR ROBERT FURNESE, Baronet [1707], of Waldershare aforesaid, s. and h. by 1st wife; *b.* 1 Aug. 1687; was M.P. for Truro, 1708-10; for New Romney (four Parls.), 1710-27, and for Kent 1727 till death in 1733, having *suc. to the Baronetcy*, 30 Nov. 1712. He *m.* firstly, Anne, da. of Anthony BALAM. She *d.* s.p.m., 29 May 1713, aged 25. He *m.*

(a) Matilda, her da., *m.* 12 March 1715, Richard (Edgcumbe), 1st Baron Edgcumbe of Mount Edgcumbe, and was ancestress of the Earls of Mount Edgcumbe.

(b) The death, 8 May 1732, of "Furnese, Lady, mother of Sir Robert Furnese" [Musgrave's *Obituary*], can only refer to her. The will of [another?] "Dame Matilda Furnese" was proved (ten years earlier) in 1722. See p. 2, note "a."

secondly [Matilda?]. She *d.* 7 April 1722.[a] He *m.* thirdly, Arabella, da. of Lewis (WATSON), 1st EARL OF ROCKINGHAM, by Catherine, da. and coheir of George (SONDES), 1st EARL OF FEVERSHAM. She *d.* 5 Sep. 1727. He *m.* lastly, 15 May 1729, at Teddington, Midx., Anne, da. of Robert (SHIRLEY), 1st EARL FERRERS, by his 2d wife, Selina, da. of George FINCH. He *d.* 7, and was *bur.* 14 March 1732/3, at Waldershare. Will pr. March 1733. His widow, who was *b.* 24 May and *bap.* 6 June 1708, at Staunton Harold, co. Leicester, *d.* 25 Feb. 1779, in Dover street, Midx., in the 72d year of her age, and the 46th of her widowhood, and was *bur.* in Grosvenor chapel, South Audley street. Will pr. April 1779.

III. 1733, to 1735. SIR HENRY FURNESE, Baronet [1707], of Waldershare aforesaid, only s. and h. by 2d wife, *b.* about 1716; matric. at Oxford (Ch. Ch.), 18 Nov. 1732, aged 16, and was *cr.* M.A., 7 Feb. 1733/4, having *suc. to the Baronetcy*, 7 March 1732/3. He *d.* unm. at Montpelier, in France, 28 March 1735, aged 19, when *the Baronetcy* became *extinct.*[b] Will pr. March 1735.

DASHWOOD:

cr. 28 June, 1707;

sometime, 1763-1781, LORD LE DESPENCER;

and, 1781-1849, DASHWOOD-KING.

I. 1707. SIR FRANCIS DASHWOOD, of West Wycombe, Bucks, Knt., 3d and yst s.[c] of Francis DASHWOOD, of Vellow Wood, Somerset, Turkey Merchant and Alderman of London,[d] (*d.* 1683), by Alice, sister of Edmund SLEIGH, Alderman and sometime (1654-55) Sheriff of London, was *b.* about 1658; was of St. Botolph's, Bishopsgate, London, Silk Merchant; acquired, about 1698, the manor of West Wycombe, Bucks, and, having been *Knighted*, at Guildhall, 29 Oct. 1702, was *cr. a Baronet*, as above, 28 June 1707. He was M.P. for Winchelsea, 1708-13; was sometime of Wanstead, Essex, and about 1720, purchased the manor of Halton, Bucks. He *m.* firstly (Lic. Fac. 13 April 1683, being then of St. Botolph's, Bishopsgate, merchant, about 25, Bachelor), Mary (then aged 18), da. of John JENNYNGS, of St. Margaret's, Westm. She, by whom he had two children, *d.* s.p.m. He *m.* secondly (Lic. Fac. 30 May 1705), Mary, 1st da. of Vere (FANE), 4th EARL OF WESTMORLAND, by Rachel, da. and h. of John BENCE, Alderman of London. She *d.* 19 Aug.

(a) The death, 7 April 1722, of "Furnese, Lady of Sir Robert, of Kent," [Musgrave's *Obituary*], can only refer to her. The will of "Dame Matilda Furnese" was proved in 1722. See p. 1, note "b."

(b) Catherine, his only sister and coheir of the whole blood, *m.* firstly, Lewis (Watson), 2d Earl of Rockingham, and secondly (as his 3d wife), Francis (North), 1st Earl of Guilford, to whom (as she *d.* s.p. 22 Dec. 1766), she devised the Waldershare estate, which is still [1905], held by his descendants. Anne, elder sister (by the half-blood), *m.* John (St. John), 2d Viscount St. John, and had issue. Selina, 3d and yst. sister (of the half-blood), *m.* 8 April 1755, Sir Edward Dering, 6th Baronet [1626], and had issue. George Furnese, Capt. in the Horse, who *d.* 15 Jan. 1741, and Henry Furnese, of Gunnersbury, many years M.P. for Romney till his death 28 Aug. 1756, were, it is presumed, cousins of these Baronets.

(c) His eldest br., Sir Samuel Dashwood, M.P. for London 1686, was Lord Mayor of that city 1702-03, and *d.* 14 Sep. 1705, aged 63, leaving issue.

(d) This Francis, was 2d s. of Francis Dashwood, of Stogumber, Somerset, and elder br. of George Dashwood, Alderman of London, who was father of Robert Dashwood, *cr. a Baronet*, 16 Sep. 1684.

1710, in her 35th year, and was *bur.* at West Wycombe. M.I. Admon. 16 Jan. 1710/1. He *m.* thirdly, 17 June 1712, at Charterhouse chapel, London, Mary, da. of Major KING (br. of Dr. KING, the late Master of Charterhouse), and by her (who was living Nov. 1717), had four children. He *m.* fourthly, 21 July 1720, Elizabeth, da. of Thomas (WINDSOR), 1st EARL OF PLYMOUTH, by his 2d wife, Ursula, da. and coheir of Sir Thomas WIDDRINGTON. He *d.* in Hanover sq., 4 Nov. 1724, and was *bur.* at West Wycombe. Will pr. 1724. His widow, by whom he had no issue, *d.* 16 Oct. 1736. Will pr. 1736.

II. 1724. SIR FRANCIS DASHWOOD, Baronet [1707], of West Wycombe and Halton aforesaid, 1st s. and h., being only s. by the 2d wife, *b.* Dec. 1708; *suc. to the Baronetcy*, 4 Nov. 1724; M.P. for Romney 1741-61 and for Weymouth 1761-63; was *cr.* D.C.L. of Oxford, 13 April 1749; Treasurer of the Chamber, 1761-62; P.C., 20 March 1761; a Lord of the Treasury; and Chancellor of the Exchequer (under the Bute Ministry), 1762-63. By the death, 26 Aug. 1762, of his maternal uncle John (FANE), 7th EARL OF WESTMORLAND and LORD LE DESPENCER, he inherited the estate of Mereworth, co. Kent, and became a coheir to that Barony, the abeyance of which was terminated in his favour, and he was summoned to the House of Lords, 19 April 1763, as LORD LE DESPENCER. He was Lord-Lieutenant of Bucks, 1763 till his death; was Master of the Great Wardrobe, 1763-65; and joint Postmaster-General, 1766 till his death; F.R.S., F.S.A., etc. He *m.*, 19 Dec. 1745, at St. Geo., Han. sq. (Lic. London to marry at Mayfair Chapel), Sarah, widow of Sir Richard ELLIS, 3d Baronet [1660], da. and coheir of George GOULD, of Iver, Bucks. She *d.* 19 Jan. 1769, at West Wycombe. M.I. at West Wycombe. He *d.* there s.p. legit., 11 Dec. 1781, aged 73, when the *Barony of Le Despencer* fell again into *abeyance* for seven years. M.I. at West Wycombe. Will pr. Jan. 1782.

III. 1781. SIR JOHN DASHWOOD-KING, Baronet [1707], of West Wycombe and Halton aforesaid, br. (of the half blood) and h. male, being s. of the 1st Baronet, by his 3rd wife; *b.* 4 Aug. 1716; entered Lincoln's Inn, 15 July 1732; matric. at Oxford (Queen's Coll.) 10 Oct. 1733, aged 17; B.C.L., 1744, having by Act of Parl., 1742, taken his mother's surname of KING, after that of DASHWOOD; was M.P. for Bishop's Castle, Jan. 1753 to 1761; *suc. to the Baronetcy*, 11 Dec. 1781. He *m.* in 1761, Sarah, sister of Blunden MOORE, of Byfleet, only da. of Edmund MOORE,[a] of Sayes House in Chertsey, Surrey, by Sarah, da. of William LEE. She *d.* 9 April 1777, aged 39. He *d.* 6 Dec. 1793, in his 78th year. Will pr. Dec. 1793.

IV. 1793. SIR JOHN DASHWOOD-KING, Baronet [1707], of West Wycombe and Halton aforesaid, 1st s. and h.; matric. at Oxford (Ch. Ch.) 21 Oct. 1783, aged 18; *suc. to the Baronetcy*, 6 Dec. 1793; was M.P. for Wycombe (nine Parls.), 1796-1831. He *m.* 29 Aug. 1789, at Carshalton, Surrey, Mary Anne, da. of Theodore Henry BROADHEAD (*formerly* BRINCKMAN), of Monk Bretton, by Mary, da. and h. of John BINGLEY, of Bolton-upon-Dearne. She *d.* 19 Jan. 1844, in Upper Montagu street. He *d.* at Halton, 22 Oct. 1849. Will pr. July 1850 and Oct. 1857.

V. 1849. SIR GEORGE HENRY DASHWOOD, Baronet [1707], of West Wycombe and Halton aforesaid, 1st s. and h., *b.* about 1790, at Bourton, co. Gloucester; ed. at Eton; matric. at Oxford, 26 Oct. 1809, aged 18; B.A., 1812; *cr.* D.C.L., 23 June 1819; M.P. for Bucks, 1832-35, and for Wycombe (six Parls.) 1837 till death; *suc. to the Baronetcy*, 22 Oct. 1849. He

(a) This Edmund was s. and h. of Sir Thomas Moore, of Sayes House aforesaid (by Elizabeth, sister of William Blunden, of Basingstoke), which Thomas was s. and h. of David Moore, also of Sayes House, by Ann, da. and h. of Thomas Agar, of the Crown Office, London, and Ann his wife (relict of Edward Phillips), sister of the celebrated **John Milton.**

m. 17 March 1823, his cousin Elizabeth, sister of Sir Theodore Henry Lavington BROADHEAD (*afterwards* BRINCKMAN), 1st Baronet [1831], da. of his maternal uncle, Theodore Henry BROADHEAD, of Monk Bretton, by Elizabeth, da. of William Gordon MACDOUGALL. He *d.* s.p., 4 March 1862, at West Wycombe park, aged 71. His widow *d.* 24 May 1889, at 49 Grosvenor sq., aged 88. Will pr. 18 July 1889, above £67,000.

VI. 1862. SIR JOHN RICHARD DASHWOOD, Baronet [1707], of West Wycombe and Halton aforesaid, next surv. br. and h., being 3d s. of the 4th Baronet, *b.* about 1792; *suc. to the Baronetcy*, 4 May 1862. He *d.* unm. 24 Sep. 1863, at Halton, aged about 71.

VII. 1863. SIR EDWIN HARE DASHWOOD, Baronet [1707], of West Wycombe aforesaid, and formerly of Nelson, in New Zealand, nephew and h. male, being only s. and h. of Edwin Sandys DASHWOOD, Capt. in the Royal Horse Guards (Blue), by Emily, da. of the Rev. Robert HARE, of Hurstmonceaux, Sussex, which Edwin (who *d.* 1846) was br. of the late and 4th s. of the 4th Baronet. He was *b.* 7 Sep. 1825; was sometime Capt. 10th Foot; *suc. to the Baronetcy*, 24 Sep. 1863. He *m.* 25 Oct. 1853, at Forglen House, Banffshire, Roberta Henrietta, 5th da. of Sir Robert ABERCROMBY, 5th Baronet [S. 1636], by Elizabeth Stephenson, da. and h. of Samuel DOUGLAS, of Netherlaw. He *d.* 8 May 1882, in his 57th year. His widow *d.* 11 Nov. 1901.

VIII. 1882. SIR EDWIN ABERCROMBY DASHWOOD, Baronet [1707], of West Wycombe aforesaid, 1st s. and h., *b.* 28 Oct. 1854, at Nelson, in New Zealand; *suc. to the Baronetcy*, 8 May 1882. He *m.* 24 Aug. 1889, at Auckland, New Zealand, Florence, only da. of Frederick NORTON, of Dargaville, in that Dominion. He *d.* s.p.m., 7 April 1893, at West Wycombe park, aged 38. His widow *m.* 2 June 1894, William Selby LOUNDES, of Whaddon Hall, Bucks, and was living 1905.

IX. 1893. SIR ROBERT JOHN DASHWOOD, Baronet [1707], of West Wycombe aforesaid, next surv. br. and h., being 3d s. of the 7th Baronet,[a] *b.* 3 June 1859, at Nelson, in New Zealand; *suc. to the Baronetcy*, 7 April 1893; sometime Captain 3d Oxfordshire Light Infantry Militia. He *m.* 25 July 1893, at St. Saviour's, Paddington, Clara Adelaide Ida Conyers, 1st da. of Major William Bayford LINDSAY, sometime of the 14th and 102d Foot.

Family Estates.—These, in 1883 (being then held by the Dow. Lady Dashwood), consisted of 4,888 acres in Bucks and 144 in Oxon. *Total.*—5,032 acres, worth £7,019 a year. *Seat.*—Wycombe Park, West Wycombe, Bucks.

WILLIAMS:

cr. 30 July 1707;

ex. 19 July 1745.

I. 1707, to 1745. NICHOLAS WILLIAMS, of Edwinsford, co. Carmarthen, Esq., 1st s. and h. of Sir Rice WILLIAMS, of the same, by his 2d wife, Mary, da. and coheir of John VAUGHAN, of Llanelly, was *cr. a Baronet*, as above, 30 July 1707. He was Sheriff of Carmarthenshire, 1697-98; was M.P. for that county (four Parls.), 1722 till death in 1745; being also sometime Lord Lieut. thereof; was Chamberlain of the Counties of Brecon, Radnor and Glamorgan, etc. He *m.* 19 June 1712, at St. Mildred's, Poultry,

(a) The 2d son, George Julius Hare Dashwood, *b.* 19 Aug. 1856, *d.* unm. 30 Nov. 1878.

London (Lic. Fac.), Mary, da. of Charles COCKS, of Worcester, by Mary, da. of John SOMERS, of Clifton-on-Severn, Attorney, sister of John, BARON SOMERS OF EVESHAM, sometime Lord Chancellor. He *d.* s.p. 19 July 1745, when the *Baronetcy* became *extinct.*[a] Will pr. 1745.

GOODERE:[b]

cr. 5 Dec. 1707;

afterwards, 1739 to 1808-09, DINELEY, *or* DINELEY-GOODERE;

ex. 1808-09.

I. 1707. EDWARD GOODERE, of Burhope, co. Hereford, Esq., s. and h. of John GOODERE, of the same, by Anne, da. of John MORGAN, of Kent, was *b.* in India, 1657; was M.P. for Evesham (three Parls.), 1708-15; for Herefordshire, 1722-27, and was *cr. a Baronet*, as above, 5 Dec. 1707.[c] He *m.* (Lic. Vic. Gen., 21 Jan. 1678/9, to marry at Bodenham, co. Hereford) Helen (then aged 18), da. and h. of Sir Edward DINELEY, of Charleton, co. Worcester, by Frances, da. of Lewis (WATSON), 1st BARON ROCKINGHAM. She *d.* in or before 1714. Will pr. 1714. He *d.* 29 March 1739, at the age of nearly 90.

II. 1739. SIR JOHN DINELEY, Baronet [1707], of Charleton aforesaid, 2d but 1st surv. s. and h,[d] *b.* probably, about 1680, served at sea in the merchant service, and subsequently, 1708, as a volunteer on board the "Diamond," but, having inherited v.p., in or shortly before 1709, the Charleton estate, being that of his maternal ancestors, took the name of DINELEY, instead of that of GOODERE. He *suc. to the Baronetcy*, but not, apparently, to his paternal estates, 29 March 1739. He *m.* before 1720, Mary, da. and h. of (—) LAWFORD, of Stapleton, co. Gloucester, s. and h. of Alderman LAWFORD, of Bristol. She, however, was divorced.[e] He, who had long been on bad terms with his br. Samuel, *d.* s.p.m.s.,[f] being strangled on board his said brother's ship the "Ruby," off Bristol, by his direction, 17 Jan. 1740/1.[g] Will pr. 1741. His divorced wife set up a fraudulent claim (as his widow), on behalf of an alleged surviving son.[h]

(a) Arabella, his niece, the only child that had issue of his br., Thomas Williams, eventually inherited his estates. She *m.* Sir James Hamlyn, 1st Baronet [1795], of Clovelly, Devon, and their son, the 2d Baronet, took the name of Williams in 1798, the *Baronetcy* becoming *extinct*, 10 Oct. 1861.

(b) No account of this Baronetcy is given in Wotton's *Baronetage* of 1741, and it is there given (vol. iv, page 278*b*) as being "extinct," while in Kimber's *Baronetage* (1771) it is stated to have become "attainted 1741."

(c) The rem., as given in the continuation of Dugdale's *List*, is to the grantee "for life with rem. to John Goodere his son and his issue male, whom failing to the heirs male of the said Edward Goodere," the grantee. It is presumed that the words "of the body" are by mistake omitted after the word "male" in both instances. It is possible that as John was the 2d son, his elder br. (slain in a duel v.p. and s.p.) may thus have been postponed to him.

(d) See note "c" above.

(e) "For adultery with Sir John Jasson" [Courthope's *Extinct Baronetage*]. She *m.* (secondly), William Rayner, or Raynes, of Whitefriars, printer, and *d.* Aug. 1757, in his lifetime. Will, as of Bath and St. Giles in the fields, Midx., pr. 6 Dec. 1757 at the Commissary Court of London.

(f) His only son lived to be of age, and to join with his father in a disentailing deed of the Charleton estates, soon after which he *d.* v.p. and s.p. in Fetter lane, London.

(g) He devised the Charleton estates, subject to his wife's dower, to the issue of his sister Eleanor, wife of Samuel Foote, of Truro. One of these sons, John Foote, took the name of Dineley, and sold the property. Another son was Samuel Foote, the celebrated actor and dramatist, who *d.* 21 Oct. 1777, aged 56.

(h) Latimer's *Annals of Bristol in the 18th Century*, pp. 233-234. See also *N. & Q.*, 9th S., v. 341.

III. 1741, Jan. **Samuel Goodere**, of Burhope aforesaid, br. and h., being 3d and yst s. of the 1st Baronet; *b.* 1687; entered the Navy 1705, serving as Lieut. through the war of the Spanish succession, but was dismissed his ship, 24 Dec. 1719, for misconduct at St. Sebastian, though in Nov. 1740, made Capt. of the "Ruby." He, apparently, had suc. to his father's unentailed estates, 29 March 1739. He *m.*, in or before 1729, Elizabeth, da. of (—) Watts, of Leauinguian and Terrew, co. Monmouth. Provoked by his brother having settled the Charleston estate on his sister's children, he contrived his murder, 17 Jan. 1740/1, as above stated, after which date accordingly, he was entitled to have *suc. to the Baronetcy*, but never assumed the same, being tried for murder (as "Samuel Goodere, Esq."), 26 March, and hanged (with his two accomplices), 15 April 1741, at Bristol, and, after dissection, *bur.* with his ancestors at Hereford.

IV. 1741, April. **Sir Edward Dineley-Goodere**, Baronet [1707], of Burhope aforesaid, 1st s. and h., *b.* 1729; *suc. to the Baronetcy*, 15 April 1741. He *d.* a lunatic and unm., March 1761, at Clapton, Midx., aged 32.

V. 1761, to 1808-09. **Sir John Dineley**, *or* **Dineley-Goodere**, Baronet [1707], of Burhope aforesaid, only br. and h., being a twin son, *b.* in 1729; *suc. to the Baronetcy*, March 1761, and sold the estate of Burhope about 1770, after which date he lived in extreme poverty, and became one of the "Poor Knights" at Windsor. He was well-known for his eccentricities. He *d.* there unm. in May 1808 or Nov. 1809,(a) when the *Baronetcy* became *extinct.*

LLOYD:

cr. 1 May 1708;

ex. 1750.

I. 1708. **Sir Charles Lloyd**, of Milfield, *otherwise* Maes-y-vellin [near Lampeter], co. Cardigan, Kt., 2d but 1st surv. s. of Sir Francis Lloyd, of the same, Comptroller of the Household to Charles I. and sometime M.P. for Cardiganshire, by his 2d wife, Bridget, da. of Richard Leigh, of Carmarthen, was *b.* at Forest Hill, Oxon, about 1662; matric. at Oxford (Jesus Coll.), 28 Nov. 1679, aged 17; Sheriff of Cardiganshire, 1688-89; was *Knighted*, 24 Nov. 1693; was M.P. for Cardiganshire, 1698-1700; and was *cr. a Baronet* as above, 1 May 1708. He *m.* firstly, Jane, da. and coheir of Morgan Lloyd, of Green Grove, co. Cardigan. She *d.* s.p.m. He *m.* secondly, in or before 1706, Frances, da. of Sir Francis Cornwallis, of Albermarles, co. Carmarthen. He *d.* 28 Dec. 1723, at Milfield aforesaid. Will pr. 1724. The will of Dame Frances Lloyd pr. 1753.

II. 1723. **Sir Charles Cornwallis Lloyd**, Baronet [1708], of Milfield aforesaid, 2d but 1st surv. s. and h., by 2d wife, *b.* about 1706, at Ludlow; admitted to Lincoln's Inn, 10 March 1719/20; matric. at Oxford (Ch. Ch.), 10 June 1721, aged 15; *suc. to the Baronetcy*. 28 Dec. 1723. He *m.* in 1727 (—), widow of (—) Jennings, of Somerset. He *d.* s.p., 25 Feb. 1728/9. Will pr. 1730. His widow *m.* George Speke and *d.* July 1754.

(a) "The papers announced his death at Windsor, in May 1808" [Burke's *Romance of the Aristocracy* (1855), vol. ii, pp. 19-35, where some curious specimens of his advertisements for a wife (24 May 1802 and 21 Aug. 1802) are given], but the date of "Nov. 1809" is his death date as given in the *Dict. Nat. Biog.*; while in Musgrave's *Obituary* the death is recorded in "Nov. 1785" (*Gent. Mag.* 1,005) of "Sir John Dineley Goodyere, Bt., Worcestershire," who apparently is meant for this same person.

III. 1729, to 1750. **Sir Lucius Christianus Lloyd**, Baronet [1708], of Milfield aforesaid, only br. and h., *b.* probably about 1710; *suc. to the Baronetcy*, 25 Feb. 1728/9; Sheriff of Cardiganshire, 1746-47. He *m.* before 1741, Anne, da. of Walter Lloyd, of Peterwell, co. Cardigan, sometime M.P. for that shire, and Attorney Gen. for Wales. He *d.* s.p., 1750, when the *Baronetcy* became *extinct.* Will pr. 1750.

CAIRNES(a):

cr. 6 May 1708;

ex. 16 June 1743.

I. 1708. **Alexander Cairnes**, of Monaghan, in Ireland, Esq., br. and h. of William Cairns (*bur.* 9 Aug. 1707, at St. Michan's, Dublin), s. of John Cairnes, of Donoghmore, co. Donegal, by Jane, da. of James Miller, M.D., of Millhugh, was a Banker in Dublin and London,(b) and was *cr. a Baronet*,(c) as above, 6 May 1708, with rem., failing issue male of his body, to "his yr. br., Henry Cairnes, of London, Merchant." He was M.P. [I.] for the county of Monaghan (three Parls.), 1709-27, and for the Borough of Monaghan, 1727 till death in 1732. He *m.* 17 Feb. 1697/8, at St. Peter le Poor, London (Lic. Fac.), Elizabeth, sister of Sir Nathaniel Gould, Turkey Merchant of London, da. of John Gould, of St. Olave's, Hart Street, London, Merchant, by Mary, his wife. She *d.* at Monaghan before 4 June 1731, when admon. was granted to her husband. He *d.* s.p.m.(d) at Dublin, 30 Oct. 1732. Will pr. [I.] 1732. Limited admon. 14 June 1739.

II. 1732, to 1743. **Sir Henry Cairnes**, Baronet [1708], br. and h. male, sometime a Merchant and Banker in London; *suc. to the Baronetcy*, 30 Oct. 1732, according to the spec. rem. of that dignity; was M.P. [I.] for the Borough of Monaghan, 1732 till death in 1743. He *m.* 10 July 1711, at St. Peter le Poor aforesaid (Lic. Fac.), Frances (niece of his brother's wife), daughter of John Gould, of Hackney, Midx., a Director of the East India Company, by Rachel, da. of Peter Gelsthorp, Citizen and Apothecary of London. He *d.* s.p. 16 June 1743, when the *Baronetcy* became *extinct*. His widow *d.* 8 and was *bur.* 11 March 1749/50, at Putney, Surrey. Will dat. 24 Aug. 1745, pr. 23 Aug. 1750.

(a) See *Mis. Gen. et Her.*, N.S., Vol. iii, pp. 356 and 358, in an elaborate pedigree of the family of Gould, pp. 355-360.

(b) "Thomas Sheridan calls him *an eminent Banker*. Dean Swift describes him as *a scrupulous puppy* and *a shuffling scoundrel* (see *Journal to Stella*, 7 June 1711)." [*Ex inform.* C. M. Tenison.]

(c) "Mr. Le Neve says he was advanced to the dignity of a Baronet of Great Britain and Ireland and paid whole fees for the former, and half fees for the latter. MSS. Vol. iii, p. 328" [Wotton's *Baronetage*, 1741]. No notice of such Irish creation is given in the *Liber Munerum Hiberniæ*, where, indeed, the only creation between 21 Nov. 1706 and 17 Oct. 1721 is that of "Deane," 10 March 1709.

(d) William Henry, his only son, *d.* unm. and v.p. Mary, Dow. Baroness Blayney [I.], his only surv. child, was at the time of his death a childless widow. She *m.* subsequently in 1734, Col. John Murray, sometime M.P. for co. Monaghan (who *d.* 29 June 1743), and *d.* 28 Aug. 1790, leaving several daughters of whom (1) Elizabeth *m.* 29 May 1754, Lieut.-Gen. Robert Cuninghame, sometime M.P. [I.] for co. Monaghan, who was *cr.* 19 Oct. 1796, Baron Rossmore [I.], and who *d.* s.p. 6 Aug. 1801; (2) Harriet, *m.* 29 Nov. 1764, William Westenra, and was mother of Warner William Westenra, who in 1801 suc. his maternal uncle abovenamed as the 2d Baron Rossmore [I.].

DE NEUFVILLE, *or* NEUFVILLE:

cr. 18 March 1708/9;

ex. presumably on death of grantee.

I. 1709, to 1720? **Robert de Neufville**, of Frankfort, in Germany, was *cr. a Baronet*, as above, 18 March 1708/9, but of him nothing further is known, and the *Baronetcy* became, presumably, *extinct* at his death.

ABERCROMBIE:

cr. 21 May 1709(a);

ex. 14 Nov. 1724.

I. 1709, to 1724. **James Abercrombie**, Esq., Capt. in the Coldstream Regiment of Guards at Edinburgh, was, it is said,(b) "natural son of the Duke of Hamilton"; was Ensign, Royal Scots, 24 May 1696; Capt., 31 May 1707, seeing much service under Marlborough and being Aide-de-Camp to the Earl of Orkney at Blenheim; Brevet Major, 1706; and subsequently Capt. and Lieut.-Col. Coldstream Guards, being *cr. a Baronet*, as above, 21 May 1709,(a) for his military services; Lieut.-Col., Royal Scots, 20 March 1711; Brevet Col., 1 Nov. 1711; and was Town Major (Lieut.-Gov.) of Dunkirk, 24 Oct. 1712 till death. He *d.* s.p.m, probably unm., 14 Nov. 1724, when the *Barontcy* became *extinct.*

ELWILL:

cr. 25 Aug. 1709;

ex. 1 March 1778.

I. 1709. **Sir John Elwill**, of Exeter, co. Devon, Knt., s. of (—) Elwill, a Grocer in that city, by (—), da. and h. of (—) Pole, of Exeter aforesaid, was *b.* probably about 1640; matric. at Oxford (Ex. Coll.), 25 March 1659, being intended for Holy Orders, but became a Merchant, at Exeter; was Receiver Gen. for Devon; M.P. for Beeralston, 1681, 1689-90, and 1695-98; Sheriff of Devon, 1699; *Knighted* at Kensington, 28 April 1696, and was *cr. a Baronet*, as above, 25 Aug. 1709. He *m.* firstly, Frances, 5th da. of Sir John Bamfylde, 1st Baronet [1641], of Poltimore, by Gertrude, da. of Amyas Coplestone. She, who was *b.* before 1664 and then living, *d.* s.p. He *m.* secondly, [Anne ?] da. of (—) Leigh, of Egham, Surrey. The will of Dame Anne Elwill, of Devon, was pr. Oct. 1716. He *d.* 25 April 1717. Will pr. May 1717.

II. 1717. **Sir John Elwill**, Baronet [1709], of Langley Park, Kent. 1st s. and h. by 2d wife; *suc. to the Baronetcy*, 25 April 1717. He *m.* Elizabeth, da. and h. of Humphrey Style, of Langley Park aforesaid. He *d.* s.p., 10 Sep. 1727. Will dat. 17 Feb. 1724/5, pr. 20 Nov. 1727. His widow *m.* (settlement 22 and 23 Aug. 1730) Henry Bartelot, of West Wickham, Kent, who, after her death, sold the estate of Langley, 12 May 1732, for £6,500. She *d.* s.p., 16 June 1731. Will pr. Dec. 1731, leaving her distant cousin, Sir Thomas Style, 4th Baronet [1627], her residuary legatee. M.I. to both at Beckenham, Kent.

(a) The date of "8 March 1710" [*Qy.* 1710/1], is given as that of this creation in the continuation of Dugdale's *List*, where it is placed next after that of "Lambert," 16 Feb. 1710 [*i.e.*, 1710/1].

(b) Musgrave's *Obituary.*

III. 1727. **Sir Edmund Elwill**, Baronet [1709], br. and h.; was for many years Comptroller of the Excise; *suc. to the Baronetcy*, 10 Sep. 1727. He *m.* Anne, da. of William Speke, of Beauchamp, Somerset. He *d.* 2 Feb. 1740. Will pr. 1740. His widow *d.* April or May 1742. Will pr. May 1742.

IV. 1740, to 1778. **Sir John Elwill**, Baronet [1709], only s. and h., *suc. to the Baronetcy*, 2 Feb. 1740; was M.P. for Guildford (three Parls.), 1747-68. He *m.* 30 Nov. 1755, at West Dean, Selina, widow of Arthur (Cole), Baron Ranelagh [I.], da. of Peter Bathurst, of Clarendon Park, Wilts, by his 2d wife, Selina, da. of Robert (Shirley), 1st Earl Ferrers. He *d.* s.p.m., 1 March 1778, and was *bur.* at Egham, Surrey, when the *Baronetcy* became *extinct.* Will pr. March 1778. His widow *d.* 9 and was *bur.* 18 Feb. 1781, at West Dean, aged 60. Will dat. 20 Aug. 1780, pr. 15 Feb. 1781.

THOROLD:

cr. 9 Sep. 1709;

ex. 1 Jan. 1737/8.

I. 1709. **Sir George Thorold**, of Harmston, co. Lincoln, Knt., 4th s. of Charles Thorold, of Harmston, Citizen and Ironmonger of London, by his 2d wife, Anne, da. of George Clarke, of London, was *b.* about 1666; was a Citizen and Ironmonger of London, and a merchant of that city; was Alderman of Cordwainer Ward, 3 May 1709, in succession to his elder br., Charles Thorold, sometime (1705-06) Sheriff of London, and was *cr. a Baronet*, as above, 9 Sep. 1709, with rem., failing heirs male of his body, to his yr. br. Samuel Thorold. He was Sheriff of London, 1710-11, and Lord Mayor, 1719-20.(a) He *m.* in 1713, Elizabeth, da. of Sir James Rushout, 1st Baronet [1661], by Alice, da. and h. of Edmund Pitt. He *d.* s.p.s. in Bloomsbury square, Midx., 29 Oct. and was *bur.* 11 Nov. 1722, at Harmston, aged 56. M.I. Will dat. 3 March 1721/2 to 28 Oct. 1722, pr. 21 Nov. 1722. His widow *m.* (as his 2d wife), 3 July 1726, George (Compton), 1st Earl of Northampton, and *d.*, his widow, 15 Jan. 1749/50, being *bur.* (with her parents) at Blockley, co. Gloucester, aged 67. Will pr. 1750.

II. 1722, to 1738. **Sir Samuel Thorold**, Baronet [1709], of Harmston aforesaid, br. and h., *suc. to the Baronetcy*, 29 Oct. 1722, according to the spec. rem. in the creation of that dignity; Sheriff of Lincolnshire, 1724-25. He *d.* unm., 1 and was *bur.* 19 Jan. 1737/8, at Harmston, when the *Baronetcy* became *extinct.* Will dat. 15 Dec. 1737, pr. 3 Jan. 1737/8.(b)

(a) His procession as Lord Mayor is thus celebrated by Pope:—

"'Twas on the day when Thorold, rich and grave,
Like Cæsar, triumphed both on land and wave."

(b) In it he devises the estate of Harmston to [his very distant cousin] "Mr. Nathaniel Thorold, now or late at Naples in Italy," with rem. in favour of the younger son of Sir John Thorold, 4th Baronet [1642]. This Nathaniel was *cr. a Baronet* as of "Harmston," 24th March 1741, a dignity which became extinct at his death, Aug. 1764.

BROWN, *or* BROWNE:

cr. 24 Feb. 1709/10([a]);

ex. presumably on death of grantee.

I. 1710, to 1711? ROBERT [but query if not ADAM] BROWN, *or* BROWNE, Esq., Lord Provost of Edinburgh, was *cr. a Baronet*, as above, 24 Feb. 1709/10([a]), but of him nothing further is known, and the *Baronetcy* became, presumably, *extinct* on his death.([b])

ERISY.

"SIR JOHN ERISY, Baronet," was admitted to Lincoln's Inn, 7 June 1710, but of him nothing more is known, and the title is presumed to have been assigned to him in error.

LAMBERT:

cr. 16 Feb. 1710/1.

I. 1711. SIR JOHN LAMBERT, of London, Knt., 1st s. of John LAMBERT, a merchant at St. Martin's, in the Isle of Rhé, in France (where he *d.* 1702), by Mary LE FEVRE, also of St. Martin's aforesaid, was *b.* 1666; ed. in England as a Protestant, at Camberwell and elsewhere; became a wealthy merchant of London, was *Knighted* in or after Sep. 1710, in which year he had advanced to the Government £400,000 and upwards, and was (consequently) at the recommendation of Robert HARLEY, Chancellor of the Exchequer, *cr. a Baronet*, as above, 16 Feb. 1710/1. He was a Director of the South Sea Company.([c]) He *m.*, in or before 1690, Madeleine, da. of Benjamin BEUZELIN, of Rouen, merchant. He *d.* 4 Feb. 1722/3. Will pr. 1723. His widow *d.* in Clarges street, Piccadilly, April 1737, aged about 70. Will pr. 1737.

II. 1723. SIR JOHN LAMBERT, Baronet [1711], 1st s. and h., *b.* 22 March 1690; *suc. to the Baronetcy*, 4 Feb. 1722/3, and was living at Pans 1741. He *m.*, in or before 1728, Anne, da. of Tempest HOLMES, a Commissioner of the Victualling Office. He *d.* 4 Sep. 1772, aged 82. His widow *d.* June 1794.

III. 1772. SIR JOHN LAMBERT, Baronet [1711], 1st s. and h., *b.* 11 Oct. 1728 and *bap.* at St. Peter le Poor, London; *suc. to the Baronetcy*, 4 Sep. 1772. He *m.*, 9 Aug. 1752, [Mary ?] da. of (—) LE NIBPS. He *d.* 21 May 1799, aged 70. Will pr. June 1799, as also in Ireland.

([a]) The date of "Nov. 1709," is given as the date of this creation in the continuation of Dugdale's *List*.

([b]) Adam Brown was Provost in 1710 and part of 1711, when he died, and oddly enough was the only Provost about that period who was not a Knight. There was no Provost of the name of *Robert* Brown anywhere near that date. [*Ex inform.* J. Balfour Paul, Lyon].

([c]) A list of the 32 members elected in Feb. 1717 (including the King, as governor) of this notorious company (founded 1702-03, 1 Anne), is given in Stow's *London* (edit. 1720), vol. v, 272. In Aug. 1720, its shares attained their maximum (£1,000 for every £100), but before Christmas it had entirely collapsed, ruining thereby many thousands of families, as well as the (in some cases innocent) directors, all of those who were M.P's being expelled from Parliament. A masterly account of this financial crash is given in Stanhope's *England, 1713 to 1783* (4th edit.), vol. ii, pp. 4-38.

IV. 1799. SIR HENRY LAMBERT, Baronet [1711], of Mount Ida, Norfolk, 2d and yst. but only surv. s. and h., *b.* in or after 1756; *suc. to the Baronetcy*, 21 May 1799. He *m.*, in 1788, Sophia, da. of Francis Xavier WHYTE. He *d.* 21 Jan. 1803. Will pr. 1803. His widow *m.* 25 Feb. 1805 (as 2d wife), Lieut.-Col. Henry Francis Fulke GREVILLE (who *d.* 13 Jan. 1816), and *d.* 21 March 1839, in Manchester square, Marylebone. Will pr. April 1839.

V. 1803. SIR HENRY JOHN LAMBERT, Baronet [1711], of Aston House, near Tetsworth, Oxon, 1st s. and h., *b.* 5 Aug. 1792; *suc. to the Baronetcy*, 21 Jan. 1803. He *m.* 7 May 1821, at St. Geo. Han. sq., Anna Maria, 2d and yst. da. of the Hon. Edward FOLEY, of Stoke Edith park, co. Hereford (yr. s. of Thomas, 1st BARON FOLEY OF WHITLEY), by his 2d wife, Eliza Maria FOLEY, da. and h. of John HODGETTS. She, who was *b.* 30 Aug. 1800, *d.* 5 March 1857. Will pr. May 1857. He *d.* at Aston House aforesaid, 17 Dec. 1858, aged 66.

VI. 1858. SIR HENRY EDWARD FRANCIS LAMBERT, Baronet [1711], of Great Malvern, co. Worcester, 1st s. and h., *b.* 7 June 1822, at Marylebone; ed. at Eton; matric. at Oxford (Balliol Coll.), 3 June 1840, aged 17; B.A., 1843; M.A., 1847; Barrister (Inner Temple), 1847; *suc. to the Baronetcy*, 17 Dec. 1858; Capt. 11th Worcestershire Rifle Vols. He *m.* 11 April 1860, at St. Geo. Han. sq., Eliza Catherine, sister and coheir of Capt. Felton William HERVEY, 13th Light Dragoons, 2d da. of Lionel Charles HERVEY, by Frances Mary, da. of Vice-Admiral Thomas WELLS. He *d.* 15 June 1872, at Great Malvern, aged 50. His widow *d.* 17 Feb. 1898, at "the Lodge," Great Malvern.

VII. 1872. SIR HENRY FOLEY LAMBERT, Baronet [1711], of Great Malvern aforesaid, 1st s. and h., *b.* 21 Jan. 1861, at 41 Green street, Midx.; *suc. to the Baronetcy*, 15 June 1872; ed. at Eton; matric. at Oxford (Ch. Ch.), 31 May 1879, aged 18; Major in Worcestershire Light Yeomanry. He *m.* 14 June 1883, at St. Geo. Han. sq., Catherine Sarah, da. of the Rev. Alfred PAYNE, Vicar of Enville, co. Stafford.

LAKE:

cr. 17 Oct. 1711.

I. 1711. BIBYE([a]) LAKE, of the Middle Temple, London, Esq., only s. and h. of Thomas LAKE, of Bishop's Norton, co. Lincoln, Barrister of the Middle Temple, by Elizabeth, da. of John STOREY, of Kniveton, co. Derby, which Thomas (who *d.* 22 May 1711, in his 54th year) was nephew and h. of Sir Edward LAKE, Baronet [I. 1661], who *d.* s.p. 18 April 1674, the said Bibye being s. and h. of Thomas LAKE (living Oct. 1670], a yr. br. (of the half blood) of the said Baronet. He was *bap.* 10 April 1684, at Bishop's Norton aforesaid, and having shortly after his father's death, represented that his said great uncle, Sir Edward, had received a warrant from Charles I, 30 Dec. 1643, for a Baronetcy with rem. to his heirs male,([b]) (which title would, had the said warrant passed the Great Seal, have devolved on him), was *cr. a Baronet*, as above, 17 Oct. 1711. He was a Bencher of the Middle Temple, London, and was Sub-Governor of the African Company. He *m.*, in or before 1713, Mary, da. and h. of William ATWELL, of London. He was *bur.* 6 April 1744, in the Temple church, aged 60, where also his widow was *bur.*, 23 Jan. 1752, both being, on the petition of their son, "Bibye LAKE, Esq.," removed in April 1760 to be *bur.* with their eldest son, the 2d Baronet, at Edmonton, Midx.

([a]) The surname of Bibye was that of the wife of Sir Edward Lake, Baronet [I. 1661], the great uncle of the grantee of 1711, who, however, was not born till more than fourteen years after her death. See vol. iii, p. 318.

([b]) See a fuller account thereof in vol. iii, p. 318, under "Lake" Baronetcy [I.], *cr.* 10 July 1661.

II. 1744. SIR ATWELL LAKE, Baronet [1711], 1st s. and h., *bap.* 9 May 1713, at St. Helen's Bishopsgate; matric. at Oxford (Jesus Coll.), 29 April 1731, aged 17; *suc. to the Baronetcy* in April 1744; was Governor of Hudson's Bay Company. He *m.* July 1740, Mary, only da. of James WINTER, of Mile End, Midx. He *d.* 10 and was *bur.* 28 April 1760, at Edmonton, Midx., aged 47. Will pr. 1760. His widow *d.* there 19 April 1782. Will pr. May 1782.

III. 1760. SIR JAMES WINTER LAKE, Baronet [1711], of "The Firs," near Tanners End, Edmonton, 1st s. and h., *b.* probably about 1745; *suc. to the Baronetcy*, 28 April 1760; was F.S.A. He *m.*, in or before 1772, Joyce, da. of John CROWTHER, of Bow, Midx. He *d.* 24 April 1807. Will pr. 1807. His widow, by whom he had thirteen children, *d.* abroad 26 July 1834, aged 88. Admon. March 1847.

IV. 1807. SIR JAMES SAMUEL WILLIAM LAKE, Baronet [1711], 1st s. and h.,([a]) *b.* in or before 1772; *suc. to the Baronetcy*, 24 April 1807. He *m.* 24 July 1807, Maria, da. of Samuel TURNER, of London. He *d.* at Ramsgate, 4 Nov. 1832. Will pr. 1833. His widow *d.* 15 March 1866, at Walmer, Kent.

V. 1832. SIR JAMES SAMUEL LAKE, Baronet [1711], 1st s. and h.,([b]) *b.* probably about 1810, *suc. to the Baronetcy*, 4 Nov. 1832; ed. at Jesus Coll., Cambridge. He *m.* 1 May 1833, at Sutton, Anne Maria, 1st da. of Admiral Sir Richard KING, 2d Baronet [1792], **G.C.B.**, by Sarah Anne, da. of Vice Admiral Sir John Thomas DUCKWORTH, 1st Baronet [1813], **G.C.B.** He *d.* 10 Dec. 1846. His widow *m.* 20 Sep. 1851, at St. Michael's, Pimlico, George Frederick MITCHELSON, M.D., of Brighton, and *d.* 17 Oct. 1869, at 7 Kensington Garden terrace, Midx.

VI. 1846. SIR ATWELL KING LAKE, Baronet [1711], 1st s. and h.; *b.* 9 April 1834, at Ramsgate; *suc. to the Baronetcy*, 10 Dec. 1846; entered the Bengal army, 1854; Lieut. 2d European Fusileers, 1856, serving in the Indian Mutiny at the Siege of Delhi, etc., as Adjutant of the 4th Irregular Cavalry; Lieut. 104th Foot, 1862; Capt. 1863, retiring in 1864. He *m.* 9 April 1870, at St. James', Norland, Frances Sarah Place, widow of Col. Richard OUSELEY, da. of William Walter JONES, of Gurrey, co. Carmarthen. She *d.* at 15 Sandford terrace, Kensington Road, Cheltenham, 15 Sep. 1896. He *d.* s.p., 15 July 1897, at East Dulwich, aged 63.

VII. 1897. SIR ST VINCENT ATWELL LAKE, Baronet [1711], nephew and h., being only s. and h. of St. Vincent David LAKE, Lieut. R.N., by Frances, da. of Peter PARTINGTON, of Croydon, which St. Vincent David (who *d.* 28 May 1865, aged 30) was br. of the late Baronet. He was *b.* 3 Jan. 1862; ed. at the Royal Naval School, New Cross, and *suc. to the Baronetcy*, 15 July 1897.([c])

([a]) The 2d s., Admiral Sir Willoughby Thomas Lake, **K.C.B.**, *d.* 18 Feb. 1847, aged 74, after a distinguished career.

([b]) The 3d s., Col. Sir Henry Atwell Lake, **K.C.B.**, Major-Gen. in the Turkish army, who distinguished himself at the Siege of Kars, 1855, *d.* 17 Aug. 1881, aged 70.

([c]) The heir presumptive (according to Burke's *Baronetage* for 1902) had, in 1902, "not been heard of for some years." His name was Arthur Johnstone Lake, *b.* 15 Oct. 1849, only surv. s. of Capt. Edward Lake, R.N., by Clara, da. of Sir William Johnstone, 7th Baronet [S. 1626], which Edward was 2d s. of the 4th Baronet. It has been ascertained that he *m.*, Dec. 1874, at Motueka, in Nelson province, New Zealand, Emily Burton, who *d.* at Christchurch there, and that he was living without male issue (having had two daughters, *b.* 1876 and 1878 respectively) in July 1903.

CALVERLEY:

cr. 11 Dec. 1711;

afterwards, 1749-77, CALVERLEY-BLACKETT;

ex. 14 Feb. 1777.

I. 1711. WALTER CALVERLEY, of Calverley, co. York, Esq., only s. and h. of Walter CALVERLEY, of the same (*d.* 10 Nov. 1691, aged 62), by Frances, da. and h. of Henry THOMPSON, of Esholt, co. York, was *bap.* 16 Jan. 1667/70, at Calverley; matric. at Oxford (Queen's Coll.), 30 June 1687, aged 17, and was *cr. a Baronet*, as above, 11 Dec. 1711. He *m.* 7 Jan. 1706/7, at St. Andrew's, Newcastle, Julia, 1st da. of Sir William BLACKETT, 1st Baronet [1685], by Julia, da. of Sir Christopher CONYERS, 2d Baronet [1628]. She *d.* 17 Sep. 1736. He *d.* 15 Oct. 1749, and was *bur.* at Calverley, aged 79.([a]) M.I.

II. 1749, to 1777. SIR WALTER CALVERLEY-BLACKETT, Baronet [1711], of Calverley and Esholt aforesaid, only s. and h., *b.* 18 Dec. 1707 and *bap.* 15 Jan. 1707/8, at Otley; matric. at Oxford (Balliol Coll.) 28 Feb. 1723/4, aged 16; assumed, in consequence of his marriage, in 1729 the name of BLACKETT after that of CALVERLEY under the will of his wife's reputed father, below mentioned; was Sheriff of Northumberland, 1731-32; M.P. for Newcastle-on-Tyne (seven Parls.), 1734 till death in 1777, having *suc. to the Baronetcy*, 15 Oct. 1749. He *m.* there, 29 Sep. 1729 (within twelve months of the death of her reputed father), Elizabeth ORDE, spinster, illegit. da. and testamentary heir of his maternal uncle, Sir William BLACKETT, 3d and last Baronet [1685]. She *d.* 21 and was *bur.* 27 Sep. 1759, at St. Nicholas', Newcastle. He *d.* s.p., in London, 14 Feb. 1777, and was *bur.* at Calverley, aged 69, when the *Baronetcy* became *extinct*.

O'CARROLL, *or* CAROLL([b]):

cr. about 1712([c]);

ex. or *dorm.*, 2 June 1835.

I. 1712?([c]) DANIEL O'CARROLL, *or* CAROLL, s. and h. ap. of John O'CARROLL, of Beaugh, co. Galway (*d.* 12 Aug. 1733), by his 2d wife, Margaret, da. of Andrew O'CREAN, *or* CREAN, of Coursfield, co. Mayo, and formerly of co. Sligo([d]); was a Capt. in Crofton's

([a]) He was author of a Diary, pub. (vol. 77) by the Surtees Society.

([b]) Most of the information in this article has been kindly supplied by G. D. Burtchaell, Office of Arms, Dublin castle.

([c]) The approximate date of this creation must be *after* he quitted the service of Spain, then at war with England, in which service he was actively employed between 1 April and 11 May 1707 (see O'Callaghan's *Irish Brigades*, pp. 232, 239, 243, 245 and 249), and before 19 Jan. 1712/3, when one of his children was *bap.* at St. Paul's, Covent Garden, as "Jane, da. of Sir Daniel Caroll, *Baronet*, and Dame Elizabeth." The date, "18 Feb. 1742," given in Beatson's *List*, and in the list in Betham's *Baronetage* is clearly an error, and refers to the date 18 Feb. 1741/2, being that on which he was made Lieut.-General.

([d]) Pedigree of Sir Daniel O'Carroll, published (in his life time) 1723 in Keating's *History of Ireland*, as also Lodge's *Irish Peerage*, 1st edit. 1754 and 2d edit. 1789, in which last (vol. iii, p. 45) see this Margaret's maternal descent from the Lords Athenry [I.]. These authorities are confirmed by the will of the said Andrew Crean, dat. 19 Jan. 1698/9, and pr. at Tuan in 1699, who mentions

regiment in the Spanish service, 1707, and, though "created by the King of Spain a knight of the Most Military Order of St. Jago, for singular services done to that crown in the time of war, he left the said service of Spain in a disgust, and afterwards had by a patent from Queen Anne, the rank of knighthood, and was under her reign Col. of a regiment of horse."(a) He "at the instance of the Duke of Ormond,"(b) was made, 1 March 1709, Lieut.-Col. and, 2 Dec. 1710, Col. of a regiment of horse (which was broke 22 Dec. 1711), being, apparently, *cr. a Baronet*, as above, about 1712,(c) though there is no patent or other record of such creation either in England or Ireland.(d) He became Brig.-General, 29 Oct. 1735; Major-General, 2 July 1739, and finally Lieut.-General, 18 Feb. 1741/2.(e) He *m.*, in or before 1712, Elizabeth, da. of Thomas JERVOISE, of Herriard, Hants, only da. of his 1st wife Elizabeth, da. of Sir Gilbert CLARKE, of Somersall, co. Derby.(f) She, who had lately arrived from Paris, *d.* in London, 30 Dec. 1728, and was *bur.* 6 Jan. 1728/9, at St. Martin's in the Fields. He *d.* 4, and was *bur.* there 12 Nov. 1750. Admon. 20 Nov. 1750, granted to his son, "Sir Daniel O'Carroll, Baronet," and under £200.

II. 1750. SIR DANIEL O'CARROLL, Baronet [1712?], 1st s. and h., *b.* probably about 1717; *suc. to the Baronetcy*, 4 Nov. 1750; was appointed Capt. in Ligonier's Horse, May 1752. He *m.* (—). He *d.* s.p.m. 30 Jan. 1758, "in the Four Courts Marshalsea, Dublin."(g)

III. 1758. SIR JOHN O'CARROLL, Baronet [1712?], of York,(h) or of Denton, co. York, and afterwards of Bath,(i) br. and h. male, *b.* 14 and *bap.* 25 Feb. 1721/2, at St. Martin's in the Fields; *suc. to the Baronetcy*, 30 Jan. 1758. He *m.* (—). He was living June 1777.(i)

(besides an only son Edward Crean, "now in Spain") his son-in-law John Carroll. The alteration of the name of "O'Crean" to "O'Connor" in Dalton's *King James' Irish Army List* (vol. i, p. 315) is an error, possibly indeed an accidental one, as the account there (though stated to be on the authority of an ancient MS.) follows in all other respects the pedigree in Keating's *Ireland*. [*Ex inform.* C. D. Burtchaell.]

(a) Sir Daniel O'Carroll's pedigree, in Keating's *History of Ireland* 1723.

(b) Lodge's *Irish Peerage*, as on p. 13, note "d."

(c) See p. 13, note "c."

(d) Either kingdom might lay claim to this Baronetcy, but it is here treated of as one of Great Britain. In the obituary of the grantee (*Gent. Mag.* and *London Mag.*) he is called "*Baronet of Great Britain*," and the Baronetcy (though under the erroneous date of 18 Feb. 1742, as to which see p. 13, note "c"), is placed in Beatson's *List* of such Baronetcies, and in that in Betham's *Baronetage* [1806], in both of which he is described as "of Denton, Yorkshire," though on what ground is unknown. Solly's *Index* [1880] follows the above, adding "s.p. 1758, extinct."

(e) "He is not to be confounded with his namesake Daniel O'Carroll, evidently an older man, also commemorated by O'Callaghan [*Irish Brigade*, p. 287] and elsewhere, who was in the *French* service, Lieut.-Col. of Berwick's Regiment, 1698, and who died in 1712." [G. D. Burtchaell].

(f) Hunter's *Familiæ minorum gentium*. [*Harl. Soc.*, xxxvii, 336].

(g) See *Pue's Occurrences*.

(h) The following notice is in *Falkner's* Journal, 6 to 18 March 1758; "New Street, York, 13 Feb. 1758, I caution anybody against buying any of the late Sir Daniel O'Carroll's property lying near Tuam, as it descends to me by entail," etc. [Signed], "John O'Carroll."

(i) *Marriages*, 1777, June 10, "John O'Carroll, Esq., son of Sir John O'Carrol [*sic*], Bart., of Bath, to Miss Elizabeth O'Carroll, da. of the late Sir Daniel O'Carroll, Bart." [*Annual Register*, 1777].

IV. 1780? SIR JOHN WHITLEY O'CARROLL, Baronet [1712?], s. and h.; *suc. to the Baronetcy* on his father's death; was British Resident at Saxe Weimar, 1804. He *m.* 10 June 1777, Elizabeth, da. and h., or coheir, of his uncle, Sir Daniel O'CARROLL, 3d Baronet [1712?] He *d.* at Frankfort-on-the-Main, 13 Jan. 1818. Admon. Jan. 1818.

V. 1818. SIR JERVOISE O'CARROLL, Baronet [1712?], 1st s. and h.; *suc. to the Baronetcy*, 13 Jan. 1818, and was living as a Baronet 2 June following.(a) He *d.* s.p.m., probably unm. at Hamburgh, 1831.

VI. 1831, to 1835. SIR JOHN WHITLEY CHRISTOPHER O'CARROLL, Baronet [1712?], br. and h. male; *suc. to the Baronetcy* in 1831. He *d.* s.p.m., presumably unm., 2 June 1835, at Hildersheim in Germany, when the *Baronetcy* became *extinct* or *dormant*.(b) Will (being then styled "Esq.") dat. 2 June 1818, pr. 8 May 1836.

FREKE:

cr. 4 June 1713;

ex. 13 April 1764.

I. 1713. RALPH FREKE, of West Bilney, co. Norfolk, Esq., as also of Rathbarry (afterwards Castle Freke), co. Cork, s. and h. of Percy FREKE,(c) of Rathbarry aforesaid (who purchased the estate of West Bilney and who was Sheriff of co. Cork, 1694, and M.P. [I.] for Clognakilty, 1692-93, 1695-99, and for Baltimore, 1703 till his death in May 1707), by Elizabeth, da. of Ralph FREKE, of Hannington, Wilts, was *b.* after 1673, and was *cr. a Baronet*, as above, 4 June 1713. He was M.P. [I.] for Clognakilty (three Parls.) 1703 till death in 1717; was Sheriff of co. Cork, 1709. He *m.* 5 March 1699, Elizabeth, da. of Sir John MEADE, 1st Baronet [I. 1703], of Ballintubber, by his 2d wife, Elizabeth, da. and coheir of Col. Daniel REDMAN, of Ballylinch, co. Kilkenny. He *d.* 1717. Will dat. 13 June 1715, pr. [I.] 1 July 1717, and [E.] May 1718. His widow *m.* (as his 1st wife) James (KING), 4th BARON KINGSTON [I.], who *d.* s.p.m.s., 28 Dec. 1761. She *d.* 6 Oct. 1750, at Ufton Court, near Reading, Berks, and was *bur.* at Michelstown, co. Cork.

II. 1717. SIR PERCY FREKE, Baronet [1713], of West Bilney and Castle Freke aforesaid, 1st s. and h., *b.* 30 April 1700; *suc. to the Baronetcy* in or before 1717; matric. at Oxford (Ch. Ch.) 27 Nov. 1717, aged 18; *cr.* M.A., 8 May 1721; was M.P. [I.] for Baltimore, 1721 till death. He *d.* unm., 10 April 1728, at Dublin, aged nearly 28. Will dat. 10 March 1727/8, pr. [I.] 1728.

(a) Will of that date of his yr. brother and successor, in which he is mentioned as a Baronet.

(b) Francis O'Carroll, who was at the Brompton Oratory in 1880, was descended from Remigius O'Carroll, a brother of the grantee. He, no doubt, was so named after Remigius Bermingham, 1st cousin to his mother, s. of Francis, Lord Athenry [I.]. There were also two other brothers of the grantee, viz., James (whose will was pr. 1764) and John.

(c) The christian name of Percy was that of his maternal grandfather, Sir Percy Smith, of Youghall, co. Cork, whose da., Dorothy, *m.* Arthur Freke, of Rathbarry, his father.

III. 1728, to 1764. SIR JOHN REDMOND FREKE, Baronet [1713], of West Bilney and Castle Freke aforesaid, only surv. br. and h.(a); *suc. to the Baronetcy*, 10 April 1728; was M.P. [I.] for Baltimore, 1728-60, and for city of Cork, 1761 till death; Sheriff of Cork, 1750; Mayor, 1753. He *m.* 16 Sep. 1739, Mary (under 14 in 1736), 4th da. and coheir of the Rt. Hon. St. John BRODRICK (1st s. and h. ap. of Alan, 1st VISCOUNT MIDLETON [I.]), by Anne, da. of Michael HILL, of Hillsborough. She *d.* at Castle Freke, 20 June 1761, and was *bur.* at Midleton, co. Cork. He *d.* s.p. 13 April 1764, when the *Baronetcy* became *extinct*.(b) Will dat. 6 Feb. 1764, pr. [I.] 1764.

CROSSE:

cr. 11 *or* 13 July 1713(c);

ex. 12 March 1762.

I. 1713. THOMAS CROSSE, of Westminster, Esq., 1st s. of Thomas CROSSE,(d) of St. Margaret's, Westm. (*d.* 1682), was *b.* 29 Nov. 1663; ed. at Westm. School (under Dr. Busby), was M.P. for Westminster (six Parls.), 1700-05 and 1710-22, and was *cr. a Baronet*, as above, 11 or 13 July 1713.(c) He *m.* Jane, da. of Patrick LAMBE, of Stoke Pogis, Bucks.(e) He *d.* 27 May and was *bur.* 1 June 1738, at St. Margaret's, Westm., in his 75th year. M.I. Will pr. 1738.

II. 1738, to 1762. SIR JOHN CROSSE, Baronet [1713], of Milbank, Westminster, 2d and yst. but only surv. s. and h.,(f) *b.* about 1700; matric. at Oxford (Ch. Ch.), 21 Feb. 1716/7, aged 16; was M.P. for Wotton Basset, 1727-34; for Lostwithiel, 1735-47, and for Westminster (as was his father), 1754-61, having *suc. to the Baronetcy*, 27 May 1738. He *m.* 15 July 1746, at St. John's, Westm., Mary GODFREY, of that parish, spinster. He *d.* s.p. at Milbank, 12 March and was *bur.* 2 April 1762, at St. Margaret's, Westminster, when the *Baronetcy* became *extinct*. Will pr. April 1762. His widow was *bur.* there, 25 Sep. 1770. Will dat. 5 June 1767 to 20 Dec. 1769, pr. 22 Oct. 1770 and 3 Nov. 1800.

(a) Ralph Freke, his next eldest br., adm. to Trin. Coll., Dublin (as Fellow Comm.), 19 May 1719, aged 17, B.A., 1724, *d.* unm. in 1727 at Richmond, Surrey.

(b) He left his estate to his eldest sister, Grace, who *m.*, June 1741, the Hon. John Evans, of Bulgaden Hall, co. Limerick (*d.* 1754), yst. s. of George, 1st Baron Carbery [I.]. Her son, John Evans, afterwards Evans-Freke, was *cr. a Baronet* [I.], 15 July 1768, and *d.* 1777, being suc. by his son, who, in 1807, became the 6th Baron Carbery [I.].

(c) In Wotton's *Baronetage* [1741] and in Dugdale's *List* it is given as 11, but in other places as 13 July 1713.

(d) Presumably the Thomas Crosse, of St. Martin's in the Fields, who had lic. (Vic. Gen.) 17 June 1663, being then about 29, bachelor, to marry Mary Lockwood, then about 29, spinster. This Thomas was probably the Thomas Crosse *bap.* 8 Feb. 1636, at Maulden, Beds.

(e) It seems not unlikely that she was the "Mrs. Anne Crosse" who *d.* in "childbed," and was *bur.* 5 Nov. 1701, in the church of St. Margaret's, Westm., in which, case however, "Anne" would be a mistake for "Jane."

(f) The 1st son, Thomas Crosse, was *bur.* 21 Aug. 1732, at St. Margaret's, Westm.

EVELYN:

cr. 6 Aug. 1713;

ex. 28 Aug. 1848.

I. 1713. JOHN EVELYN, of Wotton, co. Surrey, Esq., 2d but only surv. s. and h. of John EVELYN, Barrister (Middle Temple) and a Commissioner of the Revenue [I.], by Martha, da. and coheir of Richard SPENCER, which John (who *d.* v.p. 24 March 1699, aged 44) was s. and h. ap. of the celebrated John EVELYN, of Sayes Court, Deptford, and of Wotton aforesaid (author of *Evelyn's Diary*, *Sylva*, etc.), was *b.* at Sayes Court, 1 and *bap.* 2 March 1681/2; matric. at Oxford (Balliol Coll.), 25 Feb. 1698/9, aged 16; suc. his said grandfather (who *d.* at the age of 86), 27 Feb. 1706; was M.P. for Helston, Dec. 1708 to 1710; Joint Postmaster Gen., 1708-15, and was *cr. a Baronet*, as above, 6 Aug. 1713. He built a library (45 feet long) at Wotton. He was a Commissioner of Customs, 1721-63; F.R.S., 1722. He *m.* 18 Sep. 1705, at Lambeth, Anne, sister of Hugh, 1st VISCOUNT FALMOUTH, 1st da. of Edward BOSCAWEN, of Worthevall, Cornwall, by Jael, da. of Sir Francis GODOLPHIN, K.B. She was *bur.* 24 Jan. 1752, at Wotton, aged 67. He *d.* 15 and was *bur.* there, 22 July 1763, aged 81. Will pr. 1763.

II. 1763. SIR JOHN EVELYN, Baronet [1713], of Wotton and Sayes Court aforesaid, 1st s. and h., *b.* 24 Aug. 1706, at Wotton; matric. at Oxford (Queen's Coll.), 28 May 1725, aged 18; was M.P. for Helston, 1727-41; for Penrhyn, 1741-47; and for Helston again, 1747 till death in 1767, having *suc. to the Baronetcy*, 15 July 1763. He was Clerk of the Green Cloth to Frederick, Prince of Wales, and subsequently to George III. He *m.* 17 Aug. 1732, at Westm. Abbey (Lic. Vic. Gen. 22 May 1731, and Lic. Fac. 13 Aug. 1732), Mary, 4th da. of his maternal uncle, Hugh (BOSCAWEN), 1st VISCOUNT FALMOUTH, by Charlote, da. of Charles GODFREY. She, who was *b.* 12 and *bap.* 21 Nov. 1705, at St. James', Westm., *d.* 15 Sep. 1749, and was *bur.* at Wotton. He *d.* 11 and was *bur.* there 19 June 1767, aged 60. Will pr. June. 1767.

III. 1767. SIR FREDERICK EVELYN, Bart. [1713], of Wotton and Sayes Court aforesaid, only s. and h., *b.* 1734; served in Elliot's Light Horse at the battle of Minden, 1759; *suc. to the Baronetcy*, 11 June 1767; was a member of the Jockey Club. He *m.* 8 Aug. 1769, at St. Marylebone, Mary, da. and h. of William TURTON, of co. Stafford. He *d.* s.p. 1 April 1812, aged 78, and was *bur.* at Wotton Will pr. 1812, in which he devised his estates to his widow. She *d.* 12 Nov. 1817, in her 72d year, and was *bur.* at Wotton. Will pr. 22 Dec. 1817, whereby she devised the Wotton and Sayes Court estates to John EVELYN,(a) her husband's 5th cousin, both being 6th in descent from George EVELYN (*d.* 1603, aged 77), who was of Kingston, Long Ditton, Godstone and Wotton, all in co. Surrey.

IV. 1812. SIR JOHN EVELYN, Baronet [1713], cousin and h. male, being 1st s. and h. of Charles EVELYN, by Philippa, da. of Fortunatus WRIGHT, of Liverpool, Capt. of Privateers which Charles (who *d.* before 1781), was only surv. s. and h. of Charles EVELYN, of Yarlington, Somerset (*d.* Jan. 1748, aged 40), br. to the 2d and 2d s. of the 1st Baronet. He was *b.* about 1758; was sometime Lieut., Portsmouth division of Marines; *suc. to the Baronetcy*, but not to the estates, 1 April 1812; was declared to be of unsound mind by inq. 28 July 1795. He *d.* unm. 14, and was *bur.* 18 May 1833, at Bexhill, Sussex, aged 75. Admon. Sep. 1833.

V. 1833, to 1848. SIR HUGH EVELYN, Baronet [1713], yst. and only surv. br. and h., *b.* 31 Jan. 1769, at Totnes, Devon; sometime an officer in the Royal Navy; *suc. to the Baronetcy*, 14 May 1833. He *m.* 12 Nov. 1836, at St. Martins-in-the-Fields, Mary, widow of James Thomas HATHAWAY, of Southwark, merchant, 1st da. of John KENNEDY, of

(a) In his issue male those estates still [1905] remain.

Sutton, co. Warwick. He *d.* s.p., at Forest hill, Sydenham, 28 Aug. and was *bur.* 9 Sep. 1848, at Wotton, in his 80th year, when the *Baronetcy* became *extinct.* Will dat. 13 June 1838 to 4 Aug. 1845, pr. (30 years after death), 28 June 1878, by his widow. She, who was *b.* at Hoxton, Midx. 1803, *d.* 5 May 1883, at Eagle house, in Forest hill aforesaid, and was *bur.* at Nunhead cemetery.

DES BOUVERIE:

cr. 19 Feb. 1713/4;

afterwards, since 1737, BOUVERIE; *since* 1747, VISCOUNTS FOLKESTONE, *and, since* 1765, EARLS OF RADNOR.

I. 1714. WILLIAM DES BOUVERIE, of St. Catherine Cree church, London, Esq., eldest of the seven sons of Sir Edward DES BOUVERIE, of Cheshunt, Herts, Turkey merchant, of London (*d.* 2 April 1694, aged 72), by Anne, da. and coheir of Jacob DE LA FORTERIE, of London, merchant, was *b.* 26 Sep. 1656, was (like his father), a Turkey merchant of London, and, having acquired a great fortune, was *cr. a Baronet*, as above, 19 Feb. 1713/4. He *m.* firstly (Lic. Vic. Gen., 12 Sep. 1682, he 26 and she 20, with consent of parent), Mary, da. of James EDWARDS, of St. Stephen's, Coleman street, London. She *d.* s.p.s. He *m.* secondly, 29 April 1686 (Lic. Vic. Gen. 27), at Hackney, Midx., Anne (then about 20), da. and h. of David URRY, of London (then deceased), by Anne (then his widow), which David was s. of John URRY, of Mill place, in the Isle of Wight. He *d.* 19 May 1717, aged 60, and was *bur.* at St. Catherine Cree church, London. M.I. Will pr. May 1717. His widow *d.* at Chelsea, 5 June 1739, aged 75, and was *bur.* at St. Catherine's aforesaid. Will pr. 1739.

II. 1717. SIR EDWARD DES BOUVERIE, Baronet [1714], 1st s. and h., *b.* about 1690; *suc. to the Baronetcy*, 19 May 1717, in which year he purchased the estate of Longford Castle, in Britford, Wilts; was M.P. (three Parls.) for Shaftesbury, 1718-34. He *m.* 7 July 1718, at Somerset House Chapel, Strand, Mary, 2d and yst. da. and coheir of John SMYTH, of Beaufort buildings, Strand, Commissioner of Excise.(a) She *d.* 3 Jan. 1721, and was *bur.* at Britford, Wilts. Will pr. 1721. He *d.* s.p. 21 Nov. 1736, at Aix, in France, and was *bur.* at Britford aforesaid. Will pr. 1736.

III. 1736. SIR JACOB DES BOUVERIE, *afterwards* (since 1737) BOUVERIE, Baronet [1714], of Longford Castle aforesaid, br. and h. male, *b.* about 1694; admitted to Middle Temple, 1708; matric. at Oxford (Ch. Ch.), 20 Oct. 1711, aged 17; was sometime a merchant in London; *suc. to the Baronetcy*, and to the family estates, 21 Nov. 1736, and by Act of Parl., 22 April 1737, took the name of BOUVERIE in lieu of that of DES BOUVERIE. He was M.P. for Salisbury, 1741-47, and Recorder thereof, 1744. He *m.* firstly, 31 Jan. 1723/4, at St. Paul's Cathedral, London, Mary, da. and h. of Bartholomew CLARKE, of Delapre Abbey, co. Northampton, by Mary, sister and h. of Hitch YOUNG, of Roehampton, Surrey. She *d.* 16 Nov. 1739, and was *bur.* at Britford, Wilts. He *m.* secondly, 21 April 1741, at Swanscombe, Kent, Elizabeth, 1st da. of Robert (MARSHAM), 1st BARON ROMNEY, by Elizabeth, da. and coheir of Admiral Sir Cloudesley SHOVEL. She was living when he was *cr.*, 29 June 1747, VISCOUNT FOLKESTONE, etc.,(b) In that peerage this *Baronetcy* then *merged*, and still [1905] so continues, the 2d Viscount being *cr.*, 31 Oct. 1765, EARL OF RADNOR.

(a) Her elder sister Anne, widow of Hugh Parker, *m.* 19 Sep. 1714, Michael (Bourke), 10th Earl of Clanricarde [I.], and was ancestress of the succeeding Earls and Marquesses.

(b) "The Countess [*i.e.*, the Countess of Yarmouth, one of the King's Hanoverian mistresses) touched £12,000 for Sir Jacob Bouverie's coronet." [Walpole's Letter to G. Montagu, 2 July 1747].

COPE:

cr. 1 March 1713/4;

ex. 30 Dec. 1821.

I. 1714. JONATHAN COPE, of Brewerne, co. Oxford, Esq., s. and h. of Jonathan COPE,(a) of Ranton Abbey, co. Stafford (M.P. for that county, 1690-94), by Susan, da. and h. of Sir Thomas FOWLER, of London, was *b.* about 1690; suc. his father (who *d.* aged 30) in 1694; was M.P. for Banbury (two Parls.), 1713-22, and was *cr. a Baronet*, as above, 1 March 1713/4. He *m.*, in or before 1717, Mary, 3d da. of Sir Robert JENKINSON, 2d Baronet [1661], of Walcot, Oxon, by Sarah, da. of Thomas TOMLINS, of Bromley, Midx. She, who was *bap.* at Charlbury, Oxon, 10 June 1690, *d.* at Bath, and was *bur.* 27 Feb. 1755 at Hanwell, Oxon. He *d.* at Orton Longueville, co. Huntingdon, 28 March, and was *bur.* 4 April 1765, at Hanwell. Will pr. 1765.(b)

II. 1765. SIR CHARLES COPE, Baronet [1714], of Brewerne and Orton Longueville aforesaid, grandson and h., being 1st s. and h. of Jonathan COPE, by his 1st wife, Arabella, da. of Henry (HOWARD), 4th EARL OF CARLISLE, which Jonathan (who was *bap.* 27 Oct. 1717, at Sarsden, Oxon, and who *d.* v.p. 2 Nov. 1763), was s. and h. ap. of the late Baronet. He was *b.* about 1743; *suc. to the Baronetcy*, April 1765, and was Sheriff of Cambridgeshire and Huntingdonshire, 1773-74. He *m.*, in 1767, Catherine, 5th and yst. da. of Sir Cecil BISSHOPP, 6th Baronet [1620], of Parham, by Anne, da. of Hugh (BOSCAWEN), 1st VISCOUNT FALMOUTH. He *d.* 14 and was *bur.* 18 June 1781, at Hanwell. Will pr. June 1781. His widow (who was *b.* 30 Nov. 1744) *m.* (as his 2d wife), 22 June 1782, at her house in Hertford street, St. Geo. Han. sq., Charles (JENKINSON), 1st EARL OF LIVERPOOL, and *d.* his widow, in Hertford street, aforesaid, 1, being *bur.* 10 Oct. 1827, at Buxted, Sussex, aged 82.

III. 1781, June. SIR CHARLES COPE, Baronet [1714], of Brewerne and Orton Longueville aforesaid, *b.* about 1770; ed. at Eton; *suc. to the Baronetcy*, 14 June 1781, and *d.* soon afterwards at Eton College, 25 Dec. 1781, in his 12th year, being *bur.* at Hanwell aforesaid. Admon. April 1789.(c)

IV. 1781, Dec. to 1821. SIR JONATHAN COPE, Baronet [1714], of Moreton Pinkney, co. Northampton, uncle of the half blood and h. male, being 2d s. of Jonathan COPE abovenamed, and eldest son by his 2d wife, Jane (relict of Capt. the Hon. Shaw CATHCART), da. of Lieut.-Gen. Francis LEIGHTON, of Wattlesborough, Salop. He was *b.* about 1758; *suc. to the Baronetcy*, 25 Dec. 1781; was a Cornet in the 21st Light Dragoons, 1782, and is said to have been LL.D.(d) He *m.* April 1778, Annabella, da. of William CANDLER, of Callan Castle, co. Kilkenny, and Acomb, co. York, sometime Capt. 10th Foot, by Mary, da. of William VAVASOUR, of

---

(a) This Jonathan was s. and h. of Jonathan Cope, of Renton Abbey (*d.* 1670 aged 43), who was 4th s. of Sir William Cope, 2d Baronet [1611], of Hanwell, Oxon.

(b) He owned the ground on which the Custom House of London stood, and let it to the Government at £1,600 a year, on a lease of 99 years.

(c) The estates devolved on his two sisters, (1), Arabella Diana, Duchess of Dorset, who *d.* 1 Aug. 1825, leaving issue; (2), Charlotte Anne, who *m.* 4 April 1791, at Stepney, George (Gordon), 5th Earl of Aboyne [S.], who, after her death, became in 1836, 9th Marquess of Huntly [S.]. She inherited the estate of Orton, Longueville.

(d) Betham's *Baronetage*, 1803.

Weston Hall, co. York. She *d.* 30 Aug. 1819, and was *bur.* at Great Malvern. He *d.* s.p.s.(a) 30 Dec. 1821, and was *bur.* in the Abbey Church there, aged 63, when the *Baronetcy* became *extinct.* Will pr. 1822.(b).

BUSWELL:

cr. 5 March 1713/4;

ex. between 1727 and 1741.(c)

I. 1714, to 1730? EUSEBIUS BUSWELL, of Clipston, co. Northampton, Esq., 1st s. and h. of Eusebius BUSWELL, formerly PELSANT, of Liddington, co. Rutland (aged 25 at the Visit. of that county in 1681, and living under the name of BUSWELL, 1706(d)). by Frances, da. of Sir Richard WINGFIELD, of Tickencote in that county, which Eusebius, was s. and h. of Sir Eusebius PELSANT, of Cadeby, co. Leicester (aged 71 in the Visit. of that county in 1681), by Anne, his 2d wife, sister of Sir George BUSWELL, Baronet (so *cr.* 7 July 1660), of Clipston aforesaid, who *d.* s.p., 10 March 1667, was *b.* at Tickencote in 1681; matric. at Oxford (Pembroke Coll.), 20 May 1698, aged 17, and was *cr. a Baronet*, as above, 5 March 1713/4. He *m.* firstly, Hester, 2d da. and coheir of Sir Charles SKRYMSHIRE, of Norbury manor, co. Stafford, by his 1st wife Hester, da. and h. of George TAYLOR, of Darwent hall, co. Derby. She *d.* s.p. 7 April 1706, and was *bur.* at Clipston. M.I. He *m.* secondly, Honora (*bap.* 23 May 1694), da. of Ralph SNEYD, of Keel hall, co. Stafford. He *d.* s.p.m.,(e) presumably, between 1727 and 1741, when the *Baronetcy* became *extinct.*(c)

CREATIONS BY GEORGE I.

1 Aug. 1714 to 11 June 1727.

BECK:

cr. 1 Nov. 1714;

ex. 12 Jan. 1764.

I. 1714. JUSTUS BECK, of the city of London, Esq., of foreign extraction, but an eminent Merchant of London, was *cr. a Baronet*, as above, 1 Nov. 1714, being the first person so created by George I. He *m.* Rachel, da. of Charles CHAMBERLAYNE, sometime (1687-88) Alderman of London. He *d.* 15 Dec. 1722, and was *bur.* at St. Nicholas' Cole Abbey, London. Admon. 21 Jan. 1722/3. His widow *d.* 1 Oct. 1734. Will dat. 4 June 1731, pr. 8 Oct. 1734.

(a) He outlived his three sons, of whom (1), Jonathan Cope, *b.* at St. John's, Dorset, matric. at Oxford (Ch. Ch.), 24 Oct. 1798, aged 18; B.A., 1802; took Holy Orders; was Rector of Wraxall and Woodborough, Wilts, and Vicar of Langridge, Somerset, and *d.* unm. 10 March 1814, at Reading, aged 34; (2), Charles Cope, *d.* unm. on board the "Hannibal," at Port Royal, 30 Sep. 1795; 3) Henry Thomas Cope, *d.* unm., being killed at Seringapatam in 1792.

(b) He devised the estate of Moreton Pinkney to his wife's nephew, Edward Candler.

(c) It is given as *existing* in Wotton's *Baronetage* for 1727, but as *extinct* in that for 1741.

(d) The M.I. to the Baronet's 1st wife, who *d.* 7 April 1706, speaks of her as "wife of Eusebius Buswell, Junior, Esq.," shewing, apparently, that his father Eusebius was then alive, and that both were then styled *Buswell.*

(e) Frances, his da. and h. (by 2nd wife), *m.* Christopher Horton, of Catton, co. Derby, and had issue.

II. 1722. SIR CHAMBERLAYNE BECK, Baronet [1714], s. and h., *suc. to the Baronetcy* 15 Dec. 1722. He, apparently, was admitted to Gray's Inn 21 Jan. 1724/5.(a) He *d.* unm., Aug. 1730.

III. 1730, to 1764. SIR JUSTUS DENIS BECK, Baronet [1714], br. and h., *b.* about 1708; *suc. to the Baronetcy* in Aug. 1730. He *d.* unm. 12 Jan. 1764, in Wood street, London, aged 56, when the *Baronetcy* became *extinct.*(b) Will pr. Jan. 1764, he being then of Essex.

AUSTEN:

cr. 16 Nov. 1714;

ex. 22 March 1741/2.

I. 1714, to 1742. JOHN AUSTEN, of Derhams [in South Mims], co. Middlesex, Esq., s. and h. of Thomas AUSTEN, of the same (living there 1683), and of Hoggesden or Hoxton in that county, by Arabella (mar. lic. 13 Oct. 1673), da. and h. of Edward FORSET, of Ashford, Midx., and of Tyburn Manor, in Marylebone, inherited the said Manor of Tyburn, or Marylebone, which he sold in 1710, to John (HOLLES), DUKE OF NEWCASTLE, was M.P. for Middlesex (three Parls.), 1701-02, 1708-10, and 1722-27, and was *cr. a Baronet*, as above, 16 Nov. 1714. He also inherited the Manor of Highbury, in Islington, which he sold in 1723, and ten years later, in 1733, he sold the reversion of the Manor of Derhams. He *d.* unm. 22 March 1741/2, and was *bur.* at South Mims, when the *Baronetcy* became *extinct.* His will as of Highgate, Midx., dat. 8 Nov. 1740, pr. 22 March 1741/2, by Mary WRIGHT, spinster, the residuary legatee.

HUMFREYS, *or* HUMPHREYS:

cr. 30 Nov. 1714;

ex. 14 June 1737.

I. 1714. SIR WILLIAM HUMPHREYS [*or* HUMFREYS],(c) Knt. and Alderman of London, only s. of Nathaniel HUMFREYS, of Candlewick street, London, Citizen and Ironmonger (who was 2d s. of William AP HUMFREY, of Penrhyn, co. Montgomery), was himself a Citizen and Ironmonger of London, being sometime (1705) Master of that Company; was an Oilman or Drysalter in the Poultry, living afterwards in Bloomsbury square; was Sheriff of London, 1704-05, being *Knighted* 26 Oct. 1704; Alderman of Cheap Ward, 29 July 1707, and of Bridge Without, 25 Jan. 1733 till his death; M.P. for Marlborough, 1715-22; Lord Mayor of London, 1714-15; officiated, 20 Oct., at the Coronation of George I, and, having entertained that King and

---

(a) The admittance, however, is that of "Chamberlayne Beck, of Old Fish Street, London, *Gent.*," whereas he was a Baronet more than two years before. Presumably, however, the "Gent." is a mistake, as the Baronet (whose mother's name was Chamberlayne) was doubtless the only Beck (then living) who had been christened "Chamberlayne."

(b) He had three brothers, Jacob, George, and Frederick, all living 4 June 1741.

(c) In the Rev. A. B. Beaven's admirable work on the *Aldermen of London*, it is stated that he wrote his name as "Humfreys," and the name is so spelled in Wotton's *Baronetage* [1727].

the Prince and Princess of Wales at the Guildhall, was *cr. a Baronet*, as above, 30 Nov. 1714. He was President of Bridewell and Bethlehem Hospitals, Lord of the Manors of Barking and Dagenham, Essex, was of Hever Castle, Kent, etc. He *m.* firstly, Margaret, da. of William WINTOUR, of Dymock, co. Gloucester, by (—), da. of Sir William BRADWELL, of Maxey, Essex. She *d.* 19 Aug. 1704, and was *bur.* at St. Mildred's, Poultry. He *m.* secondly, 6 Jan. 1705, at Knightsbridge chapel, Ellen, widow of Col. Robert LANCASHIRE, of London, merchant. She, by whom he had no issue, *d.* 25 March 1732. Will pr. 1734. He *d.* 26 Oct. and was *bur.* 6 Nov. 1735, at St. Mildred's aforesaid.(a) Will pr. 1735.

II. 1735, to 1737. SIR ORLANDO HUMFREYS, *or* HUMPHREYS, Baronet [1714], only s. and h., by 1st wife, *suc. to the Baronetcy*, 26 Oct. 1735. He *m.* in or before 1725, Ellen, da. and coheir of Robert LANCASHIRE and Ellen his wife, both abovenamed. He *d.* s.p.m.s.,(b) 14 June 1737, when the *Baronetcy* became *extinct*. Will pr. 1737. His widow *d.* 3 April 1745. Will pr. 1745.

EYLES:

cr. 1 Dec. 1714;

afterwards, 1745-68, EYLES-STILES;

ex. 1 Nov. 1768.

I. 1714. FRANCIS EYLES, of London, Esq., br. of Sir John EYLES, of South Brome, Wilts, who (though not a Freeman and not having ever been Sheriff) was, from Sep. to Dec. 1688, Lord Mayor of London, both being sons of John EYLES, of Wilts, Woolstapler, was a Citizen and Haberdasher and an eminent Merchant of London; Sheriff, 1710-11; Alderman of Bridge without, 23 Jan. 1711 till his death in 1716, and was *cr. a Baronet*, as above, 1 Dec. 1714. He was many years a Director of the East India Company, as also of the Bank of England, of which he was sometime Governor. He *m.* Elizabeth, da. of Richard AYLEY, of London, Merchant. He *d.* 24 May and was *bur.* 5 June 1716 at St. Helen's, Bishopsgate. Will pr. June 1716. His widow *d.* 6 and was *bur.* 22 April 1735 at St. Helen's aforesaid.

II. 1716. SIR JOHN EYLES, Baronet [1714], 2d but 1st surv. s. and h.,(c) Citizen and Haberdasher of London; was M.P. for Chippenham (three Parls.) 1713-27, and for London, 1727-34; was, in 1715, a Commissioner of the estates forfeited in the recent Jacobite rising; *suc. to the Baronetcy*, 24 May 1716; was Alderman of Vintry, 19 June 1716, and of Bridge without, 22 July 1737 till his death, at which date he was "Father of the City"; Sheriff of London, 1719-20; was a Director and sometime Governor of the Bank of England; Sub-Governor of the South Sea Company, Feb. 1720/1, being subsequently a trustee of the estates of the (then) late Directors of that

(a) See *Her. and Gen.*, vol. v, p. 487, for an account of his funeral from his house in Bloomsbury sq.

(b) His only son, Robert, *d.* but a few months before him, 17 Jan. 1736/7.

(c) His yst. br., Sir Joseph Eyles, also Citizen and Haberdasher of London, was Sheriff of that city 1724-25, being *Knighted* during office, 9 Dec. 1694, and was Alderman of Cheap, 6 Feb. 1738/9 till his death, 8 Feb. 1739/40, having been sometime M.P. for Devizes, 1722-27; for Southwark, 1727-34, and for Devizes, again, 1734 till death. He *m.* Sarah, da. of Alderman Sir Jeffery Jefferies, sometime [1699-1700] Sheriff of London. She *d.* 20 April 1761, leaving issue.

Company(a); Lord Mayor of London, 1726-27; Joint Postmaster-General, 1739-44. He purchased the estate of Gidea Hall, in Havering, co. Essex, and, pulling down "the fine old mansion there, erected the house now [1861] standing"(b) in the "elegant manner"(c) of eighteenth century buildings. He *m.* his cousin, Mary, da. of Joseph Haskins STILES, of London, by Sarah, 1st da. of Sir John EYLES, Lord Mayor of London (1688), br. to the 1st Baronet. She *d.* 14 and was *bur.* 23 Nov. 1735, at St. Helen's aforesaid. He *d.* 11 March 1744/5. Will pr. 1745.

III. 1745. SIR FRANCIS HASKINS EYLES-STILES, Baronet [1714] of Gidea Hall aforesaid, *formerly* EYLES, only s. and h., who, under the will of his maternal uncle, Benjamin Haskins STYLES, of Moor Park, in Rickmansworth, Herts (who *d.* unm. 4 April 1739), had assumed the name of STILES after that of EYLES. He was F.R.S., 1742; *suc. to the Baronetcy*, 11 March 1744/5, and a few months later, in Oct. 1745, sold the Gidea Hall estate. He was a Commissioner for Victualling, 26 Jan. 1762. He *m.*, probably about 1735, Sibella (*bap.* 1 Dec. 1711, at Astbury, co. Chester), da. of the Rev. Philip EGERTON, D.D., Rector of Astbury, by Frances, da. of John OFFLEY. He *d.* at Naples, 26 Jan. 1762. Admon. 8 May 1765, and 27 Feb. 1769. His wife survived him, but *d.* before 23 April 1763, when her admon. as "formerly of Battersea, Surrey, but late of the city of Naples, widow," was granted to her son.

IV. 1762, to 1768. SIR JOHN HASKINS EYLES-STILES, Baronet [1714], of Hampstead, Midx., only s. and h., *b.* 16 April 1741, *suc. to the Baronetcy*, 26 Jan. 1762. He *d.* unm. 1, and was *bur.* 5 Nov. 1768, at St. Helen's, Bishopgate, aged 27, when the *Baronetcy* became *extinct*.(d) Admon. 5 Dec. 1768.

SMYTH:

cr. 2 Dec. 1714;

ex. 2 Oct. 1811.

I. 1714. JAMES SMYTH, of Isfield, co. Sussex, Esq., only s. and h. of Alderman Sir James SMYTH,(e) citizen and draper of London, Lord Mayor of that city, 1684-85 (*d.* 9 Dec. 1706, in his 73d year), by his 2nd wife, Elizabeth (*m.* June 1682), da. and coheir of Arthur SHIRLEY, of Isfield aforesaid, was *b* about 1686; matric. at Oxford (Ball. Coll.), 16 Sep. 1702, aged 16, and, having suc. his father in Dec. 1706, was *cr. a Baronet*, as above, 2 Dec. 1714; and was Sheriff of Sussex, 1714-15. He *m.* Mirabella, da. of Sir Robert

(a) See p. 10, note "c," *sub* "LAMBERT" as to this company. The name of John Eyles is not among the Directors thereof for 1717, but that of "Francis Eyles, Esq." appears therein, possibly by mistake. John Eyles, the 2d Baronet, however, had suc. as a *Baronet* shortly before that date, while his father, *Francis* (who was not unlikely to have been a Director), was a Baronet as early as 1714. There was indeed another Francis Eyles, of Earnshill, Somerset (*d.* Dec. 1735), who was nephew of the 1st Baronet, but it seems improbable that he is the person indicated.

(b) *N. & Q.*, 2d S., xii, 483.

(c) Morant's *Essex*, I, 67.

(d) Mary, his only surv. sister, *b.* 16 Jan. 1745, *m.*, in or before 1766, her cousin Philip Egerton, of Oulton, co. Chester (*d.* 1786, aged 54), and was *bur.* 19 Dec. 1821, at Little Budworth, being mother of Sir John Grey-Egerton, 8th Baronet [1617], who *suc. to that Baronetcy*, 23 Sep. 1814.

(e) This James was 2d s. of Sir Robert Smyth, of Upton, Essex, *cr. a Baronet*, 30 March 1665. See vol. iii, p. 9, note "b."

LEGARD, one of the Masters in Chancery. She *d.* 21 Feb. 1714, in her 30th year. He *d.* 28 Feb. 1716/7, in his 32d year. Both were *bur.* with his parents at Westham, Essex. M.I. Will pr. March 1717.

II. 1717. SIR ROBERT SMYTH, Baronet [1714], of Isfield aforesaid, and of Fornham, Suffolk, only s. and h., *b.* about 1709; *suc. to the Baronetcy*, 28 Feb. 1716/7. He *m.* 23 Sep. 1731, Louisa Caroline Isabella, yst. da. of John (HERVEY), 1st EARL OF BRISTOL, by his 2d wife, Elizabeth, da. and h. of Sir Thomas FELTON. She *d.* 11 May 1770, aged 55, and was *bur.* at Westham aforesaid. He *d.* 10 Dec. 1783, aged 74, and was *bur.* there. Will pr. Jan. 1784.

III. 1783, to 1811. SIR HERVEY SMYTH, Baronet [1714], of Isfield and Fornham aforesaid, only s. and h., *b.* 1734; sometime Page of Honour to George II; aide-de-camp to Gen. WOLFE at the siege of Quebec, 1759, becoming afterwards Colonel in the Foot Guards. He *suc. to the Baronetcy*, 10 Dec. 1783. He *d.* unm. 2 Oct. 1811, aged 77, when the *Baronetcy* became *extinct*.(a) Admon. Nov. 1711.

PAGE:

cr. 3 Dec. 1714;

ex. 4 Aug. 1775.

I. 1714. GREGORY PAGE, of Greenwich, co. Kent, Esq., s. of Gregory PAGE, of London, merchant, one of the Directors of the East India Company (living 1690), was *b.* about 1669, being in 1690, a brewer; was M.P. for New Shoreham (three Parls.), 1708-13 and 1715 till death: and was *cr. a Baronet*, as above, 3 Dec. 1714. He *m.* (Lic. Vic. Gen. 21 Jan. 1689/90), he of Greenwich, brewer, about 21, and she of St. Augustine's, London, about 17, Mary, da. of Thomas TROTMAN, late citizen of London, deceased, and Mary, his wife. He *d.* 25 May, and was *bur.* (in linen) 2 June 1720, at Greenwich. Will pr. June 1720. His widow *d.* at Greenwich, 4 March 1728/9, and was *bur.* thence in a vault in Bunhill Fields, Midx. M.I.(b)

II. 1720, to 1776. SIR GREGORY PAGE, Baronet [1714], of Greenwich aforesaid, 1st s. and h.;(c) *suc. to the Baronetcy*, 25 May 1720. He purchased in 1723 the estate of Wricklemarsh, in Charlton, co. Kent. He *m.* (mar. lic. 26 May 1721) Martha, 3d da. of Robert KENWARD, of Kenwards in Yalden, co. Kent. She *d.* 30 Sep. and was *bur.* 7 Oct. 1767, at Greenwich. He *d.* s.p. 4 and was *bur.* there, 14 Aug. 1775, aged about 80, when the *Baronetcy* became *extinct*.(d) Will pr. 12 Aug. 1775.

(a) His only sister Anna Mirabella Henrietta, *b.* 1738, *m.* 1761 William Beale Brand, of Polsted Hall, Suffolk.

(b) The following is part of the monumental inscription:—"In 67 months, she was tapp'd 66 times, had taken away 240 gallons of water, without ever repining at her case, or ever fearing the operation."

(c) "Thomas Page, Esq.," the only other son, was *bur.* 4 Nov. 1763, at Greenwich.

(d) He left his estates to his great nephew, Sir Gregory Turner, 3d Baronet [1733], of Ambrosden, who thereupon took the name of Page before that of Turner. He was s. and h. of Sir Edward Turner, 2d Baronet (*d.* 31 Oct. 1766), who was s. and h. of Sir Edward Turner, 1st Baronet (so *cr.* 24 Aug. 1733), by Mary (*bur.* at Greenwich, 18 Feb. 1723/4), only sister of the testator.

FRYER:

cr. 21 Dec. 1714(a);

ex. 11 Sep. 1726.

I. 1714, to 1726. JOHN FRYER, Esq., Alderman of London, sometime Citizen and Pewterer, but afterwards (19 July 1720) Fishmonger of that city, was Alderman of Queenhithe, 7 Feb. 1709/10, till his death, and was *cr. a Baronet*, as above, 21 Dec. 1714.(a) He was Sheriff of London, 1715-16, and Lord Mayor, 1720-21; was a Director of the South Sea Company, and purchased an estate at Wherwell, Hants. He *m.* firstly, before 1700, (—). She *d.* 12 Nov. 1718.(b) He *m.* secondly, (—). She *d.* 17 Aug. 1723. He *m.* thirdly, 11 March 1724/5, at Lincoln's Inn Chapel, Isabella, da. of Sir Francis GERARD, 2d Baronet [1620], of Harrow, by Isabel, da. of Sir Thomas CHEEKE. He *d.* s.p.m.s.,(c) 11 Sep. 1726, of gout in the stomach, at his seat at Wherwell aforesaid, when the *Baronetcy* became *extinct*. Will pr. 1726. His widow *m.* 11 May 1728, at St. Antholius, London, as his 2d wife, Henry (TEMPLE), 1st VISCOUNT PALMERSTON [I.], who *d.* 10 June 1757, aged 84. She *d.* 11 Aug. 1762, at North end, Hammersmith. Will pr. 1762.

LOWTHER:

cr. 6 Jan. 1714/5;

ex. 22 Dec. 1763.

I. 1715. WILLIAM LOWTHER, of Swillington, co. York, Esq., 1st s. and h. of Sir William LOWTHER, of the same, sometime (1695-96) M.P. for Pontefract (who *d.* 7 Dec. 1705, aged 66), by Catharine, da. of Thomas HARRISON, of Dancers hill, Herts, was *b.* probably about 1665; admitted to Gray's Inn, 14 Dec. 1682; was (v.p.) Sheriff of Yorkshire, 1697-98, being M.P. for Pontefract (seven Parls.), 1701-10 and 1715 till death, and was *cr. a Baronet*, as above, 6 Jan. 1714/5. He *m.* Amabella, da. of Banastre (MAYNARD), 3d BARON MAYNARD OF ESTAINES, by Elizabeth, da. of Henry (GREY), 10th EARL OF KENT. He *d.* 6 March 1728/9. His widow *d.* 8 Aug. 1734.

II. 1729, to 1763. SIR WILLIAM LOWTHER, Baronet [1715], of Swillington aforesaid, 1st s. and h., *suc. to the Baronetcy*, 6 March 1728/9; was M.P. for Pontefract, 1729-41. He *m.* firstly, in 1719, Diana, da. of Thomas CONDON, of co. York. She *d.* 1 Jan. 1736. He *m.* secondly, 17 Aug. 1736, at Brotherton, co. York, Catherine, da. of Sir William RAMSDEN, 2d Baronet [1689], by Elizabeth, da. of John (LOWTHER), 1st VISCOUNT LONSDALE. He *d.* s.p., 22 Dec. 1763, when the *Baronetcy* became *extinct*.(d) Will pr. 1764. His widow *d.* 5 Jan. 1778. Will pr. 1778.

(a) The date on the Patent Rolls is 21 Dec., though the creation is generally ascribed to 13 Dec. 1714.

(b) Musgrave's *Obituary*.

(c) His only son, John Fryer (by his 1st wife), *d.* 16 Aug. 1724, aged 24, at Wherwell, the funeral sermon being preached by John Ball [*N. & Q.*, 9th Series, vol. viii, p. 507]. A daughter *d.* 25 Oct. 1731. See note "b" above.

(d) He left his estates to his cousin, the Rev. William Lowther, Rector of Swillington and Prebendary of York, who was s. and h. of his uncle, Christopher Lowther (*d.* 1718), yr. br. of the 1st Baronet. This William was *cr. a Baronet*, 22 Aug. 1764, and was father of William, *cr.* Earl of Lonsdale in 1807.

CAREW:

cr. 11 Jan. 1714/5;

ex. 19 Aug. 1762.

I. 1715. NICHOLAS CAREW, of Beddington, co. Surrey, Esq., only surv. s. and h. of Sir Francis CAREW,(a) of the same (*d.* 29 Sep. 1689, aged 26), by Anne, da. of William BOTELER, was *b.* 6 Feb. 1686/7; was M.P. for Haslemere, 1708-10 and 1714-22, and subsequently for Surrey, 1722 till death, and was *cr. a Baronet*, as above, 11 Jan. 1714/5. He *m.* in or before 1712, Anne, da. of Nicholas HACKET, of Bucks. He *d.* at Beddington, 18 March 1726/7, aged 40. Admon. 7 April 1727 and 4 March 1775. His widow *m.*, June 1728, William CHETWYND, sometime M.P. for Wootton Basset. She *d.* at Marlborough, on her journey to Bath, Feb. 1739/40.

II. 1727, to 1762. SIR NICHOLAS HACKET CAREW, Baronet [1715], of Beddington aforesaid, 2d but only surv. s. and h., *b.* in or after 1716; *suc. to the Baronetcy* 18 March 1726/7. He *m.*, April 1741, Katherine, da. of John MARTIN, of Overbury, co. Gloucester, sometime M.P. for Tewkesbury. She *d.* 18 March 1762. He *d.* s.p.m.,(b) a few months later, 19 Aug. 1762, when the *Baronetcy* became *extinct*. Will pr. 1762.

JANSSEN, JANNSEN, *or* JANSON:

cr. 11 March 1714/5;

ex. 8 April 1777.

I. 1715. SIR THEODORE JANSON [*or* JANSSEN], of Wimbledon, co. Surrey, Knt., 1st s. of Abraham JANSSEN (who was 1st s. of Theodore JANSSEN DE HEEZ, of Angoulême, in France), was *b.* about 1658, "removed, in 1680, into England with a considerable estate,"(c) was naturalised by Act of Parliament, and became a merchant of London, residing at St. Stephen's, Walbrook; *Knighted*, 26 Feb. 1697/8, and was, "at the special request of the Prince of Wales"(c) [afterwards George II], *cr. a Baronet*, as above, 11 March 1714/5. He purchased the manor of Wimbledon, about 1715; was M.P. for

(a) The paternal great grandfather of this Francis was Sir Nicholas Throckmorton, s. of another Sir Nicholas Throckmorton, by Anne, da. of Sir Nicholas Carew, **K.G.**, sister of Sir Francis Carew, of Beddington. This first named Nicholas took the name of Carew on inheriting the estate of Beddington from his maternal uncle, the said Sir Francis Carew, who *d.* unm., 16 May 1611, aged 81.

(b) He devised his estates in favour of his only surv. da., Catherine (as long as she continued unm.), with various remainders, in consequence of which, on her death, unm., 3 March 1769, they devolved on Richard Gee, grandson of Richard Gee, of Orpington, by Philippa, sister of Sir Francis Carew abovenamed, the father of the 1st Baronet. This Richard took the name of Carew by Act of Parl., and *d.* unm., 28 Dec. 1816, leaving the estates to Anne Paston Gee, widow, relict of his br., William Gee, who *d.* 28 March 1828, devising them to her maternal cousin, Benjamin Hallowell, subsequently Sir Benjamin Hallowell Carew, **G.C.B.**, on whose death, 2 Dec. 1834, they devolved on his son, Charles Hallowell Carew, Capt. R.N. [*Coll. Top. et Gen.*, vol. v, p. 174], who sold the Beddington estate.

(c) Wotton's *Baronetage* [1741] from information supplied by the first Baronet, whose grandfather, Theodore, is stated to have been youngest son of "the Baron de Heez, who in the troubles of the Netherlands opposed the Duke of Alva, was Gov. of Brussels, was taken prisoner and beheaded, and all his estates confiscated." This family is not to be confounded with that of I'anson or Janson, Baronets, so *cr.* 6 May 1652.

Yarmouth, April 1717 till expelled 31 Jan. 1721, as being one of the Directors of the South Sea Company, on the collapse of which, in 1720, he was ruined, and his estates sold.(a) He *m.* 26 Jan. 1697/8, at Christ Church, Newgate street, London, Williamsa, da. of Sir Robert HENLEY, of the Grange, Hants, by Catherine, da. of Sir Anthony HUNGERFORD. She *d.* 2 Sep. 1731. He *d.* 22 Sep. 1748, aged nearly 90, and was *bur.* at Wimbledon. Admon. 7 Oct. 1748, and April 1820.

II. 1748. SIR ABRAHAM JANSSEN, Baronet [1715], 1st s. and h., was M.P. for Dorchester, April 1720 to 1722; *suc. to the Baronetcy*, 22 Sep. 1748. He *d.* unm. 19 Feb. 1765, and was *bur.* at Wimbledon. Will pr. 1765.

III. 1765. SIR HENRY JANSSEN, Baronet [1715], br and h., *suc. to the Baronetcy*, 19 Feb. 1765. He *d.* unm. at Paris, 21 Feb. 1766.

IV. 1766, to 1777. SIR STEPHEN THEODORE JANSSEN, *or* JANNSEN, Baronet [1715], br. and h., citizen and stationer of London, being a merchant in that city, and sometime, 1747-54, M.P. thereof, Alderman of Bread street, 1748-65; Sheriff, 1749-50; Lord Mayor, 1754-55, but became insolvent in 1756.(b) He was, subsequently, Chamberlain of London, 1765 to 1776. He *suc. to the Baronetcy*, 21 Feb. 1766. He *m.* Catherine, da. of Col. SOULGERE, *or* ST. LEGER, of the island of Antigua. She *d.* 25 Oct. 1757. He *d.* s.p.m. 8 April 1777, and was *bur.* at Wimbledon, when the *Baronetcy* became *extinct*.

KNELLER, *rectius* KNILLER:

cr. 24 May 1715;

ex. 19 Oct. 1723.

I. 1715, to 1723. SIR GODFREY KNELLER [*rectius* KNILLER], of Whitton,(c) [near Hounslow], co. Middlesex, Knt., 3d s. of Zacharias KNILLER, of Lubeck in North Germany, Portrait Painter, formerly of Eisleben in Thuringia (*d.* 4 April 1675), by Lucia BEUTEN, his wife, was *b.* 8 Aug. 1646, at Lubeck; was ed. at first for a military career, but in 1668 applied himself to painting, coming to England in or soon after 1675, where his fame as a portrait painter was soon established. He was *Knighted*, 3 March 1691/2, being then "Principal portrait painter in Ordinary" (an office which he held till his death), and was *cr. a Baronet*, as above, 24 May 1715. He *m.* 23 Jan. 1703/4, at St. Bride's, London, Susanna GRAVE, widow, da, of the Rev. John

(a) See, as to his integrity in the South Sea bubble, the account rendered by him 20 June 1720. [Manning and Bray's *Surrey*, vol. iii, p. 269]. See p. 10, note "c," under "LAMBERT" Baronetcy [1711], for a notice of this Company.

(b) It is stated [Manning and Bray's *Surrey*, vol. iii, p. 270, note "f"], that he, "like his father, became unfortunate in business, was made a bankrupt and had his certificate, but [that] he devoted three-quarter of an income allowed him by his relations to the gradual payment of those debts that had not been fully paid, and when he was chosen Chamberlain of London paid the full amount with interest." He had been owner of the Battersea and French enamel works carried on at York House, Battersea, of which many specimens were sold in 1756 at the sale of his effects as an insolvent at his house in St. Paul's churchyard.

(c) "Kneller's house at Whitton still [1892] exists, though much altered. It is known as "Kneller Hall," and is now [1892] used as the School of Military Music." [*Dict. Nat. Biogr.*]

CAWLEY,(a) Archdeason of Lincoln and Rector of Henley-on-Thames. He *d.* s.p. legit.,(b) at his house in great Queen street, Midx., 19 Oct., and was *bur.* in his garden at Twickenham, 7 Nov. 1723, in his 78th year. M.I. at Westm. Abbey. Will dat. 27 April to 24 Oct., and pr. Dec. 1723. His widow was *bur.* 11 Dec. 1729, at Twickenham aforesaid. Will pr. 1729.

WARRENDER:

cr. 2 June 1715.

I. 1715. GEORGE WARRENDER, of Lochend, co. Haddington, Esq., s. of George WARRENDER, by "Margaret CUNNINGHAME, a relation of Sir David CUNNINGHAME, of Milncraig, Baronet [S.], and, by her mother, descended of the family of MACDOWAL, of Frewch,"(c) was *b.* about 1658; was left an infant at his father's death; "was put out to business as a merchant, came to be a very considerable dealer in foreign trade, and acquired, with a fair character, an handsome estate(c)"; is sometimes (though doubtless erroneously) said to have been *cr. a Baronet* [S.] in 1705, or May 1705,(d); was a zealous supporter of the Protestant cause, and L. Provost of Edinburgh, 1707 and 1714, and was undoubtedly *cr. a Baronet* [G.B.], 2 June 1715. He was M.P. for Edinburgh, 1715 till his death. He *m.* firstly, in or before 1686, Margaret, da. of (—) LAWRIE, of Edinburgh, Merchant. He *m.* secondly, Grizel, daughter of Hugh BLAIR, also of Edinburgh, Merchant. He *d.* in London, 4 March 1721/2, in his 65th year, and was *bur.* in the Dissenters' burial ground at Bunhill Fields. M.I. Will pr. 1721.

II. 1722. SIR JOHN WARRENDER, Baronet [1715], of Lochend aforesaid, 1st s. and h., being only s. by 1st wife, *b.* about 1686; *suc. to the Baronetcy*, 4 March 1721/2; supported the Government in the rising of 1745, and obtained the grant of several estates accordingly. He *m.*, in 1720, Henrietta, da. of Sir Patrick JOHNSTON, sometime L. Provost of Edinburgh and M.P. [S.] thereof, 1703-06. He *d.* 13 Jan. 1772, in his 87th year.

III. 1772. SIR PATRICK WARRENDER, Baronet [1715], of Lochend aforesaid, 2d but only surv. s. and h.(e) *b.* 7 March 1731; an officer in the Army, serving at the battle of Minden (1 Aug. 1759), being sometime in the Horse Guards, but afterwards Lieut.-Col. of the 11th Dragoons; was M.P. for Haddington burghs, 1768-74; King's Remembrancer of the Court of Exchequer, 1771-91; *suc. to the Baronetcy*, 13 Jan. 1772. He *m.* in 1780, H. BLAIR, spinster. He *d.* 14 June 1799, aged 68. Admon. April 1811. His widow *d.* 8 May 1838, aged 79.

IV. 1799. SIR GEORGE WARRENDER, Baronet [1715], of Lochend aforesaid, 1st s. and h., *b.* 5 Dec. 1782, at Dunbar; *suc. to the Baronetcy*, 14 June 1799, and soon afterwards matric. at Oxford (Ch. Ch.), 23 Oct. 1799, but was afterwards of Trinity Coll., Cambridge, and M.A., 1811, of that Univ.; was M.P. for Haddington burghs, 1807-12; for Truro, 1812-18; for Sandwich, 1818-26; for Westbury, 1826-30; and for Honiton, 1830-32; was a Lord of the Admiralty, 1812-22; a Commissioner of the Board of Control, 1822-28; P.C., 4 Feb. 1822; F.R.S.; Lieut.-Col. of the Berwickshire Militia. He purchased the picturesque estate of Clifden, Bucks. He *m.* 3 Oct. 1810, at St. James', Westm.,

(a) This John was son of William Cawley the Regicide.

(b) Agnes, his illegit. da., *m.* (—) Huckle, and was mother of Godfrey Kneller Huckle, who inherited most of his fortune.

(c) Wotton's *Baronetage*, edit. 1741, *ex inform* of the 2d Baronet.

(d) See vol. iv. p. 432.

(e) George Warrender, the 1st son, Major in the Horse Guards, served during the greater part of the Seven Years' War, and *d.* v.p. and unm., in Germany, aged 30.

Anne Evelyn, 2d da. of George Evelyn (BOSCAWEN), 3d VISCOUNT FALMOUTH, by Elizabeth Anne, da. and h. of John CREWE. He *d.* s.p. 21 Feb. 1849, at 63 Upper Berkeley street, Marylebone, aged 66.(a) Will pr. March and July 1849. His widow, who was *b.* 23 Nov. 1791, in St. James' square, *d.* 5 March 1871, at Versailles, near Paris, in her 80th year.

V. 1849. SIR JOHN WARRENDER, Baronet [1715], of Lochend aforesaid and of Bruntsfield House, co. Edinburgh, br. and h., *b.* March 1786; sometime Lieut. 1st Foot Guards, and Capt. in the Army; *suc. to the Baronetcy*, 21 Feb. 1849. He *m.* firstly, 10 April 1823, Julian Jane, 4th da. of James (MAITLAND), 8th EARL OF LAUDERDALE [S.], by Eleanor, d. and h. of Anthony TODD. She, who was *b.* 10 Oct. 1791, *d.* 19 May 1827, aged 35. He *m.* secondly, 25 June, 1831, Frances Henrietta, 2d da. of Richard Pepper (ARDEN), 1st BARON ALVANLEY, by Anne Dorothea, sister of Edward, 1st BARON SKELMERSDALE, da. of Richard WILBRAHAM-BOOTLE. She *d.* s.p.m., 20 Feb. 1852, at Malaga, aged 60. He *d.* 21 Jan. 1867, at Bruntsfield House, in his 81st year.

VI. 1867. SIR GEORGE WARRENDER, Baronet [1715], of Lochend and Bruntsfield House aforesaid, only s. and h., by 1st wife, *b.* 7 Oct. 1825, at Edinburgh; ed. at Eton; sometime Capt. in the Coldstream Guards; *suc. to the Baronetcy*, 21 Jan. 1867. He *m.* 13 July 1854, at St. George's, Han. sq., Helen, only da. and h. of Sir Hugh PURVES-HUME-CAMPBELL, 7th Baronet [S. 1685], of Marchmont, by Margaret, da. of John SPOTTISWOODE. She *d.* 11 March 1875, at Bruntsfield House, aged 40. He *d.* 13 June 1901, at 87 Eaton square, aged 75, and was *bur.* in the Grange Cemetery, Edinburgh. Property sworn at £456,138, the personalty (E. and S.) being £391,507.

VII. 1901. SIR GEORGE JOHN SCOTT WARRENDER, Baronet [1715], of Lochend and Bruntsfield House aforesaid, 2d but 1st surv. s. and h.,(b) *b.* 31 July 1860; entered the Royal Navy, serving in the Zulu War 1879 (medal and clasp), and in China, 1900; Captain R.N.; *suc. to the Baronetcy*, 13 June 1901; **C.B.**, 1902. He *m.* 6 Feb. 1894, at St. Paul's, Knightsbridge, Ethel Maud, 5th and yst. da. of Anthony (ASHLEY-COOPER), 8th EARL OF SHAFTESBURY, by Harriet Augusta Anne Seymourina, da. of George Hamilton (CHICHESTER), 3d MARQUESS OF DONEGALL [I.]. She was *b.* 16 Dec. 1870.

Family Estates.—These, in 1883, consisted of 2,260 acres in Roxburghshire; 1,089 in Haddingtonshire, and 74 in Midlothian. *Total*—3,423 acres, worth £6,561 a year. *Principal Seat*—Bruntsfield House, co. Edinburgh.

TENCH:

cr. 8 Aug. 1715;

ex. 2 June 1737.

I. 1715. FISHER TENCH, of Low Leyton, co. Essex, Esq., 5th but only surv. s. (out of nine sons) of Nathaniel TENCH, of the same (*d.* 2 April 1710, aged 78), by his 2d wife Anne, sister and h. of Thomas FISHER, da. of Thomas FISHER, Alderman of London, was *b.* about 1674; was Sheriff of Essex, 1711-12; M.P. for Southwark (two Parls.), 1713-22; and was *cr. a Baronet*, as above, 8 Aug. 1715. He *m.* in or before 1697, Elizabeth, da. of Robert BIRD, of Herts, one of the Ancients of Staple Inn, London. He *d.* 31 Oct., and was *bur.* 9 Nov. 1736, at Leyton, aged 64. His widow *d.* 4 and was *bur.* there 13 March 1737/8, aged 63. M.I.

(a) He was an amateur musician of considerable celebrity, and took an active part in all matters connected with the opera. He was also somewhat of a *bon vivant*, whereby he acquired the nickname of "Sir Gorge Provender."

(b) John Warrender, Capt. Gren. Guards, the 1st s., was *b.* 5 March 1859, at Lochend, and *d.* unm., v.p., 12 July 1894, at Tunbridge Wells.

V

II. 1736, to 1737. **Sir Nathaniel Tench**, Baronet [1715], of Low Leyton aforesaid, only s. and h. *b.* there 30 Aug. and *bap.* 4 Sep. 1697; matric. at Oxford (Trinity Coll.), 2 Aug. 1716, aged 18; *suc. to the Baronetcy*, 31 Oct. 1736. He *d.* unm. 2 and was *bur.* 9 June 1737, in his 40th year, at Leyton, when the *Baronetcy* became *extinct.*[a] M.I.

SAINT JOHN:

cr. 10 Sep. 1715;

ex. Sep. 1756.

I. 1715, to 1756. **Francis Saint John**, of Longthorpe, co. Northampton, Esq., 3d but 1st surv. s. and h. of Francis Saint John, of the same (living 1697), being 2d s. by his 2d wife, Mary (*m.* May 1674), da. of Dannett Foorth, Alderman of London, was *b.* probably about 1680; admitted to Lincoln's Inn, 22 July 1697; was Sheriff of Northamptonshire, 1714-15; and was *cr. a Baronet*, as above, 10 Sep. 1715. He *m.* (Lic. Fac. 4 July 1712) Mary, 1st da. and coheir of Sir Nathaniel Gould,[b] of Stoke Newington, Midx., Turkey Merchant, by Frances, da. of Sir John Hartopp, 3d Baronet [1619] of Freathby, co. Leicester. She *d.* 8 Dec. 1720, at Stoke Newington, and was carried thence, 12, for burial in the country. He *d.* s.p.m.[c] Sep. 1756, when the *Baronetcy* became *extinct*. Will pr. 3 Sep. 1756.

CHAPLIN:

cr. 19 Sep. 1715;

ex. 23 May 1730.

I. 1715. **Robert Chaplin**, of the Inner Temple, London, Esq., being also of Well, co. Lincoln, 3d s. of Sir Francis Chaplin, sometime (1677-78) Lord Mayor of London, by Anne, da. of Daniel Huett, of Essex, was admitted to Gray's Inn, 3 Aug. 1675, being then a citizen and merchant of London; was *cr. a Baronet*, as above, 19 Sep. 1715, with a spec. rem., failing heirs male of his body, to his nephew, Porter Chaplin. He was one of the Directors of the South Sea Company, and M.P. for Grimsby 1715, till expelled from the House of Commons, 28 Jan. 1720/1, when in 1720 that Company collapsed.[d] He *m.* (—), da. of (—) Harrington. She *d.* before him. He *d.* s.p.m., 1 July 1728. Admon. 8 Feb. 1728/9, as of Well, co. Lincoln, to his da. Anne, wife of James Bateman.[e]

([a]) Jane, his sister, *bap.* 30 June 1704, at Low Leyton, *m.* Adam Sorseby, of Chesterfield, and *d.* s.p. 18 May 1752, being *bur.* at Leyton. Another sister is said to have *m.* 6 March 1739, (—) Cowley, of Herts.

([b]) See pedigree of Gould in *Mis. Gen. et Her.*, new series, vol. iii, pp. 355-359.

([c]) Of his two daughters (1) Frances, *d.* unm. 19 May 1794, aged 82, at Welwyn, Herts, and was *bur.* at Longthorpe. M.I. (2) Mary, *m.* Sir John Bernard, 4th Baronet [1662], of Huntingdon, and *d.*, his widow, 21 Sep. 1793, at Hillingdon, Midx., leaving issue.

([d]) See p. 10, note "c," under "Lambert" Baronetcy [1711], for a notice of this Company.

([e]) They were *m.* 21 Sep. 1721; she *d.* at Bath 7 and was *bur.* 19 March 1733 at Well aforesaid. Her husband was yr. br. to William Bateman, *cr.* 12 July 1725, Viscount Bateman and Baron Culmore [I.]

II. 1728, to 1730. **Sir John Chaplin**, Baronet [1715], of Tathwell, co. Lincoln, great nephew and h. male, being only s. and h. of Porter Chaplin, of Tathwell, by Anne, da. and coheir of Richard Sherwin, of London, which Porter (who was *bur.* at Tathwell, 27 July 1719), was 1st s. and h. of John Chaplin, of Tathwell, Sheriff of Lincolnshire 1690 (*d.* 11 Nov. 1714, aged 56), elder br. of the grantee. He was *b.* about 1711; *suc. to the Baronetcy*, 1 July 1728, under the spec. rem. in its creation. He *m.* 26 March 1730, (—), da.[a] of William Morris, of Fernham, near Farringdon, Berks. He *d.* s.p.m.[b] 23 May, and was *bur.* 6 June 1730, at Tathwell, aged 19, when the *Baronetcy* became *extinct.*[c] Will pr. Nov. 1730.

BYNG:

cr. 15 Nov. 1715;

afterwards, since 1721, Viscounts Torrington.

I. 1715. **Sir George Byng**, of Southhill, co. Bedford, Knt., 1st s. of John Byng, of Wrotham, Kent (who sold that estate in 1666), by Philadelphia, da. of (—) Johnstone, of Loans, Surrey, was *b.* 27 Jan. 1663/4, at Wrotham; served both in the Army and Navy; Captain R.N., 1688; Rear-Admiral 1703, distinguishing himself at Malaga and at Gibraltar, in 1704; was *Knighted*, 22 Oct. 1704; M.P. for Plymouth (five Parls.), 1705-21; Admiral of the Blue, 1708; a Lord of the Admiralty, 1709-21; Admiral of the White, 1711; in command to defend the coast against the Jacobite insurgents of 1715; and was *cr. a Baronet*, as above, 15 Nov. 1715; Commander-in-Chief in the Baltic, 1717, and in the Mediterranean, 1718-21, defeating 31 July 1718 the Spanish Fleet, off Cape Pesaro; was Plenipotentiary to Fez and Morocco, 1718, and to the Princes and States of Italy, 1718-21; Treasurer of the Navy, 1720-24; Rear Admiral of Great Britain, 1720; P.C., 3 Jan. 1721. He *m.* 5 March 1690/1, at St. Paul's, Covent Garden (Lic. Vic. Gen. same date) Margaret, da. of James Master, of East Langdon, Kent, by Joyce, da. of Sir Christopher Turner, of Milton Erneys, Beds, one of the Barons of the Exchequer. She was living when he was *cr.* 21 Sep. 1721, BARON BYNG OF SOUTHHILL, co. Bedford, and VISCOUNT TORRINGTON,[d] co. Devon. In that peerage this *Baronetcy* then *merged*, and still (1905) so continues. See *Peerage*.

See fuller particulars in *Peerage*, under "Torrington."

([a]) Her sister, Henrietta Maria, *m.* Sir Joseph E. Moore, 4th Baronet [1675].

([b]) Anne, posthumous da. and h., *b.* 4 Jan. 1731/2, *m.* 3 March 1750/1 Arthur Gregory, of Styvechale, co. Warwick.

([c]) His uncle and h. male (who, apparently, was not included in the spec. rem. of the Baronetcy), Thomas Chaplin, of Blankney, co. Lincoln, and Tathwell aforesaid, was ancestor (in the male line) of the family still (1904) settled there.

([d]) It is singular how popular as a peerage title was the town of Torrington. Only two years before this creation the *Barony of Torrington* had become extinct by the death, 27 May 1719, of Thomas Newport, who had been so *cr.* 20 June 1716. That creation was but two months [!] after the *Earldom of Torrington* had become extinct, by the death, 14 April 1716, of Arthur Herbert, the incompetent Admiral who had been so *cr.* 29 May 1689. This last creation was but seven months, after an earlier *Earldom of Torrington*, had become extinct, by the death, 6 Oct. 1688, of Christopher (Monck), 2d Duke of Albemarle and Earl of Torrington, whose father, the celebrated Gen. George Monck, had been so. *cr.* 7 July 1660.

SLOANE:

cr. 3 April 1716;

ex. 11 Jan. 1753.

I. 1716, to 1753. **Hans Sloane**, of Chelsea, co. Middlesex, M.D., 7th and yst. s. of Alexander Sloane, of Killileagh, or White's Castle, co. Down, in Ireland, by Sarah, da. of the Rev. (—) Hicks, D.D., sometime Chaplain to Archbishop Laud, was *b.* there 10 April, 1660; studied Medicine at Paris and at Montpelier; was M.D. at the Univ. of Orange, July 1683; F.R.S., 21 Jan. 1685; Fellow of the Coll. of Physicians 12 April 1687, and after fifteen months in Jamaica (where, being a great botanist, he collected 800 species of plants) settled in 1689 in Bloomsbury square, and acquired a very extensive practice; Sec. to the Royal Society, 1693-1712, of which he was Vice-President, 1712, and President (on the death of Sir Isaac Newton), 1727-40; Physician to Christ's Hospital (to which he was a generous benefactor), 1694-1730; *cr.* M.D. by the Univ. of Oxford, 19 July 1701; purchased the manor of Chelsea, Midx., in 1712; was Physician Gen. to the Army, 1714, and was *cr. a Baronet*, as above, 3 April 1716; President of the College of Physicians, 1719-35; First Physician to George II, in 1727, and retired from general practice in 1741. He *m.* (Lic. Fac. 9 May 1695) Elizabeth, widow of Fulk Rose, of Jamaica, Physician, da. and coheir of John Langley, Alderman of London, by Elizabeth, da. and coheir of Richard Middleton, also Alderman of London. She *d.* 27 Sep. and was *bur.* 1 Oct. 1724, at Chelsea, in her 67th year. M.I. He *d.* s.p.m.s. 11, and was *bur.* 18 Jan. 1753 at Chelsea, when the *Baronetcy* became *extinct.*[a] Will pr. 1753.[b]

DIXWELL:

cr. 11 June 1716;

ex. 14 Jan. 1757.

I. 1716, to 1757. **William Dixwell**, of Coton Hall, co. Warwick, Esq., s. and h. of Brent Dixwell, of the same (who *d.* 10 June 1690, aged 24), by Anne, da. of John Sandys, of Loveline, co. Worcester, was *b.* probably about 1688, and was *cr. a Baronet*, as above, 11 June 1716; was Sheriff of Warwickshire, 1715-16. He *m.* in 1712, Mary, da. of Sir Roger Cave, 2d Baronet [1641], of Stanford, by his 2d wife, Mary, da. of Sir William Bromley, K.B. She *d.* a year afterwards, 11 Feb. 1712/3. aged 20, and was *bur.* at Churchover. M.I. He *d.* s.p. 14 Jan. 1757, when the *Baronetcy* became *extinct*. Admon. as of St. Mary Abchurch, London, widower, to William Dixwell Grimes, Esq., and Anna Maria, wife of William Cracroft, nephew and niece and only next-of-kin.

([a]) Of his two surv. daughters and coheirs (1) Sarah, *m.* George Stanley and was mother of William Stanley, who *d.* young and was *bur.* (with his maternal grandmother) at Chelsea, 21 Nov. 1724, and of the Rt. Hon. Hans Stanley, who *d.* s.p. 13 Jan. 1780; (2) Elizabeth, *m.* 25 July 1717 Charles (Cadogan), 2d Baron Cadogan of Oakley, and was ancestress of the Earls Cadogan, who eventually inherited the whole of the Sloane estates.

([b]) He bequeathed his valuable collections to the nation (for the sum of £20,000, less than half what they had cost him), which subsequently were placed in the British Museum. He also devised his botanic garden at Chelsea to the Apothecaries Company.

DUTRY:[a]

cr. 19 June 1716;

ex. 20 Oct. 1728.

I. 1716, to 1728. **Dennis** [*or* **Dionysius**] **Dutry**, of London, Esq., eldest of the six sons of John Dutry,[b] of Amsterdam, Merchant (*d.* there in his 90th year), by his 2d wife, "Geertruda Deyman, of an ancient family of Amsterdam,"[a] lived may years in France, but settled in London about 1690, where he became a Merchant and was *cr. a Baronet*, as above, 19 June 1716. He was a director of the East India Company and resided at Putney, in Surrey. He *m.* in London, Mary, (*b.* at Bordeaux, in France), da. of Hillary Renau, formerly of Bordeaux, Merchant, but subsequently (1688), of London. He *d.* s.p. 20 Oct. 1728, when the *Baronetcy* became *extinct*. Will pr. 1728. His widow *m.*, in 1734, Gerard Vanneck, of Austin Friars, London, Merchant (who *d.* s.p. 17 Aug. 1750), and *d.* "an ornament to her sex" in March 1743. Will p. 1743.

PERROTT, *or* PERROT:[e]

1716, *or* 1717[c] to 1759?

"Sir James Perrot," one of the children of "Richard Perrott," by "Anne, da. of Gabriel Smith, of the Brookhouse, in Cheshire," is alleged (though apparently untruly) to have been "employed in many capacities by the Government, and, on his relinquishing a balance due to him for the redemption of British slaves" is alleged to have been "*cr. a Baronet*, 1 July 1716,[c] with limitation to the eldest son of his brother Richard and his heirs male, but not permitted to take rank from the original grant of this dignity to Sir Francis Perrott,[d] Knight and Baronet, 29 June 1611."[e] This alleged grant of 1611 was, however, undoubtedly fictitious.

([a]) See an account of this family, in Wotton's *Baronetage*, 1st edit. 1727.

([b]) This John was son of John Dutry, of Thounin, in the province of Guienne in France, said to have been son of "one of the Prime Ministers at the Court of Governante of the Netherlands, the Dutchess of Parma," but to have been disinherited by his father for having become a Protestant. See note "a" above.

([c]) The date, 1 July 1717, is assigned to the Perrott creation in "*the list of all the Baronets from their first institution*," given in Kimber's *Baronetage* [1771], presuming the grantee there called "*Robert* Perrot, of Richmond, Surrey, Esq." (whose Baronetcy was then [1771] "claimed by Sir Richard, who has no patent"), to be the same person as the "Sir *James*" in the text. This date of 1717 is copied in Courthope's *List of all the Baronetcies of England*, but inasmuch as the date of 1 July 1716, is that of the precedency granted to Sir Richard Perrott by the Royal Warrant of 3 Jan. 1767, the date of 1717 is presumably an error for 1716. No creation of a Baronetcy of Perrot under either date is to be found in Wotton's *Baronetage* [1741].

([d]) *Francis* is apparently meant for *Thomas*, it being stated (see note "e" below) that Sir Thomas Perrott, who *m.* Dorothy, d. of Walter (Devereux), Earl of Essex, and who *d.* s.p.m., "was *cr. a Baronet*, 29 June 1611, but died before his patent was made out." Not only, however, is there no warrant for such creation, but the will of the said Sir Thomas Perrott was pr. 1594, and in 1595 his relict was the wife of the Earl of Northumberland, more than fifteen years before this alleged creation.

([e]) There is no notice of any Baronetcy of Perrot in Wotton's *Baronetage* [1727 or 1741] or anywhere else till 1771, when it first appears in the Appendix to vol. iii of Kimber's *Baronetage* [1771], pp. 458-467, from which the passages within inverted commas are taken. Kimber's notice contains an account

No locality is assigned to this James, neither can the date of his death or any other particular be ascertained about him. It is probable that he is meant for the same person(a) as *Robert* Perrot mentioned next below.

---

by "Mr. T. L." [*i.e.*, Thomas Lowndes, one of the booksellers whose names appear in the title page to that work], which purports to give "a short account of Sir Richard and his family, from a curious pedigree left by him in the hands of the late Mr. Kimber." This mendacious account of the family is, for the most part, the authority for the statements in the text, as above. The earlier portion is stated to be based on a pedigree (deducing the family from "Brutus, who first inherited this land, which after him was called Britain about 116 years before the birth of Christ"), which purposes to be made by one Owen Griffiths, who was wounded in Carew Castle, in 1650, by the side of his master, Sir James Perrott, "Marquis of Nerberth," etc. There was, however, no siege of Carew Castle in 1650 (which indeed had surrendered in 1644), neither was there any Marquess of Narbeth, though the pedigree (which, of course purports to have been compiled at some date *after* 1650) is dedicated to him. This Sir James Perrott, who is stated in one part of this account to have had a warrant from Charles I for his creation as "Marquis of Narbeth, Earl and Viscount Carew, and Baron Perrott," and to have been in command at Carew Castle in 1650 is, however, stated elsewhere therein, to have died in 1641, though (as a matter of fact) his will was pr. as early as May 1637. Thomas, elsewhere called Francis (who *d.* in or before 1594), elder br. of this James, is said to have been *cr. a Baronet* in 1611, though that date is more than fifteen years after his death (see p. 33, note "d"). This Sir Thomas had in reality but *one* "da. and sole heir" [*Top. and Gen.* ii, 501], Penelope, who *m.* (1) Sir Thomas Gower, and (2) Sir Robert Naunton, but another da. is here (falsely) assigned to him, *viz.*, Dorothy, who is alleged to have *m.* her cousin, James Perrott, and to have been ancestress of the (so called) Baronet of 1767, said, in her right, to quarter the arms of "Devereux, Earls of Essex." The said James is stated to be s. of Thomas, s. of Owen Perrott (*d.* 1597), who is said to have been a yr. br. of Sir John Perrott, **K.B.**, the Lord Deputy of Ireland (father of Sir Thomas Perrott, the alleged Baronet of 1611), both being sons of Sir Thomas Perrott, of Haroldston, co. Pembroke.—No such Owen Perrott, however, nor any such Dorothy ever existed. (See E. L. Barnwell's *Notes on the Perrott Family*, 1867, p. 62). This James Perrott, said to have been in right of his mother, "Lord of Wellington under Dinmer, co. Hereford," is stated to have had three sons. by this apocryphal Dorothy, *viz.* (1) Sir Herbert Perrott [whose will was pr. Sep. 1683]; (3) James Perrott, who *d.* 1683, and was *bur.* at Haverfordwest; and (2) Francis [called a few lines lower "Thomas"] Perrott, of Upper Bignall Hill, who is stated to have been father of Richard, the father of James Perrott, stated therein to have been *cr. a Baronet*, 1 July 1716, and of Richard, father of "Sir Richard Perrot, the present [1771] Baronet."

The above genealogy is thus spoken of as early as 1811 in Fenton's well-known *Historical Tour through Pembrokeshire*, "The pedigree this charlatan Baronet delivered in, is a most curious travesty of the genuine one appertaining to that family * * * and may throw some light on the history of a man, who blazed on the town about thirty-five years ago, and practised his imposture so successfully that there exists a *fiat* of his present majesty, dated 3 Jan. 1767 * * * for his taking rank and title from 1 July 1716." T. C. Banks (in his *Baronia Angl. Conc.*, vol. ii, p. 1167) speaks (1) of this warrant as "declaratory of honours that were never granted," and (2) of the pedigree as a compilation that "one would imagine was rather the fruit of a disordered mind than the produce of a serious research and faithful representation."

(a) This view is adopted in Burke's *Baronetage* (1902), but there is no such person as a *Robert* Perrott, in the pedigree supplied by Sir Richard to Kimber's *Baronetage* [1771], the said Richard being therein stated to have succeeded his uncle, *James* Perrott, the grantee in the Baronetcy.

"ROBERT PERROT, of Richmond, Surrey, Esq.," stated to have been *cr. a Baronet*, 1 July 1717,(a) and whose death, as "*Sir Robert Perrot, Bart.*," is stated to have taken place at Brussels, 29 May 1759.(b) No such Robert PERROTT, however, is mentioned in Sir Richard's pedigree (see p. 33, note "e"), and no patent, sign manual, docquet, nor any other document exists to indicate that any person named James, or Robert PERROT, was created, or was intended to be created, a Baronet in 1716 or 1717. A Royal Warrant, however, dated 3 Jan. 1767, was obtained,(c) in which it is stated that "to avoid all doubts and disputes about the rank and precedency of Sir Richard PERROTT, Baronet" (whose relationship, however, to any former Baronet is not indicated), the place, rank, precedency, etc., of a Baronet, to commence from 1 July 1716, are granted to him and the heirs male of his body. This grant of the *precedency* of a Baronetcy of 1 July 1716, made by a Royal Warrant, dated more than fifty years later, will (though more properly belonging to the date of the said warrant, 3 Jan. 1767) be dealt with (for the sake of convenience) under the date of 1 July 1716.

PERROTT, *or* PERROT:
Royal warrant, *dated* 3 Jan. 1767,(d)
of the precedency of a Baronetcy of 1 July 1716.

I. 1767. RICHARD PERROT, one of the sons of Richard PERROT, of Mardol, in Shrewsbury, distiller, by Rebecca

---

(a) See p. 33, note "c."

(b) *Gent. Mag. for* 1759. In that publication for 1769 is the death in Nov. of "*Sir Richard Perrot, Dublin.*" This last person, however, is not styled a Baronet. It is to be observed, however, that the then [1771] Baronet is spoken of as "*Sir Richard Perrott*," as early as 24 Oct. 1758 (see p. 33, note "c"), while it is stated in J. G. Nichols's article (see note "c" below), that "he suc. as 2d Baronet in 1731.".

(c) See an able article in the *Her. and Gen.* (vol. viii, pp. 314-324 (by its accomplished editor, John Gough Nichols, F.S.A., a most acute genealogist), entitled "*Sir Richard Perrott, a soi-disant Baronet.*" The words used therein, as applied to the Royal warrant of 3 Jan. 1767, are, that it was "surreptitiously obtained"; and the grantee is styled "one of the most daring pretenders to title and pedigree in the last [*i.e.*, the eighteenth] century." The matter is fully dealt with in that article, and the proceedings described therein appear to justify the strong language used above.

(d) According to the Royal warrant, dated 3 Jan. 1767, and signed "H. S. Conway," whereby "to avoid all doubts and disputes about the rank and precedency of our trusty and well beloved subject Sir Richard Perrott, Baronet," it is declared that he "and the heirs male of his body lawfully begotten, shall have and enjoy in all places, assemblies and meetings, the place, rank, pre-eminence, precedency, privileges and immunities of, or belonging to the degree of a Baronet of this our Realm, and to take place and commence as from 1 July 1716." No Royal warrant, it is believed, ever has or ever can create a *hereditary* dignity (such as that of a Baronetcy or Peerage), and though such warrant can direct letters patent of creation to be issued, or can refer to any such patent that had previously been passed, this [most extraordinary] warrant does neither. The effect of this Royal warrant is, apparently, not to *create a Baronetcy*, but to give to its recipient and "the heirs male of his body" *the style and precedency of a Baronet* of the creation of 1 July 1716. See J. G. Nichols's article (note "e" above), as to the obtaining of this document. As to the date of 1 July 1716 or 1 July 1717, which is that of a Baronetcy alleged to have been conferred on James Perrot and Robert Perrott, respectively, see text, pp. 33 and 35, under these respective dates.

da. of Isaac WYKE, of Wacton, co. Hereford,(a) was *b.* probably in or shortly before 1716, and is said to have *suc. to a Baronetcy* conferred on his uncle, *James* PERROT, 1 July 1716, with a spec. rem. in his favour.(b) The date of his succession to this alleged Baronetcy is stated to have been in 1731,(c) but a notice (*Gent. Mag.*, 1759) of the death at Brussels, 29 May 1759, of a "Sir *Robert* PERROT, Bt.," coupled with an alleged creation (see above) on 1 July 1717 [*not*, however, 1716], as a Baronet, of "*Robert* PERROT, of Richmond, Surrey, Esq., now claimed by Sir Richard, who has no patent" (see *List of all the Baronets* in Kimber's *Baronetage* [1771]), rather suggests that *Robert*(d) (not *James*) was the uncle he purported to succeed and that 1759 (not 1731) was the date of such succession. It is to be observed that there is no reference in this warrant to any Baronetcy of the date of 1 July 1716 having ever been granted, nor to the Christian name [*Qy.* James or Robert?] or surname [*Qy.* Perrot?] of the grantee, but the date is that of the Baronetcy alleged by the grantee of the warrant of 1767 (b) to have been conferred on his uncle "Sir James Perrot," with a special remainder to himself. This Richard *Perrot* is stated to have been "of a military genius and in service in East India before he was 14 years old," and to have received from Frederick, King of Prussia, a [most extraordinary] commission (called in J. G. Nichols's article [see p. 35, note "c"] a "*pretended* commission"), dated 24 Oct. 1758, in which that King "confided solely to him the sole care of his intended marine," with instructions to destroy the ships of the Empress Queen. the King of Sweden, and the Grand Duke of Tuscany. The comment added thereto is that "A Lord High Admiral of Great Britain could not have been vested with more extraordinary powers."(c) He however procured a Royal warrant (said to have been "surreptitiously obtained,"(e) dated 3 Jan. 1767 (in which he is styled "SIR RICHARD PERROTT, BARONET"), whereby, to avoid all doubts about his rank or precedency, he and the heirs male of his body are granted the rank, precedency, privileges, etc., of a Baronet,

---

(a) In the pedigree put forth by him (as to which see p. 33, note "c") his mother is said to be "Rebecca, da. of Isaac Wyke, of Wacton Court, in Herefordshire, Esq., paternally descended from Wyke, a Knight, to whom William the Conqueror granted divers lands," etc. No description or place of residence is given to his father (said in Burke's *Baronetage* for 1902 to have been "of Broseley, Salop"), but these particulars have been supplied by an article in the *Gent. Mag.* for Feb. 1770, entitled "*Particulars of the noted Perrot, who presented the Flint petition*," where it is stated that "The pretended Baronet is plain D—k P—t, the second son of one P—t, a decayed Distiller, of Mardol, in Shrewsbury: his elder brother an Apothecary, but now practises as a Physician at Tewkesbury, by virtue of a diploma from Leyden."

(b) According to the recipient's account (as to the value of which see p. 33, note "e," *circa* finem) printed in Kimber's *Baronetage* [1771], and, apparently according to that account alone.

(c) The words in J. G. Nichols's article (see p. 35, note "c") are, "He succeeded. we are told, as 2d Baronet in 1731," but it does not appear therein *where* "we are told" of this fact.

(d) No such Robert, however, appears in the pedigree (see note "c" above), and the [marvellous] commission (printed therewith) signed by Frederick, King of Prussia, and dated 24 Oct. 1758, speaks of him [at that date] as "Sr Richard Perrott." Possibly, however, as the commission is in French, and as neither the word "Chevalier" nor that of "Baronet" is used, the "Sr" does not necessarily indicate that he was either.

(e) See J. G. Nichols's article, p. 35, note "c" as to this obtainment.

to commence from 1 July 1716.(a) He also claimed to have been at the battle of Culloden in 1745 "in personal attendance on the Duke of Cumberland," and to have been *cr. a Baron* by Louis XV of France "with the privilege of the *tabouret* to his Lady and the wives of his successors."(b) A very different account of his career previous to 1770 is given elsewhere.( ) He, undoubtedly, presented a loyal address 8 Jan. 1770 from "the Bailiffs, Corporation and borough of Flint" to the young Prince of Wales, expressive of their disapproval of petitions for the dissolution of Parliament(d); and his house "in Gloucester View, Park lane," was not long after "dismantled" by one of the Wilkes mobs and its "costly effects" burned, though "in compensation he received a grant of the *ancient manor of Cheslemere* (wherever that may be)," etc.(b) He *m.* (when, apparently, nearer 70 than 60) 3 March 1782, at Haddington, Margaret Jemima FORDYCE, of Inveresk, spinster, said to have been da. of Capt. William FORDYCE, Royal Marines, Gentleman of the Bedchamber to George III. He *d.* in 1796,(e) and for about fifty years after his death nothing appears about this Baronetcy.(f) His widow, to whom a pension had been granted in 1789, was living at 25 Warren street, Fitzroy square, Marylebone, 7 Dec. 1803.(g)

(a) See p. 35, note "d," as to the Royal warrant. It may be observed that (probably from inadvertence) nothing is said therein about the style of a Baronet, but possibly the style of "Sir" may be considered as included among the "privileges" belonging to that degree.

(b) See J. G. Nichols's article (as on p. 35, note "c") where it is observed that "To the initiated in Court etiquette this statement will appear scarcely less ridiculous than the appointment to be Lord High Admiral of Prussia. The privilege of the *tabouret* (or to be seated on a stool in the Royal presence) was confined to the Duchesses of France and the wives of grandees of Spain, and attempts to extend it to titular Princesses were jealous resisted. See the *Memoires du Duc de Saint Simon*."

(c) *i.e.*, In the article in the *Gent. Mag.* for Feb. 1770 (as to which see p. 36, note "a," where several very discreditable transactions as to swindling women out of their fortune as well as character are recounted, and it is added that at Worcester "he passed for a Knight of the Order of the Eagle of Prussia—that was his travelling title there," and that "in 1760 he passed at Beverley, in Yorkshire, for Admiral to his Prussian Majesty, and pretended a commission to purchase shipping for that monarch, but Lord Rockingham, suspecting the impostor, obliged him to decamp."

(d) The following comments thereon occur in the Historical Chronicle of the *Gent. Mag.* for Jan. 1770:—"The concurring accounts that are published in the papers of an infamous adventurer under the above name [*i.e.* that of *Sir Richard Perrot, Bart.*] involve a mystery how such a man could procure an address, and what means he could make use of to obtain countenance at Court to present it." See J. G. Nichols's article, p. 35, note "c."

(e) Burke's *Baronetage* (1847), as quoted in J. G. Nichols's article (see p. 35, note "c"), but the date of death is omitted in later editions, *e.g.*, those of 1871 and 1902.

(f) The Baronetcy appears in Burke's *Baronetage* of 1847 for, apparently, the first time, being certainly absent in that of 1841. It is not in Debrett's *Baronetage* of 1819, 1824 or 1840, nor in Playfair's *Baronetage* (1809), nor (as an existing creation) in Betham's *Baronetage* (1805), but in that work it is given in the list of creations (under 1767, "with precedency from 1 July 1716"), being printed *in italics* to signify that it was then *extinct*, being, presumably, so considered after the death of the grantee of the warrant of the precedency of a Baronetcy of 1767.

(g) Letter of that date in Bigland's collection (R.B.G. 48, pp. 10-14) in the College of Arms.

II. 1796. SIR EDWARD BINDLOSS PERROTT, Baronet [1767],(a) of Plumstead, Kent, 1st s. and h., b 1 Sep. 1784; *suc. to the Baronetcy*(a) in 1796. He *m.* 10 May 1810, at St. Swithin's, Winchester, Louisa Augusta, da. (*Qy.* illegit.) of Nicholas BAYLY, Col. 1st Foot Guards, br. of Henry (PAGET, *formerly* BAYLY) 1st EARL OF UXBRIDGE. He *d.* 24 March 1859, at Plumstead, aged 74. His widow *d.* there 15 Jan. 1860, aged 81.

III. 1859. SIR EDWARD GEORGE LAMBERT PERROTT, Baronet [1767],(a) of Brook Hall house in Plumstead aforesaid, 1st s. and h.; *b.* 10 May 1811; Ensign East Kent militia, 1833; Capt. 1839, retiring 1854; *suc. to the Baronetcy*,(a) 24 March 1859; raised the 9th Kent (Plumstead) Artillery Vols. He *m.* 13 Oct. 1847, Emma Maria, only da. of Charles Evelyn HOUGHTON, Commander R.N. She *d.* 15 June 1878, at Plumstead, in her 68th year. He *d.* there 4 June 1886, in his 76th year. Will dat. 3 July 1878, pr. 23 Sep. 1886.

IV. 1886. SIR HERBERT CHARLES PERROTT, Baronet [1767],(a) of Brook Hill house aforesaid, 1st s. and h., *b.* 26 Oct. 1849; ed. at Ipswich School; sometime Ensign 21st Kent Rifle vols., and Capt. reserve of officers; afterwards Lieut.-Col., commanding 3d Buffs, East Kent, reg. of militia; *suc. to the Baronetcy*,(a) 4 June 1886; C.B. (Civil), 1902, for services connected with the Transvaal war. He *m.* 10 Dec. 1901, at St. Peter's, Eaton square, Ethel Lucy, 1st da. of Marcus Stanley HARE, Capt. R.N., by Matilda Jane, da. of William TOLLEMACHE, of Harrington, co. Northampton.

D'AETH:

cr. 16 July 1716;

ex. April 1808.

I. 1716. THOMAS D'AETH, of Knowlton, co. Kent, Esq., as also of North Cray place in that county, s. and h. of Thomas D'AETH, of London, merchant, by Elhanna (*m.* Oct. 1669, *d.* 1738, aged 86), da. of Sir John ROLT, of Milton Earnest, Beds, was *b.* probably about 1670; was M.P. for Canterbury, 1708-10, for Sandwich, 1715-22, and was *cr. a Baronet*, as above, 16 July 1716. He *m.* firstly, about 1704, Elizabeth, sister and h. (in 1707) of Sir John NARBOROUGH, Baronet [1688], of Knowlton aforesaid, da. of Admiral Sir John NARBOROUGH, by Elizabeth, da. of John HILL. She *d.* in childbirth of her twelfth child, 24 June 1721, in her 39th year, and was *bur.* at St. Margaret's, Westm. He *m.* secondly, Jane, da. of Walter WILLIAMS, of Dingeston, co. Monmouth. He *d.* 4 Jan. 1745. Will pr. 1745.

II. 1745. SIR NARBOROUGH D'AETH, Baronet [1716], of Knowlton aforesaid, 1st s. and h. by 1st wife; *suc. to the Baronetcy*, 4 Jan. 1745. He *m.*, about 1740, Anne, da. of John CLARKE, of Blake Hall, Essex. He *d.* 8 Oct. 1773. Will dated 15 Feb. 1771, pr. 24 Jan. 1774.

(a) See p. 35, note "d."

III. 1773, to 1808. SIR NARBOROUGH D'AETH, Baronet [1716], of Knowlton aforesaid, only s. and h., *b.* about 1750; matric. at Oxford (Ch. Ch.), 5 Feb. 1768, aged 18; *suc. to the Baronetcy*, 8 Oct. 1773. He *d.* unm. April 1808, when *the Baronetcy* became *extinct*.(a) Will pr. May 1808 and Jan. 1844.

DECKER:

cr. 20 July 1716;

ex. 18 March 1748/9.

I. 1716, to 1749. MATTHEW DECKER, of London, Esq., s. of (—) DECKER, of Amsterdam (of a family, which, being Protestant, had fled from, Flanders at the time of the Spanish persecution under the Duke of ALVA), was *b.* there about 1679, but, coming to England in 1702, became a merchant of London; was M.P. for Bishopscastle, 1719-22; and was *cr. a Baronet*, as above, 20 July 1716. He was one of the directors of the East India Company, and settled at Richmond, Surrey,(b) being Sheriff of that county, 1728-29. He *m.* before 1717, Henrietta, da. of the Rev. Richard WATKINS, D.D., Rector of Wickford, co. Warwick. He *d.* s.p.m.s.(c) 18 and was *bur.* 25 March 1749, at Richmond, aged 70, when *the Baronetcy* became *extinct*.(d) Will pr. 1749. His widow *d.* 4 and was *bur.* 12 May 1759, at Richmond, aged 80.

MILNER:

cr. 26 Feb. 1716/7.

I. 1717. WILLIAM MILNER, of Nun-Appleton Hall, co. York, Esq., 1st s. and h. ap. of William MILNER, of the same, and of Beeston and Bolton Percy in that county, Alderman and sometime (1697) Mayor of Leeds, cloth merchant (*d.* 23 Dec. 1740, aged 78), by Mary, da. of Joshua IBBESTON, also sometime Mayor of Leeds, was *b.* probably in or soon after 1696; is said to have been ed. at Eton and at Cambridge(e); admitted to the Middle

(a) The Knowlton estate devolved on his cousin, George William Hughes, s. of William Hughes, of Betshanger, Kent, by his 2d wife, Harriet, 1st of the five daughters and coheirs of Josiah Hardy, Consul at Cadiz, by Harriet, 5th and yst. sister (but the only one that had issue) of Sir Narborough D'Aeth, 2d Baronet.

(b) At Richmond "he had the first in England that was brought to maturity of the East and West India plant called *the Annanas*, or Pine Apple, so famous for its incomparable taste and beauty" [Wotton's *Baronetage*, 1741].

(c) Matthew Decker, his son, was *bur.* at Richmond, 25 March 1717. Of the three daughters (1) Catherine, *m.* 3 May 1744 at St. James', Westm., Richard (Fitzwilliam), 6th Viscount Fitzwilliam of Meryon [I.], and *d.* 7 Feb. 1786. (2) Henrietta Maria, *m.* 30 May 1737, at Richmond (as his 1st wife), the Hon. John Talbot, but *d.* s.p. and v.p. Sep. 1747. (3) Mary, *m.* Dec. 1738, William Crofts, of Saxham, Suffolk. He is said to have left £60,000 to his only surviving child.

(d) He was a great philanthropist, and his entertainment of "the Great and the Poor" is set forth fully in his obituary notices, in one of which it is aptly remarked of his vast wealth that he "enjoys it still, for he shared it with the poor."

(e) Foster's *Yorkshire Families*.

Temple, 9 July 1713; and was v.p. *cr. a Baronet*, as above, 26 Feb. 1716/7. He was M.P. for York 1722-34, and was Grand Master of the English Freemasons, 1728. He *m.* Elizabeth (*b.* 1700), da. of Sir William DAWES, 3d Baronet [1663], Archbishop of York [1714-24], by Frances, da. of Sir Thomas DARCY, 1st Baronet [1660], of St. Osith's. He *d.* 23 Nov. 1745 in the parish of St. Geo. Han. sq. Admon. 8 March 1745/6. His widow *d.* 9 March 1782, aged 82, and was *bur.* at Bolton Percy. Will pr. April 1782.

II. 1745. SIR WILLIAM MILNER, Baronet [1717], of Nun-Appleton aforesaid, only s. and h., *b.* probably about 1725; *suc. to the Baronetcy*, 23 Nov. 1745, being then at Venice; subscribed £100 towards the defence of Yorkshire against the Jacobite insurgents; Sheriff of Yorkshire, 1747-48; Receiver Gen. of Excise (annual salary £2,500), 29 Nov. 1748. He *m.* 30 April 1747, at Midgham, Berks, Elizabeth, 3d and yst. da. and coheir of Rev. the Hon. George MORDAUNT (5th s. of John, 1st VISCOUNT MORDAUNT OF AVALON), being his 2d da. by his 3d wife, Elizabeth, da. of Lieut.-Col. COLLYER, Lieut.-Gov. of Jersey. He *d.* 8 Nov. 1774, and was *bur.* at Leeds. Will pr. Nov. 1774. His widow *d.* 1785. Will pr. Sep. 1785.

III. 1774. SIR WILLIAM MORDAUNT MILNER, Baronet [1717], of Nun-Appleton aforesaid, 2d but 1st surv. s. and h., *b.* 6 Oct. 1754; possibly ed. at Winchester, 1770-73; *suc. to the Baronetcy*, 8 Nov. 1774; was Lord Mayor of York, 1787 and 1790, and was M.P. for that city (five Parls.), 1790 till death in 1811. He *m.* in 1776, Diana, da. of Humphrey STURT, of Critchill, Dorset, by Mary, da. and h. of Charles PITFIELD of Hoxton, Midx. She *d.* at Exeter, 15 Jan. 1805. He *d.* 9 Sep. 1811, in his 57th year, and was *bur.* at Bolton Percy. Will pr. 1811.

IV. 1811. SIR WILLIAM MORDAUNT STURT MILNER, Baronet [1717], of Nun-Appleton aforesaid, 1st s. and h., *b.* there 1 Oct. 1779; ed. at Eton; matric. at Oxford (Ch. Ch.), 19 Feb. 1798, aged 18; sometime in the Yorkshire Militia; *suc. to the Baronetcy*, 9 Sep. 1811; Sheriff of Yorkshire, 1717-18. He *m.* firstly, 13 July 1803, at St. Geo. Han. sq., Selina, da. of the Rt. Hon. Theophilus CLEMENTS, of Ashfield, co. Cavan, by his 2d wife, Catherine, da. of the Rt. Hon. John BERESFORD. She *d.* s.p.m., 28 May 1805. He *m.* secondly, 28 May 1809, Harriet, 1st da. of Lord Edward Charles Cavendish BENTINCK (yr. s. of William, 2d DUKE OF PORTLAND), by Elizabeth, da. of Richard CUMBERLAND, the well-known dramatist. He *d.* 25 March 1855, at Nun-Appleton, aged 75. Will pr. May 1855. His widow, who was *b.* 9 April 1787, *d.* 31 Dec. 1862, aged 75.

V. 1855. SIR WILLIAM MORDAUNT EDWARD MILNER, Baronet [1717], of Nun-Appleton aforesaid, 1st s. and h. by 2d wife, *b.* there 20 June 1820; ed. at Eton; matric. at Oxford (Ch. Ch.), 30 May 1838, aged 17; B.A., 1841; M.A., 1844; was, v.p., M.P. for York, 1848-57, having *suc. to the Baronetcy*, 25 March 1855. He *m.* 16 April 1844, Georgiana Anne, sister of Richard George, 9th EARL OF SCARBROUGH, 3d da. of Frederick LUMLEY-SAVILE, of Tickhill Castle, co. York, by Charlotte, da. of George BERESFORD, Bishop of Kilmore. He *d.* at Nun-Appleton, 12 Feb. 1867, aged 46, and was *bur.* at Tadcaster. His widow, who had been raised to the rank of the daughter of an Earl, by Royal warrant, dated 1857, *d.* 2 Feb. 1877, at 48 Eaton square.

VI. 1867. SIR WILLIAM MORDAUNT MILNER, Baronet [1717], of Nun-Appleton aforesaid, 1st s. and h., *b.* 10 May 1848, in Eaton place; ed. at Eton; matric. at Oxford (Ch. Ch.), 23 May 1866, aged 18; *suc. to the Baronetcy*, 12 Feb. 1867; was sometime Captain in the East Yorkshire Militia. He *d.* unm. at Cairo, 14 April 1880, in his 32d year.

VII. 1880. SIR FREDERICK GEORGE MILNER, Baronet [1717], of Nun-Appleton aforesaid, br. and h., *b.* 7 Nov. 1849; ed. at Eton; matric. at Oxford (Ch. Ch.), 30 May 1868, aged 18; B.A., 1873; *suc. to the Baronetcy*, 14 April 1880; was M.P. for York, 1883-85, and for the Bassetlaw Division of Notts since 1890; P.C., 1900. He *m.* 19 Oct. 1889, at Nun-Appleton, Adeline Gertrude Demson, 2d da. of William BECKETT, of Meamood Park, co. York, by Helen, da. of William (DUNCOMBE), 2d BARON FEVERSHAM. She was *b.* 14 May 1859.

Family Estates.—These, in 1883, consisted of 5,491 acres in the West Riding of Yorkshire, valued at £8,977 a year. *Seat.*—Nun-Appleton, near Tadcaster, co. York.

PERROTT:

cr. 1 July 1717, *or* 1 July 1716, *see* under 1716.

ELTON:(a)

cr. 31 Oct. 1717.

I. 1717. ABRAHAM ELTON, of the city of Bristol, Esq., s. of Isaac ELTON, of St. Philip and St. Jacob's, Barton Regis, Bristol, Citizen and Freeholder of Bristol (*bur.* 31 March 1695, at St. Philip's aforesaid,(b) by his 1st wife, Elizabeth (*bur.* there 28 Nov. 1677), was *bap.* 3 [?] July 1654, at St. Philip's; went to sea, 1672, but settled at Bristol as early as 1680, where for many years he was at the head of the commerce of that city.(c) He was President of the "Gloucestershire Society," 1689; admitted to Merchant Venturers, 1690; Sheriff of Bristol, 1702; Master of the Merchant Venturers, 1708; Mayor of Bristol, 1710; and having bought the estate of Clevedon Court, Somerset, in 1709, and that of Whitestaunton, in that county, in 1714 (the manor house itself not till 1723), as well as other properties in Somerset, Gloucestershire and Wilts, was Sheriff of Gloucestershire, 1716, and, taking an active part against the Jacobite rising in 1715, was *cr. a Baronet*, as above, 31 Oct. 1717. He was M.P. for Bristol, 1722-27, and a staunch supporter

(a) Much of the information in this article has been kindly supplied by Ambrose Elton, 1st s. of the present (the 8th) Baronet.

(b) The family were settled in this parish as early as 1608, when their name first appears in the parish register in a baptism (24 Feb.) of "Mary, da. of Thomas Elton, Dr. of Physic." This Dr. Thomas Elton, who *d.* at Bath, 1618, left a large family (mostly *bap.* at Bristol), and makes his brother, Ambrose Elton, of the Hazles, near Ledbury, one of his executors. One of his sons, Richard Elton, of Bristol (*bap.* 29 April 1610 in the same parish), was Col. of the London Train bands, and was afterwards Deputy Gov. of Hull, being a well known Puritan, as were most of his Bristol kindred. They, according to Wotton's *Baronetage* [1741] (who states it to be "*ex inform.* Ab. Elton, Bar., 1727"), were "of an ancient family, till lately of the Hazle in Herefordshire, and Gloucestershire." This letter, dated 26 Sep. 1725 [*sic*], is written in the third person, and is [1905] among the *Addit. MSS.* [24,120, fo. 301] in the British Museum. The date of "1727" as ascribed to it in Wotton's *Baronetage* [second edition 1741] means, no doubt, that the information was given for the first edition of that work, which was issued in 1727.

(c) "He was pioneer of its Brassfoundaries and Ironfoundaries, and was owner of its principal weaving industry, as well as of its Glass and Pottery works, besides largely contributing to the shipping of the port." [See note "a" above].

of Walpole. He *m.* 11 Sep. 1676, at St. Philip's aforesaid, Mary, da. of Robert JEFFERIES, of Pile Green, co. Gloucester. He *d.* at his house in Small street, Bristol, 9 Feb. 1727/8, and was *bur.* "with great pomp" at St. Philip's aforesaid. Will pr. 14 March 1727/8 and 5 June 1728. His widow *d.* in Small street, Bristol, 25 April 1728, and was *bur.* with him. Will pr. 6 May 1728.

II. 1728. SIR ABRAHAM ELTON, Baronet [1717], of Clevedon Court aforesaid, 1st s. and h., *bap.* 30 June 1679, at St. John's the Baptist, Bristol; Sheriff of Bristol, 1710; Master of the Merchant Venturers, 1719; Alderman and sometime (1719) Mayor of Bristol; M.P. for Taunton, 1724-27, and for Bristol, 1727, till death 1742; *suc. to the Baronetcy,* 9 Feb. 1727/8. He *m.* 14 May 1702, at Westbury, Wilts (settl. 12 May 1702) Abigail, da. of Zachary BAYLY, of Charlcot House, near Westbury aforesaid, and of Northwood Park, near Glastonbury, Somerset, by Abigail, da. of (—) COOKE. She was *bur.* at St. Nicholas, Bristol. He *d.* 20 Oct. 1742, and was *bur.* at Clevedon, aged 63. Will pr. 1743.

III. 1743. SIR ABRAHAM ELTON, Baronet [1717], of Clevedon Court aforesaid, 1st s. and h., *b.* at Bristol, 1703; Sheriff thereof, 1728; Mayor, 1742; *suc. to the Baronetcy,* 20 Oct. 1742, and to the Clevedon estate, having previously, on the death of his grandparents in 1728, succeeded to others (of very considerable value), all of which last he alienated.(a) He *d.* unm., 29 Nov. 1761, at Bristol, and was *bur.* at Clevedon, aged 58. Will pr. 1762.

IV. 1761. SIR ABRAHAM ISAAC ELTON, Baronet [1717], of Clevedon Court aforesaid, br. and h., being 3d and yst. s. of the 2d Baronet,(b) *b.* 1717 at Bristol; admitted to the Inner Temple, 4 March 1735, and to Lincoln's Inn, 19 July 1742; Barrister, 24 Nov. 1742; Town Clerk of Bristol, 1753-86; *suc. to the Baronetcy,* 29 Nov. 1761; Master of the Merchant Venturers, 1767; and many years Chairman of the Somerset Quarter Sessions. He *m.* 26 Dec. 1747, at Bristol, Elizabeth, da. of James READ, merchant of that city. She *d.* before 1771. He *d.* at Bath, 5 Feb. 1790, and was *bur.* at Clevedon, aged 73. Will pr. Feb. 1790.

V. 1790. SIR ABRAHAM ELTON, Baronet [1717], of Clevedon Court aforesaid, only s. and h., *b.* 23 March and *bap.* May 1755, at Bristol; matric. at Oxford (Queen's Coll.), 9 April 1772, aged 17; B.A., 1775; incorp. at Cambridge (Christ's Coll.), 1778; M.A., 1778; took Holy Orders, and was, in 1786, and for some years subsequently, Minister and Lecturer at West Bromwich, co. Stafford; *suc. to the Baronetcy,* 5 Feb. 1790; and was many years Chairman of the Somerset Quarter Sessions. He *m.* firstly, 7 Nov. 1776, Elizabeth, 1st da. of Sir John DURBIN, of Walton Manor house, Somerset, sometime (1777 and 1778) Mayor of Bristol, by Elizabeth, da. and h. of John COLLETT, of Bristol. She *d.* 29 March 1822, and was *bur.* at Clevedon, aged 65. He *m.* secondly, 29 March 1823, at Clifton, Mary, 1st da. of William STEWART, of Castle Stewart, co. Wigton, by Euphemia, da. of Kenneth MACKENZIE, *styled* LORD FORTROSE, s. and h. ap. of William, the 5th and attainted EARL OF SEAFORTH [S.]. He *d.* at the Royal Hotel, Clevedon, 23 Feb. 1842, and was *bur.* at Clevedon, aged 86. Will pr. April 1842. His widow *d.* s.p. 6 Dec. 1849, at Clevedon, and was *bur.* there, aged 76. Will pr. Jan. 1850.

(a) The estates of Whitestaunton and Winford, which had been purchased by the 1st Baronet, were not included, and they had been left by him to his 2d surv. son, Jacob Elton, Mayor of Bristol, 1733, whose descendant (in the male line) still (1905) owns the former.

(b) Jacob Elton, Captain R.N., the 2d son, *d.* s.p. 29 March 1745, being slain in a most bravely contested sea fight with the French. M.I. in Bristol Cathedral.

VI. 1842. SIR CHARLES ABRAHAM ELTON, Baronet [1717], of Clevedon Court aforesaid, 1st s. and h.,(a) *b.* 31 Oct. 1778, at St. James' Barton, Bristol, and *bap.* at St. James' there; ed. at Eton; was, in 1796, an officer in the 48th Foot, serving in Holland in 1799, under the Duke of York; Capt. 1809; was Lieut.-Col. of the Somerset militia; *suc. to the Baronetcy,* 23 Feb. 1842. He *m.* 27 Feb. 1804, at St. Michael's, Bristol, Sarah, 1st da. of Joseph SMITH, of Berkeley crescent, Bristol, merchant (sometime, 1794, Mayor of Bristol), by Sarah, da. of Michael POPE, of Whitsun Court, Bristol. She, who was *b.* at Whitsun Court, 1 Oct. 1782, and *bap.* there, *d.* 14 March 1830, and was *bur.* at Clevedon, aged 48. He, who was a good classical scholar and a poet,(b) *d.* 1 June 1853, at the house of his son-in-law (the Rev. Edward Douglas TINLING), in the Royal crescent, Bath, and was *bur.* at Clevedon, aged 74. Will pr. Aug. 1853.

VII. 1853. SIR ARTHUR HALLAM ELTON, Baronet [1717], of Clevedon Court aforesaid, 3d but 1st surv. s. and h.,(c) *b.* 19 April 1818, at Belle View place, Clifton, and *bap.* there; ed. at Blundell's school, Tiverton, and at Sandhurst; was, in Oct. 1836, an officer in 14th Foot, retiring 1841; *suc. to the Baronetcy,* 1 June 1853; Sheriff of Somerset, 1857-58; M.P. for Bath (Liberal interest) from April 1857 to May 1859; Capt. 1st Somerset Artillery Volunteers, 1860. He *m.* firstly, 10 June 1841, at Southampton, Rhoda Susan, widow of James Charles BAIRD, Capt. 15th Hussars, 2d da. of James WILLIS, of Atherfield and of Freshwater house, Isle of Wight, by Flora, da. of William WYNCH, of the East India Service, Secretary to the Nabob of Arcot. She, who was *b.* 16 May 1809, at Atherfield, and *bap.* at Freshwater aforesaid, *d.* 1 Nov. 1873, at Staunton house, Bournemouth, and was *bur.* at All Saints', East Clevedon, aged 63. He *m.* secondly, 20 Nov. 1876, at Weare, Somerset, Eliza, widow of the Rev. William MATHIAS, Incumbent of Burtle, Somerset, da. of Edward Austice STRADLING, of Bridgwater, by Eliza, da. of (—) ANSTICE. He, who was author of some works of fiction, and of several political pamphlets, and who was for sometime associated with the *Saturday Review*, *d.* s.p.m.,(d) 14 Oct. 1883, aged 65, at Clevedon Court, having never recovered from the shock of a fire which greatly damaged that house (destroying the greater part of his library and most of the west wing) some eleven months before, and was *bur.* at All Saints', East Clevedon. His widow, by whom he had no issue, *d.* 5 Jan. 1884, at 39 Kensington square, in her 63d year, and was *bur.* at All Saints' aforesaid.

VIII. 1883. SIR EDMUND HARRY ELTON, Baronet [1717], of Clevedon Court aforesaid, nephew and h. male, being only s. and h. of Edmund William ELTON, of Florence, a painter of considerable merit, by his 1st wife Lucy Maria, da. of the Rev. John Morgan RICE, of the Manor house, Tooting, Surrey, which Edmund William, who *d.* 2 Dec. 1859, aged 36, was next br. to the late Baronet. He was *b.* 3 May 1846, at Royal York crescent, Clifton,

(a) His only sister, Julia Maria, *m.* in Jan. 1807, Henry Hallam, the well-known Historian (*d.* 21 Jan. 1859, aged 81), and was mother of Arthur Henry Hallam (*bur.* with his maternal ancestors at Clevedon), whose early death, 15 Sep. 1833, aged 22, is commemorated by Tennyson (though nearly twenty years later) in the well known "*In Memoriam.*"

(b) "His most important work was his *Specimens of the Classic Poets, in a chronological series from Homer to Tryphiodorus; translated into English verse.* This collection contains passages from sixty ancient poets, viz., thirty-three Greek and twenty-seven Latin, the translations of which are of much merit. His characters of the poets prefixed to each specimen are written in a spirit of nicely descriminating criticism." [*Annual Reg.*, 1853].

(c) The two elder sons, Abraham and Charles, were drowned v.p. in boyhood, while bathing in the Bristol Channel, 20 Sep. 1819.

(d) Of his two surv. daughters and coheirs (1) Laura Beatrice, *m.* 3 Jan. 1864, George Louis Monck Gibbs, of Belmont, in Wraxall, co. Somerset (who *d.* 26 Nov. 1881), and has issue; (2) Mary Agnes, *m.* 7 July 1868, her cousin, the 8th Baronet, as in the text.

and *bap.* at Clifton; ed. at Bradfield Coll., Berks, and at Jesus Coll., Cambridge; *suc. to the Baronetcy,* 14 Oct. 1883; Sheriff of Somerset, 1895; Hon. Lieut.-Col. 1st Batt. Gloucester Artillery Vols.; originator and sole designer of the "*Elton ware.*"(a) He *m.* 7 July 1868, at All Saints', East Clevedon, Mary Agnes, 2d and yst. da. and coheir of his uncle, Sir Arthur Hallam ELTON, 7th Baronet [1717], by his 1st wife Rhoda Susan, da. of James WILLIS, all abovenamed.

Family Estates.—These, in 1883, consisted of 4,200 acres in Somerset, mis-stated in Bateman's *Great Landowners*, 1883, as 2,411, and there stated to be worth £8,206 a year. *Seat.*—Clevedon Court, near Bristol, Somerset.

BRIDGES:

cr. 19 April 1718;

sometime, 1868-75, BARON FITZWALTER OF WOODHAM WALTER;

ex. 27 Nov. 1899.

I. 1718. BROOK BRIDGES, of Goodneston, co. Kent, Esq, 1st s. and h. of Brook BRIDGES,(b) of the same, and of Grove, co. Midx., Auditor of the Imprest. of the Treasury, purchaser of the Goodneston estate, and builder of the mansion there (*b.* 2 Jan. 1643(c), and *d.* 23 Dec. 1717, aged 74), by Mary (*m.* 18 Nov. 1672, at St. Barth.-the-Less, London), da. of Sir Justinian LEWEN, was *b.* 12 Aug. 1679;(c) admitted to the Middle Temple, London, 25 April 1713, was (like his father) one of the Auditors of the Imprest., and was *cr. a Baronet,* as above, 19 April 1718; F.R.S. He *m.* firstly, 23 June 1707, at the Chapel Royal, Whitehall, Margaret, sister of Robert, 1st BARON ROMNEY, da. of Sir Robert MARSHAM, 4th Baronet [1663], by Margaret, da. and h. of Thomas BOSVILLE. He *m.* secondly, Mary, da. of Sir Thomas HALES, 2d Baronet [1660], of Blaksbourne, by Mary, da. of Sir Charles PYM, 1st Baronet [1663]. She *d.* 6 July 1724. He *d.* 16 March 1727/8, aged 48. Will pr. 1728.

II. 1728. SIR BROOK BRIDGES, Baronet [1718], of Goodneston Park in Goodneston aforesaid, 1st and only surv. s. and h., by 1st wife, *b.* there 12 March 1708/9;(c) matric. at Oxford (Ch. Ch.), 10 June 1726, aged 17; *suc. to the Baronetcy,* 16 March 1727/8; was Sheriff of Kent, 14 Dec. 1732, till his death five months later. He *m.*, about 1732, his cousin, Anne, da. and coheir of Sir Thomas PALMER, 4th Baronet [1621], of Wingham, by his 1st wife, Elizabeth, da. of Sir Robert MARSHAM, 4th Baronet [1663], abovenamed. He *d.* 23 May 1733, aged 24. Will pr. 1733. His widow, who was *bap.* 26 July 1714, at Wingham, *m.* in 1737, Lieut.-Colonel the Hon. Charles FEILDING (who *d.* 6 Feb. 1745/6), and *d.* 16 Feb. 1742/3. Admon., as of St. James', Westm., 20 March 1742/3 and 30 March 1767.

(a) This handsome decorative pottery made by himself at Clevedon Court, has been awarded seven International first class gold medals, besides several others at minor exhibitions. He was, in Dec. 1900, elected a member of the *Arts and Crafts Society*, on the motion of (the well-known) Walter Crane.

(b) This Brook Bridges, the 2d s. of Col. John Bridges, of Alcester, co. Warwick, was yr. br. of John Bridges, of Barton Segrave, co. Northampton, father of John Bridges, the well-known historian of that county, who *d.* 1724, aged 58, his work being published in 1791, sixty-seven years after his death.

(c) The following notes, probably written by the 1st Baronet, are at the back of the engraved title of an Oxford New Testament, 1675:—" . . . oke Bridges, Andr, borne 21 Janny 1643; Brook Bridges his sonn was borne 12 Augt 1679; Jno Bridges, yonger sonn, borne 2 July 1682; Brooke Bridges, grandson to ye Auditor was borne at Goodnestone 12 March 1708/9." [*Ex inform.*—Ernest Axon, Reference Library, King Street, Manchester].

III. 1733. SIR BROOK BRIDGES, Baronet [1718], of Goodneston Park aforesaid, posthumous s. and h., *b.* 17 Sep. 1733, at Whitehall, and *suc. to the Baronetcy* on his birth; was M.P. for Kent, Nov. 1763 to 1768, and 1768-74; and Receiver-General of the Land Tax of that county. He *m.* 11 June 1765, at St. Geo. Han. sq., Fanny, only surv. da. and h. of Edmund FOWLER,(a) of Graces, in Little Baddow and of Danbury, Essex, by Elizabeth, da. of (—) PATESHALL, of Worcester. He *d.* 4 Sep. 1791, in Portman square, and was *bur.* at Goodneston, aged nearly 58. Will pr. Sep. 1791. His widow, who was *b.* 5 and *bap.* 29 Dec. 1746, at Little Baddow, *d.* 16 March 1825, aged 78, and was *bur.* at Goodneston. Will pr. April 1825.

IV. 1791. SIR BROOK WILLIAM BRIDGES, Baronet [1718], of Goodneston Park aforesaid, and of Woodham Walter, co. Essex, *formerly* WILLIAM BRIDGES, 3d but 1st surv. s. and h.,(b) *b.* 22 June 1767, at Goodneston; took the Christian name of *Brook* before that of *William*, by lic. from the Bishop of the diocese.(c) He was in the Royal Navy, becoming, eventually, Commander. He *suc. to the Baronetcy,* 4 Sep. 1791. He *m.* firstly, 14 Aug. 1800, at Bexley, co. Kent, Eleanor, da. and eventually coheir of John FOOTE, of Lombard street, London, Banker. She *d.* 29 Jan. 1806. Will pr. May 1832. He *m.* secondly, 15 Dec. 1809, Dorothy Elizabeth, 1st da. of Sir Henry HAWLEY, 1st Baronet [1795], of Leybourne Grange, Kent, by his 1st wife, Dorothy, da. and h. of John ASHWOOD. She *d.* 17 May 1826. He *d.* 21 April 1829, in Albemarle street, aged 61, and was *bur.* at Goodneston. Will pr. May 1829.

V. 1829. SIR BROOK WILLIAM BRIDGES, Baronet [1718], of Goodneston Park and Woodham Walter aforesaid, 1st s. and h., *b.* 2 June 1801, at Goodneston; ed. at Winchester, 1814; matric. at Oxford (Oriel Coll.), 13 Feb. 1819, aged 17; B.A., 1822; M.A., 1827; *suc. to the Baronetcy,* 21 April 1829; M.P. for East Kent, Feb. to July 1852, and (three other Parls.) 1857 till *cr. a Peer* in 1868. He claimed in 1841 the *Barony of Fitzwalter* (*cr.* 1295), and proved himself heir to a moiety (and probably to the entirety) thereof. The abeyance however was not terminated in his favour,(d) though some twenty-

(a) This Edmund (who *d.* 25 July 1751, aged 50) was s. and h. of Christopher Fowler, of Hackney, Midx., by Frances, da. and coheir of Henry Mildmay, of Graces aforesaid, and Mary, his wife, sister and coheir of Benjamin (Mildmay), Lord Fitzwalter (1295), who was *cr.*, in 1730, Earl Fitzwalter. On his death, s.p., 29 Feb. 1756, Fanny Fowler (afterwards Lady Bridges) became (in right of her said grandmother, Frances Mildmay) one of the three coheirs of that ancient Barony.

(b) Brook Bridges, the 1st s., was *b.* 14 Aug. 1766, and *d.* v.p. 9 July 1781.

(c) Presumably this was done at Confirmation, but there is no indication as to the date, which was probably after the death (9 July 1781) of his elder br. Brook. There is a curious note on this *ecclesiastical* "assumption of a new christian name" in Betham's *Baronetage* [1803], which, however, in Foster's *Baronetage* is stated to have been done by Act of Parliament. An instance of change of baptismal name is entered in the parish register of St. Finn Barr's Cathedral, Cork, under 21 Sep. 1761, being that of Lieut. Robert St. George Caulfield, 93d Foot, then presented for confirmation, who was permitted by the Bishop to change his name of *Robert St. George* to that of *William*, and was confirmed as William.

(d) A vulgar proverb says that "Kissing goes by favour," and the Whig Ministry of the early Victorian period were scrupulously careful not to allow any considerations of Equity or Desert to prevent the extension of this sound maxim to the domain of abeyances. Sir Brooke's politics were Tory and this ensured the rejection of his claim, and it mattered not at all that the abeyance of numerous Baronies (*e.g.* Beaumont, Braye, Camoys, Hastings, etc.), were, at or about the same time terminated, these being in favour of Whig claimants (notwithstanding the fact that the said Baronies had been for centuries unheard of and that the fortunate claimants in most cases represented a very small fraction of them), while in *this* case the Barony of Fitzwalter had continued uninterruptedly from 1295 to 1756, and the claimant (who in all probability was heir to the entirety) was undoubtedly the representative of a moiety thereof.

seven years later he was *cr.*, 17 April 1868, BARON FITZWALTER OF WOODHAM WALTER, co. Essex. He *m.* 4 July 1834, his cousin Fanny, 1st da. of Lewis CAGE, of Milgate in Bersted, Kent, by Fanny, da. of Sir Brook BRIDGES, 3d Baronet [1718]. She *d.* 28 Oct. 1874, at Goodneston Park, aged 81. He *d.* there s.p. 6 Dec. 1875, aged 74, when the *Peerage* became *extinct.*

VI. 1875. SIR BROOK GEORGE BRIDGES, Baronet [1718], of Goodneston Park aforesaid, only br. and h., *b.* there 12 Oct. 1802; matric. at Oxford (Oriel Coll.), 22 May 1821, aged 18; B.A., 1825; in Holy Orders; Rector of Orlingbury, co. Northampton, 1827-53; Rector of Blanckney, co. Lincoln, 1853-78. He *suc. to the Baronetcy*, 6 Dec. 1875. He *m.* 15 Nov. 1832, at St. Marylebone, Louisa, 4th da. of Charles CHAPLIN, of Blanckney aforesaid, by Elizabeth, da. and h. of Robert TAYLOR, M.D. She *d.* 21 Jan. 1884, at Goodneston, aged 88. He *d.* there s.p. 1 April 1890, aged 87.(a)

VII. 1890. SIR THOMAS PYM BRIDGES, Baronet [1718], cousin and h. male, being 2d but 1st surv. s. of the Rev. Brook Henry BRIDGES, M.A., Rector of Danbury and of Woodham Ferrers, co. Essex, by Jane, da. of Sir Thomas Pym HALES, 4th Baronet [1660], which Brook Henry (who *d.* 20 Sep. 1855, aged 86) was yr. br. of the 4th and 2d s. of the 3d Baronet. He was *b.* 22 Oct. 1805; ed. at Winchester; matric. at Oxford (Ch. Ch.), 6 Nov. 1823, aged 18; B.A., 1828; was in Holy Orders; Rector of Danbury aforesaid, 1855 till death; *suc. to the Baronetcy*, 1 April 1890. He *m.* 14 June 1831, Sophia Louisa, da. of Sir William Lawrence YOUNG, 3d Baronet [1769], by Louisa, da. of William TUFNELL. She *d.* 4 Jan. 1850. He *d.* s.p.m. 28 Feb. 1895, at Danbury Rectory, aged 89. Will pr. in Ireland and resealed in London, at £2,874.

VIII. 1895, to 1899. SIR GEORGE TALBOT BRIDGES, Baronet [1718], cousin and h. male, being 4th and yst. but last surv. s. of the Rev. Brook Edward BRIDGES, Vicar of Lenham and Incumbent of Wingham, co. Kent, by Harriet, da. and coheir of John FOOTE, of Lombard street, London, Banker, abovenamed, which Brook Edward (who *d.* 23 April 1825, aged 45) was yr. br. of the 4th and 3d s. of the 3d Baronet. He was *b.* 10 May(b) 1818, at Ramsgate, and was ed. at a school there; practised Law till 1845, when he entered the Jesuit Novitiate, taking Holy Orders in 1853, and going as a Missionary to India in 1858, where he remained till his death forty-one years later. He *suc. to the Baronetcy*, 28 Feb. 1895. He *d.* unm. 27 Nov. 1899, at Bhosawne, near Bombay, in the Deccan of Hindustan, and was *bur.* there, aged 81, when the *Baronetcy* became *extinct.*

BLACKWELL:

cr. 16 July 1718;

ex. 9 May 1801.

I. 1718. SIR LAMBERT BLACKWELL, of Sprowston Hall, co. Norfolk, Knt., one of the younger of the seventeen children of Captain John BLACKWELL, of Mortlake, co. Surrey (an active Parliamentary officer, 1650-58, but living long afterwards, 1688, as Governor of Pennsylvania), by Elizabeth, da. of James SMITHSBY, was, in 1697, made Knight Harbinger and Gentleman of the Privy Council, being *Knighted*, 18 May 1697. From 1698 to 1705 he was Envoy to Tuscany and Genoa, residing at Genoa; was M.P. for Wilton, 1708-10; was one of the Governors of the South Sea Company in

(a) On his death the coheirship to the Barony of Fitzwalter devolved on his only sister, Eleanor, widow of the Rev. Henry Western Plumptree, and at her death, 24 Jan. 1892, on her issue.

(b) Not *Aug.* (as in Foster's *Baronetage*) 1883. This and the rest of the information about this Baronet since his admission to the Jesuit Society has been kindly supplied by the Rev. John George MacLeod, of the Jesuit College, Manresa House, Roehampton, Surrey.

1717,(a) and was *cr. a Baronet*, as above, 16 July 1718. He *m.* before Feb. 1697/8, probably about 1700, Elizabeth, 2d da. of Sir Joseph HERNE, of London, Merchant, by Elizabeth, da. of Sir John FREDERICK, sometime (1661-62) Lord Mayor of London. He *d.* 27 Oct. 1727. Will pr. 1727. His widow, who was *b.* 24 May and *bap.* 11 June 1678, at St. Olave's, Old Jewry, *d.* 12 Oct. 1729. Will pr. 1729.

II. 1727. SIR CHARLES BLACKWELL, Baronet [1718], of Sprowston aforesaid, only s. and h.; *b.* probably about 1700; *suc. to the Baronetcy*, 27 Oct. 1727. He *m.*, in or before 1721, Anne, da. of Sir William CLAYTON, 1st Baronet [1732], of Marden, co. Surrey, by Martha, da. of John KENRICK, of London, Merchant. He *d.* 18 July 1741. Admon. as of St. James', Westm., 5 Aug. 1741. His widow *m.* 19 Aug. 1742, at the Chapel Royal, Whitehall (Lic. Fac. 18), as his 1st wife, the Rev. John THOMAS, D.C.L., then Rector of Bletchingley, Surrey, afterwards (1768), Dean of Westminster, and (after her death) Bishop of Rochester (1774-93), who *d.* 22 Aug. 1793. She *d.* 7 July 1772.

III. 1741, to 1801. SIR LAMBERT BLACKWELL, Baronet [1718], of Sprowston aforesaid, only s. and h., *b.* about 1732; matric. at Oxford (Ch. Ch.), 26 April 1750, aged 17; *suc. to the Baronetcy*, 18 July 1741. He *m.* Amelia, widow of Michael POPE, of Whitsun Court, Bristol, da. of Col. MARTIN.(b) He *d.* s.p., 9 May 1801, aged 69, when the *Baronetcy* became *extinct*. He left "all his estate, with his valuable collection of paintings, books, coins, etc., to William FOSTER, Junior, Esq., of Norwich."(c)

OUGHTON:

cr. 27 Aug. 1718;

ex. 4 Sep 1736.

I. 1718, to 1736. ADOLPHUS OUGHTON, of Tachbrooke, co. Warwick, Esq., s. and h. of Adolphus OUGHTON, of Fillongley and Great Harborough, in that county, by Mary, da. of Richard SAMWELL, of Upton, co. Northampton, was *b.* about 1685; matric. at Oxford (Trin. Coll.), 19 March 1701/2, aged 17; admitted to Middle Temple, 1703; was M.P. for Coventry (four Parls.), 1715, till death in 1736, and, having been proxy for H.R.H. the Duke of York on his instalment as Knight of the Garter (30 April 1718), was *cr. a Baronet*, as above, 27 Aug. 1718. He was Colonel of the 8th Dragoons, 1733, and was a Brig. General 1735. He *m.* firstly, his cousin Frances, widow of Sir Edward BAGOT, 4th Baronet [1627], da. and h. of Sir Thomas WAGSTAFFE, of Tachbrooke aforesaid, by Frances, da. of Richard SAMWELL abovenamed. She *d.* in or before 1714. Her admon., as of Tachbrooke, 24 July 1714. He *m.* secondly, Elizabeth, da. of John BABER, by Mary, da. and coheir of Sir Thomas DRAPER, Baronet [1660], of Sunninghill Park, Berks. He *d.* s.p. legit.(d) 4 Sep. 1736, when the *Baronetcy* became *extinct*. Will pr. 1737. His widow *d.* in or before 1749. Her admon. as "of Sunninghill Park, Berks, widow," granted 29 April 1749, to her br. and next of kin "John BABER, Esq."

(a) See p. 10, note "c," under "LAMBERT" Baronetcy [1711] for a notice of this Company.

(b) The following inscription is written on the back of a miniature now (1905) at Clevedon Court, Somerset, by Marianne Smith, sister of Sarah, wife of Sir Charles Abraham Elton, 6th Baronet [1717]:—"Amelia, da. of Colonel Martin, wife of Michael Pope, of Whitsun Court, Bristol, married secondly Sir Lambert Blackwell, Bt. My grandmother. M.S."

(c) *Annual Register* for 1801.

(d) His illegit. son, Lieut.-Gen. Sir James Adolphus Oughton, K.B., Colonel 55th Foot, *d.* 14 and was *bur.* 16 April 1780, in Bath Abbey. Dame Mary Oughton, the widow, *d.* 20 Dec. 1793.

FELLOWS:

cr. 20 Jan. 1718/9;

ex. 26 July 1724.

I. 1719, to 1724. JOHN FELLOWS, of Carshalton, co. Surrey, Esq., Deputy Governor of the South Sea Company,(a) was *b.* about 1671; was a merchant in London, purchased (for £3,500) Dr. Ratcliffe's house in Carshalton, and was *cr. a Baronet*, as above, 20 Jan. 1718/9. He *d.* s.p., presumably unm., 26 July, and was *bur.* 5 Aug. 1724, at Carshalton, aged 53, when the *Baronetcy* became *extinct.*(b) Will pr. 1724.

CHARDIN?

cr. 28 May 1720;

ex. 26 April 1755.

I. 1720, to 1755. JOHN CHARDIN, of the Inner Temple, London, Esq., s. and h. of Sir John CHARDIN, the well known Eastern traveller, Court Jeweller, and sometime (1684) Envoy to Holland, by Esther (*m.* 17 Nov. 1681), da. of (—) DE LARDINIERE PEIGNÉ, sometime a Counsellor of Parl. at Rouen, was *bap.* at Greenwich, 6 Oct. 1687; admitted to the Inner Temple, London, and having suc. his father (who *d.* aged 70), 25 Dec. 1713,(c) was, presumably, for his father's services, *cr. a Baronet*, as above, 28 May 1720. He purchased before 1741 the estate of Kempton Park, in Sunbury, Midx.(d) He *d.* unm. 26 April, and was *bur.* 10 May 1755, in Westm. Abbey (under his father's monument), aged 67, when the *Baronetcy* became *extinct*. Will dat. 18 July 1747 to (—) 1753, pr. 28 April 1755.

BLUNT:

cr. 17 June 1720.(e)

I. 1720. JOHN BLUNT, of [St. Michael's, Cornhill] London, Esq., residing at Stratford in Westham, co. Essex, s. of Thomas BLUNT, of Rochester (formerly of Strood), co. Kent, Shoemaker (who was freeman of Rochester, by purchase, 1 Sep. 1655, and who was *bur.* at St. Nicholas' in that city, 28 March 1703),(f) by Isabella, da. of Thomas BLACKE, of Frindsbury in

(a) See p. 10, note "c," under "LAMBERT" Baronetcy [1711], for a notice of this Company.

(b) "Edward Fellowes, Esq.," was *bur.* at Carshalton, 23 Jan. 1730/1. He was a Master in Chancery and br. of the Baronet.

(c) His monument at Westm. Abbey has this appropriate inscription, "nomen sibi fecit eundo."

(d) That estate he is said to have presented as early as 1746 to his nephew (son of his sister Julia), Sir Philip Musgrave, 6th Baronet [1611] of Edenhall, who certainly held it after his death, and who *d.* there, 5 July 1795, aged 84.

(e) "In Salmon's chronology the names of Blunt, Chapman, and Colby or Coleby, stand created Baronets on June 13 [1720], and Oswald Mosley on the 29th of the same month." [Continuation of Dugdale's *Catalogue of Baronets*, 1812].

(f) The entry there is "Thomas Blunt, Shewmaker, a Baptist, put into ye ground, March ye 28, 1703."

that county,(a) was *b.* 24 July 1665, and *bap.* at St. Nicholas', Rochester(b); was free of the Merchant Taylors' Company, 5 May 1689, and a Liveryman, 11 March 1691; was a Freeman of Rochester (by patrimony), 25 June 1698; practised sometime in London as a Scrivener; was Common Councilman for Cornhill Ward, 1717, being then a leading merchant and a Director of the South Sea Company,(c) and was *cr. a Baronet*, as above, 17 June 1720. In Aug. following he was "fined" for refusing to be Master of the Merchant Taylors' Company, in which month the shares of the South Sea Company (in which he was deeply involved) were at their highest price, but before Christmas it had collapsed, and he (as were the other Directors) was compelled to render the value of his estate, which, in his case, was £183,349 10s. 8¾d.(d) Twelve years later, *viz.* in 1732, he was fined by the Court of Chivalry for usurping the Arms of the family of Blount, of Sodington.(e) He *m.* firstly, 16 July 1689, Elizabeth, da. of (—) COURT, of co. Warwick. She *d.* 22 March 1707/8, and was *bur.* at Moorfields, Midx. He *m.* secondly, 22 (articles dat. 15) Dec. 1713, Susanna, widow of Benjamin TUDMAN, of Lombard street, formerly widow of John BANNER, of St. Peter le Poor Salter, da. of Richard CRADDOCK, sometime Governor of Bengal. He *d.* at Bath, 24 Jan. 1732/3, aged 67, and was *bur.* at Moorfields. Will dat. 13 Feb. 1731/2 to 15 Jan. 1732/3, pr. 3 Feb. 1732/3. His widow, by whom he had no issue, *d.* 8 and was *bur.* 16 Sep. 1743, aged 76, at St. Vedast, Foster lane, with her first husband. Will as of Westham, Essex, dat. 27 Nov. 1742, pr. 10 Sep. 1743.

(a) Their marriage, 27 March 1654, is thus recorded at Stroud, co. Kent, "Thomas Blunt, of Strood, Shoemaker (the son of John Blunt, of St. Sepulchre's, London, Upholder), and Isabella Blacke, of Frindsbury (da. of Thomas Blacke, yeoman), after three times being published." This entry (interesting as illustrative of the *status* of the alleged male descendants of the ancient Counts of Guisnes) carries the grantee's pedigree as far back as to his grandfather, whereas his very *parentage* had been ignored in all the Baronetages of the eighteenth and of the nineteenth century. In the first edition [1727] of Wotton's *Baronetage*, he is indeed said to have been "descended from the ancient family of the Blunts in Shropshire," but these words are omitted (probably not without a good reason) by the careful editor of that work in his second [1741] edition. In Debrett's *Baronetage* [1840] it is said that "this family is supposed to be descended from a junior branch of the Blounts of Sodington, which was seated at Eye and Stretton, co. Hereford," but in Burke's *Baronetage* of 1871, the father of the grantee (*viz.*, "Thomas Blunt, of Rochester," ignored in the 1841 edition), appears, together with the positive statement that "This is a branch of the ancient and eminent family of Blunt or Blount," called (in earlier editions) "Le Blount, descended from the Earls of Guisnes." Finally in Burke's *Baronetage* for 1902 the grantee's father is said to have been "Thomas Blunt, *or Blount*, of Rochester, Kent, *and formerly of Eye, Herefordshire*," but as we now find that this Thomas Blunt was a shoemaker at Stroud or Rochester from 1654 till his death in 1703, and was the son of John Blunt of St. Sepulchre's, London, "Upholder," there does not seem much probability of his ever having figured as "*Thomas Blount*, of Eye," co. Hereford. There is indeed a conjectural pedigree among Bigland's MSS., preserved in the College of Arms [R.B.G., vol. ii), deducing this Thomas (the Baptist shoemaker) from the well known (Roman Catholic) family of Blount, of Eye, co. Hereford, but it does not agree with the pedigree of that family in the *Visit. of Herefordshire*, 1634.

(b) There are no entries of births or baptisms of this family at St. Nicholas', Rochester, prior to that of 24 July 1665, the births of the three elder children (Thomas, Elizabeth, and Joane, 30 March 1655, 21 Feb. 1657, and 25 Oct. 1660), being entered among the baptisms of Stroud.

(c) See p. 10, note "c," under "LAMBERT" Baronetcy [1711] for a notice of this Company.

(d) "The public indignation was pointed chiefly against Sir John Blunt, as Projector, and against [the Earl of] Sunderland and Aislabie as heads of the Treasury . . . . The character of Blunt himself was that of a dishonest and now ruined man." [Stanhope's *England*, as on p. 10, note "c."]

(e) He appealed therefrom, and a day was appointed for the hearing, but no further proceedings took place, possibly on account of his death, a few months later, in Jan. 1732/3.

II. 1733. SIR HENRY BLUNT, Baronet [1720], of St. Lawrence, Pountney, London, 2d but 1st surv. s. and h.,(a) by 1st wife, *b.* 6 Dec. 1696; *suc. to the Baronetcy*, 24 Jan. 1732/3. He *m.*, March 1724, Dorothy, sister and coheir of John NUTT, of Leatherhead, Surrey, 1st da. of William NUTT, of Lime street, London, and Walthamstow, Essex, Citizen and Grocer of London, by Dorothy, da. of Ralph HAWKINS, of Walthamstow, Citizen and Brewer of London. She *d.* 12 Oct. 1756 at Walthamstow. Will dat. 26 Feb. 1745, pr. 20 Nov. 1756. He *d.* 12 and was *bur.* 20 Oct. 1759 at Walthamstow, aged 62. Will dat. 30 Jan., pr. 15 Oct. 1759.

III. 1759. SIR CHARLES WILLIAM BLUNT, Baronet [1720], 3d but 1st surv. s. and h., *b.* 4 and *bap.* 24 Sep. 1731, at St. Lawrence Pountney; admitted to the Middle Temple, of which he is said to have subsequently been Bencher; *suc. to the Baronetcy*, 12 Oct. 1759; was "of Clery, Hants,"(b) as also of Pullah, near Calcutta in India. He *m.* 22 July 1767, at St. George's, Queen's square, Midx., Elizabeth PEERS, spinster, elder sister and coheir of Sir Richard SYMONS, Baronet [1774], da. of Richard PEERS, of Croydon, Surrey, Alderman of London, by Anna Sophia, da. and coheir of Richard SYMONS, of the Mynde, co. Hereford. He *d.* 29 Aug. 1802, in his 72d year, at his house at Pullah abovenamed, and was *bur.* at Calcutta. M.I. in St. John's, Calcutta. Will dat. 22 May 1802, pr. 2 March 1803. He "left £100,000, threequarters of which he bequeathed to his eldest son."(c) His widow *d.* 17 Jan. 1836, aged 91, and was *bur.* at Croydon. Will dat. 7 Nov. 1826, pr. 22 Feb. 1836.

IV. 1802. SIR CHARLES RICHARD BLUNT, Baronet [1720], 1st s. and h., *b.* 6 Dec. 1775, at Odiham, Hants; was in the Bengal Civil Service of the India Company, obtaining v.p., "a situation therein worth £4,000 a year"(c), probably that of "Judge and magistrate of the Zillah of Beerb-hoom in Bengal."(d) He *suc. to the Baronetcy*, 29 Aug. 1802; was subsequently (before 1826) of Heathfield Park and Ringmer, Sussex, and was M.P. for Lewes (four Parls.), 1831 till his death. He *m.* 20 March 1824, at St. Marylebone, Sophia, widow of Richard AUCHMUTY, of the Bengal Civil Service, da. of Richard BAKER, M.D. He *d.* at Eaton place, Pimlico, 29 Feb. 1840, aged 65, and was *bur.* at Heathfield. M.I. Will dated 1 Dec. 1838, pr. 27 March 1840. His widow *d.* 14 Aug. 1862.

V. 1840. SIR WALTER BLUNT, Baronet [1720], of Heathfield Park aforesaid, only s. and h., *b.* 16 March, and *bap.* 19 April 1826, at Heathfield; *suc. to the Baronetcy*, 29 Feb. 1840; matric. at Oxford (Ch. Ch.), 31 May 1844, aged 18. He *d.* unm. at Heathfield Park, 13 July 1847, aged 21, and was *bur.* at Heathfield. Will, dated 16 March, pr. 25 July 1847.

VI. 1847. SIR CHARLES WILLIAM BLUNT, Baronet [1720], of Heathfield Park aforesaid, cousin and h. male, being 1st s. and h. of Richard Charles BLUNT, of Bretlands, in Chertsey, Surrey, by Eliza Forbes, da. of William Forbes MERCER, of Potter Hill, co. Perth, Major Commandant at Bengal, which Richard Charles (who *d.* 16 Jan. 1846, aged 59, and was *bur.* at Chertsey) was 2d s. of the 3d Baronet. He was *b.* 22 Nov. 1810, at Calcutta; ed. at Trinity Coll., Cambridge; B.A., 1834; M.A., 1845; Barrister (Middle Temple), 1835; *suc. to the Baronetcy* and the Heathfield estate, 13 July 1847; Sheriff of Sussex, 1873. He *d.* unm., 5 Nov. 1890, in his 80th year.

VII. 1890. SIR WILLIAM BLUNT, Baronet [1720], of Heathfield Park aforesaid, cousin and h. male, being 2d but 1st surv. s. and h.(e) of William BLUNT, Bengal Civil Service, by Eliza, da. of Goddard

(a) John Blunt, his elder br., *b.* 23 July 1694, living in the East Indies, 1727, *d.* unm. and v.p.

(b) Betham's *Baronetage* [1803], where that place is assigned as his "*Seat.*"

(c) *Annual Register*, 1802.

(d) Playfair's *Baronetage* [1811].

(e) His elder br., Charles Blunt, *b.* 1 Jan. 1824, who was in the Civil Service, Burmah, *m.*, but *d.* s.p. 1884.

RICHARDS, of Bath, a General in the East India Company's Service, which William (who *d.* 1859, aged 78), was 3d s. of the 3d Baronet. He was *b.* 25 June 1826; was in the Bengal Civil Service, 1846-75; *suc. to the Baronetcy* and the Heathfield estate, 5 Nov. 1890, and sold the latter a few years afterwards. He *m.* firstly, in 1852, Margaret, da. of Capt. SCOTT, R.N. She *d.* 1854. He *m.* secondly, 3 Nov. 1857, Henrietta Georgina Josephine, da. of the Rev. Robert Green JESTON, Rector of Avon Dassett, co. Warwick, by Louisa, da. of the Rev. Powell Colchester GUISE, Vicar of Elmore, co. Gloucester. She *d.* 6 Feb. 1892. He *d.* s.p., suddenly, Dec. 1902, aged 76. Will pr. at £8,819.

VIII. 1902. SIR JOHN HARVEY BLUNT, Baronet [1720], of the Priory, Lamberhurst, Kent, br. and h., *b,* 1 Jan. 1839; sometime Capt. 1st Batt. Royal Dublin Fusiliers; serving with the 1st Batt. Royal Welsh Fusiliers through the Indian Mutiny, 1857-59; was at the taking of Futteghur, and subsequent operations on the Ramgungar and Gogra, and at the siege and capture of Lucknow (medal and clasp). He *suc. to the Baronetcy*, Dec. 1902. He *m.* 28 April 1870, Susan, da. of P. HOAD.

MOSLEY, *or* MOSELY(a):

cr. 18 June 1720(b);

ex. 22 Sep. 1779.

I. 1720. OSWALD MOSELY, *or* MOSLEY, of Rolleston, co. Stafford, Esq., 1st s. and h. ap. of Oswald MOSLEY,(c) of Ancoats, co. Lancaster, and Rolleston aforesaid, sometime (1699-1700) Sheriff of Staffordshire, by Mary, da. of William YATES, of Stanley House, Blackburn, Barrister, was *bap.* 11 Aug. 1674, at the College Church of Manchester; matric. at Oxford (Oriel Coll.), 19 Jan. 1690/1, aged 16; admitted to Gray's Inn, 22 June 1691; was Sheriff of Staffordshire, 1714-15, and was v.p. *cr. a Baronet*, as above, 18 June 1720.(b) He suc. his father in the family estates, in Sep. 1726, and by the death, 26 July 1734, of his father's 1st cousin, Dame Anne BLAND (widow of Sir John BLAND, 4th Baronet [1642]), da. and h. of his uncle, Sir Edward MOSLEY, of Hulme, suc. to that estate and to the manor of Manchester. He was builder of the first Exchange erected in that town. He *m.* 4 Feb. 1702/3, at Worksop, Notts, Elizabeth, 1st da. of John THORNHAUGH, of Fenton, Notts, by Elizabeth, da. of Sir Richard EARLE, 1st Baronet [1629]. She was *b.* 10 July 1671, and was *bur.* at Rolleston.(d) He *d.* at St. James', Bath, 2, being carried thence and *bur.* 10 June 1751, at Rolleston, in his 77th year. Will pr. 1751, and again, at Chester, 12 March 1753.

II. 1751. SIR OSWALD MOSLEY, Baronet [1720], of Rolleston and Ancoats aforesaid, Lord of the Manor of Manchester, 1st s. and h., *b.* 21 April 1705 (see the Dukinfield Nonconformist Register), and *suc. to the Baronetcy*, 2 June 1751. He *d.* unm. 26 Feb. 1757, in his 52d year, and was *bur.* at Rolleston.

(a) Most of the information in this article is taken from the *Mosley Family*, by Ernest Axon, printed by the Chetham Society, 1902.

(b) See p. 48, note "e," as to this creation being, possibly, on *29* June 1720.

(c) This Oswald (*bap.* 1 Sep. 1639 and *bur.* 2 Sep. 1726, aged 87) was s. and h. of Nicholas Mosley, of Ancoats, a Royalist (*bap.* 26 Dec. 1611 and *bur.* 28 Oct. 1672), the elder br. of Sir Edward Mosley, who inherited the Hulme and Manchester estates, on the death, in 1665, of his distant cousin, Sir Edward Mosley, 2d and last Baronet [1640]. These two brothers were sons of Oswald Mosley, of Ancoats (*d.* 9 Nov. 1630, aged 47), who was s. of Anthony Mosley, of Manchester, Clothier (*d.* 25 March 1607, aged 70), the yr. br. of Sir Nicholas Mosley, of Hough, co. Lancaster, sometime (1599-1600) Lord Mayor of London, whose son, Rowland Mosley, was father of Sir Edward Mosley, *cr. a Baronet*, 20 July 1640, the father of the 2d and last Baronet (of that creation) abovenamed.

(d) "Mrs. Elizabeth Mosley" was *bur.* at Manchester in 1708, but she is described as "spinster," and if that be her correct description, she cannot be this person.

III. 1757, to 1779. SIR JOHN MOSLEY, Baronet [1720], of Rolleston and Ancoats aforesaid, Lord of the Manor of Manchester, only br. and h.; admitted to Lincoln's Inn, 4 Feb. 1725/6; ed. at Trin. Coll., Cambridge; B.A., 1727; M.A., 1735; in Holy Orders; Rector of Rolleston [1777-79], and of Fenton, both abovenamed, having *suc. to the Baronetcy*, 26 Feb. 1757. He *d.* unm. 22 Sep. 1779, and was *bur.* at Rolleston, when the *Baronetcy* became *extinct.*(a) Admon. 15 Oct. 1779, to Elizabeth TRAFFORD, widow, sister and next of kin.(b)

COLBY(c):

cr. 21 June 1720(d);

ex. 23 Sep. 1729

I. 1720, to 1729. THOMAS COLBY, of Kensington, co. Middlesex, Esq., 4th but only surv. s. and h. of Philip COLBY, of the same, by Elizabeth (*m.* 3 July 1666, at St. Albans abbey, Herts), 2d da. and coheir of William FLEWELLIN, *or* LLEWELLIN, Alderman of London, was *b.* probably about 1670; was one of the Commissioners of the Royal Navy,(d) and was *cr. a Baronet*, as above, 21 June 1720. He, who was M.P. for Rochester, Jan. 1724 to 1727, built the stately brick mansion called "Colby house," in High street, Kensington.(e) He *d.* unm., 23 Sep. 1729, and was *bur.* with his parents at Kensington, when the *Baronetcy* became *extinct.*(f) Will pr. 1729.

(a) The estates devolved on his cousin and heir male John Parker Mosley, s. and h. of Nicholas Mosley, of Manchester (*bur.* there 12 March 1733/4), who was s. of Nicholas Mosley, of London, Apothecary (*b.* at Ancoats 1654, and *d.* 1697), who was yr. br. of Oswald Mosley, the father of the 1st Baronet [1720]. This John Parker Mosley, was *cr. a Baronet*, 8 June 1781, as "of Ancoats, co. Lancaster."

(b) She, who *m.* Humphrey Trafford, of Trafford, co. Lancaster, *d.* s.p. at York, 16 Oct. 1786, aged 72.

(c) See *Visit. of Norfolk*, 1583, as continued by the *Norfolk Arch. Soc.* [vol. i of pedigrees, p. 98, pub. 1878]. The parents of the Baronet and his uncle "Thomas Colby, Esq." [living about 1707], are commemorated on a monument at Kensington, but no dates are given thereon. The burial at Kensington of "Mr. Philip Colby," 4 Sep. 1666, is probably that of the Philip Colby, who *m.* there 8 Feb. 1635/6, "Rebecca Trubellvile," and whose children were *bap.* there from 1638 to 1649. The "Philip Colby, gent.," who was *bur.* there 7 Dec. 1692, was, presumably, the Baronet's father.

(d) Wotton's *Baronetage* (1727). The creation is given in Courthope's *List* as 18 June 1720. See p. 48, note "e," as to its being, possibly, on 13 June 1720.

(e) This was pulled down about 1873 by Albert Grant, the notorious "Company Promoter," who erected an enormous residence on its site, which not long afterwards (about 1883) was sold by his creditors, and the site built over with countless small residences.

(f) "He left a large fortune, part of which (I suppose that which came from Alderman Flewellin) went to the Bullocks [his maternal aunt Mary Flewellin, *m.* Thomas Bullock, of Shipdam, Norfolk, and had issue], part went to *his kinsman*, as he terms him, Thomas Colby, Esq., Commissioner of the Royal Navy at Plymouth. Sir Antonio Brady inherited property from his great grandmother, a da. and coheir of Thomas Colby, Esq., mentioned in Sir Thomas Colby's will."—[Note by Rev. Frederic Thomas Colby, D.D., F.S.A., etc., in his "*Appendix to Colby of Great Torrington*" [1880].

CHAPMAN(a):

cr. 27 June 1720(b);

ex. 9 Feb. 1785.

I. 1720. SIR WILLIAM CHAPMAN, of London, Knt., yr. s. of Sir John CHAPMAN, Lord Mayor of London (1688-89),(c) by his 2d wife, Elizabeth, sister of Thomas WEBB, *otherwise* WOOD, da. of Anthony WEBB, of Hackney, was *b.* probably about 1670; suc. his elder br., James CHAPMAN, in Nov. 1698; was a merchant of London, a director of the South Sea Company;(d) was *Knighted* 4 Oct. 1714, and was *cr. a Baronet*, as above, 27 June 1720.(b) He *m.*, probably about 1705, Elizabeth, 3d surv. da. and coheir of his abovenamed maternal uncle, Thomas WEBB, *otherwise* WOOD, Clerk of the Kitchen to William III, by Susanna, his wife. She, who was *bap.* at Chelsea, 30 July 1685, was *bur.* 21 June 1733, at St. Peter le Poor, London. He *d.* 7 and was *bur.* 13 May 1737, at St. Peter's aforesaid. Will pr. 1737.

II. 1737. SIR JOHN CHAPMAN, Baronet [1720], of Cockenhatch, in Barkway, Herts, 1st s. and h., *b.* probably about 1710; *suc. to the Baronetcy*, 7 May 1737; was Sheriff of Herts, 1759-60; M.P. for Taunton, 1741-47. He *m.* firstly, Dec. 1736, Rachel, da. and coheir of James EDMONDSON. She *d.* in or before 1764. Admon. as of St. James', Westm., 15 July 1764. He *m.* secondly, Sarah, da. of (—). He *d.* s.p. 29 Jan. 1781. Will pr. Feb. 1781. His widow *d.* 15 March 1800, and was *bur.* at Barkway. Will pr. April 1800.

III. 1781, to 1785. SIR WILLIAM CHAPMAN, Baronet [1720], of Loudham Park in Ufford, co. Suffolk, br. and h., *bap.* 1 Oct. 1714, at St. Peter le Poor aforesaid; Sheriff of Suffolk, 1767-68; *suc. to the Baronetcy*, 29 Jan. 1781. He *m.* firstly, 8 Dec. 1759, Mary, da. of (—) NEWMAN, of Ham Abbey, Essex. She was *bur.* at Ufford, 19 Oct. following. He *m.* secondly, 1 Aug. 1767, Anne, da. and coheir of the Rev. Benjamin LANY, Rector of Mulbarton, Norfolk. He *d.* s.p. in London 9 and was *bur.* 19 Feb. 1785 at Ufford, when the *Baronetcy* became *extinct*. Will pr. Feb. 1785. His widow *d.* 9 and was *bur.* 18 March 1796 at Ufford aforesaid. Will pr. April 1796.

SANDERSON, *or* SAUNDERSON:

cr. 19 July 1720;

ex. 30 Oct. 1760.

I. 1720. SIR WILLIAM SAUNDERSON [*or* SANDERSON], of [East] Combe in Greenwich, co. Kent, Knt., Usher of the Black Rod, only s. of Ralph SANDERSON, "a Capt. in the West Indies, and Capt. of several ships of war in the Dutch War,"(e) by Ephrim, da. of (—) GARRETT, of Norfolk,

(a) A good account of this family by R. E. Chester Waters, is in Howard's *Mis. Gen. et Her.*, new series, vol. i. pp. 5-8.

(b) See p. 48, note "e," as to the date of this creation being, possibly, 13 June 1720.

(c) This is the Lord Mayor, whose death (17 March 1688/9, aged 55) was (according to Macaulay's *England*) caused by "fits" brought on through the state of mind caused by the appearance before him, in the previous December, of the notorious Lord Chancellor Jeffreys, who had been "dragged into the Justice room followed by a raging multitude" after his capture at Wapping. This seems improbable, and does not agree with the high character given to him by "the famous Dr. Scott, Rector of St. Giles'-in-the-Fields," printed in Wotton's *Baronetage*, 1741. See also *Mis. Gen. et Her.*, as in note "b" above.

(d) See p. 10, note "c," under "LAMBERT" Baronetcy, 1711, for a notice of this Company.

(e) Wotton's *Baronetage* [1727 and 1741].

III. 1808. CHARLES (GREY), EARL GREY, etc., and 3d Baronet [1746], nephew and h., being s. and h. of Charles (GREY), 1st EARL GREY (so *cr.* 11 April 1806), br. to the late Baronet. He suc. his father in the peerage 14 Nov. 1807, and *suc. to the Baronetcy*, on the death of his uncle, 30 March 1808. In that peerage this *Baronetcy* then *merged*, and still (1905) so continues. See *Peerage*.

HARBORD:

cr. 22 March 1745/6;

afterwards, since 1786, BARONS SUFFIELD.

I. 1746. SIR WILLIAM HARBORD, K.B., of Gunton, co. Norfolk, *formerly* William MORDEN, 1st s. of John MORDEN,(a) of Suffield, co. Norfolk (*d.* 27 Oct. 1726, aged 59), by Judith, sister and coheir of Harbord Cropley HARBORD, of Gunton, in that county (1st da. of William CROPLEY, of Haughley, Suffolk, by Catherine, da. of Sir Charles HARBORD), was *b.* about 1697; was M.P. for Beeralston, Feb. to April, 1734; for Dunwich, Feb. 1738 to 1741, and for Beeralston again, 1741-54, having taken by Act of Parl., 1742, the name of HARBORD instead of that of MORDEN on inheriting the estates of his maternal uncle, Harbord Cropley HARBORD aforesaid. He was K.B., 20 Oct. 1744, and was *cr. a Baronet*, as above, 22 March 1745/6. He *m.* 25 April 1732, Elizabeth, da. and coheir of Robert BRITIFFE, of Baconsthorpe, Norfolk. He *d.* 17 Feb. 1770, aged 73. Will pr. March 1770. His widow *d.* 8 Aug. 1777.

II. 1770. SIR HARBORD HARBORD, Baronet [1746], of Gunton aforesaid, *formerly* Harbord MORDEN, 1st s. and h., *b.* at Thorpe, co. Norfolk, 15/26 Jan. 1734, and took the name of HARBORD instead of MORDEN (as did his father) eight years afterwards; was M.P. for Norwich (six Parls.), Dec. 1756 to 1786; *cr.* D.C.L. of Oxford, 5 July 1759; *suc. to the Baronetcy*, 17 Feb. 1770. He *m.* 7 Oct. 1760, at Middleton, co. Lancaster, Mary, 1st da. and coheir of Sir Ralph ASSHETON, 3d Baronet [1660], of Middleton, by his 2d wife, Eleanor, da. and coheir of the Rev. John COPLEY, of Batley. She was living when he was *cr.*, 21 Aug. 1786, BARON SUFFIELD of Suffield, co. Norfolk. In that Peerage this *Baronetcy* then *merged*, and still [1905] so continues. See *Peerage*.

DANVERS:

cr. 4 July 1746;

ex. 21 Sep 1796.

I. 1746. JOSEPH DANVERS, of Swithland, co. Leicester, Esq., as also of Prestcote and Chilton, Oxon, s. and h. of Samuel DANVERS, of Swithland aforesaid, by Elizabeth,(b) da. of (—) MOREWOOD, of Overton, co. Derby, was *b.* about 1697(c); was Sheriff of Leicestershire, June to Dec. 1721;

(a) See J. J. Muskett's *Manorial Families of Suffolk* (vol. ii) for an account of the family of Morden.

(b) This Elizabeth *m.* as her 2d husband, John Danvers, of Prestcote and Chilton, Oxon, who *d.* s.p., in July 1721, being *bur.* at Cropredy, aged 70, leaving his lands to his wife's son, Joseph Danvers, afterwards (1746) *cr.* a Baronet, as above.

(c) A baptism occurs at Stoke Newington, Midx., of "Joseph, s. of Mr. Samuel Danvers," on 5 Jan. 1667/8, which, however, clearly does *not* refer to him.

M.P. for Boroughbridge, 1722-27; for Bramber, 1727-34; and for Totnes, 1734-47. F.R.S., 1724; was one of the Court of the Royal African Company, 1731, 1732. He *m.* 7 Dec. 1721, at St. Paul's Cathedral, London, Frances, da. of Thomas BABINGTON, of Rothley Temple, co. Leicester, by his 2d wife, Margaret, da. and coheir of Henry HALL, of Gretford, co. Lincoln. She *d.* 4 Feb. 1752. He *d.* 26 and was *bur.* 30 Oct. 1753, at Swithland, aged 56. Will pr. 1754.

II. 1753, to 1796. SIR JOHN DANVERS, Baronet [1746], of Swithland, Prescote, and Chilton aforesaid, only s. and h., *b.* about 1722, *suc. to the Baronetcy*, 26 Oct. 1753; Sheriff of Leicestershire, 1755-56. He *m.* Mary, da. and coheir of Joel WATSON, of Clapham, Surrey, by Sarah, da. of Sir Edmund HARRISON, of Ickford, Bucks. He *d.* s.p.m.s.(a), 21 Sep. 1796, aged 73, when the *Baronetcy* became *extinct*. Will pr. 1796.(b) His widow *d.* in or shortly before 1800. Will pr. Nov. 1800.

GOOCH:

cr. 4 Nov. 1746.

I. 1746. WILLIAM GOOCH, Esq., Governor of Virginia, 2d and yst. s. of Thomas GOOCH, of Yarmouth (*d.* 1688), by Frances, da. and coheir of Thomas LONE, of Worlingham, co. Suffolk, was *b.* at Yarmouth 21 Oct. 1681; served in all the wars during the reign of Queen Anne as also in subduing the Jacobite rising of 1715; was Lieut.-Gov. of Virginia for twenty-two years, 1727-49; was, in 1740, Col. of an American regiment, being, as such, wounded at the siege of Carthagena, and was *cr. a Baronet*, as above, 4 Nov. 1746, with a spec. rem., failing heirs male of his body, to his elder br. Thomas GOOCH, then Bishop of Norwich. He was made Major-General in 1747. He *m.* Rebecca, da. of Robert STAUNTON, of Hampton, Midx. He *d.* s.p. at Bath, 17 Dec. 1751, in his 71st year, and was *bur.* (with his mother) at Yarmouth. M.I. Will pr. 1752. His widow *d.* 1755. Will pr. Feb. 1775.

II. 1751. SIR THOMAS GOOCH, Baronet [1746], Lord Bishop of Ely, 1st br. and h., *b.* 19 Jan. 1674/5, at Worlingham; ed. at Yarmouth Grammar School; admitted to Gonville and Caius Coll., Cambridge,(c) 5 May 1691; Scholar, Oct. 1691; B.A., 1694; M.A., 1698; Fellow, 1698-1714; B.D., 1706; D.D., 1711; Head of his College (as "Master,") 1716, till his death in 1754, Vice-Chancellor of that Univ., 1717-20.(d) He was domestic Chaplain to Henry COMPTON, Bishop of London; Chaplain to Queen Anne; Rector of St. Clements, Eastcheap, London, 1714-32; Archdeacon of Essex, 1714-37; Lecturer at Gray's Inn, 1716; Canon-Residentiary of Chichester, 1719-39; Canon of Canterbury, 1730-38; Bishop of Bristol, June 1737 to Oct. 1738(e); Bishop of Norwich, 1738-48; and Bishop of Ely, 1748 till death. He (who in 1743 purchased the

(a) His surv. da. and h., Mary, *m.* 8 March 1792, as his 1st wife, the Hon. Augustus Richard Butler, who accordingly took the name of Butler-Danvers. She *d.* 10 May 1802, leaving an only child, George John, who in 1847 became 5th Earl of Lanesborough [I.], and who *d.* s.p. 7 July 1866, aged 71.

(b) In F. N. Macnamara's *Danvers Family* [1895] is a letter from "Sir John Danvers, Baronet, of Swithlands, to John Danvers, of New Court," dat. 26 Dec. 1782, saying that in case his own daughter died without issue male, he had left him all his property (save some £2,000 or so in legacies) absolutely. This devise, however, never took effect.

(c) See Venn's *Gonville and Caius College* (vol. iii, pp. 115-125) for a good account of him.

(d) During that period he was fired at, his conduct towards Bentley, Professor of Divinity (a strong Whig), having excited the animosity of the Whig party.

(e) At Bristol, however, he "stayed so short a time as never to have visited his diocese" [Cole's MSS., as quoted in Venn's work, see note "c" above].

estate of Benacre, Suffolk) *suc. to the Baronetcy*, 17 Dec. 1751. He *m.* firstly, in or before 1720 (probably in 1714), Mary, sister to Thomas SHERLOCK, Bishop of London (1748-61), da. of William SHERLOCK, D.D., Dean of St. Paul's (1691-1707). She was *bur.* at St. Clement's, Eastcheap, but removed thence in Feb. 1754 to Caius Coll. chapel. He *m.* secondly, in or before 1730, Hannah, da. of Sir John MILLER, 2d Baronet [1705], of Chichester, by his 3d wife, Elizabeth, da. of Sir William MEUX, 2d Baronet [1641]. She *d.* March 1746.(a) He *m.* thirdly,(b) 17 Feb. 1747/8, at his chapel in Ely House, Holborn (lic. Lond. same date, she about 40, spinster), Mary, da. of Hatton COMPTON, Lieut. of the Tower (grandson of the 2d EARL OF NORTHAMPTON), by (—), da. of (—) NICHOLAS. He *d.* at Ely House, Holborn, 14, and was *bur.* 21 Feb. 1754 in the chapel of Caius Coll., aged 79. Will dat. 24 Jan. 1750, pr. 25 Feb. 1754. His widow, by whom he had no issue, *d.* 14 May 1780.

III. 1754. SIR THOMAS GOOCH, Baronet [1746], of Benacre aforesaid, 1st s. and h., by 1st wife, *b.* about 1721, in London; ed. for six years at Wymondham school, Norfolk, admitted, as pensioner, 9 July 1737 to Caius Coll., Cambridge, aged 16; scholar, 1737-42; B.A., 1741; M.A., 1742; *suc. to the Baronetcy*, 14 Feb. 1754. He, by the death in 1761 of his maternal uncle, Thomas SHERLOCK, Bishop of London, inherited a fortune of about £150,000. He *m.* firstly, in 1743, Ann, widow of (—) BATES, da. and coheir of John ATWOOD, of Saxlingham. She *d.* 5 April 1767. He *m.* secondly, in Nov. 1772, Phœbe, widow of Horatio BIRTLES, Consul at Genoa, and sometime Gov. of Grenada, da. of Isaac NORTON, of London. He *d.* 10 Sep. 1781, at Tunbridge Wells, aged about 60. Will pr. Nov. 1781. His widow *d.* 1 June 1793, aged 55. Will pr. July 1793

IV. 1781. SIR THOMAS GOOCH, Baronet [1746], of Benacre aforesaid, 1st s. and h. by 1st wife, *b.* 1745, *suc. to the Baronetcy*, 10 Sep. 1781; Sheriff of Suffolk, 1785. He *m.* 23 Dec. 1766, Anna Maria, da. and h. of Thomas HAYWARD, of Weybridge, Surrey, founder's kin to William of WAYNFLEET, the founder of Mag. Coll., Oxford. She *d.* 28 Sep. 1814, aged 72. He *d.* 7 April 1826, at Benacre Hall, aged 80. Will pr. Oct. 1826.

V. 1826. SIR THOMAS SHERLOCK GOOCH, Baronet [1746], of Benacre aforesaid, 1st s. and h., *b.* 2 Nov. 1767, in Westminster; matric. at Oxford (Ch. Ch.), 24 Oct. 1785, aged 17; B.A., 1789; was M.P. for Suffolk (seven Parls.), Feb. 1806 to 1830; Chairman of the Quarter Sessions, etc.; *suc. to the Baronetcy*, 7 April 1826. He *m.* 12 May 1796, Marianne, 3d da. [and coheir ?] of Abraham WHITAKER, of Stratford, Essex, and of Lyston House, co. Hereford.(c) He *d.* at Benacre House, 18 Dec. 1851, aged 84. Will pr. Feb. 1852. His widow *d.* 19 April 1856, at Aldborough Manor, Yorkshire, aged 85. Will pr. Aug. 1856.

VI. 1851. SIR EDWARD SHERLOCK GOOCH, Baronet [1746], of Benacre aforesaid, 1st s. and h., *b.* at Holbecke, Suffolk, 1802; ed. at Westm. School; sometime, 1819-37, an officer in the 14th Dragoons, retiring as Captain; was M.P. for East Suffolk (three Parls.), Feb. 1846 till death, having *suc. to the Baronetcy*, 18 Dec. 1851. He, in 1851, was made Provincial Grand Master of the Freemasons, an office he held till his death. He *m.* firstly, 23 Jan. 1828, in Paris, Louisa Anna Maria, 2d da. of Sir George Beeston PRESCOTT, 2d Baronet [1794], by Catherine Creighton, da. of Sir Thomas MILLS. She *d.* s.p.m., 24 Feb. 1837. He *m.* secondly, 1 May 1839, Harriet, 3d da. of James

(a) With her "he lived but an uneasy life, she being both peevish and unhealthy" [Cole's MSS., *ut supra*].

(b) "This was more of vanity to ally himself with the Compton family than anything else, for the lady had but one eye, was horridly plain and immensely ill-tempered. His vanity displayed itself by his displaying his wife's arms on his carriage, instead of those of his See" [Cole's MSS. as on p. 91, note "e."].

(c) In *N. & Q.*, 8th s., xii, 329, it is stated that he was "of Stratford, Essex, and Lyster [*sic*] House, Herefordshire, a drysalter," and that his three daughters were Charlotte, Countess of Stradbroke, Diana, Lady Hamlyn-Williams, and Marianne, Lady Gooch."

Joseph HOPE-VERE, of Craigie, co. Linlithgow, by Elizabeth, da. of George (HAY), 7th MARQUESS OF TWEEDDALE [S.]. He *d.* 8 Nov. 1856, at Benacre Hall. Will pr. Dec. 1856. His widow *m.* 30 June 1858, at St. Geo. Han. sq., John ST. LEGER, Major 14th Dragoons (who *d.* 20 Oct. 1868), and *d.* 17 Oct. 1883, at 42 Charles street, Berkeley sq., aged 64.

VII. 1856. SIR EDWARD SHERLOCK GOOCH, Baronet [1746], of Benacre aforesaid, 1st s. and h., by 2d wife, *b.* 16 May 1843, at Beacon Hill, near Woodbridge, Suffolk; *suc. to the Baronetcy*, 8 Nov. 1856. He *m.* 9 Oct. 1866, at Tattingstone, Suffolk, Ellen Emily, 1st da. of Robert Augustus Hankey HIRST, of Tattingstone Place, and of Down Grange, Hants. He *d.* s.p., 27 May 1872, at Benacre Hall, aged 29. His widow *m.* 28 July 1873, at St. Geo. Han. sq. (as 2d wife), George Thompson GREAM, M.D., Physician to the Princess of Wales, of Frogmore Lodge, St. Albans, Herts, who *d.* 20 July 1888, aged 75, at the Drive, Brighton, and was *bur.* (near his 1st wife) at Aldenham, Herts. She living 1905.

VIII. 1872. SIR FRANCIS ROBERT SHERLOCK LAMBERT GOOCH, Baronet [1746], of Benacre aforesaid, br. and h., *b.* 8 Sep. 1850 at Southwold; ed. at Eton; *suc. to the Baronetcy*, 27 May 1872; Lieut.-Col. West Suffolk militia. He *m.* 16 July 1872, Sarah Annie, da. of G. A. SUTHERLAND. She *d.* 28 Oct. 1879, at Norwood, Surrey. He *d.* s.p.s., 13 Aug. 1881, at Benacre Hall, aged 30.

IX. 1881. SIR ALFRED SHERLOCK GOOCH, Baronet [1746], of Benacre aforesaid, br. and h., being 4th and yst. s. of the 6th Baronet, *b.* 20 Dec. 1851 at Southwold; ed. at Eton; sometime Lieut. 3d Middx. militia; *suc. to the Baronetcy*, 13 Aug. 1881; Sheriff of Suffolk, 1885 He *m.* 27 May 1880, Alice Elizabeth, 1st da. of Edward WILLIAMS, of Honeycombe, near Calstock, Cornwall, by Emma, da. of (—) WHITE. She, from whom he was separated, *d.* 27 Nov. 1895, at Dawlish, Devon. He *d.* 24 Feb. 1899, at Henstead Hall, near Lowestoft, aged 57. Will pr. at £168,223, net personalty £35,958.

X. 1899. SIR THOMAS VERE SHERLOCK GOOCH, Baronet [1746], of Benacre aforesaid, only s. and h., *b.* 10 June 1881; *suc. to the Baronetcy*, 24 Feb. 1899. He *m.* 10 July 1902, Florence Meta, yst. da. of James Finucane DRAPER, of St. Heliers, Jersey.

Family Estates.—These, in 1883, consisted of 7,186 acres in Suffolk, worth £3,090 a year. *Seat.*—Benacre Hall, near Wangford, Suffolk.

PEPPERELL:

cr. 15 Nov. 1746(a);

ex. 6 July 1759.

I. 1746, to 1759. WILLIAM PEPPERELL, of Massachusetts, in North America, Esq., s. of William PEPPERELL (who emigrated from Tavistock, Devon, to the isle of Shoals, Massachusetts, and *d.* 1734, having "from a penniless fisherman" become "a great shipowner and merchant"(b)), by Margaret, da. of (—) BRAY, was *b.* 27 June 1696, at Kittery Point, Maine; was engaged in shipbuilding, and was an active officer in the Maine militia, of which he was Colonel in 1722; was a member of

(a) The date of this patent is given as "10 Aug. 1745" in Playfair's *Baronetage* [1811] under the account of the Baronetcy conferred on the grantee's grandson, 29 Oct. 1774.

(b) *Dict. Nat. Biogr.*

the Council of Massachusetts, 1727 till his death, and was in 1745 made Commander-in-Chief of the troops of the United provinces attacking the French at Cape Breton, and effecting the capture of Louisburg ("the Dunkirk of America") after a forty-nine days' siege, 1745. He was made Colonel, and finally (Feb. 1759) Lieut.-Gen. in the King's army, and was *cr. a Baronet*, as above, 15 Nov. 1746.(a) He *m.* 6 March 1723, Mary, da. of Grove HIRST, of Boston, in New England. He *d.* s.p.m.s.(b) 6 July 1759, at Kittery aforesaid, aged 63, when the *Baronetcy* became *extinct*. Will pr. Nov. 1768. His widow, who survived him thirty years, *d.* 25 Nov. 1789.

FETHERSTONHAUGH:

cr. 3 Jan. 1746/7;

ex. 24 Oct. 1846.

I. 1747. MATTHEW FETHERSTONHAUGH, Esq., 1st s. and h. ap. of Matthew FETHERSTONHAUGH, twice Mayor of Newcastle (*d.* 17 Feb. 1762, aged, it is said, 102), by (—), da. and eventually h. of Robert BROWNE, was *b.* about 1715, and having, by the death, 17 Oct. 1746, of Sir Henry FETHERSTON, 2d and last Baronet [1660], suc. to Hassenbrooke manor in Stanford le Hope, Essex, and other considerable estates, said to be worth £400,000, was, in compliance with the wish of the deceased, *cr. a Baronet*, as above, 3 Jan. 1746/7. He in 1747, purchased the estate of Uppark, and in 1767 that of Ladyholt, both in the parish of Harting, Sussex. He was M.P. for Morpeth, Nov. 1755 to 1761, and for Portsmouth, 1762, till death; was F.R.S. 1752. He *m.* 24 Dec. 1746, at St. Anne's, Soho, Sarah, only da. of Christopher LETHIEULLIER, of Belmont, Middx. He *d.* at Whitehall, 18 and was *bur.* 26 March 1774, at Stanford le Hope, aged 59. M.I., in which he is described as of Fetherstonhaugh Castle, co Northumberland. Will pr. March 1774. His widow *d.* 27 Aug. 1788. Admon. May 1790.

II. 1774, to 1846. SIR HENRY FETHERSTONHAUGH, Baronet [1747], of Uppark aforesaid, etc., only s. and h., *b.* there 22 Dec. 1754; matric. at Oxford (Univ. Coll.), 11 May 1772, aged 17; *suc. to the Baronetcy*, 18 March 1774; M.P. for Portsmouth (three Parls.), 1782-96. He *m.* 12 Sep. 1825, at Uppark, Mary Anne BULLOCK, spinster, of Orton, Essex. He *d.* s.p. at Uppark, 24 Oct. 1846,(c) in his 92d year, when the *Baronetcy* (which he had enjoyed 72 years) became *extinct*.

WILLIAMS:

cr. 4 April 1747;

ex. 2 Feb. 1784.

I. 1747. HUTCHINS WILLIAMS, of Clapton, co. Northampton, and of Grey Friars, in Chichester, co. Sussex, Esq., 1st s. and h. of William Peere WILLIAMS, of Greyfriars aforesaid, and of Broxbourne, Herts, an eminent Barrister and Law Reporter, by Anne, da. of Sir George HUTCHINS, sometime a Commissr. of the Great Seal, was *b.* at St. Andrew's, Holborn, about

(a) See p. 93, note "a."

(b) His only son, Andrew Pepperell, *d.* unm. and v.p. in 1751 in his 26th year. His only da., Elizabeth, *m.* Nathaniel Sparhawk, a merchant of New England, and their 2d s., William, took the name of Pepperell in 1759, on inheriting the estates of his maternal grandfather, and was *cr. a Baronet*, 9 Nov. 1774, but the title became again extinct on his death, 18 Dec. 1816.

(c) The date of his death was the same as that of the burial (100 years before) of Sir Henry Fetherston, 2d and last Baronet [1660], from whom his father had derived his estates, who *d.* 17 and was *bur.* 24 Oct. 1746.

1701; matric. at Oxford (Queen's Coll.), 4 Jan. 1724/5, aged 24; suc. his father, 10 June 1736, and was *cr. a Baronet*, as above, 4 April 1747. He *m.* in 1726, Judith, da. and h. of James BOOTH, of Theobalds, Herts. She *d.* 6 June 1754, and was *bur.* at Clapton aforesaid. Admon. 10 May 1771. He *d.* 4 Nov. 1758 at Chichester, and was *bur.* with his wife at Clapton. Will dat. 6 Sep. and pr. 15 Nov. 1752.

II. 1758. SIR WILLIAM PEERE WILLIAMS, Baronet [1747], of Clapton and Greyfriars aforesaid, 1st s. and h., *b.* probably about 1730; ed. at Winchester, 1744-48, and at Clare Hall, Cambridge; M.A., 1759, having *suc. to the Baronetcy*, 4 Nov. 1758; was M.P. for Shoreham, Dec. 1758 till death. He, who was an officer in the Army, *d.* unm., being slain at Butelot, 27 April 1761, at the attack of Belleisle. M.I. written by Thomas Gray, the Poet. Will pr. 1761.

III. 1761, to 1784. SIR BOOTH WILLIAMS, Baronet [1747], of Clapton and Grayfriars aforesaid, br. and h., *b.* about 1735 at Chichester; matric. at Oxford (Lincoln Coll.) 7 Oct. 1757, aged 22; *suc. to the Baronetcy*, 27 April 1761; Sheriff of Northamptonshire, 1764-65. He *m.* 18 May 1763, at Kingston-on-Thames, Anne, 1st surv. da. of the Rev. Claudius FONNERAU, of Christchurch Park, near Ipswich, sometime Rector of Clapton aforesaid, by Anne, da. of the Rev. William BUNBURY, Rector of Catworthy, co. Huntingdon. He *d.* s.p. 2 Feb. 1784, and was *bur.* at Clapton, when the *Baronetcy* became *extinct*.(a) Will pr. May 1784. His widow, who was *b.* 8, and *bap.* 30 July 1731, at Clapton, *d.* at Colchester, Aug. 1799, and was *bur.* at Clapton aforesaid.

GIFFORD:

1747 to 1823.

As to the alleged statement [in *Gent. Mag.* for 1747] that "SIR THOMAS GIFFORD, of Castle Jordan, co. Meath, was *cr. a Baronet*, July 1747," see vol. iii, p. 169, under the Baronetcy of that designation, *cr.* 4 March 1660/1, which became *extinct* 4 May 1662, but which was *assumed* July 1747 to Sep. 1823.

IBBETSON:

cr. 12 May 1748;

sometime, 1861-69, SELWIN;

afterwards, 1869-1902, SELWIN-IBBETSON;

and, 1892-1902, BARON ROOKWOOD;

ex. 15 Jan. 1902.

I. 1748. HENRY IBBETSON, of Leeds, co. York, Esq., 4th, but 2d surv. s.(b) of James IBBETSON, of the same, merchant, Lord of the Manor of Denton, co. York (*d.* 1739, aged 64) by Elizabeth, da. and coheir of John NICHOLSON, M.D., of York, was *b.* about 1708, and having raised a corps of

(a) The estate of Greyfriars, Chichester, passed to his sister Ann, who *m.* 4 Feb. 1758, at Chichester, the Rev. William Fonnerau, of Christchurch Park, Ipswich, and had issue.

(b) His elder br., Samuel Ibbetson, inherited the estate of Denton, but *d.* s.p.m., 1762-68, leaving a da. and h., Alice, Countess of Shipbrook [I.], who *d.* s.p. 23 Sep. 1808.

one hundred men during the Rising of 1745, and having been Sheriff of Yorkshire, 1746-47, was *cr. a Baronet*, as above, 12 May 1748. He *m.* firstly, 3 Dec. 1735, or 23 Dec. 1736, at Rawmarsh, Catherine, 4th da. of Francis FOLJAMBE, of Aldwark, by Mary, da. of Thomas WORSLEY. She, who was *b.* 21 July, and *bap.* 18 Aug. 1717, *d.* s.p. 17 Oct. 1740. He *m.* secondly, 6 Oct. 1741, Isabella, sister and coheir of Ralph CARR, of Crocken Hall, Durham, 1st da. of Ralph CARR, of the same, by Margaret, da. of Nicholas PAXTON, of Durham. She *d.* 2 June 1757. He *d.* at York, 22 June 1761, aged 53. Will pr. 1762.

II. 1761. SIR JAMES IBBETSON, Baronet [1748], of Leeds aforesaid, 1st s. and h., *b.* about 1747; *suc. to the Baronetcy* 22 June 1761. He apparently(a) *suc.* shortly afterwards, on the death s.p.m. of his uncle, Samuel IBBETSON, to the estate of Denton, co. York. He was Sheriff of Yorkshire, 1769-70. He *m.* in 1768, Jane, da. and h. of John CAYGILL, of Skay, near Halifax, co. York, by Jane, sister of Thomas SELWIN, of Down Hall, in Hatfield Broad-oak, Essex, da. of William SELWIN, of London, Merchant. He *d.* 4 Sep. 1795, aged 48, and was *bur.* at Denton. His widow *d.* at Down Hall, 21 Aug. 1816, aged 72, and was *bur.* at Hatfield Broad-oak. M.I. Will pr. 1816.

III. 1795. SIR HENRY CARR IBBETSON, Baronet [1748], of Leeds aforesaid, 1st s. and h., *b.* about 1769; served as Captain 3d Dragoon Guards in Flanders, under the Duke of York; *suc. to the Baronetcy*, and, apparently,(a) to the estate of Denton (which he certainly possessed in and after 1808), 4 Sep. 1795; Sheriff of Yorkshire, 1803-04; Lieut.-Col. 4th Regt. of West Yorkshire Militia. He *m.* 22 November 1803, at Kirkby Overblow, co. York, Alicia Mary, only da. of William Fenton SCOTT, of Woodhall in that county. He *d.* s.p., 5 May 1825, in Conduit street, aged 56. Will pr. July 1825. His widow *d.* 12 May 1858, at Pontefract, aged 76.

IV. 1825. SIR CHARLES IBBETSON, Baronet [1748], of Denton Park, co. York, *formerly* Charles SELWIN, br. and h.; *b.* 26 Sep. 1779. He, by royal license, 18 Feb. 1817, took the name of SELWIN in lieu of that of IBBETSON, on inheriting the estates of his maternal great uncle, Thomas SELWIN, of Down Hall aforesaid. He *suc. to the Baronetcy* and to the estate of Denton, 5 May 1825, when (having thereby forfeited the Selwin estates) he resumed his patronymic of IBBETSON. He *m.* 4 Feb. 1812, at Walcot, Somerset, Charlotte Elizabeth, 1st da. of Thomas STOUGHTON, of Ballyhorgan, co. Kerry, by Jane, relict of John HANBURY, of Pontypool, da. of Morgan LEWIS, of St. Pierre, co. Monmouth. She *d.* 15 Jan. 1827. Will pr. April 1836 and July 1839. He *d.* 9 April 1839, at Denton park, in his 60th year. Will pr. July 1839.

V. 1839. SIR CHARLES HENRY IBBETSON, Baronet [1748], of Denton park aforesaid, 1st s. and h.,(b) *b.* 24 July 1814; *suc. to the Baronetcy*, 9 April 1839; sometime cornet in the Yorkshire Hussars (retiring 1843); Major in the 5th West York Militia. He *m.* 23 Dec. 1847, at Chevening, Kent, Eden, widow of Percival PERKINS, of Usworth place, Durham, da. of J. George THACKRAH, or THACKREH. He *d.* s.p.,(c) at Denton park, 6 July 1861, aged 46. His widow *m.* 9 July 1867, her husband's cousin (the 7th Baronet), whom see.

(a) It is, however, not certain whether that estate might not have devolved on Alice, Countess of Shipbrook [I.], the da. of its late owner, and not have reverted to the Ibbetson family till her death s.p., 23 Sep. 1808. She, however, is never mentioned in her father's will, dat. 11 Nov. 1762, and pr. 11 May 1768.

(b) His only br., Frederick James Ibbetson, Lieut. Queen's Bays, *d.* unm. 31 Jan. 1853, aged 30.

(c) Laura, his only sister, who *m.* 8 April 1845, Marmaduke Wyvil, and had issue, inherited the estate of Denton.

VI. 1861. SIR JOHN THOMAS SELWIN, Baronet [1748], of Down Hall, Essex, aforesaid, uncle and h. male, being 4th and yst. s. of the 2d Baronet; *b.* about 1784; *suc.* to the estate of Down Hall, 5 May 1825, on the accession of his brother to the Baronetcy and to the Ibbetson estates, when, by royal license, 5 Aug. 1825, he took the name of SELWIN, in lieu of that of IBBETSON; *suc. to the Baronetcy*, 6 July 1861. He *m.* 8 Sep. 1825, Isabella, 2d da. of Gen. John LEVESON-GOWER, of Bill hill, Berks (grandson of the 1st EARL GOWER), by Isabella Mary, da. of Philip BOWES-BROKE, of Broke Hall, Suffolk. She *d.* 24 Sep. 1858, aged 55. He *d.* 20 March 1869, at Down Hall, aged 85.

VII. 1869, to 1902. SIR HENRY JOHN SELWIN-IBBETSON, Baronet [1748], of Down Hall aforesaid, only s. and h., *b.* 26 Sep. 1826; ed. at St. John's, Coll., Cambridge; B.A., 1849: M.A., 1852; was M.P. for South Essex, 1865-68; for West Essex, 1868-85; and for the Epping Division, 1885-92, having taken his patronymic of IBBETSON after that of SELWIN, on the occasion of his second marriage, 9 July 1867, with Dame Eden IBBETSON, and having *suc. to the Baronetcy*, 20 March 1869. He was Under-Sec. to the Home Department, 1874-78; Financial Sec. to the Treasury, 1878-80; P.C., 1885; second Church-Estate Commissioner, 1885-92; Chairman of the Quarter Sessions. After sitting twenty-seven years continuously in the House of Commons he was *cr.*, 18 June 1892, BARON ROOKWOOD OF ROOKWOOD HALL AND DOWN HALL, co. Essex. He *m.* firstly, 18 Jan. 1850, at St. Geo., Han. sq., Sarah Elizabeth, 1st surv. da. and coheir of John Singleton (COPLEY), BARON LYNDHURST, three times (1827-30, 1834-35, and 1841-46) Lord Chancellor of England, by his 1st wife, Sarah Garey, da. of Charles BRUNSDEN. She, who was *b.* 16 March 1821, *d.* 25 June 1865, at 8 St. George's terrace, Queen's Gate. He *m.* secondly, 9 July 1867, at St. James', Westm. (as her 3d husband, Eden, widow of his cousin, Sir Charles Henry IBBETSON, 5th Baronet [1748], (whom see), on which occasion he took the name of IBBETSON after that of SELWIN, as abovestated. She *d.* 1 April 1899, at 62 Prince's Gate. Will pr. at £72,962 gross, the net personalty being £54,764. He *m.* thirdly, 5 Sep. 1900, at St. Michael's, Chester sq. (being then nearly 74), Sophia Harriet, 1st da. of, Major Digby LAWRELL, of Jersey. He *d.* s.p. in London, 15 Jan. 1902, aged 75 when the *Peerage* as well as the *Baronetcy* became *extinct*.(a) Will pr. at £106,268, the net personalty being £48,140. His widow living 1905.

Family Estates.—These, in 1883, consisted of 2,098 acres in Essex and Yorkshire, worth £3,090 a year.

LAWRENCE:

cr. 17 Jan 1747/8;

afterwards, 1749-56, WOOLLASTON;

ex. 30 Dec. 1756.

I. 1748. SIR EDWARD LAWRENCE, Knt., of St. Ives, co. Huntingdon, s. and h. of Rev. Paul LAWRENCE, Minister of Tangmere, co. Sussex, by Jane, sister of Thomas PALMER, of Angmering, Sussex;(b) was *Knighted*, 21 Jan. 1700/1; Gent. Usher to Queen Anne, 1703; M.P. for Stockbridge, 1705-10; F.R.S. 1708; and was *cr. a Baronet*, as above, 17 Jan. 1747/8, with a spec. rem., failing heirs male of his body, to his great-nephew, Isaac WOOLLASTON. He *d.* s.p.m., probably unm.,(c) 2 March 1748/9, or 2 May 1749. Will pr. 1749.

(a) Of his two sisters (1) Isabella Mary, *m.* 14 April 1859, Edmund Calverley, of Oulton Hall, co. York, and *d.* 6 June 1895, leaving issue; (2) Gertrude Louisa Jane, *m.* 17 June 1863, the Rev. Edward Capel Cure, M.A.

(b) Le Neve's *Knights*, p. 472.

(c) The relict [*sic*] of Sir Edward Lawrence is said to have *d.* 19 Oct. 1723,

II. 1749. SIR ISAAC WOOLLASTON, Baronet [1748], of Loseby, co. Leicester, great-nephew and h, being s. and h. of Isaac WOOLLASTON, of Loseby, by Sarah (marr. lic. London, 21 Nov. 1692, he 18 and she 17, with consent of their respective mothers, the fathers being dead), da. of (—) LAWRENCE, which Isaac (*b.* 1673 and *d.* 1736) was s. and h. of Josiah WOOLLASTON (*d.* 1689, aged 37), by Elizabeth (*m.* in or before 1673), sister of Sir Edward LAWRENCE, the late Baronet. He *suc. to the Baronetcy* in 1749, under the spec. rem. in its creation. He *m.* Sarah Rowland, widow of (—) GATTAR, da. and h. of (—) MARCH, of Haddenham, in the Isle of Ely.(a) He *d.* 13 Oct. 1750. Admon. 3 May 1751, and 19 Nov. 1755. His widow *d.* 13 Oct. 1753.

III. 1750, to 1756. SIR ISAAC LAWRENCE WOOLLASTON, Baronet [1748], of Loseby aforesaid, only s. and h., *suc. to the Baronetcy*, 13 Oct. 1750. He *d.* an infant, 30 Dec. 1756, when the *Baronetcy* became *extinct*.(b) Admon. 6 May 1757.

VANNECK:

cr. 14 Dec. 1751;

afterwards, since 1796, BARONS HUNTINGFIELD [I.].

I. 1751. JOSHUA VANNECK, of Putney, co. Surrey, Esq., yr. s. of Cornelius VANNECK, Paymaster of the Land Forces of the United Provinces, was *b.* at the Hague, Holland; came over to London 1722, where, in partnership with his elder br. Gerard VANNECK (who settled there in 1718, and *d.* s.p. in 1750), he obtained a large fortune in commerce, and was *cr. a Baronet*, as above, 14 Dec. 1751. He purchased the estate of Heveningham, in Suffolk. He *m.* in or before 1732, Marianne, da. of (—) DAUBUZ, of Putney aforesaid. She *d.* 1750. He *d.* 6 March 1777.

II. 1777. SIR GERARD VANNECK, Baronet [1751], of Putney and Heveningham aforesaid, 1st surv. s. and h.;(c) was a merchant in London; M.P. for Dunwich (four Parls.), 1768-90, having *suc. to the Baronetcy*, 6 March 1777. He *d.* unm. 22 May 1791. Will pr. June 1791.

III. 1791. SIR JOSHUA VANNECK, Baronet [1751], of Heveningham aforesaid, only surv. br. and h., *b.* 31 Dec. 1745; was a merchant of London; M.P. for Dunwich (eight Parls.), 1790-1816, and *suc. to the Baronetcy*, 22 May 1791. He *m.* 27 Sep. 1777, at St. Peter le Poor, London, Maria, 2d da. of Andrew THOMPSON, of Roehampton, Surrey, by Harriet, da. of Col. John BUNCOMBE, of Goathurst, Somerset. She was living when he was *cr.* 7 July 1796, BARON HUNTINGFIELD OF HEVENINGHAM HALL [I.], in which peerage this *Baronetcy* then *merged* and still (1905) so continues. See PEERAGE.

(a) Courthope's *Extinct Baronetage*.

(b) Of his two sisters, both minors at his death (1), Sarah, inherited the estate of St. Ives and those in the Isle of Ely. She *m.* in 1765, Taylor White, and was mother of Thomas Woollaston White, *cr. a Baronet*, 20 Dec. 1802. (2), Anne, inherited the estate of Loseby. She *m.* in 1772, Sir Thomas Folke, and had issue.

(c) Gerard William Vanneck, another son, apparently an elder one, was *bap.* 3 Oct. 1742 at Putney, and *bur.* there 9 Sep. 1743.

GIBBONS:

cr. 21 April 1752.

I. 1752. WILLIAM GIBBONS, of Barbadoes, Esq., sometime Speaker of the House of Assembly there, and Governor of that Island, whose parentage is unknown, was *cr. a Baronet*, as above, 21 April 1752. He *m.* in or before 1717, Frances, da. of Robert HALL, of Barbadoes. She *d.* there 20 April 1758, aged 64. He *d.* there May 1760. Will pr. Feb. 1766.

II. 1760. SIR JOHN GIBBONS, Baronet [1752], of Stanwell Place in Stanwell, Midx., 1st s. and h., *b.* about 1717, who v.p., had, in 1754, purchased that estate; was M.P. for Stockbridge, 1754-61, and for Wallingford, 1761-68, having *suc. to the Baronetcy*, May 1760; was made **K.B.**, March, and installed May 1761. He was *cr.* D.C.L. of Oxford, 3 July 1761. He *m.* in or before 1749, Martha, da. of the Rev. Scawen KENRICK, D.D., Rector of St. Martin's-in-the-Fields. He *d.* 9 July 1776, aged 59, at Stanwell. Will pr. 1777. His widow d. 14 May 1807, at Bath, in her 81st year. Will pr. 1807.

III. 1776. SIR WILLIAM GIBBONS, Baronet [1752], of Stanwell Place aforesaid, *b.* 5 and *bap.* 15 May 1749, at St. Margaret's, Westm.; matric. at Oxford (Merton Coll.), 25 April 1766, aged 16; B.A., 1769; *cr.* D.C.L., 9 June 1773; *suc. to the Baronetcy*, 9 July 1776; a Commissioner of the Sick and Hurt Office, 1789. He *m.* 3 Sep. 1771, Rebecca, sister of Sir Charles WATSON, 1st Baronet [1760], 1st da. of Vice-Admiral Charles WATSON, by Rebecca, da. of John Francis BULLER, of Morval. She *d.* 26 April 1811. He *d.* 26 Nov. 1814, aged 65. Will pr. 1815.

IV. 1814. SIR JOHN GIBBONS, Baronet [1752], of Stanwell Place aforesaid. 1st s. and h., *b.* 8 Jan. 1774; matric. at Oxford (Merton Coll.), 23 June 1792, aged 17; B.A., 1794; *suc. to the Baronetcy*, 26 Nov. 1814; Colonel West Middlesex Militia. He *m.* 27 Oct. 1795, at Stanwell, Elizabeth, da. of Richard TAYLOR, of Charleton house, Midx. She *d.* 20 Oct. 1835 at Brompton, Midx. He *d.* 25 March 1844, at Stanwell Place, aged 70. Will pr. 1845.

V. 1844. SIR JOHN GIBBONS Baronet [1752], of Stanwell Place aforesaid, grandson and h., being 1st s. and h. of John GIBBONS, M.A. (Oxford), of Wratting Park, co. Cambridge, by his 1st wife, Charlotte, da. of his great uncle, Sir Charles WATSON, 1st Baronet [1760] abovenamed, which John (who *d.* v.p. 31 Jan. 1841, aged 38) was 1st s. and h. ap. of the late Baronet. He was *b.* 30 Aug. 1825, at Wratting Park aforesaid; matric. at Oxford (Ball. Coll.), 30 March 1843, aged 17; B.A., 1846; M.A., 1849; having *suc. to the Baronetcy*, 25 March 1844; sometime Major West Midx. Militia. Sheriff of Midx., 1891. He *d.* unm. 6 Jan. 1893, at Stanwell Place, aged 67. Will pr. at £8,731 personalty.

VI. 1893. SIR CHARLES GIBBONS, Baronet [1752], of Stanwell Place aforesaid, br. and h., *b.* at Rome, 13 Jan. 1828; entered the Royal Navy, retiring as Captain, 1877, having served in the Black Sea during the Crimean war (medal, clasp and Turkish medal), 1854-56; was a Government emigration officer, 1868-79; *suc. to the Baronetcy*, 6 Jan. 1893. He *m.* 5 April 1864, Lydia Martha, sister of Gen. Sir John DORAN, **K.C.B.**, 4th da. of John DORAN, of Ely House, co. Wexford, Major 18th Foot, by Georgina, da. of Robert HUGHES, of Ely House aforesaid.

Family Estates.—These, in 1883, consisted of 2,695 acres in Midx., Yorkshire, Berks and Staffordshire, worth £3,710 a year. *Seat.*—Stanwell Place, near Staines, Midx.

KNOLLYS:

cr. 1 April 1754;

ex. 29 June 1772.

I. 1754, to 1772. FRANCIS KNOLLYS, the younger, of Thame, co. Oxford, Esq., only s. of Richard KNOLLYS, by his 1st wife Elizabeth, da. and coheir of Humphrey THAYER, Commissioner of Excise, and nephew of Francis KNOLLYS, of Thame aforesaid, sometime M.P. for Oxford (who *d.* unm. 24 June 1754), was *b.* about 1722; matric. at Oxford (St. John's Coll.) 27 July 1739, aged 17; *cr.* M.A., 19 April 1744, and D.C.L., 17 July 1756, having been *cr. a Baronet*, as above, 1 April 1754; Sheriff of Oxon, 1757-58; M.P. for Reading, 1761-68. He *m.* in 1756, Mary, da. and h. of Sir Robert CATER, *formerly* KENDALL, of Kempston, Beds., Alderman and sometime (1737-38) Sheriff of London, by Mary, his wife. He *d.* s.p. 29 June, and was *bur.* 7 July 1772, at St. Lawrence's, Reading, when the *Baronetcy* became *extinct*. Will pr. July 1772. His widow *d.* 19 Dec. 1791, aged 63. Will pr. Dec. 1791.

LAMB:

cr. 17 Jan. 1755;

afterwards, 1770-1853, BARONS MELBOURNE [I.];

and subsequently, 1781-1853, VISCOUNTS MELBOURNE [I.];

ex. 29 Jan. 1853.

I. 1755. MATTHEW LAMB, of Brocket Hall, in Bishop's Hatfield, Herts, Esq., yr. br. of Robert LAMB, Bishop of Peterborough, (1764-69) both being sons of Matthew LAMB, of Southwell, Notts, Attorney, land agent to the family of Coke, of Melbourne, co. Derby, was *b.* 1705; admitted to Lincoln's Inn, 26 Jan. 1725/6; Barrister, 26 April 1733; Solicitor to the Revenue of the Post Office, 1738, King's Counsel, 1754, and Counsel for the Board of Trade and Plantations. He was executor, in 1735, to his uncle, Peniston LAMB,(a) from whom he inherited a large fortune; was M.P. for Stockbridge, 1741-47, and for Peterborough (four Parls.), 1747 till his death in 1768; purchased, in 1746, the Brocket estate (where he rebuilt the mansion), and was *cr. a Baronet*, as above, 17 Jan. 1755. He *m.* in or before 1747, Charlotte, sister and h. of George Lewis COKE, of Melbourne, co. Derby (who *d.* unexpectedly in 1751), being da. of Thomas COKE, of the same, P.C., Vice-Chamberlain to Queen Anne. He *d.* 6 Nov. 1768, and was *bur.* at Bishop's Hatfield, aged about 63. Will pr. Nov. 1768, his property being estimated at nearly a million, of which one half was personalty.(b)

II. 1768. SIR PENISTON LAMB, Baronet [1755], of Brocket Hall and of Melbourne aforesaid, only s. and h., *b.* in Red Lion square, 29 Jan. and *bap.* 9 Feb. 1744/5, at St. George the Martyr, Midx., *suc. to the Baronetcy*, 6 Nov. 1768; was admitted to Lincoln's Inn, 12 June 1769; M.P. for Ludgershall (three Parls.), 1768-84; for Malmesbury, 1784; and for Newport (Isle of Wight), 1790-93, being a supporter of Lord NORTH's Ministry. He *m.*

(a) He, who was *b.* at Southwell, Notts, was admitted, 7 Oct. 1708, to Lincoln's Inn, where he *d.* 29 Jan. 1735, being "an eminent land conveyancer, reputed worth £100,000" [*Hist. Reg.*].

(b) He was "the confidential adviser of Lord Salisbury and Lord Egmont, and according to Hayward (*Celebrated Statesmen*, i, 332), feathered his nest at their expense" [*Dict. Nat. Biog.*]. The old Marchioness of Salisbury (widow of the 1st Marquess) used to say the rise of the Lamb family was from the plunder of the Earls of Salisbury.

13 April 1769, at the Bishop of Peterborough's house, in Great George street, St. Geo., Han. sq., Elizabeth, da. of Sir Ralph MILBANKE, 5th Baronet [1661], by Elizabeth, da. of John HEDWORTH. She was living when he was *cr.* 8 or 28 June 1770 LORD MELBOURNE, BARON OF KILMORE, co. Cavan [I.], and subsequently, 11 Jan. 1781, VISCOUNT MELBOURNE OF KILMORE, co. Cavan [I.] In these peerages this *Baronetcy* then *merged* till all these honours became *extinct*, by the death of the 3d Viscount and 4th Baronet, 29 Jan. 1853. See "PEERAGE."

WINNINGTON:

cr. 15 Feb. 1755.

I. 1755. EDWARD WINNINGTON, of Stanford Court, co. Worcester, Esq., s. of Edward WINNINGTON,(a) of Broadway, co. Worcester, by Sophia (who *d.* Feb. 1770), da. of (—) BOOTE, of Wantage, Berks, was *b.* at Wantage, about 1728; matric. at Oxford (Trin. Coll.), 15 May 1746, aged 18, and was *cr. a Baronet* as above, 15 Feb. 1755. He was M.P. for Bewdley (two Parls.) 1761-74. He *m.* in or before 1749, Mary, da. of John INGRAM, of Ticknell and Bewdley aforesaid. He *d.* 9 Dec. 1791. Will pr. May 1792.

II. 1791. SIR EDWARD WINNINGTON, Baronet [1755], of Stanford Court aforesaid, only s. and h.; *b.* 14 Nov. 1749; matric. at Oxford (Ch. Ch.), 30 Oct. 1767, aged 17; M.P. for Droitwich (six Parls.) Nov. 1777 till death in 1805; *suc. to the Baronetcy*, 9 Dec. 1791. He *m.* 13 Sep. 1776 (spec. lic.) Anne, yst. da. of Thomas (FOLEY), 1st BARON FOLEY OF KIDDERMINSTER (1776), by Grace, da. and coheir of George (GRANVILLE), BARON LANSDOWN OF BIDEFORD. She *d.* 9 Dec. 1794. He *d.* 9 Jan. 1805, aged 55. Will pr. 1805.

III. 1805. SIR THOMAS EDWARD WINNINGTON, Baronet, [1755], of Stanford Court aforesaid, 1st s. and h., *b.* about 1780, at Marylebone; ed. at Eton; matric. at Oxford (Ch. Ch.) 6 Feb. 1798, aged 18; *suc. to the Baronetcy*, 9 Jan. 1805; was Sheriff of Worcestershire, 1806-07; M.P. for Droitwich, 1807-16; for Worcestershire, 1820-30; for Droitwich (again), 1831-32; and for Bewdley, 1832-37. He *m.* 11 Nov. 1810, Joanna, da. of John TAYLOR, of Moseley Hall, in King's Norton, co. Worcester. He *d.* 24 Sep. 1839, at Stanford Court, aged 66. Will pr. March 1840. His widow *d.* 23 Dec. 1853, in Suffolk street, Pall Mall. Will pr. Jan. 1854.

IV. 1839. SIR THOMAS EDWARD WINNINGTON, Baronet [1755], of Stanford Court aforesaid, 1st s. and h., *b.* 11 Nov. 1811, at Moseley Hall aforesaid; ed. at Eton; matric. at Oxford (Ch. Ch.), 27 May 1830, aged 18; B.A., 1833; M.P. for Bewdley, 1837-47, and 1852-68, having *suc. to the Baronetcy*, 24 Sep. 1839; Sheriff of Worcestershire, 1851-52. He *m.* 21 June 1842, at St. Geo. Han. sq., Anna Helena, 1st da. of Sir Compton DOMVILE, 1st Baronet [1815], by his 2d wife, Helena Sarah, da. of Michael Frederic TRENCH, of Heywood, Queen's County. He *d.* 18 June 1872, at 8 Petersham terrace, Kensington, aged 61. His widow *d.* 28 March 1883, at 116 Queen's Gate, aged 66. Will pr. 6 Aug. 1883, under £14,000.

(a) This Edward was 2d s. of Francis Winnington, of Broadway, sometime (1747) M.P. for Droitwich, who was 2d s. of Sir Francis Winnington, Solicitor-Gen. to Charles II. (*d.* 1 May 1700, aged 65), by Elizabeth, sister and coheir of Edward Salwey, of Stanford Court, co. Worcester. The issue male of their eldest s., Salwey Winnington (*d.* 6 Nov. 1736), became extinct on the death of his s., Thomas Winnington, Paymaster-Gen. of the Forces, 23 April 1746, aged 46.

V

V. 1872. SIR FRANCIS SALWEY WINNINGTON, Baronet [1755], of Stanford Court aforesaid, 2d but 1st surv. s. and h.,(a), *b.* there 24 Sep. 1849; sometime Ensign, 66th Foot; *suc. to the Baronetcy*, 18 June 1872; Sheriff of Worcestershire, 1894. He *m.* 5 Feb. 1879, at All Saints', Ennismore Gardens, Jane, 1st da. of Lord Alfred SPENCER-CHURCHILL (2d s. of George, DUKE OF MARLBOROUGH), by Harriet Louisa Esther, da. of Frederick (GOUGH-CALTHORPE), 4th BARON CALTHORPE. She was *b.* 2 Feb. 1858.

Family Estates.—These, in 1883, consisted of 4,196 acres in Worcestershire, and 426 in Herefordshire. *Total.*—4,622 acres, worth £6,418 a year. *Seat.*—Stanford Court, near Worcester.

SHEFFIELD:
cr. 1 March 1755.

I. 1755. CHARLES SHEFFIELD, of Normanby, co. Lincoln, Esq., *formerly* Charles HERBERT, was illegit. son of John (SHEFFIELD), 1st DUKE OF BUCKINGHAM AND NORMANBY, by Frances(b) (then or afterwards) wife of the Hon. Oliver LAMBART (yr. s. of Charles, 3d EARL OF CAVAN [I.], da. of (—) STEWART. He was *b.* probably about 1706 (when his mother(c) would be aged 22, was "under the tuition of Mons. Brezy, at Utretcht," in Aug. 1716, and (under the will, dated 2 Aug. 1716, and pr. 28 March 1721, of his abovenamed putative father) took the name of SHEFFIELD, instead of HERBERT.(d) He (under the said will) inherited, on the death, 30 Oct. 1735, of the 2d and last Duke (at his age of 19), the considerable estates of both of these Dukes, in Lincolnshire and elsewhere, and was *cr. a Baronet*, as above, 1 March 1755. He *m.* 25 April 1741, Margaret Diana, da. of Gen. Joseph SABINE, sometime Gov. of Ghent and Gibraltar. She *d.* 7 Jan. 1762, in Buckingham House, St. James' Park, which shortly afterwards was sold by her husband for £21,000 to George III. He *d.* 5 Sep. 1774. Will pr. July 1775.

II. 1774. SIR JOHN SHEFFIELD, Baronet [1755], of Normanby aforesaid, *b.* about 1743; matric. at Oxford (Ch. Ch.) 7 Feb. 1760, aged 17; *suc. to the Baronetcy*, 5 Sep. 1774. He *m.*, 3 April 1784, Sophia Charlotte, 1st da. of William DIGBY, D.D., Dean of Durham (br. of Henry, 1st EARL DIGBY), by Charlotte, da. of Joseph Cox. He *d.* s.p., 4 Feb. 1815, aged 72. Will pr. 1815. His widow *d.* 15 Dec. 1835. Will pr. March 1836.

III. 1815, Feb. 4. SIR ROBERT SHEFFIELD, Baronet [1755], of Normanby aforesaid, br. and h., *b.* about 1758; matric. at Oxford (Ch. Ch.), 25 Jan. 1775, aged 17; B.A., 1774; M.A., 1781; took Holy Orders; *suc. to the Baronetcy*, 4 Feb. 1815. He *m.* firstly, in or before 1785, Penelope, da. of Sir Abraham PITCHES, of Streatham, Surrey. He *m.* secondly, in or before 1797, Sarah Anne, da. of the Rev. Brackley KENNET, D.D., a son, presumably, of Brackley KENNET, the cowardly Lord Mayor of London, 1779-80. He *d.* a few days after his brother, 26 Feb. 1815. Will pr. 1815. His widow *d.* 14 Sep. 1858, at Holly Hill, Hartfield, Sussex, aged 83.

(a) Thomas Edward Winnington, the 1st s., *b.* 9 Jan. 1848, at Stanford Court, ed. at Eton, matric. at Oxford (Ch. Ch.), 1 May 1867, aged 19; *d.* there unm. and v.p., in April 1869, aged 21.

(b) She is called in Playfair's *Baronetage* (1811), "S. C. Stewart, afterwards Mrs. Lambert." Her christian name, however, was undoubtedly Frances. See note "b" below.

(c) See Col. Chester's note to her burial, 11 Jan. 1750/1, aged 66, in his *Registers of Westminster Abbey.*

(d) It is just possible that the matric. at Oxford (Ch. Ch.) 5 Sep. 1721 of "Charles Herbert, son of John, of Westminster, Esq., [*sic*] aged 18," may refer to him.

IV. 1815, Feb. 26. SIR ROBERT SHEFFIELD, Baronet [1755], of Normanby aforesaid, 1st s. and h., being only s. and h. by the 1st wife, *b.* 25 Feb. 1786, at Streatham aforesaid; *suc. to the Baronetcy*, 26 Feb. 1815; Sheriff of Lincolnshire, 1817-18, and sometime Chairman of the Kirton Quarter Sessions. He *m.*, 8 Dec. 1818, Julia Brigida, da. of Sir John NEWBOLD, Chief Justice of Madras. He *d.* 7 Nov. 1862, at Normanby Park, aged 76. His widow *d.* 28 Oct. 1875, at Thornhill, East Grinstead, Sussex, in her 76th year.

V. 1862. SIR ROBERT SHEFFIELD, Baronet [1755], of Normanby Park aforesaid, 1st s. and h., *b.* there 8 Dec. 1823; ed. at Eton; matric. at Oxford (Ch. Ch.), 26 May 1841, aged 17; entered Royal Horse Guards (Blue), 1842; Captain, 1849, retiring 1861, with brevet rank of Major; *suc. to the Baronetcy*, 7 Nov. 1862; Sheriff of Lincolnshire, 1872. He *m.* 30 Jan. 1867, at Appleby, co. Lincoln, Priscilla Isabella Laura, 3d da. of Lieut.-Col. Henry DUMARESQ, Royal Engineers, by Elizabeth Sophia, sister of Robert Herbert, 3d EARL OF LANESBOROUGH [I.], da. of the Hon. Augustus Richard BUTLER-DANVERS, He *d.* 23 Oct. 1886, at 4, Brock street, Bath, aged 62. His widow *m.* 15 March 1890, Lieut.-Col. Thomas Astell ST. QUINTIN, 8th Hussars, and *d.* 30 May 1900, at "Wavendon," Ascot, Berks.

VI. 1886. SIR BERKELEY DIGBY GEORGE SHEFFIELD, Baronet [1755], of Normanby Park aforesaid, only s. and h., *b.* 19 Jan. 1876, in Grosvenor street, London; *suc. to the Baronetcy*, 23 Oct. 1886; ed. at Eton; Captain of the Lincolnshire Imperial Yeomanry; Hon. Attaché to the Embassy at Paris, 1897.

Family Estates.—These, in 1883, consisted of 9,370 acres in Lincolnshire, worth £13,480 a year; besides 150 acres there, rented at £191, held by the then Baronet and "another." *Seat.*—Normanby Park, near Brigg, co. Lincoln.

MANN:
cr. 3 March 1755;
ex. 2 April 1814.

I. 1755. HORACE MANN, Esq., British Envoy [1740-86] to Tuscany, 2d s. of Robert MANN, of Linton, co. Kent, formerly a merchant, of London (*d.* 12 March 1752), by Eleanor, da. and h. of Christopher GUISE, of Abbots Court, co. Gloucester, was *b.* about 1701; was appointed in 1737, assistant to the Envoy Extraordinary and Minister Plenipotentiary to Tuscany, being in 1740 (himself) appointed to that post, and *cr. a Baronet*, as above, 3 March 1755, with a spec. rem., failing heirs male of his body, to his brother Geoffrey [Galfridus] MANN. He, very shortly afterwards, by the death 16 Dec. 1755, of his eldest br., Edward Louisa MANN, at Linton, suc. to that estate, which, however, he made over to his nephew and successor, Horace MANN, in 1779 or 1786.(a) He was made **K.B.**, 25 Oct. 1768. He *d.* unm. at Florence, where he had resided forty-nine years, 6 Nov. 1786, aged about 85,(b) and was *bur.* at Linton. Will pr. 8 May 1787.

(a) In Betham's *Baronetage* (1805) stated to be in 1779, but in Playfair's *Baronetage* (1811) stated to be in 1786.

(b) The series of letters during forty-five years (1741-86) between himself and Horace Walpole (who had paid him a visit at Florence 1740-41) is well known, more especially those of Walpole—but those of Mann give, perhaps, the best account of the last days of Prince Charles Edward Stuart, who after 1775 resided at Florence.

II. 1786, to 1814. SIR HORACE MANN, Baronet [1755], of Linton aforesaid, nephew and h., being 2d but only surv. s. of Geoffrey MANN, of Boughton Malherbe and Egerton, co. Kent, sometime M.P. for Maidstone, by Sarah, da. of John GREGORY, of London, was *b.* 2 Feb. 1743/4; ed. at Peterhouse, Cambridge, and *cr.* M.A., 1763, *per literas regias*; was *Knighted* 1768 when acting as proxy at the installation of his uncle abovenamed, as a Knight of the Bath; was M.P. for Maidstone (two Parls.) 1774-84, and for Sandwich (four Parls.) 1790-1807; *suc. to the Baronetcy*, 6 Nov. 1786. He *m.* 13 April 1765, Lucy, da. of Baptist (NOEL), 4th EARL OF GAINSBOROUGH, by Elizabeth, da. of William CHAPMAN. She *d.* at Nice, 2 Feb. 1778. He *d.* s.p.m.,(a) 2 April 1814, aged 70, when the *Baronetcy* became *extinct*. Will pr. 9 Jan. 1816.

CAVENDISH:(b)
cr. 7 May 1755;
afterwards, since 1804, BARONS WATERPARK [I.]

I. 1755. HENRY CAVENDISH, of Doveridge, co. Derby, Esq., 1st s. of William CAVENDISH, of the same, by Mary, da. of Timothy TYRRELL, of Shotover, Oxon, and of Oakley, Bucks, and Elizabeth, his wife, da. and h. of James USSHER, Archbishop of Armagh, was *b.* 13 April 1707; matric. at Oxford (Univ. Coll.), 17 Aug. 1724, aged 17; Sheriff of Derbyshire, 1741; went to Ireland during the Vice-Royalty of his kinsman, William (CAVENDISH), 3d DUKE OF DEVONSHIRE; was made Teller of the Exchequer [I.]; Collector for Cork, 1743; Commissioner of Revenue [I.], 1747, and was *cr. a Baronet*, as above, 7 May 1755. He was M.P. [I.] for Tullagh, 1756-60, and for Lismore, 1761-68 and 1776; was P.C. [I.], 9 June 1768. He *m.* firstly, 9 June 1730, at the Chapel Royal, Whitehall (articles and lic. Lond. 8), Anne (then aged 23), da. and h. of Henry PYNE, of Waterpark, co. Cork, by Anne, da. of Sir Richard EDGCUMBE, **K.B.**, which Henry was s. of Sir Richard PYNE, sometime (1695-1709) Chief Justice of the King's Bench [I.]. She was living 1737. He *m.* secondly, 4 Oct. 1748 (Lic. 3), Catherine, widow of Sir Richard MEADE, 3d Baronet [I. 1703], 2d da. of Henry PRITTIE, of Dunalley, co. Tipperary, by Elizabeth, da. and h. of Col. James HARRISON, of Cloghjordan, in that county. He *d.* 31 Dec. 1776. Will dat. 5 Dec. 1776, pr. [I.] 1 Jan. 1777. His widow *d.* 21 March 1779, aged 69. Will dat. 20 Feb. and pr. [I.] 12 April 1779.

II. 1776. SIR HENRY CAVENDISH, Baronet [1755], of Doveridge aforesaid, 1st s. and. h. by 1st wife, *b.* 29 Sep. 1732; was v.p. M.P. [I.] for Lismore, 1764-68 and 1776, M.P. [G.B.] for Lostwithiel, 1768-74, and *suc. to the Baronetcy*, 31 Dec. 1776; he was also again M.P. [I.] for Lismore, 1783-90; for Killybegs, 1790-97; and for Lismore (again), 1798-1801, and was a firm supporter of the Irish Union; P.C. [I.], 1 July 1779; Receiver General [I.], in that year, and sometime Vice-Treasurer [I.]. He *m.* 12 Aug. 1757, Sarah, da. and h. of Richard BRADSHAW, of Cork, by Deborah, da. of William THOMPSON, of that city. She, who

(a) He had three daughters, all of whom married in his lifetime, but the estate of Linton was inherited by his nephew, James Cornwallis (*b.* 20 Sep. 1778), 1st s. of his sister, Catherine, by James Cornwallis, Bishop of Lichfield, and afterwards (1823) 4th Earl Cornwallis. He thereupon took the name of Mann only, by royal lic., 9 April 1814, and (ten years later) suc. his father, 20 Jan. 1824, as 5th Earl Cornwallis. He *d.* s.p.m.s. 21 April 1852, when all his honours became extinct.

(b) Much of the information in this article was supplied by G. T. Burtchaell, Office of Arms, Dublin, from a pedigree there registered.

(c) This William was descended from Henry Cavendish, of Doveridge, illegit. son of Henry Cavendish, of Chatsworth, co. Derby (*d.* s.p. legit. 12 Oct. 1616, aged 67), the elder br. of William, 1st Earl of Devonshire.

was *b.* 1 April 1740, was, in consideration of her husband's political services, *cr.* 15 June 1792, BARONESS WATERPARK of Waterpark, co. Cork [I.], with rem. of that Barony to the heirs male of her body by her said husband. He *d.* 3 Aug. 1804, at the Black rock, near Dublin, in his 72d year. Will pr. [I.] 1804. His widow, the *suo jure* Baroness, *d.* 4 Aug. 1807, at her house in York place. Will pr. 1807.

III. 1804. SIR RICHARD CAVENDISH, Baronet [1755], of Doveridge aforesaid, 1st s. and h., *b.* 13 July 1765; M.P. [I.] for Portarlington, 1790-97; *suc. to the Baronetcy*, 3 Aug. 1804; F.S.A. He *m.* 6 Aug. 1789, Juliana (£20,000), 1st da. and coheir of Thomas COOPER, of Mullaghmast Castle, co. Kildare, niece to Thomas BERNARD, sometime (1794-1806) Bishop of Limerick. She was living when, by the death of his mother, 4 Aug. 1807, he became BARON WATERPARK [I.]. In that peerage this *Baronetcy* then *merged*, and still (1905) so continues. See *Peerage.*

JOHNSON,(a) *or* JOHNSTON.(b)
cr. 27 Nov. 1755.

I. 1755. WILLIAM JOHNSON, *or* JOHNSTON,(a) of New York, in North America, Esq., yst. s. of Christopher JOHNSON,(c) *or* JOHNSTON, of Smithstown, co. Meath, by Anne, sister of Vice-Admiral Sir Peter WARREN, **K.B.**, da. of Michael WARREN, of Warrenstown in that county, was *b.* 1715, at Smithstown, went in 1738 to America to manage an estate of his said uncle on the Mohawk river, and embarking in trade with the Indian tribes acquired a great ascendancy over them, and was chosen by the Mohawks as their "Sachem." In 1744, was Col. of the Six Nations; in 1746 was Commissary for Indian affairs; in 1748, was in command of the New York Colonial forces; in April 1750, a member of the Governor's Council; and in April 1755, "sole superintendent of the affairs of the six united nations," with the rank of Major-General. As such, at the head of the provincial forces, he defeated the French, under Baron Dieskau, at Lake George. For this he had the thanks of Parliament, a grant of £5,000, and was *cr. a Baronet*, as above, 27 Nov. 1755. His appointment as "sole superintendent" was renewed in March 1756, and was held by him till his death, with a salary of £600. In 1759 he was second (afterwards first) in command at the capture of Fort Niagara, and in 1760 led the Indians in the advance on Montreal and the conquest of Canada. In the Indian war which followed, in 1763, his influence was greatly felt, and he succeeded in making a successful treaty with the Indians in 1768 at Fort Stanwix. For his Canadian services, he was granted 100,000 acres on the north bank of the Mohawk, where in 1764 he built "Johnson Hall," three miles from Fort Johnson. He *m.* in 1739, Mary, [*sic*](d) da. of John DE WISSENBERGH, of Montreal, a German settler on the Mohawk. She, by whom he had three children, was living 1742, but *d.* soon afterwards. He is said to have *m.* secondly (on her deathbed) a young Dutch woman, by whom he had many children.(e) He *d.* at Johnson Hall aforesaid, 11 July 1774, aged 59. Will pr. Feb. 1776.

(a) See p. 104, note "b."

(b) In the will of Warren Johnston, br. of the 1st Baronet, pr. 1785, the name is spelt "Johnston" [*Ex inform.* Lieut.-Col. G. H. Johnston, of Markethill, co. Armagh].

(c) The grandfather of this Christopher is said to have been "Thomas, 1st s. of John O'Neill, of Dungannon, co. Tyrone, in Irish called MacShane (son of John), becoming, in English, John-son" [*Ex. inform.* G. D. Burtchaell, see note "a" above].

(d) *Dict. Nat. Biog.* The lady's name is often (but apparently in error) given as "Frances."

(e) He subsequently had no less than eight illegitimate children by Molly Brandt, sister of the famous War Chief of the Mohawks.

II. 1774. SIR JOHN JOHNSON, Baronet [1755], of Johnson Hall aforesaid, s. and h., *b.* 1742; *Knighted*, v.p., 22 Nov. 1765, at St. James'; *suc. to the Baronetcy*, 11 July 1774; and suc. his cousin and brother-in-law, Col. Guy JOHNSON, in 1783, as Superintendent of the Indian affairs, which post he held till his death; was Chief of the Canadian Militia, and was in command of a regiment known as "Johnson's Greens" during the American war; was sometime of Guyot, co. Lincoln, and of Twickenham, Midx., in England. He *m.* 30 June 1773, Mary, da. of John WATTS, President of the Council of New York. She *d.* 17 Aug. 1815. He *d.* 4 Jan. 1830, at St. Mary's, Montreal, in Canada, aged 88.

III. 1830. SIR ADAM GORDON JOHNSON, Baronet [1755], of Canada, but sometime of Twickenham, Midx., 3rd, but 1st surv. s. and h. male,(a) *b.* 5 May 1781; Lieut.-Col. 6th Battalion Militia; *suc. to the Baronetcy*, 4 Jan. 1830. He *d.* unm. 21 May 1843, aged 62.

IV. 1843. SIR WILLIAM GEORGE JOHNSON, Baronet [1755], of St. Matthias, near Montreal, in Canada aforesaid, nephew and h. male, being 1st s. and h. of Col. John JOHNSON, of Point Olivier, Montreal, by Mary Diana (*m.* 10 Feb. 1825), da. of Richard DILLON, also of Montreal, which John (who *d.* 23 June 1841, aged 58) was yr. br. of the late and 6th s. of the 2d Baronet. He was *b.* 19 Dec. 1830, *suc. to the Baronetcy*, 21 May 1843; was Lieut. Royal Artillery, 1848-54. He *m.* 30 March 1889, Elizabeth, only da. of Richard Hancock BROWN, of Bowdon, co. Chester.

WHITE:

cr. 6 May 1756;

afterwards, since 1763, RIDLEY;

and, since 1900, VISCOUNTS RIDLEY.

I. 1756. MATTHEW WHITE, of Blagdon, co. Northumberland, Esq., 1st and only surv. s. and h. of Matthew WHITE, of the same, and Elizabeth, da. and coheir of John JOHNSON, of Bebridge, and Newcastle, both in the same county, was *b.* about 1727; matric. at Oxford (Univ. Coll.), 29 April 1746, aged 19; was Sheriff of Northumberland, 1756-57, and was, on presenting a petition from that county to the King, *cr. a Baronet*, as above, 6 May 1756, with a spec. rem., failing heirs male of his body, to those of his sister Elizabeth, wife of Matthew RIDLEY, of Heaton, co. Northumberland. He *d.* unm. 21 March 1763, and was *bur.* at All Saints', Newcastle-upon-Tyne.

II. 1763. SIR MATTHEW WHITE RIDLEY, Baronet [1756], of Blagdon aforesaid, nephew by the sister, being 2d s. of Matthew RIDLEY, of Heaton, co. Northumberland, sometime (1747-74) M.P. for Newcastle-on-Tyne, and 1st s. and, eventually, heir(b) of his 2d wife, Elizabeth (*d.* 4 May 1764), sister of the late Baronet, da. of Matthew WHITE, of Blagdon. He was *b.* 28 Oct. 1745, at St. John's, Newcastle, and *suc. to the Baronetcy*, 21 March 1763, according to the spec. rem. in its creation; matric. at Oxford (Ch. Ch.),

(a) His eldest br., Lieut.-Col. William Johnson, *m.* in 1802, Susan, sister of Sir William de Lancy, **K.C.B.**, and *d.* 11 Jan. 1812, aged 36, leaving three daughters, of whom two *d.* unm., and the other (Charlotte) *m.* 27 April 1820, Alexander, Count Balmain, Russian Commissioner at St. Helena (during Napoleon's captivity there), and *d.* in 1824. Col. Johnson's widow *m.* in 1815, Gen. Sir Hudson Lowe, **K.C.B.**, Governor of that island. The next br., Warren Johnson, Major 60th Rifles, *d.* in 1801.

(b) It is to be observed that though he was, in 1763, heir apparent of his mother, he was not actually her heir till a year later, viz., on her death, 4 May 1764.

27 Feb. 1764, aged 18; was M.P. for Morpeth, 1768-74, and for Newcastle-on-Tyne, 1774-1812, being, in all, nine Parls. On the death of his father, 8 April 1778 (his elder br. of the half-blood, Richard RIDLEY, having *d.* previously 19 Oct. 1762, aged 26), he suc. to the family estate of Heaton, co. Northumberland. He *m.* 12 July 1777, Sarah, sister and h. of William COLBORNE, of West Harling, co. Norfolk, da. of Benjamin COLBORNE, of Bath. She *d.* 7 Aug. 1806. He *d.* 9 April 1813, aged 67. Will pr. June 1813.

III. 1813. SIR MATTHEW WHITE RIDLEY, Baronet [1756], of Blagdon and Heaton aforesaid, 1st s. and h.,(a) *b.* 18 April 1778, at Marylebone; matric. at Oxford (Ch. Ch.), 24 April 1795, aged 17; B.A., 1798; M.P., for Newcastle (eight Parls.), 1812 till death in 1836; *suc. to the Baronetcy*, 9 April 1813. He *m.* 13 Aug. 1803, Laura, yst. d. of George HAWKINS. He *d.* 14 July 1836, at Richmond, aged 58. Will pr. Aug. 1836. His widow *d.* 22 July 1864, at 25 Upper Brook street, aged 81.

IV. 1836. SIR MATTHEW WHITE RIDLEY, Baronet [1756], of Blagdon and Heaton aforesaid, 1st s. and h., *b.* 9 Sep. 1807, at Heaton; ed. at Westm. School; matric. at Oxford (Ch. Ch.), 20 June 1825, aged 17; B.A., 1828; *suc. to the Baronetcy*, 14 July 1836; Sheriff of Northumberland, 1841; M.P. for North Northumberland, 1859-68; Lieut.-Col. Northumberland Yeomanry. He *m.* 21 Sep. 1841, at Ampthill, Beds, Cecilia Anne, 1st da. and coheir of James (PARKE), BARON WENSLEYDALE, by Cecilia Arabella Frances, da. of Samuel Francis BARLOW, of Middlethorpe, co. York. She *d.* 20 April 1845, at Blagdon. He *d.* there 25 Sep. 1877, aged 70.

V. 1877. SIR MATTHEW WHITE RIDLEY, Baronet [1756], of Blagdon and Heaton aforesaid, 1st s. and h., *b.* 25 July 1842, at 10 Carlton House Terrace; ed. at Harrow; matric. at Oxford (Balliol Coll.), 12 Oct. 1861, aged 19; Scholar, 1861-65; B.A. and 1st Class Classics, 1865; Fellow of All Souls' Coll., 1865-74; M.A., 1867; admitted to Inner Temple, 1864; was M.P. for North Northumberland, 1868-85 (contesting the Hexham Division, 1885), and for North Lancashire (Blackpool Division), 1886-1900, having *suc. to the Baronetcy*, 25 Sep. 1877; Col. of the Northumberland Yeomanry Cavalry; and (1873-95) Chairman of the Quarter Sessions. He was Under Secretary to Home Department, 1878-80; Financial Secretary to Treasury, 1885-86; P.C., 1892; Secretary of State for Home Department, 1895-1900; an Ecclesiastical Commissioner, 1895 till death. He *m.* 10 Dec. 1873, at St. Geo. Han. sq., Mary Georgiana, 1st da. of Dudley (COUTTS), 1st BARON TWEEDMOUTH OF EDINGTON, by Isabella, da. of the Right Hon. Sir James Weir HOGG, 1st Baronet [1846]. She, who was *b.* 25 Sep. 1850, *d.* at 10 Carlton House Terrace, 14 March 1899 (of blood poisoning), and was *bur.* in her father's vault at Kensal Green. He was (within two years of her death) *cr.* 17 Dec. 1900 "VISCOUNT RIDLEY AND BARON WENSLEYDALE OF BLAGDON AND BLYTH(b) both in the county of Northumberland." In that peerage the *Baronetcy* then *merged* and still (1905) so continues.(c)

(a) Nicholas William Ridley, the 2d son, took the name of Ridley-Colborne, by Royal Lic., 23 June 1802, under the will of his maternal uncle, William Colborne, and was *cr.* 15 May 1839, Baron Colborne of West Harling, Norfolk, which peerage became extinct on his death, s.p.m.s., 5 May 1854, aged 50.

(b) Such is the extraordinary way in which the *Gazette* notice ("Whitehall, Dec. 17" [1900]) declares the title, though it is impossible to deduce therefrom whether the designation "of Blagdon and Blyth" applies to the Viscountcy as well as to the Barony, or to the Barony only.

(c) He, however, enjoyed his peerage but a short time, as he *d.* (in his sleep) at Blagdon, 28 Nov. 1904, aged 62, and was *bur.* at Stannington.

SMITH:

cr. 31 Oct. 1757;

afterwards, since 1778, BROMLEY;

being for a short time, 1803-08, PAUNCEFOTE-BROMLEY.

I. 1757. GEORGE SMITH, of the town and county of Nottingham, and of East Stoke, in the said county, Esq., 1st s. and h.(a) of Abel SMITH, of East Stoke aforesaid, a Banker of Nottingham, by Jane, da. of George BEAUMONT, of Chapelthorpe, co. York, was *b.* 1714-15, and, having suc. his father in Dec. 1756, was *cr. a Baronet*, as above, 31 Oct. 1757. He was Sheriff of Notts, 1758-59. He *m.* 18 Aug. 1747, Mary, da. and h. of William HOWE,(b) of Beckenham, co. Lincoln, by Elizabeth, 3d da. and coheir of William PAUNCEFOTE, of Carswell in Newent, and of Preston, co. Gloucester, which William PAUNCEFOTE (aged circa 12 in the Visit. of that county 1682), *d.* 1710. She, who was *b.* 3 Nov. 1725, *d.* 18 May 1761, and was *bur.* at East Stoke. He *m.* secondly, 23 Feb. 1768, Catherine, 1st da. of the Rev. William VYSE, Rector of St. Philip's, Birmingham, and Archdeacon of Salop, by Catherine, da. of Richard SMALLBROOKE, sometime (1731-49) Bishop of Lichfield. He *d.* 5 Sep. 1769, and was *bur.* at East Stoke. Will pr. 1769. His widow *d.* s.p. 21 Feb. 1786, and was *bur.* there. Will pr. 1786.

II. 1769. SIR GEORGE SMITH, *afterwards* (1778-1803) BROMLEY, and (1803-08) PAUNCEFOTE-BROMLEY, Baronet [1757], of East Stoke aforesaid, 2d and yst. but only surv. s. and h. by 1st wife; *b.* 18 Aug. 1753, at St. Nicholas, Nottingham; *suc. to the Baronetcy*, 5 Sep. 1769; was Sheriff of Gloucestershire, 1775. He, by royal lic., 7 Feb. 1778, took the name of BROMLEY, in lieu of that SMITH, by direction of Robert BROMLEY, of Abberley, co. Worcester, first cousin to his mother, being surv. s. and h. of William BROMLEY of the same (*d.* 1769, aged 79), by Sarah, 2d da. and coheir of William PAUNCEFOTE, abovenamed. By the death unm. (10 March 1803, aged 72) of this Robert BROMLEY, he became heir to his mother's maternal grandfather, the abovenamed William PAUNCEFOTE, and by royal lic., 6 April 1803, took the name of PAUNCEFOTE, which he appears to have used before that of BROMLEY. He *m.* 8 Jan. 1778, at Rugeley, co. Stafford, Esther, da. of Assheton (CURZON), 1st VISCOUNT CURZON OF PENN, by his 1st wife Esther, da. and h. of William HANMER, of Hanmer, co. Flint. He *d.* 17 Aug. 1808, aged nearly 55. Will pr. Dec. 1808 and Jan. 1848.(c) His widow, who was *b.* 24 Dec. 1758, *d.* 7 Nov. 1839 at Stoke Park, aged 80. Admon. Nov. 1839.

III. 1808. SIR ROBERT HOWE BROMLEY, Baronet [1757], of East Stoke aforesaid, only s. and h., *b.* there 28 Nov. 1778; entered the Royal Navy, 1791, becoming Vice-Admiral of the Red, 1848; of the Blue, 1851, and of the White, 1854, having *suc. to the Baronetcy*, 17 Aug. 1808, Sheriff of

(a) Of his two yr. brothers (1) John Smith (bap. 5 May 1716), was a merchant in London, being grandfather of Robert Smith (3d s. of Thomas Smith, of Gedling, Notts), which Robert took the name of Pauncefote, 20 Jan. 1809, under the will of his cousin the 2d Baronet [1757], whose estate of Preston, co. Gloucester, he inherited, and *d.* 1843, aged 55, being father of Julian, *cr.* Baron Pauncefote, 18 Aug. 1899, (2) Abel Smith, of Nottingham, banker, who *d.* 12 July 1788, aged 70, being father of five sons, of whom Robert was the 1st Baron Carrington.

(b) This William was only surv. s. of Lieut.-Gen. Emmanuel Scrope Howe, by Ruperta, illegit. da. of the famous Prince Rupert (cousin of Charles I), the said Emmanuel being yr. br. of Scrope, 1st Viscount Howe [I.], both being sons of John Grubham Howe, of Langar, Notts, by Annabella, illegit. da. and testamentary coheir of Emmanuel (Scrope), Earl of Sunderland.

(c) He left the estate of Preston, co. Gloucester (which had belonged to the Pauncefote family) to his cousin Robert Smith (see note "a" above), who accordingly took the name of Pauncefote.

Notts, 1816-17. He *m.* 8 June 1812, Ann, 2d da. and coheir of Daniel WILSON, of Dallam Tower, Westmorland, by his 2d wife Sarah, da. and h. of Samuel HARPER, of Heath, co. York. He *d.* at East Stoke, 8 July 1857, aged 78. Will pr. 1857. His widow *d.* 6 March 1873, at 58 Park street, Grosvenor square, aged 86.

IV. 1857. SIR HENRY BROMLEY, Baronet [1757], of East Stoke aforesaid, 2d but 1st surv. s. and h.,(a) *b.* there 6 Dec. 1816; sometime Capt. 48th Foot; *suc. to the Baronetcy*, 8 July 1857; Capt. Commandant 3d Notts Rifle Volunteers, 1850. He *m.* firstly, in 1848, Charlotte Frances Anne, widow of Edward HENEAGE, 3d da. of Col. Lancelot ROLLESTON, of Watnall Hall, Notts, by his 1st wife, Caroline, da. of Sir George CHETWYND, 1st Baronet [1795]. She *d.* 29 Jan. 1853. He *m.* secondly, 2 Feb. 1856, Georgiana Anne, 3d and yst. da. and coheir of Vere FANE, of Little Penton Hall, co. Lincoln (grandson of Thomas, 8th EARL OF WESTMORLAND), by Elizabeth, da. of Charles CHAPLIN, of Blankney in that county. He *d.* 21 Sep. 1895, at Stoke Hall, in his 79th year. Will pr. at £32,925. His widow living s.p., 1905.

V. 1895. SIR HENRY BROMLEY, Baronet [1757], of East Stoke aforesaid, only s. and h. by 1st wife, *b.* 6 Aug. 1849; sometime Lieut. 27th Foot; *suc. to the Baronetcy*, 21 Sep. 1895; Capt. Notts Yeomanry Cavalry, and well known as a first-rate sportsman. He *m.* 23 Jan. 1873, at Stoke aforesaid, Adela Augusta, only child of Westley RICHARDS, of Ashwell, co. Rutland. He *d.* 11 March 1905, at Stoke Hall, aged 55. His widow living 1905.

VI. 1905. SIR ROBERT BROMLEY, Baronet [1757], 1st s. and h.,(b) *b.* 4 Jan. 1874; was in the Foreign Office service; Attaché at Washington, 1897-1901; Private Secretary to the Secretary of State for the Colonies, 1901-03; Administrator and Treasurer of St. Kitts and Nevis, in the West Indies, 1903; *suc. to the Baronetcy*, 11 March 1905. He *m.* 24 Feb. 1900, at St. John's Church, Washington, his cousin,(c) Lilian, 3d da. and coheir of Julian (PAUNCEFOTE) BARON PAUNCEFOTE OF PRESTON (then Ambassador to the United States of America) by Selina Fitzgerald, da. of William CUBITT, of Catfield, Norfolk.

LADE:

cr. 17 March 1758;

ex. 10 Feb. 1838.

I. 1758. JOHN LADE, of Warbledon, co. Sussex, Esq., formerly John INSKIP, s. and h. ap. of Edward INSKIP, of Uckfield in that county (*d.* 28 May 1764, aged 63), by his 1st wife, Philadelphia (*d.* 24 Nov. 1732, aged 30), da. and coheir of Vincent LADE, of Warbleton aforesaid, elder br. of Sir John LADE, 1st Baronet [1731], to whose estates (though not to whose title, which was inherited by another grandnephew of the deceased), he suc. on his death, 30 July 1740,(d) when, apparently, he took the name of LADE, in lieu of that of INSKIP; was M.P. for Camelford, 1754-61, and was *cr. a Baronet*, as above, 17 March 1758. He *m.* about 1755, Anne, sister of Henry THRALE, M.P. for Southwark, da. of Henry THRALE, brewer. He *d.* 21 April 1759 from the amputation of his leg, which had been broken by a fall from his horse. Will pr. 1759. His widow *d.* 22 April 1802, at St. Michael's, St. Albans, Herts, aged about 69. Admon. April 1802.

(a) The 1st son, Robert Bromley, M.P. for South Notts 1849-50, *d.* unm. and v.p., 30 Dec. 1850, at Stoke Hall, in his 35th year.

(b) The 2d son, Maurice Bromley-Wilson (*b.* 27 June 1875), having suc. in 1882 to the estate of Dallam Tower, co. Westmorland (formerly that of his grandfather's maternal grandfather, Daniel Wilson, abovenamed) took by royal lic. 4 Feb. 1897, the name of Wilson after that of Bromley, in compliance with the will of his cousin, Edward Hugh Wilson, who *d.* s.p. 8 Dec. 1886.

(c) See p. 108, note "a."

(d) See p. 70, note "a," under "LADE" Baronetcy, *cr.* 11 March 1730/1.

II. 1759, to 1838. SIR JOHN LADE, Baronet [1759], of Warbleton aforesaid, posthumous s. and h., *b.* 1 Aug. 1759, at Westm., and *suc. to the Baronetcy* on his birth; matric. at Oxford (Ch. Ch.), 15 Nov. 1776, aged 17; was well known as a "whip" and in sporting circles; was a prisoner in the King's Bench for debt in 1814; received (jointly with his wife) an annual pension of £300 from the Prince Regent for his life. He *m.* in or before 1789, Lætitia SMITH.(a) She *d.* at Egham, Surrey, 5 May 1825. He, having squandered all his fortune, *d.* s.p. 10 Feb. 1838, at Egham Hythe, Surrey, aged 78, when *the Baronetcy* became *extinct*. Will pr. Feb. 1838.

WILMOT:

cr. 15 Feb. 1759.

I. 1759. EDWARD WILMOT, of Chaddesden, co. Derby, M.D., Physician in Ordinary to the King, 2d(b) s. of Robert WILMOT, of the same (*d.* 8 Feb. 1683), by Joyce, da. and eventually coheir of William SACHEVERELL, of Staunton, co. Leicester, was *b.* 29 Oct. 1693 at Chaddesden aforesaid; ed. at St. John's Coll., Cambridge; B.A. and Fellow, 1714; M.A., 1718; and M.D., 1725; member of the College of Physicians, London, 1725; Fellow, 1726; Censor 1729 and 1741, being Harveian orator, 1735; F.R.S., 1730; practised in London as a Physician from 1725; Physician to Caroline, the Queen Consort, 1731; to the Prince of Wales, and in 1737 to George II; Physician-Gen. to the Army, 1740, and was *cr. a Baronet*, as above, 15 Feb. 1759. In 1760 was Physician to George III, but rétired from London next year. He *m.* in or before 1731, Sarah Marsh, da. of Richard MEAD, M.D., Physician in ordinary to George II, by his 1st wife, Ruth (*d.* Feb. 1719), da. of John MARSH, of London, Merchant. She *d.* 11 Sep. 1785, aged 83. Her admon. Jan. 1786. He *d.* 21 Nov. 1786, at Heringstone, and was *bur.* at Monkton, Dorset, aged 93. M.I. Will pr. Dec. 1786.

II. 1786. SIR ROBERT MEAD WILMOT, Baronet [1759], of Chaddesden aforesaid, only s. and h., *b.* 13 Sep. 1731; *suc.* to the *Baronetcy*, 21 Nov. 1786. He *m.* 13 May 1759, Mary, da. and h. of William WOOLLET, of Harbledown, Kent, by Mary, da. and coheir of William ROBERTS, of the same, He *d.* 9 Sep. 1793, in his 62d year. Admon. July 1795. His widow *d.* 18 March 1811. Will pr. 1811.

III. 1793. SIR ROBERT WILMOT, Baronet [1759], of Chaddesden 1st s. and h., *b.* 5 July 1765; matric. at Oxford (Univ. Coll.), 21 Nov. 1784, aged 19; *suc. to the Baronetcy*, 9 Sep. 1793. He *m.* firstly, 29 March 1796, Lucy, 1st da. of Robert GRIMSTON, of Neswick, co. York, by his 2d wife, Elizabeth, da. of (—). She, who was *bap.* 20 Aug. 1772, at St. Martin's, Micklegate, York, and whose issue became coheir to her br. John GRIMSTON, of Neswick (who *d.* s.p. 7 Jan. 1846, aged 70), *d.* May 1812. He *m.* secondly 26 May 1817, Bridget, widow of Major-Gen. Robert CRAUFURD, da. of Henry HOLLAND, of Hans Place, Chelsea. He *d.* 13 July 1842, aged 77. Will pr. Sep. 1842. His widow *d.* 30 Dec. 1844, at Brighton, aged 70. Will pr. June 1845.

(a) "He married a woman named Smith, who had been a servant at a house in Broad street, St. Giles', whose inhabitants were not endowed with every virtue" [Robinson's *The Last Earls of Barrymore*], where also her dance in 1789 with the Prince of Wales is mentioned.

(b) The 1st s., Robert Wilmot, Barrister, *m.* but *d.* s.p. 1755. The 3d s., Sir Nicholas Wilmot, of Osmaston, co. Derby, Serjeant at Law, was ancestor of the Wilmot, Baronets, so *cr.* 1772, and of the Eardley-Wilmot, Baronets, so *cr.* 1821.

IV. 1842. SIR HENRY SACHEVERELL WILMOT, Baronet [1759], of Chaddesden aforesaid, 2d but 1st surv. s. and h. by 1st wife,(a) *b.* 11 Feb. 1801; ed. at Rugby, 1812; entered the Royal Navy, becoming Commander R.N., 1864, having *suc to the Baronetcy*, 13 July 1842; Sheriff of Derbyshire, 1852. He *m.* 13 Dec. 1826, Maria, 1st da. of Edward Miller MUNDY, of Shipley Hall, co. Derby, by Nelly, da. of F. BARTON. She *d.* 24 Dec. 1865, at Chaddesden Hall, aged 50. He *d.* at Brighton, 11 April 1872, aged 71.

V. 1872. SIR HENRY WILMOT, Baronet [1759], of Chaddesden aforesaid, 2d but 1st surv. s. and h.,(b) *b.* 3 Feb. 1831; entered the Army, 1849; Capt. Rifle Brigade, 1855; served in the Indian Mutiny, 1857-58, receiving the *Victoria Cross* (medal and clasp) for personal bravery at Lucknow; Judge Advocate General to the Forces during the Chinese war, 1860-61. He was Lieut.-Col. of the Derbyshire Rifle Volunteers, 1863-81; M.P. for Derbyshire (three Parls.), Jan. 1869 to 1885, having *suc. to the Baronetcy*, 11 April 1872; **C.B.**, 1881; **K.C.B.**, 1897. He *m.* 15 July 1862, at St. Geo. Han. sq., Charlotte Cecilia, da. of the Rev. Frederic Harry PARE, by Geraldine, da. of Lord Henry FITZGERALD and Charlotte, *suo jure* BARONESS DE ROS. She *d.* 5 May 1891, at Chaddesden Hall, aged 58. He *d.* s.p. 7 April 1901, at Bournemouth, aged 70. Will pr. at £109,173 gross.

VI. 1901. SIR RALPH HENRY SACHEVERELL WILMOT, Baronet [1759], of Chaddesden aforesaid, nephew and h., being only s. and h. of the Rev. Arthur Alfred WILMOT, B.A., Rector of Morley-cum-Smalley, co. Derby, by Harriet Cecilia, da. of the Rev. Alleyne FITZHERBERT, Rector of Warsop, Notts, which Arthur (who *d.* 19 May 1876, aged 31) was 4th and yst. s. of the 4th Baronet. He was *b.* 8 June 1875; sometime Lieut. Coldstream Guards, serving in the Transvaal war, 1900; *suc. to the Baronetcy*, 7 April 1901.

CUNLIFFE:

cr. 26 March 1759.

I. 1759. SIR ELLIS CUNLIFFE, of Liverpool, co. Lancaster, Knight. s. and h. of Foster CUNLIFFE, of Saighton, co. Chester (which he had purchased in 1755), and of St. Peter's, Liverpool, merchant, by Margaret, da. of Robert CARTER, Alderman of Lancaster, was *b.* 12 April 1717; was a successful and enterprising merchant of Liverpool, and M.P. for that town (two Parls.) Dec. 1755 till death; was *Knighted* 18 April 1756, and having suc. his father (who *d.* aged 72) 11 April 1758, was *cr. a Baronet*, as above, 26 March 1759, with a *spec. rem.*, failing heirs male of his body to his br., Robert CUNLIFFE. He *m.* 19 Dec. 1760, Mary, da. of Henry BENNET, of Moston, co. Chester. He *d.* s.p.m.,(c) 16 Oct. 1767, at Lostwithiel, co. Cornwall (said to have been on his journey to Italy), aged 50, and was *bur.* in the chapel at Cherton Heath, co. Chester. M.I. Will pr. Nov. 1767. His widow *d.* 8 Oct. 1814. Will pr. 1814.

(a) The 1st s., Roberts Robert Wilmot, *b.* 2 July 1799, was an officer in the 2d Dragoon Guards, and *d.* unm. and v.p. 24 Feb. 1822. The 5th s., John Wilmot (who after Nov. 1856), was the 2d surv. s. of his parents, having suc. to the estate of Neswick, co. York, by the death of his maternal uncle. John Grimston abovenamed, took by Royal lic., 21 July 1860, the name of Grimston in lieu of that of Wilmot.

(b) The 1st son, Robert Edward Eardley Wilmot, *b.* 29 Jan. 1830, *d.* unm. and v.p 22 Oct. 1861.

(c) He left two daughters and coheirs (1) Mary, *m.* Sir Drummond Smith, of Tring park, Herts, and *d.* 17 Feb. 1804; (2) Margaret Elizabeth, *m.* William Gosling, of Roehampton Grove, Surrey.

II. 1767. SIR ROBERT CUNLIFFE, Baronet [1759], of Saighton aforesaid and of Pickhill, co. Denbigh, br. and h. male, *b.* 17 March 1719; *suc. to the Baronetcy*, 16 Oct. 1767, according to the *spec. rem.* in the creation of that dignity; Sheriff of Cheshire, 1776. He *m.* 1762, Mary, da. of Ichabod WRIGHT, of Nottingham, banker, by Elizabeth, da. of John WILDBORE, of the same. He *d.* 1778, aged 59. Will pr. 1778. His widow, who was *b.* 6 Dec. 1721, *d.* 19 Feb. 1791.

III 1778. SIR FOSTER CUNLIFFE, Baronet [1759], of Acton Park, near Wrexham, co. Denbigh, only s. and h., *b.* 8 Feb. 1755; *suc. to the Baronetcy* in 1778; Sheriff of Denbighshire, 1787-88. He *m.* 1 Oct. 1781, Harriet, da. of Sir David KINLOCH, 5th Baronet [S. 1686], of Gilmerton, by Harriet, da. of Sir Archibald COCKBURN, 7th Baronet [S. 1627], of Langton. She *d.* 9 Sep. 1830. He *d.* 15 June 1834, aged 79. Will pr. Aug. 1834.

IV. 1834. SIR ROBERT HENRY CUNLIFFE, Baronet [1759], of Acton Park aforesaid, 2d but 1st surv. s. and h.(a), *b.* 22 April 1785, at Chester; entered the military service of the Bengal E.I.C., 1798; was Colonel of the 4th Bengal Native Infantry, 1828, becoming finally (1851), Lieut.-General in that service, having been *Knighted* v.p. 18 Nov. 1829; *suc. to the Baronetcy*, 15 June 1834, and made **C.B.**, 1838. He *m.* firstly, in India, 16 Dec. 1805, Louisa, widow of Arthur FORREST, Major in the Madras service. She *d.* 4 May 1822. He *m.* secondly, also in India, 2 April 1825, Susan Emily, 2d da. of Col. John PATON, Commissary General of the Bengal army. She *d.* 11 Nov. 1856, at Craven Hill, Bayswater. He *d.* at Acton park, 10 Sep. 1859, aged 74.

V. 1859 SIR ROBERT ALFRED CUNLIFFE, Baronet [1759], of Acton Park aforesaid, grandson and h., being 1st s. and h. of Robert Ellis CUNLIFFE, East India service, by Charlotte Maria Jane, da. of Walter or Ilted HOWELL, which Robert (who *d.* v.p., 31 March 1855, aged 47) was 1st s. and h. ap. of the late Baronet, by his 1st wife. He was *b.* 17 Jan. 1839; ed. at Eton; Lieut. Scots Fusileer Guards, 1857, retiring as Captain, 1862; having *suc. to the Baronetcy*, 10 Sep. 1859; Sheriff of Denbighshire, 1868; Lieut.-Col. 3d Batt. Royal Welsh Fusileers Militia, 1872; M.P. for Flint Boroughs, 1872-74, and for the Denbigh district, 1880-85. He *m.* firstly, 5 Aug. 1869, at Goosetrey, Eleanor Sophia Egerton, only da. of Col. Egerton LEIGH, of the West Hall, High Leigh, co. Chester, by Lydia Rachel, da. and coheir of John Smith WRIGHT, of Bulcote lodge, Notts. She *d.* 13 March 1898,(b) in her 51st year, at Acton park. He *m.* secondly, 5 Jan. 1901, at St. Barnabas, Pimlico, Cecilie Victoria, 2d and yst. da. of Lieut.-Col. the Hon. William Edward SACKVILLE-WEST (6th s. of the 5th EARL DE LA WARR), by Georgina, da. of George DODWELL, of Kevinsfort. He *d.* suddenly 18 June 1905, at his Chambers in Sloane street, aged 66. His widow, who was *b.* 18 Feb. 1865, living 1905.

VI. 1905. SIR FOSTER HUGH EGERTON CUNLIFFE, Baronet [1759], of Acton Park aforesaid, 1st s. and h. by 1st wife, *b.* 17 Aug. 1875; ed. at Eton and New College, Oxford; B.A., 1898; Fellow of All Souls' College, Oxford; *suc. to the Baronetcy*, 18 June 1905.

Family Estates.—These, in 1883, consisted of 2,025 acres in Denbighshire, etc., worth £4,150 a year. *Residence.*—Acton park, near Wrexham, co. Denbigh.

(a) The 1st s., Foster Cunliffe, afterwards (in right of his wife) Cunliffe-Offley, of Madeley, co. Stafford, was *b.* 12 April 1782; ed. at Rugby, 1794; was M.P. for Chester, 1831-32, and *d.* v.p. and s.p. 19 April 1832, aged 50.

(b) According to the *Church Times* of 25 March 1898 (where she is described as "Lady Eleanor Sophia Cunliffe"), she "entered Paradise, Sunday the 13th inst."

GIDEON:

cr. 21 May 1759;

afterwards, 1789-1824, EARDLEY,

and BARON EARDLEY OF SPALDING [I.];

ex. 25 Dec. 1824.

I. 1759, to 1824. "SAMPSON GIDEON, Junior, Esq.,"(a) of Spalding, co. Lincoln, only s. and h. ap. of Sampson GIDEON, of the same, of Belvidere, near Erith, co. Kent, and of Stepney, Midx., a Jewish stockbroker, of great political influence,(b) and immense wealth (whose father, Rowland GIDEON, who became a Freeman of London, had emigrated from Portugal), by Jane, da. of Charles ERMELL, was *b.* 10 Oct. 1745, and being (like his sisters) brought up in the Christian faith, was ed. at Tunbridge school and at Eton, and was, through his father's influence (whose religion was supposed to preclude him from being thus honoured), *cr. a Baronet*, as above, 21 May 1759, at the age of 13. He suc. his father, 17 Oct. 1762 (who *d.* at the age of 63), in estates said to be worth £580,000; was M.P. for Cambridgeshire, (two Parls.), Feb. 1771 to 1780; for Midhurst, Nov. 1780 to 1784; for Coventry (two Parls.), 1784-96, and for Wallingford, 1796-1802. He, by Royal lic., July 1789, took the name of EARDLEY instead of GIDEON,(c) the name of Eardley being that of his wife's grandmother, whom, however, she did not represent. He was shortly afterwards *cr.*, 24 Sep. 1789,(d) BARON EARDLEY OF SPALDING [I.]. He *m.* 6 Dec. 1766, at St. George the Martyr, Queen sq., Midx., Maria Marowe (then a minor), 1st da. of the Right Hon. Sir John Eardley WILMOT, sometime (1766-71) Lord Chief Justice of the Common Pleas, by Sarah, da. of Thomas RIVETT, of Derby. She *d.* in Arlington street, Midx., 1 March 1794, and was *bur.* at Berkswell, co. Warwick.(e) M.I. He *d.* s.p.m.s.,(f) at 10 Marine parade, Brighton, 25 Dec. 1824, in his 80th year, when *all his honours* became *extinct*. Will pr. Feb. 1825.

(a) This description (as also all the subsequent ones that are placed within inverted commas) is the one given in the Gazette notice, as abstracted in the *Annual Register* of the year indicated. The date of the Gazette notice for the creation of Gideon is 19 May 1759.

(b) He was a financier on a large scale, raising in 1745, as much as £1,700,000 for the Government, in 1749 effecting the consolidation of the National Debt and raising various loans during the seven years war which began in 1756.

(c) "A ridiculous step to remove some part of the prejudice against him" [as being of Jewish origin], but "the cloven foot is sadly exposed by the preservation of *Sampson*." [Forde to the Duke of Rutland, 12 Aug. 1786]. His *wife* was grand-daughter of Robert Wilmot, by Elizabeth, da. and h. of Edward *Eardley*, of Eardley, co. Stafford, but inasmuch as Lady Gideon had a brother, John Wilmot, afterwards Eardley (whose son was *cr. a Baronet* in 1821), he (and not his said sister) represented the family of Eardley.

(d) See a good deal about this creation in the letters of the then Viceroy of Ireland, in the *Fortescue Papers*, vol. i. [Hist. MSS. Com., 13th report, Appendix, part iii.].

(e) A column in the *Gent. Mag.* is devoted to the most heated praises of her virtues.

(f) Both his sons *d.* unm. and v.p., *viz.* (1) Sampson Eardley, *b.* 29 Dec. 1770, who *d.* unm. at Belvidere, 21 May 1824, and (2) Lieut.-Col. William Eardley, *b.* 22 May 1775; ed. at Rugby and at Ch. Ch., Oxford; M.A., 1791; who *d.* 17 Sep. 1805, and was *bur.* at Berkswell, co. Warwick. Of his three daughters and coheirs (1) Maria Marowe, *m.* Lord Say and Sele; (2) Charlotte Elizabeth, *m.* Sir Cuthing Smith, 2d Baronet [1802]; and (3) Selina, *m.* John Walbanke Childers,

YEA:

cr. 18 June 1759;

ex. 31 Aug. 1864.

I. 1759. WILLIAM YEA, of Pyrland, in the parish of Taunton, St. James', co. Somerset, Esq., as also of Oakhampton, in Wiveliscombe, and of Stone, in Brompton Ralph, in that county, 3d but last surv. s. of David YEA, of the same, by Joan, da. and h. of Nathaniel BREWER, of Tolland, co. Somerset, suc. his elder br. David YEA, in Dec. 1758, and was *cr. a Baronet*, as above, 18 June 1759; Sheriff of Somerset, 1760-1. He *m.* in or before 1756, Julia, 1st da. of Sir George TREVELYAN, of Nettlecombe, Somerset, by Julia, da. of Sir Walter CALVERLEY, 1st Baronet [1711], of Calverley. Her will pr. July 1791. He *d.* 25 Nov. 1806. Will pr. 1807.

II. 1806. SIR WILLIAM WALTER YEA, Baronet [1759], of Pyrland aforesaid, grandson and h., being 1st s. and h. of William Walter YEA, by Jane, da. of Francis NEWMAN, of Cadbury House, Somerset, which William Walter (*b.* 8 Oct. 1756, at Oakhampton), was 1st s. and h. ap. of the late Baronet, but *d.* v.p. 27 Dec. 1804, aged 48. He was *b.* 19 April 1784, at Foiston House, Bishops Hull, Somerset; ed. at Eton; matric. at Oxford (Brasenose Coll.), 6 Nov. 1802, aged 18; *suc. to the Baronetcy*, 25 Nov. 1806. He *m.* 24 June 1806, Anne Hechstetter, 4th da. of David Robert MICHELL, of Kingston Russell and Dewlish, Dorset, by his 2d wife Eleanor, da. of Edward POORE, sometime M.P. for Sarum. He *d.* s.p.m.s.,(a) 20 May 1862, aged 78.

III. 1862, to 1864. SIR HENRY LACY YEA, Baronet [1759], of Pyrland aforesaid, br. and h., *b.* at Pyrland Hall, 18 Nov. 1798, being 4th and yst. s. of the 1st Baronet; *suc. to the Baronetcy*, 20 May 1862. He *d.* unm. 31 Aug. 1864, at Taunton, aged 65, when the *Baronetcy* became *extinct*.

GLYN:

cr. 29 Sep. 1759.

I. 1759. SIR RICHARD GLYN, Knt., Lord Mayor of London, only surv. s. of Robert GLYN, citizen of London (*d.* 1746, aged 73, being *bur.* at Ewell, Surrey), by Anne, da. of (—) MAYNARD, was *b.* about 1712; was a citizen and salter of London; Alderman of Dowgate, 22 Feb. 1750 till his death; Sheriff of London, 1752-53, being *Knighted* during office 22 Nov. 1752, and was Lord Mayor 1758-59, being *cr.* D.C.L. of Oxford, 3 July 1759, and *cr. a Baronet*, as above, 29 Sep. 1759, during office, the payment of the usual fees being remitted. He was one of the principal merchants and bankers in London;(b) was M.P. for that city, Nov. 1758 to 1768, and for Coventry, 1768 till death; was Col. of the Orange Regiment of the City Militia; President of the Hospitals of Bridewell and of Bethlehem. He *m.* firstly, 8 June 1736, Susanna, da. and h. of George LEWEN, of Ewell, Surrey (*d.* 1 April 1743), nephew and h. of Sir William LEWEN, of the same, some-

(a) He (besides daughters and a son who died in infancy) had two sons who *d.* unm. and v.p., *viz.* (1) Lacy Walter Giles Yea, *b.* in Park Row, Bristol, 20 May 1808; ed. at Eton; ensign, 37th Foot, 1825, becoming Lieut.-Col. 9 Aug. 1850, and Brevet Col. 28 Nov. 1854, distinguishing himself at Alma, and being killed while leading the assault on the Redan, in the Crimean War, 18 June 1855; (2) Raleigh Henry Yea, *b.* 2 June 1817; ensign, 13th Foot, 1835, retiring as Lieut. 1841. He *d.* at Weymouth 1 Feb. 1855 (not four months before his brother) from an accident received, when out shooting in Nov. 1854.

(b) "Was an oylman in Hatton Garden, but ultimately became a Banker."

time (1717-18) Lord Mayor of London.(a) She *d.* 4 Feb. 1751. He *m.* secondly, March 1754, Elizabeth, 1st da. and coheir of Robert CARR, of Hampton, Midx., a silkman on Ludgate hill, London, who styled himself a Baronet (9th Baronet [S. 1637]),(b) only child by his 1st wife, Grace, da. of Thomas BIGGE, of Newcastle-on-Tyne. He *d.* 1 Jan. 1773, aged 60. M.I. at Ewell. Will pr. Jan. 1773. His widow *d.* 14 April 1814. Will pr. 1814.

II. 1773. SIR GEORGE GLYN, Baronet [1759], of Ewell aforesaid, 2d but 1st surv. s. and h. by 1st wife,(c) *b.* in Hatton Garden, London, about 1739; ed. at Westminster School; admitted to Lincoln's Inn, 5 May 1757; matric. at Oxford (Lincoln Coll.) 15 March 1758, aged 18; B.A., 1760; M.A., 1763; Barrister (Inner Temple), 1761; *suc. to the Baronetcy*, 1 Jan. 1773; Col. of the 3d Regiment of the Surrey Militia. He *m.* firstly, in or before 1769, Jane, yst. da. of the Rev. Walkin LEWES, M.A., of Tredered, co. Pembroke. She *d.* 4 Sep. 1790, aged 47, and was *bur.* at Ewell.(d) M.I. He *m.* secondly, 11 June 1796, Catherine, yst. da. and coheir of the Rev. Gervas POWELL, of Lanharan, co. Glamorgan. He *d.* 4 Sep. 1814. Will pr. 1814. His widow *d.* 15 Dec. 1844, aged 74. Will pr. Jan. 1845.

III. 1814. SIR LEWEN POWELL GLYN, Baronet [1759], of Ewell aforesaid, 3d but 1st surv. s. and h., being 1st s. by the 2d wife, *b.* 14 Aug. 1801; *suc. to the Baronetcy*, 4 Sep. 1814. He *d.* at Bath, unm., 28 July 1840, aged 38. Admon. Jan. 1845.

IV. 1840. SIR GEORGE LEWEN GLYN, Baronet [1759], of Ewell aforesaid, br. and h., *b.* there 20 Sep. 1804; ed. at Westm. school; matric. at Oxford (Ch. Ch.), 30 March 1824, aged 18; took Holy Orders; was Vicar of Ewell, 1831, to his death in 1885; and sometime Chaplain to the Earl of Shaftesbury; *suc. to the Baronetcy*, 28 July 1840. He *m.* firstly, 8 Sep. 1838, Emily Jane, 1st da. of Josiah BIRCH, of Lancashire and of St. Petersburgh. She *d.* at Ewell, 26 July 1854, aged 38. He *m.* secondly, 5 May 1859, at Hove co. Sussex, Henrietta Amelia, 1st da. of Richard Carr GLYN, of the Bengal Civil Service. He *d.* at Ewell, 7 Nov. 1885, in his 82d year. Will pr. over £21,000. His widow *d.* there 25 Nov. 1903. Will pr. at £24,165.

V. 1885. SIR GEORGE TURBERVILL GLYN, Baronet [1759], of Ewell aforesaid, 1st s. and h., by 1st wife, *b.* there 22 April 1841; matric. at Oxford (Pemb. Coll.), 6 May 1862, aged 22, migrating to Mag. Hall; *suc. to the Baronetcy*, 7 Nov. 1885. He *d.* unm. 19 May 1891, aged 50, at 6 Montagu terrace, Richmond Hill, Surrey. Admon. 19 Aug. 1891, at £4,199.

VI. 1891. SIR GERVAS POWELL GLYN, Baronet [1759], of Ewell aforesaid, br. of the half blood and h., being 3d s. of the 4th Baronet and 1st s. by his 2d wife; *b.* at Ewell, 8 Oct. 1862; ed. at Winchester; matric. at Oxford (New Coll.), 15 Oct. 1881, aged 19; B.A., 1885; M.A., 1891; F.R.G.S.; *suc. to the Baronetcy*, 19 May 1891. He *m.* 19 April 1898, at St. James', Paddington, Dorothy, da. of Edmund Charles HISLOP, of Clapham park, Surrey, by Maria, da. of Charles ROMER, subsequently wife of Surgeon-Major H. D. S. COMPIGNÉ, M.D., of Gloucester terrace, Hyde Park.

(a) It is uncertain which of the two wives of her father was her mother *viz.* (1) Susanna, sister of Sir Robert Godschall; or (2) [—], sister of Henry Drax

(b) See vol. ii, p. 429, under "KERR," Baronetcy [S.], *cr.* 31 July 1637.

(c) His yr. br. of the half blood, Richard Carr Glyn (1st s. of the 2d wife of the 1st Baronet), was *cr. a Baronet*, 22 Nov. 1800, as "of Gaunts, Dorset."

(d) Richard Lewen Glyn, the only son of his mother that survived infancy, was *b.* at Bath, 1769; matric. at Oxford (Corpus Coll.), 9 July 1787, aged 17; B.A., 1790; was Major in the Army (81st Foot), and *d.* unm. at St. Domingo, 5 July 1795, aged 25. M.I. at Ewell.

COLEBROOKE:

cr. 12 Oct. 1759.

I. 1759. JAMES COLEBROOKE, of Gatton, co. Surrey, Esq., 2d s. of James COLEBROOKE, Citizen and Mercer of London, "a great money scrivener in Threadneedle street,"(a) afterwards of Arno's grove in Southgate, Midx., and Chilham Castle, Kent (*b.* 12 May 1680, at Arundel, and *d.* 18 Nov. 1752), by Mary, da. of (—) HUDSON, was *b.* 21 July 1722; ed. at Leyden Holland; was a Banker in London; purchased, in Nov. 1751, the estate of Gatton abovenamed for £23,000, was M.P. thereof April 1751 till death; and was *cr. a Baronet*, as above, 12 Oct. 1759, with a spec. rem., failing heirs male of his body, to his yst. br., George COLEBROOKE, of Southgate, Midx.(b) He *m.* 7 May 1747, Mary, 1st da. and coheir of Stephen SKINNER, of Leyton and Walthamstow, Essex. She, who was *b.* 12 Aug. 1728, *d.* in childbirth 14 and was *bur.* 20 May 1754, at Chilham aforesaid. He *d.* s.p.m.(c) 10 May 1761, aged 38, and was *bur.* there. Will pr. 1761.

II. 1761. SIR GEORGE COLEBROOKE, Baronet [1759], of Gatton aforesaid, yst. br.; *b.* 14 June 1729; ed. at Leydon Univ.; was a Merchant and Banker of London; M.P. for Arundel (three Parls.), 1754-74; *suc. to the Baronetcy*, 10 May 1761, under the spec. rem. in the limitation thereof, and purchased, at the same date, the Gatton estate from his nieces, which, however, he sold in 1774. He was also partner under the style of "Sir George Colebrooke & Co.," in a Bank at St. Mary's, Dublin, in 1764, which after being in difficulties since 1770, stopped payment in 1773,(a) when he became bankrupt.(d) He was Dep. Chairman of the East India Company, 1768; Chairman thereof, 1769, 1711 and 1772; F.S.A.; author of several literary works. He *m.* 23 July 1754, Mary, da. and h. of Patrick GAYNER, of Antigua, by Mary, da. of (—) LINCH. He *d.* at Bath Easton, Somerset, 5 July 1809, in his 81st year. Will pr. 1809. His widow *d.* 13 Aug. 1818, at Hampstead, aged 79. Will pr. 1818.

III. 1809. SIR JAMES EDWARD COLEBROOKE, Baronet [1759], of "Colebrook park," Tunbridge Wells, Kent, 3d but 1st surv. s. and h.,(e) *b.* 7 July 1761; joint Chirographer of the Court of Common Pleas, 1768 to death; sometime senior Merchant on the Bengal establishment; Persian translator there; a Judge of Appeals at Moorshedabad; and Provisional Member of the Council in Bengal; *suc. to the Baronetcy*, 5 July 1809. He *m.* 31 Jan. 1820, Louisa Anne, widow of Capt. Henry STUART, da. of George COLEBROOKE. He *d.* s.p. legit., 5 Nov. 1838, at Tunbridge Wells, Kent, aged 77. Will pr. Jan. and May 1839. His widow *m.* (for her 3d husband) 15 April 1841, James BREMBRIDGE, of Tunbridge Wells (who survived her), and *d.* 28 May 1867, at Horsham.

IV. 1838. SIR (THOMAS) EDWARD COLEBROOKE, Baronet [1759], of Ottershaw Park, in Chertsey, co. Surrey, and of Abington House, near Crawford, co. Lanark, nephew and h., being only surv. s. and h. of Henry Thomas COLEBROOKE, joint Chirographer of the Court of Common Pleas (1768 till

(a) *Ex inform.* C. M. Tenison.

(b) It seems odd that the eldest br. should have been passed over. This was Robert Colebrooke, of Chilham Castle, Kent, M.P. for Malden (three Parls), 1741-61; Minister to the Swiss Cantons, 1762-64. He *d.* s.p. at Soissons in France, 10 May and was *bur.* 26 June 1785 at Chilham.

(c) James Colebrooke, only s., *d.* an infant (six days after his mother), 20 May 1754. Of the two daughters and coheirs (1), Mary, *b.* 10 March 1750, *m.* (as 1st wife) Sir John Aubrey, 6th Baronet [1660], and *d.* s.p.s. 14 June 1781. (2), Emma, *b.* 22 Dec. 1754, *m.* 7 Oct. 1771, Charles (Bennet) 4th Earl of Tankerville, and had issue.

(d) His examination as a bankrupt is given in the *London Mag.* (1774) xliii, pp. 202 and 254.

(e) George Colebrooke, the 2d s., *b.* 6 Aug. 1759, Capt. in the Somerset Militia, *m.* June 1805 Belinda, da. of Joseph Edwards, but *d.* s.p.m. and v.p., 22 April 1809.

death), a celebrated Sanscrit scholar, sometime Judge at Mirzapoor, Member of the Bengal Council, and President of the Board of Revenue, by Elizabeth, da. of Johnson WILLIAMSON, of Portman sq., which Henry Thomas (who *d.* 10 March 1837, aged 71) was next br. to the late Baronet. He was *b.* 19 Aug. 1813; ed. at Eton; *suc. to the Baronetcy*, 5 Nov. 1838; was M.P. for Taunton (two Parls.), 1842-52; for Lanarkshire (three Parls.), 1857-68; and for North Lanarkshire (three Parls.), 1868-85; Lord-Lieut. of that county, 1869 till death; a Commissioner of Endowments [S.], 1872; Hon. D.C.L. of Glasgow, 1873. He *m.* 15 Jan. 1857, at St. Paul's, Knightsbridge, Elizabeth Mary, 2d da. of John RICHARDSON, of Kirklands, co. Roxburgh. He *d.* at 14 South street, Park lane, 11 Jan. 1890, aged 76. His widow *d.* at 18 St. James' place, 26 Oct. 1896.

V. 1890. SIR EDWARD ARTHUR COLEBROOKE, Baronet [1759], of Abington House, co. Lanark, aforesaid, 1st s. and h., *b.* Oct. 1861, at Ottershaw park abovenamed; mat. at Oxford (Ch. Ch.), 21 May 1880, aged 18; Lieut. Lanarkshire Yeomanry Cavalry, 1882; *suc. to the Baronetcy*, 11 Jan. 1890; sometime Private Secretary to the Viceroy of Ireland. He *m.* 7 June 1889, at St. Peter's, Vere street, Marylebone, Alexandra Harriet, 7th da. of Gen. Lord Alfred Henry PAGET (5th s. of Henry William, 1st MARQUESS OF ANGLESEY), by Cecilia, da. and coheir of George Thomas WYNDHAM. She was *b.* 31 March 1865, Queen Alexandra (then Princess of Wales) being her sponsor.

Family Estates.—These in 1883 consisted of 29,604 acres in Lanarkshire (worth £9,282 a year), and 419 in Surrey. *Total.*—30,023 acres, worth £9,986 a year. *Seat.*—Abington House, co. Lanark.

FLUDYER:

cr. 14 Nov. 1759.

I. 1759. SIR SAMUEL FLUDYER, Knt., Alderman of the City of London, 1st s. and h. of Samuel FLUDYER, of Frome, Somerset, and of London, Clothier,(a) by Elizabeth, da. of Francis DE MONSALLIER, a French Protestant refugee, was *b.* about 1705; "was a Blackwell Hall factor of the first eminence," who, "by great industry, a spirit of enterprise acquired prodigious wealth"(b); was a member of the Companies of the Tylers, Bricklayers, and finally of the Clothworkers; Alderman of Cheap ward, 26 June 1751 till death; M.P. for Chippenham (two Parls.), 1754 till death; Sheriff of London, 1754-55, being *Knighted* (during office), at Kensington, 19 Sep. 1755, on presenting an address to the King on his safe return from Hanover, and was *cr. a Baronet*, as above, 14 Nov. 1759, with a spec. rem., failing heirs male of his body, to his brother, Thomas FLUDYER, of London, Esq.(c) He was subsequently Lord Mayor, 1761-62, the King and Queen, who had witnessed his procession, being entertained at Guildhall, 9 Nov. 1761,

(a) He "followed the clothing business in London" [Kimber's *Baronetage*, 1770]. Admon. of the goods of Samuel Fludyer, of St. Martin's, Ironmonger lane, London, was granted 1716, to Elizabeth, the widow.

(b) See *City Biography* (2d edit., 1800), where it is stated [probably with much exaggeration] that "his origin was so low as to be employed in attending the pack-horses, which were formerly used to bring cloth from the West country to London."

(c) This Thomas Fludyer (also a London Merchant of note) was *Knighted*, 9 Nov. 1761, at the banquet given by his br., the then Lord Mayor, to the King. He (who was F.R.S., 1767, and F.S.A., 1769) was M.P. for Bedwyn, 1767-68, and for Chippenham, 1768-69. He *m.* Mary, da. of Sir George Champion, of Lee aforesaid, sometime (1737-38) Sheriff of London. She was *bur.* at Lee, 9 Dec. 1761. He *d.* s.p.m., 19 March 1769, at Hackney, leaving a da., Mary, Baroness Dacre.

with unusual magnifience at his inauguration dinner.(a) His conduct, however, was, shortly before his death, "reprehended, in the most severe terms," by Lord Chancellor Camden as to "a contraband trade he had carried on in scarlet cloth," and "as the assignee of a bankrupt."(b) He *m.* firstly, Jane, da. of (—) CLERKE, of Westminster. She *d.* s.p., at St. Michael's Bassishaw, London, 15 and was *bur.* 25 March 1757, at Lee, co. Kent, aged 53. He *m.* secondly, 2 Sep. 1758, at the Chapel in Somerset House, Strand, Caroline, 1st sister and coheir of George Bridges BRUDENELL, M.P. for Rutland, da. of the Hon. James BRUDENELL (br. of George, 3d EARL OF CARDIGAN), by Susan, da. of Bartholomew BURTON, of North Luffenham, co. Rutland. He *d.* of apoplexy 21 and was *bur.*, "in linen," 24 Jan. 1768, at Lee aforesaid, aged 63. M.I. Will pr. Feb. 1768.

II. 1768. SIR SAMUEL BRUDENELL FLUDYER, Baronet [1759], of 1st s. and h., by 2d wife, *b.* 8 Oct. 1759; *suc. to the Baronetcy,* 21 Jan. 1768; M.P. for Aldborough, June 1781 to 1784. He *m.* 5 Oct. 1786, Maria, da. of Robert WESTON, by his maternal aunt, Louisa, da. of the Hon. James BRUDENELL abovenamed. She *d.* 23 Nov. 1818. He *d.* 17 Feb. 1833, at Felixstowe, Suffolk, aged 73. Will pr. April 1833.

III. 1833. SIR SAMUEL FLUDYER, Baronet [1759], of Felixstowe aforesaid, only s. and h., *b.* 31 Jan. 1800, at Uffington Hall, co. Lincoln; matric. at Oxford (Ch. Ch.), 16 Oct. 1817, aged 17; *suc. to the Baronetcy,* 17 April 1833. He *d.* unm. 12 March 1876, aged 76.

IV. 1876. SIR JOHN HENRY FLUDYER, Baronet [1759], of Ayston Hall, co. Rutland, cousin and h. male, being 3d and yst. s.(c) of George FLUDYER, of Ayston aforesaid (M.P. for Chippenham, 1783-1802, and for Appleby, 1818-19, Sheriff of Rutland, 1814-15), by Mary, da. of John (FANE), 9th EARL OF WESTMORLAND, which George (who *d.* 15 April 1827, aged 65) was br. to the 2d and yst. s. of the 1st Baronet. He was *b.* 19 Dec. 1803, at Thistleton, co. Rutland; ed. at Westm. School, and at St. John's Coll., Cambridge; B.A., 1826; M.A., 1827; took Holy Orders, 1826; Rector of Ayston, 1834 till death; *suc. to the Baronetcy,* 12 March 1876. He *m.* 7 May 1832, at All Souls', Marylebone, Augusta, 3d and yst. da. of Sir Richard BOROUGH, 1st Baronet [1813], of Basildon, Berks, by Anna Maria, da. of Gerard (LAKE), 1st VISCOUNT LAKE. She *d.* 10 April 1889, at Ayston Hall, aged 80. He *d.* there 4 Aug. 1896, in his 93d year. Will pr. at £9,810 personalty.

V. 1896. SIR ARTHUR JOHN FLUDYER, Baronet [1759], of Ayston Hall aforesaid, 2d but 1st surv. s. and h.,(d) *b.* 12 Oct. 1844; sometime Lieut.-Col. 3d Battalion Northamptonshire Militia, *suc. to the Baronetcy,* 4 Aug. 1896. He *m.* 9 Sep. 1876, Augusta Frances, 3d da. and coheir of his maternal uncle, Sir Edward Richard BOROUGH, 2d and last Baronet [1813], by Elizabeth, da. of William (ST. LAWRENCE), 2d EARL OF HOWTH [I.].

Family Estates.—These, in 1883, consisted of 2,638 acres in Rutland, 1,774 in Monmouthshire, 312 in Berks, 102 in Wilts, 9 in Leicestershire, and 6 in Lincolnshire. *Total.*—4,841 acres, worth £6,951 a year. *Seat.*—Ayston Hall, near Uppingham, co. Rutland.

(a) See *Ann. Reg.*, 1761 (p. 245) for a full account of this banquet.
(b) See p. 117, note "b."
(c) Of his elder brothers, who both *d.* unm. (1), George Fludyer, Lieut.-Col. Grenadier Guards, *d.* Feb. 1856, aged 58. (2), William Fludyer, Lieut.-Gen., *d.* 28 Jan. 1863, aged 61.
(d) His elder br. Charles FLUDYER, Lieut.-Col. Grenadier Guards, *d.* s.p., 14 Jan. 1895, aged 54.

WATSON:

cr. 21 March 1760;

sometime, 1887-88, WATSON-COPLEY;

ex. 30 Sep. 1904.

I. 1760. "CHARLES WATSON, Esq., only s. of Charles WATSON, Esq.(a) decd., late Vice-Admiral of the Red Squadron of His Majesty's fleet, and Commander-in-Chief of His Majesty's ships in the East Indies"(b) (which Charles *d.* at Calcutta, 16 Aug. 1757 in his 44th year), by Rebecca, 1st da. of John Francis BULLER, of Morval, co. Cornwall, was *b.* 9 June 1751, at Bradfield, Berks, and was, "in consideration of the many great and eminent services rendered unto His Majesty by [the said] Charles WATSON deceased,"(b) *cr. a Baronet,* as above,(c) 21 March 1760, at the age of 8 years; matric. at Oxford (Ch. Ch.), 11 Oct. 1769, aged 18; B.A., 1772; Fellow of All Souls' College, Oxford; M.A., 1778. He was of Swaffham Prior, co. Cambridge, before 1800, in which year his mother died there,(d) and was, subsequently, of West Wratting park, in that county. He *m.* 16 July, 1789, at St. Geo. Han. sq., his cousin, Juliana, 2d da. of Sir Joseph COPLEY, 1st Baronet [1778], of Sprotborough (formerly Joseph MOYLE), by Mary, da. of John Francis BULLER abovenamed. She *d.* 24 May 1834, in New Cavendish street, Marylebone. He *d.* 26 Aug. 1844, at West Wratting park aforesaid, aged 93. Will pr. Oct. 1844.

II. 1844. SIR CHARLES WAGER WATSON, Baronet [1760], of West Wratting park aforesaid, 3d and yst. but only surv. s. and h.,(e) *b.* 4 Jan. 1800; ed. at Eton; matric. at Oxford (Ch. Ch.), 1 Nov. 1819, aged 19; B.A., 1823; M.A., 1826; *suc. to the Baronetcy,* 26 Aug. 1844. He *m.* 19 June 1827, Jemima Charlotte, 1st da. of Charles Garth COLLETON, of Haines Hill, Berks, by (—), afterwards "COUNTESS MOREL DE CHAMPEMONT." He *d.* 30 Dec. 1852, aged 52, at Stradishall. Admon. Aug. 1853. His widow *d.* 16 April 1877, at St. Leonard's-on-Sea, aged 69.

III. 1852. SIR CHARLES WATSON, *afterwards* (1887-88) WATSON-COPLEY, Baronet [1760], of West Wratting park aforesaid, 1st s. and h., *b.* there 6 April 1828; sometime in the 71st Foot, retiring as Lieut. in 1853, having *suc. to the Baronetcy,* 30 Dec. 1852. By royal lic., 12 March 1887, he took the name of COPLEY, after that of WATSON, on succeeding to the estate of Sprotborough, co. York, under the will of his father's maternal uncle, Sir Lionel COPLEY, 2d Baronet [1778]. He *m.* 12 May 1854, at Genoa, Georgina, 3d da. of the Rev. Robert TREDCROFT, M.A., Preb. of Chichester, and Rector of Tangmere, Sussex, by Charlotte, da. of Lieut.-Gen. Sir John CLAVERING, K.B. He *d.*,

(a) This Charles Watson, *b.* 1714, was son of the Rev. John Watson, D.D., Preb. of Westminster (*d.* 1724), by (—), da. of Alexander Parker, Merchant, and Prudence his wife, who by her 1st husband, Capt. Charles Wager, R.N., was mother of Admiral the Right Hon. Sir Charles Wager, sometime First Lord of the Admiralty, by whose influence he obtained early promotion. He distinguished himself greatly at the engagements off Finisterre, 3 May 1747 (under Anson), and 14 Oct. following (under Hawke), while his subsequent services in India are set forth in his M.I. at Westm. Abbey, in these words:—"Gheriah taken, Feb. 13, 1756; Calcutta freed, Jan. 11, 1757; Chandernagore taken, March 23, 1757;" these last achievements being only a few months before his death on 16 August following.
(b) See p. 113, note "a," under "GIDEON." The date of the Gazette notice of the creation of Watson is 22 March 1760.
(c) In the later Baronetages the grantee is described as "of Fulmer, Bucks."
(d) See also Lysons' *Mag. Brit.* [1808], under Cambridgeshire.
(e) The 1st son, Charles Watson, *b.* 1790, *d.* the same year; the 2d son, another Charles Watson, *b.* 1761 at Westm.; ed. at Eton; matric. at Oxford (Ch. Ch.), 21 Dec. 1809, aged 18; *d.* unm. and v.p., 1810.

s.p.m.s., 6 April 1888, somewhat suddenly, at Cannes, in France, on his 60th birthday. Will pr. 12 Oct. 1888. His widow *d.* 27 Jan. 1892, at 8 Petersham Terrace, Queen's Gate, Hyde Park, leaving personalty over £19,000.

IV. 1888, to 1904. SIR WAGER JOSEPH WATSON, Baronet [1768], br. and h. male, *b.* 27 June 1836, at West Wratting park aforesaid; matric. at Oxford (Univ. Coll.), 15 Nov. 1855, aged 19; B.A., 1859; M.A., 1863; *suc. to the Baronetcy,* 6 April 1888. He (who was the last survivor of eight grown up children, who all *d.* unm.) *d.* unm., at 100 Victoria street, Westminster, 30 Sep. and was *bur.* 5 Oct. 1904, at Kensal Green cemetery, aged 68, when the *Baronetcy* became *extinct.*(a) Will pr. at £96,578.

CREATIONS BY GEORGE III.

25 Oct. 1760 to 31 Dec. 1800,

when, owing to the Union with Ireland, 1 Jan. 1801, the creation of Baronetcies of Great Britain (as well as of Baronetcies of Ireland) ceased, and was succeeded by that of Baronetcies of the United Kingdom.

ASGILL:

cr. 16 April 1761;

ex. 1823.

I. 1761. SIR CHARLES ASGILL, Knt., Alderman of London, s. of Charles ASGILL, of Barford, Oxon,(b) *b.* about 1713; rose from the position of an "out-door collecting clerk at a Banking House in Lombard street, to the first department in the house";(c) was a Citizen and Skinner of London, and a considerable Merchant and Banker;(d) was Alderman of Candlewick ward, 7 April 1749 till he resigned, 1 July 1777; Sheriff of London, 1752-53, being *Knighted* during office, 22 Nov. 1752; Lord Mayor, 1757-58, and was *cr. a Baronet,* as above, 16 April 1761, being the first so honoured by the new King. He *m.* firstly in 1752, Hannah (£25,000), da. of Henry VANDERSTAGEN, of London, Merchant, when "he immediately joined his name to the firm."(c) She *d.* 6 and was *bur.* 13 Feb. 1754, at St. Bartholomew's-by-the-Exchange, London. He *m.* secondly, Sarah, da. of Daniel PRATTVILL, Merchant, of London, sometime "Sec. to Sir Benjamin Keene's Embassy to the Court of Spain."(b) He *d.* 15 and was *bur.* 21 Sep. 1788, at St. Bartholomew's aforesaid, aged 75, "worth upwards of £160,000."(c) His widow *d.* 6 June 1816. Will pr. 1816.

II. 1788, to 1823. SIR CHARLES ASGILL, Baronet [1761], only s. and h. by 2d wife, *b.* about 1760; entered the 1st Foot Guards, 1778, becoming Capt. in 1781. As such he was taken prisoner at Yorktown in Virginia, Oct. 1781, and (in retaliation for an American officer having been hanged) was condemned to death. He was, however, released a month later. He *suc. to the Baronetcy,* 15 Sep. 1788; was Equerry to the Duke

(a) His yr. br. Rev. Cecil Estcourt Benyon Watson, M.A. (Oxford), *d.* unm., at Sistra Legano in Italy, 28 May 1903, aged 64, but one year before him.
(b) Playfair's *Baronetage* [1811].
(c) Betham's *Baronetage* [1803].
(d) See Hilton Price's *London Banker's* (p. 123), under "Nightingale."

of York, with whom, as Lieut.-Col. in the Guards (which he became in 1790), he served through the campaign in Flanders; was active in suppressing the Irish rebellion in 1798, becoming finally (4 June 1813), General, and being Col. of the 85th Foot, 1806, and of the 11th Foot, 1807. He *m.* 28 Aug. 1790, Sophia Charlotte, 6th and yst. da. of Admiral Sir Chaloner Ogle, 1st Baronet [1816], by Hester, da. and coheir of John THOMAS, D.D., Bishop of Winchester. Her admon. May 1824. He *d.* s.p., 1823, when the *Baronetcy* became *extinct.* Will pr. Aug. 1823.

HESKETH:

cr. 5 May 1761;

sometime, 1792-96, JUXON;

afterwards, 1867-72, and since 1876, FERMOR-HESKETH.

I. 1761. THOMAS HESKETH, of Rufford [near Ormskirk], co. Lancaster, Esq., 3d but 1st surv. s. and h. of Thomas HESKETH, of the same, sometime (1722-27) M.P. for Preston, by Martha, da. and coheir of James St. Amand, of St. Paul's, Covent Garden, and Elizabeth, his wife, the only child that had issue of Sir William JUXON, 1st Baronet [1660], of Little Compton, co. Gloucester, was *b.* 21 Jan. 1726/7; suc. his father, 18 April 1735; matric. at Oxford (Ch. Ch.), 29 Oct. 1743, aged 17, and was *cr. a Baronet,* as above, 5 May 1761, with a spec. rem., failing heirs male of his body, to his br., Robert HESKETH. He *m.* Harriet,(a) da. and coheir of Ashley COWPER, Clerk of the Parl., by Dorothy, da. of John OAKES. He *d.* s.p., 4 March, 1778, aged 51. Will pr. 1778. His widow, who was *bap.* 12 July 1733, at Hertingfordbury, Herts, *d.* 10 Jan. 1807, at Clifton, near Bristol. Will pr. 1607.

II. 1778. SIR ROBERT HESKETH, *afterwards* (from 1792), JUXON, Baronet [1761], of Rufford aforesaid, *b.* there 23 April 1728; was sometime a Wine Merchant at Bristol; *suc. to the Baronetcy,* 4 March 1778. He, in 1792, assumed the name of JUXON, in lieu of HESKETH, being that of his mother's maternal uncle, Sir William JUXON, 2d Baronet [1660], whose heir he was. He *m.* 19 April 1748, at Preston, co. Lancaster, Sarah, da. of William PLUMBE, of Wavertree, in that county. She *d.* 1792. He *d.* 30 Dec. 1796, and was *bur.* 7 Jan. 1797, at St. Martin's-in-the-Fields, aged 68. Will pr. Jan. 1797.

III. 1796. SIR THOMAS DALRYMPLE HESKETH, Baronet [1761], of Rufford aforesaid, grandson and h., being 2d but only surv. s. and h. of Thomas Hesketh, by Jacintha, da. of Hugh DALRYMPLE, Attorney-Gen. of Grenada, which Thomas (who *d.* v.p. 13 Jan. 1781, aged 32) was 1st s. and h. ap. of the late Baronet. He was *b.* 13 Jan. 1777., at New York, in America; *suc. to the Baronetcy,* 30 Dec. 1796. He *m.* firstly, Feb. 1798, Sophia, only da. of the Rev. Nathaniel HINDE, Vicar of Shiffnall, Salop. She *d.* 8 Feb. 1817. He *m.* secondly, 15 Sep. 1821, at Broadwater, Sussex, Louisa ALLEMAND, Spinster. She *d.* 6 Sep. 1832, at Lausanne. He *d.* 27 July 1842, at Rufford Hall, aged 65. Will pr. Aug. 1842.

IV. 1842. SIR THOMAS HENRY HESKETH, Baronet [1761], of Rufford aforesaid, 1st s. and h., by 1st wife; *b.* 11 Feb. 1799; *suc. to the Baronetcy,* 27 July 1842. He *m.* 3 April 1824, at Cheltenham, Annette Maria, da. of Robert BOMFORD, of Rahinston, co. Meath, by Maria, da. of the Hon. James MASSY-DAWSON, 2d s. of Hugh, 1st BARON MASSY OF DUNTRILEAGUE [I.]. He *d.* 10 Feb. 1843, aged nearly 44. His widow *d.* 17 Dec. 1879.

(a) Lady Hesketh was first cousin and a favourite correspondent of William COWPER, the Poet.

V. 1843. SIR THOMAS GEORGE HESKETH, *afterwards*, since 1867, FERMOR-HESKETH, Baronet [1761], of Rufford aforesaid, and of Easton Neston, co. Northampton, only s. and h., *b.* 11 Jan. 1825, at Rufford Hall; matric. at Oxford (Ch. Ch.), 9 June 1843, aged 18; *suc. to the Baronetcy*, 10 Feb. 1843; Sheriff of Lancashire, 1848; Col. of the 2d Lancashire Militia, 1852-72; M.P. for Preston (three Parls.), 1862-72. Having inherited the estate of Easton Neston abovenamed, by the death of his wife's brother below-mentioned, he and his *second* son (afterwards the 7th Baronet), took by royal lic., 8 Nov. 1867, the name of FERMOR before that of HESKETH. He *m.* 10 March 1846, at St. Geo. Han. sq., Anna Maria Isabella, elder of the two sisters and coheirs of the 5th and last EARL OF POMFRET (who *d.* s.p., 8 June 1867), da. of Thomas William (FERMOR), 4th EARL OF POMFRET, by Amabel Elizabeth, da. of Sir Richard BOROUGH, 1st Baronet [1813]. She, who was *b.* 2 Jan. 1828, *d.* 25 Feb. 1870, at Easton Neston. He *d.* 20 Aug. 1872, at Rufford Hall, aged 47.

VI. 1872. SIR THOMAS-HENRY-FERMOR HESKETH, Baronet [1761], of Rufford aforesaid, 1st s. and h., *b.* 9 Jan. 1847, at Misterton Hall; *suc. to the Baronetcy*, 20 Aug. 1872. He *d.* unm. 28 May 1876, aged 29.

VII. 1876. SIR THOMAS-GEORGE FERMOR-HESKETH, Baronet [1761], of Rufford and Easton Neston aforesaid, *formerly*, 1849-67, Thomas George HESKETH, br. and h., *b.* 9 May 1849; sometime in the Rifle Brigade, retiring as Lieut.; *suc. to the Baronetcy*, 28 May 1876; Hon. Col. 4th Batt. Liverpool Reg. of Militia; Sheriff of Northamptonshire, 1881. He *m.* 22 Dec. 1880, at Belmont, San Francisco, Florence Emily, da. of William SHARON, of San Francisco, Senator of Nevada.

Family Estates.—These in 1883, consisted of 9,394 acres in Lancashire, 5,784 in Northamptonshire, and 15 in the North Riding of Yorkshire. *Total.*—15,193 acres, worth £31,633 a year. *Seats.*—Rufford Hall, near Ormskirk, co. Lancaster, and Easton, near Towcester, co. Northampton.

DELAVAL:

cr. 1 July 1761;

afterwards, 1783-1808, BARON DELAVAL OF REDFORD [I.];

and, 1786-1808, BARON DELAVAL OF SEATON DELAVAL [G.B.];

ex. 17 May 1808.

I. 1761, to 1808. JOHN HUSSEY DELAVAL, of Ford, co. Northumberland, Esq., 2d s. of Francis Blake DELAVAL, of Seaton Delaval and Ford Castle, co. Northumberland, and of Doddington, co. Lincoln (*d.* Dec. 1752), by Rhoda, da. of Robert APREECE, of Washingley, co. Huntingdon, and Sarah, his wife, da. and eventually sole heir of Sir Thomas HUSSEY, 2d Baronet [1611], of Honington and of Doddington aforesaid, was *b.* about 1728; was M.P. for Berwick, Jan. 1765 to 1774, and 1780 till *cr.* a Peer [G.B.] in 1786, and was *cr. a Baronet*, as above, 1 July 1761. He suc. to the family estates on the death, 7 Aug. 1771, of his elder br., Sir Francis Blake DELAVAL, K.B. He *m.* firstly, 2 April 1750, in Duke Street chapel, Westm., his cousin, Susanna, widow of John POTTER, Under Sec. of State, da. of R. ROBINSON, by Margaret, sister of Francis Blake DELAVAL abovenamed, da. of Edward DELAVAL. She *d.* in Hanover square 1 and was *bur.*, with great pomp, 11 Oct. 1783, in Westm. Abbey (as a Peeress) as "the Right Hon. Susanna, Lady Delaval." He was about that period, viz., by King's letters, dat. 24 Sep., and by patent, 17 Oct. 1783, *cr.* BARON DELAVAL OF REDFORD, co. Wicklow [I.], being subsequently *cr.*, 21 Aug. 1786, BARON DELAVAL OF SEATON DELAVAL, co. Northumberland [G.B.]. In these peerages this *Baronetcy* then *merged*, and so continued till *all his honours* became *extinct* at his death, s.p.m.s., 17 May 1808. See *Peerage*.

BAYNTUN-ROLT:

cr. 7 July 1762;

ex. 12 Aug. 1816.

I. 1762. EDWARD BAYNTUN-ROLT, of Spye Park [near Calne], co. Wilts, Esq., *formerly* Edward ROLT, 2d s. of Edward ROLT, of Sacombe, Herts (admitted to Lincoln's Inn, 14 Oct. 1702, and *d.* 1722, being s. and h. of Sir Thomas ROLT, of the same,(a) President of India), by Anne, sister and h. of John BAYNTUN, of Spye Park aforesaid, and Bromham, Wilts, da. of Henry BAYNTUN, of the same, by Anne, sister and coheir, of Charles (WILMOT), 3d EARL OF ROCHESTER, was *b.* about 1710, and having by the death, in 1717, of his maternal uncle, John BAYNTUN abovenamed, inherited Spye Park and other estates, took the name of BAYNTUN before that of ROLT; was M.P. for Chippenham (five Parls.), 1737-68; Groom of the Bedchamber to Frederick, Prince of Wales, 1746; Surveyor of the Duchy of Cornwall, 1751; and was *cr. a Baronet*, as above, 7 July 1762. In 1787 was one of the Council to George, Prince of Wales. He *m.*, before 1743, Mary, da. of (—) POYNTER, of Herriard, Hants. He *d.* Jan. 1800, aged 90. Will pr. March 1800, and again 1816.

II. 1800, to 1816. SIR ANDREW BAYNTUN-ROLT, Baronet [1762], of Spye Park aforesaid, only surv. s. and h.,(b) *b.* probably about 1745; *suc. to the Baronetcy* in Jan. 1800, and was Sheriff of Wilts, 1802-03. He *m.* 29 June 1777, Mary Alicia, 1st surv. da. of George William (COVENTRY), 6th EARL OF COVENTRY, by his 1st wife, Maria, da. of John GUNNING. She, who was *b.* 9 Dec. 1754, and whose marriage was dissolved by Act of Parliament, 1783, *d.* 8 Jan. 1784. He is said to have subsequently *m.* Anna Maria MAUDE.(c) He *d.* s.p.m. or s.p.m.s.,(d) 12 Aug. 1816, when the *Baronetcy* became *extinct*.

PAUL:

cr. 3 Sep. 1762;

ex. 16 Dec. 1820.

I. 1762. SIR ONESIPHORUS PAUL, of Rodborough, co. Gloucester, Knt., 2d s. of Nicholas PAUL (who was s. of the Rev. Onesiphorus PAUL, M.A., Vicar of Warnborough, Wilts), by Elizabeth, da. of Thomas DEAN, of Woodchester, co. Gloucester, was *b.* about 1705; was an extensive woollen manufacturer at Woodchester, where, in Aug. 1750, he entertained Frederick, Prince of Wales; was Sheriff of Gloucestershire, 1760-61, being *Knighted*, 17 Dec. 1760, at St. James', on presenting an address to the King from that county, and was *cr. a Baronet*, as above, 3 Sep. 1762. He *m.* firstly, in or before 1737, Jane, da. of Francis BLACKBURN, of Richmond, co. York, by Alice, da. of Thomas COMBER, D.D., Dean of Durham. She d. 26 May 1748, and was *bur.* at Woodchester. He *m.* secondly, Catharine, da. and coheir of Frances FREEMAN, of

(a) See *Genealogist*, N.S. (vol. xvii, pp. 145-149), for an account of him and his ancestry, correcting that in Le Neve's *Knights*, and referring to "the excellent pedigree" of his descendants in Cussan's *Herts*, under Sacomb.

(b) An elder son, "John Bayntun, son of Edward, of Spye Park, Wilts, Baronet," matric. at Oxford (St. John's Coll.), 2 July 1766, aged 23.

(c) Burke's *Extinct Baronetage*.

(d) "Andrew Bayntun, son of Andrew, of Bath, Baronet," matric. at Oxford, 10 Oct. 1815, aged 18. If he was legitimate, he must have *d.* s.p.m. and v.p. within ten months of that date, for the estates devolved on his da. and h., Mary Barbara, *b.* about 1778, who *m.*, in 1797, Rev. John Starky, D.D., and had issue.

Norton Malreward, co. Somerset. She *d.* s.p.s., 20 Oct. 1766, and was *bur.* at Woodchester, in her 58th year. M.I. Will pr. Aug. 1767. He *m.* thirdly, Sarah, widow of John TURNER, of King's Stanley, co. Gloucester, da of John PEACH, of Woodchester. He *d.* at Rodborough, 21 Sep. 1774, aged 69, and was *bur.* at Woodchester. Will pr. Oct. 1774. His widow *d.* April 1801, and was *bur.* at Little Ilford, co. Essex.

II. 1774, to 1820. SIR ONESIPHORUS PAUL, *afterwards* (1780-1820) SIR GEORGE ONESIPHORUS PAUL, Baronet [1762], of Rodborough aforesaid, only surv. s. and h., by 1st wife, *b.* 9 Feb. 1745/6; matric. at Oxford (St. John's Coll.), 8 Dec. 1763, aged 17; *cr.* M.A., 12 Dec. 1766; *suc. to the Baronetcy*, 21 Sep. 1774. He, by royal lic., 9 Feb. 1780, took the additional name of GEORGE; was Sheriff of Gloucestershire, 1780-81. He *d.* unm. 16 Dec. 1820, at Hill House, Rodborough, aged 74, when the *Baronetcy* became *extinct*.(a) Will pr. 1821.

DUNDAS:

cr. 16 Nov. 1762;

afterwards, since 1794, BARONS DUNDAS OF ASKE;

since 1838, EARLS OF ZETLAND, and

since 1892, MARQUESSES OF ZETLAND.

I. 1762. LAWRENCE DUNDAS, of Kerse, co. Stirling, Esq., as also of Upleatham and Aske, co. York, 2d s. of Thomas DUNDAS, of Fingask, co. Perth (*d.* 1762), by Bethia, da. of John BAILLIE, of Castlecarry, co. Stirling, was *b.* probably about 1710), was Commissary Gen. and Contractor to the Army, 1748-59, acquiring thereby a large fortune; was M.P. for Linlithgow burghs, 1747 till unseated in March 1748; for Newcastle-under-Lyme, Dec. 1762 to 1768; and for Edinburgh, 1768-80, and Feb. 1781 till death 7 months later, being *cr. a Baronet*, as above, 16 Nov. 1762, with a spec. rem. failing heirs male of his body, to his elder br., Thomas DUNDAS, of Fingask aforesaid; P.C., 9 Oct. 1771; Vice-Admiral of Shetland and Orkney. He *m.* 9 April 1738, Margaret, only da. of Alexander BRUCE, of Kennet, Brig.-General, by Mary, da. of Robert (BALFOUR), LORD BALFOUR OF BURLEIGH [S.]. He *d.* 21 Sep. 1781, at Aske Hall, co. York, leaving an estate of £16,000 a year, and "a fortune of £900,000 in personalties and landed property."(b) Will pr. Oct. 1781. His widow *d.* 11 Oct. 1802, aged 87.

II. 1781. SIR THOMAS DUNDAS, Baronet [1762], of Kerse and Aske aforesaid, only s. and h., *b.* 16 Feb. 1741, and *bap.* at Edinburgh; was M.P., for Richmond, March 1763 to 1768, and for Stirlingshire (five Parls.), 1768, till raised to the Peerage in 1794; *suc. to the Baronetcy*, 21 Sep. 1781, and was Lord Lieut. of Orkney and Zetland, 1794. He *m.* 14 May 1764, in Grosvenor street, St. Geo. Han. sq., Charlotte, 2d da. of William (FITZWILLIAM), 1st EARL FITZWILLIAM (3d Earl [I.]), by Anne, da. of Thomas (WATSON-WENTWORTH), 1st MARQUESS OF ROCKINGHAM. She, who was *b.* 25 July 1745, was living when he was *cr.* 13 Aug. 1794, BARON DUNDAS OF ASKE, co. York. In that peerage this *Baronetcy* then *merged*, and still so continues, the 2d Baron being *cr.* 2 July 1838, EARL OF ZETLAND, and the 3d Earl (4th Baron and 5th Baronet) being *cr.* 22 Aug. 1892, MARQUESS OF ZETLAND. See *Peerage*.

(a) The estate of Rodborough passed to his cousin, John Dean PAUL, who was *cr. a Baronet*, 2 Sep. 1821.

(b) *Annual Register*, 1781.

LLOYD:

cr. 26 Jan. 1763;

ex. 19 Aug. 1769.

I. 1763, to 1769. "HERBERT LLOYD, of Peterwell, co. Cardigan, Esq.,"(a) yr. s. of Walter LLOYD, of Voelallt, by (—), da. and h. of Daniel EVANS, of Peterwell aforesaid, was *b.* 1719; matric. at Oxford (Jesus Coll.), 15 March 1737/8, aged 18; Barrister (Inner Temple), 1742; suc. to Peterwell on the death, 27 June 1755, of his elder br., John LLOYD; was M.P. for Cardigan, 1761-68, and was *cr. a Baronet*, as above, 26 Jan. 1763. He *m.* firstly, 20 May 1742, (—), da. of (—) BRAG, of Essex, with whom he had £15,000. He *m.* secondly, 14 Aug. 1769,(b) a few days before his death, Anne, said to be widow of Richard STEDMAN, of Strata Florida [but *qy.* if not "widow of (—) BACON, Esq."(b)] yst. da. of William POWELL of Nanteos.(c) He *d.* s.p., 19 Aug. 1769, and was *bur.* at Peterwell, aged 50, when the *Baronetcy* became *extinct*.(d) Will pr. June 1771. His widow *d.* July 1778.

SMYTH, *or* SMITH:

cr. 27 Jan. 1763;

ex 19 May 1849.

I. 1763. "JARRIT SMITH, of the City of Bristol, Esq.,"(a) only s. of John SMITH, of Bristol, was *b.* about 1692, and having, by marriage, become possessed, about 1741, of the estate of Long Ashton, co. Somerset, was M.P. for Bristol (two Parls.) March 1756 to 1768, and was *cr. a Baronet*, as above, 27 Jan. 1763. He *m.* 8 Feb. 1731/2, at Barrow Gurney, co. Somerset, Florence, widow of John PIGOTT, of Brockley, co. Somerset (who *d.* s.p., 20 April 1730), sister and coheir (18 July 1741) of Sir John SMYTH, *or* SMITH, 3d and last Baronet [1641], of Long Ashton aforesaid, being 4th da. of Sir John SMYTH, *or* SMITH, 2d Baronet [1641], by (—), da. and coheir of Sir Samuel ASTREY, of Henbury, co. Gloucester. She, who was *b.* 2 Aug. 1701. *d.* 10 and was *bur.* 17 Sep. 1767, at Henbury. He *d.* 24 Jan. 1783, aged nearly 92. Will pr. April 1783.

II. 1783. SIR JOHN HUGH SMYTH, Baronet [1763], of Long Ashton aforesaid, 1st s. and h., *b.* probably about 1735; *suc. to the Baronetcy*, 24 Jan. 1783. He *m.* 1 Sep. 1757, Elizabeth, da. and h. of Henry WOOLCHURCH, of Sodbury and Pucklechurch, co. Gloucester. He *d.* s.p. 30 March 1802. Will pr. 1802. His widow *d.* 30 March 1825. Will pr. April 1825.

III. 1802. SIR HUGH SMYTH, Baronet [1763], of Long Ashton aforesaid, nephew and h., being 1st s. and h. of Thomas SMYTH, of Heath House in Stapleton, co Gloucester, by Jane, da. and h. of Joseph WHITCHURCH, of Heath House aforesaid, which Thomas (who *d.* 11 March 1800), was only br. to the late Baronet. He was *b.* 3 July 1772, at Pucklechurch; matric. at Oxford (Oriel Coll.), 15 Dec. 1790, aged 18; *suc. to the Baronetcy*, 30 March

(a) p. 113, note "a," under "GIDEON." The date in the *Gazette* notice of the creation of Lloyd is 18, that of Smith is 22 Jan., and that of Blakiston, Fleming and Mayne is 15 April 1763.

(b) *Annual Register*, 1769 [marriages].

(c) This William was son of Sir Thomas Powell, sometime (1688) one of the Judges of the Court of King's Bench.

(d) The estate of Peterwell devolved on his nephew (son of his 1st sister Elizabeth), John Adams, who sold the same and *d.* at Brompton, 2 June 1817, in his 71st year.

1802. He *m.* 20 May 1797, Margaret, 5th da. of CHRISTOPHER WILSON, D.D., Bishop of Bristol. She *d.* s.p. 30 Nov. 1819. He is sometimes said to have *m.* subsequently in 1822, Elizabeth HOWELL, spinster. He *d.* s.p. 28 Jan. 1824, aged 51. Will pr. 1824.

IV. 1824, to 1849. SIR JOHN SMYTH, Baronet [1763], of Long Ashton aforesaid, only br. and h., *b.* 9 Feb. 1776, at Stapleton aforesaid; matric. at Oxford, (Worcester Coll.), 29 June 1793, aged 17; B.A., 1797; *suc. to the Baronetcy*, 28 Jan. 1824. He *d.* unm. 19 May 1849, aged 73, when the *Baronetcy* became *extinct.*(a) Will pr. July 1849.(b)

BLAKISTON, *or* BLACKISTON:

cr. 22 April 1763.

I. 1763. "SIR MATTHEW BLACKISTON [*sic*, but *Qy.* BLAKISTON], Knt.,"(c) Alderman of London, s. of George BLAKISTON, of London, by (—), da. of Matthew HALE, also of London, was *b.* about 1702; was Citizen and Grocer of London, and a considerable merchant in that city; Alderman of Bishopsgate, 23 May 1750,(d) till discharged 20 June 1769; was Sheriff, 1753-54; *Knighted*, at Kensington, 8 June 1759, on the occasion of the coming of age of George, Prince of Wales; was Lord Mayor, 1760-61, and was *cr. a Baronet*, as above, 22 April 1763. He was Col. of the Green Regt. of the London Militia. He *m.* firstly (—), da. of Rev. Charles HALL, of Halsay, co. York.(e) He *m.* secondly, Mrs. Mary BLEW, of Chelsea, Midx. She *d.* s.p. 8 and was *bur.* 13 Jan. 1754, at St. Martin's-in-the-Fields. He *m.* thirdly (being then of St. Olave's Jury, London), 8 April 1760, at St. James', Westm., Annabella, da. of Thomas BAYLEY, of Hampton Court, Midx., and of Coventry, by Bridget, da. of Sir Wolston DIXIE, 3d Baronet [1660]. He *d.*, in Jermyn street, 14 and was *bur.* 21 July 1774, at St. Martin's-in-the-Fields, aged 72. Admon. 14 July 1774. His widow *m.* 25 Aug. 1776, Hugh CANE, Lieut.-Col. 5th Dragoon Guards. She *d.* at Winterton, Berks, 9 June, 1783.

(a) The title and property, worth £30,000 a year, were, however, claimed a few years after the death of the 4th Baronet by a clever impostor, styling himself "*Sir Richard Hugh Smyth*, Baronet," and claiming to be s. and h. of Sir Hugh Smyth, the 3d Baronet, by Jane Vandenbergh, who was *m.* 19 May 1796, and who *d.* in giving him birth, 2 Feb. 1797, at Warminster, Wilts. His real name, however, proved to be *John Provis*, son of a carpenter at Warminster. On the death of the 3d Baronet in 1824, his alleged father, he claimed to have had the right to succeed him. His evidence, supported by an intricate series of perjuries and forged documents, was found false, Aug. 1853, when he was sentenced, at the Gloucester Assizes, to twenty years' transportation. He apparently derived much knowledge of the Smyth family by having *m.* in 1814 one of the domestic servants at Ashton Court. [See *Annual Reg.* for 1853, pp. 308-330, for an elaborate account of this celebrated trial, entitled "Smyth *v.* Smyth and others."]

(b) The estates devolved on Florence, the elder of his two sisters and coheirs. She was *b.* 27 May 1769; *m.* (as his 2d wife), 11 May 1799, John Upton, of Ingmire Hall, co. York (*d.* 3 Jan. 1832), took the name of Smyth in 1849, and *d.* 15 July 1852, aged 83, being suc. by her grandson, John Henry Greville Upton, who accordingly took the name of Smyth in 1852, and was *cr. a Baronet* (as of Long Ashton, Somerset), 25 April 1859, a dignity which became extinct on his death, 27 Sep. 1901.

(c) See p. 125, note "a," under "LLOYD."

(d) His election was petitioned against, on the ground of his being disqualified by not residing in the city, but was confirmed.

(e) By her he is said to have had a son, Charles George Blakiston, who *d.* unm. and v.p., in 1758. It is possible that the burial of "Margaret Blackston, woman," 19 Aug. 1725, at St. Martin's-in-the-Fields (where his 2d wife and he himself was buried), may refer to this wife.

II. 1774. SIR MATTHEW BLAKISTON, Baronet [1763], only surv. s. and h., by 3d wife, *b.* 1761 at the Mansion House, London, during his father's Mayoralty; *suc. to the Baronetcy*, 14 July 1774. He *m.* Sep. 1782, Anne, 1st da of John ROCHEFORT, of Cloghrenane, co. Carlow, by Dorothea, da. of Thomas BURGH, of Bert, co. Kildare. He *d.* 20 Sep. 1806, aged 45. Admon. Oct. 1806. His widow *d.* 27 Nov. 1862, at Torquay, Devon, in her 102d year.

III. 1806. SIR MATTHEW BLAKISTON, Baronet [1763], of Sandybrook Hall, in Ashbourne, co. Derby, 1st s. and h., *b.* 13 May 1783, at Athlone; *suc. to the Baronetcy*, 20 Sep. 1806. He *m.* 12 April 1810, Lucy, 1st da. of James MANN, of Linton Place, Kent, by Lucy, da. of Sir Horace MANN. He *d.* 23 Dec. 1862 (a month after his mother), at Sandybrook Hall aforesaid, aged 79. His widow *d.* there 29 Dec. 1871, aged 84.

IV. 1862. SIR MATTHEW BLAKISTON, Baronet [1763], of Sandybrook Hall aforesaid,(a) 1st s. and h., *b.* 15 Jan. 1811, at Bath; ed. at Trinity College, Dublin; B.A., 1836; M.A., 1839; *suc. to the Baronetcy*, 23 Dec. 1862. He *d.* unm., at Sandybrook Cottage, Ashbourne, 3 Dec. 1883, in his 73d year, and was *bur.* at Ashbourne.

V. 1883. SIR HORACE NEVILE BLAKISTON, Baronet [1763], nephew and h., being 1st s. and h. of the Rev. Horace Mann BLAKISTON, Vicar of Benhall, Suffolk (1840-75) by Charlotte, da. of the Rev. William Henry Galfridus MANN, Vicar of Bowdon, Cheshire, which Horace last named, who *d.* 9 Feb. 1878, aged 58, was yr. br. of the late Baronet, and 4th s. of the 3d Baronet. He was *b.* 2 Aug. 1861, and *suc. to the Baronetcy*, 3 Dec. 1883.

FLEMING:

cr. 22 April 1763;

ex. 5 Nov. 1763.

I. 1763. April to Nov. "JOHN FLEMING, of Brompton Park, co. Middlesex,"(b) Esq., s. of Robert FLEMING, Lieut. in [his brother's] Major-Gen. James FLEMING'S Regt. of Foot (*d.* in or before May 1749), by Anne, his wife, was *b.* about 1701, and was *cr. a Baronet*, as above, 22 April 1763. He *m.* (settlement 3 July 1753) Jane, only da. of William COLEMAN, of Garnhay, Devon, by Jane, sister of Edward, 8th DUKE OF SOMERSET, da. of Sir Edward SEYMOUR, 5th Baronet [1611]. He *d.* s.p.m.s.,(c) (a few months after his creation), 5 Nov. 1763, aged 61, when the *Baronetcy* became *extinct*. His remains (together with those of his only son, who *d.* four weeks before him) were removed from South Audley chapel and deposited, 21 Feb. 1764, in Westm. Abbey. M.I.(d) Will dat. 18 June 1763, pr. 21 Nov. 1763, 18 June 1776. His widow *m.* March 1770 (spec. lic.), in Upper Brook street, St. Geo. Han. sq. (as his 2d wife), Edwin LASCELLES, who was *cr.* 9 July 1790, BARON HAREWOOD, co. York, and who *d.* s.p. 25 Jan. 1795. She *d.* at 16 Portman street, Midx., 11 and was *bur.* 19 April 1813, at Westm. Abbey, aged 81. Will dat. 22 Feb. 1811, pr. 14 May 1813, 9 May 1821, and 31 May 1824.

(a) The estate of Sandybrook was sold either by him, shortly after his succession to the Baronetcy, or by the Executors or Trustees of his uncle, the 4th Baronet.

(b) See p. 125, note "a," under "LLOYD." The word "Esq." is (presumably by mistake) omitted in the notice of Fleming.

(c) He had four daughters, of whom three *d.* unm., and the other, Seymour Dorothy *m.* 20 Sep. 1775, Sir Richard Worsley, 7th Baronet [1611], who *d.* s.p., 5 Aug. 1805.

(d) See copy of this M.I. in Kimber's *Baronetage* [1770], vol. iii, p. 476.

MAYNE:

cr. 22 April 1763;

afterwards, 1776-94, BARON NEWHAVEN [I.];

ex. 28 May 1794.

I. 1763, to 1794. "WILLIAM MAYNE, of Marston Mortein, Beds, Esq.,"(a) one of the twenty-one children of William MAYNE, of Powis Logie, co. Clackmannan, being 4th s., 1st by his 2d wife, Helen, da. of William GALBRAITH, of Balgair, was *b.* 1722; was for many years a merchant in the family house at Lisbon, but returned in 1751, and having acquired by his marriage, in 1758, considerable property in Ireland, was M.P. [I.], for Carysfort, 1760-64, and was *cr. a Baronet*, as above, 22 April 1763; P.C. [I.], March 1766; M.P. for Canterbury, 1774-80, and for Gatton(b) (two Parls.) 1780-90, being *cr.* 26 July 1776, BARON NEWHAVEN OF CARRICKMAYNE, co. Dublin [I.].(c) He *m.* in 1758, Frances,(d) sister and coheir of John (ALLEN), 3d VISCOUNT ALLEN OF STILLORGAN [I.], yst. da. of Joshua, the 2d Viscount, by Margaret, da. of Samuel DU PASS. He *d.* s.p.s. 28 May 1794, aged 72, at his house in Duke street, Dublin, when *all his honours* became *extinct*. Admon. June 1800. His widow *d.* in Charles street, 4 and was *bur.* 9 March 1801, at St. James', Westm.

HORTON:

cr. 22 Jan. 1764;

ex. 2 March 1821.

I. 1764. "WILLIAM HORTON, of Chaderton, co. Lancaster,"(e) Esq., 1st s. and h. of Thomas HORTON, of the same, Gov. of the Isle of Man (*d.* 18 March 1757, aged 71), by Anne, da. and coheir of Richard MOSTYN, of London, Merchant, was *b.* probably about 1715; was Sheriff of Lancashire, 1764-65, and was *cr. a Baronet*, as above, 22 Jan. 1764. He *m.* in 1751, Susanna, da. and h. of Francis WATTS, of Barnes Hall, co. York. He *d.* 25 Feb. 1774. Will pr. April 1774.

II 1774. SIR WATTS HORTON, Baronet [1764], of Chaderton aforesaid, 1st s. and h., *b.* 17 Nov. 1753; *suc. to the Baronetcy*, 25 Feb. 1774; Sheriff of Lancashire, 1775-76. He *m.* 3 June 1778, Henrietta, 3d sister of Edward, 12th EARL OF DERBY, da. of James STANLEY, *styled* [in error] LORD STRANGE, by Lucy, da. and coheir of Hugh SMITH. He *d.* s.p.m. 13 Nov. 1811, aged 58. Admon. June 1831, Dec. 1833 and May 1844. His widow, who was *b.* 1756, *d.* at Bath, 1830. Admon. June 1831 and Aug. 1844.

(a) See p. 125, note "a," under "LLOYD."

(b) His estate there, which commanded the borough election was sold in 1789 for £80,000.

(c) His spirited speech in the House of Commons when (during the American War) Burke boasted of being in intercourse with Franklin (then in open revolt) is in Wraxall's *Memoirs* (edit. 1884), vol. ii, p. 34.

(d) Mrs. Delany, writing in Feb. 1755, calls her "a little lively sort of a Fairy not very conversant with the great world."

(e) See p. 113, note "a," under "GIDEON." The date in the Gazette notice for the creation of Horton and Rodney is 21 Jan., that of Moore, 28 Jan.; that of Amyand, Duncan and Gordon, 9 Aug.; that of Lowther, 17 Aug.; and that of Pigot, 23 Nov. 1764. The word "Esq." is (presumably by mistake) omitted in the notice of Horton.

III. 1811, to 1821. SIR THOMAS HORTON, Baronet [1764], of Chaderton aforesaid, br. and h. male, *b.* 21 July 1758 [*Qy.* if not LL.B., of Cambridge (Trinity Coll.), 1782]; was in Holy Orders; Vicar of Badsworth, co. York. He *m.* 28 July 1779, Elizabeth, elder sister of his brother's wife, being 1st sister of the EARL OF DERBY abovenamed. She, who was *b.* 1748, *d.* 13 April 1796. He *d.* s.p.m. 2 March 1821, aged 62, when the *Baronetcy* became *extinct*.

RODNEY:

cr. 22 Jan. 1764;

afterwards, since 1782, BARONS RODNEY OF RODNEY STOKE.

I. 1764. "GEORGE BRIDGES RODNEY, Esq., Vice-Admiral of the Blue,"(a) 2d but 1st surv. s. of Henry RODNEY, of Walton-on-Thames, Surrey, sometime a Capt. in Holt's Marines, by Mary, 1st da. and coheir of Sir Henry NEWTON, Judge of the Court of Admiralty, is said to have been *bap.* 13 Feb. 1718/9 at, St. Giles'-in-the-Fields;(b) ed. at Harrow, but, in July 1732, entered the Navy as "King's letter boy;" Lieut. 1739; Capt. 1742; distinguished himself in the victory off Cape Finesterre in Oct. 1747; Gov. of Newfoundland, 1749-50; Rear-Admiral, 1759; reduced Martinique, in Feb. 1762, taking possession of St. Lucia, Grenada, and St. Vincent; Vice-Admiral, 21 Oct. 1762, being *cr. a Baronet*, as above, 22 Jan. 1764; Governor of Greenwich Hospital, 1765-70; was M.P. for Saltash, May 1751 to 1754; for Okehampton, Nov. 1759-1761; for Penhryn, 1761-68; for Northampton, 1768-74 (at which election he is said to have been nearly ruined by expending £30,000), and finally, for Westminster, 1780 till raised to the peerage in 1782; was Rear-Admiral of Great Britain, Aug. 1771; Admiral, 29 Jan. 1778; was, in 1779, Commander-in-Chief of the Fleet on the Leeward Islands station, defeating, in Jan. 1780, a Spanish squadron, and relieving the siege of Gibraltar, for which he received the thanks of Parliament, and was made **K.B.** (supernumerary), 14 Nov. 1780. In 1781 he captured the Dutch island of St. Eustatius, but his crowning victory was the defeat of the French Fleet under Count de Grasse, 12 April 1782,(c) off the Leeward Islands, for which he was *cr.*, 19 June 1782, BARON RODNEY OF RODNEY STOKE, co. Somerset, with an annuity of £2,000, which, in 1793, was extended to his successors in that title. He *m.* firstly, 2 Feb. 1753, at Portland chapel, Marylebone, Jane, sister of Spencer, 8th EARL OF NORTHAMPTON, da. of the Hon. George COMPTON, by Mary, da. and h. of Sir Berkeley LUCY, 3d and last Baronet [1618]. She, who was *b.* 11 Jan. 1730, at Lisbon, *d.* 28 Jan. 1757 and was *bur.* at Old Alresford, Hants. He *m.* secondly, in or before 1765, Henrietta, da. of John CLIES, of Lisbon, Merchant. She, who was *b.* about 1739, at Lisbon, was living when he was raised to the peerage, as abovestated, 19 June 1782. In that peerage this *Baronetcy* then *merged*, and still [1905]-so continues. See "Peerage."

(a) See p. 128, note "e," under "HORTON."

(b) *Dict. Nat. Biog.* No such entry, however, appears in the copious extracts from these Registers in the College of Arms, London. His parents had, in 1715, a child, "Maria Constantia," *b.* 25 Sep. and *bap.* 7 Oct. at St. Margaret's, Westm., and another in 1719, "Catherine," *b.* 26 Dec., in Warwick Court, and *bap.* 20 Jan. 1719/20, at St. Andrew's, Holborn.

(c) "Brave Rodney made the French to rue,
The twelfth of April '82."

MOORE:

cr. 28 Jan. 1764;

ex. 16 Jan. 1780.

I. 1764. "HENRY MOORE, of Jamaica, Esq.,"(a) 1st and only surv. s. and h. of Samuel MOORE, of the same, by Elizabeth, sister and coheir of Samuel LOWE, of Goadby, co. Leicester, was *b.* 1713; ed. at Eton and at Leyden Univ.; was Member in several Parls. in Jamaica, being, in 1752, Member of Council; in 1753, Island Secretary; and from 1756 to 1762, Lieut.-Governor of that island, and was *cr. a Baronet*, as above, 28 Jan. 1764. In July 1765 was made Governor of New York, where he thenceforth resided. He *m.* 13 Dec. 1751, Catharine Maria (sister of Edward LONG, the Historian of Jamaica), da. of Samuel LONG, of Longueville in Jamaica, Member of Council for that island, by Mary, da. of Bartholomew TATE, of DELAPRE, co. Northampton. He *d.* at New York, 11 Sep. 1769, aged 56. Will pr. June 1770. His widow, who was *b.* 2 Dec. 1727, *m.* Richard VINCENT, and *d.* 8 June 1812, in England.

II. 1769, to 1780. SIR JOHN HENRY MOORE, Baronet [1764], only s. and h., *b.* in 1756; *suc. to the Baronetcy*, 11 Sep. 1769. He *d.* unm. 16 Jan. 1780, when the *Baronetcy* became *extinct*.(b) Will pr. as "of Bucks," Feb. 1780.

AMYAND:

cr. 9 Aug. 1764;

afterwards, since 1771, CORNEWALL.

I. 1764. "GEORGE AMYAND, of London, Merchant."(a) one of the sons of Claudius AMYAND, Surgeon-in-Ordinary to George II (*d.* 6 July 1740), by Mary, his wife, was *b.* 26 Sep. and *bap.* 15 Nov. 1720, at St. James', Westm.; was a London Merchant, trading principally with Hamburgh; M.P. for Barnstaple, 1754, till death in 1766; one of the assistants to the Russia Company, 1756; a Director of the East India Company, 1762,(c) and was *cr. a Baronet*, as above, 9 Aug. 1764. He *m.* in or before 1748, Anna Maria, da. of John Abraham KORTEEN, of Hamburgh, Merchant. He *d.* 16 and was *bur.* 23 Aug. 1766, at Carshalton, Surrey, aged 45. His widow *d.* 30 June and was *bur.* there 7 July 1767, aged 42. Her will pr. July 1767.

II. 1766. SIR GEORGE AMYAND, *afterwards* (1771), CORNEWALL, Baronet [1764], of Crookham, Beds, and (after 1771), of Moccas Court, co. Hereford, 1st s. and h., *b.* 8 Nov. 1748; matric. at Oxford (Ch. Ch.), 6 April 1766, aged 17; *cr.* M.A., 14 March 1769, and D.C.L., 8 July 1773, having *suc. to the Baronetcy*, 16 Aug. 1766. He, by royal lic., 5 July 1771, took the name of CORNEWALL, in lieu of that of AMYAND, in consequence of his approaching marriage. He was M.P. for Herefordshire

(a) See p. 128, note "c," under "HORTON."

(b) He was author of some juvenile poems.

(c) According to "F. G. H. Price" [*N. & Q.*, 5th S., iv, 397], "in 1762, there was a Banking firm in London styled Sir George Amyand, Staples and Mercer, carrying on business in Cornhill, near to Gracechurch street. In 1776, this firm became Staples, Baron Dimsdale & Co., 50 Cornhill, which now [1875] flourishes under the style of Dimsdale & Co." Either the date "1762" or the "Sir" is apparently, incorrect, for the Baronetcy dates from 1764, and no previous Knighthood was apparently conferred. In Price's *London Bankers* (p. 52) the firm in 1762 is described as "*Messrs.* Amyand, Staples and Mercer."

V

(six Parls. in all), 1774-96, and 1802-07. Colonel of the Herefordshire Militia, 1805. He *m.* 18 July 1771, Catherine, da. and h. of Velters CORNEWALL, of Moccas Court aforesaid. He *d.* 26 Aug. or Sep. 1819, in his 71st year, and was *bur.* at Moccas. Will pr. 1820. His widow *d.* 27 March 1835. Will pr. May 1835.

III. 1819. SIR GEORGE CORNEWALL, Baronet [1764], of Moccas Court aforesaid, 1st s. and h., *b.* 16 Jan. 1774, and *bap.* at St. Geo. Han. sq.; matric. at Oxford (Ch. Ch.), 27 April 1792, aged 18; Col. of the Herefordshire militia; *suc. to the Baronetcy* in Aug or Sep. 1819. He *m.* 26 Sep. 1815, Jane, only da. of William NAPER, of Loughcrew, co. Meath (br. to James, 1st BARON SHERBORNE), by Jane, da. of the Rev. Ferdinando Tracy TRAVELL, of Upper Slaughter, co. Gloucester. He *d.* 27 Dec. 1835, at Moccas Court, in his 62d year. Will pr. Feb. 1836. His widow *d.* there, 13 Feb. 1853, aged 64. Will pr. May 1853.

IV. 1835. SIR VELTERS CORNEWALL, Baronet [1764], of Moccas Court aforesaid, 1st s. and h., *b.* there 20 Feb. 1824; matric. at Oxford (Ch. Ch.), 19 Oct. 1842, aged 18; *suc. to the Baronetcy*, 27 Dec. 1835; Sheriff of Herefordshire, 1847; Major of the Militia of that county, 1855-59. He *d.* unm. 14 Oct. 1868, aged 44.

V. 1868. SIR GEORGE HENRY CORNEWALL, Baronet [1764], of Moccas Court aforesaid, br. and h., *b.* there 13 Aug. 1833; ed. at Rugby, and at Trinity Coll., Cambridge; B.A. 1856; M.A., 1871; in Holy Orders; Rector of Moccas since 1861; *suc. to the Baronetcy*, 14 Oct. 1868. He *m.* 4 June 1867, Louisa Frances, only da. of Francis BAYLEY, Judge of the Westm. County Court (yr. s. of the Right Hon. Sir John BAYLEY, 1st Baronet [1834], and sometime [1830-34] a Baron of the Court of Exchequer), by his 1st wife, Elizabeth, da. of Alexander MACDONALD, of London. She *d.* 2 Feb. 1900.

Family Estates.—These, in 1883, consisted of 6,946 acres in Herefordshire and 368 in Beds. *Total.*—7,314 acres, worth £8,104 a year. *Seat.*—Moccas Court, near Weobley, co. Hereford.

DUNCAN:

cr. 9 Aug. 1764;

ex. 1 Oct. 1774.

I. 1764, to 1774. "WILLIAM DUNCAN, of Marybone [co. Middlesex], M.D.,"(a) yr. s.(b) of Alexander DUNCAN, of Lundie, co. Angus, by Isabella (*m.* 1702), da. of Sir Patrick MURRAY, 2d Baronet [S. 1673], of Ochtertyre, was *b.* probably about 1715; was M.D. of St. Andrew's College, Scotland, 4 May 1751; Licentiate of the Coll. of Physicians, London, 30 Sep. 1756; Physician-in-Ordinary to George III, soon after his accession, and was *cr. a Baronet*, as above, 9 Aug. 1764; F.R.S., 1771. He *m.* 5 Sep. 1763, Mary, 1st da. of Sackville (TUFTON), 7th EARL OF THANET, by Mary, da. and coheir of William (SAVILE), 2d MARQUESS OF HALIFAX. He *d.* s.p. at Naples, 1 Oct. 1774, and was *bur.* at Hampstead, Midx., when the *Baronetcy* became *extinct*. Will pr. Oct. 1775. His widow, who was *b.* 1723, *d.* 5 July 1806. Will pr. 1806.

(a) See p. 128, note "c," under "HORTON."

(b) His elder br., Alexander Duncan, of Lundie, was grandfather of Adam Duncan, the celebrated Admiral, who won the battle of Camperdown, 11 Oct. 1797, and was accordingly *cr.* Viscount Duncan of Camperdown.

GORDON:

cr. 21 Aug. 1764;

ex. 9 May 1831.

I. 1764. "SIR SAMUEL GORDON, at [*sic*] Newark-upon Trent, Knt."(a) s. of Samuel GORDON,(b) by Eleanor, da. of (—) MAGENNIS, was "bred up in Physic;(b) settled at Newark-upon-Trent; was Sheriff of Notts, 1761-62; *Knighted*, 18 March 1761, and was *cr. a Baronet*, as above, 21 Aug. 1764. He *m.* in or before 1747, "Elizabeth BRADFORD, niece and heir to Sir Matthew JENISON,(c) of Newark-upon-Trent." He was *bur.* 29 April 1780, at Newark. Admon., as of "Branston, co. Lincoln," 15 July 1780. His widow *d.* 29 March and was *bur.* 4 April 1799, at Newark.

II. 1780, to 1831. SIR JENISON WILLIAM GORDON, Baronet [1764], of Haverholme Priory, co. Lincoln, only s. and h., *bap.* 30 Sep. 1747, at Newark-upon-Trent; *suc. to the Baronetcy* in April 1780; Sheriff of Lincolnshire, 1783-84; Vice-Lieut. of that county, 1803; Patent Customer of the Port of Newcastle-upon-Tyne. He *m.* Oct. 1781, Harriet Frances Charlotte, 2d da. of the Hon. Edward FINCH-HATTON (6th s. of Daniel, EARL OF WINCHILSEA), by Elizabeth, da. and coheir of Sir Thomas PALMER, 4th Baronet [1621]. She, who was *b.* 19 Feb. 1752, *d.* 11 June 1821. He *d.* s.p. 9 May 1831, at Haverholme Priory aforesaid, aged 83, when the *Baronetcy* became *extinct*. Will pr. Nov. 1831.

LOWTHER:

cr. 22 Aug. 1764;

afterwards, since 1802, VISCOUNTS LOWTHER;

and since 1807, EARLS OF LONSDALE.

I. 1764. "The REV. WILLIAM LOWTHER, M.A., of Swillington, Yorkshire,"(d) Clerk in Holy Orders, only s. and h. of Christopher LOWTHER, of Little Preston in that county, by Elizabeth, da. of Daniel MAUDE, of Alverthorpe, which Christopher (who *d.* 1718) was yr. br. of Sir William LOWTHER, Baronet (so *cr.* 6 Jan. 1714/5), and uncle of the 2d and last Baronet of that creation. He was *b.* 10 July 1707; ed. at Trinity Coll., Cambridge; B.A., 1730; M.A., 1734; incorp. at Oxford, 9 July 1734; in Holy Orders; Rector of Swillington; and Vicar of Wetton, co. York, 1742; Preb. of York, 1754; and having by the death, 22 Oct. 1763, of his cousin, Sir William LOWTHER, 2d and last Baronet [1715], suc. to the family estate of Swillington, was *cr. a Baronet*, as above, 22 Aug. 1764. He *m.* 31 Dec. 1753, Anne, da. of the Rev. Charles ZOUCH, Vicar of Great Sandal, co. York, by Dorothy, da. of Gervase NORTON, of Wakefield. She *d.* 3 April 1759. He *d.* 15 June 1788, in his 81st year. Will pr. 1788.

II. 1788. SIR WILLIAM LOWTHER, Baronet [1764], of Swillington aforesaid, 1st s. and h., *b.* 29 Dec. 1757; was M.P. for Carlisle, 1780-84; for Cumberland, 1784-90, and for Rutland, 1796-1802, having *suc. to the*

(a) See p. 128, note "c," under "HORTON."

(b) Kimber's *Baronetage* [1770]. His father's name is not given in the *Baronetages* of Betham or Playfair, though all three works state him to be a descendant of Thomas Gordon, who settled in Ireland *temp.* James I.

(c) An elaborate account of the Jenison family is in Playfair's *Baronetage* [1811], in a note to this Baronetcy, but the parentage of this Knight does not appear therein, though it is stated that in 1677 his namesake, another Matthew Jenison (probably a relative) purchased the Augustine Friars, in Newark.

(d) See p. 113, note "a," under "GIDEON." The date of the Gazette notice of the creation of Lowther is 17 Aug., and of Pigot, 23 Nov. 1764.

Baronetcy, 15 June 1788; entered the army, 1794, becoming finally, 1800, Lieut.-Col. He *m.* 12 July 1781, at St. James', Westm., Augusta, 1st da. of John (FANE), 9th EARL OF WESTMORLAND, by his 1st wife, Augusta, da. of Lord Montague BERTIE, yr. s. of Robert, 1st DUKE OF ANCASTER. She, who was *b.* 18 Sep. 1761, was living when, on the death, 24 April 1802, of his cousin James (LOWTHER), EARL OF LONSDALE (so *cr.* 24 May 1784), he became the 2d VISCOUNT LOWTHER OF WHITEHAVEN, under the spec. rem. in the creation of that dignity, 26 Oct. 1797. He was subsequently *cr.* 7 April 1807, EARL OF LONSDALE. In those peerages this *Baronetcy* then *merged*, at the dates abovementioned, and still so continues. See *Peerage.*

WILLIAMS.

EDWARD WILLIAMS, of Langoed Castle, Brecknockshire, Esq., is (erroneously) stated to have been *cr. a Baronet*, as above, in Banks's continuation of Dugdale's *List*. See, as to him, vol. ii, p. 224, notes "c" and "d," under "WILLIAMS," *cr.* 4 May 1644.

PIGOT:

cr. 5 Dec. 1764;

sometime, 1766-77, BARON PIGOT OF PATSHULL [I.].

I. 1764. "GEORGE PIGOT, Esq., late Governor of Fort St. George,"(a) Madras, in East India, 3d but 1st surv. s. of Richard PIGOT, of Westminster (*bap.* at Hodnet, Salop, 6 Oct. 1679, and *d.* 31 Dec. 1729), by Frances (Tirewoman to Caroline, the Queen Consort), da. of Peter GOODE, of St. Anne's, Soho, was *b.* 4 and *bap.* 31 May 1719, at St. Martin's-in-the-Fields; became a Writer to the East India Company, 1736; was Governor of Madras (for the first time), 1755-63, being, shortly after his resignation, *cr. a Baronet*, as above, 5 Dec. 1764, with a spec. rem., failing his issue male, to his two brothers, Robert PIGOT and Hugh PIGOT,(b) respectively; was M.P. for Wallingford, Jan. 1765 to 1768, and for Bridgnorth, 1768 till his death in 1777; was *cr.* LL.D. of the University of Cambridge, 3 July 1779. Having purchased the estate of Patshull, co Stafford (for, it is said, £100,000), he was raised to the Irish peerage, being *cr.* 18 Jan. 1766, BARON PIGOT OF PATSHULL, *co. Dublin* [I.]. In April 1775 he was again made Governor of Madras, resuming office at Fort St. George in Dec. 1775, but, being at variance with the Council, was actually arrested at their command in Aug. 1776, and *d.* unm. and s.p. legit.,(c) in [illegal] confinement at the Company's Garden House, near Fort St. George, 11 May 1777, aged 58, when the *peerage* became *extinct*.(d) Will pr. 5 Feb. 1778.

(a) See p. 128, note "c," under "HORTON."

(b) This Hugh Pigot became an Admiral, and *d.* 15 Dec. 1792, leaving an only son, General Sir Henry Pigot, G.C.M.G., who *d.* s.p. 7 June 1840, aged 89.

(c) Besides a da., Sophia, who *m.* 14 March 1776, the Hon. Edward Monckton, he had two illegit. sons, viz. (1), Gen. Richard Pigot, Col. of the 4th Dragoon Guards, who *d.* 22 Nov. 1868, aged 94; and (2), Admiral Sir Hugh Pigot, K.C.B., who *d.* 30 July 1857, aged 82.

(d) The celebrated "Pigot Diamond" (weighing 188 grains), was disposed of by lottery under Act of Parliament, July 1800, for £23,998; sold at Christie's in May 1802, for 9,500 guineas, and again in or soon after 1818, for £30,000, to Ali Pasha, at whose deathbed in Feb. 1822, it was by his order crushed to powder.

II. 1777. Sir Robert Pigot, Baronet [1764], of Patshull, co. Stafford, br. and h., *b.* 20 Sep. 1720; served in the 31st Foot at the battle of Fontenoy in 1745; was in command of the 38th Foot at the battle of Bunkers Hill, 17 June 1775, and was, for his services there, made Colonel thereof; Major General 1777, and Lieut.-General 1782. He was M.P. for Wallingford, 1768-72, and *suc. to the Baronetcy*, under the spec. rem. 11 May 1777. He *m.* 18 Feb. 1765, at St. Anne's, Soho, Anne, sister of Sir John Allen-Walsh, 1st Baronet [I. 1775], only da. of Allen Johnson, of Kilternan, co. Dublin, by Olivia, da. of John Walsh, of Ballykilcavan, in Queen's County. She *d.* July 1772, and was *bur.* at Patshull. He *d.* 11 Aug. 1796, aged 75. Will pr. 1797.

III. 1796. Sir George Pigot, Baronet [1764], of Patshull aforesaid, 1st s. and h., *b.* 29 Oct. 1766. He raised in 1794, a regiment (the 130th) of which he was made Colonel Commander, and with which he served in the Peninsula; was Colonel, 1800; Major-General, 1805; Lieut.-General, 1812, and General 1825, having *suc. to the Baronetcy*, 11 Aug. 1796; Sheriff of Staffordshire, 1825-26. He *m.* 18 July 1796, at Patshull, Mary Anne, da. and coheir of the Hon. John Monckton, of Fineshade Abbey, co. Northampton (yr. s. of John, 1st Viscount Galway [I.]), by Anne (*m.* 21 Jan. 1766), da. of (—) Adams. She *d.* 30 Oct. 1833. He *d.* at Patshull, 24 June 1841, aged 74. Will pr. Oct. 1841.

IV. 1841. Sir Robert Pigot, Baronet [1764], of Patshull aforesaid, and of Branches Park, co. Cambridge, 2d but 1st surv. s. and h., *b.* at Patshull, 1801; was M.P. for Bridgnorth 1832-37, and Feb. 1838 to 1853 (six Parls. in all), and *suc. to the Baronetcy*, 24 June 1841. He *m.* firstly, 5 Oct. 1826, at Hale, Mary, 2d da. of William Bamford, of Bamford Hall, co. Lancaster. She *d.* s.p. 5 Sep. 1847. He *m.* secondly, 22 Jan. 1850, at Stetchworth, co. Cambridge, Emily Georgiana Elise, elder da. of Samuel Yate Benyon, of Ash Hall, Salop, and Stetchworth Park, co. Cambridge. He *d.* 1 June 1891, in his 90th year, at Hillside, Bracknell, Berks. His widow, who received the red ribbon of the Legion of Honour for her work with the Ambulance, 1870-71, living 1905.

V. 1891. Sir George Pigot, Baronet [1764], of Warfield-Grove, near Bracknell, Berks, 1st and only surv. s. and h. by 2d wife; *b.* 15 Dec. 1850, at Moulton Paddocks, Suffolk; *suc. to the Baronetcy*, 1 June 1891. He *m.* 19 Aug. 1879, at St. Matthew's, Hatchford, Alice Louisa Raynsford, 2d da. of Sir James Thompson Mackenzie, 1st Baronet [1890], of Glen Muick and Kintail, by Mary, da. of Charles Du Pre Russell, of the Bengal Civil Service.

MILDMAY:

cr. 5 Feb. 1765;

ex. 8 Aug. 1771.

I. 1765, to 1771. "William Mildmay, of Moulsham Hall, co. Essex, Esq.,"(a) only s. of William Mildmay, Chief of the East India Company's factory at Surat, by Sarah, da. of (—) Willcox, Judge in the Civil Court there, was *b.* about 1705; ed. at Emman. Coll., Cambridge; M.A. of that University (Comitiis Regiis), 1728; admitted to Middle Temple, of which he subsequently was a Bencher; was one of the two Commissioners, 1750-56, accredited to Paris to settle the disputes as to Nova Scotia, St. Lucia, Tobago, etc., and, having inherited by the death, 29 Feb. 1756, of his distant cousin, Benjamin (Mildmay), Earl Fitzwalter,

(a) See p. 113, note "a," under "Gideon." The date of the Gazette notice of the creation of Mildmay is 5 Feb.; of Major, 8 July; of Mawbey, 27 July; and of Knowles, 19 Oct. 1765.

considerable estates in Essex, served in the Militia of that county, and was *cr. a Baronet*, as above, 5 Feb. 1765. He *m.* Anne, 1st da. of Humphrey Mildmay, of Shawford, Hants, by Lætitia, da. and h. of Holyday Mildmay, of Shawford aforesaid. He *d.* s.p., 8 Aug. 1771, at Bath. Will pr. Sep. 1771. His widow *d.* 28 March 1796.(a) Will pr. April 1796.

MAJOR:

cr. 15 July 1765;

afterwards, since 1781, Henniker;

and, since 1800, Barons Henniker [I.].

I. 1765. "John Major, of Worlingworth Hall, co. Suffolk, Esq.,"(b) as also of Thornham Hall, in that county, only surv. s. and h. of John Major, of Bridlington, co. York (who *d.* at sea, 1709, aged about 40), by Elizabeth, da. of the Rev. Richard Tennant, Rector of Carnaby and Boynton, co. York, was *b.* 17 May 1698, at Bridlington; was senior elder brother of the Trinity House, 1741 81; Sheriff of Suffolk, 1754; M.P. for Scarborough, 1761-68, and was *cr. a Baronet*, 15 July 1765, as above, with spec. rem., failing heirs male of his body, to his son in law, "John Henniker, Esq."(b) He *m.* 20 Jan. 1723/4, at Bridlington, Elizabeth, only da. of Daniel Dale, of that town, merchant. She *d.* 1780. Admon. as "of St. Olave's, Hart street, London," 15 Nov. 1780. He *d.* s.p.m. 22 Feb. 1781, aged 82, both being *bur.* at Worlingworth. His will pr. March 1781.

II. 1781. Sir John Henniker, Baronet [1765], of Newton Hall in Great Dunmow, co. Essex, of Stratford-upon-Slaney, co. Wicklow, and of Thornham Hall aforesaid, son-in-law of the above, and s. and h. of John Henniker, of London, Russian Merchant, Freeman of Rochester, by Hannah, da. of John Swanson, of London, was *b.* 15 June 1724; was Sheriff of Essex, 1758; Lieut. and Deputy Warden of Waltham Forest, 1760; M.P. for Sudbury, 1761-68, and for Dover, 1774-84; *suc. to the Baronetcy*, 22 Feb. 1781, in consequence of the spec. rem. of that dignity. He *m.* 24 Feb. 1746/7, at St. Paul's Cathedral, London, Anne, elder da. and coheir(c) of Sir John Major, 1st Baronet [1765], and Elizabeth his wife, both abovenamed. She *d.* 18 July 1792, and was *bur.* at Rochester Cathedral. He was *cr.* 30 July 1800, BARON HENNIKER OF STRATFORD-UPON-SLANEY, co. Wicklow [I.]. In that peerage this *Baronetcy* then *merged*, and still [1905] so continues, the 5th Baron and 6th Baronet being *cr.* 13 July 1866, BARON HARTISMERE, co. Suffolk [U.K.]. See *Peerage*.

MAWBEY:

cr. 30 July 1765;

ex. 28 Aug. 1817.

I. 1765. "Joseph Mawbey, of Botleys [in Chertsey], co. Surrey, Esq.,"(b) 2d and yst. s. of John Mawbey, of Raunston, or Ravenstone, co. Leicester (*d.* 4 Sep. 1754, in his 62d year), by his 1st wife Martha, da. of Thomas Pratt, of Raunston, was *b.* there 2 Dec. 1730; was,

(a) The estate of Moulsham, which she held for life, then passed to her niece Jane, 1st da. and coheir of her br., Carew Mildmay, wife of Sir Henry Paulet Saint-John-Mildmay (formerly Saint-John), 3rd Baronet [1772].

(b) See p. 134, note "a," under "Mildmay."

(c) Elizabeth, the other coheir, *m.* 18 July 1767, at Waltham, co. Essex, as his 3d wife, Henry (Brydges), 2d Duke of Chandos, and *d.* s.p. his widow, 30 March 1813, aged 82, at Major House, near Twaite, Suffolk.

at the age of 17, taken into partnership by his maternal uncle, Joseph Pratt (*d.* 1754), in an extensive malt distillery and vinegar business at Vauxhall, which (together with his elder br. John Mawbey, who *d.* s.p.s. 22 June 1786, aged 61), he carried on till 1775, the profits being sufficient "to yield more than £600,000 per annum to Government in duties."(a) He was Sheriff of Surrey, 1757-58; M.P. for Southwark (two Parls.), 1761-74; and for Surrey (three Parls.), June 1775 to 1790.(b) He bought the estate of Botleys in 1763, rebuilt the mansion there, and was *cr. a Baronet*, as above, 30 July 1765. He *m.* 21 Aug. 1760, Elizabeth, sister and h. of Joseph Pratt (who *d.* May 1766), da. of Richard Pratt, of Vauxhall, his cousin german. She *d.* at Botleys, 19 and was *bur.* 26 Aug. 1796, at Chertsey. M.I. He *d.* at Botleys, 16 June 1798, and was *bur.* at Chertsey, aged 67.(c) Will pr. 1798.

II. 1798, to 1817. Sir Joseph Mawbey, Baronet [1765], of Botleys aforesaid, only surv. s. and h., *b.* probably about 1770; *suc. to the Baronetcy*, 16 June 1798. He *m.* 9 Aug. 1796, Charlotte Caroline Maria, da. and coheir of Thomas Henchman, of Littleton, co. Middlesex, and only child by his 1st wife. He *d.* s.p.m. 28 Aug. 1817, when the *Baronetcy* became *extinct*, the estate of Botleys being sold soon after his death. Will pr. 1818. His widow *d.* at Ramsgate, Aug. 1832, aged 57. Will pr. Feb. 1833.

KNOWLES:

cr. 31 Oct. 1765.

I. 1765. "Charles Knowles, Admiral of the Blue,"(d) a reputed son of Charles Knollys, titular 4th Earl of Banbury,"(e) was *b.* 1704; entered the Navy, March 1718; Lieutenant 1730; acted as Surveyor and Engineer of the Fleet in the expedition to Carthagena, 1741; Governor of Louisbourg, 1746-48, reduced Fort Louis in St. Domingo, but was unsuccessful in an attack of Cuba; Rear-Admiral of the White, 1747; defeated a Spanish Fleet in Sep. 1748, but was reprimanded by a Court Martial in Dec. 1749, for mismanagement in the action. He was M.P. for Gatton, Nov. 1749 to 1752; was Governor of Jamaica, 1752-58; Vice-Admiral of the Blue, 1755, and Admiral thereof 1760, being *cr. a Baronet*, as above, 31 Oct. 1765. Rear-Admiral of Great Britain, Nov. 1765 to Oct. 1770, when he accepted office under the Empress of Russia as President of the Admiralty, and resided for five or six years at St. Petersburgh. He was of Lovel Hill, near Windsor, Berks. He *m.* firstly, 22 Dec. 1740, Mary, sister of Sir John Gay Alleyne, 1st Baronet [1769], da. of John Alleyne, of

(a) Betham's *Baronetage* [1803] where, also, are copious extracts from parish registers, etc., relating to this family.

(b) Wraxall in his *Historical Memoirs* [vol. i, pp. 265-266], says that "he spoke with great good sense though not with brilliancy," but that "from some unfortunate circumstances in his private life, never could obtain a patient or a candid hearing in Parliament." In 1780 he, "like Wilkes, refused to concur in the vote of thanks to Lord Cornwallis," on the ground of its giving approbation to the American War. In 1784, however, he had joined the party of Pitt. He is thus spoken off in *The Rolliad* in the lines which commiserate the trials of the Speaker (Charles Wolfran Cornewall).

"There Cornewall sits, and ah! compelled by fate,
Must sit for ever, through the long debate,
Painful pre-eminence! he hears, 'tis true,
Fox, North and Burke—but hears *Sir Joseph* too."

(c) He was author of several poems and treatises, and a contributor to the *Gent. Mag.* and other periodicals.

(d) See p. 134, note "a," under "Mildmay."

(e) *Dict. Nat. Biogr.*, where an admirable account of his career (than which few have been "the subject of more contention or of more contradictory estimates") is given by Professor J. K. Laughton.

Barbadoes, by Mary, da. of William Terrill. She was *bur.* 16 March 1741/2, aged 21. He *m.* secondly, at Aix la Chapelle, 29 July 1750, Maria Magdalena Theresa, da. of Henry Francis, Comte de Bouget. He *d.* at his house in Bulstrode street, Marylebone, 9 Dec. 1777, in his 74th year. Will pr. 1778. His widow, who was *b.* in Germany, *d.* at Shrewsbury, and was *bur.* 15 March 1796. Admon. April 1797.

II. 1777. Sir Charles Henry Knowles, Baronet [1765], of Lovel Hill aforesaid, only surv. s. and h.,(a) by 2d wife, *b.* 24 Aug. 1754, at Kingston in Jamaica; entered the Navy, 1768; Lieut., 1775; *suc. to the Baronetcy*, 9 Dec. 1777; was wounded in the action off Grenada, 6 July 1779; Capt. 1782; took a distinguished part, as Capt. of the "Goliath" (seventy-four guns), in the battle off Cape St. Vincent, 14 Feb. 1797; Rear-Admiral 1799; Vice-Admiral, 1804; Admiral, 1810; G.C.B. (extra), 20 May 1820. He *m.* 10 Sep. 1800, Charlotte, 1st da. of Charles John Johnstone, of Ludlow, by Mary, da. of John Beddoe. He *d.* 28 Nov. 1831, aged 77. Admon. Jan. 1832. His widow, who was *b.* 2 June 1782, *d.* 9 June 1867, at Ryde.

III. 1831. Sir Francis Charles Knowles, Baronet [1765], 1st s. and h., *b.* 10 June 1802; ed. at Trinity Coll., Cambridge; B.A., 1825; M.A., 1828; *suc. to the Baronetcy*, 28 Nov. 1831; Barrister (Lincoln's Inn), 1834; F.R.S. He *m.* 26 May 1831, at St. Geo. Han. sq., Emma, 4th da. of Sir George Pocock, 1st Baronet [1821], by Charlotte, da. of Edward Long, Judge of the Admiralty Court in Jamaica. He *d.* 19 March 1892, aged 89, at 50 York street, Marylebone, and was *bur.* at St. Nicholas' Cemetery, Guildford. His widow *d.* 1 Dec. 1894, at Ryde, aged 90.

IV. 1892. Sir Charles George Frederick Knowles, Baronet [1765], only s. and h., *b.* 14 March 1832; entered the Navy, 1845; Capt., 1842; serving in the Burmese War, 1852-53; being in command in the Niger Expedition, 1864; and rendering valuable services in the Newfoundland Fisheries, 1871-72, and at St. Croix, 1880; Rear-Admiral, 1889; Vice-Admiral, 1894, having *suc. to the Baronetcy*, 19 March 1892. He *m.* firstly, 19 July 1861, at St. John's, Keswick, Elizabeth, only child of John Chapman, of Cleveland square, Hyde Park. She obtained a divorce, 25 July 1876.(b) He *m.* secondly, 14 June 1882, Mary Ellen, da. of Cathcart Thomson, of Halifax, Nova Scotia, (by (—), da. of the Hon. Joseph Howe, Lieut.-Governor of that colony. She *d.* 5 July 1890.

CORNISH:

cr. 1 Feb. 1766;

ex. 30 Oct. 1770.

I. 1766, to 1770. "Samuel Cornish, of Sharnbrooke, co. Bedford, Esq., Vice-Admiral of the Blue,"(c) whose parentage is unknown, "is said to have risen from a very humble origin, to have served his apprenticeship on board a collier, to have been afterwards in the East India Company's service, and to have entered the Navy as

(a) Edward Knowles, the 1st s. (only child by 1st wife), *b.* 1741, *d.* unm. and v.p. in 1762, being lost at sea when in command of the "Peregrine" sloop.

(b) By his 1st wife he had two sons, both of whom *d.* s.p. and v.p., viz. (1), John St. John Knowles, Capt. 2d Batt. Royal Irish Regt., *b.* 9 June 1862, *m.* 29 Sep. 1883, and *d.* 9 Feb. 1892; (2), Charles Alfred FitzGerald Knowles, *b.* 5 Feb. 1864, *d.* unm. 10 March 1890.

(c) See p. 113, note "a," under "Gideon." The date of the Gazette notice of Cornish is 1 Feb.; that of Moore, 10 March; that of Pringle, and of East, 3 June, that of Burrell, 15 July, that of Cheere and of Andrews, 19 July, that of Thomas, 6 Sep., and that of Wolff, 18 Oct. 1766, being in some few cases *after* the date usually assigned to the patents by which they were created.

an able seaman."(a) He was made Lieut. R.N., 16 Nov. 1739, served in the Expedition to Carthagena, 1741; took part in the action off Toulon, 11 Feb. 1743/4; was Rear-Admiral of the White, 1759; assisted at the reduction of Pondicherry in 1761, and shortly afterwards defeated the Spaniards in Manilla Bay; and (jointly with Gen. Draper) took possession of the Philippine islands in 1762, being, 21 Oct. 1762, made Vice-Admiral of the Blue, and *cr. a Baronet*, as above, 1 Feb. 1766. He was M.P. for New Shoreham (two Parls.), Dec. 1765 till death; was F.R.S. He *d.* unm., 30 Oct. and was *bur.* 4 Nov. 1770, at St. Margaret's, Westm., when the *Baronetcy* became *extinct*.(b) Will pr. Nov. 1770.

MOORE:

cr. 4 March 1766;

ex. 2 Feb. 1779.

I. 1766, to 1779. "JOHN MOORE, Esq., Rear-Admiral of the Red,"(c) 3d s. of Rev. Henry MOORE, D.D., Rector of Malpas, co. Chester (yr. s. of Henry, 3d s. of Henry, 3d EARL OF DROGHEDA [I.]), by Catharine (relict of Admiral Sir George ROOKE), da. of Sir Thomas KNATCHBULL, 3d Baronet [1641], was *b.* 24 March 1718; ed. at Whitchurch Grammar School; entered the Navy, 1729; Lieut. 1738; Captain, 1743; distinguished himself, under Hawke, in the action off Finisterre, 14 Oct. 1747; was in command at the reduction of Guadeloupe, in 1759; Rear-Admiral, 1762, and was *cr. a Baronet*, as above, 4 March 1766. He was for three years Commander-in-Chief at Portsmouth; Vice-Admiral, 1770; **K.B.**, 18 May 1770; Admiral, 29 Jan. 1778. He *m.* about 1756, Penelope, da. of Gen. William MATTHEW, Governor of the Caribbee islands. He *d.* s.p.m.s., 2 Feb. 1779, aged 60, when the *Baronetcy* became *extinct*. Will pr. March 1779. His widow *d.* 8 Aug. 1785. Will pr. Feb. 1786.

PRINGLE:

cr. 5 June 1766;

ex. 18 Jan. 1782.

I. 1766, to 1782. "JOHN PRINGLE, Dr. of Physick,"(c) of Pall Mall, in St. James', Westminster, 4th and yst. s. of Sir John PRINGLE, 2d Baronet [S. 1683], of Stichill, by Magdalen, da. of Sir Gilbert ELIOTT, 1st Baronet [S. 1666], of Stobbs, was *b.* 10 April 1707; ed. at the Universities of St. Andrew's, Edinburgh, and Leyden, at which last he became M.D., 20 July 1730; was Professor of Moral Philosophy at Edinburgh, 1733-44; Fellow of the College of Physicians there, 1735; Physician to the Army in Flanders, 1742, and to the Forces, 1744; to H.R.H. the Duke of Cumberland, 1749; to the Queen Consort's household, 1761; to the said Queen herself, 1763, and to the King in 1774, having been *cr. a Baronet*, as above, 5 June 1766. He was Licentiate of the Coll. of Physicians, London, 1758, and Fellow, 1763; F.R.S., 1745; being on the Council, 1753, and President, 1772-78. He *m.* 14 April 1752, Charlotte, 2d da. of [—] OLIVER, M.D., of Bath. She *d.* 29 Dec. 1753, aged 25. He *d.* s.p. 18 and was *bur.* 31 Jan. 1782, at St. James', Westm., aged 74, when the *Baronetcy* became *extinct*. Will pr. Feb. 1782.

(a) *Dict. Nat. Biogr.*

(b) He left a large fortune (acquired by the Manilla prize money and in the East Indies) to his nephew, Samuel Pitchford, then Capt. R.N., who took the name of Cornish, and became subsequently an Admiral.

(c) See p. 137, note "c," under "CORNISH."

EAST:

cr. 5 June 1766;

ex. 11 Dec. 1828.

I. 1766. "WILLIAM EAST, of Hall place [in Hurley, co. Berks], Esq.,"(a) only s. and h. of William EAST, of the same, and of the Middle Temple, London, Barrister at Law, by Anne, da. of Sir George COOKE, of Harefield, Middlesex, Chief Prothonotary of the Common Pleas, was *b.* 27 Feb. 1737/8, and was *cr. a Baronet*, as above, 5 June 1766. He was Sheriff of Berks, 1766-67. He *m.* firstly, 29 June 1763, at Olveston, co. Gloucester, Hannah, 2d da. of Henry CASAMAJOR, of Tokington, in that county by Elizabeth, da. of Henry WHITEHEAD, of the same. He *m.* secondly, 28 July 1768 (—), da. of (—) JACKSON. He *d.* 12 Oct. 1819, at Hall Place, in his 82d year. Will pr. 1819.

II. 1819, to 1828. SIR GILBERT EAST, Baronet [1766], of Hall Place aforesaid, 1st s. and h., *b.* 17 April 1764, at Hurley; admitted to Middle Temple 16 Nov. 1769; matric. at Oxford (Queen's Coll.), 1 July 1783, aged 19; *suc. to the Baronetcy*, 12 Oct. 1819. He was Sheriff of Berks, 1822-23. He *m.* 10 May 1788, Eleanor Mary, da. of William JOLLIFFE, of Petersfield, by Eleanor, da. and h. of Sir William HYLTON, *formerly* MUSGRAVE, 5th Baronet [S. 1638]. He *d.* s.p. 11 Dec. 1828, aged 64, when the *Baronetcy* became *extinct*.(b) Will pr. Feb. 1829. His widow *m.* (as his 1st wife) 31 March 1834, in Green street, St. Geo. Han. sq. (spec. lic.), the Hon. John Craven WESTENRA (who *d.* 5 Dec. 1874, aged 76), and *d.* 17 Dec. 1838.

BURRELL:

cr. 15 July 1766;

afterwards, since 1796, BARONS GWYDIR;

sometime, 1828-70, LORDS WILLOUGHBY DE ERESBY.

I. 1766. "MERRICK BURRELL, of West Grinstead Park, co. Sussex, Esq.,"(a) 2d son of Peter BURRELL, of Langley Park, in Beckenham, co. Kent, by Isabella, da. of John MERRICK, of Stubbers, in North Ockendon, Essex, was *bap.* 5 Nov. 1699; was a merchant in London; Director and sometime Governor of the Bank of England; M.P. for Marlow, 1747-54; for Grampound, 1754-68; for Haslemere, 1774-80; and for Bedwyn, 1780-84, being *cr. a Baronet*, as above, 15 July 1766, with spec. rem. failing heirs male of his body to his nephew," "Peter BURRELL, of Beckenham, Kent, Esq."(a) He *d.* unm. 6 April 1787, aged 87. Will pr. April 1787.

II. 1787. SIR PETER BURRELL, Baronet [1766], of Langley Park aforesaid, great nephew and h. male, being only s. and h. of Peter BURRELL, of the same, Surveyor of Crown Lands, by Elizabeth, da. and coheir of John LEWIS, of Hackney, which Peter (who *d.* 6 Nov. 1776) was s. and h. of another Peter BURRELL, also of Langley Park (*d.* 16 April 1756, aged 64), elder br. of the 1st Baronet. He was *b.* 16 July 1754, in Upper Grosvenor street, St. Geo. Han. sq.; was M.P. for Haslemere, Nov. 1776 to 1780, and for Boston (three Parls.), March 1782 to 1796, and being (in right of his wife) appointed Deputy Great Chamberlain of England, was *Knighted*, 6 July 1781, at St. James', and *suc. to the Baronetcy*, under the spec. rem., 6 April 1787. He *m.* 23 Feb. 1759, at her mother's house in Berkeley square, Priscilla Barbara Elizabeth, 1st da. of Peregrine (BERTIE), 3d DUKE OF ANCASTER AND KESTEVEN,

(a) See p. 137, note "c," under "CORNISH."

(b) The Hall Place estate devolved on his nephew, East George Clayton, afterwards Clayton-East, 2d son of Mary, his only sister (of the half blood), by Sir William Clayton, 4th Baronet [1732]. He was *cr.* a Baronet, 17 Aug. 1838.

by Elizabeth, da. and h. of William BLUNDELL, of Basingstoke. She, who was *b.* 15 Feb. 1761, and who, on the death, 8 July 1779, of her br. the 4th Duke, became one of the two coheirs of the office of Great Chamberlain, and in whose favour (18 March 1780) the BARONY OF WILLOUGHBY DE ERESBY was terminated, was living when her husband (her deputy in that great office) was *cr.*, 16 June 1796, BARON GWYDIR of Gwydir, co. Carnarvon.(a) In that peerage this *Baronetcy* then *merged*, and still [1905] so continues, the 2d and 3d Barons becoming in 1828 to 1870, LORDS WILLOUGHBY DE ERESBY. See *Peerage*.

CHEERE:

cr. 19 July 1766;

ex. 28 Feb. 1808.

I. 1766. "SIR HENRY CHEERE, Knt.,"(b) of St. Margaret's, Westm., presumably s. of John CHEERE, of Clapham, Surrey (*bur.* there 27 Sep. 1756), and Sarah, his wife, was *b.* about 1703; was mentioned as "cousin" in the will of Sir John CHARDIN, Baronet [so. *cr.* 1720], dated 18 July 1747; was the principal Statuary of his period, having a large practice; F.S.A., 1750; was *Knighted* 10 Dec. 1760, on presenting an address to the King on his accession, being at that time a Deputy-Lieut. of Midx., and was *cr. a Baronet*, as above, 19 July 1766.(c). He *m.* in or before 1730, Helen, da. of Sauvignon RANDALL. She *d.* Oct. 1769, and was *bur.* (with several of her children) at Clapham, Surrey. He *d.* at St. Margaret's, Westm., 15 and was *bur.* 29 Jan. 1781, at Clapham, aged 77. Will pr. Jan. 1781.

II. 1781, to 1808. SIR WILLIAM CHEERE, Baronet [1766], 1st surv. s. and h., *b.* about 1730; was in Holy Orders; *suc. to the Baronetcy*, 15 Jan. 1781; was of White Roding, Essex, where he *d.* unm., 28 Feb., and was *bur.* 9 March 1808, at Clapham, aged 78, when the *Baronetcy* became *extinct*.(d) Will pr. 1808.

ANDREWS:

cr. 19 Aug. 1766;

ex. 27 Feb. 1822.

I. 1766. "JOSEPH ANDREWS, of Shaw, co. Berks, Esq.,"(b) s. and h. of Joseph ANDREWS, of Shaw Place, in Shaw aforesaid, Paymaster of the Forces (who purchased Shaw Place in 1749, and *d.* April 1753, aged 62), by his 1st wife, Elizabeth, da. of Samuel BEARD, of Newcastle-under-Line, was *b.* 30 Oct. 1727, and *bap.* at his father's house in St. George's, Blooms-

(a) A good specimen of a "petticoat" peerage, the title being taken not from any of his own or his ancestors' possessions, but from a part of those of his wife in right of her great-grandmother, Mary, da. and h. of Sir Richard Wynn, 4th Baronet [1611], of *Gwydir*, co. Carnarvon. As he was but 42 when so created, it was not improbable that the title might have devolved on his issue male by a second marriage, which issue would have had no descent from the ancient family of Wynn, of Gwydir, thus commemorated.

(b) See p. 137, note "c," under CORNISH.

(c) He, apparently, is the first Sculptor who was *cr. a Baronet*. Sir Godfrey Kneller, the Painter, had been previously, 24 May 1715, so honoured.

(d) He left a large fortune to the two daughters of his br. Charles Cheere, who was *bur.* 14 Sep. 1799, at Clapham, aged 64. One of these *m.*, in 1789, Charles Madryll, of Papworth, co. Cambridge, who, consequently, took the name of Cheere.

bury, by Dr. Earle, a Dissenting Minister; was Major in the Berks Militia, and was *cr. a Baronet*, as above, 19 Aug. 1766, with a spec. rem., failing heirs of his body, to his brother, James Pettit ANDREWS. He *m.* firstly, 9 May 1762,(a) Elizabeth, da. of Richard PHILLIPS, *or* PHIPPS, of Tarrington, co. Hereford. He *m.* secondly, Elizabeth, da. of Col. DALRYMPLE. He *d.* s.p. at Shaw Place, 29 Dec. 1800, and was *bur.* 7 Jan. 1801, at Shaw, aged 73. Will pr. Jan. 1801. His widow *d.* at Hyde Park Corner, 2 Jan. 1804 [*Qy.* 1803]. Will pr. 1803 [*Qy.* 1804 or 1805].

II. 1880, to 1822. SIR JOSEPH ANDREWS, Baronet [1766], of Shaw Place aforesaid, nephew and h., being 1st and only surv. s. of James Pettit ANDREWS, Police Magistrate of Middlesex, by Anne, da. of the Rev. Thomas PENROSE, Rector of Newbury, Berks, which James (who *d.* 5 Aug. 1797), was br. of the half blood to the 1st Baronet, being s. of Joseph ANDREWS abovenamed, by his 2d wife, Elizabeth (*m.* 21 March 1734/5), da. of John PETTIT, of St. Botolph's, Aldgate, London. He was *b.* 22 Sep. 1768, and *bap.* at Shaw aforesaid; entered the 1st Regt. of Foot Guards, 1785; Lieut., 1792; serving in Flanders, 1793; *suc. to the Baronetcy*, 29 Dec. 1800; Col. of the Newbury Volunteers. He *d.* unm. 27 Feb. 1822, aged 53, when the *Baronetcy* became *extinct*.(b) Will pr. 1822.

THOMAS:

cr. 6 Sep. 1766.

I. 1766. "GEORGE THOMAS, of Yapton Place, co. Sussex, Esq., Governor of the Leeward Islands,"(c) s. of William THOMAS,(d) the only s. of Col. John THOMAS, who commanded the Barbadoes Regiment, and greatly distinguished himself at the taking of St. Christophers in 1690; was nine years (1738-47), Governor of Pennsylvania, and thirteen years (1753-66) Governor of the Leeward Islands, and, having purchased the estate of Yapton, was *cr. a Baronet*, as above, 6 Sep. 1766, resigning the Governorship 18 Dec. following. He *m.* Lydia, da. of John KING, of Antigua. He *d.* 31 Dec. 1774, in Upper Brook street. Will pr. 1775.

II. 1774. SIR WILLIAM THOMAS, Baronet [1766], of Yapton Place aforesaid, only s. and h.; Sheriff of Sussex, 1761-62; *suc. to the Baronetcy*, 31 Dec. 1774. He *m.* Margaret, da. and h. of William SYDERFFE, of Dean street, Soho. She *d.* 1763, aged (it is said) 69. He *d.* 28 Dec. 1777, at Bath. Will pr. 1778.

(a) It has been stated that they were *m.* at St. Paul's Cathedral, London, but no marriage whatever appears to have been celebrated there between 1758 and 1877. Possibly this marriage has been confused with the second marriage of Joseph Andrews, the Baronet's father, which took place there 21 March 1734/5.

(b) On 13 July 1822, died "At Shaw Place near Newbury, Mrs. Elizabeth Ann Andrews, only sister to the late Sir Joseph Andrews, Baronet, and the last of his name and family." [*Annual Register*, 1822]. This same Elizabeth Anne is, stated in Betham's *Baronetage* [1803] to be "wife of Charles Henry Hunt, Esq., late of Goldicoth, in Worcestershire." She, however, resumed her patronymic on succeeding to the Shaw estate shortly before her death, and *d.* s.p., aged 52, being suc. therein by the Rev. Dr. Penrose, Vicar of Writtle.

(c) See p. 137, note "c," under "CORNISH."

(d) The affiliation of the grantee is given in Debrett's *Baronetage* for 1819, though, oddly enough, it is omitted in the later edition, for 1840, and replaced by the vague words "was descended from a Monmouthshire family." The *father's* name does not appear in Burke's *Baronetage* (1905), nor in Foster's *Baronetage*, 1883, though each work gives that of the "distinguished" *grandfather*. With greater consistency both father and grandfather are omitted in the older Baronetages of Kimber, Betham and Playfair.

V

III. 1777. SIR GEORGE THOMAS, Baronet [1766], of Yapton Place aforesaid, and afterwards of Dale Park, near Arundel, Sussex, only s. and h.; *b.* probably about 1740; *suc. to the Baronetcy*, 28 Dec. 1777; was M.P. for Arundel (two Parls.), 1790-97; raised a Regiment of Fencible Cavalry called the Sussex, of which he was Colonel. He *m.* firstly, in or before 1777, at Geneva, Mdlle. SALES, of Pregny-la-Tour. He *m.* secondly, 20 Dec. 1782, Sophia, da. of Admiral John MONTAGU, by Sophia, da. of James WROUGHTON, of Wilcot. He *d.* 6 May 1815. Will pr. 1815. His widow, by whom he had no issue, *d.* 21 Oct. 1854, in Lower Belgrave street, aged 95. Will pr. Oct. 1854.

IV. 1815. SIR WILLIAM LEWIS GEORGE THOMAS Baronet [1766], of Dale park aforesaid, and Penthis hill, in the Isle of Wight, only s. and h., by 1st wife, *b.* 9 Sep. 1777, at Geneva; matric. at Oxford (Ch. Ch.), 21 Oct. 1795, aged 18; *suc. to the Baronetcy*, 6 May 1815. He *m.*, in or before 1802, Elizabeth, da. of Richard WELSH. She *d.* 21 Jan. 1848, at Weymouth. He *d.* there 23 Aug. 1850, aged nearly 73. Will pr. March 1851.

V. 1850. SIR WILLIAM SIDNEY THOMAS, Baronet [1766], 2d but 1st surv. s. and h.,[a] *b.* 1807 at Whippingham, in the Isle of Wight; entered the Navy, 1820; Commander, 1842; Captain (on the retired list), 1860, having *suc. to the Baronetcy*, 23 Aug. 1850. He *m.* firstly, 29 May 1843, at Clifton, Thomazine Oliver, da. of Henry HAYNES, Captain R.N. She *d.* 6 March 1853. He *m.* secondly, 18 Aug. 1856 (also) at Clifton, Fanny Louisa, yst. da. of John COULSON, of Clifton wood. He *d.* 27 April 1867, at the Grange, Great Malvern, co. Worcester, aged 59. His widow, by whom he had no issue, *d.* 9 Nov. 1870, at Portishead, Somerset, aged 51.

VI. 1867. SIR GEORGE SIDNEY MEADE THOMAS, Baronet [1766], 2d but 1st surv. s. and h., by 1st wife, *b.* 12 Feb. 1847, at Weymouth; ed. at the Royal Naval School, New Cross; *suc. to the Baronetcy*, 27 April 1867; admitted as Pensioner at Caius Coll., Cambridge, 1 Oct. 1867, residing there three terms. He *m.* 9 May 1874, Edith Margaret, 1st da. of Morgan Hugh FOSTER, **C.B.**, of Brickhill, Beds.

WOLFF:[b]

cr. 27 Oct. 1766;

ex. 3 Feb. 1837.

I. 1766. "JACOB WOLFF, of Townhill [*Qy.* Cams Hall, near Fareham], co. Southampton, Esq.,"[c] and afterwards of Chulmleigh, Devon, Baron of the Holy Roman Empire, 2d and only surv. s.[d] of Charles Godfrey WOLFF, of Narva in Livonia (*d.* 1783, aged 83), by Anne Elizabeth, da. of Peter VON ITTER, Inspector of the farms of the King of Prussia, was *b.* 27 Jan. 1739/40 (O.S.), at Moscow: came to England for his education in Aug. 1754; suc., in Dec. 1759, to the fortune of his uncle, Baron Jacob WOLFF (who, since 1727, had been Resident for the British Court at St. Petersburgh); was *cr. a Baron of the Holy Roman Empire*, by the Emperor Francis, in July, 1761, and having been naturalised in England, was *cr. a Baronet*, as above, 27 Oct. 1766.[a] He *m.* 11 Dec. 1766, Anne, only da. of the Right Hon. Edward WESTON, of Somerby Hall, co. Lincoln, Secretary of State [I.], by his 2d wife, Anne, da. of John FOUNTAYNE, of Melton, co. York. He *d.* of apoplexy, in Hammet street, Taunton, 10 and was *bur.* 28 Jan. 1809, at Wookey, Somerset, aged nearly 69. Admon. May 1809. His widow *d.* 13 March 1815. Will pr. 1815.

(a) George Thomas, the 1st son, Midshipman in the "Leander," *d.* unm. and v.p., at Trincomalee, 11 July 1820.

(b) Much of the information in this article is taken from a memorandum in a family bible in possession of C. Wontner Smith, 13 Aubert Park, Highbury, Middlesex, 20 Jan. 1888, who kindly sent a copy thereof to the compiler of this work.

(c) See p. 137, note "c," under "CORNISH."

(d) "Charles Godfrey Wolff, a Baron of the Holy Roman Empire," was *cr.* D.C.L. by the University of Oxford, 9 July 1793. This was apparently a brother of the 1st Baronet, who, like him, had, possibly, been *cr.* a Baron of the Holy Roman Empire. See Playfair's *Baronetage* [1811], but the account there seems inaccurate. That Baron (though of the same name) most certainly could not be the "Charles Godfrey Wolff, born at Narva in 1701, and died in 1783, aged 83," who was father of the 1st Baronet.

II. 1809, to 1837. SIR JAMES WILLIAM WESTON WOLFF, Baronet [1766], Baron of the Holy Roman Empire, only s. and h., *b.* 24 Nov. 1778, and *bap.* 1 Jan. 1779, at Crediton, Devon; *suc. to the Baronetcy*, 10 Jan. 1809. He *m.* 4 Jan. 1800, Frances, da. of Joseph ADKINS, of co. Lincoln. He *d.* s.p. 3 Feb. 1837, at Lyndhurst, Hants, aged 58, when the *Baronetcy* became *extinct*. Will pr. April 1837.

PERROTT:

Royal warrant *dated* 3 Jan. 1767,

with precedency of 1 July 1716.

See, as to this anomalous Baronetcy, pp. 33-38 *ante*, under 1716.

CHAMPNEYS:

cr. 26 Jan. 1767;

afterwards, 1831-39, MOSTYN-CHAMPNEYS;

ex. 21 Nov. 1839.

I. 1767. "THOMAS CHAMPNEYS, of Orchardleigh, co. Somerset, Esq.,"[b] 3d but 1st surv. s. and h. of Richard CHAMPNEYS, of the same, and of Cams, in Fareham, Hants (who was elected, but apparently did not serve as, Sheriff of Somerset, 1727, and who *d.* 1761), by his 2d wife, Jane, sister and eventually sole heir of Anthony Langley SWYMMER, da. of Anthony SWYMMER, of Jamaica, was *bap.* 9 Oct. 1745, at Fareham; matric. at Oxford (Ch. Ch.), 16 May 1764, aged 18, and was *cr. a Baronet*, as above, 26 Jan 1767. He was Sheriff of Somerset, 1775-76, after which date he resided for ten years on his estates in Jamaica. He *m.* firstly, 5 July 1768, Caroline Anne, da. of Richard COX, of Quarley, Hants, and Bartlett's buildings, London, by Carolina, da. of Sir William CODRINGTON, 1st Baronet [1721]. She *d.* 2 July 1791, at Orchardleigh. He *m.* secondly, Henrietta, da. of Humphrey MINCHIN, of Stubbington, Hants. He *d.* in that county, 2 July 1821, aged 75. Will pr. 1822. His widow *d.* s.p. at Bath, 4 Jan. 1827, aged 74. Will pr. April 1827.

(a) The original patent of creation was on sale (for 30s.) at James Coleman's, 22 High street, Bloomsbury, in March 1869.

(b) See p. 113, note "a," under GIDEON." The date of the Gazette notice for Champneys is 13 Jan.; for Foley, 27 June; for Hort, 8 Sep.; for Dennis, 19 Sep., and for Burnaby, 24 Oct. 1767.

II. 1821, to 1839. SIR THOMAS SWYMMER CHAMPNEYS, *afterwards*, since 1831, MOSTYN-CHAMPNEYS, Baronet [1767], of Orchardleigh aforesaid, only s. and h. by 1st wife, *b.* 21 May 1769; *suc. to the Baronetcy*, 2 July 1821; took the name of MOSTYN before that of CHAMPNEYS on succeeding to the estates of his wife's brother, Sir Thomas MOSTYN, 6th Baronet [1660], who *d.* s.p. 7 April 1831. He *m.* 21 April 1792, at St. Geo., Han. sq., Charlotte Margaret, 2d da. of Sir Roger MOSTYN, 5th Baronet [1660], of Mostyn, by Margaret, da. and h. of the Rev. Hugh WYNNE. He *d.* s.p., 21 Nov. 1839, at Orchardleigh, aged 70, when the *Baronetcy* became *extinct*. Admon. Dec. 1840. His widow *d.* 12 Dec. 1845, at Gloddaeth, near Conway, aged 78. Will pr. Jan. 1846.

FOLEY:

cr. 1 July 1767;

ex. 7 March 1782.

I. 1767, to 1782. "RALPH [*rectius* ROBERT-RALPH] FOLEY, of Thorpe Lee [co. Surrey], Esq.,"[a] also described as of Halstead Place, co. Kent,[b] 4th s. of Robert FOLEY, by Mary, da. of the Rev. Ralph MACKLAND, which Robert was 2d s. of Philip FOLEY, of Prestwood, co. Stafford, 3d s. of Thomas FOLEY, of Whitley Court, co. Worcester (*d.* 1 Oct. 1677, aged 61), ancestor of the BARONS FOLEY, was *b.* about 1727; was sometime a Banker in Paris, and was *cr. a Baronet*, as above, 1 July 1767. He *m.* before 1771, Dorothy, only da. of Thomas HINCHCLIFFE, of Hinchcliffe, co. York. He *d.* in London, s.p., 7 and was *bur.* 14 March 1782, at Eastham, co. Essex, aged 55, when the *Baronetcy* became *extinct*. His widow *d.* 19 Jan. 1804, aged 84. M.I. at Eastham. Her admon. March 1804.

HORT:

cr. 8 Sep. 1767.

I. 1767. "JOHN HORT, of Castle Strange, co. Middlesex, Esq.,"[a] 2d s. of the Most Rev. Josiah HORT, Archbishop of Tuam, 1741-51 (*d.* 14 Dec. 1751), by Elizabeth (*m.* 19 Feb. 1725/6), da. and coheir of the Hon. William FITZMAURICE, of Gallane, co. Kerry,[c] br. of Thomas, 1st EARL OF KERRY [I.], was *b.* 8 Aug. 1735, in Ireland; ed. at Trinity Coll., Dublin, B.A., 1752; LL.B., 1757, being incorporated at Oxford (Ch. Ch.), 17 Nov. 1758; admitted to Lincoln's Inn, 24 Oct. 1759; was Consul-Gen. at Lisbon, 1767, and was *cr. a Baronet*, as above, 8 Sep. 1767. He was afterwards (presumably on the death s.p. in 1786 of his elder br., Josiah George HORT) of Hortland, co. Kildare. He *m.* (Lic. Prerog. [I.] 20 Oct. 1789) Margaret, only da. of Sir Fitzgerald AYLMER, 6th Baronet [I. 1622], by Elizabeth, da. and h. of Fenton COLE, of Silver Hill, co. Fermanagh. He *d.* 23 Oct. 1807, aged 72. Will pr. 1807. His widow *d.* 15 Sep. 1843, in her 78th year. Will pr. Oct. 1843.

(a) See p. 143, note "b," under "CHAMPNEYS."

(b) "Halstead Place, co. Kent," is given as his residence in Kimber's *Baronetage* [1771]. There is no trace of the family at Thorpe in Surrey.

(c) The wife of this William, being mother of the said Elizabeth, was Deborah, da. of Sir John Brookes, 1st Baronet [1676].

II. 1807. SIR (JOSIAH) WILLIAM HORT, Baronet [1767], of Hortland aforesaid, 1st s. and h., *b.* 6 July 1791; ed. at Trinity Coll., Cambridge; M.A., 1812; *suc. to the Baronetcy*, 23 Oct. 1807; was Sheriff of co. Kildare, 1818, and M.P. for that county, May 1831 to Dec. 1832. He *m.* 31 March 1823, at Bathwick, Somerset, Louisa Georgiana, 2d surv. and yst. da. and coheir of Sir John CALDWELL, 5th Baronet [I. 1683], Count of the Holy Roman Empire, by Harriett, da. and coheir of Godfrey MEYNELL, of Yeldersley and Bradley, co. Derby. She, who was *b.* between Aug. 1794 and Aug. 1795, *d.* 6 May 1856, at Berne. He *d.* suddenly, 24 Aug. 1876, at 91 Ebury street, Pimlico, aged 85. Will pr. [I.], 22 Nov. 1876.

III. 1876. SIR JOHN JOSIAH HORT, Baronet [1767], of Hortland aforesaid, 1st s. and h., *b.* 14 Jan. 1824 in Dublin; entered the Army, 1840; Lieut. 61st Foot, 1842; Capt. 4th Foot, 1846; Major, 1854, serving in the Crimean Campaign, 1854-56 (medal and three clasps); Lieut.-Col., 1856; Lieut.-Col. 36th Foot, 1857; Col. in the Army, 1861; Lieut.-Col. 44th Foot, 1866; Major-Gen., 6 March 1868; Lieut.-Gen., 10 Aug. 1872; **C.B.**, 1873; *suc. to the Baronetcy*, 24 Aug. 1876; retired with the rank of General, 1881. He *d.* unm. (from injuries by having been run over by a cab eighteen months before), 5 Jan. 1882, at 35 Merrion square, Dublin, in his 58th year. Will pr. [I.] 12 June 1882.

IV. 1882. SIR WILLIAM FITZMAURICE JOSIAH HORT, Baronet [1767], of Hortland aforesaid, br. and h., *b.* 20 Jan. 1827, at Boulogne; ed. at the Military Coll. at Woolwich; admitted to King's Inns, Dublin, 1847; Barrister, Hilary, 1852; Resident Magistrate at Tuam, co. Galway, 1854-58, and at Kilkenny, 1858-82; *suc. to the Baronetcy*, 5 Jan. 1882. He *m.* firstly, 2 June 1866, Harriett Lydia, 1st da. of the Rev. Charles Butler STEVENSON, Rector of Callan, co. Kilkenny, by his 1st wife, Harriet Mary Anne, da. of James GRAHAM, of Rickardy Hall and Bannock Lodge, co. Cumberland. She *d.* 28 June 1870. He *m.* secondly, in 1874, Catherine Anne Villiers, 1st da. of John WADE, of St. Canice's Cottage, co. Kilkenny, by Deborah, da. of William BARTON, of Grove, co. Tipperary. He *d.* s.p. 18 Sep. 1887, at Hortland aforesaid, aged 60. His widow living 1905.

V. 1887. SIR FENTON JOSIAH HORT, Baronet [1767], of Hortland aforesaid, br. and h., *b.* 29 March 1836; entered the Army, 1857, serving in the Ceylon Rifles, and in the 13th Light Infantry, and being sometime Lieut.-Col. and Hon. Col. 3d Batt. Royal Inniskilling Fusileers Militia; *suc. to the Baronetcy*, 18 Sep. 1887. He *d.* unm. 4 Feb. 1902, at Leggs, co. Fermanagh, aged 65.

VI. 1902. SIR ARTHUR FENTON HORT, Baronet [1767], cousin and h. male, being 1st s. and h. of the Rev. Fenton John Anthony HORT, D.D., Lady Margaret Professor of Divinity at Cambridge and sometime (1852-82), Vicar of St. Ippolyts, Herts, by Fanny Henrietta, da. of Thomas John Dyson HOLLAND, of Heighington, co. Lincoln, which Fenton John Anthony (who *d.* 30 Nov. 1892, aged 64) was only s. and h. of Fenton HORT, of Cheltenham (*d.* 18 March 1873, aged 78), yr. s. of the 1st Baronet. He was *b.* 15 Jan. 1864; ed. at Trinity Coll., Cambridge; B.A., 1st Class Classics, 1885; M.A. and Fellow, 1888; *suc. to the Baronetcy*, 4 Feb. 1902. He *m.* 20 Aug. 1894, Helen Frances, da. of the Rev. George Charles BELL, Head Master of Marlborough College, by Elizabeth, da. of Edward MILNER.

Family Estates.—These, in 1878, consisted of 2,284 acres in co. Kildare, 973 in co. Cavan, 851 in Queen's County, and 285 in co. Fermanagh. *Total.*—4,393 acres, worth £2,234 a year, but the total amount of acres as given in Bateman's *Great Landowners* in 1883 is but 3,956, though the value is estimated as above.

DENIS, *or* DENNIS:

cr. 28 Oct. 1767;

ex. 12 June 1778.

I. 1767, to 1778. "PETER DENNIS [*or* DENIS], of [St. Mary's] Blackmonstone in Romney Marsh, Kent,"(a) Capt. R.N., s. of the Rev. Jacob DENIS (*b.* at La Rochefoucault in Angoulême, but who fled from France when aged 18, at the revocation of the Edict of Nantes, took Holy Orders and settled at Chester and finally at Wexford, where he *d.* before 1746), by Martha (*b.* in Manchester and *d.* a widow 11 July 1746, aged 77), da. of (—) LEACH, was *b.* 1713 in Chester,(b) being the eleventh child of twelve children; was Lieut. R.N., 1739; sailed round the world with Anson, 1740-44; Post Captain, 1745; took part in the action by Anson off Cape Finesterre in May 1747, and in the unsuccessful expedition against Rochefort by Hawke, in 1757; captured a French gunboat in 1758; was in the action under Hawke in Quiberon Bay in Nov. 1759; formed part of the escort of the Princess [afterwards Queen Consort] Charlotte to England in 1761, and having been M.P. for Heydon, in Yorkshire (two Parls.), 1754-68, was *cr. a Baronet*, as above, 28 Oct. 1767. He was made Rear-Admiral of the Blue, Oct. 1770; Vice-Admiral thereof, 1775, and finally Vice-Admiral of the Red. He purchased a property at Valence, near Westerham, co. Kent. He *m.* 2 Sep. 1750, Elizabeth (known previously as "Miss POPPET"), illegit. da. of John James HEIDEGGER (said to have been a Swiss Count), Manager of the Opera in London. She *d.* 30 Dec. 1765, aged 44, and was *bur.* in the new burial ground of St. George the Martyr, Midx. M.I. He *d.* s.p. 12 June 1778, aged 65, and was *bur.* there, when the *Baronetcy* became *extinct*. M.I. Will pr. 1778.

BURNABY:

cr. 31 Oct. 1767.

I. 1767. "SIR WILLIAM BURNABY [Knt.], Rear-Admiral of the Red,"(a) 3d s. of John BURNABY, of Kensington, Midx. (living 1718), by his 2d wife, Clara(c) (marr. lic. Fac., 7 May 1700), da. of Sir Edward WOOD, sometime Envoy Extraordinary to Sweden, was *b.* probably about 1710; was Capt. R.N.; *Knighted* at St. James', 9 April 1754; Rear-Admiral, 1762, and finally Vice-Admiral of the Fleet; Commander-in-Chief in Jamaica and in the Gulf of Mexico, assisting in settling the colony of Pensacola; was of Broughton Hall in Broughton Pogis, Oxon; was Sheriff of Oxon, 1755-56, and was *cr. a Baronet*, as above, 31 Oct. 1767. He *m.* firstly, in or before 1746, Margaret, widow of Timothy DONOVAN, of Jamaica. She *d.* 11 Feb. 1757. He *m.* secondly, Grace, da. of Drewry OTTLEY, of Bedford Row, Holborn. He *d.* 1776 or 1777. Admon. 5 April 1777. His widow *d.* 3 March 1823, at Stoke Cottage, near Guildford, aged 84. Will pr. 1823.

II. 1777? SIR WILLIAM CHALONER BURNABY, Baronet [1767], of Broughton Hall aforesaid, 1st s. and h., by 1st wife, *b.* 1746; Capt. R.N.; *suc. to the Baronetcy* in 1776 or 1777. He *m.* 28 June 1783, at St. Margaret's, Westm., Elizabeth, 2d da. of Crisp MOLYNEUX, of Garboldesham,

(a) See p. 143, note "b," under "CHAMPNEYS."
(b) *N. & Q.*, 8th s., ii, 29, and 7th s., xii, 43. See also Kimber's *Baronetage* [1771], where the grantee's birth is stated to have been at Chester and not at Blackmanstone, in Kent, as stated by "M.R." in *N. & Q.*, 8th s., as above.
(c) Her mother, another Clara, was sister to John Robinson, Bishop [1714-1723] of London.

Norfolk, by Catherine, da. and h. of George MONTGOMERIE, of Chippenham Hall, co. Cambridge. He *d.* 19 Feb. 1794, aged 48. Admon. March 1794. His widow *d.* 28 Feb. 1816, in her 55th year.

III. 1794. SIR WILLIAM CRISP HOOD BURNABY, Baronet [1767], of Broughton Hall aforesaid, only s. and h., *b.* probably about 1788, *suc. to the Baronetcy*, 19 Feb. 1794; ed. at the Royal Naval Academy; entered the Navy, 1806; served as Lieut. in many actions, becoming finally, 1814, Commander. He resided chiefly at Bermuda, where (1814-16) he was Commander of the "Ardent," prison ship. He *m.* there, 2 May 1818, Eleanor, widow of Joseph WOOD, of Long House, Bermuda. He *d.* s.p., 1 Aug. 1853, at Bermuda. His widow was living there many years later, and *d.* apparently in 1880.(a)

IV. 1853. SIR WILLIAM EDWARD BURNABY, Baronet [1767], cousin and h. male, being 1st s. and h. of Edward Augustus Cæsar BURNABY, Capt. R.N., by Emma, da. of (—) MACLOW, of Edinburgh, which Edward (who *d.* 11 March 1843, aged 80) was 2d s. (1st s. by 2d wife) of the 1st Baronet. He was *b.* July 1824, at Chelsea, Midx.; matric. at Oxford (Exeter Coll.), 9 Feb. 1843, aged 18; *suc. to the Baronetcy*, 1 Aug. 1853. He *m.* Oct. 1845, Caroline, da. of William REECE, of Lower Hall, Ledbury, co. Hereford. She *d.* 17 Oct. 1857, at Marlborough Hill, St. John's Wood, Midx. He *d.* s.p. at his residence, Boulogne-sur-mer, 19 Aug. 1881, aged 57.

V. 1881. SIR HENRY BURNABY, Baronet [1767], br. and h., *b.* 1829; Lieut. R.N., 1853, retiring 1859; *suc. to the Baronetcy*, 19 Aug. 1881, but is said not to have assumed the title.(b) He *m.* in 1853, Carmen Maria, only child of Senor Mariano TORRENTE, of Madrid.

PRICE:

cr. 13 Aug. 1768;

ex. 18 Oct. 1788.

I. 1768. "CHARLES PRICE, Esq.,"(c) of Rose Hall, in St. Thomas' in the Vale, in the island of Jamaica, formerly Speaker of the House of Assembly there, 1st s.(d) of Col. Charles PRICE, of Rose Hall aforesaid(e) (*d.* 23 May 1730, aged 52), by Sarah, da. of Philip EDMUNDS, of Jamaica, was *b.* 20 Aug. 1708, probably at St. Catherine's, Jamaica; matric. at Oxford (Trin. Coll.), 21 Oct. 1724, aged 16; was for thirty-one years (1732-63) a member of the Assembly at Jamaica, having been Speaker, 1746 to 1763, and thrice thanked for his services, being known as "the Jamaica Patriot"; was also, for sometime, Judge of the Supreme Court, *custos* of St. Catherine's, and Major-Gen. of all the Island Militia; and was, on his retirement, *cr. a Baronet*, as above, 13 Aug. 1768. He *m.* in or before 1733, Mary, da. of (—) SHARPE. He *d.* 26 July 1772, in Jamaica, aged 64, and was *bur.* at the Decoy in that island. M.I.

(a) She is given as living in Dod's *Baronetage* for 1880, but is omitted in that for 1881.
(b) Dod's *Baronetage* for 1905.
(c) See p. 113, note "a," under "GIDEON." The date of the Gazette notice for the creation of Price is 13 Aug. 1768.
(d) The 3d s., John Price, of Worthy park, Jamaica (*d.* 4 Feb. 1734), was grandfather of Rose Price, *cr. a Baronet*, 30 May 1815.
(e) This estate he inherited from his elder uterine br., Thomas Rose, s. of Col. William Rose, by Sarah, who was afterwards wife of Francis Price, and by him grandmother of the 1st Baronet.

II. 1772, to 1788. SIR CHARLES PRICE, Baronet [1768], of Rose Hall aforesaid, 1st s. and h., *b.* about 1733; matric. at Oxford (Trin. Coll.), 14 May 1752, aged 19; member of the Assembly at Jamaica, 1753 to 1775; Speaker (in succession to his father), 1763 to 1775; *suc. to the Baronetcy*, 26 July 1772; Major-Gen. of the Militia in that island. He *m.* Elizabeth Hannah, widow of John WOODCOCK, da. of John GUY, of Berkshire House, Jamaica, Chief Justice of that Island. She *d.* 1771. He *d.* s.p. 18 Oct. 1788, at Spanish town, Jamaica, when the *Baronetcy* became *extinct*.(a)

BURRARD:

cr. 3 April 1769;

sometime, 1795-1840, BURRARD-NEALE.

I. 1769. HARRY BURRARD, of Walhampton, co. Southampton, Esq., 1st s. and h. of Paul BURRARD, of the same, many years M.P. for Lymington(b) (*d.* 30 May 1735, aged 57), by Lucy, da. of Sir Thomas DUTTON-COLT, Envoy to the Courts of Dresden, Hanover, etc., was *b.* 1707; Gentleman Usher to the Prince of Wales, 1728; Collector of the Customs of London; Bowbearer and Riding Forester in the New Forest, Hants; M.P. for Lymington for forty-three successive years (six Parls.), 1741 to 1778; and was *cr. a Baronet*, as above, 3 April 1769, with a spec. rem., failing heirs male of his body to his brothers, William BURRARD, of Lymington aforesaid, Esq., and George BURRARD, of the Isle of Jersey, Esq., respectively. He *m.* firstly, in 1731, Alicia, da. of John SNAPE, Farrier to William III. She *d.* Sep. 1737. He *m.* secondly, in 1754, Mary Frances, da. of James CLARKE, of Wharton, co. Hereford. She *d.* Sep. 1777. He *d.* s.p.s., 12 April 1791, in his 85th year. Will pr. May 1791.

II. 1791. SIR HARRY BURRARD, *afterwards* (1795-1840) BURRARD-NEALE, Baronet [1769], of Walhampton aforesaid, nephew and h. male, being 1st s. and h. of Lieut.-Col. William BURRARD, by his 2d wife, Mary da. of Joseph PEARCE, M.D., of Lymington, which William (who *d.* Nov. 1780) was next surv. br. to the 1st Baronet. He was *b.* 16 Sep. 1765, and entered the Naval Service; was M.P. for Lymington, 1790-1802, 1806-07, 1812-23, and 1832-35, having *suc. to the Baronetcy*, 12 April 1791, under the spec. rem. in the creation thereof. By royal lic., 8 April 1795, he (in consequence of his forthcoming marriage) took the name of NEALE. In 1797 he distinguished himself at the Mutiny of the Nore, by bringing off his ship, the "San Furenzo," under a hot fire (for which he received the thanks of the City of London), and is said, in the course of his naval career, to have taken or destroyed no less than twenty of the enemies' ships. He was a Lord of the Admiralty, 1804-07; and finally, 1810, an Admiral. He entertained, on two occasions, 1801 and 1804, George III and his Queen, at Walhampton, and had, in 1825, the command of the Mediterranean Fleet. He was Groom of the Bedchamber to George III and William IV, and acted as one of the Pall Bearers at the funeral, in 1837, of the latter; **K.C.B.**, 1815; **G.C.B.**, 1822; **G.C.M.G.**, 1824-26, being re-appointed in 1832. He *m.* 15 April 1795, Grace Elizabeth, da. and coheir of Richard NEALE, of Shaw House in Melksham, Wilts, by Grace, da. and coheir of George GOLDSTONE, of Goldstone, Salop. He *d.* s.p., 7 Feb. 1840, aged 74. Will pr. March 1840. His widow *d.* 21 Dec. 1855, at Lee, co. Kent, in her 83d year.

(a) His yr. br. Rose Price, who was of the Temple, London, is sometimes (incorrectly) said to have *suc. to the Baronetcy*. He, however, *d.* s.p., before his brother, the 2d Baronet, in May 1768.
(b) Save for about forty years (1698-1701, 1713-22, 1727-41, 1778-80, 1802-06, 1807-12 and 1823-28), Lymington was represented in Parliament by the family of Burrard from 1679 to 1835.

III. 1840. SIR GEORGE BURRARD, Baronet [1769], of Walhampton aforesaid, br. and h., *b.* 6 April 1769, at Lymington; matric. at Oxford (Trinity Coll.), 12 Oct. 1786, aged 17; B.A. (Merton Coll.), 1790; M.A., 1793; in Holy Orders, being Chaplain to four successive Sovereigns, George III, George IV, William IV and Queen Victoria; Rector of Yarmouth and Vicar of Shalfleet, both in the Isle of Wight, 1801; Rector of Fobbing, Essex, 1801; Vicar of Middleton Tyas, co. York, 1804 till death, and Rector of Burton Coggles, co. Lincoln, 1822 till death; *suc. to the Baronetcy*, 7 Feb. 1840. He *m.* firstly, 18 Sep. 1804, Elizabeth Anne, da. and h. of William COPPELL, of Jamaica. She *d.* 11 April 1815. He *m.* secondly, 1 May 1816, Emma, da. of Rear Admiral Joseph BINGHAM, by Sarah, da. of Admiral Sir William PARKER, 1st Baronet [1797], of Harburn, co. Warwick. He *d.* 17 May 1856, at Walhampton aforesaid, aged 87. Will pr. Sep. 1856. His widow *d.* 2 June 1879, at the Mount, Yarmouth, Isle of Wight, aged 81.

IV. 1856. SIR GEORGE BURRARD, Baronet [1769], of Walhampton aforesaid, 1st s. and h., being only surv. s. by the 1st wife, *b.* 13 Oct. 1805; M.P. for Lymington, 1828-32; *suc. to the Baronetcy*, 17 May 1856. He *m.* 3 Jan. 1839, Isabella, da. of Sir George DUCKETT, 2d Baronet [1791], by his 1st wife, Isabella, da. of Stainbank FLOYD. He *d.* s.p. (being drowned while bathing at Lyme Regis), 7 Sep. 1870, aged 64. His widow, who was *b.* in Spring Gardens, 1813, and *bap.* at St. Martin's-in-the-Fields, *d.* 7 Dec. 1876, after a long illness.

V. 1870. SIR HARRY BURRARD, Baronet [1769], of Walhampton aforesaid, br., of the half-blood, and h., being s. of the 3d Baronet by his 2d wife; *b.* 13 Oct 1818; *suc. to the Baronetcy*, 7 Sep. 1870. He *m.* 5 Aug 1845, Mary Standley, yst. da. of J. ALLEN, of Blackheath, co. Kent. He *d.* 15 April 1871, at Hastings, aged 52. His widow *d.* 25 Nov. 1875, at the Mount, Yarmouth, Isle of Wight, aged 51.

VI. 1871. SIR HARRY PAUL BURRARD, Baronet [1769], of Walhampton aforesaid, only s. and h., *b* 5 Sep. 1846; sometime, 1866-71, an officer in the 60th Foot, retiring as Lieut.; *suc. to the Baronetcy*, 15 April 1871. He *m.* firstly, 28 March 1872, at St. John's, New Brunswick, Margaret, 2d da. of John ANDERSON, of Rothesay, and of St. John's aforesaid. She *d.* s.p., 22 April 1885, at Ringwood, Hants. He *m.* secondly, 18 Oct. 1888, Jane Eleanor Frances, 1st da. of Lieut.-Col. Bernard George Griffin BEALE, of Farningham, co. Kent.

HUME:

cr. 4 April 1769;

ex. 24 March 1838.

I. 1769. ABRAHAM HUME, of Wormleybury [in Wormley], co. Hertford, Esq., Commissary General of the Army, 4th and yst. s. of Robert HUME, *otherwise* HOME, formerly of Berwick, but subsequently of London (*d.* 1732), by Hannah, da. of (—) CURTIS, of Mile-end, Midx., was *b.* about 1703, was Commissary General of the Forces; M.P. for Steyning, 1747-54, and for Tregony, 1761-68; suc. to the estate of Wormleybury aforesaid in 1765, on the death of his elder br., Alexander HUME (who had purchased the same in 1739), and was *cr. a Baronet*, as above, 4 April 1769. He *m.* 2 Oct. 1746, Hannah, yst. da. of Sir Thomas FREDERICK, sometime Governor of Fort St. David in the East Indies, by Mary, da. of (—) MONCKEIFF. She *d.* 23 Jan. 1771, in Hill street, Berkeley square, and was *bur.* at Wormley. He *d.* 10 Oct. 1772, and was *bur.* there, aged 69. M.I. Will pr. Oct. 1772.

II. 1772, to 1838. SIR ABRAHAM HUME, Baronet [1769], of Wormleybury aforesaid, 1st s. and h., b. in Hill street, 20 Feb. 1749 [O.S.], *suc. to the Baronetcy*, 10 Oct. 1772; Sheriff of Herts, 1774-75; M.P. for Petersfield, 1774-80, and for Hastings, 1807-18; suc. to the family estate of Fernyside in Coldingham, by the death in 1785 of his father's 1st cousin, Elizabeth ROBERTSON, widow, da. and h. of Alexander HOME, of Fernyside (*d.* 1736), eldest br. of Robert HUME, *otherwise* HOME abovenamed. He was F.S.A, as also F.R.S., being at the time of his death the senior member of that Society. He *m.* 25 April 1771 (spec. lic.), at her father's house in Amen Corner, Paternoster Row, St. Michael's Ludgate, London, Amelia, sister of Francis Henry, 8th and last EARL OF BRIDGWATER, only da. of John EGERTON, D.D., Bishop of Durham (1771-87), by his 1st wife, Anne Sophia, da. of Henry (GREY), DUKE OF KENT. She, who was *b.* 25 Nov. 1754, *d.* 8 and was *bur.* 16 Aug. 1809, at Wormley. M.I. He *d.* s.p.m.(a) at Wormleybury, 24 March 1838, in his 90th year, when the *Baronetcy* became *extinct*. Will pr. May 1838.

BERNARD:

cr. 5 April 1769;

sometime, 1811—1876, BERNARD-MORLAND;

ex. 8 May 1883.

I. 1769. FRANCIS BERNARD, of Nettleham, co. Lincoln, Esq., Governor of His Majesty's Province of the Massachusetts Bay in America, only s. and h. of Rev. Francis BERNARD,(b) Rector of Brightwell, Berks, by Margaret, one of the four daughters and coheirs(c) of Richard WINLOWE, of Lewknor, Oxon, was *b.* about 1712; ed. at Westm. School, becoming a Collegian in 1726; matric. at Oxford (Ch. Ch.), 12 June 1729, aged 17; B.A., 1733; M.A., 1736; *cr.* D.C.L., 2 July 1772; Barrister, and subsequently Bencher of the Middle Temple; High Steward of Lincoln and Recorder of Boston in that county; Governor of New Jersey, Jan. 1758 to 1760; Governor of Massachusetts Bay, 1760-70, being, in consequence of his firmness in carrying out the views of the Home Government, *cr. a Baronet*, as above, 5 April 1769. In 1771 he inherited the estate of Nether Winchendon, Bucks.(c) He *m.* in 1741, Amelia, 2d da. of Stephen OFFLEY, of Norton Hall, co. Derby, being 1st da. by his 2d wife, Anne, sister of John, 1st VISCOUNT BARRINGTON OF ARDGLASS [I.], da. of Benjamin SHUTE. She, who was *b.* 27 July 1717, *d.* 26 May 1778, and was *bur.* at Aylesbury. Admon., 11 May and 6 July 1779. He *d.* 16 June 1779 at Aylesbury, and was *bur.* there, aged 67. Will pr. July 1779.

(a) Of his two daughters, both of whom *d.* v.p. (1) Amelia, Baroness Farnborough, *d.* s.p., Jan. 1837, aged 66; (2) Sophia, Baroness Brownlow of Belton (whose husband was subsequently *cr.* Earl Brownlow), *d.* 21 Feb. 1814 (four years after her marriage), leaving issue one son, John Hume Brownlow, afterwards styled Viscount Alford, who took the name of Egerton, and was father of the 2d and 3d Earls Brownlow.

(b) This Francis was only s. and h. of Francis Bernard, of Reading (*d.* 1715), s. and h. of Francis (*d.* 1680), s. and h. of Thomas Bernard, of the same (*d.* 1628, at a great age), who was yr. br. of Baldwin Bernard, of Abington, co. Northampton, and of Francis Bernard, whose son, Robert Bernard, was *cr. a Baronet*, 1 July 1662, a dignity that became extinct in 1789.

(c) Mary, sister of Mrs. Bernard (the grantee's mother), *m.* John Tyringham, of Nether Winchendon, Berks, by whom she had Jane, only da. and h., who *m.* William Beresford, and *d.* a widow and s.p. in 1771, leaving the estate of Nether Winchendon to her maternal 1st cousin, the said Sir Francis Bernard.

II. 1779. SIR JOHN BERNARD, Baronet [1769], of Nether Winchendon aforesaid, 2d(a) but 1st surv. s. and h., *b.* probably about 1746; was in the Naval Service at Boston, in America, till the outbreak of the American War, serving afterwards in the West Indies; *suc. to the Baronetcy*, 16 June 1779. He *d.* unm. at Dominica, 16 Aug. 1809.

III. 1809. SIR THOMAS BERNARD, Baronet [1769], of Nether Winchendon aforesaid, br. and h., *b.* 27 April 1750, at Lincoln; ed. at a school in New Jersey and at Harvard University; Barrister (Middle Temple), 1780, practising chiefly as a conveyancer; was many years a Governor, being from 1795 to 1806 Treasurer, and subsequently a Vice-President of the Foundling Hospital; was a great promoter of the School for the Indigent Blind (1800), the Fever Institution (1801), and of divers other charitable foundations; also of the Royal Institution (chartered 1800), of that for the Promotion of Fine Arts in the U.K. (1806), of the Alfred Club(b) in Albemarle street (1808), etc., being well-known as a philanthropist. In 1801 he was *cr.* M.A. by the Archbishop of Canterbury; LL.D., by the Univ. of Edinburgh; and made Chancellor of the Diocese of Durham, where he set on foot a Collegiate School for the Training of Teachers. He *suc. to the Baronetcy*, 16 Aug. 1809. He *m.* firstly, 11 May 1782, Margaret, da. and coheir of Patrick ADAIR. She *d.* 6 Jan. 1813, and was *bur.* in the chapel of the Foundling Hospital. He *m.* secondly, 15 June 1815, at St. Geo. Han. sq., Charlotte Matilda, 5th da. of Sir Edward HULSE, 2d Baronet [1739], by Hannah, da. of Samuel VANDERPLANK. He *d.* s.p. at Leamington, co. Warwick, 1, and was *bur.* 10 July 1818, in the chapel aforesaid, aged 68. Will pr. July 1818. His widow *d.* 20 July 1846. Will pr. Aug. 1846.

IV. 1818. SIR SCROPE BERNARD-MORLAND, Baronet [1769], of Nether Winchendon aforesaid, and of Askett lodge, in Great Kimble, Bucks, br. and h., *b.* 1 Oct. 1758, at Pestel Amberg, New Jersey, America; ed. at Harrow; matric. at Oxford (Ch. Ch.), 13 April 1775, aged 16; obtaining several College and University prizes; B.A., 1779; M.A., 1781; and D.C.L., 1788; being admitted into the College of Advocates, London, 3 Nov. 1789, and becoming, in 1795, Judge of the Episcopal Court of Durham. He had previously, 1782 and 1787, been Private Secretary to the Viceroy of Ireland, and was, 1787, Gentleman of the Black Rod [I.]. In 1785, was Secretary to the Commission of Enquiry into Public Offices, and from 1789 to 1803 was Under-Secretary of State to the Home Department; M.P. for Aylesbury (three Parls.), Feb. 1789 to 1807, and for St. Mawes (six Parls.), 1806-30; was partner in the bank of his wife's father. He, by Royal lic., 8 May 1789, took the name of TYRINGHAM in addition to that of BERNARD, and subsequently, 15 Feb. 1811, took the name of BERNARD-MORLAND. He *suc. to the Baronetcy*, 1 July 1818. He *m.* 26 July 1785, at St. Geo. Han. sq., Hannah, only child of William MORLAND, of Lee, co. Kent, surgeon, subsequently of Pall Mall, Westm., banker, and sometime M.P. for Taunton. She *d.* 4 March 1822, at Pall Mall, in her 60th year, and was *bur.* at Kimble. Will pr. 1823. He *d.* 18 April 1830, aged 71, and was *bur.* there. Will pr. Aug. 1830.

V. 1830. SIR FRANCIS BERNARD-MORLAND, Baronet [1769], of Askett Lodge, in Great Kimble aforesaid, 3d but 1st surv. s. and

(a) The 1st son, Francis Bernard, was *b.* at Lincoln about 1744; ed. at Westm. School; matric. at Oxford (Ch. Ch.), 21 May 1761, aged 17; B.A., 1766; was a British naval officer at Boston in America, where he *d.* unm. and v.p., May 1770.

(b) "A club house for literature, from which all gaming, drinking and party politics were to be excluded," of which he is said to have been "the originator." [*Nat. Dict. Biogr.*, where, however, by a strange blunder, it is spoken of as "the *Albert* Club."] See some amusing notices of its constituency in Peter Cunningham's *London* [1850], where it is said that "it was formerly known by its cockney appellation of [the] *Half-read*" [Club].

h.,(a) *b.* in Bolton street, 7 June, and *bap.* 7 July 1790, at St. Geo. Han. sq.; matric. at Oxford (Brasenose Coll.), 14 July 1806, aged 16; *suc. to the Baronetcy*, 18 April 1830, but was gazetted as Bankrupt, March 1832. He *d.* unm. at Askett Lodge, 23 Jan. 1876, aged 85, and was *bur.* at Kimble.

VI. 1876, to 1883. SIR THOMAS TYRINGHAM BERNARD, Baronet [1769], of Nether Winchendon aforesaid, br. and h., *b.* in Bolton street, 15 Sep. and *bap.* 11 Oct. 1791, at St. Geo. Han. sq.; ed. at Eton; matric. at Oxford (Ch. Ch.), 1 Feb. 1810, aged 18; Sheriff of Bucks, 1816-17; Lieut.-Col. of the Bucks Militia; M.P. for Aylesbury, 1857-65; *suc. to the Baronetcy*, 23 Jan. 1876. He *m.* firstly, 26 July 1819, at Aston Clinton, Bucks, Sophia Charlotte, da. and h. of David WILLIAMS, of Sarratt, Herts (styling himself 10th Baronet of the creation of 4 May 1644), by Sarah Sophia, da. and coheir of the Rev. John Fleming STANLEY, of Barlands, co. Radnor. She *d.* 15 May 1837. He *m.* secondly, 12 Oct. 1840, at St. Pancras, Midx., Martha Louisa, 2d da. and coheir of William MINSHULL, of Kentish town, Midx. She *d.* s.p. 18 April 1855. He *m.* thirdly, 28 July 1864, Ellen, widow of Henry ELWES, of Marchham park, Bucks. She, by whom he had no issue, *d.* 6 Nov. 1869. He *d.* s.p.m.s.,(b) 8 May 1883, in his 92d year, at Cadogan Lodge, Carlyle square, Chelsea, when the *Baronetcy* became *extinct*. Will pr. 24 July 1883, over £48,000.

ALLEYNE:

cr. 6 April 1769.

I. 1769. JOHN GAY ALLEYNE, of Four Hills, in the island of Barbadoes, Esq., Speaker of the House of Assembly there, 2d s. of John ALLEYNE,(c) of the same, Barrister (*d.* at Bath, 1730), by Mary, da. of William TERRILL, of Cabbage Tree Hall in that island, and Rebecca, his wife (to whom she was heir), da. and coheir of Col. John SPIRE, of Mount Steadfast, was *b.* 28 April 1724; suc. to the family estates, on the death (at the age of 16) of his elder br., Reynold ALLEYNE; was M.P. (annually elected), in the house of Assembly at Barbadoes, 1757-67, and Speaker, 1767-97; being *cr. a Baronet*, as above, 6 April 1769. He *m.* firstly, 19 Oct. 1746, Christian, 4th da. and coheir of Joseph DOTTIN, of Black Rocks, Barbadoes, by Ann, da. and h. of Edward JORDAN. She *d.* s.p. 1782. He *m.* secondly, 29 June 1786, Jane Abel, da. of his paternal uncle, Abel ALLEYNE, of Mount Steadfast, by Mary, da. of (—) WOODBRIDGE, of Kensington, Barbadoes. She *d.* 1800. He *d.* 1801, aged 77. Will pr. 1802.

II. 1801. SIR REYNOLD ABEL ALLEYNE, Baronet [1769], of Alleynedale Hall, Barbadoes, only surv. s. and h., by 2d wife, *b.* 10 June 1789; *suc. to the Baronetcy* in 1801. He *m.* 30 Sep. 1810, Rebecca, 3d and yst. da. of John ALTON, of Harrow, Barbadoes. She *d.* 5 June 1860 at Barton under Needwood, co. Stafford. He *d.* there 14 Feb. 1870, in his 81st year.

(a) Of his elder brothers, one, Thomas, *d.* in infancy, but William, the eldest, who was *b.* 7 July 1786, was Sheriff of Bucks, 1811, and *d.* unm. and v.p., at Caen, in Normandy, 21 Nov. 1820, aged 34.

(b) By his 1st wife he had David Williams Bernard, *b.* 5 Dec. 1830, and *bap.* at St. James', Westm., who *d.* unm. and v.p., 23 Dec. 1853, and was *bur.* at Nether Winchendon. (1), Lætitia Charlotte, 1st da., *b.* 11 Sep. 1820, and *bap.* at Sarratt; *m.* 5 Sep. 1850 (as his 1st wife), her cousin, Francis Bernard Pigott, and *d.* v.p. 17 Dec. 1865, at Neufchatel, leaving issue. (2), Sophia Elizabeth, *b.* 8 July 1829, and *bap.* at St. James', aforesaid; *m.* 13 June 1861, at Winchendon, Joseph Napier Higgins, Q.C., and had issue.

(c) This John was son of Reynold Alleyne, Chief Judge of the Bridge Court in Barbadoes, by Elizabeth, da. and coheir of John Gay.

III. 1870. SIR JOHN GAY NEWTON ALLEYNE, Baronet [1769], of Chevix, co. Derby, 1st s. and h., *b.* 8 Sep. 1820, in Barbadoes; Warden of Dulwich College, 1845-1851, and sometime President of the Steel and Iron Institute; *suc. to the Baronetcy*, 14 Feb. 1870. He *m.* 11 March 1851, at Tissington, co. Derby, Augusta Isabella, 3d da. of Sir Henry FITZHERBERT, 3d Baronet [1784], by Agnes, da. of the Rev. William BERESFORD, Rector of Sonning, Berks.

YOUNG:

cr. 2 May 1769.

I. 1769. "WILLIAM YOUNG, Esq, Lieut. Governor of the Island of Dominica,"(a) s. of William YOUNG, of the West Indies, a Physician (said to have emigrated from Scotland after the rising of 1715), by Margaret (*m.* 1720), da. of (—) NANTON, of Antigua, was *b.* 1725, was Lieut. Governor of Dominica and, having in 1767 purchased the Manor of Delaford, in Iver, Bucks, was *cr. a Baronet*, as above, 2 May 1769. He *m.* firstly, Sarah, sister of Sir William FAGGE, 5th Baronet [1660], da. of Charles FAGGE, by Elizabeth, da. of William TURNER, of Whitefriars, Canterbury. She, who was a minor and unm. in 1739, *d.* s.p. He *m.* secondly, in 1747, Elizabeth, only child of Brook TAYLOR, of Bifrons, Kent, D.C.L., Sec. to the Royal Society, by Elizabeth, da. of (—) SAWBRIDGE, of Ollantigh, Kent. He *d.* 8 April 1788, aged 63. Will pr. July 1788. His widow, who was *b.* 1729, *d.* 12 July 1801, at the Abbey House, Chertsey, Surrey.

II. 1788. SIR WILLIAM YOUNG, Baronet [1769], of Delaford aforesaid, only s. and h., by 2d wife, *b.* at Charlton, Kent, about 1750; matric. at Oxford (Univ. Coll.), 26 Nov. 1768, aged 18, "where he acquired some academical distinction;"(b) *suc. to the Baronetcy*, 8 April 1788; sold the estate of Delaford in 1790, and rented the stately mansion of Hartwell House, Bucks, until about 1807,(c) when he was succeeded therein by Louis XVIII of France. He was M.P. for St. Mawes (four Parls.), 1784-1806, and for Buckingham, 1806-07; was F.R.S. and F.S.A., and from 1807 till his death was Governor of Tobago. He *m.* firstly, 12 Aug. 1777, at St. George the Martyr, Queen square, Midx., Sarah, da. and coheir of Charles LAWRENCE,(d) by Mary da. of (—) MIHIL. She *d.* 6 Jan. 1791, in Great George street, Westm. He *m.* secondly, 22 April 1793, at St. Geo. Han. sq., Barbara, da. of Richard TALBOT, of Malahide Castle, co. Dublin, by Margaret, *suo jure* BARONESS TALBOT OF MALAHIDE [I.], da. of James O'REILLY. He *d.* at Tobago, 10 Jan. 1815,(e) in his 66th year. His widow *d.* s.p. 1 Feb. 1830.

(a) See p. 113, note "a," under "GIDEON." The date of the Gazette notice for Young is 22 March 1769.

(b) Lipscomb's *Bucks*, vol. ii, 324.

(c) The cause of his leaving is thus "painfully adverted" to in some verses he sent from "Tobago, Oct. 1814," to Sir George Lee, 6th Baronet [1660], from whom he had rented Hartwell House:—

"When sudden, on one hapless day,
A calamity happened so grievous, that yet
T'were painful to write, tho' I can not forget,
What from Hartwell then forced me away."

(d) This Charles is said to have been s. of Capt. Thomas Lawrence, R.N., Governor of Greenwich (*b.* 1680), Betham's *Baronetage* [1803], and "great grand-nephew of Henry Lawrence, the Lord President of Cromwell's Council in 1653." [Burke's *Baronetage*, 1905].

(e) The date of his death is often given as "10 Jan. 1811," but it is clear that he was alive in Oct. 1814 (see note "c" above), and his death "10 Jan. 1815, aged 66," is recorded in the *Annual Reg.* of that year.

III. 1815. **Sir William Lawrence Young**, Baronet [1769], of Marlow, Bucks, 1st s. and h., *b.* in London, about 1778; matric. at Oxford (Brasenose Coll.), 15 Nov. 1794, aged 16; *suc. to the Baronetcy*, 10 Jan. 1815. Lieut.-Col. of the Bucks Militia. He *m.* 21 Dec. 1805, Anna Louisa, sister of John Jolliffe Tufnell, of Langley, Essex, da. of William Tufnell, by Anna, da. of John Close, of Easby, co. York. He *d.* 3 Nov. 1824, at Hastings, aged 46. Will pr. Feb. 1825. His widow *d.* 4 March 1844. Will pr. March 1844.

IV. 1824. **Sir William Lawrence Young**, Baronet [1769], 1st s. and h., *b.* 29 Sep. 1806; *suc. to the Baronetcy*, 3 Nov. 1824; sometime Lieut. 8th Hussars; M.P. for Bucks (three Parls.), 1835 till death. He *m.* 27 March 1832, Caroline, da. and coheir of John Norris, of Hughenden, Bucks, where, subsequently, he resided, and where he *d.* 27 June 1842, aged 35. Will pr. Aug. 1842. His widow *d.* 16 Feb. 1871, at 80 Inverness terrace, Hyde Park, aged 57, having long survived her two elder sons, as below.

V. 1842. **Sir William Norris Young**, Baronet [1769], 1st s. and h., *b.* 15 Jan. 1833, at Fulford, near York; *suc. to the Baronetcy*, 27 June 1842; ed. at Charter House; 1st Lieut. 23d Foot (Royal Welsh Fusileers), 1852. He *m.* 10 March 1854, at Egg Buckland, Devon, Florence, 2d da. of Erving Clarke, of Efford Manor, in that county, by Anne Lætitia, da. of Paul Treby Treby, *formerly* Ourry, of Plympton. He *d.* s.p., being killed, at the battle of Alma, 20 Sep. 1854, aged 21. M.I. at Charter House Chapel, London. His widow *m.* 10 April 1860, at Plympton St. Mary, Devon, John Soltau, and *d.* 13 Aug. 1894.

VI. 1854. Sep. **Sir George John Young**, Baronet [1769], br. and h., *b.* 1 March 1835, at Hughenden aforesaid; was Lieut. in the Royal Artillery; *suc. to the Baronetcy*, 20 Sep. 1854, and *d.* unm., of cholera, before Sebastopol, a month later, 22 Oct. 1854, aged 19. Admon. May 1855.

VII. 1854. Oct. **Sir Charles Lawrence Young**, Baronet [1769], only surv. br. and h., *b.* 31 Oct. 1839, at Hughenden House aforesaid; ed. at Cheltenham College; *suc. to the Baronetcy*, 22 Oct. 1854; matric. at Oxford (New Coll.), 23 March 1858, aged 18; B.A., 1862; Barrister (Inner Temple), 9 June 1865; a Commissioner of Copyholds, 1876-77; Vice-Chairman of the Grand Trunk Railway of Canada, 1879 till death; an excellent amateur actor and author of several plays, etc.(a) He *m.* firstly, 11 Aug. 1863, at St. Michael's, St. Albans, Herts, Mary Florence, yr. da. of Henry Hayman Toulmin, of Childwickbury, Herts, by Jemima Brodie, da. of Alexander Harper. She *d.* at Childwickbury 21 July 1870, aged 25. He *m.* secondly, 3 Aug. 1871, at Redbourne, Herts, Margaret Alice Mary, 1st da. of the Rev. William Serocold Wade, Vicar of Redbourne. He *d.* 12 Sep. 1887, at Hatfield Priory, near Chelmsford, aged 47, and was *bur.* at Hughenden, Bucks. Will, dated 5 Aug. 1871, pr. Oct. 1887, above £9,330. His widow living 1905.

VIII. 1887. **Sir William Lawrence Young**, Baronet [1769], 1st s. and h., by 1st wife, *b.* 3 Aug. 1864; ed. at Charterhouse; *suc. to the Baronetcy*, 12 Sep. 1887; County Councillor, London, 1895. He *m.* 12 April 1887, at the Roman Catholic Church, Chelmsford, Helen Mary, 7th da. of the Hon. Henry William Petre, of Springfield lawn, Essex, by Mary Anne Eleanor, da. of Richard Walmesley.

(a) *e.g.*, "Jim the Penman," acted at the Haymarket, 25 March 1886, etc.

HARLAND:

cr. 13 March 1771;

ex. 16 Aug. 1848.

I. 1771. "**Robert Harland**, of Sproughton [near Ipswich], co. Suffolk,"(a) Rear-Admiral of the Blue, only s. of Capt. Robert Harland, R.N., of Sproughton aforesaid, and of Highgate, Midx. (living May 1736, and, subsequently, *bur.*, as was his wife, at St. Pancras, Midx.), by Frances, da. of (—) Clyatt, was *b.* 1715; entered the Navy, Feb. 1728/9; Lieut., 1741/2; Capt., 1744/5, taking part in Hawke's brilliant victory over the French, under L'Etenduère, 14 Oct. 1747; was Rear-Admiral of the Blue, 18 Oct. 1770, and was *cr. a Baronet*, as above, 13 March 1771. He was Commander-in-Chief in the East Indies, 1771-75; Vice-Admiral of the Red, 1778 and second in command of the Channel Fleet, 1778-1779; was Admiral of the Blue, 8 April 1782, and a Member of the Board of Admiralty, March 1782 to Jan. 1783. He purchased the estates of Belstead and Wherstead, co. Suffolk. He *m.* firstly, 15 May 1736, (—), da. of (—) Marlow, of Ipswich. She (a fortune of £20,000) *d.* s.p. He *m.* secondly, in 1749, Susanna (a fortune of £40,000), da. of Col. Rowland Reynold, of London, by (—), da. and h. of Col. John Duncombe. He *d.* at Sproughton, 21 Feb. 1784, aged 69. Will pr. March 1784. His widow *d.* 7 Feb. 1805, at Wherstead Park, Suffolk. Admon. Feb. 1805.

II. 1784, to 1848. **Sir Robert Harland**, Baronet [1771], of Wherstead Park and Sproughton aforesaid, only s. and h., by 2d wife, *b.* 1765; Cornet Royal Reg. of Dragoons, 1781-84; *suc. to the Baronetcy*, 21 Feb. 1784; Lieut.-Col. West Suffolk Militia. He pulled down the house at Sproughton and built a handsome one at Wherstead, called Wherstead Lodge. He *m.* May 1801, Arethusa, da. and h. of Henry Vernon, of Great Thurlow, Suffolk (br. to Francis, Earl of Shipbrook [I.]), by Elizabeth, da. of Thomas Payne, of Hough, co. Lincoln. He *d.* s.p., 16 Aug. 1848, aged 83, at Whetstead Park, when the *Baronetcy* became *extinct*. Will pr. Nov. 1848. His widow *d.* there, 30 March 1860, aged 82.

COCKS:

cr. 7 Oct. 1772;

afterwards, since 1784, Barons Sommers(b) of Evesham;

and sometime, 1821-83, Earls Sommers.(b)

I. 1772. "**Charles Cocks**, of Dumbleton,(c) co. Gloucester, Esq.,"(d) being also of Castleditch in Eastnor, co. Hereford, 1st s. and h. of John Cocks, of the same (*d.* 24 June 1771), by Mary, da. and h. of the Rev. Thomas Cocks, of Castleditch aforesaid, was *b.* there, 29 June and *bap.* 3 July

(a) See p. 113, note "a," under "Gideon." The date of the Gazette notice for Harland is 19 Feb. 1771.

(b) See, as to this spelling, "*The Complete Peerage*, by G.E.C.," vol. vii, p. 166, note "b."

(c) The estate of Dumbleton devolved on the father of the grantee by the death, 4 March 1765, of his cousin, Sir Robert Cocks, 4th and last Baronet [1662], of Dumbleton aforesaid. See vol. iii, p. 243, note "a."

(d) See p. 113, note "a," under "Gideon." The date of the Gazette notice for Cocks, Blake, St. John, Wilmot, Wright (of Venice), Lyde, and Leigh (which last did not pass the Seals till 15 May 1773) is 19 Sep., that for Sutton being 25 of the same month, and that for Wright (of Georgia), 5 Dec. 1772, this last being duplicated (apparently in error) 9 Jan. 1773.

1725 at Eastnor; was M.P. for Reigate (six Parls.), 1747-84; Clerk of the Deliveries of the Ordnance, 1758, and was *cr. a Baronet*, as above, 7 Oct. 1772, being Clerk of the Ordnance that same year. He *m.* firstly, 8 Aug. 1759, at St. Geo. Han. sq., Elizabeth, sister of Edward, 1st Baron Eliot of St. Germans, 5th da. of Richard Eliot, of Port Eliot, co. Cornwall, by Harriett, illegit. da. of the Rt. Hon. James Craggs. She, who was *b.* and *bap.* at St. Germans, 3 May 1789, *d.* 1 and was *bur.* 8 Jan. 1771, at North Mimms, Herts. He *m.* secondly, 20 May 1772, at St. Marylebone, Anne, sister of the Rt. Hon. Reginald Pole-Carew, da. of Reginald Pole, of Stoke Damerell, Devon, by Anne, da. of Francis Buller, of Morval, co. Cornwall. She was living when he was *cr.*, 17 May 1784, LORD SOMMERS,(a) BARON OF EVESHAM, co. Worcester. In that Barony this *Baronetcy* then *merged*, and still [1905] so continues, the 3d Baron being *cr.* 17 July 1821, EARL SOMMERS, a dignity which became *extinct*, 26 Sep. 1883.

BLAKE:

cr. 8 Oct. 1772.

I. 1772. "**Patrick Blake**, of Langham, co. Suffolk, Esq.,"(b) 1st s. and h. of Andrew Blake, of St. Kitts and Montserrat in the West Indies (*d.* in London 1760-62), by Marcella, da. of (—) French, of Ireland (which Andrew was 2d s. of Patrick Blake-Fitz-Peter, formerly of Cummer, co. Galway, who emigrated to the West Indies, and *d.* 23 Feb. 1720 in his 38th year), was *b.* probably about 1730 (being under age in 1745); was M.P. (three Parls.) for Sudbury, 1768-84, and was *cr. a Baronet*, as above, 8 Oct. 1772. He *m.* about 1765, Annabella, 2d da. of the Rev. Sir William Bunbury, 5th Baronet [1681], by Eleanor, da. of Thomas Graham, of Holbrook Hall, Suffolk. She, who was *b.* Feb. 1745, was divorced by Act. of Parl., April 1773.(c) He *d.* 1 July 1784. Will dat. 3 June, pr. 24 July 1784.

II. 1784. **Sir Patrick Blake**, Baronet [1772], of Langham aforesaid, 1st s. and h., *b.* about 1768; sometime an officer in the 10th Dragoons; *suc. to the Baronetcy*, 1 July 1784. He *m.* 12 Aug. 1789, Maria Charlotte, only da. of James Phipps, of St. Kitts aforesaid. He *d.* s.p. 25 July 1818. Will pr. 1819. The will of his widow pr. 1823.

III. 1818. **Sir James Henry Blake**, Baronet [1772], of Great Ashfield, near Ixworth, co. Suffolk, and of Langham aforesaid, br. and h., *b.* 1770; *suc. to the Baronetcy*, 25 July 1818. He *m.* 13 Feb. 1794, at St. Geo. Han. sq., Louisa Elizabeth, sister of Henry, 3d Viscount Gage of Castle Island [I.], 2d da. of the well known General, the Hon. Thomas Gage, by Margaret, da. of Peter Kemble. She *d.* 21 Jan. 1832, aged 66, at the Priory, near Bury St. Edmunds. He *d.* there three months later, 21 April 1832, aged 62. Will pr. May 1832. M.I. to both at Ixworth.

IV. 1832. **Sir Henry Charles Blake**, Baronet [1772], of Ashfield aforesaid and of Bardwell, co. Suffolk, 1st s. and h., *b.* 23 Nov. 1794; *suc. to the Baronetcy*, 21 April 1832. He *m.* firstly, 2 Aug. 1819, Mary Anne, only da. of William Whitter, of Midhurst, Sussex. She *d.* 20 April 1841. He *m.* secondly, 15 Feb. 1849, at St. Peter's, Eaton square, Louisa, widow of the Rev. George Augustus Dawson, 3d da. and coheir of Sir Thomas Pilkington, 7th Baronet [S. 1635], at Chevet, co. York, by Elizabeth Anne, da. of William Tufnell. He *d.* 22 Jan. 1880, at Ashfield Lodge, co. Suffolk, aged 85. His widow, by whom he had no issue, *d.* 28 Dec. 1881, at Bury St. Edmunds.

(a) See page 155, note "b."

(b) See page 155, note "d," under "Cocks."

(c) She *m.* secondly, George Boscawen, of St. Peter's, in the Isle of Thanet, grandson of the 1st Viscount Falmouth), who was *b.* 4 Sept. 1745, and who was sometime Capt. 1st troop of Horse Grenadiers, and M.P. for St. Mawes, 1768-74, and for Truro, 1774-80.

V. 1880. **Sir Patrick James Graham Blake**, Baronet [1772], of Bardwell and Ashfield aforesaid, grandson and h., being only s. of the Rev. Henry Bunbury Blake, Rector of Hessett, co. Suffolk, by Frances Marian, only da. of Henry James Oakes,(a) of Nowton Court, near Bury St. Edmunds, which Henry Bunbury (who *d.* v.p. 20 April 1873, in his 53d year), was 1st s. and h. ap. of the late Baronet. He was *b.* 23 Oct. 1861, at Hessett Rectory; ed. at Cheltenham College; *suc. to the Baronetcy*, 22 Jan. 1880; sometime Lieut. 3d Suffolk Militia. He *m.* 18 Oct. 1883, at St. Peter's, Eaton square, Emma Gertrude, only da. of Thomas Pilkington Dawson,(b) of Groton House, Suffolk, by Emma, da. of James King King, of Staunton Park, co. Hereford.

SAINT-JOHN, *or* ST. JOHN:

cr. 9 Oct. 1772;

afterwards, since 1790, St. John-Mildmay.

I. 1772. "**Paulet St. John**, of Farley [Chamberlayne], co. Southampton, Esq.,"(c) as also of Dogmersfield Park, in that county, 1st s. and h. of Ellis St. John, *formerly* Mews, of Farley aforesaid, by his 2d wife Martha (*m.* 31 Jan. 1703), da. and eventually h. of Edward Goodyear, of Dogmersfield Park abovenamed (which Ellis took the name of St. John in lieu of that of Mews,(d) and *d.* 19 Jan. 1729), was *b.* 7 April 1704; matric. at Oxford (Oriel Coll.), 15 July 1722, aged 17; Sheriff of Hants, 1727-28; was M.P. for Winchester 1734-41, for Hants 1741-47, and for Winchester (again) May 1751 to 1754; Mayor of Winchester, 1772; and was *cr. a Baronet*, as above, 9 Oct. 1772. He *m.* firstly, 2 Aug. 1731, Elizabeth, only surv. da. of Sir James Rushout, 2d Baronet [1661], by Arabella, da. of Sir Thomas Vernon. She *d.* s.p. 21 Dec. 1733. He *m.* secondly, 1 Oct. 1736, Mary, widow of Sir Halsewell Tynte, 3d Baronet [1674], da. of John Waters,(e) of Brecon, by Jane, da. and coheir of Francis Lloyd, of Crickadarn, one of the Judges of North Wales. She *d.* 17 Dec. 1758, at Farley. Admon. 2 May 1759. He *m.* thirdly, 13 Feb. 1761, Jane, widow of William Pescod, Recorder of Winchester, da. and h. of R. Harris, of Silksted, Hants. He *d.* 8 June 1780, aged 76. Will pr. July 1780. His widow, by whom he had no issue, *d.* 26 Jan. 1791. Will pr. Feb. 1791.

II. 1780. **Sir Henry Paulet St. John**, Baronet [1772], of Dogmersfield Park and Farley aforesaid, 1st s. and h. by 2d wife, *b.* about 1737; ed. at Winchester, 1750-54; matric. at Oxford (New Coll.), 15 Oct. 1755, aged 18; *cr.* M.A., 5 July 1759; *Knighted*, v.p., 24 Dec. 1760; M.P. for Hants (two Parls.), Feb. 1772 to 1780; *suc. to the Baronetcy*, 8 June 1780. He *m.* 27 Oct. 1763, Dorothea Maria, da. and coheir of Abraham Tucker, of Betchworth Castle, Surrey. She *d.* 26 May 1768, aged 26. He *d.* 8 Aug. 1784, aged 46. Admon. Sep. 1784.

(a) See *Mis. Gen. et Her.*, 4th S., i, pp. 45-55 for an elaborate pedigree of Oakes.

(b) This Thomas was s. of the Rev. George Augustus Dawson, by Louisa, afterwards 2d wife of Sir Henry Charles Blake, 4th Baronet [1772], all abovenamed.

(c) See p. 155, note "d," under "Cocks."

(d) He was s. and h. of Ellis Mews, sometime (1689) Mayor of Winchester (*d.* 1709), by Christian (*m.* 4 Oct. 1666, and *d.* 12 Feb. 1680), da. of Oliver St. John, of Farley aforesaid. He *m.* firstly, 6 Dec. 1699, Frances (heir to her br. Oliver St. John, who *d.* unm. 20 May 1699, aged 20), only da. of his maternal uncle, Oliver St. John, of Farley aforesaid. She, however, *d.* s.p. 25 March 1700, when he, in right of his mother, the abovenamed Christian, became a representative of the St. John family.

(e) See an account of this family of Waters in the *Her. and Gen.*, vol. ii, p. 336.

III. 1784. SIR HENRY PAULET ST. JOHN, *afterwards*, since 1790, ST. JOHN-MILDMAY, Baronet [1772], of Dogmersfield Park and Farley aforesaid, only s. and h., *b.* 30 Sep. 1764; *suc. to the Baronetcy*, 8 Aug. 1784. Sheriff of Hants, 1787-88. By royal lic. 8 Dec. 1790, he took the name of MILDMAY after that of ST. JOHN, in compliance with the will of his wife's great uncle, Carew Hervey MILDMAY,(a) of Marks Hall,(b) in Hornchurch, co. Essex, and of Hazelgrove, in Queen's Camel, Somerset (who *d.* s.p.s. 16 Jan. 1784, aged 93, being, apparently, the last heir male of the MILDMAY family), whose estates he accordingly inherited. By the death, 28 March 1796, of his said wife's paternal aunt, Anne, widow of Sir William MILDMAY, Baronet (so *cr.* 1765), of Moulsham Hall, co. Essex, he inherited that estate also. He was M.P. for Westbury, 1796-1802; for Winchester, 1802-07, and for Hants, 1807 till death. He *m.* 22 June 1786, Jane, 1st da. and coheir of Carew MILDMAY,(c) of Shawford House, Hants, and Stoke Newington, Midx, by Jane, da. of William PESCOD, Recorder of Winchester. He *d.* 11 Nov. 1808, aged 44. Will pr. 1809. His widow, by whom (besides three daughters) he had eleven sons, survived him nearly fifty years, and *d.* 6 May 1857, in Eaton square, aged 93.

IV. 1808. SIR HENRY ST. JOHN CAREW ST. JOHN-MILDMAY, Baronet [1772], of Dogmersfield Park and Moulsham Hall aforesaid, 1st s. and h., *b.* 15 April 1787, at Twyford, Hants; ed. at Winchester, 1798-1802, and possibly also at Eton; matric. at Oxford (Ch. Ch.), 28 Jan. 1805, aged 17; M.P. for Winchester, 1807-18, and *suc. to the Baronetcy*, 11 Nov. 1808; was a Knight of the Order of St. Joachim.(d) He *m.* firstly, 7 Aug. 1809, Charlotte, 1st da. of the Hon. Bartholomew BOUVERIE (2d s. of William, 1st EARL OF RADNOR), by Mary Wyndham, da. of the Hon. James Everard ARUNDELL. She, who was *b.* 2 Dec. 1788, *d.* 5 Aug. 1810. He *m.* secondly, at Würtemburg, in 1815, Harriet, his deceased wife's yr. sister, being the divorced(e) wife of Archibald John (PRIMROSE), 4th EARL OF ROSEBERY [S.]. She, who was *b.* 14 Oct. 1790, *d.* at Nice, 9 Dec. 1834. He *d.* 7 Jan. 1848, in Halkin street, Belgrave square, aged 60, having shot himself in a fit of temporary insanity. Will pr. March and June 1848.

V. 1848. SIR HENRY BOUVERIE PAULET ST. JOHN-MILDMAY, Baronet [1772], of Dogmersfield Park aforesaid, 1st s. and h., and only child by 1st wife, *b.* 31 July 1810; entered the Army, 1828; Capt. 2d Dragoon Guards, 1837, retiring as Major in 1859; *suc. to the Baronetcy*, 7 Jan. 1848. Sheriff of Hants 1849, and sometime Lieut.-Col. of the Hants Yeomanry Cavalry. He *m.* 26 Feb. 1851, at St. Geo. Han. sq., Helena, 2d da. and coheir of Charles (SHAW LEFEVRE), VISCOUNT EVERSLEY OF HECKFIELD (Speaker of the

(a) He was elder br. of Humphrey Mildmay, father of Carew Mildmay, of Shawford House, Hants, who *d.* s.p.m. 1768, being father of Dame Jane St. John-Mildmay. See note "c" below.

(b) Marks Hall was pulled down in 1808, and in 1854 the estate was sold to the Crown.

(c) He was s. and h. of Humphrey Mildmay (see note "a" above), by Lætitia, da. and h. of Halliday Mildmay, of Shawford House, Hants, and of Stoke Newington (Mildmay Park), Midx. These estates, on his death s.p.m. 29 June 1768, passed to his 1st da. Jane, then four years old, afterwards Dame Jane St. John-Mildmay. She subsequently (16 Jan. 1784) inherited the Marks Hall estate in Essex, and that of Hazlegrove, in Somerset, and finally (28 March 1796) that of Moulsham, co. Essex, as stated in the text.

(d) "This order owns its foundation to no crowned head, but has been recognised both in Great Britain and abroad as an order of Knighthood. It was founded in 1755, and derives its chief claim to notice from having numbered Lord Nelson amongst its members." [F. Townsend's "*Calendar of Knights from 1760*" (1828), p. xxv.]

(e) The cause of divorce was *crim. con.*, 1813-15, with her said br. in law and future husband, the 4th Baronet (as in the text), for which the damages obtained by the Earl were £15,000.

House of Commons 1839-57), by Emma Laura, da. of Samuel WHITBREAD, of Southill, Beds. She *d.* 15 Sep. 1897, at Dogmersfield Park, aged 74. He *d.* there 16 July 1902, in his 92d year, and was *bur.* at Dogmersfield. Will pr. at £20,175, the net personalty being £18,016.

VI. 1902. SIR HENRY PAULET ST. JOHN-MILDMAY, Baronet [1772], of Dogmersfield Park aforesaid, 1st s. and h., *b.* 28 April 1853; ed. at Eton; an officer in the Army, serving in the Egyptian War, 1882 (medal and clasp), and in the Suakim Expedition, 1885; sometime Major in the Grenadier Guards, retiring 1894; *suc. to the Baronetcy*, 16 July 1902.

Family Estates.—These, in 1883, consisted of 7,562 acres in Hants, and 6,075 in Essex. *Total.*—10,883 acres, worth £15,031 a year. *Principal Seat.*—Dogmersfield Park, near Winchfield, Hants.

WILMOT:

cr. 10 Oct. 1772;

sometime, 1834-41, and 1871-87, WILMOT-HORTON.

I. 1772. "SIR ROBERT WILMOT, of Osmaston next Derby, co. Derby, Knt.,"(a) 1st s. and h., of Robert WILMOT, of the same (*d.* Sep. 1738), by Ursula, da. and coheir of Sir Samuel MAROW, Baronet [so *cr.* 1679], of Berkswell, co. Warwick, was *b.* at Derby, about 1708; matric. at Oxford (Magdalen Coll.), 13 Feb. 1724 5, aged 16; B.A. (from Ch. Ch.), 3 March 1728 9; Resident Sec. in England of the Viceroy of Ireland, 1736; *Knighted*, at St. James', 30 May 1739, and represented Prince Frederick of Hesse at the ensuing installation of the Knights of the Garter; Deputy Sec. to the Lord Chamberlain of the Household, 1758 (till his death), and was *cr. a Baronet*, as above, 10 Oct. 1772, with a spec. rem., failing issue male of his body, to [his illegitimate son] Robert WILMOT. He *m.* (after the birth of his sons) Elizabeth, da. of Thomas FOOTE.(b) He *d.* s.p. legit., suddenly, but a few weeks after his creation, at his villa in Little Ealing, Midx., 14 Nov. 1772.(c) Will pr. Dec. 1772. His widow, Elizabeth, *d.* March 1811.(c)

II. 1772. SIR ROBERT WILMOT, Baronet [1772], of Osmaston aforesaid, illegit son, *b.* about 1752; *suc. to the Baronetcy*, under the spec. rem., 14 Nov. 1772; was Sheriff of Derbyshire, 1796-97. He *m.* firstly, 23 Feb. 1783, Juliana Elizabeth, widow of the Hon. William BYRON, 2d da. of Admiral the Hon. John BYRON, by Sophia, da. of John TREVANNION. She *d.* 18 March 1788. He *m.* secondly, 15 March 1795, Mary Anne, da. and h. of Charles HOWARD, of Pipe Grange, co. Stafford. He *d.* 23 July 1834, at the Parks, Great Malvern, aged 82. Will pr. Oct 1834. His widow *d.* 28 Oct. 1862, at Rosebank, Great Malvern, aged 86.

(a) See p. 155, note "d," under "COCKS."

(b) In Betham's *Baronetage* [1803], followed by that of Playfair, it is stated that he *m.* "Elizabeth, da. of Thomas Foote, Esq.," and that "their only surviving children are Robert, the present Baronet, William, and one da. Elizabeth." Matriculations at Oxford are recorded of (1), James Wilmot (Merton Coll.), "son of Robert, of Westminster, Baronet," 5 April 1781, aged 26 [*sic.*, but query if not 16]; and of (2) William Wilmot (Ch. Ch.), "son of Robert, of St. James', Westm., Baronet," 21 April 1785, aged 18; B.C.L., 1803. The death, 2 Oct. 1769, of the "Lady of Sir Robert Wilmot, Baronet," is recorded in the *Annual Reg.* of 1769, but there was no *Baronet* of that name at that date, and it is possible if "Knight" be substituted for "Baronet," that a first wife of this Baronet [1772], who in 1769 was but a Knight, may be indicated.

(c) Debrett's *Baronetage* [1819]. The date of the death of the 1st Baronet is sometimes given as *12 Dec.* 1772.

III. 1834. SIR ROBERT JOHN WILMOT-HORTON, Baronet [1772], of Osmaston aforesaid, and of Catton Hall, co. Derby, 1st s. and h., being only child by 1st wife, *b.* 21 Dec., 1784; ed. at Eton; matric. at Oxford (Ch. Ch.), 27 Jan. 1803, aged 18; B.A., 1806; M.A., 1815; was M.P. for Newcastle-under-Lyne (two Parls.), 1818-30, having by royal lic., 8 May 1823, taken the name of HORTON after that of WILMOT, under the will of his wife's father, Eusebius HORTON; P.C., 23 May 1827; Under Sec. for the Colonies, 1827-28; Governor of Ceylon, 1831-37; was *Knighted*, 22 June 1831; G.C.H., 1831, and *suc. to the Baronetcy*, 23 July 1834. He *m.* 1 Sep. 1806, Anne Beatrice, 1st da. and coheir of Eusebius HORTON, of Catton Hall aforesaid, by Phœbe, da. of (—) DAVENPORT. He *d.* 31 May 1841, at Sudbrooke Park, near Petersham, aged 56.(a) Will pr. June 1841. His widow *d.* 4 Feb. 1871, at Catton Hall, in her 84th year.(b)

IV. 1841. SIR ROBERT EDWARD WILMOT-HORTON, *afterwards* (1842-71) WILMOT, and *finally* (after 1871) WILMOT-HORTON, Baronet [1772], of Osmaston aforesaid, 1st s. and h., *b.* 29 Jan. 1808 at Catton Hall aforesaid; ed. at Eton; matric. at Oxford (Ch. Ch.), 2 Nov. 1826, aged 18; *suc. to the Baronetcy*, 31 May 1841, and took the name of WILMOT (only) by Royal Lic. 11 Jan. 1842; Sheriff of Derbyshire, 1846. On the death of his mother, and his succession to the Catton estate, he, by Royal lic. 11 May 1871, resumed his former surname of WILMOT-HORTON. He *m.* 20 March 1842, in Albemarle street, Margaret, widow of Robert ALGEO, yst. da. of the Rev. Andrew KERSTEMAN, of Brenchley, co. Kent, Rector of Bermondsey. He *d.* s.p., at Catton Hall, 22 and was *bur.* 25 Sep. 1880, at Croxall, aged 72. His widow *d.* 20 June 1893, at 63 Sloane street, Chelsea, aged 85.

V. 1880. SIR GEORGE LEWIS WILMOT-HORTON, Baronet [1772], of Osmaston and of Catton Hall aforesaid, only surv. br. and h., being 4th and yst. s. of the 3rd Baronet, *b.* 8 Nov. 1825; ed. at Eton and at Trin. Coll., Cambridge; B.A., 1847; M.A., 1850; in Holy Orders; Rector of Garboldisham, Norfolk, 1850-76; *suc. to the Baronetcy*, 22 Sep. 1880. He *m.* 24 July 1849, at Trinity church, Marylebone, Frances Augusta, da. of Henry Pytches BOYCE, by Amelia Sophia, da. of George (SPENCER), DUKE OF MARLBOROUGH. He *d.* s.p. 24 Oct. 1887, at Catton Hall aforesaid, aged nearly 62. Will pr. Dec. 1887, under £51,000. His widow *d.*, suddenly, 4 Feb. 1893, at Cannes.

VI. 1887. SIR ROBERT RODNEY WILMOT, Baronet [1772], cousin and h. male, being only s. and h. of Montagu WILMOT, of Norton House, near Swansea, co. Glamorgan, sometime in the Ceylon Civil Service, by Sarah Frederica, da. of Thomas EDEN, of the Bryn, co. Glamorgan, which Montagu (who *d.* 8 Nov. 1880, aged 75), was yst. s. of the 2d Baronet by his 2d wife. He was *b.* 20 June 1853; ed. at Eton; matric. at Oxford (Pembr. Coll.), 19 April 1873, aged 19; was sometime Lieut. Derbyshire Yeomanry cavalry; *suc. to the Baronetcy* (but not to the family estates) 24 Oct. 1887. He *m.* firstly, 28 Dec. 1880, at the English church, Nice, Flora Mildred, sister of Dudley Francis, 7th EARL OF GUILFORD, only da. of Dudley NORTH, *styled* LORD NORTH, by Maria, da. of Rev. the Hon. Robert EDEN. She, who was *b.* 7 June 1860 and who had a royal warrant, 6 April 1861, of the precedency of the da. of an Earl, *d.* 1 March 1886, at Norton House aforesaid. He *m.* secondly, 19 April 1888, Eleanor Georgiana, 1st da. of the Hon. Hugh Henry HARE (yr. s. of the 2d EARL OF LISTOWEL [I.]), by Georgiana Caroline, da. of Col. Birnie BROWNE, Bengal artillery. She was *b.* 8 April 1861.

Family Estates.—These, in 1883 (as owned by the 5th Baronet), consisted of 3,710 acres in Derbyshire, 750 in Staffordshire, 731 in Northamptonshire, 621 in Cheshire, and 224 in Leicestershire. *Total*, 6,036 acres, worth £12,055 a year.

(a) A man of cultivated tastes, who took great part in the political and social questions of his day, and was a voluminous political pamphleteer. He is perhaps best known as having been trustee, with Col. Doyle, for the destruction of Byron's *Memoirs.*

(b) She was the subject of Byron's graceful lines, "She walks in beauty."

WRIGHT:(a)

cr. 12 Oct. 1772;(b)

ex. or *dorm.*, in or shortly before 1812.

I. 1772. "SIR JAMES WRIGHT, Knt., His Majesty's President to the Republic of Venice,"(c) whose parentage is not known, but who was of Woodford, co. Essex,(d) was, having previously been *Knighted*, *cr. a Baronet*, as above, 12 Oct. 1772.(b) He *m.* Catherine, 1st da. of Sir William STAPLETON, 4th Baronet [1679], by Catherine, da. and h. of William PAUL. She *d.* 6 Jan. 1802, at Bath, in her 70th year. He *d.* 1803. Will pr. 1804.(e)

II. 1803, to 1812? SIR GEORGE WRIGHT, Baronet [1772], only s. and h., *suc. to the Baronetcy* in 1803. He *m.*, 3 June 1796, (—), da. and h. of Charles MACLANE, of Okingham, Berks. He *d.* in or before 1812, presumably s.p.m., when the *Baronetcy* became *extinct* or *dormant*. Will pr. 1812. Admon. of "DAME REBECCA WRIGHT, Berks," apparently his widow, granted April 1819.

LYDE:

cr. 13 Oct. 1772;

ex. 25 June 1791.

I. 1772, to 1791. "LYONEL LYDE, of Ayott St. Lawrence, co. Hertford, Esq.,"(c) 2d s. of Lyonel LYDE, sometime Mayor of Bristol (*d.* March 1744, aged 62), being 1st s. by his 2d wife Anna Maria, da. of (—), was *b.* 9 May 1724 at St. Mary's, Redcliffe, Bristol, and was *cr. a Baronet*, as above, 13 Oct. 1772. Sheriff of Herts, 1768-69. He *m.* in 1747, Rachel, 1st da. and coheir of his paternal uncle, Cornelius LYDE, of Ayot St. Lawrence aforesaid (*d.* 11 July 1747, aged 60), by his 2d wife Rachel, da. of Cornelius WITTENOM, of London. He *d.* s.p. 25 and was *bur.* 30 June 1791 at Ayott aforesaid, aged 67, when *the Baronetcy* became *extinct.*(f) Will pr. July 1791. His widow, who was *b.* 17 Feb. 1728, at St. Bride's, Fleet street, *d.* 22 March 1814, at Islington, Midx., aged 86. Will pr. 1814.

(a) Owing presumably to the confusion of two persons each named James Wright, being created Baronets in the same year, this creation is often omitted, but a short account of it is given in Betham's *Baronetage* [1804], vol. iii, appendix, p. 11. See also *N. & Q.*, 5th series, xi, p. 349, and xii, pp. 18 and 58.

(b) This is the date given (being, presumably the correct one) in the *Royal Kalendar* for 1787. The date of the Gazette notice is 19 Sep. 1772, the name being placed between those of Wilmot and Lyde, of which the patents were 10 and 13 Oct. 1772 respectively.

(c) See p. 155, note "d," under "COCKS."

(d) "Near Woodford Bridge is a patent manufactory of artificial slate, belonging to Sir James Wright, Bart. Archbishop Moore's first wife, was the sister of the late Sir James Wright, Bart., Resident at Venice." [*N. & Q.*, 5th series, xii, 18].

(e) The will of Dame Sarah Wright (possibly a second wife of this Baronet and his widow), was pr. 1810.

(f) He left the estate of Ayott St. Lawrence to his nephew, Lyonel Poole (s. of his sister, Anna Maria, by Chauncy Poole, of Shirehampton, co. Gloucester), who took the name of Lyde by Royal licence 19 July 1792. After his death s.p. it passed to the husband of his said sister (Anna Maria, who had *d.* before him Sep. 1791), Levy Ames, sometimes (1789) Mayor of Bristol, who also took the name of Lyde, and was living 1818 with issue. The estate still (1905) belongs to the Ames family.

SUTTON:

cr. 14 Oct. 1772.

I 1772. "RICHARD SUTTON, of Norwood Park, co. Nottingham, Esq.,"(a) 2d surv. s. of the Rt. Hon. Sir Robert SUTTON, **K.B.**, sometime Ambassador to Holland, Constantinople and Paris (*d.* 1746, aged 75), by Judith, Dow. COUNTESS OF SUNDERLAND, da. and coheir of Benjamin TICHBORNE (yr. br. of Henry, BARON FERRARD OF BEAULIEU [I.]), was *b.* 31 July 1733; ed. at Westminster School and at Trin. Coll., Cambridge; M.A., 1752; admitted to the Middle Temple, 21 Aug. 1754; was M.P. for St. Albans, 1768-80; for Sandwich, 1780-84, and for Boroughbridge, 1784-96; Under Sec. of State, Aug. 1766 to Sep. 1772, and having, in 1772, by the death s.p. of his elder br., John SUTTON, of Norwood Park aforesaid, suc. to the family estates, was on quitting office *cr. a Baronet*, as above, 14 Oct. 1772. He was first Commissioner of the Privy Seal, Feb. to Nov. 1768, and a Lord of the Treasury, 1780-82. He *m.* firstly Susanna, sister of Claude, 1st Baronet [1805], 1st da. of Philip Champion DE CRESPIGNY, Proctor to the Court of Arches, by Anne, da. of Claude FONNERAU. She *d.* s.p. 12 June 1766, in Red Lion square, Midx. He *m.* secondly, in or before 1770, Anne, da. and coheir of William Peere WILLIAMS, of Cadhay, Devon, by Elizabeth, da. and coheir of Peter SEIGNORET, of Greenwich and of Vevay in Switzerland. She *d.* 2 Dec. 1787. He *m.* thirdly, 8 April 1793, at St. Geo. Han. sq., Margaret, da. of John PORTER, of Wandsworth, Surrey, by Catherine, da. of his paternal uncle, Lieut.-Gen. Richard SUTTON, of Scrofton, Notts. He *d.* 10 Jan. 1802, aged 68. Will pr. 1802. His widow, by whom he had no issue, *d.* 3 Jan. 1824. Will pr. 1824.

II. 1803. SIR RICHARD SUTTON, Baronet [1772], of Norwood Park aforesaid, and of Skeffington Hall, co. Leicester, grandson and h., being only s. and h. of John SUTTON, by Sophia Frances, da. of Charles CHAPLIN, of Tathwell, co. Lincoln, which John, who *d.* v.p., 15 Sep. 1801, aged about 31, was 1st s. and h. ap. of the late Baronet. He was *b.* 16 Dec. 1798, at Brant Broughton, co. Lincoln, and *suc. to the Baronetcy*, 10 Jan. 1802; was ed. (Fellow Commoner, 22 Oct. 1816) at Trin. Coll., Cambridge; M.A., 1818. "A long minority husbanded the family estates, already large, to such an extent that he was considered one of the most wealthy men in the country." In hunting and shooting "it was maintained by his friends he never had an equal." He was Master of Foxhounds of the Burton Hunt in Lincolnshire as early as 1822, and subsequently in Rutland (Cottesmore Park), and at Quorn Hall (which he purchased for £12,000 in 1848) in Leicestershire, doing "everything *en prince*,"(b) and being said to have "spent upwards of £300,000 in pursuit of fox-hunting.(c) He *m.* (the day after he came of age) 17 Dec. 1819, Mary Elizabeth, 1st da. of Benjamin BURTON, of Burton Hall, co. Carlow, by Anne, da. of Thomas MAINWARING, of Goltho, co. Lincoln. She *d.* 1 Jan. 1842, at "Hake's Hotel." He *d.* of *angina pectoris*, at "Cambridge House," 94 Piccadilly, London,(d) 14 and was *bur.* 21 Nov. 1855, at Linford, Notts, aged 56. Will pr. Dec. 1855.

III. 1855. SIR JOHN SUTTON, Baronet [1772], of Norwood Park and Skeffington Hall aforesaid, 1st s. and h., *b.* 18 Oct. 1820, at Sudbrooke Holme, co. Lincoln, *suc. to the Baronetcy*, 14 Nov. 1855; Sheriff of Notts. 1867. He *m.* 23 Aug. 1844, Emma Helena, 1st da. of Col. SHERLOCK, **K.H.**, of Southwell, Notts. She *d.* Jan. 1845. He *d.* s.p., 5 June 1873, aged 52.

(a) See p. 155, note "d," under "COCKS."
(b) *Annual Register*, 1855, where is a good account of his career.
(c) F. Boase's *Modern English Biography, since 1850*.
(d) "No. 94 [Piccadilly] was formerly Egremont House, then Cholmondeley House, now [1850] the Duke of Cambridge's" [Cunningham's *London*, 1850]. H.R.H. the 1st Duke of Cambridge *d.* there 8 July 1850. It was after the death of Sir Richard Sutton (to whose family it and a considerable part of that district belonged), rented by Viscount Palmerston [I.], the Prime Minister, till his death in 1865, and subsequently (as now [1905]) by "The Naval and Military Club."

IV. 1873. SIR RICHARD SUTTON, Baronet [1772], of Norwood Park and Skeffington Hall aforesaid, br. and h., *b.* 21 Oct. 1821 at Sudbrooke Holme aforesaid; entered the Royal Navy, and subsequently, 1841, the 1st Life Guards; Lieut., 1844-45; Sheriff of Leicestershire, 1861; Master of the Skeffington hounds till death; *suc. to the Baronetcy*, 5 June 1873. He *m.* firstly, 18 May 1845, at Brant Broughton, co. Lincoln, Anne, 1st da. of the Rev. Henry HOUSON, Rector of Brant Broughton and of Great Coates, co. Lincoln. She *d.* s.p., 8 July 1846, or 1848. He *m.* secondly, 29 July 1851, at St. Geo. Han. sq., Harriet Anne, 1st da. of his maternal uncle, William Fitzwilliam BURTON, of Burton Hall, co. Carlow, by his 1st wife, Mary, da. of Sir John POWER, 1st Baronet [1836], of Kilfane. He *d.* 2 Oct. 1878, at St. John's Park, Ryde, in his 57th year. His widow *d.* there, 22 March 1901, aged 72.

V. 1878. SIR RICHARD FRANCIS SUTTON, Baronet [1772], of Benham park, near Newbury, Berks, 1st s. and h., *b.* 20 Dec. 1853, at Skeffington Hall aforesaid; *suc. to the Baronetcy*, 2 Oct. 1878; Sheriff of Berks, 1887. He *m.* 5 April 1888, at St. Peter's, Eaton Square, Constance Edith, 7th da. of Sir Vincent Rowland CORBET, 3d Baronet [1808], of Acton Reynold, Salop, by Caroline Agnes, da. of Vice-Admiral the Hon. Charles Orlando BRIDGEMAN, yr. s. of the 1st EARL OF BRADFORD. He *d.* of peritonitis, 25 Feb. 1891, at St. John's park, Ryde, aged 37. Will pr. at £115,973 personalty. His widow *m.*, 30 July 1895, at St. Peter's, Cranley Gardens, the Rev. Hubert Delaval ASTLEY, M.A., some time Rector of Elsborough, and was living 1905.

VI. 1891. SIR RICHARD VINCENT SUTTON, Baronet [1772], of Benham park aforesaid, posthumous s. and h., *b.* 26 April 1891, and *suc. to the Baronetcy* at his birth.

Family Estates.—These, in 1883, consisted of 4,890 acres in Lincolnshire, 3,756 in Berks, and 694 in Notts. *Total.*—9,340 acres, worth £15,500 a year. *Principal Seat.*—Benham Park, near Newbury, Berks.

WRIGHT:(a)

cr. 8 Dec. 1772;

ex. possibly in, but probably after, 1837.

I. 1772. "JAMES WRIGHT, Esq., Governor of His Majesty's Province of Georgia in America,"(b) s. of Robert WRIGHT, Chief Justice of South Carolina, formerly of Sedgfield, co. Durham,(c) was *b.* probably about 1725; was admitted to Gray's Inn, 14 Aug. 1741, as "James WRIGHT, of Charlestown in South Carolina, Gent.;" was Attorney-General, Chief Justice, and subsequently, 1761 to 1783, Governor of that Province, and was *cr. a Baronet*, as above, 8 Dec. 1772. He *m.*, in 1740, Sarah, only da. and h. of James MAIDMAN, Capt in the Army. She was drowned on her voyage to England, 1763. He *d.* 1786 Will, as of Fludyer street, Westm., dat. 24 Jan. to 1 May 1784, pr. 22 April 1786.

II. 1786. SIR JAMES WRIGHT, Baronet [1772], 1st s. and h., *b.* about 1747; *suc. to the Baronetcy*, 1786. He *m.* Mary, da. of John SMITH, sometime Governor of South Carolina. He *d.* s.p. 16 Sep. 1816 in his 70th year.

(a) This Baronetcy is, oddly enough, omitted both in Betham's *Baronetage* [1803], and in that of Playfair [1811], though there can be little doubt it was then in existence and indeed as late as 1837, and possibly later.
(b) See p. 155, note "d," under "COCKS."
(c) Burke's *Baronetage* [1841].

III. 1816, to 1837. SIR JAMES ALEXANDER WRIGHT, Baronet [1772], great nephew and h., being 1st s. and h. of James Alexander WRIGHT, of Charlestown in North America, by Caroline Mary, da. of John SIMMONDS, *or* SIMMONS, of South CAROLINA, which James Alexander (who *d.* 1803) was 1st s. of Alexander WRIGHT (an American Loyalist who finally settled at St. Mary's, Jamaica, and *d.* 1794, aged 43), who was 2d s. of the 1st Baronet. He was *b.* 28 July 1799, at Charlestown; ed. at the University of Edinburgh; *suc. to the Baronetcy*, 16 Sep. 1816; admitted, 15 Nov. 1819, to Lincoln's Inn, being then aged 20, and was re-admitted, 17 June 1825, when aged 25. He *d.* unm. Sep. 1837, aged 38, when, possibly, the *Baronetcy* became *extinct*.

IV. 1837. SIR JOHN WRIGHT, Baronet [1772], cousin of the above, was, if then surviving,(a) h. male, being 1st s. and h. of John Izard WRIGHT, by Mary, da. of Ralph IZARD, which John IZARD (who *d.* 1821) was br. to James Alexander WRIGHT, father of the late Baronet. He is said to have *suc. to the Baronetcy* in Sep. 1837, and was apparently living unm. 1861,(b) but of him (save that he was undoubtedly alive in 1821) or of any future devolution of this Baronetcy nothing further that seems trustworthy is known.(c)

LEIGH:

cr. 15 May 1773;

ex. about 1870.(d)

I. 1773. "EGERTON LEIGH, Esq., His Majesty's Attorney-General of South Carolina,"(e) 1st s. and h. of Peter LEIGH, formerly High Bailiff of Westminster, but, subsequently, Chief Justice of South Carolina (*d.* there 22 Aug. 1759, and was *bur.* at Charlestown, aged 49), by Elizabeth, da. of William LATUS, of Manchester, was *b.* 11 Oct. 1733; was a Member of the Council, Surveyor-General and Attorney General of South Carolina, and was *cr. a Baronet*, as above, 15 May 1773. He *m.* 15 Jan. 1756, Martha (*b.* 13 March 1738), da. of Francis BREMAR, of South Carolina, by Martha, da. of John LAURENS, of the same. He *d.* in England before May 1788. His widow *d.* 10 Jan. 1801.

(a) "It is supposed that he was surviving in 1821" [Foster's *Baronetage* (1883), in "Chaos," p. 708].
(b) Burke's *Baronetage* [1861]. In Foster's *Baronetage*, as above, it is mentioned that his succession is acknowledged in Burke's *Baronetage* "in Sep. 1837, although Debrett of that period omitted the title, doubtless on the supposition that it had become extinct." If, however, it was so omitted by Debrett "of that period," it is fully acknowledged in Debrett's *Baronetage*, of 1840, where Sir John's succession "in Sep. 1837" is duly set out.
(c) In Whitaker's List of Baronets from 1871 to 1879 Sir Alexander Wright is given as his successor, being presumably the Alexander Wright, who was his only brother.
(d) 1870 (with a query) is the date assigned to the extinction in Solly's *Titles of Honour*. The 3d Baronet is inserted in Dod's *Baronetage* for 1873, but omitted in that for 1874.
(e) See p. 155, note "d," under "COCKS." The Gazette notice for this Baronetcy was as long back as 19 Sep. 1772.

II. 1785? SIR EGERTON LEIGH, Baronet [1773], of Rugby Hall, co. Warwick, 3d but 1st surv. s. and h., *b.* probably in but certainly not before 1760(a); *suc. to the Baronetcy* on the death of his father. He *m* 13 May 1788, Theodosia Beauchamp (called "Mrs. BEAUCHAMP"), widow of Capt. John DONELLAN,(b) (who was hung 1 April 1781, for the murder of his said wife's brother), sister and h. of Sir Theodosius Edward Allesley BOUGHTON, 7th Baronet [1641], who was murdered as aforesaid, da. of Sir Edward BOUGHTON, 6th Baronet [1641], of Lawford Hall, co. Warwick, by his 2d wife Anna Maria, da. and coheir of John BEAUCHAMP, of co. Warwick. He *d.* s.p.m.s.(c) 27 April 1818. Will pr. 1818. His widow *m.* 10 Feb. 1823, as his 2d wife (Barry Edward O'MEARA, Surgeon R.N., the attendant of Napoleon at St. Helena (*d.* 3 June 1836, aged 50), and *d.* 14 Jan. 1830.

III. 1818, to 1870? SIR SAMUEL EGERTON LEIGH, Baronet [1773], of Brownsover House, co. Warwick, nephew and h., being only s. and h. of Sir Samuel Egerton LEIGH, by (—), da. of (—) GREIG, of St. Giles' in the Fields, which Samuel (who was *b.* 1 March 1770; *Knighted*, 1793; and *d.* 11 Dec. 1796 at Edinburgh) was next yr. br. of the late and 4th s. of the 1st Baronet. He was *b.* in Edinburgh, 10 Nov. 1796, and *suc. to the Baronetcy*, 27 April 1818. He was apparently, living 1866,(d) and appears to have *d.* unm. about 1870,(e) when the *Baronetcy* became *extinct*.

HUGHES:

cr. 17 July 1773.

I. 1773. "RICHARD HUGHES, Esq., Comptroller of the Navy, residing at Portsmouth,"(f) 1st s.(g) of Richard HUGHES, formerly of Deptford, Capt. R.N., and Commissioner of the Navy at Portsmouth Dockyard (*d.* 11 Nov. 1756, aged 86), by Mary, da. of Isaac LOADER, was *b.* about 1708; was Capt. R.N., in 1729, and subsequently (like his father) Commissioner of the Navy at Portsmouth Dockyard, where he entertained George III with great magnificence, and was consequently *cr. a Baronet*, as above, 17 July 1773. He *m.*, in or before 1729, Joanna, da. of William COLLYER, of Deptford, Capt. R.N. He *d.* 23 Sep. 1779, aged 71. M.I.(h) Will pr. Oct. 1779.

(a) His next elder br. was born 18 Dec. 1759, and the next yr. one 1 March 1770. Sisters were born 5 Dec. 1762, 29 July 1764, 1 Feb. 1766, 30 Sep. 1767, and 8 Dec. 1768. His age almost precludes him from being the Egerton Leigh who was B.A. (Sidney Sussex Coll.), Cambridge, 1775.
(b) See vol. ii, p 122, note "a."
(c) Theodosia Malsbury, *b.* 19 Dec. 1792, his only surv. da. and h., *m.* Aug. 1811, John Ward, who took the additional surname of Boughton-Leigh in 1831, and had issue.
(d) Walford's *Baronetage* for 1866, but his name does not appear in the edition for 1871.
(e) See p. 164, note "d."
(f) See p. 113, note "a," under GIDEON. The date of the "Gazette" notice for Hughes and Palliser is 15 July 1773.
(g) His yr. br., Robert Hughes, became Rear-Admiral, 18 Oct. 1770, and *d.* at Bath, 19 Jan. 1774. An account of his services is given in Playfair's *Baronetage* [1811].
(h) This inscription is given in full in Betham's *Baronetage* [1803], though it is not stated where it is situated. He is called therein "one of the principal officers and commissioners of his Majesty's navy," and the date of his death is given "September xxiii, MDCCLXXX"—but *query* if not a mistake for "MDCCLXIX."

V

II. 1779. SIR RICHARD HUGHES, Baronet [1773], 1st s. and h., *b.* at Deptford, "where part of his patrimonial fortune is situated,"(a) in 1729; ed. at the academy at Portsmouth, 1739, and joined his father's ship in 1742, becoming Rear-Admiral in 1780; Vice-Admiral in 1790; and Admiral in 1794. He was at the reduction of Pondicherry, 1760-61; was Commander-in-Chief at Halifax, Nova Scotia, 1778-80, and again, 1789-92, having *suc. to the Baronetcy*, 23 Sep. 1779, and having been second-in-command at the relief of Gibraltar in 1782 (in which year he captured a French 64-gun ship), and Commander-in-Chief in the West Indies, 1784-1786.(b) He, who was of East Bergholt Lodge, Suffolk,(a) *m.*, about 1760, Joanna, da. of William SLOANE, of South Stoneham, Hants (nephew of Sir Hans SLOANE, Baronet, so *cr.* in 1716), by his 3d wife, Elizabeth, da. of John FULLER, of Rose Hill, Sussex. He *d.* s.p.m.s.,(c) 5 Jan. 1812, aged 82. Will pr. 1812.

III. 1812. SIR ROBERT HUGHES, Baronet [1773], of East Bergholt aforesaid, br. and h. male, *bap.* 17 Sep. 1739, at Wickham, near Southampton; Scholar of Winchester, 7 Jan. 1751 to 1757; matric. at Oxford (Trin. Coll.), 30 March 1757, aged 17; Demy of Mag. Coll., 1758-67; B.A., 1761; M.A., 1763; in Holy Orders; Rector of Trimley St. Mary and Weston, Suffolk, 1769, for thirty-four years, till death in 1814; having *suc. to the Baronetcy*, 5 Jan. 1812. He *m.* firstly, in or before 1768, Gratiana, da. of Thomas MANGLES, of Devon. He *m.* secondly, 1798, Bethia, da. of Thomas HISCUTT. He was *bur.* 4 June 1814, aged about 74. Will pr. 1814.

IV. 1814. SIR RICHARD HUGHES, Baronet [1773], of East Bergholt aforesaid, 1st s. and h., by 1st wife, *b.* 2 June 1768; ed. at Trin. Coll., Cambridge; B.A., 1789; M.A., 1796; in Holy Orders; Vicar of Walkhampton, Devon, before 1800 till his death; *suc. to the Baronetcy* in June 1814. He *m.* 8 Dec. 1798, Sarah Perring, da. of the Rev. Richard SLEEMAN, Vicar of Tavistock, Devon. He *d.* 3 Jan. 1833, at East Bergholt, aged 64. Admon. Feb. 1833. His widow *d.* 15 July 1848, at East Bergholt Lodge. Will pr. Sep. 1848.

V. 1833. SIR RICHARD HUGHES, Baronet [1773], of East Bergholt aforesaid, 1st s. and h., *b.* 10 Oct. 1803 at Walkhampton; ed. at Trin. Coll., Cambridge; M.A. 1833, having *suc. to the Baronetcy* 3 Jan. 1833; Barrister, Middle Temple. He *d.* unm. at Dorking, Surrey, 16 May 1863, aged 59.

VI. 1863. SIR EDWARD HUGHES, Baronet [1773], of East Bergholt aforesaid, br. and h., *b.* 31 Mar. 1807; *suc. to the Baronetcy*, 16 May 1863. He *d.* unm. 8 Aug. 1871 at Lindfield, Sussex, in his 65th year.

VII. 1871. SIR FREDERICK HUGHES, Baronet [1773], of Dunkeld, Victoria, in Australia, cousin and h. male, being 2d but last surv. s. of the Rev. Robert HUGHES, Vicar of Westfield, Sussex, by Judith, da. of Robert PORTEUS, which Robert HUGHES (who *d.* 1828) was next br., of the whole blood, to the 4th Baronet. He was *b.* 1816; ed. at the Grammar School, Bury St. Edmunds; settled in Australia, and *suc. to the Baronetcy* 8 Aug. 1871. He *m.* in or before 1847, Matilda, da. of Edward YATES. He *d.* s.p.m. 1 Feb. 1889, in his 73d year, at Dunkeld aforesaid.

(a) Betham's *Baronetage* [1803].

(b) He appears to have been an amiable easy-tempered man without much energy or force of character. Lord Nelson, who (when subordinate to him) twice disagreed with his measures, writes of him as "'a fiddler,' living in a boarding house at Barbadoes, not much in the style of a British Admiral," and not giving "himself that weight that an Admiral ought to do." [*Dict. Nat. Biogr.*] He translated Addison's *Spectator* into French.

(c) Both his sons *d.* v.p. and unm., *viz.* (1) Robert Hughes, Capt. R.N., who *d.* 1810, and (2) John Thomas Hughes, Professor of Civil Law in Jamaica, who *d.* 22 Dec. 1802. Louisa, the 1st da., *d.* unm., and Rose Mary, the 2d da., *m.* in 1784, Major John Browne, 67th Foot (grandson of the 1st Earl of Altamont [I.]), who *d.* 1814, leaving issue.

VIII. 1889, Feb. SIR THOMAS COLLINGWOOD HUGHES, Baronet [1773], of East Bergholt aforesaid, uncle of the half blood and h. male, being s. of the 3d Baronet by his 2d wife. He was *b.* 12 Aug. 1800; ed. at Downing College, Cambridge; B.A., 1829; in Holy Orders; sometime Vicar of Cerne Abbas, Dorset, and of South Tawton, Devon; Rector of Little Billing, co. Northampton, 1872 till death; *suc. to the Baronetcy*, 1 Feb. 1889. He *m.* firstly 31 May 1820, Elizabeth St. John, da. and coheir of Robert BUTCHER, of Upland Grove, near Bungay, Suffolk. She *d.* 12 July 1879. He *m.* secondly 20 April 1881, Mary Agnes Winwood, 1st da. of Sir William SMITH, 3d Baronet [1809], of Eardiston, by Susan, da. of Admiral Sir George William PARKER, 2d Baronet [1797]. He *d.* 22 May 1889 (less than four months after his predecessor), in his 89th year at Little Billing Rectory. His widow *m.* Nov. 1890, Robert Halliday GUNNING, M.D., President of the Royal Physical Society of Edinburgh and "Grand Dignitary of the Empire of Brazil," who *d.* 22 March 1900. She was living 1905.

IX. 1889, May. SIR ALFRED HUGHES, Baronet [1773], of East Bergholt aforesaid, formerly of Norton, co. York, 3d but 1st surv. s. and h. male, *b.* 3 Jan. 1825; sometime an officer in the 33d Foot; *suc. to the Baronetcy*, 22 May 1889. He *m.* 4 Sep. 1851, Mary, da. of Col. John SMITH, of Ellingham Hall, Norfolk. He *d.* suddenly, 1 April 1898, aged 73, at East Bergholt Lodge. Will pr. at £2,053 gross and £434 net. His widow living 1905.

X. 1898. SIR ALFRED COLLINGWOOD HUGHES, Baronet [1773], of East Bergholt aforesaid, 2d but 1st surv. s. and h.,(a) *b.* 12 May 1854; *suc. to the Baronetcy*, 1 April 1898. He *m.* in 1880, Elsie, da. of John JOHNASSON, of Queen's Gate, Knightsbridge.

PALLISER:

cr. 6 Aug. 1773;

sometime, 1796-98, WALTERS;

ex. 3 Aug. 1868.

I. 1773. "HUGH PALLISER, Esq., Comptroller of the Navy,"(b) of Deptford, co. Kent, only s. of Hugh PALLISER, of North Deighton, co. York, Capt. in the Army (wounded severely at the battle of Almanza in 1707), by Mary, da. of Humphrey ROBINSON, of Thicket Priory in Cottingworth, co. York, was *b.* 26 Feb. 1722/3, at Kirk Deighton; entered the Navy in 1735, under the command of his maternal uncle, Nicholas ROBINSON; Lieut. R.N., 1741; Commander, 1746; was most severely wounded in 1748, "in a desperate action in the Mediterranean."(c) He was Governor of Newfoundland, 1764-69; Comptroller of the Navy, 1770-75, being *cr. a Baronet*, as above, 6 Aug. 1773, with a spec. rem., failing heirs male of his body, to his sister's son, George Robinson WALTERS. About that date he purchased the estate of "The Vache," in Chalfont St. Giles, Bucks. He was M.P. for Scarborough 1774, till he resigned in 1779, and for Huntingdon, 1780-84; was Rear-Admiral and Lieut.-Gen. of Marines, 1775; one of the Lords of the Admiralty, 1775-79;

(a) His elder br., Harry Scott Hughes, d. unm. and v.p., in California, 17 May 1888, aged 35.

(b) See p. 165, note "f," under "HUGHES."

(c) Playfair's *Baronetage* [1811], where it is added that these wounds, "after subjecting him to ceaseless tortures, eventually brought him to his end," and for the last sixteen years of his life rendered him unable to lie down in bed. It is conjectured, in the *Dict. Nat. Biog.*, that this pain may have "rendered him irritable, and led to his quarrel with Keppel." In that work, however, there is no mention of this "desperate action." The wounds, whether received during action or not, were, however, undoubtedly caused by the explosion of an arm-chest.

Vice-Admiral, 1778, being, as such, 3d in command under Admiral Keppel in the engagement with the French Fleet in July 1778. Here he acted very insubordinately, and, having subjected Keppel to a Court-martial (whose decision was entirely in Keppel's favour), was himself acquitted of actual misconduct by another Court-martial (which appears to have been a "packed" one), though never restored to office. He was, however, made, in 1780, Governor of Greenwich Hospital, a post he held till his death, and he became Admiral in 1787. He *d.* unm. at "The Vache," 19 March 1796, aged 73, and was *bur.* at Chalfont St. Giles.(a) M.I. Will pr. April 1796.

II. 1796. SIR HUGH PALLISER WALTERS, *afterwards*, from 1798, PALLISER, Baronet [1773], of Barnyforth, co. Wexford, and of Lee, co. Kent, great nephew, being 1st s. of George Robinson WALTERS, Capt. R.N., by Mary, da. and coheir of John ORFEUR, which George (who was named in the patent of the Baronetcy, 6 Aug. 1773, as abovestated, but who *d.* 9 Dec. 1789, before his uncle, the grantee) was only s. and h. of William WALTERS, Major in the Army (*d.* 28 Feb. 1789, aged 83), by Rebecca, 1st sister of the 1st Baronet. He was *b.* at Ross, co. Wexford, 27 Oct. 1768, and *suc. to the Baronetcy*, 19 March 1796, by virtue of the spec. rem. By royal lic., 13 Dec. 1798, he took the name of PALLISER instead of WALTERS. He *m.* 18 Jan. 1790, at Queen square chapel, Bath, Mary, yst. da. and coheir of John YATES, of Oldham, co. Essex. He *d.* at Troyes in Champaign, 17 Nov. 1813, aged 45. Admon. Aug. 1814. His widow *d.* 5 Aug. 1823.

III. 1814, to 1868. SIR HUGH PALLISER, Baronet [1773], of Castletown House, near Churchtown, and of Portobello, co. Wexford, only s. and h., *b.* 8 March 1796, *suc. to the Baronetcy*, 17 Nov. 1813. He *d.* unm. 3 Aug. 1868, aged 72, at Castletown aforesaid, when the *Baronetcy* became *extinct*.(b)

COOTE:(c)

cr. 18 May 1774;(d)

sometime, 1774-1800, EARL OF BELLAMONT [I.]

I. 1774. "CHARLES COOTE, EARL OF BELLAMONT, of the Kingdom of Ireland,"(e) who had been so *cr.* 4 Sep. 1767 was *cr. a Baronet*, as above, 18 May 1774,(d) with a spec. rem., failing heirs male of his

(a) This estate he left to his illegit. son, George Palliser, who sold it in June 1825, and *d.* 1829.

(b) "A person calling himself a cousin of the late Baronet and claiming to have succeeded to the title," wrote a letter to the editor of Debrett's *Baronetage* [1870]. See *Her. and Gen.*, vol. vi, p. 272. No such cousin could, however, have been entitled to the Baronetcy. The late Baronet was an only son, and the 2d Baronet had but one brother, William Walters, *b.* at Ross, 12 Feb. 1773, who *d.* unm., 23 Sep. 1798 at St. Vincent's.

(c) Most of the information in this article has been kindly furnished by G. D. Burtchaell, of the Office of Arms, Dublin Castle.

(d) This is often (though erroneously) considered an Irish creation, and as such is (wrongly) included in the list thereof in the *Liber Munerum Hiberniæ*.

(e) See p. 113, note "a," under "GIDEON." The date of the Gazette notice for Coote is 29 April, for Clayton, Edmonstone, Hanmer, Symonds, Lemon, Blake, Folkes, Jones, Montgomery, Gibbs, Raymond, and Smyth, 3 May 1774.

body, to [his illegit. son] "Charles COOTE, of Donnybrook, co. Dublin, Esq."(a) He *d.* s.p.m.s. legit.,(b) 20 Oct. 1800, aged 62, when his peerage honour became extinct. Will, etc., dated 9 June 1800, pr. [I.] 1802, by Charles COOTE, principal and residuary legatee. For fuller particulars of him, see "PEERAGE."

II. 1800. SIR CHARLES COOTE, Baronet [1774], sometime of Donnybrook aforesaid, but afterwards of Baggott street, Dublin, illegit. s. by "Rebecca PALMER, *otherwise* SHELDON,"(c) *b.* 1765(d); *suc. to the Baronetcy*, by virtue of the spec. rem., 20 Oct. 1800. He *m.* in or before 1798 (—), da. of (—) RICHARDSON.(e) He is also said(f) to have *m.*, Nov. 1814, Caroline Elizabeth, 2d da. of John WHALLEY. He *d.* 25 May 1857, aged about 92. Will, etc., dated 21 Oct. 1856, pr. [I.] 9 June 1857, under £6,000.

III. 1857. SIR CHARLES COOTE, Baronet [1774], of Rathmines, Dublin, s. and h., *b.* 1798;(d) *suc. to the Baronetcy*, 25 May 1857. He *m.* in 1846, Helena Melefont, widow of (—) SMITH, da. of Anthony O'RYAN, M.D. He *d.* 5 Nov. 1861, at Sandycove, co. Dublin. Will dated 10 May 1861, pr. [I.] 24 Dec. 1861, by his widow.

IV. 1861. SIR CHARLES ALGERNON COOTE, Baronet [1774], of Dublin, only s. and h., *b.* 1847; *suc. to the Baronetcy*, 5 Nov. 1861; sometime Lieut. in the Kilkenny Militia; Licenciate of the Royal Coll. of Surgeons [I.], 1883.

CLAYTON:

cr. 19 May 1774;

ex. 10 Aug. 1839.

I. 1774. "RICHARD CLAYTON, of Adlington, co. Lancaster, Esq.,"(a) 1st s. and h. of John CLAYTON of the same, by Elizabeth, da. of the Rev. (—) GOODWIN, D.D., Rector of Tankersley, co. York (which John who was living 1772, but dead before May 1774, was yr. br. of Richard CLAYTON,

(a) See page 168, note "e," under "COOTE."

(b) The Earl in his will (9 June 1800) mentions no less than twelve illegitimate children (four of whom were sons) the offspring of five different mothers. To one of these sons, Charles Coote (afterwards the 2d Baronet), he leaves £1,000, but excludes him from the entail of his estates in the counties of Monaghan and Cavan, which he settles on his three sons (1) Charles Coote, then aged 18, and a Fellow Commoner of Trinity College, Dublin, (2) Richard Coote, then aged 16, and (3) Thomas Coote, then aged 12, successively. The descendants of this Charles Coote, who was of Bellamont Forest, co. Cavan (being Sheriff of that county 1807), became extinct on the death s.p. of his last surviving son, Major-General Charles George Henry Coote, of Carrickacromin, co. Cavan, who was Sheriff (as above) 1880.

(c) So styled in the Earl's will, dated 9 June 1800.

(d) Charles Coote (styled in the note to the *Graduati Cantab.* as "*Baronettus*") was M.A. (Trin. Coll.), Cambridge, 1811. Probably, however, the person thus indicated was Sir Charles *Henry* Coote, the 9th Baronet [I. 1621], who was *b.* Jan. 1792, and *suc. to the Baronetcy* in March 1802.

(e) "The Earl in his will [9 June 1800] says of his natural da. Jane [who *m.* Ralph Dawson, of Tanna, co. Monaghan] that hers was *the only marriage of my natural children as to which I was consulted or my approbation sought or obtained.* So, possibly, the [future] Baronet's marriage was distasteful to his father, and hence the estates were not left to him. These Baronets never had any land" [G. D. Burtchaell, see p. 168, note "c"].

(f) Debrett's *Baronetage* (1824), where it is added that he had a son by this wife, born 6 Sep. 1815.

Y

Lord Chief Justice of the Common Pleas [I.], who *d.* s.p. at Adlington, 8 July 1770, aged 68), was *b.* at Manchester about 1745; matric. at Oxford (Bras. Coll.), 15 April 1763, aged 18; Barrister (Inner Temple) 1771, Bencher in 1803, having been *cr. a Baronet*, as above, 19 May 1774, with a spec. rem., failing heirs male of his body to those of his father, then late deceased. He was F.S.A.; was Recorder of Wigan, 1815-28; Constable of Lancaster Castle, and British Consul at Nantes. He *m.* in 1780, Anne, da. of Charles WHITE, of Manchester. He *d.* s.p.m.,(a) at Nantes, 29 April 1828. Will pr. Dec. 1828.

II. 1828, to 1839. SIR ROBERT CLAYTON, Baronet [1774], of Adlington aforesaid, br. and h. male, *b.* 1746, sometime Major 17th Reg. of Infantry, being at his death the Senior Major in the Army; *suc. to the Baronetcy*, according to the spec. rem. in its creation, 29 April 1828. He *m.*, in 1780, Christophera, da. of the Rev. Roger BALDWIN, D.D., Preb. of Carlisle [1764-1801], and Rector of Aldingham. He *d.* s.p., at Adlington Hall, 10 Aug. 1839, in his 93d year, when the *Baronetcy* became *extinct*. Will pr. Nov. 1839. The will of his widow was pr. July 1848.

EDMONSTONE:

cr. 20 May 1774.

I. 1774. "ARCHIBALD EDMONDSTONE, of Duntreath, co. Stirling, Esq.,"(b) 1st s. and h. of Archibald EDMONSTONE, of Duntreath aforesaid, and of Red Hall, co. Antrim, by his 2d wife Anne (*m.* 1716), sister of John, 4th DUKE OF ARGYLL [S.], da. of the Hon. John CAMPBELL, of Mamore, was *b.* 10 Oct. 1717, at Silver Banks, in co. Dumbarton; admitted to the Middle Temple, 5 Dec. 1737; was M.P. for Dumbartonshire (three Parls.), 1761-80; for Ayr burghs (two Parls), 1780-90, and for Dumbartonshire, again, 1790-96, being *cr. a Baronet*, as above, 20 May 1774. He *m.* firstly, in or before 1762, Susanna Mary, da. of Roger and sister of Benjamin HARENE, of Footscray place, Kent. She *d.* 4 and was *bur.* 11 April 1776, at St. Marylebone. He *m.* secondly, 28 April 1778, at St. Geo. Han. sq., Hester, 2d da. of Sir John HEATHCOTE, 2d Baronet [1733], of Normanton, by Bridget, da. of Thomas WHITE. She *d.* s.p. 1796. He *d.* 20 July 1807, aged 89. Will pr. 1807.

II. 1807. SIR CHARLES EDMONSTONE, Baronet [1774], of Duntreath aforesaid, 3d but 1st surv. s. and h.,(c) by 1st wife, *b.* 10 Oct. 1764; matric. at Oxford (Ch. Ch.), 10 May 1780, aged 16; B.A., 1784; Barrister (Linc. Inn), 1788; one of the six Clerks in Chancery, 1797-1807; M.P. for Dumbartonshire, 1806-07, and for Stirlingshire (three Parls.), 1812-21, having *suc. to the Baronetcy*, 20 July 1807. He *m.* firstly, 1 June 1794, Emma, sister of the 1st BARON SKELMERSDALE, 5th da. of Richard WILBRAHAM, *afterwards* WILBRAHAM-BOOTLE, by Mary, da. and h. of Richard BOOTLE, of Lathom House, co. Lancaster. She *d.* 30 Nov. 1797. He *m.* secondly, 5 Dec. 1804, Louisa, 3d da. of Beaumont (HOTHAM), 2d BARON HOTHAM OF SOUTH DALTON [I.], by Susanna, da. of Sir Thomas HANKEY. He *d.* 1 April 1821 at Brighton, aged 56. Will pr. 1821. His widow, who was *b.* 9 Oct. 1778, *m.* Jan. 1832, at Trinity church, Marylebone, Charles WOODCOCK, of Park Crescent, Portland place, and *d.* 30 Aug. 1840.

(a) Henrietta, his only da. and h., *b.* 12 Feb. 1782, *m.* 1 Dec. 1803, Lieut.-Gen. Robert Browne, who by royal lic. 6 April 1829, took the additional name of Clayton, and *d.* 10 March 1845, leaving issue.

(b) See page 168, note "e," under "COOTE."

(c) Of his two elder brothers, both of whom died unm. and v.p., (1) Archibald Edmonstone, Lieut. 1st Reg. of Foot Guards, *d.* July 1780; (2) William Archibald Edmonstone, East India service, living, apparently, 1801.

III. 1821. SIR ARCHIBALD EDMONSTONE, Baronet [1774], of Duntreath aforesaid, 1st s. and h., being only s. by the 1st wife, *b.* in Great Russell street, 12 March and *bap.* 10 April 1795 at St. George's, Bloomsbury; ed. at Eton; matric. at Oxford (Ch. Ch.), 21 Oct. 1813, aged 18; B.A., 1816; *suc. to the Baronetcy*, 1 April 1821. He *m.* 10 Oct. 1832, at Astbury, co. Chester, Emma, 2d da. of his maternal uncle, Randle WILBRAHAM, of Rode Hall, by his 1st wife, Lætitia, da. and h. of the Rev. Edward RUDD. He *d.* s.p. 15 March 1871, at 34 Wilton place, aged 76.(a) His widow, who was *b.* 28 July and *bap.* 10 Sep. 1804 at Astbury, *d.* 25 May 1891.

IV. 1871. SIR WILLIAM EDMONSTONE, Baronet [1774], of Duntreath aforesaid, br. of the half blood and h., being 2d s. of the 2d Baronet and 1st s. by his 2d wife; *b.* 29 Jan. 1810 at Hampton, Midx.; entered the Royal Navy and was wounded (by pirates) in the Archipelago in 1826; Commander, 1841; Inspector of the Coast Guard, 1844-52; Commander of the St. George guard ship at Devonport, 1852-59; Commodore on the West Coast of Africa, 1859, becoming eventually (1876) Vice-Admiral on the retired list. He was naval aide-de-camp to Queen Victoria; was **C.B.** in 1863, and *suc. to the Baronetcy*, 15 March 1871. He was M.P. for Stirlingshire, 1874-80. He *m.* 13 July 1841, at Zante, Mary Elizabeth, da. of Lieut. Col. John Whittle PARSONS, **C.M.G.**, sometime British Resident in that island. He *d.* 18 Feb. 1888, at 11 Ainslie place, Edinburgh, aged 78. His widow *d.* 11 Aug. 1902, at Cramond house, Midlothian.

V. 1888. SIR ARCHIBALD EDMONSTONE, Baronet [1774], of Duntreath aforesaid, only s. (out of nine children) and h., *b.* 30 May 1867, at Woolwich; matric. at Oxford (Ch. Ch.), 23 Jan. 1886, aged 18; *suc. to the Baronetcy*, 18 Feb. 1888; sometime Lieut. 3d Batt. Argyll and Sutherland Highlanders' Militia. He *m.* 30 Nov. 1895, at St. Paul's, Knightsbridge, Ida Agnes, only da. of George Stewart FORBES, of Aslown (2d s. of Sir Charles FORBES, 3d Baronet [1823]), by Henrietta Maria, da. of the Hon. Humble Dudley WARD.

Family Estates.—These, in 1883, consisted of 9,778 acres in Stirlingshire, worth £7,677 a year, exclusive of minerals, returned at £8,451 a year. *Principal Seats.*—Colzium, near Kilsyth, and Duntreath Castle, near Strathblane, both in co. Stirling.

HANMER:

cr. 21 May 1774;

sometime, 1872-81, BARON HANMER OF HANMER AND FLINT;

I. 1774. "WALDEN [sometimes called Job Walden] HANMER, of Hanmer, co. Flint, Esq.,"(b) only s. and h. of Job HANMER, Bencher of Lincoln's Inn (*d.* 2 March 1739), by Susanna, da. and h. of Thomas WALDEN, of Simpson place, Bucks, was *bap.* 19 March 1717; ed. at Eton; admitted to Lincoln's Inn, 27 June 1732; matric. at Oxford (Balliol Coll.), 12 June 1736, aged 18; Barrister (Linc. Inn), 1741; Bencher, 1757; and Treasurer, 1774. M.P. for Sudbury (two Parls.), 1768-80; suc. to the Hanmer estate on the death of his cousin Humphrey HANMER, in April 1773; D.C.L. (Oxford), 7 July 1773; and was *cr. a Baronet*, as above, 21 May 1774; Sheriff of Flintshire, 1785-86. He *m.* in or before 1747, Anne, yst. da. and coheir of Henry Vere GRAHAM, of Holbrook Hall, co. Suffolk, by Catharine, da. and coheir of Samuel WARNER, of the same. She *d.* 2 Feb. 1778, and was *bur.* at Simpson, Bucks. He *d.* 20 Oct. 1783, aged 66, and was *bur.* there. Will pr. Nov. 1783.

(a) He was author of some poems and travels.

(b) See page 168, note "e," under "COOTE."

II. 1783. SIR THOMAS HANMER, Baronet [1774], of Hanmer aforesaid, 1st s. and h., *b.* 5 April 1747; admitted to Linc. Inn, 12 Feb. 1765; *suc. to the Baronetcy*, 20 Oct. 1783; Steward of the Lordship of Englefield, co. Flint. He *m.*, 3 Dec. 1779, Margaret, 1st da. and coheir of George KENYON, of Peel, co. Lancaster, by his 1st wife, Margaret, da. of Thomas BANKS, of Wigan. He *d.* at Bettisfield park, co. Flint, 4 Oct. 1828, aged 81. Will pr. Nov. 1828. His widow *d.* there 6 Nov. 1830.

III. 1828. SIR JOHN HANMER, Baronet [1774], of Hanmer and Bettisfield park aforesaid, grandson and h., being 1st s. and h. of Thomas HANMER, Lieut.-Col. of the Flintshire Militia, by Arabella Charlotte, 1st da. and coheir of Thomas Skip Dyott BUCKNALL, of Hampton Court, Midx. (by Jane Charlotte Elizabeth, da. of John WYNDHAM, of Cromer, co. Norfolk), which Thomas (who was *b.* 12 April 1781; admitted to Rugby, 1789; matric. at Oxford [Ch. Ch.], 29 Nov. 1799; admitted to Lincoln's Inn, 15 Feb. 1800, and who *d.* v.p. 5 Nov. 1818, aged 37), was 1st s. and h. ap. of the late Baronet. He was *b.* 22 and *bap.* 26 Dec. 1809, at Hanmer; ed. at Eton; matric. at Oxford (Ch. Ch.), 3 Dec. 1827, aged 17; *suc. to the Baronetcy*, 4 Oct. 1828; was Sheriff of Flintshire, 1832-33; M.P. for Shrewsbury, 1832-37; for Hull, 1841-47; and for Flint burghs (six Parls.), 1847-72, being *cr.*, 1 Oct. 1872, BARON HANMER OF HANMER AND FLINT, both in co. Flint. He *m.*, 3 Sep. 1833, at Grendon, co. Warwick, Georgiana, 2d da. of Sir George CHETWYND, 2d Baronet [1795], by Hannah Maria, da. of John SPARROW. She *d.* 21 March 1880, in her 67th year, at Bettisfield park. He *d.* s.p., 8 March 1881, at Knotley park, co. Kent, aged 71, when *the peerage* became *extinct*.

IV. 1881. SIR WYNDHAM EDWARD HANMER, Baronet [1774], of Hanmer and Bettisfield Park aforesaid, br. and h., *b.* 24 Dec. 1810; sometime Capt. in the Royal Horse Guards and Major in the Army; *suc. to the Baronetcy*, 8 March 1881; Sheriff of Flintshire, 1885. He *m.* firstly, 10 March 1842, Marie Louise Victoire, 2d and yst da. of Sir John CONROY, 1st Baronet [1837], by Elizabeth, da. of Major-Gen. FISHER. She *d.* 9 Feb. 1866. He *m.* secondly, 2 Oct. 1877, Harriet Frances, 1st da. of Col. the Hon. Henry HELY-HUTCHINSON (br. of the 3d EARL OF DONOUGHMORE [I.]), by Harriet, da. of William WRIGHTSON, of Cuxworth, co. York. He *d.* 25 Aug. 1887, at Bettisfield Park, aged 76. His widow, who was *b.* 28 April 1826, living 1905.

V. 1887. SIR EDWARD JOHN HENRY HANMER, Baronet [1774], of Hanmer and Bettisfield Park aforesaid, only s. and h., by 1st wife, *b.* 15 April 1843; *suc. to the Baronetcy*, 25 Aug. 1887. He *m.* 31 Oct. 1865, Mary Elizabeth, da. of Col. Richard Tottenham FOSSE. He *d.* 3 May 1893, at St. Leonard's-on-Sea, aged 50. His widow living 1905.

VI. 1893. SIR WYNDHAM CHARLES HENRY HANMER, Baronet [1774], of Hanmer and Bettisfield Park aforesaid, only s. and h., *b.* 17 Sep. 1867, at Woburn, Beds; ed. at Eton; matric. at Oxford (Ch. Ch.), 24 April 1888, aged 20; *suc. to the Baronetcy*, 3 May 1893; Sheriff of Flintshire, 1902. He *m.* 16 April 1890, at St. Mary's, Whaddon, co. Buckingham, Essex, 1st da. of William Selby LOWNDES, of Whaddon Hall and Winslow in that county, by Jessie Mary, da. of Lieut.-Gen. Lechmere WORRALL.

Family Estates.—These, in 1883, consisted of 7,318 acres in Flintshire, 2,593 in Denbighshire, 879 in Bucks, 869 in Beds, and 1 in Salop. *Total.*—11,660 acres, worth £14,823 a year. *Seats.*—Bettisfield Park and Hanmer Hall, co. Flint, and Redbrook, near Whitchurch, Salop.

SYMONDS, *or* SYMONS:

cr. 23 May 1774;

ex. July 1796.

I. 1774, to 1796. "RICHARD SYMONDS, of the Meend, co. Hereford, Esq.,"(a) *formerly* Richard PEERS, only s. and h. of Richard PEERS, of Croydon, Surrey, Alderman of London, by Anna Sophia, da. and coheir of Richard SYMONS, of the MEEND aforesaid (which he purchased about 1740), Citizen of London, was *b.* about 1744, at St. Michael's Queenhithe, London; matric. at Oxford (Queen's Coll.), 21 Jan. 1762, aged 18; took the name of SYMONS, instead of that of PEERS, on inheriting the estate of his maternal grandfather abovenamed; was M.P. for Hereford (three Parls.), 1768-84, and was *cr. a Baronet*, as above, 23 May 1774. He *d.* unm., July 1796, when the *Baronetcy* became *extinct*.(b) Will pr. July 1797.

LEMON:

cr. 24 May 1774;

ex. 13 Feb. 1868.

I. 1774. "WILLIAM LEMON, of Carclew [in Milor], co. Cornwall, Esq.,"(a) 1st s. and h. of William LEMON,(c) of the same, by Anne, da. of John WILLYAMS, of Carnanton, in that county, was *b.* 1748, at Truro; matric. at Oxford (Ch. Ch.), 11 Jan. 1765, aged 16; was M.P. for Penrhyn, 1770-74, and for Cornwall (eleven Parls.), 1774, till death in 1824, being *cr. a Baronet*, as above, 24 May 1774. He *m.* in or before 1774, Jane, sister of Sir Francis BULLER, 1st Baronet [1789] da. of James BULLER, of Morval, co. Cornwall, by his 1st wife, Jane, da. of Allen (BATHURST) 1st EARL BATHURST. She *d.* 16 Jan. 1823, at Whitehall, aged 76. Will pr. 1824. He *d.* 11 Dec. 1824, at Carclew, aged 76. Will pr. April 1825.

II. 1824, to 1868. SIR CHARLES LEMON, Baronet [1774], of Carclew aforesaid, 2d and yst. but only surv. s. and h.,(d) *b.* 1784; matric. at Oxford (Ch. Ch.), 21 Oct. 1803, aged 19; M.P. for Penrhyn, 1807-12, and 1830-31; for Cornwall, 1831-32, and for West Cornwall (six Parls.), 1832-41 and 1842-57; was Sheriff of Cornwall, 1827-28, having *suc. to the Baronetcy*, 11 Dec. 1824; Hon. M.A., Cambridge, 1833; Deputy Warden of the Stannaries, 1852. He *m.* 5 Dec. 1810, Charlotte Anne, 4th da.

(a) See p. 168, note "e," under "COOTE."

(b) Mary, his sister and h. (who survived him forty years and *d.* 17 Jan. 1836, aged 91), *m.* 22 July 1767, Sir Charles William Blunt, 3d Baronet [1720], and was ancestress of the succeeding Baronets. She did not, however, inherit the estate of the Meend, which devolved on her maternal cousin, Thomas Raymond, who took the name of Symons accordingly.

(c) He was s. of another William Lemon (Sheriff of Cornwall, 17), who established the fortune of the family, by having obtained from Frederick, Prince of Wales, "a grant for a term of years of the dues on all minerals and metals (tin excepted) which he might cause to be discovered within the Duchy Lands of Cornwall and Devon," it being through his "thorough knowledge in mining and spirited exertions entirely owing that the mines in Cornwall were first worked upon a large scale, and to an extent unparalleled in that county." [Playfair's *Baronetage*, 1811].

(d) William Lemon, his elder br., *b.* 1774, *d.* unm. and v.p., March 1799.

of Henry Thomas (FOX-STRANGWAYS), 2d EARL OF ILCHESTER, by his 1st wife, Mary Theresa, da. of Standish GRADY. She, who was *b.* 7 Feb. 1784, *d.* 27 May 1826, in Manchester square, aged 42. He *d.* s.p.s.,(a) 13 Feb. 1868, aged about 84, when the *Baronetcy* became *extinct.*

BLAKE:

cr. 25 May 1774;

ex. 10 Sep. 1860.

I. 1774. "FRANCIS BLAKE, of Twisel Castle [in Norham], co. Durham, Esq.,"(b) only s. and h. of Robert BLAKE, of the same (formerly of Ireland), by Sarah (heiress of that estate), 3d da. of Sir Francis BLAKE, of Ford Castle, Northumberland (by Elizabeth, da. and h. of William CARR, of Ford Castle aforesaid), was *b.* about 1709; matric. at Oxford (Lincoln Coll.), 1 July 1725, aged 16; took an active part in support of the Government in the Jacobite rising of 1745; was F.R.S., 1746; being said to have been well versed in mathematics, and was *cr. a Baronet*, as above, 25 May 1774. He *m.* in or before 1734, Isabel, da. and coheir of Samuel AYTON, of West Herrington, in Houghton-le-Spring, co. Durham. She *d.* 25 May 1741 in her 31st year. He *d.* at Tinmouth, 29 March 1780, aged 72, and was *bur* with her at Houghton aforesaid. M.I.

II. 1780. SIR FRANCIS BLAKE, Baronet [1774], of Twisel Castle aforesaid, 2d but 1st surv. s. and h.(c), *b.* about 1737; *suc. to the Baronetcy*, 29 March 1780. He raised a reg. of infantry called *the Gold Spinks* and expended £80,000 in beginning the building of a Castle [Fowberry Tower?] on the banks of the Till, which he never finished. Sheriff of Northumberland, 1784-85. He *m.* 15 April 1772, Elizabeth, da. and coheir, eventually sole h. of Alexander DOUGLAS, Head of the British settlement at Bussorah in Persia, by Elizabeth, his wife, a native of that country. He *d.* 22 May 1818, aged 81. His widow *d.* 23 March 1823, in Sloane street, Chelsea, aged 73, and was *bur.* in Northumberland.

III. 1818, to 1860. SIR FRANCIS BLAKE, Baronet [1774], of Twisel Castle and Fowberry Tower aforesaid, 1st s. and h., *b.* about 1775, at Heston, Midx.; sometime Col. in the North Fencible regiment of infantry(d); *suc. to the Baronetcy*, 22 May 1818; M.P. for Berwick (five Parls.), Dec. 1820 to 1826, and March 1827 to 1834. He *m.* Jane, da. of William NEALE, which lady *d.* 3 April 1827, only ten days after her mother-in-law, also in Sloane street, being *bur.* with her. Her husband was then "left a widower without issue."(e) He *d.* s.p. legit. 10 Sep. 1860, aged 85, when the *Baronetcy* became *extinct.*(f)

(a) Charles William Lemon, his last surv. child, *b.* 10 May 1813, was drowned when at school at Harrow, 18 April 1826, a month before the death of his mother.

(b) See p. 168, note "e," under "COOTE."

(c) His elder br., Robert Blake, "a youth of extraordinary promise and expectation," *d.* 25 Jan. and was *bur.* 1 Feb. 1754, in Westm. Abbey, aged 20 [see Playfair's *Baronetage*, 1811]. Strange to say, though his burial and age are mentioned in Col. Chester's wonderful work on the registers of that Abbey, his identification is not given in the note thereto.

(d) "Greatly to the detriment of his private fortune" [Playfair, as above].

(e) Burke's *Baronetage*, 1841.

(f) In Dod's *Baronetage* for 1861 (but in no subsequent one) he is said to have been succeeded by his son, "by the da. of Mr. William Neale, viz., SIR FRANCIS BLAKE, 4th Baronet, *b.* 1825; *m.* in 1853 the 2d da. of the late Rev. Roddam Douglas, of Thorganby." This Francis however (who was apparently an illegit. son of this Baronet) is presumably the "Francis Blake, of Carlisle, Esq.," whose 1st son, Francis Douglas Blake, matric. at Oxford, 15 Jan., 1875 aged 18.

FOLKES:

cr. 26 May 1774;

afterwards, since, apparently, 1860, Ffolkes;

I. 1774. "MARTIN FOLKES [*otherwise* MARTIN BROWNE FOLKES],(a) of Hillington Hall, co. Norfolk, Esq.,"(b) only s. and h. of William FOLKES, Barrister-at-Law and Registrar of the Alienation Office, by his 2d wife, Mary, da. and h. of Sir William BROWNE, M.D., of King's Lynn, Norfolk, sometime President of the College of Physicians, which William FOLKES (who *d.* 9 April 1773) was yr. br. and h. male of Martin FOLKES, President of the Royal Society (who *d.* s.p.m., 28 June 1754, aged 64), both being sons of Martin FOLKES, by Dorothy, 2d da. and coheir of Sir William HOVELL, of Hillington aforesaid. He was *b.* May 1749; was early in life F.S.A., and was *cr. a Baronet*, as above, 26 May 1774; Sheriff of Norfolk, 1783-84; Major of a Brigade of Cavalry in the Norfolk Yeomanry, and M.P. for King's Lynn (eight Parls.), 1790-1821. He *m.* 28 Dec. 1775, Fanny, 2d and yst. da. and coheir of Sir John TURNER, 3d Baronet [1727], of Warham, by Frances, da. and coheir of John NEALE. She *d.* 30 Nov. 1813. He *d.* 11 Dec. 1821, in Mansfield street, Marylebone, aged 72. Will pr. 1822.

II. 1821. SIR WILLIAM JOHN HENRY BROWNE FOLKES, Baronet [1774], of Hillington Hall aforesaid, 4th but only surv. s. and h.,(c) *b.* 20 Aug. 1786 at Hillington Hall; ed. at Jesus Coll., Cambridge; B.A., 1810; M.A., 1813; *suc. to the Baronetcy*, 11 Dec. 1821. M.P. for Norfolk, 1830-32, and for West Norfolk, 1832-37. He *m.* 21 April 1818, at Florence, Charlotte Philippa, sister of the 1st BARON ORANMORE AND BROWNE [I.], 5th da. of Dominick Geoffrey BROWNE, of Castle Macgarrett, co. Mayo, by Margaret, da. and h. of the Hon. George BROWNE. He *d.* 24 March 1860, at Hillington, aged 73. His widow *d.* 23 Dec. 1882, at Congham Lodge, near Castle Rising, in her 85th year.

III. 1860. SIR WILLIAM HOVELL BROWNE FFOLKES,(d) Baronet [1774], of Hillington Hall aforesaid, grandson and h., being 1st s. and h. of Martin William Browne FOLKES, by Henrietta Bridget, da. of General Sir Charles WALE, **K.C.B.**, which Martin (who *d.* v.p. 24 July 1849, aged 30), was 1st s. and h. ap. of the late Baronet. He was *b.* 21 Nov. 1847, at Congham Lodge aforesaid; *suc. to the Baronetcy*, 24 March 1860; ed. at Harrow and at Trin. Coll., Cambridge; B.A., 1868; Sheriff of Norfolk, 1876; M.P. for King's Lynn, 1880-85. He *m.* 6 April 1875, at Congham, Norfolk, Emily Charlotte, 3d da. of Robert ELWES, of Congham House, by Mary Frances, da. of the Rev. Richard LUCAS, Rector of Edith Weston, Rutland.

Family Estates.—These, in 1883, consisted of 8,111 acres in Norfolk, worth £10,139 a year. *Principal Seat.*—Hillington Hall, near King's Lynn, Norfolk.

(a) Under the last designation he is returned to all Parliaments.

(b) See page 168, note "e," under "COOTE."

(c) Martin William Browne Folkes, the 1st son, *d.* v.p. and unm. in 1798, aged 20.

(d) This grotesque spelling of the name thus appears to have originated at or about this time, in which the hallucination was common that because the capital "f" was formerly written "ff" (instead of "F"), it therefore denoted that the letter was duplicated.

JONES:

cr. 27 May 1774;

ex. 3 May 1791.

I. 1774, to 1791. "WILLIAM JONES, of Ramsbury Manor, Wilts, Esq.,"(a) *formerly* William LANGHAM, yr. br. of Sir James LANGHAM, 7th Baronet [1660], being s. of William LANGHAM, of Rance, co. Northampton, by Mary, da. of Anthony DROUGHT, Merchant, was *b.* about 1737, at Barrowden, co. Rutland; matric. at Oxford (Lincoln Coll.), 26 Oct. 1753, aged 16; B.C.L. 1760, and having, in Aug. 1767 *m.* the heiress of the Ramsbury estate, took the name of JONES instead of LANGHAM, and was *cr. a Baronet*, as above, 27 May 1774. He *m.* Aug. 1767, Elizabeth, 1st da. and coheir of William JONES, of Ramsbury manor aforesaid, by (—), da. of Michael ERNLE, of Brimslade park, Wilts. He *d.* s.p. 3 May 1791, in Cavendish square, when the *Baronetcy* became *extinct.* Will pr. May 1791.(b) The will of "Dame Elizabeth JONES" [probably his widow], was pr. April 1800.

MONTGOMERY:

cr. 28 May 1774;

ex. 9 July 1831.

I. 1774. "WILLIAM MONTGOMERY, of Macbiehill [Magbiehill] co. Tweeddale, North Britain, Esq.,"(a) 1st s. and h.,(c) of William MONTGOMERY, of the same, Advocate, by Barbara, da. of Robert RUTHERFORD, of Bowland, was *b.* 19 Nov. 1717, was M.P. [I.], for Ballynakill (three Parls.) 1769, till death (d), and was *cr. a Baronet*, as above, 28 May 1774. He *m.* firstly, 1 July 1750, Hannah, 2d da. and coheir of Alexander TOMKYNS, of Prehen, co. Londonderry. She was living Aug. 1753. He *m.* 9 Jan. 1761, Anne, da. of Henry WATT [WALL, *or* EVATT], of Mount Lewis, in Ireland. She *d.* 19 June 1777. He *d.* 25 Dec. 1788, aged 71, at Dublin.

II. 1788, to 1831. SIR GEORGE MONTGOMERY, Baronet [1774], of Magbiehill aforesaid, 2d but 1st surv. s. and h.,(e) being 1st s. by the 2d wife; *b.* 1765; *suc. to the Baronetcy*, 25 Dec. 1788; M.P. for Peeblesshire, from March 1831, till his death a few months later. He *d.* unm. 9 July 1831, aged 16, when the *Baronetcy* became *extinct.* Will pr. Oct. 1831.

(a) See p. 168, note "e," under "COOTE."

(b) The Ramsbury estate passed eventually to Sir Francis Burdett, 5th Baronet [1618], whose mother Eleanor (*d.* 30 May 1783), was sister of Dame Elizabeth Jones, being 2d and yst. da. and coheir of William Jones, of Ramsbury.

(c) His yr. br. Sir James Montgomery, Lord Advocate of Scotland 1766, was *cr. a Baronet*, 16 July 1801.

(d) He is possibly identical with William Montgomery, M.P. [I.] for Augher, 1761-69, but that borough is in a different county.

(e) His elder br. of the half blood, William Stone Montgomery, Capt. 9th Foot, *b.* 4 Aug. 1754, *d.* unm. and v.p. 8 July 1777, of wounds received near Fort Ann, in America. His yr. br. of the whole blood, Robert Montgomery, Col. 19th Foot, *b.* 26 Feb. 1767, *d.* unm. 6 April 1803, being killed in a duel with Capt. Macnamara.

GIBBS, *or* GIBBES:

cr. 30 May 1774.

I. 1774. "PHILIP GIBBS, of Springhead in Barbadoes, Esq.,(a) 1st but only surv. s. and h. of Philip GIBBS,(b) of the same (*d.* Dec. 1763, aged 52), by Elizabeth, da. of John HARRIS, was *b.* 7 March 1730/1; admitted to the Middle Temple, London, 28 July 1755, and was *cr. a Baronet*, as above, 30 May 1774. He was of Fackley [*Qy.* Tackley], Oxon.(c) He *m.* 1 Feb. 1753, Agnes, da. and h. of Samuel OSBORNE, of Barbadoes. She *d.* Jan. 1813. He *d.* June 1815, aged 84. Will pr. 1816.

II. 1815. SIR SAMUEL OSBORNE GIBBES, Baronet [1774], of New Zealand, grandson and h., being only s. and h. of Samuel Osborne GIBBS, *or* GIBBES, by (—), da. of (—) BISHOP, of Exeter, which Samuel (who *d.* v.p. at Grenada in Jan. 1807), was 2d and yst. s. of the late Baronet.(d) He was *b.* 27 Aug. 1803, and *suc. to the Baronetcy*, in June 1815; was Member of the Legislative Council of New Zealand, 1856. He *m.* firstly, 28 Sep. 1825, at Cremorgan, Queen's County, Ireland, Margaret, 1st da. of Henry MOORE, of Cremorgan, by Anne, da. of Mark SCOTT, of Mohubber, co. Tipperary, elder br. of John, 1st EARL OF CLONMELL [I.]. She *d.* 20 June 1847. He *m.* 1848, Anne, da. of Richard PENNY, of Dorsetshire. He *d.* 13 Nov. 1874, aged 71. His widow living 1905, at Auckland, in New Zealand.

III. 1874. SIR EDWARD OSBORNE GIBBES, Baronet [1774], of New Zealand, 4th but 1st surv. s. and h.,(e) being 1st s. by 2d wife, *b.* Nov. 1850; *suc. to the Baronetcy*, 13 Nov. 1874; Assistant Secretary Educat. Depart. in New Zealand. He *m.* in 1879, Sarah, da. of John MITCHELL, Capt. New Zealand Militia.

RAYMOND:

cr. 31 May 1774;

afterwards, since 1788, BURRELL.

I. 1774. "CHARLES RAYMOND, of Valentine House [in Barking], co. Essex, Esq.,"(a) s. and h. of John RAYMOND, of Marple, Devon, by Anna Maria, da. of Samuel TANNER (*d.* May 1723), of Clyst St. Mary, in that county (and Isabella, his wife, da. of Peter CORSELLIS, of Flanders), was *bap.* 22 April 1713, at Withycombe Raleigh, Devon, and having established himself in the county of Essex, being Sheriff thereof, 1771-72, was *cr. a Baronet*, as above, 31 May 1774, with a spec. rem. failing heirs male of his body to "William BURRELL, of Beckenham, co. Kent, Esq., and the heirs male of his body by Sophia,

(a) See p. 168, note "e," under "COOTE."

(b) This Philip (father of Philip, the 1st Baronet) was s. and h. of another Philip Gibbs (*d.* 6 Oct. 1726, aged 39), the s. and h. of another Philip Gibbs (*d.* July 1697), the s. and h. of another Philip Gibbs, who emigrated from Somersetshire to Jamaica about 1635, and *d.* there 1648.

(c) Playfair's *Baronetage*, 1811.

(d) The 1st son, Philip Gibbes (the 6th "Philip" in lineal succession, see note "b" above), was a Member of the Council of Barbadoes. He *m.* 19 March 1807, Maria, da. of Robert Knipe, of New Lodge, near Berkhampstead, but *d.* v.p. and s.p. 14 Dec. 1812.

(e) Of his elder brothers who all *d.* unm. and v.p. (1) Philip Gibbes, *b.* 24 Aug. 1826, *d.* in India in 1850, aged 24; (2) Henry James Gibbes, *d.* 1861, aged 27; (3) Robert Gibbes, *d.* 1864, aged 28.

da. of the said Charles RAYMOND."(a) the grantee. He *m.* Sarah, 1st da. of Thomas WEBSTER, of Bromley, co. Kent. She *d.* 15 and was *bur.* 20 April 1778, at Barking, aged 55. He *d.* s.p.m.(b) 24 and was *bur.* there 29 Aug. 1788, aged 75, worth £200,000.(c) Will pr. 1788.

II. 1788. SIR WILLIAM BURRELL, Baronet [1774], of West Grinstead Park, Sussex, and of Valentine House aforesaid, son-in-law of the grantee, was 2d surv. and yst. s. of Peter BURRELL (*d.* 16 April 1756), of Langley Park in Beckenham, co. Kent, and of London, merchant (br. of Sir Merrik BURRELL, who was *cr. a Baronet*, 15 July 1766), by Amy, da. of Hugh RAYMOND, of Saling Hall, Essex, was *b.* 10 Oct. 1732 in Leadenhall street, and *bap.* at St. Peter le Poor, London; ed. at St. John's Coll., Cambridge; LL.B., 1755; LL.D., 1760; Fellow of the College of Advocates, London, 3 Nov. 1760, practising chiefly in the Admiralty Court; Chancellor of Worcester, 1764, and subsequently of Rochester; M.P. for Haslemere, 1768-74; a Commissr. of Excise, 1771-87; F.R.S. and F.S.A., and an indefatigable antiquary.(d) He *suc. to the Baronetcy*, 24 Aug. 1788 on the death of his wife's father, in accordance with the spec. rem. in the creation. He *m.* 13 April 1773, Sophia, 1st da. and coheir of Sir Charles RAYMOND, 1st Baronet 1774, by Sarah, da. of Thomas WEBSTER, all abovenamed. He, who had been partially paralysed since Aug. 1787, *d.* 20 Jan. 1796, at Deepdene, near Dorking, Surrey, aged 63, and was *bur.* at West Grinstead. M.I. at Cuckfield, Sussex. Will pr. Feb. 1796. His widow, who was a Poetess and a Dramatist, *m.* 23 May 1797 at St. Marylebone, the Rev. William CLAY, and *d.* at West Cowes, Isle of Wight, 20 June 1802, aged about 52. Will pr. 1812 [*Qy.* 1802].

III. 1796. SIR CHARLES MERRIK BURRELL, Baronet [1774], of Knepp Castle, co. Sussex, and of West Grinstead Park aforesaid, 1st s. and h., *b.* 24 May 1774 in Golden square, London; *suc. to the Baronetcy*, 20 Jan. 1796; was M.P. (Conservative interest) for New Shoreham for fifty-five years (sixteen Parls.), 1806 till death in 1862, being then the "father" of the House of Commons. He *m.* 4 July 1808, at St. Geo. Han. sq., Frances ILIFFE, *otherwise* WYNDHAM, spinster, illegit. da. of George O'Brien (WYNDHAM), 3d EARL OF EGREMONT. She *d.* 28 Sep. 1848, at Knepp Castle. He *d.* there 4 Jan. 1862, aged 87.

IV. 1862. SIR PERCY BURRELL, Baronet [1774], of Knepp Castle and West Grinstead Park aforesaid, 2d but 1st surv. s. and h.,(e) *b.* 10 Feb. 1812, in Grosvenor place; matric. at Oxford (Ch. Ch.), 8 July 1830, aged 18; *suc. to the Baronetcy*, 4 Jan. 1862; M.P. for New Shoreham (four Parls.), Feb. 1862, till death 1876. He *m.* 26 Aug. 1856, at St. Geo. Han. sq., Henrietta Katherine, 1st da. of Vice-Admiral Sir George Richard BROOKE-PECHELL, 4th Baronet [1797], by Katherine Annabella, 2d and yst. da. and coheir of Cecil (BISHOPP), LORD DE LA ZOUCHE. He *d.* s.p., 19 July 1876, in his 65th year, at 44 Belgrave square. His widow *d.* 4 March 1880, at Hyeres in France.

V. 1876. SIR WALTER WYNDHAM BURRELL, Baronet [1774], of Knepp Castle and West Grinstead Park aforesaid, br. and h., *b.* 26 Oct. 1814; *suc. to the Baronetcy*, 19 July 1876; M.P. for New Shoreham, Aug. 1876 to Nov. 1885. He *m.* 10 June 1847, at St. James', Westm., Dorothea,

(a) See p. 168, note "e," under "COOTE."

(b) Of his daughters (1) Sophia *m.* 13 April 1773, William Burrell, as in the text; (2) Juliana, *m.* Henry Boulton, of Leatherhead, Surrey, and was living 1788; (3) Anna Maria, *m.* 29 June 1781, at Barking, Thomas Newte, and *d.* at Bristol Hot Wells, 19 Aug. 1783, aged 27. M.I. at Barking.

(c) Presumably acquired by merchandise.

(d) His useful and laborious collections for a history of the county of Sussex, in twenty-four folio MSS. volumes, were left by him to the British Museum, and are of the utmost value.

(e) His elder br., Charles Wyndham Burrell, *d.* 11 July 1827, aged about 17.

da. of the Rev. John Applethwaite JONES, Vicar of Burleigh-on-the-Hill, Rutland. He *d.* at West Grinstead Park, 24 Jan. 1886, aged 71, and was *bur.* at Shipley. Will pr. 2 May 1886, above £65,000. His widow *d.* 8 Feb. 1891, at Ockendon House, Cuckfield, Sussex, aged 63.

VI. 1886. SIR CHARLES RAYMOND BURRELL, Baronet [1774], of Knepp Castle and West Grinstead Park aforesaid, 1st s. and h., *b.* 29 March 1848, at Burleigh-on-the-Hill aforesaid; ed. at Mag. Coll., Cambridge. Capt. Royal Sussex Militia, 1872-81; *suc. to the Baronetcy*, 24 Jan. 1886. He *m.* 22 July 1872, Etheldreda Mary, 1st da. of Sir Robert LODER, 1st Baronet [1887], by Maria Georgiana, da. of Hans BUSK. He *d.* 6 Sep. 1899, at Knepp Castle, aged 51. Will pr. at £43,448 gross and £38,382 net personalty. His widow living 1905.

VII. 1899. SIR MERRIK RAYMOND BURRELL, Baronet [1774], of Knepp Castle and West Grinstead Park aforesaid, only s. and h., *b.* 14 May 1877, at Knepp Castle, sometime Lieut. 1st Royal Dragoons, serving in the Transvaal war, 1899-1901; *suc. to the Baronetcy*, 6 Sep. 1899. He *m.* 11 Feb. 1901, Wilhelmina Louisa, da. of Walter WINANS, of Surrenden Park, Kent, and of Baltimore, in Maryland.

Family Estates.—These, in 1883, consisted of 9,294 acres in Sussex, worth £9,367 a year. *Seats.*—Knepp Castle and West Grinstead Park, near Horsham, and Ockendon house, in Cuckfield, all in co. Sussex.

SMITH, *or* SMYTH:
cr. 1 June 1774;

afterwards, since 1862, SMITH-MARRIOTT.

I. 1774. "JOHN SMYTH, of Sydling St. Nicholas,(a) co. Dorset, Esq.,"(b) 1st s. and h. of Henry SMITH, *or* SMYTH, of New Windsor, Berks (*d.* 31 Jan. 1768, aged 54), by Mary, da. of John HILL, was *b.* 10 April 1744; ed. at Harrow and at Mag. Coll., Cambridge(c); Sheriff of Dorset 1772-73, and was *cr. a Baronet*, as above, 1 June 1774. He was *cr.* D.C.L. of Oxford, 4 July 1780, and was M.A. (being then called of Trin. Coll.), Cambridge, 1789(d); F.S.A. and F.R.S. He *m.* firstly, in or before 1770, Elizabeth, da. and h. of Robert CURTIS,

(a) This estate was purchased by Sir William Smith, Alderman and sometime (1741-42) Sheriff of London, who *d.* s.p.s. 6 March 1751/2, aged 66. He was 2d cousin to the Baronet's grandfather (George Smith), being s. of Robert Smith, of Langham in Chard (*d.* 1691), of William Smith, of Lyme Regis, Merchant (*d.* 1677, aged 46), s. of Robert Smith, of Ilminster (*d.* 1655, aged 55), which Robert was father also of George Smith, of West Dewlish, Somerset (*d.* 1700, aged 76), father of John Smith, of the same (*d.* 1729, aged 70), father of George Smith (*d.* 1730), father of Henry, the father of the 1st Baronet. See pedigree in Hutchins's *Dorset*, vol. i, p. 168 [edit. 1861].

(b) See p. 168, note "e," under "COOTE."

(c) Playfair's *Baronetage* [1811], where it is added he "afterwards took the degree of A.M." This, however, was not till 1789, more than twenty years later, and he is then called of Trin. Coll. See note "d" below.

(d) The word "Baronettus" is put as a note in the *Graduati Cantab.* to the John Smith, of Trin. Coll., who was "A.M." in 1789. The 1st Baronet's son, John, afterwards the 2d Baronet, was then 19, and it is just possible that (as the father was ed. at Mag. Coll., see text and note "c" above) it may refer to him.

of Wilsthorpe in Greatford, co. Lincoln, Barrister (*d.* 10 March 1743/4, aged 43), by Elizabeth, da. of John WYLDBORE, of Peterborough. She *d.* 13 Feb. 1796, in Grosvenor street, and was *bur.* at Sydling. M.I. He *m.* secondly, 1 Jan. 1800, Anna Eleanora, da. of Thomas MORLAND, of Court Lodge, in Lamberhurst, co. Kent. He *d.* 13 Nov. 1807, at Sydling, aged 63. Will pr. 1808. His widow *d.* s.p. in or before 1817. Will pr. Dec. 1817.

II. 1807. SIR JOHN WYLDBORE(a) SMITH, Baronet [1774], of Sydling aforesaid, and of Down House, near Blandford, Dorset, only surv. s. and h., by 1st wife, *b.* 19 May 1770; *suc. to the Baronetcy*, 13 Nov. 1807; Sheriff of Dorset, 1814-15. He *m.* 13 May 1797, Elizabeth Anne, 2d da. and coheir of the Rev. James MARRIOTT, D.C.L., Rector of Horsemonden, Kent (*d.* 31 July 1809, aged 61), by (—), da. of (—) BOSWELL. She *d.* 27 Feb. 1847,(b) aged 77, at Down house, Dorset. He *d.* 19 Feb. 1852, in his 82d year. Will pr. May 1852.

III. 1852. SIR JOHN JAMES SMITH, Baronet [1774], of Sydling aforesaid, 1st s. and h., *b.* 10 April 1800, in Hereford street, St. Geo. Han. sq.; ed. at Winchester and at Trin. Coll., Cambridge; Col. of the Dorset militia, 1846-52; *suc. to the Baronetcy*, 19 Feb. 1852. He *m.* 11 Nov. 1828, at Somerton Erleigh, Somerset, Frances, 1st da. of John Frederick PINNEY, of Somerton House. He *d.* s.p., 2 Sep. 1862, in Berkeley square, aged 62. His widow *d.* 1 June 1895, at the house of her brother, Col. PINNEY, aged 92, and was *bur.* at Sydling. Will pr. 7 Aug. 1895, at £33,962.

IV. 1862. SIR WILLIAM MARRIOTT SMITH-MARRIOTT, Baronet [1774], of Sydling and Down House aforesaid, br. and h., *b.* 31 Aug. 1801 in Portman street, Marylebone; took by royal lic. 15 Feb. 1811, in compliance with the will of his maternal grandfather, the name of SMITH-MARRIOTT, instead of that of SMITH; ed. at Trin. Coll., Cambridge; B.A., 1825; M.A., 1829; in Holy Orders; Rector of Horsemonden, Kent, 1825 till death in 1864, having *suc. to the Baronetcy*, 2 Sep. 1862. He *m.* firstly, 29 Dec. 1825, at Benenden, Kent, Julia Elizabeth, 4th da. of Thomas Law HODGES, of Hempsted place, by Rebecca, posthumous da. and h. of Sir Roger TWISDEN, 6th Baronet [1666], of Bradbourne, Kent. She *d.* 11 March 1842. He *m.* secondly, 11 April 1844, at Blandford, Dorset, Frances, 3d da. of Robert RADCLYFFE, of Foxdenton Hall, co. Lancaster, and Hyde Manor House, Dorset, by Mary, da. of Thomas PATTEN, of Bank, co. Lancaster. He *d.* 4 Oct. 1864, at Horsemonden Rectory, in his 64th year. His widow *d.* s.p., 30 Sep. 1900, at "Twysden," in Kilndown, Kent, in her 98th year.

V. 1864. SIR WILLIAM HENRY SMITH-MARRIOTT, Baronet [1774], of Sydling and Down House aforesaid, 1st s. and h., by 1st wife, *b.* 7 Aug. 1835, at Horsemonden Rectory aforesaid; ed. at Harrow; matric. at Oxford (Balliol Coll.), 12 Dec. 1854, aged 19; *suc. to the Baronetcy*, 4 Oct. 1864; Sheriff of Dorset, 1875. He *m.* 12 Dec. 1868, at Thornton, Bucks, Elizabeth Dorothy, 4th da. of the Hon. Richard CAVENDISH, of Thornton Hall (yr. s. of Richard, BARON WATERPARK [I.]), by Elizabeth Maria Margaret, da. and h. of Thomas HART. She, who was *b.* 3 July 1841, *d.* at (her sister's house) Markeaton Hall, co. Derby, 25 March 1904, and was *bur.* at Blandford St. Mary, Dorset.

Family Estates.—These, in 1883, consisted of 3,893 acres in Dorset, worth £3,985 a year. *Principal Seat.*—Down House, near Blandford, Dorset.

(a) So named from his maternal great uncle, Matthew Wyldbore, many years M.P. for Peterborough, who *d.* unm. and left the bulk of his property to this family.

(b) Not, as generally stated, 1844.

JENNINGS-CLERKE:
cr. 26 Oct. 1774;

ex. 1788.

I. 1774, to 1788. "PHILIP JENNINGS-CLERKE, of Duddlestone Hall, co. Salop, Esq.,"(a) *formerly* Philip JENNINGS, probably s. of Philip JENNINGS(b) (*d.* in or before 1742), by his 2d wife, Dorothy (*m.* 1721 and living 1742), relict of (—) CLERKE, which Philip, was s. of Edward JENNINGS (*b.* 1647), elder br. of Admiral Sir John JENNINGS,(b) one being the 5th and the other the 15th child of Philip JENNINGS, of Duddlestone Hall aforesaid, was *b.* about 1722, and matric. at Oxford (Oriel Coll.), 7 Nov. 1739, aged 17. He took the name of CLERKE between 1760 and 1774; is described (on his first return to Parliament in 1768) as Lieut.-Col. of the Horse Guards,(c) and was *cr. a Baronet*, as above, 26 Oct. 1774. He was M.P. for Totnes (four Parls.), 1768 till death. He *m.* in or before 1758, Anne, da. of (—) THOMPSON.(b) He *d.* s.p.m.s.,(d) 14 Jan. or 22 April 1788,(e) when *the Baronetcy* became *extinct.* Will pr. 1788, also [I.] 1789. The will of his widow pr. Jan. 1798.

WINTRINGHAM:(f)
cr. 7 Nov. 1774;

ex. 10 Jan. 1794.

I. 1774, to 1794. "SIR CLIFTON WINTRINGHAM, Knt., of Dover street, in the parish of St. George's Hanover square,"(a) only s. of Clifton(g) WINTRINGHAM, M.D., of York (who *d.* there 12 March 1748), by his 1st wife Elizabeth, da. of Richard NETTLETON, of Earls Heaton, in Dewsbury, was *b.* about 1712, at York; ed. at Trin. Coll., Cambridge; M.B. 1734, and M.D. 1749; joined the Army Medical Service about 1735; Joint Physician to the Forces, 1756; Physician in Ordinary to Geo. III in 1762, and was *Knighted* 11 Feb. 1762. Fellow of the Coll. of Physicians 25 June 1763, being Censor in 1770, and was *cr. a Baronet*, as above, 7 Nov. 1774, with a spec. rem., failing heirs male of his body, to "Jarvis CLIFTON,(h) Esq., 2d son of

(a) See p. 113, note "a," under "GIDEON." The date of the Gazette notice for Jennings-Clerke is 20 Oct., and that for Wintringham, Duntze, and Pepperell is 29 Oct. 1774.

(b) See Cussan's *Herts* (Edwinstree Hundred, p. 196, and see also Col. Chester's Westm. Abbey Registers, p. 365), where is an abstract of the Admiral's will, dated 18 Nov. 1742, pr. 30 Dec. 1743.

(c) *Gent. Mag.* He, however, does not appear in the *Army List* for 1774.

(d) His s., John Edward Jennings, who matric. at Oxford (Merton Coll.), 15 Dec. 1774, aged 16, and was B.A., 1779, *d.* v.p. and s.p.m., probably unm. His da. *m.* (as 2d wife) Thomas Duncombe, of Duncombe Park, co. York, by whom she had an only child, Frances, wife of the Rt. Hon. Sir George Rose and mother of Field Marshal Lord Strathnairn.

(e) The date of 14 Jan. is that in the *Annual Register* and other periodicals, but that of 22 April is given both by Courthope and Burke in their *Extinct Baronetages*.

(f) See pedigree in Hunter's *Familiæ Minorum Gentium*, p. 487. [Harl. Soc., vol. 38, p. 487].

(g) As to the name of Clifton, Gertrude, da. of *Clifton* Rodes (s. of Sir Francis Rodes, 1st Baronet [1641]), *m.* Rev. William Wintringham, Vicar of East Retford, and was mother of *Clifton* Wintringham, the father of the Baronet.

(h) He, if, as is probable, one of the sons of the 4th Baronet, must have been about the same age or even older than the grantee, and must have *d.* unm. and before him. If, however, he was Gervase Clifton, 1st s. and h. ap. of Sir Gervase Clifton, the 6th Baronet, that Gervase, who was *b.* in or after 1766, *d.* in 1779, but inasmuch as he was, at his birth, h. ap. to a much older Baronetcy (*viz.*, one of 1611), there would have been no object in putting him in remainder to one created more than 160 years later.

Sir Jarvis CLIFTON, Bart., of Clifton, Notts."(a) He was Physician General to the Forces, 5 Dec. 1786; F.R.S., 23 Dec. 1792,(b) being also a Member of the *Société Royale de Medécine de France*. He *m.* Anne RICHARDSON. He *d.* s.p. after a long illness, 10 Jan. 1794, in his 83d year, at his house in the Upper Mall, Hammersmith, when the *Baronetcy* became *extinct*. M.I. in Westminster Abbey. Will pr. Jan. 1794. His widow, who is said to have *m.* in 1800, (—) GATHAN, *d.* at Twickenham in 1805, aged 85.

DUNTZE:

cr. 8 Nov. 1774.

I. 1774. "JOHN DUNTZE, of Tiverton,(c) co. Devon, Esq.,"(a) s. of John DUNTZE, of Exeter, merchant (living 1742), by Elizabeth, relict of Nicholas MUNCKLEY, of Exeter (who *d.* 1730), da. of James HAWKER, of Luppit, Devon, was *b.* probably about 1735, was a merchant at Exeter; was M.P. (twenty-seven years) for Tiverton (— Parls.), 1768 till death in 1795, and was *cr. a Baronet*, as above, 8 Nov. 1774. He *m.* in or before 1765, Frances, da. of Samuel LEWIS. He *d.* 5 Feb. 1795, and was *bur.* at Rockbeare, Devon. M.I. Will pr. March 1795. His widow *d.* 31 March 1801, and was *bur.* there. Will pr. 1802.

II. 1795. SIR JOHN DUNTZE, Baronet [1774], of Tiverton aforesaid, 1st s. and h., *b.* about 1765; *suc. to the Baronetcy*, 5 Feb. 1795; was, for nearly thirty years, Receiver-General of the Land and Assessed Taxes of Devon. He *m.* 5 June 1804, at Tiverton, Dorothy, 2d da. of Sir Thomas CAREW, 6th Baronet [1661], of Haccombe, by Jane, da. of the Rev. Charles SMALLWOOD. She *d.* 4 Nov. 1806. He *m.* secondly, in 1808, Elizabeth, elder sister of his late wife. He *d.* 21 June 1830, at Tiverton, aged 65. Will pr. Sep. 1830, Sep. 1833, and Sep. 1848. His widow *d.* 1 June 1832. Admon. Sep. 1833.

III 1830. SIR JOHN LEWIS DUNTZE, Baronet [1774], of Exeleigh House, Starcross, Devon, 2d and yst. but 1st surv. s. and h.,(d) being only s. by 2d wife, *b.* 16 Aug. 1809, at Tiverton; ed. at Eton; sometime Lieut. 7th Dragoon Guards; *suc. to the Baronetcy*, 21 June 1830. He *m.* 15 March 1834, at Michaelstone, co. Monmouth, Elizabeth, da. of the Rev. James COLES, Rector of that parish. He *d.* s.p., 7 Sep. 1884, at Exeleigh House aforesaid, aged 75. His widow *d.* there 23 Nov. 1892.

IV. 1884. SIR GEORGE ALEXANDER DUNTZE, Baronet [1774], cousin and h. male, being only s. and h. of the Rev. Samuel Henry DUNTZE, by Frances, da. of the Very Rev. Joseph PALMER, Dean of Cashel, which Samuel (who *d.* 15 Oct. 1855, aged 55) was 1st s. of James Nicholas DUNTZE, Paymaster-Gen. of the Forces in Sicily (*d.* 22 Sep. 1846), the 2d s. of the 1st Baronet. He was *b.* 27 Jan. 1839; *suc. to the Baronetcy*, 7 Sep. 1884. He *m.* 31 July 1869, Harriette Elizabeth Isabella, yst. da. of R. Lloyd THOMAS, an officer of the 10th Foot.

(a) See p. 181, note "a," under "JENNINGS-CLERKE."
(b) *Dict. Nat. Biogr.* The date of 13 Jan. 1742/3, is given in Munk's *Roll of Physicians*, but this presumably applies to the father, who was then living at the age of 53.
(c) In the list in Betham's *Baronetage* [1805], he is described as "of Rockbere House, Devon."
(d) His elder br. of the half blood was *b.* 1 Oct. 1806 [Playfair's *Baronetage*, 1811], *d.* v.p. and s.p.

PEPPERELL:

cr. 9 Nov. 1774;

ex. 18 Dec. 1816.

I. 1774, to 1816. "WILLIAM PEPPERELL, of Boston, in the province of Massachusetts, in America, Esq.,"(a) *formerly* William SPARHAWK, 2d s. of Nathaniel SPARHAWK, of New England, merchant, by Elizabeth, da. and h. of Sir William PEPPERELL, Baronet [so *cr.* 15 Nov. 1746], of Massachusetts aforesaid, having on the death, 6 July 1759, of his said maternal grandfather inherited his estates, took the name of PEPPERELL, instead of that of SPARHAWK, and was *cr. a Baronet*, as above, 9 Nov. 1774. His American estates, however, were subsequently, confiscated in the War of Independence. He *m.* 13 Nov. 1767, Elizabeth, da. of Isaac ROYALL, a member of the King's Council at Massachusetts. He *d.* s.p.m.s.,(b) 13 Dec. 1816, when the *Baronetcy* became *extinct*. Will pr. 1817.

WARREN:

cr. 1 June 1775;

ex. 27 Feb. 1822.

I. 1775, to 1822. "JOHN BORLACE [*rectius* BORLASE] WARREN, Esq.,"(c) of Little Marlow, Bucks, as also of Bockmers, in Medmenham in that county (both of which he sold in 1781), of Stratton Audley, Oxon, and Stapleford Hall, Notts, 1st s. and h.(d) of John Borlase WARREN, of the same (*d.* 6 May 1763, aged 63), by Bridget, da. and coheir of Gervase ROSELL, of Radcliffe-upon-Trent, Notts, was *b.* 2 Sep. and *bap.* 5 Oct. 1753, at Stapleford; ed. at Winchester, 1768; admitted to Emmanuel Coll., Cambridge, 23 Sep. 1769; B.A., 1773; M.A., 1776; was M.P. for Marlow, 1774-84; for Nottingham, Nov. 1797 to 1860, and for

(a) See p. 181, note "a," under "JENNINGS-CLERKE."
(b) William Royall Pepperell, his only son, *b.* 5 July 1775 at Boston, in America, matric. at Oxford (Ch. Ch.), 18 Feb. 1794, aged 18, and *d.* the next year, 27 Sep. 1798, unm.
(c) See p. 113, note "a," under "GIDEON." The date of the Gazette notice for Warren and Boyd is 31 May, and for Leith and Etherington, 11 Nov. 1775.
(d) In the able account of him in the *Dict. Nat. Biogr.*, some curious mistakes occur. He is called "4th" son, and it is stated that "as a lad, young Warren was intended for the church," and that "the death of his elder brother changing his prospects, changed also his views, and on 24 April 1771 he was entered on the books of the Marlborough guardship in the Medway as *an able seaman*. From this time his residence at Cambridge was curiously intermittent." He, however, never had an elder brother, being born but ten months after the marriage (14 Nov. 1752, at Risley, co. Derby), of his parents, and inasmuch as, at the age of 9, he, by his father's death, came into considerable estates and a large fortune, he is not likely to have contemplated taking holy orders, indeed in early life he was considered a great "buck" or "dandy," and his predilections were nautical. Also, his mother's name was Bridget (not "Anne"), and it was his *great* grandfather (not his grandfather), who by marriage with Anne (not "Alice") Borlase, brought the estates of Little Marlow and Medmenham, Bucks, and of Stratton Audley, Oxon, into the family, she being yst. sister and coheir (not "only da. and heiress") of Sir John Borlase, the 2d and last Baronet [1642].

Bucks, March 1807 to 1812, having been, soon after he came of age, *cr. a Baronet*, as above,(a) 1 June 1775. About this time he purchased Lundy Island, which he sold in 1777, when he joined the Navy "in earnest,(b) becoming Lieut., 1778; Captain, 1781; Commander, 1784. He was made Groom of the Bedchamber to H.R.H. the Duke of Clarence in 1787. On 23 April 1794, being then in command of a frigate squadron, he captured three French vessels, for which service he was made **K.B.**, 30 May 1794 (becoming consequently **G.C.B.** in 1815), and later in that year, June to Oct. 1794, had charge of the naval arrangements to support the French Royalists in their expedition to Quiberon bay. In 1796 "he destroyed, captured or recaptured no fewer than 220 sail,"(b) and in Oct. 1798 intercepted and defeated the French fleet off Ireland; his last naval service being the capture of a French 74 gun ship in 1806. He was Rear-Admiral, 1799; Vice-Admiral, 1805, and Admiral, 31 July 1810. He was P.C., 8 Sep. 1802, and was Ambassador to the Court of Russia, 1802 to 1804, being finally Commander in Chief on the North American station, 1813 to 1814. He was *cr.* D.C.L. of Oxford, 16 June 1814. He *m.* 12 Dec. 1780, at St. Geo. Han. sq., Caroline, yst. da. of Lieut.-Gen. Sir John CLAVERING, **K.B.**, by Diana, da. of John (WEST), 1st EARL DELAWARR. He *d.* s.p.m.s.(c) at Greenwich Hospital (when on a visit), 27 Feb. 1822, and was *bur.* at Stratton Audley aforesaid, aged 68, when the *Baronetcy* became *extinct*. Will pr. 1822. His widow *d.* 28 Dec. 1839, at Stapleford Hall, Notts, and was *bur.* with him. Will pr. Feb. 1840.

BOYD:

cr. 2 June 1775;

ex. Feb. 1889.

I. 1775. "JOHN BOYD, Esq.,"(d) of Danson, co. Kent,(e) only s. of John Augustus BOYD, of London, by Lucy (*m.* 3 Jan. 1717), da. of Judge PETERS, of the island of St. Christopher, was *b.* 29 Dec. 1718; matric. at Oxford (Ch. Ch.), 16 Feb. 1736/7, then aged 18, and was *cr. a Baronet*, as above, 2 June 1775. He *m.* firstly, 27 June 1749, Mary, da. of William BUMSTED, of Upton, co. Warwick. He *m.* secondly, 1 Aug. 1766, Catherine, da. of the Rev. John CHAPONE, of Charlton, co. Gloucester. He *d.* 24 Jan. 1800. Will pr. Feb. 1800. His widow *d.* 8 March 1813.

(a) "Being by the death of his father the representative of the Borlase family, the Baronetcy [*cr.* 4 May 1642; *ex.* 1 Feb. 1688/9] was restored [*i.e.* created afresh] in his person" [*Dict. Nat. Biogr.*] He, however, though he inherited all the Borlase estates, was but a coheir of that family. See p. 183, note "d," and see (more fully) vol. ii, p. 170, note "a," under "BORLASE."
(b) *Dict. Nat. Biogr.*, where his former fitful career in the Navy, beginning as early as 1771 (see note "b" above), is given in full.
(c) George John Borlase Warren, Ensign in the Coldstream Guards, the 1st, but last surv. son, *b.* 12 Aug. 1783, at Little Marlow, *d.* unm. and v.p., being slain at the landing of the troops at Aboukir, 8 March 1801, aged 17. Frances Maria, Baroness Vernon, the only surv. da. and h., who inherited not only her father's estates, but those of Sir George Warren, **K.B.**, of Poynton, in Cheshire, and who, accordingly, took the name of Warren, *d.* 17 Sep. 1837, aged 53, leaving issue.
(d) See p. 183, note "c," under "WARREN."
(e) This estate "was vested by an Act of Parl. in John Boyd, Esq.," who soon afterwards erected thereon "a most elegant mansion of Portland stone and gave it the name of Danson Hill" [Playfair's *Baronetage*, 1811]. What his services had been to the Government whereby, apparently, he obtained this grant and the subsequent Baronetcy, is unknown.

II. 1800. SIR JOHN BOYD, Baronet [1775], of Danson aforesaid, 1st s. and h. by 1st wife, *b.* 27 Oct. 1750, at Bath; matric. at Oxford (Ch. Ch.) 8 June 1768, aged 17; *cr.* M.A., 3 Nov. 1772; M.P. for Wareham, 1780; *suc. to the Baronetcy*, 24 Jan. 1800, and shortly afterwards sold the Danson estate. He *m.* 26 Feb. 1784, Margaret, 5th da. and coheir of the Hon. Thomas HARLEY, sometime (1767-68) Lord Mayor of London (3d son of the 3rd EARL OF OXFORD AND MORTIMER), by Anne, da. of Edward BANGHAM. He *d.* 30 May 1815, aged 64. His widow *d.* at Isleworth, 20 Nov. 1830, aged (also) 64. Will pr. Dec. 1830.

III. 1815. SIR JOHN BOYD, Baronet, [1775], 1st s. and h., *b.* 5 June 1786, *suc. to the Baronetcy*, 30 May 1815. He *m.* 22 Sep. 1818, Harriet, 2d da. (whose issue became heir) of Hugh BOYD, of Ballycastle, co. Antrim, sometime (1794-96) M.P. [I.] for that county, by Rose, da. and coheir of Alexander BOYD, of Ballycastle aforesaid, by Anna Maria, da. of Archibald (ACHESON), 1st VISCOUNT GOSFORD [I.]. He *d.* 19 Jan. 1855, at Boulogne-sur-Mer, aged 68. His widow *d.* 27 April 1864, at 9 Eaton square, in her 72d year.

IV. 1855. SIR JOHN AUGUSTUS HUGH BOYD, Baronet, [1775], 1st s. and h., *b.* 30 July 1819; entered the Royal Navy and was at the taking of St. Jean d'Acre, 1840; Lieut., 1845; *suc. to the Baronetcy*, 19 Jan. 1855. He *m.* 14 May 1850, Honora Mary, 3d da. of Charles Biggs CALMADY, of Langdown Hall, Devon. He *d.* 7 Aug. 1857, aged 38. Admon. Dec. 1857. His widow *d.* 7 March 1875, at Ballycastle aforesaid.

V. 1857. SIR HARLEY HUGH BOYD, Baronet [1775], of Drumawillen, Ballycastle, co. Antrim, only s. and h., *b.* 2 Nov. 1853; *suc. to the Baronetcy*, 7 Aug. 1857. He *d.* unm. 2 June 1876, aged 22, on board the "Teuton," off the coast of St. Helena.

VI. 1876, to 1889. SIR FREDERICK BOYD, Baronet [1775], of the Manor House, Ballycastle, uncle and h. male, *b.* 13 Aug. 1820 in Westm.; ed. at Charterhouse; matric at Oxford (Univ. Coll.), 30 May 1839, aged 18; B.A. and 4th Class Classics, 1843; in Holy Orders; Rector of Wouldham, Kent, 1854; Rector of Holwell, Beds, 1865-75; *suc. to the Baronetcy*, 2 June 1876. He *m.* firstly, 1 Aug. 1864, Katherine Mary, only child of William Henry BEAUCLERK, of Leckhampstead, Bucks, by his 1st wife, Catherine Frances, da. of George (ASHBURNHAM), 3d EARL OF ASHBURNHAM. She *d.* 3 Aug. 1867. He *m.* secondly, 24 Jan. 1872, Alice Emily Barbara, da. of the Rev. Heneage DRUMMOND, by Cecil Elizabeth, da. of Andrew Mortimer DRUMMOND. He *d.* s.p.m. Feb. 1889, at Ballycastle aforesaid, aged 68, when the *Baronetcy* became *extinct*. His widow *d.* 23 Feb. 1890, at Maple's Hotel, Dublin.

LEITH:

cr. 21 Nov. 1775;

afterwards, since 1877, LEITH-BUCHANAN.

I. 1775. "ALEXANDER [sometimes called ALEXANDER CHARLES GEORGE] LEITH, of Burgh St. Peter, co. Norfolk, Esq.,"(a) s. of Alexander LEITH, Commander of the Artillery at the siege of Havanna, and there slain, 1763, by Anne, relict of John MILET, of co. Antrim, was Lieut.-Col. 88th Foot; M.P. for Tregony, 1774-80, and was, presumably for his military services, *cr. a Baronet*, as above, 21 Nov. 1775. He *m.* firstly, Margaret, widow of (—) WREN, da. of Thomas HAY, of Huntington, Senator of the College of Justice [S.]. By her he had no issue.(b) He *m.* secondly, 1 March 1775 (—), da. of Gen. Sir John COPE, **K.B.**,(b) by Jane, yr. da. and coheir of Anthony (DUNCOMBE), BARON FEVERSHAM OF DOWNTON.(c) He *d.* 3 Oct. 1780, in Jamaica, of excessive fatigue while commanding an Expedition to the Spanish Main. Will pr. April 1782.

(a) See p. 183, note "c," under "WARREN."
(b) Playfair's *Baronetage*, 1811.
(c) *N. & Q.*, 9th S., vi, 133.

II. 1780. SIR GEORGE ALEXANDER WILLIAM LEITH, Baronet [1775], of Burgh St. Peter aforesaid, 1st and only surv. s. and h. by 1st wife, *b.* about 1765; *suc. to the Baronetcy*, 3 Oct. 1780, having been appointed Ensign, 88th Foot, and having served in Jamaica in 1779. In 1786 he was at Madras, and served during the whole of the subsequent war, at the sieges of Bangalor and Sevendroog, the storming of Tippoo's lines and the surrender of Seringapatam; was Governor of Penang, 1800-06, becoming finally, 1819, Major-Gen. in the Army, and Col. of the 9th Royal Veteran Battalion. He *m.* 10 Dec. 1798, Albinia, yst. da. of Thomas Wright VAUGHAN, of Moulsey, Surrey. He *d.* 25 Jan 1842, in Portman Street, Marylebone, aged 76. Will p. Feb. 1842. His widow *d.* eight days later, 2 Feb. 1842, Will pr. March 1842.

III. 1842, Jan. SIR ALEXANDER WELLESLEY WILLIAM LEITH, Baronet [1775], 1st s. and h., *b.* 30 Oct. 1806; *suc. to the Baronetcy*, 25 Jan. 1842. He *m.* Oct. 1832, Jemima Jean, 2d da. of Hector Macdonald BUCHANAN, of Ross, co. Dumbarton. He *d.*, shortly after his parents, 3 April 1842, aged 35. His widow, who had assumed the name of LEITH-BUCHANAN instead of that of LEITH, *d.* 6 Aug. 1877, at 41 Melville street, Edinburgh, aged 70.

IV. 1842, April. SIR GEORGE HECTOR LEITH, *afterwards*, from 1877, LEITH-BUCHANAN, Baronet [1775], 1st s. and h., *b.* 10 Aug. 1833; *suc. to the Baronetcy*, 3 April 1842; sometime, 1855-59; Captain 17th Light Dragoons; Major 1st Batt. Dumbartonshire Rifle Volunteers, 1860. On the death of his mother in 1877 and his succession to the estates of her family, he assumed the name of LEITH-BUCHANAN instead of that of LEITH. He *m.* firstly, 1 March 1856, at Hove, Sussex, Ella Maria, 1st da. of David Barclay CHAPMAN, of Downshire House, Roehampton, Surrey. She *d.* s.p.m., 10 Feb. 1857, in Charlotte square, Edinburgh, aged 23. He *m.* secondly, 24 April 1864, Eliza Caroline, da. and h. of Thomas TOD, of Drygrange, near Melrose. She *d.* 1 May 1899, at 18 Great Stuart street, Edinburgh. He *d.* at Ross Priory, co. Dumbarton, 29 Sep. 1903, aged 70.

V. 1903. SIR ALEXANDER WELLESLEY GEORGE THOMAS LEITH-BUCHANAN, Baronet [1775], of Ross Priory and Drygrange aforesaid, 1st s. and h., *b.* 5 Dec. 1866; *suc. to the Baronetcy*, 29 Sep. 1903. He *m.* 19 Jan. 1888, at Craufurdland Castle, Kilmarnock, Maude Mary, da. of Alexander GRANT, of Glasgow, merchant.

Family Estates.—These, in 1883, consisted of 1,778 acres in Dumbartonshire, 1,315 in Roxburghshire, 1,314 in Stirlingshire, and 128 in Berwickshire. *Total.*—4,535 acres; worth £3,837 a year.. *Principal Seats.*—Ross Priory, co. Dumbarton, and Drygrange, near Melrose.

ETHERINGTON:

cr. 22 Nov. 1775;

ex. 16 Aug. 1819.

I. 1775 to 1819. "HENRY ETHERINGTON, of Kingston-upon-Hull [co. York, Esq.,(a) only s. and h. of Henry ETHERINGTON, of the same, merchant, by Jane, da. of (—) PORTER, had an estate at North Ferriby, near Hull, and was *cr.* a Baronet as aforesaid, 22 Nov. 1775. He *m.* 1 June 1773, Maria Constantia, 4th da. of Sir Thomas CAVE,(b) 5th Baronet [1641], of Stanford, by Elizabeth, da. and h. of Griffith DAVIES, M.D. He *d.* s.p., 16 Aug. 1819, when *the Baronetcy became extinct.* Will pr. 1819.

(a) See p. 183, note "c," under "WARREN."
(b) In Playfair's *Baronetage* [1811], she is (erroneously) called the "da. of Sir Thomas Carr, Baronet, and sister of the present Sir Charles." This error is repeated in the *Gent. Mag.* for 1819. See *N. & Q.*, 7th S., xi, 193.

HAMILTON:

cr. 24 or 26 Aug. 1776.

I. 1776. "JOHN HAMILTON, of Marlborough House, Portsmouth, co. Southampton, Esq., Captain of His Majesty's ship Hector,"(a) 3d s. of John HAMILTON, of Chilston, or Bocton place, near Lenham, Kent (Sheriff of Kent, 1719), by Mary, da. of John WRIGHT, M.D., of London (which John HAMILTON was s. and h. of William HAMILTON, of Chilston aforesaid, yr. br. of James, 6th EARL OF ABERCORN [S.]), was *b.* 21 Feb. 1725/6, at Chilston; entered the Royal Navy, serving on the Newfoundland station, 1764-69; was sent to Quebec in 1775, and, for his gallant conduct during the siege thereof, received the thanks of Parl. and was *cr. a Baronet*, as above, 24 or 26 Aug. 1776. He was Commander of a guard ship at Portsmouth, 1776-78, and subsequently, for two years, Admiral on the Jamaica station. He *m.* 4 Oct. 1763, Cassandra Agnes, 3d da. of Edmund CHAMBERLAYNE, of Maugersbury, co. Gloucester. He *d.* 24 Jan. 1784, aged 57. Will pr. March 1784. His widow *d.* 26 Oct. 1821. Will pr. 1821.

II. 1784. SIR CHARLES HAMILTON, Baronet [1776], 1st s. and h., *b.* 25 May 1767; entered the Royal Navy, 1776, and *suc. to the Baronetcy*, 24 Jan. 1784; was at the sieges of Bastia, Calvi and San Fiorenzo in 1794; in command on the coast of Holland in 1779, and at the reduction of Goree in 1800; Rear-Admiral, 1810; Vice-Admiral, 1814; Governor of Newfoundland, 1818-24; Admiral, 1830; **K.C.B.**, 29 Jan. 1833. He was also M.P. for St. Germans, Feb. to June 1790; for Dungannon, Nov. 1801 to June 1802, and June 1803 to 1806; and for Honiton, 1807-12. He *m.* 19 April 1803, at Brompton chapel (spec. lic.) Henrietta Maria, da. of George DRUMMOND, of Stanmore, Midx., banker of London, by Martha, da. of the Hon. Thomas HARLEY, sometime Lord Mayor of London. He *d.* 14 Sep. 1849, at his residence, Iping, near Midhurst, Sussex, aged 82. Will pr. Sep. 1849. His widow *d.* 10 March 1857. Will pr. March 1857.

III. 1849. SIR CHARLES JOHN JAMES HAMILTON, Baronet, [1776], of Iping aforesaid, only s. and h., *b.* 3 April 1810; ed. at Charterhouse; *suc. to the Baronetcy*, 14 Sep. 1849; sometime (1854) Major Scots Fusileer Guards, distinguished himself at the battle of the Alma, Sep. 1854, but retired in 1855 as Lieut.-Colonel; **C.B.**, 1855. He *m.* 14 Dec. 1833, Catherine Emily, 2d da. of William Henry WYNNE, of Dublin, by Eleanora Emilia, da. of Sir Samuel BRADSTREET, 3d Baronet [I. 1759]. She *d.* 25 May 1879, in Devonshire place, Marylebone, aged 66. He *d.* there s.p., 23 Jan. 1892, aged 81. Will pr. at £188,242.

IV. 1892. SIR EDWARD ARCHIBALD HAMILTON, Baronet [1776 and 1819], of Iping aforesaid, cousin and h., being only s. and h. of John James HAMILTON, Lieut. 83d Foot, by Favoretta, da. of Panton CORBETT, of Longnor Hall, Salop, which John James (who *d.* v.p. 2 Nov. 1847, aged 29) was 1st s. and h. ap. of Admiral Sir Edward Joseph HAMILTON, 1st Baronet [1819], **K.C.B.** (*d.* 20 March 1851, aged 79), who was 2d son of the 1st Baronet of the creation of 1776. He was *b.* 26 Jan. 1843, and *suc. to the Baronetcy* [1819] on the death of his grandfather abovementioned, 20 March 1851; was sometime, 1865-67, Capt. in the Coldstream Guards; Hon. Col. 2d Vol. Batt. Cameronians. He *suc. to the Baronetcy* [1776] on the death of his cousin abovementioned, 23 Jan. 1892. He *m.* 28 May 1867, at Hengoed church, Salop, Mary Elizabeth, only da. of Joseph GILL, of Trewerne, Salop, and Burley, co. York.

Family Estates.—These, in 1883 (being those of the 3d Baronet), consisted of 2,969 acres in Sussex and Pembrokeshire, valued at £2,785 a year. *Seat.*—Iping, near Midhurst, Sussex.

(a) See p. 113, note "a," under "GIDEON." The date of the Gazette notice for Hamilton is 6 July, for Winne, Mackworth, Laroche, Peyton and Baker, 24 Aug., and for Eden, 10 Sep. 1776.

WINN, *or* WINNE:

cr. 14 Sep. 1776;

afterwards, since 1777, ALLANSON-WINN, *or* WINN-ALLANSON;

and since 1797, LORDS HEADLEY, BARONS ALLANSON AND WINN OF AGHADOE [I.].

I. 1776. "GEORGE WINNE, of Little Warley, co. Essex, Esq., late one of the Barons of His Majesty's Court of Exchequer in Scotland,"(a) only s. and h. of Pelham WINN, of South Ferraby, co. Lincoln, by Elizabeth, da. of the Rev. Gilbert WIGHTON (which Pelham was s. of George WINN, 2d s. of Sir George WINN, 1st Baronet [1660], of Nostell, co. York), was *b.* 1725; admitted to Lincoln's Inn, 24 Feb. 1743/4; Barrister, 1755; suc. to the estate of Little Warley (by the death of his cousin, Mark WINN) in 1763; was one of the Barons of the Exchequer in Scotland, 1761 to 1766; and was *cr. a Baronet*, as above, 14 Sep. 1776. Having, by the death of his cousin Charles ALLANSON,(b) suc. to the estate of Bramham Biggin, near Tadcaster, co. York, he, by royal lic. 20 Feb. 1777, took the name of ALLANSON, which he used, apparently before that of WINN. He was M.P. for Ripon (three Parls.), Sep. 1789 till death, 9 April 1798. He *m.* firstly, 12 April 1765, at Wragby, co. York, Anne, 4th da. of his cousin, Sir Rowland WINN, 4th Baronet [1660], of Nostell, by Susanna, da. of Charles HENSHAW, of Eltham, Kent. She, who was *bap.* 31 Dec. 1734 at Wragby, *d.* s.p.m. 9 Oct. 1774. He *m.* secondly, 24 June 1783, at St. Geo. Han. sq., Jane, 1st da. and coheir of Arthur BLENNERHASSETT, of Ballyseedy, co. Kerry, by Jane, da. of (—) GIRARDOT. She was living when he was *cr.*, 14 Nov. 1797, LORD HEADLEY, BARON ALLANSON AND WINN OF AGHADOE, co. Kerry [I.]. In that peerage this *Baronetcy* then *merged*, and still [1905] so continues. See "*Peerage.*"

MACKWORTH:

cr. 16 Sep. 1776.

I. 1776. "HERBERT MACKWORTH, of the Gnoll [near Neath], co. Glamorgan Esq.,"(a) as also of Glen Usk, co. Monmouth, only s. and h. of Herbert MACKWORTH, of the same, many years (1739-65) M.P. for Neath (*d.* 20 Aug. 1765, aged 77), by Juliana, da. of William (DIGBY), 5th BARON DIGBY OF GEASHILL [I.], was *b.* 1 Jan. 1736/7, at Coleshill, co. Warwick; matric. at Oxford (Magdalen Coll.), 15 Dec. 1753, aged 16; B.A. 1757; M.A., 1760; Barrister (Lincoln's Inn), 1759; M.P. for Cardiff (five Parls.), Jan. 1766 to 1790, and was *cr. a Baronet*, as above, 16 Sep. 1776. He was Col. of the Glamorgan Militia, a Vice-President of the Marine Society, and F.R.S. He *m.* in 1759, Elizabeth, only da. of Robert TREFUSIS, of Trefusis, Cornwall, by Elizabeth, da. of Gilbert AFFLECK, of Dalham, Suffolk. He *d.* of blood poisoning, 25 Oct. 1791, aged 54.(c) Will pr. Oct. 1791. His widow, who was *b.* 24 Jan. 1738, *d.* 19 Dec. 1799. M.I. at St. Cuthbert's, Wells, Somerset. Will pr. Feb. 1800.

(a) See p. 187, note "a," under "HAMILTON."
(b) This Charles was only s. and h. of William Allanson, whose sister Elizabeth *m.* the Rev. Gilbert Wighton, and was maternal grandmother of George Winn, the grantee.
(c) Caused by the non-extraction of a thorn. Full particulars are given in Playfair's *Baronetage* [1811].

II. 1791. SIR ROBERT HUMPHREY MACKWORTH, Baronet [1776], of Gnoll aforesaid, 1st s. and h., *b.* 16 Nov. 1764; *suc. to the Baronetcy*, 25 Oct 1791. He *m.* 6 Dec. 1792, Mary Anne, da. of Nathaniel MYERS, of Neath, and of Richmond, Surrey. He *d.* s.p. 13 Sep. 1795, in his 31st year. Will pr. 1795. His widow, to whom he devised Gnoll Castle(a) and other estates, *m.* 14 Sep. 1797, Capel Hanbury LEIGH, of Pontypool, co. Monmouth (who *d.* 28 Sep. 1861), and *d.* 27 June 1846.

III. 1794. SIR DIGBY MACKWORTH, Baronet [1776], of Glen Usk aforesaid, br. and h., *b.* 14 May 1766, at Marylebone; matric. at Oxford (Magdalen Coll.), 17 July 1788, aged 22, and was *cr.* D.C.L., 18 June 1799, having *suc. to the Baronetcy*, 13 Sep. 1794; Lieut.-Col. of the Oxford City Loyal Volunteers, 1798 and 1803-04. He *m.* firstly, in 1788, at Cadoxton, co. Glamorgan, Jane, da. and h. of the Rev. Matthew DEERE, of Cadoxton Place, by Margaret, da. and coheir of Anthony MADDOCKS, of Cefn-yd-fa, co. Glamorgan. She *d.* 11 Jan. 1808. Admon. Oct. 1821. He *m.* secondly, 10 July 1821, Philippa, sister of Sir Robert AFFLECK, 4th Baronet [1782], 3d da. of the Rev. James AFFLECK, Rector of Finedon, co. Northampton, by Mary, da. of (—) PROCTOR. He *d.* 2 May 1838, aged 71. Will pr. May 1838. His widow *d.* s.p., 18 July 1851, in Upper Bedford place, Bloomsbury, aged 84. Will pr. July 1861.

IV. 1838. SIR DIGBY MACKWORTH, Baronet [1776], of Glen Usk aforesaid, 1st s. and h., *b.* 13 June 1789, at Oxford; entered the Army, serving through the Peninsular War, and at Waterloo, becoming finally, 1851, Colonel; sometime Aide-de-Camp to Lord Hill; **K.H.**, 1832; *suc. to the Baronetcy*, 2 May 1838. He *m.* firstly, 16 Sep. 1816, Marie Alexandrine Ignatie Julie, only da. of Gen. and the Baroness DE RICHEPANSE, and niece to the Duc DE DAMAS-CRUX. She *d.* 1818. He *m.* secondly, 3 April 1823, Sophia Noel, da. of James MANN, of Egerton Lodge, Lenham, Kent, by Lucy, da. and coheir of Sir Horatio MANN, 2d and last Baronet [1755], of Linton in that county. He *d.* 23 Dec. 1852, at Glen Usk, aged 63. Will pr. Dec. 1852. His widow *d.* 5 Jan. 1882, at 5 Litfield Place, Clifton, by Bristol, aged 81.

V. 1852. SIR DIGBY FRANCIS MACKWORTH, Baronet [1776], of Glen Usk aforesaid, 1st s. and h., being only s. by 1st wife, *b.* 7 July 1817, at the Chateau de Beauval, Manières, near Cambrai, in France; ed. at Stanmore, Midx.; sometime, 1834-44, Ensign 90th Foot; *suc. to the Baronetcy*, 23 Dec. 1852. He *m.* in 1840, Mathilde Eleanor Eliza, 2d da. of Lieut.-Col. PEDDLE, **K.H.**, 90th Light Infantry. He *d.* 8 Sep. 1857, at Douglas, Isle of Man, aged 40. Will pr. Nov. 1857. His widow living 1905.

VI. 1857. SIR ARTHUR WILLIAM MACKWORTH, Baronet [1776], of Glen Usk aforesaid, 1st s. and h., *b.* 5 Oct. 1842, at Chatham; *suc. to the Baronetcy*, 8 Sep. 1857; Lieut. Royal Engineers, 1861; Capt. 1873; Major 1881, serving, in 1882, in the Egyptian Campaign (3d Class Medjidie); Lieut.-Col. 1882, and Col. 1886, commanding the Royal Engineers in the South Wales district, 1883-88; in the West Indies, 1888-89, and at Aldershot, 1894-99. He *m.* 18 Oct. 1865, at the British Embassy, Paris, Alice Kate, yr. da. of Joseph CUBITT, of Park street, Westminster, Civil Engineer.

Family Estates.—These, in 1883, consisted of 1,861 acres in Monmouthshire, and 1,342 in Glamorganshire. *Total.*—3,203 acres, worth £3,649 a year. *Seat.*—Glen Usk, near Bridgend, South Wales.

(a) See, as to the Gnoll estate, Playfair's *Baronetage*, [1811].

LAROCHE:

cr. 17 Sep. 1776;

ex., or *dormant*, on death of grantee, 1803-05.

I. 1776, to 1804? "JAMES LAROCHE, of Over, in the parish of Almondsbury, co. Gloucester, Esq.,"(a) yr. s. of John LAROCHE, of Englefield Green, Surrey, sometime (1727-52), M.P. for Bodmin (*d.* 20 April 1752), by Elizabeth, da. of Isaac GARNIER, of Westminster, a well-known Apothecary, was *b.* in Pall Mall and *bap.* 24 June 1734, at St. James', Westm.; had estates in Cornwall and South Wales; was M.P. for Bodmin, 1768-80, and was *cr. a Baronet*, as above, 17 Sep. 1776. He *m.* firstly, Dec. 1764, Elizabeth Rachel Anne, widow of (—) ARCHIBALD, da. and h. of William YEOMANS, of Antigua. She, by whom he had no issue, *d.* 27 Jan. 1781. Will pr. 1 Feb. 1781. He *m.* secondly, Elizabeth, da. of (—). He *d.*, presumably s.p. legit.,(a) between March 1803 and March 1805, aged about 70, when the *Baronetcy* became *extinct* or *dormant*. Will as "of Pyle, co. Glamorgan, Baronet," dated 27 March 1803, pr. 1 March 1805, by his widow, and executrix.(b)

PEYTON:

cr. 18 Sep. 1776.

I. 1776. "HENRY PEYTON, of Doddington, in the isle of Ely [co. Cambridge], Esq.,"(a) 1st s. and h. of George DASHWOOD,(c) (*d.* March 1762), by Margaret, da. of Sir Sewster PEYTON, 2d Baronet [1667], and sister of Sir Thomas PEYTON, 3d and last Baronet [1667], of Doddington aforesaid, having suc. on the death, 29 June 1771, of his said maternal uncle to the above estate,(d) took the name of PEYTON instead of that of DASHWOOD, by Act of Parl. 1771, and was *cr. a Baronet*, as above. 18 Sep. 1776. He was M.P. for Cambridgeshire, June 1782 till his death in 1789. He *m.* Dec. 1771, Frances, sister of John, 1st EARL OF STRADBROKE, 1st da. of Sir John ROUS, 5th Baronet [1660], by Judith, da. and h. of John BEDINGFELD. He *d.* May 1789. Will pr. 1789. His widow *d.* 27 May 1808. Will pr. 1808.

II. 1789. SIR HENRY PEYTON, Baronet, [1776], of Doddington aforesaid, and of Swift's House, near Bicester, Oxon, 1st s. and h., *b.* 1 July 1779, at Narborough Hall, near Swaffham, Norfolk; *suc. to the Baronetcy*, May 1789; matric. at Oxford (Ch. Ch.), 27 Jan. 1797, aged 17; *cr.* M.A., 2 May 1800; M.P. for Cambridgeshire for a few months (after a severe contest) May to June 1802; Sheriff of that county, 1808-09; was a keen sportsman and a first rate "whip," being a member of the old "Four-in-hand-Club." He *m.* 7 July 1803, at St. Geo. Han. sq., Harriet, widow of James BRADSHAW, of Portland place, da. of James FITZHUGH. He *d.* 24 Feb. 1854, at Swift's House aforesaid, aged 74. Will pr. June 1854. His widow *d.* there 26 Aug. 1857, aged 83.

III. 1854. SIR HENRY PEYTON, Baronet, [1776], of Doddington, and of Swift's House aforesaid, only s. and h., *b.* 30 June 1804, in Grafton street, St. Geo. Han. sq.; ed. at Harrow; matric. at Oxford (Ch. Ch.),

(a) See p. 187, note "a," under "HAMILTON."

(b) In his will, though he leaves all his personalty to his wife, he devises all his estates in Cornwall and elsewhere to "my son, James Laroche, Esq., now an Ensign in H.M.'s 46th Regt. of Foot," and there is nothing in it to throw doubt on his legitimacy, which indeed the word "Esq." (if used properly) would imply.

(c) This George was s. of Lieut.-Col. George Dashwood, by Angelina, da. of Sir Algernon Peyton, 1st Baronet [1667], of Doddington, being br. of Sir Robert Dashwood, 1st Baronet [1684], of Kirtlington.

(d) See vol. iv, p. 41, note "b."

29 April 1822, aged 17; sometime an officer in the 1st Life Guards; M.P. for Woodstock, 1837-38; *suc. to the Baronetcy*, 24 Feb. 1854. He *m.* 18 April 1828, Georgiana Elizabeth, 2d da. of Christopher BETHELL-CODRINGTON, of Dodington, co. Gloucester (*styling* himself a Baronet [1721]), by Caroline Georgiana Harriett, da. of Thomas (FOLEY), 2d BARON FOLEY OF KIDDERMINSTER. He *d.* 18 Feb. 1866, at Swift's House aforesaid, aged 61. His widow *d.* there, a few months later, 6 Nov. 1866, aged 67.

IV. 1866. SIR ALGERNON WILLIAM PEYTON, Baronet, [1776], of Doddington and of Swift's House aforesaid, 2d but only surv. s. and h., *b.* 13 April 1833, at Woodstock, Oxon; entered the Army, 1851; Capt. 1st Life Guards, 1856; *suc. to the Baronetcy*, 18 Feb. 1866; Sheriff of Oxon, 1870-71. He *m.*(a) 24 Nov. 1870, at St. Peter's, Onslow Gardens, Laura Sarah, yst. da. of Daniel Hale WEBB, of Wykeham park, Oxon. He *d.* s.p., 25 March 1872 (of a fit) at the King's Arms Hotel, Bicester, aged 39. His widow *m.* 30 Jan. 1878, at St. Peter's, Eaton square, Arthur (ANNESLEY), 11th VISCOUNT VALENTIA [I.], and was living, as his wife, 1905.

V. 1872. SIR THOMAS PEYTON, Baronet [1776], of Doddington and of Swifts House aforesaid, cousin and heir, being 2d but last surv. s.(b) of the Rev. Algernon PEYTON, Rector of Doddington, co. Cambridge, by Isabella Anne, da. of Thomas HUSSEY, of Galtrim, in Ireland, which Algernon (who *d.* 1 Nov. 1868, aged 82) was 2d s. of the 1st Baronet. He was *b.* 9 July 1817; ed. at Addiscombe; entered the Army, 1838, serving in the Madras service, and obtaining, in 1873, the honorary rank of Major General. He *suc. to the Baronetcy*, 25 March 1872, and was Sheriff of Oxon 1881. He *m.* 3 Nov. 1852, at Bellary, in India, Lucy, da. of William WATTS, of the Madras Civil Service. He *d.* 18 Feb. 1888, at Swifts House aforesaid, aged 70. His widow living 1905.

VI. 1888. SIR ALGERNON FRANCIS PEYTON, Baronet [1776], of Doddington and of Swifts House aforesaid, 1st s. and h., *b.* 24 Nov. 1855; Lieut. 11th Hussars, 1876, retiring as Capt.; *suc. to the Baronetcy*, 18 Feb. 1888; sometime Lieut. Col. Oxon Yeomanry; Sheriff of Oxon, 1896. He *m.* 11 Jan. 1888, at St. Geo., Han. sq., Ida Fanny, 3d da. of James MASON, of Eynsham Hall, Oxon.

Family Estates.—These, in 1883, consisted of 1,977 acres in Oxon, 1,375 in Cambridgeshire, and 606 in Huntingdonshire. *Total*—3,958 acres, worth £6,793 a year. *Residence.*—Swifts House, near Bicester, Oxon.

BAKER:

cr. 19 Sep. 1776;

afterwards, since 1882, RHODES.

I. 1776. "GEORGE BAKER, Dr. of Physic and Physician in Ordinary to Her Majesty,"(c) being also of Loventor in Totnes, Devon, s. of the Rev. George BAKER, Archdeacon of Totnes and Vicar of Modbury, Devon, by (—), da. of Stephen WESTON, D.D., Bishop of Exeter, was *b.* in Devon about 1723; ed. at Eton and at King's Coll., Cambridge, of which he was sometime a Fellow; B.A., 1745; M.A., 1749; M.D., 1756; Fellow of the

(a) It is stated in Dod's *Baronetage* for 1866, that he had "*m.* in 1864 (—) da. of (—) Isherwood." No mention, however, of this marriage is made in subsequent editions of that work or, apparently, elsewhere.

(b) The eldest son, Algernon Francis Peyton, *b.* at Secunderabad in the East Indies, 27 Sep. 1814; matric. at Oxford (Mag. Coll.), 18 April 1874; took Holy Orders, and was Rector of Lachford, Suffolk, 1845 till his death, unm., 19 Jan. 1853.

(c) See p. 187, note "a," under "HAMILTON."

Coll. of Physicians, London, 1757, of which, subsequently, he was for many years (1785-90, 1792-93, and 1795) President. He at first practised at Stamford, co. Lincoln, but removed about 1761 to London, becoming successively Physician to the household of the Queen Consort, Physician in Ordinary to herself, in or before 1776, and finally to the King, having been *cr. a Baronet*, as above, 19 Sep. 1776. F.R.S., F.S.A., and a first rate Greek and Latin Scholar. He retired from practice 1798. He *m.* 28 June 1768, at St. James', Westm., Jane, da. of Roger MORRIS, of York, by his 2d wife, Elizabeth, da. of Philip JACKSON, of London, Turkey Merchant, and Jane his wife, da. of Sir Peter VANDEPUT. He *d.* 15 and was *bur.* 24 June 1809, at St. James' aforesaid, in his 87th year. M.I. Will pr. 1809. His widow *d.* 13 July 1813. Will pr. 1813.

II. 1809. SIR FREDERICK FRANCIS BAKER Baronet [1776], of Loventor aforesaid, only s. and h., *b.* in Jermyn street, 13 May and *bap.* 17 June 1772, at St. James', Westm.; matric. at Oxford (Balliol Coll.), 4 Feb. 1791, aged 18; B.A., 1792; M.A., 1796; *suc. to the Baronetcy*, 15 June 1809. F.R.S. and F.S.A. He *m.* in July 1814, Harriet, 3d da. of Sir John SIMEON, 1st Baronet [1815], by Rebecca, da. of John CORNWALL, of Hendon, Midx. He *d.* 1 Oct. 1830, at Hastings, aged 58, through a blow from one of the fans of a windmill. Will pr. Oct. 1830 and March 1846. His widow *d.* 15 Nov. 1845, in Wilton crescent. Will pr. Feb. 1846.

III. 1830. SIR GEORGE BAKER, Baronet [1776], of Loventor aforesaid, 1st s. and h., *b.* 16 June 1816 in Paris; *suc. to the Baronetcy*, 1 Oct. 1830; matric. at Oxford (Ch. Ch.), 14 May 1834, aged 17; B.A. and 3d Class Classics, 1837; admitted to Lincoln's Inn, 7 March 1836. He *m.* firstly, 2 June 1840, at St. Geo. Han. sq., Mary Isabella, 2d da. of Robert Nassau SUTTON (yr. s. of Sir Richard SUTTON, 1st Baronet [1772]), by Mary Georgiana, da. of John MANNERS-SUTTON, of Kelham, Notts. She *d.* 6 May 1855, at Northerwood, near Lyndhurst. He *m.* secondly, 16 Nov. 1858, at St. John's, Paddington, Augusta Catherine, 2d da. of Sir Robert FITZWYGRAM, *formerly* WIGRAM, 2d Baronet [1805], by Selina, da. of Sir John Macnamara HAYES, 1st Baronet [1797]. He *d.* 27 Aug. 1882, at Woodhouse, near Axminster, Devon, aged 66. His widow, by whom he had no issue, *d.* there 13 Nov. 1893. Will pr. over £28,000 personalty.

IV. 1882. SIR FREDERICK EDWARD RHODES, Baronet [1776], *formerly* Frederick Edward BAKER, of Ticehurst, Sussex, 1st s. and h., by 1st wife, *b.* 12 July 1843, in Brook street, Grosvenor square; ed. at Harrow; took by royal lic., 29 Oct. 1878, the name of RHODES, instead of that of BAKER, on the application of his father (his Committee), under the will of George Ambrose RHODES, of Bellair, in Heavitree, co. Devon, on the death, 6 April 1877, of the tenant for life of that estate; *suc. to the Baronetcy*, 27 Aug. 1882.

EDEN:

cr. 19 Oct. 1776;

merged, 4 Sep. 1844, in the Baronetcy of EDEN, *cr.* 13 Nov. 1672.

I. 1776. "ROBERT EDEN, Esq., Governor of Maryland,"(a) in North America, 2d s. of Sir Robert EDEN, 3d Baronet [1672], of West Auckland, by Mary, da. of William DAVISON, of Beamish, was *b.* about 1741, and, having been appointed, 10 Sep. 1776, Governor of Maryland, was *cr. a Baronet*, as above, 19 Oct. 1776. He *m.* 26 April 1763, Caroline, sister and coheir of Frederick (CALVERT), 7th BARON BALTIMORE [I.], 1st da. of Charles, 6th Baron, by Mary, da. of Sir Theodore JANSSEN, 1st Baronet [1714]. He *d.* 2 Sep. 1784. Will pr. 1784. The will of his widow was pr. 1803.

(a) See p. 187, note "a," under "HAMILTON."

II. 1784. SIR FREDERICK MORTON EDEN, Baronet [1776], of Truir, co. Durham, 1st s. and heir, *b.* about 1767, at Ashted, Surrey; matric. at Oxford (Ch. Ch.), 19 April 1783, aged 16; B.A. 1787; M.A., 1789; having *suc. to the Baronetcy*, 2 Sep. 1784; Barrister (Middle Temple), 1791. He *m.* 10 Jan. 1792, at St. Geo. Han. sq., Anne, da. and h. of James Paul SMITH, of New Bond Street. She *d.* 14 July 1808. He *d.* 14 Nov. 1809. Will pr. 1810.

III. 1809. SIR FREDERICK EDEN, Baronet [1776], of Truir aforesaid, 3d but 1st surv. s. and h., *b.* about 1798; *suc. to the Baronetcy*, 14 Nov. 1809; was an Ensign in the 85th Foot. He *d.* unm., being slain in action near New Orleans, 24 Dec. 1814. Admon. Feb. 1818.

IV. 1814. SIR WILLIAM EDEN, Baronet [1776], of Truir aforesaid, br. and h., *b.* 31 Jan. 1803; ed. at Eton; matric. at Oxford (Ch. Ch.), 10 Nov. 1821, aged 18; *suc. to the Baronetcy* [1776], 24 Dec. 1814; was Custos Brevium of the Court of King's Bench. He *m.* 23 April 1844, at Wherwell, Hants, Susanna Harriet, yst. da. of Col. William IREMONGER, of Wherewell Priory, by Pennant, da. of Rice THOMAS, of Coed Helen, co. Carnarvon. She was living when he, on the death, 4 Sep. 1844, of his cousin, Sir Robert JOHNSON-EDEN, 5th Baronet [1672], *suc. to the Baronetcy* which had been conferred, 13 Nov. 1672, on their common ancestor, Robert EDEN, of West Auckland, co. Durham. In that title this *Baronetcy* then *merged*, and still [1905] so continues.

DOUGLAS:

cr. 23 Jan. 1777.

I. 1777. CHARLES DOUGLAS, of Carr, co. Perth, Captain in the Royal Navy, 3d s. (but 1st s. who left male issue) of Charles DOUGLAS,(a) of Kinglassie, is said to have served in early life in the Dutch Navy, but was in that of England in Feb. 1746/7, being Lieut. in 1753, and Capt. in 1759. For his gallant relief, 6 May 1776, of Quebec, then closely blockaded, by forcing his passage through the ice, he was *cr. a Baronet*, as above, 23 Jan. 1777. In July 1778 he was in the action off Ushant, being Capt. of the Fleet, under Rodney; contributed to the victory off Dominica over Count de Grasse, 12 April 1782, gained in a great measure by his ship breaking the French line, for the planning of which manœuvre he is sometimes (but apparently in error) given the credit. From 1783 to 1786, he was Commander-in-Chief on the Halifax station, becoming in 1787, Rear-Admiral. He was the author of many improvements in the art of naval gunnery. He *m.* firstly, a Dutch lady, who *d.* 1769, possibly Jane, da. of John BAILLIE, which lady, however (possibly a 3d(b) wife), is sometimes given as his only wife.(c) He *m.*, in or before 1777,(d) Sarah, da. of John WOOD. She *d.* 16 and was *bur.* 23 Aug. 1779, at Gosport, Hants. He *m.* finally, 19 Nov. 1781 (spec. lic.), at the house of Mr. WARING, in Marylebone street, St. James' Westm., Jane GREW, of Gosport. He *d.*, somewhat suddenly, 17 March 1789, at Edinburgh.(e) Will pr. 1789.

(a) The descent of this Charles from Sir Archibald Douglas, of Kirkness, a yr. s. of William, Earl of Morton [S.], who *d.* 1606, is set out in Debrett's *Baronetage* for 1840, but is not given in the older ones of Betham and Playfair.

(b) See p. 194, note "c."

(c) Debrett's *Baronetage*, 1840, and Foster's *Baronetage*, 1883.

(d) One of their children, Ann Irwin, was *bap.* as da. of Sir Charles Douglas, Baronet, and Sarah, 14 Dec. 1777, at Gosport.

(e) See full particulars of his death together with a long account of his whole career in Playfair's *Baronetage* [1811].

II. 1789. SIR WILLIAM HENRY DOUGLAS, Baronet [1777], s. and h.; *suc. to the Baronetcy*, 17 March 1789; was an officer in the Royal Navy, becoming finally (1808) Rear Admiral. He *d.* unm. 25 May 1809, at Chelsea.(a) Will pr. 1809.

III. 1809. SIR HOWARD DOUGLAS, Baronet [1777], next surv. br. (possibly of the half blood) and h. male,(b) *b.* 1 July 1776, being stated to have been *b.* at Gosport(c); ed. at Woolwich; Lieut. Royal Artillery, 1794; Capt., 1804; was in command at Quebec, and employed on a mission to the Cherokees, 1797; served with Congreve's mortar brigade, 1803-04; was Commandant and Inspector General of Instruction at the Military College, High Wycombe, 1804 till 1820, but fought as Lieut.-Col. at Corunna (medal with clasp) in Jan., and at Flushing in July 1809, having *suc. to the Baronetcy*, 25 May 1809. From 1811 to 1812 he again served in Spain, being entrusted with a mission to report on the state of the Spanish troops. He became Colonel in 1814; Major General, 1821; Gov. of New Brunswick, 1823-29, where he founded the University of Fredericton; Lord High Commissioner of the Ionian Islands, 1835-40; Lieut. Gen. in the Army 1837, and finally, 1851, General; being Col. of the 99th Foot, 1841-51, and of the 15th Foot, 1851 till death. **C.B.**, 1814; **K.C.B.**, 1821, **G.C.M.G.**, 1835, and **G.C.B.** (Civil), 1841, being also a Knight of the Order of Charles III of Spain. He was also F.R.S., in 1812; F.R.G.S., and D.C.L., 1 July 1829, of Oxford; was Groom of the Bedchamber to H.R.H. the Duke of Gloucester, and was M.P. for Liverpool, 1842-47. He was author of several valuable and scientific works on military and naval subjects. He *m.* July 1799, Anne, da. of James DUNDAS, of Edinburgh. She *d.* 12 Oct. 1854, at 15 Green street, Mayfair, and was *bur.* at Boldre, near Lymington, Hants. He *d.* 9 Nov. 1861, at Tunbridge, Wells, and was *bur.* at Boldre aforesaid, aged 85. Will pr. under £16,000 personalty.

IV. 1861. SIR ROBERT PERCY DOUGLAS, Baronet, [1777], 4th but 1st surv. s. and h.,(d) *b.* 29 Aug. 1805, at High Wycombe, Bucks; entered the Army, 1820; Lieut.-Col. 29th Foot; sometime Assistant Adjutant General to the Forces; Col. of the 98th Foot, 1864, becoming finally, 1874, General in the Army, retiring in 1877; Lieut.-Gov. of Jersey, 1858-63; Lieut.-Gov. of the Cape of Good Hope, 1863-68; having *suc. to the Baronetcy*, 9 Nov. 1861. He *m.* firstly, in 1840, Anne, da. and h. of Lieut.-Col. George Henry DUCKWORTH (s. and h. ap. of Sir John Thomas DUCKWORTH, 1st Baronet [1813]), by Penelope, da. of Robert FANSHAWE, Capt. R.N. She *d.* 7 Feb. 1855, at Limerick. Admon. April 1855. He *m.* secondly, 23 Oct. 1856, at Harrow-on-the-Hill, Louisa, da. of Robert LANG, of Moor Park, Farnham, Surrey. He *d.* 30 Sep. 1891, at Hurst, near Bournemouth, aged 86. His widow living 1905.

V. 1891. SIR ARTHUR PERCY DOUGLAS, Baronet, [1777], of Wellington, New Zealand, 3d but 1st surv. s. and h., by 1st wife,(e) *b.* 1845; sometime (1866), Lieut., Royal Navy; Under Secretary for Defence in New Zealand; *suc. to the Baronetcy*, 30 Sep. 1891. He *m.* 16 Nov. 1871, Mary Caroline, yst. da. of the Rev. William FOSTER, M.A., of Stubbington House, near Fareham, Hants.

(a) His age at death is said in the *Annual Register* to have been 81, but that is apparently an error.

(b) An elder br. Charles is said to have left female issue.

(c) *Dict. Nat. Biog.*, where his mother is said to have been Sarah, da. of James Wood (which Sarah was undoubtedly *m.* in or before 1777, and then living, see p. 193, note "d"), and his aunt, by whom he was brought up, to have been "Mrs. Helena Baillie, of Olive Bank, Musselburgh." This last statement, however, points to his mother having been Jane Baillie abovementioned, whose marriage must, in that case, have been *subsequent* to that of Sarah.

(d) Of his elder brothers, who all *d.* unm. (1) Charles Douglas, Major 61st Foot, *d.* 29 July 1847, at Umballa; (2) James Douglas, was killed in Afghanistan in 1841; (3) Howard Douglas, *d.* in the West Indies, 11 Aug. 1820, on board H.M.S. "The Tartar."

(e) Of his elder brothers (1) Howard Douglas *d.* 1854, aged 12; (2) Robert Stopford Sholto Douglas, an officer in the 60th Foot, *d.* unm. 1 Jan. 1875, aged 31.

HOOD:

cr. 20 May 1778;

afterwards, since 1782, BARONS HOOD OF CATHERINGTON [I.];

and, since 1796, VISCOUNTS HOOD OF WHITLEY [G.B.].

I. 1778. "SAMUEL HOOD, of Catherington, co. Southampton, Esq.,"(a) 1st s. of the Rev. Samuel HOOD, Vicar of Butley, Somerset, and Prebendary of Wells, by Mary, da. of Richard HOSKINS, of Beaminster, Dorset, was *b.* 12 Dec. 1724, and *bap.* 2 Jan. 1724/5, at Butley; entered the Royal Navy, 1740; Lieut. 1746; Commander, 1754; Capt., 1756; was employed, 1757-59, in the blockade of the French coast, capturing, 21 Feb. 1759, a French frigate (the "Bellona") of thirty-two guns; was, 1778-80, Commissioner of the Navy at Portsmouth, being *cr. a Baronet*, as above, 20 May 1778, on the occasion of the King's visit there. He became Rear-Admiral of the Blue, 26 Sep. 1780, and having greatly distinguished himself in Rodney's victory over the French fleet, under Count de Grasse, off Dominica, 12 April 1782, was raised to the peerage of Ireland as below stated. He *m.* 25 Aug. 1749, at Portsmouth, Susanna, da. of Edward LINZEE, many times Mayor of that town, by Anne, da. and finally coheir of Robert NEWNHAM, of Portsmouth. She, who was *b.* 19, and *bap.* there 20 June 1726, was living when he was *cr.*, 12 Sep. 1782 (Privy Seal, 28 May previous), BARON HOOD OF CATHERINGTON [I.]. In that peerage this *Baronetcy* then *merged*, and still [1905] so continues, the grantee being subsequently *cr.*, 1 June 1796, VISCOUNT HOOD OF WHITLEY, co. Warwick [G.B.]. See *Peerage*.

BICKERTON:

cr. 29 May 1778;

afterwards, 1823-32, HUSSEY-BICKERTON;

ex. 9 Feb. 1832.

I. 1778. "SIR RICHARD BICKERTON, Knt., Captain in His Majesty's Navy,"(a) 3d s. of Henry BICKERTON, Lieut. 4th Dragoon Guards, by Mary, da. of (—) DOWDAL, of Carrickfergus, was *b.* 23 June and *bap.* 4 July 1727, at St. Mary Magdalen, Bridgnorth, Salop; was ed. at Westm. School; entered the Royal Navy, 1739; Lieut., 1746; Capt., 1756, being *Knighted*, 24 June 1773, for steering the King's barge at a naval review off Plymouth, and was *cr. a Baronet*, as above, 29 May 1778, on the occasion of the King's visit to Portsmouth. He assisted in the second relief of Gibraltar, 1781; was Commander in the East Indies, 1782-84, assisting Sir Edward Hughes in his achievements there, was (for a short time) Commander-in-Chief in the Leeward Islands, 1786-87, becoming Rear-Admiral of the White, 1787, and Vice-Admiral, 1796; being also Port Admiral at Plymouth till his death. He, who was of Upwood, co. Huntingdon, was M.P. for Rochester 1790 till death. He *m.* 2 Jan. 1758, at St. Margaret's, Westm., Mary Anne, sister and heir to Lieut.-Gen. Vere Warner HUSSEY, of Wood Walton, 1st da. of Thomas HUSSEY, of Wrexham, co. Denbigh. He *d.* of apoplexy, 25 Feb. 1792, aged 64, and was *bur.* at Upwood. Will dat. 9 Aug. 1780, pr. 19 Jan. 1793. His widow, who was *b.* 11 and *bap.* 18 May 1740, at Wrexham, *d.* 29 Aug. 1811.

(a) See p. 113, note "a," under "GIDEON." The date of the Gazette notice for Hood and Bickerton is 20 April, for Heron, Wombwell, James, Lloyd, Coghill, Taylor, Riddell, Hawkins, Jebb, Elliot and Lippincott is 25 July, for Copley 18 Aug., and for Gunning 27 Oct. 1778.

II. 1792, to 1832. SIR RICHARD BICKERTON, *afterwards*, 1823-32, HUSSEY-BICKERTON, Baronet [1778], of Upwood aforesaid, 1st and only surv. s. and h., *b.* 11 Oct. 1759 at Southampton, entered the Royal Navy, 1771; Lieut., 1777; Commander, 1779; was in command in the action off Martinique, 29 May 1781; *suc. to the Baronetcy*, 25 Feb. 1792, became Rear-Admiral, 1799, and finally, 1810, Admiral, being employed on the coast of Egypt, 1801 (Turkish Order of the Crescent, 8 Oct. 1801), and second in command under Nelson, 1804-05. He was Commander-in-Chief at Portsmouth, 1812-14; **K.C.B.**, 2 Jan. 1815; Lieut.-Gen. of Marines, 1818, and General of Marines (in succession to William IV.), June 1830. By royal lic., 16 May 1823, he took the name of HUSSEY before that of BICKERTON. He was also a Director of Greenwich Hospital, M.P. for Poole, 1807-12, and F.R.S. He *m.* 25 Sep. 1792 in Antigua, Anne, da. of James ATHILL, of that island, M.D. He *d.* s.p. at his residence in the Circus, Bath, 9 and was *bur.* 16 Feb. 1832 at Bath Abbey, aged 72, when the *Baronetcy* became *extinct*. Will pr. Aug. 1832. His widow *d.* there 2 March 1850, aged 81. Will pr. April 1850.

ELLIOT, ELLIOTT, *or* ELIOT:

cr. 25 July 1778;

ex. 7 Nov. 1786.

I. 1778, to 1786. "SIR JOHN ELLIOT, of Peebles, Knt., Dr. of Physic,"(a) s. of (—) ELLIOT, ELLIOTT, *or* ELIOT, a Writer to the Signet, by (probably) a da. of (—) DAVIDSON, was *b.* in Edinburgh, 1736, ed. there and in France and Holland, and having obtained a good sum of prize money as surgeon on board a privateer, took the degree of M.D., 6 Nov. 1759, at the Univ. of St. Andrew's; was admitted a Licentiate to the Coll. of Physicians, London, 30 Sep. 1772, being said to have obtained £5,000 a year by his practice in that city, was *Knighted*, 31 May 1776; became Physician in ordinary to George, Prince of Wales, and was *cr. a Baronet*, as above, 25 July 1778.(b) He *m.* 19 Oct. 1771, at St. Pancras, Midx., Grace (then "a young beauty"), yr. da. of Hew DALRYMPLE, LL.D., Advocate, Attorney-Gen. of Grenada. She, by whom he had no issue, was divorced (damages £12,000) in 1774.(c) He *d.* s.p. legit., while on a visit to Brocket Hall, Herts, 7 Nov. 1786, aged about 50, and was *bur.* at Bishops Hatfield, when the *Baronetcy* became *extinct*. M.I. erected by his uncle, William DAVIDSON, of Muirhouse. Will pr. Nov. 1786.

HAWKINS:

cr. 25 July 1778.

I. 1778. "CÆSAR HAWKINS, of KELSTON, co. Somerset, Esq.,"(a) as also of Pall Mall, Westminster, s. of Cæsar HAWKINS, Surgeon, by Anne, da. of (—) BRIGHT, was *b.* 10 Jan. 1711; admitted to the Company of

(a) See page 195, note "a," under "HOOD."

(b) A curious anecdote of the slight esteem the King had for him is in Munk's *Physicians*, an estimate confirmed by a statement [*Dict. Nat. Biog.*] that "the stores of medical knowledge in his mind were small indeed."

(c) The cause was *crim. con.* with Viscount Valentia [I.], afterwards *cr.* Earl of Mountmorris [I.]. The lady, known as "Mrs. Eliot," who subsequently intrigued with George, Prince of Wales, and many others, *d.* near Sevres, 16 May 1823, at the age (as stated) of 63, which, however, would make her but 11 at her marriage in 1771. See full account of her in the *Dict. Nat. Biog.*, and in *N. & Q.*, 3d S., x, 161.

Surgeons, 1 July 1735, being on the Livery, 19 Aug. 1736, and Demonstrator of Anatomy, 1736-37; Surgeon to St. George's Hospital, 1735 to 1774; Surgeon to the Prince of Wales, and to one of the troops of Guards; Serjeant-Surgeon to George II, 7 Sep. 1747, which post he held also to George III, and, having purchased the said estate of Kelston, was *cr. a Baronet*, as above, 25 July 1778. He *m.* in or before 1738, Sarah, only da. of John COXE, of London. He *d.* 13 Feb. 1786, aged 75. Will dat. 8 June 1785, pr. 14 March 1786. His widow *d.* at Bath, 17 March 1800, aged 82, and was *bur.* at Kelston. M.I. Will pr. April 1800.

II. 1786. SIR CÆSAR HAWKINS, Baronet [1778], of Kelston aforesaid, grandson and h., being 1st s. and h. of John HAWKINS, by Anne, da. and coheir of Joseph COLBORNE, of Hardenhuish House, Wilts, which John, who *d.* v.p. at Bath, 7 May 1785, aged 41, was 3d but 1st surv. s. of the late Baronet. He *suc. to the Baronetcy*, 13 Feb. 1786; was ed. at Eton; at which school he *d.*, 10 July 1793, aged 12.

III. 1793. SIR JOHN CÆSAR HAWKINS, Baronet [1778], of Kelston aforesaid, br. and h., *b.* 9 Feb. 1782.; ed. at Winchester, 1792, and subsequently at Eton; *suc. to the Baronetcy*, 10 July 1793; matric. at Oxford (Ch. Ch.), 23 Oct. 1799, aged 17, and was *cr.* M.A., 23 June 1802. Sheriff of Somerset, 1807-08. He sold the estate of Kelston, and resided at Weymouth. He *m.* 11 Aug. 1804, Charlotte Cassandra, 1st da. of William SURTEES, of Hedley, co. Northumberland. She *d.* at Weymouth, 14 Oct. 1855, and was *bur.* at Preston, Dorset, in her 74th year. He *d.* at Frenchay, co. Gloucester, 9 Nov. 1861, aged 79.

IV. 1861. SIR JOHN CÆSAR HAWKINS, Baronet [1778], grandson and h., being only s. and h. of John Cæsar HAWKINS, by Louisa Georgiana Lætitia, da. of Thomas Bourke RICKETTS, of Combe, co. Hereford, which John (who *d.* v.p. 8 Jan. 1845, aged 39) was 1st s. and h. ap. of the late Baronet. He was *b.* 27 Jan. 1837; matric. at Oxford (Oriel Coll.), 20 March 1855, aged 18; B.A., 1858; M.A., 1861; *suc. to the Baronetcy*, 9 Nov. 1861; took Holy Orders; Vicar of St. Pauls' Chatham, 1863-64; of Westcott, Surrey, 1864-66; Rector of St. Albans, Herts, 1866-68; of Chelmsford, 1878-80; Hon. Canon of St. Albans, 1878. He *m.* 7 July 1863, at Christchurch, Paddington, Mary Catherine, yst. da. of Thomas Ellames WITHINGTON, of Culcheth Hall, co. Lancaster.

HERON:

cr. 25 Aug. 1778;

ex. 29 May 1854.

I. 1778. "THE RT. HON. RICHARD HERON, [4th and] yst. s. of Robert HERON, of Newark-upon-Trent, Notts, Esq.,"(a) (who *d.* 10 Aug. 1753, aged 66), by Elizabeth, da. of Thomas BRECKNOCK, of Thorney Abbey, co. Cambridge, was *b.* 1726; adm. to Lincoln's Inn, 30 Jan. 1748/9; a Commissr. of Bankruptcy, 1751; Remembrancer in the Exchequer, 1754; M.P. for Lisburn [I.], 1776-83; Chief Secretary for Ireland, 1777-80, and P.C. [I.], 25 Jan. 1777, and was *cr. a Baronet*, as above, 25 Aug. 1778, with a spec. rem., failing heirs male of his body, to "Thomas HERON, of Chilham Castle, co. Kent, Esq., 1st surv. s. and heir male [ap.] of the said Robert HERON."(a) He *m.* Jane, widow of Stephen THOMPSON, da. and coheir of Abraham HALL, M.D. He *d.* s.p. 18 Jan. 1805 at his house in Grosvenor square, aged 78.(b) Will pr. 1805. His widow *d.* 8 Sep. 1814, aged 91. Will pr. 1815.

(a) See p. 195, note "a," under "HOOD."

(b) In 1798 he completed a genealogy of the family of Heron of Newark.

V

II. 1805, to 1854. SIR ROBERT HERON, Baronet [1778], afterwards of Stubton Hall, co. Lincoln, nephew and h., being only surv. s. of Thomas HERON, of Chilham Castle, Kent, Recorder of Newark, by his 1st wife Anne, da. of Sir Edward WILMOT, 1st Baronet [1759], of Chaddesden, which Thomas (who *d.* 28 April 1794, aged 61), was elder br. of the late Baronet. He was *b.* at Newark, 27 Nov. 1765; ed. at St. John's Coll., Cambridge; *suc. to the Baronetcy*, 18 Jan. 1805, by virtue of the spec. rem., and suc. to considerable estates in Lincolnshire on the death, 19 Jan. 1813, of his uncle, the Rev. Robert HERON, of Grantham; was Sheriff of Lincolnshire, 1809-10; M.P. for Grimsby (in the Whig interest) 1812-18, and for Peterborough Nov. 1819 to 1847, in all nineteen Parls. He *m.* 9 Jan. 1792, at Cottesmore, co. Rutland, Emily, 2d da. and coheir of Sir Horace MANN, 2d Baronet [1755], by Lucy, da. of Baptist (NOEL), 4th EARL OF GAINSBOROUGH. She *d.* 12 Dec. 1847. He *d.* s.p. at Stubton Hall, somewhat suddenly, 29 May 1854, aged 88, when the *Baronetcy* became *extinct*.(a) M.I. at Stubton. Will pr. Dec. 1854.

WOMBWELL:

cr. 26 Aug. 1778.

I. 1778. "GEORGE WOMBWELL, of Wombwell [in the West Riding of] co. York, Esq.,"(b) 1st s. and h. of Roger WOMBWELL, of Barnsley, co. York, Grocer (*d.* at sea 1740, aged 32), by Mary, da. of Francis CHADWICK, was *bap.* at Barnsley, 11 June 1734; was a Merchant in London; Director and for two years Chairman of the East India Company; M.P. for Huntingdon, 1774 till death, and, having purchased the estate of Wombwell (formerly that of his ancestors) was *cr. a Baronet*, as above, 26 Aug. 1778. He *m.* 4 June 1765, Susanna, sister and h. of Sir Walter RAWLINSON, of Stowlangtoft, Suffolk (who *d.* s.p. 30 March 1805, in his 70th year), da. of Sir Thomas RAWLINSON, Alderman and sometime (1753-54) Lord Mayor of London, by Dorothea, da. of the Rev. Richard RAY, Vicar of Haughley, Suffolk. He *d.* at Beckenham, Kent, 2, and was *bur.* 17 Nov. 1780 at Haughley aforesaid, aged 46. Will pr. 1780. His widow, who was *b.* before 6 Nov. 1744, *d.* in London 27 Sep. and was *bur.* 8 Oct. 1816, at Haughley. Will pr. Oct. 1816 and June 1846.

II. 1780. SIR GEORGE WOMBWELL, Baronet, [1778], of Wombwell aforesaid, only s. and h., *b.* 14 March 1769; *suc. to the Baronetcy*, 2 Nov. 1780; ed. at Trinity Coll., Cambridge; M.A., 1790; Sheriff of Yorkshire, 1809-10. He *m.* firstly, 19 July 1791, at St. Geo. Han. sq., Anne, 2d da. and coheir of Henry (BELASYSE), 2d and last EARL FAUCONBERG, by his 1st wife Charlotte, da. of Sir Matthew LAMB, 1st Baronet [1755]. She, who was *b.* 27 Dec. 1768, and who inherited the family estate of Newburgh, co. York, *d.* 7 July 1808, in her 40th year, and was *bur.* at Stowlangtoft. Admon. Jan. 1809. He *m.* secondly, in or before 1813, Eliza, yst. da. of T. E. LITTLE, of Hampstead. He *d.* 28 Oct. 1846, in Eaton square, aged 77. Will pr. Feb. 1847. His widow *d.* 21 March 1856, in Chesham place, aged 65. Will pr. April 1856.

III. 1846. SIR GEORGE WOMBWELL, Baronet, [1778], of Wombwell and Newburgh aforesaid, 1st s. and h., by 1st wife; *b.* 13 April 1792, at 15 George Street, Hanover Square; well known on the turf and in fashionable society; *suc. to the Baronetcy*, 28 Oct. 1846. He *m.* 23 June 1824 (spec. lic.) at her father's house in Grosvenor Place, Georgiana, yst. da. of Thomas Orby HUNTER, of Croyland Abbey, co. Lincoln. He *d.* in George Street aforesaid, 14 Jan. 1855, aged 62, and was *bur.* at Coxwold, co. York. His widow *d.* 10 May 1875.

(a) His "*Notes*," printed in 1851, contain many curious matters. The work is reviewed somewhat savagely by Croker in the *Quarterly Review* (1852), xc, 206.
(b) See p. 195, note "a," under "HOOD."

IV. 1855. SIR GEORGE ORBY WOMBWELL, Baronet, [1778], of Wombwell and Newburgh aforesaid, 1st s. and h., *b.* 23 Nov. 1832, in George Street aforesaid; ed. at Eton; sometime Cornet 17th Lancers, and promoted to be Lieut. for his gallant conduct at the battle of Balaklava (taking part in the famous charge of the Light Brigade, with the Earl of Cardigan, to whom he was then aide-de-camp), but retired in 1855; *suc. to the Baronetcy*, 14 Jan. 1855; Sheriff of Yorkshire, 1861. He *m.* 3 Sep. 1861, Julia Sarah Alice, 1st da. of George Augustus Frederick (VILLIERS), 6th EARL OF JERSEY, by Julia, da. of the Rt. Hon. Sir Robert PEEL, 2d Baronet [1800]. She was *b.* 11 May 1842.(a)

Family Estates.—These, in 1883, consisted of 13,226 acres in the North Riding of Yorkshire, valued at £14,500 a year. *Principal Seat.*—Newburgh Park, near Easingwold, Yorkshire.

JAMES:(b)

cr. 27 Aug. 1778;

ex. 16 Nov. 1792.

I. 1778. "WILLIAM JAMES, of Park Farm place, in Eltham, co. Kent, Esq.,"(c) was *b.* about 1721 at Milford Haven; went to sea at the age of twelve; was in command of a ship at the age of twenty; was captured by the Spaniards and imprisoned for many years; was employed by the East India Company to repress piracy on the Malaba coast, being in 1751, commander-in-chief of their marine forces, and capturing, 2 April 1755, Severndroog Castle, the chief fortress on that coast; returned to England, 1759; was for twenty years a director of the East India Company; Deputy Master of Trinity House, fifteen years; a Governor of Greenwich Hospital; M.P. for West Looe 1774 till death, and F.R.S. He purchased the Park Farm estate, and was *cr. a Baronet*, as above, 27 Aug. 1778. He *m.* in or before 1765, Anne, 1st da. and coheir of Edmond GODDARD, by Elizabeth, da. and h. of John GODDARD, of Hartham, Wilts.(d) He, who had long been in ill-health, *d.* on his daughter's wedding day, 16 and was *bur.* 22 Dec. 1783, at Eltham, aged 62. Will dated 2 June 1780, pr. Dec. 1783. His widow *d.* 9 Aug. 1798. Will pr. Sep. 1798.

II. 1783, to 1792. SIR EDWARD WILLIAM JAMES, Baronet [1778], of Park Farm place aforesaid, only s. and h., *b.* about 1774; *suc. to the Baronetcy*, 16 Dec. 1783. He *d.* unm. 16 and was *bur.* 24 Nov. 1792, at Eltham, aged 18, when the *Baronetcy* became *extinct*.(e)

(a) Of their two sons, who both *d.* unm. and v.p. (1) George Wombwell, Lieut. Kings' Own Rifle Corps, *d.* 16 Jan. 1889, at Meerut, India, aged 23; (2) Stephen Frederick Wombwell, B.A. (Trin. Hall), Cambridge, Lieut. Yorkshire Hussars Yeomanry Cavalry, went, as Capt. in the Imperial Yeomanry, to the South African War, and *d.* of enteric fever, 1 Feb. 1901, at Vryburg, aged nearly 34.
(b) See H. H. Drake's *Hundred of Blackheath*, p. 190, note 7.
(c) See p. 195, note "a," under "HOOD."
(d) See an extensive pedigree in Burke's *Commoners* [1838], vol. iv, p. 329.
(e) Elizabeth Anne, his only surv. sister and h., *m.* (on the day of her father's death) 16 Dec. 1783 (at her age of 18), Thomas Boothby Parkyns, *cr.* 8 Oct. 1795, Baron Rancliffe [I.], and had issue. She was *bur.* 28 Jan. 1797 with her parents, at Eltham.

COPLEY:

cr. 28 Aug. 1778;

ex. 4 Jan. 1883.

I. 1778. "JOSEPH COPLEY, of Sprotborough, co. York, Esq., grandson and h. of the late Sir Godfrey COPLEY, Baronet,"(a) *formerly* Joseph MOYLE, s. of Joseph MOYLE,(b) (living 1710, aged 31) by Catherine, only surv. da. and h. of Sir Godfrey COPLEY, 2d and last Baronet [1666], of Sprotborough aforesaid (*d.* s.p.m.s. 9 April 1709), having suc. to the estates of his mother's family on the death, 20 Dec. 1766, of his distant cousin, Lionel COPLEY, of Sprotborough aforesaid, took by Act of Parliament 1768, the name of COPLEY instead of that of MOYLE, and was *cr. a Baronet*, as above, 28 Aug. 1778. He *m.* in or before 1767, Mary (under age in 1745), da. of John Francis BULLER, of Morval, Cornwall, by Rebecca, da. of Sir Jonathan TRELAWNY, 3d Baronet [1628], Bishop of Winchester. He *d.* 11 April 1781. Will pr. April 1781 and 1791. His widow *d.* 3 March 1787. Will pr. March 1787.

II. 1781. SIR LIONEL COPLEY, Baronet [1778], of Sprotborough aforesaid, 1st s. and h., *b.* about 1767; *suc. to the Baronetcy*, 11 April 1781. M.P. for Tregony, 1796-1802. He *d.* unm. 4 March 1806, aged 39. Will pr. 1806.

III. 1806. SIR JOSEPH COPLEY, Baronet [1778], of Sprotborough aforesaid, br. and h., *b.* about 1769, at Southampton; matric. at Oxford (Ch. Ch.), 23 Oct. 1786, aged 17; *suc. to the Baronetcy*, 11 April 1781. He *m.* 23 May 1799, Cecil, the divorced wife of the 1st MARQUESS OF ABERCORN, *formerly* Lady Cecil HAMILTON (she having been raised by royal warrant, 27 Oct. 1789, to the precedence of the da. of an Earl), 7th da. of Rev. the Hon. George HAMILTON, Canon of Windsor, by Elizabeth, da. of Lieut. Gen. Richard ONSLOW, which George, was 3d s. of James, 3d EARL OF ABERCORN [S.] She, who was *b.* 15 March 1770, *d.* 19 June 1819. He *d.* 21 May 1838, at Whitehall yard, in his 70th year. Will pr. Nov. 1838.

IV. 1838, to 1883. SIR JOSEPH WILLIAM COPLEY, Baronet [1778], of Sprotborough aforesaid, only s. and h., *b.* 27 July 1804, in Marylebone; matric. at Oxford (Ch. Ch.), 25 April 1823, aged 18; *suc. to the Baronetcy*, 21 May 1838; Sheriff of Yorkshire, 1843. He *m.* 19 Nov. 1831, at Brockelsby, co. Lincoln, Charlotte, da. of Charles (ANDERSON-PELHAM), 1st EARL OF YARBOROUGH, by Henrietta Anna Maria Charlotte, da. of the Hon. John BRIDGEMAN-SIMPSON. She, who was *b.* 20 Oct. 1810, and who was extra woman of the bedchamber to Queen Victoria, *d.* 15 Aug. 1875. He *d.* s.p. 4 Jan. 1883, at 35 Duke street, St. James', aged 78, when the *Baronetcy* became *extinct*.(c) Will pr. 7 April 1883, over £86,000.

(a) See p. 195, note "a," under "HOOD." It is to be observed that the Gazette notice for this creation is dated 18 Aug., whereas that for Lloyd, Coghill, Taylor, Riddell, Jebb and Lippincott, whose creations are posterior, is dated as early as 25 July.
(b) This Joseph Moyle was 2d s. of Sir Walter Moyle, of Bake, co. Cornwall, Sheriff of that county 1671, who *d.* Sep. 1701.
(c) He devised his estates in Yorkshire and Cornwall, subject to the life interest of his sister, to his cousin, Sir Charles Watson, 3d Baronet [1759], grandson of his paternal aunt Juliana, by Sir Charles Watson, 1st Baronet [1759]. He took the name of Copley after that of Watson, by Royal lic. 12 March 1887, and *d.* soon afterwards, s.p.m. 6 April 1888, aged 60.

LLOYD:

cr. 29 Aug. 1778;

afterwards, since 1831, BARONS MOSTYN.

I. 1778. "EDWARD LLOYD, of Pengwern, co. Flint, Esq.,"(a) yr. s. of John LLOYD, of Pontryffyd, in that county (who purchased that estate in 1686, and *d.* May 1729), by Rebecca, da. and h. of William OWEN, of Plas Issa, was *b.* about 1710; was Sheriff of Flintshire, 1768-69; is said to have been Secretary for War, and was *cr. a Baronet*, as above, 29 Aug. 1778, with a spec. rem., failing issue male of his body to his nephew, "Bell LLOYD,(b) of Bodfach, co. Montgomery, Esq."(a) He *m.* firstly, Anna Maria, da. and h. of Edward *or* Evan LLOYD, of Pengwern aforesaid. He *m.* secondly, 3 July 1774, at Portland Chapel, Marylebone, Amelia, da. of the Rt. Hon. Sir William YONGE, 4th Baronet [1661], of Colyton, Devon, by his 2d wife Anne, da. and coheir of Thomas (HOWARD), 7th BARON HOWARD OF EFFINGHAM. He *d.* s.p. 26 May 1795, in his 85th year, and was *bur.* at the Cathedral of St. Asaph. Will pr. July 1795. His widow *d.* in or before 1831. Will pr. July 1831.

II. 1795. SIR EDWARD PRYCE LLOYD, Baronet [1778], of Pontryffyd and Bodfach aforesaid, grandnephew and h., being 1st s. and h. of Bell LLOYD,(b) of the same, by Anne, da. and h. of Edward PRYCE, of Bodfach aforesaid, which Bell (who *d.* 6 May 1793, aged 63) was only s. and h. of William LLOYD, of Pontryffyd (*m.* 1726 and *d.* 1730), elder br. of the 1st Baronet. He was *b.* 17 Sep. 1768, and *suc. to the Baronetcy*, according to the spec. rem., 26 May 1795. He was Sheriff of Flintshire, 1796-97; of Carnarvonshire, 1797-98, and of Merionethshire, 1804-5; was M.P. for the Flint burghs, 1806-07; for Beaumaris, 1808-12, and (again) for the Flint burghs (five Parls., 1812-31). He *m.* 11 Sep. 1794, Elizabeth, sister and coheir of Sir Thomas MOSTYN, 6th and last Baronet [1660], of Mostyn, co. Flint (who *d.* 7 April 1831), 3d da. of Sir Roger MOSTYN, 5th Baronet [1660], by Margaret, da. and h. of the Rev. Hugh WYNNE, LL.D., Prebendary of Salisbury. She was living when he was *cr.* 10 Sep. 1831 (on the occasion of the Coronation of William IV), BARON MOSTYN of Mostyn, co. Flint. In that peerage this *Baronetcy* then *merged*, and still [1905] so continues. See *Peerage*.

COGHILL:

cr. 31 Aug. 1778.

I. 1778. "JOHN COGHILL, of Coghill Hall [near Knaresborough, in the West Riding of co. York, Esq.,"(a) *formerly* John CRAMER, of Bellaville, co. Meath, 1st s. and h. of Balthazar John CRAMER, by Judith, da. of Brinsley (BUTLER), 1st VISCOUNT LANESBOROUGH [I.], which Balthazar (who *d.* 18 June 1741), was 1st s. and h. of Oliver CRAMER, of Ballyfoyle, co. Kilkenny, by Hester, sister of the Right Hon. Marmaduke COGHILL, sometime (1735-38) Chancellor of the Exchequer [I.], da. of Sir John COGHILL, of Coghill Hall aforesaid, and of Drumcondra, co. Dublin. He was *b.* 14 July 1732, and inherited the estates of his maternal great uncle, the abovenamed Marmaduke COGHILL (who *d.* unm. 9 March 1738), though he did not assume the name of COGHILL, instead of CRAMER, till many years later, *viz.*, at some period between 1775 and 1778;(c) was M.P. [I.] for Belturbet, 1754-60, 1761-68 and 1776; was

(a) See p. 195, note "a," under "HOOD."
(b) His mother, Frances, was da. of Bell Jones, of Plas Mawr, co. Flint, Secretary to the Board of Ordnance, who was *bur.* (as was his wife, the said Frances, 29 Nov. 1722) at St. Peter's ad Vincula, Tower of London, 3 Dec. 1725.
(c) "He was returned to Parliament [I.] on each occasion as *Cramer*, and so appears in the lists of Members down to the Dissolution in 1776." [G. D. Burtchaell]. He was, however, *cr. a Baronet* in 1778 as *Coghill*.

cr. LL.D. of Dublin (*honoris causâ*), 1762, and was *cr. a Baronet*, as above, 31 Aug. 1778. He subsequently, by the death, s.p., 28 July 1789, of his cousin Hester, Dowager COUNTESS OF CHARLEVILLE [I.] (at whose request, it is said, he, in her lifetime, assumed the name of COGHILL), widow of Sir John COGHILL, Baronet [so *cr.* 24 March 1781], inherited other estates of the Coghill family, and became their representative.(a) He *m.* 17 Oct. 1754 (Lic. Prerog. [I.] 15 Oct.), Maria, sister of Sir John HORT, 1st Baronet [1767], 4th da. of the Most Rev. Josiah HORT, Archbishop of Tuam [1742-51], by Elizabeth, da. and coheir of the Hon. William FITZMAURICE. He *d.* 8 March 1790, at Bath, aged 57. Will pr. May 1790. His widow *d.* 14 Dec. 1815. Will pr. 1816.

II. 1790 SIR JOHN THOMAS CRAMER-COGHILL, Baronet, *afterwards*, 1807 to 1817, COGHILL [1778], of Coghill Hall aforesaid, 1st s. and h., *b.* 2 Feb. 1766, in Westminster; matric. at Oxford (St. John's Coll.), 10 May 1784, aged 18; *suc. to the Baronetcy*, 8 March 1790, and by royal lic., 7 June 1807, took the name of COGHILL only. He *d.* unm., 21 May 1817, aged 51. Will pr. 1817, as also in Ireland.

III. 1817. SIR JOSIAH COGHILL(b) CRAMER-COGHILL, *afterwards* COGHILL, Baronet [1778], of Ballyduff, co. Kilkenny, only br. and h., *b.* 1773; entered the Royal Navy, serving, as Lieut., in the expedition to Egypt (Egyptian medal), as Capt. in a sanguinary action off the coast of Malay, was in command at Walcheren, becoming Rear-Admiral of the Blue, 23 Nov. 1841, and Vice-Admiral of the Red, 30 Oct. 1849. He *suc. to the Baronetcy*, 21 May 1817, and by royal lic., a few days later, 7 June 1817, took the name of COGHILL only. He *m.* firstly, in March 1803, Sophia, da. of James DODSON, an officer of the Customs. She *d.* s.p.m., in Normandy, in 1817. He *m.* secondly, 27 Jan. 1819, Anna Maria, 1st da. of the Rt. Hon. Charles Kendal BUSHE, sometime (1822-41) Lord Chief Justice of the King's Bench [I.], by Anne, sister of Philip CRAMPTON, 1st Baronet [1839], da. of John CRAMPTON, of Dublin. She *d.* 10 March 1848, at Cheltenham. He *d.* at Kenilworth House, in that town, 20 June 1850, in his 78th year. Will pr. July 1850.

IV. 1850. SIR (JOHN) JOSCELYN COGHILL, Baronet [1778], of Drumcondra, co. Dublin, and of Glen Barrahane, near Castle Townshend, co. Cork, 1st s. and h., by 2d wife, *b.* 11 Feb. 1826, at Ballyduff House, co. Kilkenny; ed. at Cheltenham, and afterwards (1842) at Rugby; sometime Lieut. 59th Foot; *suc. to the Baronetcy*, 20 June 1850; Sheriff of co. Dublin, 1859. He *m.* 18 Feb. 1851, at St. Peter's Dublin (Lic. Dublin), his cousin, Katherine Frances, 2d da. of John (PLUNKET), 3d BARON PLUNKET OF NEWTON, by Charlotte, da. of the Rt. Hon. Charles Kendal BUSHE abovenamed. She, who was *b.* 17 March 1827, *d.* at Interlachen, 25 Aug. 1861, and was *bur.* at Lucerne.(c) M.I.

Family Estates.—These, in 1878, consisted of 4,564 acres in co. Kilkenny; 1,269 in co. Meath, and 472 in co. Dublin. *Total.*—6,305 acres, worth £4,552 a year.

(a) This Hester was da. and h. of James Coghill, Registrar of the Prerog. Court [I.], 2d and yst. s. of Sir John Coghill, of Coghill Hall, abovementioned, but who *d.* s.p.m. 4 Sep. 1734, about three years before his elder br. Marmaduke Coghill, also abovenamed. Her second husband, John Mayne, took the name of Coghill, and was *cr. a Baronet*, 24 March 1781, which dignity became extinct on his death, 14 Nov. 1783.

(b) He was christened *Coghill* when his father's surname was *Cramer*, and was always known as Sir Josiah-Coghill Coghill. There is a story of a countryman saying, when he heard the Baronet's name called as a Grand Juror at Kilkenny, "I dunno what put *the two cockles* on him" [G. D. Burtchaell].

(c) Their eldest son, Nevill Josiah Aylmer Coghill, Lieut. 24th Foot, *d.* unm. and v.p., being slain at Isandlwana, in the Zulu war, 22 Jan. 1879, in his 27th year.

TAYLOR:

cr. 1 Sep. 1778;

ex. 18 May 1815.

1778. "JOHN TAYLOR, of Lysson Hall, in the Island of Jamaica, Esq.,(a) 2d s. of Patrick TAILZOUR afterwards TAYLOR, by Martha, da. of George TAYLOR, of Camanas in that island (which Patrick, who settled in Jamaica, assumed the name of TAYLOR after his marriage),(b) was *cr. a Baronet*, as above, 1 Sep. 1778. He was F.R.S. He *m.* 17 Dec. 1778, at St. Marylebone, Elizabeth Godden, da. and h. of Philip HOUGHTON, of Jamaica. He *d.* 8 May 1786. Will pr. May 1787. His widow *d.* in or before 1821.(c) Will pr. May 1821 and May 1856.

II. 1786, to 1815 SIR SIMON RICHARD BRISSETT TAYLOR, Baronet, [1778], 2d and yst. but only surv. s. and h., *b.* 15 Oct. 1783; *suc. to the Baronetcy*, 8 May 1786. He *d.* unm. 18 May 1815, aged 31, when *the Baronetcy* became *extinct*.(d) Will pr. July 1815, Jan. 1816, and July 1839.

RIDDELL:

cr. 2 Sep. 1778.

I. 1778. "JAMES RIDDELL, of Ardnamurchan and Sunart, co. Argyll, Doctor of Laws,"(a) 3d s. of George RIDDELL, of Kingloss, co. Linlithgow (living 1718), by Christiana, da. of Andrew PATERSON, of Kirkton, was Superintendent-General to the British Fishery Society (resigning in 1758); F.S.A., LL.D. (Edinburgh), 27 Feb. 1767, and was *cr. a Baronet*, as above, 2 Sep. 1778. He *m.* firstly, 7 Feb. 1754, Mary, da. and h. of Thomas MILLES, of Billockby Hall, Norfolk, by his 3d wife, Helen, da. of Major FERRIOR, of Hemsby, sometime M.P. for Norfolk. By her he had five children. He *m.* secondly, in 1775, Sarah, widow of John SWINBURNE, da. and h. of Thomas BURDON, of Durham, by (—), da. and h. of Henry FOSTER, of co. York. He *d.* 2 Nov. 1797. Will pr. March 1798. His widow, by whom he had no issue, *d.* in Great Pulteney street, Bath, 5, and was *bur.* 16 June 1817, in Westm. Abbey, aged 86. Will pr. July 1817.

(a) See p. 195, note "a," under "HOOD."

(b) Playfair's *Baronetage* [1811], where the descent is deduced from the family of Tailzour, "originally of Norman extraction, who settled in Scotland early in the fourteenth century," though [oddly enough] "the first we find on record is Robert Tailzour, of Tailzourtown, who married Mary, da. of Sir Alexander Strachan, *Baronet*"! and therefore could not have lived before the seventeenth century, when that dignity was first created. There is, however, no mention in this pedigree of that celebrated "*Knyghte who wedded the Taylzeour's daughter*" (commemorated in the *Book of Ballads by Bon Gaultier*) whose armorial ensigns (borne presumably in right of his alliance with that illustrious race) were:—

"A goose, regardant, proper
Hissing on an azure shield."

(c) See *N. & Q.*, 9th S., xi, 309, as to an engraving of his picture (by J. Smart) and that of his wife (by Sir Joshua Reynolds) "from an original picture in the possession of Robert Graham, Esq., of Gartmore," presumably the husband of Ann, one of the Baronet's sisters.

(d) Of his four sisters (1) Anna Susanna, *b.* 20 March 1781, *m.* 6 March 1810, George Watson and had issue; (2) Elizabeth, *b.* 7 Sep. 1782, *m.* 17 Jan. 1805 William Mayne, and had issue; (3) Maria, *b.* 20 Oct. 1784; (4) Martha, *b.* 22 March 1786.

II. 1797. SIR JAMES MILLES RIDDELL, Baronet, [1778], of Ardnamurchan and Sunart aforesaid, grandson and h., being 1st s. and h. of Thomas Milles RIDDELL, of Larbart, co. Stirling, by Margaretta, da. of Col. Dugald CAMPBELL, of Lochnell, co. Argyll, which Thomas (who *d.* v.p. 17 July 1796, aged about 40, was 1st s. and h. ap.(a) of the late Baronet. He was *b.* 3 June 1787, at Shaw Park, co. Clackmannan; *suc. to the Baronetcy*, 2 Nov. 1797; matric. at Oxford (Ch. Ch.) 19 Oct. 1804, aged 17; B.A., 1807. He *m.* 22 March 1822, at Hulton chapel, in Runcorn, co. Chester, Mary, yst. da. of Sir Richard BROOKE, 5th Baronet [1662], by Mary, da. of Sir Robert CUNLIFFE, 2d Baronet [1759]. He *d.* 28 Sep. 1861, at Brook House, Leamington, aged 74. His widow *d.* there 30 Jan. 1866.

III. 1861. SIR THOMAS MILLES RIDDELL, Baronet [1778], of Strontian, co. Argyll, 1st but only surv. s. and h., *b.* 25 Dec. 1822, in Edinburgh; sometime in the 7th Dragoon Guards, serving in the Kaffir War; *suc. to the Baronetcy*, 28 Sep. 1861. He *m.* 16 July 1851, Mary, da. of John HODGSON, of St. Petersburg. He *d.* s.p. 18 July 1883, at Strontian, in his 61st year. His widow *d.* there suddenly 22 July 1897.

IV. 1883. SIR RODNEY STUART RIDDELL, Baronet [1778], cousin and h. male, 1st surv. s. and h. of Campbell Drummond RIDDELL, Colonial Treasurer and Member of the Council in New South Wales, by Caroline Stuart (*m.* 3 April 1830, at Ceylon), da. of the Hon. John RODNEY, which Campbell (who *d.* 27 Dec. 1858, aged 62), was yr. br. to the 2d Baronet. He was *b.* 7 March 1838; served in the New Zealand War, 1863-65 (medal); was Capt. 70th Foot, 1874-80; served in the Afghan War, 1878-80 (medal), and in the Suakim campaign, 1885, retiring in 1885, as Lieut.-Col. in the Army, having *suc. to the Baronetcy*, 18 July 1883.

Family Estates.—These, in 1883, consisted of 54,418 acres in Argylshire, worth £3,672 a year.

GUNNING:

cr. 3 Sep. 1778.

I. 1778. "SIR ROBERT GUNNING, **K.B.**, of Eltham, co. Kent,"(b) 1st s. of Robert GUNNING, of Ireland (*d.* 1750 in London), by Catherine, da. of John or Thomas EDWARDS, also of Ireland, was *b.* 8 June 1731; was Envoy to the Court of Denmark, 1765-71; to that of Prussia, 1771, and to that of Russia, 1772, where he was invested as **K.B.**, 2 June 1773 (becoming, consequently, in 1815, **G.C.B.**), being, after his return home, *cr. a Baronet*, as above, 3 Sep. 1778. He purchased the estate of Horton, co. Northampton, before 1782.(c) He *m.* firstly, 1 April 1752, Elizabeth, da. of John HARRISON, of Grantham. She *d.* s.p. a few days later 14 April 1752. He *m.* secondly, 14 Feb. 1757, Anne, only da. of Robert SUTTON, of Scrofton, Notts, by Anne,

---

(a) His yr. br. (the only one who survived infancy) George James Riddell, of Loddon Stubbs, Norfolk, matric. at Oxford (Mag. Coll.), 21 Feb. 1778, aged 19. Was Lieut. in the 2d troop of the Horse Grenadier Guards, and *d.* unm. and v.p., being slain in a duel 22 April, and *bur.* 2 May 1783, in Westm. Abbey, aged 24.

(b) See p. 195, note "a," under "HOOD." It is to be observed that the Gazette notice for this creation is dated 27 Oct., whereas that for Jebb and Lippincott, whose creations are posterior, is dated as early as 25 July.

(c) In 1782 (Dec. 20) died "Mrs. Gunning, mother of Sir Robert Gunning, of Horton, co. Northampton." [*Gent. Mag.*]

da. of C. THROCKMORTON. She *d.* 30 June 1770.(a) He *d.* 22 Sep. 1816, in his 86th year. Will pr. 1816.

II. 1816. SIR GEORGE WILLIAM GUNNING, Baronet [1778], of Horton, co. Northampton, only s. and h., by 2d wife, *b.* 15 Feb. 1763; was Fellow Commoner of Trin. Coll., Cambridge, at age of 16; gained the declamation prize; B.A., 1783; M.A., 1787. He was M.P. for Wigan, June 1800 to 1802; for Hastings, 1802-06, and for East Grinstead, March to June 1812, and 1812-18. He *suc. to the Baronetcy*, 22 Sep. 1816. He *m.* 10 Feb. 1794, Elizabeth Diana, 2d da. of Henry (BRIDGEMAN), 1st BARON BRADFORD, by Elizabeth, da. and h. of John SIMPSON. She, who was *b.* 5 June 1764, *d.* 5 May 1810. He *d.* 7 April 1823, at his house in Saville Row, aged 60. Will pr. 1823.

III. 1823. SIR ROBERT HENRY GUNNING, Baronet [1778], of Horton aforesaid, 1st s. and h., *b.* there 26 Dec. 1795; ed. at Harrow; *suc. to the Baronetcy*, 7 April 1823; Sheriff of Northamptonshire Feb. 1825, but did not act, and again 1841-42; M.P. for Northampton, 1830-31. He *d.* unm., in Oxford terrace, Hyde Park, 22 Sep. 1862, aged 66.

IV. 1862. SIR HENRY JOHN GUNNING, Baronet [1778], of Horton aforesaid, next surv. br. and h.,(b) *b.* there 17 Dec. 1797; ed. at Charterhouse; matric. at Oxford (Balliol Coll.), 8 May 1816, aged 18; B.A., 1820; M.A., 1822; took Holy Orders; Rector of Knockyn, Salop, 1822-25; Incumbent of Horton, 1826-33; Rector of Wigan, 1833-64, and Rural Dean, having *suc. to the Baronetcy*, 22 Sep. 1862. He *m.* firstly, 27 Sep. 1827, at St. Geo. Han. sq., Mary Catherine, 2d da. of William Ralph CARTWRIGHT, of Aynho, co. Northampton, by his 1st wife, Emma, da. of Cornwallis (MAUDE), 1st VISCOUNT HAWARDEN [I.]. She *d.* 25 May 1877, at Horton, aged 77. He *m.* secondly (when above 82 years of age), 23 Oct. 1879, at Great Houghton, co. Northampton, Frances Rose, 1st da. of Rev. the Hon. William Henry CHURCHILL, Rector of that parish (6th s. of the 1st BARON CHURCHILL OF WYCHWOOD), by his 1st wife, Elizabeth Rose, da. of Thomas THORNHILL, of Woodleys, Oxon. He *d.* 30 June 1885, at St. Peter's Aldwinckle, co. Northampton, aged 87. His widow, who was *b.* 28 May 1840, living 1905.

V. 1885. SIR GEORGE WILLIAM GUNNING, Baronet [1778], of Horton aforesaid, only s. and h. by 1st wife; *b.* 10 Aug. 1828, at Aynho; matric. at Oxford (Brasenose Coll.), 10 June 1877, aged 18; B.A. 1851; M.A., 1854; sometime Major, Northants and Rutlands Militia; *suc. to the Baronetcy*, 30 June 1885. He *m.* 15 May 1851, at Almondsbury, co. Gloucester, Isabella Mary Frances Charlotte, 1st da. of Lieut.-Col. William Chester MASTER, of Knole Park in that county, by Isabella Margaret, da. of the Hon. Stephen DIGBY, yr. s. of the 5th BARON DIGBY OF GEASHILL [I.]. He *d.* at Horton, of blood poisoning, 21 and was *bur.* there 24 Oct. 1903, aged 75. His widow living 1905.

VI. 1903. SIR FREDERICK DIGBY GUNNING, Baronet [1778], of Horton aforesaid, 2d but 1st surv. s. and h., *b.* 13 Nov. 1853; ed. at Radley College; *suc. to the Baronetcy*, 24 Oct. 1903.

Family Estates.—These in 1883, consisted of 3,853 acres in Northamptonshire, 159 in Bucks, and 97 in Lancashire, besides 2,737 acres in the counties of Longford and Roscommon (worth £1,437 a year). *Total.*—6,846 acres, worth £7,443 a year. *Principal Seat.*—Horton House, near Northampton.

(a) In the same month and year but twenty days before (2 June 1770) died another Mrs. Gunning, *viz.*, Bridget, widow of John Gunning (first cousin to the Baronet's father), and mother of the celebrated beauties the Duchess of Hamilton and the Countess of Coventry.

(b) His elder br. George Orlando Gunning, Lieut. 10th Hussars, d. unm. and v.p., being killed at the battle of Waterloo, 18 June 1815, aged 18.

JEBB:

cr. 4 Sep. 1778;

ex. 2 July 1787.

I. 1778, to 1787. "RICHARD JEBB, of Trent place,(a) near East Barnet, co. Middlesex, Dr. of Physic,"(b) s. of Samuel JEBB, M.D., a well known Physician, of Stratford le Bow, Essex (*d.* 9 March 1772 at Chesterfield, aged about 78), by Jane, da. of Patrick LAMB, of London, was *bap.* 30 Oct. 1729 at West Ham, Essex; matric. at Oxford (St. Mary's Hall), 8 April 1747, aged 17, but being a non-Juror took no degree; was M.D. (Marischal College), Aberdeen, 23 Sep. 1751; Licentiate Coll. of Physicians, London, 24 Feb. 1755, becoming Fellow 30 Sep. 1771; Censor, 1772, 1776, and 1781, and Herveian Orator, 1774; Physician to Westminster Hospital, 1754-62, and to St. George's Hospital, 1762-68; F.S.A., 1765, and F.R.S., being *cr. a Baronet*, as above, 4 Sep. 1778. His fees from private practise amounted to 20,000 guineas in three years, 1779-81.(c) Physician in ordinary to the Prince of Wales, 1780, and to the King 16 Dec. 1786. He *d.* unm. of a fever (caught while attending two of the Princesses) in Great George street, 2 and was *bur.* 4 July 1787 in Westm. Abbey in his 58th year, when the *Baronetcy* became *extinct*. M.I. Will (in which he describes himself as "of Lamb's Conduit street,"(d) dat. 23 Feb. to 2 July 1787, pr. 12 July 1787.

LIPPINCOTT:

cr. 7 Sep. 1778;

ex. 23 Aug. 1829.

I. 1778. "HENRY LIPPINCOTT, of Stoke Bishop, co. Gloucester, Esq.,(a) only s. and h. of Henry LIPPINCOTT, of Culmstock, Devon (*d.* 1745), by Mary, da. of Timothy PEPERELL, of Culmstock aforesaid, was *bap.* there 14 Sep. 1737; was a merchant of Bristol; Sheriff of that city, 1768 and 1770, and sometime M.P. thereof. Having, by marriage, acquired the Stoke Bishop estate, he was Sheriff of Gloucestershire, 1776-77, and was *cr. a Baronet*, as above, 7 Sep. 1778; was M.P. for Bristol 1780 till death. He *m.* 10 Sep. 1774, at Westbury-on-Trim, Catherine ("£3,000 a year"), da. and h. of Charles JEFFERIES, of Bristol, by Catherine, sister and h. (20 July 1765) of Sir Robert CANN, 6th and last Baronet [1662], da. of Sir William CANN, 5th Baronet [1662], of Stoke Bishop aforesaid. He *d.* 30 Dec. 1780, aged 43. Will pr. March 1781. His widow *d.* in or before 1797. Admon. July 1797.

II. 1781, to 1829. SIR HENRY CANN LIPPINCOTT, Baronet, [1778], of Stoke Bishop aforesaid, only s. and h., *b.* 5 June 1776; *suc. to the Baronetcy*, 30 Dec. 1780; matric. at Oxford (Oriel Coll.), 29 Jan. 1794, aged 17; *cr.* M.A., 13 May 1797. He *d.* unm., s.p. legit.(e) 23 Aug. 1829, in Portman square, Marylebone, aged 53, when the *Baronetcy* became *extinct*. Will pr. Sep. 1829.

(a) When Enfield chase was disforested he was granted a Crown lease of 385 acres, "which he converted into a park, and built thereon a convenient residence to which he gave the name of *Trent Place*, in commemoration of his successful treatment of the Duke of Gloucester, when seriously ill at Trent some years previously" [Munk's *Physicians*, corrected by the *Dict. Nat. Biogr.*].

(b) See page 195, note "a," under "HOOD."

(c) *Dict. Nat. Biogr.*

(d) His character by Dr. Lettson, "who knew him well," is in Munk's *Physicians*.

(e) In 1810 he was tried for rape. His illegit. son, Robert Cann Lippincott, of Over Court, co. Gloucester, *b.* about 1828; ed. at Eton; matric. at Oxford (Ch. Ch.) 19 May 1836, aged 18.

RUMBOLD:

cr. 27 March 1779.

I. 1779. "THOMAS RUMBOLD, Esq., Governor of Madras,"(a) 3d s. of William RUMBOLD, of the East India Company's Naval Service (*d.* at Tellicherry, 15 Aug. 1745), by Dorothy Maud, da. of Richard CHENEY, of Hackney, was *b.* 15 and *bap.* 25 Jan. 1735/6, at Low Leyton, Essex; entered the East India Company's Service in 1752; was at the siege of Inchinopoli, the retaking of Calcutta; was Aide-de-Camp to Clive at the battle of Plassey (where he was wounded), 1759; was M.P. for Shoreham, Nov. 1770 to 1774, for Shaftesbury, 1774-75, and 1780-81; for Yarmouth (Isle of Wight) April 1781 to 1784, and for Weymouth, 1784-90; was sometime Chief of Patna, and, in 1777, Governor of Fort St. George, Madras, and, having in 1778, purchased the estate of Walton Wodhall, Herts, was (shortly after the surrender of Pondicherry) *cr. a Baronet*, as above, 27 March 1779, "as a public acknowledgment of the prudence and vigor of those exertions, which, at that time, essentially contributed to the preservation of the British power in the Carnatic."(b) He *m.* firstly, 22 June 1756, at Madras, Frances, da. and coheir of James BERRIMAN, of Madras, by Frances, da. of Richard ASPINWALL, of Liverpool. She was *bur.* 22 Aug. 1764, at Calcutta. He *m.* secondly, 2 May 1772, Joanna, sister of Edward (LAW), 1st BARON ELLENBOROUGH, da. of Edmund LAW, D.D., Bishop of Carlisle, by Mary, da. of John CHRISTIAN. He *d.* at his house in Queen Anne street, Westm., 11 Nov. 1791, aged 55, and was *bur.* at Walton-at-Stone, Herts. M.I. Will pr. Dec. 1791. His widow *d.* 4 Jan. 1823. Will pr. 1823.

II. 1791. SIR GEORGE BERRIMAN RUMBOLD, Baronet [1779], 2d but 1st surv. s. and h.,(c) by 1st wife, *b.* 17 Aug. 1764, at Fort William, Calcutta; *suc. to the Baronetcy*, but not to the Hertfordshire estate,(d) 11 Nov. 1791; was Resident Minister at Hamburg to the Hanse towns, 1803-05, being however, in spite of his official position, there arrested by the French Government, 25 Oct. 1804, and imprisoned, though but for three days, at Paris. He *m.* 26 Nov. 1783, at Fort William, Caroline, only child of James HEARN, of Shanskill, co. Waterford, by Mary, da. of (—) TAYLOR. He *d.* 15 Dec. 1807, at Koenigsberg, in Germany, aged 43. Admon. June 1811. His widow *m.* 11 Oct. 1809, at St. James', Westm., Admiral Sir William Sidney SMITH, **G.C.B.** (who *d.* 26 May 1840, aged 75), and *d.* at Paris, 16 May 1826, being *bur.* at Père-la-Chaise there. Admon. Dec. 1826.

III. 1807. SIR WILLIAM RUMBOLD, Baronet [1779], 1st s. and h., *b.* 22 May 1787, or 20 May 1788; *suc. to the Baronetcy*, 15 Dec. 1807. He *m.* 13 July 1809, at Castle Donington, Harriet Elizabeth, sister (whose issue in Nov. 1850 became coheir) of the 2d and last BARON RANCLIFFE [I.], 4th da. of Thomas Boothby (PARKYNS), 1st BARON RANCLIFFE [I.], by Elizabeth Anne, da. of Sir William JAMES, 1st Baronet [1778], of Park Farm place, co. Kent. She, who was *b.* 1 July 1789, in Arlington street, Westm., *d.* in India, 8 Sep. 1830. He *d.* 24 Aug. 1833, at Hyderabad, and was *bur.* there, aged about 46. Admon. March 1834, Aug. 1838, and May 1842.

IV. 1833. SIR CAVENDISH STUART RUMBOLD, Baronet [1779], 2d but 1st surv. s. and h., *b.* 26 Aug. 1815, at Calcutta; *suc. to the Baronetcy*, 24 Aug. 1833. He *m.* in 1836, Mary Harcourt, widow of James Dawes, BARON DE FLASSONS, in France (who *d.* s.p. 1831), da. and coheir of Rear-Admiral Thomas Moore MUNDY, by Judith, da. of John HAMMOND, of

(a) See p. 113, note "a," under "GIDEON." The date of the Gazette notice for Rumbold is March, that of Bastard is Sep., and those of Basset and Farmer is Oct. 1779.

(b) M.I. at Walton-at-Stone.

(c) Richard Rumbold, the 1st s., was Capt. in the 1st Reg. of Guards, served with distinction at the Reduction of Pondicherry in Oct. 1778, but *d.* unm. and v.p. 14 June 1786, aged 26. M.I. at Walton-at-Stone.

(d) This was sold by the executors of the late Baronet, chiefly for the benefit of his 2d wife and her family.

Scoulton, Hull. She, who was *b.* at Northwold, 19 Dec. 1810, *d.* at Norwich, 9 May 1850, and was *bur.* at Northwold.(a) Will pr. June 1850. He *d.* s.p. at Nice, 27 March 1853, aged 37.

V. 1853. SIR ARTHUR CARLOS HENRY RUMBOLD, Baronet [1779], br. and h., *b.* 25 Sep. 1820, in India; ed. at Sandhurst; joined the 51st Foot in 1837; sometime Capt. 70th Foot, serving with the Osmanli Cavalry during the Russian war; 4th Class Medjidie, with rank of Colonel in the Ottoman Army; Stipendiary Magistrate in Jamaica, 1848-55, having *suc. to the Baronetcy*, 27 March 1853; President of Nevis, 1857-63; President of the Council of the Virgin Islands, 1865 till death. He *m.* firstly, 1 Jan. 1846, Antoinette Rose, only child of Commandant Antoine DE KERVEN, Lieut.-Gov. of Guadeloupe. She *d.* s.p., 27 Nov. 1867, at Tortola, from the effects of an earthquake. He *m.* secondly, 18 Aug. 1868, at Trinity church, Hammersmith, Helen Eliza, 1st da. of Edward HOPEWELL, of the Grove, Walthamstow. He *d.* at the Government House, St. Thomas, in the Virgin Islands, 12 June 1869, aged 48. His widow living 1905, as the Lady Superior of the Convent of the Sacred Heart, Malta.

VI. 1869. SIR ARTHUR VICTOR RAOUL ANDUZE RUMBOLD, Baronet [1779], posthumous s. and h., *b.* 24 July 1869 at Abington Abbey, co. Northampton, and *suc. to the Baronetcy* on his birth. He *d.* 16 June 1877, in his 8th year, at the residence of his uncle, William RUMBOLD, Villa Fabbricotti, Montrighi, Florence.

VII. 1877, June. SIR CHARLES HALE RUMBOLD, Baronet [1779], uncle and h., being 4th s. of the 3d Baronet, *b.* 12 Oct. 1822; *suc. to the Baronetcy*, 16 June 1877, but *d.* unm. two months later, 28 Aug. 1877, at the Cape of Good Hope.

VIII. 1877, Aug. SIR HORACE RUMBOLD, Baronet [1779], br. and h., *b.* 2 July 1829, entered the Diplomatic Service, 1849; was Attaché and Secretary of Embassy to several countries; Minister in Chile, 1872-78; having *suc. to the Baronetcy*, 28 Aug. 1877; Minister at Berne, 1878-79; to the Argentine Republic, 1879-80; to Sweden, 1880-84, and to Greece, 1884-86; **K.C.M.G.**, 1886; Envoy to the Hague, 1888-96; **G.C.M.G.**, 1892; Ambassador at Vienna, 1896-1900; P.C., 1896; **G.C.B.**, 1896. He *m.* firstly, 15 July 1867, Caroline Burney, da. of George HARRINGTON, of Washington in America, sometime Minister of the United States to Berne. She *d.* 26 Dec. 1872. He *m.* secondly, 8 July 1881, at Trinity Church, Sloane street, Louisa Anne, widow of St. George Francis Robert CAULFIELD, Capt. 1st Life Guards, only da. of Thomas Russell CRAMPTON, of London, Civil Engineer.

BASTARD:

Gazetted, Sep. **1779**,

but never passed the Seals.

"WILLIAM BASTARD, Esq., of Kitley, co. Devon,"(b) 3d but 1st surv. s. and h., of Pollexfen BASTARD of the same (*bur.* at Yealmpton, Devon, 12 March 1732/3), by Bridget, da. of John (POULETT), 1st EARL POULETT, was *b.* 1, and *bap.* 5 Sep. 1727, at Yealmpton; matric. at Oxford (Ch. Ch.), 18 May 1747, aged 18, and having, when a French fleet was apparently about to land at Plymouth, conducted, at his own risk, the numerous French prisoners there confined to Exeter (no troops being available), was *gazetted a Baronet*, as above, 4 or 24 Sep. 1779, but the warrant never passed the Seals. He *m.* in or before 1756, Anne, da. of Thomas WORSLEY, of Hovingham, co. York. She *d.* 1765. He *d.* 1782, leaving issue male, which still (1905) continues seated at Kitley.

(a) *East Anglian Notes and Queries* (new series), vol. v, 238.

(b) See p. 207, note "a," under "RUMBOLD."

BASSET:

cr. 24 Nov 1779;

afterwards, 1796-1835, BARON DE DUNSTANVILLE;

ex. 14 Feb. 1835.

I. 1779, to 1835. "FRANCIS BASSET, Esq.,"(a) of Tehidy, co. Cornwall, 1st s. and h. of Francis BASSET, of Terley, co. Northampton, and afterwards (1756-69) of Tehidy, by Margaret, da. of Sir John ST. AUBYN, 3d Baronet [1671], was *b.* at Walcot, 9 Aug., and *bap.* 7 Sep. 1757, at Charlbury, Oxon; ed. at Harrow and afterwards at Eton; *suc.* his father in the family estates, Nov. 1769, and was *cr. a Baronet*, as above, 24 Nov. 1779, when aged 22. He was M.P. for Penryn (three Parls.), 1780-96, being also Recorder of that town. He was *cr.* M.A., of Cambridge (King's Coll.), 1786. He *m.* firstly, 16 Aug. 1780, at St. Marylebone, Frances Susanna, da. and finally coheir of John Hippesley COXE, of Stoneaston, co. Somerset. She was living when he was *cr.* 14 June 1796, BARON DE DUNSTANVILLE OF TEHIDY, co. Cornwall. In that peerage this *Baronetcy* then *merged* till both became *extinct* on his death, s.p.m.(b) 14 Feb. 1835, aged 74.

FARMER:

cr. 19 Jan. 1780.

I. 1780. "GEORGE [sometime called George William] FARMER, Esq., 1st son of the late George FARMER, Commander of His Majesty's ship the 'Quebec,'(a) by Rebecca,(c) da. of William FLEMING, of Wootton or Witton, co. Norfolk, Capt. in the Navy," was born about 1762, and was for his father's services (who was blown up with his ship 6 Oct. 1779, after a desperate engagement with a French frigate of the greatly superior force of forty guns) *cr. a Baronet*, as above, 19 Jan. 1780, at the age of 17, being then a Midshipman in the Navy. He "afterwards fixed his residence at Mount Pleasant, in Sussex."(d) He *m.* 14 Oct. 1786, Sophia, 3d da. of Richard KENRICK, of Nantelwyd, co. Denbigh. He *d.* 26 May 1814. Admon. (of Wilts) Aug. 1815. His widow *d.* 17 Sep. 1845.

II. 1814. SIR GEORGE RICHARD FARMER, Baronet [1780], only s. and h., *b.* 28 Dec. 1788; *suc. to the Baronetcy*, 26 May 1814. He *m.* 3 May 1823, his cousin, Irene, da. of George Farmer ELLIS, of Mill Lodge, Youghal, co. Cork, by Irene, da. of George FARMER, Capt. R.N., sister of the 1st Baronet. He *d.* suddenly, in London, 1 June 1855, aged 66. His widow *d.* 8 Sep. 1862, at Reading, Berks, aged 61.

III. 1855. SIR GEORGE FARMER, Baronet [1780], 1st s. and h., *b.* 3 June 1829; *suc. to the Baronetcy*, 1 June 1855; was sometime in the Tasmanian police force, but finally settled at Point Henry, near Geelong, Victoria, in Australia. He *m.* firstly, 7 May 1863, in Tasmania, Elizabeth Amelia, only surv. da. of Thomas WATSON, of Swansea, co. Glamorgan, and of

(a) See p. 207, note "a," under "RUMBOLD."

(b) Frances, his only da. and h. by his 1st wife, became on his death, Baroness Basset of Stratton, co. Cornwall, a dignity which had been conferred on him 30 Nov. 1797, with a spec. rem. in her favour, but which became extinct on her death unm. in Jan. 1855, aged 73.

(c) This Rebecca died 19 June 1782, her pension devolving on her children [*London Mag.* 1782]. It would seem that, on her husband's death, she had a pension of £200 a year, and that "each of eight children and a ninth not yet born," had one of £25 [*Dict. Nat. Biogr.*].

(d) Playfair's *Baronetage* [1811]. In Betham's *Baronetage* [1804] his "Seat" is given as "Clairville, Sussex."

Tasmania. She *d.* 3 Aug. 1874. He *m.* secondly, 26 Feb. 1878, Mary Anne, da. of Edward Duffen ALLISON, M.D., of London. He *d.* 1 Dec. 1883, aged 74. His widow living 1905.

IV. 1883. SIR GEORGE RICHARD HUGH FARMER, Baronet [1780], 2d and yst. but only surv. s. and h. by 1st wife, *b.* 5 June 1873, at Bacchus Marsh, near Melbourne, Australia; *suc. to the Baronetcy*, 1 Dec. 1883. He, who appears to have resided at Line Drift, Fort Peddie, South Africa, *d.* unm. 1891, aged 18.

V. 1891. SIR RICHARD HENRY KENRICK FARMER, Baronet [1780], uncle and h., *b.* 11 Aug. 1841; *suc. to the Baronetcy* in 1891, being then resident at Worcester in the United States of America. He *m.* in 1878, Jane, 4th da. of Robert SMYTH, of Mountford lodge, co. Cork.

BARKER:

cr. 24 March 1781;

ex. 14 Sep. 1789.

I. 1781, to 1789. "SIR ROBERT BARKER, Knt., of Bushbridge [near Godalming], co. Surrey,"(a) only s. of Robert BARKER, M.D., sometime of Hammersmith, Midx. (*bur.* there 1745), but formerly of Drayton, Salop, by Hannah, da. of (—) WHITEHEAD, of Coleman street, London, was *b.* about 1732, at St. Anne's, Soho; became an officer in the East India Company's service 1749; was Capt. in the Artillery at Chandernagore and Plassey, 1758; accompanied, as Major, the expedition to the Philippine islands and distinguished himself at the capture of Manilla in Oct. 1762, for which he was *Knighted*, at St. James', 16 April 1764, receiving, in that year, the local rank of Colonel in the King's army, and in 1770 that of Brigadier General in the Company's service, being in the same year made Provincial Commander in Chief at Bengal and signing as such, in May 1772 (at the instance of the Nabob of Oude), the treaty of Fyzabad with the Rohillas against the Mahrattas. Disagreeing with the measures of Warren Hastings (Governor of Bengal, 1772, and Governor General of India, 1773) he quitted India about 1774; was M.P. for Wallingford, 1774-80, and, though he never spoke in Parl., was "for his consistent vote with the Government"(b) *cr. a Baronet*, as above, 24 March 1781. F.R.S. He *m.* 4 Nov. 1780, at Bolsover, co. Derby, Anne, only child of Brabazon HALLOWES, of Glapwell, in Bolsover, and of Dethick Hall, in Ashover, in that county. He *d.* s.p. at Bushbridge 14, and was *bur.* 28 Sep. 1789 at Hammersmith, when *the Baronetcy* became *extinct*. Will pr. Oct. 1789. The will of Dame Anne BARKER pr. 1806.

BANKS:

cr. 24 March 1781.

ex. 19 June 1820.

I. 1781, to 1820. "JOSEPH BANKS, of Revesby Abbey, co Lincoln, Esq.,"(a) only s. and h. of William BANKS, of the same (*d.* 1761, aged 42), by Sarah, da. of William BATE, of Fausson, co. Derby, was *b.* in Argyle street, 13 Feb. 1743/4; ed. at Harrow, 1753, and at Eton, 1756; matric. at Oxford (Ch. Ch.), 16 Dec. 1760, aged 17, being sub-

(a) See page 113, note "a," under "GIDEON." The date of the Gazette notice of Barker, Banks, Ingilby, Craufurd, Quin, André, Sykes, Coghill, and Mosley is 24 March, and that of Middleton 4 Sep. 1781.

(b) *Dict. Nat. Biogr.*

sequently, 21 Nov. 1771, *cr.* D.C.L. thereof; was an eminent Botanist, and undertook long voyages in pursuit of natural history, going to Newfoundland in 1766, accompanying Cook in his voyage round the world, 1768-71, and going to Iceland in 1772; F.R.S., 1766, of which Society he was subsequently, for above forty years (1778 till his death), President. He purchased the estate of Spring Grove, in Hounslow, Midx., in 1779 (where he sometimes entertained the King and Royal family), and was *cr. a Baronet*, as above, 24 March 1781; Sheriff of Lincolnshire, 1794-95; **K.B.**, 1 July 1795, becoming, consequently, **G.C.B.** in 1815; P.C., 29 March 1797; Commissioner of the Board of Trade, 1797; President of the Royal Institution at its foundation, 1799-1800. He *m.* 23 March 1779, at St. Andrew's, Holborn, Dorothy, 1st da. and coheir of William Western HUGESSEN, of Provender in Norton, co. Kent, by Thomazine, da. of Sir John HONYWOOD, 3d Baronet [1660]. He *d.* s.p. at his house in Soho square, 19 June 1820, aged 76, when the *Baronetcy* became *extinct*. Will pr. Sep. 1820. His widow, who was *b.* 8 Nov. 1758, *d.* in or before July 1828. Will pr. July 1828.

ANDRE;

cr. 24 March 1781;

ex. 11 Nov. 1802.

I. 1781, to 1802. "WILLIAM LEWIS ANDRÉ, Esq., of Southampton, Hants, Capt. in His Majesty's 26th Reg. of Foot,"(a) yr. and only br. of the well-known Major John ANDRÉ (hung, as a spy, at Tappan, New York, 2 Oct. 1780, aged 30), both being sons of Anthony ANDRÉ, of Clapton, Midx., merchant of London (*d.* 14 April 1769) by Marie Louise, da. of Paul GIRARDOT, of Paris, was *bap.* 25 Nov. 1760, at St. Martin's Outwich, London; was Capt. in the 26th Foot; accompanied his brother to America, in consideration of whose death in his country's cause, he was *cr. a Baronet*, as above, 24 March 1781. He *d.* unm. at Deans Leaze, Hants, 11 Nov. 1802, in his 42d year, when the *Baronetcy* became *extinct*.(b) Will, as of Bath, dat. 11 Aug. 1801, pr. 9 Dec. 1809.

COGHILL:

cr. 24 March 1781;

ex. 14 Nov. 1785.

I. 1781, to 1785. "JOHN COGHILL, of Richings [in the parish of Iver], co. Buckingham, Esq.,"(a) *formerly* John MAYNE, a Major in the Army, assumed, in consequence of his marriage, the name of COGHILL, and having purchased in 1776, the said estate of Richings, was M.P. for Newport, 1780 till his death, and was *cr. a Baronet*, as above, 24 March 1781. He *m.* in or after 1764, Hester, Dow. COUNTESS OF CHARLEVILLE [I.], only surv. da. and h. of James COGHILL,(c) LL.D., Registrar of the Prerog.

(a) See p. 210, note "a," under "BARKER."

(b) Of his three sisters and coheirs, who all *d.* unm., having long survived him, living at 23 Circus, Bath, and being well known in the intellectual and fashionable world, (1), Mary Hannah, the survivor, *d.* 3 March 1845, aged 93, leaving a fortune of £95,000. (2), Ann Marguerite (the "tuneful Anna" of Miss Seward), *d.* in or shortly before Aug. 1830. (3), Louisa Catherine, *d.* 25 Dec. 1835, aged 81.

(c) See under "COGHILL," Baronetcy, *cr.* 31 Aug. 1788.

Court [I.], by Mary, sister of Thomas PEARSON, of Rathmore, co. Meath. He *d.* s.p. 14 and was *bur.* 22 Nov. 1785, at Aldenham, Herts, when the *Baronetcy* became *extinct*. Will pr. Dec. 1785. His widow, who in 1786, sold the estate of Richings, *d.* s.p. at Isleworth, Midx., 28 July, and was *bur.* 7 Aug. 1789, at Aldenham aforesaid, devising her estates to her cousin, Sir John COGHILL, 1st Baronet [1788], *formerly* John CRAMER. Will pr. 1789.

INGILBY:

cr. 8 June 1781;

ex. 14 May 1854.

I. 1781. "JOHN INGILBY, of Ripley, in the West Riding of co. York, Esq.,(a) illegit. s. of Sir John INGLEBY, *or* INGILBY, 4th and last Baronet [1642], of Ripley aforesaid (who *d.* s.p. legit., 3 Aug. 1772), by Mary WRIGHT, was *b.* 1758, and having suc., by devise, to his said father's estates in 1772, was *cr. a Baronet*, as above, 8 June 1781. Sheriff of Yorkshire, 1782-83; M.P. for East Retford, 1790-96. He *m.* 25 Oct. 1780, at Kettlethorpe, co. Lincoln, Elizabeth, da. and h. of Sir Wharton AMCOTTS, 1st Baronet [1796], *formerly* Wharton EMERSON, by Anna Maria, sister and h. of Charles AMCOTTS, 1st da. of Vincent AMCOTTS, both of Kettlethorpe. She, who was *b.* June 1763, took by Royal Lic., 3 Oct. 1800, the name of AMCOTTS before that of INGILBY, on inheriting the Kettlethorpe estates on the death of her mother, 1 July 1800. She *d.* 21 Sep. 1812. Will pr. 1812. He *d.* 13 May 1815 in his 58th year.

II. 1815, to 1854. SIR WILLIAM AMCOTTS-INGILBY, Baronet [1781], of Ripley and Kettlethorpe aforesaid, *formerly* William INGILBY, 3d but only surv. s. and h., *b.* at Ripley, 20 June 1783, and *became a Baronet* [1796] on the death, 26 Sep. 1807, of his maternal grandfather, Sir Wharton AMCOTTS, 1st Baronet [1796], in consequence of a spec. rem., in his favour, in the creation of that dignity, 11 May 1796.(b) He assumed the name of AMCOTTS before that of INGILBY, on the death of his mother, 21 Sep. 1812 which was confirmed to him by royal lic., 11 April 1822; *suc. to the Baronetcy* [1781], which had been conferred on his father, 8 June 1781 (as above stated), and to the Ripley estate, on the death of his said father, 13 May 1815. He was M.P. for East Retford, 1807-12, for Lincolnshire (four Parls.), Dec. 1823 to 1832, and for the Lindsey Division, 1833-35, having been Sheriff of Yorkshire, 1821-22. He *m.* firstly, at Maple Hayes, co. Stafford, 18 April 1822, Louisa, da. of John ATKINSON, of Maple Hayes. She *d.* 22 July 1836, at Frankfort, aged 34. He *m.* secondly, 27 July 1843, at St. Margaret's, Westm., Mary Anne, only child of John CLEMENTSON, of Abingdon street, Serjeant-at-Arms to the House of Commons, by Eliza, da. of Sir Thomas TURTON, 1st Baronet [1796]. He *d.* s.p. at the house of his father-in-law, in Abingdon street, Westm., 14 May 1854, aged 70, when *both the Baronetcies* [1781 and 1796] became *extinct*.(c) His widow *d.* 22 Dec. 1902, aged 84.

(a) See p. 210, note "a," under "BARKER."

(b) He was at that date (11 May 1796) a younger son, his eldest br., John Ingilby, *b.* 12 Aug. 1781 (who *d.* Dec. 1799), being alive and the then heir ap. to the Baronetcy of Ingilby, which had been conferred on their father (as stated) in 1781, fifteen years before the creation of the Amcott's Baronetcy in 1796.

(c) He devised the Ripley estate to his cousin, John Henry Ingilby, s. and h. of the Rev. Henry Ingilby (*d.* 4 Sep. 1833, aged 72), who was (like testator's father) an illegit. s. of the 4th and last Baronet [1842]. This John Henry Ingilby, being then of Ripley, was *cr. a Baronet* 26 July 1866.

CRAUFURD:

cr. 8 June 1781;

sometime, 1812-39, GREGAN-CRAUFURD.

I. 1781. "ALEXANDER CRAUFURD, Esq.," of Kilbirney, [co. Stirling], in North Britain,(a) 1st s. and h. of Quentin CRAUFURD, of Newark, co. Ayr,(b) Justiciary Baillie for the west seas of Scotland (*d.* 1749), was *b.* about 1729, and was *cr. a Baronet*, as above, 8 June 1781. He *m.* 30 May 1760, Jane, da. of James CROKATT, of Luxborough, Essex. She *d.* 6 May 1794 in Clarges street. Will pr. Jan. 1795. He *d.* 15 Dec. 1797. Will pr. April 1798.

II. 1797. SIR JAMES CRAUFURD, *afterwards* 1812-39, GREGAN CRAUFURD, Baronet [1781], of Kilbirney aforesaid, 1st s. and h.,(c) *b.* 11 Oct. 1761; was British Resident at Rotterdam, 1778; Secretary of Legation at Copenhagen, 1793; *suc. to the Baronetcy*, 15 Dec. 1797; Resident Minister at the Hanse towns, 1798; Minister at Copenhagen, 1802. By royal lic., 25 June 1812, he took the name of GREGAN, before that of CRAUFURD. He *m.* 2 March 1792, Maria Theresa, sister of Henry, 3d VISCOUNT GAGE OF CASTLE ISLAND [I.], 1st da. of Gen. the Hon. Thomas GAGE, by Margaret, da. and h. of Peter KEMBLE. She, who was *b.* 4 April 1762, *d* 21 April 1832, at Hastings, aged 70. Will pr. June 1832. He *d.* 9 July 1839, in his 78th year. Will pr. July 1839.

III. 1839. SIR GEORGE WILLIAM CRAUFURD, Baronet [1781], of Burgh Hall, near Boston, co. Lincoln, 3d but 1st surv. s. and h.,(d) *b.* 10 April 1797, in Bryanston square, Marylebone; ed. at King's Coll., Cambridge, of which he was sometime Fellow; B.A., 1820; M.A., 1832; in Holy Orders; Chaplain in Bengal to the East India Company, 1822-33; Divinity Lecturer, King's College, 1831-38; Vicar of Burgh and Winthorpe, co. Lincoln, 1838-45; *suc. to the Baronetcy*, 9 July 1839; was Rector of Scremby, co. Lincoln, 1862, till death in 1881. He *m.* firstly, 15 Feb. 1843, at Ockham Park, Surrey, Hester, sister of William, 1st EARL OF LOVELACE, 1st da. of Peter (KING), 7th BARON KING OF OCKHAM, by Hester, da. of Hugh (FORTESCUE), 1st EARL FORTESCUE. She, who was *b.* 2 May 1806, *d.* 18 March 1848, at Pisa, and was *bur.* at Leghorn. He *m.* secondly, 3 May 1849, at Worthing, Barbadoes, Martha, widow of William COOKE, of Burgh House, co. Lincoln, da. of John HOLLAND, of Carrington House in that County. She *d.* s.p. 5 July 1845, at Burgh Hall aforesaid, after a long illness. He *d.* 24 Feb. 1881, at Pau, in South France, aged 84.

IV. 1881. SIR CHARLES WILLIAM FREDERICK CRAUFURD, Baronet [1781], 1st and only surv. s. and h., by 1st wife, *b.* at Rome, 28 March 1847; sometime Lieut. Royal Navy; *suc. to the Baronetcy*, 24 Feb. 1881. He *m.* 23 Nov. 1870, at West Firle, Sussex, Isolda Caroline, 1st da. of Standish Prendergast (VEREKER), 4th VISCOUNT GORT OF LIMERICK [I.], by Caroline Harriet, da. of Henry Hall (GAGE), 4th VISCOUNT GAGE OF CASTLE ISLAND [I.]. She was *b.* 5 April 1852.

(a) See p. 210, note "a," under "BARKER."

(b) Quentin Craufurd, the 2d son, *b.* 22 Sep. 1743, who was an author of some little note, assisted on one occasion the escape of the unfortunate Queen of France, Marie Antoinette, and *d.* at Paris, 12 Nov. 1819.

(c) Two of his yr. brothers were distinguished officers, viz., (1), Lieut.-Gen. Sir Charles Gregan-Craufurd, **G.C.B.**, who *d.* s.p., in April 1821, aged 58; and (2), Major-Gen. Robert Craufurd, who was slain at the assault of Ciudad Rodrigo, 24 Jan. 1812, aged 48.

(d) Of his two elder brothers (1), Thomas Gage Craufurd, an officer in the Guards, was killed at Hougoumont, 18 June 1815. (2), Lieut.-Col. Alexander Charles Craufurd, *m.*, but *d.* s.p., 12 March 1838, aged 45.

SYKES:

cr. 8 June 1781.

I. 1781. "FRANCIS SYKES, of Basildon, co. Berks, Esq.,"(a) 4th and yst. s.(b) of Francis SYKES, of Thornhill, co. York (*d.* 5 April 1766, aged 73), by Martha, da. of (—) FEARNLEY, was *bap.* at Thornhill 25 Feb. 1732; entered the East India Company's service in 1749, and acquired a considerable fortune in India, where he was sometime Gov. of Cossimbazar, Bengal; purchased, about 1770, the manor and park of Basildon, Berks, wherein he erected a stately mansion; was M.P. for Shaftesbury, May 1771 till unseated in April 1775, as also 1780-84; for Wallingford (four Parls.), 1784 till death, being also High Steward of that town, and was *cr. a Baronet*, as above, 8 June 1781. He *m.* firstly, 7 Feb. 1766, Catherine, da. of John RIDLEY. She *d.* 30 Dec. 1768, and was *bur.* at Calcutta. He *m.* secondly, 2 Sep. 1774, Elizabeth, 1st da. of William (MONCKTON, *afterwards* MONCKTON-ARUNDELL), 2d VISCOUNT GALWAY [I.], by Elizabeth, da. of Joseph DA-COSTA-VILLA-REAL. He *d.* 11 Jan. 1804, aged 71. Admon. April 1804. His widow, who was *b.* 20 July 1754, *m.* 16 Feb. 1805 at St. Geo. Han. sq., as his 2d wife, Sir Drummond SMITH, 1st Baronet [1804], of Tring Park, Herts (who *d.* 22 Jan. 1816), and *d.* 2 July 1835. Will pr. July 1835.

II. 1804, Jan. SIR FRANCIS WILLIAM SYKES, Baronet [1781], of Basildon Park aforesaid, 1st s. and h., by 1st wife, *b.* about 1767, at Fort William, Bengal; matric. at Oxford (Queen's Coll.), 14 Oct. 1785, aged 18; M.P. for Wallingford, March 1794 to 1796, and Colonel of the Berks Militia; *suc. to the Baronetcy*, 11 Jan. 1804. He *m.* 10 Nov. 1798, Mary Anne, 1st da. of the Hon. Major HENNIKER (2d s. of John, 1st BARON HENNIKER OF STRATFORD-UPON-SLANEY [I.]), by Mary, da. of John PHŒNIX, of Rochester. She *d.* of scarlet fever (caught while nursing one of her children, who *d.* of the same), 27 Feb. 1804, at Elberfeld in Germany, in her 25th year, and was *bur.* at Basildon. He *d.* a few days later, 7 March 1804, of the same disease, and was *bur.* with her. Will pr. 1804.

III. 1804, March. SIR FRANCIS WILLIAM SYKES, Baronet [1781], of Basildon Park aforesaid, 1st s. and h., *b.* 8 Aug. 1799; *suc. to the Baronetcy*, 7 March 1804; ed. at St. John's Coll., Cambridge; M.A., 1819. He sold the estate of Basildon. He *m.* 8 Aug. 1821, Henrietta, da. of Henry VILLEBOIS, of Marham Hall, Norfolk, and of Gloucester place, Marylebone. He *d.* 6 April 1843, at Lennox lodge, Hayling Island, Hants, aged 43. Will pr. April 1843. His widow *d.* 15 May 1846, at Little Missenden.

IV. 1843. SIR FRANCIS WILLIAM SYKES, Baronet [1781], 1st s. and h., *b.* at Basildon Park, 10 June 1822; sometime in the 97th Foot, but afterwards, 1843-44, Lieut. 2d Life Guards, having *suc. to the Baronetcy*, 6 April 1843. He *d.* unm. 1 Jan. 1866, aged 43, at his residence, "Isenhurst," near Mayfield, Sussex.

V. 1866. SIR FREDERICK HENRY SYKES, Baronet [1781], br. and h., *b.* at Basildon Park, 12 Feb. 1826; entered the Army, 1844; sometime Capt. 11th Hussars and Royal Horse Guards Blue; *suc. to the Baronetcy*, 1 Jan. 1866. He *m.* 5 Jan. 1867, Caroline, da. of M. J. BETTESWORTH, of Hayling, Hants. He *d.* s.p.m., 20 Jan. 1899, in his 73d year, at 7 Chesham place, Brighton. His widow living 1905.

(a) See p. 210, note "a," under "BARKER."

(b) Of his three elder brothers (1) William Sykes, was of Ackworth Park, co. York, *m.* but *d.* s.p. Oct. 1777, aged 68; (2) John Sykes, of Strand on the Green, Midx., *d.* s.p., probably unm., 2 March 1792, aged 81; (3) Richard Sykes, of Chichester, who survived him, *m.* but *d.* s.p.s. 30 Nov. 1808, at West Cowes, aged 81.

VI. 1899. SIR HENRY SYKES, Baronet [1781], br. and h. male; *b.* 9 Dec. 1828; sometime an officer in the Royal Navy, but subsequently Capt. 1st Dragoons, serving in the Crimean War (medal); *suc. to the Baronetcy*, 20 Jan. 1899.

MOSLEY:

cr. 8 June 1781.

I. 1781. "JOHN MOSLEY [sometimes called JOHN PARKER MOSLEY], of Ancoats [near Manchester], co. Lancaster, Esq.,"(a) 1st s. and h. of Nicholas MOSLEY, of Manchester, merchant (*bur.* there 12 March 1733/4), by Elizabeth, da. of William PARKER, of Derby, was *b.* 1732, and was *cr. a Baronet*, as above, 8 June 1781; Sheriff of Lancashire, 1786-87. By the death, 23 Sep. 1799, of his distant cousin,(b) Sir John MOSLEY, 3d and last Baronet [1720] of Rolleston, co. Stafford, he suc. to that estate and to the Lordship of the manor of Manchester, in accordance with his will of Sir Oswald MOSLEY, 2d Baronet [1720]. He *m.* 7 Sep. 1760, Elizabeth, da. of James BAYLEY, of Withington, co. Lancaster, by Anne, da. of Samuel PEPLOE, D.D., Bishop of Chester. She *d.* in London, Oct. 1797. He *d.* at Rolleston, 29 Sep. 1798, aged 66. Will pr. Nov. 1798.

II. 1798. SIR OSWALD MOSLEY, Baronet, [1781], of Rolleston and Ancoats aforesaid, grandson and h., being 1st s. and h. of Oswald MOSLEY, of Bolesworth Castle, co. Chester, by Elizabeth, da. and h. of the Rev. Thomas TONMAN, Rector of Little Badworth in that county, which Oswald (who matric. at Oxford [Brasenose College], 11 Nov. 1779, aged 18, and who *d.* v.p. 27 July 1789, aged 28) was 1st s. and h. ap. of the late Baronet. He was *b.* 17 March 1785, at Moston, co. Chester; *suc. to the Baronetcy*, 29 Sep. 1798; ed. at Manchester School and (1799) at Rugby; matric. at Oxford (Brasenose Coll.) 30 June 1802, aged 17; *cr.* M.A., 18 June 1806, and D.C.L., 5 July 1820; was M.P. for Portarlington, 1806-07; for Winchelsea, 1807-12; for Midhurst, Feb. 1817 to 1818; and for North Staffordshire, 1832-37, having been Sheriff of Staffordshire, 1814-15. He, by agreement, 24 June 1845, sold for £200,000 the manor and manorial rights of Manchester to the Corporation of that town.(c) He *m.* 31 Jan. 1804, Sophia Anne, 2d da. of Sir Edward EVERY, 8th Baronet [1641], by Mary, da. of Edward MORLEY, of Horsley, co. Derby. She *d.* 8 June 1859, at Rolleston Hall, aged 79. He *d.* there 24 May 1871, aged 86.

III. 1871. SIR TONMAN-MOSLEY, Baronet, [1781], of Rolleston aforesaid, 2d but 1st surv. s. and h.,(d) *b.* 9 July 1813, at Rolleston Hall; ed. at Magdalen Coll., Cambridge; sometime Lieut. 6th Dragoons; *suc. to the Baronetcy*, 24 May 1871; Sheriff of Staffordshire, 1874. He *m.* 4 Feb. 1847, at Alfreton, co. Derby, Catherine, da. of the Rev. John WOOD, of Swan hall, co. Derby. He *d.* 28 April 1890, aged 76. His widow *d.* 22 April 1891, at 47 Prince's gate, London. Will pr. at £6,643.

IV. 1890. SIR OSWALD MOSLEY, Baronet, [1781], of Rolleston aforesaid, 1st s. and h., *b.* 25 Sep. 1848; ed. at Eton; *suc. to the Baronetcy*, 28 April 1890; Sheriff of Staffordshire, 1894. He *m.* 22 Jan. 1873, at

(a) See p. 210, note "a," under "BARKER."

(b) See p. 52, note "a," under "MOSLEY," Baronetcy, *cr.* 18 June 1720, as to this relationship.

(c) It was formally conveyed to that body (who had, in 1815, refused to give £90,000 for it) by deed, dated 5 May 1846, just 250 years after the purchase thereof, in 1596, by Sir Nicholas Mosley.

(d) Oswald Mosley, the 1st son, *b.* 2 Dec. 1804; ed. at Eton; matric. at Oxford (Brasenose Coll.), 18 June 1822, aged 17, *m.* but *d.* s.p. and v.p. 25 Sep. 1856, at Rolleston hall, aged 51.

St. Mary's, Bryanston square, Elizabeth Constance, 2d da. of Sir William WHITE, of Carag lodge, Killarney, and of Gloucester place, Portman square, Marylebone, sometime (1834-35) Sheriff of Cork, by Sarah, da. of Richard Johnson LOCKETT, of Macclesfield.

Family Estates.—These, in 1883, consisted of 3,446 acres in Staffordshire; 207 in Bucks, and 50 in Derbyshire. *Total*—3,703 acres, worth £7,500 a year. *Seat.*—Rolleston Hall, near Burton-upon-Trent, co. Stafford.

QUIN:

cr. 8 June 1781;

afterwards, since 1800, BARONS ADARE [I.];

since 1816, VISCOUNTS MOUNT-EARL [I.];

and since 1822, EARLS OF DUNRAVEN AND MOUNT-EARL [I.].

I. 1781. "VALENTINE RICHARD QUIN, of Adare, co. Limerick, Esq.,"(a) 1st s. and h. ap. of Windham QUIN, of the same (*d.* 17 April 1789), by Frances, da. of Richard DAWSON, of Dawson's grove, co. Monaghan, was *b.* 30 July 1752; matric. at Oxford (Magdalen Coll.), 31 May 1769, aged 16, and was, v.p., *cr. a Baronet*, as above, 8 June 1781. He was M.P. [I.] for Kilmallock, 1799-1800, and bought two seats (for himself and a nominee) to support the Union with Ireland.(b) He *m.* firstly, 24 Aug. 1777, Frances Muriel, da. of Stephen (FOX-STRANGWAYS), 1st EARL OF ILCHESTER, by Elizabeth, da. and h. of Thomas HORNER. She, who was *b.* Aug. 1755, was living when he was *cr.* 31 July 1800, BARON ADARE of Adare [I.], being subsequently *cr.* 5 Feb. 1816, VISCOUNT MOUNT-EARL [I.], and finally, 5 Feb. 1822, EARL OF DUNRAVEN AND MOUNT-EARL [I.]. In those peerages this *Baronetcy* then *merged* and still (1905) so continues. See *Peerage*.

MIDDLETON:

cr. 23 Oct. 1781;

sometime, 1805-13, BARON BARHAM;

afterwards, since 1813, NOEL;

since 1838, BARONS BARHAM, *and since* 1841, EARLS OF GAINSBOROUGH.

I. 1781. "CHARLES MIDDLETON, Esq., Comptroller of His Majesty's Navy,"(a) 2d s. of Robert MIDDLETON, Collector of Customs at Bo'ness, co. Linlithgow by Helen, da. of Charles DUNDAS, of Arniston, co. Midlothian, was *b.* at Leith, 14 Oct. 1726; was Lieut. R.N., 1745; Post Capt., 22 May 1758; distinguished himself in 1761 by destroying a great number of French privateers, when in command of the "Emerald" frigate (twenty guns), receiving accordingly the thanks of the Assembly of Barbadoes; was from 1778 to 1790, Comptroller of the Navy, and was *cr. a Baronet*, as above, 23 Oct. 1781, with a spec. rem. of that dignity, failing heirs male of his body to "Gerard Noel EDWARDES, of Ketton, co. Rutland, Esq., and his issue male by Diana, his wife, da. of the said Charles MIDDLETON."(a) He was M.P. for Rochester, 1784-90; Rear-Admiral, 1787; Vice-Admiral, 1793, and Admiral, 1795; was one of the Lords of the Admiralty, 1794-95, being ten years later (when nearly 80) for a few

(a) See p. 210, note "a," under "BARKER."

(b) "His object is to be created a Baron," was the terse comment of the Marquess Cornwallis, then [1798-1801], Viceroy of Ireland.

months, May 1805 to Feb. 1806, First Lord of the Admiralty,(a) and being *cr.* 1 May 1805, BARON BARHAM of Barham Court and Teston, co. Kent, with a spec. rem. of that dignity, failing heirs male of his body, to his da., Diana, and the heirs male of her body. He *m.* 21 Dec. 1761, at St. Martin's-in-the-Fields, Margaret, da. of James GAMBIER, Barrister-at-Law, and Warden of the Fleet Prison, by Mary, da. of (—) MEAD. She *d.* 10 Oct. 1792, at Teston. He *d.* s.p.m., 17 June 1813, at Barham Court, aged 87.(b) Will, in which he left £10,000 apiece to each of his fourteen grandchildren, pr. Aug. 1813, and again Jan. 1848.

II. 1813. SIR GERARD NOEL NOEL, Baronet [1781], of Exton Park, co. Rutland, *formerly* Gerard Noel EDWARDES, son-in-law of the above, being only s. and h. of Gerard Anne EDWARDES, of Welham Grove, Essex, by Jane, sister of Henry, 6th and last EARL OF GAINSBOROUGH [of the creation of 1682], da. of Baptist (NOEL), 4th EARL OF GAINSBOROUGH. He was *b.* 17 July 1759, at Tickencote, co. Rutland, and was M.P. for Maidstone, 1784-88, and for Rutland (fifteen Parls), July 1788 to 1808, and Aug. 1814 till death in 1838, having by royal lic., 5 May 1798, taken the name of NOEL instead of EDWARDES, under the will of his abovenamed uncle, Henry, 6th EARL OF GAINSBOROUGH, whose estates (*viz.*, Exton Park and other considerable property), he inherited. He *suc. to the Baronetcy*, 17 June 1813, under the spec. limitation of that dignity. He was Sheriff of Rutland, 1812-13. He *m.* firstly, 21 Dec. 1780, at St. Geo. Han. sq., Diana, da. and h. of Charles (MIDDLETON), 1st Baron BARHAM, by Margaret, da. of James GAMBIER, all abovenamed. She, who, on the death of her father, 17 June 1813, suc. as *suo jure* BARONESS BARHAM, and who was mother of eleven sons and five daughters, *d.* 12 April 1823, at her seat, "Fairy Hill," near Swansea, in her 61st year, and was *bur.* at Teston. Admon. May 1823. He *m.* secondly (a few days later), 4 May 1823, Harriet, da. of the Rev. Joseph GILL, Vicar of Scraptoft, co. Lincoln. She *d.* s.p. 11 Aug. 1826, aged 41. He *m.* thirdly, 11 Aug. 1831 (at the age of 72), at Milton, near Gravesend, Isabella Evans RAYMOND. He *d.* at Exton Park, 25 Feb. 1838, aged 78, and was *bur.* at Exton. Will pr. April 1838. His widow, by whom he had no issue, *d.* 9 June 1867, at her residence, Ville Neuve, Morlaix, France, aged 74.

III. 1838. CHARLES NOEL (NOEL), BARON BARHAM, 3d Baronet [1781], *formerly* Charles Noel EDWARDES, 1st s. and h., by 1st wife, *b.* 2 Oct. 1781; suc. to the peerage, as BARON BARHAM, on the death of his mother, 12 April 1823, and *suc. to the Baronetcy*, on the death of his father, 25 Feb. 1838, which accordingly became then *merged* in that Peerage, and still (1905) so continues. He was *cr.* 13 Aug. 1841, EARL OF GAINSBOROUGH. See *Peerage*.

LOVETT:

cr. 23 Oct. 1781;

ex. 30 Jan. 1812.

I. 1781, to 1812. JONATHAN LOVETT, of Liscombe, co. Buckingham, Esq., 1st s. and h. of Jonathan LOVETT, of the same, and of Kingswell, co. Tipperary, sometime Sheriff of co. Tipperary, by Eleanor, da. of Daniel MANSERGH, of Macrony, co. Cork, was *b.* probably about 1730; suc. in 1770 to considerable estates in Ireland on the death of his great uncle, Verney LOVETT; expended large sums in the reparation of the Mansion house at Liscombe, and was *cr. a Baronet*, as above, 23 Oct. 1781. He

(a) This was on the resignation of his relative, the well-known Henry (Dundas), 1st Viscount Melville, and it would seem that his peerage, as also "the appointment, was due to Mr. Pitt's desire to lessen the force of the blow which had struck down his friend." [*Dict. Nat. Biog.*].

(b) He and his wife's relatives, the Gambiers, were among the earliest members of the "Evangelical" party in the Church of England.

was Sheriff of Bucks, 1782-83. He *m.* probably about 1775, Sarah, only da. of Jonathan DARBY, of Leap Castle, in King's County, by Susanna, da. of Robert LOVETT, of Dromoyle, in the said county. He *d.* s.p.m.,(a) 30 Jan. 1812, when the *Baronetcy* became *extinct*. Will pr. 1812. His widow *d.* in May 1836. Will pr. Oct. 1836.

TURNER:

cr. 8 May 1782;

ex. 1 Feb. 1810.

I. 1782. "CHARLES TURNER, of Kirkleatham [in Cleveland], co. York, Esq.,"(b) only s. and h. of William TURNER,(c) of the same (*d.* 12 Aug. 1774, aged 76), by Jane (*m.* 9 Feb. 1724/5), 2d sister and coheir of Charles BATHURST, of Clintz and Scutterskelfe, in that county, da. of Charles BATHURST, of the same, was *b.* about 1726; Sheriff of Yorkshire, 1759-60; M.P. (three Parls.) for York, 1768, till death in 1783, and was *cr. a Baronet*, as above, 8 May 1782.(d) He *m.* firstly, Elizabeth, 2d da. and coheir of William WOMBWELL, of Wombwell, co. York, by Margaret, da. of Sir Thomas STANDISH, 2d Baronet [1677], of Duxbury. She, who was *bap.* at Darfield, 23 Aug. 1731, *d.* s.p. and was *bur.* 18 June 1768, at Kirkleatham. He *m.* secondly, 11 Oct. 1771, Mary, da. of James SHUTTLEWORTH, of Gawthorp, co. Lancaster, by Mary, da. of Robert HOLDEN, of Aston, co. Derby. He *d.* 26 Oct. and was *bur.* 3 Nov. 1783, at Kirkleatham, aged 57. Will dated 1781, and republished 1782. His widow *m.* 4 Nov. 1784, at Aston-upon-Trent, co. Derby, as his 2d wife, Sir Thomas GASCOIGNE, 8th Baronet [S. 1635], of Parlington, co. York (who *d.* s.p.s. 12 Feb. 1810), and *d.* in childbirth, at Parlington, 1 Feb. 1786. Admon. 4 Feb. 1786, at York.

II. 1783, to 1810. SIR CHARLES TURNER, Baronet, [1782], of Kirkleatham aforesaid, only s. and h., *b.* at York 28 Jan., and *bap.* 25 Aug. 1773, at Kirkleatham; *suc. to the Baronetcy*, 26 Oct. 1783; was M.P. for Hull, 1796-1802. He *m.* 2 Sep. 1796, Teresa, 2d da. of Sir William GLEADOWE-NEWCOMEN, 1st Baronet [I. 1781], formerly William GLEADOWE, by Charlotte, *suo jure* VISCOUNTESS NEWCOMEN [I.], da. and h. of Charles NEWCOMEN, of Carrickglass, co. Longford. He *d.* s.p. 1, and was *bur.* 19 Feb. 1810, at Kirkleatham, aged 37, when the *Baronetcy* became *extinct*. Will pr. 1810. His widow, to whom he left all his estates absolutely, *m.* 21 July 1812, Henry VANSITTART, of Foxley, Berks (who *d.* s.p.m. 22 April 1848), and *d.* 1840.(e)

(a) His eldest and last surv. s., Robert Turville Jonathan Lovett, was admitted to Rugby School, Jan. 1786, but *d.* unm. and v.p. 22 Nov. 1806.

(b) See p. 118, note "a," under "GIDEON." The date of the Gazette notice for Turner was 20 April; for Drake and Affleck, 28 May and for Brisco, Apreece, and Vane, 4 June 1782.

(c) An account of the Turner family by "W.D.B.," is in the *Top. and Gen.*, vol. i, pp. 505-509. Among its members was Sir William Turner, Lord Mayor of London, 1669, who *d.* s.p., and was *bur.* at Kirkleatham, 22 March 1692/3.

(d) He "one of the most eccentric men that ever sat in Parl., accepted a Baronetcy from the Marquis of Rockingham . . . to commemorate, as he said, the era of a virtuous Minister and Administration attaining to power, and not from any impulse of personal vanity or desire of title." [Wraxall's *Hist. Memoirs*, vol. ii, p. 267. Edit. 1884.]

(e) She, by her second marriage, left "an only child Theresa Vansittart, who *m.* about 1840, her relative Arthur Newcomen, Esq." [see note "c" above].

FLETCHER:

cr. 20 May 1782;

afterwards, since 1903, AUBREY-FLETCHER.

I. 1782. HENRY FLETCHER, of Cleahall, co. Cumberland, Esq., as also of Ashley Park, in Walton-on-Thames, co. Surrey, 7th s. of John FLETCHER, of Cleahall aforesaid, being 6th s. by his 2d wife Isabella, da. and coheir of John SENHOUSE, of Netherhall in that county, was *b.* about 1727; joined the East India Company's naval service, being from 1759 to 1766 a Commander, and becoming 1766-84, a Director of that Company; was M.P. for Cumberland (seven Parls.) 1768-1802, and was *cr. a Baronet*, as above, 20 May 1782, on the conclusion of the American War, which he had uniformly opposed. He *m.* Oct. 1768, Catherine, da. and h. of John LINTOT,(a) of Southwater, Sussex, by Elizabeth, da. of Sir John AUBREY,(b) 3d Baronet [1660], of Llantrithyd, co. Glamorgan. He *d.* 29 March 1807, aged about 80, at Ashley park aforesaid. Will pr. 1807. His widow *d.* 17 Oct. 1816, aged 86. Will pr. 1816.

II. 1807. SIR HENRY FLETCHER, Baronet, [1782], of Ashley Park aforesaid, only s. and h., *b.* 4 Feb. 1772; *suc. to the Baronetcy*, 29 March 1807, and pulled down a great part of the house at Ashley park. Sheriff of Cumberland, 1810-11. He *m.* 19 March 1801, Frances Sophia, 10th da. of Thomas Wright VAUGHAN, of Woodstone, co. Lincoln. He *d.* 10 Aug. 1821, at Ashley park, aged 49. Will pr. 1821. His widow *d.* there 9 Feb. 1828. Will pr. March 1828.

III. 1821. SIR HENRY FLETCHER, Baronet, [1782], of Ashley Park aforesaid, 1st s. and h., *b.* 18 Sep. 1807; *suc. to the Baronetcy*, 10 Aug. 1821; matric. at Oxford (New Coll.) 18 March 1826, aged 18. He *m.* 26 June 1834, Emily Maria, 2d da. of George BROWNE, Member of the Council of Bombay. He *d.* 6 Sep. 1851, at Ashley Park, in his 44th year. Will pr. Oct. 1851. His widow *d.* 30 Jan. 1888, at 40 Brunswick Place, Hove by Brighton, aged 72.

IV. 1851. SIR HENRY FLETCHER, *afterwards*, since 1903, AUBREY-FLETCHER, Baronet [1782], of Ashley Park aforesaid, 1st s. and h., *b.* there 24 Sep. 1835; *suc. to the Baronetcy*, 6 Sep. 1851; Ensign, 69th Foot, 1853: Lieut., Grenadier Guards, 1855-59; Cornet in Westmorland and Cumberland Yeomanry, 1859-61; Major in the Surrey Rifle Volunteers, 1859-65, and afterwards Lieut.-Col. Commanding Sussex Volunteer Infantry Brigade. He was M.P. for Horsham, 1880-85, and for Mid Sussex since 1885; was Groom in Waiting to Queen Victoria, 1885-86; C.B. (Civil), 1900; P.C., 1901; took the name of AUBREY before that of FLETCHER, by royal lic., 1 Jan. 1903, having on the death in Dec. 1901, of Charles Aubrey AUBREY, of Dorton House, Bucks, suc. to the estates of that family in Glamorganshire (*i.e.* Llantrihyd, etc.), in Bucks (*i.e.* Dorton, Boarstall, etc.), and in Oxon, under the will of Sir John AUBREY, 6th Baronet [1660], who *d.* as long ago as 1 March 1826.

(a) He was son of Bernard Lintot, the well-known bookseller.

(b) It was through this match that some 135 years later, the 4th Baronet in 1901, suc. to the Aubrey estates in Bucks, Oxon and Glamorganshire, and took the additional name of Aubrey.

DRAKE:

cr. 28 May 1782;

ex. 19 Nov. 1789.

I. 1782, to 1789. "Rear-Admiral FRANCIS SAMUEL DRAKE,"(a) 3d s. of Sir Francis Henry DRAKE, 4th Baronet [1622], of Buckland, Devon (*d.* 26 Jan. 1739/40, aged 46), by Anne, da. of Samuel HEATHCOTE, of Hursley, Hants, was *bap.* at Buckland, 14 Sep. 1729; entered the Royal Navy, and after much creditable service, became Rear-Admiral of the Blue, Sep. 1780, and, as such, was in command of the van of the fleet under Rodney in the battle off Dominica, 12 April 1782, being consequently, a few weeks later, *cr. a Baronet*, as above, 28 May 1782. He became Vice-Admiral of the Red, Sep. 1787, and was on 14 Aug. 1789, a few months before his death, a Lord of the Admiralty, being sometimes (though probably erroneously) said to have been M.P. for Plymouth in that year. He *m.* firstly, Elizabeth, da. of (—) HAYMAN, of Kent. He *m.* secondly, 23 Jan. 1788, Pooley, da. of Lieut.-Col. George ONSLOW, by Jane, da. of the Rev. Thomas THORPE. He *d.* s.p., 19 Nov. 1789, aged 60,(b) when the *Baronetcy* became *extinct*. Admon Dec. 1789. His widow *m.* Arthur ONSLOW, Serjeant-at-Law, and *d.* 10 Dec. 1810.

PALK:

cr. 19 June 1782;

afterwards, since 1880, BARONS HALDON.

I. 1782. ROBERT PALK, of Haldon House, in Haldon, co. Devon, Esq., s. of Walter PALK, of Ashburton in that county, by (—), da. of (—) ABRAHAM, was *b.* Dec. 1717, at Ambrooke, co. Devon; matric. at Oxford (Wadham Coll.), 15 April 1736, aged 18; took Deacon's Orders, and went to Madras as Chaplain to the E.I.C., but entering the Civil Service, was a member of the Council in 1753; was Governor of Madras, 1763-67, concluding, 11 Nov. 1766, a pusillanimous treaty with the Nizam of the Deccan.(c) He was M.P. for Ashburton Dec. 1767 to 1768; for Wareham, 1768-74, and for Ashburton (again), 1774-87 (in all five Parls.), being *cr. a Baronet*, as above, 19 June 1782. He *m.* 11 Feb. 1761, Anne, da. of Arthur VANSITTART, of Shottesbrooke Park, Berks, by Martha, da. of Sir John STONHOUSE, 3d Baronet [1670], of Radley. He *d.* 29 April 1798, aged 80. Will pr. June 1798.

II. 1798. SIR LAWRENCE PALK, Baronet [1782], of Haldon House aforesaid, only s. and h., *b.* about 1766 at Madras; matric. at Oxford (Ch. Ch.), 29 March 1784, aged 18; M.P. for Ashburton, March 1787 to 1796, and for Devon, 1796-1812 (in all five Parls.), having *suc. to the Baronetcy*, 29 April 1798. He *m.* firstly, 7 Aug. 1789, at St. Geo. Han. sq., Mary, 1st da. of John (BLIGH), 1st EARL OF DARNLEY [I.], by Theodosia, da. and h. of Edward (HYDE), 3d EARL OF CLARENDON. She *d.* 4 March 1791. He *m.* secondly, 15 May 1792, at St. Marylebone, Dorothy Elizabeth, da. of Wilmot (VAUGHAN), 1st EARL OF LISBURNE [I.], by his 2d wife, Dorothy, da. of John SHAFTO. He *d.* 20 June 1813, aged 47. Will pr. 1815. His widow *d.* 15 Feb. 1849, in Bruton street, Berkeley square, aged 84.

(a) See p. 218, note "b," under "TURNER."

(b) He is frequently confused with his next elder brother, Francis William Drake, who was *bap.* 22 Aug. 1724, at Buckland, who was also a Vice-Admiral (sometime Gov. of Newfoundland), who *d.* but two years before him.

(c) "Palk Strait, which separates Ceylon from India, was named after him." In 1755 he formed "a lifelong friendship" with Col. Stringer Lawrence (the Commander of Fort St. George when besieged, 1758-59, by the French), who "on his death in 1775 left all his property to Palk's children," the only son, Lawrence, having been so called after him [*Dict. Nat. Biogr.*].

III. 1813. SIR LAWRENCE VAUGHAN PALK, Baronet [1782], of Haldon House aforesaid, 1st s. and h., *b.* 24 April 1793, at St. Geo. Han. sq.; ed. at Eton; matric. at Oxford (Ch. Ch.), 29 Jan. 1812, aged 18; *suc. to the Baronetcy*, 20 June 1813; was M.P. for Ashburton (four Parls.), 1818-31. He *m.* 9 Dec. 1815, Anna Eleanora, widow of Edward HARTOPP, of Dalby House, co. Leicester, 1st da. of Sir Bourchier WREY, 6th Baronet [1628], by his 1st wife, Anne, da. of Sir Robert PALK, 1st Baronet [1782], abovenamed. She *d.* 25 Jan. 1846. Admon. May 1846. He is said(a) to have *m.* subsequently Phillipe Anne VICTOIRE, who *d.* 1855. He *d.* 16 May 1860, at Haldon House, aged 67.

IV. 1860. SIR LAWRENCE PALK, Baronet [1782], of Haldon House aforesaid, 1st s. and h., *b.* 5 Jan. 1818, in London; ed. at Eton; M.P. for South Devon, Feb. 1854 to 1868, and for East Devon, 1868-80 (six Parls. in all), having *suc. to the Baronetcy*, 1860. He *m.* 15 May 1845, at Rufford, co. Lancaster, Maria Harriett, da. of Sir Thomas Henry HESKETH, 4th Baronet [1761], by Annette Maria, da. of Robert BOMFORD. She was living when he was *cr.* 29 May 1880, BARON HALDON of Haldon, co. Devon, in which peerage this *Baronetcy* then *merged*, and still (1905) so continues.

AFFLECK:

cr. 10 July 1782.

I. 1782. "CAPTAIN EDMUND AFFLECK,"(b) an officer of the Royal Navy, of Colchester, co. Essex, 9th s. of Gilbert AFFLECK, of Dalham Hall, co. Suffolk, sometime (1722-27 and 1737-41) M.P. for Cambridge, by Anna (*m.* 3 Nov. 1705, in Westm. Abbey), da. of John DOLBEN, of Finedon, co. Northampton (br. to Sir Gilbert DOLBEN, 1st Baronet [1704]), was *b.* 19 April 1725, entered the Royal Navy, becoming Lieut. 1745; Post Captain 1757; distinguished himself in Rodney's encounter with the Spanish Squadron off Cape St. Vincent, 16 Jan. 1780; in the repulse of the French, 26 Jan. 1782, at St. Christophers, and still more so, the following April, in the action off Dominica, when his prompt action, in passing through a gap in the enemy's line, contributed greatly to the victory. He was accordingly *cr. a Baronet*, as above, 10 July 1782, with a spec. rem. failing heirs male of his body, to the heirs male of the body of his father. He became Rear-Admiral of the Blue, 1784, and of the Red, 1786. He, who was of Finringhoe Hall, co. Essex, was M.P. for Colchester, Oct. 1787 till his death. He *m.* firstly, Esther, widow of Peter CREFFIELD, da. of John RUTH. She *d.* 15 Dec. 1787. He *m.* secondly, 14 May 1788, at St. Marylebone, Margaret, widow of William SMITHERS, of Colchester, da. and coheir of (—) BURGESS, of New York in America. He *d.* s.p. 19 Nov. 1788, aged 63. Will dat. 28 June, and pr. 24 Nov. 1788. His widow (being then of Chiswick, Midx.), *m.* 15 Aug. 1792, John MACKINNON, of Glasgow, Major 63d Foot.

II. 1788. SIR GILBERT AFFLECK, Baronet [1782], of Dalham Hall aforesaid, nephew and h., being s. and h. of John AFFLECK, of the same, sometime (1743-61), M.P. for Suffolk, and (1767-68) for Agmondesham, by Sarah, da. and h. of James METCALFE, of Hoxton, Beds, which John (who *d.* 17 Feb. 1776, aged 64) was elder br. of the late Baronet, was *b.* 24 Dec. 1740, and *suc. to the Baronetcy*, 19 Nov. 1788, under the spec. rem. of that dignity. He *m.* 18 July 1796, Mary, widow of Richard VASSALL, of Jamaica, da. of Thomas CLARK, of New York. He *d.* s.p. 17 July 1808, aged 67. Will dat. 28 Jan. 1779, pr. 7 Oct. 1808. His widow *d.* in South street, Park lane, Feb. 1835, aged 86.

(a) Dod's *Baronetage*, 1860.

(b) See p. 218, note "b," under "TURNER."

V

III. 1808. SIR JAMES AFFLECK, Baronet [1782], of Dalham Hall aforesaid, cousin and h. male, being 1st s. and h. of the Rev. James AFFLECK, M.A., Vicar of Finedon, co. Northampton, and Prebendary of Southwell, by Mary, da. of (—) PROCTOR, of Clay Coton, co. Northampton, which James (who d. Nov. 1784, aged 68) was elder br. of the 1st Baronet, being the 5th s. of his father. He was *b.* 29 April 1759; was for thirty-eight years Lieut.-Col. 16th Dragoons, and finally Lieut.-Gen. in the Army, having *suc. to the Baronetcy*, 17 July 1808, under the spec. rem. of that dignity. He *d.* unm. 10 Aug. 1833, at Dalham Hall, aged 74, and was *bur.* at Dalham. Will dat. 2 Jan., pr. 25 Sep. 1833, under £39,000.

IV. 1833. SIR ROBERT AFFLECK, Baronet [1782], of Dalham Hall aforesaid, br. and h., *b.* 27 Jan. 1763; ed. at Westm. (where he was sometime Capt. of the School); matric. at Oxford (Ch. Ch.), 26 June 1783, aged 18; B.A., 1787; M.A., 1790; in Holy Orders; Vicar of Westow, co. York, 1796-1833; Rector of Treswell, Notts, 1796-1837; Prebendary of York, 1802; Vicar of Doncaster, 1807-17, and Vicar of Silkstone, co. York, 1817-37, having *suc. to the Baronetcy*, 10 Aug. 1833, under the spec. rem. of that dignity. He *m.* 16 May 1800, Maria, 2d da. of Sir Elijah IMPEY, of Newick Park, Sussex, sometime Chief Justice of Bengal, by Mary, da. of [—] READE. She *d.* 12 March 1825. He *d.* at Dalham Hall, 7 May 1851, aged 88.

V. 1851. SIR GILBERT AFFLECK, Baronet, [1782], of Dalham Hall aforesaid, 1st s. and h., *b.* 9 June 1804; *suc. to the Baronetcy*, 7 May 1851. He *m.* 20 Dec. 1834, at St. Geo. Han. sq., Everina Frances, sister of Leslie ELLIS, Fellow of Trinity Coll., Cambridge, 1st da. of Francis ELLIS, of the Royal Crescent, Bath. He *d.* s.p., 18 Nov. 1854, at his residence in Calverley Park, Tunbridge Wells, aged 50. His widow *m.* 1 July 1858, at St. Geo. Han. sq., as his 2d wife, Rev. William WHEWELL, D.D. (the well known) Master of Trinity College, Cambridge (who *d.* there 6 March 1866, aged 72), and *d.* 1 April 1865.

VI. 1854. SIR ROBERT AFFLECK, Baronet, [1782], of Dalham Hall aforesaid, br. and h., *b.* 28 July 1805, at Retford, Notts; *suc. to the Baronetcy*, 18 Nov. 1854; was Sheriff of Suffolk, 1875. He *m.* 9 April 1850, at Welton, co. Northampton, Maria Emily, 1st da. of Edmund Singer BURTON, of Churchill in that county. He *d.* 9 Oct. 1882, at Dalham Hall, aged 77. His widow *d.* 9 Nov. 1902, at the Midland Grand Hotel, St. Pancras, London, aged 76. Will pr. at £22,722 net.

VII. 1882. SIR ROBERT AFFLECK, Baronet, [1782], of Dalham Hall aforesaid, 1st s. and h., *b.* 4 March 1852, at St. Peter Port, Guernsey; ed. at Eton; matric. at Oxford (St. John's Coll.) 9 June 1871, aged 19; *suc. to the Baronetcy*, 9 Oct. 1882. He sold the Dalham Hall estate (a famous sporting property) to Cecil Rhodes, the founder of "Rhodesia," in South Africa, who, however, died shortly afterwards. He *m.* 7 March 1886, at St. Stephen's, Gloucester Road, London (by spec. lic. at two o'clock p.m.) Julia Georgina, 2d da. of John Sampson PRINCE, of 20 Queen's Gate Gardens.

Family Estates.—These, in 1883, consisted of 2,913 acres in Suffolk; 734 in Essex; 113 in Cambridgeshire, and 4 in Huntingdonshire. *Total.*— 3,764 acres, worth £4,776 a year. *Seat.*—Dalham Hall, near Newmarket.

BRISCO:

cr. 11 July 1782.

I. 1782. "JOHN BRISCO, of Crofton Place [near Wigton], co. Cumberland, Esq.,"(a) 1st s. and h. of the Rev. John BRISCO, D.D., of Crofton Place aforesaid, Rector of Orton and Vicar of Aspatria, in that

(a) See p. 218, note "b," under "TURNER."

county (*d.* 19 April 1771, aged 70), by Catherine, da. of John HYLTON, of Hylton, was *b.* 15 May 1739; was Sheriff of Cumberland, 1778-79, and was *cr. a Baronet*, as above, 11 July 1782, with a spec. rem., failing heirs male of his body to his br. Horton BRISCO, a Colonel in the East Indian service. He *m.* 8 July 1776, Caroline Alicia, 2d da. and coheir of Gilbert Fane Fleming, by Camilla, da. of Charles (BENNET), 2d EARL OF TANKERVILLE. He *d.* at Bath, 27 Dec. 1805, and was *bur.* 3 Jan. 1806, in Bath Abbey, aged 66. M.I. Will pr. Feb. 1806. His widow *d.* 27 Dec. 1822. Will pr. 1823.

II. 1805. SIR WALTER BRISCO, Baronet, [1782], of Crofton Place aforesaid, 1st s. and h., *b.* 17 May 1778, at St. Marylebone; matric. at Oxford (Ch. Ch.) 26 Oct. 1797, aged 19; B.A., 1800; admitted to Inner Temple, 12 Feb. 1801, and migrated to Lincoln's Inn, 19 Nov. following; *suc. to the Baronetcy*, 27 Dec. 1805; Sheriff of Cumberland, 1813-14. He *m.* 18 Nov. 1806, Sarah Lester, 1st da. of Robert LADBROOK.(a) She *d.* 28 Aug. 1861. He *d.* 1 Oct. 1862, aged 84.

III. 1862. SIR ROBERT BRISCO, Baronet, [1782], of Crofton Place, otherwise called Crofton Hall, aforesaid, 2d but 1st surv. s. and h., *b.* there 17 Sep. 1808; ed. at Midhurst School; Captain in the Westmorland and Cumberland Yeomanry, 1843; *suc. to the Baronetcy*, 1 Oct. 1862; Sheriff of Cumberland, 1868. He *m.* 10 July 1832, Annie Drewry, 3d da. of George RIMINGTON, of Tynefield House, Cumberland. She *d.* 14 Aug. 1875, at Castle View, Penrith, aged 63. He *d.* 23 Dec. 1884, at Crofton Hall, aged 76.

IV. 1884. SIR MUSGRAVE HORTON BRISCO, Baronet, [1782], of Crofton Hall aforesaid, 1st s. and h., *b.* 11 Aug. 1853, at "The Oaks," Dalston, Cumberland, ed. at Winchester, *suc. to the Baronetcy*, 23 Dec. 1884. He *m.* 27 June 1867, at Feniscowles, co. Lancaster, Mary Elizabeth, widow of Richard Newsham PEDDER, Captain 10th Hussars, 1st da. of Sir William Henry FEILDEN, 2d Baronet [1846], by Mary Elizabeth, da. of James Balfour WEMYSS.

Family Estates.—These, in 1883, consisted of 3,540 acres in Cumberland, worth £5,229 a year. *Seat.*—Crofton Hall, near Wigton, co. Cumberland.

APREECE:

cr. 12 July 1782;

ex. 30 Dec. 1842.

I. 1782. "THOMAS HUSSEY APREECE, of Washingley, co. Huntingdon, Esq.,"(b) as also of Cranham Hall, Essex, and of Honington, co. Lincoln, 1st s. and h. of Thomas Hussey APREECE, of the same (*d.* about 1762), by Dorothy, da. and coheir of Sir Nathan WRIGHT, 3d Baronet [1661], of Cranham aforesaid, was *b.* 15 Nov. 1744, in Leicester Fields, Midx., and having distinguished himself, when Captain of the Huntingdonshire Militia, for his gallant defence of Alnwick, against Paul JONES, the noted pirate, was *cr. a Baronet*, as above, 12 July 1782. He *m.* 15 April 1771, at St. James', Westm., Dorothea, yst. of the two daughters and coheirs of Shuckburgh ASHBY, of Quenby Hall, co. Leicester, by Elizabeth, da. and h. of Richard HINDE, of Cold Ashby, co. Northampton. She, who was *b.* 8 Jan. 1750, in Micklegate, York, *d.* 26 Dec. 1822. He *d.* at his seat, Effingham House, Surrey, 27 May 1833, aged 88. Will dat. 12 June 1830, pr. (with four codicils) 22 June 1833.

(a) In the *Annual Reg.* for 1806, the lady is described as "Miss Lester, 1st da. of Mrs. Cooper, of Hammersmith," and she is also called "Miss Lester" in Playfair's *Baronetage* [1811], and "Miss Sarah Lester" in Debrett's *Baronetage* [1840].

(b) See p. 218, note "b," under "TURNER."

II. 1833, to 1842. SIR THOMAS GEORGE APREECE, Baronet [1782], of Washingley, etc., aforesaid, 2d but only surv. s. and h.,(a) *b.* 19 Aug. 1791; Sheriff of Cambridgeshire and Hunts. 1818-19; *suc. to the Baronetcy*, 27 May 1833. He *d.* unm., 30 Dec. 1842, aged 51, at Margate, Kent, when the *Baronetcy became extinct*. Will, in which (not having mentioned a single relative) he left all his property to St. George's Hospital, Hyde Park Corner, pr. (after litigation), 21 Nov. 1849.

VANE:

cr. 13 July 1782;

afterwards, 1794-1813, VANE-TEMPEST;

ex. 1 Aug. 1813.

I. 1782. "REV. HENRY VANE, D.D., of Long Newton, co. Durham,"(b) 2d and yst. s. of George VANE, of the same (*d.* 25 July 1750, aged 65), by Anne, da. of William MACHON, of Durham, was *b.* about 1725; ed. at Trinity Coll., Cambridge, of which he was sometime a Fellow; B.A., 1749; M.A., 1753; LL.D., 1761; was in Holy Orders; Prebendary of Durham, 1758 till death; and was *cr. a Baronet*, as above, 13 July 1782, though he did not suc. to the family estate till the death of his elder br., Lionel VANE (who *d.* unm. at Ferryhill, near Durham), 20 Feb. 1793. He *m.* Frances, da. and h. of John TEMPEST, of Sherburne, co. Durham. He *d.* 7 June 1794, aged 69. Will pr. Jan. 1795, Feb. 1853, and July 1854. His widow *d.* 19 Jan. 1795, near Darlington. Will pr. March 1795.

II. 1794, to 1813. SIR HENRY VANE-TEMPEST, Baronet [1782], of Long Newton aforesaid and of Wynyard, co. Durham, only s. and h., who by royal lic., 25 Jan. 1771, took the name of TEMPEST after that of VANE, and was M.P. for Durham, 1794-1800, *suc. to the Baronetcy*, 7 June 1794. He *m.* 25 April 1799 (spec. lic.), at her mother's house in Hanover Square, Anne Catharine, *suo jure* COUNTESS OF ANTRIM [I. 1785], who on the death of her father, 29 July 1791, had suc. to that Earldom (under the spec. rem. in its recent creation), 1st da. and coheir of Randal William (MACDONNELL), MARQUESS OF ANTRIM [I.], by Letitia, da. of Hervey (MORRES), 1st VISCOUNT MOUNTMORRES [I.]. He *d.* s.p.m.(c) 7 Aug. 1813, when the *Baronetcy* became *extinct*. Will pr. Feb. 1819, Aug. 1820 and Feb. 1839. His widow *m.* 24 May 1817 (spec. lic.) in Bruton street, St. James', Westm., Edmund PHELPS (who by royal lic., 27 June 1817, took the name of MACDONNELL only, and who *d.* at Rome, 30 May 1852, aged 72), and *d.* in Park lane, Midx., 30 June, and was *bur.* 7 July 1834 at St. James', Westm., aged 58. Will pr. Aug. 1853 and July 1854.

(a) His elder br., Shuckburgh Ashby Apreece, *b.* 17 Dec. 1773; *m.* 3 Oct. 1799, Jane, da. and h. of Charles Kerr, but *d.* s.p. and v.p. 6 Oct. 1807.

(b) See p. 218, note "b," under "TURNER."

(c) Frances Anne Emily, his only da. and h., *b.* 17 Jan. 1800, inherited his large estates, including the valuable coal mines at Seaham. She *m.* (as his 2d wife) 3 April 1819, Charles (Stewart, afterwards Vane), 3d Marquess of Londonderry [I.], who accordingly was *cr.* 18 March 1823, Earl Vane and Viscount Seaham, with rem. to the heirs male of his body by her. She *d.* his widow 20 Jan. 1865, and her eldest son, who had suc. his father, 6 March 1854, as Earl Vane, suc. his elder br. (of the half blood) 25 Nov. 1872, as 5th Marquess of Londonderry [I.].

KENT:(a)

cr. 16 Aug. 1782;

ex. 8 April 1848.

I. 1782. SIR CHARLES KENT, Knt., of Fornham St. Genevieve, co. Suffolk, *formerly* Charles EGLETON, s. and h. of Sir Charles EGLETON, of London, sometime (1742-43) Sheriff of that city (*d.* 25 April 1769, aged 69), by Sarah, (*m.* 29 Jan. 1742/3), sister and heir of Thomas KENT, of Camberwell, Surrey (*d.* unm. 15 May 1766, aged 57), only da. of Samuel KENT,(a) of Fornham St. Genevieve aforesaid, Purveyor of Chelsea Hospital, was *b.* about 1744; assumed the name of KENT instead of that of EGLETON, on inheriting the estates of his maternal grandfather; being *Knighted*, 16 Sep. 1771; was Sheriff of Suffolk, 1781-82, and was *cr. a Baronet*, as above, 16 Aug. 1782. He was M.P. for Thetford, 1784-90. He *m.* in or before 1783, Mary, 1st of the two daus. and coheirs of Josias WORDSWORTH,(b) of Wadworth, co. York, and Sevenscore, co. Kent, by Ann, da. and h. of Arthur ROBINSON, Collector of the Customs at Sunderland. He *d.* at Grantham, co. Lincoln, 14 March 1811, aged 67, and was *bur.* at Wadworth aforesaid. Will pr. 1811. His widow, who was *b.* 1751, *d.* at Poynton House, near Grantham, 17 Sep. 1817, aged 67. Admon. Feb. 1818.

II. 1811. SIR CHARLES EGLETON KENT, Baronet [1782], of Fornham, and of Poynton House aforesaid, only s. and h., *b.* 4 March 1784, at St. Geo. Han. sq.; matric. at Oxford (Ch. Ch.), 21 Oct. 1802, aged 18; *cr.* M.A., 26 June 1805; *suc. to the Baronetcy*, 14 March 1811. He *m.* 4 March 1813, Sophia Margaret, 3d da. of William (LYGON), 1st EARL BEAUCHAMP, by Catharine, da. of James DENN. She *d.* at Peterborough House, Parsons green, Fulham, Midx., 16 and was *bur.* 22 Nov. 1834, at Fulham, aged 45. Admon. March 1835. He *d.* there, a few weeks later, 5 and was *bur.* 11 Dec. 1834, at Fulham, aged 50. M.I. Will pr. 1835.

III. 1834, to 1848. SIR CHARLES WILLIAM EGLETON KENT, Baronet, [1782], of Fornham and Poynton House aforesaid, only s. and h., *b.* 15 Feb. 1819; *suc. to the Baronetcy*, 5 Dec. 1834; entered the Life Guards, 1839; Capt., 1844. He *d.* unm. at the Barracks, Regent's Park, 8 and was *bur.* 15 April 1848, at Fulham, aged 29, when the *Baronetcy* became *extinct*. M.I.

GEARY:

cr. 17 Aug. 1782.

I. 1782. FRANCIS GEARY, of Polesden(c) in Great Bookham, co. Surrey, Admiral of the White, s. of Francis GEARY, of Cheddington, Bucks, and Arcall Magna, Salop, by Judith, da. and h. of Robert BARBER, Citizen of London, was *bap.* 14 Oct. 1709; entered the Naval Service, 1727; Lieut., 1734; Capt., 1742; Rear-Admiral of the White, 1758; Vice-Admiral of the Blue, 1762; and of the Red, 1770, being then Commander-in-Chief at Portsmouth; Admiral of the Blue, 1775, and of the White, 1778; was for some months, in 1780, in command of the Channel Fleet, but retired from ill-health, and, having in his earlier career (though he never had the opportunity of distinguishing himself in any great action), effected several gallant captures, was *cr. a*

(a) See "*Genealogist*" (orig. series, vol. ii, pp. 185-192) for a full account of the family of Kent.

(b) See Hunter's *Familiæ Minorum Gentium* for elaborate pedigree of Wordsworth.

(c) This estate he had purchased for £5,500 in March 1747, being then Capt. of the "Culloden."

Baronet, as above, 17 Aug. 1782.(a) He *m.* 20 Sep. 1748 (settlement 3 Sep.), Mary, da. of Philip BARTHOLOMEW, of Oxonhoath in West Peckham, and of West Malling, both co. Kent, and only child by his 2d wife, Mary, da. of Leonard THOMAS, of Lamberhurst, Kent. She *d.* 20 Aug. 1778. He *d.* 7 Feb. 1796, aged 86, both being *bur.* at Great Bookham. Will dat. 14 Feb. 1792, pr. 1 March 1796.

II. 1796. SIR WILLIAM GEARY, Baronet [1782], of Polesden aforesaid, 2d and yst. but only surv. s. and h.,(b) *bap.* 23 Sep. 1756; matric. at Oxford (Mag. Coll.), 15 June 1773, aged 16; *cr.* M.A., 11 May 1776; *suc. to the Baronetcy*, 7 Feb. 1796, and sold the Polesden estate in 1804 having suc. to that of Oxonhoath abovenamed, by gift of his maternal uncle, Leonard BARTHOLOMEW; was M.P. for Kent, 1796-1806, and 1812-18, and a Director of Greenwich Hospital. He *m.* 15 Jan. 1810, Henrietta, widow of Edward DERING, da. and coheir of Richard NEVILLE, *formerly* JONES, of Furnace, co. Kildare. He *d.* 6 Aug. 1825 at Oxonhoath Park, aged 68.(c) Will pr. Oct. 1825. His widow *d.* 18 Jan. 1871, at Marden Vicarage, aged 91.

III. 1825. SIR WILLIAM RICHARD POWLETT GEARY, Baronet [1782], of Oxonhoath aforesaid, 1st s. and h., *b.* 13 Nov. 1810; *suc. to the Baronetcy*, 6 Aug. 1825; matric. at Oxford (Ch. Ch.), 30 May 1827, aged 17; M.P. for West Kent, 1835 to Feb. 1838. He *m.* 14 July 1835, at St. James', Westm., Louisa, only da. of the Hon. Charles Andrew BRUCE (yr. s. of Charles, 5th EARL OF ELGIN [S.]), by his 2d wife, Charlotte Sophia, da. of Thomas DASHWOOD. She, who was *b.* April 1810, *d.* 7 Aug. 1870, at 128 Harley street, Marylebone. He *d.* s.p.m., at Oxonhoath, 19 Dec. 1877, aged 67.

IV. 1877. SIR FRANCIS GEARY, Baronet [1782], of Oxonhoath aforesaid, only br. and h. male, *b.* there 12 Oct. 1811; matric. at Oxford (Ch. Ch.), 29 June 1829, aged 17; B.A., 1833; admitted to Inner Temple, 18 April 1833, aged 21; Barrister, 30 April 1841; *suc. to the Baronetcy*, 19 Dec. 1877. He *m.* firstly, 11 March 1852, at Melton Mowbray, Mary Isabella, da. of Sir Francis GRANT, the well known painter, President of the Royal Academy, 1866-78, by his 2d wife, Isabella, da. of Richard NORMAN and Elizabeth Isabella, da. of Charles (MANNERS), 4th DUKE OF RUTLAND. She *d.* s.p. 19 Jan. 1854. He *m.* secondly, 5 Aug. 1856, at St. Geo. Han. sq., Fanny Isabella, 3d da. of Andrew Redmond PRIOR, by Catherine, da. of Sir John CALL, 1st Baronet [1791]. He *d.* 1 April 1895, at 14 Warwick sq., Pimlico, aged 83. His widow *d.* 13 and was *bur.* 16 Jan. 1901, at West Peckham, Kent.

V. 1895. SIR WILLIAM NEVILL MONTGOMERIE GEARY, Baronet [1782], of Oxonhoath aforesaid, only s. and h., by 2d wife, *b.* 7 April 1859; ed. at Eton; matric. at Oxford (Ch. Ch.), 12 Oct. 1877, aged 18; B.A. and M.A., 1886; Barrister (Inner Temple), 1884; *suc. to the Baronetcy*, 1 April 1895; was Attorney-Gen. to the Gold Coast of Africa, 1895-97; author of several legal and other treatises.

Family Estates.—These, in 1883, consisted of 2,843 acres in Kent, worth £5,077 a year.

(a) "Admiral Geary's name appears frequently in Walpole's letters during 1781, but seldom with much credit, except that on one occasion he relieved Gibraltar. He was one of the members of the court-martial which tried Admiral Byng" [note to Wraxall's *Hist. Memoirs* (edit. 1884, vol. i, p. 266), by Henry B. Wheatley, F.S.A., the editor thereof].

(b) The 1st son, Francis Geary, matric. at Oxford (Balliol Coll.), 19 May 1770, aged 18, was a Cornet in Gen. Burgoyne's Light Dragoons, *d.* unm. and v.p., being slain in conflict with the insurgents in America, 13 Dec. 1776, aged 24. M.I. at Great Bookham.

(c) See *Annual Reg.* for 1825 for some account of him and of his somewhat curious political views.

PARKER:

cr. 13 Jan. 1783;

ex. 13 March 1869.

I. 1783. "VICE-ADMIRAL SIR PETER PARKER,"(a) Knt., 3d s.(b) of Rear-Admiral Christopher PARKER (who commanded the "Speedwell" in Jan. 1712, and *d.* at a great age, in Henry street, Dublin, 1 Feb. 1765), was *b.* in 1721, probably in Ireland; entered the Naval service, and was Capt. R.N., 1747; took part in the reduction of Belle Isle in 1761; was *Knighted*, 10 June 1772, when proxy for Sir John MOORE, at the installation of Knights of the Bath; distinguished himself greatly, when Commodore of the "Bristol," in a stubborn, most sanguinary, but unavailing action off Charlestown in June 1776, and took Rhode Island a few months later; Rear-Admiral of the Blue, 1777; and Vice-Admiral of the Blue, 1779, and of the White, 1780; being Commander on the Jamaica station, 1777 till 1782, when he conveyed to England the Count de Grasse and the other French officers who had been taken prisoners at Rodney's famous victory, 12 April 1782, and was *cr. a Baronet*, as above, 13 Jan 1783. He, who was of Bassingborne, co. Essex, was M.P. for Seaford, 1784 till void in 1786, and for Maldon, Feb. 1787 to 1790; was Admiral of the Blue, 1787, and of the White, 1794; Commander-in-Chief, at Portsmouth, 1793-99, and finally, 1799, Admiral of the Fleet. He was also Deputy Grand Master of the Society of Freemasons. He *m.* in or before 1761, Margaret, da. of Walter NUGENT. She *d.* 18 and was *bur.* 25 Jan. 1803, at St. Margaret's, Westm. He *d.* at his house in Weymouth street, Marylebone, 21 and was *bur.* 28 Dec. 1811, at St. Margaret's aforesaid, at the age of 90, after eighty years service in the Navy. Will pr. 1811.

II. 1811. SIR PETER PARKER, Baronet [1783], grandson and h., being 1st s. and h. of Vice Admiral Christopher PARKER, by Augusta Barbara Charlotte, da. of Admiral the Hon. John BYRON, which Christopher, who *d.* v.p. 26 May 1794 aged 33, was 1st s. and h. ap. of the late Baronet. He was *b.* 1785; entered the Navy when young; was Lieut. R.N., 1801; Commander, 1804; Capt., 1805; distinguishing himself in several brilliant skirmishes; *suc. to the Baronetcy*, 21 Dec. 1811. He *m.* 11 Feb. 1809, Marianne, 1st da. of Sir George DALLAS, 1st Baronet [1798], by Catharine, da. of Sir John BLACKWOOD, 2d Baronet [I. 1763], and Dorcas his wife, *suo jure* BARONESS DUFFERIN AND CLANEBOYE [I.]. He was slain, 30 Aug. 1814, in a rash attack on the American Camp at Bellaire, near Baltimore, and was *bur.* 14 May 1815, "at five o'clock in the morning," at St. Margaret's, Westm., aged 29. Will pr. 1814. His widow *m.* 15 Aug. 1818, Michael BRUCE, of Geneig, Scotland.

III. 1814. SIR PETER PARKER, Baronet [1783], 1st s. and h., *b.* 2 Nov. 1809; *suc. to the Baronetcy*, 30 Aug. 1814; was a Commander in the Royal Navy. He *d.* unm. in London, 17 March 1835, aged 25. Will pr. April 1835.

IV. 1835, March. SIR JOHN EDMUND GEORGE PARKER, Baronet [1783], uncle and h., *b.* 18 Dec. 1788; Captain, Royal Artillery;(c) *suc. to the Baronetcy*, 17 March 1835, but *d.* unm. eight months afterwards, 18 Nov. 1835, aged 46.

(a) See p. 113, note "a," under "GIDEON." The date of the Gazette notice for Parker, Whalley-Gardiner and Graham is 28 Dec. 1782; for Sykes and Dalling, 4 March; and for Guise and Hamond, 20 Dec. 1783, though with respect to the last two, the patents for which are said to have been 9 and 18 Dec. 1783 respectively, there is apparently some mistake.

(b) The 2d son, George Parker (*d.* in the Isle of Man, 1791), was father of Admiral Sir George Parker, **K.C.B.** (1837), who *d.* 24 Dec. 1847, aged about 80.

(c) According to Debrett's *Baronetage* [1840], he was Capt. *in the Royal Navy* and his Christian names were "John Ely."

V. 1835, (Nov.) to 1869. SIR CHARLES CHRISTOPHER PARKER, Baronet [1783], yst. and only surv. br. and h., *b.* 16 June 1792, in Harley street, Marylebone; entered the Navy, 1804; Lieut. R.N., 1811, and served that year in an attack off Cape Talliat; Commander, 1815; Capt., 1822; Rear-Admiral, 1852; Vice-Admiral, 1857, and Admiral, 1863, having *suc. to the Baronetcy*, 18 Nov. 1835. He *m.* 19 Sep. 1815, Georgiana Ellis PALLMER, spinster. He *d.* s.p., suddenly, at Clifton, by Bristol, 13 March 1869, in his 77th year, when the *Baronetcy* became *extinct*. His widow *d.* 11 July 1878, at 3 Kensington Park Road, in her 84th year.

WHALLEY-GARDINER:

cr. 14 Jan. 1783;

afterwards, 1787-1868, WHALLEY-SMYTHE-GARDINER;

ex. 6 Oct. 1868.

I. 1783. "JOHN WHALLEY-GARDINER, Esq.,"(a) of Roche Court, in Fareham, co. Southampton, *formerly* John WHALLEY, of Tackley, Oxon, 1st s. and h. of Robert WHALLEY, M.D., of Blackburn, Governor of Blackburn Grammar School, 1739-69 (*d.* 3 April 1769, aged 55), by Grace, da. and h. of Bernard GARDINER, D.C.L., sometime (1702-26) Warden of All Souls' College, Oxford, (2d s. of Sir William GARDINER, 1st Baronet [1660]), was *b.* 26 May and *bap.* 22 June 1743, at St. Giles', Oxford, matric. at Oxford (Oriel Coll.), 22 Oct. 1760, aged 17; B.A., 1764; took by royal lic. 11 Nov. 1779, the name of GARDINER after that of WHALLEY, on succeeding to the Roche Court estate, by the death (20 Oct. 1779), and under the will of his mother's first cousin (paternally) Sir William GARDINER, 3d and last Baronet [1660]; was M.P. for Westbury, 1780-84, and was *cr. a Baronet*, as above, 14 Jan. 1783, with a spec. rem., failing heirs male of his body to his two brothers James WHALLEY and Thomas William WHALLEY respectively. He was Sheriff of Hants, 1785-86. He, by Royal lic., 1787, took the name of SMYTHE between those of WHALLEY and GARDINER, having by the death of Barbara SMYTHE, spinster,(b) his mother's first cousin (maternally) succeeded to the estate of Cuddesden, Oxon. He was *cr.* D.C.L. of Oxford, 4 July 1793. He *m.* 7 July 1787 [*Qy.* at Bath], Martha, da. of Benjamin NEWCOMBE, D.D., Dean of Rochester, 1767-75. He *d.* s.p. 18 Nov. 1797, aged 54. Will pr. Jan. 1798.(c) His widow, who long survived him, *d.* 19 July 1840, at Tackley Park, Oxon, in her 75th year. Will pr. Sep. 1840.

(a) See p. 227, note "a," under "PARKER."

(b) This Barbara Smythe, who *d.* at the age of 75, was da. and h. of Sebastian Smythe (*d.* 6 Dec. 1752, aged 75), brother of Grace, wife of Bernard Gardiner, D.C.L. (and, by him mother of Grace, wife of John Whalley, parents of the 1st Baronet), both being children of Sir Sebastian Smythe, of Cuddesden, Oxon (*Knighted* 11 July 1685), a Bencher of the Inner Temple, who *d.* 21 July 1733, aged 89

(c) His feats in the way of drinking are thus commemorated in the ballad called "*The Cape Hunt*" [*Wiccamical Chaplet*, ed. by Geo. Huddesford, 1804] giving an account of a grand carousal:—

"And sooth to say, no Squire, nor Knight
Who wore on heel a spur,
Could keep his seat or stand upright,
Save SIR JOHN GARDINER.—
Ne'er shall we see his Peer again,
None like him now there be!
He drank to death *five* Aldermen,
And Oxford taylors three."

II. 1797. SIR JAMES WHALLEY-SMYTHE-GARDINER, Baronet [1783], of Roche Court aforesaid and of Clerk Hill, in the parish of Whalley, co. Lancaster, next br. and h., *formerly* James WHALLEY, *bap.* 1 Oct. 1748, at St. Giles', Oxford; matric. at Oxford (Mag. Coll.), 28 July 1764, aged 15; B.A., 1768; M.A., 1781; admitted to the Middle Temple, 30 Nov. 1768; succeeded to the estate of Clerk Hill aforesaid on the death, 20 Feb. 1780, of his uncle James WHALLEY, Bencher of the Middle Temple,(a) and was Sheriff of Lancashire 1783-84. He *suc. to the Baronetcy* under the spec. rem. of that dignity, as also to the Roche Court and other estates, 18 Nov. 1797, when he assumed the additional names of SMYTHE-GARDINER, after that of WHALLEY. He *m.* firstly, 28 Oct. 1784, at Middleton, co. Lancaster, Elizabeth, 2d da. and eventually coheir of Richard ASSHETON, D.D., Warden of Manchester, and Rector of Middleton aforesaid, by Mary, da. and coheir of William HULLS, of Freelands, in Bromley, co. Kent. She *d.* 8 Sep. 1785, aged 24. He *m.* secondly, 3 Dec. 1789, at Croston, co. Lancaster, Jane, 1st da. of Robert MASTER, D.D., Rector of Croston aforesaid, by Elizabeth, da. and coheir of John WHALLEY, of Blackburn. He *d.* 21 Aug. 1805, at Clerk Hill aforesaid, and was *bur.* at Whalley, aged 56. Will pr. 1805. His widow, who was *b.* 31 May and *bap.* 29 June 1765, at Croston, *d.* at Clerk Hill 5 and was *bur.* 12 Jan. 1843, at Whalley.

III. 1805. SIR JAMES WHALLEY-SMYTHE-GARDINER, Baronet [1783] of Roche Court aforesaid, 1st s. and h., being only s. by 1st wife, *formerly* James WHALLEY, *b.* 2 Sep. 1785, at Clerk Hill aforesaid; matric. at Oxford (Brasenose Coll.), 28 Jan. 1804, aged 18; *cr.* M.A. 18 June 1806, having *suc. to the Baronetcy*, 21 Aug. 1805, and assumed the additional names of SMYTHE-GARDINER, after that of WHALLEY; Sheriff of Hants, 1810-11. He *m.* 17 Aug. 1807, Frances, sister of Sir Oswald MOSLEY, 2d Baronet [1781], 2d da. of Oswald MOSLEY, of Bolesworth Castle, co. Chester, by Elizabeth, da. and h. of the Rev. Thomas TONMAN. He *d.* 22 Oct. 1851, aged 66. His widow, who was *b.* at Bolesworth Castle, 24 June and *bap.* 20 Aug. 1788, at Malpas, *d.* at Roche Court 13 Dec. 1855. Will pr. Jan. 1856.

IV. 1851, to 1868. SIR JOHN BROCAS WHALLEY-SMYTHE GARDINER, Baronet [1783], of Roche Court, and, after 1861, of Clerk Hill aforesaid,(b) 2d and yst. but only surv. s. and h.,(c) *b.* 16 March 1814; *suc. to the Baronetcy*, 22 Oct. 1851. He *m.* in 1861, Mary Harriet, widow of James Archibald FORREST, Capt. 5th Fusileers, and formerly widow of William STEVENS, of Southampton, da. of (—) ADAMS. He *d.* s.p.m.,(d) 6 Oct. 1868, at Roche Court, aged 54, when the *Baronetcy* became *extinct*. His widow *d.* 22 Aug. 1870, in her 46th year, at 45 South street, Grosvenor square.

(a) This James Whalley, who *d.* unm., aged 75, was son of John Whalley, of Blackburn, co. Lancaster, and nephew of James Whalley, of Great Harwood, in that county, who purchased, about 1715, the Clerk Hill estate (presumably because it was situated in *Whalley*) and who devised it to him.

(b) This estate (as to which see note "a" above), was left by the 2d Baronet to his 2d s. (1st s. by 2d wife) Robert Whalley, who *d.* unm. 16 Nov. 1840, aged 50, being succeeded therein by his yr. br. the Rev. John Master Whalley, Rector of Slaidburn. He *d.* s.p.s., 27 Oct. 1861, aged 68, when it was claimed by his sister (of the whole blood) Elizabeth Jane, wife of Samuel Jellicoe. The Court of Chancery, however, decided in favour of the heir male (though of the half blood) the 4th Baronet (as above) who died possessed thereof, but it was sold in June 1871 (three years after his death) by the trustees of his da. and heir.

(c) The 1st son James Whalley-Smythe-Gardiner, *b.* 5 Sep. 1812; matric. at Oxford (Brasenose Coll.), 20 Jan. 1831, aged 18, and *d.* unm. and v.p. 11 Oct. 1837.

(d) Mabel Katherine, his only da. and h., *b.* 6 Aug. 1863, inherited the Roche Court estate, and *m.* 13 Jan. 1887 (as his 1st wife) Henry Feildem Rawstorne, by whom she had two daughters, the elder of whom *d.* unm. and under age, from an accidental fall down a cliff.

GRAHAM:

cr. 15 Jan. 1783.

I. 1783. "JAMES GRAHAM, Esq.,"(a) of Netherby, near Carlisle, co. Cumberland, 2d s. but (within two weeks of his father's death) heir male of the Rev. Robert GRAHAM, D.D., of Netherby aforesaid (who had inherited that and other considerable estates in 1757),(b) by Frances, his cousin, da. of Sir Reginald GRAHAM, 4th Baronet [1662] of Norton Conyers, which Robert (who *d.* 2 Feb. 1782, aged 72), was 2d s. of William GRAHAM, D.D., Dean of Carlisle and Wells (*d.* Feb. 1711/2), who was yr. br. of Richard, 1st VISCOUNT PRESTON OF HADDINGTON [S.], both being sons of Sir George GRAHAM, 2d Baronet [1629] of Esk. He was *b.* at Naworth Castle, 22 April 1761, and *bap.* at Brampton, co. Cumberland; matric. at Oxford (Mag. Coll.), 11 March 1778, aged 17, being *cr.* M.A. 2 June 1782, and was *cr. a Baronet*, as above, 15 Jan. 1783. He was Sheriff of Cumberland Feb. to June 1786,and again 1795-96; was M.P. for Ripon (three Parls.), Oct. 1798 to 1807.(c) He *m.* 9 June 1785, at St. James', Westm., Catharine, 1st da. of John (STEWART), 7th EARL OF GALLOWAY [S.], by his 2d wife Anne, da. of Sir James DASHWOOD, 2d Baronet [1684] of Kirtlington. He *d.* 13 April 1824, at Netherby, aged nearly 63, and was *bur.* at Arthured, co. Cumberland. M.I. Will pr. May 1825. His widow, who was *b.* 18 March 1765, *d.* 20 Sep. 1836. Will pr. Sep. 1836.

II. 1824. SIR JAMES ROBERT GEORGE GRAHAM, Baronet [1783], of Netherby aforesaid, 1st s. and h., *b.* 1 June 1792; matric. at Oxford (Ch. Ch.), 8 June 1810, aged 18; sat in no less than fourteen Parls. for eight different constituencies during forty-three years, being M.P. for Hull, 1818-20, on the Whig interest, at the "cost of £6,000," and without any help from his father, who "was a Tory"(d); for St. Ives, 1820-21; for Carlisle, 1826-29; for Cumberland, Jan. 1829 to 1832; for East Cumberland, 1832-37; for Pembroke, Feb. 1838 to 1841; for Dorchester, 1841-47; for Ripon, 1847-52, and finally for Carlisle (again), 1852 till death, having *suc. to the Baronetcy*, 13 April 1824; was P.C., 22 Nov. 1830; and First Lord of the Admiralty, with a seat in the Cabinet, 1830-34; was *cr.* LL.D. of Cambridge (Trinity Coll.), 1835; Rector of Glasgow Univ., 1840; Home Secretary of State, 1841-46; one of the Council of the Duchy of Lancaster, 1847; First Lord of the Admiralty (again), 1852-55; **G.C.B.** (Civil), 1854. He *m.* 8 July 1819, Fanny, "a famous beauty,"(d) yst. da. of Col. James CALLENDER, afterwards CAMPBELL, of Craigforth, co. Stirling, and Ardkinglass, co. Argyll, by his 3d wife Elizabeth, da. of Alexander (MACDONNELL), 5th EARL OF ANTRIM [I.]. She *d.* after a long illness, 25 Oct. 1857, at the Pavilion Parade, West Cowes, aged 63. He *d.* 25 Oct. 1861, at Netherby, aged 69, and was *bur.* at Arthured aforesaid.(d)

(a) See p. 227, note "a," under "PARKER."

(b) This was under the will of his cousin Catharine, Dowager Baroness Widdrington. See vol. ii, p. 70, note "f," under "GRAHAM" Baronetcy, *cr.* 29 March 1629.

(c) He, possibly, is the James Graham of Jesus College, Cambridge, who became M.A. of that Univ. in 1811, and who is stated (in the note to the *Graduati Cantabrigienses*, edit. 1856,) to have been "*Baronettus.*"

(d) *Dict. Nat. Biog.*, where full particulars of his career are given, by Professor (afterwards Bishop) Creighton, not altogether in accordance with the long and laudatory account in the obituary of the *Annual Register* of 1861. He seems to have been active, clever, well-read and most conscientious as a Statesman, effecting when in office several much needed reforms, but was singularly unpopular, having "the manner of a dandy," a "style stiff and pompous," and "the impatience of an aristocratic Whig." His unpopularity was at its height in 1844, when he underwent "attacks from all sides, of which the cartoons in *Punch* are abiding memorials," caused by his authorising, as Home Secretary, the opening of certain letters at the Post Office containing the treasonable correspondence of some foreign refugees. In this, however, "he had done nothing more than previous

III. 1861. SIR FREDERICK ULRIC GRAHAM, Baronet [1783], of Netherby aforesaid, 1st s. and h., *b.* 2 April 1820 at Marylebone; ed. at Eton; matric. at Oxford (Ch. Ch.), 30 May 1838, aged 18; was attaché to the Embassy at Vienna, Jan. 1842, and subsequently served in the 1st Life Guards; *suc. to the Baronetcy*, 25 Oct. 1861; Sheriff of Cumberland, 1866-67. He *m.* 26 Oct. 1852, at St. Martin's in the Fields, Jane Hermione, 1st da. and coheir of Edward Adolphus (SEYMOUR, *afterwards* ST. MAUR), 12th DUKE OF SOMERSET, by Jane Georgiana, da. of Thomas SHERIDAN. He *d.* 8 March 1888, at 40 Park lane, Hyde Park, in his 68th year. His widow, who was *b.* 1 Jan. 1832, living 1905.

IV. 1888. SIR RICHARD JAMES GRAHAM, Baronet [1783], of Netherby aforesaid, 1st s. and h., *b.* 24 Feb. 1859; sometime Lieut. in the Argyll and Sutherland Highlanders, and subsequently in the 4th Royal Highlanders; *suc. to the Baronetcy*, 8 March 1888; Sheriff of Cumberland, 1894. He *m.* firstly, 8 July 1886, at St. Paul's, Knightsbridge, his cousin, Olivia, yst. da. of Lieut. Gen. Charles BARING, Coldstream Guards, by Helen, da. of the Rt. Hon. Sir James Robert George GRAHAM, 2d Baronet [1783] abovenamed. She *d.* s.p., 8 July 1887. He *m.* secondly, 27 June 1889, at St. Geo. Han. sq., his cousin, Mabel Cynthia, 3d da. of William Ernest (DUNCOMBE), 1st EARL OF FEVERSHAM, by Mabel Violet, another da. of the Rt. Hon. Sir James Robert GRAHAM, 2d Baronet [1783] abovenamed. She was *b.* 4 Feb. 1869.

Family Estates.—These, in 1883, consisted of 25,270 acres in Cumberland, 105 in the West Riding of Yorkshire, besides 33 in Dumfriesshire. *Total.*—25,408 acres, worth £26,821 a year. *Seat.*—Netherby Hall, near Carlisle.

DALLING:

cr. 11 March 1783;

ex 16 Feb. 1864.

I. 1783. "LIEUT. GEN. JOHN DALLING, of Burwood, co. Surrey,"(a) s. of John DALLING, of Bungay, co. Suffolk, by Anne, da. of Col. William WINDHAM, of Ersham House (near that town), co. Norfolk, was *b.* about 1731; entered the Army; was Col. of the 60th Foot, 1776; Governor of Jamaica, 1777-82; Lieut.-Gen. in the Army, 1782; Col. of the 37th Foot, 1783, and was *cr. a Baronet*, as above, 11 March 1783. He was Commander in Chief at Madras, 1784-86, becoming a full General in the Army 1796. He *m.* firstly, Elizabeth, da. of Philip PINNOTH. She *d.* s.p.s. He *m.* secondly, in or before 1770, Louisa, da. of Excelles LAWFORD, of Burwood aforesaid. He *d.* 16 Jan. 1798, aged 67. Will pr. 1798. His widow *d.* 28 March 1824.

II. 1798, to 1864. SIR WILLIAM WINDHAM DALLING, Baronet [1783], of Ersham House aforesaid, 5th but 1st surv. s. and h., by 2d wife,(b) *b.* in 1774; sometime Lieut. 3d Foot Guards; *suc. to the Baronetcy*, 16 Jan. 1798; Sheriff of Norfolk, 1819-20. He *d.* unm. 16 Feb. 1864, aged 89, when the *Baronetcy* became *extinct*.

Home Secretaries; he had not acted on his own motion but at the request of the Foreign Secretary, Lord Aberdeen, who thought it his duty to help foreign governments by discovering plots that were being hatched in England. But Lord Aberdeen held his tongue and allowed the whole storm to burst on Graham."

(a) See p. 227, note "a," under "PARKER." The description in Betham's *Baronetage* (1801) in regard to the Baronetcy of Dalling is as "of Orval, Surrey," which place is also given as the "seat" of the 2d Baronet.

(b) Charles Lawford Dalling, one of his four elder brothers, matric. at Oxford (Exeter Coll.) 19 Oct. 1787, aged 15, being described as son of "John. of Kingston, Isle of Jamaica, Baronet."

SYKES:

cr. 28 March 1783;

sometime, 1801-23, MASTERMAN-SYKES.

I. 1783, March. "REV. MARK SYKES, D.D., of Sledmere [near Malton], co. York,"(a) 2d s. of Richard SYKES, of Hull, merchant (*b.* 1658, living 1711), by his 1st wife, Mary, da. and coheir of Mark KIRKBY, of Sledmere aforesaid, *b.* April and *bap.* 9 May 1711 at Hull, ed. at Peterhouse, Cambridge; B.A., 1733; M.A., 1749; D.D., 1761; was Rector of Roos, co. York, and Proctor in Convocation for that diocese; suc. to the family estate on the death, s.p., of his elder br., Richard SYKES (sometime, 1752-53, Sheriff for co. York), and was *cr. a Baronet*, as above, 28 March 1783, six months before his death. He *m.* 14 Feb. 1735, at Ely, Decima, da. of Twyford WOODHAM, of Ely. He *d.* 14 Sep. 1783, aged 72, and was *bur.* at Roos. His widow *d.* 9 March 1793.

II. 1783, Sep. SIR CHRISTOPHER SYKES, Baronet [1783], of Sledmere aforesaid, only s. and h., *b.* 23 May 1749 at Roos; matric. at Oxford (Brasenose Coll.), 5 Nov. 1767, aged 18; *cr.* M.A., 16 June 1770, and D.C.L., 9 July 1773; *suc. to the Baronetcy*, 14 Sep. 1783; M.P. for Beverley, 1784-90. He *m.* 23 Oct. 1770, at Northenden, co. Chester, Elizabeth, da. of William TATTON, of Wythenshaw, co. Chester, by Hester, sister and heir (1780) of Samuel EGERTON, da. of John EGERTON, of Tatton park in that county. He *d.* 17 Sep. 1801, aged 52. Will pr. 1807. His widow, who was *b.* 25 April 1748, at Wythenshaw, *d.* 27 July 1803. Will pr. 1804.

III. 1801. SIR MARK MASTERMAN-SYKES, Baronet [1783], of Sledmere aforesaid, and of Settrington, co. York, *formerly* Mark SYKES, 1st s. and h., *b.* 20 Aug. 1771; matric. at Oxford (Brasenose Coll.), 10 May 1788, aged 16; assumed the name of MASTERMAN before that of SYKES on his marriage, 11 Nov. 1795; Sheriff of Yorkshire, 1795-96; *suc. to the Baronetcy*, 17 Sep. 1801; M.P. for York (three Parls.), 1807-20. He *m.* firstly, 11 Nov. 1795, Henrjetta, da. and h. of Henry MASTERMAN, of Settrington aforesaid. She *d.* July 1813. He *m.* secondly, 2 Aug. 1814, Mary Elizabeth, sister of Wilbraham EGERTON, of Tatton Park, only da. of William EGERTON, *formerly* TATTON, of Wythenshaw, by his 2d wife, Mary, da. of Richard WILBRAHAM-BOOTLE. He *d.* s.p. 16 Feb. 1823, aged 51. Will pr. 1823. His widow *m.* 16 Sep. 1834, at St. James, Westm., Dugdale Stratford DUGDALE, of Merivale, co. Warwick, and *d.* 26 Oct. 1846.

IV. 1823. SIR TATTON SYKES, Baronet [1783], of Sledmere aforesaid, br. and h., *b.* 22 Aug. 1772 at Wheldrake, co. York; ed. at Westm. School, 1784-88; matric. at Oxford (Brasenose Coll.), 10 May 1788; was, at first, articled as an Attorney, but began sheep-farming in 1803, holding his 58th sale of sheep in 1861, being also one of the largest breeders of blood stock in the country; was an owner of racehorses from 1803 till his death, 60 years later, and for more than 40 years a Master of Foxhounds.(b) He *suc. to the Baronetcy*, 16 Feb. 1823, and was Sheriff of Yorkshire, 1828-29. He *m.* 19 Jan. 1822, at Ingleby manor, co. York, Mary Anne, 2d da. of Sir William FOULIS, 7th Baronet [1619], by Anne, da. of Edmund TURNOR. She, who was *bap.* at Ingleby, 31 Oct. 1792, *d.* 1 Feb. 1861 at Sledmere, aged 68. He *d.* there, 21 March 1863, aged 90.

(a) See p. 227, note "a," under "PARKER."

(b) He was "present at the St. Leger race 74 years running, 1789-1862 [and] the winner [thereof] in 1846 was called after him *Sir Tatton Sykes.*" [Boase's *Modern English Biography.*]

V. 1863. SIR TATTON SYKES, Baronet [1783], of Sledmere aforesaid, 1st s. and h., *b.* 13 March 1826 at Westoe, co. York; matric. at Oxford (Ch. Ch.), 17 Oct. 1844, aged 18; *suc. to the Baronetcy*, 21 March 1863; Sheriff of Yorkshire, 1869-70. He *m.* 3 Aug. 1874, at Westm. Abbey, Jessica Anne Christina, 1st da. of the Rt. Hon. George Augustus Frederick CAVENDISH-BENTINCK, sometime (1875-80) Judge Advocate General (grandson to the 3d DUKE OF PORTLAND), by Prudence Penelope, da. of Col. Charles Powell LESLIE, of Glaslough, co. Monaghan. She was *b.* 4 July 1852.

Family Estates.—These, in 1883, consisted of 34,010 acres in the West Riding of Yorkshire, worth £35,870 a year. *Seat.*—Sledmere House, near Malton, co. York.

GUISE:

cr. 9 Dec. 1783.

I. 1783. "JOHN GUISE, of Highnam Court [in Churcham], co. Gloucester, Esq.,"(a) 1st surv. s. and h. of Henry GUISE, of Upton St. Leonards in that county (*d.* 23 Oct. 1749), by Mary, sister and coheir of Henry COOKE, of Highnam Court aforesaid, da. of Edward COOKE, of the same (which Henry GUISE was s. of William GUISE, of Winterbourne (*d.* 28 Aug. 1716, aged 68), s. of Henry GUISE, of the same, the yr. br. of Christopher GUISE, 1st Baronet [1661], of Elmore, co. Gloucester), was *bap.* at Gloucester, 25 May 1733; was Sheriff of Gloucestershire, 1768-69, and Lieut.-Col. of the Gloucestershire Militia, and (the *Baronetcy* conferred on his great grand-uncle, Christopher GUISE, 10 July 1661, having become *extinct*, 6 April 1783) was (a few months later) *cr. a Baronet*, as above, 9 Dec. 1783. He was *cr.* D.C.L. of Oxford, 3 July 1793. He *m.* 28 June 1770, Elizabeth, da. and h. of Thomas WRIGHT, of Laurence lane, London, by Elizabeth, da. and coheir of William WOODFORD, M.D., of Epsom, Surrey, which Thomas was yr. br. to Sir Martin WRIGHT, sometime, 1740-55, one of the Justices of the King's Bench.(b) He *d.* 2 May 1794, in his 61st year. Will pr. June 1794. His widow *d.* 1808. Will pr. 1808.

II. 1794. SIR BERKELEY WILLIAM GUISE, Baronet [1783], of Highnam Court aforesaid, 1st s. and h., *b.* 14 July 1775; ed. at Eton; matric. at Oxford (Ch. Ch.), 24 Jan. 1794, aged 18; *cr.* M.A., 29 Oct. 1796, and (long afterwards) D.C.L., 12 June 1823; *suc. to the Baronetcy*, 2 May 1794, and by the death, 8 June 1807, of Jane, wife of the Hon. Shute BARRINGTON, D.D., Bishop of Durham (sister and h. of Sir William GUISE, 5th and last Baronet [1661]), to the family estates of Elmore Court and Rendcombe, co. Gloucester.(c) In 1814 he disputed the will of his mother's cousin, Thomas WRIGHT (to whom he was heir at law), who disposed of his vast property to strangers.(b) He was M.P. for Gloucestershire (seven Parls.), Feb. 1811 to 1832, and for East Gloucestershire, 1832 till death in 1834; was Verderer of the Forest of Dean. He *d.* unm. 23 July 1834, aged 59. Will pr. Sep. 1834.

III. 1834. SIR JOHN WRIGHT GUISE, Baronet [1783], of Elmore Court and Rendcombe aforesaid, br. and h., *b.* 20 July 1777 at Highnam Court aforesaid; Ensign, 70th Foot 1794 and, subsequently, 3d Foot Guards 1795; serving in Spain 1800, in Egypt 1801, in Hanover 1805, and in the Peninsula 1812-14, receiving a cross for his conduct at Fuentes d'Onor, Salamanca, Vittoria and Nive; **K.C.B.**, 13 Sep. 1831; *suc. to the Baronetcy*, 23 July 1834; was Col. of the 87th Foot, 1847 till death; General in the army, 11 Nov. 1851; **G.C.B.**, 10 Nov. 1862. He *m.* 12 Aug. 1815, Charlotte Diana, yst. da. of John VERNON, of Clontarf Castle, co. Dublin, by Elizabeth, da. of Joseph [not Henry] FLETCHER, of Dublin. She *d.* 5 Feb. 1835 at Rendcombe. He *d.* 1 April 1865, at Elmore Court, in his 88th year.

(a) See p. 227, note "a," under "PARKER."

(b) See *N. & Q.*, 8th S., vol. vi, p. 233, for a good account of this family of Wright, and of the lawsuit arising on the death (14 March 1814, aged 87) of Thomas Wright, the last surv. child of the Judge.

(c) See vol. iii, p. 219, note "b."

IV. 1865. SIR WILLIAM VERNON GUISE, Baronet [1783], of Elmore Court and Rendcombe aforesaid, 1st s. and h.; b. 19 Aug. 1816, in Holles Street, Marylebone; sometime an officer in the 75th Foot; *suc. to the Baronetcy*, 1 April 1865, Lieut.-Col. South Glouc. Militia, 1868-80; Sheriff of Gloucestershire, 1872. He *m.* 27 June 1844, at Tiberton, co. Hereford, Margaret Anna Maria, 1st da. of the Rev. Daniel LEE-WARNER, of Tiberton Court in that parish and of Walsingham Abbey, Norfolk, by Anne, da. and coheir of Francis William Thomas BRYDGES, of Tiberton Court aforesaid. He *d.* 24 Sep. 1887, at Elmore Court, aged 71. Will pr. under £50,000. His widow *d.* 10 Nov. 1903, at Coombe House, Westbury-on-Trim, aged 82.

V. 1887. SIR WILLIAM FRANCIS GEORGE GUISE, Baronet [1783], of Elmore Court aforesaid, 2d but 1st surv. s. and h.,(a) b. 14 Dec. 1851; ed. at Eton; sometime Lieut.-Col. and afterwards Hon. Col. of the (3d batt.) Gloucestershire militia; *suc. to the Baronetcy*, 24 Sep. 1887; Sheriff of Gloucestershire, 1893. He *m.* 23 Aug. 1887, at St. Mark's, North Audley Street, Ada Caroline, 2d da. of Octavius Edward COOPE, of Rochetts, near Brentwood, Essex.

Family Estates.—These, in 1883, consisted of 2,087 acres in Gloucestershire, valued at £4,002 a year.

HAMOND:

cr. 18 Dec. 1783;

afterwards, since 1873, HAMOND-GRÆME.

I. 1783. "SIR ANDREW SNAPE HAMOND, Knt.,"(b) Captain in the Royal Navy, only s. of Robert HAMOND, of Blackheath, Kent, shipowner (*d.* 1775, aged 70), by Susanna, da. and h. of Robert SNAPE, of Blackheath, and niece of Andrew SNAPE, D.D., Provost of King's College, Cambridge, was *b.* 17 Dec. 1738, at Blackheath; entered the Navy, 1753; Lieut. R.N., 1759; Commander, 1765; Capt., 1770, being in command on the North American station in the expedition to the Chesapeake, 1777, and in the defence of Sandy Hook in July 1778, for which service he was *Knighted* at St. James', 15 Jan. 1779; was Lieut.-Gov. of Nova Scotia, 1781-82, and Commander-in-Chief at Halifax till 1783, when he was *cr. a Baronet*, as above, 18 Dec. 1783, with a *spec. rem.*, failing heirs male of his body, to "Andrew Snape DOUGLAS,(c) Esq., Capt. in His Majesty's Navy."(b) He was Commander-in-Chief at the Nore, 1785-88; Commissioner, 1793, and Comptroller, 1794, of the Navy till 1806, when he retired on an annuity of £1,500. He was sometime of Holly Lodge, Berks, but subsequently of Hamond Lodge, near Lynn, co. Norfolk, and was M.P. for Ipswich, 1796-1806. He *m.* 8 March 1779, Anne, da. and h. of Major Henry GRÆME, of Hanwell Heath, co. Midx., and of Gorthey, co. Perth, sometime Lieut.-Gov. of St. Helena, by Anne, da. and coheir of Henry DOUGHTY, of Broadwell, co. Gloucester. He *d.* 12 Sep. 1828, in his 90th year. Will pr. Sep. 1828. His widow *d.* 7 Sep. 1838. Admon. Sep. 1838.

(a) The 1st son, Anselm Edward Henry Guise, *b.* 26 Sep. 1847, *d.* v.p. unm. and under age, 8 April 1863.

(b) See p. 227, note "a," under "PARKER."

(c) He was nephew of the grantee, being s. of his eldest sister, Lydia, by William Douglas, of Springfield, near Edinburgh, was *b.* 8 Aug. 1761; entered the Navy at the age of 10 and was made Capt. at the age of 19 for his services at the siege of Charlestown; was *Knighted*, 13 Sep. 1789; severely wounded in the action of 1 June 1794, and distinguished himself greatly in that of 23 June 1795. He *d.* 4 and was *bur.* 12 June 1797 at Fulham, in his 36th year. Will pr. June 1797. He left an only son, Andrew Snape Douglas, *b.* at Portsmouth, 6 Jan. 1788, sometime Sec. of Embassy in the Netherlands.

II. 1828. SIR GRAHAM EDEN HAMOND, Baronet [1783], only s. and h., *b.* 30 Dec. 1799, in Newman street, Marylebone; entered the Navy in his 6th year in Sep. 1785; was present at the victory of 1 June 1794; Lieut. R.N., 1796; Capt. 1798; was at the battle of Copenhagen, 2 April 1801; effected several captures of Spanish frigates and was at the reduction of Flushing in 1809; C.B, 4 June 1815; Rear-Admiral, 1825, and having been charged with the delivery of the treaty of separation between Brazil and Portugal, was made Knight Commander of the Portuguese Order of the Tower and Sword; *suc. to the Baronetcy*, 12 Sep. 1828; **K.C.B.**, 13 Sep. 1831; was Commander-in-Chief on the South American station, 1834-38; Vice-Admiral, 1837; **G.C.B.**, 5 July 1855, and Admiral of the Fleet, 10 Nov. 1862. He *m.* 30 Dec. 1806, Elizabeth, da. of John KIMBER, of Fowey, co. Cornwall. He *d.* 20 Dec. 1862, at his residence, Norton Lodge, Freshwater, Isle of Wight, aged 62. His widow *d.* there, 24 Dec. 1872, in her 89th year.

III. 1862. SIR ANDREW SNAPE HAMOND, *afterwards*, from 1873, HAMOND-GRÆME, Baronet [1783], of Norton Lodge aforesaid, 1st s. and h., *b.* 3 Oct. 1811 at Freshwater aforesaid, entered the Navy about 1825, becoming in due course Rear-Admiral in 1864 and Vice-Admiral 1870, having *suc. to the Baronetcy*, 20 Dec. 1862. By royal lic., 3 April 1873, he took the name of GRÆME after that of HAMOND. He *m.* 13 Nov. 1844, at Otaheite, Mary Anne, 2d da. of Edward MILLER, of Cambridge, British Consul at Otaheite, niece of Gen. MILLER. He *d.* 21 Feb. 1874 at Norton Lodge aforesaid, aged 62. His widow living 1905.

IV. 1874. SIR GRAHAM EDEN WILLIAM GRÆME HAMOND-GRÆME, Baronet [1783], of Norton Lodge aforesaid, *formerly* HAMOND, 1st s. and h., *b.* 20 Aug. 1845, at Tahiti; took [together with his father] the name of GRÆME after that of HAMOND by Royal lic. 6 April 1863; sometime Lieut. 16th Lancers, serving with the 3d Dragoon Guards, 1867-68, in Abyssinia; *suc. to the Baronetcy*, 21 Feb. 1876. He *m.* 3 Aug. 1876, at St. Geo. Han. sq., Evelyn Emma Murray, 1st da. of Major Robert Bartholomew LAWES, of Old Park, Dover, and of No. 9 Clarges street.

BARROW:

cr. 22 Jan. 1784;

afterwards, since 1789, CRAWLEY-BOEVEY.

I. 1784. "CHARLES BARROW, of Hygrove [*i.e.*, Highgrove in Minsterworth], co. Gloucester, Esq.,"(a) only s. and h. of Charles BARROW,(b) of the island of St. Christopher's, Merchant (*bap.* 13 Sep. 1681, at Awre, co. Glouc., and *d.* 3 March 1743/4), by Elizabeth, da. of (—) HARRIS, Lieut. Gov. of the Leeward islands, was *b.* 1708 at St. Christopher's; was Recorder of Tewkesbury; M.P. for Gloucester (seven Parls.), Nov. 1751 till death in 1789, being a firm supporter of the measures of FOX; was *cr.* D.C.L. of Oxford 2 July 1754, and was *cr. a Baronet*, as above, 22 Jan. 1784, with a *spec. rem.*, failing

(a) See p. 113, note "a," under "GIDEON." The date of the Gazette notice for Barrow, Morshead, Rycroft, Smith, Lombe, Durrant, Pepys, Wood, Fitzherbert and Beevor is 20 Dec. 1783.

(b) Much information about the families of Barrow and Crawley is given in Arthur W. Crawley-Boevey's "*The Perverse Widow, Catharina, wife of William Boevey, Esq., of Flaxley Abbey, co. Gloucester,*" pub. by Longman's, 4to, 1898. The grantee was grandson of Thomas Barrow, of Field Court, in Hardwick, co. Gloucester, who was son of Thomas Barrow, of Awre in that county (living 1641) being doubtless a descendant of the family of "Berowe," of Field Court and Awre aforesaid, whose pedigree was recorded in the Heralds' Visitation of Gloucestershire, 1623.

heirs male of his body, to "Thomas CRAWLEY-BOEVEY,(a) of Flaxley Abbey, co. Gloucester, Esq."(b) He *m.* about 1728, Mary, da. of Daniel RANDALL, of Gloucester. She *d.* 7 April 1778, aged 70. M.I. at Minsterworth. He *d.* s.p. legit.(c) 10 Jan. 1789, in his 81st year, and was *bur.* at Minsterworth. M.I. Will dat. 10 Aug. 1787, pr. 5 Sep. 1789 and 1 June 1821.

II. 1789. SIR THOMAS CRAWLEY-BOEVEY, Baronet [1784], of Flaxley Abbey aforesaid,(d) 1st s. and h. of Thomas CRAWLEY-BOEVEY, of Flaxley Abbey (*d.* 20 Nov. 1769, aged 60), by Susanna, sister and h. of Rev. John LLOYD, D.D., Rector of Stowe-nine-Churches, and Vicar of Heyford, co. Northampton, only da. of John LLOYD, of London. He was *b.* 14 Feb. and *bap.* 13 March 1743/4, at Flaxley; matric. at Oxford (Pembroke Coll.), 27 April 1762, aged 18; suc. to the Flaxley Abbey estate on the death of his father in Nov. 1769, and (twenty years later) *suc. to the Baronetcy* 10 Jan. 1789 (though to none of the estates of the late Baronet) under the *spec. rem.* in the creation of that dignity. He was presented with the freedom of the city of Gloucester, 21 Sep. 1792. He *m.* 20 Feb. 1769, at St. Michael's, Gloucester, Anne, 2d da. (whose issue became coheir) of the Rev. Thomas SAVAGE, of Broadway, co. Worcester, and of Field Court in Hardwicke, co. Gloucester, by Eleanor, da. and h. of Thomas BARROW, of Field Court abovenamed, uncle to the 1st Baronet. She *d.* 10 and was *bur.* 17 Sep. 1816 at Flaxley. He *d.* there 11 and was *bur.* there 18 Aug. 1818, aged 74. Will pr. Sep. 1818.

III. 1818. SIR THOMAS CRAWLEY-BOEVEY, Baronet [1784], of Flaxley Abbey aforesaid, 1st s. and h., *b.* 28 Nov. and *bap.* 1 Dec. 1769, at Flaxley; Sheriff of Gloucestershire, 1808-09, as also, 1831-32, having *suc. to the Baronetcy*, 11 Aug. 1818. He *m.* 28 Oct. 1807, Mary Albinia, 1st da. of Sir Thomas Hyde PAGE, Capt. Royal Engineers, by his 2d wife, Mary Albinia, da. of John WOODWARD, of Ringwould, Kent, Capt. 70th Foot. She *d.* 16 Feb. 1835, aged 50. He *d.* at Flaxley Abbey, 10 Jan. 1847, aged 77. Will pr. 1877. Both *bur.* at Flaxley.

IV. 1847. SIR MARTIN HYDE CRAWLEY-BOEVEY, Baronet [1784], of Flaxley Abbey aforesaid, 2d but only surv. and h., *b.* 25 May 1812, at Wootton Lodge, near Gloucester; matric. at Oxford (Trinity Coll.), 26 March 1831, aged 18; *suc. to the Baronetcy*, 10 Jan. 1847. Verderer of the Forest of Dean, 1847; Capt. Gloucester Yeomanry Cavalry, 1854; Capt. 12th Gloucester Rifle Volunteers. 1860. He *m.* 9 June 1836, at Bath, his 2d cousin, Elizabeth, 1st da. of the Rev. George William DAUBENY, of Seend House Wilts, by Elizabeth, da. of the Rev. Charles CRAWLEY, B.C.L., Rector of Stowe-nine-Churches, co. Northampton, yr. br. of the 2d Baronet abovenamed. He *d.* at Flaxley Abbey, 14 Oct. 1862, aged 50. His widow, who was *b.* 6 Dec. 1814, *d.* at Flaxley Cottage, 9 Aug. 1892. Both *bur.* at Flaxley.

(a) The *wife* of this Thomas was 1st cousin once removed to the grantee, her mother Eleanor being da. of Thomas Barrow, his paternal uncle.

(b) See p. 235, note "a."

(c) He devised all his property to his illegit. da., "Mary Caroline Barrow," then under 21. She *m.* Charles Evans, of Gloucester, and *d.* a widow 29 May 1837, leaving issue, of whom the survivor, Edmund Barrow Evans, *d.* s.p. 26 July 1868.

(d) The estate of Flaxley Abbey, granted by Henry VIII to the family of Kingston, came about 1660 to that of Boevey, and was devised by William Boevey (who *d.* s.p. 1692, aged 35) to Thomas Crawley after the death of his widow. This lady ("*the Perverse widow*" mentioned in note "b" above) died 21 Jan. 1726, aged 56, when the devise took effect, and the said Thomas Crawley took the additional name of Boevey and *d.* Feb. 1741, being father of Thomas Crawley-Boevey (who *d.* Nov. 1769) and grandfather of (another) Thomas Crawley-Boevey, the 2d Baronet. The mother of Thomas Crawley, the devisee, was Mary (wife of another Thomas Crawley, who *d.* at Twickenham in March 1714), 1st cousin of the testator, being da. (though not heir or coheir) of David Bonnell, of Isleworth, by Anne, sister of James Boevey, testator's father.

V. 1862. SIR THOMAS HYDE CRAWLEY-BOEVEY, Baronet [1784], of Flaxley Abbey aforesaid, 1st s. and h., *b.* there 2 July 1837; Ensign 69th Foot, 1857; Lieut., 1863, retiring in 1865, having *suc. to the Baronetcy*, 14 Oct. 1862; Verderer of the Forest of Dean, 1873; Sheriff of Gloucestershire, 1882; sometime Hon. Colonel 2d Vol. Batt. Glouc. Regiment. He *m.* 25 July 1865, at Eastington, co. Glouc., Frances Elizabeth, only da. of the Rev. Thomas PETERS, Rector of Eastington, by Frances, da. of the Rev. John Adey CURTIS-HAYWARD, of Quedgeley House in that county.

MORSHEAD:(a)

cr. 22 Jan. 1784;

ex. 17 March 1905.

I. 1784. "JOHN MORSHEAD, of Trenant Park [in Duloe], co. Cornwall, Esq.,"(b) 2d but 1st surv. s. and h. ap. of William MORSHEAD, of Cartuther and Trevarbin in that county, sometime (1753) Sheriff of Cornwall (*bur.* 4 May 1784 at St. Neot, aged 62), by Olympia,(c) sister and heir (1780) of Sir Christopher TREISE, da. of John TREISE, of Lavithan Blisland, in that county, was *bap.* 4 Aug. 1747, at Menheniot, Cornwall, matric. at Oxford (Oriel Coll.), 15 May 1766, aged 18; M.P. for Callington, 1780-84, and for Bodmin, 1784-1802, and was *cr. a Baronet*, as above, 22 Jan. 1784. He was Surveyor-Gen. to the Prince of Wales, 1796; L. Warden of the Stannaries, 1798-1800, and Col. of the Devon and Cornwall Miners, 1799. He alienated all his estates, 1809-11. He *m.* 17 April 1778, at St. Marylebone, Elizabeth, 1st da. and coheir of Sir Thomas FREDERICK, 3d Baronet [1723], by Elizabeth, da. of Peter BATHURST. He *d.* 10 April 1813, aged 65, and is said to have been *bur.* in the Isle of Man(d). Will pr. Dec. 1815 and Nov. 1846. His widow *d.* 17 Jan. 1845, at Richmond, Surrey, at a great age, and was *bur.* at Paddington. Will pr. Feb. 1845.

II. 1813. SIR FREDERICK TREISE MORSHEAD, Baronet [1784], of Pigmy Hall, Cumberland,(e) 1st s. and h., *b.* 1 Jan. 1783; *bap.* at St. Marylebone; sometime an officer in the Coldstream Guards; *suc. to the Baronetcy*, 10 April 1813. He *m.* 15 Nov. 1821, at Carlisle, Jane, 2d da. of Robert WARWICK, of Warwick Hall, co. Cumberland. He *d.* 8 July 1828, aged 45, at his residence, "Derwent Lodge," Keswick, and was *bur.* at Keswick. Will pr. Jan. 1829. His widow *d.* 19 May 1832, at Carlisle, and was *bur.* at Wetherel Carlisle.

III. 1828, to 1905. SIR WARWICK CHARLES MORSHEAD, Baronet [1784], of Forest Lodge, in Binfield, Berks, and afterwards of Tregaddick Blisland, Cornwall, only s. and h., *b.* 26 Nov. 1824, and *bap.* at Crosthwayte, near Keswick; *suc. to the Baronetcy*, 8 July 1828; Cornet 6th Dragoons, 1845; Capt., 1850-53, and was A.D.C. to the Viceroy of Ireland. He *m.* firstly, 8 June 1854, at St. Geo. Han. sq., Selina Anne, 3d da. of the Rev. William VERNON-HARCOURT, of Nuneham Park, Oxon, Canon of York, by Matilda Mary, da. of Col. William GOOCH. She *d.* 14 Sep. 1883, at Forest Lodge aforesaid, and was *bur.* at Binfield. He *m.* secondly, 2 June 1887, at Waltham St. Laurence, Berks, Sarah Elizabeth, 2d da. of Montagu WILMOT, of Norton House, co. Glamorgan, by Sarah Frederica, da. of Thomas EDEN. He *d.* s.p. 17 March 1905, aged 80, at Forest Lodge aforesaid, and was *bur.* at Blisland, Cornwall, when the *Baronetcy* became *extinct*. His widow living 1905.

(a) Much of the information in this article has been supplied by Reginald Glencross, Barrister, owner of the estate of Lavithan abovenamed.

(b) See p. 235, note "a," under "BARROW."

(c) She was *bap.* 18 May 1726, at Blisland, and was *bur.* 7 March 1811, at St. Neots, Cornwall.

(d) Vivian's "*Visitations of Cornwall,*" where, however, he is said to have *d.* in 1812.

(e) So styled in a deed, dated Oct. 1815, in possession of Reginald Glencross—see note "a," above.

RYCROFT:

cr. 22 Jan. 1784.

I. 1784. "THE REV. RICHARD RYCROFT, D.D., of Calton, co. York,"(a) *formerly* Richard NELSON, only surv. s. of John NELSON, of Calton aforesaid and of Hatton Garden, London, by Mary, da. of (—); was *b.* Nov. 1736, at St. Andrew's, Holborn; ed. at Cath. Hall, Cambridge; B.A., 1758; M.A., 1761; D.D., 1773, having by royal lic., 28 Dec. 1758, taken the name of RYCROFT, instead of that of NELSON; was Rector of Penshurst, Kent, and (1773) of Patching with West Tarring, Sussex; purchased the manor of Bokesell, or Bowsell, in Kent, in 1778, and was *cr. a Baronet*, as above, 22 Jan. 1784. He resided at Farnham, Surrey. He *m.* 13 Feb. 1759, Penelope, yst. da. of the Rev. Richard STONHEWER, LL.D., Rector of Houghton le Spring, Durham. He *d.* 5 July 1786, in his 50th year. Will July 1786. His widow *d.* 13 Feb. 1821, at her house in Curzon street, Mayfair, in her 88th year. Will pr. 1821.

II. 1786. SIR NELSON RYCROFT, Baronet [1784], of Farnham, Surrey, 3d but 1st surv. s. and h.,(b) *b.* 15 Feb. 1761; *suc. to the Baronetcy*, 5 July 1786. He *m.* firstly, 11 July 1791, at St. Geo. Han. sq., Charlotte, yst. da. of Henry READ, of Crowood, Wilts. She *d.* 28 May 1803, at Fir Grove, Farnham. He *m.* secondly, 3 May 1808, Margaret, yst. da. of Robert MANDEVILLE. He *d.* suddenly, of apoplexy, at Cheltenham, 1 Oct. 1827, aged 66. Will pr. Nov. 1827. His widow *d.* s.p., 30 March 1835, in Curzon street, Mayfair. Will pr. June 1835.

III. 1827. SIR RICHARD HENRY CHARLES RYCROFT, Baronet [1784], of Farnham aforesaid, and afterwards of Manydown Park, near Basingstoke, Hants, 2d but 1st surv. s. and h., by 1st wife, *b.* 21 Dec. 1793, at Southampton; *suc. to the Baronetcy*, 1 Oct. 1827. He *m.* 18 May 1830, Charlotte Anne Josephine, 1st da. of William TENNANT, of Little Aston Hall, co. Stafford, by Maria Charlotte, da. of Charles (PELHAM), 1st BARON YARBOROUGH. He *d.* 21 Oct. 1864, at Manydown Park aforesaid, in his 71st year. His widow *d.* 3 Oct. 1874, at "Everlands," near Sevenoaks, Kent, aged 69.

IV. 1864. SIR NELSON RYCROFT, Baronet [1784], of Manydown Park aforesaid, and afterwards of Kempshott Park, near Dummer, Hants, 1st s. and h., *b.* 11 March 1831 at Brighton; ed. at Eton; sometime an officer in the 85th Foot; *suc. to the Baronetcy*, 21 Oct. 1864; Sheriff of Hants, 1881; sometime Lieut.-Col. com. and afterwards Hon. Col. 3d Batt. Hants Reg. Militia; purchased the manor and estate of Dummer, Hants. He *m.* 27 July 1858, at St. Paul's Episcopal Church, Dundee, Juliana, 1st da. of Sir John OGILVY, 9th Baronet [S. 1626], of Baldovan, by his 1st wife, Juliana Barbara, da. of Lord Henry HOWARD. He *d.* 30 March 1894, at Kempshott Park aforesaid, aged 63. Will pr. at £85,949 gross and £50,052 net. His widow living 1905.

V. 1894. SIR RICHARD NELSON RYCROFT, Baronet [1784], of Dummer House, Hants, 1st s. and h., *b.* 12 Dec. 1859; ed. at Eton and at Trin. Coll., Cambridge; sometime Lieut. Rifle Brigade; Capt. 3d Batt. Hants Militia, and served with the Imperial Yeomanry, 1899-1900, in the Transvaal war, having *suc. to the Baronetcy*, 30 March 1894. Sheriff of Hants, 1899. He *m.* 11 Feb. 1886, at Eggesford, Devon, Dorothea Hester Bluett, 4th da. of Isaac Newton (WALLOP, *formerly* FELLOWES), 5th EARL OF PORTSMOUTH, by Eveline Alicia Juliana, da. of Henry John George (HERBERT), 3d EARL OF CARNARVON. She was *b.* 27 Jan. 1863.

(a) See p. 235, note "a," under "BARROW."
(b) His yr. br., Sir Henry Rycroft, was Knight Harbinger to the Court, 1816, till his death, s.p., 3 Oct. 1846, aged 70.

SMITH:

cr. 22 Jan. 1784(a);

afterwards, 1821-57, DODSWORTH;

and, since 1857, SMITH-DODSWORTH.

I. 1784. "JOHN SILVESTER SMITH, of Newland Park, in the West Riding of the County of York, Esq.,(b) as also of Birthwait, in that county, only s. and h. of John SMITH, of the same (*d.* 1746), by his 2d wife, Anne, da. of Christopher HODGSON, of Westerton (which John was s. of John SMITH, of Ecclesfield, by Priscilla, da. of (—) SILVESTER), was *b.* 1734, and was *cr. a Baronet*, as above, 22 Jan. 1784. He *m.* 20 July 1761, Henrietta Maria, da. (whose issue became coheir) of John DODSWORTH, of Thornton Watlass, co. York, by Henrietta, sister of Matthew HUTTON, Archbishop of Canterbury, da. of John HUTTON, of Marske. He *d.* 15 June 1789, aged 55,

II. 1789. SIR EDWARD SMITH, *afterwards*, since 1821, DODSWORTH, Baronet [1784], of Newland Park aforesaid, 1st s. and h., *b.* 13 Aug. 1768; *suc. to the Baronetcy*, 15 June 1789; was sometime Lieut. 4th Dragoon Guards; Capt. 105th Foot, 1793-95; suc. to the estate of Thornton Watlass aforesaid on the death of his maternal uncle, Frederick DODSWORTH, D.D., Canon of Windsor [1783-1821], when, by Royal lic., 21 May 1821, he took the name of DODSWORTH instead of that of SMITH. He *m.* 22 Sep. 1804, Susanna, yst. da. of Col. Henry DAWKYNS, of Standlynch Park, Wilts, by Juliana, da. of Charles (COLYEAR), 2d EARL OF PORTMORE [S.]. She *d.* 13 March 1830 at Newland Park aforesaid. He *d.* s.p. 31 Dec. 1845, aged 77, at Thornton Hall, near Bedale, aged 67.

III. 1845. SIR CHARLES SMITH, *afterwards*, 1846-57, DODSWORTH, Baronet [1784], of Thornton Watlass and Newland Park aforesaid, yst. and only surv. br. and h.,(c) *b.* 22 Aug. 1775; sometime Lieut. 2d Light Dragoons; *suc. to the Baronetcy*, 31 Dec. 1845, and by Royal lic., 12 March 1846, took the name of DODSWORTH instead of that of SMITH. He *m.* 8 June 1808, Elizabeth, only child of John ARMSTRONG, of Lisgoole, co. Fermanagh, by Sophia, da. of Cadwallader (BLAYNEY), 9th BARON BLAYNEY OF MONAGHAN [I.]. She *d.* 12 June 1853. He *d.* 28 July 1857, at Thornton Hall aforesaid, aged 81.

IV. 1857. SIR MATTHEW SMITH-DODSWORTH, Baronet [1784], of Thornton Watlass and Newland Park aforesaid, 4th but 1st surv. s. and h.(d); *b.* 6 Feb. 1819, at Thornton Hall aforesaid; entered the Army 1837, becoming Capt. R.A., 1846; *suc. to the Baronetcy*, under the surname of SMITH-DODSWORTH, 28 July 1857. He *m.* 23 Sep. 1852, at St. Margaret's, Whalley

(a) An account of this Baronetcy (under the spelling of "Smyth") is given in Courthope's *Extinct Baronetcies* [1835], it being there stated to have been *cr.* on 22 *Dec.* [not Jan.] 1784 and to have become *extinct* on the death, s.p., of Edward, the 2d Baronet, "circa 1823, æt. circa 55." In the chronological list of creations, however, in that work the creation of "Smith, now Dodsworth, of Newland Park, York," is [rightly] given as on "22 *Jan.* 1784" (between the creations of Rycroft and Lombe), but is followed (strange to say) after seven others by the creation on "22 *Dec.* 1784" of "Smyth, of Newland Park, York," this last creation being printed in type that denotes it to be then [1835] extinct. This duplicate creation in *Dec.* 1784 as also its [supposed] extinction, "circa 1823," seem palpable errors.
(b) See p. 235, note "a," under "BARROW."
(c) His next elder br., the Rev. George Smith, Vicar of Erchefont, Alderbury and Farley with Pitton, Wilts, was *b.* 25 Sep. 1772, and *d.* unm. 1811.
(d) Of his elder brothers, who all *d.* unm. and v.p., (1) John Dodsworth, Major in the Army, *b.* 27 June 1809, *d.* 11 May 1852; (2) Edward Frederick Dodsworth, *b.* 1811, *d.* 1833; (3) Charles Dodsworth, an officer in the Royal Navy, *b.* 2 Aug. 1812, *d.* 18 Feb. 1832.

Range, Manchester, Anne Julia, yst. da. of Col. John CROWTHER, K.H., of Brotherton, co. York, by Eliza, da. and coheir of Thomas Pulleyn MOSLEY, of Burley, in Wharfedale. He *d.* 30 April 1858, at Torquay, aged 39. His widow *d.* 26 Feb. 1890, at Cowling Hall, near Bedale, co. York.

V. 1858. SIR CHARLES EDWARD SMITH-DODSWORTH, Baronet [1784], of Thornton Watlass and Newland Park aforesaid, 1st s. and h., *b.* 27 June 1853, at Otterington, co. York; *suc. to the Baronetcy*, 30 April 1858; ed. at Eton; matric. at Oxford (Balliol Coll.) 18 Oct. 1871, aged 18. He *m.* 5 March 1889, at Kirkby Wiske, co. York, Blanche, 3d da. of the Hon. George Edwin LASCELLES (yr. s. of the 3d EARL OF HAREWOOD), by Louisa Nina, da. of William David (MURRAY), EARL OF MANSFIELD. He *d.* s.p., 5 Aug. 1891, at Thornton Watlass aforesaid, aged 38. His widow, who was *b.* 6 Jan. 1864, living 1905.

VI. 1891. SIR MATTHEW BLAYNEY SMITH-DODSWORTH, Baronet [1784], br. and h., *b.* 26 Oct. 1856, at Otterington aforesaid; matric. at Oxford (Univ. Coll.), 16 Oct. 1875, aged 18; B.A. (St. Alban Hall) 1879; *suc. to the Baronetcy*, but not to the estates, 5 Aug. 1891. He *m.* 8 Nov. 1887, Agnes Elizabeth, only da. of John CROWDIER.

Family Estates.—These, in 1883, consisted of 4,042 acres in the North and West Ridings of Yorkshire, worth £5,464 a year, exclusive of mineral rents. *Principal Seat.*—Thornton Watlass, near Bedale, co. York.

LOMBE:

cr. 22 Jan. 1784;

afterwards, since 1817, JODRELL.

I. 1784. "JOHN LOMBE, of Great Melton, co. Norfolk, Esq.,"(a) *formerly* John HASE, 1st s. of John HASE, of Great Melton aforesaid, by Mary, da. (whose issue became heir) of Edward LOMBE,(b) of Weston, in that county, was *b.* about 1731; took the name of LOMBE instead of that of HASE, by Act of Parl. 1762, on succeeding to the estates of his maternal uncle, Edward LOMBE (sometime, 1714, Sheriff of Norfolk), was Sheriff of Norfolk, 1772-73, and was *cr. a Baronet*, as above, 22 Jan. 1784, with a *spec. rem.*, failing heirs male of his body, "to his brother, Edward HASE, of Sall, in the said county of Norfolk, Esq. [failing whom] to the heirs male [of the body] of Vertue, wife of Richard Paul JODDRELL, of Saxlingham, in the same county, niece of the said John LOMBE, Esq."(a) He *d.* unm., 27 May 1817, at Great Melton Hall, aged 86. Will pr. 1817.

II. 1817. SIR RICHARD PAUL JODRELL, Baronet [1784], of Great Melton aforesaid, great nephew of the above, being 1st s. of Richard Paul JODRELL, of Saxlingham, Norfolk (sometime, Jan. 1794 to 1796, M.P. for Seaford), by Vertue, his wife, both abovenamed, he being then heir male of his said mother (who *d.* 23 March 1806, aged 50), 1st da. and coheir of Edward HASE, the grantee's brother, also abovenamed, which said Edward had *d.* s.p.m.,

(a) See p. 235, note "a," under "BARROW."
(b) Of this family was the well known Sir Thomas Lombe, Alderman and sometime (1727-28) Sheriff of London, who introduced the process of "silk-throwing into England, receiving, in 1732, a grant of £14,000 from Parl. for such service. He *d.* 3 Jan. 1738/9, worth £120,000, leaving two daughters and coheirs, viz. (1) Mary, *m.* 24 April 1749, James (Maitland), 4th Earl of Lauderdale [S.], and (2) Hannah, *m.* 2 June 1740 (as his 2d wife), Sir Robert Clifton, 5th Baronet [1611], of Clifton, Notts. He was s. of Henry Lombe, of Norwich, worsted weaver (*d.* 1695), s. of Edward Lombe, who was said to have been uncle to Edward Lombe, the maternal grandfather of the 1st Baronet.

4 May 1804, aged 70. He was *b.* 26 June 1781, at Marylebone; ed. at Eton; matric. at Oxford (Mag. Coll.), 1 July 1799, aged 18; B.A., 1804; M.A., 1804; Barrister, 1803; *suc. to the Baronetcy*, 27 May 1817, under the spec. rem. in the creation thereof, on the death of his mother's paternal uncle, the grantee. He was Sheriff of Norfolk, 1822-23. By the subsequent death of his father, 26 Jan. 1831, he suc. to Sall and other family estates. He *m.* 12 Dec. 1814, Amelia Caroline KING, spinster, illegit. da. of Robert (KING), 2d EARL OF KINGSTON [I.]. She *d.* 18 Jan. 1860, at 64 Portland Place. He *d.* there 14 June 1861, in his 80th year.

III. 1861. SIR EDWARD REPPS(a) JODRELL, Baronet [1784], of Sall Park, Norfolk, and Nethercote Place, Oxon, 2d but 1st surv. s. and h.,(b) *b.* 20 June 1825 at Marylebone; ed. at Eton; matric. at Oxford (Queen's Coll.), 1 Feb. 1843; B.A. (New Inn Hall) 1848; M.A. (Queen's Coll.) 1849; in Holy Orders; Rector of Saxlingham, Norfolk, 1855-61; *suc. to the Baronetcy*, 14 June 1861; founded a Scholarship at Queen's Coll., Oxford, 1866. He *m.* 10 June 1852, at Trinity Church, Tunbridge Wells, Lucinda Emma Maria, da. of Robert T. GARDEN, of River Lyons, King's County. He *d.* s.p. 12 Nov. 1882 at 21 Portland Place, aged 57.(c) His widow *d.* 1 March 1888, aged 63.

IV. 1882. SIR ALFRED JODRELL, Baronet [1784], of Bayfield Hall, near Holt, co. Norfolk, cousin and h. male, being 2d and yst. s.(d) of Edward JODRELL, Major 16th Foot, by Adela Monckton, da. of Sir Edward BOWYER-SMIJTH, 10th Baronet [1661], of Hill Hall, Essex, which Edward JODRELL (who *d.* 27 Jan. 1868, aged 54) was 1st s. of Edward JODRELL (*d.* 1853) next br. to the 2d Baronet. He was *b.* 13 Aug. 1847; *suc. to the Baronetcy* (but not to the family estates), 12 Nov. 1882, and was Sheriff of Norfolk, 1887. He *m.* 25 Feb. 1897, at Trinity Church, Folkestone, Jane, 3d da. of James Walter (GRIMSTON), 2d EARL OF VERULAM, by Elizabeth Joanna, da. of Major Richard WEYLAND. She was *b.* 12 Dec. 1848.

Family Estates.—These, in 1883 (being those of the 3d Baronet), consisted of 4,100 acres in Norfolk; 1,436 in Oxon and 436 in Derbyshire. *Total.*—5,972 acres, worth £6,735 a year.

DURRANT:

cr. 22 Jan. 1784.

I. 1784. "THOMAS DURRANT, of Scottow, co. Norfolk, Esq.,"(e) s. and h. of Davy DURRANT, of the same [B.A., 1724; M.A., 1729 (Caius Coll.), Cambridge], by his 1st cousin, Margaret (*d.* 1742), da. and h. of Thomas DURRANT, also of Scottow (*d.* 1727), was *b.* about 1722, was Sheriff of Norfolk, 1784-85, and was *cr. a Baronet*, as above, 22 Jan. 1784. He *m.*, in or

(a) The name of "Repps" commemorates his descent from John Repps, of Matisham, Norfolk, whose da. and h., Vertue, *m.*, April 1754, Edward Hase, of Sall, in that county (br. of the grantee), and was mother of Vertue, the mother of this (the second) Baronet.
(b) The 1st son, Richard Paul Hase Jodrell, *b.* 3 Aug. 1818; matric. at Oxford (New Coll.), 15 Jan. 1836, aged 17; *m.* but *d.* s.p. and v.p., 12 Nov. 1855, aged 37.
(c) On his death the estates of Sall Park, in Norfolk and Nethercote House, Oxon, devolved on his only sister Amelia Vertue, who had *m.*, 18 June 1842, Charles Fitzgerald Higgins, of Westport, co. Mayo. She, by royal lic., 1883, took the name of Jodrell and *d.* 15 Sep. 1890, leaving issue.
(d) The eldest son, Edward Jodrell, of Bayfield Hall abovenamed, sometime an officer in the 13th Foot, *b.* 15 Oct. 1845, *d.* unm. (a few months before the 3d Baronet), 17 March 1882.
(e) See p. 235, note "a," under "BARROW."

before 1773, Susanna, 1st da. of Hambleton CUSTANCE, of Weston, Norfolk, by Susanna, da. and h. of John PRESS, Alderman of Norwich. He *d.* 6 Sep. 1790, aged 68. Will pr. Oct. 1790. His widow *d.* 9 Dec. 1833, aged 82. Will pr. Jan. 1834.

II. 1790. SIR THOMAS DURRANT, Baronet [1784], of Scottow aforesaid, 2d but 1st surv. s. and h., *b.* 1775; *suc. to the Baronetcy*, 6 Sep. 1790. He *m.* 28 Sep. 1799, Sarah Crooke, da. of Henry STEENBERGEN, of the island of St. Christopher. He *d.* 22 May 1829, aged about 54. Will pr. Oct. 1829. His widow *d.* July 1845. Will pr. July 1845.

III. 1829. SIR HENRY THOMAS ESTRIDGE DURRANT, Baronet [1784], of Scottow aforesaid, only s. and h., *b.* 4 May 1807, at Harpenden, Herts; *suc. to the Baronetcy*, 22 May 1829. He *m.* firstly, 23 June 1830, Agnes Sophia Katharine, da. of Robert MARSHAM, of Stratton Strawless, Norfolk, by Frances Anne, da. of John CUSTANCE, of Weston House, Norfolk. She *d.* in childbirth, 28 April 1831, at Scottow Hall, in her 19th year. He *m.* secondly, 31 Jan. 1833, at Sprowston, Norfolk, Diana Julia, 4th da. of Sir Josias Henry STRACEY, 4th Baronet [1818], of Rackheath, by Diana, da. of David SCOTT, of Dunniland. He *d.* 16 May 1861, at Scottow Hall, aged 54. His widow *d.* 9 Feb. 1867, aged 55, at Highnam, Hurst Green, the house of her brother in law, the Rev. George LUXFORD.

IV. 1861. SIR HENRY JOSIAS DURRANT, Baronet [1784], of Scottow aforesaid, 1st s. and h., by 2d wife, *b.* 2 Sep. 1838, at Bognor, Sussex, *suc. to the Baronetcy*, 16 May 1861. He *m.* 30 April 1863, at Brussels, Alexandrina Charlotte, da. of Gen. Sir Robert BARTON, **K.C.H.** He *d.* s.p.m., 6 April 1875, at Mentone, aged 36, leaving his estates to his widow for her life with rem. to his daughters. His widow *m.* 15 July 1884, at St. Mary Abbott's, Kensington, Lieut.-Col. Arthur BLUNDELL (who *d.* 1891), and was living 1905.

V. 1875. SIR WILLIAM ROBERT ESTRIDGE DURRANT, Baronet [1784], only br. and h. male, *b.* 19 Aug. 1840; ed. at Eton; Ensign 15th Foot, 1858; Lieut. 1860, till he retired; *suc. to the Baronetcy* (but to none of the estates), 6 April 1875, and resided in Australia. He *m.* in 1862, Emily, da. of (—) STREET, of Australia.

Family Estates.—These, in 1883, being those of the 3d Baronet, consisted of 2,835 acres in Norfolk, valued at £4,904 a year.

PEPYS:

cr. 22 Jan. 1784;

sometime, 1830-49, LESLIE;

afterwards, since 1849, BARONS COTTENHAM,

and, since 1850, EARLS OF COTTENHAM.

I. 1784. "LUCAS PEPYS, Doctor of Physic, of Brook Street, Grosvenor Square [co. Middlesex], Physician Extraordinary to His Majesty,"[a] 2d and yst. s. of William PEPYS, of Lombard Street, London, banker (*d.* Sep. 1743, aged 44), by his 2d wife, Hannah, relict of Alexander WELLER, da. of Richard RUSSELL,[b] M.D., of Lewes, Sussex, was *b.* 24 May, and *bap.* 8 June 1742, at St. Mary's Woolnoth; ed. at Eton; matric. at Oxford

(a) See p. 235, note "a," under "BARROW."

(b) This Dr. Russell, who took the degree of M.D. at Rheims, in 1738, practising at Ware, in Herts and at Brighton, acquired considerable eminence by his work on the use of sea water in glandular diseases. He died at Reading, 5 July 1771.

(Ch. Ch.), 3 July 1760, aged 18; B.A., 1764; M.A., 1767; Bachelor of Medicine, 1770; Doctor of Medicine, 1774; having been made a member of the Medical Society at Edinburgh, 22 Feb. 1765, and practising as a Physician both in London and Brighton. He was Physician to the Middlesex Hospital, 1767-77; was Fellow of the College of Physicians, London, 1775, was several times Censor, and for ten years (1788-98) Treasurer thereof; was Physician Extraordinary to the King in 1777, and was *cr. a Baronet*, as above, 22 Jan. 1784, with *a spec. rem.*, failing heirs male of his body, to his brother "William Weller PEPYS, of Ridley, in the co. Pal. of Chester, Esq., one of the Masters in the High Court of Chancery." He attended George III for his mental disorder, 1788-89, as also in 1804, having been in 1792 made Physician in Ordinary to the King, in 1794 Physician Gen. to the Army, and for fifteen years President of an Army Medical Board, which had the direction of all medical affairs and the appointment of all the Physicians in the Army, but which (not unnaturally) was broken up in 1809 on his (and his colleagues') refusal to proceed to Walcheren to report on the fever there raging. He was President of the College of Physicians, 1804-10; F.S.A., 1770, and F.R.S., 1780. He resided as early as 1784 at Box Hill, Surrey. He *m.* firstly, as her second husband, 30 Oct. 1772,[a] at Brighton, Jane Elizabeth, *suo jure* COUNTESS OF ROTHES [S.], widow of George Raymond EVELYN, and only da. of John (LESLIE), EARL OF ROTHES [S.], by his 1st wife Hannah, da. of Matthew HOWARD, of Thorpe, co. Norfolk. She, who was *b.* 5 May 1750, and who suc. to the peerage on the death of her brother, 18 July 1773, *d.* in Upper Brook Street, 2 June 1810, aged 60. He *m.* secondly, 29 June 1813, at St. Geo. Han. Sq., Deborah, da. of Anthony ASKEW, M.D. (the well known classical scholar), by his 2d wife Elizabeth, da. of Robert HOLFORD, one of the Masters in Chancery. He *d.* 17 June 1830, at his house in Park Street, Grosvenor Square, aged 88. Will pr. July 1830. His widow, by whom he had no issue, *d.* 21 June 1848, at Cheltenham, aged 84. Will pr. Aug. 1848.

II. 1830. THE HON. SIR CHARLES LESLIE, Baronet [1784], of Juniper Hill in Boxhill, Surrey, 1st s. and h. of his father by his 1st wife (to whom, however, he was not heir), appears to have always borne the surname of his mother; was *b.* 28 Sep. 1774, at Brighton; matric. at Oxford (Ch. Ch.) 31 Jan. 1793, aged 19; was sometime in command of a troop of the 7th Dragoons; *suc. to the Baronetcy*, 17 June 1830. He *d.* unm., 4 Feb. 1833, aged 58. Will pr. March 1833.

III. 1833. THE HON. SIR HENRY LESLIE, Baronet [1784], of Juniper Hill aforesaid, only br. and h., appears to have always borne the surname of his mother; was *b.* 21 Sep. 1783, at Brighton; ed. at St. John's Coll., Cambridge; M.A. 1802; in Holy Orders and Rector of Sheephall, Herts, 1806; Rector of Wetherden, Suffolk, 1809; Preb. of Exeter, 1809; Chaplain to the King, 1809, retaining all his preferments till his death. He *suc. to the Baronetcy*, 4 Feb. 1833. He *m.* 15 Feb. 1816, Elizabeth Jane, yst. da. of the Rev. James Ray OAKES,[b] Vicar of Thurston and Rector of Tostock and Rattlesden, all co. Suffolk, by Elizabeth, da. of Rev. James TYRELL, of Thurlow in that county, Vicar of Thurston aforesaid. She *d.* a few months later, 12 Dec. 1816. Admon. Nov. 1843. He *d.* s.p. 8 July 1849, at Juniper Hill, aged 65. Will pr. Jan. 1850.

IV. 1849. CHARLES CHRISTOPHER (PEPYS), BARON COTTENHAM, and Baronet [1784 and 1801], 1st cousin and h. male, being 2d s. of Sir William Weller PEPYS, 1st Baronet [1801], by Elizabeth, da. of the Rt. Hon. William DOWDESWELL, which William Weller PEPYS was elder br. to Sir Lucas PEPYS, 1st Baronet [1784]. He was *b.* 29 April 1781, and was (on being made Chancellor of Great Britain) *cr.* 20 Jan. 1836, BARON COTTENHAM of

(a) Mrs. Boscawen thus writes of Dr. Pepys, to Mrs. Delany, 30 Sep. 1772, on the announcement of this intended marriage, "I believe he is a gentleman by birth and certainly by education and manners; his character, too, is excellent."

(b) See a good pedigree of the family of Oakes, in the *Mis. Gen. et Her.*, 4th S., vol. i, pp. 44-51.

Cottenham, co. Cambridge. He *suc. to the Baronetcy* [1801], conferred on his father (23 June 1801) on the death, 5 Oct. 1845, of his elder br. the 2d Baronet, and *suc. to the Baronetcy* [1784], conferred on his uncle (22 Jan. 1784), on the death, 8 July 1849, of his 1st cousin, the 3d Baronet, as abovementioned, under the *spec. rem.* in the creation of that dignity. In that Peerage this *Baronetcy* then *merged* and still [1905] so continues, the 1st Baron being shortly afterwards *cr.* 11 June 1850, EARL OF COTTENHAM, etc. See "*Peerage.*"

WOOD:

cr. 22 Jan. 1784;

afterwards, since 1866, VISCOUNTS HALIFAX OF MONK BRETTON.

I. 1784. "FRANCIS WOOD, of Barnsley, co. York, Esq., 2d son of Francis WOOD, late of Barnsley aforesaid Esq., dec^d,"[a] (which Francis *d.* 30 Aug. 1775, aged 78), by his 1st wife Mary Dorothy, da. of the Rev. Charles PALMER, D.D., Rector of Long Marston and Preb. of York, was *bap.* 2 Jan. 1729, at Barnsley, was *cr. a Baronet*, as above, 22 Jan. 1784, with *a spec. rem.* failing heirs male of his body, "severally to the Rev. Henry WOOD,[b] of the same place, D.D., 1st s. of the said Francis WOOD, deceased, and to the heirs [male of the body] of the said Francis WOOD, deceased."[a] He *m.* 5 June 1779, at St. James', Westm., Elizabeth, da. and h. of Anthony EWER, of Swine in Holderness, co. York, and of the Lea, in Watford, and of Bushey Hall, Herts. He *d.* s.p. 1 July 1795, aged 66. Will pr. Dec. 1795. The will of his widow pr. Dec. 1796.

II. 1795. SIR FRANCIS LINDLEY WOOD, Baronet [1784], of Bowling Hall, near Bradford, and of Hemsworth and Hickleton, co. York, nephew and h., being 1st s. and h. of Charles WOOD, of the same,[c] Capt. in the Royal Navy, by Caroline, da. and coheir of Thomas Lacon BARKER, of Otley, co. York, which Charles (who *d.* 9 Oct. 1782, aged 51, of wounds received in action off Madras), was yst. br. of the grantee. He was *b.* 16 Dec. 1771; ed. at Emmanuel College, Cambridge; B.A., 1793; M.A., 1796, having *suc. to the Baronetcy*, 1 July 1795, according to the *spec. rem.* in the creation thereof; was Sheriff of Yorkshire, 1814-15. He *m.* 15 Jan. 1798, Anne, 1st da. and coheir of Samuel BUCK, of New Grange and Park Hill, near Firbeck, co. York, Recorder of Leeds. She *d.* 11 Jan. 1841, at Hickleton, co. York. He *d.* there 31 Dec. 1846, and was *bur.* at Hickleton. Will pr. May 1847.

III. 1846. SIR CHARLES WOOD, Baronet [1784], of Bowling Hall aforesaid, and of Hickleton Hall, near Doncaster, co. York, 1st s. and h.; *b.* 20 Dec. 1800, at Pontefract, and *bap.* at Hemsworth; ed. at Eton; matric. at Oxford (Oriel Coll.), 28 Jan. 1818, aged 17; B.A. and double first class, 1821; M.A., 1824; was M.P. for Great Grimsby, 1826-31; for Wareham, 1831-32; for Halifax, 1832-65, and for Ripon, 1865-66, in all twelve Parls.; was

(a) See p. 235, note "a," under "BARROW."

(b) This Henry Wood, who was ed. at Jesus Coll., Cambridge, B.A., 1748; M.A., 1752, and D.D., 1755, was of Hemsworth Manor, co. York, and was Rector of Hemsworth and Vicar of Halifax. He *m.*, but *d.* s.p.s., 27 Oct. 1790, aged 64.

(c) This estate, formerly that of the family of Lindley, was devised to him by his father's 2d cousin, Thomas Pigot (*d.* s.p. 1770, aged 78), son of George Pigot, of Preston, co. Lancaster, by Elizabeth (sister of Francis Lindley, of Bowling Hall, whose issue all *d.* unm.), only da. of Francis Lindley, of Bowling Hall aforesaid (age 32 at the visit. of Yorkshire in 1665), whose sister Elizabeth *m.* William Simpson, of Babworth, Notts, and was mother of John Simpson, who had issue, and of Elizabeth, 3d wife of Henry Wood, of Barnsley (*d.* 4 May 1720, aged 74), and mother of Francis Wood, who was father of the 1st Baronet [1784], and of the said Charles Wood.

Joint Secretary to the Treasury, 1832-34; Secretary to the Admiralty, 1835-39; Chancellor of the Exchequer, 1846-52; P.C., 1846; and *suc. to the Baronetcy*, 31 Dec. 1846; President of the Board of Control for India, 1852-55; First Lord of the Admiralty, 1855-58; **G.C.B.** (Civil), 19 June 1856; Sec. of State and President of the Council for India, 1859-66. He *m.* 30 July 1829, at St. Geo. Han. sq., Mary, 5th da. of Charles (GREY), 2d EARL GREY, by Mary Elizabeth, da. of William Brabazon (PONSONBY), 1st BARON PONSONBY OF IMOKILLY. She was living when he was *cr.* 21 Feb. 1866, VISCOUNT HALIFAX OF MONK BRETTON, co. York. In that peerage this *Baronetcy* then *merged*, and still [1905] so continues. See *Peerage*.

FITZHERBERT:

cr. 22 Jan. 1784.

I. 1784. "WILLIAM FITZHERBERT, of Tissington, co. Derby, Esq.,"[a] 1st s. and h.[b] of William FITZHERBERT, of the same, sometime (1762-72) M.P. for Derby and a Lord of Trade and Plantation (*d.* 2 Jan. 1772, aged 60), by Mary, da. of Littleton Poyntz MEYNELL, of Bradley, co. Derby, was *b.* 27 May 1748; was *cr.* M.A. of Cambridge (St. John's Coll.), 1770; admitted to Lincoln's Inn, 14 June 1773, becoming subsequently a Barrister; was Recorder of Derby; Gentleman Usher to George III, and was *cr. a Baronet*, as above, 22 Jan. 1784.[c] He *m.* 14 Oct. 1777, at St. George's, Bloomsbury, Sarah, only da. of William PERRIN, of Jamaica. He *d.* 30 July 1791, aged 43. Will pr. Dec. 1791. His widow *d.* 6 March 1795. Will pr. March 1795.

II. 1791. SIR ANTHONY PERRIN FITZHERBERT, Baronet [1784], of Tissington aforesaid, 1st s. and h., *b.* 21 July, and *bap.* 18 Aug. 1779 at St. Geo. Bloomsbury; *suc. to the Baronetcy*, 30 July 1791. He *d.* unm. 2 April 1798, aged 18. Will pr. June 1798.

III. 1798. SIR HENRY FITZHERBERT, Baronet [1784], of Tissington aforesaid, yst. br. and h., *b.* 4 and *bap.* 16 Aug. 1783 at St. Geo. Bloomsbury; *suc. to the Baronetcy*, 2 April 1798; ed. at St. John's Coll., Cambridge; M.A., 1804; admitted to Lincoln's Inn, 25 Jan. 1805; Barrister, 1808; Sheriff of Derbyshire, 1815-16. He *m.* 27 Dec. 1805, at Ashbourne, co. Derby, Agnes, 2d and yst. da. of the Rev. William BERESFORD, Rector of Sonning, Berks. He *d.* 1 June 1858, at Tissington Hall, aged 74. His widow *d.* 25 Nov. 1863, at West Farleigh, Kent, in her 81st year.

IV. 1858. SIR WILLIAM FITZHERBERT, Baronet [1784], of Tissington aforesaid, 1st s. and h., *b.* 2 June 1808; ed. at Charterhouse, London; *suc. to the Baronetcy*, 1 June 1858; Sheriff of Derbyshire, 1866. He *m.* 20 Feb. 1836, at Barbadoes, Anne, 2d da. of Sir Reynold Abel ALLEYNE, 2d Baronet [1769], of Alleyndale Hall in that Island, by Rebecca, da. of John OLTON, of Harrow, in Barbadoes. She *d.* 14 Dec. 1864, in Curzon street, Mayfair. He *d.* 12 Oct. 1896, aged 88, at Tissington Hall. Will pr. at £203,168 personalty.

(a) See p. 235, note "a," under "BARROW."

(b) His yr. br. Alleyne Fitzherbert, was *cr.* Baron St. Helens, a dignity which became extinct at his death, 19 Feb. 1839, aged 85. The name of Alleyne was that of his maternal grandmother, Judith, da. of Thomas Alleyne, of Barbadoes, wife of Littleton Poyntz Meynell.

(c) It appears from the long and laudatory obituary notice of him in the *Gent. Mag.* for 1795 (vol. lxi, p. 777), quoted in Betham's *Baronetage* [1804], that having "began his services at St. James' as a Gentleman Usher" he "attained the seniority to which it has been the custom to annex the dignity of a Baronet," but that subsequently been summoned by the Lord Chamberlain, when at a great distance from London, "for one day's attendance," he, after performing "his duty, immediately gave in his resignation."

V

V. 1896. SIR RICHARD FITZHERBERT, Baronet [1784], of Tissington aforesaid, 3d but only surv. s. and h.,(a) b. 12 April 1846; ed. at St. John's Coll., Cambridge; B.A., and took Holy Orders, 1870; M.A., 1874; Rector of Warsop, Notts, 1872-96; *suc. to the Baronetcy*, 12 Oct. 1896. He *m.* 10 Oct. 1871, Mary Anne, da. of Edward ARKWRIGHT, of Hatton, co. Warwick.

Family Estates.—These, in 1883, consisted of 5,846 acres in Notts, 2,914 in Derbyshire, 418 in Kent, and 7 in Staffordshire. *Total.*—9,185 acres, worth £14,199 a year. *Principal Seats.*—Tissington Hall, near Ashbourne, co. Derby; Nettleworth Manor, near Mansfield, Notts, and West Farleigh, co. Kent.

BEEVOR:

cr. 22 Jan. 1784.

I. 1784. "THOMAS BEEVOR, of Hethel, co. Norfolk, Esq.,"(b) 1st s. of Thomas BEEVOR, of Norwich, by his 3d wife, Hester, da. of John SHARPE, of that city; was *b.* 25 Oct. 1726; was, presumably, the Thomas BEEVOR, who was B.A. of Cambridge (Trinity Coll.), 1745; was a great agriculturist; and was *cr. a Baronet*, as above, 22 Jan. 1784. He *m.* 7 July 1750, Elizabeth, da. and h. of Miles BRANTHWAITE, of Hethel aforesaid. She *d.* 31 Jan. 1794.(c) He *d.* Jan. 1814, aged 87. Will pr. 1814.

II. 1814. SIR THOMAS BEEVOR, Baronet [1784], of Hethel aforesaid and of Hargham, Norfolk, 1st s. and h., *b.* 15 Nov. 1753; *suc. to the Baronetcy*, Jan. 1814. He *m.* 24 Aug. 1795, Anne, da. and h. of Hugh HARE, of Hargham aforesaid. He *d.* 10 Dec. 1820, aged 67. Will pr. July 1821.

III. 1820. SIR THOMAS BRANTHWAITE BEEVOR, Baronet [1784], of Hargham aforesaid, only s. and h., *b.* 7 April 1798 at Old Buckenham, Norfolk; *suc. to the Baronetcy*, 10 Dec. 1820. He *m.* firstly, 9 Dec. 1819, Elizabeth Bridget, 2d da. of Richard LUBBOCK, M.D., of Norwich. She *d.* 23 Nov. 1831, at Hargham, aged 29. He *m.* secondly, 4 Sep. 1832, Martha, da. of Archibald HERDIMENT, of Old Buckenham aforesaid. She *d.* 25 Oct. 1843. He *m.* thirdly, 15 March 1845, Mary, da. of F. DAVIES. She *d.* 1878. He *d.* 6 April 1879, at Yarmouth, aged 81.

IV. 1879. SIR THOMAS BEEVOR, Baronet [1784], of Hargham aforesaid, 1st s. and h., being only s. by 1st wife, *b.* there 23 Aug. 1823; ed. at Univ. Coll., London; admitted to the Inner Temple, 24 March 1843, and to Lincoln's Inn, 1 May 1845, becoming, subsequently, a Barrister. He *suc. to the Baronetcy*. 6 April 1879. He *m.*, 10 Dec. 1850, at St. James', Dover, Sophia Jane, widow of Isaac Jermy JERMY,(d) da. of the Rev. Clement CHEVALLIER, M.A., Rector of Badingham, Suffolk. He *d.* 18 Aug. 1885, at Hingham, Norfolk, aged 61. His widow *d.* 22 Feb. 1890.

(a) Of his elder brothers, who both *d.* unm. and v.p., (1) William Cromwell Fitzherbert, 16th Hussars, *d.* 24 Jan. 1874, aged 32; (2) Beresford Fitzherbert, *d.* 25 May 1872, aged 28.

(b) See p. 235, note "a," under "BARROW."

(c) According to Debrett's *Baronetage* [1840] she *d.* 21 July 1810.

(d) This Isaac, together with his father of the same name, Isaac Jermy formerly Preston, Recorder of Norwich (who took the name of Jermy, 6 Sep. 1838, on succeeding to the estate of Stanfield, Norfolk) was murdered at Stanfield Hall, 28 Nov. 1848, (his wife, the abovenamed Sophia Jane, being wounded at the same time), by John Blomfield Rush, who, after a six days' trial, was hanged 14 April 1849.

V. 1885. SIR HUGH REEVE BEEVOR, Baronet [1784], 2d but 1st surv. s. and h.,(a) *b.* 31 Oct. 1858 at Hingham aforesaid; ed. at Felstead Grammar School, Essex. Member Royal College of Surgeons and L.S.A., 1882; Resident Medical Officer at King's College Hospital, London, 1882-83; M.B., London, 1884, and subsequently M.D.; *suc. to the Baronetcy*, 18 Aug. 1885. Fellow of the Royal College of Physicians. He *m.* 22 June 1894, Emily Georgina, 1st da. of Sir William FOSTER, 2d Baronet [1838], of Norwich, by his 1st wife Georgina, da. of Richard ARMIT, of Monkstown, co. Dublin.

Family Estates.—These, in 1883, consisted of 2,386 acres in Norfolk, worth £2,193 a year.

KENYON:

cr. 28 July 1784;

afterwards, since 1788, BARONS KENYON OF GREDINGTON.

I. 1784. "The Rt. Hon. LLOYD KENYON,"(b) of Gredington in Hanmer, co. Flint, Master of the Rolls, 2d but 1st surv. s. and h., of Lloyd KENYON, of Gredington (*d.* 30 Sep. 1773, aged 77), by Jane, da. and coheir of Robert EDDOWES, of Eagle Hall, co. Chester, was *b.* 5 Oct. 1732, at Gredington; ed. at Ruthin Grammar School; articled, for five years, to an Attorney at Nantwich; admitted to the Middle Temple, 7 Nov. 1750; Barrister, 7 Feb. 1756; M.P. for Hindon, 1780-84, and for Tregony, 1784-88; Chief Justice of Chester, 1780; Attorney-General (without ever having been Solicitor-General), March 1782 to April 1783, and again Dec. 1783 to March 1784, being made Master of the Rolls, 30 March 1784; P.C., 2 April 1784, and *cr. a Baronet*, as above, 28 July 1784. He *m.* 16 Oct. 1773, at Deane, co. Lancaster, his cousin Mary, 3d da. of George KENYON, of Peel Hall, co. Lancaster, Barrister, by Peregrina, yst. da. and coheir of Robert EDDOWES abovenamed. She was living when he, having been appointed, 4 June 1788, Chief Justice of the King's Bench, was a few days later, *cr.* 9 June 1788, LORD KENYON, BARON OF GREDINGTON, co. Flint. In that peerage this *Baronetcy* then *merged*, and still [1905] so continues. See *Peerage*.

SMYTH:

said (in error) to have been *cr.* 22 Dec. 1784;

and to have become *extinct* about 1823.

See p. 239, note "a," under "SMITH," *cr.* 22 Jan. 1784.

(a) The eldest son Thomas Edward Beevor, *d.* unm. and v.p. 6 Aug. 1879, aged 25, at Colorado, in America.

(b) See p. 113, note "a," under "GIDEON." The date of the Gazette notice for Kenyon is 24 July 1784.

SINCLAIR:

cr. 14 Feb. 1786.

I. 1786. "JOHN SINCLAIR, Esq., of Ulbster,"(a) co. Caithness, 3d but only surv. s. and h. of George SINCLAIR, of the same, Heritable Sheriff of Caithness (*d.* 31 Aug. 1770, at Edinburgh), by Janet, sister of William, EARL OF SUTHERLAND [S.], da. of William GORDON, *afterwards* SUTHERLAND, *styled* LORD STRATHNAVER. He was *b.* 10 May 1754, at Thurso Castle, co. Caithness; ed. at the High School, Edinburgh, and afterwards at the Univs. of Edinburgh, Glasgow, and Oxford; matric. at Oxford (Trinity Coll.), 26 Jan. 1775, aged 20; Advocate, 1775; admitted to Lincoln's Inn, 22 March 1774, becoming a Barrister, 9 May 1782; was M.P. for Caithness, 1780-84, 1790-96, 1802-1806, and 1807-11, but that county being only alternately represented, he was, while its representation ceased, M.P. for Lostwithiel, 1784-90, and for Petersfield, 1797-1802. He was *cr. a Baronet*, as above, 14 Feb. 1786, with a *spec. rem.*, failing heirs male of his body, to those of his two daughters respectively by his late wife. In that year he made an extensive journey (exceeding 7,500 miles) in the north of Europe. He was LL.D. of Glasgow Univ., 1788; F.A.S. and F.R.S. In 1791 he effected the establishment of a Society [S.] for improvement of British wool, and in 1794 that of a "Board of Agriculture," of both of which he was the first President. In 1794 he raised a regiment of Fencibles, being the first ever levied for *general* service. He was a Director of the Bank of Scotland in 1796, as also of the British Fisheries, and was made P.C. 29 Aug. 1810.(b) He was also Cashier of the Excise [S.]. He *m.* firstly, 26 March 1776, at St. Martin's in the fields, Sarah, da. and h. of Alexander MAITLAND, of Stoke Newington, Midx. She *d.* s.p.m. 15 May 1785. He *m.* secondly, 6 March 1788, at St. Geo. Han. Sq., Diana Jane Elizabeth, 1st da. of Alexander (MACDONALD), 1st BARON MACDONALD OF SLATE [I.], by Elizabeth Diana, da. of Godfrey BOSVILLE. He *d.* at his house in George Street, Edinburgh, 21, and was *bur.* 30 Dec. 1835, at Canongate, aged 81. His widow, by whom he had twelve children,(c) *d.* at Edinburgh 22, and was *bur.* 26 April 1845, at Canongate aforesaid, aged 74.

II. 1835. SIR GEORGE SINCLAIR, Baronet [1786], of Thurso, co. Caithness, 1st s. and h., by 2d wife, *b.* 23 Aug. 1790; ed. at Harrow and the Univ. of Gottingen, being arrested, with his tutor, at Paris, in Oct. 1806, though not long detained captive; was M.P. for Caithnesshire (six Parls.), 1811-12, 1818-20, and 1831-41, having *suc. to the Baronetcy*, 21 Dec. 1835. He *m.* 1 May 1816, Catherine Camilla, sister of Lionel William John (TALMASH, *afterwards* TOLLEMACHE), EARL OF DYSART [S.], 2d da. of Sir William TALMASH, *formerly* MANNERS, 1st Baronet [1793], *styled* LORD HUNTINGTOWER, by Catherine Rebecca, da. of Francis GREY. She, who was *b.* 5 Nov. 1792, and who was raised to the rank of the da. of an Earl by Royal warrant 6 Nov. 1840, *d.* 17 March 1863. He *d.* 9 Oct. 1868 in George street, Edinburgh, aged 78.

III. 1868. SIR (JOHN GEORGE) TOLLEMACHE SINCLAIR, Baronet [1786], of Thurso aforesaid, 2d(d) but only surv. s. and h., *b.* 8 Nov. 1824 in Prince's street, Edinburgh; sometime page of honour to Queen Victoria and an officer in the Scots Fusileer Guards; *suc. to the Baronetcy*, 9 Oct. 1868;

(a) See p. 113, note "a," under "GIDEON." The date of the Gazette notice for Sinclair is 4 Feb. 1786.

(b) No less than seven pages (4to) are devoted to an eulogium of him and of his services in the cause of Agriculture, Health, Finance, Statistical Philosophy, etc., in Playfair's *Baronetage* [1811].

(c) Among these children were (1) Catherine, *b.* 17 April 1800, and *d.* unm. 6 Aug. 1864, who was well known as the authoress of *Modern Accomplishments*, *Modern Society*, *Holiday House*, and other novels; (2) John Sinclair, D.D., many years Archdeacon of Middlesex and Vicar of Kensington, who *d.* unm. 22 May 1875, aged 77, having been more than thirty years Treasurer of the National Education Society.

(d) Dudley Sinclair, the 1st son, *d.* unm. and v.p. 1844, aged 26.

M.P. for Caithnesshire (three Parls.), 1869-85. He *m.* 22 Nov. 1853, at Raintor, co. Durham, Emma Isabella Harriett, 1st of the three sisters and coheirs (21 Feb. 1878) of William Standish STANDISH, of Duxbury Park, co. Lancaster, and Cocken Hall, co. Durham, being da. of William Standish STANDISH, *formerly* CARR, of the same, by Sarah, da. of Richard JENKINS, of Beachley Lodge, co. Gloucester. She was divorced 4 July 1878.(a)

Family Estates.—These, in 1883, consisted of 78,053* acres in Caithnesshire, worth £12,833 a year, exclusive of quarries rented at £1,378. *Seat.*—Thurso Castle, co. Caithness.

MACPHERSON:

cr. 27 June 1786;

ex. 12 Jan. 1821.

I. 1786, to 1821. "JOHN [*misprinted* JAMES] MACPHERSON, of Calcutta [in the province of Bengal], Esq.,"(b) 2d and yst. s.(c) of the Rev. John MACPHERSON, D.D. (Aberdeen Univ.), Minister of Sleat in the Isle of Sky, and formerly of Barra (*d.* 1765, in his 56th year), by Janet, 1st da. of Donald MACLEOD, of Bernera in Harris, accompanied his maternal uncle, Capt. MACLEOD, to India, arriving at Madras 1767; conducted some successful diplomatic negotiations with the Nabob of the Carnatic, and was in 1773 made Paymaster to the Army there; was M.P. for Cricklade (two Parls.) April 1779 to 1782, and for Horsham 1796-1802; was a member of the Supreme Council at Bengal, 1781 to 1782 (a time of great emergency), and was for a short time, 1785 to Sep. 1786, Governor General of India, receiving the thanks of the Court of Directors for his able administration(d) and being *cr. a Baronet*, as above, 27 June 1786. He retired to Frant, in Sussex, where he raised a company of Militia, of which he was Captain. He *d.* unm. at an advanced age, 12 Jan. 1821, at Brompton Grove, Midx., when the *Baronetcy* became *extinct*. Will pr. 1821.

COLQUHOUN:

cr. 27 June 1786.(e)

I. 1786, June. "JAMES COLQUHOUN, of Luss, Esq.,"(b) co. Dumbarton, *formerly* James GRANT, 4th but 2d surv. s. of Sir James COLQUHOUN, *subsequently* (after 1719) GRANT, 6th Baronet [S. 1625], (*d.* 16 Jan. 1746-7), by Anne, only child of Sir Humphrey COLQUHOUN, 5th

(a) She *d.* 1889.

(b) See p. 113, note "a," under "GIDEON." The date of the Gazette notices for Macpherson, Colquhoun, Douglas, Shirley, Green, Rowley, Corbet, Vane-Fletcher, Hoare, Hunter-Blair, and Farrell-Skeffington is 10 June 1786.

(c) His eldest br., the Rev. Martin Macpherson, M.A. (Aberdeen Coll.), suc. his father as Minister of Sky in 1766. He *m.* Mary Mackinnon, of Corrychatican, and is mentioned by Dr. Johnson in the *Tour to the Hebrides* as being "with his sister [Isabel] distinguished by politeness and accomplishments. By him [writes the Doctor] we were invited to Ostig."

(d) More than eleven pages (4to) in Playfair's *Baronetage* [1811] are devoted to his career, with the conclusion that "feeble is the testimony of our praise to his multifarious merits." He and his "multifarious merits" are, however, altogether ignored in the *Dict. Nat. Biog.*

(e) The *Baronetcy* [S.], which had been granted 30 Aug. 1625 to John Colquhoun, of Luss, the ancestor of this James, passed (under the regrant of that dignity to the 5th Baronet, on 29 April 1704), to his elder br., Ludovic Grant, and was inherited by that brother's descendants of the name of Grant, who still (1905) possess that dignity, but the estate of Luss, which by an entail of the 5th Baronet was never to be united with the estates of Grant, passed to the said James, according to that entail, denuded of the ancient Baronetcy of Colquhoun.

Baronet [S. 1625] of Luss aforesaid, was *b.* 22 Feb. 1714 and having (when in 1735 the fee expectant of the Grant estates had been made over to his then only surv. elder brother, Ludovic, the eldest brother, Humphrey, having shortly before *d.* unm., in Sep. 1732) *suc.* to the estate of Luss (under the deed of entail thereof in 1704 by his said maternal grandfather, Sir Humphrey COLQUHOUN, which, after some dispute, was confirmed to him by legal decision in 1738); assumed the name of COLQUHOUN, instead of GRANT.(a) He served with the 42nd Foot ("Black Watch") in Flanders; was at the battle of Dettingen, June 1743, becoming, finally, Major in the army, and being *cr. a Baronet*, as above, 27 June 1786, five months before his death. He built the mansion of Rossdhu. He *m.* 12 April 1740, at Edinburgh, Helen, sister of William, EARL OF SUTHERLAND [S.], 1st da. of William GORDON, *afterwards* SUTHERLAND, *styled* LORD STRATHNAVER, by Catherine, da. of William MORISON, of Prestongrange. He *d.* 16 Nov. 1786, at Rossdhu, aged 72. His widow *d.* 7 Jan. 1791.

II. 1786, Nov. SIR JAMES COLQUHOUN, Baronet [1786], of Luss aforesaid, 1st s. and h., *b.* 28 July 1741; Advocate, 30 Dec. 1765; Sheriff Depute of Dumbartonshire, 1775; a Principal Clerk of Session, 1779; *suc. to the Baronetcy*, 16 Nov. 1786. He *m.* 22 July 1773, at Edinburgh, Mary, yst. of the two daughters and coheirs of James FALCONER, of Monktown, co. Edinburgh, by Jane, da. of David (FALCONER, 5th LORD FALCONER OF HALKERTON [S.]. He *d.* 23 April 1805, at Edinburgh, aged 63. Will pr. 1807. His widow *d.* 12 April 1833.

III. 1805. SIR JAMES COLQUHOUN, Baronet [1786], of Luss aforesaid, 1st s. and h., *b.* 28 Sep. 1774; was a Captain in the army, 1796; was M.P. for Dumbartonshire, 1799-1806, having *suc. to the Baronetcy* 23 April 1805. He *m.* (contract 11 June 1799) Janet, da. of the Rt. Hon. Sir John SINCLAIR, 1st Baronet [1786] of Ulbster, by his 1st wife Sarah, da. and h. of Alexander MAITLAND. He *d.* 3 Feb. 1836, after a long illness, aged 61. His widow, whose issue male was in rem. to the Baronetcy granted to her father 14 Feb. 1786 (but five months before the creation of the Baronetcy enjoyed by her husband), *d.* 21 Oct. 1846, at Rossdhu, aged 65.

IV. 1836. SIR JAMES COLQUHOUN, Baronet [1786], of Luss aforesaid, 1st s. and h., *b.* 7 Feb. 1804, in Edinburgh; *suc. to the Baronetcy*, 3 Feb. 1836; M.P. for Dumbartonshire, 1837-41; Lord Lieut. of that county, 1837. He *m.* 14 June 1843, Jane, 2d da. of Sir Robert ABERCROMBY, 5th Baronet [S. 1636], of Birkenbog and Forglen, by Elizabeth Stephenson, da. and h. of Samuel DOUGLAS. She *d.* eleven months later, 3 May 1844. He was drowned in Loch Lomond, 18 and was *bur.* 28 Dec. 1873, in the chapel of Rossdhu, aged 69.

V. 1873. SIR JAMES COLQUHOUN, Baronet [1786], of Luss aforesaid, only s. and h., *b.* 30 March 1844, at Edinburgh; ed. at Harrow, and at Trin. Coll., Cambridge; B.A., 1868; M.A., 1871; *suc. to the Baronetcy*, 18 Dec. 1873. He *m.* firstly, 8 Dec. 1875, at St. Thomas' Episcopal Church, Edinburgh, his 1st cousin, Charlotte Mary Douglas, yst. da. of William MONRO, Major 29th Foot, by Elizabeth, da. of Sir Robert ABERCROMBY, 5th Baronet [S. 1636], abovenamed. She *d.* s.p.m., 9 and was *bur.* 17 Jan. 1902, at

(a) See p. 249, note "e." It is, however, not altogether clear whether on his father's death, 16 Jan. 1746/7, he did not assume the Nova Scotia Baronetcy of Colquhoun [S. 1625], or, at all events, whether it was not wrongly attributed to him; indeed, Sir Robert Douglas, in his *Baronage* [S.], allows the title of Baronet not only "to *both* these brothers but even to Colquhoun, of Tillyquhoun as heir male of the 1st Baronet, so that in that work the Nova Scotia Baronetcy [of 1625] is actually divided into three portions all conferring the same rank and title" [*Her. and Gen.*, vol. v, p. 91]. See also vol. ii of this work, pp. 293-296.

Rossdhu. He *m.* secondly, in 1905, Ivie Muriel Ellen, only da. of Major Ivies Maclean URQUHART.

Family Estates.—These, in 1883, consisted of 67,041 acres in Dumbartonshire, worth £12,845 a year. *Principal Seats.*—Rossdhu House, Ardencaple Castle, and Arrochar House, all in co. Dumbarton.

DOUGLAS:

cr. 27 June 1786;

sometime, 1822-85, SCOTT-DOUGLAS.

I. 1786. "SIR JAMES DOUGLAS, Knt., Admiral of the White,"(a) being of Springwood Park, in Kelso, co. Roxburgh, yr. s. of George DOUGLAS, of Friarshaw, in that county, Advocate, Solicitor of the Tithes [S.], by Elizabeth, da. of Sir Patrick SCOTT, 2d Baronet [S. 1671], of Ancrum, was *b.* about 1703; entered the Royal Navy; Capt. 1743/4; was M.P. for Orkney and Shetland (two Parls.), 1754-68; was a member of the Court Martial that tried Admiral Byng, Jan. 1757, and having been sent home with news of the capture of Quebec (13 Sep. 1759), was *Knighted* 16 Oct. 1759; was Commander-in-Chief off the Leeward Islands 1760-62, capturing Dominica in 1761, and serving as second in command at the reduction of Martinique in 1762; was Rear-Admiral, 1762; Vice-Admiral, 1770; Admiral, 1778, and was (a year before his death) *cr. a Baronet*, as above, 27 June 1786. He *m.* firstly, in 1753, Helen, da. of Thomas BRISBANE, of Brisbane, co. Renfrew. She *d.* 20 March 1766, at Springwood Park. He *m.* secondly, Helen, 6th da. of John (BOYLE), 2d EARL OF GLASGOW [S.], by Helen, da. of William MORISON. He *d.* 2 Nov. 1787, aged 84. His widow *d.* s.p. 17 Oct. 1794, in Portman square, Marylebone.

II. 1787. SIR GEORGE DOUGLAS, Baronet [1786], of Springwood Park aforesaid, 1st s. and h., by 1st wife, *b.* 1 March 1754 or 1755, at Springwood Park; was an officer, 21st Foot and 1st Foot Guards, 1771-89; M.P. for Roxburghshire (four Parls.), 1784-1806, having *suc. to the Baronetcy*, 2 Nov. 1787. He *m.* 16 Oct. 1786, Elizabeth (niece of his step-mother), 1st da. of John (BOYLE), 3d EARL OF GLASGOW [S.], by Elizabeth, da. of George (Ross), LORD ROSS OF HALKHEAD [S.]. She *d.* in London 15 Feb. 1801, in her 42d year. He *d.* 4 June 1821, in Edward street, Portman square, aged about 67. Admon. Aug. 1821.

III. 1821. SIR JOHN JAMES DOUGLAS, afterwards (since 1822) SCOTT-DOUGLAS, Baronet [1786], of Springwood Park aforesaid, only s. and h., *b.* 18 July 1792; sometime Capt. 15th Hussars, serving in the Peninsula, being present at Waterloo and receiving a medal; *suc. to the Baronetcy*, 4 June 1821. By royal lic., 10 July 1822, he took the name of SCOTT before that of DOUGLAS, in consequence of his intended marriage. He *m.* 15 Aug. 1822, at St. Geo. Han. sq., his cousin Hannah Charlotte, da. and h. of Henry SCOTT, of Belford, co. Roxburgh. He *d.* 24 Jan. 1836, at Boulogne-sur-Seine, near Paris, aged 43. His widow *m.* 19 Dec. 1837, at St. James', Westm., William SCOTT-KERR, of Chatto, co. Roxburgh (who survived her) and *d.* at Paris 29 April 1850.

IV. 1836. SIR GEORGE HENRY SCOTT-DOUGLAS, Baronet [1786], of Springwood Park aforesaid, only s. and h., *b.* 19 June 1825, at Edinburgh, and *suc. to the Baronetcy*, 24 Jan. 1836; sometime (1850-51), Capt. 34th Foot; Major (1862) of Roxburgh Rifle Volunteers, and Brig.-General of "the Royal Company of Archers," *i.e.*, the Royal Body Guard of Scotland; M.P. for Roxburghshire, 1874-80. He *m.* 1 Nov. 1851, at Gibraltar, Mariquita Juana Petronila, 1st da. of Don Francisco Sanchez Serrano DE PINA, of Gibraltar aforesaid. He *d.* suddenly 26 June 1885, at Springwood Park, aged 60. His widow living 1905.

(a) See p. 249, note "b," under "MACPHERSON."

V. 1885. SIR GEORGE BRISBANE DOUGLAS, Baronet [1786], of Springwood Park aforesaid, *formerly* SCOTT-DOUGLAS, 2d but 1st surv. s. and h.,(a) *b.* 22 Dec. 1856, at Gibraltar; ed. at Harrow and at Trin. Coll., Cambridge; B.A., 1877; M.A., 1881; *suc. to the Baronetcy*, 26 June 1885, when he discontinued the use of the name of SCOTT-DOUGLAS, and resumed that of DOUGLAS only.

Family Estates.—These, in 1883, consisted of 5,568 acres in Roxburghshire, worth £6,771 a year. *Seat.*—Springwood Park, near Kelso, co. Roxburgh.

SHIRLEY:

cr. 27 June 1786;

ex. 26 Feb. 1815.

I. 1786. "THOMAS SHIRLEY, of Oat Hall [*i.e.*, Ote Hall, in Wivelsfield],(b) co. Sussex, Esq., Governor of the Leeward Carribbee islands,"(c) 3d but only surv. s.(d) of Gen. William SHIRLEY, sometime (1755-56) Commander-in-Chief of the Army in North America, and subsequently (1758) Governor of the Bahama islands (*d.* 24 March 1771, at Boston, in New England, aged 77), by Frances, da. of Francis BARKER, of London, was *b.* 30 Dec. 1727 (registered at Wivelsfield),(e) and was, when only 16, a Capt. in the Army; was appointed Governor of the Bahama islands, 28 Nov. 1767; of Dominica, 3 Feb. 1774; of the Leeward islands, 9 May 1781; was Col. of the 91st Foot, 1781, and was *cr. a Baronet*, as above, 27 June 1786. He became Lieut.-Gen., 18 Oct. 1793, and General, 8 Jan. 1798, about which date he sold the Ote Hall estate. He *m.* 4 June 1768, at Rivenhall, Essex, Anna Maria, 1st da. of Thomas WESTERN, of Rivenhall aforesaid, by Anne, da. of Robert CALLIS. She, who was *b.* 21 Nov. 1737, *d.* in Dominica, 1777. He *d.* at Bath 18 and was *bur.* 26 Feb. 1800, in the Abbey there, aged 72. M.I. Will pr. March 1800.

II. 1800, to 1815. SIR WILLIAM WARDEN SHIRLEY, Baronet [1786], 2d but only surv. s. and h.,(f) *b.* 4 Aug. 1772 in the Bahama Islands, was an officer in the Royal navy; *suc. to the Baronetcy*, 18 Feb. 1800. He *d.* unm. 26 Feb. 1815, and was *bur.* at Rivenhall aforesaid, aged 42, when the *Baronetcy* became *extinct*.(g) Will pr. 1815.

(a) The eldest son James Henry Scott-Douglas, *b.* 27 May 1853, B.A. (Trin. Coll.), Cambridge, 1876; Lieut. 21st Royal Scots Fusileers, *d.* unm. and v.p., being killed in Zululand, 3 July 1879.

(b) The estate of Ote Hall was acquired by the marriage of Elizabeth, da. and h. of John Godman, of that place, with William Shirley, of London, merchant (who *d.* at Clapham, Surrey, 1701), by whom she was mother of Gen. William Shirley, the father of the grantee [see Evelyn P. Shirley's *Stemmata Shirleiana*].

(c) See p. 249, note "b," under "MACPHERSON."

(d) Of his two elder brothers, who both *d.* unm. and v.p., (1) William Shirley, Sec. to Major-Gen. Braddock, was killed with him in a bloody battle with the French and Indians in Ohio, in America, in 1756, aged 35; (2) John Shirley, Captain in the army, died of camp fever at Oswego, in America, in 1755, aged 30.

(e) It is generally stated that he was born at Boston in New England, but it is expressly stated in Shirley's reliable work quoted in note "b" above, that the birth is registered at Wivelsfield, so that the presumption (though by no means the certainty) is that he was born there.

(f) His eldest brother, Thomas Western Shirley, Capt. R.N., *b.* in the Bahama Islands 1770, *d.* of fever, 6 Oct. 1794 at Weymouth, and was *bur.* there.

(g) "By his decease s.p. the ancient family of the Shirleys of Sussex, who had flourished at Wiston, Preston, West Grinstead and Ote Hall, all in that county, for 12 [!] generations, became extinct in the male line, the female [line] being till the year 1844 represented by the Rt. Hon. Charles Callis Western, Baron Western of Rivenhall" [*Stemmata Shirleiana*, as in note "b" above].

GREEN:

cr. 27 June 1786;

ex. 1826.

I. 1786. "WILLIAM GREEN, Esq., Chief Engineer at Gibraltar,"(a) 1st s. of Farbridge(b) (*Qy.* Fairbridge, but sometimes called Godfrey) GREEN, of Durham, by Helen, sister of Adam SMITH, of Aberdeen, was *b.* 4 April 1725 at St. Martin's in the Fields(b); was ed. by his mother's relatives at Aberdeen; made cadet gunner, 1737, and practical engineer, 1743; served with the Engineers in Flanders and Brittany, 1745-48; Chief Engineer in Newfoundland, 1755; was wounded at Quebec, 1759; was for 22 years (1761-83) in service at Gibraltar; Col. in the army, 1777; distinguished himself greatly as Chief Engineer during the famous siege of Gibraltar, 1779-83, and received the thanks of Parl. He had become Major-Gen. in 1781, and was *cr. a Baronet*, as above, 27 June 1786. He was Lieut.-Gen. 1793, and full General 1798, retiring in 1803 and living at Brambleberry House, Plumstead (or "at Marass,")(c) co. Kent. He *m.* 26 Feb. 1754, Miriam, da. of Lieut.-Col. Justly WATSON, of the Engineers, son of Col. Jonas WATSON, who was killed at the siege of Carthagena, when in command of the Royal Artillery. She *d.* 21 June 1782, and was *bur.* in Broadway Chapel, Westm. He *d.* 11 Jan. 1811 at Bifrons, near Canterbury (the house of his da. Miriam, wife of Major Oliver NICHOLLS), aged 85, after seventy years' service, and was *bur.* at Plumstead. M.I. Will pr. 1811 and 1839.

II. 1811, to 1826. SIR JUSTLY WATSON GREEN, Baronet [1786], of Marass, co. Kent, 1st but only surv. s. and h., *b.* 8 Oct. 1755, at Newfoundland; sometime an officer in the 1st Royals; *suc. to the Baronetcy*, 11 Jan. 1811. He *d.* unm. at Chichester, late in the year 1826,(d) aged 71, when the *Baronetcy* became *extinct*. Admon. Jan. 1827.

ROWLEY:

cr. 27 June 1786.

I. 1786. "JOSHUA ROWLEY, Esq., Rear Admiral of the Red,"(a) 2d s. of Sir William ROWLEY, K.B., Admiral of the Fleet (*d.* 1 Jan. 1768, aged about 78), by Arabella, da. and h. of George DAWSON, Capt in the Army (killed at the siege of Gibraltar, 1727), was *b.* 1 May 1734, in Dublin, entered the Royal Navy; Lieut. 1747; was in command of a reinforcement to the West Indies, and made Rear-Admiral of the Blue, 1779, being in the action off Grenada, 6 July 1779, and in those off Martinique, April and May 1780; was in command on the Jamaica Station 1782-83, and, being then Rear-Admiral of the Red, was *cr. a Baronet*, as above, 27 June 1786. He became Vice-Admiral of the White, 24 Sep. 1787. He was of Tendring Hall, Suffolk. He *m.* 18 April 1759, at St. Stephen's, Coleman street, London, Sarah, da. and h. of Bartholomew BURTON, of Petersham, Surrey, a Director of the Bank of England. He *d.* at Tendring Hall, 26 Feb. 1790, aged 55. Will pr. March 1790. His widow, by whom he had seven sons,(e) *d.* 26 Dec. 1812. Will pr. 1813.

(a) See p. 249, note "b," under "MACPHERSON."

(b) Ped. recorded in Coll. of Arms. The father of the grantee is called "Walter" in the *Dict. Nat. Biogr.*

(c) Betham's *Baronetage* [1804].

(d) The entry of his death in the *Gent. Mag.* is between 12 Nov. and 15 Dec. 1826.

(e) Of these sons (1) Bartholomew Samuel Rowley, Admiral of the Blue and Commander-in-Chief in Jamaica, *b.* 10 June 1764, *d.* 7 Oct. 1817; (2) Charles Rowley, Admiral of the White and G.C.B., *b.* 16 Dec. 1770, was *cr. a Baronet*, 21 March 1836. Yet another Baronetcy, also for naval services, had been conferred on this family, *viz.*, 2 Nov. 1813, on Josiah Rowley, then Capt. R.N. (afterwards Admiral), he being first cousin of the two abovenamed, and nephew of the grantee of 1786. This dignity became extinct 10 Jan. 1842.

V

II. 1790. SIR WILLIAM ROWLEY, Baronet [1786] of Tendring Hall aforesaid, 1st s. and h., b. 10 Feb. 1761, in Argyll street; *suc. to the Baronetcy*, 26 Feb. 1790; was Sheriff of Suffolk, 1791-92, and M.P. for that county (four Parls.), 1812-30. He *m.* March 1785, at St. Marylebone, Susanna Edith, 3d da. of Admiral Sir Robert HARLAND, 1st Baronet [1771], by his 2d wife Susanna, da. of Col. Rowland REYNOLD. He *d.* 20 Oct. 1832, at Tendring Hall aforesaid, in his 72d year. Will pr. March 1833. His widow *d.* at an advanced age, 21 Jan. 1850, at Holbecke Hall, Suffolk. Will pr. March 1850.

III. 1832. SIR JOSHUA RICKETTS ROWLEY, Baronet [1786], of Tendring Hall aforesaid, 2d but 1st surv. s. and h.,(a) *b.* probably about 1790; entered the Royal Navy, and became eventually, 1855, Vice-Admiral of the Blue, having *suc. to the Baronetcy*, 20 Oct. 1832. He *m.* 10 Aug. 1824, at St. Marylebone, Charlotte, only da. of John MOSELEY, of Great Glemham House, Suffolk. He *d.* s.p. 18 March 1857, at 61 Wimpole street, Marylebone. His widow *d.* 11 Dec. 1862.

IV. 1857. SIR CHARLES ROBERT ROWLEY, Baronet [1786], of Tendring Hall aforesaid, br. and h., *b.* 5 May 1800; sometime Capt. Gren. Guards; *suc. to the Baronetcy*, 18 March 1857. He *m.* 14 Sep. 1830, Maria Louisa, only da. of Joshua (VANNECK), 2d BARON HUNTINGFIELD [I.], by his 1st wife, Frances Catherine, da. of Chaloner ARCEDECKNE. She, who was *b.* 29 Sep. 1811, *d.* 16 March 1878. He *d.* at Tendring Hall aforesaid, 8 Sep. 1888, aged 88.

V. 1888. SIR JOSHUA THELLUSSON ROWLEY, Baronet [1786], of Tendring Hall aforesaid, 2d but 1st surv. s. and h.,(b) b. 8 Feb. 1838; *suc. to the Baronetcy*, 8 Sep. 1888. Hon. Col. 2d Vol. Batt. Suffolk Reg. He *m.* 19 Oct. 1887, at St. Stephen's, South Kensington, Louisa Hèlene (then Maid of Honour to Queen Victoria), 3d da. of William (BROWNLOW), 2d BARON LURGAN, by Emily, da. of George Henry (CADOGAN), 5th EARL CADOGAN. She was *b.* 13 Oct. 1861.

Family Estates.—These, in 1883, consisted of 7,324 acres in Suffolk and 1,292 in Essex. *Total.*—8,616 acres, worth £11,608 a year. *Seat.*—Tendring Hall, near Stoke by Nayland, Suffolk.

CORBET, *late* DAVENANT:

cr. 27 June 1786;

ex. 31 March 1823.

I. 1786, to 1823. "CORBET CORBET, *late* DAVENANT, of Stoke-upon-Tern, and Adderley, co. Salop, Esq.,"(c) only s. and h. of Thomas DAVENANT, of Clearbrooke, in Pembridge, co. Hereford, by Anne, sister and heir (7 May 1750) of Sir Henry CORBET, 6th and last Baronet [1627], of Stoke and Adderley aforesaid, only da. of Sir Robert CORBET, 4th Baronet [1677], was *b.* probably in Parliament Street, Westm., 6 Feb. 1752; ed. at Trinity Coll., Cambridge; B.A., 1774; M.A., 1777; and having suc. to the estates of his maternal ancestors, took the name of CORBET, instead of that of Davenant, by Royal lic., 20 Jan. 1783, and was *cr. a Baronet*, as above, 27 June 1786. He *m.* in 1772, at Wrenbury, co. Chester, Hester Salusbury (*b.* 6 Feb. 1753), yst. da. of Sir Lynch Salusbury COTTON, 4th Baronet [1677], of Comberme, by Elizabeth, da. of Rowland COTTON, of Etwall, co. Derby. He *d.* s.p., after three days' illness, 31 March 1823, at Cambridge, aged 71, when the *Baronetcy* became *extinct*.(a)

(a) The eldest son William Barrington Harland Rowley, *b.* 9 March 1787, *m.* in 1819, Marianne, da. of J. Hart, but *d.* s.p. and v.p. before 1832.

(b) The eldest son William Arcedeckne Rowley, *b.* 30 Dec. 1836, *d.* v.p. unm. and under age, 20 Jan. 1853.

(c) See p. 249, note "b," under "MACPHERSON."

VANE-FLETCHER:

cr. 27 June 1786;

afterwards, since about 1790, FLETCHER-VANE.

I. 1786, June. "LYONEL WRIGHT VANE-FLETCHER, of Hutton in the Forest, co. Cumberland, Esq.,"(b) *formerly* VANE, 1st s. and h. of Walter VANE-FLETCHER, *formerly* VANE, of the same, by his 1st wife, Mercy, da. of Samuel WRIGHT, of Wanstead, Essex (which Walter, who inherited the Hutton estates on the death in 1761 of his next elder br.,(c) Henry FLETCHER, *formerly* VANE, took the name of FLETCHER after that of VANE and *d.* 1 March 1775, aged 82), was *b.* 28 June 1723, at Rotterdam, and having suc. to the Hutton estates on the death of his father was (a few weeks before his death) *cr. a Baronet*, as above, 27 June 1786. He *m.* in Aug. 1758, at St. Andrew's, Holborn,(d) Rachael, da. of David GRIFFITH, of Llandkennen, co. Carmarthen. He *d.* 19 July 1786, aged 63. Will pr. Jan. 1787. His widow *d.* Jan. 1802.

II. 1786, July. SIR FREDERICK VANE-FLETCHER, *afterwards* FLETCHER-VANE, Baronet [1786], of Hutton and of Armathwaite, co. Cumberland, 1st s. and h., *b.* 27 Feb. 1760 at Harrow-on-the-Hill, Midx.; *suc. to the Baronetcy*, 19 July 1786; was Sheriff of Cumberland, 1788-89; M.P. for Winchelsea, Oct. 1792 to 1794; for Carlisle, 1796-1802, and for Winchelsea, again, 1806-07. He *m.* 9 March 1797, at St. George the Martyr, Queen square, Midx., Hannah, da. of John BOWERBANK, of Johnby, co. Cumberland. He *d.* March 1832, aged 72. His widow *d.* 17 Dec. 1861, aged 93.

III. 1832. SIR FRANCIS FLETCHER-VANE, Baronet [1786], of Hutton and Armathwaite aforesaid, 1st s. and h., *b.* 29 March 1797 in Great Ormond street, Midx.; *suc. to the Baronetcy*, March 1832; was Sheriff of Cumberland, 1837-38. He *m.* 10 April 1823 (spec. lic.), at her father's house, St. Leonard's Lodge, Horsham, Sussex, Diana Olivia, 3d da. of Charles George BEAUCLERK, by Emily Charlotte, da. of William OGILVIE. He *d.* 15 Feb. 1842 at Frankfort-on-the-Maine, aged 44. His widow *d.* 9 Feb. 1875 at Burton Hall, Christchurch, in her 69th year.

IV. 1842. SIR HENRY RALPH FLETCHER-VANE, Baronet [1786], of Hutton aforesaid, 1st s. and h., *b.* 13 Jan. 1830 at Hutton Hall; *suc. to the Baronetcy*, 15 Feb. 1842; ed. at Eton; matric. at Oxford (Ch. Ch.), 15 June 1848, aged 18; Sheriff of Cumberland, 1856; Colonel of the Westmorland and Cumberland Yeomanry. He *m.* 12 April 1871, at the Chapel of Maxwelton, near Thornhill, co. Dumfries, Margaret, 1st surv. da. of Thomas Stewart GLADSTONE, of Capenoch in that County.

Family Estates.—These, in 1883, consisted of 7,194 acres in Cumberland, worth £5,102 a year. *Seat.*—Hutton Hall, near Penrith, co. Cumberland.

(a) He devised the estate of Adderley to Richard Corbet, 2d s. of Sir Andrew Corbet, 1st Baronet [1808], of Moreton Corbet, Salop, a very distant cousin, though one in the male line, of his mother. The rest of his property he left to the family of Cotton, being that of his wife.

(b) See p. 249, note "b," under "MACPHERSON."

(c) The eldest br., George Vane, inherited the paternal estates at Long Newton, co. Durham, and was father of Henry Vane, *cr. a Baronet*, 13 July 1782, being ancestor of the Vane-Tempest family. Their mother was Catherine, da. of Sir George Fletcher, 2d Baronet [1641], of Hutton aforesaid, which estate subsequently devolved on her 2d son Henry, and finally on her 3d son Walter (father of the grantee of 1786) as in the text above.

(d) Betham's *Baronetage*, 1804.

HOARE:

cr. 27 June 1786.

I. 1786. "RICHARD HOARE, of Barn Elms [in the parish of Barnes] co. Surrey, Esq.,"(a) 1st s. and h. of Sir Richard HOARE, of the same, Goldsmith and Banker of London, sometime (1745-46) Lord Mayor of London (*d.* 12 Oct. 1754, aged 45), being only s. by his 1st wife Sarah, da. of James TULLY, was *b.* 7 March 1734/5, was a partner in 1754 in the family bank in Fleet street, and was *cr. a Baronet* (a year before his death), as above, 27 June 1786. He *m.* firstly, 20 March 1756, Anne, da. and coheir of his paternal uncle, Henry HOARE, of Stourhead, Wilts(b), (*d.* 8 Sep. 1785, aged 80), by his 2d wife, Susan, da. and h. of Stephen COLT, of the Isle of Thanet. She *d.* 5 May 1759. He *m.* secondly, 7 May 1761, Frances Anne, da. of Richard ACLAND, Merchant of London, by Anne, da. of Peter BURRELL, of Beckenham, Kent. He *d.* 11 Oct. 1787, aged 52. Will pr. 1787. His widow *d.* 20 Sep. 1800. Admon. Nov. 1800.

II. 1787. SIR RICHARD COLT HOARE, Baronet [1786], of Stourhead aforesaid, 1st s. and h., being only s. by 1st wife, was *b.* 9 Dec. 1758; entered the family banking house (37 Fleet street, London) at an early age, but quitted it, when entrusted by his maternal grandfather with the Stourhead property. After the death of his wife, in 1785, he devoted himself chiefly to travelling, antiquarian research and topography(c). He *suc. to the Baronetcy*, 11 Oct. 1787; F.L.S., F.A.S., F.R.S., etc. Sheriff of Wilts, 1805. He *m.* 28 Aug. 1783, Hester, only da. of William Henry (LYTTLETON), 1st BARON LYTTLETON OF FRANKLEY, by Mary, da. of James MACARTNEY. She *d.* 22 Dec. 1785. He *d.* s.p.m.s.,(d) 19 May 1838, in his 80th year, at Stourhead, and was *bur.* at Stourton. M.I. at Salisbury Cathedral. Will pr. July 1838.

III. 1838. SIR HENRY HUGH HOARE, Baronet [1786], of Stourhead aforesaid, and of Wavendon, Bucks, br. of the half blood and h. male, being 2d s. of the 1st Baronet, *i.e.*, 1st s. by his 2d wife, *b.* 27 Sep. 1762; was partner (finally senior partner) in the family banking house; *suc. to the Baronetcy*, and the family estates, 19 May 1838. He *m.* 25 Aug. 1784, Maria Palmer, sister of Sir John PALMER-ACLAND, 1st Baronet [1818], 3d da. of Arthur ACLAND, of Fairfield, Somerset, by Elizabeth, da. of William OXENHAM. He *d.* of gout, 17 Aug. 1841, at Wavendon House, Berks, in his 80th year. Will pr. Oct. 1841. His widow *d.* 31 Jan. 1845. Will pr. March 1845.

(a) See p. 249, note "b," under "MACPHERSON."

(b) The estate of Stourhead had been bought in 1720 from the family of Stourton by his father, Henry Hoare, Goldsmith and Banker of London, who *d.* soon afterwards, 19 March 1724/5, aged 58.

(c) His extensive "*History of Modern Wiltshire*," (14 parts folio, usually bound in six vols.), deals with the southern portion only. He published also "*Ancient History of North and South Wiltshire*," 2 vols., 1812-21, and various other topographical and architectural works.

(d) His only child Henry Richard Hoare; *b.* 17 Sep. 1784; matric. at Oxford (Ch. Ch.) 3 May 1803, aged 18, *m.* 20 Feb. 1808, Charlotte, da. of Sir Edward Dering, 7th Baronet [1626], and *d.* v.p. and s.p.m., 18 Sep. 1836, aged 52, leaving a da. and h., Anne, who *m.* 26 March 1835, Sir George Benvenuto Buckley Mathew, **K.C.M.G.**, and *d.* 17 Jan. 1872, leaving issue. She, however, though the heir at law to her grandfather, did not inherit the Stourhead estate, which was entailed on the heir male.

IV. 1841. SIR HUGH RICHARD HOARE, Baronet [1786], of Stourhead aforesaid, and Lillingston Dayrell, Bucks, 2d but 1st surv. s. and h., *b.* 27 Nov. 1787; *suc. to the Baronetcy*, 17 Aug. 1841. He *m.* 22 April 1819, Anne, da. of Thomas TYRWHITT-DRAKE, of Shardloes, in Amersham, Bucks, by Anne, da. of the Rev. William WICKHAM, Rector of Garsington, Oxon. She *d.* 23 March 1847, in Eaton square. Will pr. April 1847. He *d.* s.p., 10 Jan. 1857, in his 70th year. Will pr. Feb. 1857.

V. 1857. SIR HENRY AINSLIE HOARE, Baronet [1786], of Stourhead, nephew and h., being s. and h. of Henry Charles HOARE, of Wavendon, Bucks, Banker of London, by Anne Penelope, relict of Capt. John PRINCE, sister of Sir Robert Sharpe AINSLIE, 1st Baronet [1804], da. of Gen. George AINSLIE, which Henry (who *d.* 15 Jan. 1852, aged 51), was next br. to the late Baronet. He was *b.* 14 April 1824, was ed. at Eton and at St. John's Coll., Cambridge; *suc. to the Baronetcy*, 10 Jan. 1857; was M.P. for Windsor, July 1865, till unseated April 1866, and for Chelsea, 1868-74. He *m.* 15 April 1845, at Hurley, Berks, Augusta Frances, 2d da. of Sir East George CLAYTON-EAST, 1st Baronet [1838], by Marianne Frances, da. of Charles BISHOP. He *d.* s.p.m.s., 7 July 1894, at 12 West Eaton place, Pimlico, aged 70, and was *bur.* at Stourton. Will pr. at £126,210 gross, and at "*nil*" net, his life being insured for £10,000. His widow *d.* 12 April 1903, at West Eaton place aforesaid, and was *bur.* at Stourton.

VI. 1894. SIR HENRY HUGH ARTHUR HOARE, Baronet [1786], of Stourhead aforesaid, cousin and h. male, being only s. and h. of Henry Arthur HOARE, of Wavendon, Bucks, by Julia LACY, da. of Thomas Veale LANE, which Henry (who *d.* 6 Nov. 1873, aged 69), was yr. br. to the 4th, being 7th s. of the 3d Baronet. He was *b.* 19 Nov. 1865; was sometime Lieut. 3d Batt. Beds. Reg. (Militia); *suc. to the Baronetcy*, 7 July 1894. He *m.* 4 Oct. 1887, Alda, da. of William Henry Purcell WESTON.

Family Estates.—These, in 1883 (belonging to the 5th Baronet), consisted of 5,996 acres in Wilts; 5,310 in Somerset, and 2,681 in Dorset. *Total.*—13,987 acres, worth £16,088 a year. It has not, however, been ascertained whether these, or any of these, devolved on the 6th Baronet or on the 5th Baronet's daughter, but the estates of the now (1905) Baronet (as given in 1883), were 1,715 acres in Devon, 1,317 in Bucks, 216 in Beds, and 10 in Essex. *Total.*—3,258 acres, worth £4,964 a year. The "*Seats*" of the present (1905) Baronet (as given in Burke's *Baronetage* for 1905) are "Stourhead [near] Bath; Wavendon [near] Woburn; and Oxenham [near] Okehampton."

HUNTER-BLAIR:

cr. 27 June 1786.

I. 1786. "JAMES HUNTER-BLAIR, Lord Provost of Edinburgh,"(a) 2d s. of James HUNTER, of Mainholm, and afterwards of Brownhill,(b) both in co. Ayr, by Anne, da. and h. of William CUNNINGHAME, of Brownhill aforesaid, was b. Feb. 1740/1; was a merchant and banker in Edinburgh, took the name of BLAIR after that of HUNTER, about 1774, in consequence of his marriage; acquired a large fortune as partner in the bank of "Sir William

(a) See p. 249, note "b," under "MACPHERSON."

(b) The eldest son, Lieut.-Col. William Hunter, of Mainholm and Brownhill aforesaid, *d.* unm. 1792, aged 52.

Forbes & Co.," Edinburgh; was King's Printer and Stationer [S.]; M.P. for Edinburgh, Oct. 1781 to 1784; Lord Provost in or before 1786, and was *cr. a Baronet*, as above, 27 June 1786. He *m.* in 1770, Jane, sister and (in 1774) heir of David BLAIR, only da. of John BLAIR, of Dunskey, co. Wigton, by Anne, sister and coheir of David, 10th EARL OF CASSILLIS [S.], da. of Sir Thomas KENNEDY, 4th Baronet [S. 1682]. He *d.* 1 July 1787, aged 46. Will pr. Oct. 1787. His widow *d.* 2 Feb. 1817. Admon. May 1818.

II. 1787. SIR JOHN HUNTER-BLAIR, Baronet [1786], of Dunskey aforesaid, 1st s. and h., *b.* probably about 1772; *suc. to the Baronetcy*, 1 July 1787. He *d.* unm. 24 May 1800.

III. 1800. SIR DAVID HUNTER BLAIR, Baronet [1786], of Blairquhan Castle, co. Ayr, br. and h., being 4th but 2d surv. of the ten sons(a) of the 1st Baronet; *b.* about 1778, in Edinburgh; *suc. to the Baronetcy*, 24 May 1800; Col. of the Ayrshire Militia, and Vice-Lieut. and Convener of that county. He *m.* firstly, 2 July 1813, Dorothea, 2d da. of Edward HAY-MACKENZIE, of Newhall and Cromartie (br. of George, 7th MARQUESS OF TWEEDDALE [S.]), by Maria, 1st da. and coheir of George (MACKENZIE), 6th LORD ELIBANK [S.]. She *d.* 22 May 1820. He *m.* secondly, 15 Jan. 1825, Elizabeth, 3d da. of Sir John HAY, 5th Baronet [S. 1635], of Smithfield, by Mary Elizabeth, da. of James (FORBES), 16th LORD FORBES [S.]. He *d.* 26 Dec. 1857, at Blairquhan Castle aforesaid, in his 80th year. His widow *d.* 3 Aug. 1859, at Caldwell, co. Ayr.

IV. 1857. SIR EDWARD HUNTER-BLAIR, Baronet [1786], of Blairquhan Castle and of Dunskey aforesaid, 2d but 1st surv. s. and h.,(b) by 1st wife; *b.* 24 March 1818, at Milton, near Maybole, co. Ayr; ed. at the Royal Naval College, Edinburgh; was sometime a midshipman; was twelve years, 1837-49, an officer in the 93d Highlanders; *suc. to the Baronetcy*, 26 Dec. 1857; Lieut.-Col. Commandant of the Ayrshire and Wigtonshire Artillery Volunteers, 1867-73. He *m.* 4 June 1850, at St. Paul's, Edinburgh, Elizabeth, da. of George WAUCHOPE, br. of William WAUCHOPE, of Niddrie, co. Midlothian. He *d.* 7 Oct. 1896, at Blairquhan Castle, aged 78. Will pr. at £7,561 personalty. His widow *d.* 5 May 1899, at Milton aforesaid.

V. 1896. SIR DAVID OSWALD HUNTER-BLAIR, Baronet [1786], 1st s. and h., *b.* 30 Sep. 1853, at Dunskey aforesaid: ed. at Eton; matric. at Oxford (Magdalen Coll.), 20 Jan. 1872, aged 18; B.A., 1876; M.A., 1879; sometime Capt. in the Ayr and Wigton Militia; took Holy Orders in the Church of Rome, and became a Monk of the Order of St. Benedict, and subsequently Master of "Hunter-Blair's Hall," Oxford, a College for Benedictine Students; *suc. to the Baronetcy* (but not to the unentailed family estates), 7 Oct. 1896.

Family Estates.—These, in 1883, consisted of 13,417 acres in Ayrshire, and 8,255 in Wigtonshire. *Total.*—21,672 acres, worth £12,892 a year, of which the Wigton rental (£4,948), and part (£811) of the Ayrshire was (at that date) the property of David, the 1st son of the (then existing, *i.e.*) 4th Baronet [Bateman's *Great Landowners*, 1883].

(a) Of these sons James Hunter-Blair, the 3d surv. one, inherited "by family settlements the estate of Dunskey" [Playfair's *Baronetage*, 1811]. He was Lieut.-Col. of the Ayrshire Militia, and M.P. for Wigtonshire (three Parls.) Aug. 1816, till his death unm. 24 June 1822, when he was suc. in the Dunskey estate by his next yr. surv. br. Forbes Hunter-Blair, sometime a partner in the bank of "Sir William Forbes & Co.," Edinburgh, who also *d.* unm. in 1833, and was suc. therein by his yr. br. Major-General Thomas Hunter-Blair, C.B., who *d.* s.p. 31 Aug. 1849, after whose death it presumably passed to his only surv. br. and heir at law, the 3d Baronet, whose son, certainly, was possessed of it.

(b) The eldest son, James Hunter-Blair, Lieut.-Col. Scots Fusileer Guards, *b.* 22 March 1817, M.P. for Ayrshire, 1852-54, *d.* unm. and v.p., being slain when in command of his Battalion, at the battle of Inkerman, 5 Nov. 1854, aged 37.

V

FARRELL-SKEFFINGTON:

cr. 27 June 1786;

afterwards, probably about 1800 to 1850, SKEFFINGTON;

ex. 10 Nov. 1850.

I. 1786. "WILLIAM CHARLES FARRELL-SKEFFINGTON, Esq., of Skeffington Hall, co. Leicester,"(a) *formerly* FARRELL, 3d but 1st surv. s. and h. of William FARRELL, of the same, Lieut. of Grenadiers in the Coldstream Foot Guards (*d.* 6 April 1777, aged 61), by his 1st wife, Mary, da. and h. of Richard ARNOLD, Deputy-Secretary at War, which William was 3d but 1st surv. s. and h. of [another] William FARRELL (*b.* in College Green, Dublin, 17 Jan. 1689), being the only surv. child of his 1st wife, Elizabeth, 1st sister and one of the two coheirs of Thomas SKEFFINGTON, *formerly* BROME,(b) of Skeffington Hall aforesaid, who *d.* s.p., 18 May 1729, aged 32. He was *b.* in Jermyn street, St. James', Westm., 24 June 1742; was sometime Capt. in the 1st Regt. of Foot Guards; Lieut.-Col. in the Army; took by Royal Lic., 11 June 1772, the name of SKEFFINGTON,(c) after that of FARRELL, but subsequently appears to have used the name of SKEFFINGTON only; was one of the Esquires to the Duke of York on his installation as a Knight of the Bath, and was *cr.* a *Baronet*, as above, 27 June 1786. He was Col. of the Leicestershire Yeomanry Cavalry, "the first Regiment of Yeomanry that was completed" which (accordingly) "received their standards in form" with great state, 22 Aug. 1794. He *m.* 9 Dec. 1765, at St. Peter-le-Poor, London, Catharine Josepha, 1st da. and, by the death of her brother, eventually coheir of Michael HUBBERT, of co. Cork, and of the Isle of Teneriffe, by Margaret, da. and coheir of (—) O'CONDON, of Ireland. She, who was *b.* at Laguna, in Teneriffe, about 1743, *d.* 26 July 1811, in her 69th year. Admon. Feb. 1828. He *d.* 21 or 26 Jan. 1815, aged 72.

II. 1815, to 1850. SIR LUMLEY ST. GEORGE SKEFFINGTON, Baronet [1786], of Skeffington Hall aforesaid, 2d but only surv. s. and h., *b.* 23 March 1771, at St. Pancras', Midx.; *suc. to the Baronetcy* in Jan. 1815; and dissipated all his fortune. He was author of several dramatic works.(d) He *d.* unm. 10 Nov. 1850, in lodgings, near the King's Bench prison (of which he had lately been an inmate) in his 80th year, when the *Baronetcy* became *extinct*.

MILLER:

cr. 3 March 1788.(e)

I. 1788. THOMAS MILLER, of Glenlee and Barskimming, both co. Ayr, Esq., President of His Majesty's College of Justice in Scot-

(a) See p. 249, note "b," under "MACPHERSON."

(b) He was only s. and h. of "Thomas Skeffington *alias* Brome" (*d.* 25 Dec. 1709, aged 45), who was 1st s. and h. of [another] Thomas Brome, of Croxall, co. Derby, who was s. of William Brome of Woodlow, co. Warwick, by Catharine, 3d sister and coheir of John Skeffington (the last heir male of the family of Skeffington of Skeffington), who *d.* s.p., 4 Nov. 1613. A very elaborate account of this family (as also of that of Farrell) is given in Betham's *Baronetage*, 1804.

(c) His father had suc. for life, with rem. to himself in tail, to the remaining moiety of the Skeffington estate, on the death, 29 June 1771, of Sir Thomas Peyton, 3d and last Baronet [1667], husband of Bridget (who *d.* s.p. Dec. 1762), the yr. sister of Thomas Skeffington, formerly Brome, and of Elizabeth, wife of William Farrell, grandmother to the grantee.

(d) His fame as a Dandy and a Poet is enshrined in Byron's *English Bards and Scotch Reviewers*:—

"And sure GREAT SKEFFINGTON must claim our praise,
For skirtless coats, and skeletons of plays," etc.

See a good account of his career in his obituary in the *Annual Register* for 1850.

(e) The date is frequently given as 19 Feb. 1788, which possibly is that of the Gazette notice.

land, yr. br. and h. of John MILLER, of Glenlee, Professor of Law at the Univ. of Glasgow (who *d.* unm. 28 Nov. 1780), both being sons of William MILLER, of Glenlee and Barskimming aforesaid, Writer to the Signet, (*d.* 1753), by Jane, da. of Thomas HAMILTON, of Shield Hall, was *b.* 3 Nov. 1717; Advocate, 17 July 1742; Steward Depute of Kirkcudbright, 1748-55; joint Principal Clerk of Glasgow, 1748; Solicitor of Excise [S.], 1755; Solicitor Gen. [S.], 1759; M.P. for Dumfries, 1761-66; Lord Justice Clerk [S.], under the style of *Lord Barskimming*; was appointed President of "the College of Justice," *i.e.*, the Court of Session [S.], 29 March 1787, as "of Barskimming, Esq.," and was *cr. a Baronet*, as above, 3 March 1788.(a) He *m.* firstly, 16 April 1753, Margaret (*bap.* at Glasgow, 10 June 1733) 1st da. of John MURDOCH, of Rosebank, Merchant, sometime Provost of Glasgow, by his 1st wife Margaret, da. of William LANG, merchant of Glasgow. He *m.* secondly, Anne, da. of John LOCKHART, of Castle Hill, co. Lanark, but by her had no issue. He *d.* 27 Sep. 1789, aged 71. The will of "Dame Anne MILLER" is pr. 1817.

II. 1789. SIR WILLIAM MILLER, Baronet [1788], of Glenlee and Barskimming aforesaid, only s. and h., by 1st wife, *b.* 12 Aug. 1755; Advocate, 3 Aug. 1777; M.P. for Edinburgh, 16 Sep. 1780, till unseated 23 March 1781; *suc. to the Baronetcy*, 27 Sep. 1789; was a Lord of Session [S.] under the style of *Lord Glenlee*, but resigned office in 1840, when about 85 years old. He *m.* 5 Nov. 1777, Grizel, da. of George CHALMERS, of Pittencrieff, co. Fife, by his paternal aunt Grizel, da. of William MILLER, of Glenlee abovenamed. She *d.* before him. He *d.* 9 May 1846, at Barskimming, aged 90.

III. 1846. SIR WILLIAM MILLER, Baronet [1788], of Glenlee and Barskimming aforesaid, grandson and h., being 1st s. and h. of Thomas MILLER, Advocate (1803), by Edwina, da. of Sir Alexander Penrose CORDON-CUMMING, 1st Baronet [1804], which Thomas (who *d.* v.p. 1827) was 1st s. and h. ap. of the late Baronet. He was *b.* 12 Sep. 1815, in Edinburgh; ed. at Eton; was sometime an officer in the 12th Lancers, was made a "Knight Commander of the Order of the Temple, in Jan. 1846,"(b) and *suc. to the Baronetcy*, 9 May 1846. He *m.* 27 April 1839, at St. Mary's, Bryanston square, Emily, 2d da. of Lieut.-Gen. Sir Thomas MACMAHON, 2d Baronet [1816], G.C.B., by Emily Anne, da. of Michael Roberts WESTROPP, of Cork. He *d.* 30 Oct. 1861, in Gloucester place, Marylebone, aged 46. His widow *d.* 8 Aug. 1892, at 9 Langhorne Gardens, Folkestone, in her 77th year.

IV. 1861. SIR THOMAS MACDONALD MILLER, Baronet [1788], of Glenlee and Barskimming aforesaid, 1st s. and h., *b.* 1 Jan. 1846, at Edinburgh; *suc. to the Baronetcy*, 30 Oct. 1861. He *m.* in 1863, Isabella Freeman Seton, da. of William ANDERSON, of Calcutta. He *d.* 4 Sep. 1875, at Folkestone, aged 29. His widow, who was adjudicated a bankrupt in Nov. 1878 (liabilities £1,785, assets £19), being then described as of Braunston, co. Northampton, and of Craven street, Strand, *m.* in 1880, Ivan Baillie GRANT, 3d Hussars (who *d.* Aug. 1903), and was living 1905.

V. 1875. SIR WILLIAM FREDERICK MILLER, Baronet [1788], of Glenlee and Barskimming aforesaid, 2d but 1st surv. s. and h.,(c) *b.* 7 April 1868; *suc. to the Baronetcy*, 4 Sep. 1875; sometime Lieut. 3d Yorkshire Reg. Militia; served in the Transvaal War with the Imperial Yeomanry; Hon. Lieut. in the Army. He *m.* 17 May 1890, at the Roman Catholic Oratory, Brompton, Mary Augusta, yst. da. of Charles John MANNING, of 15 Princes Gardens, by Louisa Augusta, da. of the Rev. Sir Augustus Brydges HENNIKER, 3d Baronet [1813].

Family Estates.—These, in 1883, consisted of 4,453 acres in Ayrshire, worth £3,823 a year. *Principal Seat.*—Barskimming, co. Ayr.

(a) See p. 259, note "d."

(b) Dod's *Baronetage* for 1861.

(c) The eldest son, William Frederic Miller, *d.* 31 Aug. 1868, aged 4½ years old, being accidentally burnt to death, at 31 Clarendon road, Notting Hill.

LAFOREY:

cr. 2 Dec. 1789;

ex. 17 June 1835.

I. 1789. "JOHN LAFOREY, Esq., Captain in the Royal Navy,"(a) 2d s. of Lieut.-Col. John LAFOREY, Governor of Pendennis Castle (*d.* 1753), by Mary, sister and h. of Jasper CLAYTON, of Fern Hill, Berks, da. of Lieut.-Gen. Jasper CLAYTON, by Juliana, da. and coheir of Sir Nicholas LOFTUS, of Fethard, co. Wexford, was *b.* about 1729; joined the naval service; was Lieut., R.N., 1748; Post Capt., 1758; took part in the reduction of Martinique, 1762, and in the action off Ushant, 1778; was Commissr. of the Navy in Barbadoes and the Leeward Islands, 1779-83, being moved to Plymouth 1783 to 1789, and *cr. a Baronet*, as above, 2 Dec. 1789. He had been passed over in a promotion of flag officers, 1787, on the ground of having accepted a civil appointment, but that decision being overruled, was made Rear-Admiral of the Red in 1789 with the seniority of 24 Sep. 1787. He was Commander in Chief in the Leeward Islands, 1789-93 and 1795 till his death in 1796, capturing Tobago April 1793. He became Vice-Admiral of the White, Jan. 1793, and Admiral of the Blue, June 1795. He *m.* in Antigua, in or before 1763, Eleanor, only surv. da. of Francis FARLEY, Colonel of the Royal Artillery, Member of the Council and one of the Judges of that island. He *d.* of yellow fever, on board a homeward bound ship, 14 and was *bur.* 21 June 1796 with military honours in the Governor's Chapel at Portsmouth, aged 67. Will pr. July 1796. His widow living 1803.

II. 1796, to 1835. SIR FRANCIS LAFOREY, Baronet [1789], only s. and h., *b.* in Virginia, 31 Dec. 1767; joined the naval service; *suc. to the Baronetcy*, 14 June 1796; resided at Whitby, Devon; was Rear-Admiral of the Blue, July 1810, becoming finally (1835) Admiral of the Blue. He held a command at the battle of Trafalgar, 1805, and was Commander-in-Chief in the Leeward islands, 1811-14; K.C.B., 1815. He *d.* unm. at Brighton, 17 June 1835, aged 67, when the *Baronetcy* became *extinct*. Will pr. July 1835.

BULLER:

cr. 13 Jan. 1790;

sometime, 1800-60, BULLER-YARDE-BULLER;

being, since 1858, BARONS CHURSTON.

I. 1790. FRANCIS BULLER, Esq., one of the Judges of the Court of King's Bench, 4th s. of James BULLER, of Morval, co. Cornwall, and of Downes, near Crediton, co. Devon, sometime (1747-65) M.P. for Cornwall (*d.* 1765), being 3d s. by his 2d wife, Jane, da. of Allen (BATHURST), 1st EARL BATHURST, was *b.* 17 March 1745/6, at Downes aforesaid; ed. at the Grammar School at Ottery St. Mary, Devon, and subsequently at Christ's Hospital (the Blue-coat School), London; admitted to Inner Temple, 1763; practised for many years (1765-72), as a Special Pleader; Barrister (Middle Temple), 1772; King's Counsel and 2d Judge of the County Palatine of Chester, Dec. 1777; and, next year, (when but 32), 6 May 1778, one of the Judges of the Court of King's Bench, where, during the illness of the Chief Justice (the Earl of Mansfield), he, practically, was head. When, however, that post became vacant in 1788, it was given to Kenyon, "a vastly inferior Lawyer,"(b) and he was solaced by being *cr. a Baronet*, as above, 13 Jan. 1790. He sat as a puisne Judge under Lord Kenyon

(a) See p. 113, note "a," under "GIDEON." The date of the Gazette notice for Laforey is 5 Nov. 1789.

(b) *Dict. Nat. Biog.*, under "BULLER."

some six years, after which he migrated into the Court of Common Pleas, 10 June 1794, till his death. He *m.* 5 Dec. 1763, at Ottery St. Mary, Devon, when only 17, Susanna, only da. of Francis YARDE, of Churston Ferrers, and Ottery St. Mary aforesaid (*d.* Jan. 1749/50, aged 46), by Elizabeth, da. of (—) NORTHLEIGH. He *d.* suddenly, at his house in Bedford square, 5 and was *bur.* (with his eldest son)(a) 12 June 1800, at St. Andrew's, Holborn, aged 54. Will pr. 1800.(b) His widow, who was *bap.* 24 July 1740 (*Qy.* at Ottery St. Mary), *d.* 21 June 1810.

II. 1800. SIR FRANCIS BULLER-YARDE-BULLER, Baronet [1790], of Lupton House, near Brixham, Devon, and of Churston Ferrers aforesaid, *formerly* BULLER-YARDE, and previously to that BULLER, 2d but only surv. s. and h., *b.* 28 Sep. 1767, and *bap.* 22 Jan. 1768, at St. Andrew's, Holborn; ed. at Winchester, 1777-79, being Scholar (Founder's Kin), 23 July 1779 to 9 March 1782, soon after which date he suc. to the estates of his mother's family, and took the name of YARDE after that of BULLER; was M.P. for Totnes, 1790-96, and, having *suc. to the Baronetcy,* 5 June 1800, he, by Royal Lic. of the 26 of that month. took the name of BULLER after that of BULLER-YARDE. He *m.* 2 June 1791, Eliza Lydia, da. and h. of John HALLIDAY, of Dilhorne Hall, co. Stafford, and of Lincoln's Inn. He *d.* abroad, 17 April 1833, aged 65. Admon. July 1836. His widow *d.* 1 Nov. 1851, at Gloucester gate, Regent's park, aged 77. Will pr. Nov. 1851.

III. 1851. SIR JOHN BULLER-YARDE-BULLER, Baronet [1790], of Lupton House and Churston Ferrers aforesaid, 2d but 1st surv. s. and h., *b.* 12 April 1799, at Dilhorne Hall aforesaid; matric. at Oxford (Oriel Coll.), 15 May 1816; B.A., and 2d Class in Classics, 1819; M.A., 1822, being *cr.* D.C.L., 9 June 1853; *suc. to the Baronetcy,* 17 April 1833; was M.P. for South Devon (six Parls.), 1835 till raised to the peerage in 1858; Lieut.-Col. of the South Devon Militia, 1845; Special Deputy Warden of the Stannaries, 1852. He *m.* firstly, 24 June 1823, Elizabeth, sister of John, 1st BARON WINMARLEIGH, da. of Thomas WILSON-PATTEN, of Bank Hall, co. Lancaster, by Elizabeth, da. of Nathan HYDE. She *d.* 20 Feb. 1857, at Lupton, aged 58. He (before his second marriage), was *cr.* 2 Aug. 1858, BARON CHURSTON of Churston Ferrers and Lupton, co. Devon, obtaining, shortly afterwards, a Royal Lic., 28 Feb. 1860, for himself and his issue to discontinue the name of BULLER, before that of YARDE-BULLER. In that peerage this *Baronetcy* then *merged,* and still (1905) so continues.

OAKELEY:

cr. 5 June 1790.

I. 1790. "CHARLES OAKELEY, of Shrewsbury, Esq.,"(c) who had been nominated in April 1790 Governor of Madras, 2d s. of the Rev. William OAKELEY, M.A., Rector of Forton, co. Stafford, and Vicar of Holy Cross, Shrewsbury (*d.* Oct. 1803, aged 66), by Christian, da. and h. of Sir Patrick STRACHAN, of Glenkindie Castle, co. Aberdeen, was *b.* at Forton, 26 Feb. 1751; ed. at Shrewsbury School; entered the service of the East India Company as a writer 1766; Secretary, 1773; Judge Advocate General and

(a) Edward Buller, the 1st son, *b.* 19 May and *bap.* 10 June 1765, at St. Margaret's, Westm., *d.* in boyhood, at St. Giles'-in-the-Fields, 3, and was *bur.* 6 Feb. 1782, at St. Andrew's, Holborn.

(b) His work on *Trials at Nisi Prius* had a great reputation, but "with all his industry, sagacity, quickness and intelligence, and notwithstanding his urbanity to the Bar, he was not a popular Judge. He was considered arrogant in his assumption of superiority, hasty in his decisions and decrees, prejudiced, severe, and even cruel in criminal trials" [Foss's *Judges of England*].

(c) See p. 113, note "a," under "GIDEON." The date of the Gazette notice for Oakeley is June, and that for Orde is July 1790.

Translator, 1777-80; President of the Committee of Revenue for the Nabob of Arcot, 1781-84; President of the Madras Board of Revenue, 1786-88, and, finally, in April 1790, nominated Governor of Madras, when he effected, at once, several important reforms in the Civil Administration, though not having full authority till March 1792; he equipped, in 1793, the successful expedition to Pondicherry, but retired from office in Sep. 1794. He had meanwhile been *cr. a Baronet,* as above, 5 June 1790. He, in 1795, settled at Shrewsbury, and subsequently (1810) at Lichfield, and was *cr.* D.C.L. of Oxford, 15 June 1825. He *m.* 19 Oct. 1777, at Fort St. George, Helena, only da. of Robert BEATSON, of Kilrie, co. Fife. He *d.* 7 Sep. 1826, at Lichfield Palace, aged 75, and was *bur.* at Forton. Mon. (by Chantrey) in Lichfield Cathedral.(a) Will pr. Oct. 1826. His widow (by whom he had fourteen children,(b) of whom ten survived him), *d.* 19 Feb. 1839, at Lichfield Palace abovenamed.

II. 1826. SIR CHARLES OAKELEY, Baronet [1790], 1st s. and h., *b.* 25 Sep. 1778, at Madras; admitted to Rugby School, 5 Feb. 1792; Sec. of Legation and Chargé d'Affaires, successively, in Bavaria, Sweden, and the United States; *suc. to the Baronetcy,* 7 Sep. 1826. He *m.* 20 March 1820, Charlotte Françoise Augusta Gisberte Ramadier, *suo jure* BARONESS DE LORMET, only child of Ramadier, BARON DE LORMET, of Meysenbrock, in the Netherlands, Col. of the 32d Reg. "de Chasseurs." He *d.* s.p.m., 30 June 1829, at Huy, in the Netherlands, aged 50. His widow *d.* 2 Oct. 1850, aged 47.

III. 1829. SIR HERBERT OAKELEY, Baronet [1790], next surv. br. and h. male, being 4th s. of the 1st Baronet; *b.* 10 Feb. 1791, at Madras; ed. at Westm. School; matric. at Oxford (Ch. Ch.), 25 April 1807, aged 16, being Student of Ch. Ch., 1807-23; B.A. and 1st Class Classics, 1811, reciting, in July of that year, a congratulatory ode of his own composition at the installation of Lord GRENVILLE as Chancellor of Oxford; M.A., 1813; in Holy Orders; was Chaplain to Dr. HOWLEY, Bishop of London, 1814 to 1826; Preb. of Lichfield, 1816-32; Preb. of London, 1816, till death; Preb. of Worcester, 1817-30; Vicar of Ealing, Midx., 1822-34; *suc. to the Baronetcy,* 30 June 1829; Dean and Rector of Bocking, Essex, 1834 till death, and Archdeacon of Colchester, 1841 till death. He *m.* 5 June 1826, at St. Margaret's, Westm., Atholl Keturah, 2d da. of the Rev. Lord Charles MURRAY-AYNSLEY, *formerly* MURRAY, Dean and Rector of Bocking aforesaid (yr. s. of John, 3d DUKE OF ATHOLL [S.]), by Alice, da. of George MITFORD, great niece and heir of Gawen AYNSLEY. She *d.* in London 26 Jan. 1844. He *d.* there 27 March 1845, aged 54. Will pr. April 1845.

IV 1845. SIR CHARLES WILLIAM ATHOLL OAKELEY, Baronet [1790], 1st s. and h.,(c) *b.* 25 Oct. 1828, at Ealing; ed. at Eton, *suc. to the Baronetcy,* 27 March 1845; matric. at Oxford (Ch. Ch.), 4 June 1846, aged 17; sometime Captain Bengal Cavalry. He *m.* 16 May 1860, at St. James', Westminster, Ellen, only child of John Meeson PARSONS, of Angley Park, near Cranbrook, Kent, and of Raymond's Buildings, Gray's Inn. She *d.* 20 June 1895, at Frittenden House, near Staplehurst, Kent, and was *bur.* at Frittenden. He *m.* secondly, 16 Sep. 1896, Elizabeth, widow of Hamilton GOODALL, da. of Henry W. TUSON.

(a) He had "assisted warmly in the establishment of the National Society's Schools, on Bell's system, in Shrewsbury and Lichfield." [*Dict. Nat. Biogr.*]

(b) The yst. of these the Rev. Frederic Oakeley, M.A., *b.* 5 Sep. 1802, at the Abbey House, Shrewsbury, ed. at Ch. Ch., Oxford, sometime, 1824-45, Fellow of Balliol College, is well-known as one of the earliest members of the "Tractarian Movement." He was Incumbent of Margaret Chapel (afterwards rebuilt as "All Saints'") Margaret street, Marylebone, 1839-45; joined the Roman Catholic Church in Sep. 1845, and was, as such, Canon of Westminster 1852, till his death 29 Jan. 1880, aged 77.

(c) The 2d son, Sir Herbert Stanley Oakeley, D.C.L. and LL.D., a well-known musician, being Professor of Music in the University of Edinburgh, 1865-91, and twenty years Hon. Composer of Music to Queen Victoria in Scotland, *d.* unm. and was *bur.* 28 Oct. 1903, aged 73, at Eastbourne.

ORDE:

cr. 9 Aug. 1790;

afterwards, since 1880, CAMPBELL-ORDE.

I. 1790. "JOHN ORDE, Esq., Governor of the Island of Dominica and Captain in the Royal Navy,"(a) yr. br. of Thomas (ORDE-POWLETT), 1st BARON BOLTON, both being sons of John ORDE, of East Orde and Morpeth, (*d.* 1784), by his 2d wife Anne, da. of Ralph MARR, of Morpeth, was *b.* 22 Dec. 1751; entered the Royal Navy 1766; was in command of a sloop at the reduction of Philadelphia, 1778, and of Charlestown in 1780, and was made Governor of Dominica in 1783 (where he restored peace and quiet), holding office for about ten years, and being *cr. a Baronet,* as above, 9 Aug. 1790. He became Rear-Admiral, 1795; Vice-Admiral, 1799; was in command of a squadron off Finisterre, 1804-5, becoming Admiral of the Blue, 1805, and finally Admiral of the White, 1810. He was M.P. for Yarmouth (Isle of Wight), Aug. 1807 to 1812. He *m.* firstly, in 1781, Margaret Emma, da. and h. of Richard STEPHENS, of Charlestown, South Carolina. She *d.* s.p.s., 13 Sep. 1790. He *m.* secondly, 3 Dec. 1793, at St. Marylebone, Jane, 1st da. of John FRERE, of Roydon, Norfolk, by Julia, da. and h. of John HOOKHAM, of Bedington, Surrey, merchant. He *d.* 19 Feb. 1824, at his house in Gloucester place, Marylebone, in his 73d year. Will pr. 1824. His widow *d.* 16 Sep. 1829. Will pr. Feb. 1830.

II. 1824. SIR JOHN POWLETT ORDE, Baronet [1790], only s. and h., *b.* 9 June 1803, in Gloucester place, Marylebone; ed. at Eton; matric. at Oxford (Ch. Ch.), 10 April 1821, aged 17; B.A., 1826; having *suc. to the Baronetcy,* 19 Feb. 1824; Captain in the Argyll and Bute Militia. He *m.* firstly, 15 June 1826, at Walton, co. Surrey, Jane, 1st da. and coheir of Peter CAMPBELL, of Kilmory House, co. Argyll, with whom he acquired that estate. She *d.* there 13 June 1829. He *m.* secondly, 14 June 1832, Beatrice, yst. da. of James EDWARDS, of Harrow, Midx., by Catherine, da. of the Rev. Edward BROMHEAD, Rector of Repham, co. Lincoln. He *d.* 13 Dec. 1878, at Kilmory House aforesaid, aged 75. His widow *d.* 29 July 1895, at 47 Connaught square, Paddington, and was *bur.* at Harrow aforesaid, aged 81. Will pr. 2 Sep. 1895 at £20,314.

III. 1878. SIR JOHN WILLIAM POWLETT ORDE, *afterwards,* from 1880, CAMPBELL-ORDE, Baronet [1790], of Kilmory House aforesaid, and of North Uist, co. Inverness, only s. and h., by 1st wife, *b.* 23 Feb. 1827, at Geneva; ed. at Eton; sometime Captain 42nd Highlanders; *suc. to the Baronetcy,* 13 Dec. 1878, and took, by Royal Lic., 16 Jan. 1880, the name of CAMPBELL (being that of his mother) before that of ORDE. He *m.* firstly, 17 July 1862, at St. Michael's, Chester Square, Alice Louisa, sister of Sir Arthur Edward MIDDLETON, 7th Baronet [1662], only da. of Charles Atkins MONCK, of Belsay, Northumberland, by Laura, da. of Sir Matthew WHITE-RIDLEY, 3d Baronet [1756]. She *d.* 7 Jan. 1883, at Kilmory House, aged 41. He *m.* secondly, 20 Dec. 1884, Louisa Charlotte Temple, 1st da. of Robert Temple FRERE, M.D., of Harley Street, by his 1st wife, Theresa Arabella Fanny, da. of the Rev. William DOWELL, Vicar of Locking, Somerset. He *d.* 12 Oct. 1897, suddenly, at Lochmaddy, aged 70. Personalty sworn at £27,670. His widow living 1905.

IV. 1897. SIR ARTHUR JOHN CAMPBELL-ORDE, Baronet [1790], of Kilmory House, North Uist aforesaid, 1st s. and h., by 1st wife, *b.* 13 April 1865; *suc. to the Baronetcy,* 12 Oct. 1897; served in the South African war as Lieut. in "Lovat's Scouts" with the Imperial Yeomanry. He *m.*, 6 Jan. 1892, May Ronald, 1st da. of John Campbell STEWART, of Fasnacloich, co. Argyll, sometime Capt., 72nd Highlanders.

Family Estates.—These, in 1883, consisted of 81,099 acres in Inverness-shire, and 4,646 in Argyleshire. *Total.*—85,745 acres, worth £6,373 a year. *Seat.*—Kilmory, near Loch-Gilp-Head, co. Argyll and North Uist, co. Inverness.

(a) See p. 262, note "c," under "OAKELEY."

MALET:

cr. 24 Feb. 1791.

I. 1791. "CHARLES WARRE MALET, Esq., Resident at Poonah, in the East Indies,"(a) 1st s. of the Rev. Alexander MALET, M.A., Preb. of Wells, Rector of Combe Flory, co. Somerset and Maiden Newton, co. Dorset (*d.* 19 Nov. 1775, aged 71), by Anne, da. of the Rev. Laurence ST. LO, D.D., Rector of Pulham, Dorset, was *bap.* 30 Dec. 1752, at Combe Flory; was, in 1770, a writer, holding, subsequently, other posts in the East India Company's service; was on a mission to the Great Mogul, who made him an Ameer of the Mogul Empire; was appointed in 1785 Resident Minister at Poonah (an office he held till 1791), and, subsequently, to the court of the Peshawar of the Mahrattas, between whom and the Nizam and the East India Company he negotiated, in June 1790, a treaty of alliance against Tippoo Sultan, being accordingly, *cr. a Baronet,* as above, 24 Feb. 1791. He was, for nine months. Acting Governor of Bombay, retiring in 1798. F.S.A. and F.R.S. He resided at Wilbury House in Newton Toney, Wilts; was Sheriff of that county, 1809-10, and Lieut.-Colonel of the Wilts Militia. He *m.* 17 Dec. 1799, Susanna, 1st da. of James WALES, of Upper Norwood, Surrey (a Portrait Painter of some note), by Margaret, da. of William WALLACE, of Dundee. He *d.* 24 Jan. 1815, aged 62. Will pr. 1815. His widow, by whom he had eight sons, *d.* 21 Dec. 1868, at Netherclay, near Taunton, in her 91st year.

II. 1815. SIR ALEXANDER MALET, Baronet [1791], of Wilbury House aforesaid, 1st s. and h., *b.* 23 July 1800, at Hartham park, Biddestone, Wilts; *suc. to the Baronetcy,* 24 Jan. 1815; ed. at Winchester; matric. at Oxford (Ch. Ch.), 19 Jan. 1819, aged 18; B.A. and 2d Class Classics, 1822; unpaid Attaché at St. Petersburgh, 1824, and at Paris, 1827; Attaché at Lisbon, 1833; Sec. of Legation at Turin, 1835, and at the Hague, 1836; Sec. of Embassy at Vienna, 1843; Envoy at Stuttgart, 1844; Minister Plenipotentiary to the Germanic Confederation at Frankfort, 1852 till its dissolution in Dec. 1866, when he retired, having been, in June 1866, made **K.C.B.** He *m.* 22 Dec. 1834, Marianne Dora, only da. of John SPALDING, of the Holme, co. Wigton, by Marianne (subsequently BARONESS BROUGHAM AND VAUX), da. of Thomas EDEN, of Wimbledon, Surrey. He *d.* 28 Nov. and was *bur.* 2 Dec. 1886, at Newton Toney, aged 86. Will pr. 5 Jan. 1887. His widow *d.* 2 Jan. 1891, at Bournemouth.

III. 1886. SIR HENRY CHARLES EDEN MALET, Baronet [1791], of Wilbury House aforesaid, 1st s. and h., *b.* 25 Sep. 1835, in Upper Brook street; ed. at Eton; entered the Grenadier Guards, 1854; serving in the Crimea (medal with clasp and Turkish medal); Lieut.-Col., 1862-70; *suc. to the Baronetcy,* 28 Nov. 1886; sometime Commander 20th Midx. Rifle Volunteers. He *m.* 18 Feb. 1873, Laura Jane Campbell, yr. da. of John HAMILTON, of Hilston park, co. Monmouth. He *d.* s.p.m. at Brighton, and was *bur.* 16 Jan. 1904, at Newton Toney, aged 68. Will pr. at £23,190. His widow living 1905.

IV. 1904. SIR EDWARD BALDWIN MALET, Baronet [1791], of Wilbury House aforesaid, only br. and h. male, *b.* 10 Oct. 1837, in Holland; ed. at Eton; matric. at Oxford (Corpus Christi Coll.), 14 April 1856, aged 18, having, previously, entered the Diplomatic Service, 10 Oct. 1854, as Attaché at Frankfort; Attaché at Brussels, 1858; at Rio de Janeiro, 1861; 2d Sec. at Washington, 1862; at Lisbon, 1865; at Constantinople, 1865-68; and at Paris, 1868; **C.B.**, 1871; Sec. of Legation at Pekin, 1871, and at Athens, 1873; Sec. of Embassy at Rome, 1875-76; and at Constantinople, 1878-79; Consul-Gen. and Minister Plenipotentiary to Egypt, 1878-83; **K.C.B.**, 1881; Envoy to Brussels, 1883; Ambassador to Berlin, 1884 to 1895, when he retired, having *suc. to the Baronetcy,* 16 Jan. 1904; P.C., 1885; **G.C.M.G.**, 26 June, 1885; **G.C.B.**,

(a) See p. 113, note "a," under GIDEON. The date of the Gazette notice for Malet and for Kennaway is Feb. 1791, that for Lushington, being April 1791.

9 Feb. 1886; Member of the Hague Court of Arbitration. He *m.* 19 March 1885, at Westm. Abbey, Ermyntrude Sackville, 2d and yst. da. of Francis Charles Hastings (RUSSELL), 9th DUKE OF BEDFORD, by Elizabeth, da. of George (SACKVILLE-WEST), 5th EARL DE LA WARR. She was *b.* 9 May 1856.

Family Estates.—These, in 1883, consisted of 2,942 acres in Wilts, Hants and Leicestershire, worth £2,700 a year.

KENNAWAY:

cr. 25 Feb. 1791.

I. 1791. "JOHN KENNAWAY, Esq., Capt. of Infantry in the service of the East India Company, and resident at Hyderabad,"(a) 3d s. of William KENNAWAY, of Exeter, merchant (*d.* 1793), by Frances, da. of Aaron TOZER, also of Exeter, was *b.* 6 March 1758, and *bap.* at Holy Trinity, Exeter; ed. at Exeter Grammar School; entered the Military Service of the East India Company at the age of 14; was Capt. in 1780, serving in the Carnatic Campaign till 1786, when he was made Aide-de-Camp to the Governor General (Cornwallis), who employed him on a mission to the Nyzam of Hyderabad, whom he induced to make a treaty with the Company against Tippoo Sultan, for which service he was *cr. a Baronet*, as above, 25 Feb. 1791. In 1792, he conducted, with success, an advantageous treaty with the said Tippoo, and became the first resident at Hyderabad till 1794, when he returned to England. He bought the estate of Escott, near Ottery St. Mary, Devon, and was Col. of the East Devon Militia. He *m.* Feb. 1797, Charlotte, 2d da. and coheir of James AMYATT, many years (1784-1806) M.P. for Southampton, by Mary, da. of John WOLLASTON. He *d.* 1 Jan. 1836, at Escott Lodge, Devon, aged 77. Will pr. Feb. 1836. His widow *d.* 1845.

II. 1836. SIR JOHN KENNAWAY, Baronet [1791], of Escott Lodge aforesaid, 1st s. and h., *b.* there 15 Dec. 1797; *suc. to the Baronetcy*, 1 Jan. 1836; Sheriff of Devon, 1866. He *m.* 28 April 1831, at Kingscote, co. Gloucester, Emily Frances, da. of Thomas KINGSCOTE, of Randalls, Surrey, by Harriet, da. of Sir Henry PEYTON, 1st Baronet [1776], of Doddington. She *d.* 16 May 1858, at Weston-super-Mare, aged 62. He *d.* at Escott Lodge, 19 Feb. 1873, aged 75.

III. 1873. SIR JOHN HENRY KENNAWAY, Baronet [1791], of Escott Lodge aforesaid, 1st s. and h., *b.* 6 June 1837, at Park Crescent, Marylebone; ed. at Harrow; matric. at Oxford (Ball. Coll.), 6 June 1856, aged 19; 1st Class, Law and Modern History and B.A., 1860; M.A., 1862; Barrister (Inner Temple), 1864; M.P. for East Devon, April 1870 to 1885, and for the Honiton Division since 1885, having *suc. to the Baronetcy*, 19 Feb. 1873; Member of the Church Discipline Commission, 1904; sometime Lieut.-Col. and afterwards Hon. Col. 3d Vol. Batt. Devon Reg. He *m.* 27 Nov. 1866, Frances, 1st da. of Archibald Francis ARBUTHNOT, of Hyde Park Gardens, by Gertrude Sophia, da. of Field Marshal Hugh (GOUGH), 1st VISCOUNT GOUGH OF GOOJERAT.

Family Estates.—These, in 1883, consisted of 4,045 acres in Devon, of the value of £5,038 a year. *Seat.*—Escott Lodge, near Ottery St. Mary, Devon.

(a) See p. 265 note "a," under "MALET."

LUSHINGTON:

cr. 26 April 1791;

I. 1791. "STEPHEN LUSHINGTON, of South-Hill Parks, Berks, Esq., Chairman of the East India Company,"(a) 2d s. of the Rev. Henry LUSHINGTON, D.D. [Oxford], Vicar of Eastbourne, Sussex (*d.* 13 Jan. 1779, aged 69), by his 1st wife, Mary, da. of the Rev. Roger ALTHAM, D.D., Archdeacon of Midx., was *b.* 17 June 1744, at Eastbourne; was sometime a Proctor in Doctors Commons; M.P. for Hedon, Dec. 1783 to 1784; for Helston, 1790-96; for St. Michael's, 1796-1802; for Penrhyn, 1802-06, and for Plympton, 1806-07; many years a Director of the East India Company, being Chairman in 1790, and was *cr. a Baronet*, as above, 26 April 1791. He *m.* 6 June 1771, Hester, 1st da. of John BOLDERO,(b) of Darrington, co. York, and subsequently of Aspenden Hall, Herts, a Banker of London, by Esther, da. of D. STONE, of Bath. He *d.* 12 Jan. 1807, aged 62. Will pr. 1807. His widow who was *b.* 1753 at Darrington, *d.* 9 Dec. 1830. Will pr. June 1831.

II. 1807. SIR HENRY LUSHINGTON, Baronet [1791], sometime of Trent Park, near Southgate, Midx., but subsequently (on the death of his maternal uncle, Charles BOLDERO) of Aspenden Hall aforesaid,(b) 3d but 1st surv. s. and h.,(c) *b.* 27 Oct. 1775, in Henrietta street, Covent Garden; ed. at Eton; *suc. to the Baronetcy*, 12 Jan. 1807; Consul-Gen. at Naples, 1815-32. He *m.* 8 April 1799, Fanny Maria, sister and coheir of Matthew Gregory LEWIS (the Poet), 1st da. of Matthew LEWIS, Under Sec.-at-War. She *d.* 26 May 1862, at 32 Montagu sq., Marylebone, aged 85. He *d.* there, 25 June 1863, aged 87.

III. 1863. SIR HENRY LUSHINGTON, Baronet [1791], of Aspenden Hall aforesaid, 1st s. and h.,(d) *b.* 10 Oct. 1803, in Bedford sq.; entered the Bengal Civil Service, 1821, becoming eventually Judge of the highest Civil and Criminal Courts in the North-west Provinces, but retiring in 1851; *suc. to the Baronetcy*, 25 June 1863. He *m.* firstly, 26 March 1825, Eliza Louisa, da. of William TROWER, of the Bombay Civil Service. She *d.* 23 May 1862.(e) He *m.* secondly, 17 June 1863, Eliza Hannah, da. of John SHELLEY. She *d.* s.p.m. 26 March 1889, at Aspenden Hall. He *d.* there, 26 Sep. 1897, in his 95th year, and was *bur.* at Aspenden.

IV. 1897. SIR HENRY LUSHINGTON, Baronet [1791], of Aspenden Hall aforesaid, only s. and h., by 1st wife, *b.* 24 Jan. 1826; ed. at Haileybury College; entered the Bengal Civil Service and became a Judge at Allahabad; *suc. to the Baronetcy*, 26 Sep. 1897. He *m.* 29 Dec. 1849, Elizabeth, da. of Anstruther CHEAPE, of Rossie, co. Fife. He *d.* at Aspenden Hall, 15 March 1898, aged 72, and was *bur.* at Aspenden. Will pr. at £10,459. His widow *d.* at 13 Broadwater Down, Tunbridge Wells, 6 June 1902. Will pr. at £7,836 gross and £7,418 net.

V. 1898. SIR ARTHUR PATRICK DOUGLAS LUSHINGTON, Baronet [1791], of Aspenden Hall aforesaid, 2d but only surv. s. and h.,(f) *b.* 19 Jan. 1861; sometime in the 26th Foot; Major 3d Dragoon Guards, and served in the Transvaal war, 1900-02, having *suc. to the Baronetcy*, 15 March 1898. He *m.* 21 Jan. 1892, Florence, 1st da. of James BURNESS, of the Lodge, Melton, Suffolk.

(a) See p. 265, note "a," under "MALET."

(b) See elaborate pedigree of Boldero in J. J. Muskett's *Suffolk Manorial Families* [1900], vol. i. pp. 176-188.

(c) The 2d surv. s., the Rt. Hon. Stephen Lushington, D.C.L., Judge of the Admiralty Court and Dean of the Arches, was well known as one of the Counsel for Queen Caroline at her trial. He *d.* 19 Jan. 1873, aged 91, leaving issue.

(d) The 2d s., Admiral Sir Stephen Lushington, G.C.B., who commanded the Naval Brigade at the Siege of Sebastopol, *d.* 28 May 1877, aged 73.

(e) *Foster's Baronetage* (1883). The date is suspiciously like that of the death of her husband's mother, on 26 (not, however, 23) May 1862.

(f) The eldest son, Henry Cartwright Lushington, *b.* 22 April 1858, *d.* v.p. in boyhood, 11 Feb. 1866.

JAMES:

cr. 28 July 1791;

afterwards, since 1884, BARONS NORTHBOURNE.

I. 1791. "WALTER JAMES JAMES, of Langley Hall [in Hempstead Norris], Berks, Esq.,"(a) as also of Denford Court in that county, *formerly* Walter James HEAD, 2d s. of Sir Thomas HEAD, of Langley Hall aforesaid, Sheriff of Berks, 1744, by Jane, da. of Rowland HOLT, of Redgrave Hall, Suffolk, which Thomas (who *d.* Oct. 1780, aged 65) was s. of Richard HEAD, of Langley Hall, whose sister, Elizabeth, *m.* John JAMES, of Denford Court aforesaid (*d.* s.p. about 1772, leaving his estates to the sons, successively, of his wife's niece, the said Elizabeth HEAD), was *b.* 8 Feb. 1759 at Westminster; matric. at Oxford (Trin. Coll.), 9 Oct. 1777, aged 18; *cr.* D.C.L., 27 June 1788; suc. in 1777 his elder br., William JAMES, *formerly* HEAD, in the estate of Denford Court, took the name of JAMES instead of that of HEAD by Act of Parl., 1778, and was *cr. a Baronet*, as above, 28 July 1791. He was Warden of the Mint, 1798. He *m.* 15 April 1780, at her father's house in New Burlington street, Jane, yst. da. of Charles (PRATT), 1st EARL CAMDEN, sometime Lord Chancellor, by Elizabeth, da. and h. of Nicholas JEFFREYS. She, who was *bap.* 23 July 1761, *d.* 1 Sep. 1825. He *d.* 8 Oct. 1829, at Freshford, Somerset, in his 71st year. Will pr. Nov. 1829.

II. 1829. SIR WALTER CHARLES JAMES, Baronet [1791], of Langley Hall aforesaid, grandson and h., being only s. and h. of John JAMES, sometime Minister Plenipotentiary to the Netherlands, by Emily Jane, da. of Walter (STEWART), 1st MARQUESS OF LONDONDERRY [I.], which John (who *d.* v.p. 4 June 1818) was 2d and yst. s.(b) but finally h. ap. of the late Baronet. He was *bap.* 8 June 1816, at St. Geo. Han sq.; *suc. to the Baronetcy*, 8 Oct. 1829; was ed. at Westm. School; matric. at Oxford (Ch. Ch.), 23 May 1833, aged 16; B.A., 1836; M.A., 1840; was M.P. for Hull, 1837-47; Sheriff of Kent, 1855. He *m.* 17 April 1841, Sarah Caroline, 5th da. and coheir of Cuthbert ELLISON, of Hebburn Hall, co. Durham, by Grace, da. and coheir of Henry IBBETSON, of St. Anthonys, co. Northumberland. She was living when he was *cr.* 5 Nov. 1884, BARON NORTHBOURNE OF BETTESHANGER, co. Kent, AND OF JARROW GRANGE, co. palatine of Durham. In that peerage this *Baronetcy* then *merged*, and still [1905] so continues. See *Peerage*.

ERSKINE:(c)

cr. 28 July 1791;

ex., 30 July 1836.

I. 1791. "Lieut.-Gen. SIR WILLIAM ERSKINE, Knt.,"(a) was of Torrie, co. Fife, being only s. and h. of Lieut.-Col. William ERSKINE of the same (*b.* 19 May 1691, wounded at Fontenoy, 1745) by Henrietta, da. of William BAILLIE, of Lamington (which William ERSKINE was 1st s. and h.

(a) See p. 113, note "a," under GIDEON. The date of the Gazette notice for James, Erskine, Martin, Boughton-Rouse, Hawkins, Call, Jackson, Woodford, Pole, Vaughan, Rich, Hudson, Tapps, Chad and Brograve (for all fifteen of which the patents are dated 28 July) is June 1791.

(b) The 1st s. Francis James, Capt. 81st Reg., *d.* unm. and v.p. 14 April 1812, being slain at Badajoz.

(c) The account, down to 1813, of these Baronets (male descendants of the 2d Lord Cardross [S.], and, of course, within the limitation of that peerage) which is given in Wood's *Douglas's Peerage* [S.], is omitted altogether in the *Scots Peerage* [1905] "founded" thereon.

of Col. the Hon. William ERSKINE, of Torrie aforesaid, a yr. s. of David, 2d LORD CARDROSS [S.]), was *b.* at Edinburgh, 27 March 1728, joined his father's regiment, the 7th Dragoons, in 1742, remaining in the army 53 years, serving in Germany, America, and Flanders (nineteen campaigns in all), becoming finally Lieut.-Gen. and Colonel of the 26th (Cameronian) Regiment of Foot. He was *Knighted* 27 July 1763 and was *cr. a Baronet*, as above, 28 July 1791. He *m.* 29 May 1767, Frances, widow of George DRUMMOND, of Blair Drummond, 4th da. of James MORAY, of Abercairny, by Christian, da. of Alexander (MONTGOMERIE), EARL OF EGLINTON [S.]. She *d.* 28 Feb. 1793, at Torrie. He *d.* there 19 March 1795, in his 67th year. Will pr. March 1796.

II. 1795. SIR WILLIAM ERSKINE, Baronet [1791], of Torrie aforesaid, 1st s. and h.; *b.* 30 March 1770; served as Major of the 15th Dragoons in Flanders and Aide-de-Camp to his father, 1793-94; ranking, finally, as Major-General, 1808, and being Colonel of the 14th Garrison battalion on half-pay. He *suc. to the Baronetcy*, 19 March 1795, and was M.P. for Fifeshire (two Parls.), 1796-1806. He *d.* unm. at Brozas, 13 Feb. 1813, aged 42. Will pr. 1813.

III. 1813. SIR JAMES ERSKINE, Baronet [1791], of Torrie aforesaid, br. and h.; *b.* 30 Sep. 1772, entered the 26th Foot in 1788, and served as Captain of Dragoons in Flanders and as Aide-de-Camp to General Vyse, 1793-94; was promoted as Major for his conduct at the battle of Catean, 26 April 1794, and was, as Lieut.-Col. of the 15th Light Dragoons, at the battle of Bergen, 2 Oct. 1799; Aide-de-Camp to the King, 1800; Lieut.-Col. 2d Dragoon Guards, 1803, and, finally, Major-Gen. in the Army, 1808. He *suc. to the Baronetcy*, 13 Feb. 1813. He *m.* 5 March 1801, Louisa, sister to the 1st MARQUESS OF ANGLESEY, 3d. da. of Henry (PAGET), 1st EARL OF UXBRIDGE, by Jane, da. of the Very Rev. Arthur CHAMPAGNE, Dean of Clonmacnoise. He *d.* s.p., in Dover street, Piccadilly, 3 March 1825, aged 52. Will pr. April 1825. His widow, who was *b.* 26 March 1777, *m.* in 1826, General the Right Hon. Sir George MURRAY, G.C.B. (who *d.* 28 July 1846, aged 74), and *d.* 23 Jan. 1842, in Belgrave square, in her 65th year.

IV. 1825, to 1836. SIR JOHN DRUMMOND ERSKINE, Baronet [1791], of Torrie aforesaid, br. and h., being 3d and yst. s. of the 1st Baronet, *b.* 5 April 1776; was in the Bengal Civil Establishment, 1792, and *suc. to the Baronetcy*, 3 March 1825. He *d.* s.p., presumably unm., 30 July 1836, aged 60, in Hanover street, Hanover square, when the *Baronetcy* became *extinct*.(a)

MARTIN:

cr. 28 July 1791.

I. 1791. "HENRY MARTIN, Esq., Comptroller of His Majesty's Navy,(b) 2d s. of Samuel MARTIN, of Antigua (*d.* Nov. 1776, aged 83), being 1st s. by 2d wife Sarah, da. of Edward WYKE, Lieut.-Gov. of Montserrat, was *b.* 28 Aug. 1733, at Shroten, Dorset, was Commissioner, and, subsequently, Comptroller of the Navy at Portsmouth, and was *cr. a Baronet*,

---

(a) He "bequeathed a collection of paintings, forty-six in number, and several Greek and Roman marbles and bronzes to the College of Edinburgh" [*Annual Register*, 1836].

(b) See p. 268, note "a," under "JAMES."

as above, 28 July 1791. He was M.P. for Southampton 1790 till death. He *m.* 26 Nov. 1761, at Iniscerra, co Cork, Elizabeth Anne, widow of St. Leger Heyward GILLMAN, of Gillmanville, co. Cork, da. of Harding PARKER, of Passage West, in that county, by Catherine, da. of John NEVILLE, of Newrath, co. Wicklow. He *d.* 1 Aug. 1794, in his 61st year. Will pr. Aug. 1794. His widow *d.* 6 March 1808.(a)

II. 1794. SIR HENRY WILLIAM MARTIN, Baronet [1791], of Lockinge, Berks, 2d but 1st surv. s. and h., *b.* 20 Dec. 1768, at Bishopstown, co. Cork; *suc. to the Baronetcy*, 1 Aug. 1794. He *m.* 23 June 1792, Catherine, da. of Thomas POWELL, of "The Chestnuts," Tottenham, Midx. He *d.* 3 Feb. 1842, in Upper Harley street, Marylebone, aged 73. Will pr. April 1842. His widow *d.* in Wiltshire, 5 Jan. 1847. Will pr. March 1847.

III. 1842. SIR HENRY MARTIN, Baronet [1791], of Lockinge aforesaid, 2d but only surv. s. and h., *b.* 3 Oct. 1801, in Weymouth street, Marylebone; matric. at Oxford (Oriel Coll.), 20 June 1820, aged 18; *suc. to the Baronetcy*, 3 Feb. 1842. He *m.* 8 March 1825, Catherine, 1st da. of his paternal uncle, Sir Thomas Byam MARTIN, **G.C.B.**, Admiral of the Fleet, by Catherine, da. of Robert FANSHAWE, Capt. R.N. He *d. s.p.* 4 Dec. 1863, at Tunbridge Wells, aged 62. His widow *d.* there 20 June 1882.

IV. 1863. SIR WILLIAM FANSHAWE MARTIN, Baronet [1791], cousin and h. male, being 1st s. and h.(b) of Sir Thomas Byam MARTIN, **G.C.B.**, Admiral of the Fleet abovenamed, by Catherine, da. of Robert FANSHAWE, Capt. R.N., Resident Commissioner at Plymouth Dockyard, which Thomas (who was *b.* at Ashted, Surrey, and *d.* 21 Oct. 1854, aged 80) was 4th and yst s. of the 1st Baronet. He was *b.* 5 Dec. 1801; entered the Royal Navy, 1813; was Rear-Admiral of the Blue, 1852; of the White, 1855; of the Red, 1856; Vice-Admiral of the Blue, 1858; of the White, 1860; of the Red, 1862; Admiral of the Blue, 1863, being placed on the retired list, 1870; but made Rear-Admiral of the United Kingdom, 19 Sep. 1878. He was Commander-in-Chief in the Mediterranean, 1860, and Naval Commander-in-Chief at Devonport, 1866. He had also been a Junior Lord of the Admiralty, 1858-59; **K.C.B.**, 28 June 1861; **G.C.B.**, 24 March 1873; having *suc. to the Baronetcy*, 4 Dec. 1863. He *m.* firstly, 25 July 1827, Anne, 4th and yst. da of William Draper (BEST), 1st BARON WYNFORD, by Mary Anne, da. of Jerome KNAPP. She, who was *b.* 13 Feb. 1808, *d.* 1 April 1837. He *m.* secondly, 21 May 1838, at Hove, Sussex, Sophia Elizabeth, 2d da. of Richard HART, of Wirksworth, co. Derby, by Caroline, da. of Robert SHUTTLEWORTH, of Barton Lodge, co. Lancaster. She *d.* 12 Nov. 1874, at Upton Grey House, near Winchfield, Hants. He *d.* there 24 March 1895, aged 93. Will pr. at £95,213.

V. 1895. SIR RICHARD BYAM MARTIN, Baronet [1791], of Upton Grey House aforesaid, 3d but only surv. s. and h., being 1st s. by 2d wife, *b.* 28 April 1841; *suc. to the Baronetcy*, 24 March 1895. He *m.* 20 July 1869, at Egg Buckland, Devon, Catharine, only child of William Beaumain KNIPE, Capt. 85th Dragoon Guards, by Elizabeth Charlotte (afterwards wife of Copleston Lopez RADCLIFFE), da. of Frind Cregoe COLMORE, of Moor End, co. Gloucester.

(a) She was mother, by her first husband, of Sir John St. Leger Gillman, Knt., *cr. a Baronet* [I.] in 1799.

(b) The 2d s., Admiral Sir Henry Byam Martin, **K.C.B.**, *d.* unm., 9 Feb. 1865, at Genoa.

BOUGHTON-ROUSE:

cr. 28 July 1791;

afterwards, since 1794, ROUSE-BOUGHTON;

merged, *1794, in the Baronetcy of Boughton, cr. 1641.*

I. 1791. "CHARLES WILLIAM BOUGHTON-ROUSE, of Rouse Lench, co. Worcester, Esq.,"(a) as also of Downton Hall, co. Salop, *formerly* Charles William BOUGHTON, 2d s. of Algernon BOUGHTON, of Poston Court, in Vowchurch, co. Hereford, by Mary, da. (but not heir nor coheir) of the Hon. Algernon GREVILLE and Catharine his wife, da. and coheir of Lord Arthur SOMERSET and Mary his wife, da. and h. of Sir William RUSSELL, Baronet (so *cr.* 8 Nov. 1660), of Laugharne, by Hester, da. of Sir Thomas ROUSE, 1st Baronet [1641], of Rouse Lench aforesaid. He was *b.* at Nicholas', Worcester, probably about 1745; went to India in the Bengal Civil Service in 1765, and was a Judge in several Courts there. Having, by the death, 30 Dec. 1768, of his distant cousin, Thomas PHILIPS-ROUSE *(formerly* Thomas PHILIPS), of Rouse Lench aforesaid,(b) (a descendant of the said Sir Thomas ROUS, 1st Baronet [1641]), suc. (under his will) to that estate, he took the name of BOUGHTON-ROUS, instead of that of BOUGHTON; was M.P. for Evesham (two Parls.), 1780-90, and for Bramber, 1796-99; Sec. to the Board of Control for Indian affairs, 1784-91. He by Royal Warrant, 18 May 1791, had licence to use the name of ROUSE, either *before* or *after* that of BOUGHTON, and was *cr. a Baronet*, as above, 28 July 1791. He *m.* 3 June 1782, at St. James', Westm., Catharine, da. and h. of William PEARCE, *otherwise* HALL, of Downton Hall aforesaid, through whom he acquired that estate. She was living when, by the death, 26 Feb. 1794, of his elder br., Sir Edward BOUGHTON, 8th Baronet [1641], of Lawford Hall, co. Warwick, he *suc.* to the Baronetcy, conferred 4 Aug. 1641, on his lineal ancestor William BOUGHTON, of Lawford aforesaid In that more ancient Baronetcy this *Baronetcy* then *merged*, and still (1905) so continues. On this occasion (though he did not inherit the Boughton estates) he assumed the name of ROUSE-BOUGHTON instead of BOUGHTON-ROUSE.

HAWKINS:

cr. 28 July 1791;

ex. 6 April 1829.

I. 1791, to 1829. "CHRISTOPHER HAWKINS, of Trewithan, co. Cornwall, Esq.,(a), 2d but 1st surv. s. and h. of Thomas HAWKINS, of the same, Col. in the Guards, sometime (1747-54) M.P. for Grampound (*d.* 1 Dec. 1770, aged 42), by Anne, da. of James HEYWOOD, of London, was *b.* May 1758, at Trewithan; was Sheriff of Cornwall, 1783-84; M.P. for St. Michael's (three Parls.), 1784-99; for Grampound (three Parls.), July 1800 to 1807; for Penryhn, 1818-20, and for St. Ives (Cornwall), May 1821 to 1828, being, in all, nine out of eleven consecutive Parls. He was, when he retired, "Father of the House of Commons," and was *cr. a Baronet*, as above, 28 July 1791. He was Recorder of Tregony, St. Ives, and of Grampound, F.R.S., F.A.S., and F. Hort. Soc. He *d.* unm.,(c) of erysipelas, at Trewithan aforesaid, 6 April 1829, aged 70, when the *Baronetcy* became *extinct*. Will pr. May 1827 and March 1842.

(a) See p. 268, note "a," under "JAMES."

(b) This Thomas was paternal grandson of E. Phillips, by Mary, da. of Sir Thomas Rous, 1st Baronet [1641], of Rouse Lench. See vol, iii, p. 108.

(c) In Betham's *Baronetage* (1803) he is (erroneously) said to have *m.*, and to have had a son "John Hawkins, of Sunbury, Esq., who *m.* (—), da. of Humphrey Sibthorpe, M.P. for Lincolnshire." This John, however, who was of Bignor park, Sussex, was the yst. *brother* (not the son) of the grantee.

CALL:

cr. 28 July 1791;

ex. 21 Oct. 1903.

I. 1791. "JOHN CALL, of Whiteford [in Stoke Climsland], co. Cornwall, Esq.,"(a) s. of John CALL, of Prestacutt in Launcells, in that county (*d.* 31 Dec. 1766, aged 62) by Jane, da. of John MILL, was *b.* 30 June 1732, at Fenny park, near Tiverton, and when his "classical education under Mr. Daddo, at Tiverton," and "under Mr. Keate, of Somerton," was "completed in his 17th year,"(b) left for India, in 1749, as Secretary to Benjamin Robins, Chief Engineer of the E.I. Company's Settlements; was a Writer on the Madras establishment, 1751, and as Engineer carried out the erection of defensive works at Fort St. David, and was (before he was 20) made Chief Engineer there, becoming, in 1757, the same at Madras; effecting in 1762 the reduction of the fortress of Vellore, and being, in 1768, Accountant-General of the Madras Presidency and a member of the Governor's Council. He, however, soon afterwards returned to England; was Sheriff of Cornwall, 1771-72; was a Commissioner to report on the management of the Crown lands, 1782, being confirmed in that office by Parliament in 1786; in 1784 he became partner in the London Banking House of Messrs. Pybus & Co.; was M.P. for Callington (three Parls.), 1784 till death, and was *cr. a Baronet*, as above, 28 July 1791. F.R.S. and F.A.S. He *m.* 28 March 1772, at St. George's, Bloomsbury, Philadelphia, 3d da. and coheir(c) of William BATTIE, M.D., of Great Russell Street, Bloomsbury, and of Kingston, Surrey, by (—) da. of Barnham GOODE, one of the under Masters of Eton College. He, who had been blind for the last seven years, *d.* of apoplexy at his house in Old Burlington street, 1 March 1801, aged 68. Will pr. 1801. His widow *d.* 29 Sep. 1822. Will pr. 1822.

II. 1801. SIR WILLIAM PRATT CALL, Baronet [1791], of Whiteford aforesaid, 1st s. and h., *b.* 28 Sep. 1781; was, presumably, ed. at Winchester, 1797-99; *suc. to the Baronetcy*, 1 March 1801;(d) was partner in the banking house of "Call, Marten & Co.," Old Bond Street; Sheriff of Cornwall, 1807-08. He *m.* 19 June 1806, Louisa Georgiana, 3d da. of George (FORBES), 5th EARL OF GRANARD [I.], by his 2d wife, Georgiana Augusta, da. of Augustus (BERKELEY), 4th EARL OF BERKELEY. She, who was *b.* Dec. 1779, *d.* 25 Jan. 1830, at Whiteford House, aged 50. He *d.* there 3 Dec. 1851, aged 70. Will pr. Jan. 1852.

III. 1851. SIR WILLIAM BERKELEY CALL, BARONET [1791], of Whiteford aforesaid, only s. and h., *b.* 10 May 1815, at Whiteford House; was partner in his father's Banking house; *suc. to the Baronetcy*, 3 Dec. 1851; Special Deputy Warden of the Stannaries, 1852. Sheriff of Cornwall, 1856. He *m.* 14 April 1841, Laura Emma, yst. da. of Charles Wright GARDINER, of Coombe Lodge, Whitchurch, Oxon. He *d.* 22 Dec. 1864, at 25 Old Bond street, aged 49.

IV. 1864, to 1903. SIR WILLIAM GEORGE MONTAGU CALL, Baronet [1791], of Whiteford aforesaid, only s. and h., *b.* 6 Feb. 1849, at 25 Old Bond street; ed. at Eton; *suc. to the Baronetcy*, 22 Dec. 1864. He *m.* in 1884, Marie Vanlentine, da. of Capt. MAULEON, of Anjou. He *d. s.p.* 21 Oct. 1903, at "The Hollies." Lee, Ilfracombe, Devon, aged 54, when the *Baronetcy* became *extinct*. His widow living 1905.

(a) See p. 268, note "a," under "JAMES."

(b) Betham's *Baronetage* [1803], as also Playfair's [1811]. These positive statements militate against the conjecture (*Dict. Nat. Biogr.*) that "it is believed that he was ed. at Blundell's School," at Tiverton.

(c) The eldest da., Anne, *m.*, as his 2d wife, Admiral Sir George Young, and the 2d da. Catherine, *m.* 1 April 1771, at St. Geo., Bloomsbury, John Rashleigh of Cornwall. Dr. Battie is said to have died worth £100,000.

(d) A stilted account of "the three days' fête at his beautiful seat (Nov. 1802) on his coming of age" is given in Betham's *Baronetage* [1803].

JACKSON:

cr. 28 July 1791;

afterwards, 1797-1902, DUCKETT;

ex. 13 May 1902.

I. 1791. "GEORGE JACKSON, of Hartham House [in Corsham], Wilts, Esq., a Judge Advocate of His Majesty's Fleet,"(a) 3d but 1st surv. s. and h. of George JACKSON, of Hill House, in Richmond, co. York, and of Ellerton Abbey, in that county (*d.* 1758, aged 70), by Hannah, da. of William WARD, of Gisborough, co. York, was *b.* about 1725; entered the Civil Service of the Navy; was Secretary to the Navy Board, and afterwards, for sixteen years, 1766-82, Secretary to the Admiralty, becoming subsequently Judge Advocate of the Fleet;(b) was M.P. for Weymouth, March 1786 to 1788, and for Colchester, Dec. 1788 till unseated April 1789, as also 1790-96, being *cr. a Baronet*, as above, 28 July 1791. He subsequently, by Royal lic., 3 Feb. 1797, took the name of DUCKETT instead of JACKSON, under the will (dated 27 Feb. 1764) of his second wife's maternal uncle, Thomas DUCKETT,(c) of Hartham House abovenamed. He *m.* firstly, 24 Sep. 1741, at St. Bennet's, Paul's Wharf, London, Mary, da. and h. of his maternal uncle, William WARD, of Gisborough aforesaid, by Frances, da. of Sir Francis VINCENT, 5th Baronet [1620]. She *d. s.p.m.s.* 1754, and was *bur.* at Islington. He *m.* secondly, 9 Sep. 1775, at St. Margaret's, Westm., Grace, widow of Robert NEALE, of Shaw House, Wilts, da. and h. of Gwyn GOLDSTONE, of Goldstone, Salop, and of London, merchant, by Grace, 1st da. (whose issue eventually became coheir) of George DUCKETT,(c) of Hartham House abovenamed. She *d.* at 15, Upper Grosvenor street, 2 March 1798, and was *bur.* in Trinity church, South Audley street. Admon. March 1798. He *d.* at the same place, 15 Dec. 1822, in his 98th year (being, it is said, the oldest householder in London), and was *bur.* at Bishop's Stortford, Herts.(d)

II. 1822. SIR GEORGE DUCKETT, Baronet [1791], of Hartham House aforesaid, *formerly*, 1777-1797, George JACKSON, only surv. s. and h., by 2d wife, *b.* 17 July 1777, in Old Palace Yard, Westm. He, when of age, joined with his father in barring the entail of the Duckett estates; was M.P. for Lymington, 1807-12, and for Plympton, Oct. to Dec. 1812; F.R.S., 1808; F.S.A.; sometime Lieut.-Col. of the West Essex Militia; *suc. to the Baronetcy*, 15 Dec. 1822; and was gazetted a bankrupt, March 1832. He *m.* firstly, 17 July 1810, Isabella, yr. da. and coheir of Stainbank FLOYD, of Shrewsbury, and of Barnard's Castle, co. Durham,(e) by Anne, da. of (—)

(a) See p. 268, note "a," under "JAMES."

(b) To commemorate the services he rendered to the celebrated navigator, Captain James Cook, "Port Jackson" in New South Wales, and "Point Jackson" in New Zealand, were so named. He "wrote a great deal in the public newspapers," and it even "has been reported that he was the celebrated *Junius*." [Duckett's "*Anecdotal Reminiscences*."]

(c) The family of Duckett is elaborately treated of in Sir G. F. Duckett's "*Duchetiana*." See p. 274, note "b."

(d) He had a residence at Roydon in that vicinity, and had taken great part in making the river Stort navigable from Bishop's Stortford, to where it joins the river Lea.

(e) By the request (made shortly before his death) of her son, Sir George Floyd Duckett, the 3d Baronet [1791], this statement is added: "She was in direct descent from Captain David Floyd, of the Navy, Groom of the Bedchamber to James II, at St. Germain." This descent, according to a privately printed history of the Floyd family, was through her father (a yr. br. of John Floyd, who became a Protestant, and *d.* in Germany, being ancestor of the Floyd, Baronets [1816]) who was a son of David Floyd, a partizan of the young Chevalier, the said David being son of the abovenamed Captain David Floyd, a follower of James II, and likewise a partizan of the old Chevalier.

Lecky, of that county. She *d.* 10 Oct. 1844, aged 64.(a) He *m.* secondly, 30 April 1846, at St. Pancras, Midx., Charlotte, widow of Joseph Laxe, da. of Edmond Seymour, of Inholmes, Berks, and of Crowood Park, Wilts. He *d.* 15 June 1856, aged 78, in Gloucester gardens, Hyde Park, and was *bur.* at Kensal Green. Admon. Aug. 1857. His widow, by whom he had no issue, *d.* in Gloucester Gardens aforesaid, 18 Nov. 1862, aged 76.

III. 1856, to 1902. Sir George Floyd Duckett, Baronet [1791], only s. and h., by 1st wife, *b.* 27 March 1811, in Spring Gardens, and *bap.* at St. Martin's in the Fields; ed. at Harrow; matric. at Oxford (Ch. Ch.), 13 Dec. 1828, aged 17; entered the Army and was sometime Major in the 87th Foot; Lieut.-Col. of the West Essex Militia; *suc. to the Baronetcy*, 15 June 1856; was an officer of Public Instruction to the French Government, 1888; Knight of the order of merit of Saxe Coburg Gotha, 1890; Knight (1st Class) of the Saxe Ernestine family order, 1893.(b) He *m.* 21 June 1845, at Hampton Court, Isabella, da. of Lieut.-Gen. Sir Lionel Smith, 1st Baronet [1838], **G.C.B.** and **G.C.H.**, by his 2d wife, Isabella Curwen (sister of the Rt. Hon. Sir Henry Pottinger, 1st Baronet [1840], **G.C.B.**), da. of Eldred Curwen Pottinger, of Mount Pottinger, co. Down. She *d.* 13 Dec. 1901. He *d.* at Cleeve House, Yatton, co. Somerset, 13 May 1902, in his 92d year, when the *Baronetcy* became *extinct*.

WOODFORD:

cr. 28 July 1791;

ex. 17 May 1828.

I. 1791. "Ralph Woodford, Esq., late [1772-74] Envoy Extraordinary to Denmark,"(c) 1st s. of Matthew Woodford, of St. Michael's, Southampton, by Mary, da. and coheir of John Brideoak, was *b.* probably about 1735; was British Resident to the Hanse Towns, 1763-72; Envoy Extraordinary to Denmark, 1772-74, and was *cr. a Baronet*, as above, 28 July 1791. He was of Carleby, co. Lincoln. He *m.* 19 May 1773, at St. Geo. Han. sq., Gertrude, da. of (—) Reesen. She *d.* 1794. He *d.* 26 Aug. 1810, and was *bur.* at Cheltenham. M.I. Admon. Dec. 1810.

II. 1810, to 1828. Sir Ralph James Woodford, Baronet [1791], of Carleby aforesaid, only s. and h., *b.* about 1784; *suc. to the Baronetcy*, 26 Aug. 1810; was Gov. of the Isle of Trinidad, 1813, till his death fifteen years later. He *d.* unm., on board "The Duke of York" packet, returning from Jamaica, 17 May 1828, aged 44, when the *Baronetcy* became *extinct*. Will pr. Nov. 1828.

(a) "She died under distressing circumstances. A wonderfully energetic woman, she was bent upon impossibilities, was taken dangerously ill, whilst prosecuting enquiries upon one of these occasions, was mismanaged, and died amongst strangers, at a distance from her family. She had been searching for *el dorado*; prosecuting enquiries for what had no existence in fact." [Duckett's *Anecdotal Reminiscences*.]

(b) He was author, in 1848, of a *Technological Military Dictionary*, in German, French, and English, for which he received the great gold medals of "Science and Art" from Austria and Russia, the gold medal "of merit" from France, and a grant of £200 from the Royal Bounty Fund. Author, also, of several genealogical works and treatises, *e.g.*, "*Duchetiana, Genealogical Memoirs of the Families of Wyndesore and Duket*" [4to 1869 and 1874]; "*The Parentage of Gundreda*" [1878], as also "*The Countess Gundreda*," 1873, and, finally, "*Anecdotal Reminiscences by an Octo-Nonogenarian*" [1894], in which is a complete list of his works.

(c) See p. 268, note "a," under "James."

POLE:

cr. 28 July 1791;

afterwards, since 1853, Van-Notten-Pole.

I. 1791. "Charles Pole, of Wolverton, Hants, Esq.,"(a) *formerly* Charles Van-Notten, only surv. s. of Charles Van-Notten, of Amsterdam and London, merchant (*d.* 1 March 1750/1, aged 48), by Susanna, da. of David Bosanquet, of London, Turkey merchant, was *b.* 14 Jan. 1735, and became a successful merchant of London. By Royal Lic. 7 March 1787, he in consequence of his marriage took the name of Pole instead of that of Van-Notten (save for purposes of commercial intercourse), and was *cr. a Baronet*, as above, 28 July 1791, with a *spec. rem.*, failing heirs male of his body, to those of his da. Susanna Pole. He was Sheriff of Hants, 1791-92. He *m.* 9 Sep. 1769, Millicent, 1st da. and coheir of Charles Pole,(b) of Holcroft, co. Lancaster, sometime (1756-61) M.P. for Liverpool, by Anne, da. and coheir of John Johnston, of co. Lancaster. He *d.* 18 June 1813, aged 78. Will pr. 1813. His widow, who was *b.* 17 Feb. 1746, *d.* 16 Nov. 1818. Will pr. 1818.

II. 1813. Sir Peter Pole, Baronet [1791], of Wolverton aforesaid, *formerly*, 1770-87, Peter Van-Notten, 1st s. and h., *b.* 25 Oct. 1770; *suc. to the Baronetcy*, 18 June 1813; was partner in the Banking House of "Pole, Thornton & Co.," which firm was dissolved in 1826; M.P. for Yarmouth (Isle of Wight), March 1819 to 1826. He *m.* 24 Dec. 1798, Anna Guildelmina, 1st da. of Richard Buller, of Cumberland street. She *d.* 25 July 1835. Will pr. March 1836. He *d.* 30 Aug. 1850, at 41 Welbeck street, aged 79. Will pr. Oct. 1850.

III. 1850. Sir Peter Pole, *afterwards*, from 1853, Van-Notten-Pole, Baronet [1791], of Wolverton aforesaid, and of Todenham, co. Gloucester, 1st s. and h., *b.* 11 Feb. 1801, in Bedford square, St. Giles in the Fields; matric. at Oxford (Bras. Coll.), 30 May 1818, aged 17; *cr.* M.A., 4 July 1821; Capt. South Hants Militia, 1824-52; *suc. to the Baronetcy*, 30 Aug. 1850. By royal lic. 11 June 1853, took the paternal name of his family, Van-Notten, before that of Pole; was Sheriff of Warwickshire, 1856. He *m.* firstly, 28 July 1825, at All Souls, Langham Place, Louisa, 4th da. of Edmond Henry (Pery), 1st Earl of Limerick [I.], by Alice Mary, da. and h. of Henry Ormsby. She, who was *b.* 2 April 1798, *d.* at Brighton, 6 Aug. 1852. Admon. Dec. 1852. He *m.* secondly, 24 Sep. 1863, at St. George's, Canterbury, Louisa, 3d da. of Samuel Lands, of the Bombay Civil Service. He *d.* at Todenham, 13 May 1887, aged 86. Will pr. 17 Aug. 1887, above £8,900. His widow, by whom he had no issue, living 1905.

IV. 1887. Sir Cecil Pery Van-Notten-Pole, Baronet [1791], of Todenham aforesaid, grandson and h., being 1st s. and h. of Cecil Charles Pole, by Frances Emma, da. of Rev. the Hon. Henry Rice, Rector of Great Rissington, co. Gloucester, which Cecil Charles (who *d.* v.p. 17 Sep. 1876, aged 46), was only s. and h. ap. of the late Baronet, by his 1st wife. He was *b.* 30 Sep. 1863; sometime Lieut. 3d Batt. Royal Fusileers Militia; *suc. to the Baronetcy*, 13 May 1887. He *m.* 27 June 1894, at Trinity Church, Twickenham, Frederica Katharine, 3d da. of Sir Thomas George Freake, 2d Baronet [1882], by Frederica Charlotte Mary, da. of Col. Frederick Maitland.

(a) See p. 268, note "a," under "James."

(b) This Charles (who *d.* Oct. 1779) was yr. br. of German Pole, of Radborne, co. Derby, both being sons of Samuel Pole, who succeeded to that estate in 1683, and *d.* 10 Feb. 1730.

VAUGHAN:

cr. 28 July 1791;

ex. 29 April 1859.

I. 1791. "Robert Howell Vaughan, of Nannau, co. Merioneth, Esq.,"(a) being also of Hengwrst in that county, 3d. s. of Robert Vaughan, of Hengwrst aforesaid, sometime (1728-29, and 1734-35), Sheriff of Merionethshire (*d.* Jan. 1750) by Janet (*m.* Dec. 1733) da. and coheir of Hugh Nannau, of Nannau aforesaid, was *b.* about 1738; suc. his elder br. Hugh Vaughan (who was Sheriff of Merionethshire, 1752) in those estates and was *cr. a Baronet*, as above, 28 July 1791. He *m.* in or before 1767, Anne, da. and h. of Edward Williames, of Ystymcollwym, co. Montgomery. She *d.* 4 March 1791. He *d.* 13 Oct. 1792. Will pr. June 1793.

II. 1792. Sir Robert Williames Vaughan, Baronet [1791], of Nannau aforesaid, 1st s. and h., *b.* about 1768 at Erbistock, co. Flint; matric. at Oxford (Jesus Coll.), 24 Nov. 1797, aged 19; *suc. to the Baronetcy*, 13 Oct. 1792; was M.P. for Merionethshire for forty-four years (twelve Parls.), 1792-1836. He *m.* Sep. 1801, Anna Maria, 3d sister and coheir (1831) of Sir Thomas Mostyn, 6th and last Baronet [1660] of Mostyn, co. Flint, da. of Sir Roger Mostyn, 5th Baronet [1660], by Margaret, da. of the Rev. Hugh Wynne, LL.D. He *d.* 22 April 1843, at Nannau, aged 75. Will pr. Sep. 1843. His widow *d.* there 30 May 1858, aged 81.

III. 1843, to 1859. Sir Robert Williames Vaughan, Baronet [1791], of Nannau aforesaid, only s. and h., *b.* 23 June 1803, at Chester; matric. at Oxford (Brasenose Coll.), 17 April 1822, aged 18; *suc. to the Baronetcy*, 22 April 1843; Sheriff of Merionethshire, 1846. He *m.* July 1835, Frances, 1st da. of Edward Lloyd, of Rhagatt in that county. She *d.* at Rug, co. Merioneth, 16 Sep. 1858, aged 47. He *d.*, in London, 29 April 1859, aged 55, when *the Baronetcy* became *extinct*.

RICH, *late* BOSTOCK:

cr. 28 July 1791.

I. 1791. "Reverend Charles Rich, *late* Bostock, of Rose Hall [*i.e.*, Roos Hall, in Beccles], co. Suffolk, LL.D.,"(a) *formerly* Charles Bostock, of Shirley, near Southampton, Hants, 2d and yst. s. of the Rev. John Bostock, D.D., Canon of Windsor (1757 till death in 1786), by Mary, da. and eventually heir of John Hopson, of Beenham, Berks, was *b.* about 1752, at Windsor; matric. at Oxford (St. John's Coll.) 30 June 1768, aged 16; took Holy Orders; B.C.L., 1776; D.C.L., 1780; took, in consequence of his marriage, the name of Rich instead of Bostock, by royal lic. 23 Dec. 1790, and was *cr. a Baronet*, as above, 28 July 1791.(b) He purchased the manor of Beenham abovenamed, in 1793, and the great tithes thereof, in 1804, in which parish his elder br. Rev. John Bostock (*d.* 1816) had a seat inherited through their mother.(c) He, in 1812, sold the estate of Roos Hall (which had long been in the Rich family), and also (about the same date) that of Waverley Abbey. He *m.*

(a) See p. 268, note "a," under "James."

(b) It is to be observed that this creation was nearly eight years before the Baronetcy of Rich [1676], which was held by his wife's father, became extinct by the death of her uncle, the 6th and last Baronet, 8 Jan. 1799. As to that Baronetcy (which was conferred 24 Jan. 1675/6, on Charles Rich, grandson of Robert, 2d Baron Rich), of which the Baronets of 1791 are (through the wife of the grantee), the representatives, see vol. iv, pp. 72-74.

(c) Playfair's *Baronetage* [1811].

4 Jan. 1783, at New Windsor, Berks, Mary Frances, da. and h. of Lieut.-General Sir Robert Rich, 5th Baronet [1676], of Roos Hall aforesaid, Claxton Abbey, Norfolk, and Waverley Abbey, Surrey, by his 1st wife Mary, sister of Peter, 1st Earl of Ludlow [I.], da. of Peter Ludlow, of Ardsallagh, co. Meath. He *d.* 12 Sep. 1824, at Shirley aforesaid, in his 73d year, and was *bur.* in South Audley street chapel. Will pr. 1824. His widow, who was *b.* 31 May 1755, *d.* 20 May 1833, in Upper Grosvenor street, in her 78th year, and was *bur.*, with her parents, in South Audley street chapel. Will pr. July 1833. M.I. to both in Millbrook church, Hants.

II. 1824. Sir Charles Henry Rich, Baronet [1791], of Shirley and Claxton Abbey aforesaid, and of Beenham Park, Berks (which last he sold in 1834), 1st s. and h., *b.* 19 April 1784; *suc. to the Baronetcy*, 12 Sep. 1824. Sheriff of Hants, 1826-27. He *m.* 6 Nov. 1806, Frances Maria, 2d and yst. da. of Sir John Lethbridge, 1st Baronet [1804], by Dorothea, da. of William Buckler. She *d.* 20 Feb. 1852, at Tunbridge Wells. He *d.* 22 Oct. 1857, aged 73, at Wallington, Surrey.

III. 1857. Sir Charles Henry John Rich, Baronet [1791], of Shirley and Claxton Abbey aforesaid, 1st s. and h., *b.* 22 Dec. 1812, at Bossington House, Hants; *suc. to the Baronetcy*, 22 Oct. 1857. He *m.* 27 Nov. 1855, at St. Marylebone, Harriet Theodosia, 1st da. and coheir of John Stuart Sullivan (Madras Civil Service), of Devonshire place, in that parish, by Selina Theodosia, da. of Thomas Paul Sandby. He *d.* 12 Dec. 1866, at 12 Nottingham place, Marylebone, in his 54th year. His widow *d.* there, 10 July 1870. Both *bur.* at Nunhead Cemetery. M.I.

IV. 1866. Sir Charles Henry Stuart Rich, Baronet [1791], of Shirley and Claxton Abbey aforesaid, and afterwards of Devizes Castle, Wilts, only s. and h., *b.* 7 March 1859, at 12 Nottingham place, and *bap.* at St. Marylebone; *suc. to the Baronetcy*, 12 Dec. 1866; ed. at Harrow and at Jesus Coll., Cambridge; F.S.A. He *m.* 27 July 1881, at Trinity Church, Tunbridge Wells, Fanny, only da. of the Rev. Joseph Page, of Little Bromley, Essex, by Mary Jane, da. of the Rev. Walter Burton Leach, of Sutton Montis, Somerset.

HUDSON:

cr. 28 July 1791;

sometime, Oct. to Nov. 1813, Hudson-Palmer,

and, since Nov. 1813, Palmer.

I. 1791. "Charles Grave Hudson, of Wanlip, co. Leicester, Esq.,"(a) (an estate he acquired by his first marriage), only s. and h. of Joseph Hudson, of Boutherbeck, near Keswick, Cumberland, sometime Consul for the Dutch at Tunis (*d.* at Port Mahon, 1754, aged 86), by Sarah, da. of William Plowman, of Leghorn, merchant, was *b.* at Tunis, 3 April 1730, was a merchant of London, and a director of the South Sea Company; Sheriff of Leicestershire, 1784-85, and was *cr. a Baronet*, as above, 28 July 1791. He *m.* firstly, 8 March 1766, Catherine Susanna, 1st da. and coheir of Henry Palmer, of Wanlip aforesaid, by Elizabeth, da. of (—) Borkett. She, who was *b.* April 1742, *d.* at Wanlip, 24 Jan. 1805. He *m.* secondly, 13 Jan. 1806, Sarah, da. of Peter Holford, a Master in Chancery. She *d.* s.p., 5 Sep. 1811. Admon. March 1812. He *d.* 24 Oct. 1813, in his 84th year. Will pr. Jan. 1814, Sep. 1827, March 1833 and May 1868.

(a) See p. 268, note "a," under "James."

II. 1813. SIR CHARLES THOMAS HUDSON-PALMER, *sometime*, Oct. to Nov. 1813, PALMER, Baronet [1791], of Wanlip aforesaid, *formerly* Charles Thomas HUDSON, 2d but 1st surv. s. and h., *b.* there 20 May 1771; matric. at Oxford (Ch. Ch.), 21 Oct. 1789, aged 18; B.A., 1794; admitted to Lincoln's Inn, 24 April 1793; assumed the name of HUDSON-PALMER, probably in 1805, on the death of his mother; *suc. to the Baronetcy*, 24 Oct. 1813, and by royal lic. (in the next month), 13 Nov. 1813, took the name of PALMER only. He *m.* 14 July 1802, Harriet, 3d and yst. da. and coheir of Sir William PEPPERELL, Baronet (so *cr.* 9 Nov. 1774), by Elizabeth, da. of Isaac ROYAL, of Massachusetts. He *d.* 30 April 1827, aged 55. Will pr. May 1827. His widow *d.* 22 Jan. 1848, aged 74, at Farnborough Hill, Hants. Will pr. Feb. 1848.

III. 1827. SIR GEORGE JOSEPH PALMER, Baronet [1791], of Wanlip aforesaid, 1st s. and h., *b.* 20 Dec. 1811; *suc. to the Baronetcy*, 30 April 1827; matric. at Oxford (Ch. Ch.), 7 April 1830, aged 18; Sheriff of Leicestershire, 1839-40. He *m.* 26 Feb. 1836, at Westonbirt, co. Glouc., Emily Elizabeth, yst da. of George Peter HOLFORD, of Westonbirt aforesaid, by Anne, da. of the Rev. Averill DANIEL, of Lifford, co. Donegal. He *d.* 22 Feb. 1866, at Wanlip Hall, aged 54. His widow *d.* in London, 6 Oct. 1871.

IV. 1866. SIR ARCHDALE ROBERT PALMER, Baronet [1791], of Wanlip aforesaid, 1st s. and h., *b.* there 1 Nov. 1838; sometime, 1860-69, Lieut. Rifle Brigade; *suc. to the Baronetcy*, 22 Feb. 1866; Sheriff of Leicestershire, 1881. He *m.* 19 Aug. 1873, at Stanton Harold, co. Leicester, Augusta Amelia, only surv. da. of Washington Sewallis (SHIRLEY), 9th EARL FERRERS, by Augusta Annabella, da. of Edward (CHICHESTER), 4th MARQUESS OF DONEGALL [I.]. She was *b.* 25 Dec. 1849.

TAPPS:

cr. 28 July 1791;

sometime, 1835-76, TAPPS-GERVIS,

afterwards, since 1876, TAPPS-GERVIS-MEYRICK.

I. 1791. "GEORGE IVISON TAPPS, of Hinton Admiral, Hants, Esq.,"(a) only s. of George Jarvis TAPPS, of North Church, in King's Langley, Herts, Barrister (*d.* 10 May 1774), by Jane, da. of J. IVISON, of Carlisle,(b) was *b.* 5 Jan. 1753, and was *cr. a Baronet*, as above, 28 July 1791; Sheriff of Hants, 1793-94. He *m.* 29 June 1790, at St. Marylebone, Sarah, sister of Sir George BUGGIN,(c) da. of Barrington BUGGIN, of St. Dunstans in the East, a director of the South Sea Company, by Anne, da. of John CHAPMAN, of London. She *d.* 11 July 1813, in Great Cumberland place, Marylebone. He *d.* 15 March 1835, at Admiral Hinton, aged 82. Will pr. Aug. 1835.

(a) See p. 268, note "a," under "JAMES."

(b) In the will of this "George Jarvis Tapps, Esq.," dat. 15 March and proved 19 May 1774, he leaves his lands to his loving wife Jane for life, with rem. to George Ivison Tapps, rem. to Jane Ivison Tapps, both in tail (with rem. to the children of John Ivison, of Charles street, shoemaker). He does not, however, speak of this George and Jane as being his children, but merely as infants now living with him, who, he states, are described in the registers of St. Margaret's, Westminster, one as "Jane Tapps" (not "Jane Ivison Tapps" as called in the will) child of George and Jane, and the other (George) as being similarly described. The omission from the register of the mother's surname of Ivison (attributed in the will to both of them before that of Tapps) is to be noted.

(c) The widow of this Sir George Buggin was *cr.* 10 April 1840, Duchess of *Inverness*, being supposed to have been ecclesiastically married, about 1831, to H.R.H. the Duke of Sussex, Earl of *Inverness*, etc.

II. 1835 SIR GEORGE WILLIAM TAPPS, *afterwards*, from Dec. 1835, TAPPS-GERVIS, Baronet [1791], of Hinton Admiral aforesaid, only s. and h., *b.* 24 May 1795; was ed. at Trin. Coll., Cambridge; B.A., 1819; M.A., 1822; admitted to Lincoln's Inn, 13 April 1815, aged 20; was (v.p.) M.P. for Romney 1826-30, and for Christchurch, 1832-33; *suc. to the Baronetcy*, 15 March 1835, and, shortly afterwards by Royal lic., 3 Dec. 1835, took the name of TAPPS-GERVIS(a) instead of TAPPS. He *m.* 20 Sep. 1825, Clara, 1st da. of Augustus Elliott FULLER, of Rose Hill and Ashdown House, Sussex, by Clara, 1st da. and coheir of Owen Putland MEYRICK, of Bodorgan, co. Anglesey. She *d.* Dec. 1831. He *d.* 26 Oct. 1842, aged 47. Will pr. Nov. 1842.

III. 1842. SIR GEORGE ELIOTT MEYRICK TAPPS-GERVIS, *afterwards*, from 1876, TAPPS-GERVIS-MEYRICK, Baronet [1791], of Hinton Admiral aforesaid, 1st s. and h., *b.* 1 Sep. 1827, at Dover; matric. at Oxford (Ch. Ch.), 4 June 1846, aged 18; *suc. to the Baronetcy*, 26 Oct. 1842. He by royal lic., 16 March 1876, took the name of MEYRICK after that of TAPPS-GERVIS, under the will of his maternal uncle, Owen John Augustus FULLER-MEYRICK, of Bodorgan, co. Anglesey, to which estate he suc.; Sheriff of Anglesey, 1848. He *m.* 4 Dec. 1849, at Ashbourne, co. Derby, Fanny, 4th da. of Christopher HARLAND, of the same, Apothecary, by Mary, da. of Thomas and Ann HARTSHORNE.(b) She *d.* 24 June 1892, at Hinton Admiral, aged 72. He *d.* there, after a long illness, 7 March 1896, aged 68. Will pr. at £19,755.

IV. 1896. SIR GEORGE AUGUSTUS ELIOTT TAPPS-GERVIS MEYRICK, Baronet [1791], of Hinton Admiral and Bodorgan aforesaid, *formerly*, 1855-76, TAPPS-GERVIS, only s. and h., *b.* 9 March 1855, at Hinton Admiral; ed. at Eton; *suc. to the Baronetcy*, 7 March 1896; was Sheriff of Hants, 1900. He *m.* 1 Oct. 1884, at Dilton Marsh, Wilts, Susan Jacintha, yst. da. of Charles Paul PHIPPS, of Chalcot, Wilts, by Emma Mary, da. of M. BENSON, of Liverpool.

Family Estates.—These, in 1883, consisted of 16,918 acres in Anglesey (inherited from the family of Meyrick); 6,660 in Sussex (inherited from the family of Fuller), and 4,286 in Hants. *Total.*—27,864 acres, worth £20,867 a year. *Principal Seats.*—Hinton Admiral, near Christchurch, Hants, and Bodorgan, co. Anglesey.

CHAD:

cr. 28 July 1791;

ex. 30 Sep. 1855.

I. 1791. "GEORGE CHAD, of Thursford, co. Norfolk, Esq.,"(c) only s. of Robert CHAD, of Wells, in that county, merchant (*d.* Dec. 1736), by Elizabeth, da. of Charles WRIGHT,(d) of Kilverstone, co. Norfolk,

(a) George Jarvis or Gervis, who *d.* 1718, aged 82, left three daughters and coheirs, of whom (1) Lydia, *m.* Sir Peter Mews, and *d.* s.p. at Hinton Admiral, 6 April 1751; (2) Agnes Maria, *m.* William Clerke, of Buckland, Herts, and *d.* 6 Jan. 1726, leaving issue; (3) Elizabeth, *m.* Richard Tapps, citizen and merchant tailor of London (will dat. 5 March 1724/5, and pr. 26 Nov. 1725), and was mother of George Jarvis Tapps, who proved her will 23 Jan. 1732/3, and *d.* 1735, being grandfather, by a son of his own name [Burke's *Baronetage*, 1903] of the grantee.

(b) This Thomas Hartshorne and Anne his wife were, at one time, footman and housemaid in the service of Dr. Taylor, of Ashbourne, the friend and frequent host of the well-known Dr. Samuel Johnson. [*Ex inform.* Rev. Francis Jourdain, sometime, 1878-98, Vicar of Ashbourne].

(c) See p. 268, note "a," under "JAMES."

(d) An elaborate account of the families of Wright of Kilverstone, and of Violett of Pinkney Hall, from whom that estate was derived, is in Playfair's *Baronetage* [1811].

was *b.* 1730; admitted in 1748 (as a Fellow Commoner) to Christ's College, Cambridge; admitted to Lincoln's Inn, 24 May 1749, becoming subsequently a Barrister; Recorder of Lynn, 1769 till 1794; inherited in 1781, by the death of his nephew Charles WRIGHT(a) (in his 31st year) the estate of Pinkney Hall, co. Norfolk, and was for thirty years, till 1792, Joint Chairman of Sessions for that county, being *cr. a Baronet*, as above, 28 July 1791. He *m.* firstly, in 1775, Sarah, da. of John ROWLLS, of Kingston, Surrey. She, by whom he had seven children, *d.* 1786, aged 38. He *m.* secondly, in 1791, Mary, da. and h. of Edward FLETCHER, of Richmond, Surrey. She, by whom he had no issue, *d.* 1794, in her 50th year, and was *bur.* at Thursford. Will pr. Dec. 1794. He *d.* 24 Nov. 1815, in his 85th year. Will pr. 1816.

II. 1815, to 1855. SIR CHARLES CHAD, Baronet [1791], of Thursford and Pinkney Hall aforesaid, 1st surv. s. and h.,(b) *b.* 24 April 1779., *suc. to the Baronetcy*, 24 Nov. 1815. He *m.* 14 June 1810, Anne, 2d da. of Edward Garth (TURNOUR), 2d Earl of Winterton [I.], by his 1st wife Jane, da. of Richard CHAPMAN, of London. She, who was *b.* 6 Dec. 1785, *d.* 2 Feb. 1832. He *d.* s.p.s., at 1 Gloucester square, Hyde Park, 30 Sep. 1855, aged 76, when the *Baronetcy* became *extinct*. Will pr. Oct. 1855.

BROGRAVE(c):

cr. 28 July 1791;

ex. 1 June 1828.

I. 1791. "BERNEY BROGRAVE, of Worstead House [in Worsted], co. Norfolk, Esq.,"(d) 1st s. and h. of Thomas BROGRAVE, of Great Badow, co. Essex (*d.* 20 April 1753, aged 61), by Julia, da. and h. of John BERNEY, of Westwick, co. Norfolk, was *b.* 10 Oct. 1726, at St. Dunstan's in the West, London, and was *cr. a Baronet*, as above, 28 July 1791. He *m.* firstly, 31 May 1761, at Great Baddow, Jane, 1st da. and coheir of Edward HAWKER, of that parish. She *d.*, at Worstead, 6 Aug. 1765, aged 34. He *m.* secondly, 23 Jan. 1769, at Norwich, Jane, da. of Matthew HALLCOTT, of Hoo, co. Norfolk. She *d.* 14 May 1793, at Waxham, co. Norfolk the day before the death of her son Thomas BROGRAVE. He *d.* in, or shortly before, 1797. Admon. March 1797.

II. 1797? to 1828. SIR GEORGE BERNEY BROGRAVE, Baronet [1791], of Worstead House aforesaid, 2d but 1st surv. s. and h., being 1st s. by the second wife, *b.* and *bap.* 4 Feb. 1772, at Worstead; *suc. to the Baronetcy*, in or shortly before 1797. He *m.* 7 May 1800, Emma Louisa, yst. da. and coheir of Edward WHITWELL, by Mary, da. of John MILNES, of Wakefield, co. York. She was divorced by Act of Parliament, 28 April 1809.(e) He *d.* s.p., 1 June 1828, aged 56, when the *Baronetcy* became *extinct*.(f) Admon. Nov. 1828.

(a) See p. 279, note "d."

(b) Robert John Chad, the 1st s. that survived infancy, *b.* 29 April 1778, *d.* unm. and v.p., near Florence in 1793 in his 21st year, and was *bur.* at Leghorn.

(c) This Baronetcy has been singularly ignored. No mention is made of it in Courthope's *Extinct Baronetage* (1835), or in Burke's (1844); neither is it in the list of extinct Baronetcies given in Debrett's *Baronetage* (1840), nor (as is mentioned in *N. & Q.*, 7th S., 11, 63) in Solly's *Hereditary Titles of Honour* [1880].

(d) See p. 268, note "a," under "JAMES."

(e) She *m.* 3 May 1809 (being a few days later), Marsham Elwin.

(f) His yr. br. Captain Roger Brograve had shot himself in 1813, and he, himself, is said in the *Ann. Register* for 1828 to have been "the last known male descendant of that ancient family" of Brograve.

KING:

cr. 18 July 1792;

afterwards, since 1888, DUCKWORTH-KING.

I. 1792. "SIR RICHARD KING, Knt., Rear-Admiral of the Red squadron of His Majesty's Fleet,"(a) 3d but 1st surv. s. of CURTIS KING, a Master in the Royal Navy, and sometime Master Attendant at Woolwich (*d.* 1 May 1745), by Mary, sister of Curtis BARNETT, Commodore, da. of Benjamin BARNETT, Lieut. R.N., was *b.* at Gosport 10 Aug. 1730; entered the Royal Navy, 1738, serving in the Mediterranean and the East Indies; Lieut., 1746; Commander, 1756, being in command at the capture of Calcutta and Hooghly; took part in the expedition to Manila in 1762; Commodore, 1779; distinguished himself greatly in the action off Sadras, 17 Feb. 1782, being, on his return to England, *Knighted* 5 June 1784; Rear-Admiral of the White, Sep. 1787; of the Red, Sep. 1790, being *cr. a Baronet*, as above, 18 July 1792; Governor of Newfoundland, 1792-94; Vice-Admiral of the Blue 1793; of the Red, 1794; Commander-in-Chief at Plymouth, 1794; Admiral of the Blue, 1795, and of the White, Feb. 1799. He was M.P. for Rochester (two Parls.), May 1794 to 1802. He *m.* 30 Nov. 1769, Susanna Margaretta,(b) da. of William COKER, of Mapowder, Dorset, by Susanna, da. of the Rev. Laurence ST. LO, D.D., Canon of Wells. She *d.* 18 Oct. 1794, at Southampton. Admon. Feb. 1801. He *d.* at his house in Devonshire place, 27 Nov. and was *bur.* 4 Dec. 1806, at St. Mary-le-bone, aged 76. Will pr. 1807.

II. 1806. SIR RICHARD KING, Baronet [1792], 1st but only surv. s. and h., *b.* 28 Nov. 1774; entered the Royal Navy 1788; Lieut., 1791; Commander, 1793; Captain, 1794; was in command of the "Achille" (twenty-four guns) at the battle of Trafalgar, Oct. 1805; *suc. to the Baronetcy*, 27 Nov. 1806; Captain of the Fleet, 1811; Rear-Admiral, 1812; **K.C.B.**, 2 Jan. 1815; Commander-in-Chief in the East Indies, 1816-20; Vice-Admiral, 1821; Commander-in-Chief at the Nore, 1833 till death. He *m.* firstly, 29 Nov. 1803, Sarah Anne, only da. of Admiral Sir John Thomas DUCKWORTH, 1st Baronet [1813], **G.C.B.**, by his 1st wife, Anne da. and h. of John WALLIS, of Lanteglos, Cornwall. She *d.* abroad 20 March 1819. Admon. Sep. 1821. He *m.* secondly, 16 May 1822, Maria Susanna, da. of Admiral Sir Charles COTTON, 5th Baronet [1641], of Maddingley, co. Cambridge, by Philadelphia, da. of Rear-Admiral Sir Joshua ROWLEY, 1st Baronet [1786]. He *d.*, of cholera, 5 Aug. 1834, at the Admiralty House, Sheerness, in his 60th year. Will pr. Sep. 1834. His widow *d.* 8 Jan. 1871, at Maddingley aforesaid, in her 81st year.

III. 1834. SIR RICHARD DUCKWORTH-KING, Baronet [1792], 1st s. and h. by 1st wife, *b.* 12 Sep. 1804, at Stoke Damerell; ed. at Eton; entered the Army, 1822; *suc. to the Baronetcy*, 5 Aug. 1834; Captain (half-pay), 1836, having in 1881 the Hon. rank of Major. He *m.* 12 May 1836, at Christ Church, Marylebone, Marianne, only da. of James BARNETT, of Dorset square. She *d.* March 1837. He *d.* s.p.s., 2 Nov. 1887, in his 84th year, at 2 Chesterfield street. Will pr. under £8,500.

IV. 1887. SIR GEORGE ST. VINCENT KING, *afterwards*, from 1888, DUCKWORTH-KING, Baronet [1792], **K.C.B.**, br. of the whole blood and h., *b.* 15 July 1809; ed. at the Naval Coll., Portsmouth; entered the

(a) See p. 113, note "a," under "GIDEON." The date of the Gazette notice for King and Stirling, is 7 July 1792.

(b) She is said in Playfair's *Baronetage* (1811) to have been the "widow of George Cornwallis Broun, Esq., a Capt. in the Army, br. to the Countess of Peterborough," who in Foster's Baronetage (1883) is called "Captain *Sir* George Cornwallis Broun." There is no mention of such marriage in the Coker pedigree as given in Hutchins' *Dorset*, where, however, it is stated that "a daughter" of Robert Coker, *brother* of the said Susanna, married "Capt. Broun."

Navy, 1824; Commander, 1834; was, serving as Captain, in the Black Sea during the Crimean war, 1854-55, being second in command of the Naval Brigade at the Siege of Sebastopol; **C.B.**, 1855; Rear-Admiral, 1867, and Vice-Admiral, 1867, being Commander-in-Chief in China and the East Indies, 1863-67; **K.C.B.**, 1873; Admiral, 1875, having the "good service" pension in 1876; was Aide-de-Camp to Queen Victoria; 3d class Medjidie and an officer of the Legion of Honour; *suc. to the Baronetcy*, 2 Nov. 1887, and by royal lic, 13 Feb. 1888, took the name of DUCKWORTH before that of KING, having, on 24 Nov. 1887, suc. to the estates of his maternal uncle, Sir John Thomas Buller DUCKWORTH, 2d and last Baronet [1813], of Weare House, near Exeter, Devon. He *m.* 16 Dec. 1847, at St. Peter's, Eaton square, Caroline Mary, sister of the 3d EARL OF PORTARLINGTON [I.], 2d da. of the Hon. Henry DAWSON-DAMER, of Milton Abbey, Dorset, by Eliza, da. of Edmund Joshua MORIATY, Captain, R.N. She, who was *b.* 3 Oct. 1818, *d.* in childbirth, 5 Dec. 1851, in Chesham Place. He *d.* at Weare House aforesaid, 18 Aug. 1891, aged 82.

V. 1891. SIR DUDLEY GORDON ALAN DUCKWORTH-KING, Baronet [1792], of Weare House aforesaid, *formerly*, 1851-88, Dudley Gordon Alan KING. 2d but only surv. s. and h., *b.* 28 Nov. 1851; sometime Capt. 69th Foot; Major, Welsh Regt.; Aide-de-Camp to the Viceroy of Ireland, 1879 and 1880; served in the Soudan, 1885 (medal, clasp and Khedive's star); *suc. to the Baronetcy*, 18 Aug. 1891; sometime Lieut.-Col. and Col. commanding 1st Volunteer Battalion Devon Regt. He *m.* 15 April 1890, Eva Mary, only da. of Major-Gen. Ralph GORE, Royal Horse Artillery.

STIRLING:

cr. 19 July 1792;

ex. 13 Feb. 1843.

I. 1792. "THE RT. HON. JAMES STIRLING, Lord Provost of Edinburgh,"(a) 1st s. of Alexander STIRLING, of the same city, Merchant, by Jean (*d.* 30 July 1810, aged 94), da. of James MOIR, of Sockfield, co. Perth, was *b.* about 1740; was partner in the Edinburgh banking house of "Mansfield, Ramsay, and Co.," becoming (1790-91) Lord Provost of Edinburgh, and, "having made some spirited exertions in favour of [the] Government at a very critical period,"(b) was *cr. a Baronet*, as above, 19 July 1792. He was twice again (1794-95 and 1798-99) Lord Provost, and was of Mansfield, in co. Ayr. He *m.* Alison, yst. da. of one of his partners, James MANSFIELD, of Edinburgh, Banker. He *d.* 17 Feb. 1805 in Queen square, Edinburgh, aged 65, and was *bur.* at Greyfriars, Edinburgh. M.I. Will pr. 1803. His widow *d.* 20 July 1823, aged 73, and was *bur.* with him. M.I.

II. 1805, to 1843. SIR GILBERT STIRLING, Baronet [1792], of Uppal, co. Edinburgh, 2d but only surv. s. and h., *b.* about 1779; entered, at an early age, the Coldstream Foot Guards, serving with that corps at the Helder and in Egypt, under Abercrombie, and in the Peninsula under Wellington, but retiring in 1812 with the rank of Lieut.-Col., having *suc. to the Baronetcy*, 17 Feb. 1805. He purchased the estate of Larbert, co. Stirling, where he *d.* unm. 13 Feb. 1843, aged 64, and was *bur.* in Greyfriars aforesaid, when the *Baronetcy* became *extinct*. M.I. Will pr. July 1844.

(a) See p. 281, note "a," under "KING."
(b) Playfair's *Baronetage* [1811].

SHORE:

cr. 27 Oct. 1792;

afterwards, since 1797, BARONS TEIGNMOUTH [I.].

I. 1792. "JOHN SHORE, Esq., of Heathcote, co. Derby,(a) 1st s. of Thomas SHORE, of Melton, co. Suffolk, Supercargo to the East India Company, by his 2d wife, Dorothy, da. of (—) SHEPHERD, a Capt. in that Company's service (*d.* 1759), was *b.* 5 Oct. 1751, in St. James's street; ed. at Harrow; embarked for India at the age of 17; was on the Provincial Council at Calcutta, 1773; on the Board of Revenue there, 1780-85; on the Supreme Council, 1786-89; taking an active part in settling the revenues of Bengal, Behar and Orissa, and was *cr. a Baronet*, as above, 27 Oct. 1792, on being made Governor-General of India, a post he held for five years, being raised to the peerage on his retirement therefrom. He *m.* 14 Feb. 1786, at Little Derham, near Exeter, Charlotte, only da. of James CORNISH, of Teignmouth, by Margaret, da. of the Rev. William FLOYER, Rector of Trusham, Devon. She was living when he was cr., 3 March 1797, BARON TEIGNMOUTH [I.]. In that peerage this *Baronetcy* then *merged*, and still (1905) so continues. See "PEERAGE."

GOULD:

cr. 15 Nov. 1792;

afterwards, since 1792, MORGAN;

and, since 1859, BARONS TREDEGAR.

I. 1792. "SIR CHARLES GOULD, Knt.,"(a) 1st s. of King GOULD, Deputy Judge Advocate of the Army (*d.* 1756), by Elizabeth, da. of Charles SHAW, of Besthorpe, co. Norfolk,(b) was *b.* 25 and *bap.* 29 April 1726, at St. Margaret's Westm.; ed. at Westm. School; matric. at Oxford (Ch. Ch.), 1 June 1743, aged 17; B.A., 1747; M.A., 1750; Barrister (Middle Temple), 1750; Judge Advocate-General, 1771-1806; *cr.* D.C.L. (Oxford), 8 July 1773; Chancellor of the Diocese of Salisbury, 1772; M.P. for Brecon, April 1778 to 1787, and for Breconshire, 1787-1806 (four Parls.); was *Knighted*, 5 May 1779, and *cr. a Baronet*, as above, 15 Nov. 1792. The following day, he, by royal lic., 16 Nov. 1792, took for himself and issue the name of MORGAN instead of GOULD, his wife having, by the death, 27 June 1792, of her brother, John MORGAN, of Tredegar, co. Monmouth, inherited that estate. P.C., 1802. He *m.* Feb. 1758, Jane, 1st da. of Thomas MORGAN, of Ruperra, co. Glamorgan (yr. br. of Sir William MORGAN, of Tredegar, **K.B.**), by Jane, da. and co-heir of Maynard COLCHESTER, of Westbury-on-Severn. She *d.* 14 Feb. 1797. Admon. June 1798. He *d.* 6 Dec. 1806, aged 80. Will pr. 1806.

II. 1806. SIR CHARLES MORGAN, Baronet [1792], of Tredegar aforesaid, *formerly*, 1760-92, Charles GOULD, 1st s. and h. *b.* 4 Feb. 1760; was M.P. for Brecon, 1787-96, and for Monmouthshire, 1796-1831 (nine Parls.); sometime Captain in the Coldstream Guards; Lieut.-Col. in the Army; having *suc. to the Baronetcy*, 6 Dec. 1806. He expended large sums on his estates and on agricultural improvements, erecting at Newport an extensive cattle market. He was *cr.* D.C.L. of Oxford, 13 June 1834. He *m.* in or before 1791, Mary Magdalen, da. of George STOREY, Capt. R.N. She *d.* 24 March 1808. He *d.* 5 Dec. 1846, at Tredegar House, in his 87th year. Will pr. Jan. 1847.

(a) See p. 113, note "a," under "GIDEON." The date of the Gazette notice for Shore is 2, and for Gould 30 Oct. 1792.
(b) The ancestry of this grantee is thus quaintly given in Betham's *Baronetage* [1811]. "The parents of the present Baronet were of good families, neither elevated nor depressed, and of respectable characters. His father's name was Gould, with the Christian name of King; his mother's name was Shaw."

III. 1846. SIR CHARLES MORGAN ROBINSON MORGAN, Baronet [1792], of Tredegar aforesaid, *formerly*, April to Nov. 1792, Charles Morgan Robinson GOULD, 1st s. and h., *b.* 10 April and *bap.* 15 May 1792, at St. Margaret's, Westm.; matric. at Oxford (Ch. Ch.), 8 May 1811, aged 19, being *cr.* D.C.L., 5 July 1848; was (when aged 20) M.P. for Brecknock, 1812-18, 1830-32, and 1835-47 (in all six Parls.); *suc. to the Baronetcy*, 5 Dec. 1846, and was Sheriff of Breconshire, 1850. He *m.* 6 Oct. 1827, at "St. Mary's, Marylebone," Rosamond, only da. of General Godfrey Basil MUNDY, by Sarah Brydges, da. of George Brydges (RODNEY), 1st BARON RODNEY, the celebrated Admiral. She was living when he was *cr.*, 16 April 1859, BARON TREDEGAR of Tredegar, co. Monmouth. In that peerage this *Baronetcy* then *merged*, and still (1905) so continues. See "PEERAGE."

MANNERS:

cr. 12 Jan. 1793;

afterwards, since 1821, TALMASH;

being sometime, 1821-40, *styled* LORDS HUNTINGTOWER;

and being, since 1840, EARLS OF DYSART [S.].

I. 1793. "WILLIAM MANNERS, of Hanby Hall, co. Lincoln, Esq.,"(a) as also of Buckminster, co. Leicester, 1st s. and h. of John MANNERS,(b) of the same, sometime (1754-74) M.P. for Newark (*d.* 22 Sep. 1792), by Louisa, who (long after his death) became, on 9 March 1821, *suo jure* COUNTESS OF DYSART [S.], being da. of Lionel (TALMASH, *or* TOLLEMACHE), EARL OF DYSART [S.], and 1st surv. sister and heir of line of Wilbraham, EARL OF DYSART [S.] (who *d.* s.p. 9 March 1821), was *b.* 1766; ed. at Harrow; and was *cr. a Baronet*, as above, 12 Jan. 1793, with a spec. rem., failing heirs male of his body, to his brothers, John MANNERS and Charles MANNERS, respectively. He was M.P. for Ilchester, April 1803 till void Feb. 1804, and, again, 1806-07. He became, 9 March 1821, *by courtesy*, LORD HUNTINGTOWER, on the accession of his mother to the peerage, at that date, as (*suo jure*) COUNTESS OF DYSART [S.], and by royal lic. (the next month), 6 April 1821, took the name of TALMASH instead of that of MANNERS. He *m.* 12 Jan. 1790, Catherine Rebecca, 3d and yst. da. of Frances GREY, of Lehena, co. Cork. He *d.* (before his mother), of apoplexy, at Buckminster Park, 11 and was *bur.* 28 March 1833, at Buckminster, aged about 66. Will pr. April 1833. His widow (Lady HUNTINGTOWER), who was authoress of some poems, *d.* at Leamington, co. Warwick, 21 March 1852, aged 85. Will pr. June 1852.

II. 1833. SIR LIONEL WILLIAM JOHN TALMASH, Baronet [1793], *styled* LORD HUNTINGTOWER, *formerly*, 1791-1821, MANNERS, 1st s. and h., *b.* 18 Nov. 1791; M.P. for Ilchester, Feb. 1827 to 1830; *suc. to the Baronetcy*, as also to the courtesy title of his father, 11 March 1833. He *m.* 23 Sep. 1819, his cousin, Maria Elizabeth, 1st da. of Sweeney TOONE, of Keston Lodge, Kent, by (—), da. of Francis GREY abovenamed. She was living when, by the death of his grandmother, 22 Sep. 1840, he became EARL OF DYSART [S.], in which peerage this *Baronetcy* then *merged*, and still (1905) so continues. See "PEERAGE."

(a) See p. 113, note "a," under "GIDEON." The date of the Gazette notice for Manners is Jan., that for Ford is Feb., and those for Baring and Smith-Burges 12 April 1793.
(b) This John was one of several illegit. children of Lord William Manners (2d s. of John, 2d Duke of Rutland), of whom seven, by Corbetta Smith, were *bap.* from 1733/4 to 1743 at St. James', Westm.

FORD:

cr. 22 Feb. 1793.

I. 1793. "FRANCIS FORD, of Ember Court [in Thames Ditton, co. Surrey], Esq.,"(a) as also of Lears in Barbadoes, only s. and h. of Francis FORD, of Lears aforesaid, a Member of Council of that island (*d.* in London, 1772), by Elizabeth, da. of John HOTHERSALL, of the Cliff, in Barbadoes, was *b.* 15 Nov. 1758, at Lears aforesaid; was ed. at Winchester, 1767-69; was a Member of Council of Barbadoes; acquired the estate of Ember Court abovenamed; was M.P. for Newcastle-under-Lyme, Feb. 1793 to 1796, and was *cr. a Baronet*, as above, 22 Feb. 1793. He *m.* 22 Jan. 1785, Mary, sister of Thomas, 1st VISCOUNT ANSON, 1st da. of George ANSON, *formerly* ADAMS, of Shugborough, co. Stafford, by Mary, da. of George (VENABLES-VERNON), 1st BARON VERNON OF KINDERTON. He *d.* in Barbadoes, 17 June 1801, aged 42. Will pr. 1801. His widow *d.* 20 Jan. 1837, at Cheltenham, aged 78. Will pr. May 1837.

II. 1801. SIR FRANCIS FORD, Baronet [1793], of Ember Court aforesaid, 1st s. and h., *b.* 15 Jan. 1787, *suc. to the Baronetcy*, 17 June 1801; matric. at Oxford (Ch. Ch.) 24 Oct. 1805, aged 18. He *m.* 4 Sep. 1817, Eliza, 2d da. of Henry BRADY, of Limerick, by Sarah, da. and coheir of John PEARSON, of Clondalkin, co. Dublin. He *d.*, after eight years painful illness, 13 April 1839, at Charlton Kings, near Cheltenham, aged 52. Will pr. May 1839. His widow *d.* 29 May 1875, at 6 Suffolk square, Cheltenham.

III. 1839. SIR FRANCIS JOHN FORD, Baronet [1793], of Ember Court aforesaid, 1st s. and h., *b.* 14 Aug. 1818; *suc. to the Baronetcy*, 13 April 1839; sometime Captain 20th Bombay Infantry. He *m.* 31 Oct. 1846, at St. Nicholas', Brighton, Cornelia Maria, 1st da. of Gen. Sir Ralph DARLING, **G.C.B.** (*d.* 2 April 1858, aged 82), by (—) da. of Lieut.-Col. John DUMARESQ. He *d.* abroad, 26 Nov. 1850, aged 32. Will pr. June 1851. His widow *d.* 21 May 1896, at "the Ridge," Hartfield, Tunbridge Wells, in her 78th year.

IV. 1850. SIR FRANCIS COLVILLE FORD, Baronet [1793], 2d and yst. but only surv. s. and h., *b.* 11 June 1850, and *suc. to the Baronetcy* a few months later, 26 Nov. 1850; was ed. at Harrow. He *m.* 25 March 1873, at Cathedine, co. Brecon, Frances Colville, 1st da. and coheir of his paternal uncle William FORD, **C.S.I.**, sometime in the Bengal Civil Service, by Catherine Margaret, da. of Major-Gen. John Anthony HODGSON, East India Service. He *d.* 16 Nov. 1890, aged nearly 40. His widow living 1905.

V. 1890. SIR FRANCIS CHARLES RUPERT FORD, Baronet [1793], 1st s. and h., *b.* (a twin with his brother) 5 April 1877, and *suc. to the Baronetcy*, 16 Nov. 1890; ed. at the grammar school at Sedbergh and at the universities of Paris and Bonn.

SMITH-BURGES:

cr. 4 May 1793;

ex. 24 April 1803.

I. 1793, to 1803. "JOHN SMITH-BURGES, Esq., of Eastham, co. Essex,"(a) *formerly* John SMITH, s. of John SMITH, of Lambeth, Surrey, and of London, merchant, by Mary, da. of Griffin RANSOM, of Lambeth aforesaid, was *b.* about 1734; was upwards of thirty years a Director of the East India Company; was Lieut.-Col. of the 3d Regt. of East India

(a) See p. 284, note "a," under "MANNERS."

Volunteers, was of Havering Bower, Thorpe Hall, and Eastham, co. Essex; took, by royal lic. 10 June 1790, the name of BURGES (being that of his wife's father), after that of SMITH, and was *cr. a Baronet*, as above, 4 May 1793. He *m.* in 1771, Margaret, da. and h. of Ynyr BURGES, of East Ham and Thorpe Hall aforesaid (*bur.* 31 Dec. 1793, at East Ham), by Margaret, formerly Margaret BROWNE.(a) He *d.* s.p. 24 April 1803, aged 69, and was *bur.* at East Ham, when the *Baronetcy* became *extinct*. M.I. there and at Havering, co. Essex. Will pr. 1803. His widow *m.* (as his 2d wife), 23 July 1816, at St. Geo. Han. sq. (spec. lic.) John (POULETT), 4th Earl POULETT, **K.T.**, who *d.* 14 Jan. 1819, aged 62. She *d.* at Brighton, 28 May, and was *bur.* 6 June 1828, at East Ham, aged 84. Will pr. Aug. 1838. M.I. at East Ham.

BARING:

cr. 29 May 1793;

afterwards, since 1866, BARONS NORTHBROOK OF STRATTON;

and, since 1876, EARLS OF NORTHBROOK.

I. 1793. "FRANCIS BARING, Esq., of London,"(b) 3d s. of John BARING, of Larkbere, near Exeter, cloth manufacturer, a merchant in the Virginia trade (*d.* Nov. 1748, aged 51), by Elizabeth, da. of John VOWLER, of Bellairs, near Exeter, was *b.* 18 April 1740, at Larkbere; was sent to the firm of Boehm, in London, to study commerce, and, though deaf from his youth, "at an early period distinguished himself by his accurate knowledge and dexterity in financial calculations,"(c) was "enabled by his affluence to assist the Minister in the various loans required from time to time,"(c) and soon became "the leading member of the monied interest,"(c) being, at the time of his death, "the first merchant in Europe."(d) He was a Director of the East India Company in 1779, and Chairman, 1792-93, during which period he was *cr. a Baronet*, as above, 29 May 1793. He was M.P. for Grampound, 1784-90; for Chipping Wycombe, Feb. 1794 to 1796; for Calne, 1796-1802, and for Chipping Wycombe, again, 1802-06. He, in 1790, purchased the estate of Stratton Park, in Micheldever, Hants, but resided chiefly at Beddington in Surrey, and in Hill street, London. He *m.* 12 May 1767, at Croydon, Surrey, Harriet, yst. da. and coheir of William HERRING, of Croydon (cousin to Thomas HERRING, sometime, 1747-57, Archbishop of Canterbury), by (—), da. of (—) DAWSON. She, who was *b.* in Lambeth Palace, 18 May 1750, *d.* 3 Dec. 1804, at Bath. He *d.* at Lee, co. Kent, 12 Sep. 1810, aged 70. Will pr. 1810. Both *bur.* at Micheldever.

II. 1810. SIR THOMAS BARING, Baronet [1793], of Stratton Park aforesaid, 1st s. and h.(e) *b.* 12 June 1772, and *bap.* at St. Margaret's

(a) The marriage of "Ynyr Burges, of St. Laurence Jury, and Margaret Browne, of St. Margaret, New Fish street," 15 Sep. 1747, at Gray's Inn chapel, doubtless refers to them.

(b) See p. 284, note "a," under "MANNERS."

(c) Playfair's *Baronetage* [1811].

(d) So styled by Lord Erskine. See *Dict. Nat. Biog.*, where it is (somewhat obscurely) stated that "By 1830 [*viz.*, twenty years after his death], a period of not more than seventy years [*Qy.* seventy years after the founding of the House], it was calculated that he [*Qy.* the House that he had founded] had earned nearly seven millions of money."

(e) The 2d son, Alexander Baring, was *cr.* 10 April 1835, Baron Ashburton, while the 3d son, Henry Baring, was father of (1) Edward Charles Baring, *cr.* 30 June 1885, Baron Revelstoke, and (2) of the well known diplomatist, Sir Evelyn Baring, *cr.* 20 June 1892, Baron Cromer; 25 Jan. 1899, Viscount Cromer; and 8 Aug. 1901, Earl of Cromer.

Pattens, London; was in the East India Company's service, 1790-1801; partner in the house of "Baring Brothers," London; M.P. for Wycombe (eight Parls.), 1806-32, and for Hants, June to Dec. 1832, having *suc. to the Baronetcy*, 12 Sep. 1810. He *m.* 13 Sep. 1794, at Calcutta, Mary Ursula, 1st da. of Charles SEALY, of Calcutta, Barrister. She *d.* at Stratton Park, 26 July 1846, aged 72. He, who "was best known for his fine taste in art and his magnificent collection of pictures,"(a) *d.* there 3 April 1848, aged 75.(b) Will pr. May 1848. Both *bur.* at Micheldever.

III. 1848. SIR FRANCIS THORNHILL BARING, Baronet [1793], of Stratton Park aforesaid, 1st s. and h., *b.* 20 April 1796, at Calcutta; ed. at Winchester (1808), and at Eton; matric. at Oxford (Ch. Ch.), 18 Jan. 1814, aged 18; B.A. and double First Class, 1817; M.A., 1821; admitted to Lincoln's Inn, 1817; Barrister, 1823; M.P. for Portsmouth (eleven Parls.), 1826-65; a Lord of the Treasury, 1830-34; Joint Sec. thereof, June to Nov., 1834, and April 1835 to 1839; P.C., 1839; Chancellor of the Exchequer, 1839-41; *suc. to the Baronetcy*, 3 April 1848; First Lord of the Admiralty, 1849-52. He *m.* firstly, 7 April 1825, at Portsmouth, Jane, 5th da. of the Hon. Sir George GREY, 1st Baronet [1814], **K.C.B.** (3d s. of Charles, 1st EARL GREY), by Mary, da. of Samuel WHITBREAD, of Bedwell Park, Herts. She, who was *b.* 20 Oct. 1804, *d.* 23 April 1838, in Belgrave square. He *m.* secondly, 31 March 1841, at St. Geo. Han. sq., Arabella Georgina, 2d da. of Kenneth Alexander (HOWARD), 1st EARL OF EFFINGHAM, by Charlotte, da. of Neill (PRIMROSE), 3d EARL OF ROSEBERY [S.]. She, who was *b.* 25 Jan. 1809, was living, when (six months before his death) he was *cr.*, 4 Jan. 1866, BARON NORTHBROOK OF STRATTON, co. Southampton. In that peerage this *Baronetcy* then *merged*, and still (1905) so continues, the 2d Baron (4th Baronet) being *cr.* 10 June 1876, EARL OF NORTHBROOK. See "*Peerage.*"

SAXTON:(c)

cr. 26 July 1794;

ex. 25 Jan. 1838.

I. 1794. "CHARLES SAXTON, Esq., of Circourt [in Deuchworth], co. Berks,"(d) 4th s. of Edward SAXTON,(e) of Goosey, Berks, and of Whitefriars, London, sometime Mayor of Abingdon (admon. 11 Sep. 1755), by Elizabeth, da. of Thomas BUSH, of Burcot, Oxon, was *b.* about 1730; entered the Navy, 1745; Lieut. on the East India station, being 1st Lieut. at the action with Conflans in 1759; Commander, 1760; Post-Captain, 1762, and, after many years service, Commissioner of the dockyard at Portsmouth, 1790-1808, being *cr. a Baronet*, as above, 26 July 1794. He *m.* 11 July 1771, at St. Geo. Han. sq., Mary, only da. of Jonathan BUSH, of Burcott aforesaid. He *d.* at Gloucester, 11 Nov. 1808. Will dat. 18 Oct. 1807, pr. 25 Nov. 1808. His widow *d.* in, or shortly before, 1823. Admon., as of "Ireland," Aug. 1823.

(a) *Annual Register*, 1848.

(b) He was the eldest of five brothers, three of whom died within a few weeks of each other, viz., he himself on 3 April; his br., Henry Baring, of Cromer, Norfolk, on 13 April; and his br., Lord Ashburton, on 13 May 1848.

(c) Much information about this family has kindly been supplied by W. H. Richardson (2 Lansdown place, Russell square, W.C.) who has made a study of the history of all families connected with Abingdon and its vicinity.

(d) See p. 113, note "a," under "GIDEON." The date of the Gazette notice for Saxton is 19 July 1794.

(e) This Edward was s. of Clement Saxton, or Sexton, of Abingdon, Currier, by Joan Justice, of Sutton, who were *m.* at St. Helen's, Abingdon, 13 Feb. 1699/700.

II. 1808, to 1838. SIR CHARLES SAXTON, Baronet [1794], of Circourt aforesaid, 1st s. and h., *b.* 2 Oct. 1773, at West Meon, Hants; ed. at Eton; matric. at Oxford (Univ. Coll.), 20 Oct. 1792, aged 19; B.A., 1796; M.A., 1799; admitted to Lincoln's Inn, 5 Dec. 1791; Barrister, 1800; Recorder of Abingdon, 1805-19, and, as such, presented in 1808 portraits of George III and Queen Charlotte to the Corporation; was Under Sec. to the Viceroy of Ireland, Sep. 1808 to 1812; *suc. to the Baronetcy*, 11 Nov. 1808. He was M.P. for Cashel, 1812-18, being returned also (though he declined to sit) for Malmesbury. He *d.* unm. at Caldicot House, Abingdon, 25 Jan. 1838, in his 65th year, when the *Baronetcy* became *extinct*.(a) Will pr. Feb. 1838.(b)

PASLEY:

cr. 1 Sep. 1794;

sometime, 1808-09, SABINE;

afterwards, since 1809, SABINE-PASLEY.

I. 1794. "REAR ADMIRAL THOMAS PASLEY,"(c) 5th s. of James PASLEY, of Craig, near Langholm, co. Dumfries (*d.* 13 April 1773, aged 78), by Magdalene, da. of Robert ELLIOT, of Middlemiln, co. Roxburgh, was *b.* 2 March 1734, at Craig; entered the Navy 1752; Lieut., 1757; Post Capt., 1771; Rear-Admiral, April 1794, and, as such, held a command, under Lord HOWE, in the famous battle of 1 June 1794, where he lost a leg, being, in consequence, granted an annual pension of £1,000, and *cr. a Baronet*, as above, 1 Sep. 1794, with a spec. rem., failing heirs male of his body, to those of his two daughters(d) respectively. He became Vice-Admiral, 1795; Commander-in-Chief at the Nore, 1798, and at Plymouth, 1799; Admiral, 1 Jan. 1801. He *m.* in or before 1776, Mary, da. of Thomas HEYWOOD, Chief Justice and Deemster of the Isle of Man. She *d.* 26 April 1788, at Avignon, in France. He *d.* s.p.m. 29 Nov. 1808, aged 74. Will pr. 1809.

II. 1808. SIR THOMAS SABINE, *afterwards*, from 1809, SABINE-PASLEY, Baronet [1794], grandson and h., being only s. and h. of John SABINE, Capt. in the Grenadier Guards (*d.* 11 Aug. 1805, aged 32), by Mary (*m.* 21 Aug. 1800), 1st da. and coheir of the late Baronet. He, who was *b.* 26 Dec. 1804, in Welbeck street, Marylebone, *suc. to the Baronetcy*, according to the spec. rem. in the creation of that dignity, 29 Nov. 1808, and by royal lic., 20 March

(a) John Saxton, his yr. br., said to have been "a Captain of Dragoons," is erroneously said [Debrett's *Baronetage*, 1840, and Burke's *Baronetage*, 1841] to have *suc.* him as 3d Baronet. This John, however, as also another brother, Clement, *d.* apparently, v.p. There is no mention of them in their father's will, dated 18 Oct. 1807, wherein Charles and his sister Mary are the only children named. There was a John Saxton, Major in the Army (whose will was dat. 14 May and pr. 5 June 1778), who was a br. of the 1st Baronet, and who, possibly, is confused with his nephew of the same name. The *Oxford Journal* (which paper was doubtless well informed as to the state of a family long resident in that neighbourhood) distinctly says, on recording the death of Sir Charles Saxton, "the title thus becoming extinct."

(b) The estates devolved on his nephew John Oliver, 1st s. of his sister Mary [not, as often stated, "Philadelphia Hannah"], wife (*m.* 19 June 1805) of Admiral Robert Dudley Oliver. This John Oliver sold Circourt and *d.* 13 Oct. 1887, at Oxendon, co. Northampton, aged 78, leaving issue.

(c) See p. 113, note "a," under "GIDEON." The date of the Gazette notice for Bowyer, Gardner, Pasley and Curtis, is 16 Aug. 1794; the two Vice-Admirals (Bowyer and Gardner) being named before Rear-Admiral Pasley.

(d) Of these, the yst. da., Magdalen, *m.* 27 Sep. 1798, Thomas Dowdeswell, of Pall Court, co. Worcester (who *d.* Nov. 1811), and *d.* s.p. 1841.

1809, took the name of PASLEY. He was ed. at the Royal Naval College, 1817; going to sea, 1818; Lieut., 1824; Commander, 1828; Capt., 1831; Superintendent of Pembroke Dockyard, 1849-54; served in the Black Sea during the Crimean War, 1854-56; Rear-Admiral, 1856; Crimean medal and 4th Class Medjidie, 1858; Superintendent of Devonport Dockyard, 1857-62; Vice-Admiral, 1863, and Admiral, 20 Nov. 1866; Commander-in-Chief at Portsmouth, 1866-69; **K.C.B.**, 24 May 1873. He *m.* 10 June 1826, Jane Matilda Lilly, 1st da. of the Rev. Montagu John WYNYARD, B.D., Rector of West Rounton, in Cleveland, by Jane, da. of Lieut.-Gen. Francis LASCELLES. She, who was *b.* 9 Nov. 1805,(a) *d.* 15 May 1869, at Shedfield House, Fareham, Hants. He *d.* there 13 Feb. 1884, in his 80th year.

III. 1884. SIR THOMAS EDWARD SABINE-PASLEY, Baronet [1794], grandson and h., being 1st s. and h. of Thomas Malcolm SABINE-PASLEY, Capt. R.N., by Emma Louisa, da. of John LOSH, of Trinidad, which Thomas Malcolm (who *d.* v.p. 20 Jan. 1870, aged 40) was 1st s. and h. ap. of the late Baronet. He was *b.* 12 Nov. 1863, at Windermere; ed. at Cavendish Coll., Cambridge (B.A., 1883), and at Sandhurst Military College; *suc. to the Baronetcy*, 13 Feb. 1884; served, as Capt. of the 1st Vol. Battalion of the Royal Berks Regt., in the Transvaal War, 1899-1900 (medal and three clasps), obtaining the brevet rank of Major. He *m.* 17 April 1890 at St. Mark's, Ettagh, King's County, Constance Wilmot Annie, 1st da. of Francis (HASTINGS), 14th EARL OF HUNTINGDON, by Mary Ann Wilmot, only child of Col. the Hon. John Craven WESTENRA. She was *b.* 10 July 1870.

BOWYER:

cr. 8 Sep. 1794;

merged April 1799

in the Baronetcy of BOWYER, *cr.* 25 June 1660.

I. 1794. "VICE-ADMIRAL GEORGE BOWYER,"(b) 3d s. of Sir William BOWYER, 3d Baronet [1660], of Denham Court, Bucks (*d.* 12 July 1767, aged 56), by Anne, da. (whose issue became coheir) of Sir John STONEHOUSE, 7th and 4th Baronet [1628 and 1670] of Radley, Berks, was *b.* 1739; Lieut. R.N., 1758; Commander, 1761; Post Capt., 1762, serving in North America and the West Indies, 1778-81; was M.P. for Queenborough, 1784-90; Rear-Admiral, 1 Feb. 1793, distinguishing himself, when in command of a ninety gun ship at Howe's victory off Ushant, 1 June 1794, where he sustained the loss of a leg; for this he received an annual pension of £1,000, was made Vice-Admiral, 4 July 1794, and was *cr. a Baronet*, as above, 8 Sep. 1794. He, on the death, 1 Jan. 1795, of his cousin, Penelope, BARONESS RIVERS, suc. to the estate of Radley, Berks, under the will of his maternal uncle, Sir James STONHOUSE, 9th and 6th Baronet [1628 and 1670], of Radley aforesaid. He *m.* firstly, 11 Nov. 1768, at Putney, Surrey, Margaret, widow of Sir Jacob Garrard DOWNING, 4th Baronet [1663], da. of the Rev. [—] PRICE, Curate of Barrington, co. Gloucester. She, by whom he had no issue, *d.* 18 Sep. 1778, at Mount Pleasant, Putney, and was *bur.* at Croyden, co. Cambridge. Admon. 22 Feb. 1781. He *m.* secondly, 4 June 1782, Henrietta, da. and h. of Admiral Sir Piercy BRETT, of Beckenham, Kent, by Henrietta, da. of Thomas COLBY, Clerk of the Cheque at Chatham. She was living, when (within eight months of his death) he, by the death, in April 1799, of his elder br., Sir William BOWYER, 4th Baronet [1660], *suc. to the Baronetcy* conferred 25 June 1660 on his ancestor Sir William BOWYER, of Denham, Bucks. In that more ancient dignity, this *Baronetcy* then *merged* and still, 1905, so continues.

(a) See pedigree of Wynyard in *Mis. Gen. et Her.*, New Series, vol. ii, p. 270.

(b) See p. 288, note "c," under "PASLEY."

GARDNER :

cr. 9 Sep. 1794 ;

afterwards, since 1800, BARONS GARDNER OF UTTOXETER [I.] ;

and since 1806, BARONS GARDNER OF UTTOXETER [U.K.].

I. 1794. "VICE-ADMIRAL ALAN GARDNER,"(a) 3d s. of William GARDNER, Lieut.-Col. 11th Dragoons, by Elizabeth, da. and coheir of Valentine FARRINGTON, M.D., of Preston, co. Lancaster, was *b.* 12 April 1742, at Uttoxeter; joined the Navy in 1755; Lieut. R.N., 1760; Commander, 1762; Post Capt., 1766; captured a large French merchant ship, 3 Nov. 1778; was one of the seconds in command at the battle of Grenada, 6 July 1779; Commander-in-Chief in Jamaica, 1786-89; a Lord of the Admiralty, 1790-95; M.P. for Plymouth (two Parls.), Feb. 1790 to 1796, and for Westminster (two Parls.), 1796-1806; Rear-Admiral, Feb. 1793, distinguishing himself in Howe's victory of 1 June 1794, and being, consequently, made Vice-Admiral 4 July, and *cr. a Baronet*, as above, 9 Sep. 1794. Admiral of the Blue, 14 Feb. 1799, and Commander-in-Chief on the coast of Ireland, Aug. 1800. He *m.* 20 May 1769, at Kingston, in Jamaica, Susanna Hyde, widow of Sabine or Samuel TURNER (who *d.* s.p.), da. and h. of Francis GALE, of Liguania, in St. Andrew's, Jamaica, by Susanna, da. of James HALL, of Hyde Hall in that island. She was living when he was *cr.*, 29 Dec. 1800, BARON GARDNER OF UTTOXETER in the peerage of Ireland, being, subsequently, *cr.*, 27 Nov. 1806, BARON GARDNER OF UTTOXETER, co. Stafford, in the peerage of the United Kingdom. In these peerages this *Baronetcy* then *merged* and still (1905) so continues. See *Peerage.*

CURTIS :

cr. 10 Sep. 1794.

I. 1794. "REAR ADMIRAL SIR ROGER CURTIS, Knt.,"(a) s. of Roger CURTIS, of Downton, Wilts, by Christobella, da. of (—) BLACHFORD, entered the Navy, 1762; Lieut. R.N., 1771; Commander, 1776; Post Capt. (through the influence of Lord Howe, "although one of the youngest masters and commanders in the fleet"), 1777 ;(b) co-operated for nearly eighteen months with the Governor of Gibraltar in the defence of that fortress and rendered most important service in the repulse of the floating batteries, 13 Sep. 1782, for which he was *Knighted*, 29 Nov. 1782. He was appointed Lord Howe's Flag Captain in 1790, and, as such, was present at the battles of 29 May and 1 June 1794,(c) was sent home with the despatches; made Rear-Admiral, 4 July 1794, and *cr. a Baronet*, as above, 10 Sep. 1794. Vice-Admiral, 14 Feb. 1799; Commander-in-Chief at the Cape of Good Hope, 1799-1803; Admiral of the Red, 23 Feb. 1803; one of the commissioners for revising the civil affairs of the Navy, 1805-08; Commander-in-Chief at Portsmouth, 1809; **G.C.B.**, 2 Jan. 1815. He *m.* in Dec. 1778, Sarah, yst. da. and coheir of Matthew BRADY, of Gatcombe House in the isle of Portsea. He *d.* 14 Nov. 1816. Will pr. 1816. His widow *d.* 11 April 1817. Will pr. 1817.

II. 1816. SIR LUCIUS CURTIS, Baronet [1794], of Gatcombe House aforesaid, 2d but only surv. s. and h.,(d) *b.* 3 June 1786; entered the Royal Navy, 1795; was in command of the "Magicienne" at the reduction of

(a) See p. 288, note "c," under "PASLEY."

(b) Playfair's *Baronetage* [1811].

(c) "His name was thus much mixed up with the questions that were raised as to the battle of 1 June 1794, and it was roundly asserted that the not following up the pursuit of the defeated enemy was due to his cautious counsels and his influence with the Commander-in-Chief." [*Dict. Nat. Biogr.*]

(d) The 1st son, Roger Curtis, *b.* 10 March 1780, was a Post Capt., R.N., but *d.* unm. and v.p., 12 July 1802.

the isle of Bourbon in the Indian ocean, 21 Sep. 1809; **C.B.**, 1815; *suc. to the Baronetcy*, 14 Nov. 1816. He became Rear-Admiral of the Blue, 28 June 1838; Vice-Admiral of the Blue, 15 Sep. 1849; of the Red, 5 March 1857; Admiral of the Blue, 2 July 1855; of the White, 30 July 1857; of the Red, 1 Nov. 1860, and finally Admiral of the Fleet, 11 June 1864, having two years before been made **K.C.B.**, 10 Nov. 1862. He *m.* 1 June 1811, Mary Figg, 1st da. of Moses Greetham, of East Cosham, Hants, Dep.-Judge Advocate of the Fleet. She *d.* 30 May 1841. He *d.* 14 Jan. 1869, at Portsdown Hill, in the parish of East Cosham, aged 82.

III. 1869. SIR ARTHUR COLIN CURTIS, Baronet [1794], grandson and h., being 2d but only surv. s. and h. of Roger William CURTIS, of the island of St. Vincent, by E. B., da. of (—) VICAT, which Roger (who *d.* v.p. 23 Sep. 1859), aged 42, was 3d but 1st surv. s. and sometime h. ap. of the late Baronet. He was *b.* 1858, at Trinidad, and *suc. to the Baronetcy*, 14 Jan. 1869. He *m.* 26 Oct. 1880, Sarah Jessie, 2d da. of Alexander DALRYMPLE, of the island of St. Vincent. He *d.* June 1898, aged 40, in British Columbia, being lost on a journey, in very rough weather, to Klondyke, his body being found in "Mud River." Will pr. at £2,210, the net personalty being £2,099. His widow *m.* 21 June 1900, Lieut.-Col. Robert Maziere BRADY, Royal Artillery, and was living 1905.

IV. 1898. SIR ROGER COLIN MOLYNEUX CURTIS, Baronet [1794], only s. and h., *b.* 12 Sep. 1886; *suc. to the Baronetcy*, June 1898.

SANDERSON :

cr. 6 Dec. 1794 ;

ex. 21 June 1798.

I. 1794, to 1798. "SIR JAMES SANDERSON, Knt., of London,"(a) s. of (—) SANDERSON, of York, Grocer, by (—), his wife (who *d.* 23 Jan. 1802, aged 85), was *b.* there 30 Dec. 1741, became clerk and afterwards partner to John JUDD, Hop Merchant, of London; was a member of the Drapers' Company, London; head of a banking house in Lombard street; Alderman of Bridge within, 1783-94; Sheriff of London, 1785-86, being *Knighted*, at St. James', during office, 6 Oct. 1786; Lord Mayor, 1792-93; M.P. for Malmesbury, Feb. 1792 to 1796,(b) and for Hastings, 1796 till death, being *cr. a Baronet*, as above, 6 Dec. 1794. He *m.* firstly, Elizabeth, 1st da. of [his partner] John JUDD, of Chelmsford, Essex, sometime (1787) Sheriff of that county. She *d.* 17 Aug. 1793, s.p.s. (when "Lady Mayoress"), at East hill, Wandsworth, Surrey, aged 50, and was *bur.* at St. Magnus', London. M.I. He *m.* secondly, Elizabeth, da. of Thomas SKINNER, sometime, 1794-95, Lord Mayor of London, by (—), da. of (—) WHITE. He *d.* s.p.m.,(c) at Wandsworth, 21 June, 1798, aged 56, and was *bur.* at St. Magnus' aforesaid, when the *Baronetcy* became *extinct.* M.I. Will pr. Aug. 1798. His widow, an "evangelical lady," *m.* (after "a scandalous intimacy formed about 1803")(d) 15 Aug. 1808, the notorious and profligate William HUNTINGTON, a dissenting preacher, who *d.* 1 July 1813, in his 69th year. She *d.* 9 Nov. 1817. Will pr. 1817.

(a) See p. 113, note "a," under "GIDEON." The date of the Gazette notice for Sanderson, Willoughby and Prescott, is 28 Nov. 1794.

(b) "Pitt offered him the honour of moving the Address to the King, which nothing but extreme vanity would have allowed him to undertake; however, it was his first and last speech in the House, for it was so full of bad grammar and bold assertions that it created general laughter." [*N. & Q.*, 8th S. xii, 73].

(c) His only da. and h. (by his 2d wife) *m.* in 1815, Richard Burdon, B.A., Fellow of Oriel College, Oxford, who, as a First Class man, and gainer of other honours, is celebrated in verse in *N. & Q.*, 7th S., xi, 249. He subsequently took the name of Sanderson after that of Burdon.

(d) *Dict. Nat. Biog.*, under "HUNTINGTON."

WILLOUGHBY :

cr. 8 Dec. 1794.

I. 1794. "CHRISTOPHER(a) WILLOUGHBY, Esq., of Baldon House, co. Oxford,"(b) only surv. s. and h. of Christopher WILLOUGHBY,(c) of Berwick Lodge, co. Gloucester, and of Bristol, merchant (*d.* 20 June 1773), by his 2d wife, Rebecca (living 1795, aged about 86), da. and h. of James FISHER, of Somerton, co. Somerset, was *b.* Nov. 1748, and *bap.* at St. Stephen's, Bristol; was *cr.* D.C.L. of Oxford, 27 June 1788, and *cr. a Baronet*, as above, 8 Dec. 1794. He *m.* firstly, 8 July 1776, Juliana, da. of the Rev. John BURVILL, of Bexley, Kent. She *d.* s.p.m. 30 April 1777, and was *bur.* at Baldon. He *m.* secondly, 29 Jan. 1789, Martha, da. of Morice EVANS, of St. James', Westm. He *d.* 5 April 1808, in his 60th year. Will pr. 1808. The will of his widow pr. May 1848.

II. 1808. SIR CHRISTOPHER WILLIAM WILLOUGHBY, Baronet [1794], of Baldon House aforesaid, 1st s. and h., by 2d wife, *b.* 2 Sep. 1793, at St. Marylebone; ed. at Eton; *suc. to the Baronetcy*, 5 April 1808; matric. at Oxford (Corpus College), 29 April 1811, aged 18. He *d.* unm. at that College, 24 June 1813, from the effects of a blow at cricket, in his 20th year.

III. 1813. SIR HENRY POLLARD WILLOUGHBY, Baronet [1794], of Baldon House aforesaid, br. and h., *b.* there 17 Nov. 1796; ed. at Eton; *suc. to the Baronetcy*, 24 June 1813; matric. at Oxford (Ch. Ch.), 27 Oct. 1814, aged 18; was M.P. for Yarmouth (Isle of Wight), 1831-32; for Newcastle-under-Lyne, 1832-34; and for Evesham (four Parls.), 1847 till death in 1865, rendering much good service in the matter of simplifying the national accounts. He *d.* unm., 23 March 1865, at 63 Lower Brook street, aged 68.

IV. 1865. SIR JOHN POLLARD WILLOUGHBY, Baronet [1794], of Baldon aforesaid, br. and h., *b.* there 21 April 1799; ed. at the Merchant Taylors' School, and at Haileybury College; serving a short time in the Navy; entered the Bombay Civil Service, 1817; Chief Sec. to the Bombay Government, 1835-46; Chief Judge of the Court of Sudder Dewanee, 1849-51; a member of the Bombay Council, 1846-51, retiring on an annuity; a Director of the East India Company, 1854; M.P. for Leominster, 1857 till appointed, in Oct. 1858, Member of the Indian (Home) Council, an office he held till his death ;(d) *suc. to the Baronetcy*, 23 March 1865. He *m.* firstly, 24 July 1822, Elizabeth, only da. of Col. James KENNEDY, **C.B.**, who *d.* at Benares, 25 Sep. 1859. She *d.* 14 Nov. 1852. He *m.* secondly, in 1854, Mary Elizabeth, 4th da of Thomas HAWKES, of Himley House, co. Stafford, sometime M.P. for Dudley. He *d.* 15 Sep. 1866, at his residence, Fulmer Grove, Bucks, aged 67. His widow living 1905.

V. 1866. SIR JOHN CHRISTOPHER WILLOUGHBY, Baronet [1794], of Baldon House aforesaid, only s. and h., by 2d wife, *b.* 20 Feb. 1859; *suc. to the Baronetcy*, 15 Sep. 1866; ed. at Eton, and at Trinity Coll., Cambridge; 2d Lieut. 6th Dragoons, 1880, being transferred the same year to the Horse Guards; served in the Egyptian and Nile Expeditions, 1882 and 1884 (medals and clasps); Capt., 1887; Major, 1895; was second in command of the forces of the Imperial South Africa Company, 1890-91; served in the Matabele Campaign, 1893-94 (medal); commanded British South Africa Company's troops

(a) The word "Charles" is, by mistake, put for "Christopher" in the *Annual Register* for 1794, quoting the Gazette notice.

(b) See p. 291, note "a," under "SANDERSON."

(c) This Christopher was 1st s. of Benjamin Willoughby, of St. Thomas, Bristol, merchant (*d.* June 1725, aged 54) who was 4th son (1st by his 2d wife) of John Willoughby, Mayor of Bristol, 1665.

(d) To him, Western India is chiefly indebted for the suppression of infanticide and of the dreadful practice of "Suttee."

which accompanied Dr. Jameson in the disastrous *raid* into the Transvaal in 1896, and was accordingly taken prisoner by the Boers, and, on his release, was sentenced to ten months' imprisonment, under the Foreign Enlistment Act. He was in Ladysmith during the siege, and was afterwards on the Staff of the Mafeking relief force.

Family Estates.—These, in 1883, consisted of 2,282 acres in Oxon, Gloucestershire, Surrey and Bucks, valued at £3,926 a year.

PRESCOTT :

cr. 9 Dec. 1794.

I. 1794. "GEORGE WILLIAM PRESCOTT, Esq., of Theobalds Park [in Cheshunt], co. Hertford," 1st s. and h. of George PRESCOTT, of the same, sometime (1771-72) Sheriff of Herts (who *d.* 20 April 1790, aged 78), by Mary, da. of Jacob ELTON, of Bristol, was *bap.* 17 Nov. 1748; was Sheriff of Herts, 1793-94, and was *cr. a Baronet*, as above, 9 Dec. 1794. He was also of Eardshaw Hall in the parish of Davenham, co. Chester. He *m.* 28 April 1774, Sarah, sister of Charles (LONG), BARON FARNBOROUGH OF BROMLEY HILL PLACE, da. of Beeston LONG, of Carshalton Park, Surrey, and Bishopsgate street, London, by Sarah, da. and h. of Abraham CROPP, of Richmond, Surrey. He *d.* "of a third stroke of apoplexy," 22 July 1801, aged 52. Will pr. 1801. His widow *d.* 18 July 1817. Will pr. 1817.

II. 1801. SIR GEORGE BEESTON PRESCOTT, Baronet [1794], of Theobalds Park aforesaid, 1st s. and h., *b.* 11 Feb. 1775; *suc. to the Baronetcy*, 22 July 1801. He *m.* firstly, 20 Aug. 1799, Catherine Creighton, 2d da. of Sir Thomas MILLS, Governor of Quebec. She *d.* 6 April 1832, at Paris. He *m.* secondly, July 1833, Flore Theodore Virginie, da. of BARON MOUCHERON. He *d.* abroad 25 Oct. 1840, aged 65. Will pr. Dec. 1840. His widow *d.* s.p., 1 Sep. 1841.

III. 1840. SIR GEORGE WILLIAM PRESCOTT, Baronet [1794], 1st s. and h. by 1st wife, *b.* 14 Nov. 1800; *suc. to the Baronetcy*, 25 Oct. 1840. He *m.* firstly, 10 July 1827, Emily, da. of Col. SYMES, of Ballyarthur, co. Wicklow. She *d.* s.p., 3 Jan. 1829. He *m.* secondly, 26 July 1845, Eliza, yst. da. of Henry HILLIAR. He *d.* at Caen, in Normandy, 27 April 1850, aged 49. His widow, who, in or before 1868, was wife of Montague DETTMAR, *d.* at 17 Grafton street, 20 Feb. 1882, aged 57.

IV. 1850. SIR GEORGE RENDLESHAM PRESCOTT, Baronet [1794], 1st s. and h. by 2d wife, *b.* in London, 27 Sep. 1846, and *suc. to the Baronetcy*, 27 April 1850; ed. at Eton; sometime, 1864-69, Sub-Lieut. 2d Life Guards; was of Isenhurst, near Mayfield, Sussex; Sheriff of Sussex, 1882-83. He *m.* 24 July 1872, at Christ Church, Lancaster Gate, Paddington, Louise Franklin, da. of Lionel LAWSON, of Brook street, Hanover square. He *d.* 29 July 1894, aged 47, at 9 Clarges street, Piccadilly, and was *bur.* at Kensal Green cemetery. Will pr. 19 Nov. 1894, at £65,104 gross, and £46,907 net.

V. 1894. SIR GEORGE LIONEL LAWSON BAGOT PRESCOTT, Baronet [1794], 1st s. and h., *b.* in Clarges street, 5 Oct. 1875; *suc. to the Baronetcy*, 29 July 1894; Lieut. 2d Life Guards.

Family Estates.—These, in 1883, consisted of 2,121 acres in Sussex, 1,113 in Kent, 511 in Flintshire, 112 in Herts, 105 in Bucks, 83 in Oxon, and 33 in Middlesex. *Total.*—4,078 acres, worth £5,465 a year. *Principal Seat.*—Isenhurst, near Hawkhurst.

(a) See p. 291, note "a," under "SANDERSON."

STEPHENS:

cr. 13 March 1795;

ex. 20 Nov. 1809.

I. 1795, to 1809. "PHILIP STEPHENS, Esq.,"(a) 3d but last surv. s. of the Rev. Nathaniel STEPHENS,(b) Rector of Alphamstone, Essex (*d.* 1730, aged 50), by Ellis, da. of Philip DEANE, of Harwich, was *b.* 11 Oct. 1723, at Bures, co. Essex; suc. his eldest br., Tyringham STEPHENS, a Commissioner of the Victualling Office (who *d.* unm., aged 55) in 1768; was of St. Faith's and Horsford, co. Norfolk, and of Fulham, co. Midx.; M.P. for Liskeard (two Parls.). Dec. 1759 to 1768, and for Sandwich (seven Parls.), 1768-1806; 2d Sec. to the Admiralty, 1759-63; 1st Sec. 1763, and was *cr. a Baronet*, as above, 13 March 1795, with a spec. rem., failing heirs male of his body, "to his nephew, Stephens HOWE, Esq.,"(a) being at the same time made one of the Lords of the Admiralty, a post he held till 1806. He *d.* unm. 20 and was *bur.* 28 Nov. 1809, at Fulham, aged 86, when the *Baronetcy* became *extinct*.(c) Will pr. 1810.(d)

CHETWYND:

cr. 1 May 1795.

I. 1795. "SIR GEORGE CHETWYND, of Brocton Hall [in Bastwick], co. Stafford, Knt.,"(a) 2d s. of William CHETWYND, of the same, by Martha, relict of Thomas HESKETH, da. of James ST. AMAND, of St. Paul's, Covent Garden, was *b.* 26 July 1739; suc. his eldest br. James CHETWYND, 1 March 1774, was Clerk to the Privy Council (an office he held above sixty years), was *Knighted* 19 Jan. 1787, and was *cr. a Baronet*, as above, 1 May 1795. He inherited the estate of Grendon Hall, co. Warwick, on the death s.p. of Lady Robert BERTIE, 17 April 1798, under the will of William Henry CHETWYND. He *m.* 5 June 1783, Jane, da. of Richard BANTIN, of Little Faringdon, Berks. He *d.* 24 March 1824, in his 85th year. Will pr. 1824. His widow *d.* 17 July 1841, aged 83. Will pr. Aug. 1843.

II. 1824. SIR GEORGE CHETWYND, Baronet [1795], of Grendon Hall(e) aforesaid, 1st s. and h., *b.* 28 July 1783, at Brocton Hall aforesaid; matric. at Oxford (Bras. Coll.), 31 May 1802, aged 18; Barrister (Lincoln's Inn), 1813; M.P. for Stafford, 1820-26; *suc. to the Baronetcy*, 24 March 1824;

(a) See p. 113, note "a," under "GIDEON." The date of the Gazette notice for Stephens is 4 March, for Chetwynd, Dryden, Salusbury, Gamon, Darell, Neave, Hawley, Pollen and Wentworth, is 11 April; for Murray, A'Court, Vanden-Bempdé-Johnstone, Hamlyn and Poore is 23 June, and for Bland-Burges, 24 Oct. 1795.

(b) An elaborate account of the family of Stephens is in Betham's *Baronetage* [1804].

(c) Lieut.-Col. Stephens Howe, his nephew, sometime M.P. for Yarmouth, who was in remainder to the Baronetcy (5th and yst. s. of his sister, Millicent, by William Howe, of Mislethorne, co. Essex), *d.* unm. at Port Royal in Jamaica, 9 July 1796, aged 37.

(d) His estates devolved on Thomas (Jones), 6th Viscount Ranelagh [I.], the husband of his illegit. da., Caroline Elizabeth Stevens, who *m.* 21 Aug. 1804, at Fulham, but who *d.*, v.p., and s.p.s. in childbed, 17 June 1805, at her father's house in the Admiralty, Whitehall.

(e) His father's estate of Brocton Hall was inherited by the *second* son William Faulkener Chetwynd, Major in the Army, who *d.* 25 April 1873, aged 85, leaving issue.

Sheriff of Warwickshire, 1828-29. He *m.* 30 Aug. 1804, Hannah Maria, 1st da. and coheir of John SPARROW, of Bishton Hall, co. Stafford, by Elizabeth, da. and coheir of Ralph MORETON. He *d.* 24 May 1850, at Grendon Hall, aged 66.(a) Will pr. July 1850. His widow *d.* 7 June 1860, at Bishton Hall aforesaid, aged 80.

III. 1850. SIR GEORGE CHETWYND, Baronet [1795], of Grendon Hall aforesaid, 1st s. and h., *b.* there 6 Sep. 1809; matric. at Oxford (Ch. Ch.), 27 Nov. 1827, aged 17; B.A., 1830; *suc. to the Baronetcy*, 24 May 1850; sometime Captain Warwickshire Yeomanry Cavalry, resigning in 1861. He *m.* 2 Aug. 1843, at St. Geo. Han. sq., Charlotte Augusta, 1st da. of Arthur Blundell Sandys Trumbull (HILL), 3d MARQUESS OF DOWNSHIRE [I.], by Maria, da. of Other Hickman (WINDSOR), 5th EARL OF PLYMOUTH. She, who was *b.* 30 June 1815, *d.* at Grendon Hall, 24 Nov. 1861, aged 46, from injuries received by a fall from her horse. He *d.* there 24 March 1869, aged 59.

IV. 1869. SIR GEORGE CHETWYND, Baronet [1795], of Grendon Hall aforesaid, 2d but 1st surv. s. and h., *b.* 31 May 1849, in Hanover square; matric. at Oxford (Ch. Ch.), 24 Jan. 1868, aged 18; *suc. to the Baronetcy*, 24 March 1869; Sheriff of Warwickshire, 1870. He *m.* 9 June 1870, at St. James', Westm., Florence Cecilia, DOW. MARCHIONESS OF HASTINGS, 3d and yst. da. of Henry (PAGET), 2d MARQUESS OF ANGLESEY, by his 2d wife Henrietta Maria, da. of the Rt. Hon. Sir Charles BAGOT, G.C.B. She was *b.* Aug. 1842.

Family Estates.—These, in 1883, consisted of 4,139 acres in Warwickshire (worth £8,699 a year), 1,066 in Monmouthshire, 833 in Staffordshire, 479 in Leicestershire, and 109 in Cheshire. *Total.*—6,626 acres, worth £12,445 a year. *Principal Seat.*—Grendon Hall, near Atherstone, co. Warwick.

DRYDEN:

cr. 2 May 1795;

merged 24 March 1874;

into the Baronetcy of TURNER, *cr.* 24 Aug. 1733.

I. 1795. "SIR JOHN DRYDEN, of Canons Ashby, co. Northampton, Knt.,"(b) *formerly* John TURNER, 6th and yst. s. of Sir Edward TURNER, 2d Baronet [1733], of Ambrosden, Oxon, by Cassandra, da. of William LEIGH, of Adlesthrop, co. Gloucester, was *bap.* 11 Nov. 1752, at Ambrosden; was ed. at Harrow, made the grand tour, and soon after entered the 1st Reg. of Foot Guards; inherited above £50,000,(c) and, having acquired the estate of Canons Ashby, on the death, 7 May 1791, of Dame Elizabeth DRYDEN, widow of Sir John DRYDEN, 7th and last Baronet [1619], of Canons Ashby aforesaid (who was uncle to his wife) took the name of DRYDEN, instead of that of TURNER; was Sheriff of Northamptonshire, 1793-94; *Knighted* 15 March 1793; raised a troop of Yeomen Cavalry, and was *cr. a Baronet*, as above, 2 May 1795. He *m.* 14 May 1781, at

(a) He was a collector of works of art and *virtu*. A catalogue of his provincial coins and tokens, by Thomas Sharp of Coventry, was printed 1834.

(b) See p. 294, note "a," under "STEPHENS."

(c) Playfair's *Baronetage* [1811], as also Betham's *Baronetage* [1804], where it is stated that "being in the heyday of youth he became one of the most fashionable young men about town; in short, he dissipated a large sum of money, in a manner not sanctioned by the approbation of his maturer judgment and riper years. Indeed, to be candid, he contracted debts, which the short possession of a large fortune did not enable him entirely to liquidate."

St. Marylebone, Elizabeth, 1st da. and coheir of Bevill DRYDEN, of Ore, near Newbury, Berks, by Mary, da. of (—) DUBBER, of Cirencester, co. Gloucester, which Bevill was yr. br. to Sir John DRYDEN, 7th and last Baronet [1619] abovenamed. He *d.* of asthma, 14 Aug. 1797, at Canons Ashby, and was *bur.* there, aged 44. Admon. May 1797. His widow, who was *b.* 18 July 1753, *m.* Godfrey SCHOLEY, of London, who *d.* 4 Jan. 1819. She, who after his death resumed the surname of DRYDEN, *d.* 5 Nov. 1824, at Margate, Kent. Will pr. 1824.

II. 1797. SIR JOHN EDMUND DRYDEN, Baronet [1795], of Canons Ashby aforesaid, 1st s. and h., *b.* 17 Sep. 1782; *suc. to the Baronetcy*, 14 Aug. 1797. He *d.* unm. 29 Sep. 1818, aged 36. Admon. Oct. 1818.

III. 1818. SIR HENRY DRYDEN, Baronet [1795], of Canons Ashby aforesaid, br. and h., *b.* 7 July 1787, in Berkeley square; matric. at Oxford (Trin. Coll.), 13 Nov. 1805, aged 18; B.A., 1809; M.A., 1812; *suc. to the Baronetcy*, 29 Sep. 1818; was in Holy Orders; Vicar of Ambrosden, Oxon (1821), and Vicar of Leeke Wootton, co. Warwick (1824). He *m.* 31 July 1817, Elizabeth, 3d da. of the Rev. Julius HUTCHINSON, of Woodhall Park, Herts, and of Owthorpe, Notts, Vicar of Layer Breton, Essex, by Frances, his wife. He *d.* 17 Nov. 1837, at Leeke Wootton, aged 50. Will pr. Feb. 1838. His widow *d.* 22 Nov. 1851, at Canons Ashby. Will pr. Dec. 1851.

IV. 1837. SIR HENRY EDWARD LEIGH DRYDEN, Baronet [1795], of Canons Ashby aforesaid, 1st s. and h., *b.* 17 Aug. 1818, at Adlesthrop, co. Gloucester; *suc. to the Baronetcy* [1795] on the death of his father, 17 Nov. 1837; ed. at Shrewsbury School (under Dr. Butler), and at Trin. Coll., Cambridge; M.A. 1839, and M.A. (*ad eundem*) of Oxford, 1840; Sheriff of Northamptonshire, 1844. He *m.* 24 Jan. 1865, at St. Peter's, Brackley, co. Northampton, Frances, 1st da. of the Rev. Robert TREDCROFT, Rector of Tangmere, Sussex, and Preb. of Chichester. She was living when, on the death 24 March 1874, of his cousin Sir Edward Henry PAGE-TURNER, 6th Baronet [1733], he suc. to the Baronetcy conferred 24 Aug. 1733, on his ancestor (in the male line) Edward TURNER, of Ambrosden, co. Oxford. In that more ancient Baronetcy this *Baronetcy* then *merged*, and still (1095) so continues, the holders continuing to use the surname of DRYDEN (possessing the estates of that family only) instead of that of TURNER.

SALUSBURY:

cr. 4 May 1795.

ex. 30 March 1868.

I. 1795. "ROBERT SALUSBURY, of Llanwern, co. Monmouth, Esq.,"(a) 1st s. and h. of Robert SALUSBURY, of Cotton Hall, co. Denbigh (*d.* 1776), by Gwendolen, da. and h. of Ellis DAVIES, of Nantyrerwheid, co. Merioneth, was *b.* 10 Sep. 1756; Sheriff of Monmouthshire, 1786-87; M.P. for that county, Aug. 1792 to 1796, and for Brecon (four Parls.), Nov. 1796 to 1812, and was *cr. a Baronet*, as above, 4 May 1795. He *m.* 16 May 1780, Catharine, da. and finally coheir of Charles VAN, of Llanwern aforesaid, by whom he acquired that estate. He *d.* 17 Nov. 1817, at Canterbury, in his 62d year. Will pr. July 1819. His widow *d.* 21 July 1836.

II. 1817. SIR THOMAS ROBERT SALUSBURY, Baronet [1795], of Llanwern aforesaid, 2d but 1st surv. s. and h., *b.* 18 May 1783; *suc. to the Baronetcy*, 17 Nov. 1817. He *m.* 1 Oct. 1833, Elizabeth Mary, only surv. child of his paternal uncle the Rev. Lynch BURROUGHS, *formerly* SALUSBURY, of Offley Place, Herts, by Jane, da. of William OFFLEY. He *d.* s.p. 14 Feb. 1835, aged 51. Will pr. April 1835. His wife survived him.

(a) See p. 294, note "a," under "STEPHENS."

III. 1835, to 1868. SIR CHARLES JOHN SALUSBURY, Baronet [1795], of Llanwern aforesaid, br. and h., *b.* 7 Feb. 1792, at Llanwern House; ed. at Trin. Hall, Cambridge; LL.B. 1815; in Holy Orders; Rector of Llanwern 1816 to death; *suc. to the Baronetcy*, 14 Feb. 1835. He *d.* unm. 30 March 1868, at Llanwern, aged 76, when the *Baronetcy* became *extinct*.

GAMON:

cr. 11 May 1795;

afterwards, since 1818, GRACE.

I. 1795. "RICHARD GAMON, of Minchenden House, co. Middlesex, Esq.,(a) only s. and h., of Richard GAMON,(b) of Datchworthbury, Herts, and of Grosvenor square (*d.* 1787, aged about 70), by Elizabeth, da. and h. of John GRACE, of the Grange, in Queen's County, was *b.* 14 Aug. 1748; was sometime an officer in the 1st Reg. of Foot Guards; was M.P. for Winchester (five Parls.), 1784-1812, in which city he chiefly resided, and was *cr. a Baronet*, as above, 11 May 1795, with a spec. rem., failing heirs male of his body, "to Richard GRACE, of Rahin, in the Queen's County, Esq."(a) He *m.* firstly, Grace, da. and coheir of Col. James JEFFREYS, or JEFFERIES, by Elizabeth (relict of Lord Augustus FITZROY, and mother of the 3d DUKE OF GRAFTON), da. of Col. William COSBY, Governor of New York. She, by whom he had no issue, *d.* 10 Aug. 1794. He *m.* secondly, 2 July 1796, Amelia, widow of Thomas Ivie COOKE, Major 20th Light Dragoons (who *d.* in Jamaica, 22 Oct. 1793), 2d da. of John (MURRAY), 3d DUKE OF ATHOLL [S.], by Charlotte, *suo jure* BARONESS STRANGE, da. and h. of James (MURRAY), 2d DUKE OF ATHOLL [S.] She, who was *b.* 3 and *bap.* 10 July 1763, at Dunkeld, *d.* at Farnham, Surrey (on her journey to Winchester), 19 Oct. 1806. He *d.* s.p.m.,(c) at Winchester, 8 April 1818, in his 70th year.(d) Will pr. 1818.

II. 1818. SIR WILLIAM GRACE,(e) Baronet [1795], of Rahin, and Boley, in Queen's County, cousin of the above, being 1st s. and h. of Richard GRACE, of the same, sometime (1790-97), M.P. [I.] for Baltimore, by Jane, da. of the Hon. John EVANS, of Bulgaden Hall, co. Limerick (yr. s. of George, 1st BARON CARBERY [I.]), which Richard (who was named in the spec. rem. of the Baronetcy, and who *d.* before the grantee 9 Jan. 1801), was 1st s. of William GRACE, of St. Germain's, in France (*d.* 23 Nov. 1777), the 2d s. of Michael GRACE, of Gracefield, otherwise Shanganagh, Queen's County (*d.* 19 Feb. 1760, aged 78), the 1st s. of Oliver GRACE, of Shanganagh aforesaid, Chief Remembrancer of the Exchequer [I.], who *d.* 8 June 1708, and who was elder br. of John GRACE(a) abovenamed, the maternal grandfather of the grantee. He

(a) See p. 294, note "a," under "STEPHENS."

(b) See Playfair's *Baronetage* [1811] for an account of the family of Gamon.

(c) Charlotte Amelia, his only da. (by his 2d wife), *b.* 12 April 1797, *d.* unm. 16 Nov. 1835.

(d) He was brother in law to three Dukes, viz., to the Duke of Grafton, br. (of the half blood) to his 1st wife; to the Duke of Atholl [S.], br. to his 2d wife, and to James (Brydges) 3d Duke of Chandos, who had *m.* (21 June 1777) his sister Anna Eliza (Gamon), by whom she was mother of the Duchess of Buckingham and Chandos.

(e) "This family was supposed to be derived from Raymond *Le Gros*, who *m.* Basilia, the sister of Strongbow, and is asserted so to be in Lodge's *Peerage of Ireland* (edit. 1754), and in *The Memoirs of the Family of Grace*, by Sheffield Grace, Esq., F.S.A. [London, 1823]. The true descent of the family has been demonstrated by Richard Langrishe, F.R.S.A.I., in papers on *The Origin of the Family of Grace of Courtstown, co. Kilkenny, and of the title to the Tullaroan estate*, in vols. xxx, 319, and xxxii, 64, of the *Journal of the Royal Society of Antiquaries of Ireland*." [*Ex inform.*, G. D. Burtchaell].

was ed. as a Fellow Commoner at Trin. Coll., Dublin. He *suc. to the Baronetcy*, 8 April 1818, under the spec. rem. in the creation of that dignity. He *m.* in or before 1817, Mary, da. of Richard DUNNE, of Carlow. He *d.* 27 Jan. 1841. Will p. [I.] 1841.

III. 1841. SIR WILLIAM GRACE, Baronet [1795], of Boley aforesaid, 1st s. and h., *b.* 6 Nov. 1817; *suc. to the Baronetcy*, 27 Jan. 1841. He *d.* unm. 23 March 1887, aged 69.

IV. 1887. SIR PERCY RAYMOND GRACE, Baronet [1795], of Boley aforesaid, br. and h. male, *b.* 11 Aug. 1831; ed. at Trin. Coll., Dublin; B.A., 1853; admitted to King's Inn, Hilary 1850; Barrister, Trin. Term 1854; Major in the Queen's County Royal Rifles; *suc. to the Baronetcy*, 23 March 1887; Sheriff of co. Dublin, 1888; Sheriff of Queen's County, 1892; a Commissioner of Nat. Education, 1888; of Irish Lights, 1889, and of the Charitable Board of Bequests, 1900. He *m.* 24 June 1874, Margaret, 4th da. of Valentine O'Brien O'CONNOR, of Rockfield, co. Dublin, and Ballykisteen, co. Tipperary, by Monica, da. of William ERRINGTON, of High Warden, Northumberland. He *d.* at Boley, 16 Aug. 1903, aged 72. His widow living 1905.

V. 1903. SIR VALENTINE RAYMOND GRACE, Baronet [1795], of Bolan aforesaid, only s. and h., *b.* 11 Jan. 1877; Capt. 4th Batt. Leinster Regiment (Militia); *suc. to the Baronetcy*, 16 Aug. 1903; Chairman of the Dublin Distillers' Company. He *m.* 21 July 1900, at the Roman Catholic Church of St. Peter and St. Edward, Palace street, Westm., Mildred Mary Eustace, 2d da. of Major John Eustace JAMESON, of Tancy House, co. Dublin, sometime (from 1795) M.P. for West Clare, by Mary Elizabeth, da. of John Bond CABBELL, of Cromer Hall, Norfolk.

Family Estates.—These, in 1878, consisted of 2,085 acres in Queen's County, worth £1,446 a year.

DARELL:

cr. 12 May 1795.

I. 1795. "LIONEL DARELL, of Richmond Hill, in the county of Surrey, Esq.,"([a]) 1st s. of Lionel DARELL, of Bedford Row, St. Andrew's, Holborn (*d.* 19 Oct. 1783, aged about 70), by Honoria, da. of Humphrey HARDWICK, Merchant and Vice-Consul at Lisbon, was *b.* at Lisbon, 25 Sep. 1742; was a Director and sometime Chairman of the East India Company, and Colonel of the 1st Regiment of "Loyal East India Volunteers;" was M.P. for Lyme Regis (three Parls.), 1780-84, and for Hedon, 1784-1802, and was *cr. a Baronet*, as above, 12 May 1795. He *m.* 30 July 1766, at St. George the Martyr, Queen square, Midx., Isabella, da. of Timothy TULLIE, of Queen square aforesaid, a Director of the East India Company. She *d.* 6 and was *bur.* 15 May 1800. He *d.* 30 Oct. 1803, after a few days' illness, with which he was seized while presiding at the East India House, aged 61. Will pr. 1803.

II. 1803. SIR HARRY VERELST DARELL, Baronet [1795], of Richmond Hill aforesaid, 1st and only surv. s. and h., *b.* 25 Dec. 1768, at Calcutta; was senior Merchant in the Bengal establishment, and Commercial Resident at Etawah and Calpee; *suc. to the Baronetcy*, 30 Oct. 1803. He *m.* 2 June 1809, Amelia Mary Anne, only da. of William BEECHER, of Howbury, Berks. He *d.* at Calpee, 13 April 1828, in his 60th year. Will pr. Oct. 1829. His widow *d.* 5 Jan. 1878, in her 88th year, at 9 Queen's Gate terrace.

([a]) See p. 294, note "a," under "STEPHENS."

III. 1828. SIR HARRY FRANCIS COLVILLE DARELL, Baronet [1795], 1st s. and h., *b.* 17 Nov. 1814, at Lucknow; *suc. to the Baronetcy*, 13 April 1828; was Major, 7th Dragoon Guards, 1847, and Lieut.-Col. (by brevet), 1848. He *d.* unm. 6 Jan. 1853, aged 38. Will pr. May 1853.

IV. 1853. SIR WILLIAM LIONEL DARELL, Baronet [1795], of Fretherne Court, co. Gloucester, br. and h., *b.* 5 Feb. 1817, in Brook street; matric. at Oxford (Ch. Ch.), 4 June 1835, aged 18; B.A., 1839; M.A., 1842; in Holy Orders; Rector of Fretherne, co. Gloucester, 1844-78; *suc. to the Baronetcy*, 6 Jan. 1853. He *m.* firstly, 29 May 1840, Mary, 1st da. of Sir Francis FORD, 2d Baronet [1793], by Eliza, da. of Henry BRADY, of Limerick. She *d.* s.p. 9 March 1842. He *m.* secondly, 18 April 1843, Harriet Mary, sister and h. of Sir Matthew Edward TIERNEY, 3d Baronet [1834], only da. of Sir Edward TIERNEY, 2d Baronet [1834], by Anna Maria, da. of Henry JONES. She *d.* 27 June 1873, at Frimley, co. Surrey. He *m.* thirdly, 7 Jan. 1880, at St. Geo. Han. sq., Fanny Julia, widow of T. Hyde CLARKE, of the Firs, Frimley, Surrey, and of 7 Upper Grosvenor street. He *d.* 1 June 1883, aged 66, at 22 Upper Brook street. Will pr. 14 July 1883, over £42,000. His widow *d.* 17 Jan. 1894, aged 63.

V. 1883. SIR LIONEL EDWARD DARELL, Baronet [1795], of Fretherne Court aforesaid, 1st s. and h. by 2d wife, *b.* 6 Sep. 1845; matric. at Oxford (Ch. Ch.), 18 May 1864, aged 18; sometime Captain, Gloucester Yeomanry Cavalry; *suc. to the Baronetcy*, 1 June 1883; Sheriff of Gloucestershire, 1887. He *m.* 26 June 1870, Helen Frances, only child of Edward MARSLAND, of Henbury Park, co. Chester.

Family Estates.—These, in 1883, consisted of 2,890 acres in Gloucestershire, Cheshire, Derbyshire, and in co. Cork, worth (in all) £3,868 a year.

NEAVE:

cr. 13 May 1795.

I. 1795. "RICHARD NEAVE, of Dagnam Park [near Romford], co. Essex, Esq.,"([a]) 1st s. of James NEAVE, of Walthamstow, Essex, and of London, Merchant (*b.* 7 Aug. 1700), by Susanna, da. of Thomas TRUMAN, Receiver-Gen. for Notts, was *b.* 22 Nov. 1731; was a merchant of Broad street, London; Director and sometime, 1750, Gov. of the Bank of England; one of the Commissioners of Public Accounts; Chairman of the London Dock Company, the West India Merchants and Ramsgate Harbour Trust; a Director of the Hudson Bay Company; and, having purchased (in 1792) the estate of Dagnam, was chosen Sheriff of Essex, 1794, but did not act, and was *cr. a Baronet*, as above, 13 May 1795; F.S.A., and F.R.S. He *m.* 14 Feb. 1761, at St. Giles'-in-the-Fields, Frances, 4th surv. da. of John BRISTOW,([b]) of Quidenham Hall, Norfolk, Governor of the South Sea Company (*d.* 1770 at Lisbon), by Anna Judith, da. of Paul FOISSIN. He *d.* 28 Jan., and was *bur.* 9 Feb. 1814 at Romford, aged 82, whence his body was removed to South Weald, Essex. Will pr. 1814. His widow *d.* 18 Jan. 1830, in Albemarle street. Will pr. Feb. 1830.

II. 1814. SIR THOMAS NEAVE, Baronet [1795], of Dagnam Park aforesaid, and formerly of Hampstead, Midx., 1st s. and h., *b.* 11 Nov. 1761, at St. Benet's Fink, London; *suc. to the Baronetcy*, 28 Jan. 1814; Sheriff of Essex, 1820-21; F.S.A., and F.R.S. He *m.* 13 June 1791, at Yateley, Hants, Frances Carolina, 4th da. of Rev. the Hon. William DIGBY, D.D., Dean of Durham (br. of Henry, 1st EARL DIGBY), by Charlotte, da. of Joseph COX. She, who was *b.* 22 Aug. 1772, at Coleshill, co. Warwick, *d.* 24 April 1835. He *d.* 11 April 1848, at Dagnam Park, aged 86.

([a]) See p. 294, note "a," under "STEPHENS."

([b]) See an account of the Bristow family in Betham's *Baronetage* (1804), under "NEAVE."

III. 1848. SIR RICHARD DIGBY NEAVE, Baronet [1795], of Dagnam Park aforesaid, 1st s. and h., *b.* 9 Dec. 1793, at St. Botolph's, Bishopsgate, London; matric. at Oxford (Ch. Ch.), 28 Oct. 1812, aged 18; B.A. (St. Mary's Hall), 1815; admitted to Lincoln's Inn, 1814; *suc. to the Baronetcy*, 11 April 1848. He *m.* 7 Aug. 1827, Mary, da. of James Everard (ARUNDELL), 9th BARON ARUNDELL OF WARDOUR, by his 2d wife, Mary, da. of Robert Burnet JONES. She, who was *b.* 28 Oct. 1809, *d.* 30 Aug. 1849, at Dagnam Park. He *d* 10 March 1868, in his 75th year, at 78 Eccleston square, Pimlico.

IV. 1868. SIR ARUNDELL NEAVE, Baronet [1795], of Dagnam Park aforesaid, 1st s. and h., *b.* 5 June 1829, in Dover street; ed. at Eton; entered the Army, 1853, and was (1857) Capt. 3d Dragoon Guards; *suc. to the Baronetcy*, 10 March 1868. He *m.* 26 Sep. 1871, at St. James', Westm., Gwyn Gertrude, yst. da. of William Lewis (HUGHES), 1st BARON DINORBEN, by his 2d wife, Gertrude, da. of Grice SMYTH, of Ballinatray, co. Waterford. He *d.* 21 Sep. 1877 at Llysdulas, co. Anglesey, aged 48. His widow, who was *b.* 20 May 1845, living 1905.

V. 1877. SIR THOMAS LEWIS HUGHES NEAVE, Baronet [1795], of Dagnam Park and Llsydulas aforesaid, 1st s. and h., *b.* 26 Jan. 1874, at Grosvenor place; *suc. to the Baronetcy*, 21 Sep. 1877; ed. at Eton and at Trin. Hall, Cambridge; Major Royal Anglesey Engineer Militia.

HAWLEY:

cr. 14 May 1795.

I. 1795. "HENRY HAWLEY, of Leybourne Grange [near Maidstone], co. Kent, Esq.,"([a]) only s. and h. of James HAWLEY, of the same, M.D. and F.R.S. (who purchased that estate in 1776, and *d.* 22 Dec. 1777, aged 71), by Elizabeth, da. of Joseph BANKS, of Revesby Abbey, co. Lincoln, was *b.* 12 Nov. 1745, at St. George's, Bloomsbury; matric. at Oxford (Oriel Coll.), 17 March 1763, aged 17; B.A., 1766; Barrister (Inner Temple), 1769, was Sheriff of Kent, 1783-84, and was *cr. a Baronet*, as above, 14 May 1795. He *m.* firstly, 10 Aug. 1770, Dorothy, da. and h. of John ASHWOOD, of Madeley, Salop. She *d.* 4 Dec. 1783. He *m.* secondly, 5 Sep. 1785, Anne, 1st da. of William HUMPHREY, of Llewyn, co. Montgomery. He *d.* 20 Jan. 1826, aged 80. Will pr. Feb. 1826. His widow *d.* 7 Nov. 1829, aged 72. Will pr. Nov. 1829.

II. 1826. SIR HENRY HAWLEY, Baronet [1795], of Leybourne Grange aforesaid, 1st s. and h., being only s. by 1st wife, *b.* 20 Oct. 1776, in Great Russell street, Bloomsbury; matric. at Oxford (Oriel Coll.), 25 June 1794, aged 17; *suc. to the Baronetcy*, 20 Jan. 1826. He *m.* 29 Nov. 1806, Catherine Elizabeth, 2d da. of Sir John Gregory SHAW, 5th Baronet [1665], by Theodosia Margaret, da. of John (MONSON), 2d BARON MONSON OF BURTON. He *d.* 29 March 1831, in London, aged 54. Will pr. April 1831. His widow *d.* 15 March 1862, in Park street, Regent's park, aged 75.

III. 1831. SIR JOSEPH HENRY HAWLEY, Baronet [1795], of Leybourne Grange aforesaid, 1st s. and h., *b.* 27 Oct. 1814, at St. Marylebone; matric. at Oxford (Oriel Coll.), 10 March 1831, aged 17, and *suc. to the Baronetcy* a few days later, 29 March 1831; Sheriff of Kent, 1844. He *m.* 18 June 1839, at St. Geo. Han. sq., Sarah Diana, 3d da. of Gen. Sir John Gustavus CROSBIE, G.C.H. and K.C.B., of Watergate, Sussex, by Frances Page, da. and h. of George THOMAS, *formerly* WHYTE, of Westergate and Yapton in that county. He *d.* s.p.m. 20 April 1875, at 34 Eaton place, in his 61st year. His widow *d.* there, 9 March 1881.

([a]) See p. 294, note "a," under "STEPHENS."

IV. 1875. SIR HENRY JAMES HAWLEY, Baronet [1795], of Leybourne Grange aforesaid, br. and h. male, *b.* 14 July 1815; *suc. to the Baronetcy*, 20 April 1875. He *m.* firstly, in 1837, Elizabeth, da. of Robert Askew SMITH, *or* Robert ASKEW, *or* Thomas ASKEW. She *d.* 22 Sep. 1871. He *m.* secondly, 5 June 1877, at St. Nicholas', Brighton, Maria Selina, 1st da. of Edward J. Morant GALE. She *d.* a few weeks later, 25 July 1877, at Chiavenna, Italy. He *d* s.p. 5 Oct. 1892, at his residence, "Hoove Lea," Hove, near Brighton, aged 77. Will pr. at £131,946 gross, and £33,489 net personalty.

V. 1892. SIR HENRY MICHAEL HAWLEY, Baronet [1795], of Leybourne Grange aforesaid, and of Tumby Lawn, near Boston, co. Lincoln, nephew and h. male, being 1st s. and h. of the Rev. Henry Charles HAWLEY, Rector of Leybourne, by Mary Elizabeth, da. of Sir Michael CUSACK-SMITH, 3d Baronet [I. 1799], by Eliza, da. of C. P. MOORE, which Henry Charles (who *d.* 16 Feb. 1877, aged 53), was yr. br. to the late Baronet, and 3d and yst. s. of the 2d Baronet. He was *b.* 25 March 1848; was ed. at Radley College, Berks; matric. at Oxford (Queen's Coll.), 29 Oct. 1867, aged 19; *suc. to the Baronetcy*, 5 Oct. 1892. He *m.* 24 Nov. 1875, Frances Charlotte, 2d da. of John WINGFIELD-STRATFORD, of Addington Park, Kent, by Jane Elizabeth, da. of Gen. Sir John Wright GUISE, 3d Baronet [1783], G.C.B.

Family Estates.—These, in 1883, consisted of 4,638 acres in Lincolnshire, 1,521 in Kent, 1,366 in Northamptonshire, and 28 in Middlesex. *Total.*—7,553 acres, worth £12,211 a year. *Principal Seat.*—Leybourne Grange, near Maidstone, Kent.

POLLEN:

cr. 15 May 1795.

I. 1795. "JOHN POLLEN, of Redenham [in Thruxton], co. Southampton, Esq.,"([a]) 1st s. and h. of John POLLEN, of Andover, sometime (1734-54) M.P. for that town, one of the Welsh Judges, and a Bencher of Lincoln's Inn (*d.* 24 July 1775), by Hester, sister of Sir Paulet ST. JOHN, 1st Baronet [1772], da. of Ellis ST. JOHN, of Farley, was *b.* about 1731; matric. at Oxford (Corpus Christi Coll.), 15 May 1759, aged 18; Barrister (Lincoln's Inn), 1770, becoming subsequently (1802) a Bencher, and was *cr. a Baronet*, as above, 15 May 1795. He *m.* firstly, 1 Feb. 1778, Louisa, da. and h. of Walter HOLT, of Redenham aforesaid. She *d.* 18 July 1798. He *m.* secondly, Charity Anne, da. and coheir of Richard SOUTHBY, of Bulford, Wilts. He *d.* 17 Aug. 1814. Will pr. 1814. His widow *d.* s.p., 13 July 1830.

II. 1814. SIR JOHN WALTER POLLEN, Baronet [1795], of Redenham aforesaid, 1st s. and h., *b.* there 6 April 1784; ed. at Eton; matric. at Oxford (Ch. Ch.), 12 Nov. 1803, aged 19; *suc. to the Baronetcy*, 17 Aug. 1814; was M.P. for Andover, 1820-31, and 1835-41, in all five Parls. He *m.* 9 Sep. 1812, Charlotte Elizabeth, only da. of the Rev. John CRAVEN, of Chilton House, Wilts, presumably by his 2d wife, Catherine (*m.* 6 July 1779), da. of James HUGHES, of Ashbury and Letcombe, Berks. He *d.* s.p. 2 May 1863, aged 79. His widow *d.* at Redenham, 7 Oct. 1877, aged 81.

III. 1863. SIR RICHARD HUNGERFORD([b]) POLLEN, Baronet [1795], of Redbourne, Wilts, nephew and h., being s. and h. of Richard POLLEN, of the same, and of Lincoln's Inn, London, by Anne, da. of Samuel Pepys

([a]) See p. 294, note "a," under "STEPHENS."

([b]) The family were connected with that of Hungerford through the marriage of Elizabeth, sister of the 1st Baronet, with George Hungerford of Studley, Wilts. She *d.* s.p. in 1816, and the name of Hungerford appears, in virtue of this alliance, to have been in great favour among her relatives as a baptismal name.

COCKERELL, of Westbourne, Midx., which Richard (who *d.* 7 Feb. 1838, aged 51) was br. of the late and 2d s. of the 1st Baronet. He was *b.* 19 Oct. 1815, in Paddington; ed. at Eton; matric. at Oxford (Ch. Ch.), 23 May 1833, aged 17; B.A., 1837; admitted to Lincoln's Inn, 1837; *suc. to the Baronetcy,* 2 May 1863. He *m.* firstly, 5 June 1845, Charlotte Elizabeth, da. of John GODLEY, of Killigar, co. Leitrim, by Catherine, da. of the Rt. Hon. Denis DALY, of Dunsandle, co. Galway. She *d.* 22 Feb. 1860. He *m.* secondly, 29 Sep. 1870, at the church of the Annunciation, Woodchester, Frances Mary, yst. da. of William Bernard AIRD. He *d.* 9 April 1881, at Clifton, by Bristol, aged 65. His widow living 1905.

IV. 1881. SIR RICHARD HUNGERFORD(a) POLLEN, Baronet [1795], of Redbourne aforesaid, 1st s. and h., *b.* 6 Oct. 1846, in Welbeck Street, Marylebone; ed. at Eton; matric. at Oxford (Ch. Ch.), 7 June 1865, aged 18; sometime Lieut.-Col. 4th Gloucester Reg. (Militia); *suc. to the Baronetcy,* 9 April 1881. He *m.* 8 June 1875, at Stoke Bishop, co. Gloucester, Frances Anne St. Aubyn, 1st da. of William Savage WAIT, of Woodborough, Somerset.

Family Estates.—These, in 1883, consisted of 3,036 acres in Hants and 1,466 in Wilts. *Total.*—4,502 acres, worth £5,444 a year. *Seat.*—Redbourne, near Chippenham, Wilts.

WENTWORTH:
cr. 16 May 1795;
ex. 10 April 1844.

I. 1795. "JOHN WENTWORTH, Esq., Lieut.-Gov. of Nova Scotia,"(b) 1st s. and h. of Mark Hunkyn WENTWORTH,(c) of Portsmouth, in New Hampshire, New England, one of the Council of that province (*d.* 28 Dec. 1785), by Elizabeth, da. of John RINDGE, of Portsmouth aforesaid, was *b.* about 1737; ed. at Harvard Univ.; M.A., 1758; was in 1766 made Gov. of New Hampshire, holding that office till the secession of the United States; D.C.L. of Oxford, 12 Aug. 1766; D.C.L. of Dartmouth College, 1773; D.C.L. of the Univ. of Aberdeen, 1773; Lieut.-Gov. of Nova Scotia, 1792-1808, and was *cr. a Baronet,* as above, 16 May 1795. He, having returned to England in 1810, after forty-six years' loyal service, was sometime of Parlut, co. Lincoln. He *m.* in or before 1774, Frances, da. of his paternal uncle, Samuel WENTWORTH, of Boston, in America, by Elizabeth, da. of (—) DERING, of New England, said to have been s. of (—) DERING, who emigrated from Kent. She *d.* 14 Feb. 1813. He *d.* at Halifax, Nova Scotia, 8 April 1820, aged 83.

II. 1820, to 1844. SIR CHARLES MARY WENTWORTH, Baronet [1795], only s. and h., *b.* 18 Jan. 1775 in New Hampshire; ed. at Westm. School; matric. at Oxford (Brasenose Coll.), 16 June 1792, aged 17; B.A., 1796; M.A., 1799; B.C.L. and D.C.L., 1806; admitted to Lincoln's Inn, 1798; Member of the Council of Nova Scotia, 1801-05; *suc. to the Baronetcy,* 8 April 1820. He *d.* unm. 10 April 1844, at Kingsend, Devon, aged 69, when the *Baronetcy* became *extinct.* Will pr. Aug. 1844.

(a) See p. 301, note "b."
(b) See p. 294, note "a," under "STEPHENS."
(c) He was 6th s. of John Wentworth, Lieut.-Gov. of New Hampshire, by Sarah, da. of Mark Hunkyn, which John was grandson of William Wentworth, of New Hampshire, said to have emigrated from Yorkshire to Boston, in New England, in 1628.

MURRAY:
cr. 3 July 1795;
sometime, 1810 (?) to 1822, MACGREGOR-MURRAY;
afterwards, since 1822, MURRAY-MACGREGOR, and MACGREGOR.

I. 1795. "JOHN MURRAY, of Lanrick, co. Perth, Colonel and Military Auditor General of Bengal,"(a) was 1st s. of Evan MURRAY, who served in the 88th Foot with much distinction in Germany, by Janet, yst. da. of John MACDONALD, of Balgony,(b) which Evan (who *d.* 1778) was yr. br. of Robert MACGREGOR, *otherwise* MURRAY, of Glencarnock, who was in command against the Government in 1745 at Culloden, both being sons of John MACGREGOR, of Glencarnock aforesaid. He was *b.* 10 April 1745; was Lieut.-Col. in the East India Company's service, Auditor General of Bengal and was *cr. a Baronet,* as above, 3 July 1795. He, in 1822, a very short time before his death took the name of MACGREGOR, being that of his paternal ancestors, before that of MURRAY. He *m.* in 1774, Anne, da. of Roderick MACLEOD, of Edinburgh, Writer to the Signet. He *d.* early in 1822, aged 77. Admon. March 1822. His widow *d.* 5 Feb. 1830, at Portobello, near Edinburgh, aged 81.

II. 1822. SIR EVAN JOHN MACGREGOR-MURRAY, *afterwards* MURRAY-MACGREGOR, Baronet [1795], of Clangregor Castle, co. Perth, only s. and h., *b.* Jan. 1785, *suc. to the Baronetcy* early in 1822 and by royal lic., a few months later, 22 Dec. 1822, took the name of MACGREGOR after that of MURRAY. He had, long previously, entered the Army; was Lieut., 15th Dragoons, 1803; Assistant Adjutant-General in Spain and Portugal, 1810; Deputy Quartermaster-General in the East Indies, 1813; Assistant Adjutant-General and afterwards Deputy Adjutant-General at Madras, 1817, being severely wounded, in Hislop's engagement, 27 Feb. 1818; **K.H.**, 1821; Colonel, 1825; Aide-de-Camp to George IV and William IV; **K.C.H.**, 1831; Major-General, 1837; Governor of Dominica, 1831; of Antigua, 1832, of Barbadoes, etc., 1836, and of Trinidad, 1839; being *cr.* **K.C.B.**, July 1838. He *m.* 28 May 1808, in London, Elizabeth, 4th da. of John MURRAY), 4th DUKE OF ATHOLL [S.] by his 1st wife Jean, da. of Charles Schaw (CATHCART), 9th LORD CATHCART [S.]. He *d.* at the Seat of Government, in Barbadoes, 14 June 1841, aged 56. Will pr. Dec. 1841. His widow, who was *b.* 14 April and *bap.* 5 May 1787, at Dunkeld, *d.* in Hanover square, London, 12 April 1846, and was *bur.* at Balquhidder.

III. 1841. SIR JOHN ATHOLL BANNATYNE MURRAY-MACGREGOR, Baronet [1795], of Clangregor Castle aforesaid, 1st s. and h., *b.* 20 Jan. 1810; *suc. to the Baronetcy,* 14 June 1841; President of the Virgin Islands, 1850. He *m.* 14 Nov. 1833, at St. James', Westm., Mary Charlotte, 3d and yst. da. and coheir of Rear-Admiral Sir Thomas Masterman HARDY, Baronet (so *cr.* 1806), **G.C.B.**, Governor of Greenwich Hospital (*d.* 20 Sep. 1839), by Louisa Emily Anne, da. of Admiral the Hon. Sir George Cranfield BERKELEY, **G.C.B.**, yr. s. of the 4th EARL OF BERKELEY. He *d.* 11 May 1851, aged 41. Will pr. Jan. 1854. His widow *d.* 29 April 1896, at Faraday House, Hampton Court, aged 83.

IV. 1851. SIR MALCOLM MURRAY-MACGREGOR, Baronet [1795], of Edinchip, near Balquhidder, co. Perth, 1st s. and h., *b.* 29 Aug. 1834; *suc. to the Baronetcy,* 11 May 1851; Lieut. R.N., 1854, serving at Sebastopol and receiving the Crimean medal; Commander, 1856; Capt., 1862, retiring 1875. He *m.* 26 Oct. 1864, at St. Geo. Han. sq., Helen Laura, da. and h. of Hugh Seymour (MCDONNELL), 4th EARL OF ANTRIM [I.], by Laura Cecilia, da. of Thomas (PARKER) 5th EARL OF MACCLESFIELD. He *d.* at Edinchip, suddenly, 31 Aug. 1879, aged 45. His widow, who was *b.* 1837, living 1905.

(a) See p. 294, note "a," under "STEPHENS."
(b) By his wife "that celebrated favourite of the Muses, the pious and charitable, Mrs. Alicia Mackenzie, aunt of Isabella, mother of Dunbar, Earl of Selkirk, and 3d da. of the brave Major Kenneth Mackenzie, of Suddy, by Isabella Paterson, da. of the Right Rev. John, Lord Bishop of Ross." [Playfair's *Baronetage,* 1811.]

V. 1879. SIR MALCOLM MACGREGOR, *or* MURRAY-MACGREGOR, Baronet [1795], of Edinchip aforesaid, 1st s. and h., *b.* 3 Aug. 1873; *suc. to the Baronetcy,* 31 Aug. 1879; entered the Royal Navy; Lieut., 1894, and subsequently Commander.

A'COURT:
cr. 4 July 1795;
afterwards, since 1828, BARONS HEYTESBURY.

I. 1795. "WILLIAM PIERCE ASHE-A'COURT, Esq., of Heytesbury, Wilts,"(a) only s. and h. of General William ASHE-A'COURT, thirty years (1751 till his death, 2 Aug. 1781) M.P. for Heytesbury, by Annabella (*m.* 22 Feb. 1746), da. and coheir of Thomas VERNON, of Twickenham Park, Midx. (which William, who was 2d s. of Pierce A'COURT, by Elizabeth, da. of William ASHE, of Heytesbury, took the name of ASHE before his patronymic of A'COURT presumably after the death, s.p., in Sep. 1768, of his elder br., Pierce ASHE-A'COURT, aged 61), in compliance with the will of his maternal uncle, Edward ASHE), was *b.* about 1747; served many years in the Army, becoming, finally, Colonel; was M.P. for Heytesbury (three Parls.), Sep. 1781 to 1790, and 1806-07, and was *cr. a Baronet,* as above, 4 July 1795. He was Lieut.-Colonel 2d Wilts Militia. He *m.* firstly, in 1769, Catherine, da. of Lieut.-Col. John BRADFORD. She *d.* s.p. 23 Sep. 1776, and was *bur.* at Cheltenham. He *m.* secondly, 30 Oct. 1777, at Salisbury, Lætitia, da. of Henry WYNDHAM, of the Close, Salisbury, by Arundel, da. of Thomas PENRUDDOCK, of Compton, Wilts. He *d.* 22 July 1817, at Heytesbury House, in his 70th year. Will pr. 1817. His widow *d.* 2 Aug. 1821.

II. 1817. SIR WILLIAM A'COURT, Baronet [1795], of Heytesbury aforesaid, 1st s. and h., by 2d wife, *b.* 11 July 1779, in the Close, Salisbury; ed. at Eton; Sec. of Legation at Naples, 1801; Sec. to Special Mission to Vienna, 1807; Envoy to the States of Barbary, 1813; to Naples, 1814; *suc. to the Baronetcy,* 22 July 1817; P.C., 1817; **G.C.B.**, 1819; Envoy to Spain, 1822; Ambassador to Portugal, 1824-28. He *m.* 3 Oct. 1808, at St. Geo. Han. Sq., Maria Rebecca, 2d da. of the Hon. William Henry BOUVERIE (yr. s. of William, 1st EARL OF RADNOR), by Bridget, da. of James (DOUGLAS), EARL OF MORTON [S.]. She, who was *b.* Oct. 1783, was living when he, having been appointed Ambassador to Russia, was *cr.* 23 Jan. 1828, BARON HEYTESBURY, co. Wilts. In that peerage this *Baronetcy* then *merged,* and still (1905) so continues. See PEERAGE.

VANDEN-BEMPDE-JOHNSTONE:
cr. 6 July 1795;
afterwards, since 1881, BARONS DERWENT OF HACKNESS.

I. 1795. "RICHARD [VANDEN](b) BEMPDÉ JOHNSTONE, Esq., of Hackness Hall, co. York,"(a) was 1st s. and h. of Lieut.-Col. John JOHNSTONE, by Charlotte Van Lore, Dow. MARCHIONESS OF ANNANDALE [S.], da. and h. of John VANDEN-BEMPDÉ, of Hackness Hall aforesaid, and of Pall Mall, Midx., merchant, which John JOHNSTONE (who *d.* of wounds received at Carthagena, 1741) was yr. s. of Sir William JOHNSTONE, 2d Baronet [S. 1700], of Westerhall. He was *b.* 21 Sep. 1732; served in the 3d Foot Guards; suc. to the Hackness estate in right of his mother (whose heir he was, she having *d.* 23 Nov.

(a) See p. 294, note "a," under "STEPHENS."
(b) "Vanden" is (presumably by mistake) omitted both in the Gazette notice as given in the *Annual Register* for 1795 and in the Parl. return.

1762), and by Act of Parl., in 1793, in accordance with the will of his abovenamed maternal grandfather, took the name of VANDEN-BEMPDÉ instead of that of JOHNSTONE, which last name, however, he, by royal lic., 1 June 1795, resumed as a final surname, and was *cr. a Baronet,* as above, 6 July 1795, with a spec. rem., failing heirs male of his body, to his br., "Charles JOHNSTONE, Esq., of Haverfordwest."(a) He was M.P. for Weymouth, 1790-96. He *m.* firstly, Nov. 1756, Catherine, da. of James AGNEW, of Bishops Auckland, co. Durham. She *d.* s.p. 1790. He *m.* secondly, in Park Street, St. Geo. Han. Sq., at the house of her uncle, Rev. James SCOTT, D.D., Margaret, da. of John SCOTT, of Charter House Sq., London. He *d.* 14 July 1807, near Scarborough, aged 75. Will pr. 1807. His widow *d.* 7 Dec. 1853, at Thirsk, aged 79.

II. 1807. SIR JOHN VANDEN-BEMPDÉ-JOHNSTONE, Baronet [1795], of Hackness aforesaid, 1st s. and h., by 2d wife, *b.* there 28 Aug. 1799; *suc. to the Baronetcy,* 14 July 1807; ed. at Rugby, 1810, and at Trin. Coll., Cambridge; M.A., 1821; was Sheriff of Yorkshire, 1824-25; M.P. for that county (two Parls.), Dec. 1830 to 1832, and for Scarborough (nine Parls.), 1832-37, and 1841, till death in 1869; was *cr.* D.C.L. of Oxford, 15 June 1841; Lieut.-Col. of the West Riding Yeomanry Cavalry, 1859. He *m.* 14 June 1825, at St. Geo. Han. Sq., Louisa Augusta, 1st da. of the Hon. Edward VENABLES-VERNON-HARCOURT, Archbishop of York, by Anne, da. of Granville (LEVESON-GOWER), 1st MARQUESS OF STAFFORD. He *d.* 24 Feb. 1869, in his 70th year, at 34 Belgrave Sq., from injuries received when out hunting. His widow *d.* a few months later, 4 Aug. 1869, at Eridge Castle, Kent.

III. 1869. SIR HARCOURT VANDEN-BEMPDE-JOHNSTONE, Baronet [1795], of Hackness aforesaid, 1st s. and h., *b.* 3 Jan. 1829, at Bishopsthorpe Palace, York; ed. at Eton; sometime Lieut. 2d Life Guards; *suc. to the Baronetcy,* 24 Feb. 1869; M.P. for Scarborough (three Parls.), March 1869 to 1880. He *m.* 27 May 1850, at St. Geo. Han. Sq., Charlotte, sister of Charles Henry, 1st BARON HILLINGDON, 2d da. of Sir Charles MILLS, 1st Baronet [1868], of Hillingdon, Midx., by Emily, da. of Richard Henry COX, of Hillingdon. She was living when he was *cr.,* 10 Oct. 1881, BARON DERWENT OF HACKNESS, in the North Riding of the county of York. In that peerage this *Baronetcy* then *merged,* and still (1905) so continues. See PEERAGE.

HAMLYN:
cr. 7 July 1795;
afterwards, 1811-1861, HAMLYN-WILLIAMS;
ex. 10 Oct. 1861.

I. 1795. "JAMES HAMLYN, Esq., of Clovelly Court, Devon, and of Edwinsford, co. Carmarthen,"(a) *formerly* James HAMMETT, being 1st s. and h. of Richard HAMMETT, by Elizabeth, da. and h. of (—) RISDEN, the said Richard being s. of another Richard HAMMETT, by Thomazine, sister to Zachary HAMLYN, of Lincoln's Inn and of Clovelly Court aforesaid, inherited the last named estate from his great uncle Zachary HAMLYN abovenamed, and by Act of Parliament took the name of HAMLYN instead of that of HAMMETT, and was *cr. a Baronet,* as above, 7 July 1795. He was M.P. for Carmarthenshire, April 1793 to 1802. He *m.* 12 June 1762, at St. Geo., Bloomsbury, Arabella, da. and coheir, eventually [1780] sole h. of Thomas WILLIAMS, of Great Russell Street, by his 1st wife (—), da. of (—) POWELL, of Derwith, co. Carmarthen, the said Arabella being niece and eventually h. of Sir Nicholas WILLIAMS, Baronet (so *cr.* 30 July 1707), of Edwinsford aforesaid, who *d.* s.p. 19 July 1745.(b) She *d.* 1797. He *d.* 28 May 1811. Will pr. 1811.

(a) See p. 294, note "a," under "STEPHENS."
(b) See p. 5, note "a," under "WILLIAMS."

II. 1811. SIR JAMES HAMLYN-WILLIAMS, Baronet [1795], of Clovelly Court and Edwinsford aforesaid, 1st but only surv. s. and h., *b.* about 1765. He, having on the death of his mother inherited the estates of her family, took v.p. by royal lic., 2 March 1798, the name of WILLIAMS as a final surname. He was M.P. for Carmarthenshire and *suc. to the Baronetcy*, 28 May 1811. He *m.* 22 June 1789, Diana Anne, 2d da. and coheir of Abraham WHITAKER,(a) of London and of Stratford, co. Essex, and Lyston House, co. Hereford. He *d.* at Clovelly Court, 3 Dec. 1829, aged 64. Will pr. March 1830. His widow *d.* 7 Sep. 1849, at Norwood, Surrey, aged 84. Will pr. Sep. 1849.

III. 1829, to 1861. SIR JAMES HAMLYN-WILLIAMS, Baronet [1795], of Clovelly Court and Edwinsford aforesaid, *b.* 1791 in Westminster; ed. at Eton; matric. at Oxford (St. Mary's Hall), 22 Oct. 1796, aged 15; *suc. to the Baronetcy*, 3 Dec. 1829; Lieut.-Col. East Devon Militia, 1846; Sheriff of Carmarthenshire, 1848; M.P. for that county, 1831, and again 1835-37. He *m.* 15 Feb. 1823, at Castlehill, Devon (the seat of her father), Mary, 4th da. of Hugh (FORTESCUE), 1st EARL FORTESCUE, by Hester, sister of George, 1st MARQUESS OF BUCKINGHAM, da. of the Right Hon. George GRENVILLE. He *d.* s.p.m.,(b) 10 Oct. 1861, at Clovelly Court, aged 70, when the *Baronetcy* became *extinct*. His widow who was *b.* 15 Sep. 1792, *d.* 12 Aug. 1874, at 39 Portland Place, in her 82d year.

POORE:

cr. 8 July 1795.

I. 1795. "JOHN METHUEN POORE, Esq., of Rushall, co. Wilts,"(a) 2d s. of Edward POORE, of Charlton, Wilts, and of Rushall aforesaid, sometime (1773-74) Sheriff of that county (*d.* 10 April 1788), by Barbara, 2d da. and finally coheir of Paul METHUEN, of Bradford, Wilts, was *b.* 8 June 1745, at Bradford, and was *cr. a Baronet*, as above, 8 July 1795, with a spec. rem., failing heirs male of his body to "his brother Edward POORE, of Wedhampton in the same county, Esq."(c) He was Sheriff of Wilts, 1797-98. He *d.* unm. 1 June 1820, at Rushall aforesaid, aged 75. Will pr. 1820.

II. 1820. SIR EDWARD POORE, Baronet [1795], of Rushall aforesaid, great nephew and h., being 1st s. and h. of Edward POORE (*d.* 17 July 1814, aged 41), by his 1st wife, Martha Anne, da. of George WOLFF, Danish Consul in London, which Edward was 1st s. and h. of Edward POORE, of Wedhampton, Wilts (*d.* 30 Dec. 1795, aged 53), who was elder br. of the grantee. He was *b.* 4 Dec. 1795; matric. at Oxford (Magdalen Coll.), 14 Oct. 1814, aged 18; *suc. to the Baronetcy*, 1 June 1820, under the spec. rem. in the creation thereof. He *m.* 6 Jan. 1818, Agnes, 3d da. of Sir John MARJORIBANKS, 1st Baronet [1815], of Lees, by Alison, da. of William RAMSAY, of Barnton. He *d.* 13 Oct. 1838, in Norfolk Street, Park Lane, in his 43d year. Will pr. March 1839. His widow *d.* 13 Oct. 1868, in the Close, Salisbury, aged 67.

III. 1838. SIR EDWARD POORE, Baronet [1795], only s. and h., *b.* 6 March 1826, in Hereford Street; *suc. to the Baronetcy*, 13 Oct. 1838; Lieut., Scots Fusilier Guards, 1844, retiring in 1848. He *m.* 18 Sep. 1851,

(a) See p. 92, note "c," under "GOOCH" as to him and his three daughters.
(b) Susan Hester, his 1st da. and coheir, *m.* 9 April 1850, Lieut.-Col. Henry Edward Fane, of Avon Tyrrell, Hants, who took the name of Hamlyn-Fane, on his wife's inheriting Clovelly Court, and *d.* 27 Dec. 1868. She *d.* 19 May 1869. Their only son *d.* unm., 10 March 1884, aged 25, and was suc. in the Clovelly estate by his yr. sister, Christine Louisa, who *m.* 11 June 1889, Frederick Gosling, who, accordingly (by royal lic.), took the name of Hamlyn only.
(c) See p. 294, note "a," under "STEPHENS."

at Chartham, Kent, Frances Elizabeth, da. of the Rev. Henry Riddell MOODY, M.A. (Oxford), of Ashley, Beds, Rector of Chartham (1822-23), and Hon. Canon of Canterbury. He *d.* 23 Nov. 1893, aged 67, in West Australia. His widow *d.* 21 April 1896, at 11 Neville Terrace, Onslow Gardens, aged 70.

IV. 1893. SIR RICHARD POORE, Baronet [1795], 1st s. and h., *b.* 7 July 1853, at Coburg, Canada West; entered the Royal Navy, serving in the Perak Expedition, 1875-76; at the bombardment of Alexandria, 1882, and in the Nile Expedition, 1885, becoming Rear-Admiral in 1903, having *suc. to the Baronetcy*, 23 Nov. 1893; was A.D.C. to the King in 1903, and an officer of the Legion of Honour. He *m.* 14 Sep. 1885, at St. Augustine's, Queen's Gate, Ida Margaret, yst. da. of the Right Hon. Richard GRAVES, Bishop of Limerick (1866-99), by Selina, da. of John CHEYNE, M.D. Physician to the Forces [I.].

BURGES:

cr. 21 Oct. 1795;

afterwards, since 1821, LAMB.

I. 1795. "JAMES BLAND BURGES, Esq, Under Secretary of State for Foreign Affairs,"(a) only s. and h. of George BURGES, Comptroller-General of the Customs [S.] (*d.* at Bath, 16 March 1786, having been formerly a Capt. in General Humprey Bland's Dragoons, which General he attended at Gibraltar when, 1749-52, Governor thereof), by Anne Whichnour, 1st da. of James (SOMERVILLE), 13th LORD SOMERVILLE [S.]. He was *b.* 8 June 1752, at Gibraltar; ed. at Westm. School; matric. at Oxford (University Coll.), 7 Jan. 1770, aged 17, and on leaving Oxford in 1773, went the grand tour; Barrister (Lincoln's Inn), Easter 1777, and a Commissioner of Bankruptcy; M.P. for Helston, Jan. 1787 to 1790; Under Secretary of State in the Foreign Department, 1789-95;(b) being Joint Commissioner of the Privy Seal, July to Nov. 1794, and being, "on retiring from the Foreign Office to make room for a personal friend of Lord Grenville,"(c) *cr. a Baronet*, as above, 21 Oct. 1795, and receiving in addition "the sinecure title and post of *Knight Marshal of the Royal Household*, with remainder to his son."(c) By royal lic. 25 Oct. 1821, he took the name of LAMB instead of BURGES, having suc. to the estate of his friend, John LAMB.(d) He was author of "*The Birth and Triumph of Love*," and of other poems and tales.(e) He *m.* firstly, 19 June 1777,

(a) See p. 294, note "a," under "STEPHENS."
(b) "During the serious riots of 1795 in London, Pitt, Nepean and Burges were the only public officials who daily appeared at the Government Offices" [*Dict. Nat. Biog.*].
(c) *Dict. Nat. Biog.*
(d) By him (a clever financier) "the scheme of the Sinking Fund, usually associated with the name of Pitt, was actually originated," to whom the project was unfolded by Burges, the friend of this John Lamb [*Dict. Nat. Biog.*].
(e) His poems, however, were not considered of the first order of merit, even in that age of very indifferent poets. The following epigram, attributed to Porson, gives him, however, the fourth place among them:—

"Poetis nos lætamur tribus—
Pye, Petro Pindar, Parvo Pybus.—
Si ulterius ire pergis,
Adde his—Sir James Bland Burges."

The three persons thus commemorated were Henry James Pye, the unpoetical "Poet Laureate" (*d.* 1813); John Wolcot, who wrote as "Peter Pindar" (*d.* 1819), and Charles Small [" *Parvus* "] Pybus, many years M.P. for Dover, author of a poem called "The Sovereign," published in 1800, and scathingly reviewed by Porson in the "Monthly Review" of that year.

Elizabeth, 2d da. of Edward (NOEL), 1st VISCOUNT WENTWORTH, by Judith, da. of William LAMB, of Farndish, co. Northampton. She *d.* s.p. 21 Jan. 1779. He *m.* secondly, 16 Dec. 1780, Anne, 3d da. of Lieut.-Col. Lewis Charles MONTOLIEU, BARON DE ST. HYPOLITE. She, by whom he had ten children, *d.* 17 Oct. 1810. He *m.* thirdly, 8 Sep. 1812, Margaret,(a) widow of Alexander FORDYCE, 2d da. of James (LINDSAY), 5th EARL OF BALCARRES [S.], by Anne, da. of Sir Robert DALRYMPLE. She, by whom he had no issue, *d.* 1 Dec. 1814. Will pr. 1814. He *d.* 13 Oct. 1824, aged 72. Admon. Nov. 1824.

II. 1824. SIR CHARLES MONTOLIEU LAMB, Baronet [1795], of Beauport, near Battle, co. Sussex, *formerly*, 1785-1821, Charles Montolieu BURGES, 2d but 1st surv. s. and h., by 2d wife, *b.* 8 July 1785 at Nantcribba Hall, co. Montgomery; *suc. to the Baronetcy*, 1 Dec. 1824, as also to the post of *Knight Marshal of the Royal Household*,(b) in which he was confirmed, 20 Jan. 1825; was for some years Lieut.-Col. of the Ayrshire Yeomanry; Sheriff of Sussex, 1829-30. He *m.* firstly, Mary, widow of Archibald MONTGOMERIE, *styled* LORD MONTGOMERIE, da. and coheir of Archibald (MONTGOMERIE), EARL OF EGLINTON [S.], by his 2d wife, Frances, da. of Sir William TWYSDEN, 6th Baronet [1611]. She *d.* 2 June 1848 in Clifford street. He *m.* secondly, 28 Oct. 1853, at Geneva, Frances, 1st da. of the Rev. William MARGESSON, of Van and Oakhurst, co. Surrey, Rector of Watlington and Vicar of Mountfield, Sussex, by Mary Frances, da. of Bryan COOKE, of Owston, co. York. He *d.* 21 March 1864, aged 78, at Beauport. His widow *d.* s.p., 1 July 1884, at 3 Cadogan place.

III. 1864. SIR ARCHIBALD LAMB, Baronet [1795], of Beauport aforesaid, grandson and h., being 1st s. and h. of Charles James Savile Montgomerie LAMB, *formerly*, 1816-21, BURGES, by Anna Charlotte, da. of Arthur GREY, of Bersted, Sussex, which Charles (who *d.* v.p. 11 Dec. 1856, aged 40) was 2d but 1st surv. s. of the late Baronet by his 2d wife. He was *b.* 5 Nov. 1845; *suc. to the Baronetcy*, 21 March 1864; entered the 2d Life Guards, 1868, becoming eventually Major, and serving with the Imperial Yeomanry in the Transvaal war; Knight of Justice of St. John of Jerusalem. He *m.* 20 March 1875, at Christ Church, Marylebone, Louisa Mary Caroline, widow of John Richard FENWICK, 2d and yst. da. of Sir Henry Thomas Estridge DURRANT, 3d Baronet [1784], by his 2d wife, Julia Diana, da. of Sir Josias Henry STRACEY, 4th Baronet [1818].

FARQUHAR:

cr. 1 March 1796.

I. 1796. "WALTER FARQUHAR, M.D.,"(c) 4th s. of the Rev. Robert FARQUHAR, Minister of Garioch, co. Aberdeen (*d.* 1787, in his 89th year), by Catherine, da. of the Rev. Walter TURING, Minister of Rayne in that county, was *b.* Oct. 1738; ed. at King's Coll., Aberdeen; M.A., and subsequently (1796) M.D., of that University; studied medicine at Edinburgh and Glasgow; Army Surgeon in Howe's expedition in 1761; but finally settled in London, practising there first as an Apothecary and subsequently as Physician, and being *cr. a Baronet*, as above, 1 March 1796. In the same year he became (3 May) Fellow of the College of Physicians at Edinburgh, and (30 Sep.) Licentiate of the College of Physicians, London, being (22 March 1800) Physician to the Prince of

(a) They had been attached to each other in early youth, he being the "Young Jamie" of the well-known poem of "Auld Robin Gray," written by Lady Anne Barnard, sister of Lady Margaret.
(b) In right of the abovementioned grant of 1795 made to his father.
(c) See p. 113, note "a," under "GIDEON." The date of the Gazette notice for Farquhar is 20 Feb; for Pellew, 12 March; for Bellingham, 21 March, and for Hippesley, Amcotts, Hartopp, Turton and Baker, 30 April 1796.

Wales. In 1813 he partially withdrew from a very extensive practise. He *m.* in 1771, Anne, widow of Dr. HARVIE, a Physician, 4th da. of Alexander STEVENSON, *or* STEPHENSON,(a) of the island of Barbadoes. She *d.* 23 Sep. 1797. He *d.* in London 21 March 1819, aged 80. Will pr. 1819.

II. 1819. SIR THOMAS HARVIE FARQUHAR, Baronet [1796], 1st s. and h., *b.* 27 June 1775; *suc. to the Baronetcy*, 21 March 1819; was a partner in the Banking House of "Herries, Farquhar and Co.," of St. James' street, London, and a Director of the Guardian Insurance Company. He purchased an estate called "Granard," in Roehampton, Surrey. He *m.* 11 July 1809, Sybella Martha, da. and h. of the Rev. Morton ROCKLIFFE, of Woodford, co. Essex, by Martha, 1st da. of the Rev. Thomas Leigh BENNETT, of Thorpe Place, co. Surrey, and Aylsham, co. Norfolk. He *d.* 12 Jan. 1836, aged 60, at King street, St. James', Westm. Will pr. Jan. 1836. His widow *d.* 20 April 1869, at 28 Upper Grosvenor street, in her 85th year.

III. 1826. SIR WALTER ROCKLIFFE FARQUHAR, Baronet [1796], 1st s. and h., *b.* in St. James' street, 4 June 1810; *suc. to the Baronetcy*, 12 Jan. 1836; was a partner in the Banking House of "Herries, Farquhar and Co." abovenamed. He purchased the estate of Polesden Lacy, near Dorking, co. Surrey, and was Sheriff of that county, 1859. He *m.* 28 Nov. 1837, at St. Geo. Han. sq., Mary Octavia, 8th and yst. da. of Henry Charles (SOMERSET), 6th DUKE OF BEAUFORT, by Charlotte Sophia, da. of Granville (LEVESON-GOWER), 1st MARQUESS OF STAFFORD. He *d.* 15 July 1900, at Polesden Lacy aforesaid, in his 91st year. Will pr. above £23,000 gross, the net personalty being *nil*. His widow, who was *b.* 16 July 1814, living 1905.

IV. 1900. SIR HENRY THOMAS FARQUHAR, Baronet [1796], 1st s. and h., *b.* 13 Sep. 1838, in Upper Brook street; ed at Harrow; *suc. to the Baronetcy*, 15 July 1900; resided at Gilmilnscroft, near Mauchline, co. Ayr. He *m.* 8 July 1862, at St. James'. Westm., Alice, 1st da. of Henry William Bouverie (BRAND), 1st VISCOUNT HAMPDEN OF GLYNDE (many years Speaker of the House of Commons), by Eliza, da. of Gen. Robert ELLICE. She was *b.* 24 March 1840.

PELLEW:

cr. 18 March 1796;

afterwards, since 1814, BARONS EXMOUTH OF CANONTEIGN;

and since 1816, VISCOUNTS EXMOUTH.

I. 1796. "CAPT. SIR EDWARD PELLEW, KNT.,"(c) 2d s. of Samuel PELLEW, of Flushing in Mylor, co. Cornwall, Commander of a Dover packet (*d.* 1764, aged 52), by Constance, da. of Edward LANGFORD, was *b.* 19 April 1757, at Dover; ed. at Truro Grammar School; entered the Navy, 1770; Post-Capt., 1780, and having in June 1793 captured a French frigate (the "Cleopatra") of 63 guns, was *Knighted*, 29 June 1793. He effected subsequently various other captures, and rescued from shipwreck, at great peril to himself, the crew of a large East Indiaman, off Plymouth, early in 1796, and was *cr. a*

(a) See an account of the family of Stevenson in Playfair's *Baronetage* (1811) under "Farquhar," where Lady Farquhar is said to be da. of Thomas (not Alexander) Stevenson, by Barbara, da. of (—) Donkyn.
(b) The 2d son, Robert Townsend-Farquhar, was *cr. a Baronet*, 21 Aug. 1821, and was grandfather of Horace Brand Farquhar, *cr. a Baronet*, 25 Oct. 1892, and subsequently *cr.* Baron Farquhar of St. Marylebone, 20 Jan. 1898.
(c) See p. 308, note "c," under "FARQUHAR."

Baronet, as above, 18 March 1796, being then, apparently, of Treverry, co. Cornwall; was M.P. for Barnstaple, 1802 till resigned in 1804; Rear-Admiral, 1804, and Commander-in-chief in the East Indies, where, in 1807, he destroyed the Dutch fleet; Vice-Admiral, 1808; Commander-in-chief in the North Sea, 1810; in the Mediterranean, 1811; Admiral of the Blue, 1814. He *m.* 28 May 1783, Susanna, 2d da. of James FROWDE, of Knoyle, Wilts. She was living when he was *cr.*, 1 June 1814, BARON EXMOUTH OF CANONTEIGN, co. Devon, being two years later, in consequence of his successful bombardment of Algiers, *cr.*, 10 Dec. 1816, VISCOUNT EXMOUTH, co. Devon. In those peerages this *Baronetcy* then *merged*, and still (1905) so continues. See "PEERAGE."

BELLINGHAM:

cr. 19 April 1796.

I. 1796. "WILLIAM BELLINGHAM, Esq.,"(a) 4th s. of Alan BELLINGHAM, of Castle Bellingham, co. Louth, Surveyor of the Port of Drogheda (*d.* 15 Jan. 1796, aged 87), by Alice, da. and coheir of the Rev. Hans MONTGOMERY, of Grey Abbey in that county, Rector of Killinshee and Vicar of Ballywater, was *b.* probably about 1756; ed. at Trin. Coll., Dublin; B.A., 1778; M.P. for Reigate, 1784-89; a Commissioner for Victualling the Navy, 1789; was Private Sec. to the Rt. Hon. William PITT, and was *cr. a Baronet*, as above, 19 April 1796, with a spec. rem., failing heirs male of his body, to those of his father. He was sometime Receiver-Gen. of the Land and Assessed Taxes for London; was a Director of Greenwich Hospital and F.S.A. He *m.* 3 Dec. 1783, Hester Frances, 4th and yst. da. of the Rev. the Hon. Robert CHOLMONDELEY, by Mary (sister to the celebrated actress, "Peg WOFFINGTON"), da. of John WOFFINGTON, of Dublin, journeyman bricklayer. He *d.* s.p. at Langley Farm, Beckenham, Kent, 27 Oct. 1826. Will pr. Dec. 1826. His widow, who was *b.* 8 July and *bap.* 2 Aug. 1763, at St. Geo. Han. sq., *d.* 27 Jan. 1844 at Dunany House, co. Louth, aged 80, and was *bur.* at Castle Bellingham. Will pr. July 1844.

II. 1826. SIR ALAN BELLINGHAM, Baronet [1796], of Castle Bellingham aforesaid, nephew and h. male, being 1st s. and h. of Alan BELLINGHAM, of Kilsaran and of Dublin, merchant, by his 1st wife, Anne, da. of John Elliott CAIRNES, of Killyfaddy, co. Tyrone, which Alan (who *d.* 5 Nov. 1800) was 2d br. of the grantee. He was *b.* 2 Feb. 1776, and (having by the death s.p. in 1822 of his great-nephew, William Henry BELLINGHAM, of Castle Bellingham, and the consequent extinction of the heirs male of the body of Lieut.-Col. Henry BELLINGHAM, 1st br. of the grantee, succeeded to the Castle Bellingham estate) *suc. to the Baronetcy*, 27 Oct. 1826, under the spec. rem. in the creation of that dignity. He *m.* 5 Nov. 1799, Elizabeth, 2d da. of the Rev. Rees Edward WALLS, of Boothby Hall, co. Lincoln. She *d.* 27 Feb. 1822. He *d.* at Chatillon sur Loire, in France, 26 Aug. 1827, aged 51. Admon. 7 Nov. 1827.

III. 1827. SIR ALAN EDWARD BELLINGHAM, Baronet [1796], of Castle Bellingham aforesaid, 1st s. and h., *b.* 8 Oct. 1800 in Dublin; ed. at Trin. Coll. in that Univ.; B.A., 1821; M.A., 1832; *suc. to the Baronetcy*, 26 Aug. 1827. Sheriff of co. Louth, 1829. He *m.* 12 Jan. 1841, at Skirbeck, co. Lincoln, Elizabeth, only child of Henry CLARKE, of West Skirbeck House. She *d.* 11 April 1887, aged 77, at Dunany House, co. Louth. He *d.* there 19 April 1889, in his 89th year.

IV. 1889. SIR ALAN HENRY BELLINGHAM, Baronet [1796], of Castle Bellingham aforesaid, 1st s. and h., *b.* there 23 Aug. 1846; ed. at Harrow and at Exeter Coll., Oxford; B.A., 1869; M.A., 1872; Barrister (Lincoln's Inn) 1875; sometime Capt. 6th Battalion Royal Irish Rifles; M.P. for co. Louth, 1880-85; *suc. to the Baronetcy*, 19 April 1889; Chamberlain to Pope

(a) See p. 308, note "c," under "FARQUHAR."

Leo XII; Commissioner of Nat. Education [I.]; Member of Senate of Royal Univ. [I.]; Sheriff of co. Louth, 1897. He *m.* firstly, 13 Jan. 1874, at "St. Thomas of Canterbury," Exton, co. Rutland, Constance Julia Eleanor Georgiana, 2d da. of Charles George (NOEL), 2d EARL OF GAINSBOROUGH, by Ida, da. of William George (HAY), EARL OF ERROLL [S.]. She, who was *b.* 19 Oct. 1847, *d.* 8 April 1891, at Castle Bellingham. He *m.* secondly, 11 June 1895, at the Roman Catholic church of "Our Lady," in St. John's Wood, Regent's Park, Lelgarde Harry Florence, yr. da. of Augustus Wykeham CLIFTON, of Lythem, co. Lancaster, by Bertha Lelgarde (*neé* HASTINGS) *suo jure* BARONESS GREY DE RUTHYN. She was *b.* 16 Feb. 1870.

Family Estates.—These, in 1883, consisted of 11,810 acres in co. Mayo (valued at only £295 a year) and 4,186 acres in co. Louth. *Total.*—15,996 acres, worth £4,586 a year. *Seat.*—Castle Bellingham, co. Louth.

HIPPISLEY:

cr. 10 May 1796;

ex. 20 March 1867.

I. 1796. "JOHN COXE(a) HIPPISLEY, Esq.,"(b) of Warfield Grove, Berks, 1st and only surv. s. of William HIPPISLEY, of Clifton, near Bristol, by Anne, 1st sister and coheir of Thomas WEBB, of Cromhall Court, co. Gloucester (*d.* s.p. 1802), da. of Robert WEBB, of the same, was *b.* about 1748; matric. at Oxford (Hertford Coll.), 3 Feb. 1764, aged 16, being twelve years later *cr.*, 3 July 1776, D.C.L.; Barrister (Inner Temple), 1771, becoming a Bencher in 1803 and Treasurer in 1816; was employed in some diplomatic commissions, 1779-80, but afterwards entered the service of the East India Company, holding important offices in the Kingdom of Tanjore, which he resigned in 1787; was Recorder of Sudbury, 1790, and M.P. for that town (five Parls.) 1790-96 and 1802-18; was again employed, 1792-95, in Italy and Germany (where he arranged the marriage, which took place 18 May 1797, of the Princess Royal with the reigning Duke of Wurtemburg), and was *cr. a Baronet*, as above, 10 May 1796. He was Sheriff of Berks, 1800-01; F.S.A. and F.R.S.; one of the first managers of the Royal Institution of Great Britain; Hon. M.A. (Trinity Coll.), Cambridge, 1811. He *m.* firstly, at Rome, early in 1789, Margaret, 2d da. of Sir John STEUART, 3d Baronet [S. 1687], of Allanbank, co. Berwick, by Margaret Agnes, da. of Charles SMITH, of Boulogne. She *d.* at Brompton, Midx., 24 Sep. 1799, aged 44, and was *bur.* at Warfield. M.I.(c) He *m.* secondly, 16 Feb. 1801, at Whatley, Somerset, Elizabeth Anne, widow of Henry Hippisley COXE, of Stoneaston, only da. of Thomas HORNER, of Mells Park, Somerset, by Elizabeth, da. of the Rev. Thomas PAGET. He *d.* 3 May 1825, in Grosvenor street in his 78th year and was *bur.* in the Temple church, London. Will pr. June 1825. His widow, by whom he had no issue, *d.* in Grosvenor place, 25 March 1843, in her 83d year. Will pr. May 1843.

(a) The name of Coxe was that of his paternal grandmother, Dorothy, only da. of William Coxe, of East Harptree, Somerset, wife of John Hippisley of Yatton, Somerset.

(b) See p. 308, note "c," under "FARQUHAR."

(c) A copy of this M.I. is given in Betham's *Baronetage* [1804] where it is stated that she was "maternally deriving her descent from William, 1st Marquis of Douglas, by the Lady Mary Gordon, da. of George, 1st Marquis of Huntley." Her mother's brother, Hugh Smith, was, indeed, *otherwise* called Hugh Seton (which may perhaps indicate a Gordon descent), but beyond that their father, Charles Smith, was a wine merchant at Boulogne, nothing more is known of the pedigree. The M.I. also quaintly records that "her body sinking to an early grave, lies interred in the chancel of this church." This same Baronetage gives a most elaborate account of the career of the 1st Baronet, whom it states to have been instrumental in calling the attention of the Prince Regent to the distressing want of means of Cardinal York, the grandson of James II.

II. 1825, to 1867. SIR JOHN STUART HIPPISLEY, Baronet [1796], of Warfield Grove, and, after 1843, of Stoneaston aforesaid, only s. and h., by 1st wife, *b.* 16 Aug. 1790, at Clifton, near Bristol; ed. at Eton; matric. at Oxford (Ch. Ch.), 1 Feb. 1810, aged 19; B.A., 1813; *suc. to the Baronetcy*, 3 May 1825. He *d.* unm., 20 March 1867, aged 76, at the Manor House, Mells, co. Somerset, when the *Baronetcy* became *extinct*.(a)

AMCOTTS:

cr. 11 May 1796;

sometime, 1807-12, INGILBY;

and, after 1812, AMCOTTS-INGILBY;

merged, 1815, in the older Baronetcy [*cr.* 1781] of INGILBY;

ex. 14 May 1854.

I. 1796. "WHARTON AMCOTTS, Esq.,"(b) of Kettlethorpe Park, co. Lincoln, *formerly* Wharton EMERSON, 2d s. of Alexander EMERSON, of East Retford, Notts, and Caistor, co. Lincoln (*d.* 1791), by Elizabeth, da. and coheir of the Rev. Thomas BOSVILLE, of co. Northampton, was *b.* 23 and *bap.* 24 Feb. 1739/40, at Hackthorne, co. Lincoln; took the name of AMCOTTS, instead of that of EMERSON, by royal lic., 13 May 1777, on succeeding to the estate of Kettlethorpe, by the death of his wife's br., Charles AMCOTTS, of the same, to whom she was heir; was M.P. for Retford (three Parls.), 1780-1802, and was *cr. a Baronet*, as above, 11 May 1796, with a spec. rem., failing heirs male of his body, to the second and other the younger sons of his daughter Elizabeth, with rem. to the heirs male of her body. He *m.* firstly, 16 April 1762, at the Chequer Chapel, Lincoln, Anna Maria, 1st da. of Vincent AMCOTTS, of Harrington and Aistrop, co. Lincoln, by Elizabeth, da. and eventually h. of John QUINCEY, M.D., of Lincoln. She, who was *b.* 11 April 1725, *d.* 1 July 1800, at East Retford, aged 75. M.I. at Harrington aforesaid. He *m.* secondly, 20 Oct. 1800, Amelia CAMPBELL, spinster, of Whitley, Northumberland, by whom he had no issue. He *d.* s.p.m. at Scarborough, 26 Sep. and was *bur.* 5 Oct. 1807 at East Retford, aged 67. Will pr. 1807.

II. 1807. SIR WILLIAM INGILBY, *after* 1812 AMCOTTS-INGILBY, Baronet [1796], of Kettlethorpe Park aforesaid, grandson by the daughter of the above, being (at the death of his maternal grandfather abovenamed), 3d but 2d surv. s. of Sir John INGILBY, 1st Baronet [1781], of Ripley, co. York, by Elizabeth, only child of Sir Wharton AMCOTTS, 1st Baronet [1796], abovenamed, was *b.* at Ripley, 20 June 1783; and *suc. to the Baronetcy* [1796], 26 Sep. 1807, according to the spec. rem. in the creation of that dignity. He, on the death of his mother, Dame Elizabeth AMCOTTS-INGILBY, 21 Sep. 1812, took the name of AMCOTTS before that of INGILBY. On the death of his father, Sir John INGILBY, 1st Baronet [1781], of Ripley, 13 May 1815, he *suc. to that Baronetcy* [1781], in which title this *Baronetcy* of AMCOTTS [1796] (being of later date) then *merged*, and so continued till both became *extinct* at his death, s.p., 14 May 1854, aged 70. See fuller particulars, page 212, under "INGILBY."

(a) Margaret Frances, his 1st sister and coheir (the only sister that married), *m.* 6 July 1806, Thomas Strangways Horner, of Mells Park, Somerset (only s. of her stepmother), and *d.* his widow, 18 Oct. 1865, leaving issue.

(b) See p. 308, note "c," under "FARQUHAR."

CRADOCK-HARTOPP:

cr. 12 May 1796.

I. 1796. "EDMUND CRADOCK-HARTOPP, Esq.,"(a) of Freathby, co. Leicester, and of Fouroaks Hall, co. Warwick, *formerly* Edmund BUNNEY, only surv. s. of Joseph BUNNEY, of Leicester, merchant, and of Newark, Notts, by Mary, sister and h. of Joseph CRADOCK, of Knytiton, co. Leicester (*d.* unm. 4 Feb. 1778), da. of Edmund CRADOCK, of the same, was *b.* 21 April 1749 at Leicester; matric. at Oxford (Univ. Coll.), 4 Nov. 1767; *cr.* M.A. 23 Jan. 1772; inherited property from the families of CRADOCK (abovenamed), and of HARTOPP (from whom his wife was maternally descended), and by Act of Parl., Michaelmas, 1777, took the name of CRADOCK-HARTOPP; was Sheriff of Leicestershire, 1781-82, and was *cr. a Baronet*, as above, 12 May 1796. He was M.P. for Leicestershire (two Parls.), Nov. 1798 to 1806, and was *cr.* 16 June 1814, D.C.L. of the Univ. of Oxford. He *m.* 7 Aug. 1777, Anne, da. of Joseph HURLOCK, Governor of Bencoolen and one of the Directors of the East India Company, h. to her mother, Sarah, 1st da. and coheir of Sir John HARTOPP, 4th and last Baronet [1619], of Freathby aforesaid.(b) He *d.* 10 June 1833, in his 85th year, at Redland, by Bristol. Will pr. Sep. 1833. His widow *d.* Sep. 1837. Will pr. March 1838 and Feb. 1839.

II. 1833. SIR EDMUND CRADOCK-HARTOPP, Baronet [1796], of Freathby and Fouroaks Hall aforesaid, 3d but 1st surv. s. and h.,(c) *b.* 17 May 1788 at Merivale, co. Warwick; ed. at Rugby, 1801; admitted to Lincoln's Inn, 1807; matric. at Oxford (Ch. Ch.), 22 Oct. 1807, aged 19; B.A., 1811; M.A., 1814; *suc. to the Baronetcy*, 10 June 1833; Sheriff of Leicestershire, 1838-39. He *m.* 23 Sep. 1824, at St. Geo. Han. sq., Mary Jane, only da. of Morton (EDEN), 1st BARON HENLEY OF CHARDSTOCK [I.], by Elizabeth, da. of Robert (HENLEY), 1st EARL OF NORTHINGTON. She *d.* 12 April 1843, at Malvern, aged 47. He *d.* s.p. at Knighton Lodge, co. Leicester, 3 April 1849, aged 60. Will pr. Oct. 1849.(d)

III. 1849. SIR WILLIAM EDMUND CRADOCK-HARTOPP, Baronet [1796], of Fouroaks Hall aforesaid, br. and h., *b.* there 2 Dec. 1794; ed. at Rugby, 1806; *suc. to the Baronetcy*, 3 April 1849; Sheriff of Warwickshire, 1853. He *m.* in 1825, Jane Mary, 1st da. of Henry Bloomfield KEANE. He *d.* 16 Oct. 1864 at Fouroaks Park, aged 69. His widow *d.* 31 Oct. 1881, at her residence in Warwick Sq., Pimlico, in her 74th year.

IV. 1864. SIR JOHN WILLIAM CRADOCK-HARTOPP, Baronet [1796], of Fouroaks Hall aforesaid, 1st s. and h., *b.* there 1829; entered the Army, 1851; Capt. 17th Lancers, 1854-67; *suc. to the Baronetcy*, 16 Oct. 1864; Lieut.-Col. Warwickshire Rifle Volunteers. He *m.* 14 Aug. 1855, at St. James', Paddington, Charlotte Frances, sister of Cardinal HOWARD, 1st da. of Capt. Edward Gyles HOWARD (nephew of Bernard Edward, DUKE OF NORFOLK), by Frances Anne, da. of George Robert HENEAGE, of Hainton, co. Lincoln. He *d.* 25 May 1888, of heart disease, at his residence, "Bodergan Firs," Bournemouth, aged 59. His widow *d.* 17 Nov. 1889, at Eastbourne.

(a) See p. 308, note "c," under "FARQUHAR."

(b) See vol. i, p. 132, note "b," under "HARTOPP."

(c) Of his two elder brothers (1), Edmund Joseph, *b.* at Florence, 8 July 1778, *d.* the next year at Bath, 29 March 1779; (2), George Harry William, *b.* at Merivale, 20 Aug. 1785, ed. at Rugby, 1797; matric. at Oxford (Ch. Ch.), 24 Oct. 1804, aged 19; B.A., 1810; M.A., 1811; assumed the name of Fleetwood before that of Cradock-Hartopp to commemorate his descent, through his mother, from that branch of the Fleetwood family that were settled at Stoke Newington, Midx. He was M.P. for Dundalk, July 1820, till his death unm. and v.p. 31 March 1824.

(d) He, apparently, devised some of his estate to his nephew, Edward Hartopp Grove, s. of his yr. sister, Emilia, by William Grove, of Shenstone Park, co. Stafford. This Edward, who was in Holy Orders, in compliance with his uncle's will, took by royal lic., 22 May 1849, the name of Cradock; was Canon of Worcester, 1848-54; D.D., 1854, and Principal of Brasenose College, Oxford, 1853, till his death, 27 Jan. 1886, aged 75.

V. 1888. SIR CHARLES EDWARD CRADOCK-HARTOPP, Baronet [1796], 1st s. and h., b. 1858; ed. at Eton; Lieut in the Scots Guards, serving in the Egyptian campaign, 1882 (medal, clasp and Khedive's star); *suc. to the Baronetcy*, 25 May 1888. He *m.* 10 June 1895, at St. Mark's, North Audley street, Millicent, 1st da. of Charles Henry WILSON, of Warter Priory, co. York.

Family Estates.—These, in 1883, consisted of 2,181 acres in Leicestershire Warwickshire and Rutland, worth £4,110 a year.

TURTON:

cr. 13 May 1796;

ex. 13 April 1854.

I. 1796. "THOMAS TURTON, Esq.,"(a) of Starborough Castle, co. Surrey, 3d and yst. s. of William TURTON, of Soundess-in-Nettlebed, Oxon, and of Kingston Lisle, Berks (who had served as an officer of the Oxford Blues in the seven years' war in Germany), by his 2d wife Jane, da. of Thomas CLARKE, M.D., of Hertford, was *b.* at Kingston Lisle, 27 Sep. 1764; ed. at Jesus Coll., Cambridge; B.A., 1787; M.A., 1790; purchased the estate of Starborough Castle, with one quarter of the manor, in 1793; was Sheriff of Surrey, 1795-96; distinguished himself during the riots of that year, and was consequently *cr. a Baronet*, as above, 13 May 1796. He was admitted to Lincoln's Inn, 24 Nov. 1801, becoming subsequently a Barrister, and was Clerk of the Juries in the Court of Common Pleas, 1806-12; was M.P. for Southwark 1806-12. He *m.* in or before 1787, Mary, da. and h. of the Rev. John MICHELL, Rector of Thornhill, co. York. She, who was *b.* 1 Aug. 1765, *d.* 28 Jan. 1837. He *d.* 1844, aged about 80. Will pr. Aug. 1844.

II. 1844, to 1854. SIR THOMAS EDWARD MICHELL TURTON, Baronet [1796], of Starborough Castle aforesaid, only s. and h., *b.* 8 Nov. 1790; ed. at Trinity Coll., Cambridge, 1809; admitted to Lincoln's Inn, 31 Oct. 1809, becoming a Barrister in 1818; Registrar of the Supreme Court of Calcutta, 1841-48; *suc. to the Baronetcy* in 1844. He *m.* firstly, 2 Nov. 1812, Louisa, 2d da. of Major-General BROWNE. She obtained a divorce in 1831.(b) He *m.* secondly, in 1842 (—), 2d da. of Capt. Edmund DENMAN, R.N. He *d.* s.p.m. (or s.p.m. legit.), 13 April 1854, at the Mauritius, on his way to England, aged 63, when the *Baronetcy* became *extinct*.(c)

BAKER:

cr. 14 May 1796.(d)

I. 1796. "ROBERT BAKER, Esq.,"(a) of Dunstable, or Upper-Dunstable House, in Richmond, co. Surrey, and of Nicholas Hayne in Culmstock, co. Devon, 3d and yst. s. of John Baker, M.D., of Richmond aforesaid, by Sarah (*m.* 1749/50, at Somerset House chapel), da. and coheir of Robert WOOD, LL.D., was *b.* 20 April and *bap.* 25 May 1754 at Richmond; was Major of the Surrey Fencible Cavalry, and, having raised and maintained a troop of 500 horse, was *cr. a Baronet*, as above, 14 May 1796.(d) He *m.* 28 May 1783, at

(a) See p. 308, note "c," under "FARQUHAR."
(b) She *m.* shortly afterwards; certainly before 1840.
(c) In his obituary in the *Annual Register*, it is stated (though, apparently, in error) that "he was three times married, and has left issue."
(d) This Baronetcy is oddly enough [erroneously] classed as a Baronetcy of *Ireland* in Lascelles' *Liber Munerum Hiberniæ*, under 1796, as "ROBERT BAKER, of Upper Dunstable, co. Surrey."

Sidmouth, Devon, Dinah, only surv. da. and h. of George HAYLEY, Alderman and sometime (1775-76) Sheriff of London, by Mary, sister of the notorious John WILKES, sometime (1774-75) Lord Mayor of that city. She *d.* March 1805. He *d.* 4 Feb. 1826, aged 71. Will pr. Feb. 1826.

II. 1826. SIR HENRY LORAINE BAKER, Baronet [1796], of Dunstable House aforesaid, 2d but 1st surv. s. and h.,(a) *b.* 3 Jan. 1787 at Nancy, in *Loraine*, France; entered the Royal Navy, 1797; was at the storming of Sumana (St. Domingo), 1807; was promoted for his conduct at the defence of Anholt in 1811; served at Guadaloupe in 1815; C.B., 4 June 1815; Captain R.N., 13 June 1815; *suc. to the Baronetcy*, 4 Feb. 1826, was promoted retired Rear-Admiral, 6 Nov. 1850, and retired Vice-Admiral, 9 July 1857. He *m.* 27 June 1820, Louisa Anne, da. of William WILLIAMS, of Castle Hall, Dorset, by Anne, sister of Sir John Colman RASHLEIGH, 1st Baronet [1831], 1st da. of John RASHLEIGH, of Penquite, Cornwall. He *d.* 2 Nov. 1859 at Dunstable House, aforesaid, aged 72. His widow *d.* there, 12 Sep. 1861, aged 60.

III. 1859. SIR HENRY WILLIAMS BAKER, Baronet [1796], only s. and h., *b.* 27 May 1821, in London; ed. at Trin. Coll., Cambridge; B.A., 1844; M.A., 1847. In Holy Orders: Curate of Great Horkesley, Essex, 1842-51; Vicar of Monkland, co. Hereford, 1851 to death; originator of the hymn book entitled *Hymns Ancient and Modern* (1860), and author of several fine hymns therein.(b) He *suc. to the Baronetcy*, 2 Nov. 1859, and *d.* unm. 12 Feb. 1877, at Horkeley House, Monkland, aged 55.

IV. 1877. SIR GEORGE (EDWARD DUNSTAN) SHERSTON(c) BAKER, Baronet [1796], cousin and h., male (great grandson of the 1st Baronet), being 1st s. and h. of Henry Sherston BAKER, Barrister, by Maria Martha, da. of John BURKE, of co. Tipperary, and of York place, Marylebone, which Henry (who *d.* 26 April 1875, aged 60) was only s. and h. of the Rev. George Augustus BAKER, Rector of Ibstone-cum-Fingest, Oxon (*d.* 4 March 1866 aged 77), 3d s. of the 1st Baronet. He was *b.* 19 May 1846. Barrister (Lincoln's Inn) 1871, having previously practised as a Special Pleader; *suc. to the Baronetcy*, 12 Feb. 1877; was an Associate of the *Institût de droit International*, 1879; Recorder of Helston, 1886-89; Recorder of Barnstaple and Bideford, 1889; one of the Examiners of Inns of Court, 1895-1901; Revising Barrister, 1899-1901; one of the Judges of County Courts, 1901.(d) He *m.* 3 June 1873, Jane Mary, da. of James FEGEN, C.B., of Ballilonty, co. Tipperary, formerly in the Royal Navy.

HAYES:

cr. 6 Feb. 1797;

ex. 23 Jan. 1896.

I. 1797. "JOHN MACNAMARA HAYES, M.D.,"(e) of Old Burlington street, Westminster, 2d s. of John HAYES, of Limerick, by Margaret, da. and coheir of Sheedy MACNAMARA, of Ballyally, co. Clare, was *b.* 1750 at Limerick; served with distinction as surgeon, and subsequently as physician, to the army during the whole of the American war; was M.D. of the Univ. of Rheims, 20 March 1784; admitted Licentiate of the Coll. of Physicians,

(a) His elder br., Robert Baker, *b.* 13 Nov. 1785, *d.* unm., June 1802.
(b) Of this publication "the most popular hymn book ever compiled, twenty million copies have been sold in or before 1892." [F. Boase's *Modern English Biography*, 1892].
(c) The name Sherston was that of his paternal grandmother, Sophia, wife of the Rev. G. A. Baker, yst. da. of Peter Sherston, of Stoberry Hill, Somerset.
(d) Author of several legal works.
(e) See p. 113, note "a," under "GIDEON." The date of the Gazette notice for Hayes is 20 Jan.; for Pechell, is 24 Feb.; for Thompson and Parker is 27 March, and for Onslow is 17 Oct. 1797.

London, 26 June 1786; Physician Extraordinary to George, Prince of Wales, 1791; Physician to the Westminster Hospital, 1792-94; Director of Hospitals to the Forces, 1793, served in the West Indies, performing that office in so satisfactory a manner that he was *cr. a Baronet*, as above, 6 Feb. 1797. He was subsequently Inspector-Gen. of the Medical Department in the Ordnance at Woolwich. He *m.* 1 May 1787, Anne, 1st da. of Henry WHITE, one of the Council of New York. He *d.* of acute laryngitis, 19 and was *bur.* 26 July 1809, at St. James', Westm., aged 59. M.I. Will pr. 1809. His widow *d.* at Cheltenham, 18 and was *bur.* 24 Jan. 1848, at St. James' aforesaid, aged 86. Will pr. Feb. 1848.

II. 1809. SIR THOMAS PELHAM HAYES, Baronet [1797], 1st s. and h., *b.* in Old Burlington street, 18 Nov. and *bap.* 17 Dec. 1794 at St. James', Westm.; *suc. to the Baronetcy*, 26 July 1809; entered the Bengal Civil Service as a Writer, 1813; was Assistant to the Collector of Behar, 1816; Officiating Collector of Behar, 1818; of Shahabad, 1819; of Sahun, 1820; Assistant to the Salt Agent and Collector of Hidgellee, Dec. 1821, returning to England, 1823. He *m.* 27 June 1840, at St. Geo. Han. Sq., Caroline Emma, widow of Lieut.-Col. Hill DICKSON, da. of Thomas STOUGHTON, of Ballyhorgan, co. Kerry. He *d.* s.p.s. at Dieppe, 5 and was *bur.* 10 Sep. 1851, at St. James', Westm., aged 56. M.I. Admon. Sep. 1851. His widow *d.* 10 Aug. 1879.

III. 1851, to 1896. SIR JOHN WARREN HAYES, Baronet [1797], only surv. br. and h., *b.* in Old Burlington St. 12 and *bap.* 24 Aug. 1799, at St. James', Westm.; ed. at Harrow; matric. at Oxford (Wadham Coll.), 17 May 1817, aged 18; B.A., 1821; M.A. 1824; in Holy Orders, 1822; Rector of Arborfield, Berks, 1839-80, having *suc. to the Baronetcy*, 5 Sep. 1851. He *m.* 10 Sep. 1844, at Strathfieldsaye, Hants, Ellen, 2d da. of George Edward BEAUCHAMP, of the Priory, in Strathfieldsaye, and of Thetford, Norfolk (2d s. of Sir Thomas BEAUCHAMP-PROCTOR, 2d Baronet [1745]), by his 1st wife, Ellen Louisa, da. of Robert William HALHED, of the Priory aforesaid. She *d.* 1849. He *d.* s.p.m.s.,(a) at "Newlands," near Wokingham (the residence of his son-in-law, John SIMONDS), 23 Jan. 1896,(b) at the great age of 97, when the *Baronetcy* became *extinct*. Will dat. 7 July 1885, pr. at £5,236.

PECHELL:

cr. 1 March 1797;

afterwards, since 1801, BROOKE-PECHELL.

I. 1797. "PAUL PECHELL, Esq, of Paggleshsam, co. Essex," (c) 3d and yst. surv. s. of Lieut.-Colonel Jacob PECHELL, *otherwise* DE PECHELS, of Owenstown, co. Kildare, by Jane (*m.* in or before 1716), da. of John BOYD, of Dublin (which Jacob, who was living 1751, aged 72, came over from France with his father, Samuel DE PECHELS, of Montauban,(d) at the revocation of the Edict of Nantes in 1685), was *b.* 12 Nov. 1724, at Owenstown aforesaid; entered the Army 1744, as Cornet in the 1st Dragoons, serving two campaigns in Flanders, and being, when Captain 36th Foot, wounded at the

(a) Besides a da., Ellen Anna, who *m.*, 23 April 1868, John Simonds abovementioned, he had a son, John Beauchamp Hayes, *b.* 1 Aug. 1848 at Arborfield, sometime (1872-80) Capt. in the 12th Lancers. He *m.* in 1878, but *d.* s.p.m. and v.p., 18 Nov. 1884, leaving three daughters and coheirs.
(b) His death on 17 Aug. 1893 is [erroneously] recorded in the *Annual Register* for that year. This is noted by "Edward H. Marshall, M.A.," in *N. & Q.* (8th s., ix, 166), who remarks that "if the Annual Register is right the newspapers are wrong."
(c) See p. 315, note "e," under "HAYES."
(d) A full account of his career and of the Pechell family is in the *Sussex Archæological Collections*, vol. xxvi, pp. 113-151 (1875).

battle of Laffeldt, 2 July 1747; was Captain in the 2d Dragoon Guards in 1751, and in the 2d Horse Grenadiers, 1754, of which he became Lieut.-Colonel in 1762, retiring from service ("receiving a lump sum(a) for his commission") 24 Jan. 1768, and (nearly thirty years afterwards) being *cr. a Baronet*, as above, 1 March 1797. He *m.* 11 Feb. 1752, Mary, only surv. da. and h. of Thomas BROOKE, of Paggleshsam aforesaid, by Frances, da. of Daniel WILMOT, of Tooting, Surrey. He *d.* 13 Jan. 1800, aged 75. Will pr. Jan. 1800. His widow *d.* nine months later, Oct. 1800. Will pr. Oct. 1800.

II. 1800. SIR THOMAS PECHELL, *afterwards* (1801-26) BROOKE-PECHELL, Baronet [1797], of Paggleshsam aforesaid, and afterwards of Aldwick, Sussex, 1st s. and h., *b.* 23 Jan. 1753, at St. Clement's, London; ed. at Westm. School; matric. at Oxford (Ch. Ch.), 30 May 1771, aged 18; B.A., 1775; M.A., 1779; Gentleman Usher to the Queen Consort, Charlotte, 1795; was an officer in the Army, becoming finally, in 1814, Major-General, having *suc. to the Baronetcy*, 13 Jan. 1800, shortly after which he, in accordance with his mother's will, took by royal lic., 22 Nov. 1800, the name of BROOKE before that of PECHELL. He was M.P. for Downton (three Parls.), April 1813 to 1818, and Feb. 1819 to 1826. He *m.* 28 April 1783, Charlotte, 2d da. of Lieut.-General Sir John CLAVERING, K.B., Commander-in-Chief in Bengal, by Diana, yst. da. of John (WEST), 1st EARL DELAWARR. He *d.* 18 June 1826, at Aldwick aforesaid, aged 73. Will pr. Dec. 1826. His widow *d.* 23 Oct. 1841, at Hampton Court Palace, aged 82.

III. 1826. SIR SAMUEL JOHN BROOKE-PECHELL, Baronet [1797], of Aldwick aforesaid, 2d but 1st surv. s. and h., *b.* 1 Sep. 1785; entered the Navy, 1796; distinguished himself in 1809 in the capture of a forty-gun French frigate; was at the reduction of Martinique, 1810, and in various other actions, becoming finally, 9 Nov. 1846, Rear-Admiral; was made C.B., 4 June 1815; *suc. to the Baronetcy*, 18 June 1826; was M.P. for Helston, 1830-31, and for Windsor, 1832-35; a Lord of the Admiralty, 1830-34, and 1839-41; K.C.H., 6 Jan. 1833; F.S.A, etc. Extra Naval Aide-de-Camp to Queen Victoria. He *m.* 15 April 1833, at her mother's house in Grosvenor square, Julia Maria, only surv. da. of Robert Edward (PETRE), 9th BARON PETRE OF WRITTLE, by Anne, da. and coheir of Philip HOWARD, br. of Edward, DUKE OF NORFOLK. She *d.* 6 Sep. 1844, in Hill street, Berkeley square. Will pr. March 1850. He *d.* there s.p., 3 Nov. 1849, in his 65th year. Will pr. Jan. 1850.

IV. 1849. SIR GEORGE RICHARD BROOKE-PECHELL, Baronet [1797], of Castle Goring, co. Sussex, br. and h., *b.* 30 June 1789 in London, entered the Navy in 1803, serving chiefly in American waters; Capt., 1822, becoming finally Rear-Admiral, 17 Dec. 1852, and Vice-Admiral, both on the retired list, 5 Jan. 1858; Gent. Usher of the Privy Chamber, 1830; Equerry to the Queen Consort, 1831; M.P. for Brighton (Whig interest) in seven Parls., 1835 till death, having *suc. to the Baronetcy*, 3 Nov. 1849. He *m.* 1 Aug. 1826, at Parham Park, Sussex, Katherine Annabella, 2d and yst. da. and coheir of Cecil (BISSHOPP), LORD ZOUCHE DE HARYNGWORTH, by Harriett Anne, da. and h. of William SOUTHWELL. He *d.* s.p.m.s.,(b) 29 June 1860, at 27 Hill St., Berkeley Sq., aged about 71. His widow, who was *b.* 1 Dec. 1791, *d.* 29 July 1871, at Hampton Court Palace.

V. 1860. SIR GEORGE SAMUEL BROOKE-PECHELL, Baronet [1797], of Alton House in Alton, Hants, *formerly* George Samuel PECHELL, cousin and h. male, being 1st s. and h. of Samuel George PECHELL, of Bereleigh, Hants, Capt. R.N., by Caroline, da. of William THOYTS, of Sulhampstead, Berks, which Samuel (who *d.* 30 Dec. 1840, aged 54) was 1st s. and h. of Augustus PECHELL, of Berkhampstead, Herts, Receiver-Gen. of the Customs (*d.* 19 Sep. 1820, aged 67), who was 2d s. of the 1st Baronet. He was *b.* 10 March

(a) *Dict. Nat. Biog.*
(b) His only son, William Henry Cecil George Brooke-Pechell, Capt in the 77th Foot, *d.* unm. and v.p., being killed in the trenches before Sebastopol, 3 Sep. 1855, aged 25.

1819, at Chalfont St. Giles, Bucks; matric. at Oxford (Trin. Coll.), 3 July 1838, aged 19; Ensign, 47th Madras Native Infantry, 1840, and subsequently Lieut.; *suc. to the Baronetcy*, 29 June 1860, when he assumed the name of BROOKE before that of PECHELL; Lieut.-Col. 4th Batt. Hants Rifle Vols., 1863; Col. 1873. He *m.* 11 Oct. 1842, at Darwhar, in India, May Robertson, 1st da. of Col. BREMNER, of the 47th Madras Infantry aforesaid. He *d.* 8 July 1897, at Alton House aforesaid, aged 78. Will pr. at £43,443. His widow living 1905.

VI. 1897. SIR SAMUEL GEORGE BROOKE-PECHELL, Baronet [1797], of Culverton House, in Alton, Hants, 1st s. and h., *b.* 16 Aug. 1852, at Oldbury, near Bridgnorth, sometime an officer in the Royal Navy; *suc. to the Baronetcy*, 8 July 1897. He *m.* 4 Dec. 1879, at Newton Valence, Hants, Constance Louisa, 2d da. of Edward Henry CHAWNER, of Newton Manor House, Capt. 77th Foot, by his 1st wife, Frances Sidney, da. of John Hampden GLEDSTANES, of Cheshunt. She obtained a divorce "*nisi*" in Nov. 1903 which, owing to his death within a year, was never made absolute. He *d.* s.p. at Wandsworth 9 and was *bur.* 12 Feb. 1904, at Alton, aged 51. His widow living 1905.

VII. 1904. SIR AUGUSTUS ALEXANDER BROOKE-PECHELL, Baronet [1797], br. and h., *b.* 31 July 1857; ed. at Edinburgh Univ.; M.B., 1881; Surgeon-Major Army Medical Staff; *suc. to the Baronetcy*, 9 Feb. 1904. He *m.* in 1888, Mabel Marion Anderson, da. of Major-Gen. George BRIGGS, of the Madras Staff Corps.

Family Estates.—These, in 1883, consisted of 2,469 acres in Essex, Hants, and co. Dublin, worth £3,107 a year.

THOMPSON:

cr. 23 June 1797;

ex. 1 July 1868.

I. 1797. "CHARLES THOMPSON, Esq., Vice-Admiral of the Blue,"(a) being presumably of Virhees, Sussex,(b) whose parentage is unknown, is said(c) to have been "descended" from Norborne (BERKELEY), LORD BOTETOURT (who *d.* unm., 1770, aged about 60), in which case he, presumably, was his illegit. son;(d) was *b.* about 1740; entered the Royal Navy, 1755; Lieut., 1761; Captain, 1772; was in command of a 74-gun ship at Chesapeake, 5 Sep. 1781, at St. Kitts in Jan. 1782, and in Rodney's action, 12 April following; was at the capture of Martinique and Guadaloupe, 1794; Rear Admiral, 12 April 1794; Vice-Admiral, 1 June 1795; was second in command at the battle off Cape St. Vincent, and, accordingly, was *cr. a Baronet*, as above, 23 June 1797. Having, however, "presumed to censure the execution of four mutineers,"(e) he was recalled, though, afterwards, 1798-99,(e) made third in command in the Channel Fleet. He was M.P. for Monmouth, 1796 till his death. He *m.* in or before 1785, Jane, da. and h. of Robert SELBY, of Bonington, near Edinburgh. He *d.* at Fareham, Hants, 17 March 1799, aged about 59. Will pr. April 1799. His widow *d.* there Feb. 1833, aged 66. Will pr. June 1833.

II. 1799 SIR NORBORNE THOMPSON, Baronet [1797], of Virhees(b) aforesaid, 1st s. and h., *b.* 23 March 1785; *suc. to the Baronetcy*, 17 March 1799. He *d.* unm. at Chelsea, 1 July 1826, aged 41. Admon. Aug. 1826.

(a) See p. 315, note "e," under "HAYES."
(b) The Baronetcy is headed "Thompson of Virhees, Sussex," in Betham's *Baronetage* [1804], only seven years after its creation.
(c) Betham's *Baronetage*, 1804.
(d) This conjecture is supported by the name of "Norborne" being given to his eldest son.
(e) *Dict. Nat. Biog.*

III. 1826, to 1868. SIR HENRY THOMPSON, Baronet [1797], only surv. br. and h., being 3d and yst. s. of the grantee, *b.* 5 Nov. 1796, at Gosport; matric. at Oxford (Oriel Coll.), 7 Dec. 1814, aged 18; B.A., 1819; M.A., 1821. In Holy Orders, and sometime Incumbent of Trinity Church, Fareham; *suc. to the Baronetcy*, 1 July 1826; Vicar of Frant, Sussex, 1844 till death; and Prebendary of Chichester, 1854. He *m.* firstly, Feb. 1828, at Portsea, Hannah Jean, 4th da. of the Hon. Sir George GREY, 1st Baronet [1814], **K.C.B.**, by Mary, da. of Samuel WHITBREAD, of Bedwell Park, Herts. She *d.* s.p.m., 5 June 1829. He *m.* secondly, 29 Oct. 1838, Emily Frances Anne, yst. da. of Ralph LEEKE, of Longford Hall, Salop. He *d.*, s.p.m.s.,(a) 1 July 1868, at Bournemouth, aged 71, when the *Baronetcy* became *extinct*. His widow *d.* 13 Sep. 1883, at "Fairview," Hawkhurst.

PARKER:

cr. 24 July 1797;

ex. 17 Nov. 1903.

I. 1797. "WILLIAM PARKER, Esq., Rear-Admiral of the Red,"(b) being, presumably, of Harburn, co. Warwick,(c) s. of Augustine PARKER, of Queenborough in the Isle of Shepey, Jurat and sometime Mayor thereof, and Commander of a yacht in the King's service (*d.* June 1783), by Elizabeth, da. of William BEAL, of Shorles, near Minster, was *b.* 1 Jan. 1743; entered the Navy, 1756; Lieut., 1766; Commander, 1773; Capt., 1777; Commander-in-chief on the Leeward Islands station, 1787-90; was in command of a 74-gun ship under Howe, 1792-94, and, on 28 May 1794, disabled a 120-gun ship (being, however, himself disabled thereby) from taking part in the action of 1 June; was Rear-Admiral, 14 July 1794; Commander-in-chief at Jamaica, 1795-96; distinguished himself, as third in command under Jervis, at the battle of St. Vincent, 14 Feb. 1797, and was accordingly *cr. a Baronet*, as above, 24 July 1797.(c) He was Commander-in-chief on the Halifax station, 1800-01, being recalled for a technical offence. He *m.* 28 Dec. 1766, Jane, 1st da. of Edward COLLINGWOOD, of Greenwich. He *d.* suddenly, of apoplexy, at his seat, Ham, co. Surrey, 31 Oct. 1802, in his 60th year. Will pr. 1803. His widow *d.* in or before 1815. Will pr. 1815.

II. 1802. SIR WILLIAM GEORGE PARKER, Baronet [1797], of Harburn aforesaid,(c) only s. and h., *b.* 19 Aug. 1787, *suc. to the Baronetcy*, 31 Oct. 1802, having previously entered the Royal Navy; Lieut. 1803; Commander, 1810; Capt., 1814.(d) He *m.* 29 Aug. 1808, Elizabeth, da. of James Charles STILL, of East Knoyle, Wilts. He *d.* 24 March 1848, at Plymouth, aged 60. Will pr. April 1848. His widow *d.* 29 April 1863, at his residence, Lansdown Villa, Plymouth, aged 76.

(a) Henry Charles Thompson, his only s. by 2d wife, *b.* 7 May 1843; matric. at Oxford (University Coll.), 11 June 1862, aged 19; *d.* unm. and v.p. 15 Jan. 1863.
(b) See p. 315, note "c," under HAYES.
(c) This Baronetcy is headed "Parker, of Harbury [*i.e.*, Harburn], co. Warwick," in Betham's *Baronetage* [1804], only seven years after its creation, and the "seat" of the then Baronet (who certainly resided there in 1818) is so described in Debrett's *Baronetage* [1840].
(d) He is said in the account of his father [*Dict. Nat. Biogr.*] to have "died a Vice-Admiral in 1848," but no such promotion is recorded in Haydn's *Dignities*, and, moreover, in his obituary in the *Ann. Reg.* (where a good account of his career is given) he is styled "Captain R.N.," as is he also in the record of the death of his widow in April 1863.

III. 1848. SIR GEORGE PARKER, Baronet [1797], 2d but 1st surv. s. and h.,(a) *b.* 1813; entered the military service of the East India Company, 1831, becoming Capt. in 1834, and subsequently Major in the 74th Bengal Native Infantry; Joint Magistrate at Meerut, and in charge of Abkaree, 1847; Cantonment Magistrate at Cawnpore, having *suc. to the Baronetcy*, 24 March 1848. He *m.* firstly, 24 Jan. 1838, Eliza Cecilia, da. of John MARSHALL, of Falmouth, sometime surgeon at Dinapore. She *d.* 5 Aug. 1843. He *m.* secondly, 10 Dec. 1846, Gertrude, yst. da. of Lieut.-Col. ELDERTON, East India Company's Service. She *d.* s.p.m., 12 May 1848. He was slain (together with Major-Gen. Sir Hugh Massey WHEELER, **K.C.B.**) 6 July 1857, in a gallant sortie for the relief of Cawnpore, during its siege, aged about 44.

IV. 1857. SIR GEORGE LAW MARSHALL PARKER, Baronet [1797], only s. and h., by 1st wife, *b.* 25 Sep. 1840; *suc. to the Baronetcy*, 6 July 1857, and entered, in that year, the military service of the East India Company at Bengal; was Lieut. in H.M.'s 3d Goorkha Regiment. He *d.* unm., 15 March 1866, at Madeira, aged 25.

V. 1866. SIR HENRY PARKER, Baronet [1797], uncle and h. male, *b.* 16 June 1822; *suc. to the Baronetcy*, 15 March 1866. He *m.* in 1848, Maria Jane, da. of Thomas HECTOR, of Toronto, in Upper Canada, and of London. He *d.* s.p. suddenly, 11 Oct. 1877, aged 55, at Toronto. His widow living 1905.

VI. 1877, to 1903. SIR MELVILLE PARKER, Baronet [1797], only surv. br. and h. male, being 4th s. of the 2d Baronet; *b.* 14 Feb. 1824; *suc. to the Baronetcy*, 11 Oct. 1877, and resided at "Knoyle" Cooksville, near Toronto aforesaid. He *m.* in 1847, Jessie, da. of Thomas HECTOR abovenamed. She *d.* 1899. He *d.* s.p.m., 17 Nov. 1903, aged 79, when *the Baronetcy* became *extinct*.

ONSLOW:

cr. 30 Oct. 1797.

I. 1797. "RICHARD ONSLOW, Esq., Vice-Admiral of the Red,"(b) 2d s. of Lieut.-General Richard ONSLOW, Governor of Plymouth, by his 2d wife Pooley, da. of Charles WALTON, of Little Bursted, Essex (br. of Vice-Admiral Sir Charles WALTON), which Richard (who *d.* 16 March 1760) was yr. br. of the Right Hon. Arthur ONSLOW (Speaker of the House of Commons [1728-61], and father of the 1st EARL ONSLOW), was *b.* 23 June 1741; entered the Royal Navy; Lieut., 1758, becoming Rear-Admiral, 1793; Vice-Admiral, 1794, and finally, 1799, Admiral. He was second in command, under Admiral Duncan, and, having distinguished himself at the battle of Camperdown, 11 Oct., was *cr. a Baronet*, as above, 30 Oct. 1797; was Lieut.-General of the Royal Marines and was made **G.C.B.**, 2 Jan. 1815. He was of Althain, co. Lancaster.(c) He *m.* 2 June 1773, Anne, da. of Matthew MICHELL, of Chitterne All Saints, Wilts, Capt. R.N. He *d.* 27 Dec. 1817, at Southampton, aged 76. Will pr. 1819. His widow *d.* 31 Jan. 1837, at Brighton, aged 85. Will pr. Feb. 1837.

(a) The eldest son, William James Parker, Lieut. in the East India service, is frequently (though erroneously) said to have *suc. to the Baronetcy*. He *m.* twice but *d.* s.p. and v.p., in 1845, aged about 35.
(b) See p. 315, note "e," under "HAYES."
(c) The Baronetcy is so headed in Betham's *Baronetage* [1804] only seven years after its creation, the 2d Baronet was living at Althain in 1822; the "seat," also, is so given in Debrett's *Baronetage* [1840].

II. 1817. SIR HENRY ONSLOW, Baronet [1797], of Althain(a) and Chitterne aforesaid, and afterwards of Hengar, near Bodmin,(b) co. Cornwall, 2d but 1st surv. s. and h.,(c) *b.* 23 April 1784; Capt., Royal Artillery, 1806, retiring on half-pay; *suc. to the Baronetcy*, 27 Dec. 1817. He *m.* 7 Feb. 1807, Caroline, da. of John BOND, of Mitcham, Surrey. He *d.* 13 Sep. 1853, at Brighton, in his 70th year. Will pr. Oct. 1853. His widow *d.* 6 Jan. 1867, at Cheltenham in her 89th year.

III. 1853. SIR HENRY ONSLOW, Baronet [1797], of Hengar and Chitterne aforesaid, 1st s. and h., *b.* 5 Oct. 1809 at Charlton by Woolwich, sometime Capt. 10th Foot; *suc. to the Baronetcy*, 13 Sep. 1853; Sheriff of Cornwall, 1857. He *m.* 21 Nov. 1848, Ellen, 6th and yst. da. of Samuel PETER, of Porthcothan, Cornwall, by Sarah, da. of (—) CARBIS. He *d.* s.p.m.s., 20 Nov. 1870, at Hengar, aged 61. His widow, who was *b.* 19 Dec. 1870, *d.* 16 Dec. 1877, at Colquite, co. Cornwall.

IV. 1870. SIR MATTHEW RICHARD ONSLOW, Baronet [1797], of Hengar and Chitterne aforesaid, br. and h. male, *b.* 12 Sep. 1810; entered the Bengal cavalry, 1825, retiring as Major; *suc. to the Baronetcy*, 20 Nov. 1870. He *m.* firstly, 1 May 1837, Eliza Antonia, 2d da. of William Newton WALLACE, Colonel of the 53d Bengal Native Infantry. She *d.* 15 June 1854. He *m.* 6 Dec. 1855, Mary, da. of J. SALTER. He *d.* 3 Aug. 1876, at Hengar, aged 65. His widow *d.* apparently in 1892.(d)

V. 1876. SIR WILLIAM WALLACE RHODERIC ONSLOW, Baronet [1797], of Hengar and Chitterne aforesaid, 1st s. and h. by 1st wife, *b.* 13 Aug. 1845, at Simla, in India; ed. at Marlborough College; entered 12th Foot, 1864; Lieut. 1868, serving in New Zealand (medal), but retired 1874; *suc. to the Baronetcy*, 3 Aug. 1876; sometime Capt. 3d Batt. of the Duke of Cornwall's Light Infantry Militia. He *m.* 11 Feb. 1873 at "Villa Mentone," Killiney, co. Dublin, Octavia Katherine, sister and coheir of Sir Charles James KNOX-GORE, 2d and last Baronet [1868], being 8th and yst. da. of Sir Francis Arthur KNOX-GORE, 1st Baronet [1868], of Belleek Manor, co. Mayo (formerly Francis Arthur KNOX), by Sarah, da. of Charles Nesbitt KNOX, of Castle Lacken.

Family Estates.—These, in 1883, consisted of 5,419 acres in Cornwall and 1,638 in Wilts. *Total.*—7,057 acres, worth £3,234 a year. *Principal Seat.*—Hengar House, near Bodmin, co. Cornwall.

KNIGHTLEY:(e)

cr. 2 Feb. 1798;

sometime, 1892-95, BARON KNIGHTLEY OF FAWSLEY.

I. 1798. JOHN KNIGHTLEY, of Fawsley, co. Northampton, Clerk in Holy Orders, br. and h. of Valentine KNIGHTLEY(f) of the same, sometime (1795-96) Sheriff of Northamptonshire (*d.* unm. 7 July 1796, aged 52),

(a) See p. 320, note "c," under
(b) He must have derived this estate from his mother's family. In 1814 Hengar was the property and occasional residence of Mathew Michell (son of Mathew Michell, Capt. R.N.), to whom it had been left by Col. Samuel Michell (*d.* 1786), whose father *m.* the 2d da. of Richard Lower, M.D., of the same. See Lysons's *Cornwall* [1814].
(c) The eldest, son Matthew Richard Onslow, *m.* 30 Nov. 1805, Sarah, da. of Hugh Seton, Lieut.-Gov. of Surat, and *d.* v.p. and s.p.m. 10 Aug. 1808, leaving two daughters and coheirs.
(d) She is given as living in Dod's *Baronetage* for 1892, but omitted in that for 1893.
(e) An elaborate pedigree of this family is in Baker's *Northamptonshire*, vol. i, pp. 381-383. See also *Mis. Gen. et Her.*, 1st S., vol. i, pp. 129-133.
(f) He matric. at Oxford (Brasenose Coll.), 19 Oct. 1762, aged 18, and was *cr.* M.A., 3 April 1767.

who was br. and h. of Lucy KNIGHTLEY, of the same, M.P. for Northampton, 1763-68, and for Northamptonshire, 1773-84, having been Sheriff of that County, 1770-71 (*d.* s.p. 29 Jan. 1791, aged 49), all three being the elder of the six sons of Valentine KNIGHTLEY,(a) of Fawsley, M.P. for Northamptonshire, April 1748 till his death (*d.* 2 May 1754, aged 35); by Elizabeth, da. and coheir of Edmund DUMMER, of Swathling in North Stoneham, Hants. was *b.* 17 Feb. 1746/7 at Fawsley; matric. at Oxford (Brasenose College), 3 May 1765, took Holy Orders; was Rector of Byfield, co. Northampton, 1777-1810, and, having suc. to the family estates on the death of his elder br., 7 July 1796 (as abovestated), was *cr. a Baronet*, as above, 2 Feb. 1798, with a spec. rem. failing heirs male of his body, to those of his yr. brother, Charles KNIGHTLEY, Clerk in Holy Orders, deceased. He *m.* 15 April 1779, at St. Geo. Han. sq., Mary, only da. and h. of John BAINES, of Layham, Suffolk, by Elizabeth, sister and coheir of James JOHNSON, D.D., Bishop of Worcester (1759-74), da. of the Rev. James JOHNSON, Rector of Long Melford, Suffolk. He *d.* s.p. in London, 29 Jan. and was *bur.* 6 Feb. 1812 at Fawsley, aged nearly 65. Will pr. 1812. His widow *d.* 21 Oct. 1830. Will pr. Oct. 1830.

II. 1812. SIR CHARLES KNIGHTLEY, Baronet [1798], of Fawsley aforesaid, nephew and h., being 1st s. and h. of the Rev. Charles KNIGHTLEY,(b) B.C.L., Rector of Preston Capes and Vicar of Fawsley, both in co. Northampton (1778 till death), by Elizabeth, da. of Henry BOULTON, of Moulton, co. Lincoln, which Charles (who *d.* 28 June 1787, aged 33), was yr. br. of the 1st Baronet. He was *b.* 30 Jan. and *bap.* 10 March 1781, at Preston Capes; ed. at Rugby; matric. at Oxford (Ch. Ch.), 19 Oct. 1799; aged 18, being many years later *cr.* D.C.L., 13 June 1834; *suc. to the Baronetcy*, 29 Jan. 1812; Sheriff of Northamptonshire, 1817-18, and M.P. for South Northamptonshire (five Parls.), Dec. 1834 to 1852. He *m.* 24 Aug. 1813, at St. Geo. Han. sq., Selina Mary, 1st da. of Felton Lionel HERVEY, of Englefield Green, Surrey, by Selina, da. and h. of Sir John ELWILL, 4th and last Baronet [1709]. She *d.* 27 July 1856, at Fawsley Park, aged 75. Will pr. Feb. 1857. He *d.* there 30 Aug. 1864, in his 84th year.

III. 1864. SIR RAINALD KNIGHTLEY, Baronet [1798], of Fawsley aforesaid, only s. and h., *b.* in Upper Brook street 22, and *bap.* 24 Oct. 1819, at St. Geo. Han. sq.; was M.P. (Conservative interest) for South Northamptonshire (nine Parls., during forty years, 1852 till raised to the peerage in 1892, having *suc. to the Baronetcy*, 30 Aug. 1864. He was *cr.* 23 Aug. 1892, BARON KNIGHTLEY OF FAWSLEY, co. Northampton. He *m.* 20 Oct. 1869, at St. Peter's, Eaton square, Louisa Mary, da. of Gen. Sir Edward BOWATER,(c) **K.C.H.**, by Emilia Mary, da. of Col. Michael BARNE, of Sotterley, Suffolk. He *d.* s.p. at Fawsley Park, 19 Dec. 1895, and was *bur.* at Fawsley, aged 76, when the *peerage* became *extinct*. Will pr. at £23,023 gross, and £4,250 net personalty. His widow, who was *b.* 25 April 1842 and *bap.* at St. Geo. Han. sq., and who was an Extra Lady-in-Waiting to H.R.H. the Duchess of Albany, was living 1905.

IV. 1895. SIR VALENTINE KNIGHTLEY, Baronet [1798], cousin and h. male, being 1st s. and h. of the Rev. Henry KNIGHTLEY,(d) M.A., Rector of Byfield and Vicar of Fawsley, 1810 till death, by Jane Diana, da. of the Rev. Philip STORY, of Lockington Hall, co. Leicester, which Henry (who *d.* 9 Sep. 1813, aged 26) was yr. br. of the 2d Baronet. He was *b.* 30 Sep. 1812, and *bap.* 17 Feb. 1813, at Charwelton, co. Northampton; ed. at Eton; matric. at Oxford (Ch. Ch.), 26 Nov. 1830, aged 18; B.A., 1834; M.A. (Lambeth degree), 1837; in Holy Orders; Rector of Preston Capes, 1836, and of Charwelton, 1837 till his death. He *suc. to the Baronetcy*, 19 Dec. 1895, and *d.* unm., at Preston Capes Rectory, 28 April 1898, aged 85.

(a) He matric. at Oxford (St. John's Coll.), 27 Sep. 1735, aged 17.
(b) He matric. at Oxford (St. Mary Hall), 21 Feb. 1771, aged 17; B.C.L. (Trinity Coll.), 1778.
(c) See *Mis. Gen. et Her.*, New Series, vol. ii, pp. 177-182.
(d) He matric. at Oxford (Ch. Ch.), 3 Feb. 1804, aged 18; B.A. 1807; M.A., 1810.

V. 1898. SIR CHARLES VALENTINE KNIGHTLEY, Baronet [1798], nephew and h., being 1st s. of the Rev. Henry Charles KNIGHTLEY, B.A. (Cambridge), Vicar of Combroke, with Compton Verney, co. Warwick (*d.* there, 14 Aug. 1884, aged 70), by Mary Maria, da. of Sylvester RICHMOND, Captain 49th Foot, which Henry was yr. br. of the late Baronet. He was *b.* 22 July 1853, at Leamington, co. Warwick; matric. at Oxford (Ch. Ch.), 23 May 1872, aged 18; B.A., 1876; Barrister (Inner Temple), 1879; *suc. to the Baronetcy*, 28 April 1798. He *m.* 26 April 1883, Juliet Claudine, da. of T. W. WATSON, of Lubenham, co. Leicester.

Family Estates.—These, in 1883 (being then the property of the 3d Baronet), consisted of 8,041 acres in Northamptonshire, worth £13,182 a year. *Seat.*—Fawsley Park, near Daventry, co. Northampton.

HAY, *otherwise* DALRYMPLE-HAY:
cr. 7 April 1798.

I. 1798. "JOHN HAY, Esq.,"(a) *formerly* John DALRYMPLE, 2d but 1st surv. s. and h. of James DALRYMPLE, M.D., of Dunragit in Glenluce, co. Wigton (*d.* 14 May 1776, aged 69), by Grace, da. of Patrick MACDOUALL, of Freugh, was *b.* 14 April 1746; was an officer in the Army, serving in the American war, and becoming finally a Colonel; suc. to the estate of Park place in Glenluce aforesaid, on the death s.p., 30 April 1794, of his wife's brother, Sir Thomas HAY, 4th Baronet [S. 1663], of Park place aforesaid; took by royal lic., 4 April 1798, the name of HAY, using it apparently after that of DALRYMPLE, and was *cr. a Baronet*, as above, a few days subsequently, 7 April 1798. He *m.* 15 April 1779, Susan, sister and h. of Sir Thomas HAY abovenamed, only da. of Sir Thomas HAY, 3d Baronet [S. 1663], by Jean, da. of John BLAIR, of Dunskey. He *d.* 12 May 1812, aged 66. His widow *d.* Jan. 1825.

II. 1812 SIR JAMES DALRYMPLE-HAY, Baronet [1798], of Park place and Dunragit aforesaid, only s. and h., *b.* 26 July 1789, at Dunragit; matric. at Oxford (Ch. Ch.), 21 Oct. 1808, aged 18; *suc. to the Baronetcy*, 12 May 1812. He *m.* firstly, 27 Sep. 1819, Elizabeth, 1st da. of Lieut.-Gen. Sir John Shaw HERON-MAXWELL, 4th Baronet [S. 1683], by Mary, da. and h. of Patrick HERON, of Heron, co. Galloway. She *d.* 10 Feb. 1821. He *m.* secondly, March 1823, Anne, 1st da. of George HATHORN, of Brunswick square, Midx., She *d.* 10 July 1838. He *d.* 19 March 1861, at Dunragit, aged 71.

III. 1861. SIR JOHN CHARLES DALRYMPLE-HAY, Baronet [1798], of Park place and Dunragit aforesaid, 1st s. and h., being only child by 1st wife, *b.* 11 Feb. 1821, in Princes street, Edinburgh; ed. at Rugby, 1833; entered the Royal Navy, 1834, served off the Cape during the first Caffre war; served in the Syrian war, being at the bombardment of Beyrout and Acre, 1839-42, and distinguishing himself in the boat attack on Tortosa, 20 Sep. 1840; was in command off the coast of China, Sep. and Oct. 1849, at the destruction of two piratical fleets; was in command in the Black Sea during the Crimean war, 1855-56, being present at the fall of Sebastopol (Syrian medal, Acre medal, War medal and Sebastopol clasp; 4th class of the Turkish order of the Medjidie); was in command in North America and the West Indies, 1857-60, becoming Rear-Admiral, 1866 (retired 1870); Vice-Admiral, 1872, and finally, 1878, Admiral, having *suc. to the Baronetcy*, 19 March 1861. He was M.P. for Wakefield, 1862-65; for Stamford, May 1866 to 1880, and for Wigton burghs, 1880-85. He was a

(a) See p. 113, note "a," under "GIDEON." The date of the Gazette notice for Hay is 20 April [*Qy.* March], for Anderson is 5 May, for Anstruther, 11 May, for Williams and Callandar, 23 June, and for Caldez, 6 Aug. 1798.

Public Works Loan Commissioner, 1862-74, being made P.C. 2 March 1874; was a Lord of the Admiralty, 1866-69; **C.B.**, 1869; **K.C.B.**, 1885; **G.C.B.**, 1902. He was also *cr.* D.C.L. (Oxford), 22 June 1870; Vice-President of the Institute of Naval Architects; F.R.S., F.R.G.S., etc. He *m.* 17 Aug. 1847, at Ettrick church, co. Selkirk, Eliza, 3d. da. of William John (NAPIER), 9th LORD NAPIER OF MERCHISTOUN [S.], by Eliza, da. of the Hon. Andrew James COCHRANE-JOHNSTONE. She, who was *b.* 26 Sep. 1822, *d.* 2 April 1901, at 108 St. George's square, Pimlico, aged 78.

ANDERSON:
cr. 14 May 1798;
ex. 21 May 1813.

I. 1798, to 1813. "RIGHT HON. JOHN WILLIAM ANDERSON, of Mill Hill, Hendon, co. Middlesex, Esq., Lord Mayor of the City of London,"(a) 2d but only s. that had issue of William ANDERSON, of Dantzic, Merchant (*b.* in Scotland and *d.* at Dantzic, 1749, aged about 50), by Lucy, da. of (—) Sheldon, was *b.* at Dantzic about 1736; was a Citizen and Glover of London; Alderman of Aldersgate, 12 Feb. 1789 till death; Sheriff of London, 1791-92; M.P. for Okehampton, 1790 till void, Feb. 1791, and for London (three Parls.), March 1793 to 1806; Lord Mayor, 1797-98, being during office, *cr. a Baronet*, as above, 14 May 1798. President of Christ's Hospital, Treasurer of the Artillery Company, a Director of the Royal Exchange Assurance Company, etc. He *m.* in 1762, Dorothy, 2d and yst. da. and coheir of Charles SIMKINS, of Devizes, Wilts, only child by his 2d wife Dorothy, da. of Henry PORTAL, of Treefolk, Hants.(b) He *d.* s.p. 21 May 1813 in his 78th year, when the *Baronetcy* became *extinct*. Will pr. 1813. His widow *d.* 9 Dec. 1817 and was *bur.* at Hendon, Midx.(b) Will pr. 1817.

ANSTRUTHER:
cr. 18 May 1798;
merged, 5 Jan. 1808,
in the Baronetcy of ANSTRUTHER [S.], *cr.* 6 Jan. 1700.

I. 1798. "SIR JOHN ANSTRUTHER, Knt., Chief Justice of the supreme court of Judicature at Fort William, in Bengal,"(a) in the East Indies, 2d s. of Sir John ANSTRUTHER, 2d Baronet [S. 1700], of Anstruther and Elie House, co. Fife, by Janet, da. of James FALL, of Dunbar, Merchant, was *b.* at Elie House, 27 March 1753; admitted to Lincoln's Inn, 12 Feb. 1774; Advocate, 30 July 1774; Barrister (Lincoln's Inn), 1779; was M.P. for Anstruther Easter burghs (two Parls.), 1783-90; for Cockermouth, 1790-96, and for Anstruther Easter burghs (again), 1796-97, and 1806 till death in 1811, taking a leading part in the impeachment of Warren Hastings; was Chief Justice in Bengal, 1796-1806; *Knighted*, 4 Oct. 1797, and was *cr. a Baronet*, as above, 18 May 1798; P.C., 19 Nov. 1806. He *m.* in or before 1784, Maria Isabella, 1st da. of Edward BRICE, of Berners street, Marylebone. She was living when, on the death, 5 Jan. 1808, of his elder br. Sir Philip ANSTRUTHER-PATERSON, 3d Baronet [S. 1700], he *suc. to the Baronetcy* [S.], which had been conferred, 6 Jan. 1700, on their grandfather John ANSTRUTHER. In that Baronetcy [S.] of an older date this *Baronetcy* [G.B.] then *merged* and still (1905) so continues. See vol. iv, p. 388.

(a) See p. 323, note "a," under "HAY."
(b) See pedigree of Simkins in *Mis. Gen. et Her.*, 3d S., v. 80.

WILLIAMS:
cr. 24 July 1798;
sometime, 1842-59, HAY-WILLIAMS.

I. 1798. "JOHN WILLIAMS, Esq., of Bodelwyddan, by St. Asaph,"(a) co. Flint, 1st s. and h. of Bennet WILLIAMS,(b) of Chester (*d.* v.p., 24 March 1786, aged 50), by Sarah, da. of Roger HESKETH, of Rossall, co. Lancaster, was *b.* 22 Dec. 1761; Sheriff of Flint, 1794-95; and was *cr. a Baronet*, as above, 24 July 1798. He *m.* 21 Oct. 1791, Margaret, da. and h. of Hugh WILLIAMS, of Tyfry, co. Anglesey. He *d.* 9 Oct. 1830, at Bodelwyddan, aged 68. Will pr. Dec. 1830. His widow *d.* 6 March 1835, aged 66.

II. 1830. SIR JOHN WILLIAMS, *afterwards* (1842-59) HAY-WILLIAMS, Baronet [1798], of Bodelwyddan and Tyfry aforesaid, 2d but 1st surv. s. and h., *b.* 9 Jan. 1794, at Bodelwyddan; *suc. to the Baronetcy*, 9 Oct. 1830, and took by royal lic., 12 May 1842, the name of HAY before that of WILLIAMS. He *m.* 8 Sep. 1842, at St. Geo. Han. sq., Sarah Elizabeth, only da. of William Pitt (AMHERST), 1st EARL AMHERST, by Sarah, relict of the 5th Earl of Plymouth, da. and coheir of Andrew (ARCHER), 2d and last BARON ARCHER OF UMBERSLADE. He *d.* s.p.m., 10 Sep. 1859, aged 65. His widow, who was *b.* 9 July 1801, *d.* 8 Aug. 1876.

III. 1859. SIR HUGH WILLIAMS, Baronet [1798], of Bodelwyddan aforesaid, br. and h. male, *b.* there 8 Jan. 1802; ed. at Rugby; Barrister (Middle Temple), 1830; *suc. to the Baronetcy*, 10 Sep. 1859; Sheriff of Denbighshire, 1862. He *m.* 16 April 1843, Henrietta Charlotte, only da. of his distant cousin, Sir Watkin WILLIAMS-WYNN, 5th Baronet [1688], of Wynnstay, co. Denbigh, by Henrietta Antonia, da. of Edward (CLIVE), 1st EARL OF POWIS. He *d.* at Bodelwyddan, 10 May 1876, aged 74. His widow *d.* 28 May 1878, at "the Brow," Rhuabon.

IV. 1876. SIR WILLIAM GRENVILLE WILLIAMS, Baronet [1798], of Bodelwyddan aforesaid and Pengwern Hall, co. Flint, 1st s. and h., *b.* 30 May 1844, in Dover street, Piccadilly; ed. at Eton; entered the Life Guards, 1863; Lieut., 1868; sometime an Officer in the 1st Royal Dragoons; *suc. to the Baronetcy*, 10 May 1876; Sheriff of Flintshire, 1882. He *m.* 16 Sep. 1884, at St. Geo. Han. sq., Ellinor Harriet, only da. of Willoughby Hart SITWELL, of Ferney Hall, Salop. She *d.* 30 April 1894. He *d.* suddenly at Pengwern Hall aforesaid, 28 Aug. 1904, aged 60.

V. 1904. SIR WILLIAM WILLOUGHBY WILLIAMS, Baronet [1798], of Bodelwyddan aforesaid, 1st s. and h., *b.* 11 Sep. 1888; *suc. to the Baronetcy*, 28 Aug. 1904.

Family Estates.—These, in 1883, consisted of 5,360 acres in Denbighshire and 4,011 in Flintshire. *Total.*—9,371 acres, worth £8,871 a year. *Principal Seat.*—Bodelwyddan, near St. Asaph, co. Flint.

(a) See p. 323, note "a," under "HAY."
(b) This Bennet was great grandson of Sir William Williams, 1st Baronet [1688], ancestor of the Williams-Wynne, Baronets, being s. of John Williams, Chief Justice of Breeon, Glamorgan and Radnor (*d.* 4 May 1787, aged 87), who was 3d s. (the 1st s. who left issue) of John Williams, of Chester, a Welsh Judge (*d.* 1735), who was 2d s. of the abovementioned Baronet.

DALLAS:

cr. 31 July 1798.

I. 1798. GEORGE DALLAS, of Petsal, co. Stafford,(a) and Upper Harley street, Marylebone, Midx., 2d s.(b) of Robert DALLAS, of Kensington, co. Midx. (*bur.* there 15 April 1796), and of Cooper's Court, St. Michael's Cornhill, London, by Elizabeth, da. of the Rev. James SMITH, Minister of Kilbirnie, co. Ayr, was *b.* 6 April 1758 in London; ed. at Geneva; went, at 18, to Bengal as a Writer in the East India Company's service; was for a few years Superintendent of the Collections at Rajeshahi, but returned to England in or shortly after 1785, and was *cr. a Baronet*, as above, 31 July 1798. He was M.P. for Newport (Isle of Wight), May 1800 to 1802. He *m.* 11 June 1788, Margaret Catherine, 4th and yst. da. of Sir John BLACKWOOD, 2d Baronet [I. 1763], by Dorcas, *suo jure* BARONESS DUFFERIN AND CLANEBOYE [I.], da. and coheir of James STEVENSON, of Killyleagh. He *d.* 14 Jan. 1833, at Brighton, aged 74(c), and was *bur.* in St. Andrew's Church, Waterloo street. M.I. Will pr. Feb. 1833. His widow *d.* 5 April 1846, in Henrietta street, Cavendish square, Marylebone. Will pr. April 1846.

II. 1833. SIR ROBERT CHARLES DALLAS, Baronet [1798], 4th and yst.(d) but only surv. s. and h., *b.* 23 Dec. 1804, at Dawlish, Devon; matric. at Oxford (Oriel Coll.), 7 July 1821, aged 16; B.A. 1825; M.A., 1829; Barrister (Lincoln's Inn), 1829; *suc. to the Baronetcy*, 14 Jan. 1833; Lieut.-Colonel of the Royal Grenada Militia, and Militia Aide-de-Camp to the Lieut.-Governor of Grenada. He *m.* 29 Sep. 1841, at St. Mary's, Bryanston square, Frances Henrietta, widow of Charles DES VOEUX, 5th and yst. da. of Edward (LAW), 1st BARON ELLENBOROUGH, by Anne, da. of George Philips TOWRY. He *d.* 2 Aug. 1874, at 55 Montagu square, in his 70th year. His widow, who was *b.* 11 Feb. 1812, *d.* 2 March 1894, at 17 Ashburn place, Cromwell road, South Kensington, in her 83d year.

III. 1874. SIR GEORGE EDWARD DALLAS, Baronet [1798], 1st s. and h., *b.* 9 Oct. 1842, in Henrietta street aforesaid; entered the Foreign Office, Dec. 1863, becoming, eventually, chief clerk thereof, but retired in 1900, having, long previously, *suc. to the Baronetcy*, 2 Aug. 1874. He *m.* 17 Sep. 1884, Felicia Mary, 1st da. of the Rev. George Earle WELBY, B.A., Canon of Lincoln, and Rector of Harrowby, co. Lincoln, by Augusta, da. and h. of the Rev. William WOODALL, of Branston and Waltham, co. Leicester.

(a) The Baronetcy is described as "Dallas of Petsall, Staffordshire" (as also is the "seat" of the 1st Baronet) in Betham's *Baronetage* [1806], only six years after its creation.

(b) His elder br., Sir Robert Dallas, sometime (1818-23), Lord Chief Justice of the Court of Common Pleas, *d.* 25 Dec. 1824, aged 78.

(c) He was, at an early age, author "of a clever poem, entitled *The India Guide*, published at Calcutta [and] said to have been the first publication which was issued from the Indian Press," and was, later on, author of several political pamphlets, *e.g.*, one in vindication of Warren Hastings [1789]; another, in defence of the Marquess Wellesley's policy in India [1806], etc., his writings being "chiefly distinguished by their elegance of style and expression" [*Dict. Nat. Biog.*].

(d) Of his three elder brothers, who all *d.* unm. and v.p. (1), William Gemmel Dallas, *b.* 11 April 1792, *d.* 7 Nov. 1799; George Dallas, *b.* 31 Dec. 1797; *d.* 14 Feb. 1816, being killed by the accidental discharge of a gun; (3), Henry Dallas, Capt. 37th Foot, *b.* 31 July 1802, *d.* 25 Dec. 1824, aged 78.

CALLANDAR, *or* CALLENDER;

cr. 1 Aug. 1798;

ex. 2 April 1812.

1798, to 1812. "JOHN CALLENDAR [*or* CALLENDER], of Westertown, co. Stirling, and of Crichton and Preston Hall and Elphinstone, in the counties of East and Mid Lothian,"(a) 3d but 1st surv. s. and h. of Alexander CALLANDAR, *or* CALLENDER, of Westertown aforesaid (*d.* April 1742, aged 31), by Margaret, da. of David RAMSAY, of Lethendie and Mungall, was *b.* Sep. 1739; served heir special to his father, 15 May 1758; was Col. in the Army; M.P. for Berwick-upon-Tweed (three Parls.), Sep. 1795 to 1807, and was *cr. a Baronet*, as above, 1 Aug. 1798. He *m.* 2 Feb. 1786, Margaret, widow of Bridges KEARNEY, da. of John ROMER, of Cherwick, co. Northumberland. He *d.* s.p., 2 April 1812, aged 72, when the *Baronetcy* became *extinct*. Will pr. 1816. His widow *d.* 22 Sep. 1815. Admon. 1815.

CALDER:

cr. 22 Aug. 1798;

ex. 31 Aug. 1818.

I. 1798, to 1818. "SIR ROBERT CALDER, Knt., Captain in the Royal Navy, and of Southwick, co. Southampton,"(a) 4th s. of Sir James CALDER, 3d Baronet [S. 1686], of Park House, near Maidstone, Kent, by his 1st wife, Alice, da. and coheir of Admiral Robert HUGHES,(b) was *b.* 2 July 1745; entered the Royal Navy, 1759, receiving, as midshipman, £1,800 as his share of the prize-money (the highest on record) for the capture of the Spanish ship "Hermione," 21 May 1762; Lieut., 1762; Capt., 1780, being in command on the Home Station, 1780-83; was Captain of the Fleet, under Jervis, in the Mediterranean, and, as such, present at the battle of St. Vincent, from which he carried home the despatches, and was *Knighted*, 3 March 1797, being *cr. a Baronet*, as above, 22 Aug. 1798; Rear-Admiral, 1799; was outmanœuvred by a French squadron, which escaped him, in Feb. 1801; became Vice-Admiral, 1804; came suddenly on the French Fleet under Villeneuve, off Finisterre, in July 1805, but declined to engage it (leaving thereby the English coast exposed); was recalled and censured for "error in judgment" in Dec. following. He became Admiral, 31 July 1810, and **K.C.B.**, 2 Jan. 1815. He *m.* in May 1779, Amelia, da. of John MICHELL, of Bayfield, co. Norfolk. He *d.* s.p. 31 Aug. 1818, aged 73, when the *Baronetcy* became *extinct*. Will pr. 1818. His widow, who, previous to his death, had become deranged, *d.* 1 Dec. 1830, at Fisherton Anger, Wilts, in her 76th year. Admon. May 1831.

FLETCHER:

cr. 24 Aug. 1798;

afterwards, since 1812, BOUGHEY, *or* FLETCHER-BOUGHEY.

I. 1798. THOMAS FLETCHER, of Newcastle-under-Lyne, and Betley Court, co. Stafford, Esq., the only child that had issue of Thomas FLETCHER, of Newcastle aforesaid, Banker (*b.* 23 Jan. 1717, at Earl Stearndale in Hartington, co Derby, and *d.* 4 Nov. 1783), by Elizabeth, da. and

(a) See p. 323, note "a," under "HAY."

(b) See vol. iv, p. 349, note "a," under "CALDER."

coheir of John FENTON,(a) was *b.* 25 Nov. 1747, at Newcastle aforesaid; Sheriff of Staffordshire, 1788-89; Major Commandant of the Newcastle Volunteers, 1798, being, in that year, *cr. a Baronet*, as above, 24 Aug. 1798. He *m.* 8 May 1781, his kinswoman, Anne, 1st da. and coheir of John FENTON,(a) of Newcastle aforesaid, by Anastasia, da. of John CRADOCK, of Betley Court aforesaid He *d.* 14 July 1812, aged 64, and was *bur.* at Betley. Will pr. 1812. His widow *d.* at Betley Court, 2 and was *bur.* 25 Oct. 1851, at Betley, aged 70. Admon. Jan. 1622.

II. 1812. SIR JOHN FENTON BOUGHEY, Baronet [1798], of Betley Court aforesaid, and of Aqualate Mere, co. Stafford, *formerly* John Fenton FLETCHER, only s. and h., *b.* 1 May 1784; matric. at Oxford (Ch. Ch.), 3 May 1803, aged 19; took, by royal lic., 16 May 1805, the name of BOUGHEY,(b) in compliance with the will of his cousin, George BOUGHEY,(c) whose estates he inherited: *suc. to the Baronetcy*, 14 July 1812; was M.P. for Newcastle-under-Lyne, 1812, and for Staffordshire, 1820 till death; was Lieut.-Col. of the North Staffordshire Militia. He *m.* 9 Feb. 1808, Henrietta Dorothy, 1st da. of Sir John CHETWODE, 4th Baronet [1700], by Henrietta, da. of George Harry (GREY), 5th EARL OF STAMFORD and 1st EARL OF WARRINGTON. He *d.* 27 June 1823, aged 39. Will pr. 1823. His widow *d.* 22 Jan. 1849, at Meretown House. Will pr. April 1849.

III. 1823. SIR THOMAS FLETCHER FENTON BOUGHEY, *or* FLETCHER-BOUGHEY, Baronet [1798], of Aqualate aforesaid, 1st s. and h., *b.* 22 Jan. 1809, at Betley; *suc. to the Baronetcy*, 27 June 1823; matric. at Oxford (Ch. Ch.), 19 April 1826, aged 17; B.A., 1829; Sheriff of Staffordshire, 1832-33. He *m.*, 27 Dec. 1832, Louisa Paulina, 7th and yst. da. of Thomas GIFFARD, of Chillington, co. Stafford, by Charlotte, sister and coheir of William, 9th EARL OF DEVON, da. of William, 2d VISCOUNT COURTENAY, *de jure* 8th EARL OF DEVON. She *d.* 10 Dec. 1879, at Aqualate. He *d.* there 6 Oct. 1880, aged 71.

(a) The families of Cradock, Fenton and Boughey were much intermingled with that of Fletcher. The 2d Baronet was doubly descended from James Fenton (living 1638), viz. (1), through his father, the 1st Baronet, whose father, Thomas Fletcher, had *m.* Elizabeth, da. of John Fenton (*d.* Oct. 1760), 2d s. of Daniel Fenton of Cheddleton, co. Stafford (by Alice, da. of (—) Boughey, of the Knoll in Audley, co. Stafford), which Daniel was the 2d son of the said James Fenton; and (2), through his mother, Ann, da. and coheir of (another) John Fenton (*d.* March 1782), who was s. of Thomas Fenton (by Ann, da. of John Cradock), the grandson or great-grandson of the said James Fenton. He had also a double descent from John Cradock, of Audley, co. Stafford (*d.* 9 Sep. 1721, aged 65, being father of Elizabeth, who *m.* George Boughey, as in note "c" below), *viz.*, (1) through his maternal grandfather, John Fenton (*d.* March 1782, as abovestated), who was s. of Thomas Fenton abovenamed, by Anne, da. of the said John Cradock, of Audley; and (2) through his maternal grandmother, Anastasia, wife of John Fenton abovenamed (*m.* 16 April 1748, and then aged 21), da. and h. of John Cradock, of Betley (*d.* 8 Feb. 1758, aged 71), by Anastasia, his wife, which John was s. and h. of the said John Cradock, of Audley.

(b) The will directs the name to be taken alone, and in that form the devisee (the 2d Baronet) seems to have used it, and possibly, but not certainly, his successors. The licence, however, to take it does not specify whether it was to be taken solely or in addition to the family name.

(c) This George Boughey, who *d.* 15 Feb. 1788, was of Audley, co. Stafford, and of the Inner Temple, London, and was the last survivor of four brothers, all of whom *d.* s.p., children of George Boughey, of Audley aforesaid, by Elizabeth (*m.* 7 Jan. 1708), da. of John Cradock, as in note "a" above. He was, consequently, 1st cousin to both of the maternal grandparents of the devisee, and not improbably a distant blood relation, through the match of Alice Boughey with Daniel Fenton, as mentioned in note "a" above.

IV. 1880. SIR THOMAS FLETCHER-BOUGHEY, Baronet [1798], of Aqualate aforesaid, 1st s. and h., *b.* 5 April 1836; ed. at Eton; matric. at Oxford (Ch. Ch.), 8 June 1854, aged 18; *suc. to the Baronetcy*, 6 Oct. 1880; Sheriff of Staffordshire, 1898-99. He *m.* 25 Aug. 1864, Sarah Arabella, only da. of Harold LITTLEDALE, of Liscard Hall, co. Chester.

Family Estates.—These, in 1883, consisted of 10,505 acres in Staffordshire, 270 in Derbyshire, 153 in Salop, and 47 in Cheshire. *Total.*—10,975 acres, worth £16,715 a year. *Seat.*—Aqualate Hall (near Newport), co. Stafford.

TROUBRIDGE:

cr. 30 Nov. 1799.

I. 1799. "THOMAS TROUBRIDGE, Esq., Captain in the Royal Navy, and of Plymouth,"(a) s. of Richard TROUBRIDGE,(b) of Cavendish street, Marylebone, by Elizabeth, was *b.* about 1758, being admitted on the foundation of St. Paul's School, London, 22 Feb. 1768, aged 10; entered the Royal Navy, 1773; Lieut., 1780; Capt., 1782; was present at the battles off Sadras and Trincomalee, 1782, and at Admiral Hughes's third and fourth actions, 1783-84, but was taken prisoner in May 1794, being, as such, present on board a French 80-gun ship at Howe's victory, 1 June 1794, who, it is said (on her capture), named him the commander thereof. In that year he was Commander of the 74-gun ship "Culloden," was present at the unsatisfactory action off the Hyeres, 13 July 1795, and led the line at the battle of Cape St. Vincent, 14 Feb. 1797, with great gallantry and determination. He, however, failed in the attack on Santa Cruz, in July following, and struck on a shoal at the battle of the Nile, 1 Aug. 1798, receiving, however, the gold medal. He ably supported Nelson's operations at Naples and Malta, in 1799; was made Knight of the Sicilian Order of St. Ferdinand and Merit, and was *cr. a Baronet*, as above,(c) 30 Nov. 1799. He was, for a few months in 1800, Captain of the Channel Fleet off Brest; was a Lord of the Admiralty, 1801-04, and was Rear-Admiral, 23 April 1804. M.P. for Yarmouth (Norfolk), 1802-06. In April 1805, was appointed to the chief command in the East India seas, which, shortly afterwards, was changed to that at the Cape of Good Hope, on his way to which, from Madras, he was drowned in the wreck of the "Blenheim" (74 guns), off Madagascar. He *m.*, about 1786, at St. Marylebone, Frances, widow of "Governor" RICHARDSON, da. of John NUTHALL. She *d.* 13 June 1798, and was *bur.* at St. Andrew's, Plymouth. He *d.* Feb. 1807, as abovestated. Will pr. 1808.

II 1807. SIR EDWARD THOMAS TROUBRIDGE, Baronet [1799], of Blomer, co. Sussex,(c) only s. and h., *b.* at Upton House, near Romsey, Hants, about 1787; entered the Royal Navy, 1797; was at the battle of Copenhagen, 1801; Lieut., 1806, assisting in the search for his father; *suc. to the Baronetcy*, in Feb. 1807; Capt., 1807; commanded the Naval Brigade at New Orleans, 1814; Commander-in-Chief at Cork, 1831-32; Naval Aide-de-Camp to William IV and Queen Victoria, 1831-41; M.P. for Sandwich (five Parls.), 1831-47; a Lord of the Admiralty, 1835-41; **C.B.**, 20 July 1838; Rear-Admiral, 23 Nov. 1841. He *m.* 19 Oct. 1810, Anna Maria, da. of Admiral Sir Alexander Forester Inglis COCHRANE, **G.C.B.** (6th s. of Thomas, 8th EARL OF DUNDONALD [S.]), by Maria, da. of David SHAW. He *d.* 7 Oct. 1852, at 11 Eaton place, London, aged about 50. Will pr. Jan. 1853. His widow *d.* 14 May 1873, at 17 Queen's gardens, Bayswater.

(a) See p. 113, note "a," under "GIDEON." The Gazette notice for Troubridge (the only Baronetcy conferred in 1799) is 23 Nov. 1799.

(b) This Richard was s. of John Troubridge, also of Marylebone, by Arabella, da. of (—) Davis, of Ham, Surrey. Many of the family were born in Bell yard, King street, St. Margaret's Westm.

(c) In the index to Playfair's *Baronetage* [1811], this Baronetcy is described as "of Blomer, co. Sussex," and that place is given as the residence of the 2d Baronet in Dod's *Baronetage* for 1852.

III. 1852. SIR THOMAS ST. VINCENT HOPE COCHRANE TROUBRIDGE, Baronet [1799], 1st and only surv. s. and h.,(a) b. 25 May 1815; Ensign 73d Foot, 1834; Lieut. 7th Royal Fusileers, 1836, serving in Gibraltar, West Indies and Canada; Capt., 1841; Major, 1850, serving in the Crimean campaign, being in the forefront at the battle of the Alma, 20 Sep., and being "Field Officer of the day" at the battle of Inkerman, 5 Nov. 1854, where he lost his right leg and left foot, remaining, however, in the battery till the battle was over; *suc. to the Baronetcy*, 7 Oct. 1852; Lieut.-Col., March 1885, but placed on half-pay six months later; **C.B.**, 1855; Victoria Cross, and Aide-de-Camp to Queen Victoria, 18 May 1855 till death; Crimean medal with clasps, Medjidie (fourth class) and Legion of Honour; Director-Gen. of Army clothing, 1855-57; Deputy-Adjutant-Gen. (Clothing Department), 1857 till death. He *m.* 1 Nov. 1855, at St. Michael's, Chester square, Louisa Jane, da. of Daniel GURNEY, of North Runcton, Norfolk, by Harriet Jemima, da. of William (HAY), EARL OF ERROLL [S.]. She *d.* 29 Aug. 1867, in Park street, Grosvenor square, aged 36. He *d.* a few weeks later; 2 Oct. 1867, at 8 Queen's gate, West Kensington, aged 52. Both *bur.* in Kensal Green Cemetery.

IV. 1867. SIR THOMAS HERBERT COCHRANE TROUBRIDGE, Baronet [1799], 2d but 1st surv. s. and h., b. 13 Sep. 1860, at North Runcton Hall aforesaid; *suc. to the Baronetcy*, 2 Oct. 1867; ed. at Wellington Coll.; Lieut. 1st Batt. King's Royal Rifle Corps, 1879; Capt., 1888, but resigned same year. He *m.* 13 July 1893, at Christchurch, Mayfair, Laura (sister of Rachel, COUNTESS OF DUDLEY), da. of Charles GURNEY.

GLYN:

cr. 22 Nov. 1800.

I. 1800. "SIR RICHARD CARR GLYN, of Gaunts [co. Wimborne] co. Dorset, Knt., late Lord Mayor of the City of London,"(b) 4th s. of Sir Richard GLYN, 1st Baronet [1759] (*d.* 1 Jan. 1773, aged 60), being 1st s. of his 2d wife, Elizabeth, da. and coheir of Robert CARR, of Hampton, co. Midx., and of Ludgate Hill, Silkman, styling himself a Baronet [S. 1637],(c) was *b.* 2 Feb. 1755; ed. at Westm. School; Citizen and Salter of London; partner in his late father's banking firm, "Hallifax, Mills, Glyn and Mitton," of London(d); Alderman of Bishopsgate, 3 Sep. 1790 to 1829, and of Bridge without, 1829 till his resignation in 1835, after having become "the father of the Corporation;" Sheriff of London, 1790-91, being *Knighted*, at St. James', 24 Nov. 1790; Lord Mayor, 1798-99, being *cr. a Baronet*, as above, the following year, 22 Nov. 1800; M.P. for St. Ives, Cornwall, 1796-1802, and a firm supporter of Pitt's Administration; President of Brudenell and Bethlehem Hospitals, and Lieut.-Col. of the North-East London Volunteers. Was of Hinton Parva and of Gaunts House in Wimborne, Dorset, which last he rebuilt. He *m.* 2 July 1785, Mary,(e) only da. of John PLUMPTRE, of Fredville, Kent, and of Nottingham, sometime (1761-74) M.P. for Nottingham, by his 2d wife, Mary, da. of Philips GLOVER, of Wispington, co. Lincoln. She *d.* 2 Aug. 1832, aged 71, in Arlington street. He *d.* there 27 April 1838, aged 83. Will pr. May 1838.

(a) His only br., Edward Norwich Troubridge, Capt., R.N., *d.* unm. and v.p., 1850, in China.

(b) See p. 113, note "a," under "GIDEON." The Gazette notice for the creation of Glyn, Kingsmill, Buxton, Elford, Holland, Milman, Peel, and Stirling, is 4 Nov. 1800.

(c) See vol. ii, p. 429, under "KERR" Baronetcy, *cr.* 31 July 1637.

(d) "A firm which has the reputation of having a larger business than any other private banking house in the city of London" [*Dic. Nat. Biog.*].

(e) She, through the families of Brooke, Killigrew, Neville, Beauchamp and Despencer, was descended from Edward III, through Constance, da. of Edmund, Duke of York, son of that King.

II. 1838. SIR RICHARD PLUMPTRE GLYN, Baronet [1800], of Gaunts House aforesaid, 1st s. and h.,(a) *b.* 13 June 1787; matric. at Oxford (Ch. Ch.), 20 Oct. 1804, aged 17; was afterwards of Brasenose Coll., and *cr.* M.A., 3 June 1818, was a Banker of London, as also a Gentleman of the Privy Chamber; *suc. to the Baronetcy*, 27 April 1838; Sheriff of Dorset, 1841. He *d.* unm. 20 Dec. 1863, at 37 Upper Brook street, aged 76.

III. 1863. SIR RICHARD GEORGE GLYN, Baronet [1800], of Gaunts House aforesaid, nephew and h. male, being 1st s. of Robert Thomas John GLYN, East India Company's service, by Frederica Elizabeth, da. of Henry HARFORD, of Down Place, Berks, which Robert (who *d.* 27 March 1836, aged 47), was next br. of the late Baronet. He was *b.* 22 Nov. 1831; matric. at Oxford (Merton Coll.), 31 May 1850, aged 18; entered the Army, 1852; serving as Capt. in the Royal Dragoons through the Crimean War; *suc. to the Baronetcy*, 20 Dec. 1863; Sheriff of Dorset, 1869; sometime Master of the Blackmoor Vale Hounds. He *m.* 30 April 1868, at Maperton, Somerset, Frances Geraldine, yst. da. of Major Henry Thomas George FITZGERALD, of Maperton House, by Elizabeth Harriet, da. of the Rev. Samuel Wildman YEATES.

Family Estates.—These, in 1883, consisted of 9,620 acres in Dorset, 83 in Somerset, and 67 in Wilts. *Total.*—9,770 acres, worth £12,893 a year. *Seat.*—Gaunts House, Wimborne, Dorset.

KINGSMILL:

cr. 24 Nov. 1800;

ex. 4 May 1823.

I. 1800. "ROBERT KINGSMILL, Esq., Admiral of the Blue Squadron of His Majesty's Fleet,"(b) *formerly* Robert BRICE, 2d s. of Charles BRICE, of Castle Chichester, near Kilroot, co. Antrim, Capt. in the Army (*d.* 1748, aged 64), by Jane, da. of (—) ROBINSON, of Newton Ardes, co. Down, was *b.* about 1730; became Lieut. R.N., 1756; Commander, 1761, in which year he captured a French 10-gun privateer; was present at the reduction of Martinique and St.Lucia, in 1762; took the name of KINGSMILL, by Act of Parl., 1766, his wife having suc. to the estate of Sidmanton, Hants, on the death of her maternal uncle, William KINGSMILL; was in command of a 64-gun ship at the action off Ushant, 27 July 1778, but quitted it "in disgust at the action of the Admiralty" in the matter of the Court-martial on Admiral KEPPEL.(c) He was M.P. for Yarmouth (Isle of Wight), Dec. 1779 to 1780, and for Tregony, 1784-90; was in command of a 90-gun ship "in the Spanish armament of 1790"(c); Rear-Admiral, 1793, Vice-Admiral, 1794; and Admiral, 14 Feb. 1799, being Commander-in-Chief on the coast of Ireland, 1793-1800, and being *cr. a Baronet*, as above, 24 Nov. 1800, with a spec. rem., failing heirs male of his body, to the heirs male of the body of his br., Edward KINGSMILL, *formerly* BRICE, then deceased. He *m.* before 1764, Elizabeth, da. and h. of Hugh CORRY, of Newtown Ardes, co. Down, by Frances, sister and coheir (sole heir of the whole blood) of William KINGSMILL, of Sidmanton aforesaid, being da. of Sir William KINGSMILL, of the same (who was aged 25 at the Visit. of Hants in 1686, and who *d.* 26 Nov. 1698), by his 1st wife, Frances, da. of Thomas COLWALL, Alderman of London. She *d.* 1783, and was *bur.* at Kingsclere, Hants. He *d.* s.p. at Sidmanton, 23 Nov. 1805, aged 74.

(f) George Carr Glyn, the 4th son, was *cr.* 14 May 1869, Baron Wolverton.

(b) See p. 330, note "b," under "GLYN."

(c) *Dict. Nat. Biog.*

II. 1805, to 1823. SIR ROBERT KINGSMILL, Baronet [1800], of Sidmanton and Castle Chichester aforesaid, formerly, 1772-86, Robert BRICE, nephew and h., being only s. and h. of Edward KINGSMILL, formerly BRICE, of Castle Chichester aforesaid, Surveyor of the Revenue at Belfast, by Katharine, da. of George SPRAIGHT, of Carrickfergus, which Edward (who *d.* 4 July 1796, aged 68) was br. to the grantee and had taken the name of KINGSMILL by royal lic. Dec. 1786.(a) He was *b.* 1772 and *suc. to the Baronetcy*, under the spec. rem. in its creation 23 Nov. 1805; Sheriff of Hants, 1811-12. He *m.* June 1796, Elizabeth, da. of Charles NEWMAN, of Calcutta. She was living 1801. He *d.* s.p.m.,(b) 4 May 1823, aged about 50, when the *Baronetcy* became *extinct*.

BUXTON:

cr. 25 Nov. 1800;

ex. 20 Jan. 1888.

I. 1800. "ROBERT JOHN BUXTON, of Shadwell Lodge, co. Norfolk, Esq.,"(c) 1st s. and h. of John BUXTON, of Channons Hall in Tybenham and of Rushford, both co. Norfolk (*d.* Feb. 1782, aged 65), by Elizabeth, da. and h. of John JACOB,(d) of Tockenham and Norton, Wilts, was *b.* 27 Oct. 1753, at Rushforth, was M.P. for Thetford, 1790-96, and for Great Bedwyn (two Parls.), Dec. 1797 to 1806, and, being a personal friend and active supporter of William Pitt, was *cr. a Baronet*, as above, 25 Nov. 1800. He *m.* 22 May 1777, at St. Geo. Han. sq., Juliana Mary, 2d da. of Sir Thomas BEEVOR, 1st Baronet [1784], by Elizabeth, da. and h. of Miles BRANTHWAYT, of Hethel, Norfolk. He *d.* "after many years of protracted suffering," 7 June 1839, at Shadwell Lodge, in his 86th year. Will pr. July 1839. His widow *d.* 5 Feb. 1843. Will pr. June 1843.

II. 1839. SIR JOHN JACOB BUXTON, Baronet [1800], of Shadwell Lodge and Tockenham aforesaid, only s. and h., *b.* at Norwich, 13 Aug. 1788; matric. at Oxford (Ch. Ch.), 29 Jan. 1807, aged 18; was M.P. for Great Bedwyn (six Parls.), March 1818 to 1832; *suc. to the Baronetcy*, 7 June 1839; Sheriff of Norfolk, 1841. He *m.* 5 Aug. 1825, at St. Geo. Han. sq., Elizabeth, 1st da. of Sir Montagu CHOLMELEY, 1st Baronet [1806], by his 1st wife Elizabeth, da. and h. of John HARRISON. He *d.* 13 Oct. 1842, aged 54, at Tunbridge Wells. Will pr. March 1842. His widow *d.* 28 Aug. 1884, at Shadwell Lodge, in her 81st year.

III. 1841, to 1888. SIR ROBERT JACOB BUXTON, Baronet [1800], of Shadwell Lodge and Tockenham aforesaid, only s. and h., *b.* in London 13 March 1829; ed. at Eton; *suc. to the Baronetcy*, 13 Oct. 1842; matric. at Oxford (Ch. Ch.), 27 May 1847; Sheriff of Norfolk, 1870; M.P. for South East Norfolk (three Parls.), April 1871 to 1885. He *m.* 4 Dec. 1865, at St. Peter's, Eaton sq., Mary Augusta Harriet, da. and h. of Lieut.-Col. John JOHNSTONE, E.I.C.S. (2d s. of James Raymond JOHNSTONE, of

(a) His connection with that family was exceedingly remote, being only through his brother's childless and then deceased wife, whose mother was one of the Kingsmill family. He, however, had presumably been constituted heir by his brother to the Kingsmill estates.

(b) Of his two daughters, Eliza Catherine, *b.* 1797, and Anna Maria, *b.* 1801, the former inherited the Sidmanton estate, and *m.* 10 June 1824, Sir John Kingsmill, of Hermitage Park, near Lucan, co. Dublin, Col. of the Battle-Axe Guards [I.], 1828-34 (*d.* 23 Oct. 1859), and *d.* 23 May 1865, having had issue.

(c) See p. 330, note "b," under "GLYN."

(d) A good account of the family of Jacob is in Betham's *Baronetage* [1804].

Alva, co. Stirling), by Caroline, da. of the Rev. Charles PANNEL. He *d.* s.p.m.,(a) 20 Jan. 1888, at Shadwell Court, aged 58, when the *Baronetcy* became *extinct*. His widow living 1905.

Family Estates.—These, in 1883, consisted of 9,309 acres in Norfolk, 801 in Wilts and 80 in Suffolk. *Total.*—10,190 acres, worth £7,260 a year. *Principal Seat.*—Shadwell Lodge, near Thetford, Norfolk.

ELFORD:

cr. 26 Nov. 1800;

ex. 30 Nov. 1837.

I. 1800, to 1837. "WILLIAM ELFORD, of Bickham, co. Devon, Esq., Lieut.-Col. of the South Devon Regiment of Militia,"(b) 1st s. and h. of the Rev. Lancelot ELFORD, of the same (who suc. thereto in 1760), Vicar of Plympton, Devon (*d.* Feb. 1782, aged 63), by Grace, da of Alexander WILLS, of Kingsbridge in that county, was *b.* about 1748; was Recorder of Plymouth; M.P. for that Borough, 1796-1806, and for Rye, July 1807 to July 1808, being a firm supporter of Pitt's administration; was many years Lieut.-Col. of the South Devon Militia and, when that regiment volunteered to serve in Ireland, was *cr. a Baronet*, as above, 26 Nov. 1800. He was elected F.R.S., 1790, was F.L.S. and was a skilful landscape painter. He *m.* firstly, 20 Jan. 1776, at Plympton St. Maurice, Mary, da. of the Rev. John DAVIES, of Plympton, by Mary, da. of John CHARD, of Tracy, co. Devon. She *d.* 1817. He *m.* secondly, in 1821, Elizabeth, widow of Col. Maine Swete WALROND, da. and coheir of Humphrey HALL, of Manadon, Devon, by Jane (*or* Elizabeth), da. of John (ST. JOHN), 10th BARON ST. JOHN OF BLETSHOE. He *d.* s.p.m.s.,(c) 30 Nov. 1837, in his 90th year, at the Priory, Totnes, Devon, when the *Baronetcy* became *extinct*. M.I. at Totnes. Admon. Jan. 1838, Nov. 1844, and Oct. 1848. His widow, by whom he had no issue, *d.* Oct. 1839 at Belair, Devon. Will pr. Dec. 1839.

HOLLAND, *formerly* DANCE:

cr. 27 Nov. 1800;

ex. 15 Oct. 1811.

I. 1800, to 1811. "NATHANIEL HOLLAND, of Wittenham, co. Berks, Esq.,"(b) as also of Cranbury House, near Winchester Hants, formerly Nathaniel DANCE, 3d s. of George DANCE, of St. Luke's, Old Street, London, Architect to the city of London (*d.* 11 Feb. 1768, aged 75), by Elizabeth (*m.* 1 March 1719/20, at Hackney), da. of (—) GOULD,

(a) Of his two daughters and coheirs (1) Maud Isabel, *m.* 18 Dec. 1901, Gerard James Barnes, of Morningthorpe, Norfolk, who, by royal lic., 26 March 1902, took the name of Buxton.

(b) See p. 330, note "b," under "GLYN."

(c) His only son Jonathan Elford, *b.* 5 and bap. 28 Nov. 1776 at Plympton St. Maurice, matric. at Oxford (Oriel Coll.), 3 June 1795, aged 18; was M.P. for Westbury, March to Nov. 1820. He *m.* in 1810, but *d.* s.p. and v.p., 11 March 1823, at Uplands, Tamerton Foliott. Of the two daughters and coheirs (1) Grace Chard, *bap.* as above, 5 Nov. 1781, *d.* unm. in 1856; (2) Elizabeth, *bap.* as above, 12 March 1782, *m.* in 1821, Gen. Sir George Pownall Adams, **K.C.H.** (who *d.* 10 June 1856, at East Budleigh, Devon, aged 77), and had issue.

of Hackney, was *b.* 18 May 1735 and *bap.* at St. Luke's aforesaid; admitted to Merchant Taylors' School in 1744; studied the art of painting in Italy; became a portrait painter of considerable distinction; was a member of the Incorporated Society of Artists in 1761, and a foundation member of the Royal Academy, but ceased to exhibit in 1776 and retired in 1790 on his marriage. He was M.P. for East Grinstead, 1790-1802; for Great Bedwyn, 1802-06, and for East Grinstead (again), 1807 till death. By royal lic., 4 July 1800, he took the name of HOLLAND "out of his great respect to Charlotte HOLLAND,(a) of Wigmore street, Cavendish square, spinster," and in the same year was *cr. a Baronet*, as above, 27 Nov. 1800. He *m.* in 1790, Harriet, widow of Thomas DUMMER, of Cranbury, Hants (who *d.* 3 June 1781, leaving her that estate, 4th da. of Sir Cecil BISHOPP, 6th Baronet [1620], of Parham, by Anne, da. of Hugh (BOSCAWEN), 1st VISCOUNT FALMOUTH. He *d.* s.p. 15 Oct. 1811, aged 76, when the *Baronetcy* became *extinct*.(b) Will pr. 1811. His widow *d.* in or before 1825. Will pr. June 1825.

MILMAN:

cr. 28 Nov. 1800.

I. 1800. "FRANCIS MILMAN, of Levaton [in Woodland], co. Devon, M.D., and Physician to His Majesty's Household,"(c) s. of the Rev. Francis MILMAN, B.A. (Oxford), Rector of East Ogwell and Vicar of Abbotskerswell, Devon (*d.* 1773, aged 69), by Sarah, da. and coheir of (—) DYER, of Levaton aforesaid, was *b.* 31 Aug. 1746, at East Ogwell; matric. at Oxford (Exeter Coll.), 5 July 1760, aged 13; B.A., 1764; Fellow, 1765-80; M.A., 1767; B. Med., 1770; D. Med., 1776; one of Dr. Radcliffe's Fellows, 1771-80; Physician to Middlesex Hospital, 1777-79; Fellow of the College of Physicians, London, 1778; Gulstonian Lecturer, 1780; Croonian Lecturer, 1781; Herveian Orator, 1782; being President of the said College, 1811 and 1812, resigning 6 Oct. 1813; Physician extraordinary to the King's household, 1785, being *cr. a Baronet*, as above, 28 Nov. 1800; Physician in ordinary to the King, 1806. F.R.S. He *m.* 20 July 1779, Frances, da. and h. of William HART, of Stapleton, co. Gloucester, by Frances, sister of William MILES, of the Grove, Pinner, Midx. He *d.* at the Grove aforesaid 24 June 1821, aged 74, and was *bur.* at Chelsea, Midx.(d) Will pr. 1821. His widow *d.* 1836, aged 81. Will pr. June 1836.

(a) It is not clear whether this lady was then alive, or if she was any relation or connection of the grantee. She probably was the Charlotte, sister of Isabella who *m.* Thomas Dummer (possibly the father of Lady Holland's first husband), which two sisters were coheirs (1729) of their br., Sir William Holland, 3d and last Baronet [1629] of Quiddenham, Norfolk.

(b) Two of his nephews were somewhat distinguished, viz., (1) Sir Nathaniel Dance (son of his eldest br. James Dance, otherwise Love, Comedian, *d.* 1774, aged 54) who, as Commander in the East India Company's service, put to flight in 1804, a French squadron, under Admiral Linois, and *d.* 25 March 1827, aged 79; (2) Col. Sir Charles Webb Dance, K.H. (s. of his yr. br. George Dance, a well known Architect, *d.* 14 Jan. 1825, aged 84), who served in the Peninsular war and was wounded at Waterloo; was "Silver Stick" at the coronation of George IV., and *d.* 13 Nov. 1844, aged 58.

(c) See p. 330, note "b," under "GLYN."

(d) "He was a courtly person of no great medical attainments" [*Dict. Nat. Biog.*].

II. 1821. SIR WILLIAM GEORGE MILMAN, Baronet [1800], of Levaton and Pinner Grove aforesaid, 1st s. and h.,(a) *b.* 19 April 1781, at St. Geo. Han. sq.; ed. at Eton; matric. at Oxford (Exeter Coll.), 22 May 1798, aged 17; B.A., 1801; *suc. to the Baronetcy*, 24 June 1821. He *m.* 23 Oct. 1809, Elizabeth Hurry, sister of Sir Edward Hall ALDERSON, sometime (1834-57), one of the Barons of the Exchequer, da. of Robert ALDERSON, Recorder of Norwich, Ipswich and Yarmouth, by (—), da. of Samuel HURRY of Yarmouth. She *d.* 13 Dec. 1853, at Pinner Grove, aged 62. He *d.* 21 Aug. 1857, at Ramsgate, aged 76. Will pr. Oct. 1857.

III. 1857. SIR WILLIAM MILMAN, Baronet [1800], of Pinner Grove aforesaid, 2d but 1st surv. s. and h.,(b) *b.* 21 Nov. 1813, at Easton-in-Gordano, Somerset; matric. at Oxford (Brasenose Coll.), 21 Jan. 1833, aged 19; B.A., 1837; Barrister (Inner Temple), 1841, going the Oxford Circuit; *suc. to the Baronetcy*, 21 Aug. 1857. He *m.* 29 Oct. 1841, at Sherington, Bucks, Matilda Frances, 1st da. of the Rev. John PRETYMAN; Rector of Sherington. He *d.* 17 June 1885, at Tenby, in his 72d year. His widow *d.* 24 May 1890, at "The Croft," Tenby.

IV. 1885 SIR FRANCIS JOHN MILMAN, Baronet [1800], 1st s. and h., *b.* 10 Aug. 1842; ed. at Woolwich Academy; entered the Royal Artillery, 1867, but retired 1870; sometime Captain and Adjutant 2d Brigade, Welsh Division, Royal Artillery; *suc. to the Baronetcy*, 17 June 1885. He *m.* 25 Aug. 1870, Katharine Grace, da. of Stephen Charles MOORE, of Barne, co. Tipperary, by Anna, da. of Lieut.-Col. Kingsmill PENNEFATHER, of New Park, in that county.

PEEL:

cr. 29 Nov. 1800.

I. 1800. "ROBERT PEEL, of Drayton Manor, co. Stafford, and of Bury, co. Lancaster, Esq.,"(c) 3d s. of Robert PEEL, of Peelfold, near Oswaldtwistle, and of Manchester, co. Lancaster (who *d.* extremely rich,(d) 12 Sep. 1795, having established at Blackburn, as early as 1764, the calico-printing firm of "Haworth, Peel and Yates," and who thus may be considered as the founder of the Lancashire cotton trade), by Elizabeth, sister of (—) HAWORTH, his partner, and da. of Edmund HAWORTH, of Walmesleyfold, in the

(a) Of his two yr. brothers (1), Lieut.-Gen. Francis Miles Milman, distinguished himself in the Peninsula wars (war medal and four clasps), and *d.* Dec. 1856, aged 73; (2), Henry Hart Milman, D.D., Dean of St. Paul's (1849-68), well known as an author of poetry, plays and historical works (*The History of the Jews*, etc.), *d.* 24 Sep. 1868, aged 77. He is celebrated by Byron, in the ode (after the style of *Cock Robin*) on the death (1821) of the Poet Keats (supposed to have been hastened by disparaging criticism), as under:—

"Who killed John Keats?
I, says the *Quarterly*,
Savage and Tartarly,
I killed John Keats.

Who shot the arrow?
The poet-priest Milman,
So ready to kill man,
And he shot the arrow."

(b) His yr. br. Robert Milman, D.D., was Bishop of Calcutta, 1867-76, and *d* 15 March 1876, aged 60.

(c) See p. 330, note "b," under "GLYN."

(d) He is said to have left £13,000 to each of his seven sons, and to his only surv. daughter.

said county, was *b.* 25 April 1750, at Peelfold; ed. at Blackburn and in London; entered his father's firm in 1773, at the age of 23, as a partner; adopted the discoveries of Arkwright as to the mechanical methods of saving human labour; purchased, in 1787, considerable estates in Lancashire, and subsequently in Staffordshire and Warwickshire, and, in conjunction with his partner, William YATES, established extensive cotton works at Tamworth; was M.P. for that town (six Parls.), 1790-1820; "armed and commanded six companies of Bury Royal Volunteers" in 1798(a) (his firm having given £10,000 "to the voluntary contribution of 1797"(a); was a warm supporter of the Pitt Administration, and of the Irish Union, and was *cr.* a *Baronet*, as above, 29 Nov. 1800. In 1802, he carried through Parliament a most useful Act as to factory legislation (he being himself at that time the employer of some 15,000 people), and in 1819 he opposed the resumption of cash payments, a measure carried in that year by his son.(a) He was a Governor of Christ's Hospital, London. He *m.* firstly, 8 July 1783, at the age of 33, Ellen, da. of William YATES, of Bury aforesaid, one of his partners. She, by whom he had six sons and five daughters, *d.* 28 Dec. 1803. He *m.* secondly, 17 Oct. 1805, at St. Geo. Han. sq., Susanna, sister of the Rev. Sir William Henry CLERKE, 8th Baronet [1660], da. of Francis CLERKE, of North Weston, by Susanna Elizabeth, da. of Thomas Henry ASHURST, of Waterstock, Oxon. She, by whom he had no issue, *d.* 10 Sep. 1824. Admon. July 1825. He *d.* 3 May 1830, aged 80, at Drayton Park, and was *bur.* at Drayton Basset. Will pr. June 1830.

II. 1830. THE RIGHT HON SIR ROBERT PEEL, Baronet [1800], of Drayton Manor aforesaid, 1st s. and h., *b.* 5 Feb. 1788, in a cottage near his father's house (then under repair), Chamber Hall, near Bury, co. Lancaster; ed. at Harrow, 1801-04; matric. at Oxford (Ch. Ch.), 21 Oct. 1805, aged 17, as a Gentleman Commoner; B.A. and double first class, 1808; M.A., 1814, being *cr.* D.C.L. 18 June 1817. He was M.P. for Cashel (a seat which his father had bought for him), April 1809 to 1812; for Chippenham, 1812-17; for Oxford University (four Parls.), June 1817 to 1829; for Westbury, March 1829 to 1830, and for Tamworth (seven Parls.), 1830 till his death twenty years later. In 1810 he seconded the Address (at the age of 22), and was Colonial Under Secretary, 1810-12; P.C., 1812, and Chief Secretary for Ireland, 1812-18, "establishing the peace preservation police, vulgarly termed *Peelers*, a body afterwards consolidated into the Royal Irish Constabulary"(a); successfully opposing Catholic emancipation, and delivering, 9 May 1817, "his first really great speech against the Catholic claims."(a) From 1818 to 1822 he was out of office, though on 24 May 1819, with respect to metallic currency, "he introduced his resolutions in a memorable speech, and upon them was founded *Peel's Act*, which provided that the Acts restraining cash payments should finally cease on 1 May 1823."(a) This was in direct opposition to his father's views, and to his own vote in 1811, as against Francis Horner's resolutions of a similar kind. He rejoined the [Tory] Ministry (under the Earl of Liverpool) in 1822 as Home Secretary, with Cabinet rank; effected some useful reforms, based on the views of Sir James Mackintosh, in "mitigating and consolidating the criminal law,"(a) but resigned office in April 1823, after the accession of Canning, "on the ground that he was opposed to Canning on Catholic emancipation."(a) In the Wellington Ministry he was Home Secretary (for the 2d time), and Leader of the House of Commons (for the 1st time), from Jan. 1828 to Nov. 1830, during which period he, on 5 March 1829, "in a great speech of over four hours' duration, introduced his bill for Catholic emancipation,"(a) although he had "on broad and uncompromising grounds"(a) vigorously opposed it during his twenty years of Parliamentary life. This measure became law 13 April following. In the same year, 1829, he created the Metropolitan Police Force.(b) He *suc. to the Baronetcy*, and to his father's vast estates, 3 May

(a) *Dict. Nat. Biog.*, in articles on the 1st and 2d Baronets written by the Hon. George Villiers Peel, grandson of the latter.

(b) These were called "Bobbies" in honour of his christian name of Robert, and sometimes (like the Force he established in Ireland) "Peelers."

1830. In the Reform Ministry of Earl Grey, "out of the twenty important domestic questions dealt with during the sessions of 1833 and 1834, he sided in no less than sixteen with the [Whig] Government."(a) On 9 Dec. 1834 he, as 1st Lord of the Treasury and Chancellor of the Exchequer, became Prime Minister, when the measure for establishing the Ecclesiastical Commission was carried, but after having "six times in six weeks suffered defeat,"(a) he resigned office, 8 April 1835, "and retiring into opposition, gradually built up a great party, which became known as the *Conservative Party* (a name first used in 1831), its policy being to maintain intact the established constitution of Church and State."(b) In 1836 he was Lord Rector of the University of Glasgow. In 1839 he was summoned, but failed, to form a Cabinet, owing to his insisting on the dismissal of some of the Ladies-in-Waiting on Queen Victoria. This "bed-chamber question" having, however, been settled in his favour, he formed a Ministry "emphatically on Protectionist principles"(c) in Aug. 1841, which lasted (save that he resigned office 9 but resumed it 20 Dec. 1845) till June 1846. During these years he (1) largely reduced indirect taxation, though he imposed a heavy income-tax; (2), re-organised the Bank of England; (3), sent a "sop," or (to use his own phrase) "a message of peace to Ireland,"(a) by increasing the grant to Maynooth College for the Irish Priesthood, from £9,000 to about £26,000, and by "establishing certain Queen's Colleges on a non-sectarian basis"(a); and (4) lastly, repealed the Act of 1828 (passed while he was a Minister), which fixed "a duty varying inversely with the price of corn—in other words a sliding scale,"(a) and "in a series of speeches delivered on 22 and 27 Jan., 9 Feb., 27 March, and 15 May [1846], expounded the theory and practice of Free Trade,"(a) modestly declaring that "the name to be associated with free trade in corn was not his own, but that of Richard Cobden."(a) This was the last tergiversation in his tortuous career, inasmuch as for the remaining four years of his life he held no office. He was F.R.S. and F.S.A., an Elder Brother of the Trinity House and a Governor of Charter House; a liberal patron of art and literature, he himself forming "a famous collection of pictures."(a) He *m.* 8 June 1820, at her mother's house in Upper Seymour street, Marylebone, Julia, only da. of Gen. Sir John FLOYD, 1st Baronet [1816], by Rebecca Juliana, da. of Charles DARKE, of Madras, Merchant. He *d.* at his house in Privy Gardens, Whitehall, 2 July 1850, from injuries by a fall from his horse (on Constitution Hill) three days before and was *bur.* 9 July following at Drayton Basset, aged 62.(d) Will pr. June 1830. His widow *d.* (being found dead in her bed) 27 Oct. 1859, in Privy Gardens aforesaid, and was *bur.* at Drayton aforesaid.

(a) See p. 336, note "a."

(b) *Dict. Nat. Biog.*, as abridged into one volume [1903].

(c) *Annual Register* [1850], in obituary notice.

(d) He had declined "the Garter," as well as a peerage (which last was offered also to, and declined by, his widow), or any other recompense for his long continued and laborious services, and (with greater consistency than Gladstone, who in his will gave a strongly suggestive hint of his wishes) a public funeral, though he died within a stone's throw of Westminster Abbey. His character and career have been thus depicted:—

"A man of high personal character and cold ungracious manners; he lacked the brilliance of his rival Canning, but possessed as much ability as is compatible with an absence of genius. He showed little originality or creative power but great receptiveness of mind. The leading measures which he passed were due either to the influence and insistence of such men as Horner, Mackintosh and Cobden, or to the pressure of circumstances in the teeth of his own opinions. He is the standard example of opportunism, and those tergiversations which earned him the hatred of his political associates now secure him the posthumous advocacy of Radical historians. Though widely different in nature, his career offers striking points of resemblance to that of his famous pupil Gladstone—both were masters of Parliamentary arts, both moved continuously from extreme Toryism to Liberalism (though a more cautious temperament and a shorter life prevented the earlier statesman from covering as much ground as the later) and both alike wrecked the party which they had led. Nevertheless,

III. 1850. Sir Robert Peel, Baronet [1800], of Drayton Manor aforesaid, 1st s. and h.,(a) *b.* 4 May 1822 in London; ed. at Harrow, 1835-41; matric. at Oxford (Ch. Ch.), 26 May 1841, aged 19; entered the diplomatic service; was attaché to the legation at Madrid, 1844-46; Secretary of legation and subsequently chargé d'affaires at Berne, 1846-50; *suc. to the Baronetcy*, 2 July 1850; was M.P. (seven Parls.) for Tamworth (in succession to his father), 1850-80 (first as "a Liberal Conservative," and afterwards as "a Liberal"); for Huntingdon, 1884-85, and for Blackburn, 1885-86 (as a Conservative), but becoming afterwards a "Home Ruler," contested Inverness in 1886, and Brighton, at a by-election in 1889, in that interest, where, being "hopelessly defeated, his political career [then] came to a disappointing close."(b) He was a Lord of the Admiralty, 1855-57; Secretary to the special mission to Russia, on the coronation of the Emperor, July 1856; P.C. [G. B. and I.], 25 July 1861, and Chief Secretary for Ireland, 1861-65; **G.C.B.**, 5 Jan. 1866; "was extensively engaged in racing from about 1856," and latterly, becoming embarrassed, "chiefly owing to his reckless extravagance,"(b) disposed of his father's fine collection of seventy-seven pictures and eighteen drawings to the National Gallery, in March 1871, for £75,000, and ceased to reside at Drayton Manor.(b) He *m.* 17 Jan. 1856, at the Royal Chapel, Whitehall, Emily, 8th and yst. da. of Field Marshal George (Hay), 8th Marquess of Tweeddale [S.], by Susan, da. of William (Montagu), 5th Duke of Manchester. He *d.* (being found dead in his bed, of hæmorrhage on the brain) 9 May 1895 at 12 Stratton street, aged 73. Will pr. at £9,096. His widow, who was *b.* 15 Nov. 1836, living 1905.

IV. 1895. Sir Robert Peel, Baronet [1800], of Drayton Manor aforesaid, only s. and h., *b.* 12 April 1867; ed. at Harrow; matric. at Oxford (Trinity Coll.), 16 Oct. 1886, aged 19; migrated to Balliol Coll., 1887; *suc. to the Baronetcy*, 9 May 1895. He *m.* in 1897, Mercedes, da. of Baron de Graffenried, of Thun, Switzerland.

Family Estates.—These, in 1883, consisted of 6,453 acres in Staffordshire, 3,075 in Warwickshire, and 395 in Lancashire. *Total.*—9,923 acres, worth £24,532 a year. *Seat.*—Drayton Manor, near Tamworth.

Peel's exploit of passing a measure of the first importance, which he had been placed in power to defeat, remains (and it is hoped may long remain) unrivalled. It may be possible to excuse his betrayal of his supporters in the matter of the corn laws by recognising his sincere, if late and sudden, conversion to a free trade policy which certainly benefited for a time the manufacturing classes from which he sprang, but it would seem impossible (had it not been attempted) to defend his admission of the Catholic claims in spite of his previous opposition and abiding convictions." [Vicary Gibbs.]

(a) Of the younger sons of the Statesman (1) The Right Hon. Sir Frederick Peel, **K.C.M.G.**, Chief Railway Commissioner, *b.* 26 Oct. 1823, living 1905; (2) Sir William Peel, **K.C.B.**, Capt. R.N., *d.* unm. 27 April 1858, aged 33; (3) John Floyd Peel, Capt. Fusileer Guards, *b.* 24 May 1827, living 1905; (4) Arthur Wellesley Peel, *b.* 3 Aug. 1829, *cr.* 9 May 1895, Viscount Peel of Sandy, co. Bedford, having been for eleven years (1884-95) Speaker of the House of Commons. See *Peerage*.

(b) *Dict. Nat. Biog.* in an article on him by G. C. Boase, where his "oratorical gifts," his "perfect command of language," and "rare powers of irony," are set forth, though it is added that "he used his abilities fitfully" and that "the want of moral fibre in his volatile character, an absence of dignity and an inability to accept a fixed political creed prevented him from acquiring the confidence of his associates or of the public."

STIRLING:

cr. 15 Dec. 1800.

I. 1800. "Walter Stirling, of Faskine, co. Lancaster [should be "co. Lanark"], Esq., Banker of London,"(a) 1st s. and h.(b) of Sir Walter Stirling, of Faskine aforesaid, Capt. R.N. (who *d.* 24 Nov. 1786, in Red Lion square, London, in his 69th year), by Dorothy (*d.* 1782, aged 45, at Drumpellier, near Glasgow), da. of Charles Willing, of Philadelphia, was *b.* 24 June 1758; was a Banker in Pall Mall, London; M.P. for Gatton, April 1799 to 1802, and (three Parls.) for St. Ives (Cornwall), 1807-20; Major Commandant of the Stroud Volunteers, 1798-1803; and was *cr. a Baronet*, as above, 15 Dec. 1800; Lieut.-Col. of "the Prince of Wales's Loyal Volunteers," 1803; a Governor of Bridewell and Bethlehem Hospitals; a Director of the Globe Insurance Company; F.R.S. and F.S.A. Sheriff of Kent, 1804. He *m.* 28 April 1794, Susanna, da. and h. of George Trenchard Goodenough,(c) of Borthwood in the Isle of Wight, Broughton Pogis, Oxon, and of Dunstalls, near Shoreham, and "The Grove," near Shooter's Hill, both in co. Kent, Commissioner of Taxes, by Anne (*m.* 4 Feb. 1769), da. of John Carter, of Portsmouth. She *d.* in childbirth, 8 and was *bur.* 22 June 1806, at St. James', Westm. He *d.* at the Albany Chambers, Piccadilly, 25 Aug. 1832, aged 74. Will pr. Sep. 1832.

II. 1832. Sir Walter George Stirling, Baronet [1800], of Borthwood aforesaid, only s. and h., *b.* 15 March and *bap.* 29 April 1802, at St. James', Westm.; matric. at Oxford (Ch. Ch.), 19 Oct. 1819, aged 17; admitted to Lincoln's Inn, 1822; *suc. to the Baronetcy*, 25 Aug. 1832. He *m.* 18 Oct. 1835, at St. Marylebone, Caroline Frances 3d and yst. da. of Field-Marshal John (Byng), 1st Earl of Stafford, by his 2d wife, Marianne, da. of Sir Walter James James, *formerly* Head, 1st Baronet [1791]. He *d.* at 36 Portman square, 1 Dec. 1888, aged 86. Will, leaving all to his wife, pr. at £63,818. His widow, who was *b.* 17 Sep. 1811, *d.* at 4 Draycott place, London, 27 May 1898, aged 87.

III. 1888. Sir Walter George Stirling, Baronet [1800], of Borthwood aforesaid, 2d and yst.(d) but only surv. s. and h., *b.* 5 Sep. 1839, at Ryde; sometime Capt., Royal Horse Artillery; Aide-de-Camp to the Viceroy of Ireland, 1869-74; sometime Governor to H.R.H. Prince Leopold, Duke of Albany; and, subsequently, Extra Groom-in-Waiting to Queen Victoria; *suc. to the Baronetcy*, 1 Dec. 1888; Hon. Col., Kent Artillery Militia. He *m.* firstly, 12 Oct. 1875, at St. John's, Wilton road, Midx., Eliza Horatia Frederica, Dowager-Viscountess Clifden of Gowran [I.], da. of Frederick Charles William Seymour, by his 2d wife, Augusta, da. of Frederick (Hervey), 1st Marquess of Bristol. She, who was *b.* 14 July 1833, and was one of the Ladies of the Bedchamber to Queen Victoria (1867-72), being Extra Lady thereof after 1872, and **V.A.**, 3d Class, *d.* after four years' illness, 23 April 1896, at "Burr's-wood" in Groombridge, Kent, and was *bur.* at Groombridge, aged 62. He *m.* secondly, 21 Feb. 1903, at St. Geo. Han. sq., Emily Frances, Dowager-Baroness De L'Isle and Dudley of Penshurst, 1st da. of William Fermor Ramsay, of Chester square, Pimlico.

[On 1 Jan. 1801, the Union with Ireland took place, after which date the creation of *Baronetcies of Great Britain* (as well as *of Ireland*) ceased, and that of *Baronetcies of the United Kingdom* began].

(a) See p. 330, note "b," under "Glyn."

(b) The 2d son, Vice-Admiral Charles Stirling, was of Woburn Farm in Chertsey, Surrey, and *d.* Nov. 1833, aged 73, leaving numerous issue.

(c) He was of founders kin to William of Wykeham, Bishop of Winchester, through the families of Southby, Trenchard, Henley, Udred, Rivett, Hatch, Bolney, Beke and Archmore (see tabular pedigree in Bethams' *Baronetage* [1804]), through the marriage of Alicia, sister of John, the Bishop's father, with John Archmore.

(d) The 1st s., Walter Stirling, Lieut. in the Coldstream Guards [1855], who had served as a Midshipman in the attack on Sebastopol in Oct. 1854 (medal, clasp, and Order of the Medjidie), *d.* unm., and v.p., at Hesse Darmstadt, 5 June 1862, aged 24.

Baronetcies of Ireland.(a)

1619—1800.

FIFTH AND LAST PART.

VIZ.,

CREATIONS,

1707—1800,

Being the creations made between 1 May 1707, the date of the Union with Scotland, and 1 Jan. 1801, the date of the Union with Ireland, when these creations (as well as those of Great Britain) ceased, and the creations of the United Kingdom began.

CREATIONS BY QUEEN ANNE,

1 May 1707 to 1 Aug. 1714.

DEANE:

cr. 10 March 1709/10;(b)

afterwards, since 1781, Barons Muskerry [I].

I. 1710. "Sir Matthew Deane, Knt., of Dromore, co. Cork,"(b) 3d s. of Moses *or* Matthew Deane, of Deane's Fort, Somerset, was *b.* about 1626, settled in Ireland, admitted a freeman of Cork, 2 Nov. 1663, and having purchased considerable estates in co. Cork, was *Knighted*, 3 Dec. 1680, and was *cr. a Baronet* [I.], as above, by patent dat. at Dublin, 10 March 1709/10 (9 Anne), the privy seal bearing date 14 Jan. previous at St. James'.(b) He *m.*

(a) See vol. i, p. 223, note "a," for acknowledgment of the kind assistance of Sir Arthur Vicars, Ulster King of Arms, and others, and more especially of the copious and accurate information given by G. D. Burtchaell (of the Office of Arms, Dublin), as to the Irish Baronetcies, and others connected with Ireland, which indeed is invaluable.

(b) The description (as well as the dates) of the grantees of these Irish Baronetcies (down to 27 July 1772), is, when placed within inverted commas (if not otherwise stated), taken from the *Liber Munerum Hiberniæ* (see vol i, p. 223, note "b"). This list, however, ceases to give full information after 27 July 1772, giving merely the *year*-date of the patent, and omitting altogether that of the Privy Seal. There is a note to the effect that the date of 1772 being "the end of

firstly, Mary, da. of Thomas Wallis, of co. Somerset. He *m.* secondly (Lic. Prerog. [I.], 15 Nov. 1680), Martha, widow of Lieut.-Col. John Nelson and formerly of Lieut.-Col. Richard Osbaldeston (killed at the siege of Gloucester, 1643), da. of Richard Boyle, D.D., Archbishop of Tuam (1638-44), by Martha, da. of John Wight, of Catherine Hill, Surrey. By her he had no issue. He *m.* thirdly (Lic. Cloyne, 1703), Dorothy, Dowager Countess of Barrymore [I.], da. and h. of John Ferrer, of Dublin and Dromore, but by her had no issue. He *d.* (within a year of his creation) 10 Jan. 1710/1, aged 84. Will dat. 10 May 1708, pr. [I.] 5 Dec. 1717.

II. 1711. Sir Robert Deane, Baronet [I. 1710], of Dromore aforesaid, 1st s. and h. by 1st wife, *suc. to the Baronetcy*, 10 Jan. 1710/1. He *m.* (Lic. Cork, 1676), Elizabeth, 1st da. and coheir(a) of Capt. Roger Brettridge, of Castle Brettridge, *otherwise* Castle Magner, co. Cork, by Jane, da. of (—) Hamby. He *d.* 14 Sep. 1712. His widow *m.* (Lic. Cork, 1714), John Bentley.

III. 1712. Sir Matthew Deane, Baronet [I. 1710], of Dromore aforesaid, s. and h., *suc. to the Baronetcy*, 14 Sep. 1712, Sheriff of co. Cork, 1714; M.P. for Charleville, 1713-14, and for co. Cork, 1728 till death in 1747. He *m.* in or before 1706, Jane, only da. of the Rev. William Sharp, of Dublin, sometimes (erroneously) said to be son of the ill-fated James Sharp, Archbishop of St. Andrew's (1661-79), who was murdered in 1679.(b) She *d.* 6 June 1732. He *d.* 11 March 1746/7.(c) Will dat. 6 Aug. 1746, pr. [I.] 23 July 1747.

IV. 1747. Sir Matthew Deane, Baronet [I. 1710], of Dromore aforesaid, 1st s. and h., *b.* about 1706 at Kilchaneck, co. Cork; matric. at Oxford (Ch. Ch.), 15 July 1721, aged 15; admitted to Middle Temple, 1 Aug. 1721. M.P. [I.] for the city of Cork, 1739 till death; *suc. to the Baronetcy*, 11 March 1746/7. He *m.* at St. Andrew's, Dublin, 31 July 1743 (Lic. Prerog. [I.] 28 July), Salisbury ("£14,000 fortune"),(d) sister and h. of Thomas Davenport Davies, Esq., of Manley and Marton, co. Chester (*d.* in Jamaica, 1741), only da. of Robert Davies, of the same (*d.* 1739), by Salisbury, da. of Nathaniel Lee, of Dernhale, in that county. He *d.* s.p.m. 10 June 1751. Will dat. 21 Jan. 1747/8 to 1 June 1751, pr. [I.] 1751. His widow *m.* Francis Barry and *d.* 14 Nov. 1755, in Dawson street, Dublin. Will pr. [I.] 1756.

V. 1751. Sir Robert Deane, Baronet [I. 1710], of Dromore aforesaid, br. and h. male, *b.* about 1707 at Kilchaneck aforesaid; matric. at Oxford (Ch. Ch.), 15 July 1721 (the same time as his abovenamed elder br.), aged 14; B.A., 1725; admitted to Middle Temple, 1721; Barrister (Dublin),

---

Lodge's Baronetage," the subsequent entries were a "Concurrent List in continuation of Lodge from Beatson, to be verified lower down on collation with the Rolls of Chancery in Ireland." This continuation, however, besides its deficiency in dates and information, is also very incorrect, Baronetcies of Great Britain being in some cases inserted therein, so that after 27 July 1772 it is no longer relied upon in this work.

(a) Of the other two daughters and coheirs (1) Jane, *m.* firstly Thomas Badham, and secondly Matthew Frend. (2) Mary, *m.* Francis Hartstonge, and was mother of Sir Standish Hartstonge, 2d Baronet [I. 1681]. See vol. iv, p. 214, where, however, the name of *Richard* is, in error, put for *Roger* Brettridge.

(b) William Sharp, the only son of the Archbishop, was *cr. a Baronet* [S.], 12 April 1683. See vol. iv, p. 321.

(c) His death is [erroneously] given as "Jan. 1742" in Musgrave's *Obituary*.

(d) It appears from her husband's will that she brought him £6,000 besides the Cheshire estates which were then (1747) of the value of £13,000. These appear to have devolved on the 1st Baron Muskerry [I.] who, in 1789, sold the greater part of them to Thomas Lowten.

Michaelmas, 1737; *suc. to the Baronetcy*, 10 June 1751; M.P. [I.] for Tallagh (two Parls.), 1757-68, and for Carysfort, 1769 till death. P.C. [I.], 9 Jan. 1768. He *m.* 24 Aug. 1738, at St. Paul's, Dublin (Lic. Prerog. [I.], 21 Aug.), Charlotte, 2d da. of Thomas TILSON, of Dublin, by Elizabeth, 1st da. and coheir of James KNIGHT. He *d.* 7 Feb. 1770, in Kildare street, Dublin. Will dat. 1 Jan. pr. [I.] 2 April 1770. His widow *d.* in or before 1798. Will pr. 1798.

VI. 1770. SIR ROBERT TILSON DEANE, Baronet [I. 1710], of Dromore aforesaid, and afterwards of Springfield Castle, co. Limerick, 2d but 1st surv. s. and h., *b.* 19 Oct. and *bap.* 29 Nov. 1745, at St. Anne's, Dublin; *suc. to the Baronetcy*, 7 Feb. 1770; M.P. [I.] for Carysfort, 1771-76, and for co. Cork, 1776 till raised to the peerage four years later; Sheriff of co. Cork, 1773; P.C. [I.], 6 March 1777; Governor of co. Limerick. He *m.* 7 June 1775, at St. Anne's, Dublin (Lic. Prerog. [I.], 6 June), Anne (£3,000 a year), da. and h. of John FITZMAURICE, by Anne, da. of (—) SHEEHY, which John was s. and h. of John FITZMAURICE, of Springfield Castle aforesaid, nephew to the 1st EARL OF KERRY [I.]. She was living when he was *cr.*, 5 Jan. 1781, BARON MUSKERRY, co. Cork [I.]. In that peerage this *Baronetcy* then *merged* and still (1905) so continues. See "PEERAGE."

GORE:

assumed in or shortly before 1711 to, possibly, 1760.

I. 1711? NATHANIEL GORE, of Artarmon in Drumcliffe, co. Sligo, and of Newtown, co. Leitrim, 4th s. of Sir Robert GORE, of Newtown aforesaid (*Knighted*, 28 Feb. 1678/9, and *d.* Dec. 1705), by Frances, da. of Sir Thomas NEWCOMEN, of Sutton, co. Dublin, which Robert was s. and h. of Sir Frances GORE, of Artarmon aforesaid (*Knighted* 8 May 1661), who was 4th s. of Sir Paul GORE, 1st Baronet [I. 1622], was *b.* 1692; became, by the death of his elder brothers in their minority, heir to the family estates, and in or before July 1711, possibly as early as 1705, after his father's death, *assumed the title of Baronet.*(a) He *m.* (Lic. Prerog. [I.], 24 July 1711, in which he is *styled* "Baronet), Lætitia, da. and h. of Humphrey BOOTH, of Dublin (nephew of Sir Robert BOOTH, of Salford, co. Lancaster, Lord Chief Justice of the King's Bench [I]), by Elinor, da. of (—) JONES. He *d.* (—).

II. 1743, to 1760? BOOTH GORE, of Artarmon aforesaid, 1st s. and h., who possibly *styled* himself, *or* was *styled* Baronet, *b.* 1712; was (possibly v.p.), Sheriff of Leitrim, 1742, being then termed "Esq.," as also was he in his marr. lic. (Prerog. [I.] 23 Dec. 1743), though the marriage is spoken of (*Exshaw's Mag.*, Jan. 1744) as that of "*Sir Booth Gore, Bart., of Ireland, to Miss Newcomen.*" He *m.* (Lic. Prerog. [I.] 23 Dec. 1743) Emilia, da. of Brabazon NEWCOMEN, of Calliaghstown, co. Louth, by Arabella, 3d da. of the Hon. Oliver LAMBART, 3d s. of Charles, 1st EARL OF CAVAN [I.]. She was living when he, some seventeen years later, was *cr. a Baronet* [I.], being styled "Esq." in the patent of that creation. See "GORE," Baronetcy [I.], *cr.* 30 Aug. 1760.

(a) Possibly, as both his father and grandfather were Knights, he considered the title to be hereditary. See somewhat analogous cases in the assumed Baronetcies of "DIXON" and "O'SHAUGHNESSY," vol. iv, pp. 198 and 224.

CREATIONS BY GEORGE I.

1 Aug. 1714 to 11 June 1727.(a)

ECHLIN:

cr. 17 Oct. 1721.(b)

I. 1721. "SIR HENRY ECHLIN, Knt., of Dublin Baron [*Qy.* late Baron] of the Exchequer [I.],"(b) 2d s. of Robert ECHLIN, of Castleboy and Ardquin, co. Down (*d.* 25 April 1657, in his 30th year), by Mary, da. of Henry LESLIE, D.D., Bishop of Meath, which Robert was s. and h. of the Rev. John ECHLIN, a free denizen of Ireland, 9 Aug. 1633, as being s. and h. of Henry ECHLIN, D.D., Bishop of Down and Connor, who emigrated from Scotland. He was *b.* at Ardquin, 1652; admitted to Trinity Coll., Dublin, 29 April 1667, aged 15; Semi-Scholar, 1667; admitted to Lincoln's Inn, 27 March 1672; to King's Inns, Dublin, 26 June 1677; 2d Serjeant-at-Law [I.], 3 Aug. 1683; Baron of the Exchequer, 20 Oct. 1690; Justice of the King's Bench, 18 March 1691/2; *Knighted*, 5 Nov. 1692; Baron of the Exchequer (again), 16 Feb. 1692/3, till removed, 8 Nov. 1714, being *cr. a Baronet* [I.], as above, by patent dat. at Dublin, 17 Oct. 1721, the Privy Seal being dat. at Kensington, 7 Aug. previous.(b) He was of Rush House, co. Dublin, of Clonagh Castle, co. Kildare, and of Castle Hacker, co. Mayo. He *m.*, probably about 1675, Agnes, da. of the Rev. William MUSSETT, *or* MUSHETT, of Belfast. He *d.* 29 Nov. 1725, aged 73. Will dat. 29 Jan. 1721/2, pr. [I.] 7 Dec. 1747.

II. 1725. SIR ROBERT ECHLIN, Baronet [I. 1721], of Rush House aforesaid, and Kenure Park, co. Dublin, grandson and h., being 1st s. and h. of Robert ECHLIN, sometime (1692-93) M.P. [I.] for Newtown (Ards.) and (1695 till death) for Newry, by Penelope, da. of Sir Maurice EUSTACE,(c) of Harristown, co. Kildare (by his 1st wife, da. of Sir Robert COLVILL), which Robert ECHLIN (who *d.* v.p., Dec. 1706) was 1st s. and h. ap. of the late Baronet. He was *b.* 13 Nov. 1699, and *suc. to the Baronetcy*, 29 Nov. 1725. He *m.* Dec. 4 1725, at Dublin, Elizabeth, da. and coheir of William BELLINGHAM, 3d s. of James BELLINGHAM, of Levens, Westmorland. He *d.* s.p.m.s.(d) 13 May 1757, at Rush, and was *bur.* there, aged 57. M.I. Will dat. 8 Feb. 1757, pr. [I.] 1757. His widow *d.* Jan. 1783, aged 72.(e)

III. 1757. SIR HENRY ECHLIN, Baronet [I. 1721], of Rush House aforesaid, nephew and h. male, being posthumous s. and h. of Henry ECHLIN, Cornet of Horse, by Rachel, relict of Col. Oliver MCCAUSLAND, da. of James HAMILTON, which Henry (who *d.* 16 Oct. 1740, aged 37) was br. to the late Baronet. He was *b.* 22 Dec. 1740; matric. at Oxford (Ch. Ch.), 3 May 1758, aged 17, and *suc. to the Baronetcy*, 13 May 1757, and a great part of the family estates, which, save a small amount in co. Kildare, he dissipated.(f) Sheriff of

(a) It seems extraordinary that for so long a space as eleven years (1710 to 1721) there should have been no creations of any Irish Baronetcy. This honour, however, was very rarely conferred by George I or George II, only indeed in three cases by the one during a reign of thirteen years, and in fourteen cases by the other during a reign of thirty-three years.

(b) See p. 340, note "b," under "DEANE."

(c) See vol. iv., p. 222, note "c."

(d) His da. and h., Elizabeth, *m.* (Lic. Dublin, 15 June, 1747) Francis Palmer, of Palmerstown, co. Mayo, and of Swords, co. Dublin, and was mother of Roger Palmer, who, by inheritance or purchase, acquired Rush House and all other the estates in co. Dublin of the Echlin family.

(e) She is said in her obituary notice in the *Gent. Mag.* to be sister of the late Countess of Derby, etc.

(f) "The family estates in Dublin, Mayo and Kildare were greatly reduced by the extravagence of the 3d and 4th Baronets and their wives, and [were] finally dissipated by the 5th Baronet." [Dod's *Baronetage*, 1905].

co. Dublin, 1762; Surveyor of the Customs at Rush, April 1788. He *m.* "Emily LA ROCHE, da. of the Governor of Martinico."(a) He *d.* s.p. and suddenly, 1799 at Balbriggan.

The Baronetcy was assumed in and after 1799 as under:—

IV bis. 1799, or 1814. SIR CHAMBRE ECHLIN, Baronet(b) [I. 1721], cousin, who (on the ground of the supposed illegitimacy of the children of his great uncle, the father of the 4th Baronet) alleged himself to be heir male, he being the 1st s. and h. of Henry Frederick ECHLIN, of New York in America, Capt. in the Army, by Anne *m.* (1787, at Shelburne in Nova Scotia), da. of John CONKLAN, of Nova Scotia, which Henry (the date of whose death(c) has not been ascertained) was 1st s. and h. of Chambre ECHLIN, Parish Clerk of St. Catherine's, Dublin, by Esther (marr. lic. at Dublin, 29 Feb. 1759), da. of Frederick NEWMAN, of Lisburne, the said Chambre (*b.* 18 March 1711, and *d.* Nov. 1776) being *second* s. of Henry ECHLIN, D.D., Vicar of St. Catherine's aforesaid (*d.* 1764), who was 2d s. of the 1st Baronet. He was *b.* 1788, at Halifax in Nova Scotia, and *assumed the Baronetcy* in 1814, on the ground of his (or, possibly, his father) having suc. thereto in 1799.(d) He *m.* before 1811, Susanna, da. of (—) BOYCE.(e) He *d.* s.p. 1823, being drowned at sea.

V bis. 1823, to 1844. SIR HENRY ECHLIN, Baronet(b) [I. 1721], of Halifax in Novia Scotia, br. and h.; *suc. to the Baronetcy*(b) in 1823, and appears, as a Baronet, in various *Directories*, 1824 to 1844. After that date nothing more is known of this assumption.(f)

(a) She is so described in the pedigree entered in Ulster's office, 16 Feb. 1806, by Robert Echlin, br. to Sir James the then Baronet. In *Pue's Occurrences* his marriage is given as being in "Sep. 1758, at Edinburgh, to Miss Roach, of Curzon street, Mayfair," but the date of the mar. lic. at Dublin, in which she is called "Elizabeth Roach, of the parish of St. Peter [Dublin], Spinster," is 28 Jan. 1762. Presumably, however, all three notices refer to the same person.

(b) According to the assumption of the Baronetcy in 1799.

(c) This Henry, in a note, written 22 Feb. 1817, in the Will book, in Ulster's office, by Sir William Betham (then Deputy Ulster), is said to have been, in 1799, "in America, and could not claim, but his son, now Sir Chambre Echlin, has adduced sufficient evidence before me to prove all these children [*i e.*, those of the father of the 4th Baronet] to be the bastards of Bridget Hickey, *alias* Byrne." The marriage licence of 5 Dec. 1765 is ignored, while the will of the said Bridget's husband (in which she is called his wife), dated 27 Jan. 1787 and pr. May 1789 [I.], which has never been disproved and which bears no sign of forgery about it, is (in the abovenamed note) called "a false and foul conspiracy to defraud the heir of his title and estates." The said Sir William Betham, in a letter to "My dear Sir Chambre," dated 12 Sep. 1814, states that he considers his right to the Baronetcy as "fully proved," and, accordingly, enters a pedigree, stating that Sir Chambre Echlin was successor to the Baronetcy on the death of Sir Henry in 1799, thus contradicting the statement in the note of 22 Feb. 1817 (as above) that Chambre's father was then (1799) alive, in which case he (and not his son) would have been so entitled. The date of death of this father is ignored, and the contradictory statements as to whether he, or his son, became a Baronet in 1799, remain.

(d) See note "h" above, *circa finem*.

(e) Playfair's *Baronetage* [1811].

(f) He had a yr. br., Joseph Echlin, but it is probable that the male issue of their grandfather, Chambre Echlin (who *d.* Nov. 1776), is now (1905) extinct.

IV. 1799. SIR JAMES ECHLIN, Baronet [I. 1721], of Clonagh Castle aforesaid, cousin and h. male, being the then 1st surv. s. of Henry ECHLIN, of the same, by Bridget (mar. lic. [I.], 5 Dec. 1765), da. of (—) HICKEY, which Henry (who was admitted to Trin. Coll., Dublin, 15 June 1723, aged 17, and who *d.* 1787), was 1st s. and h.(a) of Henry ECHLIN, D.D., Vicar of St. Catherine's, Dublin, and Vicar-Gen. of the diocese of Tuam (*d.* 4 Nov. 1764), who was 2d s. of the 1st Baronet. He, who was *b.* 1769,(b) *suc. to the Baronetcy* in 1799. He *m.* (Lic. [I.], 2 Feb. 1788) Jane, da. of his paternal uncle Chambre ECHLIN, of Kilrush House, co. Dublin (*d.* 1776 aged 65) by Esther, da. of Frederick NEWMAN, of Lisburne. He *d.* 18 Feb. 1833, and was *bur.* at Caddanstown, co. Kildare. Will dat. 16 Dec. 1830, pr. [I.] 20 Feb. 1836.

V. 1833. SIR FREDERICK HENRY ECHLIN, Baronet [I. 1721], of Clonagh Castle aforesaid, 1st s. and h., *b.* 4 March 1795; *suc. to the Baronetcy*, 18 Feb. 1833, but in consequence of the costs of a "famous suit" in the Irish Equity Court of Exchequer, lasting from 1827 to 1850, all his estate was sold and he himself became "a pauper."(c) He, who, "like his grandfather" Henry ECHLIN, was "half witted,(c) *d.* unm. 27 May 1871, aged 76.

VI. 1871. SIR FERDINAND FENTON ECHLIN, Baronet [I. 1721], br. and h., *b.* 10 March 1798, at Clonagh Castle aforesaid; ed. in Austria(d); *suc. to the Baronetcy*, 27 May 1871. He *m.* 10 Nov. 1841, Mary, only da. of William J. CAVANAGH, of Grangebeg, co. Westmeath. She *d.* May 1869. He *d.* 4 July 1877, aged 79.

VII. 1877. SIR THOMAS ECHLIN, Baronet [I. 1721], of Dublin, 1st s. and h., *b.* 8 Nov. 1844, at Clonagh; sometime a private in the Royal Irish Constabulary; *suc. to the Baronetcy*, 4 July 1877.

BURDETT:

cr. 11 July 1723;(e)

afterwards, since 1840, WELDON.

I. 1723. "THOMAS BURDETT, Esq., of Dunmore, co. Carlow,"(e) 2d but 1st surv. s. and h. of Thomas BURDETT,(f) of the Old Castle at Garrahill in that county; sometime (1662) Sheriff for co. Carlow (will dat. 2 Jan. 1685, pr. [I.] 16 Aug. 1701), by Catherine (*m.* 2 July 1653), da. of Sir Robert KENNEDY, 1st Baronet [I. 1665] of Mount Kennedy, co. Wicklow, was *b.* 14 Sep. 1668 at Garrahill; admitted to Trin. Coll. Dublin, as a pensioner, 29 Sep. 1685, aged 18; Sheriff of co. Carlow, 1701; M.P. [I.] for that county, 1704-13, for Carlow borough, 1713-14, and for co. Carlow (again), 1715 till death;

(a) From the *second* son, Chambré Echlin, derived the rival claimant, see above.

(b) This was proved at the Summer Assizes of 1789 at Athy, as also was the marriage of his mother (Bridget) two years previous thereto. He was, accordingly, 16 Jan. 1790, put into possession of his father's estate of Clonagh, which had been claimed by his cousin, Chambré Echlin. A similar claim by another Chambré Echlin (who had assumed the Baronetcy) was non-suited in 1814, with £196 costs. See memorial of Sir James Echlin [the 4th] Baronet, to Ulster King of Arms, now [1905] in Ulster's Office, Dublin.

(c) In Burke's *Vicissitudes of Families*, 3d series [1863], pp. 8-12, is an account of the extreme poverty of the then Baronet and of his br. (and future successor) Ferdinand Fenton Echlin.

(d) Dod's *Baronetage*, 1879.

(e) See p. 340, note "b," under "DEANE."

(f) This Thomas was 1st s. and h. of Robert Burdett, Merchant and Alderman of London, by Mary, da. of (—) Wright, also Alderman thereof, which Robert obtained, in 1630, grants of upwards of twenty town lands in co. Carlow. This Robert is (without any valid proof) sometimes asserted [Playfair's *Baronetage*, 1811, etc.] to be identical with Robert Burdett, 2d s. of Sir Francis Burdett, 1st Baronet, [1618], of Foremark, co. Derby.

Volunteered to raise a regiment of Foot at his own expense in 1715, and wes *cr. a Baronet* [I.], as above, by patent dat. at Dublin, 11 July 1723, the privy seal being dat. at St. James', 31 Dec. 1722, with a spec. rem. failing heirs male of his body, to those of "Anne Weldon, his sister, wife to Walter WELDON, of Raheen, in the Queen's County, Esq."(a) He was Governor of co. Carlow, 1725 till death. He *m.* firstly (as her 3d husband), probably about 1700, Honora, DOWAGER COUNTESS OF ARDGLASS [I.], widow of Francis CUFF, sometime M.P. [I.] for co. Mayo (who *d.* 26 Dec. 1694, aged 38), sister of Murrough (BOYLE), 1st VISCOUNT BLESSINGTON [I.], da. of Michael BOYLE, D.D., Archbishop of Armagh (1678-1702) and sometime Lord Chancellor [I.], by his 2d wife Mary, da. of Dermot (O'BRIEN) 5th BARON INCHIQUIN [I.]. She, by whom he had no issue, *d.* in Dublin, and was *bur.* in St. Patrick's in that city, 14 Nov. 1710. He *m.* secondly, in or before 1715, Martha, 4th da. of Bartholomew VIGORS, Bishop of Ferns and Leighlin [1691-1721], by Martha, da. of Constantine NEALE, of New Ross, co. Wexford. He *d.* 14 April 1727, aged 58. Will dat. 15 April 1724, pr. [I.] 8 March 1727/8.

II. 1727. SIR WILLIAM VIGORS BURDETT, Baronet [I. 1723], of Dunmore aforesaid, only s. and h., by 2d wife, *b.* 8 June 1715, *suc. to the Baronetcy*, 14 April 1727. He *m.* firstly, before Aug. 1739, (—), niece of Robert JONES, of Mount Kennedy, co. Wicklow, whose will was dat. 16 Aug. 1739. She (whose only s., Thomas, *d.* 1 March 1755) *d.* 22 Feb. 1768. He *m.* secondly, 5 Oct. 1769, Henrietta, widow of Terence O'LOGHLIN, sister of Murrough, 4th EARL OF INCHIQUIN and 1st MARQUESS OF THOMOND [I.], 3d da. of the Hon. James O'BRIEN, by Mary, da. of William JEPHSON, dean of Kilmore. She *d.* 17 Nov. 1797. He *d.* 17 Dec. 1798, aged 83.

III. 1798. SIR WILLIAM BAGENAL BURDETT, Baronet [I. 1723], 1st surv. s. and h., by 2d wife; *bap.* 16 July 1770; matric. at Oxford (Magdalen Coll.), 17 May 1790, aged 19;(b) *suc. to the Baronetcy*, 17 Dec. 1798. He *m.* firstly, in Great Prescott street, London, 7 March 1800, Maria, da. of the Rev. Henry James REYNETT, D.D., by Mary, da. of the Rev. Gilbert KENNEDY. She, by whom he had three sons living in 1811,(c), *d.* 5 July 1816. He *m.* secondly, 18 July 1820, at Rochdale, Esther, 1st da. and coheir of Thomas SMITH, of Castleton Hall, co. Lancaster. He *d.* s.p.m.s.,(d) at Cheltenham, 14 Dec. 1840, aged 70. Will pr. Jan. 1841. His widow *d.* there, 1 Jan. 1845. Will pr. Feb. 1845.

IV. 1840. SIR ANTHONY WELDON, Baronet [I. 1723], of Raheen, *otherwise* Rahinderry, Queen's County, and of Kilmorony, co. Kildare, cousin, being 3d. s., but eldest existing h. male, of the Rev. Anthony WELDON, Rector of Athy, co. Kildare, by his 2d wife, Anne, da. of John COGHLAN, which Anthony (who *d.* 1803, aged 73) was 3d s. of Arthur WELDON, of Rahinderry aforesaid, s. and h. of Walter WELDON, of the same, sometime (1692-1715), M.P. [I.] for Carlow (*d.* 16 May 1728/9), by Anne, sister of Sir Thomas BURDETT, 1st Baronet [I. 1723] abovenamed. He was *b.* 16 June 1781, at St. John's Abbey, Athy; served in the Madras Artillery, and received, in 1855, the local rank of

(a) See p. 340, note "b," under "DEANE."

(b) In Foster's *Alumni Oxon.*, though the date is given as "1790," he is described as "Sir Vigors William Burdett, *Bart*," and spoken of as the 2d Baronet, whose marriage in 1769 (being, actually, a year *before* this matriculator was *born*) is set forth. The same date is given in Col. Chester's MS. copy of these matriculations (unfortunately changed from a chronological to an alphabetical arrangement, so that there is no means, if there be an error in the date, of correcting such error), but the entry there (and Col. Chester gives the entries *as they are in the original*) is "Burdett, Vigors William (son of William, Baronet), aged 19," which implies that he had not at that date succeeded to his father's title, and shews that his father was named William, and not (as was the father of the 2d Baronet) Richard. Unless, therefore, the date is wrong, the entry (though the name "Vigors" is given to the son instead of to the father) must apply to the 3d (and not to the 2d Baronet.

(c) Playfair's *Baronetage* [1811].

(d) Helen, his only surv. da. and h. (by 1st wife), *m.*, in 1831, Capt. Henry Bell, of Woolsington, Northumberland, who *d.* s.p.

Colonel in the East Indies, having been Sheriff of Queen's County, 1839, and having *suc. to the Baronetcy*, 14 Dec. 1840, according to the spec. rem. in the creation thereof.(a) He *m.* 4 Jan. 1824, Harriett, yst. da. of Colonel Thomas HOCKLEY, of Bury St. Edmunds, Suffolk. He *d.* 21 Dec. 1858, aged 77, at Rahinderry aforesaid. His widow was *bur.* 7 Jan. 1864, at St. John's aforesaid.

V. 1858. SIR ANTHONY CROSSDILL WELDON, Baronet [I. 1723], of Rahinderry and Kilmorony aforesaid, 2d but 1st surv. s. and h.,(b) *b.* 16 March 1827; entered the Madras Army, 1843, retiring as Lieut. in 1854; *suc. to the Baronetcy*, 21 Dec. 1858; Sheriff of Queen's County, 1861. He *m.* 12 June 1862, at St. John's, Paddington, Elizabeth Caroline Thomasina, 1st surv. da. of Arthur KENNEDY, Lieut.-Col. 18th Hussars, by Mabella, relict of Kenrick Morres HAMILTON-JONES, da. of Major Charles HILL, of Bellaghy Castle, co. Derry. He *d.* 14 Jan. 1900, at Kilmorony aforesaid, aged 72. His widow living 1905.

VI. 1900. SIR ANTHONY ARTHUR WELDON, Baronet [I. 1723], of Rahinderry, *b.* 1 March 1863, in Oxford square, Paddington; ed. at Charterhouse, and at Trinity Coll., Cambridge; B.A., 1884; Major and Hon. Lieut.-Col. 4th Batt. Leinster Regt. (Royal Canadians); Aide-de-Camp. to Commander-in-Chief (Viscount Wolseley), 1895-1900, and served through the South African war, 1899-1900 (medal with clasps); D.S.O., 1900, having *suc. to the Baronetcy*, 14 Jan. 1900. He *m.* 11 Feb. 1902, at St. Peter's, Eaton square, Winifred, da. of Lieut.-Col. J. E. VARTY-ROGERS, sometime of the Royal Dublin Fusileers, one of the Gentlemen-at-Arms, by Georgiana Florence, da. of (—) COOKE.

Family Estates.—These, in 1878, consisted of 2,498 acres in Queen's County, and 292 in co. Kildare. *Total.*—2,790 acres, worth £2,206 a year.(c) *Seats.*—Kilmorony, near Athy, co. Kildare, and Rahinderry, Queen's County.

FOWNES:

cr. 26 Oct. 1724;(d)

ex. 5 April 1778.

I. 1724. "SIR WILLIAM FOWNES, Knt., of Dublin, Alderman,"(d) s. of (—); was Sheriff of Dublin, 1697-98; was in 1698 appointed co-Ranger of Phœnix Park, Dublin, and of all the parks, chases, and woods in Ireland, an office he resigned in Nov. 1704; was Alderman of Dublin, 21 April 1699; M.P. [I.] for Wicklow (borough), 1704-13; Sheriff of co. Wicklow, 1707; was Lord Mayor of Dublin,(e) 1708-09, being *Knighted* [I.] during office, 17 May

(a) In the *Dublin Gazette*, 22 Jan. 1841, is the certificate "of W. Betham, Ulster," that the male issue of the grantee failed on the death of his grandson, 14 Dec. 1840, and that Anthony Weldon was entitled to the Baronetcy.

(b) The eldest son, Arthur Weldon, *d.* unm. and v.p., July 1853.

(c) The acreage and valuation of the Irish estates in 1878 is from *The Landowners of Ireland*, by U. H. Hussey de Burgh [1878]. In it "the valuation of the property for taxation purposes, and not the rental, is given. In 1878 the rental might be approximately ascertained by adding one-third to the valuation." [G. D. Burtchaell].

(d) See p. 340, note "b," under "DEANE."

(e) As several Lord Mayors of Dublin are among the Irish Baronets, the following note by G. D. Burtchaell, Office of Arms, Dublin, shewing the constitution of that Corporation is added:—

"Previous to the Municipal Reform Act, 1840, the Corporation of Dublin consisted of the Lord Mayor, elected annually by the Aldermen from among themselves. The senior Alderman who had not passed the Chair was, as a rule, elected, and was liable to a fine if he refused to take office. Two Sheriffs, elected annually from the Freemen. Twenty-four Aldermen, elected for life from the

1709, and was *cr. a Baronet* [I.], as above, by patent dat. at Dublin, 26 Oct. 1724, the Privy Seal being dat. at Kensington, 7 Aug. previous.(a) He, who became "Father of the city" of Dublin, July 1733, *d.* 3 April 1735, and was *bur.* at St. Andrew's, Dublin. Will, as "of Island bridge, co. Dublin," dat. 8 April 1734, pr. [I.] 1735.

II. 1735, to 1778. SIR WILLIAM FOWNES, Baronet [I. 1724], of Woodstock,(b) co. Kilkenny, grandson and h., being only s. and h. of Kendrick FOWNES, sometime (1713) Sheriff of co. Wicklow, by Elizabeth, da. and h. of Col. Stephen SWEETE, of KILKENNY, which Kendrick (who *d.* v.p., 13 Oct. 1717), was only s. and h. ap. of the late Baronet. He was *b.* 1709, in Dublin; admitted to Trinity Coll., Dublin, as a Fellow Commoner, 26 Sep. 1726, aged 17; LL.D., *honoris causâ*, 1754, having *suc. to the Baronetcy*, 3 April 1735; was M.P. [I.] for Dingle Iconsh, 1749-60, for Knocktopher, 1761-76, and for Wicklow (borough), 1776 till death; Sheriff of co. Kilkenny, 1755; P.C. [I.], 1760, being removed 7 May 1770. He *m.* 23 Dec. 1739, at Kill, co. Kildare (Lic. Prerog. [I.] 19 Dec.), Elizabeth, 5th da. of Brabazon (PONSONBY), 1st EARL OF BESSBOROUGH [I.], by his 1st wife, Sarah, relict of Hugh COLWILL, da. of James MARGETSON. She was *bap.* 26 Sep. 1719. He *d.* s.p.m.,(c) at Woodstock, 5 April 1778, when the *Baronetcy* became *extinct*. Will dat. 4 Nov. 1773, pr. [I.] 3 Dec. 1778. His widow *d.* July 1778, at Rosanna, co. Wicklow.

CREATIONS BY GEORGE II.

11 June 1727 to 25 Oct. 1760.

HAMAN:

cr. 19 Nov. 1727;

ex. 26 Jan. 1727/8.

I. 1727, to 1728. "JOHN DICKSON HAMMAN [*rectius* HAMAN], Esq., of Woodhill, in the county [of the city] of Cork,"(a) only s. of John HAMAN (will pr. 4 Aug. 1718), was *cr. a Baronet* [I.], as above, by patent dat. at Dublin, 19 Nov. 1727, the Privy Seal being dat. at St. James', 21 July previous. He *m.* Elizabeth, 2d da. of Sir Thomas PRENDERGAST, 1st Baronet [I. 1699], of Gort, co. Galway, by Penelope, da. of Henry CADOGAN, of Liscartan, co. Meath. He *d.* s.p., 26 Jan. 1727/8, a few months after his creation. Will dat. 10 Jan. 1727/8, pr. [I.] 5 March 1730/1. His widow, who, on 23 Sep. 1730, became heir to her br., Sir Thomas PRENDERGAST, 2d and last Baronet [I. 1699], *m.* 21 Nov. 1728 (Lic. Cork) Charles SMYTH, of Limerick (M.P. [I.] thereof for forty-five years), who *d.* 18 Aug. 1784, by whom she was mother of John, 1st VISCOUNT GORT [I.].

Sheriff Peers; the senior Alderman was styled, but not officially, "Father of the City." The Common Council, comprising the Sheriff Peers (those who had served, or fined for the office of Sheriff), and ninety-six representatives of the Civic Guilds. Of the latter, the Trinity Guild, or Guild of Merchants was the most important, having thirty-one representatives. From it the Sheriffs were generally, but not invariably chosen. The Lord Mayor and Sheriffs came into office on 30 September."

(a) See p. 340, note "b," under "DEANE."

(b) Woodstock was part of the large estates, co. Kilkenny, inherited from his maternal grandfather, who had purchased them in 1702 from the Trustees of Forfeited Estates.

(c) Sarah, his only da. and h., *m.* 28 May 1765, William Tighe, of Rosanna, co. Wicklow, and had issue.

MOLYNEUX:

cr. 4 July 1730:

I. 1730. "THOMAS MOLYNEUX, Esq.,(a) State Physician of Dublin,"(b) 5th s. of Samuel MOLYNEUX, of Castle Dillon, co. Armagh, Chief Engineer of Ireland, by Anne, da. and h. of William DOWDALL, of Mount Town, co. Meath, which Samuel (who *d.* 1692) was 3d but 1st surv. s. of Daniel MOLYNEUX, sometime (1597-1632) Ulster King of Arms, was *b.* 14 April 1661; ed. at Christ Church School, Dublin; admitted to Trinity Coll., Dublin, as Fellow Commoner, 8 Sep. 1676, aged 15; B.A. 1680; M.D. 1687, having studied medicine at Leyden; was F.R.S., 1686; Fellow Coll. of Physicians [I.], being Hon. Fellow, 1692-98; M.P. [I.] for Ratoath, 1695-99; Regius Professor of Physic at Dublin, 1717; Physician General to the Army [I.], 16 June 1718; Physician to the State, 1725, being *cr. a Baronet* [I.], as above, by patent dat. at Dublin, 4 July 1730, the Privy Seal being dat. at Windsor, 16 June previous. He *m.* (mar. lic. 13 May 1694) Catherine, da. of Ralph HOWARD, M.D., of Shelton, co. Wicklow (Regius Professor of Physic at Dublin), by Catherine, da. of Roger SOTHEBY, of Wicklow. He *d.* 19 Oct. 1733, aged 72. Will dat. 18 Sep. 1733, pr. [I.] 9 Jan. 1733/4. His widow (by whom he had four sons and eight daughters), *d.* 18 Dec. 1747.

II. 1733. SIR DANIEL MOLYNEUX, Baronet [I. 1730], of Dublin, 3d but 1st surv. s. and h.,(c) *b.* 1708; admitted to Trin. Coll., Dublin, as Fellow Commoner, 9 July 1723, aged 15; B.A., 1727; M.A., 1730; *suc. to the Baronetcy*, 19 Oct. 1733; F.R.S. 1735; "a member of the celebrated academy, *Della Crusca*, at Florence," as also "a very learned man, fond of study."(d) He *d.* unm. 1738, aged 30. Will dat. 2 Oct. 1738, pr. [I.] 3 May 1739.

III. 1738. SIR CAPEL(e) MOLYNEUX, Baronet [I. 1730], only surv. br. and h., *b.* 1717; ed. at Trinity Coll., Dublin; B.A., 1737, being thirty-one years later *cr.* (*honoris causâ*) LL.D. in 1768; *suc. to the Baronetcy* in 1738; Sheriff of co. Armagh, 1744; was M.P. [I.] for Clogher, 1761-68, for the Univ. of Dublin, 1769-76, and for Clogher (again) 1776-83; P.C. [I.], 15 July 1776. He suc. to the family estate of Castle Dillon abovenamed on the death, 21 March 1759, of Lady Elizabeth Diana ST. ANDRÉ, formerly wife of his first cousin, the Rt. Hon. Samuel MOLYNEUX (*d.* s.p. 1728), of Castle Dillon aforesaid. He erected there in 1760 "the most costly park gates, perhaps, at that time in the three kingdoms," and subsequently "built a fine obelisk near his park to commemorate the revival of our [I.] Constitution in 1782."(d) He *m.* firstly, 22 Aug. 1747, at Somerset House chapel, Strand, Midx., Elizabeth, sister of Sir William EAST, 1st Baronet [1766], da. of William EAST, of Hall place, in Hurley, Berks, by Anne, da. of George COOKE, of Harefield, Midx. She *d.* at Arbour Hill, Dublin, 15 Jan. 1757. He *m.* secondly, 20 Aug. 1766, Elizabeth, only da. of Lieut. Gen. John ADLERCRON (*formerly* TRAPAUD), sometime Commander-in-Chief in the East Indies, by Elizabeth, da. of Bartholomew ARABIN. He *d.* at Castle Dillon, Aug. 1797, in his 80th year. Will dat. 21 April 1792, pr. [I.] 2 Sep. 1797. His widow *d.* at Bath, Nov. 1800. Will pr. [I.] 1801.

(a) Frequently (though erroneously) said to have been *Knighted* in June 1695. None of the family were Knights, though the founder is often called *Sir* Thomas and the grantee's father, *Sir* Daniel.

(b) See p. 340, note "b," under "DEANE."

(c) Of his elder brothers (1) Samuel *d.* young; (2) William was killed, 28 May 1813, by a leaden image falling on him in a garden near Dublin, aged 14.

(d) Playfair's *Baronetage* [1811].

(e) The name "Capel" was probably in honour of Elizabeth Diana, da. of Algernon (*Capel*), 2d Earl of Essex, who *m.* in 1717, as her 1st husband, the Right Hon. Samuel Molyneux, and who, in his right, held the Castle Dillon estate from 1728 till her death in 1759.

IV. 1797. Sir Capel Molyneux, Baronet [I. 1730], of Castle Dillon aforesaid, 2d but 1st surv. s. and h., by 1st wife, b. 30 March 1750; ed. at Trinity Coll., Dublin; B.A., 1771; "distinguishing himself at College by obtaining many premiums;"(a) *suc. to the Baronetcy* in Aug. 1797; Sheriff of co. Armagh, 1805. He *m.* 19 June 1785, in Gloucester street, Dublin (Lic. Dublin, June 1785), Margaret, 1st da. of Sir Neale O'Donel, 1st Baronet [I. 1780], of Newport, co. Mayo, by Mary, da. of William Coane, of Ballyshannon, co. Donegal. He *d.* s.p., 3 Dec. 1832, at his house in Merrion square, Dublin, aged 82. Will pr. June 1837.

V. 1832. Sir Thomas Molyneux, Baronet [I. 1730], of Castle Dillon aforesaid, br. of the half blood and h. male, being 4th s. of the 3d Baronet and the 1st son by 2d wife. He was *b.* 26 Dec. 1767; entered the Army, and having "served with much credit under Sir Charles Grey in the West Indies," retired on half-pay before 1811,(a) but became, eventually, 27 May 1825, Lieut.-General. He *suc. to the Baronetcy*, 3 Dec. 1832. He *m.*, in or before 1813, Elizabeth, da. of Thomas Perring. He *d.* at Dublin, 26 Nov. 1841, aged 73. Will pr. Dec. 1842.

VI. 1841. Sir George King Adlercron Molyneux, Baronet [I. 1730], of Castle Dillon aforesaid, only s. and h., being "only legit. child,"(b) *b.* 17 Oct. 1813; Sheriff of co. Armagh, 1837; *suc. to the Baronetcy*, 26 Nov. 1841. He *m.* 6 July 1837, Emma, da. of (—) Green. He *d.* 25 Jan. 1848, aged 34. His widow *m.* 13 July 1849, at All Souls', Langham place, Marylebone, William Edward Fox, M.D., of Brislington, Somerset (who survived her), and *d.* 11 Nov. 1874, at Clifton, near Bristol, in her 61st year.

VII. 1848 Sir Capel Molyneux, Baronet [I. 1730], of Castle Dillon aforesaid, only s. and h., *b.* there 1841; *suc. to the Baronetcy* 25 Jan. 1848; Sheriff of co. Armagh, 1864. He *m.* 15 Jan. 1863, at Valencia Church, co. Kerry, Mary Emily Frances, 1st da. of Sir Peter George Fitzgerald, 1st Baronet [1880], of Valencia, by Julia, da. of Peter Bodkin Hussey. He *d.* s.p.m.,(c) 24 Jan. 1879, at Castle Dillon, aged 37. His widow living 1905.

VIII 1879. Jan. Sir John William Henry Molyneux, Baronet [I. 1730], cousin and h. male, being 2d s.(d) of John Molyneux, of Gavel Hill, Salop, by Ella, da. of (—) Young, which John was yr. br. of the 5th and 4th Baronets, and yr. s. of the 3d Baronet. He was *b.* 28 Jan. 1819; ed. at Trinity Coll., Cambridge; B.A. and 27th Wrangler, 1841; took Holy Orders; Hon. Canon of Ely, 1875, and Vicar of Sudbury, Suffolk, till death; *suc. to the Baronetcy*, 24 Jan. 1879, a few weeks before his death. He *m.* 21 April 1842 at Lezayre, Isle of Man, Louisa Dorothy, yst. da. of John Christian, of Milntown, Deemster of that island, by Susanna, da. of Lewis Robert Allen, of Bath. She *d.* 15 Feb. 1877. He *d.* 5 March 1879, at Sudbury Vicarage, aged 60.

IX. 1879 March. Sir John Charles Molyneux, Baronet [I. 1730], 1st s. and h., *b.* 27 June 1843; ed. at Bradfield Coll., Berks, and at Christ's Coll., Cambridge; LL.B., 1867; took Holy Orders, 1867; Curate of Horsmonden, Kent, 1876-80; of Barcheston (sole charge), co. Warwick,

(a) Playfair's *Baronetage* [1811.]

(b) Foster's *Baronetage*, 1883. In the obituary of his father (*Gent. Mag.*, 1842) four sons and six daughters are attributed to that Baronet by his said wife. The three elder of each were, however, illegitimate. Of the sons (1) Thomas Molyneux Willliams, **K.H.** [1836], is stated (erroneously) to have *suc. to the Baronetcy*. He was Major in the Army, 1826; Lieut. Gen. 1866, and *d.* apparently in 1871; (2) John, "late Capt. 37th Reg;" (3) William, Lieut. R.N.; (4) George.

(c) His only da. and h., Julia Elizabeth Mary, *m.* 14 Aug. 1897, William John Talbot, of Mount Talbot, co. Roscommon, and has issue.

(d) The eldest son, Rev. Capel Molyneux, B.A. (Cambridge), having first been in the Army, took Holy Orders, and became a well known preacher, being Curate of Woolwich, 1842-50; Incumbent of the Lock Chapel, Harrow road, 1850-60, and Vicar of St. Paul's, Onslow square, 1860-72. He *d.* s.p.m., 27 Dec. 1877, at Cannes, aged 73.

1880-86; Vicar of Portesham, Dorset, 1886, having *suc. to the Baronetcy*, 5 March 1879. He *m.* firstly, 15 April 1873, Fanny, da. of Edward Jackson, of Walsoken House, Wisbeach. She *d.* 23 April 1893. He *m.* secondly, 31 Jan. 1895, Ada Isabel, yst. da. of Rev. Abraham Farley Wynter, B.A. (Oxford), Rector of Barnadiston, Suffolk.

Family Estates.—These, in 1883 (after an "unsatisfactory correction" by the 9th Baronet), consisted of 6,726 acres in Queen's County (worth only £952 a year), 6,009 in co. Armagh (worth £4,598 a year), 2,226 in co. Kildare, 1378 in co. Limerick, and 221 in co. Dublin (this last being, presumably, worth £1,918(a)) a year). *Total.*—16,560 acres, worth £10,000 a year.
In 1878 these estates consisted of 5,463 acres in Queen's County (worth only £952 a year), 3,416 acres in co. Armagh (worth £4,598 a year), 2,426 in co. Kildare (worth £1,530 a year), and 1,388 in co. Limerick (worth £1,002 a year). *Total.*—12,693 acres, worth £8,082 a year.(b) *Seat.*—Castle Dillon, co. Armagh.

BAYLY:

cr. 4 July 1730;

afterwards, since 1782, Lords Paget de Beaudesert,

since 1784, Earls of Uxbridge;

and since 1815, Marquesses of Anglesey.

I. 1730. "Edward Bayly, Esq., of Placenewyd [Plas-Newydd], co. Anglesey and Mount Bagenall, co. Louth,"(c) only s. and h. of Nicholas Bayly, Governor of the Isle of Arran [I.], sometime (1661-66), M.P. [I.] for Newry, by Dorothy (sometimes called Anne), formerly Dorothy Hall, apparently da. and h. of (—) Hall,(d) which Nicholas was s. and h. of Lewis Bayly, D.D., Bishop of Bangor (1616-31), by Anne, da. of Sir Henry Bagenall, of Newry Castle, etc., in Ireland, and of Plas-Newydd aforesaid. He was M.P. [I.] for Newry (two Parls.), 1704-14, and having suc. on the death, in 1712, of his cousin, Nicholas Bagenall, to the estates in co. Anglesey and in Ireland held by that family; Sheriff of co. Down, 1730, and was *cr. a Baronet* [I.], as above, by patent dat. at Dublin, 4 July 1730, the Privy Seal being dat. at Windsor, 16 June previous. He *m.* (Lic. [I.] 28 Aug. 1708), Dorothy, da. of the Hon. Oliver Lambart (3d s. of Charles, 1st Earl of Cavan [I.], by his 2d wife, Eleanor (*m.* in 1677), only child of Simon Creane, *or* Crane, of the Furrows, Great Forest, co. Dublin. He *d.* 28 Sep. 1741, and was *bur.* at Delgany, co. Wicklow. Will, as of "Tinny park, co. Wicklow," dat. 10 Oct. 1741 pr. [I.] 1742. His widow *d.* 16 Aug. 1745, and was *bur.* at Delgany.

(a) The sum of £1,918 for the co. Dublin estates (the value of which is not given in the return) is the balance required to make up the whole of the estates to £10,000, at which they were estimated by the 7th Baronet [See Bateman's *Great Landowners*, edit. 1883].

(b) See p. 347, note "c," under "Burdett."

(c) See p. 340, note "b," under "Deane."

(d) In her funeral certificate [I.] the entry runs thus: "*Dame* Dorothy Hall was *m.* to Mr. Bayly, of (—), and was interred in St. Michael's church, Dublin," 5 March 1713/4. [*N. & Q.*, 7th S., vi, 168, *et seq.*, see also 6th S., v, 386]. This description seems as if she was the relict of Sir (—) Hall, but that conjecture is refuted by the arms, which are those of Bayly (*Gules*, a chevron, *vaire*, between 3 martlets, *or*) impaling Hall. The coat of Hall is also given as a quartering to the Earl of Uxbridge in Edmondson's *Baronagium* [1784, vol. vi, p. 23b], where there is a large pedigree of the Bagenall and Bayly families. It is to be noted that these arms are totally different from the arms of Bayly (*Azure*, 9 estoiles, *or*), generally attributed to this family, but see *N. & Q.*, 3d S., iii, 91 and 259, as to the arms used by the Bishop of Bangor. The arms of Edward Bayly are recorded in Ulster office in 1715, quartering Bagenall and Hall, which confirms the fact of his mother being the heiress of Hall.

II. 1741. Sir Nicholas Bayly, Baronet [I. 1730], of Plas-Newydd and Mount Bagenall aforesaid, 1st s. and h., *b.* in co. Anglesey in 1709; admitted to Trinity Coll., Dublin, as Fellow Commoner, 12 July 1726, aged 18; was M.P. for co. Anglesey (four Parls.), 1734-41, 1747-61, and April 1770 to 1774, having *suc. to the Baronetcy*, 28 Sep. 1741; was Lord Lieut. of that county, 1763. He *m.* firstly, 19 April 1737, at St. Geo. Han. sq., Caroline, da. and h. of Brig.-Gen. Thomas Paget, Governor of Minorca, by Mary, da. and coheir of Peter Whitcombe, of Great Braxted, Essex, sometime merchant at Constantinople, which Thomas was the only son that had issue of the Hon. Henry Paget,(a) yr. s. of William, Lord Paget de Beaudesert. She *d.* 7 Feb. 1766, at Plas Newydd, and was *bur.* at Llanldwen, co. Anglesey. Admon. 22 Aug. 1766. He *m.* secondly, Anne, da. of (—) Hunter. He *d.* at his house in Bond street, Midx., 9 Dec. 1782, aged, presumably, 72,(b) and was *bur.* at Llanldwen aforesaid. Will pr. 15 Jan. 1783. His widow *d.* 18 May 1818. Admon. Nov. 1819.

III. 1782. Henry (Paget), Lord Paget de Beaudesert, and a Baronet [I. 1730], 2d but 1st surv. s. and h.(c) by 1st wife, *b.* 18 June and *bap.* 16 July 1744, at St. Geo. Han. sq.; *suc.* (in right of his mother) 17 Nov. 1769 *to the Barony of Paget de Beaudesert*, and was so sum. by writ 13 Jan. 1770. By royal lic., 29 Jan. 1770, he took the name of Paget instead of that of Bayly. He *suc. to the Baronetcy*, 9 Dec. 1782, which then became *merged* in this *Barony* and still (1905) so continues. He was subsequently *cr.*, 19 May 1784, Earl of Uxbridge, his son and h., the 2d Earl and 4th Baronet [I. 1730], being *cr.*, 4 July 1813, Marquess of Anglesey. See *Peerage*.

FORSTER:

assumed between 1738 and 1767 to 1787 or 1794.

I. 1766? Nicholas Forster, of Tullaghan, co. Monaghan, s. and h. of John Forster,(d) of the same, sometime (1715) Sheriff of that county (*d.* 1738), by Elizabeth, da. of the Rev. Andrew Montgomery, of Carrickmacross, co. Monaghan, was *b.* 1713, and having

(a) Thomas and his sister Dorothy, wife of Sir Edward Irby, 1st Baronet [1704] were children of the second wife (Mary) of this Henry Paget, who *m.* firstly Anne, da. of Robert Sandford, of Sandford, Salop. This first wife, Anne, who *d.* 15 and was *bur.* 19 Dec. 1683 in St. Michan's church, Dublin, had issue seven sons, of whom three, Rupert, Charles and James (the 7th son) were living at her death (funeral entry in Ulster's office), but all of whom *d.* s.p. The second wife (mar. lic. Dublin, 29 March 1684) was Mary, da. of Col. Hugh O'Rorke, sometime (1689), Sheriff of co. Leitrim, by Joan, 1st da. of Humphrey Reynolds, of Loughscur in that county, and Russell his wife, da. of Sir James Ware, senior [*Ex. inform.* G. D. Burtchaell].

(b) His age, according to his coffin plate [Collins's *Peerage*, edit. 1812], was "75," which, as his parents were not married till 1708, must be a mistake.

(c) The eldest son, Edward Bayly, *d.* unm. and under age 1756, and was *bur.* at Portsmouth.

(d) This John Forster (whose will, dat. 26 Nov. 1738, was pr. [I.] 6 Jan. 1738/9) was s. and h. of the Rev. John Forster (*b.* 1646; admitted to Trinity Coll., Dublin 6 July 1664, aged 18, and *d.* 1704), who was s. of Capt. John Forster, who had a grant of 4,394 acres (including Tullaghan) in co. Monaghan, under the Act of Settlement 1667, and who *d.* in 1676. He (without any valid proof) is sometimes stated to have been identical with John, 4th s. of Sir Humphrey Forster, 1st Baronet [1620], who *d.* 1663, aged 68, and whose 4th son John is said to have *d.* s.p.m. 1674. That Baronetcy [E.] became *extinct* in 1711, and, is presumably the one assumed, as above, in 1738, so that this assumption would have been more correctly placed under the *English* Baronetcy, *cr.* 20 May 1620, *ex.* Dec. 1711.

suc. to the family estate on the death of his father in 1738, *assumed the title of Baronet* in or after the above date, but before his marriage in 1767; Sheriff of co. Monaghan, 1739. He *m.* firstly, in 1738, Charlotte, 3d da. of John Foster, of Dunleer, co. Louth, by Elizabeth, da. of William Fortescue, of Newragh, in that county. By her he had nine children who lived to be of age. He *m.* secondly in Jan. 1767, Hester, widow of Charles Tisdall, of Charlesfort, co. Meath, da. of Oliver Cramer, by Deborah, da. of Henry Rudkin. He *d.* at Tullaghan, July 1783, and was *bur.* at Tedavnet. Will, in which he is described as "*Baronet*," dat. 15 Feb. 1782, pr. [I.] 7 Feb. 1784.

II. 1783, to 1787. Sir Anthony Forster, Baronet(a) [I.], of Tullaghan aforesaid, 2d but 1st surv. s. and h. male,(b) *b.* 1745; sometime Lieut.-Col. of the 54th Foot; *assumed the Baronetcy* in 1783, on his father's death. He *d.* unm., at Halifax, Nova Scotia, 4 Nov. 1787, when, probably, the *assumption of this Baronetcy* ceased. Will, in which he is described as "Baronet," dat. 17 July 1784, pr. [I.] 24 April 1788.

III. 1787, to 1794. Thomas Forster, of Tullaghan aforesaid, br. and h. male, *b.* 3 Sep. 1751; was in Holy Orders. He, possibly, on the death of his elder br. in 1787, *assumed the Baronetcy*. Anyhow, however, "dropping all disproved claims in connection with the Aldermaston family in Berkshire,"(c) *i.e.*, with the Baronetcy [E.] granted to that family, 20 May 1620, he was *cr. a Baronet* [I.], 15 Jan. 1794. See that dignity.

COOKE:

cr. 28 Dec. 1741;

ex. 10 Feb. 1758.

I. 1741, to 1758. "Samuel Cooke, Esq., of Dublin, Alderman,"(d) s. of Sir Samuel Cooke, Brewer, sometime (1712-13 and 1713-14) Lord Mayor of Dublin (*d.* 28 Aug. 1726), by Mary, da. of Michael Christian of that city, Merchant, was, like his father, a brewer; was Sheriff of Dublin, 1730-31; Alderman, 22 Feb. 1731/2; Lord Mayor (for the first time), 1740-41, and was *cr. a Baronet* [I.], as above, by patent dat. at Dublin, 28 Dec. 1741, the Privy Seal being dat. at St. James' 18 Nov. previous. He was M.P. [I.] for Dublin, 16 Nov. 1749 till death, and was Lord Mayor (for the second time), 14 Dec. 1749 to 1750. He *m.* at St. Anne's, Dublin (Lic. Dublin, 10 June 1726), Judith, 2d da. of John Trench, D.D., Dean of Raphoe, by Anne, da. of Richard Warburton, of Garryhinch, in Queen's County. He *d.*

(a) According to the assumption of that dignity in or after 1738.

(b) The eldest son, John Forster, *b.* 1743, *m.* 5 July 1777, Sophia, da. of Alexander Wynch, Governor of Madras, and *d.* s.p.m. and v.p., 5 Oct. 1780. Will pr. [I.] 1780.

(c) Letter, dat. 19 Oct. 1842, written by the Rev. Sir Thomas Forster, 1st Baronet [I. 1794], printed in Shirley's *History of co. Monaghan*, p. 223.

(d) See p. 340, note "b," under "Deane."

s.p.m.,(a) 10 Feb. 1758, when the *Baronetcy* became *extinct*. Will, in which he directs his burial to be at St. James', Dublin, dat. 30 March 1737, pr. [I.] 27 April 1758, by Anne COOKE, his only surv. child. His widow *d.* in Anne Street, Dublin, 25 Nov. 1770.

O'CARROLL, *or* CARROLL ;

said (erroneously) to have been *cr.* 18 Feb. 1742.(b)

See O'CARROLL, *or* CARROLL, *cr.* [G.B.] about 1712.

COLTHURST :

cr. 3 Aug. 1744.

I. 1744. "JOHN COLTHURST, the younger, commonly called JOHN CONWAY COLTHURST, Esq., of Ardrum, co. Cork,"(c) 1st s. and h. ap. of John COLTHURST, of Ardrum and Ballyally, sometime (1734-57) M.P. [I.] for Tallagh, and (1738) Sheriff of co. Cork (*d.* 12 July 1756, aged 78), by his 1st wife, Alice, da. and h. of James CONWAY, of Cloghane, co. Kerry, was v.p., *cr. a Baronet* [I.], as above, by patent dat. at Dublin, 3 Aug. 1744, the Privy Seal being dat. at Kensington, 28 June previous. He was M.P. [I.] for Doneraile, 1751 to 1760; for Youghal, 1761-68; and for Castle Martyr, 1769 till death. He *m.* in 1741, Charlotte, 3d and yst. da. of Thomas (FITZMAURICE), 1st EARL OF KERRY [I.], by Anne, sister of Henry, EARL OF SHELBURNE [I.], only da. of Sir William PETTY. She *d.* 9 Oct. 1774. He *d.* at Ardrum, 19 Sep. 1775. Will dat. 25 Aug. 1775, pr. [I.] 15 March 1776.

II. 1775. SIR JOHN CONWAY COLTHURST, Baronet [I. 1744], of Ardrum aforesaid, 1st s. and h., *b.* probably about 1743; *suc. to the Baronetcy*, 19 Sep. 1775. He *d.* unm. (of wounds received five days previously, in a duel with Dominick TRANT), 15 Feb. 1787, at Old Connaught, near Bray.(d) Will dat. 13 Feb., pr. [I.] 6 March 1787.

III. 1787. SIR NICHOLAS COLTHURST, Baronet [I. 1744], of Ardrum aforesaid, br. and h.; was M.P. [I.] for St. Johnstown (Longford), 1783-90, and for Castle Martyr, 1791 till death, having *suc. to the Baronetcy*, 15 Feb. 1787; Sheriff of co. Cork, 1788. He *m.* 8 (Lic. 1) May 1788, Harriet, 2d da. of the Right Hon. David LA TOUCHE, of Marlay, co. Dublin, by Elizabeth, da. of George MARLAY, D.D., Bishop of Dromore. He *d.* at St. Stephen's Green, Dublin, July 1795. Will dat. 10 May, pr. [I.] 30 Sep. 1795. His widow *m.* in 1798, Lieut.-Gen. GRAY, and *d.* 1841.

(a) His only son, Samuel, living 30 March 1737, *d.* unm. and v.p. The only da. Anne, *m.*, after her father's death, Walter Weldon, of Kilmorony, co. Kildare (as his second wife), and *d.* 4 Dec. 1809, aged 83, leaving daughters and coheirs, of whom Mary, the eldest, *m.*, in 1786, Thomas Trench, Dean of Kildare. Their 3d son, Thomas Trench, of Millicent, co. Kildare, took by royal lic., 10 May 1850, the name of Cooke [*Ex inform.* G. D. Burtchaell].

(b) See p. 13, note "c."

(c) See p. 140, note "b," under "DEANE."

(d) "Notwithstanding the laudable efforts of the Sheriffs those two days past, to prevent an affair of honour, the gentlemen met this day near Bray about three o'clock, and each discharged three case of pistols. Counsellor D. T [—] was twice shot through the coat, and Sir John C [—] received a ball in his breast, of which he is since dead" [*Walker's Hibernian Magazine*].

IV. 1795. SIR NICHOLAS CONWAY COLTHURST, Baronet [I. 1744], of Ardrum aforesaid, only s. and h., *b.* Jan. 1789; *suc. to the Baronetcy*, July 1795; was sometime Capt. 68th Foot; M.P. for City of Cork (four Parls.) 1812 till death, and Col. of the Cork Militia. He *m.* 11 (Lic. 6) Nov. 1819, his cousin Elizabeth, da. and h. of Col. George VESEY, of Lucan, co. Dublin, by Emily, da. of the Right Hon. David LA TOUCHE abovenamed. He *d.* 6 Jan. *or* 22 June 1829, at Leamington, aged 40.

V. 1829. SIR GEORGE CONWAY COLTHURST, Baronet [I. 1744], of Ardrum aforesaid, 1st s. and h., *b.* 1824; *suc. to the Baronetcy*, in 1829; ed. at Harrow; matric. at Oxford (Ch. Ch.), 20 Oct. 1841, aged 17; Sheriff of co. Cork, 1850; M.P. for Kinsale (three Parls.), June 1863 to 1874. He *m.* 16 (Lic. 6) Jan. 1846, at Blarney, co. Cork, Louisa Jane, only da. and h. of St. John JEFFREYS, of Blarney Castle. He *d.* suddenly 24 Sep. 1878, at Buxton, aged 54. His widow living 1905.

VI. 1878. SIR GEORGE ST. JOHN COLTHURST, Baronet [I. 1744], of Ardrum and Blarney Castle aforesaid, only s. and h., *b.* 1850; ed. at Harrow; sometime Lieut. 43d Foot and A.D.C. to the Viceroy of Ireland; *suc. to the Baronetcy*, 24 Sep. 1878; Sheriff of co. Cork, 1884. He *m.* 27 Aug. 1881, at Cork Cathedral, Edith Jane Thomasina, only surv. child of Jonas MORRIS, of Dunkathel, co. Cork, sometime Capt. 1st Royal Dragoons, by Ellen, da. and h. of Silver Charles OLIVER, of Inchera, co. Cork.

Family Estates.—These, in 1878,(a) consisted of 31,260 acres in co. Cork, worth £9,664 a year. *Principal Seats.*—Blarney Castle and Ardrum, both co. Cork.

WOLSELEY :

cr. 19 Jan. 1744/5.

I. 1745. "RICHARD WOLSELEY, Esq., of Mount Arran,(b) [*afterwards* Mount Wolseley], co. Carlow,"(c) yst. br. of Sir William WOLSELEY, 5th Baronet [1628], of Wolseley, co. Stafford, being 3d s. of Capt. Richard WOLSELEY, of Mount Arran aforesaid, many years (1703-13 and 1715-24) M.P. [I.] for co. Carlow, by Frances (mar. lic. 16 Jan. 1688/9) da. and h. of John BURNISTON, of Dublin, which Richard (who suc. to his father's Irish estates, and *d.* 1724) was yst. s. of Sir Charles WOLSELEY, 2d Baronet [1628]. He was *b.* Feb. 1696; was M.P. [I.] for co. Carlow 1727-60 and 1761-68, and was *cr. a Baronet* [I.], as above, by patent dat. at Dublin 19 Jan. 1744/5, the Privy Seal being dat. at St. James' the 2d of the same month. He *m.* firstly (Lic. Prerog. [I.], 25 Feb. 1722/3), Anne, widow of [—] SMITH. She *d.* s.p. He *m.* secondly (Lic. Dublin 5 May 1727), Alicia, widow of William ROGERSON, 4th da. of Sir Thomas MOLYNEUX, 1st Baronet [I. 1730], by Catherine, da. of Ralph HOWARD, M.D. He *d.* 8 April 1769 in St. Stephen's Green, Dublin, aged 73. Will dat. 6 and pr. [I.] 28 April 1769. His widow *d.* 17 Aug. 1778, in Molesworth street, Dublin. Will dat. 27 March 1772, pr. [I.] 10 Sep. 1778.

(a) See p. 347, note "c," under "BURDETT."

(b) Mount Arran, near Tullow, anciently Crosslow (*rectius* Crossecloghe), was so named about 1670-80 by Richard (Butler), Earl of Arran, Viscount Tullogh, etc. [I.], who was so *cr.* 13 May 1662, and who *d.* 25 Jan. 1685/6, s.p.m.s., being suc. in this estate by his nephew, Charles Butler, also *cr.*, 8 March 1693, Earl of Arran, etc. [I.], who sold it, before 1703, to Richard Wolseley. In the ordnance map the hill on the townland of "Mount Wolseley or Crosslow" is [incorrectly] called "Mount Aaron."

(c) See p. 140, note "b," under "DEANE."

II. 1769. SIR RICHARD WOLSELEY, Baronet [I. 1745], of Mount Wolseley aforesaid, 1st s. and h. by 2d wife,(a) *b.* 10 Jan. 1729; *suc. to the Baronetcy*, 8 April 1769. He *m.* 31 Jan. 1775, at St. Thomas', Dublin, Letitia, da. and h. of Anthony MARLAY,(b) of Celbridge, co. Kildare, by Martha, da. and h. of William USSHER, of Dublin. He *d.* 28 July 1781, at St. Catherine's, Dublin, aged 82. Will dat. 6 Jan. 1774, pr. [I.] 27 Nov. 1781. His widow *d.* suddenly (being found dead in her bed), Aug. 1788, in Kilkenny. Will dat. 26 Sep. 1787, pr. [I.] 20 March 1789.

III. 1781. SIR WILLIAM WOLSELEY, Baronet [I. 1745] of Mount Wolseley aforesaid, only surv. s. and h.,(c) *b.* 26 Jan. 1775 in Dublin; *suc. to the Baronetcy*, 28 July 1781; matric. at Oxford (Christ Church), 17 Oct. 1792, aged 17; B.A., 1795. He *d.* unm. 30 Aug. 1819, aged 44. Will pr. 1820.

IV. 1819. SIR RICHARD WOLSELEY, Baronet [I. 1745], of Mount Wolseley aforesaid, cousin and h. male, being 1st s. and h. of Col. Clement WOLSELEY, of Wolseley Lodge, co. Carlow, sometime (1770) Sheriff of that county, by Catherine, da. of Arthur ST. GEORGE, D.D., Dean of Ross, which Clement (who *d.* 1811) was br. of the 2d and yr. s. of the 1st Baronet. He was *b.* 15 June 1760; was B.A. (Trin. Coll.) Dublin, 1782; M.A., 1809; took Holy Orders and was Precentor of Down, 1796-1823; *suc. to the Baronetcy*, 30 Aug. 1819. He *m.* firstly, at Ballybeg, co. Wicklow, August 1786, Mary Anne, da. of the Rev. Jeremiah SYMES, of Ballybeg aforesaid, by Jane, da. of Thomas MEADE, of Dublin. He *m.* secondly, Mary, da. of William Richard MIDDLEMORE, of Grantham, co. Lincoln. He *m.* thirdly, Elizabeth, da. of William SMITH, of Golden Bridge House, co. Dublin, by Martha, da. of Robert COLLINS. He *d.* s.p. 3 May 1852, at "Wolseley House," Cheltenham, in his 92d year. His widow *d.* 15 July 1880, at "Moosaphia Cottage," Kingstown, aged 84.(d)

V. 1852. SIR CLEMENT WOLSELEY, Baronet [I. 1745], of Mount Wolseley aforesaid, nephew and h., being only s. and h. of John Rogerson WOLSELEY, Major in the Army, by Mary, da. of Arthur BAILLIE, of Kilbride, co. Carlow, which John was next br. to the late Baronet. He was *b.* 27 Oct. 1794, at Summer Hill, co. Dublin; was an officer in the 80th Foot, and served in India; Major of the Carlow Militia; *suc. to the Baronetcy*, 3 May 1852; was Sheriff of co. Carlow, 1852. He *m.* 30 April 1833, at Cheltenham, Elizabeth, 1st da. of Peter VAN-HOMRIGH, sometime (1826-30) M.P. for Drogheda. He *d.* 30 Oct. 1857, at Brussels, aged 63. His widow *d.* 25 April 1889, at Bath, aged 85, and was *bur.* at Tullow.

VI. 1857. SIR JOHN RICHARD WOLSELEY, Baronet [I. 1745], of Mount Wolseley aforesaid, 1st s. and h., *b.* 24 June 1834, in Upper Mount street, Dublin; Ensign in Royal Irish Foot, 1854, serving as Lieut. during part of the Crimean war (Crimean and Turkish medals), but retiring, from ill health, in Jan. 1856; *suc. to the Baronetcy*, 30 Oct. 1857; Sheriff of co. Carlow, 1861. He *m.* 6 Dec. 1859, at Rockbarton, co. Limerick, Frances Annabella, yst.

(a) The 3d son, Rev. William Wolseley, Rector of Tullycorbet, co. Monaghan (formerly Capt. in the 8th Hussars, serving in the Seven Years' War, and distinguishing himself by taking a standard at the battle of Dettingen), *d.* 1800 at a great age, being grandfather (through his fifth son, Garnet Joseph Wolseley, Major 25th Borderers, who *d.* 1840, aged 62), of the well known Field Marshal, Viscount Wolseley, and being great great grandfather (through his eldest son) of the 9th Baronet, who suc. to that title in 1890.

(b) This Anthony was br. of Richard Marlay, Bishop of Waterford, both being sons of Sir Thomas Marlay, Lord Chief Justice of the King's Bench [I.], who was br. of George Marlay, Bishop of Waterford.

(c) Three elder brothers all *d.* young and v.p., viz., (1) Richard Ussher Wolseley, *b.* 8 April, *bap.* at St. Thomas, Dublin, 7 May 1766; *d.* 5 May 1770 in Sackville street, Dublin; (2) a son, *b.* 27 March 1767; (3) Anthony Ussher Wolseley, *bap.* 23 Sep. 1772, at St. Thomas aforesaid.

(d) She for the last six years of her life was, together with the widows of the 5th and 6th Baronets, one of three dowager ladies of this family.

da. of Arthur BLENNERHASSET, of Ballyseedy, co. Kerry, by Frances Deane, da. of Henry Deane GRADY. He *d.* suddenly, s.p.m.,(a) 20 June 1874, at Mount Wolseley aforesaid, aged nearly 40. His widow living 1905.

VII. 1874 SIR CLEMENT JAMES WOLSELEY, Baronet [I. 1745], of Mount Wolseley aforesaid, br. and h. male, *b.* 25 July 1837, at Sandbrook, co. Carlow; Barrister (Inner Temple), 1860; admitted to King's Inns, Dublin, Hilary 1860; Barrister, 1863; *suc. to the Baronetcy*, 20 June 1874; Major of the King's County Militia, 1878 to death; Sheriff of co. Carlow, 1883. He *m.* 12 Sep. 1872, Constance Louisa, 1st da. of Lieut. Gen. Robert Parker RADCLIFFE, Royal Artillery, by (—), da. of Col. Sir John Head BRYDGES. He *d.* s.p. at Mount Wolseley, 16 Oct. 1889, aged 52. His widow *d.* 18 Aug. 1899, at 10 Lower Grosvenor place, London.

VIII. 1889. SIR JOHN WOLSELEY, Baronet [I. 1745], Dean of Kildare, 1st cousin once removed and h. male, being 1st s. and h. of Lieut. Arthur WOLSELEY, by Jane, da. of Arthur GRIFFITHS, of Tregarron, co. Cardigan, which Arthur (who *d.* 28 May 1842, aged about 70) was uncle to the 5th and yr. br. of the 4th Baronet. He was *b.* 9 June 1803; ed. at Trinity Coll., Dublin; B.A. 1826; M.A. 1832; in Holy Orders; Rector of St. Michael's, Portarlington, Queen's County, 1839; 3d Canon of Kildare, 1849, and Dean of Kildare, 1859, till death, having *suc. to the Baronetcy*, 16 Oct. 1889. He *m.* 13 Oct. 1832, Anne, only da. of John MAUNSELL, of Portarlington aforesaid and Carrickoreely, co. Limerick, Barrister, by his 1st wife, Anne, da. and h. of Edward WEBSTER, of Whitehall, co. Dublin. She *d.* 14 Dec. 1860. He *d.* s.p. 26 and was *bur.* 30 Jan. 1890, at Portarlington, aged 86.

IX. 1890. SIR CAPEL CHARLES WOLSELEY, Baronet [I. 1745], 2d cousin twice removed and h. male, being 1st and only surv. s. of William Charles WOLSELEY, Major 6th Foot, by Annie, da. of the said William's paternal uncle, the Rev. Capel WOLSELEY, Rector of Trinity, Salford, which William (who *d.* 28 Nov. 1878, aged 43) was 1st s. of the Ven. Cadwallader WOLSELEY, Archdeacon of Glendalough (*d.* 4 Nov. 1872, aged 66), who was 1st s. of the Rev. William WOLSELEY, Rector of Glenarm and Dunaghy, the 1st s. of the Rev. William WOLSELEY,(b) Rector of Tullycorbet, co. Monaghan (*d.* 1800 at a great age), yr. br. of the 2d and 3d s. of the 1st Baronet. He was *b.* 24 Aug. 1870; ed. at the Sandhurst Military College; sometime Lieut. "The Queen's" regiment; British Vice-Consul at Archangel; *suc. to the Baronetcy*, 26 Jan. 1890.

Family Estates.—These, in 1883 (belonging to the 7th Baronet) consisted of 2,547 acres in co. Carlow, and 2,643 in co. Wexford. *Total.*—5,190 acres, worth £3,800(c) or £3,027 a year. The estates of the 8th Baronet were, in 1878 (eleven years before he suc. to that title), 1,412 acres in King's County, Queen's County, co. Wexford and co. Tipperary, worth £762.(c) *Seat.*—Mount Wolseley, near Tullow, co. Carlow.

SOMERVILLE :

cr. 14 June 1748 ;

afterwards, since 1863, BARONS ATHLUMNEY [I.]

I. 1748, June. "SIR JAMES SOMERVELL [*rectius* SOMERVILLE], Knt., of Dublin, Alderman,"(d) only s. of Thomas SOMERVILLE, merchant and (in 1716) Alderman of Dublin (*d.* 23 and was *bur.* 25 July 1718, at St. Audoen's, Dublin) by his 1st wife, Katherine, da. of James KING, of Corrard, co. Fermanagh, entered the Corporation of Dublin as a representative of the Trinity Guild, or "Guild of Merchants," 1717;(e) was a Merchant of Dublin; Sheriff,

---

(a) Of his five daughter and coheirs, the eldest, Ada Frances Alice, *m.* 18 June 1885, Lieut.-Col. Charles Bradford Harries Jenkins, who, by royal lic. 15 Nov. Nov. 1894, took the name of Wolseley before that of Jenkins.

(b) See p. 356, note "a."

(c) According to the Irish return of 1878, as to which see p. 347, note "c," under "BURDETT."

(d) See p. 340, note "b," under "DEANE."

(e) See p. 347, note "e," under "FOWNES."

1720-21; suc. to the estates of his maternal uncle, James KING, 2 March 1726; Alderman of Dublin, 16 May 1729; M.P. [I.] for that city, 1735 till death; Lord Mayor, 1736-37, being *Knighted* 9 Sep. 1737, and *cr. a Baronet* [I.], as above, by patent dat. at Dublin, 14 June 1748, the Privy Seal being dat. at St. James' 12 May previous. He *m.* 2 Feb. 1713/4, at St. Audoen's aforesaid (Lic. Dublin, 30 Jan.), Elizabeth, da. of William (not Thomas) QUAILE, Alderman and sometime (1718-19), Lord Mayor of Dublin. She *d.* 10 and was *bur.* 11 Nov. 1725, at St. Audoen's. He *d.* a few months after his creation, 16 and was *bur.* 18 Aug. 1748, at St. Audoen's aforesaid. Will dat. 12 Aug. 1740, pr. [I.] 24 Feb. 1748/9.

II. 1748, Aug. SIR QUAILE SOMERVILLE, Baronet [I. 1748], of Dublin and of Flemingstown, co. Meath, 1st s. and h., *bap.* 14 March 1714: elected a representative of the Trinity Guild, Dublin, 1738:(a) Sheriff of the City of Dublin, 1741-42: Sheriff of co. Meath, 1743; *suc. to the Baronetcy,* 16 Aug. 1748. He *m.* firstly, 19 Feb. 1740 (Lic., Dublin, 18), Mary, da. and h. of George WARBURTON, LL.D., Master in Chancery, by Hannah, da. of (—) SMITH, of Drommenagh, co. Fermanagh. She *d.* 28 Feb. 1748. He *m.* secondly, (Lic. Prerog. [I.], 11 April 1755), Sarah, 1st da. of Thomas TOWERS, of Archerstown, co. Meath, one of the six Clerks [I.], by Martha, sister and h. of James RILEY, da. of Edward RILEY. He *d.* 5 Dec. 1772, at Brownstown, co. Meath. Will dat. 10 April 1769, pr. [I.] 20 Dec. 1772. The will of his widow dat. 18 March 1780, pr. [I.] 1789.

III. 1772. SIR JAMES QUAILE SOMERVILLE, Baronet [I. 1748], of Flemingstown aforesaid, and Somerville, co. Meath, 1st s. and h., by 1st wife, *b.* probably about 1742, *suc. to the Baronetcy,* 5 Dec. 1772. He *m.* (Lic. Prerog. [I.], 16 June 1770) Catherine, 1st da. of Sir Marcus LOWTHER-CROFTON, 1st Baronet [I. 1758], of the Mote, co. Roscommon, by Katharine, sister and h. of Sir Edward CROFTON, 4th Baronet [I. 1661], of the Mote aforesaid, da. of Sir Edward CROFTON, 3d Baronet [I. 1661]. She, who was *b.* 6 June 1753, *d.* 1775. He *d.* between Aug. and Dec. 1800. Admon. [I.] 21 May 1802.

IV. 1800. SIR MARCUS SOMERVILLE, Baronet [I. 1748], of Somerville aforesaid, 1st s. and h., *b.* probably about 1775, was M.P. for co. Meath (ten Parls.), Aug. 1800, till his death in 1831, having *suc. to the Baronetcy* late in 1800. He *m.* firstly, 1 Oct. 1801, Mary Anne, da. and h. of Sir Richard GORGES-MEREDYTH, Baronet [I. *cr.* 1787], *formerly* Richard GORGES, by Mary, da and h. of Arthur Francis MEREDYTH, of Dollardstown, co. Meath. He *m.* secondly, (Lic. Prerog. [I.]), 7 April 1825, his cousin, Elizabeth, 1st da. of Piers GEALE, of Clonsilla, co. Dublin, by Elizabeth, da. of Marcus Lowther CROFTON, 3d s. of Sir Marcus Lowther CROFTON, 1st Baronet [I. 1758] abovenamed. He *d.* abroad, 11 July 1831. Admon. Feb. 1834. His widow *m.* 26 July 1841, at the Vice Regal Lodge, Dublin, Hugh (FORTESCUE), 2d EARL FORTESCUE, the then Viceroy of Ireland (who *d.* 14 Sep. 1861, aged 78), and *d.* 4 May 1896, at 68 Brook Street, in her 92d year.

V. 1831. SIR WILLIAM MEREDYTH SOMERVILLE, Baronet [I. 1748], of Somerville aforesaid, 1st s. and h., by 1st wife, *b.* about 1803: matric. at Oxford (Ch. Ch.), 18 Feb. 1822, aged 19; *suc. to the Baronetcy,* 11 July 1831: M.P. for Drogheda (three Parls.), 1837-52, and for Canterbury (three Parls.), 1854-65: Under Sec. to the Home Department, 1846-47; Chief Sec. for Ireland, 1847-52; P.C. [G.B.] 22 July, and [I.] 16 Aug. 1847. He *m.* firstly, 22 Dec. 1832, by spec. lic., at Hamilton Place, St. Geo. Han. Sq., Maria Harriet, yst. da. of Henry (CONYNGHAM), 1st MARQUESS CONYNGHAM [I.], by Elizabeth, da. of Joseph DENISON. She *d.* s.p.m.s., 3 Dec. 1843. He *m.* secondly, 16 Oct. 1860, at the British Embassy, Paris, Maria Georgiana Elizabeth, only da. of Herbert George JONES, Serjeant-at-Law, by Maria Alicia, da. of Sir George William LEEDS, 1st Baronet [1812]. She was living when he was *cr.* 14 Dec. 1863, BARON ATHLUMNEY of Somerville and Dollardstown, co. Meath [I.], being shortly afterwards *cr.* 3 May 1866, BARON MEREDYTH of Dollardstown, co. Meath [U.K.]. In these peerages this *Baronetcy* then *merged,* and still (1905) so continues. See PEERAGE.

(a) See p. 357, note "e"

MORRES:

cr. 24 April 1758;

afterwards, 1815-29, DE MONTMORENCY;

ex. 14 April 1829.

I. 1758. "SIR WILLIAM EVANS MORRES, Knt., of [Kilcreene], co. Kilkenny,"(a) 2d s.(b) of Francis MORRES, of Castle Morres, in that county, by Catharine, da. and h. of Sir William EVANS, Baronet [I., *cr.* 1683], appears to have suc. to the estates of his maternal grandfather abovenamed: was M.P. [I.] for Kilkenny(c), (two Parls.), 1752-68, and for Newtown, 1768 till death; was Sheriff of Kilkenny City, 1736-37; Sheriff of co. Kilkenny, 1741: Mayor of Kilkenny 1754-55, being *Knighted,* 28 May 1755, and was *cr. a Baronet* [I.], as above, by patent dat. at Dublin, 24 April 1758, the privy seal being dat. at St. James, 29 March previous. He *m.* firstly, 2 June 1737, Margaret, sister and h. of Charles HAYDOCK, da. of Josias HAYDOCK, of Kilkenny and of Buslick, co. Tipperary, by Mary (subsequently wife of Sir John STAPLES, 5th Baronet [I. 1628]), da. of (—) GOSLIN. She *d.* 22 Aug. 1753. He *m.* secondly, 1 July 1755, Maria Juliana, da. and coheir of William RYVES, of Upper Court, co. Kilkenny (s. of Sir Richard RYVES, one of the Barons of the Exchequer, [I.]), by Anne, da. of John CLAYTON, Dean of Kildare (1708-25). He *d.* 11 Oct. 1774, at Bath, in his 64th year. His widow, living 1811,(d) *d.* at a great age in 1812.

II. 1774. SIR HAYDOCK EVANS MORRES, Baronet [I. 1758], of Kilcreene aforesaid, 1st s. and h., being only s. by 1st wife, *b.* probably about 1740: was Mayor of Kilkenny, 1766-67; M.P. [I.] for Kilkenny (two Parls.), 1769, till his death in Dec. 1776, having *suc. to the Baronetcy,* 11 Oct. 1774. He *m.* 23 July 1772, Frances Jane Gorges, da. and h. of Ralph GORE, of Barrowmount, co. Kilkenny, by Elizabeth, da. and h. of Henry GORGES, of Somerset, co. Londonderry. He, who was "a man of social habits and highly popular in his native country,"(c) *d.* s.p.,(e) Dec. 1776. Will dat. 24 Dec. 1776, pr. [I.] 31 Jan. 1777. His widow *m.* 10 Feb. 1778, William GORE, of St. Valerie, co. Wicklow, and of Woodford, co. Leitrim, who *d.* 2 April 1815, aged 70.(f)

III. 1777, to 1829. SIR WILLIAM RYVES MORRES, *afterwards,* 1815-29, DE MONTMORENCY, Baronet [I. 1758], of Upperwood, *or* Upper, court, co. Kilkenny, br. of the half-blood and h. male, being 2d s., the only s. by the 2d wife, of the 1st Baronet, *b.* 7 Nov. 1763: *suc. to the Baronetcy,* Dec. 1777; was M.P. [I.] for Newtown, 1785-90, took by royal lic. 17 June 1815, together with four of his cousins(g), the name, stated

(a) See p. 340, note "b," under "DEANE."

(b) The eldest son, Hervey Morres, was *cr.,* 4 May 1756, Baron, and 29 June 1763, Viscount Mountmorres [I.], and the 3d son, Redmond Morres, was father of Lodge Evans Morres, *cr.* 31 July 1800, Baron Frankfort of Galmoye [I.] and 22 Jan. 1816, Viscount Frankfort de Montmorency [I.].

(c) See G. D. Burtchaell's *M.P's for Kilkenny,* pp. 141 and 162.

(d) Playfair's *Baronetage* [1811].

(e) Mary, his sister of the whole blood and h., *m.* April 1770, Clayton Bayly, of Gowran.

(f) Their grandson, John Ralph Ormsby-Gore, was *cr.,* 14 Jan. 1876, Baron Harlech.

(g) These were (1) Francis Hervey (Morres), 3d Viscount Mountmorres [I.]; (2), Lodge Evans (Morres), 1st Baron Frankfort of Galmoye [I.] (afterwards *cr.* [22 Jan. 1816] Viscount Frankfort de Montmorency [I.]); (3), Reymond Hervey Morres, "Esq.," and (4), Henry Francis Morres, "Esq."

to be "their ancient and original surname of DE MONTMORENCY," instead of that of MORRES.(a) He *d.* unm. 14 April 1829, aged 66, when the *Baronetcy* became *extinct.* Will dat. 13 April and pr. [I.] 2 June 1829.(b)

LOWTHER-CROFTON:

cr. 12 June 1758;

afterwards, since 1784, CROFTON;

and since 1817, BARONS CROFTON OF MOTE [I.].

I. 1758. "MARCUS LOWTHER-CROFTON, Esq., of the Mote, co. Roscommon,"(c) *formerly* Marcus LOWTHER, 2d s. of George LOWTHER, of Kilrue, co. Meath, sometime M.P. [I.] for Ratoath (*d.* June 1716), by Jane, sister of Marcus, 1st EARL OF TYRONE, 3d da. of Sir Tristram BERESFORD, 3d Baronet [I. 1665], assumed the name of CROFTON about 1745 on the death of his wife's brother, Sir Edward CROFTON, 4th Baronet [I. 1661], of the Mote aforesaid (to whom she was heir), was M.P. [I.] for Ratoath, 1753-60, for Roscommon Borough, 1761-68, and for Ratoath (again) 1769-76, and was *cr. a Baronet* [I.], as above, by patent dat. at Dublin, 12 June 1758, the privy seal being dat. at Kensington, 24 May previous. Sheriff of co. Roscommon, 1760. He *m.* 9 Sep. 1743, Katherine, sister and heir of Sir Edward CROFTON, 4th Baronet [I. 1661], only da. of Sir Edward CROFTON, 3d Baronet [I. 1661], by Mary, da. of Anthony NIXON, of Dublin. She, who was *b.* 12 June 1721, *d.* 9 April 1767. He *d.* 16 Jan. 1784 Will dat. 24 Dec. 1773, pr. [I.] 24 June 1788.

II. 1784. SIR EDWARD CROFTON, Baronet [I. 1758], of the Mote aforesaid, 1st surv. s. and h., *b.* 11 Oct. 1748; M.P. [I.] for co. Roscommon, 1768, but unseated, and subsequently (three Parls.) 1776 till death in 1797: Sheriff of co. Roscommon, 1773, having *suc. to the Baronetcy,* 16 Jan. 1784; Col. of the Roscommon Militia. He *m.* 13 April 1767, Anne, or Armida, da. and h. of Thomas CROKER, of Backweston, or Baxtown, co. Kildare, by Anne, da. and coheir of William RYVES, of Upper Court, co. Kilkenny, s. of Sir Richard RYVES, one of the Barons of the Exchequer [I.]. He, who had distinguished himself for his zeal in repressing the riots in the counties of Galway and Roscommon, *d.* of a rapid consumption at Bristol, 30 Sep. 1797, aged 48. His widow, who was *b.* 11 Jan. 1751, was within three months of his death, *cr.* 1 Dec. 1797, BARONESS CROFTON OF MOTE, co. Roscommon [I.], a peerage having been intended for her late husband. She *d.* 12 Aug. 1817, aged 66.

III. 1797. THE HON. SIR EDWARD CROFTON, Baronet [I. 1758], of the Mote aforesaid, 1st s. and h., *b.* 23 Oct. 1778; *suc. to the Baronetcy,* 30 Sep. 1797. He *m.* 12 Sep. 1801, Charlotte, 5th da. of John (STEWART), 7th EARL OF GALLOWAY [S.], by his 2d wife, Anne, da. of Sir James DASHWOOD, 2d Baronet [1684]. He *d.* at Mote Park, having committed suicide, 8 Jan. 1816, aged 37. His widow, who was *b.* 7 Aug. 1777, *d.* May 1842. Will pr. Jan. 1843.

(a) See *Complete Peerage,* by G.E.C., vol. iii, p. 401, note "c," under "FRANKFORT," and see (more especially) "THE MONTMORENCY IMPOSTURE" in J. Horace Round's *Feudal England* [1895], where the subject is exhaustively handled, the article concluding with these words:—"The house of Morres has no more right by hereditary descent to the name and arms of de Montmorency than any of the numerous families of Morris, or, indeed, for the matter of that, the family of Smith." See also the *Quarterly Review* for Oct. 1893 (vol. 177, p. 392), in an able article on the PEERAGE, where it is said that "indeed no one knows what the descent was" —"even Sir Bernard [Burke] no longer venturing so much as to hint [in his *Peerage*] at the presumed descent."

(b) In it he devises all his estate in trust for his "illegitimate son, William Morress [*sic.*], now called William De Montmorency, Esq."

(c) See p. 340, note "b," under "DEANE."

IV. 1816. SIR EDWARD CROFTON, Baronet [I. 1758], of the Mote aforesaid, 1st s. and h., *b.* 1 Aug. 1806, *suc. to the Baronetcy,* 8 Jan. 1816, and, next year, at the age of 11, *suc. to the Peerage* on the death of his grandmother abovenamed, 1 Aug. 1817, as BARON CROFTON OF MOTE, co. Roscommon [I.]. In that peerage this *Baronetcy* then *merged,* and still (1905) so continues. See PEERAGE.

BURTON:

cr. 2 Oct. 1758;

ex. 2 Oct. 1902.

I. 1758. "SIR CHARLES BURTON, Knt., of Dublin, Alderman,"(a) 5th s. of Benjamin BURTON, of Burton Hall, co. Carlow, Banker and Alderman of Dublin, many years (1703-27), M.P. [I.] and sometime (1706-07), Lord Mayor of that city (*d.* 28 May 1728), by Grace, da. of Robert STRATFORD, of Belan, co. Kildare; entered the Corporation of Dublin as representative of the Trinity Guild, 1732;(b) Sheriff of Dublin, 1733-34; Alderman, 3 Nov. 1748; M.P. [I.] thereof, 1749-60, being *Knighted,* 9 Jan. 1749-50; Lord Mayor, 1752-53, and was *cr. a Baronet* [I.], as above, by patent dat. at Dublin, 2 Oct. 1758, the privy seal being dat. at Kensington, 29 Aug. previous. He was first President of the Court of Conscience, Dublin, on its establishment, 29 Sep. 1760. He *m.* (Lic. Prerog. [I.]), 9 Sep. 1731) Margaret, 1st da. of Richard MEREDYTH, of Shrowland, co. Kildare, called(c) 2d Baronet [I. 1660], by Sarah, da. and coheir of Jeffery PAUL, of Bough, co. Carlow. He *d.* in Dublin, 6 June 1775, being then senior Alderman and "Father of the City of Dublin."(b) Will dat. 5 Jan. 1773, pr. [I.] 16 June 1775. His widow *d.* in Marlborough Street, Dublin, Jan. 1788, aged 89.

II. 1775. SIR CHARLES BURTON, Baronet [I. 1758], of Pollerton, co. Carlow, only s. and h., Capt. and afterwards (1777) Major in the 18th (Lord Drogheda's) Light Dragoons; *suc. to the Baronetcy,* 6 June 1775. He *m.* 11 Aug. 1778 (Lic. Dublin), Catherine, 3d da. and coheir of John (CUFFE), 2d BARON DESART [I.], by Sophia, da. and h. of Brettridge BADHAM. He *d.* April 1812. Will pr. [I.] 1813. His widow was *bur.* 10 Oct. 1827, at Rutland Church, in Urglin, co. Carlow.

III. 1812. SIR CHARLES BURTON, Baronet [I. 1758], of Pollerton aforesaid, 1st s. and h., *b.* 17 May 1779, in North Great George Street, Dublin, *suc. to the Baronetcy,* April 1812; Sheriff of co. Carlow, 1820. He *m.* Aug. 1807, Susanna, only da. of Joshua Paul MEREDYTH (br. of Barry Colles MEREDYTH, who in 1808 assumed the Baronetcy [I. 1660] as 7th Baronet)(c) by Elizabeth, da. of John BONHAM. He *d.* at Pollerton 6 and was *bur.* 10 Jan. 1830, at Rutland Church aforesaid, aged 50.

IV. 1830. SIR CHARLES BURTON, Baronet, [I. 1758], of Pollerton aforesaid, only s. and h., *suc. to the Baronetcy,* 6 Jan. 1830. He, who was of weak intellect, *d.* unm., 17 and was *bur.* 21 May 1842, at Rutland Church aforesaid, aged 30. Admon. [I.] June 1842, for £13,846.

(a) See p. 340, note "b," under "DEANE."

(b) See p. 347, note "e," under "FOWNES."

(c) See under "MEREDYTH" Baronetcy [I.], *cr.* 20 Nov. 1660. This Richard Meredyth (*b.* 1667 and admitted to Trin. Coll., Dublin, 5 June 1685, aged 18) was son of Robert, yst. *brother* of the grantee, and not as was pretended, a son of the grantee himself, who *d.* Feb. 1664-5, two years before such birth. The existence of the Baronetcy after the death of the grantee is disallowed by Sir A. Vicars, Ulster.

V. 1842, to 1902. Sir Charles William Cuffe Burton, Baronet [I. 1758], of Pollerton (which name he changed to Pollacton) aforesaid, cousin and h. male, being 1st s. and h. of Benjamin Burton, Lieut. 19th Lancers, by Grace Anne, da. and h. of William Roberts, of Gloucester Place, Marylebone, which Benjamin (who *d.* 1834) was yr. br. of the 3d, and 3d s. of the 2d Baronet. He was *b.* 13 Jan. 1823, in Marylebone; matric. at Oxford (Brasenose Coll.), 9 June 1841, aged 18; *suc. to the Baronetcy*, 17 May 1842; Lieut. 1st Dragoons, 1845, retiring 1849; Sheriff of co. Carlow, 1851. He *m.* 15 Dec. 1861, at St. Geo. Han. Sq., Georgiana Mary, only da. of David Haliburton Dallas, by Mary Anne, da. and h. of James Whiting Yorke, which David was s. of Lieut.-Gen. Sir Thomas Dallas, K.C.B. He *d.* s.p. at Pollacton aforesaid, 2 Oct. 1902, in his 80th year, and was *bur.* in Killeshin Cemetery, Queen's County, when the *Baronetcy* became *extinct.*(a) Will dat. 6 July 1882, pr. at £62,347. His widow *d.* at Pollacton, 15 March 1904.

COOPER:

cr. 3 Oct. 1758;

ex. 8 Aug. 1761.

I. 1758, to 1761. "William Cooper, LL.D., of Dublin,"(b) s. of Thomas Cooper, was *b.* about 1689; admitted to King's Inns, Dublin, as an Attorney of the King's Bench [I.]; was Chief Examiner in Chancery [I.], 1723-56; M.P. [I.] for Hillsborough, 1733, till death in 1761; Seneschal of the Manor of Newcastle [I.], 1736; one of the Masters in Chancery [I.], 26 Feb. 1739/40, till his resignation in 1754, and was *cr. a Baronet* [I.], as above, by patent dat. at Dublin, 3 Oct. 1758, the privy seal being dat. at Kensington, 15 Sep. previous, with a spec. rem., failing heirs male of his body, to those of his brother, "Thomas Cooper,(c) Esq., deceased."(b) He *m.* Elizabeth, da. of (—) Forster. He *d.* s.p.s.(d) 8 Aug. 1761, when the *Baronetcy* became *extinct.*(e) Will dat. 24 Nov. 1760, pr. 20 Aug. 1761. His widow *d.* Oct. 1766. Will dat. 6 June 1763, pr. [I.] 13 Oct. 1768.

(a) Grace Ellen, elder of the two daughters and coheirs of his yst. br., Col. Adolphus William Desart Burton, C.B. (who *d.* 11 Feb. 1882, aged 55), *m.* 16 Sep. 1890, Sir Francis Charles Edward Denys, 3d Baronet [1813], who by royal lic., 1905, took the additional name of Burton.

(b) See p. 340, note "b," under "Deane."

(c) This Thomas Cooper *d.* 15 Aug. 1755. Admon. [I.] 29 Aug. 1755. His son, Thomas Cooper, for a few weeks the heir presumptive to the Baronetcy, was Registrar of the Court of Chancery [I.], 1745. The latter *m.* 1 Nov. 1744, Anne, da. of Richard Warren, of Grangebeg, co. Kildare, but *d.* s.p., 20 Dec. 1758. Will pr. [I.] 29 Dec. 1758.

(d) His only child, Thomas Cooper, *b.* in co. Westmeath, 1712, entered Trin. Coll., Dublin, 28 Feb. 1728/9, aged 16; B.A., 1733; Barrister (Dublin), Trin., 1738; *d.* v.p. and unm., 13 Dec. 1741.

(e) His grand niece, Catherine Rothe, spinster (only da. of his niece, Catherine, the da. of his br., Thomas Cooper, *m.* Dec. 1748, and *d.* Aug. 1767, by her husband, Richard Rothe, of Butler's Grove, co. Kilkenny), was *b.* 1757, assumed the name of Cooper, and *m.* 27 Dec. 1774, Hon. Pierce Butler (2d s. of the 1st Earl of Carrick [I.]), who then assumed the name of Cooper, and *d.* s.p. 5 May 1825, aged 74. She *d* 20 Feb. 1833. The estates then passed to Harman Herring, who thereupon assumed the name of Cooper. He was 1st surv. s. of Darby Herring, who was in remainder to them under the will of the 1st Baronet.

BRADSTREET:

cr. 14 July 1759.

I. 1759. "Simon Bradstreet, Esq., Counsellor at Law, of Dublin,"(a) 1st s. and h. of Simon(b) Bradstreet, of Port Lahane, co. Tipperary, by (—), was *b.* 1693; entered Trin. Coll., Dublin, 6 Jan. 1707/8, aged 15; Scholar, 1710; B.A., 1712; Barrister, (Dublin), 11 May 1720, and was *cr. a Baronet* [I.], as above, by patent dat. at Dublin, 14 July 1759, the privy seal being dat. at Kensington, 26 June previous. He was of Kilmainham, co. Dublin. He *m.*, in or before 1728, Ellen, 3d da. of his paternal uncle, Samuel(b) Bradstreet, of Tinnescolly, co. Kilkenny, by Elizabeth, da. of Charles Agar, of Gowran, co. Kilkenny. He *d.* 26 April 1762, aged 69, and was *bur.* at Clondalkin, co. Dublin. M.I. Will dat. 2 Nov. 1760, pr. [I.] 5 May 1762. His widow *d.* at Kilmainham, 25 and was *bur.* 26 Oct. 1779, at Clondalkin, aged 82. Admon. [I.] 27 Nov. 1779.

II. 1762. Sir Simon Bradstreet, Baronet [I. 1759], of Kilmainham aforesaid, 1st s. and h., *b.* 22 March and *bap.* 7 May 1728,(c) at St. Nicholas Within, Dublin; admitted to Middle Temple, London, 5 July 1750; Sheriff of co. Dublin, 1760; Barrister (Dublin), 1761; *suc. to the Baronetcy*, 26 April 1762. He *m.* 9 Oct. 1759 (Lic. 8), Anne, 4th da. of the Rt. Hon. Sir Henry Cavendish, 1st Baronet [1755], by his 1st wife, Anne, da. and coheir of Henry Pyne, of Waterpark, co. Cork. He *d.* s p m.(d) at Kilmainham, and was *bur.* 16 Dec. 1773, at Clondalkin, aged 45.(c)

III. 1773. Sir Samuel Bradstreet, Baronet [I. 1759], of Stacumnie, near Celbridge, co. Kildare, br. and h. male, admitted to Middle Temple, London, 29 Jan. 1753; Barrister (Dublin), Hilary, 1758; Recorder of Dublin, 14 July 1766, being, as such, admitted within the Bar, 23 Jan. 1767; *suc. to the Baronetcy* in Dec. 1773; M.P. for Dublin (two Parls.), 1776 to 13 Jan. 1784, when he was made Fourth Justice of the Court of King's Bench [I.], being the first "Fourth Justice" that had ever been appointed. He *m.* 19 (Lic. 14) Jan. 1771, Elizabeth, da. and h. of James Tully, M.D., of Dublin, by Bridget, sister (whose issue became coheir) of Edmund Netterville, of Longford Castle, co. Galway, da. of Patrick Netterville, of Longford. He *d.* 2 May 1791, at his seat at Booterstown, co. Dublin. Will dat. 19 Oct. 1790, pr. [I.] 7 May 1791. His widow *d.* 25 Dec. 1799. Will pr. [I.] 1801.

IV. 1791. Sir Simon Bradstreet, Baronet [I. 1759], of Stacumnie aforesaid, 1st s. and h., *b.* 25 Nov. 1772, at Mespil, Upper Leeson Street, Dublin; admitted to Gray's Inn, London, 2 Feb. 1789; *suc. to the Baronetcy*, 2 May 1791. He *m.* 1 Jan. 1808 (Lic. Dublin, Dec. 1807), Clare Margaret, da. of John Murphy, of Fleet Street, Dublin. He *d.* 25 Oct. 1853, at Clontarf, in his 83d year. His widow *d.* 12 Nov. 1869.

V. 1853. Sir John Valentine Bradstreet, Baronet [I. 1759], of Castilla, in Clontarf, co. Dublin, 1st s. and h., *b.* 23 Sept. 1815, at Stacumnie aforesaid; *suc. to the Baronetcy*, 25 Oct. 1853. He *m.* 8 Nov. 1836, Josefa, da. of Don Vincente Xavier de Vinuesa, of Burgos, in Spain. She *d.* 7 Feb. 1879. He *d.* s.p., 21 Nov. 1889, at Castilla aforesaid, aged 74.

(a) See p. 340, note "b," under "Deane."

(b) This Simon and Samuel were sons of John Bradstreet, of Blanchville Park, co. Kilkenny, and Margaret, his wife.

(c) *Ex inform.* C. M. Tenison. The age of 29 as stated (*Journal of the Association for the Preservation of the Memorials of the Dead in Ireland*, vol. iii, p. 436) to be in the Vestry books at Clondalkin is clearly wrong, and should apparently be 45.

(d) Eleanor Catherine, his da. and h., *m.* 5 Jan. 1782, William Hore, of Harpers town, co. Wexford (slain by rebels 20 June 1798), and *d.* 1849, leaving issue.

VI. 1889. Sir Edmund Simon Bradstreet, Baronet [I. 1759], of Castilla aforesaid, and of St. Jean de Luz, France, only br. and h., *b.* 24 Aug. 1820; *suc. to the Baronetcy*, 21 Nov. 1889. He *m.* Jan. 1846, Emily Matilda Sophia, da. of General the Chevalier Victor Marion de Gaja, of Las Courtines, Castelonaudary, France, by Matilda, da. of Lord Robert Stephen FitzGerald, 6th s. of James, 1st Duke of Leinster [I.]. She *d.* 25 June 1883. He *d.* 30 March 1905, at Woodbrook, near Port Arlington, aged 84.

VII. 1905. Sir Edward Simon Victor Bradstreet, Baronet [I. 1759], only s. and h., *b.* 1856; admitted to Trin. Coll., Dublin, 1874; *suc. to the Baronetcy*, 30 March 1905. He *m.* in 1888, Fortunée, da. of (—) Fiori, of Bougie, Algeria.

Family Estates.—These, in 1878,(a) consisted of 2,696 acres in co. Galway (worth £804 a year), 21 in the city of Dublin (worth £356 a year), and 16 in co. Dublin (worth £121 a year). *Total.*—2,733 acres, worth £1,281 a year.

RIBTON:

cr. 21 April 1760;

ex. 5 April 1901.

I. 1760. "Sir George Ribton, Knt., of [the Grove, in] Stillorgan, co. Dublin,"(b) 1st s. and h. of William Ribton, of Sillough [Sollough ?], in Fingall, co. Dublin, by Anne, da. of (—) (who *d.* his widow, 1757-58), was admitted to the Corporation of Dublin as representative of the Trinity Guild, 1732(c); Sheriff, 1738-39; Alderman, 25 April 1743; Mayor, 1747-48, being *Knighted* 30 Sep. 1747, on coming into office, and was *cr. a Baronet* [I.], as above, by patent dat. at Dublin, 21 April 1760, the privy seal being dat. at St. James' on the 2d of the same month. He *m.* in or before 1740, Anne, da. of (—) Fisher, of Sollough [Sillough ?], co. Dublin. He *d.* at Bath, 9 March 1762. Will dat. 29 Jan., pr. [I.] 23 March 1762.

II. 1762. Sir George Ribton, Baronet [I. 1760], of the Grove aforesaid and afterwards of Landscape, in Rathfarnham, co. Dublin, only s. and h., *b.* 25 May 1740; *suc. to the Baronetcy*, 9 March 1762; Sheriff of co. Dublin, 1773. He *m.* firstly (Lic. Dublin, 4 March 1768), Mary, 2d da. of John Grogan, of Johnstown, co. Wexford, by Catherine, da. of Andrew Knox, of Rathmacnee, in that county. She *d.* s.p.m. in Francis Street, Dublin, 1 Feb. 1781. He *m.* secondly (Lic. Dublin, 1781), Jane, da. and heir or coheir of John Sheppey, of Rockfield, co. Dublin, by Jane, da. of the Rev. Edward Drury, D.D. He *d.* 1806, aged 66. Will pr. [I.] 1806.

III. 1806. Sir John Sheppey Ribton, Baronet [I. 1760], of Woodbrook, near Bray, co. Dublin, 2d but 1st surv. s. and h., by 2d wife,(d) *b.* 7 Feb. 1797; *suc. to the Baronetcy* in 1806; served for nine years in the Rifle Brigade in the Peninsular Wars and in America, being four times wounded; Sheriff of co. Dublin, 1824. He *m.* firstly, 9 April 1818 (Lic. Dublin), Mary Anne, da. and h. of Jeremiah Hayes, of Killuragh, co. Limerick. He *m.* secondly, 20 (Lic. Prerog. [I.] 16) Jan. 1841, Emily, widow of Walter Hussey Hill, only da. of Thomas Quinan. He *d.* 1 May 1877, at 48 Ebury Street, Pimlico, aged 80. His widow *d.* 16 Jan. 1887, from the effects of a carriage accident, at Woodbrook aforesaid.

(a) See p. 347, note "c," under "Burdett."

(b) See p. 340, note "b," under "Deane."

(c) See p. 347, note "e," under "Fownes."

(d) His elder br., George Ribton, *d.* April 1796.

IV. 1877, to 1901. Sir George William Ribton, Baronet [I. 1760], of Grey Fort, Kilcool, co. Wicklow, 2d but 1st surv. s. and h., being 1st s. by 2d wife,(a) *b.* 16 Aug. 1842, at Woodbrook aforesaid, ed. at Cheltenham College; *suc. to the Baronetcy*, 1 May 1877. He *m.* 22 June 1869, Elizabeth, widow of Francis Kennedy, Capt. 77th Foot, only child of Christopher Sanders, of Deer Park, co. Cork, by Elizabeth, relict of William Broomhead, of Newcastle-on-Tyne. He *d.* s.p., 5 April 1901, at Grey Fort aforesaid, aged 58, when the *Baronetcy* became *extinct*. His widow living 1905.

Family Estates.—These, in 1878,(b) consisted of 1,146 acres in co. Limerick, and 77 in co. Dublin. *Total.*—1,223 acres, worth £1,594 a year.

GORE:

cr. 30 Aug. 1760;

afterwards, since 1804, Gore-Booth.

I. 1760. "Booth Gore, Esq., of Artarman, [in Drumcliffe] co. Sligo,"(c) who, possibly, like his father, styled himself or was styled a Baronet,(d) 1st s. and h.(e) of Nathaniel Gore, of the same and of Newtown Gore, co. Leitrim, styling himself a Baronet as early as 1711,(d) by Lætitia, da. and h. of Humphrey Booth, of Dublin (nephew of Sir Robert Booth, of Salford, co. Lancaster, Lord Chief Justice of the King's Bench [I.]), was *b.* 1712; was Sheriff of co. Leitrim, 1742; was of Lissadell, co. Sligo, and was Sheriff of that county, 1771, having been *cr. a Baronet*, as above, by patent dat. at Dublin, 30 Aug. 1760, the privy seal being dat. at St. James' as early as 14 Feb. 1758. He *m.* (Lic. Prerog. [I.], 23 Dec. 1743) his cousin,(f) Emilia (then of St. Michan's, Dublin, spinster), da. of Brabazon Newcomen, of Calliaghstown, co. Louth, by Arabella, 3d da. of the Hon. Oliver Lambart, 3d s. of Charles, 1st Earl of Cavan [I.]. He *d.* at Lissadell, 22 July 1773, aged 61. His widow *d.* Nov. 1778, at Bath, and was *bur.* there.

II. 1773. Sir Booth Gore, Baronet [I. 1760], of Lissadell aforesaid, and of Huntercombe House, 1st s. and h., *suc. to the Baronetcy*, 22 July 1773; Sheriff of co. Sligo, 1785. He, by the death, in Feb. 1789, of his paternal uncle, John Booth, *formerly* Gore, of Salford, co. Lancaster, inherited that estate, formerly the property of the family of Booth. He *d.* unm. 17 June 1804, at Huntercombe aforesaid. Will pr. 1806.

III. 1804. Sir Robert Newcomen Gore, *afterwards* Gore-Booth, Baronet [I. 1760], of Lissadell and Salford aforesaid, only br. and h., *suc. to the Baronetcy*, 17 June 1804, and took (a few weeks later) by royal lic., 30 Aug. 1804, the name of Booth after that of Gore. Sheriff of co. Sligo, 1806. He *m.* 19 Nov. 1804, Hannah, da. of Henry Irwin, of Streamstown, co. Sligo, by Ann, da. of (—) Stewart. He *d.* 23 Oct. 1814.

(a) His elder br., of the half-blood, John Hayes Ribton, *b.* 7 Feb. 1819, *d.* unm. and v.p., 21 May 1844.

(b) See p. 347, note "c," under "Burdett."

(c) See p. 340, note "b," under "Deane."

(d) See p. 342, as to this assumption by Nathaniel Gore, and as to the possibility of the same dignity being, as early as 1743, assumed by, or attributed to, Booth Gore, the grantee of 30 Aug. 1760.

(e) The 2d son, John, took the name of Booth in or before 1746, in which year he was Sheriff of co Dublin. He inherited the estate of Salford, co. Lancaster, under the will, dat. 30 Dec. 1756, of his cousin, Robert Booth, of Salford aforesaid. He *d.* unm., Feb. 1789.

(f) His paternal grandmother, wife of Sir Robert Gore, was Frances, da. of Sir Thomas Newcomen, of Sutton, near Dublin.

IV. 1814. SIR ROBERT GORE-BOOTH, Baronet [I. 1760], of Lissadell aforesaid, 1st s. and h., *b.* 25 Aug. 1805, at Bath; *suc. to the Baronetcy,* 23 Oct. 1814; ed. at Westminster School, and at Queen's Coll., Cambridge; M.A., 1826, being admitted in 1834 to an *ad eundem* degree by the University of Dublin; was M.P. for co. Sligo (seven Parls.), 1850, till death, and Lord Lieut. of that county, 1871. He *m.* firstly, 23 March 1827, Caroline, 2d da. of Robert Edward (KING), 1st VISCOUNT LORTON [I.], by Frances, da. of Laurence (PARSONS), 1st EARL OF ROSSE [I.]. She *d.* s.p., 13 Jan. 1828, at Southampton, aged 21. He *m.* secondly, 2 April 1830, in Dublin, Caroline Susan, 2d da. of Thomas GOOLD, of Merrion Sq., Dublin, a Master in Chancery, by Elizabeth, da. of the Rev. Brinsley NIXON, Rector of Painstown, co. Meath. She *d.* 16 Jan. 1855, in Dublin. He *d.* 21 Dec. 1876, at Lissadell, aged 71.

V. 1876. SIR HENRY WILLIAM GORE-BOOTH, Baronet [I. 1760], of Lissadell aforesaid, 2d and yst. but only surv. s.(a) by 2d wife, *b.* 1 July 1843: ed. at Eton; Sheriff of co. Sligo, 1872; *suc. to the Baronetcy,* 21 Dec. 1876. He *m.* 29 April 1867, at Tickhill, co. York, Georgiana Mary, only da. of Col. Charles John HILL, of Cotgrave, Notts, by Frances Charlotte Arabella (precedency warrant, 1857, as an Earl's daughter), sister of the 9th EARL OF SCARBROUGH, da. of Frederick SAVILE, *formerly* LUMLEY, of Tickhill Castle. He *d.* 13 Jan. 1900, at San Moritz, aged 56. His widow living 1905.

VI. 1900. SIR JOSSLYN AUGUSTUS RICHARD GORE-BOOTH, Baronet [I. 1760], of Lissadell aforesaid, 1st s. and h., *b.* 25 Feb. 1869; *suc. to the Baronetcy,* 13 Jan. 1900; Sheriff of co. Sligo, 1904.

Family Estates.—These, in 1883, consisted of 31,774 acres in co. Sligo, valued at £16,774 a year, and (—) acres in Lancashire, valued at £572 a year. *Total* of annual value, £17,346. *Seat.*—Lissadell, co. Sligo.

CREATIONS BY GEORGE III.

25 Oct. 1760 to 31 Dec. 1800.

when, owing to the Union with Ireland, 1 Jan. 1801, the creation of Baronetcies of Ireland ceased, being succeeded by that of Baronetcies of the United Kingdom of Great Britain and Ireland.

YORKE:

cr. 13 April 1761;

ex. 30 Sep. 1776.

I. 1761, to 1776. "WILLIAM YORKE, Esq., of Dublin, Chief Justice of the Common Pleas" [I.],(b) was *b.* about 1700; was ed. at Charterhouse School; was Justice of the Common Pleas [I.], 23 Feb. 1742/3, and Chief Justice, 19 Feb. 1753, till his resignation in 1761, having been one of the three Commissioners of the Great Seal in 1740. He was P.C. [I.] and Chancellor of the Exchequer [I.] 1761-63, and was *cr. a Baronet,* as above, by patent dat. at Dublin, 13 April 1761, the privy seal being dat. at St.

(a) His elder br. of the full blood, Robert Newcomen Gore-Booth, *b.* about 1831, matric. at Oxford (Ch. Ch.), 20 May 1850, aged 19; *m.* but *d.* s.p. and v.p., 29 Oct. 1861, aged 30.

(b) See p. 340, note "b," under "DEANE."

James', 28 March previous. He *m.* (Lic. Prerog. [I.], 10 Sep. 1744) Charity, widow of William COPE, of Loughgall, co. Armagh, 4th da. of the Rev. Rowland SINGLETON (br. of the Rt. Hon. Henry SINGLETON, sometime, 1754-59, Master of the Rolls [I.]), by Elizabeth, da. of John GRAHAM, of Drogheda. He *d.* s.p. at Brentford, Midx., from an overdose of laudanum accidentally taken, 30 Sep. 1776, aged 76,(a) and was *bur.* in the Charterhouse Chapel, London, when the *Baronetcy* became *extinct.* Will pr. 1776. His widow *d.* 6 and was *bur.* with him 8 May 1779, aged 72. Will pr. [I.] 1779. M.I. to both of them.

O'FLAHERTY:(b)

1762(?) to 1808.

JOHN O'FLAHERTY, of Lemonfield, co. Galway, 2d s. of Murrough Morgan O'FLAHERTY, of the same, by Jane, da. of Theobald (BOURKE), 6th VISCOUNT MAYO [I.], was *b.* about 1726; suc. his elder br., Brian O'FLAHERTY in 1750 in the family estate, "served with honour and applause as Capt. in the 65th Regiment of Foot; was one of the party which composed the forlorn hope at the taking of Martinique [Feb. 1762] and Guadaloupe, and, for his gallant conduct, was rewarded with a company. *In the Commission* [1762?] he is *styled Baronet.* In a subsequent Commission of the Peace, 15 Jan. [1779], 19 Geo. III, he is *styled Knight,* but neither he nor his successor seems to have cared much about either title."(c) He (being then called "Knight") was Sheriff of co. Galway, 1800. He *m.* 18 July 1764, Mary, da. of the Rev. Thomas ROYSE, of Nantenan, co. Limerick, by Annabella, da. of (—) RUSSELL.(d) He *d.* 1808, aged 82 (leaving an only s. and h., Thomas Henry O'FLAHERTY, *b.* 3 June 1777, who *m.* but *d.* s.p.s., 16 June 1848, having never assumed the title), when the *Baronetcy* attributed to the said John *ceased.*

MAY:

cr. 30 June 1763.

ex. 1834.

but assumed for a short time, in or shortly before 1887.

I. 1763. "JAMES MAY, Esq., of Mayfield, co. Waterford,"(e) 1st s. and h. of James MAY, of the same, sometime M.P. [I.] for co. Waterford (*d.* 1735), by Lætitia, da. of William (PONSONBY), 1st VISCOUNT DUNCANNON [I.], was *b.* about 1724; was Sheriff of co. Waterford, 1752, and M.P. [I.] for that county (six Parls.), Oct. 1760 till 1798, when he resigned, "because of his extreme age," having been *cr. a Baronet* [I.], as above, by patent dat. at Dublin, 30 June 1763, the privy seal being dat. at St. James, 19 April previous. He *m.*

(a) There is a full account of this event in the *Annual Register* for 1776.

(b) The discovery of this assumption is due (as indeed is almost all that is valuable in the account here given of these Irish Baronetcies) to G. D. Burtchaell, of the Office of Arms, Dublin.

(c) See *O'Flaherty's West Connaught,* ed. by James Hardiman for the Irish Archæological Society, 1846, p. 417, and note "h."

(d) "Sir John O'Flaherty, Baronet, and Lady O'Flaherty, his *Sposa.* He was a plain agreeable country gentleman. Her Ladyship was to the full as *plain,* but not quite so agreeable." [Sir Jonah Barrington's *Personal Sketches of his own times,* 1827.]

(e) See p. 340, note "b," under "DEANE."

his cousin, Anne, da. of Thomas MOORE, of Marlfield, co. Tipperary, by Mary,(a) sister of Stephen, 1st VISCOUNT MONTCASHELL [I.], da. of Richard MOORE, of Cashel, co. Tipperary (1st cousin of the said Thomas MOORE), by Elizabeth his wife, da. of William (PONSONBY), 1st VISCOUNT DUNCANNON [I.] abovenamed. She *d.* Jan. 1792, and was *bur.* at Christ Church, Waterford. He *d.* 7 Nov. 1811, at May Park [*Qy.* Mayfield], co. Waterford, at a great age, and was *bur.* at Christ Church aforesaid. Will dat. 2 July 1803 to 26 Sep. 1810, pr. [I.] 11 Jan. 1812.

II. 1811. SIR (JAMES) EDWARD MAY, Baronet [I. 1763], of Mayfield aforesaid, 1st s. and h., was Sheriff of co. Waterford, 1781; M.P. [I.] for Belfast, 1798-1800, and M.P. [U.K.] for the same (five Parls.), 1801, till his death; *suc. to the Baronetcy,* 7 May 1811. He is said(b) to have *m.* (and probably after the birth of his children did marry) Elizabeth, da. of Francis LUMLEY, of Passage, co. Waterford (will pr. 1768), by his 2d wife (*m.* 1740) Catherine, da. of Lionel IZOD. He *d.* s.p. legit.,(c) 23 July 1814. The admon. of "Dame Elizabeth MAY, Midx.," granted July 1835, probably refers to his widow.

III. 1814. SIR HUMPHREY MAY, Baronet [I. 1763], of Maypark [*Qy.* Mayfield], co. Waterford, br and h., Collector of the Revenue at Waterford; Sheriff of co. Waterford, 1798; *suc. to the Baronetcy,* 23 July 1814.(d) He *m.* (Lic. Dublin, 1 July 1784) Jane, da. of the Rev James GRUEBER, by Dorcas, da. of John SMYTH, of Violetstown, co. Westmeath. He *d.* s.p., early in 1819.(e) Will dat. 13 Feb. 1792, pr [I.] 2 March 1819. His widow *d.* 30 Sep. 1834. Will dat. 9 Oct. 1828 pr. [I.] 9 May 1835.

(a) This is the statement of the 1st Baronet as to his wife's ancestry. Her mother is frequently (in error) said to have been da. of George King, of Kilpeacon, co. Limerick. That George King *m.* her paternal aunt, Margaret Moore (her will pr. 1755), and *d.* s.p. 1722.

(b) Playfair's *Baronetage* [1811].

(c) It is [erroneously] stated in Burke's *Extinct Baronetage* that the title became extinct at his death. The four children, by the said Elizabeth Lumley, ascribed to him in Playfair's *Baronetage* [1811] were doubtless, illegitimate. These were "two sons, Stephen, and the Rev. Edward, Rector of the Parish of Belfast, and two daughters," *i.e.,* (1) Anne, who *m.* 8 Aug. 1795, at St. Marylebone, George Augustus (Chichester), 2d Marquess of Donegall [I.], and (2) Elizabeth, who *m.* Thomas Verner, of Church Hill, co. Armagh. As to the sons abovenamed (1) Sir Stephen Edward May, *b.* about 1781, was Collector of Customs at Belfast, and M.P. thereof, 1814-18, being returned as "Sir Stephen May, Baronet, in the place of his father." He was, however, subsequently *Knighted* 20 April 1816, by the Viceroy [I.]. He (according to Dod's *Knightage,* 1844) "claims also to be a Baronet of Ireland, which title it is said his grandfather, Sir James May, received in 1763." He *d.* at Bath, 28 Oct. 1845, aged 64. (2) Edward May, matric. at Oxford (St. Mary Hall), 21 March 1800, aged 17, as son of "Edward, of Mayfield, Ireland, Esq.," being afterwards (as stated above) Rector of Belfast. Sir Arthur E. Vicars, Ulster King of Arms, kindly sends the following extracts (from the Betham correspondence in his possession) from a letter of Sir James May, giving an account of his family, as under—"Mayfield, Jan. 9th 1809. Ann Moore was my wife and mother of all my children, which consisted of five sons and two daughters. I lost one son in the American war, three of them are maryed. James Edward, my eldest, who has children, the two next, Humphrey May and Thos. May, are long maryed but have not had a child: the daughter of James Edward May is maryed to the Marchioness (*sic*) of Donegall, and youngest to Mr. Verner of the County of Down." The following is from a letter of "C.L.T." (*i.e.,* the Hon. Charles Ludlow Tonson), dated Dec. 20, 1808:—"Edward May, Esq., Member for Belfast, and eldest son of Sir James May, Bart., is married to the daughter of . . . Lumley, Esq., of the Co. Cork, and widow of . . . They have no children, but before marriage they had a daughter, Anna May, the present Marchioness of Donegal. Humphrey May another son of Sir James May, Bart., lives at a country seat near Waterford, is married but has no issue."

(d) See statement on p. 369, note "c."

IV. 1819, to 1834. SIR GEORGE STEPHEN MAY, Baronet [I. 1763], only surv. br. and h., being 5th and yst. s. of the 1st Baronet(a); was *b.* about 1763; matric. at Oxford (as "Stephen, son of James, of Clonegham, co. Waterford, Baronet"), 4 April 1781, aged 18; Barrister (Dublin), 1784; *suc. to the Baronetcy* in 1819, being "at that date, [indeed as early as 1803] and till his death in 1834, of unsound mind."(b) He *d.* a lunatic and unm. in Swift's Hospital, Dublin, in 1834,(c) when the *Baronetcy* became *extinct.* Admon. 1839.

This Baronetcy was assumed, in 1886, till his death in Jan. 1887, by THOMAS PAINE MAY,(c) a British subject, sometime Assistant Treasurer of the United States at New Orleans and Col. in the Army, "lately [1885] of Maylawn, Louisiana, in the United States of America." He, who was *b.* 17 July 1842, was the only surv. s. of Thomas MAY, of Maylawn aforesaid, s. and h. of Patrick MAY, of Ballinalack, co. West-

(a) This George Stephen has a legacy in his father's will, 2 July 1803, "in case he should recover from his malady." He is omitted in Playfair's *Baronetage* [1811], where only four sons are given, viz., the two elder as in the text, and "(3) Thomas May, Esq., who *m.* Miss Carr, but has no issue; (4) Charles May, Esq., *d.* unmarried." This Charles is doubtless the son who was slain unm. and v.p. "being lost in the American War" (see p. 368, note "c"), and who accordingly is not mentioned in his father's will, dated 2 July 1803. His brother, Thomas May (B.A. [Dublin] 1777, M.A., 1786), was in Holy Orders and Rector of Clonmel. He *m.* (Lic. Dublin, 1779) Brabazon, da. of the Rev. Thomas Carr, D.D., by his 2d wife, Anne, da. of William Wall, of Coolnamucky, co. Waterford. He *d.* s.p., 1810. Admon. [I.] 1811. The will of his widow, dat. 13 Nov. 1816, was pr. [I.] 7 May 1819.

(b) See statement in note "c," below.

(c) See his claim to this Baronetcy in the "*Times*" newspaper for 23 May 1885, as below:—"Reward of £100.—Whereas Sir James May, of Mayfield, Representative in Parliament for the County of Waterford, was, in the year 1763, created a Baronet of Ireland, with limitation to the heirs male of his body lawfully begotten, and the said Sir James May had five sons, the issue of his marriage, namely, James Edward, Humphrey, Thomas, Charles, and George Stephen, and dying in or about the year 1811, was succeeded by his eldest son called Sir Edward May, at whose death, three years subsequently, the title devolved on Sir Humphrey May as third baronet, and was enjoyed by him until his decease in 1819, when (his next brother, Thomas, having predeceased without issue in 1809, and the existence of Charles May, next in succession, or any issue male of his body, being ignored) the baronetcy was reputed to, rather than assumed by, George Stephen May, the fifth and youngest son of the 1st baronet, who at that date (1819) and till his death in 1834 was of unsound mind.

And whereas in certain suits in the Court of Chancery in Ireland, dating from or about the year 1814 to 1844, and known as "May versus May, Carew, Medlicott, and others," "May versus Pennefather and others," "May v. Medlicott," and "Marjoribanks versus Medlicott"—the objects of which were, amongst others, the distribution of and otherwise dealing with the estate of the said Sir James May under the terms of his marriage settlement and will—in all of which proceedings, as in the decrees made thereon, the aforesaid Charles May is treated as having died without issue and intestate, though the evidences, if any, upon which that position was supported and maintained do not appear to have been preserved and cannot now be found.

And whereas Thomas Paine May, a subject of Her Majesty the Queen, but lately of Maylawn, Louisiana, in the United States of America, claims (as the only surviving son of Thomas May, of Maylawn aforesaid, deceased, who was the son and heir of Patrick May, of Ballinalack, in the County of Westmeath, deceased) to be the great grandson and heir-at-law of the aforesaid Charles May.

Now notice is hereby given that—as it is required by Sir Bernard Burke, C.B.,

meath, s. of Charles MAY,(a) 4th s. of Sir James MAY, the 1st Baronet [I. 1763]. He stated himself to have *suc. to the Baronetcy*, as 6th Baronet [I. 1763] [presumably on the death of his father], in 1852, but not to have assumed the title till 1886. He *m.* in 1866, Mary, only da. of Miles TAYLOR, Rep. for Louisiana in the United States Congress. He *d.* as "SIR THOMAS MAY, Baronet, of Mayfield, Waterford, and of Maylawn, St. John Baptist, Louisiana, U.S.A.,"(b) 11 Jan. 1887, at Charles Street, St. James Sq., London.

With respect to this claim of "Sir Thomas May," Sir Bernard Burke, Ulster King of Arms, in reply to a letter, dat. 13 Oct. 1886, from Messrs. Deane and Nash, Solicitors, 14 South Square, Gray's Inn, requesting him to insert in his forthcoming *Baronetage* an account of this Baronetcy, taken from Debrett's *Baronetage* (as by them enclosed) wrote that he was "unable to comply with their request," adding that "the Baronetcy of May, of Mayfield, co. Waterford, created 30 June 1763, is extinct."

BLACKWOOD:

cr. 1 July 1763;

afterwards, since 1807, BARONS DUFFERIN AND CLANEBOYE [I.];

since 1871, EARLS OF DUFFERIN [U.K.];

and since 1888, MARQUESSES OF DUFFERIN AND AVA [U.K.].

I. 1763. "ROBERT BLACKWOOD, Esq., of Ballyliddy, *i.e.*, Ballyleidy, in the Upper Claneboye], co. Down,"(c) 1st s. and h. of John, or James BLACKWOOD, of the same (attainted in the Parl. of James II., 1689), by Ursula *or* Anne (*d.* 12 Sep. 1741), da. of Robert HAMILTON, of Killyleagh, was *b.* 5 Nov. 1694, and was *cr. a Baronet* [I.], as above, by patent dat. at Dublin, 1 July 1763, the privy seal being dat. at St. James', 19 April previous. He *m.* firstly, in 1719, Joyce, sister of Joseph, 1st EARL OF MILLTOWN [I.], da. of Joseph LEESON, of Dublin, brewer, by Margaret, da. of Andrew BRICE, sometime Sheriff of Dublin. He *m.* secondly, in 1729, Grace, only da. of Isaac MACARTNEY, sometime (1690) Sheriff of co. Antrim, by Grace, sister and h. of John HALTRIDGE, sometime (1703-27) M.P. [I.] for Killyleagh. He *d.* 1774. Will pr. [I.] 1774. His widow *d.* 30 Dec. 1788.

LL.D., Ulster King of Arms, that evidence rebutting the assumption of the death without issue male and intestate of the said Charles May be produced to his satisfaction—the sum of ONE HUNDRED POUNDS will be paid to any one who shall give such INFORMATION as will lead to the proof that the said CHARLES MAY DID NOT DIE WITHOUT ISSUE MALE as alleged.

Application to be made to Stephen Tucker, Esquire, Somerset Herald, Heralds' College, London: Arthur L. Barlee, Esq., Solicitor, No. 30, Westland-row, Dublin; or to us.

DEANE, CHUBB, and Co., Solicitors to the said Thomas Paine May

No. 14, South-square, Gray's inn, London, W.C."

(a) This Charles May in reality, however, *d.* unm. and v.p. before 2 July 1803. See p. 369, note "a."

(b) See cutting [kindly furnished by C. M. Tenison, of Hobart, Tasmania] from an Irish newspaper [*Qy.* the *Irish Times*] of 12 Jan. 1887, where he is thus described in his obituary, it being added that he was "fortified by the rites of the Roman Catholic church." He left two sons, viz., (1) Thomas May, *b.* 31 Jan. 1871, and (2) John May, *b.* 19 March 1872.

(c) See p. 340, note "b," under "DEANE."

II. 1774. SIR JOHN BLACKWOOD, Baronet [I. 1763], of Ballyleidy aforesaid, 1st s. and h., by 1st wife, *b.* 1722; was M.P. [I.] for Killyleagh, 1761-68: for Bangor, 1769-76: for Killyleagh (again), 1776-83 and 1783-90: for Bangor (again), 1790-97, and finally (third time) for Killyleagh, 1798, till his death in 1799, being a firm opponent of the proposed Union [I.], and having *suc. to the Baronetcy* in 1774. He *m.* (Lic. 22 May 1751) Dorcas, 1st da. and coheir of James STEVENSON,(a) of Killyleagh aforesaid, by Anne, da. of Gen. Nicholas PRICE, of Hollymount. He *d.* 27 Feb. 1799, aged 77. Will dat. 24 July, 1792, pr. [I.] 1799. His widow, who was *b.* 1726, was, in consideration of the political services of her son, at his request, *cr.*, 31 July 1800, BARONESS DUFFERIN AND CLANEBOYE OF BALLYLEIDY AND KILLYLEAGH, co. Down [I.], with rem. of that Barony to the heirs male of the body of her late husband. She *d.* in Hinde Street, Marylebone, 8 and was *bur.* 18 Feb. 1807, at St. Marylebone, aged 81. Will pr. Feb. 1807.

III. 1799. SIR JAMES STEVENSON BLACKWOOD, Baronet [I. 1763], of Ballyleidy aforesaid, 2d but 1st surv. s. and h.,(b) *b.* 8 July 1755; was M.P. [I.] for Killyleagh (three Parls.), 1788-1800, being (unlike his father) a firm supporter of the Union [I.], and obtaining a peerage for his mother, and £15,000 on the disfranchisement of Killyleagh. He, who *suc. to the Baronetcy* 17 Feb. 1799, was Sheriff of co. Down, 1804, and became on the death of his mother, 8 Feb. 1807, BARON DUFFERIN AND CLANEBOYE OF BALLYLEIDY AND KILLYLEAGH, co. Down [I.], in which peerage this *Baronetcy* then *merged*, and still (1905) so continues, the 5th peer and 2d Baronet being *cr.* in 1871, EARL OF DUFFERIN, and in 1888, MARQUESS OF DUFFERIN AND AVA. See PEERAGE.

COTTER:

cr. 11 Aug. 1763.

I. 1763. "JAMES COTTER, Esq., of Rockforest, [near Mallow], co. Cork,"(c) 1st s. and h. of James COTTER, of Ann Grove in that county, by Margaret, da. of George MATTHEW, of Thurles, Major in the Army (and Mary, relict of Simon EATON, da. of Sir Richard ALDWORTH), which James (who was executed 7 May 1720, for high treason in supporting the Jacobite cause) was s. and h. of Sir James COTTER, of Ann Grove aforesaid, Col. of Dragoons and Commander-in-Chief of the Irish forces of James II (*d.* June 1705), was *b.* about 1714; ed. at Trin. Coll., Dublin; B.A., 1736; was M.P. [I.] for Askeaton, 1761-68, and was *cr. a Baronet* [I.], as above, by patent dat. at Dublin, 11 Aug. 1763, the privy seal being dat. at St. James, 19 April previous. He *m.* in 1746 (Lic. Cork) Arabella COSBURNE [*sic* but *recte* CASAUBON], widow of William CASAUBON, of Carrig, co. Cork, da and coheir of the Rt. Hon. John ROGERSON, Chief Justice of the King's Bench [I.], by Elizabeth, da. of Stephen LUDLOW. He *d.* 9 June 1770, and was *bur.* at Carrigtohill. M.I. Admon. [I.] 30 July 1770. His widow *d* at Mallow, April 1793.

(a) This James was only s. and h. of Col. Hans Stevenson, by Anne, da. and eventually sole h. of James Hamilton, of Neilsbrook, co. Antrim, who was nephew of (his issue becoming heir to) James Hamilton, *cr.* 4 May 1622, Viscount Claneboye, co. Down [I.], a peerage which became extinct, 12 Jan 1675, on the death of the grantee's grandson, 2d Earl of Clanbrassil [I.], and 3d Viscount Claneboye [I.]. Hence the title of "Claneboye" was added to that of Dufferin in the creation of 1800.

(b) The eldest son, Robert Blackwood, *b.* 1752, was M.P. [I.] for Killyleagh (two Parls.), 1776, till his death unm. and v.p., 31 Jan. 1785, through a fall from his horse, near Belfast. The 7th and yst. s., Vice-Admiral Sir Henry Blackwood, was *cr. a Baronet*, 1 Sep. 1814.

(c) See p 340, note "b," under "DEANE."

II. 1770. SIR JAMES LAURENCE COTTER, Baronet [I. 1763], of Rockforest aforesaid, 1st s. and h., *b.* about 1748; ed. at Westm. School; matric. at Oxford (Ch. Ch.), 18 June 1766, aged 18, becoming a student of that College: B.A., 1770; admitted to Lincoln's Inn, 2 Aug. 1766; *suc. to the Baronetcy*, 9 June 1770; was M.P. [I.] for Taghmon, 1771-76; for Mallow, 1783-90, and for Castle Martyr (two Parls.), 1790-1800; Sheriff of co. Cork, 1781; Col. of the Mallow Militia. He *m.* firstly, 16 Nov. 1772, Anne, only da. of Francis KEARNEY, of Garretstown, near Kinsale, co. Cork, by Mary, da. and h. of Maurice ROCHE, of Dunderron, co. Cork. She *d.* s.p., 1773. He *m.* secondly (Lic., Cloyne, 1785), Isabella, widow of George BRERETON, of Carrigslaney, co. Carlow, da. of the Rev. James HINGSTON, of Aglish, co. Cork, Preb. of Donoughmore, by Catherine, da. and h. of the Rev. Benezer MURDOCK, Rector of Kilshanick. He *d.* 9 Feb. 1829, aged about 80. His widow *d.* April 1832.

III. 1829. SIR JAMES LAURENCE COTTER, Baronet [I. 1763], of Rockforest aforesaid, 1st s. and h., by 2d wife, *b.* probably about 1780; was M.P. for Mallow, 1812-18, having *suc. to the Baronetcy*, 9 Feb. 1829. He *m.* 1 Jan. 1820, Helena Trydell, 3d da. and coheir of James LOMBARD, of Lombardstown, co. Cork, by Anne, da. of John Townsend BECHER, of Creagh, in that county. He *d.* 31 Dec. 1834. His widow *d.* 1 June 1870, at Eastly Mallow.

IV. 1834. SIR JAMES LAURENCE COTTER, Baronet [I. 1763], of Rockforest aforesaid, only s. and h., *b.* 4 April 1828, at Cork; *suc. to the Baronetcy*, 31 Dec. 1834; ed. at Trin. Coll., Dublin; B.A., 1849; Ensign 27th Foot, 1848-49; one of the Corps of Gentlemen-at-Arms, 1850; Capt., London Militia, 1852; Capt., 5th Midx. Militia, 1853; Capt. Tower Hamlets Militia, 1863; Sheriff of co. Cork, 1882. He *m.* firstly, 14 June 1851, Julia Emily, da. of Frederick Albert LOINSWORTH, M.D., Inspector-Gen. of Hospitals, Calcutta. She *d.* 5 Feb. 1863, at Midleton Park, Queenstown, co. Cork. He *m.* secondly, 30 April 1864, at St. John's, Homerton, London, Jane Vargott, da. of William K. MAUGHAN of Sedgwick House, Midx. He *d.* 10 Oct. 1902.

V. 1902. SIR JAMES LAURENCE COTTER, Baronet [I. 1763], of Rockforest aforesaid, grandson and h., being 1st s. and h. of James Lombard COTTER, Lieut. Gloucester Reg., by Clare Mary, da. of Thomas SEAGRAVE, Capt. Royal Marines, which James, who *d.* v.p., 12 April 1893, aged 33, was 2d and yst., but at one time h. ap. of the late Baronet.(a) He was *b.* 11 July 1887, and *suc. to the Baronetcy*, 10 Oct. 1902.

Family Estates.—These, in 1878,(b) consisted of 7,873 acres in co. Cork, worth £2,143 a year, together with land (acreage not given) in Cork city, worth £318 a year, the total rental being £2,461 a year.

BROOKE:

cr. 3 Jan. 1764;

ex. 7 March 1785.

I. 1764, to 1785. "ARTHUR BROOKE, Esq., of Colebrooke [near Brookborough], co. Fermanagh,"(c) 1st s. and h of Henry BROOKE, of the same, sometime M.P. [I.] for that county (*d.* 14 July 1761), by Lettice (marr. lic., 29 March 1711), sister of Sir Charles BURTON, 1st Baronet [I. 1758], da. of Benjamin BURTON, sometime Lord Mayor of Dublin,

---

(a) The 1st son, Sir Ludlow Cotter, *b.* 11 June 1853, at Dublin; ed. at Cheltenham Coll., was *Knighted* at Windsor, 12 Dec. 1874 (as the eldest son of a Baronet), and *d.* unm. and v.p., 23 Nov. 1882, at Rockforest, aged 29. Great objections were made to this Knighthood as a matter of right in a legal point of view, though granted in the patent of Baronetcy, and it has since this date [1882] been rarely, if ever, conferred.

(b) See p. 347, note "c," under "BURDETT."

(c) See p. 340, note "b," under "DEANE."

was possibly B.A. (Trin. Coll.), Dublin, 1746: was Sheriff of co. Fermanagh, 1752; M.P. [I.] thereof (three Parls.), 1761-83, and for Maryborough, 1783, till death, and was *cr. a Baronet* [I.], as above, by patent dat. at Dublin, 3 Jan. 1764, the privy seal being dat. at St. James, 24 Oct. 1763: Gov. of co Fermanagh; P.C. [I.] 15 May 1770. He *m.* firstly, 6 Aug. 1751, Margaret, sister of William Henry, 1st EARL CLERMONT [I.], only da. of Thomas FORTESCUE, of Randalstown, co. Louth, by Elizabeth, da. of James HAMILTON, of Tullymore, co. Down. She, who was *b.* 27 March 1728, *d.* 22 Sep. 1756, at Bath. He *m.* secondly, 21 Sep. 1775, at the Palace, Clogher, Elizabeth, da. of (—) FOORDE, and a near relation of John GARNETT, Bishop of Clogher (1758-82). He *d.* s.p.m.s.,(a) in Sackville Street, Dublin, 7 March 1785, when the *Baronetcy* became *extinct*.(b) Admon. [I.] to his widow, 21 May 1785.

BLUNDEN:

cr. 12 March 1766.

I. 1766. "JOHN BLUNDEN, Esq., of [Castle Blunden, formerly Clonmorne, co.] Kilkenny,"(c) only surv. s. and h. of John BLUNDEN, of the same, M.P. [I.] for Kilkenny, 1727, till his death (8 Jan 1752), by his 1st wife, Martha, sister of John, 1st BARON DESART [I.], da. of Agmondisham CUFFE, a distinguished member of the Irish Bar, was admitted to the Middle Temple, 16 Nov. 1739; Barrister (Dublin), Michaelmas 1744; was Mayor of Kilkenny, 1753-54; M.P. [I.] for Kilkenny city (two Parls.), 1761-76, and Recorder thereof, and was *cr. a Baronet* [I.], as above, by patent dat. at Dublin, 12 March 1766, the privy seal being dat. at St. James', 31 Jan. previous. He *m.* (Lic. Dublin, 25 Feb. 1755/6), Lucy Susanna, da. of his maternal uncle, the said John (CUFFE), 1st BARON DESART [I.] abovenamed, by his 2d wife, Dorothea, da. of Lieut.-Gen. Richard GORGES. He *d.* at Castle Blunden, Jan. 1783. Will dat. 8 June 1782, pr. [I.] 14 Feb. 1783.(d) His widow *d.* 27 April 1812.

II. 1783. SIR JOHN BLUNDEN, Baronet [I. 1766], of Castle Blunden aforesaid, 1st s. and h., *b.* 15 Aug. 1767; *suc. to the Baronetcy*, Jan. 1783; Mayor of Kilkenny, 1801-02: Sheriff of co. Kilkenny, 1805 and 1813. He *m.* firstly (Lic., 26 Jan. 1786), Frances, da. and h. of John ROBBINS, of Ballyduffe, co. Kilkenny, by Frances, da. of Capt Francis SHANLEY. She *d.* 12 Jan. 1808, in Green Park Place, Bath. He *m.* secondly, in 1812, Hester, da. of John HELSHAM, of Leggetts Rath, co. Kilkenny, by Mary, only child of John BLUNT, of Kilkenny. He *d.* s.p., 1 March 1818, aged 50.

III. 1818. SIR JOHN BLUNDEN, Baronet [I. 1766], of Castle Blunden aforesaid, nephew and h., being 1st s. and h. of William Pitt BLUNDEN, by Harriet, da. of Thomas POPE, of Popefield, in Queen's County, which William (who *d.* 17 April 1817, aged 56) was 2d s. of the 1st Baronet. He was *b.* 21 Dec. 1814, in Kilkenny, and *suc. to the Baronetcy*, 1 March 1818; was admitted to King's Inns, Dublin, Easter 1836; Barrister (Dublin), Hilary 1840, having been admitted to Lincoln's Inn, 3 April 1838; was Sheriff of Kilkenny city, 1843-44, and of co. Kilkenny, 1847, and a first-rate sportsman in the hunting field. He *m.* 22 April 1839, at St. Geo. Han. Sq., Elizabeth, 3d and yst. da. of Major John KNOX, of Mount Falcon, in Castlerea, co. Mayo, by his 2d wife, Catherine, da. of

---

(a) Besides two sons, Henry and Arthur, both living in 1755, both of whom *d.* young, he had, by his 1st wife, two daughters and coheirs, *viz.* (1) Selina, who *m.*, 24 April 1769, Thomas (Vesey), 1st Viscount de Vesci [I.], and (2) Lætitia Charlotte, who *m.*, 19 July 1774, Sir John Parnell, 2d Baronet [I. 1766], both of whom had issue.

(b) His nephew, Henry Brooke of Colebrooke abovenamed, was *cr. a Baronet* 7 Jan. 1822.

(c) See p. 340, note "b," under "DEANE."

(d) In it he desires that he may not be buried till his body begins to putrify or his head be severed from his body, and that the burial should be "without ceremony in the round part of the wood where the laurel is planted, and the ditch of water surrounds it."

V

Richard CHALONER, of Kingsfort, co. Meath. He *d.* 27 Jan. 1890, aged 75. His widow *d.*, apparently, in or before 1901.(a)

IV. 1890. SIR WILLIAM BLUNDEN, Baronet [I. 1766], of Castle Blunden aforesaid, 1st s. and h., *b.* 25 July 1840 in Dublin; admitted a Fellow Commoner to Trin. Coll., Dublin; Scholar (Science), 1860; B.A., 1862; Medical Scholar, 1874; Bach. Med., 1876; having been admitted to King's Inns, Dublin, 1863; L.R.C.S. [I.], 1876, and L. Med. K.Q.C.P. [I.], 1877; sometime resident at Waitara, near Taranaki, in New Zealand, where he practised as a Physician; *suc. to the Baronetcy,* 27 Jan. 1890; Sheriff of co. Kilkenny, 1904, during the King's visit to Ireland. He *m.* in 1879, Florence Caroline, da. of Henry SHUTTLEWORTH, of New Plymouth, in New Zealand.

Family Estates.—These, in 1878,(b) consisted of 1,846 acres in co. Kilkenny, worth £1,385 a year.

SAINT-GEORGE:

cr. 12 March 1766.

I. 1766. "RICHARD SAINT-GEORGE, Esq., of Athlone, co. Westmeath,"(c) as also of Woodsgift, co. Kilkenny, 2d s. of George SAINT-GEORGE, of Woodsgift aforesaid, many years (1723-60) M.P. [I.] for Athlone (*d.* 23 Dec. 1762, in his 80th year), by Elizabeth (marr. lic., 16 June 1715), sister of John, 1st EARL OF DARNLEY [I.], da. of Thomas BLIGH, of Rathmore, co. Meath, was *b.* about 1720; suc. his elder br., Henry SAINT-GEORGE, sometime (1761-63) M.P. [I.] for Athlone (who *d.* unm., aged 47) in July 1763; was M.P. [I.] for Athlone (four Parls.), 1763, till death in 1789, and was *cr. a Baronet* [I.], as above, by patent dat. at Dublin, 12 March 1766, the privy seal being dat. at St. James', 31 June previous. He *m.* 27 July 1764, Sarah, only da. of Robert PERSSE, of Roxburgh, co. Galway, by Elizabeth, da. of Sir William PARSONS, 2d Baronet [I. 1677]. He *d.* 25 Feb. 1789, at Woodsgift aforesaid. Will dat. 17 Feb. pr. [I.] 16 June 1789. His widow *d.* in Merrion Sq., Dublin, July 1798.

II. 1789. SIR RICHARD BLIGH SAINT-GEORGE, Baronet [I. 1766], of Woodsgift aforesaid, 1st s. and h., *b.* 5 June 1765; *suc. to the Baronetcy,* 25 Feb. 1789; was M.P. [I.] for Athlone (three Parls.), 1789-1800, taking a prominent part against the Union [I.], and being said to have declined a Peerage; Sheriff of co. Roscommon, 1790; Secretary of the Order of St. Patrick, being invested, 15 Feb. 1793, at Dublin Castle. He *m.* firstly, 10 Feb. (Lic. Dublin 4 Jan.) 1799, Harriet da. of the Rt. Hon. Thomas KELLY, of Kellyville, Queen's County, sometime (1784-1801) Justice of the Court of Common Pleas [I.], by Frances, da. of James HICKEY, of Carrick-on-Suir. She *d.* s.p.m. He *m.* secondly, in April 1807, at Abbert, co. Galway, Bridget, 1st da. of Theophilus BLAKENEY, of Abbert, sometime M.P. [I.] for Athenry, by Margaret, da. of John STAFFORD, of Gillstown, co. Roscommon. He *d.* at Cork, 29 Dec. 1851, aged 86, being then one of the few survivors of the Irish Parl. His widow *d.* Dec. 1866.

III. 1851. SIR THEOPHILUS JOHN SAINT-GEORGE, Baronet [I. 1766], 1st surv. s. and h., by 2d wife, *b.* 5 Oct. 1816; was Sheriff of co. Kilkenny, 1839; *suc. to the Baronetcy,* 29 Dec. 1851, and, having settled in Natal, South Africa, was made, in 1852, an Assistant Magistrate there, raising the troop of the Natal Carbiniers of which he was Colonel. He *m.* firstly, 11 Jan. 1836, Caroline Georgiana, 2d da. of Joseph Andrew DE LATOUR, of Hexton House, Herts, by Caroline, da. of William YOUNG, illegit. s. of Patrick (MURRAY), 5th LORD ELIBANK [S.]. She *d.* 1842. He *m.* secondly, 11 Nov. 1847, at Churchtown, co. Waterford, Maria, 1st da. of John POWER, of Churchtown aforesaid, by Alice, da. of Thomas LALOR, of Cregg, co. Tipperary. He *d.* 27 July 1857, at Pietermaritzburg, aged 40. His widow *d.* 5 Sep. 1893.

(a) She is mentioned as living in Dod's *Baronetage* for 1901, but omitted in that for 1902.
(b) See p. 347, note "c," under "BURDETT."
(c) See p. 340, note "b," under "DEANE."

IV. 1857. SIR RICHARD DE LATOUR SAINT-GEORGE, Baronet [I. 1766], 1st s. and h., by 1st wife, *b.* 2 April 1837; *suc. to the Baronetcy,* 27 July 1857; was a Capt. in the Bengal Artillery. He *d.* unm., at Landor, Upper Provinces, India, 14 Oct. 1861, aged 24.

V. 1861. SIR JOHN SAINT-GEORGE, Baronet [I. 1766], br. of the half-blood and h. male, being 3d s. of the 3d Baronet, and the 1st s. by his 2d wife; *b.* 3 April 1851; *suc. to the Baronetcy,* 14 Oct. 1861; ed. at Trin. Coll., Dublin; sometime, 1872-75, in the 18th Foot, but exchanged as Lieut. in 1875 to the 71st Foot (Highland Light Infantry), and resigned in 1882. He *m.* 1 Dec. 1894, Rose, 3d da. of Sir George BERKLEY, K.C.M.G. [1893], by (—), da. of Francis GARFORD.

Family Estates.—These, in 1878,(a) consisted of 974 acres in co. Kilkenny, worth £543 a year, besides 720 in King's County (attributed to Lady St. George), worth £232 a year.

PARNELL(b):

cr. 3 Nov. 1766;

afterwards, since 1841, BARONS CONGLETON.

I. 1766. "JOHN PARNELL, Esq., of Rathleague, Queen's County,"(c) only surv. s. and h. of John PARNELL,(d) of the same, Justice of the King's Bench (1722 till his death, 2 July 1727), by Mary, sister of William WHITSHED, sometime (1714-27) Chief Justice of the King's Bench [I.], da. of Thomas WHITSHED, was *b.* probably about 1720; ed. at Trin. Coll., Dublin; B.A., 1740; Barrister (King's Inns, Dublin), Hilary 1744; Sheriff of Queen's County, 1753; M.P. [I.] for Maryborough (three Parls.) 1761 till death, and was *cr. a Baronet* [I.], as above, by patent dat. at Dublin, 3 Nov. 1766, the privy seal being dat. at St. James', 25 Sep. previous. He *m.* (Lic. Prerog. [I.], 7 March 1744/5) Anne, sister of Bernard (WARD), 1st VISCOUNT BANGOR [I.], 2d da. of Michael WARD, of Castle Ward, co. Down, sometime (1727-59) Justice of the King's Bench [I.], by Anna Catherina, da. of James HAMILTON, of Bangor, co. Down. He *d.* 14 April 1782, at Chester. Will dat. 28 March and pr. [I.] 17 July 1782. His widow *d.* April 1795.

II. 1782. SIR JOHN PARNELL, Baronet [I. 1766], of Rathleague aforesaid, only surv. s. and h., *b.* probably about 1746; ed. at Trin. Coll., Dublin; B.A., 1766; Barrister (King's Inns, Dublin), Hilary 1774, becoming a Bencher in 1786; was M.P. [I.] for Bangor, 1767-68; for Inistiogue, 1777-83, and for Queen's County, 1783-1800, being M.P. [U.K.] for the last (during ten months), Jan. 1801, till his death; a Commissioner of Revenue [I.],(e) 1780

(a) See p. 347, note "c," under "BURDETT."
(b) See G. D. Burtchaell's *M.P.'s for Kilkenny,* p. 170.
(c) See p. 340, note "b," under "DEANE."
(d) This John Parnell was yr. br. of Thomas Parnell, D.D., Archdeacon of Clogher, the well-known Poet (*d.* s.p.s., July 1717, aged 38), both being sons of Thomas Parnell, of Dublin (*d.* 1686), who emigrated from Congleton, in Cheshire (of which place his father, Tobias Parnell, gilder and painter, had been Alderman, and his grandfather, Thomas Parnell, mercer and draper, had been sometime (1620-21) Mayor, which town accordingly furnished the title of the Peerage granted in 1841 to his descendant.
(e) "He continued in the industrious discharge of the duties of this station for ten years under [3] successive administrations (Rutland, Buckingham and Westmorland) with unshaken steadiness. Upon the arrival of Earl Fitzwilliam, in 1795, he appeared to totter in his office; he, however, despised a stubborn consistency and cheerfully co-operated with Mr. Grattan and the other members of

suc. to the Baronetcy, 14 April 1782; was Chancellor of the Exchequer [I.], 1785, till removed in Jan. 1799 for his opposition to the proposed Union [I.], receiving, however (after it had taken place), £7,500 for the loss of the "pocket borough" of Maryborough. He had been made P.C. [I.], 24 Jan. 1786. He *m.* 19 July 1774 (Lic. Prerog. [I.], 13), Lætitia Charlotte, da. and coheir of the Rt. Hon. Sir Arthur BROOKE, Baronet [I., 1763], by his 1st wife, Margaret, da. of Thomas FORTESCUE, of Randalstown, co. Louth. She *d.* in Dawson Street, Dublin, Nov. 1783. He *d.* suddenly, 5 Dec. 1801, in Clifford Street, and was *bur.* in the Bayswater Road burial ground of St. Geo. Han. Sq., M.I. Will pr. [I.] 1802.

III. 1801. SIR JOHN AUGUSTUS PARNELL, Baronet [I. 1766], 1st s. and h., *b.* May 1775, being a cripple and dumb from his birth; *suc. to the Baronetcy,* but not to the estates, 5 Dec. 1801. He *d.* unm., 30 July 1812, aged 37.

IV. 1812. SIR HENRY BROOKE PARNELL, Baronet [I. 1766], of Rathleague aforesaid, br. and h., *b.* 3 July 1776; ed. at Eton (possibly, also [1792] at Winchester) and at Trin. Coll., Cambridge; was M.P. [I.] for Maryborough (in the last Irish Parl.), 1798-1800; suc., on the death of his father, 5 Dec. 1801, to the estates of the family, by Act of Parl. [I.], May 1789, in consequence of his elder brother's disabilities; was M.P. for Queen's County, April to June 1802; for Portarlington, July to Dec. 1802; for Queen's County again (ten Parls.), Feb. 1806 to 1832, and for Dundee (three Parls.), April 1833, till *cr.* a peer in 1841, taking an active part in favour of the Catholic Emancipation and Free Trade; Commissioner of the Treasury [I.], 1806-07; *suc. to the Baronetcy,* 30 July 1812; Member (and subsequently Chairman) of the Finance Committee, 1828; P.C., 27 April 1831; Sec. at War, 1831, till dismissed in 1832; Treasurer of the Navy, 1835; Paymaster of the Forces, 1835, and Paymaster-Gen. 1836, till death. He *m.* 17 Feb. 1801, Caroline Elizabeth, 1st da. of John (DAWSON), 1st EARL OF PORTARLINGTON [I.], by Caroline, da. of John (STUART), 3d EARL OF BUTE [S.]. She was living when he (ten months before he committed suicide) was *cr.*, 18 Aug. 1841, BARON CONGLETON of Congleton, co. Chester. In that peerage this *Baronetcy* then *merged,* and still (1905) so continues. See PEERAGE.

STEELE:

cr. 12 Feb. 1768;

sometime, 1862-72, STEELE-GRAVES.

ex. or *dormant,* 29 June 1876.

I. 1768. "RICHARD STEELE, Esq., of Dublin,"(a) s. of Richard STEELE, of (—), co. Cork, by (—), da. of (—) HART, of that county, settled at Hampstead, near Dublin, and was *cr. a Baronet* [I.], as above, by patent dat. at Dublin, 12 Feb. 1768, the privy seal being dat. at St. James', 5 Jan. previous. He was M.P. [I.] for Mullingar (two Parls.), 1766-76, and was *cr.* LL.D. of Dublin Univ., *honoris causa,* 1770. He *m.* firstly, in 1731, Jane, da. of Francis ARMESTEAD, of Cork, Merchant. He *m.* secondly, 16 Sep. 1756 (Lic. Prerog. [I.], 13), Margaret SMITH, of Henry Street, Dublin, spinster, da. of Robert SMITH, of Gibblestown, Scotland. He *d.* Feb. 1785 in Dominick Street, Dublin. Will dat. 6 Jan. 1780, pr. [I.] 3 March 1785.

the [late] opposition who then came into power; he thus secured his continuance in office" which he consequently held during the administration of Fitzwilliam, of Camden, and part of that of Cornwallis. [Playfair's *Baronetage,* 1811]. He was "a plain, frank, cheerful and convivial man," and "in his extensive patronage his disinterestedness was almost unparalleled." [*Dict Nat Biogr.*, quoting Barrington's *Memoirs of Ireland.*]
(a) See p. 340, note "b," under "DEANE."

II. 1785. SIR PARKER STEELE, Baronet [I. 1768], of Hampstead aforesaid, 2d but 1st surv. s. and h., by 1st wife, *b.* probably about 1735; served as 2d Lieut. in the 23d Fusileers during the Seven Years' War in Germany, being at the Battle of Minden (1759), and being wounded at the taking of Hesse Cassel; was aide-de-camp in 1763 to the Viceroy [I.]; Capt. in 29th Foot, 1764, serving many years in America; *suc. to the Baronetcy,* Feb. 1785. He *m.*, Nov. 1773, Maria, da. of John VERITY, of Bowling Hall, co. York. He *d.* at Ranelagh road, co. Dublin, 13 May 1787. Will dat. 14 April, pr. [I.] 6 June 1787. The will of his widow was pr. [I.] 1809.

III. 1787. SIR RICHARD STEELE, Baronet [I. 1768], of Hampstead aforesaid, 1st s. and h., *b.* 4 Aug. 1775; *suc. to the Baronetcy,* 13 May 1787; entered the army, 1723; Capt. 4th Reg. of Dragoon Guards, 1795, being, when in command thereof against the rebels [I.] severely wounded, 19 June 1798, at Ovidstown, co. Kildare; Sheriff of co. Dublin, 1820. He *m.* 20 March 1798, at Bath, Frances Mary Collette, yr. da. of Edward DALTON, of Grenanstown, co. Tipperary, COUNT D'ALTON in the Holy Roman Empire, and Lieut.-Gen. in the Imperial army (killed 24 Aug. 1793, at the battle of Hoondscoote, near Dunkirk), by Mary, da. of John MACCARTHY. He *d.* 2 Aug. 1850, at St. Stephen's Green, Dublin, aged nearly 75. Will pr. Aug. 1850. His widow, who was *b.* at Vienna, 27 Dec. 1783, *d.* 18 July 1857, at Weymouth, and was *bur.* at Radipole, Dorset. Will pr. Oct. 1857.

IV. 1850. SIR JOHN MAXWELL STEELE, *afterwards* (from 1862), STEELE-GRAVES, Baronet [I. 1768], of Mickleton Manor, co. Gloucester, 2d but 1st surv. s. and h.,(a) *b.* 4 May 1812 in Dublin; matric. at Oxford (Brasenose Coll.), 22 June 1829, aged 18; admitted to Lincoln's Inn, 1831; *suc. to the Baronetcy,* 2 Aug. 1850; took by royal lic., 30 July 1862, in consequence of his marriage, the final name of GRAVES; Sheriff of co. Gloucester, 1866; Capt. 16th Gloucester, Rifle Vols., 1860; Major North Gloucester Militia, 1862. He *m.* 31 July 1838, at Mickleton, co. Gloucester, Elizabeth Anne, 1st da. and coheir of John GRAVES, who *d.* 1818, a year before his elder br., the Rev. Morgan GRAVES, of Mickleton Manor aforesaid, both being sons of the Rev. Richard Morgan GRAVES, D.D., of the same. He *d.* s.p.m.,(b) 25 Sep. 1872, at Mickleton, Manor House, aged 60. His widow *d.* 29 Sep. 1877,(c) at Weston-super-Mare, aged 60.

V. 1872, to 1876. SIR FREDERICK FERDINAND (d)ARMSTEAD STEELE, Baronet [I. 1768], uncle and h. male, being 4th and yst. s. of the 2d Baronet, *b.* 25 March 1787 in Dublin; *suc. to the Baronetcy,* 25 Sep. 1872, and recorded his pedigree at Ulster Office, Dublin, 12 Oct. following.(e) He *m.* firstly, 24 Oct. 1809, Anne, only da. of Robert EVERED, of Bridgwater, Somerset. She *d.* 19 Aug. 1844. He *m.* secondly, 4 March 1863,

(a) The 1st son, Richard Steele, *b.* 12 June 1802, *d.* unm. and v.p., 1824. The 3d and yst. s., Lieut.-Col. Edward STEELE, C.B., (83d Foot), *d.* s.p., 4 Aug. 1862, aged 48.
(b) His only da. and h., Frances Elizabeth, *m.* 30 Nov. 1871, her cousin, Francis Robert Steele Bowen, s. of the Rev. Christopher Bowen, by her paternal aunt, Katharine Emily, da. of the 3d Baronet. He, who took the name of GRAVES, *d.* 16 July 1876, his wife having *d.* 16 Aug. 1874.
(c) The death, a few weeks later, 27 Nov. 1877, of the Dowager Baroness Graves [I.] is not to be mistaken for that of the Dowager Lady Steele-Graves, as in the text.
(d) He was so named after Frederick the Great, King of Prussia, and his br., Prince Ferdinand, under both of whom his father had served.
(e) This pedigree was verified by his own declaration and that of his niece, Sarah Steele, spinster, 1st da. of his elder br., the Rev. Robert Steele, Rector of Mundsley, and Tyringham, Norfolk. She testified to the death, s.p., of three of her four brothers (Parker, *d.* 1861, Robert, *d.* 1833, and Armstead, *d.* 1840), and that the remaining br. (Richard, who *d.* 1840) left an only son, Richard, who *d.* unm. in 1865.

Anne Mary, da. of Samuel GARDNER, of Red Hill House, Sheffield. He *d.*, it is presumed, s.p.m.s.,(a) 29 June 1876, at Grove cottage, Keynsham, Somerset, aged 89, when the *Baronetcy* became *extinct* or *dormant*. His widow *d.* s.p., 30 June 1897, at 10 Camden Crescent, Bath.

FREKE:

cr. 15 July 1768;

afterwards, since 1807, *or previously*, EVANS-FREKE;

and, since 1807, BARONS CARBERY [I.].

I. 1768. "JOHN FREKE, Esq., of Castle Freke, co. Cork,"(b) formerly John EVANS, 2d s. of the Hon. John EVANS, of Bulgaden Hall, co. Limerick, by Grace, sister and h. (13 April 1764) of Sir John Redmond FREKE, 3d Baronet [1713], of Castle Freke aforesaid, and only da. of Sir Ralph FREKE, 1st Baronet [1713], of West Bilney, co. Norfolk, which John EVANS (who was Sheriff of co. Limerick, 1743, and who *d.* 1758) was 4th s. of George (EVANS), 1st BARON CARBERY [I.]. He assumed the name of FREKE instead of EVANS in or before June 1765, was authorised so to do by act of Parl., 7 June 1766, and was *cr. a Baronet* [I.], as above, by patent dat. at Dublin, 15 July 1768, the privy seal being dat. at St. James', 17 June previous. He suc. his elder br., George EVANS, of Bulgaden Hall aforesaid, in 1769; was M.P. [I.] for Baltimore (two Parls.), 1769, till death; was Sheriff of co. Wexford (being then of Merville, in that county), 1774. He *m* 15 (Lic., 9) June 1765, Elizabeth, 2d and yst. da. of Arthur (GORE), 1st EARL OF ARRAN [I.], by Jane, da. and h. of Richard SAUNDERS, of Saunders Court, co. Wexford. She *d.* Sep. 1776, at Marville, co. Wexford. He *d.* 20 March 1777. Will dat. 8 Feb. and pr. [I.] 20 Nov. 1777.

II. 1777. SIR JOHN FREKE, Baronet [I. 1768], of Castle Freke aforesaid, 1st s. and h., *b.* 11 Nov. 1765, or 1766; *suc. to the Baronetcy*, 20 March 1777; was M.P. [I.] for Donegal (borough), 1784-90, and for Baltimore (two Parls.), 1790-1800. He *m.* 25 Jan. 1783, at Saunders Court, co. Wexford, Catherine Charlotte (*b.* Sep. 1766), 3d da. of his maternal uncle, Arthur Saunders (GORE), 2d EARL OF ARRAN [I.], by his 1st wife, Catherine, da. of William (ANNESLEY), 1st VISCOUNT GLERAWLEY [I.]. She was living when, by the death, 4 March 1807, of his cousin, John (EVANS), 5th BARON CARBERY [I.], he suc. to that title as BARON CARBERY [I.], when, if not previously, he assumed the name of EVANS-FREKE. In that peerage this *Baronetcy* then *merged*, and still (1905) so continues. See PEERAGE.

(a) By his 1st marriage he had (besides a son named Smith, who *d.* young), two elder sons (twins). Parker and Robert Evered, *b.* 1810, at Wellington, Somerset. These, in 1830, *i.e.*, "seventy-five years ago [Burke's *Baronetage*, 1905] went to the West Indies and have not since been heard of," presumably dying there, s.p. and v.p., "having, it is supposed, perished during a visitation of cholera in the West Indies" [Dod's *Baronetage*, 1905]. In the pedigree recorded by their father in 1872 he gives no information whatever about them save only their names.

(b) See p. 340, note "b," under "DEANE."

LOFTUS:

cr. 16 July 1768;

ex. 12 March 1864.

I. 1768. "EDWARD LOFTUS, Esq., of Mount Loftus,(a) co. Kilkenny,"(b) as also of Richfield, co. Wexford, and Drummabish, co. Tyrone, illegit. s. of Nicholas (LOFTUS), 1st VISCOUNT LOFTUS OF ELY [I.] (who *d.* 31 Dec. 1763, aged 76), was *b.* about 1742; was Capt. in Gen. Conway's Reg. of Foot; was, possibly, *cr.* LL.D., *honoris causâ*, 1766, by the Univ. of Dublin, and was *cr. a Baronet* [I.], as above, by patent dat. at Dublin, 16 July 1768, the privy seal being dat. at St. James', 17 June previous. He was M.P. [I.] for Jamestown, 1761-68; Sheriff of co. Tyrone, 1777, and of co. Wexford, 1784. He *m.* 18 March 1758 (being then described as *the Hon. Capt. Loftus*), Anne, 1st da. and coheir of the Rev. Paul READ, Rector of Leckpatrick, co. Tyrone, by Elizabeth,(c) da. of the Rev. James HAMILTON, of Tullybrick and Castlehill, co. Down. He was *bur.* 17 May 1818, at Powerstown, co. Kilkenny, aged 76. Will dat. 28 July 1800, pr. [I.] 1822. His widow *d.* (a few months later) and was *bur.* 3 Aug. 1818, at Powerstown, aged (also) 76.

II. 1818. SIR NICHOLAS LOFTUS, Baronet [I. 1768], of Mount Loftus and Richfield aforesaid, 1st s. and h., *b.* 1763; Sheriff of co. Kilkenny, 1801; of co. Wexford, 1805; Major, Kilkenny Militia, 1801; Lieut.-Col., 1810; *suc. to the Baronetcy*, May 1818. He *d.* unm. 16 and was *bur.* 18 Aug. 1832, at Powerstown, aged 69. Will dat. 1 May 1831, pr. [I.] May 1834.(d)

III. 1832, to 1864. SIR FRANCIS HAMILTON LOFTUS, Baronet [I. 1768], of Mount Loftus and Richfield aforesaid, only surv. br. and h., being 4th and yst. s. of the 1st Baronet,(e) *b.* 1778; Capt. in the Kilkenny Militia, 1804; *suc. to the Baronetcy*, 16 Aug. 1832. He *d.* unm. 12 and was *bur.* 22 March 1864, at Powerstown, aged 86, when the *Baronetcy* became *extinct*. Will dat. 24 Dec. 1857, pr. [I.] 9 June 1864, devising (subject to certain legacies) all his real and personal estate to Mary MURPHY, "a reputed da. of my late br., Lieut. Edward LOFTUS, 4th Royal Irish Dragoon Guards, now the wife of my land agent, Matthew MURPHY."(f)

(a) Originally Dunroe, in the parish of Powerstown, but, when acquired by John Eaton from Viscount Galmoy [I.], called "Mount Eaton," and, subsequently, when acquired by Viscount Loftus [I.], "Mount Loftus."

(b) See p. 340, note "b," under "DEANE."

(c) This Elizabeth *m.* secondly, Dr. Ferguson, and *d.* in Jervis Street, Dublin, Oct. 1776.

(d) He makes bequests to John, Harriet, Charlotte and Susan, who had taken the name of Loftus "at my desire," being children of Charlotte Meany, widow of Stephen Meany, late Lieut. 87th Foot.

(e) Of his two next elder brothers (1) Lieut. Edward Loftus, 4th Royal Irish Dragoon Guards, had *d.* s.p., legit. before 1832, and (2) Henry Loftus, Cornet in the Army, had *d.* s.p. before 1832.

(f) Her son, John Murphy, who suc. accordingly to the estates of Mount Loftus and Richfield, was Sheriff of co. Kilkenny, 1873, and *d.* 1881, leaving issue, who have assumed the name of Loftus. It is stated, in Walford's *County Families*, that this was "under the will of Sir F. Loftus, Bart.," but there is no such direction or suggestion in the said Will.

NUGENT:

cr. 18 July 1768;

ex. Aug. 1799.

I. 1768. "JAMES NUGENT, Esq., of Donore, co. Westmeath,"(a) 1st s. and h. of Thomas NUGENT, of the same (*d.* Sep. 1758), by Mary (*m.* 1724, and *d.* Oct. 1788, aged 86), da. of James DALY, of Carrownekelly, co. Galway, was *b.* probably about 1730, and was *cr. a Baronet* [I.], as above, by patent dat. at Dublin, 18 July 1768, the privy seal being dat. at St. James', 17 June previous, with a spec. rem., failing heirs male of his body, to his br., Peter NUGENT. He *m.* firstly, 13 Feb. 1761, Catherine, 1st da. and coheir of Robert KING, of Drewstown, co. Westmeath, by Anne, da. of the Rev. Thomas KING, Prebendary of Swords. She *d.* 1787. He *m.* secondly (Lic. Prerog. [I.] 2 April 1878), Frances, da. of John NUGENT, of Ballynecarrow, co. Westmeath, by Mary, da. of Nicholas COYNE, of Coyneville. He *d.* s.p., 29 March 1794. Will dat. 14 June 1793, pr. [I.] 16 July 1796. His widow *m.* 2 April 1802, (—) JOHNSON, a General in the Austrian Service.

II. 1794, to 1799. SIR PETER NUGENT, Baronet [I.1793], of Donore aforesaid, br. and h., *b* about 1745. *suc. to the Baronetcy*, 29 March 1794, according to the spec. rem. in the creation thereof. He *m.* 28 May 1785, Mary, widow of (—) ROGERS. He *d.* s.p. in London, Aug. 1799, and was *bur.* at Stanwell, Midx., aged 54, when the *Baronetcy* became *extinct*.(b) Will dat. 29 Sep. 1794 to 15 Sep. 1797, pr. [I.] 29 Sep. 1799. His widow *d.* at Bath, 24 Feb. 1831, aged 93. Will pr. March 1831.

O'BRIEN:

1768 (or before) to 1798.

"SIR PAUL O'BRIEN, Baronet," is stated to have *d.* at Lisbon in Nov. 1768 [*Ann. Reg.*, 1768], and "SIR PAUL O'BRIEN of the co. of Meath" is stated to have *d.* at Lisbon, Oct. 1768 [*Freeman's Journal*, Dublin].

"SIR EDWARD UNICK O'BRIEN, Baronet," is stated to have *d.* at Sion, near Cork, Nov. 1798 [*Walker's Hibernian Magazine*].

The explanation of this designation is probably that the representation of the Baronetcy [I.] conferred by the titular James III, 19 Jan. 1723, on "John O'BRIEN, *or* O'BRYAN," a Colonel of Foot (subsequently, 21 July 1733, Minister from that King to France), was inherited by both of the above, successively.

(a) See p. 340, note "b," under "DEANE."

(b) His nephew, Thomas FitzGerald, 2d but 1st surv. s. of his sister Christina, by Pierce FitzGerald, of Baltinoran, suc. to the estate of Donore, and assumed the name of Nugent. He was suc. by his son, Percy, *b.* 29 Sep. 1797, who, having by royal lic. taken the name of Nugent, was *cr. a Baronet*, under that name, 30 Sep. 1831.

JOHNSTON(a):

cr. 27 July 1772;

ex. Feb. 1841.

I. 1772. "RICHARD JOHNSTON, Esq., of Gilford, co. Down,"(b) 1st s. and h. of Richard JOHNSTON,(c) of the same, sometime Sheriff of co. Armagh (1733), co. Down (1735), and co. Monaghan (1738) (who was *b.* 6 March 1710, and *d.* at Gilford, 11 Feb. 1758), by Catherine (*m.* 1737, and *d.* Sep. 1794, aged 85), da. and h. of the Rev. John GILL, Rector of Aghnamullen, co. Monaghan, was *b.* 1 Aug. 1743; Sheriff of co. Down, 1765, and of co. Armagh, 1771, and was, for his services against the insurgents (known as *Hearts of Oak* and *Hearts of Steel*) *cr. a Baronet* [I.], as above, by patent dat. at Dublin, 27 July 1772, the privy seal being dat. at St. James', 29 June previous.(b) He was M.P. [I.] for Kilbeggan, 1776, and for Blessington (two Parls.), 1783, till death. He *m.* Oct. 1764 (Lic. Dublin), Anne, sister of Sir William ALEXANDER, 1st Baronet [1809], 2d da. of William ALEXANDER, of Dublin, Merchant, by Mary, da. of (—) PORTER, of Vicarsdale, co. Monaghan. He *d.* 22 April 1795. Will dat. 10 Dec. 1794, pr. [I.] 24 June 1795.

II. 1795, to 1841. SIR WILLIAM JOHNSTON, Baronet [I. 1772], of Gilford aforesaid, only s. and h., *b.* 18 July 1765; Sheriff of co. Down, 1788; *suc. to the Baronetcy*, 22 April 1795. He *d.* unm., Feb. 1841, in Bryanston Sq., and was *bur.* at St. Marylebone, aged 65, when the *Baronetcy* became *extinct*.(d) Admon. March 1841.

COOTE:

The next entry in the list of Irish Baronetcies in the *Liber Munerum Hiberniæ* (as to which see p. 340, note "b," under DEANE) is as under:—

"1774. CHARLES COOTE, EARL OF BELLAMONT, with rem. in default of his issue male to Charles COOTE, of Donybrook, co. Dublin, and the heirs male of his body."

This, however, was not an Irish Baronetcy but one of Great Britain, the patent being dat. at Westminster, 18 May 1774. See p. 168.

(a) Much information in this article has been kindly supplied by Col. G. H. Johnston, of Markethill, in North Ireland, from a printed memoir of the Johnston and Magill families, made for the 2d Baronet.

(b) See p. 340, note "b," under "DEANE."

(c) This Richard was s. and h. of Sir William Johnston, by Nichola Anne, da. of Sir Nicholas Acheson, 4th Baronet [S. 1628], which William (who *d.* 22 Sep. 1722) inherited the Gilford estate on the death, in 1699, of his maternal uncle, Sir John Magill, Baronet [I.], so *cr.* 18 Nov. 1680. See vol. iv, p. 218, note "d," under "Magill."

(d) The Gilford estates devolved on his two sisters or their representatives, *viz.*, (1) Mary Anne, *b.* 17 Jan. 1769, *m.* 6 Feb. 1794 (Lic., 1 Feb.), John Henry Burges, of Woodpark, co Armagh, and had issue; (2) Catherine, *b.* 20 Aug. 1777, *m.* (Lic., 2 March 1799) Joseph Mason Ormsby, sometime M.P. for Gory.

da. of Anthony Dwyer abovenamed. He *m.* secondly, in 1820, his 2d cousin, Anne Matilda, 1st da. of Richard Waller, of Castle Waller, co. Tipperary, by Maria Theresa, da. of Capt. Theobald Bourke, uncle of the 1st Baronet. He *d.* 1839.

IV. 1839, to 1873. Sir Richard Donnellan de Bourgho, *or* de Burgo, Baronet [I. 1785], of The Island, Castle Connell aforesaid, 1st s. and h., by 2d wife, *b.* 1 April 1821; *suc. to the Baronetcy* in 1839; Major in the Limerick Militia, 1855; Sheriff of co. Limerick, 1855. He *m.* 8 Aug. 1844, Catherine, yst. da. of Brooke Brasier, of Ballyellis, co. Cork, by Ellen, da. and coheir of Henry Mitchell, of Mitchellsfort in that county. He *d.* s.p., 26 Jan. 1873, aged 51, at Ballyellis aforesaid, the seat of his wife's brother, Kilner Brasier (from the effects of a fall a few days previous, while out hunting), when the *Baronetcy* became *extinct.* Will pr. 24 June 1873, under £1,000. His widow, who long survived him, *d.* apparently in 1895.(a)

GODFREY:

cr. 17 June 1785.(b)

I. 1785. "William Godfrey, Esq.,"(b) of Bushfield, co. Kerry,(c) 1st s. and h. of John Godfrey, of the same (will dat. 30 Oct. 1781, pr. [I.] 12 Oct. 1782), by Barbara, da. of the Rev. (—) Hathway and Mary, his wife, da. of Thomas (Coningsby), Earl Coningsby, was Sheriff of co. Kerry, 1780; M.P. [I.] for Tralee, 1783-90, and for Belfast, 1792-97, and was *cr. a Baronet* [I.], as above, 17 June 1785, the privy seal being dat. 2 May previous.(b) He *m.* 15 Aug. 1761, Agnes, only da. of William Blennerhassett, of Elm Grove, co. Kerry, by Mary, da. of John Morley, of Cork. He *d.* 23 Jan. 1817.

II. 1817. Sir John Godfrey, Baronet [I. 1785], of Bushfield aforesaid, 1st s. and h., *b.* 16 June 1763; sometime Lieut.-Col. of the Kerry Militia; *suc. to the Baronetcy*, 23 Jan. 1817. He *m.* 26 Nov. 1796, at Cromore, co. Antrim, Eleanor, 1st da. of John Cromie, of Cromore, by Anne, da. of Thomas Thompson, of Greenmount, in that county. He *d.* 21 Jan. 1841, aged 77. His widow *d.* 1852, aged 81.

III. 1841. Sir William Duncan Godfrey, Baronet [I. 1785], of Kilcoleman Abbey, formerly called Bushfield aforesaid, 1st. s. and h., *b.* 30 Aug. 1797 at Lisburn, co. Antrim; Sheriff of co. Kerry, 1830; *suc. to the Baronetcy*, 21 Jan. 1841. He *m.* 14 Oct. 1824, at the British Embassy, Paris, Maria Theresa, 2d da. of John Coltsmann, of Flesk Castle, co Kerry. He *d.* 20 Sep. 1873, aged 76. His widow *d.* 6 March 1883, aged 77.

IV. 1873 Sir John Fermor Godfrey, Baronet [I. 1785] of Kilcoleman Abbey aforesaid, 1st s. and h., *b.* in London, 3 Oct. 1828: sometime Lieut. 2d Dragoon Guards; Sheriff of co. Kerry, 1861; *suc. to the Baronetcy*, 20 Sep. 1873. He *m.* 7 Aug. 1856, Mary Cordelia, only surv. da. of Thomas White Scutt, of Clapham House, in Litlington, Sussex. He *d.* 19 Feb. 1900, aged 71. His widow living 1906.

V. 1900. Sir William Cecil Godfrey, Baronet [I. 1785], of Kilcoleman Abbey aforesaid, 1st s. and h., *b.* 21 July 1857; sometime Lieut. 24th Foot, serving in the Zulu War, 1879 (medal and clasp); *suc. to the Baronetcy*, 19 Feb. 1900. He *m.* firstly, 10 Feb. 1885, Adela Maud Gethin, only surv. child of Frederick John Henry Fownes Hamilton, by Frances Catherine,

(a) She appears in Dod's *Baronetage* for 1895 but not in that for 1896.
(b) See p. 382, note "a," under "Hamilton."
(c) See list in Betham's *Baronetage* [1805], vol. v, p. 51.

only da. of Richard Gethin, of Earlsfield, co. Sligo. She *d.* s.p.m., 14 Aug. 1890. He *m.* secondly, 21 Nov. 1901, Mary Henrietta, 1st da. of Richard John Leeson-Marshall, of Callinafercy, co. Kerry, by Zeena, da. of the Ven. Ambrose Power, Archdeacon of Lismore, 4th s. of Sir John Power, 1st Baronet [1886].

Family Estates.—These, in 1878,(a) consisted of 5,986 acres in co. Kerry, and 106 in co. Cork. *Total.*—6,092 acres, worth £3,303 a year. This estate, then consisting of 6,331 acres was granted by Charles II, 30 June [1667], 19 Car. II, to Major John Godfrey for his services against the rebels in 1641, which donation is, in Sir William Petty's *Reflections on Matters in Ireland*, stated to have been "by no means an equivalent for the Major's services." This John was father of William, father of John, the father of (another) John (*d.* 1712), who was father of John (*d.* 1782), the father of the 1st Baronet.

STAUNTON:

cr. 31 Oct. 1785(b);

ex. 10 Aug. 1859.

I. 1785. "George Leonard Staunton, Esq.,"(b) of Cargin, co. Galway, (c) as also of Clydagh in that county, only s. and h. of Col. George Staunton, of the same (*d.* 3 May 1780, aged 80), by Margaret, da. of John Leonard, of Carra, co. Galway, was *b.* 10 April 1737, at Cargin; ed. at the Jesuit College, Toulouse, and at the School of Medicine, Montpelier, where he became M.D. in 1758; practised as a Physician in the West Indies; Sec. to the Governor of Dominica; purchased an estate in Grenada, where he became Attorney-Gen., Member of the Council, Col. of the Militia and aide-de-camp to the Governor (Macartney), being, after the capitulation of Grenada in 1779, sent as a hostage to Paris. In 1782 he accompanied the Gov.-Gen. of India (Macartney) as Secretary, effecting, among other services, a treaty of peace with Tippoo Sultan, signed 11 March 1784, for which he received a life annuity of £500 from the East India Company and was *cr. a Baronet* [I.], as above, 31 Oct. 1785, the privy seal being dat. the 3d of the same month.(b) He was F.R.S., Feb. 1787 and D.C.L. of Oxford, 16 June 1790, being then "of Smuens, [*sic*] Bucks." In 1792 he was Sec. to the Ambassador (Macartney, again) in the Embassy to China.(d) He *m.* 22 July 1771, at Salisbury, Jane, da. of Benjamin Collins, of Milford House, near Salisbury, Banker (an eminent printer), sometime M.P. for that city, by his 2d wife, Mary, da. of John Cooper, of Salisbury. He *d.* of paralysis, at his house, Devonshire Street, Marylebone, 14 and was *bur.* 23 Jan. 1801, in Westm. Abbey, aged 63. Will pr. 1802. His widow *d.* 16 and was *bur.* 24 June 1823, at St. Marylebone, in her 71st year. M.I.

II. 1801, to 1859. Sir George Thomas Staunton, Baronet [I. 1785], of Cargin and Clydagh aforesaid, and of Leigh Park, near Havant, Hants, only surv. s. and h., *b* 26 May 1781 at Milford House abovenamed; accompanied his father to China in 1792, acquiring a perfect knowledge of the Chinese language and literature; writing, subsequently, several works relating to that kingdom; admitted to Trin. Coll., Cambridge, as Fellow Commoner, 1797; Writer in the East India Company's factory at Canton, 1798; Supercargo, 1804; Interpreter, 1808, and Chief of the Factory, 1816, having *suc. to the Baronetcy*, 14 Jan. 1801; F.R.S., 28 April 1803; Joint "King's Commissioner of Embassy" to Pekin, 1816; *cr.* D.C.L. of Oxford Univ.,

(a) See p. 347, note "c," under "Burdett."
(b) See p. 382, note "a," under "Hamilton."
(c) See list in Betham's *Baronetage* [1805], vol. v, p. 51.
(d) He was an able diplomatist, whose career was described by his son (privately printed, at Havant, 1823), and who himself published in 1797 an account of the Earl of Macartney's Embassy to China.

3 June 1818; M.P. for St. Michael's, Cornwall, 1818-26; for Heytesbury, 1830-32; for South Hampshire, 1832-35, and for Portsmouth (four Parls.), 1838-52; Joint Founder of the Royal Asiatic Society, 1823, to which he gave 3,000 vols. of Chinese works. He *d.* unm., 10 Aug. 1859, at his house, 17 Devonshire Street, Marylebone, aged 78, when the *Baronetcy* became *extinct.*(a)

RICHARDSON:

cr. 30 Aug. 1787(b);

afterwards, since 1830, Richardson-Bunbury.

I. 1787. "William Richardson, Esq.," of Augher, co. Tyrone,(c) s. and h. of St. George Richardson, of the same, sometime (1755-60) M.P. [I.] for Augher, by Elizabeth, 1st da. (all of whose brothers *d.* s.p.), of Benjamin Bunbury, of Mount William, co. Tipperary (*d.* 1765), was M.P. [I.] for Augher, 1783-90, and for Ballyshannon, 1798-1800; Sheriff of co. Tyrone, 1789, and was *cr. a Baronet* [I.], as above, 30 Aug. 1787, the privy seal being dat. 21 July previous.(b) He *m.* firstly, Mary, widow of Carey Hamilton, da. and coheir of William Newburgh, of Balyhaise, co. Cavan, by Lætitia, da. and coheir, of Brockhill Perrott, of Castle Bagshaw, co. Cavan. She *d.* in or before 1775. s.p.m. He *m.* secondly (Lic., 20 April 1775) Eliza Richardson, spinster. He *d.* 29 Oct. 1830. Will pr. as of "Dorset," Nov. 1830.

II. 1830. Sir James Mervyn Richardson-Bunbury, Baronet [I. 1787], of Kilfeacle, co. Tipperary, and of Augher aforesaid, 1st s. and h. by 2d wife, *b.* 1781; took by royal lic., 20 April 1822, the name of Bunbury (being that of his paternal grandmother) after that of Richardson; *suc. to the Baronetcy*, 29 Oct. 1830; was Sheriff of co. Tyrone, 1831. He *m.* 23 June 1810, Margaret, 2d da. of John Corry Moutray, of Favor Royal, co. Tyrone, by Mary Anne Catherine, da. of Major Ambrose Upton, 13th Dragoons. He *d.* 4 Nov. 1851, at Augher Castle, aged 70. His widow *d.* 1870.

III. 1851. Sir John Richardson-Bunbury, Baronet [I. 1787], of Kilfeacle and Augher aforesaid, 1st s. and h., *b.* 10 Oct. 1813 at Castle Hill, co. Tyrone; matric. at Oxford (St. Alban's Hall) 21 Oct. 1830, aged 17; B.A., 1834; in Holy Orders; *suc. to the Baronetcy*, 4 Nov. 1851. He *m.* 5 Dec. 1838, Maria, da. of William Anketell, of Anketell Grove, co. Monaghan, by Sarah, da. of John Waring Maxwell, of Finnebrogue, co. Down. She *d.* 2 March 1888, at 10 Catherine Place, Bath, aged 73.

Family Estates.—These, in 1878,(d) consisted of 789 acres in co. Tipperary and 635 in co. Tyrone. *Total.*—1,424 acres, worth £1,079 a year.

(a) He left his estates to his two cousins, George Staunton Lynch and Capt. Henry Cormick Lynch, 2d and 3d sons of Mark Lynch, of Duras Park, co. Galway (*d.* 1822), being the 1st and 2d sons by his 2d wife (his cousin), Victoire, da. of Richard Wolsey Cormick, of Wolsey Park, in the Island of Grenada, by his paternal aunt, Lucy Barbara, sister of the 1st Baronet. Both of these took the name of Staunton after that of Lynch, the latter, who inherited Leigh Park and the English estates, *d.* a few months after testator, leaving issue, while the former, who inherited Clydagh and the Irish estates, *d.* 4 April 1882, leaving issue.
(b) See p. 382, note "a," under "Hamilton."
(c) See list in Betham's *Baronetage* [1805], vol. v, p. 51.
(d) See p. 347, note "c," under "Burdett."

CARDEN:

cr. 31 Aug. 1787(a);

I. 1787. "John Craven Carden, Esq.,"(a) of Templemore, co. Tipperary,(b) 1st s. and h. of John Carden, of the same (will dat. 10 Dec. 1766, pr. [I.] 1774), by Elizabeth (mar. lic., 1747), da. and h. of the Rev. Robert Craven (Chaplain to the Earl of Chesterfield), by Rose, da. of Thomas Otway of Lissenhall, co. Tipperary, was *b.* about 1758; raised and commanded the 30th Regiment of Light Dragoons (reduced 1802), and was *cr. a Baronet* [I.], as above, 31 Aug. 1787, the privy seal being dat. 23 July previous.(a) He *m.* four times, viz., firstly, 23 (Lic. 22) Jan. 1776, Mary, 3d da. of Arthur (Pomeroy), 1st Viscount Harberton [I.], by Mary, da. of Henry Colley, of Castle Carbury, co. Kildare. She, who was *b.* 19 March 1757, *d.* (before her father's elevation to the peerage) 28 Sep. 1778. He *m.* secondly, 2 May 1781, (Lic., Dublin), at the Speaker's House, Dublin, Sarah, da. of John Moore, of Drumbanagher, co. Armagh. He *m.* thirdly, 14 (Lic. 9) Feb. 1788, Frances Maria (*b.* 16 Jan. 1769), sister of Warner William (Westenra), 2d Baron Rossmore [I.], da. of Henry Westenra, by Harriet, da. and coheir of Col. John Murray. Her will pr. 1807. He *m.* fourthly, between 1802 and 1811, Anne, Dow. Viscountess Monck of Ballytrammon [I.], da. of Henry Quin, M.D., of Dublin, by Anne, da. of Charles Monck, of Grange Gorman, co. Dublin. He *d.* 21 Nov. 1820, at Templemore Priory, in his 63d year. His widow, by whom he had no issue, *d.* 20 Dec. 1823.

II. 1820. Sir Arthur Carden, Baronet [I. 1787], of Templemore Priory aforesaid, 2d but 1st surv. s. and h., by 1st wife,(c) *b.* March 1778; sometime Capt. 4th Dragoon Guards; *suc. to the Baronetcy*, 21 Nov. 1820; Sheriff of co. Tipperary, 1820. He *m.* (Lic., 10 Feb. 1801) Mary, da. of Thomas Kemmis, of Shane Castle, Queen's County, by Anne, da. of Henry White. He *d.* s.p., 4 March 1822, aged 43. His widow *m.* Capt. Joseph Smith, 28th Foot, of Mount Butler, co. Tipperary (whom she survived), and *d.* there, 20 June 1867, in her 85th year.

III. 1822. Sir Henry Robert Carden, Baronet [I 1787], of Templemore Priory aforesaid, br. of the half blood and h., being 5th and yst. s., the only s. by the 3d wife(d) of the 1st Baronet, *b.* 8 Feb. 1789; sometime, 1807, Lieut. 1st Reg. of Dragoons; served under the Duke of Wellington in the Peninsula and at Waterloo; *suc. to the Baronetcy*, 4 March 1822; Sheriff of co. Tipperary, 1824. He *m.*, 10 March 1818, Louisa, only child of Frederick Thompson, of Woodville, Queen's County, sometime (1810) Sheriff of that county, by Sarah, da. of William Smyth, of Borris in Ossory, in Queen's county. He *d.* 23 March 1847, aged 58.

IV. 1847. Sir John Craven Carden, Baronet [I. 1787], of Templemore Priory aforesaid, 1st s. and h., *b.* there 1 Dec. 1819; ed. at Eton; sometime Lieut. 8th Hussars; *suc. to the Baronetcy*, 23 March 1847; Sheriff of co. Tipperary, 1849. He *m.* firstly, 23 July 1844, Caroline Elizabeth Mary, da. of Sir William Mordaunt Sturt Milner, 4th Baronet [1717], by his 2d wife, Harriet Elizabeth, da. of Lord Edward Charles Cavendish-Bentinck. She *d.* s.p.m., 5 Nov. 1850, being accidentally shot in the grounds of Templemore Priory, aged 27. Admon., Dec. 1850. He *m.* secondly, 21 June 1852, at St. John's Episcopal Church, Edinburgh, Julia Isabella, only da. of Admiral Charles Gepp Robinson, of Viewbank, Oban, co. Argyll. He *d.* 22 March 1879, suddenly, from heart failure, aged 59. His widow living 1906.

(a) See p. 382, note "a," under "Hamilton."
(b) See list in Betham's *Baronetage* [1805], vol. v, p. 51.
(c) The 1st son, John Carden, *b.* April 1777, *d.* unm. and v.p. before 1811.
(d) His next elder brother, of the half blood (the only son by the 2d wife), Annesley Carden, Cornet in the 7th Dragoon Guards, *d.* unm. and v.p., before 1811.

V. 1879. SIR JOHN CRAVEN CARDEN, Baronet [I. 1787], of Templemore Priory aforesaid, 1st s. and h., by 2d wife, *b.* there 30 Jan. 1854; ed. at Eton and at the Univ. of Cambridge; *suc. to the Baronetcy*, 22 March 1879; Sheriff of co. Tipperary, 1882. He *m.* 10 Feb. 1891, Sybil Martha, only surv. da. and h. of Col. Valentine BAKER (afterwards Lieut.-Gen. in the Turkish Army, and known as "Baker Pasha"), by Fanny, only child of Frank WORMALD, of Potterton Hall, Aberford.

Family Estates.—These, in 1878,[a] consisted of 7,856 acres in co. Tipperary, worth £9,317 a year.

DES VOEUX:

cr. 1 Sep. 1787.[b]

I. 1787. "CHARLES DES VOEUX, Esq.,"[b] (*more correctly*) CHARLES PHILIP VINCHON DES VOEUX[c], of Indiaville, Queen's County,[d] 1st s. of the Rev. Marin Anthony Vinchon DES VOEUX, of Portarlington, in that county, formerly of Bacquecourt, in Normandy (author of several religious and polemical works; will dat. 24 March 1785, pr. [I.] 13 June 1793), by his 2d wife[e] Charlotte (marr. lic., Dublin, 8 Oct. 1739), da. of James D'EXOUDUN, was *b.* probably about 1744; entered the East India Company's service; was Governor of Masulipatam and second in command at Madras; was M.P. [I.] for Carlow, 1783-90, and for Carlingford, 1790-97, and was *cr. a Baronet* [I.], as above, 1 Sep. 1787, the privy seal being dat. 24 July previous.[b] He was of Woodhall, co. York. He *m.* (Lic., Dublin, 13 Nov. 1778) Mary Anne, 3d da. of the Very Rev. Arthur CHAMPAGNE, Dean of Clonmacnois, by Mary Anne, da. of Major Isaac HAMON. He *d.* Aug. 1814. Will pr. 1815.

II. 1814. SIR CHARLES DES VOEUX, Baronet [I. 1787], of Indiaville aforesaid, 1st s. and h., *b.* 5 Sep. 1779; Capt. 20th Foot, serving in Holland, under the Duke of York, and losing his right leg at the battle of Alkmaar; *suc. to the Baronetcy*, Aug. 1814. He *m.* firstly, June 1801, at Bradford, Christina, yst. da. of Richard HIRD, of Rawdon, co. York. She *d.* July 1841. He *m.* secondly, 13 Dec. 1842, at All Souls, Marylebone, Cecilia, 2d and yst. da. of Charles Ingoldsby (PAULET), 13th MARQUESS OF WINCHESTER, by Anne, da. of John ANDREWS. He *d.* 28 Sep. 1858, at Sillwood House, Brighton, aged 79. His widow, who was *b.* 12 Nov. 1806, *d.* 23 Aug. 1890, at Oldfield Lodge, Maidenhead, Berks, and was *bur.* in St. Luke's church there. Will pr. 6 Oct. 1890, over £25,000.

III. 1858. SIR HENRY WILLIAM DES VOEUX, Baronet [I. 1787], of Drakelow, co. Derby, 2d but 1st surv. s. and h.,[f] by 1st wife, *b.* 16 Dec. 1806; ed. at Rugby, 1819; entered the Army, retiring in 1861 as Lieut.-Col.; was sometime Gentleman-Usher-Daily-Waiter to Queen Victoria, but resigned in 1859, having *suc. to the Baronetcy*, 28 Sep. 1858. He, who after

(a) See p. 347, note "c," under "BURDETT."
(b) See p. 382, note "a," under "HAMILTON." The grantee is, however, called in his father's will "Charles *Philip Vinchon* des Voeux."
(c) So named in his father's will.
(d) See list in Betham's *Baronetage* [1805], vol. v, p. 51.
(e) His 1st wife (marr. lic., Dublin, 3 May 1736), was Mary Louisa Quergroode de Challais. His 3d wife (marr. lic., Dublin, 1770) was Hannah Pain, who survived him. Her will dat. 8 Oct. 1794, pr. [I.] 6 Oct. 1795.
(f) The eldest son, Charles Des Voeux, *b.* 29 April 1802, at York; ed. at Rugby, 1815; matric. at Oxford (Oriel Coll.), 8 Feb. 1821, aged 18; B.A., 1825; admitted to Lincoln's Inn 1825; was Sec. of Legation at Brussels. He *m.* but *d.* s.p. and v.p. at Brussels in Aug. 1833.

his marriage in 1839 resided chiefly at his wife's dower house, Drakelow, co. Derby, was Sheriff of that county, 1864. He *m.* 16 July 1839, at St. Geo. Han. Sq., Sophia Catherine, widow of Sir Roger GRESLEY, 8th Baronet [1611], of Drakelow aforesaid, yst. da. of George William (COVENTRY), 7th EARL OF COVENTRY, by his 2d wife, Peggy, da. and coheir of Sir Abraham PITCHES. He *d.* s.p., 4 Jan. 1868, at Drakelow, aged 61. His widow, who was *b.* 30 Nov. 1801, *d.* 29 March 1875.

IV. 1868. SIR FREDERICK ASSHETON DES VOEUX, Baronet [I. 1787], br. of the half blood and h., being 3d s. of the 2d Baronet and only s. by 2d wife; was *b.* 1818; *suc. to the Baronetcy*, 4 Jan. 1868; sometime Lieut. Coldstream Guards, retiring 1871. He *d.* unm. 3 March 1872, at 5 Albert Terrace, Knightsbridge, aged 53.

V. 1872. SIR HENRY DALRYMPLE DES VOEUX, Baronet [I. 1787], cousin and h. male, being 1st s. and h. of the Rev. Henry DES VOEUX, Chaplain to the 1st Marquess of Anglesey, by his 1st wife, Frances, da. and h. of Daniel DALRYMPLE, of Barrow, co. Derby, which Henry (who *d.* at Interlaken, 30 Sep. 1857, aged 70) was 2d s. of the 1st Baronet. He was *b.* 1824 at Carlton, Notts; ed. at Harrow; matric. at Oxford (Balliol Coll.), 27 May 1841, aged 18; B.A., 1845; M.A., 1847; Fellow of All Souls College, 1847-64; *suc. to the Baronetcy*, 3 March 1872; Sheriff of co. Carlow, 1879. He *m.* 13 Aug. 1863, at St. Geo. Han. Sq., Alice Magdalen Grey, 7th and yst. da. of Thomas (EGERTON), 2d EARL OF WILTON, by his 1st wife, Mary Margaret, da. of Edward (STANLEY), 12th EARL OF DERBY. He *d.* s.p.m., 20 Jan. 1894, at 46 Grosvenor Place, aged 73. His widow, who was *b.* 13 Sep. 1842, living 1905.

VI. 1894. SIR CHARLES CHAMPAGNE DES VOEUX, Baronet [I. 1787], br. and h. male, *b.* 26 Nov. 1827; *suc. to the Baronetcy*, 20 Jan. 1894. He *m.* 9 Nov. 1853, Katharine, da. of Thomas Watkins RICHARDSON, of Clifton by Bristol. She *d.* 3 March 1895.

Family Estates.—These, in 1878,[a] consisted of 722 acres in co. Carlow, worth £685 a year, and 1,037 (belonging to the representatives of Major Thomas Des Voeux) in Queen's County, worth £926 a year.

LESLIE:

cr. 3 Sep. 1787[b];

ex. 21 Nov. 1818.

I. 1787, to 1818. "EDWARD LESLIE, Esq.,"[b] of Tarbert, co. Kerry,[c] 1st s. and h. of the Rt. Rev. James LESLIE, D.D., Bishop of Limerick (*d.* 24 Nov. 1770), by Joyce, sister and coheir of Thomas LYSTER, da. of Anthony LYSTER, both of Lysterfield, co. Roscommon, was *b.* 1744; matric. at Oxford (Wadham Coll.), 29 June 1765, aged 18; *cr.* M.A., 19 April 1769; Barrister (Middle Temple), 1777; "suc. to the estates of his ancestors, as also to Huntingdon, co. Carlow, and Johnstown, co. Wexford"[d]; M.P. [I.] for Old Leighlin, 1787-90, and having assisted "in quelling disturbances in 1786 and 1787,"[d] was *cr. a Baronet* [I.], as above, 3 Sep. 1787, the privy seal being dat. 25 July previous.[b] He, in 1802-03, raised a corps of cavalry "from his tenantry at Tarbert, of which he was appointed Capt. Commandant."[d] He *m.* 29 (Lic., Dublin, 23, and settlement 29) July 1773, Anne, 1st da. and coheir of Hugh CANE, of Dowdstown, co. Kildare, Lieut.-Col. 5th

(a) See p. 347, note "c," under "BURDETT."
(b) See p. 382, note "a," under "HAMILTON."
(c) See list in Betham's *Baronetage* [1805], vol. v, p. 51.
(d) Playfair's *Baronetage* [1810].

Dragoons, by his 1st wife,[a] Louisa,[b] da. of Edward RIGGS, of Riggsdale, co. Cork. He *d.* s.p.m.[c] at Weymouth, 21 Nov. 1818, aged 4, when the *Baronetcy* became *extinct*. Will dat. 10 to 12 May 1786, pr. 10 March 1819. His widow *d.* 26 July 1825, at Bath.

MANNIX:

cr. 4 Sep. 1787[d];

ex. 1822.

I. 1787, to 1822. "HENRY MANNIX, Esq.,"[d] of Richmond, co. Cork,[e] s. of Henry MANNIX, of Cork (*d.* July 1777), by Mary, da. of Noblet JOHNSON, of that city (*d.* Feb. 1783), was *b.* 1740; Barrister (Dublin), Michaelmas 1763, and being "an active magistrate, was, for his services,"[f] *cr. a Baronet* [I.], as above, 4 Sep. 1787, the privy seal being dat. 26 July previous.[d] He *m.* 20 May 1764, in Cork, Elizabeth, da. of John PARKER, of Youghal, co. Cork, by Penelope, da. of George WALLIS, of Curryglass, in that county. He *d.* s.p. legit.[g] at Eastwood, near Tenby, co. Pembroke, 1822, when the *Baronetcy* became *extinct*. Will dat. 16 Aug. 1820 to 1 Feb. 1822, pr. [I.] 19 Dec. 1822. His wife survived him.

GORGES-MEREDYTH:

cr. 5 Sep. 1787[d];

ex. Sep. 1821.

I. 1787, to 1821. "RICHARD GORGES-MEREDYTH, Esq.,"[d] of Catherine's Grove, co. Dublin,[e] formerly Richard GORGES, only s. and h. of Hamilton GORGES, of the same, sometime (1761-69) M.P. [I.] for Swords, by Catherine (*m.* 27 April 1734), da. of John KEATINGE, which Hamilton (who *d.* 8 April 1786) was 2d s. of Richard GORGES, of Kilbrue, co. Meath. He was *b.* in Clifford Street, 7, and *bap.* 14 May 1735, at St. James', Westm.; matric. at Oxford (Brasenose Coll.), 11 July 1752, aged 17, and was *cr.* M.A., 17 Feb. 1756; admitted to Lincoln's Inn, 12 Nov. 1756; was M.P. [I.] for Enniskillen (two Parls.), 1768-76, and for Naas, 1787-90; assumed the additional surname of MEREDYTH on his marriage in 1775, and was *cr. a Baronet* [I.], as above, 5 Sep. 1787, the privy seal being dat. 27 July previous.[d] He *m.* 2 (Lic., Dublin, 1) March 1775, Mary, da. and h. of Arthur Francis MEREDYTH, of Dollardstown, co. Meath, by Mary, his wife. He *d.* s.p.m.,[h] Sep. 1821, aged 86, when the *Baronetcy* became *extinct*. Will dat. 21 Jan. 1803, pr. [I.] 24 July 1834.

(a) He *m.* for his 2d wife, Annabella, widow of Sir Matthew Blakiston, 1st Baronet [1763].
(b) She was sister to Edward Riggs, whose da. and h., Anne, *m.* Sir John Miller, 1st Baronet [1778].
(c) His da. and h., Catherine Louisa, *m.* 16 June 1807, Lord Douglas Gordon-Hallyburton (br. of George [Gordon], 9th Marquess of Huntly [S.]), and *d.* his widow, 2 Oct. 1851. She inherited part of her father's estates, the other part devolving on Robert Leslie, the heir male.
(d) See p. 382, note "a," under "HAMILTON."
(e) See list in Betham's *Baronetage* [1805], vol. v, p. 51.
(f) Playfair's *Baronetage* [1810].
(g) After making provision for his wife and for Maria, his illegit. da. by "Mary Banks, *alias* Mrs. Axford, residing at Eastwood, near Tenby," he devises his estates between his two illegit. sons (by the said Mary Banks), Henry Mannix and William Mannix equally.
(h) Mary Anne, his da. and h., *m.* Sir Marcus Somerville, 4th Baronet [I. 1748], and had issue.

NEWPORT:

cr. 25 Aug. 1789[a];

ex. 15 Feb. 1859.

I. 1789. "JOHN NEWPORT, Esq.,"[a] of Newpark, co. Kilkenny,[b] 1st s. and h. of Simon NEWPORT, of Waterford, Banker, by Elizabeth, da. of William RIALL, of Clonmell, co. Tipperary, was *b.* 24 Oct. 1756; ed. at Eton and at Trin. Coll., Dublin; Barrister (Dublin), Michaelmas, 1780; partner, with his brother William, in his father's bank at Waterford, which subsequently, under the name of "Simon Newport, Sir John Newport and William Newport," failed in 1820[c]; took part in the convention of Volunteer Delegates in Nov. 1783 at Dublin, and was *cr. a Baronet* [I.], as above, 25 Aug. 1789, the privy seal being dat. 18 July previous,[a] with a spec. rem., failing heirs male of his body, to his br., "William Newport, Esq.,"[a] of Waterford. He was M.P. for Waterford (nine Parls.), Dec. 1803 to 1832;[d] was, for a short time, 25 Feb. 1806 to May 1807, Chancellor of the Exchequer [I.],[e] P.C. [I.], 25 July 1806; was *cr.* D.C.L. of the Univ. of Oxford, 3 July 1810, and was Comptroller Gen. of the Exchequer [U.K.] (the first person appointed to that post), 11 Oct. 1834 to Sep. 1839, retiring with an annual pension of £1,000. He *m.*, 1 Oct. 1784, Ellen, da. of Shapland CAREW, of Castleboro, co. Wexford, by Dorothy, da. and coheir of Isaac DOBSON. He *d.* s.p., at Newpark, 9, and was *bur.* 15 Feb. 1843, at Waterford Cathedral, aged 86.[f] Will dat. 26 Aug. 1842, pr. [I.] April 1843.

II. 1843, to 1859. SIR JOHN NEWPORT, Baronet [I. 1789], of Newpark aforesaid, nephew and h., being 2d but 1st surv. s.[g] of William NEWPORT, of Waterford, Banker, and 1st s. by 2d wife, Mary (*m.* Sep. 1792), only da. of (—) CAMPART, niece to (—) VERE, Banker in Birchin Lane, London, which William[h] (who was *b.* 3 March 1758 and *d.* June 1820, at Waterford) was br. of the 1st Baronet. He was *b.* Aug. 1800; was in Holy Orders; *suc. to the Baronetcy*, 9 Feb. 1843, according to the spec. rem. He *d.* unm., in Little Ryder Street, St. James, Westm., 15 Feb. 1859, aged 58, when the *Baronetcy* became *extinct*.[i] Will dat. 8 April 1843 to 30 Jan. 1846, pr. 5 March 1859, re-sealed [I.] June 1860, under £10,000.

(a) See p. 382, note "a," under "HAMILTON."
(b) See list in Betham's *Baronetage* [1805], vol. v, p. 51.
(c) *Ex inform.* C. M. Tenison, of Hobart, Tasmania.
(d) He had been elected in 1806 for St. Mawes in Cornwall, but preferred to sit for Waterford.
(e) The Exchequers of Great Britain and Ireland were not united till 1817.
(f) He "was a staunch Whig and a steady supporter of Catholic emancipation, a man of considerable ability and of great industry, but lacking in judgment. Owing to the pertinacity with which he pushed his inquiries in the House of Commons, he acquired the nickname of the *Political Ferret*." [*Dict. Nat. Biogr.*]
(g) The eldest son (the only son by the 1st wife, Sarah, da. of Lt.-Col. George Gilman, *m.* Feb. 1783, *d.* in Portugal, July 1790) was Simon George Newport, Lt.-Col. 10th Hussars. He who was *b.* May 1785 was ed. at Eton; matric. at Oxford (Brasenose Coll.), 6 Nov. 1802, aged 17, *d.* s.p. before Feb. 1843.
(h) This William is erroneously made [Burke's *Baronetages*, 1844 to 1850] to have *suc. to the Baronetcy* in 1843, but the death of the 1st Baronet and the succession of his nephew John to that dignity were noted at the time in Ulster's Office.
(i) His yst. br., William Newport, *b.* Feb. 1805, ed. at Christ's Coll., Cambridge, admitted to Lincoln's Inn, 19 May 1824, is sometimes, erroneously, said to have *suc. to the Baronetcy* [Burke's *Baronetages*, 1859 to 1863]. He, however, *d.* before his brother, who, in his obituary notice [*Ann. Reg.*, 1859] is spoken of as the "only surviving son of the late William Newport, Esq., of Waterford."

BATESON-HARVEY:

cr. 26 Aug. 1789[a];

afterwards, 1825-70, BATESON;

ex. 15 April 1870.

I. 1789. "ROBERT BATESON HARVEY, Esq.,"[a] of Killoquin, co. Antrim,[b] 2d s. of Richard BATESON, of Londonderry (*b.* at Garstang, co. Lancaster, *d.* at Londonderry, Nov. 1766), being 1st s. by 2d wife, Elizabeth (*m.* 19 Aug. 1742, in Derry Cathedral, *d.* 3 Jan. 1789, aged 59, *bur.* at Langley), sister and h. of David HARVEY, of Marylebone, Midx. (who *d.* 1 July 1788, aged 73), da. of Robert HARVEY, of Londonderry aforesaid, took by royal lic., 16 Sep. 1788, the name of HARVEY after that of BATESON, having inherited the large property of his maternal uncle, the said David HARVEY; purchased on the 30th of the same month the estate of Langley abovenamed, and was *cr. a Baronet* [I.], as above, 26 Aug. 1789, the privy seal being dat. 18 July previous, with a spec. rem., failing heirs male of his body to those of his father, Richard BATESON, deceased. He *d.* s.p. legit.[c] 5 June 1825, in his 78th year, at Langley Park aforesaid. Will pr. Nov. 1825.

II. 1825, to 1870. SIR ROBERT BATESON, Baronet [I. 1789], of Castruse, co. Donegal, nephew and h., being 1st s. and h. of Thomas BATESON, of Londonderry, by his 2d wife, Margaret, da. of the Rev. Joseph DOUGLAS, co. Antrim, which Thomas (who was living 1789) was elder br. of the half blood of the 1st Baronet,[d] being 1st s. of Richard BATESON abovenamed by his 1st wife, Sarah, da. of (—) MCCLINTOCK, of co. Donegal. He was *b.* about 1793, was Sheriff of co. Donegal, 1822, and *suc. to the Baronetcy*, 5 June 1825, under the spec. rem. of that dignity. He *m.* Feb. 1819, Eliza, 2d da. of Anthony HAMMOND, of Hutton Bonville, co. York, by Jane, da. of John CLOSE, of Easby Hall, co. York. She *d.* 1867. He *d.* s.p. 15 April 1870, at Castruse aforesaid, in his 78th year, when the *Baronetcy* became *extinct*.

HAYES:

cr. 27 Aug. 1789.[a]

I. 1789. "SAMUEL HAYES, Esq.,"[a] of Drumboe Castle, co. Donegal,[b] only surv. s. of Challis[e] HAYES, Vice Consul at

(a) See p. 382, note "a," under "HAMILTON."
(b) See list in Betham's *Baronetage* [1805], vol. v, p. 51.
(c) His illegit. son, Robert Harvey, *b.* 1 Feb. 1791, inherited Langley Park and most of his property; was Sheriff of Bucks, 1828, and was father of Robert Bateson Harvey, *cr. a Baronet*, 28 Nov. 1868.
(d) The 1st Baronet had also a yr. br. (of the whole blood), George Bateson, Capt. 3d Reg. of Guards, who *d.* April 1789, and was *bur.* at Clifton by Bristol, leaving issue (besides daughters) two sons, both of whom *d.* unm. before 1811. [Playfair's *Baronetage*, 1811.]
(e) So called in Playfair's *Baronetage* [1811], but called Charles in Burke's *Baronetage* [1905].

Lisbon (where he was murdered by his own servant in 1737), by Deborah, da. of (—) HOLDITCH, of Totnes, Devon (which Challis was s. of Challis HAYES, of Bridgwater, Somerset, merchant), was *b.* 1737, and having acquired by marriage the estate of Drumboe Castle abovenamed, was *cr. a Baronet* [I.], as aforesaid, 27 Aug. 1789, the privy seal being dat. 18 July previous. He *m.* in or before 1773, Mary, da. and h. of William BASIL, of Drumboe Castle abovenamed and of Wilton Park, Bucks. He *d.* at Clifton by Bristol, 21 July 1807,[a] aged 70. Will pr. 1807.

II. 1807. SIR SAMUEL HAYES, Baronet [I. 1789], of Drumboe Castle aforesaid, only s. and h., *b.* Feb. 1773, sometime Capt. in the 1st Life Guards; *suc. to the Baronetcy*, 21 July 1807. He *m.* (Lic. Prerog. [I.], 12 Aug. 1803) Elizabeth[b] (*b.* 6 July 1779), 1st da. of Sir Thomas LIGHTON, 1st Baronet [I. 1791], by Anne, da. of William POLLOCK. He *d.* 16 Sep. 1827, aged 54. Will pr. Dec. 1828. His widow *d.* 18 Jan. 1848.

III. 1827. SIR EDMUND SAMUEL HAYES, Baronet [I. 1789], of Drumboe Castle aforesaid, only s. and h., *b.* 2 July 1806 in Dublin; ed. at Trin. Coll., Dublin; B.A., 1827; M.A., 1832; *suc. to the Baronetcy*, 16 Sep. 1827; M.P. for co. Donegal (nine Parls.), 1831-60. He *m.* 3 July 1837, Emily, 1st da. of the Hon. Sir Hercules PAKENHAM, K.C.B., (yr. s. of the 2d BARON LONGFORD [I.]), by Emily, da. of Thomas (STAPLETON), LORD LE DESPENCER. He *d.* 30 June 1860, aged nearly 54. His widow *d.* 21 April 1883, at Purbrook Lodge, Cosham, Hants, aged 64.

IV. 1860. SIR SAMUEL HERCULES HAYES, Baronet [I. 1789], of Drumboe Castle aforesaid, 1st s. and h., *b.* there 3 Feb. 1840, ed. at Harrow; entered the Army, 1858; Lieut. 2d Life Guards, 1862; Capt., 1857, retring in 1872, having *suc. to the Baronetcy*, 30 June 1860; Sheriff of co. Donegal, 1884. He *m.* 25 July 1878, at St. Ann's, Meon-Glas, co. Donegal, Alice Anne, 4th da. of James (HEWITT), 4th VISCOUNT LIFFORD [I.], by his 2d wife Lydia Lucy, da. of the Rev. John Wingfield DIGBY. He *d.* s.p.m., 7 Nov. 1901, at Funchal, Madeira, aged 61. Will pr. at £10,222. His widow, who was *b.* 16 Sep. 1854, living 1905.

V. 1901. SIR EDMUND FRANCIS HAYES, Baronet [I. 1789], of Drumboe Castle aforesaid, only br. and h., *b.* there 1850; ed. at Harrow; *suc. to the Baronetcy*, 7 Nov. 1901. He *m.* in 1900, Alice, da. of Judge WILKINSON, of New South Wales.

Family Estates.—These, in 1878,[c] consisted of 22,825 acres in co. Donegal, worth £6,356 a year.

(a) The name of Hayes was rendered notorious about this date by the conduct of an Irish knight (not, apparently, a relative of this family), Sir Henry Brown Hayes, who at the Cork Assizes, 6 April 1801, was found guilty of "feloniously carrying away with intent to marry her, Mary Pike," and was condemned to death, though subsequently transported. The lady often erroneously called Penrose was a Quaker heiress, and the affair gave rise to several facetious verses. See *N. & Q.*, 6th s., IX, 10, 118 and 314.
(b) Called, erroneously, "Anne" in the marr. lic., though not in the recorded pedigree. Anne Lighton, *b.* 27 Aug. 1789, would have been but 14 in 1803.
(c) See p. 347, note "c," under "BURDETT."

HODSON:

cr. 28 Aug. 1789[a]

I. 1789. "ROBERT HODSON,[b] Esq.," of Hollybrook, co. Wicklow"[a] as also of Greenpark, *otherwise* Tuitestown, co. Westmeath, only s. and h. of William HODSON,[c] of Tuitestown aforesaid (*d.* at Bath, 2 Aug. 1768, aged 41), by Eleanor, da. of Robert ADAIR,[d] of Hollybrook aforesaid, was *b.* 1747; Sheriff of co. Westmeath, 1776; of co. Wicklow, 1786, was *cr. a Baronet* [I.], as above, 28 Aug. 1789, the privy seal being dat. 18 July previous. He was subsequently Sheriff of co. Cavan, 1791. He was Lieut.-Col. of the Cavan Militia, and had command of the town of Wicklow during the rebellion of 1798. He *m.* firstly, 11 April 1774, Anne, da. and h. of his maternal uncle, Forster ADAIR, of Hollybrook aforesaid, by Anne, da. of Sir George RIBTON, 1st Baronet [I. 1759]. She, who was *b.* 11 Feb. 1757, *d.* s.p.s.,[e] 27 June 1790, and was *bur.* at St. Canice, Westmeath. He *m.* secondly, in 1799, Jane, 1st da. of Brent NEVILLE, of Ashbrook, co. Dublin, by Frances, da. of James DANCE. He *d.* 19 July 1809, aged 62. The will of the widow was pr. Feb. 1852.

II. 1809. SIR ROBERT ADAIR HODSON, Baronet [I. 1789], of Hollybrook and Greenpark aforesaid, 1st surv. s. and h., being 1st s. by 2d wife, *b.* 14 March 1802; *suc. to the Baronetcy*, 19 July 1809; Sheriff of co. Wicklow, 1825, and of co. Westmeath, 1827. He *d.* unm., 19 Oct. 1831, aged 29.

III. 1831. SIR GEORGE FREDERICK JOHN HODSON, Baronet [I. 1789], of Hollybrook House and Greenpark aforesaid, yst. br. and h., *b.* 26 Oct. 1806, in Dublin; *suc. to the Baronetcy*, 19 Oct. 1831; Sheriff of co. Wicklow, 1834; of co. Cavan, 1839, and of co. Westmeath, 1846. He *m.* 15 (marr. lic. [I.], 4) Sep. 1852, Meriel Anne, 3d da. of his maternal uncle, the Rev. Richard NEVILLE, Rector of Clonpriest, co. Cork, by Anne, da. of Col. William GORE. He *d.* 2 April 1888, at Holybrook House aforesaid, aged 81. His widow living 1905.

IV. 1888. SIR ROBERT ADAIR HODSON, Baronet [I. 1789], of Hollybrook House and Greenpark aforesaid, 1st s. and h., *b.* 29 Sep. 1853; ed. at Haileybury Coll.; *suc. to the Baronetcy*, 2 April 1888; Sheriff of co. Cavan, 1889, and of co. Wicklow, 1891; Lieut.-Col. commanding 4th Batt. Irish Fusileers Militia.

Family Estates.—These, in 1878,[f] consisted of 4,121 acres in co. Cavan, 1,211 in co. Wicklow, 720 in co. Westmeath, and 367 in co. Meath. *Total.*—6,419 acres, worth £4,427 a year.

(a) See p. 382, note "a," under "HAMILTON."
(b) In the "promotions" for 1789 in the *Ann. Reg.* of that year, the grantee is (strangely) called "Robert Hodson Barry."
(c) This William Hodson, the fourth in succession of that name, was great great grandson of John Hodson, Bishop of Elphin, 1667-86.
(d) A pedigree of Adair of Hollybrook is in Playfair's *Baronetage* [1811], under "HODSON."
(e) Of her two sons, the eldest, *b.* 1776, *d.* an infant, and the other, William Robert, *b.* 1779, *d.* 1780.
(f) See p. 347, note "c," under "BURDETT."

TALBOT:

cr. 31 March 1790[a];

ex. 10 June 1850.

I. 1790. "CHARLES HENRY TALBOT, Esq.,"[a] of Belfast, co. Antrim,[b] as also of Mickleham, co. Surrey, 2d s. of Major-Gen. Sherington TALBOT, of Evesham, co. Worcester, by his 1st wife, Elizabeth, da. of Henry MEDGET, which Sherington (who *d.* 18 Nov. 1766, aged 67) was 3d s. of William TALBOT, D.D., sometime (1722-30) Bishop of Durham (the ancestor of the EARLS TALBOT, who, since 1856, became EARLS OF SHREWSBURY), was *b.* 30 Oct. 1720; suc. his elder br., the Rev. William TALBOT, M.A., Vicar of Kineton, co. Warwick, and Rector of St. Giles, Reading (who *d.* s.p., 2 March 1774, aged 56), and was *cr. a Baronet* [I.], as above, 31 March 1790, the privy seal being dat. 12 of the same month. He *m.* 26 Feb. 1749/50, at the Temple Church, London, Anne, only child of Thomas HASSELL, of St. Pancras, Midx. He *d.* 10 June 1798, aged 77. Will pr. June 1798. The will of his widow was pr. 1810.

II. 1798. SIR CHARLES TALBOT, Baronet [I. 1790], of Belfast and Mickleham aforesaid, 1st s. and h., *b.* in Bedford Row, 8 Nov. and *bap.* 5 Dec. 1751 at St. Andrew's, Holborn; *suc. to the Baronetcy*, 10 June 1798; M.P. for Weobley, 1800-02; for Rye, 1803-06, and for Bletchingley, 1812 till death, having inherited the estate of Chart park, in Dorking, Surrey, in 1802, from Elizabeth CORNEWALL, widow, da. and h. of his paternal uncle, Henry TALBOT, of Chart park aforesaid, a Commissioner of the Revenue. He *d.* unm., 3 Nov. 1812, aged nearly 61. Will pr. 1812.

III. 1812, to 1850. SIR GEORGE TALBOT, Baronet [I. 1790], of Chart Park aforesaid, only br. and h., *b.* in Bedford Row, 14 March, and *bap.* 13 April 1761 at St. Andrew's, Holborn; sometime Lieut. in the 3d Reg. of Guards; *suc. to the Baronetcy*, 3 Nov. 1812. He *m.* June 1787, at Walcot, near Bath, Anne, da. of the Rev. Nathaniel PRESTON, of Swainstown, co. Meath, by his 2d wife, Mary, da. of the Hon. Henry HAMILTON, 3d s of Gustavus, 1st VISCOUNT BOYNE [I.]. He *d.* s.p.m.,[c] 10 June 1850, at 21 Grosvenor Square, aged 89, when the *Baronetcy* became *extinct*.

LIGHTON:

cr. 1 March 1791[d];

I. 1791. "THOMAS LIGHTON, of Merville, co. Dublin, Esq.,"[a] as also of Longfield, co. Tyrone, and of Clara, in the Barony of Gowran, co. Kilkenny, s. of John LIGHTON, of Rasperry Hill, in the Barony of Comber, co. Derry (*b.* 17 July 1722, being s. of John LIGHTON, formerly of Glasgow), by Elizabeth, da. of John WALKER, of Tisdern, co. Tyrone, was sometime a tradesman at Strabane,[e] afterwards a soldier in East India, and finally became

(a) See p 382, note "a," under "HAMILTON."
(b) See list in Betham's *Baronetage* [1805], vol. v, p. 51.
(c) He had two daughters, Mary Anne, *b.* 10 April 1788, at Walcot by Bath, and Charlotte Georgina.
(d) The dates of creation and descriptions of the Baronets [I.] from 1791 to 1800 are supplied by G. D. Burtchaell from the Register of Baronets in the Office of Ulster King of Arms, Dublin. The privy seals were all dated at St. James's, the patents at Dublin. See p. 382, note "a," under "HAMILTON."
(e) *Ex inform.* C. M. Tenison, of Hobart, Tasmania. See also the obituary notice in the *Ann. Reg.* for 1805 (p. 496), where there is an interesting account of the whole of his career, and his rise from poverty to affluence.

a Banker in Dublin ;(a) Sheriff of co. Dublin, 1790 ; M.P. [I.] for Tuam, 1790-97, and for Carlingford, 1798-1800, and was *cr. a Baronet* [I.], as above, 1 March 1791, the privy seal being dat. 9 Feb. previous.(b) He was Sheriff of co. Tyrone, 1801. He *m.* 11 Dec. 1777, Anne, da. of William POLLOCK, of Strabane aforesaid. She, who was *b.* 6 June 1760, *d.* 1804. He *d.* at Dublin, 27 April 1805. Will pr. 1806.

II. 1805. SIR THOMAS LIGHTON, Baronet [I. 1791], of Merville aforesaid, 1st s. and h., *b.* 19 May 1787 ; *suc. to the Baronetcy,* 27 April 1805. He *m.* 14 Dec. 1811, at St. Paul's, Covent Garden, (being then of that parish, bachelor), Sylvia (then a minor), da. of John BRANDON, of St. Giles' in the Fields. He *d.* 11 May 1816, aged nearly 29.

III. 1816. SIR THOMAS LIGHTON, Baronet [I. 1791], of Merville aforesaid, only s. and h., *b.* 1814 ; *suc. to the Baronetcy,* 11 May 1816, and *d.* soon afterwards in 1817, after Jan., aged 3.

IV. 1817. SIR JOHN LEES LIGHTON, Baronet [I. 1791], uncle and h., being 3d and yst. s. of the 1st Baronet, *b.* 1 Jan. 1792 ; was in Holy Orders ; Rector of Donaghmore, co. Donegal, 1816, till death ; *suc. to the Baronetcy* in 1817. He *m.* 23 Jan. 1817, Mary Hamilton, 2d da. of Christopher John PEMBERTON, M.D., of Newton, co. Cambridge, by Eleanora, da. of James HAMILTON, of Woodbrook, Strabane. She *d.* 28 June 1826, aged 28, and was *bur.* at Donaghmore. He *d.* 5 April 1827, aged 35, and was *bur.* there. M.I. Will pr. Feb. 1828.

V. 1827. SIR JOHN HAMILTON LIGHTON, Baronet [I. 1791], 1st s. and h., *b.* 20 May 1818 ; *suc. to the Baronetcy,* 5 April 1827 ; ed. at St. John's Coll., Cambridge ; B.A., 1839. He *d.* unm., 29 April 1844, aged 25. Will pr. Nov. 1844 and June 1852.

VI. 1844. SIR CHRISTOPHER ROBERT LIGHTON, Baronet [I. 1791], br. and h., *b.* 28 May 1819, at Earlsgift, co. Tyrone ; ed. at St. John's Coll., Cambridge ; B.A., 1843 ; M.A., 1846, taking Holy Orders, 1845 ; *suc. to the Baronetcy,* 29 April 1844 ; Vicar of Ellastone, co. Stafford, 1848 till death. He *m.* 2 June 1843, Mary Anne Elizabeth, only da. of the Rev. Digby Joseph Stopford RAM, of Brookville, co. Cork, by Penelope, da. of Christmas Paul WALLIS, of Renny, in that county. He *d.* 12 April 1875, at Ellastone aforesaid, aged 55. His widow *d.* 22 March 1902.

VII. 1875. SIR CHRISTOPHER ROBERT LIGHTON, Baronet [I. 1791], of Brockhampton Court, co. Hereford, 1st s. and h., *b.* 4 July 1848, at Hookfield Grove, Epsom, Surrey ; ed. at Repton School and at Trin. Coll., Cambridge ; B.A., 1871 ; admitted to Lincoln's Inn, 23 Nov. 1870 ; Barrister, 26 Jan. 1874, going the Oxford circuit ; *suc. to the Baronetcy,* 12 April 1875 ; Sheriff of Herefordshire, 1885. He *m.* 6 April 1880, at Kensington Church, Helen Frances, 1st da. of James HOULDSWORTH, of Coltness, co. Lanark, by Katherine Jane, da. of the Rev. Henry Walter MCGRATH, Canon of Manchester.

Family Estates.—These, in 1878,(c) consisted of 945 acres in co. Galway, worth £219 a year, and 88 in co. Tyrone, worth £213 a year. *Total.*—1033 acres, worth £432 a year.

(a) The firm at the time of his death was known as "Lighton, Needham and Shaw," Robert Shaw, who afterwards, in 1821, was *cr. a Baronet,* being one of the partners. The Bank, then in Foster Place, Dublin, was in 1836 taken over by the Royal Bank of Ireland.

(b) See p. 429, note "d," under "LIGHTON."

(c) See p. 347, note "c," under "BURDETT."

FORSTER :

cr. 15 Jan. 1794(a) ;

ex. 21 Jan. 1904.

I. 1794. "THOMAS FORSTER, of Tullaghan, co. Monaghan, Clerk,"(a) 3d s. of Nicholas FORSTER, of the same, who *assumed the title of Baronet*(b) (being so styled when Sheriff of co. Monaghan, 1739), by his 1st wife, Charlotte, da. of John FOSTER, of Dunleer, co. Louth, was *b.* 9 Sep. 1751 ; ed. at Trin. Coll., Dublin ; Scholar, 1772 ; B.A., 1773 ; M.A., 1813 ; was in Holy Orders ; suc. to the family estates, 4 Nov. 1787 (being heir male to his elder br., Anthony FORSTER, *styling himself Baronet*), when possibly he himself may have assumed that title ; anyhow, about ten years later he was *cr. a Baronet* [I.], as above, 15 Jan. 1794, the privy seal being dat. 9 Dec. previous.(a) He *m.* at Wicklow (Lic., Dublin, Oct. 1786) Dorcas, only da. of the Ven. George HOWSE, M.A., Archdeacon of Down (1742-70), by Lætitia, da. of the Rev. John WYNNE, D.D. She *d.* 23 Dec. 1828. He *d.* 3 Dec. 1843, at Coolderry, co. Monaghan, aged 92, and was *bur.* at Ballinode in that county.

II. 1843. SIR GEORGE FORSTER, Baronet [I. 1794], of Coolderry aforesaid, only s. and h., *b.* 21 March 1796, at Baronstown Glebe, co. Louth ; ed. at Trin. Coll., Dublin ; B.A., 1817 ; M.A., 1833 Sheriff of co. Monaghan, 1817 ; *suc. to the Baronetcy,* 3 Dec. 1843 ; was M.P. for co. Monaghan (three Parls.), 1852-65. He *m.* firstly, May 1817, Anna Maria, 1st da. of Matthew FORTESCUE, of Stephenstown, co. Louth, by Mary Anne, 1st da. of John MCCLINTOCK, of Drumcar, in that county. She *d.* 2 May 1848. He *m.* secondly, 20 March (Lic. Prerog. [I.], 6 Feb.) 1855, his cousin, Charlotte Jane, yst. da. of William Hoare HUME, of Humewood, co. Wicklow, by Charlotte Anna, only da. of Samuel DICK, and Charlotte his wife, sister of Sir Thomas FORSTER, 1st Baronet [I. 1794]. He *d.* 4 April 1876, at 63 Fitzwilliam Square, Dublin, and was *bur.* at Ballinode, aged 80. M.I. at Tedavnet. His widow *d.* s.p., 9 Aug. 1889, at 63 Fitzwilliam Square aforesaid. Will pr. over £93,000.

III. 1876. SIR THOMAS ORIEL FORSTER, Baronet [I. 1794], of Coolderry aforesaid, 1st s. and h., by 1st wife, *b.* 7 June 1824 at Dundalk ; sometime Capt. 77th Foot ; Lieut.-Col. Commandant 5th Royal Irish Fusileers Militia, 1855-84 ; Sheriff of co. Monaghan, 1860 ; *suc. to the Baronetcy,* 4 April 1876 ; C.B. (civil), 1881. He *m.* 15 Jan. 1862, Mary Elizabeth Alice, 3d da. and coheir of Thomas Span (PLUNKET), 2d BARON PLUNKET, Bishop of Tuam, Killala and Achonry, by Louisa Jane, da. of John William FOSTER, of Fane Valley, co. Louth. He *d.* s.p., 28 Dec. 1895, at his residence, Ballymascanlan House, near Dundalk, aged 71. Will pr. at £2,512. His widow living 1905.

IV. 1895, to 1904. SIR ROBERT FORSTER, Baronet [I. 1794], of Coolderry aforesaid, only br. and h., *b.* 27 April 1827, at Dundalk ; sometime Hon. Major 5th Batt. Royal Irish Fusileers Militia ; *suc. to the Baronetcy,* 28 Dec. 1895. He *m.* 9 Aug. 1866, Mary Frances, 1st da. of Ralph SMYTH, of Newtown, co. Louth, by Anna, da. of the Rev. Charles CRAWFORD, Vicar of St. Mary's, Drogheda. She *d.* 30 March 1903. He *d.* s.p. in Dublin, 21 Jan. 1904, aged 76, when the *Baronetcy* became *extinct.*(c)

(a) See p. 429, note "d," under "LIGHTON."

(b) See pp. 352-53 for an account of the Baronetcy assumed from about 1766 by the family of Forster, of Tullaghan.

(c) Of his two sisters (1) Emily Isabella, *m.* 3 May 1847, Samuel Usher Roberts, C.B., who *d.* 11 Jan. 1900, leaving issue ; (2) Catherine Dorcas, *m.* 19 July 1852, Spencer George Augustus Thursby, Capt. 1st Royals (who *d.* 6 June 1871), and *d.* 21 May 1889, leaving issue.

PAUL :

cr. 20 Jan. 1794.(a)

I. 1794. "JOSHUA PAUL, of Paulville, in the county of Carlow, Esq.,"(a) as also of Ballyglan, co. Waterford, and Tinoran, co. Wicklow, 1st s. and h. of Christmas PAUL, of the same, sometime (1741-48) M.P. [I.] for the city of Waterford, by Ellen, only da. and h. of Robert CAREW, of Ballynamona, co. Waterford, and Castleboro, co. Wexford, was, for what service is unknown,(b) *cr. a Baronet* [I.], as above, 20 Jan. 1794, the privy seal being dat. 10 Dec. previous.(a) He *m.* in 1771, Sarah, da. and coheir of William GUN, of Kilmorny, co. Kerry, by Elizabeth, 1st da. and coheir of Isaac DOBSON. He *d.* 15 April 1799. Will pr. [I.] 1799. His widow *d.* Dec. 1824.

II. 1799. SIR JOSHUA CHRISTMAS PAUL, Baronet [I. 1794], of Paulville, Ballyglan, and Tinoran aforesaid, 1st s. and h., *b.* 4 Dec. 1773 ; *suc. to the Baronetcy,* 15 April 1799. He *m.* 16 April 1811, Elizabeth, yst. da. of Henry WALLIS, of Drishane Castle, co. Cork, by his paternal aunt, Elizabeth, da. of Christmas PAUL abovenamed. She *d.* 16 April 1836. He *d.* s.p. at Dublin, 22 Aug. 1842, aged 68.

III. 1842. SIR ROBERT JOSHUA PAUL, Baronet [I. 1794], of Paulville, Ballyglan, and Tinoran aforesaid, nephew and h., being only s. and h. of William Gun PAUL, Barrister, by Marianna, da. of Edward MOORE, of Mooresfort, co. Tipperary, which William (who *d.* May 1833) was br. of the late Baronet. He was *b.* 2 April 1820, ed. at Trin. Coll., Dublin ; B.A., 1841 ; *suc. to the Baronetcy,* 22 Aug. 1842 ; Sheriff of co. Carlow, 1844, and of co. Waterford, 1846. He *m.* 16 (Lic. Prerog. [I.] 14) Nov. 1848, Anne, 1st da. of William BLACKER, of Woodbrook, co. Wexford, by Elizabeth Anne, sister of Robert Shapland (CAREW), 1st BARON CAREW [I.], da. of Robert Shapland CAREW, of Castleboro aforesaid. She *d.* May 1858. He *d.* 9 May 1898, at Ballyglan aforesaid, aged 78.

IV. 1898. SIR WILLIAM JOSHUA PAUL, Baronet [I. 1794], of Paulville, Ballyglan, and Tinoran aforesaid, 1st s. and h., *b.* 20 June 1851 ; ed. at Trin. Coll., Cambridge ; B.A., 1875 ; M.A., 1878 ; Resident Magistrate [I.], 1880 ; *suc. to the Baronetcy,* 9 May 1898. He *m.* 16 June 1880, at Gatton, co. Surrey, Richenda Juliet, 4th da. of Henry Edmund GURNEY, of Nutwood, in that county, by Jane, 1st da. of Henry BIRKBECK, of Keswick Old Hall, Norfolk.

Family Estates.—These, in 1878,(c) consisted of 2,894 acres in co. Wicklow, 1,401 in co. Carlow, 708 in co. Kerry, and 243 in co. Waterford. *Total.*—5,246 acres, worth £3,468 a year.

BOND :

cr. 21 Jan. 1794(a) ;

ex. 3 March 1823.

I. 1794. "JAMES BOND, of Coolamber, co. Longford, Esq.,"(a) 2d s. of the Rev. James BOND, Presbyterian Minister of Corboy, co. Longford (*d.* Sep. 1762), by Catherine, da. of the Rev. Thomas WENSLEY, of Lifford, co. Donegal, was *b.* 11 June 1744, at Newtown, co. Longford ; was M.P. [I.] for Naas, 1790-97, and was *cr. a Baronet* [I.], as above, 21 Jan. 1794, the privy seal being dat. 11 Dec. previous.(a) He *m.* 27 July 1770, Anne, widow

---

(a) See p. 429, note "d," under "LIGHTON."

(b) He, however, was [see Playfair's *Baronetage,* 1811] "a Justice of the Peace for co. Waterford."

(c) See p. 347, note "c," under "BURDETT."

of Richard EYRE, of the East India Company's service, da. of William HORNBY, Governor of Bombay. She *d.* 3 July 1809. He *d.* 2 June 1820. Will dat. 26 July 1813, with three codicils, pr. [I.] 10 May 1822, by his da., Louisa wife of Holwell WALSHE.

II. 1820, to 1823. SIR THOMAS BOND, Baronet [I. 1794], of Coolamber aforesaid, 2d but only surv. s. and h.,(a) *b.* at Bombay, 27 Oct. 1776 ; *suc. to the Baronetcy,* 2 June 1820. He *m.* 4 April (settlement, 25 March) 1803, Louisa Sarah, da. of John READ, of Porchester, Hants, and Mary, his wife. He *d.* s.p.(b) in Kildare Street, Dublin, 3 March 1823, aged 46, when the *Baronetcy* became *extinct.*(c) His widow *m.* July 1824, Patrick Kavanagh GIBBONS, of Dublin, Attorney.

SHEE(d) :

cr. 22 Jan. 1794(e) ;

ex. 25 Jan. 1870.

I. 1794. "GEORGE SHEE, of Dunmore, co. Galway, Esq.,"(e) and afterwards of Lockleys, Herts, 1st s. and h. of Anthony SHEE, of Castlebar, co. Mayo (*d.* 15 Feb. 1783, aged 72), by Margaret (*m.* 1748), da. of Edmund BURKE, of Curry, co. Mayo, was *b.* Jan. 1754, "spent many years in the East Indies,"(f) and was *cr. a Baronet* [I.], as above, 22 Jan. 1794, the privy seal being dat. 14 Dec. previous.(e) He was Surveyor-Gen. of the Ordnance [I.], April 1797 to 1799 ; was M.P. [I.] for Knocktopher (two Parls.), 1798-1800, receiving £1,137 as compensation for the loss of that seat, at the Union [I.] ; was Sec. to the Treasury [I.], 1799-1800 ; Under Sec. for the Home Department, 1800-03, and for War and Colonies, 1806-07 ; Receiver-Gen. of the Customs [I.], 12 Nov. 1801. He *m.* 2 July 1784, Elizabeth Maria, da. of James CRISP, of Dacca, in the East Indies, "nearly allied to the family of BURNISH, of Worcestershire."(k) He *d.* at Brighton, 3 Feb. 1825, aged 71. Will pr. May 1825. The will of his widow ("Herts") pr. Oct. 1838.

II. 1825, to 1870. SIR GEORGE SHEE, Baronet [I. 1794], of Dunmore aforesaid and of Mudiford, Hants, 1st s. and h., *b.* 14 June 1785 ; ed. at St. John's Coll., Cambridge ; B.A., 1806 ; M.A., 1811 ; *suc. to the Baronetcy,* 3 Feb. 1825 ; Sheriff of co. Galway, 1828 ; Under Sec. for Foreign Affairs, 1830-34 ; Minister Plenipotentiary to Berlin, Oct. 1834 to July 1835, and to Stuttgart, 1835-44. He *m.* firstly, 5 Feb. 1808, Jane,

---

(a) His three brothers all *d.* unm. and v.p. ; James Hornby Bond (the eldest), *d.* June 1792 ; Samuel Bond, *b.* 3 June 1781, *d.* before 1804, and William Bond, *b.* 9 Sep. 1787, *d.* before July 1813.

(b) Of his two sisters (1) Anne Wensley, *b.* 24 Jan. 1774, *m.* 24 Dec. 1792, as his 1st wife, the Hon. Christopher Hely-Hutchinson, and *d.* 30 March 1796, leaving an only child, John, who *d.* unm. 1842 ; (2) Louisa, *b.* 13 April 1778, *m.* firstly, John Miller, of Russell Sq., Bloomsbury, and secondly, Holwell Walshe, of Dublin, Barrister. She *d.* May 1835, leaving two daughters and coheirs by her first, and three by her second husband.

(c) "His name nevertheless appears in the list of Baronets in the Irish directories as '*Bond, Thomas ; Longford,*' down to the year 1837. He was, in 1845, resuscitated as '*Thomas Lonsford Bond,*' apparently a compound of his christian name and address. Burke makes a similar mistake in the *Extinct Baronetage,* but '*Thomas*' is the only name given to him by his father, when recording his pedigree, and in his will and the subsequent proceedings thereon." [G. D. Burtchaell.]

(d) See as to this family, G. D. Burtchaell's *M.P.'s of Kilkenny,* p. 192.

(e) See p. 429, note "d," under "LIGHTON."

(f) Playfair's *Baronetage,* 1811.

1st da. of William YOUNG, of Hexton House, Herts. She *d.* 1832. He *m.* secondly, in 1841, Sarah, 3d da. of Henry BARRET, of Denton, Norfolk. She *d.* 12 Aug. 1866, at 38 Grosvenor Place. He *d.* there s.p., 25 Jan. 1870, in his 85th year, when the *Baronetcy* became *extinct.*(a)

O'REILLY:

cr. 23 July 1795(b);

afterwards, since 1812, NUGENT.

I. 1795. "HUGH O'REILLY, of Ballinlough, co. Westmeath, Esq., Lieut.-Col. of the County Militia,"(c) 1st s. and h. of James O'REILLY, of the same, by Barbara, 2d and yst. sister of John NUGENT, of Dysert, co. Westmeath, Lieut.-Gov. of Tortola (who *d.* unm. 1811), da. of Andrew NUGENT, of Dysert and Tulloughan,(c) was *cr. a Baronet* [I.], as above, 23 July 1795, the privy seal being dat. 11 June previous.(b) He, by royal lic., 11 Sep. 1812, took the name of NUGENT only, in compliance with the will of his maternal uncle the said John NUGENT. He *m.* in or before 1790, Catherine Mary Anne, da. and h. of Charles MATHEW, of Thurles, co. Tipperary, by Anne, da. of James MORRES, of Rosetown, in that county, 4th s. of Sir John MORRES, 3d Baronet [I. 1631]. He was living 1820.(d)

II. 1825? SIR JAMES NUGENT, Baronet [I. 1795], of Ballinlough aforesaid, formerly, till 1812, James O'REILLY, 1st s. and h., *b.* probably before 1790; *suc. to the Baronetcy* on his father's death. He *m.* 8 Jan. 1811, Susan Victoria Regina Mary, only da. of C. P. D'ARABET, Baron of the Holy Roman Empire. He *d.* s.p. 26 April 1843, at Bagnéres de Bigorre, Pyrenees. Will pr. Aug. 1843. His widow *d.* 19 April 1862, at Paris.

III. 1843. SIR JOHN HUGH NUGENT, Baronet [I. 1795], of Ballinlough aforesaid, Count of the Holy Roman Empire, formerly, till 1812, John Hugh O'REILLY, only surv. br. and h., *b.* 5 April 1800; sometime Major in the Austrian service: Chamberlain to the Emperor of Austria, by whom he was *cr.* COUNT OF THE AUSTRIAN EMPIRE: *suc. to the Baronetcy*, 26 April 1843; Sheriff of co. Westmeath, 1850. He *m.* 18 Oct. 1842, Lætitia Maria, 1st da. of Charles Whyte ROCHE, of Ballygran, co. Limerick, by Letitia, 1st da. of John WHYTE, of Leixlip. He *d.* 16 Feb. 1859, at Ballinlough Castle, aged 58. His widow living 7 Nov. 1884, as administatrix to her son, Andrew Greville Nugent.

IV. 1859. SIR HUGH JOSEPH NUGENT, Baronet [I. 1795], of Ballinlough aforesaid, COUNT OF THE AUSTRIAN EMPIRE, 1st s. and h., *b.* 29 Dec. 1845; *suc. to the Baronetcy*, 16 Feb. 1859. He *d.* unm., 23 Oct. 1863, aged 17, being accidentally shot, near Stoke by Neyland, Suffolk, where he was at school.

V. 1863. SIR CHARLES NUGENT, Baronet [I. 1795], of Ballinlough aforesaid, COUNT OF THE AUSTRIAN EMPIRE, br. and h., *b.* 7 Feb. 1847; *suc. to the Baronetcy*, 23 Oct. 1863: Cornet, 17th Lancers, 1866; Lieut., 1868, retiring 1869. He *m.* 15 Nov. 1871, at Berkswell, co. Warwick,

(a) The estates (11,206 acres in co. Galway, valued, in 1878, at £4,502 a year) devolved on his nephew, George Edward Dering, son of Robert Dering, of Lockleys, Herts, by Lætitia (*m.* 4 June 1829, *d.* 19 June 1852), the only married da. of the 1st Baronet.

(b) See p. 429, note "d," under "LIGHTON."

(c) See p. 410, note "b," under "NUGENT."

(d) *Ex inform.* W. D. Pink. His sister, Margaret, was *cr.*, 26 May 1831, Baroness Talbot de Malahide [I.].

Emily Ruth Eades, 1st da. of Thomas WALKER, of Berkswell Hall, and of 21 Park Lane, Midx., by Ruth, da. of John EADES, of Delph, co. Stafford.

Family Estates.—These, in 1878,(a) consisted of 4,692 acres in co. Westmeath and 683 in co. Meath. *Total.*—5,375 acres, worth £4,172 a year.

TYDD:

cr. 24 July 1795(b);

ex. 1803.

I. 1795, to 1803. "JOHN TYDD, of Lamberton, Queen's County, Esq.,"(b) 1st s. and h. of Frend TYDD, by Eliza, da. of Pierce MOORE, of Loran, and Cremorgan, Queen's County, was ed. at Trin. Coll., Dublin: Scholar, 1762; B.A., 1764; Barrister (Dublin), Hilary, 1772; M.P. [I.] for Maryborough, 1776-83; for Ardfert, 1783-90: for Ballinakill, 1790-97, for Clogher, 1798, and for Fore, 1798-1800, having been *cr. a Baronet* [I.], as above, 24 July 1795, the privy seal being dat. 12 June previous.(b) He *m.* May 1772, Diana, da. of Benjamin BUNBURY, of Kilfeacle, co. Tipperary, by Mary, da. of John KELLY, of Maryborough. He *d.* s.p., 1803, and was *bur.* at St. Anne's, Dublin, when the *Baronetcy* became *extinct.* Will pr., 1803. His widow *d.* 22 Oct. 1821, at her house in Rivers Street, Bath. Will pr. 1821.

HOPKINS:

cr. 25 July 1795(b);

ex. 11 May 1860.

I. 1795. "FRANCIS HOPKINS, of Athboy Lodge, co. Meath, Esq.,"(b) only s. and h. of Francis HOPKINS,(c) of Athboy (*d.* 30 July 1789, aged 75), by his 1st wife, Martha (*m.* 29 Sep. 1755), da. of Walter BURTON, one of the Six Clerks [I.], was *b.* 2 Aug. 1756; ed. at Trin. Coll., Dublin; was a Barrister (Dublin), Michaelmas, 1781; put to flight, in 1794, 2,000 insurgents (being severely wounded in the fray) and was *cr. a Baronet* [I.], as above, 25 July 1795, the privy seal being dat. 13 June previous.(b) He was M.P. [I.] for Kilbeggan, 1798-1800. He *m.* (Lic., 1 May 1811) Eleanor, da. of Skeffington THOMPSON, of Rathnally, co. Meath. He *d.* 19 Sep. 1814, and was *bur.* at Rathnally, aged 58. Will dat. 17 Dec. 1813, pr. [I.] 12 Nov. 1814. His widow living Nov. 1837.

II. 1814, to 1860. SIR FRANCIS HOPKINS, Baronet [I. 1795], of Athboy aforesaid, and of Rochfort, co. Westmeath, only s. and h., *b.* 28 May 1813 at Athboy: *suc. to the Baronetcy*, 19 Sep. 1814; matric. at Oxford (Ch. Ch.), 27 June 1830, aged 17; Sheriff of co. Westmeath, 1854. He *d.* unm. at Madeira, 11 May 1860, aged nearly 47, when the *Baronetcy* became *extinct.*(d)

(a) See p. 347, note "c," under "BURDETT."

(b) See p. 429, note "d," under "LIGHTON."

(c) He was s. of Francis Hopkins (*d.* 1744), who was 2d s. of "James Hopkins, Esq., the first of the family who settled in Ireland, coming over with Cromwell" [Ped. reg. in Ulster's Office]. This Francis is incorrectly stated [Playfair's *Baronetage*, 1811] to have been a yr. s. of Ezekiel Hopkins, Bishop of Derry, 1681-90, who *d.* 19 Jan. 1690, and who had no son named "Francis." [*Ex inform.* G. D. Burtchaell].

(d) Of his two sisters (1) Anna Maria, *m.* 7 Aug. 1835, Loftus Tottenham, of Glenfarne Hall, co. Leitrim; (2) Eleanor Frances, *m.* 22 June 1838, George Johnstone.

MEREDYTH:

cr. 26 July 1795.(a)

I. 1795. "SIR JOHN MEREDYTH, Knt., of Carlandstown, co. Meath,"(a) only s. and h. of Thomas MEREDYTH,(b) of Newtown, co. Meath (*d.* 1773), by Alicia, sister of the Rt. Hon. Philip TISDALL, Attorney-Gen. [I.], da. of Richard TISDALL, was *b.* after 5 Oct. 1740: Barrister (Dublin) Hilary, 1775; Sheriff of co. Meath, 1783; *Knighted*, 1783, and was *cr. a Baronet* [I.], as above, 26 July 1795, the privy seal being dat. 15 June previous.(a) He *m.* 15 Aug. 1769, Helen, da. of William ENGLISH, of Springfield, co. Tipperary. He *d.* at Calcutta, 27 Oct. 1799, and was *bur.* in the Southpark Street burial ground there.

II. 1799. SIR THOMAS MEREDYTH, Baronet [I. 1795], of Carlandstown aforesaid, 1st s. and h., *b.* July 1770; ed. at Trin. Coll., Dublin; B.A., 1789; took Holy Orders: *suc. to the Baronetcy*, 27 Oct. 1799. He *d.* unm., Jan. or Feb. 1815, aged 44.

III. 1815. SIR HENRY MEREDYTH, Baronet [I. 1795], of Carlandstown aforesaid, br. and h., *b.* June 1775; ed. at Trin. Coll., Dublin; B.A., 1794; LL.B. and LL.D., 1804; Barrister (Dublin) Trinity 1797; *suc. to the Baronetcy* in 1815; King's Counsel, 18 Feb. 1822; Bencher, Hilary 1832; Judge of the Admiralty Court [I.], 1831-38, and an Ecclesiastical Commissioner [I.]. He *m.* in 1800 (Lic. Ferns), Editha, da. of George LE HUNTE, of Artramont, co. Wexford, by Alice Mary, da. of (—) CORRY. She *d.* 1853. He *d.* 2 May 1859, in Rutland Sq., Dublin, aged nearly 84.

IV. 1859. SIR HENRY MEREDYTH, Baronet [I. 1795], of Carlandstown aforesaid, only s. and h., *b.* 1802 in Dublin: ed. at Trin. Coll., Cambridge; B.A., 1825; was Sheriff of co. Meath, 1836; *suc. to the Baronetcy*, 2 May 1859. He *m.* 4 June (Lic. Prerog. [I.], 29 May) 1828, Mary Anne, only da. of William Evans Morres BAYLY,(c) of Norelands, co. Kilkenny, by Mary Anne, da. and h. of Charles SAVAGE, of Ardkeen, co. Down. She *d.* 1855. He *d.* 4 Aug. 1889, aged 87.

V. 1899. SIR HENRY BAYLY MEREDYTH, Baronet [I. 1795], of Norelands aforesaid, grandson and h., being 1st s. and h. of Henry William MEREDYTH, Lieut. 7th Hussars, sometime (1862) Sheriff of co. Kilkenny, by Harriet Anne, da. of the Rev. William LE POER TRENCH, which Henry, who *d.* v.p. at Guernsey, 6 Nov. 1878, aged 49, was only s. and h. ap. of the late Baronet. He was *b.* 14 Jan. 1863, at Ardnagashel, co. Cork, sometime Lieut. West Somerset Yeomanry Cavalry, and North Irish Division R.A.; Sheriff of co. Kilkenny, 1888; *suc. to the Baronetcy*, 4 Aug. 1889. He *m.* firstly, 27 Oct. 1886, Kathleen, only child of Robert Patrick O'HARA, of Raheen, co. Galway, by Frances, da. of Lieut.-Col. Gervase POWER, 3d s. of Sir John POWER, 1st Baronet [1836]. She was

(a) See p. 429, note "d," under "LIGHTON."

(b) This Thomas was s. of another Thomas Meredyth, of Newtown (*d.* 13 Jan. 1731), s. of Charles Meredyth, of the same, Major in the Army (*d.* 1710), s. of Sir Thomas Meredyth, of Dollardstown, co. Meath (*d.* 1677), who was yr. br. of the Rt. Hon. Sir Robert Meredyth, of Greenhills, co. Kildare (father of Sir William Meredyth, *cr. a Baronet* [I.], 20 Nov. 1660), both being sons of Richard Meredyth, Bishop of Ferns and Leighlin, 1589-97.

(c) This William was s. of Clayton Bayly, of Gowran, co. Kilkenny, by Mary, 2d da. of Sir William Evans Morres, 1st Baronet [I. 1758].

divorced in 1894. He *m.* secondly, 21 April 1897, at Christ Church, Mayfair,(a) Mildred Beatrice, yst. da. of Edmund B. LIEBERT, sometime an officer in the 18th Hussars.

Family Estates.—These (all of which were inherited by the 5th Baronet from his maternal ancestors of the name of Bayly and Savage) consisted, in 1878,(b) of 3,217 acres in co. Kilkenny, 3,071 in co. Down, and 128 in co. Kildare. *Total.*—6,416 acres, worth £6,509 a year.

BAKER:

cr. 1796.

"ROBERT BAKER, of Upper Dunstable, co. Surrey," is (erroneously) stated in the *Liber Munerum Hiberniæ* to have been *cr. a Baronet* [I.] in "1796," but this is manifestly an error for the creation, 14 May 1796, of "ROBERT BAKER, Esq., of Dunstable, or Upper Dunstable House, in Richmond, co. Surrey," as a Baronet [G.B.]. The mistake is curious, as the grantee does not appear to have been in any way connected with Ireland.

BURKE:

cr. 5 Dec. 1797.(c)

I. 1797. "THOMAS BURKE, of Marble Hill [*formerly* Gorteenacuppogue, near Longhrea], co. Galway, Esq.,"(c) s. and h. of John BURKE, of the same (*d.* 1793, aged 80), by Mary, da. and h. of (—) CARROLL, of Killoran (which John was s. and h. of Thomas BURKE, of Gorteenacuppogue aforesaid), was *cr. a Baronet* [I.], as above, 5 Dec. 1797, the privy seal being dat. 9 Oct. previous.(c) He *m.* April 1774, Christian, da. of James BROWNE, of Limerick. He *d.* 1813.

II. 1813. SIR JOHN BURKE, Baronet [I. 1797], of Marble Hill aforesaid, only s. and h., *b.* about 1782; entered the Army, becoming in 1804 Lieut.-Col. of the 98th Foot; *suc. to the Baronetcy*, in 1813; was M.P. for co. Galway (two Parls.), 1830-32, Sheriff, 1838, and, subsequently, Vice-Lieut. of that county. He *m.* 18 May 1812, at St. James', Westm., Elizabeth Mary, 1st da. of the Rt. Hon. John CALCRAFT, of Rempstone Hall, Dorset (illegit. s. of John CALCRAFT, of Ingress, Kent), by Elizabeth Mary, da. and coheir of Sir Thomas Pym HALES, 4th Baronet [1660]. He *d.* 14 Sep. 1847, at Ely Place, Dublin, in his 66th year. Will pr. Nov. 1847. His widow, who was *b.* 9 July 1791, *d.* 27 Jan. 1859, at Dublin.

III. 1847. SIR THOMAS JOHN BURKE, Baronet [I. 1797], of Marble Hill aforesaid, 1st s. and h., *b.* 7 June 1813; sometime Capt. 1st Dragoons; *suc. to the Baronetcy*, 14 Sep. 1847; M.P. for co. Galway (five Parls.), May 1847 to 1865. He *m.* 21 Feb. 1857, Mary Frances, 2d da. of Anthony Francis (NUGENT), 9th EARL OF WESTMEATH [I.], by Anne Catherine, da. and coheir of Malachy DALY. He *d.* at Marble Hill, 9 Dec. 1875, aged 62. His widow, who was *b.* 3 Oct. 1831, *d.* 2 Sep. 1892, aged 61.

(a) The marriage thus celebrated in a church of the Established Church was (though legal) protested against as being non-canonical, the divorced wife being alive.

(b) See p. 347, note "c," under "BURDETT."

(c) See p. 429, note "d," under "LIGHTON."

V

IV. 1875. SIR JOHN CHARLES BURKE, Baronet [I. 1797], of Marble Hill aforesaid, 1st s. and h., *b.* 7 Feb. 1858; ed. at Sandhurst College; *suc. to the Baronetcy*, 9 Dec. 1875; 2d Lieut. 20th Hussars, 1879. He *d.* unm., 16 Aug. 1880, at Newbridge, Ireland, in his 23d year.

V. 1880. SIR HENRY GEORGE BURKE, Baronet [I. 1797], of Marble Hill aforesaid, br. and h., *b.* 30 Dec. 1859; *suc. to the Baronetcy*, 16 Aug. 1880; ed. at the Oratory and at Trin. Coll., Dublin; B.A., 1879; Lieut. Connaught Rangers Militia, 1881-85; Sheriff of co. Galway, 1883.

Family Estates.—These, in 1878,(a) consisted of 25,258 acres in co. Galway and 2,230 in co. Roscommon. *Total* —27,488 acres, worth £8,339 a year.

JERVIS-WHITE-JERVIS:

cr. 6 Dec. 1797.(b)

I. 1797. "JOHN JERVIS-WHITE-JERVIS, of Bally Ellis, co. Wexford, Esq.,"(b) as also of Belcamp, near Coolock, co. Dublin, *formerly* John JERVIS-WHITE, 1st s. and h. of John JERVIS-WHITE, of Bally Ellis aforesaid,(c) Barrister (*d.* 12 July 1793), by Elizabeth, da. of George WHITBOURNE, of Dublin, was *b.* 10 June 1765; was a Barrister (Dublin), Trinity, 1791(d); took, by royal lic., 6 Nov. 1793, the name of JERVIS after his own surname; raised a corps of Riflemen in co. Wexford in 1796 to support the Government, and was *cr. a Baronet* [I.], as above, 6 Dec. 1797, the privy seal being dat. 10 Oct. previous. He subsequently, in 1803, raised a like corps in co. Somerset. He *m.* firstly, 1 June 1789, Jane, 1st da. of Henry NISBETT, of Aghmore, co. Longford, by Elizabeth, da. of George WRIGHTSON, Alderman of Dublin. He *m.* secondly, in 1828, Mary, da. of Thomas BRADFORD, of Sandbach, co. Chester. He *d.* in 1830, aged 65. His widow married[?] her late husband's nephew, John JERVIS-WHITE, LL.D., of Ferns, co. Wicklow, Barrister (who *d.* s.p. 1873) and *d.* 15 July 1879, aged 77, at Cambridge Terrace, Hyde Park.

II. 1830. SIR HENRY MEREDYTH JERVIS-WHITE-JERVIS, Baronet [I. 1797], of Bally Ellis and Belcamp aforesaid, 2d but 1st surv. s. and h.(e) by 1st wife, *b.* 20 Nov. 1793 at Belcamp; entered the Royal Navy and became Commander; *suc. to the Baronetcy* in 1830; Sheriff of co. Dublin, 1837. He *m.* 16 Dec. 1818, Marian, da. of William CAMPBELL, of Fairfield, co. Ayr, by his 2d wife, Catherine, da. of William GUNNING, br. of Sir Robert GUNNING, 1st Baronet [1778]. She *d.* 8 March 1861, at Blackgang Chine, Isle of Wight. He *d.* 17 March 1869, in Dublin, aged 75.

III. 1869. SIR HUMPHREY CHARLES JERVIS-WHITE-JERVIS, Baronet [I. 1797], of Bally Ellis and Belcamp aforesaid, 2d but 1st surv. s. and h.,(f) *b.* 1 Jan. 1821; *suc. to the Baronetcy*, 17 March 1869. He *m.* 22 May 1875, at St. Mary Magdalen's, Munster Sq., Regent's Park, Kate Evelyn

(a) See p. 347, note "c," under "BURDETT."
(b) See p. 429, note "d," under "LIGHTON."
(c) This John was s. and h. of another John Jervis-White, of Bally Ellis (*d.* 7 Nov. 1769, aged 69), who was only s. and h. of John White, of Bally Ellis (*d.* Oct. 1723), by Catherine, only surv. da. and h. of Sir Humphrey Jervis, Lord Mayor of Dublin, 1681-82. Her descendants assumed the name of Jervis before that of White.
(d) He was not, however, "LL.D." as is stated in Foster's *Baronetage* [1883].
(e) The 1st son, John, was *b.* at Hertford, 23 April 1790, and *d.* v.p., 26 Jan. 1803.
(f) The 1st son, Rev. John Jervis-White-Jervis, B.A., *b.* 16 Sep. 1819, *m.* but *d.* s.p. and v.p., 23 Nov. 1863, at Nice.

D'Aubin, da. of James MCKAIN, of Pembroke, as also of Bordeaux and Paris. He *d.* s.p., 23 July 1887, at Hastings in his 67th year. His widow *d.* 18 March 1895, at Littlehampton, Sussex.

IV. 1887. SIR JOHN HENRY JERVIS-WHITE-JERVIS, Baronet [I. 1797], of Bally Ellis and Belcamp aforesaid, nephew and h., being 1st s. and h. of Henry JERVIS-WHITE-JERVIS, of Felixtow, co. Suffolk, Capt. and Hon. Col. Royal Artillery, sometime (1859-80) M.P. for Harwich, by Lucy, 1st da. of John Chevallier COBBOLD, sometime (1847-68), M.P. for Ipswich, which Henry, who *d.* 22 Sep. 1881, aged 56, was next br. of the late Baronet. He was *b.* 4 July 1857; entered the Royal Artillery, becoming finally Lieut.-Col., serving in 1879 in the Zulu War, and in the Transvaal, 1899, but retired in 1903; *suc. to the Baronetcy*, 23 July 1887. He, shortly afterwards, *m.* 9 Aug. 1887, at St. Philip's and St. James', Cheltenham, his second cousin, Margaret Frances Lockhart, yst. da. of Capt. George Gunning John CAMPBELL, Royal Horse Artillery, Madras.

Family Estates.—These, in 1878,(a) consisted of 1,216 acres in co. Wexford, valued at £711, besides 2 acres in the city of Dublin, valued at £1,568 a year, which last then belonged to the father of the 4th Baronet

---

MULLINS:

cr. 7 Dec. 1797(b);

afterwards, since 1800, BARONS VENTRY, co. Kerry [I.].

I. 1797. "THOMAS MULLINS, of Burnham, co. Kerry, Esq.,"(b) 1st s. and h. of William MULLINS, of the same (*d.* 3 May 1761, aged 71), by Mary, da. of George ROWAN, of Mahara, co. Derry, was *b.* 25 Oct. 1736, and was (for what services is unknown) *cr. a Baronet* [I.], as above, 7 Dec. 1797, the privy seal being dat. 11 Oct. previous.(b) He *m.* 5 Oct. 1755, Elizabeth, da. of Townsend GUNN, of Rattoo, co. Kerry, by Elizabeth, da. of Conway BLENNERHASSET, of Castle Conway, in that county. She was living when he was *cr.*, 31 July 1800, BARON VENTRY(c) of Ventry, co. Kerry [I.]. In that peerage this *Baronetcy* then *merged*, and still (1906) so continues. See PEERAGE.

(a) See p. 347, note "c," under "BURDETT."
(b) See p. 429, note "d," under "LIGHTON."
(c) His son and successor, not approving of the name of "Ventry," presented in Feb. 1824 a memorial to the Viceroy [I.], setting forth that he was anxious to change the title by which his peerage was designated, "inasmuch as it is obnoxious to a disagreeable and unpleasant interpretation in continental languages, and would expose memorialist to contempt and ridicule rather than confer that degree of honour and respect which would otherwise attach to a nobleman of the United Kingdom when travelling abroad. That, Memorialist being descended from an ancient family seated centuries ago at Burnham, in the county of Norfolk, and having likewise inherited from his ancestors an estate in the county of Kerry, called Burnham, is desirous to change his title of Lord Baron Ventry and in lieu thereof to be henceforward designated, known and called by the title of Lord Baron Burnham, of Burnham in the county of Kerry." He therefore prayed his Excellency to recommend to His Majesty to grant him royal licence and authority "that he and the other persons in remainder to the said peerage may have, hold and enjoy the privileges conferred in and by the said letters patent by the style, name and title of Lord Baron Burnham of Burnham in lieu of those of Lord Baron Ventry of Ventry." [*Ex inform.* G. D. Burtchaell.]

BROWNE:

cr. 8 Dec. 1797(a);

sometime, 1835-69, DE BEAUVOIR;

ex. 5 Sep. 1890.

I. 1797. "JOHN EDMOND BROWNE, of Palmerstown, co. Mayo, Esq.,"(a) as also of Johnstown, co. Dublin, 2d s. of Dominick BROWNE,(b) of Breaffy, co. Mayo (*d.* 1776, aged 75), by his 2d wife, Anne, da. of John DARCY, of Gurteen, co. Galway, was *b.* 1 Oct. 1748; admitted to Lincoln's Inn, 26 June 1778; Barrister, 1784; Sheriff of co. Mayo, 1791; Capt. of the South Mayo Militia, taking an active part in suppressing the Irish rebels, and was *cr. a Baronet* [I.], as above, 8 Dec. 1797, the privy seal being dat. 12 Oct. previous.(a) He *m.* (Lic. Prerog. [I.], 20 Dec. 1792) Margaret, 2d da. of Matthew LORINAN, of Ardee, co. Louth, by Lucy, 2d da. of Francis LUCAS, of Greenan, co. Monaghan. He *d.* 5 Sep. 1835, at his residence, Holles Street, Dublin, in his 87th year.(c) His widow *d.* 13 March 1843, at Willesden House, Shepherd's Bush, Midx., in her 66th year.

II. 1835. SIR JOHN EDMOND DE BEAUVOIR, Baronet [I. 1797], of Johnstown aforesaid, and of East Harling Hall, co. Norfolk, formerly (1794-1826) John Edmond BROWNE, 1st s. and h., *b.* 10 Dec. 1794; sometime an officer in the 26th Foot; took by royal lic., 14 Oct. 1826, the name of DE BEAUVOIR, instead of BROWNE, in consequence of his marriage; was *Knighted*, 9 March 1827, as the s. and h. ap. of a Baronet;(d) M.P. for Windsor, 1835, till unseated 6 April following; *suc. to the Baronetcy*, 5 Sep. 1835. He *m.* firstly, in 1825 or 1826, Mary, widow of Admiral MACDOUGAL, da. and h. of Richard WRIGHT, of East Harling Hall aforesaid, and said to be "sole next of kin to the Rev. Peter DE BEAUVOIR."(e) She *d.* 11 Feb. 1831. He *m.* secondly, 16 March 1867, Lætitia, da. of the Rev. Charles MANN, of Denvir Hall, Norfolk, Rector of Southery, in that county, by his 2d wife, Susanna, da. of Admiral MACDOUGAL abovenamed. He *d.* s.p., 29 April 1869, in Upper Gloucester Place, Marylebone, aged 74. His widow *d.* probably in 1885.(f)

III. 1869, to 1890. SIR CHARLES MANLEY BROWNE, Baronet [I. 1797], of Johnstown aforesaid, yst. and only surv. br. and h., *b.* 1 March 1806; sometime Capt. Durham Artillery Militia; *suc. to the Baronetcy*, 29 April 1869. He *m.* in 1840, Jane, da. of Thomas Macaulay CRUTTWELL, of Perrymead Lodge, near Bath. She (who appears to have been divorced) *d.* in 1863. He *d.* s.p.s.,(g) 5 Sep. 1890, aged 84, and was *bur.* from 58 Gloucester Crescent, Hyde Park, at Kensal Green cemetery, when the *Baronetcy* became *extinct*.

(a) See p. 429, note "d," under "LIGHTON."
(b) This Dominick was s. and h. of Andrew, who was s. and h. of another Dominick, both of Breaffy aforesaid, the last being 3d and yst. s. of Sir John Browne, 1st Baronet [S. 1636], of the Neale, and consequently br. to Sir George Browne, 2d Baronet, ancestor to the Barons Kilmaine [I.], and to Col. John Browne, ancestor to the Marquesses of Sligo [I.].
(c) See *Gent. Mag.*, 1835, p. 427.
(d) See p. 372, note "a," under "COTTER," for a similar case as late as 1874.
(e) Burke's *Baronetage*, 1841.
(f) Her name appears in Dod's *Baronetage* for 1885, but is absent in the one for 1886.
(g) His only son, John, *b.* 14 April 1841, *d.* unm. and v.p., 1877.

BRABAZON:

cr. 16 Dec. 1797(a);

ex. 24 Oct. 1840.

I. 1797. "ANTHONY BRABAZON, of New Park, co. Mayo, Esq.,"(a) 1st s. and h. of George BRABAZON, of the same (*d.* 29 March 1780), by Sarah (*d.* Aug. 1797), da. of Dominick BURKE, of Clorough, co. Galway, was *b.* probably about 1750, and was, for what services is unknown, *cr. a Baronet* [I.], as above, 16 Dec. 1797, the privy seal being dat. 13 Oct. previous.(a) He *m.* March 1774,(b) Anne, 1st da. of the Rt. Hon. Sir Capel MOLYNEUX, 3d Baronet [I. 1730], by his 1st wife, Elizabeth, da. of William EAST, of Hall Place, Berks. He *d.* 3 July 1803, and was *bur.* at Kilconduff, near Swinford. Will pr. [I.] 1805. His widow survived him many years.

II. 1803, to 1840. SIR WILLIAM JOHN BRABAZON, Baronet [I. 1797], of Newpark, *otherwise* Brabazon Park aforesaid, 2d but only surv. s. and h., *suc. to the Baronetcy*, 3 July 1803; Sheriff of co. Mayo, 1826; M.P. for that county, 1835 till death. He *d.* unm., 24 Oct. 1840, at Brabazon Park aforesaid, when the *Baronetcy* became *extinct*.(c) Will dat. 20 Jan. 1840.

MACARTNEY:

cr. 4 Jan. 1799.(a)

I. 1799. "SIR JOHN MACARTNEY, of Lish, co. Armagh, Knt.,"(a) 2d s. of William MACARTNEY, of Belfast, many years (1747-60) M.P. [I.] for that town (*d.* 1797), by Catherine, da. of Thomas BANKES, was M.P. [I.] for Fore, 1793-97, and for Naas, 1798-1800; was "in consequence of his energetic exertions in the promotion of the inland navigation of Ireland, *Knighted* at the opening of the Grand Canal Docks,"(d) 29 April 1796, and was *cr. a Baronet* [I.], as above, 4 Jan. 1799, the privy seal being dat. 25 June previous.(a) He was Deputy Chief Remembrancer of the Exchequer [I.]. He *m.* firstly (Lic. Prerog. [I.], 26 Feb. 1778), Anne, da. of Edward SCRIVEN, by Elizabeth, da. of John BARCLAY, of Dublin. By her he had seven children. He *m.* secondly, 4 (Lic. Prerog. [I.], 3) Nov. 1794, Catherine, da. of the Rt. Hon. Walter HUSSEY-BURGH, Chief Baron of the Exchequer [I.], 1782-83, by Anne, da. of Thomas BURGH, of Bert, co. Kildare. He *d.* 29 May 1812. His widow, by whom also he had issue, *d.* 17 Sep. 1840, in her 70th year.

(a) See p. 429, note "d," under "LIGHTON."
(b) He is erroneously stated in Foster's *Baronetage* [1883] to have *m.* in 1776 Anne, elder da. and coheir of George William Molyneux, by Catherine, da. of Richard Gore, the said George William being 2d son of Sir Capel abovenamed. Sir Anthony's own statement, 2 March 1799, is "I married Anne Molyneux, eldest da. to the late Sir Capel Molyneux." [*Ex inform.* G. D. Burtchaell.]
(c) Of his two sisters (1) Anne Mary, *m.* Hercules Sharpe, of Oaklands, in Westfield, Sussex, and had a son, William John Sharpe, who, by royal lic., 23 April 1841, took the name of Brabazon, as did in like manner, 9 Aug. 1847, H. B. Sharpe, presumably his brother; (2) Sarah, *m.* (as his 2d wife) Henry Francis (Roper-Curzon), 14th Baron Teynham, and *d.* s.p., 28 June 1854.
Catherine, sister of the 1st Baronet, *m.* (as his 2d wife) Luke Higgins, of Castlebar, co. Mayo, by whom she had an only son, Hugh Brabazon Higgins, Capt. 15th Hussars, who, having suc. to Brabazon Park and other estates of his mother's family, took by royal lic., 15 Sep. 1852, (Dublin Gazette) the name of Brabazon, and *d.* 1864, leaving issue. [*N. & Q.*, 9th s., viii, 314.]
(d) Playfair's *Baronetage*, 1811.

II. 1812. Sir William Isaac Macartney, Baronet [I. 1799], of Lish aforesaid, 1st s. and h., by 1st wife, *b.* 25 Oct. 1780; ed. at Trin. Coll., Dublin; B.A., 1801; M.A., 1812; having *suc. to the Baronetcy*, 29 May 1812; in Holy Orders; Rector of Desertegny, in the diocese of Derry, till his death. He *m.* 28 May 1818, Ellen, illegit. da. of Sir John Barrington, 9th Baronet [1611]. He *d.* 31 July 1867, at Linsford Glebe, Buncrana, co. Donegal, aged 86. His widow *d.* 7 Sep. 1875, in Londonderry.

III. 1867. Sir John Macartney, Baronet [I. 1799], of Jolimont, Mackay, Queensland, in Australia, 1st s. and h., *b.* 10 Oct. 1832; *suc. to the Baronetcy*, 31 July 1867. He *m.* 1 Sep. 1865, Catherine, 2d da. of Alexander Miller, of Merindindi, Victoria. She *d.* May 1904.

SMITH, *or* SMYTH:

cr. 28 Aug. 1799(a);

afterwards, 1808-36, Cusack-Smith, *and since* 1836, Cusac-Smith.

I. 1799. "Micheal [*sic*] Smyth, of Newtown, in the King's County, Esq., one of the Barons of the Exchequer [I.],"(a) only s. and h. of William Smith, of Newtown aforesaid (*d.* 1747, and was *bur.* at Geashill), by Hester, da. of (—) Lynch, was *b.* 7 Sep. 1740; ed. at Trin. Coll., Dublin; scholar, 1757; B.A., 1759; LL.B., 1777; Barrister (Dublin), Hilary 1769, becoming a Bencher, Hilary 1794; M.P. [I.] for Randalstown, 1783-93; a Baron of the Exchequer [I.], 1793-1801, and was *cr. a Baronet* [I.], as above, 28 Aug. 1799, the privy seal being dat. 10 of the same month;(b) Master of the Rolls [I.], 23 June 1801, till he resigned in June 1806, and P.C. [I.], 21 Aug. 1801. He *m.* firstly, in 1765, Mary Anne, da. of James Cusack, of Ballyronan, co. Wicklow, and Coolmines, co. Dublin, by Angelina, da. and h. of (—) Cruise, of Ballyronan aforesaid. She *d.* 23 June 1798. He *m.* secondly, Eleanor, da. of his first cousin, Michael Smith, Clerk of the Island of St. John, America. He *d.* 17 Dec. 1808, aged 68. Will pr. [I.] 1809. His widow, who was *b.* 1784, *d.* 24 Nov. 1825.

II. 1808. Sir William Cusack-Smith, Baronet [I. 1799], of Newtown aforesaid, formerly William Smith, 1st s. and h., being only s. by 1st wife, *b.* 23 Jan. 1766, in Dublin; matric. at Oxford (Ch. Ch.) as Gentleman Commoner, 26 Nov. 1783, aged 17; B.A., 1786; admitted to Lincoln's Inn, 1784; Barrister (Dublin), Trinity, 1788; LL.D. (Dublin), 1793; "admitted as an Advocate in the Spiritual Court"(c); was M.P. [I.] for Lanesborough, 1794-97; King's Counsel [I.], 1796. By royal lic., 12 March 1800, he took the name of Cusack (being the patronymic of his deceased mother) before that of Smith; Solicitor-General [I.], 6 Dec. 1800,(d) till 27 Dec. 1801, when he became a Baron of the Exchequer [I.],(e) which post he held till his death; Bencher of King's Inns, Dublin, 1802; F.R.S.; *suc. to the Baronetcy*, 17 Dec. 1808. He

(a) See page 429, note "d." under "Lighton."

(b) William Smith, afterwards the 2d Baronet, writes to Sir Chichester Fortescue, Ulster King of Arms, as under: "The Lord Lieut. has been pleased to direct that my father should precede all other Baronets created at the same time. I presume there can be no doubt that this has been done accordingly. I have in my possession my Lord Castlereagh's letter communicating to me the direction of the Lord Lieutenant."

(c) *Annual Register* (Obituary), 1836, and Playfair's *Baronetage*, 1811.

(d) He, when Solicitor-General, and his father, when Baron of the Exchequer, went the same circuit together, early in 1801, as the two Judges of Assize.

(e) He became so in succession to Peter Metge, not (though it is often so stated) to his father, whose successor was the Rt. Hon. St. George Daly, Prime Serjeant. [*Ex inform.* G. D. Burtchaell].

m. 13 Aug. 1787, Hester, 1st da. of Thomas Berry, of Eglish Castle, King's County, by Frances, da. and h. of Knight Berry, of the same. She *d.* 4 June 1832. He *d.* 21 Aug. 1836, at Newton aforesaid, aged 70.

III. 1836. Sir Michael Cusac(a)-Smith, Baronet [I. 1799], of Newtown aforesaid, 1st s. and h., *b.* 21 Dec. 1793; sometime an officer in the 3d Light Dragoons and 11th Hussars; *suc. to the Baronetcy*, 21 Aug. 1836. He *m.* in 1820, Eliza, 2d da. of C. R. Moore. She *d.* June 1828. He *d.* 16 May 1859, at Leybourne Rectory, Kent, the house of his son-in-law, Rev. Henry Charles Hawley.

IV. 1859. Sir William Cusac-Smith, Baronet [I. 1799], 1st s. and h., *b.* 1822; sometime an officer in the 10th Royal Wurtemberg Lancers; *suc. to the Baronetcy*, 16 May 1859.

CHINNERY:

cr. 29 Aug. 1799(b);

ex. 20 Aug. 1868.

I. 1799. "Broderick Chinnery, of Flintfield, co. Cork, Esq.,"(c) 3d and yst. s.(d) of the Rev. George Chinnery, of Midleton, co. Cork (will dat. 13 Jan. 1753, pr. [I.] 23 April 1755), by Eleanor, da. of Dr. William Whitfield, and Catherine, his wife, sister of Alan (Brodrick), 1st Viscount Midleton [I.], da. of Sir St. John Brodrick, was *b.* probably about 1740; Barrister (Dublin), Easter 1763; M.P. [I.] for Castlemartyr, 1783-90, and for Bandonbridge (two Parls.), 1790-1800, being M.P. [U.K.] for Bandonbridge aforesaid (two Parls.), 1801-06; Sheriff of co. Cork, 1786, and was *cr. a Baronet* [I.], as above, 29 Aug. 1799,(b) the privy seal being dat. 12th of the same month. He *m.* firstly, Feb. 1768, his cousin, Margaret, da. and h. of Nicholas Chinnery, of Flintfield aforesaid, by Barbara, da. of Roger O'Callaghan, of Derrygallon, co. Cork. She *d.* 1 Oct. 1783. He *m.* secondly, 2 July 1789, Alice, 4th da. of Robert Ball, of Youghal, co. Cork, by Mary, da. of Bent Croker. He *d.* May 1808. Will dat. 17 July to 12 Sep. 1807, pr. [I.] 19 Jan. 1809 and [E.] April 1809 and Nov. 1834. His widow, who was *b.* 1760, *d.* 1833. Admon. [I.], 18 Jan. 1834.

II. 1808. Sir Broderick Chinnery, Baronet [I. 1799], of Flintfield aforesaid, 3d but 1st surv. s. and h., being yst. s.(e) by the 1st wife, *b.* 29 May 1779; *suc. to the Baronetcy*, May 1808. He *m.* 25 Feb. 1803, Diana Elizabeth, yst. da. of George Vernon, of Clontarf Castle, co. Dublin, by Elizabeth, relict of (—) Hughes, da. of (—). She *d.* 16 June 1824. He *d.* 19 Jan. 1840, aged 60. Will dat. 9 Jan. 1840, pr. Feb. 1840, and [I.] 18 March 1841.

III. 1840, to 1868. Sir Nicholas Chinnery, Baronet [I. 1799], of Flintfield aforesaid, and of 18 Hyde Park Sq., Paddington, only s. and h., *b.* 7 July 1804, at Bath; ed. at Queen's Coll., Cambridge; B.A., 1826; M.A., 1829; in Holy Orders; *suc. to the Baronetcy*, 19 Jan. 1840 He *m.* 27 March 1843, at St. Peter's, Dublin, his 1st cousin once removed, Anna, da. of the Rev. John Fane Vernon of Aubawn, co. Cavan, by Frances,

(a) He appears to have altered the spelling of Cusack to Cusac.

(b) This is the date given in Playfair's *Baronetage*, 1811, and, as it is the day after the creation of Smith, the royal warrant whereof was 10 Aug., two days before that for this creation, it seems most probable.

(c) See p. 429, note "d," under "Lighton."

(d) His eldest br., George Chinnery, Bishop of Cloyne, *d.* s.p. 20 Aug. 1780.

(e) Of the two elder sons (1) Nicholas Chinnery, matric. at Oxford (Trin. Coll.), 15 Feb. 1787, aged 18, *d.* unm., 1790, aged 21; (2) George Chinnery, *d.* Aug. 1797, aged 23.

da. of John Kearney, D.D., Bishop of Ossory, 1806-13. She and he perished together, 20 Aug. 1868, being (with Lord and Lady Farnham [I.] and twenty-eight others) burned to cinders by an explosion of petroleum, caused by a terrific accident on the London and North Western Railway, near Abergele, in North Wales, and were *bur.* there. On his death s.p.m.(a) aged 64 (20 Aug. 1868, as aforesaid), the *Baronetcy* became *extinct*.

GILLMAN:

cr. 1 Oct. 1799;(b)

ex. 1815.

I. 1799, to 1815. "Sir John St. Leger Gillman, of the city of Cork, Knt.,"(c) as also of Carriheen, co. Cork, 1st and only surv. s. of St. Leger Heyward Gillman, of Carriheen aforesaid, (*d.* 4 Nov. 1757), by Elizabeth Anne, da. of Harding Parker, of Hillbrook, co. Cork, was *b.* 21 Nov. 1756; ed. at Trin. Coll., Dublin; Barrister (Dublin), Trinity 1784; *Knighted*, 1796, and was *cr. a Baronet* [I.], as above, 1 Oct. 1799, the privy seal being dat. 13 Aug. previous. He *m.* 10 June 1790, Hannah, da. of Sir Thomas Miller, 5th Baronet [1705], by his 1st wife, Hannah, da. of (—) Black, Alderman of Norwich. She *d.* 30 May 1803. He *d.* s.p.m.s.,(c) at Bath, 1815, aged 58, when the *Baronetcy* became *extinct*. Will pr. 1817.

WHEELER-DENNY-CUFFE:

cr. 30 Dec. 1800;(b)

afterwards, 1820? *to* 1853, Denny-Wheeler-Cuffe;

and since 1853, Wheeler-Cuffe.

I. 1800. "Jonah Wheeler-Denny-Cuffe, of Leyrath, co. Kilkenny, Esq.,"(b) 1st s. and h. of Sir Richard Wheeler-Denny-Cuffe,(d) of Leyrath aforesaid, by Rebecca (*m.* 10 Dec. 1768), 1st da. of Eland Mossom, of Mount Eland, co. Kilkenny, Recorder of Kilkenny, which Richard (who *d.* June 1797, at Leyrath), *formerly* Richard Wheeler, was s. and h. of Jonah

(a) Anne Elizabeth Frances Margaretta, his only da. and h., *m.* 23 Aug. 1864, James Robert Alexander Haldane, D.D., Bishop of Argyll and the Isles, 1883-1906, who consequently, by royal lic., 29 July 1864, took the name of Chinnery *after* that of Haldane. He, by a subsequent royal lic., 2 Sep. 1878, took the said name of Chinnery *before* his patronymic of Haldane, and *d.* Feb. 1906, aged 63, leaving issue.

(b) See p. 429, note "d," under "Lighton."

(c) Of his sons (1) George Gillman *d.* young; (2) John St. Leger Gillman, *b.* 25 Jan. 1794, at Walcot, near Bath; matric. at Oxford (Balliol Coll.), 14 May 1812, aged 18, but *d.* unm. and v.p. soon afterwards, 25 Oct. 1812. Of his daughters (1) Hannah Anne, *d.* young; (2) Hannah Elizabeth, *m.* 30 Aug. 1835, the Rev. J. D'Arcy Preston, M.A.; (3) Margaret Emily; (4) Frances.

(d) He is stated in Foster's *Baronetage* [1873] to have been *Knighted* 8 Dec. 1768, and in Playfair's *Baronetage* [1811] to have been *Knighted* by the Duke of Portland, when Viceroy [I.]. This Viceroyship was from April to Sep. 1782, but this Richard, in his son's entrance to Lincoln's Inn, 17 May 1790, is described as "Wheeler Cuffe, *Esq.*," so that his Knighthood appears to have been subsequent to either date.

Wheeler,(a) of Leyrath aforesaid (*d.* 28 Jan. 1776), by Elizabeth (*m.* 22 Dec. 1743), da. and coheir of Denny Cuffe, of Sandhill, co. Carlow (br. of John, 1st Baron Desart [I.]), and, having inherited the estates of his mother's family, assumed the additional surnames of Denny-Cuffe. He was *b.* about 1769; admitted to Lincoln's Inn, 17 May 1790; was Sheriff of co. Kilkenny, 1797, and was *cr. a Baronet* [I.], as above (being the last person who received an *Irish* Baronetcy), 30 Dec. 1800, the privy seal being dat. as long previous as 14 Aug. 1799.(b) Sometime after his creation he transposed the names of Wheeler and Denny, and took for his surname that of Denny-Wheeler-Cuffe. He was Mayor of Kilkenny, 1823-24. He *m.* 31 Jan. 1814, Elizabeth, da. of William Browne, of Browne's Hill, co. Carlow, by Charlotte, da. of Joseph Deane (Bourke), 3d Earl of Mayo [I.], and Archbishop of Tuam. He *d.* 9 May 1853, at Leyrath, in his 84th year. His widow *d.* 15 Jan. 1871, at "The Rocks," co. Kilkenny.

II. 1853. Sir Charles Frederick Denny Wheeler-Cuffe, Baronet [I. 1800], of Leyrath aforesaid, 2d but 1st surv. s. and h., *b* 1 Sep. 1832; *suc. to the Baronetcy*, 9 May 1853; ed. at Sandhurst; Capt. 66th Foot, 1857; Brigade-Major of the Queen's troops at Malta, 1858-60, and served in the Indian Mutiny campaign, 1858-59 (medal); Major in the Army, 1859, retiring from the Army, 1862; Sheriff of co. Kilkenny, 1863. He *m.* 2 July 1861, at Affane, co. Waterford, Pauline Villiers-Stuart, spinster, illegit. da. of Henry (Villiers-Stuart), Baron Stuart de Decies, by Madame de Ott. She *d.* s.p., 5 July 1895.

Family Estates.—These, in 1878, consisted of 1,738 acres in co. Kilkenny, valued at £1,388 a year.

(a) This Jonah was 4th in descent from Jonah Wheeler, D.D., Bishop of Ossory, who *d.* 19 April 1640, in his 97th year.

(b) See p. 429, note "d," under "Lighton."

Jacobite Baronetcies.

created 11 Dec. 1688 to 31 Jan. 1788.

Being (1) those made by JAMES II after his dethronement, 11 Dec. 1688, till his death, (2) those made by his son and successor, TITULAR JAMES III (the Chevalier de St. George), 16 Sep. 1701 till his death, and (3) finally those made by that Prince's son and successor, TITULAR CHARLES III (Prince Charles Edward), 1 Jan. 1766, till his death, 31 Jan. 1788, when such creations ceased inasmuch as neither Baronetcies nor Peerages were conferred by that Prince's brother and successor, TITULAR HENRY IX (Cardinal York), on whose death, 13 July 1807, the male descendants of the Stuart Kings became *extinct*, and the assumption of the royal title ceased.

These creations, whether English, Scotch or Irish, are in the subjoined account classed together chronologically, and it must be borne in mind that the Act of Union with Scotland, in 1707, was not acknowledged by these Princes so that the creations made by them after that date still continue as *of England* or *of Scotland*, and not (as was the case in the creations by the Constitutional Sovereigns) as *of Great Britain*.

An account of these creations, of which till recently very little was known, has been admirably set forth by the Marquis of Ruvigny and Raineval in a work entitled "The Jacobite Peerage, Baronetage, Knightage, and Grants of Honour" (1 vol., pp. 268, Edinburgh, T.C. and E.C. Jack, 1904), with genealogical notes by its author. To this work the reader is referred for fuller particulars than those that are here given, and to it the Editor is for the most part indebted for the information set forth below.

CREATION BY JAMES II.

After his dethronement, 11 Dec. 1688, till his death, 16 Sep. 1701.(a)

ASHTON [E.]:(b)

cr. in or shortly before Nov. 1692.

"(—) ASHTON, s. and h. of John ASHTON [of St. Paul's, Covent Garden, Midx.], sometime Clerk of the Closet to Mary of Modena,"(c) the Queen Consort, by Mary (marr. lic. Vic. Gen. 15 Dec. 1685, he about 32 and she about 19), da. of Edward RIGBY, of London, mercer (which lady *d.* at St. Germains, 1694), the said John(d) having been executed at Tyburn, 28 Jan. 1690/1, for high treason in adhering to James II (declaring on the scaffold that he was a Protestant and was glad to lose

(a) It seems probable that James II (who created after his dethronement about 10 English, 5 Scotch, and 11 Irish peerages) conferred more Baronetcies than this one, though the record of such creations has, apparently, perished.

(b) The whole of the information in this article has been supplied by W. D. Pink.

(c) Ruvigny's *Jacobite Peerage, Baronetage, Knightage, and Grants of Honour* [1904]. See remarks thereon, in text above, lines 18 to 24.

(d) This John Ashton was son of Andrew Ashton, a Royalist Captain in 1644 (*bur.* 1679, at Fernworth), who mentions him in his will (pr. at Chester, 1679/80), and who was 3d son of Thomas Ashton, of Penketh, co. Lancaster, who *d.* 1645.

his life in the service of one "from whom he had received favours for 16 years past"), was *b.* between 1687 and 1691, and, at a very early age, was *cr. a Baronet* [E.], by the exiled King, James II, in or shortly before Nov. 1692.(a) He *d.* probably soon afterwards.(b)

CREATIONS BY THE TITULAR KING JAMES III.

16 Sep. 1701 to 1 Jan. 1766.

LALLY [I.]:

cr. 7 July 1707.

"GERARD LALLY, 2d s. of Thomas LALLY, *or* O'MULLALLY,(c) of Tullaghnadaly, co. Galway (will 7 June 1677), by Jane, sister of Theobald, 7th VISCOUNT DILLON [I.],"(d) da. of Capt. Robert DILLON, of Loughglyn, co. Roscommon, was an officer in the Army of James II, but, after the surrender of Limerick, 3 Oct. 1691, retired to France, becoming eventually, 28 Oct. 1708, Lieut.-Col. of Dillon's Regiment, being that of his maternal uncle. He was *cr. a Baronet* [I.], as above, 7 July 1707, by patent dat. at St. Germain-en-laye, and was, 20 Feb. 1734, made Brig.-General in the French Army, with a promise of being made "Maréchal-de-Camp" at the next promotion, with the precedency of 1719. He *m.* 18 April 1701, at Romano, in Dauphiny, in the diocese of Vienne, Anne Mary, da. of Charles Jacques DE BRESSAC, SEIGNEUR DE LA VACHE. He *d.* at Arras, Nov. 1737, leaving male issue.(e)

(a) "Mrs. Ashton, wife to him lately executed, with her son, went to France, and at her arrival at Paris King James made him a Baronet." [Luttrell's *Diary*, 8 Nov. 1692.].

(b) Of his brothers, John the eldest, was *bur.* 30 June 1686, at St. Faith's, London; Edward was *bur.* there 20 May 1689, as also another child (unnamed) 11 Aug. 1691, the father being there buried on the day of his death. The only child, apparently, who reached maturity was Mary Ann Isabella, who *m.* the Rev. Richard Venn, M.A., Rector of St. Antholin's, London, and who *d.* 25 Jan. 1762, leaving issue.

(c) See an article by "G.D.B." in *N. & Q.*, 9th S, x. 453, as to this family, shewing their descent from William O'Mullally, Archbishop of Tuam, 1573-95.

(d) See Ruvigny's *Jacobite Creations*, as on p. 446, note "c."

(e) The right to this Baronetcy devolved on and appears to have been assumed by (1) his only s. and h., Thomas Arthur Lally, who is accordingly set forth as the 2d Baronet in Ruvigny's *Jacobite Creations*, see p. 446, note "c"). He was *b.* at Romano and *bap.* there, 15 Jan. 1702. He was a distinguished military officer, and as Colonel of a newly-raised Irish infantry regiment served through the campaign of 1745, and was accordingly *cr.*, 16 Jan. 1745/6 (by the titular King James III), EARL OF MOENMOYNE, VISCOUNT BALLYMOLE and BARON TOLLENDALLY [I.], being about the same time *cr.* or recognised by Louis XV as COUNT OF LALLY and BARON OF TOLLENDAL in France. He was executed in Paris, 9 May 1766, by decree of the *Parlement de Paris*, leaving (by Felicité, his wife, da. of John Crofton, of co. Longford) an only s. and h., (2) Trophime Gerard Lally, 2d Count of Lally in France, etc., *b.* in the parish of St. Lawrence, Paris, 10 March 1751, Deputy of the *Noblesse* of Paris to the States General, 1789, who, many years later, was *cr.* by Louis XVIII, 19 Aug. 1815, MARQUIS DE LALLY-TOLLENDAL, and a Peer of France. He *d.* in Paris, s.p.m., 11 March 1830, in his 80th year, when the issue male of the grantee of 1707 became *extinct*.

RONCHI [E.]:

cr. 24 July 1715.

"JOSEPH RONCHI, was *cr.* 24 July 1715, *a Knight and Baronet* [E.], with rem. to the heirs male of his body."(a) He *d.* (—).(b)

SHERLOCK [I.]:

cr. 9 Dec. 1716.

"SIR PETER SHERLOCK, Knt., was *cr.*, 9 Dec. 1716, *a Knight and Baronet* [I.], with rem. to the heirs male of his body."(a) He, apparently, was the Peter (Don Pedro) SHERLOCK, of Madrid, in Spain, Colonel of the Spanish Regiment de Ultonia, who was *b.* in co. Waterford, *m.* Mary (Donna Maria), da. of (—) RONAN, and who *d.* in or before 1751 (will pr. [I.] 1751), leaving a son, Don Juan SHERLOCK, Captain in the said regiment before 1761, and Colonel in 1765. This Peter was son of James (Don Diego) SHERLOCK, of Balyna, co. Wexford (will dated 16 June 1696, pr. [I.] 1698), by Eleanor (Donna Leonora), da. of Walter TALBOT, of Ballynamona, co. Wexford, the said James being s. of Peter SHERLOCK (2d s. of James SHERLOCK, of Gracedieu, co. Waterford), by Joane, da. of Sir George SHERLOCK. [*Ex inform.* G. D. Burtchaell, the pedigree being registered in Ulster's office, Dublin.] "He appears to have been engaged in commerce, there being repeated allusions to his *barques*. As late as May 1716 he is spoken as *Mr.* Sherlock." [*Ex inform.* W. D. Pink.] The death of "SIR RICHARD SHERLOCK, BARONET," 15 June 1730, is recorded in Musgrave's *Obituary*, but his connection, if any, with this grantee has not been ascertained.

REDMOND [E.]:

cr. 20 Dec. 1717.

"SIR PETER REDMOND, Knight of the Order of Christ,"(a) of Portugal, s. of Michael REDMOND, of the Hall, co. Wexford, by Catherine, da. of Peter SHERLOCK, of Gracedieu, co. Waterford, was "*cr.*, 20 Dec. 1717, *a Knight and Baronet* [E.], with rem. to heirs male of his body."(a) On 1 Jan. 1718 he was appointed (by the titular James III) Consul-Gen. for Portugal, and on 15 Dec. 1721 was *cr.* BARON [REDMOND] [I.], with rem. to heirs male of his body. He *m.* Anne, 1st da. of Robert PARKER, of Templeogue, co. Dublin. He *d.* probably before 26 March 1732,(c) leaving male issue.(d)

(a) See Ruvigny's *Jacobite Creations*, as on p. 446, note "c."

(b) Presumably the same Joseph Ronchi, who was *cr. a Baronet* [E.] by the same titular King, 5 Oct. 1722, whom see.

(c) On that date his four daughters, probably being then orphans, had a declaration of their noblesse. These were (1) Elizabeth Bridget, who *m.* James Nugent, styling himself a Baronet [I. 1622], see vol. i, p. 231; (2) Frances, and (3) Anna, both living unm. in Paris, 1763; (4) [—] who *d.* young.

(d) The right to the Baronetcy devolved on his only s., John Redmond, Knight of the Order of Christ of Portugal, and of the Military Order of St. Louis of France, Maréchal de Camp, in the French army, 1763, when he registered his pedigree in Ulster's office, Dublin. [*Ex inform.* G. D. Burtchaell].

WOGAN [I.]:

cr. 1719.

"SIR CHARLES WOGAN, 2d s. of William WOGAN, of Rathcoffy, and Anne(a) GAYDON, his wife,"(b) was [it is said(b)] *b.* about 1698,(c) and, having taken part in the Rising of 1715, was taken prisoner at Preston, 14 Nov. 1715, his trial for high treason being fixed for 5 May 1716, but with seven others (out of fifteen who essayed to do so) escaped, the day previous, from Newgate to France, where he served in the Dillon Regiment till 1718; was, 27 April 1719, instrumental in releasing "in a romantic manner" the Princess Mary Clementina Sobieska from the Castle of Innspruck, where, on her way to be married to the titular King James III, she had been imprisoned by the Emperor of Germany, he being in reward "*cr. a Knight and Baronet* [I.], with rem. to his heirs male,"(b) and having, 13 June 1719, "the title of Roman Senator"(b) conferred on him by the Pope. He entered the Spanish service; was at the relief of Santa Cruz, from the siege, by the Moors, in 1723; was before 1730 Brig.-General and Governor of La Mancha; was Governor of Barcelona in 1750, and "General de Brigade." He *d.* s.p.m., probably unm., in Spain, soon after 1752.(d)

(a) This Anne was da. of John Gaydon, by (—), da. of (—) Sutton, which John was s. of Nicholas Gaydon, by Bridget, sister of Richard [Talbot], Duke of Tyrconnell [I.], da. of Sir William Talbot, 1st Baronet [I. 1623].

(b) See Ruvigny's *Jacobite Creations*, as on p. 446, note "c."

(c) If (as stated in Ruvigny's *Jacobite Creations*, see p. 446, note "c") he was "*b.* about 1698," his parentage (which is by no means certain) could not possibly be as given in the text and in Count O'Kelly's *Famille de Wogan* [Paris, 1896], inasmuch as William Wogan, who was s. of Nicholas Wogan, of Rathcoffy, co. Kildare, by Catherine, da. of Jenico (Preston) Viscount Gormanstown [I.], and who (by Anne Gaydon) is there given as father of the Baronet ("*b.* about 1698"), *d.* in or before 1672, when his br., John Wogan, took out admon. to him as he did in 1690 to their mother, Catherine Wogan, otherwise Preston. This John (not William) Wogan, who was Sheriff of co. Kildare, 1687 and 1688, and M.P. [I.] for that county in King James' Parliament of 1689, and who was apparently the eldest son (transmitting the estate to his descendants) is, strangely enough, ignored in O'Kelly's work. He *m.* Judith, da. of Anthony O'Moore, of Balyna, co. Kildare, and was succeeded by his s. Nicholas Wogan, who *m.* Rose, da. and coheir of Sir Neill O'Neill, 2d Baronet [I. 1666]. This Nicholas is stated in O'Kelly's work, (very confusingly) to have been a *brother* of Sir Charles, the grantee. [*Ex inform.* G. D. Burtchaell].

(d) The limitation being to "heirs male" the right to this dignity is stated to have devolved on his nephew (1) Edward Wogan, a yr. s. of his br., Patrick Wogan, of Richardstown, being his 1st s. by his 3d wife. This Edward *d.* s.p. at Manila, 1771-82, and was suc. by his brother (2) Francis Wogan, or de Wogan, *bap.* 1 June 1720 at Clane, co. Kildare; distinguished himself with the Irish Brigade at the Battle of Lauffeld, 2 July 1747; was naturalised in France, Feb. 1764; was a Knight of the Order of St. Louis, and was living 1781. His 1st surv. s. and h., (3) Edward John Peter de Wogan, *b.* 29 March 1778, at Dinan, *d.* 1854, leaving issue; (4) Emile Edward de Wogan, *b.* at Dinan, 13 March 1817, Knight of the Legion of Honour, 11 Aug. 1850, *d.* in Paris, 23 June 1891, leaving an only s. and h., (5) Emile Tannequy de Wogan, *b.* 23 Nov. 1850, and living 1904. These five persons (and their wives and issue) are set out in full as the 2d, 3d, 4th, 5th and 6th Baronets in Ruvigny's *Jacobite Creations*. See p. 446, note "c." It is, however, doubtful whether Edward Wogan, who assumed the title in or soon after 1752, was the heir male of his father, Patrick Wogan, who, by his 1st wife, Mary Dempsey, had several children.

RONCHI [E.]:

cr. 5 Oct. 1722.

"JOSEPH RONCHI was *cr. a Knight* [*Qy. and Baronet*] [E.], with rem. to heirs male of his body."(a) He *d.* (—).(b)

O'BRIEN, *or* O'BRYAN [I.]:

cr. 19 Jan. 1723.

"JOHN O'BRIEN, *or* O'BRYAN,"(a) was appointed, 13 Oct. 1717, a Colonel of Foot,(c) and was *cr.*, 19 Jan. 1723, *a Knight and Baronet* [I.]." He was, 21 July 1733, appointed Minister at the Court of Paris, and had, 19 Sep. 1736, "full powers to treat with the Court of Madrid."(a) He *d.* (—).(d)

MACLEOD [S.]:

cr. 5 Sep. 1723.

"JOHN MACLEOD, of Glendale and Meidle,"(a) in the Isle of Skye, 1st s. and h. of Alexander MACLEOD, of the same (who retired to France but *d.* at a great age at Ebost, in Skye aforesaid), by his 2d wife Christina, da. of John MACLEOD, of Drynoch, was *b.* probably about 1700; was sometime Page to the titular James III, by whom he was, 5 Sep. 1723, "*cr. a Knight and Baronet* [S.], with rem. to his heirs male."(a) He is sometimes said to have taken part in the Rising of 1745. In 1770 he emigrated to America. He *m.* in or before 1748, Margaret, da. of Lachlan MACQUEEN, of Totorome, in Skye. He *d.* (—), in North Carolina, America, aged 75.(e)

(a) See Ruvigny's *Jacobite Creations*, as on p. 446, note "c."

(b) It seems, however, that "24 July 1715, Bar le Duc," is the date of a warrant for a Baronetcy to Joseph Ronchi, in which case one may presume that the patent of 5 Oct. 1722 to Joseph Ronchi refers to the same person and to this warrant. There are several persons of the name of Ronchi mentioned in the *Stuart Papers*. Joseph Ronchi was probably a br. of Don Pietro Ronchi, Arch-priest of St. Vincent in Bologna, and of Don Giacomo Ronchi, Almoner to Queen Mary [wife of James II] at St. Germain's. In a letter from that Queen, dated 18 Jan. 1694, she refers to this Don Petro Ronchi and *his brothers who have been long attached to my service. Calendar of Stuart Papers*, part i, p. 83, *History MSS. Commission*. [*Ex inform.* W. D. Pink].

(c) He probably is the "[—] O'Bryan" who was appointed, 30 Dec. 1717 "to go to Vienna." There was, however, a "Colonel Daniel O'Bryan," *b.* 1683 (also in the diplomatic service of the titular James III) who was appointed, 15 Nov. 1745 "to be minister to the Court of Paris," and who had, 7 Feb. 1746, "full powers to treat with the Court of Madrid." [Ruvigny's work as above, under *Diplomatic Appointments*], and who eventually 11 Oct. 1746, was *cr.* Earl of Lismore [I.].

(d) See p. 380 as to a "*Sir Patrick O'Brien, Baronet*," who *d.* in 1768, and as to a "*Sir Edward Unick O'Brien, Baronet*," who *d.* in 1798, both of whom were not improbably descended from this grantee, and consequently assumed the style of "Baronet."

(e) The limitation of this dignity was to "heirs male," but the right thereto would devolve on the heirs male *of the body* as under: (1) William Macleod, 2d but 1st surv. s. and h., *b.* about 1750; ed. at Edinburgh, and M.D. of that Univ.; *d.* 10 Aug. 1811, at Borline, in Skye, aged 61; (2) John Macleod, 2d but 1st surv. s. and h., Physician to the Forces in Spain when only 21; *d.* s.p. at Portsmouth,

HIGGINS [I.]:

cr. 6 May 1724.

"DR. HIGGINS, 1st Physician to the King of Spain, was, 6 May 1726, *cr. a Knight and Baronet*" [I.](a). He *d.* (—).(b)

ROBERTSON [S.]:

cr. (as alleged) 1725.

"ALEXANDER ROBERTSON, of Struan, 13th Chief of Clan Robertson, 2d but 1st surv. s. and h. of Alexander ROBERTSON, of the same (*d.* 1687), by his 2d wife, Marion, da. of Gen. BAILLIE, of Letham,"(a) was *b.* about 1668; ed. at St. Andrew's Univ., which (having suc. to the family estate) in 1687 he left, and "joined Dundee"(a) (much against his mother's wishes), for which he was attainted in 1690, and his estates confiscated. He fled to France, returning in 1703 on the accession of Queen Anne, from whom he obtained a pardon. He joined in the Rising of 1715, was taken prisoner at Sheriffmuir, 16 Sep. 1715, but again escaped to France and was again attainted in 1716. He was "in 1725 said to have been *cr. a Knight and Baronet* [S.], with rem. to his heirs male."(a) He returned to Scotland in 1731 and joined in the Rising of 1745 and fought at Prestonpans, being then about 77. He, who was "a poet of some note,"(a) *d.* s.p., presumably unm., 18 April 1749, aged 81, and was *bur.* at Struan.(c)

1814; (3) Bannatyne William Macleod, br. and h., was M.D., and in the Indian Medical service, being Inspector-Gen. of Army Hospitals in Bengal; C.B.; *d.* 1856; (4) Harry John Bannatyne Macleod, only s. and h., *b.* 1824; Col. Royal Artillery; *d.* at Edinburgh, 1877; (5) Bannatyne Macleod, 1st s. and h., *b.* at Hobart, Tasmania, 1860; ed. at Edinburgh and at Clare Coll., Cambridge; M.A.; Barrister (Inner Temple), 1894; Collector and District Magistrate at Madras, 1897; living 1905. These four persons (and their wives and issue) are set out in full as the 2d, 3d, 4th, 5th and 6th Baronets in Ruvigny's *Jacobite Creations*. See p. 446, note "c."

(a) See Ruvigny's *Jacobite Creations*, as on p. 446, note "c."

(b) There was a Thomas Higgins, or Higgons, who was made a Gentleman Usher of the Privy Chamber, 27 Oct. 1701, and was *Knighted* 13 Sep. 1713, being Secretary of State, 24 Dec. 1713 to July 1715. He possibly was the grantee, but there is no evidence of his having been a physician, neither is the Christian name of the grantee known. This Thomas was one of three Jacobite brothers, sons of Sir Thomas Higgons, diplomatist and author, who died 1691. The elder br. George Higgons, was mortally wounded by a bailiff in 1697, and the yst. one Bevill Higgons, historian and poet, *d.* 1735, aged 65.

(c) The limitation being to heirs male, the right to this dignity, as also to the Struan estate, would devolve on his cousin, Duncan Robertson, fourth in descent from Robert Robertson, 10th of Struan, who was great grandfather of the grantee. Duncan's estate was, however, seized by the Crown in 1752, as he had not been, by name, included in the last Act of indemnity. He was suc. by (2) Col. Alexander Robertson, his s. and h., who obtained a restoration of the estates in 1784, and *d.* unm. 1822, being suc. by his cousin and h. male, (3) Alexander Robertson, 5th in descent from Robert Robertson, 10th of Struan above mentioned. He was infeft in the Barony of Struan, 23 June 1824, and *d.* 20 March 1830, being suc. by (4) Major-Gen. George Duncan Robertson, C.B., Knight of the Austrian Order of Leopold, who *d.* 1 July 1842, aged 76, who was suc. by his only s. and h., (5) George Duncan Robertson, *b.* 26 July 1816, Lieut. 42d Highlanders, who

ROBERTSON [S.]:

cr. 10 May 1725.

"ALEXANDER ROBERTSON, of Fascally, co. Perth, s. and h. of Alexander ROBERTSON, of the same,"(a) (who *d.* March 1712), was, 18 May 1725, *cr. a Knight and Baronet* [S.], with rem. to heirs male.(a) He *d.* 1732.(b)

SHERIDAN(c) [I.]:

cr. 17 March 1726.

"THOMAS SHERIDAN, only s. and h. of Thomas SHERIDAN,(d) sometime Private Secretary to James II, by, it is said,(e) a natural da. of that King,"(a) (which Thomas *d.* shortly before 13 Nov. 1712), was Envoy to Prince James Sobieski, 3 Jan. 1723, and was, 17 March 1726, *cr. a Knight and Baronet* [I.]. He was Under Governor to Prince Charles, titular Prince of Wales, 4 June 1727, and was "one of the seven who accompanied that Prince to Scotland in July 1745,"(a) escaping after the Battle of Culloden from Arisaig to Rome, 4 May 1746, where shortly afterwards he *d.* s.p.,(f) 25 Nov. 1746.

d. s.p., 3 April 1864, being suc. by his uncle, (6) Alexander Gilbert Robertson, *b.* 6 March 1805, and *d.* 16 Oct. 1884, who was suc. by his 1st s. and h., (7) Alexander Alasdair Stewart Robertson, of Struan, *b.* 6 Nov. 1863, who, styling himself "Struan Robertson," was living 1905. These seven persons (and their wives and issue) are set out in full as the 2d, 3d, 4th, 5th, 6th, 7th and 8th Baronets in Ruvigny's *Jacobite Creations*. See p. 446, note "c."

(a) See Ruvigny's *Jacobite Creations*, as on p. 446, note "c."

(b) The limitation of this dignity was to heirs male, but the right thereto would devolve in the first place on the heir male *of the body* as under: (1) George Robertson, of Fascally, s. and h., who, on the retreat of the Jacobite Army from Stirling, in Feb. 1745/6, joined Prince Charles, at Perth. He was served heir to his father in 1764, and is said to have been the last of the direct male line "of Fascally," which estate, about 1770, was sold to the Duke of Atholl [S.].

(c) See vol. iii, p. 322, under "SHERIDAN," in the notes to that article.

(d) This Thomas was fourth of the eight sons of the Rev. Denis Sheridan, of Togher, co. Cavan, being yr. br. of the half blood to William Sheridan, D.D., Bishop of Kilmore, 1681 (till deprived in 1691), and to Patrick Sheridan, D.D., Bishop of Cloyne, 1679, till death, 22 Nov. 1682. He was *b.* at St. John's, Trim, co. Meath, 1647; admitted to Trin. Coll., Dublin, 7 Jan. 1660/1, aged 14; B.A., 1664; Fellow, 13 April 1667; Collector of Customs, Cork, 1671; Commissioner of the Revenue [I.], 1687; followed James II into exile, to whom he was Private Secretary and Commissioner of the Household.

(e) This lady, however, is elsewhere called (with more probability) "an English lady, da. of (—) Jones." She has been conjectured to have been a niece of Father Petre.

(f) He is erroneously stated in O'Callaghan's *Irish Brigades* (p. 373) to have left a son, "the Chevalier Michel de Sheridan, or Sir Michael Sheridan." That Michael, however, was evidently the "Michael Sheridan, Col. of Horse in the French service, 1765," who is thus entered in the pedigree (see vol. iii, p. 322, note "d"), and who was *b.* 1715, was Mareschal de Camp, and in 1770 Knight of St. Louis. He was s. of Daniel Sheridan (*d.* 1732), one of the five sons of James Sheridan, yr. br. of Thomas, father of the grantee. The statement in the *Dict. Nat. Biogr.* that Thomas, the grandfather of the well-known Richard Brinsley Sheridan, was a son of this James, is untrue. None of the five sons were named Thomas, and the Thomas next above mentioned entered Trin. Coll., Dublin, 18 Oct. 1707, as son of *Patrick* Sheridan, whose connection with the family is uncertain. [*Ex inform.* G. D. Burtchaell.]

GRÆME [S.]:

cr. 6 Sep. 1726.

"JOHN GRÆME, 1st s. and h. of James GRÆME, of Newton, Solicitor-General [S.], 1688 (*d.* between 1737 and 1740), by Elizabeth, da. of Robert MORAY, of Abercairney, was, 6 Sep. 1726, *cr. a Knight and Baronet* [S.], in reward for his services at the Court of Vienna, and the same day was appointed Minister of that Court."(a) In April 1727 he was for a short time Chief Secretary of State to the titular James III, as, also, subsequently, 1759-63, having been *cr.* 20 Jan. 1760, LORD NEWTON, VISCOUNT OF FALKIRK, and EARL OF ALFORD(b) [S.]. He *d.* "apparently s.p.,"(a) in the Scots College, Paris, 3 Jan. 1773, at a great age.

O'GARA [I.]:

cr. 2 May 1727.

"LIEUT.-COL. OLIVER O'GARA,"(a) s. of John O'GARA, by Mary, da. of Charles O'CONNOR, of Belanagar, co. Roscommon, was M.P. [I.] for Sligo, in the Irish Parl. of James II (1689), was in command of a Reg. of Infantry at Aughrim, 12 July 1691, on behalf of James II, whom he joined in France in 1692, being made Lieut.-Col. of Foot Guards, and subsequently Col. of the Queen's Dragoons, and being, 2 May 1727, *cr. a Knight and Baronet* [I.], with rem. to heirs male of his body.(a) He *m.* in or before 1692, Elizabeth(c) (not as usually called, Mary), widow of Richard FLEMING, of Staholmock, da. of Randall (FLEMING), BARON OF SLANE [I.], being only child of his 1st wife, Eleanor, da. of Sir Richard BARNEWALL, 2d Baronet [I. 1622]. He *d.* (—), having had four sons,(d) some of whom survived him, though none, apparently, assumed the Baronetcy.

HELY [I.]:

cr. 28 June 1728.

"SIR JOHN HELY, Knt., was, 28 June 1728, *cr. a Knight and Baronet* [I.], with rem. to the heirs male of his body."(a) He *d.* (—).

(a) See Ruvigny's *Jacobite Creations*, p. 446, note "c."

(b) "The preamble speaks of his family having been out with Montrose and as having greatly contributed to the victory of Alford." See note "a" above.

(c) In the pedigree entered in 1756 by her son Charles O'Gara, she is called "Elizabeth," but there is no reference to any previous marriage.

(d) These were (1) John Patrick O'Gara, *bap.* at St. Germain's, 25 Oct. 1692, Brigadier in the Spanish service; (2) James Oliver O'Gara, *bap.* as aforesaid, 15 Dec. 1694, Col. of the Hibernia Regiment in Spain; (3) [—] O'Gara, Lieut.-Col. of the Irlandia Regiment in Spain; made a Commander of the Spanish Order of Calatrava for his conduct at the Battle of Veletri, in Italy, in 1743; (4) Charles O'Gara, *bap.* as aforesaid, 16 July 1699, "Majestatum Imperialium Camerarius actualis," 1756, Count of the Holy Roman Empire and Knight of the Golden Fleece, who *d.* s.p. in opulent circumstances at Brussels, 1775, or 1776, or possibly 1785.

FORESTER [S.]:

cr. 31 March 1729.

"SIR JOHN FORESTER, Knt.,"(a) who is spoken of as "*Sir* John" as early as 9 Dec. 1714 in a letter from the Duke of Berwick to the titular James III, and who, presumably, was "the Sir John FORESTER who (under the cipher name of M. Fisher) is frequently mentioned as a trusted agent in the *Stuart Papers*, 1714-16,"(a) was, 31 March 1729, *cr. a Knight and Baronet* [S.], with rem. to the heirs male of his body.(a) He *d.* (—).

CONNOCK [E.]:

cr. 22 Feb. 1732.

"WILLIAM CONNOCK, Esq. (grandson of George CONNOCK,(b) *b.* 1575, a yr. s. of the family of CONNOCK, of Treworgy, co. Cornwall), was, 22 Feb. 1732, *cr. a Knight and Baronet* [E.], with rem. to his grandson, Joseph CONNOCK, son of the deceased Sir Timon CONNOCK, Knt., *as a mark of the royal favour for Sir Timon's loyal services*."(a) He *d.* (—).(c)

WORTH [I.]:

cr. 12 Sep. 1733.

"PATRICK WORTH, Esq., of the Kingdom of Ireland, Lieut.-Colonel in the service of His Imperial and Catholic Majesty, and Town Mayor of Ghent, was, 12 Sep. 1733, *cr. a Knight and Baronet* [I.]."(a) He *d.* (—).

FORSTAL [I.]:

cr. 22 Jan. 1734.

"SIR MARK FORSTAL,(d) was, 22 Jan. 1734, *cr. a Knight and Baronet* [I.]."(a) He was s. of James FORSTALL, of Molennahouna, co. Kilkenny, by Helen,(e) da. of Peter DEN, of Thomastown, co. Kilkenny. He was living in Spain when he registered his pedigree in Ulster's office, 2 March 1735. He *d.* (—).

(a) See Ruvigny's *Jacobite Creations*, as on p. 446, note "c."

(b) This George is mentioned in the will of his uncle, Richard Connock, dat. 11 Dec. 1619, as Capt. George Connock. He had a da., *bap.* 20 Nov. 1614, and a son, Richard, about to be called to the Bar, who possibly may have been the grantee's father. See Vivian's *Visitations of Cornwall*.

(c) The right to this Baronetcy devolved on and appears to have been assumed by this Joseph Connock, who "is said to have derived the title of Count of Alby, in the Holy Roman Empire, from his mother, and to have been *cr.* Marquis of Albevill" (see note "a" above), her mother being da. of Sir Ignatius WHITE, *or* VITUS, 1st Baronet [1677], Count of Alby and Marquis d'Albeville, in the Holy Roman Empire. See vol. iv, pp. 87-88, note "e," under "WHITE."

(d) "A Sir Mark *Forester* writes to the Duke of Mar, from Calais, 24 Feb. 1716. *Query*, if not the Sir Mark *Forstal* who was made a Baronet [I.] 22 Jan. 1734." See note "a" above.

(e) This Helen, *m.* subsequently, Edmund Butler, of the family of Cahir, by whom she had a son, Richard Butler, living 1735.

RAMSAY [S.]:

cr. 23 March 1735.

"ANDREW MICHAEL RAMSAY, Knight of the Military Order of St. Lazarus in France, and Governor of the King's nephew, the Prince of Turenne, was, 23 March 1735, *cr. a Knight and Baronet* [S.], with rem. to the heirs male of his body."(a) He *d.* (—).

LUMISDEN [S.]:

cr. 5 Jan. 1740.

"JOHN LUMISDEN, 1st s. of Andrew LUMISDEN, sometime Rector of Duddingston, and afterwards (1727-33) Bishop of Edinburgh, by Catharine CRAIG, of Riccarton, was, 5 Jan. 1740, *cr. a Knight and Baronet* [S.]."(a) He *m.* in or after 1716 (having been tutor to her son), Mary, widow of William (GORDON), 6th VISCOUNT KENMURE [S.], sister of Robert, 5th EARL OF CARNWATH [S.], da. of Sir John DALZELL, by Harriet, da. of Sir William MURRAY, 1st Baronet [S. 1664]. He *d.* s.p. in France, 1751. His widow *d.* 16 Aug. 1776, at Terregles, sixty years after the death of her 1st husband.

MACGREGOR, *otherwise* DRUMMOND [S.]:

cr. 14 March 1740.

"ALEXANDER MACGREGOR, *otherwise* DRUMMOND, of Balhaldies,"(a) s. of Duncan MACGREGOR, of the same, *b.* about 1660, assumed, in consequence of his own name being proscribed by the Government, the name of DRUMMOND; was, for political reasons in 1704, on the death of the last chief of Clan Gregor without issue, elected to the Chieftainship of the Clan Gregor, but the fact was kept secret; was a distinguished Jacobite and was engaged in most of the plots of the time for the restoration of the *House of Stuart*, and was, 14 March 1740, "*cr. a Knight and Baronet* [S.], with rem. to the heirs male of his body."(a) He *m.* 1686, Margaret, sister of John CAMERON, *cr.*, 27 Jan. 1717, by the titular James III, LORD LOCHIEL [S.], da. of the celebrated Sir Ewen CAMERON, of Lochiel, by his 2d wife, Isabel, da. of Sir Lauchlan MACLEAN. He *d.* at Dunblane, 1 March 1749, aged 89.(b)

(a) See Ruvigny's *Jacobite Creations*, as on p. 446, note "c."

(b) The right to this Baronetcy would devolve (1) on his 1st s. and h., William Macgregor, *otherwise* Drummond, of Balhaldies aforesaid, who was *b.* 1698, and was, like his father, a noted Jacobite, taking part in the Rising of 1715, being in several Jacobite commissions, and (though he took no part in the Rising of 1745), being attainted and exempted by name from the Act of Indemnity, 1747. He *d.* near Paris, 1765. His only s. and h., (2) Alexander John William Oliphant Macgregor, *otherwise* Drummond, of Balhaldies aforesaid, *b.* in Paris, 26 Sep. 1758, returned to England; was Capt. 65th Foot, and *d.* 1794. His 1st s. and h., (3) William Oliphant Macgregor, *otherwise* Drummond, of Balhaldies aforesaid, *b.* 1782, was Major in the 77th Foot, and *d.* s.p 1810, being suc. by (4) his next br. and h., Donald Macgregor, *otherwise* Drummond, of Balhaldies aforesaid, which estate was (75 years later) sold on 16 Sep. 1885. These four persons, (with their wives and issue), are set out in full as the 2d, 3d, 4th and 5th Baronets in Ruvigny's *Jacobite Creations*. See p. 446, note "c."

MACDONELL [S.]:

cr. 6 June 1743.

"ALEXANDER MACDONELL, 16th Chief of Keppoch, 1st s. and h. of Col. MACDONELL, 15th Chief of Keppoch (*d.* 1730-36), by Barbara, da. of Sir Donald MACDONALD, of Sleat,"(a) was *b.* 1694-98, served ten years in the French Army; was sent in 1743 by the Scottish Jacobites on a mission to the titular King James III, by whom, 6 June 1743, he was "*cr. a Knight and Baronet* [S.], with rem. to his heirs male."(a) On the arrival of Prince Charles in Scotland in 1745 he was one of the first to join him at Glenfinnan. He *m.* about 1722, Jeane, sister of Dugald STEWART, *cr.*, by the titular James III, BARON APPIN [S.], 6 June 1743, da. of Robert STEWART, 8th Chief of Appin, by Anne, da. of Sir Duncan CAMPBELL, of Lochnell. He *d.* 16 April 1746, being slain at the Battle of Culloden. His widow *d.* after 1757.(b)

GAYDON [I.]:

cr. 29 July 1743.

"SIR RICHARD GAYDON, Knt., Major General of our forces, and at present Lieut.-Colonel of Dillon's Regiment in the service of his Most H.M.C.M."(a) having been one of the four gallant Irishmen,(c) who assisted the Princess Mary Clementina Sobieski in escaping, 29 April 1719, from the Castle of Innspruck, was *Knighted* June 1719, being also a Knight of St. Louis in France, and was, 29 July 1743, *cr. a Knight and Baronet* [I.],(a)" with rem. to the heirs male of his body."(a) He *d.* (—).

(a) See Ruvigny's *Jacobite Creations*, as on p. 446, note "c."

(b) The limitation of this dignity was to "heirs male," but the right thereto would devolve, in the first place, on the heirs male *of the body* as under: (1) Ranald Macdonell, 1st s. and h., *b.* about 1735-36, Lieut. 78th Highlanders, 1759, serving in Jamaica and America, and retiring as Major. He, about 1759, obtained a lease of the family estates, which had been forfeited in 1746. He *d.* 1788; (2) Alexander Macdonell, 1st s. and h., *b.* in Jamaica, 29 Oct. 1772, and became Major in the 1st Royals. He *d.* unm. in Barbadoes, 25 June 1808; (3) Richard Macdonell, only br. and h., *b.* at Keppoch, 29 Nov. 1780, Lieut. 92d Highlanders. He *d.* unm., of yellow fever, at Up Park Camp, Jamaica, 14 Aug. 1819; (4) Alexander Macdonell, only uncle and h. male, *b.* at Keppoch about 1742-43; sometime Major in the Glengarry Fencibles; emigrated to Canada and settled in Prince Edward's Island, where he *d.* 1820; (5) Chichester Macdonell, 1st s. and h.,(*) who *d.* s.p.m.s. at Greenock, in 1838, when the legitimate male issue of the grantee became *extinct*, and "the Chiefship of Keppoch devolved on Angus Macdonell" (*b.* 5 July 1801), s. and h. of Donald (*b.* 1 May 1761), 3d s. of Angus (*b.* 21 July 1726), illegit. s. of Ranald, the s. and h. of the grantee. The five persons above mentioned, heirs of the body to the grantee (with their wives and issue), are set out in full as the 2d, 3d, 4th, 5th and 6th Baronets in Ruvigny's *Jacobite Creations*. See p. 446, note "c."

(*) The 2d and yst. son, John Macdonell (who is often, though erroneously, said to have *d.* at Baltimore, U.S.A., in 1824, leaving issue), *d.* unm. of cholera, at Montreal, in 1832.

(c) These were John Missett, Capt., and Edward O'Toole, Cornet in Dillon's Regiment (both of whom were Knighted at the same time), who, with him, assisted their kinsmen, Sir Charles Wogan (made a Baronet [I.] on that date, by the titular King James III) in this enterprise.

BUTLER [E.]:

cr. 23 Dec. 1743.

"JAMES BUTLER, was, 23 Dec. 1743, *cr. a Knight and Baronet* [E.], for special service in that country,"(a) [*sic*, though no country is previously named]. The grantee was not improbably either (1) James BUTLER, "Hipparchus in exercitu Regis Christianissimi, 1733," 3d s. of Edmund BUTLER, by Jane, da. of Edmund COMMEN, of co. Waterford, or (2) James BUTLER, Knight of the Military Order of St. Louis, of France, s. of Thomas BUTLER (of the Dunboyne family), by Elizabeth, da of Philip COMERFORD.(b) He *d.* (—).

MACDONALD, *or* MACDONELL [I. or S.]:

cr. 1745.

"JOHN MACDONALD, *or* MACDONELL, stated(c) to have been *brother's son to the Earl of Antrim*,"(a) being "one of the seven who accompanied Prince Charles to Scotland in 1745, and served under him down to Culloden,"(a) is said to have been by him *cr. a Baronet* [I. or S.]. He *d.* (—).

WARREN [I.]:

cr. 3 Nov. 1746.

"COLONEL RICHARD WARREN, 3d [but should be 2d] s. of John WARREN, of Corduff, co. Dublin [living 1733], by his 1st wife, Mary, da. of Richard JONES,"(a) but should be "of Richard LONG,(d) was sometime engaged in commercial pursuits at Marseilles; entered Lally's Regiment with honorary rank of Capt.; was in command of a French vessel sent to assist Prince Charles, with which he landed at Stonehaven in Oct. 1745, being made Colonel, 12 Nov. following; distinguished himself at the siege of Carlisle, and finally escorted in safety that Prince in a 36-gun frigate when escaping from Moidart to Roscoff, in Brittany, and was accordingly *cr. a Baronet* [I.], 3 Nov. 1746, receiving a pension of 1,200 livres from Louis XV. He served both in the Army of the titular King James III and in the French Army, being finally, 1760, Major-General in the one, and, 1762, *Marechal de Camp* in the other; was a Knight of St. Louis of France, Aug. 1755, and Governor of Belle Isle, 1763-75, where he *d.* unm., 21 June 1775.

(a) See Ruvigny's *Jacobite Creations*, as on p. 446, note "c."

(b) *Ex inform.*, G. D. Burtchaell.

(c) As to this statement, it is to be noted that the 1st Earl of Antrim who *d.* 1636 left but two sons, of whom (1) Randal, the 2d Earl and 1st Marquess, *d.* s.p. 1682, while (2) Alexander, 3d Earl, *d.* 1699, leaving an only son, Randal, 4th Earl, who *d.* 1721, leaving but one son. "The Chevalier Johnstone refers to him [*i.e.*, this grantee] contemptuously as *Macdonell*, an *Irishman*." See p. 446, note "c."

(d) In the pedigree reg. in 1745, in Ulster's Office by Thomas Warren, the 1st brother of the grantee, he, the said Richard, is called the 2d son (William, James, and John being the 3d, 4th, and 5th sons), and the mother is called da. of Richard *Long*, not of Richard *Jones*. This corrects the account in the Rev. Thomas Warren's *Warren Family* [1902], which is that followed by Ruvigny, see p. 446, note "c." [*Ex inform.*, G. D. Burtchaell].

HAY [S.]:
cr. 31 Jan. 1747.

"COLONEL WILLIAM HAY was, 31 Jan. 1747, *cr. a Knight and Baronet* [S.]."(a) He *d.* (—).

RUTLEDGE [I.]:
cr. 23 Dec. 1748.

"WALTER RUTLEDGE, *Armateur*, of Dunkirk, s. of James RUTLEDGE, Esq. (of the family of Rutledge, of the province of Connaught), by Juliana, da. of Sir Thomas BLAKE, Knight Baronet [I.]."(a) had, 5 July 1745, a declaration of his *noblesse* from [the titular] King James III, and, was, 23 Dec. 1748, (for his services to Charles [titular] Prince of Wales) "*cr. a Knight and Baronet* [I.], with rem. to the heirs male of his body."(a) He *d.* (—).

O'SULLIVAN, *or* SULLIVAN [I.]:
cr. 9 May 1753.

"JOHN WILLIAM O'SULLIVAN (of the O'Sullivans of Munster), *b.* in co. Kerry, 1700; ed. in Paris for the Catholic Priesthood"(a); served in the French Army in Corsica in 1739, and afterwards in Italy; was in 1744 admitted to the Household of Prince Charles Edward, to whom he was Adjutant-General, landing with him, 5 Aug. 1745, at Lochnanuagh, and being his chief adviser, civil and military, through the whole campaign. He was in joint command of the 900 Highlanders who captured Edinburgh, 16 Sep. 1745; was the leader of the "Irish Party," and Quartermaster-General of the Prince's Army, with whom he remained, after the defeat at Culloden till his escape, effecting his own, 1 Oct. 1746, and being *Knighted* by the titular King James III between 19 Dec. 1746 and 17 April 1747,(b) and subsequently, 9 May 1753, "*cr. a Knight and Baronet* [I.], with rem. to heirs male of his body."(a) He *m.* Louisa, da. of Thomas FITZGERALD. He *d.* (—), leaving male issue.(c)

(a) See Ruvigny's *Jacobite Creations*, as on p. 446, note "c."

(b) He is said to have been previously *cr.* DUKE OF MUNSTER, by Prince Charles Edward, who acted as Regent for his father, the titular King James III. The tradition as to this is given under O'SULLIVAN in Ruvigny's *Jacobite Creations*, see p. 446, note "c."

(c) The right to the dignity would have devolved (1) on his only s. and h., Thomas Herbert O'Sullivan, an officer in the Irish Brigade in the French service, but afterwards one in the British service, serving through the American War, 1783, when he entered the Dutch service, continuing therein till his death in Holland in 1824; (2) John William Thomas Gerald O'Sullivan, ed. at Montreal, settled in the United States and became a naturalised American citizen, being Consul to the Barbary States. He *d.* May 1825, being shipwrecked; (3) William O'Sullivan, 1st s. and h., Lieut. in the Navy of the United States, and *d.* unm., being lost at sea: (4) John Louis O'Sullivan, br. and h., *b.* at Gibraltar, Nov. 1813, ed. at Westm. School, and was sometime (1854-58) American Minister at Lisbon. He *d.* s.p., 24 March 1895, in New York, when the issue male of the grantee became *extinct*. The four persons abovementioned (with their wives and issue), are set out in full in Ruvigny's *Jacobite Creations*, as on p. 446, note "c."

CONSTABLE [E.]:
cr. 17 Sep. 1753.

"JOHN CONSTABLE, Esq.,"(a) was, "for his services to Henry [titular] Duke of York,"(a) 17 Sep. 1753, "*cr. a Knight and Baronet* [E.], with rem. to heirs male of his body."(a) He was for many years Major-domo of the Household to the titular King James III, and was living Jan. 1766, when he was dismissed by the titular King Charles III.

CREATIONS BY THE TITULAR KING CHARLES III.
1 Jan. 1766 to 31 Jan. 1788.(b)

HAY [S.]:
cr. 31 Dec. 1766.

"JOHN HAY, Portioner of Restalrig, near Edinburgh,"(a) an estate he had acquired by his marriage in Dec. 1727, 2d s. of Alexander HAY, of Huntingdon and East Lothian, Sheriff Deputy of Haddington, by Mary, da. of (—) GORDON, of Lismore, was Substitute Keeper of the Signet, 1725-41 and 1742-44; Fiscal, 1732-34, and Treasurer, 1736-46: joined Prince Charles on his landing in Scotland, 1745, to whom he was Treasurer, and afterwards, 1746, Secretary; serving through the campaign. but being blamed for neglect of duty as Quartermaster, on the eve of the battle of Culloden; was attainted, 1746, and continued in Prince Charles' service, by whom, when titular King, he was in Jan. 1766, appointed Major-domo of the Household, and was, 31 Dec. 1766, "*cr. a Knight and Baronet* [S.], with rem. to his heirs male."(a) He, however, was dismissed, 8 Dec. 1768, and returned in 1771 to Scotland. He *m.* Dec. 1727, Anne, da. and h. of James ELPHINSTONE, of Restalrig abovenamed. He *d.* in Scotland, 6 Dec. 1784, leaving male issue.(c)

(a) See Ruvigny's *Jacobite Creations*, as on p. 446, note "c."

(b) Very few dignities were conferred by this Prince, only one peerage (the Dukedom of Albany [S.], conferred on or before 24 March 1783, on his illegit. da., Charlotte, whom he also "invested with the green ribbon, as K.T.," on St. Andrew's Day, 1784), and two Baronetcies [S.], viz., Hay and Stewart, as above. He is also alleged, though, apparently without any valid authority, to have created (presumably in 1745) when [titular] Prince Regent, two other Peerages, viz., the Dukedom of Munster [I.], conferred on John William O'Sullivan, and the Viscountcy of Frendraught [S.], conferred on James Crichton. See Ruvigny's *Jacobite Creations* (as on page 446, note "c"), under "O'SULLIVAN," for the former, and see *Scots Peerage* (1906), under "FRENDRAUGHT," for the latter.

(c) The limitation of the dignity was to "heirs male," but the right thereto would devolve in the first instance on the heirs male *of the body* as under: (1) Alexander Hay, only s. and h., *d.* s.p., 1791 (who is set out in Ruvigny's *Jacobite Creations* as the 2d Baronet). He was suc. by his cousin and h. male (2) Thomas Hay (set out, as above, as the 3d Baronet), 1st s. and h. of Alexander Hay, of Mordington, who was s. and h. of Thomas Hay, of Huntingdon (a Senator of the College of Justice, *styled* Lord Huntingdon), who was elder brother of the grantee. He, on 13 April 1825. *suc. to the Baronetcy* [S.], of Hay, *cr.* 22 Feb. 1703, as the 5th Baronet of that creation, in which, accordingly, the representation of the grantee of 1766 then vested, and still (1906) so continues.

STEWART "[G.B.]"(a):
cr. 4 Nov. 1784.

"COLONEL JOHN ROY STEWART,"(b) s. of Donald STEWART, by his 2d wife, Barbara, da. of John SHAW, of Rothiemurchus (which Donald was s. of John STEWART, the last Laird of Kincardine), was *b.* at Knock, co. Kincardine, 1700; was Lieut. and Quartermaster in the Scots Greys, but being engaged in a Jacobite plot, fled to France and joined the French Army. In 1745 he joined Prince Charles at Blair Atholl, raised the Edinburgh Regiment, and was in command thereof at Culloden, where he was wounded; was afterwards in the Household of Prince Charles, and was, with him, imprisoned at Paris, in 1748. He afterwards retired to Holland, but rejoined the Prince at Ancona, and accompanied him when titular King, to Rome in Jan. 1766, being made Major-domo of the Household in Dec. 1768, and was "*cr. a Baronet of Great Britain*(a) 4 Nov. 1784, with rem. to the heirs male of his body."(b) He was living Jan. 1788, when he received a pension of £1,250 in lieu of £750 a year left him (as Major-domo) by the late titular King. He, who was a poet and one of the best swordsmen of his day, *m.* an Italian lady, and left issue.(c)

INDEX TO THE JACOBITE BARONETCIES, 1688—1788.

(a) "It is so in the patent, but surely only by an oversight, as the Union with Scotland in 1707 was not recognised by the exiled House of Stuart." See Ruvigny's *Jacobite Creations*, as on p. 446, note "c."

(b) See Ruvigny's *Jacobite Creations*, as on p. 446, note "c."

(c) The right to the dignity would have devolved on his s. and h., [—] Stewart, a Colonel in the Papal service, who, in 1848, was in command of the Pope's Artillery He, accordingly, is set forth as the 2d Baronet in Ruvigny's *Jacobite Creations*, as on p. 446, note "c."

p. 1; line 10, *for* "28 March 1735," *read* "17, or 18, March, 1734/5"; line 19, *after* "within," *add* "He (as was Sir John Huband, 1st Baronet [1660]) was one of the ten original directors of the Bank of England, 27 July 1694, under Sir John Houblon, the Governor. He, by successful dealings in Change Alley, founded on information from correspondents in every part of Europe, became a millionaire"; line 23, *after* "54," *add* "and was *bur.* 8 Dec., at Waldershare"; lines 23 and 24, *for* "*d.* s.p.m.(a) 8 May 1732,(b)" *read* "by whom he had no male issue,(a) *d.* 7 and was *bur.* at Waldershare, 17 April 1722.(b) Will (as relict of Sir Henry Furnese, Baronet) dat. 21 March 1720/1, pr. 4 May 1722, by her son Anthony BALAM"; line 28, *after* "firstly," *add* "about 1708"; last line, *after* "BALAM." *add* "by his stepmother, Matilda, da. of Sir Thomas VERNON, all three abovementioned"; note "a," line 1, *for* "her," *read* "their"; line 3, *conclude* "She was *bur.* at Waldershare, 28 March 1721, aged 22"; note "b," *dele* and *insert*, in lieu thereof, "The entry in Musgrave's *Obituary* of the death, 7 April 1722, of *Furnese, Lady of Sir Robert* [*sic*], *Kent*, doubtless refers to her. There is also therein an entry of the death, 8 May 1732, of "*Furnese, Lady, mother of Sir Robert Furnese*, which, inasmuch as such mother had then been dead thirty-seven years and her successor (the second wife and widow of Sir Henry) had been dead ten years, is inexplicable."

p. 2; line 1, *dele* "[Matilda?]" *to* "Arabella," and *insert* "8 July 1714, Arabella, 6th"; line 3, *for* "*d.* 5," *read* "who was *b.* 15 March 1693, *d.* 6 and was *bur.* at Waldershare, 19"; line 5, *for* "7," *read* "14"; line 6, *for* "14," *read* "19"; *for* "will pr. March 1733," *read* "M.I. Will dat. 2 June 1732, pr. 20 March 1732/3.(a)"; line 15, *dele* "Montpelier" *to* "1735," *and insert* "Marseilles (not Montpelier, 17, or 18 March 1734/5"; line 16, *for* "Will pr. March 1735," *read* "He was *bur.* 3 July 1735, at Waldershare. M.I. Will dat. 18 May 1734, pr. 26 April 1735, by his cousin, Henry FURNESE, Esq., of St. Geo. Han. sq."; note "a," *dele* and *insert* in lieu thereof, "Much information about this family, and many abstracts of wills, including the interesting one of Catherine, Countess of Guilford (pr. 1767), the heiress thereof (which throws much light thereon), has kindly been given by Hamilton Hall, of Fordcombe, near Tunbridge Wells"; note "b," *commence* as under "The date of 17 is given in his M.I., but that of 18 March 1735 in the Parish Register"; line 1, *after* "blood," *add* "*b.* 1715"; line 3, *for* "to whom," *read* "who"; *for* "she devised," *read* "*suc.* her in"; line 6, *for* "3d and," *read* "(probably posthumous)"; *for* "April," *read* "May"; line 8, *for* "Henry," *read* "his brother Henry"; line 9, *for* "were, it is presumed, cousins of these," *read* "are called cousins, by the second and 3d."

p. 5; note "a," line 3, *for* "name," *read* "additional name."

p. 10; in margin, *for* "1710 to 1711?" *read* "1710 to 1720?"; line 4, *dele* "(but query if not Adam)"; line 5, *for* "Esq.," *read* "a Colonel in the Saxon army, though generally, but erroneously, called"; between lines 13 and 14, *insert* "*afterwards, since* 1905, GREY"; note "b" *conclude thus* "Clearly, however, Adam Brown, who was not elected Provost till Michaelmas 1710, some months later than this creation, was not the grantee. He was again so elected in Michaelmas 1711, and *d.* shortly afterwards 16, being *bur.* (with great pomp) 18 Oct. 1711, in the Greyfriars, Edinburgh; his will, 6 Oct. 1712, in the Edinburgh Commissariot, being given up to his eldest son, William Brown, Ensign in Orkney's Foot, whose will (he being then Captain in Sinclair's Foot) was recorded as above, 10 Feb. 1744. The identification of the grantee is given in Musgrave's *Obituary*, where his creation is spoken of as that of *Brown, Robert, Chiliarcha* [*sic*], *Saxon, Baronettus Anglus, 1710; Gazette. 4669.* [*Ex inform.* James R. Anderson, 84 Albert Drive, Crosshill, Glasgow]."

p. 11; line 25, *after* "LAMBERT," *add* "*afterwards, since* 1905, GREY"; line 29, *after* "Yeomanry," *add* "He, by royal lic., June 1905, took the name of GREY instead of that of LAMBERT, after the death (29 Jan. 1905) of Katherine, widow of George Harry (GREY), 7th EARL OF STAMFORD, 3d and last EARL OF WARRINGTON, who *d.* s.p. 2 Jan. 1883, having devised (after his widow's death) his estates at Enville, etc., co. Leicester, to the said Lady LAMBERT, then Catherine Sarah PAYNE, spinster."

p. 13; note "c," *conclude* "See, also, p. 87 below."

p. 21; line 22, *after* "will," *add* "in which he leaves all to *Mrs. Mary Wright, now living with me.*"

p. 24; note "d," *commence* "The mansion at Blackheath was built by his guardians."

p. 37; note "f," last line, *for* "of precedency," *read* "which granted the precedency of a Baronetcy."

p. 42; line 24, *for* "1717," *read* "17 Feb. 1718"; line 27, *after* "Sessions," *add* "He entered and signed his pedigree, 22 Nov. 1784, at the College of Arms"; line 28, *for* "Bristol," *read* "St. James', Bristol"; lines 28 and 29, *dele* "merchant" *to* "1771," *and insert* "of Stanton Drew, Somerset (*bur.* 25 Aug. 1760), Merchant of Bristol. She *d.* 8 and was *bur.* 11 April 1755 at Stanton, aged 30"; line 35, *for* "and was in," *read* "before 1784, when he was as also in"; line 37, *after* "1776," *add* "probably in Bristol"; line 40, *after* "She," *add* "who was *b.* 2 Sep. 1756, at St. Nicholas', Bristol."

p. 63; line 26, *for* "*b.* about 1708," *read* "*bap.* 27 Aug. 1710, at Horsham"; line 29, *for* "76," *read* "74."

p. 69; note "c," *conclude* "He appears in 1774 as *Sir Timothy Tallboy and Mrs. G . . . s*, in the notorious *Tete-a-tete Portraits, Town and County Mag.*, vi, 177. [See *N. & Q.*, 10th S., iv, 343]."

p. 72; line 22, *for* "da.," *read* "posthumous da."; line 23, *for* "da. and heir," *read* "illegit. da. (by Alice BODEN)."

p. 79; line 11, *for* "Rothorpe," *read* "Owthorpe."

p. 82; line 14, *after* "1853," *add* "His widow *d.* 11 March 1860, at Hastings, aged 62."

p. 83; last line, *conclude* "Will dat. 24 March 1744, pr. at York, 25 Sep. 1747."

p. 84; line 4, *after* "10," *add* "or 25"; line 7, *for* "10 Sep. 1768," *read* "in Sep. 1758"; line 11, *after* "M.I.," *add* "Will dat. 18 Dec. 1779, pr. 3 March 1783."

p. 87; lines 8, 11 and 12, *for* "Harmeston," *read* "Harmston."

p. 89; note "a," *conclude* "whose surname she by deed poll assumed. He, however, was sentenced, 21 Dec. 1905, to five years penal service, for endeavouring to procure the murder of his lawful wife, who, having obtained a decree of divorce *nisi*, delayed to make it absolute (which was not so made till 9 April 1906), thereby precluding him from a remarriage."

p. 98; line 24, *for* "in or before 1732," *read* "20 Feb. 1731/2, at St. Martin's, Outwich, London."

p. 109; line 33, *for* "Warbledon," *read* "Warbleton."

p. 110; line 4, *after* "17," *add* "As a ward of his uncle, Mr. THRALE, he came under the notice of the celebrated Dr. Johnson, who wrote some 'lively, satirical and too prophetic verses on his coming of age.' [*Ann. Reg.*, 1838.] He entered eagerly into all the follies of the day(c)"; *add* (as note "c") "He appears, in 1778, as *the Libertine Lad and Miss B . . . s* [*i.e.*, Sir John Lade and Miss Maria B . . . s], in the *Tete-a-tete Portraits, Town and County Mag.*, vol. x, 513. [See *N. & Q.*, 10th S., iv, 344]"; note "a," *conclude* "She is spoken of as the *Amazonian Lætitia*, who created a sensation by riding astride on horseback, looked like Diana, and drove a

curricle and four with supreme skill. Rumour said that she had lived at St. Giles's as the mistress of *Sixteen-string Jack*, a highwayman, who was hanged in 1774. [W. H. Wilkins's *Mrs. Fitzherbert and George IV*, 1905]."

p. 111; line 26, *conclude* "He *m.* 12 Dec. 1905, at St. Jude's, South Kensington, Ada Marion, 2d and yst. da. of Frederick Henry (MAITLAND), 13th EARL OF LAUDERDALE [S.], only child by his 2d wife, Ada Twyford, da. of the Rev. Henry Trail SIMPSON, Rector of Adel, co. York. She was *b.* 21 June 1884."

p. 112; line 8 from bottom, *after* "66," *add* "Will pr. at £63,088."

p. 113; line 3, *for* "1789," *read* "July 1789"; line 4, *after* "and," *add* "*subsequently*, Sep. 1789 to 1824."

p. 116; between lines 2 and 3, *insert* "*afterwards*, since 1906, BARON COLEBROOKE OF STEBENHEATH."

p. 117; line 20, *conclude* "She was living when he was *cr.*, 20 Feb. 1906, BARON COLEBROOKE OF STEBENHEATH, co. Middlesex, in which Peerage this Baronetcy then *merged*. See *Peerage*."

p. 133; line 13, *after* "above," *add* "2 Nov. 1764."

p. 136; note "c," *conclude* "In 1780 he figures as *Sir J. Hogstie and Mrs. Fl . yd* [*i.e.*, Floyd] in the *Tete-a-tete Portraits, Town and County Mag.*, vol. xii, p. 513. [See *N. & Q.*, 10th S., iv, 462]."

p. 149; last line, *for* "pr.," *read* "dat. 2 March 1771, pr. 21."

p. 155; line 29, *for* "*extinct*," *read* "*extinct*(aa)," and *add* (as note "aa"), "The Baronetcy was apparently claimed by Henry Harland, the well-known novelist, only child of American parents, sometime settled at St. Petersburg, where he was *b.* 1 March 1861. He *m.* Aline Merrian, an American lady, but *d.* s.p. at San Remo, 10 Dec. 1905, aged 44. According to his obituary in *The Times* (22 Dec. 1905), 'he believed himself to be a DORMANT BARONET [*sic*] of the United Kingdom [*sic*], in direct descent from a son of Admiral Sir Robert Harland [created a Baronet of *Great Britain*, 13 March 1771], who [*sic*, meaning, presumably, whose said son] had emigrated to America about 1770, and whose descendants had been careful not to claim the title when the Baronetcy was supposed to expire in 1848, lest by the laws of the State of Connecticut, in which they had large landed property, they should lose a proportion of their estates.'"

p. 156; note "c," *conclude* "They figure in 1779 as *The Seducing Captain and the Abandoned Wife* in the *Tete-a-tete Portraits, Town and County Mag.*, vol. xi, p. 625. [See *N. & Q.*, 10th S., iv, 462]."

p. 168; *transpose* lines 29 and 30.

p. 169; line 20, *conclude* "He *m.* (—), who in 1905 was in the Adelaide Hospital, Dublin."

p. 176; line 26, *after* "derry," *add* "by Hannah, da. of Samuel FOLEY, Bishop of Down, 1694-95."

p. 194; line 39, *for* "living 1905," *read* "*d.* 11 Nov. 1905, at St. George's Lodge, Winchester, aged 85."

p. 202; line 24, *for* "He *m.* firstly, in March 1803, Sophia, da. of James," *read* "was Sheriff of co. Dublin, 1831. He *m.* firstly, 31 Aug. 1803, at Fort St. George, Madras, Sophia, da. of John.(bb)" *Insert* (as note "bb") "This John was son of James Dodson, F.R.S. See *Genealogist*, N.S., xxi, 195, in 'Notes to Marriages at Fort St. George'"; line 3 from bottom, *conclude* "He *d.* 29 Nov. 1905, in his 80th year, at Glen Barrahane aforesaid"; *add*—

V. 1905. SIR EGERTON BUSHE COGHILL, Baronet [1778], of Glen Barrahane aforesaid, 2d but 1st surv. s. and h.,(c) *b.* 7 Feb. 1853; ed. at Haileybury; *suc. to the Baronetcy* 29 Nov. 1905. He *m.* 11 July 1893, at Castlehaven, co. Cork, his cousin Elizabeth Hildegarde Augusta, yr. da. of Lieut.-Col. Thomas Henry SOMERVILLE, of Brisbane, co. Cork, by Adelaide Eliza, da. of Sir Josiah COGHILL, 3d Baronet [1778], by his 2d wife.

p. 207; note "b," *conclude* "He appears in 1777 as *The Shaftesbury Nabob and Miss K...ghl...y* in the *Tete-a-tete Portraits, Town and County Mag.*, vol. vii, p. 625. [See *N. & Q.*, 10th S., iv, 343]."

p. 211; line 4, *for* "President," *read* "President(d)," and *add* (as note "d") "He appears in 1773 as *the Circumnavigator and Miss B . . n*, in the *Tete-a-tete* Portraits, *Town and Country Mag.*, vol. v, p. 457. [See *N. & Q.*, 10th S., iv, 343]."

p. 214; line 12, *for* "1781," *read* "1781(c)," and *add* (as note "c") "He appears in 1776 as *The Disappointed Nabob and Miss R . . d*, in the *Tete-a-tete Portraits, Town and County Mag.*, vol. viii, p. 289. [See *N. & Q.*, 10th S., iv, 343"; line 23, *for* "1785," *read* "1785(d)," and *add* (as note "d") "He appears in 1789 as *The Treacherous Guest and the Ungrateful Wife* (*i.e.*, Mrs. Parslow) in the *Tete-a-tete Portraits, Town and County Mag.*, vol. xxi, p. 531. [See *N. & Q.*, 10th S., iv, 522]."

p. 237, line 8, *conclude* "She *d.* at Flaxley Abbey 24 and was *bur.* 28 Nov. 1905, at Flaxley, in her 64th year"; last line, *for* "His widow living 1905," *read* "His will, above £44,000 gross, and above £29,000 net personalty, pr. (after litigation) Feb. 1906, by the widow."

p. 241; note "a," line 4, *for* "this (the second)," *read* "the second, and grandmother of this (the third)."

p. 246; line 6, *conclude* "He *d.* 4 Jan. 1906, at Tissington Hall, aged 59. His widow living 1906," *add thereto*—

VI. 1906. SIR HUGO MEYNELL FITZHERBERT, Baronet [1784], of Tissington aforesaid, 1st s. and h., *b.* 3 July 1872; ed. at Eton and at Trinity Coll., Cambridge; B.A., 1891; sometime Lieut. 8th Hussars; Master of the North Cornwall Hunt, 1905; *suc. to the Baronetcy*, 4 Jan. 1906.

p. 249; line 12, *for* "12," *read* "13"; line 26, *dele* "at an advanced age, 12 Jan. 1821"; line 28, *for* "when," *read* "13 and was *bur.* 25 Jan. 1821, at St. Anne's, Soho, aged 77. M.I. At his death."

p. 261; line 33, *for* "1800-60," *read* "1800-58."

p. 267; line 3, for "Parks," *read* "Park."

p. 283; *insert* between lines 21 and 22, "*sometime*, after 1906, VISCOUNT TREDEGAR."

p. 284; line 12, *after* "continues," *add* "the 2d Baron being *cr.* in Jan. 1906, VISCOUNT TREDEGAR"; line 20, for "22," *read* "23"; lines 37 and 38, *for* "1791," *read* "1794"; note (b), line 2, *after* "Smith," *add* "or Smyth, da. of an apothecary at Shrewsbury."

p. 287; line 31, *for* "Deuchworth," *read* "Denchworth"; line 33, *after* "London," *add* "Malt Distiller"; *before* "admon." *insert* "*d.* 3 June."

p. 295; line 27, *for* "DRYDEN," *read* "DRYDEN,(aa)" *and add* (as note "aa") "This is one of the few (only nineteen in all) Northamptonshire families whose pedigree is given in the *Victorian History of Northamptonshire* [*Genealogical vol.*, ed. by Oswald Barron, F.S.R., 1906]. Seven of these pedigrees relate to Baronets, *viz.*, Dryden (1619 and 1795), Wake (1621), Isham (1627), Palmer (1660), Langham (1660), Robinson (1660), and Knightley (1798)."

p. 314; line 5, *after* "Millicent," *read* "Florence Eleanor"; line 6, *conclude* "She was divorced (decree '*nisi*' being made absolute) 27 Nov. 1905(e)"; *add as note* "e," "This was for misconduct with Henry Arthur Mornington (Wellesley), 3d Earl Cowley, whom she *m.* next month, 14 Dec. 1905, at Colombo. There had been a previous petition for her divorce, which was, however, dismissed in 1900."

p. 321; note "e," line 1, *for* "An," *read* "Pedigree in the *Victorian History of Northamptonshire* [1906]. See above, under the Corrigenda to p. 295. There is also an."

p. 330; line 26, *for* "co. Wimborne," *read* "in Wimborne."

p. 346; line 18, *for* "(—)," *read* "Catherine Sympson[aa]"; and *add* (as note "aa") "*Ex inform.* G. D. Burtchaell, from the *Fisher MSS.* in the Office of Arms, Dublin."

p. 347; line 21, *after* "1900," *add* "Sheriff of Queen's County, 1906; Vice-Chamberlain to the Viceroy [I.], 1906."

p. 362; note "e," line 2, *for* "*m.*," *read* "[which Thomas *m.*"; *for* "1767," *read* "1767]."

p. 372; line 7, *after* "Militia," *add* "On the death, in 1797, of Sir Riggs Falkiner, 1st Baronet [I. 1778], he became head of *Falkiner's Bank*, Cork, thenceforth styled *Cotter and Kellett*, which failed in 1807 for £420,000, and which paid but 10s. in the pound, when finally wound up in 1826, though it was stated that the assets at the time of failure were worth 40s. in the pound."

p. 389; 4 lines from bottom, *for* "*m.*," *read* "*m.* firstly"; last line, *conclude* "He *m.* secondly, 7 Feb. 1906 (when in his 83d year), at the Roman Catholic Church of 'Our Lady,' Grove Road, St. John's Wood, Algitha Maud, only da. of Sir [Henry] Daniel Gooch, 2d Baronet [1866] by Mary Kelsall, da. of Joseph Rodney Croskey, of Philadelphia."

p. 392; line 29, *after* "previous," *add* "He was head of *Falkiner's Bank*, Cork, which, after his death in 1797 (Richard Kellett, father of the 1st Baronet [1801], having been a partner therein as early as 1775), became *Cotter and Kellett*, and as such, failed in 1807. See p. 372 under Cotter, 2d Baronet [I.] 1763."

p. 396; line 6, *after* "1804," *add* "was one of the Sheriffs of the City and County of Londonderry,[g] 1826-27, being Mayor of that city, 1832-33"; *add as note* "g," "The jurisdiction of the city extended over the county till the Municipal Reform Act, after which the Sheriff for the *County* was appointed by the Crown. [*Ex inform.* G. D. Burtchaell]."

p. 427; line 3, *for* "and," *read* "was sometime (1768) of Lincoln's Inn Fields, Midx., Surgeon"; lines 5 and 6, *for* "in or before 1773, Mary, da. and h.," *read* "17 April 1768, Mary, 1st surv. da. (whose issue became heir or coheir)"; line 7, *after* "Bucks," *add* "by Frances, 1st da. of William Dowdeswell, of Pull Court, co. Worcester. She, who was *b.* 11, and *bap.* 26 July 1739, at St. Anne's, Soho, *d.* before April 1779."

p. 447; note "e," line 6, *for* "and was accordingly *cr.*," *read* "being aide-de-camp at Falkirk"; *after* "1745/6," *add* "and was, probably soon after that date, *cr.*"

p. 451; note "c," line 10, *after* "by," *add* "his s. and h."

INDEX

TO THE SURNAMES OF THE SEVERAL HOLDERS OF THE

BARONETCIES OF GREAT BRITAIN AND THOSE OF IRELAND, CREATED BETWEEN 1 May 1707 and 31 Dec. 1800,

including not only the surnames of the grantees themselves, but also those of their successors, to which is added the local (or, failing that, the personal) description of each grantee. The name of any Peerage dignity held with a Baronetcy is not included, neither is the surname of the holder of any Baronetcy when conjoined with a Peerage, if such surname is different[a] from that of the grantee or of any Commoner (his successor) who possessed the Baronetcy.

PAGE

---

[a] See vol. i, p. 263, note "a."

PAGE

PAGE

V

NOTICE

AS TO THE

Complete Baronetage,

BY

G. E. C.

Vol. i., Baronetcies, English, 1611 to 1625, and Irish, 1618 to 1625, created by James I.; (issued April 1900, to Subscribers, at 14s.); price, after publication, £1 1s. net.

Vol. ii., Baronetcies, English, Irish and Scottish or Nova Scotia, created by Charles I., 1625 to 1649; (issued May 1902, to Subscribers, at £1 1s.); price, after publication, £1 11s. 6d. net.

Vol. iii., Baronetcies, as next above, created 1649 to 1664, including those created by the Lord Protector in 1657 and 1658; (issued Aug. 1903, to Subscribers, at £1 1s.); price, after publication, £1 11s. 6d. net.

Vol. iv., Baronetcies, as next above, created 1665 to 1707, the date of the Union with Scotland, when the creation of English and Scottish or Nova Scotia Baronetcies ceased and that of Baronetcies of Great Britain commenced; (issued December 1904, to Subscribers, at £1 1s.); price, after publication, £1 11s. 6d. net.

Vol. v., Baronetcies of Great Britain and Ireland, 1707 to 1800, when, after the date of the Union with Ireland, 1 Jan. 1801, the creation of such Baronetcies ceased and that of Baronetcies of the United Kingdom commenced. Also "Jacobite Baronetcies," 1688—1788, *cr.* by the titular Kings of the House of Stuart; (issued April 1906, to Subscribers, at £1 1s.); price, after publication, £1 11s. 6d. net.

The above Volumes give an account of all Baronetcies created through a period of about 190 years (*viz.*, from the institution of that order in 1611 down to 1800); during 82 years of which period (1625-1707) they were of *three* Kingdoms, and during 100 years (1618-25 and 1707-1800) of *two*. After 1800, however (*viz.*, since the Irish Union, 1 Jan. 1801), they are much easier dealt with, being of *one* Kingdom only, *viz.* "the United Kingdom of Great Britain and Ireland."

The price of these five volumes, if purchased together, is £5 5s. net. Apply to Messrs. William Pollard & Co. Ltd., Publishers, North Street, Exeter.

The age (81 this month) and infirmities of the Editor make it probable that he will not see any future Volumes through the press. Should, however, he be able to do so, they will be issued (as were the last four volumes) at £1 1s. to subscribers, the price, after publication, being raised to £1 11s. 6d. net.

April 1906.

INDEX

Index

TO THE FIVE VOLUMES OF THE

"Complete Baronetage"

1611—1800.

BY

G E. C

TOGETHER WITH AN

Appendix

CONTAINING SOME FEW SUCH BARONETCIES WHICH, INADVERTENTLY, ARE OMITTED, OR WHICH HAVE BEEN IMPERFECTLY DEALT WITH, IN THE FIVE VOLUMES PREVIOUSLY ISSUED.

EXETER :
WILLIAM POLLARD & Co. Ltd., NORTH STREET
1909.

CONTENTS.

PREFACE.

During the period here treated of, 1611 to 1800, there existed no less than four different series of Baronetcies, each of a separate Kingdom, *viz.* (1) Baronetcies of *England*, 22 May 1611 to 30 April 1707; (2) those of *Ireland*, 30 Sep. 1619 to 31 Dec. 1800; (3) those of *Nova Scotia or Scotland*, 28 May 1625 to 30 April 1707; and (4) those of Great Britain, 1 May 1707 to 31 Dec. 1800. Since this last date, *i.e.*, after the Union with Ireland, 1 Jan. 1801, *all* Baronetcies are of *one* and the same realm, *viz.*, that of *the United Kingdom of Great Britain and Ireland*, the arms and pedigrees of all grantees being duly registered in the College of Arms, London, under the Royal Warrant of 3 Dec. 1783, which previously had applied to the Baronetcies of Great Britain only. It is thus manifest that it is a much easier matter to deal with the creations in and after 1801 than with those which were created during the two centuries previous to that date.

The surname of the grantee, as also of every successor to the dignity (not being a Peer) is given in this index, but the Peerage title held by any Baronet is omitted.

The index itself is formed by the fusing together the five separate indexes to the five volumes of the *Complete Baronetage*, 1611 to 1800, *edited by G.E.C.* This was carried out at the cost of W. H. Weldon, C.V.O., Norroy King of Arms, who in so doing was able to correct several inaccuracies in the former indexes.

Grantees of the same name are arranged in chronological order, inasmuch as the designation (and, in several cases, even the surname) of the grantee does not, *of necessity* devolve with the dignity.

G.E.C.

NOTE.

It is proposed, if the health of the Editor (now, 1909, in his 85th year) should permit, to conclude this volume with a general Corrigenda to the five volumes already issued of the *Complete Baronetage to 1800.* In this Corrigenda such information as is already given in the "APPENDIX" will not be repeated, though a reference thereto will in all cases be given.

Since this Index was printed the legitimacy of Capt. John Twisden, R.N., son of Lieut. William Twisden, R.N., who was the 2d son of the 5th Baronet [1666], has been established by a judgment of the Court of Probate, 5 July 1909. This John (who died in 1853, aged 86) would accordingly (at the age of 12) have been entitled on the death, 5 Oct. 1779, of his uncle, Sir Roger Twisden, 6th Baronet [1666], to that dignity, and his grandson and heir male would accordingly be now (1909) so entitled. The succession to the Baronetcy from 5 Oct. 1779 to 1 Jan. 1841 (which was presumed to have followed that of the Bradbourne estate) and its extinction at the last named date would likewise be invalidated.

Index to the Baronetage, 1611 to 1800,

comprising ALL THE BARONETCIES of the Kingdoms of ENGLAND, IRELAND, SCOTLAND and GREAT BRITAIN, from the institution of that dignity, 22 May 1611, until 1 January 1801 (the date of the Union with Ireland), after which date all Baronetcies are of *one* Kingdom only, viz., "the UNITED KINGDOM OF GREAT BRITAIN AND IRELAND."

[The letters "I." and "S." (within square brackets), placed immediately after the surname of the Grantee, denote respectively that the creation was either one of IRELAND (30 Sep. 1619 to 30 Dec. 1800), or of SCOTLAND, otherwise NOVA SCOTIA (28 May 1625 to 24 April 1707). When no such letters are given, all creations, before 1 May 1707 (the date of the Union with Scotland), are of ENGLAND, and all, after that date, of GREAT BRITAIN.

The abbreviations "*cr.*," "*ex.*," "*dorm.*" and "*forf.*" stand respectively for "created," "extinct," "dormant" and "forfeited."

The above Baronetcies (1611 to 1800) are fully dealt with in the "*Complete Baronetage*, edited by G.E.C." (5 vols., 1906), to which, consequently this list forms, also, an index, and to which the figures at the end of each creation (*e.g.*, "ii. 98" meaning *vol.* ii., *page* 98, of that work) refer.

An Index to the JACOBITE BARONETCIES (1688 to 1784) created by the exiled Kings of the House of Stuart is given, separately, at the end hereof.]

(a) See Appendix; this Baronetcy (or supposed Baronetcy) being either omitted in *The Complete Baronetage*, 1611 to 1800, by G.E.C., or a somewhat important incident, not given therein, being added.

(a) See p. 1, note "a."

(a) See p. 1, note "a."

(a) See p. 1, note "a."

(a) See p. 1, note "a."

(a) See p. 1, note "a."

(a) See p. 1, note "a."

(a) See p. 1, note "a."

(a) See p. 1, note "a."

(a) See p. 1, note "a."

(a) See p. 1, note "a."

(a) See p. 1, note "a."

(a) See p. 1, note "a."

(a) See p. 1, note "a."

(a) See p. 1, note "a."

(a) See p. 1, note "a."

(a) See p. 1, note "a."

INDEX TO THE JACOBITE BARONETCIES,

created by the exiled Kings of the House of Stuart, between 11 Dec. 1688 and 4 Nov. 1784, when such creations ceased.(a)

Notice.—The Act of Union with Scotland not being recognised by these Kings, there are no creations of Great Britain, so that all these creations are either of England, Scotland, or Ireland, denoted respectively by "[E.]," "[S.]" and "I.]."

(a) This list is compiled from the *Jacobite Peerage, Baronetage, Knightage, and Grants of Honour*, compiled by the Marquis of Ruvigny and Raineval, published at Edinburgh (T. C. and E. C. Jack), 1904. In this most valuable work will be found a full account of these grantees and their descendants. It may be observed that after the "Rising" of 1745 there are very few creations, and after the death, 1 Jan. 1766, of the titular James III, only one Peerage and two Baronetcies were conferred by his successor, viz., the Dukedom of Albany, conferred 24 March 1783, on his daughter; the Baronetcy of Hay, 31 Dec. 1766, on John Hay, many years his personal attendant and then Major Domo of the Household; and the Baronetcy of Stewart, 4 Nov. 1784, on Col. John Roy Stewart, then and for many years previous Major Domo of the Household.

APPENDIX

Appendix,

containing alphabetical list of such Baronetcies (created 1611 to 1800) as are omitted (and some few that are imperfectly dealt with) in "*The Complete Baronetage*, 1611 *to* 1800, *by G.E.C.*," mentioned on page 1.

ABERCROMBY [S.]:

cr. 20 Feb. 1635/6. [See Vol. ii., p. 417.]

ALEXANDER, the 1st Baronet, registered arms in 1674, was living 1678, as a Commissioner for Banffshire, but *d.* before 13 Dec. 1684. The date of his third marriage, 22 Aug. 1668, is confirmed in the Baird Genealogical collections; so that JAMES, the 2d Baronet, the eldest child thereof, born in 1669, could not (as stated in Playfair's *Baronetage*) have married in 1645, or have taken a share in the troubles of Charles I. [*Ex inform.* James R. Anderson.]

BALLENTINE:

cr. before 1679.

A creation of a Baronetcy of this name is, in some measure, implied by a certificate, dated 7 Nov. 1679, at the College of Arms, London, that no *record* of any Baronetcy or Knighthood is recorded, since the Restoration in 1660, as having been granted to JOHN BALLENTINE, of Northumberland or Cumberland.

BARCLAY(a) [S.]:

cr. about 1660?

"SIR DAVID BARCLAY, of Cullairne, Baronet" [S.]. It is stated in the "*Index to Services of Heirs*" that in 1702, John BARCLAY was served heir to his father, John BARCLAY, who *d.* Jan. 1684, which John was son of SIR DAVID BARCLAY, of Cullairnie, Baronet.

BATHURST:

cr. 15 Dec. 1643. [See vol. ii., p. 239.]

This Baronetcy was claimed(b) in 1908 by Dwight Laurence Bathurst, of Colorado, as being the heir male of the body of the 5th Baronet, as under:—

(a) The notices of four Baronetcies [S.], viz., BARCLAY, DRUMMOND, GRAY, and MURE were supplied in Nov. 1902 by James R. Anderson, of Glasgow.

(b) The claim of Charles Bathurst, a bookseller (*b.* 15 Nov. 1711) to the title, was that his father, John Bathurst, citizen and pewterer of London (*d.* 1719) was (as seems by his will to have been the case) a son of Robert Bathurst (aged 38 in 1682 and *d.* 30 May 1692), 4th s. of the 1st Baronet. This Robert signed the pedigree of 1682, giving the names of twelve of his children, that of John not being among them, but as he is said to have had sixteen children, and as the youngest child in 1682 was only nine months old, "John" may have been one of the four younger children, born after that date. The issue male of Robert (aged 14 in 1682), the *eldest* s. of the above-named Robert, became *extinct* 28 Feb. 1765 on the death of Robert Bathurst, of Cleyhall in Lechlade, aged 67, s. and h. of the last-named Robert (*d.* 6 Oct. 1726, aged 59), who was s. and h. of Robert Bathurst (aged 38 in 1682), 4th s. of the 1st Baronet. See the Monumental Inscriptions to these three Robert Bathursts at Lechlade. Charles Bathurst, the bookseller, *d.* s.p.m.s. 21 July 1786, leaving a da. and heiress, Elizabeth, who *m.* William Woodman, of Bristol, goldsmith, and *d.* about 1815, leaving issue; her husband being living there 1825, aged 46.

V. 1695? SIR FRANCIS BATHURST, Baronet [1643], *bap.* 11 Feb. 1675 at Lechlade, co. Glouc.; aged about 6 in the Visitation of that county, 1682; *suc. to the Baronetcy* before (probably long before) 1719 on the death of his brother who had succeeded thereto in 1688.(a) He obtained a grant of 200 acres in New Georgia, 7 Oct. 1734, and, embarking on the 31st, landed there 3 Jan. 1734/5 with his wife, three daughters and younger son. He *m.* before 1713, Frances (*bap.* 3 May 1679 at Cumnor, Berks), da. of his maternal uncle, Rev. William PEACOCK, M.A. (Oxford), Vicar of Cumnor aforesaid, 1682 to 1728. His wife *d.* at Savannah, Jan. 1736/7. He himself *d.* soon afterwards, before 1741,(b) having possibly *m.* (as a 2d wife) Mary PEMBER, widow.

VI. 1738? SIR LAURENCE BATHURST, Baronet [1643], 1st s. and h., *bap.* 3 Mar. 1713, at Lechlade, co. Glouc.; adm. to Westminster School, June 1821, aged 8; King's scholar, 27 Feb. 1727, but ran away in 1728 and being kidnapped, was stripped of his "quality ensigns"(c) and sold to a family named Walker, near Philadelphia, in Pennsylvania. He was from 1735, till 1781, "Teacher" in a family named Roberts, in Montgomery County, being known as "Baronet Bathurst."(c) He *m.* 12 June 1741, at the first Presbyterian Church, Philadelphia, Anne ROBERTS (*b.* 18 Feb. 1723), by whom (besides two daughters) he had five sons (Allen, John, Henry, Benjamin and Laurence), *b.* between 1742 and 1757. He *d.* in Montgomery County, Pennsylvania, 1793.

VII. 1793. JOHN BATHURST, 2d but 1st surv. s. and h., *b.* 12 June 1744, living at Honybrook, Chester County, Pennsylvania, 1816, *d.* there s.p.m. Jan. 1820.

VIII. 1820. LAURENCE BATHURST, of Bald Eagle Valley, Howard township, in Cruter County, Pennsylvania, yst. and only surv. br. and h. male, *b.* 22 Aug. 1757, at Germanstown, Pennsylvania; entered "Washington's Guard" in 1776 and served in the war of the Revolution; was a leading Methodist; had a grant of 900 acres on the Ridore river in Canada in 1816. He *m.* at Barren Hill Church, near Germanstown, 7 April 1782, Rebecca ARCHIBALD, of Pennsylvania, by whom he had eleven children. He *d.* 17 Feb. 1845 at Howardstown aforesaid, aged 88.

IX. 1845. ARCHIBALD BATHURST, 1st s. and h., *b.* 4 April 1783. He *m.* 21 Feb. 1802, Hannah BAITMAN. He *d.* 6 Mar. 1856 in Cruter County aforesaid, and was *bur.* in Old Curtin burying ground.

(a) Their father *d.* in 1688. Their mother (*m.* Aug. 1670, at Cumnor, Berks) *d.* in 1712. Sir Francis was in 1719 their only living child. See Chancery Suit of that date.

(b) Wotton's *Baronetage*, published in 1741, wherein his death and the succession of his son, Laurence, to the Baronetcy are mentioned.

(c) See Memoirs of Jonathan Roberts, Senator U.S.A., pub. in 1812, who (as also his father) was a pupil of this Laurence Bathurst.

X. 1856. LAURENCE BATHURST, only s. and h., *b.* 29 Dec. 1802 in Cruter County aforesaid. He *m.* firstly, in 1827, Sarah Cox, who *d.* s.p.m. He *m.* secondly, in 1831, Catherine MACMULLEN. He *d.* 6 Mar. 1856, aged 53 years 2 months and 24 days, and was *bur.* as aforesaid.

XI. 1856. REUBEN ARCHIBALD BATHURST, s. and h., by 2d wife, *b.* 26 Jan. 1832, in Cruter County, aforesaid. He *m.* firstly 20 Mar. 1856, Kate CARTER, who *d.* s.p.m. He *m.* secondly, 8 Mar. 1861, Sarah THOMAS. He *d.* 4 Feb. 1897, at Lone Tree, Cass, Missouri.

XII. 1897. DWIGHT LAURENCE BATHURST, of Pueblo, Colorado, s. and h. by 2d wife, *b.* 14 Aug. 1866, who claims to be the 12th Baronet [1643] as above. He *m.* 24 May 1899, Alice HENRY, and has a son, *b.* 8 Sep. 1904, all three being alive in 1908.

BENNET:

cr. in or before 1660.

In the Calendar of State Papers for 1660 is a warrant to create "RICHARD BENNET" a Baronet, with rem. to his brother, Sir Humphrey BENNET. *Query*, if "Richard" is not a mistake for "Thomas." THOMAS BENNET, of Babraham, co. Cambridge (elder br. of Sir Humphrey BENNET, of Shalden, Hants, *Knighted* before Dec. 1645), was *cr. a Baronet* 22 Nov. 1660. These, however, had as their eldest br., Richard BENNET, of Kew, Surrey, who *d.* s.p.m. in April 1658. Though this Richard is *bur.* at Babraham, 29 April 1658, as "Richard Benet, *Esq.*, of Chancery Lane, Middlesex," it may possibly refer to him for there is at Babraham a monumental inscription as follows:—"Here lie buried RICHARD & THOMAS BENET, two brothers, and *both of ym Baronetts*. They lived together & were brought up together at schoole, at ye university & at Inns of Court. They married two sisters, ye daughters & heirs of Levinus Munk, Esq.

Sir Richard } died { Aprill ye 12, 1658 } aged { 63.
Sir Thomas } died { June ye 28, 1667 } aged { 71."(a)

BINGHAM(b) [S.]:

cr. 7 June 1634. [See Vol. ii., p. 398.]

HENRY, the 1st Baronet, was Sheriff of co. Galway as early as 1607 and, presumably, for co. Mayo, 1639; was M.P. [I.] thereof July to Nov. 1634 and 1639, till discharged owing to illness. He *d.* before 27 Jan. 1658/9, and was *bur.* in the chapel of Castlebar. Admon. [I.] of that date granted to a creditor. The will of his widow, Catherine, dat. 31 Oct. 1673, was pr. at Tuam, 21 July 1674. GEORGE, the 2d Baronet, was Sheriff of co. Mayo, 1662, 1663, 1678 and 1679, being Custos Rotulorum of the same, 1 Aug. 1663. He *d.* in 1682, before 1 June, when his son, HENRY, the 3d Baronet, was made Custos Rotulorum of co. Mayo. He was Sheriff thereof 1684, 1685 and 1694. He *m.* firstly (Lic. Dublin, 3 Feb. 1677/8), Jane, da. of Sir James CUFFE, of Ballinrobe, co. Mayo, by Alice, da. of Rev. the Hon. Ambrose AUNGIER, D.D. He *m.* secondly, Lettice,

(a) See Add. MSS. 5,802, fo. 37, in the British Museum.

(b) *Ex inform.* G. D. Burtchaell, Athlone Pursuivant of Arms, Office of Arms, Dublin, to whom the Editor is indebted for innumerable corrections, additions and emendations to the Irish pedigrees, of which his knowledge is unrivalled,

da. of Charles BINGHAM, of Newbrook, co. Mayo, by Mary, da. of Henry BLENNERHASSETT, of Castle Hassett, co. Fermanagh. JOHN, the 5th Baronet, was *b.* about 1696; adm. to Trin. Coll., Dublin, as Pensioner, 26 Nov. 1713, aged 17; Sheriff of co. Mayo (v.p.) 1721. He *d.* at Castle Bar, July 1749. His widow *d.* at Bath, Feb. 1761. JOHN, the 6th Baronet, was M.P. [I.] for co. Mayo, 30 Oct. 1749 till his death the next year, 10 Oct. 1750. CHARLES, the 7th Baronet, was Sheriff of co. Mayo, 1756.

BLUNDELL(a) [I.]:

cr. 13 Oct. 1620. [See Vol. i., p. 224.]

FRANCIS, the 1st Baronet, was undoubtedly a yr. br. of Sir George BLUNDELL, of Cardington, Beds (who acquired that estate by marriage with the heiress of John GASCOIGNE), both being sons of John BLUNDELL. See a pedigree of fifteen generations, certified by Richard St. George, Norroy, 1619, in Ulster's Office. His widow *m.* Nicholas WHITE, of Dublin, Alderman, whose will was pr. [I.] 11 Sep. 1645. She *m.* thirdly, Lieut.-Col. LITTELL. She *d.* 25 and was *bur.* 29 Nov. 1671, in Christ Church, Dublin. Funeral entry (ignoring her 2d husband) in Ulster's Office. Admon. [I.] 3 Nov. 1677. GEORGE, the 2d Baronet, *d.* between 22 Jan. 1673/4 and 8 May 1676. Admon. [I.] 8 May 1676. The marr. lic. for the first marriage of FRANCIS, the 3d Baronet, is dated 24 Dec. 1670; that for his second marriage [Dublin], 19 Dec. 1675. His M.I. is at Monasteroris. MONTAGUE the 4th Baronet, was *bap.* 19 June 1689, at St. Margaret's, Westm.

BOURKE(a) [I.]:

cr. about 1645? [See Vol. ii., p. 272.]

JAMES, the 3d Baronet, was living 5 Dec. 1707. See Exchequer Bill, "Lawless *v.* Bourke," in which it is alleged that the "said Sir James being mightily indebted in London was forced to abscond himself, and having sold his estate in Ireland and spent the money he got for the same, and having no other estate in any part of the world, nor any money or other income, and being not bred to any manner of business whereby he might get his livelihood, was in a most perishing condition in London for two or three months, and had nothing in the world to support him but the charity of his countrymen, and the said Sir James, being continually hunted by bailiffs up and down the said city of London did make an escape and came for Ireland." Various "shady" transactions are alleged against him. He subsequently stated that he was going again to London with the Duke of Ormonde, and was to be made a Captain of Horse.

BOURKE(a) [I.]:

cr. about 1646;

ex. before Jan. 1652/3.

"SIR JOHN BOURKE, Knt. and Baronet [I.], and Dame Margaret his wife," on 29 Jan. 1652/3, preferred a petition against Hugh CONNOR [Chancery Proceedings], and a decree was made thereon 9 Oct. 1654. This Margaret was relict of Walter BERMINGHAM, of Dunfert, co. Kildare (who *d.* 13 June 1638), and da. of Gerald FITZMAURICE, of Galye, co. Kerry, and the above-named John was probably "SIR JOHN BOURKE, Mayor of Limerick," who in 1646 was "attended on" by "the Herald of Arms, vested in his coat of office." See Richard Billings' *History of the Confederate War*, 1641-48.

(a) See page 65, note "b."

BRIGGS:

cr. 12 Aug. 1641. [See Vol. ii., p. 134.]

In Playfair's *Baronetage* [1811] "SIR JOHN BRIGGS, now abroad, the 6th and present Baronet," is stated to have been son of Sir Hugh BRIGGS, the 5th Baronet, and to have two sons, viz., (1) Clement, an officer in the army, a widower, without issue, and (2) John, of Blackheath, an officer in the navy, who *m.* Tamar Priscilla SCUDAMORE, and had a son, John Henry Lindsay Scudamore BRIGGS.

BROWN:

cr. 14 Dec. 1699. [See Vol. iv., p. 180.]

This Baronetcy was (1901-1908) claimed(a) by CHARLES WILLIAM WOOLFE CLIFTON-BROWNE, son of Col. W. L. CLIFTON-BROWNE, sometime Consul at Liberia, who was great grandson of the Very Rev. William Laurence BROWNE, D.D. and LL.D., Principal of Mareschal College, Aberdeen, and Dean of the Thistle and Chapel Royal, said to be descended from a yr. s. of the 1st Baronet. He was ed. at University Coll. School, London, and was sometime Lieut. in the 4th East Surrey Rifles. He *m.* in 1889, Maud Mary PAYNE. The 3d Baronet is said to have been in the Rising of 1745.

BURDETT(b) [I.]:

cr. 11 July 1723. [See Vol. v., p. 345.]

The parentage assigned to Thomas BURDETT, father of the grantee, in Playfair's *Baronetage* [1811] is "quite incorrect, and the alleged grants of upwards of twenty townlands in Carlow are a pure fiction." This Thomas was son of George BURDETT, M.A., Dean of Leiglin [1668-71], to whom he (being then "of Garrahill") took out admon. 3 Nov. 1671 in the Diocesan Court of Leighlin. Betham suggests the Dean to have been son or grandson of Thomas BURDETT (2d s. of Thomas BURDETT, who *d.* 15 July 1591), the uncle of Sir Thomas BURDETT, the 1st Baronet [1618], of Bramcote. Anyhow, the 1st Baronet [I. 1723] by his will dat. 1724, left the ultimate remainder of his estates to Sir Robert BURDETT, the 3d Baronet [1618], of Bramcote.

CAREW(c):

cr. 9 Aug. 1641. [See Vol. ii., p. 126.]

The issue male of the 3d Baronet, JOHN, (who was born at Roscrow in St. Minver, Cornwall, and *bap.* 6 Nov. 1635 at St. Minver), became *extinct* on the death of his grandchild, Coventry, the 6th Baronet, 24 Mar. 1748, when the title (often erroneously supposed to have become *extinct* at that date) devolved as under:—

(a) His claim first appears in Dod's *Peerage*, etc., for 1901, and is continued to the present date [1909] from which work these particulars are taken.

(b) See p. 65, note "b."

(c) The whole of the information in this article and the note thereto is furnished by Reginald M. Glencross, M.A., LL.B. (Trin. Coll.), Cambridge, a most accurate and acute genealogist. Much of it is contained in two articles by him entitled "The Carew Baronets of Antony, co. Cornwall," pub. July 1907 and Jan. 1909 in *The Genealogist*, N.S., Vols. xxiv. and xxv., giving an account of the descendants (hitherto ignored or most imperfectly given) of Thomas Carew, 3d surv. s. of Sir Alexander, the 2d Baronet, being the ancestor of the 7th and 8th Baronets.

VII. 1748. SIR JOHN CAREW, Baronet [1641], second cousin and h. male, being 1st and h. of John CAREW, formerly of Liskeard, co. Cornwall, and afterwards of West Harrowbear in Calstock, in that county, by Sarah, his wife, which John (who succeeded his only br., Alexander CAREW in that estate in or soon after Aug. 1735, and whose will., dat. 7 May 1744, was pr. 14 Oct. 1745) was 2d and yst. s. of Thomas CAREW, of West Harrowbear aforesaid (*bap.* 14 May 1640; *m.* 14 Nov. 1665 and *d.* between 26 Dec. 1684 and 28 Mar. 1686) who was 3d s. of Sir Alexander CAREW, the 2d Baronet. He was *bap.* 24 May 1708 at Liskeard; matric. at Oxford (Pembroke Coll.) 1 July 1726, aged 17; B.A., 1730; M.A., 1733; was in Holy Orders; Curate of Lanlivery, Cornwall, 20 Sep. 1731; Rector of Black Torrington, Devon, May 1737, till his death in 1762; *suc. to the Baronetcy* 24 Mar. 1748. He *d.* s.p., presumably unm., in 1762. Admon. 25 Aug. 1762 (Bishop of Exeter's Court) to his br., Thomas CAREW, one of the next of kin.

VIII. 1762, to 1799. SIR ALEXANDER CAREW, Baronet [1641], next br. and h., *bap.* 9 May 1715 at Liskeard aforesaid; matric. at Oxford Balliol (College), 20 May 1735, aged 19; B.A., 1738/9; in Holy Orders; Vicar of Faccombe, Hants, in 1744, and Vicar of St. Wenn, Cornwall, 1743, till his death in 1799; *suc. to the Baronetcy* in 1762; was a lunatic in 1765. He *d.* s.p. presumably unm., and was *bur.* 3 July 1799 at Blisland, aged 84, when the issue male of his grandfather and apparently the *Baronetcy* itself became *extinct*.(a)

(a) His three younger brothers all *d.* unm., viz.: Thomas Carew, of Saltash, surgeon, who was *bur.* at St. Stephen's, Saltash, 26 Jan. 1797, aged 76; William Carew, *bur.* 13 April 1730 at Liskeard, aged 6 years, and Joseph Carew, *bap.* 25 Oct. 1720, sometime Lieut. of H.M.S. "Assistance," whose will, dat. 25 Nov. 1752, was pr. 30 Mar. 1754.

Of the seven sons of ALEXANDER, the 2d Baronet, (1 and 2), Richard and Alexander were *bap.* together, 28 Oct. 1632, and *d.* young; (3), John, *bap.* 6 Nov. 1635, at St. Minver, co. Cornwall, succeeded as 3d Baronet, his male issue becoming *extinct* 24 Mar. 1748; (4), Wymond, *bap.* 15 May 1638 as aforesaid, was residing at Smyrna as a merchant in 1664, and *d.* s.p., apparently unm.; will dat. 8 Aug. 1664, pr. 5 May 1665 by his mother. (5), Thomas, *bap.* 14 May 1640, as aforesaid, whose issue male is dealt with in the text. (6), Richard, *bap.* 21 April 1641, as aforesaid, who was of Abertanet, Salop, and M.P. for Saltash, 1689 till his death s.p., being *bur.* 18 Sep. 1691. Will dat. 22 Aug. 1691, pr. 20 Jan. 1691/2. (7), Alexander (second of that name), whose date and place of baptism is not known; was of Smyrna, and is named in the will of his br., Wymond, in 1664. He *d.* unm. Admon. 19 Feb. 1673.

Of the younger sons of RICHARD, the 1st Baronet, all being by Grace (*m.* 1617), his 2d wife (1), John, *born* 3 and *b.* 7 July 1622, at Antony; matric. at Oxford (Gloucester Hall) 9 Mar. 1637/8, aged 15; admitted to Inner Temple, 1640; M.P. for Tregony, 1647-53, and, being one of the regicide Judges, was executed at Charing Cross, 15 Oct. 1660. (2), Wymond, *b.* 28 Aug. and *bap.* 23 Sep. 1623 at Antony; *bur.* there 9 Aug. 1624. (3), Sir Thomas Carew, of Barley, Devon, *bap.* 19 July 1624, at Antony; M.P. for Callington, 1658; for St. Michael's, 1660, and for Exeter 1680; *Knighted*, 21 July 1671. He *m.* about 1660, Elizabeth, da. of John Cooper, of Exeter, by whom he had five sons, as below. He was *bur.* 29 July 1681, at St. Thomas', Exeter. Will pr. 1682 at Exeter Consistory Court. (4), Richard, of Barley aforesaid, *bap.* 18 June 1626 at Antony. Will dat. 2 Oct. 1685, pr. 15 Nov. 1686, 8 Oct. 1690, and 31 July 1699 at Exeter. (5), Joseph, of Aleppo, *bap.* 11 Jan. 1628, at Antony. Will dat. 20 April 1674, pr. 20 Feb. 1674/5. (6), Robert, of St. Margaret's, Lothbury, London, *bap.* 16 Sep. 1627 at Antony; *d.* unm. and was *bur.* 8 Jan. 1654/5, at St. Margaret's aforesaid. Nunc. will dat. 2, pr. 30 Jan. 1654/5. Another br. named Anthony is given in Vivian's *Visitations of Cornwall* and is there said to have *m.* "Anna, da. of John Arundell, of Lanherne." Now inasmuch as this match must have taken place in or before 1623, (as in the Heralds' Visitation of Dorset of that year, "Anna," da. of John Arundell, of Chidiock, Dorset, "*alias* Arundell of Lanherne," is mentioned as

CHALMERS [S.]:

cr. 24 Nov. 1664. [See Vol. iii., p. 348.]

This Baronetcy was claimed in March 1907 by HOWARD CHALMERS, a young married man from Winnipeg, as son and heir of HENRY ROBERT CHALMERS, of the Public Drawing Office, Bank of England, London, E.C., lately deceased, who by letter, dated 5 Dec. 1904, stated himself to be son of CHARLES BOORN CHALMERS, only s. of Capt. SIR CHARLES WILLIAM CHALMERS, R.N. (by Isabella, relict of Capt. SCOTT), only s. of SIR ROBERT CHALMERS, R.N. (by Mary, da. of Surgeon Major BOORN), adding that the said Robert's "right to the Baronetcy [1792 to 1807] was never questioned." According to this letter the grantee was succeeded by his grandson, Charles CHALMERS, who matriculated arms at the Lyon Office "about 1760, and who was served heir to his grandfather." The brother of this Charles was SIR GEORGE CHALMERS, the well-known painter, who *d.* 1792, leaving a daughter, and was succeeded by the abovenamed ROBERT CHALMERS, his nephew, s. of Capt. JOHN CHALMERS, another grandson of the grantee.

The statements above given need proof.

CHAMBERS:

cr. 24 Oct. 1663. [Misplaced in Vol. iv., p. 225, which see.]

A warrant [*State Papers, Domestic*, 1660-70] dated 24 Oct. 1663 for creating "[—] CHAMBERS, a Baronet" [*Qy.* I.], probably refers to SIR RICHARD CHAMBERS, who *d.* before 31 Oct. 1694, having *m.* Mariana de Villa Labos of Xeres in Spain. She was living in London, as his widow, 23 April 1695.

COCKBURN [S.]:

cr. 24 May 1671. [See Vol. iv., p. 282.]

The second marriage of JAMES, the 3d Baronet, to Phœbe SHARMAN was by lic. (Cork), 1779. By it their three sons born before that date were legitimated [S.]. JAMES, the 5th Baronet, who in 1800 succeeded his brother of the half blood, was *b.* probably about 1770, but was legitimated [S.] by his parents' marriage in 1779 abovenamed. On his death in 1841 the *Baronetcy* became *extinct* or *dormant*.

"uxor Antho. Carew, de Antony,") it is quite clear that the Anthony mentioned could not be a son (though possibly he was a brother) of Richard, the first Baronet, whose s. and h. (the 2d Baronet) was aged but 10 in 1620. The marriage of "Anne, da. of Richard Hoblyn," on "26 July 1664," to John Carew, another of the sons of the 1st Baronet, is also impossible as the said John (the Regicide) was executed four years *before* that date.

The five sons of Sir Thomas Carew, of Barley abovenamed (s. of the 1st Baronet) appear to have all *d.* without issue, viz., (1), John, *d.* young, *bur.* 16 May 1662 at S. Thomas', Exeter. (2), Thomas, *b.* about 1663; was of Barley aforesaid; M.P. for Saltash, 1700-05; *bur.* at St. Thomas aforesaid. Will dat. 29 March, pr. 24 May 1705. (3), Richard, *b.* about 1664; matric. at Oxford (Exeter Coll.), 18 Mar. 1683/4, aged 19; admitted to Middle Temple, 1684; will dat. 15 Nov. 1713, pr. 4 Nov. 1714, at Consistory Court, Exeter. (4), Henry, of St. Thomas, Exeter, under age in 1686; one of the four Tellers of the Exchequer. Will dat. 13 Mar. 1698, pr. 20 Jan. 1698/9. (5), Joseph, of Exeter, *d.* unm. Admon. Nov. 1692.

COOPER [S.]:

cr. 1646. [See Vol. ii., p. 445.]

The date of 1646, as given in Edmondson's list of the Baronets of Scotland is more likely to be correct than that of 1638, which appears to be a misappropriation of that of Cooper of Ratling Court. (See *The Genealogist*, O.S., vol. i., p. 334 [1877]). In that volume (pp. 257-266) is an article on "Cooper of Gogar," supplementing one in the *Her. and Gen.* (vol. viii., p. 193), which furnishes a negative reply to the query, "Was a Baronetcy ever conferred on a Cooper of Gogar?" The writer thereof was that very able and acute genealogist, R. R. Stodart, Lyon Clerk Depute, 1863-86. Some thirty years later, in *The Genealogist*, N.S., vol. xxiv. (pp. 89-96), is an article on this Baronetcy by "St. David M. Kemeys-Tynte," in which are given the full particulars of the finding of the Scottish Jury, 1 Aug. 1775, that Grey COOPER was entitled to the Baronetcy. In this, the opinion of the claimant's counsel, Sir John Dalrymple (afterwards a Baron of the Court of Exchequer [S.]) is set forth, viz., that such a Baronetcy *did* exist, though (by his own shewing) it was never applied to any of the ancestors of the claimant.

CORNWALL, *or* DE CORNEWALL:

assumed in or before 1747 till 1756.

"SIR ROBERT DE CORNEWALL, Baronet," appears among the M.P's elected for Leominster, 1747, and, according to the strange account given below, had, beforehand, obtained a sign manual from George II. to use that style, so that his return, as such, should not be inoperative on the ground of "no person being to be found of that name and distinction." He, who was *b.* in 1700, was of Benington, co. Hereford, being 3d but 1st surv. s. and h. of Vice Admiral Charles CORNEWALL, *afterwards* CORNWALL,(a) of the same (*d.* 9 Nov. 1718, aged 49), by his 2d wife, Dorothy, da. of Thomas HANMER, of Hanmer, co. Flint.(b) He, on the strength of his father having (as it was alleged) been promised a Baronetcy in 1716 by George I., *assumed a Baronetcy* many years after the death in 1718 of his said father, but before (probably long before) 1738, and was thus described when Sheriff for Radnorshire, Feb. to Nov. 1738, and when elected M.P. for Leominster in 1747, for which he sat till 1754. He *d.* unm. 11 April 1756,(c) his death being thus noticed in the *London Mag.* for that year (p. 196): "Sir Robert de Cornewall, Bart. dying without issue the title and estate descend to Counsellor Cornewall, of the Temple." His will, dat. 8 April 1756, in which he describes himself as "Sir Robert de Cornewall, of Berrington Castle, co. Hereford, Baronet," was pr. 22 of that month by the abovenamed nephew and residuary legatee, Charles Wolfran CORNWALL, *afterwards* (1780-89) Speaker of the House of Commons, who, however, never assumed the Baronetcy.(d)

(a) This Charles most certainly never assumed the Baronetcy said to have been promised to him in 1716, but was *bur.* 27 Nov. 1718 in Westm. Abbey as "The Rt. Hon. Charles Cornwall, Esq., Vice Admiral," etc. His will also was pr. *as such* by his son, the abovenamed Robert, who likewise was *not* styled a Baronet in the probate thereof.

(b) A tabular pedigree of the family is in the *Mis. Gen. et Her.*, 2d S., v. 78, and a full account of its members is given in "*The House of Cornewall*," compiled by the Earl of Liverpool and the Rev. Compton Reade [Jakeman & Carver, Hereford, 1908]. The account therein, however, as to the assumption of this Baronetcy is singularly incorrect, it being stated that the grantee [*sic*] (who *d.* in 1718) was created a Baronet by George II. [*sic*] but *d.* before the patent was signed."

(c) In *Faulkner's Journal* for July 1753 [*sic*] the death [in error] is recorded of "Sir Robert de Cornewall at Berington Castle, co. Hereford, Bart., M.P., a bachelor; heir, his nephew, a minor," but in *Exshaw's Magazine* for 1756 is a circumstantial account of his death on 4 April 1756.

(d) He, who was only son of testator's youngest brother, Jacobs Cornwall, was *b.* 15 June 1735; admitted to Lincoln's Inn, 28 Jan. 1755; Speaker of the House of Commons 1780, till his death (s.p.) 2 Jan. 1789. He sold the estate of Berrington which for ten generations had been in his family in the direct male line.

AS TO THE ASSUMPTION OF THE BARONETCIES OF CORNWALL AND PERROTT.

The following curious extract(a) from *The Calendar of Home Office Papers*, 1766-1769, throws some light on these extraordinary assumptions:—

Law Officers' Entry Book, 1762-1795.

"1766, Dec. 26. Encloses a paper received from a Gentleman who styles himself SIR RICHARD PERROTT, setting forth his claim to the dignity of a Baronet, although his ancestors for the reasons therein contained did not take out the patent under the Great Seal or even obtain the sign manual from the King. At the same time in two votes (enclosed) of the House of Commons, when the Gentleman was in Parliament,(b) he has the title of *Sir Richard Perrott.* He now asks His Majesty to grant him a warrant of rank and precedence *as a Baronet* from 1 July 1716, when the dignity was first intended to be granted to his uncle, James [*sic*] Perrott.(c) Desires the Attorney General to state his opinion and, in case he shall see no reasons against complying with the request, to prepare a warrant for the purpose."

The following is also entered:—"ADMIRAL CORNWALL, when he sailed to the Mediterranean, had it given him in charge, in company with JAMES PERROTT, Esq., by George I. to redeem all British subjects who should be found in slavery in the Barbary States. They expended in that expedition a much larger sum than ever they received and often solicited the balance in the King's lifetime, and afterwards the late King(d), who while at Hanover, to make them some return for their services and losses created them Baronets with precedency from the 1st of July 1716: but, though promised the patent at the expense of the Crown, found, on their application here for the warrant, before they could obtain them with the limitation as stipulated (viz., that of the Admiral, in default of heirs male, to his relation(e) SIR ROBERT DE CORNWALL, late Member of Leominster, and his heirs male—and that of *James Perrott*, in [a like] default, to his nephew, *Richard Perrott*, son of his brother, Richard Perrott, and his heirs male), it would cost them a considerable sum, and unwilling to expend a further sum they never was [*i.e.*, were] taken out, yet *the Admiral and James Perrott bore the title to their deaths*,(f) and the Admiral's successor, *Sir Robert de Cornwall*, was elected Member for Leominster *under that title*, but on a rumour that it would be deemed a false return no person being to be found of that name and distinction, he applied to the late Duke of Grafton, his friend, who undertook to obtain a sign manual from the late King before the sitting of the House, a copy of which you have here subjoined, which the Duke carried to the King, who signed it—the validity of the election, when that was known, was never disputed. *After the death of Sir James Perrott*, his *nephew*

(a) This was supplied by a well-known antiquary, the Rev. A. B. Beaven, M.A., who writes that though it "seems to be somewhat Thucydidean in the length of its sentences and its *Anakolouthia*, it is copied verbatim."

(b) This, however, is one of the many false statements with which this extraordinary document bristles, inasmuch as Richard Perrott *never was* in Parliament.

(c) An account of the Perrott Baronetcy is in "*The Complete Baronetage*, 1611-1800, by G.E.C." (vol. ii., p. 33, note "c"), from which it will be seen that there is great confusion between this *James* and a certain *Robert* Perrott, of Richmond, Surrey, stated to have been *cr. a Baronet* 1 July 1717. The whole matter is ably dealt with by the well-known John Gough Nichols, in the *Her. and Gen.* (vol. viii., pp. 314-324), where "Sir Richard Perrott," who assumed the title, is styled "one of the most daring pretenders to title and pedigree in the last [*i.e.*, the eighteenth] century."

(d) "The late King" in 1766 was George II., who also is defined as coming "after" George I.'s (the grantor's) "lifetime," but George II. did not succeed to the Crown till June 1727, about nine years *after* the death of Vice-Admiral Cornwall, one of the two alleged grantees.

(e) This "relation" was actually no other than his *son*, Robert, who assumed the Baronetcy, though not for some time after the grantee's death, as above stated.

(f) This is certainly false as far as Cornwall is concerned. See p. 70, note "a."

Richard, according to the intention of the limitation, *was reputed the Baronet* and bore the title ever since, and in the dispute in the House of Commons which commenced 4 March 1761 with Charles Fitzroy Scudamore, Esq., was therein treated, styled and reputed as *Sir Richard Perrott*."

COURTENAY, *or* COURTNEY(a) [I.]:

cr. 20 Dec. 1621.

[*Delete* the account in Vol. i., p. 229 and lines 1 to 4 on p. 230. *Insert* as under.]

I. 1621. "GEORGE COURTNEY, Esq., of Newcastle, co. Limerick," sometimes called GEORGE OUGHLTRED COURTENAY, 4th of the seven sons of Sir William COURTENAY, of Powderham, Devon (one of the undertakers in 1585 for the plantation of Ireland), by his 1st wife, Elizabeth, da. of Henry (MANNERS), EARL OF RUTLAND, was *b.* about 1580-85, and was *cr. a Baronet* [I.] by Privy Seal dat. Westminster 10 Dec. 1641, but no patent was ever enrolled,(b) and he is described as an "Esq." as late as 1 Nov. 1641, when his son, William, was *Knighted*. He *m.* in or before 1616, Catherine, da. of Sir Francis BERKELEY, of Askeaton, co. Limerick, by Katharine, da. of Adam LOFTUS, Archbishop of Dublin and Lord Chancellor [I.]. He *d.* 5 March 1644. Admon. [I.] as "Esq.," 20 July 1658, to his son Francis.

II. 1644. SIR WILLIAM COURTENAY, of Newcastle aforesaid, *called also* WILLIAM OUGHTRED COURTENAY, 1st s. and h., *b.* 1616; had livery, 20 March 1638, of the estate of his maternal uncle, Henry BERKELEY; was *Knighted* v.p. 1 Nov. 1641 by the Lord Justices [I.]. He *m.* (settlement 22 Nov. 1639) Margaret, d. of Sir William FENTON, by Margaret, da. of Maurice FitzEdmund FITZGIBBON. He *d.* s.p.s.(b) 4 Feb. 1651/2.

III. 1652. FRANCIS COURTENAY, of Newcastle aforesaid, br. and h., *b.* 1617; was a Colonel in the army. He *never assumed the Baronetcy.* He *m.* in 1658, Frances, 1st da. of Richard (BOYLE), 2d EARL OF CORK [I.], by Elizabeth, da. and h. of Henry (CLIFFORD), 5th EARL OF CUMBERLAND. He *d.* 20 March 1659/60. Funeral entry [I.]. Will dat. 18 Jan. 1658/9 (at which date he had no issue), pr. 1660 [I.]. His widow *m.* April 1662 (as his 1st wife), Wentworth (DILLON), 4th EARL OF ROSCOMMON [I.] (who *d.* 18 Jan. 1684), and was living 17 June 1665, but *d.* before Nov. 1674.

IV. 1660, to 1700? SIR WILLIAM COURTENAY, of Newcastle aforesaid, *called also* WILLIAM OUGHTRED COURTENAY, only s. and h., *b.* in 1659 or 1660, and, apparently, *assumed or was credited with the Baronetcy.* His claim, 8 Aug. 1663 [by, presumably, his guardian] to 8,971 acres in co. Limerick as "Sir William Courtney, son of Francis, brother of Sir William, son of George,"(c) was heard by the Court of Claims, Dublin, on Monday, 16 Aug. 1663, and "dismist to law." Nothing more is known of him.(d) The Limerick attainders by James II. in 1689 include "Francis Courtney, Esq., James Courtney, Esq., and Richard Courtney, Esq., sons of Sir William."(e)

(a) See p. 65, note "b," under "BINGHAM."

(b) His only child, George Courtenay, *d.* s.p. and v.p. [MSS. Trinity Coll., Dublin, "F. 3, 23"].

(c) Nineteenth Report of the Deputy Keeper of the Public Record Office [I.], 1887. There is clearly a clerical error in the abstract of these decrees in identifying him with Sir William Courtenay of Powderham.

(d) He is often stated to have *m.* Joan, da. of Sir Thomas Southwell, of Castle Mattress, co. Limerick, by Elizabeth, da. of William Starkey, of Dromolen, co. Clare. That lady, however, *m.* as his 1st wife and for her only husband (settlement 21 Sep. 1678), *Richard* Courtenay, 3d s. of Sir William Courtenay of Powderham.

(e) See vol. i., p. 230, note "a."

CURTIUS:

cr. 2 April 1652.

[*Delete* the account in Vol. iii., p. 12, and *insert* as under.]

I. 1652. "WILLIAM CURTIUS, then Resident, for His Majesty, with Gustavus, King of Sweden, and the Princes of Germany," was *cr. a Baronet* 2 April 1652, having been "employed for many years, by King Charles I. and King Charles II., as Resident with the Princes of Germany, during which time he did several considerable services to the said Kings and others of the royal family, and to many of the English nation."(a) By sign manual of Charles II., dat. 1 Nov. 1654, it appears that £14,255 was due to him for salary and other allowances. This was unsatisfied at his death in 1678.(a)

II. 1678, to 1700? SIR CHARLES CURTIUS, Baronet [1652], 1st s. and h., *suc. to the Baronetcy* in 1678. He was living 12 Dec. 1688, when he assigned the debt due to his father (as above) to his yr. br., Adolph Curtius, and presumably was so on 15 Dec. 1693, when the said Adolph Curtius, as "Esq.," petitioned the Crown for the same. Nothing is known of the family after that date.

DAWNAY:

cr. 19 May 1642.

[*Delete* the account of the 2d Baronet as also note "d" in Vol. ii., p. 176, and *insert* as under.]

II. 1644, July to Nov. SIR THOMAS DAWNAY, Baronet [1642], of Cowick aforesaid, only surv.(b) s. and h.; *bap.* 23 April 1644 at Sessay; *suc. to the Baronetcy*, 13 July 1644, and was *bur.* 4 Nov. 1644 at Sessay, when the *Baronetcy* became *extinct*.(c)

DE VIC:

cr. 3 Dec. 1649.

[*Delete* the account of the 2d Baronet in Vol. iii., p. 11, and *insert* as under.]

II. 1671, to 1688. SIR CHARLES DE VIC, Baronet [1649], only surv. s. and h., *suc. to the Baronetcy*, 20 Nov. 1671, and pr. his father's will, 15 Feb. 1671/2. He served in Ireland, 1675-78, as Ensign and Lieut. in a Regiment of Guards; Captain in Sir William King's Regiment in March 1684/5; in Colonel Theodore Russell's in Sep. 1685, and subsequently in Colonel Anthony Hamilton's [*Ormonde MSS.*, vol. i., pp. 429, 446; vol. ii., p. 224]. He *m.* in or before 1673(d). He *d.* s.p.m.(e) 17 March 1688, at Downpatrick, Ireland, when the *Baronetcy* became *extinct*. M.I. there.

(a) "Petition of Adolph Curtius, son of Sir William Curtius, Baronet," 15 Dec. 1695, claiming £14,000 due from the Crown to his father. [House of Lords MSS., vol. i., N.S., pp. 5-7.]

(b) The first child, John, was *bap.* 6 Dec. 1642, and *bur.* 14 March 1643/4, both at Snaith.

(c) See vol. ii., p. 176, note "e."

(d) Ann, their child, was *bap.* 25 Aug. 1673 at St. Michan's, Dublin, and *bur.* there 1 Aug. 1674.

(e) See vol. iii., p. 11, note "a."

DICK [S.]:

cr. about 1638, 1642 or 1646 ?

[*Insert* in Vol. ii., p. 449, between lines 16 and 17 as under.]

After the death, 19 Dec. 1655, of the well-known Sir William Dick, of Braid, the grantee (or supposed grantee) of the Baronetcy, it was, apparently, *assumed*, though somewhat fitfully, as under :—

II.* 1655. SIR ALEXANDER DICK, Baronet [S.], of Craighouse, near Edinburgh, 2d but 1st surv. s., though not heir male of his father. He had a pension of £132 to him and his descendants by royal warrant, Nov. 1674 (confirmed by James II.), but before long, however, he was ruined and had protection in 1681 against arrest. He *d.* before 1695.

III.* 1690 ? ANDREW DICK, s. and h., who presumably survived his father, but who is never styled "Sir," was an Advocate. He *m.* 11 Oct. 1683, Clara, sometimes called "Honble. Clara *Ruthven*," da. of James (BAILLIE), 2d LORD FORRESTER [S.], by his 2d wife, Jean, da. of Patrick (RUTHVEN), EARL OF BRENTFORD. He *d.* in or before 1698. His widow *m.* (—) MURRAY, of Spot.

IV.* 1698 ? LEWIS DICK, sometimes called SIR LEWIS DICK, Baronet [S.], br. and h., but who as "Mr. Lewis Dick." was served heir to his brother in 1698. He was a Captain in the army.

V.* 1710 ? SIR ALEXANDER DICK, Baronet [S.], s. and h.(a) He *m.* Margaret, da. of Patrick SCOT, of Rossie. He *d.* s.p.m.s.(b) probably before April 1736, but certainly before 1760. Some years after his death the service to this Baronetcy of 1768 was issued to Sir John Dick as in the text of Vol. ii., p. 449.

DOWDALL [I.]:

cr. 24 Nov. 1663. [See Vol. iv., p. 227.]

The warrant for the creation of this Baronetcy is dat. 24 Nov. 1663, so that the statement of Betham that it was created by James II is, apparently, erroneous.

DRAKE:

cr. 2 Aug. 1622. (See Vol. i., p. 208.]

This Baronetcy did not become extinct on the death of the 5th Baronet, 22 Feb. 1794, but in the event of Francis Henry Drake, nephew of that Baronet, being (as was presumably the case) illegitimate would have devolved as below :—

(a) According to the memorial of Janet and Anne, his two daughters [probably before April 1736, but certainly before 1760] to the Lords Commissioners of H.M.'s Treasury, stating that they were "daughters of Sir Alexander Dick, Baronet," and that they were "the only descendants now in life of Capt. Lewis Dick," son of Sir Andrew Dick, of Craighouse. One of these ladies, Janet, *m.* 1 April 1736, as his first wife, Sir Alexander Dick, 3d Baronet [S. 1707], of Prestonfield, and *d.* s.p.m., 26 Oct. 1760, leaving two daughters who had a pension of £132.

(b) Patrick, his only son, *d.* s.p. and v.p.

VI. 1794, to 1810. SIR JOHN SAVERY DRAKE, Baronet [1622], cousin and h. male, being only s. and h. of John DRAKE, Collector of Customs, and sometime Mayor of Plymouth (*d.* 1753, aged 44), by Anne SPICER, of Farway (*m.* Aug. 1736), which John was s. of the Rev. Bamfield DRAKE, B.A., Rector of Farway (*d.* June 1729, aged 59), who was a s. of Joseph DRAKE, of Buckland Monachorum (*d.* Oct. 1708), who was yr. s. of the first Baronet. He was *b.* about 1740 ; was Lieut. 33d Foot ; received the Freedom of Glasgow ; *suc. to the Baronetcy*, 22 Feb. 1794 ; became insane, and *d.* unm. March 1810, when the *Baronetcy* became *extinct*.

DRUMMOND [S.](a):

cr. about 1640 ?

SIR JOHN DRUMMOND, of Carnock. It is stated in Douglas' *Baronage* [S.] (edit. 1798, p. 571), that he is "*said to have been a Baronet*" [S.]. He was s. of Sir Alexander DRUMMOND, of Carnock and Bannockburn, by Elizabeth, da. of Sir Alexander HEPBURN, of Waughton. He sold the lands of Carnock to Sir Thomas Nicolson, and was slain at the battle of Alford in 1645, *ex parte Regis*. He *m.* (—), da. of (—) ROLLOCK, of Duntreath. "Whether he left any children is uncertain, but either at his death in 1645 or soon after, the honours of Carnock sunk into the family of Hawthornden," descendants of his great grandfather.

EARLE:

cr. 2 July 1629. [See Vol. ii., p. 76.]

This Baronetcy, which apparently became *extinct* on the death of the 4th Baronet, 18 Aug. 1697, was claimed in 1900, and *assumed* in or before 1905, by the REV. WILLIAM EARLE, M.A. (Dublin), Curate of St. Clement Danes, 1895. He stated himself to be son of SIR GEORGE EARLE, 9th Baronet, by Cecilia, da. of Ralph STONE, of Carnew Castle, co. Wicklow, which George was son of SIR ROBERT EARLE, 8th Baronet, s. of SIR WILLIAM EARLE, 7th Baronet, son (or possibly grandson, by a son named John) of SIR ROBERT EARLE, 6th Baronet, son of SIR WILLIAM EARLE, 5th Baronet, who is said to have been a younger son of the 1st Baronet. The existence of these five Baronets is unknown. The claimant was ed. at Trin. Coll., Dublin ; B.A., 1882 ; M.A., 1892 ; in Holy Orders, 1882 ; Curate of Carnteel, co. Tyrone, 1882-83 ; of Currin, co. Managhan, 1883-87 ; of Tallow, co. Waterford, 1887-89 ; of St. James', Leicester, 1890-91 ; of Sunbury, Middlesex, 1891-95, and of St. Clement Danes, 1895. He (who was styled by Judge Addison "*a self-appointed Baronet*") was committed in April 1905 at Southwark County Court for twenty-one days in default of paying a bill at 5s. a month [*Daily Express*, 14 April 1905].

GORDON [S.]:

cr. 28 May 1625. [See Vol. ii., p. 280.]

The 10th Baronet, who was a Roman Catholic and a generous supporter of that Church, and who "in his early days was occupied largely with industrial undertakings, but during the past twenty-five years led the life of a recluse" [*Morning Post*, 5 March 1908], *d.* unm. at Letterfourie, 4 March 1908, aged 83, when the *Baronetcy* again became *dormant*. Will pr. above £22,000 personalty.

(a) See p. 63, note "a," under "BARCLAY."

GRENVILLE:

cr. 9 April 1630. [See Vol. ii., p. 78.]

The death of this Baronet, generally said to be in 1658, was on 31 Oct. 1659. See a letter to Sir Edward Hyde from one John Forde, dated at Bruges "All Saints' Day, 1659," saying he had heard by an express from Ghent that Grenville died there "yesterday." [*Clarendon MSS.*, in the Bodleian Library, Oxford, communicated by the Rev. W. D. Macray, Ducklington Rectory, Witney.]

GRAY [S.](a):

cr. about 1640 ?

SIR WILLIAM GRAY, of Pittendrum, is called "KNIGHT BARONET' [S.], both in *Crawfurd's Peerage* [S.] and in *Douglas' Peerage* [S.], edit. 1764, p. 316. He was living 1641, being father of WILLIAM GRAY, slain 1660, who, by Anne, his wife, "Mistress of Gray," da. and heir of line of Andrew (GRAY), LORD GRAY [S.], had a son, PATRICK GRAY, who in 1663 (on the death of his maternal grandfather abovenamed) became LORD GRAY [S.].

HASILRIGG, *or* HESILRIGE:

cr, 21 July 1622. [See Vol. i., p. 203.]

The following remarkable notices relate to the wife of Sir Robert Hesilrige, the 8th Baronet, who was disinherited, and who succeeded to the title (but not to the estates) on his father's death, 23 April 1763 :—"1768, April 29. Mr. Ralph Inman is requested to make quest for '*a very poor unfortunate lady, at Roxbury*.' Lady Hesilrige, wife of [Robert] the son of Sir Arthur Hesilrige, who is enquired for, Mr. Jonathan Ormston (Sir Arthur's trustee), and who must make proof of her marriage." "1768, Nov. 18. Letter to Lady Hesilrige at Boston. Interest due on the death of her father [in-law], Sir Arthur Hesilrige, on £500 legacy . . . Sir Arthur left his estate to the youngest of five sons. He is not yet of age. Your son, as he will have the title ought to have the estate likewise." [*Mr. Carr Ellison's Mss.*, p. 95 ; Report xv., Appendix x., *Hist. Mss. Commission* ; quoted in *The Ancestor*, vol. i., p. 260, April 1902.]

HUBAND:

cr. 2 Feb. 1660/1. [See Vol. iii., p. 158.]

The title was assumed and the estate claimed about 1785 by JOHN HAYES HUBAND, of Dublin, an officer of the Revenue (*b.* 25 Aug. and *bap.* 7 Sep. 1724 at St. Luke's Dublin), as great great grandson and heir male of TEVEREY HUBAND, who was yr. br. of the 1st Baronet, and who under the will, dat. 19 April 1671, of his mother, Ann, d. and h. of Gervase TEVEREY, of Stapleford, Notts, inherited the manor of Twiford and Greenhill, co. Derby. This Tevery Huband is alleged to have been father of EDWARD HUBAND, of Hobery Green, in Inkbury, co. Worcester (*bur.* 27 Aug. 1670 at Inkbury), father of EDMUND HUBAND, of Dublin, tanner (*bur.* 4 June 1719 at St. Luke's, Dublin), father of FRANCIS HUBAND, of Mill Street, Dublin, brewer (*bap.* 3 March 1694 at St. Nicholas Without, Dublin, and *d.* intestate before 9 Feb. 1727/8), who by Anne (*m.* 11 May 1723, at St. Andrew's Dublin), da. of John HAYES, of co. Wicklow, was father of the claimant. The pedigree, even if proved, would give no claim to the title unless under a special remainder to collaterals, and is discredited as to the date of 1670 being that of

(a) See p. 63, note "a," under "BARCLAY."

the burial of claimant's great grandfather, inasmuch as "John Hughband," of Mill Street, Dublin, tanner, brother of Edmund Hughband (who can be identified as the claimant's grandfather) in one of his two wills, dat. 1 Nov. 1689, and proved in Dublin, 25 Jan. 1689/90, makes his father one of his executors, which father was according to claimant's pedigree, buried 27 Aug. 1670. The claimant *m.* in or before 1754 (apparently as his first wife), Mary, da. of Thomas CHALKE, of Dublin. He *d.* s.p.m.(a) 20 Jan. 1805. In his will, dat. 27 Sep. 1802, pr. [I.] 25 March 1805, he styles himself "JOHN HAYES HUBAND, ESQ., now SIR JOHN HAYES HUBAND, BARONET, of the city of Dublin," and states that he was legally entitled as heir male to the Ipsley estate in Warwickshire, but had not means to establish his right thereto. He calls his wife "Mary Anne Huband, otherwise Byrne," and her mother "Edith Byrne, otherwise Huband". [*Ex inform.* G. D. Burtchaell, Athlone Pursuivant.]

HUTCHINSON [I.]:

cr. 11 Dec. 1782. [See Vol. v., p. 410.]

This Baronetcy became *extinct* on the death unm. of Sir EDWARD SYNGE-HUTCHINSON, 3 Nov. 1906, aged 76.

I'ANSON:

cr. 6 May 1652. [See Vol. iii., p. 14.]

SIR JOHN I'ANSON, 7th and last Baronet, *suc. to the Baronetcy*, Nov. 1799, and *d.* s.p.m. 3 March 1800, aged 66, being *bur.* in Tunbridge Church. M.I. On his death the *Baronetcy* became *extinct*.

IBBETSON:

cr. 2 June 1748. [See Vol. v., p. 97.]

This Baronetcy, which apparently became *extinct*, 15 Jan. 1902, on the death of the 7th Baronet (who, in 1892, had been *cr.* BARON ROOKWOOD), was claimed and assumed in 1907 as under, an advertisement appearing in *The Times* newspaper of 13 Dec. 1907 to the effect that George Broun Ibbetson, of 7 Clovelly Mansions, Teddington, Middlesex, has assumed the Baronetcy conferred in 1748 on Henry Ibbetson, of Leeds, co. York, and will henceforth "be known as SIR GEORGE BROUN IBBETSON, BARONET, and by that name and designation only." This claim is commented upon in the *Daily Mail* newspaper of 14 Dec. 1907, in which the claimant states that "my claim is perfectly direct : my great great grandfather was first cousin to the first Baronet." This then being the ground of the claim, it is manifest, that, even allowing the pedigree to be as stated, it gives no right to the Baronetcy which was created as above, with the usual remainder to *heirs male of the body* of the grantee.(b)

JERMY:

cr. Nov. 1663.

"ROBERT JERMY, of Norfolk," had a "warrant for a Baronetcy, Nov. 1663 [*Collection of State Papers*, 1660-70]. Nothing more is known of him.

(a) Mary, apparently his only child, *b.* 18 and *bap.* 25 Sep. 1754, at St. Catherine's, Dublin, was living 27 Sep. 1802.

(b) The enrolment of the patent has been searched by Reginald M. Glencross and the certainty of that fact has thus been ascertained.

KIEVIT :

cr. 6 Sep. 1667.

" SIR [*Qy.* Sieur ?] JEAN KIEVIT " had a *warrant for a Baronetcy* 6 Sep. 1667 [Entry Book 23, p. 548; *Collection of State Papers* (*Domestic*)]. He was probably the same person as " SIEUR KIEVITT," whose ship, the " St. John," of Rotterdam and Stettin, laden with wine and bound from France to Hamburg, was brought into Plymouth as a prize, and was ordered to be restored to him, 3 July 1667. [*Ib.*](a)

Possibly identical with JOHN NICHOLAES KIEVIT, of Rotterdam, whose da., Deborah Speelman, widow, was raised to the rank of a Baronet's widow, 9 Sep. 1686. See vol. iv., p. 142.

LAURIE [S.] :

cr. 27 March 1685. [See Vol. iv., p. 332.]

This Baronetcy, which presumably became *extinct* on the death of the 6th Baronet, 7 Jan. 1848, was assumed on the ground of a descent in the male line from the third son of the 1st Baronet by HENRY ALFRED LAURIE, of the Civil Service, who claimed to have succeeded his brother, " SIR CHARLES LAURIE " therein in 1894, both being sons of COL. JOHN LAURIE, R.A. (who did not assume the title), by Julia Susan, da. of Capt. Alexander PITFORD, 67th Regiment. No third son, but only two are attributed to the 1st Baronet in Playfair's *Baronetage* [S.], of whom Walter, the youngest, became the 3d Baronet. The claimant first appears in Dod's *Baronetage* for 1899. He was *b.* 1845; *m.* firstly, 1873, Alice Mary, da. of Capt. Edmund Charles CROWLY, 3d Madras Cavalry. She *d.* 1885. He *m.* secondly, 1890, Alice Elizabeth, da. of Thomas OAKELEY, of Oakeley, Salop.

LEKE, *or* LEAKE :

cr. 22 May 1611. [See Vol. i., p. 8.]

This Baronetcy, which apparently became *extinct* on the death, 17 July 1736, of the fourth holder, Nicholas (Leke), 4th Earl of Scarsdale, was assumed from probably about 1780 till 1816, by the owner of Quebec Castle, near East Dereham, Norfolk, which, in an engraving about 1780, is said to be the seat of " SIR JOHN ODINGSELLS LEAKE, BARONET," who on his M.I. at St. Stephen's, Norwich, in 1816 is styled " SIR JOHN ODINGSELLS LEEKE, BARONET." He was probably the son of the Rev. Robert Leeke, Rector of Great Snoring, 1734-1762 (*d.* 2 July 1762), son presumably of John Odingsells Leeke (*b.* 1672), an attorney at Epperstone in 1703, and afterwards (1726) at Worksworth, co. Derby, who was the only son of John Leeke (nunc. will dat. 3 July 1673, pr. 2 Nov. 1674), by Elizabeth, da. and h. of Emanuel Odingsells. This John was yr. br. of Drewell Leeke, of the Chantry in Newark, both being sons of Nicholas Leeke, of Hedley, co. York, a yr. br. of Sir Francis Leeke, who was *cr. a Baronet* in 1663, the title becoming *extinct* in 1681. The said Nicholas and Francis were sons of William Leeke, of the Chantry aforesaid (*d*; 1650), who was a yr. br. of Francis Leeke, *cr. a Baronet* in 1611, and *cr.* Earl of Scarsdale in 1645, which dignities became *extinct* in 1736. (See *Her. and Gen.*, vol. vii., pp. 495-500, and *Notes & Queries*, 6th S., vol. viii., p. 448; vol. ix., pp. 16, 57 and 297.). Sir John *d.* 5 Feb. 1816, aged 69. Will pr. in P.C.C. His widow, Elizabeth, *d.* 13 Oct. 1818, both *bur.* at St. Stephen's, Norwich. M.I. It is possible that this assumption was made on the ground that the grant of Baronetcy was (as has sometimes, though erroneously, been supposed) made to Sir Francis Leke, *father* of the grantee, but this is *disproved* by a deed, dated 5 Sep. (1624), 22 James I., between " Sir Francis Leeke, the Elder, *Knt.*, and Sir Francis Leeke, Knt. and *Baronet*, his son and heir." [Addit. MSS., 6,700, p. 194.] Besides that, in his patent of creation, 6 Oct. 1624, as Baron Deincourt (his father being still alive) he (the son) is styled " Baronet."

(a) See p. 65, note " b," under " BINGHAM."

LIVINGSTON [S.] :

cr. 20 July 1663. [See Vol. iv., p. 333.]

This Baronetcy, which became apparently *extinct* or *dormant* on the death, in 1810, of Sir Alexander Campbell [born Livingston], 4th Baronet [S. 1663], of Ardkinglass, co. Argyll, was assumed as under :—

V. 1810, to 1831. JAMES CALLANDER, of Craigforth, co. Stirling, s. and h. of John CALLANDER, of the same, a Scottish antiquary (*d.* 14 Sep. 1789, " at a good old age "), by Mary, sister of Sir James CAMPBELL, 3d Baronet [S. 1685], da. of Sir James LIVINGSTONE, 2d Baronet [S. 1685], was *b.* 21 Oct. [O.S.] 1745; ed. at the High School, Edinburgh; Ensign, 51st Foot, 1759, serving in the Seven Years' War; was afterwards Colonel and was at Naples as Inspector-General, and subsequently, till 1802, at the Ionian Islands. He was one of the English detained in France by Napoleon, being there when in 1810 he succeeded to the estate of Ardkinglass on the death of his cousin, the 4th Baronet, when he *took the name of Campbell and, assuming also the Baronetcy*,(a) styled himself SIR JAMES CAMPBELL, Baronet [S. 1685]. He *m.* firstly, in 1768, Christian, yst. da. of George FORBES, of Hitchener, Hall, Surrey. She *d.* 1771. He *m.* secondly, Harriet DATENS, spinster. She *d.* 17 Aug. 1773. He *m.* thirdly, Sep. 1777, Elizabeth Helena, (*b.* 17 June 1747), da. of Alexander (MAC-DONNELL), 5th EARL OF ANTRIM [I.], by his 2d wife, Anne, d. and h. of Charles Patrick PLUNKET. She *d.* 1796. He presumably *m.* in or before 1810, " Madame Lina Talina SASSEN," a French lady, whom he sent over to Scotland as his Commissioner, describing her as his " beloved wife." [Anderson's " *Scottish Nation.*"] The Court of Session found this marriage " not proven," but awarded her £300 a year, which, however, was, on appeal to the Lords, reversed. She for the rest of her life, which ended within a fortnight of his, brought various actions against him, suing *in formâ pauperis*. He *d.* May 1831, aged 85, leaving male issue, none of whom, however, assumed the Baronetcy.

MACDONALD [S.] :

cr. 14 July 1625. [See Vol. ii., p. 292.]

The merger of this Baronetcy, 7 July 1773, with the BARONY OF MACDONALD OF SLATE, co. Antrim [I.], conferred at the abovenamed date on the 9th Baronet, did not last longer than 13 Oct. 1832, when the 3d Baron and 11th Baronet *d.*, leaving issue male by a lady whom he subsequently married. That marriage, according to the law of Scotland, legitimated such issue, and the heirs male thereof were by it entitled to the *Scottish* Baronetcy, and are so now (1909), though not (according to the English and Irish law) to the *Irish* Barony. This Baronetcy, however, they have never assumed.

(a) There can be no doubt of this fact. The life of Sir James Campbell was published in 1832 (2 vols., 8vo), being his memoirs, by himself, though, according to Anderson's *Scottish Nation* (1864), it was " a work not remarkable for the accuracy of its facts." In Burke's *Landed Gentry* [edit. 1849, vol. iii., p. 54] an account is given of his first three marriages (as in the text) and of his issue, his grandson, James Henry Callander, being then of Craigforth and Ardkinglass, but no mention is made of the assumption of the Baronetcy in 1810, nor is there any allusion to the fourth and last wife, if indeed she was one.

MACKENZIE [S.] :

cr. 21 May 1628. [See Vol. ii., p. 355.]

Notwithstanding the forfeiture of this Baronetcy by its devolution, 14 Sep. 1763, on the attainted heir male of the body of the grantee, it was assumed from 1826 to 1848, and it was not till Jan. 1882 that the issue male of the grantee became *extinct*. Subject to the attainder the right of descent was as below :—

VI. 1763. GEORGE MACKENZIE, *sometime* (1731-1745), EARL OF CROMARTY [S.], cousin and h. male, being s. and h. of John, 2d EARL OF CROMARTY [S.], who was elder br. to Sir Kenneth MACKENZIE, 3d Baronet [S. 1628], to whom the *novo damus* of that dignity was granted in 1704. He *suc. his father*, 20 Nov. 1731, in the *Earldom of Cromarty* [S.], which became *forfeited* by his attainder in 1746. On the death of Sir Kenneth MACKENZIE, 5th Baronet [S. 1628], of Tarbat, and 3d Baronet [S. 1704], of Roystoun, he *suc. to those Baronetcies* which in consequence of his attainder *became thereby forfeited*. He *d.* 28 Sep. 1766, aged about 63.

VII. 1766. JOHN MACKENZIE, *styled* LORD MACLEOD, s. and h., *b.* 1727, *d.* s.p. 2 April 1789.

VIII. 1789. KENNETT MACKENZIE, of Cromarty, cousin and h. male, being s. and h. of Capt. the Hon. Roderick MACKENZIE (living 1745), yr. br. of the attainted Earl, being 2d s. of John, 2d EARL OF CROMARTY [S.]. He *d.* s.p.m. 4 Nov. 1796, when the issue male of the 1st Earl became *extinct*.

[See fuller particulars under " CROMARTY " Earldom [S.], *cr.* 1704.]

IX. 1796. ROBERT MACKENZIE, of Milnmount,(a) cousin and h. male, and as such entitled, but for their forfeiture, to the Baronetcies [S. 1628 and 1704], which he never assumed. He was s. of Alexander MACKENZIE, of Ardlock, co. Ross, by Margaret, da. of Robert SUTHERLAND, of Langwell, co. Caithness, which Alexander (who *d.* in 1772) was s. and h. of John MACKENZIE, of the same (*d.* 1726), s. and h. of Alexander MACKENZIE, also of Ardlock, who was yr. br. of George, 1st EARL OF CROMARTY [S.], both being sons of Sir John MACKENZIE, 1st Baronet [S. 1628]. of Tarbat. He was *b.* 1743; was a Lieut.-Col. in the East India Company's service. He *m.* firstly, Margaret, sister of John MACKENZIE, of Bayfield. She, from whom he was separated, *d.* s.p. 1787. He *m.* secondly, in or before 1801, Katharine, da. of Col. SUTHERLAND, of Uppat, co. Sutherland, by Elizabeth, da. of William BAILLIE, of Rodshall. He *d.* 1809.

X. 1809. ALEXANDER MACKENZIE, *afterwards* (1826), SIR ALEXANDER MACKENZIE, Baronet [S. 1628 and 1704](b). 1st s. and h., by 2d wife, *b.* 16 May 1802; *suc.* his father, 1809; was an officer in the 48th Bengal Native Infantry; was served by a Scottish Jury, at Tain, 17 Aug. 1826, heir male to George (MACKENZIE), 1st EARL OF CROMARTY [S.], brother to his great grandfather, and thereupon *assumed the Baronetcies* [S.], to which, but for their forfeiture, he would have been entitled in 1809 at his father's death. He *d.* unm.(c) at Calcutta, 28 April 1841, aged 38. Will pr. Dec. 1842.

XI. 1841. SIR JAMES SUTHERLAND MACKENZIE, Baronet [S. 1628 and 1704],(b) br. and h., *b.* 1805. He *assumed the Baronetcies* on his brother's death, 28 April 1841. He *d.* unm. at Kensington, 24 Nov. 1858, aged 53.

(a) Most of the particulars concerning him and his successors have been kindly supplied by Lieut. E. M. Mackenzie, of Melbourne, Victoria.

(b) According to the assumption, after the service in 1826, of the Baronetcy, notwithstanding the forfeiture in Sep. 1763.

(c) The following marriage, given in the *Gent. Mag.* for Feb. 1812 cannot rightly refer to him, as he was then but nine years of age : " Sir Alexander Mackenzie, of Arock, co. Ross, to Miss Geddes Mackenzie."

XII. 1858, to 1882. JOHN MACKENZIE, cousin and h. male, being 1st surv. s. of Kenneth MACKENZIE, of Ledbag, by his 2d wife, Elizabeth, da. of (—) MACKAY, of Oldeney, which Kenneth was br. to Robert MACKENZIE [No. IX.] abovementioned, both being sons of Alexander MACKENZIE, of Ardloch, great grandson of the 1st Baronet, [S. 1628], of Tarbat. He suc. his cousin, 24 Nov. 1858, in the representation of the 1st Baronet, but *never assumed the forfeited Baronetcies* [S. 1628 and 1704]. He *m.* twice, but *d.* s.p. Jan. 1882, when the *issue male of the 1st Baronet* [S. 1628], of Tarbat, became *extinct*.(a)

MAPLES :

cr. 30 May 1627. [See Vol. ii., p. 22.]

[Substitute the following account for the one given as above.]

I. 1627. " THOMAS MAPLES, of Stow, co. Huntingdon, Esq.," whose parentage and career is unknown, was *cr. a Baronet*, as above, 30 May 1627. He *m.* Agnes, da. of (—). She *d.* 26 Aug. 1624, and was *bur.* at Stow. M.I. He *d.* 13 Feb. 1634/5, and was *bur.* there. M.I. His will dat. 29 Dec. 1634, pr. 7 March 1634/5, and confirmed 13 June 1635.

II. 1635, to 1650. SIR THOMAS MAPLES, Baronet [1627], only s. and h., to whom his father leaves £300 a year for life, praying that he may be endued " with more grace and temperance than he hitherto hath shewed " ; living 13 June 1635. He *d.* s.p. before 1655, when a deed of sale of a house at Colchester was executed by his nephews and coheirs, Thomas Rouse and John Stewkley.(b)

MARSHALL [S. and E.] :

cr. 1658. [See Vol. iii., p. 325.]

[Substitute the following account for the one above given.]

I. 1658. May to Aug. COL. WILLIAM MARSHALL, s. of Charles MARSHALL, of St. Ninian's, Stirling (where the family had long been seated), was for his fidelity to the late King (Charles), for whom he raised a regiment and suffered two years' imprisonment, *cr. a Baronet* [S. and E.] as above, by patent dat. at Brussels, 21 May 1658 [Stodart's *Scottish Arms*, vol. ii., p. 384], of which (though there is no record in the Great Seal Register) a copy has been privately printed, stating the dignity to be " infra regnum nostrum Angliæ et Scotiæ," and to be granted " sibi et heredibus suis in perpetuum, nepotibus æque et filiis." He *d.* at Ghent, a few months later, Aug. 1658, aged 56.(c)

(a) The collateral heirs male of the grantee of 1628 are presumably the Mackenzie Baronets [S. 1703], of Scatwell, and they appear to have assumed the same (in addition to their own Baronetcy) notwithstanding its forfeiture. This heirship is, however, only on the presumption of the failure of the male issue of James Mackenzie, of Keppoch, a yr. son of Alexander Mackenzie, of Ardloch, yr. br. of George, 1st Earl of Cromarty [S.], both being sons of the 1st Baronet [S. 1628] of Tarbat. This James had four sons, (1) Alexander, (2) Simon, (3) George (who *d.* aged 109), (4) Colin. Of these four, the 3 elder *m.* and had issue.

(b) Of his sisters, (1) Elizabeth (*d.* before 1655) was mother of Thomas Rouse, her heir, living 1655; (2) Agnes (*d.* before 1655) was mother of John Stewkeley, living 1636. [*Ex inform.* J. Horace Round.]

(c) Pedigree of Busk, with account of the family of Marshall, of Stirling. Privately printed.

II. 1658. Aug. GEORGE MARSHALL, s. and h., *never assumed the Baronetcy.* He settled about 1661 on lands granted to him on the river Sackville, in the provinces of Colchester, Hampshire and Halifax, in Nova Scotia.

III. 1710? WILLIAM MARSHALL, s. and h., *never assumed the Baronetcy.* He *m.* in or before 1750, and *d.* 1772.

IV. 1772, to 1816. CHARLES S. MARSHALL, only s. and h., *never assumed the Baronetcy.* He sold the estate in Nova Scotia and *d.* s.p. in 1816, being lost at sea on his voyage to England, when the *Baronetcy* became, in all probability, *extinct.*(a)

MAXWELL [S.]:

cr. 30 June 1663. [See Vol. iii., p. 340.]

The 2d Baronet did not die s.p. (as above stated), but was succeeded on his death in 1694, by his son as below.

III. 1694. SIR GEORGE MAXWELL, Baronet [S. 1663], s. and h. by first wife, was by Inq., 21 Nov. 1699, found seized of 9 merks of the lands of "Orchzeardtowne," in the parish of Buitle, co. Kirkcudbright. He, styling himself as of Orchardtoun, Baronet, states in a petition presented between 1703 and 1712 to the Duke of Ormond, Lord Lieutenant of Ireland,(b) that "going abroad to improve himself by travell, he hapned to be in France after the 10th day of Aprill, 1689, but never served in any plot against their late Majesties," that he returned to Scotland 3 years since and deported himself with all duty and loyalty, that he had a small estate in Ireland at his entering upon his travels and he wants Her Majesty's lycence to goe into Ireland in order to the recovery of his right." He *m.* between April 1708 and 20 July 1715, Mary, Dow. VISCOUNTESS MONTAGU, 1st da. of William (HERBERT), 1st MARQUESS OF POWIS, by Elizabeth, da. of Edward (SOMERSET), 2d MARQUESS OF WORCESTER. He *d.* s.p., 22 Feb. 1719/20, "at Archerton in Scotland," according to his Admon., 12 March 1719/20, to his widow. This was revoked, and his will dat. 20 July 1715 as "of Cowdray, Sussex, Baronet," pr. 14 June 1720 in P.C.C. by Mungo Maxwell, Esq., the executor.(c) His widow *d.* 30 Oct. 1744, or 1745,(d) and was *bur.* at Bruges. M.I. Will dat. 23 May 1738, pr. 31 Oct. 1745.

IV. 1720. [*Qy.*] "SIR GEORGE MAXWELL, of Orcharton," *d.* 28 Dec. 1746 [*Scots Mag.*, p. 98], probably heir male above.

* * * * * * *

(a) Of his two sisters and coheirs, (1) Rachel, *b.* 1750, *m.* firstly, Col. Faesch, 60th Regiment, who *d.* s.p. She *m.* secondly, about 1786, Joseph Edward Green, (who *d.* 1812 in Paris, aged 72), and *d.* 10 Dec. 1823, leaving an only surv. child, Maria, who was wife (April 1814) of Hans Busk, of Glennadder, co. Radnor. They had issue. (2) Mary, *b.* 1753, *m.* (—) Westcombe, and had issue, extinct in the second generation. See p. 81, note "c."

(b) The Duke of Ormond was Lord Lieutenant [I.], 1703-04, 1704-05, 1710-11, and 1711-12, and as the petition is endorsed and referred to the Lord Justices, "it must have been during one of his absences from Ireland." [*Ex inform.* G. D. Burtchaell, Athlone Pursuivant.]

(c) The will leaves all to Mungo Maxwell, 1st son of Robert Maxwell, of Golston, in the Stewartry of Kirkcudbright, by his 2d wife (— Lindsey), but if the said Mungo die under 21, then his next younger brother of the whole blood is to take his place. No other relations are mentioned.

(d) 30 Oct. 1745, according to the date of her M.I., of which a copy is given in the *Top. and Gen.*, Vol. ii., p. 535.

VII? [——] to 1786. "SIR ROBERT MAXWELL, Baronet, of Orchardtown," *d.* 21 Sep. 1786 [*Scots Mag.*, p. 467], is said to have been the 7th and last Baronet.(a) "Lady Maxwell," his relict, *d.* at Helmington Hall, Durham, April 1807 [*Hibernian Magazine*].

MEREDITH [I.]:

cr. 20 Nov. 1660. [See Vol. iii., p. 306.]

This Baronetcy became (in reality) extinct on the death of the grantee, without issue, in Feb. 1664/5, but was assumed more than 140 years later on the strength of a bogus pedigree recorded in Ulster's Office in 1808, in which the assumer of the title was (falsely) represented as the 7th Baronet, great grandson of the first Baronet.(b) It continued to be so assumed till the death s.p.m.s., 8 Oct. 1904, of "Sir" Edward Henry John Meredyth, the 10th Baronet [I. 1660] according to the fictitious descent in the above-mentioned pedigree. In Dec. 1904, Ulster King of Arms (Sir Arthur E. Vicars) disallowed the assumption of this title on the grounds that there was no proof that the 1st Baronet left issue. It was, however, assumed as below—

IX. 1904. SIR GEORGE AUGUSTUS JERVIS MEREDYTH, Baronet [I. 1660](c), cousin and h. male, being 2d but only surv. s. and h. of Charles Burton MEREDYTH, Major Royal Marines, by Maria (*m.* 1 Oct. 1822, at St. Mary's, Lambeth), da. of Henry JERVIS, which Charles Burton (who *d.* 14 Feb. 1865, aged 84) was yr. br. of the (so called) 8th and 9th Baronets. He was *b.* 11 Dec. 1831; left Ireland in 1850; was sometime in the police force, and is said to have been a cabman at Hobart Town, Tasmania, where he resided subsequently. He *assumed the Baronetcy* in Oct. 1904. He *m.* firstly, 7 June 1854, Ellen LAMPTON, who *d.* 5 Aug. 1903, leaving male issue. He *m.* secondly, 23 Feb. 1905, at Melbourne, Australia, Eliza, da. of (—) HURN.

MOWATT [S.]:

cr. 3 June 1664.(d) [See Vol. iii., p. 346.]

To the account above given of these obscure Baronets it may be added that one of them, presumably the 4th Baronet, Sir Alexander MOWAT, *m.* Antonatta [*Qy.* WINWOOD]. At all events the admon. of "DAME ANTONATTA MOWAT, late of London, widow," was granted, 18 Jan. 1723/4, at Dublin, to her son, [Sir] "Winwood Mowat, of Bewmares, co. Anglesey, Baronet."

(a) The Baronetcy of Orchardton, extinct or dormant, was about to be claimed by the heir in 1805, but the estate having been sold the idea was given up." [Anderson's *Scottish Nation*, Edinburgh, 1860, vol. iii., p. 128.]

(b) Richard Meredyth, of Shrewland, co. Kildare, was not *b.* in 1657, and was not a son of William, *cr. a Baronet* [I.] in 1660, but was *b.* at Shrewland in 1667, being s. of Robert Meredyth, 3d and yst. s. of Sir Robert Meredyth, of Shrewland (*d.* 17 Oct. 1668), the father of the 1st Baronet, which Baronet *d.* s.p. in 1665, two years *before* this Richard was born. He never assumed the title of Baronet, neither did any of his sons, nor did his grandson, Richard, though he and they are styled in the pedigree of 1808, as 2d, 3d, 4th, 5th and 6th Baronets. It was not till the bogus pedigree was recorded in 1808 that Barry Colles Meredyth, nephew and h. male of the so styled 6th Baronet, assumed the title.

(c) According to his assumption of that dignity.

(d) *Ex inform.* G. D. Burtchaell, Athlone Pursuivant.

V? 1715? SIR WINWOOD MOWAT, Baronet [S. 1664], presumably s. and h. of Alexander, 4th Baronet, by Antonatta, abovenamed, was living as a Baronet 18 Jan. 1723/4. He *m.* Elizabeth, yr. da. of William JEPHSON, Dean of Lismore [1690-1720], by Anne, relict of Capt Samuel HARTWELL, da. of Redmond BARRY, of Rathcormac, co. Cork. He *d.* s.p. before 9 June 1739, the date of the will of his widow, Dame Elizabeth MOWAT, pr. [I.], 30 May 1740.

[The title was assumed as late as 9 May 1829. See Vol. iii., p. 346.]

MURE [S.]:

temp. Car. I.(a)

SIR WILLIAM MURE, of Rowallan, in Scotland, is described as "KNIGHT BARONET" in the service of William MURE his son, 13 April 1658. See "*The Historie and Descent of the House of Rowallan*" [Glasgow, 1825, p. 95.]

NUGENT [I.]:

cr. 11 Jan. 1621/2. [See Vol. i., p. 230.]

This Baronetcy was *forfeited* in 1691 by the attainder of Sir Thomas, the 3d Baronet, who *d.* s.p., probably about 1710, certainly before Nov. 1726, when his widow died. It was assumed, however, as under(b):—

VI. 1710? SIR JOHN NUGENT, Baronet [I. 1622],(c) "of Farragh," br. and h. male, being 2d. s. of the 2d Baronet, *assumed the title.* He became a priest and *d.* unm. in France.

V. 1720? SIR RICHARD NUGENT, Baronet [I. 1622],(c) br. and h. male, Colonel in the Irish Brigade in the French service; *assumed the title.* He *m.* Anne, da. of Sir Richard NAGLE, Attorney General [I.], 1686-90, Principal Secretary of State and sometime Speaker of the House of Commons [I.], by Joanna, da. of Thomas KEARNEY. He *d.* s.p. at St. Germain, in France, about 1732.

VI. 1732? SIR JAMES NUGENT, Baronet [I. 1622],(c) of "Taghmore," cousin and h. male, being 1st s. and h. of Christopher NUGENT, of Dardistown, co. Meath (M.P. for Fore, 1689, in the Parl. [I.] of James II, Col. of Cavalry and subsequently a General in the service of France), by Bridget, da. of Robert (BARNEWALL), BARON TRIMLESTOWN [I.], which Christopher (who *d.* 3 June 1731 at St. Germain-en-laye) was s. and h. of Francis NUGENT, of Dardistown aforesaid (will dat. 3 Aug. 1678, pr. 15 Sep. 1686), 2d s. of the 1st Baronet. He was *b.* probably shortly before 1703; was Col. of "Nugent's Regiment" in the service of France, 1716 to 1732,(a) and was a Knight of the military Order of St. Louis in that kingdom.(b) He *m.* Elizabeth Bridget, da. of Peter REDMOND, of the Hall, co. Wexford, Knight of the Order of Christ in Portugal, by Anne, da. of Robert PARKER. He *d.* s.p.m.(c) 12 Dec. 1739, at St. Germain aforesaid.

(a) See p. 63, note "a," under "BARCLAY."

(b) *Ex inform.* G. D. Burtchaell, Athlone Pursuivant.

(c) Subject to the forfeiture of 1691.

VII. 1739, to 1783. SIR PETER WALTER CHRISTOPHER NUGENT, Baronet [I. 1622],(d) br. and h. male, *b.* at St. Germain's aforesaid about 1703, being aged 70 or thereabouts, 28 April 1773(a); was in the French service; Lieut.-Col. of Fitz-James's (formerly Nugent's) Cavalry; Brigadier-General, 1745; Field Marshal, 1748; Lieut.-General, 1762.(a) He *d.* s.p., probably unm., at St. Germain's aforesaid, 14 Feb. 1783, when the *Baronetcy* apparently became *extinct.*(e)

PERROTT:

alleged date, 1 July 1716 or 1717. [See Vol. v., pp. 33, 35 and 143.]

Besides the above references see also in this Vol. (pp. 8-10) under "CORNWALL" or "DE CORNEWALL."

PYE:

warrant 22 Dec. 1662.

"SIR ROBERT PYE, of Berkshire," *i.e.*, of Faringdon in that county, 1st s. and h. of Sir Robert PYE, of the same, Auditor of the Exchequer (*d.* 20 May

(a) Among the Betham MSS. in Ulster's Office is a list in French of the officers of the name of Nugent who were in the French service since 1690. Among them is "*Jacques Nugent, Chevalier Baronet*, Colonel du Regiment de Nugent, depuis 1716, jusque au 1732; mort a St. Germains le 12 Dec. 1739," as also "*Pierre Gualtier Christophe Nugent, Chevalier Baronet*, Lieut.-Colonel du Regiment de Fitzjames Cavalerie (auparavant Nugent), Brigadier des armées du Roi le 1 May 1745; Marechal de Camps le 10 Mai 1748; Lieut.-General le 25 Juillet 1762 mort a St. Germains le 14 Feb. 1783." This last is spoken of as "*Paul* Walter Christopher Nugent, Baronet," in the Cusack pedigree printed in M. Laine's *Archives de la Noblesse de France* [Paris, 1808, Vol. i., *Cusack*, p. 20], and as "Lieut.-Gen. in the armies of the King [of France]; born at St. Germain en laye; aged 70 or thereabouts, 28 April 1773," when he signed the "Certificate de Noblesse" of Marie Madelaine Josephe Aglaé de Cusack. "Paul" is evidently a mistake for "Pierre," *i.e.*, Peter.

(b) His military services are set forth in O'Callaghan's *Irish Brigade*, p. 153.

(c) Anna Johanna, his only da., *m.* July 1761, Edmund Rothe.

(d) Subject to the forfeiture of 1691.

(e) His yst. br., Patrick, had *d.* s.p. before 1764. He had four uncles, John, Walter, Patrick and Thomas, of whom Walter was slain at Aughrim in 1691. No issue of any of these is known. Patrick became Lieut.-Col. in Berwick's Regiment in the French service in 1706, and *d.* in France, while Thomas was a Captain in FitzJames's Regiment in the French service.

2), by Mary, da. and coheir of John CROKER, of Battisford, co. Gloucester, elder br. of Sir John PYE, of Hone, co. Derby, 1st Baronet (1665); took an active t in the civil wars at first for the Commonwealth, but subsequently for the toration; obtained a *warrant*, 22 Dec. 1662, *for a Baronetcy*,(a) but no patent passed and neither he nor any of his issue ever assumed it.(b) He *d.* 1701, ring male issue.

RAMSAY [S.]:

cr. 23 June 1669. [See Vol. iv., p. 273.]

The 1st Baronet *d.* v.p. in 1680 and was succeeded as below:—

1680, to 1709. SIR ANDREW RAMSAY, Baronet [S. 1669], of Abbotshall, co. Fife, s. and h., *suc. to the Baronetcy* in 1680. He was served heir in 1690 to his grandfather, Sir Andrew RAMSAY, a Lord of Session under the style of Lord Abbotshall, who *d.* 17 Jan. 88, aged 69. He *d.* in 1709, apparently s.p., and was *bur.* at Abbotshall, when e *Baronetcy*, presumably, became *extinct*.

RICHARDSON [S.]:

cr. 13 Nov. 1630. [See Vol. ii., p. 380.]

On the death, 12 April 1821, of SIR JOHN CHARLES RICHARDSON, 3th(c) Baronet [S. 1630], JOHN STEWART-RICHARDSON, of Pitfour, was on 9 Jan. 837 served his heir male, and on 27 May following was entered in Lyon's Office S.] as a Baronet, and is ancestor of the succeeding Baronets as now (1909) ecognised. This service of 1837 was, however, protested against by Arthur George STEWART-RICHARDSON, who claimed the Baronetcy since 1821 for the eirs male of the body of his great great grandfather, James RICHARDSON (of whom e in 1877 became the representative), the said James being stated to be a brother not of a cousin, as is the case of the line of Pitfour) of Sir George RICHARDSON, Baronet [so styled in the service of 1837], who *d.* in 1768, and who was ancestor f the succeeding Baronets down to 1821. The claimant wrote, 23 Dec. 1907, as follows:—"It is not my intention for the time being to contest the Baronetcy with the present holder, but I have lodged a copy of my family tree with the Lyon King of Arms as a formal protest." Those who, according to this pedigree (printed by the claimant), were entitled to the Baronetcy after the death of the 13th Baronet in 1821, were as under:—

(a) Calendar of State Papers, 1660—1670.

(b) His great great grandson, Henry James Pye, of Faringdon (*b.* 10 Feb. 1744/5, *d.* 11 Aug. 1813), was Poet Laureate. To him apply the lines:—

"Poetis nos lætamur tribus,
Pye, Petro Pindar, Parvo Pybus," etc.

See Vol. v., p. 307, note "e," under "BURGES."

(c) His predecessors, the 12th, 11th, 10th and 9th Baronets are generally, though erroneously, styled the 11th, 10th, 9th and 8th Baronets respectively. The 7th Baronet, Robert, *d.* in 1752, s.p., but it was not till 1783 that James Richardson assumed the title and registered arms in the Lyon Office as "*Sir James Richardson, Baronet.*" Now the father of this James, viz., George Richardson (*b.* at Forganderry, co. Perth, 1691, and *bur.* 28 Dec. 1768, at Greyfriars, Edinburgh) survived the 7th Baronet sixteen years, and, granting that the title was rightly assumed by his son in 1783, would himself have been the 8th Baronet after 1752, till his death in 1768. Indeed in the subsequent service of the heirship to this title, 9 Jan. 1837, he is styled "*Sir George Richardson, Baronet,*" though he certainly never assumed that title.

XIV. 1821. JOHN RICHARDSON, of Perth, only son that had issue of William RICHARDSON, of Forganderry, co. Perth (*b.* there 14 July 1717, and living 1764), by Janet BEAT (*m.* there 10 Nov. 1750), which William was the eldest son that had issue(a) of James RICHARDSON, of Forganderry aforesaid (*b.* there 1692, and living there 1731), who was the only br. that had issue of Sir George RICHARDSON, 8th Baronet [S. 1630],(b) who *d.* 1768, being ancestor of the 9th, 10th, 11th, 12th and 13th Baronets. He was *b.* 10 Aug. 1758, at Forganderry and on the death of his cousin, the 13th Baronet, 12 April 1821, became *entitled to that Baronetcy*, which, however, he never assumed. He *m.* Anne GLEIG. He *d.* 1 Dec. 1835, at Perth, aged 77.

XV. 1835. ALEXANDER RICHARDSON, of Perth, only s. and h., *b.* there 3 May 1793; was *entitled to the Baronetcy*, 1 Dec. 1835, but never assumed the same. He *d.* unm. 14 March 1874, aged 81.

XVI. 1874. WILLIAM RICHARDSON, cousin and h. male, being 2d but 1st surv. s. and h., and the only s. that had issue of Patrick RICHARDSON, of Bridgend House, Perth, by Janet (*m.* 1805, at Perth), da. of John RUSKIN, of Edinburgh, which Patrick (*b.* 3 Nov. 1773, at Perth, and *d.* there 26 July 1824) was the only s. that had issue of James RICHARDSON, of Perth (*b.* 10 Jan. 1720, at Forganderry, *d.* 5 Jan. 1772), yr. br. of William, father of John, who in 1821, was entitled to become the 14th Baronet as above stated, both being sons of James RICHARDSON, of Forganderry aforesaid. He was *b.* at Perth, 1807, and became *entitled to the Baronetcy* 14 March, 1874, but never assumed the same. He *m.* firstly, Mary, da. of John CAPPS. He *m.* secondly, Eleanor, da. of John BOLDING. He *d.* in London, 1876.

XVII. 1876. WILLIAM GEORGE RICHARDSON, 1st s. and h., only s. by first wife,(c) *b.* 3 July 1838, at 7 Radnor Place, Paddington; became *entitled to the Baronetcy* in 1876, but did not assume the same. He *m.* 29 April 1872, at 22, King street, Aberdeen, Margaret Knight, da. of John MONSON, of Fingusk. He *d.* 15 July 1877.

XVIII. 1877. ARTHUR GEORGE STEWART RICHARDSON, only s. and h., became *entitled to the Baronetcy* 15 July 1877, but did not assume the same; was living at Buluwayo in Rhodesia, Oct. 1907.

SANDYS:

cr. 17 March 1663/4.(d)

"SIR THOMAS SANDYS, of Kent," had a warrant for a Baronetcy, 17 March 1662/3 [Calendar of State Papers, 1660-70]. Nothing more is known of him.

(a) Of the two younger sons, James was the ancestor of the present [1909] claimant, while Peter (*b.* at Forganderry, 29 Aug. 1731, *m.* 20 Feb. 1756, M. Miller), had two sons, viz., (1) James, *b.* 24 Feb. 1757, *m.* 17 Aug. 1781, Katherine Hepburn and had a son, William Richardson, *b.* 8 Aug. 1782, at Forganderry, and (2) Colin, *b.* 1759. Failing male issue of any of these, the line of Pitfour, represented by the present [1909] holder of the dignity may possibly be the collateral heirs male of the grantee of 1630, though it is alleged that, even then, there are other branches of the family senior to that of Pitfour.

(b) See as to this George, being the 8th Baronet, p. 86, note "c."

(c) His yr. br. (the only son by the 2d wife), Henry Adair Richardson, was a Director of the Anglo-Egyptian Bank. He *m.* Frances.

(d) The information in this article was furnished by G. D. Burtchaell, Athlone Pursuivant.

SHORT:

assumption in or before 1661.(a)

In June 1661 there was an information against CAPT. EDWARD SHORT, of Newington Butts, [Surrey], of whom it was said that "he has *usurped the title of Baronet*" [Calendar of State Papers, 1660-70]. Admon. of "EDWARD SHORT, *alias* SIR EDWARD SHORT, Knt., of Newington Butts, Surrey," was granted 6 June 1661 to Richard Mason, principal creditor.(b) Revoked, 3 Feb. 1664/5, and admon. granted to Dame Anne Bryers, principal creditor.

SUTTON:

in or before 1663 to, or after, 1685.(a)

"SIR EDWARD SUTTON, KNT. AND BARONET," had a confirmation of an order, granting him lands in co. Kildare from the Duke of Ormonde, Lord Lieutenant of Ireland, 4 May 1663 [*Ormonde MSS.*, App., 8th Rep., Hist. MSS. Com., p. 504*b*], as also 4 July 1663, to recover by distress the amount due to him by Lieut. Richard Thompson. [*Ibid.*, p. 529*b*.] On 27 July 1663, he was decreed by the Court of Claims, as an "Innocent Protestant," to be entitled, as an Incumbrancer, to 200 acres in co. Kildare. In *The Book of Survey and Distribution* these 200 acres comprise the lands of Killballymerin, in the parish of Cloncurry and Barony of Ikeathy, with part of the adjoining common, but no grant was ever enrolled. He is there styled "*Sir*," without the addition of Baronet. He petitioned the Lord Lieutenant [I.], 8 July 1664, for a custodian of lands in Meath [*Ormonde MSS.*, App., 9th Rep., Hist. MSS. Com., p. 142*b*]. He petitioned as "*Knight and Baronet*" in Oct. 1666, to be satisfied out of concealed lands [Act of Settlement, Lit. C., p. 178, P.R.O., Ireland]. Lord Preston wrote to him from Paris, 5 May 1685 [*Graham MSS*, App. 7th Rep., Hist. MSS. Com., p. 326*b*]. He was possibly a yr. s. of Gilbert SUTTON, of Richardstown, in the said Barony of Ikeathy, who *d.* 30 March 1631, leaving Gerald SUTTON, his son and heir, then aged 8. There is a petition from him about the same date [*i.e.*, 5 May 1685], where he states that "he married the widow of Sir Thomas LUCAS, who owed a debt of £1,500 on which he [petitioner] has for 26 years paid interest at 10 per cent. She is deceased. The petitioner has lost his income and cannot pay. Lords Ormond and Inchiquin, when with the army about Dublin and Drogheda, had of his wife's chattels to the value of £3,000. In 1641 Charles I gave him a warrant for an Irish viscountcy." [*Graham MSS.*, App. 7th Rep., Hist. MSS. Com., p. 409*b*.]

Note.—This Sir Thomas LUCAS *m.* (Lic. Jan. 1628/9) Anne, da. of Sir John BYRON, and made his will 11 March 1648/9, pr. 26 Aug. 1650. She *d.* 22 and was *bur.* 24 May 1679 in St. Peter's, Drogheda. Funeral entry at Ulster's Office, where, however, is no mention of her second marriage to this Edward Sutton, which, nevertheless, was undoubtedly a fact.

(a) See p. 87, note "d," under "SANDYS."

(b) His burial does not appear to be recorded in the registers of St. Mary's, Newington, but there is a baptism there, 13 Nov. 1659, of Mary, da. of "Edward Short, *Esq.*"

TALBOT, *or* TALBOTT [I.]:

cr. 4 Feb. 1622/3.(a) [See Vol. i., pp. 247-248.]

forfeited, 1691;

extinct (together with Earldom of Tyrconnell [I.]), 12 March 1752.

[The account given in G.E.C.'s *Complete Baronetage* as above is faulty, and the following should be substituted for it]:—

I. 1623. "WILLIAM TALBOTT, Esq., of Carton, co. Kildare," son of Patrick TALBOT, by Genet, da. of Thomas, "f. BARTH.-f. GERALD," which Patrick was 3d s. of William TALBOT, of Robertstown, co. Meath, a yr. s. of Thomas TALBOT, of Malahide (*d.* 23 July 1487), by his 2d wife, Elizabeth BUCKLEY.(b) He was Recorder of Dublin, 16 July 1602, and was admitted to the Freedom of that city by special grace, but was removed in 1605 for refusing to take the oath of Supremacy; was admitted to the King's Inns, Dublin, 24 July 1607; was committed to the Tower for refusing to deliver his opinion on the doctrine of Suarez, touching the deposing and killing of Kings; was M.P. [I.] for co. Kildare, 1613-15, and was *cr. a Baronet* [I.], as above, by patent dat. 4 Feb. 1622/3 at Dublin, the privy seal being dat. 16 Dec. 1621 at Westminster. He *m.*, probably about 1605, Alison, da. of John NETTERVILLE, of Castletowne, co. Meath, by Margaret, da. of Luke NETTERVILLE, of Dowth, in that county. He *d.* 16 March 1633/4, and was *bur.* 1 April 1634, in the church of Maynooth in the parish of Larraghbrene, leaving eight sons(c) and eight daughters. Funeral certificate [I.]. Will dat. 12 March 1633/4, pr. [I.] 6 Nov. 1636.

II. 1634. SIR ROBERT TALBOT,(d) Baronet [I. 1623], of Carton aforesaid, 1st s. and h., *b.* probably about 1610(e); *suc. to the*

(a) The information in this article was furnished by G. D. Burtchaell, Athlone Pursuivant.

(b) This descent is according to a pedigree entered by Thomas Molyneux, Ulster, in the Office of Arms [I.], which is confirmed by the will of the 1st Baronet (dat. March 1633/4), in which he entails the principal portions of his estate, after the provisions made for his own issue in the marriage settlement of his eldest son, on his cousins, John Talbot, *of Robertston*, and Richard Talbot, brother of the said John. The generally received pedigree, that he was son of Robert Talbot, 3d son of Sir Thomas Talbot, of Malahide, is certainly incorrect, though given by Sir William Betham in a pedigree of about 1820. According to a pedigree lodged in Ulster's Office, about 1820, the parents of the Baronet were *Robert* Talbot and (—) Luttrell, the said "Robert being a younger son of Talbot of Robertstown, co. Meath, being son or grandson of William Talbot, of Robertstown, 3d son of Thomas Talbot, of Malahide, who *d.* 13 July 1487, by his 2d wife, Elizabeth Buckley."

(c) Of the eight sons, Robert, John, Garrett, James, Thomas, Peter, Gilbert and Richard, the third son, Garrett, *m.* before March 1633/4, and was father of William, who became the head of the family in May 1691; the sixth son, Peter, b. 1620, was Roman Catholic Archbishop of Dublin, 1669-80, was arrested on suspicion of being concerned in the Popish plot, and *d.* in prison, 1680. The eighth and youngest son, Richard (the well known "lying Dick Talbot"), was *b.* 1630; was *cr.* 20 June 1685, Earl of Tyrconnell [I.], with a spec. rem., and was *cr.*, 30 March 1689, by James II, after his expulsion, Duke of Tyrconnell [I.].

(d) It was so usual in the seventeenth and eighteenth centuries to name the eldest son after the paternal grandfather, that his name of "Robert" tends to support the 1720 pedigree, that Robert, not Patrick, was the name of the father, of the 1st Baronet. Moreover, of the eight sons of that Baronet, not one was named "Patrick."

(e) The dates of birth of his eight sisters are unknown, but as the sixth son was born 1620, it is probable that he (Robert), the eldest, was *b.* ten years before him.

Baronetcy, 16 Mar. 1633/4; M.P. [I.] for co. Wicklow, June to Oct. 1634.(a) He *m.* Grace, da. of George (CALVERT), 1st BARON BALTIMORE [I.], by Anne, da. of George MYNNE. He *d.* 21 Oct. 1670. Inq. p.m. Admon. [I.], 13 May 1671.

III. 1670, to 1691. SIR WILLIAM TALBOT, Baronet [I. 1623], of Listarton, co. Meath, only s. and h., *suc. to the Baronetcy*, 21 Oct. 1670; was Secretary of the Colony of Maryland, 1670-71; Master of the Rolls [I.], 22 April 1689, till removed in 1690; M.P. [I.] for co. Meath in the Parl. of James II, 1689, and P.C. [I.]. He *m.* (articles 10 Nov. 1683) Anne, widow of Lucas (DILLON), 6th VISCOUNT DILLON OF COSTELLO [I.], 1st da. of Richard (NUGENT), 1st EARL OF WESTMEATH [I.], by Mary, da. of Sir Thomas NUGENT, Baronet [I. 1622]. He *d.* s.p. 18 May 1691, at Galway, and having been attainted the same year (1691), as "of Kilkarty [*recte* Liscarton], Baronet," the Baronetcy was *forfeited*. His widow's claim to dower was entered with the trustees of forfeited estates [I.] in 1700. Her will dat. 14 July 1710, pr. [I.] 1711.

IV. 1691. WILLIAM TALBOT, of Haggardstown, co. Louth, 1st cousin and h. male, being s. and h. of Garrett TALBOT, by Margaret, da. of Henry GAYDON, of Dublin, the said Garret (who *d.* before June 1685), being 2d s. of the 1st Baronet. He was *b.* about 1643; was decreed "Innocent" by the Court of Claims [I.], 27 July 1663, and restored in counties Louth and Dublin; was M.P. for Louth in the Parl. [I.] of James II in 1689; was attainted in 1691, but *suc. to the right to the Baronetcy*, 18 May 1691, subject to his own attainder and that of the late Baronet abovementioned. A few months later, on the death, s.p.m., 14 Aug. 1691, of his uncle, Richard (TALBOT), EARL (though better known as DUKE) OF TYRCONNELL [I.], he *suc. to the right to that Earldom*, under the spec. rem. in its creation,(b) 20 June 1685, and accordingly styled himself "*Comte* (or *Conde*) *de Tyrconnell*," *i.e.*, EARL OF TYRCONNELL [I.], residing chiefly in France or Spain. He *m.* Mary, da. of Nicholas WHITE, of Clonmel, Alderman and M.P. [I.] 1689 (in the Parl. of James II) for that town. He *d.* 26 Dec. 1724, in his 82d year.

V. 1724, to 1752. RICHARD FRANCIS TALBOT, *styling himself* EARL OF TYRCONNELL I.], etc., and 5th Baronet [I. 1623], grandson and h., being only s. and h. of Richard TALBOT, *styling himself* VISCOUNT BALTINGLASS, by Charlotte, his cousin, da. and coheir of Richard (TALBOT), 1st EARL (though better known as DUKE) OF TYRCONNELL [I.], which so styled Viscount Baltinglass, who was s. and h. ap. of William (TALBOT), *styling himself* EARL OF TYRCONNELL [I.] next abovenamed, *d.* v.p. He was *b.* 1710, and *suc. to the right to the said titles*, 26 Dec. 1724. He *m.* Madeleine DE LYS. He *d.* s.p. 12 March 1752, at Berlin, when *all the abovenamed titles* became *extinct*. His widow *d.* at Paris, 2 Nov. 1759.

(a) On 30 Oct. 1634, Bryan Byrne was elected M.P. [I.] for co. Wicklow, "*vice* Talbot deceased," but the word "deceased" is probably an error. [*Ex inform.* W. D. Pink.]

(b) The limitation of this Earldom was to the heirs male of the body of the grantee, failing which, to his nephews, "Sir William Talbot, of Carton, Baronet, and William Talbot, of Haggardstone, Esq.," in like manner.

TOWRIS, *or* TOURS:(a)

temp. Car. II.

"SIR JOHN TOWRIS, Knt. and Baronet," occurs two or three tin in the State Papers (Domestic) of Charles II, and appears to have been sentenc to be hanged, drawn and quartered in April 1666, "for forging the sign man of the King," but to have been respited, when a warrant for his transportati was issued. He "is described as *Knt. and Baronet* in the royal sign man (cclxvii, 38 and 39), so there can be no doubt about it. He signs uniformly TOWR but in the petition is described as SIR JOHN TOURS. The only suggestion I c make is that he is an unrecorded son of Sir Charles ST. ETIENNE (DE LA TOU Baronet [S. 1629], but I can find no account of these De la Tours in Moreri."(b)

TERRY, *or* TIRRY [I.](a)

warrant 20 June 1627.

"DAVID TERRY, fitz Edmund," of Cork, received by King's letters, dat. at Westminster, 20 June 1627 (State Papers [I.] of Charles I) an order for his *creation as a Baronet* "in virtue of his services performed for the King and for his other merit." No patent was ever enrolled, and presumably none was ever passed.(c) He was s. and h. of Edmund TERRY, or TIRRY, of Cork (who *d.* 30 Nov. 1603), and was himself Alderman of Cork and M.P. [I.] for that city, 1613-15. He was "recommended" by Sir William St. Leger, the Lord Lieutenant [I.], 7 Dec. 1629, as having been "prominent in the service of the King" (*State Papers* [I.]).

TULP, *or* TULIP:

cr. 23 April 1675.

ex. or *dorm.* probably about 1690.

I. 1675, to 1690? SIR RICHARD TULP, *or* TULIP,(d) of Amesterdam in Holland, Knt., who as "DIDRIGH TULP, Meestersknaep of Holland, and West Friesland, and Director of the Dutch East India Company," had been *Knighted*, 5 Nov. 1674, in the King's bedchamber at Whitehall, was *cr. a Baronet*, as above, 23 April 1675, a dignity which, presumably, became *extinct* or *dormant* at his death.

(a) *Ex inform.* Rev. A. B. Beaven, M.A.

(b) Letter to the said A. B. Beaven, Dec. 1908, from Wm. A. Shaw, Litt. D.

(c) A similar case to that of Courtenay [I.], 10 Dec. 1621, and of Chevers [I.], 25 June 1623.

(d) He is called "TULIP" in the Calendar of State Papers for 1675, but "TULPE" when Knighted in 1674.

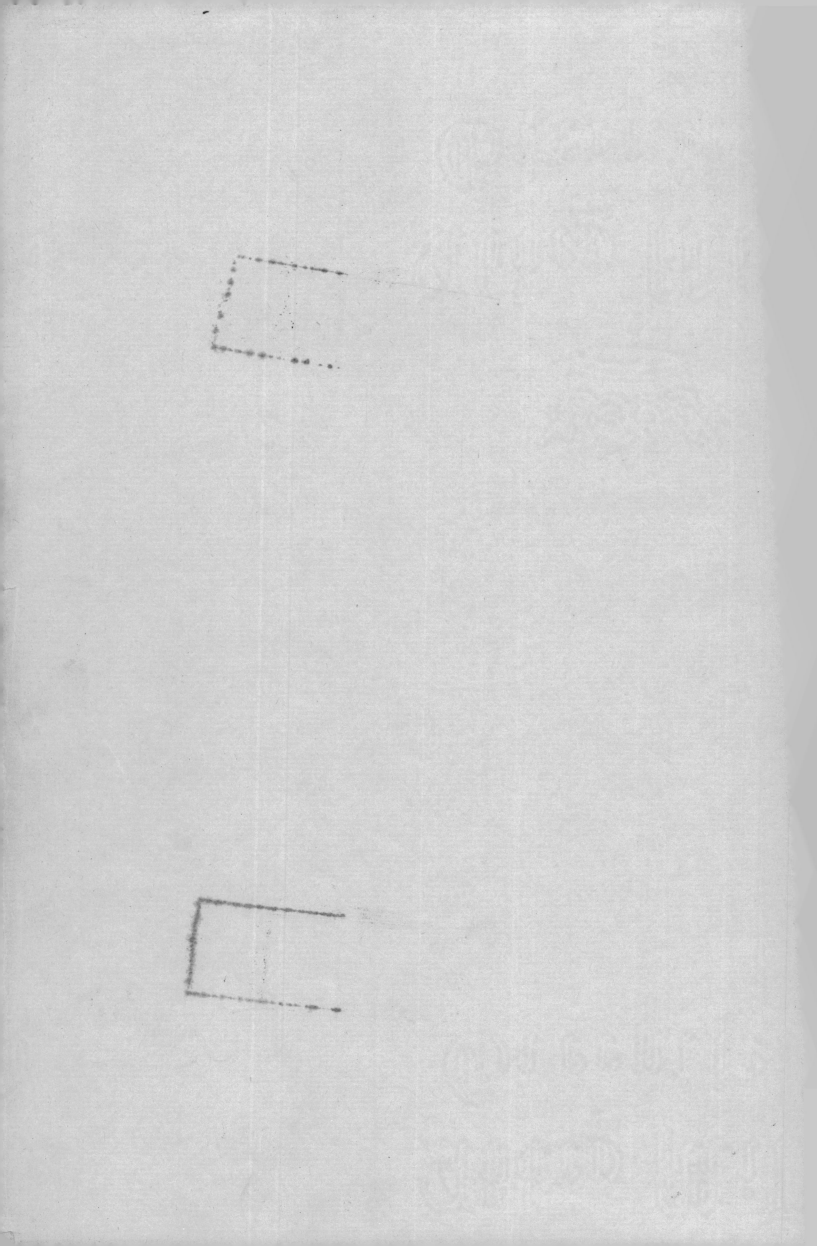